WHO'S WHO
IN
PENNSYLVANIA

A BIOGRAPHICAL DICTIONARY OF LEADING LIVING MEN AND WOMEN OF THE STATES OF PENNSYLVANIA, NEW JERSEY, DELAWARE, MARYLAND AND WEST VIRGINIA

VOLUME 1

1939

COMPILED AND EDITED UNDER THE DIRECTION OF
ALBERT NELSON MARQUIS

CHICAGO
THE A. N. MARQUIS COMPANY
1939

Copyright, 1939, by
THE A. N. MARQUIS COMPANY

PREFACE

It has been the aim of the publishers to gather into a single handy volume, brief, dependable personality sketches of the leading men and women of the various localities herein represented. The need of such a compilation long has been apparent, and it is confidently believed, that the need has been consummated in these pages in very large measure. Here are listed and biographically photographed 13,127 men and women who have "achieved" not only for themselves and their respective communities, but many of them also for the nation.

It long has been recognized that a printed compilation of certain authentic personal data pertaining to these leaders, following the pattern of WHO'S WHO IN AMERICA for the whole country, would constitute an invaluable book of ready reference, not only for the wide-awake editor of today and the future student of present-day activities, but also for the up-to-date public in general.

Various biographical compilations covering local fields, all more or less fugitive in character, have made their appearance from time to time. With but few exceptions they have been so incomplete and valueless as to fail of wide public acceptance. For this reason the publishers of WHO'S WHO IN AMERICA have felt it an obligation to make available their unique facilities for the production of sectional biographical reference books such as the present volume.

For the building of this new volume every proper source of available names has been drawn upon, and every reasonable effort has been made to procure the requisite data from persons deemed eligible for inclusion in keeping with the discriminating standard fixed for admission. Nevertheless, a few names which should have been included are missing; but in almost every instance the omission is not due to inadvertence or lack of effort on the part of those responsible for the preparation of material for the book. As a rule, such omissions are the result of failure on the part of the persons invited to provide the necessary facts. However, the great majority of such invitations were promptly accepted, and other helpful cooperative courtesies were freely extended. For these grateful thanks are hereby extended. Notwithstanding the impediments and handicaps encountered during construction, this volume may lay just claim to greater completeness, a greater degree of accuracy and a more dependable and authoritative record of outstanding *living* men and women of an exceedingly important section of the country—a section whose economic, civic, social and other interests, if not identical, are nevertheless closely related—than has ever before been attained.

As a matter of course the present volume carries the life-sketches of all residents of territory covered by this compilation who are listed in WHO'S WHO IN AMERICA. The national volume confines itself solely to nation-wide notables. As a natural consequence there will here be found many names of outstanding prominence locally which could not be given a place in the volume devoted to the whole country. The number of those listed in WHO'S WHO IN AMERICA living in this territory is only slightly above 4,000, whereas the total number listed in this volume is 13,127.

Special care has been taken to secure accuracy. In every possible instance the facts were procured at first hand, and the sketches in printed form (galley proofs) were submitted for verification and correction just before going to press. In this painstaking way authenticity has been safeguarded.

Admission to these pages have been confined to living subjects only, because the purpose from the very first has been to provide for easy reference a dictionary of contemporaries, and to mirror the current progress and history as reflected in the life-statistics of worthwhile people. The men and women whose life-histories are here presented are largely, those who guide and control the activities and welfare of wide areas of our country, in all important avenues of private, public, business and intellectual endeavor.

In the daily work and turmoil of life, one finds but little opportunity, outside of his own intimate circle, to become acquainted with those whose personalities are of most interest. The reader can doubtless think of many leading citizens concerning whose activities he would like to procure dependable information such as is indicated by the following queries: Where and when was he born, where and how educated? What the predominating characteristics of his home life? What his religious, social, and political environment, and what have been the chief steps of his career? By consulting these pages the desired information may be found.

It is believed that this volume has been so compiled (under a new arrangement) as to largely overcome serious disadvantages inherent in the majority of so-called localized biographical volumes. The boundary of no single state, under modern conditions, can prescribe reference utility for a biographical volume intended for use in libraries, business offices, schools, publication offices and other reference centers. Under modern conditions, individuals may even live in one state and carry on their daily occupations in another; and certainly the varied contacts of life today are intimately interwoven throughout several more or less contiguous states.

As a direct result of these conditions a biographical volume limited to a single state is not a satisfactory reference tool. As the publishers of this volume are concerned entirely with the production of useful biographical reference books, they have decided, though the expense of doing so may be considerable, to produce only books that will serve reference requirements most effectively.

Extensive investigations have demonstrated that only by the covering of appropriate areas, rather than by taking a mere sales advantage of totally inappropriate states lines, can such a service be rendered. Despite the obviously greater expense involved, it was decided to provide such a coverage in this compilation, and at no greater expense to purchasers.

Therefore, this volume covers an appropriate area—a grouping of more or less contiguous states—as well as the titled state itself. This area-coverage has been carefully established, following a careful study of the inter-relations now prevailing in the section involved.

Consequently, the user of the volume is given biographical coverage of the localities most closely related to him, and is not placed at the disadvantage of having to lay aside the volume because of the non-coverage of individuals a few hundred miles away who happen to be living beyond a state line, but nevertheless intimately related to the life of his own vicinity. By this arrangement, it is obvious that no inconvenience can result to the reader, as all sketches are alphabetically listed, and, as has been stated, the very considerable addition to the compiling and production expense has been absorbed by the publishers. Naturally there is a reason for making this added expenditure which is believed to be both sound and entirely practicable. The publishers are interested in producing standard reference books in the future years, as they have produced such books throughout the past half-century, and they hope that the added expenditure will aid in clearly defining an advantageous difference between merely transitory volumes without substantial standing, and those which endeavor, first of all, to serve highly useful reference needs.

To make dependable a volume such as this it is necessary that it should be impartial, and inclusion in it unpurchasable. Not a single sketch in the book has been paid for, nor inserted for any financial consideration whatsoever.

With a view to revisions, as time and necessity make advisable, suggestions for improvement, changes in biographical data, notices of deaths, and changes of address as they occur are invited.

For Index by States,
See Pages 995 to 1040.

ABBREVIATIONS

The following abbreviations are frequently used in this book:

A.A.	Degree of Associate of Arts.
A.A.A.	Agricultural Adjustment Administration.
A.A.A.S.	American Association for the Advancement of Science.
A.a.g.	Assistant adjutant-general.
A. and M.	Agricultural and Mechanical.
A.A.O.N.M.S.	Ancient Arabic Order of the Nobles of the Mystic Shrine (Masonic).
A.A.S.R.	Ancient Accepted Scottish Rite (Masonic).
A.B.C.F.M.	American Board of Commissioners for Foreign Missions (Congregational).
A.B. (also B.A.)	Bachelor of Arts.
A.C.	Analytical Chemist; Air Corps; Army Corps.
Acad.	Academy; Academic.
A.C.P.	American College of Physicians.
A.C.S.	American College of Surgeons.
A.C.S.A.	American Schools of Architecture.
Actg.	Acting.
A.d.c.	Aide-de-camp.
Add.	Additional.
Adj.	Adjutant; Adjunct.
Adj.Gen.	Adjutant General.
Adm.	Admiral.
Adminstr.	Administrator.
Adminstrn.	Administration.
Adv.	Advertising; Advocate; Advisory.
A.E.	Agricultural Engineer.
A.E. and P.	Ambassador Extraordinary and Plenipotentiary.
A.E.F.	American Expeditionary Forces.
A.F.D.	Doctor of Fine Arts.
A.F. and A.M.	Ancient Free and Accepted Masons.
A.F. of L.	American Federation of Labor.
Agr.	Agriculture.
Agrl.	Agricultural.
Agt.	Agent.
a. i.	ad interim.
A.I.A.	American Institute of Architects.
Ala.	Alabama.
A.L.A.	American Library Association.
A.L.I.	American Library Institute.
Am.	American.
A.M. (also M.A.)	Master of Arts.
A.M.A.	American Medical Association.
A.M.E.	African Methodist Episcopal.
Am. Inst. E.E.	American Institute of Electrical Engineers.
Am. Soc. C.E.	American Society of Civil Engineers.
Am. Soc. M.E.	American Society of Mechanical Engineers.
A.N.A.	Associate National Academician.
Anat.	Anatomical.
Ann.	Annual.
Anthrop.	Anthropological.
Antiq.	Antiquarian.
A.O.H.	Ancient Order of Hibernians.
Appmt. or Apptmt.	Appointment.
Apptd.	Appointed.
Apts.	Apartments.
A.Q.M.	Assistant quartermaster.
A.R.A. Assn.	Am. Relief Administration Assn.
A.R.C.	Am. Red Cross.
Archæol.	Archæological.
Archtl.	Architectural.
Ariz.	Arizona.
Ark.	Arkansas.
Arty.	Artillery.
A.S.	Air Service.
A.S.S.C.	Air Service Signal Corps.
Assn.	Association.
Asso.	Associate; Associated.
Asst.	Assistant.
Astron.	Astronomical.
Astrophys.	Astrophysical.
Atty.	Attorney.
Aug.	August.
Av.	Avenue.
b.	Born.
B.A. (also A.B.)	Bachelor of Arts.
B.Agr.	Bachelor of Agriculture.
Bapt.	Baptist.
B.Arch.	Bachelor of Architecture.
B.B.A.	Bachelor of Business Administration.
Batln., Batt. or Bn.	Battalion.
B.C.	British Columbia.
B.C.E.	Bachelor of Civil Engineering.
B.Chir.	Bachelor of Surgery.
B.C.L.	Bachelor of Civil Law.
B.C.S.	Bachelor of Commercial Science.
Bd.	Board.
B.D.	Bachelor of Divinity.
B.Di.	Bachelor of Didactics.
B.E.	Bachelor of Education.
B.E.F.	British Expeditionary Force.
Bet.	Between.
B.F.A.	Bachelor of Fine Arts.
Bibl.	Biblical.
Bibliog.	Bibliographical.
Biog.	Biographical.
Biol.	Biological.
B.J.	Bachelor of Journalism.
Bk.	Bank, Book.
Bks.	Barracks.
B.L. (or Litt.B.)	Bachelor of Letters.
Bldg.	Building.
Blk.	Block.
B.L.S.	Bachelor of Library Science.
Bn.	Battalion.
B.O.	Bachelor of Oratory.
Bot.	Botanical.
Boul.	Boulevard.
B.P.	Bachelor of Painting.
B.P.E.	Bachelor of Physical Education.
B.P.O.E.	Benevolent and Protective Order of Elks.
B.Pd. (or Pd.B.)	Bachelor of Pedagogy.
B.Py.	Bachelor of Pedagogy.
Br.	Branch.
Brig.	Brigadier; Brigade.
Brig. Gen.	Brigadier General.
Brit.	British; Britannica.
Brit.Assn.Adv.Sci.	British Association for the Advancement of Science.
Bro.	Brother.
B.S. (also S.B. or Sc.B.)	Bachelor of Science.
B.S. in Ry. M.E.	Bachelor in Railway Mechanical Engineering.
B.S.A.	Bachelor of Agricultural Science.
B.S.D.	Bachelor of Didactic Science.
B.Th.	Bachelor of Theology.
Bull.	Bulletin.
Bur.	Bureau.
Bus.	Business.
Bvt.	Brevet.
Bvtd.	Brevetted.
B.W.I.	British West Indies.
C.A.	Central America.
C.A.C.	Coast Artillery Corps.
Calif.	California.
Can.	Canada.
Cantab.	of or pertaining to Cambridge University, Eng.
Capt.	Captain.
Cath.	Catholic.
Cav.	Cavalry.
C.E.	Civil Engineer.
C.E.F.	Canadian Expeditionary Forces.
Ch.	Church.
Ch.D.	Doctor of Chemistry.
Chem.	Chemical.
Chem.E.	Chemical Engineer.
Chirurg.	Chirurgical.
Chmn.	Chairman.
C.I.C.	Commander in Chief.
Civ.	Civil.
Climatol.	Climatological.
Clin.	Clinical.
Clk.	Clerk.
C.L.S.C.	Chautauqua Literary and Scientific Circle.
C.M.	Master in Surgery.
Co.	Company; County.
C.O.	Commanding Officer.
C.O.F.	Catholic Order of Foresters.
Col.	Colonel.
Coll.	College.
Colo.	Colorado.
Com.	Committee.
Comd.	Commanded.
Comdg.	Commanding.
Comdr.	Commander.
Comdt.	Commandant.
Commd.	Commissioned.
Commn.	Commission.
Commr.	Commissioner.
Com. Sub.	Commissary of Subsistence.
Con.	Consolidated.
Condr.	Conductor.
Conf.	Conference.
Confed.	Confederate.
Congl.	Congregational; Congressional.
Conglist.	Congregationalist.
Conn.	Connecticut.
Cons.	Consulting.
Concertm.	Concertmaster.
Consol.	Consolidated.
Constl.	Constitutional.
Constn.	Constitution.
Constrn.	Construction.
Contbd.	Contributed.
Contbg.	Contributing.
Contbns.	Contributions.
Contbr.	Contributor.
Conv.	Convention.
Coop.	Coöperative.
Corpl.	Corporal.
Corpn.	Corporation.
Corr.	Correspondent; Corresponding; Correspondence.
Cos.	Companies; Counties.
C.O.T.S.	Central Officers' Training School.
C.P.A.	Certified Public Accountant.
C.P.H.	Certificate of Public Health.
C.S.	Christian Science.
C.S.A. (or C.S. Army)	Confederate States Army.

xi

ABBREVIATIONS—Continued

C.S.B.	Bachelor of Christian Science.
C.S.D.	Doctor of Christian Science.
C.S.N. (or C.S. Navy)	Confederate States Navy.
C.S.R.	Certified Shorthand Reporter.
Ct.	Court.
C.T.	Candidate in Theology.
C.W.S.	Chemical War Service.
Cyclo.	Cyclopedia.
d.	Daughter.
D.Agr.	Doctor of Agriculture.
D.A.R.	Daughters of the American Revolution.
D.C.	District of Columbia.
D.C.L.	Doctor of Civil Law.
D.C.S.	Doctor of Commercial Science.
D.D.	Doctor of Divinity.
D.D.S.	Doctor of Dental Surgery.
Dec.	December.
Deg.	Degree.
Del.	Delaware; Delegate.
Dem.	Democratic.
D. Eng. (also Dr. Engring., or E.D.)	Doctor of Engineering.
Denom.	Denominational.
Dep.	Deputy.
Dept.	Department.
Dermatol.	Dermatological.
Desc.	Descendant.
D.H.L.	Doctor of Hebrew Literature
Dir.	Director.
Disch.	Discharged.
Dist.	District.
Div.	Division; Divinity.
D.Litt. (also L.H.D.)	Doctor of Literature.
D.M.D.	Doctor of Medical Dentistry
D.O.	Doctor of Osteopathy.
D.P.H. (also Dr.P.H.)	Diploma in Public Health, or Doctor of Public Health. or Doctor of Public Hygiene.
Dr.	Doctor.
D.R.	Daughters of the Revolution.
D.R.E.	Doctor of Religious Education.
D.Sc. (or Sc.D.)	Doctor of Science.
D.S.C.	Distinguished Service Cross.
D.S.M.	Distinguished Service Medal.
D.S.T.	Doctor of Sacred Theology.
D.T.M.	Doctor of Tropical Medicine.
D.V.M.	Doctor of Veterinary Medicine.
D.V.S.	Doctor of Veterinary Surgery.
E.	East.
E. and P.	Extraordinary and Plenipotentiary.
Eccles.	Ecclesiastical.
Ecol.	Ecological.
Econ.	Economic.
Ed.	Educated.
E.D. (also D.Eng., or Dr. Engring.)	Doctor of Engineering.
Ed.B.	Bachelor of Education.
Ed.D.	Doctor of Education.
Edit.	Edition.
Ed.M.	Master of Education.
Edn.	Education.
Ednl.	Educational.
E.E.	Electrical Engineer.
E.E. and M.P.	Envoy Extraordinary and Minister Plenipotentiary.
Egyptol.	Egyptological.
Elec.	Electrical.
Electrochem.	Electrochemical.
Electrophys.	Electrophysical.
E.M.	Engineer of Mines.
Emer.	Emergency.
Ency.	Encyclopædia.
Eng.	England.
Engr.	Engineer.
Engring.	Engineering.
Engr. O.R.C.	Engineer Officers' Reserve Corps.
Engr. R.C.	Engineer Reserve Corps.
Engrs.	Engineers.
Entomol.	Entomological.
e.s.	Eldest son.
Ethnol.	Ethnological.
Evang.	Evangelical.
Exam.	Examination; Examining.
Exec.	Executive.
Exhbn.	Exhibition.
Expdn.	Expedition.
Expn.	Exposition.
Expt.	Experiment.
Exptl.	Experimental.
F.	Fellow.
F.A.	Field Artillery.
F.A.C.P.	Fellow American College of Physicians.
F.A.C.S.	Fellow American College of Surgeons.
F.E.	Forest Engineer.
Feb.	February.
Fed.	Federation.
Fgn.	Foreign.
Fla.	Florida.
Frat.	Fraternity.
F.R.C.P.	Fellow Royal College of Physicians (England).
F.R.C.P.E.	Fellow Royal College of Physicians of Edinburgh.
F.R.C.S.	Fellow Royal College of Surgeons (England).
F.R.S.E.	Fellow Royal Society of Edinburgh.
Ft.	Fort.
G.-1 (or other number)	General Staff Officer No.
Ga.	Georgia.
G.A.R.	Grand Army of the Republic.
G.D.	Graduate in Divinity.
g.d.	Granddaughter.
Gen.	General.
Geneal.	Genealogical.
Geod.	Geodetic.
Geog.	Geographical; Geographic.
Geol.	Geological.
Geophys.	Geophysical.
G.H.Q.	General Headquarters.
Gov.	Governor.
Govt.	Government.
Grad.	Graduated; Graduate.
g.s.	Grandson.
Gt.	Great.
Gynecol.	Gynecological.
Hdqrs.	Headquarters.
H.G.	Home Guard.
H.I.	Hawaiian Islands.
H.M.	Master of Humanics.
H.Ty. (or H.T.)	Hawaiian Territory.
Hist.	Historical; Historic.
Homœ.	Homœopathic.
Hon.	Honorary; Honorable; Honorably.
Ho. of Reps.	House of Representatives.
Hort.	Horticultural.
Hosp.	Hospital.
Hts.	Heights.
Hydrog.	Hydrographic.
Ia.	Iowa.
Ida.	Idaho
Ill.	Illinois.
Illus.	Illustrated.
Inc.	Incorporated; Inclusive
Ind.	Indiana, Independent.
Ind. Ty.	Indian Territory.
Inf.	Infantry.
Ins.	Insurance.
Insp.	Inspector.
Insp.Gen.	Inspector General.
Inst.	Institute.
Instn.	Institution.
Instr.	Instructor.
Instrn.	Instruction.
Internat.	International.
Intro.	Introduction.
I.O.B.B.	Independent Order of B'nai B'rith.
I.O.G.T.	International Order of Good Templars.
I.O.O.F.	Independent Order of Odd Fellows.
Jan.	January.
J.B.	*Jurum Baccalaureus.*
J.C.B.	*Juris Canonici* Bachelor.
J.C.L.	*Juris Canonici Lector.*
J.D.	Doctor of Jurisprudence.
J.g. (or Jr.g.)	Junior Grade.
Jour.	Journal.
Jr.	Junior.
J.S.D.	Doctor of Juristic Science.
Jud.	Judicial.
J.U.D.	*Juris Utriusque Doctor:* Doctor of Both (Canon and Civil) Laws.
Kan.	Kansas.
K.C.	Knight of Columbus.
K.C.C.H.	Knight Commander of Court of Honor.
K.P.	Knight of Pythias.
K.T.	Knight Templar
Ky.	Kentucky.
La.	Louisiana.
Lab.	Laboratory.
Lang.	Language.
Laryngol.	Laryngological.
Lbr.	Lumber.
L.H.D.	Doctor of Letters of Humanity.
L.I.	Long Island.
Lit.	Literary; Literature.
Lit.Hum.	*Literae Humanores* (classics. Oxford Univ., Eng.).
Litt.B. (or B.L.)	Bachelor of Letters.
Litt.D.	Doctor of Letters.
LL.B.	Bachelor of Laws.
LL.D.	Doctor of Laws.
LL.M. (or M.L.)	Master of Laws.
L.O.M.	Loyal Order of Moose.
L.R.C.P.	Licentiate Royal Coll. Physicians.
L.R.C.S.	Licentiate Royal Coll. Surgeons.
L.S.A.	Licentiate Society of Apothecaries.
Lt. (or Lieut.)	Lieutenant.
Lt.Col.	Lieutenant Colonel.
Lt.Gen.	Lieutenant General.
Lt.Gov.	Lieutenant governor.
Ltd.	Limited.
Luth.	Lutheran.
m.	Married.
M.A. (or A.M.)	Master of Arts.
Mag.	Magazine.
M.Agr.	Master of Agriculture.
Maj.	Major.
Maj.Gen.	Major General.
Mass.	Massachusetts.
Math.	Mathematical.
M.B.	Bachelor of Medicine.
M.B.A.	Master of Business Administration.
M.C.	Member of Congress, Medical Corps.
M.C.S.	Master of Commercial Science.
Mcht.	Merchant.
Md.	Maryland.
M.D.	Doctor of Medicine.
M.Di.	Master of Didactics.
M.Dip.	Master in Diplomacy
Mdse.	Merchandise.
Me.	Maine.
M.E.	Mechanical Engineer; Methodist Episcopal.
Mech.	Mechanical.

ABBREVIATIONS—Continued

M.E. Ch	Methodist Episcopal Church.	N.Ph.D	Doctor of Natural Philosophy.	Psychiat	Psychiatrical.
Med	Medical.	Nov	November.	Psychol	Psychological.
Med. O.R.C.	Medical Officers' Reserve Corps.	Nr	Near.	Pub	Public; Publisher; Publishing; Published.
Med. R.C	Medical Reserve Corps.	NRA	National Recovery Administration.	Publ	Publication.
M.E.E.	Master of Electrical Engineering.	N.S	Nova Scotia.	Pvt	Private.
Mem	Member.	N.T	New Testament.	Py.B	Bachelor of Pedagogy.
Met	Metropolitan.	Numis	Numismatic.		
Metall	Metallurgical.	N.W	Northwest.	Q.M.	Quartermaster.
Meteorol	Meteorological.	N.Y	New York (state).	Q.M.C.	Quartermaster Corps.
Meth	Methodist.			Q.M.Gen.	Quartermaster General.
Metrol	Metrological.	O	Ohio.	Q.M.O.R.C.	Quartermaster Officers' Reserve Corps.
M.F.	Master of Forestry.	Obs	Observatory.	Q.M.R.C.	Quartermaster Reserve Corps.
M.F.A.	Master of Fine Arts (carries title of Dr.)	Obstet	Obstetrical.	Quar	Quarterly.
		Oct	October.	Que	Quebec (province).
Mfg	Manufacturing.	O.E.S.	Order of the Eastern Star.		
Mfr	Manufacture; Manufacturer.	Ofcl	Official.	q.v.	quod vide (which see).
Mfrs	Manufacturers.	Okla	Oklahoma.		
Mgr	Manager.	Ont	Ontario.	(R.)	Reserve.
M.I.	Military Intelligence.	Ophthal	Ophthalmological.	(R.F.)	Reserve Force.
Mich	Michigan.	O.Q.-M.G.	Office of Quartermaster General.	R.A.M.	Royal Arch Mason.
Micros	Microscopical.			R.C.	Roman Catholic; Reserve Corps.
Mil	Military.	O.R.C.	Officers' Reserve Corps.	R.C.S.	Revenue Cutter Service.
Mineral	Mineralogical.	Ore	Oregon.	Rd.	Road.
Minn	Minnesota.	Orgn	Organization.	R.D.	Rural Delivery.
Miss	Mississippi.	Ornithol	Ornithological.	R.E.	Reformed Episcopal.
M.I.T.	Massachusetts Institute of Technology.	O.S.B.	Order of Saint Benedict.	Rec	Recording.
		O.T.	Old Testament.	Ref	Reformed.
M.L. (or LL.M.)	Master of Laws.	O.T.C.	Officers' Training Camp.	R.F.D	Rural Free Delivery.
M.Litt.	Master of Literature.	Otol	Otological.	Regt	Regiment.
Mlle	Mademoiselle (Miss).	O.T.S.	Officers' Training School.	Regtl	Regimental.
Mme	Madame.	O.U.A.M.	Order United American Mechanics.	Rep	Republican; Representative
M.M.E.	Master of Mechanical Engineering.	Pa	Pennsylvania.	Rept	Report.
Mng	Managing.	Pass	Passenger.	Res. or (Res.)	Reserve.
Mo	Missouri.	Path	Pathological.	Ret	Retired.
Mont	Montana.	Pd.B. (or B.Pd.)	Bachelor of Pedagogy	Rev	Review; Reverend; Revised.
M.P.	Methodist Protestant.	Pd.D	Doctor of Pedagogy.	R.F.C.	Reconstruction Finance Corpn.
M.Pd	Master of Pedagogy.	Pd.M	Master of Pedagogy.		
M.P.E.	Master of Physical Education.	P.E.	Protestant Episcopal.	Rhinol	Rhinological.
		Pe.B.	Bachelor of Pediatrics.	R.I.	Rhode Island.
M.P.L.	Master of Patent Law.	P.E.N.	Poets, Playwrights, Editors, Essayists and Novelists (Internat. Assn.)	R.M.S.	Railway Mail Service.
M.R.C.P.	Member Royal College of Physicians.			Röntgenol	Röntgenological.
		Penol	Penological.	R.O.S.	Royal Order of Scotland.
M.R.C.S.	Member Royal Coll. Surgeons.	Pharm	Pharmaceutical.	R.O.S.C	Reserve Officers' Sanitary Corps.
M.R.E.	Master of Religious Education.	Pharm.D	Doctor of Pharmacy.		
		Pharm.M	Master of Pharmacy.	R.O.T.C.	Reserve Officers' Training Corps.
M.S. (or M.Sc.)	Master of Science.	Ph.B	Bachelor of Philosophy.		
M.S.F	Master of Science of Forestry.	Ph.C	Pharmaceutical Chemist.	R.P.	Reformed Presbyterian.
M.S.T.	Master of Sacred Theology.	Ph.D	Doctor of Philosophy; Doctor of Pharmacy.	R.R.	Railroad.
Mt	Mount.			R.T.C.	Reserve Training Corps.
Mtn	Mountain.	Ph.G	Graduate in Pharmacy.	Ry	Railway.
Mus	Museum; Musical.	Phila	Philadelphia.		
Mus.B	Bachelor of Music.	Philol	Philological.	s	Son.
Mus.D. (or Mus.Doc.)	Doctor of Music.	Philos	Philosophical.	S	South.
Mus. M	Master of Music.	Photog	Photographic.	S.A.	South America.
Mut	Mutual.	Phys	Physician, Physical.	San	Sanitary.
M.V.M	Massachusetts Volunteer Militia.	Phys. and Surg	Physicians and Surgeons.	S.A.R.	Sons of the Am. Revolution.
		Physiol	Physiological.	S.A.T.C.	Students' Army Training Corps.
M.W.A	Modern Woodmen of America.	P.I.	Philippine Islands.		
		Pl	Place.	Savs	Savings.
Mycol	Mycological.	P.-M.	Paymaster.	S.B. (also B.S. or Sc.B.)	Bachelor of Science.
N	North.	Polit	Political.	S.C.	South Carolina; Sanitary Corps.
N.A	National Academician; North America; National Army.	Poly	Polytechnic.		
		Pomol	Pomological.	Sc.D. (or D.Sc.)	Doctor of Science.
N.A.D	National Academy of Design.	P.Q.	Province of Quebec.	S.C.D	Doctor of Commercial Science.
Nat	National.	P.R.	Porto Rico.	Sch	School.
Nav	Navigation.	Prep	Preparatory.	Sci	Science; Scientific.
N.B.	New Brunswick.	Pres	President.	S.C.V.	Sons of Confederate Veterans.
N.C.	North Carolina.	Presbyn	Presbyterian.	S.C.W	Society of Colonial Wars.
N.D.	North Dakota.	Presdl	Presidential.	S.D	South Dakota.
N.E.	Northeast, also New England.	Prin	Principal.	S.E.	Southeast.
N.E.A.	National Educational Association.	Proc	Proceedings.	Sec	Secretary.
		Prod	Produced (for production of play).	Sect	Section.
Neb	Nebraska.			Seismol	Seismological.
Nev	Nevada.	Prof	Professor.	Sem	Seminary.
N.G.	National Guard	Prog	Progressive.	Sept	September.
N.G.N.Y	National Guard of New York.	Propr	Proprietor.	Sergt	Sergeant.
N.H.	New Hampshire.	Pros. Atty	Prosecuting attorney.	S.I.	Staten Island.
N.J.	New Jersey.	Pro Tem	Pro tempore (for the time being).	S.J.	Society of Jesus (Jesuit).
N.M.	New Mexico.			S.J.D.	Doctor Juristic Science.
				S.M.	Master of Science.

ABBREVIATIONS—Continued

Soc.	Society.	Th.M	Master of Theology.	U.S.N.R.F.	United States Naval Reserve Force.
Sociol	Sociological.	Theol	Theological.	U.S.P.H.S.	United States Public Health Service.
S. of V.	Sons of Veterans.	Topog.	Topographical.		
S.O.R.C.	Signal Officers' Reserve Corps.	Tp. (or Twp.)	Township.	U.S.R.	United States Reserves.
S.O.S.	Service of Supply.	T.P.A.	Travelers' Protective Assn.	U.S.R.C.S.	U.S. Revenue Cutter Service.
Spl.	Special.	Tr.	Training.	U.S.S.R.	Union of Soviet Socialist Republics.
Splty.	Specialty.	Trans	Transactions; Transferred.		
Sq.	Square.	Transl.	Translation, Translations.	U.S.V.	United States Volunteers.
Sr.	Senior.	Treas.	Treasurer; Treasury		
S.R.	Sons of the Revolution.	Twp. (or Tp.)	Township.	V.	vice.
S.R.C.	Signal Reserve Corps.	Ty. (or Ter.)	Territory.	Va.	Virginia.
S.S.	Sunday School, Steamship.	Typog.	Typographical.	Vet.	Veteran; Veterinary.
St.	Saint; Street.			Vice-pres. (or v.p.)	Vice-president.
Sta.	Station.	U.	University.	Vis.	Visiting.
Statis	Statistical.	U.B.	United Brethren in Christ.	Vol.	Volunteer; Volume.
S.T.B.	Bachelor of Sacred Theology.	U.C.T.	United Commercial Travelers.	Vs.	Versus (against).
S.T.D.	Doctor of Sacred Theology.	U.C.V.	United Confederate Veterans.	Vt.	Vermont.
S.T.L.	Licentiate in Sacred Theology; Lector of Sacred Theology.	U.D.C.	United Daughters of the Confederacy.	W.	West.
		Univ.	University.	Wash.	Washington (state).
		U.P.	United Presbyterian; Union Pacific.	W.C.T.U.	Woman's Christian Temperance Union.
Supt.	Superintendent.				
Surg.	Surgical.	Urol.	Urological.	W.D.C.	War Department Citation.
S.W.	Southwest.	U.S.	United States.	W.I.	West Indies.
Symph	Symphony.	U.S.A.	United States Army.	Wis.	Wisconsin.
T. and S.	Trust and Savings.	U.S.C.G.	United States Coast Guard.	W.Va.	West Virginia.
Tech.	Technical; Technology.	U.S.C.T	U.S. Colored Troops.	Wyo.	Wyoming.
Technol.	Technological.	U.S.H.G.	United States Home Guard.		
Temp.	Temporary, Temperance.	U.S.M.C.	United States Marine Corps.	Y.M.C.A.	Young Men's Christian Assn.
Tenn.	Tennessee.	U.S.M.H.S.	United States Marine Hospital Service.	Y.M.H.A.	Young Men's Hebrew Assn.
Ter. (or Ty.)	Territory.			Yrs.	Years.
Tex.	Texas.	U.S.N.	United States Navy.	Y.W.C.A.	Young Women's Christian Association.
T.H. (or H.T.)	Territory of Hawaii.	U.S.N.A.	United States National Army.		
Th.D.	Doctor of Theology.	U.S.N.G.	United States National Guard.	Zoöl.	Zoölogical.

PRINCIPAL RAILWAY ABBREVIATIONS

A.,B.& A. Ry.	Atlanta, Birmingham & Atlantic Ry.	C.,St.P.,M.&O.Ry.	Chicago, St. Paul, Minneapolis & Omaha Ry.	N.,C.& St.L. Ry.	Nashville, Chattanooga & St. Louis Ry.
A.C.L. R.R.	Atlantic Coast Line R.R.	C.Vt. Ry.	Central Vermont Ry.	N.P. Ry.	Northern Pacific Ry.
A.& P. Ry.	Atlantic & Pacific Ry.	C.& W.I. R.R.	Chicago & Western Indiana R.R.	N.& W. Ry.	Norfolk & Western Ry.
A.,T.& S.F. Ry.	Atchison, Topeka & Santa Fe Ry.			N.Y.C.&H.R.R.R.	New York Central & Hudson River R.R.
B.& A. R.R.	Boston & Albany R.R.	D.& H. Co.	Delaware & Hudson Co.	N.Y.C. R.R.	New York Central R.R.
B.& M. R.R.	Boston & Maine R.R.	D.,L.& W. R.R.	Delaware, Lackawanna & Western R.R.	N.Y.,C.&St.L.R.R.	New York, Chicago & St. Louis R. R.
B.& O. R.R. Co.	Baltimore & Ohio R.R. Co.				
B.& O.S.-W. R.R.	Baltimore & Ohio Southwestern R.R.	D.& R.G. R.R. Co.	Denver & Rio Grande R.R. Co.	N.Y.& N.E. Ry.	New York & New England Ry.
B.,R.& P. Ry.	Buffalo, Rochester & Pittsburgh Ry.	G., C.& S.F. Ry.	Gulf, Colorado & Santa Fe Ry.	N.Y.,N.H.& H.R.R.	New York, New Haven & Hartford R.R.
C.& A.R.R.	Chicago & Alton R. R., now Alton Ry. Corpn.	G.,M.& N. R.R.	Gulf, Mobile & Northern R.R.	N.Y.,O.& W. Ry.	New York, Ontario & Western Ry.
C.,B.& Q. Ry. Co	Chicago, Burlington & Quincy Ry. Co.	G. N. Ry.	Great Northern Ry.		
		G.T. Ry.	Grand Trunk Ry.	O.S.L. R.R.	Oregon Short Line R.R.
C.,C.,C.& St.L.Ry.	Cleveland, Cincinnati, Chicago & St. Louis Ry.	G.W. Ry. of Can	Great Western Ry. of Canada.	O.-W.R.R.& N.Co.	Oregon-Washington R. R. & Navigation Co.
C.& E.I. R.R.	Chicago & Eastern Illinois R.R.	H.V. Ry.	Hocking Valley Ry.	Pa. R.R.	Pennsylvania R.R.
		I.C. R.R.	Illinois Central R.R.	Penna. Co.	Pennsylvania R. R. Co.
C.& G.T.Ry.	Chicago & Grand Trunk Ry.	I.G.N. R.R.	International Great Northern R.R.	P.& L. E.R.R.	Pittsburgh & Lake Erie R.R.
C.G.W. Ry.	Chicago Great Western Ry.			P.,C.,C.& St.L. R.R.	Pittsburgh, Cincinnati, Chicago & St. Louis R.R.
C.,H.& D. Ry.	Cincinnati, Hamilton & Dayton Ry.	K.C.S. Ry.	Kansas City Southern Ry.	P.M. R.R.	Pere Marquette R.R.
C.,I.& L. Ry.	Chicago, Indianapolis & Louisville Ry.	L.A.& S.L. R.R.	Los Angeles & Salt Lake R.R.	P.& R. Ry.	Philadelphia & Reading Ry.
C., M.& St.P.Ry.	Chicago, Milwaukee & St. Paul Ry.	L.E.& W. R.R.	Lake Erie & Western R.R.	S.A.L. Ry.	Seaboard Air Line Ry.
		L.I. R.R.	Long Island R.R.	St.L.& S.F. R.R.	St. Louis & San Francisco R.R.
C.& N.P. R.R.	Chicago & Northern Pacific R.R.	L.& N. R.R.	Louisville & Nashville R.R.	S.P. Co.	Southern Pacific Co.
C.N. Ry.	Canadian Northern Ry.	L.S.& M.S. Ry.	Lake Shore & Michigan Southern Ry.		
C.& N.-W. Ry.	Chicago & Northwestern Ry.	L.V. R.R.	Lehigh Valley R.R.	T.& P. Ry.	Texas & Pacific Ry. Co.
C. of Ga. Ry.	Central of Georgia Ry.			U.P. R.R.	Union Pacific R.R.
C.& O. Ry.	Chesapeake & Ohio Ry.	M.C. R.R.	Michigan Central R.R.	W.& L. E. Ry.	Wheeling & Lake Erie Ry.
C.P. Ry.	Canadian Pacific Ry.	M., K.& T. Ry.	Missouri, Kansas & Texas Ry.	W.C. Ry.	Wisconsin Central Ry.
C.,R.I.& P. Ry.	Chicago, Rock Island & Pacific Ry.	M.& O. R.R.	Mobile & Ohio R.R.	W.P.R.R. Co.	Western Pacific R.R.Co.
		Mo.P. Ry.	Missouri Pacific Ry. (now Missouri Pacific R.R.)	W.S. R.R.	West Shore R.R.
C.R.R. of N.J.	Central Railroad of New Jersey.	M.& St.L. R.R.	Minneapolis & St. Louis R.R.		
C.& S. Ry. Co.	Colorado & Southern Ry. Co.	M.,St.P.& S.S.M. Ry.	Minneapolis, St. Paul & Sault Ste. Marie Ry.	Y.& M.V. R.R.	Yazoo & Mississippi Valley R.R.

ADDENDA

Received Too Late for Insertion in Regular Order in the Body of the Book.

CARR, John Robert, Christian Science lecturer; b. Durham, N.C., July 7, 1878; s. Dr. Albert Gallatin and Annie (Parrish) C.; student Homer Mil. Sch., Oxford, N.C., 1893-95; A.B., U. of N.C., 1900; M.D., Johns Hopkins, 1904; grad. work, U. of Heidelberg, Germany, and Vienna, 1906-07; m. Florence Lee Heitter, Oct. 12, 1914. Interne and asst. resident surgeon Johns Hopkins Hosp., 1900-04; later resident physician and surgeon Union Protestant Infirmary, Baltimore; now Christian Science practitioner; mem. Bd. of Lectureship of First Ch. of Christ, Scientists, Boston. Mem. Phithotomy Med. Soc., Order of Gimghoul, Phi Beta Kappa, Zeta Psi. Democrat. Contbr. to church pubis. Home: Greene Manor Apts., Germantown, Philadelphia, Pa. Office: 726 Integrity Bldg., Philadelphia, Pa.

CHEEK, Leslie, Jr., museum dir.; b. Nashville, Tenn., Oct. 28, 1908; s. Leslie and Mabel (Wood) C.; S.B., Harvard, 1931; B.F.A., Yale U., Dept. Architecture, 1935; m. Mary Tyler Freeman, June 3, 1939. Naval science instr., Culver Mil. Acad., summer, 1929; stage designer University Players, Cape Cod, summer, 1930; instr. art history, Lake Forest Acad. of Architecture and Landscape Architecture, summer, 1931; instr. architecture, Coll. of William & Mary, 1935-36, asst. prof., 1936-37, head Dept. Fine Arts, 1937-38; dir. Baltimore Museum of Art since 1939. Mem. accessions com. Va. Museum of Art, Richmond, and State of Va. Art Commn. Mem. Am. Assn. Univ. Profs., Phi Beta Kappa, Pi Eta, Speakers' Club, Hasty Pudding, Iktinos Soc. Club: Gibson Island (Md.). Contbr. to mag. of Art. Home: 3908 N. Charles St. Address: Baltimore Museum of Art, Baltimore, Md.

CIOTTI, Hector Joseph, lawyer; b. Baltimore, Md., Jan. 22, 1898; s. Andrew and Agnes (Vincenti) C.; A.B., Loyola Coll., Baltimore, 1919, M.A., 1922; LL.B., U. of Baltimore, 1927; spl. courses Georgetown and Johns Hopkins univs., 1918; m. Priscilla J. Ciupinska, June 4, 1924; children—Agnes, Priscilla Ann. Sec. and dir. Guaranty Co. of Md., 1922-25; treas. and dir. Cambridge Apts. Co., 1925-27; admitted to Maryland bar, 1927; asst. gen. counsel Md. Casualty Co., 1927-31; asst. solicitor Baltimore City since 1931; official rep. Baltimore City, visiting 14 countries and participating in trial of cases in courts of Poland, Lithuania and Russia, 1935; also admitted to practice before U.S. Supreme Ct., U.S. Bd. of Tax Appeals and all state and federal cts. in Md.; prof. law, U. of Baltimore, since 1936. Dir. Frank L. Wight Distilling Co., Ashburton Improvement Assn. Pres. and dir. St. Leo's Italian Orphan Asylum. Mem. Real Estate Board of Baltimore, Am. Bar Assn., Baltimore Bar Assn.; comdr. and organizer Italian Post of Baltimore No. 106 of Am. Legion, also past judge advocate for dept. of Md. Democrat. Mem. K.C. Club: University (Baltimore). Home: 3501 Rosedale Rd., Ashburton, Baltimore. Office: 309 Court House, Baltimore, Md.

GIBSON, Robert Murray, judge; b. Duncansville, Pa., Aug. 20, 1869; s. William James (D.D.) and Elizabeth (Murray) G.; student Pa. State Coll.; A.B., Washington and Jefferson Coll., 1889; m. Lorena G. Core, Oct. 4, 1897. U.S. dist. judge, Western Dist. of Pa., by apptmt. of President Harding, since July 29, 1922. Republican. Presbyn. Mason. Home: 6101 Stanton Av. Address: Federal Bldg., Pittsburgh, Pa.

HEPBURN, Joseph Samuel, chemist; b. Phila., Pa., Aug. 25, 1885; s. Samuel Martin and Mary Minor Weight (Danenhower) H.; A.B., Central High Sch. of Phila., 1903, A.M., 1908; B.S. in Chemistry, U. of Pa. 1907, M.S., 1907; Ph.D., Columbia U., 1913; M.D., Hahnemann Med. Coll. and Hosp. of Phila., 1934; unmarried. Scientific asst. Food Research Lab., Bur. of Chemistry, U.S. Dept. Agr., 1907-08, asst. chemist, 1908-12 and 1913-20; fellow in biol. chemistry, Columbia, 1912-13; instr. chemistry Hahnemann Med. Coll. and Hosp. of Phila., 1920-22, lecturer, 1922-25, asso. prof., 1925-39, prof. since 1939; research asso. in gastroenterology since 1937; cons. biol. chemist Broad Street Hosp.; in charge basal metabolism and sec. of staff Women's Homeopathic Hosp. Sec., treas. and mgr. Hahnemann Research Foundation; historian, master of archives and mgr. Associated Alumni Central High Sch.; mgr. Evang. Edn. Soc. of P.E. Ch. Mem. Am. Chem. Soc. (councilor 1925), Am. Soc. Biol. Chemists, Pa. Chem. Soc. (gov.), Acad. Natural Sciences of Phila., Physiol. Soc. of Phila., Franklin Inst. (sec. sect. physics and chemistry 1909-23; mem. com. on science and the arts in charge of medal awards since 1919), Sigma Xi, Pi Upsilon Rho, City Hist. Soc. of Phila. (pres. and dir.); fellow Nat. Gastroenterological Assn.; hon. asso. mem. Am. Inst. Homeopathy. Awarded Longstreth medal, 1911, certificate of Merit, 1921, both from Franklin Inst. Republican. Episcopalian (accounting warden and vestryman St. John's Ch., North Liberties). Co-author (with Wm. A. Pearson) : Physiological and Clinical Chemistry, 1925, 2d edit., 1938. Author or co-author 110 papers in scientific and med. jours. and govt. documents. Home: 2045 N. Franklin St. Office: 235 N. 15th St., Philadelphia, Pa.

HUBBARD, Thomas Foy, civil engr.; b. Baltimore, Md., Sept. 14, 1898; s. Thomas Matthew and Mary Ann (Plummer) H.; student Baltimore Poly. Inst., 1912-16; B.E., Johns Hopkins U., 1921; m. Rose Elizabeth Hicks, Nov. 26, 1924; children—Thomas Hicks, John Gardner, James Hugh. Instr., Rock Hall High School, 1917; private, S.A.T.C., 1918; field engr., Baltimore City Water Dept., 1921-22; bldg. supt., Public Improvement Commn., 1923; instr., Forest Park High School, 1924; instr., Johns Hopkins U., 1925-32; asso. in civil engring. since 1932. Coincident with above; sec. Johns Hopkins Alumni Assn., 1926-36; engr. Pa. State Highway Commn., 1926; struct. engr. with H. G. Perring, 1929-32; exec. sec. Md. State Planning Com., 1934-38; asso. consultant, Nat. Resources Com., since 1934. Methodist. Member, Masons, Tau Beta Pi, Sigma Xi, Am. Soc. Planning Officials; asso. mem. Am. Soc. Civil Engineers. Clubs: Engineers (Baltimore), Johns Hopkins, Miles River Yacht (St. Michaels, Md.). Home: 3324 Ellerslie Av., Baltimore, Md.

LEWIN, John Henry, lawyer; b. Parkton, Md., May 13, 1898; s. Frank Parr and Corinne (Hooper) L.; grad. Tome Sch. for Boys, Port Deposit, Md., 1916; A.B., Johns Hopkins, 1920; LL.B., cum laude, Harvard, 1923; m. Janet Gordon Keidel, Feb. 11, 1938; 1 son, John Henry. Admitted to Md. bar, 1923, also bar Court of Appeals of Md. and U.S. Supreme Court; asso. with Hershey, Machen, Donaldson & Williams, Baltimore, 1923-25, Armstrong, Machen & Allen, 1925-33; lecturer, Law Sch. U. of Baltimore; asst. city solicitor for Baltimore, 1925-27; peoples counsel before Md. Pub. Service Commn., 1929-33; chief trial and enforcement sects., A.A.A., 1933-35; acting gen. counsel, Federal Security Agency, 1939; spl. asst. to U.S. atty. gen. since 1935. Served in S.A.T.C., 1918. Mem. Am., Md. and Baltimore bar assns., Am. Law Inst., S.A.R., Cum Laude Soc. of Tome Inst., Alpha Delta Phi, Omicron Delta Kappa. Democrat. Episcopalian. Clubs: Bachelor's Cotillion, Wranglers Law (Baltimore), L'hirondelle (Ruxton, Md.). Home: 1114 St. Paul St., Baltimore, Md. Office: Dept. of Justice, Washington, D.C.

MACFARLANE, Catharine, M.D.; b. Phila., Pa., Apr. 7, 1877; d. John J. and Nettie Ottinger (Huston) Macfarlane; student U. of Pa., 1893-95; M.D., Woman's Med. Coll. of Pa., 1898; unmarried. Interne Woman's Hosp., Phila., 1898-99; private practice, Phila. since 1899; instr. in obstetrics, Woman's Med. Coll., 1899-1900, prof. of gynecology since 1922; gynecologist Woman's Hosp., Phila., 1908-38; gynecologist in chief Woman's Med. Coll. Hosp. since 1922; gynecologist and obstetrician Phila. Gen. Hosp. since 1922. Awarded grant by A.M.A. for research on value of early examination for cancer, 1938, 39. Fellow Am. Coll. Surgeons, Coll. of Physicians of Phila. (1st woman mem.); mem. A.M.A., Pa. State Med. Soc., Phila. County Med. Soc., Am. Med. Women's Assn., Med. Women's Internat. Assn., Am. Assn. Univ. Women. Republican. Presbyn. Clubs: Women's University, Cosmopolitan (Phila.). Author: Textbook of Gynecology for Nurses, 1908. Home: 5808 Greene St. Office: 701 Medical Arts Bldg., Philadelphia, Pa.

MURPHY, Ray Dickinson, life ins.; b. Springfield, Mass., Feb. 28, 1887; s. William Henry and Lida Coreille (Sibley) M.; A.B., Harvard, 1908; m. Elizabeth Chapin, June 24, 1911; children—Chapin Taylor (dec.), Lambert (dec.), Elizabeth Coreille, Ray Bradford. Actuary Mass. Mutual Life Ins. Co., 1908-10, Hartford Life Ins. Co., 1910-13; with Equitable Life Assurance Soc. since 1913, beginning as asst. actuary, later asso. actuary and 2d v.p., v.p. and actuary since 1936. Pres. Council of Social Agencies, Montclair, N.J., 1938-40; trustee Montclair Convalescent Home, Montclair Art Museum; formerly trustee Montclair Community Chest. Mem. Actuarial Soc. of America (pres. 1938-40), Phi Beta Kappa, Pi Eta Club. Republican. Conglist. Clubs: Harvard (New York); Faculty (Cambridge, Mass.); Upper Montclair (N.J.) Country. Author (with P. C. H. Papps): Construction of Mortality Tables from the Records of Insured Lives (textbook), 1922. Contbr. to Transactions of Actuarial Soc. of America. Home: 28 Godfrey Rd., Upper Montclair, N.J. Office: 393 Seventh Av., New York, N.Y.

RODGERS, Decatur Hedges, judge; b. Taxahaw, S.C., Aug. 13, 1890; s. James Farnsworth and Mary Beall (Hedges) R.; A.B., Ogden Coll., Bowling Green, Ky., 1910; LL.B., U. of Va., 1913; m. Annie Leitch Lancaster, Aug. 24, 1917; children—Decatur Hedges, Nathan Lancaster, James Beall, William Leitch, Mary Ann. Adj. prof. of mathematics, Ogden Coll., 1909-10;

admitted to bar of W. Va. and Federal courts, 1913; instr. in law, U. of W.Va., 1912-13; asst. pros. atty., Berkeley County, W.Va., 1921-25; apptd. judge 23d Judicial Circuit, W.Va., 1925, for term 1925-26, elected, 1926, and re-elected 1928, 1936. Organizer Berkeley County Council Boy Scouts and pres., 1930-35; v.p. Shenandoah Valley Council Boy Scouts, 1933-35; mem. Employment Com. for W.Va., 1930; W.Va. del. to Nat. Conf. Social Work, Minneapolis, 1931, Phila., 1932; mem. Berkeley County Welfare Bd., 1932-35; mem. Re-employment Com. for Berkeley County, 1933-34; W.Va. del. to Washington White House Conf., 1933, White House Conf. on Child Welfare, 1934; mem. Berkeley County advisory com. of Nat. Youth Adminstrn., 1935; mem. com. on edn. and training W.Va. Conf. of Social Workers, 1938-39; pres. Berkeley County Commn. for Jewish Relief, 1939. Awarded Silver Beaver, Boy Scouts of America. Served in O.T.C., Camp Lee, during World War. Mem. W.Va. Bar Assn., W. Va. Judicial Assn. (v.p. 1939), Order of Coif, Raven Soc., Phi Alpha Delta. Republican. Presbyterian (trustee). Mason. Club: Rotary (Martinsburg, W.Va.). Home: 1025 W. King St., Martinsburg, W.Va.

WILSON, William Bruce, clergyman; b. Baltimore, Md., Nov. 5, 1901; s. John B. and Bessie Armitage (Bruce) W.; A.B., Muskingum Coll., New Concord, O., 1921, D.D., 1937; Th.M., Xenia Theol. Sem., St. Louis, Mo., 1924; grad. student, Washington U., 1922-24, U. of Pittsburgh, 1925-26; m. Jane Allison, of Ford City, Pa., June 17, 1924; 1 son, James Allison. Ordained to ministry United Presbyn. Ch., May 10, 1924; pastor Chartiers U.P. Ch., Pittsburgh, Pa., 1924-27, Coraopolis (Pa.) U.P. Ch., 1927-37; asso. sec. Bd. Am. Missions of U.P. Ch., 1937-38, gen. sec. since 1938. Mem. Home Missions Council, Tau Kappa Alpha. Republican. Contbr. to religious jours. Home: 325 Clearview Av., Crafton, Pittsburgh, Pa. Office: Publication Bldg., 9th St., Pittsburgh, Pa.

BIOGRAPHIES

An asterisk (*) following a sketch indicates that it could not be verified.

A

AARON, Marcus, mfr.; b. Pittsburgh, Pa., Dec. 14, 1869; s. Louis I. and Mina (Lippman) A.; ed. prep. dept. Western U. of Pa.; matriculated in the Univ. and left soon afterwards on account of illness; LL.D., U. of Pittsburgh, 1924; m. Stella Hamburger, Nov. 23, 1898; children—Marcus Lester, Fannie Hamburger. Pres. Homer Laughlin China Co., mfrs. semi-vitreous tableware; pres. Newell Co., Newell Bridge & Ry. Co. (Newell, W. Va.). Mem. Bd. of Public Edn., Pittsburgh, since 1911, pres. since 1922; mem. State Bd. of Edn. of Pa., 1916-21; mem. State Council of Edn., 1921-23; trustee Carnegie Inst., Carnegie Inst. Tech., Carnegie Library. Mem. bd. Union of Am. Hebrew Congregations; trustee Jewish Publ. Soc.; pres. Rodef Shalom Congregation, Pittsburgh, since 1930. Republican. Home: 5564 Aylesboro Av. Office: Union Trust Bldg., Pittsburgh, Pa.

AARON, Sister Mary Cyril, coll. dean; b. Clarion, Pa.; d. Thomas Ledwith and Suzanne (Burgoon) A.; A.B., Seton Hill Coll., Greensburg, Pa., 1924; M.A., Fordham U. N. Y., 1925; summer school student Notre Dame U. 1921, 1922, Columbia U., 1929-'31, U. of Pittsburgh, 1930-'33. Secondary school teacher, public schools, Clarion Co., Pa., 1908-10; entered religious order of Sisters of Charity, 1910; secondary school teacher, parochial schools, Pittsburgh, 1910-12; with Seton Hill Coll., Greensburg, Pa., since 1924, as asso. prof. of psychology and logic, 1924-25, asso. prof. of edn., since 1925, dean since 1929. Dir. Seton Hill Coll. Alumnae Corpn. Mem. Nat. Cath. Edn. Assn. (eastern regional rep.), Nat. Assn. of Deans of Women (mem. social com.), Sisters of Charity of Greensburg, Pa. Republican. Catholic. Address: Seton Hill Coll., Greensburg, Pa.

AARONSON, Robert Howard, Jr., insurance; b. Bordentown, N. J., Jan. 15, 1902; s. R. Howard and Ada Estelle (Wells) A.; B.S., Princeton U., 1923; LL.B., S. Jersey Law Sch., Camden, N. J., 1930; m. Margaretta Harrison, Oct. 14, 1933; 1 dau., Susan Grundy. Began as clk. in ins. office, 1923; mem. firm R. H. Aaronson & Son, 1928-37, propr. of bus. since 1937; sec. and treas. Penn Producing Co., cranberry growers; dir. Bordentown Banking Co., Bordentown Bldg. & Loan Assn. Served as sec.-treas. Bordentown Bus. Assn.; Chamber of Commerce, both since 1931. Mem. Bordentown Police Pension Commn. and sec. since 1938. Trustee Bordentown Library Assn., First Bapt. Ch. of Bordentown. Mem. Nat., N.J. State and Burlington Co. assns. of ins. agts. Independent Republican. Baptist. Mason (32°, Shriner). Clubs: Yapewi Aquatic (Bordentown); Gateway (Princeton) Princeton (Trenton); Sunnybrae Golf (Yardville); Forsgate Country (Jamesburg) Home: 20 Prince St. Office: 205 Farnsworth Av., Bordentown, N.J.

ABBETT, Leon; chmn. of bd. and pres. Am. Business Shares, Inc. Address: 1 Exchange Place, Hoboken, N.J.

ABBOTT, Alfred Theodore, manufacturer; b. Phila., Pa., July 28, 1880; s. Theodore and Alvina Ro (Sewig) A.; ed. pub. schs. and Drexel Inst. Tech.; m. Ethel Wegefarth, April 3, 1913 (died 1932). Pres. A. Theo. Abbott & Co., mfrs. of decorative fabrics; pres. Abbott Mfg. Co. Mem. Rice Leaders of the World. Republican. Presbyterian. Mason. Clubs: Union League (Phila.), Whitemarsh Valley Country (Chestnut Hill). Inventor: Sunpruf Kapock decorative fabrics, radio grille cloth, Aquapruf treatment for decorative fabrics, Eezee-Rack for decorative displays. Home: Kenilworth, Philadelphia. Office: 23d and Allegheny Av., Philadelphia, Pa.

ABBOTT, Edwin Milton, lawyer; b. Phila., Pa., June 4, 1877; s. Theodore and Alvina A.; prep. edn. Central High Sch., Phila.; LL.B., U. of Pa., 1896, hon. N.Ph.D.; m. Florence H. Wilson, Nov. 9, 1905; children—Emilie Ferry (Mrs. Fred Ella), T. H. Wilson. Admitted to Pa. bar, 1896; has served as counsel in 138 homicide cases and many criminal and civil suits; chief counsel in fight of commuters in and about Phila. against the railroads; mem. Pa. Ho. of Rep., 1911-12; chmn. Commn. on Revision of Criminal Laws, State of Pa., 1912-15, 1917-25; minority nominee for judge of Court of Common Pleas, 1913. Apptd. spl. asst. city solicitor, Feb. 1924, and assigned as spl. counsel to Gen. Smedley D. Butler, dir. of Pub. Safety, prosecuted over 600 padlock cases successfully; atty. Dept. of Justice of Pa., assigned to Banking Dept., 1931-35; apptd. spl. counsel Dept. of Pub. Safety, Phila., Feb. 1936; counsel for Director Pub. Safety Elliott; gen. counsel for Sesqui-centennial; counsel for Boys' Week Council (chmn. Safety First Com.); dir. Allied Youth. Pres. Oak Lane Park Improvement Assn. During World War organized first Home Defense League in America; govt. appeal agt.; chmn. Legal Advisory Bd.; Pres. Pa. Branch Civil Legion. Mem. Am. Bar Assn. (vice chmn. sect. on criminal justice and law enforcement), Am. Inst. Criminal Law and Criminology (sec. 10 yrs.), Pa. State Bar Assn. (chmn. com. on criminal law 8 yrs.), Phila. Bar Assn., Hist. Soc. of Pa., Law Acad., Poet Laureate League. Presbyn. (deacon). Mason (32°, Shriner), Artisan; mem. Knights of Malta. Clubs: Lawyers' (dir.); Manufacturers and Bankers, Century Veterans, Sagamore, Shrine, Varsity Athletic, Skytop, Old York Road Country, Veteran Athletes. Author: Thoughts in Verse, 1922; The Law and Religion, 1938. Contbr. poems, lyrics, legal articles and articles on law enforcement; wrote words and music of "Alma Mater Red and Blue" (U. of Pa. song); poems have appeared in many anthologies. Home: 708 64th Av., Oak Lane Park, Phila. Office: 926 Land Title Bldg., Philadelphia, Pa.

ABBOTT, Fred Walter, civil engr.; b. Chicago, Ill., Nov. 20, 1872; s. Arthur Augustin and Ella Maria (Heffron) A.; ed. public and private schools, Chicago, Ill.; m. Blandina Sealella, June 29, 1932. With Sax & Abbott, Phila., civil engrs., 1898-1914; cons. engr. Horace Trumbauer, Phila., architect, 1914-18; asst. gen. mgr. Chester Shipbuilding Co., Chester, Pa., 1918-20; cons. engr. Ritter & Shay, Phila., architects, 1920-32; engr. Publicker Commercial Alcohol Co. and subsidiary cos., Phila., Pa., since 1932, chief engr. since 1937. Life mem. Am. Soc. Civil Engrs., Art Alliance, Phila. Mason. Home: 407 Westview Av. Office: 1800 W. Lehigh Av., Philadelphia, Pa.

ABEL, R. L.; prof. petroleum refinery, U. of Pittsburgh Sch. of Mines. Address: U. of Pittsburgh, Pa.

ABELL, Frank Dale; pres. First Nat. Bank of Morristown. Address: Morristown, N.J.

ABELL, Richard Gurley, instr. anatomy; b. Phila., Pa., Jan. 24, 1904; s. Edward Walter and Bertha Maria (Halsey) A.; A.B., Swarthmore Coll., 1926; A.M., U. of Pa., 1930, Ph.D., same, 1934; m. Ellen Degray Yerzley, April 9, 1928; 1 dau., Margaret Lessing (b. Swarthmore, Pa., March 27, 1932). Engaged as instr, zoology, U. of Pa., 1928-30; fellow in anatomy, Med. Sch., U. of Pa., 1930-36; instr. in anatomy, Med. Sch., U. of Pa. since 1936. Mem. Am. Assn. Anatomists, Physiol. Soc. of Phila., Sigma Xi. Awarded John Lockwood Memorial Fellowship by Swarthmore Coll., 1932-33; awarded prize for research by U. of Pa. Chapter Sigma Xi, 1936. Mem. Religious Soc. Friends. Contbr. research articles to anat., physiol. and med. jours. Home: The Croydon, 241 S. 49th St., Philadelphia, Pa.

ABERCROMBIE, Ronald Taylor, physician; b. Baltimore, Md., Jan. 19, 1879; s. John (Morrison) and Elizabeth Sarah (Daniel) A.; student Maupins Prep. Sch., 1896-97; A.B., Johns Hopkins, 1901, M.D. 1905; m. Jennie Scott Waters, Nov. 21, 1906; children—Francis Waters (dec.), Margaret Waters (Mrs. Arthur L. Nelson), Katharine Gordon (Mrs. McCord Sollenberger). Dir. of physical edn., Johns Hopkins, 1905; resident physician, Church Home and Infirmary, 1905, 06; physician in charge, Christ Church Dispensary, 1907-12; dispensary surgeon, Johns Hopkins Hosp., 1906-26; instr., bacteriology and pharmacology, Woman's Med. Sch., 1907-09; coroner at large, Baltimore, Md., 1908-12; instr., school hygiene, Johns Hopkins, summers 1911, 12; associated with a brother, David T. Abercrombie, founder of Abercrombie & Fitch, sporting goods, New York, since 1896. Organized first student military unit at Johns Hopkins in 1916, later a unit of R.O.T.C.; contract surgeon Med. Corps, U.S. Army, 1918. Mem. A.M.A., A.A.A.S., Am. Pub. Health Assn., Med. and Chirurg. Faculty of Md., Baltimore City Med. Soc., Md. and Va. Hist. Socs., Municipal Art Soc., Phi Gamma Delta. Democrat. Presbyterian. Clubs: Maryland, Elkridge, Johns Hopkins, St. Andrew's Soc. (Baltimore, Md.); Wianno (Osterville, Mass.); Home: 10 Whitfield Rd. Office: Johns Hopkins Univ., Baltimore, Md.

ABERLE, Gustave Carl, hosiery mfg.; b. Phila., Pa., Dec. 24, 1889; s. Fredrick C. and Margret (Fox) A.; student U. of Pa, 1908-12; m. Emily Rebecca Brown, of Germantown, Phila.,

Mar. 28, 1932; 1 son, Gustave Carl; children of wife by former marriage—Evelyn (Mrs. Robert Haag), Frank Aberle, Emily Aberle. Began as apprentice in hosiery mill, 1913, treas. H. C. Aberle Co., 1934-38, vice-pres., 1932-38, pres. and sole owner Aberle Inc. since 1938. Served as sergt. World War. Dir. Osteopathic Hosp. Republican. Episcopalian. Mason (32°). Club: Huntington Valley Country. Home: Washington Lane, Jenkintown, Pa. Office: A & Lippincott Sts., Philadelphia, Pa.

ABERLE, Harry C., pres. H. C. Aberle Co.; b. Phila., Pa., Apr. 7, 1876; s. Frederick and Amanda (Reinhardt) A.; student Pierce Sch., Phila., and Phila. Textile Sch.; m. Mabel Lizbeth Price (dec.); children—Harry, Betty; m. 2d, Ruth Carlotta Greene, Aug. 23, 1926; children—John, Carl, Dick. Formerly v.p. Fidelity Knitting Mills; treas. 1574-36 Market St. Corpn.; now pres. H. C. Aberle Co., Phila.; dir. Ninth Bank and Trust Co., 1616 Walnut St. Realty Corpn., Greensboro Full Fashioned Hosiery Co. Mason. Club: Union League (Phila.). Home: White Hall, Lenox Rd., Jenkintown, Pa. Office: Clearfield, Lippincott, Water and B Sts., Philadelphia, Pa.

ABERLY, John, clergyman, educator; b. Albrightsville, Pa., Sept. 18, 1867; s. John and Catharine (Oberkercher) A.; grad. Fairview Acad., Brodheadsville, Pa., 1884; A.B., Gettysburg (Pa.) Coll., 1888, A.M., 1891, D.D., 1905, LL.D., 1936; m. Alice Strauss, 1889; children—Amy Strauss (Mrs. R. M. Dunkelberger), Frederick Heyer. Ordained ministry Luth. Ch., 1890; missionary in India, 1889-1923; in charge Theol. Training Instn., Guntur, India; pres. Luth. Mission 8 yrs. and mem. Nat Missionary Council of India, Burma and Ceylon 10 yrs.; prof. missions, Luth. Theol. Sem., Maywood, Ill., 1923-26; pres. Luth. Theol. Sem., Gettysburg, since 1926, also prof. systematic theology. Mem. Phi Beta Kappa. Author: Bible Biographies, 1910; Commentary on Romans, Madras, India, 1912; Commentaries on the Prophets, 1917; Life of Christ, 1921; Telugu Bible Dictionary, 1923—all in Telugu. Address: Theological Seminary, Gettysburg, Pa.*

ABERSOLD, George William; mem. staff Ohio Valley Gen. and Wheeling hosps. Address: 36 14th St., Wheeling, W. Va.

ABERSOLD, John Russell, univ. prof.; b. Pittsburgh, Pa., June 4, 1902; s. John Henry and Mary (Mack) A.; A.B., U. of Pa., 1922, LL.B., Law Sch., 1925, M.A., 1929, Ph.D., 1931; m. Ruby Lou McFadden, Dec. 22, 1926. Instr. in business law, Wharton Sch., U. of Pa., 1925-37, asso. prof. since 1937. Mem. Theta Xi. Republican. Presbyterian. Mason. Club: Cynwyd (Cynwyd, Pa.). Author: A Survey of Commercial Arbitration in Pa., 1927. Co-author: A Statistical Study of Civil Litigation in the Philadelphia Courts, 1932; Studies in Judicial Administration, 1933; Bankruptcy Administration and Proposed Remedies, 1933. Home: 5 W. Windemere Terrace, Lansdowne, Pa. Office: 404 Logan Hall, Univ. of Pennsylvania, Philadelphia, Pa.

ABESHOUSE, Benjamin Samuel, surgeon, urologist; b. New Haven, Conn., Feb. 7, 1901; s. Abraham and Ida (Golden) A.; grad. New Haven High Sch., 1918; Ph.B. cum laude, Yale (Sheffield Scientific Sch.), 1921; M.D., Yale Med. Sch., 1924; m. Carolyn M. Kehrman, June 19, 1927; children—Ellen Ruth, George Alan, Jane Carol. Interne Sinai Hosp., Baltimore, 1924-25, asst. surgeon, 1925-26, surgical resident, 1926-27; associated in private practice with Dr. A. E. Goldstein, Baltimore, 1927-30; in practice limited to genito-urinary diseases, Baltimore, since 1930; instr. genito-urinary pathology, U. of Md. Med. Sch., since 1927. Mem. Baltimore Med. Soc., Medico-Chirurg. Faculty of Md., A.M.A., Am. Urol. Assn., Am. Neisserian Assn., Phi Alpha. Democrat. Mem. Reform Jewish Temple. Author: Genito-Urinary Diseases in Famous People (or Troubled Waters), 1939. Contbr. over 40 articles to med. jours. Home: 5601 South Bend Rd. Office: 100 W. Monument St., Baltimore, Md.

ABRAHAM, James William, retired coal and coke operator; b. Fayette Co., Pa., Oct. 15, 1866; s. Aaron Jones and Eliza (Jackson) A.; ed. Georges Creek Acad., Fayette Co., Pa.; m. Juliet Conner, Oct. 14, 1903; children—Evelyn (Mrs. Francis C. Benson), Mary Louise, Jean (Mrs. Joseph C. Burwell), James E., Juliet (Mrs. Allan B. Williams). Employed in store and then with H. C. Frick Coke Co. as store mgr., 1887-1901; organized Newcomer Coke Co., 1902; pres. and gen. mgr. South Fayette Coke, 1904, Banning-Connellsville Coke Co., Wineland-Gilmore Coal & Coke Co., Mapletown Coal Co., Producers Coke Co.; vice-pres. and dir. Nat. Bank of Fayette Co., 1929-32; now vice-pres. Fayette Title & Trust Bldg. Corpn.; pres. Carter Ice Cream Co. Served as pres. Uniontown Sch. Bd., 1912-16; pres. Fort Necessity Chapter S.A.R., 1932-33; chmn. Fort Necessity Memorial Park, 1932-35. Pres. Uniontown Hosp. Assn.; vice-pres. Library Assn. Republican. Protestant. Mason (32°, Shriner). Club: Uniontown Country (charter mem.). Home: 50 W. Main St., Uniontown, Pa.

ABRAHAM, Paul James, lawyer; b. Smithfield, Fayette Co., Pa., Aug. 8, 1887; s. James W. and Emma (Core) A.; student California (Pa.) State Teachers Coll.; B.S., Bucknell U., 1910, A.M., 1913; LL.B., U. of Pittsburgh, 1913; m. Caroline Lauffer, Sept. 8, 1923; 1 dau., Caroline Lauffer. Teacher rural schs., Fayette Co., Pa., 1903-04; prin. Seventh Ward Sch., Greensburg, Pa., 1910-11; instr. in English, Carnegie Inst. Tech., Pittsburgh, 1911-13; admitted to Pa. bar, 1914, and since in gen. practice of law, Greensburg; solicitor for county controller of Westmoreland Co., Pa., 1928-36; dir. and sec. Keystone Laundry, Greensburg, since 1924. Served as 1st lt. 60th Inf., 5 Div., U.S. Army, with A.E.F. 1917-19. Decorated with Verdun medal and Silver Star medal, 9th Inf. Brigade, Fifth Div. Mem. exec. com. Westmoreland-Fayette Council, Boy Scouts America; interested in Y.M.C.A. and Salvation Army. Mem. Am. Legion (chmn. com. on Scouting; chmn. Boy Scout com. Dept. of Pa.), Delta Sigma. Republican. Methodist. Mason (32°, Shriner). Clubs: Rotary, Greensburg Country. Home: 536 N. Maple Av. Office: Safe Deposit and Trust Bldg., Greensburg, Pa.

ABRAHAMS, Robert David, lawyer, writer; b. Phila., Pa., Sept. 24, 1905; s. William and Anne (David) A.; LL.B., Dickinson Sch. of Law, 1925; m. Florence Kohn, Nov. 21, 1929; children—Richard Irving, Roger David, Marjorie. Admitted to Pa. bar, 1925; sec. to commr. gen. to Europe for Sesqui-Centennial Expn., 1925; asst. city solicitor, 1927-32; editor The Independent (weekly), 1932; consul at Phila. for Dominican Republic since 1931; asst. chief counsel Legal Aid Soc. of Phila. since 1933. Dir. Community Health Center. Mem. Nat. Lawyers Guild (dir. Phila. Chapter), Phila. and Pa. bar assns., Tau Epsilon Rho. Ind. Democrat. Jewish religion. Mason. Clubs: Philmont Country, Phila. Consular. Author: Come Forward (verse), 1928; New Tavern Tales (Fiction), 1930; The Pot Bellied Gods (verse), 1932; Handbook of Pennsylvania Collection Practice (legal, M. J. Meyer, co-author), 1931. Contbr. verse and prose to Saturday Evening Post, Esquire, Ken, Judge and other nat. mags. since 1937; contbr. to law jours. Home: 6340 N. 7th St. Office: 700 Bankers Securities Bldg., Philadelphia, Pa.

ABRAMS, Dorothy A., librarian; b. Wells, N.Y.; d. William Lee and Ruby (Morrison) A.; grad. Gloversville (N.Y.) High Sch., 1914; B.S., Kansas State Teachers Coll., 1919; certificate New York State Library, 1921; M.A., Teachers Coll., Columbia U., 1934. Reference asst., Kansas State Teachers Coll., 1919-20, U. of N.D., 1921-23; asst. librarian Emporia (Kan.) Public Library, 1923-24; librarian Paterson (N.J.) State Teachers Coll. since Sept. 1925; instr. summer library sch., Ocean City, N.J., summers, 1927-31, Trenton State Teachers Coll., summers, since 1933. Mem. Am. Library Assn., N.J. State Library Assn. (sec.), N.J. State Edn. Assn. Chmn. of Library Sect. of Eastern States Conf. of Teachers Colleges. Protestant. Home: 24 Arlington Av., Hawthorne, N.J. Address: State Teachers Coll., Paterson, N.J.

ABRAMS, Lawrence Brundige, gen. sales mgr.; b. Orange, N.J., June 4, 1890; s. Herbert Thomas and Anna Josephine (Mead) A.; B.S., U. of Mich., 1912; m. Ida Graulich, Dec. 29, 1914; children—Lawrence Brundige, Jr., Margaretta Gunther. Employed as engr. tests, A. S. Cameron Steam Pump Works, 1912-13; hydraulic engr., Ingersoll Rand Co., Cleveland, O., 1914-16; engr. pump tests, A. S. Cameron Steam Pump Works, Phillipsburg, N.J., 1916-17; engr. F. S. Hardesty cons. engr., Washington, D.C., 1917-21; mgr. Ingersoll-Rand Co. office, Washington, D.C., 1921-26; mgr. Ingersoll-Rand Co. of N.E., Boston, Mass., 1927-33; gen. sales mgr. Ingersoll-Rand Co., N.Y. City since 1935. Mem. Soc. Am. Mil. Engrs., Am. Soc. Naval Engrs., Delta Tau Delta. Republican. Presbyn. Clubs: Downtown Athletic (New York); Corinthian Yacht (Marblehead, Mass.). Home: 376 Ridgewood Av., Glen Ridge, N.J. Office: 11 Broadway, New York, N.Y.

ABRAMSON, Maurice, artist; b. Bayonne, N.J., Mar. 4, 1908; s. Abram and Adele (Slugh) A.; ed. Bayonne High Sch., 1921-25, Nat. Acad. Design Art Sch., 1930-35; unmarried. Has followed profession as artist since 1935; cartoonist for theatre mags. Exhibited 108th Annual Exhbn. of Nat. Acad. Design, New York, 1933; N.J. Gallery, Newark; Woman's Club, Jersey City, N.J. Represented by mural "The American Dream" in main bldg. Bayonne Pub. Library. Awarded second Hallgarten prize for painting at 112th annual exhbn. of Nat. Acad. Design., 1937. Home: 729 Av. A, Bayonne, N.J.

ACHESON, Alexander Wilson, lawyer; b. Washington, Pa., Oct. 19, 1885; s. Ernest Francis and Jannie B. (Stewart) A.; A.B. cum laude, Washington and Jefferson Coll., Washington, Pa., 1907; LL.B., Harvard Law Sch., 1910; m. Jennie Chase Belmore, Nov. 22, 1910; children—Ernest Francis, Flora Belmore. Admitted to Washington Co. and Pa. Supreme Court bar, 1910, and since practiced at Washington, Pa.; solicitor for Children's Aid Soc. of Washington Co., Pa., since 1922. Trustee and counselor Washington and Jefferson Coll. since 1935. Mem. Pa. Bar Assn. (regional dir. 6th zone, 1938-39), Washington Co. Bar Assn. (pres., 1936-37), Men's Union of Washington Presbytery of Presbyterian Ch. (pres., 1936-37), Phi Kappa Psi, Phi Beta Kappa. Ind. Republican. Presbyterian. Club: Bassett (Washington, Pa.). Home: 75 Acheson Av. Office: 411 Washington Trust Bldg., Washington, Pa.

ACHESON, Marcus Wilson, Jr., lawyer; b. Allegheny, Pa., August 27, 1873; s. Marcus Wilson and Sophie Duff (Reiter) A.; grad. Shady Side Acad., Pittsburgh, 1890; A.B., Washington and Jefferson, 1894, A.M., 1897; m. Margaret Hawkins, June 14, 1902; children—Marcus W., Jane, William G. Hawkins, George Hawkins, David. Admitted to bar, Dec. 14, 1895, since in practice at Pittsburgh; mem. firm of Patterson, Sterrett and Acheson, 1901-13, Sterrett and Acheson, 1913-29, Sterrett, Acheson and Jones since 1929. Pres. Legal Aid Soc. of Pittsburgh since 1908, convening First Conf. of Legal Aid Socs., Pittsburgh, Nov. 10, 1911; pres. Nat. Alliance Legal Aid Socs., 1914-16, Nat. Assn. Legal Aid Orgns., 1931-36, Pittsburgh Housing Assn., 1928-35, Fed. of Social Agencies of Pittsburgh and Allegheny County, 1930-34; chmn. Community Council of Pittsburgh, 1932-34; mem. bd. of dirs. Public Charities Assn. of Pa.; member Com. on Business and Housing of President's Conf. on Home Building and Home Ownership, 1931; pres. Allegheny Cemetery; chmn. Pittsburgh Regional Labor Bd., 1935. Trustee Washington and Jefferson Coll. and Shady Side Acad. Mem. Am. Law Inst., Phi Beta Kappa. Drew Pittsburgh Graded Tax Law, 1913. Home: 1060 Morewood Av. Office: Henry W. Oliver Bldg., Pittsburgh, Pa.

ACKER, Eleanor Beatrice, artist, designer; b. Camden, N.J., June 12, 1907; d. Charles Henry and Christine (Trench) A.; student Northeast Sch., Camden; grad. Collingswood (N.J.) High Sch., 1925; grad. Sch. of Industrial Art, Phila., 1925-29; student Moore Inst. and School of Design for Women, 1930, also Graphic Sketch Club, Philadelphia, several yrs. under Earl Horter. Began as etcher, wood block printer and painted in oils and water colors, 1931, free lance work until 1938; designer with Gladys E. Eisenhardt, creator of industrial designs, N.Y. City, since 1939. Exhibited (by invitation) Art Inst., Chicago, Harrisburg, Pa. and Wilmington, Del., Pa. Acad. Fine Arts, Print Club Phila., etc. Prints in permanent collection, Graphic Sketch Club. Received Bok Award for Aquatint, Graphic Sketch Club, 1934; spl. prize color print Studio Club, Nashville, 1935; 1st water color prize and purchase of water color "The Consistory" for Collingswood (N.J.) Public Library, 1935; hon. mention for black and white, 1st Southern Exhibition of N.J. Artists, 1936. Mem. Am. Artists Professional League; former mem. Plastic Club, Lantern and Lens Guild of Women Photographers (Philadelphia). Home: 109 Lawnside Av., Collingswood, N.J. Office: 132 E. 19th St., New York, N.Y.

ACKERMAN, Garret N., banker; b. Paskack, N.J., Nov. 9, 1856; s. Nicholas B. and Hannah A.; ed. Husbroucks Inst., Jersey City, and Packards Business College, New York; m. Margaret Ackerman, 1869 (died 1934); 1 dau., Helen (Mrs. Garret A. Van Valen). Began as partner of Ackerman Bros., general mdse., Woodcliff Lake, N.J., 1875, continued until retirement in 1936; pres. and dir. First Nat. Bank, Westwood, since 1920. Served as township clerk, school clerk and co. freeholder; mayor Woodcliff Lake, 1917-31. Democrat. Mem. Reformed Ch. Home: Woodcliff Lake, N.J. Office: Westwood, N.J.

ACKERSON, Henry E., Jr.; judge Circuit Court since 1924. Address: Jersey City, N.J.

ACKLEY, Clarence E(merson), acting supt. public instruction; b. Caldwell, O., Mar. 28, 1887; s. Samuel and Sarah (McGarry) A.; A.B., Oberlin Coll., 1910, A.M., 1913; student Teachers Coll., Columbia, summer 1924; Ph.D., U. of Pittsburgh, 1933; m. Hallie Grace Radcliff, June 25, 1910; children—Vivien Lucile (Mrs. William Dick), Robert Radcliff. Supt. of schools, Chesterland, O., 1910-12; teacher of English, Helena (Mont.) High Sch., 1913-14, Louisville (Ky.) High Sch., 1914-18; supt. of schools, Anchorage, Ky., 1918-20, Winchester, Ky., 1920-22, Ashland, Ky., 1922-28; head supervisor of schools, Jacksonville, Fla., 1928-30; teacher of English, Overbrook Jr. High Sch., Pittsburgh, 1930-35; dir. of professional licensing Dept. of Pub. Instrn., 1935-36, dir. of administration and finance, 1936-38, dep. supt. of pub. instrn., 1938-39, acting supt. pub. instrn. since May 29, 1939; lecturer on school adminstrn., U. of Fla., summers 1925, 28, State Teachers Coll. (Richmond, Ky.), U. of Ky., summer 1926, U. of Pittsburgh, summers 1933, 38, 39, Pa. State Coll., 1937, 38, 39. Chmn. Bd. of State Teachers Coll. Presidents of Pa., State Council of Edn. of Pa., Pa. Pub. Sch. Employees Retirement Bd. Mem. N.E.A., 1910-39, Am. Assn. of School Administrators since 1910, Pa. Edn. Assn., 1930-39, Am. Assn. of Univ. Profs., Phi Delta Kappa, Phi Sigma Pi. Baptist. Pres. Kiwanis Club, Winchester, Ky., 1920-21. Author: Constitutional Limitations on Legislation for Common Schools, 1933. Contbr. to Yearbook of School Law, 1934-39; also numerous articles on school law in American School Board Journal, The Nations Schools, etc. Home: 130 Cohassett St., Pittsburgh, Pa. Office: Dept. of Public Instruction, Harrisburg, Pa.

ACKLEY, David B.; chief of staff Mercer Hosp.; attending surgeon N.J. State Hosp. for Epileptics. Address: 21 N. Clinton Av., Trenton, N.J.

ADAIR, Watson Black, lawyer and referee in bankruptcy; b. Osborne, Pa., May 29, 1875; s. James and Martha Louise (Black) A.; ed. U. of City of New York, 1892-93; LL.B., U. of Pittsburgh Law Sch., 1900; unmarried. Admitted to Pa. bar, 1900 and engaged in gen. practice of law at Pittsburgh; a referee in bankruptcy of U.S. Dist. Ct. since 1920. Served with Army Field Service of Am. Red Cross in France, 1918. Borough solicitor and later pres. Sch. Bd., Edgeworth Borough. Mem. Am., Pa. State, Allegheny Co. bar assns., Nat. Assn. Referees in Bankruptcy (past pres.), Nat. Bankruptcy Conf. Republican. Clubs: Duquesne (Pittsburgh); Allegheny Country (Sewickley). Home: 214 Quaker Rd., Sewickley, Pa. Office: 604 Federal Bldg., and 743 Gulf Bldg., Pittsburgh, Pa.

ADAMIC, Louis, writer; b. village of Blato, Austria (now Yugoslavia), Mar. 23, 1899; s. Anton and Ana (Adamic) A.; student Gymnasium, Ljubljana, Yugoslavia, 1910-13; m. Stella Sanders, June 15, 1931. Came to U.S., 1913, naturalized, 1918. Served in U.S. Army during World War. Awarded Guggenheim fellowship, 1932-33; awarded a grant-in-aid, Rockefeller Foundation, 1937, Carnegie Foundation, 1939. Mem. Authors' League of America; mem. bd. of trustees Foreign Language Information Service. Author: Dynamite, 1931; Laughing in the Jungle, 1932; The Native's Return, 1934; Grandsons, 1935; Cradle of Life, 1936; The House in Antigua, 1937; My America, 1938. Contbr. articles and fiction to mags. Address: R.F.D. 1, Milford, N.J.

ADAMS, Comfort Avery, electrical engr.; b. Cleveland, Nov. 1, 1868; s. Comfort Avery and Katherine Emily (Peticolas) A.; S.B., Case Sch. of Applied Science, Cleveland, 1890, E.E., 1905, Dr. Engring., 1925; student mathematics and physics, Harvard, 1891-93; m. Elizabeth Challis Parsons, June 21, 1894; children—John, Clayton Comfort. Asst. in physics, Case School of Applied Science, 1886-90; designing engr., 1890-91; instr., 1891-95, asst. prof., 1896-1905, prof. elec. engring., 1906-16, Lawrence professor of engineering, Harvard U., 1914-35, Gordon McKay prof. of elec. engring., 1935-36, emeritus since 1936; dean Harvard Engring. Sch., 1919; chmn. div. engring. Nat. Research Council, 1919-21. Consulting engr. for Am. Tool & Machine Co., Boston, 1905-30, The Okonite Co., 1915—, Okonite Callender Cable Co., 1925—, Babcock and Wilcox Co., 1926—, Gen. Electric Co., 1927-32, Budd Manufacturing Co., 1934—. Member International Jury of Awards (department electricity), St. Louis Expn., 1904. Unitarian. Fellow Am. Acad. Arts and Sciences, Am. Inst. Elec. Engrs. (pres. 1918-19), A.A.A.S.; mem. Nat. Acad. of Sciences, Instn. Elec. Engrs., Verein Deutscher Elektrotechniker, Société Francaise des Electriciennes, Am. Soc. Civil Engrs., Am. Soc. Mech. Engrs., Soc. Promotion Engineering Education, American Physical Soc., American Welding Soc. (pres. 1919-20), Am. Bur. of Welding (dir. 1919-36), Engring. Foundation (chmn. welding research com. since 1936), Am. Engring. Council, Am. Engring. Standards Com. (chmn. 1918-20). Mem. John Fritz Medal Bd. of Award (pres. 1922), Edison Medal Bd. of Award (chmn. 1920). Chmn. Gen. Engring. Com. of Council Nat. Defense, during war period, also as chmn. Welding Com. of Emergency Fleet Corpn. Clubs: Engineers' (Philadelphia); Engineers (New York); Harvard Faculty (Cambridge, Mass.); Cedarbrook Country. Author: Dynamo Design Schedules; also articles on kindred subjects. Received 1st award of Miller medal, "for conspicuous contributions to the art of welding," 1929. Home: 436 W. Stafford St., Philadelphia, Pa.

ADAMS, Earl Dabney, dir. of purchases Wheeling Steel Corpn.; b. Wheeling, W.Va., May 5, 1878; s. Charles Dabney and Lewellen (Hull) A.; student prep. sch., 1893-95; m. Emma Bailey Forbes, Jan. 31, 1914 (died 1935). Began as clk. Jacob Snider Sons, wholesale heavy hardware, 1895; clk. Pa. R.R., Am. Sheet & Tin Plate Co.; asst. mgr. Pope Tin Plate Co.; purchasing agt. Wheeling (W.Va.) Steel & Iron Co.; dir. of purchases Wheeling Steel Corpn. since 1920, Consumers Mining Co., Harmarville, Pa., since 1920. Mem. S.A.R. Republican. Protestant. Mason, Elk. Clubs: Three Springs Farm (Ohio County, Wheeling, W.Va.); Fort Henry, Wheeling Country (Wheeling); Duquesne (Pittsburgh, Pa.); Rolling Rock (Ligonier, Pa.). Home: Orchard St. Office: 1134-40 Market St., Wheeling, W.Va.

ADAMS, Edwin Plimpton, prof. physics; b. Prague, Jan. 23, 1878; s. Edwin Augustus and Caroline Amelia (Plimpton) A.; B.S., Beloit Coll., Wis., 1899, Sc.D., 1931; M.S., Harvard, 1901, Ph.D., 1904; studied univs. of Berlin, Göttingen, Trinity Coll., Cambridge U.; unmarried. Became prof. physics, Princeton, Sept., 1906. Mem. Am. Physical Soc., Am. Math. Soc., Beta Theta Pi, Am. Philos. Soc. Clubs: University, Harvard, Princeton (New York); Royal Societies (London). Home: Princeton, N.J.*

ADAMS, Edwin Wesley, associate supt. of schools; b. Phila., Pa., Aug. 1, 1886; s. Edwin Lincoln and Mae Lydia (Emery) A.; grad. Central High Sch., Phila., 1905; student Sch. of Pedagogy, Phila., 1905-07; B.S., Temple U., 1914, Ed.D., 1928; A.M., U. of Pa., 1922; m. Ella Virginia Hulsizer, June 30, 1909. Teacher in Phila. elementary schools, 1907-11; critic teacher and lecturer in edn. and psychology, 1911-14; prin. Phila. elementary schools, 1914-18, 1919-21; dist. supt., Phila., 1921-24; prin. Phila. Normal Sch. and dir. Div. of Teacher Edn., 1924-30; asso. supt. of Phila. Public Schs. since 1930; lecturer in edn., U. of Pa., 1917-18; Cleveland City Normal Sch., summer 1920; Temple U., 1924, 25; Pa. State Coll., 1926, 27. Served as 1st lt., U.S. Army, in charge clin. psychol. examinations, Camp Upton, 1918. Mem. Phila. Com. on Prevention of Blindness, Mayor's Scholarship Com., Phila. Dir. White-Williams Foundation, Child Guidance Clinic, Phila. Shut-in Soc. Mem. Phila. Teachers Assn., Pa. State Edn. Assn., N.E.A., Dept. of Sch. Adminstrs., Phi Delta Kappa. Republican. Presbyterian. Club: Schmen's (Phila.). Author: Community Civics, 1920; Conduct and Citizenship, 1926; An Analysis of Teaching, 1929; Our Democracy, 1939. Home: Cambridge Apt. Office: 21st and Parkway, Philadelphia, Pa.

ADAMS, Enoch H.; surgeon-in-chief Centre Co. Hosp. Home: N. Allegany St., Bellefonte, Pa.

ADAMS, George J.; chief of corporate work Pa. R.R. Office: Broud St. Station Bldg., Philadelphia, Pa.

ADAMS, Harold; chmn. bd. Northern Bank & Trust Co. Address: Lancaster, Pa.

ADAMS, Herbert C.; editor Parkersburg News. Address: care Parkersburg Pub. Co., Parkersburg, W.Va.

ADAMS, Jessie French, librarian; b. Tuckerton, N.J.; d. Charles Edwin and Ellen Marie (French) A.; student pub. sch. and high sch., Atlantic City, N.J., N.J. Library Commn. Summer Sch., 1907. Library apprentice Atlantic City Free Pub. Library, Atlantic City, N.J., 1905-10, asst. librarian, 1910-20, librarian since 1920. Mem. Am. Library Assn., N.J. Library Assn., Atlantic County Hist. Soc. Presbyn. Clubs: Soroptimist, Woman's, Business & Professional Women's (Atlantic City). Contbr. articles to newspapers and mags. Home: 2823 Arctic Av., Atlantic City, N.J.

ADAMS, John Stokes, lawyer; b. Philadelphia, Pa., Mar. 22, 1864; s. Greenfield and Josephine Lippincott (Stokes) A.; prep. edn., Christ's Ch. Sem., Lexington, Ky.; grad. Emerson Inst., Washington, D.C., 1880; A.B., U. of Pa., 1884, LL.B., 1886; m. Heloise Zelina Root, Apr. 23, 1890; children—Henry Clay, Randolph Greenfield, John Stokes. Admitted to Pa. bar, 1886, and practiced since at Philadelphia; mem. firm of Adams, Childs, McKaig and Lukens; lecturer on law of mines, U. of Pa. Law Sch., 1907-29; chmn. bd. Integrity Trust Co. since 1927; director Ridge Avenue Passenger Ry. Co., Ellis, Stone & Co. (Greensboro, N.C.). Mem. Am. Bar Assn., Pa. Bar Assn., Bar Assn. Philadelphia, Am. Hist. Assn., Phi Kappa Psi, Phi Beta Kappa. Democrat. Club: University. Author: The Law of Mines and Mining in the U.S. (with D. M. Barringer), 1897. Editor: An Autobiographical Sketch by John Marshall, 1937. Home: 325 S. 43d St. Office: 700 Integrity Bldg., Philadelphia, Pa.

ADAMS, Leason Heberling, physical chemist; b. Cherryvale, Kan., Jan. 16, 1887; s. William Barton and Katherine (Heberling) A.; B.S., U. of Ill., 1906; m. Jeannette Blaisdell, Jan. 25, 1908; children—Leason Blaisdell, William Muirhead, Madeline Jeannette, Ralston Heberling. Industrial chemist with Morris & Co. and M. P. Ry. Co., 1906-08; research, technologic br., U.S. Geol. Survey, 1908-10; research, Geophysical Lab., Carnegie Instn., Washington, D.C.

since 1910, acting dir., 1936-37, dir. since 1938. Fellow American Physical Soc., Geol. Soc. America; mem. Am. Chem. Soc., Am. Ceramic Soc., Seismological Soc. America, Philos. Soc. Washington (pres. 1929), Geol. Soc. Washington, Washington Acad. Sciences (pres. 1932), Mineral Soc. (London), Sigma Xi, Phi Lambda Upsilon. Awarded Edward Longstreth medal, Franklin Institute, for process for annealing glass, 1924. Club: Cosmos. Home: Bradley Boul. and Burdette Rd., Bethesda, Md. Office: 2801 Upton St., Washington, D.C.*

ADAMS, Marjorie Nickles, painter; b. Shippensburg, Pa., Oct. 11, 1898; d. William Alfred and Merenda (Clippenger) Nickles; ed. Shippensburg Teachers Coll., 1916-17, Pa. Museum and Sch. of Industrial Art, 1917-21, Chester Springs Art Sch., summers 1921-22, Pa. Acad. of Fine Arts, 1922-25; m. Edgar Frick Adams, Aug. 12, 1924; 1 son, Edgar Nickles (b. Jan. 7, 1927). Portrait painter (especially children), landscape painter; private teacher of art. Exhibited at Acad. of Fine Arts, Centennial in Phila., Phila. Art Club, Phila. Plastic Club, traveling exhibitions under Academy Fellowship. Awards: 1st prize, Chester Springs Water Color Show, 1922; 1st prize, Phila. Plastic Club, 1927; European Traveling Cresson Scholarship, Pa. Acad. of Fine Arts, 1924; two 1st prizes for life studies offered by John Lewis, pres. of Acad. of Fine Arts, 1923. Chmn. Pub. Schs. Art Com., Swarthmore. Mem. Fellowship of Pa. Fine Arts Acad., Phila. Art Alliance. Republican. Episcopalian. Home: 1 Drexel Rd., Swarthmore, Pa.

ADAMS, Martin Ray, coll. prof.; b. Blountville, Tenn. Aug. 6, 1892; s. Eugene Vaden and Matilda Catherine (Akard) A.; ed. King Coll., Bristol, Tenn., 1908-10; A.B., Roanoke Coll., 1912, A.M., 1912; student Columbia U., summers, 1914, 1920, U. of Calif., summer, 1922; A.M., Princeton, 1923, Ph.D., Princeton, 1927; m. Charlotte Schroder, of Charleston, S.C., Sept. 3, 1927; 1 son, Bernard Augustus. Instr. English, Mt. Pleasant (N.C.) Collegiate Inst., 1912-15, Roanoke Coll., Salem, Va., 1915-18; asst. prof. English, U. of S.D., 1919-22, Goucher Coll., 1924-26; prof. English, Franklin and Marshall Coll., Lancaster, Pa., since 1927. Served in hosp. corps U.S.N., 1918-19. Mem. Modern Lang. Assn. of America, Am. Assn. Univ. Profs., Phi Sigma Kappa. Democrat. Lutheran. Contbr. publs. Modern Lang. Assn. of America, also lit. mags. and journs. Home: 582 School Lane, Lancaster, Pa.

ADAMS, Paul David, constrn. engr.; b. Newark, N.J., May 23, 1893; s. James Cooley and Harriet C. (Cooley) A.; C.E., Princeton, 1915; m. Elizabeth Woolsey Fooks, Apr. 2, 1923; 1 son, David Paul. Began as asst. engr., then res. engr., E. I. Dupont de Nemours Co. at Parlin, N.J., 1916-20, asst. constrn. mgr. same at Wilmington, Del., 1920-23; organized Adams-Faber Co., bldg. constrn., White Plains, N.Y. and Upper Montclair, N.J. and pres. and dir. since 1923; dir. Bank of Montclair, Montclair, N.J.; trustee Montclair Bldg. & Loan Assn. Mem. Phi Beta Kappa, Cloister Inn Club (Princeton U.). Republican. Episcopalian. Clubs: Fellsbrook (pres.), Country (Essex Fells); Rotary (Montclair); Princeton (New York). Home: Stewart Rd., Essex Fells, N.J. Office: 241 Lorraine Av., Upper Montclair, N.J.

ADAMS, Rayford Kennedy, M.D., neuropsychiatrist; b. Monroe, N. C., Feb. 22, 1886; s. Henry B. and Fannie (Person) A.; student Duke U., Durham, N.C., 1904-07, U. of N.C., Chapel Hill, N.C., 1908-10; M.D. Jefferson Med. Coll., Phila., Pa., 1912; m. Mary Belle King, Nov. 2, 1918; children—Rayford Kennedy, Jr., Elizabeth Houston, Mary Belle. Resident physician, Mercer Hosp., Trenton, N.J., 1912-13; mem. staff, N.J. State Village for Epileptics, 1913-15; mem. staff State Hosp., Raleigh, N.C., 1915-29; sr. resident physician, N.J. State Village for Epileptics, Skillman, N.J. since 1929. Certified as Specialist in Neurology and Psychiatry by Am. Bd. Neurology and Psychiatry. Mem. Am. Med. Assn., Med. Soc. of N.J., Somerset Co. Med Soc., Neuropsychiatric Soc. of N.J. (exec. council), Sigma Nu, Phi Chi, Theta Nu Epsilon. Methodist. Home: Lakeside Lodge, Skillman, N.J.

ADAMS, Rowland Keedy, judge; b. Waynesboro, Pa., July 10, 1889; s. Joseph Clagett and Barbara E. (Keedy) A.; A.B., St. Johns Coll., Annapolis, Md., 1911; LL.B., U. of Md., Baltimore, 1914; m. Elva F. Hoffman, Apr. 15, 1918: children—Marja Dorothy, Rowland Keedy. Admitted to Md. bar, 1914; in practice of law since 1914; formerly mem. law firms Johnson & Adams, Marchant, Adams & Hargest, Adams & Hargest; deputy states atty., Baltimore, 1924-27; asso. judge Supreme Bench of Baltimore City since Mar. 1, 1934. Successively 2d lt., 1st lt. and capt., U.S. Inf., May, 1917-Dec., 1918. Mem. bd. regents U. of Md. Mem. Am. Bar. Assn., Md. State Bar Assn., Baltimore City Bar Assn. Democrat. Lutheran. Club: Wednesday Law (Baltimore). Home: 1808 Fairbank Road. Office: Court House, Baltimore, Md.

ADAMS, Russell Vroom, investment banker; b. Plainfield, N.J., Jan. 22, 1888; s. Frederick Coe and Julia (Vroom) A.; student Plainfield (N.J.) Pub. Sch., 1896-98; Montclair, (N.J.) Pub. Sch., 1898-1900, Newark (N.J.) High Sch., 1900-04, N.Y.U. (financial course), 1905-09; m. Harriet Stratemeyer, Oct. 20, 1915; children—Russell Vroom, Patricia Stratton, Camilla Anne, Edward Stratemeyer. Municipal bond salesman J. S. Reppel & Co., Newark, N.J., 1904-12, mem. of firm, 1912-25; partner Adams & Mueller, investment bankers, Newark, N.J., since 1925. Mem. N.Y., Newark (N.J.) Chambers of Commerce, N.J., Essex Co. Bankers' Assns. Republican. Presbyterian. Clubs: Baltusrol Golf (Springfield, N.J.); Rotary (Newark, N.J.); Maplewood (N.J.) Country; N.J. Bond (pres., Newark, N.J.); New York Municipal Bond; Essex, Down Town (Newark, N.J.). Home: 48 N. Terrace, Maplewood, N.J. Office: 24 Commerce St., Newark, N.J.

ADAMS, Viers Wilson, head, Johnstown Center; b. Braddock, Pa., Jan. 29, 1909; s. Frank Thompson and Minnie Blanche (Morrow) A.; A.B., U. of Pittsburgh, 1930, A.M., same, 1934; m. Zella Frances Wallace, July 18, 1932. Engaged as asst. to the head of the Johnstown Center, U. of Pittsburgh, Johnstown, Pa., 1930-36, head of the Johnstown Center since 1936. Mem. Omicron Delta Kappa, Theta Chi, Phi Delta Kappa. Received George Wharton Pepper Award (U. of Pittsburgh) 1930. Republican. Presbyterian. Mason. Club: Rotary of Johnstown. Home: 43 Venango St., Johnstown, Pa. Office: 218 Central High Sch., Johnstown, Pa.

ADDICKS, Lawrence, consulting engr.; b. Phila., Mar. 3, 1878; s. of Charles Henry and Mary Knox (Buzby) A.; U. of Pa., spl. course; B.S. in Mech. and Elec. Engring., Mass. Inst. Tech., 1899; m. Mary Maulsby O'Brien, June 20, 1899; 1 dau., Madeleine. Supt. Chrome (N.J.) plant, U.S. Metals Refining Co., 1905-14; consulting engr. since 1914. Mem. Naval Consulting Bd. Mem. Am. Soc. Mech. Engrs., Am. Inst. Mining Engrs., Am. Soc. for Testing Materials, Electrochem. Soc. (past pres.), Mining and Metall. Soc. America; fellow Am. Inst. Elec. Engrs.; mem. Instn. of Mining and Metallurgy (London). Episcopalian. Club: Chemists', Mining (New York). Author: Copper Refining, 1921. Home: Bel Air, Md.

ADDIE, Charles Edward Barton, professor of dentistry; b. London, Eng., Dec. 11, 1881; s. Thomas Kitchen and Millicent (Nicholson) A.; came to U.S., 1909, naturalized, 1917; m. Lyle Carroll, Jan. 28, 1908; 1 son, Charles Barton. Began as dental apprentice, 1898; in practice of gen. dentistry since 1903, specialist in orthodontia since 1918, instr. dentistry, Temple U., Phila., Pa., 1913-16, asst. prof., 1916-18, prof. orthodontics and crown bridge work since 1918. Fellow Am. Coll. Dentists; mem. Phila. Co. Dental Soc. (past pres.), Pa. State Dental Soc. (past v.p.), Garretsonian Surg. Soc. (past pres.), Child Emer. Health State Com., Am. Acad. for Promotion of Children's Dentistry, A.A.A.S., Blue Key, Omicron Kappa Upsilon, Xi Psi Phi. Republican. Episcopalian. Mason. Home: 1005 Kenwyn St., Philadelphia, Pa.

ADDIS, Charles Matthaei, pres. Refiners Lubricating Co.; b. Newark, N.J., Jan. 16, 1890; s. John Henry and Liberty (Valleire) A.; grad. Barringer High Sch., Newark, 1908; B.S. in Chemistry, Lafayette Coll., 1912; post-grad. work, Columbia U., 1914; m. Jane Lewis Miller, Sept. 24, 1919; children—Patricia (dec.), Elizabeth. Began as chemist U.S. Cast Iron Pipe & Foundry Co., 1912; teacher sciences, Newark (N.J.) High Schs., 1913-14; mgr. advertising New York Lubricating Oil Co., 1914-20; v.p. Nat. Lubricants Co., 1920-23; pres. and dir. Refiners Lubricating Co. since 1923. Served with Essex Troop of N.J. on Mexican Border, 1916; mem. Norton Harjes Ambulance Corps, A.E.F. (with French Army), 1917-19. Mem. Soc. Automotive Engrs., Chi Phi, Theta Nu Epsilon. Republican. Presbyn. Mason. Clubs: Downtown Athletic (New York); Mountain Lakes Club; Mountain Lakes Riding (Mountain Lakes, N.J.); Green Mountain Horse Assn. (Rutland, Vt.). Home: 90 Hanover Road, Mountain Lakes, N.J. Office: 601 W. 26th St., New York, N.Y.

ADDISON, Joseph, lawyer; b. Glenn Dale, Md., July 25, 1885; s. Francis Girault and Ellen Moylan (Bowie) A.; LL.B., Georgetown U., Washington, D.C., 1908, LL.M., 1909; m. Marguerite Waring Clagett, Apr. 24, 1915; children —Katherine Duckett, Joseph, William Baruch. Gen. practice at Baltimore, Md., since 1909; asso. with law firm Barton, Wilmer, Ambler & Stewart, Baltimore, Md., to 1919, partner Barton, Wilmer, Bramble, Addison & Semans since 1919; gen. counsel and dir. People's Drug Stores, Inc., Washington, D.C. Mem. Am., Md. State, Baltimore City, D.C. bar assns. Episcopalian. Clubs: Merchants (Baltimore, Md.); University (Washington, D.C.). Home: Glenn Dale, Md. Office: Mercantile Trust Bldg., Baltimore, Md.

ADDISON, William H(enry) F(itzgerald), anatomist; b. Whitby, Ont., Can., Apr. 23, 1880; s. John Hardill and Harriet Matilda (Rowe) A.; B.A., University of Toronto, 1902, M.B., 1905, M.D., 1917; studied in Europe seven summers, in spring of 1928 in Madrid with Ramón y Cajal and in spring of 1934 with Rio Hortega; m. Eleanor Corkhill Adams, Dec. 25, 1905; 1 dau., Agnes Eleanor. With U. of Pa. since 1905, demonstrator of normal histology and embryology until 1912, asst. prof., 1912-19, prof. since 1919. Fellow A.A.A.S., Coll. of Phys. of Phila.; mem. Am. Assn. Anatomists, Am. Soc. Naturalists, Phila. Zoöl. Soc., Phila. Acad. Nat. Sciences, Phila. Pathol. Soc., Marine Biol. Lab. (Wood's Hole), Mass.), Am. Physiol. Soc., Sigma Xi, Phi Beta Pi. Episcopalian. Editor: Villiger's Brain and Spinal Cord (4th edit.), 1931; Piersol's Normal Histology (15th edit.), 1932. Contbr. papers in scientific jours. on the microscopic structure of tissues and organs, including the brain. Address: Univ. of Pa. School of Medicine, Philadelphia, Pa.

ADE, Lester Kelly, educator; b. Trout Run, Pa., July 27, 1890; s. Gottlieb E. and Emma (Kelly) A.; grad. Muncy (Pa.) Normal Sch., 1909, Commercial Coll., Williamsport, Pa., 1910; A.B., Bucknell U., 1921, A.M., 1924; Ph.D., New York Univ., 1931; A.M., Yale U., 1932; LL.D., Bucknell, 1935; Litt.D., Temple U., 1936; L.H.D., Beaver Coll., 1938; Guggenheim fellow in education, 1925-26; m. Alverta Lightfoot, March 19, 1921. Teacher and principal elementary and secondary schs., Lycoming Co., 1910-22; supt. schs. Muncy, 1922-27; dean of State Teachers Coll., West Chester, Pa., 1927-28; prin. State Normal Sch., New Haven, Conn., 1928-35; supt. of pub. instrn., State of Pa., since 1935. Served in inf., U.S.A., with A.E.F. in Siberia, World War. Pres. and chief exec. officer Pa. State Council of Edn.; chmn. Pa. Pub. Sch. Employees' Retirement Bd.; also ex-officio member various state boards. Past pres. N.E. Teacher-Preparation Assn.; sec. Eastern States Assn. of Professional Schs. for Teachers; mem. Progressive Edn. Assn., New Edn. Fellowship, N.E.A., Nat. Soc. Study Education, A.A. A.S., Am. Edn. Research Assn., Phi Delta Kappa, Sigma Alpha Epsilon, and Kappa Delta Pi frats. Episcopalian. Clubs: Graduate (New Haven); Howard Club of Knights-Templar (Williamsport); University (Harrisburg). Author: An Educational Survey of Lycoming County,

1922; Marking Systems in Use in the Arts Colleges of Pa. (paper), 1926; Comparative Study of Policies and Programs of Municipal Teacher-Preparation Institutions in the U.S., 1928; Provisions in the State Teachers Colleges of Pa. for Laboratory-School Experience in Teaching (thesis), 1931; Teacher-Preparation Curricula in the U.S., England, France and Germany (essay), 1932; also numerous articles, reports and published addresses on edn. Home: 931 N. Front St. Office: State Education Bldg., Harrisburg, Pa.

ADER, Kenneth Lawrence; b. Rahway, N.J., July 18, 1911; s. William and Iva (Lawrence) A.; B.S., Rutgers U., 1934; m. Mildred Ainge, June 19, 1937. In employ Merck & Co., mfg. chemists, Rahway, N.J., since 1935, now accountant in price control dept. Serving in Chem. Warfare Sch., O.R.C. First pres. Rahway Jr. Chamber of Commerce, 1935. One of organizers and now mem. Rahway Young Republicans; mem. Rep. Co. Com. Mem. Lambda Chi Alpha, Rahway High Sch. Alumni (v.p.). Republican. Presbyn. Club: Junior Chamber of Commerce of Rahway (dir.). Leader of dance orchestra since 1928, having played some important engagements. Home: 1163 Jefferson Av. Office: Merck & Co., Rahway, N.J.

ADERTON, Alphonso Lamaraux, business exec.; b. Savilton, N.Y., Nov. 10, 1876; s. Thomas Jefferson and Mary Edsall (Lockwood) A.; student Newburg (N.Y.) Free Acad., 1890-94; m. Elsie Gildersleeve, June 10, 1903; children—Elsie Aileen, Thomas Radcliffe, Victor. Clerical work, 1894-98; clerk, Newburgh, N.Y., Post Office, 1899-1914; pres. N.Y. States Assn. of Post Office Clks., 1906-08; business supt. N.Y. State Sunday School Assn., 1914-17; asst. business supt. Internat. Sunday School Assn., 1917-19; sec. and mgr. Hockenbury System, Inc., Harrisburg, Pa., 1919-27; pres. Bellvue Park Assn., Harrisburg, Pa., 1924-26; v.p. Aderton, Johnson and Mayer, Inc., Harrisburg, Pa., 1927-33; v.p. and mgr. Aderton-Johnson Assos., Harrisburg, Pa., since 1933; gen. agt. U.S. Life Ins. Co. since 1935; dir. Hanover Thrift Corpn., Gettysburg Thrift Corpn., Carlisle Thrift Corpn., Mechanicsburg Community Credit Co., Huntingdon Co. Thrift Co., Thrift Investment Corpn. of Pittsburgh, Chambersburg Thrift Corpn. Served in Spanish-Am. War, 1898-99. Mem. United Spanish War Vets. Mason. Club: Rotary (Harrisburg, Pa.). Home: 1512 North St. Office: 75 Union Trust Bldg., Harrisburg, Pa.

ADKINS, William H., judge; b. Talbot Co., Md., July 21, 1862; s. Isaac L. (M.D.) and Mary E. (Hughlett) A.; B.A., Johns Hopkins, 1882; B.L., U. of Md., 1883; m. Mary H. Dawson, Oct. 8, 1891; children—Leonard Dawson, Edith Dawson. Began practice at Easton, 1883; apptd. asso. judge 2d Jud. Circuit of Md., Aug. 1906, and elected, Nov. 1907, for term of 15 yrs.; apptd. chief judge 2d Jud. Circuit and asso. judge Court of Appeals of Md., Mar. 1919, and elected Nov. 1919, for term of 15 yrs. Democrat. Episcopalian. Home: Easton, Md.

ADLER, Charles, II, inventor; b. Baltimore, Md., June 20, 1899; s. Harry and Carolyn (Frank) A.; grad. The Park Sch., Baltimore, 1917; student Johns Hopkins, 1917-19; m. Alene Steiger, June 10, 1925; children—Amalie Carol, Harry, II. Began as railroad station helper, 1919; signal engr. Md. & Pa. R.R., 1923; v.p. The Adler Safety Control Co., 1927. Inventor of vehicular sound detector for operation of traffic signals; safety filament lamp; color design lenses; speed control signal system; coordinated intersection signal and speed control; rotating stop-sign railway-highway crossing signal. Served in S.A.T.C., during World War. Affiliated mem. Assn. Am. Railroads; mem. Inst. Traffic Engrs. Club: Baltimore Press. Contbr. nat. newspapers and mags. Home: 2401 Ken Oak Rd. Office: Mt. Royal Station, Baltimore, Md.

ADLER, Cyrus, college pres.; b. Van Buren, Ark., Sept. 13, 1863; s. Samuel and Sarah (Sulzberger) A.; A.B., U. of Pa., 1883, A.M., 1886, Litt.D., 1930; Ph.D., Johns Hopkins U., 1887; L.H.D., Hebrew Union College, 1925, Phi Beta Kappa from the Univ. of Pa. in 1933; m. Racie Friedenwald, Sept. 1905. Fellow, instr., and asso., Semitic langs., Johns Hopkins, 1884-93; librarian Smithsonian Instn., 1892-1905, asst. sec. same, 1905-08; curator of historic archæology and historic religions, U.S. Nat. Mus., 1889-1908; president Dropsie College for Hebrew and Cognate Learning, Philadelphia, since 1908; acting pres. Jewish Theol. Sem. of America (N.Y. City), 1916-24, pres. since 1924. Mem. Bd. Pub. Edn., Phila., 1921-25; pres. trustees, Free Library of Philadelphia; mem. bd. overseers Gratz College-Hebrew Education Society, Philadelphia. Special commissioner of Chicago Expedition to Turkey, Egypt, Tunis, Algiers, Morocco, 1890-92; U.S. del. to Conf. on an Internat. Catalogue of Scientific Lit., 1898 (internat. council). Mem. Am. Philos. Soc.; (v.p.), Am. Oriental Soc. (pres. 1923), Am. Jewish Hist. Soc. (ex-pres.), Washington Acad. of Sciences, etc. Clubs: Cosmos (Washington, D.C.); University, Philobiblon, Oriental (Phila.). Has written many articles on Semitic philology, Assyriology, Oriental archæology, comparative religion, bibliography, Am. Jewish history, etc. One of editors Jewish Encyclopedia; editor so-called Jefferson Bible, American Jewish Year Book, 1899-1906, and Jewish Quarterly Review, published by Dropsie College; chairman board editors New Jewish Translation of the Bible; chmn. Jewish Classics Com. of Jewish Publication Soc. America; pres. Am. Jewish Com., 1929—; mem. council of The Jewish Agency for Palestine; mem. bd. govs. Hebrew Univ. in Jerusalem; trustee Am. Schs. of Oriental Research; mem. exec. bd. Boy Scouts of America; chmn. Army and Navy Com., Jewish Welfare Board. Author: Told in the Coffee House—Turkish Tales (with Allan Ramsay), 1898; Jacob H. Schiff, His Life and Letters, 1928; Memorandum on the Western Wall, prepared for the Spl. Commn. of the League of Nations on behalf of the Jewish Agency for Palestine, 1930. Lectures, selected papers, addresses by Cyrus Adler, collected and published by his colleagues and friends on the occasion of his 70th birthday, Sept. 13, 1933, with a bibliography. Home: 2041 N. Broad St., Philadelphia, Pa.

ADLER, Francis Heed, ophthalmologist; b. Phila., Pa., Feb. 4, 1895; s. Dr. Lewis H. and Emma Augusta (Heed) A.; A.B., U. of Pa., 1916, M.A., 1918, M.D., 1919; m. Sara Erdman, June 27, 1917 (died Dec. 26, 1937); children—Francis Erdman, Jeanne. Cons. surgeon Wills Hosp., Phila., since 1937; prof. ophthalmology, U. of Pa., since 1937. Fellow Am. Coll. Surgeons; mem. A.M.A., Am. Ophthal. Soc., Am. Acad. Ophthalmology and Otolaryngology, Coll. of Physicians of Phila., Phi Delta Theta. Republican. Episcopalian. Clubs: Union League, Phila. Cricket, Rittenhouse (Phila., Pa.). Author: Clinical Physiology of the Eye, 1933; numerous clin. and scientific articles. Asso. editor of The Archives of Ophthalmology. Home: 7360 Huron Lane, Mt. Airy, Pa. Office: 313 S. 17th St., Philadelphia, Pa.

ADOLPHE, Albert Jean, artist; b. Phila, Pa., Feb. 17, 1865; s. Anthony and Mary (Weaver) A.; ed. Central High Sch., Phila.; pupil Pa. Acad. Fine Arts; Sch. of Industrial Art of Pa. Mus.; École des Beaux Arts, Paris; studied with Gérome and Whistler, Paris, de Vriendt in Antwerp. Former instr. in interior decoration, Drexel Inst., also at Sch. Industrial Art, and scenic artist, Acad. of Music, Phila.; instructor at La France Art Institute: has served as artist for various cos. engaged in interior decoration; supplied decorations for steamships St. Louis and St. Paul, of the Am. Line. Exhibited at Glass Palais, Munich; Salons des Artists Francais, Paris; Art Inst. Chicago; Chicago Expn. also Acad. Fine Arts, Art Club, Graphic Sketch Club, Phila. Sketch Club, Imps Club—all of Phila. Awarded Charles Toppan Prize, Pa. Acad. Fine Arts, 1891; hon. mention, Chicago Expn., 1893, Paris Salon, 1899, gold medal, Art Club of Phila., 1904, and hon. mention, same, 1921; Stotesbury prize, Phila., 1916, for "Americanization Through Art." Mem. Alumni Assn. Sch. of Industrial Arts, Pa. Mus.; hon. mem. Graphic Sketch Club, Imps Club (Phila.). Free Thinker. Home: 2616 W. Montgomery Av. Studio: 1811 N. Etting St., Philadelphia, Pa.

AFFELDER, Estelle May; b. Williamsport, Pa., July 14, 1875; d. Barney and Pauline (Fleishman) May; student Pittsburgh Pub. Sch., 1887-88; grad. Bishop Bowman Inst., Pittsburgh, Pa., 1893; m. Louis Jacob Affelder, Jan. 12, 1899 (died Apr. 8, 1930); children—Louise May (Mrs. Emanuel M. Davidove), Katherine, Paul B. Mem. Pa. State Council for the Blind (apptd. by Gov. Pinchot), 1932-36, exec. com. of pub. affairs div., and of group work div. of Fed. of Social Agencies, budget com. of Community Fund. Trustee Rodef Shalom Congregation, Pittsburgh, Pub. Health Nursing Assn., Irene Kaufmann Settlement, Emma Kaufmann Camp; dir. Nat. Fed. of Settlements. Mem. Alpha Epsilon Phi (patroness since 1923). Republican. Jewish religion. Club: Concordia (Pittsburgh). Address: 5825 Bartlett St., Pittsburgh, Pa.

AFFLERBACH, Calvin Eugene, educator; b. Tohickon, Pa., Oct. 11, 1896; s. John Frank and Emma Strawn (Atherholt) A.; student Perkasie (Pa.) High Sch., 1910-13, Keystone State Normal Sch., Kutztown, Pa., 1913-15; A.B., Dickinson Coll., Carlisle, Pa., 1920, A.M. (hon.), 1926; M.A., Columbia U. Teachers Coll., 1925; Ed.D., New York U. Sch. of Edn., 1939; m. Mamie Anna Louise Hartman, June 4, 1932. Prin. Warwick Twp. High Sch., Chester Co., Pa., 1915-17; teacher mathematics, Kutztown (Pa.) High Sch., 1920-22; supervising prin. Felton (Del.) High Sch., 1922-23; county supervisor, State Dept. of Pub. Instrn., Georgetown, Del., since 1923; instr., U. of Del. Summer Sch., Newark, Del., summers 1926-30. Served as apprentice seaman, U.S.N.R.F., 1918. Mem. N.E.A., Del. State Edn. Assn., Sussex Co. Teachers Assn. (pres. 1930-31), Am. Legion (dept. comdr. 1933-34), Alpha Chi Rho, Phi Delta Kappa. Reformed Ch. Mason (Royal Arch; past grand high priest, Past Grand Master, Grand Council Royal and Select Masters; K.T.), Odd Fellow. Home: 12 S. King St. Office: Court House Annex, Georgetown, Del.

AGAR, William Macdonough, headmaster; b. N.Y. City, Feb. 14, 1894; s. John Giraud and Agnes Louise (Macdonough) A.; grad. The Newman Sch., Lakewood, N.J., 1912; B.S., Princeton, 1916; A.M., 1920, Ph.D., 1922; m. Alida Stewart Carter, May 6, 1922; children—Alida Marie, Sylvia Carter, Catherine Macdonough, John Herbert Michael. Geologist Anaconda Copper Co., Butte, Mont., 1922-23; instr. in geology, Yale, 1923-26, asst. prof., 1926-28; asst. prof. of geology, Columbia, 1928-35; headmaster and trustee The Newman Sch., Lakewood, N.J., since 1935. Served as sous chef Service Sanitaire (Etats) Unis No. 16 (Am. Field Service), 1917; 1st lt. Air Service (pilot), U.S.A., with A.E.F., 1917-18. Decorated Croix de Guerre (France). Mem. Geol. Soc. America, Mineral Soc. America, Soc. Econ, Geologists, Am. Inst. Mining and Metall. Engrs., A.A.A.S., Sigma Xi. Democrat. Roman Catholic. Club: Princeton (N.Y. City). Compiled: Geology from Original Sources (with R. F. Flint and C. R. Longwell), 1929. Revised Pirsson and Schuchert's Textbook of Geology (with others), 1929. Contbr. articles on geology to tech. jours. Mem. editorial advisory board and contbr. articles and reviews to The Commonweal. Address: The Newman School, Lakewood, N.J.

AGEE, Howard Hibbs, rate engr.; b. Cheshire, O., June 25, 1888; s. Alva and L. Grace (Hibbs) A.; B.S. in E.E., Pa. State Coll., 1910; grad. study and asst. in elec. engring., Mass. Inst. Tech., 1910-11; m. Mabelle E. Williams, Oct. 16, 1912. Elec. engr. Power Construction Co., Shelburne Falls, Mass., 1911-13, elec. engr., D.C. and Wm. B. Jackson, cons. engrs., Chicago and Boston, 1913-17; engr. Philadelphia Electric Co., 1917-18; consulting engr. with Thomas Conway, Jr., on electric gas and ry. properties, 1919-26; chief engr. with Gillette & Malcomson on valuations and reports, 1926-27; cons. engr. for utilities, 1927-28; rate engr. Public Service Electric & Gas Co. since 1928. Served as capt., Engring Corps, U.S.A., France, with tech. bd.; later with commn. to negotiate peace, in charge Liaison Sect., Engring. Dept., War Damage Bd. Mem. Am. Inst. E.E., Am. Soc. Mech. Engrs., Am. Soc. Mil. Engrs.,

Edison Electric Inst. (mem. rate com.), Am. Gas Assn. (mem. and past chmn. rate com.), Assn. Edison Illuminating Cos. (mem. rate com.), Sigma Chi, Eta Kappa Nu, Phi Kappa Phi. Presbyn. Clubs: Essex (Newark); Baltusrol Golf (Springfield, N.J.). Contbr. articles to tech. mags. Home: 565 High St. Office: 80 Park Pl., Newark, N.J.

AGGER, Eugene Ewald, prof. economics; b. Cincinnati, O., Dec. 4, 1879; s. Peter Nicholas and Johanna (Sess) A.; grad. Hughes High Schs., Cincinnati, 1898; A.B., U. of Cincinnati, 1901, A.M., 1902; Ph.D., Columbia, 1907; m. May C. Hessler, June 4, 1908; children—Carolyn Eugenia, Donald. Successively lecturer in economics, asst. prof. and asso. prof., Columbia, 1907-26; prof. economics and head of dept., also dir. bur. econ. and business research, Rutgers U., since 1926. Lecturer Am. Inst. Banking since 1917; asst. dir. div. of analysis and research Federal Reserve Bd., 1917-18; asst. to pres. Nat. City Bank, New York, 1918-20; editorial writer Standard Daily Trade Service, 1920-21. Asso. dir. Grad. Sch. of Banking, Am. Inst. Banking, 1935; dir. management division, asst. administrator, consultant, Resettlement Administration, Washington, since 1935; commr. N.J. State Housing Authority since 1936. Mem. Board of Edn., Tenafly, N.J., 1920-29. Mem. Am. Economic Assn., Am. Statis. Association, Phi Beta Kappa. Presbyn. Author: The Budget in the American Commonwealth, 1907; Organized Banking, 1918; Banking in New Jersey, 1930; Banking and the New Deal, 1934; Money and Banking, 1939. Editor of Am. edition Henry Clay's Economics for the General Reader, 1918. Home: Hillcrest, New Brunswick, N.J.

AHL, A(ugustus) William, educator, author; b. Germany, Sept. 6, 1886; s. William and Dorothy A.; A.M., Susquehanna U., Selinsgrove, Pa., 1912; grad. Breklum Sem., Germany, 1908; Ph.D., Vanderbilt U., 1920; spl. student Peabody Coll. for Teachers, Nashville, Tenn., 1921-22; m. Henrietta Paulsen, Apr. 15, 1910; children—William G., Hildegard Dorothea. Ordained Luth. ministry, at Schenectady, N.Y., 1909; pastor Herkimer, N.Y., 1909-10, Baltimore, Md., 1910-16, Nashville, Tenn., 1916-22; instr. Vanderbilt U., 1921-22; prof. Greek lang. and lit., Thiel Coll., Greenville, Pa., 1922-27; prof. Greek and ancient history, Susquehanna U., Selinsgrove, Pa., since 1927. Mem. Am. Philol. Assn., Classical Assn. of the Atlantic States, Classical League, Am. Oriental Soc., Philos. Soc. Gt. Britain, Acad. Letters and Science (Naples), Pi Gamma Mu. Author: Outline of Persian History, 1922; Bible Studies in the Light of Recent Research, 1923. Home: Selinsgrove, Pa.

AIKEN, Gerald Randolph, lawyer; b. Baltimore, Md., Jan. 14, 1903; s. Albert Allen and Lula Edith (Richards) A.; LL.B., U. of Md. Law Sch., Baltimore, Md., 1925; m. Maude McDonald, Oct. 24, 1926; 1 dau., Ann. Admitted to Md. bar, 1924 and since engaged in gen. practice of law at Baltimore; mem. firm Aiken and Krieger since 1937; trial counsel for Md. Casualty Co., Baltimore, Md., 1924-34; asst. U.S. atty. for Dist. of Md. since 1934. Mem. Am. Bar Assn., Md. State Bar Assn., Bar Assn. of City of Baltimore. Democrat. Club: University. Home: 20 Dutton Av., Catonsville. Office: Baltimore Trust Bldg., Baltimore, Md.

AIKEN, William J.; in gen. practice of law since 1915. Office: 2005 Law & Finance Bldg., Pittsburgh, Pa.

AIKENS, H. Hayes; exec. v.p. Phila. Suburban Transportation Co. Home: 25 E. Park Road, Llanerch, Pa. Office: 69th St. Terminal, Upper Darby, Pa.

AIKMAN, Everett M.; surgeon E. I. du Pont de Nemours & Co., Edge Moor and Newport plants. Address: E. I. du Pont de Nemours & Co., Edge Moor, Del.

AILMAN, Mildred Amelia, librarian; b. Thompsontown, Pa., Aug. 13, 1900; d. Jerome Thompson and Ninette (McCleery) Ailman; grad. State College (Pa.) High Sch., 1918; A.B., Pa. State Col., 1922; B.S., Simmons Coll., Sch. of Library Science, 1925; student summers U. of Chicago, 1933, Pa. State Coll., 1936, 37, 39; unmarried. Circulation asst. Pa. State Coll. Library, 1922-24; librarian, Westminster Coll., New Wilmington, Pa., since 1925. Mem. Am. Library Assn., Am. Assn. Univ. Women, Theta Upsilon. Republican. Lutheran. Home: 143 W. Fairmount Av., State College, Pa. Address: Westminster College, New Wilmington, Pa.

AIRES, Benjamin Harrison, civil engr.; b. Baltimore, Md., Nov. 15, 1888; s. Andrew Jackson and Clarissa (Miller) A.; grad. Carnegie Inst. Tech. (night sch.), 1925; m. Lillian Elizabeth Yedele, Dec. 22, 1920; 1 son, Edward Andrew. Rodman Washington, Baltimore & Annapolis Ry., 1907-09; rodman, later party chief, Reding & Howard and J. Spence Howard, Baltimore, Md., 1909-13; survey party chief, E. V. Coonan & Co., Baltimore, Md., 1913-17; inspector, estimator and valuation work P. & L.E. R.R. Co., 1917-22; private practice as civil engr., 1922-24 and since 1934; mem. firm Aires & Pettay, civil engrs., 1924-26, Aires, Stone & Pettay, 1926-34. Neighborhood commr. Boy Scouts of Mt. Lebanan Twp., Allegheny Co., Pa.; chmn. camp maintenance com. Allegheny Co. Council, Boy Scouts of America. Mem. Nat. Soc. Professional Engrs., Pa. Soc. of Professional Engrs. (sec. Pittsburgh chapter), Nat. Geog. Soc., Phi Nu (past dir. Carnegie Inst. Tech. night sch. chapter). Awarded Silver Beaver by Boy Scouts of America, 1936. Lutheran (sec. Grace Evang. Lutheran Ch., Pittsburgh). Club: Kiwanis of Pittsburgh (dir.). Home: 114 Marlin Drive E., Mt. Lebanon Twp., Allegheny Co., Pa. Office: 610 Maloney Bldg., Pittsburgh, Pa.

AITKIN, Austin King, advertising exec.; b. Trenton, N.J., July 5, 1887; s. James Stuart and Evelyn (Fontaine) A.; student Tome Sch., Port Deposit, Md., 1906, Princeton U., 1906-08; m. Mary Madeleine Harding, Feb. 2, 1911 (died Nov. 4, 1933); children—Doris Harding (Mrs. William Miller Hawkins), Stuart King; m. 2d, Annette Kathleen Peck, June 14, 1937. Adv. mgr. Trenton Potteries Co., Trenton, N.J., 1910-16; partner Dippy & Aitkin, adv. agency, Phila., 1916-20; formed, 1920, The Aitkin-Kynett Co., Phila., adv. agency, and since partner. Served as industrial investigator for Draft Bd. during World War. Republican. Presbyterian. Clubs: Union League, Racquet, Poor Richard, Phila. Country (Phila.); Colonial (Princeton, N.J.). Home: 28 State Rd., Bala-Cynwyd, Pa. Office: 1400 So. Penn Sq., Philadelphia, Pa.

AKELEY, Archibald P(aul), supt. county schs.; b. Russell, Pa., May 18, 1886; s. Lester O. and Emma (Rhodes) A.; ed. Grove City Coll., 1910-15, Mansfield State Teachers Coll., 1926-29, St. Bonaventures, 1932-33; m. Doris Heymann, Dec. 31, 1918; children—John Wilder, James Douglas. Engaged in teaching, 1905-11; prin. high sch., Costello, Pa., 1911-15; asst. supt. co. schs., 1915-18; supt. schs. Potter Co., Pa. since 1918. Chmn. Potter Co. Red Cross. Dir. Coudersport Pub. Library, Lock Haven State Teachers Coll. Pres. Potter Co. Hist. Soc. Republican. Presbyterian (stated clk. Bd. Elders First Ch.). Mason (33°). Clubs: Rotary, Golf. Home: 709 N. West St., Coudersport, Pa.

AKERS, Oscar Perry, prof. mathematics; b. Trenton, Mo., June 16, 1872; s. James and Eliza E. (Kackley) Akers; A.B., U. of Colo., 1900, A.M., 1902; Ph.D., Cornell U., 1905; Göttingen U., 1913-14; m. Ella M. Tarr, July 16, 1896. Student Engring. Sch. Univ. of Colo., 1900-01; Oliver scholar, Cornell U., 1902-04; asst. in Dept. of Mathematics, same 1904-05; asst. prof. mathematics, 1905-07, prof. since 1907, Allegheny Coll. (now also sec. of faculty); on leave of absence to study and travel in Europe, 1913-14. Mem. Am. Math. Soc., A.A.A.S., Circolo Matematico di Palermo, Sigma Xi, Omicron Delta Kappa, Delta Tau Delta. Contbr. to mags. and periodicals on math. topics. Home: 360 N. Main St., Meadville, Pa.

ALBERT, Charles Elwood, educator; b. Pen Argyl, Pa., Jan. 10, 1883; s. Urbanus and Sarah Hannah (Jones) A.; grad. high sch., Pen Argyl, 1901; C.E., Lafayette Coll., 1908; grad. work, Pa. State College and N.C. State College; LL.D., Southwestern, Memphis, Tenn., 1937; m. Jeanne Marstiller, Sept. 1, 1915; children—Charles Elwood, Jeanne Marstiller. Teacher high sch., Pa., 1909-11; prof. mathematics, Davis and Elkins Coll., Elkins, W.Va., 1911-13; instr. in mechanics, Pa. State Coll., 1913-16; civ. engr. Camden (N.J.) Iron Works, 1916-20; instr. in mechanics, Drexel Inst. (night sch.), Phila., 1920-22; dean and prof. mathematics, Davis and Elkins Coll., 1922-35, acting pres., July 1, 1935-July 6, 1936, pres. since 1936. Pres. Bd. of Edn., Randolph County, W.Va., July 1, 1933—. Mem. W.Va. Acad. Science (pres. 1934-35), Alpha Tau Omega, Chi Beta Phi. Democrat. Presbyn. Mason. Home: 10 Boundary Av., Elkins, W.Va.

ALBIG, Reed H.; pres. Nat. Bank of McKeesport. Office: McKeesport, Pa.

ALBINSON, J. Warren, clergyman; b. Bloomfield, N.J., Nov. 10, 1896; s. Thomas Henry and Margot (Murphy) A.; Ph.B., St. Stephen's Coll. of Columbia U., 1917; A.B., Upsala Coll., East Orange, N.J., 1921; student Gen. Theol. Sem., N.Y. City, 1925, N.Y. Univ. Grad. Sch., 1926-28; D.D., St. Paul's Coll., Turners Falls, Mass., 1928; m. Virginia Ross Caldwell, Feb. 25, 1930; 1 dau., Margot Louise. Ordained to ministry Episcopal Ch., deacon, 1923, priest, 1924; rector, Butler, N.J., 1920-30, Pompton Lakes, N.J., 1922-30, Ringwood Manor, N.J., 1922-30; rector Cecil County Cooperative Parish of chs. at Aikin, Port Deposit, and Elkton, Md., since 1930; founder of cooperative parish plan for work in rural field of Episcopal Ch. which has developed largest rural parish to date in entire Anglican Communion; treas. bd. religious edn., Diocese of Newark, 1928-30; pres. eccles. ct., Diocese of Easton since 1933; nominated for bishop of Diocese of Easton, 1939, and withdrew after five ballots. Served as inf. officer, U.S.A., 1917-19; now capt. inf., U.S.A., inactive; comdg. officer C.C.C. camps in Wash., Calif. and Pa., 1933-35. Dir. and treas. Cecil Co. Children's Aid Soc. since 1930. Sec. and treas. Northern Convocation, Diocese Easton, 1939—. Vice-pres. supreme council Pi Alpha. Democrat. Mason. Odd Fellow. Clubs: Rotary, East End Tennis (Elkton); Tome Golf (Port Deposit). Author: The New Priesthood, 1930; Four Confirmation Lectures for Adults, 1932. Contbr. articles to religious journs. Home: 105 Bridge St., Elkton, Md.

ALBION, Robert Greenhalgh, prof. of history, author; b. Malden, Mass., Aug. 15, 1896; s. James Francis and Alice Marion (Lamb) A.; A.B., Bowdoin Coll., 1918; A.M., Harvard, 1920, Ph.D., 1924; m. Jennie Barnes Pope, Aug. 16, 1923. Teaching fellow, Harvard, 1920-22; with Princeton U. since 1922, as instr. in history, 1922-24, asst. prof., 1924-28, asso. prof., 1928-39, prof. of history since 1939, dir. of summer session and asst. dean of the faculty since 1929. Served as 2d lt. Inf., 159th Depot Brigade, 1918. Trustee Wooster Sch. Elected hon. life mem. Soc. for Nautical Research (Eng.); awarded David A. Wells prize, Harvard, 1926. Mem. Am. Hist. Assn., Assn. Am. Historians, Econ. History Soc., Am. Naval Foundation, Theta Delta Chi, Phi Beta Kappa. Republican. Club: Princeton (New York). Author: Forests and Sea Power: The Timber Problem of the Royal Navy, 1926; Introduction to Military History, 1929; Brief Biographies (with others), 4 vols., 1929-31; History of England and the British Empire (with W. P. Hall), 1937; Square Riggers on Schedule, 1938; The Rise of New York Port (1815-60), 1939. Editor: Philip Vickers Fithian: Journal, 1775-1776 (with L. Dodson), 1934. Contbr. numerous articles to Dictionary of Am. Biography; also to Ency. of Social Sciences and Saturday Review of Lit. Home: 69 Harrison St., Princeton, N.J.; (summer) South Portland, Me.

ALBRIGHT, Charles (Clinton), highway engr.; b. Brinfield, Ind., May 20, 1879; s. John Wallace and Sophia Emily (Bower) A.; grad. Marion (Ind.) High Sch., 1897; B.S. in civil engring., Purdue U., Lafayette, Ind., 1903, C.E., 1908; m. Adda Mable Robinson, June 22, 1904; children—Mary Mildred (Mrs. Paul W. Jones), Helen Louise (Mrs. Robert R. Duff). Rodman on engring. corps B. & O. R.R., 1902-03; asst., same, Newark, O., 1903-04; asst. engr. southern lines A.,T. & S.F. Ry., 1904-08; instr. in civil engring., U. of Ill., Urbana, Ill., 1908-09; successively asst. prof., asso. prof., prof. of civil engring., Purdue U., Lafayette, Ind., 1909-24;

founder and in charge Purdue summer surveying camp, 1914-19; dir. Purdue Road Sch., 1921-24; dir. grad. highway engring., Ia. State Coll., Ames, Ia., summer 1922; with Pa. Dept. of Highways, Harrisburg, Pa., since 1924, successively as asst. engr., office engr., twp. engr., cost engr., acting state mgr. highway planning survey; registered Professional Engr., Ind. Served as pvt., Ind. N.G., 1897-98; mem. O.T.S., Ft. Sheridan, Ill., 1918. Mem. City Council, Lafayette, Ind., 1920-24. Mem. Am. Ry. Engring. Assn., Soc. Am. Mil. Engrs., Am. Assn. State Highway Officials; hon. mem. Contour Soc., Triangle Fraternity (Purdue). Republican. Methodist. Mason. Home: 1319 N. 15th St. Office: Pa. Dept. of Highways, Harrisburg, Pa.

ALBRIGHT, Denton M(orris), educator; b. Black Rock, Pa., Aug. 20, 1893; s. Albert Pious and Theresa Jane (Miller) A.; A.B., Albright Coll., 1915; A.M., Columbia Univ., 1922; m. Ethel Mary Jane Varner, June 25, 1926; children—Ellen Jane, Denton Morris, George Albert, Mary Carolyn. Teacher, Altoona (Pa.) High Sch., 1915-17; supervising principal, Spring Grove, Pa., 1917-18; teacher, Harrisburg (Pa.) Tech., 1918-24; principal, Kittanning (Pa.) High Sch., 1924-26; supt. of schs., Rochester, Pa., 1926-34, Lewiston, Pa., 1934-38, Crafton, Pa., since 1938; mem. summer sch. faculty, Geneva Coll., Beaver Falls, Pa., 1930-35, Juniata Coll., Huntingdon, Pa., 1937-38. Mem. Am. Legion, Y.M.C.A. (dir.), Chamber of Commerce (dir.), N.E.A., Assn. Am. Sch. Adminstrs., Nat. Soc. for Study of Edn., Phi Delta Kappa. Republican. Methodist. Mason (Shriner). Address: 17 Emerson St., Crafton, Pa.

ALBRIGHT, Louis Francis, physician; b. Camden, N.J., May 9, 1906; s. Louis Harry and Mary Frances (Parker) A.; B.S., Hahnemann Sch. of Sci., Phila., Pa., 1926; M.D., Hahnemann Med. Coll., Phila., Pa., 1930; m. Roberta Lambert Clayton, Oct. 1, 1932; children—Mary Louise, Barbara Ann. Interne Ann May Memorial Hosp., Spring Lake, N.J., 1930-31; physician in gen. practice of medicine at Spring Lake, N.J., since 1931, specialist in internal medicine and diagnosis since 1934; attdg. asso. physician, Firkin Memorial Hosp., Neptune, N.J., 1931-39, chief out-patient dept., 1936-39, attdg. physician in charge hematology, out-patient dept., 1936-39; attdg. asso. physician, Monmouth Memorial Hosp., Long Branch, N.J., 1936-39; attdg. physician in charge, Hematology Clinic, 1936-39; consultant in medicine, Riverview Hosp., Red Bank, N.J., since 1935. Served as pres. bd. health, Spring Lake, N.J., since 1931; sch. physician, Spring Lake since 1931. Fellow Am. Coll. Physicians; mem. A.M.A., N.J. State Med. Soc. Republican. Episcopalian. Clubs: Spring Lake Bathing and Tennis. Home: 118 Madison Av., Spring Lake, N.J.

ALBRIGHT, Raymond Wolf, coll. prof.; b. Akron, Pa., July 16, 1901; s. Richard Lausch and Margaret Garman (Wolf) A.; student Albright Coll., 1918-21; B.D., Evang. Sch. of Theology, 1922; A.B., Franklin and Marshall Coll., 1923, A.M., 1924; B.D., Reformed Theol. Sem., 1924; Th.D., Div. Sch. of the P.E. Ch., 1933; univ. scholar in history and religions, U. of Pa., 1928-29; fellow Carl Schurz Memorial Foundation in Germany, 1937; m. Mary Catherine Sherr, June 18, 1924 (died 1932); children—Winifred Louise, Raymond Jacob; m. 2d, Caroline Elizabeth Ayer Rising, of Phila., Pa., June 9, 1933; 1 stepson, Hawley Knox Rising. Ordained deacon in the Evang. Ch., 1921, elder, 1923; pastor at Berkshire Heights, Lebanon, and Matamoras, Pa., 1922-1927; prof. of ch. history, Evang. Sch. of Theol., Reading, Pa., since 1926; prof. of grad. ch. history, Temple U., since 1935; dean of Reading Sch. of Leadership Training. Dir. Reading Council of Christian Edn.; mem. gen. conf. of the Evang. Ch. Mem. Am. Soc. of Ch. History, Berks County Hist. Society, Pa., German Soc., Hist. Soc. of Evang. Ch. (v.p., trustee, curator), Lambda Chi Alpha, Alpha Pi Omega, Phi Upsilon Kappa. Club: Torch. Author: History of Religious Education in Evangelical Church, Cleveland, O., 1932. Home: 1524 Palm Av. Office: Evangelical School of Theology, Reading, Pa.

ALBRIGHT, William Foxwell, orientalist; b. Coquimbo, Chile, May 24, 1891; s. Rev. Wilbur Finley and Zephine Viola (Foxwell) A.; A.B., Upper Ia. U., 1912, Litt.D., 1922; Ph.D., Johns Hopkins, 1916, D.H.L., Jewish Theol. Sem. of America, Jewish Inst. of Religion, 1936; Th.D., Univ. of Utrecht (Netherlands), 1936; m. Ruth Norton (Ph.D.), Aug. 31, 1921; children—Paul Norton, Hugh Norton, Stephen Foxwell, David Foxwell. Prin. high sch., Menno, S.D., 1912-13; instr. in Semitics, Johns Hopkins, 1916-17, Johnston scholar, 1917-18; Thayer fellow, Am. Sch. Oriental Research, Jerusalem, 1919-20, acting dir., 1920-21, dir. 1921-29, 1933-36; W.W. Spence prof. Semitic langs., Johns Hopkins, since 1929. Richards lecturer U. of Va., 1931; Carew lecturer Hartford Theol. Sem., 1931; Coleman lecturer Lafayette Coll., 1937. Dir. archæol. expdns., Gibeah of Saul (1922-23, 33), Tell Beit Mirsim (1926, 28, 30, 32), Bethel (1927, 34), Moab (1924, 33), Petra (1934); archæol. adviser, Danish Shiloh Expdn. (1929), Bethzur (1931). Vice-pres., chmn. com. on Sch. in Jerusalem, and editor Bulletin, Am. Schs. of Oriental Research. Mem. Am. Council Learned Socs (chmn. com. Mediterranean antiquities 1931-33, vice chmn. 1939), Am. Philos. Soc. (research com. since 1936; council 1938-41), Archæol. Inst. America, Am. Oriental Soc. (pres. 1935-36), Soc. Biblical Lit. (pres. 1939), Linguistic Soc. America, Palestine Oriental Soc. (pres. 1921-22, 1934-35), Phi Beta Kappa; hon. mem. Inst. Oriental Studies of Hebrew Univ. Del. Internat. Congress of Orientalists, Oxford, 1928, Leiden, 1931, Rome, 1935, Brussels, 1938 (mem. consultative com. since 1931, chmn. U.S. delegation 1935). Methodist. Author: Excavations at Gibeah of Benjamin, 1924; The Spoken Arabic of Palestine (with E. N. Haddad), 1927; The Archæology of Palestine and the Bible, 1932, 3d rev. edit., 1935; The Excavation of Tell Beit Mirsim, vol. I, 1932, IA, 1933, II, 1938; The Vocalization of the Egyptian Syllabic Orthography, 1934; Recent Discoveries in Bible Lands, 1936. Contbr. over 200 papers and several hundred reports and reviews on archæol., Bibl. and oriental subjects. Home: 2305 Sulgrave Av., Baltimore, Md.

ALBRIGHT, William H., treasurer of state of N.J. since 1934. Home: Woodbury, N.J.

ALBUM, Leon, rabbi; b. Zeimel, Kurland, Apr. 27, 1880; s. Rabbi Isaac Mendel and Hannah (Israelson) A.; scion of the rabbinical family of Katzenellenhaugen and medical family of Mandelstam; came to U.S., 1898, naturalized, 1901; ed. Valozin and Jerusalem seminaries and U. of Chicago and Stanford U. (A.B. 1907); m. Amelia Sobel, Sept. 6, 1908; children—Mildred, Selma, Manuel Moses. Rabbi Temple Keneseth Israel, San Francisco, Calif., 1900-08, Temple Uptown Torah, New York, 1909-17, Temple Shaari Zedeck, Phila., since 1918. Served with Jewish Welfare Bd. during Spanish-Am. War, 1898; visiting chaplain of Jewish Welfare Bd. to Camps Lee, Mead and Dix during World War. Mem. Bd. Jewish Ministers of Phila., Stanford Alumni Assn. Club: Stanford University (Phila.). Asso. editor San Francisco Times and San Francisco Emanuel, 1900-08; asso. editor Elmira Sunday Telegram, 1910; contbr. to Hapisgo (Hebrew jour.); contbr. poems and articles to various publs. Address: 5332 Columbia Av., Philadelphia, Pa.

ALCOCK, John Leighton, owner John L. Alcock & Co.; b. Market Drayton, Shropshire, England, May 9, 1868; s. Thomas Goodall and Charlotte Elizabeth (Leighton) A.; ed. Peter St. Grammar Sch., Manchester, England; m. Edith Allen, June 17, 1896. Owner John L. Alcock & Co.; officer and dir. many organizations. Home: 208 E. Joppa Road, Towson, Md. Office: Munsey Bldg., Baltimore, Md.

ALDEN, Carroll Storrs, college prof.; b. Medina, O., Mar. 15, 1876; s. Ezra Judson and Helen Frances (Storrs) A.; Beloit Coll., 1894-97; B.A., Yale, 1898, Ph.D., 1903; m. Meeta Campbell, d. Maj. Gen. William Montrose Graham, U.S. Army, Oct. 21, 1911. Assistant in English, Yale U., 1901-03; instr. in English, Grinnell Coll., 1903-04; instr. in English, 1904-19, prof., 1919—, head dept. of English, history and govt., 1924—, U.S. Naval Acad. Episcopalian. Editor: Jonson's Bartholomew Fair, 1904; Some Recent Essays and Poems, 1925. Author: A Guide to Annapolis and the Naval Academy (with W. O. Stevens), 1910; A Short History of the United States Navy (with others), 1911; Life and Letters of George Hamilton Perkins, 1914; Composition for Naval Officers (with W. O. Stevens), 1918; American Submarine Operations in the War, 1920; Makers of Naval Tradition (with Ralph Earle), 1925; Writing and Speaking—A Handbook for Naval Officers, 1927; Lawrence Kearny—Sailor Diplomat, 1936. Contbr. to Dictionary of American Biography and Am. Year Book. Home: 3 Porter Rd., U.S. Naval Academy, Annapolis, Md.

ALDEN, Ezra Hyde, retired ry. official; b. Bridgewater, Mass., Jan. 26, 1866; s. Ezra Hyde and Mary Esther (Smith) A.; ed. Bridgewater pub. schs., 1870-82; m. Hattie C. Hathaway, June 28, 1892; children—Esther Hyde, Olive Hathaway (Mrs. Roy Frank Larson), Philip Merriam, Margaret Wheeler, Francis Carter. Clerk and stenographer, Boston, 1882-91; with Norfolk and Western Ry. Co. from 1891 to retirement Mar. 1, 1936, successively as chief clerk to sec., 1891-1905, sec. and asst. treas., 1905-20, financial vice pres., 1920-36. Sec. of Pa. Soc. of Order of Founders and Patriots of America since 1937. Republican. Swedenborgian. Club: Union League (Phila.). Home: 6385 Woodbine Av., Philadelphia, Pa.

ALDERFER, Harold Frederick; prof. polit. science, Pa. State Coll. Address: State College, Pa.

ALDERMAN, Lewis R., educator; b. Dayton, Ore., Oct. 29, 1872; s. A. L. and Charlotte (Odell) A.; ed. McMinnville Coll.; A.B., U. of Ore., 1898; Ph.D., American U. Washington, 1933; LL.D., Linfield Coll., McMinnville, Ore., 1938; m. Alice Barber 1899 (dec.); children—Mrs. Fanny Ruth Tait, Robert Barber, John Clement; m. 2d, Lola E. Lake, 1924. Taught school; county supt. schs., Yamhill Co., Ore., 1904-07; city supt. schs., Eugene, 1907-08; asso. in dept. of edn., U. of Ore., 1908-10; state supt. pub. instrn., Ore., 1910-13; supt. of schs., Portland, 1913-19; with Army Ednl. Corps, in France and Germany, 1919; ednl. adviser U.S. Navy, 1919-24; mem. Survey Staff for survey New York pub. schs., 1924; senior specialist in adult edn., U.S. Office of Education, Washington, D.C., since 1925; also instr. evening classes, George Washington U., 1929-32; director of edn. programs Federal Emergency Relief Adminstrn. and Works Progress Adminstrn. since 1933. Mem. bd. of regents American Univ. since 1935. Mem. Acacia Fraternity. Mason, Odd Fellow. Club: Cosmos. Author of ednl. bulls. Lecturer on ednl. subjects; contbr. on ednl. topics. Home: 507 E. Thornapple St., Chevy Chase, Md. Address: U.S. Office of Education, Washington, D.C.

ALDERSON, Joseph Newman, state adminstr. Works Progress Adminstrn.; b. Alderson, W.Va., June 8, 1887; s. Joseph Newman and Alethea Lillie Ellis (Putney) A.; student Allegheny Inst., 1894-1900, Alderson (W.Va.) Acad., 1900-01, Pantops Acad., Charlottesville, Va., 1902-04, Dunsmore Business Coll., Staunton, Va., 1907-08; m. Frances Lucile Richardson, Feb. 15, 1911; children—Frances Alethea, Alice Todd. Teller First Nat. Bank, Alderson, W.Va., 1910-14; postmaster, 1914-23; mcht., 1923-35; also pres. and gen. mgr., Western View Land Co., Alderson, W.Va., 1925-37; dir. dist. 3, Works Progress Adminstrn. of W.Va., 1935-37, state adminstr. since 1937; sec. Alderson Realty Co., Alderson, W.Va. Served as recorder, Alderson, W.Va., and mem. City Council. Mem. and pres. Alderson Sch. Bd. and Monroe County Sch. Bd. Pres. Chamber of Commerce, Alderson. Democrat. Presbyn. (trustee Alderson Ch.). Mason. Modern Woodman. Home: Riverview Terrace. Office: Peoples Exchange Bldg., Charleston, W.Va.

ALDRICH, Moriel Simeon (Col.), ins. broker; b. New York, N.Y., Mar. 20, 1894; s. Edwin Moriel and Bella Florence (Hall) A.; student Pub. Sch. No. 76 and No. 77, New York, 1901-08; grad. DeWitt Clinton High Sch., 1912;

studied Cornell U., 1912; m. Marguerite Mahan, Dec. 24, 1918; children—Virginia Lee, Edwin Moriel, William Thomas. Began as cow puncher, 1912; tutor in Calif., 1913; asst. supt. Am. Ice Co., New York, 1913; receiving clerk C. P. Rogers Co., New York, 1914; billing clerk Adams Express Co., New York, 1914; mgr. account dept. Camp Upton, L.I., 1915-16; commissary supt., Newport News, Va., 1916-17, Nitro, W.Va., 1918; proprietor and gen. mgr. Merchandise and trucking business, 1919-21; salesman of office supplies, Charleston, W.Va., 1922; editor and asst. mgr. Dixie Motor Bus Guide, 1923; founder, 1923, and mgr. W.Va. Bus Assn., 1923-39; state agent Am. Fidelity & Casualty Co., 1928-39; regional mgr. Markel Service, 1930-39; gen. mgr. South Hills Bus Lines, 1932-37; pres. M. S. Aldrich & Associates, Inc. Dir. W.Va. Assn. Police Civil Service Commission, Inc.; pres. Charleston Civil Service Police Commn.; pres. Kanawha Valley Safety Council. Mem. W.Va. State Chamber of Commerce (former dir.), Charleston Chamber of Commerce (dir.). Republican. Christian Scientist. Mason (Shriner), Elk, Moose. Clubs: Kanawha Country, Meadow Brook Country (Charleston); Coral Gables (Fla.) Country; Southern W.Va. Automobile (vice-pres.), W.Va. State Automobile (pres.). Home: 1575 Lee St. Office: 412 Charleston Nat. Bank Bldg., Charleston, W.Va.

ALDRIN, Edwin Eugene, aviator, aviation consultant; b. Worcester, Mass., Apr. 12, 1896; s. Carl J. and Anna (Nelson) A.; A.B., Clark U., 1915; grad. study Worcester Poly. Inst., 1916; M.S., Mass. Inst. Tech., 1917, D.Sc., 1928; grad. U.S. Air Corps Engring. Sch., McCook Field, Dayton, O., 1920; m. Marion G. Moon, Mar. 22, 1924; children—Madeline Ross, Fay Anne, Edwin E. Commd. 2d lt. C.A.C., U.S.A., Oct. 26, 1917, 1st lt., Jan. 6, 1918; detailed to Signal Corps, Aviation Sect., 1918; asst. chief Airplane Sect., Engring Div., McCook Field, 1919; comdg. officer 28th Bombardment Squadron, P.I., 1922-24; sec. Air Service Engring. Sch., McCook Field, 1924-26, asst. comdt., 1927-28; capt., Mar. 6, 1928; resigned, Nov. 12, 1928; maj. Specialist R.C. since Feb. 1929; aviation mgr. Standard Oil Development Co., July 1928-Jan. 1929; formerly aviation mgr. Standard Oil Co. of N.J.; formerly pres., v.p., dir. and gen. mgr. Stanavo Specification Bd., Inc. U.S. Army pilot and transport pilot. Licensed professional engr. State of N.Y. Gov. Aeronautical Chamber of Commerce; formerly pres. Daniel Guggenheim Medal Fund; tech. adviser Guggenheim Safe Aircraft Competition; mem. advisory com., aeronautical course, Mass. Inst. Tech.; mgr. Internat. Flying Team, Nat. Air Races, 1932. Flights made in Hawaii, Philippines, China, Siam, France, England, Belgium, Holland and Germany, 1922-24; flew the first Am. airplane, 1929, to make business tour of Europe; holds several cross-country airplane speed records; made transatlantic round trip on airship Hindenburg. Mem. aviation com. Merchants' Assn. of New York; charter mem., mem. council, fellow, former treas. and v.p. Institute of Aeronautical Sciences, Incorporated; member visiting com. Dept. of Mech. Engring., Mass. Inst. Tech. Asso. fellow Royal Aeronautical Soc.; mem. Am. Soc. M.E., Soc. Automotive Engrs., Am. Soc. for Testing Materials (mem. tech. com. on gasoline, tech. com. on motor oils), Nat. Aeronautic Assn. (v.p. 1938), Aero Club of France, Sigma Xi, Kappa Phi, Am. Legion (past vice comdr. Air Service Post 501). Decorated Commendatore Order of Crown of Italy. Contbr. papers on aircraft fuels. Supervised revision of C. N. Monteith's Simple Aerodynamics, 1925. Home: 25 Princeton Pl., Upper Montclair, N.J. Office: 30 Rockefeller Plaza, New York, N.Y.

ALEXANDER, Andrew S., lawyer; b. Putnam Co., W.Va., Aug. 7, 1867; s. William A. and Leonora C. A.; LL.B., W.Va. Univ. Law Coll., 1890; m. Susan Mann, Dec. 24, 1904; children—Andrew S., Leonora (Mrs. Charles P. Orr), Mathew M. Admitted to W.Va. bar and engaged in gen. practice of law at Charleston; served as prosecuting atty. of Putnam Co. and judge Ct. Common Pleas, Kanawha Co. Democrat. Presbyn. Mason. Home: Kanawha St. Office: Security Bldg., Charleston, W.Va.

ALEXANDER, Fay Knight, physician; b. Pine Island, Minn., May 13, 1903; s. M. William and Florence Alice (Perkins) A.; B.S., U. of Minn., 1926, M.B., same, 1928, M.D., same, 1929; m. B. Leone Furtney, of Rochester, Minn., July 8, 1931; children—F. Knight, William Putnam. Interne U. of Pa. Hosp., 1928-30; fellow and asso., X-ray dept., U. of Pa., 1930-35; dir. dept. of radiology, Chestnut Hill Hosp. since 1935. Diplomate Am. Bd. Radiology. Mem. Coll. of Phys. of Phila., Phila. Roentgen Ray Soc., Sigma Nu, Nu Sigma Nu. Unitarian. Club: Philadelphia Cricket. Home: East Gravers Lane. Office: 8835 Germantown Av., Philadelphia, Pa.

ALEXANDER, George Milton, pub. utility executive; b. near Morgantown, W.Va., November 10, 1867; s. John and Caroline (Conn) A.; LL.B. and B.S., W.Va. U., 1892; m. Gertrude Jamison, June 22, 1892; children—Virginia (Mrs. Robert E. Barnes), Edward Eugene. Admitted to W.Va. bar and began practice at Fairmont; prosecuting atty. Marion Co., W.Va., 1895-1900; pres. Bd. of Edn., Fairmont Independent Sch. Dist., 1911-1919. Served as capt., Ordnance Dept., U.S.A., World War. Mem. W.Va. State Bar Assn., U.S. Chamber Commerce, Phi Beta Kappa, Phi Sigma Kappa. Christian Scientist. Mason, Odd Fellow, Elk. Clubs: Maryland (Baltimore); Pittsburgh Athletic. Home: 639 Benoni Av. Office: Deveny Bldg., Fairmont, W.Va.*

ALEXANDER, James Herbert; mem. law firm Alexander & Clark. Address: Warren, Pa.

ALEXANDER, James Waddell, mathematics; b. Sea Bright, N.J., Sept. 19, 1888; s. John White and Elizabeth A.; B.S., Princeton, 1910, M.A., 1911, Ph.D., 1915; studied univs. of Paris and Bologna; m. Natalia Levitzkaja, Jan. 15, 1917; children—Irina, John. Began as instr. in mathematics, Princeton, 1911, asst. prof., 1920-25, asso. prof., 1926-28, prof., 1928-33, prof. Institute for Advanced Study since 1933. Served as capt. tech. staff, Ordnance Dept., U.S. Army, 1917-18. Mem. Nat. Acad. Sciences, Am. Philos. Soc., Am. Math. Soc., Math. Assn. America, A.A.A.S., Phi Beta Kappa. Awarded Bocher prize, Am. Math. Soc. 1929. Clubs: Am. Alpine, Quadrangle, Nassau. Contbr. to math. publs. Home: 29 Cleveland Lane, Princeton, N.J.*

ALEXANDER, John H., M.D.; mem. surg. staff Allegheny Gen. Hosp.; surgeon Pa. R.R. Address: 200 9th St., Pittsburgh, Pa.

ALEXANDER, Maitland, clergyman; b. New York, Apr. 8, 1867; s. Henry M. and Susan M. (Brown) A.; A.B., Princeton, 1889, A.M., 1892; McCormick Theol. Sem., Chicago, 1889-90; grad. Princeton Theol. Sem., 1892; D.D., Lafayette, 1897; LL.D., Worcester U., 1900; m. Madelaine F. Laughlin, Apr. 17, 1906; children—Maitland Alexander, Alexander Laughlin, Madelaine Laughlin, Charles Beatty. Ordained Presbyn. ministry, 1892; pastor Long Branch, N.J., 1893-97, Harlem, N.Y., 1897-99, 1st Ch., Pittsburgh, 1899-1927 (emeritus). Moderator Presbyn. Gen. Assembly, 1914. Republican. Clubs: Pittsburgh, Duquesne, Allegheny Country, University, Pittsburgh Golf; New York Yacht, Links (New York); Gulf Stream Golf, Tarratine Yacht (commodore). Home: Sewickley, Pa.

ALEXANDER, Park Jacobus, lawyer; b. Bridgeport, O., April 12, 1879; s. William and Sarah Jane (Park) A.; A.B., Washington and Jefferson Coll., 1900, A.M., 1904; LL.B., Harvard, 1903. Admitted to the Pa. bar, and practicing atty. in Pittsburgh since 1904; gen. counsel Fidelity Trust Co. Served as lt. coast arty., later instr. in arty. fire, U.S. Army, with A.E.F., during World War. Trustee Washington and Jefferson Coll., Presbyn. and University Hosps. (Pittsburgh). Mem. Am. Pa., and Allegheny Co. bar assns., Beta Theta Pi. Republican. Presbyterian. Mason. Clubs: University, Duquesne, Pittsburgh Athletic, Oakmont Country. Home: University Club. Office: Park Bldg., Pittsburgh, Pa.

ALEXANDER, Ralph Irwin, mech. engr.; b. Keene, N.H., July 31, 1890; s. George Herbert and Lucy Francis (Dexter) A.; grad. Templeton High Sch., Baldwinsville, Mass., 1909; B.S. in M.E., R.I. State Coll., Kingston, R.I., 1913; m. Ethel Isabelle Thomas, Oct. 15, 1915; children—John Clifford, Eunice Elizabeth (died), Harold David. Began as test engr. York Mfg. Co., York, Pa., 1913; instr. mech. engring., U. of Me., Orono, Me., 1917-18; head instructormechanical engring. dept., Rensselaer Poly. Inst., Troy, N.Y., 1918-20; plant engr. Strathmore Paper Co., Woronoco, Mass., 1920-21; engr. in charge design and construction of power station A. N. Pierson, Inc., Cromwell, Conn., 1921-22; chief engr. Lehigh Stone Co. and Victor Oolithic Stone Co., Kankakee, Ill., and Bloomington, Ind., 1922-24; cons. engr. Messrs. Ophuls & Hill, New York, 1924-28; mech. engr. Celanese Corpn. of America since 1928. Mem. Am. Soc. Mech. Engrs., Beta Phi (charter mem.), Phi Kappa Phi. Republican. Conglist. Club: Western Md. Motor (Cumberland, Md.). Home: 181 E. Main St., Frostburg, Md. Office: Celanese Corpn. of America, Cumberland, Md.

ALEXANDER, William E., banker; b. Whitestown, Pa., Jan. 16, 1896; s. William H. and Edith (McGowan) A.; student high sch., Slippery Rock, Pa., 1909-12; m. Abbie Posey, Aug. 21, 1922; children—Grace Martha, William E. Employed by B.&O. R.R., New Castle, Pa., 1912-17; banking since 1920; v.p. and dir. The Fulton Nat. Bank, Lancaster, Pa., since 1934. Served with 5th F.A., 1st Div., U.S. Army, with A.E.F., 1917-19. Dir. Welfare Fed., Lancaster (Pa.) Y.M.C.A (treas.), Lancaster Free Pub. Library; v.p. Recreation and Playground Assn. Mem. Lancaster Chamber of Commerce (state counsellor since 1938, pres. 1937-38), Lancaster Co. Bd. of Pub. Assistance (sec. since 1938). Republican. Elder Reformed Ch. Club: Rotary (Lancaster, Pa.). Home: 735 N. Reservoir St. Office: Penn Sq., Lancaster, Pa.

ALEXANDER, William Fontaine, ins. agency; b. Jefferson Co., W.Va., Mar. 19, 1873; s. William Fontaine and Anne Catherine (Henkle) A.; student Charles Town (W.Va.) Acad., 1885-90; m. Cicely deG. Woolley, Nov. 29, 1898; children—Cicely Fontaine (Mrs. John Harkey Reiter), Anne Catherine (Mrs. Talbott Winchester Jenkins). Studied law in office of Forrest W. Brown, Charles Town, W.Va., 6 years; admitted to W.Va. bar, 1894 and engaged in gen. practice of law at Charles Town, 1894-96; mem. firm Washington, Alexander & Cooke, ins. agts., Charles Town, W.Va., since 1906. Mem. W.Va. Assn. of Ins. Agents. Democrat. Episcopalian. Mason. Kiwanis. Home: George St., Charles Town, W.Va.

ALFORD, Leon Pratt, engineer, editor; b. Simsbury, Conn., Jan. 3, 1877; Emerson and Sarah Merriam (Pratt) A.; B.S. in Electrical Engineering, Worcester Poly. Institute, 1896, M.E., 1905, Dr. of Engineering, 1932; m. Grace A. Hutchins, January 1, 1900; 1 son, Ralph I. Shop foreman McKay Metallic Fastening Assn., Boston, 1896-97, McKay-Bigelow Heeling Assn., 1897-99; production supt. McKay Shoe Machinery Co., 1899-1902; mech. engr. United Shoe Machinery Co., Boston, 1902-07; engring editor American Machinist, 1907-11, editor in chief, 1911-17; editor Industrial Management, 1917-20, Management Engineering, New York, 1921-23, Mfg. Industries, 1923-28; v.p. Ronald Press Co., 1928-34; asst. engr. in charge mfg. costs, Federal Communications Commn., 1935-37; prof. administrative engring., New York Univ., since 1937. Past vice-president and member research coms. American Engring. Council which produced repts. on Waste in Industry, Twelve-Hour-Shift in Industry, Safety and Production in Industry and Tech. Changes in Mfg. Industries. Mem. Am. Soc. Mech. Engrs. (past v.p.), Inst. of Management (past pres.), Institut Scientifique d'Organisation et de Gestion, Nat. Association Cost Accountants, Sigma Xi. Melville Gold Medalist, 1927; Gantt Gold Medalist, 1931. Methodist. Club: Engineers. Author: Bearings and Their Lubrication, 1912; Laws of Management, 1928; Life of Henry Laurence Gantt, 1934. Editor: Artillery and Artillery Ammunition, 1917; Management's Handbook, 1924; Cost and Production Handbook, 1934. Home: 9 Mountain Av. N., Montclair, N.J. Office: New York University, University Heights, New York, N.Y.

ALFORD, Newell Gilder, cons. mining engr.; b. Phila., Pa., Dec. 11, 1887; s. Reuben Gilder and Mary Ellen (DuBree) A.; grad. Friends Central Preparatory Sch., 1906; A.B., Swarthmore Coll., 1909; B.S., U. of Pittsburgh, 1933, E.M., 1934; m. Caroline Farren Atkinson, June 27, 1912; children—Newell Gilder, Frances Lydia. With engrng. corps U.S. Coal & Coke Co., Gary, W.Va., summers, 1907-08; by-product oven work, Ill. Steel Co., Joliet, 1909; with St. Bernard Mining Co., Earlington, Ky., 1910-20, mine supt. and asst. chief engr., 1913-19, chief engr., Apr. 1920, asst. to pres. and chief engr., to Oct. 1920; mem. firm and v.p. Howard N. Eavenson & Associates, cons. mining engrs., Pittsburgh, 1920, firm name changed, Oct. 1, 1935, to Eavenson and Alford, Apr. 1, 1937, to Eavenson, Alford & Auchmuty; sec., treas., gen. mgr. and dir. Clover Splint Coal Co., Inc.; treasurer and director Air Cleaning & Sizing Co. Enlisted in U.S.A., Sept. 1917, discharged as sergt. 309th Engrs., Apr. 1919. Mem. Am. Inst. mining and Metall. Engrs., Engrs. Soc. Western Pa., Mining Soc. of Nova Scotia, Coal Mining Inst. of America (v.p.), Canadian Mining Inst., W.Va. Mining Inst., Ky. Mining Inst., Ill. Mining Inst., Am. Mining Congress (chmn. com. mech. mining), Kentucky Historical Assn., Soc. War of 1812, Am. Legion, Delta Upsilon, Book and Key (Swarthmore). Mem. Soc. of Friends. Mason. Author of numerous pamphlets, brochures, articles, etc., about mining. Home: 314 S. Homewood Av. Office: Koppers Bldg., Pittsburgh, Pa.

ALGEO, Albert Melvin; b. Cecil Twp., Washington Co., Pa., Mar. 27, 1878; s. Samuel S. and Martha (Stewart) A.; student Washington (Pa.) pub. schs. and Washington Business Coll.; m. Coila Stemple, of Wellington, O., Dec. 20, 1917. Began career in glass industry as stenographer Hazel Glass Co.; supt. Hazel Plant No. 1, Washington, Pa., upon orgn. Hazel-Atlas Glass Co. and served many years, dist. mgr. in charge Pa. plants, 1924-34, v.p. and spl. sales mgr., 1934-Jan. 3, 1938; dir. Citizens Nat. Bank, Washington, Pa., Washington Mold and Foundry Co., Pacific Coast Talc Co., Los Angeles, Calif. Dir. Washington Hosp. Assn., Washington Community Chest; mem. of council Boy Scouts. United Presbyn. (formerly pres. bd. trustees Second United Presbyn. Ch.). Clubs: Bassett (charter mem.), Washington County Golf and Country (Washington, Pa.). Address: 10 Wilmont Av., Washington, Pa.

ALLBECK, Montraville M(cHenry), clergyman; b. near Muncy, Pa., Oct. 3, 1873; s. John Gottlieb and Effie (DeWald) A.; student Lycoming County Normal Sch., Muncy, Pa., 1889-90, Missionary Inst., Selinsgrove, Pa., 1891-94, Susquehanna U., Selinsgrove, 1894-97, D.D., 1919; m. Lida Belle Schwartz, Sept. 15, 1897; children— Willard Dow, Marian Lenore (Mrs. Myron D. Harnly). Teacher in public schools, Pa., 1889-91; ordained to ministry United Luth. Ch., 1897; pastor Millville, Pa., 1897-99, Berwick, Pa., 1899-1904, Monessen, Pa., 1904-08, Monongahela, 1908-19, Zelienople, Pa., 1919-32, Scottdale, Pa., 1932-39; retired 1939; recording sec. Pittsburgh Synod, 1907, statistical sec., 1916-19. Dir Susquehanna U., 1926-35; mem. bd. dirs. Zelienople Orphans Home, 1921-36; dir. Synodical Bd. Home Missions, 1914-21, 1936-39 (now a mem.). Mem. Phi Mu Delta. Charter mem. Zelienople Rotary. Author: Annals of the Allbecks: A History and Genealogy, 1930. Contbr. to Luth. periodicals. Home: Scottdale, Pa.

ALLDERDICE, Norman, machinery mfr.; b. McKeesport, Pa., Feb. 16, 1894; s. Taylor and Ellen (Hansell) A.; ed. pub. schs.; m. Hester S. Semple, Dec. 16, 1936. Began with open hearth dept. Carnegie Steel Co., Pittsburgh, 1911; supt. open hearth dept. Nat. Tube Co., 1916-21; mgr. Pittsburgh office Manning, Maxwell & Moore, Inc., 1921-27; pres. and treas. Arch Machinery Co., 1927-37; pres. Auto-Tite Joints Co., 1921-38; v.p. Gen. Am. Transportation Corpn., 1934-37; special agent Frank M. Knox Co. since 1936. Republican. Clubs: Duquesne (Pittsburgh); Cloud (New York); Blind Brook, Allegheny Country, Edgeworth, Rolling Rock, Siwanoy, Annandale Country (Pasadena, Calif.). Home: Sewickley Heights, Pa. Office: 30 Rockefeller Plaza, New York, N.Y.

ALLEBACH, Leroy, lawyer; b. New Bethlehem, Pa., July 25, 1880; s. Anson Milo and Clara Cornelia (Jacox) A.; student pub. schs., New Bethlehem, Pa., 1886-96, Clarion (Pa.) State Normal Sch., 1899-1900, Grove City (Pa.) Coll., 1901-03; LL.B., U. of Mich., Ann Arbor, Mich., 1904-06; m. Telle Tomlin Thompson, Feb. 19, 1917; 1 son, Newton Webster. Admitted to W.Va. bar, 1906, and since practiced at Charleston, W.Va.; asst. gen. atty. N.Y. Central R.R. Co.; pres. and dir. Ashley Bread Co., Triple State Electric Co., Nu Way Co., Security Bldg. Co., Charleston, W.Va.; v.p., sec. and dir. Elite Laundry Co., Charleston; v.p., treas. and dir. The Sylvania Corpn., Charleston; dir. and gen. counsel First Nat. Bank, New Bethlehem, Pa., The Meadow River Lumber Co., Rainelle, W.Va., The Bank of Rainelle, W.Va. Mem. Charleston Common Council, 1918. Chmn. Charleston Housing Authority. Mem. Am. Bar Assn., W.Va. Bar Assn., Charleston Bar Assn. Republican. Episcopalian. Mason (32°, K.T., Shriner), Elk. Home: 1342 MacCorkle Av. Office: 1105 Security Bldg., Charleston, W.Va.

ALLEMAN, Frank; consulting surgeon, Lancaster Gen. Hosp. Address: 420 W. Chestnut St., Lancaster, Pa.

ALLEMAN, Gellert, chemist; b. Littletown, Pa., July 23, 1871; s. Monroe John and Elizabeth (Gilfillan) A.; B.S., Pa. Coll. (Gettysburg), 1893, Sc.D., 1925; Ph.D., Johns Hopkins, 1897; U. of Berlin, 1911-12; m. Katharine Constable Spencer, July 7, 1902; children —Gellert Spencer, Robert Gilfillan. Instr. chemistry, U. of Me., 1897-98, Washington U., St. Louis, 1898-1902; prof. chemistry, Swarthmore Coll., since 1902, on leave of absence since 1928. Men. advisory board Chemical Warfare Service. Fellow Society of Chemical Industry (London), A.A.A.S., Chem. Soc. (London), Deutsche Chemische Gesellschaft; mem. Am. Chem. Soc., Am. Electrochem. Soc., Franklin Inst. (bd. mgrs.; v.p.). Clubs: Racquet (Phila.); Chemists' (New York). Visited various European universities, 1927-28. Home: Wallingford, Pa.

ALLEMAN, Herbert Christian, theologian; b. Bloomsburg, Pa., May 13, 1868; s. Benjamin F. (D.D.) and Charlotte (Benson) A.; A.B., 1st honor, Pa. Coll., Gettysburg, 1887; grad. Luth. Theol. Sem., Gettysburg, 1891; U. of Pa., 1908-11; D.D., Temple U., 1907; m. Julia Suesserott, July 8, 1897; 1 son, Benson Suesserott. Ordained Luth. ministry, 1891; pastor Trinity Ch., Chambersburg, Pa., 1891-96, College Ch., Gettysburg, Pa., 1896-1900, Messiah Ch., Phila., 1900-11; prof. O.T. lit. and theology, Luth. Theol. Sem., since 1911. Trustee Luth. Publ. Soc., Phila., 1900-11; mem. bd. of Publication of United Luth. Ch.; incorporator Presbyn. Ministers' Fund. Mem. Soc. Bibl. Lit. and Exegesis, Phi Gamma Delta, Phi Beta Kappa. Democrat. Author: The Gist of the Sermon, 1905: The Book—A Brief Introduction to the Bible, 1908; Prayers for Boys, 1925; The Old Testament—A Study, 1934; The New Testament —A Study, 1934; New Testament Commentary, 1936. Home: Gettysburg, Pa.

ALLEN, Albert L(eroy), gen. insurance and specialized service; b. Holden, Mass., Aug. 25, 1887; s. George L. and Fanny J. (Richardson) A.; ed. pub. schs. and high sch.; m. Alice L. von Keller, June 20, 1916; children—Barbara Heath, Albert Leroy, Jr., Heath Ledward. Employed with various concerns, 1902-12; with Mass. Employes Ins. Assn. (now Liberty Mutual) and State Insurance Fund of N.Y., 1912-15; asso. with State Insurance Fund, Harrisburg, Pa., 1915-19; pres. and treas. Albert L. Allen Co., Inc., gen. ins. and specialized workmen's compensation service, Allen Registry Bureau, specialized accident ins., Harrisburg, Pa., since 1919; dir. Harrisburg Gas Co., Department Reports Co., Capital Landing Field Co., E. O. Dare & Son Agency, H. F. Oves Agency. Served as chmn. workmen's compensation com. Pa. State Chamber of Commerce; past dir. Harrisburg Chamber of Commerce; gen. campaign chmn. Harrisburg Welfare Campaign, 1938; mem. bd. govs. Harrisburg Welfare Assn., Council Boy Scouts. Mem. Harrisburg Ins. Agts. Assn. (past pres.). Mem. bd. govs. Harrisburg Motor Club; past pres. Lions Club. Republican. Mason (K.T., 32°, Shriner, Tall Cedars). Clubs: Harrisburg, Zembo Luncheon, Pennsylvania Soc., Y.M.C.A., Country, Rotary. Home: 2936 N. Second St. Office: Allen Bldg., 319 N. Second St., Harrisburg, Pa.

ALLEN, Alexander John, research in physics; b. Glenwood Springs, Colo., Oct. 4, 1900; s. Alexander and Leah (Blotiaux) A.; A.B., U. of Colo., 1923; A.M., N.U. Univ., 1926, Ph.D., same, 1929; m. Katherine Burns, Oct. 31, 1929. Began as lab. asst., U. of Colo., 1922-23; elec. engr. Mountain States Telephone Co., Denver, Colo., 1923-24; instr. physics, N.Y. Univ., 1926-28, research asso., 1929; Fellow Bartol Foundation, Franklin Inst., 1929-30; research physicist, Cancer Research Labs., U. of Pa. Grad. Sch. of Medicine, 1930-35; chief physicist, Biochem. Research Foundation of Franklin Inst. since 1935. Fellow A.A.A.S., Am. Phys. Soc. Mem. Franklin Inst., Sigma Xi, Sigma Phi Epsilon. Home: 660 Parrish Rd., Swarthmore, Pa.

ALLEN, Charles Laurel, journalism; b. Berwick, N.D., July 5, 1902; s. Charles and Sarah Ellen (Lowry) A.; A.B., U. of N.D., 1924; A.M., U. of Ill., 1927; Ph.D., Columbia, 1940; m. Lida Mae Grace, June 16, 1926; 1 son, Charles Richard. Served as printer, reporter, editor, Mouse River Farmers Press, Towner, N.D., 1914-19; reporter, makeup man, Jamestown (N.D.) Daily Alert, 1920-22; teacher printing, U. of N.D., 1923-24; teacher printing and English, Jefferson Jr. High Sch., Minneapolis, 1924-25; asst. in journalism, advancing to prof. journalism, U. of Ill., 1925-37; visiting prof. journalism, Northwestern U., 1937; dir. dept. of journalism, Rutgers U., and exec. sec. N.J. Press Assn. since 1937; dir. of accounting and cost finding Nat. Editorial Assn., 1933-35, dir. of research, 1934-36. Mem. council on research Am. Assn. of Schs. and Depts. of Journalism since 1936. Mem. Am. Assn. Teachers of Journalism (pres. 1938-40), Phi Beta Kappa, Delta Sigma Rho, Sigma Delta Chi. Republican. Presbyterian. Mason. Author: Country Journalism, 1927; Journalist's Manual of Printing, 1928. Home: 38 N. 8th St., New Brunswick, N.J.

ALLEN, Clarence Eugene; pastor First Methodist Ch., Warren, Pa. Home: Market and Second Av., Warren, Pa.

ALLEN, David Kell, clergyman; b. Cadiz, O., May 23, 1896; s. Walter Lowrie and Elizabeth (Long) A.; ed. Geneva Coll., 1915-17; A.B., Coll. of Wooster (O.), 1922; S.T.B., Western Theol. Sem., Pittsburgh, 1925; Ph.D., U. of Edinburgh, Scotland, 1928; m. Esther A. Symons, June 16, 1926; children—Marjorie Symons, Robert Mark. Ordained to ministry Presbyn. Ch., 1925; pastor, Poke Run, Pa., 1925-26, Erie, Pa., 1928-33; pastor First Ch., Johnstown, Pa., since 1933. Pres. of ministerial assns. of Erie, 1932-33, Johnstown, 1937-38; mem. judicial comm. of Synod of Pa. Served as pvt. inf. U.S.A., 1917-19, with A.E.F. in France, Italy, Austria and Jugo-Slavia. Served as moderator Blairsville Presbytery, 1938-39. Mason. Home: 133 Second Av., Johnstown, Pa.

ALLEN, Edward Monington, educator; b. Dover, N.J., May 23, 1899; s. David Frederick and Lottie B. (Worman) A.; B.S., Lafayette Coll., 1922; grad. study, Princeton, 1922-23, Columbia, 1927-29; m. Elsie Jeanette Burn, Dec. 22, 1923; 1 dau. Diane Elaine. Teacher of English, High sch., Brooklyn, N.Y., 1923-24; dir. academic dept. Calhoun (Ala.) Sch., 1924-27; lecturer in history, Coll. City New York, 1927-30; asst. to editor Records of Civilization Series, Columbia U. Press, 1927-29; editor Annual Report Am. Gas Assn., 1928; headmaster and trustee Mohegan Lake (N.Y.) Sch., 1930-34; mgr. book service dept., Internat. Textbook Co. since 1937; prof. of publishing U. of Scranton since 1937. Army Y.M.C.A. sec., Camp Dix, N.J., 1917-18. Mem. Am. Hist. Assn., Assn.

Mil. Schs. and Colls. of U.S., Assn. Colls. and Prep. Schs. of Middle Atlantic States and Md., Schoolmasters Assn. N.Y., Alpha Chi Rho, Phi Upsilon Kappa. Republican. Presbyn. Author: America's Story as Told in Postage Stamps, 1930; The Author's Handbook, 1938. Home: 1744 Capouse Av., Scranton, Pa.

ALLEN, Edward Riley, chemist; b. Pana, Ill., July 28, 1884; s. John Daniel and Mary (Mulholland) A.; B.S., U. of Ill., Urbana, Ill., 1906; Ph.D., Cornell U., 1913; m. Dora Christine Christner, May 31, 1910; children—Mary Genevieve (Mrs. Charles N. Mellowes), Dorothy Christine. Scientific asst. U.S. Dept. of Agr., Washington, D.C., 1906-10; research chemist and biologist, div. of soil technology, Ohio Agrl. Exptl. Sta., Wooster, O., 1913-15, asso. in charge of div., 1915-17; asso. in bio-chemistry, Sch. of Medicine, Washington U., St. Louis, Mo., 1917-19, visiting investigator, Mo. Bot. Gardens, 1917-19; research chemist, dye works, E. I. du Pont de Nemours & Co., Wilmington, Del., 1919-23, pigment plant, Newark, N.J., 1923-27, tech. dir. pigment plant since 1927. Mem. Am. Chem. Soc., Am. Inst. Chemists, Sigma Xi. Presbyterian. Club: Chemists (New York). Home: 15 Crest Acres, Summit, N.J. Office: 256 Vanderpool St., Newark, N.J.

ALLEN, Fred Clay, pharmacist; b. Lima, W.Va., Apr. 18, 1888; s. Stephan A. and Dorcas (Stoneking) A.; Ph.G., Valparaiso U., Valparaiso, Ind., 1909; m. Mary Jo. Berry, June 15, 1928; children—Ann Clay and Fred Clay. Began as pharmacist Ohio Valley Drug Co., Wheeling, W.Va., 1909; pres. and mgr. Royal Drug Store, retail druggists, since 1920; dir. Pendleton County Bank, Elk View Improvement Co. Mayor of Marlinton, 1928-32; mem. W.Va. State Senate, 1936-40. Served with A.E.F. in France, World War. Received W.Va. Pharmacy award, 1937. Mem. W.Va. State Bd. of Pharmacy; pres. W.Va. State Pharmaceutical Assn., 1933, W.Va. Affiliated Sportsmen's Assn., 1934; mem. Am. Legion, Pocahontas Bd. of Trade. Democrat. Mason (Shriner), Elk. Club: Pocahontas County Rod and Gun (Marlinton). Address: Marlinton, W.Va.

ALLEN, George Henry, coll. prof.; b. Grand Rapids, Mich., July 28, 1876; s. George Roderick and Viola (Miller) A.; A.B., U. of Mich., Ann Arbor, Mich., 1898, A.M., 1899, Ph.D., 1904; m. Wilifred Morris, Jan. 1, 1907 (died Mar. 28, 1931); 1 son, George Edmund Morris; m. 2d. Ilène Martin, Dec. 20, 1932. Instr. and asst. prof. Latin, U. of Cincinnati, 1904-11; rep. of Bur. of Univ. Travel, Berlin, Germany, 1911-14; mgr. Bur. of Univ. Travel, Newton, Mass., 1920-21, rep. in Paris, France, 1921-29; prof. Latin and fine arts, Lafayette Coll., Easton, Pa., since 1929. Served as translator for Mil. Intelligence Dept., Gen. Staff, U.S. Army, during World War. Mem. Classical Assn. of Atlantic States, Alliance Francaise, Delta Upsilon, Phi Beta Kappa. Democrat. Episcopalian. Club: Lafayette Coll. Faculty (Easton, Pa.). Home: 120 McCartney St. Office: Lafayette Coll., Easton, Pa.

ALLEN, Henry Butler, sec. and dir. Franklin Inst.; b. Greenfield, Mass., July 20, 1887; s. Franklin and Nettie (Lee) A.; student Amherst (Mass.) Coll., 1905-08; Metall. Engr., Sch. of Mines, Columbia, 1911; m. Ione A. Ralli, May 29, 1915; children—Ione, Julia, Margaret, Lois Elizabeth. U.S. examiner iron and steel in N.Y. State, 1912-13; metall. engr. Henry Disston & Sons, Inc., 1913-17 and 1922-26, chief metallurgist, 1926-35; v.p. Dodge Steel Co., 1920-22; administrative sec. and dir. Franklin Inst., Phila., since 1935. Served as capt. Ordnance Dept., U.S. Army, A.E.F., 1917-20. Pres. Physics Club, 1936-37; v.p. Franco-Am. Inst. of Science, Internat. Benjamin Franklin Soc.; asso. trustee Board of Grad. Edn. and Research, U. of Pa.; mem. council Phila. Council Boy Scouts of America; mem. advisory board Phila. Ordnance Dist. Mem. Am. Iron and Steel Inst., Am. Inst. Mining and Metall. Engrs., Am. Soc. of Metals, Franklin Inst., Am. Inst. of N.Y., Am. Assn. of Museums, Am. Soc. for Testing Materials, Newcomen Soc., Electrochemical Soc. (Phila. sect.), Benj. Franklin Internat. Soc., S.R., British Iron and Steel Inst., Ex-Members' Assn. Squadron A (New York), Delta Kappa Epsilon. Decorated Chevalier of the Legion of Honor (France). Republican. Unitarian. Clubs: Rittenhouse, Engineers, Cricket, University, Franklin Inn, Penn Club, Contemporary, Rotary. Home: 8112 St. Martin's Lane, Chestnut Hill, Pa. Office: Benjamin Franklin Parkway at 20th, Philadelphia, Pa.

ALLEN, Henry Elisha, educator; b. Orange, N.J., June 13, 1902; s. Elisha Hubert and Jane Elizabeth (Durand) A.; student Gilman Country Sch., Roland Park, Md., 1913-17, The Hill Sch., Pottstown, Pa., 1917-20; A.B., Yale, 1924; M.A., U. of Chicago, 1929, Ph.D., 1930; resident study in Turkey and the near east, 1929-30; m. Helen Elizabeth Davis, June 18, 1927; children—Lenore Elizabeth, Carolyn Ruth. Began as master in English, The Hill Sch., Pottstown, Pa., 1924-26; instr. in religion, Lafayette Coll., Easton, Pa., 1930-31, asst. prof., 1931-37, asso. prof. since 1937. Dir. Social Service League of Easton, Pa.; v.chmn., United Council for Civic Betterment. Dir. Nat. Council on Religion in Higher Edn. (N.Y. City). Mem. Am. Oriental Soc., New Orient Soc. of America, Nat. Assn. of Biblical Instrs., Family Welfare Assn. of America, Skull and Bones, Elizabethan Club (Yale), Psi Upsilon. Republican. Presbyterian. Club: Faculty of Lafayette Coll., Easton, Pa. Author: The Turkish Transformation, 1935 and articles to jours. on modern Turkey and the religion of Islam; contbr. ed. Jour. of Bible and Religion. Lecturer on Islam at Haskell Inst., U. of Chicago, 1933. Home: 159 Shawnee Av., Easton, Pa.

ALLEN, (William) Hervey, author; b. Pittsburgh, Pa., Dec. 8, 1889; s. William Hervey and Helen Ebey (Myers) A.; U.S. Naval Acad., 1910-11; B.Sc., U. of Pittsburgh, 1915, Litt.D., 1934; studied Harvard, 1920-22; m. Ann Hyde Andrews, June 30, 1927; children—Marcia Andrews, Mary Ann, Richard Francis. Instr. English, Porter Mil. Acad., Charleston, S.C., 1920, 21; instr. English, high sch., Charleston, 1922-24; with dept. of English, Columbia University, 1924-25; lecturer on Am. Lit., Vassar College, 1926-27; lecturer on modern poetry, Bread Loaf (Vt.) Sch. of English and Writers' Conf., 1930, 31. Midshipman U.S. Navy, 1909-10; 2d lt. 18th Pa. Inf., on Mexican border, 1916; 1st lt. 111th Inf., 28th Div., A.E.F., 1917-19, World War; wounded in action, Aug. 1918; instr. English, French Mil. Mission. Fellow Royal Soc. of Arts; mem. Nat. Inst. Arts and Letters, Md. Hist. Soc., Poetry Soc. America, MacDowell Colony, Poetry Soc. of South Carolina (founder), Sigma Chi, Omicron Delta Kappa. Clubs: Players (New York); Hamilton Street (Baltimore); Surf (Miami Beach, Fla.); Chesapeake Bay Yacht. Author: Wampum and Old Gold, 1921; The Bride of Huitzil, 1922; Carolina Chansons (with Du Bose Heyward), 1922; The Blindman, 1923; Earth Moods, 1925; Towards the Flame, 1926; Israfel (biography of E. A. Poe), 1926; Poe's Brother (with Thomas Ollive Mabbott), 1926; New Legends, 1929; Sarah Simon, 1929; Songs for Annette, 1929; Anthony Adverse, 1933; Action at Aquila, 1937. Home: Bonfield Manor, Oxford, Talbot Co., Md.

ALLEN, Howard Bushnell; prof. edn. W.Va. U. Address: West Virginia U., Morgantown, W.Va.

ALLEN, James Edward, college pres.; b. Hebron, Va., June 13, 1876; s. Peter Woodward (M.D.) and Fannie Blunt (Scott) A.; A.B., Hampden-Sydney, 1898, LL.D., 1923; studied U. of Va., summers 1902, 1903; grad. student in Latin, Johns Hopkins, 1903-05; m. Susan H. Garrott, June 18, 1910 (now dec.); children—Jas. Edward, Joseph Garrott, Robert Alfriend, Charles Garrott, Frances Blunt (dec.), Carter Randolph; m. 2d, Mrs. Parke D. Carter, June 11, 1927. Prin. schs., Phoebus, Va., 1900-01; v.prin. and instr. Latin, high sch., Newport News, 1901-03; instr. modern langs., Deichman Prep. Sch., Baltimore, 1904-05; instr. Latin, Notre Dame Coll., Md., 1905; prin. high sch. and instr. German, Newport News, 1905-06; prof. French and German, Davis and Elkins College, W.Va., 1906-09; pres. Davis and Elkins Coll., 1910-35; pres. Marshall Coll., Huntington, W.Va., since July 1, 1935. Mem. N.E.A., Am. Philol. Assn., Randolph County Hist. Soc. (v.p. 1932), Am. Geog. Soc., Phi Beta Kappa, Kappa Delta Pi. Democrat. Presbyn.; mem. com. of Christian Edn. Synod of W.Va., moderator of the Synod, 1934; mem. Southern Assn. of Presbyn. Colleges. Was "Four Minute Man," during the war. Clubs: Social, Literary, Rotary (pres. 1922-23). Contbr. on ednl. topics. Author of The Minimum Salary of a Rural Presbyterian Pastor, 1930. Home: Huntington, W.Va.

ALLEN, James Marshall, physician; b. Clinton Corners, N.Y., Oct. 14, 1901; s. James Clapp and Anna Euhert (Tousey) A.; A.B., Williams Coll., Williamstown, Mass., 1923; M.D., Columbia U. Coll. Phys. & Surgs., 1927; m. Eleanor Elizabeth Dunning, July 2, 1935; children—James Marshall, Jr. Interne Fifth Av. Hosp., New York, 1927-29; engaged in gen. practice of medicine at Passaic, N.J., since 1930. Dir. Passaic Chapter Am. Red Cross, Y.M.C.A. of Passaic. Mem. Passaic Co. Med. Soc., Passaic Practitioners Club (pres.), Exchange Club of Passaic, Zeta Psi, Nu Sigma Nu. Republican. Presbyn. Clubs: Passaic Tennis, City (Passaic); Williams (New York). Direct desc. of Priscilla and John Alden through maternal grandmother. Home: 26 Kent Ct. Office: 657 Main Av., Passaic, N.J.

ALLEN, Junius, artist; b. Summit, N.J., June 9, 1898; s. James Junius and Martha Gaunt (Woodward) A.; student Kingsley Sch., Essex Fells, N.J., 1914-17, N.Y. Sch. of Fine and Applied Arts, 1921-22, Nat. Acad. Design, 1922-24 (pupil of G. W. Maynard, C. Hawthorne, G. E. Browne, A. W. Woelfle). Studio manager Am. Desatype Co., New York City, 1919. Served in 302d Field Signal Batt., A.E.F., 1917-19. Represented by "Metropolis," Montclair (N.J.) Art Mus.; "A Memory," Summit (N.J.) High Sch. Awarded bronze medal, Plainfield (N.J.) Art Assn.; medal of award, Montclair Art Assn.; same, Am. Artists' Professional League; 3d Hallgarten prize, Nat. Acad. Design; lay members' prize, Salmagundi Club (New York); first prize, N.J. Gallery; hon. mention, New Rochelle (N.Y.) Art Assn. Associate Nat. Academician; mem. Allied Artists America, Artists' Fund Soc., Am. Artists Professional League, Salmagundi Club (chmn. art com.), Montclair Art Assn. (mem. art com.), Summit Art Assn. (hon., chmn. exhbn. com.). Home: 18 Fenwood Rd., Summit, N.J.*

ALLEN, Leah Brown, prof. of astronomy; b. Providence, R.I., Nov. 6, 1884; d. Samuel F. and Abby L. (Willey) Allen; A.B., Brown U., 1907; A.M., Wellesley Coll., 1912; grad. student U. of Pa., 1919-20, U. of Calif., 1924-25; unmarried. Computer, Lick Observatory, 1907-09; laboratory asst., Wellesley Coll., 1909-12, instr., 1912-19, 1920-24, asso. prof., 1926-27; Martin Kellogg research fellow, Lick Observatory, 1925; asso. prof. of astronomy, Hood Coll., Frederick, Md., 1927-28, prof. since 1928. Fellow A.A.A.S.; mem. Am. Astron. Soc. Congregationalist. Address: Hood College, Frederick, Md.

ALLEN, Leslie, steel mfr.; b. Allentown, Pa., Sept. 13, 1894; s. John and Ella A. (Schuman) A.; C.E., Lehigh U., Bethlehem, Pa., 1916; m. Elizabeth Abbot, Apr. 6, 1931; children—John Leslie, Judith. Mgr. Carnegie Works, McClintic-Marshall Co., 1924-28, Buffalo (N.Y.) Works, 1928-31; became mgr. works Pittsburgh Dist., Bethlehem Steel Co., 1931. Mem. Pittsburgh Chamber of Commerce, Employers' Assn. of Pittsburgh. Clubs: Duquesne, Longue Vue Country (Pittsburgh); Buffalo (N.Y.) Canoe. Home: 6684 Kinsman Rd. Office: 1224 Oliver Bldg., Pittsburgh, Pa.

ALLEN, Ned Bliss, univ. prof.; b. Carbondale, Ill., Dec. 30, 1899; s. Carlos Eben and Maude (Willsey) A.; student pub. schs., Carbondale, Ill., 1905-17, Phillips Andover Acad., Andover, Mass., 1917-18; A.B., Dartmouth Coll., Hanover, N.H., 1922; B.A., St. John's Coll., Oxford U., Eng., 1926; Ph.D., U. of Michigan, Ann Arbor, Mich., 1931; m. Alice Katherine Hall, June 25, 1930; children—Emily Willsey, Janet Hall. Teacher Spanish and French, Ky. Mil. Inst., Lyndon, Ky., 1923; instr. English, U. of Southern Calif., Los Angeles, Calif.,

ALLEN

1927-28, part-time instr. English, U. of Mich., Ann Arbor, Mich., 1928-31; asso. prof. English, U. of Del., Newark, Del., since 1931. Served in S.A.T.C., 1918. Mem. Modern Lang. Assn., Nat. Council of Teachers of English, Am. Assn. Univ. Prof., Pleiad (Dartmouth), Phi Beta Kappa, Phi Kappa Phi, Kappa Kappa Kappa. Rhodes Scholar from N.D., 1923-26. Club: Faculty (Newark, Del.). Author: The Sources of Dryden's Comedies, 1935; several articles on Shakespeare scholarship. Address: Newark, Del.

ALLEN, Philip Meredith, pres. P. M. Allen Adv. Agency; b. Germantown, Phila., Pa., Feb. 14, 1893; s. Col. Ralph Wheelock Pomeroy and Frances Lillian (Spooner) A.; student Germantown (Pa.) Acad., 1901-11, Knox Coll., Galesburg, Ill., 1912-15; m. Marie Hanifen Dobbins, June 6, 1924; 1 son, Ralph Wheelock Pomeroy III. Reporter Phila. Press, Ledger, 1915-18; reporter, spl. writer and correspondent Phila. North American, 1919-22; chief copy staff Clark-Whitcraft, Inc., Phila., Pa., 1922-24; established, 1924, P. M. Allen Adv. Agency, and since pres. Served as private, 1st Pa. Cavalry on Mexican Border, 1915-16; served as cadet major Air Service, U.S. Army, during World War. Gov. War Library and Mus., Phila. Mem. Franklin Inst., Pa. Hist. Soc., Geneal. Soc. Pa., Am. Legion, Pa. Soc. S.A.R., Mil. Order of Loyal Legion of U.S. Republican. Soc. of Friends. Clubs: Union League, Aviation, Pylon Aviation, Pastorius (Phila.). Contbr. articles on early Am. furniture, wrought iron, aviation to Saturday Evening Post and other nat. mags. Home: Berry Pomeroy, Blue Bell, Pa. Office: 18 W. Chelten St., Philadelphia, Pa.

ALLEN, Rena, educator; b. Rumson, N.J., Mar. 15, 1888; d. Charles T. and Miriam E. (Gaskill) A.; grad. Rumson pub. schs., 1906, N.J. Teachers Coll., 1909; B.S., Teachers Coll., Columbia, 1924, M.A., 1933; unmarried. Teacher Woodbridge (N.J.) pub. schs., 1909-19, Indiana Normal Sch., Ft. Wayne, Ind., 1919-22, Detroit (Mich.) Teachers Coll., 1922-23, Horace Mann Sch., Columbia U., 1923-24; dir. student teaching and asso. prof. edn., U. of Del., since 1924; teacher Horace Mann Sch., summers, 1920, 21 and 22; dean of women, U. of Del., summer sch., since 1932; assisted in survey, Stamford, Conn., 1923-24. Dir. Del. Safety Council. Mem. N.E.A., Am. Assn. Univ. Women, Am. Assn. Univ. Profs., Progressive Edn. Assn., Soc. Study of Edn. Republican. Presbyn. Home: 504 Tisdale Pl., Woodbridge, N.J. Address: University of Delaware, Newark, Del.

ALLEN, Robert Gray, congressman; b. Winchester, Mass., Aug. 24, 1902; s. Arthur Harrison and Sally (Gray) A.; student Phillips Academy, Andover, Mass., 1916-22, Harvard, 1922-25; m. Katharine Hancock Williamson, 1925; children—Katharine Hancock, Robert Gray. With Walworth Co., 1925-37, salesman, 1925-29, sales mgr., 1925-37; mem. 75th and 76th Congresses (1937-41), 28th Pa. Dist. Democrat. Episcopalian. Elk, L.O.O.M., Eagle. Rotarian. Home: Walnut av., Greensburg, Pa.

ALLEN, Roy Morris, cons. scientist; b. Coleville, Pa., Feb. 12, 1882; s. William Letchworth and Mollie Elizabeth (White) A.; grad. Butler (Pa.) High Sch., 1898; m. Gertrude May Child, June 14, 1910; children—Rev. Paul Child, Rev. David William, Howard Thomas, Florence Louise. Partner, Reliance Telephone & Mfg. Co., Butler, Pa., 1900-09; supervising engr., research labs., Bell System, New York City, 1909-25; pvt. cons. work, Bloomfield, N.J., since 1925. Engaged in design and supervision of submarine detection apparatus under joint control of Western Electric Co. and U.S. Navy Dept. during World War. Fellow N.Y. Micros. Soc. (past pres.), Am. Micros. Soc.; mem. Am. Soc. for Testing Materials, Am. Inst. M.E., Am. Foundrymen's Assn., N.Y. Acad. of Sciences. Independent Republican. Baptist. Author: A Manual of the Microscope, 1939; The Microscope in Elementary Cast Iron Metallurgy, 1939. Address: 126 Berkeley Av., Bloomfield, N.J.

ALLEN, Samuel S., Jr., neurologist; instr. neurology, U. of Pittsburgh; neurol. surgeon St. Francis, Allegheny Gen. and Eye and Ear hosps. Address: 3509 Fifth Av., Pittsburgh, Pa.

ALLEN, Wendell D.; mem. Md. State Bd. of Edn., term expires 1942. Address: 1111 Lexington Bldg., Baltimore, Md.

ALLEN, Wilbert M.; pres. Central Union Co.; also dir. many companies. Home: 70 Alken Ridge, St. Clairville, O. Office: Central Union Bldg., Wheeling, W.Va.

ALLEN, William Franklin, congressman; b. Bridgeville, Del., Jan. 19, 1883; s. William Franklin and Mollie (Smith) A.; ed. pub. schs., Seaford, Del.; m. Mary Addie Davis, Apr. 16, 1905; children—William Franklin, Layton Robert, Doris. Telegrapher, 1901-21; fruit and produce dealer 1921-27; pres. Allen Package Co., 1927-37; real estate operator, 1927-37; pres. Allen Oil Co., 1927-32; pres. Allen Petroleum Corpn. since 1932; member 75th Congress (1937-39), Del. at large; mem. Del. State Senate, 1925-27. Democrat. Methodist. Mason (Shriner). Clubs: Democratic (Seaford), Democratic (Wilmington). Home: Seaford, Del.

ALLEN, William G.; mem. surg. staff Hamot Hosp. Home: 943 W. 6th St. Office: 217 W. 8th St., Erie, Pa.

ALLEN, William Warden, pres. First Nat. Bank of South Charleston; b. Argentum, Ky., Feb. 26, 1892; s. Edward and Margaret Katherine (Warden) A.; ed. Greenup (Ky.) grade sch., 1898-1905, high sch., 1906-09; unmarried. Began as bank clk., Greenup, Ky., 1909; asst. cashier Citizens State Bank, Greenup, 1911-13, Day & Night Bank, Charleston, W.Va., 1914-15; note teller Charleston Nat. Bank, 1915-17; sec. Charles Ward Engring. Works, Charleston, 1918-30; pres. First Nat. Bank, South Charleston, W.Va., since 1936; v.p. and dir. The Allen Co., South Charleston, since 1936. Kanawha Co. Relief Adminstr., Charleston, 1932-34; asst. state relief adminstr., Charleston, 1935-36. Republican. Methodist. Mason (Shriner). Club: Lions (South Charleston, W.Va.). Home: 1403 Jackson St., Charleston, W.Va. Office: South Charleston, W.Va.

ALLIS, Oswald Thompson, theologian; b. Wallingford, Pa., Sept. 9, 1880; s. Oscar H. and Julia W. (Thompson) A.; A.B., U. of Pa. 1901; B.D., Princeton Theological Seminary, 1905; A.M., Princeton University, 1907; Ph.D., from Univresity of Berlin, 1913; D.D., Hampden Sydney College, 1927"; m. Ruth Robinson, Sept. 21, 1927; children—Julia Thompson, Constance Ruth. Instructor Semitic philology, Princeton Theol. Sem., 1910-22, asst. prof., 1922-29; prof. O. T. history and exegesis, Westminster Theol. Sem., 1929-30, prof. of O. T., 1930-1936. Editor Princeton Theol. Rev., 1918-29; asso. editor Evangelical Quarterly (Edinburgh), 1930—. Mem. American Oriental Soc., Am. Bible Soc. (versions com.), S.R. Republican. Presbyn. Contbr. to Biblical and Theological Studies; also articles in the Princeton Theol. Rev., etc. Address: Care Pennsylvania Co., 15th and Chestnut Sts., Philadelphia, Pa.*

ALLIS, Paul Mitten, physician; b. Wyalusing, Pa., Apr. 6, 1891; s. Ned H. and Augusta (Mitten) A.; M.D., U. of Pa. Med. Sch., 1913; grad. study U. of Pa. Med. Sch., 1917-18, also, Vienna, Berlin and London, 1924-26; m. Mary Thompson, Nov. 16, 1918. Engaged in gen. practice of medicine at Lewistown, Pa., 1915-21, specializing in diseases of eye, ear, nose and throat since 1926; mem. surg. staff, Lewistown Hosp. since 1918. Mem. Am., Pa. State, and Mifflin Co. med. assns., Am. Acad. Ophthalmology and Otolaryngology, Phi Alpha Sigma. Republican. Protestant. Home: Milroy, Pa. Office: 6 N. Brown St., Lewistown, Pa.

ALLISON, James Boyd, Jr., educator; b. Punxsutawney, Pa., Jan. 28, 1901; s. James Boyd and Elizabeth (Robinson) A.; grad. Punxsutawney High Sch., 1919; B.S., Pa. State Coll., 1923; Ph.D., Iowa State Coll., 1927; m. Dorothy Lewis, Dec. 31, 1926; children—Marjorie Ann, Dorothy Jean. Graduate asst., Iowa State Coll., 1923-26, industrial fellow, 1926-27; instr. biochemistry, Rutgers U., 1927-29, asst. prof. biochemistry since 1929. Mem. A.A.A.S., Am. Chem. Soc., Alpha Zeta, Sigma Xi, Phi Lambda Upsilon, Phi Kappa Phi, Gamma Sigma Delta; asso. mem. New York Acad. Science. Presbyn. (elder New Brunswick Ch.). Club: University Outing (New Brunswick). Home: 409 Grant Av., Highland Park, N.J.

ALLISON, James Breadner, army officer; b. York, S.C., Sept. 15, 1873; s. Dr. James B. and Susan Baldwin (Meek) A.; B.S., C.S. Mil. Acad. (now The Citadel), Charleston, 1895; m. Katherine Steel Johnson, Aug. 16, 1913 (died Dec. 12, 1928). Apptd. 2d lt. U.S. Army, Oct. 10, 1898; promoted through grades to col. Signal Corps, May 9, 1921; apptd. major gen., chief signal officer, January 1, 1935; retired from active service, Sept. 15, 1937. Served in Mexico, 1914; organized and trained troops at Ft. Leavenworth, Kan., World War. Awarded D.S.M. Presbyn. Mason. Clubs: Army and Navy (Washington, D.C.); Chevy Chase (Md.); Ft. Monmouth (N.J.) Club; Rumson (N.J.) Country. Home: Chevy Chase Club, Chevy Chase, Md. Address: Munitions Bldg., Washington, D.C.

ALLISON, James Waters, banker; b. Richmond, Va., June 10, 1894; s. James Waters and Minnie Clemens (Jones) A.; student Nolley's Sch., Richmond, Va., 1906-09; grad. Woodberry Forest (Va.) Sch., 1912; B.S., Columbia U., 1916, student Law Sch., 1916-17; m Anne Hopkins Hope, Oct. 7, 1932; stepchildren—Samuel Gregory Hope, Neville Monroe, Peter. Clk. trust dept. The First Nat. Bank of Richmond, Va., 1919-22, asst. trust officer, 1922-28 (bank became First and Merchants Nat. Bank of Richmond, 1926), trust officer, 1928-34, v.p. and trust officer, 1934-36; v.p. Equitable Trust Co., Wilmington, Del., since 1936, dir. since 1937. Ensign, U.S.N.R.F., 1917-19, lt. jg., 1919. Clubs: Vicmead, Commonwealth (Richmond, Va.); Columbia University (New York); Wilmington (Del.) Country. Home: "Rokeby," Wilmington, Del. Office: 901 Market St., Wilmington, Del.

ALLISON, Jonathan David, trustee of estate; b. Salona, Pa., Aug. 19, 1872; s. Henry Clay and Agnes Montgomery (Bennison) A.; ed. pub. schs.; m. Josephine Wilson, May 2, 1901. Employed with various concerns, 1890-96; with Red Run Coal, Lumber & Brick Cos. 1897-1900, supt., later sec., treas. and gen. mgr., 1902-12; organized Ralston Coal Co. and dir., 1912-17; became one of executors Charles S. Green Estate, 1911, and has continued since; built Green Home for Aged Ladies and mgr. since 1914. Dir. Lycoming Co. Crippled Childrens Soc. Trustee and treas. Roaring Branch M.E. Ch. Republican. Presbyn. Mason (K.T., 32°, Shriner). Clubs: Masonic, Shrine, Texas-Blockhouse Fish and Game (pres.). Home: Roaring Branch, Pa.

ALLISON, Wesley L.; otorhinolaryngologist Mercy Hosp. Home: 1224 Farragut St. Office: 500 Penn Av., Pittsburgh, Pa.

ALLISON, David B(acharach), surgeon; b. Phila., Pa., July 11, 1891; s. Millard Fillmore and Rae (Bacharach) A.; grad. Atlantic City High Sch., 1910; M.D., Jefferson Med. Coll., 1914; m. Katherine Bothwell, Nov. 1, 1921. Surgeon, Atlantic City, N.J., since 1914; formerly asst. beach surgeon, asst. police and fire surgeon, asst. surgeon Atlantic City Hosp.; now attending surgical chief Atlantic City Hosp.; med. dir. and surgical chief Betty Bacharach Home; attending surgeon Atlantic Co. Hosp. for Tuberculosis; consulting surgeon Atlantic Co. Hosp. for Mental Diseases; surgeon Jewish Seaside Home; pres. Atlantis Bldg. & Loan Assn. Served as lt. j.g., U.S.N.R.F. during World War; now lt. comdr. Diplomate Am. Bd. Surgery. Fellow Am. Coll. Surgeons; Internat. Coll. Surgeons; mem. A.M.A., Atlantic Co. Med. Soc. (past pres.), N.J., Med. Soc., N.J. Hosp. Assn., Assn. Mil. Surgeons (past pres. N.J. Chapter), Vets. of Foreign Wars, Am. Legion; hon. mem. Atlantic City Beach Patrol, N.J. Firemen's Assn., Police Benefit Assn. Republican. Reformed Jewish religion. Mason (32°, Shriner), Tall Cedars, Elk, Moose. Clubs: Phila. Medical; New Bedford Yacht; Tuna (Atlantic City). Home: 104 S. Charles St., Atlantic City, N.J.

ALLMAN, Drue Nunez, floriculturist; b. Phila., Pa., Sept. 30, 1893; s. Herbert D. and Mildred

ALLMAN C. (Nunez) A.; student Princeton U., 1911-12; B.S. in agr., Cornell U., 1915, M.S. in agr., 1920; m. Blanche A. Oppenheimer, Oct. 14, 1917; children—Herbert D., William B. Instr. horticulture, Nat. Farm Sch., Pa., 1915-19; instr. floriculture and vegetable culture, Cornell U., 1919-20; engaged in commercial flower growing and breeding as owner and mgr. Allman Nurseries, since 1920; specializes in snapdragon breeding, originator of several varieties; lecturer on flowers and hort. subjects. Dir. Nat. Farm Sch., Doylestown, Pa. Mem. Soc. Am. Florists, Alpha Sigma Phi. Clubs: Phila. Art Alliance, Phila. Florists. Contbr. to hort. and trade jours.; writer on garden subjects, Phila. Inquirer, 1934-37. Now cooperating with state expt. stations, chem. and elec. equipment companies in research: growing plants under electric lights, growing plants in cinders and gravel without soil, testing effects of various chemicals on root growth, automatic feeding and watering of florists' plants. Address: 8040 Rowland Av., Philadelphia, Pa.

ALLMAN, Justin Paul, wholesale merchant; b. Phila., Pa., June 28, 1873; s. David and Pauline (Kayser) A.; ed. pub. schs.; m. Viola Hirsh, June 5, 1900 (died July 6, 1933); children—Henry Hirsh, Charles Kayser, Robert Justin; m. 2nd, Hortense Wolf, June 30, 1936. Began in wallpaper business, 1899; mem. of firm Kayser & Allman, Inc., wholesale wall papers, since 1894. Hon. pres. Fed. of Jewish Charities of Phila., Nat. Wall Paper Wholesaler's Assn.; pres. Decorative Trades Assn. Jewish religion. Mason; trustee Pa. Grand Lodge Endowment Fund for Masonic Homes, Freemasons Memorial Hosp. Clubs: Reciprocity (hon. pres. Nat., pres. Phila.), Philmont Country, 100 Club of Phila. (treas.). Home: 235 S. 15th St. Office: 1709 Walnut St., Philadelphia, Pa.

ALLNER, F. A.; v.p. Pa. Water & Power Co. Home: 908 W. Belvidere Av. Office: Lexington Bldg., Baltimore, Md.

ALLPORT, James H., mining engr.; pres. First Nat. Bank of Barnsboro, Rich Hill Coal Co. Address: Barnsboro, Pa.

ALLWEIN, A. Francis, development engr.; b. Phila., Pa., Apr. 11, 1895; s. Jerome Adam and Sophia (Schaefer) A.; grad. Northeast High Sch., Phila., 1912; B.S. in elec. engring., U. of Pa., 1916; m. Mary M. McCluskey, June 22, 1929; children—Janet Elizabeth (deceased), Edward Francis. Test engr. Gen. Electric Co., Schenectady, N.Y., 1916-19; instr. in mech. engring., U. of Pa., 1919-26; teacher Drexel Inst. Evening Sch., 1920-31; research engr. Atwater Kent Mfg. Co., 1926-30; development engr. on industrial instruments, Leeds & Northrup Co., Phila., 1930-31; dist. rep. for H. A. DeVry, Inc., Chicago, 1931-35; development eng. Brown Instrument Co., Phila., since 1935. Mem. Am. Inst. Elec. Engrs., Am. Soc. for Metals. Republican. Roman Catholic. Club: Phila. Engineers. Home: 714 Carpenter Lane, Germantown, Philadelphia, Pa.

ALMOND, Linda Stevens (Mrs. Huston B. Almond), author; b. Seaford, Del.; d. William Henry and Julia Catherine (Donoho) Stevens; ed. Mrs. Sutton's and Miss Roney's Sch. for Girls, Phila., Pa.; m. Huston Berley Almond, Oct. 6, 1909. Contbr. to Youth's Companion, Child Life. St. Nicholas and other mags. Democrat. Episcopalian. Author: Peter Rabbit Books, beginning 1921—Peter Rabbit's Easter; When Peter Rabbit Went To School; Peter Rabbit's Birthday; Peter Rabbit Goes A-Visiting; Peter Rabbit and Jack the Jumper; Peter Rabbit and the Little Boy; Peter Rabbit and Little White Rabbit; Peter Rabbit and the Old Witch Woman; Peter Rabbit and the Tiny-Bits; Peter Rabbit Goes A-Fishing; Peter Rabbit and the Two Terrible Foxes; Peter Rabbit's Holiday; also Little Glad Heart, 1921; Mary Redding Takes Charge, 1926; Peter Rabbit and the Little Girl; Peter Rabbit's Picnic; Buddy Bear Series; Penny Hill Stories; Gleelup—the Gnome Tales. Contbr. to mags. Home: 30 Benezet St., Chestnut Hill, Philadelphia, Pa.

ALPERS, Bernard Jacob, neurologist and psychiatrist; b. Salem, Mass., Mar. 14, 1900; s. Samuel and Bessie (Swift) A.; student Harvard, 1917-19; M.D., Harvard Med. Sch., 1923; Sc.D. Med., U. of Pa., 1930; m. Dr. Lillian Sher, Sept. 11, 1927; children—Paul Joel, David Herschel. Began as physician, 1930, and since in practice as neurologist and psychiatrist; prof. neurology, Jefferson Med. Coll., Phila., Pa., since 1938. Diplomate in Neurology and Psychiatry, Am. Bd. of Psychiatry and Neurology; mem. Am. Neurol. Assn. (asst. sec.), Am. Psychiatric Assn., Assn. for Research in Nervous and Mental Diseases, Coll. of Physicians of Phila., Phila. Neurol. Soc. (sec.), Phila. Psychiatric Soc., Phila. Co. Med. Soc. Mem. Brith Sholem. Jewish religion. Club: Harvard (Phila.). Home: 500 Oak Rd., Merion, Pa. Office: 111 N. 49th St., Philadelphia, Pa.

ALSENTZER, Harry August, Jr., asso. prof. chemistry; b. Phila., Pa., Feb. 6, 1898; s. Harry August and Alice (Koch) A.; B.S. in Chem., U. of Pa., 1920, Ph.D., same, 1926; m. Esther Elizabeth Spencer, Aug. 26, 1922; children—Harry A. III, John Spencer. Engaged as instr. chemistry, U. of Pa., 1920-26, asst. prof. chemistry, 1926-36, asso. prof. chemistry since 1936. Mem. A.A.A.S., Am. Chem. Soc., Electrochem. Soc., Sigma Xi, Alpha Chi Sigma. Republican. Lutheran. Club: Lenape (Philadelphia). Home: 2201 N. 13th St., Philadelphia, Pa.

ALSTON, Robert S.; surgeon Germantown and Stetson hosps. Address: 121 W. Walnut Lane, Philadelphia, Pa.

ALTER, George Elias, lawyer; b. Springdale, Pa., May 8, 1868; s. Elias and Martha (Ferson) A.; ed. pub. schs.; (LL.D., Lafayette 1921); read law in office of William Yost, Pittsburgh; m. Diana J. Swanton, Sept. 11, 1902; children—Georgia (dec.), Diana (dec.), Kathleen E., Helen Martha (dec.), Frances E., Geo. E., Jr., David S. Admitted to Pa. bar, 1893, and began practice at Pittsburgh; mem. Pa. Ho. of Rep. 1908-14 (speaker, 1913-14); mem. Commn. on Revision of Tax and Corpn. Laws, 1911-12, Commn. to Revise and Codify the Law of Decedents' Estates, 1915-17, Commn. on Constl. Amendment and Revision, 1919-20; atty. gen. of Pa., term Dec. 14, 1920-Jan. 16, 1923; mem. firm of Alter, Wright & Barron. Pres. Pa. Bar Assn., 1924-25; mem. council of Am. Law Inst., 1923—; mem. Commn. on Uniform State Laws, 1927-32. Republican. Methodist. Clubs: Duquesne, University, Oakmont Country, Long Vue. Home: 314 S. Dallas Av. Office: First National Bank Bldg., Pittsburgh, Pa.*

ALTMEYER, George; chmn. bd. Union Nat. Bank. Home: 2303 Jenny Lind St. Office: 900 Market St., McKeesport, Pa.

ALTMEYER, Walter Seddon, pres. Crown Chocolate Co.; b. McKeesport, Pa., June 24, 1884; s. George and Isabella (Seddon) A.; grad. McKeesport High Sch., 1901; home study, U. of Chicago, 1908-15; m. Gladys Greenlee, of Washington Co., Pa., Aug. 6, 1908. With Crown Chocolate Co. since 1907, successively clerk, bookkeeper, operating engr., chief engr., mgr., and sec., pres. and dir. since 1908; v.p. and dir. Krantz Brewing Co.; treas. and dir. The Seddon Co.; sec., treas. and dir. Tube City Brewing Co.; dir. Union Nat. Bank, The Stallings Co. Republican. Mason (K.T.), Elk. Clubs: Youghiogheny Country, Rotary (McKeesport). Home: 1601 Coursin St. Office: 900 Market St., McKeesport, Pa.

ALTMILLER, Charles Henry, mining engr., anthracite coal; b. Hazelton, Pa., Mar. 15, 1898; s. Justus Emerald and Etta (Drissell) A.; grad. Hazelton pub. schs., 1917; student Bethlehem (Pa.) Prep. Sch., 1917-18, Lehigh U., 1918-20; E.M., U. of Pittsburgh, 1923; m. Annie Louise Crawford, of Pittsburgh, June 2, 1926; 1 son, Charles Henry; m. 2d, Mary Katherine Moser Mills, of Shamokin, Pa., June 4, 1938; 1 dau., Marcia Moser Mills. Engring., 1907-36; anthracite coal business since 1925; vice-pres. Union Improvement Co.; vice-pres. and dir. Cranberry Improvement Co.; engr. and dir. Buck Mountain Coal Mining Co.; treas. and dir. Diamond Coal Land Co.; vice-pres. and dir. Penmar Shares Co. Served in R.O.T.C., 1918. Mem. Hazelton Chamber of Commerce (pres. 1935), Hazelton Exchange Club (dist. gov., pres. 1934), Izaak Walton League (Pa. v.p. since 1936), Soc. of Engrs., Delta Tau Delta. Lutheran. Elk. Club: Beaver Run Hunting and Fishing (Pike Co., Pa.). Address: Hazelton, Pa.

ALVIN, G(uerino) W., surgeon; b. Salerno, Italy, Jan. 25, 1885; s. John and Philomena (Galasso) A.; brought to U.S., 1893; student U. of Pittsburgh, 1907-10; M.D., U. of Louisville, 1911; m. Jeanette Sunseri, Oct. 29, 1913; children—Flora, John, Mary, Dorothy, Salvatore, Lillian. Asst. surgeon U.S. Marine and Pub. Health Hosp., 1911-12; chief of staff, gynecologist and obstetrician, St. Joseph's Hosp., 1913-19, Pittsburgh Hosp., 1918-21; med. dir., chief surgeon and gynecologist, Belvedere Gen. Hosp. since 1921. Served as capt. Med. Res. Corps, U.S.A. Decorated Knight of the Order of Crown of Italy. Venerable local lodge and State Dep. Juvenile Lodges, Sons of Italy. Mem. Am. and Allegheny Co. med. assns., Internat. Coll. Surgeons. Republican. Mem. K.C. Clubs: Stanton Heights Country, Italian Professional of Pittsburgh (financial sec.). Home: Churchill Rd., Wilkinsburg, Pa. Office: 541 Paulson Av., Pittsburgh, Pa.

ALWYNE, Horace, prof. of music; b. Lancashire, Eng., Oct. 13, 1891; s. Thalberg and Mary (Whittaker) A.; holder Sir Charles Hallé Memorial Scholarship, 1909-12; goldmedallist and grad. with distinction, Royal Manchester Coll. of Music, Eng., 1912, hon. fellow, 1924; studied with Prof. Max Mayer (Eng.), and Prof. Michael von Zadora (Berlin); m. Mildred S. Avery. Dir. of music, Manchester (Eng.) Grammar Sch., 1911-12; head piano dept., Skidmore Sch. of Arts, Saratoga Springs, N.Y., 1914-21; asso. prof. music, Bryn Mawr Coll., 1921-27, prof. and head dept. since 1927. Made first pub. appearance at age of 11, first appearance with orchestra at 13; has appeared in concerts extensively in Europe and America, including recitals in Berlin and Vienna; appeared as soloist with Hallé Orchestra and B.B.C. Orchestra, Eng., with Phila. Orchestra three times, with N.Y. Philharmonic, Detroit Symphony two times, Russian Symphony five times, and as composer, conductor and pianist with Detroit Symphony; also many appearances with well-known quartettes. Mem. bd. dirs. Phila. Settlement Music Sch. since 1933; pres. Phila. Soc. for Contemporary Music, 1928-29. Home: Orchard Way, Rosemont, Pa. Office: Bryn Mawr Coll., Bryn Mawr, Pa.

AMADON, Roger S(hirley); prof. veterinary physiology, U. of Pa. Address: U. of Pennsylvania, Philadelphia, Pa.

AMBERG, Richard Hiller, editor and pub. newspaper; b. New York, N.Y., June 5, 1912; s. Max W. and Irma (Hiller) A.; A.B. magna cum laude, Harvard, 1933; m. Janet Katharine Law, June 18, 1938. In employ Gulf Refining Co., 1933-35; with ins. co., Newark, N.J., 1935-37; propr., editor and pub. Oil City Blizzard, daily evening newspaper, Oil City, Pa. since 1937. Organized Coll. Div. Rep. Nat. Com., 1932. Mem. Oil City Chamber of Commerce, Titusville Chamber of Commerce, Lions. Dir. Oil City Chapter Nat. Aeronautical Assn. Mem. Am. and Pa. Newspaper Publishers assns. Ensign, U.S. Naval Reserve. Republican. Congslist. Clubs: Harvard (New York); Press (Erie); Wanango Country, National Republican (New York). Home: Woodland Heights. Office: 221 Sycamore St., Oil City, Pa.

AMBLER, Charles Henry, college prof.; b. New Matamoras, O., Aug. 12, 1876; s. Lutellus and Ella Rebecca (Wells) A.; grad. W. Liberty (W.Va.) State Normal Sch., 1900; A.B., W.Va. U., 1904, A.M., 1905; Ph.D., U. of Wis., 1908; m. Helen Mary Carle, Sept. 4, 1920; children—Mary Elizabeth, Helen Louise. Prof. history and polit. science, Randolph-Macon Coll., Ashland, Va., 1908-17; prof. history, W.Va. Univ., 1917—, also head dept. of history since 1929. Prof. summer sessions, U. of Tex., 1918, 20 and 24; visiting prof. Ohio State Univ., 1928-29; pres. Ashland (Va.) Sch. Bd., 1908-

17, Monongalia County (W.Va.) since 1932. Editor John P. Branch Hist. Papers, 1908-17; editor Letters and Papers of R. M. T. Hunter, Diary of John Floyd; Siviter, Anna Pierpont, Recollections of War and Peace, 1861-1868, (1938); Sheriff Pleasants Co., W.Va., 1900-01. Methodist. Mem. Am. Hist. Assn., Am. Polit. Science Assn., Miss. Valley Hist. Assn., Am. Geog. Soc., Sigma Nu, Phi Beta Kappa, Tau Kappa Alpha. Mason, Odd Fellow, Maccabee. Author: Sectionalism in Virginia from 1777 to 1861, 1910; Thomas Ritchie—A Study in Virginia Politics, 1912; Life of John Floyd, 1918; A History of Transportation in the Ohio Valley with Special Reference to Waterways 1932; A History of West Virginia, 1933; George Washington and the West, 1936; Francis H. Pierpont, Union War Governor of Virginia and Father of West Virginia, 1937; West Virginia Stories and Biographies, 1937; also pamphlets and articles. Home: 128 Simpson St., Morgantown, W.Va.

AMBLER, Mason Gaither, lawyer; b. Winchester, Va., Aug. 27, 1876; s. Benjamin Mason and Nannie L. (Baker) A.; grad. several schs., U. of Va., and law course same univ.; m. Isabella, d. Dr. Robert L. Brown, June 22, 1921. Admitted to W.Va. bar, 1899; mem. firm Van Winkle & Ambler, 1904-21; now mem. Ambler, McCluer & Ambler. Mem. W.Va. Com. on Uniform State Laws, 1910-16; trustee Sinking Funds City of Parkersburg. Chmn. of Red Cross Civil Service Relief Com. for Wood and Wirt Counties during World War. Mem. Am. Bar Assn., W.Va. Bar Assn. (chmn. exec. council 1924-25; pres. 1927-28), Delta Psi; life mem. Am. Law Inst. Democrat. Episcopalian. Contbr. Am. Bar Journal and other legal mags. Home: Parkersburg, W.Va.

AMBRUSTER, Howard Watson, chemical engr.; b. Germantown, Pa., Aug. 12, 1878; s. Watson and Emma Elizabeth (Earley) A.; ed. Germantown Acad., 1887-94, U. of Pa., 1894-98; B.S. in economics, U. of Pa., 1939; m. Florence Ursula Favreau, June 15, 1910; children—Watson, Joseph Favreau (dec.), Albert Miller (dec.). Reporter Phila. Evening Telegraph, 1896-97; football coach Rutgers U., New Brunswick, N.J., 1898; clk. clearing house, Phila. Stock Exchange, 1899; constrn. engr. Va. Portland Cement Co., Craigsville, Va., 1900; editorial writer, exchange editor Phila. Times, 1901; sec., dir. Gen. Artificial Silk Co., Phila., 1902-04; with rayon, textile and chemical industries, 1905-12; organizer, sec. and dir. Frohman Chem. Co., Sandusky, O., 1913-18; gen. mgr. Hemingway & Co., Bound Brook, N.J., 1919-21; mem. bd. operators Sherwin-Williams Co., Cleveland, 1920; cons. engr. for arsenical and insecticide industries, N.Y. City, 1921-32, Westfield, N.J., since 1932. Made survey of world's arsenical supply, showing relation to boll weevil control, 1921; rebuilt and reorganized arsenical plant, Nat. Chem. Co., Pittsburg, Calif., 1924, and directed warehouse distribution of its calcium arsenate in cotton states, 1925-26; announced menace of the arsenical spray residue problem, 1926; entered pharm. industry to supply pure ergot to med. profession, 1927; took various legal steps to compel enforcement of Pure Food and Drug Act and false advertising laws, since 1928; has frequently appeared before congressional coms., grand juries and radio and platform audiences; lectured at Columbia University, University of Pennsylvania and New York University, 1935-37. Mem. 7th Regt., N.Y.N.G., Am. Protective League during World War. Mem. Crop Protective Inst. of Nat. Research Council, Franklin Inst., Am. Chem. Soc., N.J. Chem. Soc., Am. Acad. Polit. and Social Science, Chemists Club, Drug and Chem. Club, S.R., Vets. 7th Regt. N.Y.N.G. Patentee of method of making arsenic acid and of the manufacture of insecticides. Presbyn. Clubs: Varsity, Gridiron. Author: Arsenic, Calcium Arsenate and the Boll Weevil, 1923; (with others) Mineral Industries, vol. 34, 1926, vol. 35, 1927; Why Not Enforce the Laws We Already Have? or How and Why Industries' Outlaws are Crucifying Harvey Wiley's Pure Food and Drug Law (with Ursula Ambruster), 2 edits., 1935. Appeared as own atty. in numerous court actions, arising out of current pub. activities, 1930-38, and in Jan. 1936 secured reversal of a N.J. Supreme Court decision from the N.J. Court of Errors and Appeals. Contbr. scientific articles to Encyclopedia Americana and mags. Address: Westfield, N.J.

AMERMAN, Ralph Alonzo, banker; b. Scranton, Pa., May 19, 1884; s. Lemuel and Mary (Van Nort) A.; prep. edn., Hill Sch., Pottstown, Pa., and Worcester (Mass.) Acad.; student Cornell U., 1903-04; m. Ada May Wrightnour, Apr. 13, 1905; children—Jean, Ralph. Began in 1904 with Spring Brook Water Supply Co.; gen. agt. for Buick, northeastern Pa., 1906-18; gen. mgr. Scranton Glass Instrument Co., 1919-23; v.p. Lincoln Trust Co., 1923-26, chmn. bd., 1926-28; pres. Dime Bank-Lincoln Trust Co., 1928-32; v.p. First Nat. Bank of Scranton since 1932; pres. Lincoln Realty Co.; v.p. Thrift & Loan Finance Co.; dir. Jessup Hill Coal Co., Megargee Bros., Industrial Thrift & Loan Corpn., Packard Lackawanna Auto Co. Served as bus. mgr., later divisional sec., Y.M.C.A., A.E.F., France, 1 yr. Trustee Keystone Junior Coll., Bucknell U., Scranton Community Welfare Assn. Mem. Kappa Sigma. Republican. Presbyn. Mason (33°, K.T., Shriner), Elk. Clubs: Scranton, Kiwanis, Scranton Canoe, Scranton Country, Abington Hills Country, Irem Temple Country, Abington Hills Hunt, Pocono Hunting and Fishing, Gatineau Rod and Gun. Home: 535 Monroe Av. Office: First National Bank, Scranton, Pa.

AMES, Frank Newton, mfr.; b. Corry, Pa., Sept. 3, 1881; s. Charles Howard and Jennie (Ferrow) A.; student high sch.; m. Jessie Elizabeth Barlow, Oct. 24, 1914; 1 son, Eli Barlow. Began as clk., 1898; now pres. Aero Supply Mfg. Co., mfrs. aircraft accessories. Episcopalian. Home: 43 W. Smith St. Office: Main St. and 5th Av., Corry, Pa.

AMES, J. Wilson, lawyer; b. Hawley, Pa., Mar. 1, 1895; s. James D. and Lucy (Millham) A.; student Hawley High Sch., Hawley, Pa., 1909-12, Swarthmore (Pa.) Prep. Sch., 1912-13; A.B., Swarthmore (Pa.) Coll., 1917; student Columbia U., summer 1917; studied law Swarthmore, Columbia U. and in office of V. A. Decker, Hawley, Pa.; m. Ethel Schiessler, June 26, 1923. Admitted to Pa. bar, 1922, and began practice in Wayne Co.; referee in bankruptcy, Wayne and Pike Counties, 1924-28; dist. atty., Wayne Co., since 1928; vice-pres. First Nat. Bank, Hawley, Pa.; pres. and treas. Hawley Water Co.; solicitor Hawley Bldg. & Loan Assn.; Hawley Borough. Served as 2d lt., 36th Inf., U.S. Army, Camp Devans, Mass., during World War. Rep. State committeeman for Wayne Co. Dir. Hawley Chamber of Commerce, Wayne Memorial Hosp., Honesdale, Pa. Mem. Dist. Atty. Assn. of Pa. (pres. 1937-38), Pa. Bar Assn., Wayne Co. Bar Assn., Am. Legion (past comdr. Hawley Post), Phi Sigma Kappa. Republican. Presbyterian (elder and supt. Sunday Sch.). Mason (K.T., Shriner), Odd Fellow. Clubs: Exchange, Honesdale Golf, Shrine (Honesdale, Pa.); Elmhurst Country (Elmhurst). Home: 523 Academy St. Office: Court House, Honesdale, Pa.

AMES, Joseph Sweetman, physicist; b. Manchester, Vt., July 3, 1864; s. Dr. George Lapham and Elizabeth (Bacon) A.; A.B., Johns Hopkins, 1886, fellow, 1887-88, Ph.D., 1890; LL.D., Washington Coll., 1907, Univ. of Pennsylvania, 1933; Johns Hopkins University, 1936; m. Mrs. Mary B. (Williams) Harrison, Sept. 14, 1899 (died 1931). Asst. in physics, 1888-91, asso., 1891-1893, asso. prof., 1893-99, prof. physics, 1899-1926, dir. Physical Lab., 1901-1926, provost, 1926-29, president, 1929-35, president emeritus since 1935, Johns Hopkins U. Honorary member Royal Institution Great Britain; fellow Am. Acad. Arts and Sciences; mem. Nat. Acad. Sciences, Am. Phys. Soc. Mem. Nat. Advisory Com. for Aeronautics since 1917 (chmn. since 1927); chairman foreign service committee of Nat. Research Council which visited France and Eng. in May and June, 1917, to study origin and development of scientific activities in connection with warfare. Home: 2 Charlcote Pl., Guilford, Baltimore, Md.

AMES, Louis Annin, mfr.; b. Island St. Helena, S.C., Sept. 5, 1866; s. Jacob Meech and Phebe (Palmer) A.; ed. pub. and high schs., Jersey City, N.J.; m. Abby Whitney Crowell, Jan. 20, 1909. Pres. Annin & Co. (flag mfrs.), Old Glory Realty Co., Theodore Crowell, Inc.; pres. Park Lane Realty Co. of N.J.; dir. Verona Trust Co. Democrat. Chmn. bd. trustees Universalist Gen. Conv., Ch. of Divine Paternity; pres. New York State Convention of Universalists, Grover Cleveland Birthplace Assn. Pres. gen. Nat. Soc. S.A.R.; gov.-gen. of Founders and Patriots of America; mem. Soc. Colonial Wars, S.R., Soc. Am. Wars, St. Nicholas Soc., N.Y. Hist. Soc., Am. Scenic and Hist. Soc. Mem. Chamber of Commerce of State of N.Y., Merchants Assn., Bd. of Trade, Fifth Av. Assn., Broadway Assn., Washington Continental Guard. Clubs: Mil. and Naval, Salmagundi, Aldine, Universalist, Advertising, Essex Fells Country, Fells Brook. Home: 85 5th Av., New York, and Essex Fells, N.J. Office: 1 E. 16th St., New York, N.Y.

AMES, William Homer, librarian; b. Pittsville, Md., Mar. 19, 1876; s. William Cree and Margaret Catherine (Demory) A.; ed. Dickinson Prep. Sch., Carlisle, Pa., 1893-97; Ph.B., Dickinson Coll., 1901; unmarried. Employed as asst. compiler Fourth Series Pa. Archives, 1901; instr. chemistry, Metzger Coll. for Young Women, Carlisle, Pa., 1901-07; prof. econs. and sociology, Irving Coll. for Young Women, Mechanicsburg, Pa., 1903; librarian, J. Herman Bosler Memorial Library, Carlisle, Pa., since 1903; librarian, Hamilton Library and Hist. Assn. of Cumberland Co., Pa., since 1928; mng. editor The Public Speaker's Magazine, 1926-32. Dir. Hamilton Library and Hist. Assn. of Cumberland Co., Pa. Mem. Sigma Alpha Epsilon. Republican. Mem. M.E. Ch. Elk. Author: One Hundred Master Speeches, 2 vols., 1922-23; The Speaker's Library, 1926. Contbr. History of the Cumberland Valley, Pa., 1930. Home: No. 1 Hamilton Apts. Office: 158 W. High St., Carlisle, Pa.

AMICK, Chester A(lbert), chemist; b. Scipio, Ind., Apr. 19, 1895; s. Albert and Rosa Belle (Amick) A.; A.B., with distinction, Ind. Univ., Bloomington, Ind., 1920, A.M., 1921; student U. of Lyon, France, 1919, Cornell U., 1925-27; m. Marcella Hoover, June 24, 1925; children—James Albert, Donald Hoover, Robert Myrl. Engaged in teaching, pub. schs. in Ind., 1913-15, 1917-18; instr. Arsenal Tech. Schs., Indianapolis, Ind., 1921-25; research chemist, Pacific Mills, Lawrence, Mass., 1927-31; dir. research, U.S. Finishing Co., Providence, R.I., 1931-32, Glenlyon Print Works, Phillipsdale, R.I., 1932-35; research chemist, Calco Chem. Co., Bound Brook, N.J., since 1935. Served as musician with Ind. N.G. on Mexican border, 1916; corpl. F.A., U.S.A., 1918-19; with A.E.F.; interpreter Army of Occupation, 1919. Fellow Am. Inst. Chemists. Mem. Am. Chem. Soc., Am. Assn. Tech. Chemists and Colorists, Soc. Dyers and Colorists (Eng.), A.A.A.S., Phi Beta Kappa, Alpha Chi Sigma, Theta Chi. Awarded Grasselli Chem. Co. fellowship, Ind. Univ., 1921; Pacific Mills fellowship, Cornell, 1926-27. Republican. Presbyn. Mason. Club: Square and Compass. Home: 121 E. Maple Av., Bound Brook, N.J.

AMMANN, Othmar Hermann, civ. engr.; b. Schaffhausen, Switzerland, Mar. 26, 1879; s. Emanuel and Emilie Rosa (Labhardt) A.; C.E., Swiss Federal Poly. Inst., Zurich, 1902, Dr. Tech. Sciences, 1930; Dr. Engring., New York University, 1931; Sc.M., Yale University, 1932; Dr. Engring., Pa. Military College, 1934; m. Lilly Selma Wehrli, July 24, 1905 (deceased 1933); children—Werner, George Andrew, Margaret; m. 2d, Klary Vogt Noetzli, 1935. Came to U.S., 1904, naturalized citizen, 1924. Investigation, design and bldg. of bridges, etc., in Europe and U.S., 1902-23; asst. chief engr. on design and constrn. Hell Gate Bridge, New York, 1912-18; cons. engr., N.Y. City, 1923-25; chief engr. of bridges, 1925-30, chief engr. Port of New York Authority since 1930, in gen. charge planning and constrn. Outerbridge Crossing and Goethals Bridge across Arthur Kill, arch bridge across Kill van Kull at Bayonne, N.J., George Washington Bridge and Lincoln Tunnel across Hudson River at New York, and other projects; mem. bd. engrs. in charge Golden Gate Bridge, San Francisco, 1929-36; chief engr. Triborough Bridge. Authority in charge of planning and construction of Triborough Bridge and Bronx-Whitestone Bridge, both across East River, N.Y. City. Mem. Am. Soc. C.E., Am. Inst. Cons. Engrs., Am. Ry. Engring. Assn., Am. Soc. Testing Materials, Inst. of Civil Engineers of Great Britain; fellow A.A.A.S. Awarded Thomas Fitch Rowland prize, Am. Soc. C.E., 1918. Protestant. Club: Engineers. Home: 272 Rockaway Av., Boonton, N.J. Office: 111 8th Av., New York, N.Y.

AMOS, Thyrsa Wealtheow, dean of women; b. Frankfort, Ind., Nov. 20, 1879; d. Joseph Bonaparte and Mary Agness (Grove) A.; Fairmount Coll., Wichita, Kan., 1903; A.B., A.M., U. of Kan., 1917; LL.D., U. of Pittsburgh, 1930. Successively teacher pub. schs., prin. elementary sch. and high sch., dean of girls, high sch., Shawnee, Okla.; instr. in psychology, U. of Kan., 1917-18; also social dir. summer session; dean of women, U. of Pittsburgh, since 1919. Mem. Am. Assn. Univ. Women, Nat. Assn. Deans of Women (pres., 1929-31), D.A.R., Phi Beta Kappa, Pi Lambda Theta, Mortar Board. Democrat. Episcopalian. Club: Twentieth Century. Lecturer, personnel work in education. Home: 166 N. Dithridge St., Pittsburgh, Pa.

AMRAM, David Werner, lawyer, referee in bankruptcy; b. Phila., Pa., May 16, 1866; s. Werner David and Esther (Hammerschlag) A.; student Rugby Acad., Phila., 1880-83; B.A., U. of Pa., 1889, LL.B. and M.A., 1889; 3 children by 1st marriage. Admitted to Pa. bar, 1889, and since practiced at Phila.; referee in bankruptcy, Phila., since 1903. Dir. or trustee numerous ednl. and pub. instns. Wrote several books and many mag. articles. Home: 136 Radnor St., Bryn Mawr, Pa. Office: 12 S. 12th St., Philadelphia, Pa.

AMRAM, Philip Werner, lawyer; b. Phila., Pa., Mar. 14, 1900; s. David Werner and Beulah (Brylawski) A.; A.B., U. of Pa., 1920; B.S.A., Pa. State Coll., 1922; LL.B. cum laude, U. of Pa., 1927; m. Emilie S. Weyl, Dec. 18, 1924; children—Mariana B., David Werner III. Admitted to Pa. bar, 1927, and since asso. with Wolf, Block, Schorr & Solis-Cohen, Phila., mem. firm since 1936; instr. Pa. practice and practice court, U. of Pa. Law Sch., since 1929. Mem. procedural rules com. Supreme Court of Pa. engaged in revision of procedural law of Pa. Served as 2d lt. inf. U.S. Army, 1918. Dir. Gratz Coll., Phila.; dir. Jewish Publ. Soc. America. Mem. Pa. and Phila. bar assns., Phi Kappa Phi, Order of Coif. Ind. Republican. Jewish religion. Club: Phila. Art Alliance. Author: Amram's Pennsylvania Common Pleas Practice (4th edit. 1936). Editor-in-chief U. of Pa. Law Review, 1926-27; lecturer and author on legal topics; active in philanthropic work in Phila. Home: Belphida Farms, Feasterville, Pa. Office: 1204 Packard Bldg., Philadelphia, Pa.

ANDERS, Howard S(chultz), M.D.; b. Norritonville, Montgomery Co., Pa., Nov. 12, 1866; s. Nathaniel H. and Regina (Schultz) A.; A.B., Central High Sch., Phila., 1885, A.M., 1892; M.D., U. of Pa., 1890; m. Mabel Gilling, Dec. 27, 1893 (died Nov. 1911); m. 2d, Maud Howland Wiggins, of Ottawa, Ill., Mar. 12, 1912. Interne Presbyn. Hosp., Phila., 1890-91; in gen. practice, Phila., since 1891; instr. clin. medicine, Medico-Chirurgical Coll. (now Grad. Sch. of Medicine, U. of Pa.), 1893-98; prof. phys. diagnosis, same, 1899-1913; attending physician Samaritan and Phila. Gen. hosps., 1898-1909; cons. cardiologist Elm Terrace Hosp., Lansdale, Pa., 1937. Sch. dir. 15th Ward, Phila., 4 yrs.; pres. bd. Lincoln Coll. Prep. Sch. since 1926; pres. Phila. Soc. Arts and Letters, 4 yrs.; pres. Pa. Soc. Prevention Tuberculosis, 1903-05. Appointed lt. comdr. Med. Res., U.S. Navy, 1918. Hon. mem. Royal Meteorol. Soc., London, Eng.; mem. Sydenham Med. Coterie, Phila. (sec. 5 yrs.). Formerly mem. med. socs., A.A.A.S., Am. Climatologic Assn., Am. Pub. Health Assn. Author: Textbook on Inductive Physical Diagnosis, 1907. Contbr. many articles to jours. on relation of dust to pub. health, epidemic influenza and weather, "failing heart," etc.; pioneer in advocating individual drinking cups (1894), anti-spitting legislation (1896), state sanatorium for consumptives (1899); active in promulgating non-political, non- socialized medical program for indigent and unemployed middle classes, 1933-38; active in improving Phila. water supply. Home: City Line and Belmont Av. Office: 1808 Pine St., Philadelphia, Pa.

ANDERS, Stanley S., banking; b. Norristownville, Pa., Oct. 12, 1886; s. George H. and Eveline (Schultz) A.; student Norristown High School and U. of Pa.; m. Elizabeth Rambo, Apr. 15, 1914 (now deceased); children—Betty R., Samuel G., Stanley S.; m. 2d, Anne Swartz, Mar. 15, 1936. With Peoples Nat. Bank, Norristown, Pa., since 1904, starting as runner, now cashier and dir.; dir., trust officer and sec. of bd. Norristown Clearing House Assn.; pres. Rambo & Reyors, hosiery mfrs., Norristown. Republican. Mason. Club: Plymouth Country. Home: 1615 DeKolb St. Office: Peoples Nat. Bank, Norristown, Pa.

ANDERSON, Archer Edward, clergyman; b. Elizabeth, N.J., Dec. 30, 1899; s. August and Charlotte (Berglund) A.; A.B., Tex. Christian U., 1934; Th.B., Dallas Theol. Sem., Dallas, Tex., 1935, Th.M., 1935, Th.D., 1937; m. Lillian M. Kissling, Nov. 4, 1925; children—Lillian Clara, Frances Helen, Archa Edwina. Student pastor, Camden Dist., N.J. Conf. M.E. Ch., 1920-21; missionary to Guatemala, C.A., under Central Am. Mission, 1923-30; ordained to ministry Presbyn. Ch. in U.S., 1931; pastor, Fort Worth, Tex., 1931-33, Cleburne, Tex., 1933-36; pastor Narbeth Presbyn. Ch., Narberth, Pa. since 1936; co-founder and first dean, Robinson Bible Inst., Penajachel, Guatemala, 1923; co-founder and first dean, Central American Bible Inst., Guatemala City, 1927; prof. doctrine, Phila. Sch. of the Bible, 1936-39; dir. Interdenominational Young Peoples Conf. of Stony Brook, L.I. since 1938. Served as pvt. Med. Corps. U.S.A., 1918-19. Mem. council, Central American Mission, Dallas, Tex. Mem. Alpha Chi. Presbyterian. Home: 112 Dudley Av., Narberth, Pa.

ANDERSON, Camilla May, psychiatrist; b. Sidney, Mont., June 21, 1904; d. Peter and Bertha (Josephson) A.; A.B., U. of Ore., 1925, M.D., 1929. Interne U. of Ore. Med. Sch. Hosp., 1929-30; asst. physician Binghampton (N.Y.) State Hosp., 1930-31; psychiatrist Trudeau Sanitarium, Saranac Lake, N.Y., 1932-33; physician in charge women's psychiatric service, Pittsburgh City Hosp., 1934-36; psychiatrist women's receiving service, Allegheny County Hosp., Woodville, Pa., Apr.-Nov. 1936; exec. sec. Pa. Mental Hygiene Com. of Pub. Charities Assn. of Pa., Phila., since Nov. 1936; asst. prof. nursing edn., Duquesne U., Pittsburgh, 1936-38; special lecturer mental hygiene, U. of Pa., since 1937; asst. psychiatrist Phila. Gen. Hosp.; lecturer in psychiatry, Temple U. Med. Sch., Phila.; private practice of psychiatry, Phila. Diplomate Nat. Bd. Med. Examiners, 1930; certified as specialist in psychiatry by Am. Bd. Psychiatry and Neurology, 1938; mem. A.M.A., Pa. Med. Soc., Phila. County Med. Soc., Am. Psychiatric Assn., Pa. Psychiatric Assn., Phila. Psychiatric Assn., Alpha Epsilon Iota. Lutheran. Author: Emotion Hygiene, The Art of Understanding, 1937. Home: 2201 Chestnut St. Office: 255 S. 17th St., Philadelphia, Pa.

ANDERSON, Carlotta Adele (Mrs. J. Scott Anderson), teacher, writer; b. N.Y. City, Mar. 15, 1876; d. Newell Willard and Emma Cathrine (Jones) Bloss; academic course, Claverack (N.Y.) Coll., 1893, post-grad. work, 1894; trained as oral teacher of deaf, Wright-Humason Sch., N.Y. City; student Columbia Univ. and Swarthmore College; B.S. in Edn., U. of Pa., 1918, M.A., 1922; Montessori method under Signora Galli-Saccenti, Rome; m. J. Scott Anderson, June 2, 1897; children—David Roy, Dorothy Scott. Teacher, Wright-Humason Sch., 1894-97; owner oral schs. for the deaf and teacher-training schs., N.Y. City, Swarthmore and Torresdale, Pa., 1901-16; organizer and directress of Torresdale House (All Saints' Ch.), the first building erected in America especially for Montessori work (teacher-training, Montessori, primary, grammar and high schs.), 1912-17; prin. academic dept. N.J. Sch. for the Deaf, and in charge of training teachers of the deaf at the N.J. State Normal Sch., Trenton, 1918-21; teacher of deaf Phila. pub. schs. since 1921. U.S. Govt. and state del. 3d Internat. Congress on Home Edn. and Parent-Teachers' Unions, Brussels, 1910. Hon. member Internat. Com. of Congresses on Home Edn. and Parent-Teacher Unions for several yrs. Founder, 1911, and first pres. Swarthmore Safe and Sane Fourth of July Assn.; pres. Swarthmore Woman's Suffrage League, 1909-12. Home: 33 Sellers Av., Millbourne, Upper Darby, Pa.

ANDERSON, Charles D., educator; b. Manistique, Mich., Apr. 14, 1893; s. Alex and Ida (Peterson) A.; B.S., Mich. State Coll., East Lansing, Mich., 1917; A.M., Teachers Coll. of Columbia U., 1922; m. Florence E. Steffy, June, 1920; 1 son, Kenneth Charles. Teacher in rural sch., Manistique, Mich., 1912-13, high sch., Traverse City, Mich., 1917-19, high sch., Dover, Del., 1919-20; prin. high sch., Newtown Sq., Pa., 1920-21; statistician N.Y. Ednl. Finance Inquiry, N.Y. City, 1921-22; head dept. sci. and secondary div., State Teachers Coll., Fredonia, N.Y., 1922-26; statistician State Dept. Pub. Instrn., Trenton, N.J., 1926-34; asst. commr. edn., State Dept. Pub. Instrn., Trenton, N.J. since 1934; taught summer schs., Fredonia State Teachers Coll., N.Y., summers 1923-24, Glassboro, N.J., summers 1926-31. Mem. N.E.A., Nat. Assn. Pub. Sch. Adminstrs., Nat. Council Sch. House Constrn., N.J. State Edn. Assn., N.J. Pub. Sch. Bus. Ofcls. Assn. Nat. Pub. Sch. Bus. Ofcls., N.J. Schmasters Club, N.J. Council Edn., Phi Delta Kappa. Republican. Presbyn. Mason. Home: 18 E. Wellington Av., Pennington, N.J.

ANDERSON, Claire Alexander, univ. prof.; b. Butler Co., Pa., Aug. 3, 1892; s. William C. and Sarah Jane (Graham) A.; student Slippery Rock State Teachers Coll.; elec. engring. dept., U. of Pittsburgh Engring. Sch.; m. Martha M. Brown, June 22, 1921; children—Margaret Louise, Miriam Brown. Teacher grade schs., 1910-14; partner in gen. mdse. business, 1914-20; design and development elec. engr. Westinghouse Electric & Mfg. Co., Pittsburgh, Pa., 1922-24; prof. elec. engring., U. of Pittsburgh, since 1924; in charge engring dept., Johnstown Center. Served in 309th Engrs., U.S. Army, France, 1918-19. Ruling elder Presbyterian Ch. Mem. Soc. for Promotion of Engring. Edn., Am. Legion. Home: 127 Fourth Av., Westmont, Pa. Office: Johnstown Center, U. of Pittsburgh, Johnstown, Pa.

ANDERSON, Clarence Edgar, business exec.; b. Barclay, Md., June 13, 1890; s. Preston R. and Elizabeth (Graham) A.; student Barclay Sch. and Beacon Business Coll.; m. Lola Jackson, Jan. 21, 1912; children—Francis Marie, Ruth Ellen. Telegraph operator Pa. R.R., Bridgeville, Del., 1908-20, station agt., Ridgely, Md., 1920-22, bookkeeper H. P. Cannon & Son, Inc., Bridgeville, Del., 1922-30, treas. since 1930; dir. Bridgeville Bldg. & Loan Assn. Trustee Bridgeville Consolidated Sch.; mem. bd. stewards Bridgeville Methodist Ch. Methodist. Mason. Club Kiwanis (Bridgeville, Del.). Home: Delaware Av. Office: Bridgeville, Del.

ANDERSON, Daniel Godwin, real estate; b. Milford, Del., Apr. 5, 1882; s. James Francis and Sarah Greer (Hall) A.; student Milford (Del.) Classical Acad., 1888-97, Milford (Del.) Pub. Sch., 1897-98; A.B., Washington Coll., Chestertown, Md., 1902; student Yale Law Sch., 1914-15; grad. Am. Acad. of Dramatic Arts, New York, 1917; m. Frances Clara Cocke, Oct. 2, 1926; children—Daniel Godwin and Frances Howe (twins), Jacqueline Hall. Prin., Millsboro (Del.) Pub. Sch., 1902-03; asst. mgr. Bronx office, New York Edison Co., New York, 1903-09; engaged in pvt. real estate transactions, Rehoboth Beach, Del., 1920-27; licensed real estate broker since 1927; owner of Daniel G. Anderson, real estate, Rehoboth Beach, Del., since 1928; v.p. Rehoboth Trust Co. Attended Plattsburg Officers Mil. Training Camp; Y.M.C.A. war work sec. as ednl. dir. Unit No. 1, Camp Dix, 1917-18. Dir. Rehoboth Air Service, Rehoboth Sch. Bd. Mem. Phi Delta Phi, Yale Adelphia Soc. (Washington Coll.; pres.). Republican. Episcopalian. Club: Kiwanis (Rehoboth Beach, Del.; past pres.); Rehoboth Beach Country, Rehoboth Indian Beach. Address: 11 Park Av., Rehoboth Beach, Del.

ANDERSON, Dwight Malcolm, lawyer; b. Aberdeen, O., Aug. 9, 1886; s. William Henry and Mary Louise (Malcolm) A.; B.S., Washington and Jefferson Coll., 1909, M.S., 1910; LL.B., U. of Pa., 1914; m. Grace N. McCoy, of Sistersville, W.Va., Aug. 5, 1915; children—Dwight Malcolm, Jr., Frank McCoy, Stephen Barry. Admitted to Pa. bar and began practice at Washington, Pa., 1914; alone in gen. practice at Donora since 1915; served as solicitor for Borough of Donora, Pa., 1918-38; solicitor for local banks for over fifteen yrs.; dir. and counsel Union Nat. Bk. Mem. Am., Pa. and Washington Co. bar assns., Phi Gamma Delta, Phi Delta Phi. Republican. Presbyterian. Mason (32°, Shriner). Club: Monongahela Valley Country (dir.). Home: 727 Thompson Av. Office: 617 McKean Av., Donora, Pa.

ANDERSON, Edmund Arnold, phys. metallurgist; b. Bridgeport, Conn., July 27, 1899; s. Leonard Hemfried and Elizabeth Mary (Hunold) A.; Ph.B., Yale, 1920, M.S., 1923; m. Katharine Jean Barber, July 30, 1927; children—Edmund Arnold, David Barber, Katharine Elizabeth. Employed as phys. metallurgist, Handy & Harman, Bridgeport, Conn., research on white gold and silver solders, 1920-21; with Research Div., New Jersey Zinc Co., Palmerton, Pa. since 1923, now chief investigator metal sect. Mem. Am. Inst. Metall. Engrs., Am. Electro Platers Soc. Republican. Congregationalist. Mason. Club: Engineers of Lehigh Valley (Bethlehem, Pa.). Home: Residence Park, Palmerton, Pa.

ANDERSON, Edwin Joseph Arthur, extension apiarist; b. St. Marys, Pa., Apr. 19, 1900; s. Walter Wilson and Elizabeth Mary (Kerner) A.; B.S., Pa. State Coll., 1924; M.S., Cornell U., 1925; m. Mary Amelia Boyer, Aug. 14, 1925; children—Ray Edwin, Grace Annabel, Leona May, Mary Elizabeth, Paul Allen. Student asst. in apiculture, Pa. State Coll., 1921-22 and 1923-24; instr. entomology, Clemson (S.C.) Coll., 1925-26; instr. entomology and beekeeping, Pa. State Coll., 1926-31, asst. prof. since 1931; editor Pa. Beekeeper since 1927. Mem. A.A.A.S., Honey Producers League, Delta Theta Sigma. Home: 307 S. Garner St., State College, Pa.

ANDERSON, H. M.; pres. York Eastern Telephone Co. Home: Muddy Creek Forks, Pa. Office: 31 S. Beaver St., York, Pa.

ANDERSON, Henry Rummel, lawyer; b. Welch, W.Va., July 23, 1903; s. Luther Colfax and Frances (Rummel) A.; A.B., O. Wesleyan U., Delaware, O., 1924; student O. State U. Law Sch., Columbus, O., 1924-25; LL.B., W.Va. Univ. Law Sch., Morgantown, 1927; m. Anne N. Semans, July 28, 1928; children—Henry Delbert, Frances Rummel. Admitted to W.Va. bar, 1927 and since engaged in gen. practice of law at Charleston; asso. with firm Rummel, Blagg and Stone since 1927, mem. firm since 1933; vice pres., sec. and dir. Spartan Gas Co., Charleston, W.Va., since 1937. Mem. W.Va. Bar Assn., City of Charleston Bar Assn., Phi Delta Phi, Beta Theta Pi. Republican. Methodist. Home: 908 Ridgemont Road. Office: Security Bldg., Charleston, W.Va.

ANDERSON, Hjalmar Sigfrid, surgeon; b. Oil City Pa., Oct. 23, 1902; s. Anders Martin and Louisa Bernadotta (Johnson) A.; grad. Oil City High Sch., 1921; B.S., Allegheny Coll., Meadville, Pa., 1925; M.D., Johns Hopkins Med. Sch., 1929; m. Mary Teresa Smith, Oct. 15, 1938. Interne St. Agnes Hosp., Baltimore, Md., 1929-32; instr. Johns Hopkins Med. Sch., 1929-32; surgeon McClung Hosp., Richmond, W.Va., 1932-33; gen. practice of medicine, Titusville, Pa., since 1933. Served as 1st lt. Med. Corps, R.O.T.C., 1929. Fellow Am. Coll. Surgeons; mem. Crawford Co. Med. Soc., Phi Kappa Psi, Alpha Chi Sigma, Phi Chi. Republican. Lutheran. Mason (K.T., 32°). Home: Sherwood Apts. Office: 121 W. Spring St., Titusville, Pa.

ANDERSON, Horace Brockman, physician; b. Moore, S.C., Nov. 14, 1890; s. James H. and Sallie (Watson) A.; ed. Wofford Coll., 1907-11, A.B., 1911; M.D., Jefferson Med. Coll., 1917; m. Lois Hutchison, June 15, 1926; children—Sallie Watson, Horace Brockman, Jr. Interne Pennsylvania Hosp., Phila., 1917-19, dir. Ayer Lab. same, 1919-20; asso. prof. pathology, U. of N.C. Med. Sch., 1920-21; pathologist and med. dir. Conemaugh Valley Memorial Hosp., Johnstown, Pa., since 1922. Served as 1st lt. Med. Corps Res., U.S.A., 1917-18. Fellow Am. Coll. Phys. Mem. Am. Med. Assn., Am. Soc. for Study Neoplastic Diseases, Am. Soc. Clin. Pathologists, Am. Heart Assn., Pa. Heart Assn., Alpha Kappa Kappa, Alpha Omega Alpha. Presbyterian. Clubs: Bachelor, Sunnehanna Country (Johnstown). Home: St. Clair Rd. Office: U.S. National Bank Bldg., Johnstown, Pa.

ANDERSON, Hugh Craig, v.p. and treas. H. J. Heinz Co.; b. Belfast, Ireland, May 1, 1871; s. James and Rosanna (Craig) A.; student pub. schs.; m. Nettie Sheppard, June 5, 1902; children—Hugh Craig, Donald Herbert. With H. J. Heinz Co. since 1887, dir. since 1913, treas. since 1920, v.p. since 1931. Home: 5812 Northumberland St. Office: care H. J. Heinz Co., Pittsburgh, Pa.

ANDERSON, Hurst Robins, coll. prof.; b. Cleveland, O., Sept. 16, 1904; s. Foster Cookman and Ora Estelle (Robins) A.; A.B., Ohio Wesleyan U., Delaware, O., 1926; student U. of Mich. Sch. of Law, Ann Arbor, Mich., 1927-28; M.S., Northwestern U. Sch. of Speech, Evanston, Ill., 1934; m. Marian Charlene Powell, Aug. 25, 1932; children—Sarah Jane, Powell Robins. Alumni sec., Ohio Wesleyan U., 1926-27; instr. English, Allegheny Coll., Meadville, Pa., 1929-31, asst. prof., 1931-38, chmn. dept. speech since 1932, asso. prof. since 1938. Mem. Am. Assn. Univ. Profs., Nat. Assn. Teachers of Speech, Sigma Alpha Epsilon, Delta Sigma Rho, Omicron Delta Kappa. Republican. Methodist Episcopalian. Club: Round Table (Meadville, Pa.). Author: Practical Speaking, 1933; contbr. to ednl. publs. Home: 204 Meadow St. Office: Allegheny Coll., Meadville, Pa.

ANDERSON, J. Fisher; in practice of law since 1911. Address: 15 Exchange Place, Jersey City, N.J.

ANDERSON, J. H.; v.p. and gen mgr. Cooper Bessemer Corpn. Address: Grove City, Pa.

ANDERSON, James Tollman; b. Beaver Co., Pa., June 19, 1872; s. George W. and Margaret (Johnston) A.; ed. pub. sch. and high sch.; m. Sarah J. Wilson, Dec. 19, 1901; children—Margaret Ruth (Mrs. John A. Waddell), Martha I. (Mrs. Howard C. Moore), Mary Louise (Mrs. John C. McCleery), James T., Jr. Engaged in business as furniture dealer and funeral dir. at Beaver, Pa., since 1899; pres. Ft. McIntosh Nat. Bank since 1936, Dollar Bldg. & Loan Assn. since 1918; dir. Rochester Thrift & Loan Assn., Penn-Beaver Hotel Co. Presbyterian, Mason (K. T., 32°, Shriner), K.P., I.O.O.F. Club: Ft. McIntosh of Beaver (v.p.). Home: 444 Dravo Av. Office: 535 3d St., Beaver, Pa.

ANDERSON, John F., M.D.; b. Fredericksburg, Va., Mar. 14, 1873; s. John Kerwin and Lucy Ella (Hundley) A.; pub. schs., Fredericksburg, Locustdale, Bowling Green, Va., and Washington; M.D., U.of Va., 1896; Pathologische Institut, Vienna; Thompson Yates Labs., Liverpool, Eng., and Liverpool Sch. of Tropical Medicine, 1899-1901; m. Lucy Temple Hundley, Nov. 6, 1899; children—John Layton (dec.), Richard Hundley, Beverley Whiting (dec.). Asst. surgeon U.S.P.H. and Marine Hosp. Service, 1898; passed asst. surgeon, 1903. On epidemic duty in connection with yellow fever, 1898; quarantine officer Dry Tortugas, 1898-99; immigrant inspr. Ellis Island, 1899; sanitary observer at Glasgow, Oporto and Liverpool, 1899-1900; sanitary attaché U.S. consulates-gen., Barcelona, Marseilles, Vienna, London and Liverpool, 1899-1901; asst. dir. Hygienic Lab., Washington, 1902-09, dir. Oct. 1, 1909-Jan. 1, 1916; dir. Research and Biol. Labs., E. R. Squibb & Sons since 1916, also v.p. Fellow A.A.A.S.; mem. Am. Assn. Pathologists and Bacteriologists; Soc. Am. Bacteriology Soc. Exptl. Medicine and Biology, A.M. A., Am. Pub. Health Assn., Assn. Am. Physicians, Phi Beta Kappa and Alpha Omega Alpha; pres. Am. Drug Mfrs. Assn. Episcopalian. Since 1902 has written many articles and bulls. presenting results of original investigations upon effects of serums, toxins and anti-toxins, typhoid fever, bacteria in milk, tubercle bacilli; the etiology of typhus fever and of measles, etc. Home: 195 College Av., New Brunswick, N.J.

ANDERSON, John Ure, sec. and treas. Pittsburgh Steel Co.; b. Youngstown, O., Dec. 12, 1891; s. Hugh and Jane (Ure) A.; ed. Rayen Sch., Youngstown, O., 1906-10; A.B., Williams, 1914; m. Gertrude Woodcock, Jan. 4, 1919; children—Mary Jean, John Ure, Jr., Marjorie, Gertrude. In employ Trumbull Steel Co., Warren, O., 1914-19, treas. 1919-25, treas. and sec., 1925-28; treas. Republic Iron & Steel Co., 1928-30, treas. Republic Steel Corpn., 1930-31; sec.-treas. National Fireproofing Corpn., 1932-37, now dir.; sec. and treas. Pittsburgh Steel Co. since 1937. Mem. Phi Beta Kappa, Delta Upsilon. Republican. United Presbyn. Mason. Home: 1441 Washington Rd., Mt. Lebanon, Pa. Office: 1600 Grant Bldg., Pittsburgh, Pa.

ANDERSON, Mildred Moore, parliamentarian; b. Adrian, Mich., Jan. 19, 1876; d. William Harrison and Jane Ann (Miller) Moore; B.L., Adrian (Mich.) Coll., 1897; m. Dr. William Anderson, Sept. 26, 1901 (died 1938); children—Mary Helen, William. Began as parliamentarian, Congress of Clubs of Pittsburgh, Allegheny Co. and many local organizations in Pa., 1908; assisted Gen. Henry M. Robert in his revision of Rules of Order and the writing of "Parliamentary Law" and "Parliamentary Practice," 1912-1923; nat. parliamentarian Nat. Council Jewish Women, 1915-21, Nat. Soc. D.A.R., 1916-36; parliamentarian Nat. Parents and Teachers Assn., 1920-29, Pa. State Fed. of Women, 1915-38; special consultant for clubs, since 1930. Dir. Aspinwall (Pa.) Pub. Schs., 1918-36. Member Pittsburgh Chapter D.A.R.; mem. Pa. Soc. Descendants of the Mayflower, Pa. Soc. of Colonial Dames, Kappa Kappa Gamma. Republican. Clubs: Twentieth Century (Pittsburgh, Pa.; hon. mem.); Woman's (Aspinwall, Pa.). Home: 211 Eastern Av. Address: Aspinwall Sta., Pittsburgh, Pa.

ANDERSON, Paul Lewis, photographic expert; b. Trenton, N.J., Oct. 8, 1880; s. Edward Johnson and Belle (Lewis) A.; E.E., Lehigh U., 1901; m. Mary Lyon Green, Aug. 22, 1910; children—Priscilla, Ruth. With Westinghouse Electric & Mfg. Co., Pittsburgh, Pa., 1901; engring. and testing depts., Sprague Electric Co., Watsessing, N.J., 1902-04; engring. dept. New York Telephone Co., 1904-07; a founder and mem. Struss-Anderson Labs., mfrs. "Kalogen" (photographic developer), of which was originator. Has exhibited photographs in leading cities of America, and in London, Hamburg and Budapest. Mem. Orange Camera Club (pres. 1938-40), Authors' League America. Author: Pictorial Landscape Photography, 1914; Pictorial Photography, Its Principles and Practice, 1917; The Fine Art of Photography, 1919; The Cub Arrives, 1927; Half-Pint Shannon, 1928; With the Eagles, 1929; A Slave of Catiline, 1930; For Freedom and for Gaul, 1931; The Knights of St. John, 1932; Swords in the North, 1935; Pugnax the Gladiator, 1939; The Technique of Pictorial Photography, 1939. Contbr. short stories to mags. Home: 36 Washington St., East Orange, N.J.

ANDERSON, Ralph Sankey, coal exec.; b. Phila., Pa., May 26, 1878; s. David Lewis and Margaret (Edwards) A.; student pub. schs. and U. of Pa.; m. Isabel Kinkade, Nov. 5, 1901; children—David Lewis II, Ruth Leigh. Began as office boy, Geo. B. Newton Coal Co., Phila., 1898, successively salesman 1899-1907, salesmanager 1907-12, v.p. and gen. sales mgr. since 1912, dir. since 1930; dir. Newton Supply Co., B. Rowland & Bros. Served as pvt., U.S. Army, Apr.-Nov. 1898. Presbyterian (treas. Bethany Temple Ch., 1905-39). Mason (32°). Clubs: Union League, Optimists, Reciprocity, One Hundred (Phila.); Seaview Golf (Absecom, N. J.). Home: 5035 Walton Av. Office: 53rd and Baltimore Av., Philadelphia, Pa.

ANDERSON, Randolph L.; cons. orthopedic surgeon Charleston Gen., Kanawha Valley, Mountain State and St. Francis hosps. Address: 1023 Quarrier St., Charleston, W.Va.

ANDERSON, Robert Franklin, prof. mathematics; b. Lancaster County, Pa.; s. Robert and

Sarah (Carroll) A; B.S., State Normal Sch., 1896, M.S., 1898; A.B., Villanova College 1896, A.M., 1900, ScD., 1908; m. Mary E. Shillow, Dec. 27, 1910; children—Mary, Jean, Ruth. Teacher in pub. schs., 1886-88; in charge dept. of English, Coll. of Commerce, Phila., 1890-91; prin. pub. schs., Langhorne, Pa., 1891-92; in charge of dept. of mathematics, Pa. Mountain Summer Assembly, summers, 1906-11; prof. mathematics, State Teachers Coll., West Chester, Pa., 1907-36, now dir. Student Activities Association of same institution. Author: (with the late Prof. David M. Sensenig) of the Sensenig-Anderson series of arithmetics; New Complete Arithmetic, 1900; Essentials of Arithmetic, 1902; Introductory Arithmetic, 1903; (with the late Dr. G. M. Philips) of the Silver-Burdett Arithmetics; (with Dr. George H. Hallett) of Elementary Algebra. Author of The Anderson Arithmetics, 1921; Arithmetic for Today (with Dr. George N. Cade), 1931; Arithmetic for Everyday Life (with Dr. Shelton Phelps), 1933; Mathematics Through Experience (with Dr. Joel S. Georges and Dr. Robert L. Morton), 1937; also several pamphlets on math. subjects. Home: West Chester, Pa.*

ANDERSON, Robert R., supervising principal; b. Delta, York Co., Pa., Mar. 26, 1883; s. James E. and Sara (Scott) A.; grad. Delta High Sch., 1900; student Millersville State Normal Sch., 1907-08, Dickinson Sem., Williamsport, 1910-11, U. of Pa., 1912-13, U. of Pittsburgh; m. Mary J. Chandlee, Dec. 26, 1914; children—Mary Louise, Isabel Chandlee. Teacher in public schools, York Co., Pa., 1903-06, Dickinson Sem., Williamsport, Pa., 1908-11; prin. Marysville (Pa.) High Sch., 1911-14, Leechburg (Pa.) High Sch., 1914-18; supervising prin., Springdale, Pa., 1918-19, Brackenridge, Pa., since 1919. Mem. N.E.A., Pa. State Edn. Assn., Dept. of Supts., Theta Pi Pi. Democrat. Methodist. Mason, Odd Fellow. Clubs: Tarentum Kiwanis; Allegheny Chamber of Commerce. Address: 1052 8th Av., Brackenridge, Pa.

ANDERSON, Robert van Vleck, geologist; b. Galesburg, Ill., Apr. 18, 1884; s. Melville Best (LL.D.) and Charlena (van Vleck) A.; B.A., Stanford, 1906; m. Gracella Rountree, Mar. 1923; children—Robert Playfair, Patricia Sage, Gracella Gurnee. Geological and zoölogical work, Japan, 1905; assistant in investigations of California earthquake for Carnegie Institution, 1906; geologic aid, assistant geologist and geologist, U.S. Geol. Survey, 1906-13; made investigations of geol. and petroleum resources of Calif., and was member Oil Land Classification Board; as consulting geologist visited many parts of world since 1911; geologist for S. Pearson & Son., Ltd., London, Eng., 1913-18; representative of U.S. War Trade Bd. in Sweden; Am. delegate on Inter-Allied Trade Com., Stockholm, 1918-19; dir. Whitehall Petroleum Corpn., Ltd., London, 1919-23, chief geologist, 1923-26. Engaged in independent scientific work, 1927-34. Collaborateur, Service de la Carte Geologique de l'Algérie, 1930-32; research in Algeria under grant from Geol. Soc. America, 1933; with Socony Vacuum Oil Co., Inc., 1934— Mem. Geol. Soc. America (chmn. Cordilleran sect. 1928), Paleontol. Soc. America, Assn. Am. Geographers, Soc. Econ. Geologists, Archæol. Inst. America, Calif. Acad. Sciences, Société Géologique de France, Sigma Xi. Unitarian. Author various reports pub. by U.S. Govt., and other scientific papers. Address: 334 Highland Av., Upper Montclair, N.J.

ANDERSON, Russell Sherwood, physician; b. Kane, Pa., July 23, 1895; s. John Vinton and Jennie Estelle (Sherwood) A.; grad. Hahnemann Sch. of Sci., Phila., 1917; M.D., Hahnemann Med. Coll. and Hosp., 1921; m. Rebecca Jane Tobin, Jan. 23, 1925; children— Mary Jane, Beatrice Lou. Interne, J. Lewis Crozier Hosp., Chester, Pa., 1921-22; in pvt. practice, Erie, Pa., 1922-23; out of practice due to ill health and spl. study, 1923-26; mem. staff, Loomas Sanatorium, Liberty, N.Y., 1926-27, and Episcopal Mission Sanatorium, Chestnut Hill, Phila., 1927-30, Mich. State Sanatorium, Howell, Mich., 1930-37; asso. med. dir. 1934-37); supt. and med. dir. Erie Co. Tuberculosis Hosp., Erie, Pa. since 1937. Served in S.A.T.C., 1918. Fellow Am. Coll. Phys., 1939. Fellow A.M.A. Mem. Am. Sanatorium Assn., Nat. Tuberculosis Assn., Pa. State and Erie Co. med. socs., Erie Co. Health and Tuberculosis Assn., Phi Epsilon Rho. Republican. Protestant. Club: Kiwanis. Home: 3915 Parkside Av., Erie, Pa.

ANDERSON, Thomas Bruce Hurt, U.S. Pub. Health Service; b. Charlottesville, Va., July 21, 1891; s. Samuel Leake and Susie Jane (Carter) A.; M.D., U. of Va., 1914; m. Mabel Lane, Nov. 18, 1915; children—Mary Sue (Mrs. Preston B. Hundley), Thomas Bruce Hurt, Charlotte Virginia, Howard Leake. With U.S. Pub. Health Service since 1915; senior surgeon since 1935; med. officer in charge marine hosp., Pittsburgh, 1928-30, New Orleans, 1930-35, Baltimore since 1935; formerly asso. prof. preventive medicine and hygiene, La. Med. Center. During World War served on coast guard cutter, 1917, in charge extra-cantonment sanitary zone, Ft. Leavenworth, 1918-19. Mem. A.M.A., Assn. Mil. Surgeons, Nu Sigma Nu. Mason. Address: U.S. Marine Hospital, Baltimore, Md.

ANDERSON, Thomas Lee, lawyer; b. Barnesville, O., Aug. 28, 1892; s. Thomas Alexander and Lee (Hilles) A.; A.B., Washington and Jefferson Coll., 1914; LL.B., U. of Pittsburgh Law Sch., 1922; m. Louise Hendry Hughes; 1 dau., Louise Lee. Engaged in newspaper work as reporter and editor, 1914-22; admitted to Pa. bar, 1922 and since engaged in gen. practice of law at Washington; asst. dist. atty. Washington Co., 1923-28. Served as 1st lieut. 21st Machine Gun Bn., U.S.A. with A.E.F., 1918-19; 1st lieut. to maj. inf. res. corps, U.S.A. to 1932. Mem. Am. Pa. State, and Washington Co. bar assns., Phi Delta Theta, Delta Theta Phi. Republican. Presbyterian. Home: Redstone Rd. Office: First Nat. Bank Bldg., Washington, Pa.

ANDERSON, Troyer Steele, asso. prof. history; b. Minneapolis, Minn., Apr. 28, 1900; s. Frank Maloy and Mary Gertrude (Steele) A.; A.B., Dartmouth, Hanover, N.H., 1922; A.M., Harvard, 1923; B.A., Oxford, Eng., 1926, D.Phil., 1929; m. Mary F. Gerould, Sept. 11, 1926; children—Kenneth Foster, Nancy Steele. Instr. in history, Brown U., Providence, R.I., 1926-28; asst. prof. history, Swarthmore (Pa.) Coll., 1928-35, asso. prof. since 1935. Served in U.S. Army, 1918. Rhodes Scholar from N.H., 1923-26. Mem. Am. Hist. Assn., Phi Beta Kappa. Democrat. Congregationalist. Author: The Command of the Howe Brothers during the American Revolution, 1936. Home: 2 Whittier Place, Swarthmore, Pa.

ANDERSON, Walter Irwin, lawyer; b. Woodbine, Pa., Oct. 27, 1897; s. Benjamin F. and Alice Rachel (Anderson) A.; student Franklin and Marshall Coll., Lancaster, Pa., 1920-22; B.A., Yale Law Sch., 1925; m. Lola M. Reed, June 25, 1929; children—Walter William, Alice Elizabeth, Joseph Reed. Admitted to York County bar, 1926; in gen. practice law at York, Pa., since 1926. Dist. atty., York County, 1934-37; dep. atty. gen., York, 1938-39. Dir. Family Service Bur., York Chapter of Am. Red Cross. Presbyn. Clubs: Kiwanis, University, Country (York). Home: 1629 Second Av., Elmwood, Pa. Office: 124 E. Market St., York, Pa.

ANDERSON, William Allison, manufacturer; b. Trenton, N.J., June 4, 1870; s. Gen. Henry Reuben and Florence (Allison) A.; student Lawrenceville (N.J.) Sch., 1883-88; unmarried. With John A. Roebling's Sons Co., wire mfrs., Trenton, N.J., since Nov. 1888, beginning as timekeeper, pres. since 1936; dir. John A. Roebling's Sons Co., Otis Elevator Co., Delaware & Hudson Co. Home: Princeton, N.J. Office: 640 S. Broad St., Trenton, N.J.

ANDERSON, William Beverly, Jr., mcht.; b. Portsmouth, O., Jan. 16, 1899; s. William Beverly and Ida (Russell) A.; A.B., O. Wesleyan U., Delaware, O., 1921; m. Lucile Richards, Oct. 6, 1922. Asso. with Anderson-Newcomb Co., dept. store, Huntington, W.Va., since 1921, treas., 1922-26, vice-pres., 1926-30, pres. since 1930; dir. First Huntington Nat. Bank since 1934. Served as vice mayor, Huntington, W.Va., 1934-36. Dir. Huntington Chamber of Commerce, W.Va. State Chamber of Commerce. Mem. Phi Kappa Psi. Republican. Methodist. Club: Executive. Home: Roland Park, Huntington. Office: 925 3rd Av., Huntington, W.Va.

ANDERSON, William Brennan, clergyman; b. Monmouth, Ill., Dec. 7, 1868; s. David and Margaret (Nelson) A.; A.B., Westminster Coll., New Wilmington, Pa., 1894, D.D., 1914; grad. Pittsburgh Theol. Sem., 1897; LL.D., Westminster, 1924; m. Mary Blanche Heidelbaugh, June 30, 1897 (died June 28, 1928); children—Gerald Howard (dec.), Lelia Blodwen (dec.), David Dean, Douglas McClure (dec.), Harriet Margaret. Ordained U.P. ministry, 1897, and went as missionary to India; pres. Gordon Coll., Rawal Pindi, 1899-1903; asso. sec. Bd. of Foreign Missions U.P. Ch. of N.A., 1909-10, 1914-16; corr. sec. same, 1916-38; retired, 1938. Moderator of General Assembly U.P. Ch., 1933-34. Republican. Author: Bible Lessons for Bible Teachers, 1901; Far North in India (with C. R. Watson), 1909; A Watered Garden, 1919. Home: 6804 Quincy St., Philadelphia, Pa.

ANDERSON, William Downs, v.p. Atlantic Refining Co.; b. Phila., Pa., Feb. 12, 1874; s. Robert and Elizabeth (Downs) A.; student Drexel Inst. and Wharton Sch. of Finance (U. of Pa.); m. Mary McBride, Oct. 1, 1904. With Atlantic Refining Co. since 1898, beginning as sec. to the sec. of co., became asst. sec., later sec., now v.p. and dir. in charge of exports. Home: 4948 Hazel Av. Office: 260 S. Broad St., Philadelphia, Pa.

ANDERSON, William Ketcham, clergyman; b. N.Y. City, Apr. 27, 1888; s. Bishop William Franklin and Lulah (Ketcham) A.; B.A., Wesleyan U., 1910, D.D., 1930; M.A., Columbia, 1913; B.D., Union Theol. Sem., 1914; m. Fanny E. Spencer (A. B. Goucher Coll. 1913), Dec. 19, 1916; children—Almeda Jane, Elizabeth Cushman, William F. II, Josephine Spencer. Taught high sch., Chattanooga, Tenn., 1910-11; pastor, Carpenter, Wyo., 1912; ordained M.E. ministry, deacon, 1915, elder, 1917; pastor Ohio State U., 1915-18; organizing sec. Ohio Council of Chs., 1919, and its 1st sec., 1919-20; field sec. for Ohio of Inter-Ch. World Movement, 1920; pastor Calvary Ch., Pittsburgh, Pa., 1920-26, First Ch., Butler, 1926-28, Franklin St. Ch., Johnstown, since 1928; exchange preacher, London, 1930. Mem. Commn. on Course of Study, M.E. Church, Commn. on Worship and Music, M.E. Ch. Mem. staff of Ohio Branch Council Nat. Defense, 1917; with Army Y.M.C.A., Camp Sherman, 1918. Trustee Wesley Foundation, Pa. State Coll.; del. of Pittsburgh Conf. to Gen. Conf. M.E. Ch., 1936; del. to uniting conf. of 3 Meth. bodies, Kansas City, Mo., 1939. Mem. Am. Hymn Soc., Phi Nu Theta. Mason. Clubs: Pocasset (Mass.) Golf; Quiz (Pittsburgh). Occasional contbr. to religious periodicals; composer of several hymn tunes and songs. Author: (with others) Athletics at Wesleyan. Home: 116 Tioga St., Johnstown, Pa.

ANDERSON, William Scott, pres. Shoe Press Corpn.; b. Huntington Co., Pa., Jan. 28, 1878; s. Rev. William Henry and Lydia (McNeal) A.; ed. pub. schs.; m. Mary Henderson, Apr. 17, 1906; 1 dau., Mary (Mrs. Amos Dotterer). Began as clerk Leas McVitty, Inc., 1895, advancing to vice-pres., 1909-14; pres. Penn Leather Co., 1914-35; pres. Shoe Press Corpn. since 1932; pres. Penn Standard Sole Cementing Process, Inc.; dir. and voting trustee Compo Shoe Machinery Corpn. Republican. Presbyterian. Club: St. Nicholas (New York). Home: 2241 N. 53d St. Office: 240 N. 3d St., Philadelphia, Pa.

ANDORN, Alvin M., sec.-treas. Penn Steel Castings Co.; b. Oct. 17, 1895; ed. pub. schs. and high sch.; unmarried. Asso. with Penn Steel Castings Co., Chester, Pa., since 1917, sec.-treas. since 1923, dir. since 1923. Home: The Warwick, Philadelphia, Pa. Office: Chester, Pa.

ANDREW, Harriet White Fisher (Harriet White Fisher), author; b. Pennline, Crawford Co., Pa.; d. Oscar A. and Hannah (Fisher) White; ed. Young Ladies' Classical Sem., Cleveland; finished at Hildesheim, Germany, 1882; m. Clark Fisher (chief engr. U.S.N.), July 20, 1898 (died Dec. 31, 1903); m. 2d, Sylvano Alfredo Andrew (lt. Argentine Navy), Apr. 27, 1912. Owner Eagle Anvil Works, Trenton, N.J., conducting business under firm name of Fisher & Norris. Presbyn. Mem. Daughters of Ohio. Mem. Am. Red Cross. Clubs: Elice Yacht, Golf (Lake Como, Italy). Author: A Woman's World Trip in a Motor Car, 1911; also stories in mags. Home: "Bella Vista," Trenton, N.J. Office: Fisher & Norris, Trenton, N.J.

ANDREW, Seymour Lansing, statistician; b. Boston, Mass., May 23, 1887; s. Samuel Worcester and Helen (Seymour) A.; student Roxbury Latin Sch., 1898-1904; A.B., Harvard, 1910; m. Katherine Murphy, May 11, 1910; children—Helen Edith, Seymour Lansing. Clerk Am. Telephone and Telegraph Co., 1910-14, foreign statistician, 1914-19, asst. chief statistician, 1919-21, chief statistician since 1921. Fellow Am. Statis. Assn.; mem. Am. Econ. Assn., A.A.A.S., Econometric Soc., Am. Political Science Assn., Acad. Political and Social Science, Social Science Research Council, Economic Club of N.Y., Controllers Institute of America, Am. Anthropol. Soc., Kappa Sigma. Episcopalian. Clubs: Harvard, Downtown Athletic, Railroad-Machinery (New York). Home: Orange, N.J. Office: 195 Broadway, New York, N.Y.

ANDREWS, Benjamin Richard, coll. prof.; b. Hector, N.Y., Dec. 31, 1877; s. Charles Thomas and Mary Elizabeth (Clark) A.; A.B., Cornell U., 1901, A.M., same, 1903; Ph.D., Teachers Coll. of Columbia U., 1909; m. Elizabeth L. Russell, July 9, 1907; children—Russell (dec.), Roger R., Benjamin R., Jr. Began as gen. sec. Cornell U. Christian Assn., 1901-02; supervisor ednl. mus. Teachers Coll. of Columbia U., 1903-05, social dir. Speyer Sch. Social Center, Teachers Coll., 1905-07, exec. sec. Sch. Household Arts, 1907-10, instr. household econs., 1910-12, asst. prof., 1912-23, asso. prof., 1923-25, prof. household econs. since 1925. Served as expert in household thrift, U.S. Dept. Agr., 1917; asso. dir. savings div., U.S. Treasury Dept., 1919. Treas. World Peaceways. Mem. exec. com. Com. on Militarism in Edn. Mem. Am. Home Econs. Assn. (sec.-treas.), Nat. Com. on Household Employment (chmn.), Phi Delta Kappa, Delta Upsilon, Sphinx Head. Presbyterian. Author: Economics of the Household, 1923, rev. edit., 1935. Editor series of fifty home econs. coll. and sch. text-books. Home: 1 Old Wood Rd., Edgewater, N.J.

ANDREWS, Carl W(illis), corpn. exec.; b. New Bethlehem, Pa., Oct. 12, 1894; s. William Marion and Melda Enna (Truitt) A.; student Kiski Prep. Sch., Saltsburg, Pa., 1910-14; B.S. in Econ., U. of Pa., 1918; m. Helen Lathrop Smith, Oct. 11, 1919; 1 son, Carl Willis. Asst. cashier, First Nat. Bank, New Bethlehem, Pa., 1919-25, v.p. and dir., 1925-36; asst. to sec., banking, Commonwealth of Pa., 1935-36; treas. and dir. Molded Materials, Inc., Ridgway, Pa., since 1936; treas. and comptroller, Stackpole Carbon Co., St. Mary's, Pa., since 1938. Republican. Baptist. Mason (32°, Shriner). Clubs: St. Marys (Pa.) Country; Elk County Country (Ridgway, Pa.). Home: 700 Hyde Av., Ridgway, Pa. Office: Tannery, St. Marys, Pa.

ANDREWS, Charles Edgar, Jr., banker; b. New Bethlehem, Pa., June 22, 1881; s. Firman L. and A. Blanche (Craig) A.; A.B., cum laude, and hon. mention in economics, Harvard Univ., 1904; m. Marjorie Eddinger, August 13, 1928. In banking business at New Bethlehem since 1905; pres. First Nat. Bank, chmn. of bd. Lincoln Investment Co. (New Bethlehem), First Nat. Bank (Rimersburg, Pa.), Sligo (Pa.) Nat. Bank, Meadow River Lumber Co. (Rainelle, W.Va.). Republican. Baptist. Clubs: Duquesne (Pittsburgh); Harvard (New York). Home: New Bethlehem, Pa.

ANDREWS, Clarence Ladelle, physician; b. nr. Farmerville, La., Jan. 5, 1882; s. Joseph Thomas Brooks and Victoria (Shute) A.; B.S., La. State U., 1908; M.D., Johns Hopkins U. Med. Sch., 1912; m. Lucile Mory Peterkin, Sept. 29, 1917. Interne, Jefferson Hosp., Roanoke, Va., 1912-13; prof. anatomy, U. of Miss., 1913-14; med. asso. Marvel Sanitarium, Atlantic City, N.J., 1914-20; asso. med. chief, Atlantic City Hosp., Atlantic City, N.J., 1924-27, chief of med. service since 1927. Fellow Am. Coll. Phys. (gov. 1935-39). Mem. A.M.A., Atlantic County and N.J. State med. socs., Kappa Sigma, Phi Chi. Republican. Baptist. Club: Kiwanis of Atlantic City (pres.). Home: Hotel President. Office: 1616 Pacific Av., Atlantic City, N.J.

ANDREWS, Dickson, lawyer; b. Meadville, Pa., June 21, 1887; s. Robert and Emma (Dickson) A.; grad. Meadville High Sch., 1904; A.B., Allegheny Coll., 1908; LL.B., Harvard, 1915; m. Lena Mae Brown, Oct. 11, 1922; 1 dau., Carol Jean. With New First Nat. Bank, Meadville, Pa., successively as clerk, bookkeeper and teller, 1908-12; admitted to Pa. bar, 1915, and since in gen. practice at Meadville, 1915-17, and since 1926; gen. practice as mem. firm McNees & Andrews, Apollo, Pa., 1919; city clerk, Meadville, 1919-26; city solicitor, Meadville, since 1924; county solicitor, Crawford Co., 1928-31. Served as an exec. Am. Nat. Red Cross, Southern Div., 1917-18; Officers Training Camp, U.S. Army, Camp Johnston, 1918. Trustee Y.W.C.A., Meadville, since 1933. Mem. Phi Beta Kappa, Phi Gamma Delta. Republican. Methodist. Odd Fellow. Home: 730 Pine St. Office: 357 Center St., Meadville, Pa.

ANDREWS, Donald Hatch, chemist; b. Southington, Conn., June 11, 1898; s. Russell Gad and Mary Boies (Hatch) A.; grad. Phillips Acad., Andover, Mass., 1916; B.A., Yale, 1920, Ph.D., 1923; unmarried. Began as research asst. in chemistry, Yale, 1923; nat. research fellow, U. of Calif., 1924-25; internat. research fellow, U. of Leiden, 1925-26; research fellow, Bartol Research Foundation, 1926-27; with Johns Hopkins U. since 1927, prof. chemistry since 1930. Mem. 1st Scientific Commn., L'Inst. Internat. de Froid. Fellow Am. Physical Soc., Royal Chem. Soc. (Eng.); mem. Am. Chem. Soc., A.A.A.S., Am. Philos. Soc., Phi Beta Kappa, Sigma Xi, Gamma Alpha, Alpha Chi Sigma, Alpha Chi Rho, Scarlet Sphinx. Republican. Conglist. Club: University. Address: Johns Hopkins University, Baltimore, Md.

ANDREWS, Ethan Allen, biologist; b. New York, Sept. 10, 1859; s. Horace and Julia Russell (Johnson) A.; Ph.B., Yale, 1881; grad. student Yale and Polytechnicum, Hanover; fellow Johns Hopkins, 1884-86, Ph.D., 1887; m. Sara Gwendolen Foulke, Mar. 17, 1894; children—Ethan Allen, John Hare Powel, Julia Gwenllian De Veau. Asst. U.S. Fish Commn., 1879-81; asst., 1887-92, asso. prof. biology, 1892-1908, became prof. Zoölogy, 1908, Johns Hopkins. Mem. Soc. Am. Zoölogists (pres., 1904), etc. Has written biol. papers in various jours. Home: 107 E. Lake Av., Baltimore, Md.*

ANDREWS, H. G.; editor Johnstown Democrat. Address: Johnstown, Pa.

ANDREWS, James Henry Millar, civil engr.; b. Belfast, Ireland, Jan. 31, 1876; s. James Walkinshaw and Mary Elizabeth (Carmichael) A.; brought to U.S., 1880; B.S., Pa. State Coll., 1898; m. Esther McKinley Bender, Nov. 16, 1904; 1 dau., Mary Carmichael. Draftsman Pa. Steel Co., 1898-1900; engr. Carlisle Mfg. Co., 1900-03; with Phila. Rapid Transit Co. since 1903, successively as asst. engr., asst. to chief engr., supt. lines and cables, engr. of distribution, engr. of way, chief engr., asst. vice-pres., and now asst. to pres. and chief engr. Served as capt. engrs. Pa. Nat. Guard; maj. 103rd Engrs., U.S. Army, 1917; lt. col. Ordnance, U.S. Army, 1918; col. Ordnance Reserve since 1920. Trustee and mem. exec. com. Pa. State Coll. Chmn. Mayor's Traffic Commn., Phila., 1928. Mem. Am. Soc. Civil Engrs., Franklin Inst., Am. Legion (comdr. Post No. 130, 1919-20), Mil. Order Foreign Wars of U.S., Mil. Order of World War, Soc. 28th Div. U.S. Army, Pa. Scotch-Irish Soc., The St. Andrews Soc. of Phila., Hist. Soc. of Pa., Sigma Alpha Epsilon. Republican. Mason. Clubs: Union League, Engineers (pres. 1927-29), Art of Phila., Phila. Cricket. Home: 1708 Harris Rd., Chestnut Hill, Pa. Office: Mitten Bldg., Philadelphia, Pa.

ANDREWS, Mary Edith, coll. prof.; b. West Newton, Pa., June 6, 1892; d. David C. Norwood and Eliza Jane (Sheele) Andrews; A.B., Oberlin Coll., 1917, A.M., 1920, grad. student, 1924-25; B.D., Chicago Theol. Sem., 1926; Ph.D., U. of Chicago, 1931; unmarried. Public school teacher, Pa., 1918-19, 1923-24; ednl. missionary, Natal, S. Africa, 1920-22, instr. in religion, Goucher Coll., 1926-32, asst. prof., 1932-38, asso. prof. since 1938, chmn. dept. of religion, since Sept. 1939. Former state treas. Md. branch, Women's Internat. League for Peace and Freedom. Mem. Am. Assn. Univ. Profs., Am. Assn. Univ. Women, Soc. Bibl. Lit. and Exegesis, Nat. Assn. Bibl. Instrs. (pres. 1938). Awarded Gilchrist-Polter Prize Fund, Oberlin Coll., 1931. Presbyterian. Author: The Ethical Teachings of Paul, 1934. Contbr. to religious journals; contbg. editor Jour. of Bible and Religion. Home: 200 E. 24th St., Baltimore, Md.

ANDREWS, Matthew Page, editor, author; b. Shepherdstown, W.Va., July 15, 1879; s. Matthew Page and Anna (Robinson) A.; A.B., Washington and Lee U., 1901, A.M., 1902, Litt. D., 1924; unmarried. Teacher private schools, Winchester, Va., 1902-04, Baltimore, 1904-11; lecturer, Colonial period U.S. history; editorial adviser, Yale Univ. Press, Chronicles of America Dept., 1923; chmn. Baltimore City George Washington Bi-Centennial Commn., 1932; Chmn. Md. Tercentenary Commn. of Baltimore, 1934. Episcopalian. Mem. Delta Tau Delta, Phi Beta Kappa. Club: University. Author: A History of the U.S., 1913; A Brief History of the United States, 1916; A Heritage of Freedom, 1918; Birth of America (play), 1920; American History and Government, 1921; The Book of the American's Creed, 1921; The Biggest Book in the World, 1925; History of Maryland—Province and State, 1929; The Founding of Maryland, 1933; Soul of Maryland—Pageant of the Founding, 1934; Virginia, The Old Dominion, 1937. Home: 849 Park Av., Baltimore, Md.

ANDREWS, Schofield, lawyer; b. New York, N.Y., Aug. 7, 1889; s. Avery De Lano and Mary Campbell (Schofield) A.; grad. St. Paul's Sch., Concord, N. H., 1906; A.B. Harvard, 1910; LL.B., U. of Pa., 1913; m. Lillian Forsyth Brown, April 21, 1921 (died May 7, 1927); children: Schofield, Stuart Brown, Stockton Avery; m. 2d, Marie D. Grant, May 9, 1929. Admitted to Pa. bar, 1913, and since practiced in Phila.; mem. firm Ballard, Spahr, Andrews and Ingersoll since 1919; dir. Central-Penn. Nat. Bank, Barber Asphalt Corpn., Salt Dome Oil Corpn. Served in U.S. Army, May, 1917, to June, 1919, as lt. col., asst. chief of staff, 90th Div., with A.E.F. Awarded D.S.M. Trustee Chestnut Hill Hosp., Pa. Sch. for the Deaf. Republican. Episcopalian. Clubs: Philadelphia, Sunnybrook Golf. Home: Chestnut Hill, Philadelphia, Pa. Office: Land Title Bldg., Philadelphia, Pa.

ANDRUS, Edwin Cowles, physician; b. Kaatsban, N.Y., Feb. 28, 1896; s. Jonathan Cowles and Margaret (De Witt) A; student Oberlin (O.) Acad. and High Sch., 1908-12; A.B., Oberlin Coll., 1916, A.M., 1917; M.D., Johns Hopkins, 1921; m. Miriam Jay Wurts, June 10, 1933. House officer, Johns Hopkins Hosp., 1921-23; fellow in medicine Nat. Research Council, London and Vienna, 1923-25; resident physician, Johns Hopkins Hosp., 1925-27; asso. in medicine, Johns Hopkins U., 1926-31, asso. prof. of medicine since 1931, asst. dean of med. faculty, 1929-34. Fellow Am. Coll. Physicians; mem. A.M.A., Am. Physiol. Soc., Am. Heart Assn., Am. Soc. Clin. Investigation, Am. Clin. and Climatol. Assn., Assn. Am. Physicians, Med. and Chirurg. Faculty of Md. Republican. Mem. Fourteen West Hamilton Street Club (Baltimore). Home: 4304 Norwood Rd. Office: 1201 N. Calvert St., Baltimore, Md.

ANDRUSS, Harvey Adolphus, coll. dean; b. Fort Worth, Tex., Feb. 19, 1902; s. Edward Hamilton and Myrtle (McDaniel) A.; A.B., U. of Okla., Norman, Okla., 1924; M.B.A., Northwestern U., Evanston and Chicago, Ill., 1928; m. Elizabeth Archibald, June 12, 1929; 1 son, Harvey Adolphus. High sch. Prin., Okla., 1921-24; head, Commerce Dept., Ponca City (Okla.) High Sch., 1924-25; lecturer, Northwestern U. Sch. of Commerce, Evanston and Chicago, Ill.,

1925-27; and supervisor, Dept. of Commerce, State Teachers Coll., Indiana, Pa., 1927-30; dir., Dept. of Business Edn. State Teachers Coll., Bloomsburg, Pa., 1930-37, dean of instruction since 1937; spl. lecturer New York Univ. Sch. of Edn., N.Y. City, 1937, and Univ. of Okla., Norman, Okla, 1939. Adviser on civil service exam., Unemployment Compensation Bd. of Review, Harrisburg, Pa., since 1937. Mem. board, Bloomsburg Hospital; chmn. Bloomsburg Chapter, Am. Red Cross; pres. exec. com. Salvation Army, Bloomsburg; pres. Alpha Alumni Assn. of Phi Beta Kappa in Pa.; mem. Kappa Delta Pi, Beta Gamma Sigma, Beta Alpha Psi, Pi Omega Pi, Gamma Rho Tau, Phi Sigma Pi, Phi Alpha Tau. N.E.A., Pa. Edn. Assn., Eastern Commercial Teachers Assn., Nat. Commercial Teachers Fed. Presbyterian. Mason (32°). Clubs: Kiwanis (mem. bd. dirs.), Bloomsburg Country (Bloomsburg, Pa.). Author: Business Law Cases and Tests, 1934; Ways to Teach Bookkeeping and Accounting, 1938; contbr. over thirty articles an monographs to yearbooks, business, ednl. and professional jours. Home: 740 E. 3d St., Bloomsburg, Pa.

ANGEL, Philip, lawyer; b. Inverness, Scotland, Sept. 4, 1905; s. Henry Esrael and Charlot (Angel) A.; brought to U.S., 1912, naturalized, 1922, grad. Huntington (W.Va.) High Sch., 1923; LL.B., W.Va. U., 1928; m. Frances Hannah Levy, Dec. 14, 1936; 1 son, Philip, II. Admitted to W.Va. bar, 1928, practiced in Huntington, 1928-33, and since practices in Charleston; mem. firm Avis & Angel; vice-pres. Acme Gas Co.; asst. U.S. atty., Southern Dist., W.Va., 1930-34. Mem. Am. Bar Assn., W.Va. Bar Assn., Kanawha County Bar Assn., Phi Sigma Delta. Republican. Hebrew religion. Club: South Moor Country (Charleston). Home: 907 Edgewood Av. Office: Charleston Nat. Bank Bldg., Charleston, W.Va.

ANGELA, Emilio Peter, sculptor; b. Italy, July 12, 1889; brought to U.S., 1895; s. Francesco and Fortunata (Podesta) A.; grad. Cooper Union Institute, N.Y. City, 1907, Nat. Acad. Design, 1910, Art Students League, 1912; studied art under A. A. Weinman, George Brewster, H. MacNeil, S. Calder, G. Bridgeman and Back; m. Maria Dughi, 1915; 1 son, Emilio. Principal works: Goose Boy and Goose Girl, Barking Sea Lions (pair), Son of the Soil (fountain pieces for estate of Joseph P. Day; portraits of J. P. Day, Mrs. P. P. Day, W. W. Renwick and Baby Angela; Flower Girl (Philadelphia Sesquicentennial); statuettes Mirthfulness, Boxer, Ecstasy, Shot Putter, Sundial and Early Bird. Awarded 1st prize in composition, 2d prize in sculpture. Mem. Nat. Sculpture Soc., Chatham Art Club. Catholic. Home: 66 Hedges Av., Chatham, N.J.

ANGELO, Emidio, artist, cartoonist; b. Phila., Pa., Dec. 4, 1903; s. Stanislaw and Laura (Alesandroni) A.; ed. pub. schs., Graphic Sketch Club, Pa. Acad. Fine Arts (European scholarship, 1927-28); married. Began as cartoonist, 1928, cartoons appearing in Saturday Evening Post, Colliers, Life; art editor Town Crier (Phila. weekly), 1930-31; cartoonist and caricaturist Public Ledger, 1932-33; then free lance cartoonist for advertising agencies; now political cartoonist Phila. Inquirer. Mem. Da Vinci Alliance, Art Alliance (Phila.); fellow Pa. Acad. Fine Arts. Republican. Lecturer on history of comic art and cartooning, also on animated cartoons. Home: 2131 Walnut St. Office: 27 S. 18th St., Philadelphia, Pa.

ANGLADA, Joseph A(ugustus), cons. engr.; b. New York, N.Y., Jan. 29, 1880; s. Joseph and Louise (Maisch) A.; E.E., Columbia U., 1899; m. Bertha Elise Fils, Nov. 12, 1901; children—Alfred, Jeanette, Grace, Charlotte. Engr. Internat. Power Co., Providence, R.I., 1900-01, U.S. Navy Equipment Dept., Brooklyn, N.Y., 1902-03; designer, Vehicle Equipment Co., Brooklyn, N.Y., 1904-06; asst. editor Horseless Age, New York, 1907-09; chief engr., G.J.G. Motor Co., White Plains, N.Y., 1910-11; engr. and designer Gibb Engring. Co., Glendale, N.Y., 1912-15, Universal Rim Co., Chicago, Ill., 1916-17; gen. mgr. Commercial Car Unit Co., Phila., 1918-19; cons. engr., New York City, since 1920 for H. H. Westinghouse, Milwaukee Locomotive Co., Anderson Motor Co., Electrocar Corpn., U.S. Industrial Alcohol Co., Standard Oil Co. (N.Y.), Anglada Motor Corpn., Nott Fire Engine Co., Hudson Motor Co., etc.; pres. Anglada Motor Co., New York, since 1928; dir. Empire Brake Co. Mem. Soc. of Automotive Engrs. (mem. council, chmn. Metropolitan Sect.), Com. on Standardization of Small Tools and Machine Elements (sec. since 1930). Republican. Christian Scientist. Clubs: City (New York); Engineers' (Phila.); Keystone Automobile, Philadelphia; Wyncote Men's (Wyncote, Pa.); Old York Road Country (Jenkintown, Pa.). Author many articles on automotive subjects. Holder several automotive patents. Home: 207 West Av., Jenkintown Pa. Office: 11 Park Pla., New York, N.Y.

ANGLOCH, Milton C.; vice-pres. and director Jones & Laughlin Steel Corpn. Home: 1 The Boul., Carrick. Office: Third Av. and Ross St., Pittsburgh, Pa.

ANNENBERG, Moses Louis, newspaper pub.; b. Insterberg, Germany, Feb. 11, 1878; s. Tobias and Sarah (Greenberg) A.; brought to U.S., 1883; ed. Chicago Pub. Schs.; m. Cecilia Friedman, Aug. 20, 1899; children—Diana, Esther, Pearl, Janet, Enid, Walter, Lita, Evelyn, Harriet. Began as newsboy in Chicago; circulation mgr. Chicago Examiner, 1904-06; newspaper distributor in Milwaukee, 1906-17; pub. Wisconsin News, 1917-19; apptd. circulation mgr. all Hearst publs., 1919, resigned, 1926, to devote time to his own pub. interests; purchased Phila. Inquirer, 1936; also pub. Daily Racing Form, N.Y. Morning Telegraph, Miami Tribune, Radio Guide, Screen Guide, Official Detective Stories; has extensive realty holdings. Clubs: Pa. Athletic (Phila.); Milwaukee Athletic. Home: Drake Hotel, Chicago, Ill. Office: Philadelphia Inquirer, Phila, Pa.

ANSCHUTZ, C. W.; pastor Germantown Covenant Presbyn. Ch. Address: 6327 Limekiln Pike, Philadelphia, Pa.

ANSON, Edward Hiram, cons. engr.; b. Ausable Forks, N.Y., Dec. 9, 1902; s. Hiram J. and Olive A. (Taylor); ed. Au Sable Forks and Keeseville (N.Y.) high schs.; B.S. in E.E., Coll. of Engring., New York U., 1925; m. Margaret Elizabeth Rogers, Oct. 31, 1925; children—Dorothy Rogers, Elizabeth Louise. Engring. asst. Gibbs & Hill, Inc., 1925-27; engr. Am. Steel & Wire Co., 1927-28; asst. catenary engr. Jackson & Moreland, 1928-31; asst. engr. Gibbs & Hill, Inc., 1931-35, engr. since 1935. Mem. N. Y. Univ. Engring. Com. on Employment. Mem. Am. Soc. Civil Engrs., Am. Ry. Engring. Assn., Assn. Am. Railroads (electrical sect.), Delta Phi, Iota Alpha. Presbyterian (trustee). Club: N.Y.U. Letter. Home: Silverbrook Road, Shrewsbury, N.J. Office: Room 490 Pennsylvania Station, New York, N.Y.

ANSPACH, Brooke Melancthon, gynecologist; b. Reading, Pa., Mar. 3, 1876; s. John Melancthon and Lydia Catharine (Bueher) A.; Lafayette Coll., class of 1896; M.D., University of Pa., 1897; hon. Sc.D., Lafayette Coll., 1936; m. Martha Brown McCormick, Nov. 1, 1906; children—Margaretta McCormick (Mrs. J. Kent Willing, Jr.), Catharine McCormick (Mrs. Geo. L. Pew). Asso. in gynecology, University of Pennsylvania until 1921; prof. gynecology, Jefferson Med. Coll., June 1921; attending gynecologist, Jefferson Med. Coll. Hosp.; cons. gynecologist, Bryn Mawr Hosp. Fellow Am. Coll. Surgeons, Coll. Physicians of Phila., Am. Gynecol. Soc. (expres.), Am. Gynecol. Club. Republican. Lutheran. Clubs: Union League, Phila. Country. Author: Gynecology, 1921. Home: 116 Mill Creek Rd., Ardmore, Pa. Office: 1827 Spruce St., Philadephia, Pa.

ANSPACH, Marshall R.; in gen. practice of law since 1923; now spl. deputy atty. gen. Address: 516 Vernon Av., Williamsport, Pa.

ANSTADT, Henry; pastor First Lutheran Ch. Home: 170 S. Second St., Chambersburg, Pa.

ANSTAETT, Herbert Bulow, librarian; b. Batavia, O., Aug. 4, 1902; s. Leonard George and Mary (Bulow) A.; B.S. in Edn., Miami U., Oxford, O., 1924; B.S., Columbia U. Sch. of Library Service, 1927, M.S. (Carnegie Fellow), 1932; m. Alice Fowler, Sept. 3, 1929; 1 dau., Dilly Ann. Asst. librarian Miami U., Oxford, O., 1924-25, asst. librarian and part time instr. English, 1925-26; asst. in main reading room, reference dept., N.Y. Pub. Library, summer 1927; librarian Franklin and Marshall Coll., Lancaster, Pa., since 1927. Mem. Am. Library Assn., Pa. Library Assn., Cliosophic Soc. (Lancaster, Pa.), Kappa Phi Kappa, Alpha Kappa Pi. Republican. Evang. and Ref. Ch. Club: Calumet (Franklin and Marshall Coll., Lancaster, Pa.). Home: 50 N. West End Av. Office: Franklin and Marshall Coll. Library, Lancaster, Pa.

ANSTINE, Harry B., mayor; b. York, Pa., Nov. 17, 1872; s. Albert W. and Clara E. (Bentz) A.; student high sch. and business coll.; m. Emma I. Becker, Dec. 17, 1895; children—Kathryn R., Margaret. Began as driver for Lafean Bros., York, Pa., 1890; bookkeeper York Cracker and Biscuit Co., Ltd., 1892-98; cashier Nat. Biscuit Co., 1898-1914; became sec.-treas. York Pretzel Bakery Co., 1914, later pres.; supervisor of census, 25th Pa. Dist., 1930; mayor of York, Pa., since 1932, present term expiring Jan. 1940. Home: 458 W. Market St. Office: 25 S. Duke St., York, Pa.

ANTHONY, Harold Elmer, zoölogist; b. Beaverton, Ore., Apr. 5, 1890; s. Alfred Webster and Anabel (Klink) A.; student Pacific U., Forest Grove, Ore., 1910-11; B.S., Columbia, 1915, M.A., 1920; D.Sc., Pacific Univ., Forest Grove, Ore., 1934; m. Edith Irwin Demerel, of N.Y. City, Apr. 5, 1916 (died 1918); 1 son, Alfred Webster; m. 2d, Margaret Feldt, of N.Y. City, February 22, 1922; children—Gilbert Chase, Marjorie Stuart. Field agent United States Biological Survey, 1910-11; staff Am. Mus. Natural History since 1911, asso. curator of mammals, 1919-26, curator since 1926. Exploration and research in N. America, Panama, Ecuador, West Indies, Chile, Africa, Burma, etc. Commd. 1st lt. F.A., Nov. 1917; capt., Sept. 1918; served in France June-Sept. 1918. Fellow New York Academy of Sciences, New York Zoöl. Soc.; mem. Am. Soc. Mammalogists (president 1935-37), National Research Council; hon. mem. Sociedad Colombiana de Ciencias Naturales. Clubs: Boone and Crockett, Englewood Field Club. Author: Indigenous Land Mammals of Porto Rico, Living and Extinct, 1918; Mammals of Porto Rico (2 vols.), 1925-26; Fieldbook of North American Mammals, 1928; also papers on mammalogy and paleontology. Scientific editor Mammals of America, 1917; comns. editor (mammals), Book of Knowledge, 1926. Home: 95 Huguenot Av., Englewood, N.J. Office: Am. Museum Natural History, New York, N.Y.

ANTHONY, Harry William, hosiery mfr.; b. Centerville, Md., Dec. 1, 1886; s. William B. and Mary Ann (Mertz) A.; student Strausstown (Pa.) Grade and Grammar Sch., 1896-1903; m. Florence L. Batteiger, Aug. 24, 1907; children—William Batteiger, Mary Batteiger (Mrs. Robert R. Harner), Gene Batteiger. Flour and feed dealer, Cressona, Pa., 1907-10; in hosiery mfg. bus. since 1910, sec. & treas. H. W. Anthony Co., Strausstown, Pa., since 1924; pres. Monroe Full Fashioned Hosiery Co., Monroe, N.C., since 1937; pres. Strausstown Nat. Bank. First Burgess, Strausstown Borough, 1914-16; pres. Strausstown Borough Sch. Bd. since 1922; mem. Pa. State Assembly, Spl. Session 1936; mem. bd. dirs. Welfare Fed. of Reading and Berks Co. (Pa.), 1931-32; mem. Berks Co. Unemployment Relief Bd., 1932-33. Democrat. Reformed Church. Mason (Shriner). Address: Strausstown, Pa.

ANTHONY, Irvin (Whittington), author; b. Philadelphia, Pa., March 5, 1890; s. Samuel and Eliza (Conquest) Anthony; B.S., U. of Pa., 1911, A.M., 1914; m. Eleanor Louisa Cooper, 1918. Author: Down to the Sea in Ships 1925; Three Ships in Azure, 1927; Paddle Wheels and Pistols, 1929; Voyagers Unafraid, 1930; Decatur, 1931; Ralegh and His World, 1934; The Saga of the Bounty, 1935; Revolt at Sea, 1937. Contbr. to leading Am. magazines and periodicals. Home: 45 H St., Seaside Park, N.J.

ANTHONY, James T.; vice-pres. Gen. Refractories Co. Home: 196 Wyoming Av., South Orange, N.J. Office: 1600 Real Estate Trust Bldg., Philadelphia, Pa.

ANTHONY, Luther B., editor; b. Fort Scott, Kan., May 9, 1876; s. Capt. Jacob Merritt and Mary (Luther) A.; largely self-ed.; m. Charlotte Sutherland, May 14, 1910; children—Grace D., Daniel S., Susan B., and Charlotte S. Formerly was an actor and entertainer; director of Drexel Orchestra, Philadelphia, Pa. 1898-99; dir. dramatics in schs. and colls., including Muhlenberg and Lafayette colls., Bucknell U., Lehigh U., until 1903. Collaborates in constrn. of plays with playwrights, mgrs., actors and novelists; founder, 1909, and editor The Dramatist (the only magazine of dramatic technology in the world); founder and pres. Institute of the Drama; for 30 years managed and installed branch offices for the Bradstreet Co. in Eastern Pa. Republican. Free Thinker. Mem. Phi. Gamma Delta. Contbr. to mags. Author: Dramatology, 1914; Eleven P.M. (with Paul M. Potter, play); Tootlums (with William H. Buckingham, play). Lectures on the drama; expert in copyright infringement litigations. Home: Eastern, Pa.; (summer) Raubsville, Pa.

ANTHONY, Richard Lewis, professor, mech. engring.; b. Lewiston, Me., Dec. 24, 1903; s. Alfred Williams and Gertrude Brown (Libbey) A.; B.S., Yale, 1925, M.E., same, 1930; grad. student Yale, 1932-35; m. Wilhelmina Groomes, Apr. 18, 1925; 1 dau., Barbara Jane. Employed as asst. engr. Connecticut Co., New Haven, Conn., 1925-27; successively grad. student, asst., instr., Yale U., 1927-35, and cons. engr., New Haven Clock Co. and Indian Motocycle Co.; mech. engr. Westcott & Mapes, Inc., 1935-37 and instr. mathematics, Hamden Hall Sch., and mech. drawing, New Haven Y.M.C.A. Jr. Coll.; prof. mech. engring. and chmn. dept., Bucknell U. since 1937. Mem. Am. Soc. Mech. Engrs., Soc. Automotive Engrs., Franklin Hall Club, Sigma Xi, Theta Xi. Republican. Baptist. Clubs: Bucknell Golf (Lewisburg); Mory's (New Haven, Conn.). Home: College Park, Lewisburg, Pa.

ANTHONY, Roy David, coll. prof.; b. Rochester, N.Y., April 2, 1884; s. Daniel Macomber and Charlotte (Finch) A.; student East High Sch., Rochester, N.Y., 1900-04; B.S., U. of Rochester, 1908; B.S. in Agr., Cornell U., 1910, M.S. in Agr., 1913, Ph.D., 1920; m. Marian Salisbury, Aug. 8, 1911; children—Gertrude Finch (dec.), David Salisbury. Asst. agronomist Am. Steel & Wire Co., 1910; instr., Cornell U., 1910-13; asso. horticulturist, N.Y. Agrl. Expt. Sta., Geneva, N.Y., 1913-19; prof. pomology, Pa. State Coll., State Coll., Pa., since 1919; conducting research in fruit growing since 1913. Fellow A.A.A.S.; mem. Am. Soc. Hort. Science, Am. Soc. Plant Physiology, Am. Assn. Univ. Profs., Phi Beta Kappa, Sigma Xi, Gamma Alpha, Alpha Zeta, Delta Theta Sigma, Psi Upsilon. Republican. Quaker. Home: 125 Hillcrest Av., State College, Pa.

ANTOPOL, William (Arnold), physician, exptl. medicine; b. Brooklyn, N.Y., April 6, 1903; s. Israel A. and Mata (Elman) A.; B.S., Coll. City of N.Y., 1923; M.D., L. I. Coll. Hosp., 1927; m. Bella Scholer, June 24, 1937. Interne Beth El Hosp., Brooklyn, 1927-28; George Blumenthal fellow in pathology, Mount Sinai Hosp., N.Y., 1928-29; Theodore Escherich fellow Mount Sinai Hosp., N.Y., 1929-30; asst. in pathology, The Mount Sinai Hosp., N.Y., 1930-36; Herbert L. Celler fellowship grant, 1930; Emanuel Libman fellowship grant for study in Leipzig and Vienna, 1932; pathologist and dir. labs., Bayonne Hosp. and Dispensary, 1930-35; cons. pathologist, Hudson Co. Tuberculosis Hosp., 1932-36; pathologist and dir. labs., Newark Beth Israel Hosp. since 1935. Served in R.O.T.C., 1920-22. Fellow A.M.A., Am. Soc. Clin. Pathologists, Acad. Medicine Northern N.J., N.Y. Acad. Medicine. Mem. Assn. Am. Pathologists & Bacteriologists, Soc. for Exptl. Biology and Medicine, Am. Pub. Health Assn., N.Y. Pathol. Soc., Harvey Soc. N.Y., Essex Co. Med. Soc., Biochem. Soc. Gt. Britain. Jewish religion. Contbr. articles and papers to med. journs. on pathological, physiological and experimental medicine. Home: 2 Custer Av. Office: Beth Israel Hospital, 201 Lyons Av., Newark, N.J.

APONICK, John J., judge; b. Nanticoke, Pa., May 27, 1899; s. Joseph and Stella (Ziolkowski) A.; B.S. in Econ., U. of Pa., 1923, LL.B., 1927; m. Zoe W. Krushefski, Nov. 22, 1932; 1 son, John J. Travelling auditor Lybrand, Ross Bros. & Montgomery, Phila., 1923-24; instr. Wharton Sch., U. of Pa., 1924-37; judge Court of Common Pleas, Luzerne Co., since 1938; dir. First Federal Savings and Loan Assn. of Wilkes-Barre, Pa. Trustee U. of Scranton, Pa.; bd. mem. Mercy Hosp., Wilkes-Barre, Pa. Mem. Am. Bar Assn., Pa. Bar Assn. K.C., Elk. Clubs: Tatra (Wilkes-Barre); Sarmation (Nanticoke). Home: Tilbury Terrace, West Nanticoke, Pa. Address: Court House, Wilkes-Barre, Pa.

APP, Austin Joseph, college prof.; b. Milwaukee, Wis., May 24, 1902; s. August Henry and Katherine (Obermaier) A.; grad. St. Frances Sem. High Sch., St. Frances, Wis., 1920; A.B., St. Frances (Wis.) Sem., 1924; A.M., Catholic Univ. of America, Washington, D.C., 1926, Ph.D., 1929; unmarried. Instr. in English, Cath. Univ. of America, and Cath. Sisters Coll., 1929-35, prof. of English and head of dept. since 1935; prof. Cath. Univ. Summer Sch., Incarnate Word Coll., San Antonio, Tex., 1936. Mem. Modern Lang. Assn., Cath. Poetry Soc. America (pres. Chesterton Cath. Poetry Soc., Scranton, Pa.). Roman Catholic. Club: Purple (Scranton). Author: Lancelot in English Literature, 1929. Contbg. editor to Words; editorial advisor, Cath. Library World. Contbr. to periodicals. Dir. Scranton Radio Forum over Station WGBI. Traveled in Europe (4 times), Mexico, Puerto Rico, Panama. Home: 343 Harrison Av., Scranton, Pa.

APP, Frank, agriculturalist; b. Buffalo Roads, Pa., Jan. 26, 1886; s. Francis S. and Sarah (Miller) A.; B.S., Pa. State Coll., 1911; Ph.D., Cornell Univ., 1919; m. Helen E. Minch, Sept. 19, 1918; children—Jean, Helen Louise, Sarah Elizabeth, Frank J., Alva Agee. Asst. agronomist, Pa. State Coll., 1911; asst. prof. agronomy, N.H. State Coll., 1911-14, Rutgers Coll., 1914-15; in charge dept. of agronomy, Rutgers, 1915-18; chief div. of agronomy and agrl. economics, N.J. State U. Agrl. Expt. Sta., 1918-23; consulting agrl. economist N.J. State Dept. Agr., 1920-23; exec. sec. N.J. Federation County Bds. Agr., 1920-23, treas., 1923-27; mem. exec. com. Am. Farm Bur. Federation; agrl. rep. Rep. Nat. Com., 1924; dir. organization, Federated Fruit and Vegetable Growers, 1924-25; vice-pres. and managing dir. of Minch Brothers, 1923-27; agricultural editor Camden Post, 1927. Mem. of New Jersey State Farm Relief Com., 1929, 30, 32; mem. Governor's Mortgage Com., N.J., 1932; pres. N.J. Farm Bureau, 1934; consultant U.S. Dept. Agr., 1934; advisor and consultant for production of perishable crops for quick freezing. Mem. bd. visitors N.J. State Coll., 1935. Mem. Am. Farm Economic Assn. (chmn. com. of investigations, 1918-20), New Brunswick Scientific Soc., Alpha Gamma Rho, Phi Kappa Phi, Lambda Chi Alpha, Sigma Xi. Republican. Asst. editor Jour. Farm Economics; agrl. adviser Porto Rican Fruit Growers, 1929-30. Author: Farm Economics, 1924; The Farmer and His Farm (in collaboration). Contbg. editor Am. Agriculturist, 1934. Contbr. numerous articles in technical jours. Home: Bridgeton, N.J.

APPEL, Joseph, designer, silk mfr.; b. Usti nad Orlici, Bohemia, Mar. 12, 1865; s. John and Anna (Blazke) A.; student High School, Usti nad Orlici, 1876-79, Textile School, Policka-Vienna, 1882-91, Commercial School, Vienna, 1886-88, École des Art Decorative, Paris, 1891-93; m. Marie Novák, July 16, 1895 (died 1927); children—Ernest Joseph, Olga Ernestine (Mrs. Reinhold Draeger), Jaroslav Josef and Otokar Václav (twins, deceased). Came to U.S. 1893, naturalized, 1907. Supt. of Lcup Silberstern, tapestry, carpets, Vienna, Austria, 1888-91; study in Paris, 1891-93; designer and supt. C. E. Meding, Paterson, N.J., 1893-98; with brother began mfr. of tie silk, Paterson, N.J., 1898; business increased from 12 to 150 looms, 1898-1936; retired 1936; formerly dir. Bank of Europe, New York, Baltic Bldg. & Loan Assn.; former treas. Nat. Bank of America, Paterson, N.J., Paterson Textile Sch. Mem. Silk Assn. of America. Presented collection of silk samples to Passaic Co. Museum and Usti nad Orlici Museum in Bohemia (now Czecho-Slovakia). Traveled extensively in Europe and America. Home: 106 Preakness Av., Paterson, N.J.

APPEL, Kenneth Ellmaker, psychiatrist; b. Lancaster, Pa., May 15, 1896; s. John Wilberforce and Ella Julia (Roberts) A.; A.B., Franklin and Marshall Coll., 1915, hon. D.Sc. from same college, 1935; A.M., Harvard University, 1916; Ph.D., 1918, M.D., 1924; m. Madeleine Hunt, Sept. 2, 1921; 1 dau., Joan. Resident phys. U. of Pa. Hosp., 1924-26; asst. phys. dept. of nervous and mental diseases, Pennsylvania Hosp., 1926-29, consultant, dept. of mental and nervous diseases, Pa. Hosp., and chief of neuro-psychiatric clinic., Out Patient Dept., Pa. Hosp., 1930; psychiatrist to Inst. of Pa. Hosp., 1930; asst. prof. psychiatry, Med. Sch. U. of Pa., and asst. psychiatrist, Pa. Univ. Hosp., since 1931; consultant psychiatrist to ednl. instns. Mem. A.M.A., Am. Psychiatric Soc., Coll. of Physicians of Phila., Phi Kappa Psi, Phi Beta Kappa, Alpha Omego Alpha. Member Reformed Ch. of America. Author: Discovering Ourselves (with Edward A. Strecker, M.D.), 1931; The Treatment of Behavior Disorders Following Encephalitis (with Earl D. Bond, M.D.), 1931; Practical Examination of Personality and Behavior Disorders—Adults and Children (with Edward A. Strecker, M.D.), 1936. Contbr. to med. jours. Home: 408 Berkley Rd., Haverford, Pa. Address: Inst. of the Pa. Hospital, 111 N. 49th St., Philadelphia, Pa. *

APPEL, Theodore Burton, M.D.; b. Lancaster, Pa. Sept. 8, 1871; s. Rev. Theodore (D.D.) and Susan Burton (Wolff) A.; A.B., Franklin and Marshall, 1889, A.M., 1892; Sc.D., 1915; M.D., U. of Pa., 1894; m. Mary, d. George and Mary (Hurford) Calder, June 18, 1900; children—Mary Calder, Susan Burton, Ellen Ellery, Theodore Burton, James Ziegler. Interne, Presbyn. Hosp., Phila., 1894-96; in practice at Lancaster; med. dir. Lancaster Gen. Hosp., 1906-20; sec. Health Com., Pa., 1927-35. Pres. Med. Soc. State of Pa., 1910 (chmn. com. on scientific work, 1899-1908; trustee, 1910-27); mem. A.M.A., Lancaster City and Co. med. socs., Chi Phi, etc. First lt. and asst. surgeon Battery C, N.G. Pa., 1905; commd. capt., Med. R.C., June 6, 1917; maj., Sept. 18, 1917; lt. col. Med. Corps U.S.A., Nov. 6, 1918; lt. col. Med. O.R.C., 1919; col., 1924. Fellow Am. Coll. Surgeons. Home: 305 N. Duke St., Lancaster, Pa. *

APPEL, Thomas Roberts, lawyer; b. Titusville, Pa., May 11, 1881; s. John W. and Ella J. (Roberts) A.; ed. Franklin and Marshall Acad., 1895-97, Franklin and Marshall Coll., 1897-1901; U. of Pa. Law Sch., 1901-02; m. Eva T. Rengier, Jan. 23, 1907; children—Roberts Rengier, Charles Rengier, Thomas Gilmore, Anthony Roberts. Admitted to Pa. bar, 1904, and since engaged in gen. practice of law at Lancaster; dir. and solicitor Lancaster Nat. Bank since 1928. Served as pres. Welfare Fed. of Lancaster Co., 1934. Dir. Tuberculosis Soc. of Lancaster Co. Mem. Phi Kappa Psi. Republican. Mem. First Reformed Church, Lancaster. Club: Hamilton. Home: 48 N. President Av. Office: 33 N. Duke St., Lancaster, Pa.

APPLE, Henry Harbaugh, college pres.; b. Mercersburg, Pa., Nov. 8, 1869; s. Thomas Gilmore (pres. Franklin and Marshall Coll., 1878-90) and Emma (Miller) A.; A.B., Franklin and Marshall Coll., 1889, A.M., 1892; grad. Theol. Sem. of Reformed Church in U.S., 1892; D.D., Lafayette, 1909; LL.D., Univ. of Pa., 1913, Univ. of Pittsburgh, 1919, Heidelberg Univ., 1925, Ursinus Coll., 1934, Franklin & Marshall Coll., 1935; m. Florence Emma Herr, Nov. 8, 1894; 1 dau., Emma (dec.). Ordained Ref. Ch. ministry, 1892; pastor St. John's Ch., Phila, 1892-98, Trinity Ch., York, Pa., 1898-1909; pres. Franklin and Marshall Coll., Lancaster, Pa., 1909-35, pres. emeritus since 1935. Pres. Philadelphia Classics, 1896, Zion Classics, 1902, Potomac Synod, 1905; mem. exec. com. Bd. Home Missions. Chaplain York City Fire

Dept. (vol. dept. of 2,000 men), 1900-09; pres. Schubert Choir. Served during World War as chmn. United War Work in Lancaster Co., chmn. Federal Labor Bd. for Lancaster Co.; chmn. Civic Com. for War Memorial. Decorated Cross of Merit by Hungarian Govt., 1934. Mem. Coll. and Univ. Council Pa., York Co. Hist. Soc., Lancaster Co. Hist. Soc., Phi Kappa Psi, Phi Beta Kappa, Am. Acad. Polit. and Social Science, Am. Philos. Soc.; pres. Assn. of Schs., Colls. and Seminaries of Reformed Ch. in U.S.; pres. Assn. Pa. Coll. Presidents, 1920-21; pres. Lancaster Chamber of Commerce, 1928-29. Republican. Clubs: Hamilton, Country. Home: Lancaster, Pa.

APPLE, Joseph Henry, college pres.; b. Rimersburg, Pa., Aug. 4, 1865; s. Rev. Joseph Henry and Elizabeth Ann (Geiger) Apple; A.B. Franklin and Marshall Coll., 1885, A.M., 1888, hon. Pd.D., 1911; LL.D., Ursinus Coll., 1916; Temple U., 1932, Franklin and Marshall Coll., 1933; m. Mary E. Rankin, Dec. 27, 1892 (died Dec. 2, 1896); children—Miriam Rankin, Charlotte Elizabeth (dec.); m. 2d, Gertrude Harner, Nov. 23, 1898; children—Mrs. Elizabeth Apple McCain, Emily Gertrude, Joseph Henry. Prin. high sch. and prof. math., Clarion and Pittsburgh, Pa., 1885-93; pres. Hood (formerly Woman's) Coll., 1893-1934, now pres. emeritus. Dir. Frederick Hotel Co. Chmn. campaign com. for new Y.M.C.A. bldg., 1906; pres. Y.M.C.A., 1908-13. Exec. sec. Forward Movement, Reformed Ch. U.S., 1919-26; pres. Potomac Synod of Reformed Ch. in U.S., 1935-36. Chmn. campaign com. Frederick County Memorial Assn., 1926; dir. Frederick Co. Free Library; mem. Md. Pub. Library Commn. since 1912, pres., 1917. Mem. Frederick County Hist. Soc. (pres.), Phi Beta Kappa, Phi Kappa Psi. Mason. Clubs: Cosmos (Washington, D. C.); Rotary (Frederick). Author: Frederick in Song and Story, 1935. Lecturer and writer. Honored by community at fortieth anniversary as pres. Hood Coll., May 12, 1933, as "oldest college president in point of service." Home: 323 N. College Parkway, Frederick, Md.

APPLE, Miriam Rankin, librarian; b. Frederick, Md., Dec. 19, 1893; d. Joseph Henry and Mary (Rankin) Apple; prep. edn., Hood Coll. Prep. Sch., 1906-10; A.B., Hood Coll., 1914; B.S., Simmons Coll., 1918; unmarried. Asst. librarian, Hood Coll., 1914-17; index and catalogue clerk office of the chief Quartermaster, with A.E.F., Tours, France, 1918-19; librarian, Hood Coll. since 1919. Mem. Md. Library Assn., Columbian Library Assn., A.L.A., Am. Assn. Univ. Women. Hood Coll. Alumnae Assn. (pres). Republican. Mem. Reformed Ch. Clubs: Zonta of Frederick (sec.), Stamp and Coin, Hood (Frederick). Home: 323 N. College Parkway, Frederick, Md.

APPLE, Ulysses Admund, clergyman; b. Radnor, Pa., Sept. 30, 1870; s. George E. and Anstina (Keely) A.; A.B., Gettysburg Coll., 1895; ed. Gettysburg Theol. Sem., 1895-98; hon. D.D. Gettysburg Coll., 1928; m. Rachel E. Dalp, June 12, 1901; children—Frances Elizabeth (Mrs. Earl L. Garrett), Edna Mae, Charlotte Grace. Began as clk. with Pa. R.R. Co., 1888; ordained to ministry Luth. Ch., 1898; pastor, Trenton, N. J., 1898-1901, Red Lion, Pa., 1901-18, Mechanicsburg, Pa., 1918-20, Annville, Pa., 1920-36; asst. Zion Ch. Lebanon, Pa., since 1937; served as sec. Western Pa. Luth. Synod, 1907-14; sec. Eastern Pa. Luth. Synod, 1926-30. Pres. bd. trustees, Tressler Orphans Home, Loysville, Pa. Trustee Clarence Miller Camp for Boys, Camp Newaka. Republican. Mem. Luth. Ch. Mason (32°). Home: 28 Hoke Av., Lebanon, Pa.

APPLEBAUM, Samuel, violinist and teacher; b. Passaic, N.J., Jan. 15, 1904; s. Michael and Fannie (Levin) A.; ed. Juilliard Sch. of Music, Inst. Mus. Art, 1922-26; post grad. study, pvt. pupil of Prof. Leopold Auer, 1926-28; m. Sadie Rothman, Aug. 14, 1927; children—Michael, Lois May. Appeared in concerts at age 12 yrs.; conductor N.J. Music Educators' Assn. String Ensemble; instr. violin, pub. schs., Newark, N.J., 1930; founder and first violinist, Newark String Quartet, giving yearly series of chamber music recitals; music critic of new recordings for mag. entitled, Violins and Violinists. Program chmn. N.J. Music Educators' Assn. Mem. Alumni Assn. Juilliard Sch. of Music. Republican. Jewish religion. Clubs: Y.M. H.A., Y.W.H.A. (Newark). Author: Primer Methods for the Violin (6 books), 1936; Violin Bowings—How and When to Teach Them. Contbr. articles to mus. mags. Home: 45 Ingraham Pl., Newark, N.J.

APPLEBY, J(ames) Randolph, Jr., lawyer; b. Jersey City, N.J., Mar. 4, 1891; s. James Randolph and Maria (DuBois) A.; ed. Columbia U., 1908-09; LL.B., N.Y. Law School, 1911; LL.M., same, 1912; m. Bessie Hodapp, Apr. 15, 1914; children—Elizabeth, J. Randolph, III, Theodore, Robert, Carolyn, Kathryn, Richard, John, Donald, William. Admitted to N.Y. bar, 1912, and engaged in gen. practice of law in N.Y. City, asso. with firm Parker, Davis, Wagner & Walton, 1912-16; admitted to N.J. bar as atty., 1913, counsellor, 1916, and engaged in gen. practice of law at South River since 1916; dir. Providers Bldg. & Loan Assn. Past pres. Chamber of Commerce. Trustee South River War Memorial Free Pub. Library, Middlesex Co. Tuberculosis League. Mem. Middlesex Co. Bar Assn., Phi Sigma Kappa. Republican. Mem. Ref. Ch. (deacon). Mason. Jr. Order United Am. Mechanics. Clubs: Lions, Laurence Brook Country of South River (dir.). Home: 232 Main St. Office: First Nat. Bank Bldg., South River, N.J.

APPLEBY, John Winfred, wholesale hardware and mill supplies; b. Mt. Union, Pa., Dec. 3, 1888; s. James Y. and Elizabeth (Walsh) A.; ed. pub. schs. of Pa. and N.Y.; m. Julia Jacobs, Nov. 20, 1912; children—Lucille, Irene, Ruth, Jeannette, Elizabeth, John Winfred. Asso. with Appleby Bros. & Whittaker Co., Harrisburg, Pa., since 1910, treas. since 1914; dir. Market St. Trust Co. Served as mem. bd. dirs. Harrisburg Sch. Bd. Dir. Harrisburg Chamber of Commerce, Y.M.C.A. Treas. Bethesda Mission. Republican. Mem. M.E. Ch. (pres. bd. trustees). Clubs: Harrisburg Rotary (pres), Hershey Country. Home: 816 N. 17th St. Office: 216 S. Second St., Harrisburg, Pa.

APPLEBY, Paul Henson, editor and pub.; b. Greene Co., Mo., Sept. 13, 1891; s. Andrew B. and Mary (Johnson) A.; A.B., Grinnell (Ia.) Coll., 1913; m. Ruth Meyer, Oct. 4, 1916; children—Margaret, Mary Ellen, Loring Troy. Pub. weekly newspapers in Mont., Minn., Ia., 1914-20; editor Iowa Mag., Waterloo, Ia., 1920-24; editorial writer Des Moines Register and Tribune, 1924-28; pub. weekly newspapers in Va., 1928-33; exec. asst. to Sec. of Agr. since 1933. Democrat. Home: 121 W. Bradley Lane, Chevy Chase, Md. Office: Dept. of Agriculture, Washington, D.C.

APPLEGATE, J. Arthur; chmn. bd. South Amboy Trust Co.; pres. Commonwealth Bank of Metuchen, Investors & Owners Bldg. & Loan Assn. Address: Perth Amboy, N.J.

APPLEGATE, John Bayles, lawyer; b. Hoboken, N.J., Oct. 9, 1900; s. Ivins Davis and Evangelyn (Parslow) A; Ph.B., Brown Univ., 1923; LL.B., Columbia U., 1926; m. Pauline Hammell, May 5, 1931; 1 dau., Judith Hammell. Served clerkship in office Lindsbury, Depue & Faulks, Newark, N.J., 1926-27; admitted to N.J. bar, as atty., 1927, as master in chancery and counsellor, 1930; engaged in gen. practice of law at Hoboken, N. J., since 1928; mem. firm Besson & Applegate, 1928-35, propr. firm since 1935. Trustee Hoboken Community Y.M. C.A., Stevens-Waldheim Forum. Mem. Am. Bar Assn., Hudson Co. Bar Assn., Delta Upsilon, S.R. Episcopalian. Mason. Clubs: Euclid Masonic, Kiwanis (Hoboken); Brown University, Delta Upsilon (New York). Home: 2 Ninth St. Office: 1 Newark St., Hoboken, N.J.

APPLEMAN, Charles Orville, plant physiologist; b. Millville, Pa., Dec. 6, 1878; s. Emanuel L. and Elizabeth Jane (Gillispie) A.; B.P.; Bloomsburg (Pa.) State Normal Sch., 1898; Ph.B., Dickinson Coll., 1903; Ph.D., U. of Chicago, 1910; m. Emma Frances Reeme, June 9, 1904; 1 dau., Katherine Reeme. Prof. biology, Lombard Coll., Galesburg, Ill., 1904-08; plant physiologist, Md. Agrl. Expt. Sta., since 1910; prof. plant physiology, U. of Md., since 1917, also chmn. of Botany and dean Grad. Sch. Fellow A.A.A.S.; mem. Am. Bot. Soc., Am. Soc. Plant Physiologists (pres. 1933), Am. Chem. Soc., Am. Soc. for Promotion of Agr., Washington Acad. Sciences, Am. Soc. Naturalists, Phi Delta Theta, Phi Beta Kappa, Sigma Xi, Alpha Zeta, Phi Kappa Phi. Democrat. Club: Indian Spring Golf. Author of numerous articles and bulls. relating to plant life. Home: College Park, Md.

APPLETON, Joseph Luke Teasdale, bacteriologist; b. Albany, N.Y., Sept. 18, 1888; s. Joseph Luke Teasdale and Margaret (Graham) A.; B.S., Hamilton Coll., 1909, hon. Sc.D., 1935; D.D.S., U. of Pa., 1914; m. Catharine Garnar, June 5, 1914; children—Catharine Jane, Joseph Luke Teasdale. Instr. chemistry, Pa. State Coll., 1910, instr. zoölogy, 1910-11; now prof. pathology School of Dentistry, U. of Pa.; consultant U.S. Pub. Health Service. Served as 1st lt. Dental Corps., U.S. Army, 1917. Mem. Phila. Mouth Hygiene Assn., Am. Dental Assn. (mem. research commn.), Internat. Assn. Dental Research, Soc. Am. Bacteriologists, A.A.A.S., Phi Beta Kappa, Sigma Xi. Home: 4001 Spruce St., Philadelphia, Pa.

APPLEYARD, Joseph, physician; b. Dunlo, Pa., Jan. 1, 1898; s. Arthur and Jane (Law) A.; ed. Grove City Coll., 1914-16, U. of Pa., 1916-18; M.D., U. of Pa. Med. Sch., 1922, grad. study, same, 1925-26; m. Kathryn Elizabeth Hoover, Nov. 25, 1927; children—Joann Jane, Jeanne Law. Interne, Lancaster (Pa.) Gen. Hosp., 1922-23; chief resident phys., Harrisburg City Hosp., 1923-24; in gen. practice of medicine, 1924-25; in practice of medicine at Lancaster, specializing in urology since 1926; mem. staff Lancaster Gen. hosp., St. Joseph and Lancaster Co. hosps., Rossmere Tuberculosis Sanitorium; exec. sec. City Bd. Health, Lancaster, Pa. Fellow Am. Coll. Surgs. Mem. Lancaster Co. Med. Soc., Pa. State Med. Soc., Omega Upsilon Phi. Republican. Protestant. Home: 606 State St. Office: 152 E. Walnut St., Lancaster, Pa.

ARBUCKLE, Howard Bell, chemist; b. nr. Lewisburg, W.Va., Oct. 5, 1870; s. John Davis Arbuckle and Elizabeth (Van Lear) A.; B.A., 1890; spl. student in chemistry, U. of Va., 1894-95; Ph.D., in Chemistry, Johns Hopkins, 1898; m. Ida Meginniss, June 4, 1896; children—Howard Bell, Adèle Taylor. Fellow Hampden-Sidney Coll., 1889-90; prof. ancient langs. Seminary West of Suwanee (foundation for U. of Fla.), 1891-94; teacher, and prof. Agnes Scott Inst. (later coll.), Decatur, Ga., 1898-1912; prof. chemistry, Davidson (N.C.) Coll., since 1913. A founder of Continental Dorset Club for registry of pure bred Dorset sheep; contbg. editor Am. Sheep Breeder, 1900-20; founder Edgewood Stock Farm and brought over selected importation of sheep from Eng., 1904. Pres. N.C. Jersey Breeders Assn., 1930. Mcm. Am. Red Poll Breeders Assn., Am. Aberdeen-Angus Breeders Assn., Continental Dorset Club (a founder), Am. Chem. Soc. (founder and ex-pres. Ga. sect., ex-pres. N.C. sect.), N.C. Acad. Science (pres. 1925), Pi Kappa Alpha (councilor princeps, 1900-05; grand councilor, 1913-33), Gamma Sigma Epsilon (honorary chemical; grand chancellor 1920-28), Phi Beta Kappa, Omicron Delta Kappa, Scabbard and Blade. Presbyterian. Clubs: Kenmore Golf (founder. was pres. 1925-30), Symposium (Atlanta, Ga.). Author: Redetermination of the Atomic Weight of Zinc and Cadmium, 1898; Laboratory Manual in Household Chemistry, 1912; The Life and Habits of the Honey Bee, 1925. Contbr. numerous articles to chem. lit. and agrl. jours. Researches in corn proteins and cellulose products; discovered pyrolene. Home: Davidson, N.C.; (summer) "Maplemont," Maxwelton, Greenbrier Co., W.Va.

ARBUTHNOT, Charles, III, merchant; b. Pittsburgh, Pa., Sept. 1, 1888; s. Charles and Caroline (Berger) A.; student Asheville (N.C.) Sch., 1901-06, Hotchkiss Sch. Lakeville, Conn., 1906-08; A.B., Yale, 1912; m. Beaumont Hazzard,

Nov. 8, 1933. With Arbuthnot-Stephenson Co., wholesale dry goods, 1912, dir. since 1933, v.p. since 1939. Dir. Pittsburgh Chamber Commerce, Pittsburgh Convention and Tourist Bur.; chmn. citizens advisory com. Pittsburgh Bur. of Police, 1937; chmn. parade com. Allegheny County Sesqui-Centennial, 1938. Served as 1st lt. 315th Inf., U.S. Army, 1917-19. Mem. Delta Kappa Epsilon. Republican. Presbyterian. Mason. Clubs: Allegheny Country (Sewickly, Pa.); Rolling Rock (Ligonier); Harvard-Yale-Princeton Club of Pittsburgh (v.p.), Yale of Pittsburgh (pres.). Home: 6423 5th Av. Office: 801 Penn Av., Pittsburgh, Pa.

ARBUTHNOT, Thomas Shaw, M.D.; b. Allegheny, Pa., Feb. 18, 1871; s. Charles and Elizabeth (Shaw) A.; A.B., Yale, 1894; M.D., Coll. Phys. and Surg. (Columbia), 1898; M.R.C.S., Eng., 1900; L.R.C.P., London, 1900; LL.D., U. of Pittsburgh, 1919; unmarried. Dean Med. Sch. of U. of Pittsburgh, 1909-18. Pres. Carnegie Hero Fund; mem. bd. Carnegie Corpn., N.Y., 1933—. Mem. A.M.A. In service in France, 1917-19. Address: 6425 5th Av., Pittsburgh, Pa.

ARCHAMBAULT, A(nna) Margaretta, artist; b. Phila., Pa.; d. Achille Lucien and Henrietta Bennett (Haupt) A.; ed. priv. sch. of Miss Mary Anna Longstreth, Phila. Dir. Phila. Sch. Miniature Painting. Has exhibited widely at exhbns. of miniatures; awarded Medal of Honor, Pa. Soc. Miniature Painters, 1922. Painted miniatures from life of Presidents Warren G. Harding and Calvin Coolidge, for the Butler Art Inst., Youngstown, O.; oil portrait of Michael Hillegas, 1st treas. of U.S., for Independence Hall collection, Phila., and for Treasury Bldg., Washington; oil portrait of Prof. Lewis M. Haupt, for Engring. Dept., U. of Pa., of Admiral Stephen Bleecker Luce for United States Naval Academy, Annapolis, Md., of Robert W. Lesley, Esq., for Merion Golf Club, of Dr. Harrison Allen, for Coll. of Physicians, Phila., Mrs. J. Willis Martin, for Strawberry Mansion, Fairmont Park, Phila., Rev. William Ashmead Schaeffer, for Lutheran Theol. Sem., Mt. Airy; miniatures of Lord Edward Strachie of England, late Hon. Archie Gordon, owned by Lady Aberdeen of Scotland. Member Pennsylvania Soc. of Miniature Painters (vice-pres.), Fellowship of Pa. Acad. of Fine Arts, Phila. Art Alliance, Hist. Soc. of Pa., Bot. Soc. U. of Pa., Bartram's Garden Assn., Church Hist. Soc., Am. Swedish Hist. Soc. (Women's Auxiliary), Huguenot Soc., The Print Club. Republican. Episcopalian. Clubs: Plastic (charter mem.), Civic. Author: Art, Architecture and Historic interests in Pennsylvania, 1924. Home: 426 S. 40th St. Studio: 1714 Chestnut St., Philadelphia, Pa.

ARCHER, Charles Homer, supt. schs.; b. Bluefield, W.Va., Sept. 9, 1888; s. John Wythe and Mary (Carr) A.; student Mercer Co. pub. schs., 1894-1905, Concord State Normal Sch., 1906-11, W.Va. U., summer, 1914; A.B., Concord State Teachers Coll.; m. Nora Cooper, Aug. 27, 1909; children—Robbie (wife of Dr. R. L. Lee), Clarence Elmer. Teacher one-room sch., 1909-10; teacher and prin. Elementary and high schs., 1911-14; supt. schs., Adkin Dist., McDowell Co., W.Va., 1914-21; on leave of absence from sch. work, 1921-22; registrar Concord State Teachers Coll., 1923-34; asst. supt. Mercer Co. schs., 1934-35, supt. since 1935. Mem. Kiwanis Internat. Com. on Pub. Affairs for U.S., 1938. Mem. Am. Assn. Sch. Adminstrs., N.E.A., "96 Club;" pres. W.Va. Assn. County Supts., 1935-36. Democrat. Methodist. Mason (K.T.; Past Master A.F.&A.M.; Past High Priest R.A.M.), Kiwanian since 1925 (past pres.; dist. gov. W.Va. Dist. Kiwanis Internat. 1933). Home: Athens, W.Va. Office: Princeton, W.Va.

ARCHER, Franklin Morse, banker; b. Camden, N.J., Nov. 27, 1873; s. Benjamin F. and Mary W. (Sloan) A.; grad. Episcopal Acad., Phila., 1890; A.B., Princeton U., 1894; LL.B., Harvard, 1897; m. Bessie M. Chandlee, June 14, 1900; children—Franklin Morse, Elizabeth C. (Mrs. Henry B. Guthrie, Jr.), Gertrude A. (Mrs. Richard L. Fitzwater, Jr.), Evan Chandlee. Admitted to N.J. bar, 1897, and practiced in Camden, 1897-1918; pres. Nat. Bank of Camden, 1918-22; pres. First Nat. State Bank of Camden, 1922-27; pres. First Camden Nat. Bank & Trust Co. since 1927; dir. Am. Dredging Co. (Phila.), Camden Fire Ins. Co., Phila. and Camden Ferry Co., Provident Mutual Life Ins. Co., West Jersey and Seashore R.R. Co. Mem. advisory com. 3d Federal Reserve Dist. of R.F.C. Dir. and treas. Cooper Hosp. Republican. Presbyterian. Clubs: Union League (Phila.); Nassau (Princeton); Tavistock Country (Haddonfield); City (Camden). Home: 570 Warwick Rd., Haddonfield, N.J. Office: Broadway and Cooper St., Camden, N.J.

ARCHER, Franklin Morse, Jr., lawyer; b. Camden, N.J., Sept. 17, 1902; s. Franklin Morse and Elizabeth (Chandlee) A.; grad. Haddonfield (N.J.) High Sch., 1918; Phillips Exeter (N.H.) Acad., 1919; A.B., Princeton, 1923; LL.B., Harvard, 1926; m. Mary Joy Reeve, Sept. 23, 1928; children—Franklin Morse, III, Mary Joy. Admitted to N.J. bar, 1927, and since practiced in Camden; mem. firm Boyle & Archer. Dir. Cooper Hosp., Camden; dir. Camden Y.M.C.A.; vice-pres. Moorestown Welfare Assn.; mem. bd. govs., Phila. Skating Club, Phila. Humane Soc. Mem. Am. Bar Assn., N.J. Bar Assn., Camden Co. Bar Assn. Republican. Presbyterian. Clubs: Rotary of Camden (pres.); Princeton Quadrangle; Moorestown Field; Princeton of Phila., Philadelphia. Home: 601 Chester Av., Moorestown, N.J. Office: First Camden Nat. Bank Bldg., Camden, N.J.

AREFORD, G. Carl, realtor; b. Carmichaels, Pa., March 9, 1887; s. Sylvanus T. and Margaret (Conner) A,; student Carmichaels (Pa.) High Sch., 1901-04, Waynesburg (Pa.) Coll., 1904-06; unmarried. Gen. mgr. LeTexo Land Co., Crockett, Tex., 1910-20; gen. mgr. Areford Coal Mining Co., Uniontown, Pa., 1920-30; partner Areford Bros., real estate brokers, Uniontown, Pa., since 1912. Mem. Fayette Greene Coal Assn. (pres. 1920-30), Uniontown Chamber of Commerce (pres. 1926-39). Democrat. Presbyterian. Clubs: Kiwanis (pres. 1928), Uniontown Country (Uniontown, Pa.). Home: 22 Ben Lomond St. Office: 62 E. Main St., Uniontown, Pa.

ARENSBERG, Francis Louis, manufacturer; b. Pittsburgh, Pa., Oct. 1, 1883; s. Conrad Christian and Flora Belle (Covert) A.; student Shady Side Acad., Pittsburgh, Pa., 1895-1900; B.S., Harvard, 1904; m. Florence Dangerfield, Dec. 28, 1908; 1 son, Alan. Began as helper in open hearth dept. Jones & Laughlin Steel Co., Pittsburgh, 1905; salesman Vulcan Crucible Steel Co., 1906-08; works mgr. McCullough-Dalzell Crucible Co., 1908-16; pres. Vesuvius Crucible Co., Swissvale, Pa., since 1916; pres. Reymer & Bros., Inc., Pittsburgh, mfg. confectioners, 1936-37. Mem. Supervisory Agency for Crucible Industry under N.R.A. Mem. Engrs. Soc. of Western Pa., Am. Ceramic Soc., Am. Refractories Inst., Ry. Bus. Assn. Republican. Presbyterian. Clubs: Pittsburgh Athletic Assn., Railway (Pittsburgh). As pres. Vesuvius Crucible Co. cooperated with U.S. Bur. of Mines in investigation of domestic clays and graphites for use in crucible industry; cooperated in development of standard crucible sizes adopted by the industry. Home: 4739 Bayard St., Pittsburgh, Pa. Office: 2216 Palmer St., Swissvale, Pa.

ARENTZ, Fred Brunjof, mgr. mfg. plant; b. Ocala, Fla., Aug. 27, 1892; s. Brunjof and Martha (Brightman) A.; B.S., U. of Rochester (N.Y.), 1914; m. Laura Gould, May 22, 1918; 1 dau., Frances Gould. Began as asst. chemist, Rochester, N.Y., 1914-16; research industrial fellowship, Columbia U., 1916; research chemist, U.S. Industrial Alcohol Co., Baltimore, Md., 1917-26; plant mgr., U.S. Industrial Alcohol Co., Newark, N.J., since 1926. Served as pres. Ironbound Mfrs. Assn., Newark, N.J., since 1936. Chmn. Newark Advisory Planning Bd. since 1939. Mem. Theta Chi. Republican. Episcopalian. Home: Tulip Lane, Short Hills. Office: 400 Doremus Av., Newark, N.J.

ARLITZ, William J., M.D.; mem. staff Christ Hosp. (Jersey City), N.J. State Hosp. (Greystone Park), North Hudson Hosp. (Weehawken), Moses Taylor Hosp. (Scranton, Pa.). Address: 107 Newark St., Hoboken, N.J.

ARMENTROUT, Aubrey Webster, surgeon; b. Rockingham Co., Va., Apr. 22, 1901; s. Walter Scott and Myrtice (Maddox) A.; A.B., U. of Ky., Lexington, Ky., 1922; M.D., Johns Hopkins U. Med. Coll., 1926; M.S. in Surgery, U. of Va. Med. Coll., Charlottesville, 1930; m. Catherine Byrer, June 8, 1935. Interne Jefferson Hosp., Roanoke, Va., 1926-27; asst. resident, 1927-28, resident, 1928-29; surgical resident, U. of Va. Hosp., University, Va., 1930-31; engaged in gen. practice of surgery at Martinsburg, W.Va., since 1933; on surg. staff Kings Daughteers Hosp. since 1933. Fellow Am. Coll. Surgeons. Mem. Am. Med. Assn., W.Va. Med. Soc., Sigma Xi, Phi Chi. Democrat. Presbyn. Mason. Clubs: Rotary, Golf (Martinsburg). Home: 1015 W. King St. Office: Public Sq., Martinsburg, W.Va.

ARMENTROUT, Walter Wardlaw, educator; b. Washington Coll., Tenn., Jan. 22, 1894; s. Cyrus Bruce and Lutetia (Moore) A.; B.S., U. of Tenn., 1916; M.S., U. of Wis., 1925; Ph.D., U. of Minn., 1930; student U. of Minn., 1927-28; m. Dorothy Henrietta Carolyn Gasch, Aug. 4, 1928; children—Steven Alexander, Sally. Teacher vocational agriculture, Bradley Co. High Sch., Tenn., 1916-18; mem. Nat. Child Labor Com., New York, 1920-22; teacher of edn., U. of Tenn., 1923, U. of W.Va., since 1924, head of dept. of agrl. economics since 1933. Served as sergeant M.C., U.S. Army; in France, Sept.-Dec. 1918, Army of Occupation in German, Dec. 1918-Sept. 1919. Mem. Am. Farm Economics Assn., Alpha Zeta. Democrat. Presbyn. Clubs: Faculty, Public Affairs (Morgantown, W.Va.). Home: North Willey St., Morgantown, W.Va.

ARMOR, James Coe, elec. engr.; b. Pittsburgh, Pa., Oct. 7, 1874; s. William Gillespie and Emma Dorothy (Miller) A.; ed. Pittsburgh pub. schs. and Duffs Coll., 1894-95; m. Grace Florence Bennett, Sept. 6, 1919. Began as office boy in real estate office, 1888; various positions in connection of mfr. and operation steam and elec. machinery, 1889-1902; research and design engring. dept. Nernst Lamp Co., 1902-05; design and research engring. dept. Nat. Electric Signalling Co., 1905-07, with charge operation transatlantic radio sta. 1906; research dept. Westinghouse Electric and Mfg. Co., 1907-11; same, Nat. Electric Signalling Co., 1911-12; transformer design engring. dept. Gen. Electric Co., 1913-20; engring. dept. Pittsburgh Transformer Co., 1920-28; with Allis-Chalmers Mfg. Co. in charge design of power transformers since 1928. Registered professional engr. in Pa. Mem. Am. Inst. Elec. Engrs., Inst. Radio Engrs. (charter mem.). Republican. Lutheran. Holds patents in radio, electric arc welding and refrigeration. Home: 652 Highland Place, Bellevue, Pittsburgh, Pa. Office: Allis-Chalmers Mfg. Co., N.S. Pittsburgh, Pa.

ARMOUR, Allison Vincent, plant and archæol. research; b. Chicago, Ill., March 18, 1863; s. George and Barbara (Allison) A.; grad. Harvard Sch., Chicago, 1880; B.A., Yale, 1884; m. Anne Louise Kelley, Dec. 10, 1885 (died April 2, 1890). Conducted 8 voyages for plant research, U.S. Dept. Agr., also several voyages in archæol. research. Vol. aid (temp. service) Naval Intelligence, World War. Awarded Meyer medal by Am. Genetic Assn. for plant exploration. Asso. fellow Davenport Coll. of Yale Univ.; hon. fellow N.Y. Acad. of Sciences. Republican. Clubs: University, Brook, New York Yacht (New York); Metropolitan (Washington); Bath (London); Yacht Club de Belgique. Home: Princeton, N.J. Office: 340 Park Av., New York, N.Y.

ARMSTRONG, Alexander, ex-atty. gen. of Md.; b. Hagerstown, Md., June 28, 1877; s. Alexander and Elizabeth Key (Scott) A.; A.B., Princeton, 1899, A.M., 1900; LL.B., U. of Pa., 1903; LL.B., U. of Md., 1923; m. Mary Rebekah Woods of Baltimore, Jan. 25, 1911 (died 1938); 1 son, Alexander. Began practice at Hagerstown, 1904; mem. firm Armstrong & Scott, 15 yrs.; now practices at Hagerstown in own name; mem. firm Armstrong, Machen & Allen, Baltimore; dir. Potomac Edison Co., Chesapeake and Potomac Telephone Co. of Baltimore City (mem. exec. com.), Blue Ridge Fire Insurance Co.; (mem. exec. com.), New Amsterdam Casualty Co.; pres. Armstrong Company of Detroit, Mich. City solicitor, Hagerstown, 1904-06; state's atty., Washington Co., Md., 1908-

ARMSTRONG — ARNOLD

12; pres. Bd. of Supervisors of Election, Washington Co., 1912-16; atty. gen. of Md., 1919-23; Rep. candidate for gov. of Md., 1923; del. at large Rep. Nat. Conv., 1924. Chmn. Baltimore City Pa. R.R. Commn., 1929-30, Commn. to Investigate Maryland's Care of Insane and Feeble Minded, 1936. Pres. Md. State Bd. Law Examiners; mem. Nat. Conf. Uniform State Laws (pres. since 1936); mem. bd. mgrs. Council of State Govts., 1936-39; mem. Lawyers Round Table; pres. Seven Sch., Inc.; mem. bd. mgrs. Training Sch. for Boys; dir. Library Assn. of Baltimore Bar, 1931-37; mem. Am. Law Inst., Am. Bar Assn. (mem. House of Dels., 1936-39), Md. State Bar Assn. (pres., 1926-27), Bar Assn. City of Baltimore, Bar Assn. of Washington Co., Md. State Bankers Assn. (pres., 1930-31), Phi Beta Kappa, S.A.R. (pres. Md. chapter 1935-37). Presbyn. Mason (33°); pres. Scottish Rite Holding Co. Clubs: Merchants, Maryland (Baltimore). Home: Boyce Av., Ruxton, Md. (P.O., Towson, R.R. 8). Offices: 15 N. Jonathan St., Hagerstown and Calvert Bldg., Baltimore, Md.

ARMSTRONG, C(harles) Dudley, cork mfr.; b. Wilkinsburg, Pa., Aug. 21, 1888; s. Charles Dickey and Gertrude Virginia (Ludden) A.; student Shadyside Acad., Pittsburgh, Pa., 1900-03, Hill Sch., Pottstown, Pa., 1903-06; B.A., Yale, 1910; m. Mary Jones Hilliard, July 1, 1916; children—Barbara Hilliard, John Larimer, Virginia Dudley, Thomas Morton, Henry Hilliard; vice-pres. and sec. Armstrong Cork Co., Lancaster, Pa., since 1937; dir. Union Nat. Bank. Chmn. bd. of trustees the Shippen School. Republican. Episcopalian. Clubs: Lancaster Country, Hamilton Fox Chapel, Pittsburgh, Duquesne (Pittsburgh). Home: Abbeville, Lincoln Highway West. Office: Lancaster, Pa.

ARMSTRONG, Clyde Allman, lawyer; b. New Kensington, Pa., June 14, 1898; s. Ulysses S. and Anna M. (Allman) A.; A.B., Westminster Coll., New Wilmington, Pa., 1919; LL.B., U. of Pittsburgh, 1922; m. Ethlyn W. Logan, Dec. 27, 1923; children—Dale Logan, Clyde Wilson, Carolyn Lee. Admitted to Pa. bar, 1922; asso. with Thorp, Bostwick & Stewart, Pittsburgh, which later became Thorp, Bostwick, Stewart & Reed; partner Thorp, Bostwick, Reed & Armstrong. Served as 2d lt. field arty., U.S. Army, 1918. Mem. bd. trustees Westminster Coll., New Wilmington, Pa. Mem. Delta Phi Sigma, Delta Theta Phi. Mem. United Presbyterian Ch. Mason (32°, Shriner). Clubs: Longue Vue, University (Pittsburgh); Williams Country (Weirton, W.Va.). Home: 2040 Beechwood Boul. Office: 2812 Grant Bldg., Pittsburgh, Pa.

ARMSTRONG, Dwight L., cork mfr.; b. Pittsburgh, Pa., June 4, 1894; s. Charles D. and Gertrude Virginia (Ludden) A.; student Hill Sch., Pottstown, Pa., 1909-13; A.B., Yale, 1917; m. Marion Gilmore Appel, Jan. 15, 1922; children—Andrew J., Charlotte A., Mary Martha. With Armstrong Cork Co., Lancaster, Pa., since 1919, successively as Pacific Coast Dist. mgr., San Francisco and Seattle, 1922-23, asst. gen. sales mgr., 1923-26, gen. sales mgr. floor div., 1928-29, vice-pres. in charge sales, 1930-32, vice-pres. and gen. mgr. glass and closure div., since 1933; dir. Armstrong Cork Co., U.S. Bung Mfg. Co. Organized Lancaster (Pa.) Welfare Fed., 1926, pres., 1926-27. Mem. Crown Mfrs. Assn. (pres., 1932-37), Cork Inst. of America (chmn. cork stopper div., 1933-37). Republican. Presbyterian. Mason. Clubs: Lancaster Country, Pine Valley Golf, Yale Club of N.Y. Home: 1271 Wheatland Av. Office: Liberty St., Lancaster, Pa.

ARMSTRONG, Edward Cooke, educator; b. Winchester, Va., Aug. 24, 1871; s. James Edward and Margaret (Hickman) A.; A.B., Randolph-Macon Coll., 1890, A.M., 1894, LL.D., 1917, Ph.D., Johns Hopkins, 1897; also univs. Paris and Berlin; L.H.D., Oberlin, 1927; m. Emerline Holbrook, June 8, 1905; 1 son, Percy Holbrook. Prof. French lang., 1897-1917, chmn. Romance dept., 1910-17, Johns Hopkins U.; prof. French lang., Princeton, 1917—. Nat. recruiting sec. for the Foyer du Soldat and nat. dir. of French instrn. in the training camps, 1918; dean Am. students and lecturer in U. of Bordeaux, 1919. Trustee Am. Univ. Union in Europe, 1919-29; sec. Am. Council Learned Societies, 1925-29, chairman, 1929-1935. Chevalier Legion of Honor. Mem. Modern Language Assn. America (pres. 1918, 19); fellow Medieval Academy America, American Academy Arts and Sciences, Am. Philos. Soc. Author: Syntax of the French Verb; French Shifts in Adjective Position; Taking Counsel with Candide; French Metrical Versions of Barlaam and Josaphat; Authorship of the Vengement Alixandre and of the Venjance Alixandre; Medieval French Roman d'Alexandre (with others), Vols. 1 and 2, 1937. Editor: Le Chevalier à l'Epeé; Elliott Monographs in the Romance Langs. and Lits. Co-editor: Modern Language Notes, 1911-15. Home: Princeton, N.J.

ARMSTRONG, Frederic Palmer, banker; b. Keyport, N.J., Nov. 29, 1887; s. Frederic Francis and Mary Emma (Sellick) A.; ed. public schools of Keyport; m. Mable Jan Schenck, Oct. 18, 1910; children—Dorothy (Mrs. James F. Humphreys), Doris (Mrs. James G. Pappas). With Keyport Banking Co. since 1903, beginning as clerk and advancing through all positions, pres. since 1929; treas. and dir. Second Keyport Loan Assn., Surf Theatre Co., Keyport Theatre Co. Sec. and treas. Monmouth Co. Bankers and Clearing House Assn. Mem. N.J. Bankers Assn. (mem. exec. com.). Republican. Mem. Reformed Ch. Clubs: Keyport Yacht; Forsgate Golf (Jamesburg, N.J.). Home: 121 Atlantic St. Office: Keyport Banking Co., Keyport, N.J.

ARMSTRONG, Thomas Fullerton, pres. Conkling-Armstrong Terra Cotta Co.; b. Perth Amboy, N.J., Aug. 31, 1869; s. Thomas and Marian (English) A.; student Hackettstown (N.J.) Sem., married, Aug. 8, 1893; children —Thomas Fullerton, John Neill. Pres. Conkling-Armstrong Terra Cotta Co. Pres. Common Council of City of Phila.; dir. of supplies in Mayor Moore's Cabinet. Trustee Temple U., Pennington Sem.; pres. Master Builders' Exchange. Mem. N.J. Soc. of Pa. (ex-pres.). Clubs: Manufacturers' (ex-pres.), Business, Rotary (Phila.). Home: 2226 Tioga St. Office: Wissahickon Av. and Junida St., Philadelphia, Pa.

ARMSTRONG, Thomas R.; in practice of law since 1905. Address: 15 Exchange Place, Jersey City, N.J.

ARMSTRONG, William Park, theologian; b. Selma, Ala., Jan. 10, 1874; s. William Park and Alice (Isbell) A.; A.B., Princeton, 1894, A.M., 1896; grad. Princeton Theol. Sem., 1897; studied U. of Marburg, 1897, U. of Berlin, 1897-98, U. of Erlangen, 1898; grad. student, Princeton Theol. Sem., 1899; D.D., Temple U., 1915; m. Rebekah Sellers Purves, Dec. 8, 1904; children—Rebekah Purves, William Park, George Purves, Anne Elizabeth, Jane Crozier, James Isbell. Ordained Presbyn. ministry, 1900; instr. N.T. lit. 1899-1903; prof. N.T. lit. and exegesis, Princeton Theol. Sem., since 1903. Democrat. Home: Princeton, N.J.

ARNER, Calvin E.; in gen. practice of law since 1893. Office: 506 Commonwealth Bldg., Allentown, Pa.

ARNER, Maurice Raymond, high school prin.; b. Salem, O., Aug. 16, 1897; s. Caleb Dickinson and Mary Ataline A.; student Greenford (O.) High Sch., 1912-14; grad. Columbiana (O.) High Sch., 1916; B.S. in edn., Ohio State U., 1926; student U. of Chicago, summer 1928; M. Ed., U. of Pittsburgh, 1937; unmarried. Teacher rural schools, Columbiana Co., O., 1919-22; teacher of mathematics, Connellsville (Pa.) High Sch., 1926-27; head mathematics dept., McKees Rocks (Pa.) High Sch., 1927-35, prin. since 1935. Mem. field staff Pa. State Christian Endeavor Assn., lecturing on religious subjects for young people; titles of lectures, "Three Faces toward the Sunset," "I will Be a Christian Whatever the Cost," "Four Fundamentals of Effective Prayer," "Worthwhile Living;" also lectures on "Effective Teaching of Mathematics," "Youth Guidance." Mem. N.E.A., Pa. State Edn. Assn., Sigma Delta Rho, Sigma Delta Sigma. Presbyterian (mem. session, teacher ladies' Bible class, McKees Rocks Ch.). Club: Lions. Home: 319 Russellwood Av. Office: Wayne Av., McKees Rocks, Pa.

ARNETT, John Hancock, physician; b. Phila., Pa., Sept. 14, 1889; s. William W. and Elizabeth (Hancock) A.; A.B., Princeton, 1912; M.D., U. of Pa., 1916; m. Katharine McCollin, June 4, 1921; children—Edward McCollin, John Hancock, Alice Frances. Interne Hosp. of U. of Pa., 1916-18; in practice of medicine, Phila., since 1920; school physician, Drexel Inst. of Tech.; chief of medical service "B," Episcopal Hosp.; asso. prof. of medicine, Grad. Med. Sch., U. of Pa., since 1934. Served as 1st lt., Med. Corps, U.S. Army, 1918. Mem. A.M.A., Phila. Coll. of Physicians. Sigma Xi, Nu Sigma Nu. Democrat. Episcopalian. Contbr. many articles to med. jours. Home: 6200 Ardleigh. Office: 2116 Pine St., Philadelphia, Pa.

ARNHOLD, George Levering, lawyer; b. Phila. Pa., Dec. 2, 1891; s. George Westerman and Augusta (Levering) A.; A.B., Central High Sch., 1911; student U. of Pa., 1911-12; LL.B., Law Sch., U. of Pa., 1915; m. Elizabeth R. Edwards, Jan. 3, 1933. Admitted to Pa. bar, 1916, and since practiced in Philadelphia; sec. Adelphia Hotel Co. Mem. Phila., Pa. and Am. bar assns. Republican. Episcopalian. Mason. Club: Sandy Run Country. Home: 521 Pelham Rd. Office: 133 S. 12th St., Philadelphia, Pa.

ARNOLD, Arthur, lawyer; b. Piedmont, W. Va., Sept. 20, 1884; s. Stewart Baldwin and Hannah (Elliott) A.; grad. high sch., Piedmont, 1903; grad. law sch., W. Va. Univ. 1906; m. Mabel Helen Shook, June 26, 1918. Admitted to W.Va. bar, 1906, and began practice at Piedmont; pros. atty. Mineral Co., W.Va., 1911-12, also 1921-25; city atty. Piedmont, 1921-35; U.S. atty., Northern Dist. of W.Va., 1926-34; Rep. nominee for judge of 21st Judicial Circuit of W.Va., 1936. Mem. Am., W.Va. and Mineral County bar assns., Pi Kappa Alpha. Republican. Episcopalian. Home: Piedmont, W.Va.

ARNOLD, Arthur D., supt. of schools; b. Westboro, Mass., Jan. 29, 1871; s. Daniel Woodward and Rebecca (Fay) A.; grad. Westboro High Sch., 1889; A.B., Dartmouth Coll., 1893, A.M., 1896; m. Claudia Arius, Mar. 12, 1896; children—Verner Arthur, Barbara Woodward (Mrs. F. J. Hutchins). Prin. Lincoln (Mass.) High Sch., 1893-94; prof. of history, Mt. Herman (Mass.) Sch., 1894-95; prin. Stoughton (Mass.) High Sch., 1895-1902, Passaic (N.J.) High Sch., 1902-32; supt. of schools, Passaic, N.J., since 1932. Trustee Passaic Pub. Library, Passaic Y.M.C.A. Mem. N.E.A., N.J. Schoolmasters Club, N.J. State Teachers Assn., Progressive Edn. Assn. (U.S. and N.J.), N.J. Council of Edn., N.J. County Council of Teachers, N.J. State Assn. Teachers of Speech, N.J. Supts. Round Table Assn., Passaic Teachers Assn., Passaic Community Council, Phi Beta Kappa, Alpha Delta Phi. Republican. Mem. Reformed Ch. Mason. Rotarian. Home: 140 Ascension St. Office: 18 Belmont Place, Passaic, N.J.

ARNOLD, Benjamin L., insurance; b. Kittanning, Pa., Aug. 29, 1888; s. Harry Andrew and Ida (Luker) A.; student Kittanning Acad., 1900-06; B.S., U. of Pa., 1910; m. Helen Ross Leason, Sept. 11, 1912; children—Isobel Ross, Benjamin Andrew. Began as business associate of Harry A. Arnold, 1910; now owner Harry A. Arnold & Son, gen. insurance; dir. Farmers Nat. Bank, Graff-Kittanning Clay Products Co.; pres. Kittanning Cemetery Co. Mem. Mid-West Penn Ins. Agents Assn., Phi Gamma Delta. Republican. Presbyterian (trustee First Presbyn. Ch.). Mason. (K.T., 32°, Shriner), K.P. Clubs: Kittanning Country, Kiwanis (pres 1924). Home: 310 N. Water St. Office: Colwell-Arnold Bldg., Kittanning, Pa.

ARNOLD, C. Russell; exec. v.p. and dir. South Phila. Nat. Bank. Home: 272 N. Lansdowne Ave., Lansdowne, Pa. Office: Second and Pine Sts., Philadelphia, Pa.

ARNOLD, Clifford Hood, physician; b. Gladwyne, Pa., Aug. 31, 1888; s. Herbert A. (M.D.) and Louise A. (Harley) A.; student U. of Pa., 1907-08; M.D., Med. Coll. of Va., 1913; m. Audrey R. Dillon, June 5, 1917; children—Louise Harley, Audrey Virginia. Interne St. Lukes Hosp., South Bethlehem, Pa., 1913-

14; in pvt. practice, Chester, Pa., 1914-16, 1919-20; in pvt. practice at Ardmore, Pa. since 1921; mem. staff Curtis Clinic, Jefferson Hosp.; dir. Lower Merion Federal Savings and Loan Assn. Served as lieut. Med. Corps, Pa. N.G., Mexican border campaign, 1914-17; capt. Med. Corps, U.S.A., 1917-19. Republican. Baptist. Mason. Home: 28 School Lane, Ardmore, Pa.

ARNOLD, D(aniel) H(arvey) Hill, lawyer; b. Beverly, W.Va., Jan. 18, 1879; s. Thomas J. and Eugenia (Hill) A.; student Davidson Coll., Davidson, N.C., 1896-98; A.B., Washington & Lee U., Lexington, Va., 1900; student U. of Mich., Ann Arbor, 1901-02; m. Mary Ann Denham, Oct. 12, 1906 (died 1909); m. 2d Rebecca Andrews, Aug. 4, 1914; children—Elizabeth Eugenia, Rebecca Andrews. Admitted to W.Va. bar, 1902, and engaged in gen. practice of law at Elkins since 1902; mem. firm Arnold & Crawford since 1938; dir. and counsel Tygarts Valley Nat. Bank, Elkins, W.Va. Past pres. Elkins Chamber of Commerce. Trustee Davis & Elkins Coll., Elkins, W.Va., 1925-38. Mem. Am. Bar Assn., W.Va. Bar Assn. (past v.p.), Randolph Co. Bar Assn. (past pres.), Kappa Alpha. Democrat. Presbyn. Mason. Home: 106 Boundary Av. Office: Arnold Bldg., Davis Av., Elkins, W.Va.

ARNOLD, Frank Atkinson; b. Westboro, Mass., June 2, 1867; s. Daniel W. and Frances (Fay) A.; high sch. and coll. preparatory edn., also spl. study; m. Harriet Eudora Gurney, Nov. 27, 1890; children—Dorothy Faye (Mrs. W. O. Graham), Hilda Gurney (Mrs. F. S. Pease), Cyril Durrell, Donald Woodward, Frank Denman, Phyllis Eudora (Mrs. C. D. Rudolph). Engaged in mercantile business to 1893; editor and publisher The Trade Monthly, Boston, 1894-97; asst. advertising manager The Christian Endeavor World, Boston, and editor Literary Bulletin, 1898-99; on staff Boston Journal, 1900; editor and gen. mgr. Dry Goods Chronicle, and Modern Merchant, New York, 1900-02; v.p., sec., sec. Colonial Press, Boston, pubs. The Suburban, 1904-07; v.p., sec. Suburban Press, New York, 1907-10; pres. same and pub. Suburban Life Mag., afterwards Countryside Mag., 1911-16; spl. lit. work for Arnold Arboretum, Boston, 1917; sec. and dir. Frank Seaman, Inc., adv. agency, New York, 1917-26; dir. of development Nat. Broadcasting Co., 1926-32; v.p. Albert Frank-Guenther Law, Incorporated, 1932-33; consultant in radio broadcasting since 1933; lecturer at Coll. of City of New York since 1930; nat. export chmn. Am. Assn. Adv. Agencies; trade adviser Nat. Foreign Trade Council; v.p. and asso. managing dir. Inst. of Pub. Relations. Conglist. Republican. Mason. Mem. Mayor's Com. on Nat. Defense (New York). Club: Advertising. Writer on subject of radio advertising; author of Broadcast Advertising the Fourth Dimension, 1931, Television Edit., 1933. Home: Upper Montclair, N.J. Office: 120 Wall St., New York, N.Y.

ARNOLD, Harrison Heikes, univ. prof.; b. Dillsburg, Pa., Mar. 25, 1889; s. Noah and Fannie (Heikes) A.; student West Chester (Pa.) State Normal Sch., 1909-11; A.B., Haverford (Pa.) Coll., 1918; M.A., Harvard, 1919, Ph.D., 1926; m. Jessie Millar Anderson, June 24, 1920; children—David Anderson, George Peter. Asst. business mgr., West Chester (Pa.) State Normal Sch., 1911-14; teacher Romance languages, Pa. State Coll., 1919-32, prof. of Spanish since 1932. Mem. Am. Assn. of Teachers of Spanish, Modern Language Assn. of America, Phi Beta Kappa, Phi Sigma Iota. Democrat. United Brethren Ch. Author: Marta y Maria por A. Palacio Valdes, 1929; contbr. numerous articles on Spanish language and literature to language jours. Address: 519 Holmes St., State College, Pa.

ARNOLD, Jesse Oglevee, physician; b. Fayette Co., Pa., Dec. 28, 1868; s. John and Mary (Oglevee) A.; ed. Southwestern State Normal, Mount Union Coll.; student Jefferson Med. Coll., 1893-97, M.D., 1897; m. Olive B. Dunn, Oct. 14, 1897; 1 dau., Mary Evelyn (Mrs. Herbert Braun). Interne Jefferson Med. Coll. Hosp., 1896-97; asso. prof. in Temple U. Med. Sch., 1904-14, clin. prof., 1914-26, prof. obstetrics since 1926. Fellow Am. Coll. Surgeons.

Protestant. Club: Phila. Medical. Author: Temple University Obstetrical Guide-Book, 3d edit., 1938. Home: 6517 N. 12th St. Office: 4149 N. Broad St., Philadelphia, Pa.

ARNOLD, John Carlisle, lawyer; b. Curwensville, Pa., Mar. 10, 1887; s. William C. and Jane (Irvin) A.; ed. U. of Pa. Law Sch., grad. 1909; m. Clare E. Platt, Sept. 17, 1913; children—Jane I. (Mrs. Charles E. Mann), John C., Jr., Daniel P., Mary L. Admitted to Pa. bar, 1910, engaged in practice at DuBois, 1910-18, at Clearfield since 1918; admitted to all courts of Pa., U.S. Dist. Court and U.S. Circuit Court of Appeals; served as solicitor Borough of DuBois, 1915, and City of DuBois, 1916-18; dist. atty. Clearfield Co., 1918-25; mem. firm Arnold & Platt, 1923-24, Hartswick, Arnold & Platt, 1924-28, Arnold & Smith, 1928-32, Arnold & Chaplin since 1932. Mem. Am. and Clearfield Co. bar assns. Republican. Methodist. Mason (32°, Shriner). Club: Acorn of DuBois. Home: 105 Elizabeth St. Office: Progress Bldg., Clearfield, Pa.

ARNOLD, John Harold, farming; b. Fayette Co., Pa., Nov. 25, 1900; s. Espy Emerson and Nancy Annette (Junk) A.; ed. high sch. Dunbar Twp., Pa., 1916-20; B.S., Pa. State Coll. 1924; unmarried. Worked on home farm of father, 1924-37, propr. and mgr. own farm since 1937; supervised thrift gardens, 1933; served as mem. Pa. Ho. of Rep., 1935-39; asst. State Exec. Officer, Pa. Agr. Conservation Program since 1937. Mem. Nat., State, County and local Grange. Democrat. Baptist. Home: Vanderbilt, Pa. Office: 140 S. 2d St., Harrisburg, Pa.

ARNOLD, Robert Samuel Lee, sales engr.; b. Paint Lick, Ky., June 8, 1897; s. Robert Lee and Mary Francis (Cochran) A.; B.M.E., U. of Ky., 1919; m. Emma Kenderdine Boehmer, Apr. 28, 1928; 1 son, Holbrook Townsend. Draftsman Ford Motor Co., 1919; sales engr. Am. Blower Co., Pittsburgh, and Columbus, O., 1920-22, mgr. domestic engr. dept., 1923; sales engr. York Heating and Ventilating Corpn., 1923-24, asst. sales mgr., 1924-26, mgr. Phila. dist., 1926-31; dist. mgr. Carrier York Corpn., 1931-33; dist. supervisor Carrier Products Corpn., 1933-34; dist. mgr. unit heater div. Herman Nelson Corpn., 1934-36; prop. Robt. Arnold Sales & Engring. Co. and pres. Lowell Air Conditioning Corpn. since 1936. Served as aviator with Unit No. 6 U.S. Navy, 1918. Mem. Am. Soc. Heating and Ventilating Engrs., Kappa Sigma, Mystic 13. Republican. Baptist. Clubs: Kiwanis (Phila.); Swarthmore (Pa.) Economic Discussion Group. Pioneer in unit heater method of heating; inventor of heating and ventilating unit for garages which introduces fresh air and removes carbon monoxide gas; author of papers and articles for tech. socs. and jours. Home: 6391 Sherwood Rd., Overbrook. Office: 409 Otis Bldg., Philadelphia, Pa.

ARNOVICH, Morris, professional baseball player; student Superior (Wis.) State Teachers Coll. Began with Superior and Hazleton baseball teams; outfielder with Phila. Nat. League Baseball Team since 1937. Mem. Nat. League All-Star Team, 1939. Address: care Phila. Nat. League Baseball Club, Philadelphia, Pa.

ARNY, Henry Vinecome, pharmaceutical chemist; b. Phila., Feb. 28, 1868; s. Louis Christian and Sarah (Shinn) A.; Ph.G., Phila. Coll. Pharmacy, 1889; studied U. of Berlin, 1893-94, U. of Göttingen, 1892-93, 1894-96, Ph.D., 1896; m. Katharine Moody Smith, Apr. 22, 1903; children—Robert Allen, Sarah Elizabeth, Malcolm Moody, Francis Vinacomb. Prof. pharmacy and dean. Coll. of Pharmacy, Western Reserve University, Cleveland, 1897-1911; prof. chemistry, 1911-37, dean, 1930-37, Coll. of Pharmacy, Columbia Univ., now retired. Editor of The Druggists' Circular, 1914-15, Year Book, Am. Pharm. Assn., 1916-22; technical editor of American Druggist since 1928. Remington medalist, 1922; Ebert medalist, 1924. Mem. com. of revision U.S. Pharmacopœia, com. of revision Nat. Formulary; pres. Am. Conf. of Pharm. Faculties, 1915-16; mem. exec. com. Am. Metric Assn., 1916-20; chmn. Nat. Conf. on Pharm. Research, 1922-29; fellow Chem. Soc.

(Eng.); member Am. Pharm. Assn. (pres. 1923-24), Am. Chem. Soc. A.A.A.S., Franklin Inst.; hon. mem. German Pharm. Soc. (Berlin), Pharm. Soc. of Great Britain. Democrat. Episcopalian. Club: Columbia Faculty (New York). Author: Principles of Pharmacy, 1909, 4th edit., 1936. Home: 135 Watchung Av., Upper Montclair, N.J.

ARONOFF, Max, musician; b. Phila., Pa., Dec. 25, 1906; s. Abraham and Rose (Zunikoff) A.; student Central High Sch., Phila., Curtis Inst. of Music, 1924-31; m. Reba Hoffstein, May 24, 1932; 1 dau., Dorothy Ann. Began as violinist at age of 7; became mem. faculty Curtis Inst. of Music, Phila., 1931; appeared as soloist of viola and with Curtis String Quartet making tours of U.S. and Europe; represented Am. music at Silver Jubilee of King George; played at White House, and for Lady Astor in London, etc. Home: 1019 Keystone Av., Upper Darby, Pa. Office: Curtis Inst. of Music, Rittenhouse Square, Philadelphia, Pa.

ARONSON, Harvey Morton, lawyer, pres. Keystone Grinder and Mfg. Co.; b. Pittsburgh, Pa., July 25, 1892; s. Samuel B. and Adelaide (Goldman) A.; student U. of Pittsburgh, 1910-13; m. Mildred Newman, June 26, 1918; children—Robert S., Edward N. Solicitor Uptown Bd. of Trade, 1914-17, Squirrel Hill Bd. of Trade, 1924, Pa. Premium Bldg. and Loan Assn. of North Side, Pittsburgh, since 1934, Garfield Premium and Loan Assn. No. 2 and No. 3 of Allegheny City, Pa., since 1934; pres. and dir. Keystone Grinder and Mfg. Co., Pittsburgh, since 1920; Sol. Associated Buyers, Inc. Served as C.P.O., U.S. Naval Res., 1917-21. Sec. and dir. Emma Farms Assn.; pres. Men's Soc. of Rodef Shalom Temple (rep. of Men's Soc. on bd. of trustees). Mem. Squirrel Hill Bd. of Trade, Allegheny Co. Bar Assn., Pa. State Bar Assn., Am. Bar Assn., Am. Legion (Post No. 5), Pi Tau Pi. Republican. Jewish religion. Mason, A. O. Fay Lodge No. 676. Clubs: Concordia, Westmoreland Country (Pittsburgh). Home: 1942 Wightman St. Office: 2108 Law & Finance Bldg., Pittsburgh, Pa.

ARONSON, I. Leonard; in gen. practice of law since 1899; officer or dir. numerous corpns. Home: 2000 Wendover St. Office: Grant Bldg., Pittsburgh, Pa.

ARROWSMITH, Harold Noel; canon-in-charge Cathedral of the Incarnation. Home: 3707 Greenway St., Baltimore, Md.

ARTER, Theodore; editor Altoona Tribune. Office: 1110 12th St., Altoona, Pa.

ARTHUR, Edmund Watts, lawyer and U.S. commr.; b. Allegheny, Pa., July 15, 1874; s. Hugh Wilson and Anna E. (Watts) A.; A.B., U. of Pittsburgh, 1895; m. Anna M. Robertson, June 26, 1902; children—Harriet (Mrs. Smyers), Anna (Mrs. Kennedy), Margaret R., Mary H., William R. Admitted to bar, 1897. Sch. dir. Cheswick Borough, Pa., 1904-20; mem. council Ben Avon Borough, Pa., since 1928; U. S. commr. Western Dist. of Pa. since 1926. Dir. Rasner & Dinger Co. Solicitor and mem. bd. dirs. Western Pa. Humane Soc. Mason (32°; Past Master). Author (vol. of essays): The Country Rambler, 1934; also newspaper and mag. articles. Home: 7438 Perrysville Av., Ben Avon, Pa. Office: 612 Magee Bldg., Pittsburgh, Pa.

ARTHUR, Herbert Spencer; vice-pres. and dir. Daily News Co. Home: 637 Walnut St., McKeesport, Pa.

ARTHUR, J(ames) Howard, banker; b. Pittsburgh, Pa., Aug. 21, 1884; s. James B. and Olive (White) A.; student Pittsburgh pub. schs. and Pittsburgh Acad.; m. Marion Cameron, Mar. 27, 1918; 1 son, William Howard. Began with Peoples Nat. Bank; with First Nat. Bank at Pittsburgh since 1902, now vice-pres. and cashier; dir. and trustee of stockholders of Nat. Erie Corpn. Dir. and ex-pres. Am. Inst. of Banking; dir. Investment Bankers Assn., mem. constitution and by-laws coms., 1925-26, state and local taxation com., 1928-29, group chairmen's com., 1928-30, business conduct com., 1933-36, gov., 1936-37. Mem. Western Pa. Group Investment Bankers Assn. (former sec. and treas., vice-chmn. and mem. exec. com.), Pittsburgh Chamber of Commerce. Clubs: Bankers (president and dir.), Duquesne, Highland Country. Home: 38 N. Harrison Av., Bellevue. Office: Wood and 5th Sts., Pittsburgh, Pa.

ARTHUR, Samuel John, clergyman; b. Barrie, Ontario, Can., Feb. 13, 1859; s. Samuel and Mary Ann (McKee) A.; student Collegiate Inst., Barrie, Toronto Bapt. Coll., 1883-88; B.D., Crozer Theol. Sem., Chester, Pa., 1895; S.T.D. and D.D., Webster Univ., Atlanta, Ga., 1931; m. Jessie May Hand, Sept. 18, 1889; children—Joletta May (Mrs. Walter D. Rhoads), Hulda Houston (Mrs. Harold M. Matthews), Jennie Wanda (Mrs. Harold C. Tefft), George Gordon (deceased), Wendell R. (deceased). Ordained to the ministry of Baptist Ch., 1888; pastor Parkdale Ch., Toronto, 1888-90, Emmanuel Ch., Schnectady, N. Y., 1891-94, Luzerne Av. Ch., West Pittston, Pa., 1895-1901, First Ch., Erie Pa., 1901-07, North Ch., Jersey City, Pa., 1907-12, Emmanuel Ch., Winnipeg, Manitoba, 1912-16; interim pastor, Avon-by-the-Sea, N.J., 1917-20; pastor Wayne Park Ch., Erie Pa., 1920-37; now interim pastor of Pa. Bapt. Convention. Home: 220 W. 18th St., Erie, Pa.

ARTHUR, William Cathcart, mfg. fasteners; b. Bellevue, Pa.; s. Hugh Wilson and Anna Elizabeth (Watts) A.; A.B., U. of Pittsburgh, 1907; LL.B., U. of Pittsburgh Law Sch., 1913; m. Sara Margaret Warrick, Sept. 16, 1918 (dec.); children—William Cathcart, James Hartford. Employed as bank clk. and high sch. instr., 1907-14; admitted to Pa. bar and in gen. practice of law at Pittsburgh, 1914-17; asst. sec. B. F. Goodrich Co., 1917-27; sec., then sec. and treas., later vice-pres. and sec., now pres. and dir. Talon, Inc. (formerly Hookless Fastener Co.), Meadville, Pa. Trustee Meadville City Hosp. Dir. and past-pres. Pa. State Chamber of Commerce; dir. Meadville Chamber of Commerce. Mem. Phi Gamma Delta. Mem. M.E. Ch. Clubs: Meadville Country (dir.); Duquesne, University (Pittsburgh); Up-Town, National Democratic (New York). Home: 608 Chestnut St. Office: Talon, Inc., Meadville, Pa.

ARTHURS, Ann C.; clin. prof. otolaryngology and chief of ear, nose and throat dept., Woman's Hosp. Address: 1831 Chestnut St., Philadelphia, Pa.

ARTHURS, Stanley M., artist; b. Kenton, Del., Nov. 27, 1877; s. Joshua M. and Nancy M. (Wright) A.; ed. Drexel Inst., Phila.; studied art under Howard Pyle, Wilmington, Del.; unmarried. Mural paintings: "Occupation of Little Rock, Ark., by Federal Troops," in governor's room, State Capitol, St. Paul, Minn.; "Landing of De Vries, at Swanendale, 1631," Univ. of Del., Newark, Del.; "The Drum Beat of a Nation," "The Crusaders," "The First Day of Peace"—all in State Capitol, Dover, Del.; life size painting of George Washington, American Club, Shanghai, China; "Arrival of Governor Printz at Fort Christina, 1642," in Gray School, Wilmington, Del. Member Architectural League of New York, Soc. Mural Painters, Salmagundi Club (New York), Wilmington Soc. Fine Arts (dir.), Franklin Inn Club (Phila.). Rotarian. Writer and illustrator hist. articles in Scribner's Mag.; 54 paintings pub. in vol. "The American Historical Scene." Home: 1305 Franklin St., Wilmington, Del.

ARZT, Max, rabbi; b. Poland, Mar. 20, 1897; s. Hyman and Anna (Grossbach) A.; brought to U.S., 1902, naturalized, 1915; B.S., Coll. City of N.Y., 1918; A.M., Columbia U., 1921; Rabbi, Jewish Theol. Sem. of America, 1921, D.H.L., same, 1934; m. Esther Podolsky, Mar. 7, 1922; children—Miriam, Aaron David, Raphael Baruch. Rabbi Temple Beth El, Stamford, Conn., 1921-24; rabbi Temple Israel, Scranton, Pa., since 1924; lecturer Jewish Theol. Sem. of America. Dir. Scranton Y.M.H.A. Council Social Agencies. President Rabbinical Assembly of America. Republican. Mason. I.O. O.F. Home: 809 Monroe Av., Scranton, Pa.

ASH, Arthur F., M.D., attending asso. ophthalmologist Christ Hosp.; cons. ophthalmologist Margaret Hague Maternity Hosp. Address: 710 Boulevard East, Weehawken, N.J.

ASH, Frank W., M.D.; attending surgeon St. Joseph's Hosp. Address: 180 Carroll St., Paterson, N.J.

ASH, William Cook, educator; b. Chester Co., Pa., April 27, 1876; s. William Rambo and Julia (Cook) A.; grad. Northeast High Sch., Phila., 1893; B.S. in Edn., U. of Pa., 1917, A.M., 1919; m. Mary Weest, Sept. 11, 1901; children—Lane Cook, Ruth. Worked in machine shop and as electrician until 1907; prin. Phila. Trades Schs. (day and evening), 1907-18; dir. of observation and prin. Model Sch., U. of Pa. Summer Sch., 1909-12; dir. summer training courses for continuation class teachers, Phila., since 1914; dir. practical arts and vocational edn., Phila. pub. schs., Dec. 1, 1918-22 also dir. vocational teacher training, U. of Pa.; prof. vocational edn. and dir. of vocational teacher training, U. of Pa., since 1922. Mem. N.E.A., Pa. State Ednl. Assn., Phila. Teachers' Assn., Nat. Soc. for Vocational Edn., Soc. Coll. Teachers of Edn., Phi Delta Kappa. Republican. Methodist. Mason (K.T.). Organized and developed vocational edn. in pub. schs. of Phila., the first city in U.S. to have a public trades sch. Home: 828 Wynnewood Rd., Philadelphia, Pa.

ASHBROOK, Frank Getz, fur animal expert; b. York, Pa., Oct. 20, 1892; s. Frank De Huff and Sarah Rebecca (Getz) A.; grad. high sch., York, 1910; B.S. in Agr., Pa. State Coll., 1914; m. Caroline Brigham McKinley, July 14, 1924. Jr. animal husbandman, Bur. Animal Industry, U.S. Dept. Agr., 1914-18; also teacher night sch., Vet. Coll., George Washington U., 1914; with French High Commn. (on leave from Dept. Agr.), 1919-20; engaged in gen. farming, Pa., 1920-21; in charge fur-bearing animal work, Div. of Fur Resources, Biol. Survey, U.S. Dept. Agr. since 1921. Commr. gen. for U.S., Fur Trade Expn. and Congress, Leipzig, Germany, May 31-Sept. 30, 1930. Served as 1st lt., inf., U.S.A., Feb. 1918-April 1919. Mem. Lambda Gamma Delta, Chi Phi. Mason. Author: Our Furry Friends, 1927; Fur Farming for Profit, 1928; Furry Friends, 1929; Rabbits for Food and Fur, 1930; also author of govt. bulls. on fur farming, etc. Home: 36 Winston Drive, Bethesda, Md. Office: Biological Survey, U.S. Dept. Agr., Washington, D.C.

ASHBURY, Howard Elmer, physician, radiologist; b. Baltimore, Md., April 26, 1880; s. Joseph Martin and Emma Bartlett (Elmer) A.; Ph.G., Md. Coll. of Pharmacy, 1899; M.D., U. of Maryland, 1903; m. Ellen Hicks, January 9, 1904; children—Howard Hicks (M.D.), Helen Bartlett. In practice of radiology, Baltimore since 1903; house surgeon Hosp. for Crippled and Deformed Children, Baltimore, 1903-08; asst. in orthopedic surgery Johns Hopkins Hosp., 1909-17; radiologist St. Joseph's Hosp. until 1936, Hebrew Hosp., U. of Md. Hosp. until 1917; consulting radiologist Vets. Adminstrn., Baltimore Regional Office. Prof. radiology, Army Med. Sch., Washington, 1917-19; lt. col. Med. Reserve Corps, U.S. Army. Mem. Am. Roentgen Ray Soc., A.M.A., Baltimore City Med. Soc., Med. and Chirurg. Faculty of Md. Democrat. Presbyterian (deacon). Mason. Home: 2515 Pickwick Rd. Office: Medical Arts Bldg., Baltimore, Md.

ASHCRAFT, Charles Edward, Jr., civil engr.; b. Highlands, Campbell Co., Ky., April 15, 1884; s. Charles Edward and Ella Louise (Toy) A.; C.E., U. of Cincinnati, 1908; m. Edna May Miller, Dec. 14, 1909; children—Charles Edward, III, Mary Virginia. Faculty asst., Coll. of Engring., U. of Cincinnati, 1906-08; jr. engr., U.S. Army Engrs., 1908-17; supt. constrn., Foundation Co. of N.Y., 1917; design engr., Imperial Irrigation Dist., Calexico, Calif., 1918; supt. constrn., Foundation Co. of N.Y., 1918; gen. supt. constrn., Baker-Dunbar-Allen Co., Pittsburgh, 1918-19; design engr., Toupet, Beil & Conley, Inc., Pittsburgh, 1919-20; chief engr., Beckwith Machinery Co., Pittsburgh, 1920-28; Pittsburgh dist. mgr., Sauerman Bros., Inc., of Chicago, 1928-30; gen. mgr. Dayton Whirley Co., Dayton, O., 1930-31; cons. engr., private practice, Pittsburgh, 1931-36; asst. engr., U.S. Army Engrs., Conchas Dam, N.M., 1936; asso. engr., U.S. Army Engrs., Pittsburgh, Pa., since 1936. Registered Professional Engr. in Pa. Mem.

Soc. Am. Mil. Engrs., Nat. Soc. Professional Engrs., Pa. Soc. Professional Engrs., Delta Tau Delta. Presbyterian. Mason. Contbr. articles to engring. jours. Home: 31 S. Grandview Av., Crafton, Pittsburgh, Pa. Office: New Post Office Bldg., Pittsburgh, Pa.

ASHCRAFT, Leon Thomas, surgeon; b. Philadelphia, Pa., Nov. 4, 1866; s. Samuel F. and Sarah (Godshall) A.; Ph.B., Dickinson Coll., Pa., 1887, A.M., 1890; M.D., Hahnemann Med. Coll., Phila., 1890; m. Eleida Bosler, June 18, 1908; children—Leon Thomas, John Joseph Bosler. Practiced in Phila. since 1890; prof. urology, Hahnemann Med. Coll. and Hosp. Home: 2039 Walnut St., Philadelphia, Pa.

ASHE, Edmund Marion, art instr.; b. New York, N.Y., June 19, 1870; s. William Nathaniel and Katherine Anne (Long) A.; ed. pub. schs. and pvt. tutors; student Met. Mus. of Art, Sch. of Art, 1887-88, Art Students League, 1888-92; m. Estelle Egbert, Sept. 5, 1893; children—Dorothy Estelle (Mrs. Charles Lewis Thompson), Edmund Marion. Illustrator on staff of Harper's mag., 1893-94; free lance contbr. to mags., 1894-1910; also illustrator of books, head of dept. of painting and design. Carnegie Inst. of Technology since 1928; represented by painters in Pa. State Coll., Carnegie Inst. and private galleries. Mem. Art Commn. for the City of Pittsburgh, Tau Sigma Delta. Democrat. Episcopalian. Home: 1241 Murdock Rd., Pittsburgh, Pa.

ASHEN, David Jacob, lawyer; b. Newark, N.J., March 30, 1906; s. Louis and Rose Leah (Jacobs) A.; ed. Columbia U., 1923-25; LL.B. cum laude, N.J. Law Sch. now Newark U., 1929; unmarried. Engaged as law clk. with Luce & Kipp, 1927-30; admitted to N.J. bar as atty., 1929, as counsellor, 1933; atty. with Luce & Kipp, Rutherford, N.J., 1930-31; mem. firm Luce, Kipp & Ashen, 1932 to 1936, Kipp, Ashen & Kipp since 1936. U.S. Conciliation Commr. since 1937. Pres. Bergen Co. Young Rep. Club, 1935-36. Mem. Bergen Co. Bar Assn., King's Bench, Phi Epsilon Pi. Republican. Mem. Jewish religion. Mason. Clubs: Lions (Rutherford); Yountakah Country (Nutley). Home: 15 E. Newell Av. Office: 10 Ames Av., Rutheford, N.J.

ASHFORD, Thomas F., Jr., pres. and dir. Second Pool Coal Co. Home: 27 Hazel Drive, Mt. Lebanon, Pa. Office: Duquesne Way and Sixth St., Pittsburgh, Pa.

ASHLEY, George Hall, geologist; b. Rochester, N.Y., Aug. 9, 1866; s. Roscoe B. and Anna (Hall) A.; M.E., Cornell Univ., 1890, A.M., 1892; Ph.D., Stanford Univ., 1894; Sc.D., Lehigh University, 1937; m. Mary E. Martin, July 11, 1895. Paleontologist, Rochester, N.Y., 1889-91; asst. geologist, Geol. Survey of Ark., 1891-93; teaching in Calif., 1894-96; asst. state geologist of Ind., 1896-1900; prof. biology and geology and curator of museum, Coll. of Charleston, S.C., 1900-03; prof. pharmacognosy, Med. Coll. State of S.C., 1901-03; asst. geologist, 1901-05, geologist, 1905-12, administrative geologist, 1912-19, U.S. Geol. Survey; state geologist of Pa., 1919—. Acting prof. geology, Vanderbilt U., 1917. Fellow A.A.A.S.; mem. Geol. Soc. Am., Geol. Soc. Washington, Washington Acad. Sciences, Pa. Acad. Sciences, Am. Inst. Mining and Met. Engrs., Coal Mining Inst. America, etc.; hon. mem. Tenn. Acad., Ind. Acad. Science, S.C. Pharm. Assn.; ex-pres. Internat. Assn. of Torch Clubs. Author of numerous geol. reports and articles in lit. and tech. jours. Home: 3037 N. Front St., Harrisburg, Pa.

ASHLEY-MONTAGU, Montagu Francis, anatomist and anthropologist; b. London, Eng., June 28, 1905; s. Charles and Mary (Plotnick) A.-M.; A.M., Cambridge (Eng.) U., 1926; U. of London, Eng., 1926; student U. of Florence, Italy, 1928-29; Ph.D., Columbia U. 1937; came to U.S., 1930, naturalized, 1939; m. Helen Marjorie Peakes, Sept. 18, 1931; children—Audrey, Barbara. Began an hon. research asst., British Mus., London, Eng., 1926; researcher, Columbia U., 1927-28, Florence (Italy) U., 1928-29; curator phys. anthropology, Wellcome Hist. Med. Mus., London, 1929-30; lecturer child growth and development, New Sch. for Social Research, N.Y., 1931; asst. prof. anatomy, N.Y.U., 1931-38; asso. prof. anatomy, Hahnemann Med. Coll., Phila., Pa., since 1938. Lecturer in physical anthropology, Acad. of Natural Sciences, Philadelphia, since 1939; lecturer in morphology, School of Architecture, Columbia, since 1939. Served as guardsman, Welsh Guards, British Army, 1919. Mem. Internat. Com. for the Standardization of Anthropometric Techniques. Hon. corr. mem. Anthrop. Soc. of Florence, Italy; mem. A.A.A.S., Am. Assn. Anatomists, Am. Assn. Phys. Anthropologists, Am. Assn. Anthropologists, Am. Ethnol. Assn., History of Science Soc., Am. Assn. Scientific Workers, Soc. for the Study of Child Growth and Development, Sigma Xi. Fellow Royal Anthrorp. Inst. of Gt. Britain and Ireland. Awarded Morris Chaim prize, N.Y., 1934. Home: 26 Narbrook Park. Office: 235 N. 15th St., Philadelphia, Pa.

ASHMAN, Louis Sidney, chmn. exec. com. and dir. Allied Charter Trust Co. Home: S. W. corner Lake Drive and Callow Av. Office: 211 E. Fayette St., Baltimore, Md.

ASHTON, Dorothy Laing, physician; b. Phila., Pa., Mar. 25, 1888; d. Taber and Margaret (Laing) A.; grad. Swarthmore Perp. Sch., 1905; A.B., Bryn Mawr Coll., 1910; M.D., U. of Pa. Med. Sch., 1921. Engaged in practice of medicine and surgery at Swarthmore, Pa. since 1922; asst. in obstetrics, Preston Retreat, Phila., 1922-27; asst. in obstetrics and gynecology, Methodist Hosp., 1922-27; asst. and asso. in gynecology, Woman's Hosp., 1922-30; clin. prof. gynecology, Woman's Med. Coll. of Pa., 1930-39; asst. in gynecology, Phila. Gen Hosp. since 1935; mem. courtesy staff, Del. Co. Hosp. since 1935. Fellow mem. Am. Coll. Surgeons; Phila. Co. Med. Soc., Pa. Med. Soc., A.M.A. Home: 502 Cedar Lane, Swarthmore, Pa.

ASHTON, Ethel V., artist; b. Phila., Pa.; d. Charles M. and Mary V. (Carey) Ashton; ed. Moore Inst. and Sch. of Design for Women and Pa. Acad. of Fine Arts; also European galleries and classes; unmarried. Exhibited paintings: Pa. Acad. of Fine Arts, Phila. Sketch Club, Art Club of Phila., Phila. Art Alliance, Art Inst. of Chicago, N.Y. Gallieries, Independent Artists, and private collections. Awarded hon. mention Phila. Art Club, 1928, Sketch Club, 1928, 1937. Mem. Moore Inst. Alumni, Phila. Art Alliance, Independent Artists, Am. Fed. of Arts. Home: Garden Court, 47th and Pine Sts. Studio: 225 S. 6th St., Philadelphia, Pa.

ASHTON, Leonard C., insurance; b. Germantown, Pa., Apr. 23, 1887; s. Taber and Margaret Shotwell (Laing) A.; student Swarthmore Coll.; A.B., Harvard U. LL.B., U. of Pa.; m. Ruth N. Potter, Jan. 27, 1917. With Provident Mutual Life Ins. Co. of Phila. since 1913, becoming sec., 1918, vice-pres. and sec. since 1929. Home: 409 Elm Av., Swarthmore, Pa. Office: 4601 Market St., Philadelphia, Pa.

ASHWORTH, Ben H., lawyer; b. Rocky Gap, Va., July 9, 1888; s. Robert Matthews and Sarah (Honaker) A.; student Concord State Coll., Athens, W. Va., 1902-05; LL.B., W.Va. U., Morgantown, W.Va., 1916; student Sorbonne U., Paris, France, 1919; unmarried. Admitted to W. Va. bar, 1916; in practice at Northfork, W.Va., 1917; in pvt. practice at Beckley, W.Va., since 1919. Served as corpl. 137th Inf., 35th Div., U.S. Army, 1917-19. Mem. W.Va. State Senate, 1924-28; city solicitor, Beckley, W.Va., since 1938. Mem. W.Va. Bar Assn., Am. Legion. Democrat. Baptist. Mason, Odd Fellow. Club: Raleigh County Country (Beckley, W.Va.). Home: 14 Heber St. Office: 58 Main St., Beckley, W.Va.

ASKEW, Sarah Byrd, librarian; b. Dayton, Ala.; d. Samuel Horton and Thyrza (Pickering) A.; ed. high sch., Atlanta, Ga.; Pratt Inst. Library Sch., 1903-04; hon. Dr. Library Science, Rutgers, 1930. Began as asst. in Cleveland Pub. Library, 1903; organizer N.J. Pub. Library Commission, 1905, and has continued with same, serving as librarian, 1913-30, sec. since 1930; reference librarian N.J. State Library, 1909-12. Library war service, 1917-19. Nat. chmn. on children's reading, Nat. Congress of Parents-Teachers, 1924-29, asso. chmn. since 1929; mem. Bd. of Edn., Trenton, since 1922. Mem. A.L.A. (vice-pres. 1938-39), N.J. Library Assn., Patrons of Husbandry, League for Creative Work (Ridgewood, N.J.). Presbyn. Clubs: Contemporary, Zonta Club. Author: (brochure) The Man, the Place and the Book, 1916. Contbr. to professional mags. Home: 234 W. State St. Address: State House Annex, Trenton, N.J.

ASPINALL, Richard, educator; b. Bolton, Eng., Dec. 1, 1881; s. Archibald James and Catherine (Barlow) A.; came to U.S., 1906, naturalized, 1911; A.B., West Va. Wesleyan Coll., Buckhannon, W.Va., 1912; D.B., Drew U., Madison, N.J., 1914; A.M., New York U., 1914, Ph.D., 1926; student Oxford U., Eng., summer 1921; m. Anne Maude Rusmisell, June 11, 1912; children—Catherine Virginia, Samuel Rusmisell. Instr. of philosophy, W.Va. Wesleyan Coll., Buckhannon, W.Va., 1914-23, sociology, Iliff Sch. of Theology, Denver, Colo., 1926-27, social psychology, Denver U. Summer Sch., 1926; pres. Western State Coll., Gunnison, Colo., 1927-30; asst. to pres., W.Va. U., Morgantown, W.Va., since 1930. Mem. N.E.A., Rotary Internat. (dist. gov. 1920-21), Phi Kappa Sigma, Kappa Delta Pi, Phi Delta Kappa. Republican. Methodist. Mason (32°; venerable master Lodge of Perfection, Morgantown, W.Va.; chaplain Grand Lodge of W.Va.). Club: Rotary (Morgantown, W.Va.). Home: 245 Waitman St., Morgantown, W.Va.

ASPLUNDH, Griffith, arboriculture; b. Bryn Athyn, Pa., May 19, 1896; s. Carl Hjalmar and Emma (Steiger) A.; student Bryn Athyn High Sch., 1911-13; Pierce Business Coll., 1913-14; B.S., Pa. State Coll., 1923; m. Myrtle Nina Elder, July 15, 1926; children—Barr Elder, Paul Scott, Leone. Tree trimming, 1914-19; in business for himself as tree surgeon, 1923-27; formed Asplundh Tree Expert Co., Inc., 1927, pres. until 1937, when business became partnership, now sr. partner; pres. Utilities Line Constrn. Co., Inc.; vice-pres. and dir. Keswick Nat. Bank. Served with 103d Engrs., 28th Div., U.S. Army, with A.E.F., 1917-19; cited for bravery. Republican. Swedenborgian. Club: Huntington Valley Country (Abington, Pa.). Home: Alden Rd., Bryn Athyn, Pa. Office: 820 Homestead Rd., Jenkintown, Pa.

ASTON, James, metallurgical engineer; b. Bury, Eng., June 14, 1876; s. Thomas and Mary (Marsden) A.; B.S. in E.E., U. of Wis., 1898, Ch.E., 1912, D.Sc., 1933; m. Ellen Gertrude Felsen, Jan. 11, 1902; children—Alice Marsden (Mrs. Wm. Schellhammer), Ruth. Brought to U.S., 1879, naturalized, 1906. In steel and foundry business, 1898-1908; research on iron alloys, U. of Wis., 1908-12; prof. metallurgy, U. of Cincinnati, 1912-15; metall. engr. U.S. Bur. of Mines, 1915-16; metallurgist A.M. Byers Co., Pittsburgh, 1916-26; prof. mining and metallurgy and head dept., Carnegie Inst. Tech., 1926-35; also cons. metallurgist A.M. Byers Co. since 1926. Inventor of process for mfr. of wrought iron, displacing hand puddling. Awarded Robert W. Hunt medal, Am. Inst. Mining and Metall. Engrs. Mem. Am. Ry. Engring. Assn., Engrs. Soc. of Western Pa., Am. Soc. for Metals, British Iron and Steel Inst., Am. Iron and Steel Inst., Am. Inst. Mining and Metall. Engrs., Am. Soc. for Testing Materials, Sigma Xi, Tau Beta Pi, Alpha Chi Sigma, Phi Lambda Upsilon. Mason. Club: University (Pittsburgh). Co-author: Johnson's Materials of Construction. Home: 7315 Perrysville Av., Ben Avon, Pittsburgh, Pa.

ASTON, John Geldart, prof. organic chemistry, Pa. State Coll. Address: State College, Pa.

ATCHISON, Clyde Shepherd, coll. prof.; b. Carnegie, Pa., June 28, 1882; s. Thomas Cunningham and Mary Jane (Shepherd) A.; A.B., Westminster Coll., New Wilmington, Pa., 1903; Ph.D., Johns Hopkins U., 1907; grad. student Mass. Inst. Tech., summer 1914, U. of Chicago, summer 1920; LL.D., Westminster Coll. 1934; unmarried. Instr. math. Williams Coll., Williamstown, Mass., 1907-11, asst. prof., 1911-12; prof. and head math. dept., Washington and Jefferson Coll., Washington, Pa., since 1912; engr. on location Erie Ry., summer 1905, 1906, engr. on constrn., summer 1911, 1912; prof. math., U. of W.Va., Morgantown, W.Va., summer sessions, 1922, 1924; on Davis Foundation Travel Fellowship (for development internat. good will), Europe, summer 1935. Served in Plattsburg Mil. Training Camp, 1916; auditor and cost accountant U.S. Shipping Bd., 1918. Consultant for Spl. Com. on Pub. Debt of City of Milwaukee, Wis., 1930. Fellow A.A.A.S.; mem. Am. Math. Soc., Math. Assn. of Am., Phi Beta Kappa. Republican. United Presbyterian (elder). Clubs: Rotary (dir.), Fortnightly (Washington, Pa.) Lectured, winter 1937-38, on Russia after spending summer 1937 traveling there; recent research pub. in magazine, "Concrete," Oct., 1937. Home: 442 E. Beau St. Office: Washington and Jefferson Coll., Washington, Pa.

ATCHISON, Thomas Cunningham, clergyman; b. Bloomfield, O., Oct. 31, 1855; s. John and Nancy (Cunningham) A.; A.B., Muskingum Coll., New Concord, O., 1878, A.M., 1881; grad. Pittsburgh (Pa.) Theol. Sem., 1881; D.D., Westminster Coll., New Wilmington, Pa., 1896; m. Mary Jane Shepherd, June 15, 1881 (died May 31, 1923); children—Clyde Shepherd, Mabel Vernon (dec.), Thomas Calvin. Pastor First U.P. Ch., Carnegie, Pa., 1881-1901, North Av. U.P. Ch., Baltimore, Md., 1901-08, First U.P. Ch., Lawrence, Mass., 1908-34. Mem. bd. ch. extension, U.P. Ch., 1885-1901, com. on denominational young people's work, 1894-98 (chmn. Saratoga Conv. 1898); moderator Synod of N.Y., 1914, 72d Gen. Assembly, Des Moines, Ia., 1930; pres. bd. dirs. Pittsburgh Theol. Sem., 1916-18, 1920-21; supt. missions Boston Presbytery since 1913. Contbr. to religion press. Home: 442 East Beau St., Washington, Pa.

ATCHLEY, Dana Winslow, physician; b. Chester, Conn., July 8, 1892; s. William Abner and Florence Albertine (Ames) A.; B.S., U. of Chicago, 1911; M.D., Johns Hopkins, 1915; m. Mary Cornelia Phister, Sept. 21, 1916; children—Dana Winslow, John Adams, William Ames. Interne Johns Hopkins Hosp., Baltimore; physician specializing in internal medicine; asso. visiting physician Presbyn. Hosp., New York, since 1925; asso. prof. of medicine, Coll. of Physicians and Surgeons, Columbia U., New York; consultant in internal medicine to Northern Westchester Hosp. (Mt. Kisco, N. Y.), Nyack Hosp. (Nyack, N.Y.), Anna Jacques Hosp. (Newburyport, Mass.), Tuxedo (N.J.) Hosp. Trustee Englewood (N.J.) Sch. for Boys. Mem. Harvey Soc., Assn. Am. Physicians, N. Y. Acad. Medicine, Am. Soc. Clin. Investigation; hon. life mem. Am. Mus. Natural History. Episcopalian. Clubs: Englewood, Englewood Field; Old Town Country (Newbury, Mass.); Century Assn. (New York). Home: 262 Oakwood Road, Englewood, N.J. Office: Presbyterian Hospital, New York, N.Y.

ATHERHOLT, Gordon Meade; vice-pres. Gulf Oil Corpn. Office: Gulf Bldg., Pittsburgh, Pa.

ATHERTON, Benjamin Rockwell, pres. Union Nat. Bank of Jersey Shore, Pa.; b. Houlton, Me., Mar. 7, 1863; s. Alexander B. and Mary E. (Barker) A.; student pub. schs., Houlton, Me., 1869-78; m. Myra E. Ellis, Sept. 30, 1915; 1 dau., Louisa M. With Ardell Lumber Co., Center Co., Pa. 1882-86, St. Lawrence Lumber Co., on Greenbriar River, W.Va., 1886-89; running engine and scaling logs, Jones Lumber Co., Philipsburg, Pa., 1889-91; engr. N.Y. Central R.R., 1891-1933; pres. Union Nat. Bank, Jersey Shore, Pa., since 1933. Mem. Brotherhood of Locomotive Engrs. Republican. Baptist (deacon First Baptist Ch., Jersey Shore, Pa., since 1906). Mason. Club: Masonic (Jersey Shore, Pa.). Home: 418 Allegheny St. Office: 222 Allegheny St., Jersey Shore, Pa.

ATHERTON, Fred Bicknell, broker; b. Scranton, Pa., Aug. 11, 1885; s. Bicknell Bennett and Amanda (Safford) A.; grad. Scranton High Sch., 1901; student Lafayette Coll., 1905-07; m. Ruth Lansing, Oct. 29, 1912; children—James Lansing, Frances. Clerk Third Nat. Bank, Scranton, Pa., 1907-09; asso. with J. H. Brooks & Co., mem. New York Stock Exchange, since 1910, as office mgr., 1910-16, partner since 1916; vice-pres. and dir. Brooks Realty Co.; dir. Lackawanna Laundry Co., Associated Laundries of Ill., Temple Coal Co.; vice-pres. and dir. East Bear Ridge Colliery Co. Mem. Sons of the

Revolution, Phi Delta Theta. Republican. Presbyterian. Clubs: Scranton, Country (Scranton); Bankers (New York). Home: 535 Jefferson Ave. Office: Brooks Bldg., Scranton, Pa.

ATHERTON, Thomas Homer, vice-pres. Fidelity-Philadelphia Trust Co.; b. Phila., Pa., Mar. 6, 1874; s. Charles and Sallie C. (Davis) A.; ed. pub. and private schs., Phila.; married; children—Thomas Homer, Mary (Mrs. George Hastings Bond). Began with Internat. Navigation Co., May 1, 1892; with Fidelity Trust Co., now Fidelity-Phila. Trust Co., since 1896, vice-pres. since Dec. 3, 1920; dir. Little Schuylkill Navigation R.R. & Coal Co. Episcopalian. Clubs: Midday, Manufacturers and Bankers, Pen (Phila.). Home: The Cambridge, Alden Park, Germantown, Phila. Office: 135 S. Broad St., Philadelphia, Pa.

ATKIN, Isaac Cubitt Raymond, banker; b. Springfield, Ont., Can., Jan. 2, 1892; s. William Isaac and Martha (Calk) A.; ed. Springfield, Ont., pub. and high schs.; m. Alice Winnifred Flanagan, Sept. 27, 1922; children—Donald Raymond, Frances Winnifred (dec.), James Blakeslee. Came to U.S., 1925, naturalized 1939. Asso. with Traders Bank of Can. and Royal Bank of Can., 1909-25; with J. P. Morgan & Co. since 1925, partner since 1939. Served as capt. in 102d Can. Inf. Batt., C.E.F., 1915-19. Decorated Mil. Cross and bar. Episcopalian. Clubs: Broad Street (New York); Baltusrol Golf, Short Hills (Short Hills, N.J.); United Services (Montreal, Can.). Home: Short Hills, N.J. Office: 23 Wall St., New York, N.Y.

ATKINS, Jacob Thurman, lawyer; b. Lower Chanceford Twp., York Co., Pa., June 1, 1879; s. Preston Geen and Barbara Amanda (Wise) A.; student Lower Chanceford (Pa.) pub. schs., 1884-96, Millersville State Normal Sch., 1899-1900, Dickinson Prep. Sch., Carlisle, Pa., 1901-02; Ph.B., Dickinson Coll., Carlisle, Pa., 1906, M.A., 1908, LL.B., Law Sch., 1908; m. Hattie Pearle McCleary, June 18, 1914; children—Preston Geen, Sue Rebecca. Admitted to Pa. bar, 1909, and since practiced at York, Pa.; asst. dist. atty., York Co., Pa., 1914-22; prothonotary, 1926-30. Dem. chmn. York Co., Pa., 1914-18. Mem. York Co., Pa., bar assn., Kappa Sigma. Democrat. Methodist Episcopal. Knight of Malta. Club: Lions (York, Pa.). Home: 120 E. Cottage Pl. Office: 36 E. Market St., York, Pa.

ATKINS, Paul Moody, economist, author; b. Boston, Mass., Apr. 3, 1892; s. Edward and Martha Moody (Williams) A.; A.B., Yale, 1914; A.M., 1915; grad. study Armour Inst., Chicago; Docteur de l'Université de Paris, 1925; m. Genevieve Bergier, June 15, 1920; children—David Pierre, Henri Bergier, Edward Moody. Cost accountant for Gray & Davis, Inc., 1915; production engr. Square D. Co., 1916; management engr. Acme Wire Co., 1916-17; cons. engr. L. V. Estes, Inc., industrial engrs., 1919-20; instr. in mfg., U. of Chicago, 1920-26; engineer-economist, Ames, Emerich & Co., 1926-30; v.p. Cornell, Linder & Co., 1931; special liquidator of securities for United States Comptroller of Currency, 1932-37; treas. and trustee Alfred P. Sloan Foundation; financial sec. to Alfred P. Sloan, Jr., and treas. New Castle Corpn., Jaxon Corpn., Rene Corpn., Marquette Corpn. and Snug Harbor Development Corpn., 1937-38; consulting economist and financial counsel since 1938; v.p. and dir. Grant & Atkins, Inc., since 1939. Served as 2d lieut. Field Artillery U.S. Army, 1918-19; instr. U.S.A. Arty. Sch., Clermont-Ferrand, France, 1918; lt. col. M. I. Res. Specialist, Am. Commn. to Negotiate Peace, Paris, 1919; Am. sec. of sub-commn. on Czecho-Slovak Affairs, Peace Conf.; pub. credit mem. of Kemmerer Financial Mission, Peru, 1931. Mem. American Economics Assn., Phi Beta Kappa, Beta Theta Pi and Pi Gamma Mu fraternities. Congregationalist. Club: Montclair Athletic. Author: Industrial Cost Accounting for Executives, 1923; A Text Book of Industrial Cost Accounting, 1924; L'Enseignement de la Comptabilité de Prix de Revient dans les Universités et Écoles Supérieures aux Etats-Unis, 1925; Factory Management, 1926; Rozpocet ve Výrobé Prumyslové, 1926; A Bibliography of Production Engineering and Factory Cost Accounting, 1927; Economic Briefs of Europe, 1927; Secondary Reserves of Banks, 1928; Economic Briefs of Latin America, 1928; Bank Secondary Reserves and Investments, 1929; The Investment of Corporation Reserves, 1929; Bank Secondary Reserve and Investment Policies, 1930. Contbr. to econ. and industrial jours. Home: 199 Inwood Av., Upper Montclair, N.J. Office: 55 Liberty St., New York, N.Y.

ATKINS, Paul Sidney, clergyman; b. Hazardville, Conn., Apr. 13, 1882; s. Isaac and Jane (Carter) A.; student Library Training Sch., Springfield, Mass., 1902-03; S.T.B. from Philadelphia Divinity School, 1918; D.D. from same school, 1937; m. Ethel Merrick Weishampel, June 8, 1907; children—Richard Knight, Jane Carter, Lesley Chapin, Elisabeth Roberts, Paul Sidney, Anne Carter, Donald Craige, Carolyn Merrick. Ordained deacon P.E. Ch., 1916, priest, 1917; curate St. Asaph's Ch., Bala, Pa., 1913-17; priest in charge Ch. of Incarnation, Morrisville, Pa., 1917-18; arch-deacon, Harrisburg, 1927-29; rector St. John's Ch., York, Pa., since 1918. Canon of St. Stephen's Cathedral, Harrisburg. Pres. York City Sch. Bd.; mem. York Bd. of Recreation. Chmn. Central Com. on Christian Social Service of the Five Dioceses of the Episcopal Ch. in Pa. Mem. Advisory Council Visiting Nurse Assn., Social Agencies Council, Pa. Pub. Charities Assn., Pa. State Conf. on Welfare. Republican. Mason. Club: Cleric (pres.). Contbr. to various religious publs. Home: 663 Linden Av., York, Pa.

ATKINSON, Ralph Waldo, elec. engr.; b. Smithland, Ia., June 16, 1887; s. Walter Edward and Dessa Flora (Waterman) A.; grad. high sch., Carroll, Ia., 1901; B.S. in E.E., Ia. State Coll., 1906, E.E., 1911; m. Elsie Lee Mercer, June 1, 1916; children—Alice Lee, George Mercer. Asst. to chief engr. Standard Underground Cable Co. (a div. of Gen. Cable Co.), 1908-23, chief elec. engr., 1923-29; dir. high voltage research, Gen. Cable Corpn., since 1929. Dir. Perth Amboy Y.M.C.A., Simpson M.E. Ch. Fellow Am. Inst. E.E. Am. Assn. for Advancement of Science; asso. Instn. E.E. (Brit.). Republican. Mason. Clubs: Engineers, New York; Rotary. Contbr. to Jour. and Proc. Am. Inst. E.E. Inventor of methods of mfg., testing, terminating and jointing high voltage electric cables. Home: 206 Watchung Fork, Westfield, N.J. Office: Gen. Cable Corpn., Perth Amboy, N.J.

ATKINSON, Sterling Krick, prof. accounting; b. Bellaire, O., Feb. 11, 1904; s. Frank G. and Amelia (Krick) A.; ed. Juniata Coll., Huntingdon, Pa., 1921-23; B.S. in Commerce, Temple U., 1926; A.M., U. of Pa., 1929; Ph.D., Columbia, 1934; m. Mildred C. Miller, Dec. 28, 1927; 1 son, Sterling Krick. With Temple U. since 1926, now prof. accounting. Mem. Nat. Assn. Cost Accountants, Am. Econ. Assn., Am. Assn. Univ. Profs., Beta Gamma Sigma, Delta Sigma Pi. Republican. Presbyterian. Contbr. to Accounting Review. Home: 324 Roberts Av., Glenside, Pa. Office: Temple University, Philadelphia, Pa.

ATKINSON, Willard Stowell, consulting engr.; b. Camden, N.J., Nov. 21, 1874; s. George Allan and Rachel (Watson) A.; ed. Camden pub. grammar sch. and by private study; m. Elizabeth Walter; children—Lillian (wife of Maj. Hanford N. Lockwood, Jr., U.S.A.), Helen (dec.). Began with Edison Electric Light Co., 1889; electric construction supt.; with Zimbars & Hunt, New York, as factory mgr. (power house supplies); dynamo designer, "L" Dynamo Co., Phila.; supervising engr. Princeton U., 1904-10; chief engr. Albro-Clem Elevator Co., 1913, Atlantic Elevator Co., to 1923; now cons. engr. for freight and passenger elevators. In charge Albro-Clem plant in production gun elevating gearing for Ordnance Dept., U.S. Army, 1918. Life mem. Am. Inst. Elec. Engrs. Registered professional elec. and mech. engr. in N.Y., Pa., and N.J. Mem. Internat. Elec. Congress, 1904; field aid U.S. Naval Consulting Bd., 1916; chmn. com. on research and engring. Elevator Mfrs. Assn. of U.S.; chmn. Pa. Elevator Bd.; mem. sectional com. on elevators Am. Engring. Standards Com., 1920. Writer various papers on elevator engring. and traffic, wire cables and drives, worm gearing, etc. Holder of patents on elec. apparatus, steel ropes and elevator devices. Home: 9 W. Walnut Av., Westmont, N.J. Office: 1612 Vine St., Philadelphia, Pa.

ATLEE, Edward Dillingham, physician; b. Wayne, Pa., Feb. 16, 1899; s. Louis William and Alice (Dillingham) A.; student Episcopal Acad., Phila., Pa., 1916; M.D., U. of Pa., 1923; m. Elizabeth Lindsay Black, Sept. 6, 1924; 1 dau., Anne Lindsay. Asst. pediatrician, out-patient dept. Pa. Hosp., Phila., Pa., 1926-34, to hosp. since 1934; instr. pediatrics, Temple U. Hosp.-Med. School., Phila., 1932-37; asst. pediatrician, out-patient dept. Bryn Mawr (Pa.) Hosp. since 1933. Fellow Am. Acad. Pediatrics; mem. Phila. Co. Med. Soc., Phila. Pediatric Soc., Pa. State Med. Soc., A.M.A. Republican. Episcopalian. Club: Aesculapian (Phila.). Author articles on pediatrics, etc. in med. jours. Home: Ardmore and Belmont Avs., Ardmore Pa. Office: 2227 Delancey St., Philadelphia, Pa.

ATLEE, John Light, surgeon; b. Lancaster, Pa., June 26, 1875; s. William Augustus and Elizabeth (Champneys) A.; A.B., Franklin and Marshall Coll., Lancaster, 1896, D.Sc, 1915; M.D., U. of Pa., 1900; m. Frances Rine Baer, June 17, 1903; children—John L. (M.D.), Frances, Elizabeth, William Augustus. Practiced at Lancaster since 1900; cons. surgeon Lancaster Gen. Hosp.; med. dir. St. Joseph's Hosp. Trustee Y.M.C.A., Franklin and Marshall Coll. Fellow A.M.A., Am. Coll. Surgeons; mem. Med. Soc. State of Pa., Lancaster Co. Med. Soc., Phi Beta Kappa, Sigma Xi, Phi Alpha Sigma, Pi Gamma Mu. Republican. Episcopalian. Clubs: University (Phila.); Hamilton, Lancaster Country. Home: Bausman, Lancaster Co. Office: 37 E. Orange St., Lancaster, Pa.

ATLEE, Washington Lemuel, pres. Delaware County Trust Co.; b. Phila., Pa., July 24, 1868; s. Charles Light and Sarah R. (Poole) A.; student pub. schs.; m. Florence Edna Hicks, June 8, 1898; 1 son, Washington Lemuel (dec.). Began in wholesale dry-goods business as stock clk., 1888; order clk. and salesman Wood Brown & Co., Phila., 1888-93; became stock clk. Columbia Mills Co., 1894; later salesman and supt. Am. Feather & Down Co.; was mgr. Woods & Logan; sec. and dir. Huston Mfg. Co., Chester, Pa., 1900-29; sec. and dir. Delaware County Trust Co., Chester, 1935-38, pres. since 1938. V.P. and dir. Excelsior Saving Fund; dir. Chester Rural Cemetery Co. Clk of Session, Third Presbyterian Ch. of Chester. Club: Rotary (Chester). Home: 2306 Providence Av. Office: Crozer Bldg., Fifth & Market Sts., Chester, Pa.

ATWELL, George Perry, clergyman; b. Clintonville, Pa., July 23, 1867; s. Robert T. and Phoebe (Scott) A.; B.S., Grove City Coll., 1895; ed. Western Theol. Sem., Pittsburgh, 1895-98; (hon.) D.D., Grove City Coll., 1912; m. Lillian Lawrence, Nov. 24, 1896. Ordained to ministry Presbyn. Ch. in U.S.A., 1898, and pastor, Glenn Willard, Pa., 1898-1903, Crafton, Pa., 1903-12, Greensburg, Pa., 1912-21; pastor Second Ch., Washington, Pa., since 1921; mem. bd. dirs. Presbyn. Book Store, Pittsburgh, Pa. Served as moderator Presbyn. Synod of Pa., 1928-29. Republican. Presbyn. Home: 411 E. Chestnut St., Washington, Pa.

ATWELL, Loyal Porter, physician and surgeon; b. Foxburg, Pa., June 24, 1899; s. Floyd and Mary (Crawford) A.; A.B., Geneva Coll., 1921; M.D., Jefferson Med. Coll., 1925; m. Hester Wilson, June 2, 1925; children—Robert Burton, Constance June. Interne St. Francis Hosp., Pittsburgh, Pa., 1925-26, engaged in pvt. practice medicine and surgery at Ambridge, Pa., 1926-28, at Beaver Falls, Pa., since 1928; mem. surgical staff, Providence Hosp., Beaver Falls, Pa., since 1928, pres. staff since 1938; mem. surg. staff, Beaver Valley Gen. Hosp., New Brighton, Pa., since 1928. Served in S.A.T.C., 1918. Mem. Am. Med. Assn., Pa. State Med. Soc., Beaver Co. Med. Soc., Nu Sigma Nu, Alpha Omega

Alpha. Republican. Presbyn. Mason (32°). Home: 1204 6th Av., Beaver Falls, Pa.

ATWILL, Lionel, actor; b. Croydon, Eng., Mar. 1, 1885; s. Alfred and Ada Emily (Dace) A.; ed. under pvt. tutor and at Mercer's Sch., London; m. Elsie Mackay, 1920; m. 2d, Mrs. Louise Cromwell MacArthur, June 1930; 1 son, John Anthony. Trained as architect; made first appearance on stage in The Walls of Jericho at Garrick Theatre, London, 1905; toured in plays of Shakespeare, Shaw, Pinero, Galsworthy, Ibsen, and several current successes; in Australia, 1910; returned to London, 1912—played in Milestones, Poor Little Rich Girl, Little Minister, Years of Discretion; came with Mrs. Langtry to U.S., 1915, and toured as Dick Marsden in Mrs. Thompson; played in New York in The Lodger, Eve's Daughter, L'Elevation, Wild Duck, Hedda Gabler, Doll's House, Tiger! Tiger!!; starred by Belasco in Deburau, The Grand Duke, The Comedian; appeared season of 1923-24 in The Heart of Cellini, later in The Outsider, and in Cæsar and Cleopatra, 1925, in Beau Gallant, 1926; directed The Squall, Lady Alone, The Adventurer, The Thief, and played in same, 1926-27; played Napoleon in play of same name, also played in revival of The Outsider, season of 1927-28; in The Silent Witness, 1931; in motion pictures, 1932-33, in Silent Witness, Dr. X, Wax Museum, Song of Songs, Nana, The Devil is a Woman, Captain Blood, The High Command (England), Three Comrades, The Great Waltz, Son of Frankenstein, Hound of the Baskervilles, The Sun Never Sets, etc. Clubs: British Commonwealth, Fencer's (New York); Green Room (London); Green Spring Valley Hunt, Maryland Yacht, Baltimore Country. Address: Eccleston, Md., and White Lodge, Pacific Palisades, Calif.

ATWOOD, Arthur R., banker; b. Champlain, N.Y., Nov. 21, 1891; s. Levi E. and Ida M. (Waters) A.; m. Florence E. Doane, July 6, 1920; 1 son, John Doane. With U.S. Treasury Dept., 1931-35; dir. and vice-pres. Colonial Trust Co., Pittsburgh, since July 1935; dir. Unity Railways Co., Miller Printing Machinery Co., Clinton Block Coal Co.; vice-pres. and sec. Freehold Bank. Capt. 367th F.A. Reserve. Presbyterian: Mason. Clubs: Duquesne, Pittsburgh Field. Home: 78 Woohaven Drive, Mt. Lebanon. Office: Colonial Trust Co., Pittsburgh, Pa.

ATWOOD, Edward A., M.D.; attending otolaryngologist Paterson Gen. Hosp. and Paterson Eye and Ear Infirmary. Address: 360 Park Av., Paterson, N.J.

ATWOOD, Horace; prof. emeritus of poultry husbandry, W.Va. U. Address: West Virginia U., Morgantown, W.Va.

AUBREY, George William, lawyer; b. Mauch Chunk, Pa., June 26, 1875; s. Thomas and Anna (Lewis) A.; LL.B., Dickinson Sch. of Law, Carlisle, Pa., 1900; m. Vernie Johnson Aubrey, Apr. 28, 1909. Admitted to Pa. bar, 1906, and since practiced at Allentown, Pa.; mem. firm Aubrey & Friedman, Allentown, since 1928; treas. and dir. Allentown Commonwealth Bldg. Co.; dir. Allentown Portland Cement Co. Presidential elector (Pa.), 1924. Trustee Dickinson Sch. of Law. Republican. Methodist Episcopalian. Clubs: Livingston, Lehigh Country (Allentown, Pa.). Home: 38 S. Fulton St. Office: 605 Commonwealth Bldg., Allentown, Pa.

AUCHTER, Eugene Curtis, horticulturist; b. Elmgrove, N.Y., Sept. 14, 1889; s. William David and Florence Monroa (Curtis) A.; B.S., Cornell U., 1912, M.S., 1918, Ph.D., 1923; m. Catherine Elizabeth Beaumont, Aug. 25, 1914. Asst. in pomology, Cornell U., 1911-12; asst. and asso. prof. of horticulture, W.Va. U., 1912-17; head dept. of horticulture, U. of Md., 1918-28; prin. horticulturist in charge div. of fruit and vegetable crops and diseases, U.S. Dept. of Agr., 1928-38, asst. chief Bureau of Plant Industry, 1935-38, chief of Bureau of Plant Industry since 1938. Mem. bd. mgrs. New York Bot. Gardens. Hon. fellow Royal Hort. Soc. of London; fellow A.A.A.S.; mem. Am. Soc. Plant Physiologists, Am. Soc. Hort. Science, Am. Genetics Assn., Sigma Xi, Phi Kappa Phi, Alpha Zeta. Clubs: Cosmos (Washington, D.C.); Rotary (College Park, Md.). Author: (with H. B. Knapp) Orchard and Small Fruit Culture, 1929; Growing Tree and Small Fruit, 1929. Home: College Park, Md. Office: U.S. Dept. of Agriculture, Washington, D.C.

AUERBACHER, Louis John, mfg. milk products; b. Phila. Pa., April 1, 1874; s. Louis Henry and Helen (Pfaff) A.; ed. Newark (N.J.) Pub. High Sch., 1886-90; m. Amy Goldbach, Aug. 8, 1897 (dec.); children—Louis, Jr., George N.; m. 2d, Henrietta Saenger, Aug. 3, 1925. Began as salesman, later mgr. E. S. Greeley & Co., elec. supplies; pres. Federal Screen Co., 1914-16; pres. Beck Flaming Lamp Co., 1908-11; pres. Ambrosia Milk Corpn., 1912-16; vice-pres. The Dry Milk Co., 1918-39; vice-pres. and dir. Casein Co. of America since 1936; dir. of Medical Relations, The Borden Co. since 1935; developed the flaming arc lamp and other elec. devices; developed the powdered milk industry; pioneered in development irradiated milk. Republican. Mason. Clubs: Roseville Athletic of Newark (past pres.); Chemists (New York City); American (Havana, Cuba). Home: 255 N. 7th St., Newark, N.J. Office: 350 Madison Av., New York, N.Y.

AUF DER HEIDE, Oscar Louis, ex-congressman; b. N.Y. City, Dec. 8, 1874; s. Carl F. and Louise A.; ed. pub. schs.; m. Mary Andras, Aug. 18, 1895; children—Carl F., Mrs. May M. Johnsen, Oscar L. Resident of West New York, Hudson Co., N.J., since age of 12; in real estate business; mem. Town Council, 1899-1902; pres. Bd. of Edn., 1903-04; mem. N.J. State Assembly, 1908-11, inclusive; mem. Bd. of Assessors, West New York, 1912-13; Mayor of West New York, 1914-17; mem. Bd. Freeholders of Hudson Co., N.J., 1915-24; mem. 69th to 72d Congresses (1925-33), 11th N.J. Dist, and 73d Congress (1933-35), 14th N.J. Dist. Democrat. Home: West New York, N.J.

AUFHAMMER, Charles H., gynecologist, Coatesville Hosp. Address: 249 E. Lincoln Highway, Coatesville, Pa.

AURAND, Orris Henry, supt. of schools; b. Lewistown, Pa. Dec. 2, 1898; s. Arthur A. and Clara V. (Kane) A.; B.S., Susquehanna U., 1921; A.M., Columbia, 1932, grad. student 1933-34; m. Edna Woolbert, Aug. 19, 1930. Supervising prin. of schools, Lehman Twp., Luzerne Co., Pa. 1921-30, Burnham Borough, Pa., 1930-34; prin. Steelton (Pa.) High Sch., 1934-35; supt. of schools, Steelton, Pa., since 1935. Served in S.A.T.C., 1918. Chmn. City Safety Com., 1936. Mem. Am. Assn. Sch. Administrs., Am. Legion, Phi Delta Kappa, Kappa Delta Pi, Phi Mu Delta. Republican. Methodist (trustee). Mason (32°), Odd Fellow, Nat. Grange. Club: Kiwanis (pres. 1939). Home: 603 Pine St. Address: Steelton Public Schools, Steelton, Pa.

AUSTIN, Charles Reuben, prof. of metallurgy; b. Manchester, Eng., Oct. 8, 1894; s. Samuel and Mary (Brundritt) A.; came to U.S. 1927; B.Sc., Coll. Tech., Manchester, Eng.; 1918; M.Sc., U. of Manchester, Eng., 1920; grad. study, U. of Wales, 1920-24, Ph.D., same, 1923; F.I.C., 1925; m. Doris A. Bowen of Llandilo, Wales, June 1930; research metallurgist with Nat. Phys. Lab., Eng., 1924-27; chief resident metallurgist, Nat. Tube Co., Pittsburgh, Pa., 1927-30; sect. engr. Research Labs., Westinghouse Electric and Mfg. Co., 1930-34; lecturer in metallurgy, Carnegie Inst. Tech., 1929-34; prof. of Metallurgy and cons. metallurgist, Pa. State Coll., since 1934. Fellow Inst. Chemistry, Gt. Britain. Mem. Inst. Metals, Iron and Steel Inst., Am. Soc. for Metals, Phi Lambda Upsilon, Sigma Gamma Epsilon, Sigma Xi. Protestant. Contbr. sci. articles and researches to tech. journs. Home: Whitehall Rd., State College, Pa.

AUSTIN, James Hannah, Jr., wholesaler lumber; b. Junction City, Kan., Oct. 25, 1882; s. James Hannah and Fanny J. (Smith) A.; grad. high sch., Kansas City, Mo., 1901; m. Bonita Pettijohn, Dec. 27, 1911; children—James, Hannah, III, David. Began as clerk and timekeepre, Kansas City, Mo., 1902; in railroad construction, Oklahoma, 1902-04; since 1904 engaged in mfr. and sale of lumber; pres. and dir. Austin Lumber Co., wholesale lumber, since 1925. Republican. Clubs: Duquesne (Pittsburgh); Allegheny Country, Edgeworth (Sewickley). Home: Sewickley, Pa. Office: Am. Bank Bldg., Pittsburgh, Pa.

AUSTIN, James Harold, M.D.; b. Phila. Pa., Sept. 22, 1883; s. James Smith and Louisa McKee (Sloan) A.; grad. Episcopal Acad., Phila., 1901; B.S., U. of Pa., 1905, M.D., 1908; m. Thelma Frances Wood, June 21, 1924; children—Thelma Frances, James Harold, John Brander, III. Began as physician, Phila., Pa., 1908; asso. research medicine and medicine, U. of Pa., 1911-17; asst. and asso. Rockefeller Inst., New York, 1919-21; prof. research medicine, U. of Pa., since 1922; editor Jour. Clin. Investigation, 1926-35; sec. Coll. of Physicians, Phila. Served successively as 1st lt. capt. and maj., Med. Corps., U.S. Army, 1917-19. Fellow Am. Coll. Physicians; mem. Am. Med. Assn., Assn. Am. Physicians, Am. Soc. Clin. Investigation, Assn. Am. Pathologists and Bacteriologists, Soc. Exptl. Biology and Medicine, Am. Soc. Biol. Chemistry, Harvey Soc. N.Y., A.A.A.S., Delta Upsilon, Phi Beta Kappa, Sigma Xi, Alpha Omega Alpha. Episcopalian. Club: University (Phila.). Contbr. to Scientific jours. on biochemistry and physiology. Home: 464 Conshohocken State Rd., Bala-Cynwyd, Pa. Office: Maloney Clinic, 36th and Spruce Sts., Philadelphia, Pa.

AUSTIN, Richard Loper, banker; b. Phila. Pa., March 28, 1859; s. John Brander and Sarah (Bell) A.; ed. Phila High Sch.; m. Lorraine Fleming, Dec. 9, 1886 (died 1912); 1 dau. Lucylle. Began as clk. Central Nat. Bank, Phila., 1876: cashier Independence Nat. Bank, 1885-89, pres., 1889-1901; v.p. Girard Nat. Bank, 1901-14, pres., 1914; an organizer Federal Reserve Bank, Phila., Nov. 1914, and Federal reserve agt. and chmn. of bd., 1914-36. Mem. bd. Y.M.C.A. of Phila.; mem. bd. trustees gen. Assembly of Presbyn. Ch., Presser Foundation. Club: Union League. Home: Union League Club. Office: 925 Chestnut St., Philadelphia, Pa.

AUSTIN, Shirley Plumer; partner Parrish & Co.; dir. Pittsburgh Stock Exchange. Home: Orchard Knoll, R.D. No. 2, Allison Park, Pa. Office: 235 Fouth Av., Pittsburgh, Pa.

AUTEN, James Ernest, pres. Barber Asphalt Corpn.; b. Berlin Twp., Knox Co., O., July 8, 1883; s. William A. and Ida (Steele) A.; ed. pub. schs. and mech. engring. course Internat. Correspondence Sch.; m. Bertha J. Harre, Dec. 17, 1908 (died July 1936); children—Hudson W., Richard L. Began with Goodrich Rubber Co., Akron, O., 1898; bookkeeper and cashier J. Parker Alexander Brick Co., Akron, 1901-03; draftsman Sterling Boiler Co., 1903-04; developing and designing pumping and elec. machinery in engring. depts. successively with William Seaver Morgan Co., and White Motor Co., Cleveland, O., H. H. Bridgewater Machine Co., Akron, Sandusky (O.) Foundry Machine Co., Rice Barton & Fails Co., Worcester, Mass., Barber Coleman Co., Rockford, Ill., Western Electric Co., Chicago, 1908-09; master mechanic Indiana Harbor (Ind.) Works, Am. Steel Foundries, 1909-11; engr. of constrn. Firestone Tire & Rubber Co., Akron, 1911-14; charge of designing new plant, later asst. to pres. Cadillac Motor Car Co., 1914-18; asst. to pres. Sampson Tractor Co., 1918-20; with Lafayette Motor Co., later gen. mgr. Nash Motor Co., Milwaukee, Wis., 1920-23; asso. with Universal Winding Co., Providence, R.I., 1933-36; pres. and dir. Gen. Asphalt Co. (now Barber Asphalt Co.) since May 1936; pres. and dir. Uintah Ry. Co.; mng. dir. Trinidad Lake Asphalt Operating Co., Ltd.; dep. chem. and dir. Trinidad Lake Petroleum Co., Petroleum Development Co. Clubs: Racquet (Phila.); Phila. Country (Dala, Pa.). Mason. Home: 6450 Sherwood Rd., Overbrook, Pa. Office: Box 2, N.J.

AVERETT, Leonard; gynecologist and obstetrician Northern Liberties, St. Luke's and Children's Hosps. Address: 2106 Spruce St., Philadelphia, Pa.

AVERY, Charles Dwight, geologist; b. Galesville, Wis., July 29, 1877; s. Henry Newell and

Catherine Seabring (Fowler) A.; student Minneapolis grammar and high sch.; academic course, U. of Minn., 1898-99; student U. of Minn. Mining Sch., 1899-1901; Engr. of Mines, Mich. Coll. of Mines, 1903; m. Myra Katherine Graham, Dec. 6, 1917; 1 dau., Nancy. Civil and mining engr., Utah, Mont., Nev. and Idaho, and Wyo., 1903-08; mineral insp. and Carey Act inspector Gen. Land Office, Dept. of Interior, headquarters, Helena, Mont., and Cheyenne, Wyo., 1908-20; geologist U.S. Geol. Survey since 1920, now sr. geologist. Mem. Am. Soc. Civil Engrs. (pres. D.C. Sect. 1927-28), Am. Assn. Petroleum Geologists, Geol. Soc. of Washington, Beta Theta Pi. Presbyn. Clubs: Federal, Pick & Hammer (Washington, D.C.). Home: 127 Chestnut Av., Takoma Park, Md. Office: 3240 Interior Bldg. North, Washington, D.C.

AVERY, George A., pastor Hope Presbyn. Ch. Address: 1733 S. Frazier St., Philadelphia, Pa.

AVINOFF, Andrey, director Carnegie Museum, advisory professor of zoölogy of Univ. of Pittsburgh; b. Tulchin, Russia, Feb. 14, 1884; s. Gen. Nicholas and Alexandra (Lukianovitch) A.; LL.M., U. of Moscow, 1905; Sc.D., U. of Pittsburgh, 1927; L.H.D., Washington and Jefferson Coll., 1934; unmarried. Specialized in entomology, and exhibited paintings since 1904; owned a noted collection of butterflies of Asia before the Revolution in Russia; served with Red Cross, World War; came to U.S., 1917; asso. curator entomology, Carnegie Mus., 1924-26, dir. since 1926. Advisory prof. zoölogy and asst. prof. fine arts, U. of Pittsburgh; councilor Am. Assn. of Museums. Mem. museum assns. of England and Germany and various learned socs. of Am. and foreign countries. Mem. Russian Orthodox Ch. Address: Schenley Apts., Pittsburgh, Pa.

AVIS, John Boyd, judge; b. Deerfield, Cumberland Co., N.J., July 11, 1875; s. John H. and Sallie (Barker) A.; ed. pub. sch., Deerfield; hon. LL.D., South Jersey Law Sch., of Camden, 1938; m. Minnie Genung Anderson, Sept. 27, 1899. Admitted to N.J. bar, 1898, and practiced at Woodbury until 1929; dir. Woodbury Trust Co. Judge U.S. Dist. Court, N.J. Dist., since 1929. Mem. N.J. Gen. Assembly, 1902-05 (speaker 1904-05); mem. N.J. State Senate, 1906-08; del. to Rep. Nat. Conv., 1912; Rep. presdl. elector, N.J., 1928. Presbyn. Mason, Odd Fellow, Moose, Forester, Red Man; mem. Grange. Home: 48 Newton Av., Woodbury, N.J. Chambers: U.S. Court House, Camden, N.J.

AVIS, S. B.; mem. law firm Avis & Angel. Address: Charleston Nat. Bank Bldg., Charleston, W.Va.

AYARS, R. D.; prof. accounting U. of Pittsburgh Sch. of Business Administration. Address: U. of Pittsburgh, Pittsburgh, Pa.

AYCOCK, Thomas Bayron; surg. consultant Springfield State Hosp., Spring Grove State Hosp. of Md. and Md. Tuberculosis Sanatorium; mem. staff U. of Md. Hosp.; chief surgeon Baltimore City Hosps.; asso. surgeon Mercy Hosp.; clin. prof. surgery, U. of Md. Sch. of Medicine. Office: 101 W. Read St., Baltimore, Md.

AYDELOTTE, Frank, college pres.; b. Sullivan, Ind., Oct. 16, 1880; s. William E. and Matilda (Brunger) A.; A.B., Ind. U., Bloomington, Ind., 1900; A.M., Harvard, 1903; Rhodes scholar from Ind. to Oxford U. 1905-07, B.Litt., 1908; LL.D., Allegheny Coll., 1923, Yale, 1928, Indiana U., 1937; D.Litt., U. of Pa., 1924, U. of Pittsburgh, 1925, Oberlin, 1926; D.C.L., Oxford U., 1937; hon. fellow, Brasenose Coll., Oxford, 1937; m. Marie Jeannette Osgood, June 22, 1907; 1 son, William Osgood. Instr. English, Southwestern State Normal School, California, Pa., 1900-01; instructor English, Indiana University, 1901-02, Louisville (Ky.) Boys' High School, 1903-05; asso. prof. English, Ind. U., 1908-15; prof. English, Mass. Inst. Tech., 1915-21; pres. Swarthmore Coll. since 1921. Am. sec. to Rhodes trustees since 1918; trustee Carnegie Foundation for Advancement of Teaching since 1922; nat. dir. War Issues Course, War Dept. Com. on Edn. and Spl. Training, 1918; trustee, Teachers' Insurance and Annuity Assn. America, 1923-27; mem. administrative bd. Institute of Internat. Edn.; chmn. ednl. advisory bd. John Simon Guggenheim Memorial Foundation since 1925; mem. div. of ednl. relations of National Research Council since 1922; trustee World Peace Foundation since 1927, Institute for Advanced Study since 1930. Mem. Modern Lang. Assn. America, American Hist. Assn., American Philosophical Soc. (mem. council 1935—), Council on Foreign Relations, American Academy Political and Social Science, Phi Beta Kappa Fraternity (mem. senate, 1931-43), Sigma Nu; pres. Assn. American Colleges, 1925; honorary mem. Am. Assn. Univ. Profs. Democrat. Clubs: Cosmos (Washington); Century (New York); Franklin Inn (Philadelphia); Harvard (Boston and New York); Athenæum (London). Author: Elizabethan Rogues and Vagabonds, 1913; College English, 1913; The Oxford Stamp, 1917. Editor: Materials for the Study of English Literature and Composition, 1914; English and Engineering, 1917; Oxford of Today (with L.A. Crosby), 1922; Honors Courses in American Colleges and Universities (Nat. Research Council), 2d edit., 1925. Home: 324 Cedar Lane, Swarthmore, Pa.

AYER, Joseph Cullen, clergyman; b. Newton, Mass., Jan. 7, 1866; s. Joseph Cullen and Caroline Eliza (Roberts) A.; ed. Harvard, Berlin, Halle and Leipzig; B.D., Episcopal Theol. Sch., Cambridge, Mass., 1887; fellow Johns Hopkins, 1899-1900; A.M., Ph.D., Leipzig, 1893; hon. S.T.D., U. of the South, 1917; D.D. from Episcopal Theological School, Cambridge, Mass., 1931; m. Cora Julia Whittaker, Jan. 11, 1894; children—Caroline Elizabeth, Richard Gordon Lawrence. Deacon, 1887, priest, 1890, P.E. Ch.; asst. Charlestown, Mass., 1887; rector S. Groveland, Mass., 1888-90, Keene, N.H., 1893-95, Nantucket, Mass., 1895-99; lecturer on canon law, Episcopal Theol. Sch., Cambridge, Mass., 1901-05; prof. ecclesiastical history, P.E. Div. Sch., Phila., since 1905; lecturer on History of Religions, U. of Pa. since 1927; rector St. Philip's Ch., Phila., 1929-36; retired. Mem. Am. Ch. Hist. Soc., Oriental Club. Editor: The World's Orators (G. C. Lee, editor-in-chief), vol. 2, vol. 3 (collaboration), and vol. 4, 1900. Author: Die Ethik Joseph Butlers, 1893; The Rise and Development of Christian Architecture, 1902; A Source Book for Ancient Church History, 1913. Also articles in revs. on canon law, music nad painting. Home: 200 St. Mark's Sq., Philadelphia, Pa.

AYERS, Hobart Bentley; pres. H. K. Porter Co.; b. Westerly, R. I., Nov. 10, 1872; s. Walter G. and Hannah M. (Bentley) A.; student Westerly High Sch. and Dartmouth Coll.; M.E., Lehigh U., 1896; m. Bessy May Randolph, June 4, 1904. Pres., gen. mgr. and dir. H. K. Porter Co. Home: 7128 Meade St. Office: 49th and Harrison Sts., Pittsburgh, Pa.

AYERS, Joseph Williams, dir. of research; b. Easton, Pa., Jan. 6, 1904; s. Charles P. and Emma (Williams) A.; B.Chem., Cornell U., 1927, student grad. sch., 1928; m. Caroline B. Stone, Oct. 6, 1934; 1 dau., Kitty Stone. Pres. Calcium Chemical Corpn. since 19—; dir. of research C. K. Williams & Co., Easton, Pa., since 1928, now also dir. of Co.; dir. New England Lime Co. Chmn. Northampton Co. Com., Nat. Economy League; mem. exec. com. and dir. Easton (Pa.) Y.M.C.A. Mem. Zeta Psi. Clubs: Country of Northampton County, Skytop Lodge, Pomfret (Easton, Pa.); Cornell (New York). Author: Numerous articles on iron oxides, paints and paint materials, colors and coloring matters, color tests, etc. in tech. jours, since 1932. Holder of five patents. Home: 22 N. 14th St. Office: 640 N. 13th St., Easton, Pa.

AYRES, Arthur Underwood, engineer; b. Mechanicsburg, Pa., June 24, 1893; s. Eugene Edmond and Ada (Underwood) A.; A.B., Swarthmore Coll., 1913; m. Emily Elizabeth Bell, 1929; children—Arthur Underwood, Marian Louise. Transmission engr. Chester Valley Electric Co., Coatsville, Pa., 1913; elec. engr. Valdosta (Ga.) Lighting Co., 1914; mgr. Electric Supply Co. of the South, Valdosta, Ga., 1914-16; motor application engr., Westinghouse Electric & Mfg. Co., East Pittsburgh, Pa., 1916; power engr. Atlantic City (N.J.) Electric Co., 1917-18; chief engr. The Sharples Corpn., Phila., since 1919. Mem. Phi Beta Kappa. Baptist. Author articles for engring. jours. Holder many patents covering centrifugal machines and processes. Home: 9 W. Hampton Rd. Office: 23d and Westmoreland Sts., Philadelphia, Pa.

AYRES, James Douglas; chmn. bd. P. McGraw Wool Co., Union Barge Line Corpn. Office: 116 Central Sq., Pittsburgh, Pa.

B

BABASINIAN, V(ahan) S(imon), chemistry; b. Marsovan, Asia Minor, Nov. 28, 1876; s. Simon and Hripsimeh (Mallian) B.; A.B., Anatolia Coll., Asia Minor, 1895; A.M., Brown U., 1903, Ph.D., 1906; unmarried. Came to U.S., 1897, naturalized citizen, 1910. Instr. in chemistry, Brown U., 1903-06; instr. in chemistry, Lehigh, 1906-09, asst. prof., 1909-11, asso. prof., 1911-22, prof. organic chemistry since 1922. With Chem. Warfare Service (research), Washington, 1918, du Pont Co., Wilmington, Del., 1919. Fellow A.A.A.S.; mem. Am. Chem. Soc., Tau Beta Pi, Sigma Xi. Republican. Conglist. Mason. Translator: Gattermann's Practical Methods of Organic Chemistry, 1914. Contbr. to Jour. Am. Chem. Soc., Industrial and Engineering Chemistry, etc. Home: 232 W. Packer Av., Bethlehem, Pa.

BABB, Maurice Jefferis, prof. mathematics; b. Marshalltown, Pa., Oct. 20, 1870; s. Hiram W. and Galena (Jefferis) B.; grad. West Chester State Normal, 1891, M.E., 1893; B.S. Haverford Coll., 1895; Ph.D., U. of Pa., 1910; m. Blanche Vincent, Nov. 27, 1898 (dec.); 1 son, Jervin J.; m. 2d, Mary Gibbons, June 11, 1920; children—Maurice J., James Gibbons, Sylvia Mary. Engaged as prin. and instr. various schs. and acads., 1891-1901; instr. mathematics, Pa. State Coll., 1901-04; instr. mathematics, U. of Pa., 1905-10, asst. prof., 1910-24, prof. since 1924. Trustee Phila. Inst. since 1912. Sec. faculty Sch. Edn. since 1924. Mem. Bd. Edn. Lower Merion Sch. District, 1912-16. Fellow A.A.A.S.; mem. Am. Math. Soc., Pa. State Edn. Assn., Phila. Sect. Assn. Teachers of Mathematics of Middle States and Md. (past pres.). Mason (K.T., 32°). Club: Lenape. Contbr. articles to math. jours. and articles to hist. mags. Home: 157 Cricket Av., Ardmore, Pa.

BABBITT, James Addison, oto-laryngologist; b. Waitsfield, Vt., Oct. 22, 1869; s. James Howard and Mary French (Abbott) B.; grad. Phillips Acad., Andover, Mass., 1889; A.B., Yale, 1893; A.M., Haverford, 1896; M.D., U. of Pa., 1898; m. Mary Abigail Adams, Sept. 11, 1895 (died Mar. 31, 1911); children—Mary Evelyn (Mrs. Alan W. Hastings), Helen Adams (Mrs. Edward L. Webster), Mary Adams; m. 2d, Marcella Stovall Hardwick, June 20, 1921; stepchildren—Marcella S. (Mrs. John Conklin), David P. Cordray. Prof. hygiene and physical edn., Haverford, retired with emeritus title, 1828; emeritus prof. clinical otolaryngology, University of Pa. School of Medicine; asso. prof. otolaryngology, University of Pa. Graduate School of Medicine; laryngologist and aurist, Laukenau Hosp.; otolaryngologist to Children's Hosp. of Mary J. Drexel Home; cons. otolaryngologist to Lankenau Hosp., Children's Hosp. of Phila., Misericordia Hosp., Fitzgerald-Mercy Hosp.; mem. courtesy staff of Bryn Mawr, Presbyn., Chestnut Hill and Episcopal hospitals. Maj. Am. Red Cross, hosp. service in France and Germany, 1917-19. Mem. U.S. Football Rules Com., 1906-25. Fellow Am. Laryngol. Assn. (sec.), Am. Otol. Soc., Am. Acad. Ophthalmology and Otolaryngology, Am. Laryngol, Rhinol. and Otol. Soc., Am. Coll. Surgeons, Coll. of Physicians of Phila.; mem. A.M.A., Phila. Laryngol. Assn., Phi Beta Kappa, Sigma Xi, Phi Gamma Delta, Alpha Mu Pi Omega. Republican. Mem. Soc. of Friends. Clubs: Union League, University, Haverford, Merion Cricket. Writer of many articles on med. subjects. Home: "Taunton," Tunbridge Rd., Haverford, Pa. Office: 1912 Spruce St., Philadelphia, Pa.

BABBOTT, Frank Lusk, educator; b. Brooklyn, N.Y., May 28, 1891; s. Frank Lusk and Lydia Richardson (Pratt) B.; A.B., Amherst Coll., 1913, LL.D., 1933; M.D., Coll. of Phys. and Surg. (Columbia), 1918; m. Elizabeth

French, Mar. 2, 1918; children—Frank L., Edward F., Lydia R., David, Elizabeth. Asst. dispensary phys. Harriet Lane Home, Johns Hopkins Hosp., 1920-21; asst. in pediatrics, Yale Med. Sch., 1921-22, instr. 1922-23; asso. in pediatrics, L.I. Coll. Hosp., 1925-27; asst. dean L.I. Coll. of Medicine, Brooklyn, 1927-31, pres. since 1931. Trustee Pratt Inst. Brooklyn Poly. Inst.; trustee Brooklyn Inst. of Arts and Sciences; v.p. Brooklyn Children's Aid Soc. Mem. Med. Soc. Co. of Kings (trustee); Alpha Delta Phi. Presbyn. Clubs: University, Century Assn. (New York); Crescent Athletic-Hamilton (Brooklyn). Home: Bernardsville, N.J. Address: 350 Henry St., Brooklyn, N.Y.

BABCOCK, Charles C., mem. law firm Babcock & Champion. Address: Atlantic City, N.J.

BABCOCK, Edward Vose; b. Fulton, N.Y., Jan. 31, 1864; s. Leaman B. and Harriet (Vose) B.; ed. pub. schs., Oswego County, N.Y.; m. 2d, Mary D. Arnold; children—Dorothy Arnold, Edward Vose, Fred Courtney. Entered lumber business as employe at Detroit; established E. V. Babcock & Co., lumber, Pittsburgh, Jan. 1, 1890; officer many lumber cos. Home: 5135 Ellsworth Av. Office: Frick Bldg., Pittsburgh, Pa.*

BABCOCK, George W.; in practice of law since 1920. Address: Hackensack, N.J.

BABCOCK, Harry Francis, clergyman; b. Blackwells, Pa., Mar. 27, 1886; s. Hiram B. and Sarah Ann (James) B.; student Williamsport Dickinson Sem., 1907-11; A.B., Pa. State Coll., 1922; student Drew Theol. Sem., Madison, N.J. 3 summers, Garrett Bibl. Inst., Evanston, Ill., 2 summers; m. Jessie B. Reed, Aug. 12, 1914; children—John Reed, Jean. Entered ministry M.E. Ch., 1911; ordained, 1914; joined Central Pa. Conf., Mar. 1912; minister Center and Sandy Ridge, Pa., 1911-13, Bakerton, Pa., 1913-16, Half Moon Ch., Stormstown, Pa., 1917-20; student pastor, State College, Pa., 1920-24; minister Beaver Memorial Ch., Lewisburg, Pa., 1924-28, First M.E. Ch., Bloomsburg, Pa., 1928-35; pastor St. Paul's M.E. Ch., State College, Pa., since 1935; dir. Wesley Foundation and vice-pres. bd. trustees since 1935. Mem. bd. of trustees Central Pa. Conf. M.E. Ch. (mem. finance com.). Dir. Williamsport Dickinson Sem. and Jr. Coll. Mem. Center Co. Conservation Com.; mem. State College Sportman's Club. Former scoutmaster. Republican. Mason (32°), Odd Fellow (past grand). Clubs: Kiwanis of Bloomsburg, Pa.; Lions of Lewisburg, Pa. (pres., 1928). Home: 345 E. Beaver Av., State College, Pa. -

BABCOCK, William Wayne, surgeon; b. E. Worcester, Otsego Co., N.Y., June 10, 1872; s. William Wayne and Sarah Jane (Butler) B.; grad. Binghamton (N.Y.) High Sch.; M.D., Coll. Phys. & Surg., Baltimore, 1893; studied summer sch., Harvard, 1893; M.D., Sch. of Medicine, U. of Pa., 1895; M.D., Medico-Chirurg. Coll., Phila., 1900; hon. A.M., Pennsylvania College, Gettysburg, Pa., 1904; LL.D. from Temple University, 1932; m. Marion C. Watters, May 14, 1918; children—Jane Butler, Catherine, Bonnie, William Wayne. Resident phys., St. Mark's Hosp., Salt Lake City, 1893-94; resident phys., Phila. Polyclinic and Coll. for Graduates in Medicine, 1895-96; house surgeon, Kensington Hosp. for Women, Phila., 1896-98; demonstrator and lecturer in pathology and bacteriology, Medico-Chirurg. Coll., Phila., 1896-1903, also during same period, curator to Pathol. Soc., Phila., 3 yrs., asst. pathologist to Phila. Hosp. 2 yrs. and pathologist to Kensington Hosp. for Women; prof. gynecology, 1903—, prof. surgery and clin. surgery, 1903-17, Temple Coll.; prof. oral surgery, Phila. Dental Coll., 1907-08; surgeon to Temple University and Philadelphia Gen. hosps., Phila. Has conducted researches leading to improved methods in surgery and invented a number of surg. instruments. Commd. capt., Med. R.C., May 9, 1917; entered service Camp Greenleaf, Ga.; regtl. surgeon 318th Field Arty., Camp Jackson, Aug. 1917; surg. chief, Gen. Hosp. No. 6, Ft. McPherson, Ga., Sept. 1917-Sept. 1919; commd. maj., Nov. 1917; lt. col., June 1918.

Fellow Am. Coll. Surgeons, Am. Assn. for Advancement of Science; mem. Am. Med. Assn., Am. Therapeutic Society (pres. 1917-18), Pathol. Soc. Phila., Am. Assn. Obstetricians, Gynecologists and Abdominal Surgeons (pres. 1933-34), Société des chirurgiens de Paris, Phi Chi, etc. Mason. Episcopalian. Clubs: Union League, Rotary, Camp Fire of America, Philadelphia Country. Author: Preventive Medicine, 1902. Co-Author: Prophylaxis, Vol. V, Cohen's System of Physiologic Therapeutics, 1903; Text Book of Surgery, 1928. Surgical editor Cyclopedia of Medicine. Home: Bala, Pa. Office 1720 Spruce St., Philadelphia, Pa.

BACH, George William, mfg. exec.; b. Germany, Apr. 18, 1877; s. Carl Christian and Elizabeth (Forster) B.; m. Emma Fries, June 5, 1906; children—Justina, Emma Georgia. Spl. marine engring. work and instr. engring., U.S. Steel Corpn., 1906-13; gen. mgr. Union Iron Works, Erie, Pa., 1913-33, Am. Sterilizer Co., Erie, since 1933; holds unlimited ocean and fresh water chief engr's. license; dir. Union Iron Works, Am. Sterilizer Co. Served in engring. dept., U.S. Navy. Mem. engring. advisory bd., Dept. of Labor and Industry, selected by and representing Pa. industry, since 1920; official Erie Community Chest, chmn. two successful campaigns, in charge industrial div.; pres. St. Vincent's Hosp., Erie.; commr. of Boyscouting; dir. Erie Philharmonic Soc. Founder Erie Tech. Fed.; mem. Am. Soc. M.E., Am. Boiler Mfrs. Assn. (ex-chmn.). Clubs: Erie, Rotary, Erie Yacht (Erie, Pa.). Has lectured and written numerous articles on tech. subjects. Interested in development of youth, boyscouting, apprentice-training, labor relations. Home: 455 Kahkwa. Office: 1230 Plum St., Erie, Pa.

BACHARACH, Herman Ilfeld, artist illustrator; b. Las Vegas, N.M., Aug. 5, 1899; s. Isaac L. and Belle (Ilfeld) B.; student N.M. Normal U., 1913-17, U. of Pa., 1917-19, Pa. Mus. Sch. of Art, 1919-23; unmarried. Books illustrated: Little Blue Man, Pinocchio, Davy and the Goblin, Don Quixote, Gulliver's Travels, Mother Goose Land, Uncle Remus Stories, Book of Humor, Seven Favorites, etc. Awards: Pinocchio listed by Graphic Arts among 50 Best Illustrated Books of Year, 1927; Pa. Mus. Alumni Award for block prints, 1936. Address: 4239 Sansom St., Philadelphia, Pa.

BACHARACH, Isaac, ex-congressman; b. Phila., Pa., Jan. 5, 1870; grad. Atlantic City (N.J.) High Sch., 1885. Pres. Bacharach Real Estate Co.; Atlantic City Lumber Co. Mem. N.J. Ho. of Rep., 1911; mem. 64th to 74th Congresses (1915-37), 2d N.J. Dist. Republican. Home: Brigantine, N.J. Office: 1704 Pacific Av., Atlantic City, N.J.

BACHELLER, Joseph Henry, banker; b. Newark, N.J., Feb. 1, 1869; s. John Collins and Harriet Amelia (Parcells) B.; ed. high sch., Newark; m. Edith Adele Smith, April 30, 1895; children—Muriel (Mrs. Donald C. Swatland), Adele (wife of Dr. Herbert A. Schulte), Joseph Henry, John Smith. Began as clk. N.Y. Life Ins. Co., 1885; in 1890 asso. with Samuel S. Dennis and later managed estate of A. L. Dennis; v.p. Ironbound Trust Co., Newark, 1907-08, pres. 1908-27 (Ironbound Trust merged with Fidelity Trust Co., 1927); v.p. Fidelity Union Trust Co., Newark, 1927-31, pres. since 1931; dir. Prudential Life Ins. Co. Alderman, Newark, 1897-1903, chmn. finance com., 1900-1903, pres. bd., 1903; mem. State Assembly, 1900-02, State Senate, 1903-05; pres. First Shade Tree Commn., 1904; comptroller City of Newark, 1905-11; mem. State Water Supply Commn., 1907-13, pres., 1913, pres. bd. of Edn., 1922-23; former trustee Newark Free Pub. Library; mem. Newark Sinking Fund Commn. since 1923; mem. Essex County Park Commn. of State of N.J. since 1926; pres. Children's Aid Soc. of Newark, N.J.; dir. Newark Y.M.C.A. Republican. Baptist. Clubs: Essex, Down Town (Newark); Baltusrol Golf, Rockaway River Country. Home: 375 Mt. Prospect Av. Office: Fidelity Union Trust Co., Newark, N.J.

BACHMAN, Albert, coll. prof.; b. Winterthur, Switzerland, July 14, 1893; s. Albert and Emily (Mehmann) B.; Ph.D. in History, U. of Zürich,

1919; Ph.D. in French, Columbia U., 1934; came to U.S., 1920, naturalized, 1931; m. Gertrude A. Reymond, June 13, 1931; children—Albert Eric, Edwin. Began as tutor in Marseilles, France, 1919-20, Leland and Gray Sem., Townshend, Vt., 1920-21; instr. U. of N.C., 1921-22, Hamline U., St. Paul, Minn., 1922-23; traveled in Japan, China and India, 1923-24; instr., asst. and asso. prof. romance langs., U. of Ariz., 1924-31; prof. French and head dept. romance langs., Gettysburg Coll. since 1931. Mem. Modern Lang. Assn. of America, Swiss Alpine Club, Tau Kappa Epsilon, Phi Sigma Iota. Republican. Lutheran. Rotarian. Home: 325 N. Stratton St., Gettysburg, Pa.

BACHMAN, Benjamin Byron, vice-pres. Autocar Co.; b. Phila., Pa., Oct. 4, 1886; s. Charles Uhler and Emma Matilda (Jacoby) B.; ed. pub. schs., Phila., Pa., night courses and home study; m. Gertrude Ennis, Oct. 16, 1907; 1 son, Paul Logan. Employed as draftsman, Enterprise Mfg. Co., 1900-02; with Falkenau Sinclair Machine Co., 1902-04; asso. with The Autocar Co., Ardmore, Pa., since 1905, vice-pres. since 1929. Mem. Am. Soc. Mech. Engrs., Soc. Automotive Engrs., Franklin Inst. Republican. Mem. Reformed Ch. Home: 6134 Nassau Rd. Office: Ardmore, Pa.

BACHMAN, David Maynard, referee in bankruptcy; b. Durham, Pa., June 23, 1876; s. R. K. and Malinda E. Bachman; A.B., Lafayette Coll., Easton, Pa., 1896, A.M., 1899; unmarried. Admitted to Pa. bar, 1900, and in practice of law at Easton, Pa., 1900-17; traveler, 1917-31; referee in bankruptcy, Phila., since 1931. Democrat. Mem. German-Reformed Ch. Clubs: University (Phila.); Pomfret (Easton, Pa.). Home: 414 S. 15th St. Office: 12 S. 12th St., Philadelphia, Pa.

BACHMAN, Frank H.; mem. firm Parrish & Co.; dir. various companies. Home: Rydal, Pa. Office: 212 S. 15th St., Philadelphia, Pa.

BACHMAN, Rowland Wilson, surgeon; b. Allentown, Pa., Aug. 28, 1895; s. David Steward and Carrie R. (Rice) B.; ed. Pa. State Coll., 1912-13, U. of Pa., 1913-15; M.D., U. of Pa. Med. Sch., 1919; m. Rose E. Johnson, Aug. 4, 1920; children—David Steward, Phyllis Ann. Interne Allentown Hosp., 1919-20; in gen. practice at Allentown since 1920; asso. surgeon Allentown Hosp. since 1925; mem. Bee Inc., auto accessories, Gaumer, Inc., candy, Alrow Farm. Served in S.A.T.C., 1917-18. Mem. Allentown Chamber of Commerce. Diplomate Nat. Bd., 1920. Mem. Am. Med. Asso., Lehigh Co. Med. Soc., Sigma Xi, Phi Rho Sigma, Am. Legion, Patriotic Order Sons of America. Republican. Lutheran. Mason. Eagle. Club: Shrine of Allentown. Home:⋅ 301 N. 2d St., Allentown, Pa.

BACHMANN, Carl George, ex-congressman; b. Wheeling, W.Va., May 14, 1890; s. Charles F. and Sophia (Neuhardt) Bachmann; student Washington and Jefferson Coll., Pa., 1908-10; A.B., W.Va. U., 1913, LL.B., 1915; m. Susan Louise Smith, July 14, 1914; children—Charles F., Gilbert S., Susan. Admitted to bar of W.Va., 1915, and began practice at Wheeling; asst. pros. atty. Ohio County, W.Va., 1917-21, pros. atty., 1921-25; mem. 69th to 72d Congresses (1925-33), 1st W.Va. Dist. Mem. Phi Sigma Kappa (W.Va.U.) Mason, Odd Fellow, K.P., Elk. Republican. Presbyn. Home: 7 Locust Av. Office: 1513 Chapline St., Wheeling, W.Va.

BACHMANN, Ernest Frederick, clergyman; b. Witten, Westphalia, Germany, July 3, 1870; s. Ernst and Helen (Naumann) B.; came to America, 1881; grad. Wagner College, 1889; grad. Luth. Theol. Sem., Mt. Airy, Phila., 1892; D.D., Muhlenberg, 1914; m. Lydia Brezing, Sept. 8, 1896; 1 son, E. Theodore. Ordained Luth. ministry, 1892; pastor Concordia Ch., Buffalo, N.Y., 1892-1906; supt. Mary J. Drexel Home and Phila. Motherhouse of Deaconesses (in one instn.) since 1906. Pres. Conf. Lutheran Deaconess Motherhouses in America; dir. Luth. Inner Mission Soc. of Phila.; a founder, trustee and sec. 10 yrs. Luth. Home for Aged, Buffalo; trustee Wagner Coll., 7 yrs.; also of Muhlenberg Coll., 1933—. Pres. of Inner Mission Bd. of United Luth. Ch. in America, 1918-30; mem. Evang. Luth. Ministerium of Pa.; mem. Deaconess Bd. of United Luth. Ch. Mem. German Soc. of Pa. Republican. Address: Mary J. Drexel Home, 2100 S. College Av., Philadelphia, Pa.

BACHRACH, Walter Keyser, real estate; b. Baltimore, Md., Jan. 29, 1888; s. David and Fannie (Keyser) B.; ed. Md. Inst. Sch. Art and Design Night School, 1901-05; grad. Baltimore Poly. Inst., 1906; m. Mildred Landis Rinehart, Nov. 17, 1920. With engring. corps, B. & O. Ry., 1907-08; entered into partnership with father (a pioneer in Am. portrait photography and founder Bachrach orgn.), 1910; took over management of original Baltimore and Washington studios and expanded chain of Bachrach Studios in South and West; brother of Louis Fabian Bachrach, present mgr. and owner of Bachrach chain; pres. Washington Management Corpn., real estate management, Washington, D.C., since 1926; dir. City Bank of Washington. Enlisted photographic sect. Air Service, U.S. Army, 1917; commd. 2d lt. aviation Sect. Signal Reserve Corps, 1918. Mason (32°). Clubs: University, Congressional Country (Washington). Home: 5415 Moorland Lane, Edgemoor, Bethesda, Md. Office 2032 Belmont Rd., Washington, D.C.

BACKENSTOE, Gerald Seler, physician and surgeon; b. Emmaus, Pa., Aug. 27, 1903; s. Dr. Martin John and Agnes (Seler) B.; B.A., Columbia U., 1923; M.D., U. of Pa., 1927; m. Harriet Susan Schwartz, Nov. 5, 1929; children—John Edwin, Harriet Susan. Med. examiner Civil Aeronautics Authority, Emmaus, Pa., since 1929; dir. Second Nat. Bank, Allentown, Pa. Hon. mem. Emmaus (Pa.) Chamber of Commerce; mem. Boy Scouts of America (five year vet.), Allentown Chamber of Commerce, Assn. of Mil. Surgeons of U.S., Lehigh Co. Med. Soc., Res. Officers' Assn. of U.S., A.M.A., Am. Air Mail Soc., Am. Philatelic Soc., Blue Ridge Aero Club, Aero Med. Assn., Phi Chi. Republican. Mem. Moravian Ch. Clubs: Rotary of Emmaus, Pa. (pres. 1937-38); National Travel (New York City); Lehigh Country (Allentown, Pa.). Address: 500 Chestnut St.; Emmaus, Pa.

BACKES, Peter; mem. law firm Backes & Backes. Address: Trenton Trust Bldg., Trenton, N.J.

BACKSTRAND, Clifford J., business exec.; b. Los Angeles, Calif., July 21, 1897; s. John Ferdinand and Christine (Scott) B.; A.B., Pomona Coll., Claremont, Calif., 1920; B.S. in economics, U. of Pa., 1921; m. Edris Powlison, 1922 (divorced 1935); 1 dau., Barbara. With Armstrong Cork Co., Floor Div., since 1921, successively as salesman, 1921-22, dist. mgr., San Francisco, 1922-27, asst. sales mgr., Lancaster, 1927-29, asst. gen. sales mgr., 1929-30, gen. sales mgr., 1930-33, gen. mgr. since 1933, dir. Armstrong Cork Co. since 1935, vice-pres. since 1938. Served in O.T.C., Plattsburg, and Camp Pike, Ark., 1918. Mem. Phi Beta Kappa, Phi Gamma Delta. Republican. Presbyterian. Mason. Clubs: Hamilton, Lancaster Country, University (Lancaster); Phi Gamma Delta (New York). Home: 1034 Woods Av. Office: Armstrong Cork Co., Lancaster, Pa.

BACON, Allen E., educator; b. Wilkes-Barre, Pa., Aug. 19, 1890; s. Charles E. and Mae (Allen) B.; grad. Lafayette Coll., Easton, Pa., 1911; post-grad. work, U. of Pa., 1931-34; m. Lucy Cushing Dame, June 21, 1921 (died 1937); 1 son, Allen; m. 2d, Dolores Anne Williams, Jan. 31, 1939. With Wilkes-Barre, Pa., public schools since 1911, as high sch. teacher, 1911-22; grade sch. principal, 1922-24; high sch. principal, 1924-34; supt. schs., since 1934. Republican. Episcopalian. Mason (Shriner). Clubs: Kiwanis, Franklin. Home: 71 Old River Rd. Office: 81 N. Washington St., Wilkes-Barre, Pa.

BACON, Arthur Daniel, retired mfr.; b. Harrisburg, Pa., July 25, 1872; s. Daniel and Anna (Clark) B.; ed. public schools of Harrisburg, and Gettysburg Coll., 1889-1900; m. Barbara Baldwin, Jan. 4, 1894; children—Anna Elizabeth (Mrs. S. Edward Moore), Beatrice (Mrs. Harold Fleisher), Arthur Daniel; m. 2d, Vania Waters, June 25, 1925. Pres. and mgr. D. Bacon Co., mfg. confectioners, Harrisburg,

Pa., 1893-1927; retired 1927; dir. Capital Bank & Trust Co. Mem. Harrisburg City Council, 1904-12; pres. Sch. Bd. for 6 years; pres. Harrisburg Library; pres. Y.M.C.A.; pres. Boy Scouts; pres. Harrisburg Masonic Temple Assn.; sec. Pa. Confectioners Assn. Republican. Methodist (trustee). Mason (33°, K.T.), past eminent grand comdr. Club: Rotary. Home: 2346 N. 2d St. Office: Room 108 Penn Harris Hotel, Harrisburg, Pa.

BACON, Clarence Everett, investment banking; b. Westbrook, Conn., Aug. 18, 1890; s. Clarence Everett and Katharine Sedgewick (Whiting) B.; student Middletown (Conn.) High Sch., 1905-09; B.S., Conn. Wesleyan U., 1913; m. Eva Peabody, Nov. 6, 1915; 1 dau., Anne Peabody. Salesman with Lee Higginson & Co., N.Y., 1914-16, Spencer Trask & Co., 1916-23; partner since 1923; dir. Spencer Trask Fund; vice-pres. and dir. Broadway Realty Co., Colo., Fluorspar Corpn. Trustee Wesleyan U., Bennett Coll., Southern Edn. Foundation, Inc., Spelman Coll. (Atlanta, Ga.), Atlanta Univ., Morehouse Coll. Served with 312th Inf., later lt. 48th Field Arty., 1917-19. Pres. bd. of dirs. Montclair Y.M.C.A., 1925-36; mem. exec. com. N.Y. State Chamber of Commerce, 1933-36; pres. bd. trustees Montclair Community Chest since 1939. Mem. S.A.R., New England Soc. of New York (dir. since 1939). Republican. Episcopalian (ex-vestryman St. Luke's Ch.). Clubs: Downtown, Downtown Athletic (New York); Montclair Athletic, Montclair Golf; Lake George (N.Y.); Sagamore Golf. Home: 16 Erwin Park, Montclair, N.J. Office: 25 Broad St., New York, N.Y.

BACON, Earl Douglas, chamber of commerce sec.; b. Belleville, N.Y., June 13, 1894; s. Joseph Niles and Harriet Leonora (Teear) B.; student Colgate Acad., Hamilton, N.Y., 1908-12, Hamilton (N.Y.) High Sch., 1912-13; A.B., Colgate U., 1917; student Cornell U., summer 1919, Columbia, summer 1921; m. Helen Frances Case, June 12, 1931. Teacher, Mill Brook Sch., Concord, Mass., 1917-18, Medina, (N.Y.) High Sch., 1919-20, Central High Sch., Cleveland, O., 1920-23; asst. sec. Cleveland Chamber of Commerce, 1923-26; sec. Lakewood (O.) Chamber of Commerce, 1926-29; sec. mgr. Elyria (O.) Chamber of Commerce, 1929-35; bureau mgr. Ohio Council of Retail Merchants, Columbus, O., 1935; exec. sec. Sharon (Pa.) Chamber of Commerce since 1936; mgr. Shenango Valley Retail Credit Co.; sec. Shenango Valley Safety Council. Corpl. Co. E, 348th Inf., U.S. Army, with A.E.F., 1918-19. Sec.-treas. Pa. Commercial Secs. Assn.; mem. Nat. Assn. of Commercial Orgn. Secs., Pa. Commercial Secs. Assn., Am. Legion, Phi Beta Kappa, Lambda Chi Alpha. Republican. Congregationalist. Elk. Clubs: University, Kiwanis (Sharon). Home: 451 Spencer Av. Office: 40 Vine Av., Sharon, Pa.

BACON, Frank N., lawyer; b. Jonesboro, Tenn., July 12, 1886; s. William M. and Amanda (Miller) B.; student U. of Tenn.; B.A., U. of Okla.; LL.B., Cumberland U.; m. Oretha Blager, Oct. 13, 1913; children—Mary, Ruth. Admitted to bar, 1913; mem. firm Mahan, Bacon & White, Fayetteville, W.Va.; pres. Fayetteville Federal Savings & Loan Assn., Home Land Co. (Fayetteville). Mem. Delta Epsilon. Republican. Methodist. Mason. Address: Fayetteville, W. Va.

BACON, George Morgan, civil engr.; b. Worcester, Mass., Mar. 28, 1872; s. George Andrew and Susan Lyman (Hillman) B.; grad. high sch., Syracuse, N.Y., 1889; B.S. in C.E., Cornell U., 1893; studied Hanover (Germany) Polytechnic, 1894; m. Isabel Gerry Dame, Feb. 5, 1898; children—Isabel Lyman (Mrs. Phillip Fox LaFollette), Dorothy York (Mrs. Lauchlin Bernard Currie), Lois Bigelow, Barbara Dame (Mrs. Philip Swain McConnell), Priscilla (Mrs. F. C. Gans). Constrn. of Boston Subway, 1894-98, Cripple Creek (Colo.) Short Line Ry., 1900; pvt. practice, Salt Lake City, Utah, 1902-24, operating in 5 states; state engr. of Utah, 1925-33. Mem. Am. Soc. C. E., Utah Soc. Engrs. (pres. 1916), Engring. Council of Utah (pres. 1925, 29), Soc. for Promotion Engring. Edn. Democrat. Episcopalian. Mason. Club: Alta

(Salt Lake City). Author: Seven Poems, 1912; Seven Sonnets, 1913. Home: Millstone, N.J.

BACON, Harry Ellicott, M.D.; b. Phila., Pa., Aug. 25, 1900; s. H. Augustus and Minnie S. (Thomas) B.; M.D., Temple U., 1925; B.S., Villanova (Pa.) Coll., 1933; m. Althea H. Wahle, June 21, 1935; children—Harry Ellicott, Andrea Perrot. Asso. prof. proctology, Grad. Hosp., U. of Pa.; asst. prof. Temple U. Med. Sch.; proctologist, St. Luke's and Children Hosp., Nat. Stomach Hosp.; consultant proctologist Paul Kimball Hosp. (Lakewood, N.J.), Mercy Hosp. Private in S.A.T.C., 1918; now 1st lt. 340th Inf. Reserve. Fellow Proctologic Soc., Am. Coll. Surgeons; mem. Phila. Co. Med. Soc.; Pa. State Med. Soc., Temple U. Med. Alumni Assn., Proctologic Soc. of Grad. Hosp. of U. of Pa. Republican. Presbyterian. Mason. Clubs: Aesculapian (Phila.), Medical of Phila. Home: 1400 Greywall Lane, Overbrook Hills, Merion, Pa. Office: 1527 W. Girard Av., Philadelphia, Pa.

BACON, John F.; surgeon York Hosp. Address: 28 S. Queen St., York, Pa.

BACON, Lee Fairchild, dean; b. Madison, Wis., Aug. 31, 1898; d. Selden and Sally Blair (Fairchild) B.; prep. edn. U. Sch. for Girls, Chicago; A.B., U. of Wis., 1920, M.A., 1928; M.A., Columbia U., 1935; student Harvard U. summer, 1938; unmarried. Instr. history, Kemper Hall, Kenosha, Wis., 1921-23; exec. advisor, student govt. assn., U. of Wis., 1926-32; dean of women, Marshall Coll., since 1934. Mem. Am. Assn. Univ. Women, W.Va. State Ednl. Assn., Am. Coll. Personnel Assn., State and Nat. Deans of Women, Delta Gamma, Phi Delta Gamma, Panhellenic. Episcopalian. Club: Aitrusa. Home: 1223 Fifth Av. Huntington, W.Va.

BACON, Leslie R(andolph), research chemist; b. Henniker, N.H., Mar. 16, 1903; s. Elgin S. and Carrie May (Farley) B.; B.S., U. of N.H., 1924; M.S., New York U., 1925, Ph.D., 1927; m. Isabelle Blair Bradley, June 15, 1929; children—John Elgin, Robert Elwin. Chemist Am. Doucil Co., Phila., 1927-31; research chemist Phila. Quartz Co., Phila., since 1931; instr. Drexel Inst. Evening Sch. since 1936. Mem. Am. Chem. Soc., Franklin Inst., Alpha Chi Sigma, Phi Kappa Phi. Home: 314 Clearbrook Av., Lansdowne, Pa. Office: 121 S. 3d St., Philadelphia, Pa.

BACON, Lewis H.; mem. surg. staff Lemos B. Warne and Good Samaritan hosps. Office: 300 Mahantongo St., Pottsville, Pa.

BACON, Raymond Charles, research chemist; b. Manila, P.I., Jan. 12, 1908; s. Raymond Foss and Edna Rose (Hine) B.; student De Pauw U., Greencastle, Ind., 1925-27; B.S. cum laude, Princeton, 1930; Ph.D., Leland Stanford U., 1933; student Agr. and Vet. Coll., Copenhagen, Denmark, 1933-35; unmarried. Research chemist Caleo Chem. Co., Bound Brook, N.J., since Oct. 1, 1935. Mem. Phi Lambda Upsilon, Sigma Xi. Episcopalian. Contbr. to Jour. Phys. Chemistry. Home: Chimney Rock Rd., Bound Brook, N.J.

BACON, Walter Austin, physician; b. Ogden, Utah, Mar. 26, 1894; s. Albert and Elizabeth Lee (Hearne) B.; grad. Delmar (Del.) High Sch., 1912; M.D., Jefferson Med. Coll., Phila., 1916; m. Dorothy Rich, Oct. 4, 1919 (died May 2, 1933); children—Emily Elizabeth (died in infancy), Dorothy Ann, William Dudson; m. 2d, Elizabeth Flock, Feb. 8, 1936. Resident physician Pottsville Hosp., 1916-17; in gen. practice, 1919-25; specialized in eye, ear, nose and throat, at New York Eye and Ear Infirmary Hosp., Bellevue Hosp., Jefferson Hosp., since 1926; chief of staff of eye, ear, nose and throat Lemos B. Warill Hosp. since 1926. Served as senior lt. Med. Corps, U.S. Navy, making 14 trips on Transport U.S.S. Siera, 1917-19. Mem. Schuylkill Co. Med. Soc., Omega Upsilon Phi. Democrat. Episcopalian (vestryman). Mason (K.T., 32°, Shriner). Clubs: Schuylkill Country, Pottsville Assembly. Home: 1601 Mahanton St. Office: 300 Mahanton St., Pottsville, Pa.

BADGLEY, Theo. J.; in practice of law since 1899. Address: 744 Broad St., Newark, N.J.

BADURA, Bernard, artist; b. Milwaukee, Wis., Sept. 22, 1896; s. Teofil and Stanistawa (Kowalska) B.; ed. Wis. State Normal Sch. of Fine and Applied Arts, Pa. Acad. of Fine Arts, 1921-25; m. Faye Swengel, July 8, 1928. Began as artist and stained glass craftsman and later a craftsman in wood; paintings exhibited in Corcoran Gallery, Washington, D.C., Nat. Acad., New York City, Pa. Acad., and Art Club, Phila., Cincinnati Mus., Conn. Acad. Fine Arts, Hartford, New Haven Paint and Clay Club, Clearwater (Fla.) Mus. Served in Aviation Corps as sergt. U.S.A., 1918-19. Awarded Toppan hon. mention and Cresson traveling scholarship, Pa. Acad., 1924; hon. mention, Conn. Acad. Fine Arts, 1934. Home: New Hope, Pa.

BADURA, Faye Ruth Swengel (Mrs. Bernard B.), artist; b. Johnstown, Pa., Oct. 28, 1904; d. William Wesley and Eleanor Gertrude (Stiver) Swengel; grad. Lock Haven High Sch.; ed. Pa. Acad. Fine Arts, Phila., 1922-26; m. Bernard Badura, July 8, 1928. Has followed profession as artist since 19—; paintings exhibited at Corcoran Art Gallery, Washington, D.C., Pa. Acad. of Fine Arts, Art Club, Phila., Nat. Acad., New York City, Cincinnati (O.) Mus., Conn. Acad. Fine Arts, Hartford, New Haven Paint and Clay Club, Clearwater (Fla.) Mus.; rep. in various pvt. collections. Awarded Cresson Traveling fellowship Pa. Acad. Fine Arts, 1925; awarded gold medal from Fellowship Pa. Acad. Fine Arts, 1936. Presbyn. Club: Pennsylvania Academy Fellowship. Home: New Hope, Pa.

BAER, George Henry, utilities exec.; b. 1872; ed. State Sch., Kutztown, Pa. Treasurer and dir. Pottstown (Pa.) Gas Water Co. since 1909; sec.-treas. and dir. West Pottsgrove (Pa.) Water Co., North Coventry (Pa.) Water Co., Pottstown Passenger Ry. Co., Bringhurst (Pa.) Trust Co., Manatawny Silk Co., Pottstown, Pa., Montgomery Lead & Zinc Mining Co., Joplin, Mo.; sec. and dir. Boyertown (Pa.) Gas & Fuel Co., Nagle Realty Co., Boyertown, Pa.; dir. Pottstown Mutual Fire Ins. Co.; sec.-treas. Mt. Zion Cemetery Corpn., Pottstown, Pa. Presbyterian. Home: 548 High St. Office: 348 High St., Pottstown, Pa.

BAER, Harry Abraham David, surgeon; b. Neff's, Pa., Jan. 23, 1888; s. Osville and Manetta (Klotz) B.; A.B., Franklin and Marshall Coll., 1908; grad. Reformed Theol. Sem., 1911; M.D., Jefferson Med. Coll., 1917; unmarried. Pastor Reformed Ch., Glade, Pa., 1911-13; in practice of medicine, Allentown, Pa., since 1920; owner and operator Baer Hosp. (for surgery and gynecology only) since 1920. Served as flight surgeon, 29th Aero Service Squadron, U.S. Army, during World War. Mem. Am., State and County Med. Socs. Address: 1648 Hamilton St., Allentown, Pa.

BAER, Ira P.; judge, Domestic Relations Ct. Address: Huntington, W.Va.

BAER, William Jacob, artist; b. Cincinnati, Ohio, Jan. 29, 1860; s. Henry and Barbara B.; m. Laura Schwenk, 1885 (died July, 1924); children—Ella Laura (Mrs. Robert S. Mounce), Marian Ethel, Laura (Mrs. John V. Breisky, dec.), Mildred (Mrs. D. Herbert Smith, dec.); m. 2d, Mrs. Henrietta F. Dixon, Aug. 15, 1929. Pupil of Munich Royal Acad., 1880-84, receiving 4 medals and one of his works being purchased by the Directors for the Acad. Painted pictures in genre and portraits in oil and taught, 1885-92; then confined himself to miniature painting, of which art he is a pioneer of the modern sch. Awarded 1st medal for miniatures and ideal paintings, New York, 1897; 1st class medals Paris Expn., 1900, Buffalo Expn., 1901, Charleston Expn., 1902, for miniatures and ideal works; hors concours, St. Louis Expn., 1904, and mem. internat. jury of awards. Treas. Am. Soc. of Miniature Painters; A.N.A., 1913; hon. mem. Calif. and Pa. Soc. Miniature Painters, Montclair Art Museum. Gold medal San Francisco Expn., 1915. Home: 75 Prospect St., East Orange, N.J.

BAESEMAN, R. Winfield, M.D.; attending ophthalmologist and otolaryngologist Raleigh Fitkin-Paul Morgan Memorial Hosp.; cons. ophthalmologist and otolaryngologist N.J. State Hosp. Address: 501 Grand Av., Asbury Park, N.J.

BAETJER, Edwin G., lawyer; b. Baltimore, Md., June 25, 1868; s. John G. and Mary A. B.; LL.B., U. of Md., 1890; unmarried. Admitted to Md. bar, 1890, and practiced since at Baltimore; dir. Safe Deposit & Trust Co. of Baltimore, Mercantile Trust Co. of Baltimore, Baltimore Transit Co., Dun-Bradstreet, Inc. Chmn. Draft Appeals Bd. and federal food administrator for Md., World War; chmn. City Service Commn., Baltimore. Trustee Johns Hopkins U., Peabody Library and Inst., McDonogh Sch. Clubs: Maryland, University (Baltimore); Links (New York). Home: 16 W. Madison St. Office: Mercantile Trust Bldg., Baltimore, Md.

BAGBY, Alfred, Jr.; in gen. practice of law since 1894. Address: 111 N. Charles St., Baltimore, Md.

BAGBY, Anne Campbell, librarian; b. Baltimore, Md.; d. Alfred, Jr., and Janet Ritchie (Campbell) B.; student Margaret Brent Grammar Sch., 1905-14, Friends Sch., Baltimore, 1914-18; A.B., Goucher Coll., Baltimore, 1918-22; certificate Pratt Inst. Sch. of Library Science, Brooklyn, N.Y., 1927; unmarried. Librarian Lower Merion Jr. High Sch., Ardmore, Pa., 1927-29; asst. cataloguer William H. Welch Med. Library, Johns Hopkins Hosp., Baltimore, 1930; librarian U. of Md. Law Sch., Baltimore, since 1931. Mem. Spl. Libraries Assn., Delta Gamma. Democrat. Baptist. Home: 2920 N. Calvert St. Office: U. of Md. Law Sch., Redwood and Greene Sts., Baltimore, Md.

BAGG, Linus W., M.D.; visiting surgeon Presbyn. Hosp. Address: 31 Lincoln Park, Newark, N.J.

BAGGER, Henry Horneman, cleryman; b. Brooklyn, N.Y., Nov. 12, 1893; s. Captain Hartvig Axel and Agnes (Horneman) B.; A.B., Muhlenberg Coll., Allentown, Pa., 1915; studied Columbia, summer 1916; B.D., Luth. Theol. Sem., Phila., 1919; A.M., Grad. Sch., University of Pa., 1919; D.D., Gettysburg Coll., 1933; m. Margaret Finck (A.B., Vassar College, 1917; A.M., Univ. of Pittsburgh, 1935), Aug. 20, 1920; children—Geoffrey Austin (dec.), Ralph William, Carol, Barbara. Instr. high school, Lebanon, Pa., 1915-16; ordained to ministry Luth. Ch., 1919; pastor St. Paul's Ch., Morgantown, W.Va., 1919-21, First English Luth. Ch., Butler, 1921-30; pres. Pittsburgh Synod Evang. Luth Ch. since 1930. Trustee Thiel Coll. (Greenville, Pa.), Bethesda Home (Meadville), Old Peoples Home (Zelienople), Orphans' Home (Zelienople), etc.; mem. and v.p. Bd. of Edn., United Lutheran Ch. in America, 1930-38, mem. exec. bd. since 1938. Democrat. Home: 199 Dewey St., Edgewood, Pittsburgh. Office: Law and Finance Bldg., 429 4th Av., Pittsburgh, Pa.

BAGLEY, Cecil Hopkins, physician; b. Bagley, Md., Aug. 17, 1893; s. Charles and Ella Virginia (McCauley) B.; A.B., Johns Hopkins U., 1917; M.D., Johns Hopkins U. Med. Sch., 1921; unmarried. Resident house officer, Johns Hopkins Hosp., 1921-22; asst. resident in surgery, Johns Hopkins Hosp., 1922-25; resident in ophthalmology, Wilmer Inst., 1925-27; asst. to Dr. W. H. Wilmer, Wilmer Inst., 1927-28; engaged in practice of ophthalmology, Baltimore, since 1928; instr. in ophthalmology, Wilmer Inst. since 1928; visiting ophthalmologist, Union Memorial Hosp., Hosp. for Women of Md., and Church Home and Infirmary. Mem. A.M.A., Southern Med. Assn., Baltimore City Med. Soc., Wilmer Residents' Assn., Phi Chi. Episcopalian. Clubs: Maryland Yacht (Baltimore); Gibson Island (Gibson Island); Miles River Yacht (Saint Michael); Havre de Grace Yacht (Havre de Grace). Home: 17 East Eager St., Baltimore, Md.

BAGLEY, Charles, Jr., surgeon; b. Sunnybrook, Md., Apr. 3, 1882; s. Charles (M.D.) and Ella V. (McCauley) B.; A.B., Loyola Coll., Baltimore, 1911; M.D., U. of Md., 1904; m. Mary Monroe Harlan, Dec. 10, 1919; children—Charles, Elizabeth Henderson. Visiting surgeon Sinai Hosp., St. Agnes Hosp., Ch. Home and Infirmary, Union Memorial Hosp., Bon Secours Hosp., Maryland General Hospital, West Baltimore General Hospital; consulting surgeon South Baltimore General Hospital, Baltimore Eye, Ear and Throat Charity Hosp., Presbyn. Eye, Ear and Throat Hosp., Franklin Square, Provident, and St. Joseph's hosps. (Baltimore), Emergency Hosp. (Annapolis), Md., Alleghany Hosp. (Cumberland) and Waynesboro (Pa.) Hosp.; asso. in exptl. neurology, Johns Hopkins; prof. neuro-surgery, Med. Dept. U. of Md. Mem. subcom. on ophthalmology, Gen. Med. Bd. of Council Nat. Defense. Fellow Am. Coll. Surgeons, Soc. Neurol. Surgeons (pres. 1931), Southern Surg. Assn.; mem. A.M.A., Med. and Chirurg. Faculty, Md., Baltimore City Med. Soc. (pres. 1930). Episcopalian. Club: Baltimore Country. Home: 17 E. Eager St. Office: The Latrobe, Baltimore, Md.

BAGNELL, Robert, minister; b. Philadelphia, Aug. 10, 1865; s. John and Eliza (Curran) B.; studied under pvt. tutors; A.M., Columbia, 1909, Ph.D., 1911; (D.D., Cornell Coll., Ia., 1905); m. Mary E. Wallace, Mar. 17, 1886; 1 son, Robert Harold. Ordained M.E. ministry, 1888; various pastorates in Ia. until 1901; pastor Met. Temple, New York, 1901-07, Janes Ch., Brooklyn, 1907-14, Park Avenue Church, Philadelphia, Pa., 1914-17, Grace Church, Harrisburg, Pa., 1917-33, First Ch., Charleston, 1933-37; now retired. Mem. Continuation Com. on Faith and Order since 1925; mem. World Conf. on Faith and Order, Laussanne, 1927, Edinburgh, 1937. Special rep. of Com. on Pub. Information, and spl. sec. of Y.M.C.A. in France and Eng., 1918. Mason (32°, K.T.). Author: Economic and Moral Aspects of the Liquor Business, 1912. Home: 243 Tulpehocken St., Germantown, Philadelphia, Pa.

BAHLKE, George Washington, ins. exec.; b. Baltimore, Md., Feb. 22, 1871. Agt. Metropolitan Life Ins. Co., Baltimore, Md., 1899-1900, asst. mgr., 1900-04, mgr., Richmond, Va., 1904-13, mgr., Baltimore, Md., since 1913; pres. Highland Park (Va.) Improvement Assn., Windsor Hills Improvement Assn.; dir. Federal Home Loan Bank, Winston-Salem, N.C. Organized War Savings Stamp Socs. during World War. Dir. City Wide Congress; mem. Baltimore Pub. Sch. Assn. (mem. gen. council), Real Estate Bd. of Baltimore (mem. civic affairs com.; dir.; mem. housing com.), Bd. of Zoning Appeals for Baltimore; chmn. Henrico (Va.) Sch. Bd. Rep. candidate for Register of Wills; former mayor Highland Park, Va. Mem. bd. of advisors, Presbyn. Home for the Aged. Mem. Grand Jurors Assn. (past pres.), Assn. of Commerce, Y.M.C.A. (dir., Richmond, Va.; chmn. finance com.), Md. League of Bldg. Assns. (pres.), Old Town Merchants & Mfrs. Assn., Baltimore Assn. of Life Underwriters, Rotary Internat. (34th dist. gov., 1923-24; mem. classification, membership, program, community service coms.; chmn. internat. service com.; organized 15 clubs in 34th dist.; mem. 34th dist. conf.; mem. credentials com. at internat. conv., 1930; mem. Rotary Foundation Promotion Com., 1934-35). Republican. Presbyterian. Mason (Shriner; Scottish Rite). Clubs: Chesapeake (Baltimore, Md.); Business Men's (organizer; dir.; Richmond, Va.); Rotary (Pikesville, Md.; hon. mem.); Rotary (Richmond, Va.; organizer, 1913; charter mem.; hon. life mem.); Rotary (Baltimore, Md.; pres., 1925-26). Assisted in campaigns for funds for S. Baltimore Gen. Hosp., Community Fund, Salvation Army, Y.M.C.A., etc., at Baltimore, Md. Office: 720 Munsey Bldg., Baltimore, Md.

BAHN, Walter David, treas. Union Trust Co. of Md.; b. New Freedom, York Co., Pa., Jan. 20, 1877; s. Milton W. and Ellen S. (Emig) B.; ed. York (Pa.) High Sch. and Bryant and Stratton Business Coll., Baltimore, Md.; m. Helen M. Wilson, Mar. 22, 1919. Began as messenger boy Pa. R.R., New Freedom, Pa.; became jr. mem. Gore and Bahn, merchants, New Freedom, 1900; sr. mem. W. D. Bahn & Co., grain and flour mill, 1902-25; mgr. Felt & Paper Co., York, Pa., several years; pres. First Nat. Bank, New Freedom, 1903-06; vice-pres. Commerce Trust Co., Baltimore, 1919-27; treas. Union Trust Co. of Md., Baltimore, since 1927; treas. and dir. Royal Realty Corpn. Dir. Baltimore Assn. Credit Men. Republican. Presbyterian. Mason (K.T., Shriner). Club: Baltimore Country. Home: 611 Edgevale Rd. Office: Baltimore and St. Paul Sts., Baltimore, Md.

BAHNEY, Luther William, metall. engr.; b. Red Bluff, Calif., Dec. 25, 1878; s. Eugene William and Harriet (Mayhew) B.; grad. Red Bluff High Sch., 1895; Ph.G., Coll. of Pharmacy, U. of Calif., 1897; Metall. Engr., Stanford U., 1911; m. Ada Hilton Ferguson, Nov. 7, 1906; children—Elizabeth Ruth (Mrs. Charles Edward Mills), Harriette Ada (Mrs. Joseph Caldwell Wylie, Jr.). Began as pharmacist, 1897; studied metall. chemistry with L. Falkenau, Inc., San Francisco, 1899-1900; assayer and chemist Selby Smelting & Lead Co., Selby, Calif., 1901-05; mgr. Xitinga Mines, Mexico, 1906; private lab., Los Angeles, 1906-07; taught metallurgy, Stanford U., 1907-11; taught metall. engring., Yale U., 1911-17; metall. engr. Scovill Mfg. Co., Waterbury, Conn., 1917-28; Research Oxygen-Free Corpn., U.S. Metals Refining Co., Carteret, N.J., 1928-38; mgr. Scomet Engring. Co. since 1938. Mem. Am. Inst. Mining and Metall. Engrs.; hon. mem. Berzelius (Yale), Sigma Xi (pres. 1912). Republican. Episcopalian. Mason. Home: 45 Georgian Court, Elizabeth, N.J. Office: Scomet Engring Co., Carteret, N.J.

BAHNSEN, Henry, pres. Am. Nat. Bank, Christian Bahnsen, Inc.; v.p. Peoples Bank & Trust Co. Address: Passaic, N.J.

BAILEY, Alanson Quigley, clergyman; b. Livonia Station, N.Y., Jan. 17, 1874; s. Alanson and Anna (Rianhard) B.; A.B., Lehigh U., 1898; B.D., Gen. Theol. Sem., 1901; m. Deborah Van Buren, Jan. 14, 1903; children—Alanson Quigley, John Swartwout, Daniel Carl, Paul Edward Dowden. Ordained Episcopal ministry, 1901, priest, 1902; missionary, Sanford, Me., 1901-02; curate St. Luke's Ch., Montclair, N.J., 1902-07; co-rector Trinity Ch., Hartwell, O., 1907-08; rector St. Paul's Ch., Jeffersonville, Ind., 1908-15, St. Simeon's Ch., Wildwood, N.J., 1915-19, Christ Ch., Shrewsbury, N.J., 1919-22, Holy Trinity Ch., Collingswood, N.J., since Apr. 1, 1922. Sec. Bd. of Social Service, Diocese of N.J., mem. Standing Com.; dean of Camden-Woodbury Convocation. Mem. Phi Beta Kappa. Independent Republican. Author: The Living Sacrifice, 1917; Essays Toward Faith, 1923; also (pamphlets) The Episcopal Church; The Holy Communion; The Sign of the Cross; The Rubrics; Confirmation. Address: 861 Haddon Av., Collingswood, N.J.

BAILEY, Arthur Low, librarian; b. Methuen, Mass., June 29, 1867; s. Frederick Henry and Mary (Low) B.; grad. Methuen High Sch., 1885; student Tufts Coll., 1894-96; B.L.S., N.Y. State Library Sch., 1898; m. Mabel Calder Dobbin, Sept. 3, 1903; 1 son, Arthur Chaplin (dec.). Reorganized New Milford Pub. Library, 1898; head of order dept., New York State Library, 1898-1904; librarian Wilmington Inst. Free Library since 1904; also dir. New Castle County Free Library, 1927—. Mem. board Delaware State Library Commn.; mem. Wilmington Council Boy Scouts of America. Mem. A.L.A., Am. Library Inst., Alumni Assn. of N.Y. State Library Sch. (pres. 1906-07), League of Library Commrs. (pres. 1909-10), Del. Library Assn. (1st pres. 1933-34), Del. Acad. of Medicine (dir.). Republican. Clubs: Wilmington Whist, Social Service, Rotary. Author: Library Bookbinding, 1916. Contbr. library publications. Address: 1503 Rodney St., Wilmington, Del.

BAILEY, Arthur Scott, author; b. St. Albans, Vt., Nov. 15, 1877; s. Windfield Scott and Harriet Sarah (Goodhue) B.; A.B., Harvard Coll., 1902; m. Estella Wright Goodspeed, Sept. 14, 1913. Editor various book publishers, 1904-16; since that time engaged in writing. Mem. Sigma Phi. Republican. Unitarian. Author of many juvenile books, magazine and newspaper articles and syndicated features. Home: 164 Watchung Av., Upper Montclair, N.J.

BAILEY, Austin, telephone engr.; b. Lawrence, Kan., June 9, 1893; s. Edgar H. S. and Aravesta (Trumbar) B.; grad. Lake Forest (Ill.) Acad., 1911; A.B., U. of Kan., 1915; Ph.D., Cornell U., 1920; m. Leola Crawford, Feb. 8, 1921; children—Nancy, Bruce, Holmes. Began as supt. apparatus dept. Corning Glass Works, 1920; prof. physics, University of Kan., 1921-22; with Am. Telephone & Telegraph Co., 1922-34, Bell Telephone Labs., 1934-37, Am. Telephone & Telegraph Co. since 1937. Served as 2d lt. Signal Corps, U.S. Army, 1917-18. Mem. Millburn (N.J.) Bd. of Edn. since 1934, 2 terms. Fellow Inst. of Radio Engrs.; mem. Am. Inst. Elec. Engrs., Sigma Xi, Alpha Chi Sigma. Republican. Presbyn. Clubs: Wyoming Civic Assn., Wyoming (Millburn). Writer of many articles pertaining to radio, etc. Holder of several U.S. and foreign patents. Home: 193 Sagamore Road, Maplewood, N.J. Office: 195 Broadway, New York, N.Y.

BAILEY, Calvin Weston, ins. official; b. Newark, N.J., Jan. 20, 1861; s. George H. and Hannah M. (Ryder) B.; ed. Newark Acad.; m. Sara Armour, May 1, 1894; 1 son, Kenneth Armour (dec.). With Am. Ins. Co., of Newark (fire), 1876, becoming asst. sec., 1906, sec., 1909, v.p., 1914, pres., 1918-35, chmn. of bd. since 1935; chmn. bd. Columbia Fire Ins. Co. (Dayton, O.), Bankers Indemnity Ins. Co., Dixie Ins. Co. (Greensboro, N.C.). Republican. Conglist. Club: Essex. Home: East Orange, N.J. Office: 15 Washington St., Newark, N.J.

BAILEY, Emmett E., architect; b. Tully Valley, N.Y., May 5, 1872; s. Willis S. and Hannah L. (Moore) B.; ed. pub. schs., Tully Valley and Tully Village, N.Y., 1877-90; archtl. student, 1897-1900; m. Zelma A. Belden, Aug. 2, 1893; children—Olive L., Clara L., Earl B., Nellie Marie, Walter O. Worked on farms summers, 1884-90; worked in lumber woods and saw mills, Mich., 1891-92; supt. bldg. constrn., Ashtabula, O., 1893-94; contracting business, 1895-1903; began as architect, 1900; established archtl. practice, Oil City, Pa., 1904, and since in practice at Oil City, specializing in banks and vault engring. One of originators Pa. Soc. for Crippled Children, pres. 1922-29, and dir., 1922-34; organizer and pres. Venango Co. (Pa.) Soc. for Crippled Children; pres. Oil City Y.M.C.A., 1920-30, dir. since 1906; chmn. Venango Co. (Pa.) Bd. of Pub. Assistance, 1937-39. Mem. Rotary (dist. gov. 33d Dist., 1924-25), A.I.A. (Pittsburgh chapter), Pittsburgh Archtl. Club, Pa. Assn. of Architects. Protestant. Mason (Commandery, Consistory, Shriner), Elk, Odd Fellow. Clubs: Rotary (Oil City, Pa.; organizer, 1919, pres., 1919-23); Shrine (Erie, Pa.); Venango Country (Reno, Pa.; charter mem.); Acacia (Oil City Pa.; charter member). Delivered hundreds of addresses to Rotary Clubs, conventions, civic organizations, Y.M.C.A.'s. Home: 46 E. Bissell Av. Office: 111 Center St., Oil City, Pa.

BAILEY, Ervin George, mech. engr.; b. Damascus, O., Dec. 25, 1880; s. George W. and Ruthetta (Butler) B.; M.E., Ohio State U., 1903; Dr. Engring., Lehigh University, 1937; m. Carrie Huntington, Aug. 23, 1904; children—George Huntington (dec.), Mrs. Katharine Louise Hoyt. Asst., later chief of testing dept. of Consolidation Coal Company, Fairmont, W.Va., 1903-07; in charge coal dept. Arthur D. Little, Inc., Boston, Mass., 1907-09; mech. engr. and partner Fuel Testing Co., Boston, 1909-15; founder and pres. Bailey Meter Co., mfrs. fluid meters and automatic combustion control devices, Cleveland, O., since 1916; pres. Fuller Lehigh Co., mfrs. pulverized coal equipment, water cooled furnaces, 1926-31; v.p. and dir. Babcock & Wilcox Co., New York, since 1930. Received Longstreth medal, Franklin Inst., 1930, Lamme medal, Ohio State Univ., 1936. Mem. Am. Soc. M.E., Am. Inst. Mining and Metall. Engrs., Soc. Naval Architects and Marine Engrs., Sigma Xi, Tau Beta Pi. Republican. Presbyterian. Clubs: Northampton County Country (Easton, Pa.); Engineers (Boston); Engineers, Railroad-Machinery (New York). Home: Green Gables, Easton, Pa. Office: 85 Liberty St., New York, N.Y.

BAILEY, Ethel H., mech. engring.; b. Houlton, Me., Aug. 18, 1896; d. Walter Burton and Anna Crane (Saunders) B.; grad. Deering High Sch., Portland, Me., 1915; ed. George Washington U., 1920, Newark Coll. Engring., 1930-31, Rutgers U. Extension, 1929-30, New Sch. For Social Research, New York City, 1930-31, Montclair State Teachers Coll., 1938-39. Began as inspr. airplanes and airplane engines, Signal Corps., U.S.A., 1917-19; with Bur. Constrn. and Repair, Aircraft Div., U.S.N., 1919-22; with L.W.F. Engring. Corpn., L.I., N.Y., 1923-24, Soc. Automotive Engrs., N.Y., 1924-26; with Art Metal Works, Newark, N.J., 1926-29; with General Electric Co., 1929-32; with Emergency Relief Adminstrn., 1933-36; with Montclair Pub. Library since 1936; assisted pres. bd. trustees of Montclair Pub. Library in obtaining grant from Carnegie Corpn. for study of cost accounting in pub. libraries in U.S., 1938; licensed professional engr. in N.J. Served as ofcl. rep. U.S. Govt. in charge testing and inspecting Liberty 12 airplane engine built by Nordyke Marmon Co., 1918. Fellow A.A.A.S. Mem. A.L.A., Am. Soc. Mech. Engrs., Soc. Am. Mil. Engrs., Nat. Assn. Professional Engrs., Nat. Federation Bus. and Professional Women. Republican. Episcopalian. Club: Cosmopolitan (Montclair). Contbr. articles to mags. Rep. America in First Internat. Conf. of Women in Sci., Industry & Commerce, Wembly, Eng., 1925; British Engineering Exhibition. Home: 17 Montclair Av., Montclair, N.J.

BAILEY, Frank R.; surgeon Western Pa Hosp. Address: 4800 Friendship Av., Pittsburgh, Pa.

BAILEY, Garland Howard, univ. prof.; b. Giatto, W.Va., Nov. 6, 1890; s. Jonathan Sims and Timandria (Godfrey) B.; B.Sc., W.Va. Univ., Morgantown, 1915; student Harvard U., 1915-16; M.D., Johns Hopkins U. Med. Sch., 1920, Dr. P.H., 1921; m. Harriett Martin, Jan. 2, 1920; 1 son, Robert Garland. Engaged in teaching, pub. schs., W.Va., 1907-10; instr. pathology, U. of Wis., 1921-22; instr. epidemiology, Harvard U., 1922-23; instr. preventive medicine and hygiene, Harvard U., 1923-25; asso. immunology, Johns Hopkins U., 1925-26, asso. prof. since 1926, actg. head dept. immunology, 1930-32. Served in S.A.T.C., 1918. Mem. A.A.A.S., Soc. Am. Bacteriologists, Am. Pub. Health Assn., Assn. Harvard Chemists, Delta Omega, Sigma Xi, Phi Beta Kappa. Democrat. Baptist. Mason. Club: Johns Hopkins. Contbr. Jour. of Immunology, Am. Jour. of Hygiene, Jour. of Infectious Diseases. Home: 2632 N. Charles St., Baltimore, Md.

BAILEY, George Albert, investment banker; b. Tamaqua, Pa., Feb. 19, 1890; s. Albert and Elizabeth Holman (Trout) B.; student Phila. Business Coll. and Coll. of Commerce, 1912; grad. Wharton Evening Sch., U. of Pa., 1919, grad. student, same, 1919-22; m. Fannie Avery, June 1921; children—Dorothy Elizabeth (deceased), George Albert. Messenger and clerk, Reading Ry., 1905-11; stenographer and gen. business, 1911-20; investment business, 1920-33, as statistical adviser and proprietor; has been proprietor George A. Bailey & Co. since 1933; vice-pres. and dir. Sovereign Investors, Inc.; dir. Sovereign Corpn. Trustee Am. Hosp. for Diseases of the Stomach. Mem. Pi Delta Epsilon. Republican. Episcopalian. Mason (32°, Shriner). Clubs: Union League, Bala Golf (Phila.). Contbr. articles on investments to periodicals. Home: 15 Narbrook Park, Narberth, Pa. Office: 1518 Walnut St., Philadelphia, Pa.

BAILEY, George B.; mem. law firm Bailey & Grimm. Address: 744 Broad St., Newark, N.J.

BAILEY, George Corbin, supt. chem. works; b. Eureka, Kan., Dec. 1, 1885; s. George Louis and Margaret (Corbin) B.; student U. of Kan., 1903-04; A.B., U. of Wis., 1909; A.M., Yale, 1914, Ph.D., 1916; m. Anita Klein, Aug. 7, 1912. Group leader in research lab., Barrett Co., Edgewater, N.J., 1917-21; dir. of lab. Nat. Aniline Co., Marcus Hook, Pa., 1921-22, group leader, Buffalo, N.Y., 1922-26; chemist Roessler & Hosslasher, Perth Amboy, N.J., 1926-30; supt. I. E. du Pont de Nemours & Co., Perth Amboy, since 1932. Sec.-treas. Perth Amboy Industrial Assn. Mem. Alpha Chi Sigma, Sigma Xi. Republican. Club: Rotary of Perth Amboy (past pres.). Home: 260 W. Jersey St., Elizabeth, N.J. Office: 71 Buckingham Av., Perth Amboy, N.J.

BAILEY, George Reily, banker; b. Harrisburg, Pa., Mar. 16, 1899; s. Edward and Elizabeth Hummel (Reily) B.; grad. Harrisburg Acad., 1916, Phillips Acad., Andover, Mass.,

BAILEY, [entry continues] 1919; B.S., Sheffield Sci. Sch., Yale, 1923; m. Elizabeth Lupton Scott, Jan. 8, 1931; children—Elizabeth Reily, Anne King, Susan Elder. With Harrisburg Nat. Bank since 1923, asst. cashier, 1925-36, vice-pres. since 1927; dir. Harrisburg Trust Co. since 1925, sec., 1926-37, vice-pres. since 1932; vice-pres. and dir. Harrisburg Gas Co., Harrisburg Rys. Co., Harrisburg Airport, Williamsport & North Branch Ry. Co.; dir. Halifax (Pa.) Nat. Bank, Magee Carpet Co., Bloomsburg, United Ice and Coal Co., Moorhead Knitting Co., Allison-East End Trust Co., Chestnut St. Market, Harrisburg. Vice-pres. and dir. Harrisburg Chamber of Commerce; mem. Pa. State Council of Edn.; chmn. Central Pa. Deposit Liquidation Com.; treas. and dir. Harrisburg Y.M.C.A. Bldg. Fund; mem. exec. and finance coms. Harrisburg Welfare Fed.; trustee Market Square Presbyn. Ch. Mem. Sons of Revolution, Pa. Scotch-Irish Soc., Newcomen Soc. of England. Clubs: Racquet (Washington, D.C.); Racquet, Yale (Phila.); Rolling Rock (Pittsburgh); St. Anthony (New York); Gibson Island (Baltimore); Eagles Mere (Pa.) Golf. Home: 1604 N. 2nd St. Office: Harrisburg Nat. Bank, Harrisburg, Pa.

BAILEY, Henry J.; pres. Desco Corpn.; officer or dir. several companies. Home: 1110 Jackson St. Office: 211 Shipley St., Wilmington, Del.

BAILEY, James B., pres. Pine Iron Works Co.; b. Pottstown, Pa., July 5, 1869; s. Charles Lukens and Emma (Doll) B.; grad. Hill Sch., 1886, Yale, 1889; m. Caroline Reily, Nov. 6, 1895; children—Georgia Reily (Mrs. Theodore Seelye), Mary Emily (Mrs. Rothwell Sheriff), Louise H. (Mrs. Thomas Laughlin). Pres. Charles L. Bailey & Co., 1899-1910; gen. mgr. Central Iron & Steel Co., 1902-12; pres. Pine Iron Works Co., Phila. and Pine Forge, Pa., Am. Pressed Steel Co.; dir. Potts Mfg. Co., Mechanicsburg, Pa. Treas. State Y.M.C.A., 1902-10; dir. Harrisburg Hosp., 1902-12; trustee Market-Square Presbyn. Ch., 1902-12; now trustee Bryn Mawr Presbyn. Ch. Mem. Cut Nail Mfrs. Assn. (pres. 1895-1904). Clubs: University, Merion Cricket (Phila.); Delta Psi (Yale). Home: Fishers Rd., Bryn Mawr, Pa. Office: 517 Commercial Trust Bldg., Philadelphia, Pa.

BAILEY, Levin Claude, lawyer; b. Quantico, Md., Feb. 7, 1892; s. John Curtis and Emma Virginia (Banks) B.; A.B., St. John's Coll., Annapolis, Md., 1911; LL.B., U. of Md., Baltimore, Md., 1913; m. Irma Aurelia Porter, of Norfolk, Va., Nov. 20, 1919; 1 son, James Porter. In practice at Salisbury, Md., since 1913, mem. firm Miles, Bailey & Williams, Salisbury, since 1925; city solicitor, Salisbury, Md., 1920-24, 1938-39; states atty., Wicomico Co., Md., 1927-34; dir. and vice-pres. Salisbury Realty Co., Del-Mar-Va Mortgage Co., Citizens Loan Co.; dir. and sec. Salisbury Ice Co. Served as capt., Co. F, 317th Inf., 80th Div., Army Line Sch. and Army Staff Coll., Langres, France, 1917-19; post adj., Trier, Germany, with Army of Occupation, 1918-19; attended first officers training camp, Fort Myer, Va., 1917. Pres. and dir. Wicomico Co. Free Library; dir. Md. Tuberculosis Assn. Mem. Am., Md. State bar assns. Democrat. Episcopalian. Elk (past exalted ruler, Salisbury, Md., Lodge 817). Home: 608 Camden Av. Office: Colonial Bldg., Salisbury, Md.

BAILEY, Neil Phillips, prof. of mech. engring.; b. Canon City, Colo., Nov. 13, 1900; s. John Newton and Mary (Phillips) B.; B.S. in mech. engring., U. of Colo., 1924; M.S. in mech. engring., U. of Ida., 1927; m. Margaret Hunsicker, Dec. 21, 1923; children—John Abner, Mary Catherine, Richard Neil. Cadet engr. Gen. Electric Co., Schenectady, N.Y., 1924-25; instr., later asst. prof., mech. engring., U. of Ida., 1925-29; with engring. dept., Wash. Water Power Co., summers 1926, 28, 29; asst., later asso., prof. of mech. engring., U. of N.C., 1929-34; prof. and head of mech. engring. dept., Ia. State Coll., 1934-35; prof. and head of mech. engring. dept., Rutgers U. since 1935. Served as private U.S. Marine Corps, on Asiatic duty, 1918-19. Mem. Am. Soc. Mech. Engrs., Soc. for Promotion of Engring. Edn., Tau Beta Pi, Sigma Xi, Sigma Tau, Acacia. Republican. Contbr. to mech. engring. and professional jours. Home: 411 S. 1st Av., Highland Park, N.J. Office: Rutgers University, New Brunswick, N.J.

BAILEY R. D.; mem. law firm Bailey & Shannon. Address: Pineville, W.Va.

BAILEY, Ralph Waldo, chemist; b. Elizabeth, N.J., Dec. 27, 1873; s. George W. and Emma M. (Blackman) B.; prep. edn. Pingry Sch., 1880-91; B.S., Princeton U., 1895; m. Nellie K. West, May 14, 1908; children—Charles Perkins, Doris West. Became chemist Grässelli Chem. Co., 1895; now pres. Stillwell & Gladding, analytical and consulting chemists. Mem. Am. Chem. Soc., Assn. Cons. Chemists and Chem. Engrs., Am. Oil Chemists Soc., Clio. Republican. Presbyterian. Clubs: Chippewa Yacht (Chippewa Bay, N.Y.). Home: 610 Tremont Av., Westfield, N.J. Office: 130 Cedar St., New York, N.Y.

BAILEY, Russell B.; mem. staff Ohio Valley Gen. Hosp.; cons. surg. State Tuberculosis Sanitarium, Hopemont, W.Va. Address: 58 16th St., Wheeling, W.Va.

BAILEY, Stacy P., pres. B-ettes Corpn. and B-ettes Co.; b. Waycross, Ga., Oct. 8, 1892; s. Dr. Theodore A. and Agnes (Parker) B.; student Ga. Sch. Tech., Atlanta, Ga., 1911-13; m. Marie Adams, Dec. 18, 1913; children—Stacy Parker, William Adams. Pres. B-ettes Co., Inc., manufacturing, DuBois, Pa., since 1935, B-ettes Corpn., DuBois, Pa., and New York, N.Y., since 1938. Methodist. Elk. Home: 89 Portland Rd., Highlands, N.J. Office: 237 W. Long Av., DuBois, Pa.; 155 E. 44 St., New York, N.Y.

BAILEY, Weldon, artist; b. Phila., Pa., Dec. 14, 1905; s. William John and Mary Frances (Epp) B.; ed. pub. schs. and high sch., Pa. Acad. of Fine Arts, Graphic Sketch Club, all of Phila. Has followed profession of artist since 1924, illustrator for leading mags. and for writings of well-known authors; art critic Phila. Record, 1931-34, Phila. Art News, season 1937-38. Exhibited at Pa. Acad. Fine Arts, Art Club, Art Alliance, Phila. Museum, Phila. Print Club, Warwick Galleries, all of Phila., Weyhe Galleries, Grand Central Galleries, both of New York City, Los Angeles Museum, Oakland (Calif.) Museum, Honolulu Acad. of Fine Arts. Represented in New York Pub. Library and pvt. collections. Awarded hon. mention, Phila. Art Dirs. Club, 1929, Mary S. Collins Prize, 1934. Mem. Fellowship of Pa. Acad. of Fine Arts. Club: Phila. Art Alliance. Home: 3017 Cottman St. Studio: 706 S. Washington Sq., Philadelphia, Pa.

BAILEY, William Seiler, lawyer; b. Harrisburg, Pa., Aug. 15, 1899; s. Charles L. and Mary Frances (Seiler) B.; student Harrisburg Acad., 1914, Chestnut Hill (Pa.) Acad., 1917; A.B., Yale, 1921; LL.B., Dickinson Law Sch. Carlisle, Pa., 1924, A.M., 1924; unmarried. Admitted to Pa. bar, 1924, and since in practice at Harrisburg, Pa.; mem. firm Bailey & Rupp; dir. Central Iron and Steel Co., Harrisburg Rys. Co. Served as 2d lt. F.A., U.S. Army, Sept.-Dec. 1918; with Pa. Nat. Guard as 2d lt. F.A., Oct.-Nov. 1921, 1st lt. F.A., 1921-1925, capt. F.A., 1925-34, capt. Cav., Brig. Hdqrs. Staff, 52d Cav. Brig., since 1937. Mem. Am., Pa. State and Dauphin Co. bar assns., Zeta Psi, Elihu. Republican. Episcopalian. Elk. Clubs: Beaufort Hunt (Harrisburg); Yale (New York). Home: 2529 N. 2d St. Office: 16 N. 2d St., Harrisburg, Pa.

BAILY, William Lloyd, architect; b. Phila., Pa., Dec. 26, 1861; s. Joshua Longstreth and Theodate Stackpole (Lang) B.; student Germantown (Pa.) Friends Sch., 1868-70, Friends Sch., Phila., 1870-75, Penn Charter Sch., Phila., 1875-80; B.S., Haverford (Pa.) Coll., 1883; student Acad. Fine Arts, Phila., 1886; m. Sarah Boyd, Apr. 27, 1893; children—William Lloyd, Livingstone Boyd, Sara Boyd (Mrs. Craig Heberton II). Mem. firm Baily & Truscott, Phila., 1890-1901; mem. Baily & Bassett, Phila., architects, 1901-31. Mem. bd. Civic & Health Assn., Ardmore, Pa.; U.S. insp. birds and animals, Port of Phila., since 1900. Pres. Friends Freedmen's Assn., Phila.; v.p. Whittier Centre and Wharton Settlement. Mem. A.I.A., Acad. Natural Sciences, Phila., Del. Valley Ornithol. Club., Am. Ornithol. Union, Pa. Audubon Soc. (treas.). Republican. Soc. of Friends. Clubs: Ozone Golf (Phila.); Merion Cricket (Haverford, Pa.). Lecturer on bird conservation; author many articles on birds; amateur artist and photographer of birds, flowers, landscapes. Home: 411 Lancaster Av., Haverford, Pa.

BAIN, Edgar Collins, metallurgist; b. nr. Marion, O., Sept. 14, 1891; s. Milton H. and Alice Anne (Collins) B.; B.Sc., Ohio State U., 1912, M.Sc., 1916; hon. Dr. Engring., Lehigh University, 1936; m. Helen Louise Cram, Feb. 18, 1927; children—Alice Anne, David. Began as chemist U.S. Bur. Standards, 1916; instr. U. of Wis., 1916-17; chem. engr. B.F. Goodrich Co., 1917; metallurgist Nat. Lamp Co. (Gen. Electric Co.), 1918-22; research metallurgist Atlas Steel Co., 1922-24, Union Carbide & Carbon Research Lab., 1924-28, U.S. Steel Corpn. since 1928, assistant to vice-pres. since Feb. 1935. Howe memorial lecturer, 1932; E. DeM. Campbell memorial lecturer, 1932. First lt., U.S.A., World War, 1918. Awarded Robert W. Hunt medal for work on nonrusting steels, 1929, Henry Marion Howe medal, for work on hardening of steel, 1931. Am. Iron and Steel Inst. medal, 1935, for work on alloy steel; Benjamin Lamme medal, Ohio State U., for eminence in engring. Fellow Am. Physics Soc.; mem. Am. Inst. Mining and Metall. Engrs., Am. Soc. for Metals (pres., dir., past chmn. N.Y. sect.), Am. Soc. for Testing Materials, Am. Soc. for Metals (v.p. 1935). Author: (with M. A. Grossmann) High Speed Steel, 1931; also many papers on steel metallurgy. Home: 7 Wilson Dr., Ben Avon Heights, Pittsburgh, Pa. Office: U.S. Steel Corpn. of Del., 436 7th Av., Pittsburgh, Pa.

BAINS, Edward, pres. Bloomsburg Hosiery Mills, Inc.; b. Phila., Pa., Aug. 2, 1874; s. Thomas Mellor and Matilda Ella (Yates) B.; student Friends Central Sch., Phila., 1882-91; m. Ethel Franklin Betts, Sept. 20, 1909. With Thomas Dolan & Co., worsted mfrs., 1891-96; sec.-treas. Phila. Wire Co., 1896-1904; organized Barger & Bains, hosiery mfrs., 1904; sec.-treas. Barger, Bains & Munn, Phila., 1904-19; pres. Bloomsburg Hosiery Mills, Inc., Germantown, Pa., since 1919; dir. Nat. Bank of North Phila., 1921-26, v.p., 1923-26. Mem. bd. mgrs. Germantown Dispensary and Hosp., Germantown Y.M.C.A. Republican. Episcopalian. Clubs: Art, Phila. Cricket (Phila.). Home: 1018 Westview St., Mt. Airy Post Office. Office: 101 W. Chelten Av., Germantown, Philadelphia, Pa.

BAIR, George Joshua, research in ceramics; b. Emporium, Pa., Aug. 26, 1905; s. William George and Harriet May (Auchu) B.; B.S., Pa. State Coll., 1927, M.S., same, 1930; D.Sc., Mass. Inst. Tech., 1936; m. Florence Ellen Donovan, Aug. 22, 1928; children—Anna Denise, Mary Cordelia. Began as asst. supt. brick plant, 1927; instr. ceramics, Pa. State Coll., 1927-31, asst. prof. 1931-36; industrial fellow Mellon Inst., 1936-37; sr. fellow, Mellon Inst. since 1937; vice-pres. Keystone Brick Co., Watsontown, Pa. Mem. Am. Ceramic Soc., Inst. Ceramic Engrs., Alpha Sigma Phi, Sigma Gamma Epsilon, Tau Beta Pi, Sigma Xi. Republican. Roman Catholic. Clubs: Faculty (Pittsburgh); Robert Kennedy Duncan (Mellon Institute). Contbr. tech. articles on ceramics to sci. journs.; contbg. author to "Engineering Opportunities," 1939. Home: 6607 Aylesboro Av., Pittsburgh, Pa.

BAIR, Henry Smyser, engineer; b. York, Pa., Apr. 2, 1889; s. Robert C. and Ella Nora (Smyser) B.; student York (Pa.) Collegiate Inst., 1901-07, Pa. State Coll., 1907-11; m. Alma May Quickel, Sept. 29, 1915. Cadet engr. York Gas Co., now Pa. Gas & Electric Co., York, Pa., 1911-15, engr. since 1927; dir. Pa. Gas & Electric Co., Interborough Gas Co., Conewago Gas Co., Peoples Light of Pittston. Mem. York Chamber of Commerce, Am. Gas Assn., Pa. Gas Assn. Republican. Protestant. Mason, Elk. Clubs: Rotary, York Country (York, Pa.). Home: 125 S. Beaver St. Office: 127 W. Market St., York, Pa.

BAIR, Lawrence Emerson, prof. of theology; b. Hegins, Pa., Apr. 16, 1884; s. Joel Ressler and Ida Sevilla (Ressler) B.; grad. Hegins High Sch., 1901; student Keystone State Normal Sch., 1901-02; A.B., Franklin and Marshall Coll., 1908, D.D., 1929; student Theol. Sem. of the Reformed Ch., 1908-11, Divinity Sch., of the U. of Chicago, 1914; A.M., Columbia, 1927; Ph.D., U. of Pittsburgh, 1939; m. Sadie I. Starr, June 6, 1911; children—Helen Maude, Laura Mary, Lawrence Edgar Starr. Ordained to the ministry of Evang. and Reformed Ch., 1910; asst. pastor St. John's Church, Shamokin, Pa., 1910-13; pastor Salem Reformed Ch., Shamokin, Pa., 1913-17; pastor Trinity Reformed Ch., Millersburg, Pa., 1917-20; pastor First Evangelical and Reformed Ch., Greensburg, Pa., 1920-39; prof. of theology, Theol. Sem. of Reformed Ch., since 1939. Mem. Phi Delta Kappa. Home: 519 W. James St., Lancaster, Pa.

BAIRD, David, Jr., ex-senator; b. Camden, N.J., Oct. 10, 1881; s. David and Christiana B.; edn., Raymond Acad., Camden, Penn Charter Sch., Philadelphia, Pa., and Lawrenceville (N.J.) Sch.; C.E., Princeton, 1903; m. Mrs. Frances H. Smith, June 21, 1930. Pres., treas. David Baird Co., lumber, Camden; pres. and dir. North Camden Bldg. & Loan Assn., Economy Bldg. & Loan Assn., Market Bldg. & Loan Assn.; pres. and dir. Smith-Austermuhl Co.; dir. 1st Camden Nat. Bank, West Jersey & Seashore R.R., N.Y & Long Branch R.R. Apptd. U.S. senator from N.J., Nov. 30, 1929, to fill unexpired term (1925-31) of Senator Walter E. Edge, resigned; nominee for gov. of N.J., 1931. Home: Faughan River Farm, Evesham Road, Marlton, N.J. Office: 425 N. Delaware Av., Camden, N.J.

BAIRD, Joseph Shannon, physician; b. Edgerton, Kan., Nov. 16, 1889; s. Robert and Emma (Shannon) B.; A.B., Coll. of Emporia, 1912; M.D., U. of Pa. Med. Sch., 1916; m. Gladys Chaplin, Oct. 5, 1921; 1 dau., Bonnie Jean. Interne West Penn Hosp., 1916-17; resident phys. Municipal Hosp., Pittsburgh, Pa., 1923-30, supt. since 1930. Served as capt. Med. Corps, U.S.A., with A.E.F., 1918-19. Mem. Allegheny Co. Med. Soc., Pa. State Med Soc., Pitts. Pediatric Soc. Fellow Pittsburgh Acad. of Medicine, Am. Acad. of Pediatrics. Presbyterian. Home: Municipal Hospital, Pittsburgh, Pa.

BAISH, Henry H., sec. retirement board; b. Adams Co., Pa., Feb. 11, 1874; s. Garrett J. and Julia A. (Pensyl) B.; M.E., Shippensburg State Normal Sch., 1895; A.B., Lebanon Valley Coll., 1901; (hon.) LL.D., Lebanon Valley Coll., 1929; m. Ruth Elder, June 20, 1910; 1 dau., Margaret Ann. Instr. pub. schs., Altoona, Pa., 1892-1908, supt. pub. schs., 1908-17; sec. Pa. Pub. Sch. Employes' Retirement Bd. since 1918. Mem. bd. trustees, Lebanon Valley Coll. Republican. Mem. United Brethren in Christ. Clubs: Explorers, Torch, Rotary (Harrisburg). Home: 2615 N. Second St. Office: Education Bldg., Harrisburg, Pa.

BAKER, Allen Langdon, univ. prof.; b. Red Bank, O., Feb. 21, 1893; s. Ernest Edward and Lenora (Langdon) B.; student Walnut Hills High Sch., Cincinnati, O., 1906-10; B. Sc., Ohio State U., Columbus, O., 1917, M.Sc., 1931; m. Elizabeth Wilson Hopkins, Dec. 5, 1917; children—Richard Hopkins, Allen Langdon. Clerk and stenographer, Cincinnati Southern R.R., Cincinnati, O., 1910-12; farming, 1912-13, 1917-20; with Agrl. Extension Service, Pa. State Coll., since 1920, successively as instructor, assistant prof., associate prof. and prof. of agrl. extension since 1928 (asst. state leader, 4-H Clubs, 1920-22, state leader since 1922). Mem. Alpha Zeta, Gamma Sigma Delta, Epsilon Sigma Phi. Methodist. Club: University (State College, Pa.). Address: State College, Pa.

BAKER, Arthur Mulford, clergyman, editor; b. Wapakoneta, O., Oct. 11, 1880; s. John Mulford and Alice Maria (Arthur) B.; A.B., Defiance (O.) Coll., 1906; grad. McCormick Theol. Sem., 1909; studied Columbia U. and Ind. U.; Ph.D., Ind. U., 1928; m. Glenna Maude Helser, June 20, 1907; children—Margaret (Mrs. Arthur M. Adams), Daniel Arthur. Ordained Presbyn. ministry, 1909; pastor Marlboro Ch., Chicago, 1908-11, Grace Ch., Milwaukee, Wis., 1911-13, First Ch., Silver City, N.M., 1913-16, First Ch., Las Cruces, 1916-17, First Ch., Martinsville, Ind., 1919-24; asst. editor Am. S.S. Union Publs., 1924-30, editor since 1930; regular contbr. S.S. lessons to jours., also on methods of teaching. Chaplain 120th Inf., U.S.A., with A.E.F., 1918-19; capt. Co. K, 151st Ind. N.G., 1923-24; chaplain O.R.C. Author: If I Were a Christian, 1930; Hoofbeats in the Wilderness, 1930; The River of God, 1930. Home: 6207 Wayne Av. Office: 1816 Chestnut St., Philadelphia, Pa.

BAKER, Charles George, lawyer; b. Morgantown, W.Va., July 4, 1890; s. George C. and Julliette (Boyers) B.; A.B., W.Va. Univ., Morgantown, 1911; LL.B., W.Va. Univ. Law Coll., 1913; m. Charlotte Blair, July 16, 1913; children—Mary Jane (Mrs. John W. Schuster), Betty Sue (Mrs. Charles S. Armistead). Admitted to W.Va., bar, 1913 and since engaged in gen. practice of law at Morgantown; mem. firm Baker & Reeder since 1937; served as asst. prosecuting atty. Monongalia Co., 1917-24; city solicitor of Morgantown, W.Va., 1925-29; circuit judge of Monongalia Co., 1929-37. Served as sergt. inf., U.S.A. in World War. Past pres. Morgantown Chamber of Commerce. Mem. W.Va. State Chamber of Commerce. First sec. local Kiwanis Club (1920-21). Mem. am., W.Va. State and Monongalia Co. bar assns., Am. Legion (hon.), Vets. Fgn. Wars, Kappa Alpha, Phi Delta Phi. Hon. Texas Ranger. Republican. Methodist (trustee First M.E. Ch.). Mason. Odd Fellow. Club: XX (Morgantown). Home: 209 S. Walnut St. Office: 170 Chancery Row, Morgantown, W.Va.

BAKER, Charles Whiting, mech. engring.; b. Johnson, Vt., Jan. 17, 1865; s. Thomas Jefferson and Mattie (Whiting) B.; ed. Vt. State Normal Sch., 1879-82; C.E., U. of Vt., 1886; m. Rebekah Wheeler, June 4, 1890; children—Jefferson Wheeler, Charles Whiting, Jr. (dec.). Employed as asso. editor Engineering News, 1887-90, mng. editor, 1890-94, editor in chief, 1894-1917; cons. editor, Engineering News-Record, 1917-20; engaged in bus. on own acct. as broker for sale bus. properties, Montclair, N.J., since 1920. Served as commr. Palisades Interstate Park of N.Y. and N.J. since 1912. Mem. Am. Soc. Mech. Engrs. (v.p. 1909-11), Machinery Club. Conglist. Author: Monopolies and the People, 1889; Pathways Back to Prosperity, 1932. Home: 20 S. Mountain Av., Montclair, N.J.

BAKER, Charles William, Jr., broker; b. New York, N.Y., Dec. 18, 1900; s. Charles William and Frances Anne (Chandler) B.; student Collegiate Sch., New York, 1905-14, St. Paul's Sch., Concord, N.H., 1914-18; A.B., Harvard, 1922; m. Elizabeth Swift Holladay, May 23, 1925; children—Elizabeth Swift, Anne Louise, Charles William III. Securities salesman Laird Bissell & Meeds, brokers in securities and commodities, Wilmington, Del., 1922-26, partner since 1926; dir. Joseph Bancroft & Sons Co., Newport Industries, Inc. Dir. Homeopathic Hosp. Assn., Wilmington. Mem. Spee Club, Varsity Club (Harvard). Republican. Episcopalian. Clubs: Wilmington, Recess, Wilmington Country, Vicmead Hunt, Delaware Turf (Wilmington, Del.); Harvard of Delaware; Bond, Harvard (Phila., Pa.); Harvard (New York). Home: Greenville, Del. Office: du Pont Bldg., Wilmington, Del.

BAKER, Colley Sharpnack, chmn. Pa. Securities Commn.; b. West Pike Run Twp., Washington Co., Pa., Jan. 16, 1890; s. Charles E. and Mary Ann (Sharpnack) B.; grad. East Washington (Pa.) High Sch., 1908; student Washington and Jefferson Coll., 1908-1912; m. Marie Elizabeth Coyle, Nov. 16, 1914; children—Robert Charles, Colley Sharpnack. While in college was reporter for Washington (Pa.) Record, Washington Democrat, editor Washington Journal; reporter Uniontown (Pa.) Morning Herald, 1911-12, 1914-17; asst. editor Tri State News Bur., Pittsburgh, 1912-14; political and financial writer and editor Phila. North American, 1917-23; editor Stroudsburg (Pa.) Record, 1923-35; mem. Pa. Securities Commn. since 1935, chmn. since 1937. Mem. Nat. Assn. of Securities Commissioners (chmn. com. on investment trusts and investment companies since 1938); mem. Eastern Region Nat. Assn. of Securities Commissioners (chmn. since 1938). Democrat. Home: 115 North St., Harrisburg, Pa.; Pocono Park, Stroudsburg, Pa. Office: Education Bldg., Harrisburg, Pa.

BAKER, Donald Gay, coll. prof.; b. Haverford, Pa., Oct. 16, 1905; s. William Wilson and Mertie Gay (Collins) B.; student Westtown (Pa.) Sch., 1920-22; A.B., Haverford (Pa.) Coll., 1926; M.A., Harvard, 1929, Ph.D., 1932; m. Margaret Searle Knapp, June 24, 1933; children—Louise Gay, Elizabeth Searle. Teacher of Latin and Greek, St. George's Sch., Newport, R.I., 1926-28; asst. prof. of Greek, Ursinus Coll., Collegeville, Pa., 1932-36, asso. prof. since 1936. Mem. Am. Inst. Archæology, Am. Philol. Assn., Phila. Classical Club. Republican. Soc. of Friends. Soccer coach at St. Georges' Sch., Harvard and Ursinus Coll. Address: Collegeville, Pa.

BAKER, Elsworth Fredrick, M.D., psychiatrist, psychoanalyst; b. Summit, S.D., Feb. 5, 1903; s. Niles Albert and Effie Anna (Cartwright) B.; ed. Regina Coll., Regina, Sask., U. of Manitoba, 1922-23; M.D., cum laude, Manitoba Med. Coll., 1928; grad. study, U. of Vienna, Royal Coll. Surgeons, Edinburgh, 1929; m. Olga Maria Bertagni, of Pisa, Italy, Feb. 5, 1931. Rotating interne, Vancouver (B.C.) Gen. Hosp., 1927-28; res. phys., State Hosp., Greystone Park, N.J., 1928-31; sr. res. phys., chief of women's service, State Hosp., Marlboro, N.J. since 1931; has spent 350 hrs. didactic and control analysis under Dr. Louis S. London, N.Y. City, 1934-38. Licentiate Med. Council of Canada. Fellow Am. Med. Assn., Am. Psychiatric Assn. Diplomate Am. Bd. Psychiatry & Neurology. Mem. A.A.A.S., N.J. Neuropsychiatric Assn., Am. Med. Assn. of Vienna. Mem. United Ch. Can. Contbr. articles to med. journs. Home: State Hospital, Marlboro, N.J.

BAKER, Everett Meade, physician; b. Valencia, Pa., June 3, 1902; s. Everett Minner and Blanche Anna (Datt) B.; ed. pub. schs. and high sch. Pittsburgh; B.S. in Chem. Engring., Grove City Coll., 1923; M.D., U. of Pittsburgh, 1927; grad. student Med. Sch. Cornell U., 1933-34; unmarried. Interne St. Francis Hosp., Pittsburgh, Pa., 1927-28; resident in obstetrics, Elizabeth Steele Magee Hosp., 1928-29, resident pathologist, 1929-30, resident surgeon, 1930-31; engaged in gen. and surg. practice in Butler Co., 1931-33; in practice gynecology and surgery at Pittsburgh since 1934. Served as res. officer med. corps U.S.A. since 1924. Fellow Am. Coll. Surgeons; mem. Pittsburgh Obstet. and Gynecol. Soc., Biol. Soc., Clin. Pathol. Soc., Beta Sigma, Nu Sigma Nu. Republican. Methodist. Mason (32°; Shriner). Home: Valencia. Office: 121 University Pl., Pittsburgh, Pa.

BAKER, Frank Eugene, broker; b. Louisville, Ill., Jan. 24, 1890; s. Michael Benton and Ella H. (Rippetoe) B.; grad. Sumner (Ill.) High Sch., 1907; student Shurtleff Coll., Alton, Ill., 1907-09; B.S., U. of Pa., 1911; m. Gladys W. Campbell, July 15, 1913; children—Gladys Campbell (Mrs. Alexander H. Reynolds, Jr.), Nan (Mrs. William Alden Eaton, Jr.), Jean Frances. Began as investment broker, 1911; since 1929 mem. firm Baker, Weeks & Harden, investment brokers, mem. N.Y. Stock Exchange; dir. Henry K. Wampole & Co.; treas. Phila. Stock Exchange. Mem. Welfare Commn. of Commonwealth of Pa.; v.p. Bd. Home Missions and Ch. Extension of M.E. Ch.; trustee and pres. bd. M.E. Hosp.; v.p. and trustee Drew U. Republican. Methodist. Mason. Clubs: Union League, Midday, Bond, Phila. Country (Phila.); Hangar, Broad St. (New York). Home: 306 Bala Av., Bala-Cynwyd. Office: 1421 Chestnut St., Philadelphia, Pa.

BAKER, Frederick Van Vliet, artist; b. New York, Nov. 6, 1876; s. Charles and Elizabeth Priscilla (Vanderpoel) B.; ed. Pratt Inst., Brooklyn, École des Beaux Arts, Colorossi, Paris; m. Maud Lillian Forsbrey, Dec. 13, 1902. Pres. Colonial Studios (Inc.) since 1906; instr. in life drawing, painting and composition, Pratt Inst. Exhibited in salons, Paris, 1901, 02, 03, also at Ghent, Vienna, Chicago, New York, etc. Asso.

Société Nationale des Beaux Arts, 1901. Home: Mountain Lakes, N.J. Address: Pratt Institute, Brooklyn, N.Y.

BAKER, George Harold, canning vegetables; b. Aberdeen, Md., Oct. 15, 1884; s. James Bramwell and Frances (Richardson) B.; grad. Bryant & Stratton Bus. Coll., 1905; Ph.B., Dickinson Coll., 1910, A.M., same, 1911; ed. Peabody Conservatory of Music, 1915-17; m. Louise Lockhart, Apr. 16, 1920; children—George Harold, Jr., James Lockhart, Barry. Engaged as teacher French and history, Conway Hall, 1910-11; entered bus. of canning vegetables, 1911; pres. G. H. Baker, Inc. since 1934; first vice-pres. First Nat. Bank, Aberdeen, Md. Served as enlisted pvt. to 1st lt. then capt., U.S.A., 1917-19, maj. U.S.A. Res., 1919. Trustee Dickinson Coll., Carlisle, Pa. Mem. Kappa Sigma. Ind. Republican. Methodist. Home: Aberdeen, Md.

BAKER, Henry Fenimore, chem. mfg. and banking, retired; b. Somerset Co., N.J., Mar. 28, 1859; s. Milton and Henrietta (Boozer) B.; Ph.G., N.J. Bd. of Pharmacy, 1876; night course Pratt Inst. Tech., 1894-95; m. Cora Warman, Nov. 15, 1887; children—Marjorie (Mrs. Frank G. Breyer), Albert Brewer, Edwin Warman, Anne Love (Mrs. Herbert J. Leimbach), Henry Fenimore, Jr., Helen Maxwell (Mrs. Charles S. Brawner). Began as drug clk., 1873, grad. pharmacist, 1876; then mem. drug firm Geo. F. Wilson & Co., Trenton, N.J.; later road salesman Bruen Bros. & Richey, N.Y., and sales mgr. Martin Kalbfleisch Chem Co., N.Y. City; then sales mgr. Gen. Chem. Co., N.Y. City; became pres. Thomsen Chem. Co., Baltimore, Md.; mem. firm Robert Garret & Sons, bankers, Baltimore, to 1918, retired from active bus., 1918; mem. bd. dirs. Hopkins Place Savings Bank. Mem. Baltimore Assn. Commerce (dir. past pres.), Baltimore Drug Exchange (past pres.), Baltimore Safety Council (dir. past pres.), Md. Tuberculosis Assn. (treas and dir.). Trustee Goucher Coll., Baltimore, Md. Past pres. Gen. Nat. Soc. S.A.R. Republican. Episcopalian. Club: Mt. Washington of Baltimore (past pres.). Home: Northway Apts. Office: 900 St. Paul St., Baltimore, Md.

BAKER, Henry Scott, univ. treas.; b. Washington, D.C., Sept. 9, 1895; s. Robert W. and Abby P. (Scott) B.; B.S. in engring., Johns Hopkins U., 1917; m. Frances I. Robinson, June 6, 1925; children—Henry Scott, Jr., Ralph Robinson. Began as engr., 1919; asst. dir. Industrial Bur., Bd. of Trade, Baltimore, Md., 1920-26; with Alex Brown & Sons, 1926-34; treas. Johns Hopkins U. since 1934, sec. bd. trustees since 1934; dir. Metropolitan Savings Bank, Baltimore, Md. since 1937. Served at First O.T.C., Fort Meyer, Va., 1917; capt. F.A., U.S.A., 1917-19, with A.E.F. in France, 1918-19. Mem. Alpha Delta Phi. Democrat. Episcopalian. Clubs: L'Hirondelle (Ruxton); Johns Hopkins, Bachelors Cotillon. Home: 805 St. Georges Rd., Baltimore, Md.

BAKER, Holmes Davenport, banker; b. Frederick, Md., Apr. 11, 1880; s. Joseph Dill and Emma Newkirk (Cunningham) B.; student Frederick Acad., 1890-95; A.B., Western Md. Coll., Westminster, Md., 1899; m. Geraldine Frost, Sept. 16, 1922; children—Geraldine Frost, Holmes Davenport (dec.), Joseph Dill, II. Began as clk. Citizens Nat. Bank, 1900, pres. since 1922; v.p. Standard Lime & Stone Co., Washington Building Lime Co. Served as 2d lt., later 1st lt., U.S.A., World War. Trustee and v.p. Buckingham Sch., Buckeystown, Md.; trustee Frederick Female Sem., Frederick Home for the Aged; mem. Md. Com. for Expenditure of Pub. Works Fund, 1933, recovery bd. for Norfolk, Va. dist., NRA, 1933; chmn. Frederick County Welfare Bd., 1933; mem. of Bowman Com. on the Structure of the Md. State Govt., 1938; mem. bd. dirs. Community Fund of Frederick, Md.; pres. Md. Bankers Assn., 1925-26; mem. exec. council Am. Bankers Assn., 1937; pres. Federated Charities of Frederick, Md.; dir. Frederick Chamber of Commerce. Democrat. Episcopalian. Clubs: Rotary (ex-pres.), Catoctin Country (Frederick); Chesapeake (Baltimore); Woodmont Rod and Gun (Hancock, Md.). Home: Frederick, Md.

BAKER, Horace Forbes, lawyer; b. Mayville, N.Y., Apr. 15, 1878; s. George Albert and Julia Brewster (Hurlbert) B.; grad. Rayen High Sch., Youngstown, Ohio, 1897; A.B., magna cum laude, Harvard Univ., 1901, LL.B. from same university, 1903; m. Jane Torrance, Apr. 16, 1914; children—Francis J. Torrance, Mary Rachel. Admitted to Pa. bar, 1904, and began practice at Pittsburgh; associated with A. O. Fording in gen. practice; asst. to gen. counsel Wabash R.R. Lines East of Toledo, 1905-08; atty. for receivers same road, 1908-12, receiver, 1912-16; gen. counsel and v.p. reorganized company, The Pittsburgh & W.Va. Ry. Co., 1917-22; gen. practice since 1917; mem. firm Baker & Watts; mem. bd. directors St. Paul Coal Co., Bostwick Steel Lath Co., Standard Sanitary Mfg. Co., Nat. Fireproofing Corpn.; trustee Dollar Savings Bank (Pittsburgh). Mem. bd. of dirs. Public Charities Assn. of Pa.; pres. Community Fund of Pittsburgh; trustee Family Society of Allegheny County; dir. Woods Run Settlement. Mem. Am., Pa. State and Allegheny Co. bar assns., Am. Civic Assn., Sigma Alpha Epsilon. Republican. Episcopalian. Mason. Clubs: Harvard of Western Pa., Harvard-Yale-Princeton, Pittsburgh, Duquesne (Pittsburgh); Allegheny Country; Edgeworth Club; Harvard (New York). Home: 1008 Beaver Rd., Sewickley, Pa. Office: Union Trust Bldg., Pittsburgh, Pa.

BAKER, John Henry, mfg. bldg. materials; b. Buckeystown, Md., Nov. 24, 1869; s. William Gideon and Susan Ellen (Jones) B.; ed. Western Md. Coll., Westminster, 1884-86, Eastman Business Coll., Poughkeepsie, N.Y., 1890; m. Lena Frances Millard, Feb. 14, 1893; children—Almira (Mrs. F. Lazelle Sawyers), Ellen (Mrs. Joseph D. Baker, Jr.). Asso. with The Standard Lime & Stone Co., Baltimore, Md. since began as sec. and treas., 1890, pres. and dir. since 1922; pres. and dir. Buckeystown Packing Co.; v.p. and dir. Citizens Nat. Bank, Frederick, Md. Sec., treas. and dir. Buckingham Sch., Buckeystown, Md.; dir. Western Md. Coll., Westminster, Md.; v.p. and mem. bd. visitors Md. Sch. for Deaf, Frederick. Democrat. Methodist. Clubs: Chesapeake (Baltimore); Rotary (Frederick). Home: Buckeystown, Md. Office: First Nat. Bank Bldg., Baltimore, Md.

BAKER, John M(aurice), lawyer; b. LeRoy, W.Va., Nov. 22, 1872; s. Dallas Monroe and Mary Eliza B.; student Fairmont State Normal Sch., Fairmont, W.Va., two terms 1892; LL.B., W.Va. Univ. Law Coll., 1896; m. Jessie M. Riley, Sept. 19, 1899; children—Clay R., Mary V. (Mrs. Roy F. Truman). Admitted to W.Va. bar, 1896; engaged in gen. practice of law at Ripley and Spencer, W.Va., since 1896; prosecuting atty. Jackson Co., 1905-09; mem. bd. edn. Spencer, W.Va., 1912-17; served as mem. W.Va. Senate, 1923-27. Mem. Am. Bar Assn., W.Va. State Bar Assn., Regional Bar Assn. Republican. Mason. Home: 203 Spring St. Office: 307 Church St., Spencer, W.Va.

BAKER, John Stewart, banker; b. Lawrence, N.Y., August 6, 1893; s. of Stephen and Mary Dabney (Payson) B.; grad. Hill Sch., 1911, Princeton, 1915; m. Marianne L. Foote, 1915. Chmn. bd. Bank of the Manhattan Co.; dir. Bank of Manhattan Safe Deposit Co., etc. Served in U.S. Navy, World War. Clubs: Baltusrol Golf, Union League, Union, Down Town Assn. Home: Short Hills, N.J. Office: 40 Wall St., New York, N.Y.

BAKER, Joseph Richardson, lawyer; b. New Hartford, N.Y., Feb. 11, 1872; s. Alonzo E. and Cordelia (Richardson) B.; A.B., Hamilton Coll., Clinton, N.Y., 1893; m. Florilla G. Richmond, February 21, 1928. Was admitted to N.Y. bar, 1896; law clerk Commn. to Five Civilized Tribes, Dept. of Interior, 1902-03; with Post Office Dept., 1903-06, Dept. of State, 1906-16; spl. agt. Dept. of State in Samoa, and vice and dep. consul at Apia, 1911; asst. solicitor Dept. of State since 1916; agt. Dept. of State, in Panama, 1917. Mem. U.S.-Panama Commn. to negotiate a treaty, 1924; commr. U.S. Gen. Claims Commn., U.S., and Mexico, 1924; del. of U.S. to Paris Conf. on Air Navigation, 1929; tech. adviser to U.S. delegation at Geneva Conf. on Red Cross and Prisoners of War, 1929; agt. Dept. of State in Germany, 1929; commr. U.S. Gen. Claims Commn., U.S. and Panama, 1933; agent of Department of State in Mexico, 1935; tech. adviser to U.S. delegation at Buenos Aires Conf. on Maintenance of Peace, 1936. Mem. Am. Soc. Internat. Law, Sigma Phi, Phi Beta Kappa. Collaborator: Commercial Laws of the World; The Laws of Maritime Warfare; The Laws of Land Warfare; Selected Topics connected with The Laws of Warfare. Prepared: The Laws of Neutrality. Clubs: University, Arts. Home: Kensington, Md.

BAKER, Maclyn Francis, M.D.; b. Irvington, N.J.; s. David and Anna (Winikus) B.; student New York U., 1916-20; M.D., Bellevue Hosp. and Med. Sch., 1924; m. Elimara Evans, 1920; children—Evan Hubert, Donn; m. 2d, Pauline Wolgemuth, 1937. Began gen. practice of medicine, 1925; attending surgeon Irvington Gen. Hosp. Fellow Am. Coll. Surgeons. Home: 987 Sanford Av. Office: 638 Stuyvesant Av., Irvington, N.J.

BAKER, Mary Neikirk, librarian; b. Keedysville, Md., Aug. 20, 1884; d. William Otterbein and Mary Susan (Neikirk) B.; A.B., Otterbein Coll., 1906; certificate, N.Y. State Library Sch., 1910. Librarian Elwood (Ind.) Pub. Library, 1910-12; asst. supt. circulation, Seattle (Wash.) Pub. Library, 1912-18, branch of same, 1920-22; library organizer, O. State Library, 1923-27; asst. to librarian in charge Central Circulation Branch, New York Pub. Library, 1928-31; librarian Osterhout Free Library, Wilkes-Barre, Pa., since 1931. Trustee Bucknell Jr. Coll., Wilkes-Barre, Pa. Mem. Pa. Pub. Library Assn. (pres. 1938-39). Presbyterian. Clubs: Wyoming Valley Women's, College (Wilkes-Barre) Mountaineers (Seattle). Home: 132 S. Franklin St. Office: Osterhout Free Library, Wilkes-Barre, Pa.

BAKER, Maurice Edward, physician and surgeon; b. Cleveland Co., N.C., Mar. 19, 1892; s. Michael J. and Dora S. (Shell) B.; B.S., U. of N.C., Chapel Hill, N.C., 1919; M.D., Jefferson Med. Coll., Phila., 1921; m. Rebecca Zieger, 1923. Physician, genito-urinary dept., Cooper Hosp., Camden, N.J., 1922-27; gynecol. dept., Jefferson Hosp., Phila., 1923-37; med. dir., Camden (N.J.) City Pub. Schs., since 1937; pres. Belleview Hosp., Camden, N.J., since 1937. Address: 1149 Kaighn Av., Camden, N.J.

BAKER, Milton Grafly, supt. Valley Forge Mil. Acad.; b. Phila., Pa., Aug. 24, 1896; s. Frank Robertson and Sallie (Dimmock) B.; student Brown Prep. Sch., 1911-14, St. John's Coll., 1915-17; m. May Porter Hagenbuch, May 24, 1924; 1 dau. Ann Porter. Supt., pres. and treas. Valley Forge Mil. Acad. since 1928. Served in U.S. Army, 1917-21; now col. comdg. 103d Cav., Pa. Nat. Guard. Mem. Valley Forge Park Commn., Pa. Soc. S.R., Mil. Order World War. Republican. Episcopalian. Mason (32°). Clubs: Union League, Art, Army and Navy (Phila.); Canadian (New York). Home: Wayne, Pa.

BAKER, Morris H., banking; b. Birchardville, Pa., July 16, 1896; s. Horace and Nellie (Morris) B.; ed. high sch., Montrose, Pa., 1912-15, Peirce Sch. of Bus., Phila., Pa., 1916; m. Dawn Drake, 1916; 1 son, Braton D. Asso. with Farmers Nat. Bank & Trust Co. of Montrose, Pa., since 1916, successively clk., bookkeeper, teller, asst. to pres., exec. vice-pres., vice-pres., cashier and dir.; pres. and dir. Montrose Beef Co., Pittston, Pa.; dir. Beach Mfg. Co. Republican. Methodist. Mason (K.T., Shriner). Clubs: Craftsman, Country. Home: 57 Lake Av. Office: Public Av., Montrose, Pa.

BAKER, Moses Haven, physician; b. Stockwell, Ind., June 4, 1883; s. Joseph Haven and Belle (Miller) B.; grad. Lafayette (Ind.) High Sch., 1902; B.S., Purdue U., 1905; student Liese Univ., Aachen, Germany, 1905-06; M.D., Johns Hopkins, 1910; m. Nita M. Cashman, June 20, 1915. Interne St. Francis Hosp., Pittsburgh, 1910-11, resident physician, 1911-12; in practice of medicine, Pittsburgh, since 1912, specializing in clinical pathology since 1914. Served as capt. Med. Corps, U.S. Army, 1917-19. Mem. A.M.A., Soc. Am. Bacteriologists, Am. Soc. Clin. Pathology, Pittsburgh

Acad. Science, Beta Theta Pi, Nu Sigma Nu. Republican. Presbyterian. Home: 6045 Bunkerhill St. Office: 121 University Place, Pittsburgh, Pa.

BAKER, Moses Nelson, editor; b. Enosburg, Vt., Jan. 26, 1864; s. Benjamin N. and Sarah M. (Wright) B.; Ph.B., U. of Vt., 1886, C.E., 1899; m. Ella S. Babbit, Aug. 22, 1889; children—Theta Helen, Will Wright (dec.), Frederick Wood, Elizabeth Wright, Ruth, Dorothea. Asso. editor Engineering News, 1887-1917, and of Engineering News-Record, 1917-32. Mem. Bd. Health, Montclair, N.J., 1894-1915, pres. 1904-15; v.p. New Jersey State Department Health, 1915-16. Member National Municipal League (chairman executive committee 1911-18), American Water Works Association. Editor: Manual of American Water Works, 1888, 1889-90, 1891, 1897; Municipal Year Book, 1902. Author: Sewage Purification in America, 1893; Sewage Disposal in United States (joint author), 1894; Sewerage and Sewage Purification, 1896; Potable Water, 1899; Municipal Monopolies (joint author), 1899; Municipal Engineering and Sanitation, 1901; British Sewage Works, 1904; Notes on British Refuse Destructors, 1905, also author Municipal Engineering Topics in Internat. Year Book, 1898, 99, and 1907—; same in Internat. Cyclo., and Nelson's Loose Leaf Encyc. Home: 53 Oakwood Av., Montclair, N.J.

BAKER, Oliver Edwin, economic and sociological geographer; b. Tiffin, Ohio, Sept. 10, 1883; s. Edwin and Martha (Thomas) B.; B.Sc., Heidelberg Coll., Ohio, 1903, M.Sc., 1904; M.A., in Polit. Science, Columbia, 1905; studied forestry, Yale U., 1907-08, agr., U. of Wis., 1908-12, economics, 1919-21, Ph.D., 1921; hon. D.Sc., Heidelberg (Ohio) College and Goettingen (Germany), 1937; m. Alice H. Crew, 1925; children—Helen Thomas, Sabra Z., Edwin Crew, Mildred Coale. With Wis. Agrl. Expt. Sta., 1910-12, U.S. Dept. Agr. since 1912; employed in research on land utilization in U.S. and farm population; in charge of preparation, and editor of Atlas of American Agriculture, issued in sects., 1914-36. Mem. Assn. Am. Geographers (pres. 1931), Am. Meteorol. Soc., Farm Economic Assn., Am. Statis. Assn., American Sociological Soc. Republican. Author: (with A. R. Whitson) The Climate of Wisconsin and Its Relation to Agriculture, 1912; (with V. C. Finch) Geography of the World's Agriculture, 1917; (with W. L. Wilson and Ralph Borsodi) Agriculture and Modern Life, 1939; also, with others, of sections of Atlas Am. Agr. Contbr. to U.S. Dept. Agr. Year Books, 1915-38, and to geographic publs. Home: College Park, Md. Office: Bureau of Agricultural Economics, Washington, D.C.

BAKER, Philip Woodell, physician; b. Castleton, Vt., May 3, 1905; s. Albert Jefferson and Minnie Eloise (Woodell) B.; B.Sc., Mass. State Coll., Amherst, Mass., 1927; M.D., Harvard U. Med. Sch., 1931; m. Alice Bacon Hopkins, Sept. 15, 1930; children—Phyllis Elizabeth, Lucille Mae. Resident physician Cooper Hosp., Camden, N.J., 1931-32; in pvt. practice of medicine at High Bridge, N.J., since 1932; sch. physician, High Bridge since 1933; attdg. surgeon, Taylor-Wharton Steel & Iron Co., High Bridge, since 1933; physician Lebanon Twp. Schs. since 1935; field physician Hunterdon Co., 1937-39. Served as 1st lt. Med. Res., 1931-36. Mem. Am. Med. Assn., N.J. State Med. Soc., Hunterdon Co. Med. Soc. (pres. 1935), Kappa Gamma Phi. Mem. Ref. Ch. Mason, K. of P. Club: Harkers Hollow Golf (Phillipsburg). Home: Church St., High Bridge, N.J.

BAKER, Ralph Dodamead, real estate, insurance; b. Camden, N.J., Mar. 24, 1887; s. James Fairfowl and Emma (Cooper) B.; student Liberty School, Camden, N.J., 1901-03, Temple Coll., Phila., 1906-08; m. Helen Nicholas, Oct. 7, 1916; children—Helen Nicholas, James Fairfowl, Stuart Gilmore. Began in father's real estate office, James F. Baker Co., Camden, N.J., 1903, partner, 1910-15, purchased business, June 30, 1915, and has since been pres.; real estate business in all branches, sales, management, appraisals, court testimony and insurance; vice-pres. Community Hotel Corpn. (owners of Walt Whitman Hotel); dir. West Jersey Title and Guaranty Co.; dir. First Camden Nat. Bank & Trust Co.; sec. Phoenix Bldg. & Loan Assn.; treas. Guarantee Bldg. & Loan Assn. Mem. Camden Co. Chamber of Commerce. Treas. Camden Home for Friendless Children. Mem. governing council of Am. Inst. of Real Estate Appraisers of Nat. Assn. of Real Estate Bds. Mem. N.J. Chapter Am. Inst. Real Estate Appraisers, Camden Co. Real Estate Bd., Nat. and N.J. Assns. of Real Estate Bds., Soc. Residential Appraisers (dir.), Camden Co. Hist. Soc. Mem. bd. trustees West Jersey Homeopathic Hosp. and Harleigh Cemetery Assn., Camden, N.J. Republican. Presbyterian. Mason (32°, Shriner), Modern Woodmen of America. Represented N.J. Highway Commn., Camden Co. Park Commn., Camden Bd. of Freeholders in acquisition of land; represented R.F.C. in appraising property in 3d Federal Dist., N.J., also Federal Deposit Ins. Corpn., Home Owners Loan Corpn. and Works Progress Adminstrn. in appraisals; appraisals in all types of property. Home: 111 Chews Landing Rd., Haddonfield, N.J. Office: 924 Broadway, Camden, N.J.

BAKER, S. Josephine, M.D.; b. Poughkeepsie, N.Y., Nov. 15, 1873; d. Orlando D. M. and Jennie Harwood (Brown) B.; M.D., Woman's Med. Coll., New York Infirmary, 1898; interne N.E. Hosp., Boston, 1898-99; Dr. P. H. Bellevue Med. Coll. (New York U.), 1917; unmarried. Asst. to commr. of health, N.Y. City, 1907-08; dir. Bur. Child Hygiene, Dept. of Health, 1908-23; consultant U.S. P.H.S., and various other orgns.; consultant Children's Bureau of U.S. Dept. Labor. Former mem. from U.S. of Health Com. League of Nations. Organized 1st bur. of child hygiene under govt. control, leading to lowest baby death rate in N.Y. City, of any large city in America or Europe. Fellow A.M.A., Am. Pub. Health Assn., New York Acad. Medicine; mem. Am. Child Health Assn. (ex-pres.), N.Y. State and N.Y. County med. socs., Authors' League America. Democrat. Unitarian. Clubs: Cosmopolitan, Women's City. Author: Healthy Mothers, 1923; Healthy Babies, 1923; Healthy Children, 1923; Child Hygiene, 1925; Fighting for Life, 1939. Formerly lecturer on child hygiene, Columbia and New York univs. Home: 148 Hodge Rd., Princeton, N.J.

BAKER, Samuel, asso. dean of corr. school; b. Smorgon, Russia, Aug. 13, 1893; s. Ephraim and Mary (Grossman) B.; student Cooper Union Inst. Tech., N.Y., 1909-13, Coll. of City of N.Y., 1913-16; came to U.S., 1907, naturalized, 1912; m. May Neidorf, Nov. 29, 1924; 1 dau., Virginia Harriet. Structural draftsman, Am. Bridge Co., N.Y., 1913-14; surveyor and designer, Pub. Service Commn., N.Y., 1914-16; designer, Pittsburgh and Lake Erie R.R., Pittsburgh, Pa., 1916-19; concrete designer, E. I. duPont de Nemours & Co., Wilmington, Del., 1919; principal, civil engring. schs., Internat. Corr. Schs., Scranton, Pa., 1919-26, dir. civil engring. schs., 1926-38, asso. dean, schs. of tech., since 1938; bridge designer, Erie R.R., N.Y., 1926. Mem. Am. Soc. C.E., Am. Ry. Engring. Assn., Soc. for Promotion of Engring. Edn., Pa. Soc. Professional Engrs., Am. Concrete Inst., Am. Assn. Engrs. Club: Scranton Tennis (Scranton, Pa.; dir., past pres.). Author: Structural Drawing, 1924; Reinforced Concrete Design, 1928; Concrete Engineers' Manual (handbook), 1930; numerous pamphlets on civil engring. subjects for Internat. Corr. Schs. Home: 1501 Quincy Av. Office: International Correspondence Schools, Scranton, Pa.

BAKER, Thomas Alexander, univ. prof.; b. Dalton, Ga., Jan. 17, 1893; s. Thomas Alexander and Winifred (Stone) B.; student Trumansburg (N.Y.) High Sch., 1906-10; B.S., Cornell U., 1914, Ph.D., 1933; m. Ruth Elizabeth Brown, Aug. 11, 1923; children—Melissa, Winifred (dec.), Phyllis. Instr. in animal husbandry, Cornell U., 1914-17, State Sch. of Agr., Cobleskill, N.Y., 1917-18; prof. of animal husbandry, U. of Del., Newark, Del., since 1919. Served as pvt. with U.S. Marines in France, 1918-19. Mem. A.A.A.S., Am. Assn. of Univ. Profs., Sigma Xi, Phi Kappa Phi, Gamma Alpha, Alpha Zeta. Presbyterian. Mason. Club: Lions (Newark, Del.). Address: 240 Orchard Rd., Newark, Del.

BAKER, Thomas Stockham, educator; b. Aberdeen, Harford Co., Md., Mar. 23, 1871; s. John H. and Cornelia E. (Stockham) B.; A.B., Johns Hopkins, 1891, Ph.D., 1895; U. of Leipzig, 1892; LL.D., U. of Del., 1924; ScD., Duquesne, 1928, Lafayette College, 1932; unmarried. Asso. in German, 1895-1900, lecturer on modern German lit., 1900-08, Johns Hopkins; prof. modern langs., 1900-08, dir., 1909-19, The Jacob Tome Inst., Port Deposit, Md.; sec. Carnegie Inst. Tech., 1919-22, pres., 1922-35, pres. emeritus and trustee since 1935; chmn. tech. com. Carnegie Coal Research Lab. Director Forbes National Bank. Mus. critic Baltimore Sun, 1895-1905. Mem. Mod. Lang. Assn. Am., Head Masters' Assn., Phi Beta Kappa. Clubs: University (Baltimore), Pittsburgh Athletic, Duquesne, University (Pittsburgh). Author: Lenau and Young Germany. Editor: Hauptmann's The Sunken Bell, 1898. Contbr. lit. and ednl. essays to mags. and newspapers. Delivered, in Paris, 1928, under auspices of Carnegie Foundation for Internat. Peace, series of articles entitled America, the Land of Realism, The American Mind, Mechanization and Standardization, The Voice of the People. Organized first, second and third internat. conferences on bituminous coal, held at Carnegie Inst. of Tech., 1926, 28 and 31. Lectured, 1933, at German univs. under auspices of Carl Schurz Memorial Foundation on "The Significance of the United States for Europe in the Twentieth Century." Home: Pittsburgh Athletic Club. Address: Carnegie Institute of Technology, Pittsburgh, Pa.

BAKER, Ulysses S. Grant, editor and newspaper pub.; b. Burlington, Pa., July 9, 1878; s. Thomas S. and Joanna (Lavin) B.; ed. pub. schs. of Pa.; m. Nora V. Stapleton, Oct. 18, 1899; children—Paul S., J. Donald. Employed as circulation mgr., Evening News, Burlington, Vt., 1901-02; ed. and pub. Evening Tribune, Toronto, O., 1902-07; ed. in chief, Daily Review, Towanda, Pa., 1907-17; purchased Evening Transcript, established 1886, and Susquehanna Weekly Ledger, established 1863, both at Susquehanna, Pa., and propr., ed. and pub. since 1917; active in civic affairs. Trustee Barnes Memorial Hosp., Susquehanna, Pa. Republican. Contbr. to many newspapers, spl. corr. for press assns., articles for mags. Lecturer on hist. and wide variety of topics over large part of N.Y. and Pa. Rep. Nat. Comm. campaign speaker, Pa., 1936. Home: 204 Jackson Av. Office: Exchange St., Susquehanna, Pa.

BAKER, Walter H.; pres. Universal Cyclops Steel Corpn. Home: LeMoyne Av. Extension, Washington, Pa. Office: Bridgeville, Pa.

BAKER, William E., judge; b. Beverly, W. Va., Feb. 25, 1873; s. Eli and Margaret Ellen (Sexton) B.; B.S., W.Va. Conf. Sem., Buckhannon, W.Va., 1893; A.B., LL.B., W.Va. U., 1896; m. Martha Ruston Davidson, Mar. 1906. Began practice at Elkins, 1896, spl. counsel late S. B. Elkins and H. G. Davis, U.S. senators; mem. Rep. State Com., W.Va., 1912-20, chmn. 1918-20; judge U.S. Dist. Court, Northern Dist. of W.Va., since Apr. 3, 1921. Republican. Presbyn. Mason (K.T., 32°, Shriner). Home: Elkins, W.Va.

BAKER, William E., pres. William E. Baker & Co. Address: Tenafly, N.J.

BAKER, William Franklin, physician; b. Phila., Pa., Oct. 12, 1878; s. Thomas and Elizabeth (Kennedy) B.; student U. of Pa., 1895-97; M.D., Hahnemann Med. Coll., Phila., 1898; grad. study U. of Heidelberg, Germany, 1901. Began as hosp. pharmacist, 1896, and supt. hosp., 1896-1912; engaged in practice of medicine at Phila. since 1898; lecturer on phys. therapy, Hahnemann Med. Coll., 1898-1938. Pres. Nat. Soc. Phys. Therapy; past pres. Phila. Co. Homeopathic Soc.; mem. Am. Pa. State, Germantown med. assns., Pi Upsilon Rho. Republican. Methodist. Mason. Home: 2131 E. Cumberland St., Philadelphia, Pa.

BAKER, William Gideon, Jr., investment banking; b. Frederick Co., Md., Dec. 21, 1874; s. William G. and Susan Ellen (Jones) B.; A.B., Western Md. Coll., 1894; A.B., Yale, 1896; LL.B., U. of Md., 1899; m. Mary Drake Sawyers, Feb. 1, 1911. Associated with Sewell S. Watts (now deceased) in firm of Baker, Watts & Co., investment bankers, Baltimore, 1900, and has since continued under same title; dir. Standard Lime & Stone Co., Baltimore Transit Co., Safe Deposit & Trust Co. of Baltimore, Baltimore Equitable Soc. Mem. New York and Baltimore stock exchanges. Trustee Enoch Pratt Free Library (formerly president and treasurer); chairman sales committee Liberty Loan, Baltimore Dist., World War; formerly v.p. Community Fund, now. mem. exec. com. Pres. Investment Bankers Assn. of America, 1918-19. Trustee Western Md. Coll., Buckingham Sch. for Boys, Children's Hosp. Sch. Member Phi Beta Kappa. Mason. Ind. Democrat. Clubs: Maryland, University, Baltimore Country, Elkridge Club. Home: "Wyndon," Towson, Baltimore Co., Md. Office: Calvert and Redwood Sts., Baltimore, Md.

BAKER, William Henry, mfg. exec.; b. York, Pa., Aug. 15, 1896; s. John Edgar and Mary Salome (Billmeyer) B.; student Tome Sch., Port Deposit, Md., 1912-17; m. Rebecca Buckingham Yeagley, June 27, 1925; children—John Edgar II, Mary Elizabeth, Rebecca Yeagley. With J. E. Baker Co., quarrying and mfg. stone products, York, Pa., since 1912, as boiler fireman, 1912-16, foreman, 1916-20, asst. gen. supt., 1920-28, safety engr. and asst. gen. supt., 1928-36, v.p. since 1936; dir. Guardian Trust Co., Marietta Gravity & Water Co., Columbia Water Co. Mem. U.S. Naval Res., Bremerton, Wash., 1918. Mem. Am. Legion (comdr. York, Pa., Post, 1921), Tall Cedars of Lebanon, Pa. Soc., Nat. Safety Council. Republican. Methodist. Mason (Zeredetha Lodge 451; Yorktown Royal Arch 304; Gethsemane Commandery 75; Zembo Temple; Harrisburg Consistory; Scottish Rite). Clubs: Lafayette, Country (York, Pa.). Home: 216 Elmwood Boul. Office: 114 N. George St., York, Pa.

BAKETEL, H(arrie) Sheridan, physician and medical editor; b. Hopedale, O., Nov. 15, 1872; s. Oliver Sherman (D.D.) and Rosie Lucretia (Mack) B.; student Phillips Exeter Acad., Exeter, New Hampshire, 1889-90; student Boston Univ., 1890-92; M.D., Dartmouth Coll., 1895; post-grad. work Harvard Med. Sch., 1895; A.M., Holston Coll., Tenn., 1908; grad. study, London and Paris; m. Corinne Phillippi Sellers, Mar. 30, 1915; children—Mary (dec.), H. Sheridan, Jr. Began practice at Derry, N.H., 1896; in practice at New York since 1910; prof. preventive medicine, Long Island Coll. Medicine, Brooklyn, N.Y., 1915-31, emeritus prof. preventive medicine since 1931; lecturer on medical economics since 1915; prof. physiol. and consultant on syphilology, First Inst. of Podiatry since 1913; editor Gaillard's Med. Jour., 1905-08; editor Med. Times, 1911-26; •cofounder, 1923, since editor Med. Economics; pres. Physiol. Labs. of Reed & Carnrick, Jersey City, since 1925; some time urologist to Long Island Coll. Hosp., Beekman Street Hosp., House of Relief of New York Hosp., Skin and Cancer Hosp., N.Y. City; cons. phys. Peekskill (N.Y.) Hosp., Western Md. Hosp., Cumberland. First lt. Med. R.C., 1912-17, maj., Med. Corps, U.S.A., 1917, 33 months' service, World War; lt. col., Med. R.C., 1919; col. since 1924. First v.p. and chmn. bd. of trustees Columbia U. Coll. of Pharmacy since 1938. Drug representative on President Hoover's Business Survey Conf., 1929-31; del. to U.S. Pharmacopœial Conv., 1930, 1940. Fellow A.M.A., Am. Coll. Physicians, Am. Public Health Assn., N.Y. Acad. Medicine; mem. Am. Urol. Assn., Am. Med. Editors Assn. (pres. 1920), Am. Pharm. Mfrs. Assn. (pres. 1929-31), Am. Chem. Soc., Soc. Med. Jurisprudence, Clin. Congress Physicians, Assn. Mil. Surgeons, N.J. and N.H. state med. socs., Manhattan Med. Soc., Med. Soc. Greater New York, Associated Physicians of L.I., Brooklyn Urol. Soc., Brooklyn Surg. Soc., Am. Pharm. Assn., St. Vincent's Assn. (London), S.A.R., Mil. Order World War, U.S. Army Reserve Officers Assn., Am. Legion, Dartmouth Medical Alumni Assn. (pres. 1922-29), Beta Theta Pi (ex-v.p.; asso. editor publ.; chmn. alumni commn.; senator 1935-38), Interfraternity Conf. (ex-sec. and ex-vice chmn.), Alpha Kappa Kappa (co-founder), Theta Nu Epsilon. Episcopalian. Mason (32°, Shriner). Clubs: Dartmouth, National Rep., Fraternity, Pilgrims, Beta Theta Pi (New York); Army and Navy (Washington); University of Jersey City; Connaught (London). Author: The Treatment of Syphilis, 1920; also many monographs. Home: (summer) Canaan, N.H.; (winter) James Island, Charleston, S.C. Office: 155 Van Wagenen Av., Jersey City, N.J.

BAKEWELL, Donald Campbell, steel mfr.; b. Salem, O., Dec. 5, 1887; s. Thomas Howard and Annie Esther (Mullins) B.; grad. Hotchkiss Sch., Lakeville, Conn., 1904; A.B., Yale, 1908; grad. study, Mass. Inst. Tech.; m. Margaret Jenifer Jennings, June 7, 1913; children—Donald Campbell (dec.), Richard Jennings, Margaret Jenifer, Dorothy Evan. Began in steel mfg. business with Penna. Co., Altoona, Pa., 1910; pres. Duquesne Steel Foundry Co., Pittsburgh, 1917-37; pres. Pittsburgh Forge & Iron Co.; v.p. Ill. Zinc Co., Blaw-Knox Co. Mem. Employers Assn. of Pittsburgh (dir.), Alpha Delta Phi. Republican. Episcopalian. Clubs: Pittsburgh, Duquesne, Allegheny Country. Home: Sewickley, Pa. Office: 2105 Grant Bldg., Pittsburgh, Pa.

BAKKEN, Herman Ernest, research dir.; b. Faribault, Minn., Sept. 13, 1892; s. Gilbert H. and Mary (Haugen) B.; prep. edn. Augustana Coll., Canton, S.D., 1906-10; A.B., St. Olaf Coll., Northfield, Minn., 1915; student U. of Minn., 1916-18; m. Helen Thomas, Dec. 24, 1919; children—Jane Audrey, Herman Ernest. Teacher, Little Falls (Minn.) High Sch., 1915-16; supt. Am. Magnesium Corpn., Niagara Falls, N.Y., 1922-29; asst. dir. of research Aluminum Co. of America, Pittsburgh, since 1928. Served as 2d lt. Chem. Warfare Service, U.S. Army, at Edgewood Arsenal, 1918-19. Mem. Am. Chem. Soc., Am. Inst. Mining and Metall. Engrs., Alpha Chi Sigma, Phi Lambda Upsilon. Republican. Presbyterian. Clubs: Longue Vue (Verona, Pa.); University (Pittsburgh). Home: 1121 Shady Av., Pittsburgh, Pa. Office: New Kensington, Pa.

BALANO, Paula H(immelsbach), artist, stained glass designer; b. Leipzig, Germany, May 10, 1877; d. John F. and Francisca (Wentzel) Himmelsbach; brought to U.S. at the age of 2 yrs.; ed. Drexel Inst., 1894-97, Pa. Acad. Fine Arts, 1897-1900, Alphonse Mucha, Paris, 1900-01; married, 1918; 1 dau., Francisca Naiade. Began as a portrait painter; began designing and making stained glass windows, 1927. Works: St. Stephen's Ch., Ch. of the Ascension, Phila.; Franciscan Monastery, Del.; King Chapel, Wilmington, Del.; Chapter House, State College, Pa. Fellow Pa. Acad. Fine Arts. Mem. Plastic Club, Phila. Episcopalian. Home: 68 Harvey St. Studio: 131 Harvey St., Philadelphia, Pa.

BALCOM, Max F., vice-pres. Hygrade Sylvania Corpn.; b. Emporium, Pa., Jan. 20, 1889; s. George F. and Sarah (Fenton) B.; grad. Emporium (Pa.) High Sch., 1905; student Bryant & Stratton Business Coll., Buffalo, N.Y., 1907; m. Besse G. Huggler, July 13, 1926; 1 dau., Martha Jean. Clerk and teller First Nat. Bank, Emporium, Pa., 1905-12; auditor and asst. treas. Angldile Scale Co., Elkhart, Ind., 1912-15; cashier Holmes Snowflake Co., Toledo, O., 1916; owner Emporium Transfer Co., 1917-18; cashier Nilco Lamp Works, Inc., Emporium, 1918-25; asst. sec. Sylvania Products Co., Emporium, 1925-31; now vice-pres. Hygrade Sylvania Corpn. (Emporium), Emporium Trust Co.; dir. Emporium Water Co., Emporium Foundation, Inc. Pres. Emporium Borough Council, 1928-30. Republican. Episcopalian. Mason. Address: Emporium, Pa.

BALDERSTON, C. Canby, prof. of industry; b. Kennett Square, Pa., Feb. 1, 1897; s. John L. and Anna E. (Marshall) B.; ed. Westtown Sch., 1912-14, Pa. State Coll., 1915-17; B.S. in Econs., U. of Pa., 1921, A.M., same, 1923, Ph.D., same, 1928; m. Gertrude Emery, July 28, 1922; children—Frederick E., Robert W. 2d. Asst. prof. industry, U. of Pa., 1925-31, prof. since 1931. Vice-pres. Industrial Relations Assn. of Phila. since 1938. Mem. exec. com., Westtown Sch.; mem. bd. mgrs. Friends Hosp., Frankford. Mem. Am. Management Assn., Am. Economic Assn., Am. Statis. Assn., Soc. for Advancement of Management, Theta Xi. Republican. Mem. Society of Friends. Clubs: Rolling Green Golf, Lenape, Ozone. Author: Managerial Profit Sharing, 1928; Profit-Sharing for Wage Earners, 1937; Group Incentives, 1930; Executive Guidance of Industrial Relations, 1935. Co-author (with Karabasz and Brecht): Management of an Enterprise, 1935; Management of a Textile Business, 1938. Home: 601 Childs Av., Drexel Hill, Pa.

BALDINGER, Albert Henry, clergyman; b. Wetzel Co., W.Va., Feb. 13, 1876; s. Henry and Sarah (Hook) B.; A.B., Westminster Coll., New Wilmington, Pa., 1900, D.D., 1923; B.D., Pittsburgh Theol. Sem., 1903; studied at Edinburgh and Glasgow univs., 1931; m. Mary Estelle Spencer, June 23, 1903; children—Wallace Spencer, Wilbur Henry, Rachel Duira, Ruth Alberta. Ordained ministry U.P. Ch., 1903; pastor successively Springdale, Pa., Spokane, Wash., and Fowler, Calif., until 1915; asso. sec. Bd. of Home Missions, U.P. Ch., Pittsburgh, 1915-17; pastor Butler, Pa., 1917-30; prof. Old Testament lit. and exegesis, Pittsburgh-Xenia Theol. Sem., Pittsburgh, since 1931. Asso. editor United Presbyterian since 1925. Mem. Commn. for Study of Christian Unity, Federal Council of Churches; mem. Com. on World Conf. on Faith and Order. Republican. Presbyn. Club: Quiz. Author: Sermons on Revelation, 1924; also brochures, The Paramount Problem of Protestantism and Broken-Down Altars; also contbr. mag. articles. Home: 41 Penshurst Rd., Ben Avon Hghts., Pittsburgh, Pa.

BALDREY, Haynsworth, sculptor, artist; b. Cortland, N.Y., Aug. 24, 1885; s. Henry and Mella (Loomis) B.; studied Syracuse U., Rinehart Sch. of Sculpture and Pa. Acad. Fine Arts; m. Lillian Maud Smith, June 18, 1910. Began as advertising artist, 1905; jewelry designer, 1919-29; short story writer, 1910-20; now engaged as watercolorist, sculptor and lecturer. Has exhibited work at New York art galleries and in cities of the East. Awarded First Rinehart Award, 3 yrs.; Montclair Art Assn. medal; first Art Center of The Oranges Awarded, 2 yrs.; first Ridgewood Art Assn. Award. New Jersey State chmn. Am. Artists Professional League, 1934-37, first v.chmn. since 1937; pres. N.J. Water Color and Sculpture Soc.; mem. Nat. Sculpture Soc. Republican. Episcopalian. Home: Newton, N.J.

BALDRIDGE, Robert M.; pres. Union Nat. Bank. Home: 2005 Jenny Lind Av. Office: 314 Fifth Av., McKeesport, Pa.

BALDRIGE, Thomas Jackson, judge; b. Hollidaysburg, Pa., Apr. 5, 1872; s. Howard Malcolm and Laura (Mattern) B.; prep. edn. Andover (Mass.) Acad.; A.B., Bucknell U., Lewisburg, Pa.; D.C.L., U. of Pa. and Bucknell; m. Anna Dean, Apr. 18, 1917. Admitted to Pa. bar, 1895, and began practice at Hollidaysburg; apptd. judge Court of Common Pleas, Jan. 13, 1910, and elected to same office, 1911 and 1921; atty. gen. of Pa., by appt. of governor, 1927-29; apptd. judge Superior Court of Pa., Jan. 18, 1929, and elected to same office November 1929, for term expiring January 1, 1940. Apptd. one of three commrs. to codify and revise laws of decedents' estates, Oct. 14, 1915. Trustee Bucknell U., and Highland Hall, Hollidaysburg. Mem. Am. Law Inst., Am. and Pa. bar assns. Republican. Baptist. Clubs: Union League, Pa. Athletic (Phila.); Harrisburg Country, Blairmont Country. Home: 620 Allegheny St., Hollidaysburg, Pa.

BALDRIGE, William Lovell, pres. and gen. mgr. E. R. Baldrige & Co.; b. Bennington, Blair Co., Pa., May 28, 1869; s. Edwin Rockefeller and Emma (Lovell) B.; student Hollidaysburg (Pa.) pub. schs.; m. Ione Bartley Condron, Mar. 10, 1891 (died 1935); children—Edwin Rockefeller, Mrs. John A. Matthews. Bookkeeper Blair (Pa.) Iron & Coal Co., 1886-89; sec.-treas. Juniata Limestone Co., 1889-91, gen. mgr., 1891-98; asst. gen. mgr. E. R. Baldrige & Co., Inc., Hollidaysburg, Pa., 1898-1914, pres. and gen. mgr. since 1914; assisted in organizing and developing Standard Refractories Co., 1913-20. Treas. Hollidaysburg (Pa.) Borough, 1896-1914; delegate to 1912 Rep. Nat. Conv. from 19th Pa.

BALDWIN, Arthur Charles, clergyman; b. Rochester, N.Y., Aug. 9, 1875; s. Charles J. and Adelaide L. (Fosdick) B.; A.B., Denison U., Granville, O., 1896. Rochester Theol. Sem., 1900; m. Nellie T. Forbes, Apr. 17, 1901; 1 son, Schuyler Forbes. Ordained Bapt. ministry, 1900; pastor Ballston Spa, N.Y., 1900-06, 1st Ch., Aurora, Ill., 1906-08, 1st Ch. Fall River, Mass., 1908-14; foreign sec. Am. Bapt. Foreign Missionary Society, 1914-15, and now member of board of managers; pastor Park Av. Baptist Ch., Rochester, N.Y., 1915-16, Chestnut St. Ch., Phila., since June 1919. Army Y.M.C.A. service, overseas, 1918-19. Del. bd. mgrs. Am. Bapt. F. M. Soc. to W. African and Congo Jubilee Conf., Sept. 1928. Mem. Sigma Chi. Republican. Clubs: Union League, Phi Alpha Clerical Club. Author: Mrs. Galeb's Boarder (serial in Christian Herald, pub. in book form, 1939). Home: 4510 Osage Av., Philadelphia, Pa.

BALDWIN, Arthur J., lawyer; b. Cortland, N.Y., Aug. 26, 1868; s. Eben R. and Caroline (West) B.; A.B., Cornell U., 1892; m. Frances Smiley, June 18, 1892. Began law practice, North Tonawanda, N.Y., 1894; in office of late James B. Dill, New York, 1897; mem. firm Dill & Baldwin, 1899, later Griggs, Baldwin & Baldwin, 1902—; sec. and dir. Miss. Glass Co., Miss. Wire Glass Co.; dir. Brooklyn Ash Removal Co., Northwestern Live Stock Co., Long Island Lighting Co., Cement Gun Co., Walsh Refractories Co., The Grosvenor Co. Mem. Delta Phi. Democrat. Methodist. Mason. Clubs: Manhattan, Engineers', Bankers. Home: 56 S. Munn Av., East Orange, N.J. Office: 225 Broadway, New York, N.Y.

BALDWIN, Calvin Benham, govt. official; b. East Radford, Va., Aug. 19, 1902; s. William Thomas and Lizzie (Worth) B.; ed. East Radford High Sch., 1917-20, Va. Poly. Inst., 1920-23; m. Louise Delp, June 25, 1924; children—Calvin Benham, Sally Worth. Shop insp. N.&W. Ry., Roanoke, Va., 1923-25, asst. to gen. foreman, 1925-28; mgr. and owner Electric Sales & Service Co., East Radford, 1928-33; asst. to U.S. sec. of agr., Washington, D.C., 1933-35; asst. adminstr. Resettlement Adminstrn. and Farm Security Adminstrn., Washington, D.C., since 1935. Democrat. Presbyn. Contbr. to periodicals. Home: 4340 E. West Highway, Bethesda, Md. Office: South Bldg., Dept. of Agriculture, Washington, D.C.

BALDWIN, Clifford Ashton, judge; b. Camden, N.J., Sept. 4, 1897; s. Clifford E. and Elizabeth (Simpson) B.; B.S., U. of Pa., 1918; m. Josie L. Sloan, Nov. 27, 1920; children—Jane Elizabeth, Clifford A., Jr., Ann. Studied law in the office of Albert E. Burling; admitted to N.J. bar as atty., 1920, as counselor, 1925; in gen. practice of law at Camden since 1920; prosecutor of the pleas of Camden Co., 1929-34; judge Camden Co. ct. of common pleas since 1937. Served in U.S.N.R.F. active duty, 1918; lt. and lt. comdr. N.J. Naval Militia since 1935. Mem. Am., N.J. State, and Camden Co. bar assns., Phi Beta Kappa, Am. Legion. Republican. Episcopalian (sr. warden St. Johns Ch., Camden). Mason (32°). Elk. Clubs: City (Camden) / Penn Athletic (Philadelphia). Home: 2114 Merchantville Av., Merchantville. Office: 728 Cooper St., Camden, N.J.

BALDWIN, Edward Hill, M.D.; cons. surgeon Homeopathic Hosp. of Essex County, St. Marys Hosp. (Passaic). Address: 83 Lincoln Park, Newark, N.J.

BALDWIN, Elizabeth Gilbert, prin. of Highland Hall; b. Wallingford, Conn., Aug. 26, 1892; d. Seymour Gilbert and Jennie (Parmelee) Baldwin; grad. Wallingford (Conn.) High Sch., 1910; A.B., Vassar Coll., 1914; grad. student Yale, 1928-32; unmarried. Teacher of history, Kemper Hall, Kenosha, Wis., 1914-15; record clerk N.Y., N.H.&H. R.R., 1916-18; worked in family lumber business, 1918-20; teacher of history, Gateway Sch., New Haven, Conn., 1920-26, Cambridge (Mass.) Haskell Sch., 1926-28; mem. History Research Council, Boston, 1927-28; asst. and prin., Oxford Sch., Hartford, Conn., 1928-32; dean, Emma Willard Sch., Troy, N.Y., 1932-33; prin., Highland Hall, Hollidaysburg, Pa., since 1934. Mem. Nat. Assn. Prins., Am. Assn. Univ. Women, Vassar Club of New Haven, Yale Library Associates. Episcopalian. Club: Pine Orchard (Pine Orchard, Conn.). Interested in farming and owns a farm in Conn. Home: Cheshire, Conn. Address: Hollidaysburg, Pa.

BALDWIN, Frank E(lmer), attorney, banking; b. Duke Center, Pa., June 4, 1866; s. John E. and Josephine A. (White) B.; ed. Chamberlain Inst., Randolph, N.Y., St. Bonaventure's Coll., Allegany, N.Y.; A.B., Law Dept. U. of Mich., 1893; (hon.) LL.D., St. Bonaventure's Coll., 1918; m. Addie G. Wolters, Nov. 14, 1895. Engaged in teaching, 1889-91; admitted to Pa. bar, 1894 and since in gen. practice of law at Austin; interested in real estate and oil business; pres. and dir. First Nat. Bank of Austin since 1913. Served as mercantile appraiser McKean Co., 1893, burgess of Austin for two terms, sch. dir. five yrs., postmaster seven yrs.; chmn. Rep. Co. Com., 1902, del. to Rep. State Convs.; elected to Pa. Senate, 1908, 1916, 1920, served as Pres. Pro Tem., 1919, 1921, re-elected to Senate, 1924, 1928; elected Auditor Gen., Pa., 1932 for term four yrs. Mem. Pa. Soc. of N.Y. Republican. Methodist. Mason (33°), I.O.O.F., K.P. Elk. Address: Austin, Pa.

BALDWIN, Harrison Rowe, sales exec.; b. Erie, Pa., June 1, 1883; s. Nelson and Sarah Elizabeth (Rowe) B.; ed. Erie High Sch., 1897-1900, Georgetown U. (law), 1909-10, U. of Pa. (law), 1910; m. Edna Estelle Packard, June 15, 1912; children—Harrison Packard, Emma Jeanne (wife of Dr. Hans Paul Kronheim). Began as news reporter, 1901; reporter Washington Times, 1909-10; state and foreign editor Phila. Ledger, 1910-12; mng. editor Reading (Pa.) News, 1912-14; with Hammermill Paper Co. since 1914, asst. advertising mgr., 1914-20, asst. sales mgr., 1920-26, sales mgr., 1926-33, v.p. in charge of sales since 1933. Ind. Democrat. Presbyterian. Clubs: Kahkwa Country, Erie, Shriners (Erie). Home: 530 Shawnee Drive. Office: Hammermill Paper Co., Erie, Pa.

BALDWIN, Henry Ward, pres. Baldwin Laboratories, Inc.; b. Punxsutawney, Pa., Feb. 17, 1890; s. Henry A. and Susan (Heltman) B.; student pub. schs.; m. Marie Hunter, Aug. 28, 1923; children—Audrey Constance, Henry Ward, David Harol, Richard Clive, Sally Ann. Pres. and dir. Baldwin Labs., Inc., Saegertown, Pa. since incorporation, 1933. Founder "Q" Club of Nat. Newspaper Representatives. Mem. Nat. Assn. Insecticide and Disinfectant Mfrs. Elk, Moose. Clubs: Erie Press, Erie Ad (Erie, Pa.); Canadian (New York). Author: Pursuing a Policy; The Road to Success. Home: The Terrace. Office: Main St., Saegertown, Pa.

BALDWIN, James H.; surgeon Methodist Episcopal Hosp. Address: 1426 Pine St., Philadelphia, Pa.

BALDWIN, Robert Dodge, prof. edn.; b. N.Y. City, Aug. 28, 1891; s. Edward Colfax and Florence Amelia (Newhouse) B.; grad. DeWitt Clinton High Sch., N.Y. City, 1909; A.B., Princeton, 1913; grad. study U. of Ore., 1914; A.M., Columbia, 1916; grad. study Stanford, 1921; Ph.D., Cornell U., 1926; m. Edna Isadore Post, Aug. 9, 1916; children—Edna Margaret, Edward Post, Robert Dodge. Prin. high sch., Bay Shore, N.Y., 1913-14; sec. Y.M.C.A., Los Angeles, Calif., 1914-15; supt. county union high sch. Arlington, Tenn., 1916-17; prof. of edn., Wash. State Normal Sch., Cheney, 1917-24; prof. rural edn., U. of Mo., 1925; pres. Central State Teachers Coll., Stevens Point, Wis., 1926-30; prof. of ednl. administration, Coll. of Edn., West Virginia Univ., 1930-31, and since 1933; supt. Haskell Indian Inst., 1931-33. Visiting specialist in rural edn., Pa. State Coll., summer 1929, and in school administration and finance, U. of Ida., summer 1936, Cornell U., summer 1939. Mem. N.E.A., Am. Assn. of Sch. Administrs., Am. Country Life Assn., Phi Delta Kappa, Phi Kappa Phi, Kappa Delta Pi. Presbyn. Author: Cheney System of Cumulative Classroom Child Study, 1919; Financing Rural Education, 1927; The Financing of Public Education in West Virginia, 1938. Address: Morgantown, W.Va.

BALDWIN, William Lester, lawyer; b. Kent Co., Md., June 21, 1894; s. William Walker and Cora (Moffett) B.; A.B., Washington Coll., Chestertown, Md., 1913; LL.B., U. of Md. Law Sch., Baltimore, 1916; (hon.) A.M., Washington Coll., 1916; m. Irene Cecile Pinney, Apr. 23, 1919; children—Miriam (dec.), William Lester, Samuel Clifford, Richard Moffett, John Gardner (dec.). Admitted to Md. bar, 1916 and since engaged in gen. practice of law at Baltimore; sec. Md. League for Nat. Defense, 1916-18; in practice alone, 1919-31; mem. firm Baldwin & Jarman since 1931. Served as ensign U.S.N.R.F. (a), 1918. Dir. Baltimore Y.M.C.A. Mem. bd. visitors and govs. Washington Coll., Chestertown, Md. Mem. Am., Md. State, Baltimore City bar assns., Barristers Club, Theta Kappa Nu. Republican. Methodist. Club: Hillendale Country (Baltimore). Home: 2942 Wyman Parkway. Office: Fidelity Bldg., Baltimore, Md.

BALL, Michael Valentine, M.D., surgeon; b. Warren, Pa., Feb. 14, 1868; s. George and Mary (Cohn) B.; high sch., Warren, Pa.; M.D., Jefferson Med. Coll., Phila., 1889; post grad. work, U. of Berlin, 1889-90; m. Grace Paterson, 1905; children—Mary, John George, Jean, William Lincoln. Began as interne German Hosp., Phila., then resident phys. Eastern State Penitentiary, 1892-95; instr. in bacteriology, Polyclinic, Phila., 1896-97; pres. Bd. of Health, Warren, 1901-07; prof. clin. pathology, New York Med. Coll. for Women, 1916-17; specializes in diseases of eye and ear. Dir. Warren Gen. Hosp. Mem. A.M.A., Acad. Natural Science of Phila., Am. Acad. Ophthalmology and Oto-Laryngology, A.A.A.S. Mason (32°, Shriner), Elk. Club: Shakespeare (Warren). Author: Essentials of Bacteriology, 1891. Home: Warren, Pa.

BALLAGH, James Curtis, univ. prof.; b. Brownsburg, Va.; s. Rev. Dr. James H. and Margaret Tate (Kinnear) B.; grad. Washington and Lee U., 1884, U. of Va., 1888; A.B. (extra ordinem), Johns Hopkins, 1894, Ph.D., 1895; LL.D., U. of Ala., 1906); m. Josephine Jackson, July 6, 1897 (died June 19, 1921); children—James Curtis Jackson, Dorothy Vaughan, Thomas Carter, Josephine de Hanmere; m. 2d, Jane Lee Moffitt, Aug. 24, 1925. Prof. of mathematics, Cox Coll., Ga., 1889; asst. prof. biology, Tulane U., 1891; asst., instr., and asso. in history, 1895-1905, asso. prof. Am. history, 1905-11, prof., 1911-13, Johns Hopkins; asst. prof. and prof. polit. science, U. of Pa., 1913—. Visiting prof. history, polit. science and foreign relations, Md. State Normal Coll., summer 1916, N.Y. City Pub. Sch. Com., winters 1919-21; also summers, history, New York U., 1921; polit. science, U. of Mich., 1925, West Virginia University, 1929; lecturer U. of Virginia Inst. Pub. Affairs, 1935; lecturer polit. science, U. of Pa., 1936, and 16 preceding summers. Author: White Servitude in the Colony of Virginia, 1895; A History of Slavery in Virginia (John Marshall prize essay), 1902; American Foreign Policy in the Orient, 1915; America's International Diplomacy, 1918. Also numerous articles in revs., encys. and biog. dictionaries. Editor: Southern Economic History, 1607-1909 (Vols. V and VI of The South in the Building of the Nation), 1910; The Letters of Richard Henry Lee, Vol. I, 1762-1778, Vol. II, 1779-1794, 1911-13; sometime co-editor Johns Hopkins Studies in Hist. and Polit. Science, and of Annals of Am. Acad. of Polit. and Social Science. Mem. Delta Psi. Home: 5864 Woodbine Av. Address: 5864 Woodbine Av., Overbrook, Philadelphia, Pa.

BALLANTINE, Stuart, radio engr.; b. Germantown, Pa., Sept. 22, 1897; s. Charles Mansfield and Mary Stuart (Beverland) B.; ed. Drexel Inst., 1917, Harvard U., 1920-21, 1923-24; m. Virginia Gregory Orbison, June 18, 1927. Research engr., Radio Frequency Labs., 1922-23; engaged in pvt. research, 1924-27; dir. research, Radio Frequency Labs., 1927-29; pres. Boonton Research Corpn., 1929-34; pres. Ballantine Labs., Inc., elec. communication apparatus, Boonton, N.J., since 1935. Served as expert radio aide, U.S.N., 1917-20. Fellow Am. Phys. Soc., Acoustical Soc. America, Inst. Radio Engrs. (pres. 1935). Mem. Radio Club of America, Franklin Inst. Awarded Morris Liebmann Memorial Award by Inst. Radio Engrs., 1931, Elliott Cresson Medal by Franklin Inst., 1934; John Tyndall Fellow at Harvard, 1923-24. Mem. Ref. Episcopal Ch. Club: Harvard (Philadelphia). Author: Radio Telephony for Amateurs, 1922. Contbr. about forty articles on elec. communication. Home: Boonton, N.J.

BALLANTYNE, Nathaniel Wallace, pres. W.Va. Fire Clay Mfg. Co.; b. Pittsburgh, Pa., Dec. 22, 1868; s. Alexander and Irene (Freeman) B.; student pub. schs. and business coll.; m. Lucie Brown, Dec. 5, 1906; children—Robert Brown, Irene Virginia, Jean Wallace. Pres. W.Va. Fire Clay Mfg. Co. Address: Diamond Bank Bldg., Pittsburgh, Pa.

BALLARD, F. L.; mem. law firm Ballard, Spahr, Andrews & Ingersoll. Office: Land Title Bldg., Philadelphia, Pa.

BALLARD, Wilson Turner, civil engring.; b. Baltimore, Md., April 21, 1893; s. Edwin Kemp and Ada Virginia (Chilcoat) B.; student Baltimore Poly. Inst., 1907-11; C.E., Cornell U., 1916; m. Susan Catherine Reaney, Nov. 29, 1921; children—Wilson Turner, Jr., Catherine Ann. Draftsman and designer, 1916; resident engr. on constrn., Stone & Webster, Boston, Mass., 1919-20; with Norton, Bird & Whitman, Baltimore, Md., 1920; engr. paving commn., City of Baltimore, 1920-22; engring. consultant to bankers in Baltimore, 1922-26; asso. then vice-pres. The J. E. Greiner Co., cons. engrs., Baltimore, 1926-33; chief engr. Pub. Works Administrn. of Federal Govt. for Md. and Del., 1933-36; spl. engring. consultant Baltimore County Metropolitan Dist., 1936-38, also highways engr. Baltimore Co., 1938; engr. Housing Authority of Baltimore, Md., since 1939. Served in First O.T.C., Ft. Myer, Va., 1917; 2d lt. then 1st lt. Engrs., U.S.A., 1918-19 with A.E.F. in France in major campaigns. Mem. and chmn. sub-com. on highways, Md. State Planning Commn. since 1935. Mem. Am. Soc. Civil Engrs. (past pres. Md. Sect. 1932). Awarded James Laurie prize for 1935. Democrat. Episcopalian (vestryman). Clubs: L'Hirondelle (Ruxton); Carrollton Hounds (Carroll Co.). Home: Ruxton. Office: 37 Commerce St., Baltimore, Md.

BALLENTINE, Floyd George, prof. Latin; Factoryville, Pa., July 9, 1878; s. John and Harriet (Gerould) B.; grad. Clarion State Normal Sch., 1894; A.B., Bucknell U., 1899; A.B., Harvard U., 1900, A.M., same, 1901, Ph.D., same, 1903; m. Grace A. Newton, Aug. 31, 1901; children—Eleanor, George Newton, Robert Gerould, Ruth. Engaged as instr. Latin, Bucknell U., 1903-04, asst. prof. Latin, 1904-15, prof. since 1915. Mem. Am. Philol. Assn., Am. Assn. Univ. Profs., Phi Gamma Delta. Republican. Baptist. Author: Hauton Timorumenos of Terence, 1910. Contbr. "Some Phases of the Cult of the Nymphs," to Harvard Studies in Classical Philology, Vol. XV. Home: Lewisburg, Pa.

BALLINGER, Robert Irving, architect; b. Md., May 22, 1892; s. Walter F. and Bessie M. (Connell) B.; grad. Germantown (Phila.) Acad., 1910; Pratt Inst., 1915; m. Frances Taylor, May 17, 1917; children—Robert I., Jean V., Walter F. II. Practiced in Phila. since 1915; mem. firm The Ballinger Co.; treas. Industrial Realty Corpn.; dir. Super-Span Patents Corpn., Phila. Housing Assn., Chestnut Street Assn., Am. Mut. Liability Ins. Co. of Boston. Designed plants of Atwater Kent Mfg. Co., Budd Mfg. Co., Victor Talking Machine Co., etc., also many chs., office bldgs., hosps. and apt. houses in eastern U.S. Mem. Am. Inst. Architects. Republican. Methodist. Mason. Clubs: Union League, Country. Home: 3027 W. Coulter St. Office: 105 S. 12th St., Philadelphia, Pa.

BALSBAUGH, Edward Marlin, coll. prof.; b. Hummelstown, Pa., Aug. 11, 1876; s. Jacob H. and Leah (Bomberger) B,; B.Ed., Shippensburg Teachers Coll., 1896; B.S., Lebanon Valley Coll., 1901; A.M., U. of Pa., 1912; extension work Lafayette Coll. and Pa. State Coll.; m. Mabelle Lucille Keck, June 30, 1903; children—Edward Francis (M.D.), Dorothy. Prin. Lansford (Pa.) High Sch., 1902-07, Lebanon (Pa.) High Sch., 1907-14; supt. of schools, Lebanon, Pa., 1914-26, Lansford, Pa., 1926-38; asso. prof., dept. of edn., Lebanon Valley Coll., since 1938. Mem. N.E.A., Pa. State Edn. Assn. Republican. Mem. United Brethren Ch. Mason. Rotarian (Lansford). Home: Annville, Pa.

BALSLEY, Charles Hammond, city official; b. Connellsville, Pa., June 30, 1870; s. James Robison and Catherine Anderson (Francis) B.; ed. pub. schs. and Duff's Bus. Coll.; m. Olive Berthena Keenan, Nov. 26, 1892; children—Raymond, Catherine Anderson. Employed as motion picture machine operator, San Francisco and Los Angeles, Calif., 1896; showed first motion pictures in State of Calif. at Orpheum Theatre, San Francisco, June 1896; with Westinghouse Electric & Mfg. Co., East Pittsburgh, Pa., 1897-99; asso. with James Robison Balsley in bldg. and contracting business, 1900-12; free lance motion picture cameraman, 1912-17; engaged in bldg. and contracting, 1917-34; county tax collector, 1934-36; city health officer and city inspr. weights and measures, Connellsville, Pa., since 1936. Mem. Connellsville Bd. of Trade; mem. Bd. of Edn., Connellsville, 1900-12. Republican. Clubs: Elks, Eagles. Home: 119 N. First St. Office: City Hall, Connellsville, Pa.

BALTHASER, Jennie M. (Mrs. Charles J. Balthaser); mem. Dem. State Com.; b. Berks Co., Pa., Dec. 6, 1895; d. George M. and Isabella (Field) Ernst; ed. pub. schs.; m. Charles J. Balthaser, June 24, 1916; children—Lillian I, Ruth F., Catherine M. Employed as telephone operator in Court House, Reading Pa., since 1935; mem. Dem. Co. Com. since 1926; mem. Dem. State Com. since 1934; pres. Womans Dem. Club of Sinking Spring; sec. Ladies of the Golden Eagle since 1924; dist. pres. Patriotic Order of Americans, 1934-35; pres. Reading Hosp. Auxiliary No. 9, Sinking Spring. Democrat. Lutheran. Home: Sinking Spring, Pa.

BALZ, George Adam; pres. Seaboard Refractories Company. Address: Perth Amboy, N.J.

BAMBERGER, Edgar S., retired merchant; b. Baltimore, Md., Feb. 14, 1883; s. Julius and Estella (Frankenheimer) B.; student Marston's University Sch., Baltimore, Md., 1896-1900; A.B., Johns Hopkins, 1903; m. Mildred D. Fox, Oct. 17, 1910 (died July 1, 1936); children—Mildred (Mrs. Marks), Jane (Mrs. August S. Bing), Ellen L.; m. 2d, Mrs. Mabel S. Bing, Nov. 12, 1937; step children—Betty Bing, August S. Bing. Began as bundle wrapper, John Wanamaker, New York, Sept. 1903; buyer and advertising mgr. Hutzler Bros., Baltimore, 1903-07; with L. Bamberger & Co., Newark, N.J., 1907-33, in various capacities, becoming vice-pres. and sec.; co-founder and vice-pres. Packard-Bamberger Co., Hackensack, N.J., 1933-37, resigned, 1937, but still dir. Trustee Inst. for Advanced Learning (Princeton, N.J.), U. of Newark. Republican. Clubs: Newark Athletic, Down Town (Newark); Mt. Ridge Country (West Caldwell, N.J.); Hollywood Golf (Deal, N.J.). Home: 100 Gregory Av., West Orange, N.J.

BAMBERGER, Florence Eilau, prof. education; b. Baltimore, Md.; d. Ansel and Hannah (Eilau) B.; B.S., Teachers Coll. (Columbia), 1914; M.A., Columbia, 1915, Ph.D., 1922; unmarried. Instr. edn., Johns Hopkins, 1916, associate, 1917, asso. prof., 1918, prof. since 1924; exec. sec. of exec. com. Coll. for Teachers, same univ., 1930; dir. Coll. for Teachers, Johns Hopkins, 1937. Mem. N.E.A., Social Science Honor Soc., Nat. Soc. Coll. Teachers of Edn., Nat. Soc. for Study of Edn., Am. Soc. Univ. Profs., Pi Lambda Theta, Pi Gamma Mu, Phi Beta Kappa. Author: The Effect of Physical Make-up of a Book on Children's Selection, 1922; Cut and Draw Stories (with G. Rawlings), 1927; Washington, Frontiersman and Planter, 1931; Guide to Children's Literature (with A.M. Broening), 1931; Reading, A Form of Living, 1938; Syllabus Guide for Observation of Demonstration Exercises, 1938. Home: Marlborough Apts., Baltimore, Md.

BAMBERGER, Henry Fischler, civil engr.; b. Phila., Pa., May 17, 1894; s. Leo and Annie (Behrend) B.; B.S. in C.E., U. of Pa. Towne Sci. Sch., 1916; C.E., same, 1931; unmarried. With engring. dept. Pa. R.R. Co. on constrn. and maintenance of way at various cities, office of engr. maintenance of way and chief engr. maintenance of way, Phila., Pa.; in charge maintenance of way constrn. Phila. to Wilmington electrification, 1925-28; asst. ry. equipment engr., Corps of Engrs. War Dept., 1928-29; associate engr. War Dept. on water supply, flood control, hydro-electric power studies on Del., Roanoke, and Conn. rivers, at Phila., Norfolk, and Providence, R.I., offices, since 1929; chief asst. in charge tech. div., Phila. Engr. Dist. Served as corpl. 103d Engrs., U.S.A., 1917-19, with 28th Div., A.E.F.; now 1st lt. Engrs. Res., U.S.A. Awarded Victory Medal with 5 clasps (U.S.); Medal City of Verdun. Mem. Nat. Soc. Professional Engrs., Pa. Soc. Professional Engrs. (sec. Phila. chapter), Soc. Am. Mil. Engrs., Enging. Alumni U. of Pa., Res. Officers Assn. of U.S., Soc. 28th Div. A.E.F., Am. Legion (past comdr. Engrs. Post), 40 Hommes et 8 Chevaux (past chef de gare). Republican. Mason (32°, Shriner). Moose. Home: 817 Roosevelt Boul., Philadelphia, Pa. Office: 900 Custom House, Philadelphia, Pa.

BAMBERGER, Leo, retired mfg. photo engraver; b. New York City, Sept. 2, 1868; s. Benjamin and Caroline (Gabriel) B.; ed. pub. schs. and high sch., New York City, and Cooper Inst.; m. Annie Behrend, June 11, 1893; children—Henry F., J. Leiter. Began career in 1884 with John C. Moss, New York, N.Y., and was coinventor and pioneer in the swelled gelatine process and soft metal halftones for photo engraving; organized Commercial Photo Engraving Co., Phila., Pa., and pres., 1898-1938, retired, 1938; asso. with Henry George, T. W. Powderly and Samuel Gompers in pub. of The Leader, N.Y. labor paper, 1886-94; one of founders Labor Day; co-founder Phila. Photo Engravers Union, A.F. of L.; served as pres. many bldg. & loan assns. in Phila.; former dir. Mfg. Photo Engravers Assn. of Phila. Mem. Internat. Photo Engravers Union, A.F. of L. Republican. Mason. Moose. Home: 817 Roosevelt Boul., Philadelphia, Pa.

BAMBERGER, Louis, merchant, philanthropist; b. Baltimore, Maryland, May 15, 1855; s. Elkan and Theresa (Hutzler) B.; hon. D.Sc., Newark College of Engineering; hon. M.A., Rutgers; hon. LL.D., Newark University; unmarried. Noted for his philanthropies; with his sister, Mrs. Felix Fuld, widow of his late partner, donated $5,000,000 for the establishment of Institute for Advanced Study at Princeton, N.J., under direction of Dr. Abraham Flexner; upon retirement from business distributed over $1,000,000 among employes; donor of Newark Mus. Bldg. (about $750,000). Home: 602 Center St., South Orange, N.J. Office: 131 Market St., Newark, N.J.

BAMFORD, Ronald, univ. prof.; b. Rochdale, Eng., Nov. 1, 1901; s. John William and Eda (Kershaw) B.; brought to U.S., 1906; B.S., Conn. State Coll., Storrs, Conn., 1924; M.S., U. of Vt., 1926; Ph.D., Columbia U., 1931; m. Florence Martha Cronin, Dec. 26, 1930; 1 son, Ronald William. Grad. asst., U. of Vt., Burlington, 1924-26, instr. botany, 1926-29; fellow Columbia U., 1929-30, grad. asst., 1930-31; asst. prof. botany, U. of Md., 1931-32, asso. prof., 1932-39, prof. since 1939. Mem. Bot. Soc. America, Sigma Xi, Phi Mu Delta. Democrat. Episcopalian. Club: Kiwanis (Prince Georges County, Md.). Home: 7 Holly St., College Heights, Hyattsville, Md.

BANCROFT, George Russell, prof. of physiol. chemistry; b. Weymouth, Digby Co., Nova Scotia, July 7, 1878; s. Rev. James William and Mary Louise (Fowler) B.; grad. Provincial Normal Coll., Truro, Nova Scotia; B.A., Acadia Univ., Wolfville, Kings Co., N.S., 1906, hon. D.Sc., 1934; A.B., Yale, 1914, Ph.D., 1917; student U. of Chicago, summer 1920, 1924, Yale Grad. Sch. of Medicine, 1929; m. Iva Myrtle Stevens, Aug. 20, 1907; children—George Herbert, Constance Lucille. Came to U.S., 1913. Prin. Freeport Schools, Freeport, Nova Scotia, 1898-99, 1900-03, 1906-07; teacher Horton Collegiate Acad., 1903-05; science master, Halifax (N.S.)

Acad., 1907-13; asst. instr., Yale, 1913-17; prof. of chemistry and physics, Transylvania U., 1917-18; asst. prof. of organic chemistry, U. of Ky., 1918-20; assoc. prof. of chemistry, W.Va. Univ., 1920-23; prof. of bio-chemistry, Sch. of Medicine, W.Va., Univ., 1923-31; prof. of physiol. chemistry and toxicology, Jefferson Med. Coll., since 1931. Served in Canadian Militia, 1910-13. Fellow Am. Inst. of Chemists (chmn. Pa. Chapter 1938-39), Am. Assn. for Advancement of Science; mem. Am. Chem. Soc., Franklin Inst., Pa. Chem. Soc., W.Va. Scientific Soc. (sec. 1922; vice-pres. 1923; pres. 1924), W. Va. Acad. of Science (pres. 1924), Ky. Acad. of Science, Nova Scotia Inst. of Science, Theta Kappa Psi. Republican. Baptist. Club: Yale (Phila.). Home: 436 Gainesboro Rd., Drexel Hill, Pa. Office: Jefferson Medical College, 1025 Walnut St., Philadelphia, Pa.

BANCROFT, John, Jr.; pres. Joseph Bancroft & Sons Co., Wilmington, Del., and Reading, Pa. Home: "Rockford," Wilmington, Del.

BANCROFT, Milton H., painter; b. Newton, Mass., Jan. 1, 1867; s. William H. and Martha (Varney) B.; prep. edn. Newton pub. schs.; student Mass. State Normal Art Sch., 1883-86; prof. in tech. studies, Swarthmore Coll., Pa., 1886-92, but continued studies irregularly in Pa. Acad. Fine Arts; supt. schs. and instr. in Pa. Acad. Fine Arts, 1892-94; studied in Colorossi, Delacluse and Julien acads., Paris, 1894-99; m. Margaret Corliss Moore, 1894; children—John Townsend, Anna Moore, Thomas Leggett. Exhibited in Société des Artistes Français, and in all large exhbns. of New York, Phila., Boston, Washington and Chicago; splty. portraits; executed mural decorations for Court of the Seasons, Panama-Pacific Expn., San Francisco. Instr. Mechanics Inst., New York. Mem. Architectural League, Salmagundi Club, MacDowell Club (New York), Phila. Sketch Club. Home: Sandy Spring, Md.

BANCROFT, Wilfred; treas. and gen. mgr. Lanston Monotype Co. Home: 716 Millbrook Lane, Haverford, Pa. Office: 24th and Locust St., Philadelphia, Pa.

BANCROFT, William Wallace, prof. philosophy; b. Chester, Pa., Feb. 6, 1893; s. William Henry and Ursula (Riffert) B.; A.B., Ursinus Coll., 1919; student Princeton Theol. Sem., 1916-20; A.M., U. of Pa., 1921; Ph.D., U. of Pa., 1931; unmarried. Began as instr. English, Ursinus Coll., Collegeville, Pa., 1925; asst. prof. English and philosophy, 1927-29, asso. prof. same, 1929-31, prof. philosophy since 1931. Mem. A.A.A.S., Am. Philos. Assn., Brit. Inst. Philosophy. Republican. Episcopalian. Author: Joseph Conrad, His Philosophy of Life, 1933. Contbr. articles to philos. journs. Home: 942 Main St., Collegeville, Pa.

BANDEL, John Martin, real estate; b. Baltimore, Md., Nov. 24, 1880; s. Martin Luther and Mary Susannah (Bancard) B.; A.B., Johns Hopkins U., 1901; m. Alice Morgan, May 10, 1910; 1 son, John Morgan. Began as civil engr.; engaged in rock quarrying, 1906, railroad construction with L.&N. R.R., 1907; construction work, Md. State Roads Commn., 1908-09; in charge of construction Baltimore Sewerage Commn., 1911-12; real estate broker since 1925; propr. Bernard B. Bandel & Co. Mem. Am. Soc. Civil Engrs., S.A.R. Independent Democrat. Unitarian. Home: Linthicum, Md. Office: Fidelity Bldg., Baltimore, Md.

BANDIERE, Charles M(aure), real estate; b. Italy, May 29, 1892; s. John and Mary B.; brought to U.S., 1896, naturalized, 1919; A.B., Central High Sch., Phila., Pa., 1910; m. Bess R. Gleason, June 2, 1920; children—John Hugh, Betty May. Engaged in bus. on own acct. as dealer in automobiles, Baltimore, 1919-38; in real estate bus. in Baltimore as pres. The Hosbach-Bandiere Co., real estate holding co., Baltimore, since 1938. Mem. Baltimore Aviation Commn. Mgr. gubernatorial campaign com. for Mayor Howard W. Jackson, Baltimore, 1938. Dir. St. Leo's Orphan Asylum, Baltimore. Independent Democrat. Roman Catholic. K.C. Home: 4703 Norwood Av. Office: 215 N. Calvert St., Baltimore, Md.

BANE, David Emulous, lawyer; b. Greene Co., Pa., Jan. 18, 1879; s. Morgan Andrew and Mary Elizabeth (Bowser) B.; desc. William B., landed with Quakers, 1687, settled in Bucks Co.; ed. pub. schs. and Madison Acad., 1898-1900, O. Northern U., 1902-03; m. Nellie Ray Ramage, Dec. 12, 1903; children—Eustace Herschell, Ruth Naomi (Mrs. Ross C. Shriver), Sarah Elizabeth, Catherine Roberta (dec.), David Morgan. Engaged in teaching 1900-07; studied law in office Cooper & Van Swearingen; admitted to Pa. bar, 1908 and since engaged in gen. practice of law in Uniontown; mem. firm Bane & Bane, with son since 1933. Served as sch. dir. in North Union Twp. and Uniontown; on Co. Bd. of View for over 26 yrs.; pres. Bd. Edn. of Uniontown, 4 yrs. Mem. Am. and Pa. bar assns. Democrat. Mem. Central Christian Ch. Mason. Home: 104 Murray Av. Office: 57 E. Main St., Uniontown, Pa.

BANE, James Clinton, lawyer; b. Coal Center, Pa., Feb. 3, 1902; s. Lawrence L. and Olive V. B.; grad. East Pike Run (Pa.) High Sch., 1918; student Duquesne U., Pittsburgh, 1918-20; LL.B., Duquesne Law Sch., 1923; m. Helen Rodd, Mar. 14, 1928; 1 son, James Clinton. Admitted to Pa. bar, 1923, and since practiced in Washington, Pa.; dist. atty. Washington Co. (Pa.) since 1936; admitted to practice in Superior and Supreme Courts of Pa., Federal Dist. Courts, U.S. Supreme Court. Mem. Washington Co. Bar Assn., Pa. Bar Assn., Dist. Attys. Assn. of Pa., Tau Delta Phi. Democrat. Episcopalian. Mason (32°, Shriner), Elk, Moose, Odd Fellow. Clubs: Arms, Washington Golf and Country, Lions (Washington, Pa.); Nemacolin Country (Beallsville, Pa.). Home: George Washington Hotel. Office: Courthouse, Washington, Pa.

BANGE, Guy Wilfred, lawyer; b. Hanover, Pa., July 4, 1880; s. Robert R. and Mary (Meredith) B.; A.B., Franklin and Marshall Coll., 1903; m. Belle Wallace Shaner, May 11, 1918; 1 son, Philip Wallace. Admitted to Pa. bar, 1909, and since practiced in Hanover; dir. First Nat. Bank of Hanover; dir. Hanover Trust Co. Dir. Hanover Gen. Hosp. Mem. Am. Bar Assn., Pa. Bar Assn., York County Bar Assn., Phi Kappa Sigma. Republican. Mem. Reformed Ch. Home: 15 Highland Av. Office: Carlisle St. and Bank Lane, Hanover, Pa.

BANGHART, Harold Lewis, estate trustee; b. Franklin, Me., Mar. 11, 1886; s. Charles Lance and Nellie Adell (Clement) B.; student Fryeburg (Me.) Acad., 1903-06, Hotchkiss Sch., Lakeville, Conn., 1906-08; A.B., Yale, 1912; m. Mary Talbott, Nov. 8, 1917. Instr. French and German, Hotchkiss Sch., Lakeville, Conn., 1912-16; estimating dept., Proctor Marble Co., Proctor, Vt., 1916; treas. Proctor Trust Co., Proctor, Vt., 1917-18; mgr. W. A. Talbott and R. B. McNair estates, Warren, Pa., 1918-38; trustee H. M. Talbott estate since 1936; dir. Warren Bank & Trust Co. Chmn. Advancement Com., Warren County Council, Boy Scouts of America; pres. Warren Pub. Library; treas. Children's Aid Soc.; trustee Y.M.C.A. Mem. Shakespeare Club, Wolf's Head, Delta Kappa Epsilon. Republican. Presbyterian (elder; supt. 1st Presbyn. Ch. Sch.). Clubs: Conewango Valley Country (Warren, Pa.); Lake Placid (Essex Co., N.Y.); Green Mountain Club (Rutland, Vt.). Home: 310 Conewango Av. Office: Warren Bank & Trust Co. Bldg., Warren, Pa.

BANKS, William Hamlin, physician; b. Mifflintown, Pa., Nov. 16, 1862; s. William and Jane Elizabeth (Hamlin) B.; ed. Lewistown (Pa.) Acad., 1880-82; M.D., U. of Pa. Med. Sch., 1889; m. Bessie Jacobs Parker, Oct. 27, 1892 (now dec.); children—Robert Parker, Jane Hamlin (wife of Capt. Albert E. Ely), William Hamlin, Jr., Kathryn Jacobs (Mrs. John E. Richardson), Hugh McAlister. Engaged in gen. practice of medicine at Mifflintown, Pa. since 1889; county med. dir., 1905-39; pres. Mifflintown Water Co. Mem. A.M.A., Pa. State Med. Soc., Juniata Co. Med. Soc. Democrat. Presbyn. Mason. Home: 29 Main St., Mifflintown, Pa.

BANKSON, Ellis Edwin, cons. engineer; b. Bethany, Ill., Apr. 18, 1884; s. William Wilhite and Margaret Laura (Vaughan) B.; B.S. in C.E., Millikin Univ., Decatur, Ill., 1907; C.E., U. of Pittsburgh, 1922; m. Lillian Marie Kerr, Sept. 19, 1912; children—Betty (Mrs. J. Clifford Bowers), Carol, Ellis Edwin. Instr., advancing to asst. prof. civil engring., U. of Pittsburgh, 1907-12; lecturer civil engring., U. of Manitoba, 1912-17; various engagements on engring. and construction work in field and office; asst. engr. advancing to partner The Chester Engineers, consultants on hydraulic and sanitary projects, Pittsburgh, Pa., since 1917. Mem. Am. Soc. Civil Engrs., Am. Water Works Assn., Sigma Alpha Epsilon. Presbyn. Mason (32°, Shriner). Contbr. papers and articles on valuation and rate-making under regulatory laws. Home: 6562 Bartlett St. Office: 1050 Century Bldg., Pittsburgh, Pa.

BANNER, Franklin Coleman, head dept. journalism, Pa. State Coll.; b. Unionville, Mo., Aug. 10, 1895; s. Winfield Scott and Rebecca (Roberts) B.; A.B. and B.J., U. of Mo., 1919, A.M., same, 1920; D. of J., U. of London (Eng.), 1925; unmarried. Employed as reporter, Kansas City Journal, 1920-22; on editorial staffs, Chicago Journal, Chicago Daily News, 1922-24, London (Eng.) Chronicle, 1925; fgn. corr. Am. newspapers, 1925; head dept. journalism, Pa. State Coll. since 1926; organized first Nat. Joint Com. of editors, pubs. and dirs. of journalism for raising standards of schs. Mem. Royal Inst. Journalists, Eng., Press Congress of World, Am. Assn. Schs. and Depts. Journalism (past v.p.), Am. Assn. Teachers of Journalism (past v.p.), Nat. Com. on Research in Journalism, Pa. State Joint Com. on Journalism for High Schs., Sch. Adv. Com. of Pa. Newspaper Pubs. Assn., Pa. Press Conf. (dir.), Am. Press Soc., Sigma Delta Chi, Pi Delta Epsilon. Methodist. Clubs: London Press (hon.); University (State College). Contbr. feature stories on travel. Home: University Club, State College, Pa.

BANNER, Roy Roscoe, educator; b. Scott County, Va., Mar. 22, 1888; s. William Marion and Martha Jane (Ramey) B.; A.B., Richmond Coll., Richmond, Va., 1910; student Columbia U., summers, 1922-25, M.A., 1925; m. Jeannette Hylton, May 10, 1911; children—Roy R., Marjorie Fox, William Patton. Began as high sch. teacher, Oak Hill, W.Va., 1914; high sch. teacher, Bramwell, W.Va., 1915-17; supt. Bramwell (W.Va.) pub. schs., 1917-24; supt. Ceredo-Kenova (W.Va.) pub. schs., 1924-33; asst. co. supt. schs., Wayne Co., W.Va., 1933-35; prin. Logan (W.Va.) Sr. High Sch., since 1935. Democrat. Baptist. Mason (32°, Shriner). Home: Logan, W.Va.

BANNEROT, Frederick George, pres. United Oil Co.; b. Freedom, Pa., Aug. 26, 1875; s. Alexander A. and Hannah (Holland) B.; student Western U. of Pa. (now U. of Pittsburgh), Class of 1896; m. Margaret Long, Apr. 5, 1898; 1 son, Frederick George. Pres. and dir. United Oil Co., United Refining Co.; v.p., treas. dir. Elk Refining Co.; dir. Tiona Petroleum Co., Emblem Oil Co. Clubs: Duquesne, Pittsburgh Athletic (Pittsburgh); Oakmont Country (Oakmont); Pittsburgh Field (Aspinwall). Home: Schenley Apts. Office: Preble Av. and Franklin St., Pittsburgh, Pa.

BANTON, Conwell, physician; b. Phila., Pa., June 10, 1875; s. Edward W. and Laura B. (Scott) B.; student Lincoln U., Pa., 1892-93; M.D., U. of Pa., 1900; LL.D., Wilberforce (O.) U., 1916; m. Elizabeth Davis, Nov. 11, 1903; 1 dau., Alice L. (Mrs. John H. Carter). In practice as physician since 1901; now med. dir. Edgewood Sanitarium, Wilmington, Del. Formerly mem. Rep. State Com. of Del. Mem. Nat. Med. Assn., Alpha Phi Alpha. Republican. Episcopalian. Mason (33°; Past Grand Master; Scottish Rite, Prince Hall, past sec. gen.). Club: Monday (Wilmington, Del.). Address: 924 French St., Wilmington, Del.

BARACH, Joseph H., M.D.; b. Lithuania, Mar. 12, 1883; s. Z. and Dora (Oppen) B.; brought to U.S., 1888; student Park Inst., Pittsburgh, 1895-99; M.D., U. of Pittsburgh, 1903; m. Edna S. Levy, Sept. 1915; children—Joseph L., Richard. Resident physician West Pa. Hosp., 1903-04, resident pathologist, 1905; pathologist Eye and Ear Hosp., 1904-09; cons. physician, dept. of health, Carnegie Inst. Tech., since 1910; asst. prof. medicine, Sch. of Medicine, U. of Pittsburgh, and med. dir. Falk

Clinic, U. of Pittsburgh, since 1930, prof. clin. medicine, Sch. of Dentistry since 1934; visiting physician Presbyn. Hosp. since 1910. Served as capt. Med. Corps, U.S. Army, 1918-19. Fellow Am. Coll. Physicians; mem. A.M.A., A.A.A.S., Sigma Xi. Republican. Clubs: Westmoreland Country, Concordia. Home: 5745 Beacon St. Office: 435 5th Av., Pittsburgh, Pa.

BARBER, Charles Williams, army officer; b. Gloucester Co., N.J., Sept. 21, 1872; s. George W. and Ellen (Taggart) B.; ed. pub. schs. and business coll.; studied law in office of Hon. H. S. Grey, atty. gen. of N.J., 1899; m. Katherine Runge, Mar. 8, 1894; 1 son. Russell George. Commd. 2d lt. 4th N.J. Inf., Spanish-Am. War, July 16, 1898; 1st lt., Sept. 27, 1898; capt., Mar. 3, 1899; hon. mustered out, Apr. 6, 1899; 1st lt. 28th U.S. Inf., July 5, 1899; hon. mustered out vol. service, May 1, 1901; commd. 2d lt. 2d Inf. U.S.A., Feb. 2, 1901; 1st lt., Nov. 11, 1901; capt. 4th Inf., Mar. 11, 1911; assigned to 3d Inf., Jan. 1, 1915; retired as maj., Sept. 1, 1916; brig. gen., N.A., July 25, 1917. Served in Philippines, 1899-1901, 1902-03, 1906-08; duty with Isthmian Canal Commn., Panama, 1908-15; Mexican border service, 1916; apptd. brig. gen. and adj. gen. of N.J., Dec. 5, 1916; in charge orgn. state troops for war, registration and selection of drafted men, etc.; comdg. 29th Div., July 28-Aug. 25, 1917; comdg. 57th Infantry Brigade, Camp McClellan, Anniston, Ala., Sept. 11, 1917; in command 57th Inf. Brig. in front line sectors and as chief of staff, Base Sect. No. 2, Bordeaux (gen. staff officer A.E.F.), June 1918-July 1919; returned to status of retired officer, Aug. 1919; brig. general retired, June 21, 1930. Special representative Atlantic Refining Co., in Mexico, 1920; gen. mgr. Antilles Molasses Co., 1920-21; pres. and dir. Charles W. Barber & Son, Inc., investment bankers, New York; dir. Schluter & Co., Inc., investment bankers; officer and dir. various industrial and financial corpns. Officer Legion of Honor (France); D.S.M. (U.S.); D.S.M. (State of N.J.). Mem. Mil. Order Carabao. Republican. Methodist. Mason. Clubs: Army and Navy (Manila and Washington), Bankers (New York). Home: Short Hills, N.J. Office: 111 Broadway, New York, N.Y.

BARBER, Charlie R.; mayor of Erie, present term expires 1940. Address: City Hall, Erie, Pa.

BARBER, J. Thomas; editor Lancaster News. Office: 8 W. King St., Lancaster, Pa.

BARBER, Samuel, composer; b. West Chester, Pa., Mar. 9, 1910; s. Dr. Samuel LeRoy and Marguerite McLeod (Beatty) B.; student Curtis Inst. of Music, Phila., 1923-32, studying piano with Isabelle Vengerova, singing with Emilio de Gogorza, composition with Rosario Scalero; grad. Curtis Inst. of Music, 1932; unmarried. Composer since 7 years of age. Compositions: Serenade for String Quartet, 1929; Dover Beach (for voice and string quartet), 1931; String Quartet in B minor, 1936; Sonata (for cello and piano), 1932; Overture to "School for Scandal" (for orchestra), 1932; Music for a Scene from Shelley (for orchestra), 1933; Symphony in One Movement (for orchestra), 1936; Adagio for Strings, 1936; Essay for Orchestra, 1937; The Virgin Martyrs (choral), 1935; also many songs. Works have been played by Nat. Broadcasting Co. Symphony Orchestra (Toscanini, condr.), Salzburg Festival, 1937 (Rodzinski condr.), Augusteo Orchestra, Rome, Italy (Molinari, condr.), and most of the major orchestras of U.S. Awards: Prix de Rome, 1935; Pulitzer Prize for Music, 1935, 1936. Home: West Chester, Pa. Address: care G. Schirmer, Inc., 3 E. 43d St., New York, N.Y.

BARBER, Theodore S.; pres. and gen. mgr. Morris Run Coal Mining Co.; also officer or dir. various other cos. Home: 171 S. Franklin St. Office: 14 S. Franklin St., Wilkes-Barre, Pa.

BARBEY, John Edward, silk mfg.; b. Reading, Pa., Jan. 28, 1890; s. John and Mary Ellen (Garst) B.; grad. Hill Sch., Pottstown, Pa., 1908; Ph.B., Yale, 1911; m. Catharine E. Quier, June 3, 1925; children—John E., Jr., Pierre G., Mary Glyde, Edwin Quier, Helen Hawley. Asso. with Vanity Fair Silk Mills, mfrs. underwear and hosiery, Reading, Pa., since 1912, gen. mgr. since 1916. Served as capt. A.S., U.S.A., 1917-18. Mem. Book and Snake, Yale. Presbyn. Clubs: Merion Cricket, Westchester Country, Berkshire Country, Wyomissing. Home: R.F.D. 2. Office: Vanity Fair Silk Mills, Reading, Pa.

BARBOUR, John Carlyle, judge; b. Haledon, N.J., Apr. 18, 1895; s. William J. and Anna (Campbell) B.; LL.B., New York Law Sch., 1917; student King's College, London Univ., England, 1919; m. Mabel Evelyn Bennett, Mar. 28, 1921; children—John Carlyle, Mary Bennett. Admitted to N.J. bar, Dec. 11, 1916, and since in practice in Clifton; pres. Clifton (N. J.) Nat. Bank since 1925; judge Circuit Court of N.J. since June 26, 1936. Mem. N.J. Assembly, 1929-32; mem. N.J. Senate, 1933-36, pres. 1936; acting gov. of N.J., 1936. Served with 312th Inf., U.S. Army, with A.E.F., 1918-19. Mem. Am. Bar Assn., N.J. State Bar Assn., Sons of Am. Revolution, Delta Theta Phi. Republican. Episcopalian. Mason (Shriner), Elk. Home: 400 Dwas Line Rd., Clifton, N.J. Address: Court House, Hackensack, N.J.

BARBOUR, Marshall R., broker; b. Pittsburgh, Pa., Jan. 7, 1891; s. John B. and Laura (Rogers) B.; A.B., Cornell U., 1914; m. Jenifer Lesslie, Apr. 30, 1921. Mem. firm John B. Barbour & Co. since 1920. Home: 1429 Browning Road. Office: 301 Magee Bldg., Pittsburgh, Pa.

BARBOUR, W. Warren, U.S. senator; b. Monmouth Beach, N.J.; s. William and J. Adelaide (Sprague) B.; grad. Browning Sch., N.Y. City, 1906; m. Elysabeth C. Carrere, Dec. 1, 1921; children—Elysabeth C., Warren, Sharon. Appointed member U.S. Senate, December 1, 1931, to fill vacancy caused by death of Dwight Morrow and elected to Senate, Nov. 1932, for term expiring 1937; elected, Nov. 1938, to fill vacancy for term ending Jan. 3, 1941. Mem. N.G.N.Y. 10 yrs. Republican. Presbyn. Clubs: Union League, Merchants, Racquet and Tennis, New York Yacht; Rumson (N.J.) Country; Metropolitan (Washington, D.C.). Home: Locust, N.J. Office: Red Bank, N.J.

BARCHUS, John Livengood, banker, merchant; b. Fayette Co., Pa., Oct. 10, 1865; s. Daniel and Barbara (Livengood) B.; student Salisbury (Pa.) Pub. Schs., 1871-79, Hagerstown (Md.) Acad., 1881-83, Bryant & Stratton Business Coll., Baltimore, Md., 1887-88; m. Mary Edna McClure, Oct. 10, 1899; children—John McClure, Dorothy, Daniel Quincy, Eleanor (dec.). Sr. mem. of firm Barchus & Livengood Co., gen. merchandising, Salisbury, Pa., 1889-1938; established Valley Bank of Salisbury, Pa., 1889-1902, then organized First Nat. Bank of Salisbury (Pa.), 1902, pres. since 1902; sec. and treas. Pa. & Md. Street Ry., Salisbury, Meyersdale, and Garrett, Pa., 1907-25; treas. Salisbury (Pa.) Coal & Lumber Co., 1909-39; dir. Twentieth Century Mfg. Co.; former dir. Citizen's Light & Power Co. of Salisbury. Mem. Borough Council, Salisbury, Pa. (pres., 1891-97); mem. and treas. Bd. of Edn. Borough Schs., 1900-05. Republican. Brethren Ch. Mason (Shriner, 32°). Address: Salisbury, Pa.

BARCLAY, Isaiah Disbrow, mfg. fertilizers; b. Cranbury, N.J., July 2, 1901; s. Ezekiel Silvers and Lizzie (Chamberlin) B.; student Peddie Sch., Hightstown, N.J., 1916-20, Colgate Univ., Hamilton, N.Y., 1920-21; m. Gladys Snedeker, June 21, 1922; children—William Snedeker, Elizabeth Chamberlin. Employed as salesman, Chamberlin & Barclay, 1921-22, mem. firm 1922-25; treas. Chamberlin & Barclay, Inc., mfrs. fertilizer, mchts. produce, farm equipment, Cranbury, N.J. since 1925; vice-pres. First Nat. Bank, Cranbury, N.J. since 1936. Republican. Presbyn. (trustee First Ch.). Mason. Club: Lions of Cranbury. Home: No. Main St. Office: Cranbury, N.J.

BARCLAY, John, Jr., banker; b. Greensburg, Pa., June 12, 1900; s. John and Rebecca (Coulter) B.; grad. Hill Sch., Pottstown, Pa., 1920; A.B., Princeton U., 1924; m. Josephine Eicher, Jan. 16, 1926; children—Rebecca Coulter II, John III. Began as clerk Barclay-Westmoreland Trust Co., 1924, successively teller, asst. treas., sec.-treas., treas. and v.p. and since 1937 pres. Mem. Greensburg City Council, 1931-36; dir. Westmoreland Hosp. Assn. Democrat. Presbyterian. Clubs: Greensburg Country; Rolling Rock (Ligonier); Pike Run Country (Jones Mills); Colonial (Princeton, N.J.); Harvard-Yale-Princeton (Pittsburgh). Home: 320 W. Pittsburgh St. Office: 1 N. Main St., Greensburg, Pa.

BARCLAY, William Kennedy, broker; b. Phila., Pa., June 27, 1868; s. John K. and Attaresta (Williams) B.; student Dr. Faires Classical Inst., Phila., 1877-84, U. of Pa., 1884-88; m. Florence Elizabeth Brunner, June 2, 1892; children—George Goddard, William Kennedy, Virginia, Marian, Charles Brunner, Florence (dec.). Began as stock broker, 1891; partner DeSilver and Barclay, Phila., 1894-1910; operated William K. Barclay Co., Phila., 1910-12; senior partner Barclay, Moore & Co., Phila., since 1912, members of N.Y. Stock Exchange, Phila. Stock Exchange, asso. mem. of New York Curb Exchange and mem. Investment Bankers' Assn. of America. Republican. Episcopalian. Clubs: Union League, Midday (Phila.); Little Egg Harbor Yacht (Beach Haven, N.J.; past commodore); Tockwogh Yacht (Fredericktown, Md.). Home: Haverford, Pa. Office: Fidelity-Philadelphia Trust Bldg., 123 S. Broad St., Philadelphia, Pa.

BARCLAY, William Kennedy, Jr., banker and broker; b. Phila., Pa., Mar. 30, 1896; s. William Kennedy and Florence Elizabeth (Brunner) B.; grad. William Penn Charter Sch., Phila., 1912; B.Economics, U. of Pa., 1916; m. Grace Maxine Westervelt, Feb. 8, 1936; 1 son, William Kennedy III. Bond trader Barclay, Moore & Co. (mems. N.Y. Stock Exchange, Phila. Stock Exchange, N.Y. Curb Exchange), 1916-17, 1919-20, partner since Jan. 1920; dir. Admiral Beatty Hotel Co. Served as lt., j.g., U.S. Navy, 1917-19. Republican. Episcopalian. Clubs: Union League (Phila.); Little Egg Harbor Yacht (Beach Haven, N.J.); Tockwogh Yacht (Frederick, Md.). Home: Wynnewood, Pa. Office: 123 S. Broad St., Philadelphia, Pa.

BARD, Guy Kurtz, lawyer; b. Lincoln, Pa., Oct. 24, 1895; s. Silas E. and Miranda S. (Kurtz) B.; grad. Denver (Pa.) High Sch., 1910; grad. Millersville State Teachers Coll., 1913; A.B., Franklin and Marshall Coll., 1916; LL.B., U. of Pa., 1922; unmarried. Learned printing trade as a boy in father's country newspaper; successively rural sch. teacher, Lancaster Co., Pa., prin., Warwick Twp. High Sch., Lititz, Pa., teacher mathematics and sch. management, Millersville State Normal Sch., supervising prin., Ephrata (Pa.) Schs.; admitted to Pa. bar, 1922, and since practiced at Lancaster, Pa.; admitted to practice Supreme Court of Pa. and U.S. and Federal courts; special asst. to U.S. atty. gen., 1934-37; U.S. atty. Eastern Pa. Dist., 1937; mem. Pa. Pub. Utility Commn., 1937-38; atty. gen. of Pa. by appmt. of Gov. Earle, 1938. Sec. Dem. Co. Com., Lancaster Co., 1920-24, chmn., 1925-34; del. at large from Pa. to Dem. Nat. Conv., Chicago, 1932 (mem. com. on resolutions, drafted prohibition repeal plank); Dem. nominee for lt. gov. of Pa., 1930. Served with U.S. Army, with A.E.F., 1918-19. Pres. bd. of trustees Millersville State Teachers Coll. Mem. Am., Pa. and Lancaster Co. bar assns., Am. Judicature Soc., Am. Acad. Polit. and Social Science, Acad. Polit. Science, Am. Legion (past comdr. Denver, Pa., post), Phi Kappa Tau. Elk (past exalted ruler). Club: Hamilton (Lancaster). Home: Denver, Pa. Office: Lancaster, Pa.

BARD, Philip, prof. of physiology; b. Hueneme, Calif., Oct. 25, 1898; s. Thomas Robert and Mary Beatrice (Gerberding) B.; student Thacher Sch., Ojai, Calif., 1913-17; A.B., Princeton U., 1923; A.M., Harvard, 1925, Ph.D., 1927; m. Harriet Hunt, June 29, 1922; children—Virginia Hunt, Elizabeth Stanton. Teaching fellow in physiology, Harvard Med. Sch., 1925-26, instr. in physiology, 1926-28; asst. prof. of biology, Princeton U., 1928-31; asst. prof. of physiology, Harvard Med. Sch., 1931-33; prof. of physiology and dir. of dept., Johns Hopkins U. Sch. of Medicine, since 1933. Served as private Am. Ambulance Service, Section Sanitaire Unit, 578, with French and Am. armies, 1917-19. Mem. Am. Physiol. Soc. (councilor 1936-39, sec. since 1939), Am. Neurological Assn., Harvey Soc., Am. Acad. Arts and Sciences, Nat. Research Council (exec. com. of Med. Div.), Nat. Bd. Med. Examiners, Assn. for Research in Nervous and Mental Diseases, Phi Beta Kappa, Tower Club (Princeton). Contbr. to physiol. and med. jours.; editor of and contbr. to Macleod's Physiology in Modern Medicine, 8th edit., 1938. Home: 38 Warrenton Rd. Address: Johns Hopkins Medical School, Baltimore, Md.

BARDGETT, Edward Russell, ry. official; b. Fort Erie, Ont., Can., Aug. 17, 1875; s. George Frederick and Jane Sartin (Daggert) B.; came to U.S., 1882, naturalized, 1900; ed. pub. schs. and Commercial Commerce Business Sch., Buffalo, N.Y., 1882-95; m. Emily Maude Jackson, Mar. 9, 1898 (deceased July 13, 1938); children—Emily Maude (Mrs. Donald H. Babbitt), Jane Jackson (Mrs. Roger H. Milne), Edward White. Successively with Northern Steamship Co., L.V. R.R., C.&A. R.R., 1894-1918; port agt., Ore & Coal Exchange, 1918-19; gen. freight agt., Cunard White Star, Ltd., 1919-30; gen. traffic mgr. Western Md. Ry. Co., 1930-33, v.p. since 1933. Pres. Pub. Library Assn., Glen Rock, N.J. Republican. Episcopalian (vestryman Christ Ch.). Mason, Shriner. Clubs: Union League (Chicago); Merchants (Baltimore); Dequesne (Pittsburgh); Lafayette (York, Pa.); Traffic (New York, Chicago, Pittsburgh, Baltimore, Detroit, York). Home: 3700 N. Charles St. Office: Standard Oil Bldg., Baltimore, Md.

BARISON, Morris E.; judge Juvenile Court. Address: Jersey City, N.J.

BARKER, Albert Winslow, artist and lecturer; b. Chicago, Ill., June 1, 1874; s. Albert Sampson and Julia (Beam) Winslow Barker; student Pa. Acad. of Fine Arts, 1890-95; A.B., Haverford Coll., 1917; A.M., U. of Pa., 1920, Ph.D., 1921; studied lithography under Bolton Brown, 1927; m. Agnes McMakin, April 20, 1904; 1 dau., Agnes Susan (Mrs. H. Walter Davis); m. 2d, Anna Ellis Roberts, 1910; 1 dau., Elizabeth Roberts (Mrs. Ernst Koch); m. 3d, Alice Paxson, July 30, 1926. Instr. Sch. of Industrial Art, Phila., Pa., 1903-13, summer sch. U. of Pa., 1921-23; dir. of art edn., Wilmington (Del.) pub. schs., 1921-29. Represented by lithographic prints in Library of Congress, New York Public Library, Baltimore Mus., Pa. Mus., Los Angeles Mus., Boston Mus. of Fine Arts, Smithsonian Instr., Corcoran Gallery (Washington, D.C.), Uffizi Gallery (Florence, Italy), Honolulu Gallery of Art, Fogg Museum. Awarded gold medal Internat. Print Makers Expn. by Print Makers Soc., of Calif., 1935. Mem. Print Makers Soc. of Calif., Phi Beta Kappa. Contbr. of articles to scientific mags. Research-work in chemistry of lithographic technique. Address: Moylan, Pa.

BARKER, H. C.; prof. physics, U. of Pa. Address: U. of Pennsylvania, Philadelphia, Pa.

BARKER, Harry, cons. engineer; b. Rutland, Vt., July 19, 1881; s. Barney and Hannah Estelle (Coburn) B.; B.S., U. of Vt., 1904; m. Marion I. Booth, Apr. 21, 1909; children—Samuel Booth, Ruth Elizabeth. Instr. in engring., U. of Vt., 1903-05; asst. engr., Vt., Ariz., Calif. and Nev., 1904-07; asso. editor Engring. News and Engring. News-Record, 1907-17; cons. engr. since 1919; mem. Barker & Wheeler, engrs., New York and Albany, N.Y.; cons. engr. to Public Service Commn. since 1925; advisory engr., Municipal Electric Utility Assn. of N.Y. since 1935; cons. engr. Tenn. Valley Authority, since 1936. Lecturer on practice of engring., U. of Vt. Served as capt. Engr. Corps, U.S.A., 1917-18. Mem. Am. Soc. M.E., Am. Inst. E.E., S.A.R., Phi Beta Kappa, Sigma Nu. Republican. Conglist. Clubs: Railroad-Machinery, Fraternity. Author: Public Utility Rates, 1917; also brochures and booklets. Contbr. articles to tech. publs. Home: 201 N. Mountain Av., Montclair, N.J. Office: 11 Park Pl., New York, N.Y.

BARKER, Lewellys Franklin, M.D.; b. Norwich, Ont., Can., Sept. 16, 1867; s. James F. and Sarah Jane (Taylor) B.; ed. Pickering Coll., Ont., 1881-84; M.B., U. of Toronto, 1890; student U. of Leipzig, 1895, univs. of Munich and Berlin, 1904; hon. M.D., U. of Toronto, 1905; LL.D., Queen's Univ., Kingston, Can., 1908, McGill Univ., Montreal, Can., 1911; University of Glasgow, Scotland, 1930; m. Lillian H. Halsey, Oct. 1903; children—John Hewetson, William Halsey, Margaret Taylor. Asso. in anatomy, 1894-97, Johns Hopkins U.; resident pathologist, Johns Hopkins Hosp., 1894-99; asso. prof. anatomy, 1897-99, pathology, 1899-1900, Johns Hopkins U.; prof. and head dept. anatomy, Rush Med. Coll. (U. of Chicago), 1900-05; prof. medicine, Johns Hopkins U. and chief phys. Johns Hopkins Hosp., 1905-1913; now emeritus prof. medicine Johns Hopkins and visiting phys. Johns Hopkins Hosp. Johns Hopkins med. commr. to P.I., 1899; mem. spl. commn. apptd. by Sec. of the Treas. to determine existence or non-existence of plague in San Francisco, 1901. Corr. mem. Budapest Royal Soc. Physicians, Medico-Chirurg. Soc. of Edinburgh, Gesellschaft für Innere Medizin und Kinderheilkunde in Wien; mem. Swedish Med. Soc.; chmn. bd. scientific dirs. Wistar Inst. of Anatomy; pres. Nat. Com. for Mental Hygiene, 1909-18, Assn. Am. Physicians, 1913, Am. Neurol. Assn., 1916, Southern Med. Assn., 1919, Assn. for Study of Internal Secretions, 1919, med. and chirurg. faculty of Md., 1923; vice-pres. A.M.A., 1917; v.p. American Society for the Control of Cancer; chairman advisory board, Federal Industrial Institution for Women, Alderson, W.Va., and of Med. Council U.S. Veterans Bur. Clubs: Maryland, Johns Hopkins (Baltimore); Century and Charaka (New York). Author: The Nervous System and Its Constituent Neurones, 1899; Translation of Werne Spalteholz's Hand Atlas of Human Anatomy, 1900; Laboratory Manual of Human Anatomy (with Dean De Witt Lewis and D. G. Revell), 1904; The Clinical Diagnosis of Internal Diseases, 1916; Tuesday Clinics at Johns Hopkins Hospital, 1922; Blood Pressure (with N. B. Cole), 1924; The Young Man and Medicine, 1927. Co-Editor: Endocrinology and Metabolism, 1922. Also numerous med. papers and addresses. Home: 208 Stratford Rd., Guilford. Office: 1035 N. Calvert St., Baltimore, Md.

BARKER, Oliver D.; urologist Parkersburg City and St. Joseph's hosps. Address: 700 Market St., Parkersburg, W.Va.

BARKER, Rodman; v.p. and dir. John Wanamaker, Phila. Home: Port Royal Av., Foxboro, Pa. Office: City Hall Square, Philadelphia, Pa.

BARKHORN, Charles Webner, M.D.; otorhinolaryngologist Newark Eye and Ear Infirmary and Presbyn. Hosp.; asso. surgeon Babies Hosp.-Coit Memorial; asso. otologist Essex County Isolation Hosp.; asst. surgeon dept. craniology Newark City Hosp. Address: 223 Roseville Av., Newark, N.J.

BARKHORN, Henry Charles, physician; b. Newark, N.J., Dec. 2, 1885; s. Charles Henry and Jennie (Hodson) B.; M.D., Cornell U. Med. Sch., 1907; m. Mariette Louise Gless, Sept. 9, 1914; children—Henry Charles, Jr., Janet Louise, Richard Edward, Mariette Amie. Engaged in practice of medicine and surgery at Newark, N.J., since 1909, specializing in diseases of ear, nose and throat since 1917. Fellow Am. Coll. Surgeons; mem. Am. Med. Assn., N.J. State and Essex Co. med. socs., Soc. of Surgs. of N.J., Acad. of Medicine of Northern N.J. (pres. 1937-39), Practitioners Club (pres. 1931-32) Doctors Club (pres. 1921-22), Essex Co. Tuberculosis League (v.p. since 1937), Cornell Med. Alumni Assn. (pres. 1928-30), St. Benedicts Prep. Alumni (pres. 1931-32). Democrat. Roman Catholic. Club: Essex County Country (West Orange). Home: 45 Johnson Av., Newark, N.J.

BARKLEY, Frederick R., newspaper corr.; b. Watertown, N.Y., May 18, 1892; s. Reuben E. and Josephine (Workman) B.; grad. high sch., Watertown, 1913; m. Claire Coyle, Nov. 22, 1916. Reporter Watertown Standard, 1913-14; asst. sporting editor Springfield Republican, 1914-15; telepragh editor Geneva (N.Y.) Times, 1915, Providence Journal and Evening Bulletin, 1916-17, Detroit Free Press, 1917-18, Detroit News, 1918-21; editor Detroit Forum, 1919-20; exec. sec. Washington City Club, 1921-23; Washington corr. Baltimore Evening Sun, 1923-38, New York Times since Jan. 8, 1938. Disclosed exclusively in newspaper and magazine articles the nature of Palmer "red raids" in Detroit. Ind. Democrat. Clubs: Nat. Press, Penguin (sec. and treas., 1924-25; president, 1925-26), Overseas Writers, White House Correspondents' Association. Author: (with Ray Tucker) Sons of the Wild Jackass, 1932. Contbr. to mags. Was author of first exposés of power and aluminum trusts to appear in "class" mags. Home: 3 Armat Drive, Bradley Hills, Bethesda, Md. Office: 717 Albee Bldg., Washington, D.C.

BARLING, Eugene Hobart, advertising; b. New York, N.Y., July 16, 1892; s. Edward Eugene and Corrinne (Howe) B.; student Barringer Sch., Newark, N.J., 1910-14, Princeton, 1917-18; m. Madeline Russell, Jan. 2, 1918; children—William Edward, Barbara Jean. Began as local representative of Star-Eagle, Newark, N.J., 1914, advertising mgr. 1916-18; special rep. Barron-Collier, Newark, 1915-16; sales mgr. United Advertising Corpn., outdoor advertising, Me., Conn., Pa., N.J., 1920-25, vice-pres., dir. and sales mgr. since 1925; dir. Federal Advertising Corpn. Served as lt. Air Corps, U.S. Army, 1917-18. Mem. Theta Phi. Republican. Episcopalian. Clubs: Newark Athletic, Baltusrol Golf, Red Bank Yacht, Newark Advertising. Contbr. to Judge and advertising periodicals. Home: Hutton Park, West Orange, N.J. Office: 354 Park Av., Newark, N.J.

BARLOW, De Witt Dukes, civil engr.; b. Phila., Pa., Oct. 4, 1880; s. Thomas Arnold and Elizabeth (Dukes) B.; B.S., Phila. High Sch., 1898; B.S. in C.E., U. of Pa., 1901; m. Elizabeth Hail Moody, May 16, 1905; children—Anne May, Esther Moody, Elizabeth Hail, De Witt D., Carlton Montague, Jean Lewis. Began practice at Phila., 1901; pres. Atlantic, Gulf & Pacific Co. since 1921; also pres. of Atlantic, Gulf & Pacific Company of Texas, North Atlantic Dredging Company, Atlantic Peninsular Holding Company. Was associate chief of Dredging Section, War Industries Board, 1918-19; chmn. Dredge Owners' Protective Orgn. since 1920. Mem. Common Council, Plainfield, N.J., 1922-23; mem. Bd. of Health, 1923-24; pres. Bd. of Edn., 1924-37; pres. Plainfield Symphony Soc.; mayor of City of Plainfield, 1937-39. Mem. bd. dirs., Metropolitan Popular Season, Inc. Chmn. N.J. Citizens Com. for the Princeton Local Govt. Survey. Asso. mem. Am. Soc. C.E.; mem. Sigma Xi. Republican. Presbyn. Clubs: Engineers, Univ. of Pa. Club (New York); Plainfield Country. Home: Plainfield, N.J. Office: 15 Park Row, New York, N.Y.

BARNARD, Chester Irving, telephone official; b. Malden, Mass., Nov. 7, 1886; s. Charles H. and Mary E. (Putnam) B.; student Harvard, 1906-09; hon. D.Sc., Rutgers U.; LL.D., Newark, U.; m. Grace F. Noera, Dec. 6, 1911; 1 dau., Frances. Began in statis. dept. Am. Telephone & Telegraph Co., 1909; commercial engr., 1913-22; asst. v.p. and gen. mgr. Bell Telephone Co. of Pa. and associated cos., 1922-23, gen. mgr., 1923-25, v.p. and gen. mgr., 1925-26, v.p. in charge operations, 1926-27; first pres. N.J. Bell Telephone Co. since 1927; dir. Fidelity Union Trust Co., Prudential Ins. Co. of America, Am. Ins. Co., L. Bamberger & Co., N.J. Bell Telephone Co. First state dir. Emergency Relief for N.J., 1931, resigned, Feb. 28, 1933, again served, Apr.-July, 1935 (resigned); chmn. State Relief Council, N.J., 1935. Founder mem. Newark Art Theatre. Tech. adviser to rate com. and operating bd. U.S. Telephone Administration, World War. Alumni trustee The Northfield Schools, Inc., Mt. Hermon, Mass.; trustee Rutgers U., Newark U.; dir. Nat. Bur. of Economic Research, Inc.; mem. Nat. Advisory Com. N.Y. World's Fair of 1939; mem. visiting com. dept. of sociology, Harvard U.; mem. bd. dirs. Newark U. Mem. Stable Money Assn. (mem. N.J. state council), Nat. Econ. League (mem. nat. council), N.J. State Chamber of Commerce, Chamber of Commerce and Civics of the Oranges and Maplewood, N.E. Soc. of Orange N.J. (counselor), Bach Soc. of N.J., Telephone Pioneers of America, Newcomen Soc. Clubs: Essex, Downtown, Newark Athletic (Newark); Harvard (New Jersey); Harvard (New York); Carteret (Jersey City); Seaview Golf (Absecon); Essex County Country, Lake Mohawk Country. Home: 333 Forest Rd., South Orange, N.J. Address: 540 Broad St., Newark, N.J.

BARNARD, Glenn Harrison, elec. engring.; b. Hemlock, N.Y., Jan. 21, 1889; s. Peter Pitts and Clara (Jerome) B.; E.E., Syracuse U., 1912; ed. First Engrs. Class U.S. Naval Acad., Annapolis, 1917; m. Evelyn Leach, Oct. 25, 1922. With General Electric Co., Schenectady, N.Y., 1912-16, asst. inspr. for U.S. Navy, Schenectady, 1916; elec. engr. Electro Dynamic Co., mfg. electric motors and generators largely for marine use, Bayonne, N.J., 1919-30, gen. mgr. and elec. engr., Electro Dynamic Works of Electric Boat Co., Bayonne, N.J., since 1930. Served as lt. U.S.N. Res., 1917-19, radio officer U.S.S. Connecticut, 1917, elec. officer U.S.S. New Mexico, 1918-19; now lt. comdr. U.S.N.R., exec. officer Seventh Batln. Mem. Am. Inst. Elec. Engrs., Soc. Naval Archts. and Marine Engrs., Am. Soc. Naval Engrs., Nat. Council Am. Ship Builders, Tau Beta Pi. Awarded Victory Medal Atlantic Fleet (U.S.); World War Medal (N.Y. State). Republican. Attend Congl. Ch. Home: 4 Howard Place, Bayonne, N.J.

BARNARD, J(ames) Lynn, educator; b. Milford, Otsego Co., N.Y., Aug. 9, 1867; s. James Taylor and Cora Ophelia (Smith) B.; grad. Cooperstown (N.Y.) High Sch., 1886; B.S., Syracuse U., 1892; Ph.D., U. of Pa., 1897; m. Jessie May Cummings, Sept. 6, 1893; children —Grover (dec.), Margaret, Frances Cummings. Prof. history and polit. science, Ursinus Coll., Collegeville, Pa., 1897-1904; field agt., New York and Phila. charity orgn. socs., 1904-06; prof. history and govt., Phila. Sch. of Pedagogy, 1906-20; dir. social studies Pa., Dept. Pub. Instrn., 1920-27; prof. polit. science and dir. social studies for teachers, Ursinus Coll., 1927. Mem. faculty, Mass. State Normal Sch., Hyannis, summer session 1914, Teachers Coll. (Columbia), 1916, U. of Pittsburgh, 1917, 18, Harvard University, 1919 and 1920, Pa. State College, 1923-32, Univ. of Pa., 1935, Western State Teachers Coll., Kalamazoo, Mich., 1937. Mem. American Acad. Polit. and Social Science, Am. Polit. Science Assn., Phi Kappa Psi, Phi Beta Kappa, Kappa Phi Kappa. Methodist. Author: Factory Legislation in Pennsylvania, 1906. Co-author: The Teaching of Community Civics (U.S. Bur. Edn.), 1915; Citizenship in Philadelphia, 1918; Our Community Life, 1926; Epochs of World Progress, 1927; Civics Readers, 3 vols., 1938. Editor and compiler: Getting a Living, 1921. Home: Collegeville, Pa.

BARNARD, Julian W., lawyer; b. Kennet Sq., Pa., Nov. 4, 1897; s. Wilson and Phebe (Walker) B.; grad. Lower Merion Twp. High Sch., Ardmore, Pa., 1913-17; student Swathmore (Pa.) Coll., 1917-18, 1919-20, Dickinson Sch. of Law, 1920-23, LL.B., 1923; m. Beatrice K. Creager, Jan. 3, 1925; children—Julian W., Joan C. Admitted to Pa. bar, 1923, and since practiced in Montgomery Co.; associated with firm Larzelere & Wright, Norristown, Pa., 1927-33; dir. and solicitor Second Saving Fund & Loan Assn.; solicitor Sumneytown Loan Assn. Served as pvt. 1st class, 158th Co., 1st Regt., U.S. Marine Corp, during World War. Solicitor of the Borough of Norristown, Pa., since 1936. Campaign mgr. for the present Judge Wm. F. Dannehower of Montgomery Co., Pa., 1933. Mem. Montgomery Co., Pa. State bar assns., Sigma Chi. Republican. Society of Friends. Home: 1600 Markley St. Office: 50 E. Penn St., Norristown, Pa.

BARNERT, Meyer, mgr. Barnert Mills; b. Paterson, N.J., July 30, 1881; s. Boas and Liebchen (Neufield) B.; E.E., Columbia U., 1904; unmarried. Began as test engr., Gen. Electric Co., Schenectady, 1904, turbine erecting engr., 1906-10; power sales engr. Cities Service Co., Joplin, Mo., 1911-18, Northern States Power Co. at Wis., Minn. and Dak. properties, 1918-25; asst. mgr. Northern States Power Co., St. Paul, Minn., 1925-30; mgr. Barnert Mills, Paterson, N.J., since 1930. Mem. Industrial Commn., Paterson. Mem. Am. Inst. Elec. Engrs. Republican. Mason, Odd Fellow, B'nai B'rith, etc. Home: 284 Ellison St. Office: Grand St. and Railroad Av., Paterson, N.J.

BARNES, Arnold Appleton, oil and gas operator; b. Charleston, W.Va., Feb. 12, 1889; s. Edwin A. and Mabel (Appleton) B.; student Lawrenceville (N.J.) Sch., 1905-08; B.S., Princeton U., 1912; m. Frances Arbuckle, Aug. 31, 1926; children—Arnold Appleton, Jr., John Arbuckle. Employed as clk. Abney Barnes Co., wholesale dry goods, Charleston, W.Va., 1912-26, sec. and dir. since 1917; independent stock broker and mgr. of properties since 1926; mem. firm Howard & Barnes, production of natural gas, Charleston, W.Va. since 1935; pres. and dir. Barnes Transportation Co., Lincoln Mineral Co.; sec., treas., dir. and gen. mgr. W.Va. Land & Improvement Co., Charleston Co., Cambridge Gas Co., Harvard Gas Co.; vice-pres. and dir. First Nat. Bank of S.C., South Charleston, since 1931. Served in civilian capacity as foreman U.S. Naval Ordnance Plant during World War. Pres. Charleston Chamber of Commerce. Dir. Charleston Red Cross. Mem. Soc. Residential Appraisers, Phi Beta Kappa. Presbyn. Mason (32°, Shriner). Clubs: Edgewood Country, Rotary (Charleston); Dial Lodge (Princeton). Home: Ridgemont Rd. Office: Kanawha Bank & Trust Bldg., Charleston, W.Va.

BARNES, Demass Ellsworth, educator; b. Gambier, O., Apr. 12, 1893; s. Thomas Ellsworth and Lydia Belle (Rolston) B.; A.B., Ohio Northern U., Ada, O., 1913; univ. scholar, Harvard, 1914-16, M.A., 1915, mem. Am. School Detachment, U. of Montpellier, France, 1919; grad. work in edn., U. of Pittsburgh Night Sch., 1930-32; m. Helen Elise Garden, June 19, 1929; 1 son, Thomas Garden. Asst. govt., Harvard, 1915-16, Radcliffe Coll., Cambridge, Mass., 1915-16 (2d half yr.); instr. history, Monson (Mass.) Acad., 1916-18, Morristown (N.J.) Sch., 1919-20, head history dept., 1920-22; head dept. social studies, Shady Side Acad., Pittsburgh, Pa., since 1922, dir. Summer Sch., 1924-38, acting headmaster, 1937-38, asst. headmaster since 1938; reader in Am. History, Coll. Entrance Exam. Bd., 1922, 1924-35, examiner Am. History, 1933, 1934, 1935. Served as 2d lt., Inf., U.S. Army, 1918-19, A.E.F., Sept. 1918-Aug. 1919, Am. Army Occupation, Jan.-Mar. 1919. Dir. Animal Rescue League, Pittsburgh. Mem. Am. Hist. Assn., Middle States Assn. History Teachers, Nat. Council of Social Studies, Hist. Soc. of Western Pa., Hist. Assn. of Pa., N.E.A., Pa. State Edn. Assn., Fgn. Policy Assn., Ohio Northern U. Alumni Assn., Harvard Club of Western Pa., Church Club of Diocese of Pittsburgh, Com. on Religious Edn. (Diocese of Pittsburgh), Civic Club of Allegheny Co. (com. on edn.). Episcopalian (vestryman Emmanuel Episcopal Ch., Pittsburgh, since 1929). Mason (Warsaw, O., Lodge 225). Office: Shady Side Academy, Fox Chapel, Pittsburgh, Pa.

BARNES, George Emerson, clergyman; b. Hersey, Mich., May 26, 1882; s. Joseph Asa and Ella Minerva (Bennett) B.; Olivet (Mich.) Coll., 1899-1901; B.A., U. of Mont., 1902; Rhodes scholar from Mont. at Oxford U., Eng., 1904-07; B.A., Christ Ch. Coll., 1907 (first honors in theology); D.D., Alma (Mich.) Coll., 1916; m. Myrtle Kendall Montague, Aug. 4, 1908; children—Kendall Montague, Allan Campbell, Robert Gaylord, Margaret Elizabeth. Ordained Presbyn. ministry, 1907; pastor Coldwater, 1907-12, 1st Ch., Battle Creek, 1912-18, 1st Ch., Flint, 1918-22, Overbrook Presbyn. Ch., Phila., Pa., since 1922. Chmn. Presbyn. War Service Commn. for Mich. and Wis., 1918; camp pastor, Camp Custer, Mich., 1918. Moderator Synod of Mich., 1915-16; mem. Home Missions Council Presbyn. Ch. U.S.A., 1913-16. Gov. 9th Dist. Rotary Clubs, 1921-22. Mem. bd. dirs. Haverford (Pa.) Prep School; sec. Assn. of Am. Rhodes Scholars; bus. mgr. Am. Oxonian; dir. Phila. Fed. of Chs.; mem. advisory board World Alliance for Friendship; mem. board of corporators of Presbyn. Minister's Fund; moderator Presbytery of Phila., 1936-38; chmn. Com. on Arrangements for Sesquicentennial Gen. Assembly, 1938; mem. Supervisory Com. on Social Edn. and Action of Presbyn. Ch. since 1936; del. to World Confs. at Oxford and Edinburgh, 1937. Republican. Mason (32°, K.T., Shriner). Clubs: Union League, Rotary; Gull Lake (Mich.) Country. Writer on religious subjects. Home: 6376 City Line Av., Philadelphia, Pa.*

BARNES, George O., public official; b. Sugar Run, Pa., Oct. 6, 1878; s. Oscar O. and Frances E. (Wright) B.; studied Valparaiso (Ind.) U., Georgetown U. Law Sch. 1 yr., Am. Inst. Banking 1 yr., accountancy 1 yr.; m. Joanna L. Kane, Sept. 2, 1908; children—George Anthony, Mary Elizabeth, Edward Oscar, Eugene Kane, Joanne. With Nat. Bank Redemption Agency, U.S. Treasury Dept., Washington, 1902-29, supt., 1920-29; asst. treas. of U.S., May 6, 1929-July 21, 1933; exec. asst. to treasurer of U.S. since Aug. 1, 1933. Republican. Catholic. Home: 608 Rolling Road, Chevy Chase, Md. Office: Treasury Dept., Washington, D.C.

BARNES, Grace, librarian; b. Tippecanoe Co., Ind., Mar. 31, 1876; d. Thomas Jefferson and Mary Havens (Mason) Barnes; B.S., Purdue U., Lafayette, Ind., 1894; B.L.S., Library Sch., U. of Ill., 1918; A.M., U. of Md., 1935; student U. of Chicago, summer 1910; unmarried. Teacher, Mrs. Starrett's Sch. for Girls, Chicago, 1910-11; asst. librarian, A. and M. Coll., Miss., 1914-15; cataloguer, U. of Ill. Library, 1915-18; head cataloguer and reference librarian, U. of Okla., 1918-19; reference librarian, U. of Mo., 1920-23; head librarian U. of Md., 1923-37; librarian, Nat. Park Coll., Forest Glen, Md., since 1938. Home: 3419 30th St., N.W., Washington, D.C. Office: National Park College, Forest Glen, Md.

BARNES, H. Edgar, asso. justice Supreme Court of Pa. Address: Philadelphia, Pa.

BARNES, Horace Richards, prof. economics; b. Haddonfield, N.J., May 8, 1887; s. Frederick Rigby and Louisa S. (Frank) B.; ed. Bucknell U., 1907-09; A.B., U. of Pa., 1911, A.M., 1913; hon. LL.D., Washington Coll., 1928; m. Laura May Hibberd, of Media, Pa., June 13, 1916; children—Elizabeth Jean, Horace Richards. Instr. Peddie Inst., 1915-16; asst. prof. Drexel Inst. Tech., 1916-18; prof. Pa. Mil. Coll., 1918-19; bursar U. of Pa., 1919-21; prof. and dir. dept. economics and business adminstrn., Franklin and Marshall Coll. since 1921, also sec. Bd. of Trustees since 1928; Harrison Scholar, U. of Pa., 1912-13, Harrison Fellow in Economics, 1913-15; econ. adviser to various firms. Served as pres. civil service bd. Lancaster Co. Dept. of Police, 1930-34; chmn. Budget Com. Lancaster Welfare Fed. for six yrs.; exec. dir. Lancaster Co. for NRA, 1933. Mem. Am. Econ. Soc., Am. Acad. Social Sci., Lancaster Co. Hist. Soc., Phi Sigma Kappa (nat. pres., 1930-32), Pi Gamma Mu. Republican. Baptist. Home: 928 Virginia Av., Lancaster, Pa.

BARNES, Howard M(artin), banker; b. Glen Gardner, N.J., Feb. 10, 1892; s. Elmer E. and Laura (Folwell) B.; ed. William Penn Charter Sch., Phila., 1909-11, U. of Pa., 1911-13, Univ. of Montpellier, France, 1918-19, Temple U. Law Sch., Phila., 1922-26; unmarried. Clerk P.&R. R.R., Phila., 1920-21; with Federal Reserve Bank, Phila., 1921-29; with Doylestown Nat. Bank & Trust Co., since 1929, exec. vice-pres. since 1929; vice-pres. and dir. White Hall Mutual Fire Ins. Assn., Chalfont Mutual Storm Ins. Assn.; asst. treas. and dir. Eddington Distilling Co. Served as lt. 28th Div., U.S. Army, 1915-19, with A.E.F., 1917-19; capt. 111th Inf., U.S. Army Reserve Corps, 1920-36. Republican. Presbyterian (trustee). Mason. Home: 115 E. State St. Office: Doylestown Nat. Bank & Trust Co., Doylestown, Pa.

BARNES, Ira Winslow, banker; b. Factoryville, Pa., Mar. 29, 1878; s. Dayton Curtis and Sarah Elminy (Woodruff) B.; student Wyoming Sem., Kingston, Pa., 1894-97; m. Louise Marian Lyon, Sept. 1, 1902; children—Curtis Lyon, Ira Winslow. With Second Nat. Bank, Wilkes-Barre, Pa., 1898-1902; cashier First Nat. Bank, Weatherly, Pa., 1902-04; asst. cashier Union Nat. Bank, Mahanoy City, Pa., 1904-06, cashier, 1906-11; asst. to the pres. Ninth Nat. Bank, Phila., May 1911, to Jan. 1912, pres., 1912-23; pres. Ninth Bank & Trust Co., since Oct. 1, 1923; dir. Commonwealth Title Co. Mem. bd. mgrs. Northeastern Hosp., Phila. Republican.

Methodist (treas. and mem. bd. trustees First Ch. of Germantown). Mason. Clubs: Union League (Phila.); Huntingdon Valley Country of Abington, Pa. (treas.). Home: 6680 Lincoln Drive. Office: Front and Norris Sts., Philadelphia, Pa.

BARNES, James, physicist; b. Halifax, Nova Scotia, Dec. 11, 1878; s. Henry Wisdom and Emma Frances (Johnson) B.; B.A., Dalhousie Coll., Halifax, 1899, M.A., 1900; 1851 exhbn. scholar, 1900-03; Ph.D., Johns Hopkins, 1904; studied Cambridge, Eng., 1914, U. of Manchester, Eng., 1915; m. Helen Wilson, July 28, 1917. Fellow, Johns Hopkins, 1903-04, instr., 1904-06; research fellow, U. of Manchester, 1915; prof. physics, Bryn Mawr Coll., 1906-31; tech. advisor, Franklin Inst. since 1931. Maj. Ordnance Res., U.S.A. Fellow A.A.A.S., Am. Physical Soc., Franklin Inst. (bd. of mgrs. 1925-30); mem. Phi Beta Kappa, Sigma Xi, Phi Kappa Psi. Presbyn. Contbr. many articles to Philos. Mag., Physical Rev., Astrophys. Jour., etc. Home: Whitehall, Haverford, Pa. Address: Franklin Institute, Philadelphia, Pa.

BARNES, James Anderson, univ. prof.; b. Prentiss, Ky., Nov. 17, 1898; s. Joseph Franklin and Emma May (Brown) B.; A.B., Ky. Teachers Coll., Bowling Green, Ky., 1924; M.A., U. of Wis., Madison, Wis., 1925, Ph.D., 1928; m. Elinor Shafer, Jan. 14, 1928. Asst. instr. in history, U. of Wis., Madison, Wis., 1924-27; asst. prof., U. of S.D., Vermilion, S.D., 1928-29; instr., Temple U., Phila., 1930-32, asso. prof. since 1932; visiting prof. in history, U. of Ky., Lexington, Ky., summer 1929, U. of Tex., Austin, Tex., summer 1936, U. of N.C., Chapel Hill, N.C., summer 1937. Served as sergt., 1st class, U.S. Army, A.E.F. in France, during World War. Mem. Am., Miss. Valley, Pa. historical assns., Alpha Delta Kappa, Pi Gamma Mu. Awarded fellowship in Am. history, U. of Wis., 1927-28; fellow The Brookings Institution, 1929-30, The Social Science Research Council, 1932-33; awarded Grant-in-Aid, The Social Science Research Council, summer 1938. Democrat. Methodist. Author: John G. Carlisle: Financial Statesman (Am. Polit. Leader Series), 1931; numerous articles to hist. jours.; contbr. to Leica Manual. Book review editor, Pennsylvania History (quarterly of Pa. Hist. Assn.). Pioneer in the use of the miniature camera as a copying instrument for the historian. Address: 429 E. Allen's Lane, Mt. Airy, Philadelphia, Pa.

BARNES, John Hampton, lawyer; b. Pittsburgh, Pa., Dec. 24, 1860; s. William Henry and Eva (Hampton) B.; A.B., Yale, 1881; studied Columbia Law Sch., 1882-83; m. Emily Leland Harrison, Apr. 21, 1892; children—Dorothy Hampton (Mrs. Jewett Newton), Sylvia Leland (Mrs. Forde Todd), Cecily Weldon (Mrs. Emile Geyelin); m. 2d, Eleanor Kearny Biddle, Apr. 14, 1904; children—Eleanor Biddle (Mrs. H. Gates Lloyd, Jr.), John Hampton. Began practice in Phila., 1883; mem. firm Barnes, Biddle & Myers; counsel Pa. R.R. Co., Girard Trust Co., Westmoreland Coal Co., Giant Portland Cement Co., Catawissa Ry. Co., Philadelphia Nat. Bank, Berwind Coal Mining Co.; dir. Phila. Nat. Bank, Phila. Contributionship for Ins. of Houses from Loss by Fire, Catawissa Ry. Co.; mgr. Phila. Savings Fund Soc. Mem. Am. Inst. of Law, Pa. Bar Assn., Phila. Bar Assn. (former chancellor), Delta Kappa Epsilon, Scroll and Key. Republican. Clubs: Philadelphia (Phila.); University, Yale (New York); Graduate (New Haven). Home: West Acres, Devon, Chester Co., Pa. Office: Morris Bldg., 1421 Chestnut St., Philadelphia, Pa.

BARNES, Morgan, headmaster; b. nr. Mercer, Pa., May 7, 1870; s. Samuel and Elizabeth (Baker) B.; A.B., Harvard U., 1891; studied U. of Berlin, 1892; LL.D. from Grove City (Pa.) College, 1933; m. Jane Dale, Sept. 15, 1904; children—Eleanor Dale (Mrs. Frederick Lovett Taft, 3d), Thomas Dale. Instr. in Latin, Grove City Coll., 1892-94, prof., 1894-96; prof. Greek, Westminster (Pa.) Coll., 1896-1903; classical master The Thacher Sch., Ojai, Calif., 1903-10; acting v. prin. Northwestern Normal Sch., Pa., 1911-14; prof. Romance langs., Grove City College, 1914-15, prof. English, 1915-17; sr. master The Thacher Sch., 1917-31, became headmaster, 1931; prof. Romance langs., Grove City Coll. since 1937. Pres. board Ojai Valley Pub. Library; pres. Ojai Chapter Am. Red Cross; dir. George Jr. Republic of Pa.; v.p. Indian Defense Assn., Santa Barbara; pres. trustees Ojai Valley Sch.; v.p. Ojai Valley Chamber of Commerce. Hon. life member California Headmasters Assn. Trustee Ojai Presbyterian Ch. Contributor to Atlantic, also newspapers; weekly column, "Quips and Countercheck," under nom de plume "Touchstone," Mercer (Pa.) Dispatch. Home: 433 N. Broad St., Grove City, Pa. Address: Casa de Piedra Ranch, Ojai, Calif.

BARNES, Morton A., clergyman; b. Plymouth, Conn., Dec. 20, 1875; s. Martin Van Buren and Mary Jane (Brooks) B.; ed. St. Stephen's Coll., 1895-99, Theol. Sem., Alexandria, Va., 1899-1902. Ordained to ministry P.E. Ch., deacon, 1902, priest, 1903; curate, St. John's, Waterbury, Conn., 1902-04; rector, Christ Ch., Fairmont, W.Va., 1904-08; rector, Grace Ch., Newark, N.J., 1908-14; rector, St. James Ch., Long Branch, N.J. since 1914; propr. and dir. Camp Nejecho, summer camp for boys, now in 27th season. Served as mem. Sch. Bd., City of Long Branch, N.J. Mem. Bd. Govs., Monmouth Memorial Hosp. Dir. Long Branch Pub. Health Nursing Assn. Mem. Sigma Alpha Epsilon. Episcopalian. Home: 15 Slocum Pl., Long Branch, N.J.

BARNES, T(homas) Ellis, securities at auction; b. Phila., Pa., July 7, 1873; s. J. Harbeson and Clara S. (Smith) B.; ed. pub. schs.; m. Malvina A. Herr, of Jersey City, N.J., Oct. 12, 1922. Engaged in business of selling stocks and bonds at auction since starting as clk., 1890, to retirement, 1925; mem. firm Barnes and Lofland, security auctioneers; dir. Phila., Germantown and Norristown R.R. Co., Plymouth R.R. Co., Citizens Passenger Ry. Co., Northern Liberties Gas Co. Republican. Episcopalian. Clubs: Union League, Philadelphia Country (Philadelphia); Merion Cricket (Haverford). Home: Haverford, Pa., also Miami Beach, Fla.

BARNES, W. Harry, physician; b. Phila., Pa., Apr. 4, 1887; s. George W. and Eliza (Webb) B.; A.B., Central High Sch., Phila., 1907; M.D., U. of Pa., 1912; grad. study, U. of Pa. Grad. Sch. of Medicine, 1920-21, U. of Paris, France, 1924, U. of Bordeaux, France, 1924; m. Martha E. Thomas, of Atlantic City, N.J., Sept. 23, 1912; children—W. Harry, Jr., Lloyd T. (M.D.), Ralph W., Leroy T., Carl L. Engaged in gen. practice of medicine at Phila., 1912-21, practice limited to diseases of ear, nose and throat since 1921. Served as actg. asso. surgeon U.S. Pub. Health Service, Boston, Mass., 1918. Mem. Am. Bd. Otolaryngology, Sigma Pi Phi. Democrat. Mem. M.E. Ch. Mason. Home: 1315 N. 15th St., Philadelphia, Pa.

BARNES, William J., M.D., attending surgeon Englewood Hosp. Address: 155 Engle St., Englewood, N.J.

BARNETT, Frank R., corpn. dir.; b. St. Thomas, Pa., May 4, 1874; s. Daniel and Margaret (Besore) B.; m. Amy E. Vance, Jan. 14, 1902. Owner, mgr. Leland Hotel, Waynesboro, Pa., 1902-08; since 1908 dir. and interested financially in Landis Tool Co., Citizens Nat. Bank & Trust Co., Waynesboro Bldg. & Loan Assn. Mem. bd. mgrs. Waynesboro (Pa.) Hosp. Republican. Trinity Reformed Church. Mason (32°, K.T., Shriner), Elk. Clubs: Waynesboro (Pa.) Country (mem. bd. dirs.); Tin Whistle's Golf (Pinehurst, N.C.). Address: 48 W. Main St., Waynesboro, Pa.

BARNETT, George Ernest, economist; b. Cambridge, Md., Feb. 19, 1873; s. Edward D. and Elizabeth (Meredith) B.; A.B., Randolph-Macon Coll., 1891; Ph.D., Johns Hopkins, 1902; unmarried. Instr., asso. and asso. prof. polit. economy, 1901-11, prof. statistics, since 1911, Johns Hopkins University. Member American Economic Association (president, 1932), Am. Statis. Assn. Am. Assn. for Labor Legislation. Author: State Banking in the United States, 1902; The Printers, 1909; State Banks and Trust Companies, 1911; Mediation, Investigation and Arbitration in Industrial Disputes (with D.A. McCabe), 1916; Machinery and Labor, 1926. Editor: A Trial Bibliography of American Trade Union Publications, 1904. Co-editor of Studies in American Trade Unionism, 1906. Home: 827 Park Av., Baltimore, Md.✦

BARNEY, Charles Neal, manufacturing exec.; b. Lynn, Mass., June 27, 1875; s. William Mitchell and Mary Louise (Neal) B.; A.B., Tufts Coll., Medford, Mass., 1895, hon. A.M., 1909; LL.B., Boston U., 1898; m. Maizie Blaikie, June 27, 1901; children—Virginia, Stuart Neal (Dec.). Began as lawyer, Boston, Mass., 1898; partner Lummus & Barney, Lynn, Mass., 1900-15, Barney & Woodruff, 1915-18; officer Worthington Pump and Machinery Corpn., Harrison, N.J., since 1918, sec.-treas. since 1931; lecturer Northeastern Law Sch., Boston, 1908-18, Boston U. Law Sch., 1911. Mayor, Lynn, Mass., 1906-07; presidential elector, Mass., 1908; chmn. legal advisory bd. for draft, Lynn, 1917. Trustee Tufts Coll., Boston, 1908-20. Mem. Am., Mass. and N.Y. bar assns., Soc. of Mayflower Descendants (N.Y.), Phi Beta Kappa, Theta Delta Chi. Republican. Universalist. Mason. Clubs: University (N.Y.); Fox Meadow Tennis (Scarsdale, N.Y.); Pacific (Nantucket, Mass.). Author: Equity and Its Remedies, 1915. Home: 15 Barclay Rd., Scarsdale, N.Y. Office: Worthington Pump and Machinery Corpn., Harrison, N.J., and 2 Park Av., New York, N.Y.

BARNHART, Frank P(ierce), lawyer; b. Johnstown, Pa., Sept. 6, 1873; s. Henry and Amanda (Bowman) B.; B.S., Indiana (Pa.) State Normal Sch., 1895; A.B., Princeton, 1902; LL.B., Dickinson Sch. of Law, 1905, A.M., Dickinson Coll., 1905; m. Gertrude Heller, Nov. 14, 1907; 1 dau., Gertrude D. (Mrs. Howard Holman, Jr.). Admitted to Pa. bar, 1906, and since practiced in Johnstown; mem. firm Barnhart & Adams; judge of Court of Common Pleas of Cambria Co., Pa., by appointment of gov., 1929-30. Mem. Pa. State Legislature, 1907-09. Mem. Am. Bar Assn., Pa. Bar Assn., Cambria Co. Bar Assn., Phi Kappa Psi. Republican. Methodist. Clubs: Princeton (Pittsburgh); Rotary (Johnstown). Home: 1522 Franklin St. Office: 402 Swank Bldg., Johnstown, Pa.

BARNHART, John Love, clergyman; b. Greensburg, Pa., July 1, 1872; s. William Rowe and Catherine (Shupe) B.; A.B., Franklin and Marshall Coll., Lancaster, Pa., 1893; student Harvard U., 1893-94; B.D., Theol. Sem. of Ref., Ch. in U.S., Lancaster, Pa., 1897; (hon.) D.D., Franklin and Marshall Coll., 1922; m. Emma A. Rupp, Sept. 27, 1898; children—Louise Gertrude (wife of Jesse S. Spangler, M.D.), William Rupp (D.D.). Ordained to ministry Ref. Ch. in U.S., 1897; pastor, West Milton, Pa., 1897-1901, Saegertown, Pa., 1901-10; pastor Christ Ch., Baltimore, Md. since 1910 ch. now known as Messiah Evang. and Ref. Ch.; served as pres. Ministerial Union of Baltimore and Vicinity, 1922; mem. exec. com. Fed. of Chs., 1922-37; pres. of Synod of Potomac Ref. Ch. in U.S., 1931. Trustee Franklin and Marshall Coll. since 1921. Mem. bd. ministerial relief of Ref. Ch. in U.S. since 1914. Republican. Mem. Evang. & Ref. Ch. Club: Inter-Church of Baltimore. Contbr. articles to religious papers. Home: 3408 Edgewood Rd., Baltimore, Md.

BARNHART, Paul Shupe, lawyer; b. Greensburg, Pa., Sept. 16, 1880; s. William R. and Catharine Sherrick (Shupe) B.; A.B., Franklin and Marshall Coll., Lancaster, Pa., 1903; student U. of Pittsburgh Law Sch., 1906-07; m. Mary Alice Breck, March 25, 1909 (died 1939); children—Eleanor Pauline, Alice Elizabeth, Catharine May. Admitted to Westmoreland County bar, 1908, and since practiced at Greensburg, Pa.; mem. firm Beacom, Barnhart & Ankney, Greensburg since 1921-30; dir. Barclay-Westmoreland Trust Co., Greensburg, 1921-33. Mem. Greensburg Bd. of Edn., 1923-35, pres., 1929-35. Republican. Mem. Reformed Ch. in U.S.A. Mason (Westmoreland Lodge 518, Greensburg; Shriner, Syria Temple, Pittsburgh). Home: 417 Harrison Av. Office: Finance Bldg., Main St., Greensburg, Pa.

BARNHART, William Rupp; prof. Biblical lit. and religion, Hood Coll. Address: Hood College, Frederick, Md.

BARNHOUSE, Donald Grey, minister, editor; b. Watsonville, Calif., March 28, 1895; s. Theodore and Jane Ann (Carmichael) B.; student U. of Chicago, Princeton, Princeton Theol. Sem., 1915-17, Grenoble, France, 1923-25; grad. student and faculty asst., U. of Pa., 1925-27, Th.M., 1927; D.D., Dallas Theol. Sem., 1933; m. Ruth Tiffany, of Huntingdon, Pa., 1922; children—Ruth Tiffany, Donald Grey, David Heath, Dorothy Grace. Ordained ministry Presbyn. Ch., 1918; pastor Tenth Presbyn. Ch., Phila., since 1927; radio preacher over Columbia Broadcasting System, 1928-32, over WOR and 100 stations, 1932. First lt. U.S.A., 1917-18. Dir. Ecole Biblique de Belgique (Brussels), 1919-21; pastor Eglise Reformee de France (Fressinieres), 1921-23. Commr. Gen. Assembly, Presbyn. Ch., 1928. Dir. Stony Brook (L.I., N.Y). Sch. for Boys. Editor Revelation (monthly mag.). Mem. Victoria Inst. (London); asso. mem. Am. Schs. of Oriental Research. Club: Union League. Author: His Own Received Him Not, But—, 1933; God's Methods for Holy Living, 1937; Life by the Son, 1938. Foreign travel and study, Europe, 1919-25, summers, 1927, 29, 30, 32, 33, 35, 36 (Russia), 1937 (under grant of Carl Schurz Foundation), 1938. Made 16 months tour of foreign mission fields in Asia, speaking in colleges, univs., etc., 1934-35. Home: 1701 Delancey St. Office: 1700 Spruce St., Philadelphia, Pa.

BARR, Floyd Walker, clergyman; b. Stephenson Co., Ill., July 24, 1886; s. Howard Foster and Amanda Jane (Walker) B.; student Interior Acad., Dakota, Ill., 1899-1903, Blackburn Coll., Carlinville, Ill., 1903-05; A.B., Coll. of Wooster, 1907, D.D., 1925; student Western Theol. Sem., 1908-09; B.D., McCormick Theol. Sem., 1911; D.D., Coe Coll., 1923; m. Julia Frances Sanner, Sept. 7, 1907; children—Margaret Jane (wife of Rev. William V. Longbrake), Julia Esther (wife of John Wycliffe McCracken). Teacher of Greek and mathematics, Coll. of Ida., 1907-08; ordained to ministry of Presbyterian Ch., June 1911; asst. minister Third Presbyn. Ch., Chicago, 1911-12; pastor First Presbyn. Ch., Sterling, Ill., 1912-15, First Presbyn. Ch., Monmouth, Ill., 1915-20, Collegiate Presbyn. Ch., Ames, Ia., 1920-22; pastor First Presbyn. Ch., Beaver Falls, Pa. since 1922. Served as religious dir. Army Y.M.C.A., Camp Dodge, 1918. Mem. Pittsburgh Presbyn, Ministers Assn., Beaver Falls Ministerial Assn., Alpha Tau Epsilon. Republican. Mason. Home: 809 Lincoln Place, Beaver Falls, Pa.

BARR, Joseph Wilson, insurance agency; b. Oil City, Pa., July 1, 1875; s. Wilson Ralya and Jennie C. (Harding) B.; ed. pub. schs. and high sch., Oil City; A.B., Amherst, 1899; m. Florence L. Byles, Jan. 16, 1913; children—Joseph Wilson, Jr., Mary Virginia (Mrs. William Kirkpatric Selden). Began as ins. clk., 1899; admitted to Pa. bar, 1903; propr. Barr's Insurance Agency since 1912; dir. Oil City Trust Co. since 1914. Served on various local bds. during World War. At various times an officer or dir. Chamber of Commerce and civic bodies. Dir. Oil City Community Fund, Community Concert Assn.; vice-pres. Forum Associates. Treas. and dir, or dir. Oil City Hosp. since 1912. Mem. bd. of dirs. Pa. Assn. of Ins. Agts. since 1926. Mem. Delta Kappa Epsilon. Republican. Episcopalian. Mason (K.T., 32°). Clubs: Amherst (New York City); Rotary, Wanango Country, Boat (Oil City). Home: 115 W. Third St. Office: National Transit Bldg., Oil City, Pa.

BARR, (Frank) Stringfellow, college president; b. Suffolk, Va., Jan. 15, 1897; s. William Alexander and Ida (Stringfellow) B.; student Tulane, 1912-13; B.A., U. of Va., 1916, M.A., 1917; Rhodes scholar, Oxford U., 1919-21, B.A., M.A.; diplôme, U. of Paris, 1922; studied U. of Ghent, Belgium, 1922-23; m. Gladys Baldwin, Aug. 13, 1921. Asst. prof. modern European history, U. of Va., 1924-27, asso. prof., 1927-30, prof., 1930-37; visiting prof. of liberal arts, U. of Chicago, 1936-37; pres. St. John's Coll. since 1937; advisory editor Va. Quarterly Rev., 1926-30, editor, 1930-34, advisory editor, 1934-37. In Ambulance Service, U.S.A., 1917; transferred to Surgeon Gen's. Office, 1918; disch. Apr. 1919. Mem. Va. Commn. on Interracial Co-operation. Mem. Alpha Tau Omega, Sigma Upsilon, Phi Beta Kappa, Raven Soc. Democrat. Episcopalian. Club: Quadrangle. Author: Mazzini—Portrait of an Exile, 1935. Contbr. articles to mags. and book revs. to New York Herald Tribune, The Nation, New Republic, etc. Home: Annapolis, Md.

BARRACLOUGH, Henry, official Presbyn. Gen. Assembly; b. Windhill, Yorks, Eng., Dec. 14, 1891; s. Joseph Heaton and Sarah Jane (Metcalfe) B.; came to U.S., 1914, naturalized citizen, 1919; ed. high schs., Yorkshire, Eng., 1902-07; m. J. Isabell Rosenberger, Nov. 9, 1921. Employed in secretarial work in Eng., 1907-14; pianist with Rev. J. Wilbur Chapman, D.D., and Charles M. Alexander, evangelists, Eng. and U.S., 1914-17; sec. to Rev. George G. Mahy, D.D., Presbyn. Gen. Assembly's Com. on Evangelism, 1919-21; mgr. Adminstrn. Dept., Office of Presbyn. Gen. Assembly since 1921; rec. sec. Trustees of Gen. Assembly Presbyn. Ch. U.S.A.; choirmaster Tioga Presbyn. Ch., Phila. since 1931; Compiler annual statistics pub. in minutes of Gen. Assembly. Served as regtl. sergt. maj., U.S.A., 1917-19, with hdqrs. detachment, 78th Div. A.E.F. Mem. Assn. Statisticians of Am. Religious Bodies (sec. since 1934), Hymn Soc. of Phila. (sec. since 1936). Republican. Presbyn. Mason. Clubs: Union League, Presbyterian Social Union (Philadelphia); Symposium (Princeton). Composer many well known hymns. Home: 8302 Cadwalader Rd., Elkins Park, Pa. Office: Witherspoon Bldg., Philadelphia, Pa.

BARRATT, Stanley, physician; b. McIntyre, Pa., Dec. 5, 1878; s. Thomas Whitford and Clythera E. (Welcher) B.; ed. Lock Haven Normal Sch., 1904-05; M.D., Hahnemann Med. Sch., Phila., Pa., 1909; m. Margaret F. Keating, May 1, 1912; children—Virginia (Mrs. Gerald F. Smith), Rachel, Thomas Keating. In employ various concerns, 1900-04; engaged in pvt. practice of medicine, Straight, Elk Co., Pa., 1910-11, in Wilcox since 1911; mem. med. staff Community Hosp., Kane, Pa.; also operated retail store since 1918. Served as mem. local sch. bd., 10 yrs. Fellow Am. Med. Assn.; mem. Pa. State Med. Soc., Elk Co. Med. Soc. Republican. Unitarian. Home: Wilcox, Pa.

BARRETT, Anthony Patrick, stock broker; b. Omaha, Neb., Dec. 23, 1889; s. Edward Barrett and Norah (Kilgallen) B.; A.B., U. of Mich., 1913: studied law U. of Alberta, Edmonton, Can., 1913-16; m. Anna Mabel Hetherington, Oct. 1915; children—Phyllis Madeleine, Constance Elaine. Sales promotion, Sherman Corpn., Montreal, and Phila., 1917-27; stock broker Baker, Weeks & Harden, Phila., 1927-37. Mem. Pa. Securities Commn. since 1937. Dem. county chmn., Delaware Co., Pa., 1934-36. Catholic. Home: 4037 Lasher Rd., Drexel Hill, Pa. Office: State Capitol, Harrisburg, Pa.

BARRETT, Arthur, pres. Barrett Machine Co.; b. Pittsburgh, Pa., May 15, 1886; s. Josiah and Elizabeth Floyd (McCreary) B.; ed. Bellevue, Pa., pub. schs., Kiskiminetas Springs Sch., 1903-04; B.S., Case Sch. of Applied Sci., Cleveland, O., 1908; m. Mary B. Templeton, Oct. 13, 1914; children—Edwin Templeton, Elizabeth, Mary Louise, Dorothy Jean. Began as shop foreman, 1908; organized Barrett Machine Co. for mfg. metal specialties, 1912, and since then pres. and dir. of same; pres. and dir. Bellevue Savings and Trust Co.; Western Pa. Bldg. and Loan Assn.; dir. Nat. Ben Franklin Fire Ins. Co. Dir. Suburban Gen. Hosp. Mem. Sigma Xi, Kappa Sigma, Tau Beta Pi. Republican. Presbyn. Mason (32°). Club: Highland Country. Home: 260 Lincoln Av., Bellevue. Office: 912 Behan St., Pittsburgh, Pa.

BARRETT, Arthur G.; surgeon St. Agnes and Franklin Sq. hosps.; surgeon-in-charge Navy Reserve Unit No. 2. Address: 701 Cathedral St., Baltimore, Md.

BARRETT, Benjamin Brooke, banker; b. King of Prussia, Pa., Nov. 13, 1884; s. Adam and Mary (Desmond) B.; ed. pub schools., Upper Merion Twp., Pa., Schissler Business Coll., Norristown, Pa., 1900-01; m. Laura Schultz Anders, Oct. 15, 1913; children—Benjamin Brooke, Donald Anders. Asst. mgr. Reading Screw Co., Norristown, Pa., 1901-18; sec. Mfrs.'s Assn. of Montgomery, Co., Pa., 1918-28; sec. Norristown Penn Trust Co., Norristown, Pa., since 1928; pres. and dir. Norris Bldg. Assn. since 1936; sec.-treas. Pa. Real Estate Exchange, Clarion Bituminous Coal Mining Co.; sec. Schuylkill Valley Lines, Inc.; dir. Norristown Water Co. Dir. Montgomery Hosp., Norristown Chamber of Commerce; trustee Y.M.C.A. Mem. Red Cross, Community Chest. Republican. Lutheran. Mason (Charity Lodge). Clubs: Union League (Phila.); Rotary (Norristown, Pa.). Home: 1503 Northview Drive, Curren Terrace. Office: Main and Swede Sts., Norristown, Pa.

BARRETT, Charles Sanborn, physicist; b. Vermilion, S. D., Sept. 28, 1902; s. Charles H. and Laura (Dunham) B.; B.S. in elec. engring., U. of S.D., 1925; Ph.D., U. of Chicago, 1928; m. Dorothy Arlina Adams, Aug. 2, 1928; 1 dau., Marjorie Arlina. Charles A. Coffin fellowship, U. of Chicago, 1927-28; asst. physicist div. of phys. metallurgy, Naval Research Lab., 1928-37; physicist metals research lab. and lecturer dept. metallurgy, Carnegie Inst. Tech., Pittsburgh, since 1932. Mem. Am. Inst. Mining and Metall. Engrs., Am. Soc. for Metals, Am. Phys. Soc., Delta Tau Delta, Gamma Alpha, Sigma Xi. Contbr. research articles and tech. papers on crystallography, X-rays, radiography by gamma rays, internal-stresses, etc., to professional jours. Address: Carnegie Inst. of Technology, Pittsburgh, Pa.

BARRETT, Don Carlos, economist; b. Spring Valley, O., Apr. 22, 1868; s. I. Merritt and Mary (Evans) B.; A.B., Earlham Coll., Richmond, Ind., 1889, A.M., 1893; A.M. Harvard, 1897, Ph.D., 1901; studied at univs. of Göttingen and Berlin, 1903-04; m. Marcia Frances Moore, Aug. 3, 1892. Prin. in secondary schools, 1889-92; instructor in history and economics, Earlham College, 1892-93; instructor in economics, Harvard, 1896-97; instr., later asst. prof. economics, Haverford (Pa.) Coll., 1897-1907, prof., 1907-34, dean of coll., 1904-08, prof. emeritus since 1934; visiting prof. economics Stanford, 1924, Princeton, 1917-18, 1926-28. Mem. Economists' Nat. Com. on Monetary Policy, American Econ. Assn., Am. Acad. Polit. and Social Science, Am. Assn. Univ. Profs., Phi Beta Kappa. Mem. Soc. of Friends. Author: The Greenbacks and Resumption of Specie Payments, 1931. Contbr. to econ. mags. Home: 5 College Circle, Haverford, Pa.

BARRETT, Dulin A., v.p. Carnegie-Illinois Steel Corpn.; b. St. Clairsville, O., Feb. 4, 1875; s. Alexander and Esther A. (Ault) B.; student grade sch. and Wheeling Business Coll.; m. Minnette Kuhn, Nov. 1, 1906. Dist. mgr. Vandergrift Dist. Plants, Am. Sheet and Tin Plate Co., 1915-28, asst. to v.p., 1929-32, v.p. in charge operations, 1932-36; v.p. in charge industrial relations Carnegie-Illinois Steel Corpn., Pittsburgh, since 1936. Clubs: Duquesne, Pittsburgh Athletic, Pittsburgh Field (Pittsburgh). Home: 1060 Morewood Av. Office: 1015 Carnegie Bldg., Pittsburgh, Pa.

BARRETT, Michael Thomas, dentist; b. Huntingdon, Que., Can., July 27, 1881; s. Dennis and Catherine (Timlin) B.; ed. acads., Can., and N.Y.; D.D.S., U. of Pa. Dental Dept., 1903; hon. M.S., Villanova, 1915; m. Della MacDonald, June 29, 1921. Came to U.S., 1900; demonstrator in prosthetic dentistry, U. of Pa., 1904-10; instr. in normal histology, same, 1910-14; instr. in oral pathology, Grad. Sch. of Medicine, U. of Pa. Discoverer of amœbæ in pyorrhea, 1914. Mem. Psi Omega, Sigma Xi. Roman Catholic. Wrote: The Protozoa of the Mouth in Relation to Pyorrhea Alveolaris (pub. in Dental Cosmos, Aug., 1914); Clinical Report on Amœbic Pyorrhea (same, Dec., 1914); The Internal Anatomy of the Teeth with Special Reference to the Pulp with its Branches; The Effects of Thymus Extract on the Early Eruption and Growth of the Teeth of White Rats; A Study of the Etiological Factors Governing Dental

Caries; etc. Address: 247 S. 16th St., Philadelphia, Pa.

BARRETT, William A., urologist; demonstrator antomy and instr. urology, U. of Pittsburgh; urologist, sr. staff, St. Joseph's Hosp. and Dispensary; asst. urologist Western Pa. Hosp. Address: 3700 Fifth Av., Pittsburgh, Pa.

BARRINGER, Brandon, banker; b. Cape May, N.J., June 11, 1899; s. Daniel Moreau and Margaret (Bennett) B.; prep. edn. Haverford (Pa.) Sch., 1908-16, Evans Sch., Mesa, Ariz., 1916-17; A.B., Princeton U., 1921; unmarried. With Pennsylvania Co. for Insurances on Lives and Granting Annuities, since 1921, as analyst, statistical dept., 1921-28, statistician, 1928-33, v.p. since 1933; pres. and dir. Standard Iron Co., Cass Co. Iron Co.; dir. Cambria Iron Co., Old Ben Coal Corpn., Second and Third Street Passenger Ry., Aldrich Pump Co., Allentown Rolling Mills, Investment Corpn. of Phila., Lehigh Valley R.R. Served in S.A.T.C., 1918. Trustee Jefferson Med. Coll., Library Co. of Phila., Fairmount Park Art Assn., Corpn. for Relief of Widows and Children; mgr. University Museum. Republican. Clubs: Philadelphia, University Barge (Phila.); Nassau, Campus (Princeton). Home: 1530 Locust St. Office: Packard Bldg., 15th and Chestnut Sts., Philadelphia, Pa.

BARRINGER, D(aniel) Moreau, Jr., investment mgr.; b. Phila., Pa., June 30, 1900; s. Daniel Moreau and Margaret (Bennett) B.; prep. edn., Haverford (Pa.) Sch., 1909-16; B.S., Princeton U., 1921; unmarried. Mining engr. Inspiration Consol. Copper Co., 1921-24; asst. to D. M. Barringer, mine valuation and engring., 1924-25; field engr. Southwest Metals Co., 1926; geologist Phelps Dodge Corpn., 1926-30; statistician, later dir., sec. and mem. exec. com. Investment Corpn. of Phila., since 1931; v.p., dir., mem. exec. com. Delaware Fund, Inc.; v.p., dir. W. S. Wasserman Co., investment mgrs.; sec. and dir. Wellington Fund, Inc., Cass Co. Iron Co., East Tex. Iron Co.; dir., Hanover Bessemer Iron & Copper Co. Served in S.A.T.C., 1918. Mem. bd. mgrs. City Parks Assn. of Phila., Hosp. of Protestant Episcopal Church in Phila. Republican. Episcopalian. Clubs: Philadelphia, University Barge of Phila. (past sec.). Home: 1530 Locust St. Office: 225 S. 15th St., Philadelphia, Pa.

BARROLL, Lewin Wethered, lawyer; b. Chestertown, Md., Nov. 22, 1888; s. Hopewell Horsey and Margaret Spencer (Wethered) B.; A.B., Washington Coll., Chestertown, Md., 1908; A.B., Yale U., 1910; LL.B., U. of Md. Law Sch., Baltimore, Md., 1912; A.M., Johns Hopkins U., 1914; m. Valerie Von D. Marbury, June 9, 1917; children—Lewin Wethered, Jr., Margaret Spencer Wethered, William L. Marbury, John Marshall, Valerie Marbury. Admitted to Md. bar, 1911, and since engaged in gen. practice of law at Baltimore; also in practice and admitted to bars, Del. and Va.; also engaged in farming about 2000 acres land in Kent Co., Md. Organized three cos. militia, 1916-17; served as capt. inf., U.S.A., 1917-18. Mem. Am., Md. State, and Baltimore City bar assns., Alpha Delta Phi. Democrat. Episcopalian: Club: Maryland (Baltimore). Home: 159 W. Lanvale St. Office: Calvert Bldg., Baltimore, Md.

BARRON, Jacob Thomas; v.p. Pub. service Electric & Gas Co. Address: 80 Park Place, Newark, N.J.

BARROW, Henry Yeaman, publisher; b. New York, N.Y., May 12, 1885; s. Harry and Lilly (Yeaman) B.; student Madison (N.J.) Acad., 1897-99, Sewanee (Tenn.) Mil. Acad., 1899-1901, U. of the South, 1901-02; m. Mollie Amolie Droescher, Nov. 4, 1918; one dau., Molly. Clerk Lackawanna R.R., New York, 1902; clerk bookkeeping dept., Prudential Life Ins. Co., Newark, N.J., 1903-05; factory supt. Jos. Middleby & Sons, Boston, 1906; advertising mgr. Sweet-Orr & Co., New York, 1907; ranching in Mont., 1908-10; with Standard Statistics Co. since Oct. 1910, now pres.; pres. Social Security Statistical Corpn. Pres. N.J. Golf Assn., 1926-28; pres. Metropolitan Golf Assn., 1926-28. Clubs: Morris County Golf (Convent, N.J.); Echo Lake Country (Cranford, N.J.). Home: 225 Orchard St., Cranford, N.J. Office: 345 Hudson St., New York, N.Y.

BARROW, William E.; pres. and gen. mgr. Joy Mfg. Co.; officer or dir. many other cos. Home: 1198 Otter St. Office: Buffalo and Third Sts., Franklin, Pa.

BARROWS, Arthur Monroe, physician; b. Irasburg, Vt., Nov. 20, 1875; s. Hamlet W. and Susan (Churchill) B.; student Battle Creek Coll., Battle Creek, Mich., 1895-96; M.D., Jefferson Med. Coll., Phila., 1901; grad. study, Mt. Sinai Hosp., Columbia U., 1926, Grad. Hosp., Phila., 1928; m. Emma May Tabram, Sept. 25, 1905; 1 dau., Virginia Churchill (Mrs. Joseph G. Blandi). Interne St. Francis Hosp., Trenton, N.J., 1902-03; engaged in gen. practice of medicine and surgery at Trenton, N.J. since 1903; asst. gynecologist, Mercer Hosp., Trenton, N.J., 1920-30, chief obstet. dept., 1928-36, chief gynecologist since 1936. Mem. Am. Med. Assn., N.J. Med. Soc. Republican. Protestant. Mason (K.T., 32°). Club: Kiwanis of Trenton. Home: 440 Hamilton Av., Trenton, N.J.

BARRY, Herbert, lawyer; b. Wilmington, N.C., Feb. 25, 1867; s. Maj. (U.S.A.) Robert Peabody and Julia Kean (Neilson) B.; prep. edn. various private schools; student U. of Va., 1884-88, B.L., 1888; m. Ethel M. Dawson, Feb. 16, 1898; children—Herbert, Eleanor, Stuyvesant. Admitted to Va. bar, 1888, N.Y. bar, 1890; mem. firm Davies, Auerbach, Cornell & Barry, 1897-1913; sr. partner, Barry, Wainwright, Thacher & Symmers since 1913. Mem. Troop A, later Squadron A, N.G.N.Y., 1891-1908; capt., 1900-08, and mem. Gov. Hughes' staff; maj. Squadron A Cav., N.Y.G., Dec. 1917; commd. maj. inf. U.S.A., May 1918; served overseas, May 1918-June 1919; hon. discharged, July 1919; subsequently commd. lt. col. 302d Regiment Cav., O.R.C., 1923, retired, 1931, with rank of col. Mem. Am. Bar Assn., Assn. Bar City of New York, New York County Bar Assn., N.Y. State Bar Assn., S.R., Soc. Colonial Wars, etc.; vice gov. The Virginians of N.Y. City; pres. Ex-members Assn. of Squadron A. Republican. Episcopalian. Clubs: University, Downtown, Essex County Country, Rock Spring. Pres. Bd. of Edn. of West Orange. Contbr. to Va. Law Review, papers on many subjects pub. in each year, 1923-37, later compiled under title Viewed with Detachment. Home: Llewellyn Park, West Orange, N.J. Office: 72 Wall St., New York, N.Y.*

BARSEL, Solomon Mordecai, rabbi; b. Tiberias, Palestine, Jan. 1, 1899; s. Pinchas and Goldie (Feinstein) B.; came to U.S., 1915, naturalized, 1922; student Beth Chasan Soffer, Safed, Palestine, 1910-15, Eron Prep. Sch., N.Y. City, 1917-19, Dropsie Coll., Phila., Pa., since 1934; Ph.G., New Jersey Coll. of Pharmacy, Newark, N.J., 1922; B.S., William & Mary Coll., Williamsburg, Va., 1932; m. Rebecca Shapiro, Jan. 11, 1914; children—Benny, Thelma. Began as rabbi Adath Jeshurun Synagogue, Newport News, Va., 1928-31, Gomley Chesed Synagogue, Portsmouth, Va., 1931-34, Bnai Jeshurun Synagogue, Phila., since 1934; pres. Strawberry Mansion Zionist Dist.; mem. exec group Phila. Zionist Orgn. Mem. Rabbinic Assembly, Bd. of Jewish Ministers, Interracial Bd. of Ministers. Won Alumni award for scholarship, 1931, 1932, The Dean's Award, Rutgers U., Newark, N.J., Branch 1932. Hebrew religion. Mason, K.P. Edited The Leader, Newport News, Va., 1928-32; contbr. to Jewish Times, Phila. Home: 2427 N. 33d St. Office: 33d St. above Diamond, Philadelphia, Pa.

BARTH, Carl G(eorge Lange), mechanical engr.; b. Christiania, Norway, Feb. 28, 1860; s. of Jacob Böckman and Adelaide Magdalene (Lange) B.; grad. High Sch., Lillehammer, Norway, 1875; grad. Tech. Sch., Horten, 1876; m. Hendrikke Jacobine Fredericksen, Mar. 4, 1882 (died Feb. 25, 1916); children—J. Christian, Carl G., I. Adelaide (dec.), Elizabeth F.; m. 2d Sophia E. Roever, Jan. 25, 1919. In machine shops, Norwegian Navy Yards; instr. in mathematics and mechanical drawing, Tech. Sch., Horten, to 1880; came to America, 1881; mech. draftsman with Wm. Sellers & Co., Phila., 1881-90, and instr. in mech. drawing, evening schs. of Franklin Inst., 1882-88; engr. and chief draftsman with Arthur Falkenau, Phila., 1890-1901; designer, Wm. Sellers & Co., 1891-95; engr. and chief draftsman, Rankin & Fritch Foundry & Machine Co., St. Louis, 1895-97; designer St. Louis Water Dept., Feb.-June, 1897; with Internat. Corr. Schs., Scranton, Pa., 1897/98; instr. in manual work and mathematics, Ethical Culture Schs., New York, 1898-99; machine shop engr. Bethlehem Steel Co., 1899-1901; there met Frederick W. Taylor, the father of scientific management, and was his prin. associate until Taylor's death in 1915; introducing Taylor system of scientific management, in machine shops, 1901-23; rep. of Tinius Olsen Testing Machine Co. in Japan, 1923-24; now retired. Expert in shop management, Ordnance Dept., U.S. Army, 1909-18, and again during World War; lecturer on scientific management Harvard U., 1911-16, and 1919-23, U. of Chicago, 1914-16. Mem. Am. Soc. M. E. (life), A.A.A.S. (life), Franklin Inst., Am. Economic Assn., Am. Acad. Polit. and Social Science, Indian Rights Assn. (life); hon. mem. Taylor Soc. Club: Engineers of Phila. (life). Address: 900 N. 63d St., Philadelphia, Pa.

BARTHOLD, William Gregory, lawyer; b. Phila., Pa., Nov. 12, 1897; s. Allen H. and Emma Agnes (Gregory) B.; ed. Bethlehem High Sch. (valedictorian), 1914; A.B., Lehigh U., 1918; LL.B., Harvard U. Law Sch., 1922; m. Frances Werkheiser, Nov. 4, 1925; children—Audre, Nancy. Admitted to Pa. bar, 1923, and since in gen. practice of law at Bethlehem; admitted to practice before Supreme and Superior Cts. and U.S. Dist. Ct.; asst. dist. atty., 1928-32; solicitor Borough of Freemansburg, 1924-38, for Sheriff Northampton Co., 1934-35, for Bethlehem Sch. Dist., 1934-38; judge Court of Common Pleas, Northampton Co. since Dec. 1938. Served as mem. Pa. Senate, 1937-38. Mem. Am., Pa., and Northampton Co. (pres.) bar assns., Phi Beta Kappa, Alpha Chi Rho. Democrat. Reformed Ch. Mason (32°), I.O.O.F. K.P., Elk. Clubs: Bethlehem; Saucon Valley Country (Friedensville). Home: 1808 Sycamore St. Office: 208 Bethlehem Trust Bldg., Bethlehem, Pa.

BARTHOLOMEW, Tracy, research engr.; b. Austin, Tex., Nov. 14, 1884; s. George Wells and Hettie Julia (Cole) B.; student Ohio State U., 1902-03; E.M., Colo. Sch. of Mines, 1906; m. Sarah Jane Anderson, Oct. 6, 1921; children—George Anderson, Jane Anderson. Construction engr. Federal Lead Co., Flat River, Mo., 1906-07; designing and test engr. Nev. Consol. Copper Co., McGill, Nev., 1907-09; gen. mgr. Alkali-Proof Cement Div. of Colo. Portland (now Ideal) Cement Co., Denver, Colo., 1909-11; mgr. Rico Tropical Fruit Co., Garrochales, P.R., 1911-21, pres. since 1921; sr. fellow Mellon Inst. of Industrial Research, Pittsburgh, Pa. since 1921; mgr. of research Duquesne Slag Products Co., Pittsburgh, since 1929. Served as capt. 374th Inf., U.S.A. 1918-19. Mem. Am. Inst. Mining and Metall. Engrs., Am. Soc. Civil Engrs., Am. Chem. Soc., Am. Ceramic Soc., Am. Soc. Municipal Engrs., Am. Soc. Testing Materials, Am. Concrete Inst., Engrs. Soc. of Western Pa., Beta Theta Pi, Phi Lambda Upsilon. Republican. Presbyterian. Mason (K.T., Shriner). Clubs: Faculty (U. of Pittsburgh); Churchill Valley Golf (Pittsburgh). Home: 1545 Beechwood Boul. Office: Diamond Bank Bldg., Pittsburgh, Pa.

BARTLE, Harvey, railway surgeon; b. Philadelphia, Pa., Oct. 5, 1874; s. George W. and Elizabeth (Rice) B.; grad. high sch., Phila., Pa., 1892; M.D., U. of Pa., 1902; m. Flora H. Dixon, June 15, 1907; 1 son, Harvey, M.D. Practiced in Phila. since 1902; chief med. examiner Pa. R.R.; president Association Pa. R.R. Surgeons. Trustee Bapt. Theol. Sem., Phila.; pres. Bapt. Union of Phila. Fellow A.M.A. (mem. council on industrial health); mem. Med. Soc. of State of Pa. and Phila. County Med. Soc., Assn. Am. Railroads (mem. med. and surg. sect.), New York and New England Ry. Surgeons Assn., Am. Industrial Physicians and Surgeons Assn., Am. Assn. Ry. Surgeons (pres.), Sigma Xi. Republican. Baptist. Mason. Club: Union League. Contbr. articles on industrial medicine. Home: 424 W.

Hortter St., Germantown. Office: 15 N. 32d St., Philadelphia, Pa.

BARTLE, Henry J(ohn), physician; b. Phila., Pa., Apr. 2, 1882; s. Henry J. and Mary (Adams) B.; B.S., Central High Sch., Phila., 1901; M.D., U. of Pa. Med. Sch., 1905; m. Doris Mears Ogram, April 16, 1913; children—Bettina Mears, Henry J. III. Interne Memorial Hosp., Roxborough, Pa., 1905-06; engaged in gen. practice of medicine at Phila., Pa., 1906, specializing in internal medicine in 1920; senior clinical asst. Jefferson Hosp., gastro-enterological dept. since 1916. Mem. Am. Gastroenterol. Assn., Coll. of Phys. of Phila., Phila. Co. Medical Assn., Alpha Omega Alpha, Sigma Xi. Republican. Episcopalian. Contbr. numerous med. articles treating mostly with gastro-intestinal conditions. Home: 141 Linwood Av., Ardmore. Office: 1930 Chestnut St., Philadelphia, Pa.

BARTLETT, Alden Eugene, clergyman; b. Boston, Mass., Dec. 13, 1872; s. Alden Eustis and Sarah Elizabeth (Jacquith) B.; B.D., Tufts Div. Sch., 1897; spl. courses, Emerson Sch. of Oratory and Harvard; (S. T. D. Lombard Coll., 1912); m. Josie S. Newman, Oct. 5, 1899. Ordained ministry, 1897; pastor Manchester, New Hampshire, 1899-1905, Stamford, Conn., 1905-07, Chicago, 1907-14, All Souls Ch., Brooklyn, N.Y., 1914-22, First Congl. Ch., Pontiac Mich., 1922-27; now known as "the joy maker," visiting chs. all over Am. on speaking tour. Republican. Mason (K.T.). Club: Tufts College. Author: The Joy Maker, 1918; Harbor Jim, 1923; Least Known America, 1925; Out-of-the-Way Places of Europe, 1928. Frequent lecturer at chautauquas and before clubs, extensive traveler in out-of-the-ordinary places. Home: Bartlett Manor, West Chester, Pa.

BARTLETT, George Griffiths, clergyman; b. Sharon Springs, N.Y., June 3, 1872; s. Edward T. and Emily S. (Pile) B.; A.B., Harvard, 1895; grad. Div. Sch. P.E. Ch., Phila., 1898; m. Cecilia Helen Neall, May 9, 1905; children—Emily Neall, Edward Totterson, George Neall. Deacon, 1898, priest, 1900, P.E. Ch.; asst., Grace Ch., New York, 1898-1902; rector Memorial Ch. of St. Paul, Overbrook, Phila., 1902-08; dean Cathedral of Our Merciful Savior, Faribault, Minn., 1908-11; rector Ch. of Our Savior, Jenkintown, Pa., 1911-15; dean and prof. Div. Sch. P.E. Ch., Philadelphia, 1915-37, retired. Home: 7520 Crittenden St., Mt. Airy, Philadelphia, Pa.

BARTLETT, J. Kemp; mem. law firm Bartlett, Poe & Claggett; dir. many companies. Home: 2100 Mount Royal Terrace. Office: Calvert & Redwood Sts., Baltimore, Md.

BARTLETT, John Walden, prof. dairy husbandry; b. Granville, N.Y., Aug. 1, 1891; s. David R. and Ida (Norton) B.; B.Sc., U. of Vt., 1914; A.M., Columbia U., 1928; Ph.D., N.Y. Univ., 1933; m. Ruth Stearns, Oct. 10, 1915 (died 1925); children—John W., Jr., Martha E.; m. 2d, Ann H. Pease, June 21, 1927. Engaged as dairyman, Dairy Extension Service of Holstein Breed Assn., 1916-22; prof. dairy husbandry, Rutgers U. since 1922; also dairy husbandman, N.J. Agrl. Expt. Sta., New Brunswick, N.J., since 1922; responsible for establishment and conduct of research in largest Holstein Breeding Expt. in the world. Past pres. New Brunswick Rotary Club; past sec. Dist. 36 Rotary Internat. Mem. Sigma Nu, Phi Delta Kappa, Alpha Kappa Pi, Sigma Psi, Alpha Zeta. Republican. Mem. Dutch Reformed Ch. Club: Union. Home: 130 N. 6th Av., New Brunswick, N.J.

BARTLETT, North Emory, executive; b. Easton, Md., May 16, 1870; s. Robert and Anne North (Emory) B.; student private and pub. schs. of Md., 1876-89; m. Bertha Kennedy, Nov. 16, 1898; children—Bertha Emory (Mrs. Robert W. Perry), Anne North (Mrs. Anne N. B. Goldsborough), Carmita deSolms (Mrs. Seth C. Hetherungton). Began as salesman Pa. Salt Mfg. Co., Phila., Pa., 1894, and successively salesman, manufacturers' agent, special sales agent, sales mgr., 1894-1927, v.p. in charge sales since 1927. Clubs: Chemists (New York); Chesapeake Bay Yacht (Easton, Md.). Home: 2125 Pine St. Office: 1000 Widener Bldg., Phila., Pa.

BARTLETT, Robert W.; pres. Ventnor City Nat. Bank. Address: Ventnor, N.J.

BARTOL, George E., Jr.; pres. C. Howard Hunt Pen Co., Phila. Bourse; dir. Central-Penn Nat. Bank. Home: Old Gulph Road, Wynnewood, Pa. Office: 7th and State Sts., Camden, N. J.

BARTON, Carlyle, lawyer; b. Baltimore Co., Md., Sept. 12, 1885; s. Randolph and Agnes Priscilla (Kirkland) B.; student Boys Latin Sch., Baltimore, 1898-1903; A.B., Johns Hopkins, 1906; LL.B., U. of Md., 1908; m. Isabel Rieman Thom, Dec. 6, 1915; children—Isabel Thom, Carlyle, Anne Lowe Rieman. Was admitted to Md. bar, 1908, and since in practice at Baltimore; now mem. firm Niles, Barton, Morrow & Yost; dir. Md. Trust Co., Hopkins Place Savings Bank, Seaboard Commercial Corpn. Asst. to counsellor Dept. of State, Washington, 1917-18. Trustee Johns Hopkins U. Chancellor Diocese of Md., P.E. Ch. Mem. Am., Md. State and Baltimore City bar assns., Alpha Delta Phi. Democrat. Episcopalian. Clubs: Maryland, Merchants. Home: Dulaney Valley Road, Towson, Md. Office: Baltimore Life Bldg., Baltimore, Md.

BARTON, George, author; b. Phila., Jan. 22, 1866; s. George and Maria (Gormley) B.; pub. sch. edn.; m. Sophia McCauley, June 14, 1893. Began newspaper work with Phila. Inquirer, 1887; sec. to collector of customs, Phila., 1898-1913; editorial writer Phila. Evening Bulletin; now editorial writer Phila Inquirer. Was sec. of joint legislature com. (Pa.) apptd. to investigate the Soldiers' Orphans' schs. of Pa., 1896. Republican. Catholic. Author: Angels of the Battlefield, 1898; Mystery of Cleverly, 1907; Adventures of the World's Greatest Detectives, 1908; Lady of the Tower, 1909; Adventures of Bromley Barnes, 1909; Real Stories of the Secret Service, 1910; In Quest of the Golden Chest, 1911; Barry Wynn—A Story of the United States Congress, 1912; Great Cases of Famous Detectives, 1913; Bell Haven Nine, 1914; Bell Haven Five, 1914; Bell Haven Eight, 1915; Bell Haven Eleven, 1915; A Young Knight of Columbus, 1916; The World's Greatest Military Spies and Secret Service Agents, 1917; Mystery of the Red Flame, 1918; Strange Adventures of Bromley Barnes, 1919; Celebrated Spies and Strange Mysteries of the Great War, 1919; The Pembroke Mason Affair, 1920; Little Journeys Around Old Philadelphia, 1925; Famous Detective Mysteries, 1926; Great Triumphs of Crime Detection, 1937. Also about 200 short detective stories in mags. and newspapers. Home: 804 N. 63d St. Office: The Inquirer, Philadelphia, Pa.

BARTON, John H(enry), chmn. mfg.; b. Flemington, N.J., Oct. 26, 1889; s. Jacob G. and Anna W. (Henry) B.; ed. high sch., Flemington, N.J., Coleman Bus. Coll., Newark, N.J.; m. Anita N. Pfleger, Aug. 9, 1911. Began as lab. worker, Yocum-Eachus Lab., Newark, N.J., 1912-18; salesman Atlas Refinery, 1913-19; asso. with National Oil Products Co., chem. mfrs., Harrison, N.J., since 1919, now pres. and dir. since 1923; vice-pres. and dir. Metasap Chemical Co., Inc.; dir. Eastern Semolina Mills, Inc., New York, West Hudson County Trust Co.; propr. and operator Barton Farms, Flemington, N.J. Republican. Baptist. Mason (K.T., Shriner). Clubs: Athletic (Newark); Canoe Brook Country (Summit); Copper Hill Country (Flemington); Maplewood Country (Maplewood, N.J.). Home: 381 Grove Rd., South Orange, N.J. Office: 1st and Essex Sts., Harrison, N.J.

BARTON, Olive Roberts (Mrs. James Lowrie Barton), writer; b. Allegheny, Pa., July 26, 1880; d. Thomas Beveridge and Cornelia (Gilleland) Roberts; sister of Mary Roberts Rinehart; grad. high sch., Allegheny, 1897, grad. study, 1898; m. Lt. Col. James Lowrie Barton, June 19, 1902; children—Eleanor Aikins (dec.), Virginia-Anne, Mary Roberts (Mrs. R. L. Brummage, Jr.). Teacher, pub. schs., Allegheny, 1898-1902, Butler, Pa., 1905-06, 1917-18; free lance writer, 1905-19; feature writer Newspaper Enterprise Assn. (Scripps Howard Syndicate), 1919-25; daily serial for children, "Adventures of the Twins"; daily editorials, features, 1925-28; daily column on child training and family management since 1928. Mem. National League of Am. Penwomen. Republican. Episcopalian. Clubs: Twentieth Century, Authors' (Pittsburgh). Author: Cloud Boat Stories, 1916; Wonderful Land of Up, 1918; Helter Skelter Land, Land of Near By, Scrub Up Land and Topsy Turvy Land (series), 1920; Story Riddles in Rime and Prose, 1928; Bramble Bush Riddles, 1930. Editorial writer. Home: Gettysburg, Pa. Office: NEA—461 8th Av., New York, N.Y.

BARTON, Randolph, Jr., lawyer; b. Baltimore, Md., Dec. 12, 1871; s. Randolph and Agnes P. (Kirkland) B.; student Mr. Carey's Sch., Baltimore; A.B., Johns Hopkins U., 1891; LL.B., U. of Md. Law Sch., Baltimore, 1893; m. Eleanor A. Morison, June 10, 1902. Mem. law firm Barton, Wilmer, Bramble, Addison and Semans, Baltimore. Democrat. Episcopalian. Home: "Airslie," Pikesville, Baltimore Co., Md. Office: 806 Mercantile Trust Bldg., Baltimore, Md.

BARTON, Samuel Goodwin, univ. prof.; b. Ivyland, Pa., Jan. 1, 1882; s. Edmund and Emma Ristine (Goodwin) B.; A.B., Temple U., 1903; Ph.D., U. of Pa., 1906; unmarried. Harrison research fellow in astronomy, U. of Pa., 1906-07; prof. math., Clarkson Coll. of Tech., Potsdam, N.Y., 1907-11; asst. prof. math. and astronomy, Swarthmore Coll., Swarthmore, Pa., 1911-13; instr. astronomy, U. of Pa., 1913-14, asst. prof., 1914-31, asso. prof. since 1931. Dir of U. S. Shipping Bd. Navigation Sch., 1917-19. Mem. Am. Astron. Soc., A.A.A.S., Am. Assn. Univ. Profs., Sigma Xi. Republican. Presbyterian. Joint author: A Guide to the Constellations, 1928; monthly newspaper articles on current astron. events since 1914, papers in science jours. and in publications of the Flower Astronomical Observatory. Home: 33 N. 61st St. Office: 3438 Walnut St., Philadelphia, Pa.

BARTON, Samuel Van Duzen, banking; b. Irvington, Ill., Sept. 27, 1873; s. Leicester Charles and Francelia (Ford) B.; ed. schs. Irvington and Centralia, Ill.; A.B., Valparaiso (Ind.) Normal, 1899; diploma econs. and law, Am. Inst. of Banking, 1914; m. Jennie Grace Farrand, June 14, 1905; children—Samuel Van Duzen, Jr. (dec.), Ruth Jeannette. Began as teacher, Irvington, Ill., 1895; prin. high sch., Benton, Ind., 1899-1900; ins. agt. and insp. Metropolitan Bldg. and Loan Assn., 1902; with Pittsburgh Lamp and Brass Co., 1902-07; teller First Nat. Bank, Crafton, Pa., 1907-16; auditor R. W. Evans & Co., Pittsburgh, 1916-23; cashier First Nat. Bank, Castle Shannon, since 1923; dir. Herzog Products Corpn. Served as speaker in World War. Pres. Castle Shannon Bd. of Trade, 1933-37. Active in Boy Scout and Ch. work. Mem. Lamda Chi Alpha. Republican. Methodist. Mason (K.T.) Clubs: Bankers (Pittsburgh); Social 36 of Crafton (charter mem. 1906). Home: 3730 Poplar Av. Office: First National Bank, Castle Shannon, Pa.

BARTON, Vola Price, coll. prof.; b. Baltimore, Md., Dec. 19, 1893; d. James Sheridan and Mary Irene (Eichelberger) B.; A.B., Goucher Coll., Baltimore, 1915; A.M., Mount Holyoke Coll., South Hadley, Mass., 1917; Ph.D., Johns Hopkins U., 1923; unmarried. Asst. in physics, Mt. Holyoke Coll., 1915-17; asst. in physics, Goucher Coll., 1917-19, instr., 1919-23, asst. prof., 1923-26, asso. prof., 1926-31, prof. since 1931, chmn. of dept. since 1932; lab. asst. Bur. of Standards, June-Sept. 1918, asst. physicist, June-Aug. 1920, research asso., July-Sept. 1924, and June-Aug. 1925. Mem. A.A.A.S., Am. Physical Soc., Am. Optical Soc., Am. Assn. Univ. Profs., Md. Acad. Sciences, Am. Assn. Physics Teachers, Phi Beta Kappa. Methodist. Home: 2500 Ken Oak Road, Baltimore, Md.

BARTON, Warren Hamilton, banker; b. New York, N.Y., June 14, 1863; s. Hamilton Whaley and Julia A. (Collins) B.; student Brooklyn (N.Y.) High Sch., 1878-81. Became importer and jobber, 1882; engaged in rose growing,

1900-21; in banking since 1918; now pres. First Nat. Bank, Madison, N.J.; dir. and chmn. exec. com. Madison Trust Co. Mem. and pres. Madison Bd. of Health 7 years; trustee and pres. Madison Pub. Library. Methodist. Club: Rotary of Madison. Home: 37 Fairview Av. Office: First Nat. Bank Bldg., Madison, N.J.

BARTOW, Harry Edwards, educator; b. Delaware Co., Pa., Sept. 11, 1877; s. Isaac Farra and Elizabeth (Edwards) B.; student Chester (Pa.) High Sch., 1891-95, Peirce Sch., Phila., 1895-98; m. Hannah Carlon, Aug. 25, 1901; 1 son, James Carlon. Accountant, office manager, 1899-1917; teacher, Peirce School, Phila., 1917-18, sec., 1918-34; dean Strayer's Business Sch., Phila., Pa., since 1935. Methodist. Odd Fellow. Author: Our Boy, 1913; The Superintendent's Guide, pub. annually since 1917; For the Superintendent, 1914-39. Co-author: Sunday-School Management, 1916. Home: 211 Pusey Av., Collingdale, Pa. Office: 807 Chestnut St., Philadelphia, Pa.

BASCOM, Florence, geologist; b. Williamstown, Mass.; d. John and Emma (Curtiss) B.; A.B., B.L., U. of Wis., 1882, B.S., 1884, A.M., 1887; Ph.D., Johns Hopkins, 1893. Instr. geology and petrography, Ohio State U., 1893-95; lecturer and asso. prof., 1895-1906, prof. geology, 1906-1928, prof. emeritus since 1928 Bryn Mawr Coll. Geol. asst., 1896-1901, asst. geologist, 1901-09, geologist, 1909-36, U.S. Geol. Survey. Asso. editor Am. Geologist, 1896-1905. Fellow Geol. Soc. America (councilor 1924-26; 2d v.p. 1930), A.A.A.S.; mem. Phila. Acad. Natural Sciences, Geog. Soc. Phila., Washington Acad. Sciences, Seismological Soc. America, Soc. of Women Geographers, Div. Geology and Geography of Nat. Research Council, Mineral. Soc. America, Inst. Mineralogy and Meteorology, England, Geol. Soc. Washington, Pick and Hammer Club, Am. Geog. Soc., Petrologist Club, Phi Beta Kappa, Sigma Xi. Joint author and author geologic folios; also bulls. and numerous papers in tech. jours. Home: (summer) North Adams, Mass., R.D. 2. Address: Bryn Mawr College, Bryn Mawr, Pa.

BASCOM, Harry Franklin, civil engring.; b. Whitehall, N.Y., July 29, 1873; s. Warren Franklin and Clara Barney (Buel) B.; C.E., Rensselaer Poly. Inst., 1896; m. Mary E. Broughton, Nov. 24, 1903; children—Warren Broughton, Franklin Buel, James Marshall. Employed as draftsman and engr. with various corpns., 1897-1901; mem. firm Lehr & Bascom, engrs., Allentown, Pa., 1901-08, mem. firm Bascom & Sieger since 1908; in gen. engring. and surveys, and engr. various boroughs in vicinity; has laid out for development a large portion of Allentown and adjacent area since 1901; constrn. engr. many large mfg. plants; pres. Sterling Improvement Co., Seroled Real Estate Co. Served as city engr. Allentown, Pa., 1903-06, 1918-24; engr. Allentown Housing Authority since 1938. Mem. Theta Xi. Republican. Episcopalian. Home: 1342 Walnut St. Office: Allentown Bank Bldg., Allentown, Pa.

BASHIOUM, H.; prof. chem. engring. and head of dept., U. of Pittsburgh Sch. of Engring. Address: U. of Pittsburgh, Pittsburgh, Pa.

BASKERVILL, William Malone, editor; b. Nashville, Tenn., Feb. 1, 1888; s. William Malone and Janie (McTyeire) B.; ed. Vanderbilt U. and U. of the South; m. Evelyn Frances Lynch, April 25, 1916; children—Dorothy Frances, Evelyn Katherine, Janie Cecelia. Began as reporter Nashville Tennessean, 1907, later with Commercial Appeal, Montgomery Advertiser and New York Journal; telegraph editor Atlanta Journla, 1910-11; news editor Asso. Press, southern div., 1911-14; asst. gen. news mgr. Internat. News Service, N.Y. City, 1919-20; asst. mng. editor New York Journal, 1921-22; mng. editor Atlanta Georgian-American, 1922-26, Baltimore News and Sunday American since 1926. Mem. Phi Beta Theta. Clubs: Rodgers Forge Country, Baltimore Country. Home: 3907 N. Charles St. Address: Baltimore News and American, Baltimore, Md.

BASKETT, George Terrell, psychiatrist; b. Gainesville, Tex., Jan. 9, 1882; s. George W. (M.D.) and Garra (McLean) B.; A.B., U. of Tex., 1904; M.D., U. of Mich. Med. Sch., 1908; m. Olive Thorne, M.D., Aug. 10, 1910. Asst. phys., St. Peter, Minn., State Hosp. for Mental Diseases, 1908-10, asst. supt., 1912-25; supt. Willmar (Minn.) State Hosp. for Mental Diseases, 1925-27; supt. Retreat Mental Hosp., Retreat, Pa., since 1927; psychiatric consultant to Nanticoke (Pa.) State Hosp. and to Pittston (Pa.) Gen Hosp. Diplomate Am. Bd. Psychiatry and Neurology. Mem. Am., Pa. State, Luzerne Co., and Lehigh Valley med. assns., Am. Psychiatric Assn., State Hosp. Assn. of Pa., State Assn. of Supts. of Pa. Mental Hosps., Alpha Tau Omega, Phi Alpha Sigma. Republican. Presbyn. Mason (K.T., Shriner). Clubs: Kiwanis (Nanticoke); Shawnee (Plymouth). Home: Retreat Mental Hospital, Retreat, Pa.

BASKETT, Olive Thorne, physician; b. Cincinnati, O., July 18, 1882; d. Alonzo Marion and Ida Belle (Ferree) Thorne; M.D., Miami Med. Coll., Cincinnati, O., 1906; m. Dr. George Terrell Baskett, Aug. 9, 1910. Interne Women's Hosp., Detroit, Mich., 1906-07; house physician Jackson (Mich.) City Hosp., 1907; asst. physician St. Peter (Minn.) State Hosp., 1908-10, 1912-25; senior physician Retreat (Pa.) Mental Hosp. since 1927; certified by Am. Bd. Psychiatry. Mem. A.M.A., Pa. State Med. Soc., Luzerne County Med. Soc. Republican. Presbyn. Address: Retreat Mental Hospital, Retreat, Pa.

BASS, Lawrence Wade, chemist; b. Streator, Ill., June 18, 1898; s. John Hiram and Sara (Leek) B.; Ph.B., Yale, 1919, Ph. D., 1922; Loomis Fellowship, 1922, and Nat. Research Fellowship, 1923; studied Tulane U., U. of Lille (France), U. of Paris, and Pasteur Inst., 1923-25; Am. Field Service fellow, 1923-25; fellow International Edn. Bd., 1925; m. Edna Maria Becker, Nov. 23, 1935. Asst. Rockefeller Inst. for Med. Research, 1925-27, asso., 1927-29; exec. asst. Mellon Inst. Industrial Research, Pittsburgh, 1929-31; asst. dir. research Borden Co., N.Y. City, 1931, dir. research, 1932-36; asst. dir. Mellon Inst., 1937—. Mem. A.A.A.S., Am. Chem. Soc., Am. Dairy Science Assn., Am. Econ. Assn., Am. Inst. Chem. Engrs., Am. Inst. Chem., Am. Pub. Health Assn., Am. Statis. Assn., Soc. Chem. Industry, Sigma Nu, Sigma Xi, Alpha Chi Sigma, Phi Lambda Upsilon. Clubs: University, Faculty (Pittsburgh); Chemists (New York). Author: Nucleic Acids (with P. A. Levene), 1931; Nucleinsäuren, Nucleotide, Nucleoside in "Bio-chemisches Handlexikon" (with same), 1933. Translator: Chemistry of Inorganic Complex Compounds, 1923. Contbr. on chem. researches and chem. economics. Mem. cons. editorial bd., Chemical Industries. Home: 4601 Bayard St. Address: Mellon Inst., Pittsburgh, Pa.

BASSETT, Carroll Phillips, consulting engr.; b. Brooklyn, N.Y., Feb. 27, 1863; s. Allen Lee and Caroline (Phillips) B.; C.E., Lafayette Coll., 1883, E.M., 1884, Ph.D., 1888; m. Margaret Condit Kinney, Apr. 14, 1904; children—Carroll Kinney, Estelle Condit, Wm. B. K. Designed and erected water works, electric light, drainage, sewerage disposal plants, in N.Y., N.J., Pa., Conn., W.Va. and S.C., 1886-1910; largely interested in water and electric ultility cos., 1900-22; consulting engineer; pres. Summit Development Co., Commonwealth Land Co., Summit Home Land Co.; dir. State Title & Mortgage Guaranty Co., First Nat. Bank and Trust Co., First Securities Co. (Summit), Firemen's Insurance Co. (Newark). Trustee N.J. Historical Society, Lafayette Coll., Y.M.C.A. (Summit); mem. exec. com. Sentinels of the Republic. Fellow Am. Geog. Soc.; mem. Am. Soc. C.E., Am. Water Works Assn., N.E. Water Works Assn., N.J., Public Utilities Assn., Phi Beta Kappa, Tau Beta Pi, Phi Delta Theta (ex-pres.), N.J. Soc. Colonial Wars, N.J. Hist. Soc., N.J. Washington Assn. Republican. Presbyn. Mason. Clubs: University (New York); Baltusrol Golf, Canoe Brook Country. Home: "Beacon Hill," Summit, N.J.

BASSETT, Lavern Clarke, physician; b. Richburg, N.Y., Sept. 25, 1879; s. Ezra Lee and Lennie Adel (Hall) B.; grad. Richburg High Sch., 1899; B.S., Alfred U., 1904; M.D., Hahnemann Med. Coll., Chicago, 1910; m. Jennie Letta Bender, June 15, 1911; 1 dau., Faith Edith (Mrs. Thomas Phillip Brechtlein). Physician, Dunellen, N.J., since 1920; mem. obstetrical staff Muhlenburg Hosp., Plainfield, N.J.; mem. auxiliary staff St. Peter's Hosp., New Brunswick, N.J. Served as 1st lt. Med Corps, U.S. Army, with A.E.F., 1918-19. Trustee Am. Sabbath Tract Soc. Mem. Am. Legion, Dunellen Chamber of Commerce, Alfred U. Alumni. Republican. Mem. Seventh Day Baptist Ch. (trustee Piscataway Ch.). Mem. Modern Woodmen of America, Patriotic Order Sons of America. Club: Rotary of Dunellen. Home: 320 New Market Rd., Dunellen, N.J.

BATAILLE, Edward Francis, editor; b. Newark, N.J., May 24, 1904; s. Louis Edward and Carolyn Agatha (Hebring) B.; ed. pub. schs., Newark; m. Mildred Catherine Ballantine, Jan. 29, 1929. With Newark Sunday Call since 1918, became reporter, 1920, editorial writer, 1931, asso. editor, 1933, editor, 1937; dir. Newark Call Printing & Pub. Co. since 1939; also editor Newark Jewish Chronicle, 1921-26, and chmn. publ. bd. N.J. Bldg. and Loan Guide and Bull., 1932-36. Mem. Am. Soc. Newspaper Editors, N.J. Press Assn., N.J. Hist. Soc., N.J. Legislative Correspondents Club. Roman Catholic. Clubs: Essex, Down Town (Newark); Nat. Press (Washington). Author: Grace Church in Newark, 1937. Home: 39 Courter Av., Maplewood, N.J. Office: 91 Halsey St., Newark, N.J.

BATCHELLER, Hiland Garfield, steel mfr.; b. New York, N.Y., Dec. 5, 1885; s. Hiland Garfield and Josephine Mary (Clements) B.; prep. edn. Glens Falls Acad., 1900-03; Ph.B., Wesleyan U., 1907; m. Jessie Jackson, Apr. 5, 1913; children—Mary Arthur (Mrs. J. Q. A. Doolittle), Betty, Hiland, Jessie. Salesman U.S. Steel Corpn., 1909-16; asst. to pres. Ludlum Steel Co., Pittsburgh, 1916-21, v.p., 1921-31, pres., 1931-38; pres. Allegheny-Ludlum Steel Corpn. since 1938; dir. N.Y. Telephone Co., State Bank of Albany, Wallingford Steel Co., Atlas Steel Co., Ltd., Forging & Casting Corpn. Trustee Rensselaer Poly, Inst. Fellow Am. Geog. Soc.; mem. Am. Iron and Steel Inst. Republican. Episcopalian. Clubs: Duquesne, Fox Chapel Golf (Pittsburgh); Fort Orange, Schuyler Meadows (Albany); Laurentian (Quebec); Bankers (New York). Home: Menand Rd., Albany, N.Y. Office: Oliver Bldg., Pittsburgh, Pa.

BATDORF, Grant David, bishop; b. at Lickdale, Pa., Apr. 30, 1874; s. William and Amelia (Sattazahn) B.; B.S., Pa. State Normal Sch., Millersville, Pa., 1893; grad. Bonebrake Theol. Sem., Dayton, O., 1898; spl. student Lehigh U. and U. of Chicago; Ph.B., Ill. Wesleyan U., 1902, Ph.D., 1910; D.D., Otterbein Coll., 1921; LL.D., Lebanon Valley College, 1936; m. Lydia A. Zellers, Apr. 25, 1894; children—Agnes Luella, Hillis Gordon. Ordained ministry U.B. Ch., 1898; pastor successively at Allentown, Harrisburg, Reading and Lancaster, Pa., until 1920, First Ch., Dayton, O.—the outstanding ch. in the denomination—, 1920-29; elected bishop, May 14, 1929, and assigned to the East Dist. Has received nearly 2,000 members into ch. fellowship and raised over $1,000,000 for ch., ednl. and benevolent enterprises. Spl. lecturer in dept. of preaching, Bonebrake Theol. Sem. Trustee Bonebrake Theol. Sem. (chmn. exec. com.; business mgr., Jan.-July 1929); pres. Ministerial Pension Fund, Pa.. State Council of Chs. Pa. Anti-Saloon League, Quincy Orphanage and Home; chmn. bd. Christian Edn. of U.B. Ch.; mem. Commn. on Ch. Union; mem. exec. com. Federal Council of Chs., also of com. on worship; trustee Lebanon Valley Coll. Mem. Pa. German Soc., Am. Geog. Soc., Dayton Chamber Commerce. Republican. Club: Dayton City. Author: The Pastor; (brochure) The Pivotal Man, 1915; Jesus' Money Gospel (brochure), 1920; Progressive Teacher Training Course (with others), 1923. Made world tour for study and lecture on foreign missions, 1936-37. Home: 1509 State St., Harrisburg, Pa.

BATDORF, Harvey Solomon, coll. adminstrator; b. Wiconisco, Pa., May 10, 1900; s. Solomon Peter and Alice Maude (Williams) B.; stud. Wiconisco (Pa.) High Sch., 1914-19; B.S., Lafayette Coll., Easton, Pa., 1928; unmarried. Clerk Miners Deposit Bank and Trust Co., Lykens, Pa., 1922-24, 1928-32; business mgr. Centennial Celebration, Lafayette Coll., Easton, Pa., 1932, asst. registrar since 1933, asst. to pres. since 1936, dir. admissions since 1938. Mem. Middle States Assn. Deans and Advisers of Men, Middle States Assn. Collegiate Registrars (v.p., 1937), Sigma Nu. Republican. Presbyterian. Mason. Clubs: Faculty (Easton, Pa.); Lafayette (New York); Hillcrest (Phillipsburg, N.J.) Address: Lafayette Coll., Easton, Pa.

BATEMAN, John, sculptor; b. Cedarville, N.J., Feb. 14, 1877; s. Joseph and Harriet (Hulings) B.; student Sch. of Industrial Art (Phila.); Pa. Acad. Fine Arts (summer scholarship abroad, 1905, 2-yr. scholarship abroad, 1906, 07); m. Caroline Ware, June 27, 1900; 1 son, John. Exhibited in Salon, Paris, and principal art centers in U.S.; latest work: Bronze Soldiers' Memorial Fountain, Doylestown, Pa.; Bronze Seal of Atlantic City; large group "Machinery" and three hist. panels, Pa. Bldg. and thirteen bronze tablets for the thirteen original states, Forum of the Founders, Sesquicentennial, Phila., 1926; seated figure Abraham Lincoln, Gillespie Schools, Phila., Pa., 1934; bust of Walt Whitman, Camden, N.J.; Peter Pan fountain Haddonfield, N.J.; 3 panels for Woodrow Wilson High Sch., Camden, N.J. (Joan of Arc, Merchant of Venice, Dante's Inferno). Hon. mention, San Francisco Expn., 1915. Mem. Nat. Sculpture Soc., Fellowship Pa. Acad. Fine Arts. Mason. Home: Haddonfield, N.J. Studio: 3d and Grant Sts., Camden, N.J.

BATEMAN, William, manufacturer; b. Ansieres, France, Mar. 16, 1863; s. Soloman and Sarah (Barker) B.; came to U.S., 1889, naturalized, 1894; married (wife now deceased); children—Doris, Florence (Mrs. George Rittenhouse Dugan). Pres. Dorence Worsted Co., Inc. (mfrs. worsted cloth); dir. Second Nat. Bank of Phila., at Frankford. Mem. Soc. Sons of St. George. Mason. Home: 4618 Adams Av. Office: 1615 Foulkrod St., Philadelphia, Pa.

BATES, Daniel Moore, industrial management; b. Wilmington, Del., Apr. 18, 1876; s. George Handy and Elisabeth Ballister (Russell) B.; B.S. in Chem. Engring., Mass. Inst. Tech., 1896; m. Bertha Corson Day, May 17, 1902; children—Bertha (Mrs. James Marshall Cole), Charles Theodore Russell, Frances Corson (Mrs. Frank Schoonmaker). Apprentice cotton dept. Pacif Mills, Lawrence, Mass., 1896-97; with Joseph Bancroft & Sons Co., Wilmington, Del., 1897-1912; agt. and gen. mgr. Lewiston Bleachery & Dye Works, Lewiston, Me., 1912-20; vice-pres. and mem. board dirs. Day & Zimmermann, Inc., in charge of industrial management, Philadelphia, Pa., 1920-28; pres. Bates, Inc., industrial management, Phila., Pa. since 1928; pres. and dir. Cold Spring Bleachery, Yardley, Pa. since 1923; dir. Day & Zimmermann, Inc., Phila., Pa., U.S. Finishing Co., N.Y. City and Norwich, Conn. Served as maj. ordnance dept., U.S.A., 1917-18; now col. F.A., U.S.A.R.F. Mem. Am. Soc. Mech. Engrs. Episcopalian. Clubs: Wilmington, Country (Wilmington); St. Anthony, Rittenhouse, Racquet, Midday (Philadelphia); St. Anthony, Merchants (New York); St. Anthony, Union (Boston). Home: R.F.D. 1, Wilmington, Del. Office: Packard Bldg., Philadelphia, Pa.

BATES, Edward Irving, publisher; b. Meadville, Pa., Nov. 27, 1904; s. Walter Irving and Marion (Sackett) B.; grad. Meadville High Sch., 1923; student Allegheny Coll., 1923-26, University Afloat (world cruise), 1926-27; m. Elinor Knight Van Scoten, Apr. 26, 1930; children—Walter Irving II, John Dodd, Edgar S. Reporter, 1927; business mgr. and treas. Tribune-Republican, 1929, sec-treas., Tribune Publishing Co., printers and publishers, 1930-34, pres. and gen. mgr., 1934-36, treas. and gen. mgr. since 1936; dir. Meadville Terminals, Tribune Pub. Co. Dir. Meadville Chapter Am. Red Cross, Meadville City Hosp. Mem. Phi Kappa Psi (sec., treas., and dir. Beta Corpn.). Republican. Baptist. Mason. Clubs: Rotary, Meadville Country, Round Table, Meadville Literary Union (sec.), Iroquois. Home: 386 Hamilton Av. Office: Federal St., Meadville, Pa.

BATES, Harry H(oward), mech. engr.; b. at Middleway (Kearneysville), W.Va., Aug. 10, 1889; s. William Grantham and Susan (Smith) B.; grad. Jefferson Acad., Middleway, W.Va., 1905; B.S., Va. Poly. Inst., 1913, M.E., 1914; m. Martha Darlington Helms, June 30, 1922; children—William Helms, Marian Helms. Observer of tests N.&W. Ry., Roanoke, Va., 1913-14, boiler house engr., power dir., 1914-16; mech. supt. E. I. DuPont de Nemours, 1916-17; mech. supt. Acme White Lead and Color Works, 1919-20; asst. chief engr. stoker dept., Westinghouse Electric & Mfg. Co., South Philadelphia, Pa., 1920-26, works engr. since 1926. Served as 1st lt. commanding 2d Railway Arty., Repair Shop, A.E.F., U.S. Army, 1917-19. Vice-pres. and dir. Taylor Hosp. pres. and dir. Chester Pike Bldg. Assn.; mem. bd. of edn., Dist. of Ridley Park, Pa. Mem. Am. Legion, A.A.A.S., Tau Beta Pi. Republican. Club: University. Contbr. articles to tech. jours. Inventions pertaining to X-ray, television, heaters, steam turbines, welding, bolting, pulverizers, gear cutting, etc. Home: 300 Glenloch Rd., Ridley Park, Pa. Office: Westinghouse Electric & Mfg. Co., South Philadelphia, Pa.

BATES, Joseph Sumner; founder and pres. Bates Chem. Co. Address: 224 Haverford Av., Swarthmore, Pa.

BATES, Madison C., prof. of English; b. Abingdon, Ill., Oct. 26, 1881; s. Madison Cauby and Minerva Emma (Latimer) B.; A.B., Williams Coll., Williamstown, Mass., 1904, A.M., 1905; A.M., Harvard, 1906; m. Helen Elizabeth Bullard, Dec. 31, 1907; children—Robert Latimer, Mary Elliott (Mrs. Edward Leach Clark). Instr. in English, U. of Ill., 1906-07; prof. of English and head of dept., S.D. State Coll., 1907-18; asst. prin., Burr and Burton Sem., Manchester, Vt., 1918-23, prin., 1923-27; dean of pre-legal dept., N.J. Law Sch., 1927-30; dean Dana Coll., Newark, N.J., 1930-36 (N.J. Law Sch. and Dana Coll. now merged with U. of Newark); prof. of English, U. of Newark since 1936. Mem. Modern Lang. Assn. America, Poetry Soc. America, Cowper Soc. (Eng.), Phi Beta Kappa. Home: 537 Summit Av., Maplewood, N.J. Office: Univ. of Newark, Newark, N.J.

BATES, Robert Sackett, editor; b. Meadville, ville, Pa., July 19, 1910; s. Walter Irving and Marion (Sackett) B.; grad. Meadville High Sch., 1927; A.B., Allegheny Coll., 1931; m. Margaret Herr, Nov. 25, 1933; children—Susan Herr, Robert Sackett. Reporter Tribune-Republican, Meadville, 1931-34, editor since 1934; pres., sec. and dir. Tribune Publishing Co., printers and pubs. Tribune-Republican, Evening Republican; dir. Merchants Nat. Bank & Trust Co., Meadville. Mem. Rep. State Com. Pres. Crawford Co. Hist. Soc.; sec. Meadville Library, Art and Hist. Assn.; dir. Meadville Y.M.C.A.; dir. Pa. Coll. Music; dir. Meadville Chamber of Commerce; chmn. Meadville Sesquicentennial Commn. Mem. Asso. Press, Pa. Newspaper Pubs. Assn., Phi Kappa Psi, Omicron Delta Kappa, Pi Delta Epsilon (journalism), Alpha Chi Sigma (chemistry). Republican. Baptist. Mason. Clubs: Lions, Country, Iroquois, Literary Union, Round Table. Home: N. Main St. Office: Federal St., Meadville, Pa.

BATES, William, surgeon; b. Phila., Pa., Apr. 11, 1889; s. Samuel Lee and Mary Sloan (Smith) B.; grad. Camden (N.J.) High and Manual Training Sch., 1908; B.S., U. of Pa., 1912, M.D., 1915; m. Marie Alice Bergstresser, June 7, 1919; children—William, Katherine Marie. Interne Univ. Hosp., 1915-17; practice of surgery since 1917; instr. in surgery, Grad. Sch. of Medicine, U. of Pa., 1921-28, asst. prof., 1928-34, prof. since 1934. Served as lt. Med. Corps, U.S. Army, 1917-19. Fellow Am. Coll. Surgeons; Fellow A.M.A.; mem. Pa. State Med. Soc., Phila. Co. Med. Soc., Internat. Coll. Surgeons, Phila. Coll. Physicians, Acad. of Surgery of Phila. Republican. Methodist. Mason. Clubs: University, Aesculapian (Phila.). Home: 2029 Pine St., Philadelphia, Pa.

BATES, William Nickerson, univ. prof.; b. Cambridge, Mass., Dec. 8, 1867; s. Charles and Anna Pamela (Nickerson) B.; grad. Cambridge Latin Sch., 1886; A.B. (with honors), Harvard, 1890, A.M., 1891, Ph.D. from same univ. 1893; Am. Sch. Classical Studies, Athens, Greece, 1897-98; m. Edith Newell Richardson, Dec. 28, 1901 (she died February 27, 1926); children—William Nickerson, Robert Hicks. Instructor Greek, Harvard, 1893-95; instr. Greek, asst. prof. and prof., U. of Pa., since 1895, head of dept. since 1910, title, professor Greek language and literature. Editor Transactions of Univ. Mus., 1904-07; editor Am. Jour. Archæology, 1908-20, editor-in-chief, 1920-24. Incorporator, 1902, recorder, 1903-09, Archæol. Inst. America; mem. mng. com. Am. Sch. Classical Studies in Athens since 1902, prof. Greek lang. and lit. and acting dir., 1905-06; del. Internat. Congress for History of Religions, Leyden, 1912. Mem. governing bd. Am. Foundation in France for Pre-historic Studies (now Am. Sch. Prehistoric Research), 1920-25. Fellow Am. Acad. Arts and Sciences; mem. Am. Philol. Assn., Oriental Club, Classical Club, Pa. Hist. Soc., Hellenic Soc. (London), Archæol. Club (Boston), Founders and Patriots America, Phi Beta Kappa Fraternity. Republican. Unitarian. Clubs: Harvard (Philadelphia); Harvard (Boston); Authors' (London). Editor Iphigenia in Tauris (of Euripides), 1904, Chinese edition, 1936. Reviser: Hertzberg's History of Greece, 1905. Wrote: (monographs) Date of Lycophron, 1895; Notes on the Theseum at Athens, 1901; The Old Athena Temple on the Acropolis, 1901; Etruscan Inscriptions, 1905; New Inscriptions from the Asclepieum at Athens, 1907; Five Red-Figured Cylices, 1908; Two Labors of Heracles on a Geometric Fibula, 1911; Euripides, a Student of Human Nature, 1930; etc.; also numerous articles in archæol. and philol. jours. Home: 220 St. Mark's Sq., Philadelphia, Pa.; (summer), Ogunquit, Me.

BATON, George Scott, consulting mining engr.; b. Phila., Pa., July 5, 1873; s. Henry C. and Amanda (Cox) B.; student Lehigh U., Bethlehem, Pa.; m. Mary H. Bickley, Nov. 19, 1903; children—Eleanor, Charles, Louise. Began as engr. Monongahela (Pa.) Coal & Coke Co., 1895; div. engr. Frick Coke Co., 1896-1900; operator Riverside Coal & Coke Co., 1900-02; then pres. and engr. Standard Coal & Coke Co., now owner George S. Baton & Co.,; also pres. Greensburg-Connelsville Coal & Coke Co., Ligonier Valley Supply Co.; chmn. of bd. Tube City Collieries, Inc. Trustee Christ Church. Mem. Pittsburgh Chamber of Commerce, Am. Soc. C.E., Am. Soc. of Mining and Metall. Engrs., Engring. Soc. of Western Pa. Clubs: University, Duquesne, Fox Chapel, Oakmont (Pittsburgh). Home: 326 S. Graham St. Office: 1100 Union Trust Bldg., Pittsburgh, Pa.

BATT, William Loren, pres. S.K.F. Industries; b. Salem, Ind.; s. George McClellan and Hettie (Markland) B.; M.E., Purdue U., 1907, Dr. Engring., 1933; m. Ruby Burroughs, Oct. 28, 1909; children—Martha L. (Mrs. Robert Abbott), Barbara B. (Mrs. Richard Bond), Jean (Mrs. Robert Y. Ritchie), William, Robert R. Assistant to Dr. W. F. M. Goss in research work, Purdue U., 1907; lab. head, Hess-Bright Mfg. Co., 1907-10, sec., 1916, until affiliation of co., 1919, with S.K.F. Industries; gen. mgr. of same, 1919-23, pres. since 1923; dir. Air Preheater Corpn., Hudson Ins. Co. Vice-pres. and dir. Swedish Chamber of Comm. of U.S. Mem. Am. Soc. Mech. Engrs. (pres. 1936), Soc. Automotive Engrs. Republican. Protestant. Clubs: Engineers (New York); Engineers, Union League (Phila.); Upper Montclair Golf, Pine Valley Golf. Home: Wyncote, Pa. Office: Front St. and Erie Av., Philadelphia, Pa.*

BATTAGLIA, Pasquale Michael, artist and teacher; b. Phila., Pa., Jan. 5, 1905; s. Rosario and Mary (Pirosa) B.; B.S. in Fine Arts in Edn., U. of Pa., 1929; B.F.A., Pa. Acad. of Fine Arts, 1933. Engaged as asst. instr. in drawing, U. of Pa., 1928-33; relief investigator, Co. of Phila., 1934-36; instr. art, Central Evening High Sch. since 1935, Holmes Jr. High Sch. since 1936. Has exhibited in all leading water color exhbns. in Phila. since 1930. Rep. in permanent collection The Pa. Acad. Fellowship. Awarded hon. mention for water color, West Chester Co. Exhbn., 1935. Mem. Pa. Acad. Fellowship, Phila. Water Color Club, Art Teachers Assn. of Phila., West Chester Co. Art Assn.,

Kappa Phi Kappa. Republican. Roman Catholic. Home and studio: 736 S. 6th St., Philadelphia, Pa.

BATTEN, Harry Albert, advertising; b. Phila., Pa.; s. George and Imogene E. (Doke) B.; ed. Phila. pub. schs.; m. Florence E. Wenzell, Feb. 25, 1933; children—Jane, Suzanne. With N. W. Ayer & Son, Inc., since 1911, advancing through printing, business and copy depts.; in charge copy production, 1928, v.p. in charge copy, 1929, dir., 1931, pres. since 1936; dir. First Nat. Bank of Phila. Served in U.S. Navy during World War. Trustee Pa. Working Home for Blind Men; dir. Phila. Orchestra Assn. Protestant. Club: Merion Cricket. Co-author of "The Written Word" and author of numerous articles on advertising and public relations. Home: Bryn Mawr, Pa. Office: West Washington Square, Philadelphia, Pa.

BATTEN, Loring Woart, clergyman; b. Gloucester Co., N.J., Nov. 17, 1859; s. Thomas G. and Emeline (Zane) B.; A.B., Harvard, 1885; B.D., Phila. Div. Sch., 1887; Ph.D., U. of Pa., 1893; S.T.D., Hobart, 1903; m. Clara B. Ware, March 18, 1886. Deacon, 1886, priest, 1887, P.E. Ch.; instr. and prof. O.T., Phila. Div. Sch., 1888-99; rector St. Mark's Ch., New York, 1899-1911. Lecturer and prof. O.T., Gen. Theol. Sem., 1904-33, now emeritus. Member Am. Oriental Soc., Soc. Bibl. Lit. and Exegesis, Oriental clubs of New York and Phila. Clubs: Century, Harvard, The Club, The Clericus, Authors' (London). Author: Old Testament from the Modern Point of View, 1889; The Hebrew Prophet, 1905; Ezra-Nehemiah in the Internat. Critical Commentary, 1913; The Relief of Pain by Mental Suggestion, 1917; Good and Evil, 1918; The First Book of Samuel, 1919; also articles in Hastings' Dictionary of the Bible and articles in Semitic and Oriental jours. and periodicals. Home: 560 Riverview Rd., Swarthmore, Pa.

BATTLE, John Rome, consulting engr.; b. St. Louis, Mo., March 30, 1889; s. Henry Samuel and Laura (Willing) B.; direct desc. Mathew Battle, who bought land in Colony of Va., 1653; grad. Blight Prep. Sch., Phila., 1906; B.S. in mech. engring., Towne Sci. Sch., U. of Pa., 1910, M.E., 1917; m. Amiee Archer Turner, May 30, 1914; children—Henrietta Riggs, John Rome. Began as cadet engr. United Gas Improvement. Co., 1910; engr. and Washington rep. Atlantic Refining Co., 1912-18; engr. and Phila. mgr. Swan & Finch Co., 1918-19; pres. and chief engr. J. R. Battle Co., Inc., consulting petroleum engrs. since 1919; pres. Gun-Fil Corpn., mfrs. lubrication equipment since 1928; formerly cons. engr. to Nat. Petroleum Marketers Assn. Mem. Am. Soc. Mech. Engrs., Am. Petroleum Inst. Democrat. Club: St. Davids Golf (Wayne, Pa.). Author: Handbook of Lubricating Engineering, 1916; Handbook Industrial Oil Engineering, 1920, 29, 38. Former asso. editor Nat. Petroleum News; contbr. articles on lubrication, liquid fuels and oil to tech. jours. Home: 39 St. Paul Road, Ardmore, Pa. Office: Otis Bldg., 16th and Sansom Sts., Philadelphia, Pa.

BATTLES, William W., pres. Battles & Co., Inc.; b. Phila., Pa., June 23, 1890; s. Frank and Lucy B. (Wait) B.; C.E., Princeton U., 1912. Pres. and dir. Battles & Co., Inc., since 1930. Home: Newton Square, Pa. Office: 1518 Locust St., Philadelphia, Pa.

BAUER, Elmer E.; pres. Allegheny Trust Co., Reibert Ice Co. Home: Glenshaw, Pa. Office: 413 Federal St., Pittsburgh, Pa.

BAUER, John, cons. economist in pub. utilities; b. of German parentage, Saratoff, Russia, Feb. 25, 1881; s. John and Elizabeth (Bartholoma) Bauer; brought to U.S. from Russia, 1892; B.A., Doane College, Crete, Neb., 1904, LL.D., 1935; B.A., Yale University, 1906; Ph.D., 1908; m. Florence Foss, Dec. 25, 1909; children—Frederick Foss, William Adams. Began as prin. pub. schs., Benkelman, Neb., 1900; teacher history, high sch., Crete, 1904-05; instr. economics, Cornell U., 1908-10, asst. prof., 1910-14; statistician Pub. Service Commn., State of N.Y., 1st Dist., 1914-16; asst. prof. economics, Princeton, 1916-17; chief of accounting div. Pub. Service Commn., State of N.Y., 1st Dist., 1917-19; utility rate adviser, City of New York, 1920-30; dir. Am. Pub. Utilities Bur. (a consulting group), New York since 1925. Served as economic consultant N.Y. Legislative Commn. on Revision of Pub. Service Commissions Law, 1929; mem. Marketing Bd. of St. Lawrence Power Development Commn. of N.Y., 1930; economic consultant to S.C. Power Rate Investigating Commn., 1931; utility rate investigator for League of Va. Municipalities, 1932-33; consultant to N.Y. Power Authority in electric distribution cost studies, 1932-33; consultant to N.C. League of Municipalities in telephone rate investigation, 1934-35; utility surveys for cities of Louisville, Ky., Pittsburgh and Boston, 1934-35; valuation expert, U.S. Dept. of Justice, 1937; economic consultant S.C. Rural Electrification Authority, 1937. Mem. Am. Econ. Assn., Nat. Municipal League, Internat. City Mgrs.' Assn., Govt. Research Assn., Pub. Ownership League of America, City Affairs Com. (New York), Tax Policy League, People's League for Economic Security, Phi Beta Kappa. Democrat. Mason. Author: Effective Regulation of Public Utilities, 1925; also (brochures) Standards for Modern Public Utility Franchises, 1930; (with Col. John P. Hogan) Report of Marketing Board to St. Lawrence Power Development Commission, 1931; (with Nathaniel Gold) Permanent Prosperity—And How to Get It, 1934; Public Utility Valuation for Purposes of Rate Control (with Gold), 1934; America's Struggle for Electric Power, 1935; Conditions and Requirements of Modern Mass Transportation in the Pittsburgh District (with A. E. Shaw), 1936; The Electric Power Industry—Development, Organization and Public Policies (with Gold), 1939; also numerous articles on pub. utility economics and pub. control of business; also contbr. to various works on these subjects. Editor Dept. on Pub. Utilities of Nat. Municipal Rev.; editorial consultant on pub. utilities, Public Management; asso. editor Public Ownership of Public Utilities and The People's Money. Home: 62 Montclair Av., Montclair, N.J. Office: 280 Broadway, New York, N.Y.

BAUER, John Conrad, chemist; b. Baltimore, Md., Feb. 21, 1902; s. Conrad and Grace (Spies) B.; grad. Baltimore City Coll., 1919; Ph.G., U. of Md. Sch. of Pharmacy, 1926, B.S., 1928; M.S., U. of Md., 1930, Ph.D., 1933; m. Katherine Barnickol, Nov. 29, 1928; 1 dau., Katherine Ann. Began as drug store clerk, Baltimore, 1914; hosp. lab. and radium technician, Howard A. Kelly Hosp., Baltimore, Coal Valley Hosp., Montgomery, W.Va., Colonial Hosp., Baltimore, 1919-26; instr. in chemistry, U. of Md., 1926-28, lecturer in physiol. chemistry and food analysis, 1928-36; chief chemist Noxzema Chem. Co., Baltimore, since 1936. Fellow Am. Inst. of Chem.; mem. Am. Chem. Soc., Am. Pharm. Soc., Md. Pharm. Soc., Phi Kappa Phi, Sigma Xi, Rho Chi. Home: 2424 Kentucky Av., Baltimore, Md.

BAUER, William G.; pres. Daily Press Pub. Co., Kane Brick & Tile Co., Keystone Commercial Corpn. Address: St. Marys, Pa.

BAUER, William J.; mem. firm John B. Barbour & Co. Home: 1155 Steuben St. Office: 336 4th Av., Pittsburgh, Pa.

BAUERNSCHMIDT, Marie Oehl von Hattersheim, civic worker; b. Baltimore, Md., Jan. 7, 1875; d. Ernest Rudolph Oehl and Caroline (Hellweg) von Hattershiem; student pub. schs., Baltimore, 1882-90; m. William Bauernschmidt, Jan. 29, 1896 (died 1934); children—Margaret Caroline (Mrs. J. Gordon Valiant III), Lt. Comdr. George William, William, Jr. Mem. bd. Home for Incurables, Baltimore, 1898-1912; Babies Milk Fund Assn., Baltimore, 1902-18; mgr. Children's Hosp. Sch., Baltimore, 1914-19; mem. mgrs. bd. Union Memorial Hosp., Baltimore, 1915-33; exec. sec. Pub. Sch. Assn., Baltimore, since 1919, which organized to get Baltimore pub. schs. out of politics and build better system pub. edn., also to stop political control of police, supervise liquor control, and improve condition of colored people; pres. N.Y. Paper Co. since 1934. Served as asso. dir. War Savings Stamps for Md., 1918-19. Democrat. Lutheran. Club: Baltimore Country (Baltimore, Md.). Home: 1 E. University Pl. Office: 1322 Fidelity Bldg., Baltimore, Md.

BAUGH, Albert Croll, prof. English; b. Philadelphia, Pa., Feb. 26, 1891; s. Horace L. and Margaret (Croll) B.; A.B., U. of Pa., 1912, A.M., 1914, Ph.D., 1915; m. Nita Emeline Scudder, June 20, 1925; children—William Scudder, Daniel. Began as asst. instr. English, U. of Pa., 1912, and has continued with same univ., prof. English since 1928; visiting prof., Stanford Univ., summer 1928, Duke U., summers 1935, 37, 39. Mem. Modern Lang. Assn. America (editorial bd.), Mediæval Acad.America (advisory bd.), Pa. Hist. Society, Phi Beta Kappa. Clubs: Franklin Inn, Lenape. Author: (with P. C. Kitchen and M. W. Black) Writing by Types, 1924; History of the English Language, 1935. Editor: William Haughton's Englishmen for My Money, 1917; Schelling Anniversary Papers, 1923; (with G. W. McClelland) Century Types of English Literature, 1925; (with P. C. Kitchen) Synonymns, Antonyms and Discriminations (in New Century Dictionary), 1927; Thomas Hardy's Return of the Native, 1928; (with A. H. Quinn and W. D. Howe) The Literature of America (2 vols.), 1929; (with N. E. McClure) Essays toward Living, 1929. Contbr, biographies in Dictionary of Am. Biography and articles in mags. Asso. editor Philological Quarterly. Home: 4220 Spruce St., Philadelphia, Pa.

BAUGHER, Jacob I., city supt. schs.; b. Black Rock, Pa., Mar. 7, 1889; s. Aaron S. and Lydia M. (Buser) B.; A.B., Elizabethtown Coll., 1923; A.M., Columbia U., 1925; Ph.D., same, 1930; m. Lillian M. Stermer, Dec. 18, 1908; children—Earl, Edwin, Galen, Naomi, Stanford, Wilfred, Norman. Engaged in teaching rural pub. schs., 1908-19; instr. mathematics, Elizabethtown Acad., 1919-21; prof. edn. and dir. extension work, Elizabethtown Coll., 1923-29; supervising prin. pub. schs., Hershey, Pa., 1930-33, supt. of schs. since 1934; dir. Demonstration High Sch., Lebanon Valley Coll., summers 1935-37; instr. Pa. State Coll., summers 1937-39; sec.-treas. Gen. Edn. Bd. Ch. of the Brethren, 1934-39; mem. com. of 3 to formulate practice teaching standards for Liberal Arts Coll. Assn. for the Advancement of Teaching for Pa. Mem. N.E.A., Nat. Assn. Sch. Adminstrn., Pa. State Edn. Assn., Pa. Anti-Tuberculosis Soc., Dauphin Co. Council Christian Edn., Phi Delta Kappa, Hershey Welfare Bd. Republican. Mem. Ch. of Brethren. Club: Hershey Civic (pres.). Contbr. to ednl. publs. Home: 305 E. Chocolate Av., Hershey, Pa.

BAUGHMAN, George W., Jr., engineer; b. Gilboa, O., Feb. 11, 1900; s. George W. and Mertie B. (Peckinpaugh) B.; B.E.E., Ohio State U., 1920, E.E., 1924; m. Cecile M. Lytel, June 30, 1928; 1 son, George W. III. Engr. Western Electric Co., New York, N. Y., 1920-23; engr. Union Switch and Signal Co. since 1923. Mem. Phi Kappa Tau, Sigma Xi, Eta Kappa Nu, Tau Beta Pi. Mason. Club: Pittsburgh Railway. Inventor in fields of railway signaling, centralized traffic control, automatic train control, control of railway brakes. Home: 103 Biddle Ave., Pittsburgh, Pa. Office: Union Switch and Signal Co., Swissvale, Pa.

BAUGHMAN, Harry Fridley, clergyman; b. Everett, Pa., Jan. 23, 1892; s. George W. and Elizabeth M. (Schafhirt) B.; A.B., Gettysburg Coll., 1910; ed. Luth. Theol. Sem., Gettysburg, 1910-13; (hon.) D.D., Gettysburg Coll., 1931; m. Joretha A. Liller, Oct. 17, 1917; 1 son, Peter Fridley. Ordained to ministry Luth. Ch., 1913, and pastor at Keyser, W.Va., 1913-18, Pittsburgh, Pa., 1918-25; pastor Trinity Ch., Germantown, Phila., Pa., since 1925. Sec. Church Papers Com., United Lutheran Ch., and mem. Bd. of Publication. Zimmerman lecturer, Gettysburg Sem. Home: 3123 Queen Lane, Philadelphia, Pa.

BAUM, Felix, physician and surgeon; b. Germany, Feb. 20, 1883; s. Alexander and Clara (Phiebig) B.; came to U.S., 1924, naturalized, 1929; M.D., Med. Sch., Heidelberg, Germany, 1908; m. Lillie Henle Hofheimer, Sept. 27, 1910; children—Dr. Otto Sigmund, Lewis F. Served as med. dir. Nat. Jewish Hosp., Denver, Colo., 1924-27; asst. prof. of medicine, U. of Colo. Med. Sch., 1924-27; in pvt. practice as physician and surgeon, Newark, N.J., since 1927;

cons. phys. Essex Mountain Tuberculosis Sanatorium, Verona, N.J.; phthisiologist, St. Mary's Hosp., Orange, N. J.; mem. med. adv. com. Deborah Sanatorium, Brown Mills, N.J. Served as capt. Med. Corps, Prussian Army to 1924. Awarded Iron Cross (Germany), 1914. Fellow Am. Coll. Chest Phys. Mem. Am. Acad. Tuberculosis Phys., Nat. Tuberculosis Assn., Internat. Union Against Tuberculosis, German Med. Soc., Acad. Medicine of Northern N.J., Essex Co. Med. Soc. Contbr. many articles on tuberculosis and related subjects to med. lit. of U.S. and Europe. Home: 765 S. Tenth St., Newark, N.J.

BAUM, Henry John, civil engring; b. Stone City, Ia., Oct. 29, 1886; s. John Kaspar and Kunigunda (Wolfschmitt) B.; B.E., State of Ia., 1908, C.E., same, 1914; m. Katharine A. Murphy, Dec. 30, 1914; 1 son, Vincent Henry. Employed as engr. in various cities and for various firms, 1908-18; prin. asst. city engr., Johnstown, Pa., 1919-21; city engr., Altoona, Pa., since 1921, also serves as chief Bur. Bldg. Inspection, mem. Park and Recreation Commn. and sec. City Planning Commn., Bd. Zoning Appeals, Traffic Planning Commn.; trustee, chmn. budget com. Altoona Community Chest. Trustee Blair Co. Branch, Pa. Assn. of The Blind. Pres. Pa. Assn. of Planning Commrs., City Engrs. Conf. Cities of 3d Class in Pa. Republican. Roman Catholic. K.C. Pres. K.C. Home Assn. Club: Lions of Altoona (past pres.). Home: 3205 Broad Av., Altoona, Pa.

BAUM, Walter Emerson, artist; b. Sellersville, Pa., Dec. 14, 1884; grad. Sellersville High Sch., 1902; art edn. Pa. Acad. of Fine Arts (student of William Trego); m. Flora Billger Barndt, Nov. 16, 1904; children—Marian Eleanor (Mrs. J. Lawrence Grim), Robert Emerson, Ruth Lynnette, Edgar Schofield. Painter of landscapes since 1910; editor of Sellersville Herald; art dir. Phila. Evening Bulletin; dir. Allentown (Pa.) Art Museum; dir. Kline-Baum Art Sch. Exhibited at Pa. Acad., Phila. Art Club, Corcoran Art Gallery (Washington, D.C.), Nat. Acad. Design (New York), Chicago Art Inst., also in galleries, etc., St. Louis, Buffalo, Fort Worth, Baltimore, San Francisco, Cleveland, etc. Represented in permanent collections of Irene Rich Art. Assn., Norfolk Va.; State College, Pa.; Phila. Water Color Club; Hazelton High Sch.; Woodrow Wilson Jr. High Sch. (Phila.); Allentown Art Museum. Awarded: bronze medal Am. Artists Exhbn., Phila., 1924; Jennie Sesnan gold medal Pa. Acad., 1925; picture purchase prize, Springville, Utah, 1933; Fellowship prize Pa. Academy, 1939; honorable mention Phila. Sketch Club, 1939. Mem. Phila. Art Alliance, Phila. Sketch Club, Germantown Art League, Fellowship of Pa. Acad. of Fine Arts, Am. Artists Professional League, Art Club of Phila., Phila. Water Color Club, Bucks-Montgomery Press League, Allentown-Bethleham Art Alliance, Pa.-German Folk Lore Soc. Mem. Sellersville Sch. Bd., Sellersville-Perkasie Joint Sch. Bd. Lutheran. Author: Two Hundred Years, an informal history of Pa.-Germans of Bucks Co., Pa. Contbg. artist for Curtis Pub. Co. Address: Sellersville, Pa.

BAUMANN, John Roland, florist; b. Rahway, N.J., Oct. 27, 1882; s. Camille Eugene and Annie (Nelson) B.; ed. Rahway (N.J.) pub. schs. and New Jersey Business Coll., Newark; m. Helen Ward, June 12, 1912; children—John Roland, Ward. Florist with C. E. Baumann, Inc., wholesale and retail florists and growers, landscape contractors, Rahway, N.J., since 1915, owner since 1916, pres. since 1931; partner Baumann Bros., Rahway, since 1921; v.p. Better Homes Bldg. & Loan Assn. of Rahway since 1925; mem. bd. mgrs. Rahway Savings Instn. since 1934. Pres. Rahway Sinking Fund Commn., 1938-39. Exec. Union Council of Boy Scouts of America since 1932. Elk. Clubs: N.Y. Florists (New York); N.J. Florists (New York); Kiwanis (Rahway, N.J.); Colonia Country (Colonia, N.J.); Ilderan Outing (Rahway, N.J.). Home: 289 Maple Ave. Office: 900 St. George Av., Rahway, N.J.

BAUR, J. Fred; pres. St. James Savings Bank. Address: 411 E. Baltimore St., Baltimore, Md.

BAUSMAN, J(ohn) W(atts) B(aer), lawyer, banker; b. Lancaster, Pa., Mar. 12, 1855; s. Jacob and Mary (Baer) B.; A.B., Lafayette Coll., Easton, Pa., 1874, A.M., 1877; m. Annette Franklin, Apr. 28, 1880 (died 1882); m. 2d, Blanche Franklin, 1892. Admitted to Pa. bar, 1877; pres. Farmers Trust Co. Trustee Bethany Home, Reading, Pa., Franklin and Marshall Coll., and Yeates Sch.; dir. Lancaster County Ry. & Light Co., Hamilton Watch Co., Pa. Glass Sand Co. and numerous pub. utility cos. Republican. Episcopalian. Mem. Delta Kappa Epsilon. Clubs: Art, Union League (Phila.); Hamilton (Lancaster); Merion Cricket (Haverford). Pres. Pa. Bankers' Assn.; exec. council Am. Bankers' Assn. Home: 325 W. Chestnut St., Lancaster, Pa.

BAUSMAN, Robert Otis, univ. prof.; b. Dayton, Ind., Judy 3, 1891; s. Andrew and Martha Jane (Crowden) B.; B.S., Purdue U., Lafayette, Ind., 1914; M.S., U. of Del., Newark, Del., 1925; Ph.D., Cornell U., 1930; m. Ruth C. Clendaniel, Oct. 9, 1919; 1 son, Robert Otis. Specialist in agrl. extension, Purdue U., Lafayette, Ind., 1914-17; agrl. extension, U. of Del., Newark, Del., 1918-27; asso. professor research and teaching agrl. econs. since 1928. Mem. Am. Econ. Assn., Am. Farm Econ. Assn., Am. Statis. Assn., Am. Assn. Univ. Profs., Alpha Gamma Rho, Epsilon Sigma Phi. Episcopalian (vestryman). Mason. Contbr. articles to tech. pubis. Home: 91 W. Park Pl., Newark, Del.

BAWDEN, George Abner, surgeon; b. Cumberland, Md., Nov. 19, 1894; s. William Henry and Henrietta (Parker) B.; student Alleghany County Acad., Cumberland, Md., 1909-12; M.D., U. of Md. Med. Sch., Baltimore, 1916; m. Blanche Irene Lober, Aug. 14, 1918; children—Shirley Irene, Olga Virginia. Interne Md. Gen. Hosp., Baltimore, 1916-17, chief surg. resident, 1917-18; engaged in gen. practice of medicine and surgery at Baltimore, Md., 1919-25, gen. surgery since 1925. Served as lt. (j.g.) to lt. Med. Corps U.S.N.R.F., 1917-21, active duty, 1918-19. Fellow Am. Coll. Surgeons; mem. A.M.A., Southern Med. Assn., Med. & Chirurg. Faculty of Md., Baltimore City Med. Soc., Theta Kappa Psi. Republican. Lutheran. Mason (32°, Shriner). K.P. Clubs: University (Baltimore); Gibson Island (Gibson Island, Md.). Home: 1517 E. North Av. Office: Medical Arts Bldg., Baltimore, Md.

BAY, Robert Parke; attending surgeon Church Home and Infirmary; chief surgeon Md. Gen. Hosp.; cons. surgeon South Baltimore Gen. Hosp., Baltimore, Union Hosp., Elkton, and Hartford Memorial Hosp., Havre-de-Grace. Address: 1800 N. Charles St., Baltimore, Md.

BAYARD, Edwin Stanton, agrl. editor; b. Kingston, O., Dec. 13, 1867; s. Samuel Peter and Martha Ellen (Lutz) B.; grad. high sch., Waynesburg, Pa.; A.B., Waynesburg Coll., 1889, A.M.; m. Mary Virginia Kerr, June 9, 1903, 1 son, Samuel Preston. Editor in chief Capper-Harman-Slocum Co., pubs. Pa. Farmer, Ohio Farmer, Mich. Farmer; mem. firm Bayard Bros., cattle breeders, Waynesburg; owner Virginia Farms, Livermore, Pa. Member United States Agrl. Conf., 1921, Nat. Livestock Com., Am. Com. Internat. Inst. of Agr. (Rome); chmn. Allegheny County Farm Bur. Trustee and mem. exec. com. Pa. State Coll. Mem. Am. Aberdeen-Angus Breeders' Assn. (dir.), Pa. Livestock Breeders' Assn. (pres.), East Liberty Chamber of Commerce (pres.), Holland Soc. of New York, Sigma Delta Chi; hon. mem. Am. Vet. Med. Assn. Alpha Zeta, Gamma Sigma Delta. Mem. Pa. N.G. Republican. Presbyn. Mason. Rotarian. Lecturer. Home: 6366 Jackson St. Office: 7301 Penn Av., Pittsburgh, Pa.*

BAYARD, Thomas Francis, ex-senator; b. Wilmington, Del., June 4, 1868; s. Thomas Francis (U.S. senator) and Louisa (Lee) B.; A.B., Yale, 1890; student law dept. Yale, 1890-1901, and in father's office, 1891-93; m. Elizabeth Bradford, d. Dr. Alexis I. du Pont, Oct. 3, 1908. Admitted to Del. bar, 1893; moved to N.Y. City, 1897, and was apptd. asst. corpn. counsel; returned to Wilmington, 1901; chmn. Dem. State Com., 1906-16; city solicitor, Wilmington,

1917-19; elected to U.S. Senate from Del., Nov. 1922, to fill vacancy for unexpired term ending Mar. 4, 1923, and for term ending Mar. 4, 1929; was the 5th mem. of family to occupy senatorial chair from Del. Episcopalian. Home: Wilmington, Del.

BAYLES, Edwin Atkinson, lawyer; b. N.Y. City, Dec. 1, 1875; s. George (M.D.) and Catharine Sequine (Johnson) B.; A.B., Columbia, 1896, A.M., 1897, LL.B., 1899; m. Madeleine Gould, Oct. 20, 1903. Admitted to N.Y. bar, 1899, Dist. of Columbia bar, 1919; former partner Chrystie, Williamson & Bayles and Williamson & Bayles, New York, and Cuthell, White, Bayles & Appel, Washington, D.C.; (retired); dir. Home Ins. Co., City of New York Ins. Co., Home Indemnity Co., Gibraltar Fire & Marine Ins. Co., Nat. Liberty Ins. Co. of America, Baltimore Am. Ins. Co., Home Fire Security Corpn. (all of N.Y. City), Ga. Home Ins. Co. Mem. Phi Gamma Delta. Republican. Episcopalian. Clubs: Essex County, Country (W. Orange, N.J.); Columbia University, Phi Gamma Delta (New York); Hyannisport (Mass.); St. Enodoc Golf, Rock (Cornwall, Eng.). Home: 27 Lake Road, Short Hills, N.J.

BAYLES, Theodore Floyd, theologian; b. West Kortright, N.Y., July 25, 1871; s. John Owen and Martha Brown (Floyd) B.; prep, edn., Stamford (N.Y.) Sem.; A.B., Union Coll., Schenectady, N.Y., 1895; grad. New Brunswick Theol. Sem., 1898; B.D., Rutgers, 1898, D.D., 1924; m. Mary Bevier, Sept. 17, 1902; children—Marthena, Theodore Bevier. Ordained ministry Ref. Ch. in America, 1898; pastor successively Gardiner, N.Y., Little Falls, Freehold and Bayonne, N.J., and Walden, N.Y., until 1924; prof. practical theology, New Brunswick Theol. Sem., since 1924. Mem. Phi Beta Kappa. Republican. Home: 1 Seminary Place, New Brunswick, N.J.

BAYLESS, Stanley Corbett, paper mfr.; b. Binghamton, N.Y., Feb. 1, 1887; s. George C. and Georgie Ellen (Healey) B.; grad. Binghamton (N.Y.) High Sch., 1905; student Union Coll., Schenectady, N.Y., 2 yrs., Class of 1909; m. Carlotta Louise Schlager, June 25, 1912; children—Stanley, Barbara. Gen. mgr. Bayless Pulp & Paper Corpn., Austin, Pa., since 1911. Republican. Mason, K.P. Address: Austin, Pa.

BAYLEY, Francis Reed, clergyman; b. Millville, N.J., Oct. 25, 1877; s. William Henry and Mary Jacobs (Sheldon) B.; A.B., Dickinson Coll., 1900, D.D., 1920; m. May S. Merryman, Dec. 17, 1903; children—Francis C., Mary Anna (Mrs. Marshall H. Barnard), John. S. Ordained Meth. ministry, 1902; admitted to Baltimore Annual Conf., M.E. Ch., 1902; served various pastorates, 1902-21; dist. supt. M.E. Ch., 1922-28; pastor Walbrook M.E. Ch., Baltimore, 1928-34; now supt. of Baltimore East Dist. Del. Gen. Conf. since 1920 (chmn. Judiciary Com. 1932-36); del. to Uniting Conf. of Methodism, 1939. Pres. and trustee Deaconess Home, Baltimore. Mem. Home Missions and Ch. Extension Bd. of M.E. Ch. Mason (K.T.) Home: 506 Evesham Av., Baltimore, Md.

BAYLEY, Paul Leverne; prof. physics Lehigh U. Address: Bethlehem, Pa.

BAYLIS, Chester; pres. Nat. Union Bank. Address: Dover, N.J.

BAYLISS, Charles William, pres. Artic Roofings, Inc.; b. Chicago, Ill., Apr. 7, 1882; s. William Thomas and Mary Clara (Addison) B.; ed. pub. schs., Milwaukee, Wis.; m. Mary Anne Bloomfield, Apr. 29, 1911; children—Mary Bloomfield, Margaret Addison, Charles William. In railroad work, later traveling freight agt., traveling salesman and sales mgr. Portland Cement Industry until 1910; mgr. street and road dept. Gen. Asphalt Co. (now The Barber Asphalt Co.), 1910-19, became v.p., 1919; pres. Artic Roofings, Inc.; dir. Glassine Paper Co., The Laguna Corpn. Mason. Clubs: Art, Bachelors Barge, Racquet, Phila. Country, Aronimink Golf. Home: 210 Pembroke Av., Wayne, Pa. Office: Edge Moor, Del.

BAYLISS, Ella Heywang (Mrs. George E. Bayliss), oil producer; b. Titusville, Pa., Apr. 22, 1889; d. Mark J. and Florence M. (Porter)

Heywang; grad. high sch., Titusville, 1907, Titusville Hosp. Nurses Training Sch., 1910; m. George E. Bayliss, Apr. 8, 1912 (died Oct. 15, 1937); children—Elizabeth, William Heywang. Individual owner since death of husband. Mem. Titusville Chamber of Commerce. Mem. Pa. Crude Oil Assn., Independent Petroleum Assn. Chmn. Ladies Auxiliary of Titusville Hosp. since 1923; chmn. Pa. Dept. Pub. Assistance, Crawford Co. since 1937. Served as alternate to Del. Dem. Conv., New York City, 1928. Mem. Y.W.C.A., Ladies Auxiliary Y.M.C.A. Mem. D.A.R. (sec. local chapter, 1927-35). Pres. Crawford Co. Pa. Fed. Woman's Clubs, 1934-36. Chmn. Pageant Com. of Titusville Diamond Jubilee of Oil, 1934; Mothers Assistance Bd. Crawford Co., 1934-37. Democrat. Presbyn. Club: Titusville Woman's (pres. 1933-35). Home: 210 E. Main St. Office: Second National Bank Bldg., Titusville, Pa.

BAYLOR, C. N., editor Hagerstown Herald and Hagerstown Mail. Address: Care Herald-Mail Co., Hagerstown, Md.

BAYLOR, John Ward, surgeon; b. Liberty Tazewell Co., Va., June 11, 1893; s. Dr. William Edwin and Eva Matilda (Thompson) B.; grad. Graham (Va.) High Sch., 1909; A.B., Washington and Lee U., 1914; M.D., Johns Hopkins, 1918; unmarried. House officer Johns Hopkins Hosp., 1918-21, asso. in otolaryngology, 1921; in private practice as surgeon, specializing in ear, nose and throat, Baltimore, since 1921; mem. staffs of Johns Hopkins Hosp., Church Home and Infirmary, Hosp. for Women of Md. Served as 1st lt. Med. Corps, U.S. Army, 1918. Mem. Phi Beta Kappa, Pi Kappa Alpha, Phi Chi. Democrat. Club: Johns Hopkins. Home: 6 E. Read St. Office: 1118 St. Paul St., Baltimore, Md.

BAZARD, Walter Scott, school supt.; b. Marienville, Pa., Nov. 16, 1893; s. John C. and Minerva (Kunselman) B.; A.B., Washington and Jefferson Coll., Washington, Pa., 1916; M. Ed., U. of Pittsburgh, 1934; m. Jean Ferguson, June 26, 1926; 1 son, Walter Scott. Teaching prin., Morris Twp. (Pa.) High Sch., 1916-17; civ. engr. Union R.R., East Pittsburgh, Pa., 1919-22; teacher of mathematics, Beaver (Pa.) High Sch., 1922-24, Center Twp. High Sch., Des Plaines, Ill., 1924-26; prin., Beaver (Pa.) Jr. High Sch., 1926-30, Midland (Pa.) High Sch., 1930-35; supt. of schs., Midland, Pa., since 1935. Served as 2d lieut., C.A.C., U.S. Army during World War; now major, U.S. Army Res. Dist. commr. Boy Scouts of America; dir. Beaver Co. (Pa.) Red Cross; mem. Am. Legion, Phi Kappa Sigma, Phi Delta Kappa. Republican. Presbyterian. Club: Rotary, Midland, (Pa.). Home: 1240 Beaver Av. Office: Public Schools, Midland, Pa.

BAZETT, Henry Cuthbert, prof. physiology; b. Gravesend, Eng., June 25, 1885; s. Henry and Eliza Ann (Cruickshank) B.; B.A. (1st class honors), Oxford, 1908, M.B., B.Ch., 1910; F.R.C.S., Eng., 1910; St. Thomas's Hosp., London, 1908-12; grad. work Harvard, 1912-13; m. Dorothy Rufford Livesey, Mar. 10, 1917; children—Hazel, Donald John. Came to U.S., 1921. Demonstrator physiology, St. Thomas's Hosp., 1911-12; Radcliffe travelling fellow, Oxford, 1912-15; fellow Magdalen Coll., Oxford, 1913-21; demonstrator pathology, Oxford, 1913-14, Christopher Welch lecturer clin. physiology, Oxford, 1918-21; prof. physiology, U. of Pa. since 1921. Served as lieut. to maj., R.A.M.C. (sr.) in Brit. Army M.C., 1915, with B.E.F. in France, 1914-18. Mem. Phi Beta Pi, Sigma Xi. Episcopalian. Mason. Club: British Officers (Philadelphia). Home: 629 Haydock Lane, Haverford, Pa.

BAZLEY, James Robert, contracting engring.; b. Oswego, N.Y., Aug. 5, 1886; s. Edward and Lodema (Jacobs) B.; student Oswego State Normal Sch., 1905-07; B.S. in mech. engring., U. of Mich., 1911; m. Alice Harman, Oct. 22, 1913; children—Jane MacBride (Mrs. Clyde Beekman Gordon), Alice Harman, James Robert, Jr. Asso. with N. J. Cuyle & Son, 1911-18; gen. mgr. Mahanoy Constrn. Co., 1918-19; founder and prop. J. Robert Bazley, Inc., Contracting Engrs., heavy excavations, foundations, road building, 1919, pres. and treas. since incorporation, 1930; 1st v.p. Miners Nat. Bank. Served as pres. Pottsville Chamber of Commerce, 1935-38; pres. Community Chest since 1935. Dir. Pottsville Hosp. Mem. Am. Soc. Mining Engrs. Presbyterian. Club: Pottsville. Home: 18th St. and Oak Rd. Address: P.O. Box 117, Pottsville, Pa.

BAZZONI, Charles Blizard, geophysicist; b. Newburgh, N.Y., Jan. 28, 1886; s. Charles Lewis and Marie Antoinette (Dayton) B.; B.Pd., N.Y. State Normal Coll., 1905; B.S., U. of Pa., 1911, M.A., 1913, Ph.D., 1914; Harrison research fellow (U. of Pa.) at U. of London, 1915-16; m. Edith Vera Harling, Dec. 31, 1918. Teacher science, high schs. of N.Y., 1905-07; instr. in physics, U. of Pa., 1910-19; research asst., King's Coll. (U. of London), 1916-17; asst. prof. physics, U. of Pa., 1919-21, prof. exptl. physics, 1921-1938; in charge geophys. exploration, Sun Oil Co., 1925-26, chief geophysicist since 1938. Capt. Corps Engrs., U.S.A., 1917-19; in command in field of Sound Ranging Serv., A.E.F.; maj. Field Arty., O.R.C. Fellow A.A.A.S., Am. Physical Soc.; mem. Franklin Inst. (mem. com. on science and the arts), Assn. Exploration Geophysicists, Am. Seismological Soc., Optical Soc. America, American Geophysical Union, Sigma Xi. Awarded gold medal, Sesquicentennial Expp., Phila., 1926. Decorated British Mil. Cross; Officer d'Académie with Palms (French); citation by Gen. Pershing. Episcopalian. Author: Text Book of Physics, 1920; Kernels of the Universe, 1927; Matter and Energy, 1931; contbr. Jour. Franklin Inst., Philos. Magazine, Physical Rev., etc. Experimenter in field of atomic physics, seismic, gravitational and elec. geographical exploration. Home: Roger's Lane, Wallingford, Pa.

BEACH, George Raimes, lawyer; b. Jersey City, N.J., Mar. 14, 1875; s. Marcus and Mary R. (Jackson) B.; LL.B., Columbia, 1897; m. Lucy McBride, Apr. 30, 1901; children—George R., Katharine L. In practice of law since 1897; has served as referee in bankruptcy, spl. master Court of Chancery, master in chancery and town counsel for Montclair; pres. Beach Land Co., mgr., v.p. and mem. bd. investment Provident Instn. for Savings, Jersey City; sec. and dir. Glen Ridge Land Co.; dir. First Nat. Bank & Trust Co. (Montclair), Colonial Life Ins. Co. of America; v.p. and mem. exec. com. N.J. State Savings Bank Assn.; trustee Glendale Cemetery Assn. Mem. Bd. of Adjustments and Town Planning Bd., Montclair; dir. Organized Aid Assn., Jersey City; trustee Montclair Community Hosp., Boy Scouts of Montclair. Alumni trustee Columbia U., 1925-31. Mem. Am. Bar Assn., N.J. State Bar Assn., Hudson Co., Bar Assn. (pres. 1922), Nat. Assn. Referees in Bankruptcy (pres.), N.J. Hist. Soc., Delta Kappa Epsilon. Pres. Alumni Fed. Columbia U., 1923-26. Democrat. Episcopalian. Clubs: Columbia University, Lawyers (New York); Carteret, Downtown (Jersey City); Montclair Golf. Home: 167 S. Mountain Av., Montclair, N.J.; (summer) Road's End Farm, Sussex, N.J. Office: 239-241 Washington St., Jersey City, N.J.

BEACH, H(arry) Prescott, lawyer; b. Hamden, Conn., Feb. 23, 1871; s. Lt. Dennis and Josephine (Jackson) B.; LL.B., Columbia, 1891; m. Laura Dolbear, Nov. 27, 1895; children—George A. H. (dec.), Prescott, Louis Dolbear, Laura Lancaster (wife of Dr. Leopold Edward Thron), Robert Treat. Began reading law in office of Joseph H. Choate, N.Y. City, Sept. 1, 1891; in gen. practice, 1895-1932; gen. counsel and v.p., Chale Realty Co., 1927-32; dir. and mem. exec. and finance coms. Morris Plan Industrial Bank of New York. Mem. Merchants Assn. of N.Y. City, 1914-32. Official arbitrator Am. Arbitration Assn.; pres. N.Y. State Bd. of Commrs. of License since 1914; pres. Seamen's Christian Assn. (N.Y. City) since 1914; vice-chmn. and dir. Seamen's House of Y.M.C.A.; mem. N.J. State, N.Y. City and Montclair Town, George Washington bicentennial coms.; mem. N.Y. City Park Assn., Essex Inst. (Salem, Mass.). Pres. and trustee The Revolutionary Memorial Soc. of N.J.; mem. Nat. Soc. Sons Am. Revolution, (past v.p. gen. nat. soc., nat. trustee and past pres. N.J. soc.), N.Y. Soc. Colonial Wars, Am. Friends of Lafayette, Anglo-Am. Records Foundation, Vet. Artillery Corps and Mil. Soc. of War of 1812, Nat. Geneal. Soc., N.Y. Geneal. and Biog. Soc. (mem. publication bd.), Geneal. Soc. of N.J. (v.p. and trustee), N.J. Archæol. Soc., Hist. Congress of N.J. (pres.) N.J. Numismatic Soc. (ex-pres.), Milford (Conn.) Hist. Soc., Phi Gamma Delta, etc. Democrat. Episcopalian (formerly mem. vestry Christ Ch., Glen Ridge, N.J.). Clubs: Nat. Arts, Phi Gamma Delta (New York); Down Town (Newark); Church Club of N.J. Author: (with others) The Story of Montclair, 1930. Contbr. on hist. and biog. topics, also short stories and poems. Home: 376 Upper Mountain Av., Montclair, N.J. Office: 550 W. 20th St., New York, N.Y.

BEACH, Sylvester Woodbridge, clergyman; b. Woodville, Miss., July 24, 1852; s. Rev. Charles and Fannie (Woodbridge) B.; A.B., Princeton University, 1876; grad. Princeton Theological Seminary, 1880; D.D. from Wooster (O.) College, 1914; m. Eleanor Orbison, Aug. 10, 1882 (died 1927); children—Mary Hollingsworth (Mrs. Frederic J. Dennis), Sylvia Woodbridge, Cyprian Woodbridge. Ordained Presbyn. ministry 1880; pastor Baltimore, Md., 1880-87, First Ch., Bridgeton, N.J., 1887-1900; in charge Am. students, work in Latin Quarter, Paris, France, 1900-05; co-pastor Am. Ch. in Paris, 1903-05; pastor First Ch., Princeton, N.J., 1905-23, now emeritus. Ex-moderator Synod of N.J. Mem. Soc. Descendents of Colonial Governors, Soc. Colonial Wars, S.R., S.A.R. Mason. Clubs: Nassau (Princeton), Princeton (New York), American (Paris). Pastor to President Woodrow Wilson and officiated at the White House, at marriage of two daughters of the President. Contbr. Princeton Rev. and other periodicals. Toured Near East, 1922, as commr. Alliance of Ref. Chs. Home: Nassau Club, Princeton, N.J., and 2885 Santa Anita Av., Altadena, Calif.

BEAL, Carleton DeCastro, clergyman; b. Chicago, Ill., Oct. 13, 1889; s. George and Lizzie (DeCrastos) B.; ed. Cushing Acad., Ashburnham, Mass., 1903-06, Harvard N. Dental Sch., 1906-07, DuBose Memorial Ch. Training Sch., Fairmount, Tenn., 1921-23; grad. U. of South, spl. course, 1923; study spl. grad. course Phila. Divinity Sch., 1923-24; m. Mary Alice Bower Eicholtz, Nov. 8, 1918; children—John Philip Eicholtz, Isabelle Margaret (Mrs. Henry L. Spahr), William Carleton, Mary Jane, Kathryn Patsy. Employed in dept. stores, Boston, Mass., 3 yrs.; successively, credit man, salesman, actor and singer, 11 yrs.; ordained to ministry P.E. Ch., deacon, May 1924, priest, Feb. 1926; rector All Saints Ch., Williamsport, Pa., 1923-26, Berwick, Pa., 1926-28; Condersport, Pa., 1928-31; retired, 1931; operates farm at Table Rock, Pa. Served as sgt. U.S.A., 1917-19. Mem. Xi Psi Phi, Am. Legion. Republican. Episcopalian. Home: R.F.D. No. 1, Biglerville, Pa.

BEAL, Frederick W.; prof. mathematics, U. of Pa. Address: U. of Pennsylvania, Philadelphia, Pa.

BEAL, George Denton, chemist; b. Scio, O., Aug. 12, 1887; s. James Hartley and Fannie Snyder (Young) B.; Ph.C., Scio Coll. Pharmacy, 1906, Pharm. D., 1907; Ph.B., Scio Coll., 1908; A.M., Columbia University, 1910; Richard Butler scholar in chemistry, same univ., 1910-11, Ph.D., 1911; Pharm. M., Philadelphia College Pharmacy, 1933; Sc.D., Mount Union College, 1933; m. Edith Downs, July 3, 1912; children—George Denton, Marjorie Downs. Asst. in chemistry, Scio Coll. Pharmacy, 1906-08; instr. in chemistry, U. of Ill., 1911-14, asso., 1914-18, asst. prof., 1918-20, associate prof. analytical and food chemistry, 1920-24, prof., 1924-26; asst. dir. of the Mellon Inst., Pittsburg, Pa., since 1926. Collaborator with com. on revision U.S. Pharmacopœia, 1920; mem. com. of revision U.S. Pharmacopœia, 11th revision (chmn. sub-com on organic chemicals; mem. U.S. Pharmacopœial Conv., 1930; chmn. sub-com. on anthraquinone drugs, Nat. Research Council, 1922-27. Trustee Mt. Union College (Alliance, O.), Phila. (Pa.) Coll. of Pharmacy and Science; dir. Pittsburgh Coll. of Pharmacy. Fellow A.A.A.S., Am. Pub. Health Assn.; mem. Am.

Chem. Soc. (chmn. medicinal div., 1938), Am. Pharm. Assn. (1st v.p. 1934-35; pres. 1936-37), Nat. Conf. on Pharm. Research, World Conf. on Narcotic Control, Pa. Pharm. Assn., Am. Soc. Testing Materials, Lambda Chi, Alpha, Sigma Xi, Alpha Chi Sigma, Phi Lambda Upsilon (nat. pres., 1917-19), Gamma Alpha. Winner Ebert prize, Am. Pharm. Assn., 1920. Republican. Methodist. Clubs: University, Univ. of Pittsbugh Faculty (Pittsburgh); Chemists' (New York). Contbr. to Jour. Am. Pharm. Assn., Jour. Am. Chem. Soc. Home: 6659 Woodwell St., Pittsburgh, Pa.

BEAL, Walter Hubert, mfg. exec.; b. Toledo, Ia.; s. Albert M. (M.D.) and Carrie (Middlekauff) B.; grad. high sch. Moline, Ill., 1912, U. of Ill., 1916; m. Dorothy Barratt, June 2, 1920; children—Walter Hubert, Richard Barratt. Began with Lycoming Mfg. Co., Williamsport, Pa., 1919, sales mgr., 1919-27, v.p., 1927-30, gen. mgr., 1930-31, became pres., 1931; pres. Auburn (Ind.) Automobile Co., 1932-34; v.p. Cord Corpn., Chicago, Ill., 1934-35; chmn. bd. N.Y. Shipbuilding Corpn., 1935-38; pres. Aviation Mfg. Corpn. and vice-pres. The Aviation Corpn. since Feb. 1938. Served as capt. Ordnance Dept., U.S. Army, World War. Mem. Delta Kappa Epsilon. Presbyn. Club: Marion Cricket. Home: 1233 Remington Rd., Wynnewood, Pa. Address: Aviation Mfg. Corpn., 420 Lexington Av., New York, N.Y.

BEALE, Leonard Tillinghast, pres. Pa. Salt Mfg. Co.; b. Philadelphia, Pa., May 28, 1881; s. Edward Fitzgerald and Maria Litchfield (Lewis) B.; student Haverford Sch., 1891-99, Princeton U., 1899-1901; M.E. and B.S., U. of Pa., 1904; m. Anna Lewis, Dec. 9, 1911; children —Frances Lewis (Mrs. Evan Randolph, Jr.), Edward Fitzgerald III, Anne. Pres. Pa. Salt Mfg. Co., and subsidiaries; dir. Pa. Co. for Insurances on Lives, Penn Mutual Life Ins. Co., Fire Assn. of Phila., Phila. Contributionship, Nat. Lead Co., Titanium Pigment Co.. Bell Telephone Co. of Pa., John T. Lewis & Bros. Co., Titan Co., Dir. Pa. Sch. for Deaf; mem. exec. com. Mfg. Chemists' Assn. Mem. Delta Psi. Republican. Episcopalian. Clubs: Philadelphia, Midday (Phila.); Chemists (New York). Home: 2025 De Lancey Pl. Office: Widener Bldg., Philadelphia, Pa.

BEALE, Wilson Thomas Moore, clergyman; b. Baltimore, Md., Sept. 27, 1876; s. Rev. David J. (D.D.) and Mary (Moore) B.; A.B., Princeton, 1899, A.M., same, 1902; grad. student Princeton Sem., 1899-1902; hon. D.D., St. John's Coll., Annapolis, Md., 1922; m. Mary Harlan, May 2, 1906; children—Mary Moore, Wilson Thomas Moore, Margaret Harlan. Ordained to ministry Presbyn. Ch., 1902; pastor at Zion, Cecil Co., Md., 1902-07; *pastor Salisbury, Md., 1907-14, Eastside Ch., Paterson, N.J., 1914-23; pastor Oak Lane Presbyn. Ch., Phila., Pa., since 1923. Trustee Presbyn. Hosp. and Magee Convalescent Hosp., Phila. Former mederator presbyteries of New Castle, Del., Jersey City, N.J., Phila. North, Pa. Moderator Synod of Pa. of the Presbyn. Ch. U.S.A., 1938-39. Life pres. class of 1902, Princeton, N.J., Sem. Republican. Mason (grand chaplain of grand lodge of Pa.) Clubs: Twentieth Century, Union League. Home: 6635 N. 11th St., Philadelphia, Pa.

BEALL, Charles Ray, engineer; b. West Lafayette, O., Dec. 8, 1882; s. Alexander Thomas and Mary Cornelia (Flagg) B.; grad. Pub. High Sch., West Lafayette, O., 1899; E.E., Ohio State U., Columbus, O., 1907; m. Annie Grant Loomis, Sept. 9, 1911. Engring. apprentice, Westinghouse Electric & Mfg. Co., East Pittsburgh, Pa., 1907-09, engr., 1909-10; engr., Union Switch & Signal Co., 1910-16, elec. engr., 1916-22, asst. chief engr., 1922-37, chief engr. since 1937. Mem. Am. Inst. Elec. Engrs. Republican. Presbyterian. Mason. Home: 1409 Walnut St., Edgewood, Pa. Office: Swissvale, Pa.

BEALL, J. Glenn, chmn. State Roads Commn.; dir. Dept. of Pub. Works. Address: Federal Reserve Bank Bldg., Baltimore, Md.

BEALL, John Thomas, Jr., real estate; b. Cumberland, Md., Nov. 25, 1881; s. John Thomas and Emma D. (Blucker) B.; student high sch.; m. Anna E. Hancock, Jan. 1, 1914; children—Elizabeth Ann, Ruth E. Pres. Hazelwood Realty Co.; sec. and dir. Hazelwood Bank; dir. Twenty-third Ward Bldg. & Loan Assn. Mason (trustee Jappa Lodge No. 608), Odd Fellow. Home: 3423 Beechwood Boul. Office: 4805 2d Av., Pittsburgh, Pa.

BEALS, C. Wearne, physician; b. St. Petersburg, Pa., Jan. 23, 1888; s. Hiram and Sara Etta (Edinger) B.; grad. Ohio Mil. Inst., 1908; grad. St. Petersburg High Sch., 1909; student U. of Cincinnati, 1909-10; M.D., Jefferson Med. Coll., 1917; M.Sc., U. of Pa., 1926; m. Margaret Ream, Feb. 20, 1919; 1 dau., Betty Ann. Interne Passavant Hosp., 1917-18; in gen. practice as physician, Coraopolis and Seneca, Pa., 1918-23; in practice of bronchoscopy, ophthalmology and otolarynogology, DuBois and St. Marys, Pa., since 1923; mem. firm Drs. Beals & Murdock. Served as 1st lt. Med. Corps, U.S. Army, 1918. Fellow Am. Coll. Surgeons; mem. A.M.A., Am. Acad. Ophthalmology and Otolaryngology, Western Pa. Eye, Ear, Nose and Throat Soc., Alpha Chi Sigma, Beta Theta Pi, Phi Beta Pi. Republican. Lutheran. Mason. Club: DuBois Country (DuBois, Pa.). Home: Sabula, Pa. Office: 41 N. Brady St., DuBois, Pa., Bille Bldg., St. Marys, Pa.

BEAM, Adam Leland, univ. prof.; b. Kincaid, Kan., Feb. 26, 1891; s. John Elwood and Minnie (Lee) B.; B.S., State Coll. of Wash., Pullman, Wash., 1915; M.S., Pa. State Coll., 1916; m. Faye Boggs, June 26, 1917; children—Richard Leland, Dorothy Faye, Robert Elwood, Betty Louise. Prof. of dairy production, Pa. State Coll. Served as 2d lt., Inf., U.S. Army (9 months overseas) during World War. Mem. Am. Dairy Science Assn., Gamma Sigma Delta, Alpha Zeta, Lambda Chi Alpha. Presbyterian. Address: 141 Ridge Av., State College, Pa.

BEAMAN, J(ames) Frank(lin), news writer and editor; b. Pueblo, Colo., Oct. 26, 1897; s. James Lincoln and Jeanette (Bowman) B.; ed. pub. sch. and high sch., Pueblo, Colo., 1904-16; m. Helen Walsh, Oct., 1918 (now dec.); 1 dau., Janet; m. 2d, Virginia Gunning, Aug. 20, 1927. Newspaper reporter at Pueblo, Colo., Cleveland, O., and Huntington, W.Va., 1915-17; asso. with United Press in various exec. positions and in various cities, 1917-28; editor various papers, 1928-36; financial editor Phila. Record, 1936-38; chief publicity activities Emergency Council State Assns., 1938; with Curtis Publishing Co., Phila., since 1939. Hon. mem. Sigma Delta Chi (journalism), O. State U., 1927. Episcopalian. Home: 100 W. Albemarle Av., Lansdowne, Pa. Office: Curtis Publishing Co., Philadelphia, Pa.

BEAMAN, William W, banking; b. Bradford Co., Pa., Sept. 8, 1885; s. John W. and Frances (Wilson) B.; ed. pub. sch. and high sch., Troy, Pa., 1891-1903; unmarried. Asso. with First Nat. Bank, Troy, Pa., since 1905, cashier, 1912-37, pres. and dir. since 1937; treas. and dir. Troy Engine and Machine Co. Served as mem. Bd. Edn., Boro Schs., Troy, Pa.; mem. Bradford Co. Bd. Sch. Dirs. Trustee Mansfield State Teachers Coll. Democrat. Presbyterian (trustee First Ch.). Mason (K.T., 32°, Shriner). Clubs: Masonic, Rotary (Troy); Corey Creek Golf (Mansfield); Country (Dallas, Pa.). Home: 170 Center St. Office: Main and Exchange, Troy, Pa.

BEAMISH, Richard Joseph, lawyer, writer; b. Scranton, Pa., Nov. 6, 1869; s. Francis Allen and Mary (Loftus) B.; ed. high sch. and Sch. of the Lackawanna, Scranton; m. 3d, Maud Weatherly, Aug. 14, 1909; children—Dorothy (Mrs. John J. Madigan), Ella (Sister M. Amator), Richard J., Elsa. Admitted to Pa. bar, 1890 and began practice at Scranton; asst. dist. atty. Lackawanna Co., 1890-93; mng. editor Scranton Free Press, 1893-97, Carbondale (Pa.) Anthracite; directing editor Philadelphia Press, 1911-20; spl. writer, Philadelphia Inquirer; polit. editor Philadelphia Record; became sec. Commonwealth of Pa., Jan. 20, 1931; chief counsel Pa. Pub. Service Commn., 1935-37; mem. Pa. Pub. Utility Commn. since 1937. Managed the presidential campaign of Judge George Gray of Delaware for Democratic nomination, 1908. Mem. Pub. Service Commn., Pa., 1926. Mem. Aero Club of Pa. Clubs: Art, Friendly Sons of St. Patrick (Phila.); National Press (Washington). Author: History of the World War (with F. A. March), 1918; America's Part in the World War (with same), 1919; Lindbergh—the Lone Eagle, 1927. Contributor of articles to Tariff Review, etc. Writer of 20 articles on industrial conditions in Europe, many reprinted by Rep. Nat. Com. in presdl. campaign, 1928; mem. Latin-Am. tour of President-elect Hoover, winter 1928-29. Home: Riverview Manor Apts., Front and Harris Sts. Address: Public Utility Commission, Capitol Bldg., Harrisburg, Pa.

BEAN, Albert Morton, supt. schs.; b. Centre Point, Montgomery Co., Pa., Sept. 15, 1888; s. Irwin Harley and Ella C (Kriebel) B.; student North Wales (Pa.) High Sch., 1901-04, Perkiomen Sch., 1904-06; A.B., Dickinson Coll., 1910, A.M., 1914; student Columbia U., Teachers Coll., 1914-15, U. of Pa. Sch. of Edn., 1919-29; m. Bessie Russell Leslie, June 30, 1923. Teacher Windber (Pa.) High Sch., 1910-12, Bethlehem (Pa.) High Sch., 1912-14; prin. elementary and Jr. schs., Camden, N.J., 1914-24; city supt. schs., Gloucester City, N.J., 1924-30; county supt. schs., Camden, N.J., since 1930. Served as sergeant, 78th Div., 312th Inf., Co. F. Mem. council Boy Scouts of America. Mem. N.E.A., N.J. Council of Edn., Camden County Coordinating Council, Am. Legion, Phi Delta Kappa, Theta Chi. Methodist. Mason. Club: Rotary. Home: 225 Windsor Ave., Haddonfield, N.J. Office: Court House, Camden, N.J.

BEAN, Arthur Nicholas, clergyman, writer; b. Riegelsville, Pa., July 18, 1877; s. Tobias Trauger and Elizabeth Clarissa Ann (Nicholas) B.; ed. Riegelsville Acad., 1892-96, Gettysburg (Pa.) Coll., 1897-1901, Luth. Theol. Sem., Gettysburg, 1901-04; hon. D.D., Gettysburg Coll., 1922; m. Ada Marguerite Horine, Dec. 12, 1907; children—Beatrice Salome, Marion Horine, Charlotte Helen Sunday (Mrs. Wilhelm Franz Goetze), Elizabeth Rebecca. Ordained to ministry of United Luth. Synod of N.Y., Oct. 14, 1904; organizer and pastor First English Luth. Ch., Paterson, N.J., 1904-27; pastor Epiphany Luth. Ch., Irvington, N.J., since 1930. Pres. Paterson Ministers' Assn., 1915-23; v.p. Paterson Council of Chs., 1920-25; exec. sec. Fed. Chs. of Passaic and Bergen Counties; founder Paterson interdenominational Good Friday services and chmn., 1914-26; active in bringing notable musicians to Paterson. Fellow Institute of American Genealogy; member New Jersey Sons Am. Revolution, Am. Flag House and Betsy Ross Memorial Assn., Pa. Soc. of N.J. (chaplain since 1928), Internat. Benjamin Franklin Soc., Internat. Goodwill Congress, World Alliance for Internat. Friendship through the Churches, 1926-28, English Speaking Union, Hist. Soc. of N.J., Passaic Co. Hist. Soc., S.A.R. (chaplain capt. Godwin Chapter, Paterson 1939), Phi Sigma Kappa. Voted one of Paterson's 10 foremost citizens in newspaper ballot, 1925. Republican. Author of books: Thoughts for This Day, 1928; Helps by the Way, 1930; The Bridges We Cross, 1938; Cords That Hold, 1939. Contbr. of syndicated articles. Editor of The Lutheran Messenger, 1912-26. Writer of songs: Alone with God, Arise, Oh My Soul, Delaware, My Own, Blossomtime, The Long Ago, Oh My Bermuda Night. Address: 211 Montclair Av., Newark, N.J.

BEAN, Oscar O., mgr. and treas. Intelligencer Co. Address: Doylestown, Pa.

BEAN, Theodore Lane, lawyer; b. Norristown, Pa., June 27, 1878; s. Col. Theodore Weber and Hannah (Heebner) B.; grad. Norristown High School, 1893; B.S., University of Pa., 1899, B.L. from same university, 1902; m. Sarah Albertson Hunter, October 14, 1903 (she died Apr. 30, 1908); children—Mary Hunter (Mrs. Richard Rogers), Elizabeth Lee (Mrs. Franklin B. Wildman, Jr.); m. 2d, Adele Cantrell, Aug. 18, 1917. Admitted to Pa. bar, 1902, and since practiced in Norristown; burgess of Norristown, 1903; asst. dist. atty., Montgomery Co., 1905; state senator, 1935-38; vice-pres. and dir.

Montgomery Nat. Bank; dir. Montgomery Trust Co.; pres. and dir. Norristown Water Co. Mem. Beta Theta Pi, Phi Delta Phi. Republican. Episcopalian. Mason (32°). Clubs: Bachelors Barge Loyal Legion, Union League, Merion Cricket, Radnor Hunt. Home: Trooper Rd., West Norriton Twp., Montgomery Co., Pa. Office: 317 Swede St., Norristown, Pa.

BEANE, John G., clergyman; b. Frostburg, Md., June 1, 1864; s. William and Mary (Brogan) B.; St. Charles Coll., Md.; St. Mary's Sch., Baltimore; S.T.B., 1893. Ordained priest R.C. Church, 1894; asst. priest St. Paul's Cathedral, Pittsburgh, 1893-1903; pastor Corpus Christi Ch., Pittsburgh since 1903. Address: 1550 Lincoln Av., Pittsburgh, Pa.*

BEANS, Robert Taney, newspaper man; b. Wheeling, W.Va.; s. William C. and Adah B.; student pub. schs. and high sch., Wheeling, W.Va.; m. Aug. 1, 1906; 1 dau., Betty Jane. Began as reporter and artist on Wheeling Register; reported, city and telegraph editor Wheeling Intelligencer to 1905; editor W.Va. Oil Review, Sistersville, 1905; returned to Wheeling Intelligencer, 1906; then editor Wheeling Telegraph; later state editor, now city editor Wheeling Intelligencer, Wheeling, W.Va. Home: Bridgeport, O. Office: Intelligencer, Wheeling, W.Va.

BEAR, Raymond R., v.p. and gen. mgr. Lehigh Portland Cement Co. Address: Allentown, Pa.

BEARD, John Adams, lawyer; b. Berks Co., Pa., June 30, 1861; s. Augustus Warren and Amanda Louise (Bechtel) B.; student Mifflinburg (Pa.) High Sch., 1877-84; m. Minerva J. Pellman, Nov. 1, 1900 (died Mar. 29, 1919). Admitted to Pa. bar, 1888, and since in practice at Mifflinburg, Pa.; v.p. Mifflinburg Bank and Trust Co.; pres. Kooltex Knitting Mills. Republican. Reformed Church. Mason (32°). Club: Accacia, Williamsport, Pa. Home: 431 Chestnut St., Mifflinburg, Pa.

BEARD, Myrtle Hafer; b. Reading, Pa., Jan. 8, 1902; d. Edward H. and Julia (Weida) Hafer; grad. Reading High Sch., 1919; m. John A. Beard; Nov. 29, 1923; children—John Amos, Jr., Janice Julia. Charge of general insurance office, Reading, Pa., 1919-25; home duties, 1925-36; sec. to chief clerk of county commrs., Berks Co., Pa., 1936-37, chief clerk since 1937 (first woman chief clerk in Berks Co.). Soprano soloist Grace Luth. Ch., 1917-22, St. Mary's Episcopal Ch., 1922-24. Pres. West Reading Dem. Women's Assn. since 1932; mem. Dem. Com. of West Reading, 1932-36. Lutheran. Home: 5 Hillside Rd., Wyomissing Hills. Office: Court House, Reading, Pa.

BEARD, William M.; pres. Westfield Trust Co. Address: Westfield, N.J.

BEARDEN, Joyce Alvin, univ. prof.; b. Greenville, S.C., Oct. 19, 1903; s. Joseph Sylvester and Annie (Haley) B.; B.A., Furman U., Greenville, S.C., 1923; Ph.D., U. of Chicago, 1926; m. Lillian Lavonia Singleton, June 6, 1923; 1 son, Alan Joyce. Fellow, U. of Chicago, 1925, asst., 1926, instr. in physics, 1926-29; asso. in physics, Johns Hopkins, 1929-32, asso. prof., 1932-39, prof. since 1939. Fellow Am. Phys. Soc., mem. Phi Beta Kappa, Sigma Xi. Baptist. Clubs: Johns Hopkins Faculty, Maryland Yacht (Baltimore, Md.). Address: 312 Southway, Baltimore, Md.

BEARDSLEE, Claude Gillette, univ. prof.; b. West Springfield, Mass., June 25, 1888; s. Clark Smith and Emma Gillette (Alvord) B.; A.B., Yale, 1909; B.D., Hartford (Conn.) Theol. Sem., 1912, S.T.M., 1913; M.A., U. of Southern Calif., 1922; Ph.D., Brown U., 1931; m. Pauline Dustin Johnson, Aug. 26, 1914 (died 1918); 1 dau., Caroline; m. 2d Louise Meech Miner, Sept. 23, 1920; children—Ruth, Betsy Remembrance, Claudia Gillette, Alvord Miner. Ordained ministry Congl. Ch., 1914; pastor Southington, Conn., 1914-20; supt. of employment, Peck, Stow & Wilcox Co., Southington, 1920-21; grad. asst., later instr. and asst. prof. philosophy, U. of Southern Calif., 1921-24; pastor Kingston, R.I., 1924-29; grad. student asst. in philosophy, Brown U., 1929-31; prof. moral and religious philosophy, also chaplain, Lehigh U., since 1931. Served as pvt., advancing to 2d lt. arty., U.S.A., 1917-19. Mem. Am. Philos. Assn., Am. Assn. Univ. Profs., Phi Kappa Epsilon, Omicron Delta Kappa. Republican. Mason. Home: 745 Delaware Av., Bethlehem, Pa.

BEARDSLEE, John Walter, Jr., theologian; b. Constantine, Mich., July 11, 1879; s. John Walter and Sarah Eliza (Armitage) B.; A.B., Hope Coll., Mich., 1898, D.D., 1913; A.M., U. of Chicago 1900; grad. Western Theological Seminary, Holland, Michigan, 1903; Ph.D., University of Chicago, 1913; D.D., Rutgers College, 1922; D.Th., Faculté libre de Théologie Protestante de Paris, 1936; m. Frances Eunice Davis, of Boston, Massachusetts, Aug. 8, 1912; children—John Walter, William Armitage, Frank Palmer, David Cromwell, Ellen. Ordained ministry Ref. Ch. in America, 1910; prof. ethics, 1905-12, prof. Latin, 1912-13, Hope Coll.; prof. N.T. lang. and lit. Western Theol. Sem., 1913-17; prof. Hellenistic Greek and N.T. exegesis, New Brunswick Theol. Sem. since 1917, pres. since 1935. Vice-pres. Bd. of Foreign Missions of Ref. Ch. in America; v.p. Gen. Synod, Reformed Ch. in America, 1937-38; mem. Phi Beta Kappa, Soc. Bibl. Lit. and Exegesis. Club: University (N.Y). Author: Nature in Fifth Century Greek Literature, 1918. Home: 25 Seminary Pl., New Brunswick, N.J.

BEARDSLEY, Edward John Gillespie, physician; b. Roxbury, Conn., May 31, 1879; s. Lewis Bulkely and Mary Agnes (Gillespie) B.; student Parker Classical Acad., Woodbury, Conn., 1892-93, Waterbury (Conn.) High Sch., 1893-96, Phila. Coll. of Pharmacy, 1896-98; M.D., Jefferson Med. Coll., Phila., Pa., 1902; m. Minerva Louise Post, June 1917; children—Mary Louise Wolcott, John Post, Richard Hunt. Interne Phila. Gen. Hosp., 1902-04, Municipal Hosp. for Contagious Diseases, 1905; externe East London (Eng.) Gen. Hosp., 1906; asso. with Jefferson Med. Coll. and Hosp., Phila., since 1906, serving in various teaching capacities, now clin. prof. medicine. Served as capt. Med. Reserve Corps, U.S. Army, June-Nov. 1917, Major to 1918, lt. col., 1918-19. Licentiate Royal Coll. Physicians of Eng.; mem. Am. Coll. Physicians, Am. Clin. Assn., Phi Alpha Sigma (nat. sec.). Republican. Address: 1919 Spruce St., Philadelphia, Pa.

BEARDSLEY, Wilfred A.; prof. Romance lang., Goucher Coll. Address: Goucher Coll., Baltimore, Md.

BEARDWOOD, Matthew, M.D., chemist; b. Cape May City, N.J., June 22, 1872; s. Matthew and Jane (Mitchell) B.; A.B., Central High Sch., Phila., 1890, A.M., 1895; M.D., Medico-Chirurg. Coll., Phila., 1894; spl. student, U. of Pa., 1906-08, U. of Edinburgh, 1909; (Sc.D., Ursinus, 1916); unmarried. In gen. med. practice, Phila., since 1895. Instr. chemistry, 1896-99, lecturer on clin. chemistry, 1899-1900, adj. prof. chemistry, 1900-14, prof. gen. chemistry and toxicology, 1914-16, Medico-Chirurg. Coll.; prof. chemistry, Ursinus Coll. since 1903. Mem. Am. Chem. Soc., A.M.A., Phila. County Med. Soc., Zeta Delta, Phi Beta Pi. Republican. Odd Fellow. Author: Students Notes on Toxicology, 1904. Home: 5500 Ridge Av., Philadelphia, Pa.

BEASON, Ross, pres. Quarterly Income Shares, Inc. Address: 15 Exchange Pl., Jersey City, N.J.

BEATTIE, Lester Middleswarth, asso. prof. English; b. New London, O., Nov. 26, 1887; s. John H. and Martha L. (Middleswarth) B.; A.B., Oberlin Coll., 1914; A.M., Harvard U., 1920, Ph.D., same, 1931; unmarried. Engaged as instr. English, Oberlin Coll., 1914-18, U. of Wis., 1919-21; asst. prof. English, Carleton Coll., 1921-23; instr. English, Tufts Coll., 1924-26, asst. prof., 1926-28; asst. prof. English, Carnegie Inst. Tech., 1928-31, asso. prof. since 1931. Served as pvt. C.A., U.S.A., 1918; 2d lt. C.A. Res. Corps, 1918-22. Mem. Modern Lang. Assn. of America, Am. Assn. Univ. Profs., Phi Beta Kappa, Phi Kappa Phi. Congist. Author: John Arbuthnot, Mathematician and Satirist, 1935. Home: 7 Olympia Place, Pittsburgh, Pa.

BEATTIE, Robert Brewster, clergyman; b. Middletown, N.Y., Sept. 19, 1875; s. Rev. Charles (D.D.) and Harriet Harris (Tobias) B.; prep. edn., Wallkill Acad., Middletown; B.A., Union Coll., Schenectady, N.Y., 1896, D.D., 1917; grad. Princeton Theol. Sem. 1899; m. Cecilia Dolson, Nov. 2, 1899; 1 son, Charles Robert. Ordained ministry Presbyn. Ch., 1899; pastor Broad Av. Presbyn. Ch., Altoona, Pa., 1899-1903, First Ch., Franklin, 1903-12, First Presbyn. Ch., East Orange, N.J., since 1912. Mem. Bd. Christian Edn. of Presbyn. Ch., U.S.A. Trustee Bloomfield Sem., Home for Aged Presbyterians (Belvidere, N.J.). Mem. Beta Theta Pi. Clubs: Essex County Country, Rock Spring Country. Home: 9 S. Munn Av., East Orange, N.J.

BEATTY, Albert McGaffey, motion picture engr. and exec.; b. Cloud Co., Kan., May 25, 1884; s. William Tracy and Mary (McGaffey) B.; ed. grammar and high school, Kansas City, Mo., and correspondence courses and night schools; m. Lillian Lidlow, Jan. 5, 1919; children—Roger Lindlar, Ruth Elizabeth. Began as clerk in wholesale drygoods store, 1901, later traveling salesman; picture theatre owner, laboratory worker, 1920-23; exec. sec. Motion Picture Chamber of Commerce of America, 1923-27; now vice-pres. United Cinema Co., New York, vice-pres. Austin K. Herba, Inc., Charlotte, N.C., pres. since 1928; sales mgr. Internat. Projector Corpn.; vice-pres. and sec. J. M. Wall Machine Co.; pres. Callaghen Publicity Film Co.; pres. Beatty & Sutphen. Served in Mo. Nat. Guard 6 years; during World War was Y.M.C.A. sec. with A.E.F. in charge of all entertainment. Mem. Soc. Motion Picture Engrs., Am. Projection Soc., Motion Picture Council. Republican. Mem. Christian Ch. Mason. Home: 142 Beech St., Nutley, N.J.

BEATTY, Henry Townsend, clergyman; b. Conshohocken, Pa., June 29, 1863; s. James and Margaret Ann (Rhoads) B.; grad. Conshohocken High Sch., 1881, Tremont Sem., Norristown, Pa., 1883; A.B., Lafayette Coll., 1887, A.M., 1890; grad. Union Theol. Sem., 1890; Ph.D., New York U., 1898; D.D., Lafayette Coll., 1909; m. Jane Dumont, of Phillipsburg, N.J., Sept. 6, 1890 (died 1934); children—Harold Dumont, Florence (Mrs. William L. Phelps), Herbert Campbell. Ordained Presbyn. ministry, 1890; pastor First Ch., Hoboken, since 1890. Apptd. chaplain with rank of 1st lt., O.R.C., 1922; now inactive. Trustees Presbytery of Jersey City since 1904. Charter mem. Delta Upsilon. Republican. Received spl. diploma at 50th anniversary of graduation from Lafayette Coll., 1937. Home: 1036 Bloomfield St., Hoboken, N.J.

BEATTY, John David; personnel officer; b. Pittsburgh, Pa., Oct. 4, 1896; s. Joseph and Sarah (Kerr) B.; student Stetson Acad., DeLand, Fla., 1911-14; B.S., Carnegie Inst. Tech., 1920, C.E., 1928; m. Mary C. Hulley, Dec., 1923; children—Marcia Jane, Marie Louise. Night supt. Dravo Contracting Co., 1920-21; high sch. prin., Bergholz, O., 1921-22; constrn. engr. Jones & Laughlin Steel Corpn., 1922-24; engr. Portland Cement Assn., 1924-26; head bur. of recommendations and sec. mining and metall. advisory bds., Carnegie Inst. Tech. since 1926; v.p., dir. Nat. Industrial Pub. Co.; treas. dir. Carnegie Tech. Credit Union. Served 2d lt. 163rd Aero Squadron, 2d Day Bombardment Group, U.S. Army, with A.E.F., 1917-18. Dir. of work Allegheny Co. Emergency Assn., 1931-32; sec. and treas. Pittsburgh Personnel Assn. Mem. Am. Soc. C.E., Engrs. Soc. of Western Pa., Theta Xi (sec. and dir. Theta Xi Club of Pittsburgh). Episcopalian. Mason. Club: Stanton Heights of Pittsburgh. Contbr. articles on personnel, etc., to jours. Home: Roseyards, R.D. 1, Valencia, Pa.

BEATTY, Joseph Moorhead, Jr., coll. prof.; b. Villa Nova, Pa., Jan. 23, 1891; s. Joseph Moorhead and Laura Milburn (Schaefer) B.; A.B., Haverford (Pa.) Coll., 1913; A.M., Harvard, 1914, Ph.D., 1917; m. Elizabeth Tatum Rhoads, June 4, 1927 (died 1928). Instr. in English, Goucher Coll., Baltimore 1917-20, asst. prof., 1920-23, asso. prof., 1923-30, prof. since 1930. Mem. Modern Lang. Assn., Am.

Assn. Univ. Profs., Haverford Soc. of Md. (v.p.), Phi Beta Kappa. Republican. Mem. Soc. of Friends. Clubs: Soc. of the Cincinnati of Pa., Founders Club of Haverford Coll. Writer of articles on literary and geneal. subjects. Home: 308 Thornhill Road, Baltimore, Md.

BEATTY, Ralph P., urologist Uniontown Hosp. and Connellsville State Hosp. Address: 42 W. Main St., Uniontown, Pa.

BEATTYS, George Davis, lawyer; b. Poughkeepsie, N.Y., July 20, 1862; s. George Hubbell and Mary Elizabeth (Davis) B.; A.B., Wesleyan U., Conn., 1885, A.M., 1888; LL.B., Columbia, 1887; m. Jessie L. McDermut, Oct. 22, 1890 (died Feb. 20, 1932); children—Frank L., Mrs. Adele M. Beatty, Mrs. Madeleine Dobbrow, Mrs. Jessie Rogers. Practiced in N.Y. City since 1887; gen. counsel Æolian Co. Mutual Bond & Mortgage Corpn.; asst. corpn. counsel Brooklyn, 1906. Mem. 7th Regt. N.Y.N.G., 5 yrs.; prize commr. E. Dist., N.Y., Spanish-Am. War. Mem. bd. mgrs. Methodist Hosp., Am. Bible Soc.; trustee John St. M.E. Ch. Trust Fund Soc. (pres.). Trustee Wesleyan U., Conn., 1905-35. Mem. Gen. Conf. of Meth. Ch., 1936. Mem. Am. Bar Assn., N.Y. State Bar Assn., Assn. Bar City of N.Y., Phi Nu Theta and Phi Beta Kappa (Wesleyan). Republican. Methodist. Mason. Home: Westfield, N.J. Office: 27-29 W. 57th St., New York, N.Y.

BEAVER, Harry C., mfr. pumps and machinery; b. McAlisterville, Pa., Aug. 13, 1876; s. Spencer F. and Minerva (Beasor) B.; ed. Juniata Coll., Huntingdon, Pa., Martin's Business Sch., Pittsburgh, Marquette Univ. Law Sch.; m. Jane Carvel, Jan. 17, 1901; children—Paul F., Winifred (Mrs. A. N. Clifton), Harry C. Began with Pa. Co., 1896; successively with U.P. R.R., Westinghouse Electric and Mfg. Co., Allis-Chalmers Mfg. Co. (Milwaukee), Stevens-Duryea Co. and Rolls-Royce Co. of America (both of Springfield, Mass.), until 1930; pres. Worthington Pump and Machinery Corpn. (Harrison, N.J.), since 1930. Conglist. Home: Longmeadow, Mass. Address: Worthington Pump and Machinery Corpn., Harrison, N.J.

BEAVER, J. Lynford, prof. of elec. engring.; b. Phoenixville, Pa., Aug. 25, 1882; s. Frank and Eleanora Shippley (Rowland) B.; Ed. M., West Chester State Teachers Coll., 1900; E.E., Lehigh U., 1904, M.S., 1921; Sc.D., Harvard, 1932; m. Henrietta Elizabeth McClatchey, Mar. 29, 1910; children—Donald P., Margaret Walker (Mrs. Alex List), Mary Elizabeth, Ann Harrison. Elec. inspr. N.Y. Fire Ins. Exchange, 1904-05; instr. of elec. engr., U. of Pa., 1905-07, Drexel Tech. Inst., 1907-13; distribution dept. Phila. Electric Co., 1917-18; asst. prof. of elec. engring., Lehigh U., 1918-25, assoc. prof., 1925-32, prof. of elec. engring. since 1932; elec. engring. dept. Phila. Electric Co., 1937. Mem. Sch. Bd. of Moravian Prep. Sch. Fellow Am. Inst. Elec. Engring.; mem. Soc. for promotion of Engring. Edn.; mem. A.A.A.S., Tau Beta Pi, Eta Kappa Nu, Theta Xi. Republican. Mem. Moravian Ch. Clubs: Torch, Engineers (Lehigh Valley). Home: 402 High St., Bethlehem, Pa.

BEAVER, William H., partner Keen & Co.; mem. N.Y. Stock Exchange. Home: Haverford, Pa. Office: 1342 Fidelity-Philadelphia Trust Bldg., Philadelphia, Pa.

BECHTOLD, Frank, Jr., chemist; b. Brooklyn, N.Y., Aug. 5, 1896; s. Frank and Franziska (Schmitt) B.; B.S. in Chemistry, Poly. Inst., Brooklyn, 1918; grad. study, Columbia U., 1919-20; m. Mary Howes, Aug. 3, 1935. Employed as supervising chemist, Doehler Die Casting Co., Brooklyn, N.Y., 1919-20; asst. chief chemist, Aluminum Die Casting Corpn., Garwood, N.J., 1921-27, United States Aluminum Co., 1928-33; chief chemist, Garwood Plant of Aluminum Co. of America, Garwood, N.J. since 1933. Mem. A.A.A.S., Am. Chem. Soc., Am. Soc. for Metals. Presbyn. Home: 8 Columbia Av., Cranford. Office: Aluminum Co. of America, Garwood, N.J.

BECHTOLD, Gustavus Henry, clergyman; b. Philadelphia, Pa., Jan. 8, 1882; s. Gustav Conrad and Magdalene (Baumgartner) B.; student Phila. pub. schs., Allentown Prep. Sch., Muhlenberg Coll., Lutheran Theol. Sem. (Phila.); D.D., Muhlenberg Coll.; m. Leona M. Wetmore, 1912; children—Esther Caroline, Gustav Henry, Austin Theodore, Leona Madaline. Pastor Church of the Atonement, Asbury Park, N.J., 1912-14; dir. Lutheran Settlement and Martin Luther Neighborhood House, Phila., 1914-22; v.p. Bd. of Social Missions of United Lutheran Ch. since 1922. Mem. bd. Children's Country Week Assn., Pa. Prison Soc., Pa. Assn. for Blind; chmn. Phila. Ednl. Week for Blind; sec. Samaritan Shelter. Address: 1228 Spruce St., Philadelphia, Pa.

BECK, Charles E., physician and surgeon; b. Stone Church, Pa., Sept. 18, 1867; s. George Ezra and Mary (Wolslayer) B.; student West Chester State Normal Sch., 1886-89; M.D., Medico-Chirurgical Med. Sch., 1893; m. Mary Jane Brands, June 9, 1897; 1 dau., Edith May (Mrs. Walter E. Emery). In gen. practice of medicine Zelienople, Pa., 1893-94, Portland, Pa. since 1894; on auxiliary staff of Gen. Hosp., East Stroudsburg, Pa., and Easton (Pa.) Hosp.; v.p. Portland Nat. Bank; postmaster, Portland, 1909-14. School dir. and pres. of town council for many years. Mem. A.M.A., Pa. State Med. Soc., Northampton County Med. Soc. (past pres.), Lehigh Valley Med. Soc. (past pres.), and county med. socs. Republican. Presbyterian (elder for many years and clerk of session). Mason (K.T., 32°, Shriner). Club: Saw Creek Hunting and Fishing (East Stroudsburg, Pa.). Address: Portland, Pa.

BECK, Charles W., Jr., engraving; b. Phila., Pa.; s. Charles W. and Julia (de Lacy) B.; student Temple U.; m. Helen Woodward, Oct. 24, 1899. With Beck Engraving Co. since beginning of active career, now pres., treas. and dir. Home: Crescent Road, Wyncote, Pa. Office: 7th and Sansom Sts., Philadelphia, Pa.

BECK, Harvey Grant, physician; b. York Co., Pa., Aug. 15, 1870; s. John F. and Matilda (Leader) B.; Ph.G., Md. Coll. Pharmacy, Baltimore, 1893; M.D., Coll. Phys. & Surgs., Baltimore, 1896; (hon.) D.Sc., Washington Coll., Chestertown, Md., 1916; m. Katherine Elizabeth Clagett, Sept. 23, 1903; children—Luther Clagett, Frances Ford. Interne Mercy Hosp., Baltimore, 1896-97; engaged in gen. practice of medicine at Baltimore since 1897; visiting physician and consultant Sinai Hosp., Mercy Hosp.; consultant Franklin Square Hosp.; visiting physician Church Home & Infirmary, Univ. Hosp., Union Memorial Hosp., Baltimore; prof. clin. medicine, U. of Md. Sch. of Medicine since 1915, Coll. of Physicians and Surgeons, Baltimore, 1910-1915. Served as mem. local draft bd., Baltimore during World War. Fellow Am. Coll. Physicians; mem. A.M.A., Am. Therapeutic Soc., Assn. for Study Internal Secretions, Southern Med. Assn., Med. & Chirurg. Faculty Md., Baltimore City Med. Soc., Biol. Soc. U. of Md., Research Soc., Phi Beta Pi. Republican. Lutheran. Mason. Club: University. Contbr. articles to med. jours. Home: 215 Northway, Guilford. Office: 100 E. 23d St., Baltimore, Md.

BECK, Herbert Huebener, prof. chemistry; b. Lititz, Pa., Nov. 15, 1875; s. Abraham R. and Joanna (Huebener) B.; ed. Beck Family Sch., 1881-91, Ulrich Prep. Sch., 1891-92; B.S., Lehigh U., 1896; grad. student Royal Tech. High Sch., Berlin, Germany, 1904; (hon.) D.Sc., Franklin and Marshall Coll., 1935; m. Gladys Thome, June 15, 1916; children—Bernard Grube, Margarita, Samuel Thome. Began as chemist Pennsylvania Soap Co., Lancaster, Pa., 1896 and continued to 1931; instr. chemistry and mineralogy, Franklin and Marshall Coll., 1901-08, prof. and head dept. since 1908; cons. chemist on food stuffs, fertilizers and brewing. Vice-pres. bd. trustees Linden Hall Sch. for Girls Jr. Coll. Mem. Am. Chem. Soc., Am. Branch Newcomen Soc. of Eng., Am. Ornithologists Union, Del. Valley Ornithol. Club: Lancaster Co. Historical Soc. (pres. since 1924), Moravian Hist. Soc. (vice-pres.), Cliosophic Soc. of Lancaster, Delta Upsilon, Tau Beta Pi. Republican. Moravian. Author: Minerals of Lancaster Co., 1912; Ornithology of Lancaster Co., 1924. Contbr. to mags. and journs. Reviewer of books. Home: 515 President Av., Lancaster, Pa.

BECK, Jean-Baptiste, prof. Romanic langs. and history of music; b. Guebwiller, Alsace, Aug. 14, 1881; s. Jean-Baptiste and Barbara (LaWurlin) B.; ed. École Alsacienne, Paris, U. of Strasbourg, Sorbonne and École des Hautes Études, Paris; Ph.D., U. of Strasbourg, 1907; m. Louise Goebel, June 15, 1912; children—Jean-Marie Baumont, Marie-Louise, Prof. Latin, École Alsacienne, 1900-02; French exchange prof., U. of Vienna, 1910; prof. Romanic langs., U of Ill., 1911-14, Bryn Mawr Coll., 1914-20, U. of Pa. since 1920; prof. history of music, Yvette Guilbert Sch., 1916-18, Columbia and Inst. Mus. Art, 1919-20, Curtis Inst. Music, 1924-1938. Organist, St. Léger, 1899, St. Gervais, Paris, 1900-02. Fellow Am. Mediæval Soc.; Fellow Am. Geog. Soc.; mem. Am. Inst. Polit. Science, Am. Musicol. Soc. (exec. bd.), Council of Learned Socs. (com. on musicology); rep. of Curtis Inst. of Music at Beethoven Centennial, Vienna, 1927. Catholic. Author: Die Melodien der Troubadours, 1908; La Musique des Troubadours, 1909; Corpus Cantilenarum Medii Aevi: he Manuscrit Cangé, 1927; he Manuscrit du Roi (in collaboration with Madame Louise Beck), 1938. Discoverer of key to translation of mediæval music. Home: 125 Radnor St., Bryn Mawr, Pa.

BECK, John Albert, petroleum refining; b. Karns City, Pa., Sept. 14, 1884; s. George and Anna Marie (Bezler) B.; m. Elva Frazier, Sept. 22, 1914; children—Mary Elizabeth, John A., Thomas F., Elva Isabel, Nettie Jane, George A., Marjorie Ann. Began as petroleum refiner, 1904; pres. and dir. Pa. Refining Co. since 1906; v.p. and dir. Pa. Coal Products Co. Republican. Lutheran. Mason. Address: Karns City, Pa.

BECK, Paul R., oil refining; b. Karns City, Pa., July 20, 1896; s. George and Anna Marie (Bezler) B.; grad. Butler City High Sch., 1914; student Washington & Jefferson Coll., 1916-18; m. Helen Katherine Smiley, Oct. 2, 1919; children—Paul Richard, Wilhelmina. With Pa. Refining Co. since 1918, beginning with gen. office work, sec. and treas. since 1924. Mem. Phi Gamma Delta. Republican. Lutheran. Mason (32°). Clubs: Rotary, Butler Country (Butler). Home: 610 E. Pearl St. Office: Pa. Refining Co., Butler, Pa.

BECK, Solomon Scott, lawyer; b. Kent Co., Md., Feb. 13, 1883; s. George and Kate Rosa (Harris) B.; student pub. schs. of Kent County, Md.; A.B., Washington Coll., 1903; LL.B., U. of Md. Law Sch., 1906; m. Mackey Perry, Dec. 9, 1909; children—S. Scott, Jr., Betty. Admitted to Md. bar, 1906; since in gen. practice of law; mem. law firm (with son) Beck & Beck since 1938; pres. Chestertown Bank of Md. Sec. and mem. bd. Visitors and Governors of Washington Coll. Mem. Md. Bar. Assn. Democrat. Episcopalian. Mason. Club: Chester River Yacht and Country (Chestertown). Address: Chestertown, Md.

BECKER, Edgar Allen, v.p. and treas. Industrial Press.; b. Baltimore, Md., Jan. 19, 1879; s. Louis and Ida L. (Zimmerman) B.; ed. private schs., Baltimore and Marston U.; married; 1 son, Edgar Louis. Began as office boy C. H. Pearson Packing Co., Baltimore, 1896; held position with C. L. Applegarth & Co., Baltimore, Adams Express Co., Baltimore, and with D. F. Kelly (now Kelly Becker & Co.), accountants; with Industrial Press, pubs., N.Y. City, since 1918, now v.p. and treas.; treas. and sec. Industrial Corpn. of N.J. Home: 249 Gardner Road, Ridgewood, N.J. Office: 148 Lafayette St., New York, N.Y.

BECKER, John Brugger, physician and surgeon; b. Harrisburg, Pa., Jan. 6, 1886; s. William F. and Nora I. (Brugger) B.; M.D., Medico-Chirurg. Coll., 1910; studies U. of Pa. Post Grad. Sch., 1926; m. Marie Meyers, June 12, 1911. Employed as stenographer, 1906; interne Medico-Chirurg. Coll. Hosp., 1910-11; engaged in gen. practice of medicine and surgery at Phila. since 1911, specializing in proctology since 1926. Served in Med. Corps U.S.N.R.F., 1918-19; lieut. Med. Corps U.S.N.R. Med. examiner Artisans Order of Mutual Protection. Pres.

Phila. Operatic Soc., 1933-34. Tenor soloist Walnut Street Presbyn. Ch., Phila. Mem. Phila. Clin. Soc. (bd. dirs. 1938). Ptolemy Soc. Republican. Presbyn. Mason. Club: Plays and Players. Home: 5211 Chester Av. Office: 1930 Chestnut St., Philadelphia, Pa.

BECKER, Joseph, corpn. exec.; b. Essen, Germany, Oct. 1, 1887; s. Johann and Maria (Duwentester) B.; ed. elementary schs., Germany; Dr. Engring., Lehigh U., 1933; m. Dorothea Molitor, Aug. 10, 1912; children—Dorothy Elizabeth (Mrs. John Woade), John Joseph, Joseph John. Came to U.S., 1910, naturalized, 1919. Coke plant operator, 1903-06; chemist in coal distillation, 1906-10; chief chemist, 1910-12; supt., 1912-15; cons. engr., 1915-20; corpn. exec. since 1920; v.p., dir. and gen. mgr. of engring. and constrn. div. Koppers Co.; v.p. Koppers United Co.; trustee Eastern Gas & Fuel Associates; dir. Comn. Coke Co., Koppers Coal Co., New England Coal & Coke Co. Awarded Walton Clark medal of Franklin Inst. Mem. Iron and Steel Inst., Engrs. Soc. Western Pa. Clubs: Duquesne, University, Pittsburgh Athletic Assn. (Pittsburgh); Oakmont Country (Oakmont, Pa.); Pittsburgh Field (Aspinwall, Pa.). Inventor of Becker coke oven and processes for recovery of byproducts in mfr. of gas and coke. Home: 910 Waldheim Rd., Sharpsburg, P.O., Pittsburgh, Pa. Office: Koppers Bldg., Pittsburgh, Pa.

BECKER, Leo V., M.D.; chief of staff Passaic County Welfare Home Hosp. Address: 69 Ward St., Paterson, N.J.

BECKER, Sylvanus A., coll. prof.; b. Northampton Co., Pa., July 12, 1879; s. Sylvanus A. and Mary A. (Meyer) B.; student high sch., Nazareth, Pa. 1898; C.E., Lehigh U., Bethlehem, Pa., 1903, M.S., 1909; m. Annie M. Reif, 1909. Asst. engr. B.& O. R. R., 1903-05, roadmaster Mo.P. R. R., 1905-06; instr. civil engring., Lehigh U., 1906-09, asst. prof., 1909-12, asso. prof. since 1912; cons. engr. since 1921. In charge highway and ry. engring. Vocational Training Sch., Camp Coppee, during World War. Mem. Am. Soc. C.E., Soc. Promotion of Engring. Edn., Engineer's Club of Lehigh Valley, Phi Sigma Kappa, Tau Beta Pi. Republican. Club: Bethlehem Country (Bethlehem, Pa.). Author: Descriptive Geometry Problem Layouts. Home: 3 E. North St. Office: Lehigh U., Bethlehem, Pa.

BECKER, Mrs. William A., pres. gen. D.A.R.; b. Westfield, N.J.; d. Ainsworth James and Susie (Baker) Hague; A.B., Smith Coll., Northampton, Mass., 1909; studied Columbia, 1911; L.H.D., Lincoln Memorial U.; m. William A. Becker, June 4, 1919. Mem. Nat. Soc. Founders and Patriots of America, Daughters of Am. Colonists, Daughters of Colonial Wars, Colonial Dames of America, Daughters of 1812, Nat. Soc. Daughters American Revolution (pres. gen.), Holland Dames of America. Presbyn. Contbr. to D.A.R. Mag. Home: 77 Prospect St., Summit, N.J.

BECKLEY, Clarence William, pres. C. Beckley, Inc.; b. Buffalo, N.Y., July 29, 1880; s. John and Elizabeth (Bley) B.; student high sch.; m. Mollie Stewart, 1906; 1 son, James Stewart. Pres. and gen. mgr. C. Beckley, Inc., since 1905; dir. De Luxe Metal Furniture Co. Warren (Pa.) Nat. Bank, Community Loan Co. of Warren (Pa.). Dir. Y.M.C.A., Warren, Pa. Mason. Club: Conewango. Home: 18 4th Av. Office: 244 Penn Av. West, Warren, Pa.

BECKLEY, Quitman F., clergyman, univ. chaplain; b. Frederick, Md., Feb. 5, 1891; s. Quitman Shields Joseph and Caroline (Kreh) B.; St. Patrick's Acad., St. Charles Coll.; J.C.B. Catholic Univ., 1915; post. grad. work in social sciences, 1915-17; LL.D., Providence Coll., 1928. Ordained to priesthood, 1915; apptd. mem. faculty Aquinas Coll., 1919; curate, later pastor St. Mary's Ch., Johnson City, Tenn. 1921-23; Western Mission Band, Dominican Order, 1923-26; curate St. Mary's Priory, New Haven, Conn., 1926; with Eastern Mission Band, Dominican Order, 1926-28; chaplain dir. Catholic activities, Princeton U. since 1928; formerly mem. faculty and trustee Providence Coll., spl. lecturer in liturgy, Westminster Choir Sch., Princeton, 1924-36. Chaplain U.S.N., later U.S.

M.C., 1917-19. Trustee Newman Sch., Lakewood, N.J., chaplain Am. Legion, 1930-36; comdr. Princeton Post, 1932. Mem. English Speaking Union, Catholic Round Table of Sciences. Ind. Democrat. Catholic. Clubs: Nassau (Princeton); Princeton (New York). Address: 121 Pyne Hall, Princeton, N.J.

BECKMAN, Irland McKnight, financial secretary; b. Erie, Pa., Sept. 28, 1897; s. William R. and Sarah King (McKnight) B.; student Yale, 1915-18; B.S. in Econ., Wharton Sch. of Finance and Commerce, U. of Pa., 1922; m. Dr. Elizabeth B. Hurlock, Dec. 21, 1931; children—Daryl Elizabeth, Gail McKnight. State bank examiner, Pa., 1923-24, 3d dep. sec. of banking, 1924-26, 2d dep. sec. of banking, 1926-34, 1st dep. sec. of banking, 1935-37, sec. of banking, 1937-39; chmn. State Banking Board, Pa., 1937-39; financial head Temple U. since Apr. 1939. Mem. Nat. Assn. of State Bank Supervisors (exec. com., 1938-39), Pa. Soc. of S.R. (Phila. Chapter). Presbyterian. Mason (Perry Lodge, Erie, Pa.; Scottish Rite). Clubs: Yale, Phila. Country (Phila.); Yale (N.Y.). Contbr. articles on banking and building and loan assns. to newspapers and mags. Home: The Cambridge, Alden Park, Germantown Philadelphia, Pa. Office: Temple University, Philadelphia, Pa.

BECKWITH, Charles Stewart, entomologist; b. Olean, N.Y., May 16, 1891; s. Charles Henry and Clementine (Porter) B.; grad. Olean High Sch., 1909; B.S., Rutgers Coll., 1914, M.S., 1924; m. Hilda Stults, Sept. 5, 1917. With N.J. Agrl. Expt. Sta. since 1914, as field entomologist, 1914-16, asst. entomologist, 1916-27, asso. entomologist, 1927-31, chief of cranberry and blueberry investigations since 1931; sec., treas. and dir. Atlantic Co. for Culture of Cranberries. Mayor of Pemberton, N.J., since 1939. Mem. A.A.A.S., Am. Assn. Economic Entomologists, Am. Cranberry Growers' Assn. (sect. treas.), Sigma Xi, Alpha Chi Rho. Republican. Presbyterian. Mason (Scottish Rite). Club: Rotary. Author: Cranberry Growing in New Jersey, 1931; Blueberry Culture, 1937. Home: Pemberton, N.J.

BECKWITH, Frank C.; chmn. bd. Hamilton Watch Co. Home: 1035 Woods Av., Lancaster, Pa.

BECKWITH, Frank Jennings, lawyer; b. Charles Town, W.Va., May 19, 1892; s Frank and Leacy (McDonald) B.; student Shenandoah Valley Acad., Winchester, Va., 1908-11; LL.B., Washington & Lee U. Law Sch., 1915; m. Margaret Shannon Denny, Aug. 31, 1935; children —Frank Denny, George Scollay. Admitted to W.Va. bar, 1915, and since engaged in gen. practice of law at Charles Town; admitted to practice before Supreme Ct. of the U.S., 1932; served as mem. W.Va. Ho. of Dels., 1921; mem. state exec. com. Am. Legion, 1921; title abstractor U.S. Forest Service, 1933; gen. receiver, circuit ct. Jefferson Co., W.Va., since 1936; mem. congl. exec. com. 2d dist. W.Va. since 1936; mem. W.Va. bd. edn., 1937-42; dir. and atty. Charles Town & Summit Point Bldg. & Loan Assn. Served as pvt. inf., U.S.A., 1918. Mem. Am. and W.Va. bar assns., Phi Kappa Sigma, Delta Theta Phi, Am. Legion. Democrat. Episcopalian. Mason. Home: 611 S. George St. Office: E. Washington St., Charles Town, W.Va.

BECKWITH, J. S., pres. Beckwith Machinery Co. Home: 6340 Darlington Rd. Office: 6550 Hamilton Av., Pittsburgh, Pa.

BEDFORD, Bruce, pres. Luzerne Rubber Co., United N.J. R.R. & Canal Co., Trenton Savings Fund Soc. Address: Trenton, N.J.

BEDFORD, Henry Pardee, lawyer; b. Newark, N.J., Jan. 4, 1887; s. Harry S. and Laura (Trenchard) B.; grad. high sch., Irvington, N.J.; studied law in office Hon. Jos. A. Beecher; m. Lela Smith, Irvington, N.J., June 27, 1910; children—Myrtle C., Henry P., Jr. Admitted to N.J. bar as atty., 1908, and since engaged in gen. practice of law at Irvington, admitted as counsellor, 1912; served as police court judge, Irvington, N.J., 1912-18; elected commr. Town of Irvington, 1922, served as commr. revenue and finance, 1924-34, town atty., 1934-35; pres.

Chancellor Trust Co. since 1932. Dir. Irvington Y.M.C.A., 10 years. Pres. bd. trustees First Christian Congl. Ch. Mem. Essex Co. Bar Assn. Republican. Conglist. Mason. Elk. Jr. O.U. A.M. Club: Kiwanis. Home: 72 Grove Av. Office: 1007 Springfield Av., Irvington, N.J.

BEDFORD, Paul, lawyer; mem. Bedford, Waller, Jones and Darling. Office: Wilkes-Barre, Pa.*

BEDROSSIAN, Edward H., physician; b. Marsovan, Armenia, Oct. 25, 1886; s. Hagop and Victoria B.; came to U.S. 1908 and naturalized citizen, 1914; A.B., Anatolia Coll., 1904; M.D., U. of Pa., 1912; m. Angele Sirvart Adourian, Apr. 28, 1920; children—E. Howard, Robert H., Doris L. Resident phys. Memorial Hosp., Phila., 1912-13, Episcopal Hosp., 1913-14, Phila. Hosp. for Contagious Diseases, 1914-15; phys. Dept. Health, Phila., 1915-18; instr. ophthalmology, Temple U. Med. Sch., 1928-33; med. examiner Civil Aeronautical Authority since 1928; ophthalmologist, Del. Co. Hosp., Drexel Hill, Pa., since 1929; med. ophthalmic tour in India, 1936-37. Served as 1st lt. Med. Corps, U.S.A., 1918-19; now lt. col. Res. Mem. Am. Med. Asso., Pa. State and Del Co. med. assns., Mil. Surgs. of America. Republican. Mem. Drexel Hill (Pa.) Presbyterian Church. Mason. Club: Lions of Chester. Home: 531 Foss Av., Drexel Hill, Pa. Office: 1737 Chestnut St., Philadelphia, Pa.

BEE, Charles Howard, physician; b. Marion Center, Pa., Feb. 7, 1875; s. Daniel H. and Elizabeth (MacChesney) B.; grad. Indiana (Pa.) State Teachers Coll., 1900; student U. of Chicago, summer 1900, U. of Michigan, 1901-03; M.D., Medico Chirurgical Coll., 1905; post grad. work at Post Grad Hosp. and Med. Sch., Chicago, 1905-24; m. Clare P. Poorman, Oct. 24, 1907; children—Daniel Harold, Mary Thresa. Began as teacher, 1892; in practice as physician, Summit, O., 1905-11, Cleveland, O., 1911-16, Marion Center, Pa., 1916-20, Indiana, Pa., since 1920; mem. of med. staff Indiana Co. Memorial Hosp. Del. to Rep. Nat. Conv., Chicago, 1936. Mem. Bd. of Edn., Indiana, for 12 years pres. 4 years. Mem. A.M.A., Pa. State Med. Soc., Indiana Co. Med. Soc. (past pres.). Methodist. Home: 555 Water St., Indiana, Pa.

BEEBE, James; surgeon Beebe Hosp., Del. Colony for Mental Defectives and Pa. R.R. Address: Lewes, Del.

BEEBE, Richard C.; mem. surg. staff Beebe Hosp. Address: Lewes, Del.

BEEDE, Victor Augustus, forester, univ. prof.; b. East Braintree, Mass., Dec. 9, 1886; s. Frank Herbert and Caroline May (Coan) B.; student New Haven (Conn.) Pub. Schs., 1900-06; A.B., Yale, 1910, M.F., Sch. of Forestry, 1912; m. Ella Small, June 26, 1912; 1 son, John Knowlton. Asst. forester, Mass. Forestry Assn., Boston, 1913; forest asst. U.S. Forest Service, Pike Nat. Forest, Colo., 1913-14; asst. state forester, Concord, N.H., 1914-16; sec. N.Y. State Forestry Assn., 1916-17; asst. mgr. Timberlands Mutual Fire Ins. Co., Portsmouth, N.H., 1917-18; woods insp., scaler, Brown Corpn., Trois Pistoles, Quebec, Can., 1918-20, local mgr. Riviere du Loup, Quebec, 1920-24, forester, Quebec City, Quebec, 1924-31, observing woods practice in pulpwood operations in Norway, Sweden, Finland, 1927; mem. faculty forestry dept., Pa. State Coll., 1931-34, asst. prof. of forest management, 1935-37, head forestry dept. and prof. forest management since 1937; substitute prof., Yale Sch. of Forestry, 1934-35. Sr. mem. Soc. Am. Foresters, Canadian Soc. of Forest Engrs., Zeta Psi, Xi Sigma Pi, Gamma Sigma Delta. Independent Democrat. Contbr. tech. articles to Journal of Forestry. Address: 512 Garner St., State College, Pa.

BEEGLE, Clifford Heath, machinery mfg.; b. Beaver Falls, Pa., Jan. 11, 1896; s. Frederick N. and Nellie Emily (Heath) B.; ed. Hill Sch., Pottstown, Pa., 1910-15, Cornell U., 1915-17; m. Frances C. Ague, July 2, 1921; children—Barbara Ann, Frederick N. II, John Ague. In employ Union Drawn Steel Co., 1914-15, in Chicago sales office, 1915; field mgr. in oil fields, Wyoming, 1917-18; with Union Drawn Steel Co., 1919-21, Pittsburgh sales mgr., 1921-23, vice-pres., 1923-29; organizer Burgess Co., Inc., mfr. oil meters, varied products and ordnance, and pres. and treas. since 1925; pres. and treas. Union Hotel Co.; pres. Beaver Refrigerator & Potteries Co.; dir. First Nat. Bank, Copperweld Steel Co., Wheeling Machine Co., Elwood Co.; dir. and sec. Strip Tin Plate Co. Pres. Beaver Falls Masonic Temple Assn.; dir. Beaver Falls Hosp., Providence Hosp., Y.M.C.A., Beaver Co. Children's Home, Salvation Army, Pa. Assn. for the Blind, St. Francis Hosp. (Miami Beach, Fla.). Mem. Soc. Automotive Engrs., Phi Sigma Kappa. Republican. Mem. Christian Ch. (Disciples). Mason (K.T., Shriner). Clubs: Lions, Beaver Valley Country (Beaver Falls); Duquesne (Pittsburgh); Woodmont Rod and Gun (Hancock, Md.); Committee of 100, Surf, Bath (Miami Beach, Fla.). Home: "Heath Manor," Patterson Heights. Office: 12th St. and 11th Av., Beaver Falls, Pa.

BEEGLE, May, concert mgr.; b. Bedford, Pa., Oct. 23, 1885; d. Thomas P. and Margaret (Keyser) B.; ed. pub. sch. and high sch. Has been mgr. Pittsburgh Orchestra Assn. since 1915; mgr. Art Soc., 1929-37; mgr. May Beegle Concerts since 1922; Pittsburgh mgr. New York Children's Theatre. Mem. League of American Pen Women. Mem. First Evangelical Lutheran Ch. Clubs: Twentieth Century, Woman's City, Tuesday Musical, Business and Professional Woman's, Civic of Allegheny County. Home: Schenley Apts. Office: Union Trust Bldg., Pittsburgh, Pa.

BEEHLER, George William, Jr., real estate; b. Philadelphia, Pa., Mar. 28, 1899; s. George W. and Amy (Bourne) B.; student Phila. Grammar Sch., 1906-14, Northeast High Sch., 1914-18; spl. courses, Temple U. and U. of Pa., 1918-39; m. Margaret H. Bowers, Nov. 14, 1923; 1 dau., Margaret Elaine. With Land Title Bank and Trust Co., 1918-21; real estate broker under own name since 1922; sec. 9 bldg. and loan assns. Served with S.A.T.C. during World War. Mem. North Phila. Realty Bd. (ex-pres.), Phila. Realty Bd. (former v.p. and mem. bd. govs.), West Phila. Realty Bd., Pa. State Assn. Real Estate Bds., Nat. Assn. Real Estate Bds., Soc. Residential Appraisers, Bldg. & Loan League of Phila., Northeast High Sch. Alumni Assn. (mem. exec. com.). Republican. Presbyn. Mason, Moose; past master Artisans Order Mutual Protection. Home: 3603 N. 21st St. Office: S.E. corner 9th and Lehigh Sts., Philadelphia, Pa.

BEER, Phares Groff, clergyman; b. Bedminster, Pa., Apr. 19, 1890; s. Edward K. and Lydia (Groff) B.; A.B., Muhlenberg Coll., 1913; ed. Temple U., 1914-15, Phila. Luth. Sem., 1914-17, Susquehanna U., 1918-22; A.M. U. of Pa., 1921; D.D., Webster U., 1932; m. Edith Moyer, Apr. 10, 1918; children—Edith Vyrtue, Ruth Minnie Lydia, Erwin Wallace (dec.), Helen Evangeline. Engaged in teaching, 1907-09, prin. sch., 1912-14; navigation inspr. Port of Phila., 1915-17; ordained to ministry Luth. Ch., 1917, and pastor Line Mountain, Pa., 1917-19, Plainfield, Pa., 1919-21; pastor Grace Ch., Allentown, Pa., since 1921, instr. English Bible, Allentown Prep. Sch., 1922-27, dean Grace Training Sch. since 1922, pastor of Good Shepherd Home, Allentown, since 1922; pres. adv. bd. Good Shepherd Home. Served as judge of election, twelfth ward, 1923-37; organizing mem. Wind Gap Fire Co. and Wind Gap Bd. of Trade. Pres. Allentown Luth. Pastoral Assn., 1938. Chmn. Rural Ch. Com. of the Ministerium of Pa., 1923-25. Democrat. Lutheran. Club: Exchange (Allentown). Compiled Bibliography of Pennsylvania History, 1917. Contbr. many articles to ch. publs. Editor Grace Herald monthly ch. mag. Home: 708 St. John St., Allentown, Pa.

BEERS, Clifford Whittingham, founder of the mental hygiene movement; b. New Haven, Conn., Mar. 30, 1876; s. Robert Anthony and Ida (Cooke) B.; Ph.B., Sheffield Scientific Sch. (Yale), 1897, hon. M.A., 1922; m. Clara Louise Jepson, 1912. In business N.Y. City, 1898-1900, 1904-06. Founder, 1908, Conn. Soc. for Mental Hygiene (first orgn. of its kind, since which similar ones have been founded in many states); founder, 1909, and sec. Nat. Com. for Mental Hygiene; visited Great Britain, France and Belgium, 1923, in interests of internat. mental hygiene movement; had pvt. audiences with King Albert and Cardinal Mercier and interviews with other leaders abroad. Founder, 1928, and since sec. Am. Foundations for Mental Hygiene; organized and became sec.-gen. 1st Internat. Congress on Mental Hygiene, held in U.S., 1930; founder, 1930, and gen. sec. Internat. Com. for Mental Hygiene; founder, 1931, and sec. Internat. Foundation for Mental Hygiene. Mem. National Institute Social Sciences; hon. mem. Am. Psychiatric Assn., Am. Orthopsychiatric Assn. and British Nat. Council for Mental Hygiene, and other mental hygiene societies. Awarded (1933) Cross of Chevalier of Legion of Honor by French Govt. in recognition of international work in mental hygiene; awarded (1933) the Gold Medal of Nat. Inst. Social Sciences for "distinguished services for the benefit of mankind"; honored (1934) by publication of presentation edition of "Twenty-five Years After —Sidelights on the Mental Hygiene Movement and Its Founder," containing about 500 25th anniversary tributes, collected by the late Dr. William H. Welch, chmn. of the Tribute Com., apptd. by Nat. Com. for Mental Hygiene in connection with the anniversary celebration. Clubs: Graduate, Berzelius (New Haven); Yale (New York). Author: A Mind That Found Itself (autobiography), 1908, 24th edit., 1939; also articles on the mental hygiene movement. Home: 171 Sherwood Place, Englewood, N.J. Office: 50 W. 50th St., New York, N.Y.

BEERS, George Pitt, ch. official; b. Emporia, Fla., Apr. 4, 1883; s. John Leonard and Catherine (Zacharias) B.; A.B., Colgate Univ., 1906, B.D., 1910, A.M., 1913, D.D., 1929; m. Alice Tupper, Aug. 24, 1910. Ordained Bapt. ministry; held pastorates in Baltimore, Springfield, Mass., and at 1st Ch., Paterson, N.J.; mem. bd. mgrs. Am. Bapt. Home Mission Soc. since Jan. 1934, exec. sec. since Oct. 1934; 1st v.p. N.J. Bapt. State Conv., 1931-35; chmn. com. on unification of young people's work, Northern Bapt. Conv., 1933-34; chmn. of Council on World Evangelization of Northern Bapt. Conv. since 1935; vice-pres. Home Missions Council since 1939; chmn. Bapt. Com. for Rehabilitation of Christian German Refugees. Mem. Phi. Beta Kappa. Home: 151 Berkeley Pl., Glen Rock, N.J. Address: 23 E. 26th St., New York, N.Y.

BEERS, Louis J., lawyer; counsel various building and loan assns.; mem. advisory bd. Springfield Av. Branch of Federal Trust Co. Address: Prudential Bldg., Newark, N.J.

BEERY, Pauline Gracia (Mrs. Warren B. Mack), prof. textile chemistry; b. Norborne, Mo., Dec. 19, 1891; d. John Perry and Dora (Woodford) B.; A.B., High Sch., Norborne, Mo., 1913; A.M., Mo. State U., 1919; Ph.D., Columbia U., 1932; grad. studies Pa. State Coll.; m. Warren B. Mack, Dec. 23, 1923. Dir. home econ. research and prof. textile chemistry, Pa. State Coll. Fellow A.A.A.S., Am. Inst. of Chemists; mem. Am. Chem. Soc., Am. Soc. for Testing Materials, Am. Assn. of Textile Chemists and Colorists, Am. Home Econs. Assn., Faraday Soc. of England, Soc. For Research in Child Development, Am. Acad. of Polit. and Social Scis., Am. Assn. Univ. Profs., Com. for Standardization of Ultimate Consumer Goods of Am. Standards Assn. Episcopalian. Home: 245 W. Hamilton Av., State College, Pa.

BEERY, Vincent Dee, clergyman; b. Minneapolis, Minn., Mar. 16, 1887; s. Abraham and Amy Blatch (Smith) B.; A.B., Wooster Coll., Wooster, O., 1913; B.D., Theol. Sem., Princeton, 1917; m. Margaretta Theodora Dickey, May 10, 1917. Engaged in teaching in Fairfield County, O., 1904-08; instr. Greek and Bible, Wooster Acad., 1913-14; ordained to ministry Presbyn. Ch. at Gallipolis, O., 1917 and pastor, Gallipolis, 1917-20, Middleport, O., 1920-23, Johnstown, Pa., 1923-28; with Presbyn. Bd. of Nat. Missions, 1928-33; pastor Patterson Memorial Ch., Phila., Pa., since 1933. Chm. Com. on United Promotion of Phila. Presbytery. Mem. Presbyn. Ministers' Assn. of Phila., Delta Sigma Rho. Republican. Presbyn. Author: Brass Tacks, 1919. Contbr. to rel. mags. Corr. at Phila. for The Presbyterian (journ.). Home: 318 N. 63d St., Philadelphia, Pa.

BEESON, Charles Edmund, vice-pres. and treas. Pittsburgh Steel Co.; b. Janesville, Wis., Feb. 28, 1869; s. John Kennedy and Ellen (Huston) B.; prep. edn. Phillips Acad., Andover, Mass.; Ph.B., Yale, 1892; m. Helen White, Apr. 10, 1902; children—Marion Ellen (Mrs. A. Verner Wasson), John Kennedy, Analana White. Sec. Pittsburgh Horse Shoe Co., 1897-99; sec. Pittsburgh Steel Hoop Co., 1899-1902; sec. Pittsburgh Steel Co. (mfrs. pig iron, blooms, billets, nails, fencing, etc.), 1902-28, v.p. and treas. since 1928; pres. Alicia Supply Co. Trustee Shady Side Acad., Homewood Cemetery. Mem. Book and Snake Soc. (Yale). Republican. Episcopalian. Mason. Clubs: Duquesne, Fox Chapel, Rolling Rock (Pittsburgh). Home: 432 Morewood Av. Office: Pittsburgh Steel Co., Pittsburgh, Pa.

BEEUWKES, C. John; mem. law firm Emory, Beeuwkes, Skeen & Oppenheimer. Address: First Nat. Bank Bldg., Baltimore, Md.

BEGGS, Frederic; mem. law firm Beggs & Grimshaw. Address: Citizens Trust Bldg., Paterson, N.J.

BEGGS, George Erle, prof. civ. engring.; b. Ashland, Ill., Apr. 23, 1883; s. Edwin and Emma (Beggs) B.; A.B., Northwestern U., 1905; C. E., Columbia, 1910; m. Frances May Ingalls, Sept. 26, 1912; 1 son, George Erle. With Princeton U. since 1914, prof. civ. engring. since 1930. Mem. Am. Soc. C.E., Am. Inst. Cons. Engrs., Phi Beta Kappa, Tau Beta Pi, Sigma Xi. Author: Live Load Stresses in Railway Bridges, 1916. Home: 201 Prospect St., Princeton, N.J.

BEGLEY, Thomas D(evlin), lawyer; b. Phila., Pa., July 4, 1903; s. William J. and Caroline M. (Devlin) B.; ed. St. Joseph's Coll., Phila., 1923-24; LL.B., Georgetown U., Washington, D.C., 1927; m. Margaret A. Moore, Feb. 19, 1936; 1 son, Thomas D., Jr. In employ Thomas Devlin Mfg. Co., 1919-22; with Rosoff Construction Co., 1927-28; admitted to D.C. bar, 1929; admitted to N.J. bar as atty., 1930, counsellor, 1939; engaged in gen. practice of law at Burlington, N. J. since 1930; dir. Burlington City Loan & Trust Co., J. T. Severns Sons Co., Inc.; dir. and sec. Enterprise Realty & Equipment Co.; served as city solicitor, Burlington, N.J. since 1931. Mem. N.J. Bar Assn., Burlington Co. Bar Assn. Republican. Roman Catholic. K.C. B.P.O.E. L.O.O.M. Clubs: Oneida Boat (Burlington); Manufacturers and Bankers (Philadelphia). Home: Talbot and Pearl Sts. Office: 333 High St., Burlington, N.J.

BEHAN, Richard Joseph, surgeon; b. Pittsburgh, Pa., 1879; s. John and Annie (O'Donnell) B.; grad. Pittsburgh High Sch., 1898; M.D., U. of Pittsburgh, 1902; studied in Europe, 1910-14; m. Esther H. Hrubesky, Jan. 20, 1913. Resident, Mercy Hosp., Pittsburgh, 1902, South Side Hosp., 1903; pathologist, St. Francis Hosp., 1904-05, asst. surgeon, 1906; asst to chair of physical diagnosis, U. of Pittsburgh School of Medicine, 1903-08, asso. prof. same, 1908; vol. asst., Royal Surg. Clinic, Berlin, 1912-13; surgeon, St. Joseph's Hosp. since 1914, City Hosp. for Tuberculosis since 1916, City Hospital, Mayview, since 1922; formerly dir. cancer dept. Pittsburgh Skin and Cancer Foundation; surgeon Leech Farm Hosp., Tuberculosis County Home and Hosp., Woodville, Pa. Capt. M.C., U.S.A. Served as surgeon 4th Reserve Hosp., Nish, Serbia, 2d Balkan War. Mem. A.M.A., Am. Coll. Surgeons (dir.), Allegheny County Med. Soc. (pres.), etc. Decorated Order of San Savar (Serbian). Member Knights of Columbus. Author: Pain, 1913; Cancer, 1938; Relation of Trauma to New Growths, 1939. Contbr. of sect. "Tumors" to Am. Med. Encyclopedia; sect. "Head Pain" to Dental Diagnosis; also numerous monographs on surgery and cancer. Home: 5710 Elgin Av. Office: Jenkins Arcade Bldg., Pittsburgh, Pa.

BEHNEY, Charles Augustus, M.D.; b. Myerstown, Pa., Oct. 7, 1891; s. Augustus and Valeria (Loose) B.; A.B., Ursinus Coll., Collegeville, Pa., 1912; M.D., U. of Pa., 1917; m.

Victoria Parks, Jan. 7, 1928; 1 son, Charles Augustus. Began as physician, 1918; asso. in obstetrics and gynecology, U. of Pa. Sch. of Medicine since 1928; asso. in gynecology, Grad. Sch. of Medicine, U. of Pa., since 1928; asst. gynecologist and obstetrician, Hosp. of U. of Pa. since 1928; gynecologist, radiological-clinical staff, Phila. Gen. Hosp. since 1928; obstetrician and gynecologist, Bryn Mawr Hosp. since 1928; gynecologist, Chestnut Hill Hosp., 1928-33, Presbyn. Hosp., Phila., since 1933; examiner in gynecology, Nat. Bd. Med. Examiners since 1926. Served as 1st lt. Med. Corps, U.S. Army, 1918-19, as asst. neuro-surgeon U.S. Gen. Hosp. Cape May, N.J., and Walter Reed Gen. Hosp. Washington, D.C. Licentiate Nat. Bd. Med. Examiners; fellow Am. Coll. Surgeons; mem. Am. Gynecol. Soc., Phila. Coll. Physicians, A.M.A., Am. Bd. Obstetrics and Gynecology, Phila. Obstet. Soc., N. Am. Obstetric and Gynecologic Club, Phila. Co. Med. Soc., Pa. State Med. Soc., Main Line Branch of Montgomery Co. Med. Soc., Pa. Acad. Science, A.A.A.S., Phila. Skating Club, Humane Soc., Alpha Kappa Kappa, Sigma Xi. Mem. Reformed Ch. Mason. Home: 543 Manor Road, Wynnewood. Office: 3722 Chestnut St., Philadelphia, Pa.

BEHREND, Ernst Richard, paper mfr.; b. Coeslin, Germany, March 29, 1869; s. Moritz and Rebecca (Wolf) B.; ed. in Dresden and Charlottenburg; m. Mary Brownell, June 1, 1907; 1 dau., Harriet Ellen. Came to United States, 1896, naturalized citizen, 1901. Engr. with Pusey & Jones Co., Wilmington, Del., later with Nekoosa Paper Co.; rep. of Am. paper mill machinery mfrs. in Eng., France, Germany and Scandinavia, 1897; founder, 1898, and pres. Hammermill Paper Co., Erie, Pa. Lt. comdr. United States Naval Reserves. Member executive com. War Activities, Erie, World War; four-minute speaker; dir. War Chest; hon. dir. Community Chest. Former pres. Hamot Hosp. Mem. Am. Soc. Mech. Engrs. Republican. Lutheran. Mason (K.T.), Odd Fellow, Elk. Clubs: Erie, University, Kahkwa Country; Chemist, New York Athletic, Bayside Yacht; Erie Yacht; Congressional Country (Washington, D.C.); Biltmore Country Club, Havana Country, Indian Harbor Yacht, Columbia Yacht, Ida Lewis Yacht. Home: East Lake Rd., Erie, Pa., and Newport, R.I. Address: Hammermill Paper Co., Erie, Pa. *

BEHREND, Moses, M.D.; b. Phila., Pa., June 6, 1877; s. Jacob and Sarah B.; M.D., U. of Pa., 1899; m. Clara Rosenbaum, Jan. 11, 1905; children—Ruth (Mrs. Merlin Hagedorn), Albert, Jeanne (Mrs. Alexander Kelberine). Practicing physician, Phila., since 1899; attending surgeon Jewish and Mt. Sinai Hosps.; thoracic surgeon Phila. Gen. Hosp. and Sanatoria of Commonwealth of Pa. Fellow Am. Coll. Surgeons; mem. A.M.A., Pa. Med. Soc., Phila. Co. Med. Soc., Internat. Coll. Surgeons, Pathol. Soc., Am. Pediatric Soc.; hon. mem. Phi Lambda Kappa, Phi Epsilon. Jewish religion. Club: Philmont Country. Address: 1738 Pine St., Philadelphia, Pa.

BEIDEMAN, Joseph Ellsworth, oculist; b. Norristown, Pa., Sept. 25, 1895; s. Elmer Ellsworth and Martha (Middleton) B.; grad. Norristown High Sch., 1913; student Lafayette Coll., 1913-15; M.D., U. of Pa., 1919; m. Rebecca Morris Balmer, June 24, 1925. Interne Presbyterian Hosp., Phila., 1919-20; interne Wills Hosp., Phila., 1920-22; in practice as oculist, Norristown, Pa., since Feb. 1922; ophthalmologist to Montgomery Hosp., Sacred Heart Hosp., Norristown State Hosp.; dir. Montgomery Trust Co.; dir. and vice-pres. Town and Country Bldg. & Loan. Mem. Montgomery Co. Med. Soc. (past pres.), Sigma Nu, Alpha Kappa Kappa. Republican. Presbyterian. Club: Plymouth Country (Norristown). Home: Port Kennedy Rd., Audubon, Pa. Office: Montgomery Trust Arcade, Norristown, Pa.

BEIDLEMAN, Harry Hursh, clergyman; b. Harrisburg, Pa., Dec. 3, 1889; s. William Calder and Elizabeth (Hursh) B.; A.B., Gettysburg Coll., 1912; ed. Gettysburg Theol. Sem., 1912-15; hon. D.D., Gettysburg Coll., 1933; m. Katharine Duncan, Nov. 6, 1918; children—Barkley, Edward Bayard. Ordained to ministry Luth. Ch., 1915, and pastor St. Paul's Ch., Frostburg, Md., 1915-22, Calvary Ch., Baltimore, Md., 1922-28; pastor St. Matthew's Ch., Hanover, Pa., since 1928. Served as Luth. camp pastor during World War. Trustee Gettysburg Coll. Mem. exec. com. Bd. Fgn. Missions of United Luth. Ch. in America. Mem. Phi Sigma Kappa. Republican. Lutheran. Mason (K.T.). Club: Country (Hanover). Home: 55 Frederick St., Hanover, Pa.

BEIERSCHMITT, Gerald Augustine, supt. of schs.; b. Mt. Carmel, Pa., Feb. 5, 1904; s. Frank Joseph and Mary Catherine (Schneider) B.; grad. St. Charles' Jr. Coll., Catonsville, Md., 1923; A.B., Holy Cross Coll., Worcester, Mass., 1925; M.A., Bucknell U., 1935; m. Dora Marie Betz, Apr. 10, 1939. Instr. German-English, Holy Cross Coll., Worcester, Mass., 1926-28; supervising prin. of schs., Centralia, Pa., 1928-34; supt. of schs., Mt. Carmel, Pa., since 1934; dir. Peoples Bldg. & Loan Assn., Mt. Carmel, Pa. V.p. Community Cooperative Concert Assn., Mt. Carmel (Pa.) Oratorio Soc.; mem. Mt. Carmel (Pa.) chapter Am. Red Cross (exec. com.), Mt. Carmel (Pa.) Tuberculosis Soc. (exec. com.), Joseph A. Holmes Safety Assn. (exec. com.), Boy Scouts of America (exec. com.), Kappa Phi Kappa. Roman Catholic. A.A.S.A., N.E.A., P.S.E.A., B.P.O.E., K.C. Clubs: Mt. Carmel Motor, Fountain Springs Country (treas., mem. bd. of govs.), Rotary (Mt. Carmel, Pa.). Home: 213 S. Oak St. Office: Roosevelt Junior High Sch., Mt. Carmel, Pa.

BEILER, Irwin Ross, prof. English Bible; b. Lima, O., Jan. 14, 1883; s. Adam Clarke and Mary Jane (Davis) B.; A.B., Ohio Wesleyan U., 1907, D.D., 1933; S.T.B., Boston U. Sch. of Theol., 1911; Ph.D., Boston University, 1918; Jacob Sleeper fellow University of Berlin, 1911-12; m. Elizabeth Kelsey Crates, June 28, 1911 (died April 4, 1934); children—Adam Clarke, Ross Crates, Dorothy Eleanor, Charles Kelsey, David Davis, Theodore Wiseman; m. 2d, Jessie A. Virtue, July 3, 1937. Acting prof. philosophy and English Bible, Allegheny Coll., 1912-13; prof. Bibl. lit., Baker U., Baldwin, Kan., 1913-18; pastor First M.E. Ch., Minneapolis, Minn., 1918-20; prof. English Bible and philosophy of religion, Allegheny Coll., since 1920. Mem. Erie Conf. M.E. Ch. Mem. Nat. Assn. Bibl. Instrs., Soc. Bibl. Lit. and exegesis, Am. Theol. Soc., Am. Assn. Univ. Profs., Round Table, Phi Gamma Delta, Phi Beta Kappa. Author: Studies in the Life of Jesus, 1936. Home: 196 Spring St. Meadville, Pa.

BEIRNE, Francis Foulke, journalist; b. Ashland, Va., Aug. 20, 1890; s. Richard Foulke and Clara Haxall (Grundy) B.; prep. edn. Gilman Country Sch. for Boys, Baltimore, 1903-08; A.B., U. of Va., 1911; B.A., Oxford Univ., England (Merton Coll.), 1914, M.A., 1919; m. Rosamond Harding Randall, Nov. 22, 1919; children—Clare Haxall, Daniel Randall. Reporter and copyreader, The Sun, Baltimore, 1914-17; with Liggett & Myers Tobacco Co., Richmond, Va., 1918-21; copyreader, The Baltimore News, 1921-23; editorial writer and columnist under name of Christopher Billopp, The Evening Sun, since 1923. Served at 1st O.T.C., Ft. Myer, 1917; commd. 2d lt. 80th Div. U.S. Army, Aug. 1917, 1st lt. Feb. 1918; with Renting, Requisition and Claims. Service, S.O.S., A.E.F., March 1918-June 1919. Trustee Gilman Country Sch. Mem. Delta Psi, Phi Beta Kappa. Rhodes Scholar from Va., 1911-14. Democrat. Episcopalian. Club: L'Hirondelle (Ruxton, Md.). Home: Ruxton, Md. Office: The Evening Sun, Baltimore, Md.

BEISLER, Henry, wholesale paper; b. New York, N.Y., Jan. 31, 1886; s. John and Lena (Carl) B.; ed. New York Public Schools; m. Louise Schillig, Aug. 28, 1910; children—Madeline L., Henry, Jr. Began as salesman, New York, 1900; pres. Beisler, Weidmann Co., Inc., wholesale paper, Belleville, N.J., since 1922; vice-pres. Atlantic Paper Tubes, Belleville. Mem. Bd. of Publ. of United Lutheran Ch. in America; dir. Children's Friend Orphan's Home, Jersey City, N.J.; pres. of bd. St. John's Luth. Ch., Jersey City, N.J. Home: 614 16th St., Union City, N.J. Office: Belleville, N.J.

BEISLER, Lawrence G., M.D.; attending surgeon Elizabeth Gen. Hosp.; asso. visiting surgeon Hosp. of St. Barnabas. Address: 1528 N. Broad St., Hillside, N.J.

BEISSER, Paul T., social worker; b. Reading, Pa., July 25, 1895; s. J. George and Mary (Pflum) B.; B.S. in econ., U. of Pa., 1916; diploma, N.Y. Sch. of Social Work, New York City, 1917; m. Miriam E. Strunk, June 24, 1919; children—Paul T., James E. Asst. employment mgr., Industrial Service Co., Boston, Mass., 1917-18; statistician Bur. of Labor Statistics, U.S. Dept. of Labor, Washington, D.C., 1918-20; field sec. N.Y. Sch. of Social Work, New York City, 1920-22; gen. sec. Henry Watson Children's Aid Soc., Baltimore, since 1925. Served as pvt., U.S. Army Ordnance Corps, 1918. Mem. Governor's Com. of Unemployment Relief, Md., 1933. Pres. Child Welfare League of America, Inc.; gen. sec. Henry Watson Children's Aid Soc. Mem. Am. Assn. of Social Workers (research sec.), Pub. Charities Assn. of Pa. (sec. Child Welfare Div.). Democrat. Lutheran. Club: Univ. (Baltimore, Md.). Pres. Md. State Conf. on Social Welfare, 1929-33; mem. White House Conf. of Children in a Democracy, 1939. Home: 707 Evesham Av. Office: 204 W. Lanvale St., Baltimore, Md.

BEITLER, Harold Bornemann, lawyer; b. Phila., Pa., Dec. 31, 1880; s. Abraham Merklee and Julia Louise (Bornemann) B.; ed. Eastburn Acad., 1891-97, under pvt. tutors, 1897-1901; student Law Sch., U. of Pa., 1898-1901; m. Ethel Haffline Eisenbrey, Oct. 16, 1906; children—Abraham Merklee, Eleanor, Anita Barbara. Admitted to Pa. bar, 1902, and since practiced in Philadelphia; partner Maxwell & Beitler, 1908-15, Dickson, Beitler & McCouch, 1915-31, Beitler & Burns since 1931. Chmn. Four Minute Men, Pa., and 3d Federal Res. Dist., 1917-19. Dir. Sleighton Farm Sch. for Girls. Mem. Am. Bar Assn., Pa. Bar Assn., Phi Delta Theta. Republican. Episcopalian. Mason. Clubs: Union League, Constitutional, Keystone Automobile (v.p.); Edgemere (Pike Co., Pa.). Home: Pennstone Road, Bryn Mawr, Pa. Office: 1421 Chestnut St., Philadelphia, Pa.

BEITLER, S. Wilmer, clergyman; b. Phila., Pa., May 21, 1877; s. Joseph and Sarah (Cade) B.; B.S., Central High Sch., Phila., 1896; student Princeton Theol. Sem., 1912-15; D.D., Hastings Coll., Hastings, Neb., 1927; m. Mary Synnott Eldridge, Jan. 18, 1916; 1 dau., Sarah. Asso. with Pioneer Suspender Co., Phila., 1898-1912, beginning as clerk and advancing to treas.; ordained to ministry of Presbyterian Ch., 1915; pastor First Presbyn. Ch., Sayre, Pa., 1915-17, First Ch., Ingram, Pa., 1917-23; pastor First Presbyn. Ch., Butler, Pa. since 1923; leader and instr. denominational Young Peoples conferences and leader of college spiritual emphasis programs. Mem. Pi Gamma Mu. Address: 405 W. Pearl St., Butler, Pa.

BELCHER, Arthur William, educator; b. Medford, Mass., June 10, 1884; s. Edward Wheatcroft and Mary Frances (Camp) B.; A.B., Harvard U., 1904; A.M., Columbia U., 1910; m. Louisa M. Norton, July 18, 1911; children—Charles Norton, Arthur Nathan. Engaged as instr. mathematics in high schs., Plymouth, Mass., Summit, N.J., Fairhaven, N.J., also Stuyvesant High Sch., N.Y. City; later instr. mathematics, East Side High Sch., Newark, N.J.; prin. South Side High Sch., Newark, N.J. since 1929. Trustee Maplewood Civic Assn., Maplewood Community Service. Mem. Ref. Ch. Mason. Co-author (with Alan Johnson); Introductory Algebra; Second Course in Algebra. Home: 682 Prospect St., Maplewood, N.J.

BELCHER, Donald Ray, statistician; b. Albion, Mich., Nov. 4, 1887; s. Sylvester H. and Margaret (Donald) B.; A.B., Kalamazoo (Mich.) Coll., 1909, A.M., Columbia, 1915; student Sorbonne U. (Paris), 1919; m. Mary Carver Williams, Aug. 9, 1921; children—Donald William, Mary Priscilla, Jonathan Thomson. Began as mathematics teacher pub. schs., 1909; prof. mathematics, Hanover (Ind.) Coll., 1910-14; instr. mathematics, Columbia, 1914-18; asst. chief statistician Am. Telephone and Telegraph Co. since 1919. With A.E.F. in France,

World War. Mem. N.J. Pension Survey Commn., 1930-32; mem. and approval officer N.J. Commn. for the Blind since 1932; pres. Westfield Bd. of Edn. Fellow A.A.A.S., Am. Statis. Assn.; mem. Inst. of Math. Statistics, Am. Math. Soc., Am. Econ. Assn., Econometric Soc., Acad. of Polit. Science. Republican. Baptist. Clubs: Economic, Town Hall, Railroad-Machinery. Home: 550 Prospect St., Westfield, N.J. Office: 195 Broadway, New York, N.Y.

BELCHER, Wallace Edward, structural engr.; b. Medford, Mass., Oct. 4, 1879; s. Edward Wheatcroft and Mary Frances (Camp) B.; B.C.E., U. of Me., 1899, C.E., 1902; A.M., Harvard, 1904; m. Elisabeth Holden, Nov. 23, 1909; children—Mary Elisabeth (Mrs. T. G. A. Henstridge), Ralph Holden, Wallace Edward. Was designing engineer of industrial and pub. utility structures, with J. G. White Engring. Co., 1906-08, H. M. Byllesby & Co., 1909-13, Westinghouse Church Kerr Co., 1915-16, Stone and Webster, 1916-19; structural engr. Dwight P. Robinson & Co. (supervising engr. Hotel Statler, Boston, Mass.; designing and supervising engr. North Station Development and Coliseum, B.&M. R.R., Boston) since 1919, co. merged into United Engrs. & Constructors. Mem. Am. Soc. C. E., Harvard Engring. Soc. Beta Theta Pi, Tau Beta Pi. Republican, Episcopalian. Mason. Clubs: Harvard (New York); Engineers (Phila.). Home: 5900 Woodbine Av., Overbrook, Pa. Office: 1401 Arch St., Philadelphia, Pa.

BELFORD, Ralph J., M.D., chief of staff and chief of surgical service Princeton Hosp.; also mem. visiting staff various hosps. Address: 88 Nassau St., Princeton, N.J.

BELIN, G. d'Andelot; pres. E. I. duPont de Nemours & Co. of Pa.; dir. many other cos. Home: Waverly, Pa. Office: 701 First Nat. Bank Bldg., Scranton, Pa.

BELIN, Henry III, mfg. exec.; b. Scranton, Pa., Feb. 9, 1901; s. Paul Beck and Lucie Sherred (Welles) B.; B.S., Yale, 1924; m. Katherine Hoffman, Sept. 29, 1925; children—Henry, Alice, Paul. Treas. Scranton (Pa.) Lace Co. since 1928; dir. and treas. Scranton Airport Corpn. since 1929; pres. Abington Nat. Bank, Clarks Summit, Pa. since 1934; dir. First Nat. Bank of Scranton,. Pa. Republican. Presbyterian. Home: Waverly, Pa. Office: Glenn St., Scranton, Pa.

BELING, Christopher C(harles), physician; b. Colombo, Ceylon, Apr. 4, 1873; s. William Wright and Maria Elizabeth (Prins) B.; grad. Wesley Coll., Colombo, 1891, Ceylon Med. Coll., 1897; L.R.C.P., L.R.C.S., Royal Coll. Phys. & Surgs., Edinburgh, Scotland, 1900; came to U.S., 1900, naturalized, 1906; m. Margaret Lucille Abbott, Nov. 21, 1905; children—Christopher Abbott (M.D.), Elaine Abbott. Connected with Govt. (Brit.) Med. Service, Ceylon, 1897-99, in charge several dist. hosps.; in pvt. practice in N.Y. State, 1900; mem. staff N.J. State Hosp. for Insane, Morris Plains, N.J., 1901-07; in private practice in Newark, N.J. since 1907; clin. asst. Vanderbilt Clinic, N.Y. City, 1907-12; in charge first Neuropsychiatric Clinic, N.J. at St. Michael's Hosp., Newark, 1908-23; attdg., neurologist, St. Michael's Hosp. and chief neuropsychiatric dept. Newark City Hosp. since 1908; cons. neuropsychiatrist to many hosps. Served on local and U.S. Advisory draft bds., 1917-1919; neuropsychiatrist to U.S. Pub. Health Service and Vets. Bur., 1919-23. Assisted in founding first Juvenile clinic and Bur. Mental Hygiene, dir. Bur., 1919-22. Fellow Am. Coll. Physicians; mem. A.M.A., Am. Neurol. Assn., Assn. for Research in Nervous and Mental Diseases, Am. Psychiatric Assn., N.J. Neuropsychiatric Assn. (past pres.), N.J. State Med. Soc., (chmn. judicial council), Morris Co. Med. Soc. (past pres.), N.Y. Psychiatric Assn., N.Y. Neurol. Soc., British Med. Assn. Contbr. many articles to med. publs. Home: 102 N. Mountain Av., Montclair, N.J. Office: 111 Clinton Av., Newark, N.J.

BELKNAP, (Almira) Fredericka, personnel dir.; b. New York, N.Y., Feb. 20, 1893; d. Chauncey and Emma Louise (McClave) B.; A.B., Barnard Coll., New York, 1915; student Columbia U.. 1915-16; A.M., N.Y.U., 1927; unmarried. Began as sec. Barnard Coll., New York, 1917; sec. Barnard Sch. for Girls, 1919-20, Am. Orchestral Soc., New York, 1920-23; dir. bur. of Appointments N.Y.U. School of Edn., 1923-29; dir. personnel bur. N.J. Coll. for Women, New Brunswick, N. J., since 1929. Served in War Camp Community Service, New York, 1918-19. Mem. Am. Coll. Personnel Assn., N.J. Guidance and Personnel Assn., Vocational Guidance Assn., Am. Assn. Univ. Women, Women's League of Rutgers Univ., Barnard Coll. Alumni Assn., Gamma Phi Beta. Clubs: New Brunswick College (New Brunswick, N.J.); Barnard of Union Co., (N.J.). Home: 153 N. 8th Av. Office: N.J. College for Women, New Brunswick, N.J.

BELKNAP, John Harrison, mgr. tech. employment and training; b. Corvallis, Ore., Feb. 17, 1892; s. Edward Milton and Elizabeth Ann (Hooper) B.; B.S. in elec. engring., Ore. State Coll., 1912; student, U. of Chicago, summer 1915; m. Inez Johnson, Sept. 16, 1914; 1 dau., Margaret Lucile. Inst. engring, physics, Ore. State Coll., 1912-19, asst. prof. elec. engring., 1919-23; with Westinghouse Electric & Mfg. Co. since 1923, as control engr., 1923-29, mgr. control engring., 1929-31, dist. engr., 1931-36, mgr. tech. employment and training since 1936. Served as 1st lt. 103d F.A., U.S. Army, 1917-18. Registered engr. in Pa. Mem. Am. Inst. Elec. Engrs., Engrs. soc. of Western Pa., Am. Mil. Engrs., Tau Beta Pi, Eta Kappa Nu, Sigma Tau, Phi Sigma Kappa. Republican. Methodist. Mason. Home: 600 Berlin Rd., Wilkinsburg, Pa. Office: 306 4th Av., Pittsburgh, Pa.

BELL, Albert Harvey, lawyer; b. Cedar Rapids, Ia., Nov. 20, 1857; s. John Robinson and Margaret (Singer) B.; student Mt. Union Coll., Alliance, O.; (hon.) LL.D., Westminster Coll., New Wilmington, Pa.; m. Mary Clarke, Mar. 19, 1885 (dec.); children—James Clarke, Mary Margaret (dec.), Albert H. (2d lieut. killed in action, 1918). Admitted to Pa. bar and since engaged in gen. practice of law at Greensburg; mem. firm Bell and Bell; dir. Barclay Westmoreland Trust Co. Served as pres. bd. dirs. Greensburg Sch. Dist. Dir. Westminster Coll., Bd. Publication of United Presbyn. Ch., Morrison Underwood Donation Fund. Democrat. United Presbyn. (mem. bd. elders). Home: 431 S. Main St. Office: Shoemaker Bldg., Greensburg, Pa.

BELL, C. Ray; mayor of Lebanon. Address: Lebanon, Pa.

BELL, Charles Herbert, merchant and miller; b. Phila., Pa., Oct. 16, 1877; s. Samuel, Jr., and Ada A. (Rees) B.; student Eastburn Acad., 1887-94; Haverford Coll., 1894-96; A.B. Harvard, 1900; m. Harriette A. Rogers, May 15, 1918; m. 2d, Evelyn Murphy, Oct. 13, 1937. Began career as merchant and miller as mem. firm, later vice-pres. Samuel Bell & Sons, 1900-31; vice-pres. then pres. The Bellson Company since 1931; pres. S. & C. H. Bell Co., Quaker City Flour Mills Co.; treas. Buffalo Flour Milling Co.; dir. Land Title Bank and Trust Co. Served as capt. Q.M.C. during World War. Dir. Phila. Chamber of Commerce, Phila. Bourse, Phila. Commercial Exchange. Republican. Presbyn. Clubs: Union League, Racquet, Country, Merion Cricket, Bachelors Barge (Phila.); Harvard (New York City). Home: Devon. Office: 996 Drexel Bldg., Philadelphia, Pa.

BELL, Enid, sculptress; b. London, England, Dec. 5, 1904; came to U.S., 1915; d. Horatio and Jean (Diack) B.; studied Glasgow (Scotland) Sch. of Art, 1919-20, St. John's Wood Sch. of Art and under Sir W. Reid Dick, London, 1920-21, Art Students League, New York, N.Y., 1921-25; m. Missak Palanchian, 1932; 1 son, John. Began as sculptress, 1927; teacher arts and crafts, drawing and painting, Miss Chapins Sch. for Girls, New York, 1929-31; teacher crafts, drawing and painting Newark Art Club, Newark, 1933-34. Has exhibited at Architectural League, Pa. Acad., Nat. Acad., Regional Art Exhbn., Brooklyn Mus., Salons of America, Paris World's Fair, etc. Prin. works: carved wood panel in post offices, Mount Holly, N.J., 1938, Boonton, N.J., 1939; 2 carved plaster panels, 2 portrait reliefs, 1 cement group and 2 carved wood panels, Union City Free Public Libraries; 3 carved wood panels, Robert Treat Sch., Newark, One-man shows Ferargil Gallery, 1929, Arden Gallery (both of New York), 1934. Received medal of award for sculpture N.J. Chapter, Am. Artists Professional League, 1933; sculpture medal Newark Art Club Exhbn., 1936; gold medal Paris World's Fair, 1938. Home: 141 Columbia Av., North Bergen, N.J.

BELL, Frank Breckenridge, steel mfr.; b. Mercer, Pa., Sept. 24, 1876; s. John W. and Hester Martin (Davitt) B.; grad. high sch., Mercer, 1892; student Grove City (Pa.) Coll., 1893; M.E., Lehigh U., 1897; m. Mary Ewing Stranahan, June 16, 1904; children—Davitt Stranahan, James Alexander, Elizabeth Ewing. Began with Clairton (Pa.) Steel Co., 1904; various positions in steel works, 1904-09; supt. Inter-Ocean Steel Co., Chicago Heights, Ill., 1909-16; pres. Kennedy-Stroh Corpn., Pittsburgh, Pa., 1916; pres. Edgewater Steel Co., Pittsburgh, since 1916; dir. Jessop Steel Co., Fidelity Trust Co. (Pittsburgh). Mem. Iron and Steel Inst., Am. Soc. for Testing Materials, Am. Soc. M.E. Republican. Presbyn. Clubs: University, Duquesne, Oakmont Country, Longue Vue Country. Home: 808 Devonshire St. Address: Box 478, Pittsburgh, Pa.

BELL, Harry Carter, banker; b. Pittsburgh, Pa., Feb. 16, 1889; s. Franklin P. and Jeanette S. (Carter) B.; student Sterrett Pub. Sch., Pittsburgh, Pa., 1895-1902; grad. Central High Sch., Pittsburgh, 1906; m. Helen Marie Porter, July 24, 1914; children—Mary Ann, Jane Marie, Richard Porter. Clerk Lloyd Real Estate Co., Pittsburgh, Pa., 1906-09; salesman J.S. & W.S. Kuku, Inc., Pittsburgh, Pa., 1909-13; asst. Pittsburgh rep. Nat. City Bank of N.Y., 1913-15; v.p. Colonial Trust Co., Pittsburgh, since 1915; dir. Eljer Co., Electric Products Co., Unity Rys. Co., Fullerton-Portsmouth Bridge Co. Republican. Presbyterian. Club: Duquesne (Pittsburgh). Home: 5619 Elgin Av. Office: 414 Wood St., Pittsburgh, Pa.

BELL, Jesse Scott, realtor; b. St. Clairsville, Pa., Nov. 10, 1875; s. James Wallace and Anna (Levegood) B.; student Dickinson Jr. Coll., Williamsport, Pa., 1894-96; m. Laurette Mussina, June 5, 1902. Began as newspaper reporter, Williamsport Sun, 1898; mgr. Evening News, 1905-09; Bell Agency, Williamsport, Pa., realtors, since 1909. Mem. Williamsport Chamber of Commerce (pres. 1923-26), Pa. Assn. of Real Estate Bds. (pres. 1923), Pa. Assn. of Planning Commrs. (pres. 1923-27). Home: 821 5th Av. Office: 47 W. 4th St., Williamsport, Pa.

BELL, John Fred, prof. economics; b. Cambridge, O., Feb. 21, 1898; s. Walter R. and Nancy (McCulloch) B.; A.B., Muskingum Coll., New Concorn, O., 1923; M.A., U. of Ill., 1924; Ph.D., 1928; m. Ruth B. Sinclair, June 22, 1929; children—Barbara Bell, Elizabeth Bell. Instr. U. of Ill., 1923-28; asst. prof. Syracuse U., 1928-29; asso. prof. Cleveland Coll. of Western Reserve U., 1929-31; prof. economics and chmn. of dept., Sch. of Commerce, Temple U., since 1931; fellow Harvard, summer 1927; visiting prof., U. of W.Va., summers of 1932, 1933. Served in R.O.T.C., 1918. Mem. Am. Econ. Assn., Am. Acad. Polit. and Social Sciences, Am. Assn. Univ. Profs., Delta Sigma Phi, Beta Gamma Sigma. Republican. Presbyterian. Home: 210 Cypress Av., Jenkintown, Pa.

BELL, John Hume, telegraph engr.; b. Ellon, Scotland, Sept. 6, 1879; s. John Nicol and Elizabeth (Jamieson) B.; student Robert Gordon's Coll., Aberdeen, 1890-94; West of Scotland Tech. Coll., Glasgow, 1902-03, Northampton Inst., London, 1903-05; m. Annie Fairbairn Buchanan, Sept. 8, 1906; children—Joanna Buchanan, Elizabeth Walker, Winifred Jamieson (Mrs. George D. Willets). Came to U.S., 1911, naturalized, 1917. Began as telegraph operator, London, 1894; served with Royal Engrs. (Signal Corps), Brit. Army, during Boer War, 1900-02; jr. engr. engring dept., Brit. Post Office Service, 1903-07, asst. engr., 1907-11; telegraph engr. Bell Telephone Labs., New York, since 1911. Trustee Village of South Orange, N.J., since

1936. Republican. Mason. Contbr. article on telegraphy to 13th edit. Encyclopædia Britannica. Home: 411 Tillou Rd., South Orange, N.J. Office: Bell Telephone Laboratories, New York, N.Y.

BELL, Laurence S., v.p. The Union Nat. Bank of Pittsburgh; b. Pittsburgh, Pa., Sept. 21, 1892; s. Morris H. and Margaret (Johnson) B.; student Pittsburgh pub. schs. and Evening Sch. of U. of Pittsburgh; m. Mary E. Angell, Feb. 6, 1917; children—Martha Jane, Mary Margaret. Asst. Nat. Bank Examiner, 1916-18; with treasury dept. Gulf Oil Corpn., 1918-22; v.p. and cashier The First Nat. Bank of Wilkinsburg, Pa., 1922-28; v.p. The Union Nat. Bank of Pittsburgh since 1928, also dir.; dir. Seyler Mfg. Co., Wilkinsburg Savings and Loan Assn. Mem. Pa. Bankers Assn. (pres.), Credit Assn. of Western Pa. (dir.), Pittsburgh Chamber of Commerce. Clubs: Edgewood Country, Duquesne (Pittsburgh). Home: 3 Scenery Rd., Wilkinsburg, Pa. Office: 4th Av. and Wood St., Pittsburgh, Pa.

BELL, Max Sibbald, ins. exec.; b. Oxford Co., Ontario, Can., Feb. 12, 1902; s. Michael C. and Mary A. (Mayberry) B.; student Ingersoll (Can.) Collegiate Inst., 1913-17; B.A., U. of Toronto (Can.), 1923; came to U.S., 1924, naturalized 1934; m. Clara M. Jackson, Aug., 1927; children—Barbara Helen, Max Sibbald. Clk. State Mutual Life Assurance Co., Worcester, Mass., 1923-26; asst. actuary Continental Am. Life Ins. Co., Wilmington, Del., 1926-29; actuary, 1929-36, v.p. and actuary since 1936. Fellow Actuarial Soc. of America. Republican. Clubs: Rotary, Wilmington Whist, University (Wilmington, Del.). Home: 2612 Harrison St. Office: du Pont Bldg., Wilmington, Del.

BELL, Robert Pierre, supt. W.Va. Industrial Sch. for Boys; b. Grantville, Calhoun Co., W.Va., June 18, 1883; s. William Edgar and Rachel Rebecca (Ferrell) B.; ed. free schools of W.Va. and Vanderbilt U., Nashville, Tenn., 1905-07; m. Katherine Leonore Steinbach, June 1, 1909; children—William Edgar, Robert Emerson, Esther Lee, Richard Steinbach. Became editor Calhoun Chronicle, Grantsville, W.Va., 1904; successively editor and gen. mgr. Point Pleasant (W.Va.) Daily Register, editor and gen. mgr. Methodist Advocate (Point Pleasant), and editor and owner The Citizen (Point Pleasant); supt. W.Va. Industrial Sch. for Boys since Oct. 3, 1933; mayor of Point Pleasant, 1914-16, city clerk, 1930-32. Democrat. Methodist. Mason (K.T.), Odd Fellow. Club: Kiwanis. Home: Point Pleasant, W.Va. Address: W.Va. Industrial School for Boys, Grafton, Taylor Co., W.Va.

BELL, Samuel Kneale, headmaster; b. Germantown, Pa., Sept. 23, 1897; s. Abraham Cook and Mattie Martha (Kelly) B.; student Lehigh U., 1916-20; A.B., Temple U., 1928; A.M., U. of Pa., 1935; m. Rachel Hamilton, June 24, 1921; 1 dau., Patricia Kneale. Engr., U.S. Naval Acad. Exptl. Research Sta., Annapolis, Md., 1921-22; chem. engr. Foote Mineral Co., Phila., 1922-23; teacher, Phila. Pub Schs., 1923-25; teacher of English, Chestnut Hill Acad., 1925-27; head of dept., 1927-36; headmaster, Abington Friends Sch., Jenkintown, Pa., since 1936. Served in U.S. Naval Reserve, 1917-18. Member Delta Upsilon, Phi Delta Kappa. Republican. Episcopalian. Mem. Wyncote (Pa.) Men's Club. Home: Wyncote, Pa. Address: Abington Friends School, Jenkintown, Pa.

BELL, Samuel Paris, lawyer; b. Grantsville, W.Va., July 23, 1870; s. William Edgar and Rachel (Ferrell) B.; ed. pub. schs.; m. Ona B. Stump, June 23, 1893; children—Myrtle (Mrs. L. C. Brecht), Holly P., Wilma (Mrs. A. M. Girard), William W., Virgil M., Mattie Eunice (Mrs. J. B. Heilmann), Samuel P., Elizabeth. Admitted to W.Va. bar, 1896, and began practice at Spencer; mem. Mathews & Bell, 1900-10, Pendleton, Mathews & Bell, 1910-19, since alone. Surveyor of lands, Calhoun Co., W.Va., 6 yrs.; Dem. nominee 3 times for judge of Circuit Court. Mem. Am. Law Inst., W.Va. State Bar Assn. (pres. 1930-31). Mem. M.E.Ch., S. Mason, Odd Fellow; chmn. bd. W. Va. Odd Fellows Home, Elkins, W. Va., since 1919, Rotarian. Former editor Calhoun Chronicle, Mountain State Odd Fellow, Methodist Laymen's Herald. Home: Spencer, W.Va.

BELL, William Hemphill; retired rear adm. Med. Corps, U.S. Navy. Address: 5 W. Blackthorn St., Chevy Chase, Md.

BELL, William Thomas, cotton goods commn.; b. Lincoln, Ala., Oct. 10, 1888; s. Alexander W. and Nancy Eugenia (Coleman) B.; A.B., Howard Coll., Birmingham, Ala., 1904-08; student Lowell Textile Sch., Lowell, Mass., 1909-11; m. Sue Kearny Hardie, May 14, 1913; children—William Thomas, Jr., Grace Hardie, Eugene Coleman. In employ Parker Cotton Mills Co., Columbia, S.C., 1911-14, asst. to vice-pres., 1914-15; with Hunter Mfg. & Commission Co., N.Y. City, 1916-33, vice-pres. and dir., 1928-33; pres. Ray Bell Mfg. Co., Selma, Ala., 1916-22; mem. firm Ketcham & Bell, cotton goods commission and selling agts., N.Y. City since 1933. Mem. bd. edn. pub. schs., Glen Ridge, N.J., since 1928, pres. bd. since 1935. Conglist. Clubs: Merchants (New York); Montclair Golf (Montclair). Home: 40 Sherman Av., Glen Ridge, N.J. Office: 22 Thomas St., New York, N.Y.

BELLAMY, Charles Robert, engineer; b. Scranton, Pa., Dec. 22, 1887; s. Charles Theodore and Eliza (Osenbach) B.; B.S. in Chem., Lafayette Coll., Easton, Pa., 1911; m. Blanche Gertrude Gardner, Oct. 12, 1910; children—Marian, Elizabeth, Robert Gardner. Cadet engr. Semet-Solvay Co., Steelton, Pa., 1911-12, research engr., 1912-13, chief chemist Indianapolis (Ind.) plant, 1913-18, asst. supt., 1918-21, chief of gas engring., Syracuse, N.Y., 1921-23; consulting engr. in private practice, New York, N.Y., 1923-29; asst. mgr. gas engring. dept., Columbia Gas & Electric Corpn. 1929-31, chief engr. gas dept. since 1931; vice-pres. Columbia Engineering Corpn., 1939. Presbyterian. Home: 37 Grover Lane, Caldwell, N.J. Office: 61 Broadway, New York, N.Y.

BELLANCA, Frank Merlo, airplane designer; b. Sciacca (Sicily), Italy, Nov. 16, 1882; s. Andrew and Concetta B.; student Post-Tech. Inst. of Physics-Mathematics, Palermo and Trapany, Italy, 1902-06; m. Claudia Boggiali, Dec. 8, 1906; children—Thea, Edi, Mirthe. Began experiments in aviation with brother, G. M. Bellanca, Taliedo, Milan, Italy, 1910, building first tractor bi-plane; built, with brother, first monoplane of modern design, Belmont Park, Long Island, N.Y., 1912; designing and asso. Bellanca Aircraft Corpn., Staten Island, N.Y., 1927-28, production mgr., 1928-29, dir. of exptl. dept., New Castle, Del., 1929-32, v.p., 1933-35, dir. of foreign sales, New York office, 1935-37; designed spl. gull-wing long distance plane for Commercial Airplane Co., Bridgeport, Conn., 1929; in 1937 designed 4 commercial planes, single and multi-engine, and 3 mil. types, twin-engine, battleship-submarine destroyer and pursuit bomber; designer and v.p. White Aircraft, Ltd., Toronto, Can., since 1938; pres. Internat. Aircraft Trading Co., Bellanca Aircraft Mfg. Co. Inventor of twin-engine with both engines in the central line of symmetry with central line of thrust, resistance and lift passing always through, or close to, central gravity line, irrespective if one or both engines are functioning; air brakes and ailerons working on airfoil vacuum; central beam fuselage construction; hydroplane torpedo chaser; etc. Chmn. Anti-Fascist Alliance. Catholic. Author: Military Superiority of the Airplane Over the Dirigible, a study, 1910; The Intellectual Movement of Today in Italy, 1912; Principles and Methods in the Labor Movement, 1916; The New Italian Immigration in the United States, 1919. Sent by Industria Sportiva, Italian mag., to first aeronautical conf., Paris, 1912. Home: 72-12 Ingram St., Forest Hills, L.I., N.Y. Office: 122 E. 42d St., New York, N.Y.

BELLANCA, Giuseppe Mario, airplane engr.; b. Sciacca, Italy, Mar. 19, 1886; s. Andrea and Concetta (Merlo) B.; teachers certificate in mathematics, Istituto Tecnico, Milan, Italy; degree in engring. mathematics, Politecnico, Milan; m. Dorothy Brown, Nov. 18, 1922; 1 son, August Thomas. Came to U.S., 1911, naturized citizen, 1929. Established lab. for spl. research in aviation, 1909; head of Bellanca Airplane Sch., Mineola, N.Y., 1912-16; cons. engr., Md. Pressed Steel Co., Hagerstown, 1917-20; cons. engr. for airplane constrn., Wright Aeronautical Corpn., Paterson, N.J., 1923-26; organizer, 1927, since pres. Bellanca Aircraft Corpn.; now pres. Bellanca Aircraft Corpn. of America; also chmn. of board and director of engineering. Designer and builder of 1st cabin monoplane in U.S.; designer and builder of transatlantic monoplane Columbia and first transpacific monoplane, "Miss Veedol." Mem. Am. Soc. M.E., Soc. Automotive Engrs., Aeronautical Chamber of Commerce, Early Birds, Quiet Birdmen. Democrat. Catholic. Contbr. tech. papers on aviation. Home: Rockland, Del. Office: Bellanca Aircraft Corpn., New Castle, Del.

BELLIS, Horace D., M.D.; attending surgeon St. Francis Hosp., N.J. State Village for Epileptics; cons. surgeon Municipal Hosp., Orthopedic Hosp. and Dispensary. Address: 437 E. State St., Trenton, N.J.

BELLOWS, Brian Chandler, telephone engring.; b. Mandan, N.D., June 10, 1884; s. Ira Chandler and Adelaide Augusta (Smith) B.; grad. Westerleigh Collegiate Inst., 1902; M.E., Cornell U., 1906; m. Florence Helen Dalton; children—Brian Chandler, John Chamberlin, Richard Macdonald. Student engr. Am. Telephone & Telegraph Co., New York, 1906-07, engr., 1907-12; traffic engr. Western Union Telegraph Co., 1912-14; service engr. Am. Telephone & Telegraph Co., 1914-20, div. traffic supt., Chicago, 1920-23; gen. toll supervisor Ill. Bell Telephone Co., Chicago, 1923-26; toll switching engr. Am. Telephone & Telegraph Co., New York, 1926-34; toll facilities dir. Bell Telephone Labs., New York, since 1934. Mem. Am. Inst. Elec. Engring., Telephone Pioneers of America, Beta Kappa. Republican. Christian Scientist. Club: Maplewood Country. Home: 12 Maryland Rd., Maplewood, N.J. Office: 463 West St., New York, N.Y.

BELTRAN, Basil R.; asso. prof. surgery, Pa. Grad. Sch.; surgeon Misericordia and Fitzgerald-Mercy hosps.; asso. surgeon Graduate Hosp. of U. of Pa.; med. dir. and surgeon Nazareth Hosp., Phila.; med. dir. and chief surgeon Eastern State Penitentiary. Address: 2109 Locust St., Philadelphia, Pa.

BEMIS, Royal Warren, physician; b. Waltham, Mass., Jan. 16, 1868; s. Royal and Susan W. (Durgin) B.; M.D., Jefferson Med. Coll., 1892; m. Gertrude L. Foster, Aug. 5, 1896; 1 dau., Marion Elizabeth. Interne at Municipal Hosp. for Contagious Diseases, Phila., Pa., 3½ years; on med. dispensary staff, St. Christopher's Hosp. for Children for 25 years; on dispensary staff Stetson Hosp., dept. ear, nose and throat for 11 years; in practice in Phila. since 1892. Served on Phila. Bd. of Pub. Health for 2¼ years. Because of present poor health has resigned from all med. assns. Republican. Methodist. Mason, I.O.O.F., Red Men. Home: 2512 N. 5th St., Philadelphia, Pa.

BEN-ASHER, Soloman, physician, cardiologist; b. Lithuania, Dec. 23, 1894; s. Morris and Ida (Slivow) B-A.; came to U.S., 1905, naturalized, 1923; B.Sc., Coll. of City of N.Y., 1919; M.D., N.Y. Univ. Med. Coll. and Bellevue Hosp., 1923; m. Naomi Ehrenkrantz, Oct. 2, 1926; children—Peninah, Hillel Mosheh. Interne, Medical Centre, Jersey City, 1923-25; engaged in pvt. practice of medicine at Jersey City, N.J. since 1925; practice limited to diagnosis and internal medicine; attending, Cardiology Dept., N.Y. Univ. Med. Coll. since 1925; physician Medical Center, Jersey City, N.J. since 1935; mem. staff Greenville Hosp., Jersey City, N.J. Served in C.W.S., U.S.A. during World War. Fellow Am. Med. Assn., Internat. Soc. Gastro-enterology; mem. Am. Heart Assn., N.J. Gastro-enterol. Assn. Jewish religion. Home: 260 Bergen Av., Jersey City, N.J.

BENCKER, Ralph B(uckley), architect; b. Phila., Pa., Dec. 24, 1883; s. John and Mary (Bowden) B.; ed. Sch. of Industrial Arts, 1900-02, Acad. Fine Arts, 1902-03, Atelier of T-Square Club, 1903-05, Temple U., 1905-07 (all of Phila.); m. Mary G. Brendel, June 24, 1907; 1 dau., Helen Wayne. Began as draftsman in office of Wilson Eyre, architect, 1900;

became connected with Price & McLanahan, 1904; admitted to partnership upon decease of Mr. Price, 1918, and title of firm changed to McLanahan & Bencker; practiced alone since June 1, 1925. Architect of bldg. representing Commonwealth of Pa., at Sesquicentennial; Wyoming Bank & Trust Co. Bldg., First Christian Ch., Tradesmen's Nat. Bank Bldg., N.W. Ayer & Son Advertising Agency Bldg., Southwestern Nat. Bank Bldg., Am. Radiator Bldg., Children's Heart Hosp., State Theatre—all Phila.; Pa. Freight Station, Chicago; Union Ry. Station, Indianapolis; Equitable Trust Co. Bldg. and M.E. Blatt Dept. Store, Atlantic City, N.J.; etc. Mem. Phila. Zoning Commn. Fellow A.I.A. (pres. Phila. Chapter); mem. Acad. Fine Arts, Pa. Mus. and Sch. Industrial Arts. Republican. Mem. First Christian Ch. Clubs: Art Club, Rotary, Philadelphia Yacht. Home: Haverford, Pa. Office: 1601 Chestnut St., Philadelphia, Pa.

BENDER, Arthur James, stock and bond broker; b. Bloomfield, N.J.; s. Charles Francis and Anna (Albinson) B.; father a Civil War vet. and for many yrs. Phila. mfr.; student pub. schs., Phila. and New York, N.Y.; m. Jessie Maude Townsend (divorced in 1911); children—Arthur James, Beatrice Maude (Mrs. Albert Allen Simpler); m. 2d, Margaretta Wilson Hobart, Sept. 1, 1921. Mgr. Dunlap & Co., Phila. and New York, 1900-08; mng. Pfaelzer & Co., Boston, N.Y., Phila., 1908-10; organized Arthur J. Bender & Co., Phila., dealers in stocks, bonds and investment securities, 1911, and since owner. Enlisted, 1918, for service in World War, but refused because of age limit. Episcopalian. Club: Bond (Phila.). Home: 214 Kent Rd., Ardmore, Pa. Office: Land Title Bldg., Philadelphia, Pa.

BENDER, Fred William, signal engring.; b. Elizabeth, N.J., Oct. 15, 1882; s. Frederick and Katherine M. (Bender) B.; ed. Battin High Sch., Elizabeth, 1894-98, Union Bus. Coll., 1898-99; m. Carolyn Agatha Blatz, Oct. 4, 1911; children—Dr. Dorothea A., Frederick R., Paul H., Thomas R., Catherine A., Joseph A. In employ The Central R.R. Co., of N.J. continuously since starting as sec. to supt. telegraph and signals, 1899, chief clk. to signal engr., 1902-18, asst. signal engr., 1918-20, signal engr. since 1920; also signal engr. N.Y. & Long Branch R.R., Mount Hope Mineral R.R., Wharton & Northern R.R., all since 1920. Mem. bd. govs. St. Elizabeth Hosp., Elizabeth, N.J. Mem. Joint Valuation Signal Com. (chmn.), N.Y. Railroad Club, Jersey Central Club (pres. 1937-38), Eastern Signal Engrs. (sec.), Assn. Ry. Elec. Engrs., Am. Ry. Guild, Central R.R. Vets. Assn., Joint Train Rules Com. of C. R.R. of N.J. and Reading Co., Assn. Am. Railroads (signal sect.), Elizabeth Music Assn., Elizabeth Philharmonic Assn. Republican. Roman Catholic. K.C. (4°). Clubs: Rotary (past pres.); Supper; Elks Glee (Elizabeth) (past pres.). Home: 349 West End Av., Elizabeth. Office: Central R.R. Co. of N.J., Jersey City, N.J.

BENDER, Harold H(erman), philologist; b. Martinsburg, W.Va., April 20, 1882; s. Isaac Lewis and Margaret Eleanor (Kline) B.; A.B., Lafayette Coll., 1903; Ph.D., Johns Hopkins, 1907; U. of Berlin, 1907-08; Phil.L.D., U. of Kansas, Lithuania, 1922; Litt.D., Lafayette Coll., 1924; m. Amelia Ashcom Hetzel, Sept. 3, 1910; 1 son, John Lewis. Univ. scholar, 1904-05, univ. fellow in Sanskrit and comparative philology, 1906-07, Johns Hopkins; instr. modern langs., 1909-12, asst. prof., 1912-18, prog. Indo-Germanic philology, 1918, chmn. dept. of Oriental langs. and lits., 1927—, Princeton. Fellow A.A.A.S.; mem. Am. Philol. Assn., Am. Oriental Soc. (dir. 1923-26, 1927-30, 1933-36, v.p. 1931-32, 1932-33, mem. exec. com. 1927-37, chmn. Com. for Promotion of Oriental Research (1934-39), Modern Language Assn. America, Modern Humanities Research Assn. (Eng.), Gesellschaft fur Deutsche Philologie (Berlin), Am. Assn. Univ. Profs. (council 1923-26), Oriental Club of Philadelphia (pres., 1923-24), Linguistic Soc. America (a founder, v.p., 1931, 1936), Altorientalische Gesellschaft (Berlin), Soc. for Advancement of Scandinavian Study, Internat. Soc. of Experimental Phonetics (London), English-Speaking Union, N.J. Soc. S.R., St. David's Soc. of New York, Phi Beta Kappa, Phi Delta Theta; mem. and former chmn. com. on Indic and Iranian studies, Am. Council Learned Socs.; mem. and collaborator Internat. Auxiliary Lang. Assn.; patron and hon. mem. Baltic Am. Soc. Trustee American School of Indic and Iranian Studies since 1934; mem. advisory board Am. Council of Learned Socs., 1935-39, Del. Internat. Congress of Orientalists, Oxford, Eng., 1928. Decorated Knight of Order of Gediminas, Grank Duke of Lithuania, 1928. Clubs: Princeton (New York); Orient (L.I.) Yacht. Contbr. to Am. and European philol. jours., various articles on grammar, syntax, accent and etymology; contbr. to Dictionary of Am. Biography, etc.; editor of etymologies, Webster's Dictionary, 1926—; writer of etymologies, and special editor, philology and linguistics, including languages and tables of languages, Webster's New Internat. Dictionary, 2d edit., 1934. Author: The suffixes mant and vant in Sanskrit and Avestan, 1910; German Short Stories, 1920; On the Lithuanian Word-Stock as Indo-European Material (in Studies in Honor of Maurice Bloomfield), 1920; A Lithuanian Etymological Index, 1921; The Home of the Indo-Europeans, 1922; The Selection of Undergraduates, 1926. Clerk of Co. Court of Berkeley Co., W.Va., 1908; draft registrar, War Dept., Princeton U., 1917; mem. House Inquiry of State Dept., 1918; German expert Dept. of Justice, 1918; Lithuanian translator Post Office Dept., 1917-18; chmn. Near East Relief Fund, Princeton U., 1918. Consulting language expert for Mergenthaler Linotype Co., 1927—. Home: 120 Fitz Randolph Rd., Princeton, N.J.; (summer) King's Highway, Orient, L.I., N.Y.

BENDER, Howard Leonard, research chemist; b. Williamstown, W.Va., Sept. 14, 1893; s. Peter Jacob and Nellie (Holtz) B.; grad. Marietta (O.) Twp. High Sch., 1911; A.B., Marietta (O.) Coll., 1917, A.M., 1918; B.S. in chem. engring., Case School of Applied Science, Cleveland, O., 1919; Ph.D., Columbia, 1923; m. Dorothy Corner, June 29, 1918; children—Rose Margaret (deceased), Nancy June, Howard Leonard. Research chemist Dow Chem. Co., Midland, Mich., 1919-21; instr. in chemistry, Marietta Coll., 1921-22; Bakelite fellow in chem. engring., Columbia, 1922-23; chemist, specializing in synthetic resins, with Bakelite Corpn., Bloomfield, N.J., since 1923. Served as engr., Reserve Corps and S.A.T.C. during World War. Fellow Inst. of Chemists; mem. Am. Chem. Soc., A.A.A.S., Nat. Rifle Assn. America. Republican. Congregationalist. Club: Lake Mohawk Country (Sparta, N.J.). Home: 7 Carteret St. Office: 230 Grove St., Bloomfield, N.J.

BENDINER, Irvin, lawyer; b. Phila., Pa., Sept. 6, 1900; s. Herman and Ray (Hartmann) B.; graduate Northeast High Sch., Phila., 1917; B.S. in Econ., Wharton Sch. of U. of Pa., 1921, M.A., Grad. Sch., 1924; LL.B., Temple U. Sch. of Law, Phila., 1925; C.L.U., Am. Coll. of Life Underwriters, Phila., 1928; m. Pauline Jacobs, May 24, 1937. Mem. firm H. Bendiner & Sons, ins. brokers, Phila., since 1919; instr. in law and ins., Temple U., Phila., 1921-30; lecturer in ins., Seth Boyden Sch. of Business, Newark, N.J., 1932-34; spl. lecturer in ins., N.Y.U., 1933-35; lecturer in ins. salesmanship, U. of Pa., 1929-37; admitted to Pa. bar, 1924, and since asso. with brothers in practice of law at Phila.; ins. consultant to sec. Banking Commn. of Pa. since 1933. Counsel to Pa. State and Philadelphia assns. of life underwriters. Served as sergt., S.A.T.C., University of Pa., 1918. Dir. Asso. Hosp. Service of Phila. Mem. Am. and Philadelphia bar assns., Am. Acad. Polit. Science, Am. Acad. Polit. and Social Science, Am. Econ. Soc., Fed. of Ins. Counsel, Am. Legion, Blue Key, Beta Gamma Sigma. Republican. Jewish religion. Lecturer, contbr. to mags. on ins. and related topics. Home: 709 W. Mt. Airy Av. Office: 942 Widener Bldg., Philadelphia, Pa.

BENEDICT, Daniel Norris, mfr. refrigerating and farm machinery; b. Quincy Twp., Franklin Co., Pa., Jan. 23, 1882; s. Daniel Mack and Isabel Price (Norris) B.; M.E., Teachers Coll., Shippensburg, Pa., 1900; m. Ethel Grace Washabaugh, Sept. 12, 1917; 1 dau., Amy Katherine. Began as teacher pub. schs., 1900; with Frick Co., Waynesboro, Pa., since 1902, treas., 1906-28, v.p. and gen. mgr. since 1928; pres. Waynesboro Knitting Co., Knickerbocker Stamping Co.; dir. various other corpns. Trustee Waynesboro Hosp. Republican. Elk. Club: Elks. Home: 203 Clayton Av. Office: Frick Co., Waynesboro, Pa.

BENEDITO, Sidney L., hotel operator; b. New Orleans, La., Apr. 30, 1884; s. Leon and Mary Louise (Schrieffer) B.; student grammar and high schs. and Spencer Coll. of Business and Accounting, New Orleans; m. Elizabeth Ann Deniger, Sept. 7, 1910. Gen. mgr. Schenley Hotel Co. and Schenley Apts. Co., Pittsburgh, 1923-31, pres. and dir. since 1931; also pres. and dir. Bellefield Co. Home: Schenley Apts. Office: Schenley Hotel, Pittsburgh, Pa.

BENEDUM, Michael Late, oil operator; b. Bridgeport, W.Va., July 16, 1869; s. Emanuel and Caroline Victoria (Southworth) B.; student pub. schs., Bridgeport; m. Sarah Nancy Lantz, May 17, 1896; 1 son, Claude Worthington (dec.). Asst. gen. mgr. land dept., South Penn Oil Co., 1889-1900; with J. C. Trees, formed Benedum Trees Oil Co., independent oil operators, employed principally in development of new properties, U.S., Mexico, S.America; pres. Benedum Trees Oil Co. since 1900, Benedum Trees Co. since 1913; dir. Colonial Trust Co. Representative on NRA Planning and Coördinating Com. under oil code, 1933; mem. Business Advisory and Planning Council U.S. Dept. Commerce, 1933. Trustee Grove City (Pa.) Coll.; dir. Western Pa. Hosp., Pittsburgh; trustee Bucknell U., Lewisburg, Pa. Mem. Am. Petroleum Inst., Chamber of Commerce of Pittsburgh. Democrat. Methodist. Mason. Clubs: Pittsburgh, Pittsburgh Country, Duquesne (Pittsburgh); Longue Vue (Vernon, Pa.); Oakmont (Pa.) Country. Home: Woodland Rd. Office: Benedum Trees Bldg., Pittsburgh, Pa.

BENEKE, George C.; mem. law firm Beneke, Callahan & Beneke. Address: Riley Law Bldg., Wheeling, W.Va.

BENET, Hugh, machine works mgr.; b. Abbeville, S.C., Aug. 20, 1892; s. William Christie and Susan (McGowan) B.; student Woodberry Forest Sch., Woodberry Forest, Va., 1907-10, U. of Wis., 1910-12; M.E., U of Va., 1914; m. Ann L. B. Shreve, Oct. 18, 1918; children—Hugh, Ann. Draftsman and rodman J. E. Sirrine Mill Engr. Co., Greenville, S.C., 1912-14; timekeeper, erecting supt., plant supt. Bartlett Hayward Co., Baltimore, 1914-18; production mgr. Tenn. Furniture Corpn., Chattanooga, 1918-21; asst. to pres. Wm. C. Robinson Oil Co., Baltimore, 1921-22; salesman, shop supt., div. mgr. Bartlett Hayward Co., Baltimore, 1922-27; mgr. Holyoke (Mass.) Works, Worthington Pump & Machinery Corpn., 1927-32, mgr. Harrison (N.J.) Works, some, since 1932. Dir. Employers Assn. of North Jersey; dir. Manufacturers Club of West Hudson. Mem. Tau Beta Pi. Clubs: Newark Athletic; Essex Fells Country (Essex Fells, N.J.); Montclair Athletic (Montclair, N.J.). Home: 36 Afterglow Av., Montclair, N.J. Office: Harrison, N.J.

BENÉT, Laura, author; b. Ft. Hamilton, New York Harbor; d. James Walker and Frances Neill (Rose) Benét; grad. Emma Willard Sch., Troy, N.Y.; A.B., Vassar Coll.; unmarried. Settlement worker, Spring St. Settlement, New York, 1916-17; placement worker Children's Aid Soc., New York, 1917; sanitary inspr. U.S. Red Cross, Augusta, Ga., 1917-19; worker St. Bartholomews House, 1925-26; sec. and asst. editor book pages N.Y. Evening Post, 1927-28, N.Y. Evening Sun, 1928-29; book review editor's asst. and book review substitute, N.Y. Times, summer 1930; writing independently since 1930. Received medal as honor poet, Nat. Poetry Center, 1936. Democrat. Episcopalian. Author: Fairy Bread (poems), 1921; Noah's Dove (poem), 1929; Goods and Chattels (fiction), 1930; Basket for a Fair (poems), 1934; The Boy Shelley (biography), 1937; The Hidden Valley (fiction), 1938. Contbr. articles, fiction and verse to many periodicals. Home: Westtown Farm House, Westtown, Pa.

BENFIELD, William Avery, clergyman; b. Mecklenburg Co., N.C., Oct. 1, 1884; s. Daniel Ferguson and Hannah A. (Robinson) B.; A.B., Davidson (N.C.) Coll., 1911; B.D., Union Theol. Sem., Richmond, Va., 1914; m. Mamie E. Bonds, Sept. 29, 1914; children—William Avery, Jr., Robert Bonds. Ordained to Presbyn. Ch. U.S., 1914; pastor, Greenville, W.Va., 1914-24; pastor Mount Pleasant and Hillsdale chs., Sinks Grove, W.Va. since 1924; stated supply, Keller Ch., Lowell, W.Va. and Pence Springs Ch., Pence Springs, W.Va.; stated clk. Greenbrier Presbytery since 1928; served as moderator Synod of W.Va., 1930-31. Democrat. Presbyn. Mason. Home: Sinks Grove, W.Va.

BENJAMIN, Charles Dow, clergyman; b. Honesdale, Pa., May 9, 1894; s. Charles Alfred and Minnie (Jansen) B.; student Allentown (Pa.) Prep. Sch., 1910-11; A.B., U. of Pa., 1915, A.M., 1916, Ph.D., 1919; student Phila. Divinity Sch., 1916; m. Grace Shaw, Feb. 6, 1910; children—Grace Helen, Janet Elizabeth, Anna Shaw. Ordained to ministry of Methodist Ch., 1920; minister Peoples M.E. Ch., Reading, Pa., 1918-19, Hulmeville M.E. Ch., 1919-22, Oak Street Ch., Norristown, Pa., 1922-25, Somerton Ch., Phila., 1925-35; minister First M.E. Ch., Bangor, Pa., 1935-39; minister Miller Memorial Methodist Ch., Phila., since 1939; research worker in Semitics, U. of Pa., 1922-35. Commn. mem. Pocono Epworth League Inst. Mem. Oriental Club of Phila. Republican. Mason. Address: 3046 N. 5th St., Philadelphia, Pa.

BENJAMIN, Frank P., lawyer, banking; b. Peckville, Pa., June 17, 1876; s. Richard S. and Emeline (Peck) B.; LL.B., Dickinson Coll. Sch. of Law, 1904; m. Mabel E. Edwards, June 1908; children—Mary Emeline, Richard Edwards, Frank P., Jr. Admitted to Pa. bar, 1904 and since engaged in gen. practice of law at Scranton; served as Dist. Atty., Lackawanna Co., 1920; pres. Scranton Lackawanna Trust Co. since 1938; dir. Scranton Mortgage Guaranty Co., First Nat. Bank; pres. U.S. Lumber Co., Mississippi Central R.R. Co. Mem. Lackawanna Co. Bar Assn., Delta Chi. Republican. Episcopalian. Club: Scranton (dir.). Home: 1660 N. Washington Av. Office: 506 Spruce St., Scranton, Pa.

BENJAMIN, Harold C., M.D.; asst. orthopedic surgeon Jersey City Med. Center; orthopedic surgeon Christ Hosp. (Jersey City), and Hudson County Hosp. (Secaucus); cons. orthopedic surgeon Margaret Hague Maternity Hosp. Address: 59 Crescent Av., Jersey City, N.J.

BENN, John Kirker, lawyer; b. Pittsburgh, Pa., July 1, 1887; s. Wallace B. and Harriet K., B.; grad. Braddock (Pa.) High Sch., 1905; LL.B., U. of Pittsburgh, 1909; m. Marion R. Miller, 1911; m. 2d, Catherine E. Hutchison, Aug. 29, 1933; 1 dau., Katherine. Admitted to Pa. bar, 1909, and since practiced in Pittsburgh; dir. Am. Gypsum Co. Republican. Presbyterian. Mason (32°, Shriner). Club: South Hills Country. Home: Mt. Lebanon, Pa. Office: Law and Finance Bldg., Pittsburgh, Pa.

BENNER, Claude Leon, ins. exec.; b. Adrian, Mich., June 27, 1892; s. John and Catherine (Ahman) B.; A.B., U. of Mich., 1919, A.M., 1920, Ph.D., Brookings Inst., Washington, D.C., 1925; m. Marion Jacklin, Nov. 8, 1924; children—Roberta, Claude, Richard Gordon. Instr. economics, U. of Mich., 1919-21; asst. prof. economics, Ia. State Coll., 1921-23; mem. research staff, Brookings Inst., Washington, D.C., 1923-25; prof. economics, U. of Del., Newark, Del., 1925-28; economist Continental Am. Life Ins., Co., Wilmington, Del., 1928-30, v.p. and dir. since 1930; lecturer in finance, Wharton Sch. U. of Pa., since 1938; dir. and mem. trust com. Equitable Trust Co., Wilmington, since 1933; dir. New Castle Mutual Ins. Co. since 1937. Mem. Am. Econ. Assn., Am. Acad. Polit. Science, Am. Statis. Assn. Republican. Club: Wilmington (Del.) Country. Author: Federal Intermediate Credit System, 1926; Ten Years of Federal Intermediate Credits, 1933. Home: 705 duPont Rd., Westover Hills. Office: duPont Bldg., Wilmington, Del.

BENNER, Thomas M., lawyer; b. Allegheny City, Pa., May 7, 1873; s. Thomas McC. and Mary (Armstrong) B.; student Ward Sch. and City High Sch.; LL.B., U. of Mich., 1896; m. Charlotte Consalus, Sept. 20, 1910. Admitted to Allegheny Co. bar at Pittsburgh, 1897; since engaged in gen. practice of law; became connected with law dept. of City of Pittsburgh, 1914, serving as asst. city solicitor and later city solicitor until 1938; trustee in bankruptcy Pittsburgh Rys. Co.; atty. for Union Spring & Mfg. Co., Eastman Kodak Stores, Inc. Mem. Am., Pa. and Allegheny County bar assns., Kappa Sigma. Republican. Methodist. Mason. Club: Duquesne. Home: 653 Morewood Av. Office: 1207 Law & Finance Bldg., Pittsburgh, Pa.

BENNER, Winthrop Webster, rubber tire mfg.; b. Minneapolis, Minn., Mar. 25, 1881; s. Webster and Clara (Hook) B.; ed. U. of Minn., 1900-03; m. Etta May Fisher, Dec. 21, 1905; 1 dau., Doris May (Mrs. Edwin J. Bognar). Vice-pres. Lee Rubber and Tire Corpn., Conshohocken, Pa. Home: Arcola, Pa. Office: Lee Rubber & Tire Corpn., Conshohocken, Pa.

BENNETT, Carey Monroe, lawyer; b. Gilmer Co., W.Va., Aug. 9, 1868; s. Alfred M. and Martha J. (Moore) B.; student Glenville State Normal Sch., Glenville, W.Va., 1887-88; LL.B., W.Va. Univ. Law Coll., 1892; m. Byrd Amfss, July 24, 1895 (dec.); 1 son, Paul Amiss; m. 2d Loretta A. Keenan, Apr. 21, 1936. Admitted to W.Va. bar, 1892 and engaged in gen. practice of law at Glenville since 1892; pres. and treas. Gilco Oil & Gas Co., Glenville, W.Va., since 1930, Valley Gas Co., Glenville, W.Va., since 1937; dir. The Oil & Gas Co. Democrat. Baptist. Home: Court St. Office: Main St., Glenville, W.Va.

BENNETT, Charles Edwin, pub. utility executive; b. Ft. Collins, Colo., May 21, 1888; s. Isaac Willis and Laura Brundage (Budrow) B.; B.S., U. of Wis., 1912; m. Mabel E. Lyons, June 16, 1915 (died 1920); 1 son, Willis Lyons; m. 2d, Helen Grow Nichols, Mar. 30, 1921; 1 son, Edwin Grow. Began as state fire prevention engr., Madison, Wis., 1912; supt. plant, Madison Gas and Electric Co., 1915; supt. gas and electric plants of same co., 1916, supt. distribution of gas and electricity, 1917, sec. and treas., 1918-20; v.p. and gen. mgr. Binghamton (N.Y.) Gas Works, 1920-30, pres. and gen. mgr., 1931-35; now pres. and dir. Mfrs. Light and Heat Co., Mfrs. Gas Co., Natural Gas Co. of W.Va., Cumberland & Allegheny Gas Co., Fayette County Gas Co., Gettysburg Gas Corpn., Greensboro Gas Co., Pa. Fuel Supply Co.; dir. Security Mutual Life Ins. Co. Mem. Am. Gas Assn., Soc. of Gas Lighting, Engr's. Soc. of Western Pa., Delta Kappa Epsilon. Republican. Episcopalian. Mason. Clubs: Pittsburgh Athletic, Duquesne (Pittsburgh); Delta Kappa Epsilon (N.Y. City); Oakmont Country. Home: 5837 Solway St. Office: Union Trust Bldg., Pittsburgh, Pa.

BENNETT, Charles Wilbur, former pres. Am. Sheet and Tin Plate Co.; b. Sylvester, Wis., Aug. 9, 1870; s. James Rush and Emily Adelaide B.; U. of Wis., 1888-92; m. Eleanore Robertson Park; 1 dau., Helen Adelaide (Mrs. King R. H. Nelson). Began as worker Marinette Iron Works, West Duluth, Minn., 1892; mech. dept., World's Columbian Expn., 1893; with Ill. Steel Co., Joliet, 1894-96; with Am. Tin Plate Co., Elwood, Indiana, from 1897, and Am. Sheet and Tin Plate Co., Pittsburgh, Pa., from 1906 until retirement, 1936, was pres. of both cos. Republican. Mason. Clubs: Duquesne, Pittsburgh Athletic, University, Pittsburgh Country, Fox Chapel Golf. Home: 6300 Darlington Rd., Pittsburgh, Pa.

BENNETT, Claude E., banking; b. Bath, N.Y., May 30, 1879; s. John R. and Catharine Elizabeth (Gray) B.; ed. pub. sch. and high sch., Bath, N.Y.; m. Florence Van Valkenburg, Sept. 18, 1912; children—Catharine Gray (wife of Dr. Wesley D. Thompson), Jane S., Barbara Van Valkenburg, Claudia Cochran. In employ Farmers and Mechanics Bank, Bath, N.Y., 1897-1904; bookkeeper Tioga County Savings and Trust Co., Wellsboro, Pa., 1904-06, treas. 1906-20, pres. since 1920; dir. First Nat. Bank; pres. Tioga Co. Bell Telephone Co., Wellsboro Hotel Co.; treas. Wellsboro Electric Co. Pres. Wellsboro Sch. Assn. Dir. Pa. State Chamber of Commerce. Mem. Pa. Bankers Association (pres.). Republican. Presbyn. Mason. Clubs: Wellsboro, Tioga Country. Home: Main St., Wellsboro, Pa.

BENNETT, Earle Ogden, lawyer; b. Asbury Park, N.J., Sept. 2, 1908; s. Warren B. and Nettie F. (Chamberlain) B.; ed. Dartmouth Coll., 1925-26; LL.B., N.J. Law Sch., 1931; m. Margaret A. Kragness, Oct. 19, 1935. Studied law in office of Gov. A. Harry Moore, Jersey City, N.J., 1931-32; admitted to N.J. bar as atty., 1932, and since engaged in gen. practice of law at Asbury Park, admitted as counsellor, 1937; master in chancery, 1937; served as police recorder, Ocean Twp., 1938-39; supreme ct. commr., 1938; instr. commercial and bus. law to employees of Jersey Central Power & Light Co. since 1938; twp. committeeman since 1938. Served in N.J.N.G., 1928-31. Dir. Asbury Park Bd. of Trade, 1934-38. Mem. bd. govs. Fitkin Memorial Hosp. Trustee Searle Non-Sectarian Home for Aged, First Presbyn. Ch. Mem. Am., N.J., Monmouth Co. bar assns., Delta Theta Phi. Lt. gov. Kiwanis of N.J. Democrat. Presbyn. Home: 1309 Woodlock Av., Wanamassa. Office: Electric Bldg., Asbury Park, N.J.

BENNETT, George Eli; visiting orthopedic surgeon Johns Hopkins Hosp., Union Memorial Hosp., Church Home and Infirmary and Hosp. for Women of Md.; med. dir. Children's Hosp. Sch. and Garrett Hosp. Dispensary; asso. prof. orthopedic surgery, Johns Hopkins U. Address: 4 E. Madison St., Baltimore, Md.

BENNETT, George Everett, physician and surgeon; b. Warren Co., Pa., July 14, 1883; s. George Washington and Ellen (Brownell) B.; M.D., U. of Pittsburgh Med. Sch., 1905; m. Mabel A. Curtis, Apr. 10, 1905 (dec.); children—Coletta A. (Mrs. Edgar J. Deissler), Clarice (dec.); m. 2d, Ellen Irvine, of Duke Center, Pa., Nov. 26, 1913. Engaged in practice of medicine and surgery at Corry, Pa., since 1905. Fellow Am. Coll. Surgs. Mem. Am., Pa. State, and Erie Co. med. assns. Republican. Mason (K.T., Shriner). Elk. Home: 47 E. Smith St. Office: 25 N. Center St., Corry, Pa.

BENNETT, George W(ayland), prof. of chemistry; b. Phila., Pa., Mar. 29, 1898; s. Joseph Alexander and Sarah Jane (Elliot) B.; B.S., Denison Univ., Granville, O., 1922; M.S., Washington and Jefferson Coll., 1924; Ph.D., Ohio State U., 1927; student U. of Pa., 1924-25, Johns Hopkins, summer 1932; m. Ethel Fetherlin, Oct. 28, 1927; children—John Joseph, Richard Bond. Asso. prof. of chemistry, Grove City (Pa.) Coll., 1927-31, prof., 1931-37; asst. prof. of chemistry and head of dept., Washington and Jefferson Coll., since 1937. Served with Hdqrs. Co., 134th F.A., 37th Div., U.S. Army, 1917-19, with A.E.F. in Meuse-Argonne and Baccarat sectors. Mem. Am. Chem. Soc., Pa. Acad. Science, Am. Legion, Sigma Xi, Phi Lambda Upsilon, Lambda Chi Alpha. Baptist. Mason. Home: 720 Donnan Av., Washington, Pa.

BENNETT, Gershon Samuel, clergyman; b. Kadina, South Australia, Sept. 8, 1882; s. Samuel and Reyna (Lawrence) B.; A.B., Hiram (O.) Coll., 1913; A.M., Columbia U., 1916; student Union Theol. Sem., New York, 1913-16; m. Edith Smith, Sept. 29, 1909; children—Raymond Gershon, Lawrence Leslie, Doris Anne. Came to U.S., 1906, naturalized, 1910. Pastor, Milang, South Australia, 1903-06; prof. Old Testament lit., Hiram Coll., 1916-18; ordained to ministry Disciples of Christ Ch., 1913; pastor Christian Ch., Minneapolis, Minn., 1918-21, West. Boul. Christian Ch., Cleveland, O., 1921-25; prof. Old Testament lit., Bethany Coll., 1925-29; pastor First Christian Ch., New Castle, Pa., since 1929. Pres. Church Council, Minneapolis, 1920-21; dean, Night Sch. of Religion, Cleveland, 1924; chmn. Emergency Relief Bd., 1932-34, Dept. of Pub. Assistance, 1938, Bd. of Appeals, 1938, all Lawrence Co.; vice chmn. State Relief Bd., Area No. 10, 1934-37; mem. advisory bd. State and Federal Labor Service since 1933; pres. New Castle Ministerial Assn., 1934; pres. Character Chest Bd., 1935-36; pres. Lawrence Co. Council Boy Scouts, 1939; mem. Nat. Council Boy Scouts of America, 1939; sec. Lawrence Co. United Pub. Welfare Agencies, 1938-39; mem. Mayors Relief Com., 1933-38; chmn. bd. dirs. New Castle Civic Music Assn., 1936; mem. New Castle Community Chest Bd., 1939; teacher Union Bible Class, Y.W.C.A., 1932-36; pres. New Castle Ch. Basketball League, 1939; mem. New Castle Parks Commn. Dir. Cleveland (O.) Childrens Home. Mem. Phi Kappa Tau, Tau Kappa Alpha. Awarded Silver Beaver by Boy Scouts of America. Republican. Mason (32°). Club: Lions. Address: 322 Park Av., New Castle, Pa.

BENNETT, Hiram Rockwell, clergyman; b. Troy, Pa., Mar. 8, 1886; s. Samuel Currier and Metta (Rockwell) B.; student Coll. City of N.Y., 1905-06; B.D., Gen. Theol. Sem., N.Y. City, 1913; m. Louise Arritta Youngs, Sept. 11, 1909; children—Allen McKean, Hiram Rockwell. Ordained deacon, P.E. Ch., 1913, priest, 1914; rector Grace Ch. (Greenville), Jersey City, N.J., 1915-19, Trinity Ch., Asbury Park, N.J., 1919-23, Christ Ch., Williamsport, Pa., 1923-35; dean Cathedral Ch. of St. John, Wilmington, Del., since 1935. Served as civilian chaplain, Camp Dix, 1918. Dir. J. V. Brown Library (Williamsport, Pa.), Lycoming County Tuberculosis Soc. Mem. Mediæval Acad. America, Phi Gamma Delta. Republican. Episcopalian (hon. canon St. Stephen's Cathedral, Harrisburg, Pa., 1931-35). Mason. Contbr. reviews and hist. articles to mags. Home: The Deanery, 2020 Tatnall St., Wilmington, Del.

BENNETT, Isaac Lee, supt. schs.; b. Circleville, W.Va., Oct. 7, 1892; s. Harman and Martha S. (Nelson) B.; grad. Bridgewater (Va.) Acad., 1921; student Bridgewater Coll., 1921 and 1925, A.B., 1925; student U. of Va., 1923-24, Madison Coll., Harrisonburg, Va., summer, 1925; m. Miss Nettie M. Waggy, Apr. 11, 1916 (died Oct. 28, 1918); 1 son, Paul Isaac; m. 2d, Lottie M. Wyant, Aug. 31, 1922; children—Emory Lee, Cornelia M., Martha F., Lottie Lorine. Teacher 1-room country sch., 1913-18; taught 2 terms while going to college; ordained to the ministry, 1917; pastor Smith Creek Brethren Churches, 1917-22; occasional evangelist since 1919; pastor Crummett Run Ch. of Brethren of Sugar Grove, W.Va., since 1925; again teacher 1-room school, 1925-31; supt. Pendleton Co. Schs. since 1931. Democrat. Mem. Brethren Ch. Home: Franklin, W.Va.

BENNETT, Lyle Hatcher (Mrs. Herman Bennett), artist, lecturer; b. Beckley, W.Va., June 24, 1903; d. John Henry and Leona Lyle (Bowman) Hatcher; grad. Beckley High Sch., 1920; student Randolph Macon Womans Coll., Lynchburg, Va., 1920-22, W.Va. Univ., 1922-23, Northwestern U., (1 semester) 1923; A.B., W. Va. Univ., 1924; m. Herman Bennett, July 23, 1927; children—John Beverly, Nancy Lyle. Teacher Beckley High Sch., 1924-25; law clerk for Judge John H. Hatcher (father), 1925-29; also studied law and admitted to W.Va. bar, 1928; has 21 trophies won in tennis tournaments between 1929-39; became interested in flower arrangement; accredited flower show judge; lecturer on list of W.Va. Garden Club; became interested in oil painting; portrait painter, also still life and landscape. State consultant for Exhbn. of Contemporary Am. Art, N.Y. World's Fair, 1939; consultant arts and crafts Kanawha County Girl Scouts of America. Exhibited: Allied Artists of W.Va., Parkersburg (W.Va.) Art Center, Clarksburg (W.Va.) Womans Club, Southern Preview of Exhbn. of Contemporary Am. Art (Richmond, Va.), Am. Artists Professional League (Bluefield, W.Va.), Nat. Exhbn. of Am. Art, New York. Mem. Allied Artists of W.Va. (pres. 1938-40), Old White Art Colony of White Sulphur Springs, W.Va., Chi Omega. Democrat. Clubs: Charleston Tennis, South Hills Garden (Charleston); W.Va. Garden, Nat. Council of State Garden Clubs. Home: 153 Abney Circle, Charleston, W.Va.

BENNETT, M(ary) Katharine Jones (Mrs. Fred Smith Bennett), philanthropist; b. Englewood, N.J., Nov. 28, 1864; d. Henry and Winifred (Davies) Jones; A.B., Elmira (N.Y.) Coll., 1885, M.A., from the same college, 1934; m. Fred Smith Bennett, July 20, 1898. President of the Woman's Board of Home Missions, Presbyn. Ch. of U.S.A. since 1909; pres. Council of Women for Home Missions, 1916-24; pres. Bd. for Christian Work in Santo Domingo, 1921-36; v.p. Bd. of Nat. Missions, Presbyn. Ch., since 1924. Mem. Assn. of Univ. Women. Clubs: Woman's, Knickerbocker Country (Englewood, N.J.). Home: 100 E. Palisade Av., Englewood, N.J.

BENNETT, Newman H.; mem. surg. staff St. Joseph's Hosp. Address: 736 Brownsville Road, Pittsburgh, Pa.

BENNETT, Virgil E., C.P.A. and economist; b. Portland, O.; s. James Madison and Sarah R. (Lowry) B.; B.S. (with hon.), U. of Pittsburgh; post-graduate work in econs.; children—Paul V. and Barbara. Served as lt., U.S.N.R. Dep. auditor gen. of Pa., 1925-29; spl. adviser to state treasurer 1929-33. Trustee Beaver (Pa.) United Presbyn. Ch. Mem. Am. Econ. Assn., Am. Accounting Assn., Pa. Soc. of N.Y. City, Am. Inst. Accountants, Delta Mu Delta. United Presbyn. Club: Pittsburgh Economic (Pittsburgh). Author articles on monetary history of U.S., naval stores accounting, water utilities, federal taxes and taxes under the Agrl. Adjustment Adminstrn.; Pa. Auditor General's Biennial Reports, 1927, 1929. Home: 200 Beaver St., Beaver, Pa. Office: Union Trust Bldg., Pittsburgh, Pa.

BENNETT, William Charles, dairy business; b. White Twp., Pa., Nov. 27, 1876; s. Michael and Charlotte (Richardson) B.; student pub. sch.; m. Laura E. Myers, May 20, 1914. Organized, 1907, and operated M. Bennett & Sons, general contractors, 1907-31; purchased Indiana Dairy Co., 1934, since pres.; dir. Textile Mills Co., Inc. Republican. Protestant. Home: 629 School St. Office: Wayne Av., Indiana, Pa.

BENNEY, George Andrew; chmn. bd. Benolite Corpn. Home: Farm Hill, Sewickley Heights, Pa. Office: Oliver Bldg., Pittsburgh, Pa.

BENNIS, David A., coal and building material; b. Germantown, Pa., Dec. 13, 1893; s. Edward F. and Kathryn T. (McCarthy) B.; A.B., St. Joseph's Coll., 1914; Civil Engr., U. of Pa., 1918; m. Helen V. Best, Apr. 14, 1920; children—Edward F., Marie Claire, Kathleen, David, Jr., John Robert. Engaged in general contracting work, 1918-23; sec. and treas. Edward F. Bennis & Sons, Inc., retail coal, fuel oil and bldg. materials since 1923. Served in U.S.N. Res., 1918-19. Roman Catholic. K.C. Clubs: Lions, Whitemarsh Valley Country, Penn Athletic. Home: 630 E. Chelten Av., Germantown. Office: 825 E. Washington Lane, Germantown, Philadelphia, Pa.

BENSINGER, C(harles) Raymond, lawyer; b. Mahoney City, Pa., May 22, 1884; s. John Calvin and Margaret (Richardson) B.; student Stroudsburg High Sch., 1899-1903; m. Lucy Roder, June 14, 1917; children—Charles, Alex. Admitted to Pa. bar, 1907, and since in practice at Stroudsburg, Pa.; v.p. and dir. First Stroudsburg Nat. Bank; dir. Worthington Mower Co., Internat. Boiler Works, Monroe Co. Water Co., Colonial Securities Co. Dir. Y.M.C.A.; vice-pres. Gen. Hosp., East Stroudsburg, Pa. Elk. Clubs: Rotary, Glen Brook Country (Stroudsburg); Wolf Hollow Country (Delaware Water Gap). Home: 28 So. Green St., East Stroudsburg, Pa. Office: 10 N. 7th St., Stroudsburg, Pa.

BENSINGER, Noel Edgar, univ. treas.; b. Chicago, Ill., Jan. 20, 1891; s. Edward James and Rilla (Lindsley) B.; A.B., Wesleyan Univ., Middletown, Conn., 1914; A.M., Harvard U., 1915, grad. study, 1916-17; m. Olga Frances Appelquest, Sept. 20, 1919. Instr. German, Carnegie Inst. Tech., Pittsburgh, 1915-16, Wesleyan Univ., 1917-18; asst. paymaster Bethlehem Shipbldg. Co., Boston, Mass., 1918-19; asst. tax accountant General Electric Co., Schenectady, N.Y., 1919-20; asst. treas. Drew Theol. Sem., Madison, N.J., 1920-28; treas. Drew Univ., Madison, N.J. since 1928; sec. Wendel Foundation. Served in A.O.T.C., Louisville, Ky., 1918. Mem. Assn. of Coll. Bus. Officers of Eastern States, Phi Beta Kappa, Phi Nu Theta. Republican. Methodist. Mason. Club: Deer Lake Assn. (Boonton, N.J.). Home: Drew Forest, Madison, N.J.

BENSLEY, Maynard G., M.D.; attending obstetrician Overlook Hosp. Address: 129 Summit Av., Summit, N.J.

BENSON, Byron David, banking; b. Passaic, N.J., Mar. 30, 1890; s. Robert D. and Harriet (Granger) B.; A.B., Princeton, 1912; m. Annie Ball, June 13, 1913; children—Dorothy (Mrs. Thomas G. Clynes, Jr.), Byron David, Anne Hathaway, Eleanor Ball. Employed successively as clk., sec., asst. treas., and sales mgr. Tidewater Oil Co., 1912-25; brokerage and investment adviser, 1925-32; asso. with Peoples Bank & Trust Co., Passaic, N.J. since 1932, vice-pres., trust officer and dir. since 1931; pres. and dir. Harben Royalty Corpn.; dir. Magor Car Corpn., Andrew McLean Corpn., Ramapo Finishing Corpn., Nat. Petroleum Co. Mem. Passaic Co. Park Commn.; trustee Passaic Gen. Hosp., First Presbyn. Ch.; dir. Passaic Y.M.C.A. Mem. Passaic Co. Bankers Assn. Republican. Presbyn. Clubs: Arcola Country (Hackensack); Princeton (New York); Nassau (Princeton). Home: 215 Passaic Av. Office: 663 Main Av., Passaic, N.J.

BENSON, C. Wesley; pres. U.S. Trust Co. of N.J., Riverside Trust Co., Peoples Park Bank. Address: 126 Market St., Paterson, N.J.

BENSON, Charles Emile, univ. prof.; b. Clinton, Ia., Sept. 9, 1881; s. Peter Emil and Anna (Peterson) B.; B.Ed., State Teachers Coll., Peru, Neb., 1911; A.B., University of Neb., 1911, A.M., 1912; Ph.D., Columbia University, 1922; m. Luella Linder, Oct. 10, 1906; 1 son, Frederic Rupert. Formerly teacher in rural schs. and prin. village schs.; supt. schs. Chelan, Wash., 1904-05, Nelson, Neb., 1907-09; fellow dept. psychology, U. of Neb., 1910-12; supt. schs., Lexington, Neb., 1912-14; prof. psychology and edn., State Normal Sch., Kearney, Neb., 1914-15; head dept. psychology, Southeast Mo. State Teachers Coll., Cape Girardeau, Mo., 1915-21; acting dean Sch. of Edn., 1922-23, and dir. of summer session, 1923, U. of Okla.; asst. prof. ednl. psychology, 1923-24, asso. prof., 1924-25, prof. since 1925, New York U., also chmn. Dept. of Educational Psychology. Ednl. adviser Berkeley Secretarial Sch., East Orange, N.J., and Berkeley-Llewellyn Secretarial School, New York City. Member bd. of trustees Harriette Melissa Mills Kindergarten Primary Sch. Commd. 1st lt. Sanitary Corps (division psychology), U.S.A., Feb. 6, 1918; served at Camp Greenleaf, Ga.; clin. psychologist, Camp Grant, Rockford, Ill.; honorably discharged, Dec. 12, 1918; retired U.S.A., 1928. Mem. N.Y. Acad. of Pub. Edn., N.E.A. (life), Nat. Soc. for Study of Edn., Coll. Teachers of Edn., Am. Psychol. Assn., Nat. Com. for Mental Hygiene, Assn. of Applied Psychologists, N.Y. Schoolmasters' Club, Phi Delta Kappa, Kappa Delta Pi, Pi Gamma Mu. Horace Mann League, Kiwanis Club (hon.), Lotos Club (New York), fellow A.A.A.S.; asso. fellow N.Y. Acad. of Medicine. Methodist. Author: The Output of Professional Schools for Teachers, 1922; Psychology for Teachers (with others), 1926, revised edit., 1933; Psychology for Advertisers (with D. B. Lucas), 1930. Home: 42 Carolin Rd., Montclair, N.J.

BENSON, Charles Prue, physician; b. Travelers Rest, S.C., Apr. 1, 1879; s. Wm. Wheeler and Cora (Hawkins) B.; M.D., Atlanta Coll. Phys. & Surgs., now Emory U. Med. Sch., 1910; m. Addie Cannon, Oct. 26, 1910; children—Ralph Cannon, Charles P., Jr., Jean Lee. After graduation engaged in gen. practice of medicine at Travelers Rest, S.C., 1911-18 and 1919-20, at Greenville, S.C., 1920-31; asso. with U.S. Vets. Adminstrn. since 1931; physician internal medicine, Vets. Adminstrn. Facility, Aspinwall, Pa. since Aug. 1937; study post grad. course Vets. Adminstrn. Facility, Washington, D.C., 1935, and at Mayo Clinic, Rochester, Minn., Oct. 1936. Served as 1st lt. then Capt. Med. Corps, U.S.A., 1918-19, in Med. Corps Res. since 1919, now lt. col. Mem. A.M.A., Southern Med. Assn. (Greenville, S.C.). Democrat. Baptist. Mason. Home: 227 Lexington Av., Aspinwall, Pa.

BENSON, Francis C., Jr.; radiologist Hahnemann Hosp.; prof. radiology Hahnemann Med. Coll. Address: 230 N. Broad St., Philadelphia, Pa.

BENSON, Joseph P.; gynecologist Adrian Hosp. Home: 128 W. Mahoning St., Punxsutawney, Pa.

BENSWANGER, William Edward, pres. Pittsburgh Baseball Club; b. New York, N.Y., Feb. 22, 1892; s. Edward B. and Kathryn (Cleere) B.; grad. Central High Sch., Pittsburgh, 1911; m. Eleanor F. Dreyfuss, June 29, 1925; 1 son, William Dreyfuss. Insurance business, 1911-31; in baseball since 1931; pres., treas. and dir. Pittsburgh Athletic Co.; sec., treas. and dir. Forbes Field Co.; dir. National League; dir. Oakland Branch, Peoples-Pittsburgh Trust Co. Served in Air Service (balloon), U.S. Army, 1918. Dir. Pittsburgh Symphony Soc. Mem. Pittsburgh Chamber of Commerce, Art Soc., Pa. Soc. of N.Y., Am. Legion; hon. mem. Phi Epsilon Pi. Republican. Masori, Elk. Clubs: Rotary, Variety, Civic, Islam Grotto, Hungry, Concordia, Musicians, Aero, Amen Corner (past pres.). Has written extensively on music; annotator for Pittsburgh Symphony since 1927. Home: 5429 Aylesboro Av. Office: 419 Flannery Bldg., Pittsburgh, Pa.

BENT, Leavitt N.; b. Framirigham, Mass., 1886; student Mass. Inst. Tech. V.p. Hercules Powder Co. Home: Philadelphia Pike, Holly Oak, Del. Office: care Hercules Powder Co., Wilmington, Del.

BENT, Quincy, v.p. Bethlehem Steel Co.; b. Steelton, Pa., July 28, 1879; s. Luther Stedman and Mary Stearns (Felton) B.; A.B., Williams Coll., Williamstown, Mass., 1901; m. Deborah Norris Brock, Jan. 4, 1910; 1 son, Horace Brock. Began work in steel plant, 1901; supt. Lebanon Furnaces, Pa. Steel Co., 1903-07, mgr. Lebanon Plant, 1907-09; asst. to pres. Md. Steel Co., 1909-16; gen. mgr. Steelton Plant, 1916-18, v.p. since 1918, Bethlehem Steel Co., also dir.; dir. Bethlehem Shipbuilding Co. Trustee Williams Coll. Mem. Am. and Brit. Iron and steel insts., Am. Soc. Mining and Metall. Engrs., Am. Acad. of Polit. and Social Science, Army Ordnance Assn., Alpha Delta Phi. Republican. Clubs: Philadelphia, Corinthian Yacht (Philadelphia); Eastern Yacht (Boston); Essex County. Home: Weyhill Farms, Bethlehem, Pa.

BENTLEY, David F., Jr., M.D.; urologist Camden County Hosp., Grenloch Cooper Hosp. Address: 406 Cooper St., Camden, N.J.

BENTLEY, Franklin Lee, prof. animal husbandry, Pa. State Coll. Address: State College, Pa.

BENTON, Herbert Elmon, clergyman; b. Vinton, Ia., July 7, 1872; s. Frederic Alphonso and Clara (Davis) B.; A.B., Tufts Coll., 1894, B.D. and A.M., 1897, S.T.D., 1924; m. Mariette Powers, June 17, 1897; children—Levi Powers (dec.), Frederic Elmon. Ordained ministry Universalist Ch., 1897; pastor successively Derby Line, Vt., Little Falls, N.Y., Riverside, Calif., Stamford, Conn., and Lowell, Mass., until 1920, Messiah Universalist Ch., Phila., Pa., since Mar. 1920. Mem. Charter Commn. of Phila. Mem. bd. dirs., Phila. Federation of Chs.; mem. exec. com. Nat. Com. on the Chs. and World Peace; mem. clergymen's adv. com. World Alliance for Internat. Friendship through the Chs.; sec. Com. of 100 Clergymen of Metropolitan Phila.; trustee Pa. Universalist Conf. Trustee Messiah Universalist Home for Aged. Mem. Foreign Policy Assn., League of Nations Assn., Delta Tau Delta. Mason. Home: 332 W. Mt. Airy Av., Philadelphia, Pa.

BENTON, Thaddeus Greene, corpn. official, lawyer; b. Washington, D.C., Mar. 23, 1900; s. William Horace and Florence May (Yeatman) B.; student Emerson Inst. and Strayers Business Coll., Washington, D.C., 1916-18; LL.B., Georgetown U., 1921; m. Ruth Elizabeth Hadley, July 21, 1923; children—Elizabeth Seymour, Thaddeus Greene. Admitted to Dist. of Columbia bar, 1921, N.Y. bar, 1928; law clk. for the Solicitor Gen. of the U.S., 1919-22; spl. asst. to the Atty. Gen. of the U.S., 1924-27; practicing atty in New York since 1927; pres and dir. Federal Oil Marketing Corpn.; Gulf States Oil and Refining Corpn., Midstates Development Corpn., Midstates Operating Corpn.; v.p. and dir. Middle States Petroleum Corpn.; Midstates Oil Corpn.; dir. treas.-sec. La. &

North-West R.R. Co. Mem. Am. Bar Assn., Delta Chi. Episcopalian. Club: Orange Lawn Tennis. Home: 249 Heywood Av., Orange, N.J. Office: 170 Broadway, New York, N.Y.

BERESFORD, Frank Moxon, physician; b. Seattle, Wash., Dec. 2, 1889; s. Spencer Moxon and Elsie (Jefferis) B.; M.S., George Washington U., Washington, D.C., 1916; B.S.M., Marquette U., 1919, M.D., same, 1919; Diplomate in Hygiene and Trop. Medicine, U.S.N. Med. Sch., Washington, D.C., 1922; grad. study, U. of Mich., 1916, U. of Calif., 1919 and 1926; m. Gail Fitch, M.D., June 29, 1915; 1 son, Spencer. Physician since 1919; asst. surg. and passed asst. surg. Med. Corps, U.S.N., 1921-25; staff mem., Mayo Clinic, 1926-27; asst. med. dir., Northwestern Mutual Life Ins. Co., Milwaukee, Wis., 1927-35; asso. med. dir., Providential Mutual Life Ins. Co., Phila., Pa., 1935-36, med. dir. since 1936. Served in U.S.N. during World War. Fellow A.M.A. Mem. Am. Pub. Health Assn., Alumni Assn. of Mayo Foundation U. of Minn., Assn. Life Ins. Med. Dirs. of America, Pa. State and Phila. Co. med. socs. Republican. Episcopalian. Home: 624 Overhill Rd., Ardmore, Pa. Office: 4601 Market St., Philadelphia, Pa.

BERG, Gustav F.; surgeon St. John's Gen. Hosp. Address: 858 Lockhart St., Pittsburgh, Pa.

BERG, John Daniel; chmn. bd. Dravo Corpn.; officer and dir. many other cos. Home: 1207 Beaver Road, Glen Osborne, Pa. Address: Pittsburgh, Pa.

BERG, Ragnar, engineer; b. Stockholm, Sweden, Mar. 10, 1886; s. Hjalmar and Marie Louise (Edberg) B.; Mining and Metall. Engr., Tech. U. of Stockholm (Sweden), 1910; came to U.S., 1911, naturalized, 1919; m. Margaret Peacock, Sept. 1, 1917; children—Margaret Louise, Hakon Harald; m. 2d, Violette Bouffard, Aug. 10, 1931. Testing engr., de Wendel Co., Hayange, France, 1911; asst. to chief engr., Crucible Steel Co., Midland, Pa., 1912-13; designer, Am. Sheet and Tin Plate Co., 1914, Bethlehem Steel Co., 1914-15; engr. Koppers Constrn. Co., 1915-24, European tech. rep., Paris, France, 1924-32, chief engr. engring. and construction div., Pittsburgh, since 1932. Mem. Inst. of Fuel (London, Eng.), Nat. Soc. of Professional Engrs. Republican. Protestant. Clubs: University, St. Clair Country (Pittsburgh, Pa.). Home: 55 Roycroft Av., Mt. Lebanon, Pa. Office: 3105 Koppers Bldg., Pittsburgh, Pa.

BERGER, Andrew Bart, banker; b. New Castle, Pa., Dec. 25, 1883; s. George Reis and Rebecca Niccolls (Gardiner) B.; grad. St. Paul's Sch., Concord, N.H., 1902, Phillips Acad., Andover, Mass., 1903; student Sheffield Sci. Sch., Yale, 1905; m. Olive Whigham Fleming, Dec. 3, 1903; children—Rebecca Bart (Mrs. Alan Stevenson Humphreys), Andrew Bart. Began as clerk Farmers Nat. Bank, Pittsburgh, 1903; partner H. N. Davis & Co., industrial engrs., 1919-23; v.p. Pa. Trust Co., Pittsburgh, 1923-26; v.p. Potter Title and Trust Co., Pittsburgh, 1926-33, pres., 1933-38; receiver 9 closed nat. banks in Pittsburgh area, including Bank of Pittsburgh, Monongahela Nat. Bank, Highland Nat. Bank, Third Nat. Bank, since Feb. 1938; dir. Potter Title & Trust Co., Pittsburgh Mallable Iron Co., Reymer Bros., Inc., P. McGraw Woolen Mills, Miller Printing Co. Served in Air Corps, U.S. Army, during World War; now col. Air Corps Reserve. Republican. Mem. S.A.R., Am. Legion, Forty and Eight. Episcopalian. Mason (33°), past comdr. in chief Pa. Consistory. Clubs: Duquesne, Fox Chapel (Pittsburgh); Rolling Rock (Ligonier). Home: 625 South Linden Av. Office: Bank of Pittsburgh, Pittsburgh, Pa.

BERGER, George Reis Bart, lawyer; b. New Castle, Pa., Mar. 31, 1887; s. George Reis Bart and Rebecca Niccolls (Gardiner) B.; grad. St. Paul's Sch., Concord, N.H., 1904; A.B., Yale, 1908; LL.B., U. of Pittsburgh, 1911; m. Margaret Lee Benham, Nov. 12, 1913; children—George Reis Bart, Margaret Benham Bart, Ann Harvy Bart, Fredericka Gardiner Bart. Admitted to Pa. bar, 1911, and since practiced in Pitts-

burgh asso. with Donald Thompson; dir. Pa. Engring. Corpn.; sec. and dir. Steel Products Co. Served as 2d lt. in Air Service Production, 1918-19. Mem. Pa. and Allegheny Co. bar assns. Republican. Episcopalian. Mason (33°). Clubs: Duquesne, Pittsburgh Golf, Fox Chapel Golf, Harvard-Yale-Princeton, Rolling Rock, Law (Pittsburgh); Army and Navy (Washington, D.C.). Home: 5516 5th Av. Office: 1220 Berger Bldg., Pittsburgh, Pa.

BERGER, G(odfrey) Fred(erick), banker; b. Buffalo, N.Y., Sept. 2, 1892; s. Godfrey William Christian and Louise (Benner) B.; grad. Buffalo (N.Y.) High Sch., 1909; student Mission House Coll., Plymouth, Wis., 1909-11, Am. Inst. Banking, 1911-14 (grad.); m. Irene Mau, Oct. 11, 1917 (divorced 1926); 1 dau., Mauri Irene (deceased); m. 2d, Lesley Turner-Brown, Apr. 15, 1932. With Citizens Bank, 1911-13, Marine Nat. Bank, 1913-14, Central Nat. Bank, 1914-15, Peoples Bank, 1915-16, all of Buffalo; with Lackawanna (N.Y.) Trust Co., 1916-17; N.Y. State bank examiner, 1917-24; with Lybrand, Ross & Montgomery, Phila., 1924-25; with Norristown-Penn Trust Co. since 1925. Mem. Am. Bankers Assn. (mem. exec. council), Pa. Bankers Assn. (chmn. trust company sect.). Faculty mem. Phila. Chapter Am. Inst. Banking and Grad. Sch. Banking. Republican. Presbyterian. Mason. Club: Whitemarsh Valley Country (Phila.). Home: 6445 Greene St., Germantown, Philadelphia. Office: Norristown-Penn Trust Co., Norristown, Pa.

BERGER, Nathan Hale, lawyer, banker; b. Brooklyn, N.Y., July 14, 1889; s. Harry Henry and Claire Paula (Firstman) B.; prep. edn. Erasmus Hall Acad. (Brooklyn); A.B., New York Univ. 1908, LL.B., 1906; m. Alice E. Zeisler, June 20, 1915; 1 dau., Claire Paula. Began practice of law, 1910; entered banking business, 1924; pres. Peoples Title & Mortgage Guaranty Co., 1926-28; v.p. Hayes Circle Nat. Bank (Newark, N.J.), 1928-30; pres. Peoples Nat. Bank & Trust Co. (Belleville, N.J.) since 1931; also pres. North Am. Building & Loan Assn., Wilson Construction Co., Reporting Corpn.; chmn. Investment Foundation. Mem. exec. bd. New York Univ. Law Sch. Mason, Elk. Club: Kiwanis. Home: 67 S. Munn Av., East Orange, N.J. Office: 60 Park Pl., Newark, N.J.

BERGEY, James Riley; pastor Third Evang. and Reformed Ch. Address: 3606 Mohawk Av., Baltimore, Md.

BERGLAND, Eric L.; b. Lexington, Ky., June 17, 1881; s. Major Eric and Lucy Scott (McFarland) B.; B.S. and E.E., Princeton U.; unmarried. Pres. Am. Pneumatic Service Co. and several other companies. Home: 1406 Woodlawn Av. Office: 837 King St., Wilmington, Del.

BERGLAND, John McFarland, physician; b. West Point, N.Y., Mar. 5, 1879; s. Eric and Lucy Scott (McFarland) B.; prep. edn., private sch., Baltimore; B.S., Princeton U., 1900; M.D., Johns Hopkins, 1904; m. Alice Lloyd Pitts, June 5, 1902; children—John McFarland, Sullivan Pitts (deceased), Eric Lloyd. Physician, Baltimore, since 1904; asso. prof. of obstetrics, U. of Md. Sch. of Medicine; lecturer in obstetrics, Johns Hopkins U. Sch. of Medicine. Fellow Am. Coll. Surgeons; mem. Med. and Chirurg. Faculty of Md. A.M.A. Southern Med. Assn. Episcopalian. Clubs: Maryland (Baltimore); Princeton (New York). Home: 229 Lambeth Rd. Office: 1014 St. Paul St., Baltimore, Md.

BERGSTRESSER, Ira F., clergyman; b. Saucon, Northampton Co., Pa., Dec. 1, 1872; s. Abraham T. and Susannah L. B.; student Keystone State Normal Sch., Kutztown, Pa., 1892-94; Ph.B., Ill. Wesleyan U., Bloomington, Ill., 1910; m. Carrie G. Newhart, Sept. 4, 1900 (deceased); children—Irene Grace (Mrs. Samuel Roth), Paul Franklin, Karl Samuel, Alma Claire; m. 2d, Katie B. Marxen, Feb. 14, 1928. Began as pub. sch. teacher, 1890; minister of East Pa. Conf., Evangelical Ch., since 1896, ordained, 1898; dist. supt. since Feb. 1933. Trustee East Pa. Conf.; has been sec. of conf.; served as del. to Quadrennial Gen. Confs.; sec. Commn. on Ch. Union; trustee Albright Coll., Reading, Pa. Mem.

Royal Arcanum. Republican. Writer of Internat. Sunday Sch. lessons for Evang. Ch. Address: 219 N. St. Cloud St., Allentown, Pa.

BERGSTROM, Albert R.; mayor of Coatesville. Address: Coatesville, Pa.

BERGY, Gordon Algy, univ. prof.; by. Caledonia, Mich., May 1, 1890; s. Emanuel and Elizabeth (Cobb) B.; Ph.C., Univ. of Mich., 1913, B.S. in Pharmacy, M.S.; m. Constance L. McCammon, June 30, 1924; 1 son, Gordon Goodrich. Prof. pharmacy, W.Va. Univ., Morgantown, W.Va., since 1916. Served in C.W.S., Development Div., Cleveland, O., during World War. Mem. Am. Chem. Soc., Am. Phar. Assn.; A.A.A.S., Am. Chemurgic Soc., W.Va. State Pharm. Assn., W.Va. Acad. Sci., Rho Chi, Phi Lambda Upsilon, Kappa Psi. Republican. United Brethren. Contbr. Am. Professional Pharmacist. Home: 317 Lebanon St., Morgantown, W.Va.

BERK, Ira Leigh, distributor Packard motor cars; b. Oldtown, O.; s. Levi and Laura (Billingsly) B.; ed. pub. sch. and high sch., Dayton, O., Miami Commercial Coll.; m. Trixie I. Boyle, June 30, 1934. With National Cash Register Co., Dayton, O., 1895-1902; with Burroughs Adding Machine Co., Detroit, Mich., 1902-1909; organized firm of Ira L. & A. C. Berk, Ltd., Sydney, Australia, 1909, for distributing motor cars and Burroughs Adding Machines in Australia and New Zealand; now dir. Ira L. & A. C. Berk, Ltd., Sydney, Australia; pres. and propr. Packard Motor Co. of Pittsburgh, distributors Packard cars for Western Pa., Northern W.Va., and Southeastern O., Pittsburgh, Pa., since 1915. Republican. Presbyn. Mason (K.T., Shriner). Clubs: Duquesne, Pittsburgh Athletic (Pittsburgh); Country (Oakmont); Longue Vue (Verona); Westchester Biltmore Country (Rye, N.Y.); Oatland Country Golf (Sydney, Australia). Home: 1224 Shady Ave. Office: 4709 Baum Blvd., Pittsburgh, Pa.

BERKEY, Charles Peter, geologist; b. Goshen, Ind., March 25, 1867; s. Peter and Lydia (Stutsman) B.; B.S., U. of Minn., 1892, M.S., 1893, Ph.D., 1897; m. Minnie M. Best, Sept. 4, 1894; children—Paul Ainsworth, Virginia Dale. Instr. in geology, U. of Minn., to 1903; tutor, instr. and asst. prof., asso. prof., and prof. geology since 1903, Columbia U. A specialist on geology applied to engineering. Employed on state surveys (geol.) of Minn., Wis. and New York; consulting geologist New York Bd. Water Supply since 1906; also consulting geologist of the Metropolitan District Water Supply Commission of Mass., Department of Water and Power of Los Angeles; consulting engineer U.S. Reclamation Bur., and Tennessee Valley Authority; petrographer and geologist on many eng. and mining problems; chief geologist Central Asiatic Expdns., Am. Mus. Natural History, since 1922; geologist Port of New York Authority; mem. U.S. Colo. River Bd. Sec. Geol. Soc. America; mem. New York Acad. Sciences (ex-pres.), Rochester Acad. Science, Geol. Soc. China, Am. Inst. Mining and Metall. Engrs., Municipal Engrs. City of New York, Am. Philos. Soc., Nat. Acad. Sciences, Phi Beta Kappa, Sigma Xi, Tau Beta Pi, Phi Gamma Delta; fellow A.A.A.S. Home: Palisade, N.J.

BERKHEIMER, Frank Evans, supervising prin. of schools; b. Williams Grove., Pa., Nov. 17, 1897; s. George Martin and Emma Jane (Evans) B.; grad. Mechanicsburg (Pa.) High Sch., 1917; A.B., Dickinson Coll., Carlisle, Pa., 1921; M.S., Pa. State Coll., 1936; m. S. Rose Huntsberger, June 21, 1927. Teacher Lemoyne (Pa.) High Sch., 1921-24, prin., 1924-31; supervising prin. public schools, Lemoyne, Pa., since 1931. Served in S.A.T. C., Oct.-Dec. 1918. Trustee Findlay (O.) Coll. Mem. N.E.A., Pa. State Edn. Assn. Democrat. Mem. Churches of God in N. America. Club: Rotary of Lemoyne. Home: 260 Walton St. Office: Market St., Lemoyne, Pa.

BERKOW, Samuel Gordon, physician; b. Egumen, Russia, Dec. 28, 1899; s. Isaac and Zelda (Gordon) B.; brought to U.S., 1905, naturalized, 1907; B.S., N.Y. Univ., 1918; M.D., N.Y. Univ. & Bellevue Hosp. Med. Coll., 1922; m. Elizabeth Doris, Mar. 13, 1930; children—Gordon Zachary, Lester Hugh, Irene Doris. Interne St. John's Hosp., New York, 1922-24; engaged in gen. practice of medicine at Perth Amboy, N.J., 1924-29, specializing in gynecology and obstetrics since 1929; mem. staff Mt. Sinai Hosp. since 1927; Perth Amboy Gen. Hosp. since 1924. Mem. A.M.A., Assn. for Study Internal Secretions, Tau Epsilon Phi. Awarded Valentine Mott Memorial Prize, surg. anatomy, by New York U., 1922. Hebrew religion. Clubs: Lions; Yacht (Perth Amboy). Author: Childless, A Study of Sterility, Its Causes and Treatment, 1937. Contbr. to med. jours. Home: 158 Kearny Av. Office: 138 Market St., Perth Amboy, N.J.

BERL, Ernst, research prof.; b. Freudenthal (formerly Austria), July 7, 1877; s. Max and Agnes B.; student chem. engring., Tech. U. of Vienna, 1894-98; Ph.D., U. of Zurich, 1901; m. Margaret Karplus, Mar. 28, 1912; children—Herbert, Walter George. Came to U.S., 1933, naturalized, 1938. Asst. U. and Tech. U. of Zurich, 1901, asst. prof., 1904-10; chief chemist rayon factory, Tubize, Belgium, 1910-14; chief chemist Austrian War Ministry, 1914-19; prof. chem. technology and electro-chemistry, Tech U. of Darmstadt, 1919-33; research prof. Carnegie Inst. Tech., since 1933. Mem. Am. Chem. Soc., Am. Inst. Chem. Engrs., Faraday Soc., Soc. Am. Mil. Engrs., Army Ordnance Assn., Am. Inst. Mining and Metall. Engrs., Nat. Research Council. Home: Schenley Apts., Pittsburgh, Pa.

BERL, Eugene Ennalls, lawyer; b. New Orleans, La., Mar. 2, 1889; s. William and Marie (Waggaman) B.; A.B., Princeton U., 1912; LL.B., Harvard, 1915; unmarried. Admitted to Del. bar, 1915, and since practiced at Wilmington, Del.; mem. firm Ward & Gray, attys.-at-law, Wilmington, Del., since 1927. Served as 1st lt., U.S. Ambulance Service, 1917-18, capt., Claims Service, 1918-19, hon. disch. 1919. Awarded Silver Star Medal with two oak leaves, U.S. Army, for service in battle in 1918. City solicitor, Wilmington, Del., 1933-35. Mem. Del. State Bar Assn., Am. Bar Assn. Democrat. Catholic. Clubs: Wilmington, Wilmington Country (Wilmington, Del.); Princeton (New York City); Army and Navy (Washington, D.C.). Home: 1303 Market St. Office: Delaware Trust Bldg., Wilmington, Del.

BERLIN, John Cook, producer of oil and natural gas; b. Elk Twp., Clarion Co., Pa., May 27, 1859; s. George Neely and Susan (Cook) B.; student Carrier Sem., Clarion, Pa., 1876-79; m. Wilda Ochs, Feb. 1885 (died Aug. 21, 1938); children—Harold O., Freda M. (Mrs. Ray W. Britton). Engaged in oil and natural gas business, Berlin & Son, with interests in oil wells in Ohio, Ill., Mich., Pa.; pres. Edenburg Oil & Gas Co.; pres. Clarion Co. Nat. Bank; v.p. Rural Telephone Co.; treas. Union Cemetery Assn. Mem. State Y.M.C.A. of Pa. Ind. Democrat. Lutheran. Maccabee, K.P. Club: Knoz Gun (Knox, Pa.). Address: Knox, Pa.

BERLIN, Joseph I., M.D.; chief eye, ear, nose and throat dept., Greenville Hosp. Address: 2600 Hudson Boul., Jersey City, N.J.

BERMAN, Aaron, realtor and builder; b. Radomisl, Kiev, Russia, Apr. 23, 1875; s. Jacob Hirsh and Ada (Chae) B.; ed. pub. and high sch., Radomisl, Russia; m. Shiphra Malin, Dec. 26, 1901; children—Henry Enoch, Naphtiel, Hannah B. (Mrs. Philip H. Damsker). Began as laborer in tannery, Titusville, Pa., 1892; soldier in Russian Army, 1895-99; private teacher, Russia, 1899-1904; returned to U.S., 1904, and engaged in real estate business; organized Berman Bros., 1907; organized William Penn Title and Trust Co. and becames pres., 1925; organized Phila. and Suburban Mortgage Guarantee Co. and became pres., 1926; pres. Berman Bros., Inc., realtors and builders; pres. Greene Manor Corpn. Founded, 1928, and since pres. West Phila. Jewish Community Center (chmn. adult adn. groups). Mem. Phila. Real Estate Bd. Republican. Jewish religion. Mason. Home: 3211 School Lane, Drexel Hill. Office: 6054 Market St., Philadelphia, Pa.

BERNARD, Ted Butler, high sch. prin.; b. Weatherford, Tex., Nov. 29, 1899; s. Jeff Davis and Rhoda Jessie (Phillips) B.; A.B., State Teachers Coll., Denton, Tex., 1927, B.S., 1927; A.M., State Teachers Coll., Greeley, Colo., 1930; Ph.D., Teachers Coll. of Columbia U., 1935; m. Ada Gertrude Barber, June 1, 1927; 1 dau., Nelma Jean. Engaged in teaching in rural schs. in Tex., 1920-27; teacher, high sch., Sherman, Tex., 1927-31; prin. high sch., Princeton, N.J. since 1932. Mem. N.E.A., N.J. Secondary Sch. Principals Assn., Kappa Delta Pi, Phi Delta Kappa. Democrat. Presbyn. Mason. Club: New Jersey Schoolmasters (Newark). Author: Secondary Education Under Different Types of District Organization, 1935. Home: 61 Jefferson Road, Princeton, N.J.

BERND-COHEN, Max, artist, lecturer, critic; b. Macon, Ga., May 7, 1899; s. Max and Tina (Golinsky) B.; B.A., LL.B., Columbia U., 1922; studied in leading art schs. of Paris and Madrid; m. Estelle Leinau Lothrop, Oct. 7, 1933. Head master Ringling Art Sch., 1932-33; head of art dept. Fla. Southern Coll. and Stanley E. Jones Foundation, Lakeland, Fla. since Sept. 1939. Exhibited at Durand-Ruel, Renaissance, Jeune Peintre galleries (Paris), 1930, Durand-Ruel, Milch, College Art Assn. (New York), 1931, Mellon Galleries, Philadelphia Artists, 1933, 129th Annual, Pa. Acad. Fine Arts (Philadelphia), 1934. Invitation exhibition Modern Museum (Madrid), 1930; selected in open competition to paint mural for Florida Bldg., Chicago Century of Progress Expn., 1933; chosen to represent Florida in All States Exhbn. (Heron Art Inst.), 1933. Awarded first prize Chester Co. Art Assn., 1934. Mem. Philadelphia Art Alliance, Zeta Beta Tau, Delta Sigma Rho. Served in S.A.T.C., Columbia U., World War. Mason. Home: Tower Farm, West Chester, Pa.

BERNER, John Nelson, general insurance; b. Phila., Pa., Mar. 24, 1896; s. John and Marie (Martin) B.; ed. public schools and Southern High Sch., Phila.; m. Adelaide T. Kraan, Aug. 13, 1924; 1 son, Jack Kraan Berner. Began as insurance clerk, Platt Yungman Co., Phila., 1909; night cashier Reading R.R., Atlantic City, 1911-17; with Phillips Co., insurance, 1919-22; with C. J. Adams Co., real estate and insurance, Atlantic City, since 1923, asst. sec. and dir. since 1930; dir. Atlantic City Fire Ins. Co. Served in U.S. Navy 1917-19; disch. as chief commissary steward. Republican. Club: Morris Guards (trustee). Home: 106 S. Troy Av., Ventnor, N.J. Office: 20 S. Tennessee Av., Atlantic City, N.J.

BERNHARD, John J.; mem. major staff, dept. of obstetrics, Allentown Hosp.; auxiliary staff Sacred Heart Hosp. Address: 1629 Turner St., Allentown, Pa.

BERNHARDY, Harry W.; chief surg. staff Rochester Gen. Hosp.; mem. surg. staff Providence Hosp. (Beaver Falls) and Beaver Valley Gen. Hosp. (New Brighton). Address: 162 Brighton Av., Rochester, Pa.

BERNHEIM, Bertram Moses, surgeon; b. Paducah, Ky., Feb. 15, 1880; s. Isaac Wolf and Amanda (Uri) B.; A.B., Johns Hopkins, 1901, M.D., 1905; post-grad. work in Europe, 1906, in U.S., 1907; m. Hilda Marcus, July 26, 1905; children—Minda, Isaac Wolfe, Peter. Practiced surgery in Baltimore since 1908, specializing in blood-transfusion, and surgery of the blood vessels; asso. prof. surgery, Johns Hopkins Med. Sch.; visiting surgeon Union Memorial Hospital, Hosp. for Women of Md., Church Home and Infirmary; asst. visiting surgeon Johns Hopkins Hospital. Maj. Med. R.C.; mem. Johns Hopkins Hosp. Base Unit, A.E.F. in France, June 1917-Feb. 1919; received citation in France. Fellow of American Coll. Surgeons, A.M.A.; mem. Medico-Chirurg. Faculty of Md. Jewish religion. Author: Surgery of the Vascular System, 1913; Blood Transfusion, Hemorrhage and the Anemias, 1917; Passed as Censored, 1918; Medicine at the Crossroads, 1939; also numerous articles dealing with surgery. Home: Pikesville, Md. Office: 1814 Eutaw Pl., Baltimore, Md.

BERNHEIM, Oscar Frederick; b. Mt. Pleasant, N.C., Nov. 16, 1868; s. Rev. Gotthardt Dellman (D.D.) and Elizabeth Crow (Clayton) B.; A.B., Muhlenberg Coll., Allentown, Pa., 1892; m. BelleGoundie Krause, May 22, 1895; children—Eleanor Elizabeth, Clayton Krause (dec.), Ruth Goundie. Learned printer's trade; pvt. sec. to Congressman C. J. Erdman, Washington, D.C., 1893-95; accountant, 1895-1907; registrar for many yrs., sec. and treas. Muhlenberg Coll. since 1907. Mem. Alpha Tau Omega. Democrat. Lutheran. Elk. Home: Muhlenberg College Campus, Allentown, Pa.

BERNHEIMER, Leo Gabe, lawyer; b. Phila., Pa., May 19, 1876; s. Seligman and Betty (Loeb) B.; student pub. schs., Phila., 1884-90; A.B., Central High Sch., Phila., 1894; B.S., Wharton Sch., U. of Pa., 1896, LL.B., Law Sch., 1899; m. Hannah Rose Nathan, Apr. 28, 1908; children—John Seligman, Leonore (Mrs. David Doskow), Leo Gabe, Betty Ray, Philip Nathan, Walter Samuel. Admitted to Pa. bar, 1899, and since in practice at Phila.; mem. firm Bernheimer & Sundheim, Phila., 1904-34. Hon. dir. Y.M.H.A. Democrat. Club: Pow Wow (Phila.). Home: 6357 Greene St. Office: 250 S. Broad St., Philadelphia, Pa.

BERNREUTER, Robert Gibbon, coll. prof.; b. Tampico, Ill., Dec. 9, 1901; s. George and Edith Wynn (Gibbon) B.; student U. of Calif., Berkeley, Calif., 1919-20; A.B., Coll. of the Pacific, Stockton, Calif., 1924; student Stanford (Calif.) U., 1925-26, 1928-29, Ph.D., 1931; m. Shirley Trimble Buell, Aug. 30, 1931. Attendant, Agnew (Calif.) State Hosp., 1924; rural sch. teacher, Capay Rancho, Calif., 1924-25; research asst. psychological clinic, U. of Hawaii, 1926-28; instr. psychology, Washington U., St. Louis, Mo., 1929-30; asst. prof. psychology, Pa. State Coll., 1931-36, asso. prof. since 1937, dir. psycho-ednl. clinic since 1931; chief div. of spl. edn., Pa. State Dept. Pub. Instrn., Harrisburg, 1936-37. Fellow A.A.A.S.; mem. Am. Psychol. Assn., Am. Assn. Univ. Profs., Pa. Assn. Clin. Psychologists (pres. 1936-37), Am. Assn. Applied Psychologists, Assn. on Mental Deficiency, Alpha Kappa Phi, Sigma Xi, Psi Chi, Kappa Phi Kappa, Phi Delta Kappa; Phi Gamma Delta, Pi Kappa Delta, Phi Sigma Pi. Author: The Personality Inventory, 1931; research articles on measurement of personality development, clin. psychology. Home: 628 N. Holmes St. Office: Pa. State Coll., State Coll., Pa.

BERNSTEIN, Mitchell, physician; b. Phila., Pa., Mar. 26, 1889; s. Henry and Rachel (Gruemann) B.; Pharm.D., Phila. Coll. Pharmacy & Sci., 1909; M.D., Jefferson Med. Coll., 1914; m. Bertha E. Buchsbaum, June 18, 1918; children—Ruth Buchsbaum, Naomi Miriam. Resident phys., Phila. Gen. Hosp., 1914-15; asst. out patient med. dispensary, Polyclinic Hosp., 1916; asst. demonstrator, Jefferson Med. Coll., 1917; instr. materia medica, Phila. Coll. Pharmacy and Sci., 1917; formerly asst. visiting physician Phila. Gen. Hosp.; asso. in medicine, Jefferson Med. Coll., Phila. since 1917; sr. attdg. phys. Jewish Hosp. since 1934. Served as phys. to Draft Bd. 1st Dist., Phila. during World War. Trustee Phila. Coll. Pharmacy and Sci. Fellow Am. Coll. Phys. Mem. Am. Med. Assn., Pathol. Soc. Phila. Republican. Jewish religion. Contbr. various topics to med. journs. Home: 7609 Mountain Av., Elkins Park, Pa. Office: 1321 Spruce St., Philadelphia, Pa.

BERNSTEIN, Ralph, M.D., dermatologist; b. Columbia, Pa., Apr. 12, 1877; s. Sigmund and Marie (Oman) B.; grad. North East High Sch., Phila., 1898; M.D., U. of Pa., 1903, Hahnemann Med. Coll., 1904; grad. work Johns Hopkins U., dept. of dermatology, 1907, Hahnemann Med. Coll. dept. of dermatology, Chicago, 1910; unmarried. Clin. asst. dermatology, Hahnemann Med. Coll., Phila., 1904-07, clin. instr., 1908-12, clin. prof. 1913-15, prof. of dermatology since 1916, lecturer on homœ. principles, 1919-27, asst. to dean, 1914-16, sec. of faculty, 1917-24; post-grad. lecturer dermatology, Phila. Acad. Medicine, 1909-12; phys. instr., House of Detention for Juveniles, Phila., 1906-12; lecturer on dermatology to med. socs., etc.; consultant Hahnemann, Women's Homœ. hosps., Phila., and Shriner's Hosp. for Children, also Crozer (Chester), West Chester Homœ., Pottstown (Pa.) Homœ. hosps., State Hosp., Allentown, etc.; consultant in dermatology to 13 hosps. in Pa., Del., N.J. Med. adviser S.A.T.C. and draft bds. during World War. Fellow Am. Coll. Physicians; mem. Nat., State and County Homœ. med. socs.; hon. mem. Union Co., Blair Co., Central Pa., and Tri-County med. socs.; mem. Am. Editors and Authors Assn., Soc. Forensic Medicine, Soc. for Investigative Dermatology, Am. Acad. Polit. Sci., A.A.A.S., Pi Upsilon Rho (nat. sec. edn. 1917-30); patron Ralph Bernstein Dermatol. Soc. Mason. Club: Pen and Pencil (hon. life mem.). Author: Solidified Carbon Dioxide in Skin Diseases, 1912; Elementary Dermatology, 1913; Ultra Violet Rays in Modern Dermatology, 1918; Notes on Dermatology for Students and Physicians, 8th edit., 1938. Contbr. many articles to med. jours. Address: 1816 Pine St., Philadelphia, Pa.

BERNSTINE, J. Bernard, M.D.; asst. prof. obstetrics, Jefferson Med. Coll.; gynecologist, Henry Phipps Inst.; asso. obstetrician and gynecologist Phila. Gen. Hosp. Address: 2007 Pine St., Philadelphia, Pa.

BERRIEN, Cornelius Roach, retired banker; b. Montclair, N.J., May 30, 1873; s. Cornelius and Margaret Elizabeth (Price) B.; B.A., Wesleyan U., Middletown, Conn., 1896, M.A., 1926; m. Grace Eleanor Beardmore, July 3, 1898; children—John Beardmore, Janet (Mrs. Donald H. Parsons), Stephen, Elizabeth (Mrs. D. Anthony D'Esopo), Geoffrey. Reporter Evening Sun, N.Y. City, 1898-1906, editorial writer, 1906-09, financial editor, 1909-13; financial editor The Sun, 1913-16; asst. sec. Central Trust Co. of New York (now Central Hanover Bank & Trust Co.), 1916-17, v.p., 1917-38. Mem. Phi Beta Kappa. Republican. Methodist. Clubs: Players; Upper Montclair Country. Home: 160 Lorraine Av., Upper Montclair, N.J. Office: 70 Broadway, New York, N.Y.

BERRY, David Walker, clergyman; b. Clokey, Pa., Oct. 7, 1869; s. William and Martha S. (Pattison) B.; A.B., Westminster Coll., New Wilmington, Pa., 1893; Th.D., Pittsburgh Theol. Sem., 1896; m. Jane Mary Graham, Sept. 30, 1896; children—Mary Gertrude (wife of James Wallace Cleland, M.D.), Martha Jane. In ministry U. Presbyn. Ch.; pastor, Mars, Pa., 1896-1902, Spokane, Wash., 1902-06; sec. Inland Empire State S.S. Assn., 1906-07; asso. pastor, Phila., Pa., 1907-08; pastor, Germantown, Phila., 1908-17; pastor First Presbyn. Ch., Millville, N.J., since 1918. Mem. bd. trustees Presbyn. Synod of N.J.; mem. com. on nat. missions; chmn. com. nat. missions Presbytery of West Jersey; pres. Millville Ministerial Assn. Club: Millville Kiwanis (charter mem.). Home: 119 N. 2d St., Millville, N.J.

BERRY, Edward Wilber, paleontologist; b. Newark, N.J., Feb. 10, 1875; s. Abijah Conger and Anna (Wilber) B.; educated privately; m. Mary Willard, Apr. 12, 1898; children—Edward Willard, Charles Thompson. Pres., treas. and mgr. Daily News, Passaic, N.J., 1897-1905; asst. in paleobotany, 1907-08, instr., 1908-11, asso., 1911-13, asso. prof. paleontology, 1913-17, prof., 1917—, dean, 1929—, provost, 1935—, Johns Hopkins U. Sr. geologist U.S. Geol. Survey, 1910—; asst. state geologist of Md. since 1917. Fellow Paleontol. Society America (pres. 1924). Geol. Soc. America (v.p. 1924), Am. Acad. Arts and Sciences, A.A.A.S., Am. Soc. Naturalists; mem Am Philos. Soc., Nat. Acad. Sciences, New York Acad. Sciences, Torrey Bot. Club, Société Géologique de France. Walker prize, Boston Soc. Natural History, 1901. Conglist. Club: Hopkins. Wrote: Lower Cretaceous of Maryland (Md. Geol. Survey), 1911; Upper Cretaceous of Maryland (same), 1916; Eocene Floras of Southeastern North America (U.S. Geol. Survey), 1916; Tree Ancestors, 1923; Paleontology, 1929; also over 500 articles on paleontol., geol. and biol. subjects in Am. and foreign scientific periodicals. Has specialized on classification and evolution of plants, particularly in Southeastern N. America, equatorial America and South America. Editor Paleobotany, Biological Abstracts; Pan Am. Geologist. Home: 19 Elmwood Road, Baltimore, Md.

BERRY, Herman C(laude); prof. materials of construction, U. of Pa. Address: U. of Pennsylvania, Philadelphia, Pa.

BERRY, Maja Leon; became vice c ancellor N.J. Court of Chancery, 1927. Home: Toms River, N.J.

BERT, Otto Frederick Herman, coll. prof.; b. New Brighton, Pa., Feb. 21, 1877; s. John Adam and Catherine Anna (Guibert) B.; B.S. Geneva Coll., Beaver Falls, Pa., 1895, A.M., 1903; student, Harvard, M.I.T.; Sc.D., Thiel Coll., Greenville, Pa., 1935; m. Mary Lavina Barbara Kepple, Dec. 26, 1903; children—Adam Kepple, Ella (Mrs. Carl G. McVicker), Peter Waldo, Mary Virginia (Mrs. Edgar J. Snyder). Began as teacher 1898; LeMoyne prof. applied math., Washington and Jefferson Coll., Washington, Pa., since 1914; dir. Washington Union Trust Co., Chartiers Housing Co. Trustee Washington sem.; dir. Lutheran Theol Sem., Phila. Fellow A.A.A.S.; mem. Math. Assn. of America, Am. Astron. Soc., Washington (Pa.) Chamber of Commerce (dir.). Republican. Lutheran. Club: Rotary (Washington, Pa.). Home: 28 N. Lincoln St. Office: Washington and Jefferson Coll., Washington, Pa.

BERTHOLF, Lloyd Millard, educator, biologist; b. Kechi, Kan., Dec. 15, 1899; s. Albert Linton and Mable Sarah (Haden) B.; grad. Spivey (Kan.) High Sch., 1917; student Friends U., Wichita, Kan., 1917-19; A.B., Southwestern Coll., Winfield, Kan., 1921; A.M., Johns Hopkins, 1922, Ph.D., 1928; m. Martha Washburn, June 15, 1921; children—Mabelyn Washburn, Max Erwin. Instr. in biology, U. of N.C. Women's Coll., 1922-24; prof. of biology, Western Md. Coll. since 1924, dean of freshmen, 1933-39, dean of faculty, since 1939. Nat. Research fellow in biology in Germany, 1930-31; Bruce fellow, Johns Hopkins, 1927-28. Served in C.A.C., U.S. Army, Oct.-Nov. 1918. Mem. Am. Soc. Zoologists, Am. Assn. Univ. Profs., A.A.A.S., N.E.A., Phi Beta Kappa, Sigma Xi, Pi Gamma Mu, Beta Beta Beta. Democrat. Methodist. Home: Uniontown Rd., Westminster, Md.

BERTOLET, John A.; chief otolaryngologist Methodist Episcopal Hosp.; consulting otolaryngologist Pa. R.R. Co. Address: 329 E. 18th St., Philadelphia, Pa.

BERTOLET, William S(chaeffer), M.D.; b. Oley, Pa., June 27, 1875; s. John B. and Amanda (Schaeffer) B.; A.B., Franklin and Marshall, 1897; M.D., U. of Pa., 1900; D.Sc., Albright Coll., 1934, Franklin and Marshall, 1935; m. Mary E. Herbine, June 27, 1905; children—John H., Mary. Began practice at Reading, Pa., 1900; med. dir. and chief on med. service Reading Hosp.; dir. Berks County Trust Co. Chmn. Med. Advisory Bd., Reading, 1917-18. Trustee Franklin and Marshall Coll. Mem. A.M.A., Am. Coll. Physicians, Phi Beta Kappa, Sigma Xi. Mem. Ref. Ch. Mason. Home and Office: 244 N. 5th St., Reading, Pa.

BERVINCHAK, Nicholas, artist; b. Black Heath, Schuylkill Co., Pa., Dec. 4, 1903; s. John and Fannie (Polinsky) B.; ed. public schools of Forrestville and Hazelton, Pa., 1910-17; completed 2-year correspondence course in art, 1932; also studied art at various evening schools and completed high school course in English at home; m. Olga Hladish, June 20, 1926; children—Nicholas, James, Marian. Worked in coal mines of Pa., 1918-24; apprentice to Paul Daubner, ecclesiastical artist, Phila., 1924-28; free-lance artist in ecclesiastical field, 1928-32; gained recognition as water color artist and etcher, 1933; art instr., Adult Ednl. Program, 1935-38; illustrated book, Minstrels of the Mine Patch, by George Korson, 1938; illustrator on Federal Writers' Project, illustrating book on Pa. anthracite, 1939. Works: murals and decorations for Mother of Sorrow Ch., Phila.; portrait etching of James B. Neale, Buck Run, Pa.; President Roosevelt, Anna Sten, etc. Exhibited at: Minn. Eastern State Expn., 1934; Chicago Century of Progress, 1934; Wanamaker's Art Gallery, Phila., 1934; Phila. Soc. Etchers and Graphic Artists, 1935; Ogunquit (Me.) Art Center, 1935, 37; Latham Foundation, 1935; Soc. Am. Etchers, New York, 1936, 38; Palm Beach Art Center, 1936; Whitney Museum of Art, 1936; Soc. of Independent Artists, New York, 1936, 37; Aqua-Chromatic Exhbn. of Water Colors, New York, 1937; Nat. Exhbn. Contemporary

Am. Prints, Stockholm, Sweden, 1937-38; Nat. Acad., New York, 1938; also one-man shows Kalamazoo, Mich., New Britain, Conn., Pottsville, Pa. Awards: 1st prize in story illustration, Minn. Eastern State Expn., 1934; hon. mention, Artists Exhbn., Pottsville, Pa., 1934, Kalamazoo Museum and Art Inst., 1938; certificate of merit, Latham Foundation, 1935. Represented in permanent collections at: Free Pub. Library, Pottsville, Pa.; Pub. Library, Kalamazoo, Mich.; Kalamazoo Inst. of Art; "Hundred Selected Prints of the Year," 1936; Library of Congress, Washington, D.C.; Pub. Library, Hazleton, Pa. Mem. Soc. of Ind. Artists of New York, Phila, Soc. of Etchers and Graphic Artists, Am. Soc. Etchers. Democrat. Mem. Ukrainian Orthodox Ch. Home: Route 1, Pottsville, Pa.

BESLER, William George, ry. chmn.; b. Galesburg, Ill., Mar. 30, 1864; s. John D. and Anna (Chapin) B.; student Mass. Inst. Tech., 1884-86; m. Effie B. Lewis, Oct. 10, 1888. Began as trainmaster's clk., C.,B.&Q. Ry., at Galesburg, 1880, and advanced to div. supt.; supt. and gen. supt. Phila. & Reading Ry., 1899-1902; gen. mgr., 1902-03, v.p. and gen. mgr., 1903-14, pres. and gen. mgr., 1914-26, chmn. bd. since Nov. 1926, Central R.R. of N.J. Clubs: Railroad, Engineers', Technology (New York). Home: Plainfield, N.J. Office: 143 Liberty St., New York, N.Y.

BESLEY, Fred Wilson, state forester; b. Vienna, Va., Feb. 16, 1872; prep. edn., public schools, Fairfax Co., Va., 1878-88; A.B., Md. Agrl. Coll., 1892; M.F., Forest Sch., Yale, 1904; hon. D.Sc., Md. State Coll. (now U. of Md.), 1914; m. Bertha Simonds, Sept. 17, 1899 (died Jan. 29, 1936); children—Florence Jean (Mrs. S. Procter Rodgers), Arthur Kirkland, Helen, Lowell. Teacher in public schools, Va., 1892-1902; forest asst. U.S. Forest Service, 1904-06; state forester of Md. since 1906. Dir. Am. Forestry Assn., Md. Development Bureau. Mem. Soc. Am. Foresters. Democrat. Presbyterian. Club: Torch (Baltimore). Home: 303 Wendover Rd. Office: 1411 Fidelity Bldg., Baltimore, Md.

BESS, Thomas, chief surgeon Potomac Valley Hosp. Address: Keyser, W.Va.

BESSON, Harlan, lawyer; b. Hoboken, N.J., July 1, 1887; s. Samuel Austin and Arabella (Roseberry) B.; student Rutgers Coll., 1903-06; LL.B., N.Y. Law Sch., 1908; m. Addie Case, May 14, 1913; 1 dau., Roberta. Admitted to New Jersey bar, 1909; now mem. firm Besson and Pellet. Town atty. Secausus, N.J., 1914-22; asst. U.S. atty., 1922-29; 1st asst. prosecutor Hudson County, N.J., 1929-32; U.S. district atty., N.J., 1932-35; now engaged in practice as mem. firm Besson & Pellet; prof. N.J. pleading and practice and federal practice and procedure, John Marshall Law Coll., Jersey City, N.J. Served as lt. inf., Mexican border, 1916; capt. U.S. Army, World War; now lt. col. Inf. Res., detailed as asst. chief of staff, G.-4, Hdqrs. 78th Div. Pres. Dept. of N.J. Reserve Officers Assn. of America, 1939-40. Mem. Delta Upsilon. Republican. Presbyn. Mason. Office: 84 Washington St., Hoboken, N.J.

BEST, Harvey D.; pres. Lanston Monotype Machine Co. Office: 24th and Locust St., Philadelphia, Pa.

BEST, Howard Richard, supt. pub. schs.; b. Neligh, Neb., Aug. 7, 1895; s. Edward Thomas and Florence May (Gilson) B.; A.B., Yankton (S.D.) Coll., 1917; A.M., U. of Neb., 1929; ed. U. of Montpelier, France, 1919-20; Ed.D., Columbia U., 1939; m. Ruth Beatrice Merrick, 1920; 1 son, Richard Junior. Engaged in teaching, pub. schs., 1917; supt. schs., Benedict, Neb., 1921-23, Wagner, S.D. 1923-29, Wayne, Neb., 1929-35; adminstr. in charge sch. system, Cranford, N.J. since 1935. Served in machine gun batln., U.S.A., 1917-19; with A.E.F. in France. Mem. N.J. Sch. Masters Club, N.Y. Sch. Masters Club, Phi Delta Kappa, Kappa Delta Pi. Presbyn. Home: 18 Central Av., Cranford, N.J.

BEST, William E.; mem. law firm McCloskey, Best & Leslie. Office: Oliver Bldg., Pittsburgh, Pa.

BEST, William Hinkle, clergyman; b. Frederick, Md., Sept. 18, 1868; s. John Thomas and Margaret Joanna (Dorsey) B.; student Frederick Coll., Frederick, Md., Randolph-Macon Acad., Front Royal, Va., 1900-03; A.B., Randolph-Macon Coll., Ashland, Va., 1906, (hon.) D.D., 1934; m. Mary I. Elliott, Nov. 18, 1897; children—William Elliott, Margaret Emma. Ordained to ministry M.E. Ch., 1899, and joined Baltimore Conf., 1897; served in regular pastorates of conf., 1897-1934; presiding elder Baltimore Dist. since 1934; served as conf. missionary sec., 1908; exec. sec. S.S. Bd., 1918-25. Dir. Md.-Del. Council of Churches. Democrat. Home: 112 Hawthorne Rd., Baltimore, Md.

BESTOR, (Horace) Paul, banker; b. Clearfield, Ia., Sept. 27, 1882; s. John Gilbert and Jennie Caldwell (Everman) B.; B.A., Tarkio Coll., 1909, LL.D., 1937; B.A., Yale University, 1910; m. Mary Rankin, Aug. 29, 1911; children—Edith Anne (dec.), Barbara Jane, Mary Lois, Paul (deceased). Teacher pub. schs., Calif., 1910-12; mem. Nat. Geog. Soc. expdn. to Peru, 1912; asst. Latin-Am. history, Yale Univ., 1912-15; mem. Mo. Ho. of Rep., 1920-22; apptd. registrar 6th Federal Land Bank District, Jan. 1922; pres. Federal Land Bank of St. Louis, 1922-29; and of Federal Intermediate Credit Bank, St. Louis, 1923-29; apptd. mem. Federal Farm Loan Bd., May 3, 1929, and designated farm loan commr., May 16, 1929, reappointed, 1931; dir. ex-officio Reconstruction Finance Corpn., Feb. 2-July 31, 1932; first land bank commr. under Farm Credit Administration, 1933. Asst. sec. Prudential Ins. Co. of America, Newark, since July 15, 1933. Mem. Nat. Drought Relief Com., 1930. Active in Red Cross and Liberty Loan work, also four-minute man, World War. Republican. Presbyn. Mason. Clubs: Yale (New York); Glen Ridge Country; Newark Athletic. Home: 436 Ridgewood Av., Glen Ridge, N.J. Office: Prudential Insurance Co., Newark, N.J.

BETHEL, Walter Augustus, army officer; b. Freeport, O., Nov. 25, 1866; s. David R. and Beccie J. (Brown) B.; grad. U.S. Mil. Acad., 1889; LL.M., Columbian (now George Washington) U., 1894; m. Elizabeth Strong, Nov. 15, 1904; children—Elizabeth, Frances (Mrs. Hugh W. Rowan), Marguerite. Commd. add. 2d lt. 4th Arty., June 12, 1889; 2d lt., June 17, 1889; 1st lt. 3d Arty., Sept. 1, 1896; capt. a.a.g. vols., May 12, 1898; hon. discharged vols., Dec. 31, 1898, capt. Arty. Corps, U.S.A., Feb. 2, 1901; promoted through grades to brig. gen., Oct. 2, 1917; apptd. judge advocate gen., rank of maj. gen., Feb. 1923, term of 4 yrs. Prof. law, U.S. Mil. Acad., 1909-14; judge advocate gen., A.E.F., May 20, 1917-Sept. 1, 1919; retired Nov. 15, 1924; counsel for U.S., Mexican Claims, Sept. 20, 1926-Nov. 1, 1931. Clubs: Chevy Chase, Army and Navy. Home: 6305 Connecticut Av., Chevy Chase, Md.

BETTMAN, Clarence Augustus, stock broker; b. Hoboken, N.J., Aug. 31, 1892; s. Christopher Augustus B.; student Plainfield (N.J.) High Sch. and New York U.; m. Marion Keyes, of Westfield, N.J., June 7, 1924; children—Marion Keyes, Margaret Keyes. Began as brokers runner, New York, 1910; successively office clerk, telephone clerk New York Stock Exchange, broker on old Curb Market (New York); chmn. bd. of govs. New York Curb Exchange since Feb. 1939. Served on U.S.S. Oklahoma, U.S. Navy, 1917-19. Trustee Rumson (N.J.) Private Sch. Republican. Presbyn. Clubs: Seabright Beach (Seabright, N.J.); Gatineau Fish and Game (Point Comfort, Quebec). Home: Rumson, N.J. Office: 74 Trinity Place, New York, N.Y.

BETTS, Emmett Albert, educator; b. Elkhart, Iowa, Feb. 1, 1903; s. Albert Henry and Grace Lou:se (Greenwood) B.; B.S., Des Moines (Ia.) U., 1925; A.M., State U. of Ia., 1928, Ph.D., 1931; m. Thelma Lucille Marshall, May 31, 1924; children—Beverly Jean, Shirley Lee, Margaret Jane. Dir. of vocational edn., Orient, Ia., Consol. Schs., 1922-24; supt. of schools, Northoro, Ia., 1925-27; research asst., U. of Ia., 1929-31; school psychologist, Shaker Heights, O., 1931-34; dir. of teacher edn., State Normal Sch., Oswego, N.Y., 1934-37; research prof. and dir. reading clinic, Pa. State Coll., since 1937. Mem. advisory bd. Pa. Assn. for the Blind; mem. advisory com. Internat. Council for Study of Exceptional Children; chmn. com. on research in reading, Nat. Conf. on Research in Elementary Sch. English. Mem. Am. Assn. Applied Psychologists, A.A.A.S., Am. Assn. Sch. Adminstrs., Am. Edn. Research Assn., Am. Psychol. Assn., N.E.A., Dept. Elementary Sch. Prins. of N.E.A., Nat. Soc. for Study of Edn., Pa. State Edn. Assn., Pa. Ednl. Research Assn., Progressive Edn. Assn., Am. Assn. Univ. Profs., Phi Delta Kappa, Psi Chi. Fellow in Distinguished Service Foundation of Optometry. Presbyterian. Home: 305 Adams Av., State College, Pa.

BETTS, George Whitefield, Jr., lawyer; b. Englewood, N.J., Feb. 14, 1871; s. George Whitefield and Margaret E. (Dominick) B.; A.B., Princeton, 1892, grad. student, 1892-95, hon. A.M., 1895; LL.B., New York Law Sch., 1895; m. Mary Howard Hall, Nov. 3, 1903; 1 son, Derick Whitefield. Admitted to N.Y. bar, 1895, N.J. bar, 1896, counsellor of State of N.J., 1899; asso. with law firm Convers & Kirlin, New York, 1895-1900; mem. firm Hunt, Hill & Betts since 1900; master of chancery of N.J.; dir. and mem. exec. com. Maritime Assn. of Port of New York; dir. Schwarzenbach Huber Co., Mannetto Hill Farm, Rodi Corpn., Union Apple Co., Thomas & Betts Co., Union Warehouse Corpn., Patrician Piece Dye Works, Pioneer Piece Dye Works. Formerly chmn. Bergen Co. (N.J.) Rep. Com.; formerly pres. now chmn. exec. com. Englewood Rep. Club; chmn. Englewood Municipal Rep. Com.; police commr. City or Englewood. Mem. Grad. Council of Princeton U.; chmn. scholarship com. Princeton Alumni Assn. of Northern N.J. Mem. Am. Bar Assn., N.Y. County Lawyers' Assn., Assn. of Bar of State of N.Y., N.J. State Bar Assn., Bergen Co. Bar Assn., Tiger Inn (Princeton U.), Whig Hall (Princeton U.). Republican. Episcopalian (warden St. Paul's Ch., Englewood). Clubs: University, Princeton, Down Town Assn., Downtown Athletic (New York); Englewood, Knickerbocker Country (Englewood, N.J.); Quogue Field, Quogue Beach (Quogue, L.I.). Home: 27 Brayton St., Englewood, N.J. Office: 120 Broadway, New York, N.Y.

BETTS, Philander, III, engineer; b. Nyack, N.Y., May 28, 1868; s. Philander, Jr., and Sarah Taulman (Demarest) B.; B.S., Rutgers Coll., N.J., 1891, M.S., 1895; E.E., Columbian (now George Washington) University, 1903, Ph.D., 1914, honorary Dr. of Engineering, 1932; m. Nancy Bell Hammer, Nov. 19, 1896; 1 son, Philander Hammer. Constructing engr. Field Engring. Co., New York, directing constrn. of some of the earliest electric lines in Newark, N.J., and Phila., 1890-93; with Westinghouse Elec. & Mfg. Co., 1893-95, elec. engr., Washington Navy Yard, 1895-1901; instr. in M.E. & E.E., Corcoran Scientific Sch., Washington, 1901-05; asst. prof., George Washington U., head of elec. engring. dept. and in charge of all mech. and elec. engring. labs., 1905-10; chief engr. Pub. Utilities Commn. N.J., 1910-34. Has served as consulting engr. in many important elec. light and power projects. Fellow Am. Inst. Elec. Engrs.; mem. Am. Soc. Mech. Engrs., Illuminating Engineering Soc., Am. Electric Ry. Assn., S.A.R. (past president N.J. Soc.), Beta Theta Pi. Mason (33°). Republican. Mem. Dutch Reformed Church. Maj. Engr. R.C., July 14, 1917; lt. col. Q.M. Corps, Mar. 18, 1918; active duty, War Dept., Washington; hon. discharged, May 31, 1919; citation by secretary of war "for efficient service in the Construction Division of the Army"; col. engr. R.C., comdr. 373d Engrs. Sr. past comdr., North Jersey Chapter Mil. Order of World War, also past comdr. N.Y. Chapter; v.p. and mem. gen. staff N.J. State Reserve Officers' Assn. (hon. v.p. for life); mem. American Legion, Sojourners (ex-pres. Manhattan Chapter). Compiler and editor of the hist. records in connection with all War Dept. construction in this country. Prominent in field of pub. service regulation, valuation and rate-making. Home: 100 Tenth Av., Belmar, N.J.

BETZ, LeRoy Drew, chem. engr.; b. Phila., Pa., Dec. 9, 1894; s. William H. and Jane M. (Drew) B.; ed. Drexel Inst., Phila., 1912-16; m. Alice Margaret Nagle, June 14, 1916; 1 son, John Drew; m. 2d, Rosalie Elizabeth Nagle, Oct. 11, 1924. Chemist Animal Oil Co., Phila., 1916-17; chemist and v.p. E. F. Drew & Co., New York, 1917-25; mem. firm and mgr. dir. W. H. & L. D. Betz, chem. engrs., Phila. since 1925. Mem. Am. Chem. Soc., Am. Soc. Mech. Engrs., Am. Water Works Assn., Am. Soc. Testing Materials. Roman Catholic. Clubs: Chemists (New York); Huntingdon Valley Country (Abingdon, Pa.). Home: Meadowbrook, Pa. Office: 235 W. Wyoming Av., Philadelphia, Pa.

BEURY, Charles E., univ. pres.; b. Shamokin, Pa., Aug. 13, 1879; s. William and Susan M. (Cockill) B.; B.A., Princeton, 1903; LL.B., Harvard, 1906; LL.D., Ursinus Coll., 1926, Lafayette Coll., 1928, Univ. of Pa., 1931, Princeton University, 1937; A.M., Hahnemann Med. Coll., 1932; D.C.L., Bucknell U., 1938; m. Ella Philson Fischer, June 27, 1906; children—Charles William (deceased), Elizabeth Philson, Marian Fischer, Nancy Lawton (dec.), Barbara, Charles Ezra. Began practice of law at Phila., 1908; associated with William A. Glasgow, Jr., 1908-21; Pres. Nat. Bank of North Philadelphia, 1921-28; chmn. bd. Bank of Phila. and Trust Co., 1928-30; pres. Temple U. since Jan. 22, 1926. Dir. Victory Loan for North Phila.; made trips to Russia and Near East for Near East Relief and Red Cross, 1917, 18, 19. Trustee Welfare Federation of Phila., Near East Relief; pres. Phila. Forum, 1928-29, 1930-31, 1938; pres. Assn. of Coll. Presidents of Pa., 1934; mem. State Council of Edn. of Pa. since Sept. 1936. Republican. Episcopalian. Clubs: Princeton, Art (Phila.); Phila. Country, Seaview Country. Traveled around the World 4 times. Author: Russia After the Revolution, 1918. Home: 112 W. Upsal St., Germantown, Pa. Address: Temple University, Philadelphia, Pa.

BEUTNER, Reinhard Heinrich, prof. pharmacology; b. Berlin, Germany, Apr. 10, 1885; s. Wilhelm and Marie (Dernburg) B.; came to U.S., 1911, naturalized citizen, 1930; Ph.D., M.D., U. of Berlin, 1926; m. Hermine Aye, of Berlin, Germany, Apr. 28, 1917; children—Karl Reinhard, Ernst H. W. Research asst., Rockefeller Inst. for Med. Research, 1911-14; connected with U. of Leiden, Holland, 1921-22; asst. prof. then prof. pharmacology, U. of Louisville, 1923-36; prof. pharmacology, Hahnemann Med. Coll., Phila. since 1936. Mem. Am. Chem. Soc., Am. Soc. for Pharmacology and Exptl. Therapy, Am. Physiol. Soc., A.A.A.S. Home: 937 W. Roosevelt Boul., Philadelphia, Pa.

BEVAN, Lynne J(ohn), cons. hydraulic engr.; b. Atlanta, Ill., Dec. 27, 1881; s. John Luther and Armada Sarah (Thomas) B.; B.S., U. of Chicago, 1903; B.S. in mining, U. of Calif., 1905; m. Elizabeth Alexandra Young, Dec. 29, 1914; children—John Alexander, Barbara Louise. Asst. engr. to John R. Freeman, cons. engr., 1905-06; asst. engr. and later prin. engr. Viele, Blockwell & Buck, cons. hydraulic engrs., 1906-27; cons. engr., specializing in water supply and water power, N.Y. City since 1928; spl. lecturer grad. course on water power engring., Poly. Inst. Brooklyn since 1934; engring. counsel U.S. Bur. Internat. Revenue and to corpns. in litigation since 1921. Mem. Town Planning Bd., Montclair, N.J., 1932-38. Mem. Am. Soc. C.E. (chmn. power div. 1929-34), Am. Water Works Assn., Montclair Soc. Engrs. (pres. 1931-32), Essex Co. Engring. Soc., Delta Upsilon (nat. pres. 1933-35, nat. treas. 1925-33 and 1935-37), Phi Beta Kappa, Sigma Xi. Republican. Baptist. Mason. Clubs: Montclair Athletic, Crestmont Golf (Montclair, N.J.); Delta Upsilon (N.Y. City). Compiler of Catalogue of Delta Upsilon, 1917; editor Calif. Jour. of Technology, 1904-05; contbr. articles to tech. jours. Home: 15 Warren Place, Montclair, N.J. Office: 7 Dey St., New York, N.Y.

BEYE, William, v.p. U.S. Steel Corpn. of Del.; b. Chicago, Ill., July 21, 1881; s. William and Nellie C. (Lombard) B.; B.L., U. of Wis., 1902; LL.B., Lake Forest Coll. of Law, 1904; m. Genevieve Ainslie, Oct. 17, 1911; 1 son, William III. Admitted to Ill. bar, Apr. 1904, and practiced in Chicago as mem. firm Knapp, Beye, Allen & Cushing and its predecessors, 1904-37; v.p. U.S. Steel Corpn. in charge industrial relations, 1937-38; v.p. and gen. counsel U.S. Steel Corpn. of Del. since 19—. Mem. Am. Bar Assn., Allegheny Co. Bar Assn., Chicago Bar Assn., Ill. Bar Assn., Chicago Law Inst., Law Club (Chicago), Psi Upsilon, Phi Delta Phi. Republican. Clubs: Duquesne, Oakmont Country, Fox Chapel (Pittsburgh); University, Chicago, Oak Park Country (Chicago); Blind Brook Country (New York). Home: Schenley Apts. Office: 436 7th Av., Pittsburgh, Pa.

BEYER, Alvin D.; pres. Alvin D. Beyer, Inc., Pleasant Mills Paper Co. Home: 1809 De Kalb St. Office: Trust Bldg., Norristown, Pa.

BEYER, Jesse William, elec. engr.; b. Walla Walla, Wash., Jan. 22, 1892; s. William Haddon and Jessie (Kevill) B.; B.S., State Coll. of Wash., Pullman, Wash., 1915; m. Alma Merschtina, Dec. 1, 1920. Began as substation operator Utah Power & Light Co., Salt Lake City, Utah, 1915; graduate student course, Westinghouse Electric & Mfg. Co., E. Pittsburgh, Pa., 1915-16; instr. elec. engring. State College of Wash., Pullman, 1916-19; mem. tech. staff Western Electric Co., New York, 1919-25; mem. tech. staff Bell Telephone Labs., Inc., New York since 1925, supervisor development open wire carrier telephones for Bell System since 1929. Mem. Am. Inst. E.E., Beta Theta Pi, Sigma Tau. Republican. Presbyterian. Mason (Boiling Spring Lodge 152). Home: 54 Van Riper Av., Rutherford, N.J. Office: 463 West St., New York, N.Y.

BEYMER, Albert Sidney, banker; b. Pittsburgh, Pa., July 28, 1863; s. Simon and Annie C. (Fracker) B.; student pub. schs., Western Univ. and Iron City Coll.; m. Nettie H. Gregg, 1892 (died 1911); m. 2d, Anne Patterson, 1918 (died 1937); children—Albert S., James Patterson. Began as bookkeeper Keystone Nat. Bank (then Keystone Bank of Pittsburgh), 1884, cashier, 1897-1914, v.p., 1914-20, pres. and dir., 1920-35, now chmn. bd. Home: Babcock Boul., Allison Park, Pa. Office: 324 Fourth Av., Pittsburgh, Pa.

BEZANSON, Anne, univ. prof.; b. Dalhousie, Nova Scotia; daughter of John Allen and Sarah Jane (Creighton) B.; came to U.S., 1901; A.B., Radcliffe Coll., Cambridge, Mass., 1915, A.M., 1916, Ph.D., 1929; research work, Harvard, 1916-18; unmarried. Dept. mgr. Gillette Razor Co., Boston, 1903-11; mem. com. on econ. research Harvard, 1920-21; co-founder, 1921, and since asso. dir. and dir., dept. of industrial research, Wharton Sch. of Finance and Commerce, U. of Pa., prof. of research, Grad. Sch. since 1929; mem. U.S. Coal Commn., 1922-23; mem. exec. com. of conf. on price research, Nat. Bur. of Econ. Research, Inc., New York since 1936. Served in War Emergency Course and Personnel Training, Bryn Mawr (Pa.) Coll., 1918-20. Mem. Am. Statis. Assn., Am. Econ. Assn., Hist. Soc. of Pa., Phi Beta Kappa. Protestant. Author many tech. articles and speeches on prices, labor conditions, the coal industry, and economics. Home: 5400 Greene St., Germantown. Office: 3440 Walnut St., Philadelphia, Pa.

BIAGI, Ernest Louis, Grand Sec. Order Sons of Italy; b. Frosinone, Italy, Apr. 5, 1902; s. Louis and Emilia (Casali) B.; Royal Tech. Sch., Rome, 1915; A.B., Royal Tech. Inst., Velletri, Rome, 1919; Royal Industrial and Commercial Inst., Terni, 1920; m. Susan A. Di Claudio, June 24, 1924; children—Amelia Lucille, Dolores Jean, Ernest Louis, Jr. Came to U.S., 1920, naturalized citizen, 1926. Successively clerk Central Bank, Jeannette, Pa.; mgr. foreign dept., First Nat. Bank, Monongahela, Pa.; asst. cashier Napoleon State Bank, Pittsburgh; editor Sentinel Press, Greensburg, Pa.; mgr. Westmoreland Pub. Co., Greensburg; now Grand Sec. Order of Sons of Italy, Phidalephia; treas. Victory Bldg. & Loan Assn. Advisor Literacy Program, Works Progress Administrn., Phila. Sec. Dante Orphanage, Concordville, Pa. Mem. Republican League of Pa. Author: Prohibition, 1926; Bazzeca, 1931. Home: 2827 S. 13th St., Philadelphia, Pa. Office: 1409 Tasker St. Philadelphia, Pa.

BIALAS, Joseph Henry, lawyer; b. Pittsburgh, Pa., Sept. 10, 1879; s. Roman Felix and Magdalena (Schnelbach) B.; LL.B., U. of Pittsburgh, 1904; m. Louise Smith, May 20, 1931. Admitted to Pa. bar, 1904, and since practiced in Pittsburgh; mem. firm Bialas & Ryan; pres. and dir. Bethlehem Labs., Inc.; treas. and dir. San Toy Mining Co. Dir. Bd. of Edn., City of Pittsburgh, Community Fund of Pittsburgh, Children's Aid Soc., Pittsburgh Orchestra Assn., Mercy Sch. of Nursing Alumni Assn., Univ. Maternity Dispensary, Conf. Cath. Charities, The Kingsley Assn.; trustee St. Paul's Cathedral; treas. Pub. Health Nursing Assn. Served capt. Judge Adv. Dept., U.S. Army, with A.E.F., during World War; disch. Apr. 20, 1919; mem. Appellate Draft Bd., Allegheny Co. during World War. Mem. Am. Legion (charter mem. East Liberty Post), Am. Bar Assn., Allegheny County Bar Assn., Pa. State Bar Assn. Republican. Catholic. Clubs: Duquesne, Oakmont, Longue Vue, University (Pittsburgh). Home: 4914 5th Av. Office: 2610 Grant Bldg., Pittsburgh, Pa.

BIANCHI, Angelo Raffaele, physician; b. Italy, Mar. 27, 1873; s. Giovani Battista and Maria (D'Anna) B.; came to U.S., 1892, naturalized, 1898; student U. of City of N.Y., 1894, L.I. Coll., N.Y., 1895-96; M.D., Baltimore U. Med. Sch., 1898; m. Antonetta Casale, 1897; children—John, Anthony, Vincent, Mary (Mrs. Thomas Marzano), Carmela (Mrs. Samuel Pecora), Marguerite. Engaged in gen. practice of medicine and surgery at Newark, N.J. Served as alderman, Newark, N.J., 1912-18. Honored as Chevalier of the Crown of Italy, 1932. Democrat. Elk. Home: 184 Hunterdon St. Office: 141 7th Av., Newark, N.J.

BIANCHI, Ovidio; in practice of law; served as mayor of Orange. Address: Orange, N.J.

BIAS (Bennett) Randolph, lawyer; b. Hamlin, Lincoln Co., W.Va., Dec. 20, 1875; s. Rolan Armstrong and Lucy (Byus) B.; ed. high sch., Marshall Coll. and W.Va. U.; m. Clothilde Gaujot, June 19, 1901; children—Bennett Randolph (deceased), Marie Marguerite (Mrs. Wallace G. Smith), Ernest Gaujot. Was teacher in public schools, 1894-95; postmaster Williamson, 1897-09; Republican nominee for Senate, W.Va., 1902; editor Mingo Republican, 1903-04; chmn. Rep. County Com., Mingo Co., 1904-08; an organizer Mingo County Bank, 1905; admitted to bar, 1910; mem. firm Wiles & Bias, 1911-20, Bias & Chafin, 1922-25, now Bias & Bias; del. at large Rep. Nat. Conv., 1924; president West Williamson Land Co.; dir. Mountaineer Hotel Corpn. Commr. from W.Va. on Uniform State Laws. Chmn. Four-Minute Men, Mingo Co., 1917-19; chmn. Legal Advisory Bd., Mingo Co., 1917-18; mem. Am. Bar Assn., W.Va. State Bar Assn. (pres. 1926), Mingo County Bar Assn., Am. Law Inst., Nat. Economic League, Williamson Chamber Commerce (ex-pres.), Phi Kappa Sigma. Episcopalian: lay deputy from W.Va. to Gen. Confs., 1922, 28, 31, 34, 37. Gov. W. Va. Kiwanis Dist., 1927. Club: University. Lecturer on "West Virginia" since 1922. Home: Williamson, W.Va.

BIBEN, Joseph Henry, editor and publisher; b. Phila., Oct. 27, 1900; s. Isaac and Jennie (Cohen) B.; B.S., U. of Pa., 1923; m. Augusta Cohen (B.A., M.A., U. of Pa.), Sept. 26, 1919; children—Elaine Ruth, Robert Lewis, Louis Henry, Harvey James. Engaged as pub. and editor Jewish papers, viz., American Hebrew, New York City since 1936, Phila. Jewish Times since 1932, Jewish Ledger, Rochester, N. Y., since 1928, Jewish Ledger, Syracuse, N.Y., since 1930, Jewish Ledger, Albany, N.Y., since 1930, Jewish Ledger, Atlantic City, N.J., since 1929, Nat. Jewish Ledger, Washington, D.C., since 1929, The Advocate, Chicago, Ill., since 1938; pres. Roto Process Co., Rochester, N.Y., 1936. Mem. Aletheophile Honorary Soc. Jewish religion. B'nai B'rith. Shrine. Clubs: Gridiron, Varsity (U. of Pa.). Home: 3 Argyle St., Rochester, N.Y. Office: Jewish Times, Philadelphia, Pa.

BICKEL, H. Rank, lawyer; b. Union Twp., Lebanon Co., Pa., July 15, 1880; s. Amos Rank and Melinda (Albert) B.; ed. public schools, Lebanon, Pa., and Lebanon Business Coll.; read law in office of Hon. Thomas H. Capp, lawyer and judge of Lebanon and Dauphin Cos., Pa., 1898-1901; m. Laura E. Helms, of Lebanon, Pa., Oct. 1, 1903; children—H. Rank, Elizabeth H. (Mrs. Philip J. Boyer). Admitted to Lebanon County bar, 1901, and since in practice at Lebanon, Pa.; practiced alone until 1937; mem. firm Bickel & Bickel, since 1937; admitted to Pa. Superior Ct., 1906, Supreme Ct., 1901; solicitor and dir. 1st Nat. Bank, Fidelity Bldg. & Loan Assn., N. Lebanon Shoe Factory, Lebanon, Pa. Mem. Pa. Bar Assn., Lebanon Co. Bar Assn. Republican. Reformed Church. Mason, Elk. Club: Hershey Country (Hershey, Pa.). Home: 308 Hathaway Park. Office: First Nat. Bank Bldg., Lebanon, Pa.

BICKEL, William Forman, treas. Harbison-Walker Refractories Co.; b. Pittsburgh, Pa., Mar. 12, 1890; s. Harry Wright and Lydia (Paulson) B.; student Shady Side Acad., 1903-09; A.B., Princeton, 1913; m. Florence Croft, Apr. 20, 1917; children—William Croft, Harry Croft, Mary Augusta. Asso. with Wilson-Snyder Mfg. Corpn., 1914-17; with Harbison-Walker Refractories Co. continuously since 1917, now treas. and dir. Trustee Carnegie Hero Fund. Dir. Shady Side Acad., Pittsburgh, Pa. Republican. Presbyn. Clubs: Duquesne, Fox Chapel Golf (Pittsburgh); Rolling Rock (Laughlintown). Home: Squaw Run Rd., Aspinwall. Office: 1800 Farmers Bank Bldg., Pittsburgh, Pa.

BIDDLE, A(nthony) J(oseph) Drexel, author, explorer, lecturer; b. W. Phila., Pa., Oct. 1, 1874; s. Edward and Emily (Drexel) B.; ed. pvt. sch., Phila., and Heidelberg, Germany; m. Cordelia Rundell Bradley, June 11, 1895. Lived in Madeira Islands, studying conditions there, returning to U.S., 1891; joined staff of Phila. Public Ledger, also contbd. to mags. and humorous jours.; revived Phila. Sunday Graphic, 1895, and became its editor; head pub. house of Drexel Biddle, 1897-1904; founder of movement known as Athletic Christianity; founder, 1907, and pres. Drexel Biddle Bible Classes (200,000 members) in U.S., England, Ireland, Scotland, W.I., W. Africa, S. Australia and Canada. Prof. on faculty of Bureau of Investigation, Training School of Department of Justice. Served in France as captain U.S. Marine Corps, 1918; now col. in U.S. Marine Corps Reserve. Commanded U.S. Marine Corps Combat Team, exhibiting at Phila. Sesqui-Centennial; instructor of individual combat, U.S. Marine Corps. Fellow Royal Geographical Society; corr. member Société Archéologique de France. Amateur boxing champion. Author: A Dual Rôle, 1894; All Around Athletics, 1894; An Allegory and Three Essays, 1894; The Froggy Fairy Book, 1896; The Second Froggy Fairy Book, 1897; Shantytown Sketches, 1898; Word for Word and Letter for Letter, 1898; The Flowers of Life, 1898; The Madeira Islands (2 vols.), 1900; The Land of the Wine (2 vols.), 1901; Do or Die, Military Manual of Advanced Science in Individual Combat (pub. by U.S. Marine Corps), 1937. Office: 112 Drexel Bldg., Philadelphia, Pa.

BIDDLE, Charles John, lawyer; b. Andalusia, Pa., Mar. 13, 1890; s. Charles and Letitia (Glenn) B.; A.B., Princeton, 1911; LL.B., Harvard U. Law Sch., 1914; m. Katharine J. Legendre, Feb. 10, 1923; children—Charles, James. Admitted to Pa. bar, 1914, and since engaged in gen. practice of law at Phila.; mem. firm Drinker, Biddle and Reath since 1925. Served in A.S. of France and A.S., U.S.A., with A.E.F., 1917-18. Dec. Legion of Honor, Croix de Guerre with four citations (France); Order of Leopold (Belgium); D.S.C. (U.S.). Mem. Phila. Council Boy Scouts of America. Trustee Pa. Instn. for Instruction of the Blind, Drexel Inst. Tech. Mem. Am., Pa., and Phila. bar assns., Soc. of Colonial Wars, Pa. Hist. Soc. Republican. Episcopalian. Clubs: Philadelphia, Sunnybrook Golf, Torresdale-Frankford Country, Phila. Gun, The Rabbit (Philadelphia); Colonial (Princeton). Home: Andalusia. Office: 1429 Walnut St., Philadelphia, Pa.

BIDDLE, Edward Macfunn, lawyer; b. Carlisle, Pa., May 29, 1886; s. Edward W. and Gertrude D. (Bosler) B.; student Dickinson Prep. Sch., 1898-1901, Dickinson Coll., 1901-04; A.B., Yale, 1906; LL.B., U. of Pa., 1909; m. Anna Hope Dale, May 20, 1922; children—Lydia Spencer, Edward Macfunn, 3d, Richard C. Dale. Admitted to Pa. bar, 1909, and began as lawyer in offices of M. Hampton Todd, Phila., later asso. with Joseph S. Clark and Charles L. McKeehan, Phila.; independent practice, Phila., 1916-21; gen. counsel Ins. Co. of N. America and affiliated and subsidiary companies; mem. bd. dirs. Fidelity & Deposit Co. of Md. Attended Plattsburg Training Camp, 1916; served as 1st lt., later capt., Ordnance Corps, and 1st lieut. Field Arty., U.S. Army, Feb.-Dec. 1918. Mem. bd. trustees Dickinson Coll.; mem. bd. dirs. Agnes Irwin Sch., Wynnewood, Pa. Mem. Am., Pa. and Phila. bar assns., Sharswood Law Club, Phi Kappa Sigma. Republican. Episcopalian. Clubs: Yale of Phila. (1st pres. 1920), Philadelphia, University Barge (Phila.); Merion Cricket (Haverford, Pa.). Home: 126 St. Georges Rd., Ardmore, Pa. Office: 1600 Arch St., Philadelphia, Pa.

BIDDLE, Francis, lawyer; b. Paris, France, May 9, 1886; s. Algernon Sydney and Frances (Robinson) B.; brought to America in infancy; student Haverford (Pa.) Sch., 1895-99, Groton (Mass.) Sch., 1899-1905; B.A. cum laude, Harvard, 1909, LL.D. cum laude, 1911; m. Katherine Garrison Chapin, Apr. 27, 1918; children—Edmund Randolph, Garrison Chapin (dec.). Admitted to Pa. bar, 1912; pvt. sec. to Justice Holmes, U.S. Supreme Court, 1911-12; associate Biddle, Paul & Jayne, Phila., 1912-15; practiced with Barnes, Biddle & Myers, Phila., since 1917, partner since 1922; special asst. U.S. atty. Eastern Dist. Pa., 1922-26; admitted to practice before Supreme Court of U.S., 1927. Chmn. Phila. br. Foreign Policy Assn. since 1924; chmn. Nat. Labor Relations Bd., 1934-35; mem. Gov. Pinchot's Commn. on Spl. Policing in Industry, 1934; mem. Phila. County Bd. of Law Examiners, 1923-32; mem. com. of censors, Phila. Bar Assn., 1923-25 and 1929-31. Mem. Bd. of Pub. Edn., Phila. Dir. Phila. Contributionship for Ins. of Houses from Loss by Fire, Pa. Com. on Penal Affairs; trustee Twentieth Century Fund (New York), Fairmount Park Art Assn. Mem. Shakspere Soc. Democrat. Mason. Clubs: Philadelphia, Phila. Country, Legal, Franklin Inn (Phila.); Harvard, Coffee House (New York). Author: Llanfear Pattern, 1927. Contbr. to legal publs. Home: 3460 W. School House Lane. Office: Morris Bldg., Philadelphia, Pa.

BIDDLE, Gertrude Bosler (Mrs. Edward W. Biddle); b. Carlisle, Pa.; d. J. Herman and Mary J. (Kirk) Bosler; A.B., Wilson Coll., Chambersburg, Pa., 1875; post-grad. work 1 yr.; hon. A.M., Dickinson Coll., Carlisle, 1917; L. H.D., Temple U., Phila., 1921; m. Edward W. Biddle, Feb. 2, 1882. Presbyn. Pres. J. Herman Bosler Memorial Library, Carlisle. Pres. State Fed. of Pa. Women, 1907-11; v.p. City Parks Assn. of Phila.; dir. Am. Planning and Civic Assn., Pub. Charities Assn. Pa., Playground and Recreation Assn. America, Phila. Branch of English Speaking Union, Art Alliance of Phila.; mem. Pa. State Council of Edn., 1924-34; mem. board of governors Phila Forum. Clubs: Civic (pres. 1915-22), New Century, Acorn (Phila.); Civic of Carlisle (founder and pres. 1898-1907), Carlisle Fortnightly. Home: Philadelphia and Carlisle, Pa.

BIDDLE, John H.; editor Huntingdon News. Address: Huntingdon, Pa.

BIDDLE, Moncure, investment banker; b. Phila., Pa., Oct. 27, 1882; s. A. Sydney and Frances (Robinson) B.; grad. Groton Sch., 1901; student Harvard, 1901-04; m. Brenda Fenollosa, June 30, 1913; children—Owen, Peyton Randolph. Began as clerk Townsend Whelen & Co., 1907; since 1931 mem. firm Moncure Biddle & Co., Pa. municipal bonds. Republican. Episcopalian. Club: Philadelphia. Home: Devon, Pa. Office: 1520 Locust St., Philadelphia, Pa.

BIDDLE, Nicholas, insurance; b. Brookline, Mass., July 30, 1893; s. Edward and Lilian Howard (Lee) B.; ed. Episcopal Acad.; grad. Princeton, 1916; m. Sarah Lippincott, Feb. 11, 1915; children—Joanna Wharton, Nicholas, Sarah Lee, John Scott, Wharton. Employed with Ins. Co. of North America, 1914-15; with Hutchinson, Rivinus & Co. gen. ins. brokers, 1915-23; established firm of Biddle, Townsend & Co., gen. ins. brokers, and mem. firm since 1923. Served with Phila. City Cav., Mexican border, 1916-7; capt. then maj. U.S.A., 1918-19, with A.E.F., in three maj. offensives; maj. U.S.A. Res. Corps, 1919-36; maj. and lt. col. Pa. Nat. Guard since 1936. Pres. Pa. Game Commn. since 1935. Trustee Abington Memorial Hosp. Vice Comdr. Mil. Order Fgn. Wars, 1930-39, comdr. since 1939. Mem. S.R., Soc. Colonial Wars (mem. council). Episcopalian. Clubs: Penn Athletic (founder-mem.), Racquet, Princeton, Huntingdon Valley Country (vice-pres.), Huntingdon Valley Hunt. Home: "Springhead," York Rd., Noble, Pa. Office: 1600 Arch St., Philadelphia, Pa.

BIDDULPH, Howard, banker; b. Montclair, N.J., June 9, 1878; s. Herbert Henry and Emma Augusta (Baldwin) B.; grad. Montclair High Sch., 1896, Cooper Inst., N.Y. City, 1898; m. Eugenia Dodge, Sept. 15, 1904; children—Howard Dodge, Cornelia. Clk. Montclair Savings Bank, 1898-1904; treas. Bloomfield Savings Instn., 1904-23, now trustee; v.p. and trustee Howard Savings Instn. since 1923; v.p. and dir. Essex County Bldg. & Loan Assn. Trustee Community Welfare Assn. Treas. N.J. Chamber of Commerce; pres. Job Haines Home for Aged People, Bloomfield Home for Aged Men and Women. Mem. Nat. Assn. Mutual Savings Banks (pres. 1931), N.J. Savings Banks Assn. (sec. 1910-29; pres. 1929-30), Collectors League of N.J., Washington Assn. of N.J., N.J. Hist. Soc. Originator of plans for modernizing mut. savings banks, and of laws governing their activities and investments. Republican. Presbyn. Clubs: Essex, Carteret Book (Newark); Glen Ridge (N.J.) Country; Lake Placid Club (N.Y.); Down Town. Home: 60 Beach St., Bloomfield, N.J. Office: 766 Broad St., Newark, N.J.

BIDWELL, Charles Clarence, prof. physics; b. Rochester, N.Y., Oct. 23, 1881; s. Charles Henry and May Isabelle (Millham) B.; A.B., U. of Rochester, 1904; Ph.D., Cornell U., 1914; m. Mary Delphina Moody, Sept. 12, 1912; children—Charles Allan, David Moody, Ruah Moody (all dec.). High sch. science teacher, 1907-10; chemist Oakes Mfg. Co., Long Island City, 1906; grad. student, asst. and instr. physics, Cornell U., 1910-16, asst. prof. physics, 1917-25, prof., 1925-27; prof. physics and head of dept., Lehigh U., since 1927, also dir. curriculum in engring. physics. Employed at U.S. Naval Experimental Lab. on submarine detection problems, World War. Fellow Am. Physical Soc.; mem. Optical Soc. America (sec. 1925-29), A.A.A.S., Soc. for Promotion Engring. Edn., Sigma Xi, Delta Kappa Epsilon. Episcopalian. Club: Lions. Author: Principles of Physics, 1922; Advanced Course in General College Physics (with P. L. Bayley), 1937. Home: Riegelsville, Pa.

BIDWELL, Marshall Spring, organist; b. Great Barrington, Mass., Dec. 24, 1893; s. Orlando Curtiss and Helen (Higley) B.; student N.E. Conservatory of Music, 1913-17; studied organ at Fontainebleau, France, with Widor and Libert, 1921; Mus.D., Coe Coll., Cedar Rapids, Ia., 1934, U. of Pittsburgh, Pa., 1935; unmarried. Became organist of First Congregational Church, Stockbridge, Mass., 1909; organist St. James Episcopal Ch., Great Barrington, Mass., 1911-13, Center Methodist Ch., Malden, Mass., 1916-19; Organist Coe Coll., Cedar Rapids, Ia., 1919-32; municipal organist of Cedar Rapids, 1930-32; organist and dir. of music, Carnegie Inst., Pittsburgh, since 1932; organist and choir dir. 3d Presbyn. Ch., Pittsburgh, since 1933; guest prof. of organ, U. of Mich., summer session, 1938. Has appeared as recitalist in prin. music centers of U.S. Awarded 1st prize for organ playing, Fontainebleau, France, 1921. Mem. Am. Guild of Organists, Kappa Gamma Psi. Republican. Presbyn. Mason. Clubs: Agora Men's, University, Musicians, Junta Men's. Address: Carnegie Institute, Pittsburgh, Pa.

BIEBER, Milton James, clergyman; b. Kutztown, Pa., Dec. 13, 1862; s. Jonathan and Bregitta (Schwoyer) B.; student Keystone State

Normal Sch., Kutztown, Pa., 1885-86; A.B., Muhlenberg Coll., 1891, A.M., 1894, D.D., 1916; student Luth. Theol. Sem., Phila., 1891-94, Neff Sch. of Oratory, Phila., 1891-94; m. Bertha L. Manning, Sept. 7, 1898. Teacher in public school, Siegfriedsdale, Pa., 1881-83; teacher in grammar school, Kutztown, Pa., 1883-84; in high sch., 1884-85; prin. Bernville (Pa.) High Sch., 1886-88; teacher of history, Normal Sch., Kutztown, Pa., 1893; ordained to ministry of Luthern Ch., 1894; pastor Mt. Joy, Pa., 1894-97, Binghamton, N.Y., 1897-1904; Luth. missionary, Eastern field, 1904-17; organized Synod of Central Canada, 1909, pres., 1909-12; missionary supt. Norwest Synod, Minneapolis, Minn., 1917-27; field sec. Northwestern Sem., Minneapolis, Minn., 1921-27; field sec. Pacific Sem., Seattle, Wash., 1927-32; acting pres., 1932-34; field sec. Phila. Sem., 1935-37; field missionary Bd. of Am. Missions, United Luth. Ch. since 1937. Mem. Pa. German Soc., Alpha Tau Omega. Home: 911 S. 60th St., Philadelphia, Pa.

BIEHL, George, editor newspaper; b. Phila., Pa., Apr. 17, 1894; s. George Washington and Thekla (Siegfried) B.; student pub. schs., Phila., Pa.; m. Annamay Usher, June 11, 1930. In employ jewelry store, 1908-12; traveling salesman various products, 1912-23; rep. weekly newspaper, 1924; editor New Jersey Herald, Union City, N.J., 1924-26; corr. N.Y. and N.J. newspapers, 1926-33; asst. supt. elections, Hudson Co., N.J., 1933; a publicity dir. campaign of Harold G. Hoffman for gov., 1934; editor Hudson News, Union City, N.J., since 1935, partner Hudson New Pub. Co. since 1935. Served as pvt. then corpl. Ry. Transportation Corps, U.S.A., 1918-19, with A.E.F. in France. Active in Rep. politics since 1924; organized State Rep. League of N.J., 1935, now trustee and state dir. Republican. Presbyterian. Home: Chadwick Road, Teaneck, N.J. Office: 708 Bergenline Av., Union City, N.J.

BIERLY, Robert Nelson, legislator, county controller; b. West Pittston, Pa., Apr. 18, 1902; s. Louis P. and Sarah A. (Woodring) B.; B.S. in C.E., U. of Pa., 1925; m. Martha E. Kohnke, June 24, 1930; children—Geneva Eleanor, Martha Marlowe, Robert. Worked on bridge constrn. as resident engr. or supt. of constrn., Whittaker & Diehl Co., Harrisburgh, Pa., 1925-32; held various state highway and federal positions in constrn. field, consisting of rds., sewers, dykes, athletic fields, sch. bldgs., airport, 1933-36; cons. engr., Wilkes-Barre, Pa., since 1936. Mem. Ho. of Rep., Commonwealth of Pa., since 1937 (mem. Ruth Legislative Commn. investigating cts. of Pa., spl. investigating com. on charges involving Gov. Earle and other civil officers); co. controller, Luzerne Co., Pa., since 1938. Mem. Pittsburgh Chamber of Commerce, Pa. Soc. of Professional Engrs., Am. Fed. of Musicians. Club: Kiwanis (Pittsburgh, Pa.). Home: 302 Montgomery Av., West Pittston, Pa. Office: County Court House, Wilkes-Barre, Pa.

BIESTER, Edward G(eorge), lawyer; b. Phila., Pa., Jan. 25, 1903; s. Edward and Anna (Ditter) B.; B.S. in Econs., U. of Pa., 1924; LL.B., Temple U. Law Sch., 1929; m. Muriel M. Worthington, Jan. 26, 1929; children —Edward G., Ann Louise, John Lee. Admitted to Pa. bar, 1929 and since engaged in gen. practice of law at Doylestown; served as asst. dist. atty. Bucks Co., 1932-37, dist. atty. since 1938; dir. and solicitor Lenape Bldg. & Loan Assn. Mem. Bucks Co. Bar Assn. Republican. Club: Doylestown Kiwanis (past pres.). Home: 84 Shewell Av., Office: Hart Bldg., Doylestown, Pa.

BIETSCH, Charles F.; gynecologist Mercy Hosp.; obstetrician Roselia Maternity Hosp. Address: 500 Penn Av., Pittsburgh, Pa.

BIGELOW, Charles A.; v.p. Hercules Powder Co. Home: Charpley School Road, Wilmington, Del.

BIGELOW, Fred A.; pres. Carpenter Steel Co. Home: Wyomissing, Pa. Office: 101 N. Bern St., Reading, Pa.

BIGELOW, Frederick Southgate, editor; b. Boston, Mass., Oct. 23, 1871; s. George Frederick (M.D.) and Rebecca Gertrude (Houghton) B.; Mass. Inst. Tech., 1890-93; m. Mary Beatrice, d. Charles Lowell, June 26, 1915; children—Charles Lowell, Gertrude Ogden, George Frederick. Asso. editor Saturday Evening Post, 1899-1929; continues as contbr. to its editorial page. Editor and compiler several text-books and other works. Mem. bd. mgrs. Hosps. of Grad. Sch. of Medicine, U. of Pa.; mem. advisory council Am. Eugenics Soc. Republican. Episcopalian. Clubs: Franklin Inn, Philobiblon (Phila.); Century (New York). Contbr. to Ladies Home Journal, Esquire, Cosmopolitan and other mags. Home: 824 Buck Lane, Haverford, Pa.; (summer) "Highfield," Chocorua, N.H.*

BIGELOW, John Ogden, judge; b. Newark, N.J., Sept. 30, 1883; s. Moses and Lila R. (Fowler) B.; A.B., Princeton, 1905; m. Elizabeth Simpson, Aug. 15, 1918. Admitted to N.J. bar, 1908; in practice at Newark, 1908-29; prosecutor of pleas Essex Co., 1922-26; counsel Pub. Utility Commn. of N.J., 1927-29; vice chancellor of N.J. since 1930. Served in U.S. Army, World War, retiring with rank of capt. Trustee Newark (N.J.) Acad. Mem. Gen. Council of Presbyn. Ch., U.S.A. Democrat. Club: Essex (Newark). Home: 465 Highland Av., Newark. Address: 1060 Broad St., Newark, N.J.

BIGELOW, Robert L.; sr. partner Bigelow & Co. Address: 15 Exchange Place, Jersey City, N.J.

BIGELOW, William Frederick, editor; b. Milford Center, O., Aug. 14, 1879; s. Alpheus Russell and Hattie (Parthemore) B.; Ohio Wesleyan U., 1899-1904, B.L., 1905, LL.D., 1927; Columbia, 1904-05; Litt.D., Kansas Wesleyan, 1930; m. (Mary) Retta Koch, Dec. 24, 1906; children—Margaret, Miriam, Mary Elizabeth. Joined staff of Cosmopolitan Mag. 1905, mng. editor, 1909-13; editor Good Housekeeping since May 1, 1913. Trustee Ohio Wesleyan Univ., American Univ. Mem. Ohio Soc. of New York, Sigma Alpha Epsilon, Phi Beta Kappa (hon.). Republican. Methodist. Mason. Home: Roselle Park, N.J. Office: 959 8th Ave., New York, N.Y.

BIGGER, Frederick, architect, town planner; b. Pittsburgh, Pa., Oct. 10, 1880; s. Thomas W. and Sara Lois (Coburn) B.; grad. U. of Pa., 1903; unmarried. Practiced at Seattle, 1908-11, Phila., 1911-13; partial practice, Pittsburgh, 1914-30; sec. Pittsburgh Art Commn., 1914-18; co-organizer, 1918, Citizens' Com. on City Plan of Pittsburgh, since exec. and town planning advisor, became mem. bd., 1923. Mem. Pittsburgh City Planning Commn., Pittsburgh Art Commn.; dir. Pittsburgh Housing Assn. Mem. Am. Inst. Architects (pres. Pittsburgh Chapter, 1930-31), Am. City Planning Inst. (pres.), Internat. Fed. for Housing and Town Planning (council). Episcopalian. Clubs: University, Union (Pittsburgh); City (New York); Phila. Sketch. Home: 600 S. Negley Av. Office: Vendergrift Bldg., Pittsburgh, Pa.*

BIGGS, John, Jr., judge, author; b. Wilmington, Del., Oct. 6, 1895; s. John and Rachel Valentine (Massey) B.; prep. edn., The Hill Sch., Pottstown, Pa.; Litt.B., Princeton; LL.B., Harvard, 1922; m. Anna Swift Rupert, Apr. 16, 1925; children—John III, Charles Rupert, Anna Swift Rupert. Admitted to Del. bar, 1922, and since practiced at Wilmington; U.S. referee in bankruptcy, Dist. of Del.; apptd. judge U.S. Circuit Ct. of Appeals for Third Circuit, Feb. 16, 1937. Enlisted in U.S. Army and served in Ordnance and Tank Corps, World War; civilian aide to sec. of war for Del., 1923-37. Mem. Am. and Del. State bar assns., Assn. Bar City of New York, Soc. Colonial Wars, S.A.R., Am. Legion. Chmn. Democratic State Com., 1930-37; chmn. Dem. delegation Dem. Nat. Conv., Chicago, 1932, Philadelphia, 1936. Presbyn. Clubs: Princeton Campus; Wilmington, Rotary Internat., Delaware Turf; Wilmington Country; Harvard (New York). Author: Demigods, 1926; Seven Days' Whipping, 1928; Delaware Laws Affecting Business Corporations (with Stewart Lynch), 1935. Contbr. to Scribner's Mag. Home: "Woodale," Wilmington. Office: Federal Bldg., Wilmington, Del.*

BIGGS, John Quincy, clergyman; b. Newton Co., Mo., Aug. 20, 1878; s. John and Dicy (Reed) B.; student Transylvania Coll., Lexington, Ky., 1903-04; B.O., Phillips U., Enid, Okla., 1912; A.B., U. of Idaho, 1919; m. Zona Davidson, 1903; children—Portia Thelma (Mrs. Walter N. Hahn), Mary Anita (Mrs. Joseph H. Ream), John Melvin. Public school teacher, 1899-1903; minister Disciples of Christ Ch. since 1902; ordained, 1903; pastor, Sumner, Ill., 1904-05, Buffalo, Mo., 1905-08, Topeka, Kan., 1921-25, Zanesville, O., 1925-29, Tonawanda, N.Y., 1929-34, Waynesburg, Pa., 1934-38, Johnstown, Pa., since 1938; prof. of oratory, public speaking and dramatics, Spokane (Wash.) U., and Tex. Christian U., Fort Worth, 1914-21. Served as voluntary chaplain during World War. Mem. Research Club of Spokane, Wash. Republican. Mason, Odd Fellow. Club: Rotary (Tonawanda, N.Y.). Address: 825 Highland Ave., Johnstown, Pa.

BIKLE, Henry Wolf, lawyer; b. Gettysburg, Pa., Oct. 20, 1877; s. Philip Melanchthon B.; D.D., and Emma J. (Wolf) B.; A.B., Pa. Coll., Gettysburg, 1897, A.M., 1900; LL.B., University of Pa., 1901; LL.D., Gettysburg (Pa.) College, 1928; LL.D., from Franklin and Marshall College, 1937; m. Lucy Leffingwell, d. George W. Cable, Sept. 14, 1910. Began practice in Phila., 1901; asst. gen. solicitor, 1907-16, asst. gen. counsel, 1916-22, gen. atty., 1922-32, gen. counsel since 1932, Pa. R.R. Lecturer on law, 1901-09, asst. prof. of law, 1909-13, prof. law (courses in constl. law and carriers), 1913-29, Law School University of Pa.; non-resident lecturer on law, Bryn Mawr Coll., 1902-04; lecturer on constl. law, Gettysburg Coll., 1906-22. Mem. Gov.'s Advisory Com. on Constl. Revision, Pa., 1935. Mem. Bd. Edn. of United Luth. Church, 1930-36. Vicepres. Association Practitioners before Interstate Commerce Commission, 1929-30, pres.; 1931-32. Fellow American Academy of Arts and Sciences; mem. Am. Law Inst., Pa. State and Am. bar assns., Pa. State Chamber of Commerce, Phi Beta Kappa, Sigma Chi. Democrat. Lutheran. Clubs: University, Rittenhouse, Legal, Bryn Mawr Polo, Phila. Cricket. Author: (with late Hon. George M. Dallas) Analytical Tables of the Law of Evidence. Contbr. Am. Law Register, U. of Pa. Law Rev., Harvard Law Rev., etc. Home: West Valley Rd., Strafford, Pa. Office: Broad Street Station Bldg., Philadelphia, Pa.

BILDER, Nathaniel, lawyer; b. New York, N.Y., May 1, 1881; s. Levy and Amalia (Garfunkel) B.; LL.B., Kent Coll. of Law, Chicago, 1905; m. Zerlina Hirsch Bilder, 1907; 1 son, Robert Martin. Admitted to N.J. bar, 1906, and practiced in Paterson, later forming partnership with David H. Bilder; since 1907 sr. mem. firm of Bilder, Bilder & Kaufman, Newark, N.J.; v.p. West Side Trust Co. (Newark), A. W. Faker, Inc.; dir. United Advertising Corpn. Trustee and dir. Y.M.H.A. and Y.W.H.A.; dir. Conf. on Jewish Charities. Mem. Am. Bar Assn., N.J. State Bar Assn. (chmn. sect. on banking laws), Essex County Bar Assn., County Lawyers Assn. Clubs: Downtown, Progress (Newark); Mountain Ridge Country. Home: 67 S. Munn Av., East Orange, N.J. Office: 60 Park Pl., Newark, N.J.

BILL, Alfred Hoyt, author; b. Rochester, N.Y., May 5, 1879; s. Edward Clark and Eliza Huline (Hoyt) B.; grad. high sch., Faribault, Minn., 1899; A.B., Yale, 1903; m. Florence Dorothy Reid, June 30, 1903; children—Alfred Reid (dec.), Florence Dorothy, Edward Clark. Instr. in English, Seabury Div. Sch., Faribault, 1910-13; treas. Bishop Seabury Mission and Shattuck Sch., Faribault, 1916-21. Served in 2d Inf., Minn. N.G., as 2d lt., 1st lt., capt. and regtl. adj., 1910-16; capt. and div. rep. Am. Red Cross, attached to 91st Div., A.E.F. 1918. Mem. Minn. Hist. Soc., Zeta Psi. Republican. Episcopalian. Clubs: Yale (New York); Nassau (Princeton). Author: The Clutch of the Corsican, 1925; Highroads of Peril, 1926; Alas, Poor Yorick!, 1927; The Red Prior's Legacy, 1929; The Wolf in the Garden, 1931; Astrophel, or the Life and Death of the Renowned Sir Philip Sidney, 1937. Home: 342 Nassau St., Princeton, N.J.

BILLETDOUX, Edmond Wood, univ. prof.; b. Hudson Falls, N.Y., Feb. 9, 1877; s. Charles A. and Harriet Viola (Baker) B.; student Drury Acad., North Adams, Mass., 1892-95; B.A. (valedictorian), Williams Coll., Williamstown, Mass., 1899, M.A., 1901; student U. of Paris and Collège de France, Paris, 1901-03; grad. study U. of Madrid, Spain, U. of Rome, Italy, 1901-03; m. Rosa Benoît LeFay, of Lorient (Morbihan), France, Sept. 13, 1903; children —Paul Edmond (dec.), Marc Raymond. Asst. in French, Williams Coll., Williamstown, Mass., 1899-1900, asst. in French and German, 1900-01, instr. Romance langs., 1903-07; asso. prof. Romance langs., Rutgers U., New Brunswick, N.J., 1907-21, prof. Spanish lang. and lit., since 1921, courses in French and Spanish in summer sch., extension, grad. sch. since 1913; prof. of French lang. and lit., N.J. Coll. for Women, New Brunswick, N.J., 1934-35. Served as lt., capt., liaison officer, 4th Sect., Gen. Staff, A.E.F., 1917-19. Mem. Modern Lang. Assn. of America, Modern Lang. Assn. of Middle States and Md., Am. Assn. of Teachers of Spanish, Am. Philol. Assn., Am. Assn. Univ. Profs., N.J. Modern Lang. Teachers Assn. (v.p. 1926-27, 1937-39, pres. 1927-29), Nat. Fed. Modern Lang. Teachers (mem. exec. com., 1926-29), Mil. Order of Fgn. Wars of U.S. (vet. companion, N.J. Chapter), Phi Beta Kappa (v.p. Rutgers Chapter 1930-31, pres. 1931-32), Phi Gamma Delta, Sigma Delta Pi. Received spl. letter of commendation from G.H.Q., A.E.F., 1919; cited by comdr.-in-chief, A.E.F., "for exceptionally meritorious and conspicuous service," 1919; awarded U.S. Victory Medal (5 bars), Williams War Medal, Rutgers U. Award (medal and citation for distinguished service), 1936, Officier d'Académie (Palmes Académiques), 1910, Officier de l'Instruction Publique, 1933. Baptist (mem. Livingston Av. Baptist Ch., 1910-39, New Brunswick, N.J.; teacher Philathea Bible Class, 1911-17; deacon since 1937). Club: Rutgers (New Brunswick, N.J.). Address: Rutgers University, New Brunswick, N.J.

BILLHARTZ, William H., banker; b. Alliance, O., Mar. 9, 1875; s. Joseph and Eliza (Miller) B.; student high sch. and Scio Coll.; m. Mabel Foust, Nov. 15, 1906 (died Mar. 1924); 1 son, William H. Pres. and dir. St. Clair Deposit Bank. Home: 915 S. Millvale Av. Office: 300 Brownsville Road, Pittsburgh, Pa.

BILLHEIMER, Stanley, clergyman; b. Shippensburg, Pa., Feb. 10, 1872; s. Thomas Charles and Emma Catherine (Ziegler) B.; A.B., A.M., Gettysburg (Pa.) Coll., 1891, D.D., 1919; student Gettysburg Theol. Sem., 1891-94; m. Ida Richardson of Washington, D.C., Dec. 13, 1904; children—John Philip, Mary Catherine (Mrs. Carlyle H. Seiler), Elinor Ruth. Ordained to ministry of United Luth. Ch. in America, Sept. 23, 1894; pastor, Georgetown, D.C., 1894-1904, York Springs, Pa., 1904-10, Norwood, Pa., 1910-24, Palmyra, Pa., since 1924. Pres. East Pa. Synod, 1914, 1924; mem. United Luth. Bd. of Publ., 1918-30; mem. United Luth. Bd. of Edn. since 1936. Has served on bds. of edn. of York Springs, Norwood and Palmyra, Pa. Trustee Gettysburg Sem., 1926-34. Active in Boy Scout work since 1911. Mem. Sigma Chi. Mason (K.T.); past master. Mem. editorial staff, The Lutheran, 1918-20; contbr. to Luth. New Testament Commentary, 1936. Home: 42 N. College St., Palmyra, Pa.

BILLIG, Thomas Clifford, lawyer, educator; b. Beaver Falls, Pa.; s. Simon Peter and Cora Eleanor (Gould) B.; student U. of Pittsburgh, 1913-14, 1921-23; B.A., Geneva Coll., Beaver Falls, 1918; M.A., U. of Pa., 1922; LL.B., Yale, 1925, J.S.D., 1928 (Sterling fellowship); m. Melba Stucky, June 16, 1927; children—Thomas Clifford, Emil Frederick Stucky, Paul Lemmer. Reporter and copyreader Pittsburgh Chronicle Telegraph, 1918, Phila. North American, 1918-20; prof. economics and head of dept., Pa. Mil. Coll., Chester, 1920-21; asst. prof. economics, Washington and Jefferson Coll., Washington, Pa., 1921-24; asso. prof. law, Washington and Lee U., 1925-26; city editor McKeesport (Pa.) Journal, 1926; admitted to Pa. bar, 1926; asst. prof. law, Cornell U., 1926-27; associated with Root, Clark, Buckner & Ballantine, N.Y. City, 1928-30; asst. counsel N.Y. Bankruptcy Investigation, 1929; actg. asso. prof. of law, Ohio State U., 1930-31; visiting prof. law, Northwestern U., summer 1931; visiting prof. law, Cornell U., summers 1927 and 1932; asso. prof. of law, W.Va., Univ., 1931-34. prof. of law, 1934-35; annotator for W.Va. Restatement of Contracts, Am. Law Inst., 1931-34; staff adviser Gov.'s Com. on Efficiency and Economy, W.Va., 1933-34; dir. of legal research NRA, Washington, D.C., 1934-35; lecturer on business law, Columbia U., summers 1934, 35; prof. law, Duke U., 1935-37; principal atty. Social Security Board since August 1936; admitted to bar of U.S. Supreme Ct., 1936; lecturer in law, Catholic U. of America since 1937; visiting prof. of law, Coll. of the City of New York, spring, 1938. Mem. Am. Assn. of Univ. Profs., Acacia, Delta Theta Phi, Pi Delta Epsilon, Order of Coif. Protestant. Mason (32°, Shriner). Clubs: Yale (New York); Yale (Washington, D.C.); Cosmos (Washington, D.C.). Author: Cases on Administration of Insolvent Estates (with Homer Franklin Carey), 1932; Equity Receiverships in Franklin Co., Ohio, 1932; Third Edition of Holbrook and Aigler's Cases on Bankruptcy, 1935, Fourth Edition, 1939; also various articles in legal and credit publs. Home: 36 Drummond Av., Chevy Chase, Md. Office: Social Security Board, Washington, D.C.

BILLIKOPF, Jacob, sociol. worker; b. Wilna, Russia, June 1, 1883; s. Louis and Glika (Katzenelenbogen) B.; student University of Richmond, Va., LL.D. from same univ., 1928; Ph.B., Univ. of Chicago, 1903; post-grad. work, same, 1902-04; Sch. of Philanthropy, New York, 1905; m. Ruth Marshall, Feb. 23, 1920 (she died August 8, 1936); children—Florence Marshall, David Marshall. Served as superintendent Jewish Settlement, Cincinnati, Ohio, 1904-05; superintendent United Jewish Charities, Milwaukee, Wis., 1905-07; supt. of United Jewish Charities, Kansas City, Mo., 1907. Active in orgn. of municipal baths, pub. night schs., free legal aid bureau, remedial loan agency and Kansas City Bd. of Pub. Welfare. Pres. Mo. State Conf. of Charities, 1911-12; served as v.p. Kansas City Bd. of Pardons and Paroles, mem. Kansas City Bd. of Pub. Welfare, and sec. Municipal Recreation Commn. Non-resident lecturer of sociology and economics U. of Mo. Dir. Jewish Ednl. Inst., Kansas City. Pres. Nat. Conf. Jewish Social Workers; exec. dir. campaign to raise $25,000,000 for Jewish war sufferers; formerly exec. dir. Fed. of Jewish Charities, Phila.; impartial chmn., Men's Clothing Industry in N.Y. City; v.p. Am. Assn. for Old Age Security; chmn. bd., N.Y. Clothing Unemployment Fund; chmn. Com. of One Hundred on Unemployment Relief, Phila., 1930-31; mem. Pa. State Welfare Commn.; mem. bd. dirs. Benjamin Franklin Memorial (Philadelphia); formerly trustee of "The Nation"; trustee of "The Survey" mags.; trustee Howard U., Washington, D.C. Mem. advisory com. New School Social Research, 1924-28; pres. Nat. Conf. of Jewish Social Service, 1933-34; apptd. impartial chmn. Govt. Regional Labor Bd. (Phila. area), 1933; exec. dir. Nat. Coordinating Com. for Aid to Refugees and Emigrants coming from Germany; dir. Labor Standards Assn., since Jan. 1, 1938. Club: City. Hon. mem. Phi Alpha, Alpha Pi Zeta. Home: Melrose Park, Pa. Office: Bankers Securities Bldg., Philadelphia, Pa.

BILLINGS, John Harland, teacher of mech. engring.; b. Orono, Ont., Can., Apr. 4, 1888; s. Samuel Martin and Eveline (Swanston) B.; B.A. Sc., U. of Toronto, 1912; M.S., Mass. Inst. Tech., 1915, Harvard, 1915; m. Anna Sibyl Stonehouse, Toronto, Ont., 1915; children—Julia Evelyn, Jean Harland, John Kimball. Came to U.S., 1913, naturalized, 1926. Teacher pub. sch., Leskard, Ont., 1906-08; asst. engr. Can. Machinery Corpn., 1912-13; instr. mech. engring., U. of Mo., 1913-14, Johns Hopkins U., 1915-16; lecturer in machine design and asst. prof., U. of Toronto, 1916-19; prof. mech. engring. and head dept., Drexel Inst. Tech. since 1919; gage engr. on fuse mfg. Russell Motor Co., summer 1916; tool engr. on aircraft motor mfg. Willys Overland Co., summer 1918; gage production rep. Imperial Munitions Bd., Ottawa, June-Oct. 1917. Fellow A.A.A.S.; mem. Soc. for Promotion Engring. Edn., Am. Soc. Mech. Engrs. (mem. exec. com. Phila. sect. 1924-30, sec.-treas. 1926-27, vice chmn. 1927-28, chmn. 1928-29), Tau Beta Pi, Pi Tau Sigma, Phi Kappa Phi. Republican. Clubs: Llanerch Country (Manoa); Drexel Men's Faculty (Phila.). Author: Applied Kinematics, 1931; Mechanics and Design of Machines, 1933. Contbr. articles to professional jours. Home: 30 Cedarbrook Rd., Ardmore, Pa.

BILOFSKY, Maxwell M., mfr.; pres. Duro-Test Corpn. Address: North Bergen, N.J.

BINDER, Louis Richard, clergyman; b. Phila., Pa., Nov. 12, 1892; s. Louis and Elizabeth (Suentzenich) B.; A.B., Bloomfield (N.J.) Coll. and Sem., 1918, B.D., 1918; A.M., Columbia, 1927; Th.M., Drew U., Madison, N.J., 1928, Ph.D., 1931; m. Johannette Leiss, Aug. 7, 1918 (deceased); m. 2d, Freda E. Erbacher, Oct. 20, 1920; children—Ruth Elizabeth, Margaret Emilie, Joan Drey. Ordained to ministry of Presbyterian Ch., Mar. 19, 1918; pastor Manhattan Park Presbyn. Ch., Irvington, N.J., 1918-22; pastor Ward Street Presbyn. Ch., Paterson, N.J., since 1922; prof. of sociology, Bloomfield Coll. and Sem., since 1932. Moderator Jersey City Presbytery, 1932-33; vice-moderator Synod of N.J., 1937-38; commr. to Gen. Assembly of Presbyn. Ch., Winona Lake, Ind., 1921, Tulsa, Okla., 1928, Denver, Colo., 1932. Dir. Bethany Home for the Aged, Irvington; vice-pres. Paterson Inter-Racial Commn., 1939. Republican. Club: Manuscript (Paterson). Author: Modern Religious Cults and Society, 1933. Home: 76 Ward St., Paterson, N.J.

BINDER, Walter J.; b. Trenton, N.J., Jan. 25, 1885; s. Frank and Catherine (Clark) B.; student State Model Sch., Trenton High Sch. and St. John's Coll.; m. Sarah Maddock, Sept. 7, 1911; children—Alice M., Kathryn C. Pres. Delaware Floor Products, Inc., and Delaware Floor Products Sales Co. since 1932. Home: 7 Belmont Circle, Trenton, N.J. Office: Christiana Av., Wilmington, Del.

BINFORD, Oriel J., gen. mgr. and dir. West Penn Cement Co.; b. Greenfield, Ind., June 3, 1877; s. Joseph L. and Susannah (Jessup) B.; B.S., Earlham Coll., Richmond, Ind.; student Indiana U., Bloomington, Ind.; m. Louise Wilson, Aug. 14, 1901; children—William W., Robert J., Louise, Marian, Marjorie. Chemist and supt. Colorado Portland Cement Co., Portland, Colo., 1900-04; supt. Pacific Portland Cement Co., Cement, Calif., 1904-06; sec., supt. and plant mgr. in El Paso and Fort Worth, Tex., and Dayton, O., for Southwestern Portland Cement Co., 1907-26; gen. mgr. West Penn Cement Co., Butler, Pa., since 1926, now also dir.; during various periods acted in advisory capacity in examinations of properties and locations of cement mfg. enterprises; v.p. and dir. Winfield R.R. Co. Mem. Butler (Pa.) Chamber of Commerce (v.p.), Community Chest Coms., Am. Soc. for Testing Materials. Clubs: Rotary (Butler, Pa.; pres.); Propeller of U.S.A.; Builders Exchange. Home: 800 E. Pearl St. Office: 233 S. Main St., Butler, Pa.

BINGHAM, Arthur W., M.D.; in practice of medicine at East Orange; mem. advisory bd. Essex County Trust Branch of Fidelity Union Trust Co. Address: 144 Harrison St., East Orange, N.J.

BINGHAM, Eugene Cook, chemist; b. Cornwall, Vt., Dec. 8, 1878; s. W. Harrison and Mary Lucina (Cook) B.; B.A., Middlebury (Vt.) Coll., 1899; Ph.D., John Hopkins Univ., 1905; D.Sc., Middlebury College, 1936; Universities of Leipzig, Berlin and Cambridge, 1905-06; m. Edith Irene Snell, June 18, 1907. Prof. chemistry, Richmond (Va.) Coll., 1906-15; asst. physicist, U.S. Bur. of Standards, 1915-16; prof. chemistry, Lafayette Coll., since Aug. 1916. Chemist, U.S. Bur. of Standards, 1918-19, on lubrication investigation. Was awarded certificate of merit by Franklin Institute, for improved form of variable pressure viscometer, 1921. Chmn. com. on plasticity Am. Soc. Testing Materials. Mem. Am. Phys. Soc., Am. Chem. Soc., Soc. of Rheology, American Association

Advancement of Science, Am. Assn. Univ. Profs., Metric Assn., Chemists' Club, Am. Inst. Chem. Engrs., Am. Inst. of Chemists, Delta Kappa Epsilon, Phi Beta Kappa, Tau Beta Pi, Alpha Chi Sigma; hon. mem. Va. Chemists' Club; sec. the Bingham Assn. Republican. Conglist. Club: Blue Mountain Club of Pa. (pres.). Author: Laboratory Manual of Inorganic Chemistry, 1911; Fluidity and Plasticity, 1921; also numerous papers pub. in Am., English and German Scientific periodicals. Inventor of instruments for the precise measurement of viscosity and plasticity. Home: 602 Clinton Terrace, Easton, Pa.

BINGLEY, George Althoff, prof. of mathematics; b. Watertown, N.Y., Nov. 12, 1888; s. John Wesley and Eva Jane (Althoff) B.; grad. Watertown High Sch., 1905; A.B., Princeton U., 1910, A.M., 1916; student Univ. of Göttingen, Germany, 1913-14; unmarried. Teacher in govt. schools, Osaka, Japan, 1910-13; instr. of mathematics, Ga. Sch. of Technology, 1918-19, U.S. Naval Acad., 1919-23; with St. John's Coll., Annapolis, Md., since 1923, as asst. prof. of mathematics, 1923-24, asso. prof. 1924-31, prof. since 1931. Served as sergt. Headquarters Co., 472d Engrs., U.S. Army, Washington, D.C., during World War. Fellow A.A.A.S.; mem. Am. Math. Assn., Phi Sigma Kappa. Received Algernon Sydney Sullivan award, 1935. Democrat. Presbyterian. Clubs: University (Baltimore); Princeton (New York); Dial Lodge (Princeton U.). Home: Brice House, Annapolis, Md.

BINING, Arthur Cecil, univ. prof., editor; b. Llanelly, Wales, Nov. 20, 1893; s. Arthur Owen and Jane (Phillips) B.; came to U.S., 1911, naturalized citizen, 1922; B.S., U. of Pa., 1927; B.D., Crozer Theol. Sem., 1927; A.M., U. of Pa., 1929, Ph.D., same, 1932; m. Inez Petry, Nov. 26, 1931. Clk. in law office, O'Brian & Henderson, Toronto, Can., 1909-11; with U.S. Steel Corpn., 1911-12, Jones & Laughlin Steel Corpn., Aliquippa, Pa., 1912-22; instr. history, Liberty High Sch., Bethlehem, Pa., 1927-28; asst. instr. history, U. of Pa., 1928-29, instr., 1929-35, asst. prof. Am. history since 1935. Mem. Edn. Alumni Assn. U. of Pa. (first v.p.), Pa. State Edn. Assn. (pres. U. of Pa. branch), Pa. Hist. Assn. (mem. council), Am. Hist. Assn., Hist. Soc. Pa., Nat. Council for Social Studies, Middle States Assn. History Teachers, Kappa Phi Kappa, Phi Delta Kappa, Pi Gamma Mu. Republican. Baptist. Club: Lenape (Philadelphia). Author: British Regulation of the Colonial Iron Industry, 1933; Pennsylvania Iron Manufacture in the Eighteenth Century, 1938. Co-author (with D. H. Bining), Teaching the Social Studies in Secondary Schools, 1935; (with A. C. Howland and R. H. Shryock), A Pageant of World History, 1939. Contbr. to hist. mags and encys. Editor: The Social Studies, Pennsylvania History, Social Studies Series; chmn. edit. bd. Educational Outlook. Home: 1112 Lindale Av., Drexel Hill, Pa.

BINKERD, Robert Studebaker; b. Dayton, Ohio, November 7, 1882; s. Oscar William and Emma (Brown) B.; Ph.B., Yale, 1904. Sec. Municipal Voters' League, Buffalo, N.Y., 1905-08, Citizens' Union, New York, 1908-09, City Club, New York, 1909-17; asst. to the chmn. Assn. of Ry. Executives, 1917-22; vice chmn. Com. on Pub. Relations of the Eastern Railroads, 1923-27; was partner investment house Jas. H. Oliphant & Co.; v.p., dir. of sales, Baldwin Locomotive Works (Phila.). Clubs: Railroad, City, Salmagundi, Yale, Bankers (New York); Racquet (Washington); Racquet, Art Club (Phila.); Rolling Green Golf (Media, Pa.); Chicago. Home: Locust Farm, South Lee, Mass.; also 1512 Spruce St., Phila. Office: Paschall Station, Philadelphia, Pa.

BINNS, Benjamin Gilbert, pres. Union Nat. Bank of Donora; b. Fayette Co., Pa., Dec. 19, 1883; s. William H. and Elma (Cope) B.; student Southwestern State Normal Sch., 1902; m. Ethel Carrick, Aug. 3, 1931; 1 stepson, Jack C. Scott. Successively asst. cashier, cashier, and v.p. First Nat. Bank of Donora, Pa.; pres. Union Trust Co. of Donora; pres. Union Nat. Bank of Donora; mem. firm Colgan & Binns, bankers, real estate, ins., Donora, Pa.; asso. with Mellbank Group. Mem. Donora Borough Council. Pres. dist. chapter, Red Cross. Mem. Washington Co. Bankers' Assn. Home: Country Club Rd., Monongahela, Pa. Office: 501 McKean Av., Donora, Pa.

BIRCH, Raymond Embree, ceramic engr.; b. McConnelsville, O., Dec. 18, 1905; s. Harold Embree Birch and Rosa (McDonald) B.; grad. high sch., McConnelsville, 1923; B. Ceramic Engring., Ohio State U., 1927, Ceramic Engr., 1937; m. Opal Martin, June 12, 1927; 1 son, Donald Martin, Ceramic engr. Carlyle Labold Co., 1927-28; research engr. Ohio State U. Expt. Sta., 1928-30; ceramic engr. Harbison-Walker Refractories Co. since 1930. Fellow Am. Ceramic Soc. (trustee 1938-41; chmn. Pittsburgh sect. 1935; chmn. refractories div. 1936); mem. Am. Inst. Ceramic Engrs. (exec. com. since 1938), Keramos (nat. pres. 1936-37), Am. Soc. Testing Materials, Soc. Glass Tech. (British), Triangle, Pi Delta Epsilon. Republican. Author of tech. articles on refractories development, mfr. and testing; holder U.S. patents on refractories and mineral uses. Home: 426 Coolidge Av., Mt. Lebanon. Office: 1800 Farmers Bank Bldg., Pittsburgh, Pa.

BIRCH, Stephen, corporation official; b. N.Y. City, Mar. 24, 1872; s. Stephen and Emily (Marshall) B.; M.E., Sch. of Mines (Columbia), 1898; m. Mary C. Rand, June 24, 1916 (she died August 4, 1930); children—Mary M. R., Stephen. Now chmn. bd. Kennecott Copper Corpn., Braden Copper Co.; pres. Alaska Steamship Co., Copper River & N.W. Railway Co.; dir. Alaska Development & Mineral Co., Bankers Trust Co., Utah Copper Co., Chicago, Burlington & Quincy Railway Company, C.&S. Ry. Co., N.P. Ry. Co., Erie R.R. Co., Nev. Northern Ry. Co. Clubs: Union, Recess, Bankers', Tuxedo, Columbia University, Piping Rock, Houvenkopf Country (New York). Home: Mahwah, N.J. Office: 120 Broadway, New York, N.Y.

BIRCH, William Dunham, vice-pres. of sales; b. Dover, N.J., Nov. 14, 1903; s. William F. and Anna Pauline (Dunham) B.; prep. edn. Phillips Acad., Andover, Mass., 1921-23; B.S., Mass. Inst. of Tech., 1928; m. Margaret Hapgood, 1930 (divorced); 1 son, Christopher; m. 2d, Helen M. Ross, 1937, 1 dau., Dagmar Anne. Automobile dealer as principal owner of Birch & Birch, Inc., Buick and Cadillac cars, Dover, N.J., 1928-38, vice-pres. since 1928; vice-pres. and sec. Dover Boiler Works since 1928, vice-pres. in charge of sales since 1938. Mem. Soc. of Mech. Engrs., Delta Kappa Epsilon. Republican. Presbyterian. Mason. Clubs: Rockaway River Country (Denville, N.J.); Lake Valhalla (Montville, N.J.); Delta Kappa Epsilon (New York). Home: 152 S. Terrace, Boonton, N.J. Office: Dover Boiler Works, Dover, N.J.

BIRCH, William F., pres. Dover Boiler Works, Am. Trust Co. Address: Dover, N.J.

BIRD, Samuel Bancroft, engineer; b. Wilmington, Del., Dec. 11, 1898; s. John Blymer and Elizabeth Richardson (Bancroft) B.; student Hill Sch., Pottstown, Pa., 1913-17; M.E., Cornell U., 1923; m. Lonsdale Miner, Nov. 26, 1923; children—Samuel Bancroft, Henry Lonsdale, John Blymer; m. 2d, Virginia Louise Anderson, Nov. 9, 1936; 1 stepson, Robert. Draughtsman Pusey & Jones Co., Wilmington, Del., 1923, estimator and salesman, 1923-25; spl. investigator Joseph Bancroft & Sons, Wilmington, Del., 1925-29, time study engr., 1929-35, research engr., 1935-37, advertising man, 1937-39, sec. since 1928, dir. since 1929; sec. Joseph Bancroft & Sons Co. of Pa. since 1929, dir. since 1928; sec. and dir. Eddystone (Pa.) Mfg. Co. since 1935; v.p., asst. sec. and dir. Bedford Springs (Pa.) Corpn. since 1936; mgr. Estate of Samuel Bancroft Jr., Inc. Trustee Del. Hosp.; dir. Wilmington Drama League. Mem. Soc. of Colonial Wars, Kappa Alpha (Northern). Republican. Episcopalian. Home: Centerville, Del. Office: Joseph Bancroft & Sons Co., Rockford, Wilmington, Del.

BIRD, William Edwin, surgeon Wilmington Gen. Hosp.; editor Del. State Med. Journal. Address: 101 W. 10th St., Wilmington, Del.

BIRDSEYE, Claude Hale, topographic engr.; b. Syracuse, N.Y., Feb. 13, 1878; s. George Frederick Hurd and Katharine Lamb (Hale) B.; A.B., Oberlin, 1901, Sc.D., 1931; post-grad. work, U. of Cincinnati and Ohio State U.; m. Grace Gardner Whitney, Nov. 23, 1904; children —Charles W., Frederick H., Florence W. Instr. in physics, U. of Cincinnati, 1901; field asst., later topographer U.S. Geol. Survey, 1901-06; surveyor Gen. Land Office, 1907-08; with U.S. Geol. Survey, 1909-29 (except when in war service), as topographer, geographer, and from Oct. 1919 to Sept. 1929, as chief topographic engr.; pres. Aerotopograph Corporation of America, 1929-32; assistant to director of U.S. Geol. Survey, 1932; chief, division of engraving and printing, U.S. Geol. Survey since 1932. Captain Corps of Engineers, U.S.A., March-July 1917; maj. July 1917-August 1918; lt. col. C.A.C., Aug. 1918-June 1919; served in France, on staff of chief of army artillery, Aug. 1917-Jan. 1919. Now col. engr., O.R.C. Decorated Officier de l'Instruction Publique (French), 1919; Daly medal (American Geog. Soc.), 1924. Mem. Am. Soc. Civil Engrs., Soc. Am. Mil. Engrs. (dir.), Am. Geog. Soc., Soc. Am. Geographers (pres. 1939), Washington Soc. Engrs. (pres. 1938), Kappa Sigma. Club: Cosmos. Explored and mapped area in vicinity of Kilauea Volcano, Hawaii, 1912; surveyed and mapped summit of Mt. Ranier, 1913; led expdn. by boat through Grand Canyon of Colorado River, 1923. Author of engring. and tech. repts. Home: 22 Grafton St., Chevy Chase, Md. Office: North Interior Dept. Bldg., Washington, D.C.

BIRDSONG, Henry Ellis, prof. journalism; b. Cooper Co., Mo., Apr. 17, 1887; s. John James and Jeston (Vaughan) B.; A.B., U. of Mo., 1912, B.J., 1913; grad. study, U. of Chicago, summers 1917, 1919; Ph.M., U. of Wis., 1924; m. Mabel Marquis, June 18, 1913; 1 dau., Virginia Jean (Mrs. David Scott Potts). Began as reporter on Kansas City (Mo.) Star, 1913-14; teacher Cooper Co. (Mo.) pub. schs., 1914-16; prin. high sch., Blackwater, Mo., 1916-17; instr. English and dir. publicity, Kan. State Teachers Coll., Emporia, 1917-22, also editor mag. and corr. newspapers; instr. journalism, U. of Wis., 1922-24; prof. journalism and head of dept., Butler U., Indianapolis, Ind., 1924-27; prof. journalism and head of dept., Temple U., Phila., since 1927. Mem. Am. Assn. Teachers of Journalism, Am. Assn. Univ. Profs., Sigma Delta Chi, Kappa Tau Alpha. Democrat. Home: 5430 Baltimore Av., Philadelphia, Pa.

BIRELY, Morris A., physician, surgeon; b. Ladiesburg, Md., Sept. 1, 1872; s. Samuel and Barbara A. (Kemp) B.; B.E., Shippensburg (Pa.) State Normal Sch. 1890; M.D., U. of Md., 1894; m. Bertha Bushey; 1 son Morris Franklin (M.D.). Physician and surgeon, Thurmont, Md., since 1894; visiting physician, Sisters of Charity, St. Joseph's Coll., Emmitsburg, Md.; pres. Mechanicstown Water Co.; dir. and surgeon Potomac Edison Co.; dir. Thurmont (Md.) Bank, Frederick (Md.) Industrial Loan Company. Mem. Frederick County Med. Soc., Med. and Chirurg. Faculty of Md., A.M.A., Southern Med. Assn. Republican. Lutheran. Mason (Shriner), Odd Fellow, K. of P. Club: Fish and Game Protective Assn. of Frederick Co., Md. Address: Thurmont, Md.

BIRELY, Morris Franklin, physician, surgeon; b. Thurmont, Md., Sept. 27, 1904; s. Morris A. and Bertha (Bushey) B.; A.B., Johns Hopkins, 1925; student Gettysburg Coll., 1921-23; M.D., U. of Md., 1929; m. Jean Harding Smith, 1931. Interne Union Memorial Hosp., Baltimore, 1929-30; surgical resident St. Agnes Hosp., Baltimore, 1930-31; private practice, Ridgewood, N.J., since 1931, specializing in ear, nose and throat. Mem. A.M.A., Passaic Co. Med. Soc., Ridgewood Med. Soc., Manuscript Club. Republican. Lutheran. Home: 170 E. Ridgewood Av., Ridgewood, N.J.

BIRKMANN, Charles John, banker; b. Phila., Pa., Oct. 27, 1889; s. John and Caroline (Snyder) B.; student Brown Prep. Sch.; m. Betty D. Hexter, Apr. 19, 1924; 1 son, Charles John. Formerly Mgr. John Birkmann Estate; partner Birkmann-Thielens Knitting Mills, Phila., 1921-24; pres. Northeast Nat. Bank of Phila. since

Feb. 18, 1928. Treas. Shriners' Hosp. for Crippled Children, Phila. Unit; mem. bd. govs. Masonic Home of Pa.; mem. Northeast Phila. Chamber of Commerce, Am. Legion. Clubs: Northeast Shrine of Phila., Tacony Lions, Torresdale-Frankford Country. Home: 5131 Roosevelt Boul. Office: 8043 Frankford Av., Philadelphia, Pa.

BIRNEY, (Herman) Hoffman, writer; b. Philadelphia, Pa., Apr. 1, 1891; s. Herman Hoffman and Elizabeth Cherrill (Boude) B.; prep. edn., high sch., Durango, Colo., and Phillips Brooks Sch., Philadelphia; student Dickinson Coll., Carlisle, Pa., 1908-12; m. Marguerite Agnes Bovington, June 14, 1930; 1 son, Herman Hoffman. Served in United States Army, with infantry, later Aviation Section, Signal Corps, Mar. 1917-Nov. 1920 advancing to 2d lt. Air Service. Mem. Phi Delta Theta. Republican. Mason. Author: King of the Mesa, 1927; The Masked Rider, 1928; Steel-dust (juvenile), 1928; Vigilantes (hist.), 1929; The Canyon of Lost Waters, 1929; Roads to Roam (travel), 1930; The Pinto Pony (juvenile), 1930; Zealots of Zion (hist.), 1931; Two Little Navajos (juvenile), 1931; Kudlu, the Eskimo Boy (juvenile), 1932; Archæological Sites in Glen Cañon of the Colorado River, 1932; Barrier Ranch (fiction), 1933; Tu'kwi of the Peaceful People (juvenile), 1933; Forgotten Cañon (fiction); Holy Murder—the Story of Porter Rockwell (biography, with Charles Kelly); Grim Journey, 1934; Eagle in the Sun, 1935; The Stranger in Black Butte, 1935; Dead Man's Trail (fiction), 1937; Mountain Chief (juvenile), 1938. Contbr. to various publs. Home: Glen Mills, Pa.

BIRRELL, George William, packer; b. Troy, N.Y., May 29, 1894; s. William and Mary Emma (Kay) B.; student high sch., Scotland, 1906-09; m. Margaret Caroline Kunzler, Nov. 13, 1920; children—Gordon William, Donald George, Dorothy Mary, Charles Frederick. Cashier and Field Clerk, Met. Life Ins. Co., Salem, Mass., and Glens Falls, N.Y., 1912-16; sales dept. Thomas G. Plant Co., shoe mfrs., Boston, Mass., 1916-17; bookkeeper Wilson & Co., Boston, 1919-20; with C. H. Kunzler Co., meat packers, Lancaster, Pa., since 1920, sec.-treas. and dir. since 1921; dir. Northern Bank & Trust Co., Industrial Bldg. & Loan Assn. Served as private, Q.M.C., U.S. Army, 1917-19. Dir. Lancaster (Pa.) Gen. Hosp. Mem. Inst. of Am. Meat Packers (dir.), Lancaster Chamber of Commerce (pres. 1933-34), Independent Meat Packers Assn. of Pa. (pres. since 1938). Presbyterian. Mason, Elk. Clubs: Kiwanis (Lancaster, Pa.; pres. 1932); Meadia Heights Golf (Lancaster, Pa.). Home: 341 N. West End Av. Office: 648 Manor St., Lancaster, Pa.

BISCOE, Alvin Blocksom, coll. prof.; b. Wilmington, Del., Dec. 25, 1900; s. Charles Edwin and Sarah Estelle (Blackwell) B.; student Wesley Collegiate Inst., Dover, Del., 1921-23; A.B., Dickinson Coll., Carlisle, Pa., 1927; A.M., Duke U., Durham, N.C., 1928; student U. of Va., Charlottesville, Va., 1928-30, Ph.D., 1932; m. Helen Marie Bowser, Aug. 30, 1930; 1 son, Alvin Blocksom. Clk. Pa. R.R., Wilmington, Del., 1917-29; head instr. economics, U. of Va., Charlottesville, Va., 1928,30, instr., summer sch., 1930, research asso. in pub. finance, 1930-31; asst. prof. economics, Bucknell U., Lewisburg, Pa., 1931-38, asso. prof. since 1938. Mem. Am. Econ. Assn., Phi Beta Kappa, Theta Chi, Tau Kappa Alpha, Delta Sigma Pi, Omicron Delta Kappa. Methodist. Co-author: State Grants-in-Aid in Virginia, 1933. Home: 114 S. Fourth St. Office: Bucknell U., Lewisburg, Pa.

BISER, Daniel Benton, govt. research; b. Laurel, Md., Dec. 1, 1893; s. Francis Henry Daniel and Mary Estelle (Benton) B.; A.B., Johns Hopkins U., Baltimore, Md., 1915, postgrad. work, 1916-17; m. Eugenia Maria Porta, May 29, 1920; children—Jean Marie, Daniel Benton, Jr. Began as constrn. foreman, George's Creek-Parker Coal Co., Frostburg, Md., 1917; utility operation and management, and engr., city of Baltimore, 1920-1929; dir. and sec. Commn. on Governmental Efficiency and Economy, Inc., Baltimore, Md., since 1929. Served as private, U.S. Army, 1918. Mem. Governmental Research Assn., Municipal Finance Officers' Assn., Am. Pub. Works Assn., Am. Soc. of Polit. and Social Science, Am. Assn. of Engrs., Tax Policy League, Nat. Municipal League. Democrat. Catholic. Clubs: University, Johns Hopkins (Baltimore, Md.). Home: 511 Stamford Rd. Office: Mercantile Trust Bldg., Baltimore, Md.

BISGYER, Gustave, social worker; b. Brooklyn, N.Y., Apr. 25, 1901; s. Joseph and Sarah (Flaumenhaft) B.; grad. Passaic (N.J.) High Sch., 1918; B.A., New York U., 1922; grad. work, Columbia U., 1922-23; m. Mary Gold, Sept. 4, 1927; children—Natalie Jane, Fronda Dora. With Educational Alliance, New York, 1919-21, Jewish Bd. of Guardians, New York, 1922; exec. dir. Jewish Ednl. Alliance, Baltimore, 1922-38, Y.M. & Y.W.H.A., Baltimore, since 1938. Mem. Am. Assn. Social Workers, Nat. Assn. Jewish Center Execs. Home: 3207 W. Rogers Av. Office: 305 W. Monument St., Baltimore, Md.

BISH, Eugene W(ilbert), prin. of schools; b. Monroe Twp., Clarion Co., Pa., Nov. 16, 1907; s. Daniel Wilbert and Effie (Lingenfelter) B.; A.B., Pa. State Coll., 1929; Ed.M., U. of Pittsburgh, 1938; m. Iris Mae Davis, July 4, 1934; 1 dau., Lois Eileen. Teacher, Canoe Twp. High Sch., Rossiter, Pa., 1929-31, prin., 1931-35; prin., Brockway Schools since 1935. Dir. Clarion-Jefferson Co. Div. of Pa. Forensic and Music League, 1939. Republican. Methodist. Mason. Baritone singer, having given concerts in Western Pa. and toured in Europe, 1928, with male chorus; won Atwater Kent Radio contest, 1931. Home: 1542 Main St., Brockway, Pa.

BISHOP, Arthur Vaughan, coll. prof.; b. Riner, Va., Mar. 28, 1883; s. William Millard and Laura Virginia (Lucas) B.; B.S., Va. Poly. Inst., Blacksburg, Va., 1906; M.A., U. of Va., Charlottesville, Va., 1911, Ph.D., 1913; m. Ellen P. Hoffman, Sept. 2, 1914. Princ., Blacksburg (Va.) High Sch., 1906-08; instr. in Latin, U. of Va., Charlottesville, Va., 1909-13, mem. Latin faculty summer sessions, 1911-24; prof. of Latin and Greek, Hollins (Va.) Coll., 1913-23, Georgetown (Ky.) Coll., 1923-28; asso. prof. of Latin, Dickinson Coll., Carlisle, Pa., 1928-29, A.J. Clarke prof. of Latin language and lit. since 1929, dean of sophomore class since 1939. Social and ednl. sec. Y.M.C.A. Camp Hancock, Augusta, Ga., summer 1918. Mem. Am. Philol. Assn., Atlantic States Classical Assn., Ky. Classical Assn. (pres., 1925-26), Phi Beta Kappa, Phi Kappa Phi. Democrat. Presbyterian (Elder, 2d Presbyn. Ch., Carlisle, Pa.). Address: 223 S. College St., Carlisle, Pa.

BISHOP, Carl, M.D.; sr. surgeon Muhlenberg Hosp. Address: 831 Madison Av., Plainfield, N.J.

BISHOP, Frederic Lendall, physicist; b. St. Johnsbury, Vt.; s. Lendall and Ellen (Bishop) B.; B.S., Massachusetts Inst. Technology, 1898; Ph.D., University of Chicago, 1905; m. Lelia Prior, Aug. 9, 1899 (died Feb. 26, 1925); 1 son, Frederic Lendall; m. 2d, Marie Thorne, Aug. 14, 1928; children—Ann Thorne, Ellen Marie. Prof. physics, U. of Pittsburgh since 1909, dean Sch. of Engring., 1909-27, Sch. of Mines, 1920-27; cons. engr., Am. Window Glass Co., Window Glass Machine Co. Editor Engineering Education. Fellow A.A.A.S.; mem. Am. Phys. Soc., Am. Inst. E.E., Soc. Promotion Engring. Edn. (sec.). Clubs: University, Field (Pittsburgh); Cosmos (Washington). Contbr. papers on engring. education, thermal conductivity, heat of dilution, electric furnaces, viscosity, mechanical mfr. of glass, etc. Home: Fox Chapel Manor, Fox Chapel Borough, Pittsburgh, Pa.

BISHOP, Frederick J., M.D.; mem. staff Scranton State, West Side, Mercy, Moses Taylor and Hahnemann Hosps.; consultant Nesbitt Memorial Hosp. Address: 327 N. Washington Av., Scranton, Pa.

BISHOP, Herman Leister, high school prin.; b. Chalfont, Pa., Dec. 29, 1894; s. Albert and Sallie (Leister) B.; student Newville High Sch., 1909-11, West Chester State Normal Sch., 1911-13; B.S., U. of Pa., 1927, A.M., 1930; m. Mabel Nyce Ruth, Dec. 14, 1918. Prin. of schools, New Britain Twp., Bucks Co., Pa., 1913-18, Upper Gwynedd Twp., 1918-20; teacher of history, Lansdale (Pa.) High Sch., 1920-27, prin. since 1927. Mem. Lutheran Brotherhood of Ministerium of Pa. (vice-pres. 1932-34, pres. 1934-36, former mem. exec. bd.). Mem. N.E.A., Pa. State Edn. Assn., Pa. State Prins. Assn., Nat. Secondary Sch. Prins. Assn. Republican. Lutheran. Club: Rotary of Lansdale (pres. 1936-37). Speaker at young peoples' and church groups. Home: Oak Park, Lansdale, Pa.

BISHOP, Howard Berkey, mfg. chemist; b. Bloomington, Ill., Jan. 24, 1878; s. Luther and Alice Jane (Berkey) B.; student Armour Inst. of Tech., Chicago, 1893-96; B.S., U. of Mich., 1900; m. Bertha Shaffner, Sept. 22, 1909; children—Vernon, Howard Berkey, Ann Poultney. Photographer, Kansas City, Mo., 1900-01; analytical chemist, 1902-10; research chemist Gen. Chem. Co., New York, 1910-17, Nat. Aniline & Chem. Co., New York, 1917-20; pres. John C. Wiarda & Co., 1921-29; pres. Sterling Products Co., mfrs. hydrofluoric acid, fluorine compounds for laundry industry since 1908; pres. N.J. Industrial Corpn. Chmn. Safety Com., Summit, N.J.; mem. N.J. State Com. Y.M.C.A.; dir. Summit Y.M.C.A. Fellow A.A.A.S.; mem. Am. Chem. Soc., Soc. Chem. Industry, Am. Inst. Chem. Engrs., Am. Inst. Chemists, Nat. Assn. Mfrs., Nat. Safety Council, Easton Bd. of Trade. Republican. Episcopalian. Mason (32°). Club: Chemists (New York). Home: 33 Prospect Hill Av., Summit, N.J. Office: 68 Bishop Rd., Easton, Pa.

BISHOP, R(ichard) E(vett), artist; b. Syracuse, N.Y., May 30, 1887; s. Richard Whitney and Minnie (Blackall) B.; M.E., Cornell U., 1909; m. Mary Helen Harrington, 1915. Elec. engr. Cutler Hammer Mfg. Co., Milwaukee, Wis., 1909-17; sec. and sales mgr. Harrington Co., Phila., 1919-33; retired from business, 1933, and took up art as a profession; specializes in etchings of wild fowl and game birds; decorator of glassware and service plates with game birds. Exhibited: Acad. of Fine Arts, Phila.; Chicago Art Inst.; Cleveland Museum of Art; Brooklyn Museum; National Acad., New York; National Museum, Washington, D.C., etc. Served as capt. Chem. Warfare Service, U.S. Army, 1917-19. Mem. bd. mgrs. Moore Inst. Art, Science and Industry. Mem. Am. Soc. Etchers, Phila. Soc. Etchers, Chicago Soc. Etchers, Print Makers of Calif., Delta Upsilon. Clubs: Rittenhouse, Sketch, Art Alliance (Phila.). Author: Bishop's Birds, 1936. Home: Spring Bank Lane, Mt. Airy, Philadelphia, Pa.

BISHOP, Ward Leslie, asso. prof. econs.; b. Portland, Ind., Apr. 6, 1902; s. Adam D. and Rose (Stone) B.; A.B., Earlham Coll., 1923; A.M., U. of Ill., 1924, Ph.D., same, 1928; m. Anna B. Lalley, Sept. 6, 1924; children—Jacqueline Ann, Barbara Jane. Engaged as asst. U. of Ill., 1924; instr. econs., U. of Ill., 1925-28; asst. prof. econs., Lehigh U., Bethlehem, Pa., 1928-31, asso. prof. since 1931; instr. in summer sessions, Pa. State Coll., 1932, W.Va. U., 1935-36; lecturer, Am. Inst. of Banking, Allentown Chapter since 1933. Mem. Am. Econ. Assn., Nat. Tax Assn. Methodist. Club: Kiwanis of Bethlehem. Home: 1401 W. North St., Bethlehem, Pa.

BISHOPP, Fred Corry, entomologist; b. Virginia Dale, Colo., Jan. 14, 1884; s. Thomas Barton and Harriet Caroline (McKay) B.; B.S., Colo. State Coll., 1902, M.S., 1926; grad. student Southern Meth. U., 1923-24; Ph.D., Ohio State U., 1932; m. Eulalie Virginia Spencer, Dec. 9, 1908; children—Harriet Eloise, Fred Thomas, Howard Spencer (dec.), Hazel Eulalie. Teaching fellow zoology and entomology, Colo. Agrl. Coll., 1902-04; asst. prof. entomology and zoology, Md. Agrl. Coll., 1904-05; spl. field agt. Bur. Entomology, U.S. Dept. Agr., 1905-08, asst. entomologist, 1908-11, entomologist, 1911-26, chief Div. of Insects Affecting Man and Animals since 1926. Fellow A.A.A.S., Entomol. Soc. of America (v.p. 1932); mem. Am. Assn. of Economic Entomologists (pres. 1937), Am. Soc. of Parisitologists (pres. 1938), Washington Acad. Sciences, Entomol. Soc. of Washington (pres. 1932), Am. Soc. Tropical Medicine, Nat. Malaria Com. (vice chmn.), Biol. Soc. of Washington, Phi Kappa Phi, Sigma Xi. Conglist. Editor section on Insects Affecting Animals of Biol. Abstracts. Home: 8014 Saratoga Av., Silver Spring, Md. Address: U.S. Dept. Agr., Washington, D.C.

BISPHAM, William Newbold, army officer; b. Warrenton, Va., May 22, 1875; s. Stacey B. and Ellen T. (Hill) B.; student Baltimore pub. schs., 1883-93, Am. Coll. Pharmacy, 1893-94; M.D., U. of Md., 1897; m. Isabelle Pinkney Gray, Jan. 2, 1900. Enlisted in U.S. Army, Oct. 4, 1899; advanced through grades to col., Oct. 3, 1926, retired, May 31, 1939; during World War commanded Med. Camp, Ft. Riley, Kan., and Camp Greenleaf, Ga.; after war commanded Lawson Gen. Hosp., Ft. Sheridan, Ill. (largest military hospital in U.S.). Mem. A.M.A., Am. Assn. Tropical Medicine, Assn. Mil. Surgeons, Nat. Malaria Com., Phi Sigma Kappa. Episcopalian. Clubs: Army and Navy, Army and Navy Country (Washington, D.C.). Home: 3700 N. Charles St., Baltimore, Md.

BISSELL, Alfred E.; partner Laird, Bissell & Meeds. Home: Westover Hills. Office: du Pont Bldg., Wilmington, Del.

BISSELL, Arthur Harry, lawyer; b. Washington, D.C., July 9, 1877; s. Arthur Harry and Fanny A. (Shelton) B.; A.B., Yale U., 1897; grad. study Columbia U. Grad. Sch., 1897-98, N.Y. Law Sch., 1899; m. Helen Manatt, May 28, 1910; children—Arthur Henry, Faith, Helen Treat, Marian. Admitted to N.Y. bar as atty., 1900, N.J. bar as atty. 1902, as counselor, 1905; in practice of law at Montclair, N.J., since 1905. Served as town recorder (police magistrate). Ind. Democrat. Conglist. Clubs: Green Mountain (N.Y. Sect.); Cosmopolitan (Montclair). Home: 133 Wildwood Av. Office: 22 S. Park St., Montclair, N.J.

BISSELL, George Perkins; b. New York, N.Y., Jan. 3, 1872; s. Champion and Josephine (Wales) B.; student Friends Sch., Wilmington; grad. Sheffield Scientific Sch. (Yale), 1890; m. Jessie Lane Elliott, Dec. 12, 1899; children—Alfred E., George P. Partner Laird, Bissell & Meeds; mem. N.Y. Stock Exchange; v.p. and dir. Del. Trust Co. (Wilmington). Dir. Wilmington Soc. Fine Arts, Wilmington Pub. Library. Home: 7 Red Oak Road. Office: du Pont Bldg., Wilmington, Del.

BITTING, William Thomas, industrial management; b. Phila., Pa., Nov. 27, 1900; s. Clarence R. and Ella G. (Dawson) B.; grad. West Phila. High Sch., 1918; C.P.A., Wharton Sch., U. of Pa., 1922; m. Judith Catharine Brophy, 1931; children—Judith, Willamena. Mem. Day & Zimmerman, Phila., 1923, Price, Waterhouse & Co., Phila., 1923-29; organized firm William T. Bitting, industrial management, Phila. and New York, 1929, and since pres.; v.p. and dir. Bitting, Incorporated.; sec. and dir. United States Sugar Corpn., Clewiston Realty and Development Corpn. Mem. Pa. Inst. of C.P.As. Home: Wynnewood, Pa. Office: 20 Exchange Pl., New York, N.Y. and Fidelity Phila. Trust Bldg., Philadelphia, Pa.

BITZER, Newton E.; chief surgeon and med. dir. St. Joseph's Hosp.; surgeon Lancaster County Hosp. Address: 236 W. Chestnut St., Lancaster, Pa.

BIXBY, Edward Welles, physician; b. Wilkes-Barre, Pa., Aug. 3, 1886; s. Charles Welles and Anne (Davis) B.; A.B., Princeton U., 1907; M.D., U. of Pa., 1911; m. Helen Lea Miner, June 1, 1916; children—Edward Welles, Hetty Lonsdale, Anne Davis, Helen Lea Miner. In pvt. practice medicine at Wilkes-Barre, Pa., since 1914; visiting physician Wilkes-Barre Gen. Hosp. since 1915, White Haven Tuberculosis Sanatorium, White Haven, Pa., since 1936. Mem. Luzerne Co. Med. Soc. (sec. 1925-32, pres. 1934), Pa. State Med. Soc. (chmn. med. sect., 1936). Republican. Presbyterian. Clubs: Westmoreland, Wyoming Valley Country (Wilkes-Barre, Pa.); University Cottage (Princeton, N.J.). Address: 292 S. Franklin St., Wilkes-Barre, Pa.

BIXLER, Edward Clinton, coll. pres.; b. Westminster, Md., Feb. 1, 1877; s. Uriah and Sarah A. (Myers) B.; A.B., Western Md. Coll., 1901, hon. A.M., 1905; Ph.D., U. of Pa., 1909; studied at Johns Hopkins, 1901-03; m. Margaret Burkhart Englar, Dec. 29, 1910; 1 dau., Ruth Cassell. Tutor Western Md. Prep. Sch., 1903-04; ordained to ministry Ch. of the Brethren, 1910; prof. ancient langs., Elizabethtown (Pa.) Coll., 1906-08; pres. and prof. ancient langs., Manchester (Ind.) Coll., 1910-11; prof. ancient langs., Bridgewater (Va.) Coll., 1911-13; prof. ancient langs. and edn., Blue Ridge (Md.) Coll., since 1913, pres. 1927-37, emeritus since 1937; dir. New Windsor (Md.) State Bank. Democrat. Home: New Windsor, Md.

BJORLEE, Ignatius, supt. sch. for the deaf; b. Freeborn Co., Minn., Dec. 9, 1885; s. Elias and Karen (Tostenson) Bjorlee; student public schools, Northwood, Iowa; B.S., St. Olaf Coll., Northfield, Minn., 1909, LL.D., 1933; M.A., and Normal fellow, Gallaudet Coll., Washington, D.C., 1910; post-grad. study, Columbia, 1916-18; m. Cornelia Cleophas, Feb. 19, 1916. Instr. N.Y. Instn. for Instrn. of the Deaf, 1910-18; supt. and prin. Md. State Sch. for the Deaf since 1918. Sec. Conf. of Execs. of Am. Schs. for the Deaf, 1919-24; sec. Conv. Am. Instrs. of the Deaf, 1920-23, pres. since 1937. Pres. Md. State Conf. of Social Work, 1926-27; pres. Francis Scott Key Council Boy Scouts of America, 1925-29; chmn. Certification Com. of Teachers and of Training Centers for Teachers of the Deaf., 1932—; mem. Juvenile Court Com. of Frederick County, Md., since 1931; gov. 34th Dist. Rotary Internat., 1929-30; chmn. Community Service Com. and mem. Aims and Objects Com., Rotary Internat., 1932-33. Mem. 22d Regt. Engrs., N.Y. Nat. Guards, 1913-17. Mem. Am. Assn. to Promote Teaching of Speech to the Deaf, Soc. of Progressive Oral Advocates, Pi Gamma Mu. Lutheran. Rotarian. Home: 242 S. Market St., Frederick, Md.

BLACK, Albert F.; pres. Farmers & Merchants Bank; officer or dir. many companies. Address: Hamlin, W.Va.

BLACK, Archibald, clergyman; b. Rothesay, Bute, Scotland, May 24, 1877; s. Hugh and Isabel (McDougall) B.; prep. edn., Rothesay Acad.; A.B., Glasgow U., 1906; student United Free Church Hall, Scotland, 1906-07; B.D., Union Theol. Sem., N.Y. City, 1909; D.D., Williams Coll., 1934; m. Ruth Hunter, May 6, 1913; children—Robert Hunter, Jean Stuart, Elizabeth Ann (dec.). Ordained ministry Presbyterian Church, 1909; minister Bedford Park Presbyn. Church, N.Y. City, 1909-14, South Congl. Ch., Concord, N.H., 1914-19; asso. minister Old South Ch., Boston, Mass., 1919-21; minister First Congl. Ch., Montclair, N.J., since 1921. Mem. Sigma Chi. Club: Montclair Golf. Author: Opening Roads, 1936. Home: 11 Plymouth St., Montclair, N.J.

BLACK, Arthur O., telephone exec.; b. Conoquenessing, Pa., May 27, 1892; s. John H. and Willie Jane (Rasley) B.; ed. common and high sch., Butler, Pa.; m. Effie Lester, Apr. 8, 1912; children—Jane Anne (Mrs. Carl L. Slear), Sara Minta, John Lester, Arthur O. Jr., Gilbert James, Carolyn Blanche. Began as toll troubleman Peoples Telephone Co. of Butler, 1910-12; central office man Pittsburgh, Bell Telephone of Pa., 1912-14; wire chief Peoples Telephone Corpn., 1914-16; engring. asst. Bell Telephone Co. of Pa., 1916-19; mgr. of plant and traffic Peoples Telephone Co. of Butler, Pa., 1919-25; gen. mgr. and sec. The Peoples Telephone Corpn., Butler, Pa., since 1925; v.p. and gen. mgr. Suburban Telephone Co., Butler, Pa., since 1937; dir. Peoples Telephone Corpn., Suburban Telephone Co. of Butler, Telephone Securities Co., Harrisville Telephone Co. Engring. rep. Chespeake & Potomac Telephone Co., with War Dept., Washington, D.C., 1917-18. Pres. and dir. Butler Twp. Sch. Bd.; mem. budget com. Community Chest; chmn. activities com. Butler Co.-Pa. Economy League. Dir. United States Ind. Telephone Assn., Pa. State Telephone and Traffic Assn., Butler Bd. of Commerce (pres. 1939), Ind. Telephone Pioneers of America (v. p.). Clubs: Kiwanis (dir. and past pres.), But-

ler Country (Butler, Pa.). Home: R. D. 5. Office: 218 S. Washington St., Butler, Pa.

BLACK, Burton Alexander, physician; b. Franklin, Pa., Apr. 16, 1876; s. Henry Burton and Susan (Likins) B.; student Allegheny Coll., Meadville, Pa.; M.D., Western U. of Pa., Pittsburgh, Pa., 1905; student N.Y. Post Grad. Med. Sch., 1909, N.Y. Eye and Ear Infirmary, 1926; grad. Wilson Coll., Chambersburg, Pa., 1937; post grad. work Carnegie Inst. Tech., 1939; m. Clare Freedland, Oct. 5, 1914; 1 dau., Martha Elizabeth. Asst. supt. and oculist Polk State Sch., Polk, Pa., 1907-26; in prvt. practice, specializing in eye, ear, nose, and throat, at Grove City, Pa., since 1926; mem. Staff Grove City Hosp. since 1926. Mem. Pa. State Med. Soc., Mercer Co. Med. Soc., Western Pa. Eye, Ear, Nose and Throat Soc. Presbyterian. Clubs: Rotary, Pitt. University, Grove City Commercial, Grove City Country (Grove City, Pa.). Home: 150 E. Pine St. Office: 217 Broad St., Grove City, Pa.

BLACK, Charles Clarke, judge; b. Mt. Holly, N.J., July 29, 1858; s. John, Jr., and Mary Anna (Clarke) B.; A.B., Princeton, 1878, A.M., 1881; student law dept. U. of Mich., 1879-80; m. Alice Greenleaf Hazen, of Flushing, L.I., N.Y., Feb. 12, 1890 (died Mar. 21, 1915); m. 2d, Helen Newbold, July 6, 1918. Admitted to the bar, 1881, and since engaged in practice at Jersey City, N.J. Mem. State Bds. Taxation and Equalization, 1891-1908, N.J. Tax Commrs., 1896, 1904; Dem. candidate for gov. of N.J., 1904; judge Circuit Ct. of N.J., 1908-14; justice Supreme Court of N.J., 1914-30, resigned. Author: Proof and Pleadings in Accident Cases, 1886; New Jersey Law of Taxation, 5th edition, 1938; Law and Practice in Accident Cases, 1900. Home: 80 Gifford Av., Jersey City, N.J.

BLACK, Eleanor Simms (Mrs. Robert Moffitt B.), artist; b. Washington, D.C., Jan. 9, 1872; d. Giles Green Craycroft and Sarah (Sollers) Simms; ed. High Sch., Washington, D.C.; Hon. Mention, Corcoran Sch. of Art; student art schs., Howard Helmick, Charles W. Hawthorne, Ossip Linde, George Elmer Browne; m. Robert Moffitt Black, Oct. 1, 1906. Engaged as supervisor of art, pub. schs. of D.C., 1899-1906; has exhibited about fifty oil paintings, most widely exhibited are "Mantle of Snow," "Balboa Park, San Diego"; important showings include Nat. Acad. of Design in New York, Pa. Acad. of Fine Arts, Phila., Pa., Biennial Exhbn. of Corcoran Gallery of Art, Washington, Southern States Art League, Asso. Artists of Pittsburgh, Gulf Galleries, Pittsburgh, Palm Beach (Fla.) Art Center. Mem. Asso. Artists of Pittsburgh, Soc. of Ind. Artists, Southern States Art League, Soc. of Washington Artists, Cordova Club of Women Painters (pres., sec., treas.). Mem. Womens Auxiliary, Am. Inst. Mining Engrs. Western Pa. Sect. (treas.). Catholic. Home: 3 Ellsworth Terrace, Pittsburgh, Pa.

BLACK, George Skinner, lawyer; b. Chambersburg, Pa., Oct. 8, 1909; s. Henry Van Tries and Mary Hazel (Skinner) B.; A.B., U. of Va., 1930; LL.B., Harvard, 1933; m. Margaret Elizabeth Hall, Sept. 28, 1935; 1 son, Jerry Hall. Admitted to Franklin Co. (Pa.) bar, 1933, and since practiced at Chambersburg, Pa.; admitted to bar of Supreme Ct. of Pa., 1936. Served as enlisted man, Troop E, 104th Cav., Pa. N.G., 1934-36, commd. 2d lt., 1936. Sec. Democratic Com. Franklin Co., Pa., since 1934. Mem. Franklin Co., Pa. bar assns., U.S. Cavalry Assn., Phi Sigma Kappa. Democrat. Episcopalian. K.P., Odd Fellow. Home: 262 Ramsey Av. Office: 12 Central Av., Chambersburg, Pa.

BLACK, Harold Lisle, prof. mathematics; b. Holton, Mich., Apr. 22, 1902; s. Benjamin F. (M.D.) and Lulu J. (Wells) B.; A.B., Albion Coll., Mich., 1923; A.M., U. of Ill., 1924, Ph.D., same, 1926; m. Grace E. Putnam, July 8, 1927; children—Jean Louise and Barbara Lucile (twins). Engaged as instr. mathematics, U. of Ill., 1926-28; prof. mathematics and head of dept., Westminster Coll., New Wilmington, Pa., since 1928. Served as treas. New Wilmington Borough Sch. Dist. Mem. Am. Math. Assn., Math. Assn. of America, Sigma Xi, Pi Mu Epsilon. Methodist. Home: 200 High St., New Wilmington, Pa.

BLACK, Helen Newbold (Mrs. Charles Clarke B.); b. Jersey City, N.J., June 17, 1887; d. Michael Taylor and Stella M. (Hager) Newbold; A.B., Barnard Coll., 1909; A.M., Columbia U., 1911; m. Charles Clarke Black, July 6, 1918. Dir. State Board of Childrens' Guardians, 1926, pres., 1935-39. Mem. bd. mgrs. Home for Aged Women, Jersey City (pres. 1933-37). Mem. Art Adv. Com., N.J. State Mus., Trenton. Mem. Hudson Co. Hist. Soc., Womans Branch N.J. Hist. Soc., N.J. Soc. Colonial Dames of America, Gamma Phi Beta. Democrat. Clubs: College, Woman's (Jersey City). Home: 80 Gifford Av., Jersey City, N.J.

BLACK, Hugh, theologian; b. Rothesay, Buteshire, Scotland, Mar. 26, 1868; ed. Rothesay Acad., Glasgow U., 1883-87, M.A., 1887, Free Church Coll., Glasgow, 1887-91; D.D., Yale, 1908, Princeton, 1911, Glasgow U., 1911; D.Litt. U. of Pittsburgh, 1917; m. Edith Margaret Kerr, June 28, 1898; children—Hugh, Margaret Grant, Isobel Stuart, Robert Kerr. Ordained 1891; minister Sherwood Ch., Paisley, Scotland, 1891-96, St. George's United Free Ch., Edinburgh, 1896-1906; came to U.S., 1906; prof. practical theology, Union Theol. Sem., New York, since 1906. Author: The Dream of Youth, 1894; Friendship, 1898; Culture and Restraint, 1900; Work, 1902; The Practice of Self-Culture, 1904; Listening to God (Edinburgh Sermons), 1906; Christ's Service of Love, 1907; The Gift of Influence (University Sermons), 1908; Comfort, 1910; Happiness, 1911; Three Dreams, 1912; According to My Gospel (Montclair sermons), 1913; The Open Door, 1914; The New World, 1915; Lest We Forget, 1920; The Adventure of Being Man, 1929. Home: Upper Montclair, N.J. Address: Union Theol. Seminary, New York, N.Y.*

BLACK, J. Leon; chmn. bd. Sussex Trust Co. Address: Milton, Del.

BLACK, Luther Allen, prof. of bacteriology; b. Macon, Ill., Mar. 14, 1903; s. Joseph Richard and Ellen Jane (Crawford) B.; B.S., U. of Ill., 1924, M.S., 1925, Ph.D., 1928; m. Margaret Savage, Sept. 6, 1927; children—Elinor Jeanette, Janice Miriam. Scholar in bacteriology, U. of Ill., 1924-25, asst. in bacteriology, 1925-26; bacteriologist diagnostic labs., Ill. State Dept. of Health, 1926-27; bacteriologist McKinley Memorial Hosp., 1927-28; instr. in bacteriology, State Coll. of Wash., 1928-29, asst. prof., 1929-30; asso. dairy bacteriologist (in charge), Wash. Agrl. Expt. Sta., 1928-30; asso. prof. of bacteriology U. of Md., 1930-35, prof. since 1935. Fellow A.A.A.S.; mem. Soc. Am. Bacteriologists (pres. Washington branch, 1938-39), Am. Pub. Health Assn., Am. Dairy Science Assn., Washington Acad. Sciences, Am. Assn. Univ. Profs., Sigma Xi, Alpha Zeta, Phi Kappa Sigma, Sigma Alpha Omicron, Phi Sigma. Author of lab. manuals in am., dairy, sanitary and pathogenic bacteriology and serology; contbr. articles to scientific jours. Home: 5 Lanhardt Rd., University Park, Md.

BLACK, Matthew Wilson, univ. prof.; b. Altoona, Pa., Apr. 14, 1895; s. William George and Della Gertrude (Yeager) B.; A.B., Pa. State Coll., 1915; A.M., Univ. of Pa., 1916, Ph.D., 1928; m. Dorothy Starr Dinsmore, June 20, 1929; 1 dau., Anne Bockée. Instr. English, U. of Pa., 1916-18, 1919-23, asst. prof., 1923-33, asso. prof., 1933-39, prof. since 1939. Private, Inf., U.S.A., 1918-19. Mem. Modern Lang. Assn., Sigma Phi Epsilon. Republican. Presbyterian. Clubs: Franklin Inn, Art Alliance (Phila.). Author: Elizabethan and 17th Century Lyrics, 1938. Home: Windridge, Berwyn, Pa.

BLACK, Ned, town planner; b. Huntingdon, Pa., Sept. 5, 1881; s. Jacob H. and Emma (Fryling) B.; C.E., Rensselaer Poly. Inst., Troy, N.Y., 1904; post grad. studies in architecture, Columbia U., 1915; m. Anne Stryker, Oct. 29, 1908; children—Robert Fryling, Jean Hatfield, Margery Ann. Power plant and pub. utility work largely with Sanderson & Porter, New York, 1902-08, 1912-16; dean civil engring., Anglo Chinese Coll. (now Fukien U.), Foochow, China, 1908-12; archtl. and bldg. work, Foochow, China, 1916-20; partner engring. firm, Black & Black, town planners, Harrisburg, Pa., since 1920; registered architect, Pa.; registered engr., Pa., N.Y. Mem. Pa. Assn. Architects, Am. Soc. C.E., Am. Soc. of Planning Officials, Sigma Xi. Socialist. Protestant. Home: 203 E. Coover St., Mechanicsburg, Pa. Office: P.O. Box 2, Harrisburg, Pa.

BLACK, Robert Moffitt, prof. of mining; b. Meyersdale, Pa., Apr. 10, 1879; s. James Stewart and Elizabeth Mary (Philson) B.; student Vanderbilt U., 1897-99; A.B., Harvard, 1901; B.S., Mich. Coll. of Mines, Houghton, Mich., 1903, E.M., 1903; student U. of Wis., 1912; m. Eleanor Rose Simms, Oct. 1, 1906. Asst. engr. N.J. and Pa. Traction Co., Trenton, N.J., 1903-04; transitman, engring. dept. Dist. of Columbia, Washington, D.C., 1904-05; mining engr. Rock Island Coal Co., Hartshorne, Indian Ter., 1905, Whitebreast Fuel Co., Chicago, 1905-07, New River & Pocahontas Consol. Coal Co., Berwind, W.Va., 1907-11, New River Co., Macdonald, W.Va., 1911; instr. civil engring., State U. of Ia., 1911-12; asst. prof. of mining, U. of Pittsburgh, 1912-17, asso. prof., 1917-20, prof. and head dept. of mining engring. since 1920. Mem. Am. Inst. Mining and Metall. Engrs., Coal Mining Inst. America (mng. dir.), Engrs. Soc. Western Pa., Am. Assn. Engrs., Am. Mining Congress, Soc. for Promotion Engring. Edn., A.A.A.S., Am. Assn. Univ. Profs., Sigma Gamma Epsilon. Methodist. Club: Faculty (Pittsburgh). Home: 3 Ellsworth Terrace, Pittsburgh, Pa.

BLACK, Russell Van Nest, planning consultant; b. Hightstown, N.J., Jan. 12, 1893; s. Lemuel and Catherine (Van Nest) B.; student Peddie Sch., Hightstown, N.J., 1909-12; B.S., Cornell U., 1916; m. Mary Todd Hedges, Apr. 24, 1923. Gen. planning practice, N.J., N.Y., Ida., Calif., 1920-25; dir. plans and surveys Phila. Regional Planning Fed., 1926-29; pvt. practice as planning consultant, city and county planning, New Hope, Pa., since 1929; dir. N.J. State Planning Bd., 1934-39; consultant Pa. State Planning Bd., 1935-39, Va. State Planning Bd., 1935-37; consultant nat. resources com., housing div., Pub. Works Adminstrn., 1933-39. Fellow Am. Soc. Landscape Architects; mem. Am. City Planning Inst. (pres. 1936-38), Am. Soc. C.E. (chmn. exec. com. city planning div., 1936-37). Protestant. Author: Planning for the Small American City, 1933; Building Lines and Future Streets, 1935; contbr. articles to tech. mags., confs. of tech. socs. Address: New Hope, Pa.

BLACK, Samuel Duncan, manufacturer; b. White Hall, Baltimore Co., Md., Aug. 2, 1883; s. Samuel Washington and Alice (Duncan) B.; ed. Baltimore Polytechnic Inst.; m. Anna Ridgely, Aug. 22, 1905; children—Elizabeth (Mrs. J. F. Apsey), Alice (Mrs. Fielding H. Lewis), Charlotte (Mrs. J. A. Murray), Samuel Duncan. With Roland Telegraphic Co., 1899-1910, successively as draftsman, elec. engr., factory supt.; one of founders of Black & Decker Mfg. Co., mfrs. portable electric tools, Towson, Md., 1910, pres. since 1910. Presbyterian. Club: Baltimore Country. Home: Stevenson Lane. Office: Black & Decker Mfg. Co., Towson, Md.

BLACK, W. P.; proctologist Mountain State Hosp. Address: 109 Capitol St., Charleston, W.Va.

BLACKBURN, Albert E., M.D.; b. Fishertown, Pa., Sept. 25, 1872; s. Uriah and Hanna B.; student Swarthmore Coll., 1891-93; M.D., Medico Chirurg. Coll., 1896; m. Myra Holliday, Nov. 7, 1900; children—Jackson M., Eliza E., Albert E. (dec.). Began as physician, 1896; resident and chief resident, Presbyterian Hosp., 1896-1900, chief out-patient med. dept., 1898-1914; med. staff, 1912-18; med. staff, Phila. Gen. Hosp., 1906-30. Pres. Pa. Bd. for Registration of Nurses, 1909-23. Mem. Phila. Co. Med. Soc., A.M.A. Clubs: Medical, West Phila. Medical Book (Phila.). Address: 706 S. Bowman Av., Merion, Pa.

BLACKBURN, George Stebbins, educator; b. Urumia, Persia, Aug. 15, 1901; s. Charles Stanley and Amy Malvina (Waring) B.; student high sch., Columbia, S.C., 1917-18; A.B., Furman U., Greenville, S.C., 1922; Ph. B., Yale, 1926; grad. University of Bordeaux, France, 1931; M.A., Middlebury French Sch., 1933; m. Elizabeth Grace Tucker Brooke, Dec. 26, 1932; children—Alfred Brooke, Elizabeth Tucker. Instr. English, Staunton Military Acad., Staunton, Va., 1922-24, English and French, Harvey Sch., Hawthorne, N.Y., 1926-28, French, Asheville (N.C.) Sch., 1928-30; Répétiteur d'anglais, École Normale, Limoges, France, 1930-31; instr. French, Hopkins Grammar Sch., New Haven, Conn., 1931-33; dir. of St. Hilda's Hall, Charles Town, W.Va., and instr. French, 1934-'8; instr. Chestnut Hill Acad., Bryn Mawr, Pa., since 1938. Mem. Carolina Playmakers, Pi Kappa Phi. Democrat. Baptist. Club: Yale (Pittsburgh). Address: Baldwin School, Bryn Mawr, Pa.

BLACKBURN, James Breckenridge, prof. of law; b. Pittsburgh, Pa., Feb. 4, 1891; s. Oliver and Anna Julia (Reed) B.; prep. edn. Mercersburg Acad., 1908-10; A.B., Princeton U., 1914; LL.B., U. of Pittsburgh, 1917; LL.M., Harvard, 1930; m. Anna Louise Miller, Aug. 18, 1917; children—James Breckenridge, Oliver Miller, William Boyd. Admitted to Pa. bar, 1919, and practiced with Rose & Eichenauer, 1919-22; trust officer Pittsburgh Trust Co., 1922-26; gen. practice Pinehurst, N.C., 1926-29; asst. prof. of law, U. of Pittsburgh, 1930-35, prof. since 1935. Served as 2d lt., F.A., U.S. Army, with A.E.F., 1917-19. Mem. Alumni Council of Mercersburg Acad. Mem. Allegheny Co. Bar Assn., Pa. Bar Assn. Democrat. Presbyterian. Mason. Clubs: Law, Duquesne (Pittsburgh); Oakmont Country (Oakmont, Pa.); Colonial (Princeton U.). Home: 322 Richland Lane. Office: 1402 Cathedral of Learning, Pittsburgh, Pa.

BLACKBURN, Lesley, lumber mfg.; b. Fishertown, Pa., Apr. 12, 1887; s. Elias and Anna D. (Furnas) B.; ed. pub. schs., Fishertown, Pa., and George Sch.; m. Nan V. Maugle, June 22, 1911; 1 dau., Barbara J. Began as clk. First Nat. Bank, Everett, Pa., 1906, cashier 1909-20; mem. firm Everett Hardwood Lumber Co., 1920-32; assisted in organizing Everett Lumber Co. and Earlston Planing Mill Co., 1932 and since then mem. of both firms; sec. Everett Real Estate Corpn.; treas. Everett Cemetery Assn.; dir. First Nat. Bank; vice-pres. Everett Cash Mutual Fire Ins. Co. Served as dir. on Everett Sch. Bd.; dir. Northern Bedford Co. Fair Assn.; pres. Everett Booster Club; treas. Bedford Co. Rep. Com. since 1934, del. to Rep. Nat. Convs., 1924 and 1936. Republican. Religious Soc. of Friends. Mason (32°, Shriner). Home: Everett, Pa.

BLACKBURN, Morris Atkinson, artist, teacher; b. Phila., Pa., Oct. 13, 1902; s. James Meyers and Emma Lotta (Brightly) B.; student Overbrook Grammar Sch., Phila., 1907-15, Phila. Trades Sch., 1915-17, Phila. Museum's Sch. of Industrial Art, 1920, Graphic Sketch Club, Phila., 1920-25, Pa. Acad. of Fine Arts, Phila., 1925-29; m. Sarah Elizabeth Thompson, May 1, 1937. Began as rivet heater, Hog Island, Phila., 1917; draftsman, Victor Talking Machine Co., Camden, N.J., 1919-24, Lincoln Furniture Co., Phila., 1924-25, Max Mazer, free lancer designer, Phila., 1925-26; designer O. E. Mertz & Co., Phila., 1926-38; instr. of furniture design and painting, Phila. Museum's Sch. of Industrial Art since 1935. Mem. Phila. Art Alliance. Awarded W 1. Emlen Cresson travelling scholarships, 1928, 1929, by Pa. Acad. of Fine Arts; murals in fresco, Mastbaum Vocational Sch., Phila., Haverford Twp. (Pa.) High Sch.; represented Phila. Museum, Wilmington (Del.) Museum, collection of Fellowship, Pa. Acad. of Fine Arts. Address: 2120 Chancellor St., Philadelphia, Pa.

BLACKFORD, George A.; mem. law firm Blackford-Hundt. Address: Board of Trade Bldg., Wheeling, W.Va.

BLACKMAN, John Hughes, Jr., life ins.; b. West Pittston, Pa., Jan. 15, 1893; s. John Hughes and May (Allen) B.; student Lawrence Acad., and Yale U., 1914; m. Emily Fuller, Nov. 24, 1917; children—Joan Lindsey, Ruth Fuller. Mgr. Eastern Pa. and Northern N.J.

dists. Mutual Life Ins. Co. of N.Y. since 1932; dir. Second Nat. Bank, Wilkes Barre, Pa. Home: R.D. 4, Dallas, Pa. Office: 426 Mulberry St., Scranton, Pa.

BLACKMORE, George Augustus, mfr. ry. equipment; b. Wilkinsburg, Pa., Jan. 7, 1884; s. George H. and Elizabeth Dorothy (Bealafeld) B.; ed. pub. schs., Wilkinsburg, and night study at colls. and corr. schs.; m. Mary Suckling Stengle, Feb. 16, 1935; children (by former marriage)—Mrs. Thelma B. Neff, Mrs. William Wallace Priest, George Stewart. Office boy, Union Switch & Signal Co., Swissvale, Pa., 1896, later stenographer gen. mgrs. office, became chief clk. engring. dept., 1900, same in N.Y. office, 1904, asst. to Eastern mgr., 1909, Eastern mgr. in charge N.Y., Atlanta and Montreal offices, 1911, gen. sales mgr., Swissvale, 1916, 2d v.p., 1917, 1st v.p. and gen. mgr., 1922, pres. since 1929; v.p. and gen. mgr. Westinghouse Air Brake Co., Wilmerding, Pa., 1932-36, pres. since July 1936; also pres. Massey Concrete Products Corpn. since Apr. 1937; pres. and dir. Union Switch & Signal Constrn. Co.; dir. A. M. Byers Co., Duff-Norton Mfg. Co., Pittsburgh Screw & Bolt Corpn., Flannery Bolt Co., Pittsburgh Coal Co., Bendix-Westinghouse Automotive Air Brake Co., Cardwell-Westinghouse Co., Westinghouse Brake & Signal Co., Ltd. (London), Canadian Westinghouse Co. of Hamilton, Ont. Clubs: Engineers' (New York); Racquet (Phila.); Pittsburgh, Duquesne, Pittsburgh Athletic, Oakmont Country, Longue Vue Country, Edgewood Country (Pittsburgh); Rolling Rock Club (Ligonier, Pa.); Chicago (Chicago). Home: Perrysville, Pa. Office: Swissvale and Wilmerding, Pa.

BLACKWELL, Ashby Carlyle, prof. chemistry; b. Lynchburg, Va., Aug. 4, 1896; s. Samuel Ashby and Minnie Lee (Doyle) B.; A.B., Randolph-Macon Coll., Ashland, Va., 1918, A.M., 1919; student Princeton U., 1920-21, U. of Chicago, summers, 1922, 23, 36 and 37; m. Harriett Cazenove Purdy, Apr. 9, 1925; 1 dau., Nancy Purdy. Instr. mathematics, Randolph-Macon Coll., Ashland, Va., 1916-19; instr. mathematics and science, Randolph-Macon Acad., Bedford, Va., 1919-20; part-time asst. in chemistry, Princeton U., 1920-21; prof. chemistry, Morris Harvey Coll., Charleston, W.Va. (moved from Barboursville, W.Va., 1935) since 1921, v.p. of coll. since 1933, chmn. natural science div. since 1938. Municipal recorder, Barboursville, W.Va., July 1, 1933-Aug. 31, 1935. Rejected three times for service during World War. Mem. Am. Chem. Soc. (dir. Kanawha Valley Sect.), A.A.A.S., W.Va. State Ednl. Assn., W.Va. Acad. Science, Chi Beta Phi (nat. pres. since May 1924), Sigma Upsilon, Tau Kappa Alpha, Pi Gamma Mu. Democrat. Methodist. Mason (Master). Writer of articles on chem. subjects. Home: 9A Brookland Court, Charleston, W.Va.

BLACKWELL, Enoch, M.D.; chief eye, ear, nose and throat dept., Mercer Hosp.; cons. ophthalmologist and otorhinolaryngologist Orthopedic Hosp. Address: 28 W. State St., Trenton, N.J.

BLACKWELL, Jefferson Davis, coll. pres.; b. Blackwell, Mo., Sept. 5, 1885; s. Aquilla and Dollie (Coleman) B.; grad. State Teachers Coll., Cape Girardeau, Mo., 1910; B.S., U. of Mo., 1914; student U. of Chicago, summer 1915; A.M., Teachers Coll., Columbia, 1923; Ph.D., Johns Hopkins, 1929; m. Salome Love, Aug. 1, 1915; children—Edith Lucile, Harold Richard, David Jefferson. Teacher rural school, Halifax, Mo., 1906-07; supt. of schs., Blodgett, Mo., 1910-12; asso. prof. agrl. edn., Tex. A. and M. Coll., 1914-17; state dir. agrl. edn. for Tex., 1917-20; asst. state dir. of vocational edn. for Pa., 1920-23; state dir. of vocational edn. for Md., 1923-35; pres. State Teachers Coll., Salisbury, Md., since 1935. Mem. Acacia, Alpha Zeta, Phi Delta Kappa. Presbyterian. Mason (K.T., Shriner). Club: Rotary of Salisbury (pres. 1939-40). Address: State Teachers College, Salisbury, Md.

BLACKWOOD, Andrew Watterson, clergyman, educator; b. Clay Center, Kan., Aug. 5, 1882; s. Thomas (M.D.) and Bella (Watterson) B.; A.B., Franklin Coll., New Athens, O., 1902; A.B., magna cum laude, Harvard University, 1905; student Princeton Theol. Seminary, 1905-06, Xenia Theological Seminary, 1906-08; D.D., University of S.C., 1918; m. Carolyn B. Philips, Apr. 6, 1910; children—Philip Thomas, Andrew W., James Russell, William Harvey. Ordained ministry United Presbyn. Ch., 1908; pastor successively Sixth U. P. Ch., Pittsburgh; First Presbyn. Ch., Columbia, S.C., and Indianola Ch., Columbus, O., until 1925; prof. English Bible, Presbyn. Theol. Sem., Louisville, Ky., 1925-30; prof. Homiletics, Princeton Theol. Sem., since 1930. Served various times as acting prof. Xenia Sem., Columbia Sem., U. of S.C. and Ohio State Summer Sch. for Pastors. Ind. Democrat. Author: Prophets—Elijah to Christ, 1917; Bible History—Genesis to Esther, 1928; The Fine Art of Preaching, 1937; also series of 10 articles on Practical Homiletics in Union Sem. Rev. Home: 52 Mercer St., Princeton, N.J.

BLACKWOOD, Edwin Neale, civil engr.; b. Ben Lomond, Mason Co., W.Va., Apr. 30, 1903; s. Charles K. and Margaret (Neale) B.; grad. Point Pleasant (W.Va.) High Sch., 1921; B.S. in C.E., W.Va. U., 1925; m. Gertrude Carman, Mar. 14, 1931; children—Mary Margaret, Edwin Neale, James Kenton. Began as draftsman, 1924; successively designer, inspector, engr., county highway engr. and plans engr.; state construction engr. in charge Div. of Construction, State Road Commn. of W.Va., since Jan. 1, 1938. Commd. lieut., U.S. Naval Reserve, 1935. Mem. W.Va. Assn. Professional Engrs., Beta Theta Pi; asso. mem. Am. Soc. Civil Engrs. Democrat. Episcopalian. Mason (Royal Arch). Home: 102 Veasey St. Office: 1340 Wilson St., Charleston, W.Va.

BLACKWOOD, James M.; chief of eye service Jameson Memorial and New Castle Hosps. Address: 446 E. Washington St., New Castle, Pa.

BLACKWOOD, Oswald, univ. prof.; b. Clay Center, Kan., Apr. 24, 1888; s. Thomas and Belle (Watterson) B.; A.B., Boston U., 1909; Ph.D., U. of Chicago, 1919; m. Gertrude Clark, Sept. 18, 1919; 1 dau., Gertrude Clark. Prof. physics, Reid Christian Coll., Lucknow, India, 1909-10; instr. physics, U. of Philippines, Manila, P.I., 1911-14; asst. prof. physics, U. of Arkansas, Fayetteville, Ark., 1919-20; asst. prof. physics, U. of Pittsburgh, 1921-24, asso. prof., 1925-27, prof. since 1928; cons. physicist, Koppers Research Co., Pittsburgh, 1925-32. Fellow A.A.A.S. (mem. council), Am. Phys. Soc.; mem. Am. Assn. Physics Teachers, Pittsburgh Physics-Chemistry Teachers Club (pres. since 1938), Sigma Xi, Beta Theta Pi. Protestant. Author: Introductory College Physics, 1938; co-author: Experimental Physics, 1934; Pittsburgh Atomic Physics, 1933. Home: 251 Lothrop St. Office: U. of Pittsburgh, Pittsburgh, Pa.

BLADEL, Edward Lee, bldg. construction; b. Rock Island, Ill., Jan. 23, 1892; s. John Phillip and Frances L. (Maucker) B.; ed. Augustana Coll., Rock Island, Ill., 1906-09, U. of Pittsburgh, 1921-23; m. Florence Eugenia Mosher, June 28, 1919 (dec.); children—Florence Yvonne, Edward Lee, Jr., John Walter; m. 2d, Marie McIntyre, of Crafton, Pa., Aug. 13, 1928; 1 son, Louis Earle. Began as sec. to purchasing agt. Rock Island Plow Co., Rock Island, Ill., 1909, sec. to gen. supt., to 1912, sec. and asst. to works mgr., 1912-16; with personnel and labor dept. John Deere Plow Co., Moline, Ill., 1916-17; mem. firm Eric Fisher Wood & Co., architects and engrs., Pittsburgh, Pa., 1920-35; in employ Rep. Nat. Com., 1936; mem. firm Smith and Bladel, architects, since 1935; pres. The Coronado Corpn. Served with 88th Div., U.S.A. and Mil. Intelligence work with A.E.F., 1917-19; active in orgn. Am. Legion, 1st treas. in France, asst. sec. Paris Conv., Mar. 1919. Mem. Am. Legion. Republican. Roman Catholic. K.C. National Guard Assn. of Allegheny Co. (sec.). Home: 52 Glenn St., Crafton. Office: 309 4th Av., Pittsburgh, Pa.

BLADES, Webster Strayer, lawyer; b. Choptank, Md., Dec. 6, 1888; s. Jehu T. and Emma W. (Patton) B.; A.B., St. John's Coll., Annapolis, Md., 1910; LL.B., Harvard Law Sch., 1915; m. Florence L. Parker, Mar. 2, 1918; children—Webster S., Alice Parker, Jehu L. Admitted to Md. bar, 1915; in gen. practice of law at Baltimore since 1915; mem. law firm Blades & Rosenfeld since 1920. Served as 1st lt., U.S. Infantry, World War; engaged in various offensives with A.E.F. Democrat. Presbyn. Mason. Home: 1423 Park Av. Office: 1206-07 Fidelity Bldg., Baltimore, Md.

BLAGG, Donald Orr, lawyer; b. Capehart, W.Va., July 31, 1886; s. Benjamin Henry and Luemma Susan (Crawford) B.; student W.Va. Univ. Law Sch., 1908-09; m. Annie Laurie Knopp, July 1, 1909; children—William Donald (dec.), Janet Annie (Mrs. Robert William Callard), Joseph Arthur, Robert Lewis, Thomas Roy. Admitted to W.Va. bar, 1909; engaged in gen. practice of law at Charleston since 1909; mem. firm Rummel, Blagg & Stone since 1925; served as city solicitor of Charleston, 1919-23, referee in bankruptcy, 1924-25. Mem. Am. Bar Assn., W.Va. State Bar Assn., Charleston Bar Assn. (pres. 1927). Republican. Methodist. Club: Kiwanis of Charleston (pres. 1926). Home: 1566 Jackson St. Office: Security Bldg., Charleston, W.Va.

BLAI, Boris, sculptor and teacher; b. Russia, July 24, 1893; s. Michael and Esther (Anatopol) B.; came to U.S., 1917, naturalized, 1931; ed. Kiev Imperial Acad. Fine Arts, Imperial Acad. Fine Arts, Leningrad, Ecole des Beaux Arts, 1912-13, Rodin Apprentice, 1913; m. Manya Gourenko, Mar. 29, 1921; 1 son, Boris. Began career as sculptor at age of 12; exhibns. in every country of Europe and in America, Annual Show Acad. Fine Arts, Pa., 1924-25, invited to Chicago Art Inst.; one man show Grand Central Galleries, New York City, 1934; asso. with R. Tait McKenzie in work, Canadian Memorial, Edinburgh, Scotland, statue of Gen. Wolfe, London; interested in Progressive Edn.; dir. of Art, Oak Lane Country Day Sch. since 1927; dir. Stella Elkins Tyler Sch. Fine Arts, Elkins Park, Pa., since 1934. Mem. Grand Central Galleries, New York, Art Alliance, Phila. Home: 4th St. & High Av., Oak Lane, Philadelphia, Pa. Office: Stella Elkins Tyler School of Fine Arts, Beach and Penrose Sts., Elkins Park, Pa.

BLAIR, Augustine Wilberforce, educator; b. Archdale, N.C., Sept. 12, 1866; s. Benjamin F. and Rachel E. (Anderson) B.; B.S., Guilford Coll., 1890; B.S., Haverford Coll., 1892, A.M., 1896; m. J. Genevieve Mendenhall, July 1, 1897 (died 1934); 1 dau., Mary (Mrs. Mower). Teacher science and history, Abington Friends Sch., Jenkinton, Pa., 1892-95; asst. chemist N.C. Expt. Station, 1897-98; chemist State of N.C., 1898-99; asst. chemist Fla. Expt. Station, 1899-1906, chemist, 1906-11; asso. soil chemist N.J. Agrl. Expt. Station, 1911-22, soil chemist since 1922; asso. prof. agrl. chemistry, Rutgers U., 1913-17, prof. since 1917. Fellow A.A.A.S.; mem. Am. Soc. Agronomy, Sigma Xi, Phi Beta Kappa, Phi Lambda Upsilon; mem.-at-large Alpha Zeta. Republican. Mem. Soc. of Friends (Quaker). Home: 202 Lawrence Av., New Brunswick, N.J.

BLAIR, John Edward, bacteriologist; b. Monroe, Me., May 30, 1899; s. John Stott and Alice Ethel (Staples) B.; A.B., Clark U., Worcester, Mass., 1920; ScM., Brown U., Providence, R.I., 1921, Ph.D., 1923; m. Lorraine Hunter Ferguson, Sept. 6, 1923; children—Donald Ferguson, Malcolm John. Instr. in biology, Brown U., 1921-22; instr. in bacteriology, Stanford U., 1923-26; bacteriologist Hosp. for Joint Diseases, New York since Jan. 1927. Fellow A.A.A.S.; mem. Soc. Am. Bacteriologists (pres. New York City Sect. 1939), Soc. Exptl. Biology and Medicine, Sigma Xi. Home: 26 Paulin Boul., Leonia, N.J. Office: Hospital for Joint Diseases, Madison Av. and 123d St., New York, N.Y.

BLAIR, John L.; pres. New Process Co. Home: 105 East St. Office: Third Av. and Hickory St., Warren, Pa.

BLAIR, Mortimer W(arren), physician; b. Phila., Pa., June 1, 1890; s. Samuel C. and Mary E. (Richardson) B.; A.B., Central High Sch., Phila., 1910; M.D., Jefferson Med. Coll., 1914; m. Olive R. Wilkinson, Feb. 27, 1917; children—Francis W., Mortimer W., Jr. Engaged in gen. practice of medicine and ophthalmology at Phila., Pa., 1915-20, specializing in ophthalmology since 1920; ophthalmologist to Roxborough Hosp. since 1926; mem. courtesy staffs Germantown and Womens Coll. hosps.; actg. asst. surg. Wills Hosp., 1917. Served as ophthalmologist to U.S.A. Base Hosp. 67 in World War. Fellow Am. Acad. Ophthalmology and Otolaryngology; mem. Am. Med. Assn., Pa. State Med. Soc., Phila. Co. Med. Soc., Vets. Fgn. Wars, Am. Legion, Lions Internat. Republican. Methodist. Mason (32°, Shriner). Clubs: Lions, Garden, Rox. Male Chorus. Cynwyd Tennis. Home: 369 Green Lane. Office: Physicians Bldg., 20th & Chestnut, Philadelphia, Pa.

BLAIR, Orland Rossini, M.D.; b. New Britain, Conn., Jan. 12, 1871; s. Charles Alfred and Ellen (Woodford) B.; student New Britain (Conn.) High Sch., 1886-90; Ph.D., Yale, 1893, M.D., Sch. of Medicine, 1896, diplomate in psychiatry, 1936; m. Emma Forest Farnham, June 19, 1923; 1 dau., Barbara Farnham. Began as interne Springfield (Mass.) Hosp., 1896; pvt. practice, Springfield, Mass., 1897-1921; asst. phys., Northampton (Mass.) State Hosp., 1921-23; asst. phys., Hillside Hosp., Clarks Summit, Pa., 1923-24, sr. asst. phys. since 1924. Served as asst. and past assistant surgeon Mass. Naval Militia, 1901-19, retired as lt. commdr., 1919; lt. M.C., U.S. Naval Res. during World War, lt. commdr. since 1918. Mem. Pa., Am. med. socs., Am. Psychiatric Assn., New England Psychiatric Soc., Am. Legion, Mil. Order of World War. Republican. Presbyterian. Mason. Address: Hillside Hosp., Clarks Summit, Pa.

BLAIR, Parr Dalton, supt. county schs.; b. Hartstown, Pa., March 28, 1877; s. John Alexander and Sarah E. (Hunter) B.; ed. Clarion State Normal Sch., 1895-97, Allegheny Coll., 1898-1900; A.B., Grove City Coll., 1905, A.M., same, 1908; grad. study, Harvard U., 1909, and U. of Pittsburgh, 1931, 32, 33; m. Alice Belle Farley, Aug. 2, 1905; children—June Alathea, Paul Dalton. Prin. schs., Spartansburg, Springboro, 1900-04; Irwin, Cambridge Springs, 1905-11; instr. Clarion State Normal Sch., summers 1898, 99, Beaver Coll., summer 1902; supt. Crawford Co. Schs. since 1911. Mem. Nat. Edn. Assn., Nat. Assn. Sch. Adminstrs., Pa. State Edn. Assn., Kappa Phi Kappa. Elder in Presbyterian Church. Mason (32°), I.O.O.F. Clubs: University, Round Table, Rotary (Meadville). Home: Meadville, Pa.

BLAIR, Ross Mitchell, publishing; b. Elizabeth, Pa., Jan. 20, 1890; s. William Henry and Alice (Ausburn) B.; ed. pub. schs., high sch. and pvt. schs.; m. Grace Campbell, June 23, 1915; children—Evelyn A., Betty H., William J., Robert P. Began as salesman on West Coast, 1908; asso. with Pittsburgh Legal Journal and Smith Bros. Co., Inc. since 1911; pres., treas., chmn. bd. dirs. Pittsburgh Legal Journal, Smith Bros. Co., Inc., Daily Law Bulletin, Campbell Loose Leaf Annotated Current Services, Inc. Mem. Pittsburgh Chamber of Commerce (state affairs com.). First v.p. Asso. Court and Commercial Newspaper Assn. of U.S.; dir. Typothetae of Western Pa., Inc. Mem. Pa. Newspaper Publisher's Assn., Allegheny Co. Newspaper Assn., Nat. Editorial Assn. Mason (32°, K.T., Shriner). Mem. U.P. Church. Home: 34 Lebanon Hills Dr., Mt. Lebanon. Office: 210 Grant St., Pittsburgh, Pa.

BLAIR, Thomas Marshall Howe, educator; b. Pittsburgh, Pa., Oct. 23, 1901; s. William Wightman (M.D.) and Margaret Kennedy (Brown) B.; student Shady Side Acad. and Arnold Sch., Pittsburgh, 1910-20, Williams Coll., 1921; B.A., U. of Pittsburgh, 1924, M.A., 1925; studied King's Coll., U. of London (Michaelmas term), 1925-26, Johns Hopkins U., 1931-34; m. Louise Colebrook, Dec. 24, 1926; children—Miranda Colebrook, Sylvia Carroll. Instr. English, Carnegie Inst. Tech., 1926-28, Western Reserve U., 1928-31; asst. Main Reading Room staff, Library of Congress, 1934-35; instr. English composition, Pa. State Coll., since 1935. Mem. State College Peace Action Com. since 1935. Mem. Modern Lang. Assn. America, Kappa Alpha, Tudor and Stuart Club (Johns Hopkins U.). Episcopalian. Club: Beaumaris Golf and Tennis Assn. (Ontario, Can.). Editor: The Unhappy Favorite, or the Earl of Essex, by John Banks (1682), 1939. Author: "A Glimpse into the Library of Congress," Library Journal, Feb. 1937. Home: Woodland Road, Pittsburgh, Pa. Address: Pennsylvania State College, State College, Pa.

BLAIR, Walter Allen, M.D.; b. Covington, Tioga Co., Pa., Feb. 29, 1888; s. Mathew Shaw and Emma Jane (Seymour) B.; A.B., Bethany Coll., 1910; M.D., Temple U., 1915; post grad. study x-ray and lab., 1919; m. Marion Tunis, June 26, 1926. Interne Charity Hosp., Norristown, Pa., 1915-16; began practice of medicine at Norristown; roentgenologist and bacteriologist to J. C. Blair Memorial Hosp., Huntington, Pa., 1919-20; in gen. practice of medicine at Chester since 1921, also 4 yrs. in Upland; urologist Taylor Hosp., Ridley Park, Pa. (pres. of staff 1937); asso. urologist Chester (Pa.) Hosp. Mem. Phila. Urol. Soc., Phila. Med. Club, Am. Legion, Beta Theta Pi, Phi Chi. Home: 207 Parkway Av. Office: 302 E. 9th St., Chester, Pa.

BLAIR, William Richards, physicist; b. Co. Derry, Ireland, Nov. 7, 1874; s. Thomas Wray and Mary (Richards) B.; came to America, 1884; grad. Kan. State Normal Sch., 1895; S.B., U. of Chicago, 1904, Ph.D., 1906; graduate Signal School of U.S. Army, 1923, Command and General Staff School of U.S. Army, 1926; m. Florence Lyon, d. Charles G. Smith, Oct. 1909; children—William Richards, Thomas Wray, Charles Lyon. Prin. high sch., Pittsburg, Kan., 1897-99; asso. in mathematics. State Normal Sch., Oshkosh, Wis., 1900-02, asst. instr. U. of Chicago, 1903-06; entered govt. service, Oct. 1906; research dir. in charge upper air research, U.S. Weather Bur., June 1907, and of Physical Lab., June 1910, and exec. officer in charge Mt. Weather Obs., Va., 1912-14; prof. meteorology, in charge aërology, U.S. Weather Bureau, 1915-17; commd. maj. Nat. Army, 1917, and assigned to Aviation Corps, with A. E.F. in France; trans. to Signal Corps, July 1918; lt. col., Feb. 1919; major in regular army, Nov. 1921, lt. col., Oct. 1934; col. Oct. 1938; retired Nov. 1938; chief of research and engring. div., Office of Chief Signal Officer, U.S. A., Washington, D.C., 1926-30; officer in charge Signal Corps. Labs. since 1930; tech. consultant, Automatic Electric Co. since 1939. Chmn. technical sub-com. Internat. Commn. for Aerial Navigation; technical advisor Internat. Wireless Commn., Paris, first half 1919; meteorologist for the "World Flight," 1924; member International Radiotelegraph Conf., Washington, 1927; member Daniel Guggenheim Com. on Aëronautical Meteorology, 1927-30. Fellow Royal Meteorology Society; member Internat. Com. for Scientific Aëronautics, Am. Phys. Soc., Philos. Soc. Washington, Am. Soc. Aëronautic Engrs. (exec. bd.), Washington Acad. Sciences, Acad. Polit. Science, Inst. of Aëronautical Sciences (founder-mem.), Phi Beta Kappa, Sigma Xi, Alpha Tau Omega, Am. Geog. Union, Nat. Research Council; fellow Am. Meteorol. Soc. Clubs: Cosmos (Washington, D.C.), etc. Home: Red Bank, N.J.; 1310 Floral St., N.W. Washington, D.C.

BLAIR, William Wightman, ophthalmologist; b. Blair, Allegheny Co., Pa., Nov. 30, 1866; s. George W. and Caroline Snowden (Wightman) B.; studied U. of Pittsburgh; M.D., Hahnemann Med. Coll. and Hosp., Phila., 1889; m. Margaret Kennedy Brown, April 16, 1895. Prof. ophthalmology emeritus, Sch. of Medicine, U. of Pittsburgh; cons. exec. surgeon Eye and Ear Hosp.; hon. librarian Lippincott Library. Fellow Am. Coll. Surgeons; mem. A.M.A., Pa. State Med. Soc., Allegheny Co. Med. Soc., Pittsburgh Acad. Medicine, Am. Acad. Otology and Ophthalmology, Am. Ophthalmol. Soc., Ophthalmol. Soc. of the United Kingdom, U. of Pittsburgh Ophthalmol. Soc. (pres.), Soc. Biol. Research of U. of Pittsburgh. Mason. Clubs: University, Rolling Rock Country. Home: Woodland Road. Office: 121 University Pl., Pittsburgh, Pa.

BLAISDELL, George Grant, pres. Zippo Mfg. Co.; b. Bradford, Pa., June 5, 1895; s. Philo C. and Sarah (Grant) B.; student Horace Mann Sch.; m. Miriam Barcroft, Feb. 21, 1923; children—Harriett Ann, Sarah Grant. Began as sec., treas., and gen. mgr. Blaisdell Machinery Co., Bradford, 1916; pres. and dir. Blaisdell Oil Co., Bradford, since 1920, Zippo Mfg. Co., Bradford, since 1934, Blaisdell Bros., New York, N.Y., since 1937. Elk. Clubs: Bradford, Pennhills (Bradford). Home: 162 Kennedy St. Office: 36 Barbour St., Bradford, Pa.

BLAKE, Charles F.; surgeon Mercy Hosp.; visiting surgeon Hosp. for Women of Md., West Baltimore Gen. and South Baltimore Gen. hosps.; prof. proctology, U. of Md. Address: 20 E. Preston St., Baltimore, Md.

BLAKE, Clinton Hamlin, lawyer and author; b. Englewood, N.J., July 26, 1883; s. Clinton Hamlin and Mary Gibson (Parsons) B.; A.B., Columbia, 1904 (class sec.), A.M. in Polit. Science, 1905, LL.B., 1906; m. Margaret Duryee Coe, June 10, 1908; children—Margaret Coe (Mrs. Theodore W. Oppel), Marion Stanley (Mrs. William G. Cullimore), Dorothy Dexter, Clinton Hamlin, Jr. Admitted to N.Y. bar, 1906, later to bars of U.S. Circuit and Dist. courts, Court of Appeals, D.C., U.S. Patent Office, and Supreme Court of U.S.; mem. Blake & Voorhees, N.Y. City; specializes in laws relating to corpns., estates, architecture and building, and unfair competition; pres. and dir. Harper-Gow Corpn.; dir. and chmn. bd. Citizens Nat. Bank & Trust Co., Englewood; mem. board of dirs. Pond's Extract Co.; dir. & mem. exec. com. National Sugar Refining Co. Special lecturer on law of architecture and building, Mass. Inst. Technology, 1921-22, 25, Columbia University, 1928, N.Y. U., 1933, and on same subject before various architectural societies; instr. in architecture N.Y. Univ., 1928. Councilman at large, pres. Common Council, Englewood, 1914-16; mayor of Englewood, 2 terms, 1916-18; resigned to enter Army. Mem. N.J. State Council of Defense, 1917-18; chmn. War Draft Bd. No. 5, Bergen Co., N.J., 1917-18; capt. Signal Corps, U.S.A., 1918-19. Former mem. exec. com. N.J. div. Am. Liberty League; former dir. and mem. exec. com. N.J. div. Assn. Against Prohibition Amendment. Mem. Am. and N.Y. State bar assns., Assn. Bar City New York, N.Y. Acad. Polit. Science, Beta Theta Pi. Republican. Clubs: University, Down Town Assn., Beta Theta Pi (New York), Knickerbocker Golf, Englewood Republican (ex-pres.), Englewood Field, Profile Golf, Wyantenuck Golf. Author: The Law of Architecture and Building, 1916-25; The Architect's Law Manual, 1924; Acquiring the Home, 1925; also many serial and spl. articles in mags. since 1915. Mem. bd. editors The Book of Englewood, 1922. Editor legal dept. Am. Architect, 1921-27 and 1934-36. Runner-up New Jersey golf champ., 1904. Home: 95 Chestnut St., Englewood, N.J.; (summer) Sugar Hill, N.H., and Great Barrington, Mass. Office: 20 Exchange Place, New York, N.Y.

BLAKE, Francis F. E., clergyman; b. Lynn, Mass.,M ar. 7, 1901; s. Walter I. and Bertha (Berry) B.; ed. Nashotah House (Wis.), 1921-27, U. of Pa., 1927-30; Th.B., Phila. Divinity Sch., 1930, Th.M., same, 1937; unmarried. Ordained to ministry P.E. Ch., deacon, 1926, priest, 1927; on staff St. Mark's Ch., Phila., Pa., since 1929; engaged as lecturer, instr., and writer on liturgies in various places; chmn. Phila. Branch of Anglican Soc. since 1936 and mem. exec. com. of same. Republican. Episcopalian. Home: 1625 Locust St., Philadelphia, Pa.

BLAKE, George H.; vice-pres. and gen. solicitor Pub. Service Corpn of N.J. Address: 80 Park Place, Newark, N.J.

BLAKELEY, George Henry, engineer; b. Livingston, N.J., Apr. 19, 1865; s. Joseph and Mary A. (Gibson) B.; B.S., Rutgers Coll., 1884, C.E. from same college, 1894, ScD., 1924; m. Grace Delia Bogart, Apr. 12, 1893; 1 son, George Bogart. Private engineering practice 1884-1888; was bridge engineer, Erie R.R., 1888-90; chief engr., Passaic Steel Co., 1890-1902, mgr. of sales, 1902-05; structural engr., 1906-08, mgr. structural steel dept., 1908-27, Bethlehem Steel Co.; v.p. same since 1927; pres. Bethlehem Steel Bridge Corpn., 1916-23; pres. McClintic-Marshall Corpn., 1931-35; dir. Bethlehem Steel Corpn., Bethlehem Steel Company,

Bethlehem Steel Export Steel Corporation. Ac-Bethlehem Shipbuilding Corpn., Bethlehem Steel Export Corporation. Actively identified with constrn. of many important bridges and bldgs., among which are Delaware River Bridge (Phila.), Peace Bridge (Niagara River, Buffalo), Golden Gate Bridge (San Francisco), Merchandise Mart (Chicago), Chase Nat. Bldg. (New York), Field Museum (Chicago); expert in devising and developing improvements in mfr. and uses of structural steel, the most important of which are broad flange structural steel sections, introduced by Bethlehem Steel Co. in 1908, and which are in gen. use in steel construction. Life trustee Rutgers Univ. Mem. American Society C.E., American Soc. Mech. Engrs., Am. Iron and Steel Inst., Chi Psi, Tau Beta Pi, Phi Beta Kappa; fellow Am. Geog. Soc. Republican. Episcopalian. Clubs: University, Lawyers', Engineers', Whitehall, Chi Psi, New York Yacht (New York); Art (Phila.); Manhasset Bay Yacht (L.I.); Saucon Valley Country (Bethlehem). Home: Fountain Hill, Bethlehem, Pa.

BLAKEMAN, William Hildreth, pub. official, writer; b. Brooklyn, N.Y., Aug. 11, 1881; s. Alexander Noel and Elizabeth Alsop (Hildreth) B.; A.B., Princeton U., 1903; B.S. in Naval Arch., Mass. Inst. Tech., 1905; m. Marguerite Louise Wilkin, Apr. 8, 1916. Employed in Cramps Shipyard, Phila., Pa., successively shipfitter, foreman, asst. to gen. supt., supt. drydock 1905-18; with Emergency Fleet Corpn. (U.S. Shipping Bd.) 1918-19; gen mgr. Union Shipbldg. Co., Baltimore, Md., 1919-22; engaged in pigment mfg., 1922-24; in ins. and gen. bus. including dir. and vice-pres. Industrial Bank of Baltimore, 1924-35; made econ. surveys of Gulf Coast region for N.Y. capitalists, 1928-29; served as Md. State Budget Dir., 1935-39; mem. Md. Intergovtl. Cooperation Commn., 1937-39; mem. State Employees Retirement Commn., 1937-39; mem. State Planning Commn., sub. com. on uniform pub. accounting, 1938-39; mem. Md. Development Bur., administrative com., 1937-39. Treas. Md. Soc. S.A.R. Mem. Mil. Order Loyal Legion, Princeton and M.I.T. alumni assns. Republican. Presbyn. Clubs: Country (Baltimore); (former mem.) Union League of Phila. Contbr. patriotic and political articles to newspapers and periodicals. Home: 308 E. Lake Av., Baltimore, Md.

BLAKESLEE, Myra Allen (Mrs. Paul Jerome Blakeslee); b. Beaver Meadows, Pa., Dec. 3, 1892; d. Dr. Charles Lesley and Daisy Deane (Farrow) Allen; ed. Lycoming Co. Normal Sch., 1908-09, Pa. State Coll., 1909-13; m. Paul Jerome Blakeslee, of Muncy, Pa., June 29, 1914. Engaged in teaching pub. schs., 1910-14; organizer Pa. Women's Suffrage Assn. in Lucerne Co. 1914-20; asst. editor Abbey Print Shop, East Orange, N.J., 1923-26; propr. and mgr. Myra A. Blakeslee, Inc., book shop, East Orange, 1926-29; organized present business of selling books direct by mail advertising, 1929. Sec. State of N.J. Good Will Commn. since 1938; 3rd v.p. Nat. Business and Professional Women's Club since 1937; chr. brd. trustees Good Government Council of N.J. since 1936, N.J. Taxpayers Assn., 1935-39, N.J. Citizens' Com. on Edn., 1935-37; pres. Service Clubs Council, 1931-32; dir. Landon Business Women's League, Eastern Div. Nat. Rep. Com., 1936; pres. Rep. Business Women of N.J. since 1935; pres. East Orange Women's Rep. Club, 1935-36; pres. N.J. Fed. Business and Professional Women's Clubs, 1932-34; pres. Business and Professional Women's Club of the Oranges, 1929-30; v.p. Citizens Forum of N.J. since 1934; mem. Essex Co. Conf. of Christians and Jews, State Women's Rep. Club, Essex Co. Women's Rep. Club; League of Women Voters of the Oranges. Republican. Home: 170 S. Clinton St., East Orange, N.J.

BLANCHARD, Charles Lester, physician; b. Dover, N.J., Oct. 13, 1900; s. John Edward and Jennie Baker (Davenport) B.; B.Sc., Lafayette Coll., Easton, Pa., 1924; student State Teachers Sch., Newton, N.J., 1920; M.D., Jefferson Med. Coll., Phila., Pa., 1928; m. Alice May Peterson, Feb. 12, 1932; children—Geraldine Ann, Valerie Jane, Jacqueline Charles. Interne Chester County Hosp., West Chester, Pa., 1928-29; engaged in gen. practice of medicine and industrial medicine at Dover, N.J. since 1929; dept. physician Dover Fire Dept.; med. dir. Dover Rescue Squad; med. adviser to bd. health of Rockaway Twp. Served as 1st lt. Med Res. since 1928. Fellow Am. Med. Assn. Mem. Assn. Mil. Surgeons of U.S., N.J. Med. Soc., Morris Co. Med. Soc., S.A.R. Republican. Methodist. Mason. Jr. Order United Am. Mechanics, Moose. Home: 396 W. Blackwell St. Office: 28 E. Blackwell St., Dover, N.J.

BLANCHARD, Maria Gertrude, librarian, instr. in library science; b. Pittsburgh, Pa., Jan. 16, 1874; d. Leonard J. and Winifred Maria (Brady) Blanchard; grad. Carnegie Library Sch., 1913; grad. Byron King's School of Oratory; A.B., U. of Notre Dame, 1927; summer student Catholic U. of America; special courses Duquesne U., U. of Pittsburgh. Branch librarian and librarian of boys and girls rooms, Carnegie Library, 1908-28; organizer and head reference dept. library, U. of Notre Dame, 1921-22; librarian and dean of women, Duquesne U., Pittsburgh, 1928-34, Univ. librarian since 1928; organized reference dept. U. of Notre Dame, Library Georgian Court Coll., Lakewood, N.J., Central Cath. Boys High Sch., Pittsburgh, Duquesne U. Library, St. Francis Coll. Library, Loretto, Pa.; instr. library science, Carnegie Library Sch., 1915-28, U. of Notre Dame, summers 1922-27, Pa. State Coll., extension, 1922-30, Seton Hill Coll. extension, 1924-25, Duquesne U. since 1928. Mem. A.L.A., Special Libraries Assn., Pa. Library Assn., Allegheny Co. Scholarship Assn., Carnegie Library School Alumni Assn., Pittsburgh Library Club, Notre Dame University Women's Club. Democrat. Roman Catholic. Home: 4506 Centre Av. Office: Duquesne University, Pittsburgh, Pa.

BLANCHET, Paul Romeo, asso. prof. French; b. Epernay, France, Sept. 4, 1879; s. Auguste and Adele (Marchal) B.; came to U.S., 1900, naturalized citizen, 1904; B.A., Chaptal Coll., Paris, 1896; M.A., U. of Paris (Sorbonne), 1900; m. Christine Bessie Passerieux, Nov. 11, 1903; children—Paul Marchal, Charles Henri. Engaged in teaching the Romance langs. since 1903; instr. French, high sch., Youngstown, O., 1903-05; master French and German, Univ. Sch., Chicago, 1905-09; head modern lang. dept., Soldan High Sch., St. Louis, Mo., 1909-17; head French Dept., Univ. Sch., Cleveland, O., 1917-22; master French, Haverford Sch., Pa., 1922-24; asso. prof. French, Pa. State Coll. since 1924. Served one yr. in French Army; now 1st lt. arty. Res. Mem. Am. Assn. of Univ. Profs., Alpha Tau Omega, Phi Sigma Iota. Awarded Officer d'Academie, 1936. Republican. Presbyn. Modern Woodmen of America. Club: University. Home: State College, Pa.

BLAND, Pascal Brooke, M.D., emeritus prof. of obstetrics; b. Monocacy, Pa., May 9, 1875; s. Caleb Harrison and Harriet Amelia B.; M.D., Jefferson Med. Coll., Phila., 1901; m. Susan Montgomery, of Phila., Dec. 27, 1906; children—Helen Buckley (Mrs. J. Hamilton Coulter), Harriet Harrison, Edward Montgomery. Interne Jefferson Med. Coll. Hosp., 1901-02, asst. gynecologist, 1902-15; asst. prof. gynecology, Jefferson Med. Coll. 1915-25, prof. obstetrics 1925-36. Cons. obstetrician or gynecologist to: Jefferson Med. Coll. Hosp.; Phila. Lying-in Hosp., St. Joseph's Hosp., Phila.; Jeanes Hosp., Fox Chase, Pa.; Delaware County Hosp., Lansdowne, Pa.; Montgomery Hosp., Norristown, Pa.; Burlington County Hosp., Mt. Holly, N.J.; Beebe Hosp., Lewes, Dela.; Pottstown Hosp., Pottstown, Pa.; Vineland Training School, Vineland, N.J. Fellow Coll. Phys. of Phila., Am. Assn. Obstetricians, Gynecologists and Abdominal Surgeons, Royal Soc. Medicine (London), Am. Coll. Surgeons; corr. mem. Clin. Soc. of Havana, Cuba; foreign corr. mem. Royal Med. Soc. of Budapest, Hungary; fellow Pan Am. Med. Assn.; first vice-pres. Internat. Coll. of Suregons; diplomate of bd. of Obstetrics and Gynecology. Mem. Am. and Phila. Co. med. assns., Med. Soc. State of Pa., Obstet. Soc. of Phila. (ex-pres.), Colonial Soc. of Pa., Academy of Fine Arts, Acad. of Natural Sciences, Pa. Hist. Soc.; A.A.A.S., Franklin Inst., Am. Acad. of Polit. and Social Science. Mason (32°). Clubs: University, Phila. Country, Union League, Rotary Internat., Alpha Kappa Kappa, Alpha Omega Alpha. Author: Textbook on Gynecology, Medical and Surgical, 1934, Textbook on Obstetrics for Students and Practitioners, 1935. Home: Bala-Cynwyd, Pa. Office: 1621 Spruce St., Philadelphia, Pa.

BLAND, Richard Howard, surety and casualty ins.; b. Baltimore, Md., Mar. 31, 1880; s. John Randolph and Maria (Harden) B.; prep. edn., University Sch., Baltimore; A.B., Harvard, 1902, LL.B., 1905; m. Mary L. Paul, Oct. 25, 1905; children—John Randolph II, Richard Howard, Frank Paul. Practical law as mem. firm Bartlett, Poe, Claggett & Bland, Baltimore 1905-16; elected v.p. and sec. U.S. Fidelity & Guaranty Co., 1916, pres., 1923-32, now chmn.; dir. Consolidated Gas, Electric Light & Power Co., Savings Bank of Baltimore, Industrial Corpn., First Nat. Bank, Fidelity & Guaranty Fire Corpn., Chesapeake & Potomac Telephone Co. Sec. Draft Bd., Baltimore County, World War. Member American Bar Association. Democrat. Episcopalian. Clubs: Maryland, Bachelors' Cotillon; Rolling Rd. Golf (Catonsville); Harvard (New York). Home: Catonsville, Md. Address: U.S. Fidelity & Guaranty Co., Baltimore, Md.

BLAND, Robert; mem. law firm Bland & Joyce; also asst. prosecuting atty. Address: Logan, W.Va.

BLANNING, Wendell Yeager, dir. Bur. Motor Carriers, Interstate Commerce Commn.; Williamstown, Pa., Nov. 13, 1888; s. William and Belle Jane (Yeager) B.; Ph.B., Dickinson Coll., Carlisle, Pa., 1912; m. Christine Anne Hoffman, Sept. 26, 1935; 1 son, Robert Wendell. Began as newspaper reporter, 1912; law librarian, 1913-24; admitted to Pa. bar, 1917, and practiced in Pa.; dir. Bur. of Pub. Convenience, Pub. Service Commn. of Pa., 1931-35; asst. dir. Bur. Motor Carriers, Interstate Commerce Commn., 1935-37, dir. since 1937. Served in inf., U.S.A., 1917-19. Mem. Alpha Chi Rho. Republican. Methodist. Mason. Author: Public Utility Regulation in Pennsylvania, 1924. Home: Williamstown, Pa. Office: Interstate Commerce Commn., Washington, D.C.

BLANSHARD, Brand, prof. philosophy; b. Fredericksburg, O., Aug. 27, 1892; s. Francis G. and Emily (Coulter) B.; A.B., U. of Mich., 1914; A.M., Columbia U., 1918; B.Sc., Oxford (Eng.), 1920; Ph.D., Harvard, 1921; m. Frances Bradshaw, 1918. Rhodes scholar, 1913-15, 1919-20; Guggenheim Fellow, 1929-30; asst. prof. philosophy, U. of Mich., 1921-25; asso. prof. philosophy, Swarthmore Coll., 1925-28, prof. since 1928; vis. prof., Columbia, 1931-32. Served with Y.M.C.A. with British Army in Mesopotamia and India, 1915-17; with A.E.F. in France, 1918-19. Mem. Am. Philos. Assn. (sec. Eastern Div., 1928-31), English Speaking Union, Phi Beta Kappa. Mem. Religious Soc. of Friends. Contbr. articles to philos. mags. and Jours. Home: 513 Ogden Av., Swarthmore, Pa.

BLANSHARD, Frances Bradshaw, dean of women; b. Fayette, Mo., May 12, 1895; d. Francis and Margaret (Rooker) Bradshaw; student Miss Copen's Sch., Northampton, Mass., 1907-12; A.B., Smith Coll., 1916; A.M., Columbia, 1918; student Univ. of Oxford (England), 1919-20; m. Brand Blanshard, Nov. 3, 1918. Teacher of English, Hollins Coll., 1918-19, Wellesley Coll., 1920-21, Ypsilanti (Mich.) State Teachers Coll., 1924-25; instr. in philosophy, Swarthmore Coll., 1925-26; acting dean of women, 1926-27, asso. dean, 1927-28, dean of women since 1928. Trustee Hollins Coll. Mem. Pa. Assn. Deans of Women, Nat. Assn. Deans of Women, Am. Philos. Assn., Phi Beta Kappa. Mem. Soc. of Friends. Clubs: Smith Coll., Womens University (Phila.). Home: 513 Ogden Av. Address: Swarthmore College, Swarthmore, Pa.

BLANTON, Darrell Elijah (Cy), professional baseball; b. Waureka, Okla., July 6, 1909. Began with Shawnee Club, 1930; pitcher Pittsburgh Nat. League Baseball Club since 1934; mem. Nat. League All-Star Team, 1937. Address: care Pittsburgh Nat. League Baseball Club, Pittsburgh, Pa.

BLANTON, James Lewis, M.D.; b. Ballsville, Va., June 1, 1899; s. Adolphus A. and Mary (Lee) B.; A.B., Randolph-Macon Coll., 1920; M.D., Med. Coll. of Va., 1924; post-grad.

BLASBAND   79   **BLESSING**

studies in pediatrics, Harvard Med. Sch., 1930; m. Bertha Jeannette Williams, Dec. 31, 1925; 1 son, James Oliver. In gen. practice of medicine, Fieldale, Va., 1924-29; in practice of pediatrics, Fairmont, W.Va., since 1930; mem. staff Cook Hosp., Fairmont State Hosp.; dir. Marion County Hosp. Service, Inc. Fellow Am. Coll. Physicians, Am. Academy Pediatrics; licentiate Am. Bd. Pediatrics; mem. A.M.A. Democrat. Methodist. Club: Rotary, Fairmont, W.Va. Home and Office: 207 Fairmont Av., Fairmont, W.Va.

BLASBAND, Alfred, banking; b. Phila., Pa., Aug. 31, 1905; s. Benjamin and Molly (Sobel) B.; ed. Central High Sch., 1920-24, U. of Pa., 1924-29; m. Gertrude Leventon, Nov. 10, 1928; children—Richard Alan, David. Sec. and treas. Bankers Securities Corpn. since 1935, also dir.; sec. and dir. Mark Store, Miami; dir. Bonwit, Teller & Co., City Stores Co., Lit Bros., Phila., Pa., Lowenstein's Memphis, Tenn., Courier-Post Co., Camden, N.J., Philadelphia Record Co., Phila., Pa., New York Post, New York City. Democrat. Jewish religion. Mason. Club: Ashbourne Country. Home: 6411 N. 13th St. Office: 1315 Walnut St., Philadelphia, Pa.

BLASINGAME, Ralph Upshaw, prof. agrl. engring., Pa. State Coll. Address: State College, Pa.

BLASS, Charles Arthur, lawyer; b. Erie, Pa., Dec. 17, 1884; s. Adam and Mary (Marks) B.; B.S. in economics, U. of Pa., 1907; J.D., U. of Mich., 1912; m. Annabelle Koehler, Dec. 30, 1907; children—Arlene Suzanne (Mrs. F. H. Dunn), Frederick Arthur. Admitted to Mich. bar, 1912, Pa. bar 1913, and since practiced at Erie, Pa.; mem. firm Craig & Blass, Erie, since 1922; asst. dist. atty., Erie Co., 1916-20, dist. atty., 1920-24. Mem. Com. on Pub. Safety (later Council of Nat. Defense), 1917-18. Republican. Lutheran. Clubs: University (founder, 1913), Erie, Kahkwa (Erie, Pa.). Home: 502 W. 7th St. Office: 802 Palace Hardware Bldg., Erie, Pa.

BLATT, A. S.; editor Easton Plain Dealer. Office: Church and Bank Sts., Easton, Pa.

BLATZ, John B.; mgr. Amalgamated Leather Companies, Inc., Wilmington, Del., since 1902, pres. and dir. since 1920. Home: 1900 Locust Street, Philadelphia, Pa. Office: Wilmington, Del.

BLATZ, William Charles, mfg. leather; b. Elizabeth, N.J., Mar. 14, 1881; s. Francis J. and Louisa (Eller) B.; student St. Benedict's Coll., Newark, N.J.; m. Edwina Keimig, May 24, 1904; children—Marie Rosalie (Mrs. Raymond Coakley), Anna Rita (Mrs. Bayard Berndt), William Charles Jeanne. Employed as tanner, 1900 and promoted through various positions to asst. supt., F. Blumenthal & Co., Wilmington, Del., later supt. then v.p. and dir., Amalgamated Leather Cos., Wilmington, Del., since 1920. Republican. Roman Catholic. Club: Wilmington (Del.) Country. Home: Fairville, Pa. Office: Amalgamated Leather Cos., Wilmington, Del.

BLAUCH, Victor Roy, supervising prin. of schools; b. Annville, Pa., July 17, 1893; s. U. Grant and Amanda (Fox) B.; grad. Annville High Sch., 1912; A.B., Lebanon Valley Coll., Annville, 1916; A.M., Columbia, 1924; m. Jennie Jones, Feb. 28, 1936; 1 dau., Mary Jeannine. Teacher of science, Brockway (Pa.) High Sch., 1916-17; prin. Leechburg (Pa.) High Sch., 1919-27; supervising prin. Leechburg Pub. Schs. since 1927. Served in Tank Corps, U.S. Army, 1917-18. Dir. Leechburg Y.M.C.A. Republican. Lutheran. Mason. Clubs: Rotary, Corinthian (Leechburg). Home: 565 2d St., Leechburg, Pa.

BLAUVELT, Bula Caswell (Mrs. Henry Scudder B.), organist; b. Jersey City, N.J.; d. Albert S. and Charlotte E. (Whitmore) Caswell; ed. Guilmant Organ Sch., N.Y. City; Inst. Mus. Art; m. Henry Scudder Blauvelt. Began professional mus. career as organist at age 19 yrs; organist various chs. in Jersey City; studios in Jersey City, Summit, and Montclair, N.J.; has given organ recitals in Jersey City, Pittsburgh, Riverside, Calif., and many other cities; now organist First Ch. of Christ Scientist, Orange, N.J.; composer of music for organ, piano, cello, violin, string quartet and voice. Mem. Am. Guild of Organists. Republican. Mem. Church of Christ Scientist: Clubs: Woman's, Music, Literary (Jersey City). Home: 57 Gardner Av., Jersey City, N.J.

BLAXTER, Henry Vaughan, lawyer; b. Derby, Eng., June 29, 1882; s. George Henry and Mary Louisa (Bishop) B.; came to U.S., 1885, naturalized, 1904; student St. Paul's Sch., Concord, N.H., 1898-1901; A.B., Harvard, 1903; LL.B., U. of Pittsburgh, 1907; m. Isabell Sloan Kennedy, Dec. 16, 1908; children—Henry Vaughan, Dorothy Bonbright, George Harold. Admitted to Pa. bar, 1907; partner in firm Lazear & Blaxter until 1917; mem. Blaxter & O'Neill, 1926-36, Blaxter, O'Neill & Houston since 1936; chmn. bd. Mackintosh-Hemphill Company; dir. and sec. American Adamite Co.; mem. bd. of dirs. Braeburn Alloy Steel Corpn., Universal Cyclops Steel Corpn., Pittsburgh Business Properties, Inc., Pittsburgh Hotels, Inc., Union Nat. Bank of Pittsburgh. Served as chmn. sub-com. on lower courts of justice of Pittsburgh Civic Assn., 1913. Trustee and v.p., Arnold School, Children's Hospital (Pittsburgh); dir. Employers Assn. of Pittsburgh, Legal Aid Soc. of Pittsburgh. Mem. Am., Pa. State and Allegheny bar assns.; asso. mem. Am. Iron & Steel Inst. Republican. Episcopalian (senior warden Calvary Ch., Pittsburgh). Clubs: Harvard-Yale-Princeton, Duquesne, Pittsburgh Golf, Fox Chapel Country (Pittsburgh); Harvard (New York). Home: 1414 Bennington Av. Office: Oliver Bldg., Pittsburgh, Pa.

BLAYDES, James Elliott, eye, ear, nose and throat specialist; b. Atoka, Tenn., June 13, 1892; s. Dr. James Elliott and Elizabeth (Boyd) B.; M.D., Vanderbilt U. Med Dept., Nashville, Tenn., 1914; m. Mabel Lucetta Hill, Dec. 7, 1922; children—James Elliott III, Nancy, Mabel Boyd. Interne Vanderbilt U. Hosp., Nashville, Tenn., 1914-15; mem. staff Bessemer (Ala.) Gen. Hosp., 1915-17; mem. house staff N.Y. Eye and Ear Infirmary, 1919-22; specialist in eye, ear, nose and throat, Bluefield, W.Va., since 1922; chief ophthalmologist and otolaryngologist St. Luke's Hosp., Bluefield, W.Va., since 1922; ophthalmologist and oto-rino-laryngologist W.Va. State Sch. for Deaf and Blind, Romney, W.Va., since 1931; v.p. Oakwood Smokeless Coal Co. since 1935; sec-treas.-mgr. Falls Mills Fishing Club since 1935. Served as 1st lt., Med. Corps, U.S. Army, 1917-19. Dir. Union Mission. Fellow Am. Coll. Surgeons; mem. A.M.A., W.Va. Med. Assn. (pres. eye, ear, nose and throat section 1937), Mercer Co. Med. Assn., Southern Med. Assn., Alpha Tau Omega, Alpha Kappa Kappa. Democrat. Presbyterian. Clubs: Kiwanis, University, Bluefield Country, Bluefield Gun, Falls Mills Fishing (Bluefield, W.Va.). Author: Blindness from the Practioner's Standpoint, 1933; Report on the Blind and Visually Handicapped in West Virginia, 1933; A Few Points in Connection with Lighting and Seeing, 1935. Home: Edgewood Road. Office: 107 Federal St., Bluefield, W.Va.

BLAYNE, Howard Samuel, author; b. Belfast, Ireland, July 19, 1869; s. Thomas and Mary C. (Murphy) B.; m. Mabel Alice Rankin, Apr. 14, 1888. Author: The Wanderers in Siberia, 1907; The Boy Captain of the Pacific, 1908; The Wanderers in Thibet, 1910; The Wanderers in Darkest Africa, 1912. Home: Philadelphia, Pa.

BLAZEK, Paul, printer and pub.; b. Czechoslovakia, Dec. 9, 1889; s. Paul and Christine (Burian) B.; ed. normal and craft schs., Czechoslovakia, Printers' Art Sch., Germany, Carnegie Tech., Pittsburgh; m. Anna Jakab, Apr. 12, 1913; children—Helen A., Milan J., Eva (Mrs. Schafer), Dusan P., Irene A. Came to U.S., 1907, naturalized, 1915. Began as printer, 1902, has been mgr. various printing concerns and owner of printing shops in New York and Pittsburgh; editor of Zivena. Home: 1716 Crosby Av. Office: 342 Boul. of Allies, Pittsburgh, Pa.

BLEAKLY, Edwin G(uy) C(ooper), lawyer; b. Wellsville, O., Oct. 5, 1865; s. William and Elizabeth (Armstrong) B.; ed. Camden grammar and high sch., 1877-80, Penn's Business Coll., Phila., 1880-91, Friends Central Sch., Phila., 1882-85; m. Ida Seymour, July 24, 1894 (deceased); 1 dau., Edith Bryan. Admitted to N.J. bar, Feb. 1890, and since practiced in Camden; mem. firm Bleakly, Stockwell, Lewis & Zink; city counsel, Camden, 1898-1900, 1901-23, 1931-37; dir. of Stockton Bldg. & Loan Assn., South Ward Bldg. & Loan Assn. Republican. Methodist. Home: 318 Cooper St. Office: 1107 N.J. Trust Bldg., Camden, N.J.

BLEAKNEY, Edward Milton, clergyman; b. Salisbury, New Brunswick, Can., July 20, 1890; s. Alexander William and Lenora (Carr) B.; B.A., Acadia Univ., 1913; B.D., Newton Theol. Sem., 1915; S.T.M., 1922; D.D., Waynesberg Coll., 1935; m. Lila Vivian Corbett, June 22, 1915; children—Vivian Lenora, Dorothy Margaret. Came to U.S., 1913, naturalized, 1921. Ordained to ministry of Baptist Ch., 1915; minister Bapt. Ch., Stoneham, Mass., 1915-19, Hyde Park, Boston, 1919-22; minister Tabernacle Bapt. Ch., Utica, N.Y., 1922-28, Mount Lebanon Bapt. Ch., Pittsburgh, 1928-37; lecturer League of Nations Assn. since 1937. Home: 125 Marlin Drive, E., Pittsburgh, Pa.

BLEAKNEY, Walker, asso. prof. physics; b. Shelocta, Pa., Feb. 8, 1901; s. Robert Wilson and Wilda (Hall) B.; B.S., Whitman Coll., 1924; ed. Harvard U., 1924-25; Ph.D., U. of Minn., 1930; grad. study, Princeton U., 1930-32; m. Dorothy Clyde Thomas, July 16, 1931. Instr. of physics, Princeton U., 1932-35, asst. prof., 1935-38, asso. prof. since 1938. Fellow Am. Phys. Soc. Mem. Phi Bata Kappa, Sigma Xi, Phi Delta Theta. Home: Princeton-Kingston Rd. Address: Palmer Laboratory, Princeton, N.J.

BLEININGER, Albert Victor, chemist; b. Polling, Bavaria, July 9, 1873; s. Francis and Lina (Pfeifer) B.; prep. edn., Munich, Germany; came to U.S., 1887; shop experience in clay industries, 1889-96; B.S. in chemistry, Ohio State U., 1901, Ceramic Engr., 1931, Lamme medal from the same univ., 1932; D.Sc., Alfred University, 1933; m. Hulda Gertrude Thomson, June 7, 1907; children—Edward Orton, Alice Vivien. Instr. in ceramics, 1901-05, asst. prof., 1905-06, asso. prof., 1906-07, Ohio State U.; asst. prof. ceramics, U. of Ill., 1907-08; chief, clay products sect. U.S. Geol. Survey, 1908-10, U.S. Bur. of Standards, 1910-11; prof. and dir. dept. ceramics, U. of Ill., 1910-12; in charge of ceramics div., Nat. Bur. of Standards, Pittsburgh, 1912-20. Chemist, Homer Laughlin China Co. since 1920. Asst., Ohio Geol. Survey, 1900-04. Chairman sub-committee on ceramic chemistry Nat. Research Council; chmn.. research com. U.S. Potters' Assn. Mem. Sigma Xi, Acacia, Alpha Chi Sigma; fellow A.A.A.S.; mem. Am. Chem. Soc. (asst. editor Abstract Jour.), Am. Ceramic Soc. (pres. 1908; editor Trans., 1905-07). Author: The Manufacture of Hydraulic Cements, 1904. Editor Collected Works of H. A. Seger, 1903. Contbr. to periodicals on the silicate industries. Home: Newell, W.Va.*

BLENKO, Walter J(ohn), lawyer; b. London, Eng., Mar. 4, 1899; s. William John and Sarah (Balman) B.; came to U.S., 1899, naturalized, 1900; B.S., Carnegie Inst. of Tech., Pittsburgh, 1921; LL.B., Duquesne U., Pittsburgh, 1924; m. Ardis L. Jones, Sept. 15, 1921; children—Walter John, Don Balman. Admitted to Pa. bar, 1924, and since practiced at Pittsburgh; mem. firm Stebbins, Blenko & Parmelee. Vice-pres. Children's Service Bureau; dir. The Community Fund of Allegheny Co., Civic Club of Allegheny Co., Pittsburgh Housing Assn. Served in Royal Air Force, British Army, 1918-19. Mem. Am. Soc..M.E., Engrs. Soc. of Western Pa., Tau Beta Pi, Sigma Alpha Epsilon. Clubs: Duquesne, University (Pittsburgh). Home: Middle Road, Allison Park, Pa. Office: Farmers Bank Bldg., Pittsburgh, Pa.

BLESSING, Riley Andrew, lawyer; b. nr. Letart, W.Va., Dec. 11, 1875; s. Calvin Thomas and Sarah Josephine (Board) B.; student Spencer (W.Va.) Normal School, 1897-98; LL.B., George Washington University, 1906; m. Delitha May Van Matre, Apr. 21, 1897; children—Leolia Genevieve (Mrs. Curtis M. Young), Beulah Gay, Robert Leslie; granddaughter, Bettie Mae

Young. School teacher, 1894-1900; clerk to county sheriff, 1900-02; admitted to D.C. and W.Va. bars, 1906; admitted to practice before U.S. Supreme Court, 1911; mem. firm Butz & Blessing, Washington, D.C., 1907-11, Musgrave & Blessing, Point Pleasant, W.Va., since 1912; mem. Lee, Blessing & Steed, Charlestown, W.Va., since 1933. Treas. Rep. County Com., 1902-04; mem. W.Va. Senate, 1912-16; asst. state tax commr., 1917-20; asst. atty. gen. W. Va., 1921-23. Mem. Am., W.Va. State and local bar assns.; life mem. Columbia-George Washington Alumni Assn. Republican. Baptist; sec. Ohio Assn. of Independent Bapt. Chs. since 1933. K.P., Woodman. Clubs: Lions, Business Men's. Home: 1 Buena Vista Pl. Office: Union Bldg., Charleston, W.Va.

BLEW, Michael James, chemical engineer; b. Wabash, Ind., Nov. 9, 1891; s. James Madison Blew and Hannah (Blew) B.; student Wabash (Ind.) Pub. Schs., 1898-1906, Wabash High Sch., 1906-10; A.B., Ind. U., Bloomington, Ind., 1915, A.M., 1916; postgraduate work, Yale, 1920-21; m. Daisy McAllister, Aug. 21, 1917; 1 dau., Mary Anna. Began as instr. chemistry dept. Ind. U., Bloomington, Ind., 1914-17; asso. prof. chemistry, U. of Louisville Med. Sch., 1919-20; instr. bacteriology, Yale, 1920-21; spl. studies, Nat. Canners Assn., Northern Ind., 1920; survey of Genesee River, Rochester, N.Y., 1920; spl. studies U.S.P.H.S., 1921; in charge experimental work, Dorr Co., Rochester, N.Y., 1921-23; san. engr. Schuylkill River Pollution Bd., Schuylkill Basin at Phila., 1923-30; instr. in municipal engring., Drexel Inst. of Tech., Phila., since 1925; consultant Camden Co. Sewage Survey Commn., 1929; in charge sewage research, stream pollution investigations, industrial waste, etc., Bureau of Engring., Phila., since 1923; consultant Capon Springs Water Co., Capon Springs, W.Va., since 1923. First lt. and capt. San. Corps with A.E.F., 1917-19, now lt. col. Officers Reserve Corps on spl. duty in connection with sewage and san. problems; instr. in mil. sanitation, summer training camps. Mem. Am. Assn. Mil. Surgeons, Am. Soc. Mil. Engrs., Reserve Officers Assn., Am. Inst. Chem. Engrs., Am. Inst. of Chemists, Am. Pub. Health Assn., Phi Chi, Alpha Chi Sigma, Sigma Xi, Order of the Boar. Registered engineer. Republican. Episcopalian. Mason, Sojourner. Author: text book on san. bacteriology for san. engrs. and articles on stream pollution and sewage and waste treatment. Address: Richmond St. and Wheatsheaf Lane, Philadelphia, Pa.

BLINN, Charles Payson, Jr., banker; b. Boston, Mass., Feb. 5, 1879; s. Charles Payson and Ida Ware (Chadbourne) B.; ed. pub. schs., Boston; m. Etta Gallison, Oct. 11, 1905; children—Marian (Mrs. Allison E. McCown, Jr.), Marjorie; m. 2d, Laura Maryland Carpenter Tappan, Apr. 13, 1937. Assistant treasurer City Trust Co., Boston, 1905-08; v.p. Nat. Union Bank, Boston, 1908-16; v.p. The Philadelphia Nat. Bank since 1916, dir. since 1926. Republican. Episcopalian. Clubs: Union League, Downtown, Merion Cricket (Philadelphia); Eastern Yacht (Marblehead, Mass.). Home: 211 Glenn Rd., Ardmore, Pa. Office: 421 Chestnut St., Philadelphia, Pa.

BLISS, Elmer Jared, Jr., pres. Regal Shoe Co.; b. Boston, Mass., May 18, 1904; s. Elmer Jared and Lina (Harding) B.; ed. Middlesex Sch., Concord, Mass., 1917-22, Harvard, 1922-26; m. Edith Sears Bartow, Nov. 29, 1934. With Regal Shoe Co., mfr. and retail sale of men's shoes since 1927, successively as jr. salesman in retail store, store mgr., mem. merchandise dept., asst. sales mgr., sales mgr., v.p. in charge operations and since 1934 pres. and dir. Mem. Southern Mass. Yacht Racing Assn. (treas. and mem. exec. com.). Republican. Episcopalian. Clubs: Harvard, Racquet and Tennis (New York); Seawanhaka Corinthian Yacht (Oyster Bay); Algonquin, Norfolk Hunt (Boston); Edgarton Yacht (Martha's Vineyard, Mass.); Spring Valley Hounds (Morristown, N.J.). Home: Blue Hill Rd., Morristown, N.J. Office: 111 8th Av., New York, N.Y.

BLISS, Robert Pratt, librarian; b. Lewisburg, Pa., Aug. 13, 1861; s. George Ripley and Mary Ann (Raymond) B.; ed. Chester Acad., Pa., Doylestown Acad., Pa.; New York Nautical Sch., New York, 1883; unmarried. Spent 1881-85 on the sea; with Delaware County Rep., Chester, Pa., 1885-93; librarian Crozer Theol. Sem., 1893-1906; asst. sec. Pa. Free Library Commn., 1906-19; chief of div. of library extension, Pa. State Library and Museum, 1919-27, retired. Camp librarian, Camp Hancock, Ga., 1917-18 (on leave). Mem. A.L.A. (life), League of Library Commns. (v.p.), Keystone State Library Assn. (sec., 1902-07, pres., 1910-11). Republican. Baptist. Club: Harrisburg. Address: Harrisburg Club, Harrisburg, Pa.*

BLISS, Sydney Rushton, pres. Bliss Silk Throwing Co.; b. Maclesfield, Eng., Nov. 19, 1878; s. Valentine and Mary Ann (Rushton) B.; brought to U.S., 1879, naturalized, 1898; grad. Paterson (N.J.) Classical Scientific Sch., 1895; m. Helen Gertrude Jones, July 27, 1912; children—Helen Jones (dec.), Mary Constance (Mrs. James Wood Johnson Carpenter), Eleanor Elizabeth, Natalie Rushton, Shirley. Began as asst. timekeeper, Paterson, N.J., 1895; with Bliss Silk Throwing Co., Scranton, Pa., since 1896, now pres.; v.p. R. D. Richardson Construction Co.; pres. North Scranton Bank and Trust Co.; v.p. Scranton Industrial Development Co. Republican. Episcopalian. Clubs: Scranton, Green Redge (Scranton); Scranton Country (Clarks Summit, Pa.). Address: 923 Electric St., Scranton, Pa.

BLISS, William Julian Albert, physicist; b. Washington, Jan. 22, 1867; s. Alexander and Ellen Taylor (Albert) B.; A.B., Harvard, 1888; certificate in elec. engring., Johns Hopkins, 1890, Ph.D., 1894; m. Edith Grantham West, Nov. 19, 1896; children—Eleanor Albert, Frances McDowell (Mrs. M. Dawson Tyson). Asst. in elec. engring, 1890-91, lecturer in physics, 1894-95, asst., 1895-98, asso., 1898-1901, collegiate prof. physics, 1901-28, Johns Hopkins, now emeritus. Fellow Am. Phys. Soc.; mem. Alpha Delta Phi. Episcopalian. Clubs: Maryland, Elkridge. Author: Manual of Experiments in Physics (with J. S. Ames), 1897. Home: 1026 N. Calvert St., Baltimore, Md.

BLIZZARD, Reese, lawyer, banker; b. Nicholas Co., W.Va.; s. James and Elizabeth (Gill) B.; grad. Glenville (W.Va.) State Normal Sch.; m. Lilly Stump; children—Reese, Roy, Pearl, Ethel; m. 2d, Fannie Holland; children—Paul, Pansy, Fannie. Served as school teacher, lawyer, newspaper owner and editor, mfr. of ice, etc.; now pres. Commercial Banking & Trust Co. Formerly circuit judge at 4th Jud. Circuit of W.Va., and U.S. dist. atty., W.Va. Mem. President's Unemployment. Com., 1931. Pres. Nat. Trotting Assn. Republican. Home: Parkersburg, W.Va.*

BLOCH, Chaim Isaac, rabbi; b. Plunge, Lithuania, Sept. 22, 1865; s. Zundel and Gitte Sarah (Meshulami) B.; grad. gymnasium, Palongen, Lithuania, 1904; rabbi, Seminary, Valozen, Poland, 1888; came to U.S., 1923, naturalized, 1928; m. Hanah Schmidt, 1890; children—Sheine Hena (Mrs. Sender Sienitzicy), Moses Leib, Max, Elias, Sheftel Jonah, Hinde Ruth (Mrs. Joseph Friedman), Abraham Philip. Rabbi, Palongen, Lithuania, 1900-05, Bausk, Latvia, 1905-23; rabbi, Jersey City, N.J., since 1923; v.p. central com. Knesseth Israel, Jerusalem, Palestine; treas. Ezras Torah Fund; dir. Orphan and Old Age Home, Jersey City, N.J. Hon. pres. Union of Orthodox Rabbis of U.S. and Can. since 1933. Author: Divrei Chibo on Moed Koton, 1935, Divrei Chibo on Megilah, 1937; Divrei Chibo on Makoth. Address: 504 Bergen Av., Jersey City, N.J.

BLOCH, Jesse A.; pres. Bloch Bros. Tobacco Co. Home: Pleasant Valley. Office: 4000 Water St., Wheeling, W.Va.

BLOCH, Julius, artist; b. Kehl, Baden, Germany, May 12, 1888; s. Nathan and Emma (Bernheimer) B.; came to U.S. 1893, naturalized, 1907; ed. Central High Sch., Phila., 1901-05, Pa. Mus. and Sch. of Industrial Art, 1905-08; Pa. Acad. of Fine Arts, 1908-12; unmarried. Represented in permanent collections in the White House by "Young Worker"; Corcoran Gallery, Washington, D.C., by "The Striker;" Phila. Mus. of Art, by "Prisoner"; Whitney Mus. of Am. Art; Pa. Acad. of Fine Arts; etc. Hon. mention Worcester Art Mus., 1934; Print Club (Phila.) Prize, 1933. Home: Malvern, Pa. Address: 10 S. 18th St., Philadelphia, Pa.

BLOCHER, Nellie K.; prof. edn., Hood Coll. Address: Hood Coll., Frederick, Md.

BLOCK, Frank Benton, surgeon; b. Phila., Pa., June 20, 1890; s. Louis B. and Reada A. (Mayer) B.; A.B., Central High Sch., Phila., 1907; M.D., U. of Pa., 1911; m. Etta N. Stauffer, May 1, 1921; children—Ruth Carolyn, Frank Benton, Robert L. Began as surgeon, 1913; surgeon to Jewish Hosp., Phila., since 1919; asso. in gynecology, Med. Sch., U. of Pa., 1913-31. Served as 1st lt., Med. Corps, U.S. Army, attached to 34th F.A. during World War. Diplomate Am. Bd. Surgery. Fellow Am. Coll. Surgeons; mem. A.M.A., Coll. of Physicians of Phila. Home: 5725 Park Av. Office: Medical Arts Bldg., Philadelphia, Pa.

BLODGETT, Francis Branch, theologian; b. Oakfield, N.Y., Feb. 27, 1875; s. Alva John and Catherine (Burt) Blodgett; B.A., Hobart Coll., Geneva, N.Y., 1899; D.D. from same coll., 1932; B.D., Episcopal Theol. Sch., Cambridge, Mass., 1902; S.T.B., Harvard, 1904; m. Mary Elizabeth Gove, Dec. 28, 1909; children—Catherine Cordelia, Mary Elizabeth. Deacon, 1902, priest, 1903, P.E. Ch.; rector Ch. of Our Redeemer, Lexington, Mass., 1902-04; canon All Saints Cathedral, Albany, N. Y., 1904-05; instr. in O.T., 1906-08, prof., 1908-21, Gen. Theol. Sem.; dean Cathedral of St. Paul, Erie, Pa., since 1921. Home: 129 W. 6th St., Erie, Pa.

BLONDHEIM, Adolphe Wiener, artist; b. Baltimore, Md., Oct. 16, 1888; s. Solomon Samuel and Bella (Wiener) B.; ed. pub. schs. and Md. Inst., Baltimore, Md., Pa. Acad. of Fine Arts, Phila., Pa.; m. Elsie Stein, June 12, 1913; 1 son, Adolphe W., Jr. Engaged as painter of portraits, and etcher since 1911, figure painter, etcher, and lithographer; instr. art, Telfair Acad., Savannah, Ga., 1921; instr. painting, Art Inst., Kansas City, Mo., 1924-26; rep. by mural, State Capitol, Jefferson City, Mo., 1922; exhbns. in leading cities. Served as sergt. engrs., U.S.A., with A.E.F. during World War. Mem. Chicago Soc. of Etchers. Awarded 2d Tappan Prize, Pa. Acad. Fine Arts, 1909, Cresson Traveling Scholarship (same), 1911, Isidor gold medal, Nat. Acad. of Design, 1918, Logan Medal for etching, Art Inst., Chicago, 1920, gold medal, Mid-Western Artists Exhbn., 1925, also silver medal for etching (same), 1925. Democrat. Jewish religion. Home: New Hope, Pa.

BLOSS, James Ramsdell, M.D., b. Ceredo, W.Va., Sept. 5, 1881; s. Hiram Wesley and Carrie Lee (Ramsdell) B.; grad. high sch., Huntington, W.Va., 1900; M.D., U. of Va., 1905; m. Garnett Lucille Coleman, Oct. 17, 1906 (died Feb. 11, 1930); m. 2d, Muessette A. Hollobaugh, July 14, 1932. Interne Chesapeake & Ohio Ry. Hosp., 1905; asst. supt. Huntington State Hosp. for the Insane, 1906-13; practiced at Huntington since 1913; obstetrician in charge of dept., C.&O. Hosp., Huntington; lecturer on obstetrics for nurses, St. Mary's Hosp., mem. attending staff same (pres. 1934); visiting staffs Memorial and Guthrie hosps., Huntington. Editor W.Va. Med. Jour., 1916-26, asst. editor, 1926-27, editor in chief, 1927-37, editor emeritus since 1937; med. examiner Mental Hygiene Commn., Cabell County, W.Va. Med. examiner Selective Draft Bd., Huntington, World War. Fellow Am. Coll. Surgeons, A.M.A. (mem. house of delegates, 1920-35; trustee 1935—), Am. Assn. Obstetricians, Gynecologists and Abdominal Surgeons (acting sec. 1935; sec. since 1936), Am. Psychiatric Assn.; mem. W.Va. Obstretric and Gynecol. Soc. (sec. treas. 1936). W. Va. State Med. Assn. (pres. 1926; chmn. maternal welfare com.), Southern Med. Assn. (mem. council 1932-38; chmn. of council, 1935; vice chairman section of obstetrics, 1935; chmn. sect. of obstetrics, 1936), Southern Assn. Ry. Surgeons, Chesapeake & Ohio Ry. Surgeons Assn., W.Va. Acad. Science, Pan-Am. Med. Assn., Central Tri-State Med. Assn. Republican. Methodist. Home: 79 Kings Highway. Office: 418 11th St., Huntington, W.Va.

BLOUGH, Elijah Robert, M.D.; b. Somerset Co., Pa., Apr. 7, 1878; s. Benjamin and Rachel (Berkey) B.; Pharm.D., Phila. Coll. Pharmacy, 1902; M.D., Eclectic Med. Coll., Cincinnati, O., 1907; m. Catherine E. Bevan, June 29, 1910. Began practice at Carrick Borough, now part of Pittsburgh, 1908; owner Carrick Pharmacy, 1908-13. Served as 1st lt. Med. Corps, U.S.A., World War. Mem. Nat. Eclectic Med. Assn. (pres. 1932-33), Pa. Eclectic Med. Assn. (ex-pres.; corr. sec.), Pa. Eclectic Med. Soc., Allegheny Co. Med. Soc., Sigma Theta. Republican. Baptist. Mason (32°), Shriner. Home: 1823 Brownsville Rd., Pittsburgh, Pa.

BLOUIN (Edmeé), Sister Marie Elise, prof. French; b. Montmagny, P.Q., Apr. 29, 1886; d. Dr. J. B. and Helmina (Dionne) B.; came to U.S. 1909, naturalized, 1929; A.B., Seton Hill Coll., 1924; A.M., McGill U., 1930; D. es Lettres (Ph.D.), Montreal U., 1934; study, summer schs., D'Youvelle Coll., 1915, U. of Pittsburgh, 1918, Coll. of New Rochelle, 1917, 1918, 1919, U. of Chicago, 1920, Western Res. U., 1925. Entered the Sisters of Charity of Mother Seton, Oct. 1911. Instr. French, St. Joseph's Acad., Greensburg, Pa. 1909-11, Jr. Coll., Seton Hill, 1912-18; head of French dept., Seton Hill Coll. since 1918; instr. Sisters' Classes, Knights of Columbus, Pittsburgh, 1918-20; hostess and instr., Sisters Coll. of Cleveland in cooperation with Western Res. U., summer 1936. Founder, 1938, and first pres. Cath. Assn. Religious Teachers Mod. Langs. Founder Le Cercle Gaulois, 1937. Mem. Societe des Profs. Francais en Amerique, Am. Assn. Teachers of French, Nat. Fed. Mod. Langs., Pa. State Mod. Lang. Teachers Assn., Sigma Kappa Phi. Roman Catholic. Home: Seton Hill Coll., Greensburg, Pa.

BLUE, Frederick Omar, lawyer; b. Grafton, W.Va., Nov. 25, 1872; s. George Frederick and Mary Martha (See) B.; ed. high sch. and under tutors; m. Margaret Jarvis Ice, Nov. 26, 1895. Began practice at Philippi, W.Va., 1893, also engaged in banking; asso. in practice at Philippi with Arthur S. Dayton, 1908-11; mem. Blue, Dayton & Campbell; dir. Charleston Nat. Bank. Mem. W.Va. Senate, 1906-10; state tax commr. of W.Va., 1911-17, also chief insp. and supervisor pub. offices of W.Va., 1911-17; mem. W. Va. Mining Strike Commn., 1912-13; state commr. of Prohibition of W.Va., 1914-17, successfully conducting litigation to Supreme Court of U.S. sustaining Webb-Kenyon Law. Mem. Am. Bar Assn., Nat. Tax Assn. Republican. Baptist. Mason (33°, Shriner). Author: When a State Goes Dry, 1916. Home: 853 Edgewood Drive. Office: Security Bldg., Charleston, W.Va.

BLUE, William Frederick, lawyer; b. Philippi, W.Va., June 29, 1897; s. Frederick Omar and Margaret (Ice) B.; student Bingham Mil. Sch., Asheville, N.C., 1915-18; LL.B., W.Va. Univ. Law Coll., 1925; m. Elizabeth Pratt, Feb. 7, 1925; children—Frederick Omar II, Nancy Elizabeth. Admitted to W.Va. bar, 1925 and since engaged in gen. practice of law at Charleston; mem. firm Blue, Dayton & Campbell since 1925. Mem. W.Va. State Bar Assn., Charleston Bar Assn., Beta Theta Pi. Republican. Baptist. Mason. Club. Edgewood Country (Charleston). Home: 916 Highland Rd. Office: Security Bldg., Charleston, W.Va.

BLUETT, Thomas; judge Municipal Court of Phila., since 1928. Address: Municipal Court, Philadelphia, Pa.

BLUM, Louis Philip, civil engring.; b. Phila., Pa., Apr. 28, 1873; s. Jacob and Catherine (Hoffman) B.; A.B., Boys' Central High Sch., Phila., 1891; m. Clara A. Mendel, Feb. 21, 1906; children—Katherine C., Louis M., George W., Howard E. In employ 8th Survey Dist., Phila., Pa., 1891-1901; asst. engr. and prin. asst. engr. in field and office, W. G. Wilkins Co., Pittsburgh, Pa., 1901-16; mem. firm Blum, Weldin & Co., civil and mining engring. and surveying, specializing in municipal work, Pittsburgh, Pa., since 1916. Mem. Engrs. Soc. of Western Pa., Am. Soc. of Civil Engrs. (mem. bd. Pittsburgh Sect.), Masonic Vets. Assn. Republican. Lutheran. Home: 3070 Watson Boul. Office: Bakewell Bldg., Pittsburgh, Pa.

BLUM, William, chemist; b. Phila., Pa., Dec. 28, 1881; s. Jacob and Catherine (Hoffman) B.; B.S., U. of Pa., 1903; Ph.D., 1908; m. Willetta Carr Bayliss, Sept. 20, 1910; 1 son, William, Instr. in chemistry, U. of Utah, 1903-08, asst. prof. 1908-09; with U.S. Bur. of Standards, Washington, since 1909, chemist since 1918. Mem. Am. Chem. Soc., A.A.A.S., Washington Acad. Sciences, Am. Electrochem. Soc. (pres. 1926); hon. mem. Am. Electroplaters' Soc., Sigma Xi. Awarded medal Inst. of Chemists, "for distinguished governmental service," 1926. Chmn. Citizens Com., Sec. 4, Chevy Chase, Md., 1916-26. Clubs: Chemists (New York); Cosmos (Washington). Author: (with G. B. Hogaboom) Principles of Electroplating and Electroforming, 1924, 2d edit., 1930; also articles on analytical and electrochemistry. Home: 215 Elm St., Chevy Chase, Md. Office: Nat. Bureau of Standards, Washington, D.C.

BLUMBERG, Harry S., metallurgist; b. Chicago, Ill., Apr. 28, 1897; s. Samuel and Gussie (Steinberg) B.; grad. Crane Coll., Chicago, 1915; m. Isabel Fromert, Aug. 19, 1930; children—John R. Joan M. Shepley. Asst. chemist, Sears Roebuck & Co., Chicago 1915-16; chemist Ill. Tool Works, Chicago, 1916-18, asst. metallurgist, 1919-20; metallurgist, Ill. Steel Corpn., South Chicago, 1920-22, A. O. Smith Corpn., Milwaukee, 1922-25, Paper & Textile Machinery Corpn., Sandusky, O., 1925-26; chief metallurgist, M. W. Kellogg Co., Jersey City, N.J., since 1926. Enlisted in U.S. Naval Reserve Force, May 1918; hon. discharged, Apr. 1919. Mem. Am. Welding Soc. (mem. filler metal specifications com.), Am. Soc. for Metals (exec. com. N.Y. chapter). Jewish religion. Contbr. to handbooks of Am. Welding Soc. and Am. Soc. for Metals. Home: 428 Lafayette St., New York, N.Y. Office: care M. W. Kellogg Co., Foot of Danforth Av., Jersey City, N.J.

BLUMBERG, Jacob, M.D.; attending surgeon Elizabeth Gen. Hosp. Address: 504 Westminster Av., Elizabeth, N.J.

BLUMBERG, Leo, engr. and univ. prof.; b. Wilmington, Del., July 22, 1894; s. Morris Karl and Gertrude (Bloch) B.; B.S. in E.E., U. of Del., Newark, Del., 1916, E.E., 1919, B.S. in M.E., 1924, M.E., 1927; student Purdue U., Lafayette, Ind., summer 1929; grad. work Temple U., Phila., Pa., since 1936; m. Julia Thelma Baum, Aug. 9, 1938. Test engr. Tabor Exptl. Lab., Wilmington, Del., 1916, Gen. Electric Co., Schenectady, N.Y., and Pittsfield, Mass., 1916-18; gen. engr. Aetna Explosives Co., New York, 1918-19; instr. mech. engring., U. of Del., Newark, Del., 1919-23, asst. prof., 1923-28, asso. prof. mech. engring. since 1928; cons. work since 1925. Served as sergt., Constrn. Div., U.S. Army, during World War. Mem. Del. Bd. of Boiler Rules since 1927. Mem. Am. Soc. M.E., Soc. for Promotion of Engineering. Edn., Am. Assn. Univ. Professors, American Legion (Post 1, Wilmington), Athenean Lit. Soc., Sigma Tau Phi, Tau Beta Pi (mem. exec. com. Wilmington chapter), Phi Kappa Phi. Clubs: Monarch, M.M.B. Soc., Young Men's Republican (Wilmington); Faculty (Newark, Del.). Home: 4 E. 14th St., Wilmington, Del. Office: University of Delaware, Newark, Del.

BLUMBERG, Nathan, M.D.; b. Phila., Pa., May 25, 1887; s. Harris and Rebecca (Kraus) B.; graduated Central High Sch., Philadelphia; M.D., Jefferson Medical Coll.; m. Rectavia Deutch, Jan. 4, 1914; children—M. Jack, Theodore Thomas. Physician and surgeon, Phila., since 1907; visiting physician Phila. Gen. Hosp.; asso. prof. of medicine, Temple University; asso. visiting physician Jewish Hospital, Philadelphia; medical director Brith Sholom; consulting physician Eastern State Penitentiary and Phila. County prisons. Served as contract surgeon, rank 1st lt., U.S. Army, 1918. Certified internist by Bd. Internal Medicine. Fellow Am. Coll. Physicians, A.M.A., Am. Coll. Chest Physicians; Mem. Phila. Co. Med. Soc., Phi Delta Epsilon. Jewish religion. Mason. Address: 1922 Spruce St., Philadelphia, Pa.

BLUMENTHAL, Hart, retired cigar mfr.; b. Phila., Pa., May 25, 1859; s. David and Eva (Baum) B.; ed. pub. schs., Phila., Peirce Commercial Coll., Phila.; m. Ida Rawitch, Jan. 29, 1882; children—Walter Hart, Ralph David (deceased). Bookkeeper, Blumenthal Bros. & Co., Phila., 1874-80; bookkeeper, Clinton, Ia., 1880-87; merchant, Blumenthal & Selig, mfrs. gas fixtures and art metal work, Phila., 1887-99; head of firm, Simon Mfg. Co., mfrs. cigars, Phila., 1901-19; retired 1919. Hon. pres. Temple Keneseth Israel since 1922 (v.p., 1924-37, pres., 1893-1939); organizer and chmn. Temple Free Library (non-sectarian); organizer and chmn. Nat. Farm Sch. (chmn. finance com.). Mem. Lincoln Fellowship of Pa., Dickens Fellowship of Pa. Awarded Diploma Medal, 1937, by Temple Keneseth Israel Alumni. Mason (Shekinah Lodge, Keystone Chapter). Address: Rittenhouse Plaza, 1901 Walnut St., Philadelphia, Pa.

BLUMER, Max A.; acting chief orthopedic surgeon Montefiore Hosp.; orthopedic surgeon Falk Clinic. Address: 3401 Fifth Av., Pittsburgh, Pa.

BLUNDON, Joseph Paul, cons. engr.; b. Riverdale, Md., June 30, 1897; s. Joseph and Fannie Petronella (Waters) B.; student LaSalle Acad., Muirkirk, Md., 1908-10, Carroll Inst., Washington, D.C., 1910-11; B.S. in C.E., U. of Md., 1915; C.E., Cornell U., 1917; m. Catherine Elizabeth Smith, Aug. 2, 1920; 1 son, Joseph Andrew. Began as inspector Washington (D.C.) Steel & Ordinance Co., 1915; held position of chief inspector with Midvale Steel Co., Nicetown, Pa. (mfrs. artillery ammunition), 1916; 1st lieut. Corps Engrs., with Constructing Q.M., U.S. Army, in design and construction of water supply system, Camp Meade, Md., 1917-18; county engr. on highway construction, Boone Co., W.Va., 1919-21; asst. div. engr. covering 10 counties on $50,000,000 construction program W.Va. State Rd. Commn., 1921-24; consulting engr. with special attention to utility rate litigation since 1924, representing cities of Toledo, Columbus and Cincinnati; mem. W.Va. Bd. of Engrs.; pres. Tri-State Utilities Corpn., Milton Water Co. Mem. Am. Soc. C.E., Am. Waterworks Assn., Soc. of Testing Materials, W.Va. Engring. Soc. (dir.). Republican. Catholic. Elk, K.C. Clubs: Cumberland Country, Cumberland Jockey; Keyser Golf. Home: 94 S. Main St. Office: 81 Orchard St., Keyser, W.Va.

BOAL, Pierre de Lagarde, diplomatic service; b. of Am. parents at Thonon-les-Bains, France, Sept. 29, 1895; s. Theodore Davis and Mathilde (de Lagarde) B.; ed. St. Paul's Sch., Concord, N. H.; m. Jeanne de Menthon, June 10, 1919. Apptd. sec. of Embassy, Dec. 20, 1919, and assigned to Mexico City; with Dept. of State, sec. Internat. Conf. on Elec. Communication, Washington, 1920; assigned to Belgrade, Dec. 1920, Warsaw, 1922; 2d sec. Legation, Berne, 1924, Lima, Sept. 1925, 1st sec., Dec. 1925; returned to Dept. of State, 1928; sec. Internat. Conf. of Am. States on Concilation and Arbitration, Washington, 1928-29; acting sec. gen. Commn. of Inquiry and Concilation of Bolivia and Paraguay, Washington, 1929; apptd. asst. chief Div. of Western European Affairs, Dept. of State, June 24, 1930, apptd. chief of same, June 20, 1931; chargé d'affaires Am. Legation, Ottawa, Can., Sept. 1932-May 1933, consul gen. Aug. 1935; assigned to Toronto, 1935 (cancelled) as counselor Legation of Ottawa, 1935; counselor Am. Embassy, Mexico City, Apr. 30, 1936; adviser Prep. Commn. for Disarmament Conf., Geneva, 1930. Served with French Army, cav. and Lafayette Flying Corps, 1914-15; capt. U.S. Air Service, overseas, Sept. 1917 to Armistice; comdr. 400th Air Squadron; in charge Am. pursuit and bombing pilots and observers attached to French air squadrons. Awarded Purple Heart, Lafayette Flying Corps ribbon, Legion of Honor, Croix de Guerre (France), Catholic. Clubs: Metropolitan (Washington); Officers' Club of 28th Div., Pa. Home: Boalsburg, Pa. Address: Am. Embassy, Mexico City, Mexico.

BOALE, John Archibald, physician; b. Leechburg, Pa., Dec. 18, 1873; s. James D. and Sarah (Armstrong) B.; M.D., U. of Pittsburgh Med. Dept., 1897. Unmarried. Asso. with Dr. John A. Armstrong, Leechburg, Pa., 1897-98; in pvt. practice alone at Vandergrift, Pa. since

1898; examiner for many of the leading life ins. cos.; vice-pres. and dir. Vandergrift Savings & Trust Co.; pres. Liberty Coal Mine Co. Served as capt. Med. Corps, U.S.A., 1918-19 located at U.S.A. Gen Hosp., Rahway, N.J. Served on Vandergrift Bd. of Health, School Bd. (past pres.) and Borough Council a total of 39 yrs., pres. of Council for 25 yrs. Mem. of Chamber of Commerce. Past comdr. Am. Legion Post. Mem. A.M.A., Pa. and Westmoreland Co. med. assns., Gen. Alumni of U. of Pittsburgh Med. Dept. Republican. Presbyn. Mason (K.T., 32°, Shriner). I.O.O.F. Elk. Club: Hill Crest Country (New Kensington). Home: 311 Longfellow St., Vandergrift, Pa.

BOARD, Fred Z.; pres. Citizens First Nat. Bank & Trust Co. Address: 54 E. Ridgewood Av., Ridgewood, N.J.

BOARDMAN, Gordon Cleis, high sch. prin.; b. Glenwood City, Wis., Apr. 7, 1901; s. Samuel Cleis and Stella (Strait) B.; B.S., U. of Minn., Minneapolis, 1927; A.M., Columbia U., 1930; m. Mabel E. Hanson, Aug. 10, 1929; children—Gordon Charles, Douglas Carter: Engaged in teaching in high schs., 1923-26; supt. schs., Brook Park, Minn., 1927-29; prin. high sch., Millville, N.J. since 1930. Trustee Millville City Library. Mem. Phi Delta Kappa, Millville Council of Fgn. Relations (past pres.). Recipient of Agnes Wilson Osborne Scholarship for study of Internat. Affairs. Methodist. Club: Kiwanis of Millville. Home: 904 E. Main St., Millville, N.J.

BOARDMAN, Samuel Ward, Jr., lawyer; b. Auburn, N.Y., Sept. 6, 1874; s. Rev. Samuel Ward (D.D., LL.D.) and Sarah Elizabeth (Greene) B.; desc. Roger Sherman, signer Declaration of Independence, Articles of Confed. and Constitution of U.S.; A.B., Maryville Coll., Maryville, Tenn., 1894; A.B., Harvard U., 1896; LL.B., N.Y. Univ. Law Sch., 1899; (hon.) LL.D., Maryville Coll., 1929; m. Charlotte Katharine Tice, May 28, 1908; children—Grace Estelle Tice, Mary Evarts, Adaline Young, Elizabeth Greene, Charlotte Katharine, Eliot. Admitted to N.J. bar as atty., 1899, as counselor, 1902, master in chancery, 1900, spl. master in chancery, 1904; settlement officer in title dept. Fidelity Trust Co., 1904-05; in practice as individual at Newark, N.J. since 1906; counsel for Cedar Grove Bldg. & Loan Assn. since 1913; counsel for Cedar Grove Twp. since 1931; sec. and treas. Cedar Grove Sch. Dist. Sinking Fund Commn.; vice-pres. Cedar Grove Improvement Assn. Served as asso. mem., Legal Advisory Bd., 1917-18. Mem. N.J. State Bar Assn. Democrat. Conglist. Mem. Bd. Proprs. of Eastern Div. of N.J. Charter mem. of Harvard Club of N.J. Home: 225 Cedar St., Cedar Grove. Office: 11 Commerce St., Newark, N.J.

BOAS, Franz, anthropologist; b. Minden, Westphalia, July 9, 1858; s. M. and Sophie (Meyer) B.; univs. of Heidelberg, Bonn and Kiel, 1877-81; Ph.D., Univ. of Kiel, Germany, 1881, M.D. honoris causa; LL.D., Sc.D., Oxford Univ., Clark University, Howard University and Columbia Univ.; Ph.D. honoris causa, University of Graz; m. Marie A. E. Krackowizer, 1887; children —Mrs. Helene Marie Yampolski, Ernst P., Mrs. Marie Franziska Michelson. Explored Baffin Land, 1883-84; assistant Royal Ethnog. Museum, Berlin, and docent of geography, Univ. of Berlin, 1885-86; investigations in N.A., Mexico, Porto Rico, 1886-1931; docent anthropology, Clark U., 1888-92; chief asst. dept. of anthropology, Chicago Expn., 1892-95, lecturer physical anthropology, 1896-99, professor anthropology, 1899-1937, prof. emeritus in residence, since 1937, Columbia University; assistant curator, 1896; curator, 1901-05, dept. anthropology Am. Mus. Natural History; hon. philologist, Bur. Am. Ethnology, 1901-19. In Mexico, 1910-12; hon. prof. National Museum of Archeology, Mexico; corr. sec. Germanistic Soc. America; pres. Emergency Soc. German and Austrian Science; mem. Nat. Acad. Sciences, Am. Philos. Soc., Am. Antiq. Soc., Am. Folklore Soc. (editor 1908-25; pres. 1931); fellow A.A.A.S. (v.p. 1895, 1907; pres. 1931), N.Y. Acad. Sciences (pres. 1910), Am. Anthrop. Soc. (pres. 1907, 1908), Am. Acad. Arts and Sciences; honorary mem. Anthropology Soc. Vienna, Société des Américanistes,

Paris, Senckenbergische Gesellschaft, Frankfurt, Geog. Soc. Göteborg, Geographical Soc. Hamburg, Geographical Society of Würzburg; honorary fellow Anthropological Institute of Great Britain and Ireland, Folk Lore Soc. of London; cor. mem. Inst. for History of Civilization (Oslo), Anthrop. socs. of Berlin (until 1939), Brussels, Florence, Moscow, Paris, Rome, Stockholm, Washington, and of Am. Numis. Soc., German Anthropol. Soc., Prussian, Munich, Danish, Vienna Acad. Scs., Leopoldina Acad. Halle, Soc. for Oriental Languages, Frankfurt; senator Deutsche Akademie, Munich. Author: The Growth of Children, 1896, 1904; Changes in Form of Body of Descendants of Immigrants, 1911; The Mind of Primitive Man, 1911, 1938; Kultur und Rasse, 1913; Primitive Art, 1927-1938; Anthrop. and Modern Life, 1928; General Anthropology (with others), 1938; also publs. on anthropometry, linguistics and anthropology of North America. Editor Columbia Univ. contbns. to Anthropology, publs. Jesup N. Pacific Expdn., Internat. Jour. Am. Linguistics, etc. Home: Grantwood, Bergen Co., N.J. Address: Columbia Univ., New York, N.Y.

BOAS, George, philosophy; b. Providence, R.I., Aug. 28, 1891; s. Herman and Sarah (Eisenberg) B.; A.B., Brown U., 1913, A.M., 1913; A.M., Harvard, 1915; studied Columbia, 1914-15; Ph.D., U. of Calif. 1917; m. Simone Brangier, June 22, 1921. Began as instr. in forensics, U. of Calif., 1915; with Johns Hopkins since 1921, asso. prof. philosophy, 1927-33, prof. of the history of philosophy since 1933. Trustee and sec. exec. bd. Baltimore Mus. of Art. Mem. Am. Philos. Assn., A.A.A.S., Am. Assn. Univ. Profs. Author: French Philosophies of the Romantic Period, 1925; Never Go Back, 1928; The Major Traditions of European Philosophy, 1928; Our New Ways of Thinking, 1930; A Critical Analysis of the Philosophy of Emile Meyerson, 1930; The Happy Beast, 1933; Philosophy and Poetry, 1933; Primitivism and Related Ideas in Antiquity (with A. O. Lovejoy), 1935; A Primer for Critics, 1937. Translator; Claude Monet (by Georges Clemenceau), 1930; Emerson, the Enraptured Yankee (by Régis Michaud), 1930. Contbr. to Harper's Mag., Atlantic Monthly. Home: Baldwin, Md.

BOBBITT, Lee Otis, sch. supt.; b. Middlety, W.Va., Aug. 25, 1883; s. Elijah and Rowena (Robinson) B.; student Summersville (W.Va.) Normal Sch., 1903-07, Marshall Coll., Huntington, W.Va., 1908-09; Ph.B., Lebanon (O.) U., 1912; A.B., Wilmington (O.) Coll., 1926; grad. study, W.Va. U., 1936-38; recommended for Pd.D., Lebanon U. and Wilmington Coll.; m. Eva Florence Grose, Aug. 9, 1916; 1 son, Lee Otis m. 2d, Flossie Baker, Jan. 13, 1921; 1 dau., Marian Charl. Teacher rural sch., 1903-07; prin. grade sch., 1908-16; supt. N. County sch., 1918-24; teacher high sch., 1925-35; supt. Summersville pub. schs., 1935-39. Sec.-treas. Dem. Exec. Com., 1920-24. Food administr., Nicholas County, World War. Mem. Phi Beta Kappa. Democrat. Baptist. Mason (Master A.F.&A.M. Lodge No. 76, 1922), Eastern Star. Club: Lions (Summersville). Address: Summersville, W.Va.

BOBBITT, Ray M., urologist St. Mary's Veterans Adminstrn. and C.&O. R.R. hosps. Address: 1139 Fourth Av., Huntington, W.Va.

BOCK, Frank J., chmn. bd. Hayes Circle Nat. Bank; pres. Sussex Fire Ins. Co., Essex Fidelity Plate Glass Ins. Co. Address: 1 Clinton St., Newark, N.J.

BOCKIUS, Morris R.; partner law firm Morgan, Lewis & Bockius; also dir. various corpns. Home: Church Lane, Germantown. Office: 2107 Fidelity-Philadelphia Trust Bldg., Philadelphia, Pa.

BODE, Frederick W.; otorhinolaryngologist Pittsburgh Hosp. Address: 507 Liberty Av., Pittsburgh, Pa.

BODINE, Helen Koues, editor; b. Elizabeth, N.J.; d. George Ellsworth and Mary Parmly (Toby) Koues; ed. Mrs. Knapp's Private Sch., Elizabeth, N.J.; m. S. Lawrence Bodine, Apr. 6, 1922. Staff editor Ladies Home Journal, 1909-14; fashion editor Vogue, 1914-16; asso. editor Good Housekeeping, as dir. fashions, architecture, building and furnishings, since 1916.

Mem. N.J. Soc. Colonial Dames of America, Acorn Club of Phila. Republican. Episcopalian. Author: (as Helen Koues) Helen Koues on Decorating the House, 1928; How to Be Your Own Decorator, 1939. Home: Newton Square, Pa. Office: Hearst Magazines, 959 8th Av., New York, N.Y.

BODINE, John Raymond, merchant, banker; b. Numidia, Pa., July 6, 1884; s. B. S. and Clara (Fahringer) B.; student Bloomsburg (Pa.) Normal Sch., 1898-99; m. Mary C. Fetterman, May 18, 1912; children—Irvin M., Harold R., Dorothy I. Sch. teacher, Cleveland Twp., 1899-1901; merchant, Newlin, Catawissa, Pa., since 1902; dir. Valley Nat. Bank of Numidia, Pa., since 1921, pres. since 1936. Mem. of corpn. Bloomsburg Hosp.; supt. Sunday Sch., mem. consistory, St. Paul's Reformed Ch., Numidia, Pa., since 1926. Mem. Columbia Co. Sunday Sch. Assn. (v.p. since 1924), Columbia Co. Supervisors and Auditors Assn. (sec. since 1914), Am. Red Cross (chmn. Roaring Creek Branch since 1923), Boy Scouts of America (council committeeman). Republican. Mem. Reformed Ch. Patriotic Order Sons of America (financial sec. Lodge 204). Address: R.D. 3, Catawissa, Pa.

BODINE, Joseph Lamb, judge; b. Trenton, N.J., Nov. 6, 1883; s. Joseph L. (M.D.) and Frances P. (Davis) B.; A.B., Princeton, 1905; LL.B., Harvard, 1908; m. Gertrude Scudder, Dec. 24, 1918; 1 son, John W. Began practice at Trenton, 1908; U.S. dist. atty., Dist. of N.J., 1919-20; U.S. dist. judge, same dist., 1920-29; justice N.J. Supreme Court since 1929. Democrat. Presbytn. Club: Trenton. Home: 146 W. State St., Trenton, N.J.

BODINE, Marc Williams, surgeon; b. Wellsboro, Pa., Feb. 4, 1899; s. Charles Williams and Ada (Sheffer) B.; grad. Phillips-Andover Acad., 1918; ed. U. of Pa., 1918-20; M.D. U. of Pa. Med. Sch., 1924; m. Martha Weare of Cedar Rapids, Ia., Nov. 3, 1928; children—Marc Williams, Jr., Martha Bodine. Interne Robert Packer Hosp., Sayre, Pa., 1924-25; fellow in surgery, Mayo Clinic, Rochester, Minn., 1925-28, first asst. in surgery, 1928-29; asso. in surgery, Guthrie Clinic and Robert Packer Hosp., 1929-32; in pvt. surg. practice at Williamsport, Pa., since 1932. Served in S.A.T.C. Fellow Am. Coll. Surgs. Mem. Am. Med. Assn., Alumni Assn. Mayo Clinic, Pa. State and Lycoming Co. med socs., Sigma Alpha Epsilon, Nu Sigma Nu. Republican. Presbyn. Home: 500 Vallamont Drive. Office: 416 Pine St., Williamsport, Pa.

BODINE, William B., mem. law firm Pepper, Bodine, Stokes & Schoch. Office: 2225 Land Title Bldg., Philadelphia, Pa.

BODINE, William Warden, v.p. United Gas Improvement Co.; b. Philadelphia, Pa., Oct. 18, 1887; s. Samuel T. and Eleanor Gray (Warden) B.; student Episcopal Acad., Phila., and St. Pauls Sch., Concord, N.H.; A.B., Harvard Coll., 1909; LL.B., U. of Pa. Law Sch., 1914; m. Angela R. Forney, Apr. 29, 1915. With United Gas Improvement Co. since 1919, now v.p. and dir. Home: "Oakwell," Villanova, Pa. Office: 1401 Arch St., Philadelphia, Pa.

BOECKEL, Richard Martin, editor; b. Philadelphia, Pa., Oct. 17, 1892; s. Richard Martin and Lennie (Ford) B.; ed. Northeast Manual Training Sch., Philadelphia; m. Florence Murheid Brewer, Jan. 10, 1916; children—Richard Martin, John Hart. Reporter Albany (N.Y.) Knickerbocker Press, 1908-09. Newburgh (N.Y.) News, 1909-10. Kingston (N.Y.) Leader, 1910-11, Poughkeepsie (N.Y.) News-Press, 1911-13; mgr. Pittsburgh Bur. Internat. News Service, 1914-16, corr. Washington Bur. of same, 1916-18; publicity dir. Industrial Bd., U.S. Dept. Commerce, 1919; corr. Washington Bur. New York Tribune, 1920-21; Washington corr. The Independent, 1922-23; co-founder, 1923, since partner and editorial dir. Editorial Research Reports, daily and weekly newspaper service. Mem. council Nat. Civil Service Reform League. Clubs: Nat. Press (Washington); Manor (Norbeck, Md.). Author: Labor's Money, 1923; Presidential Politics, 1928; "New Influences on the Daily Newspaper" (Paul Block Foundation Lecture at Yale), 1938. Home: Norbeck, Md. Office: 1013 13th St. N.W., Washington, D.C.

BOENNING, Henry D.; partner Boenning & Co.; also officer or dir. various other cos.; mem. bd. govs. Phila. Stock Exchange. Home: Emlen St., corner Creisheim Road, Chestnut Hill. Office: 1606 Walnut St., Philadelphia, Pa.

BOERICKE, Garth Wilkinson, M.D.; b. San Francisco, Calif., Aug. 12, 1893; s. William and Kate (Fay) B.; student U. of Calif., 1912-14; M.D., U. of Mich., 1918; m. Aurilla Mae Shively, May 30, 1923. Interne San Francisco Gen. Hosp., 1918-19; instr. in internal medicine, U. of Mich. Homœ. Med. Sch., 1919-21; asst. clin. prof. homœpathy, U. of Calif., 1921-26; prof. materia medica and therapeutics, Hahnemann Med. Coll., Philadelphia, Pa., since 1926; dir. Hering Research Lab., same coll. Mem. Am. Inst. Homœopathy (pres.), Pa. State Homœ. Assn. (pres. 1935), Beta Theta Pi, Alpha Sigma. Democrat. Swedenborgian. Clubs: Hahnemann, Oxford Medical. Author: Principles of Homœopathy, 1929. Contbr. to Jour. Am. Inst. Homœopathy; editor Hahnemann Monthly since 1935. Home: 525 Kenilworth Rd., Merion, Pa. Office: 235 N. 15th St., Philadelphia, Pa. *

BOETTCHER, Henry Ferdinand, univ. prof.; b. Chicago, Ill., Aug. 7, 1903; s. Henry R. and Olga (Krohmer) B.; Ph.B., U. of Chicago, 1926, M.A., 1928; M.F.A., Yale, 1935; unmarried. Instr. English, Allegheny Coll., Meadville, Pa., 1928-31, asst. prof. drama, 1935-36; prof. and head dept. of drama, Carnegie Inst. Tech. since 1936. Member Nat. Theatre Conf. Amer. Ednl. Drama Assn., Am. Assn. Univ. Profs. Home: 120 Ruskin Av. Office: Carnegie Institute of Technology, Pittsburgh, Pa.

BOETTGER, Theodore; chmn. bd. United Piece Dye Works. Address: Lodi, N.J.

BOGARDUS, James Furnas, asst. prof. geography, U. of Pa.; b. New York, N.Y., March 26, 1896; s. Joseph A. and Elizabeth (Furnas) B.; B.A., Swarthmore Coll., 1921; Ph.D., U. of Pa., 1927; m. Catharine Longstreth, Dec. 19, 1924; children—James Furnas, Katrina Jans, Edward Longstreth. Instr. econs., U. of Cincinnati, 1921-22, Swarthmore Coll., 1922-23; instr. geography, U. of Pa., 1923-30, asst. prof., 1930-35; dep. sec. Dept. Forests and Waters, Pa., 1935-36, sec., 1936-39; mem. Pa. State Planning Bd., 1936-39; pres. Navigation Comn. for Del. River and its Navigable Tributaries, 1936-39; chmn. Water and Power Resources Bd. of Pa., 1936-39; mem. San. Water Bd. Dept. Health of Pa.; chmn. Pa. State Forest Comn. Mem. Assn. of Am. Geographers, Phi Beta Kappa, Delta Sigma Rho, Kappa Phi Kappa, Kappa Sigma. Democrat. Mem. Society of Friends. Club: Penn Athletic (Philadelphia). Author: Europe a Geographic Survey, 1934. Contbr. to mags. and journs. Home: 114 Cornell Av., Swarthmore, Pa.

BOGER, Robert C.; pres. Boger & Crawford and Boger & Crawford Spinning Mills. Home: 1201 Fillmore St. Office: J and E. Venango Sts., Philadelphia, Pa.

BOGGS, John Lawrence, supervisor of ins. claims; b. Perth Amboy, N.J., Nov. 16, 1865; s. John Lawrence and Cornelia Bell (Paterson) B.; student pvt. schs., Perth Amboy, N.J., 1876-83, St. Paul's Sch., Garden City, L.I., N.Y., 1881-83; m. Christina Marie Newton, Feb. 11, 1892; children—Cornelia Paterson (Mrs. Gilbert MacKie Milligan; dec.), Christina Newton (Mrs. George L. Lewis). Began as clk. Wall St. Nat. Bank, New York, 1883; clk. actuarial dept. The Mutual Benefit Life Ins. Co., Newark, N.J., 1884-1911, sect. head, 1912, supervisor of claims since 1912; pres. East Jersey Bd. of Proprietors, Perth Amboy, N.J., since 1922; dir. Perth Amboy (N.J.) Gas Light Co. since 1917, v.p. since 1936; sec. and trustee Perth Amboy Savings Instn. since 1899. Organized battery of arty. in N.G. during World War; mem. of Mayor's Com. on Defense, Newark, N.J. Mem. exec. and historic coms. Newark Constn. Sesquitennial Com., 1938; mem. bd. edn., Perth Amboy, N.J., 1927-30. Trustee and treas. St. Barnabas Hosp., Newark, N.J., since 1900. One of founders S.A.R., 1889, and senior mem.; one of founders N.J. Soc. S.A.R., sec. 1889-92, v.p. 1915-16. Mem. N.J. Hist. Soc. (treas. 1910-37, trustee since 1910); mem. N.J. Soc. of Colonial Wars, N.J. Soc. of War of 1812, Soc. of Friends of Lafayette. Republican. Episcopalian (vestryman, treas. Grace Episcopal Ch., Newark, N.J., since 1928). Club: Bay Head (N.J.) Yacht. Descendent of William Paterson, signer of Constn., and Capt. James Lawrence, is much interested in history and recently offered collection of documents revealing fights, ambitions, scandals of N.J., N.Y., and Pa. at pub. auction in N.Y. Home: 311 Mt. Prospect Av., Newark, N.J.; (summer) Bay Head, N.J. Office: 300 Broadway, Newark, N.J.

BOGGS, L. G.; editor Fairmont West Virginian. Address: care Fairmont Newspaper Pub. Co., Fairmont, W.Va.

BOGGS, Samuel Whittemore, geographer; b. Coolidge, Kan., March 3, 1889; s. Charles Fairman and Lillian Louise (Whittemore) B.; B. Litt., Berea Coll., Berea, Ky., 1909; student Yale U., 1912-13; A.M., Columbia U., 1924; m. Amy Burt Bridgman, Aug. 16, 1916; children—Mary Lillian, Barbara Bridgman. Sec. to Pres. Wm. G. Frost, Berea Coll., Berea, Ky., 1909-12; geog. research, map compilation, editorial work, part time, 1913-19, full time since 1919; editor maps World Missionary Atlas, 1921-24; geographer U.S. Dept. State since 1924; mem. U.S. Geog. Bd., 1924-34, chmn. exec. com., 1927-34; mem. Federal Bd. Surveys and Maps since 1926; tech. adviser Am. delegation, Conf. for Codification of Internat. Law, The Hague, 1930; official del. Internat. Geog. Conf., Cambridge, Eng., 1928, Paris, 1931, Warsaw, 1934. Fellow Royal Geog. Soc. (Eng.), A.A.A. S.; mem. Assn. Am. Geographers, Am. Geog. Soc., Soc. Am. Archivists. Presbyn. Club: Cosmos (Washington). Contbr. articles to geog. and sci. jours. Home: 219 Elm St., Chevy Chase, Md.

BOHLEN, Francis Hermann, lawyer, educator; b. Chestnut Hill, Pa., July 31, 1868; s. John an Priscilla (Murray) B.; grad. St. Paul's Sch., Concord, N.H., 1884; LL.B., U. of Pa., 1892, LL.D., 1930; m. Margaret Tiers Woodville, Oct. 17, 1892; children—Priscilla (Mrs. Stephen Bonsall Brooks), Francis Hermann, Mary Ellen (Mrs. Richard Tilghman); m. 2d. Ingrid Kleen, June 23, 1913; 1 son, John. W. A. Wellow University of Pa. Law School, 1893-95, lecturer, 1898-1901, asst. prof. law, 1901-05, prof. of law, 1905-14, Algernon Sydney Biddle prof., 1914-25, 1928-38, prof. emeritus since 1938; Langdell prof. law, Harvard University, 1925-28. Sec. Industrial Accident Com. State of Pennsylvania, 1911-15; counsel to Workmen's Compensation Bd., Pa., 1915-22, and to State Workmen's Ins. Fund, 1915-23; dir. Pa. Wire Glass Co. Dir. Assn. Against Prohibition Amendment, 1931. Mem. Delta Psi. Club: Philadelphia. Author: Cases on Torts, 1915; Studies in the Law of Torts; also essays on Evidence and Workmen's Compensation. Reporter Law of Torts for Am. Law Institute, 1923. Address: University of Pa., Philadelphia, Pa.

BOK, Curtis; president judge Court of Common Pleas since 1937. Address: 1415 Delancey St., Philadelphia, Pa.

BOK, Mary Louise Curtis (Mrs. Edward Bok); b. Boston, Mass., Aug. 6, 1876; d. Cyrus Herman Kotzschmar and Louise (Knapp) Curtis; ed. pub. schs. and Ogontz Sch.; L.H.D., U. of Pa.; Mus.D., Williams College; m. Edward William Bok, Oct. 22, 1896; children—William Curtis, Cary William. Pres. Settlement Music Sch. of Phila., 1912-26; founded and endowed The Curtis Inst. of Music, 1924, and since pres. Decorated Knight 1st class, Order of Merit (Austria); Chevalier's Cross of Order of Polonia and Restituta (Poland). Republican. Presbyn. Clubs: Art Alliance, Print, Cosmopolitan (Phila.); Cosmopolitan (New York). Home: Merion Station, Pa.

BOLAND, Patrick J., congressman; b. Scranton, Pa.; s. Christopher T. and Frances (Biglin) B.; ed. St. Thomas Coll., Scranton; m. Sarah Jennings, Nov. 24, 1908; Children—Frances Joseph, John Jennings, Lenore, Christopher, Eileen; m. 2d, Veronica Barrett, Oct. 27, 1931; children—Patrick J., Eugene. Began work as a carpenter; now member firm of Boland Brothers, general contractors. Mem. 72d to 75th Congresses (1931-39), 11th Pa. Dist. Former mem. City Council, Scranton, and county commr., Lackawanna Co., Pa. Democrat. Mem. Knights of Columbus, Knight of St. George, Lackawanna Bowling Assn., B.P.O. Elks. Club: Good Fellowship. Home: 734 Clay Av., Scranton, Pa. *

BOLARD, John A., lawyer; b. nr. Meadville, Pa., Oct. 4, 1867; s. Frederick D. and Celia (Hayes) B.; ed. Waterford Acad., 1887-89; LL.B., U. of Mich. Law Sch., 1892; m. Mary Jane Cowan, Aug. 4, 1894 (died 1934); children—Frederick Cowan (dec.), Celia F., Katherine (Mrs. D. C. Dunn), George L. Admitted to Pa. bar, 1892 and since engaged in gen. practice of law at Meadville; mem. Pa. Ho. of Rep., 1919 and 1921. Mem. Erie and Crawford Co. bar assns. Republican. Methodist. Mason. Rotarian. Home: 603 Venango Av. Office: National Bank Bldg., Cambridge Springs, Pa.

BOLES, Russell Sage, physician; b. Phila., Pa., Sept. 27, 1889; s. George Howard and Rhoda (Borden) B.; M.D., U. of Pa. Med. Sch., 1912; post grad. study, Berlin and Halle, Germany, Vienna, Austria, 1914; m. Mary McNeely, Nov. 29, 1916; children—Mary Laird, Russell Sage. Began practice medicine, Phila., 1914; visiting physician Phila. Gen. Hosp. since 1916; consultant in gastro-enterology U.S. Vets. Bur., Phila., since 1920; asso. in medicine, U. of Pa. since 1920; chief dept, of gastro-enterology, Bryn Mawr (Pa.) Hosp. since Jan. 1, 1938. Served as lt., Med. Corps, U.S. Navy, during World War. Mem. Am. Gastro-Enterological Assn. (sec. since 1933), Penn Valley Assn. (dir.), A.M.A., Am. Coll. Physicians, Phila. Coll. Physicians, Pa. State Med. Soc., Phila. Co. Med. Soc. Republican. Episcopalian. Author numerous articles on internal medicine and gastro-enterology. Home: Bryn Mawr and Woodbine Avs., Penn Valley, Narberth, Pa. Office: Rittenhouse Plaza, 19th and Walnut Sts., Philadelphia, Pa.

BOLGER, James Henry, manufacturer; b. Hydeville, Vt., Oct. 31, 1889; s. Thomas and Naomi Irene (Wiswell) B.; ed. Bangor public schools and Easton Sch. of Business; m. Helene Ann Heard, Apr. 8, 1921; children—James Henry, Carol Annette, William Thomas, Helene Ann, Robert John. With Bolger-Heller Slate Co., mfrs. of structural, roofing, electrical, sanitary and blackboard slate; since 1908, successively as stenographer, sales mgr., sec., and since 1925 treas. and gen. mgr.; pres. and treas. Lehigh Structural Slate Co.; dir. First Nat. Bank in Bangor. Served in U.S. Navy, 1917-18. Mem. Pa. Slate Mfrs. Assn. (pres. 1938-39), Am. Legion. Mem. United Evangelical Ch. Mason. Elk. Home: 352 S. 2d St. Office: Bolger-Heller Slate Co., Bangor, Pa.

BOLGER, Robert Vincent, judge; b. Phila., Pa., Apr. 24, 1891; s. Peter and Ann M. (McDermott) B.; grad. Central High Sch., Phila., 1911; student Wharton Sch., U. of Pa., 1911-12; LL.B., U. of Pa., 1915; unmarried. Admitted to Pa. bar 1916, and practiced in Phila.; asst. U.S. atty. Eastern Dist. of Pa., 1920-24, 1934-37; apptd. judge Orphan's Court, Phila. Co., 1937, elected for term, 1937-47. Mem. Phila. Co. Bd. Law Examiners, 1936-37. Democrat. Roman Catholic. Home: 25 W. Phil Ellena St. Office: 430 City Hall, Philadelphia, Pa.

BOLGIANO, Louis Paul, Sr., lawyer; b. Baltimore, Md., Jan. 21, 1890; s. John and Sophie (Hennighausen) B.; LL.B., U. of Md. Law Sch., 1913; m. Amanda Rice, Nov. 11, 1915; children—Louis Paul, Jr., Duane Ridgely. Admitted to Md. bar, 1912 and since engaged in gen. practice of law at Baltimore in individual practice; dir. City Savings Bank, Baltimore, F. M. Bolgiano, Inc., Washington, D.C.; vice-pres. and dir. Duraflex Co., Baltimore; pres. and dir. Home Bldg. Co., Baltimore; dir. Parks-Hull Automotive Corpn., Baltimore, Homeland-Willow Bldg. Assn., Baltimore; interested in art and began oil painting, 1935, attended Martenet's Sch. of art and paintings accepted for exhbn. by local juries and those of other cities. Dir. The Anchorage, Baltimore. Mem. Am., Md. State and Baltimore City bar assns., Commercial Law League of America, Baltimore Y.M.C.A., Kappa Sigma, Phi Delta Phi, English Speaking Union. Methodist.

Odd Fellow. Clubs: Shakespeare (pres.), Lions of Baltimore (pres.). Home: 4411 Norwood Rd. Office: Court Sq. Bldg., Baltimore, Md.

BOLGIANO, Ralph, pres. Duraflex Corpn.; b. Baltimore, Md., Oct. 19, 1888; s. John and Sophie (Hennighausen) B.; student pub. schs. and Baltimore Poly. Inst.; M.E., Cornell U., 1909; m. Edith Bolgiano, Apr. 20, 1918. With Duraflex Corpn. since 1921, now pres.; also dir. several companies. Home: 408 Baltimore Av., Towson, Md. Office: 3200-14 Dura St., Fairfield, Baltimore, Md.

BOLLMAN, William Henry, clergyman; b. Buffalo, N.Y., June 9, 1895; s. William and Emilie (Dieckman) B.; grad. Masten Park High Sch., Buffalo, 1912; A.B., Mission House Coll., Sheboygan, Wis., 1917; B.D., Theol. Sem. of the Reformed Church, Lancaster, Pa., 1920; grad. student Lehigh U., 1931-32; D.D., Franklin and Marshall Coll., 1935; m. Ruth Betty Coxon, Sept. 30, 1922; children—Mary Ellen, William Harbaugh. Ordained to ministry of Reformed Ch. in U.S., Aug. 1920; pastor Livingston Av. Reformed Ch., New Brunswick, N. J., 1920-27, Christ Reformed Ch., Bethlehem, Pa., 1927-32; First Reformed Ch., Lancaster, Pa., since 1932. Mem. bd. of Bd. of Ministerial Pensions and Relief, Reformed Ch. in U.S. since 1924, vice-pres. of bd. since 1935. Mem. Phi Kappa Sigma, Masons. Clubs: Rotary (Bethlehem and Lancaster). Home: 44 E. Orange St., Lancaster, Pa.

BOLTE, G. Arthur; sr. mem. firm Bolte & Miller. Address: 1516 Atlantic Av., Atlantic City, N.J.

BOLTON, Elmer Keiser, chem. dir. E. I. du Pont de Nemours and Co.; b. Philadelphia, Pa., June 23, 1886; s. George G. and Jane E. (Holt) B.; A.B. Bucknell U., 1908, hon. D.Sc., 1932; A.M., Harvard, 1910, Ph.D., 1913; student Kaiser Wilhelm Inst. für Chemie, Berlin, Germany, 1913-15; m. Marguerite L. Duncan, Dec. 6, 1916; children—Duncan G., Marjorie L., Elmer K. With E. I. du Pont de Nemours and Co. since 1915, successively asst. mgr. Lodi Works, mgr. organic div. of chem. dept., dir. chem. sect. of dyestuffs dept., asst. chem. dir. of chem. dept., 1929-30, chem. dir. same dept. since 1930; dir. Bayer-Semesan Co. Trustee Bucknell University. Mem. Am. Chemical Soc. (dir. 1936-38), Am. Inst. Chemical Engrs., Soc. Chem. Industry, Deutsche Chemie Gesellschaft, Assn. Dirs. of Industrial Research, Phi Kappa Psi, Alpha Chi Sigma. Clubs: Wilmington, Wilmington Country, du Pont Country, Harvard. Home: 2310 W. 11th St. Office: Nemours Bldg., Wilmington, Del.

BOLTON, Thaddeus Lincoln, psychologist; b. Sonora, Ill., July 27, 1865; s. William and Amelia Sophia Charlotte (Dort) B.; A.B., University of Michigan, 1889, Ph.D., from Clark U., 1894; m. Martha Louise Busse, Sept. 6, 1921; 1 son, Peter Oughtred (dec.). Instr., later prof. psychology, U. of Neb., 1900-10; prof. psychology, Tempe (Ariz.) Normal Sch., 1910-13, U. of Mont., 1913-17, Temple U., Phila., 1917-37, now emeritus. Trustee Sch. of Occupational Therapy. Fellow A.A.A.S., mem. Am. Psychol. Assn., Sigma Xi, Alpha Tau Omega, Tau Psi Xi. Republican. Conglist. Was editor Univ. of Neb. Studies; founder, and for 3 yrs. editor Ariz. Jour. Edn.; contbr. to Am. Jour. Psychology, Psychol. Rev., Jour. of Philosophy, Kraepelin's Psychologische Arbeiten, Jour. of Vocational Psychology. Conducted extensive research upon value of sugar as a food. Home: Narberth, Pa.

BOLWELL, Robert Whitney, coll. prof.; b. N.Y.C., Oct. 10, 1891; s. Charles and Caroline Sophie (Peach) B.; A.B., Western Reserve U., 1916; M.A., Columbia, 1917, Ph.D., 1921; m. Sara Adelina Russell Worden. Lecturer in English, 1918, instr., 1919, Columbia; asst. prof. dept. of English, 1920, asso. prof., 1923, prof. of Am. lit., 1929, George Washington Univ., also dir. of summer seccions, 1930, advisor to foreign students, 1930, chmn. of the Graduate Council, 1939. Member American Dialect Society, Modern Language Assn. America, Am. Assn. Univ. Profs., Phi Beta Kappa, Sigma Nu. Clubs: Federal Schoolmen's, Cosmos. Author: At Large in Germany, 1915; After College—What? 1916; The Life and Works of John Heywood, 1921. Edited The Renaissance, English Lit. Series, 1929. Contbr. to Dialect Notes, (Am. Dialect Soc.), Jour. of English and Germanic Philology, Dictionary of Am. Biography, Am. Literature Quarterly, etc. Home: "Southport," Silver Spring, Md.

BOMBASSEI-FRASCANI, Giorgio M., Royal Vice-Consul of Italy; b. Florence, Italy, June 29, 1910; s. Alfredo and Margherita (Tidone) B.-F.; Dr. in Law and Polit. Sciences, U. of Florence (Italy); unmarried. Asst. prof. economics, U. of Florence, Italy, 1931-32; entered Italian Consular Diplomatic Service, 1933, vice-consul of Italy at Alexandria, Egypt, 1934-36, vice-consul of Italy at Pittsburgh since Aug. 1936. Clubs: Pittsburgh Athletic, Rolling Rock Hunt (Ligonier, Pa.) Home: 166 N. Dithridge St. Office: 715 Grant Bldg., Pittsburgh, Pa.

BOMBERGER, Christian Martin, pub. and editor; b. Lititz, Pa., Mar. 17, 1884; s. Christ H. and Elizabeth (Hess) B.; student Lititz High Sch., 1900-02, Franklin and Marshall Acad., 1902-04; A.B., Franklin and Marshall Coll., 1908; m. Edith Graff, Aug. 1915; children—Jacob Graff, Amos Hess. Taught country school, Warwick Twp., Lancaster Co., Pa., 1902-03. Reporter Public Ledger, Phila., 1908; served successively on Pittsburgh Press, United Press Assns. of Pittsburgh and New York and Greensburg Tribune; founded Jeannette News-Dispatch, 1914; pres. and treas. Jeannette Pub. Co.; pres. and treas. Wosco, Inc.; dir. First Jeannette Bank & Trust Co.; dir. Jeannette Thrift Co. Pres. Jeannette Chamber of Commerce, 1925; dir. Jeannette Pub. Library; pres. Bushy Run Battlefield Commn. since 1928. Mem. Pa. German Soc., Western Pa. Hist. Soc. Republican. Mem. Reformed Ch. Mason (32°), Elk. Clubs: Kiwanis (pres. 1923-24), Greensburg Country. Author: Christian Bomberger, Pioneer, 1922; Bomberger Chronicles, 1935; Battle of Bushy Run, 1928; George Washington, Mason, 1932; Twelfth Colony Plus, 1934. Home: Eschelbronn. Address: Jeannette, Pa.

BOMBERGER, John Henry Augustus, II, clergyman; b. Norristown, Pa., May 24, 1895; s. Augustus Wight and Mary (Kratz) B.; grad. Norristown High Sch., 1913; A.B., Ursinus Coll., Collegeville, Pa., 1917; student Harvard Grad. Sch., 1919-20; B.D., Va. Theol. Sem., Alexandria, 1923; m. Anna Laura Gottwals, June 16, 1923; children—Nancy Gottwals, John Henry Augustus, III. Teacher, high sch., 1917-19; scout exec. Boy Scouts of America, 1919-20; ordained to ministry of Episcopal Ch., 1923; now rector St. Matthew's Episcopal Ch., Wheeling, W.Va. Dir. Family Service Assn., Wheeling; chmn. dept. of Christian edn., Diocese of W.Va. Clubs: Rotary, Twilight, Fort Henry, Country, Cedar Rocks Golf (all of Wheeling). Home: 13 Walnut Av., Woodlawn, Wheeling, W.Va.

BOMBERGER, Richard Watson, educator; b. Boonsboro, Md., Oct. 13, 1896; s. Harvey Smith and Helen Virginia (Smith) B.; grad. high sch., Boonsboro, 1915; B.A., Franklin and Marshall Coll., 1920; M.A., U. of Va., 1926 (work done in summer sessions); m. Catharine Downs Schnebly, Aug. 1, 1923; 1 son, Richard Watson. With Donaldson Sch., 1920-31, English master, 1920-28, headmaster, 1928-31; dean of Franklin and Marshall Coll. since 1931. Served as pvt. Coast Arty., U.S.A., 1918-19. Mem. Phi Kappa Psi. Republican. Episcopalian. Address: Franklin and Marshall Coll., Lancaster, Pa.

BOND, Carroll Taney, judge; b. Baltimore, Md., June 13, 1873; s. James and Elizabeth (Lyon) B.; grad. Phillips Acad., Exeter, N.H., 1890; A.B., Harvard Univ., 1894; LL.B., Univ. of Md., 1896; LL.D., Johns Hopkins University, 1929; unmarried. Admitted to Md. bar, 1896, and practiced at Baltimore until 1911; asso. judge Supreme Bench, Baltimore City, 1911-24; appointed to fill vacancy as asso. judge Court of Appeals, of Md., Apr. 1924, until election 1926, chief judge Nov. 1924; elected Nov. 1926, for full term of 15 yrs., and designated chief judge. Served as corpl. and 1st sergt. 5th Maryland Regiment, U.S. Volunteers. Spanish-Am. War. Trustee Peabody Inst., Provident Hosp. (colored); mem. Littleton-Griswold Fund Com. of Am. Hist. Assn.; dir. Legal History Soc. Mem. Phi Beta Kappa. Democrat. Protestant. Clubs: Maryland, Gibson Island. Home: 3507 N. Charles St., Baltimore, Md.

BOND, Charles Martin, prof. of religion; b. Marion, Kan., Aug. 31, 1889; s. Robert Little and Mary Ann (Fritzinger) B.; grad. The Peddie School, Hightstown, N.J., 1913; A.B., Colgate U., Hamilton, N. Y., 1917, D.D., 1938; B.D., Crozer Sem., Chester, Pa., 1921; A.M., U. of Pa., 1921; student U. of Chicago Divinity Sch., 1924-25, and 3 summer quarters; m. Elizabeth Stults, Sept. 17, 1919; children—Charles Farrington, Mary Elizabeth, William Earl Glendening, Henry Symnes, Barbara Jane. Ordained to ministry of Baptist Ch., 1921; pastor Bapt. Tabernacle, Wilkes-Barre, Pa., 1919-22; university student pastor, Ohio Univ., Athens, 1922-24; prof. of religion, Bucknell U., since 1925. Served as Y.M.C.A. war work sec., with A.E.F. in England, France and Russia, 1917-19. Fellow Nat. Council on Religion in Higher Edn.; mem. Pa. Sabbath Sch. Assn. (mem. ednl. advisor com.), Student Christian Movement (mem. regional council), Nat. Assn. Bibl. Instrs., Religious Edn. Assn., Beta Theta Pi, Phi Beta Kappa. Author of pamphlet, The Liberal Arts College Functioning in the Field of Religion, 1935; also articles in Religious Edn., Crozer Quarterly, etc. Home: 309 S. 6th St., Lewisburg, Pa.

BOND, Earl Danford, psychiatrist; b. St. Paul, Minn., Jan. 25, 1879; s. Johnathan Danford and Martha (Bunker) B.; A.B., Harvard, 1900, M.D., 1908; m. Grace Lee Newson, Aug. 4, 1909; children—Douglas Danford, Ann Sharpless. At McLean Hospital, 1908-12; was instr. in neuropathology, Harvard Med. Sch., 1912-13; clin. dir. and pathologist, Danvers (Mass.) State Hosp., 1912-13; med. dir. dept. for mental and nervous diseases, Pa. Hosp., Philadelphia, 1913-30; prof. psychiatry, Grad. Sch. Medicine, U. of Pa., vice dean, 1937, pro. psychiatry, U. of Pa., since 1930; med. dir. Inst. for Mental Hygiene since 1930; lecturer Bryn Mawr Coll. Served as capt., later maj., Med. Corps, U.S.A., Sept. 1917-Mar. 1919. Mem. Phila. Child Guidance Clinic, State Welfare Commn. of Pa. Mem. Am. Psychiatric Assn. (pres. 1930), Coll. Physicians Phila., Phi Beta Kappa. Received Philadelphia award, 1932. Republican. Unitarian. Clubs: Harvard, Lenape, Tredyffrin Country. Co-Author: The Treatment of Behavior Disorders Following Encephalitis (with Dr. K. E. Appel), 1931. Contbr. to Am. Jour. Psychiatry, Mental Hygiene. Home: Old Lancaster Rd., Bryn Mawr, Pa. Office: 111 N. 49th St., Philadelphia, Pa.

BOND, Edward Johnson, insurance; b. Petersburg, Va., Oct. 18, 1888; s. Edward Johnson and Lelia (Seabury) B.; prep. edn. Boys' Latin Sch., Baltimore, Md., 1898-1903; B.S., Va. Mil. Inst. Lexington, Va., 1908; m. Mabel Holle, Oct. 20, 1921; 1 son, Edward Johnson III. Began in insurance business with Md. Casualty Co., Baltimore, 1908, first v.p., 1920-37, pres. since 1937. Fellow Casualty Actuarial & Statis. Soc. Democrat. Clubs: Maryland, Baltimore Country. Home: 701 University Parkway. Office: Maryland Casualty Co., 40th St. and Keswick Road, Baltimore, Md.

BOND, Frank Alexander, chain mfr.; b. Pittsburgh, Pa., Oct. 9, 1883; s. Alan Alexander and Elizabeth Marguerite (Babylon) B.; m. Leila Adah Stokey, Nov. 24, 1904; children—Donald Alan, Leila Frances, Kenneth Gordon. Sec. and gen. mgr. Standard Chain Co., Pittsburgh, 1913-17; pres. Nat. Chain Co., Marietta, O., 1917-19; v.p., sec. and dir. McKay Co., chain mfrs., Pittsburgh, since 1920. Member Soc. Automotive Engrs., Am. Soc. of Metals, Am. Welding Soc. Republican. Presbyterian. Clubs: Duquesne, Pittsburgh Athletic Assn. (Pittsburgh); Kahkwa (Erie, Pa.). Home: 5845 Phillips Av. Office: 1005 Liberty Av., Pittsburgh, Pa.

BOND, Harley Donovan, coll. dean; b. Lost Creek, W.Va., Sept. 26, 1897; s. Luther A. and Josie (Romine) B.; A.B., Salem Coll., Salem, W.Va., 1923; grad. student Columbia U., summers 1927-28; A.M., W.Va. Univ., Morgantown, 1930; m. Marcella Randolph, June 11, 1924; children—Richard Randolph, Nellie

BOND, Jo. Engaged in teaching, high sch., Sardis, W.Va., 1923-24; teacher, high sch., Lost Creek, W.Va., 1924-27, supt., 1927-29; prof. biology, Salem Coll., Salem, W.Va., 1930-35, dean since 1935. Served in S.A.T.C., 1918. Mem. A.A.A.S., W.Va. Acad. Sci., Salem College Hon. Soc., Am. Legion. Democrat. Seventh Day Baptist. Mason. Home: 126 Liberty St., Salem, W.Va.

BOND, Sirus Orestes, coll. pres.; b. Hackers Creek, Upshur Co., W.Va., Aug. 12, 1877; s. Levi Davis and Victoria (Arnold) B.; A.B., Salem (W.Va.) Coll., 1904; A.B., W.Va. U., 1909; A.M., Columbia, 1913, grad. study, 1913-14; Pd.D., Alfred (N.Y.) U., 1924; m. Venie Hagerty, Aug. 9, 1904. Teacher in rural schs., prin. elementary and high schs. until 1914; acting pres. Glenville (W.Va.) State Normal Sch., 1914-15; supervisor schs., Shepherdstown Dist. W.Va., and prof. edn. Shepherd Coll. State Normal Sch., 1915-19; pres. Salem Coll. since 1919; instr. in teachers institutes since 1913; mem. firm Bonds' Green Acres Hereford Farm, breeders of pure-bred Hereford cattle since 1901. World vice-pres. Christian Endeavor, 1923-28; pres. Seventh Day Baptist Gen. Conf., 1925. Mem. N.E.A., Nat. Soc. for Study Edn., W.Va. Edn. Assn., Pi Gamma Mu. Democrat. Seventh Day Baptist. Kiwanian. Author: Salem College, Its Past, Present and Future, 1924. Home: Salem, W.Va.

BOND, Walter Loucks, piano mfr. and merchant; b. York, Pa., Jan. 3, 1889; s. William S. and Sallie (Loucks) B.; B.S. in economics, U. of Pa., 1909; m. Ethel B. Bossert, July 25, 1912; 1 son, William Henry. Began as sec. to pres. Weaver Piano Co., Inc., 1909, asst. treas. 1916-19, sec. and treas. since 1919. Dir. Mfrs. Assn. of York, Asso. Retail Credit Men, York Symphony Orchestra. Republican. Lutheran. Clubs: Rotary, Country. Home: 719 Madison Av. Office: E. Philadelphia and Broad Sts., York, Pa.

BOND, William S.; pres. Weaver Piano Co. Home: 924 W. Market St. Office: Broad and Walnut Sts., York, Pa.

BONINE, Chesleigh Arthur, geologist; b. Sorrento, Fla., Mar. 25, 1888; s. Joel Carter and Lola (Hemery) B.; ed. Central High Sch., Washington, 1904-08; E.M., Lehigh U., 1912; grad. study Johns Hopkins; m. Beulah Whiteman, Nov. 22, 1913; 1 dau., Ann. Field work, U.S. Geol. Survey, until 1917; cons. oil and gas work since 1917, in N.M., N.D., Mont., Okla., Ky., Pa., Wyo., etc.; instr. geology, Lehigh U., 1917-18; with Pa. State Coll. since 1918, prof. geology and head of dept. of geology and mineralogy since Jan. 1923; coöperating geologist, State Geological Survey of Pa. Mem. Soc. Economic Geologists, Am. Inst. Mining and Metallurgical Engineers, Phi Delta Theta, Tau Beta Pi, Sigma Xi, Sigma Gamma Epsilon. Democrat. Presbyn. Author bulls. of U.S. Geol. Survey and numerous repts. Home: R.F.D. 1, State College, Pa.

BONNELL, Charles Augustus, lawyer; b. Glen Gardner, N.J., Oct. 13, 1875; s. Augustus and Mary M. (Martenis) B.; grad. Mondalia Acad., Glen Gardner, N.J., 1891; ed. Rider Coll., Trenton, N.J., 1893-94; m. Blanche Diefendorf, Oct. 13, 1907; 1 dau., Blanche N. Admitted to N.J. bar as atty., 1904, as counsellor, 1907; engaged in gen. practice of law at Cape May Ct. Ho., N.J., since 1905; admitted to practice in all state cts. and U.S. cts.; served as solicitor Middle Twp., 12 yrs., Upper Twp., 10 yrs., City Stone Harbor, 4 yrs., Borough Woodbine, 9 yrs.; dist. supt. Transfer Bureau, N.J., 23 yrs.; supreme ct. comr. and spl. master in chancery; dir. E.F.H. Corpn., Stone Harbor Hotel Corpn., Cape May Co. Lumbermen's Assn., all of Cape May C. H., Villa Hotel Corpn., Villas, N. J., Acme Amusement Co., Wildwood, N.J. Served as mem. dft. bd., 1917-19. Mem. Am. Bar Assn., N.J. State Bar Assn., Cape May Co. Bar Assn., Cape May Co. Rep. Club, Young Men's Rep. Club. Republican. Lutheran. I.O.O.F. Home: Hand Av., Cape May Court House, N.J.

BONNELL, Robert Owen, banker; b. Vincennes, Ind., March 4, 1891; s. George W. and Nancy R. (Root) B.; A.B., U. of Redlands (Calif.), 1931; studied law at Georgetown U., 1918-19; m. Hettie List Hazlett, June 23, 1923; children—Edwina Hazlett, Robert Owen, Jr. Sec.-mgr. Chamber of Commerce and Merchants and Mfrs. Assn., Redlands, Calif., 1915; gen. mgr. Northern Calif. Counties Assn., 1917; mrg. new business dept. Industrial Finance Corpn. (New York), 1919-22; v.p. and gen. mgr. 1st Industrial Bank of Denver, 1922-25; 1st v.p. Industrial Savings Trust Co. (St. Louis), 1925-29; pres. Public Bank of Maryland since 1929; dir. Union Trust Co., Hopkins Place Savings Bank. Enlisted in U.S. Navy, 1917; served as chief yeoman, later lt. (j.g.), World War. Mem. Bd. Visitors and Govs. and of exec. com. St. Johns Coll., Annapolis. Trustee and mem. exec. com., Commn. on Governmental Efficiency and Economy of Baltimore, 1934-36. Pres. Western Morris Plan Bankers Assn., 1923-28, Nat. Morris Plan Bankers Assn., 1928-30, 1934-35; pres. Assod. Hospital Service of Baltimore, Inc., 1937-39; pres. Baltimore Community Fund, 1934-36; pres. Baltimore Assn. of Commerce, 1939-40; state chmn. Nat. Economic League, 1932-36, mem. nat. organization exec. com. of same, 1934-36, 1939, vice-chmn., 1935-36, also mem. nat. council; chmn. Rep. Nat. Finance Com. for Md., 1936-39, and Md. representative on Rep. Program Com. Mem. Pi Chi. Republican. Clubs: Rotary (pres. 1935-36), Merchants, Elkridge Kennels. Home: 200 Tuscany Rd. Office: 15 E. Fayette St., Baltimore, Md.

BONNER, Francis Anthony, investment banker; b. Bryn Mawr, Pa., Dec. 22, 1899; s. Francis Henry and Alice Elizabeth (Kelly) B.; prep. edn., Hasbrouck Inst., Hasbrouck Heights, N.J.; Dickinson High Sch.; student Fordham U., New York U., Columbia; unmarried. Pres. Bonner & Bonner, inc., investment bankers, N. Y. City. Clubs: Bankers, Downtown Athletic, Carrollton (New York); Montclair Golf, Green Brook Country (Montclair). Home: 350 Upper Mountain Av., Upper Montclair, N.J. Office: 120 Broadway, New York, N.Y.

BONNER, John Joseph, Diocesan supt. schs., b. Phila. Pa., Nov. 2, 1890; s. Hugh A. and Susan M. (Fleming) B.; grad. Roman Catholic High Sch., Phila., 1908, grad. St. Charles Sem., Overbrook, Pa., 1912; A.B. and Th.D., U. of Propaganda, Rome, Italy; LL.D., Villanova Coll., 1929. Ordained priest R.C. Ch., 1917; served as chaplain, U.S.A., World War, 1918-19; asst. prin. and teacher, Roman Catholic High Sch., Phila., 1919-23; pastor St. Bernard's Ch., Easton, Pa., 1923-24; dean and teacher, Immaculata Coll., 1924-26; diocesan supt. schools, Phila., since 1926. Pres. Cath. Edn. Assn. of Pa.; treas. gen. of Nat. Catholic Ednl. Assn. Home: St. Joseph's Hosp., 16th St. and Girard Av. Office: 19th and Wood Sts., Philadelphia, Pa. *

BONNERT, O. G. F., county supt. of schools; b. Rasselas, Elk Co., Pa., April 27, 1885; s. John V. and Elizabeth M. (Markert) B.; grad. Wilcox (Pa.) High Sch., 1903; grad. Clarion State Teachers Coll., 1908; post grad. work, Grove City Coll., 1917-18, Pa. State Coll., 1933-34; m. Sue M. Thomas, Aug. 2, 1928; children—Eileen M. and O. G. F., 2d. Teacher elementary schools, 1903-06; prin. Straight (Pa.) High Sch., 1909-12, Benezett (Pa.) High Sch., 1912-15, Portland Mills (Pa.) High Sch., 1915-16; asst. supt. Elk Co., Pa., Schools, 1916-34; county supt. of schools since 1934. Pres. Elk Co. Tuberculosis Soc.; chmn. Christmas Seals Sale; mem. exec. com. Agrl. Extension Assn., Ridgway, Pa. Mem. Patrons of Husbandry, Kiwanis, K. of C. Composer of many musical selections. Address: 130 South St., Ridgway, Pa.

BONNESEN, Charles Henry, judge; b. Wheeling, W.Va., Sept. 27, 1903; s. Charles Henry and Dora Lee (Allen) B.; A.B., Ohio Wesleyan U., Delaware, O., 1926; LL.B., W.Va. U., Morgantown, 1930; m. Jane M. Potter, Sept. 22, 1934; 1 son, Charles Henry, III. Admitted to W.Va. bar, 1930; associate of Tom B. Foulk, 1930-39; judge Municipal Court, Wheeling, W. Va., since July 1, 1933. Dir. and treas. Wheeling-Ohio Co. Chapter, Am. Red Cross. Mem. Am. Bar Assn., W.Va. Bar Assn., Ohio Co. Bar Assn., Sigma Chi, Phi Alpha Delta, Theta Alpha Phi. Republican. Presbyn. Home: 32 Carmel Road. Office: Central Union Bldg., Wheeling, W.Va.

BONNET, Frederic, Jr., chemist; b. St. Louis, Mo., Feb. 28, 1878; s. Frederic and Philippine (Dirlam) B.; grad. St. Louis (Mo.) High Sch., 1896; B.S., Wash. U., St. Louis, Mo., 1899; M.S., Harvard, 1902, Ph.D., 1903; m. Annie Howard Binns, June 24, 1908; children—Charles Frederic, Philip Dirlam, Elsie Ferrar (Mrs. Frederic Wentworth Muller), David Dudley, Robert Hugh, Richard William. Instr. in chemistry, State U. of Ia., Iowa City, Ia., 1903-04; instr. in chemistry, Worcester (Mass.) Poly. Inst., 1904-09, asst. prof., 1909-13, prof., 1913-18; chief chemist U.S. Ammonium Nitrate Plant, Perryville, Md., 1918; dir. exptl. lab. Atlas Powder Co., Wilmington, Del., 1918-25; chemist Am. Viscose Corpn., Marcus Hook, Pa., since 1925. Mem. Am. Chem. Soc., A.A.A.S., Am. Assn. Textile Chemists and Colorists, Am. Soc. for Testing Materials, Sigma Xi. Republican. Home: 9 Du Pont St., Ridley Park, Pa. Office: Am. Viscose Corpn., Marcus Hook, Pa.

BONNIWELL, Eugene Cleophas, judge; b. Phila, Pa., Sept. 25, 1872; s. Evander Berry and Elizabeth (Doherty) B.; grad. U. of Pa. Law Sch., 1893; m. Madeleine Helene Cahill, June 5, 1900 (dec.); children—Eugene C., Robert Budd, John Green, Bernard Leonard, Madeleine Helene, Alfred Eugene, Eleanor Mary; m. 2d, Roberta Curry Ranck, Aug. 28, 1934. Admitted to Pa. bar, 1893 and engaged in gen. practice of law at Phila.; elected Judge Municipal Ct., 1913 and has served continuously, re-elected 1923 for term, 1933-43; pres. Firemens Assn. Pa., 1915-21, chmn. exec. com., 1921-31; Dem. nominee for gov., 1918, 1926; for justice Supreme Ct., 1921. Mem. S.A.R. (pres. Pa. soc. 1919, chancellor gen. Nat. Soc., 1921-23), Order of Lafayette (chancellor gen.), Mil. Order of Pulaski (capt. gen.), Order of Washington (chancellor gen.), S.R., Soc. War of 1812, Sons of Union Vets. of Civil War, Middle Atlantic Assn. Amateur Athletic Union (pres. 1938). Honored as Chevalier della Ordona Corona della Italia (Italy, 1924), Comdr. Order Danilio I (Montenegro, 1919), Chevalier Polonæ Restituta (Poland, 1931). Democrat. Catholic. K.C., Moose. Clubs: Penn Athletic, Valley Green Canoe, Reciprocity, One Hundred. Home: 101 W. Carpenter Lane, Philadelphia, Pa.

BONOMO, Michael J., M.D.; asst. surgeon Newark City Hosp.; asso. surgeon Newark Memorial Hosp.; attending surgeon Columbus Memorial and North Newark Hosps. Address: 587 S. 10th St., Newark, N.J.

BOOCOCK, Cornelius Brett, educator; b. Jersey City, N.J., April 21, 1898; s. William Henry and Maud (Brett) B.; grad. Nichols Prep. Sch., Buffalo, N.Y., 1916; A.B., Rutgers, 1920; studied Harvard, summer 1923; m. Ruth Allen, June 6, 1925; children—Catharyn Rombout, Cornelius Brett, Margaret Allen. Instr. Polytechnic Prep. Country Day Sch., Brooklyn, N.Y., 1920-27; headmaster Troy Country Day Sch., 1927-30; headmaster Collegiate Sch., N.Y. City, 1930-34; asso. headmaster Haverford Sch., 1934-37, headmaster since 1937. Served in U.S. Navy, 1918. Mem. Country Day Schs. Assn. and Headmasters' Assn., Delta Phi. Republican. Presbyn. Clubs: Merion Cricket, Mantoloking (N.J.) Yacht. Home: Haverford Sch., Haverford, Pa.

BOOK, William Ira, prof. physics, U. of Pa. Address: U. of Pennsylvania, Philadelphia, Pa.

BOOKSTABER, Philip David, rabbi; b. New York, N.Y., Feb. 12, 1892; s. David and Pearl (Mueller) B.; B.S., Coll. of the City of N.Y., 1911; M.S., Columbia U., 1913; diploma, N.Y. Sch. for Social Work, 1913; student George Washington U., Washington, D.C., 1913-14; rabbi, Hebrew Union Coll., Cincinnati, O., 1924; Ph.D., U. of Cincinnati, 1924; Litt.D. (hon.), Gettysburg (Pa.) Coll., 1937; m. Grace A. Rosenberg, 1918 (died 1918). Spl. agt. U.S. Dept. of Labor, 1914-16; exec. dir. Y.M.H.A., Louisville, Ky., 1916-17; head resident Jewish Settlement, Cincinnati, O., 1917-19; instr. Hebrew Union Coll., 1919-20; asst. rabbi, Rockdale Temple, Cincinnati, O., 1919-24; quiz instr., U. of Cincinnati (O.), 1920-24; rabbi, Reform Temple, Harrisburg, Pa., since 1924. Chaplain, O.R.C. Dir. Harrisburg (Pa.) Hosp.; nat. delegate, ex-committeeman Boy Scouts of America (dir. official tour to Internat. Boy Scout Jamboree, Vogelenzang-Bloemendaal, Holland, 1937); mem. Asso. Charities of Harrisburg, Pa., State and Nat. youth coms. Dep. Nat. chaplain and state chaplain, Jewish War Veterans, mem. Philos. and Psychol. Soc., Sigma Alpha Mu, Pi Tau Pi, Delta Sigma Rho. Awarded Scoutmaster's Key, Silver Beaver award in scouting. Jewish religion. Club: Rotary (Harrisburg, Pa.). Author: Creative Personality, 1925; Judaism and the American Mind, 1939; contbr. to mags. Home: Hotel Harrisburger. Office: Front and Seneca Sts., Harrisburg, Pa.

BOOKSTAVER, Barnet Seymour, M.D.; b. Russia, 1887; s. David and Pearl (Geller) B.; M.D., Bellevue Hosp. and Med. Coll., 1908; m. Anna F. Bockar, June 11, 1911. Began practice medicine, 1908; licensed health officer, State of N.J. since 1937. V.p. J. D. Bookstaver Agency, Inc. Pres. Bd. of Health, 1932-33; dir. of Health since 1932; chief med. inspector of schs. since 1932; police and fire dept. surgeon since 1932 (all of Teaneck). Organizer and pres. Jewish Community Center of Teaneck; trustee and hon. sec. Riverside Synagogue, N.Y. City. Booster organization to Am. Legion; hon. sergt. Vets. Foreign Wars. Mem. Phi Delta Epsilon, Lebanon Hosp. Alumni. Mason, Elk. Home: 193 Norma Road, Teaneck, N.J. Office: 865 West End Av., New York, N.Y.

BOOKWALTER, George Ralph, pres. Boyd N. Park, Inc.; b. Mendon, O., Aug. 18, 1892; s. Harrison S. and Margaret (Stevens) B.; m. Doris Dawson, June 4, 1918. Supt. pub. schs. Texhoma, Okla., 1919-21; sec. and treas. Boyd N. Park, Inc., Franklin, Pa., 1927-35, pres. and dir. since 1935; v.p. and dir. Franklin (Pa.) Community Bank since 1935; pres. and dir. Inter-City Credit Bur. since 1938. Major U.S. Army Res. Mem. Franklin Better Business Club (pres.), Franklin Chamber of Commerce (dir., former chmn. retail trades div.), Ft. Venango Res. Officers Assn. (ex-pres.), Am. Legion (ex-post comdr.). Methodist (trustee, mem. official bd. First M.E. Ch., Franklin, Pa.). Clubs: Franklin, Kiwanis (dir., ex-pres.). Home: 420 9th St. Office: 1252 Liberty St., Franklin, Pa.

BOOMHOWER, William Gibson, clergyman; b. Berne, N.Y., Jan. 15, 1891; s. Frank and Ada (Gibson) B.; student Hartwick Acad., Cooperstown, N.Y., 1909-11, Hartwick Theol. Sem., 1911-14, D.D., 1928; m. Mildred Elze, June 26, 1920; 1 dau., Jessie Elze. Ordained to ministry Lutheran Ch., 1914; pastor Rhinebeck, Dutchess Co., and Brunswick, Rensselaer Co., N.Y., 1914-19; gen. sec. of religious edn., N.J. State Sun. Sch. Assn. 1919-20; pastor Troy, N.Y., 1920-22, Cobleskill, N.Y., 1922-29, Jersey City, N.J., 1929-35, Phila., Pa. since 1935. Republican. Mason. Home: 5143 Race St., Philadelphia, Pa.

BOOMSLITER, George Paul, prof. mechanics, W.Va. U. Address: West Virginia U., Morgantown, W.Va.

BOONE, Charles Guthrie, plant mgr.; b. Chrisman, Ill., Sept. 16, 1878; s. Thomas M. and Rebecca (Guthrie) B.; student Chrisman (Ill.) pub. schs., 1884-94, Northwestern Acad., Evanston, Ill., 1899-1900; B.S., U. of Ill., Urbana, Ill., 1906; m. Mabel Bush, June 15, 1909; children—Eleanor Rebecca (Mrs. William A. Stone), Frances Guthrie (Mrs. James Miller), Thomas Jared (dec.), Miriam Guthrie, Charles Guthrie. Mech. engr. Cleveland Cliff Iron Co., Ishpeming, Mich., 1906-18; mech. supt. E. I. Dupont de Nemours & Co., 1918-22, asst. mgr., 1922-24; plant mgr. Pa. Salt Mfg. Co., Natrona, Pa., since 1924; dir. First Nat. Bank of Natrona. Pres. bd. of govs. Allegheny Valley Hosp.; v.p. and dir. Allegheny Valley Y.M.C.A. Republican. Presbyterian. Mason. Club: Brackenridge Heights Country (Tarentum, Pa.). Address: 41 Locust St., Natrona, Pa.

BOOTH, Albert Edward, oil producer; b. Bradford, Pa., July 18, 1887; s. Albert Bamber and Margaret Dorcas (Bovaird) B.; student Bradford (Pa.) pub. schs., 1893-1905, Princeton U., 1909; m. Myrtle Winslow Brooks, Apr. 8, 1925; 1 dau., Gretchen. Managing partner M. D. Booth & Co., independent oil producer, Bradford, Pa., since 1934; dir. Kendall Refining Co.; dir. Bovaird Supply Co., 1st chmn. petroleum advisory bd., Sch. of Mineral Industries, Pa. State College, 1915. Served as 2d lieut., 29 F.A., 3d O.T.C., U.S. Army, 1917-18. Mem. Northwestern Pa. Oil Producers Assn. (pres. 1924-32); Pa. Grade Crude Oil Assn. (dir.). Republican. Presbyterian. Clubs: Bradford (sec. and treas. since 1936), Pennhills, Valley Hunt (Bradford, Pa.). Home: 270 Jackson Av. Office: 12 Chestnut St., Bradford, Pa.

BOOTH, Cecil Oliver; prof. prosthetic dentistry, U. of Pittsburgh. Address: U. of Pittsburgh, Pittsburgh, Pa.

BOOTH, George, physician; b. Pittsburgh, Pa., Jan. 16, 1901; s. Harry John and Ella (Youngson) B.; B.S., Allegheny Coll., 1922; M.D., Harvard U. Med. Sch., 1926; m. Adelaide Earley Reech, Oct. 4, 1936; children—Albert Gustave Reech, Letitia Emilie Reech, Edward Ernest Reech II, John Earley Reech. Interne, West Pa. Hosp., 1926, Peter Bent Brigham Hosp., Boston, Mass., 1927-28; in gen. practice of medicine at Pittsburgh, Pa., since 1929; instr. medicine, U. of Pittsburgh Med. Sch.; staff phys. West Pa. Hosp.; chief of diabetic service, Childrens Hosp., Pittsburgh, and dir. Renziehauser Memorial Ward and Clinic, same. Fellow Am. Coll. Phys.; mem. A.M.A., Allegheny Co. Med. Soc., Pittsburgh Acad. of Medicine, Soc. for Biol. Research of U. of Pittsburgh, Pittsburgh Clin. and Pathol. Soc., Sigma Alpha Epsilon, Alpha Chi Sigma. Republican. Methodist. Mason. Club. Pittsburgh Athletic. Home: 1340 Bennington Av. Office: Medical Arts Bldg., Pittsburgh, Pa.

BOOTH, Isaac Walter, railway exec.; b. Phila., Pa., Apr. 1, 1883; s. Isaac Johnson and Helen Alois (Cullen) B.; student Phila. Central High Sch., 1898-99, Chester (Pa.) Commercial Coll., 1900-01, U. of Pa. Evening Sch., 1911-14; m. Myrtle T. Crossan, June 7, 1916; children—John Filbert (dec.), Robert Emrey. With Norfolk and Western Ry. at Phila. since 1902, successively as stenographer and clerk, 1902-09, chief clerk, 1909-14, sec. and asst. treas., later asst. sec. and cashier, 1914-20, sec. and asst. treas., 1920-36, v.p. and sec. 1936-38, v.p. since 1939; dir. Norfolk and Western Ry. Co. and subsidiaries, Phila. Nat. Bank, Mutual Fire, Marine and Inland Ins. Co. Former v.p., pres. and mem. exec. com. Ry. Treasurers Assn. Mem. Pi Delta Epsilon. Republican. Episcopalian. Mason. Clubs: Union League, Penn Athletic (Phila.); Old York Road Country (Jenkintown, Pa.); Roanoke (Va.) Country. Home: 8205 Elberon Av. Office: 1419 Broad St. Station Bldg., Philadelphia, Pa.

BOOTH, John A(very), lawyer; b. Rockford, Ill., June 1, 1901; s. Frederick Louis and Rosa Lena (Koeller) B.; ed. Ind. Univ., 1918-19; LL.B., N.J. Law Sch., Newark, 1923; m. Marie Katherine Christensen, July 2, 1932; children—Nancy Marie, John Avery, Jr. Employed as clk. and asst. custodian, Nat. Surety Co., N.Y. City, 1920-22; law clk. in office Coult & Smith, Newark, N.J., 1922-24; admitted to N.J. bar as atty., 1924, as counsellor and master in chancery, 1928; settlement officer Essex Title Guaranty & Trust Co., 1925-26; organized Morris & Essex Title Guaranty & Mortgage Co. and sec., treas. and dir., 1926-37; engaged in practice of law in Caldwell, N.J., to 1934, in Montclair, N.J., since 1931, asso. with Boyd & Dodd, Montclair, since 1931, also in pvt. practice; dir. Grover Cleveland Bldg. & Loan Assn., Caldwell, N.J.; formerly recorder, Caldwell, N.J.; now recorder, Essex Fells. Mem. exec. com. Council Social Agencies, Montclair. Trustee West Essex Community Fund, Grover Cleveland High Sch. Scholarship Fund, Caldwell, N.J. Mem. Am., N.J. State, and Essex Co. bar assns., Beta Theta Pi. Republican. Conglist. Mason, Elk. Clubs: Country (Essex Fells); Kiwanis of Caldwell (past pres.); Officers of Army and Navy (New York). Home: Rensselaer Rd., Essex Fells. Office: 483 Bloomfield Av., Montclair, N.J.

BOOTH, Leland, exec. farm bur.; b. Barbour Co., W.Va., Dec. 31, 1899; s. George and Maggie (O'Brien) B.; B.S. in Agr., W.Va. Univ., Morgantown, W.Va., 1924; m. Winifred Marie Viquesney, May 23, 1924; 1 dau., Betty June. Asso. with West Virginia Farm News, Morgantown, W.Va. since 1924, mgr., 1924-39, editor since 1927; sec. W.Va. Farm Bur., Morgantown, W.Va., since 1930, treas. since 1929. Mem. Tau Kappa Epsilon. Republican. Methodist. Contbr. farm jours. Home: Hopecrest. Office: Oglebay Hall, Morgantown, W.Va.

BOOTH, Miriam B, supervisor of English; b. Doylestown, O., Apr. 13, 1894; d. Eli Jacob Van Rensellar and Catharine Eliza (Hester) B.; A.B., Ohio Wesleyan U., Delaware, O., 1916; A.M., Middlebury (Vt.) Coll., 1933; summer sch. student Columbia U., 1923, 1937, New York U., 1928; student U. of Chicago, Jan.-June 1929; unmarried. Teacher of English, Cardington, O., 1916-18, Tiffin, O., 1918-20, Central High Sch., Erie, Pa., 1920-24; head of English dept., East High Sch., Erie, 1924-31, asst. prin., 1931-38; supervisor of secondary sch. English, Erie, Pa., since 1938. Mem. N.E.A., N.E.A. Dept. of Secondary Edn. (mem. com. on motion pictures), N.E.A. Dept. Secondary Sch. Prins., Nat. Council of Teachers of Eng. (Pa. rep. on pub. relations com.), Nat. Conf. on Research in English, Pa. State Edn. Assn. (mem. com. on speech edn.). Republican. Methodist. Club: College Women's (Erie, Pa.). Contbr. to ednl. jours.; speaker before teacher orgns. Home: 640 W. 9th St., Erie, Pa.

BOOTH, Osborne; T. W. Phillips prof. of Old Testament, Bethany Coll. Address: Bethany, W.Va.

BOOTH, William Wallace, lawyer; b. Pittsburgh, Pa., Nov. 2, 1896; s. Harry J. and Ella M. (Youngson) B.; grad. Charleroi (Pa.) High Sch., 1915; B.S. in Economics (cum laude), U. of Pittsburgh, 1918, LL.B., 1922; m. Adelaide Lanz, June 27, 1925; children—William Wallace, James Youngson, Cynthia Skelton. Admitted to Pa. bar, 1922, and since practiced in Pittsburgh; partner of firm Reed, Smith, Shaw & McClay, Pittsburgh; sec. Anchor Box and Lumber Co., Von Broco Steel Plate Engraving Co.; dir. William M. Bailey Co., Rowmor Corpn. Served in Air Service, U.S. Army, 1918-19. Mem. Am. Bar Assn., Pa. Bar Assn., Sigma Alpha Epsilon, Phi Delta Phi, Beta Gamma Sigma. Republican. Methodist. Mason (32°, K.T., Shriner). Clubs: Duquesne, Longue Vue, University (Pittsburgh). Home: 826 Amberson Av. Office: 747 Union Trust Bldg., Pittsburgh, Pa.

BOOTH, Winfield Scott, clergyman; b. Phila., Pa., Nov. 18, 1882; s. Adin and Ella M. (Clark) B.; A.B. summa cum laude, Bucknell U., 1908, A.M., same, 1910; B.D., Crozer Theol. Sem., 1911, M.Th., same, 1923; (hon.) D.D., Bucknell U., 1931; m. Evora Pearl Mailey, Dec. 23, 1913; children—Winfield Scott, Jr., Paul Mailey. Ordained to ministry Alpha Bapt. Ch., Phila., Pa., June 8, 1911; asso. pastor, Alpha Ch., Phila., Pa., 1908-10; pastor, Harrisburg, Pa., 1911-17, Collingswood, N.J., 1917-26; exec. sec. Bapt. Extension Soc. of Newark, N.J., and vicinity since 1926, a Class A. Bapt. City Mission Soc. Served as chaplain with rank capt., U.S.A. during World War, promoted for meritorious service aboard U.S. Transport "Princess Matoika." Trustee Internat. Bapt. Sem., East Orange, N.J. Asso. clk. East Bapt. Assn. Mem. Alumni Assn. Crozer Theol. Sem. (pres. 1938), Delta Sigma (Bucknell). Pres. Phila. Ministers Conf., 1923-24. Republican. Baptist. Mason. Artisan. Author: Materials for Modern Preaching, (yr. pub.) 1939. Home: 244 W. Passaic Av., Rutherford. Office: 158 Washington St., Newark, N.J.

BOOTHBY, Willard S.; v.p. E. H. Rollins & Sons, Inc. Home: 101 W. Mermaid Lane, Chestnut Hill. Office: 1528 Walnut St., Philadelphia, Pa.

BOOZAN, William E.; chief attending ophthalmologist and otorhinolaryngologist St. Elizabeth and Alexian Brothers hosps. Address: 1139 E. Jersey St., Elizabeth, N.J.

BORDEN, Albert Greene, life insurance; b. New York, N.Y., June 16, 1878; s. William and Mary G. (Whittemore) B.; ed. Dearborn-Morgan Private School, Orange, N.J.; m. Katharine Smith Talcott, June 5th, 1914; 1 son, Albert Greene and stepchildren, Thayer Talcott, Judith Talcott (Mrs. Russell Y. Smith), Katharine William Talcott. Began as architect, 1893; asso. with The Equitable Life Assurance Soc., New York, since 1894, now 2d vice-pres.; pres. Borden Mining Co. Served as mem. former Essex Troop, later 1st Squadron, Nat. Guard of N.J. (now 102d Cavalry), as private and advancing to captain, 1900-17. Mem. New Eng. Soc. of N.Y. Republican. Presbyterian. Clubs: Century Assn. (New York); Bankers (New York); Orange Lawn Tennis (South Orange); Rock Spring Golf (West Orange). Home: 204 Vose Av., South Orange, N.J. Office: 393 7th Av., New York, N.Y.

BORDEN, Bertram Harold, commn. merchant; b. N.Y. City, Oct. 3, 1868; s. Matthew C.D. and Harriet (Durfee) B.; ed. pvt. schs., N.Y. City; m. Mary Lavinia Owen, Jan. 23, 1896. Began business with father in Bliss, Fabyan & Co., dry goods commn., 1888; pres. Am. Printing Co., since 1912, M.C.D. Borden & Sons, Inc., since 1923, Borden Mills, Inc., since 1924. Pres. bd. edn. Borough of Rumson, Monmouth Co., N.J. Mem. N.E. Soc. of City of N.Y. Republican. Episcopalian. Clubs: Rumson Country (Rumson); Merchants, Union League (New York). Home: "The Riverlands," Rumson, N.J. Office. 90 Worth St., New York, N.Y.*

BORDEN, William S., insurance; b. Groveville, N.J., Feb. 1, 1893; s. Edward and Susan (Lewis) B.; grad. Trenton (N.J.) High Sch., 1911; A.B., Princeton, 1915; m. Lida Scheidnagel, Dec. 28, 1920; children—William S., Barbara Louise, Walter J. Social worker Children's Aid Soc., Essex County, N.J., 1915-17; real estate and insurance, Trenton, N.J., since 1919; Mercer County dir. of finance, 1922-31; pres. W. S. Borden Co. Served as capt. field arty., U.S. Army, 1917-19. Sec. War Memorial Commn., Trenton. Chmn. Rep. Com. for Mercer County; aide-de-camp to Gov. Hoffman, 1935-38; pres. Rep. Vets. Assn. of N.J. Dir. Trenton Leisure Hour Sch. Mem. Nat. Assn. Ins. Agents, Terrace Club (Princeton). Republican. Methodist. Mason (Shriner), Elk. Club: Yardley Country. Home: 924 Edgewood Av. Office: 103 W. Hanover St., Trenton, N.J.

BORDLEY, James, Jr., surgeon Hosp. for Women of Md. and Union Memorial Hosp. Address: 330 N. Charles St., Baltimore, Md.

BORG, Charles H(arry), real estate; b. Town of Union, N.J., Sept. 24, 1891; s. Franz A.J.C. and Wilhelmina (Futterer) B.; ed. pub. schs. and high sch., Town of Union; m. A. Marie Haldenwang, May 25, 1916 (died 1935); children—Charles H., Jr., Muriel Marie, Robert Halden. Began as messenger in Wall St., 1906; mem. N.Y. Curb Exchange, 1912-29: engaged in real estate and ins. bus. as Chas. H. Borg, Inc., and pres. and treas. since 1927; pres. and treas. Hudrividge Realty Corpn., Urban Investing Corpn.; pres. Magna Vista Holding Corpn.; treas. Sicomac Realty Co.; re-elected to membership N.Y. Curb Exchange, 1938. Republican. Presbyn. Mason. Club: Country (Arcola). Home: 386 Walnut St., Englewood, N.J. Office: 210 Main St., Hackensack, N.J.

BORG, John, newspaper publisher; b. Union Hill, N.J., May 24, 1883; s. Frank A. and Minna (Futterer) B.; ed. Public School and High Sch., Union Hill, N.J., 1888-97; m. Hazel M. Gowen, Apr. 15, 1905; children—Donald G., Dorothy V. (Mrs. Frank W. Packard). Began as messenger boy 1897; in banking business, 1906-20; pres. Callahan Zinc-Lead Co., 1920-26; pres. Bergen Evening Record, 1926-39; commr. Port of New York Authority since 1938. Mem. Am. Inst. Mining and Metall. Engrs. Republican. Mem. Reformed Ch. Mason, Elk. Home: 282 Prospect Av. Office: 295 Main St., Hackensack, N.J.

BORIE, Charles Louis, architect; b. Phila., Pa., June 9, 1870; s. Beauveau and Patty Duffield (Neill) B.; student St. Paul's Sch., Concord, N.H. 1884-88; B.S., U. of Pa., 1892; m. Helen Sewell, Oct. 1892, (died Nov. 1928); children—C. Louis, 3d, W. J. Sewell, Henry Peter, Beauveau, 3d; m. 2d Carrie Tyson Drayton, June 1934. Began practice in 1904; now mem. of firm Zantzinger & Borie, Phila.; prin. works: Masonic Homes, Elizabethtown, Pa., Valley Forge (Pa.) Chapel; Phila. Divinity Sch., dormitories at Princeton and Sheffield Scientific Sch. (Yale); dormitories and Adminstrn. Bldg. of U. of Chicago; St. Paul's Ch., Chestnut Hill, Pa.; Pa. Mus. of Art; Dept. of Justice Bldg., Washington, D.C. Trustee Library Co. of Phila., University Mus. of Phila., U. of Pa.; chmn. Council of Am. Acad. in Rome, Smithsonian Gallery of Art Commn. (Washington, D.C.); mem. Commn. of Fine Arts (Washington, D.C.) Fellow A.I.A.; mem. Am. Acad. Arts and Letters, Nat. Inst. of Arts and Letters. Episcopalian. Home: Rydal, Pa. Office: Architects Bldg., Philadelphia, Pa.*

BORLAND, Andrew Allen, prof. dairy husbandry; b. Sandy Lake, Pa., June 11, 1878; s. Adam C. and Sarah Ann (Carmichael) B.; B.S., Pa. State Coll., 1909; M.S., U. of Wis., 1910; m. Jessie E. Canon, Oct. 12, 1910; children—Gerald Canon, Margaret Eleanor. Engaged in teaching, pub. schs., Pa., 1898-1905; asst., dairy husbandry research, Pa. State Coll., 1910-11; prof. animal and dairy husbandry in charge dept., U. of Vt., 1911-15; prof. dairy husbandry extension in charge, Pa. State Coll., 1915-19, prof. dairy husbandry in charge of dept. since 1919. Served as mem. Bd. Edn., Burlington, Vt., 1913-15. Mem. Bd. Civic Planning, State College, Pa., since 1930. Trustee Westminster Foundation, State College, Pa. Mem. A.A.A.S., Am. Dairy Sci. Assn. (v.p. 1920-22, pres. 1922-24, pres. Eastern Div. 1925), Phi Kappa Phi, Gamma Sigma Delta, Delta Sigma Rho, Alpha Zeta, Delta Theta Sigma. U.S. Del. to 8th Worlds Dairy Cong., London, Reading, Edinburgh, Glasgow, 1928. Presbyn. Mason. Mem. com. management, Journal of Dairy Science since 1932. Contbg. editor, Pennsylvania Farmer since 1923. Contbr. many articles and bulls. on dairy cattle feeding and management. Home: 310 S. Burrowes St., State College, Pa.

BORLOSO, Alfred Nunzio, coll. prof.; b. Sessa Aurunca, Italy, July 27, 1901; s. Nunzio and Maria (Petricone) B.; came to U.S., 1924, naturalized, 1929; Litt.D., Royal U. of Naples, 1922, Ph.D., 1923; A.M., Columbia U., 1928, Ph.D., 1929; m. Violette M. Aiello, Nov. 5, 1929; children—Jacqueline Violette, Marylin Gioia. Prof. classical letters, Royal Inst., Sessa, Italy 1921-22; prof. Latin and Greek, Royal Coll., Sessa, Italy 1922-24; instr. Italian, N.Y. Univ., 1928-29; head Italian dept., N.J. State Teachers Coll., Paterson, since 1937. Served as mem. Bd. Edn., City of Paterson, since 1938; Mem. Bd. of Libraries, City of Paterson, 1930-32; Pres. literary soc., Dante Alighieri. Mem. N.J. Coll. Teachers Assn., Am. Italian Teachers Assn., Am. Assn. of Correspondents of Fgn. Newspapers, Columbia Alumni Assn. Roman Catholic. Clubs: Italian (Paterson); Art and Letters (New York). Author: Eterno Femminin Gentile, 1924; Lucilio, 1922; Com'E'Bella Giovinezza (musical comedy), 1922; Lucilius and the Latin Satyre, 1928; Barcarola (musical comedy), 1934; Democracy and Fascism, 1935; Pena Capitale, 1936; Roman Matrons, 1937; As They Say It in Italy, 1939. Contbr. many articles to mags. and jours. of Italy and America. Am. corr. Il Mattino daily newspaper of Italy. Home: 274 8th Av., Paterson, N.J.

BORNEMAN, Henry Stauffer, lawyer; b. Allentown, Pa., Mar. 22, 1870; s. Joseph H. and Esther (Stauffer) B.; grad. West Chester State Normal Sch., 1889; LL.B., U. of Pa. Law Sch. 1894; m. Martha E. Ide, June 22, 1897; children—Helen Ide, Joseph Ide; m. 2d, Rose Weller Smith, Feb. 4, 1924. Admitted to Pa. bar, 1894, and since engaged in gen. practice of law at Phila. Pres. Presbyn. Hist. Soc.; sec. Pa. German Soc. Republican. Presbyn. Mason (active in Grand Lodge of Pa.). Club: Union League (Phila.). Author: Early Freemasonry in Pennsylvania, 1931; Pennsylvania German Illuminated Manuscripts, 1938. Home: 6387 Overbrook Av. Office: 1018 Real Estate Trust Bldg., Philadelphia, Pa.

BORNSCHEUER, Albert A.; demonstrator in surgery, U. of Pittsburgh; plastic surgeon St. Francis Hosp. Home: 121 University Pl., Pittsburgh, Pa.

BOROW, Benjamin, physician; b. Bethlehem, Pa., Feb. 14, 1894; s. Max and Bella (Sprinz) B.; ed. Fargo Coll., Fargo, N.D., 1909-13, N.D. Agrl. Coll., 1913; M.D., U. of Pa. Med. Sch., 1917; grad. study, U. of Vienna, Austria, 1929-30; m. Beatrice Aronson, Apr. 27, 1922; children—Edward, Maxwell. Interne Phila. Gen. Hosp., 1917-18; engaged in gen. practice of medicine and surgery at Bound Brook, N.J., since 1919; treas. and dir. Bound Brook Hosp. Served as lt. Med. Corps, U.S.A., during World War. Mem. Am. Med. Assn., N.J. State Med. Soc. Republican. Jewish religion. Mason, Elk. Home: 574 Watchung Drive. Office: 507 Church St., Bound Brook, N.J.

BOROW, Maurice, M.D.; b. Fargo, N.D., June 1, 1902; s. Max Abraham and Elizabeth (Prince) B.; grad. Lincoln Sch., Fargo, 1916, Fargo Coll. Acad., 1920; student U. of Pa., 1920-21; B.S., U. of Ala., 1924; M.D., Temple U., 1927; unmarried. Began gen. practice of medicine, 1927; mem. staffs: Post Grad. Hosp. of New York, Bound Brook Hosp., Somerset Hosp.; county physician, County of Somerset, 1933-39. Fellow A.M.A.; mem. Acad. Medicine of Newark, Essex Co. Pathol. Soc., Congress of Obstetrics and Gynecology, Temple, Ala. Soc. of Mid West, Somerset Co. Med. Soc., N.J. State Med. Soc. Clin. Soc. Elizabeth Gen. Hosp., Kappa Nu, Phi Delta Epsilon. Republican. Jewish religion. Mason, Elk. Club: Newark Athletic. Home: Warren Twp. Office: 507 Church St., Bound Brook, N.J.

BORST, George Hermann, real estate management and sculpturing; b. Phila., Pa., Feb. 9, 1889; s. Albert William and Emma (Tadd) B.; grad. Central Manual Training High Sch., Phila., 1907; grad. Pa. Acad. Fine Arts, 1928; m. Susan Patten Armstrong, June 26, 1914. Began in building business, 1907; became mem. firm George and Borst, Phila., contractors and builders, 1910; organized 20th Century Storage Warehouse Co., and built warehouse, 1917, pres. 1917-24, pres. and chmn. bd. since 1924; pres. 20th Century Realty Co. Took up sculpturing, studying abroad in Paris, Florence and Rome. Works: Bronze Memorial Boy Scout Fountain on Common at Plymouth, N.H.; Bronze and Marble Memorial to Dr. Philip H. Goepp, Acad. of Music, Phila.; Bronze Memorials in Camp Pasquaney and Camp Onaway, N.H. Awards: Stewardson prize, Stimson prize, Cresson traveling scholarship (to Europe). Fellow Pa. Acad. Fine Arts. Republican. Episcopalian. Clubs: Union League, Kiwanis (Phila.). Home: 201 Walnut Av., Wayne, Pa. Office: 3120 Market St., Philadelphia, Pa.

BORTON, George W., pres. and gen. mgr. Pa. Crusher Co.; b. Rancocas, N.J., Nov. 6, 1870; s. George B. and Susan (Wills) B.; student Westtown (Pa.) Friends Sch. and Cornell U.; m. Elizabeth Action Lippincott, Sept. 14, 1898; 1 dau., Gertrude L. (Mrs. Zane). Engr. Charles Edgerton, constrn. work, 1895-98; with Borton-Tierney Co., 1898-1912; pres. and gen. mgr. Pa. Crusher Co., Phila., since 1904. Mem. Am. Soc. M.E., Am. Inst. M.E., Soc. of Industrial Engrs. Franklin Inst. Clubs: Phila. Engineers (Phila.); Barrel Island Gun. Home: 246 Harvey St., Germantown. Office: Liberty Trust Bldg., Philadelphia, Pa.

BORTONE, Frank, M.D.; attending thoracic surgeon Hudson County Tuberculosis Hosp.; attending surgeon Christ Hosp.; cons. surgeon Margaret Hague Maternity Hosp. Address: 2765 Hudson Boul., Jersey City, N.J.

BORTZ, Edward Le Roy, physician; b. Greensburg, Pa., Feb. 10, 1896; s. Adam Franklin and Anna (Wineman) B.; ed. Pa. State Coll., 1915-16; A.B., Harvard, 1920, M.D., Harvard Med. Sch., 1923; m. Margaret Welty, Dec. 27, 1926: 1 son, Walter Michael II. Interne The Lankenau Hosp., Phila. 1923-25; in practice of internal medicine at Phila. since 1926; chief med. service-B, The Lankenau Hospital; asso. prof. medicine, Grad. Sch. of U. of Pa. Lt. comdr. U.S.N.R., 4th Naval Dist. Fellow Am.

Coll. Phys. (gov. for Eastern Pa.); mem. Phila. Co. Med. Soc. (mem. bd. dirs., chmn. com. on med. edn.), Phila. Coll. Phys. (chmn. com. on scientific business); Pa. State Med. Soc. (chmn. commn. for study pneumonia control). Honored by Meritorious Award from Commonwealth of Pa., 1939. Republican. Presbyterian. Clubs: Union League, Penn Athletic (Phila.); Whitemarsh Valley Country (Chestnut Hill, Pa.). Home: 2021 W. Girard Av., Philadelphia, Pa.

BOSLER, Lester Comly, mech. engring.; b. Ogontz, Pa., April 29, 1884; s. Joseph and Cynthia (Green) B.; B.S. in M.E., U. of Pa., 1905, M.E., 1932; m. Marion Watson, Oct. 7, 1908; children—Lester Comly, William Joseph Watson. In employ Phila. Rapid Transit Co. in various exec. positions, 1905-16; steam engr. Midvale Steel & Ordnance Co., 1916-21; mech. engr. Madeira, Hill & Co., 1921-38; mech. engr. Coleman & Co., Phila., since 1938; pres. and dir. Automatic Appliances, Inc., distributors anthracite coal burners, Phila., since 1928. Mem. Am. Soc. Mech. Engrs., Phi Kappa Psi. Republican. Unitarian. Club: Engineers (Phila; past pres. and mem. bd.). Home: 445 W. Price St. Office: 123 S. Broad St., Philadelphia. Pa.

BOSSARD, James Herbert Siward, sociologist; b. Danielsville, Pa., Sept. 29, 1888; s. John Henry and Augusta Minerva (Oplinger) B.; A.B., Muhlenberg Coll., Allentown, Pa., 1909; A.M., University of Pa., 1911, Ph.D., 1918; m. Miriam Corrine Ritter, June 30, 1914; m. 2d, Dorothy M. Lemle, May 14, 1929; children—Barbara, Constance. Served as professor of history and social science, Muhlenberg Coll., 1911-17; lecturer on sociology, Lafayette Coll., 1917-18; prof. sociology and economics same coll., 1918, head dept. of economics and sociology, 1918-20; asst. prof. sociology Wharton Sch., U. of Pa., 1920-25, prof. since 1925; dir. William T. Carter Foundation for Child Helping, U. of Pa. since 1938. Taught summers at U. of Calif., 1929, 30, 33, 35. Pres. West Phila. Community Conf., 1922-1925. Dir. survey of Northampton Co., Pa., for Interch. World Movement, 1919; dir. survey Collegiate Schs. of Business, 1929-31. Dir. Pa. Com. on Penal Affairs; dir. child welfare div. Pub. Charities Assn. Pa.; dir. Univ. Settlement House, Social Service Dept. of U. of Pa. Hosp., Maternal Health Center; pres. Eastern Sociol. Conf., 1934-35; pres. Pennsylvania Birth Control Federation; mem. Phila. Commn. on Federal Housing Projects, Pa. State Probation Commn. Mem. Am. Acad. Polit. and Social Science, Am. Sociol. Soc. (mem. exec. com.); Am. Council of Learned Societies, Population Assn. of America, Am. Assn. Univ. Professors, Alpha Tau Omega, Pi Gamma Mu. Republican. Episcopalian. Clubs: Manufacturers, Bankers (Phila.); The Lenape, The Contemporary. Author: The Churches of Allentown, 1918; Problems of Social Well-Being, 1927. Co-Author: Education for Business, 1931. Editor and Co-Author: Man and His World, 1932; Social Change and Social Problems, 1934, rev. edit., 1938. Spl. editor Annals of Am. Acad. Polit. and Social Science, Nov. 1921, Sept. 1925, Sept. 1930, Sept. 1932, Nov. 1934, Nov. 1937. Contbr. articles to mags. Home: 28 Baily Road, Lansdowne, Pa.

BOSTOCK, Edward Crary, manufacturer; b. Chicago, Ill., Oct. 29, 1884; s. Edward Crary and Mary Elizabeth (Jungé) B.; B.S., Acad. of the New Ch., 1905; m. Madeline Glenn, Sept. 3, 1913; children—Joan, Annette (Mrs. Ralph Raynor Brown), Edward Crary, Zara, Robert Morris, Bernice, Ruth, Peter Glenn. Employed as mgr. Pleasantville Water Co., 1907-10; treas. Acad. of the New Ch., 1910-17; sec. and asst. treas. The Pitcairn Co., Phila., since 1917; pres. Pittsburgh Valve & Fittings Co., 1931-36; pres. and dir. Michigan Sugar Co., mfrs. beet sugar, since 1933; pres. Bryn Athyn Supply Co. Pres. Bryn Athyn Borough Council. Dir. The Acad. of the New Ch., Gen. Ch. of the New Jerusalem. Republican. Gen. Ch. of the New Jerusalem. Clubs: Union League (Phila.); Detroit (Detroit, Mich.); Saginaw (Saginaw,

Mich.). Home: Bryn Athyn. Office: 1616 Walnut St., Philadelphia, Pa.

BOSTON, William Theodore, supt. county schs.; b. East New Market, Md., May 29, 1909; s. James E. and Margaret E. (Phillips) B.; A.B., Washington Coll., Chestertown, Md., 1930; m. Sarah Elizabeth Bassett, Nov. 13, 1932; 1 dau., Marilyn Lou. Prin. sch., Eldorado, Md., 1930-31; teacher, Sem. Sch., Cambridge, Md. 1931-34; teacher, high sch., Cambridge, Md., 1934-35; prin. Cambridge Sem. Sch., 1935-38; supt. Dorchester County Schs. since 1938. Mem. Dorchester Chapter Am. Red Cross (v.p.), County Council Social Agencies, Bd. Dorchester Co. Md. Childrens Aid Soc., Dorchester County Recreational Council, Council Local Troop Boy Scouts of America. Mem. N.E.A., Am. Assn. Sch. Adminstrs., Nat. Vocational Guidance Assn., Phi Sigma Tau (now Lambda Chi Alpha). Baptist. Club: Rotary of Cambridge. Home: 305 Belvedere Av., Cambridge, Md.

BOSTWICK, Roy Grier, lawyer; b. Du Bois, Pa., June 18, 1883; s. Charles Edgar and Elizabeth Rebecca (Grier) B.; A.B. and A.M., Bucknell U., Lewisburg, Pa., 1905; LL.B., U. of Pa. Law Sch., 1908; m. Marie Louise Leiser, Nov. 28, 1912. Admitted to Pa. bar, 1908 and since engaged in gen. practice at Pittsburgh; mem. firm Brown, Stewart and Bostwick, 1909-21, Thorp, Bostwick, Reed & Armstrong, Pittsburgh, since 1921; vice-pres. and dir. Wilkinsburg Bank, Arcade Land Co.; sec. and dir. Wilkinsburg Hotel Co. Served as chief Div. of Analysis and chief Div. of Complaints, Nat. War Labor Bd., Washington, D.C., during World War. Trustee Bucknell U., First Presbyn. Ch.; pres. and trustee Family Soc. of Allegheny Co.; mem. exec. com. Presbyn. Union of Pittsburgh. Sec. Law Library Com. of Allegheny Co. Mem. Am., Pa., Allegheny Co. bar assns., Am. Judicature Soc., Am. Mus. of Natural History (New York), Kappa Sigma, Theta Delta Tau, Phi Kappa Sigma. Republican. Presbyterian. Mason (K.T., 32°, Shriner). Clubs: Duquesne, University, Harvard-Yale-Princeton (Pittsburgh); Longue Vue Country (Verona, Pa.); Pittsburgh Field (Aspinwall, Pa.); Wilmas (Wilkinsburg, Pa.); Union League (New York). Home: 718 North Av., Wilkinsburg. Office: 2812 Grant Bldg., Pittsburgh, Pa.

BOSWELL, George Elmer, clergyman; b. Phila., Pa., June 22, 1892; s. Charles and Sophia (Eust) B.; prep. edn. Brown Coll. Prep. Sch.; A.B., U. of Pa., 1916; S.T.B., Pa. Divinity Sch., 1918; m. Mary Virginia Brady, June 12, 1918; children—Mary Virginia, Jane Elizabeth. Ordained to ministry of Episcopal Ch., 1918; asst. rector Ch. of Resurrection, Phila., 1918-19; rector St. Thomas Ch., Glassboro, and Chapel of Good Shepherd, Pitman, N.J., 1919-21; rector Holy Trinity Ch., Hillsdale, N.J., 1921-29; rector St. James Ch., Bristol, Pa., since 1929. Mem. Sch. Bd. of Hillsdale for 2 years. Republican. Mason. Club: Exchange (Bristol, Pa.). Home: 829 Radcliffe St., Bristol, Pa.

BOSWELL, John Edward, lawyer; b. Ocean City, N.J., May 23, 1905; s. Andrew C. and Elizabeth (Stevens) B.; student Ocean City (N.J.) High Sch., 1920-24, U. of Pa., 1924-26; LL.B., Dickinson Law Sch., Carlisle, Pa., 1929; m. Kathryn N. Heil, June 5, 1930; children—Barbara Ann, Bette K. Asso. with Andrew C. Boswell in gen. practice of law at Ocean City, N.J., 1932-36; mem. of firm Boswell & Boswell, Ocean City, N.J., since 1936. City solicitor, Ocean City, N.J., since 1936; mem. N.J. State Ho. of Rep., 1937, 1938. Mem. Theta Chi. Republican. Methodist. Clubs: Kiwanis (Ocean City, N.J.); Am. Automobile of South Jersey (ex-v.p.). Home: 44 E. Surf Rd. Office: Bourse Bldg., Ocean City, N.J.

BOSWORTH, Edwin Carpenter, educator; b. Foxboro, Mass., Mar. 13, 1890; s. Arthur Holbrook and Annie Frances (Keyes) B.; grad. Foxboro (Mass.) High Sch., 1907; Ph.B., Brown U., Providence, R.I., 1911, M.C.S., 1927; m. Lucinda Eliza Jeffrey, May 15, 1912; children—Lucinda Caroline, Anne Frances (Mrs. John Gillis Adair Jr.), Ruth Margaret (Mrs. Chester Cornelius Hustead). Prof. of Mathematics Le-

land U., New Orleans, La., 1911-12; prof. of commerce, Y.M.C.A., Detroit, Mich., 1912-14; dean Pace Inst. Sch. of Accounting, Detroit, 1914-17, Pace Inst., Washington, D.C., 1917-22, Benjamin Franklin U., Washington, D.C., since 1925. Trustee Bethesda Presbyn. Ch. Mem. Nat. Geneal. Soc., Am. Accounting Assn., Phi Beta Kappa, Phi Alpha Delta, Sigma Phi Epsilon. Democrat. Presbyn. Co-author: Manual of Charting, 1923. Descendant of John Howland and Elizabeth Tilley, who came to America on the Mayflower. Home: 4625 Rosedale Av., Bethesda, Md.

BOTHWELL, Edgar C., v.p. Gulf Oil Corpn.; also officer or dir. many other cos. Home: 120 Beech St., Edgewood. Office: Gulf Bldg., Pittsburgh, Pa.

BOTHWELL, Edward G.; in gen. practice of law since 1915. Office: 1405 Commonwealth Bldg., Pittsburgh, Pa.

BOTSET, Holbrook Gorham, physicist, petroleum production research; b. Plymouth, Ind., Oct. 23, 1900; s. Frederick William and Mary Lena (Gorham) B.; student Mishawaka (Ind.) High Sch., 1914-18; B.S. in chem. engring., Purdue U., Lafayette, Ind., 1922; m. Elizabeth Keith, Sept. 19, 1931. Physicist, Standard Chem. Co., Pittsburgh, 1922-26; part time instr. in chemistry, Carnegie Inst. Tech., 1925-29; asst. chief chemist, Radium Dial Co., Pittsburgh, 1926-27, chief chemist, 1927-28; industrial fellow, Mellon Inst., Pittsburgh, 1928-29; physicist, Gulf Research & Development Co., Pittsburgh, since 1930. Fellow A.A.A.S.; mem. Am. Chem. Soc., Pittsburgh Physical Soc., Phi Lambda Upsilon. Republican. Episcopalian. Author and co-author numerous papers on tech. subjects. Home: Waldheim Rd., Fox Chapel. Office: Gulf Research & Development Co., Pittsburgh, Pa.

BOUCHELLE, J. F.; judge 13th Judicial Circuit. Address: Charleston, W.Va.

BOUGHTON, Fred Grant, clergyman; b. Bowling Green, O., June 29, 1868; s. Elon Galusha and Melinda Addie (Davis) B.; grad. high sch., Norwalk, O., 1885; A.B., Denison U., 1894; grad. Rochester Theol. Sem., 1897; D.D., Grand Island (Neb.) Coll., 1925, Rio Grande (Ohio) Coll., 1925; m. Margaret Louise Pearce, Sept. 1, 1897; children—Theodore Carey (dec.), Donald Clarke, Helen Mary, Margaret Faith. Ordained ministry Bapt. Ch., 1897; successively pastor Saxton's River, Vt., Cambridge and Warren, Ohio, until 1906; professor philosophy and French, also registrar, McMinnville (now Linfield) Coll., McMinnville, Ore., 1906-17; secretary Denison University, 1917-22; president Sioux Falls College, 1922-26; prof. philosophy, Denison U., 1926-30; pastor Central Bapt. Ch., Woodbury, N.J., since 1930. Corr. sec. Ohio Bapt. Education Soc., 1917-22. Registrar S.A. T.C., Denison U., 1918. Mem. Phi Gamma Delta. Republican. Baptist. Home: 74 E. Centre St., Woodbury, N.J.

BOUGHTON, Guy C.; consulting surgeon Hamot Hosp. and Infants Home and Hosp.; mem. staff St. Vincent's Hosp.; chief surgeon Gen. Electric Co. (Erie works). Address: 263 W. 9th St., Erie, Pa.

BOULDEN, Philip Asbury, bishop; b. Elkton, Md., Jan. 15, 1872; s. Charles Henry and Anna (Redding) B.; A.B., Lincoln U., Pa., 1901, A.M., 1905; S.T.B., Lincoln U. Theol. Sem., 1905; m. Eleanor Dorsey, Apr. 1, 1908. Ordained to ministry Union Am. M.E. Ch., 1901; served as pastor of chs. in Del. and Pa., 12 yrs.; elected bishop, 1914, assigned to Mich. and Ont., Can., and all mission area Ala., Miss. and Ga., 1914-34; bishop over first dist. Md., Del., Pa., second dist. covering N.Y., N.J., and N.E. states since 1934. Mem. Lincoln U. Alumni Assn. Republican. Mason (32°). Home: 1928 Federal St., Philadelphia, Pa.

BOULTON, Harry; pres. Penn. Gen. Casualty Co., Penn. Gen. Fire Ins. Co. Home: Clearfield, Pa. Office: 242 S. 13th St., Philadelphia, Pa.

BOUVE, Clement L(incoln), register of copyrights, lawyer; b. Hingham, Mass., May 27, 1878; s. Edward Tracy and Delphine (Dolores) B.; prep. education, private schools, Germany and Switzerland, 1886-90, Roxbury (Mass.) Latin Sch., 1891-95; A.B., Harvard University, 1899; Harvard Law Sch., 1900-02; m. Mary McLean, Sept. 10, 1906; children—Margaret, Warren Lincoln, Mary Elizabeth. Admitted to Mass. bar, 1903; sec. to Edward H. Strobel, adviser to Siamese Govt., 1903-04; asst. dist. atty., city and dist. of Manila, P.I., 1905-08; engaged in practice of internat. and of federal law, Washington, D.C., 1909-36; register of copyrights since August 1, 1936. Commr. for U.S. on Mixed Claims Commn., U.S. and Panama, 1916-17; asst. agt. for U.S., Gen. and Spl. Claims Commns., U.S. and Mexico, 1924-25, agt., 1926-31; tech. adviser, Internat. Aeronautic Conf., Washington, Dec. 1928; mem. bd. advisers, Harvard Research in Internat. Law, 1928, 29. Served as capt., later maj. and chief of staff, F.A., U.S.A., A.E.F., 1917-19. Mem. Am. Bar Assn., American Society Internat. Law, Society Colonial Wars, Society Officers of World War, American Legion, Loyal Legion. Republican. Unitarian. Clubs: Cosmos, Harvard, Chevy Chase (Washington); St. Botolph (Boston). Author: Laws Governing the Exclusion and Expulsion of Aliens from the United States, 1912; also numerous articles on internat. and aviation law. Home: 109 Shepherd St., Chevy Chase, Md. Office: Copyright Office, Library of Congress, Washington, D.C.

BOVEY, William Harbaugh, lawyer; b. Hagerstown, Md., May 22, 1895; s. Martin Luther and Roxa Bella (Harbaugh) B.; grad. Mercersburg (Pa.) Acad., 1913; Litt.B., Princeton U., 1917; LL.B., U. of Md. Law Sch., Baltimore, Md., 1922; unmarried. Admitted to Md. bar, 1922, and since practiced at Hagerstown; admitted to bar of Supreme Ct. of U.S., 1936. Served as volunteer, Am. Field Service with French Army, 1917; private, A.E.F., 1917-19. Mem. Bar Assn. of Washington Co. (sec. since 1923), Md., Del. and D.C. State Elks Assn. (pres. 1928-29), Am. Legion. Awarded Croix de Guerre, France, 1918. Republican. Presbyterian. Elk. Home: 39 Broadway, Hagerstown, Md. Office: 109 W. Washington St., Hagerstown, Md.

BOVING, Charles B(rasee), clergyman; b. Harrisonville, Mo., Nov. 26, 1871; s. George Joseph and Mary Stuart (Cordell) B.; A.B., Westminster Coll. (Mo.), 1891, A.M., 1895, D.D., 1909; grad. Princeton Theol. Sem., 1895; m. Mary Louise Woodbridge, Nov. 6, 1895; children—Louise Woodbridge (Mrs. George W. Baumhoff, Jr.), Eleanor Russell (Mrs. D. Franklin Manning). Ordained Presbyn. ministry, 1893; pastor, Lamar, Mo., 1893-98; pastor-at-large Lafayette- Springfield, Mo., 1898-99, Webb City, Mo., 1899-1905, Hannibal, Mo., 1905-11; pres. Westminster Coll., 1911-14; pastor Bowling Green, Ky., 1914-18; Moberly, Mo., 1918-24, Sidney St. Ch. (now Peters Memorial), St. Louis, Mo., 1924-27; field rep. Presbyn. Bd. of Pensions, Phila. since 1927. Trustee Westminster Coll., 1919-27; state pres. Mo., Christian Endeavor Union, 1907-08, pastor counsellor, 1919-27. Mem. Beta Theta Pi. Republican. Mason (32°). Address: 372 S. Highland Av., Pittsburgh, Pa.

BOWDEN, Garfield Arthur, chem. research; b. Dec. 19, 1880; s. John and Agnes (Lukey) B.; grad. Normal Sch., Platteville, Wis., 1901; B.S., U. of Chicago, 1913; post-grad. work, U. of Chicago and U. of Cincinnati; m. Lucy E. Bell, Sept. 10, 1902; children—Paul Webster, Isabel Agnes. Prin. State Graded Sch., Revere, Minn., 1901-02, high sch., Pepin, Wis., 1902-06; in charge science and math. depts., high sch., Winona, Minn., 1906-08; head of science dept. Twp. High Sch., Waukegan, Ill., 1908-11, asst. prin., 1915-17; asst. prof. methods of science teaching, Teachers Coll., Normal (Ill.) U., 1917-18; head of science dept. University Sch., Cincinnati, 1918-37; head of chem. research and ednl. depts. A. S. Boyle & Co., Inc., Cincinnati, O., and Jersey City, N.J., and for Am. House Products, Jersey City, N.J.; asst. prof. methods of science teaching, N.C. State Teachers Coll., Raleigh, summers 1924-27. Mem. A.A.A.S., Central Assn. Science Teachers, Am. Chem. Soc., Schoolmasters Club (Cincinnati), Cincinnati Astron. Soc., Cincinnati City Beautiful Assn., Torch Club,

Phi Delta Kappa. Presbyn. Author: General Science, 1923; Foundations of Science, 1931. Home: 139 N. Arlington Av., East Orange, N.J. Office: 1934 Dana Av., Cincinnati, O.; and 257 Cornelison Av., Jersey City, N.J.

BOWE, Dudley Pleasants; obstetrician-in-chief Bon Secours Hosp.; attending obstetrician St. Agnes Hosp.; visiting obstetrician Church Home and Infirmary, Md. Gen. Hosp., Mercy Hosp. and Hosp. for Women of Md., University Hosp.; instr. in obstetrics U. of Md. Med. Sch. Fellow Am. Coll. Surgeons, A.M.A.; mem. Southern Med. Assn., Med. and Chirurgical Faculty of Md. Address: 2 W. Read St., Baltimore, Md.

BOWEN, Harry; chmn. bd. Pocahontas Fuel Co., Inc. Address: Freeman, W.Va.

BOWEN, John C.; v.p. Lehigh Portland Cement Co. Home: 1027 N. 18th St., Allentown, Pa.

BOWEN, Josiah Slicer, M.D., public health official; b. Baltimore, Md., Apr. 28, 1882; s. Josiah Slicer and Rebecca Norma (Mears) B.; grad. Marston's Univ. Sch., Baltimore, 1899; M.D., U. of Md., 1903; m. Mrs. Elizabeth A. Buffington (nee Thompson), Feb. 28, 1910. Medical practice, Baltimore, since 1904; dep. state health officer for Baltimore County since 1914; dep. state and county health officer, Baltimore County since 1924. Mem. Md. State Legislature, 1912. Mem. Med. and Chirurg. Faculty of Md. (former vice-pres. and pres.; mem. house of dels. and bd. of councillors; mem. legislative com. and former chmn.), Baltimore Co. Med. Assn., A.M.A., Am. Pub. Health Assn., Md. Acad. Medicine and Surgery. Democrat. Episcopalian. Mason, K. of P., Jr. Order United Am. Mechanics. Home: 1710 South Rd., Mt. Washington, Baltimore, Md. Office: Towson, Baltimore Co., Md.

BOWEN, Samuel Bispham, paints mfr.; b. Woodstown, N.J., Mar. 30, 1855; s. Smith and Martha Stokes (Bispham) B.; student pub. schs., Phila., and Lawrenceville (N.J.) Sch.; 1870-72; m. Emma Virginia Wright, Apr. 7, 1880; children—Helen Marie (widow of Parson Dexter), Samuel, Virginia Wright (Mrs. Harold F. McNeil), Laurence, Sue Kingsley (Mrs. Walter A. Carl). Began as engr. in factory Pecora Paint Co. (founded by Smith Bowen, 1862), mfrs. paints, Phila., 1872, chemist, 1875-77, bookkeeper, 1877-80, salesman, 1880-1912, pres. 1912-30, chmn. bd. dirs. since 1930. Life trustee Lawrenceville (N.J.) Sch. since 1921; trustee Lingnan U., Canton, China. Fellow Phila. Mus. of Art; mem. Acad. of Fine Arts, Franklin Inst. Hist. Soc. of Pa., Pa. Son of N.J. Acad. of Natural History, New York City. Republican. Episcopalian (vestryman and rector's warden St. Peter's Ch., Germantown, Pa.). Clubs: Union League, Philadelphia Cricket (life), Country, Manheim Cricket (Phila.); U.S. Seniors' Golf Assn. (Rye, N.Y.), Monterey Peninsula Golf (Monterey, Calif.). Home: Alden Park Manor. Office: 4th and Sedgley Av., Philadelphia, Pa.

BOWER, Catharine Ruth, prof. of nursing edn.; b. Phila., Pa.; d. Frederick Evans and Harriet (Harris) Bower; A.B., Bucknell U., Lewisburg, Pa., A.M., hon. Sc.D.; grad. U. of Pa. Hosp. Sch. of Nursing; unmarried. Formerly nurse, U. of Pa. Hosp.; supervisor of operating rooms, Western Pa. Hosp., Pittsburgh; dir. of nurses Western Pa. Hosp. Sch. of Nurses; now prof. of nursing edn., U. of Pa. Chmn. Pa. State Bd. of Examiners for Registration of Nurses. Past pres. Pittsburgh League of Nursing Edn.; mem. Pa. League of Nursing Edn. (past pres.), Nat. League of Nursing Edn. (vice-pres.), Am. Nurses Assn., Pa. Nurses Assn., Am. Red Cross Nursing Service, Am. Assn. Univ. Women. Home: The Fairfax, 43d and Locust Sts., Philadelphia, Pa.

BOWER, Elizabeth B.; prof. chemistry, Hood Coll. Address: Hood Coll., Frederick, Md.

BOWER, John O.; clin. prof. surg. research, Temple U.; surgeon St. Luke's, Children's, Phila. Gen. and Northeastern hosps.; cons. surgeon Riverview Hosp., Norristown. Address: 2008 Walnut St., Philadelphia, Pa.

BOWER, Joseph Augustus, banker; b. Denver Colo., Sept. 2, 1880; s. William Alexander and

Sarah Anne (Berry) B.; grad. Detroit Business U., 1900; m. Emma Anna Wuelfing, Aug. 22, 1906; children—Phyllis Louise (Mrs. Arthur H. Lamborn, Jr.), Robert Alexander, Joseph Wuelfing, Barbara Ann. Admitted to Mich. bar, 1901, and began practice at Detroit; 1st jr. officer, later v.p. Detroit Trust Co., 14 yrs., 1901-16; pres. Hale & Kilburn Co., mfrs., Phila., 1916-17; v.p. Liberty Nat. Bank (now New York Trust Co.), New York, 1917-29, resigned; pres. Chemical Securities Corpn., 1929-32; exec. v.p. Chemical Bank & Trust Co., 1932—; pres. Detroit Internat. Bridge Co.; dir. Commercial Investment Trust, Panhandle Corpn. Life mem. bd. of trustees, Rutgers U., since 1938. Dir. Nat. Industrial Conf. Bd. Mem. Acad. Polit. Science, Am. Geog. Soc., Council of Foreign Relations, Foreign Policy Assn. Decorated officer of the crown (Belgium), 1938. General business mgr. Alien Property Custodian, World War. Republican. Catholic. Clubs: Recess, Union League (New York); Fishers Island (N.Y.); Baltusrol (N.J.) Golf; Montclair Assn., Montclair (N.J.) Golf; Boca Raton (Fla.). Home: 136 Upper Mountain Av., Montclair, N.J. Office: 165 Broadway, New York, N.Y.

BOWERMAN, Arthur L.; chmn. bd. Lincoln Nat. Bank; v.p. Eagle Fire Ins. Co. Address: 18 Washington Place, Newark, N.J.

BOWERS, Archibald Claude, pres. Pa. Rubber Co.; b. Davis Co., Ky., Nov. 15, 1887; s. Clifford Tillman and Mary Jane (Ridgeway) B.; self-educated; m. Bessie M. Saylor, Oct. 25, 1917. Began as factory supt. Inland Rubber Co., Chicago, 1921; v.p. and factory mgr. Mason Tire & Rubber Co., Kent, O., 1923-28; v.p. and factory mgr. Pa. Rubber Co., Jeannette, Pa., 1928-36, v.p. and gen. mgr., 1936-37, pres. and gen. mgr. since 1937. Mason. Club: Greensburg (Pa.) Country. Home: 905 Summit Av., Greensburg, Pa. Office: Chambers Av., Jeannette, Pa.

BOWERS, Charles H., school supt.; b. Saxton, Pa., Oct. 17, 1886; s. George L. and Ellen (Smeltzer) B.; student Millersville (Pa.) Normal Sch., 1910-12; A.B., Franklin and Marshall Coll., Lancaster, Pa., 1919; A.M., Cornell U., 1930; m. Beulah Mumaugh, June 29, 1911; children—Frances, Quentin H. Teacher rural schs., Hopewell, Pa., 1909-10; prin. Salisbury Twp. High Sch., Gap, Pa., 1912-14; supervising prin., Hopewell (Pa.) Boro Pub. Schs., 1914-17, Camp Hill (Pa.) Pub. Schs., 1919-23, Portage (Pa.) Twp. Pub. Schs., 1924-33; dist. supt., Nanty Glo (Pa.) Boro Pub. Schs., since 1933; teacher Millersville (Pa.) Normal, spring 1919; prin. local normal schs., Hopewell, New Enterprise, Everett, Pa., summers 1912-17. Mem. Lions Internat. (pres. Nanty Glo Club), N.E.A., Pa. State Edn. Assn., Phi Delta Kappa. Republican. Episcopalian. Mason (Summit Lodge 312, Ebensburg, Pa.; Williamsport, Pa., Consistory, Scottish Rite). Club: Nanty Glo (Pa.) Rod and Gun. Author: An Analysis of Teacher Participation in the Administration of High Schools in Cambria County, Pa., 1930. Home: 1076 Vine St. Office: Wagoner and Davis St., Nanty Glo, Pa.

BOWERS, Elsworth Vachel, coll. prof.; b. Delaware Co., O., Jan. 21, 1879; s. John Henry and Mary E. (Wright) B.; Ph.B., Otterbein Coll., Westerville, O., 1901; A.M., Ohio State U., 1922, Ph.D., 1929; m. Stella B. Martin, June 26, 1912. Engaged in teaching, pub. schs. in O., 1901-06; supt. schs. Tippecanoe City and Galion, O., 1906-24; prof. psychology, Marshall Coll., Huntington, W.Va., since 1924. Mem. Am. Psychol. Assn., Midwestern Psychol. Assn., W.Va. State Edn. Assn., Kappa Delta Pi. Methodist. Mason (32°). Home: 525 Sixteenth St., Huntington, W.Va.

BOWERS, Frank Lester, manufacturer; b. Point Marion, Pa., July 2, 1886; s. David Marshall and Loretta (McClain) B.; student Point Marion (Pa.) Pub. Sch. and Point Marion High Sch.; m. Asia Lee Sadler, Nov. 14, 1904; children—Theodore Marshall, Edwin Sadler, Frank Lester. Began as partner McClain Sand Co., Point Marion, Pa., 1910, now sec.-treas. and gen. mgr.; pres. and dir. Ohio Valley Sand Co., Point Marion Bridge Co.; treas. and dir. Marion Motor Co.; dir. Standard Sand and Gravel Co. Mem. Point Marion (Pa.) Borough Council,

1917-24, Pa. State Legislature, 1926-32; dir. Point Marion Sch. Dist. 1925-38. Republican. Christian Ch. Mason (32°, Shriner, K.T.), Elk, Odd Fellow. Clubs: Rotary (Point Marion, Pa.); Uniontown Country (Uniontown, Pa.). Home: 29 Main St. Office: First Nat. Bank Bldg., Point Marion, Pa.

BOWES, Edward ("Major"), radio programs; b. San Francisco, Calif.; s. John M. and Amelia (Ford) B.; ed. public schools, San Francisco and private tutors; hon. LL.D., Villanova Coll., 1939; m. Margaret Illington (deceased). Began radio career with "Major Bowes' Family Hour," 1925; originated Major Bowes Amateur Hour, 1934, voted most popular on air 1935; mng. dir. Capitol Theatre and other theatres, New York; v.p. and dir. Moredall Realty Corpn.; exec. dir. Edmar Enterprises, Tyro Productions, Inc., Laurel Hill Productions. Clubs: Cloud, Sleepy Hollow Country, Catholic, Monmouth Beach. Yacht clubs: Fairway (New York); Mobile, Bucaneer (Mobile, Ala.); Norris (Knoxville, Tenn.); Austin (Tex.); Inlet Yachting Center Fleet (Atlantic City, N.J.); Fairhaven (N.J.); Green Bay (Wis.); Sarnia (Mich.); Port Huron, St. Clair River Yachting Assn. (Port Huron, Mich.); Erie (Pa.); Racine (Wis.); New Bedford (Mass.); Galveston (Tex.); Pontiac, Oakland County Boat (Pontiac, Mich.); Gull Lake (Battle Creek, Mich.); Saginaw Bay (Bay City, Mich.); Corinthian (Tiburon, Calif.); St. Paul (Minn.); Lorain (O.); Oshkosh (Wis.); Everett (Wash.); Duluth (Minn.). Author of Verses I Like (poems). Home: Rumson, N.J. Office: 1697 Broadway, New York, N.Y.

BOWIE, Clarence K.; mem. law firm Bowie & Burke. Address: Mercantile Trust Bldg., Baltimore, Md.

BOWIE, William Cleveland, editor; b. Brunswick, Md., Apr. 8, 1906; s. Grover Cleveland and Grace Lauretta (Rockwell) B.; grad. Martinsburg (W.Va.) High Sch., 1924; student Potomac State Prep. Sch., Keyser, W.Va., 1924-25; A.B., Pa. State Coll., 1929; m. Anita Irene Hite, Sept. 22, 1934. Began as reporter Martinsburg (W.Va.) Journal, 1927; reporter Wheeling Intelligencer, 1927-30; copy desk man and reporter Baltimore (Md.) Evening Sun, 1930-39; editor The Register, Point Pleasant, W.Va., since 1930. Mem. Phi Delta Theta. Democrat. Episcopalian. Home: 1500 Kanawha St. Office: 209 Main St., Point Pleasant, W.Va.

BOWLBY, Harry Laity, clergyman; b. nr. Asbury, N.J., Jan. 26, 1874; s. Robert Melroy and Elizabeth (DeHart) B.; A.B., Princeton, 1901, A.M., 1903; grad. Princeton Theol. Sem., 1904; D.D., Washington (Tenn.) Coll., 1917; m. Bertha H. Watson, Nov. 6, 1909; 1 dau., Bertha Virginia. Ordained Presbyn. ministry, 1904; pastor First Ch., Altoona, Pa., 1905-13; gen. sec. Lord's Day Alliance of the U.S., 1913. Rep. Bd. of Christian Edn., Presbyn. Ch. in U.S.A., in the Lord's Day Alliance Bd. of Mgrs. Life mem. Oregon Trail Memorial Assn.; mem. bd. dirs. Allied Patriotic Socs. of America. Service with Y.M.C.A. in mil. camps, 1917-18. Mem. Com. Religious Edn. in Pub. Schs., N.Y. City. Mem. Presbyn. Union (New York), New England Society, Nat. and N.J. S.A.R., Friars Alumni Assn. Princeton Theol. Sem. (pres. bd. trustees), Cliosophic Soc. (Princeton), Pi Gamma Mu; hon. mem. Federal Employees Soc. of N.Y.; lt. gov. for N.J. of Pi Gamma Mu. Del. to Fifteenth (Quadrennial) Council of the Alliance of Churches holding the Presbyterian System, 1937. Republican. Mason. Clubs: Clergy, Aldine, Fraternities. Editor of Lord's Day Leader. Author numerous articles on Sabbath and Sunday subjects. Contbr. to religious publs. Home: 25 N. 20th St., E. Orange, N.J. Office: 156 5th Av., New York, N.Y.

BOWLES, Harry H., M.D.; attending surgeon Overlook Hosp. Address: 36 Woodland Av., Summit, N.J.

BOWMAN, Addison Moore, lawyer; b. Camp Hill, Pa., Apr. 16, 1880; s. Henry N. and Jennie M. (Kline) B.; student Harrisburg Acad., and Shippensburg State Normal Sch.; LL.B., Dickinson Sch. of Law, 1906; m. Mabel E. Huber, Sept. 15, 1904; 1 son, Addison M. Admitted to practice before Cumberland Co., Pa. Superior Ct., Pa. Supreme Ct. and U.S. Dist. Ct., 1905; chief burgess Camp Hill, Pa., 1903-05; deputy register of wills, Cumberland Co., 1903-05; referee in bankruptcy since 1913; Chmn. Rep. County Com. Mem. Cumberland Co. Bar Assn. (pres. 1935-36), Delta Chi. Club: Rotary. Author: Daniel Drawbaugh, Inventor; The Northern Raid of the Confederates; Title Searching in Pennsylvania. Co-author: The Law and the Motorist in Pennsylvania. Home: 30 N. 26th St., Camp Hill, Pa. Office: 14 W. High St., Carlisle, Pa.

BOWMAN, Ethel; prof. psychology, Goucher Coll. Address: Goucher Coll., Baltimore, Md.

BOWMAN, Harry Lake, univ. prof.; b. Phila., Pa., May 17, 1889; s. Harry and Emma Louise (Lake) B.; B.S. in C.E., Pa. State Coll., 1911; S.M. in C.E., Mass. Inst. Tech., 1914; m. Anna Florence Foster, Sept. 18, 1915; children—Claire Elvira, Margaret Emma, Edward Henry. Began as draftsman Am. Bridge Co., 1911-15 (on leave for grad. work at M.I.T. and instr. civil engring., Purdue, 1915); prin. asst. to C.E. Smith, cons. engr., St. Louis, Mo., 1915-18; asst. engr. Phila. & Reading R.R., 1918-19; instr. civil engring., asst. prof., asso. prof., Mass. Inst. Tech., 1919-26; prof. civil engring., Drexel Inst. Tech., Phila., since 1926; cons. engr. since 1919; registered professional engr. Mem. Am. Soc. C.E., Am. Concrete Inst., Soc. for Promotion Engring. Edn., Sigma Xi, Tau Beta Pi, Phi Kappa Phi, Alpha Tau Omega, Theta Tau. United Presbyn. Co-author (with Hale Sutherland): Structural Theory, 2d edit., 1935; Structural Design, 1938. Home: 704 Shadeland Av., Drexel Hill. Office: Drexel Inst. Tech., Philadelphia, Pa.

BOWMAN, Isaiah, univ. pres.; b. Waterloo, Ont., Can., Dec. 26, 1878; s. Samuel Cressman and Emily (Shantz) B.; grad. State Normal Coll., Ypsilanti, Mich., 1902; B.Sc., Harvard, 1905; Ph.D., Yale University, 1908, hon. M.A., 1921; hon. M.Ed., Mich. State Coll., 1927; hon. Sc.D., Bowdoin College, 1931; LL.D., Dartmouth, Charleston, Dickinson and U. of Pa., 1935, U. of Wis. and Harvard, 1936, Queen's U., 1937; m. Cora Olive Goldthwait, June 28, 1909; children—Walter Parker, Robert Goldthwait, Olive. Asst. in physiography Harvard, 1904-05; instr. in geography, State Normal Coll., Ypsilanti, 1903-04; instr. in geography, 1905-09, asst. prof., 1909-15 Yale U., dir. Am. Geog. Soc., N.Y., 1915-35; pres. Johns Hopkins Univ. since July 1, 1935. Special lecturer in geography, Wesleyan Univ., 1907-09; U. of Chicago, 1908. Leader first Yale South Am. Expdn., 1907; geographer and geologist. Yale Peruvian Expdn., 1911; leader expdn. to Central Andes, under auspices Am. Geographical Society, 1913. Chmn. National Research Council, 1933-35; vice chmn. Science Advisory Board, 1933-35. Chief territorial specialist Am. Commn. to Negotiate Peace, 1918-19; and mem. various territorial commissions of the Peace Conf., Paris, 1919; physiographer U.S. Dept. Justice in Red River boundary dispute; mem. bd. Yale Pub. Assn., 1920-25. Pres. Social Science Abstracts, Inc., 1929-31; mem. bd. dirs., Council on Foreign Relations, Woods Hole Oceanographic Instn., Woodrow Wilson Foundation, Institute of Current World Affairs, American Geographical Soc. of N.Y. (councilor 1935); pres. Internat. Geog. Union, 1931-34; mem. Am. Philos. Soc. (councilor 1935), Assn. Am. Geographers (pres. 1931), Nat. Acad. Sciences; hon. corr. mem. Geog. Soc. La Paz, Bolivia, Hispanic Soc. America, Royal Geog. Soc., London, Swedish Soc. Anthropology and Geography (foreign member, 1939), geog. socs. of Phila., Berlin, Finland, Jugoslavia, Rome, etc.; fellow Am. Academy Arts and Sciences. Livingstone gold medal, Royal Scottish Geog. Soc., 1928; Bonaparte-Wyse gold medal of Geog. Soc. of Paris, 1917, for explorations in and publications of S. America; gold medal, Geog. Soc., Chicago, 1927; Civjic medal, Geog. Soc. of Belgrade, 1935; Henry Grier Bryant gold medal, Geog. Soc. of Phila., 1937. Clubs: Explorers (ex-secretary and ex-v.p.), Century (New York); Cosmos (Washington, D.C.). Author: Forest Physiography, 1911; South America, 1915; The Andes of Southern Peru, 1916; The New World—Problems in Political Geography, 1921; Desert Trails of Atacama, 1923; An American Boundary Dispute, 1923; The Mohammedan World, 1924; International Relations, 1930; The Pioneer Fringe, 1931; Geography in Relation to the Social Sciences, 1933; Design for Scholarship, 1936; also various publs. in U.S. Geol. Survey and many papers on S. Am. geography and land settlement. Co-editor and part author of Human Geography; editor and collaborator for Limits of Land Settlement, 1937. Home: Oak Place. Address: Johns Hopkins University, Baltimore, Md.

BOWMAN, John Gabbert, educator; b. Davenport, Ia., May 18, 1877; s. John R. and Mary A. (Gabbert) B.; A.B., State U. of Ia., Iowa City, 1899, A.M., 1904; LL.D., Coe College, 1912, Univ. of Miss., 1914, Boston Univ., 1927, Rutgers Univ., 1933, Univ. of Pa., 1934; Litt.D., Oglethorpe U., 1924; Litt.D., U. of Ia., 1934; m. Florence Ridgway Berry, June 29, 1908; children—John R., Florence. Newspaper work, 1899-1901; instr. English, State U. of Ia., 1902-04, Columbia, 1905-07; sec. Carnegie Foundation for the Advancement of Teaching, New York, 1907-11; pres. State U. of Ia., 1911-14; dir. Am. Coll. of Surgeons, 1915-21; chancellor U. of Pittsburgh, 1921—. Trustee Nat. Bd. Med. Examiners (Phila.), 1915-31; consultant on hosps. U.S. Treasury Dept., 1921-23. Dir. Pittsburgh Chamber of Commerce, 1922-26; dir. Forbes Nat. Bank. Chmn. bd. Pittsburgh Chem. Warfare Procurement Dist. Clubs: The Players (New York); Cosmos (Washington); University, Duquesne, Pittsburgh Athletic, Longue Vue Golf (Pittsburgh). Contbr. to mags. and author "The World That Was." Home: 155 N. Dithridge St. Address: University of Pittsburgh, Pittsburgh, Pa.

BOWMAN, John William; partner Bowman & Co.; pres. Moorhead Knitting Co.; dir. various other companies. Home: 2030 N. 3rd St. Office: 316 Market St., Harrisburg, Pa.

BOWMAN, Joseph Hunt, engineer; b. Pittsburgh, Pa., Dec. 29, 1891; s. Joseph William and Clara A. (Shepperson) B.; student Washington & Jefferson Acad., Washington, Pa., 1906-10; M.E., Pa. State Coll., 1914; m. Mildred Busser, April 30, 1921; children—Joseph Hunt, Hamilton Busser. Began as engr. Steel Corpn., 1912; pres. Am. Steel Band Co., Pittsburgh, since 1920. Served as aviator in French Army during World War. Mem. Sigma Alpha Epsilon. Episcopalian. Mason. Clubs: Duquesne, Longue Vue (Pittsburgh). Home: 630 S. Linden Av. Office: Bowman Bldg., Pittsburgh, Pa.

BOWMAN, Robert Townsend, pres. Solfo Paint & Chem. Co.; b. Trenton, N.J., Apr. 18, 1898; s. Robert Klotz and Rhoda (Townsend) B.; ed. Lawrenceville (N.J.) Sch., Model Sch., Trenton, and Rutgers U.; m. Anne Perrine Bowman, June 11, 1921; 1 dau., Margaret Roebling. Pres. Solfo Paint & Chem. Co., Custom Made Paint Co.; dir. Trenton Banking Co. Dir. Trenton Chamber of Commerce (president), N.J. State Chamber of Commerce. Protestant. Clubs: Engineers (pres.), Trenton Country; Essex (Newark). Home: 413 W. State St. Office: 821 Pennington Av., Trenton, N.J.

BOWMAN, Willard Eugene, editor; b. at Hartford City, Ind., Sept. 5, 1890; s. Aurelius A. and Mary C. (Russell) B.; grad. Hartford City High Sch., 1907; m. Mary Pauline Smith, July 30, 1912; children—Mary Elizabeth, Margaret Pauline, Richard Eugene. Began as reporter Hartford City Times Gazette, 1907; publicity work for Ind. State Rep. Comm., etc., 1914-16; news editor and editorial writer Detroit Journal, 1916-20; Washington corr. for Toledo Blade, Detroit Journal and Newark (N.J.) Star-Eagle, 1920-22; mng. editor Newark Star-Eagle, 1922-30, editor, 1930-35; exec. v.p. and publicity dir. L. Bamberger & Co., 1935-37; editor Newark (N.J.) Star-Eagle since 1937. Mem. N.J. Alcoholic Beverage Commn., 1933, Gov.'s Sch. Survey Commn. (N.J.), 1932. Clubs: Newark Advertising, Downtown (Newark); Crestmont Golf (West Orange, N.J.). Home: 576 Lincoln Av., Orange, N.J. Office: Newark Star-Eagle, Newark, N.J.

BOWN, Charles Elmer, lawyer; b. Pittsburgh, Pa., Feb. 18, 1875; s. Charles Tytherleigh and Louisa Amanda (Alter) B.; student Harvard,

1894-96, Pittsburgh Law Sch., 1896-98; m. Anne Louise Hay, June 16, 1909; children—Julia Isabelle (Mrs. Robert H. Barth), Anne Louise (dec.), Olive Lynda, Charles Tytherleigh II. Admitted to Pa. bar, 1898 and since in gen. practice law at Pittsburgh; has served as asst. city solicitor and spl. counsel in utility matters for city of Pittsburgh; counsel for Lake Erie and River Canal Bd. and Traction Conf. Bd.; vice-pres., dir. and counsel South Hills Trust Co. Mem. Am., Pa. and Allegheny Co. bar assns. Republican. Episcopalian. Mason. Club: Harvard-Yale-Princeton (Pittsburgh). Home: 6210 Wellesley Av. Office: 918 Berger Bldg., Pittsburgh, Pa.

BOWNE, C. B., editor Montclair Times. Address: 11 Park St., Montclair, N.J.

BOYCE, Charles Prevost, investment banker; b. Baltimore, Md., Apr. 7, 1895; s. Frederick Grayson and Rebecca Latimer (Millar) B.; student pub. schs., Baltimore, Baltimore City Coll., Johns Hopkins (class of 1917); m. Caroline Ellicott, Dec. 11, 1920; children—Caroline Ellicott, Anne Allen, Charles Prevost, Patricia Ayers. Bond salesman, Robert Garrett & Sons, Baltimore, 1916-17, 1919-20; mem. firm Turner, Boyce & Co., Baltimore, 1920-21; admitted to partnership Stein Bros. (established 1853), 1921, which then became Stein Bros. & Boyce, investment bankers, Baltimore, New York, Louisville, Hagerstown-York, Md.; pres. and dir. Bayway Terminal Corpn.; dir. Kingsport Press, Inc., New York, Nat. Bondholders Corpn., New York, Lord Baltimore Hotel. Dir. Md. Sch. for Blind, Baltimore; trustee Franklin Square Hosp. Served in 1st R.O.T.C., Ft. Myer, Va., 1917; 2d lt., F.A., 80th Div. and later 1st lt., Tank Corps, U.S. Army, with A.E.F., 1917-19. Mem. bd. govs. Investment Bankers Assn. of America and chmn. its Federal Taxation Com. Democrat. Presbyterian. Clubs: Baltimore Country, Elkridge, Chesapeake, Merchants, Baltimore Bond, Racquet, Maryland, Bachelors Cotillon (Baltimore); Broad Street Club (New York City); Fishers Island (N.Y.). Home: 2 Beechdale Rd. Office: 6 S. Calvert St., Baltimore, Md.

BOYCE, Fred Grayson, Jr., banker; b. Baltimore, Md., Nov. 24, 1877; s. Fred Grayson and Rebecca Latimer (Millar) B.; grad. U. of Md.; m. Sophie Rose Meredith, Nov. 24, 1914; children—Kate Meredith, Sophie Meredith, C. Meredith. Vice-pres. and dir. Mercantile Trust Co. of Baltimore (Md.), Merchants & Miners Transportation Co. (Baltimore, Md.); dir. Fidelity & Guaranty Fire Corpn., Metropolitan Savings Bank, Real Estate Trust Co. Dir. Finney-Howell Research Foundation. Clubs: Maryland, Baltimore Country, Elkridge, Merchants, Bachelors Cotillon (Baltimore, Md.); Eastern Point Yacht, Bass Rocks Golf (Bass Rocks, Mass.); Essex Co. (Manchester, Mass.); St. George's Soc. (Baltimore, Md.). Home; 4102 Greenway, Guilford, Md. Office: 200 E. Redwood St., Baltimore, Md.

BOYCE, Gray Cowan, teacher of history; b. San Francisco, Calif., Feb. 19, 1899; s. William Thomas and Jessie Irene (Cowan) B.; A.B., U. of Calif., 1920, A.M., 1921, Ph.D., 1925; student Harvard, 1922-23, Université de Grenoble, summer 1925, Université de Gand, 1925-26; unmarried. Instr. in history, Princeton U., 1926-29, asst. prof. of history since 1929; prof. of history, Ohio State U., summer, 1938. Served in S.A.T.C., 1918. Mem. Mediæval Acad. of America, Am. Hist. Assn., Am. Assn. Univ. Profs. Democrat. Clubs: Nassau (Princeton, N.J.); Princeton (New York); Cercle des Alumni (Brussels, Belgium). Author: English-German Nation in the University of Paris During the Middle Ages, 1927; The University of Prague (with W. H. Dawson), 1937. Editor (with Dana C. Munro) and contbr. to Guide to the Study of Medieval History by L. J. Paetow, rev. edit., 1931. Contbr. to Am. Hist. Rev., Speculum, etc. Home: 401 1903 Hall, Princeton, N.J. Summer: 3201 Bayo Vista Av., Alameda, Calif.

BOYCE, Heyward E., banker; b. Baltimore, Md., Apr. 9, 1882; s. Frederick G. and Rebecca (Millar) B.; LL.B., U. of Md., 1902; m. Amabel Lee George, June 28, 1905; children—Heyward E., Rebecca Latimer, John George, Elizabeth Lee, Henrietta Cowman. With Wilson, Colston & Co., bankers and brokers, Baltimore, 1898-1908; mem. firm Colston, Boyce & Co., 1908-18; pres. Drovers and Mechanics Nat. Bank, 1921-30; pres. Md. Trust Co. since 1930; pres. and dir. Md. Trust Co. since 1930; trustee Eastern Sugar Associates (Puerto Rico); dir. Brager-Eisenberg, Inc. (Baltimore), Davis Coal & Coke Co., Md. Title & Guarantee Co. Mem. Md. Hist. Soc. (treas.), S.R. Clubs: Maryland, Bachelors Cotillon, Baltimore Country (pres.). Home: 4 Club Rd., Roland Park. Office: Md. Trust Bldg., Baltimore, Md.

BOYCE, William Graham, chmn. bd. Porcelain Enamel & Mfg. Co.; b. Baltimore, Md., 1885; s. Fred G. and Rebecca (Latimer) B.; student schs. and Wolfe's Sch.; A.B., Johns Hopkins U., 1905; LL.B., U. of Md. Law Sch., 1907; m. Elise Gillet, 1908. Chmn. bd. and treas. Porcelain Enamel & Mfg. Co.; dir. many companies. Home: 1214 N. Calvert St. Office: Union Trust Bldg., Baltimore, Md.

BOYCE, William H., ex-congressman; b. Sussex Co., Del., Nov. 28, 1855; s. James H. and Sarah J. (Otwell) B.; m. Emma E. Valliant, Oct. 25, 1882; children—Valliant (dec.), James I. (dec.). Practiced law, Georgetown, Del., 1887-97; pres. bd. edn., 1883-86, town commrs., 1895-97, Georgetown; prin. pub. schs., Laurel, Del., 1875-80, high schs., Oxford, Md., 1880-81; recorder deeds Sussex Co., Del., 1881-86; chmn. Sussex Co. Dem. Com., 1893-97; sec. of state, of Del., 1897, resigned; del. Dem. Nat. Conv., 1896, 1924; asso. justice Supreme Court of Del., 1897-1909, resident in Sussex Co.; reappointed 1909, resident in Kent Co., and state judicial reporter, 1909-21; retired, June 15, 1921; mem. 68th Congress (1923-25), at large Del.; mem. Com. on Rivers and Harbors. Former pres. Del. Citizens' Assn.; pres. Elizabeth W. Murphey Sch. for indigent white children in Kent and Sussex counties; dep. P.E. Gen. Conv., 1904, 28. Former capt. Del. N.G. Episcopalian. Home: Dover, Del.

BOYD, Charles Parker, manufacturer; b. Boston, Mass., Aug. 24, 1887; s. Charles Marshall and Jennie Eliza (Parker) B.; student Volkman Sch., Boston, Mass., 1906, Phila. Textile Sch., 1907-08; m. Marion Leslie Knott, Sept. 28, 1909; children—Leslie (Mrs. George P. Adams), Charles Marshall II, Marion, Jennie Eliza, Charles Parker, Natalie. Apprentice Am. Woolen Co., Boston, 1908-10; with Nat. Shawmut Bank, Boston, 1910-12; with Jeremiah Williams & Co., 1912-31, partner, 1917-31; dir. Beacon Mfg. Co., Swannanoa, N.C., since 1912, pres. since 1934; founded, 1931, and since pres. Charles P. Boyd & Co., Inc., Phila., originally in wool business, now mfr. metal stamping. Served in Field Service, U.S. Army, 1917-18. Republican. Episcopalian. Clubs: Racquet, British Officers (Phila.); Corinthian Yacht (Marblehead, Mass.). Home: Route 2, Kennett Square, Pa. Office: Water and Tasker Sts., Philadelphia, Pa.

BOYD, Clare Mary Constance Shenehon, artist, art-teacher; b. Minneapolis, Minn., July 28, 1895; d. Francis C. and Kate (Cross) Shenehon; B.A., U. of Minn. Arts Coll., 1918; student Minneapolis Sch. of Art, 1919-21, 24; studied at Art Students League of N.Y. 1921-23, Academie Montparnasse, Paris, 1924-25, New York U. Grad. Sch., Inst. of Fine Arts, 1938; m. Fiske Boyd, May 1, 1926; 1 dau., Sheila Shenehon. Began career as artist and teacher, Minneapolis Sch. of Art, 1924; instr. painting and history of architecture, Florentine Sch., Florence, Italy, 1926-27; head art dept. and art history, Kent Pl. Sch., Summit, N.J., since 1931; co-owner and operator (with husband), Pinehaven, Plainfield, N.H. (summer retreat for artists, amateurs and students). Exhibited: Minneapolis Art Inst., 1920-24; Minn. State Fair, 1921; Attic Club, Minneapolis, 1923; Women's University Club, N.Y. City, 1923; Argent Galleries, N.Y. City, 1934; Pa. Acad. Fine Arts, 1935; Montclair (N.J.) Mus., 1937; N.J. Regional Exhibit, Trenton, 1937, 38; N.J. Preview for the N.Y. World's Fair Exhbn. of Contemporary Art, Newark Mus., 1939; 1-man show, Summit (N.J.) Art Assn., 1939. Mem. Kappa Kappa Gamma. Home: 6 Norwood Av. Address: Kent Place Sch., Summit, N.J.

BOYD, D. Knickerbacker, architect, structural standardist; b. Phila., Jan. 5, 1872; s. David, Jr., and Alida Visscher (Knickerbacker) B.; ed. Friends' Central Sch., Rugby Acad., Phila., Pa. Acad. Fine Arts, Spring Garden Inst., Phila., and U. of Pa.; m. Elizabeth Hörnli Mifflin, Sept. 10, 1896; children—Barbara Mifflin (Mrs. Lawrence C. Murdoch), Lysbeth Knickerbacker (Mrs. Henry P. Borie). Practiced Phila. since 1892; designer Carnegie Library Bldg., Phila., chs., factories, apartment bldgs., schs. and suburban homes. Lecturer and writer on constrn. economics, archtl. adviser Structural Service Bur.; consultant on bldg. codes, zoning, production and application of bldg. materials and on informational publications. During World War, chief materials information sect., U.S. Housing Corpn., U.S. Dept. of Labor and rep. on War Industries Board. Editor Structural Service Book, Jour. A.I.A. Mem. correlating com. on legislation and administration of President's Conf. on Home Building and Home Ownership. Fellow Am. Institute Architects (ex-sec., ex-v.p.); mem. coms. on building regulations and on pub. information and structural service of Phila. chapter A.I.A.; ex-pres. Pa. State Assn. A.I.A., Phila. Chapter A.I.A.; ex-pres. Phila. Building Congress; v.p. Am. Constrn. Council (cons. on apprenticeship and better building); mem. Phila. com. Better Homes in America; mem. exec. com. Zoning Fed. of Phila.; mem. Archtl. League of New York, Am. Federation of Arts (ex-dir.), N.E.A., Phila. Housing Assn., Regional Plan of Phila. (advisory com.), Com. to Revise Building Code of Philadelphia, Civil Legion, War Industries Bd. Assn., S.R.; hon. mem. N. Texas Chapter, A.I.A. Pa. state archtl. advisor Home Owners Loan Corpn.; administrative asst. Pa., Works Progress Adminstrn.; co-ordinator of exhibits, N.Y. State Worlds Fair Commn.; advisor on building industry relations, Russell Sage Foundation. Episcopalian. Clubs: Art, Nameless, T Square (Phila.); Lotos (N.Y. City). Home: Chestnut Hill Apts., Phila., and 53 W. 33d St., New York, N.Y. Offices: 17th and Sansom Sts., Philadelphia, Pa.; and Empire State Bldg., New York, N.Y.

BOYD, David Hartin, physician; b. Allegheny, Pa., Feb. 17, 1880; s. Thomas Hartin and Sarah Martha (McKee) B.; A.B., Washington and Jefferson Coll., Washington, Pa., 1902; M.D., Harvard Med. Sch., 1906; m. Janet Mabon, Sept. 23, 1922; 1 son, Thomas Hartin II. Interne Allegheny Gen. Hosp., 1906-07; pediatrician Children's Hosp., Allegheny Gen. Hosp., Presbyterian Hosp., Columbia Hosp.; asst. prof. pediatrics U. of Pittsburgh Med. Sch.; in gen. practice at Pittsburgh since 1908, specializing in pediatrics since 1921. Served as capt., M.C., U.S.A., 1917-19. Dir. Children's Service Bur. Licentiate Am. Bd. Pediatrics; fellow Am. Acad. Pediatrics; mem. A.M.A., Pittsburgh Acad. of Medicine, Pittsburgh Pediatric Soc. Republican. Presbyterian. Club: Oakmont Country. Home: 5700 Lynne Haven Rd., Pittsburgh, Pa. Office: Westinghouse Bldg., Pittsburgh, Pa.

BOYD, Elmer B.; editor Home News and Times. Address: 127 Church St., New Brunswick, N.J.

BOYD, (Samuel) Fiske, artist; b. Phila., Pa., July 5, 1895; s. Peter Keller and Lydia (Fiske) B.; student Pa. Acad. of Fine Arts, 1913-16, Art Students League of New York, 1922-24; m. Clare Mary Constance Shenehon, May 1, 1926; 1 dau., Sheila Shenehon. Artist (paintings, prints, drawings), since 1923. Exhibits: Daniel Group, New York, 1923-29; Brownell-Lambertson Gallery, New York, 1931; Rehn Gallery, New York, 1935; Am. Print Makers, New York, 1927; Fifty Prints of the Year, Am. Inst. Graphic Arts, 1927, 29, 31; Whitney Museum, 1932; Sesqui-Centennial Expn., Phila., 1926; Century of Progress, Chicago, 1934; New York World's Fair, 1939; Golden Gate Internat. Expn., 1939. Works in permanent collections: Metropolitan, Whitney, Boston, Baltimore, Addison Gallery (Andover), Philips Memorial Gallery, John Herron Inst. (Indianapolis), Art Assn. of Newport. Murals: Summit (N.J.) Post Office.

BOYD, George M.; prof. obstetrics Pa. Grad. Sch.; cons. obstetrician Phila. Gen. Hosp. and Preston Retreat. Address: 1909 Spruce St., Philadelphia, Pa.

BOYD, Harry Burton, clergyman; b. Chicago, Ill., Mar. 10, 1882; s. Joseph Warren and Minnie (Brock) B.; B.A., cum laude, Centre Coll., Ky., 1908, D.D., 1928; B.D., McCormick Theological Sem., 1911; D.D., Hastings (Neb.) Coll., 1922; LL.D., Univ. of Dubuque, 1928; m. Margaret Elizabeth Denham, Oct. 10, 1911; 1 son, Leslie Randolph. Ordained Presbyn. ministry, 1911; pastor successively Denton, Tex., Olean, N.Y., Iowa City, Ia., until 1918, Park Ch., Erie, Pa., 1919-28, Arch. Street Presbyn. Church, Philadelphia, 1928-37, First Presbyn. Church, Indiana, Pa., since 1937. Chaplain 313th Engrs., 88th Div., U.S.A., 1917-18; sr. chaplain 88th Div., A.E.F., 1918-19; organized first sch. of chaplains held in U.S. Army, Camp Dodge, Ia., Oct. 1917; organized ednl. work of 88th Div., A.E.F., Jan. 1, 1919, enrolling 3,000 students; hon. discharged June 19, 1919. Pres. bd. dirs. U. of Dubuque; v.p. Pa. Lord's Day Alliance; trustee and v.p. U.S.S. Niagara Assn.; del. Pan-Presbyn. Alliance, 1928; commr. Gen. Assembly, 1921 and 1932; del. to Federal Council of Chs., 1932 and 1934; chmn. Phila. Prohibition Emergency Com., 1933; trustee Pa. Anti-Saloon League, 1935, v.p. since 1938. Mem. Am. Acad. Polit. and Social Science, Am. Legion, Phi Delta Theta. Republican. Mason (33°). Clubs: Ingleside, Kiwanis. Preacher before schools and colls.; contbr. to religious press. Address: 134 S. 6th St., Indiana, Pa.

BOYD, J. Cookman; in gen. practice of law since 1888. Address: 2 E. Lexington St., Baltimore, Md.

BOYD, James O(gelvie), lawyer; b. Paterson, N.J., June 22, 1885; s. James O. and Elizabeth (Boyd) B.; ed. N.Y. Univ. 1912-15, N.Y. Law Sch., class of 1916; m. Martha Gibbs, Mar. 25, 1908; children—Edna Mae, James William. Admitted to N.J. bar as atty., 1917, counsellor, 1923; engaged in gen. practice of law at Newark since 1918; served as dep. commr. Workmans Compensation Bur. of Dept. Labor of N.J., 1918-23; trial atty. for Pub. Service Corp. of N.J. since 1923. Mem. Essex County Bar Assn. Republican. Baptist. Mason. Home: 142 Inwood Av., Upper Montclair. Office: 80 Park Pl., Newark, N.J.

BOYD, Julian Parks, librarian, editor; b. Converse, S.C., Nov. 3, 1903; s. Robert Jay and Melona (Parks) B.; A.B., Duke U., 1925, A.M., 1926; student U. of Pa., 1928; m. Grace Welch, Dec. 21, 1927; children—Julian P., Kenneth Miles. Began as editor Wyo. Hist. and Geol. Soc., Wilkes-Barre, Pa., 1928; mem. N.Y. State Hist. Assn., dir., 1932-34; mem. Hist. Soc. of Pa., asst. librarian, 1934-35, librarian and editor, 1935—. Mem. Pub. Archives Commn., Am. Hist. Assn., N.Y. Hist. Soc., Am. Antiq. Soc., Soc. Am. Archivists (treas.), Mass. Hist. Soc., Phi Beta Kappa, Lambda Chi Alpha. Club: Franklin Inn. Editor: The Susquehanna Title Stated and Examined, 1928; The Susquehanna Company Papers (4 vols.), 1930; Miner's Essays of Poor Robert the Scribe, 1930. Editor (with Carl Van Doren); Indian Treaties printed by Benjamin Franklin, 1938. Author: (with Roy F. Nichols) Syllabus of Social and Economic History of the U.S., 1928. Home: 53 Merbrook Lane, Merion, Pa. Office: 1300 Locust St., Philadelphia, Pa.

BOYD, Kenneth Bray; obstetrician-in-chief Md. Gen. Hosp.; visiting gynecologist and obstetrician U. of Md. Hosp., Mercy Hosp. and Hosp. for Women of Md.; asso. obstetrician Baltimore City Hosp.; asso. in gynecology, U. of Md. Address: 104 W. Madison St., Baltimore, Md.

BOYD, Marcus, pres. Boiler Tube Co. of America; b. Glasgow, Scotland, Oct. 29, 1883; s. William and Mary Johnston (Binnie) B.; brought to U.S., 1888, and citizen upon naturalization of parent; grad. Shadyside Acad., Pittsburgh, Pa., 1903; m. Elsie McCutcheon, Apr. 2, 1909; children—Mary Louise, Marcus, Catherine Taylor, Lindsay (Mrs. T. Burt O'Bryon), Elsie. Began career as bank clk., 1904; vice-pres. Chandler-Boyd Supply Co., 1910-19; pres. Boiler Tube Co. of America, fabricators and jobbers of boiler tubing, Pittsburgh, since 1919. Served as 1st lt., Inf., U.S. Army, during World War. Republican. Presbyterian. Clubs: Duquesne (Pittsburgh); Montour Heights Country (Moon Twp., Pa.). Home: R.F.D. 2, Coraopolis, Pa. Office: Boiler Tube Co. of America, Pittsburgh, Pa.

BOYD, Pliny Arthur, sales executive; b. Amesbury, Mass., Mar. 10, 1876; s. Pliny Steel and Mary Jane (Allen) B.; grad. Cushing Acad., Ashburnham, Mass., 1894; A.B., Brown U., Providence, R.I., 1898; m. Estelle Newton, Apr. 28, 1903; children—Helen Vanderveer (Mrs. Dean Wilson Marquis), John Newton, Frances Westevelt (Mrs. Edward Canby). With Black & Boyd Manufacturing Co., gas and electric fixtures, New York, 1898-1914, beginning as draftsman and becoming manager cost department and dir.; with Everett & Barron Co., shoe dressings and dyes, Providence, R.I., since 1914, sec. and dir. since 1937; pres. and dir. Bloomfield Coal & Supply Co.; vice-pres. and director Everett & Barron, Ltd., Canada, Automatic Ladder Co. Served with Battery B, R.I. Volunteers in Spanish-Am. War. Treas. and dir. Bloomfield Community Chest. Fellow Am. Geog. Soc.; mem. Nat. Economic League, Acad. of Polit. Science, Delta Upsilon. Republican. Presbyterian. Home: 30 Clarendon Place. Office: Trust Co. Bldg., Bloomfield, N.J.

BOYD, Richard N., chem. engr.; b. Bethlehem, Pa., Apr. 7, 1893; s. James W. and Emily (Noble) B.; student Scranton (Pa.) High Sch., 1905-09; Chem. Engr., Lehigh U., Bethlehem, Pa., 1915; m. Marguerite Rudolph, June 26, 1918; 1 dau., Nancy Rudolph. Mine surveyor Hudson Coal Co., Scranton, Pa., 1909-11; chemist Trojan Powder Co., Allentown, Pa., 1915-16, supt. acid plants, 1916-18, asst. works mgr., 1918-21, gen. supt., 1921-26, asst. dir. research since 1926. Mem. Am. Chem. Soc. (chmn. local sect., 1923, sec., 1936), Sigma Chi, Tau Beta Pi. Republican. Episcopalian. Mason. Clubs: Oakmont Tennis, Lehigh Country (Allentown, Pa.). Home: 1843 Hamilton St. Office: Trojan Powder Co., Allentown, Pa.

BOYD, Roy Martin; in gen. practice of law since 1917. Office: Lincoln Liberty Bldg., Philadelphia, Pa.

BOYD, Thomas Y., pres. Honesdale Dime Bank, partner C. E. & T. Y. Boyd; b. Boyd's Mills, Pa., July 7, 1868; s. Thomas Y. and Elizabeth (Mitchell) B.; student Lowell's Business Coll.; m. Helen E. Bennett, Jan. 27, 1932. One of organizers, becoming sec. mgr., Big Eddy Telephone Co.; partner firm C. E. & T. Y. Boyd, automobile dealer, Honesdale, Pa., since 1914; pres. and dir. Honesdale Dime Bank. Commr.'s clk., Wayne Co., Pa., 4 yrs.; sheriff, Wayne Co., 4 yrs.; register of wills, Wayne Co., 8 yrs. Mem. Wayne Co. Agrl. Soc. (dir.), Protection Engine Co. No. 3. Mason (Wayne Co. Royal Arch Chapter; Savona Commandery; Shriner, Irem Temple, Wilkes-Barre, Pa.). Club: Lions' (Honesdale). Home: 72 High St. Office: Honesdale Dime Bank, Honesdale, Pa.

BOYD-CARPENTER, educator, author; b. North of Ireland, Oct. 1881; s. Sir William (bishop Ch. of England) and Lady Charlotte (Piers) Boyd-Carpenter; B.A., LL.B., Yorkshire U., 1900; M.A., Cambridge, 1903; LL.D., Berlin, 1904; m. Mrs. T. C. Hornbrook, 1917. Active in 5 parliamentary elections for Conservative Unionist Party, 1900-10; examiner for Scotch Bd. of Edn., 1904-09; parliamentary legal counsel, House of Lords, 1907-11; etc.; spent many yrs. in Oriental countries and traveled widely studying conditions there; first came to U.S. in 1915, naturalized, 1920; lecturer at Univ. of Communications, Peking, 1921-24, also at the Law School, Peking, 1923-26, and in Tokyo; lecturer at U. of Va., 1926, Johns Hopkins, 1926-27, Georgetown U., 1927-30; prof. polit. science, Georgetown U., since 1930, also prof. Asiatic langs. and history; prof. Fordham since 1929. Member Am. Acad. Polit. and Social Science, Am. Soc. Internat. Law, Japan Asiatic Soc., Chinese Social and Polit. Science Assn. Clubs: Chevy Chase (Md.); Grolier, Town Hall (New York); Royal Socs. (London); Peking Club (Peiping, China); also Stoke Poges Club. Author: Political Background of the French Revolution, 1911; Syndicalism—A Study, 1913; Elements of International Law, 1919; Elements of Political Science, 1920—all pub. in London. Translator: The Leather Seller of Samarcand, 1934; When I Came to You, 1935; Wayfarers Note Book, 1936. Contbr. to mags. on Oriental and polit. subjects. Home: 6 Bei Shui Fu Hutung, Peiping, China, also 4 W. Melrose St., Chevy Chase, Md.*

BOYDEN, Alan Arthur, asso. prof. zöology; b. Milwaukee, Wis., June 16, 1897; s. Arthur Wellesley and Carrie Elizabeth (Wheeler) B.; ed. Beloit Coll., Wis., 1916-19; A.B., U. of Wis., 1921, Ph.D., same, 1925; m. Mabel Josephine Gregg, Sept. 15, 1923; children—Alan Arthur, Jr., Douglas Gregg, Mabel Maxon, Cornelia Wheeler. Teaching asst. in zöology, U. of Wis., 1920-25; instr. zöology, Rutgers U., New Brunswick, N.J., 1925-26, asst. prof., 1926-30, asso. prof. since 1930; lecturer in zöology, U. of Calif., 1929-30. Served in Wis. N.G., 1913-16, U.S.A., 1918. Mem. A.A.A.S., Am. Soc. Zöologists, Am. Eugenics Soc., Genetics Soc. America, N.Y. Acad. Scis., Phi Beta Kappa, Sigma Xi, Phi Sigma, Gamma Alpha. Republican. Mem. Dutch Reformed Ch. Home: Lincoln St., Stelton, N.J.

BOYER, Calvin S., judge; b. Springtown, Pa., Apr. 8, 1876; student pub. schs., Springtown Acad. and Millersville State Normal Sch.; studied law, U. of Mich. Judge 7th Judicial Dist., Pa., since 1930, present term expiring 1942. Home: Doylestown, Pa.

BOYER, Carl, dir. Wagner Free Inst. Science; b. Phila., Pa., Jan. 21, 1884; s. Charles Sumner and Ella Harriet (Talbot) B.; ed. Central Manual Training Sch., Phila., Pa., 1898-1901; m. Mabel Allsop, Sept. 18, 1907; children—Carl, Jr., Ruth Alice (Mrs. Joseph Almeida), Doris Talbot. Employed as lab. worker, Automatic Telephone Switch Co., 1901-03, Leeds & Northrup Co., 1903-05; asst. to dir. Wagner Free Inst. of Science, Phila., 1905-24, curator, 1925-28, dir. since 1928; dir. and mem. exec. com. Illustrated Catalog N. Am. Devonian Fossils; mem. Pa. State Adv. Bd. Federal Writers Project in Pa. Mem. A.A.A.S., Acad. Natural Sciences, Phila., Pa. Library Club, Phila. Bot. Club, Spl. Libraries Council Phila. and Vicinity, Phila. Natural History Soc. (treas.). Republican. Episcopalian. Home: 415 E. Hortter St., Philadelphia, Pa. Office: 17th St. and Montgomery Av., Philadelphia, Pa.

BOYER, Carl Wright, prof. edn.; b. Mt. Carmel, Pa., Nov. 26, 1897; s. Charles C. and Margaret (Wright) B.; A.B., Muhlenberg Coll., 1923; A.M., N.Y. Univ., 1924, Ph.D., 1930; Nov. 30, 1928; children—Carl Wright, Jr., Marjorie Ellen. Teacher in various high schs., 1917-25; instr. in edn., Lafayette Coll., 1925-26; instr. education, Muhlenberg College, 1926-28, asst. prof., 1928-30, prof. edn. since 1930; dir. div. radio broadcasting since 1937; ednl. dir. Lehigh Valley Broadcasting Co., WCBA, WSAN. Served in U.S.A. with A.E.F. in Siberia, 1918-19. Mem. Assn. Coll. Teachers of Edn., Am. Assn. Univ. Profs., Pa. State Edn. Assn., Phi Kappa Tau, Phi Delta Kappa, Kappa Phi Kappa (mem. Nat. Council since 1936), Am. Legion (past post comdr.). Pres. Lehigh Co. Taxpayers League, 1936-37; moderator radio forums, 1937-39; dir. Kappa Phi Kappa, nat. radio edn, project, 1939-41. Republican. United Lutheran. Mason. Home: 1513 Turner St., Allentown, Pa.

BOYER, Daniel B., merchant, banker; b. Boyertown, Pa., Oct. 2, 1889; s. James Keely and Annie Charlotte (Stetler) B.; student Boyertown (Pa.) pub. schs., 1895-1902, Hill Sch., Pottstown, Pa., 1902-07; B.S., Haverford

(Pa.) Coll., 1911; m. Blanche M. Reigner, of Reading, Pa., Mar. 9, 1918; children—Daniel B., Mary Elizabeth, James Keely. Clerk Boyertown Nat. Bank, 1911-12; salesman Kuhn Investment Bankers, Phila., 1912-13; mng. J. & H. K. Boyer, Boyertown, Pa., 1913-19; succeeded to ownership D. B. Boyer & Co., department store, Boyertown, Pa., 1919 (this business started in 1805 by great-grandfather, D. B. Boyer, after whom Boyertown was named); pres., treas. Penn-Berks Investors, Reading, Pa., since 1929; v.p. and dir. Nat. Bank of Boyertown, Pa., since 1933; dir. Boyertown Burial Casket Co. since 1913; dir. Peerless Heater Co., Boyertown Savings & Loan Assn.; trustee Boyer estate, spending much time managing real estate interests. Served as lt., 28th Div., A.E.F., 1918-19. Mem. Am. Legion. Republican. Lutheran. Clubs: Rotary (Boyertown, Pa.); Seaside Park (N.J.) Yacht; Brookside Country (Pottstown, Pa.). Home: "Mt. Pleasant." Office: Phila. and Reading Av., Boyertown, Pa.

BOYER, Emery Homer; b. Johnstown, Pa., May 16, 1878; s. John and Catharine (Bowser) B.; ed. pub. schs., Johnstown; m. Fannie J. Davis, Sept. 10, 1908; 1 dau., Mildred Ruth. Began business career selling papers, 1890-95; served as apprentice in bakery of C. H. Harris, 1895-98; in employ Cambria Steel Co., 1898-1900; became mem. firm with C. H. Harris, bakery, 1901, pres. and dir. The Harris-Boyer Co. Inc., Johnstown, Pa., since 1934; dir. Johnstown Bank and Trust Co. Mem. Chamber of Commerce. Dir. and vice-pres. Family Welfare Soc., Cambria Co. Chapter Am. Red Cross since 1930, chmn., 1933-38. Republican. Methodist (pres. bd. trustees Calvary M.E. Ch. since 1918). Mason (K.T., 32°, Shriner). Club: Rotary (Johnstown, Pa.). Home: 146 F St. Office: 139 Fairfield Av., Johnstown, Pa.

BOYER E(rnest) Albert, sheriff; b. Northampton, Pa., Sept. 4, 1897; s. Thomas A. and Laura B. (Odenwelder) B.; grad. Franklin and Marshall Acad., 1916; student Franklin and Marshall Coll., Lancaster, Pa., 1916-17; grad. Bliss Elec. Sch., Washington, D.C., 1920; m. Dora R. Newhard, June 26, 1926; children—E. Albert, John Thomas, Joanne Newhard. In employ Roller-Smith Co. at Bethlehem, Pa., plant, 1920-23; engaged in elec. contracting on own acct., 1923-27; in employ Pa. Power & Light Co., 1927-32; chief dep. sheriff, Northampton Co., 1932-36, sheriff since 1936. Served in Inf., F.A., and M.C., U.S.A., 1917-19, with A.E.F. and Army of Occupation. Mem. Northampton Co. Hist. and Geneal. Soc., Pa. German Soc., Pa. German Folklore Soc., Am. Legion, Forty and Eight, Vets. of Fgn. Wars. Democrat. Reformed. Mason. Clubs: Kiwanis, Pomfret (Easton, Pa.); Catasauqua (Catasauqua, Pa.). Author: (in preparation) Biographical History of the Sheriffs of Northampton Co. Home: 220 Howertown Rd., Northampton, Pa. Office: Court House, Easton, Pa.

BOYER, Francis, mfg. chemist; b. Penllyn, Pa., June 21, 1893; s. Henry C. and Nathalie Chauncey (Robinson) B.; prep. edn., Groton (Mass.) Sch., 1906-12; student Harvard, 1912-15, Cambridge U. Eng., 1919; m. Mary Holmes, Jan. 25, 1928; children—John Francis, Markly Holmes, Mary Robinson. V.p. and dir. Smith, Kline & French Labs., Phila.; dir. Smith, Kline & French, Inc., I. Edwards Co. Served as 1st lt., 101st F.A., 26th Div., U.S. Army, with A.E.F., during World War. Republican. Home: Route 4, Norristown, Pa. Office: 105 N. 5th St., Philadelphia, Pa.

BOYER, Frank P(eter), supt. county schs.; b. Cowan, Pa., Nov. 15, 1887; s. David J. and Jennie C. (Hursh) B.; A.B., Susquehanna U., Selinsgrove, Pa., 1914, A.M., 1916, (hon.) Pd.D., 1932; A.M. in Edn., Columbia U., 1925; m. Sara E. Edmunds, June 30, 1918; children—David, Eugenia, Spencer, Winston, John, Vincent. Served as prin. grammar sch., Mazeppa, Pa., 1907-12, high sch. Lewis Twp., Pa., 1914-22; supervising prin. schs. Mifflinburg, Pa., 1922-30, supt. county schs. of Union Co., Pa., since 1930; first sealer of weights and measures, Union Co., 1912-13; instr. Summer Normal for Teachers, Defiance, Pa., 1916-17; instr. Susquehanna U. Summer Sch., 1929-38. Mem. Union Co. Hist. Soc. (pres. 1930), Patriotic Order Sons of America (pres. Union Co., 1928-29). Republican. Mason (32°). Author: History of Public Schools of Union County, 1939. Home: 200 Green St., Mifflinburg, Pa.

BOYER, George Milton, M.D.; b. Damascus, Md., May 22, 1872; s. Milton and Elizabeth (Purdum) B.; student Damascus pub. schs., 1878-92, Shenandoah Normal Coll., 1893-94; M.D., George Washington U. Med. Sch., Washington, D.C., 1902; m. Annie M. Bowman, Dec. 24, 1902; children—Susan Elizabeth, Milton McKendree, George Wesley, Annie Mary. Teacher, later prin. pub. schs., Travilla, Md., 1894-98; in gen. practice of medicine since 1902; mem. staff Sibley Memorial Hosp. (Washington, D.C.), Montgomery Co. Gen. Hosp. (Olney, Md.), Frederick City Hosp. Vice-pres. and dir. Bank of Damascus. Served as med. officer, World War, hon. discharged with rank of major. Trustee Damascus High Sch. Mem. A.M.A., Montgomery Co. Med. Soc. (pres. 1938), Md. Med. and Chirug. Faculty. Democrat. Methodist (trustee Damascus Ch.). Address: Damascus, Md.

BOYER, John Redman Coxe, vegetable oil mfg. and refining; b. Phila., Pa., Nov. 9, 1863; s. William Henry and Sarah Anne (Coxe) B.; student Newton Grammar Sch., West Phila., Pa. 1875-83; m. Florence Elizabeth Tuthill, Oct. 28, 1903; children—John Redman Coxe, Franklin Tuthill Brewster, Elizabeth Adams (Mrs. Cecil Mackie Hopkins). Began in linseed oil mfg. business, West Phila., Pa., 1883; pres. Oil Products Corpn., Singac, N.J., 1925-30; pres. Boyer Oil Mfg. Co., Indianapolis, Ind., 1914-16; pres. Cross Hill (S.C.) Oil Co., 1918-20; pres. Bishopville (S.C.) Oil Co., 1918-20; retired 1930. Served as private, Pa. N.G., 5 yrs. Republican. Episcopalian. Mason (Polar Star Lodge, New York). Club: Belmont Cricket (West Phila., Pa.). Address: South Finley Av., Basking Ridge, N.J.

BOYER, Philip A., educator; b. Phila., Pa., May 20, 1886; s. Philip A. and Emma A. (Acker) B.; student Phila. Sch. of Pedagogy, 1903-05; A.B., Temple U., Phila., 1912; A.M., U. of Pa., 1915, Ph.D.; 1920; m. Gertrude B. Stone, June 30, 1908; children—Philip A., Vincent S. Teacher, Phila. Pub. Schs., 1905-15, prin. elementary schools, 1915-23, prin. Jr. High Sch., 1923-25, dir. ednl. research, Phila. since 1925; teacher grad. schs. edn., summers, U. of Pa., 1922-36, 1939, Duke U., 1920-21, 1937-38. Dir. leadership training, Phila. Council, Boy Scouts of America. Mem. Am. Ednl. Research Assn. (pres. 1934), Am. Assn. Sch., Adminstrs., Nat. Soc. Study of Edn., Phi Delta Kappa. Club: Phila. School Men's (pres. 1936-38). Author: Boyer Speller, 1929; Learning Guide in General Science, 1934; Progress Arithmetics, 1937; Review of Research, 1939. Contbr. articles to ednl. mags. Home: 6320 Lawnton Av. Office: Parkway and 21st St., Philadelphia, Pa.

BOYER, Robert; surgeon and med. dir. Northwestern Gen. Hosp. Address: 1513 W. Girard Av., Philadelphia, Pa.

BOYER, Samuel P., physician and legislator; b. Somerset Co., Pa., Aug. 30, 1881; s. Peter and Susan (Walker) B.; student Teachers' Coll., California, Pa., 1902; B.S., Ohio Northern U., Ada, O., 1905; M.D., U. of Pittsburgh Med. Sch., 1916; m. Florence Belle Curry, 1922. Teacher Pa. High Schs., 1906-12; asso. obstetrician Conemaugh Valley Memorial Hosp., Johnstown, Pa., since 1922. Mem. Pa. Ho. of Rep., 1934-36, since 1936. Chmn. State Com. on Conservation and Edn. of State Fed. of Sportsmen's Clubs. Mem. Cambria Co. Med. Soc., Pa. State Med. Soc., A.M.A. Republican. Clubs: Civic, Sportsmen's (Johnstown, Pa.). Address: 163 Fairfield Av., Johnstown, Pa.

BOYKIN, S. F.; v.p. and treas. Coca Cola Co. Home: 1002 Berkeley Road. Office: du Pont Bldg., Wilmington, Del.

BOYLAN, James E., Jr.; in gen. practice of law since 1923; local counsel B.&O. and Western railroads. Address: Westminster, Md.

BOYLAN, Matthew A., utilities exec.; b. Bloomingdale, N.J., July 16, 1880; s. Andrew and Bridget (O'Connell) B.; student Pratt Inst., Brooklyn, N.Y., 1909-12; m. Elizabeth C. Naylor, Oct. 28, 1903; 1 dau., Beatrice. Worked in gen. store, 1899-1902; in utility business since 1902; gen. mgr. Morris & Somerset Electric Co., Morristown, N.J., 1912-25; gen. mgr. Jersey Central Power & Light Co., Asbury Park, N.J., 1925-27; v.p. South Kansas Gas Co., Chanute, Kans., 1927-28; v.p. and gen. mgr. Scranton-Spring Brook Water Service Co., Scranton, Pa., since 1928, dir. since 1936; v.p. Peoples Gas Co., Miami Beach, Fla.; v.p. and dir. Carbondale Gas Co., Pa. Water Service Co., Wyoming Co. Gas Co.; v.p. and dir. Scranton and Spring Brook R.R. Co.; dir. Winton Water Co., subsidiaries of Scranton-Spring Brook Water Service Co. Served in Spanish-Am. War, 1898. Mem. Am. Gas Assn., Pa. Gas Assn. (2d v.p. since 1938), Chamber of Commerce, Community Chest. Roman Catholic. Clubs: Kiwanis (Scranton, Scranton Country, Lackawanna Motor (Scranton, Pa.). Home: 635 Jefferson Av. Office: 135 Jefferson Av., Scranton, Pa.

BOYLE, Alexander Robert Mills, corpn. exec.; b. Glasgow, Scotland, Apr. 30, 1888; s. Alexander and Margaret (McLean) B.; student Kent Road School, Glasgow, 1894-1903, Univ. of Manitoba, 1915-16; C.P.A., by examination of Am. Inst. of Accountants, 1920; m. Bernadette Giguère, July 29, 1933; children—Bernadette Janet, Alexander Robert Mills. Began as office boy, 1903; in various occupations until 1916; served with corps of Engrs., Canadian Army, 1916-18; with Touche Niven Co., New York, 1919-25; sec., treas. and dir. Lehn & Fink Products Corpn., drugs and chemicals, New York and Bloomfield, N.J., since 1925. Mem. Am. Inst. of Accountants, Dominion Assn. of Chartered Accountants, Inst. of Chartered Accountants of Manitoba. Republican. Presbyterian. Mason. Clubs: Wee Burn Country (Darien, Conn.); Canadian (New York). Home: Darien, Conn. Office: 192 Bloomfield Av., Bloomfield, N.J.; 683 Fifth Av., New York, N.Y.

BOYLE, Charles Joseph, lawyer; b. Johnstown, Pa., Aug. 29, 1895; s. Michael Patrick and Margaret Honora (Dowling) B.; student Johnstown (Pa.) High Sch., 1911-13, St. Francis Coll. Prep. Sch., 1913-15, Cath. U. of America, Washington, D.C., 1915-17, Wharton Bus. Sch., Univ. of Pa., 1918-19; A.B., Univ. of Mich., 1920; LL.B., Univ. of Mich. Law Sch., 1923; unmarried. Employed as accountant, Dowling & Co., Inc., 1923; admitted to Pa. bar, 1923 and since engaged in gen. practice of law at Johnstown, Pa.; asso. with firm Sharkey, Widmann and Sharkey, 1924-25; in practice alone, 1925 to 1927; asso. with Edward T. Stibich, Esq., Johnstown, Pa., since 1927; dir. and counsel, Dowling & Co. Wholesale Grocery, Inc. Served in Inf., U.S. Army, 1918, in R.O.T.C. 1918-19. Mem. bd. dirs. local chapter Red Cross, council Boy Scouts. Mem. Pa. State, and Cambria Co. bar assns., Am. Legion (past comdr. Johnstown Post), U. of Mich. Alumni Assn. (sec.), Gamma Eta Gamma. Democrat. Roman Catholic. K.C. (4°), Elk (past Exalted Ruler Johnstown Lodge). Clubs: Sunnehanna, Rotary, Pennsylvania Society. Home: 224 Walnut St. Office: Johnstown Bank & Trust Bldg., Johnstown, Pa.

BOYLE, H. Cotter; surgeon Sacred Heart and Allentown hosps. Address: 1435 Hamilton St., Allentown, Pa.

BOYLE, Hugh Charles, bishop; b. Johnstown, Pa., Oct. 8, 1873; s. Charles and Ann (Keelan) B.; ed. St. Vincent's prep. sch., coll. and sem., Beatty, Pa., 1888-98. Ordained R.C. priest, 1898; asst. St. Aloysius Ch., Wilmerding, Pa., until Jan. 1903; asst. St. Paul's Cathedral and new St. Paul's Cathedral, 1903-09; supt. parish schs., diocese of Pittsburgh, 1909-16; pastor St. Mary Magdalene's Ch., Homestead, Pa., 1916-21; consecrated bishop of Pittsburgh, June 29, 1921. Home: 116 N. Dithridge St., Pittsburgh, Pa.

BOYLE, Orrin Edwin, lawyer; b. Allentown, Pa., June 12, 1891; s. John Aspinwall and

Minnie Elmira (Boyer) B.; student Allentown Prep. Sch., 1910-12, Mu lenberg Coll., 1912-14; LL.B., U. of Pa. Law Sch., 1917; m. Beatrice Sarah Gehringer, Jan. 22, 1916; children—Barbara Gehringer (Mrs. Donald MacKenzie), Orrin Edwin, Jr. (dec.), Robert Bruce Reno, Patricia Ann Boyer. Admitted to Pa. bar, 1919, and since engaged in gen. practice of law at Allentown; served as U.S. commr., 1920-24; dist. atty. Lehigh Co., Pa., 1924-28; dir. Lehigh Valley Ice Co. Mem. Am., Pa., and Lehigh Co. (past pres.) bar assns., Alpha Tau Omega, Delta Theta Phi, Patriotic Order Sons of America (past nat. pres., past state pres., founder and dir. Minute Men). Past pres. John Hay Assn. Republican. Mem. Reformed Ch. Mason (32°), Elk (past exalted ruler). Home: 35th and Congress Sts. Office: 539 Hamilton St., Allentown, Pa.

BOYNTON, Henry Cook, metallurgist; b. Willisboro, N.Y., Apr. 16, 1874; s. Orville Abram and Martha Luella (Cook) B.; grad. Plymouth (Mass.) High Sch., 1893; A.B., Harvard, 1900, S.M., 1901, Sc.D., 1904; m. Mary Allison Manter, June 11, 1902; children—Rosamond (Mrs. Philip Sherman Mumford), Paul Manter, Henry Cook. Asst. in geology, Harvard, 1900-01, asst. in metallurgy and metallography, 1901-02, instr., same, 1902-06; metallurgist with John A. Roebling's Sons Co., Trenton, N.J., since 1906. Mem. Am. Inst. Mining and Metall. Engrs., Am. Soc. Testing Materials, Am. Soc. for Metals, Brit. Iron and Steel Inst. Carnegie Research Scholar, 1905-07. Republican. Presbyterian. Mason (32°, Shriner). Clubs: Engineers (Trenton); Harvard (New York); Harvard (Phila.). Contbr. articles on metallurgy of steel to Harpers Mag. and to professional jours. Home: 935 Carteret Av. Office: 640 S. Broad St., Trenton, N.J.

BRACELAND, Francis J(ames), psychiatrist; b. Phila., Pa., July 22, 1900; s. John Joseph and Margaret (L'Estrange) B.; A.B., LaSalle Coll., Phila., 1926; M.D., Jefferson Med. Coll., Phila., 1930; m. Hope Van Gelder Jenkins, June 1, 1938. Resident physician Jefferson Hosp., Phila., 1930-32; asst. physician Pa. Hosp. for Mental Disease, 1932-35; asst. physician Burgholzli Hosp., Zurich, Switzerland, 1935-36; asst. physician Nat. Hosp., Queens Square, London, 1936; clin. dir. Pa. Hosp., 1936-37; psychiatrist Inst. of Pa. Hosp., Phila., since 1937; psychiatrist Pa. Hosp.; asst. psychiatrist Phila. Gen. Hosp.; consultant in chief to St. Joseph's and Babies hosps.; consultant psychiatrist Misericordia, Mercy, Fitzgerald hosps. and St. Edmonds Home for Crippled Children; instr. in psychiatry, U. of Pa. Med. Sch.; asst. prof. of psychiatry, Grad. Sch. of Medicine, U. of Pa., since 1939. Lt., U.S.N.R. Diplomate Am. Bd. Psychiatry; fellow A.M.A., Coll. of Physicians of Phila.; mem. Am. Coll. of Physicians, Am. Psychiatric Assn., Phila. Psychiatric Soc., Phila. Neurological Soc., Phila. Med. Club. Republican. Roman Catholic. Club: Penn Athletic (Phila.). Address: 111 N. 49th St., Philadelphia, Pa.

BRACEY, Altamont H.; mem. surg. staff Stevens Clinic Hosp. Address: Welch, W.Va.

BRACKEN, John Robert, univ. prof.; b. Duquesne, Pa., Aug. 25, 1891; s. Edward Spear and Margaret (Caughey) B.; B.S., Pa. State Coll., 1914; M.L.D., U. of Mich., 1935; m. Margaret Baird, July 25, 1917. Landscape architect, Pittsburgh, 1914-16; professional landscape architecture and city planning, Phila., 1916-24; assistant professor landscape extension, Pennsylvania State College, 1924-26, professor landscape architecture and head of division since 1926. Served in U.S. Army, 1919. Mem. Am. Soc. Landscape Architects, Am. Assn. Univ. Profs., Scarab, Alpha Zeta, Pi Gamma Alpha. Presbyterian. Mason. Address: 126 E. Nittany Av., State College, Pa.

BRACKETT, William Savage, chem. engr.; b. Cunnyngham, Pa., Oct. 27, 1898; s. William Walker and Esther L. (Savage) B.; grad. New Britain (Conn.) High Sch., 1916; B.S., Middlebury (Vt.) Coll., 1920; M.S. in Chem. Engring., Mass. Inst. Tech., 1923; m. Emily Millard, June 27, 1925; children—William Savage, Eleanor Millard, Millard Brackett (dec.). With Carbide & Carbon Chemicals Corpn. since 1923, beginning as chem. engr., chief chem. engr. since 1938. Mem. S.A.T.C., World War. Mem. Am. Inst. Chem. Engrs., Delta Kappa Epsilon. Republican. Conglist. Club: Edgewood Country (Charleston). Home: Upper Ridgeway Road. Office: 437 East Av., South Charleston, W.Va.

BRADBURY, Robert Hart, chemist; b. Philadelphia, Sept. 25, 1870; s. Robert and Margaret C. (Hart) B.; A.B., Central High Sch., Phila., 1887; Ph.D., U. of Pa., 1893; m. Mabel Bradner, June 27, 1901; children—Robert Hart, Mabel Campbell. Asst. chemist, Cambria Iron Co., 1889; chemist S. P. Wetherill Paint Co., 1891-92; prof. chemistry, Central Manual Training Sch., Phila., 1893-1907; head Dept. of Science, Southern High Sch., Phila., 1907-30; retired. Consulting chemist, Am. Chem. Paint Co. Lecturer on phys. chemistry, Dept. of Philosophy, U. of Pa., 1894-95. Mem. Am. Chem. Soc., Franklin Inst. Author: An Elementary Chemistry, 1903; A Laboratory Manual of Chemistry, 1903; An Inductive Chemistry, 1912; Laboratory Studies in Chemistry, 1912; A First Book in Chemistry, 1922, 3d edit. revised, 1938; New Laboratory Studies in Chemistry, 1923; Looseleaf Work-book for the Chemistry Laboratory, 1934. Republican. Home: Warner Rd., Colonial Village, Wayne, Pa.

BRADBURY, Samuel, M.D.; b. Germantown, Phila., Apr. 30, 1883; s. Samuel and Martha Washington (Chapman) B.; Northeast Manual Training Sch., Phila.; M.D., U. of Pa., 1905; m. Althea Norris Johnson, Sept. 26, 1914; children—Samuel, Emily Carey, Althea Norris, Wilmer Johnson. With Germantown Hosp. (Philadelphia) and Pa. Hospital (Philadelphia) until 1911; asst. visiting phys. City Hosp., New York, 1912-17, visiting phys. 1917-24; asst. visiting phys. Bellevue Hosp., 1924-27; chief in medicine, Cornell Clinic, and asst. prof. clin. medicine, Cornell U. Med. Coll., New York, 1921-27; cons. phys. New York Infirmary for Women and Children, 1924-27; dir. Out Patient Dept., Pa. Hosp., Phila., since 1927; chief of service, Germantown Hosp., Phila. Commd. 1st lt. Medical R.C., Mar. 1916; capt. M.C., U.S.A., Oct. 19, 1918; served in France, July 1917-Apr. 1919; former maj. M.C., U.S.R. Mem. A.M.A., Med. Soc. State of Pa., Phila. County Med. Soc., Coll. of Physicians of Phila., American Climatol. and Clin. Assn., Acad. Medicine of New York (fellow in internal medicine), A.A.A.S., Harvey Society, Am. Legion, Phi Kappa Psi and Phi Alpha Epsilon fraternities. Republican. Presbyn. Club: Mask and Wig (Phila.). Author: Internal Medicine—Treatment, 1923; (monograph) What Constitutes Adequate Medical Service? (pub. 1927, by The Com. on Dispensary Development of the United Hosp. Fund of New York); also contbr. to Nelson's Loose Leaf Medicine, Cyclopedia of Medicine and Text Book of Medicine by Am. Authors, Adequate Medical Care, 1937. Home and Office: 151 W. Coulter St., Germantown, Philadelphia, Pa.

BRADDOCK, (James) Harold, public relations counsel; b. Paterson, New Jersey, November 2, 1885; s. James and Alice V. (Steele) Braddock; spl. student Harvard Univ., 1906-08, 1909-10; m. Helena Hunziker, Oct. 10, 1912; children—Helena Marie (Mrs. John Lemp), James Harold, Richard Reed. Staff member of the New York Bureau of Municipal Research, 1910-13; a founder, and vice-president of American City Bur., 1913-17; directed organization of community orgns. in 25 cities, 1913-17; asso. dir. 1st Red Cross, War Fund, summer 1917; dir. Library War Council by apptmt. of Sec. of War, autumn 1917; dir. Mil. Entertainment Council, by apptmt. of same, also dir. Smileage Div. War Dept. Commn. on Training Camp Activities, 1917-18; dir. savings div. War Loan Orgn., Treasury Dept., by apptmt. of Sec. of Treasury, 1918-19; dir. Rep. Nat. Ways and Means Com., in N.J., 1919-27; chmn. ednl. relations com., N.J. Bell Telephone Co., in charge tech. employment and training, 1927-32; pub. relations dir. N.J. Sch. Survey Commn., 1934; pub. relations counsel numerous other instns., corpns., associations, spl. groups and individuals, 1919—. Mem. pub. relations com. N.J. State Normal Coll., Newark. Considered an authority upon ednl. and public relations. Unitarian. Clubs: Harvard (New York); Harvard (N.J.); Nat. Press (Washington, D.C.). Occasional contbr. to Annals of Am. Acad. Polit. and Social Science and other publs. Home: Montclair, N.J. Office: 165 Broadway, New York, N.Y.*

BRADFORD, Avery J.; receiver of Bank of Pittsburgh and a number of other banks; also dir. various companies. Home: 326 S. Dallas Av. Office: 226 Fourth Av., Pittsburgh, Pa.

BRADFORD, Charles Elmer, pres. Charles Bradford Co.; b. Kirby Post Office, Pa., Apr. 13, 1885; s. John Gordon and Sarah Ellen (Guthrie) B.; student Carnegie Inst. Tech.; unmarried. Mgr. J. E. Edmundson Co., 1910-19; organized, 1919, Charles Bradford Co., McKeesport, Pa., and since pres. and dir. Mason (32°). Home: 1140 Lincoln Way. Office: 514 Walnut St., McKeesport, Pa.

BRADFORD, Frederick Alden, coll. prof.; b. Danbury, Conn., Oct. 4, 1897; s. Frederick Alden and Bessie Potter (Nash) B.; student Case Sch. of Applied Science, 1915-17; A.B., U. of Mich., 1921, A.M., 1923, Ph.D., 1926; m. Margery Mary Felgate, Aug. 18, 1926. Asst., later instr. in economics, U. of Mich., 1920-23, and 1924-26; asst. prof. of economics, Southern Meth. U., 1923-24; asst. later asso. prof. of economics, Lehigh U., 1926-35, prof. since 1935, head of dept. of finance since 1936. Served in U.S.N.R.F., 1918-19. Mem. Am. Economic Assn., Royal Economic Soc. (Eng.), Phi Beta Kappa, Zeta Psi. Republican. Mem. research div. of Nat. Com. (head of banking and currency sec.), during 1936 presidential campaign. Author: Money and Banking, 1934. Contbr. articles and reviews on finance; mem. bd. of editors Am. Econ. Review, 1932-34. Home: 1201 Eaton Av. Office: Lehigh U., Bethlehem, Pa.

BRADFORD, Louis Jacquelin, coll. prof.; b. Dinard, France (of Am. parents), June 1, 1888; s. Louis Colyer and Katherine Allen (Sanders) B.; came to U.S., 1888; B.S., Swarthmore (Pa.) Coll., 1911; M.E., Cornell U., 1916; m. Edith Cuthbert Fleming, June 24, 1916. Instr. mech. engring., Swarthmore (Pa.) Coll., 1911-12; computor Worthington Pump & Machinery Co., Harrison, N.J., summer 1912; instr. machine design, Cornell U., 1912-16, acting asst. prof., 1916-17; in charge testing sect. Naval Aircraft Factory, Phila., Pa., 1918-19; asst. prof. machine design, Pa. State Coll., 1919-22, asso. prof., 1922-23, prof. and in charge div. since 1924. Mem. Sigma Xi, Pi Tau Sigma. Republican. Episcopalian. Co-author: (with P. B. Eaton) Machine Design, 1926; numerous articles on various phases of lubrication. Home: 602 Pugh St. Office: 213 Main Engineering Bldg., State Coll., Pa.

BRADFORD, Mark A.; surgeon South Side Hosp. Address: 529 Liberty Av., Pittsburgh, Pa.

BRADFORD, Thomas Nash, wholesale and retail mcht.; b. New Bedford, Mass., Feb. 1, 1895; s. Frederick Alden and Bessie Potter (Nash) B.; student East High Sch., Cleveland, O., 1910-14, U. of Fla., Gainesville, Fla., 1914-16; m. Ruth Gertrude Paisley, Dec. 27, 1919; children—Thomas Paisley, Margaret Ann, Ruth Mary. Began as clk. in office Valley Camp Coal Co., Cleveland, O., 1920-23, coal salesman, 1923-25, mgr. store operations, Valley Camp Coal Co., Wheeling, W.Va., 1925-27; treas. Valley Camp Stores Co., Wheeling, 1927-32, pres. and treas. since 1932; vice-pres., treas. and mgr. Pa. & W.Va. Supply Corpn., Wheeling, since 1933; dir. Valley Camp Coal Co., Cleveland, O., since 1931. Served as ensign U.S. Naval Res., 1917-19. Mem. Pi Kappa Alpha. Republican. Presbyn. Mason. Club: Fort Henry (Wheeling). Home: 51 Haddale Av., Wheeling. Office: Triadelphia, W.Va.

BRADFUTE, John Harold, service engr.; b. Cedarville, O., Aug. 26, 1893; s. William and Ola E. (Lott) B.; student high sch., Washington, O., 1905-09, business coll., Columbus, O., 1909-10, corr. sch., 1910-16, Duquesne U., Pittsburgh, Pa., 1930-37; m. Elsie Marie Jackson, June 22, 1914; children—Jeannette Olive, Carol Marie, John Harold. Agt. Otis Elevator

BRADLEY

Co., Columbus, O., 1915-18, asst. service mgr., Cleveland, O., 1918-19; partner B. & P. Electric Repair Co., Cleveland, O., 1919-24; mgr. Otis Elevator Co., Youngstown, O., 1924-29; service mgr. Westinghouse Electric Elevator Co., Pittsburgh, 1930-33, service engr. since 1933; secretary Lake Sanoma, Inc., since 1938. Member Inter-Club Council (president 1939), Boy Scouts of America (chmn. Conestoga div. since 1937), Council of Orgns. Republican. Presbyterian. Mason. Club: Kiwanis (pres. 1937), Syria Automobile (Pittsburgh; dir.). Author: Elevator Safety, 1937. Home: 260 Cedar Boul., Mt. Lebanon, Pa. Office: 1503 Gulf Bldg., Pittsburgh, Pa.

BRADLEY, Aubrey Ottarson, chemist; b. Wickliffe, O., Apr. 26, 1896; s. George Howe and Isabelle (Ottarson) B.; B.A., Ohio Wesleyan U., 1917; M.S., Ohio State U., Columbus, O., 1918, Ph.D., 1925; m. Esther Katherine Rockey, July 19, 1919; children—Joan Esther, Donald Rockey, Daniel Burr. Chemist Ault & Wiborg Co., Cincinnati, O., 1919-20; chemist Cincinnati Chem. Works, 1920-23; asso. with E. I. Du Pont de Nemours & Co., Wilmington, Del., since 1925, supt. Azo Dept. (dyeworks) since 1939. Served as pvt., Research Div., Chem. Warfare Service, U.S. Army, 1918. Mem. Am. Chem. Soc., Sigma Xi, Phi Gamma Delta, Phi Beta Kappa, Phi Lambda Upsilon. Republican. Methodist. Club: Du Pont Country (Wilmington, Del.). Home: 2015 Monroe Pl. Office: P.O. Box 389, Wilmington, Del.

BRADLEY, Edward Sculley, univ. prof.; b. Phila., Pa., Jan. 4, 1897; s. Stephen Edward and Annette Evelyn (Palmer) B.; A.B., U. of Pa., 1919, M.A., 1921, Ph.D., 1927; m. Margaret Cashner, June 11, 1921; children—Deborah Ann, Alison. Instr. English, U. of Pa., 1919-26, asst. prof., 1926-37, asso. prof. since 1937, asst. dir. Extension Sch. since 1928. Served as seaman, U.S. Navy, during World War. Mem. bd. of mgrs. Apprentices' Library, Phila., since 1929. Mem. Phi Beta Kappa, Beta Sigma Rho, Alpha Chi Rho. Soc. of Friends. Author: George Henry Boker, Poet and Patriot, 1927; Henry Charles Lea, A Biography, 1931; editor: Nydia, A Tragic Play, 1929; Sonnets of George H. Boker, 1929; author numerous articles in popular and tech. mags. Home: 730 Vernon Rd., Mt. Airy. Office: U. of Pennsylvania, Philadelphia, Pa.

BRADLEY, Francis; v.p. Midvale Co. Home: Coulter and Fox Sts. Office: Nicetown, Philadelphia, Pa.

BRADLEY, James Anthony, educator; b. Boston, Mass., May 1, 1892; s. Edward J. and Mary (Ferris) B.; grad. Boston Latin Sch., 1910; A.B., Harvard Coll., 1914; A.M., Harvard Grad. Sch., 1920; m. Eileen Margaret Harrington, Feb. 25, 1922; children—Eileen Margaret, James Anthony. Chemist Mass. State Infirmary, 1914-16; Instr. Tufts Coll. Med. and Dental Sch., 1916-18; chemist Grasselli Chem. Co., 1920-22; successively instr., asst. prof., asso. prof., now dean and asso. prof. chemistry, Newark Coll. of Engring., since 1922. Worked on explosives for U.S. Navy, Indian Head, Md., 1918. Mem. Am. Chem. Soc., Soc. for Promotion Engring. Edn., Eastern Assn. Deans and Advisors of Men, Assn. Harvard Chemists, Alpha Chi Sigma. Catholic. Clubs: Essex County Torch, Harvard of N.J. Home: 122 Indian Run Parkway, Union, N.J.

BRADLEY, Joseph Gardner, coal operator; b. Newark, N.J., Sept. 12, 1881; s. William Hornblower and Eliza (Cameron) B.; grad. St. Mark's Sch., Southboro, Mass., 1898; A.B., Harvard, 1902, LL.B., 1904; m. Mabel Bayard Warren, Nov. 4, 1905; children—Mabel Bayard, Joseph Gardner. Admitted to bar but has devoted attention to resources of W.Va.; pres. Elk River Coal & Lumber Co., Gauley Coal Land Co., New Gauley Coal Corpn., Bank of Widen, W.Va.; pres. Buffalo Creek & Gauley R.R. Co., Clay Co. (W.Va.) Bank; dir. Dauphin Deposit Trust Co. (Harrisburg, Pa.), Central Iron & Steel Co., Harrisburg Bridge Co., Underwood Elliott Fisher Co.; trustee of J. D. Cameron Trust. Secured the creation of W.Va. constabulary and the W.Va.

gross sales tax law; led coal operators in effecting revision of W.Va. mining law in the interest of safety. Del. Rep. Nat. Conv., Chicago, 1916, Kansas City, Mo., 1928; chmn. Rep. Exec. Com., Clay Co., W.Va.; member W.Va. Constitutional Commission, 1930; member W.Va. Library Commission, 1934-35; member National Council Y.M.C.A.; chmn. W.Va. State Y.M.C.A.; trustee Boston Library Soc.; dir. Southern States Industrial Council. Mem. Nat. Coal Assn. (pres. 1921-22), W.Va. Coal Assn. (pres. 1916-39), Am. Mining Congress (pres. 1927-28), Am. Inst. Mining and Metall. Engrs., Pa. Bar Assn., W.Va. Bar Assn., American Bar Assn., Alpha Delta Phi. Episcopalian. Clubs: Somerset, Tennis and Racquet, Brookline Country (Boston); Union, University, Harvard, Racquet (New York); Philadelphia; Metropolitan (Washington); Norfolk Hunt. Home: Dundon, Clay Co., W.Va.

BRADLEY, Luke C.; pres. Consolidated Electric & Gas Co., also officer or dir. many other pub. utility companies. Home: 130 East End Av., New York, N.Y. Office: 26 Exchange Place, Jersey City, N.J.

BRADLEY, Michael Joseph, congressman; b. Phila., May 24, 1897; s. Dennis Joseph and Hannah (McCarthy) B.; ed. parochial sch. and pub. high sch., Phila.; m. Emily Anguili, July 6, 1919; children—Raymond, Marian, Cathaine, Edward. Telegrapher, 1914-17; security and brokerage business, 1921-34; dep. ins. commr. of Pa., 1935-37; mem. 75th Congress (1937-39), 3d Pa. Dist. Mem. Phila. Dem. Co. Exec. Com. Served overseas in U.S.N., 1917-19. Mem. Am. Legion, Commercial Telegraphers Union. Democrat. Roman Catholic. K.C. Home: 2406 E. Hazzard St., Philadelphia, Pa.*

BRADLEY, Paul Russell; b. Chicago, Ill., Mar. 2, 1896; s. Thomas Eddy Dunham and Lizzie (Russell) B.; grad. Lake Forest (Ill.) Acad., 1913; student Northwestern U., 1913-14; A.B., Washington and Jefferson Coll., Washington, Pa., 1918; m. Lois Arrowsmith, Nov. 24, 1932. Owner Automatic Canteen Co. of Pittsburgh, Pa., since 1930. Served in Am. Ambulance Service with French Army, 1917-1919. Republican. Presbyterian. Clubs: Rotary of Metropolitan, Pittsburgh Athletic Assn., Chartiers Heights Country (Pittsburgh, Pa.). Home: Dartmouth Rd., Thornburg. Office: 2040 W. Liberty Av., Pittsburgh, Pa.

BRADLEY, Robert Holmes, v.p. Prudential Ins. Co. of America. Address: 763 Broad St., Newark, N.J.

BRADLEY, Vincent P., realtor; b. Trenton, N.J., Jan. 20, 1889; s. John and Elizabeth (Gallagher) B.; ed. parochial schools of Newark, Trenton, N.J., and Los Angeles, Trenton Public Evening Schools and Temple U. Law Sch., Phila.; m. Mary E. Wolfahrter, 1918; m. 2d, Elizabeth T. Wilmot, 1920. With W. M. Dickinson Co., real estate and insurance, Trenton, N.J., since 1905, beginning as office boy and advancing to clerk, salesman, mgr. and since 1922 partner; dir. and mem. advisory com. Mercer Trust Co. (branch of Trenton Trust Co.); sales consultant Nat. Assn. Real Estate Bds. Mem. N.J. Real Estate Commn., 1920-30, 1933-36; jury commr. for Mercer Co., 1936-39. Democrat. Roman Catholic. Mem. Dem. League, Trenton. Home: 50 Perdicaris Place. Office: 145 E. Hanover St., Trenton, N.J.

BRADLEY, Will, artist, author; b. Boston, July 10, 1868; s. Aaron and Elizabeth (Rowland) B.; spl. student at Harvard; m. Alice Gray, Aug. 29, 1888. First attracted attention by posters and book covers made in Chicago, 1893-94; went to Springfield, Mass., 1895, started the Wayside Press and pub. Bradley, His Book; has designed several type faces, a number of houses and much furniture; ex-art dir. Century Mag. and Colliers. Lecturer on typography and the use of color. Club: Players. Author: Peter Poodle, Toymaker to the King, 1906; Castle Perilous, or Once Upon a Time, Tales of Noodleburg; The Wonder Box, 1916; Spoils (drama), 1923; Launcelot and the Ladies, 1927. Home: Short Hills, N.J.

BRADLEY, William Carl, merchant, pres. Hurlock Water Co.; b. Preston, Md., May 17, 1864;

BRADSHAW

s William Spry and Emily (Hopkins) B.; ed. Preston (Md.) Grammar Sch., 1876-78; m. Laura Virginia Williams, Dec. 10, 1890 (died 1930); 1 son, Leland Alvin. Began as wheelwright and blacksmith, Preston, Md., 1878; funeral dir., Hurlock, Md., 1893-1912; owner W. C. Bradley & Son, merchants, Hurlock, Md., since 1893; established Hurlock Water Co., 1908, and since pres.; dir. County Trust Co., Hurlock, since 1915, pres. since 1932. Pres. Hurlock (Md.) Pub. Library; dir. Cambridge (Md.) Hosp. Elk, Modern Woodman. Club: Rotary (Cambridge, Md.). Address: Hurlock, Md.

BRADLEY, William Nathaniel, physician; b. Felton, Del., Aug. 19, 1871; s. John and Catherine Ann (Bostick) B.; student Phila. Manual Training Sch., 1885-88; Ph.G., Phila. Coll. of Pharmacy, 1892; M.D., U. of Pa., 1894; m. Marion Agnes Butsch, June 8, 1911 (died 1937); children—Marion Audrey, Jean Claire. Began as apprentice in pharmacy, 1888; began practice as physician in Phila., 1894; instr. in pediatrics, U. of Pa. Med. Sch., 1919-29, asso. in pediatrics, 1924-37; prof. of pediatrics, Grad. Sch., U. of Pa., since 1937; pediatrist to Phila. Gen. Hosp. since 1919; pediatrist to Howard Hosp.; consulting pediatrist Wills Hosp., Municipal Hosp. of Phila.; med. dir. Artisans Order for Mutual Protection. Dir. Starr Center Assn., Phila. Child Health Soc. Mem. Coll. of Physicians of Phila., A.M.A., Phila. Co. Med. Soc., Am. Acad. Pediatrics, Phila. Pediatric Soc. (dir.). Republican. Presbyterian. Clubs: Penn, Rotary (Phila.). Address: 1725 Pine St., Philadelphia, Pa.

BRADSHAW, Guy Read, prof. physics; b. Glens Falls, Oct. 1, 1890; s. George Monroe Brown and Elma Mary (Read) B.; A.B., Oberlin Coll., 1917; A.M., U. of Cincinnati, 1918; grad. study, Harvard U., 1918-22, N.Y. Univ., summers 1928-32; B.Pd., Edinboro (Pa.) State Teachers Coll., 1911; m. Kathryn Gordon, June 20, 1923. Engaged in teaching, high sch., 1912-14; asst. in physics, Harvard U., 1918-22, Radcliffe Coll., 1919-22; prof. physics, Thiel Coll., Greenville, Pa., since 1922. Fellow A.A.A.S. Mem. Am. Assn. Physics Teachers, Illuminating Engring. Soc., Pa. State Edn. Assn., Phi Delta Kappa, Delta Sigma Phi. Republican. Presbyn. Club: Lions of Greenville. Home: 299 Clinton St., Greenville, Pa.

BRADSHAW, John Hammond, surgeon; b. Boston, Mass., Oct. 6, 1860; s. Franklin Emmons and Ann Lovisa (Hammond) B.; student Ripon (Wis.) Coll., 1876-80; M.D., Coll. Physicians and Surgeons, N.Y. City, 1884; m. Lena Swasey Patterson, Sept. 3, 1894 (died 1928); 1 son, John Hammond. House physician Orange Memorial Hosp., 1883-90, attending surgeon, 1890-1900, cons. surgeon since 1920; cons. surgeon Jersey City Med. Center since 1933. Fellow Am. Coll. Surgeons; mem. A.M.A., N.J. Med. Soc., Essex Co. Med. Soc., Orange Med. Soc., N.J. Soc. Surgeons, Clin. Soc. Republican. Presbyterian. Club: Shongon (Dover, N.J.). Contbr. articles on med. history of N.J. and many articles on med. ethics to med. jours. Home: 27 High St., Orange, N.J.

BRADSHAW, Thompson; mem. law firm Bradshaw, McCreary & Reed. Address: Beaver, Pa.

BRADSHAW, William Aiken Sr., physician; b. Pittsburgh, Pa., June 7, 1892; s. Charles Lincoln and Ida (Aiken) B.; grad. West Sunbury (Pa.) Acad., 1911; student Mount Union Coll. Alliance, O., 1911-14, B.S., 1916; student Western Reserve U. Med. Sch., Cleveland, O., 1914-15; M.D., U. of Pittsburgh, 1918; m. Helen Logan, Oct. 28, 1922; children—Helen Marie, William Aiken, Betty Jane. Interne Mercy Hosp., Pittsburgh, Pa., 1918-19; practice of internal medicine since 1919; mem. staff Columbia Hosp., Wilkensburg, Pa., since 1923; asst. prof. of medicine, U. of Pittsburgh, since 1928; mem. staff Presbyterian Hosp., Pittsburgh, since 1938. Fellow A.M.A.; mem. Pittsburgh Acad. Medicine, Allegheny Co. Med. Soc., Biol. Soc. of U. of Pittsburgh, Alpha Tau Omega, Nu Sigma Nu. Republican. Presbyterian. Club: Longue Vue Country (Pittsburgh). Home: 1315 Beechwood Boul. Office: 121 University Place, Pittsburgh, Pa.

BRADWAY, Florence Dell, art instr., artist; b. Phila., Pa., Oct. 16, 1896; d. William Layton and Florence (Dell) Bradway; grad. Phila. High Sch. for Girls, 1914; student Phila. Sch. of Design for Women, 1914-18; unmarried. Mem. faculty Phila. Sch. of Design for Women since 1919. Exhibited at Pa. Acad. of Fine Arts, Corcoran Gallery of Art (Washington, D.C.), Nat. Acad. Design (New York), also smaller galleries. Address: 6549 Wyncote Av., Germantown, Philadelphia, Pa.

BRADY, Alfred Spates, Jr., M.D.; b. Fairmont, W.Va., Dec. 27, 1904; s. Alfred Spates and Grace Emaline (Mabie) B.; student Tome Sch., Port Deposit, Md., 1918-24; Ph.B., Yale Coll., 1928; B.S., W.Va. U., 1932; M.D., New York U. and Bellevue Hosp. Med. Coll., 1934; m. Eunice Flynn, July 26, 1929; 1 dau., Nancy Carolyn. Began as physician, 1936, practice limited to internal medicine; chief of med. service (active staff) St. Francis Hosp., also sec. med. staff. Served as 1st lt., O.R.C., Med. Corps (resigned). Asso. fellow Am. Coll. Physicians; mem. A.M.A., Am. Heart Assn., Kanawha Med. Soc. (sec.-treas.), Phi Kappa Sigma, Phi Beta Pi. Republican. Presbyn. Home: 4005 Staunton Av. Office: 240 Capitol St., Charleston. W. Va.

BRADY, George Moore, lawyer; b. Baltimore, Md., Feb. 2, 1882; s. James Henry and Katherine Taylor (Hunter) B.; A.B., Loyola Coll., 1900; LL.B., M.A. and Ph.D., Georgetown U.; LL.M. and J.D., Catholic U.; m. Ellen Latimer Atkinson, Apr. 7, 1920; children—Ellen Atkinson, George Moore, Emily Niernsee, James H. T., George Atkinson. In practice as atty. since 1903, was asso. with Lambert & Baker, Washington, D.C.; now mem. of firm Maloy, Brady & Yost, Baltimore, Md.; formerly teacher, Gonzaga Coll., Washington, D.C.; and lecturer in U. of Baltimore; served in office of Col. Hilary Herbert, former Sec. of Navy, Washington, D.C. Dir. Children's Hosp. Sch., Inc., Children's Rehabilitation Inst., Inc. Mem. Am., Md. State, Baltimore City bar assn. Democrat. Catholic. Club: Maryland (Baltimore, Md.). Home: 101 St. Johns Rd. Office: 1403 Fidelity Bldg., Baltimore, Md.

BRADY, S. Proctor; pres. Poole Foundry & Machine Co. Home: 3908 N. Charles St. Office. Woodberry, Baltimore, Md.

BRAHAM, William Walter, judge; b. Youngstown, O., Oct. 28, 1893; s. Robert Renwick and Olive (Wilkin) B.; A.B., Westminster Coll., New Wilmington, Pa., 1915; LL.B., U. of Pittsburgh, 1922; m. Selina Whitla, Jan. 18, 1927; children—Isabel Whitla, William Walter, James Whitla. Admitted to Pa. bar, 1922; mem. firm Aiken & Braham, New Castle, Pa., 1923-32, Braham, Coban & Berry, New Castle, since 1932. Judge, Lawrence Co., Pa., 1936-38, pres. judge since 1938. Served as sergt., 1st Class, Med. Dept., U.S. Army, during World War. Trustee Westminster Coll., New Wilmington, Pa. Mem. Am. Legion (comdr. Post 343, 1927-28). Republican. United Presbyterian. Clubs: Rotary, Field (New Castle, Pa.). Home: 126 Hazelcroft Av. Office: New Castle, Pa.

BRAINARD, Edward Heaton, glass mfg.; b. Salem, O., Apr. 2, 1867; s. Ira F. and Frances (Heaton) B.; student Phillips Acad., Andover, Mass., 1885-88; m. Adelaide Boyle, Oct. 6, 1890; children—Frances (Mrs. Lawrence Allderdice), Adelaide (Mrs. Frederick Bullard), Ira F. II, Margaret. Began business career as clk., 1888; engaged in business of provisions and iron and steel until 1921; engaged in mfg. glass since 1920, v.p. Westmoreland Glass Co., Pittsburgh, since 1938. Republican. Episcopalian. Clubs: Duquesne, Fox Chapel Golf (Pittsburgh); Essex County (Manchester, Mass.); Ormond (Fla.) Golf. Home: Woodland Rd. Office: 1011 Diamond Bank Bldg., Pittsburgh, Pa.

BRAINERD, Arthur Alanson, illuminating engr.; b. Durham, Conn., Apr. 6, 1891; s. Alanson Virgil and Alice Luella (Kelsey) B.; B.S., Ohio U., Athens, O., 1915; student U. of Mich. Grad Sch., 1922-23; m. Zella Elizabeth Knoll, May 23, 1916; children—Alice Elizabeth, Henry Alanson. Tester and insp. Hartford (Conn.) Electric Light Co., 1915-16; in commercial dept. Manchester (Conn.) Electric Co., 1916-18; head elec. dept., State Trade Sch., Danbury, Conn., 1918-20; instr. elec. engring., U. of N.H., 1920-24; asst. illuminating engr. Phila. Electric Co., 1924-28, illuminating engr., 1928-34, engr. and dir. Lighting Service Div. since 1934. Created floodlighting effects for Edison Bldg., Phila., 1927, Art Museum, Phila., 1929, etc. Won James H. McGraw award, 1927, for best paper of year on an engring. subject. U.S. rep. on cons. Internat. Commn. on Illumination; mem. bd. of judges for the prize award in illumination, Beaux Arts Inst., 1934; del. to Internat. Commn. of Illumination, The Hague, Holland, 1939; mem. Elec. Industry Com. on Handbook of Interior Wiring Design, representing Edison Electric Inst.; exec. sec. U.S. Nat. Comm. of Internat. Comm. on Illumination. Mem. Nat. Electric Light Assn., Illuminating Engring. Soc. (chmn. lighting service com.), Soc. for Elec. Development, Illuminating Engring. Soc. Republican. Methodist. Mason. Contbr. to mags. Home: 128 Willows Av., Norwood, Pa. Office: 900 Sansom St., Philadelphia, Pa.

BRAISTED, William Clarence, surgeon gen. U.S. Navy (retired); b. Toledo, O., Oct. 9, 1864; s. Frank and Helen Maria (Fiske) B.; Ph. B., U. of Mich., 1883; M.D., with honors, Med. Dept., Columbia U., 1886; LL.D., U. of Mich., 1917, Jefferson Med. Coll., Phila., 1918; D.Sc., Northwestern U., 1918; F.R.C.S., Edinburgh, 1919; m. Lillian Mulford Phipps, Apr. 2, 1886. Served Bellevue Hosp., New York, 2½ yrs.; practiced, Detroit, 1888-90; entered Navy as asst. surgeon, Sept. 26, 1890; promoted passed asst. surgeon, Sept. 26, 1893; surgeon, Mar. 3, med. insp., Oct. 20, 1913. Has served on many vessels and at many naval hosps.; twice instr. in surgery Naval Medical Sch.; fitted out and equipped the hosp. ship Relief, 1904. Represented Med. Dept. in Japan during Russo-Japanese War; asst. chief Bur. of Medicine and Surgery, 6 yrs., 1906 to 1912, and assisted in reorganization of same and of med. service of the Navy; served with Dr. Rixey as attending phys. at White House, President Roosevelt's administration, 1906-07; fleet surgeon, Atlantic fleet, July 1, 1912-14; surgeon-gen. and chief Bur. of Medicine and Surgery, Feb. 1914-21, rank of rear admiral. Pres. Coll. of Pharmacy and Science, Phila., since 1921; dir. Union Trust Co., Washington, D.C. Mem. A.M.A. (pres. 1919-20). Assn. Mil. Surgeons of U.S. (pres. 1912-13); hon. fellow Am. Coll. Surgeons (bd. govs.), etc. Mem. bd. dirs. Columbia Hosp. for Women; pres. bd. visitors Govt. Hosp. for Insane, Washington, D.C. Mem. exec. com. central com. and war relief bd., Am. Red Cross, 1914-20. Retired from Navy after 30 yrs.' service, Nov. 1920, with rank of rear admiral. Awarded D.S.M. for service in Navy in the World War; decorated by Emperor of Japan, and with Order of Bolivar by pres. of Venezuela. Home: West Chester, Pa.*

BRAITMAYER, Otto Ernest, former v.p. Internat. Business Machines Corpn.; b. Washington, D.C., July 8, 1873; s. John Ernest and Josephine (Tanner) B.; LL.B., Nat. U. Sch. of Law, 1895, LL.M., 1896; m. Kathleen Ketcham, Apr. 21, 1897; children—Margaret Esther (Mrs. Charles K. West, dec.), Kathleen (Mrs. Alexander D. Shaw), Josephine (Mrs. John M. Demarest), Jane; m. 2d, Marian Winifred Schoeffel, Feb. 14, 1929; children—Anne, John Watson. Sec. and office asst. to Herman Hollerith, inventor of punched card method of electric tabulation, Washington, D.C., 1889-1911; asst. gen. mgr. Tabulating Machine Co., N.Y. City, 1911-21, v.p., 1921-25; v.p. Internat. Business Machines Corpn., 1925-39, retired Apr. 1, 1939; dir. Weston Elec. Instrument Corpn. (Newark, N.J.). Dir. Nat. Assn. Mfrs., Merchants Assn., Am. Soc. Sales Execs., Am. Statis. Assn., Am. Management Assn. (all of N.Y. City). Mason. Clubs: Lotos, Bankers, Hardware, New York Yacht (New York); Bayside (L.I., N.Y.) Yacht; Kittansett, Beverly Yacht (Marion, Mass.); Capital Yacht (Washington). Home: 202 Crest Rd., Ridgewood, N.J.; (summer) Marion, Mass. Office: 590 Madison Av., New York, N.Y.

BRAKELEY, George Archibald, educator, publicist; b. Dunellen, N.J., July 13, 1884; s. Peter Winter, M.D., and Helen (Davis) B.; grad. high sch., Plainfield, N.J., 1903; A.B., Princeton, 1907; hon. A.M., U. of Pa., 1926; m. Lillian Field Fay, July 7, 1911; children—George Archibald, Barbara. Reporter, later editor Jersey City (N.J.) Journal, 1908-11; reporter, asst. city editor, asst. mng. editor New York Sun, 1911-17; editor New York Sunday Sun, 1917-19; mng. editor Red Cross Mag., 1919; v.p. John Price Jones Corpn. of N.Y., 1919-26, dir. since 1926; vice-provost in charge administration U. of Pa., 1926-31, administrative vice-pres. of University since 1931; dir. Jones and Brakeley, Inc. Trustee Chestnut Hill Acad., Springside School for Girls, Moore Sch. of Elec. Engineering, Pa. Sch. of Social Work. Mgr. Morris Foundation, Graduate Hosp.; mem. advisory bd. Cox Research Inst. Spl. asst. to dir. advertising and publicity, Liberty Loan Com., 2d Federal Res. Dist., 1918-19. Mem. S.R., Art Alliance of Phila. (dir.). Episcopalian. Clubs: Rittenhouse, Lenape, Princeton, Sunnybrook Golf (Phila.); University of Pa. (New York); Pretty Brook Tennis, Nassau Gun, Stony Brook Hunt (Princeton, N.J.). Home: 300 W. Highland Av., Chestnut Hill. Office: 3446 Walnut St., Philadelphia, Pa.

BRAM, Israel, M.D.; b. Phila., Pa., July 6, 1883; s. Simon and Rebecca (Goldfarb) B.; student Phila. Pub. Schs., Temple U., Phila., U. of Pa.; M.D., Medico Chirurg. Coll., Phila., 1909; m. Frances Silver; children—Norma, Marjorie, Ernest, Roberta. Began as physician, 1909; research in goiter and glandular diseases, Phila. since 1911; established Bram Inst. for Goiter and Glandular Diseases, 1925; instr. in clin. medicine, Medieo Chirurg. Coll., 1911-15, Jefferson Med. Coll., Phila., 1917-27. Mem. A.M.A., Pa. State Med. Assn., Phila. Co. Med. Assn., Assn. for Study of Internal Secretions, Am. Assn. for Study of Goiter, N.Y. Endocrinological Assn. Jewish religion. Club: Medical (Phila.). Author: four books on goiter for med. profession, 1920, 1924, 1928, 1936. Contbr. 160 articles on goiter and glandular diseases to med. jours. Home: Upland, Pa. Office: 1633 Spruce St., Philadelphia, Pa.

BRAMBLE, Charles Clinton, coll. prof.; b. Centreville, Md., Aug. 17, 1890; s. James and Matilda Shane (Erdman) B.; Ph.B., Dickinson Coll., 1912, A.M., 1913; Ph.D., Johns Hopkins U., 1917; m. Edith S. Rinker, Dec. 27, 1916; children—Mary Matilda, Barbara Jane, James Henry. Instr., Montclair Acad., 1912-13; lecturer mathematics, Bryn Mawr Coll., 1915-16; instr. dept. mathematics, U.S. Naval Acad., 1917-19; asst. prof. mathematics, Postgrad. Sch. U.S. Naval Acad., 1919-27, prof. since 1927. Lieutenant commander U.S.N.R. Fellow A.A.A.S; mem. Am. Math. Soc., Math. Assn. of America, Theta Chi, Phi Beta Kappa. Methodist. Home: 145 Monticello Av., Annapolis, Md.

BRAMER, Samuel Eugene; b.Phila., Pa., July 4, 1885; s. Hirsch and Cecile (Mandel) B.; student pub. schs.; m. Beatrice Brown, June 25, 1933; 1 dau., Mrs. Cecile Kahn. With Copperweld Steel Co. since 1915, now pres. and gen. mgr. Home: 554 Briar Cliff Road, Pittsburgh, Pa. Office: Glassport, Pa.

BRAMHALL, Fay Beaumont, elec. engring.; b. Camptown, Pa., Jan. 25, 1897; s. Martin Luther and Mabel (Beaumont) B.; B.S., Pa. State Coll., 1919; ed. Columbia U., 1922-25; m. D. Caryl Connolly, Aug. 22, 1936; 1 dau., Astrid Beaumont. Began as radio engr., 1919; with engring. dept., Western Union Telegraph Co., 1920-25; engr. in charge of transmission lab., Western Union Telegraph Co., N.Y. City since 1925; patentee automatic printing devices for telegraph systems and transmission devices. Mem. Am. Inst. Elec. Engrs. Republican. Presbyn. Club: Wire Club of New York (vice-pres.). Contbr. tech. articles to sci. journs. Home: Bramhall Hall, R.F.D. No. 4, New Brunswick, N.J. Office: 60 Hudson St., New York, N.Y.

BRAMMER, Fred Emerson, physician; b. Lawrence Co., O., Nov. 26, 1889; s. Oliver Edward and Sarah Elizabeth (Ashworth) B.; student Valparaiso (Ind.) University, summer 1909, 1911-12, Ohio Univ., summer 1914, 1915-16, Rio Grande (Ohio) Coll., summer 1917; taught elementary, later high sch., 8 terms, 1908-17;

M.D., U. of Cincinnati Med. Coll., 1921; m. Olive Ann Cofer, Apr. 27, 1918; children—Melba Pauline, Joseph Oliver, Ruth Ann, Doris Marie. Interne Christ Hosp., Cincinnati, O., 1921-22; engaged in gen. practice of medicine in Huntington, W.Va., 1922-27; physician for Youngstown Mines Corpn., Youngstown Sheet & Tube Co., at Dehue, W.Va., since 1927; also engaged in pvt. practice at Dehue. Served as pvt. Med. Corps, U.S.A., 1917-18; 1st lt. Med. Res. Corps, 1926, capt. since 1930. Mem. Am., Southern, W.Va. State, Logan Co. med. assns., Assn. Mil. Surgeons, W.Va. Obstet. Soc., W.Va. Soc. of Industrial Surgeons, Res. Officers Assn., Phi Beta Pi. Republican. Mason. Home: 149 Ninth Av., Huntington, W.Va.; also Dehue, W.Va. Office: Dehue, W.Va.

BRANCH, Edward Douglas, historian; b. Houston, Tex., July 7, 1905; s. Edward Thomas and Daisy Caroline (Lindley) B.; student U. of Tex., 1922-23, Ohio State U., 1925-26; A.B., U. of La., 1924, A.M., 1925, Ph.D., 1928; unmarried. Instr. in English, Okla., Agrl. and Mech. Coll., 1925; asso. prof. of social science, La. Poly. Coll., 1926-27; fellow Social Science Research Council, 1928-29; editor ency. div. P. F. Collier and Son Co., 1929-32; asso. prof. of history, Purdue U., 1932; asso. prof. history and English, Mont. State U., 1933-35; prof. of history, U. of Pittsburgh, since 1935. Mem. Am. Hist. Assn., Miss. Valley Hist. Assn., Pa. Hist. Assn., Hist. Soc. Western Pa., Am. Mil. Hist. Foundation, Sons of the Whiskey Rebellion, Phi Beta Kappa. Unitarian. Author: The Cowboy and His Interpreters, 1926; The Hunting of the Buffalo, 1929; Westward—The History of the American Frontier, 1930; The Sentimental Years, 1934; Travelways of Western Pennsylvania, 1939. Mng. editor Frontier and Midland, 1933-35, asso. editor since 1935. Contbr. articles and revs. to hist. and lit. jours. Home: 4338 Bigelow Boul., Pittsburgh, Pa.

BRAND, Franklin Marion, lawyer; b. Monongalia Co., W.Va., Mar. 13, 1880; s. James Clarke and Mary Alice (Fleming) B.; A.B., W.Va. Univ., 1906; LL.B., W.Va. Univ. Law Sch., 1907; m. Myrtle Otella Core, Nov. 12, 1910; children—James Core, Mary Kathryn (Mrs. Thomas E. Boggess) B., Freda Louise. Began as teacher pub. schs., 1899-1907; admitted to W.Va. bar, 1907 and engaged in gen. practice of law at Morgantown, W.Va., 1907-13; with legal dept. Am. Telegraph & Telephone Co. in N.Y. City, 1913-14; mem. W.Va. Ho. of Rep., 1919; mayor, Westover, W.Va. 1918, 1926; served as divorce commr. Monongalia Co., 1921-36; engaged in gen. practice of law at Morgantown, W.Va., since 1914. Mem. Sigma Nu. Republican. Methodist. Mason, Odd Fellow, Jr. Order United Am. Mechanics. Home: 52 East St. Office: 162 Chancery Row, Morgantown, W.Va.

BRAND, Millen, author; b. Jersey City, N.J., Jan. 19, 1906; s. Elmer and Carrie Esther (Myers) B.; A.B., Columbia, 1929; Litt.B., Columbia Sch. of Journalism, 1929; m. Pauline Leader, of Bennington, Vt., Nov. 10, 1931; children — Elinor, Jonathan, Emily (dec.), Daniel. Copywriter New York Telephone Co., 1929-37; instr. in fiction writing, New York U., since 1939. Mem. Authors' League, League of Am. Writers. Author: The Outward Room, 1937; The Heroes, 1939. Contbr. to mags. Home: New Hope, Pa.

BRAND, Thurlow Weed; prof. anatomy, U. of Pittsburgh. Adress: U. of Pittsburgh, Pittsburgh, Pa.

BRANDES, Elmer Walker, plant pathologist; b. Washington, D.C., July 15, 1891; s. Frederick and Emma (Pangburn) B.; B.S., Mich. State Coll., 1913, M.S., 1915; student Cornell U., 1916-17; Ph.D., U. of Mich., 1919; m. Grace Newbold, 1915; children—Elizabeth Pangburn, Ann Newbold, Margaret (dec.), William Frederick. Research asst. Mich. State Coll., 1914; plant pathologist Porto Rico Agrl. Expt. Sta., 1915-16; 2d lt. Am. Exped. Forces, France, 1918; pathologist U.S. Dept. Agr., 1919-22, sr. pathologist-in-charge Office of Sugar Plants, 1923-27, agrl. explorer, 1928; principal pathologist-in-charge division of sugar plant investigations, Bureau of Plant Industry, U.S. Department Agriculture, 1928—. Sugar expert Pan Pacific Food Conservation Congress, Honolulu, 1924. Organizer and officer Internat. Soc. Sugar Cane Technologists, general chairman, 1935-38; has been dir. of various scientific expeditions in C. and S. America, Asia and Pacific Islands; leader U.S. Dept. Agr. airplane explorations, New Guinea, 1928. Hon. mem. Proefstation voor de Java-Suikerindustrie, Pasoeroean, Java; fellow A.A.A.S., Am. Phytopath. Soc.; mem. Bot. Soc. Washington, Washington Acad. Science, Sigma Xi. Republican. Lecturer on geography and ethnology. Author numerous scientific papers on tropical crops, diseases of plants, bot., ethnol. and geog. subjects. Clubs: Cosmos, Chevy Chase. Home: 6310 Ridgewood Av., Chevy Chase, Md.

BRANDES, George Henry, coll. prof.; b. Oswego, N.Y., Apr. 10, 1895; s. George Charles and Anna (Polz) B.; B. Chem., Cornell U., 1918, Ph.D., 1925; m. Rhea May Stamm, June 17, 1928; children—George Stanley, Janet Elaine. Instr. in chemistry, Cornell U., 1920-26; asst. prof., Muhlenberg Coll., Allentown, Pa., 1926-27, prof. since 1927. Served as sergt., M.C., U.S. Army, during World War; service at Rockefeller Inst., Yale Army Lab. Sch., Base Hosp., Camp Meade, Md., 1918-19. Mem. Am. Chem. Soc., Sigma Gamma Epsilon, Phi Kappa Phi, Alpha Chi Sigma, Sigma Xi. Lutheran. Address: 331 N. Broad St., Allentown, Pa.

BRANDON, J. Campbell, lawyer; b. Butler, Pa., July 17, 1884; s. W. D. and Clara (Campbell) B.; ed. Mercersburg (Pa.) Acad., 1901-02; A.B., Princeton, 1906; student Harvard Law Sch., 1906-08; m. Kathleen Walker, June 11, 1914; children—J. Campbell, Virginia, John W. II. Admitted to Pa. bar, 1909 and since engaged in gen. practice of law at Butler; mem. firm Brandon and Brandon, Butler, Pa., since 1909; admitted to practice before Pa. Supreme and Superior cts. and Supreme Ct. of the U.S. Served with Y.M.C.A. in A.E.F., 1918-19. Mem. Am. and Pa. bar assns. Republican. Presbyterian. Mason. Clubs: Country (Butler, Pa.); Harvard - Yale - Princeton (Pittsburgh). Home: 608 McKean St. Office: 704 Savings and Trust Bldg., Butler, Pa.

BRANDON, James Bird, clergyman; b. Halifax Co., Va., Jan. 1, 1877; s. Allen Bird and Amanda (Farmer) B.; converted and joined Baptist Ch. at age of 12; student Downington Industrial Sch. and Coll., 1904-07; Lincoln U., Chester Co., Pa., 1907-10; A.M., Afro-Am. Sch. of Corr., Washington, D.C., 1916; D.D., Va. Theol. Sem. and Coll., 1921; m. Sarah Ann Johnson, June 29, 1899 (dec.); 1 dau., Eva (dec.); m. 2d, Julia C. Washington, Aug. 9, 1936. Ordained to ministry Bapt. Ch., 1907; an organizer and pastor First Bapt. Ch., Sharon Hill, Pa., 1903-04; pastor, Ocean City, N.J., 1906-10; instr. Seybert Inst., 1910-12; pastor Antioch Ch., North Glenside, Pa., 1912-23; missionary W. Coast, Africa, 1923-25; lecturer and evangelist, 1925-27; pastor Pine St. Bapt. Ch., Scranton, Pa., since 1927; studied law course in corr. sch. of law, 1920 and 1924; broadcast negro spirituals over WGBI, Scranton, 1935-36. Trustee and mem. Abington Bapt. Assn. Treas. and mem. Pa. State Conv. since 1929, Central Bapt. Assn. of Pa. since 1929; corr. sec. and treas. Direct Fgn. Mission Conf. of America. Awarded gold medal by Bapt. Ministers Conf., Phila., 1921; gold medal by Zion Bapt. Ch., Liberia, Africa, 1925; served as vice-pres. Bapt. Ministerium of Scranton. Mem. Scranton Chamber of Commerce since 1928, Internat. Relation Bd., Ch. League of America. Republican. Baptist. Author: Four Magnanimous Sermons, 1916; The Comforter, 1918; Liberia, Her Customs, Habits, Industry and Natives, 1927. Made observation trip around continent of Africa, 1936; preached in oldest Baptist Ch., Southampton, Eng. Home: 613 Pine St., Scranton, Pa.

BRANDON, John Welsh, mfg. exec.; b. Butler, Pa., June 4, 1881; s. W. D. and Clara Bell (Campbell) B.; A.B., Washington and Jefferson Coll., Washington, Pa., 1902; m. Helen G. Walker, Oct. 6, 1907 (dec.); m. 2d, Katharine Gillespie, May 11, 1937. Began business career as bank clk., 1902; asst. treas. Butler Savings and Trust Co., 1921-22; treas. Spang & Co., mfrs. oil well tools, Butler, Pa., since 1922; dir. Butler Savings & Trust Co. Republican. Presbyterian. Mason. Home: 704 N. McKean St. Office: 120 Etna St., Butler, Pa.

BRANDON, Washington D., lawyer; b. Butler Co., Pa., Nov. 1, 1847; s. John Welsh and Ruth-ann Catharine (Beighley) B.; student Witherspoon Inst., Butler, Pa., 1863-65; A.B., Washington and Jefferson Coll., Washington, Pa., 1868, (hon.) LL.D., 1937; m. Clara B. Campbell, May 27, 1875 (dec.); children—Margaret (dec.), Elora (Mrs. Robert L. James), John W., J. Campbell, Howard Allan (dec.); m. 2d, Mrs. Florence C. Bleakley, Dec. 30, 1926. Admitted to Pa. bar, 1871, and engaged in gen. practice of law at Butler continuously since 1871; admitted to practice before Pa. Superior and Supreme cts. and U.S. Dist. Ct.; mem. firm Brandon and Brandon, Butler, Pa., since 1909; pres. and dir. Butler Land and Improvement Co.; dir. Butler Savings and Trust Co.; pres. North Side Cemetery Assn.; for many yrs. active as dir. and counsel large corpns. Charter mem. and many yrs. dir. Butler Y.M.C.A.; former dir. Western Theol. Sem., Pittsburgh. Mem. Delta Tau Delta. Republican. Presbyterian (for over 60 yrs. elder First Presbyn. Ch.). Home: 519 N. Main St. Office: Savings and Trust Bldg., Butler, Pa.

BRANDT, David Dickson, high sch. prin.; b. Big Spring, Pa., Sept. 22, 1878; s. David Enos and Sadie Rupp (Schopp) B.; student Piper's Sch., Newton Twp. Cumberland Co., Pa., 1886-92, Shippensburg (Pa.) High Sch., 1892-95; A.B., Lebanon Valley Coll., Annville, Pa., 1904; B.D., Union Biblical Sem., Dayton, O., 1907; m. Emma Francis Engle, Sept. 5, 1907; children—Charles Richard, Doris Elise (Mrs. George M. Houck), Marian Lenore (Mrs. Galen B. Schubauer). Minister, Ch. of the United Brethren in Christ, Riverside, Calif., 1906; student pastor, New Carlisle, O., 1906-07, Beloit, Wis., summer 1907; teacher math., Shenandoah Collegiate Inst., Dayton, Va., 1907-10; prin. Hershey High School, 1910-11, resigned after re-election to become pastor, Schuylkill Haven, Pa., 1911-13, Reading, Pa., 1913-16; dean lit. dept., Shenandoah Collegiate Inst., 1916-21; teacher of social science, Mechanicsburg (Pa.) High Sch., 1921-24, prin. since 1924; owner Ridomae Nurseries, Hampden Twp., Cumberland Co., Pa., since 1924. Mem. Nat., Pa. State ednl. assns., Co. Prins. Assn., Business Men's League of Mechanicsburg (Pa.). Republican. Ch. of the United Brethren in Christ. Mason (Royal Arch); 32°; Sublime Prince Royal Secret). Home: 3-6 Trindle Rd. Office: High and Simpson Sts., Mechanicsburg, Pa.

BRANDT, Joseph August, publisher; b. Seymour, Ind., July 26, 1899; s. Theodore and Sophia (Schroer) B.; A.B., U. of Okla., 1921; B.A., U. of Oxford, Eng., 1923, M.A., same, 1926, B.Litt., same, 1924; grad. study, U. of Budapest, summer 1922; m. Sara Maude Little, Oct. 3, 1927; children—Brenda, Joseph Theodore. Began as reporter, newspapers in Okla.; city editor, Tulsa (Okla.) Tribune, 1924-28; dir. U. of Okla. Press, 1928-38; sec. and dir., Princeton Univ. Press since 1938; mng. editor, Books Abroad, 1928-38; editor, The Sooner Magazine, 1928-33. Author: Toward the New Spain, 1933. Served in S.A.T.C. Mem. Phi Beta Kappa, Delta Tau Delta, Sigma Delta Chi. Democrat. Lutheran. Club: Nassau (Princeton). Home: 55 Westcott Rd. Office: William and Charlton Sts., Princeton, N.J.

BRANNAN, Dorsey, surgeon, urologist; b. Grafton, W.Va., Dec. 2, 1893; s. Andrew Jackson and Anette Agusta (Carrico) B.; A.B. and B.S. in Agr., W.Va. Univ.; M.D., Johns Hopkins U. Med. Sch., 1921; m. Estelle Hamilton, Sept. 19, 1918; children—Jack, Billy, Mary Lucille. Interne Johns Hopkins Hosp., 1921-23; asst. in pathology Singer Memorial Research Lab. of Alleghany Gen. Hosp., Pittsburgh, 1923-26; asst. in surgery and urology Strong Memorial Hosp., Univ. of Rochester Sch. Medicine and Dentistry, 1926-27; engaged in pvt. practice surgery and urology at Morganstown, W.V., since 1927. Fellow Am. Coll. Surgeons, Am. Med. Assn.; mem. W.Va. State Med. Assn., Phi Beta Kappa, Rotary Internat. Home: 304 Wilson Av. Office: 403 High St., Morgantown, W.Va.

BRANNAN, William Forrest, pres. Anchor Post Fence Co.; b. Montpelier, O., Nov. 25, 1893; s. Melvin C. and Emma (Cannon) B.; grad. Bryan High Sch., 1914; student Wooster Coll., Ohio, 1914-17; m. Marjorie Case, Aug. 1, 1919; children—Pauline, Robert Russel, Majorie Marie, Kathrine, Barbara. Began as salesman, 1919; now pres. and dir. Anchor Post Fence Co., Baltimore; dir. Anchor Post Fence Co. of Calif., Am. Fence Construction. Served as pilot, Naval Flying Corp with rank of ensign, World War. Democrat. Presbyn. Clubs: Baltimore Country, Merchants (Baltimore). Home: Ruxton, Md. Office: Kane St. and Eastern Av., Baltimore, Md.

BRANSFIELD, John William, M.D.; b. Portland, Conn., June 25, 1888; s. John and Catherine (Butler) B.; student Wesleyan U., Middletown, Conn., 1907-09; M.D., U. of Pa., 1913; unmarried. Practicing physician and surgeon, Phila., since 1913; clin. prof. surgery, Womans Coll. of Pa., 1923-24; was med. dir. St. Agnes Hosp.; surgeon St. Vincent's Hosp. and Am. Oncologic Hosp. Served as lt., M.C., U.S. Army, with A.E.F., during World War; now lt. M.R.C., Fellow Am. Coll. Surgeons, Coll. Physicians of Phila.; mem. Founders Group Am. Bd. Surgery, Am. Bd. Plastic Surgery; mem. A.M.A., Pa. State and Phila. Co. med. socs., Acad. of Surgery, Phila., Phi Chi. Catholic. Clubs: Racquet, Medical, Phila. Country, Physicians, Motor (Phila.). Address: 2101 Spruce St., Philadelphia, Pa.

BRANSOME, Edwin Dagobert, pres. Vanadium Corpn. of America; b. Phila., Pa., June 18, 1893; s. Dagobert Emile and Marie (Dowd) B.; student Rockhill Acad., Ellicot City, Md., 1906-08, Ursinus Coll., Pa., 1908-12; m. Margaretta Homans O'Sullivan, Feb. 10, 1932; children—Joseph DeWitt, Margaretta Homans, Edwin Dagobert. Partner in firm of Reid Waples Co., contractors, Phila., 1913-17; with Gen. Motors Co., New York, 1919-21; v.p. and gen. mgr. Wilson Welder & Metals Co., 1921-30; co-ordinator of business relations for Air Reduction Co., Inc., 1930-35; pres. Vanadium Corpn. of America since 1935. Served as Aviation Cadet, later pilot, lt., U.S.N., 1917-19. Clubs: Leach, Cloud, Racquet and Tennis (New York); Rumson (N.J.) Country. Home: Rumson, N.J. Office: 420 Lexington Av., New York.

BRAST, Edwin A.; pres. Parkersburg Pub. Co., Fairground Land Improvement Co. Home: Chancellor Hotel, Parkersburg, W.Va.

BRATNEY, Bertrand Herbert, lawyer; b. St. Louis, Mo., May 3, 1894; s. Theodore S. and Sarah (Mitchel) B.; Washington U., 1912-16; LL.B., St. Louis U., 1917; studied Columbia, 1922-23; unmarried. Admitted to Mo. bar, 1917, and began practice in St. Louis; liquidated Equitable Surety Co. for 5 yrs., and served as counsel for Commercial Casualty Ins. Co. of N.J.; moved to N.Y. City, 1922; gen. solicitor Nat. Surety Co. of New York to 1929; apptd. deputy supt. insurance, and rehabilitor same co., Apr. 29, 1932; vice-pres. Md. Casualty Co. since Jan. 1, 1935. Mem. legislative com. Citizens Union, N.Y. City, 1922-25. Mem. New York County Lawyers' Assn., S.A.R., Sigma Chi. Conglist. Mason. Clubs: Lawyers (New York); Glen Ridge Country; Baltimore Country; Merchants (Baltimore). Home: "Brethney," near Glenelg, Md. Office: Maryland Casualty Company, Baltimore, Md.

BRATNEY, John Frederick, retired telephone exec.; b. Preston, Ill., Oct. 8, 1880; s. Theodore Stillman and Sarah (Mitchel) B.; graduate Preparatory School of Washington U., St. Louis, 1899; B.S. in E.E., Washington Univ., 1903; study Benton College Law, St. Louis; m. Grace Gunn, July 9, 1910 (divorced). Chief engr., Bell Telephone Co. of Mo., St. Louis, 1905-10; dist. supt. of plant, Mo. & Kan. Telephone Co., Kansas City, Mo., 1910, gen. supt. traffic, 1911-15, gen. commercial supt., 1915-17; asst. to operating vice-pres. Southwestern Bell Telephone System, St. Louis, 1917-20; rate engr., Am. Telephone & Telegraph Co., N.Y. City, 1920-28, gen. commercial problems engr., 1928-29; asst. tech. rep. in Europe, with hdqrs. in London, for Am. Tel. and Tel. Co. and Bell Telephone Labs., Inc., 1929-34; at New York hdqrs. of Am. Tel. & Tel. Co., 1934, and telephone rep. at Washington, D.C., for same, 1935-36 Mem., Am. Inst. E.E., Am. Statis. Soc., Telephone Pioneers of America, Empire State Soc., S.A.R.; former fellow Royal Soc. of Arts (London) and former mem. various coms. of Comite Consultatif International des Communications Telephoniques a Grande Distance, Paris. Republican. Presbyn. Mason. Clubs: University (New York); Glen Ridge Country (N.J.); Nantucket (Mass.) Yacht; Bath and Tennis Club, (Palm Beach, Fla.); former mem. various social and civic clubs in U.S. and England, including American, Royal Automobile, Woodcote Country, Regency and Gargoyle (London). Home: 105 Ridgewood Av., Glen Ridge, N.J. Address: 195 Broadway, New York, N.Y.

BRAUDE, Bennett Arthur, surgeon; b. Shamokin, Pa., Nov. 21, 1889; s. Abner and Reba (Morningstar) B.; student Pa. State Coll., 1907, Bucknell U., Lewisburg, Pa., 1907; M.D., Jefferson Med. Coll., Phila., 1914; post grad. work gynecology, Harvard, 1923; m. Rita Salome Mills, April 5, 1917; children—Suzanne Patricia, Bennett Arthur, II. Began as physician, 1914; interne, Roosevelt Hosp., Phila., 1910-11, Atlantic City (N.J.) Hosp., 1914, Phila. Gen. Hosp., 1915; chief resident Memorial Hosp., Johnstown, Pa., 1916-17, asso. medicine, 1917-21, asso. gynecology, 1921-23, asso. surgery, 1923-33, chief surgeon since 1934. Pres. staff Memorial Hosp. Served as 1st lt. M.C., U.S. Army, 1917, capt., 1918-19. Pres. Johnstown Surg. Soc.; fellow Am. Coll. Surgeons; mem. Pa. Med. Soc., A.M.A. Republican. Lutheran. Mason (32°, Shriner, K.T., Knights of Constantine). Club: Sunnehanna Country (Johnstown). Home: 122 Tioga St., Westmont, Pa. Office: 811 U.S. Nat. Bank Bldg., Johnstown, Pa.

BRAUFF, Herbert Davenport, publisher; b. Chattanooga, Tenn., May 31, 1890; s. William Sidney and Minnie (Papineau) B.; student Chattanooga (Tenn.) Pub. Schs., 1896-1903, Baylor Sch., Chattanooga, 1907-08, McCallie Sch., Chattanooga, 1908-09; m. Laura F. Ellis, July 26, 1924; children—Mary Frances, Dorothy Ann. Began as newspaperman, Chattanooga (Tenn.) Times, 1907-12; reporter Detroit (Mich.) Free Press, 1913-14; reporter Detroit (Mich.) Tribune, 1914-15; reporter New York (N.Y.) Evening Post, 1915; reporter Phila. (Pa.) Press, 1916; reporter, copy reader Pittsburgh (Pa.) Gazette-Times, 1916-20; editor Johnstown (Pa.) Leader, 1921; editorial writer Phila. Public Ledger, 1921; staff man, Asso. Press, 1922; v.p. and editor Reading (Pa.) Tribune, 1923-25; gen. mgr. Altoona (Pa.) Tribune, 1925-28; pres. and pub. Vandergrift (Pa.) News since 1928; gen. mgr. Scranton (Pa.) Sun, 1931-32; owner and operator The Nanticoke News, Nanticoke, Pa., 1931-35; helped in consolidation of Johnstown (Pa.) Democrat and Johnstown (Pa.) Tribune, 1935; pres. Vandergrift Federal Savings & Loan Assn.; v.p. Vandergrift Thrift Corpn. Served as pvt. San. Detachment, 107th F.A., Pa. Nat. Guard, 1917-19. V.p. Westmoreland Co. Council Boy Scouts of America; mem. of bd. Vandergrift (Pa.) chapter Am. Red Cross. Republican. Methodist. Clubs: Pen and Pencil (Phila.); Kiwanis, Hill Crest Country (Vandergrift, Pa.)). Home: 134 E. Adams Av. Office: 149 Columbia Av., Vandergrift, Pa.

BRAUN, Arthur E., banker; b. Pittsburgh, Pa. Pres. Farmers Deposit Nat. Bank, Pittsburgh, Reliance Life Ins. Co. of Pittsburgh, Suburban Rapid Transit St. Ry. Co., Farmers Deposit Trust Co.; v.p. Am. Window Glass Co.; dir. Harbison-Walker Refractories Co., Pittsburgh Spring & Steel Co., Radio Corpn. America, Pittsburgh Coal Co., Allegheny Steel Co. Pres. Pittsburgh Skin and Cancer Foundation; trustee Falk Foundation; chmn. board Penna. Coll. for Women; member Citizen's Committee on City Plan; board managers Buhl Foundation; trustee University of Pittsburgh; Carnegie Inst. of Tech.; dir. Western Pa. Hosp. Clubs: University, Duquesne, Fox Chapel. Home: Warwick Terrace, Morewood Heights, Pittsburgh, Pa. Office: Farmers Deposit Nat. Bank, Pittsburgh, Pa.

BRAUN, Carl J, Jr.; treas. Philadelphia Co. Home: 166 N. Dithridge St. Office: 435 Sixth Av., Pittsburgh, Pa.

BRAUN, Ernest Rutherford, Jr., merchant; b. Pittsburgh, Pa., March 11, 1900; s. Ernest Rutherford and Cora Elizabeth (Dice) B.; grad. Pittsburgh Acad., 1917; B.S., Colgate U., 1921; m. Kathryn Florence Stephens, April 28, 1925; children—Grace Louise, Ernest Rutherford III. Salesman Braun Baking Co., 1921-24, sales mgr. and dir., 1924-25, sec., 1925-35, pres. since 1935. Dir. Pa. Bakers Assn. since 1933, pres., 1938; dir. Colgate Alumni Corpn., 1935-37. Mem. Phi Gamma Delta, Pi Delta Epsilon, Skull and Scroll (Colgate). Republican. Mem. United Presbyn. Ch. Club: Shannopin Country (Ben Avon, Pa.). Home: 306 S. Home Av., Avalon, Pa. Office: 1712 Island Av., Pittsburgh, Pa.

BRAUN, Herbert, clergyman; b. Phila., Pa., Aug. 4, 1902; s. Robert and Anna Mary (Moon) B.; B.S. in Econ., Wharton Sch., U. of Pa., 1924; Th.B., Princeton Theological Seminary, 1928, Th.M., Pittsburgh Theol. Sem., 1930; S.T.D., Temple University, Philadelphia, 1935; m. Mary Evelyn Arnold, June 2, 1928; children—Robert Arnold, Loisann. Began as teacher in high sch., West Chester, Pa., 1924-25; ordained to ministry U. Presbyn. Ch., 1928; stated supply at Evans City, Pa., asst. North Side Pittsburgh, Pa.; stated supply, Third Ch., Phila., Pa.; pastor Dales Memorial Ch., Phila., since 1928; mem. Bd. Fgn. Missions of U. Presbyn. Ch. of N.A. Served in R.O.T.C., 1920-22. Trustee Westminister Coll., New Wilmington, Pa. Mem. Edn. Com. Phila. Council Christian Edn.; chmn. budget com. Phila. Presbytery; pastoral counsellor Germantown Branch Christian Endeavor; sec. Geneva Cleric. United Presbyterian, past moderator Phila. Presbytery. Mason (Past Master). Club: Warfield (Princeton, N.J.). Home: 1963 W. 69th Av., Philadelphia, Pa.

BRAUNLICH, Alice Freda, prof. of classics; b. Davenport, Ia., Feb. 1, 1888; d. Henry Uchtorf and Emilie Hedwig (Hoering) Braunlich; A.B., U. of Chicago, 1908, A.M., 1909, Ph.D., 1913; unmarried. Research asst., U. of Chicago, 1913-14; instr. in Latin and German, Frances Shimer Sch., Mount Carroll, Ill., 1914-16, instr. in Latin, 1916-18; instr. in Latin, Davenport (Ia.) High Sch., 1918-20; asst. prof. of Latin, Goucher Coll., 1920-26, asso. prof., 1926-33, asso. prof. of Latin and Greek, 1933-34, prof. of classics since 1934. Mem. Am. Philol. Assn., Archæol. Inst. America, Classical Assn. Atlantic States, Am. Assn. Univ. Profs., Phi Beta Kappa. Democrat. Unitarian. Contbr. to Am. Jour. Philology, etc.; contbr. poems to Sewanee Review. Home: 3002 St. Paul St., Baltimore, Md.

BRAUNSTEIN, Baruch, rabbi, lecturer; b. New Castle, Pa., March 3, 1906; s. Peter and Esther (Pazer) B.; student Western Reserve U., 1922-23; B.Sc., Ohio State U., 1926; M.H.L. and Rabbi, Jewish Inst. of Religion, 1930; Ph.D., Columbia, 1933; m. Gladys Belinky, June 19, 1928. Rabbi, Beth Sholom Congregation, New York, 1927-29; religious counselor Columbia U., 1929-34; rabbi, The Temple, Wheeling, W.Va., 1934-36; mem. exec. staff Emergency Peace Campaign since 1936; special lecturer, U. of Beirut, Syria; fellow Nat. Council of Religion in Higher Edn.; Guggenheim fellow Jewish Inst. of Religion. Mem. Central Conf. Am. Rabbis, Soc. of Biblical Lit. and Exegesis, Zionist Orgn. of America, Forum Soc., Am. Com. of Internat. Student Service, Jewish Pub. Soc., Delta Sigma Rho. Mem. B'nai B'rith. Author: The Chuetas of Majorca, 1936. Contbr. articles to Am. and European mags. and newspapers. Lecturer on political and religious topics. Home: 4301 Chestnut St. Office: 614 Commonwealth Bldg., Philadelphia, Pa.

BRAY, Mabel Evelyn, prof. musical edn.; b. Madison, N.J.; d. Edward Ashley and Priscilla (Haire) Bray; ed. Detroit (Mich.) High Sch., Michigan Sem. (Kalamazoo), U. of Mich. (summers), Detroit Conservatory of Music, Thomas Normal Sch. of Music and New Sch. of Methods

(Chicago). Began as singer, 1900; supervisor of music, Moorhead, Minn., 1903-04, Carlisle, Pa., 1904-06; head dept. music, Cheney (Wash.) State Teachers Coll., 1906-08, St. Louis (Mo.) Teachers Coll., 1908-12; conducted experiments in music edn., Westfield (N.J.) pub. schs., 1912-19; head dept. music, Trenton (N.J.) State Teachers Coll. since 1920; pres. N.J. Dept. of Music, 1937-39, dir., 1939-40; research council Music Educators Nat. Conf.; mem. Nat. Vocal Com. Speaker Anglo-Am. Music Conf., Lausanne, Switzerland, 1929 and 31; also at many musical and ednl. meetings in U.S. Lecturer Rutgers U., Northwestern U., Syracuse U., Columbia U. and New York U. Mem. Sigma Alpha Iota, Gamma Sigma. Republican. Episcopalian. Club: N.J. Federated Music Clubs (dir.). Author: The Phono-Song Series, 1922. Co-Author: The Music Hour Series, 1929. Mag. writer, 5 yrs.; contbr. music articles to "The Designer." Editor N.J. State Music Dept. Bulletin, 2 yrs. Home: 822 Riverside Av., Trenton, N.J.

BRAZER, Clarence Wilson, architect; b. Philadelphia, Pa., March 13, 1880; s. Christopher and Julia Wilson (Stackhouse). B.; graduated in architecture, Drexel Inst., Phila., and town planning, Columbia U.; studied architecture in offices in Phila. 4 yrs., also 4 yrs. in office of Cass Gilbert and Van Pelt Atelier of Soc. Beaux Arts Architects, New York, and in Europe; m. Mary Ella Mendenhall, of Phila., April 25, 1905; 1 son, Wilson M.; m. 2d, Esther Stevens, June 30, 1937. Began practice at Asbury Park, N.J., 1902; established office at New York, 1905, Chester, Pa., 1918. Principal works: Delaware Co. Court House, Media, Pa.; Citizens Savings Bank, Fort George Presbyn. Ch., N.Y. City; War Memorial Bridge, Swarthmore, Pa.; World War Monument, Lansdowne, Pa.; residence of A. K. Ford, Minneapolis, Minn.; Trinity P.E. Ch., Syracuse, N.Y.; Deshong Memorial Mus. and Park, Chester, Pa.; many schs., banks, instns., residences, chs. and pub. buildings, including decoration and furnishings. Has restored several important colonial buildings. Mem. Pa. State Bd. Examiners of Architects, 1919-37 (pres. 1926-31), Nat. Council Architectural Registration Bds. (pres. 1929-31). Mem. Phila. Chapter Am. Inst. Architects, Pa. State Asso. of Architects (pres. 1928-30), Architectural League of New York, Am. City Planning Inst., Soc. for Preservation N.E. Antiquities, Hist. Soc. of Pa., Delaware County Hist. Soc. (pres. 1927-37), Tri-State Regional Planning Federation, S.A.R., Am. Philatelic Soc. Republican. Mason. Clubs: Collectors' of New York (gov. since 1932), New York Rotary (historian 1918-32); Chester. Author: U.S. Stamp Essays and Proofs (hist. cat.); Course in Architectural Practice for International Correspondence Schools; also many articles in antiques mags. and philatelic mags. Office: 415 Lexington Av., New York, N.Y.; and 421 Market St., Chester, Pa.

BREAKEY, Edward Paul, entomologist; b. Phillipsburg, Kan., July 5, 1900; s. John R. and Winifred (McManus) B.; B.S., U. of Kan., 1924, A.M., 1927; student U. of Mich., 1925-26; Ph.D., Ohio State U., 1932; m. Edith Caroline Woollett, Jan. 1, 1928; children—Edward Paul, Ellen Jean. Teacher, Williamsburg (Kan.) High Sch., 1922-23; mem. Kan. U. Biol. Survey, 1924; field entomologist, Entomol. Commn. of Kan., 1924-26, Wis. State Dept. of Agr., 1927-30; asst. Ohio Biol. Survey, 1930-32; Crop Protection Inst. fellow in entomology, Ohio State U., 1932-36; industrial fellow, Mellon Inst. for Industrial Research, 1936-37, senior industrial fellow since 1937. Fellow A.A. A.S.; mem. Am. Assn. Econ. Entomologists, Entomol. Soc. of America, Kan. Entomol. Soc., Sigma Xi, Gamma Sigma Delta, Phi Sigma. Republican. Methodist. Contbr. articles to professional jours. Home: 1019 Pennsylvania Av., Oakmont, Pa. Office: Mellon Inst., Pittsburgh, Pa.

BREAM, Henry T.; B.S., Gettysburg (Pa.) Coll.; A.M., Columbia U. Football coach and instr. phys. edn., Gettysburg Coll. Address: 317 N. Stratton St., Gettysburg, Pa.

BRECKENRIDGE, John E., retired chemist; b. Palmer, Mass., May 4, 1873; s. John A. and Harriet A. (Kellogg) B.; student Palmer (Mass.) High Sch., 1888-92; B.A., Yale, 1896; m. Amy G. Edgar, Oct. 26, 1898; children—Marion Edgar, Harriet Amelia (Mrs. W. S. Roeder). Began as chemist, Carteret, N.J., 1896; dir. chemical control Am. Agrl. Chem. Co., New York, 1896-1931; retired, 1931, and entered welfare work; municipal dir. Emergency Relief Administrn., Woodbridge, N.J., 1931-34, in recreational work, 1934-38. Mayor, Woodbridge, N.J., 1923-24, clk. of sessions since 1914. Republican. Presbyterian (pres. bd. trustees). Club: Rotary (Woodbridge, N.J.; sec. since 1933). Address: 181 Green St., Woodbridge, N.J.

BREDER, Charles Marcus, Jr., biologist; b. Jersey City, N.J., June 25, 1897; s. Charles Marcus and Albertine Louise (Agathe) B.; grad. Central High Sch., Newark, N.J., 1918; hon. D.Sc.; m. Ruth B. Demarest, Nov. 18, 1918; children—Charles Marcus III, Richard Frederick; m. 2d, Ethel Lear Snyder, Apr. 17, 1933. Scientific asst. and fishery expert U.S. Bur. Fisheries, 1919-21; aquarist N.Y. Aquarium, 1921-25, research asso., 1925-33, asst. dir. 1933-37, acting dir. since 1937; rep. of Am. Museum of Natural History, Marsh-Darien expdn., 1924; with marine lab., Carnegie Inst., Dry Tortugas, 1929; Bacon expdn., Bahamas, 1930, 32, 33; Atlantis West Indian expdn., 1934; research asso. Am. Museum Natural History, since 1926, Bingham Oceanographic Foundation, Yale U., since 1933. Awarded A. Cressy Morrison prize, N.Y. Acad. Science, 1925. Fellow N.Y. Zoöl. Soc., A.A.A.S., N.Y. Acad. Science (sec. section biology, 1939); mem. Am. Fisheries Soc., Am. Soc. Ichthyologists and Herpetologists (pres. 1932), Am. Soc. Zoölogist, Ecol. Soc. of America, Sigma Xi, Beta Lambda Sigma. Republican. Author: Field Book of Marine Fishes of the Atlantic Coast, 1929. Contbr. to Bulletin of N.Y. Zoöl. Soc. and numerous tech. jours. Home: Ramapo Av., Mahwah, N.J. Office: Aquarium, New York, N.Y.

BREED, Charles Henry, educator; b. Pittsburgh, Pa., Mar. 11, 1876; s. Henry Atwood and Cornelia (Bidwell) B.; prep. edn., Shady Side Acad., Pittsburgh; A.B., Princeton University, 1899, A.M., 1902; Ed.D. from Lafayette Coll., Easton, Pa., 1928; m. Frances deForest Martin, June 10, 1903; children—Anne Martin (Mrs. Robert Longdon Bentley, Jr.), Elizabeth Leiper (Mrs. Edward C. Marshall), Henry Atwood. Teacher of Latin, Lawrenceville (N.J.) Sch., 1899-1923; organizer, 1923, headmaster until 1927, Providence (R.I.) Country Day Sch.; headmaster Blair Acad. since 1927. Served as lt., Dept. Justice, U.S., World War. Mem. Am. Classical League, Classical Assn. of Atlantic States, Headmasters' Club, Phila. Dist. Headmasters' Assn., Phi Beta Kappa. Republican. Presbyn. Clubs: Nassau (Princeton); Princeton (New York). Address: Blair Academy, Blairstown, N.J.

BREEDEN, Waldo (Preston), lawyer; b. Santa Fe, N.M., Sept. 3, 1876; s. Col. William and Mary Grace (Baker) B.; desc. from Chief Justice John Marshall and Pres. James Madison; Ph.B., U. of Chicago, 1897; LL.B., U. of Pa. Law Sch., 1903; m. Wilhelmina Jane Orr, Sept. 30, 1912; children—Juanita (Mrs. Robert J. Hester Jr.), Preston Waldo. Admitted to Pa. bar, 1905 and since engaged in gen. practice of law at Pittsburgh; admitted to practice before all cts. of Pa. and Dist. Ct. of the U.S.; dir. Monongahela Bldg. & Loan Assn., Am. Food Products Co., Purity Products Co. Served in U.S. Army during Spanish-Am. War; on staff Maj. Gen. Matthew Calbraith Butler, comdr. 1st Div., 2d Army Corps, May-Nov. 1898. Mem. Am. and Pa. bar assns. Republican. Presbyterian. Odd Fellow. Author: Our American Government, 1933; The Great Depression, 1935. Home: Mt. Troy and Evergreen Rds., Ivory Avenue, Extension. Office: 603 Law & Finance Bldg., Pittsburgh, Pa.

BREEN, Frank J.; pres. Standard Fire Ins. Co. Address: 39 N. Clinton Av., Trenton, N.J.

BREENE, Edmond C.; mem. law firm Breene & Jobson; officer or dir. many other companies. Home: Maple Av., Hasson Heights. Office: First Nat. Bank Bldg., Oil City, Pa.

BREG, W(illiam) Roy, exec. sec. Allied Youth, Inc.; b. St. Paul, Minn., Jan. 31, 1888; s. William Grobe and Martha Elizabeth (Knowland) B.; ed. pub. grade and high schs., Dallas, Tex.; m. Lonnie O. Henry, July 12, 1911; children—Frances Viola, William Roy. Asso. with banking and bond business, 1907-15; gen. agent life ins. co., 1915-16; Tex. mgr. Deming Investment Co., Dallas, 1916-17; gen. sec. Tex. Christian Endeavor Union, 1917-19; Southwestern sec. United Soc. of Christian Endeavor, hdqrs. Dallas, 1919-23; dir. religious edn., City Temple, Dallas, 1923-25; gen. sec. Kan. Christian Endeavor Union, 1925-28; Southern sec. Internat. Soc. Christian Endeavor, hdqrs. Chattanooga and Atlanta, 1928-31; exec. sec. Allied Youth, Inc., since 1931. Mem. research Council on Problems of Alcohol since 1937; trustee Internat. Soc. of Christian Endeavor since 1933; pres. Internat. Christian Endeavor Field Secs., 1919-21. Mem. A.A.A.S., Dept. of Secondary Sch. Prins. of N.E.A., Sch. Pub. Relations Assn. Presbyterian. Contbr. Journal of N.E.A., Christian Herald and other jours., mng. editor The Allied Youth. Speaker before schs., etc., on alcohol and other youth problems. Home: 401 Sonora Rd., Bethesda, Md. Office: 1201 16th St. N.W., Washington, D.C.

BRÉGY, Edith M(aurice), artist; b. Phila., Pa.; d. Francois Amédée and Katherine (Maurice) B.; ed. Phila. Sem., Pa. Sch. Industrial Art, Pa. Acad. Fine Arts, Phila. Sch. of Design, Moore Inst.; unmarried. Teacher special art class, Girard Coll. since 1922; private teaching at studio. Represented in Herron Art Inst., Indianapolis, Ind.; Moore Inst., Phila.; Coll. of William and Mary, Williamsburg, Va. Mem. bd. dirs. Pa. Acad. Home: 1722 Pine St. Studio: 34 S. 17th St., Philadelphia.

BRÉGY, Katherine Marie Cornelia, author, lecturer; b. Philadelphia, Pa.; d. F. Amédée and Kate (Maurice) B.; special student U. of Pa.; hon. Litt.D., D'Youville Coll., Buffalo, N.Y., 1920, Holy Cross Coll., Worcester Massachusetts, 1927. Mem. Poetry Society of America (pres.), Philadelphia Art Alliance, Alliance Française. Decorated Officer d'Académie, 1924, Officer de l'Instruction Publique, 1928 (France); awarded Leahy prize, Commonweal Mag., for best essay on Dante, 1927. Author: The Poets' Chantry, 1912; The Little Crusaders (play), 1919; Poets and Pilgrims, 1925; Bridges (verse) 1930; From Dante to Jeanne d'Arc (essays), 1933; Ladders and Bridges (verse), 1936. Contbr. essays and verse to America, Catholic World, Commonweal, Dublin Review, etc. Lecturer. Home: 1722 Pine St., Philadelphia, Pa.

BREHMAN, A. Balfour; pres. Union Traction Co. of Phila. Home: Green Hill Farms, Overbrook. Office: 1000 Mitten Bldg., Philadelphia, Pa.

BREITIGAN, James Hershey, banker; b. near Mount Joy, Lancaster Co., Pa., Aug. 1, 1885; s. Daniel M. and Ida J. C. (Hershey) B.; student Hossler's Public School, Mount Joy, Pa., 1902, Elizabethtown (Pa.) Coll., 1903-05; Lewis Hotel Training School, Washington, D.C., 1938-39; m. Emma Minnich Miller, June 14, 1908 (died 1935); m. 2d, Luella Grace Fogelsanger, June 17, 1938. Stenographer and bookkeeper Wellington Starch Co., Lititz, Pa., 1905-07; with Farmers Nat. Bank, Lititz, Pa., since 1907, as teller, 1907-08, asst. cashier, 1909-10, cashier, 1911-31, vice-pres. and trust officer since 1932; treas. and dir. Lititz Community Hotel Co., 1929-30; former treas. and dir. Stiffel-Freeman Safe Co. and Acme Metal Products Co., Lititz, Pa.; former dir. Thomas Wagon Co., Lititz, Corpn. Funding & Finance Co., Reading, Reading Mutual Life Ins. Co. Chmn. Lancaster Co. Liberty Loan, 1917-19; registrar local bd. Lancaster Co. Conscription Registration, 1917-18; price reporter U.S. Food Adminstrn., 1917-19; treas. Lititz War Chest, 1917-19. Mem. bd. Lititz Community Chest, 1928-31. Dir. Lititz Chamber of Commerce, 1928-33; mem. Nat. Council U.S. Chamber of Commerce, 1928-33; del. to U.S. Chamber of Commerce Conv., Washington, D.C., 1929. Mem. Lancaster Chapter Am. Inst. of Banking (mem. bd. of govs., 1916-27; vice-pres. 1926; pres. 1927; mem.

advisory bd. 1928-39; del. to nat. convs., Boston 1920, New York 1922, Cleveland 1923, Kansas City 1925, Phila. 1928); mem. Am. Inst. Banking (mem. nat. extension and membership com. 1928), Pa. Bankers Assn. (key banker for Lancaster Co. for Agrl. Commn. 1924-30). Charter mem. Lititz Rotary Club (dir. 1925-29; treas. 1925; sec. 1926; vice-pres. 1927; pres. 1928; del. to Internat. Conv., Minneapolis, 1928). Mem. Lititz Ch. of the Brethren (mem. bldg. com.; trustee; treas.; Sunday Sch. supt. 1938-39; mem. bd. Christian edn.; mem. auditing com.); mem. Nat. Council Men's Work since 1936. Mem. Elizabethtown Coll. Alumni Assn. (pres. 1938-39, former solicitor and treas.). Republican. Home: 405 S. Broad St. Office: 6 E. Main St., Lititz, Pa.

BREITSTEIN, Moses Lewis, otolaryngologist; b. Richmond, Va., Nov. 18, 1894; s. Harry and Emily (Spiegel) B.; prep. edn., public schs., Richmond, Va.; student U. of Mich., summer 1914; A.B., U. of Richmond, 1915; M.D., Johns Hopkins, 1919; Post grad. student Univ. of Vienna, 1921-22; m. Dorothy Labenberg, Sept. 5, 1925; children—Harry Charles, Dorothy. Interne Bellevue Hosp., New York 1919-20; asst. Johns Hopkins Hosp., 1920-21; otolaryngologist, Baltimore, since 1922; instr. of otolaryngology, Johns Hopkins; mem. staffs Union Memorial Hosp., Hosp. for Women of Md.; attending surgeon Baltimore Eye, Ear and Throat Hosp.; otologist Baltimore Health Dept. Served in Med. Reserve Corps, 1917-18. Fellow Am. Coll. Surgeons; mem. A.M.A. Med. and Chirurg. Faculty of Md., Am. Acad. Otolaryngology. Jewish religion. Clubs: Johns Hopkins, Suburban (Baltimore). Asso. editor of Internat. Med. Digest. Contbr. to med. jours. Home: 2405 W. Rogers Av. Office: 1213 Eutaw Place, Baltimore, Md.

BREITWIESER, Thomas John, educator; b. Jasper, Ind., Sept. 19, 1886; s. John Conrad and Kateryn (Baitz) B.; B.S., Central Normal Coll., Danville, Ind., 1909; A.B. and A.M., Ind. Univ., Bloomington, Ind., 1913, Ph.D., 1931; student Teachers Coll., Columbia U., 1913-14, N.Y. U., 1927-29; m. Anita Van Vliet, Sept. 23, 1916; 1 dau., Edna Ruth. Began as rural sch. teacher, Ind., 1904; rural sch. teacher 3 yrs.; prin. high sch., Hobbs, Ind., 1908-10; asst. prof. of psychology, State Normal Sch., Terre Haute, Ind., 1914-17; dean of faculty, Ball State Teachers Coll., Muncie, Ind., 1919-26; dir. teacher training, State Teachers Coll., East Stroudsburg, Pa., since 1926; v.p. and dir. East Stroudsburg Nat. Bank; treas. and dir. Keystone Bldg. and Loan Assn. Served as 1st lt., M.C. U.S. Army, during World War as psycholog. examiner and ednl. dir. of rehabilitation work, Camp Pike, V.p. Monroe Co. Sabbath Sch. Assn.; v.p. Monroe Co. Children's Aid Soc.; dir. Monroe Co. Crippled Children's Assn.; chmn. industrial com. East Stroudsburg Merchants Assn. Republican. Presbyterian. Mason (32°). Club: Kiwanis of Stroudsburg (pres.). Home: 80 Analomink St., East Stroudsburg, Pa.

BRENEMAN, Paul Bruce, prof. mechanics and materials of construction, Pa. State Coll. Address: State College, Pa.

BRENGLE, Henry Gaw, banker; b. Baltimore, Md., Feb. 25, 1866; s. James Shriver and Millicent Anne (Gaw) B.; A.B., Harvard, 1887; unmarried. Began in banking business with H. L. Gaw & Co., Phila., 1887; pres. Phila. Trust Co., 1918-26; pres. Fidelity-Phila. Trust Co., 1926-37. Clubs: Philadelphia, Rittenhouse (Phila.); University (New York). Home: Radnor, Pa. Office: Broad and Walnut Sts., Philadelphia, Pa.

BRENNAN, Cornelius Patricius, clergyman and Child Welfare Dir.; b. Shenandoah, Pa.; s. Edward J. and Nellie Frances (McGonigle) B.; student Mt. St. Mary's Coll., Md.; A.B., Phila. Theol. Sem., Overbrook, Pa.; A.M., Ph.D., Royal and Pontifical Univ. of Santo Tomas, Manila, P.I. Ordained priest Roman Catholic Ch., in Phila.; named domestic prelate with title of Monsignor by Pope Pius XI, Sept. 1933; secretary to Bishop of Jaro, P.I., 1925-32; Vicar-General of Jaro Diocese, P.I., 1932-33;

dir. Diocesan Charities, Archdiocese of Phila. since 1934; dir. of Cath. Children's Bureau, Inc.; rector All Saints Chapel, Phila. Gen. Hosp.; dir. Alliance of Cath. Women, Archdiocese of Phila. Mem. rural extension unit Pa. State Dept. of Welfare. Home: 3445 Walnut St. Office: 1706 Summer St., Philadelphia, Pa.

BRENNAN, John Harold, judge; b. Wheeling, W.Va., Oct. 2, 1884; s. James Bernard and Frances (Smith) B.; prep. edn., public schools, Sistersville and Wheeling; A.B., Washington and Jefferson Coll., 1904, A.M., 1908, LL.D., 1933; LL.B., Harvard, 1907; m. Arielle MacMillan, July 30, 1913; 1 son, John Harold. Admitted to W.va. bar, 1907, and began practice at Wheeling; city solicitor, Wheeling, 1913-17; exec. sec. Food Adminstrn. for W.Va. during World War; judge 1st Judicial Circuit of W.Va. since 1924. Mem. W.Va., Ohio County and Am. bar assns., Am. Law Inst., Order of Coif, Beta Theta Pi, Theta Nu Epsilon, Phi Beta Kappa. Republican. Clubs: Fort Henry, Country, Twilight, Blue Pencil, Elks (all Wheeling); Williams Country (Weirton, W.Va.). Home: Highland Park. Office: Court House, Wheeling, W.Va.

BRENNAN, John Patrick, physician; b. Poultney, Vt., Dec. 13, 1893; s. Patrick and Margaret (McCarty) B.; Ph.B., U. of Vt., Burlington, Vt., 1915; M.D., Jefferson Med. Coll., Phila., Pa., 1918; m. C. Ethel Tiedeken, Nov. 9, 1921; children—John Patrick, Jr., James Edward, Christine Ethel. Resident physician, St. Joseph's Hosp., Phila., 1918-19; res. physician and surgeon in ear, nose and throat dept., Columbia Med. Center, N.Y. City, 1929-31; engaged in gen. practice of medicine, North Adams, Mass., 1919-23, in Camden, N.J., 1923-29; specialist in diseases of ear, nose and throat, Camden, N.J., since 1931; mem. staff Cooper Hosp. (Camden, N.J.), Camden Co. Gen. Hosp. (Lakeland, N.J.). Mem. Am Med. Assn., N.J. State Med. Soc., Camden Co. Med. Soc. Roman Catholic. Club: Merchantville Country. Home: 14 Church Rd., Merchantville, N.J. Office: 429 Cooper St., Camden, N.J.

BRENNAN, Kenneth; editor The Enterprise. Address: Burlington, N.J.

BRENTANO, Arthur, bookselling; b. Hoboken, N.J., Apr. 20, 1858; s. Emil and Sara (Loewenthal) B.; ed. pub. schs., Evansville, Ind., and Jan. 30, 1890; children—Rowena LanFranco, Cincinnati, O.; m. Rowena M. L. LanFranco, Emily (Mrs. Edward A. Hermann), Arthur, Marion (Mrs. Franklyn Kingsland Oakes). Began with Brentano's, Inc., N.Y. City, 1873, pres. since 1915. Pres. Brentano's Société Anonyme, Paris; one of founders Am. Canoe Assn. Republican. Home: 224 Midland Av., East Orange, N.J. Office: 586 Fifth Av., New York, N.Y.

BRENTLINGER, John Moore, industrial engring. mgr.; b. Smithfield, Ky., Dec. 31, 1883; s. William Allen and Mollie Nareissa (Kenny) B.; grad. Cherokee Co. High Sch., Columbus, Kan., 1903; B.S. in E.E., Kan. U. Lawrence, Kan., 1910; m. Anna Frances Swezey, Apr. 8, 1916; children—John Moore, Anne (dec.); stepchildren—William Francis Swezey, Fleming Swezey, Frank Roxbury Swezey, Dorothy Swezey (Mrs. G. Dudley Gray). Electrician, Columbus (Kan.) plant, E. I. du Pont de Nemours & Co., 1910-12, power test engr., Wilmington, Del., 1912-15, Hopewell, Va., 1915-17, power supt., Hopewell, Va., 1917-18, engr., Wilmington, and Chile, S.A., 1918-19, chief industrial engr., Deepwater, N.J., since 1919, mgr. industrial engineering division, Wilmington, Del. Mem. bd. of dirs. Liberty Finance Corporation, Consol. Cemeteries Corpn.; dir. and treas., Boys' Club of Wilmington, Del., Inc. Mem. Am. Soc. M.E., Kan. U. Alumni Assn., Tau Beta Pi. Republican. Methodist. Clubs: Concord Country, Kiwanis (Wilmington, Del.). Home: 5 Cragmere Rd. Office: 12064 du Pont Bldg., Wilmington, Del.

BRESSLER, Harry Samuel, editorial cartoonist; b. Austria, Jan. 7, 1893; brought to U.S., 1901; s. Isaac and Rebecca (Ginsberg) B.; student N.Y. City pub. schs., 1901-06. Stuyvesant High Sch., 1907-10, Nat. Acad. Design, 1911-

12, Art Students League, 1913-17; spl. courses, Columbia U., 1920-23; m. Frances Bibo, July 4, 1920; children—Harry Bibo, Edward Charles. Began as advertising artist, 1912; cartoonist Universal Film Co., 1914-16, Paramount Pictures, 1916-18, New York Times, 1919, King Features Syndicate, 1919-28, Dayton Daily News, 1929-1932, New York Mirror, 1934-35, Geo. M. Adams Syndicate, 1936; sole owner and editor Bressler Editorial Cartoons, supplying more than 40 daily newspapers in U.S., since 1937. Official editorial cartoonist Dem. Nat. Com., 1928. Winner in Poster contest, 3d U.S. Liberty Loan. V.p. Spring Valley Community Center, 1934-35. Mem. Newspaper Guild of N.Y., Graphic Arts Guild, Cartoonists Guild of America; mem. cartoonist council Nat. Foundation for Infantile Paralysis. Jewish religion. Club: Newspaper Guild (New York). Home: 521 Ogden Av., West Englewood, N.J. Office: Times Bldg., New York, N.Y.

BRESTELL, Rudolph Emile, clergyman; b. New York, N.Y., July 4, 1873; s. Major Charles and Maud Henrietta (Thacher) B.; prep. edn., Hayden Acad., N.Y. City; B.A., St. Stephen's Coll., Annandale, N.Y., 1895, M.A., 1898; B.S.T., Gen. Theol. Sem., 1898; D.D., St. Stephen's Coll. of Columbia U., 1929; m. Bessie Maud Craske, Nov. 9, 1899. Deacon, 1898, priest, 1899, P.E. Ch.; curate Ch. of the Advocate, Philadelphia, Pa., 1898-1901; rector Trinity Ch., Ambler, Pa., 1901-03; curate St. Martin's in the Field, Wissahickon Heights, Phila., 1903-04; curate St. Paul's Ch., Camden, N.J., 1904-05, rector since 1905. Mem. N.G.N.Y., 1891-94; chaplain 3d Inf., N.J. N.G., 1906-13. Examining chaplain and diocese sec. Bd. of Missions, N.J.; del. Gen. Conv. P.E. Ch., 7 times since 1913. Trustee Cathedral Foundation, St. Stephen's Coll. (Columbia U.). Mem. Phi Beta Kappa, Sigma Alpha Epsilon. Republican. Home: Merchantville, N.J.

BRETHERICK, Arthur Paul, lawyer; b. Armley, Yorkshire, England, May 20, 1897; s. Joseph Paul and Jane Ann (Olivant) B.; came to U.S., 1904, naturalized, 1913; student Phila. and Darby (Pa.) pub. schs., 1903-10, Banks Business Coll. (night school), 1913-16; LL.B., Temple U. (night school), Phila., 1928; m. Ida Miller Cooper, Jan. 30, 1918; children—Arthur Paul, Phyllis Rowena, Donald Williams. With firm of Brown & Williams, lawyers, Phila., Pa., since Feb. 3, 1913, beginning as office boy and successively clerk, stenographer, private sec., office mgr. and atty.; admitted to Pa. bar, 1927. Served in U.S.N.R.F. during World War. Borough solicitor, Darby, Pa., since 1933; pres. Darby Borough Sch. Bd. since 1929; mem. Pa. State Legislature since 1939. Pres. Soc. of Sons of St. George (Phila. charitable orgn.). Mem. Delaware Co. Bar Assn.; Am. Legion (Collingdale Post). Republican. Mason, Odd Fellow, Artisans Order of Mutual Protection. Clubs: Lawyers (Phila.); Lansdowne Country (Lansdowne, Pa.). Home: 12 Golf Rd., Darby, Pa. Office: 1421 Chestnut St., Philadelphia; 304 Darby Trust Bldg., Darby, Pa.

BREVILLIER, Edwin Henry, manufacturer; b. Erie, Pa., Feb. 27, 1878; s. Frederick and Charlotte M. (Walther) B.; student U. of Pa., 1897-1900; m. Georgia Dean French, of Erie, Pa., May 14, 1910; 1 son, Frederick Charles. Asso. with father in wholesale grocery business, Erie, Pa., 1900-06; with Union Iron Works, Erie, Pa., since 1906, v.p. and dir. since 1934. Mem. bd. mgrs. Erie Cemetery Assn. Mem. Phi Delta Theta. Republican. Evangelical Ch. Clubs: Erie, Kahkwa Country (Erie, Pa.). Home: 934 W. 9th St. Office: Union Iron Works, Erie, Pa.

BREWER, Charles Philip, lawyer; b. Vineland, N.J., Aug. 26, 1882; s. Charles and Maria Pendleton (Cooke) B.; g.s. Judge Nicholas B., Gen. Philip St. George C., U.S.A.; nephew Gen. J. E. B. Stuart, late C.S.A.; LL.B., Yale, 1908; m. Muriel Fisher, July 6, 1921; children—Ray H. (dau.), Charles P., Jr., Richard T. Admitted to N.J. bar as atty., 1905, as counselor, 1908; spl. master in chancery, supreme ct. commr., supreme ct. examiner; in individual practice of law at Vineland, since 1905; served as police judge Borough of Vine-

BREWER, land, N.J., 1906, 1926-33. Served as capt. Dept. Judge Adv. Gen., U.S.A. during World War. Mem. bd. mgrs. Vineland Pub. Library. Scoutmaster, Troop 6, Vineland, N.J., 1914-24. Mem. N.J. State Bar Assn, Cumberland County Bar Assn., (pres. 1920), Am. Legion (county comdr. 1925). Episcopalian (sr. warden Trinity Ch.). Home: 716 Plum St. Office: 631 Landis Av., Vineland, N.J.

BREWER, Frank Dodge, banker; b. Glen Ridge, N.J., Oct. 3, 1885; s. Abijah R. and Margaret P. (Whipple) B.; grad. Montclair (N.J.) High Sch., 1906; B.S., Princeton U., 1910; m. Amy M. Brown, Apr. 3, 1913; children—Russell B., Chandler R. Clerk Seaboard Nat. Bank, New York, 1910-11, Brown Brothers & Co., 1911-12; with Glen Ridge Trust Co. since 1912, beginning as teller and advancing to treas. and dir., then vice-pres. and since 1929 pres.; dir. Glen Ridge Bldg. & Loan Assn., Dodge-Davis Mfg. Co. (Bristol, N.H.), Watchung Title & Mortgage Guaranty Co. (Montclair, N.J.). Trustee Convalescent Home, Verona, N.J. Mem. Cap and Gown, Princeton U. Republican. Congregationalist (former trustee). Former trustee Glen Ridge Country Club. Home: 36 Sherman Av. Office: 222 Ridgewood Av., Glen Ridge, N.J.

BREWER, Ralph Emmet, research chemist; b. Chariton, Ia., Jan. 16, 1893; s. William Eli and Edith Jane (Huntley) B.; grad. Indianola (Ia.) High Sch., 1913; A.B., Simpson Coll., Indianola, Ia., 1917; student Ia. State Coll., Ames, Ia., 1917-19; M.S., Purdue U., Lafayette, Ind., 1920; student U. of Chicago, summer 1921; Ph.D., U. of Minn., Minneapolis, Minn., 1928; m. Marguerite Brown, Dec. 19, 1931; children—Lee Roy, Donald Richard. Instr. chemistry, Ia. State Coll., Purdue U., U. of Minn., 1917-29; chief mng. eng. and plant supt. Lehigh Briquetting Co., Dickinson, N.D., 1929-30; asst. prof. chemistry, U. of Minn., Minneapolis, Minn., 1930-32, research chemist, 1932-35; research chemist and chem. engr., U.S. Bureau of Mines, Pittsburgh, since 1935. Served in Chem. Warfare Service, U.S. Army, 1918. Fellow A.A.A.S.; mem. Am. Chem. Soc., Sigma Xi, Gamma Alpha, Alpha Chi Sigma, Epsilon Sigma, Phi Lambda Upsilon. Methodist. Mason. Home: 206 Forest Hills Rd., Wilkinsburg, Pa. Office: 4800 Forbes St., Pittsburgh, Pa.

BREWER, Robert Wellesley Antony, cons. mech. engr.; s. John Sherren B.; student U. of Leeds, Eng.; came to U.S., 1915, naturalized, 1925; m. Ellen Elizabeth Curtis, 1916. Cons. mech. engr. and aviation consultant since 1902, in London to 1914, subsequently in U.S.A., in Phila., since 1922; pres. Aircraft Engine & A. D. Corpn., Phila., 1929-31. Served as capt., British Army, 1914-19; officer in charge of munitions in U.S.A., 1915-19. Fellow Soc. of Engrs. (mem. council 1907-14); asso. fellow Inst. of Aeronautical Sciences; hon. mem. Pacific Coast Gas Assn.; mem. Inst. of Automobile Engrs. (mem. council 1907); asso. mem. Inst. of Civil Engrs. Awarded Gold Medal of Soc. of Engrs., Bessemer Premium (three times), six silver trophies. Author: Art of Aviation, 1910; Motor Car Construction, 1919, 1928; Art of Carburation, 1937; articles on aviation, liquid fuel, automobiles, radio devices. Holds more than 30 patents on above arts. Address: Huntingdon Valley, Pa.

BREWER, William Russell, banker; b. Rockville, Md., Apr. 6, 1880; s. John Buchanan and Virginia Fletcher (Russell) B.; prep. edn., Rockville Acad., 1893-98; LL.B., Nat. U. Law Sch., Washington, D.C., 1907; m. Maude Stalnaker, Aug. 17, 1910; 1 dau., Virginia Russell (Mrs. W. Earle Cobey). Began as teller Montgomery Nat. Bank, Rockville, Md., 1899; vice-pres. Liberty Trust Co., Cumberland, Md., 1921-26, pres. since 1926; dir. Potomac Edison Co. Served as private Co. K, 1st Regt., Md. Nat. Guard, Apr.-July 1898; corpl. 5th Co., U.S. Vol. Signal Corps, July-Nov. 1928. Mem. Bd. of Edn., Allegany County, Md.; dir. Cumberland Chamber Commerce. Democrat. Episcopalian. Mason. Clubs: Kiwanis, Cumberland Country. Home: Windsor Rd. Office: Liberty Trust Co., Cumberland, Md.

BREWSTER, Benjamin Harris, Jr., pres. Baugh & Sons Co.; b. Phila., Pa., Oct. 22, 1872; s. Benjamin Harris and Mary (Walker) B.; student Brown's Sch., Phila., Columbia Prep. Sch., Washington, D.C., William Penn Charter Sch., Phila., U. of Pa., 1891; m. Elizabeth Baugh, Oct. 22, 1894; children—Daniel Baugh (dec.), Nancy (Mrs. Francis White), Benjamin Harris, 3d. Entered employ of Baugh & Sons Co., Phila., 1892, sec. 1892-1901, v.p. 1901-28, pres. since 1928; also pres. Baugh & Sons Co. (Baltimore), Baugh Chemical Co. (Baltimore); Baugh & Sons Co. of Ohio; chmn. exec. com. Union Trust Co. of Md.; dir. Davis Coal and Coke Co., Eutaw Savings Bank, Baltimore. Served as col. on staff of Gov. Goldsborough of Md. Vice-pres. bd. of trustees Sheppard & Enoch Pratt Hosp.; mem. advisory bd. Womens Hosp. of Md. Mem. Soc. of Descendants of the Signers of the Declaration of Independence. Democrat. Episcopalian. Clubs: Metropolitan (Washington, D.C.); Maryland (Baltimore); Green Spring Valley Hunt (Garrison, Md.). Home: Stevenson, Md. Office: 25 S. Calvert St., Baltimore, Md.

BREWSTER, Benjamin Harris, III, mfr.; b. Narbeth, Pa., Feb. 13, 1900; s. Benjamin Harris, Jr., and Elizabeth (Baugh) B.; grad. Gilman Sch., Baltimore, Md., 1917; A.B., Princeton U., 1921; m. Priscilla McIlvaine, Oct. 31, 1921; children—Benjamin Harris, IV, William McIlvaine. Second v.p. The Baugh Chem. Co., Baugh & Sons Co., The Baugh & Sons Co., Baugh & Sons Co. of Ohio, 1921-33, v.p., 1933-38, 1st v.p. since 1938, mem. bd. dirs. and exec. com. since 1921; mem. bd. dirs. and exec. com. Maryland Trust Co. since 1931. Served with U.S. Marine Corps, 1918; mem. State Aviation Commn. of Md. since 1928 (reappointed twice). Episcopalian. Clubs: Maryland, Merchants (Baltimore); Green Spring Valley Hunt (Garrison, Md.); Ivy (Princeton, N.J.). Racquet and Tennis (N.Y. City). Home: Brooklandville, Md. Office: 25 S. Calvert St., Baltimore, Md.

BREWSTER, C. Barton; pres. Provident Title Co.; also officer or dir. various other companies. Home: 8715 Shawnee St., Chestnut Hill. Office: 1201 Chestnut St., Philadelphia, Pa.

BREWSTER, Ethel Hampson, coll. prof.; b. Chester, Pa., July 3, 1886; d. Joseph Fergus and Emma Jane (Hampson) B.; A.B., Swarthmore Coll., 1907; A.M., U. of Pa., 1911, Bennett fellow in classics, 1912-14, Ph.D., 1915; student, Sch. of Classical Studies, Am. Acad. in Rome, 1926-27; unmarried. Instr. in Latin, French and English, high sch., Chester, Pa., 1907-09; head of dept. classics, high sch., West Chester, Pa., 1909-12; instr. in Latin, Vassar Coll., 1914-16; asst. prof. Greek and Latin, Swarthmore Coll., 1916-24, also dean of women, 1921-28, asso. prof., 1924-28, prof. and chmn. of dept. classics since 1928, acting dean of the coll., 1932-1933; member American Philological Assn., Archæol. Inst. America, American Assn. University Profs., Am. Assn. Univ. Women, Phi Beta Kappa. Democrat. Contbr. to philol. and ednl. jours. Home: West House, Swarthmore, Pa.

BREWSTER, William, civil engring.; b. Plymouth, Mass., June 9, 1878; s. James B. and Martha (Stoddard) B.; B.S. in M.E., Mass. Inst. Tech., 1898; m. Mary Southgate, Oct. 1, 1904; children—William Jr., Walter Southgate, Mary Baylies (Mrs. Fanning Miles Hearon). Draftsman Otis Elevator Co., Boston and Plymouth, Mass., 1898-1900; engaged in tobacco bus. in Cuba, 1901-03; 1st asst. engr., Dept. of Public Works, Republic of Cuba, 1903-05; supt. with contractor highway constrn., Havana and Pinar del Rio, Cuba, 1905-08; with Underwriters Salvage Co., New York City, 1908-09; with highway dept. Borough of Manhattan, N.Y., 1910-14; supt. E. H. Brown, Inc., on bridge and rd. constrn., N.Y. and N.J., 1915-17; mech. engr., Gillespie Loading Co., Morgan, N.J., 1917-19; with U.S. Bur. Pub. Rds., Charleston, W.Va., since 1919, sr. highway engr.; vice-pres. and dir. Lewisburg Ice Cream Co.; pres. and dir. General Lewis Hotel Co., Lewisburg, W. Va. Trustee Pilgrim Soc., Plymouth, Mass. Mem. Am. Soc. Civil Engrs., Am. Assn. Engrs.,

Soc. of Mayflower Descs. Unitarian. Mason (K.T., Shriner). Elk. Club: Elks (Charleston). Home: 2440 Kanawha St. Office: 1340 Wilson St., Charleston, W.Va.

BRICKER, Sacks; clin. instr. rhinolaryngology, Temple U.; asso. otorhinolaryngologist Jewish Hosp.; rhinolaryngologist Temple U. Hosp. Address: 1101 W. Wyoming Av., Philadelphia, Pa.

BRIDGE, Edward Mervin, physician; b. Hazardville, Conn., Dec. 10, 1901; s. Howard Stephen and Alice (Parsons) B.; B.S., Northwestern U., Evanston, Ill., 1923; M.D., Harvard U. Med. Sch., 1926; m. Ruth Reynolds, 1928; children—Seth Reynolds, William Mervin, Ann Elizabeth, Judith Allen. Interne Mass. General Hosp., Boston, 1926-27; Johns Hopkins Hosp., Baltimore, 1927-28; asst. in pediatrics, Johns Hopkins U. Med. Sch., 1928-31, asso. in pediatrics since 1931. Mem. Am. Pediatric Soc., Soc. for Pediatric Research, Internat. League Against Epilepsy. Presbyn. Home: 2709 Cheswolde Rd., Baltimore, Md.

BRIDGE, Josiah, geologist; b. Norwood, O., July 17, 1890; s. Herbert Sage and Therese (Hill) B.; A.B., University of Cincinnati, 1913; M.S., U. of Chicago, 1917; Ph.D., Princeton, 1929; m. Lucy Atwater Brown, June 5, 1918; children—Herbert Sage, Richard Benedict, James Andrew. Asst. in geol. dept., U. of Cincinnati, 1913-14; instr. in geol. lab., Mo. Sch. of Mines, 1914-15; geologist Standard Oil Co. of Calif., 1919-20; asst. prof. of geology Mo. Sch. of Mines, 1920-24, asso. prof., 1925-30; paleontologist U.S. Geol. Survey since 1930. Served as 2d lt., U.S. Army, 1917-18, 1st lt., 1918-19. Mem. Geol. Soc. America, Paleontological Society America, Sigma Xi. Home: 40 Columbia Av., Takoma Park, Md. Office: National Museum, Washington, D.C.

BRIDGES, Henry Percival, v.p. Pa. Glass Sand Corpn.; b. Hancock, Md., Jan. 24, 1878; s. Robert and Priscilla (Breathitt) B.; grad. Hancock (Md.) High Sch., 1895, Hampden-Sydney Coll., Va., 1900; grad. Bryant & Stratton Business Coll., 1902; LL.D., U. of Md. Law Sch., 1907; m. Shelly Thomas, May 22, 1922; children—Henry Perival, Shelly Powell. Practiced law in Baltimore, 25 yrs.; in glass sand business with Nelson Perin to 1924, bought Mr. Perin out, 1924, and left Baltimore, running business up to 1927; consolidated 6 cos. into Pa. Glass Sand Corpn., 1927, and since v.p. and dir.; chmn. bd. Hancock Bank. Democrat. Presbyn. (elder Hancock Ch.). Clubs: Maryland (Baltimore); sec., treas. and gov. Woodmont Rod and Gun, Hancock, Md. (visited by 6 presidents of U.S.). Home: Hancock, Md.; also Johnson City, Tenn. Office: Berkeley Springs, W.Va.

BRIDGES, William Arthur, M.D.; b. Cleveland Co., N.C., Oct. 28, 1880; s. Asbury Newton and Sarah Ann (Harrill) B.; B.S., Wake Forest Coll., 1913; M.D., U. of Md., 1915; m. Serena Selfe, July 20, 1918. Interne Baltimore City Hosps., 1915-16; asst. physician Eudowood Sanatorium, Towson, Md., 1916-18; examiner chest dept. and tuberculosis Hosp., U.S.A. Med. Corps, 1918-19; ward work, Camp Wadsworth, S.C.; spl. Lt. Hosp., 1919; physician Federal Bd. for Vocational Edn., Sept.-Nov. 1919; med. dir. Md. Tuberculosis Assn., 1919-20; supt. Eudowood Sanatorium since Jan. 1, 1921; asst. physician Tuberculosis Dispensary, Johns Hopkins Hosp., 1920-29; clinician Md. Tuberculosis Assn., part time since 1929. Mem. Md. Tuberculosis Assn. (dir. since 1937), N.C. Soc. of Baltimore (pres. 1935-36), Baltimore Co. Med. Assn., (pres. 1924), Med. and Chirurg. Faculty of Md., Nat. Tuberculosis Assn., Am. Sanatorium Assn., Baltimore Co. Pub. Health Assn.; fellow A.M.A., Am. Coll. Chest Physicians. Independent Democrat. Baptist (deacon). Club: Rotary (pres. 1936-37). Address: Towson, Md.

BRIEN, Donald Gray, wholesale and retail men's shoes; b. Boston, Mass., Jan. 20, 1895; s. William C. and Abbie (Hiltz) B.; student pub. schs. and High Sch. of Commerce, Boston, Mass.; m. Louise Lerch, July 27, 1932; 1 son, Robert Lerch. Engaged in business of wholesale and retail men's shoes since 1913; pres.

Brien, Smith and Royer, Inc., Greensburg and McKeesport, Pa., since 1914; treas. Brien Co. Served in U.S.N. during World War. Republican. Episcopalian. Home: 536 Briarcliff Rd. Office: 1251 Union Trust Bldg., Pittsburgh, Pa.

BRIGGS, Charles Albert, lumber mfg.; b. Forest Co., Pa., Apr. 26, 1876; s. George L. and Eliza (Walton) B.; ed. country schs.; m. Lucy Belle Ball, Sept. 12, 1901. Began as laborer in lumber camps, foreman, 1893, later gen. supt.; part owner and gen. mgr. various cos.; pres. and gen. mgr. Charles A. Briggs Lbr. and Mfg. Co., wholesale flooring, trim and structural lumber, Scottdale, Pa., since 1932. Republican. Methodist. Mason (K.T., 32°, Shriner). Club: Masonic. Home: Scottdale, Pa.

BRIGGS, Frankland, lawyer; b. Trenton, N.J., June 28, 1877; s. Frank O. (senator of N.J., 1907-13) and Emily Agnes (Allison) B.; student State Model Sch., Trenton, N.J., 1886-94; A.B., Princeton U., 1898; LL.B., Harvard, 1901; m. Anne Cochran Hollifield, Nov. 5, 1903 (died Nov. 17, 1938). Admitted to N.Y. bar, 1901, and began practice in New York City; atty. for Fidelity Trust Co., Newark, N.J., 1903-09; returned to New York practice, 1909; with legal dept. New York Telephone Co., 1913-27; vice-pres., dir. and gen. counsel N.J. Bell Telephone Co. since 1927; mem. bd. mgrs. Howard Savings Instn. Trustee N.J. Hist. Soc. Mem. Soc. of Colonial Wars, Sons of the Revolution. Republican. Clubs: Essex (Newark, N.Y.); Princeton (New York). Home: 560 Mt. Prospect Av., Newark, N.J. Office: 540 Broad St., Newark, N.J.

BRIGGS, George Weston, clergyman, educator; b. North Branch, Mich., Sept. 21, 1874; s. David C. and Emily E. (Weston) B.; B.S., Northwestern U., 1902, M.S., 1905; fellow U. of Calif., 1911-12, Johns Hopkins, 1914-15; grad. study, Columbia, 1922-23; m. Annie Mabel Montgomery, July 22, 1903 (died May 19, 1904); m. 2d, Mary Ames Hart, Dec. 24, 1907; children—David Keith, George Selden, Esther Emily, Janet Mary. Teacher pub. schs., in Mich., 1891-96; began to preach, 1896, ordained ministry M.E. Ch., 1904; missionary in India, 1903-25; prof. English lit., Reid Christian Coll., India, 1908-09; asst. prof. mathematics, Coll. of the Pacific, 1912-14, and prin. of acad., 1913-14; asso. prof. English Bible and philosophy, Goucher Coll., 1914-15 (leave of absence from missionary work); mem. faculty Drew U. since 1925, was prof. history of religions and lecturer in mathematics in Brothers Coll. (a part of Drew Univ.). Dir. and sec. Internat. Save the Children Fund. Served as military chaplain Non-Conformist British Troops in India, 1907-08, 1916-19. Exec. sec. Representative Council of Missions, United Provinces, India, and mem. Indian Nat. Representative Council of Missions, 1919-21. Mem. Am. Oriental Soc., Am. Anthrop. Assn., Delta Sigma Rho. Mason. Club: Oriental (New York) Author: The Chamars, 1920; Gorakhnath and the Kanphata Yogis, 1937. Home: 75 Green Village Rd., Madison, N.J.*

BRIGGS, Leon W., v.p. Superior Steel Corpn.; b. Phila., Pa., Aug. 18, 1895; s. George W. and Anna M. (Cole) B.; B.A. Swarthmore Coll.; m. A. Ina Carey, Oct. 15, 1919. V.p. Superior Steel Corpn. since 1936. Home: Schenley Apts. Office: Grant Bldg., Pittsburgh, Pa.

BRIGHAM, Carl Campbell, prof. psychology; b. Marlboro, Mass., May 4, 1890; s. Charles Francis and Ida (Campbell) B.; grad. Marlboro High Sch., 1908; Litt.B., Princeton, 1912, A.M., 1913, Ph.D., 1916; m. Elizabeth Duffield, Feb. 10, 1923; 1 dau., Elizabeth Hollister. Began as coll. instr., 1916; asst. to chief, Federal Bd. for Vocational Edn., 1919-20; asst. prof. psychology, Princeton, 1920-24, asso. prof., 1924-27, prof. since 1928. Adviser Canadian Mil. Hosps., 1917; 1st lt. Tank Corps, 1917-18. Mem. A.A.A.S., Am. Psychol. Assn. (sec. 1929-31), Social Science Research Council. Clubs: Nassau, Quadrangle (Princeton); Princeton (New York). Author: Two Studies in Mental Tests, 1917; Study of American Intelligence, 1923; Study of Error, 1932. Contbr. to scientific publs. Home: 114 Mercer St., Princeton, N.J.

BRIGHT, Alan, registrar; b. Pittsburgh, Pa., Feb. 19, 1888; s. John Graham and Duty (Mendenhall) B.; B.S. in Elec. Engring., Carnegie Inst. Tech., 1911; m. Helen Emilie Demmler, Nov. 23, 1916; children—Martha, Thomas, Frederick, Lois. Illuminating engr., specialist in outdoor illumination, Macbeth-Evans Glass Co., 1911-17; illuminating engr. Westinghouse Lamp Co., 1917-18; registrar, Carnegie Inst. Tech. since 1918. Dir. Y.M.C.A., Pittsburgh; dir. Allegheny Co. Scholarship Assn.; v.p. bd. dirs. Avonworth Sch. Dist. Mem. Am. Assn. Collegiate Registrars (nat. treas. 1928-30, pres.. 1935-36), Beta Theta Pi, Phi Kappa Phi. Republican. Methodist. Home: 134 Oliver Av., Ensworth, Pa. Office: Carnegie Inst. of Technology, Schenley Park, Pittsburgh, Pa.

BRIGHT, Stanley, lawyer; b. Pottsville, Pa., Apr. 2, 1880; s. Joseph Coleman and Jane Linn (Irwin) B.; student Lawrenceville (N.J.) pub. schs.; A.B., Princeton U., 1902; LL.B., U. of Pa. Law Sch., 1905; m. Sarah Hood Gilpin, of Philadelphia, June 3, 1909; children—Stanley, Joseph Coleman, Sarah Gilpin (Mrs. Robert Burkham), Louisa (Mrs. William Henry Peace, 2d), J. Gilpin. Admitted to bar, 1905; pres. Bright & Co., Reading, Pa.; partner J. C. Bright Co. Mem. Family Welfare Assn. of America. Mem. Zeta Psi. Republican. Clubs: Rittenhouse, Racquet (Philadelphia). Home: Cedar Hill Farm. Office: 8th and Elm Sts., Reading, Pa.

BRIGHTMAN, Harold Warren, dept. store exec.; b. Fall River, Mass., Nov. 5, 1889; s. Charles P. and Abbie Jane B.; A.B., Harvard U., 1911; m. Florence Pennington, Jan. 28, 1914; children—Emerson Eliot, Robert Lloyd. Successively, stock boy, credit office, asst. to gen. mdse. mgr., divl. mdse. mgr., Wm. Filene's Sons Co., Boston, Mass., 1911-24; divl. mdse. mgr., Abraham & Straus, Brooklyn, N.Y., 1924-28, Gimbel Bros., N.Y., 1928-31; basement mdse. mgr., L. Bamberger & Co., Newark, N.J., 1931-36, gen. mdse. mgr. since 1936, vice-pres. and dir. since 1937. Chmn. bd. trustees, Nat. Consumer-Retailer Council. Chmn. Consumer Relations Com., dir. Mdse Div., Nat. Retail Dry Goods Assn. Mem. N.J. Hist. Soc., N.J. Rep. Club, Alpha Phi Sigma. Republican. Methodist. Mason. Clubs: Essex, Downtown (Newark); Harvard of N.Y. and N.J.; Bay Head Yacht (mem. regatta com.). Contbr. many articles and many pub. addresses on subject of cooperation and better understanding between Business and the Consuming Public. Home: 140 Forest Av., Glen Ridge. Office: L. Bamberger & Co., Newark, N.J.

BRILE, Lawrence Miller, mfg. sheet aluminum; b. Spokane, Wash., Feb. 12, 1893; s. John Jonas and Minnie (Geiger) B.; student Louisville (Ky.) Male High Sch., 1907-11, Jefferson Sch. of Law (Louisville), 1911-13; m. Fannie Mollie Rosenthal, Feb. 26, 1913; children—Ruth Elizabeth, Bernice Elaine, Betty Lou. Employed in office work, 1911-13; sales mgr. U.S. Reduction Co., East Chicago, Ind., 1913-16; v.p. United Smelting & Aluminum Co., New Haven, Conn., 1916-19; pres. Brile & Ratner, Inc., N.Y. City, 1920-23; sales mgr. National Smelting Co., Cleveland, O., 1923-26; pres. Fairmont Aluminum Co., rollers and mfg. sheet aluminum, Fairmont, W.Va., since 1926. Dir. Fairmont Y.M.C.A., Red Cross, Chamber of Commerce, Community Chest, all of Fairmont, W.Va. Pres. bd. govs. Jewish Student Foundation, W.Va. Univ., Morgantown, W.Va. Hon. pres. W.Va. Council of B'nai B'rith; first vice-pres. dist. number 3 B'nai B'rith (1939). Republican. Jewish religion. Clubs: Kiwanis, Elks (Fairmont). Author: (verse) Israel and Other Poems (for pub. 1939). Contbr. verse. Lecturer and pub. speaker. Home: 435 Walnut Av. Office: Speedway, Fairmont, W.Va.

BRILLHART, David H., engring. exec.; b. York Co., Pa., Nov. 16, 1885; s. David Y. and Mary Alice (Herbst) B.; student Juniata Coll.; C.E., Lehigh U., Bethlehem, Pa.; m. Elizabeth Lehr, Nov. 11, 1923; children—Elizabeth Lehr, Mary Irene, David W., Andrew L. With engring. dept. C. & N.-W. Ry., 1906-09; engr. Griffin Carwheel Co., 1909-12; chief estimator, supt. and gen. mgr. Bethlehem (Pa.) Fabricators, 1912-19; pres. Brillhart Bros. Contracting Co., Bethlehem, Pa., 1919-23; pres. F. H. Clement & Co., engrs. and contractors, Bethlehem, Pa., since 1923; pres. E. P. Wilbur Trust Co., 1934-35; pres. Union Bank & Trust Co. of Bethlehem, Bethlehem Globe Times Pub. Co., Packer Coal Co.; dir. Times Pub. Co., East Sugar Loaf Coal Co., Bethlehem Hotel Corpn. Pres. bd. of trustees St. Luke's Hosp., Bethlehem, Pa.; dir. Bethlehem and Allentown (Pa.) Children's Home, Northampton Co. Tuberculosis Soc.; dir. and vice chmn. Northampton Co. Dept. of Pub. Assistance; vice chmn. Bethlehem Community Chest Drive; trustee First Presbyn. Ch. of Bethlehem. Mem. Bethlehem Chamber of Commerce (dir.; ex-pres.), Northampton Economy League (dir.). Presbyterian. Clubs: Bethlehem, Rotary, Waldheim (Bethlehem, Pa.); Saucon Valley Country (dir.). Home: Windfield, Bath Rd. Office: Union Bank Bldg., Bethlehem, Pa.

BRINDLE, Harry; mem. law firm Brindle & Brindle. Address: Hagerstown, Md.

BRINKER, William Earle, Jr., chem. engr.; b. Wilkinsburg, Pa., Mar. 14, 1906; s. William Earle and Clara Marguerite (Kendall) B.; grad. Wilkinsburg (Pa.) High Sch., 1924; B.S. in Chem. Engring., U. of Pittsburgh, 1928, grad. student, 1929-38; m. Dorothea E. Anderson, Sept. 2, 1931; children—Nathalia Dorothea, William Scott, John Anderson. Thermal engr. Dressler Tunnel Kilns, Inc., Cleveland, O., 1928-29; instr. chem. engring., U. of Pittsburgh, 1929-35, asst. prof., 1935-37, asso. prof. since 1937; industrial fellow, Mellon Inst. Industrial Research, 1936-37. Mem. Am. Inst. Chem. Engrs., Am. Chem. Soc., Phi Gamma Delta, Omicron Delta Kappa, Sigma Tau, Sigma Xi, Phi Lambda Upsilon. Republican. Presbyterian. Club: Faculty (U. of Pittsburgh). Home: 516 Franklin Av., Wilkinsburg, Pa.

BRINKMANN, Heinrich Wilhelm, asso. prof. mathematics; b. Hannover, Germany, Nov. 29, 1898; s. Christian and Else (Heimsoth) B.; came to U.S., 1910; A.B., Stanford (Calif.) U., 1920; A.M., Harvard 1923, Ph.D., 1925; m. Elizabeth Kellogg, June 18, 1932; 1 dau., Betsy Jane (adopted 1938). Instr. mathematics, Harvard, 1924-27, asst. prof., 1927-33; asso. prof. mathematics, Swarthmore (Pa.) Coll., since 1933. Mem. Am. Math. Soc., Math. Assn. America. Home: 512 N. Chester Rd., Swarthmore, Pa.

BRINLEY, Charles Edward, pres. Baldwin Locomotive Works; b. Phila., Pa., Feb. 25, 1878; s. Charles A. and Mary Goodrich (Frothingham) B.; grad. Groton (Mass.) Sch., 1896; A.B., Yale, 1900; Ph.B., Yale Scientific Sch., 1901; m. Helen Frazier, June 6, 1908; children—Mary Frothingham, Charles Edward (deceased), William West Frazier, George. With Am. Pulley Co. since July 1901, beginning as timekeeper, vice-pres., 1908-19, pres., 1919-39, chmn. of bd. since 1939; acting v.p. Baldwin Locomotive Works, Sept.-Dec. 1938, pres. and dir. since Jan. 1, 1939; chmn. of bd. Midvale Co., Pelton Water Wheel Co.; pres. Baldwin-Southwark Corpn., Standard Steel Works Co., Whitcomb Locomotive Co.; dir. Gen. Steel Castings Corpn., Liberty Mutual Ins. Co., Phila. Mfrs. Mutual Fire Ins., Co., United Gas Improvement Co., Phila. Electric Co.; trustee Penn Mutual Life Ins. Co.; mem. bd. mgrs. Western Saving Fund Soc. Trustee Drexel Inst. of Tech. Mem. Am. Soc. Mech. Engrs. Republican. Episcopalian. Clubs: Sunnybrook Golf (Flourtown, Pa.); Midday (Phila.). Home: Montgomery Av., Chestnut Hill, Philadelphia. Address: Paschall Post Office, Philadelphia, Pa.

BRINTON, Anna Shipley Cox (Mrs. Howard Haines Brinton), educationalist; b. San Jose, Calif., Oct. 19, 1887; d. Charles E. and Lydia Shipley (Bean) Cox; A.B., Stanford University, 1909, Ph.D., 1917; LL.D., Mills College, 1937; m. Howard Haines Brinton, July 23, 1921; children—Lydia Shipley, Edward, Catharine Morris, Joan Mary. Instructor in Latin, College of the Pacific, 1909-12, Stanford, 1912-13; student Am. Acad. in Rome, 1913-14; instr., later prof. Latin, Mills Coll., 1916-22; with Friends student relief in Germany, 1920; prof. Latin, Earlham Coll., 1922-28; acting prof. classics, Stanford, summers, 1927, 28; prof. archæology, Mills Coll., 1928-36, dean of the faculty, 1933-36;

research fellow, Woodbrooke, Selly Oak Colleges, Eng., 1931-32; asso. dir., Pendle Hill Graduate Center for Religious and Social Studies since 1936. Member American Philological Association; Friends of Far Eastern Art. Member Soc. of Friends. Author: Maphaeus Vegius and his Thirteenth Book of the Aeneid, 1930; Descensus Averno (fourteen woodcuts from the illustrated Virgil of Sebastian Brant), 1931; A. Pre-Raphaelite Aeneid, 1934. Contbr. articles in Classical Jour., Art and Archæology, Friends' periodicals, etc. Home: Pendle Hill, Wallingford, Pa.

BRINTON, Caleb C.; in practice of law since 1895. Address: Carlisle, Pa.

BRINTON, Christian, art critic, lecturer; b. Homestead Farm, W. Chester, Pa., Sept. 17, 1870; s. Joseph Hill and Mary (Herr) Brinton; B.A., Haverford (Pa.) Coll. (Phi Beta Kappa), 1892, M.A., 1906, Litt.D. from Haverford Coll., 1914; studied universities of Heidelberg and Paris, and École du Louvre. Asso. editor The Critic, 1900-04; advisory editor Art in America, 1915. Mem. Kunsthistorisches Institut, Florence. Associate of American Scandinavian Foundation; mem. American-Russian Inst., Phila. Fellow Pa. Museum of Art; mem. Internat. Jury of Awards, Dept. of Fine Arts, San Francisco Expn., 1915. Decorated, 1917, by King Gustav V, of Sweden, Knight of the Royal Order of Vasa; by King Albert of Belgium, Officer of Order of the Crown, 1931. Mem. of the Belgian League of Honor. Dir. foreign art, Sesquicentennial Internat. Expn., Phila., 1926. Clubs: The Players (New York); The Centaur (London). Author: Modern Artists, 1908; Catalogue, the Ignacio Zuloaga Exhibition, 1909; Die Entwicklung der Amerikanischen Malerei (Berlin), 1910; Masterpieces of American Painting (Berlin, Germany, and New York City), 1910; Catalogue, The Walter Greaves Exhibition, 1912; Catalogue, The Scandinavian Exhibition, 1912; La Peinture Américaine (Paris), 1913; Catalogue, The Constantin Meunier Exhibition, 1913; Introduction to History of Russian Painting, 1916; Catalogue, The Swedish Exhibition, 1916; Impressions of the Art at the Panama-Pacific Exposition, 1916; Catalogue, The Ignacio Zuloaga Exhibition, 1916; Catalogue, The Boris Anisfeld Exhibition, 1918; Catalogue, The Official Exhibition of War Paintings and Drawings by British Artists, 1919; Catalogue, Nicolas Roerich Exhibition, 1920; Introduction to History of Scandinavian Art, 1922; Catalogue, The Russian Exhibition, 1923; Catalogue, The Ivan Mestrovic Exhibition, 1924; Catalogue, The Italian Exhibition, 1926; Catalogue, Soviet Russian Art Exhibition, New York, 1929; Catalogue, The Belgian Exhibition, 1930; The Face of Soviet Art, 1934; Catalogue, The Soviet Art Exhibition, 1934; The Poster in Time and Space, 1937; Gustavius Hesselius, 1938. Contr. Iconographic Dictionary of Art; articles on art to Internat. Studio, Art in America, L'Art et les Artistes, La Renaissance, Mag. of Art, Vanity Fair, Scandinavian Review, etc. Home: Quarry House, West Chester, Pa.

BRINTON, Clarence Cresson, pres. Germantown Trust Co.; b. Phila., Pa., Apr. 1, 1877; s. Robert Morton and Octavia Eliza (Fosdick) B.; student Germantown (Pa.) Acad., 1886-93; A.B., U. of Pa., 1897; m. Mary Merrick Williams, June 20, 1936. With transportation dept. Pa. RR., Phila., 1897-99; junior clk. Germantown (Pa.) Trust Co., 1899-1903, receiving teller, 1903-06, paying teller, 1906-10, asst. treas., 1910-11, sec. and treas., 1911-13, v.p. and treas., 1913-24, v.p., 1924-25, pres. and dir. since 1925. Vice-pres. bd. of trustees Germantown Acad.; vestryman St. Luke's Ch., Germantown, 1910-35, accounting warden, 1915-35. Mem. Loyal Legion, Mayflower Soc., Colonial Soc. of Pa., Hist. Soc. of Pa., Acad. of Fine Arts, Acad. of Natural Sciences. Republican. Episcopalian. Clubs: University, Germantown Cricket, Phila. Country (Phila.). Home: The Kenilworth, Alden Park, Germantown. Office: Chelten and Germantown Avs., Philadelphia, Pa.

BRINTON, Henry Longfellow, newspaper editor; b. Oxford, Pa., Aug. 29, 1903; s. Douglas Emerson and Hettie (Hickman) B.; grad. Oxford High Sch., 1921; grad. State Teachers Coll.,

West Chester, Pa., 1925; student Temple U., Phila., summers 1922, 24, winter 1930-31, U. of Pa., winters 1925-26, 1931-32, Social Service Seminar, New York, summer 1925; m. Helen Elizabeth Coxe, Aug. 20, 1927; children—Henry Coxe, Alice Carey. School teacher Chester Co. and Bucks Co., Pa., 1921-23; elementary prin., Willow Grove, Pa., 1925-26; social service work and teacher, New York, summer 1925, newspaper reporter Daily Local News, West Chester, Pa., 1926-31, mng. editor since 1931. Dir. Chester County Council, Boy Scouts of America. Mem. Tri-State Hist. Soc. (pres. since 1937), Phi Nu Delta. Republican. Presbyterian. Home: 323 S. Walnut St. Office: 12 S. High St., West Chester, Pa.

BRINTON, Howard Haines, dir. grad. school; b. West Chester, Pa., July 24, 1884; s. Edward and Ruthanna Haines (Brown) B.; B.A., Haverford (Pa.) Coll., 1904, M.A., 1905; M.A., Harvard, 1909; Ph.D., U. of Calif., 1925; m. Anna Shipley Cox, July 23, 1921; children—Lydia Shipley, Edward, Catharine Morris, Joan Mary. Instr. Friends Boarding Sch., Barnesville, O., 1906-08, Pickering Coll., Newmarket, Ont., Can., 1909-15; prof. mathematics, Guilford (N.C.) Coll., 1915-19, acting pres., 1917-18, dean, 1918-19; publicity dir. Am. Friends Service Com., 1919-20; dir. of child feeding in plebiscite area, Upper Silesia, 1920-21; prof. physics, Earlham Coll., 1922-28; prof. religion, Mills Coll., 1928-36; lecturer in Biblical lit. Bryn Mawr Coll. since 1936; dir. Pendle Hill Grad. Sch. for Religious and Social Study, Wallingford, Pa., since 1936, acting dir. and lecturer, 1934-35. Swarthmore lecturer, London, Eng., 1931; research fellow and lecturer, Woodbrook Coll., Selly Oak Coll., Eng., autumn 1931; lecturer in philosophy, Haverford Coll., spring 1932; William Penn lecturer, Phila., 1932, 38, lecturer in history religion, Bryn Mawr Coll., Pa., 1934-35. Mem. Am. Philos. Assn., Soc. Bibl. Lit. and Exegesis, Phi Beta Kappa. Mem. Soc. Friends. Author: Vocal Ministry and Quaker Worship, 1929; The Mystic Will, A Study of the Philosophy of Jacob Boehme, 1930; Creative Worship, 1931; A Religious Solution to the Social Problem, 1934. Editor and contbr. to "Children of Light" (studies in honor of Rufus M. Jones), 1938; Divine-Human Society, 1938. Contbr. religious articles. Home: Pendle Hill, Wallingford, Pa.

BRINTON, Jasper Yeates, judge; b. Phila., Pa., Oct. 5, 1878; s. John Hill (M.D.) and Sarah (Ward) B.; grad. Episcopal Acad., Phila., 1894; A.B., U. of Pa., 1898, LL.B., 1901; hon. A.M., Washington Coll., 1915; m. Alice B. McFadden; children—John, Pamela; m. 2d, Geneva Febiger, Sept. 10, 1927. Admitted to Pa. bar 1901, and began practice at Phila.; mem. firm Conlen, Brinton & Acker, 1901-21. Assistant United States attorney, Eastern Dist. of Pa., 1904-12; sometime counsel Pa. Dept. Labor and Industry; apptd. solicitor U.S. Shipping Bd., 1921; justice Court of Appeals, Mixed Courts of Egypt since 1921. Maj., judge adv. gens'. dept., O.R.C., 1917, detailed to service in provost marshal gen'.s office, Washington, D.C.; judge adv. and renting, requisition and claims officer, rank of lt. col., France and Eng., Mar. 1918-Aug. 1919; mem. Am. Mil. Mission to Armenia, 1919; lt. col., O.R.C.; certificate meritorious service; Legion of Honor (France). Former mgr. Pa. House of Refuge and pres. Pa. Child Labor Assn. Mem. Am. Bar Assn., Am. Soc. Internat. Law, Internat. Law Assn., Phi Kappa Sigma, Phi Beta Kappa (1933). Republican. Clubs: Coffee House (New York); Alexandria (Egypt) Sporting. Author: The Mixed Courts of Egypt, 1930. Contbr. to Am. Jour. Internat. Law, Current History, etc. Home: 1423 Spruce St., Philadelphia, Pa., and Cour d' Appel Mixte, Alexandria, Egypt.

BRISCO, Norris Arthur, college prof.; b. Napanee, Ont., July 23, 1875; s. Robert McIntyre and Mary (Ham) B.; A.B., Queen's U., Kingston, Ont., 1898 (first class honors in history), A.M., 1900 (first class honors and Gowan research scholarship in polit. science); scholarship in economics, Columbia, 1902, Schiff fellow in economics, 1903-04; Ph.D., Columbia, 1907; Fellow Royal Hist. Soc., 1909-14; m. May Bartlett, June 29, 1907; children—Norris B.,

Ruth, Margaret. Tutor in history, 1905-07, instr. in economics, 1907-15, Coll. City of New York; prof. polit. economy and sociology and head of dept., 1915, prof. commerce and head dept. of economics, sociology and commerce, 1916, dir. Sch. of Commerce, 1917-20, State U. of Iowa; prof. of merchandising and director New York U. Sch. of Retailing since 1920, dean, 1928. Member American Economic Association, Eta Mu Pi (hon. mem.), Artus and Delta Sigma Pi fraternities. Republican. Episcopalian. Mason. Club: Authors' (London). Author: The Economic Policy of Robert Walpole, 1907; Economics of Business, 1913, Japanese edit., 1915; Economics of Efficiency, 1914, Japanese edit., 1916; Fundamentals of Salesmanship, 1916; Retail Salesmanship, 1920; Retail Salesmanship Source Book, 1920; (with John W. Wingate) Retail Buying, 1925; Retail Receiving Practice (with same), 1925; Principles of Retailing (with others), 1927; Retail Credit Procedure (with others), 1929; Store Salesmanship (with O. P. Robinson and Grace Griffith); Store Management, 1931; Retail Accounting (with Dr. C. K. Lyons), 1934; Retailing, 1935; (with John W. Wingate) Buying for Retail Stores, 1937; (with John W. Wingate) Elements of Retail Merchandising, 1938. Editor of Retailing Series, 1925; editor of Canada sect., Book of Knowledge, 1911-14; editor Efficiency Society Jour., 1915-17; editor Medium Priced Retailing series, 1937. Contbr. to scientific and business publs. Home: 33 Norwood Av., Summit, N.J.

BRISCOE, Philander B.; mem. law firm Briscoe & Jones. Address: Union Trust Bldg., Baltimore, Md.

BRISTOL, Edward Newell, book publisher; b. Morris, Conn., April 22, 1860; s. Alva Myron and Mary (Judd) B.; editor Williston Sem., Easthampton, Mass., and under pvt. tutors; m. Minna Baumgarten, Dec. 29, 1885 (died 1929); children—Arthur Edward, Lucy Friederike (Mrs. Edward N. Goodwin), Herbert Greene, Ralph Buffum. Began as agt. for Henry Holt & Co., New York, 1882, dir. and sec. same, 1903-18, v.p. and gen. mgr., 1918-26, pres. since 1926; v.p. Glen Ridge (N.J.) Realty Co. Mem. bd. dirs. Nat. Book Publishers' Assn. Mem. Borough Council, Bd. of Edn. and trustee Pub. Library. (all of Glen Ridge). Mem. Am. Hist. Assn., Metropolitan Mus. of Art., Am. Polit. Science Assn. Conglist. Clubs: City, Players (New York); Glen Ridge Country. Home: 64 Melrose Pl., Montclair, N.J. Office: 257 Fourth Av., New York, N.Y.

BRISTOL, Leverett Dale, M. D., health dir.; b. Chicago, June 2, 1880; s. Bishop Frank Milton (M.E. Ch.) and Nellie (Frisbie) B.; B.S., Wesleyan U., Middletown, Conn., 1903; M.D., Johns Hopkins, 1907; Dr. P.H., Harvard, 1917; m. Addie Louise Knox, June 27, 1907; children —Corabelle (Mrs. Richard Osborn Rice), Adelaide (Mrs. Livingston Lord Satterthwaite), Leverett Frisbie. Practiced in St. Paul, 1908-13; asso. prof. bacteriology, Syracuse U., 1913-14; prof. bacteriology, U. of N.D., and dir. state health labs., 1914-16; fellow and asst. Harvard Med. Sch., 1916-17; state commr. health, Me., 1917-21; prof. preventive medicine and pub. health, U. of Minn., 1922-23; dir. N.Y. State Health Demonstrations, 1923-29; health dir. Am. Telephone & Telegraph Co., since 1929. Surgeon (maj.) U.S. Public Health Service Reserve, World War. Mem. Committee on Neighborhood Health Development, New York; chmn., Lower West Side Dist. Health Com., New York; mem. bd. of dirs., New York Tuberculosis and Health Asso.; mem. exec. com. N.J. Tuberculosis League; vice-pres. N.J. Health and Sanitary Assn.; chmn. com. on industrial·diseases, N.J. Health and Welfare Conf. Trustee Wesleyan U., 1919-24. Mem. A.M.A., Am. Pub. Health Assn., A.A.A.S., Nat. Tuberculosis Assn., Am. Assn. of Industrial Physicians and Surgeons, Industrial Health Council, A.M.A.; honorary mem. Safety Engineers of Can.; mem. Sigma Xi, Phi Betta Kappa, Alpha Delta Phi, Alpha Kappa Kappa. Republican. Methodist. Contbr. numerous articles on med. subjects. Home: 19 Yale Terrace, Montclair, N.J. Office: 195 Broadway, New York, N.Y.

BRISTOW, William Harvey, educator; b. Nettleton, Mo., Oct. 9, 1897; s. Thomas Benjamin and Elizabeth May (Bacon) B.; grad. Breckenridge (Mo.) High Sch., 1916; B.S., Warrensburg (Mo.) State Teachers Coll., 1920; A.M., Teachers Coll., Columbia U., 1922, Ed.D., 1936; grad. student U. of Pa., 1934-35; m. Rosa Leah St. Clair, June 17, 1923; children—William Harvey, Elizabeth Anne, Rosemary St. Clair. Teacher, Breckenridge, Mo., 1916-17; prin. Knob Noster, Mo., 1919-20, Quapaw, Okla., 1920-21; dir. boys' work, Whittier House, Jersey City, N.J., 1922-23; supervising prin., Milford, Pa., 1923-25; asst. dir. secondary edn., Pa. Dept. Pub. Instr., 1925-30, dir., 1930-31, dep. supt. and dir. curriculum bureau, 1931-36; teacher summers, Teachers Coll., Warrensburg, Mo., 1920, Okla. U., 1923, Cornell U., 1933, George Washington U., 1936; specialist, conservation edn., U.S. Office of Edn., 1936; gen. sec. Nat. Congress of Parents and Teachers, 1936-38; forum leader U.S. Office of Edn., 1938-39; supervisor Training Sch., State Teachers Coll., Mansfield, Pa., 1939; dean of instrn., State Teachers Coll., Shippensburg, Pa., since June 1, 1939; lecturer on edn. at Ala., Okla., Ark. Univs., Pa. State Coll., Western Teachers Coll. Organizer first state program of emergency edn.; charter mem. Pa. State Employees Credit Union (mem. 1st bd. dirs.); organized Pa. Secondary Sch. Prins. Groups. Served in S.A.T.C., Ft. Sheridan, Ill., and Warrensburg, Mo., 1918. Mem. N.E.A. (Depts. Secondary Sch. Prins., Instrs. and Supervisors, Adult Edn.), Am. Assn. Sch. Adminstrs. (mem. 1940 Yearbook Commn.), Am. Adult Edn. Assn. (council of 100), Nat. Com. on Co-ordination in Secondary Edn., Joint Com. of N.E.A. and Am. Library Assn., Am. Ednl. Resarch Assn., Soc. for Study of Edn., Pa. State Edn. Assn., Pa. Hist. Soc., Curriculum Soc., Nat. Council of Parent Edn., Consumers Advisory Com. of Better Business Bureau, Phi Delta Kappa, Kappa Phi Kappa, Phi Sigma Pi, Kappa Delta Pi. Republican. Presbyterian. Mason. Clubs: Torch (Harrisburg, Pa.); Federal Schoolmen's (Washington, D.C.); West Shore Country (Camp Hill, Pa.). Author (thesis) A State Program of Secondary Education; Curriculum and Research Studies; editor Pa. Courses of Study; asso. editor Jr.-Sr. High Sch. Clearing House; asso. editor Adult Edn. Bulletin; contbr. World Book Encyclopedia; contbr. to ednl. jours. and yearbooks. Address: State Teachers College, Shippensburg, Pa.

BRITAN, Joseph Taylor, clergyman; b. Bethlehem, Ind., Feb. 11, 1873; s. George W. and Mary A. (Taylor) B.; A.B., Hanover (Ind.) Coll., 1897, A.M., 1900, D.D., 1913; student Lane Theol. Sem., Cincinnati, O., 1898-99, Auburn (N.Y.) Theol Sem., 1899-1901; student Hanover (Ind.) Coll., 1893-97; m. Annie Spencer George, Dec. 31, 1908. Teacher pub. sch., New Washington, Ind., 1892-93; prin. Union Acad., Anna, Ill., 1897-98; ordained to ministry of Presbyn. Ch., 1902; home missionary, Utah, 1901-03; asst. minister Central Presbyn. Ch., New York, 1903-06; pastor South Presbyn. Ch., Yonkers, N.Y., 1907-09, Central Presbyn. Ch., Columbus, O., 1909-25, First Presbyn, Ch., West Palm Beach, Fla., 1925-29; supply Summit Presbyn. Ch., Germantown, Pa., 1929-30; chaplain Presbyn. Hosp., Philadelphia, since 1930. Moderator Synod of Ohio, 1921. Mem. Eugene Field Soc., Nat. Assn. Authors and Journalists, Sigma Chi. Republican. Club: Union League (Philadelphia). Author: The Program of Peace, 1935; The Sunny Side of the Sick Room, 1939; also poems in Crown Anthology of Verse, 1937-38; contbr. poems and articles to papers and church mags. Home: 210 S. 39th St. Office: 51 N. 39th St., Philadelphia, Pa.

BRITT, Lillian Ann (Mrs. Robert A. Heinsohn), concert soprano; b. Live Oak, Fla.; d. Henry Hardy and Eliza Laetitia (Chesnutt) Britt; B.M., Flora MacDonald Coll. Conservatory, Red Springs, N.C., vocal study with Margaret Hecht, Atlanta, Ga., Conservatory; Guiseppe Agostini, Temple U.; m. Robert A. Heinsohn. Concert soprano, identified with music feds. and clubs in South, 1920-27; since 1930 associated with sister Nell Britt in recitals, specializing in costume recitals depicting different periods of Am. History; also lecturer on current books since 1936. Served as mem. Ga. State Dem. Com.; rec. sec. Ga. State Fed. Women's Clubs; vice-pres. bd. directors Talullah Falls Sch., Ga. Mem. Phila. Art Alliance, D.A.R.; hon. life mem. Worth Co., Ga., Confederate Vets. Assn., Saturday Morning Music Club, Macon, Ga., Kiwanis Club, Sylvester, Ga. Democrat. Presbyterian. Home: The Cambridge, Alden Park, Philadelphia, Pa.

BRITTAIN, James M.; partner law firm MacCoy, Brittain, Evans & Lewis; also dir. various companies. Office: Provident Trust Bldg., Philadelphia, Pa.

BRITTEN, Edwin F., Jr., pres. Monroe Calculating Machine Co. Address: 555 Mitchell St., Orange, N.J.

BRITTINGHAM, Thomas Evans, Jr.; pres. Mid Northern Investment Co.; officer or dir. many companies. Home: R. F. D. 1. Office: Delaware Trust Bldg., Wilmington, Del.

BROADDUS, Randolph Gwinn, surgeon; b. Chance, Va., Sept. 25, 1896; s. Julian G. and Elizabeth W. (Barksdale) B.; student Danville (Va.) Mil. Inst., 1909-13; M.D., Med. Coll. of Va., Richmond, Va., 1917; m. Ferne Halloran; children—Ferne Randolph, Virginia Gwinn. Interne Stetson Hosp., Phila., 1917; with U.S. Pub. Health Service, Alexandria, Va., 1919-20; in gen. practice of medicine, Chance, Va., 1920-22; mem. staff Hinton (W.Va.) Hosp., has served as sec. and treas.; mem. staff Raleigh Gen. Hosp., Beckley, W.Va., since 1929, now pres.; sec. and treas. Hinton Clinic. Served as 1st lt., M.R.C., 1917-18, at Evacuation Hosp. 29, 1918-19. Fellow Am. Coll. Surgeons, A.M.A.; mem. Am. Legion, Phi Beta Pi. Democrat. Episcopalian. Mason (32°, Shriner), Elk, Moose. Clubs: Black Knight Country (Beckley, W.Va.); Willow Wood Country (Hinton, W.Va.). Home: Hinton, W.Va. Office: Beckley, W.Va.

BROCK, Thomas Sleeper, clergyman, educator; b. Bridgeboro, N.J., Jan. 22, 1874; s. James Edwards and Suanna (Sleeper) B.; Ph.B., Ill. Wesleyan U., 1898; grad. New Brunswick (N.J.) Theol. Sem., 1908; B.D., Temple University, 1911, S.T.D., 1912; m. Carrie R. Iszard, Apr. 8, 1897; children—C. Lester, Dorothy Mae; m. 2d, Harriet G. Harper, March 15, 1932. Ordained ministry M.E. Ch., 1898; pastor successively at Lambertville, Burlington, Vineland, Camden and Atlantic City, N.J.; now supt. of Trenton District; also prof. homiletics, Sch. of Theology, Temple U., since 1924. Trustee Pennington (N.J.) Sem. Mem. Phi Beta Kappa, Delta Kappa Epsilon. Republican. Mason. Home: 236 Chestnut Av., Trenton, N.J.

BROCKBANK, John I., health officer; b. Kerseys, Pa., Feb. 3, 1858; s. William and Susannah (Kemmerer) B.; student Normal Sch., Edinboro, Pa., 1880, Baltimore U. Med. Sch., 1886; m. Marietta Faust, June 26, 1887; children—Leo R., Thomas William. Teacher pub. schs., Clearfield Co., Pa., 1878-84; in gen. practice of medicine at DuBois, Pa., since 1887; health officer, DuBois, since 1928. Coroner, Clearfield Co., Pa., 1902-04; mem. DuBois (Pa.) Bd. of Edn., 20 yrs.; mem. Non-Sectarian Pub. Library Bd. since orgn., 1922. Mem. Clearfield Co. Med. Soc. Republican. Roman Catholic. K.C. (Past Grand Knight). Club: Acorn (DuBois, Pa.). Address: 102 N. State St., DuBois, Pa.

BROCKWAY, Chauncey E., lawyer and banker; b. W. Williamsfield, O., Aug. 14, 1884; s. Emerson B. and Sara (Mowry) B.; A.B., Bucknell U., Lewisburg, Pa., 1907, A.M., 1908; m. Bessie Taylor, July 23, 1912; children—Robert T., Philip E., Frederic W. Admitted to Pa. bar, 1908, and since engaged in gen. practice of law at Sharon; mem. firm Brockway, Whitla and McKay, Sharon, Pa., since 1933; dir. First Nat. Bank, Sharon, Pa., since 1926, pres. since 1933; solicitor Sharon Sch. Dist. since 1926; dir. Shenango Valley Water Co. Served as past pres. and dir. Sharon Chamber of Commerce. Mem. Am., Pa., and Mercer Co. (pres. 1938) bar assns., Sigma Chi. Republican. Baptist. Clubs: Kiwanis, Country (Sharon, Pa.); Bankers (Pittsburgh). Home: 319 Buhl Boul. Office: First Nat. Bank Bldg., Sharon, Pa.

BRODEN, Edwin H., mfg. exec.; b. Cleveland, O., Nov. 13, 1877; s. Oscar F. and Caroline Jane (Cannell) B.; ed. grade and high sch., Cleveland, O., and spl. studies at Yale; m. Helen M. Rauch, July 3, 1901 (died 1913); 1 son, Edwin Rauch; m. 2d, Carolyn Elizabeth Miller, July 21, 1915; children—Richard Guffey, Willard Cannell. Engr. Brown Hoisting & Machine Co., Cleveland, 1894-95; chief draftsman H.P. Nail Co., 1895-98, Lake Shore Dist., Am. Steel & Wire Co., Cleveland, 1898-1901; asst. constrn. engr. Nat. Steel & Wire Co., New Haven, Conn., 1901-05; with Am. Steel & Wire Co. since 1905, as draftsman Newburgh Wire Works, 1905-06, chief draftsman Allentown (Pa.) Works, 1906-07, engr. attached to vice-pres. and gen. supt's. office, Pittsburgh, 1907, asst. supt. Rankin (Pa.) Works, 1907-13, supt. Braddock (Pa.) Works, 1913-16, supt. Rankin Works 1916-25, supt. Rankin and Braddock Works, 1925-28, mgr. Pittsburgh Dist. wire mills, 1928-33, mgr. Pittsburgh Dist. since 1933. Mem. Am. Soc. Mech. Engrs., Am. Iron & Steel Inst., Wire Assn. Republican. Presbyterian (trustee Edgewood, Pa., Ch.). Clubs: Metropolitan (Pittsburgh); Monongahela Valley Golf (Washington Co., Pa.); Edgewood (Pa.). Home: 132 Hawthorne St., Edgewood, Swissvale P.O. Pa. Office: 826 Frick Bldg., Pittsburgh, Pa.

BRODESSER, Frederick Anthony, state purchase commr. of N.J.; b. Elizabeth, N.J., Mar. 18, 1893; s. Christian Frederick and Rosa (Reif) B.; grad. Battin (N.J.) High Sch.; student Union Business Coll. and New York Law Sch.; m. Eleanor M. Furman, Oct. 2, 1936. Real estate and insurance since 1920; asst. sec. N.J. Senate, 1920-23; clerk House of Assembly, N.J., 1924-31, 1934-35; apptd. state purchase commr. for N.J., Jan. 20, 1936, for term 1936-41. Served as lt. Inf., U.S. Army, 1918-19; with A.E.F. Republican. Elk. Club: Suburban Golf (Union, N.J.) Office: 1143 E. Jersey St., Elizabeth, N.J.

BRODHEAD, George Milton, clergyman; b. Brodheadsville, Pa., May 21, 1857; s. Hon. Charles D. and Rachel (Keller) B.; A.B., Wesleyan U., Conn., 1882, A.M., 1885; D.D., Am. Univ., Washington, D.C., 1902; m. Clara, d. Rev. Dr. John F. Chaplain, 1887; children—Frank Chaplain, Rachel (wife of Rev. Samuel MacAdams), Charles Daniel, George Milton. Ordained ministry M.E. Ch., 1883; pastor, Moore's, Pa., 1882-85, Mt. Airy, Phila., 1885-88, E. Allegheny Av. Ch., Phila., 1888-91, Millersburg, Pa., 1891-94, Downingtown, 1894-95, Bethlehem, 1895-1900, Chestnut Hill, Phila., 1900-04, Fletcher Ch., Phila., 1904-07, Central Ch., Phila., 1907-10, Summerfield Ch., Phila., 1910-13, Bristol, Pa., 1913-16, Sayers Memorial Ch., Phila., 1916-24, Devereux Memorial Ch., 1924-27, Kensington Ch. since 1927. Chmn. Draft Bd., June 22, 1917-19. Mem. Psi Upsilon, Mystic Seven. Republican. Club: Union League. Home: 236 Winona Av., Germantown, Philadelphia, Pa.

BRODSTEIN, Ellis, lawyer; b. Phila., Pa., Jan. 4, 1896; s. Joseph and Anna (Rose) B.; student Reading (Pa.) High Sch., 1908-12; A.B., Lehigh U., Bethlehem, Pa., 1916; LL.B., U. of Pa. Law Sch., 1920; unmarried. Admitted to Berks Co. (Pa.) bar, 1920, Supreme Ct. of Pa., Superior Ct. of Pa., U.S. Dist. Ct., U.S. Circuit Ct. of Appeals, 1921; practiced under own name at Reading, Pa., since 1920. Served as sergt., 1st Class, M.C., U.S. Army, during World War; hon. disch., 1919. Dir. Kesher Zion Hebrew Sch., Kesher Zion Synagogue. Mem. Pa. Bar Assn. (rep. 23d Judicial Dist.; legal biography com.), Jewish Community Council (pres. 1936-38). Pi Lambda Phi. Republican. Jewish religion. B'nai B'rith (Lodge 768). Club: University (Reading, Pa.). Home: 25 S. 11th St. Office: Berks Co. Trust Bldg., Reading, Pa.

BRODY, Morton S.; attending urologist St. Peter's Gen. and Middlesex Gen. hosps.; mem. urol. dept. New York Post-Grad. Med. Sch. and Hosp. Address: 75 Livingston Av., New Brunswick, N.J.

BROEDEL, Max, educator; b. at Leipzig, Germany, June 8, 1870; s. Louis and Henrietta (Frenzel) B.; ed. Acad. Fine Arts, Leipzig; U. of Leipzig, 1886-90; came to U.S., 1894; m. Ruth Marian Huntington, Dec. 31, 1902; children—Elizabeth, Ruth (dec.), Carl, Elsa. Med. illustrator, anatomy and physiology, Leipzig, until 1893; Johns Hopkins Hosp., Baltimore, Md., until 1911; instr., Johns Hopkins, 1907-11, became asso. prof. of art as applied to medicine and head of dept. Evang. Lutheran. Home: 320 Suffolk Rd., Guilford, Baltimore, Md.

BROEK, John Yonker, clergyman; b. Coopersville, Mich., Sept. 13, 1880; s. Rev. Dirk and Anna (Jonker) B.; student Hope Coll., Holland, Mich., 1895-1901; A.B., Alma (Mich.) Coll., 1903; grad. New Brunswick (N.J.) Theol. Sem., 1906; D.D., Central Coll., Pella, Ia., 1925, Alma Coll., 1933; m. Florence Brewster Tubbs, Oct. 17, 1916; 1 dau. Margaret Shotwell. Ordained ministry Ref. Ch. in America, 1906; pastor Grand Av. Ch., Asbury Park, N.J., 1906-08, Trinity Ch., Plainfield, N.J., since 1908; organized 2 new chs. in Plainfield; del. to Gen. Synod 18 times. Pres. bd. trustees Classis of Newark (N.J.) since 1918, chmn. Ch. Extension Com. same since 1912; mem. Bd. Domestic Mission since 1912 and mem. exec. com. since 1919, Ref. Ch. of America; trustee of N.J. Christian Endeavor Union since 1921, Lord's Day Alliance of U.S. since 1932, Central Coll. since 1932; mem. bd. supts. New Brunswick Theol. Sem. since 1922, pres. 1924. Pres. Classis of Newark, 1911, 1923, 1932, 1937; pres. Particular Synod of New Brunswick, 1921. Del. to Fed. Council of Churches, 1938. Mem. Netherlands-American Foundation, N.J. Hist. Soc., Mich. Hist. Soc., Am. Tract Soc. (life), Lake Wentworth Assn. (Wolfeboro, N.H.), Zeta Sigma. Republican. Clubs: Lions, Country (Plainfield); Alma, Clergy (New York). Wrote: Manual of Classis of Newark, 1928; History of Trinity Reformed Church, Plainfield, N.J., 1931; 75th Anniversary of Trinity Reformed Church, 1938; The Jaques Family, 1935. Contbr. to Christian Intelligencer; has published 60 sermons, Seven Words from the Cross, The Ambassadors for Christ, etc. Home: 633 W. 7th St., Plainfield, N.J.

BROENING, William Frederick, lawyer; b. Baltimore, Md., June 2, 1870; s. Henry Jacob and Catherine (Petri) B.; LL.B., U. of Md., 1898; m. Josephine Marie Grauel, Sept. 6, 1905; children—William F., K. Ethel, E. Calvin (dec.). Practiced at Baltimore since 1898; mem. Robinson & Broening, 1912-18. Mem. City Council, Baltimore, 1897-99; mem. Ho. of Rep., Md., 1902; elected state's atty. for Baltimore City, Nov. 1911, term of 4 yrs., and reëlected Nov. 1916; mayor of Baltimore, 1919-23 and 1927-31; chmn. Maryland State Industrial Accident Commn. Dir. Gettysburg Theol. Sem. Republican. Lutheran. Past Supreme Dictator Loyal Order of Moose; Md. dir. Moose Vocational Inst., Mooseheart, Ill. Mason, Odd Fellow, K.P., Elk. Home: 3600 Fairview Av. Office: Equitable Bldg., Baltimore, Md.

BROGAN, Thomas J., judge; grad. St. Francis Xavier Coll., N.Y., 1900; LL.B., St. Johns College, Fordham, N.Y., 1912. Admitted to N.J. bar, 1912, and practiced in Jersey City; corpn. counsel, 1921-32; asso. justice N.J. Supreme Court, 1932-33, chief justice since March 1933. Address: 15 Exchange Pl., Jersey City, N.J.

BROKAW, Christopher A.; visiting surgeon Elizabeth Gen. Hosp. and Dispensary. Mem. clin. staff St. Elizabeth Hosp. Address: 1405 North Av., Elizabeth, N.J.

BROMBACHER, William George, physicist; b. Cleveland, O., Feb. 23, 1891; s. Henry and Elizabeth, B.; A.B., Lake Forest (Ill.) Coll., 1915, A.M., 1917; Ph.D., Johns Hopkins, 1922; m. Eunice M. Le Vien, Sept. 20, 1920; children—Nancy Jean, Mary Le Vien. Physicist, aeronautic instrument sect., Nat. Bureau of Standards since 1922, chief since 1926. Served in U.S. Army, 1918; now lt. comdr. U.S. Navy Reserve. Fellow Inst. of Aeronautical Sciences, Am. Phys. Soc.; mem. Philos. Soc. of Washington, Washington Acad. of Sciences, Am. Meteorol. Soc. Unitarian. Author of numerous articles on aeronautic instruments. Home: 6314 Ridgewood Av., Chevy Chase, Md. Office: Nat. Bureau of Standards, Washington, D.C.

BROMER, Edward Sheppard, theologian; b. Schwenksville, Pa., March 19, 1869; s. Albert and Catherine (Sheppard) B.; Ursinus Coll., Collegeville, Pa., 1890, D.D., 1905; B.D., Yale Div. Sch., 1893; grad. fellowship same, 1893-94; m. Flora Keelor Schwenk, 1890; children—Edna, Henry Earl, Frances Catharine. Ordained ministry Ref. Ch. in U.S., 1894; pastor successively Orwigsburg, later First Ch., Lebanon, Pa., until 1905; prof. N.T., lang. and exegesis, Ursinus Sch. of Theology, 1905-06; pastor First Ch., Greensburg, Pa., 1906-20; prof. practical theology, Theol. Sem. Ref. Ch. in U.S., Lancaster, Pa., since 1920. Mem. Am. Acad. Polit. and Social Science (Phila.), Cliosophic Soc. (Lancaster). Mason. Home: 519 W. James St., Lancaster, Pa.

BROMWELL, Richard E.; v.p. Baltimore Life Ins. Co. Address: Charles & Saratoga Sts., Baltimore, Md.

BRONK, Detlev W., physiologist, physicist; b. N.Y. City, Aug. 13, 1897; s. Mitchell and Marie (Wulf) B.; A.B., Swarthmore, 1920; studied U. of Pa., 1921; M.S., U. of Mich., 1922, Ph.D., 1926, hon. Sc.D., Swarthmore, 1937; m. Helen A. Ramsey, Sept. 10, 1921; children—John Everton Ramsey, Adrian Mitchell. Exec. sec. Phila. Food Administrn., 1918; asst. power engr. Phila. Electric Co., 1920; instr. in physics, U. of Pa., 1921; same, U. of Mich., 1921-24, instr. in physiology, 1924-26; asst. prof. physiology and biophysics, Swarthmore, 1926-27, asso. prof., 1927-28, prof., 1928-29, dean of men, 1927-29; fellow Nat. Research Council, at Cambridge and London, 1928-29; Johnson prof. biophysics and dir. Eldridge Reeves Johnson Foundation for Med. Physics, U. of Pa. since 1929, dir. Inst. of Neurology since 1936, prof. neurology, Grad. Sch. of Medicine since 1937; Weir Mitchell lecturer, Phila Coll. Physicians, 1938; Hughlings Jackson lecturer, McGill Univ., 1938. Asso. editor Jour. of Cellular and Comparative Physiology, Proc. Soc. Exptl. Biology and Medicine, Jour. of Applied Physics, Am. Jour. Physiology, Jour Neurophysiology, Biol. Abstracts. Mem. Nat. Research Council (exec. com., div. physics). Ensign U.S. Naval Aviation Corps, 1918-19. Fellow A.A.A.S., American Physical Soc.; mem. Am. Philos. Soc., Am. Physiol. Soc., British Physiol. Soc., Optical Soc. America, Soc. Exptl. Biology and Medicine, Phila. Neurol. Soc. Am. Neurol. Assn., Sigma Xi, Phi Kappa Psi, Delta Sigma Rho, Sigma Tau, Phi Beta Kappa; hon. mem. Harvey Soc., Soc. Anesthetists; cor. mem. Soc. Philomath. de Paris. Baptist. Clubs: Rittenhouse, Franklin Inn (Phila.); Cosmos (Washington, D.C.). Contbr. to Am. and British scientific jours. Home: Hill House Farm, Media, Pa. Office: University Hospital, Philadelphia, Pa.

BRONK, Isabelle, college prof.; b. Duanesburg, Schenectady Co., N.Y.; d. Abram and Cynthia (Brewster) B.; ed. Brockport (N.Y.) State Normal Sch., Wellesley, 1878-81, Germany and France, 1883-84, U. of Leipzig, Sorbonne, and Collège de France, 1889-91; Ph.B., Ill. Wesleyan U., 1893; Ph.D., U. of Chicago, 1900; studied summers at Bibliothèque Nationale and U. of Grenoble, and in Paris and Madrid, 1910-11. Fellow in Romance langs., U. of Chicago, 1898-1900, asst. in Romance langs. and lits. and head of Beecher House, U. of Chicago, 1900-01; asst. prof. French lang. and lit., 1901-02, prof. and head of Romance dept., 1902-27, prof. emeritus since 1927, Swarthmore College. At present vitally interested in the work of Women's International League for Peace. Member of modern lang. assns. of America, Middle States, Md., and Pa., Am. Assn. Univ. Profs., Am. Assn. Univ. Women, Colonial Dames America, Phi Beta Kappa. Author: Paris Memories, 1927. Editor of Pioésies diverses, by Antoine Furetière, 1908. Contbr. to Modern Lang. Notes, Modern Lang. Jour., Nation, New York Evening Post, Education, School and Society, etc. Home: Swarthmore, Pa.

BRONK, Mitchell, clergyman, editor; b. Manchester, N.Y., Nov. 24, 1862; s. Abram and Cynthia (Brewster) B.; A.B., U. of Rochester, 1886, D.D., 1913; studied Union Theol Sem., 1887-89, univs. of Leipzig, Jena, Berlin, Geneva, 1889-91; grad. Crozer Theol. Sem., Chester, Pa., 1892; A.M., New York U., 1896; m. Marie Wulf, Oct. 15, 1896; children—Detlev Wulf, Isabelle. Ordained Bapt. ministry, 1893; pastor Ascension Ch., New York, 1893-1900, First Ch., Bayonne, N.J., 1900-12, 2d. Ch., Troy, N.Y., 1912-19, 1st Ch., Stoneham, Mass., 1919-24; editor adult Sunday sch. publications, Am. Baptist Publ. Soc. since 1924, and book editor since 1931. Mem. Am. Acad. Polit. and Social Science, Soc. Bibl. Lit. and Exegesis, Editorial Div. of Internat. Council of Religious Edn., Am. Oriental Soc., Religious Edn. Assn., Soc. Mayflower Descendants, S.A.R., Delta Kappa Epsilon. Mason. Author: Pillars of Gold, 1926; Light in the Valley, 1932; Zechariah, in the American Commentary Series, 1935; Manchester Boys, 1937. Contbr. numerous articles, short stories, transls. to newspapers and mags. Home: 6325 Ross St., Germantown, Philadelphia. Office: 1703 Chestnut St., Philadelphia, Pa.

BROMSTEIN, Jesse B.; v.p. and gen mgr. Trojan Powder Co. Home: 1801 Hamilton St. Office: 17 N. 7th St., Allentown, Pa.

BROOKE, Francis John, Jr., clergyman; b. Clarksburg, W.Va., March 29, 1890; s. Francis John and Elizabeth Gay (Bentley) B.; A.B., Hampden Sydney Coll., Hampden Sydney, Va., 1911; B.D., Union Theol. Sem., Richmond, Va., 1916; grad. student Bib. Sem. in N.Y. City, 1921; (hon.) D.D., Hampden Sydney Coll., 1926; m. Elizabeth B. Baird, Sept. 25, 1919; 1 son, Francis John III. Engaged in teaching, high sch., Charles Town, W.Va., 1911-13; ordained to ministry Presbyn. Ch. of U.S., 1916; pastor, Gormania, W.Va., Bayard, W.Va., Thomas, W.Va., 1916-21, Wytheville, Va., 1921-27; pastor Ruffner Memorial Presbyn. Ch., Charleston, W.Va., since 1927. Mem. com. on stewardship and finance, Presbyn. Ch. U.S.A.; mem. Gen. Com. Army and Navy Chaplain. Chmn. Am. Red Cross, Wythe Co., Va., 1922-26; chmn. Near East Relief, Wythe Co., Va., 1922-25. Served as chaplain W.Va. Senate, 1935. Mem. bd. trustees Davis-Stuart Orphanage, Lewisburg, W.Va., Mountain Retreat Assn., Montreat, N.C. Home: 1700 Quarrier St., Charleston, W.Va.

BROOKE, Francis Mark, investments; b. Phila., Pa., June 19, 1883; s. Francis M. and Adelaide (Vogdes) B.; grad. DeLancey Sch., 1902; B.S., Princeton U., 1906; m. Nanna Sturges, June 11, 1907; children—Anita Sturges (Mrs. David McMullin, 3d), Marion Marie (Mrs. Caleb Rodney Layton, 3d), Francis Mark, 3d. Began as bond salesman with H. N. Noble & Co., Phila., 1906-08; with Edward Lowber Stokes, 1908-12; senior mem. Brooke, Stokes & Co., Phila., since 1912; dir. Bearing Co. of America, Pa. Joint Stock Land Bank, Great Lakes Utility Co. Mem. Colonial Soc., Colonial Club of Princeton (pres. 1906), Phi Kappa Psi. Republican. Protestant. Clubs: Rotary, Radnor Hunt, Merion Cricket. Home: Morris Av., Bryn Mawr, Pa. Office: 15th and Locust Sts., Philadelphia, Pa.

BROOKE, George, iron and steel mfr.; b. Phila., Pa., July 15, 1873; s. George and Mary Baldwin (Irwin) B.; Ph.B., U. of Pa., 1889; m. Lucile Polk, Aug. 1914 (died 1934); 1 dau., Elizabeth Muhlenberg (Mrs. Thomas Phipps). Began as clk. E. & G. Brooke Iron Co., Birdsboro, Pa., 1891, now sec. and dir.; v.p. and dir. Birdsboro (Pa.) Steel Foundry & Machine Co., First Nat. Bank, Birdsboro. Clubs: Phila., Rabbit (Phila.); Clambake (Newport, R.I.). Home: Ithan, Pa. Office: Birdsboro, Pa.

BROOKE, George III, steel mfr.; b. Birdsboro, Pa., July 7, 1888; s. Edward and Anne Louise (Clingan) B.; student Hill Sch., Pottstown, Pa., 1900-02, DeLancey Sch., Phila., 1902-08, U. of Pa., 1908-11; unmarried. Treas. and dir. E. & G. Brooke Iron Co., Birdsboro, Pa., since 1933, Birdsboro (Pa.) Water Co. since 1930; asst. treas. and dir. Birdsboro Steel Foundry & Machine Co., E. & G. Brooke Land Co. Served as pvt., 1st Troop, Phila. City Cavalry, Mexican Border, 1916; as 1st lt., 163d F.A. Brigade, 88th Div., at Camp Dodge, Ia. and A.E.F., 1917-19. Pres. Town Council, Birdsboro, Pa. Dir. Birdsboro (Pa.) Y.M.C.A. Mem. Delta Psi. Republican. Episcopalian. Clubs: Racquet (Phila.); Radnor Hunt (Malvern, Pa.); Rose Tree Fox Hunting (Media, Pa.); Reading (Pa.) Country. Author: With the First

City Troop on the Mexican Border, 1917. Address: Birdsboro, Pa.

BROOKE, John A.; prof. orthopedic surgery, Hahnemann Med. Coll.; chief orthopedic dept. Hahnemann Hosp.; orthopedist Children's Homeopathic and Broad St. hosps., Phila. Address: 1431 Spruce St., Philadelphia, Pa.

BROOKE, Robert Edward, iron and steel mfr.; b. Birdsboro, Pa., July 7, 1872; s. Edward and Annie (Clymer) B.; prep. edn., Emerson Inst., Washington, D.C., 1884-89, St. Paul's Sch., Concord, N.H., 1889-91; Ph.B., Sheffield Scientific Sch., Yale, 1894; m. Comelia Lausdale Ewing, Jan. 22, 1898; children—Robert Clymer, Maskell Ewing, John Louis Barde, Comelia Lausdale. Blast furnace clerk, later asst. mgr., E. & G. Brooke Iron Co., Birdsboro, Pa., 1894-99, treas., 1899-1933, pres. since 1933; v.p. Birdsboro (Pa.) Steel Foundry & Machine Co., 1898-1912, pres., 1912-34, chmn. of bd. since 1934; treas. E. & G. Brooke Land Co.; pres. Birdsboro Water Co. Dir. Birdsboro Sch. Bd., 1896-1922. Dir. Children's Aid Soc. of Pa. Mem. St. Elmo Club of New Haven, Conn. Republican. Episcopalian. Clubs: Phila. Racquet, Rabbit (Phila.); Reading (Pa.) Country. Address: Birdsboro, Pa.

BROOKS, Alonzo Beecher, naturalist; b. French Creek, W.Va., May 6, 1873; s. Adolphus and Josephine (Phillips) B.; student W.Va. country schs., 1880-94; business course, W.Va., Wesleyan Coll., 1900; B.S. in Agr., W.Va. U., 1912; m. Nellie R. Coburn, June 22, 1899. Began as farmer, 1885; surveyor, 1890-95, school teacher, 1895; forester W.Va. Geol. Survey, 1910-11, W.Va. Expt. Station, 1913-15, W.Va. State Dept. Agr., 1916-17; forest pathologist U.S. Dept. Agr., 1917-21; chief game protector, State of W.Va., 1921-28; naturalist, Oglebay Inst. since 1928. Mem. Soc. Am. Foresters, Upper Ohio Valley Hist. Soc. (pres.), Phi. Beta Kappa, Kappa Alpha. Republican. Presbyn. Club: Wheeling Rotary. Home: Oglebay Park, Wheeling, W.Va.

BROOKS, Betty Watt (Mrs. Stanley Truman B.), research asso.; b. Wellesley, Mass., Apr. 3, 1902; d. Thomas Thompson and Barbara Jane (Hunter) Watt; A.B. (with honors), Wellesley (Mass.) Coll., 1922, A.M., 1923; Ph.D., U. of Pittsburgh, 1934; m. Stanley Truman Brooks (Ph.D.), Apr. 30, 1927; children—Stanley Hunter Watt, Barbara Inda, Anne Fleming. Research asst., Sta. for Exptl. Evolution, Carnegie Instn. of Washington, Cold Spring Harbor, N.Y., 1923-25; asst. instr. botany, U. of Pittsburgh, 1925-28; asst. prof. botany, Pa. Coll. for Women, 1928-30; research asso., Carnegie Mus., Pittsburgh, Pa., since 1930; mem. Carnegie Mus. Expdns., Newfoundland, summers 1937 and 1938, 3 mos. study Brit. Mus. of Natural History, London, Eng., 1938. Fellow A.A.A.S.; mem. Bot. Soc. of America, Am. Malacol. Union, Am. Soc. Parasitologists, Am. Micros. Soc., Boston Soc. of Natural History, Pittsburgh Authors Club, Pittsburgh Wellesley Club, Wellesley Coll. Alumnae, Malacalogical Soc. of London, Quax, Chi Omega, Phi Sigma. Awarded grant from A.A.A.S. for study at Nat. Mus., Washington, D.C., 1935. Republican. Episcopalian. Contbr. articles to scientific mags. and journs. Home: 6637 Dalzell Pl. Office: Carnegie Museum, Pittsburgh, Pa.

BROOKS, Earl H.; v.p. New Amsterdam Casualty Co. of N.Y. Home: 3227 Vickers Rd., Forest Park, Baltimore, Md. Offices: 227 St. Paul Pl., Baltimore, Md.; and 60 John St., New York, N.Y.

BROOKS, Edward Schroeder, ex-congressman; b. York, Pa., June 14, 1867; s. John H. and Mary A. (Schroeder) B.; ed. York County Acad. and York Collegiate Inst.; m. Emma J. Eimerbrink, 1890; children—Karl S., Mary M. Mem. City Council, York, 3 terms; treas. York Co., 1903-06; mem. Rep. State Com., Pa., 1917-18; mem. 66th and 67th Congresses (1919-23), 20th Pa. Dist.; postmaster of York, 1925-34. Mem. Sons of Vets. Lutheran. Mason, K.P. Home: York, Pa.

BROOKS, Frank Faber, banker; b. Cleveland, O., Dec. 12, 1873; s. Joseph Judson and Henrietta (Faber) B.; grad. Williston Sem., Prep. Sch., Easthampton, Mass., 1892; Ph.B., Yale, 1896; m. Mary Leet Williams, June 4, 1904; children—Martha Shields (Mrs. Alexander Laughlin Robinson), Frank Faber, Jr., Joseph Judson, II. Began as clerk Pa. Trust Co., Pittsburgh, Pa., 1896, trust officer, 1900-1903; trust officer Colonial Trust Co., Pittsburgh, 1903-1914; v.p. and cashier, First Nat. Bank at Pittsburgh, 1914-1918, v.p., 1918-28, pres. since 1928; dir. First Nat. Bank at Pittsburgh, Peoples-Pittsburgh Trust Co., of Pittsburgh, Pa. Industries, Inc., Pa. Bankshares & Securities Corpn., Pittsburgh Steel Co., United Engring. & Foundry Co., Columbian Enameling & Stamping Co. (Terre Haute, Ind.), Woodings-Verona Tool Works, Pittsburgh Testing Lab., P. McGraw Wool Co., Nufer Cedar Co., Kittanning Iron & Steel Co. Mem. Clearing House Com. of Pittsburgh Clearing House Assn. Dir. Pittsburgh Chamber of Commerce; treas. and dir. Pittsburgh Conv. & Tourist Bureau; dir. The Community Fund; pres. and dir. Pittsburgh Commn. for Industrial Expansion; dir. and mem. finance com. Carnegie Hero Fund Commn.; Class A dir. Fed. Reserve Bank of Cleveland. Mem. Assn. of Reserve City Bankers, Am. Bankers Assn., Pa. Bankers Assn. Clubs: Duquesne, Pittsburgh, Allegheny Country, Rolling Rock, Harvard-Yale-Princeton (Pittsburgh). Home: Shields, Allegheny County, Pa. Office: First National Bank at Pittsburgh, Fifth Av. and Wood St., Pittsburgh, Pa.

BROOKS, George G., retired exec.; b. Scranton, Pa., Nov., 13, 1870; s. Reese G. and Mary Ann (Morgan) B.; grad. Wyoming Sem., 1890, Cornell U., 1894; m. Grace B. W. Williams, June 4, 1898; children—James W., Eleanor M. B. (Mrs. R. A. Robertson III), Elizabeth (Mrs. M. R. Greer), George G., Charles W. Employed as chief engr. coal cos., 1894-1902; vice-pres. and treas. Latrobe (Pa.) Water Co., 1902-28; treas. Consumers Water Co., 1912-28; v.p. Internat. Corr. Schs., Scranton, Pa., 1915-38; dir. Internat. Ednl. Pub. Co., Scranton, Pa., 1918-38; v.p. Daly West Mining Co., 1917-28, Paragon Plaster & Supply Co., 1916-38, McClure, Brooks Co., 1924-28; treas. and dir. East Bar Ridge Coal Co., 1916-24; dir. Lackawanna Trust Co., 1915-33, Merchants & Mechanics Bank, 1906-15, First Nat. Bank, 1915-34, Scranton-Lackawanna Trust Co., 1926-34, Scranton Lace Co., 1908-38, Consumers Ice Co., 1907-38, Ames Baldwin Wyoming Shovel Co., 1934-38, Temple Anthracite Coal Co., 1927-38, Oakfield Gypsum Products Co., 1914-38; mem. N.Y. Stock Exchange firm of J.W. Brooks & Co., 1908-38; treas. Brooks Realty Co., 1918-38. Served as gen. chmn. N.E.Pa. Red Cross Campaign, 1918, United War Charities, 1918. Dir. Sch. Bd., Dunmore, Pa.; chmn. Old Age Pension Bd. Lackawanna Co.; pres. Cemetery Assn. of Dunmore; trustee Wyoming Sem., Kingston, Pa., Lackawanna Hosp., Pa. Oral Sch., Cornellian Assn. Republican. Episcopalian. Home: 1549 Jefferson Av., Scranton, Pa.

BROOKS, Harold King, lawyer; b. Mill Run, Pa., Dec. 21, 1887; s. Charles King and Sadie (Van Horn) B.; student Alden Acad., Meadville, Pa., 1910-11; A.B., Allegheny Coll., Meadville, 1915; LL.B., U. of Pittsburgh, 1922; unmarried. Teacher and prin. grade schs., 1904-10; teacher and athletic coach high schs., 1915-18; admitted to Pa. and U.S. bars, 1922, and since in gen. practice with Cornelius D. Scully (now mayor), Pittsburgh. Served in 72nd Inf., 11th Div., U.S. Army, 1918-19. Mem. Am., Pa. and Allegheny Co. bar assns., Am. Legion, Phi Kappa Psi, Delta Theta Phi. Democrat. Mason. Home: 6319 Glenview Pl. Office: 602 Frick Bldg., Pittsburgh, Pa.

BROOKS, John B(irt), lawyer; b. Crawford Co., Pa., Mar. 29, 1871; s. Amaziah and Mary (Ross) B.; A.B., U. of Mich., 1895, LL.B., 1896; m. Genevieve Wilbur, 1899; children—Annette (Mrs. T. D. Hacker, now deceased), Helen (Mrs. Walter Carey), Robert W. Admitted to Pa. bar, 1897 and practiced in Erie, Pa.; mem. firm Brooks, Curtze & Silin. Mem. Pa. legislature, 1899; chmn. bd. trustees Edinboro State Teachers Coll.; pres. Pa. Bar Assn., 1932. Democrat. Presbyterian. Mason. Clubs: Erie, Kahkwa Country (Erie). Home: 512 W. 6th St. Office: Erie Trust Bldg., Erie, Pa.

BROOKS, John H.; mem. firm J. H. Brooks & Co.; officer or dir. various companies. Home: 424 Jefferson Av. Office: Brooks Bldg., Scranton, Pa.

BROOKS, Robert Clarkson, college prof.; b. Piqua, O., Feb. 7, 1874; s. James Eugene and Jennie Margaret (Kiser) B.; A.B., Ind. U., 1896; President White fellow, Cornell U., 1897-98; traveling fellow, univs. of Halle and Berlin, 1898-99; Ph.D., Cornell, 1903; Dr. rer. pol. honoris causa, U. of Berne, 1935; m. Elizabeth Hewson, Sept. 4, 1900; 1 son, Robert Clarkson. Instr., Cornell U., 1899-1904; Joseph Wharton prof. economics, Swarthmore Coll., 1904-08; prof. polit. science, U. of Cincinnati, 1908-12, Swarthmore (Pa.) Coll., Sept. 1912—; summer schools, U. of Calif., 1916; Cornell U., 1921. Field dir. Am. Red Cross, League Island Navy Yard, 1918-19. Mem. American Political Science Assn., Franklin Inn Club (Philadelphia). Democrat. Author: Corruption in American Politics and Life, 1910; Teachers' Salaries and Cost of Living, 1913; Government and Politics of Switzerland, 1918; Political Parties and Electoral Problems, 1923; Reading for Honors at Swarthmore, 1927; Civic Training in Switzerland, 1930; Deliver Us from Dictators!, 1935. Contbr. to econ. and polit. science mags. Home: Swarthmore, Pa.*

BROOKS, Rodney J.; pres. Tongue, Brooks & Zimmerman, Inc.; officer or dir. many companies. Home: 115 E. Melrose Av. Office: 213 St. Paul Pl., Baltimore, Md.

BROOKS, Stanley Truman, curator sect. Carnegie Mus.; b. Mound City, Kan., Oct. 4, 1902; s. Dr. Stanley Homer and Inda (Fleming) B.; A.B., U. of Kan., Lawrence, Kan., 1926; M.S., U. of Pittsburgh, 1927, Ph. D., 1929; m. Betty Pauline Watt (Ph.D.), Apr. 30, 1927; children—Stanley Hunter Watt, Barbara Inda, Anne Fleming. Asst. instr., U. of Kan., 1925-26; asst. in zoology, U. of Pittsburgh, 1926-28; custodian in charge Sect. of Recent Invertebrates, Carnegie Mus., Pittsburgh, Pa., 1928-30, actg. curator, 1930-32, curator Sect. of Recent Invertebrates since 1932; mem. Carnegie Mus. Expdns. to Newfoundland, summers 1934, 1936-38. Fellow A.A.A.S.; mem. Am. Micros. Soc., Am. Ecol. Soc., Am. Soc. of Parasitologists, The Malacological Union, Am. Museums Assn., Acad. Natural Sciences, Phila., Am. Geog. Soc., Kan. U. Alumni Assn., N.Y. Acad. Sciences, Twentieth Century Club of Boston, Authors Club Pittsburgh, Kan. U. Alumni of Pittsburgh (pres.), The Malacological Soc. of London, Sigma Xi, Phi Sigma. Awarded Carnegie Foundation Grant-In-Aid for Study and Travel in Europe, 1938 (spent in Germany and Eng.). Republican. Mem. Christian Ch. Author: Above The Smoke (verse), 1936; contbr. scientific papers and articles and popular articles on science and travel. Lecturer on science, travel, and poetry before clubs in many large cities and over radio. Home: 6637 Dalzell Pl. Office: Carnegie Museum, Pittsburgh, Pa.

BROOKS, Thomas R.; mem. firm J. H. Brooks & Co.; also officer or dir. various companies. Home: Scranton Club. Office: Brooks Bldg., Scranton, Pa.

BROOKS, William E., clergyman; b. Phila., Pa., Aug. 9, 1875; s. John and Sarah Jane (McDevitt) B.; A.B., Westminster Coll., New Wilmington, Pa., 1900, Litt.D., 1935; A.M., Princeton, 1904; grad. Princeton Theological Sem., 1904; D.D., Lafayette, 1916, Univ. of Dubuque, 1916; LL.D., Waynesburg (Pa.) Coll., 1938; m. Jeanette Steele Stewart, Oct. 12, 1904; children—S. Stewart, Jeanette Steele (Mrs. Frederick H. Thompson), Margaret Hamilton. Ordained Presbyn. ministry, 1904; pastor East Kishacoquillas Ch., Reedsville, Pa., 1904-09, 1st Ch., Allentown, Pa., 1909-24, 1st Ch., Morgantown, W.Va., 1924—; dir. Army Y.M.C.A. and acting chaplain, Camp Crane, 23 mos., 1917-19; nat. chaplain U.S.A. Ambulance Service Assn.; mem. Gen. Council Presbyn. Ch., U.S.A., 1929-35; pres. W.Va. Council of Social Welfare, 1931-32. Mem. Phi Beta Kappa. Recommended for D.S.M. Author: Lee of Virginia. Contributing editor The Presbyterian Banner. Contbr. poems and articles to leading mags. Home: 316 Allison Av., Morgantown, W.Va.; (summer) Orleans, Mass.

BROOME, Edwin Cornelius, school supt.; b. Central Falls, R.I., Oct. 5, 1874; s. Robert and Margaret (Monkhouse) B.; Ph.B., Brown U., 1897, A.M., 1898, Ed.D., 1927; Ph.D., Columbia, 1902; Diploma in Edn., Teachers' Coll. (Columbia), 1902; LL.B., St. Lawrence U. Law Sch., 1907; LL.D., Ursinus Coll., 1925; Juniata Coll., 1934; L.H.D., University of Pa., 1934; Litt.D., R.I. Coll. Edn., 1930; Sc.D., Temple University, 1937; m. Grace Wells Rhoads, June 1, 1909; children—Edwin Cornelius, John Rhoads. Teacher High Sch., Pawtucket, R.I., 1897-98; prin. high sch., Seymour, Conn., 1898-1900; fellow Teachers College, Columbia University, 1900; supt. schs., Rahway, N.J., 1902-06; instr. Adelphi College and supt. Elementary Department, Adelphi Acad., 1906-09; lecturer Brooklyn Institute and for Brooklyn Teachers Assn., 1908-09; supt. schs., Mt. Vernon, N.Y., 1909-13, E. Orange, N.J., 1913-21, Philadelphia, 1921-38; supt. emeritus since July 1, 1938; now atty. at law and lecturer, Temple U. Lecturer under New York Bd. of Edn., 1902-13; on sch. administration, U. of Wis., summer, 1916, Ohio State U., summer 1920. Gen. supervisor of field work Army Ednl. Corps., A.E.F., Nov. 1918-July 1919. Mem. Nat. Com. on C.M.T.C., 1922; participated in survey of N.Y. City schs., 1924-25; mem. White House Conf., on Child Health and Protection, 1930. Presbyn. Mem. N.E.A. (chmn. commission on curriculum, Dept. of Superintendence, 1926-29; pres. of Department of Superintendence, 1931-32), N.Y. State Council of Sch. Supts. (pres. 1912), Pa. State Ednl. Assn., Alumni of Teachers Coll. (pres. 1915-17), Phi Delta Phi, Phi Delta Kappa, Phi Beta Kappa. Alumni trustee Teachers Coll., 1924-26; mem. bd. dirs. Y.M.C.A. (Phila); trustee Welfare Fed. of Phila. Mason. Presbyterian. Author: A Historical and Critical Discussion of College Admission Requirements, 1903; Conduct and Citizenship (with Edwin Adams), 1926; Health and Happiness Series (with Dr. S. Weir Newmayer), 1928. Awarded medal Columbia U., 1932, "for distinguished service in education." Home: 217 E. Sedgwick St., Mt. Airy, Philadelphia. Office Packard Bld., Philadelphia, Pa.

BROOMELL, I(saac) Norman, dentist; b. Chester Co., Pa., Nov. 25, 1858; s. Isaac and Rachel B.; ed. Friends' Central Sch., Phila., 1875-78, A.M., 1878; D.D.S., Pa. Coll. Dental Surgery, 1879; LL.D., 1939; m. Lidia T. Seabury, 1884 (now dec.); 1 son, Willard Seabury (dec). Began Phila., 1881; was professor dental anatomy and histology, Pa. Coll. Dental Surgery, and dean dental dept., Medico-Chirurg. Coll., Phila.; prof. dental anatomy and histology, and dean Phila. Dental Coll., 1918—; also dean Temple U. Dental Sch. (Phila Dental Coll.). Mem. bd. dirs. Nat. Research Inst. Fellow Am. Acad. Dental Surgery, Am. Coll. Dentists; mem. Nat., Pa. and N.Y. dental socs., Acad. Stomatology, Nat. Assn. Dental Teachers, Soc. Dentaire de France, Psi Omega, etc. Republican. Clubs: Art, Pelham, Manufacturers and Bankers. Author: Anatomy and Histology of the Mouth and Teeth (with Philipp Fischelis), 1898. Compiler and Editor: Practical Dentistry by Practical Dentists, 1908. Home: 252 West Hortter St., Germantown. Office: Medical Arts Bldg., Philadelphia, Pa.

BROSKY, Frank James, musician; b. Pittsburgh, Pa., Feb. 3, 1889; s. Charles and Mary B. B.; ed. conservatory, Prague, Bohemia, 1903-05; conservatory, Leipzig, Germany, 1905-08; (hon.) Mus.D., Duquesne U., Pittsburgh, 1926; m. Martha McCook, July 29, 1925; 1 dau., Martha Mary. Began as concert violinist, 1908; asso. with Nickish, Strauss, Mahler, Paur, and Sevcik, in Europe; taught in a number of instns.; served as dean of Sch. of Music, Duquesne U., 1936-37; now devoting time to pvt. work; dir. sec. and treas. S. A. Lykens Co.; dir. American Development Co. Served in mil. intelligence div., U.S. Army, 1918; honored by complimentary letter from Lt. Col. A. G. Campbell of Gen. Staff. Republican. Roman Catholic. Clubs: Pittsburgh Athletic, Musicians (Pittsburgh). Composer of over fifty musical numbers; contbr. to mags. on mus. subjects. His violin is a Pietro Guarnerius used by the late Cezar Thompson. Home: 351 S. Fairmount Av. Office: 5930 Kentucky Av., Pittsburgh, Pa.

BROTEMARKLE, Robert Archibald, coll. prof. and personnel officer; b. Lonaconing, Md., Nov. 12, 1892; s. Clinton and Laura J. (Somerville) B.; student Mercersburg (Pa.) Acad., 1910-12; A.B., Princeton U., 1916, A.M., 1918; student Princeton Theol. Sem., 1916-18; Ph.D., U. of Pa., 1923; m. Bernice W. Rorer, Sept. 28, 1919; children—Richard Gordon, Alene Frances. Instr. psychology, U. of Pa., 1919-27, asst. prof. psychology, 1927-35, asso. prof. since 1935, coll. personnel officer since 1926. Served as chaplain, U.S. Army, 1918-19. Fellow A.A.A.S.; mem. Am. Physol. Assn., Assn. of Cons. Psychologists (pres. 1937), Am. Assn. for Applied Psychology (vice-pres.; chmn. cons. sect. 1938-39), Pa. Assn. Clin. Psychologists (vice-pres. 1938-39), Am. Coll. Personnel Assn. (vice-pres. 1935), Eastern Assn. of Coll. Deans and Advisers of Men (pres. 1936). Presbyterian. Mason (32°). Clubs: Lenape (U. of Pa.); Princeton (Phila.). Home: 1431 Comly St. Office: 116 College Hall, University of Pennsylvania, Philadelphia, Pa.

BROUGH, Charles Young, proprietor Schmuck Co.; b. Hanover, Pa., May 8, 1882; s. John Henry and Ida May (Young) B.; student Cascadillo Sch., Ithaca, N.Y., 1899-1900, Cornell U., 1900-05; m. Mary Blanche Schmuck, Sept. 2, 1908; 1 son, Henry Schmuck; m. 2d, Anna Louise Hershey, May 18, 1931; children—John Andrew, Charles William. Plant supt. J. S. Young & Co., Hanover, Pa., 1905-08; asst. gen. mgr. and supt. constrn. Hanover & McSherrytown Water Co., Hanover, Pa., 1908-13; Partner Schmuck Co., retail lumber and bldg. materials, Hanover, Pa., 1913-29, sole proprietor since 1929; dir. First Nat. Bank of Hanover, Hanover Trust Co. Dir. Hanover Gen. Hosp. Republican. Lutheran. Clubs: Arcadian, Hanover (Pa.) Country. Home: 190 Stock St. Office: Railroad and Wall Sts., Hanover, Pa.

BROUGHTON, Levin Bowland, coll. dean; b. Pocomoke City, Md., Mar. 29, 1886; s. William Thomas and Alice Mary (Bowland) B.; B.S., U. of Md., 1908, M.S., 1911; Ph.D., Ohio State U., 1926; m. Laurise McDonnell, Dec. 27, 1911; children—Elinor C., Levin Barnett. Asst. chemist Md. Agrl. Expt. Sta., 1908-11; asst. prof. chemistry, U. of Md., 1911-14, asso. prof., 1914-18, prof. agrl. chemistry, 1918-29, prof. of chemistry and state chemist since 1929; dean Coll. of Arts and Sciences since 1938. Mem. Am. Chem. Soc. (councillor 1937-38), Assn. Official Agrl. Chemists (v.p. 1939; mem. Com. "B," since 1936, chmn. 1939), Phi Kappa Phi, Sigma Xi, Alpha Chi Sigma, Kappa Alpha. Protestant. Club: Rotary. Address: College Park, Md.

BROUZAS, Christopher George, univ. prof., librarian; b. Keramidion, Greece, July 12, 1895; s. George Chris and Kalliope (George) B.; came to U.S., 1912, naturalized, 1928; A.B., Tri-State Coll., Angola, Ind., 1920; A.M., Colgate U., 1921; student U. of Va., summer 1921, New York State Coll. for Teachers, Albany, N.Y., 1922, U. of Chicago, summers, 1923, 24; Ph.D., U. of Ill., 1926; m. Florence Knight, Sept. 12, 1923; 1 son, George. Asst., Tri-State Coll., 1919 (part-time); prof. of Latin, Greek and history, Broaddus Coll., Philippi, W.Va., 1921-23; asst. in classics, U. of Ill., 1923-25, research fellow, 1925-26; asst. prof. of Latin and Greek, W.Va. Univ., 1926-29, asso. prof., 1929-35, prof. of classics and univ. librarian since 1935. Mem. State Curriculum Revision Com. in Latin. Mem. Classical League, Classical Assn. Middle West and South, Am. Philol. Assn., Am. Library Assn., Vergilius, Deutsche Chemische Gesellschaft, Soc. Chem. Industry (Eng.), W.Va. Acad. Science (treas.), W.Va. Library Assn. (pres.), Eta Sigma Phi. Republican. Presbyterian. Club: Kiwanis International. Author of many translations from Greek and Roman poets, also original poems; contbr. articles to professional jours. Home: 1000 Grand St., Morgantown, W.Va.

BROWN, Arlo Ayres, university pres.; b. Sunbeam, Mercer Co., Ill., April 15, 1883; s. Robert Ayres and Lucy Emma (Sanders) Brown; A.B., Northwestern U., 1903; B.D., Drew Theol. Sem., 1907; grad. student, Union Theol. Sem., Northwestern U.; D.D., Cornell Coll., Ia., 1921; LL.D., Syracuse University, 1927; Litt.D. from University of Chattanooga, 1929; LL.D., Northwestern U., 1938; m. Grace Hurst Lindale, Feb. 14, 1914; children—Arlo Ayres, Robert Lindale. Pastoral charges M.E. Ch., 1903-12, deason 1907, elder 1909; asso. pastor Madison Av. Ch., New York, 1907-09; pastor Mount Hope Church, New York, 1909-12; agt. Bd. of Foreign Missions, M.E. Ch., in Jerusalem, 1912-13; exec. sec. Newark Dist. Ch. Soc., 1913-14; supt. teacher training Bd. of Sunday Schs., M.E. Ch., 1914-21; pres. University of Chattanooga, 1921-1929; pres. of Drew University since 1929. Enlisted in Training Sch. for Army Chaplains, June 1, 1918; commd. 1st lt., chaplain, 318th Engrs., 6th Div., A.E.F., Aug. 29, 1918; sr. chaplain same, Dec. 21, 1918; capt., March 26, 1919; hon. discharged June 12, 1919; captain chaplain, O.R.C., 1921-24, major chaplain, 1924-34. Chmn. exec. com. Internat. Council Religious Edn. since 1939; pres. Methodist Edn. Assn., 1939-40; mem. Commn. on Conference Courses of Study of M.E. Church, University Senate of M.E. Church; mem. Appraisal Commn. of Laymen's Foreign Missions Inquiry, 1931-32. Mem. Phi Beta Kappa. Republican. Mason. Clubs: Rotary (Madison); Aldine, University (New York); University (Evanston, Ill.). Author: Studies in Christian Living, 1914; Primer of Teacher Training, 1916; Life in the Making (co-author), 1917; A History of Religious Education in Recent Times, 1923; Youth and Christian Living, 1929. Address: Drew University, Madison, N.J.

BROWN, Arthur Edward, head master; b. Union Station, Licking Co., O., May 17, 1876; s. Nicholas Comly and Rachel Ellen (Park) B.; student Ohio Wesleyan U. preparatory dept., 1895-96, Doane Acad., Granville, O., 1896-98, Denison U., Granville, O., 1898-99; A.B., Ohio Wesleyan U., Delaware, O., 1902; student Boston U., 1904-05, Harvard, 1905-07; Ph.D., Pa. Coll., Gettysburg, Pa., 1918; m. Mabel Warner Stoddard, Oct. 22, 1907; children—Philip Stoddard, Virginia (Mrs. Charles S. House), Alice Park, Arthur Edward, Nicholas Comly, III. Teacher country sch., Licking Co., O., 1893-95; supt. of schs., Caldwell, O., 1902-04; teacher, Rindge Manual Training Sch., Cambridge, Mass., 1905-07; teacher, University Sch., Cleveland, O., 1907-08, William Penn Charter Sch., Phila., 1908-12; head master Harrisburg (Pa.) Acad. since 1912. Mem. Harrisburg Chamber of Commerce, Headmasters' Assn., Sigma Alpha Epsilon. Republican. Methodist. Mason. Clubs: University, Rotary, Harrisburg Country (Harrisburg, Pa.). Home: 2995 N. Front St. Office: Harrisburg Academy, Harrisburg, Pa.

BROWN, Arthur Emlen, pres. Brown & Bailey Co.; b. Phila., Pa., May 29, 1885; s. David J. and Anne Emlen (Bangs) B.; student Friends Sch., Phila., 1893-99, Westtown (Pa.) Boarding Sch., 1899-1903, Haverford (Pa.) Coll., 1903-07; m. Helen LaDora Jefferis, Jan. 21, 1921; children—Frances Pittfield, Arthur Emlen. With Brown & Bailey Co., Phila., since 1907, v.p. and sales mgr., 1923-38, pres. and sales mgr. since 1938, dir. since 1912; dir. Fidelity Storage & Warehouse Co. Sec. of trustees Germantown (Pa.) Preparative Meeting of Friends. Mem. Folding Paper Box Assn. of America (Dir.). Republican. Soc. of Friends. Club: Salesmanagers (Phila.) Home: Kitchens Lane, Mt. Airy. Office: 417 N. 8th St., Philadelphia, Pa.

BROWN, Arthur Henry, clergyman; b. Hoboken, N.J., July 26, 1887; s. Oliver Allen and Helen Jeannette (Stover) B.; A.B., Dickinson Coll., 1907; B.D., Drew Theol. Sem., 1910; grad. study, Union Theol. Sem., N.Y. City, 1910-11, Columbia U., 1910-11; hon. D.D., Dickinson Coll., 1938; m. Ruth Gardner Latimer, Nov. 20, 1934. Ordained to ministry Meth. Ch., 1911; mem. Newark Conf. since 1911; served as pastor various chs., Jersey City, Leonia, Weehawken, Ridgefield Park and Orange, all in N.J.; pastor Meth. Ch., Ridgewood, N.J., since 1937. Served as chaplain, U.S.A., 1918-19, sr. chaplain 80th

Div. A.E.F. Mem. Beta Theta Pi. Methodist. Home: 109 Prospect St., Ridgewood, N.J.

BROWN, Benjamin B.; partner law firm Brown, Jackson & Knight; dir. several companies. Home: 127 Alderson St. Office: Kanawha Valley Bldg., Charleston, W.Va.

BROWN, Benjamin Nields, lawyer; b. Wilmington, Del., March 30, 1900; s. George T. and Isabel (Morrisson) B.; student Wilmington Friends Sch., 1906-17; A.B., Princeton U., 1921; LL.B., U. of Pa. Law Sch., 1924; m. Rowan McHugh, May 15, 1929; 1 son, Benjamin Nields. Admitted to bar, 1924, and in practice, 1924-29; in charge title ins. dept. Equitable Trust Co., Wilmington, Del., 1929-33; in practice law at Wilmington since 1933. Dir. of pub. safety, Wilmington since 1936. Mem. Del. State Bar Assn., Am. Bar Assn., Princeton Elm Club, Hare Law Club (U. of Pa.), Phi Delta Phi. Republican. Presbyterian. Club: Wilmington (Del.) County. Home: 1900 Field Rd. Office: Equitable Bldg., Wilmington, Del.

BROWN, Bishop, dir. retail training; b. Stratford, N.H., March 28, 1889; s. William Riley and Sarah Ella (Bishop) B.; grad. Tilton (N. H.) Acad., 1908; A.B., Dartmouth Coll., 1912; m. Ruth Wales Randall, Aug. 28, 1929. Hotel mgr., 1913-17; salesman Houghton Mifflin Co., Boston, 1919-21; asst. employment mgr., Jordan Marsh Co., Boston, 1921-25; store mgr. C. F. Hovey Co., Boston, 1925-28, Jay's, Inc., Boston, 1928-29; prof. store management, U. of Pittsburgh, 1929-35; dir. Research Bur. for Retail Training, U. of Pittsburgh since 1935; chief of business edn. Commonwealth of Pa. since 1937. Served as 1st sergt. Ambulance Corps, U.S.A., with A.E.F., 1917-19; attended officers sch. in France and commd. 1st lt. Decorated with Croix de Guerre (French). Dir. personnel group Nat. Retail Dry Goods Assn.; mem. Sigma Chi. Methodist (trustee Franklin M.E. Ch.). Author: Handbook of Business Administration (with W. J. Donald), 1931. Contbr. articles to Retailing and other trade pubs. Home: Lindsay Lane, Ingomar, Pa.

BROWN, Carleton, philologist, educator; b. Oberlin, O., July 15, 1869; s. Justus Newton and Hattie Augusta (Sparhawk) B.; A.B., Carleton Coll., Minn., 1888; studied Andover Theol. Sem., 1890-93; Grad. Sch., Harvard N., 1900-03, A.M., 1901, Ph.D., 1903; m. Emily L. Truesdell, June 7, 1893; children—Margery Lorraine, Wendell Edwards (des.), Truesdell Sparhawk; m. 2d, Beatrice Daw, Aug. 13, 1918; children—Emily Parker Lawless, Beatrice Carleton (dec.), Carleton Justus. Ordained Unitarian ministry, 1894; pastor Unity Ch., St. Cloud, Minn., 1894-97; Helena, Mont., 1897-1900; instr. in English, Harvard, 1903-05; asso. in English, 1905-07; asso. prof. English, 1907-10, pro. English philology, 1910-17, Bryn Mawr Coll.; prof. English, U. of Minn., 1917-21; prof. English, Bryn Mawr College, 1921-27; prof. English, New York U., 1927-39. Sec. Modern Lang. Assn. America, 1920-34, pres., 1936; fellow Mediæval Acad. of America, Nat. Acad. Arts and Sciences; mem. Phi Beta Kappa, Phi Kappa Psi. Arthur: A study of the Miracle of Our Lady Told by Chaucer's Prioress, 1910. Compiler: A Register of Middle English Religious and Didactic Verse, Part I, 1916, Part II, 1920; Religious Lyrics of the XIVth Century, 1924; English Lyrics of the XIIIth Century, 1932. Editor: Venus and Adonis and other poems, 1913; Uoems by Sir John Salusbury and Robert Chester, 1914; The Stonyhurst Pageants, 1920; Chaucer's Pardoner's Tale, 1935. Home: Upper Montclair, N.J. Address: New York University, New York, N.Y.

BROWN, Charles Leonard, M.D., prof. medicine; b. Metropolis, Ill., Apr. 27, 1899; s. William Andrew and Martha V. (Wallace) B.; B.S., U. of Okla., 1919, M.D., 1921; m. Ruth MacAllister Jamieson, June 9, 1928; children—Janet Jamieson, Martha Ann. Med practice Oklahoma City, 1921-22; resident pathologist Children's Hosp., Boston, 1923-24; house officer in medicine Peter Bent Brigham Hosp., Boston, 1922-23, resident pathologist, 1924-25, resident physician, 1925-27, jr. asso. in medicine, 1927-28; physician Univ. Hosp., Ann Arbor, Mich., 1928-35; head dept. medicine, Temple U. Hosp., Phila., since 1935; instr. pathology, Harvard, 1923-25, teaching fellow in medicine, 1925-27, instr., 1927-28; asst. prof. internal medicine, U. of Mich., 1928-29, asso., 1929-35; prof. medicine, Temple U., Phila., since 1935. Mem. revision com. U.S. Pharmacopeia XI. Fellow Am. Coll. of Physicians; mem. Am. Soc. Clin. Investigation, Central Soc. Clin. Research, A.A.A.S., A.M.A., Pa. State Med. Soc., Mass. State Med. Soc. (non-resident), Physiol. Soc. of Phila., Phila. Co. Med. Soc., Phila. Coll. Physicians, Laennec Soc. of Phila., Am. Gastro-Enterological Assn., Am. Therapeutic Soc., Phi Beta Pi. Contbr. articles to med. jours. Home: 325 N. Bowman Av., Merion, Pa. Office: 3401 N. Broad St., Phila., Pa.

BROWN, Charles Lincoln, judge; b. Phila., Pa., July 6, 1864; s. Charles and Amanda (Marple) B.; student Brown Sch., Phila., Lehigh U., Bethlehem, Pa.; LL.B., U. of Pa. Law Sch., 1891; m. Susanna Stiles Hemphill, Apr. 28, 1892; 1 dau., Hazel Hemphill. Admitted to Pa. bar, 1891, and since in practice at Phila.; counsel State Dairy and Food Commn., 1901-13; elected judge Municipal Court of Phila., 1913, for term, 1914-24, reelected for terms, 1924-34, 1934-44; apptd. pres. judge, 1914-24, re-elected by Bd. of Judges, 1929, 1934, 1939; as pres. judge organized administrative divs. and depts. of Municipal Court, planned and established functions of Petition, Delinquent, Probation, Employment depts. Elected mem. Common Council, Phila., 1891, 1893, 1903, to Select Council, 1894; mem. State Senate, 1896; chmn. Rep. City Com., 1906-07; del. to Rep. Nat. Conv., 1916, 1936, alternate del., 1920. Mem. State Advisory Council of Pa. Com. on Penal Affairs of Pub. Charities Assn. Mem. Pa. Bar Assn., Phila. Bar Assn., Hist. Soc. of Pa. Republican. Baptist. Mason. Clubs: Manufacturers and Bankers, Art, Penn. Athletic, Clover (Phila.). Home: 1426 Mt. Vernon St. Office: Room 506, City Hall, Philadelphia, Pa.

BROWN, Charles Walker, pres. Western Md. Ry.; b. Fort Gaines, Ga., Jan. 10, 1880; s. Walter Alexander and Mollie Elizabeth (Walker) B.; m. Virginia F. McGuire, Nov. 28, 1936. Rodman with C. of Ga. Ry, 1898-1900; transitman B.&O. R.R. Co., 1900-03, resident engr., 1903-04; asst. engr. A.C.L. R.R., 1904-06, engr. of roadway, 1906-08; locating engr. C. of Ga. R.R., 1908-09; supt. Hall Parker Contracting Co., 1910-11; engr. maintenance of way Lehigh and New England R.R., 1911-13, asst. supt., 1913-17, supt., 1917-27, gen. supt., 1927-30; gen. mgr. Western Maryland Ry., 1930-33, v.p. and gen. mgr., 1933-34, pres. since 1934; also pres. numerous subsidiaries; pres. Maryland Smokeless Coal Co., Somerset Coal Co., Western Md. Investment Co. Home: 315 Suffolk Rd., Guilford. Office: 502 Standard Oil Bldg., Baltimore, Md.

BROWN, Chester Timothy, physician; b. Tuckerton, N.J., Oct. 25, 1882; s. Timothy W. and Susan L. (Blackman) B.; B.Sc. Rutgers Coll., New Brunswick, N.J., 1903; M.D., Johns Hopkins Med. Sch., Baltimore, Md., 1907; m. Della L. Conger, Nov. 23, 1909; 1 son, Conger. Interne New York City Hosp., 1907-08; med. supervisor, Prudential Ins. Co. of America, Newark, N.J., 1909-18, asst. med. dir., 1918-21, asso. med. dir., 1921-34, med. dir. since 1934. Mem. A.M.A., Assn. of Life Ins., Med. Dirs. of America, Nat. Assn. Industrial Physicians and Surgeons, Beta Theta Pi, Phi Beta Kappa. Republican. Mem. Dutch Ref. Ch. Clubs: Union (New Brunswick); Cartaret (Trenton). Home: 102 N. 6th Av., New Brunswick. Office: 763 Broad St., Newark, N.J.

BROWN, Clarence Montgomery, business exec.; b. New York, N.Y., Dec. 1, 1868; s. Nicholas Francis and Louise Benner (Bell) B.; LL.B., U. of Pa., 1895; m. Luella Conwell, Apr. 2, 1902; children—Howard Benner, Lorna Conwell (Mrs. E. Wayne Haley), Robert Montgomery, Janet Danby (Mrs. William G. Guernsey). Engaged as conveyancer, 1882-95; attorney for corporations, 1895-1931; chairman board dirs. Pittsburgh Plate Glass Co. since 1931; president C. H. Wheeler Manufacturing Company; dir. Insurance Company of North America, Central-Penn Nat. Bank, Loyal Hanna Coal and Coke Company, Southern Alkali Corporation. Republican. Episcopalian. Clubs: Union League, Science and Art, Midday, Cricket, Whitemarsh Valley Golf (Phila.); Rockefeller Center (New York); Seaview Golf (Absecon, N.J.); Boca Raton (Fla.) Club; Ribault (Jacksonville, Fla.). Home: Chestnut Hill, Pa. Office: 1616 Walnut St., Philadelphia, Pa.

BROWN, Donaldson, v.p. Gen. Motors Corpn.; b. Baltimore, Md., Feb. 1, 1885; s. John Willcox and Ellen (Turner) B.; B.S. in E.E., Va. Poly. Inst., 1902; grad. study Cornell U., 1903; m. Greta du Pont Barksdale, June 20, 1916; children—Hamilton Barksdale, Frank Donaldson, Bruce Ford, Greta Barksdale, John Vaughn Willcox, Keene Claggett. In elec. dept. B.&O. R.R. Co., 1903; gen. mgr. Baltimore sales office Sprague Electric Co., 1904-08; in sales dept. E. I. duPont de Nemours & Co., 1908, gen. mgrs. office, 1912, asst. treas., 1914, treas., 1918-21, dir. since 1921; v.p. Gen. Motors Corpn. since 1921, in charge finance, 1921-29, chmn. finance com., 1929, vice chmn. since 1937. Mem. Am. Acad. Polit. and Social Science, Acad. Polit. Science, Phi Kappa Phi, Delta Phi. Republican. Episcopalian. Clubs: Economic, Metropolitan (New York); Baltimore (Baltimore); Fishers Island (Fishers Island, N.Y.); Wilmington (Del.) Country. Home: Port Deposit, Md. Office: 1775 Broadway, New York, N.Y.

BROWN, Edgar, botanist; b. Ontario Co., N.Y., Sept. 25, 1871; s. Amos C. and Emma L. (Smith) B.; Ph.B., Union Coll., N.Y., 1895; m. Harriet V. Tefft, Aug. 14, 1902; m. 2d, Elizabeth D. Gould, June 6, 1934. Botanist in charge seed testing labs. U.S. Dept. Agr., 1902-38, principal botanist. Mem. Washington Acad. Science, Phi Gamma Delta, Sigma Xi. Mem. Soc. of Friends. Club: Cosmos. Author of bulls. Dept. of Agr. Home: Lanham, Md.

BROWN, Edgar Field, banker; b. Baltimore, Md., May 13, 1897; s. Harry Tevis and Dora Augusta (Depkin) B.; student pub. schs., Baltimore, 1903-11, Baltimore Poly. Inst., 1912-13, Baltimore Business Coll., 1913-14, Pace and Pace, Baltimore, 1915-16, spl. courses Johns Hopkins U., 1926-27; m. Ardelle M. Clifford, June 24, 1927 (divorced 1939). Clk. First Nat. Bank of Baltimore, 1915-16, Title Guarantee & Trust Co., Baltimore 1916-1918-23, New Amsterdam Casualty Co., Baltimore, 1916-17; asst. secy. Century Trust Co., Baltimore, 1923-29; asst. sec., asst. treas. Baltimore Trust Co., 1929-34; asst. sec. and asst. treas. Baltimore Trust Corpn., 1934-39, sec.-treas. since 1939; v.p. Baltimore Mortgage Co. since 1934, Key Realty Corpn. since 1935; treas. Newark (N.J.) Distributing Terminals, Inc., since 1932, Baltimore Co., since 1934, Baltimore Gillet Co. since 1934; treas. and dir. Home Owners Finance Co., Baltimore, since 1938; sec.-treas. Baltimore Realty Trust, Inc., and Fiscal Mortgage Co. since 1939. Served as private, 1st class, 32d Machine Gun Bn., U.S. Army, during World War. Baptist. Mason (Concordia Lodge 13, Baltimore). Club: Rodgers Forge Golf and Country (Towson, Md.). Home: 3706 N. Charles St. Office: Baltimore Trust Bldg., Baltimore, Md.

BROWN, Ellis Yarnall, Jr., mfr.; paper mill machinery; b. Phila., Pa., Sept. 6, 1880; s. Ellis Yarnall and Sarah Elizabeth (Willits) B.; prep. edn.. Haverford (Pa) Coll. Grammar Sch.; A.B., Haverford Coll., 1901; m. Mary Downing Godley, Apr. 29, 1911; children—Ellis Yarnall III, Thomas Downing, Francis Godley, Richard Willits. Apprentice Pa. Steel Co., Steelton, Pa., 1901; since 1902 with Dowingtown (Pa.) Mfg. Co., mfrs. paper mill machinery, now v.p., treas. and dir; v.p. and dir. Dowingtown Nat. Bank. Pres. Dowingtown Borough council. Mem. Triangle Soc. of Haverford Coll. Republican. Soc. of Friends. Club: Dowingtown Business. Address: Dowingtown, Pa.

BROWN, Ford Keeler, educator; b. at Port Townsend, Wash., February 25, 1895; s. David E. and Mary (Ford) B.; grad. Tacoma (Wash.) High Sch., 1912; A.B., U. of Wash., 1920; D. Phil., Oxford Univ.; m. Zenith J. (nee) Jones; 1 dau., Janet Calvert. Asst. prof. of English, U. of Wash., 1923-24; asso. prof. of

English, St. John's Coll., 1925-29, prof., 1929-39, tutor since 1939. Rhodes Scholar from Wash., 1920; Guggenheim Fellow, 1928. Mem. Phi Kappa Sigma, Phi Beta Kappa. Club: 14 West Hamilton St. (Baltimore). Home: 243 King George St., Annapolis, Md.

BROWN, Francis Shunk, lawyer; b. Phila., June 9, 1858; s. Charles (many yrs. mem. Congress) and Elizabeth (Shunk) B.; g.s. Francis R. Shunk, gov. of Pa., and g.g.s. of William Findlay, gov. of Pa. and U.S. senator; grad. Wilmington Conf. Acad., Del.; LL.B., U. of Pa., 1879; LL.D., Lafayette, 1915; m. Lizzie Hamm, Apr. 1883; children—Francis Shunk, Anna Haines. In law practice, Phila., since 1879; mem. firm Brown & Williams; special counsel Tax Commn. of Pa., 1909-11; pres. bd. dirs. City Trusts of Philadelphia; attorney general of Pa., 1915-19. Mem. American Bar Assn., Pa. Bar Assn., Philadelphia Bar Assn. (ex-chancellor), Lawyers' Club of Phila. (pres.), Sons of Delaware, Scotch-Irish Soc. of Pa., Friendly Sons of St. Patrick, Am. Acad. Polit. and Social Science, Hist. Soc. Pa., Acad. Polit. Science of New York, etc. Clubs: Art (past pres.), Penn. Overbrook Golf, Chesapeake Cruising, Elk River Yacht. Home: 5927 Drexel Rd. Office: 1005 Morris Bldg., Philadelphia, Pa.

BROWN, Francis Shunk, Jr., judge; b. Phila., Pa., Dec. 3, 1891; s. Francis Shunk and Elizabeth (Hamm) B.; student Haverford (Pa.) Sch.; Ph.B., Lafayette Coll., Easton, Pa., 1913; LL.B., U. of Pa. Law Sch., 1916; m. Janet Ramsey McKeen, Feb. 10, 1917; children—Francis Shunk III, Maxwell McKeen. Admitted to Phila. bar, 1916; asso. with Simpson, Brown and Williams (subsequently Brown and Williams), Phila., 1916-27; asst. dist. atty., Phila. Co., 1923-26; judge ct. of common pleas number 4, Phila. Co., 1928-37, re-elected, 1937, for second ten year term. Served as pvt., U.S. Army, 1917-18, rising to capt., Adj. Gen.'s Dept., 1918; hon. disch., 1918. Alumni trustee Lafayette Coll., Easton, Pa., 1933-38. Mem. Gen. Alumni Bd. and Alumni Council of U. of Pa., 312th F.A. Assn. (mem. exec. com.), Phila. Pa. and Am. bar assns., Artisans' Order of Mutual Protection (William Patton Assembly 70), Am. Legion, Zeta Psi, Phi Delta Phi. Republican. Episcopalian. Elk (Phila. Lodge 2). Clubs: Penn Athletic (mem. bd. of govs.), Union League, Constitutional, Socialegal, Lawyers (Phila.). Home: 6809 Cresheim Rd. Office: 442 City Hall, Philadelphia, Pa.

BROWN, Frederick Lane, physician; b. Somerville, N. J., Jan. 13, 1883; s. James, Jr., and Gertrude Potter (Lane) B.; A.B., Princeton U., 1905; M.D., Coll. of Phys. & Surgs. of Columbia U., 1910; m. Esther May Suydam, June 15, 1912; children—Phoebe Esther (Mrs. Louis Stannard Baker), Frederick Lane, Jr. Interne, Bellevue Hosp., New York, 1910-12; engaged in gen. practice of medicine at New Brunswick, N.J., since 1912; mem. med. staff, St. Peter's Hosp., New Brunswick; chief of med. div., med. staff, Middlesex Hosp., New Brunswick, N.J.; mem. bd. mgrs. New Brunswick Savings Instn. since 1934. Mem. bd. dirs. Chamber of Commerce, New Brunswick, N.J. Fellow Am. Coll. Physicians; mem. N.J. Med. Soc., A.M.A. Republican. Dutch Ref. Ch. Mason. Address: 67 Livingston Av., New Brunswick, N.J.

BROWN, Gabriel Scot, mfr.; b. Dreher Twp., Wayne Co., Pa., Nov. 10, 1870; s. Thomas Mitchell and Jane (Lorimer) B.; prep. edn., Hillman Acad., Wilkes-Barre, Pa.; C.E., Princeton, 1894; m. Grace Little, Oct. 14, 1896; children—Elizabeth, Frances, Mary Little, Lorimer Hager, Thos. Mitchell. Pres. Alpha Portland Cement Co., 1914-34, now chairman of the board; director Yale & Towne Manufacturing Company, First Nat. Bank, Easton. Past president Portland Cement Assn. Mem. Am. Soc. Mech. Engrs., Am. Soc. for Testing Materials, Princeton Engring. Assn. Republican. Presbyn. Home: 720 Meixel St. Office: First Nat. Bank Bldg., Easton, Pa.

BROWN, George Adelbert, real estate; b. Cleveland, O., Oct. 21, 1882; s. David and Clara Alice (Kelly) B.; m. Jessie Luella Marker, Sept. 7, 1904; children—Eldiva Mae Bauer, Jessie Louise Clerihue. Title examiner Potter Title & Trust Co., 1901-16, settlement officer, 1916-18; supervisor real estate Phila. Co., Pittsburgh, since 1934. Exec. sec. Titusville (Pa.) Chamber of Commerce, 1918-21; exec. sec. Pittsburgh Real Estate Bd., 1922-24, now mem. bd. of govs. Club: South Hills Country. Home: 1307 Tennessee Av., Dormont, Pa. Office: 435 Sixth Av., Pittsburgh, Pa.

BROWN, George Earl, supt. of schools; b. Toronto, Kan., Feb. 12, 1883; s. George Washington and Mary Janette (Watkins) B.; grad. Kan. State Teachers Coll., Emporia, 1906; student Ind. U., 1907-08; A.B., Colo. State Teachers Coll., Greeley, 1912; A.M., Denver U., 1919; A.M., Columbia, 1926; m. Hazel Marie Harris; children—Mary-Lou Watkins (Mrs. Rhea Keith Blakely), Robert William. Began as rural school teacher, Coffey Co., Kan., 1900; prin. of schools, LeRoy, Kan., 1902-05; asst. prin., Rockport, Ind., 1906-07; supt. of schools, Garden City, Kan., 1907-13, Wenatchee, Wash., 1914-16, Greeley, Colo., 1916-29, Bisbee, Ariz., 1929-31; state commr. of edn., State of Wyo., spring of 1900; supt. of schools, Ocean City, N.J., since 1931. Pres. Colo. Edn. Assn., 1928. Mem. N.E.A., Am. Assn. of School Adminstrs., N.J. Council of Edn., N.J. Edn. Assn., South Jersey Schoolmen's Assn., Yellow Dogs. Republican. Methodist. Mason. Rotarian (gov. Dist. 50, 1936-37). Home: 228 Atlantic Av. Office: City Schools, Ocean City, N.J.

BROWN, George Harold, research engr.; b. North Milwaukee, Wis., Oct. 14, 1908; s. James Clifford and Ida Louise (Siegert) B.; B.S., U. of Wis., 1930, M.S., same, 1931, Ph.D., same, 1933; m. Julia Elizabeth Ward, Dec. 26, 1932; children—James Ward, George Harold, Jr. Employed as research engr., RCA Mfg. Co., Camden, N.J., 1933-37; mem. firm Godley & Brown, cons. radio engrs., 1937; research engr. RCA Mfg. Co., Camden, N.J., since 1938; lecturer on radio antennas, First Annual Broadcast Engrs. Conf., O. State U., 1938. Asso. Inst. Radio Engrs. Mem. A.A.A.S., Sigma Xi, Tau Beta Pi, Pi Tau Pi Sigma, Kappa Eta Kappa. Awarded Wis. Pub. Utilities Assn. Fellowship, 1930-31; U. of Wis. Regents Fellowship, 1931-33. Presbyterian. Contbr. fifteen papers of theory and design of radio antennas. Home: 500 Chews Landing Road, Haddonfield, N.J. Office: RCA Mfg. Co., Camden, N.J.

BROWN, George W., Jr., banker; b. Phila., Pa., Dec. 5, 1886; s. George W. B.; student pub. schs., North East Training Sch. and Pierce Business Coll., Phila.; m. Hanna R. Shelly, Aug. 1908; 1 son, George W. III. With Excelsior Trust Co., Phila., 1902; successively teller Nat. Security Bank, asst. to pres. Logan Trust Co., chief examiner Pa. Dept. of Banking, v.p. Nat. Bank of Commerce, Phila., mgr. Phila. agency Reconstruction Finance Corpn.; now pres. Integrity Trust Co., Phila.; dir. Commonwealth Title Co. Republican. Episcopalian. Mason. Clubs: University, Union League, Bank Officers (Phila.); Merion (Pa.) Cricket. Home: Cambridge, Alden Park, Germantown. Office: 16th and Walnut St., Philadelphia, Pa.

BROWN, Harry Fletcher, chemist; b. Natick, Mass., July 10, 1867; s. William H. and Maria F. (Osgood) B.; A.B., Harvard U., 1890, A.M., 1892; hon. D.Sc., University of Delaware, 1930; m. Florence M. Hammett, Oct. 26, 1897. Chief chemist at U.S. Naval Torpedo Sta., Newport, R.I., 1893-1900; engaged in the investigation and development of smokeless powder in the Navy Dept.; gen. supt. Internat. Smokeless Powder & Chem. Co., 1900-04; dir. of mfr. smokeless powder, E. I. duPont de Nemours & Co., 1904-15, v.p. in charge smokeless powder dept. 1915-19, now v.p. and dir. E. I. duPont de Nemours & Co.; vice-pres. and dir. Christiana Securities Co.; mem. bd. of mgrs. Wilmington Savings Soc.; dir. Equitable Trust Co. Trustee U. of Del. Mem. Am. Chem. Soc., Nat. Edn. Assn. Home: 1010 Broome St. Office: Du Pont Bldg., Wilmington, Del.

BROWN, Harry Jay, newspaper corr.; b. Washington, D.C., Nov. 29, 1877; s. Stephen C. and Frances C. (Holder) B.; ed. high sch.; m. Claire Rigby, Dec. 8, 1900. Washington corr. since 1897; corr. Portland Oregonian, 1900-20, variously corr., Tacoma (Wash.) News and Ledger, Anaconda (Mont.) Standard, Helena (Mont.) Record, Inland-Herald, Spokane, Wash.; now corr. Salt Lake Tribune, Boise (Idaho) Statesman, Spokane (Wash.) Spokesman-Review and Oakland (Calif.) Tribune. Asst. to dir. of publicity in Rep. presidential campaign, 1924; dir. of publicity in Congressional and Senatorial campaign, 1926; asst. to chmn. Rep. Nat. Com. in presidential campaign, 1928; asst. dir. of publicity Rep. Nat. Com., 1936. Clubs: Gridiron (pres. 1928), Nat. Press. Home: 6412 Ridgewood Av., Chevy Chase, Md. Office: Transportation Bldg., Washington, D. C.

BROWN, Helen Elizabeth, lawyer; b. Terre Haute, Ind., Dec. 14, 1899; d. Charles Edgar and Helen (Kelly) B.; student Barnard Coll., 1919-21; LL.B., U. of Md. Law Sch., 1926; unmarried. Engaged in newspaper work for Fort Worth Record and Dallas Dispatch, 1918; mem. editorial staff Fort Worth Press, working in City Hall, 1921-22; engaged in covering courts for Baltimore Post, 1922 (first woman in that position for Baltimore newspaper); admitted to Md. bar, 1926; in gen. practice of law at Baltimore since 1926; jr. mem. law firm Ingram & Brown since 1927. Chmn. Workmen's Compensation Dept. of Md. State Roads Commn., 1935-39. Mem. Am. Bar Assn., Women's Bar Assn. of Baltimore (ex-pres.), Phi Delta Delta; formed first orgn. of women members of Bar in Md. known as Inez Milholland Law Club, 1927; founder and first pres. Business and Professional Women's Council, 1928, again pres., 1930-32. Republican. Episcopalian. Clubs: Women's City, Barnard (Baltimore). Home: 1734 Bolton St. Office: 16 St. Paul St., Baltimore, Md.

BROWN, Henry P., Jr.; asst. prof surgery Pa. Grad. sch.; asso. in surgery, U. of Pa.; surgeon and chief Out Patient Clinic, Pa. Hosp.; surgeon Children's and Presbyn. hosps. Address: 1930 Chestnut St., Philadelphia, Pa.

BROWN, Henry Seymour, clergyman; b. Rochester, N. Y., Nov. 2, 1875; s. John Milton and Cordelia Jane (Fletcher) B.; prep. edn., Lyons Twp. High Sch., La Grange, Ill.; A.B., U. of Tex., 1897; grad. Princeton Theol. Sem., 1900; D.D., Blackburn Coll., Carlinville, Ill., 1917; m. Emma Slee Underhill, June 25, 1907; children—Fletcher Gridley, Katherine Underhill, Henry Seymour. Ordained Presbyn. ministry, 1900; asst. pastor South Park Ch., Newark, N.J., 1900-02, Tabernacle Ch., Phila., Pa., 1902; pastor successively First Ch., East Aurora, N.Y., First Ch., East Cleveland, O., Lake View Ch., Chicago, until 1918; supt. Ch. Extension Bd., Presbytery of Chicago, 1918-37, exec. sec., 1923-37; v.p. Princeton Theol. Sem. since Sept. 1937; member Department of Ch. Coöperation and Union of Gen. Assembly Presbyn. Ch. Republican. Home: 48 Mercer St. Address: Princeton Theological Seminary, Princeton, N.J.

BROWN, Henry Wilson, hardware mcht.; b. Punxsutawney, Pa., Nov. 7, 1896; s. George Copper and Adda (Wilson) B.; student Punxsutawney (Pa.) High Sch., 1911-15, U. of Pa., 1915-19; m. Hazel Lockard, May 10, 1920; children—Henry Lockard, Jeanne W. Began as clk. in hardware store and operated a coal mine, 1919; asso. with father in hardware business since 1919; treas. and dir. Punxsutawney (Pa.) Hardware Co. since 1922; treas. and dir. Punxsutawnay Brewing Co. since 1920; treas. Neal Granite and Marble Co. Served as sergt. Am. Ambulance Corps, France 1917, 1st sergt. Camp Greenleaf, Ga., 1918-19. Trustee John A. Weber Memorial Sch. Mem. Am. Legion, Sigma Phi Epsilon. Republican. Baptist. Mason (32°, Shriner). Elk. Clubs: Country, Army and Navy, Elks, Masons. Home: 109 Church St., Punxsutawney, Pa.

BROWN, Herbert V., mfr.; b. Hartland, N.Y., Aug. 12, 1887; s. George C. and Mary Jane (Booth) B.; grad. Lockport (N.Y.) High Sch., 1904; E.E., Syracuse (N.Y.) U., 1908; m. Maude A. Sherwood, June 6, 1911. With Pneumelectric Machine Co. as testing engr. and later in sales, 1908-16; organized Cherrytree Machine Co., 1916, later name changed to Brown Equipment Co. and then through merger to Brown-Fayro Co., mfrs. mining machinery, gray iron castings, fabricated steel, Johnstown, Pa.; now pres. Brown-Fayro Co. Mem. Tau Beta Pi. Republican. Catholic. Club: Sunnehanna Country. Home: 623 Luzerne St. Office: 940 Ash St., Johnstown, Pa.

BROWN, Howard Benner, lawyer; b. Phila., Pa., Mar. 20, 1903; s. Clarence Montgomery and Luella (Conwell) B.; grad. Hotchkiss Sch., Lakeville, Conn., 1922; B.S., Princeton U., 1926; LL.B., U. of Pa., 1929; m. Elizabeth Fitch, Sept. 15, 1934; 1 son, Edward Benner. Admitted to Pa. bar, 1930, and since practiced at Phila.; dir. and asst. sec. The Pitcairn Co., Phila., investments; dir. and asst. sec. 49 W. 37th St. Corpn.; dir. and sec. West Chelten Corpn.; dir. Parkside Realty Co., Pittsburgh Valve and Fittings Corpn., C. H. Wheeler Mfg. Co.; asst. sec. Southern Minerals Corpn. Mem. Phila. Stock Exchange. Mem. Phila. Bar Assn., Phi Gamma Delta, Phi Delta Phi. Republican. Episcopalian. Club: Midday (Phila.). Home: Eastern Av., Chestnut Hill. Office: 1616 Walnut St., Philadelphia, Pa.

BROWN, Hylton Roller, mech. engr.; b. Williamsburg, Pa., May 11, 1895; s. George Williams and Emma Patterson (Roller) B.; B.S., Pa.. State Coll., 1916, M.E., 1923; m. Rosina Warden Cole, Oct. 2, 1922; children—Hylton Roller, Meryl Louise, Shirley Joy. Flour mill engr. Washburn Crosby Co., Buffalo, N.Y., 1916; in charge Eastern Dist., War Emergency Campaign for dust explosion prevention, U.S. Dept. Agr., 1917-19; with U.S. Grain Corpn., 1919-20; with U.S. Dept. of Agr. since 1920, successively engaged in dust explosion prevention in industrial plants, Dept. rep. Am. Standards Assn., Nat. Fire Protection Assn., Nat. Fire Waste Council of U.S. Chamber of Commerce, now chief of dust explosion sect., Chem. Engring. Research Div. Mem. A.A.A.S., Pa. State Alumni Assn. (sec. Washington chapter), Pi Kappa Alpha. Presbyn. Mason. Writer numerous papers and publs. on dust explosion prevention in industrial plants, venting dust explosion pressure and use of inert Gas for Explosion Prevention. Home: 9410 2d Av., Silver Spring, Md. Office: U.S. Dept. of Agr., Washington, D.C.

BROWN, J(ames) Douglas, economist; b. Somerville, N.J., Aug. 11, 1898; s. James and Ella M. (Lane) B.; A.B., Princeton, 1920, A.M., 1921, Ph.D., 1928; m. Dorothy Andrews, of Eugene, Ore., June 18, 1923; children—Martha Jane, Dorothy Andrews, James Douglas, Elizabeth Andrews. Instr. Princeton U., 1921-23, 1926-27, dir. industrial relation sect. since 1926, asst. prof. economics, 1927-1934, professor of economics since 1934. Instructor, New York Univ., 1923-25; visiting assistant prof., U. of Pa., 1932-33. Served in A.E.F., Med. Detachment, 167th Inf., 42d Div., U.S.A., World War. Mem. President's Emergency Com. for Employment, 1930-31, Advisory Com. on R.R. Employment to Federal Co-ordinator of Transportation, 1933-35; participant Princeton Survey of N.J. State Govt., 1932. Dir. N.J. Conf. of Social Work since 1933; staff consultant President's Com. on Economic Security, 1934-35; tech. advisor N.J. Social Security Commn., 1935-36, assisting in drafting of N.J. unemployment ins. law; cons. economist Social Security Bd. since 1936; chmn. Adv. Council on Social Security since 1937. Mem. Am. Econ. Assn., Am. Statis. Assn., Am. Assn. for Labor Legislation, Am. Management Assn., Internat. Industrial Relations Inst., Phi Beta Kappa. Presbyn. Author: (with Eleanor Davis) The Labor Banking Movement in U.S., 1929; (with others), Facing the Facts, an Economic Diagnosis, 1932; also articles on industrial relations. Joint author or editor of repts. on industrial relations, pub. by industrial relations sect., Princeton, since 1926. Home: 148 Mercer St., Princeton, N.J.

BROWN, James Richard, surgeon; b. Hinton, W.Va., Mar. 11, 1905; s. Euel A. and Elizabeth (Coffey) B.; student U. of Richmond, Va., 1923-25; M.D., Med. Coll. of Va., Richmond, Va., 1929; m. Bertha Ingle, May 30, 1929; children—Betty Anne, Peggy Marie, James Richard II. Mem. of staff St. Mary's Hosp., and C.&O. Ry. Employees Hosp., Huntington, since 1931. Fellow Am. Coll. Surgeons; mem. Cabell Co., Med. Soc., W.Va. State Med. Soc., Phi Beta Pi. Club: Exchange. Home: 612 10th Av. Office: 1119 6th Av., Huntington, W.Va.

BROWN, James Robert, clergyman, mfr.; b. Allentown, Pa., Aug. 16, 1866; s. James Robert and Laanna L. (Beers) B.; A.B., Muhlenberg Coll., Allentown, 1887; B.D., Theol. Sem., Lancaster, Pa., 1890; m. Helen E. Mohn, July 28, 1889; children—Raymond Bishop, John Robert, Jasper Roger, Mary (Mrs. Earl T. Hilbert), James Albert, Emma Catherine (Mrs. Raymond B. Hilbert) Miriam Fietta (Mrs. Alfred Ibach), Henry Arthur. Ordained to ministry Reformed Ch. in U.S.; pastor Rebersburg, Pa., 1890-96, Schwarzwald Congregation, Jacksonwald, Pa., 1896-1913; helped organize, 1921, Mt. Penn Trust Co., pres. 1921-38; organized Easterly Woolen Co., 1909, and since treas.; helped organize Lewisburg (Pa) Mills, 1914, since treas. Burgess St. Lawrence, Pa., 1927-33. Treas. Exeter Twp. Sch. Bd., 1914-20. Mem. P.O.S. of A. Democrat. Mem. Evangelical and Reformed Church. Mason (33°, Shriner, Potentate Rajah Temple, Reading, Pa., 1932). Address: Esterly, Pa.

BROWN, James Tyler, investment analyst; b. Rockville, Ind., Nov. 8, 1904; s. Charles John and Grace Mae (LeFever) B.; A.B., DePauw U., Greencastle, Ind., 1926; M.B.A., Harvard, 1928; m. Frances Louise Tremper, Sep. 7, 1934. Began as asst. prof. accounting and finance U. of Ore., 1928-29; treas. dept. L.S. Ayres & Co., Indianapolis, Ind., 1929; mgr. cost dept. Peerless Motor Car Co., Cleveland, O., 1929-30; investment analyst Wood, Struthers & Co., New York, N.Y., 1930-37; mgr. statistical dept. Shields & Co., New York, N.Y., 1937-38; investment analyst Mellon Securities Corpn., Pittsburgh since 1938. Capt. 393d Inf., U.S. Army (res.). Mem. Am. Statis. Assn., N.Y. Soc. of Security Analysts, DePauw U. (Rector Scholar), Beta Theta Pi. Republican. Presbyterian. Mason. Clubs: Edgeworth (Sewickley, Pa.); Harvard (New York). Home: 1200 Beaver Rd., Sewickley, Pa. Office: Mellon Securities Corpn., 525 William Penn Pl., Pittsburgh, Pa.

BROWN, Jane Hays, library orgn.; b. Carnegie, Pa., Oct. 8, 1887; d. Robert Henry and Eliza Thaw (Kirkwood) B.; A. B., Agnes Scott Coll., Decatur, Ga., 1908, fellow, same, 1908-09; certificate, Emory Library Sch., Atlanta, Ga., 1912, Cleveland (O) Training Sch., 1914; grad. study, Slade Sch. of U. of London, 1936, Emory Univ. Grad. Sch., 1938. Engaged as co. librarian, Crisp Co., Cordele, Ga., 1911-12; first asst. and children's librarian, various branches, Cleveland (O.) Pub. Library, 1912-14; first asst. and supervisor children's work, Pub. Library, Lakewood, O., 1914-18; reference librarian and instr., Pub. Library, Harrisburg, Pa., 1919-20; librarian, Pub. Library, Kittanning, Pa., 1923-24; field worker, Pa. State Library Commn., 1924-26; county librarian, Atlantic County, N.J. since 1926. Served in Am. Library Assn. War Service, 1918-19; U.S.A. and U.S.N. Library Service, 1920-22. Mem. Am. Library Assn., Am. Assn. Univ. Women, N.J. Library Assn. Republican. Presbyn. Home: 400 Park Rd. Office: Atlantic County Library, May's Landing, N.J.

BROWN, John Arthur; in practice of law since 1908. Office: Land Title Bldg., Philadelphia, Pa.

BROWN, John D. M.; Florence T. Saeger prof. English literature. Home: 1620 Walnut St., Allentown, Pa.

BROWN, John F.; judge 20th Judicial Circuit of W.Va. Address: Elkins, W.Va.

BROWN, John Jacob, officer corpn.; b. Tyler, Tex., Jan. 19, 1873; s. John A. and Emma A. (Sanford) B.; ed. pvt. schs.; m. Mary Katherine McCoole, 1922. Constrn. engr. for Consolidated Compress Co., Tex., 1895; later associated with Henry R. Worthington Pump Co. of New York as specialist on development of hydraulic equipment for compressing cotton; when latter became part of Internat. Steam Pump Co., made gen. Western mgr., headquarters at Chicago; became v.p. Wheeler Condenser and Engring. Co., New York, 1907, elected pres., 1918; during World War, acted as chmn. Condenser Com., War Industry Board and a mem. Non-ferrous Metals Com.; upon consolidation of Wheeler Condenser and Engring. Co. and Power Specialty Co. as Foster Wheeler Corpn., became chmn. bd. latter; dir. Fidelity Union Trust Co., Cranford Trust Co., Foundation Foreign, Liberty Mutual Ins. Co. Mem. Am. Soc. Mech. Engrs., Soc. Naval Architects and Marine Engrs., New York Southern Soc. Clubs: Engineers, Bankers, New York Yacht, Recess, Baltusrol Golf, Abenakee; Boco Raton. Home: Cranford, N.J.; also Biddeford Pool, Me. Office: 165 Broadway, New York, N.Y.

BROWN, John Tabelé, Jr., corpn. official; b. Phila., Pa., Nov. 6, 1886; s. John Tabelé and Henrietta Elethea (Lehman) B.; student Chestnut Hill Acad., Phila., 1894-1903; B.S., U. of Pa., 1907; m. Elizabeth Richardson Pugh of Germantown, Pa., Sept. 28, 1912; 1 dau., Lois Newbold. Began as order clk., Haines Jones & Cadbury Co., Phila., 1907-12, treas., 1912-27; asst. treas. Hajoca Corpn., Phila., mfrs. and wholesalers plumbing & heating supplies, 1927-32, treas. since 1932; treas. Titan Building & Loan Assn. Mem. Nat. Assn. of Credit Men (past nat. dir.), Phi Beta Kappa. Republican. Presbyterian. Home: 118 Heacock Lane, Wyncote, Pa. Office: 31st St. and Walnut St. Bridge, Philadelphia, Pa.

BROWN, J(ohn) Thompson, vice-pres. E. I. du Pont de Nemours Co.; b. Baltimore, Md., June 8, 1882; s. John Willcox and Ellen Turner (Macfarland) B.; B.S., Va. Poly. Inst., 1902; student Cornell U., 1902-03; m. Yolande de Vignier, April 23, 1914; children—John Willcox, Robert Mott, Odile de Vignier (dec.), John Glenn, Mary Turner, Ysabel de Vignier. With E. L. du Pont de Nemours & Co. since 1903, beginning as draftsman and advancing through engring., operating and managerial positions, vice-pres. since 1929; dir. E. I. du Pont de Nemours & Co., Canadian Industries, Ltd., Remington Arms Co., Inc. Mem. Delaware State Bd. of Charities, Trustee Episcopal Ch. Sch. Foundation, Tower Hill Sch. Assn. Mem. Delta Phi, Omicron Delta Kappa. Episcopalian. Clubs: Wilmington, Wilmington Country, Du Pont Country (Wilmington). Home: Montchanin, Del. Office: Du Pont Bldg., Wilmington, Del.

BROWN, Joseph Baily, lawyer; b. Owen Co., Ky., Nov. 7, 1886; s. Knox and Adeline Crittenden (Watson) B.; A.B., Centre Coll., Danville, Ky., 1907; grad. study Georgetown U. Law Sch , Washington, D.C., 1909-11; LL.B., U. of Pittsburgh Law Sch., 1912; m. Helen Blish, Dec. 25, 1919; children—Knox, Louise Joslin, Helen Elizabeth. Admitted to Pa. bar, 1912, and since in practice at Pittsburgh, specializing in patent law; asso. with F. W. H. Clay, 1912-14, with Frederick W. Winter, 1914-19; mem. firm Winter & Brown, 1919-23, Winter, Brown & Critchlow, 1923-26, Brown & Critchlow, 1926-33, Brown, Critchlow & Flick, Pittsburgh, since 1933. Served with Dept. of State, 1918-19, sent abroad, 1918, to collect information as to enemy practices in relation to patent and trademark matters. Del. of U.S. to conv. Internat. Union for Protection of Industrial Property, The Hague, 1925. Trustee Centre Coll., Danville, Ky. Mem. Am. Patent Law Assn. (pres. 1936-38), Am. Bar Assn. (chmn. patent sect. 1934-36), Pittsburgh Patent Law Assn., Beta Theta Pi, Phi Alpha Delta. Presbyterian. Clubs: Duquesne, Oakmont Country, Field Pittsburgh); Cosmos (Washington, D.C.). Home: 404 S. Linden Av. Office: First Nat. Bank Bldg., Pittsburgh, Pa.

BROWN, Joseph J.; in practice of law since 1913. Office: Land Title Bldg., Philadelphia, Pa.

BROWN, Karl Kinder, pres. First Nat. Bank of Seaford; b. Seaford, Del., Sept. 20, 1896; s. William H. and Mary E. (Kinder) B.; student Seaford (Del.) Grade and High Sch., 1904-16; m. Anna May Carter, Aug. 8, 1918; children—Mary Carter, Karl Kinder. Began as clk., First Nat. Bank of Seaford, Del., 1916, asst. cashier, 1929-35, v.p., 1935-37, dir. since 1935, exec. v.p., 1937-39, pres. since 1939; treas. Central Realty Co., Seaford, Del. Served as corp., U.S. Army, 1918. Mem. Seaford Town Council, 1931-

34, treas., 1933. Steward St. Johns M.E. Ch., Seaford. Republican. Methodist. Mason. Club: Kiwanis (Seaford, Del.). Home: 315 Pine St. Office: High and Cannon Sts., Seaford, Del.

BROWN, Kenneth Rent, chemist; b. Pendleton, Ind., July 30, 1896; s. Calvin Fletcher and Mary (Rent) B.; grad. Pendleton (Ind.) High Sch., 1914; A.B., Swarthmore (Pa.) Coll., 1918; m. Rae Anita Horrobin, Aug. 21, 1920; children—Kenneth Horrobin, Richard Calvin, Robert Winfield. With Atlas Powder Co., mfrs. explosives, cellulosic products, etc., Tamaqua, Pa., since May 20, 1918, as chemist in Exptl. Lab., 1918-26, asst. dir., 1926-28, acting dir., 1928-30, and dir. Research Lab. since 1930. Mem. Am. Chem. Soc., Am. Inst. Chem. Engrs., Soc. of Chem. Industry, Am. Soc. Testing Materials, Electrochem. Soc., Sigma Xi, Phi Beta Kappa, Phi Kappa Psi. Republican. Clubs: Chemists (New York); Mahoning Valley Country (Lehighton, Pa.). Home: 118 Market St. Office: Research Laboratory, Atlas Powder Co., Tamaqua, Pa.

BROWN, Lawrence Greeley, physician; b. Hyman, S.C., Feb. 1, 1886; s. Ellison and Elizabeth (Eady) B.; M.D., Howard Univ. Med. Sch., Washington, D.C., 1914; grad. student, Columbia U., 1923, Surg. Inst. of Chicago, 1926; m. Lavinia E. Brown, Oct. 7, 1916; 1 dau., adopted, Landonia. Interne Freedmen's Hosp., Washington, D.C., 1914-15; engaged in gen. practice of medicine and surgery at Elizabeth, N.J., since 1915; pres. of staff, head of div. of medicine, Community Hosp., Newark, N.J.; courtesies, Alexian Brothers Hosp., Elizabeth, N.J., Beth Israel Hosp., Newark, N.J. Has served on many coms. and commns. for social betterment. Mem. A.M.A., Nat. Med. Assn., Interstate Post-Grad. Med. Assembly, Assn. Former Internes Freedmen's Hosp., Zeta Boulé. Republican. Baptist. Mason. K.P. Clubs: Howard Alumni of North Jersey. Home: 173 Madison Av., Elizabeth, N.J.

BROWN, Lewis Sarle, teacher voice and ch. music; b. West Edmeston, N.Y., June 3, 1893; s. Lewis Lamont and Ida Florence (Sarle) B.; student Utica (N.Y.) Conservatory of Music, 1920-23, U. of Mich., Ann Arbor, Mich., 1933; B.S.M., Southwestern Bapt. Theol. Sem. Sch. Sacred Music, 1925; studied voice under Robert Lawrence, Phila., 1925-36, Frank La Forge, N.Y. City, 1936, and others; m. Daisy Adams, June 3, 1926; children—Lewis Sarle, Abigail, Rioda Ann. Began as teacher of piano and ch. organist, 1912; dir. Sch. Sacred Music of Eastern Bapt. Theol. Sem., Phila., and prof. voice and ch. music since 1926. Republican. Baptist. Home: 130 Woodside Av., Narberth, Pa. Office: 1814 S. Rittenhouse Sq., Philadelphia, Pa.

BROWN, Lillian Olive, prof. of mathematics; b. Summit Station, Pa., Oct. 14, 1883; d. Jared S. and Sarah Ann (Berkheiser) Brown; grad. Keystone State Normal Sch., Kutztown, Pa., 1904; A.B., Dickinson Coll., 1908; A.M., Columbia, 1914; unmarried. Instr. mathematics, Hood Coll., 1908, now prof. and head dept. Mem. A.A.A.S., Math. Assn. America, Am. Assn. Univ. Profs., Nat. Council Teachers of Mathematics, Phi Beta Kappa. Democrat. Mem. Reformed Ch. Home: 328 Lindbergh Av., Frederick, Md.

BROWN, Mace, professional baseball; pitcher Pittsburgh Nat. League Baseball Club; mem. Nat. League All-Star Team, 1938. Address: care Pittsburgh Nat. League Baseball Club, Pittsburgh, Pa.

BROWN, Margaret Christine, college pres.; b. St. Lambert, P.Q., Can., Sept. 1, 1891; d. James Gentles and Sarah (Gibson) Brown; grad. St. Lambert Acad., Can., 1908; student Sch. for Teachers, Macdonald Coll., Can., 1908-09, Sch. of Phys. Edn., Chautauqua, N.Y., 1912, Sch. of Phys. Edn., McGill U., Montreal, 1920-21; B.S. in Edn., Rutgers U., 1930, Ed.M., 1936; unmarried. Teacher of elementary grades, Montreal Pub. Schs., 1909-12, teacher of phys. edn., 1912-21; teacher phys. edn., State Summer Normal Sch., Rutgers U., 1926-32; asst. dir. and registrar, Newark Normal Sch. of Phys. Edn. and Hygiene, 1921-26; dean and supervisor of student teaching, Panzer Coll. of Phys. Edn. and Hygiene, East Orange, N.J., 1926-32, pres. since 1932. Chmn. Nat. Com. on Women's Gymnastics; del. Internat. Fed. of Gymnastics, Berlin, 1936, Prague, 1938; adviser student sect. Am. Assn. for Health, Phys. Edn. and Recreation; ednl. chmn. Business and Professional Women's Club of the Oranges. Mem. N.J. Phys. Edn. Assn., Supervisors of Student Teaching, Nat. Soc. of Coll. Teachers of Edn. Author several articles and studies in professional lit. Home: 139 Glenwood Av. Office: Panzer College of Physical Education and Hygiene, East Orange, N.J.

BROWN, Martin, lawyer; b. Sherrard, W.Va., Sept. 1, 1871; s. Frederick M. and Sarah E. (Davidson) B.; B.C.S., Scio Coll. (now Mount Union Coll., Ohio), 1892, student summer 1903; student W.Va. Univ., Morgantown, 1894, 1902-03; m. Delora M. Dorsey, March 31, 1905; children—Homer Thayer (dec.), Jeannette Dorsey (wife of Dr. J. M. McCuskey), Genevieve. Engaged in teaching pub. schs. and high sch., 1895-1901; admitted to W.Va. bar, 1904, admitted to practice before Supreme Ct. of Appeals, W.Va., 1904, before Supreme Ct. of U.S., 1918; engaged in gen. practice of law at Moundsville, W.Va. since 1903; mem. firm Parsons & Brown, 1904-08; city solicitor, Benwood, 1914-22; served as mem. W.Va. Ho. of Dels., 1915-17; city solicitor Moundsville, 1908-12; pres., dir. and counsel Marshall County Bank, Moundsville, W.Va., since 1935; counsel for large local corpns. and has appeared in many important cases. Mem. Am., W.Va. State and Marshall Co. bar assns., Nat. Aeronautical Assn. of U.S.A. Republican. Methodist. Mason. Elk. K.P. Clubs: Moundsville Country, Marshall County Country (Moundsville). Home: 1117 E. Seventh St. Office: Marshall County Bank Bldg., Moundsville, W.Va.

BROWN, Neill S. III, wholesale paper dealer; b. Nashville, Tenn., May 24, 1873; s. Neill S. Jr. and Suzanne E. (Walton) B.; ed. Brookville (Md.) Acad., Va. Midland Acad. (Culpeper, Va.), Emerson Inst. (Washington, D.C.), Georgetown Coll. (Washington, D.C.); m. Gertrude M. Wagner, July 24, 1911; children—Neill S. IV, Ann Howard. Began as stenographer, 1890; vice-pres. R. P. Andrews Paper Co., Washington, D.C., 1897-1908; sales mgr. D. of C. Paper Co., 1908-14; vice-pres. West Penn Paper Co., Pittsburgh, 1914-18; since 1923 pres. Gen. Paper & Cordage Co., Pittsburgh, wholesale dealers in printing and wrapping papers; dir. Phoenix Glass Co. Episcopalian. Clubs: Edgeworth (Sewickley); Duquesne (Pittsburgh). Home: Shields, Pa. Office: 1411 Brighton Place, Pittsburgh, Pa.

BROWN, Oscar, lawyer; b. Phila., Pa., Sept. 2, 1905; s. Julius and Elizabeth (White) B.; A.B., Central High Sch., Phila.; LL.B., Temple U. Law Sch., Phila., 1926; unmarried. Admitted to Pa. bar, 1926, and since engaged in gen. practice of law at Phila.; mem. firm Welsh and Bluett, 1926-27, Welsh and Brown, 1927-32, in practice alone at Phila. since 1932; asst. dist. atty. Phila. Co., 1932-36. Mem. Am., Pa. State and Phila. bar assns., Lawyers Club of Phila., Pa. Soc., Friendly Sons of St. Patrick. Republican. Jewish religion. B'nai B'rith. Mason. Club: Green Valley Country. Home: 1936 Pine St. Office: 1700 Bankers Securities Bldg., Philadelphia, Pa.

BROWN, Owen Clarence, clergyman, editor; b. Cato, Kan., July 25, 1871; s. Israel Keys and Edith Eva (Johnson) B.; ed. Kan. Normal Coll., Ft. Scott, Kan., 1892, 97, 98; B.A., Ottawa (Kan.) U., 1902, M.A., 1909, D.D., 1919; B.D., Newton Theol. Instn., 1905; m. Lois C. Gates, July 12, 1899; 1 son, Carl Newton. Ordained Bapt. ministry, 1899; pastor Bronson, Kan., 1899-1902, Mt. Auburn Ch., Cambridge, Mass., 1904-05, First Ch., Emporia, Kan., 1905-07; First Ch., Lawrence, Kan., 1907-17; editor adult S.S. publs., Am. Bapt. Publ. Soc., 1917-24; editor in chief, same, 1924-33, sec. dept. of religious edn., 1928-33, exec. sec., 1933-38, special rep. since 1938. Republican. Home: Lansdowne, Pa. Office: 1701 Chestnut St., Philadelphia, Pa.

BROWN, Paul Goodwin, engineer; b. Red Oak, Ia., 1871; s. Isaac W. and Helen (Goodwin) B.; prep. edn., Wyoming Sem., Kingston, Pa.; student Cornell U., 1892-93; m. Antoinette Knapp, 1924. Pres. Keystone State Corpn. since 1925. Mem. Am. Soc. C.E., Western Soc. Engrs., Delta Kappa Epsilon. Clubs: Racquet, Cornell, Engineers, Phila. Country (Phila.); Engineers, Links, Whist, Turf and Field, United Hunts (New York); Seaview Golf (Absecon, N.J.); Boca Raton (Fla.); Gulf Stream Golf (Delray Beach, Fla.). Home: Boca Raton, Fla. Office: 1321 Arch St., Philadelphia, Pa.

BROWN, Perc Summers, vice-pres. Nat. Oil Products Co.; b. Ft. Bayard, N.M., Oct. 15, 1895; s. Edward and Alta Veronica (Summers) B.; ed. in public schools of Portland, Ore.; m. Marie Beach, Aug. 21, 1917; children—Bruce Langdon, Gordon Summers. With Albers Bros. Milling Co., 1910-22, beginning as office boy, Portland, Ore., 1910, advanced to mgr., Tacoma, Wash., 1919-21, mgr., Seattle, Wash., 1921-22; vice-pres. Ryer Grain Co., Seattle, 1922-26; pres. and dir. Brown-Jeklin & Co., mfrs. agents, Seattle, since 1927; vice-pres. and dir. Nat. Oil Products Co., Harrison, N.J., since 1933; vice-pres. and dir. The Vitab Corpn., Emeryville, Calif., Vitex Labs., Inc., Harrison, N.J., Nopco Chem. Co., Harrison. Served as private, 2d and 1st lt., 23d Machine Gun Battalion, U.S. Army, 1917-19. Pres. Kiwanis Club of Seattle, 1932. Republican. Clubs: Bankers (New York); Montclair Golf (Montclair, N.J.); Newark Athletic (Newark, N.J.); Bohemian (San Francisco). Home: 498 Ridgewood Av., Glen Ridge, N.J. Office: National Oil Products Co., Harrison, N.J.

BROWN, Ralph C.; prof. Biblical lit., W.Va. Wesleyan Coll. Address: Buckhannon, W.Va.

BROWN, Ralph Leigh, engring. exec.; b. Joliet, Ill., Aug. 14, 1890; s. Thomas James and Anna (Leigh) B.; B.S., U. of Colo., 1911, M.E., same, 1921; m. Eleanor Beatty Oliver, Aug. 17, 1912; 1 dau., Ann Elizabeth. Employed as night supt., Merchant Mills, Colo. Fuel & Iron Co., Pueblo, Colo., 1911-12; steel inspr. with R.W. Hunt Co., Chicago, Ill., 1912-13; draftsman and engr. Youngstown Sheet & Tube Co., 1913-16; mech. engr., Colo. Fuel & Iron Co., Pueblo, Colo., 1916-20; supt. constrn., gas engr., Semet Solvay Co., Syracuse, N.Y., 1920-25; pres. and dir. N.J. Coal & Tar Co., v.p. and dir. Pa. Coal & Tar Co., v.p. and dir. Disco Co., v.p. and dir. Internat. Coal Carbonization Co., all of N.Y. City, 1925-32; cons. engr. in New York, N.Y., 1932-34; engring. exec. with C. R. Vanneman, cons. engr., Albany, N.Y., since 1934. Mem. Beta Théta Pi, Vulcan. Republican. Episcopalian. Home: 9 Mendl. Terrace, Montclair, N.J. Office: 4 Irving Place, New York, N.Y.

BROWN, Ralph N., health officer; b. Farmington Twp., Warren Co., Pa., July 22, 1867; s. Paul W. and Harriet L. (Newman) B.; student pub. schs.; m. Etta M. Burgett, Feb. 7, 1889; children—Paul B., Ira R. Postmaster, Lander, Pa., 1889-93; sheriff Warren Co., Pa., 1904-07; state health officer of Pa., 1915-35; health officer, Warren Borough, Pa., since 1917. Mem. Com. of Pub. Safety for Warren Co., 1917. Pres. bd. of trustees and dir. I.O.O.F. Orphans Home, Meadville, Pa., 1913-39. Republican. Methodist. Home: 417 Water St. Office: Municipal Bldg., Warren, Pa.

BROWN, Raymond Joseph, editor; b. Hoboken, N.J., Mar. 31, 1889; s. James Francis and Ellen Agnes (McHale) B.; student Coll. of St. Francis Xavier, New York, 1904-06, Stevens Inst. Tech., Hoboken, 1906-08; m. Irene Angela Keenan, Apr. 10, 1918; 1 dau., Grace Agnes. Began as reporter Hudson Observer, Hoboken, 1908; reporter Newark (N.J.) Star, 1909-10, New York World, 1910-11, New York Press, 1912-13; news editor Pathé News, 1914-15; film editor Pathé Exchange, Universal Film Mfg. Co. and Metro Pictures Corpn., 1915-17; free lance mag. writer, 1917-23; asso. editor Popular Science Monthly, 1923-25; mng. editor, 1925-30, editor since 1930; editor Outdoor Life since 1934; editorial dir. The Sportsman, 1937; dir. Popular Science Pub. Co. Served in U.S.A. Camp Dix and Camp Lee, Va., 1918. Democrat. Clubs: Players (New York); Shackamaxon Country (Westfield, N.J.); Artists and Writers Golf Assn. Home: 217 Audley St., South Orange, N.J. Office: 353 4th Av., New York, N.Y.

BROWN, Revelle Wilson, ry. official; b. Carlyle, Ill., Aug. 5, 1883; s. Porter W. and Mary A. (Randall) B.; student high sch.; m. Carolyn B. Holdener, Dec. 9, 1903; children—Mrs. Mary Vickery, Pauline, Ralph. V.p. in charge operation and maintenance Reading Co. and Central R.R. of N.J. since 1935. Home: Drake Hotel. Office: Reading Terminal, Philadelphia, Pa.

BROWN, Richard Lewis, librarian; b. Anderson, S.C., July 11, 1901; s. John Thomas and Annie Irene (Cobb) B.; student Berea (Ky.) Acad., 1922-24; B.S., U. of S.C., Columbia, S.C., 1929, grad. student, 1929-30, summer 1938; A.B. in library science, Emory U. Library Sch., Atlanta, Ga., 1931; unmarried. Library asst. U.S. Vets. Hosp., Oteen, N.C., 1921-22; student asst., Berea (Ky.) Coll. Library, 1922-24, U. of S.C. Library, Columbia, S.C., 1925-30; reference asst. Pub. Library, Newark, N.J., June-Oct. 1931; reference librarian, Reading (Pa.) Pub. Library, 1931-37; librarian, The Citadel, Charleston, S.C., 1937-38, librarian, Muhlenberg Coll., Allentown, Pa., since Aug. 1938. Mem. Am. Library Assn., Pa. Library Assn., Special Libraries Assn., Delta Sigma Pi. Republican. Club: Kiwanis (Allentown, Pa.). Home: 2346 Tilghman St., Allentown, Pa.

BROWN, Richard P., chmn. of bd. Brown Instrument Co.; b. Phila., Pa., Sept. 26, 1884; s. Edward and Fannie (Harding) B.; student William Penn Charter Sch., Phila., 1892-1903, Drexel Inst., Phila., 1903-05; m. Edith Gillette, Oct. 5, 1918; children—Anita G., Richard P. Began with Edward Brown & Son, mfrs. industrial measuring instruments, Phila., 1905; organized successor, Brown Instrument Co., Phila., 1910, and pres., 1910-36, chmn. bd. since 1936; v.p. and dir. Minneapolis-Honeywell Regulator Co., Minneapolis, Minn., since 1935; dir. Atlantic Elevator Co., Nat. Bank of Germantown (Pa.) and Trust Co., Savings Fund Soc. of Germantown, pres. Scientific Apparatus Mfrs. Assn., 1933-34, handling code NRA. Mem. Am. Soc. M.E., Am. Inst. E.E. Republican. Episcopalian. Clubs: Union League, Racquet, Phila. Country, Phila. Cricket; Sunnybrook Golf (Phila.). Home: 3830 Oak Rd. Office: Wayne and Roberts Avs., Philadelphia, Pa.

BROWN, Samuel Horton, Jr., M.D.; b. Phila., Nov. 16, 1878; s. Samuel Horton and Cecelia Elizabeth (Greaney) B.; ed. high sch., 1893-94, De Lancey Prep. Sch., 1895; M.D., U. of Pa., 1899; m. Margaret Julia Linnane, June 21, 1916; children—Samuel Horton III, Mary Elizabeth, James Linnane, Franklin Luburg. Resident phys. Howard Hosp., 1899-1900; formerly affiliated with Northern and Southern Dispensaries, Phila., University, Episcopal, St. Christopher's, Mt. Sinai and Pennsylvania hosps.; now ophthalmologist St. Luke's and Children's Hosp., Am. Hospital for Diseases of the Stomach. Fellow College Physicians, Phila.; mem. Pa. State Med. Assn., Northern Med. Assn. (pres. 1907), Am. Acad. Ophthalmology and Oto-Laryngology. Club: Penn. Asso. editor Am. Year-Book of Medicine and Surgery, 1904-05, Therapeutic Review, 1904, Annals of Ophthalmology, 1904-06, Am. Medicine, 1906. Editor: Hughes' Practice of Medicine (7th, 8th and 9th edits.), 1904-06. Author: Eczema, Its Causes, Diagnosis and Treatment, 1906; History of Will's Hospital, Philadelphia (with William C. Posey), 1931; also various papers, revs., etc., on med. subjects. Editor: Weekly Roster and Med. Digest. Home: 10 E. Newfield Way, Bala-Cynwyd, Pa. Office: 1930 Chestnut St., Philadelphia, Pa.

BROWN, Samuel T.; treas. Koppers Co.; also officer or dir. many other companies. Home: 149 Dickson Av., Ben Avon. Office: 609 Koppers Bldg., Pittsburgh, Pa.

BROWN, Stanley L.; sr. surgeon and sr. orthopedic surgeon West Jersey Homeopathic Hosp. Address: 517 Cooper St., Camden, N.J.

BROWN, Sydney MacGillvary, univ. prof.; b. Marblehead, Mass., Aug. 10, 1895; s. Harrison Clifford and Ella Muriel (MacGillvary) B.; student Boston Latin Sch., 1910-13; B.A., Bowdoin Coll., Brunswick, Me., 1916; B.A., Brasenose Coll., Oxford, Eng., 1921, M.A., B.Litt., 1930; m. Eleanor Blanche Aldridge, June 19, 1919; 1 son, Douglas MacGillvary. Asst. prof. of European history, Lehigh U., Bethlehem, Pa., 1923-25, asso. prof., 1925-30, prof. since 1930. Joined British Royal Air Force, 1916; awarded Distinguished Flying Cross. Mem. Alpha Delta Phi, Phi Beta Kappa. Episcopalian. Author: Medieval Europe, 1932, revised edit., 1935; England (with E. Wingfield Stratford), 1938; The Royal Pedant, 1939. Contbr. hist. articles. Home: Bethlehem, Pa.

BROWN, Theodore Franklin, lawyer; b. Carroll Co., Md., Jan. 16, 1885; s. Nelson A. and Ellen J. (Maus) B.; grad. Westminster (Md.) High Sch., 1902; LL.B., Lincoln-Jefferson U., Hammond, Ind., 1909; m. Florence G. Myers, Dec. 20, 1906; 1 dau., Mildred Marie (Mrs. Geo. L. Gassman, Jr.); m. 2d, Laura E. Schaeffer, June 10, 1933. Public school teacher, Carroll Co., Md., 1902-10; admitted to Md. bar, 1910, and since practiced in Westminster; police justice, Westminster, 1912-16; states atty. for Carroll Co., 1920-35; dir. Farmers & Mechanics Nat. Bank, Sykesville State Bank. Mem. Am. Bar Assn., Md. Bar Assn., Carroll County Bar Assn. Republican. Mem. Reformed Ch. Mason, K. of P. Club: Westminster, Kiwanis. Home: 76 Pennsylvania Av. Office: Court St., Westminster, Md.

BROWN, Thomas Herbert, judge; b. New York, N.Y., Nov. 3, 1883; s. Thomas and Margaret (Cunningham) B.; LL.B., New York U., 1904; also several extension course, same univ.; 1st wife died Aug. 3, 1937; children—Thomas H., Marjorie H., Edward H.; m. 2d, Gladys O. Brown, Sept. 8, 1939. Admitted to N.J. bar, 1904; asst. prosecutor of pleas, Hudson County, 1918-23; judge Hudson Co. Ct. of Common Pleas since 1929, now president judge. Republican. Mason. Home: 280 Harrison Av., Jersey City, N.J.

BROWN, Thomas Joseph, S.J., prof. chemistry; b. Batavia, N.Y., Apr. 10, 1891; s. John S. and Margaret E. (Keefe) B.; B.S., Canisius Coll., Buffalo, N.Y., 1914; A.M., Woodstock Coll., Md., 1918. Joined Society of Jesus (Jesuits), 1914, prof. chemistry, Brooklyn Coll., Brooklyn, N.Y., 1920-21, Georgetown U., Washington, D.C., 1921-23; prof. chemistry, St. Joseph's Coll., Phila., Pa. since 1927. Mem. Am. Chem. Soc. Roman Catholic. Home: 18th and Thompson Sts., Philadelphia, Pa.

BROWN, Thomas Kite, Jr., coll. prof.; editor; b. Westtown, Pa., Mar. 19, 1885; s. Thomas Kite and Caroline (Cadbury) B.; diploma William Penn Charter Sch., Phila., 1902; A.B., Haverford (Pa.) Coll., 1906, A.M., 1907; grad. student U. of Pa., 1907-09; grad. student Harvard, 1909-12, Ph.D., 1920; grad. student U. of Berlin, Germany, 1909; m. Helen Wheeler Barnes, June 1, 1915; children—Thomas Kite III, Arthur Ellis. Instr. and asst. prof. German, Haverford (Pa.) Coll. with 3 yrs. leave for study at Harvard, 1908-19; exec. dir. Am. Assn. for Organizing Family Social Work, New York, 1919-20; organization and civic work, 1920-23; editor with John C. Winston Co., Phila. since 1923; asst. prof. German, U. of Pa., Phila., since 1927; dir. and pres. Back Log Camp, Inc. Served as chmn. Phila. Race St. Forum Com. since 1933. Mem. Modern Lang. Assn., Linguistic Soc. of America, Am. Dialect Soc., Goethe Soc., Cum Laude Soc., Phi Beta Kappa. Soc. of Friends. Editor: Bulletin of Friends Hist. Assn. since 1932; (with William Dodge Lewis and Henry Seidel Canby) The Winston Simplified Dictionary; (with William Dodge Lewis) The Winston Simplified Dictionary for Schools; (with William J. Pelo and Violet Bender) The Secretary's Handbook. Translator of A. Jorns, Studien über die Sozialpolitik der Quäker, under the title The Quakers as Pioneers in Social Work, pub. 1931. Home: 226 Dickinson Av., Swarthmore, Pa. Office: College Hall, U. of Pa. Phila., also Care John C. Winston Co., 1010 Arch St., Philadelphia, Pa.

BROWN, Thomas MacEwen; b. Pittsburgh, Pa., Aug. 20, 1897; s. James and Bella (MacEwen) B.; student pub. schs.; m. Susanna G. Large; children—James Duncan, Donald M., Robert M. Vice-pres. Duncan & Porter Co., 1928-38; propr. Tom Brown Builders' Supplies (successor to Heppenstall & Marquis Co.), Pittsburgh, since 1938; pres. Pittsburgh Builders' Exchange, 1935-37, now dir.; v.p. Chem. Lime Co., Inc., Pittsburgh, since 1938, also dir., pres. Chem. Sales Corpn., Pittsburgh, since 1938; also propr. Neville Lime Co., Pittsburgh. Club: Butler Country. Home: 28 Mayfair Drive, Mt. Lebanon, Pa. Office: 1428 Oliver Bldg., Pittsburg, Pa.

BROWN, Thomas Richardson, M.D.; b. Baltimore, Md., Sept. 11, 1872; s. Thomas R. and Harriet (Carrington) B.; grad. Baltimore City Coll., 1889; A.B., Johns Hopkins, 1892, postgrad. work, 1892-93; M.D., Johns Hopkins Med. Sch., 1897; m. Jean McComb Albert, Nov. 27, 1902; 1 dau., Eleanor Albert. Practiced in Baltimore, 1899—; associate prof. medicine, Johns Hopkins; physician in charge div. of digestive diseases, and visiting phys., Johns Hopkins Hosp.; attending physician, Union Memorial Hosp., Women's Hosp., Ch. Home and Infirmary, Bon Secours Hosp. Democrat. Episcopalian. Mem. A.M.A., M.d. Med. and Chirurg. Faculty, Alpha Delta Phi, Assn. Am. Physicians, Am. Gastroenterol. Assn., etc. Club: Maryland. Home: 14 Whitfield Rd., Guilford. Office: 12 E. Eager St., Baltimore, Md.

BROWN, Wade Hampton, medical research; b. Sparta, Ga., Oct. 18, 1878; s. George Rives and Laura Virginia (Brown) B.; B.S., U. of Nashville, 1899; grad. student U. of Chicago, 1902-03; M.D., Johns Hopkins, 1907; m. Beth Gillies, Oct. 29, 1908; children—Wade Gillies, Elspeth, Wade Hampton. Instr. pathology, U. of Va., 1907-08; instr. same, U. of Wis., 1908-10, asst. prof., 1910-11; prof. pathology, U. of N.C., 1911-13; with Rockefeller Inst. since 1913, asso. mem., 1914-22, mem. scientific staff for medical research since 1922. Mem. Assn. American Physicians, American Soc. Pathologists and Bacteriologists, Am. Soc. for Exptl. Pathology, Am. Soc. for Pharm. and Exptl. Therapeutics, Soc. for Exptl. Biology and Medicine, A.A.A.S., Sigma Xi, Nu Sigma Nu. Democrat. Presbyn. Contbr. of more than 75 papers in med. procs. and jours.; has specialized in study of biology of syphilitic infections, constitutional factors and physical environment in relation to heredity and disease. Home: 34 Westcott Road, Princeton, N.J.

BROWN, Warren Wilmer, writer; b. Elkton, Md., June 2, 1884; s. Thomas Bond and Mary Amanda (Smith) B.; student Elkton (Md.) Sch., 1890-93, Baltimore City Coll., 1897-1901, U. of Md., Baltimore, 1901-04; m. Mary Arrean Taft, Apr. 11, 1906; children—Sara Eugenia (Mrs. Arthur J. Connor), Frances Arrean. Reporter, Baltimore News, 1906 to 1924, gen. assignment man, 1906-10, critic of the arts, 1910-24; founded the mag. Gardens, Houses and People, Baltimore, Md., 1924, and since editor. Asst. dir. Baltimore (Md.) Museum of Art, 1924-33. Author: Lament of the Holly (dramatic poem); numerous articles for arts mags.; translator Le Songe d'un Soir d'Amour by Henri Bataille. Edited spl. Baltimore edition of Art and Archæology, 1925. Literary executor for Lizette Woodworth Reese, poet, 1935-36; contbr. several poems to mags. Home: 1400 Homestead St. Office: 18 E. Lexington St., Baltimore, Md.

BROWN, Willard Dayton, clergyman; b. Seward, N.Y., Feb. 15, 1874; s. William and Irene (Moore) B.; A.B., Union Coll., Schenectady, N.Y., 1900; grad. Theol. Sem., New Brunswick, N.J., 1903; studied Teachers Coll. (Columbia) D.D., Hope Coll., Holland, Mich., 1921; m. Eva Van Woert, Apr. 19, 1896 (died Feb. 10, 1929); m. 2d, Mabel Frances Cronk, Aug. 1, 1931. Ordained ministry Reformed Church in America, 1903; pastor Middleton, N.J., 1903-05, North Ref. Ch., Passaic, N.J., 1905-20; sec. Progress Campaign Com., Ref. Ch. in America, 1919-20; gen. sec. Bd. of Edn. ch., since Aug. 1920; mem. Publication Council, Christian Intelligencer and Mission Field (contributing editor); mem. Council of Church Bds. of Edn.; trustee Theol. Sem. Ref. Ch. in America. Mem. Phi Beta Kappa, Delta Upsilon. Republican. Preacher at Am. Ch., The Hague, Netherlands, 1914. Author: History of the Reformed Church in America. Home: Closter, N.J. Office: 25 E. 22d St., New York, N.Y.

BROWN, William Alger, lawyer; b. Lawton, W.Va., Sept. 8, 1899; s. Wm. Alger and Henrietta (Hughes) B.; student Greenbrier Mil. Sch., 1912-15, Woodberry Forest (Va.) Sch., 1915-19, Univ. of Va., 1919-27; m. Kathryn Linkenhoker, May 10, 1933; 1 son, William Alger, Jr. Admitted to W.Va. bar, 1928 and since engaged in gen. practice of law at Hinton; asso. with R. F. Dunlap, 1928-34, in practice alone since 1934; dir. and atty. First Nat. Bank of Hinton; vice-pres. Branch Coal & Coke Co., Coal Run Coal Co.; dir. Laurel Creek Coal Co.; vice-pres. Greenwood Coal Co. Mem. Am. Bar Assn., W.Va. State Bar Assn., Summers Co. Bar Assn. (pres.), Delta Psi, Skull & Keys. Republican. Episcopalian. Clubs: Rotary (past pres.), Willow Wood (Hinton); St. Anthony (New York). Home: Maple St. Office: Ballengee St., Hinton, W.Va.

BROWN, William Griffee, lawyer; b. Harrisonville, O., July 19, 1864; s. William H. and Araminta (Hypes) B.; student Mason City (W. Va.) graded schs., 1870-76; B.S., National Normal U., Lebanon, O., 1889; m. Margaret Groves, Nov. 16, 1889; children—Heber H., D. Ama Margaret (Mrs. Charles J. Smith), Reginald W., Mabel Evangeline (Mrs. Marshall Rowe); m. 2d, Eva Cutlip, Nov. 6, 1937. Teacher in common, high and normal schs., 1884-1902; admitted to Okla. bar, 1902; mem. law firm of Brown & Eddy since 1908; prosecuting atty., Nicholas Co., W.Va., 1904-08. State commr. of prohibition, 1921-26 and 1929-32. Republican. Methodist. Club: Lions (Summersville). Address: Summersville, W.Va.

BROWN, W(illiam) Norman, indologist; b. Baltimore, Md., June 24, 1892; s. George William and Virginia Augusta (Clark) B.; student Prep. Sch., Hiram (O.) Coll., 1905-07, Hiram Coll., 1907-08; A.B., Johns Hopkins, 1912, fellow, 1913-15, Ph.D., 1916; Harrison research fellow, U. of Pa., 1916-19; Johnston scholar, Johns Hopkins, 1919-22; studied Sanskrit at Benares, India, 1922-23; m. Helen Harrison, June 29, 1921; children—Norman Harrison, Ursula. Acting head of Sanskrit department, Johns Hopkins, 1921-22; prof. English, Prince of Wales Coll., Jammu, India, 1923-24; editor Johns Hopkins Half-Century Directory and asst. alumni director, 1924-26; fellow by courtesy Johns Hopkins University, 1925-26; associate in Sanskrit, Johns Hopkins, 1925-26; prof. Sanskrit University of Pa. since 1926; editor Jour. of Am. Oriental Society since 1926; fellow on the John Simon Guggenheim Memorial Foundation, 1928-29; curator of Indian art, Phila. Mus. Art since 1931; pres. American School Indic and Iranian Studies, Inc. Successively cadet U.S. Naval Aviation Corps, cryptographer with Mil. Intelligence Bur. and spl. agt. with U.S. Naval Intelligence, 1918. Mem. American Oriental Society (director), American Council Learned Societies (chmn. committee on Indic and Iranian studies), Linguistic Soc. America, India Soc. (London), Phila. Oriental Club, Phi Beta Kappa, Delta Upsilon. Author: The Pancatantra in Modern Indian Folklore, 1919; The Indian and Christian Miracles of Walking on the Water, 1928; The Story of Kalaka, 1933; Illustrated and Descriptive Catalogue of the Miniature Paintings of the Jain Kalpasutra as executed in the Early Western Indian style, 1934. Contbr. to numerous learned and popular publs. Home: Moylan, Pa. Address: University of Pennsylvania, Philadelphia, Pa.

BROWN, Wilson, naval officer; b. Phila., Pa., 1882; s. Wilson and Sarah Ann (Cochran) B.; student Penn Charter Sch., Phila., 1899; grad. U.S. Naval Acad., 1902; m. Lydia Ballou Chappell, Aug. 4, 1924. Commd. ensign, U.S.N., 1902, and advanced through the grades to rear adm., 1936; comdg. training squadron, Scouting Force, U.S.S. New York, 1936-37; supt. U.S. Naval Acad., Annapolis, Md., since 1938. Episcopalian. Clubs: Army and Navy, Chevy Chase, N.Y. Yacht. Address: U.S. Naval Academy, Annapolis, Md.

BROWN, Wyatt, bishop; b. Eufaula, Ala., Feb. 14, 1884; s. Eugene L. and Serena (Hoole) B.; B.A., U. of the South, 1905 (valedictorian), B.D., 1908; Litt.D., University of Alabama, 1915; D.B., St. John's Coll., 1921, Univ. of the South, 1933; LL.D., Dickinson College, Carlisle, Pa., 1933; m. Laura Little, Sept. 5, 1911; children—Wyatt, Charles Matthews, Laura Serena, Bertram III. Deacon, 1908, priest, 1909, P.E. Ch.; asst. St. John's Ch., Montgomery, Ala., 1908-09; rector All Saints' Ch., Mobile, Ala., 1909-13, Trinity Ch., Asheville, N.C., 1913-15, Ch. of the Ascension, Pittsburgh, Pa., 1915-20, Ch. of St. Michael and All Angels, Baltimore, Md., 1920-28; lecturer on Pastoral Theology, Va. Theol. Sem., 1927-28; dean St. Paul's Cathedral, Buffalo, N.Y., 1928-31; elected bishop of Harrisburg, Jan. 27, 1931; consecrated bishop St. Stephen's Cathedral, Harrisburg, Pa., May 1, 1931. Dep. to Gen. Conv., 1919, 25, 28; mem. Gen. Bd. Missions, 1917-19. Mem. Phi Delta Theta. Democrat. Mason (K.T.); Grand Prelate Grand Commandery K.T. of Pa., 1935-37. Club: Harrisburg Country. Author: Chasing Foxes and Other Sermons. Home: Bishopscourt. Address: 321 N. Front St., Harrisburg, Pa.

BROWN, Zaidee, librarian; b. Burdett, N.Y., Oct. 27, 1875; d. Edmund Woodward and Martha Day (Coit) B.; A.B., Leland Stanford, 1898; N.Y. State Library Sch., Albany, N.Y., 1901-02; unmarried. Prin. Castelleja Hall (girls' sch.), Palo Alto, Cal., 1898-99; taught in High Sch., Pueblo, Colo., 1899-1901; asst. N.Y. State Library Sch., 1902-03; classifier and cataloguer, Pub. Library, Brookline, Mass., 1903-05, and asst. librarian, 1905-08; library organizer, Ednl. Extension Div., N.Y. State Edn. Dept., 1908-10; agt. Mass. Free Pub. Library Commn., 1910-14; librarian, Pub. Library, Long Beach, Calif., 1914-22; librarian State Teachers Coll., Montclair, N.J., since 1928. Mem. P.B. K. Conglist. Lecturer N.Y. State Library Sch., and instr. in its summer sch., 1923-26; lecturer Sch. of Library Service, Columbia U., 1927-28. Editor Lantern Lists (reading lists for libraries); editor Standard Catalog for High School Libraries and Supplement, 1926-27. Author: Library Key (an aid in using books and libraries), 1928, revised edit., 1936. Address: Upper Montclair, N.J.

BROWN, Zenith J(ones) (Mrs. Ford K. Brown; writes under pseuds., Leslie Ford and David Frome), author; b. Smith River, Del Norte County, Calif., 1898; d. Milnor and Mary Francis (Watkins) Jones; A.B., U. of Wash., 1921; m. Ford K. Brown; 1 dau., Janet Calvert. Episcopalian. Club: Hamilton Street Club (Baltimore). Author: (under pseud. "David Frome") Murder of an Old Man, 1929; In at the Death, 1929; The Hammersmith Murders, 1930; The Strange Death of Martin Green, 1931; Two Against Scotland Yard, 1932; The Man from Scotland Yard, 1933; The Eel Pie Murders, 1933; Scotland Yard Can Wait, 1933; Mr. Pinkerton Goes to Scotland Yard, 1934; Mr. Pinkerton Finds a Body, 1934; Mr. Pinkerton Grows a Beard, 1935; Mr. Pinkerton, an Omnibus, 1935; Mr. Pinkerton Has the Clue, 1936; The Guilt Is Plain, 1937; The Black Envelope, 1937, Mr. Pinkerton at The Old Angel, 1939 (under pseud. "Leslie Ford"); The Sound of Footsteps, 1932; By the Watchman's Clock, 1932; Murder in Maryland, 1933; The Clue of the Judas Tree, 1933; The Strangled Witness, 1934; Burn Forever, 1935; Ill Met by Moonlight, 1937; The Simple Way of Poison, 1937; Three Bright Pebbles, 1938; Reno Rendezvous, 1939; The Town Cried Murder, 1939; False to Any Man, 1939. Contbr. stories to mags. Home: 243 King George St., Annapolis, Md.

BROWNBACK, John Harold, coll. prof.; b. Trappe, Pa., Sept. 19, 1897; s. Edwin Goodwin and Mary Virginia (Beaver) B.; A.B., Ursinus Coll., 1921, Sc.D., 1937; student Grad. Sch., U. of Pa., 1921-26; m. Lois Hook, Sept. 1, 1923. Instr. zoology, U. of Pa., 1921-26; asst. prof. biology, Ursinus Coll., 1926-28, asso. prof., 1928-36, prof. since 1936. Served with U.S.N.R.F., 1917-19. Democrat. Lutheran. Address: Collegeville, Pa.

BROWNBACK, Russell James, lawyer; b. Norristown, Pa., Oct. 1, 1893; s. Henry March and Augustine Marguerite (Lowe) B.; grad. William Penn Charter Sch., Phila., 1912; B.S. in Economics, Wharton Sch., U. of Pa., 1917, LL.B., Law Sch., 1922; m. Harriet Marple Wills, Oct. 20, 1928; 1 son, Russell James. Admitted to Pa. bar, 1922, and since practiced in Norristown, Pa.; admitted to practice before Supreme Court of U.S., 1935; dir. Montgomery Trust Co., March-Brownback Stove Co. Served as 2d lt., later 1st lt., Inf., U.S. Army, 1917-19; capt. Inf. Reserve to 1938. Mem. Am. Bar Assn., Montgomery Co. Bar Assn., James Wilson Law Club, Am. Legion, Montgomery Co., Hist. Soc., Delta Sigma Phi. Republican. Mem. Union League, Phila. Home: 823½ W. Main St. Office: 41 E. Main St., Norristown, Pa.

BROWNE, Charles, ex-congressman; b. Phila., Pa., Sept. 28, 1875; s. William Hardcastle and Alice (Beaver) B.; A.B., Coll. of N.J. (now Princeton U.), 1896, A.M., 1899; M.D., U. of Pa., 1900; U. of Berlin, 1902-03; m. Georgeanna Gibbs, April 30, 1913; children—Colston Hardcastle, Anthony DeHoojes, Archibald Ayres, Charles Brown. Began practice at Princeton, N.J., 1906; overseer of poor, Princeton, 1913-16; mayor of Princeton, 4 terms, 1916-23; pres. bd. trustees Princeton Hosp., 1919-28; mem. 68th Congress (1923-25), 4th N.J. Dist.; mem. bd. Pub. Utility Commrs., N.J., since Mar. 1925. Dir. 1st Nat. Bank (Princeton), Delaware & Bound Brook R.R. Co. Mem. Borough Council Princeton, N.J., 1933-35; mem. N.J. House of Assembly, 1936-39. Assistant to surgeon Old Point Comfort Army Hospital, Spanish-American War, 1898; student Plattsburg Camps, 1915-16; commd. 1st. lt. Med. Corps, U.S.A., 11, 1917; capt., Sept. 1918; comdt. U.S. Army Convalescent Hosp. No. 1, at Lawrenceville, N.J. Mem. bd. mgrs. N.J. State Home for Women; mem. Grad. Council Princeton U. Mem. Am. Inst. of Polit. and Social Science. Democrat. Presbyn. Author: Gun Club Cook Book, 1930. Clubs: University, Princeton, Racquet and Tennis (New York); University, Racquet, Princeton (Phila.). Home: Princeton, N.J.

BROWNE, Vere B.; v.p. Allegheny Steel Co. Home: Tarentum, Pa. Office: Breckenridge, Pa.

BROWNELL, Eleanor Olivia, sch. principal; b. New York, N.Y., Jan. 25, 1876; d. Silas B. and Sarah S. (Sheffield) Brownell; student Brearley Sch., New York, 1889-93; A.B., Bryn Mawr Coll., 1897; grad. student Columbia, 1898-99; 2 adopted daughters, Sylvia Ann Shipley, Mary Sheffield Shipley. Mem. Local Sch. Bd., New York, 1898-1905; state and student sec. Y.W. C.A., 1905-07; prin. New School, Utica, 1908-11; prin. Shipley Sch., Bryn Mawr, Pa., since 1911; dir. Sch. of Occupational Therapy, Phila. Pres. Headmistresses Assn. of East, 1928-32; mem. exec. com. Dem. Women's Luncheon Club of Phila. Democrat. Mem. Soc. of Friends. Clubs: Cosmopolitan, Acorn (Phila.); Cosmopolitan, Bryn Mawr (New York). Address: The Shipley School, Bryn Mawr, Pa.

BROWNLEE, Roy Hutchison, chemist; b. Alexis, Ill., Dec. 12, 1876; s. James Hutchison and Martha Jane (Barclay) B.; A.B., Monmouth (Ill.) Coll., 1898; grad. student Johns Hopkins U., 1898-99, U. of Calif., summer 1901; Ph.D., U. of Chicago, 1906; m. Martha Wilomine Tarnow, Sept. 14, 1904; 1 dau., Elizabeth Tarnow. Prof. natural scis., Occidental Coll., Los Angeles, Calif., 1900-01; lecture asst. dept. of chemistry, U. of Chicago, 1901-03; instr. chemistry, U. of Chicago High Sch., 1903-07; chemist and asst. supt. paraffine dept. Standard Oil Co. of Ind., 1907-12; fellow Mellon Inst. and prof. chemistry U. of Pittsburgh, 1912-14; pres. and dir. R. H. Brownlee Lab., Pittsburgh, since 1914; dir. and vice-pres. two development cos. and an oil refinery and dir. Thermatomic Carbon Co., 1922-24; inventor several processes for oil refining, welding and cutting of metals and carbon black processes. Mem. Am. Chemical Soc., A.A.A.S., Sigma Xi. Republican. Home: 4200 Parkman Av. Office: 223 Fourth Av., Pittsburgh, Pa.

BROWNMILLER, Roy Edwin, sec. of highways; b. Schuylkill Haven, Pa., Mar. 5, 1890; s. Thomas D. and Fianna (Gehert) B.; student pub. schs.; m. Minerva Hasenauer, Nov. 25, 1916; 1 son, Ronald E. Mem. Pa. Ho. of Reps., 1922-23; county commr., Schuylkill County, Pa., 1923-35; dep. sec. of highways, Harrisburg,

Pa., 1935-38, sec. of highways since 1938. Chmn. Pa. Publicity Commn., Bridge and Tunnel Commn. of Pa.; mem. Pa. Turnpike Commn., Pa.-N.J. Joint Toll Bridge Commn., Pa.-N.Y. Joint Toll Bridge Commn., State Geographic Bd. Mason, Odd Fellow. Club: Carlisle Country. Home: 400 N. 18th St., Pottsville, Pa. Office: 500 North Office Bldg., Harrisburg, Pa.

BROYLES, William Anderson, prof. agrl. edn.; b. Delaware Co., Ind., Oct. 2, 1879; s. Joseph Alfred and Eliza (Reeder) B.; B.S., Tri State Coll., Angola, Ind., 1905; A.B., Ind. U., Bloomington, Ind., 1908; A.M., U. of Wis., Madison, Wis., 1914; Ph.D., U. of Ill., Urbana, Ill., 1924; m. Bertha Lee, Sept. 2, 1908. Engaged in teaching and prin. high schs., 1899-1916; prof. agrl. edn., Agrl. & Mech. Coll. of Texas, Coll. Sta., Tex., 1916-20; prof. agrl. edn. Pa. State Coll. since 1920. Mem. Gamma Sigma Delta, Phi Delta Kappa, Alpha Tau Alpha. Presbyterian. Club: University (State College, Pa.). Author: Workbook in Field Crops, 1939; Workbook in Fruit Growing, 1934; Workbook in Poultry Husbandry, 1930; National Computing Fan, 1936. Home: 355 E. Foster Av., State College, Pa.

BROZA, Stanley Alexander ("Stan Lee B."), dir. radio programs; b. Phila., Pa., Oct. 19, 1897; s. A. H. and Tessie (Alexander) B.; ed. pub. schs., Abington (Pa.) High Sch. and business coll., Phila., Pa.; m. Esther Mallis, Jan. 1, 1923; children—Elliot, Stanley Alexander. Began business career in sales and advtg. depts. of Roth Mfg. Co.; engaged in radio broadcasting, Phila., since 1924. Jewish religion. Clubs: Art Alliance (Phila.); Friars (New York). Home: Sugartown and Fairfield Rds., Devon, Pa. Office: WCAU, 1622 Chestnut St., Philadelphia, Pa.

BRUBAKER, Merlin Martin, research chemist; b. Northfield, Minn., May 14, 1901; s. Delmer Dawson and Maud (Spear) B.; B.S., Carleton Coll., Northfield, Minn., 1923; M.S., U. of Ill., 1926, Ph.D., 1927; m. Clara Ellen Robinson, Oct. 11, 1927; 1 son adopted, Robert. Instr. of chemistry, U. of Ill., 1923-25, Carr fellowship in chemistry, 1926-27; research chemist E. I. du Pont de Nemours & Co., Exptl. Sta., Wilmington, Del., 1927-33, research supervisor since 1933. Mem. Am. Chem. Soc., A.A.A.S., Gamma Alpha, Sigma Psi, Phi Kappa Phi, Phi Lambda Epsilon. Conglist. Home: 107 North Rd., Lindamere, Wilmington, Del.

BRUCE, Howard, banker; b. Richmond, Virginia, Aug. 31, 1879; s. Albert C. and Mary (Howard) B.; preparatory education, Maguire's Sch., Richmond; C.E., Virginia Mil. Institute, 1897; m. Mary Graham Bowdoin, Oct. 26, 1912; children—Mary Howard, Julia Morris, Rosalie Calvert. Successively cadet engr. East River Gas Co., asst. supt.; asst. supt. New Amsterdam (Ind.) Gas Co.; asst. engr. Consol. Gas Co. of N.Y.; engr. of constrn., same and affiliated cos., 1902-07; gen. mgr. Bartlett, Hayward & Co., 1907-09; v.p. and gen. mgr. The Bartlett Hayward Co., 1909-17; pres. and gen. mgr., 1917-28, chmn. bd. from 1928 until consolidation of company with The Koppers Co.; chmn. bd. Baltimore Nat. Banks; dir., mem. exec. com. and chmn. bd. Worthington Pump & Mchy. Corpn., New York; dir. Internat. Mercantile Marine Co., U.S. Lines Co.; trustee Koppers United Co.; Md. Casualty Co., Safe Deposit & Trust Co. (Baltimore), Md. Dry Dock Co. B.&O.R.R. Co., Glenn L. Martin Co. Mem. Dem. Nat. Com. from Md. since 1926. Episcopalian. Clubs: Maryland, Chesapeake, Merchants, Elkridge Fox Hunting, Elkridge-Harford Hunt, Inc. (Baltimore). Home: "Belmont," Elkridge, Md. Office: care Baltimore Nat. Bank, Baltimore, Md.

BRUCE, James, corpn. exec.; b. Baltimore, Dec. 23, 1892; s. William Cabell and Louise Este (Fisher) B.; Litt.B., Princeton, 1914; LL.B., U. of Md., 1916; m. Ellen McHenry Keyser, May 24, 1919; children—Ellen McHenry, Louise Este. Vice-pres. Atlantic Exchange Bank, 1921-26, Internat. Acceptance Bank, 1926-27, Chase Nat. Bank, 1927-31; pres. Baltimore Trust Co., 1931-33; financial advisor to bd. dirs., Home Owners Loan Corpn., Washington, Sept. 1933-Dec. 1934; v.p. Nat. Dairy Products Corpn. since Jan. 1935; dir. Commercial Credit Co., Md. Casualty Co., Republic Steel Co., C., R.I.&P. Ry., Standard Gas & Electric Co., Am. Airlines, Inc., Columbia Oil and Gas Co., Utilities Equities Corpn., Federal Home Loan Bank of N.Y. Capt. U.S. Field Arty., World War. Episcopalian. Clubs: Maryland, Elkridge (Baltimore); Racquet and Tennis, Creek, Recess, Brook, River (New York). Home: Eccleston, Md. Office: 230 Park Av., New York, N.Y.

BRUCE, Louise Este (Mrs. William Cabell Bruce), civic leader; b. Baltimore, Md.; d. William Alexander and Louise (Este) Fisher; ed. The Misses Hall's Sch., Baltimore; m. William Cabell Bruce, Oct. 15, 1887; children—William Fisher (dec.), James, William Cabell (dec.), David K. E. Mgr. Y.W.C.A., Baltimore, 1891-1916; an organizer and mgr. Colored Branch of Y.W.C.A., 1896; chmn. all coms. to raise $400,000 for the erection of a new building for the Y.W.C.A., 1914; mem. adv. bd. of Com. on Work for Colored People, 1915-16; mem. of com. to admit women as students in Johns Hopkins Med. Sch.; mem. bd. mgrs. Harriet Lane Home (Johns Hopkins Hosp.), 1908-28, hon. mem. since 1928; pres. Woman's Auxiliary of Emmanuel Ch., Baltimore, 1915-16; chmn. Emmanuel Ch. Branch of the Cathedral League of Md.; mem. exec. bd. Md. Council of Defense, Woman's Sect., 1916; mem. Baltimore Women's Preparedness and Survey Commn., 1917-19; mem. food production com. Md. Council of Defense; mem. of women's com. of Nat. War Savings Commn., Baltimore; mem. Soldiers and Sailors Memorial Assn., 1918; mem. Md. Tercentenary Commn.; chmn. finance dept. Woman's Sect. of Md. Council of Defense; mem. Commn. for Erection of Memorial to Lafayette, 1917; treas. of Women's Liberty and Victory Loan Com. of Md.; treas. Assn. for Promotion of Univ. Edn. of Women; mem. St. Thomas P.E. Ch., Garrison Forest (chmn. Church Service League, 1932; pres. Woman's Auxiliary, 1933; chmn. Parish Council, 1938); mem. Md. Branch Nat. Cathedral in Washington; del. Nat. Conv. for the Study and Prevention of Tuberculosis, 1917; past vice-pres. Garden Club of America (mem. bd. associates); v.p. Friends of The Library, Johns Hopkins U., since 1934; mem. bd. dirs. Robert E. Lee Memorial Assn., Stratford, Va., since 1931; one of founders Gilman County Sch. for Boys. Mem. Md. Branch of English Speaking Union, Md. Soc. of Colonial Dames of America (former v.p.), Daughters of the Cincinnati, Md. Hist. Soc., Va. Hist. Soc., La. Hist. Soc., Instructive Visiting Nurse Assn. of Baltimore (past v.p.), Amateur Gardners' Club of Baltimore (twice pres.), Needlework Guild of America (past nat. v.p.; hon. pres. Baltimore Branch). Democrat. Clubs: Sulgrave, Senate Ladies Luncheon (Washington, D.C.); Town Club (Baltimore). Home: Ruxton Post Office, Baltimore, Md.

BRUCE, W(illiam) Cabell, ex-senator; b. Staunton Hill, Charlotte Co., Va., Mar. 12, 1860; s. Charles and Sarah (Seddon) B.; Norwood (Va.) High Sch. and Coll., 1875-78); U. of Va., 1879-80; LL.B., U. of Md.; LL.D., Hampden-Sydney Coll., Va.; LL.D., Loyola College, Baltimore, Md., 1930; m. Louise E., d. of Judge William A. Fisher, Oct. 15, 1887; children—James, David K.E. Mem. law firm Fisher, Bruce & Fisher, Baltimore, 1887-1903, 1908-10. Mem. of Md. Senate, 1894-96 (pres. 1896); head of Baltimore Law Dept., 1903-08 (resigned); mem. Baltimore Charter Commn., 1910; general counsel Public Service Commn. of Md., 1910-22, and for term 1929-35; mem. U.S. Senate, term 1923-29. Democrat. Episcopalian. Author: Benjamin Franklin, Self-Revealed (2 vols.), 1918 (awarded Pulitzer prize, as best biography of year); Below the James, 1918; John Randolph of Roanoke (2 vols.), 1923; Seven Great Baltimore Lawyers, 1931; Recollections, 1931; Imaginary Conversations with Franklin, 1933; also 3 compilations of essays and addresses. While at University of Virginia, in competition with Woodrow Wilson and others, was awarded medal as best debater of Jefferson Lit. Soc., and medal for best essay; was co-editor U. of Va. Mag. Home: Ruxton, Md.

BRUCK, Samuel, physician; b. Russia, Dec. 23, 1885; s. Tobias and Rhoda (Spare) B.; brought to America, 1887, naturalized, 1907; A.B., Central High Sch., Phila., Pa., 1903; M.D., U. of Pa. Med Sch., 1907; m. Ellen B. Shearer, Mar. 30, 1911; children—Arthur, Phoda Nina. Interne Jewish Hosp., Phila., Pa., 1907-09, asst. pediatrist, 1909-15, asst. radiologist, 1915-30, radiologist since 1930; radiologist, Northeastern Hosp. since 1920, Northern Liberties Hosp. since 1918; sec. staff and mem. bd. dirs. Northern Liberties Hosp. since 1918. Served in Med. Corps, U.S.A. Army Res. during World War. Mem. A.M.A., Radiol. Soc. of N.A., Phila. Co. Med. Soc., Phila. Roentgen Ray Soc., Med. League (sec. 1924-29, pres., 1930). Jewish religion. B'Nai Brith. Home: 2104 Pine St., Philadelphia, Pa.

BRUEN, James H., investment banker; b. Rockaway, N.J., June 24, 1886; s. James Wright and Emma (De Hart) B.; student Rockaway (N.J.) Pub. Schs., 1893-1903; m. Edna Derry, Oct. 14, 1914; children—Jean Robertson, James Harvey, William Derry. With Nat. Union Bank, Dover, N.J., 1904-19; then asso. with William A. Read & Co., New York, and later with Dillon, Read & Co., now representative Riter & Co. Pres. Morristown (N.J.) Bd. of Edn., Morristown (N.J.) Y.M.C.A. Mem. S.A.R. Republican. Presbyterian. Mason (Past Master, Acacia Lodge, Dover, N.J.). Club: Rotary (Morristown, N.J.). Home: 50 Morris Av. Office: 42 Park Pl., Morristown, N.J.

BRUGH, Benjamin Franklin, surgeon; b. Va., May 15, 1889; s. Ollin U. and Maria Ann (Farrow) B.; A.B., Roanoke Coll., Salem, Va., 1911; M.D., Med. Coll. of Va., Richmond, Va., 1915; m. Minnie Karnes, Sept. 12, 1916; children—Louise Elizabeth, Jack Caxon. Began as surgeon, 1918; in practice at Montgomery, W.Va.; v.p. and dir. Laird Memorial Hosp., pres. Fincastle Realty Co. Fellow Am. Coll. of Surgeons; mem. Phi Beta Pi. Democrat. Presbyterian. Mason (32°, Shriner). Club: Rotary (Montgomery, W.Va.). Address: 324 6th Av., Montgomery, W.Va.

BRUHNS, George Frederick William, (pen name Arthur Bruhns, in Europe), conductor and composer; b. Bunzlau, Silesia, Germany, Apr. 10, 1874; s. August and Marie (Schmidt) B.; came to U.S., 1910, naturalized, 1918; ed. Royal Conservatory, Dresden, composition under Felix Draeseke, theory under Hugo Riemann, then under Camille Saint-Saëns, Paris, France; m. Mrs. Jenny Westervelt Bennet Fett, Sept. 28, 1907 (died Feb. 22, 1938). Composed music for Don Juan's Last Wager for Sir Martin Harvey, London; conductor grand opera in Hamburg, Altenburg, Stuttgart and other cities; travelled with many singers as accompanist and coach; composer about sixty numbers pub. by leading houses in Europe and U.S.; among the well known are "American Rhapsody," "Valley Forge," symphonic poem, American Heroes National March, prologue and fugue, "The King Can Do No Wrong" and many songs; Love Romance for orchestra introduced in many pictures. Mem. Am. Soc. Composers, Authors and Pub. of Music, Societé des Auteurs, Compositeurs et Editeurs de Musique, Asso. Musicians of New York City (Local 802). Republican. Lutheran. Home: 27 Grove St., Cranford, N.J.

BRUMBACH, Claude A., woolen cloth mfr.; b. Esterly, Pa., July 9, 1895; s. William D. and Edwina (Jack) B.; student (Schuylkill Sem. and Phila. Textile Sch. (Class of 1914); m. Marguerite Mason, Jan. 16, 1922; children—Barbara, Mason. Worked in all depts. of woolen mill; since 1925, v.p. A. J. Brumbach, Inc., mfrs. woolen cloth, suitings and cloakings, Esterly, Pa. Served as 1st class sergt. Inf., U.S. Army, during World War. Mem. Am. Legion, Patriotic Order Sons of America. Republican. Reformed Ch. Mason (32°, Shriner). Clubs: University, Washington Library, Berkshire Country (Reading, Pa.). Address: Esterly, Pa.

BRUMBACH, William D., woolen mfr.; b. Esterly, Pa., June 11, 1866; s. Albert J. and Sarah (Dunckel) B.; student Palatinate Coll., Meyerstown, Pa.; m. Edwina Jack, 1890; children—Amy Jack, (Mrs. Harry Morse Shaffer), Claude A., William C. Began as clk in father's woolen mill; now pres. A. J. Brumbach, Inc.,

Esterly, Pa.; dir. Reading Cold Storage Co., Manatawny Fire Ins. Co. Mem. Hist. Soc., Patriotic Order Sons of America. Republican. Reformed Ch. Clubs: Reading Country, Wyomissing (Reading, Pa.). Address: Esterly, Pa.

BRUMBACK, Lynn Hamilton; mem. staff Washington County Hosp., Hagerstown, Md., and Waynesboro (Pa.) Hosp. Address: 170 W. Washington St., Hagerstown, Md.

BRUNE, Herbert Maxwell, Jr., lawyer; b. Baltimore, Md., Oct. 8, 1901; s. Herbert Maxwell and Lucy (Fisher) B.; student Gilman Country Sch., Baltimore, Md., 1910-18; A.B., Williams Coll., Williamstown, Mass., 1922; LL.B., Harvard Law, 1925; post grad. work, Heidelberg (Germany) U., 1925-26; m. Elaine Josephine Milbourne, Dec. 3, 1923. Asso. with law firm Brune, Parker, Carey & Gans (later Brown & Brune), Baltimore, Md., 1926-35, mem. of firm, 1932-35; counsel, Md. State Dept. of Legislative Reference, Annapolis, Md., 1927; mem. of firme Brune & Gordon, Baltimore, Md., since 1935; mem. character com. of Court of Appeals of Md. on admissions to bar, 1936-37; asso. prof. of law, U. of Md., Baltimore, Md., 1937-38. Served in S.A.T.C., U.S. Army, 1918. Mem. Md. State Old Age Pension Commn., appointed to draft Pension Act, 1935; mem. Md. Democratic Speakers Com., 1936; candidate for Democratic nomination for Gov. of Md., withdrawing to run as Independent candidate, 1938; helped organize Taxpayers League Baltimore Co. and Citizens League Baltimore (mem. council), 1938-39. Mem. Baltimore City, Md. State bar assns., Am. Bar Assn. (state chmn. Jr. Bar Conf., 1935-37), Am. Judicature Soc., Nat. Municipal League, Am. Assn. for Social Security, Phi Beta Kappa, Phi Delta Theta, Order of the Coif. Democrat. Episcopalian. Clubs: Merchants (Baltimore, Md.); L'Hirondelle (Ruxton, Md.); Williams (New York City). Author: Motor Vehicle Law of Maryland, 1928; Maryland Corporation Lawyer, 1933, supplement, 1935. Co-author: Tiffany, Outlines of Real Property, 1930. Mem. bd. trustees Md. Law Review, 1936-38. Home: Rolandvue, Ruxton, Md. Office: 1708 First Nat. Bank Bldg., Baltimore, Md.

BRUNER, John W.; chief surgeon Bloomsburg Hosp.; visiting surgeon Berwick Hosp. Address 346 Market St., Bloomsburg, Pa.

BRUNNER, Henry Sherman, univ. prof.; b. Reading Pa., Mar. 12, 1898; s. Harry Keely and Emma Bentz (Sherman) B.; B.S. Pa. State Coll., 1920, M.S., 1930; m. Vivian Erica Jenkin, Sept. 1, 1928; children—Gay, Robin. Farmer, Boyertown, Pa., 1920-29; teacher of agrl., Oley Twp. High Sch., Berks Co., Pa., 1930-34; instr. in agrl. edn., Pa. State Coll., 1934-36, asso. prof., 1936-37, prof. of agrl. edn. and head dept. of rural edn. since 1937. Served as 2d lt., Inf., U.S. Army, 1917-18. Mem. Sigma Chi, Alpha Zeta, Alpha Tau Alpha, Thespians, Scabbard and Blade, Delta Theta Sigma, Kappa Gamma Psi, Phi Kappa Phi, Gamma Sigma Delta. Mason. Charter mem. and violinist Reading (Pa.) Symphony Orch.; student leader Pa. State Coll. Symphony Orchestra, 1919-20; organizer and conductor, Pa. State Future Farmers of America Band. Address: 527 Holmes St., State College, Pa.

BRUNOT, John B., pres. Irwin Gas Coal Corpn.; b. Greensburg, Pa.; m. Nov. 6, 1878; s. Hilary J. and Mary (Bissell) B.; student Grove City (Pa.) Coll. and U. of Mich.; m. Alice E. Turner, Aug. 26, 1903; children—John B., Mary Alice, William T. Admitted to Mich. bar, 1902, Pa. bar, 1903; v.p. Operators Fuel Agency, Inc., 1917-37; pres. Irwin Gas Coal Corpn., Greensburg, Pa., since 1938. Mem. Bushey Run Battlefild Commn., 1935-37. Home: 206 Briar Hill Drive. Office: 121 N. Main St., Greensburg, Pa.

BRUNS, William Frederick, physician; b. Catlettsburg, Ky., Apr. 12, 1866; s. Frederick and Christine (Strohmeyer) B.; student U.S. Naval Acad., Annapolis, Md., 1883-85; M.D., Eclectic Med. Coll., Cincinnati, O., 1888; grad. study, N.Y. Polyclinic, N.Y. City, 1894-95; children—Henry Frederick, Nellie Irene (Mrs. W. H. Bromley). Engaged in gen. practice of medicine since 1888, at Ceredo, W.Va., since 1897; vice-pres. and dir. First Nat. Bank of Kenova, W.Va., since 1930. Served as councilman, Ceredo, W.Va., 1938-39; pres. Ind. Sch. Dist. of Ceredo-Kenova, 1903-12; mem. W.Va. Ho. of Dels., 1923-25. Mem. W.Va. State and Cabell Co. med. socs. Republican. Methodist. Mason. Home: 390 W. First St. Office: 373 W. First St., Ceredo, W.Va.

BRUNSTETTER, Max Russell, educational pub.; b. Delano, Pa., Feb. 2, 1902; s. Frank Howard and Lulu May (Appleman) B.; student Gettysburg (Pa.) Coll., 1918-20; A.B., Dickinson Coll., Carlisle, Pa., 1922; A.M., U. of Pa., 1928; Ph.D., Teachers Coll. (Columbia), 1930 (fellow); m. Frances Jenks Worstall, Oct. 6, 1923; children—Jane Buckman, Richard Worstall, George Worstall, Frank Howard. Teacher Bordentown (N.J.) Mil. Inst., 1922-23; teacher, later prin. Millville (N.J.) High Sch., 1923-28; ednl. research asso. Erpi. Classroom Films, Inc., producers of talking pictures for schs., 1930-36; mng. editor Bureau of Publs., Columbia Univ. Teachers Coll. since 1936. Mem. N.E.A., Theta Chi, Phi Delta Kappa. Republican. Presbyn. Author: Business Management in School Systems of Different Sizes, 1931; How to Use the Educational Sound Film, 1937; (brochures) Introduction to French pronunciation and Diction (with René and Paule Vaillant), 1934; Introduction to Spanish Pronunciation and Diction (with C. V. Cusachs), 1934. Editor: Educational Talking Picture, 1935. Contbr. articles to ednl. mags. Home: 12 Raymond Av., Rutherford, N.J. Address: 525 W. 120th St., New York, N.Y.

BRUNYATE, William Lawrence, lawyer; b. Cape May, N.J., Feb. 15, 1883; s. Dr. Edwin Richard and Eliza Ann (England) B.; desc. of well known English family of that name; grad. Atlantic City High Sch., 1901; Ph.B., Dickinson Coll., 1905, A.M., 1909; LL.B., Harvard, 1909; m. Ella May Chandler, Oct. 10, 1911; children—William Chandler, Ruth Winifred. Admitted to N.J. bar, 1911, and since practiced at Newark; gen. counsel for Nat. Oil Products Co. and its subsidiaries, Harrison, N.J., since 1920; dir. N.J. Realty Co., N.J. Title Ins. Co. Served on Special Draft Bd. during World War. Mem. Am. Bar. Assn., N.J. Bar Assn., Essex Co. Bar Assn. Mason. Home: 221 Grove Road, South Orange, N.J. Office: 605 Broad St., Newark, N.J.

BRUSH, Alvin G(eorge), chmn. bd. dirs.; b. Dunton, L.I., N.Y., Sept. 16, 1896; s. Walter H. and Florence L. (Styles) B.; B.C.S., New York U., 1921; m. C. Jean Williams, June 16, 1925; 1 dau., Barbara Jean. Accountant Nat. Aniline Chem. Co. (New York), 1919-22; partner Smith, Brush & Co., accountants (New York), 1923-32; pres. R. L. Watkins Co., mfrs. of Dr. Lyons tooth powder (New York), 1933-34; pres. Affiliated Products Co., cosmetic mfrs., 1934-35; chmn. of bd. Am. Home Products, mfrs. drugs and household items, since 1935. Served with Naval Reserve, U.S. Navy, 1918. Certified Public Accountant, State of N. Y. Mem. N.Y. State Soc. of C.P.A. Republican. Mason. Clubs: Union League (New York); Cherry Valley Country (Long Island). Home: 78 Kilburn Rd., Garden City, N.Y. Office: American Home Products Co., Jersey City, N.J.

BRUSH, Warren David, wood technologist; b. Newcomerstown, O., Apr. 7, 1881; s. Perry Decatur and Mary Emmeline (Washburn) B.; B.S. magna cum laude, Baldwin-Wallace Coll., Berea, O., 1905; A.M., U. of Mich., Ann Arbor, 1908; Ph.D., Am. Univ., Washington, D.C., 1930; m. Lola Roberta Huffman, Oct. 31, 1914; children—Mary Warren, James Whitney. Engaged as instr., U. of Mich., 1906-08; wood technologist, U.S. Forest Service since 1908, known as an authority on characteristics, structure, properties and uses of woods both native and fgn. Sr. mem. Soc. Am. Foresters; mem. Sigma Xi. Club: Kenwood Golf and Country (Bethesda, Md.). Home: 14 Hesketh St., Chevy Chase, Md. Office: 930 F St., Washington, D.C.

BRUST, William T.; mem. exec. com. and dir. Hammermill Paper Co. Home: 1504 E. Lake Road, Erie, Pa.

BRUTON, Paul Wesley, prof. of law; b. Woodland, Cal., Aug. 1, 1903; s. Philip and Nancy (Gilstrap) B.; student Woodland (Cal.) Pub. Schs., 1911-22, Sacramento (Cal.) Jr. Coll., 1922-24; A.B., U. of Calif., Berkeley, Calif., 1929, LL.B., 1929; J.S.D., Yale Law Sch., 1930; m. Margaret Perry, Sept. 2, 1931; children—Margaret Watson, David Philip. Admitted to Calif. bar, 1930, to practice before U.S. Supreme Ct., 1935; instr. law, Yale U., 1930-32; asso. prof. law, Duke U., Durham, N.C., 1932-35; atty. U.S. Treas., 1935-37; visiting asso. prof. of law U. of Pa., 1937-38, asso. prof of law since 1938. Mem. Phila. Juristic Soc., Order of the Coif, Phi Beta Kappa, Delta Theta Phi. Democrat. Clubs: Lenape (Phila.); Castine (Me.) Golf. Home: 505 Chestnut Lane, Wayne, Pa. Office: U. of Pa. Law Sch., Philadelphia, Pa.

BRUUN, Johannes Hadeln, research chemist; b. Sweden, Nov. 8, 1899; s. Karl and Thora (Wager) B.; student Tech. Univ. of Finland, 1917-18; diplom-ingeniör, Royal Inst. of Tech., Trondheim, Norway, 1923; Ph.D., Johns Hopkins, 1929; m. Mildred M. Hicks, May 1, 1930. Came to U.S., 1924, naturalized, 1934. Research chemist, Kongsberg Vaabenfabrikk, Norway, 1923-24; research chemist Am. Aniline, Inc., Lock Haven, Pa., 1924-25, plant chemist, 1925-26, supt., 1926-27; research fellow Nat. Bureau of Standards, Washington, D.C., 1927-28, research asso., 1928-29, sr. research asso., 1929-32; research chemist Sun Oil Co., Phila., 1932-34, mgr. exptl. div. since 1934. Served as lt. in Chem. Warfare, Norway, 1923-24. Mem. Am. Chem. Soc. (mem. exec. com. Washington, D.C., 1930-32), Am. Petroleum Inst., Pa. Chem. Soc., Washington Acad. Sciences, Sigma Xi. Republican. Episcopalian. Clubs: Springhaven Country (Wallingford, Pa.); Rolling Green Golf (Springfield, Pa.). Holder of patents on chemical subjects. Contbr. many articles on isolation of pure hydrocarbons from petroleum, etc., to scientific jours. Home: 423 Riverview Rd., Swarthmore, Pa. Office: Sun Oil Co., Norwood, Pa.

BRYAN, Charles Egbert, orchard operator; b. Washington, D.C., Aug. 18, 1872; s. Samuel Magill and Melissa Ann (Shipley) B.; student Washington (D.C.) Pub. Schs., 1883-90, St. Paul's Sch., Garden City, N.Y., 1890-92; A.B., Harvard, 1896; m. Cora Taft, June 7, 1897; m. 2d, Susan Meriwether, of St. Louis, Mo., Sept. 18, 1929. Rights of Way agt., Am. Telephone & Telegraph Co., St. Louis, Ill., 1896-97; spl. agt. Chesapeake & Potomac Telephone Co., Washington, D.C., 1897-98, commercial mgr., 1898-1901, treas., 1901-04, gen. commercial supt., 1904-14; v.p. and gen. mgr. Md. Telephone Co. (merged with Chesapeake & Potomac Telephone Co., 1908), Baltimore, 1908-14; retired, 1914; owner and operator Mt. Pleasant Orchards, Havre de Grace, Md., since 1914; dir. and mem. exec. com. Chesapeake & Potomac Telephone Co. Mem. advisory bd. Public Works Admstrn. for Md. Mem. Md. State Hort. Soc (pres.), Middle Atlantic Fruit Growers' Conf. (chmn). Address: Mt. Pleasant Orchards, Havre de Grace, Md.

BRYAN, J(ames) Wallace, lawyer; b. Cambridge, Dorchester Co., Md., Feb. 27, 1884; s. D'Arcy P. and Nannie Phelps (Wallace) B.; A.B., Johns Hopkins, 1903 (Phi Beta Kappa, and Kappa Alpha, Southern), Ph.D., 1908; LL.B., U. of Md., 1905; m. Juliette Anne Ligon, July 2, 1935; 1 dau., Anne D'Arcy. Admitted Md. State bar, 1905; sec. com. on corpns. Md. Ho. of Delegates, 1908; mem. firm of Lemmon & Clotworthy, 1909-14, now practicing alone; legal adviser, U.S. Commn. on Industrial Relations, 1915. Lecturer on jurisdiction and procedure of federal courts, and law of admiralty and shipping, Baltimore U. Sch. of Law, 1908-11, and Baltimore Law School, 1911-13; on law of carriers and common law pleading, Uuniversity of Maryland School of Law, since 1913; on commercial law and accountancy, in Johns Hopkins U. since 1916. Trustee Commn. on Governmental Efficiency and Economy, Baltimore, 1929-34, vice chairman, 1929-31. Consular agent of Peru, Baltimore, 1918-20; asst. resident auditor Emergency Fleet Corpn., 1918;

expert accountant, Q.M.C., assigned to Gen. Staff, 1918-19. Certified pub. accountant, Md., 1917. Mem. Am. Judicature Soc. (council), Am. Polit. Science Assn., American Bar Assn. (mem. special com. on Child Labor Amendment to Federal Constitution; mem. standing com. on Public Utility Law), Maryland and Baltimore bar associations, Md. Assn. of Certified Public Accountants (pres. 1927-28). Democrat. Episcopalian. Clubs: Bachelors' Cotillon, Baltimore Country, Johns Hopkins, Merchants'. Author: The Development of the English Law of Conspiracy, 1909; Students' Text on Federal Jurisdiction and Procedure, 1911; Admiralty, Carriers, Shipping, 1914; also numerous monographs, articles and book reviews. Home: Roland Park Apts., Roland Park, Md. Office: Mercantile Trust Bldg., Baltimore, Md.*

BRYAN, Joseph Harker, physician; b. Newark, N.J., Dec. 15, 1865; s. James Rogers and Lydia (Harker) B.; student Haverstraw (N.Y.) Mountain Inst., 1880-83; A.B., NY.U., 1886; M.D., N.Y. Homoe. Med. Coll., and Flower Hosp., 1890; m. Irene Dobbins, Oct. 25, 1904; children—James Edward, Katharine Louise (Mrs. Robert L. Shank), Joseph Harker, Jr. Gen. practice of medicine, New York, 1890-92, Asbury Park, N.J., since 1892. Mem. N.J. State Bd. of Med. Examiners, 1918-34 (pres., 1922-23). Pres. Bd. of Trustees, First M.E. Ch., Asbury Park, N. J. Fellow Am. Coll. Physicians; mem. Am. Inst. of Homeopathy, N.J., State Homoe. Soc., Asbury Park (N.J.) Chamber of Commerce (pres., 1915-16), Phi Beta Kappa, Delta Upsilon. Republican. Methodist. Address: 221 Asbury Ave., Asbury Park, N.J.

BRYAN, Robert Raymond, clergyman; b. Hookstown, Pa., Mar. 21, 1889; s. Robert M. and Isabelle (Swaney) B.; A.B., Westminster Coll., New Wilmington, Pa., 1910; A.M., Princeton U., 1915; grad. Princeton Sem., 1916; grad. study Columbia U., U. of Neb., Union Sem.; D.D., Sterling Coll., 1923. Teacher Sterling Coll., Sterling, Kan., 1910-13; ordained United Presbyn. ministry, 1916; pastor First Ch., Erie, Pa., 1916-22; asso. pastor Shadyside Ch., Pittsburgh, 1922-23; pastor Central Ch., Omaha, 1923-30, Presbyn. Ch. of the Messiah, Paterson, N.J., since 1930. Served as chaplain with rank of 1st lt., Camp Meade, Md., 1918. Mem. Presbyn. Bd. Foreign Missions, 6 yrs.; pres. Nat. Young People's Christian Union of United Presbyn. Ch., 1 yr. Home: 185 E. 33d St., Paterson, N.J.

BRYAN, Wilbur Aaron, high sch. prin.; b. Port Murry, N.J., Feb. 23, 1894; s. Albert and Annie (Atchley) B.; Ph.B., Lafayette Coll., Easton, Pa., 1915; m. Mazie Brown, April 3, 1920; children—Wilbur Lowell, Robert Sedgwick, Tremaine Ann (dec). Engaged as instr. physics dept., Lafayette Coll., 1915-17; teacher, high sch., Cliffside Park, N.J., 1917-18, Hackettstown, N.J., 1918-19, Wenonah (N.J.) Mil. Acad., 1919-20; prin. high sch., South River, N.J. since 1920; sec. Providers Bldg. & Loan Assn. of South River, N.J. since 1926. Served as 2d lt. Signal Corps, U.S.A., 1918. Mem. N.E.A., N.J. Schoolmasters Club, Phi Beta Kappa. Republican. Methodist. Mason. Home: 154 George St., South River, N.J.

BRYANS, Henry Bussell, exec. vice-pres. Phila. Electric Co.; b. Phila., Pa., March 26, 1886; s. Henry M. and Ella (Lonergan) B.; A.B., Central High Sch., Phila., 1903; B.S., in M.E., U. of Pa., 1907; m. Ada Matilda Trinkle, May 1, 1911; children—Henry Trinkle, Robert Trinkle. During entire business career has been continuously employed with The United Gas Improvement Co. or one of its asso. cos. since entering their employ as mech. engr., 1907; gen. supt. Phila. Suburban-Counties Gas & Electric Co., 1927-28, asst. gen. mgr., 1928; asst. gen. mgr. and vice-pres. in charge of operations, Phila. Electric Co., 1928-38, exec. vice-pres. since Oct. 25, 1938; exec. vice-pres. and dir. Deepwater Light and Power Co., Electric Realty Corpn., Phila. Electric Power Co., Phila. Hydro-Electric Co., Phila. Steam Co., The Susquehanna Electric Co., Susquehanna Power Co., Susquehanna Utilities Co.; dir.: Conowingo Land Company of Cecil Co., Howard Improvement Co., Sowego Water and Power Company. Mem. Am. Inst. Elec. Engrs., Am. Soc. Mech. Engrs., Franklin Inst., Hist. Soc. of Pa., Pa. Soc. of New York. Republican. Presbyn. Mason. Rotarian. Clubs: Rotary, Engineers, Union League, Art (Phila.); Aronimink Golf (Newtown Square Pa.); Plymouth Country (Norristown, Pa.). Home: Germantown Pike, R.F.D. No. 3, Norristown. Office: 1000 Chestnut St., Philadelphia, Pa.

BRYANT, Donald Reid, lawyer; b. Bangor, Me., Oct. 14, 1894; s. William Cullen and Charlotte (Fanton) B.; ed. U. of Me., 1912-13; LL.B., U. of Valparaiso, Ind., 1917; ed. Columbia U., 1919-20; m. Denise Destribats, May 6, 1921; children—Donald Reid, Jr., Patricia Miriam. Admitted to N.J. bar as atty., 1920, as counsellor, 1924; apptd. spl. master in chancery, 1937, supreme ct. commr., 1938; engaged in gen. practice of law at Trenton, N.J. since 1920; dist. supervisor N.J. Transfer Inheritance Tax Bur. since 1933. Served as pvt. to 2d lt. Signal Corps, U.S.A., 1917-19, with A.E.F. in France, retired acct. disability. Mem. Mercer County Bar Assn., Sigma Alpha Epsilon. Republican. Roman Catholic. Home: 115 Reading Av. Office: Trenton Trust Bldg., Trenton, N.J.

BRYSON, John Frampton, physician and banker; b. Watsontown, Pa., May 7, 1870; s. William and Mary (Nicely) B.; student State Normal Sch. and Jefferson Med. Coll. (Phila.); m. Ella Dora Balliet, May 11, 1904; 1 son, Dr. John Chalmers. In practice medicine, Girardville, Pa. Pres. First Nat. Bank of Girardville. Mason (Shriner, K.T.). Club: Fountain Springs Country. Address: 218 W. Main St., Girardville, Pa.

BUCCIERI, Agostino Rocco, college professor; b. Italy, Aug. 15, 1893; s. Salvatore and Rosa (Marsico) B.; came to U.S., 1911, naturalized, 1922; student Indiana (Pa.) State Normal Sch., 1916-18, Bethany (W.Va.) Coll., 1918-20; A.B. in edn., U. of Pittsburgh, 1923, A.M., 1931; diploma, Istituto Interuniversitario Italiano Roma, Italy, 1936; m. Julia Settino, 1920; children—Mary Frances, Agostino Rocco, Julius Samuel, Gloria Joan. Prof. of Romance langs., Bethany (W.Va.) Coll., 1918-20, Pittsburgh Acad., 1920-24, Washington and Jefferson Coll., 1924-26; prof. of Romance langs., Duquesne U., Pittsburgh, since 1929. Mem. Modern Lang. Assn. of America. Home: 900 Brookline Boul., Pittsburgh, Pa.

BUCHANAN, David Rea, executive; b. Independence Twp., Washington Co., Pa., Feb. 22, 1890; s. William H. and Winifred E. (Rea) B.; student Independence Twp. Schs.; grad. Washington Bus. Coll., 1906; m. Mary Ellen McClain, Sept. 9, 1914; children—Lois Norene, William Rea. Bookkeeper Beaver (Pa.) Refining Co., 1907-08; bill clerk, Pa. R.R., 1908-09; note teller Washington (Pa.) Trust Co., 1909-17; sec. Leonard Petroleum Co., Washington, Pa., since 1917, Leonard Oil & Gas Co. since 1917, Lenco Petroleum Co., Washington, Pa., since 1927; treas. Leonard Oil Development Co., Washington, Pa., since 1926, now also dir. Republican. Presbyterian. Mason (R.A.M., Shriner). Clubs: Washington Co. Golf and Country (Washington, Pa.); Nemacolin Country (Beallsville, Pa.). Home: 200 N. Wade Av. Office: 48 N. Main St., Washington, Pa.

BUCHANAN, Edwin P.; asst. prof. surgery, U. of Pittsburgh; mem. surg. staff Mercy Hosp. Address: Mercy Hosp., Pittsburgh, Pa.

BUCHANAN, Malcolm Griswold, vice-chancellor of N.J.; b. Trenton, N.J., March 10, 1881; s. Henry Clay and Mary Elizabeth (Griswold) B.; grad. State Model Sch., 1896; A.B., Princeton, 1900; LL.B., Harvard, 1903; m. Lily Butler, of Washington, June 9, 1906; 1 dau., Lily Butler; m. 2d, Lucy Baldwin Walradt Kennedy, July 8, 1931. Admitted to N.J. bar, 1904, and began practice at Trenton; mem. James & Malcolm G. Buchanan, 1904-16; apptd. v.-chancellor Court of Chancery of N.J., 1919, reapptd. 1926 and 1933, for term ending 1940; dir. Real Estate Title Co. of N.J. Mem. Am. and N.J. State bar assns. Republican. Episcopalian. Mason (32°, Shriner). Clubs: Trenton; Nassau (Princeton); Princeton (New York); Harvard (Phila.). Home: 8 Newlin Rd., Princeton, N.J. Office: State House, Trenton, N.J.

BUCHANAN, Mary; prof. ophthalmology, Woman's Med. Coll.; chief ophthalmologist, Hosp. of Woman's Med. Coll. of Pa.; ophthalmologist Woman's Hosp. and Southern Home for Friendless Children; consultant Woman's Dept., Norristown (Pa.) State Hosp. Address: 1737 Chestnut St., Philadelphia, Pa.

BUCHANAN, Robert Hutcheson; pres. Wyoming Valley Colleries Co. Home: 600 Clay Av. Office: Bowman Bldg., Scranton, Pa.

BUCHANAN, Scott, coll. dean; b. Sprague, Wash., March 17, 1895; s. William D. and Lillian E. (Bagg) B.; A.B., Amherst Coll., 1916; Rhodes Scholar Balliol Coll. Oxford U., Eng., 1919-21; Ph.D., Harvard U., 1925; m. Miriam Thomas, Feb. 1921; 1 son, Douglas. Sec. Amherst Christian Assn., 1916-17; instr. Greek, Amherst Coll., 1917-18; instr. philosophy, Coll. City of N.Y., 1924-28; asst. dir. People's Inst., N.Y. City, 1925-29; prof. philosophy, Univ. of Va., 1929-36; dean St. John's Coll., Annapolis, Md. since 1937. Served in U.S.N.R.F., 1918-19. Trustee St. John's Coll., Annapolis, Md. Mem. Am. Philos. Assn., Am. Math. Assn., Delta Upsilon. Congregationalist. Home: 139 Market St., Annapolis, Md.

BUCHER, George Heisler, pres. Westinghouse Electric & Mfg. Co.; b. Sunbury, Pa., July 24, 1888; s. John Beard and Hannah (Heisler) B.; grad. Pratt Inst., Brooklyn, N.Y., 1909; m. Bertha I. Rhoads, Dec. 26, 1911; children—Martha Elizabeth (Mrs. Jules W. Beuret, Jr.), Ruth Rhoads, Alma Rhoads, Irene Rhoads, George David. Grad. engring. student Westinghouse Co., East Pittsburgh, 1909-11; export dept., Westinghouse Co. (since 1919 Westinghouse Electric Internat. Co.), New York, 1911-20, asst. to gen. mgr., 1920-21, asst. gen. mgr., 1921-32, v.p. and gen. mgr., 1932-34, pres. and gen mgr., 1934-36, pres. since 1934; v.p. and Eastern dist. mgr. Westinghouse Electric & Mfg. Co., New York, 1935-36, exec. v.p., Pittsburgh, 1936-38, pres. since 1938; dir. Westinghouse Electric & Mfg. Co., Can. Westinghouse Co., Ltd. Mem. Am. Inst. Elec. Engrs. Clubs: Pittsburgh Athletic, University, Duquesne (Pittsburgh); Lawyers (New York); Electrical Manufacturers; Lake Mohawk Country (Sparta, N.J.). Home: 841 Osage Rd., Mt. Lebanon, Pittsburgh, Pa. Office: 306 4th Ave., Pittsburgh, Pa.

BUCHER, John Emery, chemist; b. Hanover, Pa., Aug. 17, 1872; s. Jacob F. and Elizabeth (Emery) B.; A.C., Lehigh U., 1891; Ph.D., Johns Hopkins, 1894; Sc.D., Brown U., 1917; m. Alcista Howard, 1896. Instr. organic chemistry, Tufts Coll., 1894-97; asso. prof. chemistry, R.I. Coll., 1897-1901; same, Brown U., 1901-15, prof. and head of dept., 1915-17; with Penman-Littlehales Chem. Co., 1917-20. Mem. Naval Consulting Bd., World War. Mem. Civil Legion. Republican. Contbr. numerous articles in professional jours. Inventor of process for nitrogen fixation, and processes for mfr. of magnesium, beryllium and aluminium. Consulting chemist, New York. Home: 57 Davenport St., North Adams, Mass. Address: 322 Main St., Fort Lee, N.J.

BUCHHOLZ, Heinrich Eward ("Ezekiel Cheever"), writer, pub.; b. Baltimore, Jan. 19, 1879; s. Heinrich and Emily (Wattenscheidt) Buchholz; educated public and private schs.; m. Nellie Gascoyne, June 6, 1905; children—Nellie G. (Mrs. Jack K. Evans), Eleanor L. Mgr. Internat. Lit. Syndicate, 1899-1905; financial editor Baltimore Evening Herald, 1905-06; spl. contbr. Baltimore Sun since 1906; editor Merchants and Manufacturers' Journal, 1909-18; owner and editor of Atlantic Educational Journal, 1911-18; editor Ezekiel Cheever's Sch. Issues since 1921; pres. Warwick & York, Inc.; mng. editor Jour. of Ednl. Psychology and Ednl. Administration and Supervision. Mng. editor Men of Mark in Maryland, 1906; editor Md. subjects in Students' Reference Library, 1908. Mem. N.E.A. Author: The Civil War, 1905; Governors of Maryland, 1906; Reconstruction, 1906; The Crown of the Chesapeake, 1907; Of What Use Are Common People?, 1923; U.S.—A Second Study in Democracy, 1926; Fads and Fallacies in Present-Day Education, 1931. Editor:

Edgar Allan Poe—A Centenary Tribute, 1910; W. & Y. Course of Study Series since 1917. Contbr. to periodicals and newspapers under pen name of "Ezekiel Cheever." Home: 2634 N. Calvert St. Office: 10 E. Centre St., Baltimore, Md.

BUCHMAN, Frank N(athan) D(aniel), clergyman; b. Pennsburg, Pa., June 4, 1878; s. Frank and Sarah A. (Greenawalt) B.; A.B., Muhlenberg Coll., 1899, A.M., 1902, D.D., 1926; grad. Mt. Airy Luth. Theol. Sem., Phila., 1902; studied Westminster Coll., Cambridge U.; unmarried. Ordained Luth. ministry, 1902; pastor Ch. of Good Shepherd, Overbrook, Pa., 1902-05; founded first Luther Hospice in America, at Overbrook, 1904; apptd. house father Luther Hosp., Phila., 1905; founded first Luther settlement in Phila., 1907; sec. Y.M.C.A., Pennsylvania State Coll., 1909-15; toured India, Korea and Japan, 1915-16, and toured Far East, 1917; extension lecturer Hartford Theological Foundation, 1916-21; became a leader in religious movement known as the Oxford Group (A First Century Christian Fellowship), 1921. Served in Europe during World War, with a flying squadron, looking after war prisoners, under Y.M.C.A.; originator of the Groups at Oxford; toured S. Africa with the Oxford Group, 1929; toured South America, 1931, Canada and U.S., 1932-33 and 1933-34; led teams totalling 2,000 in Scandinavian countries, 1934-35; in furtherance of a Spiritual Front of Oslo States, visited Holland with team of 2,000 from Great Britain and Scandinavia for nat., demonstration in Utrecht, 1937. Club: Lake Placid. Address: Allentown, Pa.; 61 Gramercy Park N., New York, N.Y.*

BUCHOLTZ, Carl, pres. Virginian Ry.; b. Baltimore, Md., Mar. 21, 1883; s. William and Alma (Hoen) B.; studied under Col. R. M. Johnson, Baltimore, 1891-94; student Loyola Coll., 1894-99; unmarried. Clk. in leaf tobacco business, 1899-1901, law office, 1901-02; machinist apprentice to supervisor of track B.&O. R.R. Co., 1902-08; maintenance of way insp. to div. engr. M.P.R.R., 1910-14; asst. engr. through grades to asst. gen. mgr. Erie R.R. Co., 1915-27, gen. mgr., 1927-32; gen. mgr., later v.p. and gen. mgr. Virginian Ry., 1933-34, pres. since 1934; pres. Loop Creek Colliery Co., Norfolk Terminal Ry. Co., dir. Norfolk & Portsmouth Belt Line R.R. Co. Mem. Am. Ry. Engrs. Assn., Ry. Signal Assn. Clubs: Town, Virginia (Norfolk); Whitehall (New York); Princess Anne Country, Norfolk Yacht and Country. Home: Monticello Hotel, Norfolk, Va., and Longgreen P. O. Baltimore Co., Md. Office: 704 Terminal Station Bldg., Norfolk, Va.

BUCHWALD, Leona Caroline, supervisor guidance and placement; b. Baltimore, Md., Jan. 4, 1892; d. Henry C. and Wilhemina F. (Feick) B.; student Baltimore Elementary schs., 1898-1904, Baltimore Prep. Sch., 1904-07, Baltimore Sr. High Sch., 1907-09; A.B., Goucher Coll., 1913; studied Harvard U., summers, 1923, 24, 25 and 26, M. Edn., 1926. Teacher English and German, Havre de Grace (Md.) High Sch., 1913-16, West Chester (Pa.) High Sch., 1916-17; head dept. of German, West Chester High Sch., 1917-18; statistical clerk War Dept., Washington, D.C., 1918-19; business girls' sec., Y.W.C.A., Baltimore, 1919-21; vocational sec., Goucher Coll., 1921-23, assisting in orgn. of vocational guidance and placement; ednl. and vocational counselor, Baltimore Pub. Schs., 1923-26, supervisor of guidance and placement since 1926; instr. ednl. and vocational guidance, Johns Hopkins U. Coll. for Teachers, winters, since 1924 and summers, 1927, 28, 29, 39; instr. ednl. and vocational guidance Rutgers U. Sch. of End., summers, 1929, 30, 32, 33, 37 and 38, Pa. State Coll., summer 1936. First v.p. Nat. Vocational Guidance Assn., 1935, chmn. program com., 1936, pres., 1936-37, mem. bd. trustees, 1937. Mem. Am. Vocational Assn., Md. Vocational Guidance Assn. (organizer 1925; pres. 4 years), League of Women Voters, Phi Beta Phi. Mem. Reformed Luth. Ch. Club: Baltimore Business and Professional Women's (an organizer; pres. 1935-37; mem. nat. advisory com. on vocational guidance). Home: 4209 Springdale Av. Office: 3 E. 25th St., Baltimore, Md.

BUCK, Charles A., steel mfr.; b. Bucksville, Pa., Mar. 14, 1867; B.S., Lehigh U., 1887, Dr. Engring., 1932. Asst. chemist, Bethlehem Steel Co., 1887-88; chemist J. I. Co. of Cuba, 1888-89; asst. chemist Bethlehem Steel Co., 1889-96, chemist, 1896-1905, chemist and supt. blast furnace, 1905-06, then becoming gen supt., now vice-pres.; pres. Bethlehem-Chile Iron Mines Corpn., also pres. Mahoning Ore & Steel Co., Address: Bethlehem Steel Co., Bethlehem, Pa.*

BUCK, Charles H.; pres. Maryland Title Guarantee Co. Home: 2900 Wyman Parkway. Office: Munsey Bldg., Baltimore, Md.

BUCK, Clayton Douglass, ex-gov.; b. in Del., Mar. 21, 1890; s. Francis N. and Margaret (Douglass) B.; prep. edn., Friends' Sch., Wilmington, Del.; student U. of Pa.; m. Alice du Pont Wilson; children—Clayton Douglass, Dorcas Van Dyke. Was engaged in road-bldg. engring. work, Del.; chief engr., Del. State Highway Dept., 1920-29; gov. of Del. 1929-37; pres. Equitable Trust Co., Wilmington. Republican. Episcopalian. Clubs: Union League, Wilmington, Wilmington Country, Home: Buena Vista, Wilmington, Del.

BUCK, Elizabeth Cooper (Mrs.); gen. mgr. Noxzema Chemical Co.; b. Greenwood, S.C., Apr. 23, 1892; d. Theodore Bartholomew and Jane Mauldin (Coc) Starnes; ed. public schools, Greenwood and Columbia, S.C.; m. Howard Dalrymple Buck, Feb. 28, 1912; children—Howard Dalrymple, George Wesley, II; m. 2d, Lt. Col. L. J. I. Barrett, Mar. 19, 1937. Sec. Traxler Real Estate Co., Greenville, S. C., 1909-12; became interested in Noxzema Chem. Co., mfrs. greaseless skin cream, 1913 (company not organized until 1917), selling, office records, personnel and mfr., gen. mgr. since 1930. Baptist. Clubs: Business and Professional Women's, Quota (Baltimore); Green Spring Valley Hunt (Garrison, Md.); St. Margaret's Hunt (Annapolis). Home: Worthington Valley, Dover Rd., Reisterstown, Md. Office: Noxzema Chemical Co., Baltimore, Md.

BUCK, Leonard Jerome, importer; b. Bethlehem, Pa., Sept. 29, 1893; s. Charles Austin and Josephine Martha (Rankey) B.; E.M., Lehigh U., Bethlehem, Pa., 1915, post grad. study, 1915-17; m. Helen Rouss, Apr. 3, 1923; children—Nancy, Martha, Charles. Began with Lehigh Coke Co., Bethlehem, Pa.; sales engr. Union Carbide & Carbon Co., New York, 1921-22; exclusive U.S. sales agt. British Am. Nickel Corpn., New York, 1922-24; v.p. Buck Kiaer & Co., New York, 1924-25; v. p. in charge ore dept. William H. Muller & Co., New York, 1925-28; pres. Leonard J. Buck, Inc., importer ores, raw materials and other metall. products for iron and steel industry, Far Hills, N.J., since 1928; dir. Ohio Ferro Alloys, Harrisburg Steel Co., Charles Broadway Rouss, Inc. Mem. Am. Iron and Steel Inst., Am. Inst. Mining Engrs., Beta Theta Pi. Catholic. Clubs: American Spaniel (New York); Somerset Hills Kennel (Far Hills, N.J.); India House (New York). Home: Far Hills, N.J. Office: 1 Newark Av., Jersey City, N.J.

BUCK, Oscar MacMillan, prof. missions and comparative religion; b. of Am. missionary parents, Cawnpore, India, Feb. 9, 1885; s. Philo M. (D.D.) and Caroline (MacMillan) B.; B.A., Ohio Wesleyan U., 1905, M.A., 1908, D.D., 1925; B.D., Drew Theol. Sem., 1908; m. Berenice Marie Baker, June 20, 1908; children—Nancy Randolph (dec.), Jean MacMillan (Mrs. George Hugh Birney, Jr.), Sara Louise. Ordained M.E. ministry, 1909; prof. Bible, Bareilly Theol. Sem., India, 1909-13; pastor in Ill., 1913-15; prof. missions and comparative religion, Ohio Wesleyan U., 1915-19; prof. missions and comparative religion, Drew Theol. Sem. (now Drew Univ.), 1920—. Sec. Commn. on Christian Higher Edn. in India, 1930-31. Author: India Beloved of Heaven (with others), 1918; Working with Christ for India (monograph), 1922; Out of Their Own Mouths, 1926; Our Asiatic Christ, 1927; India Looks to Her Future, 1930; Christianity Tested, 1934. Address: Drew University, Madison, N.J.

BUCK, Pearl Sydenstricker (Mrs. Richard J. Walsh), author; b. Hillsboro, W.Va., June 26, 1892; d. Absalon and Caroline (Stuiting) Sydenstricker; A.B., Randolph-Macon Woman's Coll., Lynchburg, Va., 1914; M.A., Cornell U., 1926; hon. M.A., Yale, 1933; m. John Lossing Buck, May 13, 1917; children—Carol, Janice; m. 2d, Richard J. Walsh, June 11, 1935; adopted children—Richard Stulting, John Stulting, Edgar Sydenstricker, and Jean Comfort. Teacher, University of Nanking, China, 1921-31, Southeastern U., Nanking, 1925-27, Chung Yang U., Nanking, China, 1928-30. Member American Academy of Arts and Letters, Phi Beta Kappa, Kappa Delta. Club: Cosmopolitan (New York). Author: East Wind-West Wind, 1929; The Young Revolutionist, 1931; The Good Earth (awarded Pulitzer prize), 1931; Sons, 1932; The First Wife and Other Stories, 1933; All Men Are Brothers (translation of the Chinese classic Shui Hu Chuan), 1933; The Mother, 1934; A House Divided, 1935; House of Earth, 1935; The Exile, 1936; Fighting Angel, 1936; This Proud Heart, 1938. Home: R.F.D. 3, Perkasie, Pa. Address: The John Day Co., 40 E. 49th St., New York, N.Y.

BUCK, Walter Hooper, lawyer; b. Baltimore, Md., Apr. 14, 1878; s. Richard Bayly and Laura Elma (Grafflin) B.; LL.B., U. of Md., 1907; m. H. Elise Vogeler, June 20, 1906; children—William G. (dec.), Walter B. (M.D.). Bank clk., 1896-1904; admitted to bar, 1907, and practiced in Baltimore; gen. counsel and dir. Union Trust Co. of Md., Buck Glass Co. Mem. council Nat. Civil Service Reform League; dir. Baltimore Criminal Justice Commn.; active in Civil Service Reform Assn. of Md. Mem. bd. visitors and govs. St. John's Coll., 1926-36, vice chmn., 1930-36. Mem. Am. Bar Assn., Md. State Bar Assn. (v.p. 1917-18), Bar Assn. of Baltimore (pres. 1923-24), Md. Judiciary Commn. (sec. 1923), S.A.R. Democrat. Episcopalian. Clubs: University, Merchants, Elkridge Fox Hunting (Baltimore). Contbr. to periodicals. Home: Brooklandville, Md. Office: Union Trust Bldg., Baltimore, Md.

BUCKE, Jacob Edward Ambrose, clergyman; b. Mt. Patrick, Pa., Nov. 3, 1875; s. Samuel Elias and Nancy Jane (Fortney) B.; B.Ed., State Teachers Coll., Lock Haven, Pa., 1897; B.D., Drew U. Sch. of Theology, Madison, N.Y., 1903; (hon.) D.D., Dickinson Coll., Carlisle, Pa., 1923; m. Linnie May Coulter, Aug. 1, 1899; children—Elizabeth Jane, M.D., (Mrs. Edgar Raymond Miller, M.D.), Rev. David Perry, Rev. Emory Stevens. Engaged in teaching pub. schs. and student pastor, 1894-1905; ordained to ministry M.E. Ch.; pastor various chs., 1905-21; dist. supt., Sunbury Dist., 1921-27; pastor, Harrisburg, Pa., 1927-34, Lock Haven, Pa., 1934-38, Shamokin, Pa., since 1938. Home: 112 E. Lincoln St., Shamokin, Pa.

BUCKEY, William Emmett, educator; b. Beverly, W.Va., Mar. 27, 1886; s. Charles N. and Rose (Cleary) B.; student elementary sch., Lodi, Calif., 1892-97, elementary and high sch., Beverly, W.Va., 1899-1906, Fairmont Normal Sch., 1909-12; M.A., West Va. U., 1920-23; student U. of Pa., summer 1912, Columbia U., summer, 1915, Harvard U., summer, 1921; m. Ada Talkington, June 15, 1915; children—William E., Sarah Rose. Teacher rural schs., W.Va., 1906-09, graded sch., Fairmont, W.Va., 1912; prin. Elementary Training Sch., Fairmont Normal Sch., 1913-17; prin. high sch., Fairmont, 1921-39; dir. summer demonstration sch., Fairmont State Teachers Coll., 4 summers. Mem. U.S. Draft Board, 1916-17. Mem. W.Va. High Sch. Prin. Assn., W.Va. Edn. Assn., Marion Co. (W.Va.) Teachers Assn. (sec-treas.), Phi Beta Kappa. Del. in attendance Kiwanis Internat. Conv., Washington, D.C., 1936, San Francisco, 1938. Republican. Methodist. Mason, Odd Fellow. Clubs: Kiwanis, Town Hall, Harvard, Rock Lake (Fairmont). Home: 804 Locust Av. Office: Loop Park, Fairmont, W.Va.

BUCKINGHAM, Edgar, physicist; b. Phila., Pa., July 8, 1867; s. Lucius Henry and Angelina Bradley (Hyde) B.; A.B., Harvard, 1887; post-grad. work same, 1887-89, U. of Strassburg, 1889-90, Ph. D., Leipsic, 1893; m. Elizabeth Branton Holstein, July 15, 1901; children—Katharine, Stephen Alvord. Asst. in physics,

Harvard, 1888-89, 1891-92, Strassburg, 1889-90; mem. faculty, Bryn Mawr Coll., 1893-99; instr. physics, U. of Wis., 1901-02; asst. physicist Bur. of Soils, U.S. Dept. Agr., 1902-05; with Bur. of Standards, 1905-37, was physicist same. Lecturer on thermodynamics, Grad. Sch. U.S. Naval Acad., 1910-12; associate scientific attaché, U.S. Embassy, Rome, Italy, 1918. Mem. Am. Soc. Naval Engrs., Philos. Soc. of Washington (pres. 1915), Acoustical Soc. of America, Newcomen Soc. Clubs: Cosmos (Washington, D.C.); Harvard (New York). Author: An Outline of the Theory of Thermodynamics, 1900; also numerous sci. articles and bulls. Home: 18 Hesketh St., Chevy Chase, Md.

BUCKINGHAM, Guy Emerson, asso. prof. education; b. Fredericktown, Pa., Mar. 18, 1899; s. William Hughes and Laura Halcyon (Baker) B.; A.B., Washington and Jefferson Coll., Washington, Pa., 1921, A.M., 1926; Ph.D., Northwestern U., Evanston, Ill., 1929; asso. mem. Advanced Sch. Edn., Teachers Coll. of Columbia U., 1938-39; m. Luna Olive Guesman, June 9, 1920; children—Mervin Baker, Betty Romaine, Walter Travis (dec.). Head of mathematics dept., high sch. South Brownsville, Pa., 1921-23; prin. high sch., Jefferson, Pa., 1923-27; asst. prof. philosophy and edn., Allegheny Coll., Meadville, Pa., 1929-36, asso. prof. since 1936. Served in S.A.T.C., 1918. Mem. A.A.A.S., Am. Assn. Univ. Profs., Am. Acad. Polit. and Social Sci., Nat. Soc. Coll. Teachers Edn., Nat. Edn. Assn., Pa. State Edn. Assn., Meadville Round Table, Beta Theta Pi, Phi Tau Gamma, Kappa Phi Kappa, Phi Delta Kappa. Republican. Presbyterian. Author: Diagnostic and Remedial Teaching in First Year Algebra, 1933; contbr. to ednl. journs. Home: 378 Meadow St., Meadville, Pa.

BUCKLER, H. Warren; pres. Md. Tuberculosis Sanatorium Commn., term expires 1941. Address: 806 Cathedral St., Baltimore, Md.

BUCKLEY, Albert Coulson, neuropsychiatrist; b. Phila., Pa., Aug. 6, 1873; s. William Coulson (M.D.) and Lucy Ann (Davis) B.; A.B., Central High Sch., Phila., 1894; M.D., Medico-Chirurg. Coll., Phila., 1897; m. Harriet Ellis Baily, 1904. Asst. neurologist, Medico-Chirurg. Hosp., 1897-1906; asso. prof. normal histology, Medico-Chirurg. Coll., 1899-1908; asso. prof. psychiatry same, 1908-17; asst. neurologist. Phila. Gen. Hosp., 1906-12; asst. phys. Friends Hospital, 1906-18; med. supt. same since 1918; alienist Phila. Orthopedic Hosp., 1912-21; prof. physiatry, Grad. Sch. of Medicine of U. of Pa. since 1919; prof. clinical psychiatry, School of Medicine, same, 1930—; neurologist Frankford Hosp., 1930; honorary consulting psychiatrist, Phila. Gen. Hosp., since 1931. Diplomate Am. Board Psychiatry and Neurology, 1936. Fellow Coll. Physicians of Phila., A.M.A.; mem. Am. Psychiatric Assn., A.A.A.S., Am. Neurol. Assn., Phila. Neurol. Soc. (pres. 1933), Phila. Psychiatric Soc. (pres. 1923, 24), Phila. Clin. Assn., Sigma Xi, etc. Author: The Basis of Psychiatry, 1920; Nursing Mental and Nervous Diseases, 1927. Home: Friends Hospital, Frankford, Philadelphia, Pa.

BUCKLEY, Oliver Ellsworth, research engr.; b. Sloan, Ia., Aug. 8, 1887; s. William Doubleday and Sarah Elizabeth (Jeffrey) B.; B.S., Grinnell Coll., 1909, D.Sc., 1936; Ph.D., Cornell, 1914; m. Clara Lane, Oct. 14, 1914; children—Katherine Lane, William Douglas, Barbara, Juliet Georgiana. Inst. Grinnell Coll., 1909, Cornell, 1910-14; employed in research dept. Western Electric Co., 1914-25; with Bell Telephone Laboratories since 1925, asst. dir. of research, Bell Telephone Labs., 1927-33, dir. of research, 1933-36, exec. vice-pres. since 1936. Served as maj. Signal Corps, A.E.F., World War, in charge Research Sect. of Div. Research and Inspection, Signal Corps, Paris. Fellow Am. Phys. Soc., A.A.A.S., Am. Inst. Elec. Engrs., Acoustical Soc. America; mem. Nat. Acad. Sciences, Franklin Inst., Sigma Xi, Phi Beta Kappa, Phi Kappa Phi. Clubs: Railroad-Machinery, Salmagundi (New York); Maplewood Country. Home: 13 Fairview Terrace, Maplewood, N.J. Office, 463 West St., New York, N.Y.

BUCKNER, Chester Arthur, prof. edn.; b. nr. Ottumwa, Ia., Jan. 28, 1885; s. Stephen Andrew and Ida Demeris (Barker) B.; A.B., U. of Ia., 1909, A.M., 1911; Ph.D., Columbia, 1918; m. Neva Grace Starrett, Apr. 25, 1911. Fellow in edn., U. of Ia., 1913-14, Columbia, 1916-17; teacher of mathematics, high sch., Clinton, Ia., 1909-10; head dept. of English, high sch., Manila, P.I., 1911-13; asst. prof. of edn., U. of Kan., 1914-16; asst. to dir., Lincoln Sch. of Teachers Coll., Columbia, 1917-19; dir. Bur. of Sch. Service, U. of Kan., 1919-20; prof. secondary edn. and head dept., U. of Pittsburgh since 1920, dir. teacher apptmt. bur., 1922-23, chmn. Sch. of Edn., 1st semester, 1924-25, dir. high sch, practice teaching, 1929-31, head div. of professional edn., 1932-35. Lecturer in edn., summers, Cornell, 1919 and 1927, U. of Wis., 1924, U. of Southern Calif., 1931. Chmn. Western Pa. Edn. Conf. since 1930; mem. advisory committee for Pa., Study of Relations of Secondary and Higher Edn., 1928-30; chmn. Com. for Revision of Pa. State Course of Study in High School English, 1935-37. Fellow A.A.A.S.; member N.E.A. (Dept. of Secondary-Sch. Principles), Am. Assn. of Sch. Adminstrs., Am. Assn. of Univ. Profs., Nat. Soc. Coll. Teachers of Edn. (mem. exec. com., 1927-30), Nat. Soc. for Study of Edn., Am. Ednl. Research Assn., Phi Delta Kappa, Kappa Phi Kappa, Acacia. Methodist. Mason. Clubs: Faculty, Pa. Schoolmasters'. Wrote Educational Diagnosis of Individual Pupils; also collaborator Libraries for Philippine Public Schools, School Survey of Wheeling, W.Va., School Survey of Wellesley, Mass. Home: 436 Sulgrave Road, Pittsburgh, Pa.

BUCKWALTER, Isaac Zimmerman, exec. newspapers and radio; b. East Earl, Pa., Aug. 2, 1898; s. Freeland Neff and Henrietta (Zimmerman) B.; ed. pub. and high schs. and bus. coll.; m. Mabel Latschar Groff, Dec. 17, 1921; children—Richard Henry, Thelma Arlene, John Marvin. Began as post office clk., 1913; bookkeeper Enterprise Telephone Co., New Holland, Pa., then asst. treas. Penn Steel and Iron Corpn., Lancaster, Pa.; engaged in newspaper business since 1920, has been gen. mgr. Lancaster (Pa.) Newspapers, Inc., since 1928; also in radio business since 1929; sec., treas. and dir. Mason Dixon Radio Group. Republican. Evang. and Reformed. Mason, Elk. Club: Kiwanis (Lancaster, Pa.). Home: 1115 Watson Av. Office: 8 W. King St., Lancaster, Pa.

BUDAHN, Louis August, supt. of schools; b. Theresa, Wis., Apr. 19, 1878; s. Herman and Sophia (Grothman) B.; grad. Spencerian Business Coll., Milwaukee, Wis., 1885, Horicon (Wis.) High Sch., 1901, State Normal Sch., Milwaukee, Wis., 1903; student U. of Wis., Madison, Wis., summers 1904-06, winter 1907; B.S., Teachers Coll., Columbia U., 1921, A.M., 1922; m. Grace Hess; children—Frances Louise (Mrs. Paul Hitchcock), Pauline Moore (Mrs. Bill Juillerat), Wanda Gunnison (Mrs. Carl Shrey), Naundice Gunnison (Mrs. John Hauser), Alice Fuller, Elizabeth Frances (Mrs. Allen House). Began as mgr. general store, Theresa, Wis., 1896; teacher rural schools, Dodge Co., Wis., 1897-99; teacher village sch., Woodland, Wis., 1899-1900; supt. Hortonville, Wis., 1903-07; head of science dept., Eau Claire (Wis.) High Sch., 1908; prin. Chippewa Falls (Wis.) High Sch., 1909; sec. and vice-pres. land and insurance company, Eau Claire, Wis., 1910-14; prin. Eau Claire High Sch., 1914-20; teachers' inst. conductor, Wis., 1915; prof. of mathematics and pedagogy, State Normal Sch., Eau Claire, Wis., 1916; survey of Baltimore Schools for Teachers Coll., Columbia, 1920-21; prin. New Brunswick (N.J.) High Sch., 1921-22; supt. of schools, Asbury-Park, N.J., 1922-24; prof. of edn. and dir. commercial teacher training, State Normal Coll., Kent, O., 1925-27; supt. of schools, Fostoria, O., 1928-30, Pottsville, Pa., 1930-39. Mem. Bd. of Edn., Eau Claire, Wis., 1913-14. Pres. Northern Wis. Teachers Assn., 1916, sec. 1917-21. Mem. N.E.A., Supt. Dept. of N.E.A. Phi Delta Kappa. Methodist. Mason (K.T.). Author: The Story of a Piece of Land. Home: 219 N. 20th St. Office: 5th and Norwegian Sts., Pottsville, Pa.

BUDD, Edward G.; pres. Edward G. Budd Mfg. Co., Budd Wheel Co., Budd Internat. Corpn. and others. Home: 157 Pelham Road, Germantown, Philadelphia, Pa.

BUDD, Thomas Allibone, univ. prof. and dean; b. Phila., Pa., June 16, 1890; s. James Marshall and Alice (Zehnder) B.; student William Penn Charter Sch., Phila., 1901-08; B.S., in Econ., U. of Pa., 1912, A.M., 1923; m. Kathryn Marie Smith, Apr. 18, 1927; 1 dau., Susan Allibone. Instr. accounting, U. of Pa., 1912-17, asst. prof., 1923-28, dir. student personnel, Wharton Sch. of Finance and Commerce, 1921-35, asso. prof. finance, 1929-36, prof. and vice-dean, Wharton Sch. since 1936. Served as ensign, Supply Corps, U.S. Naval Res. Force, during World War. Mem. Am. Academy of Political and Social Science, Am. Econ. Soc., Pi Gamma Mu and Phi Kappa Psi fraternities. Episcopalian. Clubs: Phi Kappa Psi of Phila. (treas. since 1932), University, Le Coin d'Or, Contemporary (Phila.); University of Pa. (New York). Co-author (with E. N. Wright): The Interpretation of Accounts, 1927: Home: 500 Valley View Rd., Merion, Pa. Office: Logan Hall, 36th St. and Woodland Av., Philadelphia, Pa.

BUDDINGTON, Arthur Francis, prof. of geology; b. Wilmington, Del., Nov. 29, 1890; s. Osmer Gilbert and Mary Salina (Wheeler) B.; Ph.B., Brown U., 1912, Sc.M., 1913; Ph.D., Princeton U., 1916, student 1916-17; m. Jene Elizabeth Muntz, Sept. 10, 1924; 1 dau., Elizabeth Jene. Instr., Brown, 1917 and 1919; petrologist, geophysical lab., Carnegie Inst., 1919-20; asst. prof. geology, Princeton, 1920-26, asso. prof., 1926-32, prof. since 1932, chmn. of dept. since 1936; asst. geologist, U.S. Geol. Survey, 1919-23, asso. geologist since 1923. Served as private Aviation Sect., Signal Corps, and sergt. 1st class Chem. Warfare Service, U.S. Army, 1918. Fellow Geol. Soc. of America (councillor since 1939), Soc. of Econ. Geologists, Am. Mineral. Soc. (councillor 1936-40), Am. Philos. Soc., A.A.A.S. Methodist. Contbr. to jours. articles on geology of Alaska, Adirondacks, Newfoundland, Cascade Mts. of Ore. Home: 178 Prospect Av., Princeton, N.J.

BUDKE, John Frederick, lawyer; b. Canonsburg, Pa., Apr. 26, 1899; s. John Frederick and Mary Helen (Harrison) B.; student Mercersburg (Pa.) Acad., 1916-19, Bethany (W.Va.) Coll., 1920-21; LL.B., U. of Va., Charlottesville, Va., 1926; m. Margaret May Heydrick, Aug. 8, 1923; children—Harriet Louise, John Frederick. Admitted to Va. bar, 1925, Pa. bar, 1927, and since practiced in Franklin, Pa.; dir., asst. counsel and mem. exec. com. Parkersburg Iron & Steel Co.; dir. Cecil Improvement Co.; dir. and counsel Drake Realty Co., Oil City, Pa. Candidate for State senator, 1938. Mem. exec. com. and Roll Call chmn. Franklin-Venango Chapter Am. Red Cross; formerly chmn. Central Relief Bd. and mem. Venango Co. Assn. for Blind, formerly pres., treas. Kiwanis Club. Mem. Am. Bar Assn., Pa. Bar Assn., Venango County Bar (mem. examining com.), Delta Upsilon, Delta Theta Pi. Presbyterian. Mason (K.T., Shriner), Elk. Clubs: Washington, Kiwanis, Elks (Franklin, Pa.). Home: Miller Park. Office: Hancock Bldg., Franklin, Pa.

BUDNITZ, Edmund; mem. Md. Public Service Commn. Address: Munsey Bldg., Baltimore, Md.

BUELL, Marjorie Henderson ("Marge"), cartoonist; b. Philadelphia Pa., Dec. 11, 1904; d. Horace Lyman and Bertha Taylor (Brown) Henderson; ed. Friends Sch., Westchester, Pa., Miss Sayward's Sch., Overbrook, Pa., Devon (Pa.) Manor Sch., and Villa Maria Convent, Immaculata, Pa.; m. C. Addison Buell, Jan. 30, 1936. Began as cartoonist, 1924; cartoonist for Public Ledger Syndicate, Saturday Evening Post, Country Gentleman, Ladies Home Journal, Life, Colliers and other mags. Creator: Little Lulu, 1935, and still running in Saturday Evening Post; book published in 1936; also writer many articles and stories for Life and Saturday Evening Post; illustrated several books. Republican. Presbyterian. Clubs: Young Republican. Author: Little Lulu, 1936. Home: Olde Mill Road, Frazer, Pa. Address: Box N, Malvern, Pa.

BUENTING, Otto Wilhelm, v.p. Westinghouse Air Brake Co.; b. Hanover, Kan., May 28, 1873;

s. John Wert and Christiana (Schmidt) B.; M.E., Purdue U., 1901; m. Harriet E. Richards, Aug. 12, 1913; children—Elizabeth, Otto William, Robert Ernst, Harriet Ann. Began as machinist apprentice on C., B.&Q. Ry. Co., 1889; inspector, foreman, later works mgr., Westinghouse Air Brake Co., 1901-17, gen. works mgr., 1917-26, v.p. in charge of mfr. since 1927; also v.p. in charge of mfr. Union Switch & Signal Co. Mem. Am. Soc. M.E. Mem. Reformed Ch. Mason (32°), Shriner. Clubs: Engineer, Longue Vue (Pittsburgh); Edgewood Country. Home: 512 East End Av., Pittsburgh, Pa. Office: Westinghouse Air Brake Co., Wilmerding, Pa.

BUERGER, Charles B.; v.p. Gulf Oil Corpn. Home: 120 Ruskin Av. Office: Gulf Bldg., Pittsburgh, Pa.

BUERMANN, Robert; chief of staff Paul Kimball Hosp.; mem. courtesy staff Raleigh Fitkin-Paul Morgan Memorial Hosp., Neptune, N.J., and Royal Pines Hosp. and Clinic, Pinewald, N.J.; consultant Point Pleasant (N.J.) Hosp. Address: 206 Madison Av., Lakewood, N.J.

BUFALINO, Charles J., lawyer; b. Pittston, Pa., Feb. 16, 1905; s. Salvatore and Luigina (Galante) B.; grad. Pittston High Sch., 1922; student U. of Pa., 1922-24; A.B., Villanova (Pa.) Coll., 1926; student U. of Pa. Law Sch., 1926-27, Temple U. Law Sch., Phila., 1927-29; m. Gaetana E. Volpe, April 23, 1930; 1 son, Charles Caesar. Admitted to Luzerne Co. bar, 1930; chief deputy prothonotary, Luzerne County, Dec. 1, 1932-Jan. 3, 1938; atty. for West Side Bank, West Pittston, Pa.; sec. Volpe Coal Co. (Pittston), Gateway Coal Co. (Forest City); sec.-treas. Lockport Brewing Co. (Lock Haven). Republican. Catholic. Club: Rotary (Pittston, Pa.). Home: 212 Wyoming Av., West Pittston, Pa. Office: 22 N. Main St., Pittston, Pa.

BUFFINGTON, Joseph, judge; b. Kittanning, Pa., Sept. 5, 1855; s. Ephraim and Margaret Chambers (Orr) B.; B.A., Trinity Coll., Conn., 1875; LL.D., Lafayette Coll., 1915, also Trinity, U. of Pittsburgh, Princeton, Washington and Jefferson Coll., Grove City Coll., Pa. Mil. Coll., Dickinson Coll., D.C.L., Mt. St. Mary's Coll.; m. Mary Alice Simonton, Jan. 29, 1885; 1 son, Joseph; m. 3d, Mary Fullerton Jones, Jan. 1, 1931 (died 1933). Admitted to bar, 1878; practiced at Kittanning, Pa., 1878-92; U.S. dist. judge, Western Dist. Pa., 1892-1904; U.S. circuit judge, 3d Circuit, since Sept. 21, 1906; sr. and presiding judge U.S. Circuit Court of Appeals. Mem. Psi Upsilon, Phi Beta Kappa. Chevalier Order of the Golden Crown (Italian); Order of the White Lion (Czechoslovakia). Republican. Episcopalian. Address: Custom House, Philadelphia, Pa.

BUFFUM, Douglas Labaree, prof. Romance langs.; b. nr. Memphis, Tenn., Nov. 10, 1878; s. Maj. Rufus Ellis and Clara (Tufts) B.; 8th generation from Robert Buffum, Salem, Mass., 1638; A.B. and A.M., U. of Va., 1898; Ph.D., Johns Hopkins, 1904; studied in French univs.; m. Lillian Imbrie, June 10, 1914; 1 son, Imbrie. Instr French, Yale, 1904-05; asst. prof. Romance langs., 1905-12, prof. since 1912, Princeton U. Prof. French, Princeton R.O.T.C. and S.A.T.C., World War. Chief examiner in French, Coll. Entrance Exam. Bd., 1916-26. Mem. Modern Lang. Assn. America, Modern Lang. Assn. Middle States (ex-pres.), Am. Assn. Univ. Profs. Sociétés des Anciens Textes Français, Zeta Psi, Phi Beta Kappa. Republican. Conglist. Clubs: Princeton (New York and Phila.); Nassau (Princeton); Graduate (New Haven); Johns Hopkins (Baltimore); Colonnade (Charlottesville, Va.). Editor: French Short Stories, 1907; Hugo's Les Misérables, 1908; Michelet's Histoire de France, 1909; Contes Français, 1915; Stories from Balzac, 1917; Stories from Mérimée, 1920; Le Roman de la Violette, 1928; Roman d'Alexandre (with others), 1937. Contbr. many articles on Old French lit. Home: 60 Hodge Rd., Princeton, N.J.

BUFORD, Robert K.; attending surgeon Charleston Gen. Hosp. Address: 1021 Quarrier St., Charleston, W.Va.

BUGBEE, Newton Albert Kendall, civil engr.; b. Minneapolis, Minn., April 21, 1876; s. Alvin Newton and Lucy Kendall (Davis) B.; ed. high sch., Templeton, Mass.; m. Florence Hancock Toms, Oct. 12, 1900; children—Jesse Albert, Catherine Toms (Mrs. Horace M. Royal), Chas. Kendall (dec.). Began as engr. Edge Moor Bridge Works, 1896; with Pottsville Bridge Co., 1898-1900, American Bridge Co., 1900-02; engaged in bus. on own acct. as Newton C. K. Bugbee & Co., structural steel, Trenton, N.J. since 1902, treas. and sec. since 1911; dir. Trenton Savings Fund Soc. Served as chmn. Rep. State Com., 1916-19. Comptroller State of N.J., 1918-30. Pres. McKinley Hosp., Trenton, N.J.; pres. N.J. Reformatory at Rahway, N.J. Mem. Am. Soc. Civil Engrs. Republican. Episcopalian. Mason (33°, Shriner). Clubs: Carteret Country (Trenton). Home: 231 W. State St. Office: 206 E. Hanover St., Trenton, N.J.

BUGHMAN, Henry Clay, Jr.; b. Pittsburgh, Pa., 1887; s. Henry Clay and Marie (Berry) B.; student St. Paul's Sch. and Yale U.; m. Bessie Woods, April 1914; children—Leonard W., Betty Berry. Pres., treas. and dir. Union Spring & Mfg. Co. since 1933. Home: Sewickley, Pa. Office: 1417 Clark Bldg., Pittsburgh, Pa.

BUKA, Alfred Joseph, physician and surgeon; b. North Side, Pittsburgh, Pa., May 1, 1882; s. Joseph and Peppi (Bernheim) B.; B.S., U. of Pittsburgh, 1904; M.D., Jefferson Med. Coll., Phila., Pa., 1908; Master Med. Science (Orthopedics), U. of Pa., 1928; m. Wilma Audre Ravensheart, Sept. 1, 1926; 1 son, Alfred Joseph. In practice medicine since 1909, specializing in orthopedics since 1928 at Pittsburgh; senior asso. orthopedics dept., Montefiore Hosp., Pittsburgh, since 1929. Fellow Am. Acad. Orthopedic Surgeons; mem. Pittsburgh Orthopedic Club, Allegheny Co. Med. Soc., Pa. State Med. Soc., A.M.A. Reformed Jewish Pulpit. Mason (Davage Lodge 374). Author 25 articles on med. subjects in various jours. Home: 2140 Wightman St. Office: 602-04 May Bldg., 119 Fifth Av., Pittsburgh, Pa.

BULL, Ernest M., pres. steamship lines; b. Elizabeth, N.J., Oct. 2, 1875; s. Archibald Hilton and Evelyn (Vandeventer) B.; B.S., Cornell U., 1898; m. Edith Upham, Oct. 3, 1899; children—Dorothy (Mrs. Edward B. Wright), Carolyn, E. Myron, Edith Arlyn. Began with A. H. Bull Steamship Co., N.Y. City, 1898, pres. since 1920; pres. A. H. Bull & Co., Inc., Bull Insular Line, Inc., Baltimore Insular Line, Incorporated, Bull Steamship Line, Forty West Street Realty Corpn., Ericsson Line, Keyway Stevedoring Co., Economical Homes Assn.; dir. Corn Exchange Bank & Trust Co. Mem. Psi Upsilon. Republican. Episcopalian. Clubs: Union League (New York); Montclair (N.J.) Golf. Home: Montclair, N.J.; also Monroe, Orange County, N.Y. Office: 115 Broad St., New York, N.Y.

BULLARD, Dexter Means, M.D., phychiatrist; b. Waukesha, Wis., Aug. 14, 1898; s. Ernest Luther and Rosalie (Means) B.; prep. edn., Friends Sch., Washington, D.C., 1913-17; Ph.B., Yale, 1920; M.D., U. of Pa., 1923; m. Anne W. Wilson, 1927; children—Dexter M., Rose H., James W. Physician in charge Chestnut Lodge Sanitarium since 1931; clin. prof. psychiatry, Georgetown U. Med. Sch.; dir. Farmers Bank & Trust Co. Served in S.A.T.C., 1918-19. Mem. Montgomery Welfare Bd. since 1935. Dir. Washington Sch. of Psychiatry. Fellow Am. Psychiatric Assn.; mem. Assn. of Research for Nervous and Mental Diseases, Am. Psychoanalytic Assn. Republican. Methodist. Contbr. to psychiatric jours. Address: Chestnut Lodge Sanitarium, Rockville, Md.

BULLEIT, Eugene Verner, lawyer; b. Harrison Co., Ind., Aug. 4, 1890; s. Paul Constantine and Sarah Jane (Marsh) B.; ed. Corydon (Ind.) pub. schs., 1896-1904, Corydon High Sch., 1904-06, New Albany (Ind.) High Sch., 1906-08; LL.B., U. of Louisville (Ky.) Law Sch., 1910; m. Mary Griffin Devol, Oct. 15, 1912; children —Edward Banister, Thomas Nelson. Newspaper reporter and desk work Indianapolis (Ind.) Star, 1910-13; social work Indianapolis Charity Orgn. Soc., 1913-17; field work Am. Red Cross, Ind. and O., 1917-20; sec. to Congressman Joseph H. Himes, 16th O. Dist., 1920-23; investigator War Frauds Sect., U.S. Dept. Justice, 1923-24; spl. asst. to atty.-gen., criminal and alien property matters, 1924-27; gen. law practice, Gettysburg, Pa., since 1928; mem. firm Bulleit and Bulleit, Gettysburg. Mem. Am., Pa. State and Adams Co. bar assns., Chamber of Commerce. Republican. Presbyterian. Elk. Club: Rotary (Gettysburg, Pa.). Home and Office: Gettysburg, Pa.

BULLINGER, Clarence Edward, coll. prof.; b. Phila., Pa., May 19, 1892; s. Edward Ralph and Mary (Pollitt) B.; student Spring Garden Inst., Phila., 1909-11, Franklin Inst., Phila. 1911-13, Drexel Inst. of Tech., Phila., 1913-18; B.S., Pa. State Coll., 1922, I.E., 1925, M.S., 1927; m. Mary Hess Engle, Aug. 26, 1922; 1 dau., Marion Engle. Registered Engineer Penna. Machinist and draftsman apprentice William Cramp Ship & Engine Bldg. Co., Phila., 1909-13, journeyman draftsman, 1913-17; journeyman draftsman N.Y. Shipbuilding Corpn., Camden, N.J., 1917-19; asst. to supt. McCawley & Co., Baltimore, Md., 1921-22; Instr., Asst. Prof., Assoc. Prof. industrial engring., Pa. State Coll., 1922-30, prof. industrial engring. since 1930, head industrial engring. dept. since 1930; while teaching spends summers with various industrial cos. Mem. Am. Soc. M.E., Soc. for Promotion of Engring. Edn., Soc. for Advancement of Management, Nat. Assn. Cost Accountants, Am. Management Assn. Republican. Methodist. Mason. Author: Planning and Layout of Industrial Plants, 1923; Engineering Economics, 1937; articles in engring. jours. Address: 637 W. Foster Av., State Coll., Pa.

BULLIS, William Francis, educator; b. Washington, D.C., Oct. 22, 1901; s. William John and Cynthia DeLay (Rowley) B.; grad. U.S. Naval Acad., 1924; grad. study, George Washington U., 1926-29; m. Lois Elizabeth Hoover, Nov. 27, 1929. Served as 2d lt. Signal Corps and instr. in mathematics, U.S. Army; then as 1st lt. 58th Inf. Brigade, Md. N.G.; aide to General Reckord and Governor Ritchie, 1926-27; 2d and 1st lt. 260th Coast Arty., D.C. N.G., 1927-29 inc., and capt. same since 1930. Instr. Pub. Schs., Washington, D.C., 1926-27, The Devitt Sch., 1928-30; prin. and owner Bullis Sch. since 1930. Mem. Washington Board of Trade, 1930-33. Mem. N.E.A., Coast Arty. Assn., D.C. Edn. Assn., Federal Schoolmen's Club, Internat. Lions Club. Methodist. Home: Silver Spring, Md.

BULLOCK, Charles Arthur, lawyer; b. Canton, Pa., Aug. 1, 1896; s. Charles Edward and Georgia (Catlin) B.; grad. Mercersburg (Pa.) Acad., 1916; B.S., U. of Pa., 1920; student U. of Pa. Law Sch., 1923-25; m. Edith Dorothy Dann, Aug. 7, 1928; children—Charles Arthur, Donna Mary. Admitted to Pa. bar, 1927 and since engaged in gen. practice at Canton, Pa.; sec. and solicitor of Canton Borough since 1937 dir. First Nat. Bank. Served with Land Unit A.S., U.S. Navy, O.T.S., Mass. Inst. Tech., Boston, during World War. Pres. Bd. Dirs. Canton Borough Schs. Chmn. Canton Red Cross; dir. Martha Lloyd Sch. (pvt.). Mem. Bradford Co. Bar Assn., Phi Sigma Kappa, Phi Delta Phi. Republican. Presbyterian. Mason (K.T.). Clubs: Hare Law, Rotary, Lycoming Hunting and Fishing, Canton Rod and Gun (Canton, Pa.). Home: 115 South Av. Office: First Nat. Bank Bldg., Canton, Pa.

BUMPUS, Lester Wilson, minister; b. Casey, Ill., Jan. 26, 1894; s. Charles Monroe and Zenith Eugenia (Jackson) B.; B. A., Shurtleff Coll., Alton, Ill., 1917; B.D., Rochester (N.Y.) Theol. Sem., 1922; M.A., Ph.D., U. of Pittsburgh, 1931; m. Martha Cora Draper, Aug. 7, 1919; children—Alberta Draper, Mary Louise, Dorothea Zenith. Student pastor First Baptist Ch., Port Byron, N.Y., 1920-22; minister First Baptist Ch., Marion, N.Y., 1922-23, First Baptist Ch., Troy, Pa., 1924-28, Oakland Baptist Ch., Pittsburgh, 1928-29; asso. minister First Baptist Ch., Pittsburgh, 1929-32; exec. and field sec. Baptist Orphanage & Home Soc. of Western Pa., Pittsburgh, since 1932; exec.

sec. Pittsburgh Baptist Assn. since 1932. Served as pvt., corpl. sergt., Co. E, 333 Inf., U.S. Army, Sept. 1917-Apr. 1918, pvt. 1st Class, Co. I, 129 Inf., 33d Div., A.E.F., May 1918-July 1919, in Am. Sch. Detachment, U. of Bordeaux, France, March-June 1919. Trustee Assn. of Baptist Homes and Hosps. Mem. Pa. Baptist Conv. (ex-officio mem. bd. of mgrs.), Northern Baptist Conv. (ex-officio mem. council on finance and promotion; mem. central com. Asso. Home Mission Agencies), Community Fund of Pittsburgh and Allegheny Co. (mem. budget com.), Fed. of Social Agencies of Pittsburgh and Allegheny Co. (chmn. com. of care of the aged), Alpha Zeta Lit. Soc. (Shurtleff Coll.). Republican. Baptist. In charge Baptist Missionary Broadcasts, KDKA and W8XK, 1934-35, 1935-36, 1936-37. Home: 3438 Kedzie St. Office: 708 Investment Blg., Pittsburgh, Pa.

BUNCE, Earl Hamlin, metallurgist; b. Wolcott, N.Y., Sept. 22, 1891; s. Frank Wright and Lillian Inez (Lamb) B.; grad. Lyndonville (N.Y.) High Sch., 1909; B.S. in chemistry, Cornell U., 1913; m. Elizabeth Margaret Hamilton, Sept. 1, 1922; children—Barbara Hamilton, Margery Hamilton, Peter Hamilton. With N.J. Zinc Co. since 1913, as metallurgist and research investigator, 1913-17, asst. chief of research div., 1918-27; chief research div. 1927-28, gen. mgr. tech. dept., Palmerton, Pa., since April 1928. Mem. Am. Soc. for Testing Materials, Am. Ceramics, Am. Electrochem. Soc., Am. Inst. Mining and Metall. Engrs., Inst. of the Rubber Industry, Oil and Colour Chemists Assn., Farady Soc., Engineers Club of Lehigh Valley, Theta Chi, Alembic. Republican. Presbyterian. Clubs: Cornell (New York); Blue Ridge Country (Palmerton, Pa.). Home: Residence Park. Office: Central Laboratory, Palmerton, Pa.

BUNN, John Franklin Jr., broker; b. Phila., Pa., Dec. 5, 1896; s. J(ohn) Franklin and Clara Cornelia (Stolpp) B.; student U. of Pa., 1920; m. Elsie R. Houpt, Oct. 1, 1925; children—Elsie Reith, Edith Standish Missimer, Elizabeth Jacquelin. Mgr. Wilkes-Barre (Pa.) Office, Harris, Forbes & Co. of N.Y., 1919-26, Phila. Office, 1926-30, mgr. N.Y. Dealers Dept. 1930-33; partner Bioren & Co., brokerage firm, Phila., mems. N.Y. and Phila. Stock Exchange, N.Y., Curb, Chicago Board of Trade, since 1933; sec. and dir. Ky. Ohio Gas Co., Ashland, Ky., since 1934. Served as 2d lt., Inf., U.S. Army, during World War. Mem. Chamber of Commerce of State of N.Y. Republican. Episcopalian. Clubs: Bond, Huntingdon Valley Country (Phila.); Bankers' (New York City), Westmoreland (Wilkes-Barre (Pa.). Home: 1603 Harris Rd., Laverock, Chestnut Hill, Pa. Office: 1508 Walnut St., Philadelphia, Pa.

BUNTING, George Avery, mfg. toilet cream; b. Bishopville, Md., Apr. 3, 1870; s. Lemuel W. H. and Jane (Long) B.; A.B., Washington Coll., Chestertown, Md., 1891, A.M., 1893; Ph. G., U. of Md. Sch. of Pharmacy, 1899; hon. D.Sc., Washington Coll., 1937; m. Nellie Bowen, Dec. 18, 1901; children—Dorothy, George Lloyd. Engaged as prin. pub. schs., Bishopville, Md., 1891-93; prin. Odessa (Del.) Acad., 1894-96; propr. Bunting's Drug Store, Baltimore, Md., 1902-22; originated Noxzema formula, 1914, inc. Noxzema Chem. Co., mfr. Noxzema greaseless skin cream, Baltimore, Md., 1917, and pres. since 1917; chmn. bd. dirs. Noxzema Chem. Co. of Can. Served as regt. sergt. Md. N.G., 1899-1900. Mem. Md. Bd. Pharmacy, 1922-34. Mem. Baltimore Chamber of Commerce; mem. bd. govs. Washington Coll., Chestertown. Mem. Am. Chem. Soc., Am. Pharm. Assn., Nat. Assn. Retail Druggists, Md. Pharm. Assn. (pres. 1915-16), Md. Acad. Sciences, Baltimore Veteran Druggists (pres. 1937), S.A.R., Eastern Shore Soc. Independent Republican. Presbyn. Mason (Scottish Rite, 32°, Shriner). Clubs: Mens of Roland Park Presbyn. Ch., University, Kiwanis (Baltimore). Home: 4412 N. Charles St. Office: 32d and Falls Cliff Rd., Baltimore, Md.

BUNTING, John James, clergyman; b. Bishopville, Md., Aug. 23, 1886; s. John W. and Joicie Annesley (Hudson) B.; student Wilmington Conf. Acad., Dover, Del., 1903-05; A.B., Dickinson Coll., 1908; D.D., U. of Md., 1933; m. Maude Gibson, Sept. 10, 1919; 1 son, John James, Jr. Became pastor at Mardela Springs, Md., 1909; ordained to ministry M.E. Ch., deacon, 1911, elder, 1913, Wilmington Conf.; served as Conf. Host, 1917; elected to conf. bd. examiners, 1918; editorial writer, 1923-25; pres. conf. Epworth League, 1927; elected to Gen. Conf., 1928, treas., 1930-35; supt. Salisbury Dist. since 1935; elected to Gen. Conf., 1936, head of delegation from Wilmington annual conf. to the Uniting Conf., Kansas City, Mo., 1939; dir. Council of Chs. of Md. Trustee Wesley Collegiate Inst., Dover, Del. Republican. Methodist. Mason. Home: 103 Elizabeth St., Salisbury, Md.

BUNTING, Martha; b. Phila., Pa., Dec. 2, 1861; d. Samuel and Susanna Lloyd (Andrews) B.; prep. edn. Friends' Sch., Darby, Pa.; B.L., Swarthmore Coll., 1881; B.S., U. of Pa., 1890, grad. student, 1890-91; student Woods Hole, summers 1891, 92, 99, Cold Spring Harbor Marine Lab., summer 1898, Johns Hopkins Med. Sch., 1893-94; Ph.D., Bryn Mawr, 1895; grad. student Columbia, 1898-99, U. of Pa. (fellow by courtesy), 1919-24, 1926-27, 1930-31; unmarried. Instr. biology and physiology and teacher of osteology, Goucher Coll., Baltimore, 1893-97; head teacher of biology, Girls' High Sch., Phila., 1897-98; teacher biology and physiology, Wadleigh High Sch., New York, 1900-12; research asst. to Dr. Edward T. Reichert, 1912-16, to Dr. John A. Kolmer, U. of Pa., 1918-19; war relief work, 1916-18; research in Am. colonial history of Pa. and N.J. and genealogical records of selected Quakers since 1931. Fellow A.A.A.S.; mem. Acad. of Science of Phila. (life), Library Co. of Phila. (owner of stock of ancestor who signed original articles, 1731), Geog. Soc. Phila. (charter and hon. mem.), Am. Assn. Univ. Women, Hist. Soc. Pa., Sigma Xi, etc. Republican. Mem. Religious Soc. of Friends. Club: Women's University (Phila.). Contbr. papers on biol. research to leading scientific jours.; articles on flowers, etc., to mags.; collaborator with Dr. Edward T. Reichert on 2 biol. monographs, Carnegie Publs. Home: The Touraine Apts., 1520 Spruce St., Philadelphia, Pa.

BURBAGE, E. E., Sr.; chmn. bd. and pres. Calvin B. Taylor Banking Co. Address: Berlin, Md.

BURCH, Henry Reed, economist; b. Phila., Pa., Feb. 5, 1876; s. Charles Edward and Eva Anna (Reed) B.; A.B., Central High Sch., Phila., 1893; grad. Sch. of Pedagogy, Phila., 1894; B.S., U. of Pa., 1900, Ph.D., 1903; univs. Halle and Jena, 1906; m. Mary Grier Stewart, July 23, 1902; 1 dau., Eleanor Stewart. Instr. English, 1903-04, prof. history and economics, 1904-06, head dept. history and economics, 1906-12, Central Manual Training Sch., Phila.; head dept. commerce and history, West Phila. High Sch. for Boys, 1912-26; head dept. history and social science, Overbrook High Sch., Phila., 1926—. Mem. commn. on Reorganization of Secondary Edn. in U.S. Mem. N.E.A., Am. Acad. Polit. and Social Science, Pa. State Edn. Assn., Nat. Com. for Teaching Citizenship, Nat. Council for the Social Studies, Nat. Economic League Assn. Hist. Teachers of Middle States and Maryland (vice-president 1922-23). Episcopalian. Clubs: University (Phila.); Salmagundi (New York). Author: Conditions Affecting Suffrage in the Colonies, 1903; Elements of Economics (with Scott Nearing), 1912; American Social Problems (with S. H. Patterson), 1918; American Economic Life, 1921; Problems of American Democracy (with S. H. Patterson), 1922. Home: 5208 Drexel Rd., Philadelphia, Pa.

BURCHFIELD, Albert Horne, mcht.; m. Clara A. Dicken; 1 son, Albert Horne. Pres. Joseph Horne Co., dept. store, Pittsburgh, Pa. Clubs: Duquesne, Pittsburgh Athletic, Longue Vue, Shannopin Country. Home: 210 Tennyson Av. Office: Penn Av. and Stanwix St., Pittsburgh, Pa.*

BURCHFIELD, Albert Horne, Jr., vice-pres. Joseph Horne Co.; b. Pittsburgh, Pa., July 3, 1903; s. Albert Horne and Clara A. (Dicken) B.; student Shady Side Acad., 1912-18, Lawrenceville (N.J.) Sch., 1919-20; B.S., Princeton, 1925; m. Clarissa Wainwright, Oct. 3, 1926; children—Nancy Clarissa, Albert Horne III, Mary Patricia. Exec. in training Joseph Horne Co. dept. store, Pittsburgh, 1926, successively buyer drapery dept., div. mdse. mgr. home furnishings dept., and vice-pres. and dir. since 1930. Dir. Pittsburgh Chamber of Commerce. Trustee Assn. Improvement of the Poor. Mem. Charter Club, Princeton Triangle Club. Republican. Episcopalian. Clubs: Duquesne, Princeton, Fox Chapel Golf, Longue Vue Golf (Pittsburgh). Home: 6839 Juniata Pl. Office: Joseph Horne Co., Pittsburgh, Pa.

BURCHINAL, William James, pres. Smithfield State Bank; b. Georges Twp., Pa., Feb. 17, 1893; s. Ross S. and Verda G. (Lowe) B.; student Douglas Business Coll., Uniontown, Pa.; m. Olive D. Tewell, Aug. 11, 1921; 1 son, William Owen. Merchandising and coal business, Fayette Co., Pa., 1919-30; mem. Pa. State Workmen's Compensation Bd., 1931-35; pres. Smithfield (Pa.) State Bank since 1936. Served as corp. 320th Supply Co., A.E.F., 1917-18. Mem. Pa. Ho. of Rep., 1923-25; dep. co. treas., Fayette Co., 1926-27. Mem. Am. Legion (chmn. Fayette Co. exec. com., 1937). Baptist. Address: Morgantown Rd., Smithfield, Pa.

BURDEN, Verne Gerard, surgeon; b. St. Mary's, Pa., Jan. 17, 1895; s. George E. and Margaret (Wiesner) B.; student U. of Pa. (coll.), 1913-15, M.D., 1919; M.S., Mayo Clinic, U. of Minn., 1925; m. Pauline W. Carr, 1928; children—Sarah Anne, Nancy Pauline, Constance Margaret. Physician and surgeon since 1921; surgeon to St. Joseph's Hosp., Phila., since 1926; surgeon to Phila. Gen. Hosp., 1928-31. Licentiate of Nat. Bd. Med. Examiners. Fellow Am. Coll. Surgeons; mem. Pa. State and Phila. Co. Med. Socs., Coll. Physicians of Phila. Republican. Catholic. Club: Union League (Phila.). Home: 265 Hathaway Lane, Wynnewood, Pa. Office: 255 S. 17th St., Philadelphia, Pa.

BURDICK, C(harles) Lalor, chem. engr.; b. Denver, Colo., Apr. 14, 1892; s. Frank Austin and Anna (Lalor) B.; B.S., Drake U., 1911; B.S., Mass. Inst. Tech., 1913, M.S., 1914; Kaiser Wilhelm Inst., Berlin, and Univ. College, London, 1914-16; Ph.D., U. of Basel, Switzerland, 1915; m. Kathleen Condon, 1924 (now dec.). Research asso. in chemistry, Mass. Inst. Tech. and Calif. Inst. Tech., 1916-17; metall. engr. Guggenheim Bros., N.Y. and Chile, 1919-24; vice-pres. and consulting engr. Anglo-Chilean Consol. Nitrate Corpn., 1924-28; asst. chem. dir. ammonia dept. E. I. du Pont de Nemours & Co., 1928-36, spl. investigator Development Dept. since 1936; holder numerous patents for chem. process. Served as 1st lt. Ordnance Div., U.S.A., 1917-18; trustee and sec. Labor Foundation; dir. Wilmington Boy's Club of America, Wilmington Soc. of Fine Arts. Mem. Am. Inst. Chem. Engrs., Am. Chem. Soc., A.A.A.S., Am. Inst. Mining Engrs., Nat. Aeronautical Assn., Phi Beta Kappa (hon.). Clubs: Gibson Island (Md.) Yacht; Wilmington, Wilmington Country, Vicmead Hunt (Wilmington, Del.). Contbr. articles to chem. jours. Home: Lancaster Pike and Baltimore Road. Office: 8056 du Pont Bldg., Wilmington, Del.

BURGER, Edward Kenneth, editor; b. Brooklyn, N.Y., Nov. 19, 1894; s. Edward and Bessie Evans (Wyckoff), B.; B.S., Poly. Inst. of Brooklyn, Coll. of Engring., 1917; m. Carolyn N. Smith, Apr. 25, 1917; children—Elisabeth Susanne (Mrs. Edward A. Mowerson), Edward Kenneth. Chemist, later manager industrial laboratory, General Chemical Co., New York, 1917-23; cons. practice, industrial engring., 1923-25; supt. Cochrane Chem. Co. of Jersey City., N.J., 1925-26; editorial and research work, Ticker Pub. Co., New York, since 1926; managing editor The Magazine of Wall Street since 1929, v.p. since 1930; dir. Ticker Pub. Co., Security Owners' Advisory Bur., Allendale Bldg. & Loan Assn.; councilman Allendale, N.J., 1929-32. Trustee Allendale Pub. Library. Mem. Alpha Chi Rho. Republican. Baptist. Home: 243 Park Av., Allendale, N.J. Office: 90 Broad St., New York, N.Y.

BURGESS, Arthur Stanley, broker; b. Phila., Pa., Oct. 19, 1884; s. George R. and Emily J. (Williamson) B.; ed. pub. schs. and Central

High Sch., Phila.; m. Jean Elizabeth Sheldon, 1915. Began with Townsend, Whelen & Co., June 1901; firm combined with Thos. A. Biddle & Co. to form Biddle, Whelen & Co. (mems. N.Y. Stock Exchange, Phila. Stock Exchange, N.Y. Curb Exchange), partner since 1934. Dir. Pa. Soc. for Prevention of Cruelty to Animals. Mem. Rittenhouse Astron. Soc. Republican. Episcopalian. Clubs: Huntingdon Valley Country, Bond (Phila.). Home: Washington Lane, Wyncote, Pa. Office: 1606 Walnut St., Philadelphia, Pa.

BURGESS, Frances Corrie; prof. geography, Marshall Coll. Address: Marshall Coll., Huntington, W.Va.

BURGESS, John Stewart, prof. sociology; b. Pennington, N.J., July 12, 1883; s. William and Clara Dwight (Goodman) B.; A.B., Princeton U., 1905; ed. Oberlin Coll., 1907-08, 1915-16; A.M., Columbia U., 1909, Ph.D., same, 1928; m. Stella C. Fisher, June 19, 1919; children—David Stewart, Vinton Douglas. Began as teacher in govt. sch., Kyoto, Japan, 1905; teacher, Princeton in Peking, China, 1909-29; prof. sociology, later chmn. dept. sociology, Yenching Univ., Peking, China, 1919-29; asso. prof. sociology, Pomono Coll., Claremont, Calif., 1930-33; prof. sociology, chmn. dept. sociology, Temple U. since 1933; chmn. of faculty, Wellesley Summer Inst. of Social Progress, 1938, 39. Dir. Internat. Inst., Phila.; trustee Princeton-Yenching Foundation. Mem. Am. Sociol. Soc., Am. Assn. Univ. Profs., Terrace Club of Princeton, Princeton Club of Phila. Awarded Laura Spelman Rockefeller Fellowship, 1926-28. Democrat. Presbyn. Home: 140 Heacock Lane, Wyncote, Pa.

BURGESS, Thomas, clergyman; b. St. Albans, Vt., Mar. 19, 1880; s. Rev. Thomas (D.D.) and Mary Turner (Sargent) B.; g.s. Alexander Burgess, D.D., bishop of Quincy; B.A., Brown U., 1902, D.D., 1925; grad. Gen. Theol. Sem., 1905; m. Catharine Elizabeth White, July 1, 1905; children—Elizabeth Howell, Thomas, Mary Cotheal, Howell White, Richard Mackie. Deacon and priest, 1905; priest in charge Emmanuel Ch., Ashland, and All Saints Ch., Mesardis, Me., 1905-09; rector Trinity Ch., Saco, 1909-14; priest in charge St. Barnabas Ch., Augusta, Me., 1914-15, Athol, Mass., 1915-19. Mem. Bd. of Missions, P.E. Ch., Me., 1911-15; chmn. Me. Missionary Commn., 1911-15; mem. Commn. on Missions, Province of N.E., 1914-19; dir. Com. on Various Races, Province of N.E., 1914-19; sec. nat. foreign-born Americans div., Dept. of Missions, P.E. Ch., 1919-30; rector All Hallows Ch., Wyncote, Pa., 1930-37; chaplain City Mission, Philadelphia, since 1937; diocesan secretary Retreat Association, 1935—. Member Alpha Delta Phi, Phi Beta Kappa. Mason. Author: Greeks in America, 1913; Foreigners or Friends (in collaboration), 1921; The Eastern Church in the Western World (in collaboration), 1928; The Celebrant's Manual, 1934. Home: Chestnut Hill, Pa.

BURGESS, William, Jr., executive; b. Trenton, N.J., June 20, 1880; s. William and Clara Dwight (Goodman) B.; student Colwyn Bay Coll., Colwyn Bay, Wales, 1889-92, State Model Sch., Trenton, N.J., 1892-96, Stewart Bus. Coll., Trenton, N.J., 1896-97, Alfred (N.Y.) U., 1906-07; m. Lucie Cecilia Taylor, June 2, 1908; children—John William, Charles Taylor. Apprentice Internat. Pottery Co., Trenton, N.J., 1898-1906, pres. since 1932; pres. and owner Hudson Porcelain Co., Trenton, N.J., 1907-10; owner Spring Water Supply Co. since 1900; developed Burgess Manor, Morrisville, Pa., real estate and ins., 1922. Elected Chief Burgess Borough of Morrisville, Pa., taking office Jan. 1, 1928. Mem. Bucks Co. Council Boy Scouts of America (council commr. since 1927). Republican. Presbyterian (elder First Presbyn. Ch., Morrisville, Pa.). Club: Rotary (Morrisville, Pa.; past pres.). Address: 771 N. Pennsylvania Av., Morrisville, Pa.

BURGWIN, Hill, lawyer; b. Pittsburgh, Pa., July 25, 1885; s. George Collinson and Mary (Blair) B.; prep. edn., St. Paul's Sch., Concord, N.H., 1900-02; A.B., Trinity Coll., Hartford, Conn., 1906; LL.B., U. of Pittsburgh, 1909; unmarried. Admitted to Pa. bar, 1910, and since practiced in Pittsburgh; mem. firm H. & G. C. Burgwin, 1913-19, Burgwin, Scully & Burgwin, 1919-35, Burgwin, Scully & Churchil since 1935; vice-pres. and trustee Dollar Savings Bank, Pittsburgh. Mem. Am. Bar Assn., Pa. State and Allegheny Co. bar assns., Soc. Colonial Wars of Pa., Psi Upsilon. Democrat. Episcopalian (mem. vestry Ch. of Good Shepherd; mem. chapter Trinity Cathedral; mem. bd. trustees and chancellor Diocese of Pittsburgh). Mason (32°). Clubs: Pittsburgh, Duquesne, University, Fox Chapel Golf, Pittsburgh Golf, Rolling Rock (Pittsburgh); University (New York). Home: 705 Devonshire St. Office: 1515 Park Bldg., Pittsburgh, Pa.

BURK, Paul Heber, fruit growing, banking; b. Tamaqua, Pa., Nov. 27, 1887; s. William Black and Sarah Catherine (Radcliffe) B.; A.B., Franklin and Marshall Coll., Lancaster, Pa., 1908, A.M., 1909; m. Marguerite Reber Templin, Dec. 9, 1911; children—Paul Heber, Jr., Joseph William, James Reber. Employed as entomologist Pa. Dept. Agr., 1909-12; cons. horticulturist, Phila., 1912-19; fruit grower, Beverly, N.J., since 1919; vice-pres. and dir. First Nat. Bank, Riverside, N.J., since 1926; pres. and dir. Co-operative Growers Assn., Beverly, N.J., since 1931. Served as chmn. governor's Emergency Farm Mortgage Com. N.J., 1932-34. Mem. Phi Kappa Sigma. Republican. Episcopalian. Home: Buttonwood Farm, Beverly. Office: First Nat. Bank, Riverside, N.J.

BURKART, Joseph Aloysius, lawyer; b. Washington, D.C., Jan. 4, 1874; s. Joseph William and Caroline (Krantz) B.; LL.B., Columbian (now George Washington) U., 1894, LL.M., 1895; m. Ada May Von Arx, June 15, 1910; children—Frank Joseph, Robert Howard, Herbert Von Arx. Practiced at Washington, D.C., since 1895; mem. firm Burkart & Quinn; pres. and counsel Am. Dairy Supply Co.; mem. advisory bd. Riggs Nat. Bank; dir. and counsel Call Carl, Inc. Mem. bar Supreme Court of U.S. since 1902. Mem. Am. Bar Assn., D.C. Bar Assn. (dir.; pres. 1927), Columbian Hist. Soc., Washington Bd. of Trade, Soc. Natives of D.C., Loyal Legion (mem. council). Elk (mem. Grand Lodge). Republican. Clubs: Nat. Press, Optimist International, Newcomers (ex-pres.); Columbia Country. Home: 6311 Connecticut Av., Chevy Chase, Md. Office: Woodward Bldg., Washington, D.C.

BURKE, Alexander E.; surgeon St. Joseph's Hosp., Phila., and Fitzgerald-Mercy Hosp., Darby. Address: 4119 Walnut St., Philadelphia, Pa.

BURKE, Daniel, lawyer; b. New Berlin, N.Y., Dec. 5, 1873; s. James and Mary S. (York) B.; student Oxford (N.Y.) Acad., 1885-89; A.B., Hamilton Coll., 1893, A.M., 1894; student New York U. Law Sch., 1894-95; LL.B., New York Law Sch., 1896; LL.D., Hamilton Coll., 1936; m. Kate Hull Bundy, Aug. 20, 1901; children—James Bundy, Agnes Bundy (Mrs. Henry W. Harding), Coleman. Admitted to N.Y. bar, 1896; established own office, 1899; mem. firm Burke & Burke since 1929; pres. of Conn. Mills, 1921-24; dir. Summit (N.J.) Trust Co., Martindale-Hubbell, Inc., North Am. Clay Co., R. T. French Co., Atlantis Sales Corpn. Trustee Hamilton Coll. (chmn. bd. since 1937), Kent Place Sch.; mgr. Am. Bible Soc. Mem. Am., N.Y. State, N.Y. City bar assns., Chi Psi, Phi Beta Kappa, Phi Delta Phi. Republican. Methodist. Clubs: Wall St., Bankers (New York); Canasawacta Country. Home: Fernwood Rd., Summit, N.J.; also Oxford, N.Y. Office: 72 Wall St., New York, N.Y.

BURKE, Edmund S.; pres. Kelly-Springfield Tire Co. Address: Cumberland, Md.

BURKE, Kenneth (Duva), author; b. Pittsburgh, Pa., May 5, 1897; s. James Leslie and Lillyan May (Duva) B.; ed. Ohio State U., Columbia; m. Lily Mary Batterham, May 19, 1919 (divorced); children—Jeanne Elspeth, Eleanor Duva, Frances Batterham; m. 2d, Elizabeth Batterham, Dec. 18, 1933; 1 son, James Anthony. Research work, Laura Spelman Rockefeller Memorial, 1926-27; music critic, The Dial, 1927-29; editorial work, Bureau Social Hygiene, 1928-29. Writer of stories, translations, critical articles, book reviews; music critic of The Nation, 1934-36; lectures on practice and theory of literary criticism, New Sch. for Social Research, 1937; lectures on psychology of literary form and on Samuel Taylor Coleridge, U. of Chicago, 1938. Winner of Dial award of $2,000 for distinguished service to Am. Letters, 1928; Guggenheim Memorial fellowship, $2,000, 1935. Author: The White Oxen, 1924; Counter-Statement, 1931; Towards a Better Life, a Series of Declamations or Epistles, 1932; Permanence and Change—Anatomy of Purpose, 1935; Attitudes Toward History (Vol. I, Acceptance and Rejection; The Curve of History; Vol. II, Analysis of Symbolic Structure), 1937. Translator: Death in Venice, by Thomas Mann, 1925; Genius and Character, by Emil Ludwig, 1927; Saint Paul, by Emile Baumann, 1929. Contbr. to leading mags. Home: Andover, N.J.

BURKE, Louis Frazier, marine insurance; b. New York, N.Y., Dec. 22, 1861; s. James Theodore and Kate (Kanelieu) B.; grad. Bayonne City (N.J.) pub. schs., 1878; m. Lottie Woodruff, June 22, 1885 (died June 10, 1934); children—Charles Theodore, Russell Woodruff, Sara Jeanette (Mrs. Ernest L. Hoppock). Began as clerk for Wm. J. Roberts, fire ins. agent, 1879; re-insurance clerk Phenix Ins. Co., 1884-88; supt. marine dept. Home Ins. Co., 1888-1906; mem. firm Geo. H. Smith & Hicks, 1906-23; gen. marine mgr. Home Ins. Co., 1927-30; sec.-treas. Atlantic Inland Assn., marine ins., since 1899. Charter mem. Insurance Soc. of N.Y. Formerly mem. bd. mgrs. Am. Marine Ins. Syndicates, U.S. Salvage Assn., Am. Inst. Marine Underwriters, Bd. of Underwriters of N.Y., Assn. of Marine Underwriters of U.S., Assn. of Average Adjusters of U.S.; formerly v.p. Am. Bureau of Shipping. Republican. Methodist. Mason (32°). Clubs: Drug and Chemical. Home: 345 Hillside Pl., South Orange, N.J. Office: 99 John St., New York, N.Y.

BURKE, Patrick Joseph, sch. supt.; b. Plains, Pa., Nov. 15, 1894; s. John E. and Mary F. (Hughes) B.; A.B., St. Thomas Coll.; M.A., Bucknell U., Lewisburg, Pa.; m. Linda E. Menichini, July 29, 1929. Prin. elementary sch., Moonachie, N.J., 1913-14; teacher Exeter, Pa., 1914-15, Plains, Pa., 1915-18; teacher high sch., Plains, 1918-28, prin., 1928-33; supt. of schs., Mt. Carmel Twp., Locust Gap., Pa., since 1933. Mem. exec. com., Holmes Safety Assn., Mt. Carmel Chapter Am. Red Cross. Mem. Kappa Phi Kappa. K. C. Club: Rotary (Mount Carmel). Address: Locust Gap, Pa.

BURKE, Robert Belle, educator; b. Pittsburgh, Pa., Oct. 16, 1868; s. Hubert D. and Annie (Sloane) B.; grad. Brown Prep. Sch., Phila., Pa.; A.B., U. of Pa., 1890, A.M., 1913, Ph.D., 1925; 1 son, Robert Buchey. Instr. in De Lancey Sch., Philadelphia, 1891-1915, Episcopal Acad., 1915-20; asst. prof. Latin, U. of Pa., 1920-26, prof. since 1926, also dean of coll., 1922-29. Mem. Linguistic Soc. America, Am. Philological Association, Philadelphia Classical Soc., Phila. Classical Club, Mediæval Academy of America, Phi Beta Kappa, Pi Mu. Episcopalian. Translator: J. Dinckel's The Poetic Calendar, 1925; Roger Bacon's Opus Majus, 1927; annotated translation of the Compendium of Robert Goulet, descriptive of the University of Paris, 1928; annotated translation of Gabriel Biel's The Power and Utility of Moneys, 1930. Home: Courtland Apt. B1, 43d and Chestnut Sts., Philadelphia, Pa.

BURKE, Robert E., lawyer; b. Morristown, N.J., July 24, 1892; s. Joseph F. and Margaret (Cavanaugh) B.; grad. Morristown (N.J.) High Sch., 1911; LL.B., Cornell U., 1915; m. Florence L. Merchant, May 10, 1918; children—Barbara M., Florence M. Admitted to N.J. bar, 1916, and began practice in office of late Judge Edward K. Mills, Morristown, becoming partner; continues alone since retirement of Judge Mills, 1924; as trustee of an estate became pres. Riker Co., mfrs. of light metal stampings, East Orange, N.J.; vice-pres. and counsel First Nat. Bank, Morristown. Served with U.S. Army, 1917-19; with A.E.F.; disch. as capt.; major F.A., N.J. Nat. Guard to 1922. Pres. Morristown Library and Lyceum; vice-pres. Morristown Library; v.p.

Morris County Children's Home; sec. Morristown Community Chest; trustee Washington Assn. Ind. Democrat. Roman Catholic. Clubs: Morristown, Spring Brook Country (Morristown); Essex (Newark, N.J.). Home: Kitchell Rd., Convent, N.J. Office: First Nat. Bank Bldg., Morristown, N.J.

BURKETT, Philip Henry, prof. and head dept. social sciences; b. Buffalo, N.Y., Dec. 30, 1876; s. John J. and Margaret (John) B.; grad. Canisius High Sch., Buffalo, N.Y., 1893; A.B., Campion Coll., Prairie du Chien, Wis., 1899, A.M., 1900; student, St. Ignatius Univ., Valkenburg, Holland, 1908, D.D., 1918; Ph.D., Fordham U. Social Science Sch.; Ph.D., Gregorian Univ., Rome, 1936. Taught ancient literature and modern English literature, Toledo and Cleveland, O., 1900-04; social work in England and Scotland, 1907-08; teacher ancient and modern English literature, Baltimore, 1908-10, Brooklyn, N.Y., 1911; dean Canisius Coll., Buffalo, N.Y., 1912-13, prin. high school, 1912-15; prof. of social sciences and head of dept., St. Joseph's Coll., Phila., since 1926. Mem. Eastern Jesuit Philos. Assn., Am. Cath. Hist. Soc. (mem. bd.). Soc. of Jesus. Roman Catholic. Author: Social Problems Analyzed; contbr. Catholic Charities Rev., Catholic World, America, Thought. Address: St. Joseph's College, Philadelphia, Pa.

BURKHOLDER, Eberly Paul, sch. supervisor; b. Ephrata, Pa., Feb. 5, 1898; s. Jacob Landis and Della (Eberly) B.; diploma high sch., Ephrata, Pa., 1916, State Teachers Coll., Millersville, Pa., 1919; A.B., Franklin and Marshall Coll., Lancaster, Pa., 1923; Ed.M., Harvard, 1934; grad. student U. of Pa., 1936; unmarried. Teacher rural schs., Lancaster Co., Pa., 1916-18; prin., Christiana (Pa.) High Sch., 1919-22, high sch., East Stroudsburg, Pa., 1923-25; supervisor Del. State Dept. Pub. Instrn., Dover, Del., since 1925; instr. U. of Del. summers, 1928, 1929, Bates Coll., 1938, 1939. Dir. Del. Safety Council. Chmn. Boy Scout Exec. Com., Sussex Co., Del., 1928-33, Jr. Red Cross, Sussex Co., 1928-33. Mem. Rotary Internat. (dist. gov. 1931-32), Del. State Edn. Assn. (pres. 1934-35). Lutheran. Odd Fellow (Sovereign Grand Rep.). Founder and editor Delaware School Journal. Address: Courthouse, Dover, Del.

BURKHOLDER, Henry Clay, lawyer; b. West Earl Twp., Lancaster Co., Pa., Jan. 7, 1898; s. Amos E. and Clara E. (Bolster) B.; student Franklin and Marshall Acad., Lancaster, Pa., 1911-14; A.B., Franklin and Marshall Coll., 1918; studied law in the offices of F. Lyman Windolph, 1920-22; student Law Sch. U. of Colo., 1922-24; m. Catherine Hartman Falck, June 12, 1936; children—John Nicholas, Henry Clay. Admitted to Pa. Supreme Court, 1925, later to U.S. Dist. Court, Interstate Commerce Commn., U.S. Vets. Bur., etc.; in practice in Lancaster, Pa., since 1925; solicitor for Sch. Dist., City of Lancaster, 1927-29; pres. judge Orphans' Court of Lancaster Co., 1937-38. Mem. Sch. Bd., Lancaster, 1933-37. Mem. Am., Pa. State and Lancaster Co. bar assns., Federal Bar Assn., Assn. of Practitioners before Interstate Commerce Commn., Am. Legion, Phi Kappa Tau, Phi Alpha Delta. Democrat. Unitarian (trustee). Mason (K.T., Shriner), Elk, Forester, Order of Ind. Americans. Clubs: Torch (Lancaster, Pa.); Potomac Appalachian Trail (Washington, D.C.). Home: 424 N. Duke St. Office: 45 N. Duke St., Lancaster, Pa.

BURKI, Albert Harry, pres. Pittsburgh Cut Flower Co.; b. Bellevue, Pittsburgh, Pa., Nov. 20, 1897; s. Fred and Ida (Voelp) B.; student business coll.; m. Evelyn Mock, June 22, 1923. Pres. Akron Fort Pitt Co., Akron, O.; throughout entire career has been associated with Pittsburgh Cut Flower Co., becoming pres. Mem. Soc. of Am. Florists (life). Mason (Mars Lodge, Syria Temple). Clubs: Pittsburgh Athletic, Rotary (Pittsburgh). Home: Burklyn Terrace, Gibsonia, Pa. Office: 116 Seventh St., Pittsburgh, Pa.

BURKY, Earl L(eRoy), physician; b. Reading, Pa., Apr. 11, 1898; s. George Franklin and Louisa (Steiner) B.; B.S., U. of Pa., 1918; M.S., 1922; M.D., Johns Hopkins, 1927; m. Mary Dixon Norris, Oct. 31, 1931; 1 dau., Mary Norris. Asso. prof. of ophthalmology, Wilmer Ophthal. Inst., Johns Hopkins, since 1937; asso. ophthalmologist, Johns Hopkins Hosp., since 1937. Home: Loch Raven, Md. Office: Johns Hopkins Hospital, Baltimore, Md.

BURLEW, Frederick Meinzer, lawyer; b. Middlesex Co., N.J., Mar. 12, 1895; s. Herbert and Louise (Meinzer) B.; Ph.B., Bucknell U., Lewisburg, Pa., 1915; LL.B., Harvard U. Law Sch., 1918; m. Margaret Bruce, Aug. 15, 1925; 1 dau., Elizabeth Anne. Admitted to N.J. bar as atty., 1919, as counselor, 1922; engaged in gen. practice of law at Matawan, N.J., since 1920; counsel for Matawan Twp., Monmouth Co., 1922-29, Madison Twp., Middlesex Co., since 1925, Borough of Matawan, N.J., 1932, Farmers & Merchants Nat. Bank of Matawan since 1922, Matawan Bldg. & Loan Assn. since 1932; sec. and dir. H. Burlew & Co., Inc., Matawan Properties, Inc. Served in Harvard Regt., 1915-16; pvt. to corpl., U.S.A., 1918-19. Mem. Am. Bar Assn., Monmouth Co. Bar Assn., Am. Legion (comdr. Matawan Post, 1923). Presbyn. Mason. Elk. Club: Civic (Matawan). Home: 61 Wyckoff St. Office: 121 Main St., Matawan, N.J.

BURLINGTON, Harry J., mfg. elevators; b. Ireland, Mar. 25, 1878; s. John J. and Anne (Kealy) B.; came to U.S., 1894, naturalized, 1900; student pub. schs., Ireland, 1884-92; Mech. Engr., Cooper Union Inst., N.Y. City, 1902; m. Ella A. Mauchet, 1902; children—Arthur J., Harry J., Jr., Ethel F. (Mrs. Harold Keahon), William E., Walter B., Alice I. Employed as telegraph operator, 1898; now engaged in bus. of mfg. electric passenger and freight elevators; propr. Burwak Elevator Co. Served as pres. N.J. Fish & Game Commn., now exec. sec. Served as capt. engrs., U.S.A., during World War. Pres. Bd. Edn., Montvale, N.J. Mem. U.S. Cath. Hist. Soc., Am. Wildlife Soc. Awarded medal as champion regtl. shooting, dec. by Gen. Leonard Wood. Democrat. Roman Catholic. K. C. Forester. Clubs: Carteret (Jersey City); Hickory Mountain, N.C. For many yrs. active in conservation of wild life. Home: 2 Grand Av., Montvale, N.J.

BURNAM, Curtis Field, surgeon, radiologist; b. Richmond, Ky., Jan. 17, 1877; s. Anthony Rollins and Margaret (Summers) B.; A.B., Central U., Ky., 1895; M.D., Johns Hopkins, 1900; m. Florence Overall, Oct. 10, 1908. Resident gynecologist, Johns Hopkins Hosp., 1900-05, later asso. gynecologist, Johns Hopkins Hosp., and asso. in gynecology Johns Hopkins Med. Sch. until 1912; surgeon and radiologist Howard A. Kelly Hosp., Baltimore; visiting physician in ray therapy, Johns Hopkins Hosp. and asso. prof. surgery, Johns Hopkins Med. Sch. Fellow Am. Coll. Surgeons; member A.M.A., Med. and Chirurg. Faculty of Md., Am. Gynecol. Soc., Am. Urol. Assn., Southern Surg. Assn., Southern Med. Assn., Am. Radium Soc., Am. Coll. Radiology. Presbyn. Club: Elkridge Hunt. Author: (with Howard Atwood Kelly) Diseases of the Kidneys, Ureters and Bladder, 1914, and of many med. papers. Office: 1418 Eutaw Pl., Baltimore, Md.

BURNAP, Robert Samuel, radio engring.; b. Monterey, Mass., July 12, 1894; s. Rev. Irving Arthur and Anne (Binnie) B.; B.S., Mass. Inst. Tech., 1916; m. Katherine Worden Decker, Sept. 18, 1926; 1 dau., Jean Isabel. Engaged as research asst., Mass. Inst. Tech., 1916-17; with Edison Lamp Works of General Electric Co., 1917-30; engr. in charge testing sect. commercial engring. dept., 1925-30, RCA Radiotron Co. Inc. later RCA Radiotron Div. RCA Mfg. Co., Inc., engr. in charge commercial engring. sect. since 1930. Served in Signal Corps, U.S.A. during World War, dischd. as master signal electrician. Asso. mem. Inst. Radio Engrs.; mem. Am. Inst. Elec. Engrs. Fellow Soc. Motion Picture Engrs. Republican. Conglist. Contbr. papers to transactions of tech. socs. and to tech. journs. Mem. bd. editors RCA Review since 1938. Home: 58 University Ct., South Orange. Office: RCA Mfg. Co., Inc., Harrison, N.J.

BURNETT, Loutellus Artigue, ins. underwriting; b. New Vernon, Pa., July 31, 1871; s. Abijah H. and Dorothy C. (Boyd) B.; grad. McElwain Inst., New Lebanon, Grove City (Pa.) Coll., 1890; m. Anna J. Marsteller, Sept. 21, 1892; children—Clifton A., Esta Mae (dec.), Dorothy Jane (Mrs. Lloyd F. Hunt). Began as dep. sheriff of Mercer County, Pa., under father, 1890-93; engaged in insurance business, Greenville, Pa., 1894-1906, organized Farmers and Merchants Trust Co., Greenville, 1901 and vice-pres. several yrs., organized three more banks and pres. for 10 yrs.; acquired control Monongahela Fire Insurance Co. of Pittsburgh, 1908, and vice-pres. and mgr. many yrs.; pres. L. A. Burnett Co., gen. agts. fire and casualty cos., Pittsburgh, since 1909; has been asso. with orgn. of more than fifty banks, loan, ins., coal, and real estate cos.; erected Loutellus Apt. Hotel, 1924 and other real estate operations. Republican. Methodist. Club: Metropolitan (Pittsburgh). Home: 5557 Raleigh St. Office: 429 Fourth Av., Pittsburgh, Pa.

BURNETT, Marguerite Hill, state dir. adult edn. and curriculum development; b. Brooklyn, N.Y.; d. Richard John and Frances Elizabeth (McCoy) Burnett; student Girls High Sch., Brooklyn, N.Y., 1900-04, Brooklyn (N.Y.) Teachers Training Coll., 1904-06, Teachers Coll. Columbia U., 1932-37; A.B., Adelphi Coll., Garden City, L.I., N.Y., 1910; M.A., Columbia U., 1913; unmarried. Teacher New York Pub. Schs., 1910-19, later supervisor immigrant edn. in evening schs.; state dir. immigrant edn., Del., 1919-26, state dir. adult edn. since 1926; dir. curriculum development Wilmington (Del.) Pub. Schs. since 1932. Summers—instr. U. of Del., 1922, lecturer Harvard, 1923, instr. U. of Calif., Southern Branch, 1926, instr. U. of Del., 1927, instr. Buffalo (N.Y.) State Teachers Coll., 1931. Mem. Nat. Com. on Pub. Edn., Teachers Coll., Columbia U., 1939. Mem. Am. Assn. of Adult Edn. (mem. adv. council since 1932), N.E.A. (pres. dept. adult edn., 1934-36), Soc. for Curriculum Study, Phi Lambda Theta. Mem. editorial bd. Adult Edn. Bull. of N.E.A. since 1934; co-editor Enriched Community Living (pub. by Del. State Div. of Adult Edn.), 1936. Home: Naamans Creed Rd. Office: Bd. of Education, Wilmington, Del.

BURNETT, Mary Clarke, univ. prof., social worker; b. London, Eng., Jan. 3, 1892; d. William Frederick and Amy Robertson (Joplin) Clarke; A.B., U. of Toronto, Can., 1914; A.M., Columbia U., 1918; came to U.S., 1917, naturalized, 1927; m. Arthur Henry Burnett, May 11, 1918. Girls' worker and headworker Central Neighborhood House, Toronto, Can., 1914-17; exec. Social Workers' Council, Social Unit Orgn., Cincinnati, O., 1918-20; head social service dept., Alameda Co. Pub. Health Center, Oakland, Calif., 1921-22; prof. social work and head dept. social work, Carnegie Inst. Tech., since 1922; dir. of training, State Emergency Relief Bd. of Pa., Harrisburg, 1934-36. Mem. Am. Assn. Social Workers, Am. Assn. Univ. Profs., Pittsburgh Fed. of Social Agencies (dir.). Author: Training for Social Work; Encyclopedia of Social Sciences, 1934. Home: 3114 Iowa St. Office: Carnegie Institute of Technology, Pittsburgh, Pa.

BURNETT, Paul Moreton, life ins.; b. Baltimore, Md., Jan. 18, 1867; s. William Thomas and Amelia (Chapman) B.; ed. Baltimore City Coll. and U. of Md.; m. Elisabeth Jackson, New 12, 1895; 1 dau., Ellinor (wife of Dr. Stewart H. Clifford). In practice of law at Baltimore with Charles J. Bonaparte, 1885-1920; counsel Mut. Life Ins. Co. of Baltimore, 1898-1920, dir. since 1900, v.p., 1915-20, chmn. bd., 1920-22, pres. since 1922; dir. Union Trust Co. Maj. inf., Md. N.G., until 1916. Treas. Burmont Hosp. for Crippled Children. Presbyn. Mason (32°). Contbr. to art and archtl. mags. Home: Charles St. and Blythewood Rd. Office: 1101 N. Charles St., Baltimore, Md.

BURNETT, W. Emory; asso. prof. surgery Temple U.; surgeon Temple U. and Phila. Gen. Hosp. Address: 3701 N. Broad St., Philadelphia, Pa.

BURNHAM, E. Lewis; b. Phila., Pa., Jan. 27, 1883; s. George and Anna G. (Lewis) B.; A.B., Harvard, 1904; C.E., Cornell U., 1907; m. Cora B. Sellers, Oct. 9, 1909; children—Alan, Joan (Mrs. John R. Covert, Jr.). Began in plant of Hooker Electrochemical Co., Niagara Falls, N.Y., 1907, left 1908 on account of health; with engring. corps Stone & Webster on Phila. & Western Ry., 1910-12; partner with Arthur Peck selling "Telegraphone" to 1914; in father's office until his death, 1924; in civic and philanthropic work and private affairs, Phila., since 1924; (v.-pres.) Berwyn Nat. Bank; dir. Hooker Electrochemical Co. Pres. Phila. Bureau of Municipal Research; pres. Pa. Sch. of Social Work. In charge war camp community service, Waco, Tex., 1917-19. Mem. A.A.A.S., Phi Delta Theta. Democrat. Clubs: University, Harvard, Cornell, Franklin Inn (Phila.); Harvard (New York). Home: Berwyn, Pa. Office: 1500 Walnut St., Philadelphia, Pa.

BURNLEY, Harry, merchant; b. Upper Darby, Pa., May 12, 1870; s. Washington and Anna (Fields) B.; student Dickinson Sem.; m. Bertha M. Manning, Oct. 12, 1892; 1 son, H. Parker. Entered employ of E. R. Curtis, gen. store, Media, Pa., 1888, proprietor gen. store since 1894; pres. Stonehurst Bldg. and Loan Assn., Media, since 1928; pres. Radnor & Haverford Horse Co. (71-yr.-old protective assn. against theft of horses) since 1933; dir. Media Title & Trust Co. until taken over by The Banking Dept.; dir. Morton Nat. Bank. Rd. commr., Marple Twp., Pa., 14 yrs. Presbyn. (mem. Springfield Presbyn. Ch.). Home: Springfield and Sproul Sts., Marple, Pa. Office: Media, Delaware Co., Pa.

BURNS, F. Highlands; chmn. bd. Maryland Casualty Co. Office: 701 W. 40th St., Baltimore, Md.

BURNS, Jesse Erwin, ins. and real estate; b. Guffey, Pa., Oct. 8, 1892; s. Thomas Clark and Maria Florence (Campbell) B.; prep. edn. North Washington Inst., 1906-09; A.B., Allegheny Coll., Meadville, Pa., 1916; m. Helen Haldena Gates, Sept. 30, 1922; children—Helen Louise, Claire Elizabeth. Prin. high sch., Patton, Pa., 1916-17; oil producer, Butler Co., Pa., 1919-22; since 1922 partner and mgr. J. R. Gates Sons' Co., Oil City, Pa., real estate and ins., also auto financing, bldg. and loan, oil producing; dir. Citizens' Banking Co., Oil City; dir. and treas. Home Savings and Loan Assn., Oil City. Served in 2d O.T.C., Ft. Oglethorpe, Ga., Aug.-Dec. 1917; commd. 1st lt. Inf., U.S. Army, 1917, capt., 1918, with 20th Machine Gun Batt., A.E.F., 1917-19. Dir. Oil City Y.M.C.A.; mem. Nat. Council Y.M.C.A. Sr. mem. Soc. Residential Appraisers; mem. Phi Delta Theta. Republican. Presbyterian (trustee and treas. Second Presbyn. Ch., Oil City). Mason (32°). Clubs: Wanango Country, Oil City Boat, Acacia, Rotary (Oil City, Pa.). Home: 152 W. 3d St. Office: 20 E. 1st St., Oil City, Pa.

BURNS, Keivin, physicist; b. Pleasant Ridge, N.B., Can., Mar. 1, 1881; s. John and Gertrude (Campbell) B.; brought to U.S., 1885; A.B., U. of Minn., 1903, Ph.D., 1910; studied in Europe, 1911, 12; m. Hazel Bunney, 1911 (died in 1917); 1 son, Keivin; m. 2d, Ruth Buchanan, 1926; children—John Buchanan, George Campbell. Asst. at Lick Obs., Calif., 1904-07, U. of Minn., 1907-10; Martin Kellogg fellow, Lick Obs., residence in Europe, 1911, 12; asst. physicist, 1913-17, asso., 1917, physicist, 1917-19, Bur. of Standards, Washington; astronomer, Allegheny Obs., Pittsburgh, since 1920, asst. dir. since 1930. Mem. Sigma Xi, Philos. Society Washington, A.A.A.S. Unitarian. Has specialized in spectroscopy; measured standard wavelengths; determined stellar velocities and distances. Home: 3444 Delaware Av. Address: Allegheny Observatory, Pittsburgh, Pa.

BURNS, Stillwell C., surgeon; b. Phila., Pa., July 19, 1875; s. William Augustus and Mary Ford (Corson) B.; M.D., Medico-Chirurg. Coll., 1898; m. Reba Eyre, May 10, 1911. Surgeon, Phila., since 1898; surgeon Baldwin Locomotive Works, 1906-30; asso. prof. surgery, Post-Grad. Sch., U. of Pa., since 1917. Served as maj. Med. Corps, U.S. Army, 1917-19. Fellow Am. Coll. Surgery, Am. Coll. Physicians. Catholic. Address: 1238 Atwood Rd., Philadelphia, Pa.

BURNS, Vincent Godfrey, clergyman; b. Brooklyn, N.Y., Oct. 17, 1893; s. James Howard and Katherine (Rossberg) B.; B.S., Pa. State Coll., 1916 (John W. White prize fellowship); A.M., Harvard, 1917; B.D., Union Theol. Sem., 1922; grad. study, Columbia, 1922-24; m. Edna Rodenberger, June 15, 1921; 1 dau., Barbara. Ordained Congl. ministry, 1920; successively pastor City Park Chapel (Presbyn.), Brooklyn, South Congl. Ch., Pittsfield, Mass., Central Christian Ch., N.Y. City, until 1929, pastor Union Ch. (community), Palisade, N.J., 1929-36; leader of the Log Cabin Shrine since Mar., 1936; radio artist, recitalist (chiefly poetry) and lecturer. Enlisted in U.S.A., 1918; commd. lt., June 5, 1918; went overseas, July 1918; grad. Saumur F.A. Sch.; served on staff of Gen. Foote, 163d F.A. Brigade. Chmn. bd. Ft. Lee Pub. Library, N.J. Mem. Am. Legion, Alpha Zeta, Delta Sigma Rho, Phi Kappa Phi. Mason, Odd Fellow, Jr. O.U.A.M. Club: Rockland County Golf (Nyack, N.Y.). Author: The Master's Message for the New Day, 1926; I am a Fugitive from a Georgia Chain Gang (with brother, Robt. Burns), 1932; I'm in Love with Life, 1933; Female Convict, 1934; also (brochures) Fosdick and the Fundamentalists, Health is Life. Editor: The Red Harvest (verse), 1930. Also editor, Youth Dreams (mag.). Contbr. to mags. Home: Palisade, N.J.

BURNS, Vincent Leo, college pres.; b. Catasauqua, Pa., May 11, 1891; s. William John and Hannah Cecilia (McGee) B.; A.B., St. Charles Sem., Philadelphia, 1917; J.C.B., Cath. Univ., Washington, D.C., 1927, A.M., 1928; D.Sc., La Salle Coll., Phila., 1935; Ph.D., U. of Pa., 1936. Ordained priest R.C. Ch., 1917; curate Holy Cross Ch., Phila., 1917-20; dean St. Charles Sem., 1920-26, Mission House Cath. Univ., 1926-28, Grad. Dept. of St. Charles Sem., 1928-31; rector Our Lady of Mercy Ch., Phila., 1931-32; prof. biology and moral theology, St. Charles Sem., 1932-35; pres. Immaculata (Pa.) Coll., 1935-36, St. Charles Sem., Overbrook, Phila. since April 1936; apptd. Domestic Prelate by Pope Pius XI, June 22, 1936. Mem. Phila. Archdiocese Sch. Bd., 1932. Trustee Catholic Summer Sch. of America. Address: St. Charles Seminary, Overbrook, Philadelphia, Pa.

BURNSIDE, Robert E.; mem. law firm Burnside, Moninger & Burnside. Address: Washington, Pa.

BURPEE, David, seedsman; b. Phila., Pa., Apr. 5, 1893; s. Washington Atlee and Blanche (Simons) B.; prep. edn., Culver (Ind.) Mil. Acad.; student Cornell U., 1913-14; m. Lois Torrance, July 18, 1938. Began as asst. to father in seed business, Phila., 1914; became gen. mgr. of the business, 1915; apptd. executor father's estate, 1915; pres. W. Atlee Burpee Co. since 1917; chmn. bd. Wm. Henry Maule Co., James Vick's Seeds, Inc.; pres. Tabor Realty Co.; dir. Market Street Nat. Bank, Integrity Trust Co. (all Phila.). Trustee Bucknell Univ., Lewisburg, Pa.; dir. Hahnemann Hosp., Abington Memorial Hosp., also Nat. Farm Sch., Phila. Mem. Am. Seed Trade Assn. (ex-pres.), Nat. Sweet Pea Soc. of Gt. Britain (v.p.), Canadian Soc. of Phila. (hon. life pres.), Colonial Soc., N.E. Soc., English Speaking Union, Pa. Soc. of New York, Pa. Sons of the Revolution, Delta Upsilon. Republican. Clubs: Union League (v.p. 1933-35), Poor Richard, Fourth Street, Harris, Penn Athletic (Philadelphia); Sphinx, Advertising (New York); Canadian (Boston); Doylestown (Pa.) Country; Huntingdon Valley Country; Huntingdon Valley Hunt; Bachelors Barge. Home: Fordhook Farm, Doylestown, Pa. Office: 18th and Hunting Park Av., Philadelphia, Pa.

BURPEE, W(ashington) Atlee, Jr., seedsman; b. Phila., Pa., Oct. 25, 1894; s. Washington Atlee and Blanche (Simons) B.; prep. edn. Doyleston (Pa.) High Sch. and Culver (Ind.) Military Acad.; Cornell Univ., 1917; m. Jeannetta Drysdale Lee, Nov. 1, 1916; children—Washington Atlee, Jeannetta Murray, Anne Catherine Atlee. Treas. W. Atlee Burpee Co., seed and bulb growers, 1918-36, vice-pres. and treas. since 1936; vice-chmn. of bd. Wm. Henry Maule Co., Phila.; treas. Tabor Realty Co.; dir. Northern Trust Co., Bailey, Banks & Biddle. Dir. Oncologic Hosp., Phila.; pres. Phila. Flower Show. Served in Officers Material Sch., U.S. Naval Reserves, U. of Pa., during World War. Mem. Pa. Hort. Soc. (dir.), Pa. Soc. of Sons of the Revolution, Soc. of War of 1812, Colonial Soc. (dir.), Hist. Soc. of Phila., Canadian Soc. of Phila. Republican. Episcopalian. Clubs: Phila. Country, Fourth Street, Union League, Merion Cricket, Bachelors Barge, Orpheus, Racquet (Phila.). Home: 1822 S. Rittenhouse Square. Office: 18th and Hunting Park Av., Philadelphia, Pa.

BURR, Anna Robeson, author; b. Phila., Pa., May 26, 1873; d. Henry Armitt and Josephine Lea (Baker) Brown; ed. pvt. schs.; m. Charles H. Burr, May 27, 1899. Author: The Autobiography—A Study, 1909; Religious Confessions, 1914; The House on Charles Street, 1923; The Great House in the Park, 1924; St. Helios, 1925; The Portrait of a Banker, 1927; Palludia, 1928; Weir Mitchell, 1929; The Same Person, 1931; Wind in the East, 1933; Alice James—Her Journal, 1934; Golden Quicksand (novel), 1936. Home: 4 Pennstone Road, Bryn Mawr, Pa.*

BURR, Charles Walts, M.D.; b. Phila., Nov. 16, 1861; s. D. Ridgway and Hannah (Walts) B.; B.S., Univ. of Pa., 1883, M.D., 1886, D.Sc. from same univ., 1933; unmarried. Neurologist, Philadelphia General Hospital, 1896-1931, and psychiatrist to same since 1931; professor of mental diseases, Univ. of Pa., 1901-31, prof. emeritus since 1931; phys. to Orthopædic Hosp. and Infirmary for Nervous Diseases since 1911. Pres. Am. Neurol. Assn., 1908, Phila. Psychiatric Soc., 1909, 10, Phila. Neurol. Soc., Pathol. Soc. of Phila.; fellow Coll. Physicians, Phila.; mem. A.M.A. Address: 1527 Pine St., Philadelphia, Pa.

BURR, M(ary) Vashti (maiden and professional name), lawyer; b. Ebensburg, Pa., Dec. 28, 1899; d. Richard Brown and Jane Ann (Craver) Burr; grad. Ebensburg High Sch., 1916; graduate Indiana (Pa.) State Teachers Coll., 1918; LL.B., Dickinson Sch. of Law, 1924; m. William V. Whittington, July 29, 1938. Teacher of science Ebensburg High Sch., 1918-19, Bedford High Sch., 1919-20; admitted to Pa. bar, 1925, Supreme Court of U.S., 1928; dep. atty. gen. of Pa., 1926-31; opened law offices in Harrisburg and Johnstown, Pa., Feb. 1931; specializes in tax matters. Founded Ebensburg Women's Republican Club, 1925, chmn. same, 1925-38, now hon. chmn.; founded Cambria Co. Council of Rep. Women, Inc., 1930, pres., 1930-38, now hon. pres.; chmn. business and professional women's com. of Pa. Rep. State Com. Mem. Am. Bar Assn. (mem. sect. of internat. and comparative law), Pa. Bar Assn. (vice chmn. com. on taxation), Dauphin Co. and Cambria Co. bar assns., Women's Professional Panhellenic Assn. (nat. pres. since 1937), Phi Delta Delta (dir.; nat. pres. 1936-38), Am. Assn. Univ. Women (Harrisburg branch), Chi Omega, Woolsack (Dickinson). Presbyterian. Author of legal articles in jours. and booklets; cons. editor "Women at Work," N.Y. World's Fair publ. Home: Ebensburg, Pa. Office: Payne-Shoemaker Bldg., Harrisburg, Pa.

BURR, Samuel Engle II, supt. of schs.; b. Bordentown, N.J., Dec. 6, 1897; s. Samuel Engle and Elizabeth Coward (Thompson) B.; diploma Bordentown (N.J.) High Sch., 1915; Litt.B., Rutgers U., New Brunswick, N.J., 1919; M.A., U. of Wis., Madison, Wis., 1925; M.A., Teachers Coll., Columbia U., 1927; Ed.D., Teachers Coll., U. of Cincinnati, 1936; m. Alice Elizabeth Gratz, June 1924; children—Evelyn Anne, Samuel Engle III. Spl. clk., Pa. R.R. Co., Trenton, N.J., 1919-21; teacher and coach, Bordentown (N.J.) High Sch., 1921-23; teacher, Jr. High Sch. No. 1, Trenton, N.J., 1923-24; prin., Lambertville (N.J.) High Sch., 1924-25; supervising prin., Lawrence Twp. Pub. Schs., Lawrenceville, N.J., 1925-27; dir. ednl. research, Lynn (Mass.) Pub. Schs., 1927-30; supt. schs., Glendale, O., 1930-34, New Castle, Del., since 1934; visiting prof. edn., St. Lawrence U., Canton, N.Y., summers 1930-33; visiting lecturer in edn., U. of Buffalo, N.Y., summers since 1934. Served in R.O.T.C., Plattsburgh (N.Y.) Barracks, May-Sept. 1918, as 2d lt., Inf., U.S. Army, Camp Grant, Ill., Sept.-Dec. 1918, 2d lt., F.A. Res., 1928-38, 1st lt., Sanitary Res., since 1938. Citizens Mil. Training Corps Aide to Sec. of War for New Castle County, Del., 1938-39; dir. Del. Safety Council since 1935, New Castle Safety Council since 1935. Mem. New Castle Co. Teachers Assn. (pres. 1937), Mercer Co. (N.J.) Teachers Assn. (pres. 1927), N.E.A., Am. Assn. Sch. Administrs., Am. Ednl. Research Assn., Childhood Edn. Assn., Progressive Edn. Assn., Del. State Edn. Assn., Mass. Schoolmasters Club, Dept. of Supervisors and Dirs. of Instrn., 40 and 8 (Americanism dir. 1938-39), Am. Legion (Comdr. New Castle Post 4, 1936, 1937; vice comdr. Dept. of Del., 1938, comdr., 1939, historian, 1936, 1937), Boy Scouts of America (troop com. for Troop 61), Social Service Club of Wilmington, Legionaires Schoolmasters Club of Del. (pres. since 1937), Res. Officers Assn. of U.S., Mil. Order of World War, Gen. Soc. of Colonial Wars (N.J. Branch), Beta Theta Pi, Kappa Delta Pi, Phi Delta Kappa. Republican. Episcopalian. Mem. K.P. (Adelphia Lodge 8). Clubs: Rotary (pres. 1938-39), New Castle (New Castle, Del.); Yapewi Aquatic (Bordentown, N.J.); Rutgers of Delaware (Wilmington, Del.; pres. 1936-37). Author: Report of the Survey of the Public Schools of Lawrence Township, 1927; What Is the Activity Plan of Progressive Education?, 1935; An Introduction to Progressive Education (The Activity Plan), 1933, revised ed. 1937; A School in Transition, 1937; Our Flag and Our Schools, 1937; numerous articles in ednl. mags. Mem. of survey staff, Survey of Social and State Support of Schs. ("The Financing of the Public Schools of Maine"), 1934, Survey of the Public Schools of Yonkers, N.Y., 1934. Home: 7 Landers Lane. Office: 9th and Delaware Sts., New Castle, Del.

BURR, Walter Harmon, engineer; b. Morrison, Ill., Feb. 6, 1879; s. Harmon E. and Alice (Kier) B.; B.S., Rose Poly. Inst., Terre Haute, Ind., 1909; m. Harriet Elizabeth Borman, July 14, 1909; 1 son, Robert B. Bookkeeper Leander Smith & Sons, Morrison, Ill., 1898-99, Dixon (Ill.) Business Coll. and Rose Poly. Inst., 1899-1905; apprentice Westinghouse Electric & Mfg. Co., E. Pittsburgh, Pa., 1905-06, service and constrn. work, 1906-15, asst. dist. engr. service dept., Westinghouse of Phila., 1915-17; asst. supt. elec. dept. Alan Wood Steel Co., Conshohocken, Pa., 1917-21; supt. elec. dept. Lukens Steel Co., Coatesville, Pa., since 1921; registered professional engr. State of Pa. Mem. Assn. Iron & Steel Engrs. (pres. 1934-35; chmn. developments com. since 1926), Coatesville Chamber of Commerce, Assn. of Iron & Steel Engrs. Republican. Presbyterian (elder Coatesville ch.). Mason (Goddard Lodge 383). Clubs: Rotary, Coatesville Country (Coatesville, Pa.). Author: Annual reports of new developments for trade jours. Home: 1216 Olive St. Office: South First Av., Coatesville, Pa.

BURRELL, David de Forest, clergyman; b. Chicago, Ill., June 29, 1876; s. David James and Clara Sergeant (de Forest) B.; A.B., Yale, 1898; B.D., Princeton Theological Seminary, 1901, fellow, 1903; D.D., University of Dubuque, 1918; m. Margaret Yonker North, Apr. 29, 1905; children—Elizabeth North, Margaret de Forest, Catharine. Ordained ministry Presbyn. Ch., 1901; asst. pastor 1st Presbyn. Ch., Germantown, Pa., 1901-02; instr., Princeton Theol. Sem., 1903-04; pastor 1st Presbyn. Ch., La Porte, Ind., 1904-07, South Orange, N.J., 1908-18; prof. English Bible, Dubuque (Ia.) Coll., 1918-20; pastor Westminster Presbyn. Ch., Dubuque, 1920-23, 1st Presbyn. Ch., Williamsport, Pa., since 1923. Mem. N.J.N.G., 1917-18. Bd. mgrs. Nat. Temperance Soc., Lord's Day Alliance of U.S.; mem. Bd. Pensions of Presbyn. Ch., U.S.A. Mem. Delta Kappa Epsilon. Republican. Club: Manufacturers (Milton, Pa.). Author: Letters From the Dominie, 1916; Belligerent Peter, 1920; David James Burrell, a Biography, 1929; also wrote booklets: The End of the Way; The Gift; How They Came to Bethlehem; The Lost Star; The Hermit's Christmas Guests; Three Little Angels. Home: 601 Hawthorne Av., Williamsport, Pa.

BURRELL, George Arthur, chemical engr.; b. Cleveland, O., Jan. 23, 1882; s. Alexander A. and Jane (Penny) B.; student Ohio State U., 1902-04; (Chem. E., Ohio State U., 1918; Sc.D., Wesleyan U., 1919); m. Mary L. Schafer, 1906; 1 daughter, Dorothy May; m. 2d, Naomi L. Schafer, June 16, 1914. Chemist with U.S. Geol. Survey, 1904-08; in charge research work, gas, mine gas, and natural gas and gasoline investigations, U.S. Bur. Mines, at Pittsburgh, 1908-16; consulting engr. petroleum and natural gas work, 1916-37; assistant to dir. Bur. of Mines, 1917; col. U.S. Army, in charge all research work, Chem. Warfare Service, 1917-18; located supply of helium gas in Tex. and organized the Government Helium program. Awarded D.S.M. (U.S.). During 1919-20 had charge construction of refineries for the Island and Raritan Refining Cos. (New York City), and many others, and was pres. Island Ref. Co. and vice-pres. and gen. mgr. Raritan Ref. Co.; now pres. Burrell Technical Supply Co., Burrell-Mase Engring. Co.; also pres. Atlantic States Gas Co.; cons. petroleum engr.; retained by Russian government to modernize natural gas industry, 1930-31. Inventor Burrell gas detector, Burrell gas analysis apparatus; co-inventor Burrell-Oberfell process of extracting gasoline from natural gas by charcoal method; designed and built many natural gasoline refineries. Mem. Am. Petroleum Inst., Nat. Gas Assn. America, Am. Chem. Soc., Natural Gasoline Assn. America, Tau Beta Pi, Sigma Xi (1935). Clubs: Field Club (Pittsburgh); Westchester Country (N.Y. City). Author: Handbook of Gasoline, 1917; Recovery of Gasoline from Natural Gas, 1925; An American Engineer Looks at Russia, 1932; and also several hundred papers and Govt. publs. on gas, gasoline, petroleum and allied subjects. Awarded Lamme medal, 1935, by Ohio State Univ., for achievements in engineering. Home: 117 W. 58th St., New York, N.Y. Office: 1942 Fifth Av., Pittsburgh, Pa.; and 50 Broadway, New York, N.Y.

BURRIS, William Paxton; univ. prof. (retired). Address: Box 991, Short Hills, N.J.

BURRITT, Norman Wyvell, surgeon; b. Bayonne, N.J., Mar. 31, 1893; s. Jacob L. and Mabel (Wyvell) B.; student Ten Broeck Acad., 1910-13, Hamilton Coll., 1913-16, Columbia Coll., 1916-17; M.D., U. of Buffalo, 1921; unmarried. Began as eye, ear, nose and throat surgeon, 1923; attending surgeon eye, ear, nose and throat Overlook Hosp., 1923-30, chief surgeon since 1930; attending surgeon eye, ear, nose and throat All Souls Hosp., 1925-34; attending bronchoscopist Newark Eye and Ear Infirmary and Bonnie Burn Sanatorium since 1934. Pres. Chatham Borough (N.J.) Bd. of Health since 1924. Mem. S.A.T.C., 1916-17. Fellow Am. Acad. Ophthalmology and Otolaryngology, Am. Coll. Surgeons; mem. Union Co. Med. Soc. (chmn. côm. on foods and drugs, 1934; chmn. pub. health com., 1935), Med. Soc. of N.J. (chmn. com. on foods and drugs, 1935-38; chmn. Sect. of Scientific Session of Eye, Ear, Nose and Throat, 1939), Delta Kappa Epilson. Republican. Presbyn. (elder). Home: 7 Elmwood Av., Chatham, N.J. Office: 30 Beechwood Road, Summit, N.J.

BURSTEIN, David I., lawyer; b. Phila., Pa., Dec. 2, 1906; s. Harry and Dora Ann (Jacobson) B.; grad. West Phila. High Sch., 1924; B.S., Wharton Sch. of Finance and Commerce, U. of Pa., 1927; LL.B., Harvard, 1930; unmarried. Law clerk, Judge Levinthal's office, 1929; admitted to Pa. bar, 1930; admitted to practice before Supreme Court of Pa., 1930, Federal Courts, 1931; mem. firm Burstein, Halpern & Modell, specializing in civil practice, Phila.; lecturer on farm law, Nat. Farm Sch., Doylestown, Pa. Candidate for judge Municipal Court, 1934. Mem. Sigma Alpha Rho. Democrt. Mason (32°, Shriner). Clubs: Showmens (Phila.); Harvard Law Assn. (Cambridge, Mass.). Home: Chestnut Arms. Office: North American Bldg., Philadelphia, Pa.

BURT, David Allan, banker; b. Wheeling, W.Va., Dec. 24, 1876; s. John Lukens and Martha (McKelvey) B.; grad. Wheeling High Sch., 1892; m. Elizabeth McLain, Oct. 16, 1901; children—David A., Martha S., Elizabeth M. (dec.), William L. Office boy, clk., paymaster, Whitaker Iron Co., Wheeling, 1892-98; chief clk. Ætna Standard Iron & Steel Co., 1899-1903; auditor, treas., pres. La Belle Iron Works, 1904-20; v.p. Wheeling Steel Corpn., 1921-23, now dir.; formed partnership with H. C. Hazlett under name Hazlett & Burt, investment bankers and brokers, 1923; dir. Fidelity Investment Assn., Woodward Iron Co., Wheeling Steel Corpn., Chesapeake & Potomac Telephone Co., Continental Roll & Steel Foundry Co. Chmn. W.Va. State Tax Commn., 1926-27; v.p. bd. govs., W.Va. U. Mem. Acad. Polit. Science, Am. Iron & Steel Inst. Republican. Presbyn. Mason. Clubs: Duquesne (Pittsburgh); Fort Henry (Wheeling). Home: Echo Point, Wheeling. Office: Wheeling Steel Corpn. Bldg., Wheeling, W.Va.

BURT, James C.; asso. prof. genito-urinary diseases, U. of Pittsburgh; genito-urinary surgeon Allegheny Gen. and St. Francis hosps. Address: 200 Ninth St., Pittsburgh, Pa.

BURT, William Nathaniel, Jr., river transportation; b. Indianapolis, Ind., June 3, 1882; s. William Nathaniel and Margaret Jane (Donnell) B.; ed. East Liberty Acad., Washington and Jefferson Coll., Washington, Pa.; m. Margaret McKinley Reed, Oct. 21, 1914; children—Dorothy Donnell, William Nathaniel 3d, George Reed, James Clark 2d, Thomas Reed. Mem. Pittsburgh Stock Exchange, 1908-35; pres. and dir. National Barge Co., Pittsburgh. Served as dir. Pub. Schs., Edgewood, Pa. Trustee C. C. Mellor Memorial Library. Mem. Phi Delta Theta. Republican. Presbyterian. Home: Edgewood. Office: Investment Bldg., Pittsburgh, Pa.

BURTIS, Philip Barrett, mgr. of sales; b. Burlington, N.J., Mar. 24, 1890; s. Harvey and Anna Stokes (Fenimore) B.; student pub. schs. of N.J. and Phila. Bus. Coll.; m. Helen E. Sharpe, Oct. 11, 1915; 1 dau., Virginia. Began in treasury dept. Cambria Steel Co., 1907 and advanced through various positions of that co. and its successors, Midvale Steel and Ordnance Co. and Bethlehem Steel Corpn.; mgr. sales, Phila. Dist., Bethlehem Steel Co. since 1938. Republican. Episcopalian. Clubs: Penn Athletic, Racquet (Phila.); Country (Merchantville, N.J.); Pine Valley Golf (Clementon, N.J.). Home: 401 W. Maple Av., Merchantville, N.J. Office: 1058 Broad St. Station Bldg., Philadelphia, Pa.

BURTON, Carroll, steel mfr.; b. Coolspring, Del., Oct. 14, 1875; s. Benjamin H. and Elizabeth E. (Perry) B.; student Temple U., Phila., 1893-97, Wharton Sch. of Accounts and Finance, U. of Pa., 1907-09; m. Sara E. Edwards, Dec. 24, 1910; 1 dau., Phyllis. Export rep. Lorain Steel Co., London, Eng., 1898-1904; Lorain rep. U.S. Steel Products Co., London, Eng., 1904-05; asst. to pres., in charge of girder rail sales, The Lorain Steel Co., Phila., Pa., 1905-09, asst. to pres., in charge operations, Johnstown, Pa., 1910-11, gen. mgr., 1912-19, gen. supt., 1919-20, pres. and gen. supt., 1920-26, pres., 1926-35; v.p. in charge Lorain Div., Carnegie-Illinois Steel Corpn., Johnstown, Pa., 1935-38, v.p. and sales mgr. in charge Lorain Div., since 1938. Vice-pres. Johnstown (Pa.) Community Chest. Mem. Am. Iron & Steel Inst. Republican. Clubs: Rotary, Bachelors, Sunnehanna Country (Johnstown, Pa., dir.); Duquesne (Pittsburgh); Engineers' (New York). Home: Bliss St. Office: 545 Central Av., Johnstown, Pa.

BURTON, Charles Wesley, Jr., mfg. fence materials; b. Baltimore, Md., Nov. 26, 1897; s. Charles Wesley and Eurith Ann Hargest (Leach) B.; A.B., St. John's Coll., 1919; C.P.A., Pace Inst. Accountancy, 1922; m. Mildred Mary Meyer, July 12, 1920; children—Charles Wesley III (dec.), Charles Lorenz, Mildred Mary, William Kenneth, Phyllis Jane. Served as chief clk. U.S. Shipping Bd., 1919-22; with Haskins & Sells, certified pub. accountants, 1922-26; asst. treas. The Rome Co., 1926-29; chief accountant, Anchor Post Fehce Co., Baltimore, Md., 1929-37, treas. since 1937; treas. and dir., Anchor Post Fence Co. of Calif.; sec., treas. and dir., Am. Fence Constrn. Co.; pres., sec. and dir., Fluid Heat, Inc.; C.P.A. in Md. since 1924; prof. accounting, U. of Md., 1924-26, Baltimore Coll. of Commerce since 1926. Served as 2d lt. inf., U.S.A., 1918-19. Mem. bd. ednl. council, Y.M.C.A. Mem. Md.

Assn. C.P.A.s, St. John's Coll. Alumni Assn., Am. Legion, Kappa Alpha. Republican. Methodist. Club: Sherwood Forest. Home: 3115 Juneau Pl. Office: 6500 Eastern Av., Baltimore, Md.

BURTON, Horace Moore, lawyer; b. Phila., Pa., Aug. 11, 1897; s. Joseph Walter and Clara Martha (Moore) B.; student Westtown (Pa.) Boarding Sch., 1910-16, Pa. State Coll., 1916-18, Temple U., Phila., 1918; m. Mildred L. Styer, Aug. 23, 1924; children—Katharine Styer, Martha Cox, Joseph Walter. Began as law clk., 1921; admitted to Phila. bar, 1924; mem. firm Scott & Burton, Phila., since 1925. Trustee Westtown Boarding Sch. Mem. Phila. Bar Assn., Delta Sigma Rho. Republican. Quaker. Club: Riverside Yacht (Essington, Pa.). Home: Primos, Pa. Office: 7 S. 15th St., Philadelphia, Pa.

BURTON-OPITZ, Russell, physician, physiologist; b. Ft. Wayne, Ind., Oct. 25, 1875; s. Charles and Anna B.; M.D., Rush Medical College, 1895; S.B., U. of Chicago, 1897, postgrad. work same, 1897-98, S.M., 1902, Ph.D., 1905; post-grad. work, U. of Vienna, 1898; m. Jeanette Jonassen, 1909; 1 dau., Arlyn. Asst. in physiology, U. of Breslau, 1898-1901; investigator Marine Biol. Sta., Naples, 1901; asst. in physiology, Harvard, 1901-02; asst., 1902-03, instr., 1903-04, adj. prof., 1904-10, asso. prof. physiology, 1909-23, admin. head dept. of physiology, 1909-11, lecturer in physiology since 1923, Columbia. Consultant physician, Cumberland Hosp.; consultant diseases of heart, Lenox Hill, Englewood, North Hudson, Holy Name, Christ, Hackensack hosps.—all of N.Y. City. Fellow A.M.A., A.A.A.S.; mem. Am. Physiol. Soc., Soc. Exptl. Medicine and Biology, Am. Soc. Naturalists, Deutsche Physiol. Gesellschaft, Am. Soc. Biol. Chemists, Medical Society of State of New York, New York Co. Med. Soc., Am. Soc. Pharm. and Exptl. Therapy, N.Y. Cardiol. Soc. (pres.), Sigma Xi, Alpha Omega Alpha (pres.). Contbr. to Am. and foreign physiol. and med. jours. Author: Text Book of Physiology, 1920; Advanced Lessons in Practical Physiology, 1920; Elementary Manual of Physiology. Home: Palisade, N.J.

BURTT, Howard, lawyer; b. Phila., Pa., Sept. 20, 1886; s. John Ingham and Elizabeth (Armstrong) B.; prep. edn. Westtown (Pa.) Boarding Sch., 1901-04; A.B., Haverford (Pa.) Coll., 1908; LL.B., U. of Pa., 1911; m. Geraldine Miller, Sept. 14, 1929; 1 son, Howard Graham. Admitted to Pa. bar, 1911, and since practiced in Phila.; mem. firm Guckes, Shrader, Burtt & Thornton. Dir. Grandom Instn. Mem. Am., Pa. and Phila. bar assns., Am. Philol. Assn., Phi Beta Kappa. Ind. Republican. Quaker. Clubs: Haverford (Phila.); Lake Placid (N.Y.). Home: 3410 Warden Drive. Office: Packard Bldg., Philadelphia, Pa.

BUSCH, Henry Paul, wholesale and mfg. druggist; b. Phila., Pa. Mar. 4, 1873; s. Henry E. and Eleanor K. (Jeffries) B.; ed. Rittenhouse Acad., 1884-89; B.S. in chemistry, U. of Pa., 1893; m. Lydia Leaming Smith, Nov. 9, 1910; 1 dau. Emilie Smith. Asso. with Shoemaker & Busch, wholesale druggists and mfg. pharmacists, Phila., since 1893, pres. 1924-29, dir. since 1924; dir. Ridge Av. Passenger Ry. Co. Mem. Fairmount Park Art Assn., City Parks Assn., U. of Pa. Mus., Acad. of Natural Scis., Phila. Soc. for the Preservation of Landmarks, Phila. Mus. of Art, Franklin Inst. Mus. Mem. Pa. Pharm. Assn., Am. Pharm. Assn., Am. Chem. Soc., A.A.A.S., Am. Geog. Soc., Nat. Geographic Soc. Geog. Soc. of Phila., Numismatic and Antiquarian Soc. (sec.), Am. Numismatic Assn., Hist. Soc. of Pa., Geneal. Soc. of Pa. (treas.), New England Soc., Welcome Soc. of Pa. (pres.), Colonial Soc. of Pa. (v.p.), Soc. of Colonial Wars, Soc. of War of 1812, Netherlands Soc., Friends Hist. Soc., Pa. Hist. Assn., Am. Swedish Hist. Foundation. Republican. Episcopalian. Clubs: Union League, University, Penn, Philadelphia Country (Phila.); Spring Lake Golf and Country. Home: 1006 Spruce St. Office: 515 Arch St., Philadelphia, Pa.

BUSCH, Miers, wholesale druggist; b. Phila., Pa., Feb. 8, 1863; s. Henry Ernest and Eleanor K. (Jeffries) B.; grad. Eastburn Sch., Phila., 1881; Ph.B., Wharton Sch., U. of Pa., 1885; unmarried. Began with Roller & Shoemaker, Phila., 1885, became mem. of firm, 1888; firm of Shoemaker & Busch, wholesale druggists, Phila., organized, 1892, became sole owner, 1922; incorporated, 1923, pres., 1923-24, vice-pres., 1924-30, pres. since 1930; dir. Pa. Salt Mfg. Co., 1921-31, 1st v.p., 1923-24, 1st v.p. and acting gen. mgr., 1924-26, pres. 1926-28; dir. Am. Acad. Music, 1913-28, 2d v.p., 1923-28; dir. Phila. Bourse since 1915, 3d v.p. since 1922; dir. Fairmount Park & Haddington Passenger Ry. Co. since 1924; dir. Green & Coates Sts. Phila. Passenger Ry. Co. since 1932; dir. Phila. and Grays' Ferry Passenger Ry. Co. since 1935, pres. since 1937. During the World War chmn. of house com. of Union League, including "The Annex," and had charge of entertainment of service men, 600,000 men having been entertained. Apptd. by Court as trustee Moore Inst. Arts, Science and Industry and served as chmn. finance com., 1921-28; trustee Free Library of Phila., dir. since 1937. Mem. Pa. Soc. Sons of the Revolution (color guard since 1924), Colonial Soc. of Pa. (mem. council, 1921-38), Welcome Soc. of Pa. (mem. council since 1926), Soc. of War 1812 in Commonwealth of Pa. (pres. since 1937), Soc. of Colonial Wars in Pa., Hist. Soc. of Pa., Genealogical Soc. of Pa., New Eng. Soc. Pa., Athenaeum of Phila., Musical Fund Soc. (pres. since 1934), Zool. Soc. Phila., Acad. Natural Sciences, City Parks Assn. of Phila., Pa. Acad. Fine Arts, Fairmount Park Art Assn., Benjamin Franklin Memorial, Pa. Mus. of Art, John Bartram Assn., Phila. Soc. for Preservation of Landmarks (vice-pres. since 1935). Mem. Nat. Wholesale Druggists Assn. (2d v.p. 1911), Pa. Pharm. Assn., Am. Pharm. Assn., Phila. Drug Exchange (vice-pres. 1924). Mem. Phila. Bd. of Trade, mem. exec. com., 1910-32, 1st v.p., 1928-32. Republican. Universalist (treas. First Universalist Ch.). Clubs: Union League, Penn, University, Bachelors Barge (pres. 1939), Phila. Country (Phila.); Duquesne (Pittsburgh). Has traveled among Windward Islands and made 4 trips to Europe. Home: 1006 Spruce St. Office: 515 Arch St., Philadelphia, Pa.

BUSER, Raymond G., pres. R. G. Buser Silk Corpn. Address: 27 Ryle Av., Paterson, N.J.

BUSH, Edgar Murray, physician; b. Hampstead, Md., Dec. 21, 1870; s. John M. and Elenora (Murray) B.; grad. Franklin High Sch., Reistertown, Md., 1891; M.D., U. of Md., 1896; m. Ida Florence Little, May 1, 1900; children—Ethel Grace (Mrs. Lewis Vollman), John Murray, Joseph Edgar (M.D.). School teacher, 1890-94; practice of medicine, Hampstead, Md., since 1896; pres. First Nat. Bank, Hampstead, 1910-25; mayor of Hampstead since 1922. Democrat. Methodist. Mason (past master). Address: Hampstead, Md.

BUSH, Henry Tatnall, banker; b. Wilmington, Del., Nov. 24, 1880, s. Walter Danforth and Rebecca Gibbons (Tatnall) B.; ed. Friends' Sch., Wilmington; m. Lydia Moore, Apr. 14, 1906 (now dec.); 1 son, Henry Tatnall; m. 2d, Marjorie L. Dingee (mother of Anne L. Dingee), May 25, 1929. Began as clerk with Harlan & Hollingsworth Corpn., Wilmington, 1897; president Farmers' Bank since 1927; director Wilmington Savings Fund Soc., Farmers Mutual Fire Ins. Co., Wilson Line, Inc., Farmers Bank of State of Del. Trustee Wilmington Free Library; dir. Wilmington Music Sch. Pres. Wilmington Chamber of Commerce, 1927. Mem. Soc. of Colonial Wars. Republican. Home: Beaver Valley, Wilmington. Office: Farmers' Bank, Wilmington, Del.

BUSH, R. G.; editor Elkins Inter-Mountain. Address: Elkins, W.Va.

BUSHNELL, Asa Smith, exec. dir. of intercollegiate athletics; b. Springfield, O., Feb. 2, 1900; s. John L. and Jessie M. (Harwood) B.; student Springfield (O.) High Sch., 1912-14, The Hill Sch., Pottstown, Pa., 1914-17; B.S., Princeton U., 1921; student Columbia U. Law Sch., 1922; m. Thelma L. Clark, Feb. 11, 1924; children—Asa Smith, 3d, Barbara Clark. Teller Morris Plan Bank, Springfield, O., 1922-23; treas. Direct Products Co., Springfield, O., 1924-25; editor Princeton Alumni Weekly, 1925-30; grad. mgr. Princeton U. Athletic Assn., 1927-37; editor Princeton Athletic News, 1932-37; exec. dir. Central Office for Eastern Intercollegiate Athletics, New York, since 1938. Asst. treas. Am. Olympic Com., 1936; mem. Am. Olympic Com., 1938-39; dir. Princeton Invitation Track Meet, 1934-38. Served as apprentice seaman, U.S. Naval Reserve Force, 1918. Mem. University Cottage Club of Princeton (bd. of govs.). Republican. Episcopalian. Home: 45 Vandeventer Av., Princeton, N.J. Office: Biltmore Hotel, New York, N.Y.

BUSHNELL, Henry Davis, lawyer; b. Parker's Landing, Pa., May 28, 1875; s. John and Susan Frances (Sellers) B.; A.B., Harvard, 1898; LL.B., N.Y. Law Sch., 1900; m. Edith Taber Johnson, June 3, 1903 (died May 17, 1904); 1 dau., Edith Johnson (Mrs. Maynard L. Harris); m. 2d, Helen Sprague Martin, Oct. 19, 1907; children—Daniel, Francis Martin. Admitted to N.Y. bar, 1900; also admitted to bar U.S. Supreme Court; practiced in various offices, N.Y. City, 1900-03; asst. atty. South Penn Oil Co., Pittsburgh, Pa., 1903-12; gen. counsel Ind. Pipe Line Co., The Buckeye Pipe Line Co., Northern Pipe Line Co., N.Y. Transit Co. (comprising northern group of pipe lines) since 1912. Trustee Montclair (N.J.) Art Assn., 1918-24. Mem. Am. Bar Assn., Washington Assn. of N.J., Montclair Art Assn. Conglist. Clubs: Montclair Golf; Harvard of New Jersey. Contbr. to jours. Home: 59 Afterglow Av., Montclair, N.J. Office: 26 Broadway, New York, N.Y.

BUSHONG, Robert Grey, lawyer; b. Reading, Pa., June 10, 1883; s. Jacob and Lillie (Roberts) B.; A.B., Yale, 1903; LL.B., Columbia, 1906; m. Helen Bowman, July 20, 1919; 1 dau., Sarah. Admitted to Pa. bar Sept. 23, 1906, and began practice at Reading. Mem. Pa. Ho. of Rep., 1909; president judge Orphans' Court of Berks County, 1914-15; del. Rep. Nat. Conv., 1916, 24; mem. 70th Congress (1927-29), 14th Pa. Dist. Republican. Episcopalian. Mason. Author: Pa. Land Law, 3 vols., 1938. Home: Sinking Spring, R.F.D. 2. Office: 526 Court St., Reading, Pa.

BUSSER, Frank Sylvester, lawyer; b. York, Pa., Aug. 9, 1870; s. William Franklin and Mary Catherine (Cox) B.; grad. York (Pa.) High Sch. 1888; LL.B., U. of Pa., 1897; m. Clara Willis Beckett, Oct. 31, 1899 (died 1937); children—Helen Eldredge (Mrs. Wallace S. Martindale Jr.), Selmon Cox (son). Admitted to bar of Phila. Co., 1897, subsequently to practice before Supreme Courts of Pa. and U.S. and many federal courts; soliciting of patents since 1889; v.p. F. W. White Co., luggage. Mem. Franklin Inst. Republican. Club: University (Phila.). Home: 720 Westview Av. Office: 2000 Girard Trust Bldg., Philadelphia, Pa.

BUSSEY, Gertrude Carman, coll. prof.; b. New York, Jan. 13, 1888; d. William George and Grace Fletcher (Trufant) B.; student Lockwood Collegiate Sch., Mt. Vernon, N.Y., 1898-1904; B.A., Wellesley (Mass.) Coll., 1908, M.A., 1910; student Columbia U., 1908-09 and 1912-13; Ph.D., Northwestern U., 1915; fellow by courtesy, Johns Hopkins U., 1917-19; studied Oxford U., 1921. Teacher, Brantwood Hall, Bronxville, N.Y., 1909-12; instr. philosophy, Goucher Coll., Baltimore, 1915-16; prof. philosophy since 1920. Mem. bd. Y.W.C.A., Baltimore Open Forum; trustee Christian Social Justice Fund; nat. pres. women's Internat. League for Peace and Freedom, 1939. Mem. Am. Philos. Assn., Am. Assn. Univ. Women, Phi Beta Kappa. Socialist. Episcopalian. Club: Hamilton Street (Baltimore). Home: 5412 Purlington Way, Baltimore, Md.

BUTCHER, Howard, Jr., stock broker; b. Philadelphia, Pa., Dec. 28, 1876; s. Howard and Mary L. (Richards) B.; grad. William Penn Charter Sch., 1893; student U. of Pa., 1894-96; m. Margaret Keen, Apr. 10, 1901; children—Howard, Margaret, Dora Keen (Mrs. P. B. Russel, Jr.), Mary Louisa (Mrs. Julian W. Hill), William Williams Keen, Florence. Bond salesman, 1901-10; partner in firms of Butcher & Sherred since 1910; mem. N.Y. Stock Exchange,

Phila. Stock Exchange (pres.); asso. mem. N.Y. Curb Exchange. Served overseas with Y.M.C.A., World War. Mem. bd. of mgrs. Phila. Orthopædic Hosp. and Infirmary for Nervous Diseases, Hosp. of U. of Pa. Mem. Zeta Psi. Republican. Episcopalian. Mason. Clubs: University, Union League, Midday, Merion Cricket; Ribaut (Fla.); Appalachian Mountain (Boston). Home: Ardmore, Pa. Office: 1500 Walnut St., Philadelphia, Pa.

BUTLER, Arthur Gray, civil engr.; b. Terre Haute, Ind., Sept. 20, 1888; s. Thomas Jefferson and Mary Elizabeth (Lee) B.; grad. Terre Haute, High Sch., 1906; B.S. in Civil Engring., Rose Poly Inst., Terre Haute, Ind., 1910, C.E., 1931; m. Marie Ingold Rhoads Sept. 25, 1912; children—Harriet Ingold (Mrs. Thomas S. Stevenson), Anne Spottswood, Mary Gray, Jean Lee. Mem. engring. corps Vandalia R.R., Logansport, Ind., 1910-12; contractor's engr. Henry Bickel Co., Louisville, Ky., 1912-17; with Byllesby Engring. and Management Corpn. as gen. supt. of constrn. Louisville Gas & Electric Co., 1917-29, mgr. Pittsburgh Branch, 1929-36; mgr. engring. and constrn. Duquesne Light Co., Pittsburgh, since 1936. Mem. bd. mgrs. Rose Poly. Inst.; trustee Pittsburgh Assn. for Improvement of Poor. Registered professional engr. in Pa. Mem. Am. Soc. Civil Engrs., Pa. Electric Assn. (chmn. engring. sect.), Engrs. Soc. Western Pa., Theta Kappa Nu. Republican. Presbyterian. Mason. Clubs: Longue Vue, University (Pittsburgh). Constructed Ohio Falls hydro development; widened Louisville and Portland Canal; also constructed gas plant, steam electric stations, substations, etc. Home: 5533 Beverly Place. Office: 435 6th Av., Pittsburgh, Pa.

BUTLER, Elmer Grimshaw, prof. biology; b. Parish, N.Y., Feb. 13, 1900; s. Frank Alexander and Elizabeth Jane (Grimshaw) B.; A.B., Syracuse U., 1921; A.M., Princeton U., 1925, Ph.D., same, 1926; m. Eleanor Brill, June 30, 1927. Engaged as instr. zoology, U. of Vt., 1921-23; fellow in biology, Princeton U., 1923-26, instr. biology, 1926-28, asst. prof., 1928-31, asso. prof., 1931-37, prof. biology, Princeton U. since 1937. Fellow A.A.A.S. Mem. Am. Soc. Zoologists (sec. since 1937), Am. Soc. Naturalists, Am. Assn. Anatomists, Phi Kappa Psi, Phi Beta Kappa, Sigma Xi. Republican. Presbyn. Home: 109 Broadmead, Princeton, N.J.

BUTLER, Eustace C.; attending surgeon Essex County Hosp., Cedar Grove, N.J. Address: 249 Bloomfield Av., Caldwell, N.J.

BUTLER, Frank Arthur, asso. prof. edn.; b. Sturgeon Bay, Wis., Feb. 7, 1894; s. Thomas and Mary (Gaeth) B.; ed. Ripon (Wis.) Coll., 1921-22; Ph.B., U. of Wis., Madison, Wis., 1924, Ph.M., 1925, Ph.D., 1928; m. Hilda M. Bressler, Nov. 27, 1930; 1 dau., Barbara Anne. Engaged in teaching pub. schs. and prin. pub. schs. and high schs., Wis., 1913-26; asso. prof. edn., Dept. Edn. and Psychology, Pa. State Coll. since 1928. Served as pvt. inf. U.S.A., 1917-19, with 89th Div. A.E.F. Mem. Nat. Edn. Assn., Pa. State Edn. Assn., Dept. Secondary Sch. Prins., Phi Delta Kappa. Republican. Author: The Improvement of Teaching in Secondary Schools, 1939; contbr. articles to ednl. journs. Home: Orlando Apts., State College, Pa.

BUTLER, George Vincent, publisher; b. Brooklyn, N.Y., July 16, 1904; s. George P. and May (Vincent) B.; A.B., Swarthmore Coll. 1925; study, Columbia U., summer 1924, nights 1930; m. Edith C. Malmgreen, Oct. 30, 1937. Publisher own group of 9 weekly newspapers in Del. Co., Pa. nr. Phila., corr. met. dailies and A.P., 1923-29; engaged in writing, publicity, editor house organ for Copper & Brass Research Assn., N.Y. City, 1930-33; production mgr. Economic Forum mag., N.Y. City, 1934; gen. mgr. N.J. Automobile Club, Newark, 1934; pub. New Jersey Autoist mag., Newark, 1933-37; head publicity dept., Carrier Corpn., air conditioning, Newark, 1935; head adv., sales promotion and publicity depts., Carrier Corpn. (Internat. Div.), 1937; publisher Florida Bound Guide, annual motoring directory since 1936; publisher Discoveries in Dining, first edit., 1939. Contbr. to gen trade mags. Mem. Phi Sigma Kappa. Republican. Methodist. Home: 378 Elmwood Av., East Orange. Office: 343 High St., Newark, N.J.

BUTLER, John Marshall, lawyer; b. Baltimore, Md., July 21, 1897; s. John Harvey and Eunice West (Riddle) B.; student Johns Hopkins U., Baltimore, Md., 1919-21; LL.B., U. of Md., Baltimore, Md., 1926; m. Marie Louise Abell, Apr. 5, 1926; children—John Marshall, Edwin Franklin Abell, Maria Louise. Asso. with law firm Venable, Baetjer & Howard, Baltimore, Md., since 1927, jr. partner since 1939. Served as private and corp. 110th F.A., 29th Div., U.S. Army, A.E.F., 1917-19. Mem. Beta Theta Pi. Republican. Methodist. Clubs: Baltimore Country, Merchants (Baltimore, Md.). Home: 221 Upnor Rd. Office: 1409 Mercantile Trust Bldg., Baltimore, Md.

BUTLER, LaFayette Lentz, business exec.; b. Park Place, Pa., Jan. 11, 1887; s. Charles Ellsworth and Sarah Elizabeth (Morris) B.; grad. Blair Acad., Blairstown, N.J., 1904; A.B., Princeton U., 1908; A.M., Harvard, 1913; m. Vivian Tolhurst, 1911 (died 1932); 1 son, Charles Tolhurst; m. 2d, Clair Fichter, Feb. 7, 1933. Instr. in English, U. of Salt Lake City, Utah, 1908-12; teacher English dept., High Sch., of Commerce, Springfield, Mass., 1913-14; asst. prof., U. of Utah, 1914-15; with Central Pa. Quarry Stripping & Construction Co. and Benjamin Iron & Steel Co., both Hazleton, now sec.-treas. of both companies; dir. Markle Banking & Trust Co. Served as film editor, Dept. of Interior, Washington, D.C., 1919. Pres. Hazleton Chamber of Commerce, 1924; trustee Hazleton Public Library. Mason (K.T.). Clubs: Hazleton Rotary (pres. 1922); Lotos (New York). Contbr. to periodicals. Home: 155 N. Laurel St. Office: Pine and Buttonwood Sts., Hazleton, Pa.

BUTLER, Mary, artist; b. Chester Co., Pa.; d. James and Rachel M. (James) B.; ed. Darlington Sem., West Chester, Pa.; art edn., Philadelphia Sch. Design for Women (Horstmann fellowship), Pa. Acad. Fine Arts; pupil of William M. Chase, Robert Henri, Edward W. Redfield, Cecilia Beaux, of Phila., Gustav Courtois, Prinet, Ingebert, Girardot, Paris, France. Has specialized on mountain and sea pictures. Represented at Pa. Acad. Fine Arts, West Chester State Teachers Coll., Teachers Coll. and Art Mus., Springfield, Mo., Art Mus., Peoria, Ill., Edmonton (Can.) Art Museum, etc. Awarded hon. mention, Buffalo Soc. Artists, 1913, 14; gold medal, Plastic Club, Philadelphia, 1918; Mary Smith prize, Pa. Acad. Fine Arts, 1925; spl. award of honor, Nat. Art Exhbn., Springville, Utah, 1926, 27; 2d prize, water colors, Plastic Club, 1929; hon. mention Eloise Egan prize, Nat. Assn. Women Painters and Sculptors. Life mem. Pa. Acad. Fine Arts; mem. Fellowship Pa. Acad. Fine Arts (hon. pres.), Phila. Water Color Club, Alumnæ Phila. Sch. Design for Women, Plastic Club, Com. of 1926 of Pa., Fairmount Park Art Assn., Print Club of Philadelphia, Am. Fed. of Arts, Am. Artists Professional League, Phila. Art Alliance; mem. Council for Preservation of Natural Beauty in Pa. Congregationalist. Clubs: New Century (hon.), Contemporary (Phila.). Home: 2127 Green St., Philadelphia, Pa.; (summer) Uwchland, Pa.

BUTLER, Philo Wilcox, wholesale heavy hardware; b. Binghamton, N.Y., Jan. 22, 1881; s. Charles and Cornelia (Wilcox) B.; student pub. and high sch., Binghamton, N.Y., 1888-97; m. Myra Somers, Nov. 26, 1910; children—Philo Wilcox, Janet (Mrs. Frank A. Simms). Sec. and dir. Gaylord & Eitapence Co., Binghamton, N.Y.; sec. and treas. Gaylord & Butler Co., wholesale distributors of supplies for steam, water and gas, Scranton, Pa., 1908-27, pres. and dir. since 1927; liquidator Spencer Heater Co., Scranton Electric Steel Co.; dir. Third Nat. Bank, Maccar Truck Co., Graff Furnace Co., Scranton Transit Co., Lake Winola Park Co. Mem. Zoning Bd. of Appeals of Scranton, Pa. Republican. Episcopalian. Club: Scranton (Scranton, Pa.); Scranton Country of Clarks Summit, Pa. (dir.). Home: 701 Jefferson Av. Office: P.O. Box No. 327, Scranton, Pa.

BUTLER, Ralph, M.D.; b. Loag, Chester Co., Pa.; s. James and Rachel M. (James) B.; B.E., West Chester State Normal Sch. (now West Chester Teachers Coll.), 1893; M.D., U. of Pa., 1900; studied diseases of ear, nose and throat, Vienna, 1901-02, Berlin, 2 mos., 1906; m. Ida Shaw, Dec. 18, 1905. Resident St. Joseph's Hosp., Phila., 1900-01; asst. aural surgeon, U. of Pa., 1902-06, instr. in otology, 1907-16, asst. prof. otology, 1916-24, prof. laryngology and vice dean of oto-laryngology, graduate School of Medicine, same university, since 1918; prof. diseases of nose and throat, Phila. Polyclinic and Coll. for Graduates in Medicine, 1912-18; otolaryngologist Lankenau Hosp. Fellow Am. Coll. Surgeons, A.M.A.; mem. Am. Otol. Soc., Am. Laryngol. Assn., Am. Laryngol., Rhinol. and Otol. Soc., Med. Soc. State of Pa., Phila. County Med. Soc., Phila. Med. Club, Alpha Kappa Kappa. Republican. Presbyn. Mason. Club: Penn Athletic. Home: Garden Court Apts., 47th and Pine Sts. Office: 1930 Chestnut St., Philadelphia, Pa.

BUTLER, Rock LeRoy, supervising prin. of schs.; b. Wellsboro, Pa., Apr. 26, 1882; s. George F. and Lydia (Bacon) B.; student Wellsboro (Pa.) High Sch., 1897-99, State Normal Sch., Mansfield, Pa., 1900-02; B.S., Grove City (Pa.) Coll., 1923; M.S., Bucknell U., Lewisburg, Pa., 1937; m. Eleanor Sullivan, Aug. 4, 1910; 1 son, Dr. William Sullivan. Teacher of rural school, Delmar Twp., Tioga Co., Pa., 1899-1900; teacher, Liberty, Pa., 1902-03; teacher, Wellsboro (Pa.) High Sch., 1903-14; supervising prin., Wellsboro, Pa., since 1914. Dir. Green Free Library, Wellsboro; treas. Tioga Co. Children's Aid Soc.; pres. Tioga Co. Am. Red Cross. Mem. N.E.A., Am. Assn. Sch. Adminstrs., Pa. State Edn. Assn., Tioga Co. Teachers Assn. (pres.), Tioga Co. Schoolmen's Club (pres.), Kappa Phi Kappa. Republican. Methodist. Mason. Club: Rotary (Wellsboro, Pa.). Home: 20 Meade St. Office: Nichols St., Wellsboro, Pa.

BUTLER, Smedley Darlington, officer U.S. M.C.; b. West Chester, Pa., July 30, 1881; s. Thomas Stalker and Maud (Darlington) B.; Haverford Sch., 1898; m. Ethel C. Peters, June 30, 1905; children—Ethel Peters (wife of Lt. John Wehle, U.S. Marine Corps), Smedley Darlington, Thomas Richard. Appointed to U.S. M.C., Apr. 8, 1898; promoted through grades to col., Mar. 9, 1919; brig. gen. (temp.), 1918-21; brig. gen., March 5, 1921; maj. gen., July 5, 1929; retired, Oct. 1, 1931. Leave of absence to act as dir. Dept. of Safety, Phila., 1924-25. Served as comdr. Camp Pontanezen, Brest, France, Oct. 15, 1918-July 31, 1919. Awarded 2 congressional medals of honor, for capture of Vera Cruz, Mexico, 1914, and for capture of Ft. Riviere, Haiti, 1917; D.S.M. (U.S.), 1919. Quaker. Lecturer. Address: Goshen Rd., Newtown Square, Pa.

BUTLER, Will George, musician, violinist, composer, educator; b. Blossburg, Pa., Jan. 31, 1876; s. William Mitchell and Eliza (Putnam) B.; grad. State Teachers Coll., Mansfield, Pa., 1898; Mus.B., Chicago Musical Coll., 1899, Mus.M., 1900; Mus.D., Grand Conservatory of Music, New York, 1905; violin pupil of Eugene Ysaye, Samuel E. Jacobson, Hamlin E. Cogswell, John C. Bostleman, D. O. Putnam, Susie Sexton-Thomson; unmarried. Prof. of music and condr. of symphony orchestra, Kan. State Normal Sch., Emporia, 1898-1904; prof. of music, Williamsport (Pa.), Dickinson Sem., 1904-14; prof. of music and condr. symphony orchestra, Mansfield (Pa.) State Teachers Coll., 1914-38; concert work and supt. Swarthmore Chautauqua, 1922-24. Directed first all-state high school orchestra (200 musicians) before Pa. State Edn. Assn., 1935. Hon. mem. Sinfonia Fraternity; mem. State Hemlocks Assn. (vice-pres.), Kappa Delta Pi, Delphic. Republican. Baptist. Mason (K.T., 32°, Shriner), Odd Fellow. Composer of many works including "Long Live America" (official anthem George Washington Bi-centennial celebration), "Old Pennsylvania of Mine" (state hymn), "Mansfield, Hail" (alma mater song of Mansfield State Teachers Coll.), "Fair Dickinson" (song of Dickinson Sem.), "Visions of Oleona" (played by composer at Ole Bull celebration to 15,000, 1920). Poet; author (verse) Destiny and Songs of the Heart. Original musical manuscripts preserved in State Capitol,

Harrisburg. Honored by Resolution of Pa. Folk Lore Soc. as "greatest living Pennsylvania composer, best loved music master, preserver of Ole Bull saga and father of a school of music which will become the basis of the folk songs of the future," 1935. Home: "Maple Manor," Blossburg, Pa.

BUTLER, William Lawrence, ry. official; b. Bayard, O., Dec. 7, 1894; s. Edwin Ruthvin and Rebecca Ann (McGhee) B.; B.S. in C.E., U. of Pa., 1918, C.E., 1925; m. Helen Elizabeth Reinhold, June 6, 1919; 1 dau., Joan Amelia. Spl. engr. and asst. to pres. Chicago, Aurora & Elgin R.R., 1922-25; exec. vice-pres., then operating mgr. for receivers of Cincinnati & Lake Erie R.R. since 1926; exec. vice-pres. Phila. & Western R.R. since 1930; v.p. Conway Corp., Phila., since 1926; exec. v.p. Schuylkill Valley Lines since 1933; v.p. Hamilton City Lines (Hamilton, O.) and v.p. Cincinnati & Lake Erie Bus Co. since 1934; gen. mgr. Lima City (O.) Street Ry. Co. since 1936. Served as 2d lt. U.S.A., June-Dec. 1918. Mem. Am. Soc. C.E., Am. Soc. Automotive Engrs., Phila. Art Alliance, Phi Sigma Kappa. Republican: Club: Aronimink Golf (Newtown Square, Pa.). Home: 460 Brookfield Rd., Drexel Hill, Pa. Office: 715 Fidelity-Philadelphia Bldg., Philadelphia, Pa.

BUTLER, William Mill, editor, author; b. Rochester, N.Y., June 21, 1857; s. Theophilus and Mary (Miller) B.; ed. common schs. and Hyde Park Commercial Coll., Scranton, Pa.; m. Helen J. Perrine, Nov. 24, 1880 (died Dec. 7, 1932). Began career on Scranton Daily Times, in 1876; appointed city editor of Wilkes-Barre Daily Record, same year, but broke down from overwork; editor of Reformer, Galt, Ont., 1877-78; then, reporter, city editor and editor in chief Rochester Post-Express, 1879-86; also served as city editor and associate editor Rochester Democrat and Chronicle; editor Home Mag., Binghamton, 1896-97; chief foreign corr. dept., Phila. Commercial Mus., 1899-1900; vice-consul and acting consul gen. for Paraguay, at Phila., 1899-1902; pub. trade jours., N.Y. City, 1905-25; in chem. business, 1925-27. Active in urging humane treatment and sanitary care of dead on battlefields during World War (address on subject before the House Com. on Mil. Affairs officially pub.). Historian of Soc. of the Genesee, N.Y., since 1913. Mem. A.A.A.S., Rochester Hist. Soc., N.Y. Zoöl. Soc. (life). Ind. Republican. Mason (32°, Shriner), K.P., Knight Golden Eagle. Author: Pantaletta (a satire on the woman's rights question), 1882; The Whist Reference Book, 1898; History of Paraguay, 1900 (awarded vote of thanks by Congress of Paraguay and $500 for this history); Democracy and Other Poems, 1920 (Democracy reprinted in 6,000 daily and weekly newspapers and set to music, in competition, by 12 Am. composers); The Sea-Serpent (comic opera), 1920; (monograph) The Human Eye Color, 1934; Rough-Riding on Olympus, A Bully Biography of Theodore Roosevelt, 1937; The Moonlight Oracle, 1939. Contributor to Centennial History of Rochester and Dictionary of American Biography. Visited South America and reported to State Dept. of U.S. a tentative offer of subsidy for a direct steamship line to Paraguay; trapped a jaguar (said to be the largest ever brought to this country) and presented it for display in New York Zoöl. Park, 1901. In 1934, N.Y. Supreme Court declared him sole and exclusive owner of Necrosan, of which U.S. Govt. had used $150,000 worth while bringing home soldier dead from Europe; still retains one-third interest. Address: Elmwood and Boyden Avs., Maplewood, N.J.

BUTT, Howard, mech. engr.; b. Sandusky, O., Apr. 9, 1890; s. Richard L. and Mary E. (Jordan) B.; M.E., Ala. Poly. Inst., 1908; m. Sally Ware, Nov. 13, 1919. City engr. in design and construction power houses, water works, etc., 1908-12; mech. engr. Babcock & Wilcox Co., N.Y. City, 1912-18, Riley Stoker Corpn., 1920-27, Rust Engring. Co., 1918-20, Air Preheater Corpn., 1927-30, Wm. Powell Co. since 1930. Mem. Am. Soc. Mech. Engrs., Iron and Steel Inst., Phi Delta Theta. Republican. Episcopalian. Clubs: Engineers, Downtown Athletic, Phi Delta Theta (New York); Spring Brook Golf (Morristown, N.J.). Home: Spring Brook Road, Morristown, N.J. Office: 50 Church St., New York, N.Y.

BUTT, William Edward, prof. econs.; b. Woodburn, Ind., Jan. 3, 1888; s. James Franklin and Lucretia (Johnson) B.; ed. Ind. Univ., 1907-09; A.B., U. of Wis., 1911, A.M., same, 1914; ed. Yale U., 1923-24, Ph.D., same, 1931; m. Inga Olson, Sept. 9, 1913; children—Olin Franklin, Althea (Mrs. S. Bruce Gilliard). Engaged as instr. econs., U. of Ky., 1913-14, asst. prof., 1914-20; asst. prof. econs., Pa. State Coll., 1920-27, asso. prof., 1927-32, prof. econs. since 1932. Mem. Am. Econ. Assn., Nat. Tax Assn., Am. Statis. Assn., Acacia. Democrat. Mason. Home: 118 W. Nittany Av., State College, Pa.

BUTTENHEIM, Harold S(inley), editor; b. Brooklyn, N.Y., Apr. 8, 1876; s. Joseph Harold and Margaret M. (Collier) B.; Jersey City (N.J.) High Sch., 1888-91; m. Margaret E., d. William O. Stoddard, Oct. 9, 1906. Associated with various trade and technical journals, 1893-1911; disposed of interests in 1911, and organized, with bro., Edgar J., The Civic Press (now the Am. City Mag. Corpn.), pubs. The American City Magazine, of which is editor; organized, 1913, The Am. City Bur. for promoting efficiency of civic and welfare orgns.; chmn. bd. Am. City Bur., Inc.; chmn. bd. Am. City Mag. Corpn. Dir. Nat. Campaign which raised over $3,000,000 for War Camp Community Service, 1917. Pres. Tax Policy League; pres. Am. Soc. of Planning Officials; pres. Citizens' Housing Council of N.Y.; chmn. Zoning Bd. of Adjustment (Madison, N.J.); dir. Am. Planning and Civic Assn., Nat. Child Welfare Assn, Civic Films, Inc.; hon. mem. Am. Inst. of Planners. Clubs: City (trustee), Nat. Arts (New York); Cosmos (Washington, D.C.). Home: Madison, N.J. Office: 470 4th Av., New York, N.Y.

BUTTERFIELD, Thomas Edward, univ. prof.; b. Jersey City, N.J., June 12, 1873; s. James and Jane (Williams) B.; M.E., Stevens Inst. Tech., Hoboken, N.J., 1895; C.E., Rensselaer Poly. Inst., Troy, N.Y., 1897; m. Susie Parker Palmer, Aug. 12, 1913; children—Thomas, John, Angelyn, Elizabeth. Asso. with Otto Gas Engine Works, Phila., 1898-1911, chief engr., 1906-11; asso. with Lehigh U., Bethlehem, Pa., since 1912, now prof. heat power engring. Served as capt., U.S. Army, 1917, maj., Coast Arty., 1918, mem. Arty. Bd., 1918. Fellow A.A.A.S.; asso. fellow Inst. of Aero. Sciences; mem. Am. Soc. M.E. (1st sec. Lehigh Valley Sect.), Soc. for Promotion of Engring. Edn., Am. Assn. Univ. Profs., Am. Legion (post comdr. Bethlehem Post, 1920), Pi Tau Sigma, Sigma Xi (pres. Lehigh U. Chapter 1938-39). Clubs: Engineers of Lehigh Valley (instrumental in orgn., 1921; mem. bd. mgrs. and successively sec., treas., v.p. and pres, Faculty Educational of Lehigh U. (pres. 1923; Bethlehem, Pa.). Author: Heat Engines, 1924; Steam and Gas Engineering, 1929, 2d edit., 1933, 3d edit., 1938; also various papers. Address: 41 W. Church St., Bethlehem, Pa.

BUTTERWECK, Joseph Seibert, educator; b. Allentown, Pa., Oct. 9, 1891; s. Wesley and Alice Jane (Seibert) B.; B.S., Univ. of Pa., 1922, M.A., 1924; Ph.D., Teachers College (Columbia University), 1926; m. Reba Godfrey, November 7, 1917; children—Marjorie Mary, Janet Marion; m. 2d, Grace Otto Thomas, Jan. 22, 1937; 1 son, Joseph Sebring. Teacher of science, Moorestown (N.J.) High Sch., 1910-14; real estate business, Camden and Moorestown, 1914-18; teacher of science, Media (Pa.) High Sch., 1918-20, prin., 1920-22; prin. Haddon Heights (N.J.) High Sch., 1922-24; asst. in research, Lincoln Sch., Columbia, 1925-26; asst. prof. of edn., Temple U., Phila., 1926-30, prof. edn. and dir. dept. of secondary edn. since 1930. Mem. N.E.A., Progressive Edn. Assn., Pa. State Edn. Assn., Phi Delta Kappa. Democrat. Baptist. Clubs: Manufacturers and Bankers. Schoolmen's of Pa. Author: Problem of Teaching High School Pupils How to Study, 1926; Orientation Course in Education (with J. C. Seegers), 1933; manual for classroom teachers (with George Muzzey, 1938). Contbr. to mags. Home: 115 W. Hortter St., Germantown, Philadelphia, Pa. Address: Temple University, Philadelphia, Pa.

BUTTERWORTH, Gordon, lawyer; b. Phila., Pa., Oct. 9, 1890; s. George and Marie Louisa (Yundt) B.; A.B., Northeast High Sch., 1908; A.B., Temple U., Phila., 1911, LL.B., Law Sch., 1915; m. Elsa Leslie Evans, June 20, 1916; 1 dau., Elsa Jane. Employed as sec. to Dr. Adam Geibel (blind musician and composer), 1909-11; studied in law office Rambo, Rambo and Mair, 1911-14; admitted to Pa. bar, 1914 and since engaged in gen. practice of law at Phila.; asso. with firm Rambo and Mair; admitted to practice before Pa. Superior and Supreme cts. and Federal cts.; dir. and counsel Overlook Hills Bldg. & Loan Assn., Torresdale Constructive Bldg. & Loan Assn., East Germantown Bldg. & Loan Assn.; trustee A. M. Kelch Bequest. Candidate for Pa. Senate on Rep. ticket, 1928. Trustee Temple U. Alumni Assn. of Montgomery Co., N.E. High Sch. Alumni Assn. Mem. Phila. Law Assn. Republican. Presbyn. (trustee Abington Ch.). Mason. Club: Penn Athletic (Phila.). Asso. in compilation of Bispham's Equity Practices. Home: Abington. Office: 1500 Walnut St., Philadelphia, Pa.

BUTTON, Forrest Clifton, prof. dairy manufactures; b. Fredonia, N.Y., July 22, 1894; s. George I. and Hattie E. (Babcock) B.; B.S., Cornell U. Coll. of Agr., 1916; M.S., Cornell U. Grad. Sch., 1926; m. Maie F. Livermore, Aug. 26, 1919; 1 son, Forrest C., Jr. Grad. asst. dept. dairy industry, Cornell U., 1917-18; san. inspr. U.S. Pub. Health Service, 1918; instr. dairy manufactures, Rutgers U., N.J. State Coll. of Agr. and Agrl. Expt. Sta., 1918-24, asst. prof., Rutgers U., 1924-28, asso. prof., 1928-34, prof. dairy manufactures since 1934. Mem. Am. Dairy Sci. Assn., Kappa Phi, Delta Sigma Phi, Sigma Xi. Independent Republican. Presbyn. Mason. Home: 308 Grant Av., New Brunswick, N.J.

BUTTS, Allison, metallurgist; b. Poughkeepsie, N.Y., Apr. 26, 1890; s. Allison and Arrie Elizabeth (Mosher) B.; student Riverview Mil. Acad., 1901-07; A.B., Princeton, 1911; S.B., Mass. Inst. of Tech., 1913; m. Charlotte Beatrice Rogers, July 31, 1918 (died Oct. 4, 1920); 1 son, Philip Guernsey; m. 2d, Eva Lillian Rogers, June 17, 1924; 1 dau., Virginia Jane. Smelter foreman U.S. Metals Refining Co., 1913-14, research chemist, 1914-16; asst. in metallurgy, Lehigh U., 1916-17, instr., 1917-20, asst. prof., 1920-28, asso. prof, 1928-38, prof. since 1938. Dir. Baby Health Station of Bethlehem, Pa., 1923-27. Mem. Am. Inst. Mining and Metall. Engrs. (chmn. Lehigh Valley sect. 1932, sec. since 1937), Electrochemical Soc., Am. Soc. for Metals, Inst. of Metals of Great Britain, Soc. for Promotion of Engring. Edn. (sec. div. of Mineral Technology since 1937), Sigma Xi. Presbyterian (pres. bd. of trustees 1st Ch., Bethlehem, Pa., 1930-32). Club: Engineers of the Lehigh Valley. Editor: Methods in Nonferrous Metallurgical Analysis. Author: Textbook of Metallurgical Problems, 1932; Engineering Metallurgy (with Prof Bradley Stoughton), 1926. Contbr. scientific articles to tech. mags.; asso. editor The Mineral Industry, 1916-27; spl. editor on metallurgy 2d edit. Webster's New Internat. Dictionary. Home: 1343 Montrose Av., Bethlehem, Pa.

BUTTS, Donald Charles A., bacteriologist, educator; b. Camden, N.J., May 11, 1897; s. William Henry and Dora Agusta (MacDonald) B.; B.S., Phila. Coll Pharmacy and Science, 1934, M.S., 1935, D.Sc., 1937; h. Kathryn Weekes Baughman, Sept. 7, 1938. Dir. Emery Lab. of Cancer Research, Hahnemann Med. Coll. and St. Luke's Hosp., Phila., 1923-36; dir. Lab. of Exptl. Immunology, St. Luke's Hosp., 1937; dir. Butts Labs., consulting work in bacteriology, chemistry, pharmacology, Phila., since 1938; prof. of pharmacology, Pa. State Coll. of Optometry, Phila., since 1937. Served with Chem. Warfare Service, U.S. Army, during World War. Fellow A.A.A.S., Am. Inst. of Chemists; mem. Soc. Am. Bacteriologists, Am. Pub. Health Assn., Am. Soc. Tropical Medicine; corr. mem. Argentine Soc. for Study of Cancer. Life mem. Masonic order. Home: 4300 Spruce St. Office: 6 S. 39th St., Philadelphia, Pa.

BUTTS, Henry Pemberton, lawyer; b. Charleston, W.Va., July 24, 1901; s. J. Fleetwood and Ida (Pemberton) B.; student U. of Pa., 1921-22; LL.B., W.Va. Univ. Law Sch., Morgantown, 1925; m. Catherine C. Stahlman, Dec. 27, 1935; 1 dau., Catherine Carroll. Admitted to W.Va. bar, 1925, and since engaged in gen. practice of law at Charleston; mem. firm Clark, Woodrow & Butts since 1933; dir. Nat. Bank of Commerce of Charleston, W.Va. Mem. Charleston and W.Va. bar assns., Sigma Chi, Phi Delta Phi. Republican. Elk. Club: Pioneer. Home: Malden Rd. Office: Union Bldg., Charleston, W.Va.

BUTZ, Charles Allabar, clergyman; b. Alburtis, Pa., Mar. 14, 1874; s. William and Hannah Floranda (Fegely) B.; prep. edn. Kutztown State Normal Sch.; A.B., A.M., Ursinus Coll., Collegeville, Pa., 1899; student Ursinus Sch. of Theology, 1899-1902; Ph.D., Central U., Indianapolis, 1919; student sociology U. of Pa., 1901-02; art student Albright Coll., 1907-08; m. Jennie Bertha Fritch, Apr. 28, 1904; children—Geraldine Euroma (Mrs. Christian Eurich), Althea Fritch (Mrs. Lloyd Long), Charles Albert Fritch. Ordained to ministry of Evangelical and Reformed Church, 1902; pastor Towamensing Charge, Carbon Co., Pa., 1902-05; Bethel Charge, Lebanon Co., Pa., 1905-08, Zion-Dryland Charge, Northampton Co., Pa., since 1908; teacher public schools, Bethlehem Twp., Pa., 1918-27; guidance dir. Sociology and Missions, Central U., Indianapolis, Ind., 1923-30. Pres. and historian Butz Family Assn., 1912-38; del. to Gen. Synod of Reformed Ch., 1926; pres. East Pa. Classis, 1921-22; director Interchurch World Movement, Northampton Co. Mem. Sons Am. Revolution (chaplain Valley Forge Chapter since 1929), Pa.-German Folk Lore Soc., Huguenot Society of Pa., Lebanon County Historical Society (former v.p.), Nat. Geog. Society, Lehigh Valley Ministerium of Reformed Ch.; Bethlehem Ministerium. Knights of Malta, Woodmen of the World, Odd Fellow. Genealogist of John Butz, Christian Fegely, Daniel Schmoyer, Peter Keiser, Philip Dresher, Philip Basters, Peter Diener, and others; artist (oil, water color, pastel), poet. Author: Songs and Praises, 1930; The Reformation Movement, 1914-16; History of East Pa. Classis of Ref. Ch. (1820-1939); Social Ramifications or Social Problems of Today; (MSS.) Genesis and Unfolding of Human Thot to the Time of Christ (MSS.); sketches of various chs. Contbr. to newspapers and church papers, contbr. Verses to Christmas Cavalcade of Verse, 1938; 1939 Rhythm and Rhyme; The Fair's Mart of Verse, 1939. Contbr. to Nat. Geneal. Soc. Publisher Church Herald, 1904-21. Home: 1337 Montrose Av., Bethlehem, Pa.

BUTZ, Reuben Jacob, lawyer, banker; b. Butzdale, Lehigh Co., Pa., Jan. 13, 1867; s. Reuben D. and Mary A. Butz; grad. high sch., Allentown, 1883; A.B., Muhlenberg Coll., Allentown, 1887, A.M., 1890; LL.D., Franklin and Marshall Coll., 1925; SS.D., Muhlenberg Coll., 1938; m. D. Florence Horn, June 11, 1914; children—Mary S., Ruth. Admitted to Pa. bar, 1889, practicing at Allentown; mem. firm Butz, Steckel & Rupp; pres. Allentown Nat. Bank since 1913. Chmn. Liberty Loan Drive, Lehigh Co., World War. Pres. bd. trustees Muhlenberg Coll. since 1913; ex-pres. board Cedar Crest College, Allentown, Pa.; mem. bd. of trustees Allentown Hosp. since 1920, Theol. Sem. of Reformed Ch. at Lancaster, Pa. Mem. Allentown Chamber Commerce (first pres.), Phi Gamma Delta. Republican. Mem. Reformed Ch. in U.S. Mason (32°), Elk. Clubs: Livingston, Lehigh Country. Home: 1629 Hamilton St. Office: Allentown National Bank Bldg., Allentown, Pa.

BUZZARD, Josiah F.; chief otolaryngologist Mercy Hosp. Address: 1110 13th Av., Altoona, Pa.

BYAM, Edwin Colby, univ. prof.; b. Chelmsford, Mass., Sept. 22, 1898; s. Lyman Andrew and Grace Maria (Hutchins) B.; student Chelmsford (Mass.) High Sch., 1912-16; A.B., Boston U. Coll. of Liberal Arts, 1920, A.M., Harvard Grad. Sch., 1921; student Université de Paris (Sorbonne), France, 1921-23, Centro de Estudios Históricos, Madrid, Spain, summer 1925, U. of Chicago, 1926; student Johns Hopkins U., 1926-27, Ph.D., 1936; unmarried. Instr. modern langs., Carnegie Inst. Tech., 1923-25; asso. prof. modern langs., U. of Del., Newark, Del., 1925-37, prof. since 1937, acting head dept. modern langs., 1926, 1929-37, head dept. since 1937. Served in Boston S.A.T.C., Oct.-Dec. 1918. Mem. Modern Lang. Assn. of America, Assn. of Teachers of French, Assn. of Teachers of Spanish, Sigma Alpha Epsilon, Phi Beta Kappa, Phi Kappa Phi. Awarded First Augustus Howe Buck Scholarship, Boston U., 1917; named Officier d'Académie (France), 1929, Chevalier de la Légion d'Honneur, 1934. Republican. Baptist. Mason. Address: U. of Delaware, Newark, Del.

BYCROFT, John Seymour Jr., banker; b. Sharon, Pa., Oct. 25, 1891; s. John Seymour and Anna (McKay) B.; student Sharon (Pa.) Pub. Schs., 1897-1905, Sharon (Pa.) High Sch., 1905-09; m. Mary Augusta Phillips, Feb. 18, 1922; 1 dau., Mary Jane. Began as clk., Carnegie Steel Co., Farrell, Pa., 1909-11; clk. McDowell Nat. Bank, Sharon, Pa., 1911-19, asst. cashier, 1919-24, cashier, 1924-27, v.p. and cashier since 1927, director since 1938. Served as 2d lt. Inf., U.S. Army, 1917-18. Dir. and pres. Sharon (Pa.) Sch. Dist. since 1934. Pres. Sharon (Pa.) chapter Am. Inst. of Banking, sec. and treas. group No. 7 Pa. Bankers Assn., Sharon Clearing House Assn.; treas. Mercer Co. Bankers Assn.; mem. Sharon (Pa.) Chamber of Commerce, Financial Advertisers Assn. (Chicago). Republican. Episcopalian. Mason (32°, Shriner), Elk. Clubs: Good Samaritan, Country, Ten Year, Mercer Co. Bridge (Sharon, Pa.), Sharon Social Fishing (Sharon, Pa. and Beaumaris, Can.); Youngstown (O.) City; Pittsburgh (Pa.) Bankers. Home: 150 Euclid Av. Office: McDowell Nat. Bank, Sharon, Pa.

BYE, Raymond Taylor, univ. prof.; b. Germantown, Phila., Pa., Jan. 30, 1892; s. Andrew Moore and May (Taylor) B.; student George Sch., 1904-10; A.B., Swarthmore (Pa.) Coll., 1914; A.M., Harvard, 1915; Ph.D., U. of Pa., 1918; m. Virginia Lippincott Higgins, Sept. 7, 1922; children—Doris Lippincott, Elinor Taylor, Florence Thorne. Instr. economics, U. of Pa., 1916-20, asst. prof., 1920-26, prof. since 1926. Chmn. race relations sect., Am. Friends Service Com., 1926-29. Mem. Am. League to Abolish Capital Punishment, Am. Civil Liberties Union. Soc. of Friends. Author: Capital Punishment in the United States, 1919; Principles of Economics, 1924; co-author: Applied Economics (with W. W. Hewett), 1928; Getting and Earning (with R. H. Blodgett), 1937; miscellaneous articles. Home: Moylan, Pa. Office: University of Pa., Philadelphia, Pa.

BYERLY, John Lester, pres. Union Nat. Bank; b. Ohl, Pa., July 4, 1892; s. Emmanuel F. and Mary Elizabeth (Burkett) B.; student Clarion (Pa.) Normal Sch.; m. July 14, 1914 (wife deceased); 1 dau., Kathryn L. Teacher pub. schs., 1911-14; store clk. and salesman, 1914-22; engaged in selling gen. store mdse., Summerville, Pa., 1922-38; dealer in John Deere farm equipment and tractors, Summerville, Pa., since 1934; pres. Union Nat. Bank, Summerville, since 1934. Mason. Home: Ohl, Pa. Office: R.F.D. 1, Summerville, Pa.

BYERS, John Frederic, mfr.; b. Edgeworth, Pa., Aug. 6, 1881; s. Alexander MacBurney and Martha (Fleming) B.; grad. St. Paul's Sch., Concord, N.H., 1900; B.A. from Yale University, 1904; m. Caroline Mitchell Morris, Dec. 6, 1905 (she died Nov. 14, 1934); children—Alexander M. III, John Frederic, Nancy Lee, Buckley Morris. Chmn. bd. A. M. Byers Co., Pittsburgh; dir. Union Nat. Bank (Pittsburgh), Union Savings Bank, Union Trust Co. (both of Pittsburgh), Westinghouse Air Brake Co., Union Switch & Signal Co., Western Allegheny R.R. Co. Trustee Carnegie Inst., Carnegie Inst. of Technology and Carnegie Library (all of Pittsburgh). Republican. Presbyterian. Clubs: Pittsburgh, Duquesne, Allegheny Country (Pittsburgh); Racquet and Tennis, Brook, Links (New York); Nat. Golf Links, Deepdale Golf. Home: Sewickley, Pa.

BYRD, Harry Clifton, univ. pres.; b. Crisfield, Md., Feb. 12, 1889; s. William Franklin and Sallie May (Sterling) B.; B.S., U. of Md., 1908; post grad. study, George Washington U. and Georgetown University (law), Western Md. Coll.; m. Katherine Turnbull, Dec. 27, 1913; children—Harry Clifton, Evelyn Westover, William, Sterling. Instr. English and history, U. of Md., 1912-13, dir. athletics, and football coach, 1913-34, asst. to pres., 1918-32, v.p., 1932-35, actg. pres., July 1935-Feb. 22, 1936, pres. since Feb., 1936. Dir. Hyattsville Realty Co.; mem. state com. Pub. Works Administrn., Md.; mem. Draft Bd., World War; trustee, Longfellow Sch. for Boys. Mem. Phi Kappa Phi, Pi Delta Epsilon, Omicron Delta Kappa. Democrat. Methodist. Mason (Shriner). Clubs: University (Washington, D.C.); University, Chesapeake (Baltimore); Rotary; Vansville Farmers' (Md.). Home: College Park, Md.

BYRER, Harry Hopkins, lawyer; b. Philippi, W.Va., Apr. 20, 1877; s. Frederick Samuel and Isabella (Woods) B.; student W.Va. Wesleyan Coll., 1897-1900; studied law in law-office of J. H. Woods, Philippi, W.Va., 1900-02; admitted to W.Va. bar, 1902; in gen. practice, 1902-09, and since 1922; pros. atty. Barbour Co., W.Va., 1909-14; asst. U.S. atty., Northern Dist. W.Va., 1914-22; B.&O. R.R. Co. since 1936. Trustee W.Va. Wesleyan Coll., 1910-19. Mem. Am. Bar Assn., W.Va. Bar Assn. (pres.), Berkeley Co. Bar Assn. Club: Rotary (past pres.). Democrat. Methodist. Address: Martinsburg, W.Va.

BYRNE, Amanda Austin; b. Lewisburg, W.Va., Apr. 28, 1866; d. Dr. Samuel Hunter and Mary Copeland (MacPherson) Austin; student Lewisburg Female Inst. (now Greenbrier Coll. for Women), 1875-84; m. William Eston Randolph Byrne, June 12, 1889; children—George Austin, Marie Louise (Mrs. Lester L. Sheets), Barbara Linn (Mrs. Daniel N. Mohler), Charlotte Virginia (Mrs. Robt. B. Mesmer), William Eston Randolph. Long active in United Daughters of the Confederacy, pres. Charleston chapter, 1924-27, pres. W.Va. div., 1917-22, corr. sec. gen., 1919-21, recording sec. gen., 1922-23, 1st v.p. gen., 1925-27, pres. gen., 1931-33; pres. Charleston Y.W.C.A., 1926-31; registrar Nat. Soc. Colonial Dames Resident in W.Va., 1904-36, became pres., 1936. Pres. Woman's Auxiliary Synod of W.Va. Presbyn. Ch. U.S., 1934-36. Democrat. Clubs: Charleston Women's (pres. 1931-32), Charleston Women's Democratic, Women's Kanawha Literary. Home: 1422 Quarrier St., Charleston, W.Va.*

BYRNE, Joseph M., Jr., pres. Merchants & Mfrs. Fire Ins. Co. Address: 45 Clinton St., Newark, N.J.

BYRNE, Sister Marie José, college dean; b. New York, N.Y., Aug. 13, 1876; d. George Philip and Louise Abigail (Kingsland) Byrne; A.B., Coll. of St. Elizabeth, Convent, N.J., 1902; A.M., Columbia, 1909, Ph.D., 1915; mem. Sisters of Charity. Instr. Greek and Latin, Coll. of St. Elizabeth, 1902-05 and 1906-08, prof. Latin and Greek, 1910-21, dean since 1921. Mem. Am. Assn. of Univ. Women, Nat. Assn. of Deans of Women, N.E.A., Classical League, Classical Assn. of Atlantic States. Translator: Considerations on Eternity (from Latin), 1920. Author: Prolegomena to an Edition of Decimus Magnus Ausonius, 1916. Address: College of St. Elizabeth, Convent Station, N.J.

BYRNSIDE, Marshall Azariah, lawyer; b. Boone Co., W.Va., June 29, 1878; s. Manasseh and Pharlenia (Casdorph) B.; student Marshall Coll., Huntington, W.Va., 1897-98, W.Va. Univ., Morgantown, W.Va., 1899-1900; m. Essie Hill, Jan. 15, 1902; children—Lois (Mrs. John Milne), John, George, Fred, Eunice (Mrs. W. A. Benfield, Jr.). Admitted to W.Va. bar, 1900, and since engaged in gen. practice of law at Madison; cashier Boone County Bank, 1918 to 1929; vice-pres. Boone Nat. Bank since 1929; dir. Madison Memorial. Trustee Kanawha Coll., Charleston, W.Va. Republican. Baptist. Writer of poetry. Club: Country (Madison). Home: Madison, W.Va.

BYRON, Robert J.; mem. law firm Byron, Longbotton, Pape & O'Brien. Office: Stephen Girard Bldg., Philadelphia, Pa.

C

CABEEN, David Clark, educator; b. Baraboo, Wis., June 24, 1886; s. Charles William and Sarah Amelia (Clark) C.; A.B., Syracuse U., 1908; A.M., Cornell U., 1919; Ph.D., U. of Pa., 1923; m. Violet Abbott, Sept. 2, 1922. Instr. in French, Dartmouth Coll., 1915-16, Cornell U., 1916-17, 1919, U. of Pa., 1919-23; asst. prof. French, Williams Coll., 1923-25; head of dept. Romance langs., Vanderbilt, 1925-38; acting prof. of French, U. of Cincinnati, 1938. Mem. 7th Inf., N.Y.N.G., 1913-15; with Am. Ambulance Corps in France, 1916; commd. 2nd Lt., adj. gen. dept., U.S.A., Aug. 15, 1917; served in France and Italy, Oct., 1917-Dec., 1918. Mem. Modern Lang. Assn., Am. Assn. Teachers of French, Phi Gamma Delta. Author: The African Novels of Louis Bertrand, 1923. Editor: Critical Bibliography of 18th Century French Lit., 1938—. Contbr. Publs. Modern Lang. Assn.; French Review, etc. Home: 716 Edmonds Av., Drexel Hill, Pa.

CABELL, Charles A.; pres. Carbon Fuel Co.; officer or dir. several companies. Home: 2104 Kanawha St., Charleston, W. Va. Office: Carbon, W.Va.

CADBURY, Benjamin, plumbing and heating supplies; b. Phila., Pa., Oct. 14, 1873; s. Joel and Anna Kaighn (Lowry) C.; prep. edn. William Penn Charter Sch., Phila., 1883-88, Spring Garden Inst., Phila., 1889; A.B., Haverford (Pa.) Coll., 1892, A.M., 1893; m. Anna M. Moore, Nov. 4, 1909; children—Joseph Moore, Benjamin Bartram. Began as filing clerk, 1893, with Haines, Jones & Cadbury Co., Phila., and has since continued with them and successor, Hajoca Corpn., Phila., wholesale plumbing and heating supplies; now sec. Overseer William Penn Charter Sch.; clerk of com. of management Friends Select Sch., Phila. Republican. Mem. Soc. of Friends. Home: 260 E. Main St., Moorestown, N.J. Office: 31st and Walnut Sts., Philadelphia, Pa.

CADBURY, William Edward, investment banker; b. Germantown, Phila., Pa., June 25, 1881; s. John W. and Rebecca (Warner) C.; prep. edn. Germantown Friends Sch., Phila., 1885-97; A.B. and A.M., Haverford (Pa.) Coll., 1902; m. Mary Yarnall Brown, May 31, 1905; children—Elizabeth Willits, William Edward, Eleanor. In wholesale grain business, 1902-08; advertising agency, 1909-11; since 1911 with Cadbury, Ellis & Haines, Phila., investment securities, now Cadbury, Ellis & Co.; mgr. Mine Hill and Schuylkill Haven R.R. Mgr. Friends Hosp., Frankford, Pa.; trustee Germantown Preparative Meeting of Friends. Mem. Soc. of Friends. Home: 408 Woodlawn Av., Germantown. Office: 1420 Walnut St., Philadelphia, Pa.

CADDEN, Anthony Vandril, M.D.; b. Midland, Md., July 23, 1903; s. John F. and S. Maitland (Sharp) C.; B.S., W.Va. U., 1927; M.D., Harvard U., 1929; m. Ella M. Cunningham, Nov. 14, 1931; children—Anthony V., John F. Began as messenger boy B.&O. R.R., Keyser, W. Va., 1916, check clk., 1917-19, weighmaster, 1919-22; resident physician Am. Legion Hosp., Battle Creek, Mich., 1930; asst. supt. Oakland Co. Sanitarium, Pontiac, Mich., 1931; staff physician, Michigan State Sanatorium, Howell, Mich., 1932-34; supt. and med. dir. Hopemont Sanatorium, Hopemont, W.Va., since 1934. Dir. W.Va. Tuberculosis and Health Assn.; mem. A.M.A., Coll. Physicians, W.Va. Med. Assn., Preston Co. Med. Soc., Phi Beta Pi (hon.). Democrat. Club: Preston Country. Contbr. to W.Va. Med. Jour., Am. Review of Tuberculosis and Tuberele (London, Eng.). Address: Hopemont, W.Va.

CADE, Seeley, pres. Jersey City Real Estate Board. Address: Jersey City, N.J.

CADOT, John Julius, plant manager; b. Salina, Kan., June 10, 1889; s. Will Cruzet and Fanny (Berks) C.; student Howe (Ind.) Mil. Sch., 1906-09; E.M., Colo. Sch. of Mines, Golden, Colo., 1915; m. India R. Drumhiller, Jan. 17, 1914. Began as miner, Homestake Mining Co., Lead, S.D., 1914; with various mining camps of S.D., Colo., and Ariz., Detroit Copper Co., Ariz. Copper Co., Hardinge Co., Inc., Salt Lake City, U., and Denver, Colo.; v.p. and treas. Hardinge Co., Inc., since 1922; v.p., treas. and works mgr. Steacy Schmidt Mfg. Co., York, Pa., since 1920. Served as 1st lt. Air Service, U.S. Army during World War; overseas in airplane mfr. Mem. Am. Inst. Mining Engrs., Sigma Nu. Republican. Episcopalian. Mason (32°, Shriner, K.T.). Clubs: Lafayette, Country, Rotary (York, Pa.). Home: 172 Peyton Rd. Office: Hardinge Co., Steacy Schmidt Mfg. Co., York, Pa.

CADWALADER, Thomas Francis, lawyer; b. nr. Jenkintown, Pa., Sept. 22, 1880; s. John and Mary Helen (Fisher) C.; student Episcopal Acad., Phila., Pa., 1889-96, St. Paul's Sch., Concord, N.H., 1896-97; A.B., U. of Pa., 1901; LL.B., U. of Md., 1903; m. Elizabeth Middleton Read, Nov. 23, 1911; children—Thomas Francis, Mary Helen, Anne Cleland, Benjamin Read. Admitted to Md. bar, 1903; practiced as sr. partner Cadwalader & Whitman, later Cadwalader, Whitman & Mason, Baltimore, 1903-16; practiced alone since 1919; trustee or agt. of various estates, individuals and charitable funds administered in Phila.; dir. Baltimore & Phila. Steamboat Co., 1904-35, pres., 1930-35. Served on Mexican border with Troop A, First Md. Cav. and in 5th Md. Inf.; mem. First R.O. T.C., Ft. Myer, Va., 1917; 2d lieut. cav., 1st lt. and capt. field arty., Camp Lee and Camp Zachary Taylor. Trustee U. of Pa., Hannah More Acad. (Reisterstown, Md.), St. Paul's Sch. for Boys (Mt. Washington, Md.), Church Home and Infirmary of City of Baltimore, Family Welfare Assn. Mem. Md. State, Harford County and Baltimore City bar assns., Delta Phi, Phi Beta Kappa. Episcopalian. Clubs: University (Phila.); Bachelors Cotillon. Home: The Mound, R.F.D., Joppa, Md. Office: Maryland Trust Bldg., Baltimore, Md.

CADWALADER, Williams Biddle, physician; b. Phila., Pa., July 9, 1876; s. Richard McCall and Christine (Biddle) C.; grad. St. Paul's Sch., Concord, N.H., 1894; student Princeton U., 1894-96; M.D., U. of Pa., 1902; m. Mildred Lee Biddle, Oct. 29, 1902; 1 dau., Christine Biddle (Mrs. Barclay Scull). Lab. asst. Pa. Hosp., 1902-05; post grad. work, U. of Vienna and U. of Munich, 1906-07; asst. to S. Weir Mitchell, M.D., in his private practice, Phila., 1906-13; ward service and dispensary Orthopædic Hosp. and Infirmary for Nervous Diseases, Phila., 1905-17; practice limited to neurology and psychiatry; with U. of Pa. since 1908, asst. in neuropatholoy and asst. instr. in neurology, 1911-12, inst., 1912-21, asso. in neurology and neuropathology, 1922-23, asst. prof., 1923-25, asst. prof. of neurology and neuropathology, 1925-29, prof. clin. neurology, 1929; on med. staffs of Bryn Mawr and Presbyn. Hosps. since 1920; dir. Mutual Assurance Co. Served as mem. 1st Troop, Phila. City Cav., during Spanish-Am. War in Porto Rico, May-Nov. 1898; mustered into service for World War, May 15, 1917; 1st lt. as neurologist to Base Hosp. No. 10, attached to Brit. Army, at La Treport, France, Feb. 1918, transferred to Base Hosp. No. 10, Chaumont, France; Apr. 1918, consultant in neuropsychiatry, Savenay and Nantes; July 1918, maj. as jr. consultant in neuropsychiatry, A.E.F., Neuchateau, France; disch. Feb. 19, 1919. Fellow Coll. of Physicians of Phila.; mem. Am. Neurol. Assn. (pres. 1938), Zoöl. Soc. of Phila. (pres. since 1926), Assn. for Research in Nervous and Mental Diseases, Phila. Neurol. Soc. (pres. 1917, 1930), Phila. Co. Med. Soc., Pa. State Med. Soc., Phila. Psychiatric Soc., A.M.A., Acad. Natural Sciences of Phila., Am. Soc. Mammalogists, Colonial Wars Soc., Delta Psi. Republican. Episcopalian. Clubs: Philadelphia, Ivy, Rabbit, Swiftwater Preserve, Parkside Angling Assn., Boone and Crockett (asso.). Author: Diseases of the Spinal Cord, 1932; contbr. many papers on neurol. subjects to med. jours. Home: Villa Nova, Pa. Office: 133 S. 36th St., Philadelphia, Pa.

CADWALLADER, James Albert, engineer; b. Milton, Pa., Oct. 9, 1889; s. Albert and Anna Louise (Supplee) C.; student Milton (Pa.) High Sch., 1902-06; B.S. in E.E., U. of Pa., 1912; m. Mary Elizabeth Schreyer, July 3, 1912; children—James Albert, Florence May. Student engr., gen. engring. dept. Bell Telephone Co. of Pa., Phila., 1912-15; field engr., Harrisburg, Pa., 1915-18; div. transmission engr., Harrisburg, Pa., 1918-21; asst. transmission engr., Phila., 1921-22; div. transmission engr., Pittsburgh, 1922-25; div. plant engr., Pittsburgh, 1925-26; engr. of transmission and outside plant, Pittsburgh, since 1926. Mem. Am. Inst. Elec. Engrs. (chmn. Pittsburgh section, 1929-30; sec. Middle Eastern Dist., 1929-31), Engrs. Soc. of Western Pa. (chmn. elec. section, 1931-32), Pittsburgh Chamber of Commerce. Republican. Presbyterian. Mason (32°; Harrisburg Consistory), Zembo Temple. Club: Pittsburgh Motor. Home: 207 Magnolia Pl., Mt. Lebanon, Pa. Office: 416 7th Av., Pittsburgh, Pa.

CADWALLADER, William Henry, r.r. equipment mfg.; b. Pittsburgh, Pa., Feb. 11, 1876; s. Thomas and Mary (White) C.; ed. pub. schs. and high sch., Wilkinsburg, Pa.; m. Margaret J. Donaldson, June 20, 1900; children—William Henry (M.D.), Margaret Ruth (Mrs. T. H. Cable), Robert T. Asso. with Union Switch & Signal Co. continuously since 1891; served in various positions, 1891-1911, and actg. asst. gen. mgr., 1911-12, asst. gen. mgr., 1912-14, gen. mgr., 1914-15, asst. to gen. sales mgr., 1915-25, asst. to vice-pres. and gen. mgr., 1925-27, actg. vice-pres., 1927-29, vice-pres., 1929-36, vice-pres. and gen. mgr. since 1936; vice-pres. Swissvale Corpn.; vice-pres. and dir. Am. Brake Co.; dir. First Nat. Bank at Wilkinsburg; dir., vice-pres. and gen. mgr., Union Switch and Signal Construction Co. Mem. Pittsburgh Chamber of Commerce. Republican. Methodist (a trustee, and treas. Mifflin Av. Ch.). Club: Edgewood Country. Home: 704 Savannah Av., Pittsburgh, Pa. Office: Union Switch & Signal Co., Swissvale, Pa.

CAFFERY, Edwin C.; judge N.J. Circuit Court. Address: South Orange, N.J.

CAFIERO, Anthony James, lawyer; b. Phila., Pa., Feb. 11, 1900; s. Stephen and Josephine (Conti) C.; student N.J. Law Sch., Newark, N.J., 1928-31; m. Hazel Koenig, Nov. 25, 1926; children—James Stephen, Andrea Ann. Engaged in real estate business, 1922-28; admitted to N.J. bar as atty., 1931, as counselor, 1935; now engaged in gen. practice of law as individual at Wildwood; served as treas. City of North Wildwood, N.J., also custodian of sch. moneys, 1926-32; clk. bd. of Chosen Freeholders of Cape May Co., N.J., since 1932; pres. Wildwood Tribune-Journal, Inc., newspaper pubs. and printers. Hon. mem. Rotary Internat. Republican. Roman Catholic. Clubs: Italian American, Sons of Italy, Republican. Home: N.W. Cor. 21st & Central Av., North Wildwood, N.J. Office: 3303 New Jersey Av., Wildwood, N.J.

CAIN, David Edward; prof. military science and tactics, Princeton U., with rank of lt. col. Address: 17 Ivy Lane, Princeton, N.J.

CAIRNES, Laura Jeannette, high sch. prin.; b. Jarrettsville, Md., Feb. 16, 1880; d. George Andrew and Cornelia Slee (Haile) C.; student Md. State Normal Sch., 1897-99; A.B., Goucher Coll., 1907; grad. study Cornell U., summer 1913, Johns Hopkins U., various summers. Engaged in teaching, country schs., 1899-1903; teacher history, Western High Sch., Baltimore, Md., 1907-23, head of dept., 1920-23; prin. Eastern High Sch., Baltimore, Md. since 1924. Mem. Nat. Edn. Assn., Am. Hist. Assn., Md. Hist. Soc., Am. Assn. Univ. Women, Phi Beta Kappa. Presbyn. Home: 4008 Roland Av., Baltimore, Md.

CAIRNS, Alexander, clergyman, lecturer; b. Belfast, Ireland, Sept. 7, 1871; s. James and Mary Jane (McMullen) C.; brought to U.S., 1873; Ph.B., Adrian (Mich.) Coll., 1897, B.D. (by correspondence), 1899, M.A., 1909, LL.D., 1926; m. Mary Annie Obee, Aug. 12, 1897; children—Ruth Esther, Grace Annie, John Alexander, Mary Margaret, William Morris. Ordained ministry, 1897; teacher in Japan, 1897-1901; pastor in U.S., 1901-06; lecturer, 1907-20; pastor High Street Presbyn. Ch., Newark, N.J., 1920-25; lecturer since 1926; columnist, 1927-29; pastor Community Ch., Bloomfield, Feb. 1933—. Mem. Linnæan Soc., Sigma Alpha Epsilon. Mason. Clubs: Wednesday, Institute Forum. Has lectured in every state of U.S. and throughout Canada. Titles of lectures: The Man Worth While; The Golden Age; Diploma and Destiny; Lincoln the Liberator; Washington the Warrior; The Martyrs of Intolerance; The Goose That Lays the Golden Eggs; etc. Home: 746 Ridge St., Newark, N.J.*

CALDER, Alexander, mfr. bags and paper; b. N.Y. City, June 10, 1886; s. James and Mary G. (Helwig) C.; grad. high sch., Glen Ridge, N.J., 1905; B.S., St. Lawrence U., Canton, N.Y., 1909; m. Adelaide Fancher Gunnison, Oct. 18, 1913; children—Alexander, Frederick Gunnison, Stanley Gunnison. Football and basketball coach, Erasmus High Sch., Brooklyn, 1909-10; pulp salesman Perkins-Goodwin Co., N.Y. City, 1911-13; with Union Bag & Paper Corpn. since 1913, salesman, 1913-20, mgr. paper and pulp dept., 1920-24, gen. sales mgr., 1924, v.p. and dir., 1925-31, pres. and mem. exec. com. since 1931; dir. Macon, Dublin & Savannah R.R. Co. Mem. Alpha Tau Omega. Clubs: Montclair Golf; Madison (Conn.) Country, Madison Yacht; Boca Raton Club (Fla.). Home: 89 Undercliff Rd., Montclair, N.J. Office: 233 Broadway, New York, N.Y.

CALDERWOOD, Alva John, coll. dean and prof.; b. New Bedford, Pa., Feb. 14, 1873; s. William and Esther Ellen (Cowden) C.; A.B., A.M., Grove City (Pa.) Coll., 1896, Ph.D., 1908, Litt.D. (hon.), 1921; A.B., Harvard, 1899; m. Leonora Neal, July 2, 1900; children—Helen Frances (Mrs. Rev. J. Stanley Harker), Esther Rebekah (dec.), John Neal. Began as prof. of English and mathematics, Grove City (Pa.) Coll., 1896-99, prof. of Latin since 1899, dean since 1914. Mem. Midwestern Ednl. Assn. of Pa. (pres., 1936), Classical Assn. of Middle Atlantic States. Republican. United Presbyterian. Clubs: Grove City (Pa.) Commercial, Grove City (Pa.) Country. Public Speaker. Address: 319 Poplar, Grove City, Pa.

CALDWELL, Albert Oscar, clergyman; b. Bogota, Columbia, S.A. (of Am. parents), Nov. 15, 1885; s. Milton E. and Susanna (Adams) C.; A.B., Coll. of Wooster (O.), 1907; B.D., Auburn (N.Y.) Theol. Sem., 1913; grad. study, Mansfield Coll., Oxford, Eng., 1914; (hon.) D.D., Coll. of Wooster, O., 1932; m. Grace Stone, Oct. 12, 1915; children—Elizabeth Adams, William Stone. Ordained to ministry Presbyn. Ch., 1913; pastor, Spencer, N.Y., 1914-18, Waverly, N.Y., 1918-29; pastor Presbyn. Ch., Titusville, Pa., since 1929. Presbyterian. Mason. Home: 209 N. Franklin St., Titusville, Pa.

CALDWELL, Joseph R.; mem. surg. staff Wheeling and Ohio Valley Gen. hosps. Address: 40 12th St., Wheeling, W.Va.

CALDWELL, Joseph Stuart, physiologist; b. nr. Knoxville, Tenn., Oct. 31, 1878; s. Andrew and Lemira J. (Crawford) C.; A.B., Maryville (Tenn.) Coll., 1902; student U. of Chicago, 1902-04, 1910-11 and 1914, A.M., 1904, Ph.D., 1914; m. Cora E. McCulloch, Sept. 2, 1905; 1 son, Stuart Andrew (died July 27, 1930). Prof. biology, Peabody Coll. for Teachers, Nashville, Tenn., 1904-11; head dept. botany, Ala. Poly. Inst. and Agrl. Expt. Station, Auburn, Ala., 1912-16; plant physiologist, Washington Agrl. Expt. Station, Pullman, Wash., 1916-18; plant physiologist in charge fruit and vegetable cultivation, Bur. Plant Industry, U.S. Dept. Agr., Beltsville, Md., since 1918; 1st v.p. Citizen's Bank of Riverdale, Md. Mem. A.A. A.S., Bot. Soc. America, Am. Soc. Hort. Science, Am. Soc. Plant Physiology, Sigma Xi, Phi Kappa Phi. Presbyn. Home: 211 W. Madison Av., Riverdale, Md. Address: Bureau Plant Industry, U.S. Dept. Agr., Horticultural Field Station, Beltsville, Md.

CALDWELL, William G.; mem. law firm Caldwell, Kline & Mead. Address: 1226 Chapline St., Wheeling, W.Va.

CALDWELL, William James, lawyer; b. Harlansburg, Pa., May 27, 1891; s. James Patterson and Elizabeth A. (Culbertson) C.; A.B., Oberlin (O.) Coll., 1913; LL.B., U. of Pittsburgh, 1916; m. Ruth O. MacEwen, Mar. 30, 1928; 1 son, James Allen. Began as lawyer, New Castle, Pa., 1916, and since engaged in civil and corporate practice; dir. and counsel Dollar Savings Assn., New Castle, Pa., since 1928. Served as pvt., U.S. Army, 1918. Chmn. bd. of trustees New Castle (Pa.) Pub. Library. Mem. Lawrence Co. (Pa.), Pa. State, Am. bar assns., Am. Legion, Sons of Am. Revolution. Republican. Presbyterian. Mason (32°). Clubs: Rotary, New Castle Field (New Castle, Pa.). Home: Wilmington Rd., R.D. No. 3. Office: 522-525 Lawrence Savings & Trust Bldg., New Castle, Pa.

CALDWELL, William Thomas, prof. chemistry, Temple U. Address: Broad St. and Montgomery Av., Philadelphia, Pa.

CALEY, Earle Radcliffe, asst. prof. chemistry; b. Cleveland, O., May 14, 1900; s. John Radcliffe and Minnie Annie (Mitchell) C.; ed. Case Sch. Applied Sci., Cleveland, O., 1918-20; B.S., Baldwin-Wallace Coll., Berea, O., 1923; M.Sc., O. State U., 1925, Ph.D., same, 1928; m. Grace Fowles Cochran, Dec. 24, 1925; children—Grace Virginia, Robert Cochran. Engaged as asst. in chemistry, Baldwin-Wallace Coll., Berea, O., 1921-23; teacher mathematics and sci., high sch., Leroy, O., 1923-24; prin. high sch., Monroeville, O., 1925-27; instr. chemistry, Princeton U., 1928-31, asst. prof. since 1931; chemist, Agora Excavation Staff, Athens, Greece, 1937. Served as mem. Bd. Edn., Princeton Twp. since 1939. Fellow A.A.A.S. Mem. Am. Chem. Soc. (sec.-treas. Princeton Sect. 1930-31, chmn. 1931-32), History of Sci. Soc., Sigma Xi, Gamma Alpha, Phi Lambda Upsilon. Republican. Presbyn. Author: The Direct Determination of Sodium, 1929; Analytical Factors and Their Logarithms, 1932. Contbr. to New Internat. Year Book for 1936, also many tech. articles to sci. journs. Home: 201 Harrison St., Princeton, N.J.

CALHOUN, Harlan M., lawyer; b. Franklin, W.Va., Oct. 25, 1903; s. Harrison M. and Virginia (Mullenax) C.; student Potomac State Sch., Keyser, W.Va., 1920-22, W.Va. Univ., Morgantown, 1922-26; m. Alberta Dorsey, Nov. 19, 1929; children—Ann Fredlock, Joseph Harlan. Admitted to W.Va. bar, 1926, and engaged in gen. practice of law with father as mem. firm Calhoun & Calhoun, Franklin, W.Va., 1926-31; in practice at Moorefield, W.Va., since 1931; served as prosecuting atty. of Hardy Co., 1932-36; judge 22d Jud. Circuit for 8-yr. term since 1937. Mem. Phi Delta Phi, Kappa Sigma, Patriotic Order Sons of America. Democrat. Methodist. Mason. Odd Fellow. Club: Lions of Moorefield. Home: Moorefield, W.Va.

CALLAGHAN, Glenn S., state youth administrator; b. Craigsville, W.Va., Dec. 26, 1898; s. David Thomas and Nancy Miriam (Rader) C.; student Glenville (W.Va.) Normal Sch., 1917-22; A.B., Fairmont (W.Va.) Normal Sch., 1926; student W.Va. U., summers 1928-31; m. Isabelle Warden Johnson, Jan. 3, 1921; children—Richard Johnson, William Thomas, Joseph Glenn, Jerry Ted. Reared on a farm; early experience in lumber mills and mines; dispatching clerk in Post Office, Glenville, W.Va., 1921-22; pub. sch. teacher, Nicholas County, 1914-19, Glenville Coll. Training Sch., 1920-21, Grafton pub. sch., 1922-27; prin. Fairview High Sch., 1927-31; prin. Calhoun County High Sch., 1931-35; state dir. adult edn. and recreation, Works Progress Adminstrn., 1935-36; state adminstr. Nat. Youth Adminstrn., Charleston, W.Va., since 1935. Mem. W.Va. State Edn. Assn., N.E.A., Kappa Delta Pi. Ind. liberal Democrat. Methodist. Home: 204 Beauregard St. Office: 1424 Kanawha St., Charleston, W.Va.

CALLAHAN, James Morton, univ. prof.; b. Bedford, Ind., Nov. 4, 1864; s. Martin I. and Sophia Oregon (Tannehill) C.; A.B., Ind. U., 1894, A.M., 1895; student U. of Chicago, 1894; Ph.D., Johns Hopkins, 1897; m. Maud Louise Fulcher, Sept. 4, 1907; children—Kathleen, Jean Louise, James M. Asst. and fellow in history and politics, Johns Hopkins U., 1895-97; acting prof. Am. history and constl. law, Hamilton Coll., 1897-98; hist. research at Washington and lecturer Johns Hopkins, 1898-1902, dir. bur. of hist. research, 1900-02; prof. and head of department of history and political science, 1902-29, research professor since 1929, also dean Coll. Arts and Sciences, 1916-1929, W.Va. U. Visiting prof. summer sessions, U. of Colo., 1918, Johns Hopkins, 1919, 22, U. of Southern Calif., 1921, 23, U. of Calif., 1925, University of Washington, 1927. President Ohio Valley Historical Association, 1913-14; hon. mem. 2d Pan-Am. Scientific Congress, 1915. Member Phi Beta Kappa (Johns Hopkins), American Hist. Assn., Am. Polit. Science Assn., Am. Soc. Internat. Law; del. Internat. Deep-Waterways Assn., 1895, Nat. Conservation Congress, 1911, Pan-Am. Institute of Geography and History, 1935. Historian, Semi-Centenl. Commn. W.Va., 1913. Author: Neutrality of the Am. Lakes, 1898; Cuba and International Relations, 1899, American Relations in the Pacific and the Far East, 1901; Confederate Diplomacy, 1901; The American Expansion Policy, 1903; Introduction to American Foreign Policy, Vol. I—The Monroe Doctrine and Inter-American Relations; The United States and Canada; American Foreign Policy in Mexican Relations; A Study in International History; Evolution of Seward's Mexican Policy; History of West Virginia; American Foreign Policy in Canadian Relations; Am. Northern Frontier Development. Also various historical monographs and reviews, and many articles for mags. and encys. (especially Ency. Americana and Cyclo. of Am. Government), and for "The South in the Making of the Nation." Editor of West Virginia University Studies in American History. Lecturer for Am. Assn. for Internat. Conciliation, 1915-18; known for extensive researches and studies in Am. foreign policy and diplomacy, especially in Anglo-Am. relations. Clubs: Cosmos (Washington, D.C.), Country. Home: 632 Spruce St., Morgantown, W.Va.

CALLAHAN, Jeremiah Joseph, coll. pres.; b. Bay City, Mich., Jan. 7, 1879; B.A., Pittsburgh Coll. of the Holy Ghost (now Duquesne U.), 1897, LL.D., 1923; studied Holy Ghost Apostolic Coll. (Cornwells Hgts., Pa.), Gregorian U. (Rome). Ordained priest R.C. Ch., 1904. Began teaching at Duquesne U., 1897; prof. St. Mary's Sem., Norwalk, Conn., 1906-1912; pastor Notre Dame Ch., Chippewa Falls, Wis., 1912-17; pres. Holy Ghost Coll., Cornwells Hgts., Pa., 1917-30; pres. Duquesne U. since 1930. Ind. Democrat. Author: Euclid or Einstein (Vol. I), 1932; The Science of Language, 1938. Home: Duquesne University, Pittsburgh, Pa.

CALLENBACH, Ernest William, prof. of poultry husbandry; b. New York, N.Y., Dec. 18, 1901; s. Johann Anton and Antonia Maria L. M. (Lohman) C.; B.S., U. of Wis., Madison, Wis., 1924; student Rutgers U., New Brunswick, N.J., 1924-25; M.S., Pa. State Coll., 1930; m. Margaret Isabelle Miller, July 21, 1927; children—Ernest William, Carl Anton, John Ivar. With Pa. State Coll. since 1925, as instr. in poultry husbandry, 1925-30, asst. prof., 1930-35, asso. prof., 1935-37, prof. since 1937. Mem. Poultry Science Assn., Alpha Gamma Rho, Alpha Zeta, Phi Kappa Phi, Lambda Gamma Delta, Gamma Sigma Delta, Sigma Xi. Republican. Pioneer in propagation of game birds and in work with laying cages; research in commercial brooding systems and effect of environment on fowls. Home: Boalsburg, Pa. Office: 106 Horticulture Bldg., State College, Pa.

CALLENDER, Clarence Newell, univ. prof.; b. Olyphant, Pa., Feb. 16, 1887; s. Samuel Newell and Margaret (Jones) C.; B.S. in Econ., U. of Pa., 1909, M.A., 1916, Ph.D., 1924; m. Ruth Hand, Nov. 25, 1914; children—Jane Hand, John Newell. Spl. agt. Bur. of Corpns., Dept. of Commerce and Labor, Washington, D.C., 1908; admitted to Philadelphia bar, 1912; prof. business law, U. of Pa. since 1924, chmn. business law dept. since 1935; mem. of bd. for examination of personnel, Bur. of Immigration and Naturalization, Dept. of Labor, Washington, D.C., 1933. Club: Lenape (Phila.). Home: 708 Beacon Lane, Merion, Pa. Office: 36th St. and Woodland Av., Philadelphia, Pa.

CALLOWAY, Walter Bowles, ry. official; b. Harrison, O., Dec. 28, 1873; s. Thomas Bond and Anna (Bowles) C.; ed. Wabash Coll., Ind.,

1890-91; m. Wilma Rhine, Oct. 6, 1903; children—Arthur Bond, Catherine. Began with C., C.,C.&St.L. Ry., 1891; various positions, pass. dept., same rd., 1894-98; division clk., 1898-1900, chief rate clk., 1900-01, adv. mgr., 1901-02, gen. pass. dept. C.,H.&D. Ry.; asst. gen. pass. agt. Cincinnati, Richmond & Muncie R.R., at Richmond, Ind., 1902-03; gen. pass. agt. Chicago, Cincinnati & Louisville R.R., at Cincinnati, 1903-04; asst. gen. pass. agt., same rd., and C.,H.&D. Ry., 1904-05; gen. pass. agt., C.,H.&D. Ry., 1905-11; asst. gen. pass. agt., Mar., Sept. 1911, gen. pass. agt., 1911-16, B.&O. Southwestern R.R.; apptd. pass. traffic mgr. B.&O. R.R., 1917; gen. pass. traffic mgr. B.&O. R.R. and Alton R.R. since Feb. 1, 1934. Mem. Phi Kappa Psi. Republican. Presbyn. Clubs: Chesapeake, Merchants. Home: 3810 Fenchurch Rd., Baltimore. Office: B.&O. Bldg., Baltimore, Md.

CALVARESE, Flaviano; v.p. Colonial Trust Co. Address: Wilmington, Del.

CALVERT, Bruce, editor and pub.; b. Clear Spring, Ind., June 7, 1866; s. William Hanson and Caroline (Ramey) C.; student Ind. State Normal Sch., Terre Haute, Ind., 1886-87; m. Harriet M. Dewey, Dec. 1891 (dec.); m. 2d Anna C. Gulbrandsen, June 22, 1912. Engaged in teaching, pub. schs., Ind., 1887-88; gen. agt. R. G. Badoux & Co., pubs., Chicago, 1888-89; traveling salesman, John E. Potter & Co., pubs., Phila., 1890; gen. mgr. Keystone Pub. Co., Phila., 1891-98; sales mgr. Taxis Co., Chicago, Ill., 1902-06; copy writer with Mallory, Mitchell & Faust, nat. adv. agency, Chicago, 1907-15; editor and pub. The Open Road (magazine) since 1908, at Mountain View, N.J., since 1926; propr. The Open Road Press, publishing and book mcht. Mem. bd. dirs. Am. Sunbathing Assn. Mem. Author's League of America, Nat. Soc. for Promotion of Rational Edn. (sec.). Founder World's League for a Sane Christmas. Former mem. old Press Club, Chicago. Lecturer. Contbr. many articles to mags. and publs., including The Federal Constitution and the Duties of American Citizenship (magazine serial), 1894; Socialism And Progress, 1908; Science And Health—Without Key to Scriptures, 1909; Rational Education, 1911; Calvert's Synthetic Shorthand and Word Analysis, 1926. Home: Mountain View, N.J.

CALVERT, George Herbert; partner Calvert, Thompson & Berger. Home: Glenshaw, Pa. Office: Oliver Bldg., Pittsburgh, Pa.

CALVERT, Philip Powell, entomologist; b. Phila., Jan. 29, 1871; s. Graham and Mary S. (Powell) C.; grad. Central High Sch., Phila., 1888; studied U. of Pa., 1888-89, 1891-95, Ph.D., 1895; Berlin, 1895-96, Jena, 1896; m. Amelia C. Smith, 1901. Instr. zoölogy, 1897-1907, asst. prof., 1907-12, prof. since 1912, U. of Pa. (studying natural history in Costa Rica on leave of absence, 1909-10). Asso. editor Entomological News, 1893-1910, editor since 1911. Mem. Council, Acad. Natural Sciences of Phila., since 1897; pres. Am. Entomol. Society (Phila.), 1899-1915; pres. Entomol. Soc. America, 1914; mem. Am. Soc. Zoölogists, Am. Soc. Naturalists, Ecol. Soc. America, Am. Philos. Soc., Am. Soc. Trop. Medicine, Sigma Xi; fellow A.A.A.S. Known as student of the Odonata (Dragonflies). Contbr. to the sect. Odonata in Biologia Centrali-Americana (edited by F. D. Godman, F.R.S.), 1901-08; also catalogues and numerous articles on the Odonata of various regions. Author: (with Amelia S. Calvert) A Year of Costa Rican Natural History, 1917. Home: Cheyney, Pa.

CALVERTON, Victor Francis (George Goetz), writer, lecturer; b. Baltimore, Md., June 25, 1900; s. Charles and Ida Janette (Geiger) C.; student Baltimore City Coll.; A.B., Johns Hopkins, 1921; unmarried. Founder, 1923, and since editor The Modern Quarterly (now The Modern Monthly); editor dept. of book review of Book League Monthly; lit. editor Ray Long and Richard R. Smith, Inc. Lecturer on sociology and history. Author: The Newer Spirit, 1925; Sex Expression in Literature, 1926; The Bankruptcy of Marriage, 1928; Three Strange Lovers (a trilogy), 1929; The New Ground of Criticism, 1930; American Literature at the Crossroads, 1931; The Liberation of American Literature, 1931; For Revolution, 1932; The Passing of the Gods, 1934; The Man Inside (novel), 1935; The Making of America, 1938. Editor of An Anthology of American Negro Literature, 1929; The Making of Man, 1931. Coeditor: Sex in Civilization, 1929; The New Generation, 1930; Woman's Coming of Age, 1931; The Making of Society, 1937. Mem. Am. Sociol. Soc., Am. Economic Assn., Am. Acad. Polit. and Social Science; hon. mem. Syndicat des Littérateurs Démocrates de France. Am. editor of La Paix Mondiale; author of monthly dept. "The Cultural Barometer" in Current History (mag.). Contbr. to the Hollywood Tribune (mag.), Current History, Forum, Psychol. Rev., Scribner's, Monde, La Paix Mondiale, etc. Home: 2110 E. Pratt St., Baltimore, Md. Office: 16 St. Luke's Place, New York, N.Y.

CALVIN, Everett Young, lawyer; b. Negley, O., Oct. 24, 1892; s. William Y. and Matilda (Hartford) C.; A.B., Mt. Union Coll., Alliance, O., 1914; student U. of Wis., Madison, Wis., 1916; LL.B., U. of Pittsburgh Law Sch., 1926; unmarried. Coach of athletics and High Sch. instr., Akron, O., Pub. Schs., 1915-16, Wheeling, W.Va., Pub. Schs., 1917-19; in automobile business, 1919-23; in practice of law at Beaver Falls, Pa., since 1926. Mem. Pa. Assembly, 1939-41. Mem. Beaver Co. Bar Assn. (pres. 1938), Beaver Co. Sportsmen's League (pres. 1936-37). Republican. Elk, Mason (32°). United Commercial Travelers. Baptist. Home: 1308 7th Av. Office: 1108 7th Av., Beaver Falls, Pa.

CAMERON, A(rnold) Guyot, editor; b. Princeton, N.J., Mar. 4, 1864; s. Henry Clay and Mina (Chollet) C.; A.B., Princeton, 1886, A.M., 1888, Ph.D., 1891; abroad, 1887-88; m. Anne Wood, d. Rev. Caleb Woodward Finley, June 21, 1899; children—Constance Guyot (Mrs. Townsend Ludington), Arnold Guyot, David Pierre Guyot, Nicholas Guyot, Stéphanie Guyot (dec.), Gerard Guyot, Yvonne Guyot. Prof. French and German langs. and their lits., Miami U., 1888-91; asst. prof. French (in charge of dept.), Sheffield Scientific Sch. (Yale), 1891-97; prof. French, John C. Green Sch. of Science, Princeton, 1897-1900; prof. Summer Sch. of New York U., 1909; on staff Wall Street Journal, 1912-16; war preparedness service, 1917; speaking mission to France, 1918; govt. service, 1919; mem. exec. bd., All-American Standards Council; a founder Soc. of Friends of de Grasse; mem. Am. Friends of Lafayette; secretary and historian of Princeton U. Class of 1886. Mem. Soc. Acad. d'Histoire Internationale, Civil Legion, S.R., S.A.R., Military Society War of 1812, Veteran Corps Artillery State of New York, Phi Beta Kappa. Republican. Presbyn. Author: The Torrens System—Its Simplicity, Serviceability and Success. Editor of textbooks; contbg. editor All-America since 1928. Contbr. to financial and econ. publs. Home: 24 Mercer St., Princeton, N.J.

CAMERON, Donald W.; mem. surg. staff Western Pa. Hosp. Address: 4800 Friendship Av., Pittsburgh, Pa.

CAMERON, James Ritchie; prof. oral surgery, Temple U. Address: Broad St. and Montgomery Av., Philadelphia, Pa.

CAMERON, Norman W., educator; b. Zion, Md., Sept. 27, 1876; s. Levi Oldham and Mary Elila (Wilson) C.; A.B. magna cum laude, Washington Coll., Chestertown, Md., 1895, A.M., 1897; Ph.D., U. of Pa., 1912; grad. student Columbia, 1916, Johns Hopkins, 1917; m. Louise Marguerite Sehrt, Aug. 11, 1920; children—Norman, Caroline May. Prin. pvt. acad., 1895-96; prin. high sch., 1897-98, and supt. of schs., Blacksburg, S.C., 1898-1901; teacher and administrative officer in ednl. system, P.I., 1901-04; supervising prin., Lewes, Del., 1905-07, Elkton, Md., 1907-09; head dept. of psychology. State Normal Sch., West Chester, Pa., 1909-13; head dept. of psychology and edn., Western State Teachers Coll., Kalamazoo, Mich., 1913-16; dir. of teacher training and prin. City Normal Sch., Baltimore, Md., 1916-24; supt. of schs., Pottstown, Pa., 1924-26, Chester, Pa., 1926-28; pres. State Teachers Coll., West Chester, Pa., 1928-35; supt. of schs., Garfield, N.J., since 1936. Mem. Garfield (N.J.) Bd. of Trade. Fellow A.A.A.S.; mem. N.E.A., Nat. Assn. Sch. Adminstrs., Progressive Edn. Assn., Nat. Soc. for Study of Edn. Acad. of Polit. and Social Science, Pa. Acad. of Science, Bergen County Chamber of Commerce, Chester County Hist. Soc., Pi Gamma Mu. Republican. Mason. Clubs: West Chester Golf and Country. Home: 65 Marsellus Place. Office: 115 Cedar St., Garfield, N.J.

CAMP, Chauncey Fairchild, coal operator; b. Waterbury, Corn., Jan. 27, 1892; s. Luzerne Munson and Julia (Hitcheock) C.; student high sch., Waterbury, Conn., Peddie Sch., Hightstown, N.J., 1910-12; m. Florence Beardsley, Mar. 27, 1918; children—Nancy Beardsley, Chauncey Fairchild 2d. In employ Henry W. Peabody & Co., New York, N.Y., 1912-15, U.S. Gypsum Co., 1916-17, General Fireproofing Co., 1917 also 1918-20; gen. Eastern Mgr. American Sign Co., New York, N.Y., 1920-22; with Producers Coal Co., Johnstown, Pa., since 1922, pres. and gen. mgr. since 1932; propr. Windber Mining Co.; pres. and maj. stockholder Sonman Run Mining Co.; pres. Breys Ferry Coal Corpn.; sec. dir. Kingston (Pa.) Brick Co.; dir. Lilly Bensercek Coal Co. Served in U.S. N.R.F., 1917-18, on U.S.S. President Lincoln until destroyed May 1918. Mem. Am Legion (Johnstown and Ebensburg Pa.) posts), Forty and Eight. Republican. Presbyterian. Elk. Home: Mayer Apts. Office: U.S. Bank Bldg., Johnstown, Pa.

CAMPBELL, Aaron Putnam, v.p. E. M. Gilbert Engring. Corpn. and The Utility Management Corpn.; b. Mason City, Ia., Feb. 5, 1885; s. Frederick Putman and Amanda (Baumbach) C.; studied (nights) U. of Ore., Eugene, Ore., U. of Wis., Madison, Wis., Internat. Corr. Schs., and Wilson Engring. Corpn.; m. Alice Cowart Page, Jan. 1, 1911 (dec.); children—John Leslie Putnam, Bruce Aaron; m. 2d, Emma M. Seas, Aug. 14, 1920. Machinist helper Dolby Machine Works, 1900, hydraulic press operator, 1901; chainman C.,B.&Q. R.R. Co., 1902; successively rodman, clk. in office of supt., chief clk. for trainmaster Ill. Div., C.,R.I.&P. Ry. Co., 1903-05; stenographer to John F. Stevens, chief engr. of Isthmian Canal Commn., Canal Zone, 1905-07; supt. in charge maintainance Cerro de Pasco Ry. Co., La Oroya Peru, S.A., 1907-10; asst. to pres. Portland Ry. Light & Power Co., 1911-13; with William P. Bonbright & Co., 1914-15; chief constrn. engr. W. S. Barstow & Co., Inc., 1915-30, v.p. and chief constrn. engr., 1930-33; v.p. E. M. Gilbert Engring. Corpn., Reading, Pa., since 1933, chief construction engr., 1933-38; v.p. in charge constrn. The Utility Management Corpn. since 1938; registered engr. in N.Y., Pa., Ind., Fla. and S.C. Asso. mem. Am. Soc. C.E.; mem. Pa. Soc. Professional Engrs., Nat. Soc. of Professional Engrs., Pa. Economy League (mem. Berks Co. com.). Mason (32°). Clubs: Berkshire Country; Iris, Los Angeles (Calif.) Athletic. Home: 1124 Belmont Av., Wyomissing, Pa. Office: 412 Washington St., Reading, Pa.

CAMPBELL, Arthur Russell, iron products mfg.; b. Manheim, Pa., May 1, 1898; s. Abraham Lincoln and Minnie Myra (Wisegarver) C.; student high sch., Columbia, Pa., 1912-16, Pa. Bus. Coll., Lancaster, Pa., 1919-20; m. Margaret Newcomer Youtz, of Mountville, Pa., Mar. 5, 1920; children—Arthur Russell, Robert Gordon, Richard Lawrence. Began as accountant, 1916; with Columbia Trust Co., Penn Dairies, Inc.; now sec., treas., and dir. Lancaster (Pa.) Iron Works, Inc.; certified pub. accountant in Pa. since 1931; dir. and sec. De Walt Products Corpn. Served in A.S., U.S.R., 1917-18, 246th Aero Squadron and 10th Detachment Bd. Airplane Production. Republican. Reformed Ch. Clubs: Hamilton, Media Heights Golf. Home: 1102 Helen Av. Office: Lancaster Iron Works, Inc., Lancaster, Pa.

CAMPBELL, C. William; mem. law firm Campbell, Wick, Houck & Thomas; dir. many corpns. Home: 800 Watson St., Coraopolis, Pa. Office: Peoples Bank Bldg., Pittsburgh, Pa.

CAMPBELL, Clyde Sparks, dentist; b. Normalville, Pa., Nov. 9, 1882; s. George W. and Ida May (Sparks) C.; D.D.S., U. of Pittsburgh Dental Sch., 1907; m. Catherine Strawn, June 14, 1922; children—George W., Kay E., Clyde Sparks, Jr. Successively, sch. teacher, book salesman, and merchant; engaged in practice of dentistry at Connellsville, Pa., since 1907. Served as mem. and dir. Connellsville Bd. of Edn. Interested in work for boys, established Camp Wildwood used by Boy Scouts. Trustee Connellsville Pub. Library. Mem. Nat. Dental Soc., Pa. State Dental Soc., Odontological Soc. of Western Pa., Dental Study Club of Connellsville, Theta Nu, Epsilon Psi Omega. Republican. Methodist. Elk, Jr. O.U.A.M. Clubs: Kiwanis, Pleasant Valley Country (Connellsville, Pa.); Pitt (Pittsburgh). Home: 520 Race St. Office: Second Nat. Bank Bldg., Connellsville, Pa.

CAMPBELL, David Bradford, lawyer; b. Canonsburg, Pa., Nov. 17, 1904; s. Charles White and Eva (Harper) C.; student Canonsburg High Sch., 1919-21, Bellfonte (Pa.) Acad., 1921-22; A.B., Colgate U., Hamilton, N.Y., 1928; LL.B., U. of Pittsburgh, 1931; m. Naomi Smith, July 22, 1929; children—Nancy Ruth, Linda Ann, David Smith. Admitted to Pa. bar, 1931, and since in practice at Canonsburg, Pa.; dir. Citizens Trust Co., Canonsburg Thrift Corpn.; sec. and dir. Holt, McConnell & Osburn, Inc. Mem. Pa. Bar Assn., Washington Co. Bar Assn., Alpha Tau Omega, Phi Alpha Delta. Republican. Presbyterian. Moose. Clubs: Bankers (Pittsburgh); Washington County Golf and Country, Yorick (Canonsburg, Pa.). Home: 218 Belmont Av. Office: First National Bank Bldg., Canonsburg, Pa.

CAMPBELL, Edward Hastings, M.D.; b. Kane, Pa., Feb. 8, 1894; s. Eddy W. and Cora (Hoyt) C.; grad. Warren (Pa.) High Sch., 1913; student pre-med. course U. of Pa., 1913-15, M.D., 1919; m. Ethel F. Hanna, Aug. 26, 1915; children—Edward G., Jean H., Thomas M. Interne Lankenau Hosp., Phila., 1920-22; in practice, Phila., since 1922, specializing in nose, throat and ear; now chief otolaryngol. dept. of Pa. Hosp., Children's Hosp. and asst. otolaryngologist, Lankenau Hosp.; asst. prof. of otolaryngology, Hosp. of U. of Pa.; cons. otolaryngologist, St. Christopher's Hosp. for Children and Naval Hosp.; asso. prof. otolaryngology, Grad. Sch. of Medicine, U. of Pa.; asst. prof otolaryngology, U. of Pa. Med. Sch. Served in S.A.T.C., 1918-19; now lt. comdr. Med. Dept. U.S. Naval Reserves. Fellow Am. Coll. Surgeons; mem. A.M.A., Pa. and Phila. Co. med. assns., Coll. of Physicians of Phila., Am. Laryngol. Assn., Am. Laryngol., Rhinol. and Otol. Soc., Am. Otol. Soc., Am. Acad. Ophthalmology and Otolaryngology, Phila. Laryngol. Soc., Phila. Pediatric Soc., Sigma Chi, Sigma Xi. Republican. Club: Phila. Country. Home: 244 Gypsy Lane, Wynnewood, Pa. Office: 1904 Spruce St., Philadelphia, Pa.

CAMPBELL, Edward W.; instr. urology, Hahnemann Med. Coll.; asst. visiting surgeon in urology Abington (Pa.) Memorial Hosp.; cons. urologist West Jersey Homeopathic Hosp. (Camden), McKinley Memorial Hosp. (Trenton), West Chester (Pa.) Homeopathic Hosp. and Riverview Hosp. (Norristown). Address: 1601 Walnut St., Philadelphia, Pa.

CAMPBELL, Ethan A.; surgeon-in-chief Taylor Hosp., Ridley Park. Address: 706 Madison St., Chester, Pa.

CAMPBELL, George Ashley, telephone research engr.; b. Hastings, Minn., Nov. 27, 1870; s. Cassius Samuel and Lydia Lorraine (Ashley) C.; B.S., Mass. Inst. Tech., 1891; A.B., Harvard, 1892, A.M., 1893, Ph.D., 1901; studied Göttingen, Vienna and Paris; m. Caroline Gillis Sawyer, 1913; children—Alexander Hovey (dec.), Ashley Sawyer. With Am. Tel. & Tel. Co., 1897-1934; with Bell Telephone Labs., 1934-35. Mem. Am. Acad. Arts and Sciences, Math. Soc., Math. Assn. America, Physical Soc., A.A.S. Distinguished Service medal, Inst. Radio Engrs., 1936; Elliott Cresson medal, Franklin Inst., 1939. Pioneering research in connection with loading, crosstalk, 4-wire repeater circuits, sidetone reduction, electric wave filters, inductive interference, antenna arrays, maximum output networks, Fourier integrals and electrical units. Republican. Conglist. Home: Upper Montclair, N.J.*

CAMPBELL, George Johnston, lawyer, editor, pub.; b. West Elizabeth, Pa., May 16, 1872; s. James Logan and Eva (Johnston) C.; A.B., Curry U., 1890; m. Ina Sylvania Conner, of Monongahela, Pa., Mar. 7, 1894; children—George Kane, Martha Virginia (Mrs. Paul C. Maher), Ruth Evelyn (Mrs. Walter W. Allen), Ina Conner. Employed as newspaper man in various capacities, 1890-1904; admitted to Pa. bar, 1904, and since engaged in gen. practice of law at Pittsburgh; admitted to practice before all cts. of Pa., U.S. Dist Ct., U.S. Treasury Dept., and the Supreme Ct. of the U.S.; managing editor Pittsburgh Legal Journal. Charter mem. Court and Commercial Newspaper Assn. Mem. Am., Pa. State, and Allegheny Co. bar assns. Republican. Presbyn. Mason (32°, Shriner). Club: Pittsburgh Athletic. Home: Wildwood, Pa. Office: 208-212 Grant St., Pittsburgh, Pa.

CAMPBELL, Harry Guy, contractor; b. Baltimore, Md., July 4, 1891; s. Harry Tyler and Florence (Mueller) C.; grad. Marston Univ. Sch., 1910; C.E., Cornell U., 1914; m. Grace M. Taber Thompson, Oct. 3, 1914; children—Lawrence Thompson, Harry Guy, Richard Lorimer, Seth James. Became inspr. Md. State Roads Commn., 1914; engr. and supt. Henry Smith Sons & Co., ship constrn., 1917-19; engr. and supt. on heavy constrn. Whiting-Turner Contracting Co., 1919-22; treas. and mng. partner Harry T. Campbell Sons Co., contractors, engrs., sand, gravel, crushed stone, Towson, Md., since 1922; pres. Towson Nat. Bank since 1933; treas. Gwynns Falls Stone Corpn., Texas Supply Co. Co-ordinator of Civil Works Adminstrn. for Baltimore County, 1933. Mem. Engrs. Council of Md., Asso. Gen. Contractors of America (dir.), Md. Assn. of Engrs. (dir.), Highway Contractors Assn. of Md. (pres. 1936-37), Am. Soc. Civil Engrs. (asso. mem.), Nat. Safety Council, Baltimore Chamber of Commerce, Nat. Mfrs. Assn., Sigma Phi Epsilon. Democrat. Episcopalian. Clubs: Rotary (Towson); Baltimore Country. Office: Harry T. Campbell Sons Co., Towson, Md.

CAMPBELL, James Alfred Garsed, banker; b. Chester, Pa., Feb. 19, 1858; s. James and Angelina (Garsed) C.; student Chester (Pa.) pub. schs., 1864-74; m. Elizabeth Hubley Mowry, Nov. 26, 1889; children—John Richardson (dec.), Margaret Mowry (Mrs. Henry G. Sweney), James Alfred Garsed. Began as bookkeeper and clerk, Mar. 2, 1874; asst. cashier Elliott, Sons & Co., private bankers, Phila., 1879-84; bookkeeper L. H. Taylor, Jr. & Co., stock brokers, Phila., 1884-85; with Delaware County Trust Co., Chester, Pa., since 1885, successively as teller, sec., v.p., pres., 1899-1938, and chmn. of bd. since 1938. Dir. Chester Hosp., Lindsay Law Library, Delaware County Hist. Soc., Family Soc. (welfare), Ruth L. Bennett Day Nursery, Pub. Health Nursing Service, all of Chester. Served as 2d lt., 2d Pa. Vol. Inf., during Spanish-Am. War; served 18 yrs. in Pa. Nat. Guard, retiring as lt. col. Trustee Pa. Mil. Coll., Alfred O. Deshong Memorial Art Gallery and Park. Mem. Order of Scottish Clans, United Spanish War Vets. Republican. Episcopalian. Clubs: Chester, Rotary (Chester, Pa.). Home: 707 E. 20th St. Office: Delaware County Trust Co., Chester, Pa.

CAMPBELL, James Harvey, life insurance; b. Pittsburgh, Pa., Apr. 21, 1869; s. James and Elizabeth (Figley) C.; grad. Monongahela (Pa.) High Sch., 1885; student Babson Inst., Wellesley, Mass., and Duff's Business Coll., Pittsburgh, Pa.; m. Alice B. Royce, 1903; children—James Harvey, Ethel Seymour (Mrs. Paul Ketterman), Donald Royse, Barbara. Began as cashier and bookkeeper, 1886; successively stenographer Frick Coal Co., cashier Aetna Life Insurance Co., Pittsburgh; special agent with Northwestern Mutual Life Insurance Co. since 1909. Pres. Bellevue High Sch.; treas. Bellevue Y.M.C.A.; treas. Home Bldg. and Loan Assn., Bellevue. Former mem. 10th Regt. Pa. and Naval Reserve, Pittsburgh. Republican. Presbyterian. Mason (32°, Shriner). Clubs: Business Men's, Y.M.C.A. Home: 153 N. Balph Av., Bellevue, Pa. Office: 1801 Clark Bldg., Pittsburgh, Pa.

CAMPBELL, John Edgar, lawyer; b. Charleston, W.Va., June 17, 1884; s. Samuel George and Cecelia (Wehrle) C.; LL.B., W.Va. Univ. Law Sch., 1906; m. Willamae Davis, Mar. 23, 1918; 1 dau., Dorothy Jane. Admitted to W.Va. bar, 1906 and since engaged in gen. practice of law at Charleston; mem. firm Campbell, McClintic & James. Mem. Beta Theta Pi, Delta Xi. Republican. Presbyn. Home: 1563 Jackson St. Office: Charleston Nat. Bank Bldg., Charleston, W.Va.

CAMPBELL, Lawrence Wilbur, commercial secretary; b. Johnstown, Pa., Nov. 2, 1893; s. Amos and Mary Elizabeth (Makin) C.; student Johnstown (Pa.) Pub. Schs., 1899-1915, Juniata Business School, Huntingdon, Pa., 1915-16. Began as automobile mechanic and salesman, Johnstown, Pa., 1916-21; radio dealer, Johnstown, 1922-31, and partner Johnstown Radio Co.; partner Amos Campbell & Sons, realtors, 1931-35; since 1935 engaged in civic work; sec. Citizens Council of Greater Johnstown, Pa. (mem. bd. of govs.); co-founder and dir. United States Flood Control Federation. Served as pvt., 78th F.A., Hdqrs. Co., 6th Div., U.S. Army, A.E.F. (detached service Chief Instr. Motor School, Lyons, France), during World War. Vice-pres. Pa. Assn. of Real Estate Bds., 1932, 33; managing dir. Johnstown Chamber of Commerce since March 9, 1936. Mem. Am. Legion (Post No. 294, Johnstown, Pa.). Republican. Dunkard. Home: 324 Market Street. Office: Chamber of Commerce, Johnstown, Pa.

CAMPBELL, LeRoy Brotzman, dir. Warren Conservatory of Music; b. Jasper, N.Y., Apr. 30, 1873; s. Frank Elbert and Celestia Eliza (Brotzman) C.; B.E., Central State Teachers Coll., Lock Haven, Pa., 1892; student Oberlin (O.) Coll., 1892-96; grad. Leipzig (Germany) Royal Conservatory Music (honor and scholarship student), 1900; Mus.D., Grove City (Pa.) College, 1925; studied in music normals in Paris, London, Leipzig, Vienna and Munich; m. Nellie Belle Baker, June 9, 1910; 1 adopted son, now in Dominican Order. Began as dir. mus. dept. State Teachers Coll., Fredericksburg, Va., 1896; founded Warren (Pa.) Conservatory of Music, 1906, and has since been its dir.; has conducted 19 summer tours to Europe, 12 being mus. normals or pilgrimages; made a one year trip around the world for mus. and ednl. research; ednl. dir. Progressive Series Coll. European Summer Teachers' Normals. Mem. Music Teachers Nat. Assn. (life), Soc. of Arts and Sciences of America, Am. Matthay Assn. (v.p.), Warren Acad. of Sciences (pres. 1918). Democrat; nominated candidate for state representative, 1937. Methodist. Rotarian. Author: The True Function of Relaxation in Piano Playing, 1922; The Unusual in London and Vicinity, 1935; also brochures on piano playing, ear training and Gothic architecture, and about 40 pub. mus. compositions. Contbr. articles to mus. publs.; has had 5 prize essays in same. Has given mus. and other lectures in 32 states and several foreign countries, including China and India. Served as judge for 114 contestants at Paris Conservatory, 1933, and again in 1937; made extensive tour as judge Nat. Piano Playing Tournament of America, 1938. Decorated Legion of Honor (France and Germany). Home: 600 5th Av., Warren, Pa.

CAMPBELL, Luther A., judge; b. Bergen Co., N.J., Nov. 28, 1872; s. Abraham D. Campbell; ed. pub. schs.; read law in office of father. Admitted to N.J. bar, 1894, and practiced with father until 1896; counsel to Hackensack, N.J., 12 yrs.; apptd. judge Circuit Court of N.J., 1914; apptd. judge Supreme Court of N.J., 1923, reapptd., 1924, 31, resigned, 1932, becoming chancellor Court of Chancery of N.J. for term expiring, Oct. 18, 1939. Democrat. Address: State House Annex, Trenton, N.J.; and 1 Exchange Place, Jersey City, N.J.

CAMPBELL, Paul E., clergyman, supt. parish schs.; b. Crabtree, Pa., Dec. 28, 1890; s. Daniel and Mary Agnes (Noonan) C.; ed. St.

Vincent Prep., Coll., and Sem., 1904-15, A.B., 1911, A.M., 1913; hon. Lit.D., Duquesne Univ., 1927; hon. LL.D., St. Vincent Coll., 1927. Ordained to ministry Roman Catholic Ch., priest, 1915; served as asst. pastor and prin. sch., 1915-26; supt. Parish Schs., R.C. Diocese of Pittsburgh since 1926; pres. Cath. Ednl. Assn. of Pa.; vice-pres. gen. Nat. Cath. Ednl. Assn. Author: Parish School Administration, 1937. Contbr. monthly articles on edn. to Homiletic and Pastoral Review since 1928. Lecturer on edn. in many large cities and at Cath. Summer Sch. of America, Cliff Haven, N.Y. Home: 5323 Penn Av., Pittsburgh, Pa.

CAMPBELL, Rolla Dacres; mem. law firm Campbell & McNeer. Office: First Huntington Nat. Bldg., Huntington, W.Va.

CAMPBELL, Strother Anderson, clergyman; b. Mineral, W.Va., Aug. 24, 1888; s. Edward Lee and Rebecca (Hudkins) C.; Ph.B., Denison U., 1915; B.D., Crozer Theol. Sem., 1918; A.M., U. of Pa., 1918; D.D., Stetson U., 1931; m. Florence Ruth Wilson, July 17, 1917; 1 son, Lachlan Leigh Campbell. Ordained Bapt. ministry, 1917; successively pastor at Buchannon, W.Va., Onancock, Va., Norfolk, Va., Tallahassee, Fla.; pastor Baptist Temple, Charleston, W.Va., since 1934. Mem. bd. mgrs. W.Va. Bapt. Conv.; bd. trustees Alderson-Broaddus Coll. Mason. Club: Kiwanis Internat. Author: Man in the Making, 1929; The Blessing of Believing, 1935; Marriage Made Christian, 1937. Home: 213 Morris St., Charleston, W.Va.

CAMPBELL, William, surgeon; b. Canada, Apr. 22, 1899; came to U.S., 1926, naturalized, 1931; M.D., C.M., Queens Univ., Kingston, Can., 1922; m. Florence Jaeger, Oct. 17, 1931. Engaged in gen. practice of medicine in Ottawa, Can., 1923-25; interne ear, nose, and throat, N.Y. Post Grad. Hosp., 1926-28; specializing in diseases of ear, nose and throat. In practice at East Orange, N.J., since 1928; attending staff Orange Memorial Hosp., Orange, N.J. Fellow Am. Coll. Surgs. Mem. Am. Otol. and Rhinol. Soc., N.J. State Surg. Soc., Clin. Soc. of Oranges, Canadian Soc. of N.Y. Republican. Presbyn. Mason (32°, Shriner). Clubs: Balfurral Golf (Springfield); Orange Lawn Tennis (South Orange). Home: 247 Wyoming Av., South Orange. Office: 144 Harrison St., East Orange, N.J.

CAMPBELL, William Fillmore, mgr. Campbell Co.; b. Joplin, Mo., Sept. 29, 1902; s. William Wilson and Edna (Fillmore) C.; grad. Amherst Coll., 1923; m. Kathryn McKinney, Apr. 10, 1924; children—Lorraine Agnes, William Fillmore. Asso. with Campbell Co. since 1924, asst. mgr., 1924-25, mgr. since 1925. Sec. Rep. Co. Com. since 1938. Chmn. Boy Scouts Council of New Wilmington, Pa., 1926; vice-chmn. Lawrence Co. (Pa.) Boy Scouts Council, 1938. Mem. Western Pa. Lumbers Dealers Assn. (pres. 1936-37; dir. since 1930; counselor to Nat. Chamber of Commerce. Club: Rotary of New Wilmington (pres. 1932). Invited to Washington, D.C., as mem. first conf. of little business men, 1938. Home: 341 Waugh Av. Office: 125 E. Neshannock Av., New Wilmington, Pa.

CAMPBELL, William Henry, Jr., lawyer; b. Scullville, N.J., Dec. 17, 1892; s. William Henry and Sophie (Willetts) C.; A.B., Rutgers Coll., 1915; LL.B., Harvard U. Law Sch., 1920; m. Elizabeth Mueller, Apr. 4, 1923; children—Patricia Faith, Shirley Willetts, William Henry 3d, Donald Frank. Admitted to N.J. bar as atty., 1921, as counsellor, 1924; engaged in gen. practice of law at Newark, N.J., since 1922; served as prosecutor of pleas Cape May Co., N.J., 1924-29; pres. Ocean City Apt.; treas. Woodland Cemetery Co.; sec. Windsor Distributors, Inc., Bon Aire Corpn., Vacuum Bread Cooling Corpn. Mem. Am., N.J. State, Essex Co. and Cape May Co. bar assns., Kappa Sigma, Patriotic Order Sons of America. Democrat. Presbyn. Mason. Club: Country (Mapplewood). Home: 11 Sagamore Rd., Mapplewood, N.J. Office: 1172 Raymond Boul., Newark, N.J.

CAMPBELL, William Montgomery, mfg. chemicals; b. New York, N.Y., Oct. 10, 1891; s. William James and Josephine L. (Kyle) C.; B.S., Columbia U., 1913; m. Doris K. Joffrion, Apr. 14, 1920; 1 son, Sandy M. Asst. mgr. Blum Bros., Phila., Pa., 1913-14; with Oakley Chem. Co., 1914-17 and 1919-21; with Magnus Chemical Co., Garwood, N.J., since 1921, pres. and dir. since 1921; pres. and dir. D I F Corpn., Garwood, N.J., since 1924. Served as lt. pilot A.S., U.S.A., 1917-19. Mem. Alpha Delta Phi. Mem. Associated Grocery Mfrs. of America, Assn. of Mfrs. Representatives. Republican. Presbyn. Mason. Clubs: Echo Lake Golf, Westfield Tennis. Home: 1030 Wychwood Rd. Office: D I F Corpn., Garwood, N.J.

CAMPBELL, William Scott, mechanical engring.; b. Dundee, Scotland, Apr. 28, 1886; s. Alexander and Jessie (Scott) C.; came to U.S., 1901, and naturalized citizen, 1909; student Brooklyn Poly. Inst., 1909-10, Temple U., 1916-17; m. Grace Knight, Sept. 6, 1913 (dec.); m. 2d, Bertha P. Bond, Feb. 14, 1922; 1 dau., Doris Jeanette. Employed as mech. draftsman Campbell Ptg. Press and Mfg. Co., 1901-04; machine designer Dodge Coal Storage Co., Phila., 1904-08; asst. chief draftsman Guarantee Construction Co., New York City, 1908-15; engr. and supervisor engring. contracts Link Belt Co., Phila., since 1915. Registered Professional Engr., Pa. Mem. Nat. Soc. Professional Engrs., Pa. Soc. Professional Engrs. Religious Soc. of Friends. Royal Arcanum. Club: Link Belt Engineers (past pres.). Home: 125 Cliveden Av., Glenside, Pa. Office: 2045 Hunting Park Av., Philadelphia, Pa.

CAMPBELL, Wilson Alexander, steel mfr.; b. Monongahela, Pa., Oct. 15, 1877; s. William Oliver and Mary Louisa (Shaw) C.; ed. Kiskiminetas Sprgs. Sch., Saltsburg, Pa., 1893-95; m. Alice Elizabeth Clause, Apr. 5, 1910; children—Lewis C., Elizabeth Ann, William Oliver II, Wilson Shaw. Began as bank messenger, 1895, then bank teller; sec.-treas. Vulcan Crucible Steel Co., Aliquippa, Pa., 1903-30, v.p., treas. and dir. since 1930. Served as capt., Am. Red Cross, with A.E.F. in France, 1918. Trustee Grove City (Pa.) Coll., Western Theol. Sem., Pittsburgh, Family Soc.; pres. and trustee Valley Hosp., Sewickley, Pa. Mem. S.A.R., Mil. Order of the Loyal Legion of U.S. Republican. Presbyterian. Clubs: Edgeworth, Allegheny Country (Sewickley, Pa.); Duquesne (Pittsburgh). Home: 211 Creek Drive, Sewickley, Pa. Office: Aliquippa, Pa.

CAMPION, John Leo; prof. German, U. of Pa. Address: U. of Pennsylvania, Philadelphia, Pa.

CAMPMAN, Clarence Carlton, M.D.; b. West Middlesex, Pa., Apr. 13, 1888; s. Frederick Albert and Minnie Rose (Jones) C.; grad. Staunton (Va.) Mil. Acad., 1905, U. of Pittsburgh, 1905-08; m. Phebe Mae Clarke, June 22, 1916; 1 son, Charles Frederick. Gen. practice at West Middlesex, Pa., since 1912; visiting physician, C. H. Buhl Hosp., Sharon, Pa., since 1914, pres. med. staff, 1932-33. Pres. Bd. of Edn., West Middlesex, Pa., 1930-38. Fellow A.M.A., Am. Coll. Physicians; mem. Mercer Co. Med. Soc. (past pres.), Pa. State Med. Soc., Am. Bd. of Internal Medicine, Phi Beta Pi. Republican. Presbyterian. Mason (Consistory, Commandery, Shriner). Home: 407 Main St. Office: 301 Main St., West Middlesex, Pa.

CANADA, William Joseph, cons. engring.; b. New Haven, Conn., Aug. 13, 1881; s. Charles Bradley and Laura Jane (Libbey) C.; Ph.B. in E.E. summa cum laude, Sheffield Sci. Sch. of Yale U., 1902; m. Irma Bimel, June 12, 1906; children—John Bradley, William Richards, Gordon Lee. Employed as elec. engr. with various concerns and inspection bureaus, 1902-13; elec. engr. Nat. Bureau of Standards, Washington, D.C., 1913-17; spl. engr. and asst. to mgr., Stone & Webster, 1919; dir. engring., Nat. Electric Light Assn., 1920-25; elec. field engr., Nat. Fire Protection Assn., 1925-28; dir. engring., Nat. Elec. Mfrs. Assn., 1928-35; engaged in bus. on own acct., engring., standardization, pub. and industrial relations and counselor since 1935; consultant-spl. engring., Chase-Shawmut Co., Wiremold Co. Served as asst. to gen. mgr. and to pres. American Internat. Shipbldg. Corpn., Hog Island, 1917-19. Mem. Rep. Co. Com. for many yrs. Mem. Internat. Municipal Signal Assn., Sigma Xi. Republican. Ch. of Christ Sci. Contbr. many articles to tech. journs. on elec. safety engring. and related subjects. Home: 31 Melrose Rd., Mountain Lakes, N.J. Office: 505 5th Av., New York, N.Y.

CANADY, Herman George, coll. prof.; b. Okmulgee, Okla., Oct. 1, 1901; s. Howard Thurman and Anna May Canady; A.B., Northwestern U., Evanston, Ill., 1927, A.M., 1928; m. Julia Elsie Witten, Aug. 16, 1934; children—Herman George, Jr., Joyce Anna. Engaged as prof. and head of dept. of psychology and philosophy, W. Va. State Coll., since 1928. Mem. Nat. Edn. Assn., Am. Teachers Assn. (chmn. dept. of psychology), Alpha Kappa Delta, Kappa Alpha Psi. Methodist. Contbr. to professional journals. Address: W.Va. State College, Institute, W.Va.

CANAN, William Truscott, city controller; b. Altoona, Pa., July 12, 1895; s. William Dean and Sarah (Oppy) C.; student Altoona High Sch., U. of Pittsburgh, La Salle Extension U., Phila., and Alexander Hamilton Inst., Phila.; unmarried. Spl. agt. Conn. Mutual Life Ins. Co., 1917-18; instr. Altoona High Sch., 1918-21; prin. Hollidaysburg (Pa.) High Sch., 1921-23; engaged in pvt. auditing practice, Altoona, since 1917; instr. Pa. State Coll., 1938; sec. James W. Runk Ins. Agency, Rose Hill Cemetery Co., L. G. Runk Federal Savings and Loan Assn.; sec.-treas. Altoona Glass Products Co.; pres. Livingston's Bakery; dir. Alliance Bldg. & Loan Assn. Auditor Altoona Sch. Dist. since 1924; city controller, Altoona, Pa., since 1924. Mem. Nat. Assn. Municipal Accounting Officials of U.S. and Can. (Pa. State chmn.), Blair Co. Hist. Soc. (pres. and trustee), League of Third Class Cities in Pa. (mem. Uniform Budget Com.). Mason (Grand Steward R. W. Grand Lodge). Clubs: Rotary, Blair Co. Pitt (Altoona); Nat. Travel; Varsity "P." Home: 1910 Third Av. Office: City Hall, Altoona, Pa.

CANCELMO, J. James; chief surgeon St. Vincent's Hosp. for Women and Children; mem. surg. staff Columbus Hosp.; asst. surgeon St. Mary's Hosp. Address: 5012 Spruce St., Philadelphia, Pa.

CANDEE, Charles Lucius, clergyman; b. Milwaukee, Wis., Jan. 16, 1874; s. William Sprague and M. Cecilia (Smith) C.; B.A., Princeton, 1895, M.A., 1898; grad. Princeton Theol. Sem., 1898; D.D., Dubuque (Ia.) Coll. and Sem., 1916; LL.D., Coll. of the Ozarks, 1934; m. Elizabeth L. Browne, May 18, 1899; children —Alice Beaver (Mrs. C. F. Backus), William Sprague. Asst. minister 4th Presbyn. Ch., Chicago, 1899-1900; ordained Presbyn. ministry, 1901; pastor Riverton, N.J., 1901-08, Am. Ch., Frankfort-on-the-Main, Germany, 1908, Westminster Ch., Wilmington, Del., 1909-25. Spl. preacher in mil. camps and under Y.M.C.A., World War; spl. preacher Am. Ch., Paris, summer 1923. Moderator Presbytery of Monmouth, 1907, Presbytery of Newcastle, 1912, Synod of Baltimore, 1924-25; mem. Presbyn. Gen. Assembly 3 times to 1924. Mem. Presbyn. Bd. of Ministerial Relief and Sustentation, 1915-28; mem. bd. trustees Synod of Baltimore; pres. bd. of trustees New Castle Presbytery. Apptd. mem. Del. State Bd. of Charities, 1928, pres., 1931-39; apptd. mem. State Commn. for the Blind, 1929, and Special Commn. to Draft Old Age Pension Law for Del., 1930; pres. Permanent Old Age Welfare Commn. of Del., 1931. Republican. Clubs: Country (Wilmington); University (Phila.). Wrote: (brochures) The English Bible; John Calvin. Home: Wilmington, Del.

CANN, Jessie Yereance, coll. prof.; b. Newark, N.J., May 17, 1883; s. Frank W. and Frances H. (Yereance) C.; A.B., Goucher Coll., 1904; student Columbia, summers, A.M., 1910, Ph.D., 1911; Mass. Inst. Tech. summer 1919, U. of Calif., 1927-28. Science teacher Belleville (N.J.) High Sch., 1904-09; head chemistry dept., Rockford (Ill.) Coll., 1911-14; instr. chemistry, U. of Ill., Urbana, Ill., 1914-17, asso. in chemistry, 1917-18; asst. prof. chemistry, Smith Coll., Northampton, Mass., 1918-19, asso. prof., 1919-29, prof. since 1929. Mem. Am. Chem. Soc., Am. Phys. Soc., A.A.A.S.,

Am. Assn. Univ. Profs., D.A.R., Sigma Xi (pres. Smith Coll. Chapter 1937-38), Phi Beta Kappa (v.p. Smith Coll. Chapter 1938-39). Republican. Methodist. Author numerous articles on phys. chemistry, electrochemistry and thermodynamics in chem. and engring. jours. Home: 112 Brunswick St., Newark, N.J. Office: Stoddard Hall, Smith College, Northampton, Mass.

CANN, John Pearce, lawyer; b. Kirkwood, Del., Sept. 9, 1881; s. Richard Thomas and Rebecca (Pearce) C.; student Kirkwood (Del.) Country Sch., 1888-95, Wilmington (Del.) Friends Sch., 1895-98, U. of Del., Newark, Del., 1898-1901, U. of Va., Charlottesville, Va., 1901-04; m. Ola Louise Worth, Mar. 26, 1908; children—Rebecca Brevard (Mrs. Eugene Arnold Ray), John Pearce. In practice at Wilmington, Del.; v.p. and dir. Newark (Del.) Trust Co.; atty. for Council of Newark (Del.). Trustee and treas., U. of Del. Mem. Beta Theta Pi. Mason. Club: Lions. Home: Newark, Del. Office: Wilmington, Del.

CANNADAY, John E(gerton), surgeon; b. Floyd, Va., Mar. 17, 1873; s. John B. and Martha Jane (Ingram) C.; student Roanoke Coll., Salem, Va., 1894-98; M.D., Univ. Coll. of Med., Richmond, Va., 1901; m. Margaret Stuart Roller, 1910; children—John Egerton, Margaret; m. 2d, Ellen Carr Tompkins, 1928; 1 son, Thomas Blanford. Supt. and surgeon Sheltering Arms Hosp., Hansford, W.Va., 1902-08; visiting surgeon Charleston Gen. Hosp., 1909-25, chief of surgical staff since 1925. Served as lt. Med. Res. Corps, U.S. Army, 1915, maj., 1917; med. aide to gov. of W.Va., 1917; active duty Camp Custer, and later U.S. Gen. Hosp., Ft. Sheridan, 1917, Camp Sherman, 1918. Dir. and trustee Charleston Gen. Hosp. and Training Sch. for Nurses. Fellow Am. Coll. Surgeons, Internat. Coll. Surgeons; mem. Southern Surg. Assn., A.M.A., W.Va. State and Kanawha County med. socs., Am. Assn. Traumatic Surgeons. Episcopalian. Clubs: Edgewood Country, Kanawha Country, Charleston Boat. Home: 2525 Kanawha St. Office: 1207 Elmwood Av., Charleston, W.Va.

CANNING, Joseph A.; pres. Loyola Coll. Address: Loyola Coll., Baltimore, Md.

CANNON, Burdelle Sittler, physician, otolaryngologist; b. Phila., Pa., Dec. 11, 1901; s. Henry Monroe and Jennie E. (Sittler) C.; student Baltimore City Coll., 1915-18; A.B., Johns Hopkins, 1921, M.D., 1925; m. Lillian E. Holden, Mar. 30, 1935. Interne Women's Hosp., Baltimore, 1925-26; resident surgeon Presbyn. Eye, Ear and Throat Hosp., 1926-28; practice, Baltimore since 1928, practice limited to ear, nose and throat; mem. staff Church Home and Infirmary, Women's Hosp., Union Memorial Hosp., Presbyn. Eye, Ear and Throat Hosp.; cons. otolaryngologist to Children's Hosp. Sch. Diplomate Nat. Bd. Med. Examiners. Mem. Baltimore City Med. Soc. (sec. nose and throat sect. 1934, chmn. of sect. 1935), A.M.A., Southern Med. Soc., Nu Sigma Nu. Republican. Methodist. Mason (past master). Clubs: Johns Hopkins (Baltimore); Algerine Hunting (Cedar Run, Pa.) Home: 5809 Kipling Court. Office: 409 Medical Arts Bldg., Baltimore, Md.

CANNON, Florence V., artist, teacher; b. Camden, N.J.; d. William H. and Catherine M. (Gercke) C.; grad. Camden High Sch.; ed. Sch. Industrial Art, Phila., Pa. Acad. Fine Arts, sculpture and painting; grad. study, Acad. Grand Chaumier, Paris, France. Has followed profession as artist since 1917; art dir. Harcum Jr. Coll. since 1932; taught water color and action life, Country Sch. Pa. Acad. Fine Arts, Chester Springs, Pa. summers since 1934; exhibited Pa. Acad. Fine Arts, Fellowship Pa. Acad. Fine Arts, Phila. Sketch, Print, Plastic, and Art clubs, Phila. Art Alliance, Am. and N.Y. water color clubs, Nat. Assn. Women Painters & Sculptors, Corcoran Art Gallery, Chicago Art Inst. and many other important exhbns. throughout U.S.; represented in permanent collections Fellowship Pa. Acad. Fine Arts and other important art assns. and pvt. collections; received many awards including First and Second Cresson Traveling Scholarships, First Toppan Prize and others. Mem. Nat. Assn. Women Painters & Sculptors, Am. Artists Professional League, also many important art assns. and socs. Republican. Club: Contemporary (Philadelphia). Home: 576 Benson St., Camden, N.J.; (summer) The Lodge, Lake Valley Farm, Chester Springs, Pa.

CANNON, Russell Ackley, mfr. steel products; b. Irvington on Hudson, N.Y., Mar. 19, 1888; s. John and Ruth (Hampton) C.; student pub. sch. and high sch.; m. Esther Bowen, Apr. 27, 1912; 1 dau., Virginia. Employed in foundry business since 1906; with Penn Seaboard Steel Co., later with Reading Steel Casting Co.; asso. with Birdsboro (Pa.) Steel Foundry & Machine Co. since 1921, v.p. since 1931. Mem. Steel Founders' Soc. of America, Am. Iron and Steel Inst., Railway Business Assn. Republican. Episcopalian. Clubs: Racquet, Philadelphia Country (Phila.); Bankers (New York). Home: 629 Sussex Rd., Wynnewood, Pa. Office: Birdsboro, Pa.

CANRIGHT, Cyril Markham, physician; b. Chengtu, China, Mar. 9, 1894; s. Harry Lee and Margaret (Markham) C., citizens of U.S.; A.B., O. Wesleyan U., Delaware, O., 1918; M.D., U. of Mich. Med. Sch., 1924; grad. study, Vienna, Austria, 1932, N.Y. Post Grad. Med. Sch., N.Y. City, 1933; m. Winifred Stoody, Sept. 7, 1923; children—Patricia Ann., Jean Margaret, Cynthia (dec.), John Markham. Interne Md. Gen. Hosp., Baltimore, Md., 1924-24, Buffalo City Hosp., Buffalo, N.Y., 1924-25; physician, Henry Ford Hosp., Detroit, Mich., 1925-26; asst. surgeon, Peking Union Med. Coll., Peiping, China, and asst. prof. surgery, Medical-Dental Coll., West China Union Univ., Chengtu, W. China, 1929-31; engaged in gen. practice of medicine and surgery at Cranford, N.J., since 1933. Pvt. Med. Detachment, 307th F.A., 78th Div., U.S.A., with A.E.F., World War. Diplomate Nat. Bd. Med. Examiners of U.S. Mem. A.M.A., Union Co. Med. Soc., Sigma Phi Epsilon, Am. Legion, Cranford Hist. Soc., Am. Med. Assn. of Vienna, China Med. Assn. Republican. Methodist. Club: Mens (Cranford). Contbr. med. articles to journs. in China and U.S. Home: 34 Springfield Av., Cranford, N.J.

CANTAROW, Abraham, M.D.; b. Hartford, Conn., Jan. 27, 1901; s. Joseph and Helen (Karp) C.; student Trinity Coll., Hartford, Conn., 1917-18; Tufts Coll., Medford, Mass., 1918-20; M.D., Jefferson Med. Coll., Phila., 1924; m. Elizabeth Stern, Aug. 1, 1932. Resident physician Jefferson Hosp., Phila., 1924-27, research fellow, 1927-29, biochemist since 1931; instr. in medicine, Jefferson Med. Coll., 1930-34, asso., 1934-37, asst. prof. medicine, 1937-39, asso. prof. since 1939. Mem. Am. Physiol. Soc., Am. Soc. Pharmacology and Exptl. Therapeutics, Soc. for Exptl. Biology and Medicine, A.A.A.S., Assn. for Study Internal Secretions, A.M.A., Phila. Coll. Physicians, Physiol. Soc. Phila., Alpha Omega Alpha. Author: Biochemistry in Internal Medicine, 1932; Calcium Metabolism and Calcium Therapy, 1931, 2d edit., 1933; Clinical Biochemistry, 1939; contbr. about 80 articles on physiol., biochem. and med. subjects to jours. Home: 2033 Delancey St. Office: Jefferson Hospital, Philadelphia, Pa.

CANTOR, Aaron Samuel, physician; b. Szagaren, Lithuania, Dec. 24, 1885; s. Louis and Sonia (Segal) C.; A.B., Central High Sch., Phila., 1903; M.D., U. of Pa., 1907; postgrad. study at univs. of Vienna, Halle and Munich, also Nat. Hosp. for Diseases of the Heart, London, Eng., 1924-25; m. Elma B. Phillips, Dec. 15, 1926; 1 dau., Sonya (dec.). Interne Phila. Gen. Hosp., 1907; asst. in dept. of pathology with Dr. Allen J. Smith, U. of Pa. Sch. of Medicine, 1907-10; in practice of medicine, Phila., 1908-12; founded Northeastern Hosp., 1909, serving as chief med. service, 1909-11; in gen. practice, Dickson City, Pa., 1912-24, Scranton, since 1925; chief cardiovascular diseases Hahnemann Hosp., Scranton, since 1925; asso. visiting chief W. Mountain Sanatorium, 1929-36; visiting physician Mid-Valley Hosp., Peckville, Pa., since 1912; consultant physician Wayne Co. Hosp., Honesdale, Pa. Served as 1st lt. M.C., U.S. Army, 1918-19, capt. Med. Res. Corps, 1919-24. Dep. commr. health, Dickson City, Pa., 1920-22; conducted investigation of graft in health dept., which resulted in its reorgn. and in passage of health ordinance by City Council, Dickson City. Trustee Scranton State Hosp., 1932-36, Jewish Fed. since 1926; chmn. bd. dirs. Jewish Home for Friendless since 1921; mem. bd. dirs. Scranton Y.M.H.A. since 1937. Fellow A.M.A., Am. Heart Assn., Am. Coll. Chest Physicians (since its inception, June 1937); mem. Lackawanna Co. Med. Soc. (chmn. scientific com. 1928-32). Jewish religion. Elk. Clubs: Mid-Valley Scientific (organizer, 1912; pres.); Jewish Medical (organizer and pres.). Author: Office Treatment of Pulmonary Tuberculosis. Home: 526 N. Webster Av. Office: Connell Bldg., Scranton, Pa.

CANTWELL, Garrett R.; supt. Krebs Pigment & Chemical Co. Address: 309 S. Maryland Av., Wilmington, Del.

CANTWELL, Harry Arthur; chief of surg. staff Union Hosp. of Cecil County, Elkton, Md.; surgeon Md. div., Pa. R.R. Co. Address: North East, Md.

CAPEN, Charles Herbert, civil and san. engr.; b. Jersey City, N.J., Nov. 1, 1895; s. Charles Howard and Sarah Adeline Sanford (Munford) C.; C.E., Cornell U., 1917; m. Ruth Crowell, Aug. 1, 1919; children—Ruth Earnly, Elizabeth Ada. Employed as asst. san. engr., N.J. State Dept. Health, 1917; 1919-25; engr. North Jersey Dist. Water Supply Commn. since 1925; mem. firm Daniels and Capen, engring. assos. for many municipalities on water and sewage problems; dir. and sec. Lake End Corpn.; dir. A.M. Capen's Sons. Active in politics in East Orange and West Orange; served on Rep. Co. Com. and several club coms. Served as asst. engr. on Naval Base Work, New York, 1918. Trustee N.J. Sect. of Am. Water Works Assn. Mem. Am. Soc. Civil Engrs., N.Y. State Sewage Works Assn., N.J. Sewage Works Assn. Received George W. Fuller award by N.J. Sect. Am. Water Works Assn., 1938. Republican. Presbyn. Mason. Club: West Orange Republican. Home: 8 Florence Pl., West Orange. Office: 31 Clinton St., Newark, N.J.

CAPEN, William Henry, elec. engr.; b. Newton, Mass., Aug. 13, 1890; s. William Henry and Hattie Ellen (Wiswall) C.; grad. Newton pub. schs., 1909; S.B. cum laude, Harvard U., 1913, M.E.E., 1914; m. Julia Raymond Schmalz, Sept. 15, 1915 (dec.); children—Priscilla Marsten, Joanne Raymond. Research and development engr. Western Electric Co., 1914-24; engr. Internat. Western Electric Co., 1924, Internat. Telephone & Telegraph Corpn., 1925; worked on various foreign assignments, 1926-29; asst. v.p. and asst. gen. tech. dir. Internat. Telephone & Telegraph Corpn. since 1929. Formerly pres. Mountain Lakes Sch. Bd. Pres. Mountain Lakes Art Assn. Fellow Acoustical Soc. America; mem. Am. Inst. Elec. Engrs., Inst. Radio Engrs., Radio Club America, Harvard Engring. Soc. Republican. Christian Scientist. Clubs: Mountain Lakes, Mountain Lakes Chamber Music Soc., Pi Eta, Harvard Downtown Lunch. Writer several tech. papers. Home: 365 Morris Av., Mountain Lakes, N.J. Office: Internat. Telephone & Telegraph Corpn., 67 Broad St., New York, N.Y.

CAPLAN, Albert Joseph, editor and pub.; b. Phila., Pa., June 2, 1908; s. Joseph and Frances (Belber) C.; B.S. in Edn., Temple U. Teachers Coll., 1929; m. Sylvia Fay Bayuk, Mar. 13, 1932; 1 dau., Judith Ann. Began as law clk., 1930-31; asso. with Bayuk Bros., brokerage, Phila., 1931-33; purchased Haddon Township News, Westmont, N.J., 1933, Oaklyn Bulletin, Oaklyn, N.J., 1934, Haddonfield News, Haddonfield, N.J., 1934, and South Jersey News; merged four papers under name The Greater South Jersey News, Collingswood, N.J., 1936; moved pub. office to Camden, N.J., 1938; editor and pub. Greater South Jersey News, pres., treas. and dir. South Jersey News Corpn. Served as dir. publicity for Young Republicans of N.J., 1934-38; Young Rep. Nat. Committeeman from N.J., 1937-38; mem. Camden Co. Young Rep. exec. com. since 1937. Publicity dir. Landon Campaign in charge N.J. and Del., 1936. Mem. Lambda Sigma Kappa, Beta Sigma Rho. Republican. Jewish religion. B'nai B'rith. Clubs:

Country (Philmont, Pa.); National Republican (New York). Author: For You and Other Poems (verse), 1925; Manuscript Making and Illuminating in the Middle Ages, 1926; Bibliography of Sir Walter Scott, 1927. Home: 7913 Montgomery Av., Elkins Park, Pa. Office: Broadway at Mickle St., Camden, N.J.

CAPLAN, Harry Nathaniel, clergyman; b. Baltimore, Md., Sept. 21, 1899; s. Max and Rebecca C.; A.B., U. of Cincinnati, 1921; Rabbi, Hebrew Union Coll., Cincinnati, 1924; m. Jean Backer, June 28, 1936. Rabbi Temple Keneseth Israel, Allentown, Pa., since 1924. Vice-pres. Peace Soc., Conference on Good Will. Jewish religion. Mason. Home: 1429 Linden St., Allentown, Pa.

CAPOLINO, Gertrude Rowan, artist; b. Phila., Pa., July 23, 1900; d. Henry A. and Laura (Goldner) Rowan; grad. Moore Inst., Phila. Sch. Design; m. J. Joseph Capolino, Jan. 13, 1928; 1 dau., Ann. Mem. faculty Moore Inst., Phila., 1924-34; teacher fashion illustration, Beaver Coll., Jenkintown, Pa., 1922-39; mem. faculty Spring Garden Inst. and Springside Sch. since 1928. Rep. in permanent collections of Moore Inst., South Phila. High Sch., for Girls, Spring Garden Inst., Friends Central Sch., Overbrook, Beach Haven Pub. Library, Wharton Sch. of U. of Pa., Penn Charter Sch., Pa. Acad. Fine Arts, etc. Awarded gold medal Spring Garden Inst., Springside Alumnæ; fellowship, Moore Inst. Asst. dir. Chestnut Hill (Pa.) Art Center. Mem. Alumnæ Moore Inst. (treas.), Germantown Art League, Phila. Water Color Club, Art Alliance, D.A.R., Print Club, Plastic Club. Address: 151 W. Highland Av., Chestnut Hill, Philadelphia, Pa.

CAPOLINO, J(ohn) Joseph, artist and art director; b. Phila., Pa., Feb. 22, 1896; s. Francis and Maria (di Nucci) C.; ed. public schs. (Phila.), Pa. Acad. of Fine Arts, 1915-20; also studied in England, France and Italy; m. Gertrude Rowan, June 13, 1928; 1 dau., Ann. Rep. by murals and pictures in Marine Corps Bldg., Phila.; Am. Inst. of Architects; Circolo Italiano, Phila.; U.S.M.C. Hdqrs., Washington, D.C.; Friends Central Sch., Overbrook, Phila.; Jenks Sch., Chestnut Hill, Pa.; Century of Progress, Chicago. Dir. of fine arts, Spring Garden Inst., Phila.; dir. Chestnut Hill (Pa.) Art Center; designed New Marine Corps standard; designed Tun Tavern Memorial Tablet, Water St., Phila. Works: official portrait of Maj. Gen. Commandant T. Holcomb, Washington, 1938; decoration, "The Marines Have Landed" Marine Corps Sch., Phila. Navy Yard; decoration for the San Francisco Fair, "Last Night of the World War," 1939; portrait of Nathan Hayward for the Franklin Institute. Awards: Two traveling scholarships, 1917-18, Toppan prize, 1918, Edw. T. Stotesbury prize, 1924, all Pa. Acad. of Fine Arts, gold medal, Spring Garden Inst.; gold medal Sesqui-Centennial Expn. Phila., 1926. Awarded commn. first lt., U.S.M.C.R., for marine corps decorations exhibited at Sesqui-Centennial, Phila., and Century of Progress, Chicago. Catholic. Fellow Pa. Acad. Fine Arts; mem. Da Vinci Alliance, Pro Cultura Italiano Soc. Beachcombers (Beach Haven, N.J.). Home: 151 W. Highland Av., Chestnut Hill, Pa.

CAPPABIANCA, John Battista Carlo Armando, gen. ins. agency; b. Naples, Italy, Mar. 20, 1894; s. Pasquale and Amalia Paterno (Asmundo) C.; came to U.S., 1926, naturalized, 1937; grad. as accountant, Naples, Italy 1912; m. Luigina Barboni, Mar. 5, 1921; children—Amalia, Antonietta, Pasqualino, Italo. Propr. and mgr. dept. store, Porto Garibaldi, Ferrara, Italy, 1921-26; in charge Italian consular agency, Erie, Pa., 1926-35; propr. John Cappabianca Ins. Agency, gen. fire and casualty ins., Erie, Pa., since 1936. Served as pvt. to lt., Italian Army, 1912-20, in war against Austrian Empire, 1915-18, in Fiume, 1918-20; received all the decorations awarded by Italian govt. during Austrian-Italian war. Hon. pres. Guglielmo Marconi Soc. of Warren, Pa., Cesare Battisti Club of Erie, Pa. Democrat. Roman Catholic. Club: Italian World War Vets. Assn. (an organizer, 1933). Home: 1618 Chestnut St., Erie, Pa.

CAPPER, Aaron, physician; b. Kolki, Russia, Jan. 31, 1897; s. Abraham and Rachel (Fried-man) C.; came to U.S. 1913, naturalized citizen, 1918; student George Washington U., Washington, D.C., 1916-17; B.S., Harvard, 1920; M.D., Jefferson Med. Coll., Phila., 1924; m. Estelle Spielman, Aug. 29, 1926; children—Stanley, Robert. Interne Jefferson Hosp., Phila., 1924-26, Von Pirquet Children's Hosp., Vienna, 1926-27; engaged in pvt. practice at Phila., specializing in pediatrics, since 1927; asso. in pediatrics, Jefferson Med. Coll. since 1927, Jewish Hosp. since 1933, St. Luke's Hosp. since 1938. Licentiate Am. Bd. of Pediatrics; mem. Phila. Co. Med. Soc., Phila. Pediat. Soc., Acad. of Pediatrics, Alpha Omega Alpha, Phi Delta Epsilon. Jewish religion. Home: 4717 Osage Av. Office: 2022 Spruce St., Philadelphia, Pa.

CAPPER, Howard M(artin), engineer; b. Woodward, Ia., Mar. 8, 1892; s. Harvey M. and Mary (Stoddard) C.; B.S. in C.E., Iowa State Coll., Ames, Ia., 1924; m. Juno Faye Farr, Oct. 29, 1918; 1 son, Howard Martin (dec.). Began as asst. engr. in charge of surveys, Capper Engring. Co., Adel, Ia., 1913; instr. in civil engring., Iowa State Coll., Ames, Ia., 1924-25; asst. engr. of twp. highways, York, Adams and Franklin Cos., Pa. Dept. of Highways, 1926-29; engr. Pa. R.R. Co., 1929-30; borough engr., Camp Hill, New Cumberland and Wormleysburg, Pa., boroughs since 1930; engr. West Shore Planning Federation, representing seven boroughs on West Shore at Harrisburg, Pa., since 1930. Served as flying machinist U.S. Navy Air Corps, during World War. Mem. Harrisburg Chapter Pa., Nat. socs. of professional engrs., Iowa Engring. Soc., Am. Legion (past finance officer); vice commdr. Cumberland Co. orgn.; chmn., radio com. for 19th congl. dist., dept. of Pa.). Republican. Presbyterian. Mason (32°), Order of Eastern Star. Clubs: National Acacia, West Shore Country (Camp Hill, Pa.); Rotary (New Cumberland, Pa.). Author of radio addresses for Am. Legion program. Mem. Camp Hill (Pa.) Fire Dept. No. 1. Home: 113 N. 20th St. Office: Municipal Bldg., 22d and Market Sts., Camp Hill, Pa.

CAPPS, Edward, university prof.; b. Jacksonville, Ill., Dec. 21, 1866; s. Stephen Reid and Rhoda S. (Tomlin) C.; A.B., Ill. Coll., 1887; Ph.D., Yale, 1891; studied in Athens and Halle, 1903-05; LL.D., Ill. Coll., 1911; Litt.D., Oberlin, 1923, U. of Mich., 1931; L.H.D., Harvard, 1924; LL.D., University of Athens, 1937 (Centenary); m. Grace Alexander, July 20, 1892; children—Rhoda (dec.), Priscilla, Edward, Alexander. Tutor in Latin, Yale, 1890-92; prof. Greek lang. and lit., U. of Chicago, 1892-1907; prof. classics, Princeton, 1907-36, now emeritus; lecturer, Inst. of Advanced Study since 1936. Trustee and chmn. mng. com. Am. Sch. of Classical Studies at Athens, Greece, since 1918; chmn. Commn. for Excavation of the Agora of Ancient Athens; chmn. trustees Athens (Greece) Coll.; trustee Near East Foundation. Lecturer on the Greek Theatre, Harvard, 1903; Turnbull lecturer on poetry, Johns Hopkins University, 1917; Am. editor Loeb Classical Library, editor-in-chief U. of Chicago Decennial Publications (29 vols.); mng. editor Classical Philology, 1906, 07. Dir. div. of Humanities, Rockefeller Foundation and Gen. Edn. Bd., 1929-30. Pres. Classical Assn. of Middle West and South, 1907-08, Am. Philol. Assn., 1914-15, Am. Assn. Univ. Profs., 1920; mem. Am. Philos. Soc., fellow Am. Acad. Arts and Sciences; hon. mem. Archæol. Soc. Athens. Am. Red Cross Commr. to Greece, 1918-19, with rank of lt. col.; E.E. and M.P. to Greece, 1920-21. Decorated Golden Cross Knight Comdr. Order of Redeemer, by King Alexander of Greece, 1919; Comdr. Order of the Phoenix, by King George II. Clubs: Century (New York); Princeton (New York and Philadelphia); Nassau (Princeton). Author: From Homer to Theocritus, 1902; Four Plays of Menander, 1910; The Greek Stage According to the Extant Dramas; The Chorus in the Later Greek Drama; The Introduction of Comedy into the City Dionysia; Chronological Studies in the Greek Tragic and Comic Poets; Epigraphical Problems in the History of Attic Comedy; The Plot and Text of Menander's Epitrepotes; Greek Comedy in the Columbia University Lectures on Greek Literature, 1911. Also sundry other articles in classical philology. Home: Princeton, N.J.

CAPUTO, Eugene A., lawyer; b. Cerisano, Cosenza, Italy, Feb. 17, 1899; s. Antonio and Raffaela (Greco) C.; came to U.S., 1909, naturalized, 1923; B.S. in Econ., U. of Pittsburgh, 1923, LL.B., 1925; m. Velma Lindway, Sept. 4, 1923; children—Phyllis, Paula. Began gen. practice of law, Ambridge, Pa., 1926; mem. Pa. Ho. of Reps., 1932-38 (chmn. Judiciary Gen. Com., 1935, 1936, 1937, 1938; mem. legislative com. investigating Pa. Liquor Control Bd., 1935; chmn. legislative com. investigating U. of Pittsburgh, 1935); borough solicitor, Ambridge, Pa., 1934-38. Mem. state adv. com. Pa. Com. on Penal Affairs; mem. Beaver Co., Pa. State bar assns., Order of Sons of Italy. Democrat. Catholic. Elk, Eagle. Home: 229 Elm Rd. Office; 621 Merchant St., Ambridge, Pa.

CARAHER, Edward Paul M., coll. pres.; b. Bayard, Ia., Oct. 15, 1898; s. Michael Joseph and Catherine (McDonald) C.; A.B., St. Francis Coll., Loretto, Pa., 1920; student Angelico U. and Acad. of St. Thomas, Rome, Italy; Ph.D., Sti Cosma e Damiano, Rome. Ordained priest Roman Catholic Ch., 1924; instr. Trinity Coll., Sioux City, Ia., 1924-26, rector, 1926-30; pres. and trustee St. Francis Coll., since 1937. Mem. Izaak Walton League of America. Democrat. Mem. K.C. Club: Pony Hills Golf (Woonsocket, S.D.). Address: St. Francis College, Loretto, Pa.

CARBIN, Edward F.; sec. Jersey City Real Estate Bd. Address: Jersey City, N.J.

CARDWELL, Edgar Parmele, physician; b. Wilmington, N.C., Sept. 6, 1899; s. Guy Adams and Ethel (Parmele) C.; M.D. U. of Va., 1923; m. Beatrice Chandler, Apr. 16, 1925; 1 son, E. Parmele. Interne Orange Memorial Hosp., 1923-24; attending otologist and asso. intracranial surgery, Newark Eye and Ear Infirmary; attending otorhinolaryngologist, Hosp. of St. Barnabas and for Women and Children; asst. attending otologist and asso. attending rhinolaryngologist, and bronchoscopist, Newark Presbyn. Hosp.; asst. attending surg., dept. rhinolaryngology and bronchoscopy, Essex Co. Isolation Hosp., Belleville; asst. attending surg., dept. cranial surgery, Newark City Hosp. Fellow Am. Coll. Surgeons, Am. Acad. Ophthalmology and Otolaryngology; mem. Am. Med. Assn., Am. Bronchoscopic Soc.; N.Y. Bronchoscopic Club; N.J. State and Essex Co. Med. Socs.; Acad. of Medicine of Northern N.J.; Clinician's Soc. of Newark. Club: Essex. Home: 402 Highland Av. Office: 47 Central Av., Newark, N.J.

CAREY, Andrew Galbraith, sales exec.; b. Baltimore, Md., Aug. 9, 1899; s. Francis King and Anne Galbraith (Hall) C.; grad. Gilman Country Sch., Baltimore, Md., 1917; A.B., Princeton, 1921; m. Lorna Underwood, June 15, 1928; children—Lorna Underwood, Andrew Galbraith. Engr. Worthington Pump & Machinery Corpn., Harrison, N.J., 1921-22; asso. with Carey Machinery & Supply Co., Baltimore, Md., since 1922, as salesman and sales mgr., dir. since 1926, v.p. since 1930; v.p. and dir. Carey Sales & Service Co., Baltimore, Md., since 1934; sec. and dir. Nat. Sugar Mfg. Co., Sugar City, Colo., since 1930. Served as cadet, U.S. Mil. Acad., 1918-19. Trustee Gilman Country Sch., Baltimore, Md. Mem. Ivy Club (Princeton). Episcopalian. Clubs: Green Spring Valley Hunt (Garrison, Md.); Maryland (Baltimore, Md.). Home: Chattolanee, Owings Mills P.O., Md. Office: 119 E. Lombard St., Baltimore, Md.

CAREY, Bruce Anderson, dir. of vocal music; b. Hamilton, Can., Nov. 16, 1876; s. George Whitfield and Sarah (Anderson) C.; grad. Hamilton (Ont.) Collegiate Inst., 1894; student Hamilton Conservatory of Music, 1894-97, Guildhall, London, Eng., Feb.-Oct., 1900; private instruction, Florence, Italy, 1908, 1910-11 (Braggiotti and Carobbi), Munich, 1911, Leipzig (Karl Straube), 1935. Mus. D., Moravian Coll. for Women, Bethlehem, Pa., May 1936; m. Ethel Ann Leitch, June 7, 1905. Came to U.S., 1922, naturalized, 1932. Began as teacher of singing, 1903; dir. Hamilton (Ont.) Conservatory of Music, 1907-18; dir. of music, Public

CAREY, (cont.) Schs., Hamilton, Ont., 1917-22; mem. faculty, Cornell U., and West Chester Coll., summers, 1918-23; dir. vocal music, Girard Coll., Phila., since 1922; mem. faculty, U. of Pa., 1927-29; dir. 6000-voice chorus for Sesquicentennial, Phila., 1926; dir. Phila. Mendelssohn Club (founded 1857), 1926-34; dir. Bach Choir, Bethlehem Pa., 1932-38. Served as lt., 91st Highlanders (Hamilton, Ont.), 1915-19. Decorated Serbian Award of Merit for war services. Republican. Presbyterian. Mason. Clubs: Art Alliance, Rittenhouse Square (Phila.). Home: 6 Cleveland Av., Narbeth, Pa. Office: Girard College, Philadelphia, Pa.

CAREY, Francis James, lawyer; b. Baltimore, Md., July 12, 1888; s. Francis King and Anne Galbraith (Hall) C.; prep. edn. Gilman Country Sch., Baltimore; A.B., Harvard, 1911; LL.B., U. of Md., 1912. Admitted to Md. bar, 1912; asso. Carey, Piper & Hall, Baltimore, 1912-14, mem. firm, 1914-16; then mem. firm Piper, Carey & Hall; now mem. firm Marshall & Carey, Baltimore. Entered 2d R.O.T.C., Ft. Meyer, Va., Aug. 1917; commd. 2d lt. field arty., and sent to schools for aerial observers and aerial gunnery; with A.E.F. France and Germany, Sept. 1918-May 1919; disch. June 9, 1919. Office: First National Bank Bldg., Baltimore, Md.

CAREY, Francis King, lawyer; b. Baltimore, Md., July 1, 1858; s. James and Susan B. C.; A.B., Haverford Coll., 1878, A.M., 1881; LL.B., U. of Md., 1880; m. Anne Galbraith Hall, Apr. 27, 1886; children—Louise (Mrs. Carey Rosett), Francis J., Margaret T. (Mrs. Percy C. Madiera, Jr.), Eleanor I. (dec.), Andrew G., Reginald S. In practice of law at Baltimore, Md., since 1880; pres. Charleston (S.C.) Ry., Gas & Electric Co., 1901-03; former mem. law firms of Steele, Semmes & Carey, and Carey, Piper & Hall; president National Sugar Manufacturing Co., Nat. Sugar Securities Co. Chmn. Md. Tax Revision Commn., 1922-24; mem. Municipal Exec. Com. after Baltimore fire of 1904; chmn. Baltimore Bar Assn. Com. for Corpn. Law, 1908; chmn. City Plan Com. constructing Fallsway Boul. Mem. exec. com. Baltimore Chapter, Red Cross, World War; mgr. Red Cross War Fund Campaign for Md., and mgr. Hoover's Food Conservation Campaign for Md.; mgr. Red Cross Japanese Relief for Md.; mem. boards of dirs. Family Welfare Association. Democrat. Episcopalian. Clubs: Maryland (Baltimore, Md.); Denver (Denver, Colo.); El Paso (Colorado Springs, Colo.). Author: Municipal Ownership of Natural Monopolies, 1901; Law of Husband and Wife (Stewart and Carey), 1881; Carey's Forms and Precedents, 1885. Home: 120 Churchwarden's Rd. Office: Calvert Bldg., Baltimore, Md.

CAREY, James 3d, lawyer; b. Baltimore, Md., Oct. 2, 1895; s. A. Morris and Margaret Cheston (Thomas) C.; A.B., Haverford Coll. 1916; LL.B., Harvard U. Law Sch., 1921; m. Mary Lewis Hall; children—James, Anne Thomas. Admitted to Md. bar, 1922, and since engaged in gen. practice of law at Baltimore; mem. firm Marshall & Carey. Served in F.H.A., U.S.A., 1917-19, with 29th Div. A.E.F. Trustee Baltimore Mus. of Art, Municipal Mus., Foreign Policy Assn. (Md. br.) Gilman Country Sch. Democrat. Clubs: Maryland, Merchants (Baltimore). Home: 606 Cathedral St. Office: First Nat. Bank Bldg., Baltimore, Md.

CAREY, Lawrence B.; pres. First Nat. Bank of Plainfield. Address: 107 Front St., Plainfield, N.J.

CARLANDER, Oswald R.; chief orthopedic surgeon Zurbrugg Memorial Hosp., Riverside, N.J.; asst. orthopedic surgeon Cooper Hosp.; orthopedic surgeon Salem County Memorial Hosp., Salem, N.J., and Camden County Gen. Hosp., Grenloch, N.J. Address: 622 Cooper St., Camden, N.J.

CARLETON, Francis Joseph; prof. mech. orthopedics, Temple U. Address: Broad St. and Montgomery Av., Philadelphia, Pa.

CARLIN, Leo; prof. law, W.Va. U. Address: West Virginia U., Morgantown, W.Va.

CARLING, George F., oral surgery; b. Phillipsburg, N.J., Apr. 4, 1879; s. Theodore and Jennie (Ferguson) C.; ed. pub. schs., Weatherly, Pa.; D.D.S., Pa. Coll. Dental Surgery; married, June 26, 1907; 1 son, Jack W. Engaged in practice of dentistry at Sayre, Pa., 1909-17 and since specializing in oral surgery; oral surgeon Lehigh Valley R.R. Co.; v.p. Merchants & Mechanics Nat. Bank, Sayre, Pa., 1916-39. Served as pres. Chamber of Commerce, 1920-25; dir. Weatherly-Sayre Traction Co.; postmaster, Sayre, Pa., 1923-34. Served as Rep. Co. Chmn., 1928-32. Oral surgeon, Robert Packer Hosp. Republican. Episcopalian. Mason (32°, Shriner). Elk. Clubs: Shepard Hills Country (pres. 1920-38), Acacia, Elks. Home: 217 S. Elmer Av. Office: Guthrie Clinic, Sayre, Pa.

CARLISLE, William Albert, coal broker; b. DuBois, Pa., Oct. 16, 1897; s. Harris Moore and Annie Lucretia (Draucker) C.; student Brady Twp. High Sch., Lutherburg, Pa., 1910-13; grad. DuBois (Pa.) High Sch., 1914; B.S. in business adminstrn., Lehigh U., Bethlehem, Pa., 1923; m. Josephine Lorenzo, May 8, 1929; children—William Albert, Lorenzo, Linda. Sch. teacher, 1915-17; weightmaster at mines, 1918-19; salesman Coal Hill Mining Co., Inc., 1923-28; since 1928 v.p. and mgr. of sales Coal Hill Mining Co., Inc., DuBois, Pa., wholesalers and distributors of anthracite and bituminous coal. Dir. DuBois Pub. Library. Mem. Am. Coal Distributors Assn. (nat. dir.), Sigma Chi. Republican. Clubs: DuBois (Pa.), Rotary (dir., past pres.), DuBois Country. Home: 525 Liberty Boul. Office: Deposit National Bank Bldg., DuBois, Pa.

CARLOCK, John Bruce, mining and mech. engr.; b. Carlock, Ill., Dec. 26, 1882; s. George Madison and Chloe (Canterbury) C.; State Normal Sch., Normal, Ill., 1895-97; State Normal Sch., Kirksville, Mo., 1897-99; Elgin (Ill.) Acad., 1899-1900; U. of Chicago, 1900-01; E.M., Lehigh, 1907; m. Sidney Jane Whiteside, Feb. 4, 1919; children—Eleanor Jane, Sidney Frances, John Bruce. Constr. engr. Bethlehem Steel Corpn., 1907-09; field engr., supt. refineries, Gen. Petroleum Corpn., Calif., 1909-14; supt. refineries, Richfield (Calif.) Oil Co., 1914-17; constr. engr. Dravo Contracting Co., Pittsburgh, 1919-21; with Jones & Laughlin Steel Corpn. since 1921, chief engr. Pittsburgh South Side Works since 1926, now chief engr. of plants. Served as maj., Chemical Warfare Service, with 1st Gas Regt., in France, Dec. 1917-Jan. 1919; comdr. rgt., Dec. 1918-Mar. 1919. Awarded Croix de Guerre (France); citation certificate and Victory Medal with six bars. Mem. American Iron & Steel Inst., American Soc. Mining and Metall. Engrs., Am. Concrete Inst., Soc. Iron and Steel Electrical Engineers, Engineers' Society of Western Pa., American Soc., Mil. Engrs., Am. Ordnance Assn., S.A.R., Am. Legion, Mil. Order World War, Beta Theta Pi, Phi Beta Kappa, Tau Beta Pi. Republican. Mem. Ch. of the Disciples. Home: 1301 Beechwood Boul. Office: 2709 Carson St., Pittsburgh, Pa.

CARLSON, C(arl) Allen, high school prin.; b. Meade Run (now Cartwright) Pa., June 22, 1892; s. John W. and Josephine (Nelson) C.; grad. Power's Sch., Mansfield, Tioga Co., Pa., 1909; student State Normal Sch., Mansfield, Pa., 1909-12, B. Ped., 1914; student Johns Hopkins, summers, 1915, 16, 18; Columbia, summer 1922; B.S., U. of Md., 1936, A.M., 1938; m. Blanche Travers, Aug. 17, 1916; 1 dau., Etta Alene. Prin. graded school, Fall Brook, Pa., 1912-13; prin. of school, Nanticoke, Md., 1913-23; vice prin. and head science dept., Wicomico High Sch., Salisbury, Md., 1923-24; prin. Delmar (Md.) High Sch., 1924-26; prin. Crisfield (Md.) High Sch. since 1926. Commd. 2d lt. Co. L, 1st Inf., Md. Nat. Guard, 1931, 1st lt., 1933. Mem. bd. Crisfield (Md.) Armory. Mem. N.E.A., Am. Assn. Sch. Adminstrs., Jr. Chamber of Commerce of Crisfield, Delphic Fraternity. Democrat. Club: Rotary. Home: Columbia Av. Office: Somerset Av., Crisfield, Md.

CARLSON, H. C(lifford), M.D., dir. student health; b. Murray City, O., July 4, 1894; s. Amos and Margaret (Bowen) C.; B.S., U. of Pittsburgh, 1918, M.D., 1920; m. Mary Ethel Brown, Sept. 12, 1918; children—H. Clifford, Mary Ruth. Interne Mercy Hosp., Pittsburgh, 1920-21, practicing physician, Pittsburgh, since 1921; dir. student health, U. of Pittsburgh since 1932. Mem. A.M.A. Republican. Presbyterian. Home: 801 Kirkpatrick St., Braddock, Pa. Office: Falk Clinic, Pittsburgh, Pa.

CARLSON, Oscar Ludwig, bldg. constrn.; b. Montclair, N.J., Nov. 1, 1894; s. Ludwig and Augusta (Lovengren) C.; B.S. in Chemistry, Lehigh U., 1916; m. Dicie E. Cuckler, Dec. 1, 1919; children—Richard Douglas, Robert Henry. Began as chem. engr. in charge R. & G. Salt Dept. of Central Chem. & Dye Co., Newark, N.J., 1919-20; asso. with The Carlson Company, bldg. constrn., Montclair, N.J. since 1920, successively, gen. mgr., treas., vice-pres., then pres. since 1929; dir. and chmn. real estate com. First Nat. Bank & Trust Co., Watchung Title & Mortgage Guaranty Co.; mem. bd. mgrs. and chmn. real estate com. Montclair Savings Bank; dir. and mem. real estate com. Nishuane Bldg. & Loan Assn.; sec. and treas. Carlson-Babcock, Inc. Served as comdr. U.S. submarine chaser 18 during World War, disch. as ensign, 1919; lt. comdr. CEC-VS U.S. Naval Res. Corps since 1936. Mem. planning bd. Town of Montclair, 1928-32; mayor, 1932-36; past pres. Chamber of Commerce. Mem. bd. trustees Newark Safety Council. Past pres. Asso. Contractors of N.J. Mem. Delta Tau Delta. Republican. Conglist. Mason. Clubs: American Legion (Montclair); Athletic (Newark); New York Lehigh of New York City (mem. bd. govs.). Home: 106 Inwood Av., Upper Montclair. Office: 89 Walnut St., Montclair, N.J.

CARLSON, Robert Charles, high sch. prin.; b. Proctor, Vt., July 28, 1887; s. Oscar and Leona (Berg) C.; A.B., Middlebury (Vt.) Coll., 1908; A.M., Columbia U., 1921; m. Helen Morrison, July 17, 1925; 1 dau., Janet MacCowan. Engaged as teacher mathematics and sci., high sch., Dolgeville, N.Y., 1909-12, Mountain Sch., Allaben, N.Y., 1912-13; head dept. mathematics, Montclair Acad., Montclair, N.J., 1913-16; head dept. mathematics, high sch., New Brunswick, N.J., 1916-25, prin. since 1925; pres. H.L. Fairchild Remedy Co. since 1935. Served as pvt. to sergt., U.S.A., 1917-19 with A.E.F. in France. Mem. New Brunswick Y.M.C.A. (dir.), Chamber of Commerce. Mem. Nat. Edn. Assn., N.J. Schoolmasters Club, N. J. Council on Edn., Am. Legion. Republican. Presbyn. Mason (K.T.). Elk. Kiwanis. Home: 8 Lafayette St., New Brunswick, N.J.

CARMAN, Charles Bloomfield, civil engr. and architect; b. Menlo Park, N.J., Oct. 15, 1885; s. Theodore F. and Louise (Osborn) C.; B.Sc., Rutgers Coll. now Univ., 1908, C.E., same, 1913; unmarried. Employed in various engring. positions, 1908-11; engaged in bus. on own acct. as civil engr. and architect in Metuchen, N.J., since 1911; licensed engr. and registered architect in N.J.; designed Lenox Pottery, Trenton, N.J., Empire Floor and Wall Tile Factory in Metuchen and in Zanesville, O., and others; vice-pres. and dir. Metuchen Amusement Corpn. Served as capt. engrs., U.S.A. during and after World War; with troops in Va. and in charge of real estate and unit cost system of Raritan Arsenal Constrn.; now maj. Engrs. Res. Mem. Am. Legion (dir. and past comdr. local post). Republican. Presbyn. Mason. Jr. O.U.A.M. Club: Craftsmens (Metuchen). Home: Metuchen, N.J.

CARMICHAEL, Thomas Harrison, M.D.; b. Phila., Jan. 27, 1858; s. William and Julia Baker (Hunter) C.; A.B., Central High Sch., Phila.; M.D., Hahnemann Med. Coll., Phila., 1887; m. Emily H. Leonard, Nov. 23, 1897; 1 son, Leonard. Interne Ward's Island Hosp., New York, 1886-87; lecturer on pharmaceutics, 1897-1908, prof. of pharmacodynamics, 1908-13, asso. prof. materia medica, 1913-19, Hahnemann Med. Coll. Mem. Am. Inst. Momœopathy (1st v.p., 1908, pres., 1911-12, trustee, 1912-13), Homœ. Med. Soc. Co. of Philadelphia (pres. 1908, 1917, trustee since 1912); ex-pres. Allen Lane Sch. Assn.; chmn. Com. on Homœ. Pharmacopœia, 1907-11, 1912, 1933-38; chmn. Com. on Revision Homœ. Pharmacopœia of U.S.,

1935; censor Sr. Mil. Med. Assn., 1917. Mem. Germantown and Chestnut Hill Improvement Assn. (chmn. auxiliary com.; chmn. com. on health, sewage and water). Mem. Germantown Hist. Soc., Pi Gamma Mu. Episcopalian; vestryman Christ Ch., and St. Michael's Ch., Germantown. Club: Oxford Medical. Address: 20 E. Gowen Av., Mt. Airy, Philadelphia, Pa.

CARNEY, Chesney M(ichael), lawyer; b. Silver Hill, W.Va., Apr. 16, 1901; s. Ellis B. and Julia H. (Jones) C.; A.B., W.Va. U., 1924, LL.B., 1926; m. Elise Gibson Washington, Sept. 23, 1933. Admitted to Harrison County, W.Va., bar, 1926; partner law firm Steptoe & Johnson, Clarksburg, since 1930; pres. Wheeling (W.Va.) Bridge Co.; dir. Community Savings & Loan Co. of Clarksburg. Mem. Am. Bar Assn., W.Va. Bar Assn., Harrison Co. Bar Assn., Order of the Coif, Theta Chi. Republican. Presbyn. Clubs: Clarksburg Rotary (pres. 1934-35), Clarksburg Country; Cheat Bridge. Home: 208 E. Main St. Office: Union Bank Bldg., Clarksburg, W.Va.

CARNEY, Francis T., chief urologist Mercy Hosp.; asso. prologist Conemaugh Valley Memorial Hosp. Address: 218 Franklin St., Johnstown, Pa.

CARNEY, William Joseph, lawyer; b. Erie, Pa., Aug. 18, 1899; s. William P. and Katherine (Pfadt) C.; A.B., Allegheny Coll., Meadville, Pa., 1921; LL.B., U. of Pittsburgh Law Sch., 1924; unmarried. Admitted to Erie Co. bar, 1924, and since practiced at Erie, Pa.; mem. firm Haughney, Carney & McLaughlin, attys. at law, Erie, Pa., since 1924. Mem. S.A.T.C. during World War; hon. disch., Nov. 1919. Counsel Sch. Dist. of City of Erie, Pa. since 1930. Mem. Pa. State Bar Assn., Erie Co. Bar Assn., Phi Delta Theta, Delta Theta Phi, Delta Sigma Rho. Republican. Catholic. K.C., Elk. Clubs: Maennerchor, Owls, Press, City (Erie, Pa.). Home: 431 E. 11th St. Office: 309 Masonic Temple, Erie, Pa.

CAROTHERS, John Allen, securities broker; b. Pittsburgh, Pa., Jan. 8, 1894; s. James and Laura Goodwin (Allen) C.; student Cornell U., 1912-14; B.S. in E.E., Carnegie Inst. Tech., 1917; unmarried. Employed as elec. engr. with Pittsburgh Transformer Co., 1919-21; asso. with James Carothers & Co., stock brokers, Pittsburgh, continuously since 1921, successively clk., cashier, mem. firm, and sr. mem. firm since 1938. Served as electrician various grades, then ensign, U.S.N., 1917-19; served as 2d lieut. to capt. Pa. N.G. since 1925. Republican. United Presbyterian. Club: University (Pittsburgh). Home: 123 University Place. Office: 2116 Farmers Bank Bldg., Pittsburgh, Pa.

CAROTHERS, Neil, economist; b. Chattanooga, Tenn., Sept. 19, 1884; s. Neil and Asenath (Wallace) C.; A.B., U. of Ark., 1905; Rhodes Scholar, Oxford U., 1904-07, Diploma in Economics, 1907; Ph.D., Princeton, 1916; m. Eileen Kathleen Hamilton, Aug. 10, 1917; children—Neil III, Hamilton, Stuart. Instr., later asst. prof. economics, U. of Ark., 1907-14; asst. prof. and preceptor in economics and finance, Princeton, 1916-19; economic expert, Dept. of State, 1919-20; engaged in banking, N.Y. City, 1920-23; prof. economics and dir. Coll. Business Administration, Lehigh University, 1923-36, Macfarlane prof. of economics and dean of College of Business Adminstrn. since 1936, also acting head dept. industrial engring., 1925-27. In charge of NRA Campaign, Bethlehem, Pa., 1933. Served as 1st lt. Aviation Sect., Signal Corps, U.S.A., 1917-18; capt. Gen. Staff, 1919. Mem. Pa. Rhodes Scholarship Selection Com.; dir. Bethlehem Family Welfare Assn. Bethlehem Chamber of Commerce; vice-pres. Economics Nat. Com. on Monetary Policy. Mem. Am. Econ. Assn., Pacific Coast Numismatic Soc. (hon. life), Omicron Delta Kappa, Alpha Kappa Psi, Kappa Sigma, Phi Beta Kappa. Democrat. Presbyn. Clubs: Bethlehem, Saucon Valley Country. Author: (with others) Economic Agencies of the World War (U.S. War Dept.), 1929; Fractional Money, 1930. Contbr. to periodicals; radio commentator. Address: Lehigh University, Bethlehem, Pa.

CARPENTER, Aaron Everly, mfr. oils and leather; b. Woodbury, N.J., Aug. 1, 1883; s. Charles Everly and Florence Rebecca (Browne) C.; prep. edn. William Penn Charter Sch., Phila.; A.B., U. of Pa., 1906; m. Elizabeth Ryder Williams, 1904 (divorced); children—Florence Rebecca (Mrs. Reginald Hugh Murray), Aaron Everly (dec.); m. 2d, Edythe Aramantha Anderson, July 6, 1914. With E. F. Houghton Co., Phila., mfrs. oils and leathers for industries since 1906, successively foreign rep., treas., 1st v.p. and treas., and pres. and gen. mgr. since 1935; v.p. and dir. E. F. Houghton & Co. of Can., Ltd.; dir. E. F. Houghton & Co. of Eng., Ltd.; mem. counseil d'administration Societe des Produits Houghton. Served at 1st lt. and capt., Inf., U.S. Army, with A.E.F. during World War; now maj. O.R.C. Mem. bd. govs. Florence Crittenton Home. Fellow Royal Geog. Soc.; mem. Sigma Alpha Epsilon. Mason (K.T.), Nat. Sojourner. Clubs: Art (Phila.); Germantown (Pa.) Cricket; Bay Head (N.J.) Yacht; Army and Navy (Washington, D.C.); Manasquan River Marlin and Tuna (Brielle, N.J.). Home: 804 Westview Av., Germantown. Office: 240 W. Somerset St., Philadelphia, Pa.

CARPENTER, Charles Azariah, official dept. commerce; b. Brooklyn, N.Y., May 21, 1888; s. Charles Baxter and Anna Therese (Reimer) C.; ed. Stevens Inst. Tech., Hoboken, N.J., 1904-06; M.E., Cornell U., 1908, grad. study 1910-11; m. M. Margaret Van Deusen, Sept. 29, 1911; children—Carolyn Margaret, William. Employed in engring. positions with various concerns, 1907-17; v.p. Valley Forging Co.; mem. firm Carpenter & Byrne; sales mgr. Hydraulic Press Mfg. Co.; propr. Chas. A. Carpenter Co., 1930-34; dist. mgr. Bur. Fgn. and Domestic Commerce of U.S. Dept. Commerce, Pittsburgh, Pa., since 1934. Served as 1st lt., Ordnance, U.S. Army, 1917-19. Mem. Pittsburgh Fed. Bus. Assn. (pres.), Spl. Libraries Assn., Gamma Alpha. Democrat. Christian Ch. Club: Cornell Alumni (Pittsburgh). Writer of many articles on tech. subjects and econs.; contbr. articles developing theory of specific speed applied to centrifugal pumps and fans, 1912. Aided in developing theory of unit heaters. Home: 5634 Hampton St. Office: New Federal Bldg., Pittsburgh, Pa.

CARPENTER, Edmund Hawks, newspaper editor, postmaster; b. Woodbury, N.J., May 28, 1890; s. James Dunton and Harriet (Fish) C.; grad. Woodbury High Sch., 1907; B.S., U. of Pa., 1911; unmarried. Began as newspaper reporter on Gloucester County Democrat, 1911; editor Gloucester County Democrat and Evening News, Woodbury, N.J., 1915-34; mayor of Woodbury, N.J., 1933-34; postmaster, Woodbury since 1934; partner Millville, N.J., Pub. Co., newspaper and printing; vice-pres. Farmers and Nat. Bank, Woodbury; vice-pres. Woodbury Trust Co. Served as 2d lt. Ordnance Dept., U.S. Army, with A.E.F., 1918. Mem. Woodbury Bd. of Edn., 1913-17. Pres. N.J. Press Assn., 1927-28. Democrat. Baptist. Clubs: Woodbury Kiwanis. Home: 135 High St. Address: 45 N. Broad St., Woodbury, N.J.

CARPENTER, Edmund Nelson, ex-congressman; b. Wilkes-Barre, Pa., June 27, 1865; s. Benjamin Gardner and Sally Ann (Fell) C.; ed. pub. schs. and Wyoming Sem.; unmarried. Prospector and miner in Western states several yrs.; spl. rep. E. I. du Pont de Nemours Powder Co., 1909-16; bought and operated mines in Chile. Republican candidate for Congress, 1918; mem. 69th Congress (1925-27), 12th Pa. Dist. Enlisted as pvt. N.G. Pa., 1893, and advanced to maj.; served in 9th Pa. Vol. Inf., Spanish-Am. War; chmn. Wyoming Valley Chapter Am. Red Cross, World War. Mem. Acad. Polit. Science, Wyoming Hist. and Geol. Soc., Naval and Mil. Order Spanish-Am. War, Mil. Order Fgn. Wars, Pa. Soc. S.R. Methodist. Clubs: Westmoreland (Wilkes-Barre); New York Yacht; Metropolitan (Washington, D.C.). Home: 54 Riverside Drive. Office: 6 W. Market St., Wilkes-Barre, Pa.

CARPENTER, Hedwig Küber (formerly Mrs. John S. Carpenter), organist and teacher piano and voice; b. New York City, July 21, 1896; d. Charles C. and Katharine (Donner) Küber; studied under various music teachers, New York City; ed. Peabody Conservatory, 1929-33; m. John S. Carpenter, Oct. 7, 1915 (div.); 1 dau., Helen June. Accompanist and dir. sch. orchestra at 13 yrs. of age; asst. to Wm. A. Goldsworthy, 1910; organist Sixth Ch. Christ. Sci., N.Y. City, 1912-16, First Ch. Christ. Scientist, York, Pa., 1929-32; teacher of piano, Daughters O.L. of Mercy Convent, York, Pa., 1932-34; teacher piano and voice, Paterson, N.J., and Elizabeth, N.J. since 1935; has appeared in pub. recitals for many yrs. Mem. Pa. Assn. of Organists. Episcopalian. Home: 521 Elizabeth Av., Elizabeth, N.J.

CARPENTER, Howard Childs, pediatrist; b. Phila., Pa., Dec. 16, 1878; s. Edward Payson and Frances Bradley (Childs) C.; student Friends' Central Sch., Phila., 1890-96; M.D., U. of Pa., 1900; unmarried. In practice pediatrics, Phila., since 1900; mem. faculty Pa. Scho. for Social and Health Work, 1919-21; asso. prof. pediatrics, Sch. of Medicine, U. of Pa., 1924-30; prof. pediatric hygiene, Grad. Sch. of Medicine, U. of Pa., 1920-29, prof. pediatrics since 1929, since 1929, vice dean for pediatrics since 1926; dir. dept. prevention of disease, Children's Hospital, Phila., since 1913, dir. Child Hygiene Assn., same, since 1922, med. dir., same, since 1930; pediatrist Grad. Hosp.; cons. pediatrist Delaware County Hosp.; consultant to Woman's Hosp. of Phila.; cons. pediatrist to Preston Retreat; dir. of service, dept. of pediatrics, Germantown Dispensary and Hosp. Pres. Children's Bur., Phila.; mem. bd. dirs. Adam and Sara Seybert Inst. for Poor Boys and Girls; mem. pediatric adv. com. U.S. Children's Bur.; mem. mng. com. Associated Med. Clinic; ex-pres. Children's Hosp. Assn. of America; ex-chmn. Children's Hosp. Section of Am. Hosp. Assn.; mem. of com. on pediatric edn. Med. Soc. of Pa. Fellow A.M.A., Am. Pub. Health Assn., Coll. of Physicians (Phila.); mem. Am. Pediatric Soc. (ex-pres.), Phila. Pediatric Soc. (awarded hon. medal 1933); Pathol. Soc. of Phila., Phila. Co. Med. Soc., Pa. Soc. Soc. of S.R., Pa. Soc. of Mayflower Desc., Colonial Soc. of Pa., Alpha Mu Pi Omega, Sigma Xi. Episcopalian. Collaborator Archives of Pediatrics; advisory editor Parents' Mag. Home: 1805 Spruce St., Philadelphia, Pa.

CARPENTER, James Donald, civil engring.; b. Harrisburg, Pa., May 18, 1892; s. Lewis H. and Clara A. (Bates) C.; B.S., Pa. State Coll., 1914, C.E., 1920; m. Isabel A. Ryder, March 15, 1917; children—Janet Louise, Isabel Adrian. Employed as insp. Ohio River work, U.S. Engrs., War Dept., 1914-15; with H. Koppers Co., 1916; asso. with Gannett, Eastman & Fleming, Inc., engrs., since 1918, sec. and mem. firm since 1928, in charge valuation and water works engring.; pres. Upper Mauch Chunk Water Co.; vice-pres. and dir. Lower Paxton Suburban Water Co.; vice-pres. Harrisburg Suburban Water Co.; dir. East McKeesport Water Co. Served as chief insp. dam at Racine, O., with U.S. Engrs., War Dept., 1917-18. Registered professional engr. in Pa. Mem. Tau Beta Pi. Presbyterian. Mason. Home: 3108 Green St. Office: 600 N. 2d St., Harrisburg, Pa.

CARPENTER, Joseph R., Jr.; v.p. Pa. Co. for Insurance on Lives and Granting Annuities. Home: 14 Summit St., Chestnut Hill. Office: S. E. cor. 15th & Chestnut Sts., Philadelphia, Pa.

CARPENTER, Rhys, author, archæologist; b. Cotuit, Mass., Aug. 5, 1889; s. William Henry and Anna Morgan (Douglass) C.; A.B., Columbia, 1908, Ph.D., 1916; B.A., Balliol Coll. (Oxford U., Eng.), 1911, M.A., 1914; studied Am. Sch., Classical Studies, Athens, Greece, 1912-13; m. Eleanor Houston Hill, Apr. 23, 1918. Instr. classical archæology, 1913-15, asso., 1915-16, asso. prof., 1916-18, prof., 1918—, Bryn Mawr Coll.; dir. Am. Sch. of Classical Studies at Athens, Greece, 1927-32. Served as 1st lt. M.I. Staff, U.S.A., 1918-19; attached Am. Commn. to Negotiate Peace, Paris, 1919. Member of the American Philosophical Society, Archæol. Institute of America, Philadelphia Oriental Club, Phi Beta Kappa; hon. mem. Greek Archæol. Soc., German Archæol. Inst., Austrian

Archæol. Inst.; corr. mem. Hispanic Soc. America. Author: Tragedy of Etarre, 1912; The Sun-thief, and Other Poems, 1914; The Plainsman, and Other Poems, 1920; The Land Beyond Mexico, 1921; The Esthetic Basis of Greek Art, 1921; The Greeks in Spain, 1925; The Sculpture of the Nike Parapet, 1929; The Humanistic Value of Archæology, 1933; The Defenses of Acrocorinth, 1935. Home: "Jerry Run," Downingtown, Pa.

CARPENTER, Robert Ruliph Morgan, vice-pres. E. I. du Pont de Nemours & Co.; b. Wilkes-Barre, Pa., July 30, 1877; s. Walter Samuel and Belle (Morgan) C.; prep. edn., Hillman Acad., Wilkes-Barre, Pa.; spl. study Mass. Inst. Tech.; m. Margaretta L. du Pont, Dec. 18, 1906; children—Louisa d'A., Renee du Pont, Robert Ruliph Morgan, William K. du Pont. Began as engr., E. I. du Pont de Nemours & Co., Wilmington, 1904, successively purchasing agt., dir. development dept., vice-pres., mem. exec. com., gen. mgr. cellulose dept., now vice-pres.; vice-pres. News Journal Co., Wilmington; Phila., Baltimore & Washington R.R. Co., Christian Securities Co., Delaware Realty Co. Pres. Homœopathic Hosp., Assn. of Wilmington. Mem. Phi Beta Epsilon. Republican. Clubs: Wilmington, Wilmington Whist, Wilmington Country, Vicmead Hunt, Wilderness, Boone and Crocket; Union League, Midday, Rittenhouse (Phila.); New York Yacht. Home: Montchanin, Del. Office: E. I. du Pont de Nemours & Co., Wilmington, Del.

CARPENTER, Walter Samuel, Jr., mfr. explosives and chemicals; b. Wilkesbarre, Pa., Jan. 8, 1888; s. Walter S. and Belle (Morgan) C.; prep. edn., Wyoming Sem., Kingston, Pa., 1902-06; student Cornell, 1906-10; m. Mary Wootten, June 3, 1914; children—Walter Samuel 3d, John W., Edmund N. 2d. Connected with E. I. du Pont de Nemours & Co., Wilmington, Del., since 1909, v.p. since 1919; director Gen. Motors' Corpn. (policy committee), Diamond State Telephone Co., Bell Telephone Co. of Pa., Wilmington Trust Co. Mem. bd. dirs. Wilmington Gen. Hosp.; trustee Wyo. Sem., Kingston, Pa. Methodist. Clubs: Wilmington, Wilmington Country; Hay Harbor; Fishers Island (Fisher's Island, N.Y.); New York Yacht. Home: 18th St. and Rising Sun Lane. Office: du Pont Bldg., Wilmington, Del.

CARPENTER, William Seal, prof. politics; b. nr. Wilmington, Del., Jan. 28, 1890; s. Harry Fisher and Sarah Gawthrop (Seal) C.; B.S., U. of Pa., 1911, A.M., 1912; Ph.D., Princeton, 1914; studied London (Eng.) Sch. of Economics and Political Science, 1919; m. Alice Myrtle Getchell, Aug. 7, 1924; 1 dau., Jane. Instr. in polit. science, U. of Wis., 1914-17; instr., asst. prof. and asso. prof. politics, Princeton, 1920-30, prof. since 1930, chmn. dept. since 1935. Served with A.E.F., 1918-19. Mem. adv. research council Bureau of Prohibition, 1931; mem. N.J. State Planning Bd. since 1937; mem. bd. of mgrs. Friends' Home for Children, Philadelphia, since 1937. Mem. Am. Polit. Science Assn., Am. Soc. Planning Officials, Kappa Alpha. Member Society of Friends. Club: Princeton (New York). Author: Judicial Tenure in the United States, 1918; Democracy and Representation, 1925; Development of American Political Thought, 1930; (with Paul T. Stafford) State and Local Government in the United States, 1936. Editor: Locke's Two Treatises of Civil Government, 1924; (with Paul T. Stafford) Readings in Early Legal Institutions, 1932. Contbr. articles and revs. in fields of law and politics. Research asso. Princeton Local Govt. Survey, 1935—. Home: Princeton, N.J.

CARR, Gene, illustrator and caricaturist; b. New York, Jan. 7, 1881; s. Charles and Sarah (Cox) C.; ed. pub. schs.; never studied art; m. Helen Stilwell, artist and writer, Aug. 22, 1906 (divorced); 1 dau., Cléanthe; m. 2d, Helen Adams Breadner, Aug. 5, 1937. Employed on New York Recorder, 1894, later on New York Herald, Philadelphia Times, New York Journal and New York World. Creator of comic series, Lady Bountiful, Phyllis, Romeo, All the Comforts of Home, the Prodigal Son, Father, Willise Wise, Stepbrothers, Bill, the Jones Boys, Flirting Flora, Reddy and Caruso, Metropolitan Movies, in the Morning World, Little Nell, Just Humans. McClure's Syndicate; with King Features since 1938. Contbr. to American Magazine, Colliers, Red Book, Cosmopolitan, Liberty, etc. Home: 143 Tenafly Rd., Englewood, N.J.

CARR, Harry Chiles, vice-pres. and treas. Bayuk Cigars, Inc.; b. St. Louis, Mo., Oct. 13, 1886; s. Harry Chiles and Alice (Zimmerman) C.; grad. St. Louis High Sch., 1903; student Columbia U., 1903-05; m. Anstes Turner, May 24, 1911; children—Harry Chiles, Anstes Valle. Began as draftsman Elliot Frog and Switch Co., 1905; sales mgr. Simmons Hardware Co., Phila., 1912-15; export mgr. Sun Oil Co., Phila., 1915-28; managing dir. European Properties Gulf Oil Co., Antwerp, Belgium, 1928-32, v.p. and treas. Bayuk Cigars, Inc., Phila., since 1936. Dir. Babies' Hosp., Phila. Republican. Episcopalian. Clubs: University (Phila.); Merion Cricket (Haverford, Pa.); India House (New York). Home: Rosemont, Pa. Office: 9th and Columbia Av., Philadelphia, Pa.

CARR, James Osgood; v.p. Allegheny Ludlum Steel Corpn. Home: 120 Ruskin Av., Pittsburgh, Pa. Office: Brackenridge, Pa.

CARR, Walter Russell, judge; b. Union, Pa., May 30, 1885; s. John Dickson and Amanda (Cooke) C.; A.B., Washington and Jefferson Coll., Washington, Pa., 1906, A.M., 1909; m. Mary Lulu Oglevee, July 24, 1912; 1 son, Philip Oglevee. Admitted to Pa. bar, 1908, and since in practice at Uniontown, Pa.; mem. firm Carr & Carr, Uniontown, since 1908; elected judge of Court of Common Pleas of Fayette Co., 14th Judicial Dist. of Pa., November, 1937. Mem. bd. trustees for the Diocese of Pittsburgh, Protestant Episcopal Ch.; trustee Uniontown Hosp. Assn. of Fayette Co., Pa., Fayette Co. Community Chest, Fayette Co. Chapter Am. Red Cross. Mem. Am. Bar Assn., Pa. Bar Assn., Fayette Co. Bar Assn., Phi Kappa Psi. Democrat. Episcopalian (sr. warden St. Peter's Episcopal Ch., Uniontown, Pa.). Mason. Home: 58 E. Berkeley St. Office: Court House, Uniontown, Pa.

CARR, William A.; mem. law firm Carr & Krauss. Office: 1113 North American Bldg., Philadelphia, Pa.

CARRELL, John B., physician; b. Warminster, Bucks Co., Pa., July 11, 1851; s. Ezra Patterson and Margaret Lang (Beans) C.; student Warminster (Pa.) Pub. Sch. and Excelsior Inst. (Hatboro, Pa.); M.D., Jefferson Med. Coll., Phila., Pa., 1876; m. Lizzie S. Danenhower, Mar. 31, 1880 (died 1922). In active practice as physician at Hatboro, Pa., 1877-1924; formerly physician Orange Home (Hatboro), St. Stephen's Home (Warminster), Emlin Inst. (Warminster). Mem. commn. of Pa. State Med. Soc. to have law enacted for State to build and equip a hosp. for restraint, care and treatment of inebriates and drug habitues, appearing before three legislatures and having law enacted, 1918. Mem. Bucks Co. (Pa.) Med. Soc. (pres. 1907), Montgomery Co. (Pa.) Med. Soc., Phila. Med. Club, S.A.R., Kappa Gamma Epsilon. Republican. Knights of Pythias. Editor Bucks Co. Med. Monthly, 1910-30; reporter and writer for local and city newspapers and jours. since 1869. At present writing history Bucks Co. medicine from 1609 to be incorporated in history of Bucks Co. for use in pub. schs. of co. Home: 36 E. Byberry Av., Hatboro, Pa.

CARRIGG, Joseph Leonard, dist. atty.; b. Susquehanna, Pa., Feb. 23, 1901; s. Thomas and Ellen (Houlihan) C.; student Laurel Hill Acad., Susquehanna, Pa., 1907-18; A.B., Niagara U., Niagara Falls, N.Y., 1922; student Albany (N.Y.) Law Sch., 1922-24, Dickinson Law Sch., Carlisle, Pa., 1924-25; unmarried. Admitted to Susquehanna Co. bar, 1926, and since practiced at Susquehanna and Montrose, Pa.; city solicitor, Susquehanna, Pa., since 1928, Great Bend, Pa., since 1934; dist. atty., Susquehanna Co., Pa., since 1936; dir. First National Bank, Susquehanna, Pa. Dir. Barnes Hosp., Susquehanna, Pa. Mem. Woolsack, Devils Own, Phi Sigma Kappa. Republican. Catholic. K.C. Home: 405 Pine St., Susquehanna, Pa. Office: Court House, Montrose, Pa.

CARRINGER, Marion Aubrey, lawyer; b. Sheakleyville, Pa., Nov. 5, 1876; s. Milo C. and Mary Amanda (Robinson) C.; student Clarion (Pa.) State Teachers Coll., 1893-95; Ph.B., Bucknell U., Lewisburg, Pa., 1900, Ph.M., 1901; m. June Herman, Dec. 10, 1919; children—Rachel Montgomery, Robert Milo, Dorothy June. Admitted to Pa. bar, 1905, and since practiced at Tionesta, Pa.; sec., treas. and dir. Jenks Development Corpn., Tionesta, Pa., Tionesta (Pa.) Water Supply Co.; dir. Forest Co. Nat. Bank, Jamieson Lumber & Supply Co., Marienville Glass Co. Dist. atty. Forest Co., Pa., 1910-19, since 1928, co. solicitor, 1919-26, govt. appeal agt., 1917-18, dep. atty-gen., 1925-26. Mem. Am. Bar Assn., Sigma Chi. Mason. Address: Tionesta, Pa.

CARRINGTON, Edward Codrington, lawyer; b. Washington, D.C., Apr. 10, 1872; s. Edward Codrington and Florida Troupe (Harrison) C.; ed. under pvt. tutors; m. Ethel Stuart Coyle, Oct. 5, 1899; m. 2d, Alice Welks Preston, Feb. 5, 1936 (died Dec. 30, 1938). Admitted to Md. bar, 1894, and began practice in Baltimore; mem. Carrington & Carrington, Baltimore and New York; specializes in corpn. law. Mem. staff of Gov. Goldsborough, with rank of col. Campaign manager for Md. for Theodore Roosevelt, primary election, 1912; del. at large, Rep. Nat. Conv., Chicago, same yr.; signed call for Progressive Nat. Conv., 1912, and later del. at large to same; mem. Progressive Nat. Com., 1912, and chmn. Progressive State Com., Md.; after presdl. election, 1912, led movement in Md. to unite Reps. and Progressives; regular Rep. nominee for U.S. Senate, 1914 (defeated); Rep. nominee for pres. Borough of Manhattan, 1931. Chmn. bd. and pres. Hudson River Navigation Corpn.; chmn. bd. Hudson River Steamboat Co.; pres. Americana Corpn.; v.p. Eastwood Corpn. Episcopalian. Clubs: City, Nat. Republican, Troy, 15th Assembly Dist. Republican (1st v.p.). Home: Loreley, Md.

CARRINGTON, William J(ohn), gynecologist; b. Jefferson City, Mo., Feb. 4, 1884; s. William T. and Mary (Holloway) C.; ed. Warrensburg (Mo.) Normal Sch., 1898-1900; A.B., U. of Mo., 1904; M.D., Jefferson Med. Coll., Phila., 1908; m. Lucy Grier, Jan. 10, 1910; children—William, Lucy, Mary Catherine, Elizabeth, Emily, Jane Randolph. Interne Jefferson Hosp., Phila., 1908-09; engaged in practice of medicine at Atlantic City, N.J., since 1910, specializing in gynecology and obstetrics since 1920; attdg. gynecologist, Atlantic City Hosp., Pine Rest, Atlantic Co. Hosp. for Mental Diseases, Atlantic City Municipal Hosp.; dir. Guarantee Trust Co. Pres. Sch. Bd. Ventnor, N.J., 1928-29; past pres. Atlantic Council Boy Scouts. Fellow Am. Coll. Surgeons, Internat. Coll. Surgeons (Geneva); diplomate Am. Bd. Gynecology and Obstetrics. Mem. A.M.A., Med. Soc. of N.J. (ex-pres.), N.J. Sanitation Assn., Phila. Obstet. and Pathol. socs., Atlantic Co. Med. Soc. (past pres.), Jefferson Alumni Assn. (past pres.), Kappa Sigma. Conglist. Kiwanis International (past internat. pres.). Contbr. to med. jours. Home: 12 S. Somerset Av., Ventnor, N.J. Office: 905 Pacific Av., Atlantic City, N.J.

CARROLL, Benjamin Saulsbury, high school prin.; b. Easton, Md., Sept. 6, 1901; s. Ulysses Frank and Annie Ellen (Ettien) C.; grad. Easton (Md.) High Sch., 1918; A.B., Western Md. Coll., Westminster, 1922; A.M., Teachers' Coll., Columbia, 1931; m. Margaret Warner Carroll, July 17, 1933. Teacher, Huntington (Md.) High Sch., 1922-23, Wicomico High Sch., Salisbury, Md., 1924-28; prin. Trappe (Md.) High Sch., 1928-35, Easton (Md.) High Sch., 1935-38, Bel Air (Md.) High Sch. since 1938. Presbyterian. Rotarian. Home: Hickory Av., Bel Air, Md.

CARROLL, Charles Jr., lawyer; b. Baltimore, Md., Apr. 27, 1903; s. Charles and Mary Clarita (Randol) C.; prep. edn., Marston's Univ. Sch., 1914-21; A.B., Princeton, 1925; LL.B., U. of Md., 1928; m. Anne Parker Dobbin, Apr. 30, 1930; children—Charles, III, Anne Parker. Admitted to Md. bar, 1928; asso. with William Pepper Constable, Baltimore, 1928-32; mem. firm Hill & Carroll, Baltimore, 1932-35; practicing alone, Ellicott City, Md., since 1935;

also asso. with Constable & Alexander, Baltimore, since 1935; dir. Patapsco Nat. Bank. Mem. Md. House of Dels. from Howard Co. since 1930. Mem. Md. Commn. to New York World's Fair, 1939. Mem. Md. Bar Assn., Rule Day Club, Princeton Quadrangle Club. Catholic. Clubs: Howard County Hunt (hon. sec. and treas.), Glenelg (Howard Co., Md.). Address: Ellicott, Md.

CARROLL, Douglas Gordon, stock broker; b. Baltimore, Md., July 14, 1882; s. Gen. John N. and Mary Randolph (Thomas) C.; student U. of Md., 1897-1900; m. Amelie Louise Hack, Mar. 31, 1910; children—Nancy Gordon (Mrs. William C. Trimble), Douglas Gordon. Began as clerk Merchants Nat. Bank, Baltimore, 1900-12; entered brokerage business, 1912; organized, 1916, and still owner Douglas G. Carroll & Co., stock brokers (members Baltimore Stock Exchange). Democrat. Episcopalian. Clubs: Maryland, Green Spring Hunt, Elkridge Hunt (Baltimore, Md); Everglades (Palm Beach, Fla.). Home: "Oakdene," Brooklandville, Md. Office: Stock Exchange Bldg., Baltimore, Md.

CARROLL, Joseph H.; obstetrician St. Francis Hosp., Roselia Foundling Asylum and Maternity Hosp.; asst. obstetrician Mercy Hosp. Address: 3710 Fifth Av., Pittsburgh, Pa.

CARROLL, Mitchel, coll. prof.; b. Phila., Pa., July 7, 1885; s. William and Anna (Davidson) C.; B.S., U. of Pa., 1915, Ph.D., 1919; Sc.D., Franklin and Marshall Coll., Lancaster, Pa., 1939; m. Nora Cashel, Mar. 16, 1918; 1 son, Kenneth Malcolm. Teacher Phila. Pub. Schs., 1909-14; asst. zoologist, U. of Pa., 1915-16, Harrison fellow in zoology, 1916-18; asst. state entomologist, N.J. State Experiment Sta., New Brunswick, N.J., 1918-20; prof. of biology and head dept. biology, Franklin and Marshall Coll., Lancaster, Pa., since 1920. Fellow A.A.A.S.; mem. Am. Assn. of Econ. Entomologists, Am. Assn. of Mammalogists, Marine Biol. Lab., Am. Genetic Assn., Am. Soc. of Geneticists, Am. Soc. of Zoologists, Am. Soc. of Parasitologists, Am. Micros. Soc., Sigma Xi. Address: 540 President Av., Lancaster, Pa.

CARROLL, Thomas B.; gynecologist and obstetrician Columbia Hosp., Wilkinsburg; cons. obstetrician St. Francis Hosp.; chief gynecol. dept. Montefiore Hosp.; gynecologist to Women's Hosp. of Pittsburgh. Address: 500 Penn Av., Pittsburgh, Pa.

CARROLL, Walter R.; mem. law firm Carroll & Taylor. Address: Camden, N.J.

CARROLL, Wayne T., gen. mgr. Western Allegheny R.R. Co., pres. Kaylor Natural Gas Co.; b. Union City, Pa., Oct. 31, 1881; s. Fletcher S. and Alice M. (Barnes) C.; student Edinboro State Teachers Coll. and Meadville (Pa.) Commercial Coll.; m. Rebecca M. Ingols, Aug. 28, 1906; children—Clark W., Alice R., Kathryn L., Lorraine M. Sch. teacher, Erie Co., Pa., 1900-05; sec. to supt. of mech. dept. Erie R.R., 1905-08; chief clk. to supt. Western Allegheny R.R., 1908-12, chief clk. to gen. mgr., 1912-16, asst. to gen. mgr., 1916-21, gen. mgr. since 1921; v.p. Kaylor Natural Gas Co., 1929-34, pres. since 1934, now also dir. Mason (Argyle Lodge 540, past master and life mem.; Butler chapter, Royal Arch.; Lorraine Commandery 87, K.T.; New Castle Consistory, Scottish Rite; Shriner, Syria Temple), Odd Fellow (past grand), K.P. (261, past chancellor). Club: Odd Fellows of Chicora (Pa.). Address: Kaylor, Pa.

CARSON, David R., banker; b. Phila., Pa., Sept. 11, 1880; s. Archibald and Anna J. (Black) C.; ed. pub. schs. of Phila.; student, U. of Pa. Evening Sch., 1904-08; m. Mary A. West, Nov. 25, 1909; children—Edward West, Rhoda Jane. Clerk B. S. Jauncy Jr. Co., Phila., 1895-99; bookkeeper, 4th Street Nat. Bank, 1899-1903; teller Central Trust and Savings Co., 1903-12; accountant Ford, Bacon & Davis, 1912-13; accountant and branch mgr. Alexander Bros., 1913-18; with Central-Penn. Nat. Bank, Phila., since 1918, beginning as asst. cashier, now v.p.; dir. Nat. Bank of Lansdowne. Republican. Presbyterian. Mason (32°, Consistory). Club: Union League (Phila). Home: Lansdowne, Pa. Office: Central-Penn. National Bank, Philadelphia, Pa.

CARSON, Edwin Ramsey, official bd. edn.; b. Oakdale, Ill., Mar. 6, 1885; s. William Henry and Mary Elizabeth (Ramsey) C.; B.S., Valparaiso (Ind.) U., 1907; A.B., Geneva Coll., Beaver Falls, Pa., 1910; grad. study U. of Chicago, summers, 1911, 1912, 1914; A.M., U. of Pittsburgh, 1930; m. Margaret Watson Bell, July 1, 1915; 1 son, Edwin Ramsey. Engaged in teaching in Ill., 1903-08; teacher high sch. Beaver Falls, Pa., 1910-12, prin., 1912-17; teacher high sch., McKeesport, Pa., 1917-18; prin. high sch., Munhall, 1918-22; teacher South Hills High Sch., Pittsburgh, 1922-32; prin. Woolslair & Andrews Elementary Schs., 1932-35; dir. Sch. Attendance Dept., Bd. Edn., Pittsburgh, since 1935. Mem. National, State, and Local edn. assns., Nat. League to Promote Sch. Attendance (v.p.). Republican. Reformed Presbyterian. Home: 272 Dixon Av. Office: Bellefield and Forbes Sts., Pittsburgh, Pa.

CARSON, Edwin Schively, clergyman; b. Phila., Pa., June 15, 1879; s. John Wallace and Hannah E. (Parry) C.; grad. Germantown Acad., Phila., Pa., 1898; A.B., Trinity Coll., Hartford, Conn., 1902; grad. Phila. Divinity Sch., 1904; m. Laura E. Jansen, Apr. 24, 1905; children—Gertrude (Mrs. J. F. Weber), Elizabeth B. (Mrs. R. J. Cavagnaro). Ordained to ministry of Episcopalian Ch., June 12, 1904; rector St. Paul Memorial Ch., Phila., 1904-13, Holy Trinity Ch., Minneapolis, 1913-16, Christ Ch., Ridgewood, N.J., since 1916. Mem. Alpha Chi Rho. Republican. Mason, Elk. Club: Rotary (Ridgewood). Home: 105 Cottage Place, Ridgewood, N.J.

CARSON, John (Joseph), consumers' counsel Nat. Bituminous Coal Commn.; b. Johnson Co., Ind., Nov. 16, 1889; s. William and Mary (Gleason) C.; student pub. and parochial schs., Indianapolis, Ind., 1895-1902, Manual Training High Sch., 1903-05; m. A. Elizabeth Groseclose, May 3, 1916; children—Mary Katherine, Elizabeth Jane, Joan. Clk. Van Camp Packing Co., 1905-10; reporter and city editor Indianapolis Sun and Ind. Daily Times, 1911-18; Washington corr. for St. Louis Globe Democrat, St. Louis Republic, Baltimore Sun, Baltimore Evening Sun, Scripps-Howard Alliance, 1918-24; sec. Senator James Couzens, 1924-36; consumers' counsel Nat. Bituminous Coal Commn. since 1937. Catholic. Club: Columbia Country (Washington, D.C.). Home: 16 Oxford St., Chevy Chase, Md. Office: Tower Bldg., Washington, D.C.

CARSON, John Renshaw, research engr.; b. Pittsburgh, Pa., June 28, 1887; s. John D. and Ada R. (Johnston) C.; prep. edn., Allegheny Prep. Sch., Pittsburgh; B.S., Princeton, 1907, E.E., 1909, M.S., 1912; grad. study Mass. Inst. Tech., 1907-08; D.Sc., Brooklyn Polytechnic Institute, 1936; m. Frances Atwell, July 22, 1913; 1 son, John R. Instr. in physics, Princeton, 1912-14; engr. transmission theory development, Am. Telephone & Telegraph Co., 1914-34; research mathematician, Bell Telephone Labs., N.Y. City since 1934; special lecturer, Mass. Inst. Tech., 1922, U. of Pa., 1925. Represented Am. Telephone & Telegraph Co. at Internat. Scientific Congress, Toronto, 1924, Paris, 1925, Como, 1927. Fellow Am. Inst. E.E., Inst. Radio Engrs.; mem. Am. Math. Soc. (former mem. council), Phi Beta Kappa. Awarded Liebmann Memorial prize, Inst. Radio Engrs., for invention in radio and contbns. to math. theory of electric circuits, 1924. Author: Electric Circuit Theory and the Operational Calculus, 1927; Elektrische Ausgleichvorgänge und Operatorenrechnung, 1929. Contbr. to Am. and foreign tech. and scientific jours. Home: New Hope, Pa. Office: 463 West St., New York, N.Y.

CARSON, Norma Bright, author; b. Phila., Jan. 7, 1883; d. Joseph C. and Emma (Moore) Bright; grad. Girls High Sch., Phila., 1901; m. Robert Carson, June 20, 1906; children—Robert Bright, Dorothy Bright. Presbyn. Editor The Book News Monthly, Phila., 1906-18; asso. lit. editor Phila. Press, 1918-20; mng. editor Photo-Play World, 1918-20; editor The Photo Drama Magazine, 1920-21; managing editor The Republican Woman, 1923-36; editor The Clubwoman's Journal since 1935; apptd. magistrate City of Philadelphia, 1932; appointed chief of juvenile div., Crime Prevention Bureau, City of Philadelphia, Feb. 1936. Author: The Dream Child and Other Poems, 1905; From Irish Castles to French Chateaux, 1910; The Nature Fairies, 1911; In the Kingdom of the Future, 1913; Boys of the Bible, 1914; Rosemary—For Remembrance, 1914; The Children's Own Story Book (with Florence E. Bright), 1916; The Fairy Housekeepers, 1917; Trueheart Margery, 1917; Poems for Little Men and Women (with Florence E. Bright), 1918. Home: 4418 Walnut St. Office: 1117 Pine St., Philadelphia, Pa.

CARSON, Roy Irwin, lawyer; b. Charleroi, Pa. Mar. 28, 1891; s. Noah T. and Laura (Sprowls) C.; ed. Washington and Jefferson Coll., Washington, Pa., 1909-13; A.B., U. of Pittsburgh Law Sch., 1916; m. Violet Lutes, May 25, 1917; children—Howard Francis, Roy Irwin. Admitted to Pa. bar, 1916, and since engaged in gen. practice of law at Charleroi, Pa.; served as solicitor for several municipalities and sch. districts; dir. and solicitor Nat. Bank of Charleroi (Pa.) and Trust Co. since 1926; mem. Borough Council, 1921-22; mem. Washington Co. Relief Bd. (chmn. 1933). Served as 2d lt., U.S. Army, 1917-18. Mem. bd. dirs. Charleroi Chamber of Commerce since its orgn. (past pres.). Mem. Pa. State and Washington Co. bar assns., Charleroi Turn Verein, Am. Legion, Forty and Eight. Republican. Methodist. Mason (K.T., Shriner), Odd Fellow, Grange. Clubs: Rotary, Nemacolin Country (Charleroi, Pa.); University (Pittsburgh). Home: 139 Fallowfield Av. Office: 408 Fallowfield Av., Charleroi, Pa.

CARSON, Waid Edwin, ophthalmologist; b. Racine, O., Aug. 8, 1876; s. Arthur M. and Cora (Lasher) Carson; A.B. Ohio Wesleyan Univ., Delaware, O., 1900; grad. student U. of Chicago, 1904; M.D., Med. Sch. of Johns Hopkins U., 1907; unmarried. Interne Allegheny Gen. Hosp., 1907-08; resident Wills Eye Hosp., 1913-14; mem. staff West Pa. Hosp., Eye and Ear Hosp., Elizabeth Steel Magee Hosp., Presbyterian Hosp.; prof. ophthalmology, U. of Pittsburgh since 1936. Served as opthalmologist, U.S. Naval Hosp., Great Lakes, Ill., during World War; lieut. med. corps, U.S. Naval Res. Fellow Am. Coll. Surgeons; certified Am. Bd. Ophthalmology; mem. Am., Pa. State, and Allegheny Co. med. assns., Pittsburgh Acad. of Medicine, Pittsburgh Ophthal. Soc., Am. Acad. Ophthalmology and Otolaryngology, Ophthal. Soc. of the United Kingdom, Phi Delta Theta. Republican. Mason. Home: Schenley Apts. Office: Jenkins Arcade Bldg., Pittsburgh, Pa.

CARTER, Allan; mem. firm Resinol Chem. Co. Home: 3902 N. Charles St. Office: 517 W. Lombard St., Baltimore, Md.

CARTER, Boake, radio news commentator; b. Baku, S. Russia, Sept. 1898; s. Thomas and Edith (Harwood-Yarred) C.; ed. Christ's Coll., Cambridge, Eng.; m. Beatrice Olive Richter, 1924; children—Michael Boake, Gwladys Sheleagh Boake. Came to America, 1920, naturalized citizen, 1933. Began as newspaper reporter, Daily Mail, London; in oil business in Mexico and Central America, 1920-23; with Tulsa (Okla.) World, Mexico City Excelsior, Phila. Evening Bulletin, Daily News, Phila., and other newspapers, until 1932; with Philco Radio & Television Corpn., Phila., since 1932; news commentator over Radio Station WCAU. Served in British Royal Air Force, World War, 1918. Clubs: Sketch, British Officers, Gibson Island Yacht, Torresdale, Delaware River Yacht. Author: Black Shirts—Black Skin, 1935; Johnnie "Q" Public; I Talk as I Like; This is Life; Hands Off the Far East; Why Meddle in the Orient? Home: Torresdale, Philadelphia. Address: Radio Station WCAU, Philadelphia, Pa.

CARTER, Carl J.; mem. surg. staff Cook Hosp. Address: 95 Fairmont Av., Fairmont, W.Va.

CARTER, Emmett Browning, consulting engr.; b. Union City, Pa., Dec. 19, 1878; s. Charles Grant and Lois (Taylor) C.; grad. Owego (N.Y.) High Sch., 1896; M.E., Cornell U., 1899; m. Bessie Wentz, Sept. 5, 1901; 1 son, Charles Wentz (dec.). Engring. inspector, U.S. Navy, 1899-1904; chief engr. Midvale Steel Co., 1904-

20; construction engr. Cambria Steel Co., 1920-22; gen. chief engr. The Barrett Co., all plants, 1922-25; in charge of design and building new plant The Tannin Corpn., N.Y. City, 1925-28; v.p. Delaware Floor Products, Wilmington, 1928-29; works mgr. Dresser Mfg. Co., Bradford, Pa., 1929-32; in private practice as consulting engr. since 1932. Licensed as professional engr. in N.Y., N.J. and Pa. Gov. Englewood (N.J.) Hosp. Mem. Am. Soc. Mech. Engrs. Republican. Episcopalian. Clubs: Cornell (New York); ex-pres. Engineers Club (Philadelphia). Home: 19 Prospect Terrace, Tenafly, N.J. Office: 2 Lafayette St., New York, N.Y.

CARTER, Ephraim Lee, propr. Pittsburgh Perco. Nut Co.; b. Stanley Co., N.C., Sept. 8, 1872; s. Robert Allen and Elizabeth Lavenia (Coble) C.; ed. pub. schs. and acad.; m. Mary Jane Henry, June 30, 1920. Employed as traveling salesman from 1892; in Pittsburgh since 1901; former treas. and half owner Fort Pitt Chocolate Co.; propr. Pittsburgh Perco Nut Co. since 1932. Democrat. Mason. Home: 5964 Baum Boul. Office: 6031 Broad St., Pittsburgh, Pa.

CARTER, George, editor; b. Smyrna, Del., July 31, 1865; s. John and Mary Hurd (Spratt) C.; ed. elementary pub. schs. and business coll.; m. Susie Etta Wyatt, 1886; m. 2d, Ann B. Foard, June 19, 1895; children—Mildred Lee (Mrs. J. Bayard Briggs), F(rancis) Bayard, G(eorge) Gray (the two sons held Rhodes scholarships at same time). Worked at printer's trade; local editor Del. Farm and Home; editorial staff New York newspaper 14 yrs.; served as reporter, city editor, later editor Wilmington Journal-Every Evening. Mem. Del. Com. of Defense, World War. Past pres. Delmarvia Press Assn.; pres. Goodwill Industries. Republican. Mason (K.T.). Clubs: Torch, The Senate. Home: "Cedarbrook," Smyrna, Del.*

CARTER, George Henry, former printer of U.S.; b. Mineral Point, Wis., Sept. 10, 1874; s. George and Mary Ann Battin (Lanyon) C.; Ph.B., U. of Ia., 1898; LL.B., George Washington U., 1920; m. Madge E. Penny, Sept. 1, 1904; 1 dau., Mrs. Madge Carter Goolsby (grandson Thomas Lanyon Carter); m. 2d, Lydia Althouse Goldecke, of New York, Dec. 1, 1938. Engaged in newspaper and printing work, Le Mars, Ia., 1890-94; proofreader and state news editor, Sioux City Tribune, 1898-99; reporter, The Nonpareil, Council Bluffs, 1899-1900, city editor, 1901-05; polit. writer and state house reporter, The Capital, Des Moines, 1905-07; asst. tel. editor, The Washington Post, 1907-09; Washington corr., 1909-10; asst. sec. and sec. Printing Investigation Commn., Washington, 1910-11; clk. Joint Com. on Printing, U.S. Congress, 1911-21; pub. printer of U.S., April 5, 1921-July 2, 1934; asst. to pres. Lanston Monotype Machine Co., Philadelphia. Chmn. U.S. Permanent Conf. on Printing, 1921-33; U.S. del. to First Internat. Congress of Master Printers, Gothenburg, Sweden, 1923, Third Internat. Congress, London, Eng., 1929. Mem. bar of U.S., D.C., and Iowa supreme courts. Hon. life mem. Internat. Printing Pressmen and Assistants' Union, United Typothetæ of America; hon. mem. Printing House Craftsmen (Washington, D.C., and Seattle, Wash.), and Typothetæ (Washington, D.C., Pittsburgh, Anthracite Dist., Pa.). Mem. Bd. of Commercial Arbitration for Graphic Arts Industries of New York. Mem. Am. Inst. Graphic Arts, Columbia Typog. Union No. 101 (Washington, D.C.), Am. Soc. Mech. Engrs., Soc. Am. Mil. Engrs., Phi Kappa Psi; 1st hon. mem. British Printing Industry Research Assn. Republican. Episcopalian. Mason (33°, K.T., Shriner), Eagle. Clubs: Nat. Press, Alfalfa (Washington, D.C.); Advertising (New York). Author of Congressional edition of Declaration of Independence and Constitution of United States, with Notes, 1934; Baron von Steubens Statute Proceedings; Congressional Printing Handbook; also various reports and articles. Home: 137 E. 38th St., New York, N.Y. Address: Lanston Monotype Machine Co., Philadelphia, Pa.

CARTER, Harvey Lewis, coll. prof.; b. Forest, Ind., Dec. 2, 1904; s. Harry Holmes and Martha Frances (Wyatt) C.; A.B., Wabash Coll., Crawfordsville, Ind., 1927; A.M., U. of Wis., Madison, Wis., 1928, Ph.D., 1938; m. Ruth Thornton, June 20, 1929; children—Harvey Thornton, Cherry. Instr. history and pub. speaking, Ursinus Coll., Collegeville, Pa., 1928-30, asst. prof., 1930-31, asso. prof. since 1931, coach of debate since 1928; on leave of absence, 1935-36, during which time univ. fellow in history, U. of Wis., Madison, Wis. Mem. Am. Commons Club, Am. Hist. Assn., Ind. Hist. Soc., Am. Assn. Univ. Profs., Tau Kappa Alpha. Democrat. Reformed Church. Contbr. numerous articles to The Dictionary of American History and to various hist. jours. Address: 17 Glenwood Av., Collegeville, Pa.

CARTER, J. Frank, twp. supt. schs.; b. Mapleton, Me., Jan. 10, 1891; s. James and Vinnie Estelle (Turner) C.; grad. Aroostook (Me.) State Normal Sch., 1910; B.S., Aurora Coll., 1917; A.M., U. of Me., Orono, Me., 1923; Ed.D., Temple U., Phila., 1931; m. Gladys Rollins, Aug. 20, 1923; 1 son, James Wallace. Served as prin. various high schs. in Me., 1910-25; prin. Haverford High Sch., Brookline, Pa., 1925-30; supt. of schs., Haverford (Pa.) Twp. Sch. Dist. since 1930; dir. Brookline Bldg. & Loan Assn., 1927-31. Served in Espionage-Intelligence Service during World War. Dir. Maine Line Fed. Chs. Life mem. N.E.A., Pa. State Edn. Assn; mem. Nat. Assn. Sch. Adminstrs., Am. Legion (dir. since 1928), Chamber of Commerce, Phi Delta Kappa, Kappa Phi Kappa. Republican. Methodist (local preacher). Mason. Club: Rotary (Ardmore, Pa.). Home: 25 Princeton Rd., Brookline, Pa. Office: Haverford High School, Upper Darby, Pa.

CARTER, James, clergyman; b. New York, Oct. 1, 1853; s. Walter and Eliza Ann (Thomson) C.; A.B., Columbia, 1882; grad. Union Theol. Seminary, 1885; D.D., Franklin and Marshall Coll., 1921; m. Emma Amelia Smuller, Sept. 30, 1885. Ordained Presbyn. ministry, 1885; stated supply and pastor Mendham, N.J., 1885-89; pastor Ch. of the Covenant, Williamsport, Pa., 1889-1905; prof. ch. history and sociology, Lincoln U., 1905-22; prof. homiletics and ch. history, 1922-28; also stated supply, Mendham, N.J., 1917-18. Asst. editor Carmina Sanctorum, 1886; mem. synodical com. on home missions and sustentation, 1890-97; traveled in Europe, 1870, 1902, and in Europe and the Orient, 1904, 1907; tour of historic study in Europe 8 months, 1911. Collaborated with Joint Com. on Organic Union of Presbyterian Ch. U.S.A. and United Presbyn. Ch. Mem. Com. on Penal Affairs of Pa., Am. Nat. Red Cross. Mem. Am. Humane Assn., Am. Bible Soc. Presbyn. Ministers Social Union (Phila.), Phi Beta Kappa, Phila. Chapter of Alumni Assn. of Columbia U., The League of Faith, Indian Rights Assn., Chester County Tuberculosis Soc. Author: Songs of Work and Worship, 1899; Walter Carter, Autobiography and Reminiscences, 1901; John Huss, the Man and the Martyr, 1915; A Century of Service, 1924; The Gospel Message in Great Pictures, 1929. Article, "Socialism," in New Schaff-Herzog Ency., 1911. Contbr. to periodicals. Club: Automobile (Phila.). Address: Lincoln University, Chester Co., Pa.

CARTER, John DeWeese, lawyer; b. Denton, Md., June 2, 1904; s. John Tilghman and Elizabeth (DeWeese) C.; grad. Caroline High Sch., Denton, Md., 1922; student Washington and Lee U. Sch. of Commerce, 1922-24; LL.B., Washington and Lee Law Sch., 1927; unmarried. Admitted to Md. bar, 1928, and since in practice at Denton; atty. for 4 of the 6 banks in Caroline County, Bd. of Edn. of Caroline Co., Albert W. Sisk & Son (largest brokers of canned goods in the world), Eastern Shore Pub. Service Co.; U.S. commr. for Dist. of Md., 1928-34. Mem. Dem. State Central Com. for Caroline Co. Mem. Caroline County, Md. and Am. Bar Assns., Phi Kappa Sigma, Phi Delta Phi, Omicron Delta Kappa, Sigma Club (Washington and Lee U.). Methodist (mem. bd. trustees First Methodist Ch., Denton). Mason (Shriner). Clubs: Rotary (past pres.); Shrine of Eastern Shore of Md., Phi Kappa Sigma of Md. (Baltimore); Easton Country Club. Address: Denton, Md.

CARTER, John H.; editor Lancaster New Era. Address: 8 W. King St., Lancaster, Pa.

CARTER, Samuel Thomson, Jr., retired lawyer; b. Yonkers, N.Y.; s. Samuel Thomson and Alantha (Pratt) C.; student Huntington High Sch., Huntington, N.Y., 1878-82; M.A., Princeton U., 1886; LL.B., Columbia U. Law Sch., 1888; m. Annie Washburn Burnham, Oct. 21, 1897; children—Gladys Burnham (dec.), Burnham, Samuel Thomson III. Admitted to the bar, 1888; law clk. Lord, Day & Lord, N.Y., 1888-92; mem. firm Carter, Jessup & Fallows, later Carter & Haskell and Carter & Smith; retired 1938; asso. counsel for N.Y. State Assembly Com. for investigation of Surrogate's Ct., N.Y. Co., 1899. Pres. and then chmn. bd. dirs. Berkshire Industrial Farm, Canaan, N.Y., since 1914; mem. advisory bd. Boy Conservation Bur. since 1934. Awarded Carnegie Hero Medal, 1928. Independent Republican. Presbyterian. Clubs: Princeton, Plainfield Country (Plainfield, N.J.). Author: Carter's Transfer Tax Law, 1902. Address: 940 Woodland Av., Plainfield, N.J.

CARTER, William Justin, lawyer; b. Richmond, Va., May 28, 1866; s. Edmund and Elizabeth (Reeves) C.; LL.B., Howard Univ. Law Sch., Washington, D.C., 1892; m. Elizabeth M. Allen, Feb. 17, 1894; children—Harlan Allen, William Justin, Jr., Thaddeus Stevens. Admitted to Pa. bar, 1894, and since engaged in gen. practice of law at Harrisburg, Pa.; served as pvt. sec. to Hon. E. E. Beidleman, lt. gov. Pa., 1921-23, examiner in Dept. Labor and Industry, Unemployment Compensation Div., 1938-39; dir. and counsel Community Bldg. & Loan Assn. Alumni trustee, Howard Univ., Washington, D.C. Democrat. Presbyterian. Mason. Home: 1831 Market St. Office: 2 Court St., corner Market St., Harrisburg, Pa.

CARTER, William T., 2d; b. Narragansett Pier, R.I., 1900; s. William E. and Lucile (Polk) C.; student Groton (Mass.) Sch.; m. Cintra Ellis, 1925. Partner Montgomery, Scott & Co. (mem. N.Y. Stock Exchange) since 1929. Home: Bryn Mawr, Pa. Office: 123 S. Broad St., Philadelphia, Pa.

CARTWRIGHT, John H., lawyer; b. Brockport, Pa., Sept. 28, 1899; s. Richard A. and Minnie J. (Kline) C.; grad. Ridgway Borough (Pa.) Grammar Sch., 1916, High Sch., 1920; B.S., Lafayette Coll., Easton, Pa., 1924; LL.B., Dickinson Sch. of Law, Carlisle, Pa., 1928; m. Margaret I. McQuone, Sept. 5, 1929. Admitted to bar, 1928, Supreme Ct. of Pa., 1929, U.S. Ct. for Western Dist. of Pa., 1929, U.S. Ct. for Middle Dist. of Pa., 1931; asso. with firm Ely & Ely, Ridgway, Pa., 1928-29; took over firm 1929 and since practiced under own name; solicitor and dir. Ridgway Bldg. & Loan Assn., Clawson Chem. Co., Clarion River Ry. Co. Solicitor for the County of Elk, Pa., Horton Twp. Sch. Dist., Elk County Institution Dist.; also solicitor for the Township of Horton; chmn. Elk Co. Bd. of Assistance; trustee and pres. Ridgway Free Library Assn. Mem. Elk Co. Bar Assn., Pa. Bar Assn., Sigma Chi (Phi chapter). Democrat. Episcopalian (mem. vestry Grace Episcopal Ch., Ridgway, Pa.). Mason (Elk Lodge 379, Elk Royal Arch Chapter 230, Orient Lodge 40); Elks (Carlisle, Pa., Lodge 578); Moose (Ridgway, Pa. Lodge 1183). Club: Elk Co. Country (Ridgeway, Pa.). Home: 244 Center St. Office: Rooms 1 and 2, Masonic Temple, Ridgway, Pa.

CARTWRIGHT, Richard A.; pres. Clawson Chem. Co.; also officer or dir. many companies. Home: 244 Center St. Office: 331 Main St., Ridgway, Pa.

CARTY, May Margaret; mem. N.J. State Bd. of Edn., present term expires 1944. Address: Jersey City, N.J.

CARTY, Virginia, dean; b. Frederick, Md., Dec. 27, 1893; d. J. W. L. and Minnie Rebecca (Dixon) C.; A.B., Hood College, Frederick, Md., 1913; teachers certificate (piano), Peabody Conservatory, Baltimore, 1914. Private teacher of piano, 1907-14; asso. prof. piano and theory, Hood Coll., Frederick, Md., 1914-24; dean Peabody Conservatory of Music, Frederick, since 1924. Alumni trustee Hood Coll. Democrat. Evangelical Reformed Ch. Clubs: Baltimore Music,

College (Baltimore). Home: 230 S. Market St., Frederick, Md.

CARVER, Clarence Johnson, coll. prof.; b. Buckingham, Pa., May 13, 1884; s. Stephen and Clara Engle (Johnson) C.; A.B., Dickinson Coll., Carlisle, Pa., 1909; M.A., N.Y.U., 1915, Ph.D., 1917; student, Colo. Coll., 1906; m. Anna Belle Zinn, June 2, 1909; children—Mervin Filler, Jean Eleanor, Grace Elizabeth, Ruth Evelyn. Began as sch. teacher, Upper Black Eddy, Pa., 1900; vice-prin. borough schs., West Grove, Pa., 1906-07; instr. in Latin, Norristown (Pa.) High Sch., 1909-11, Paterson (N.J.) High Sch., 1911-18; vocational guidance sec., Internat. Com. Y.M.C.A., U.S. and Can., 1918-20; asso. prof. of English and Bible, Dickinson Coll., Carlisle, Pa., 1920-21, asso. prof. of Edn., 1921-24, prof. of Edn. since 1924, dir. of teacher placement and student employment since 1928, sec. of faculty since 1929; mem. Teachers Coll. Faculty, Syracuse (N.Y.) U., summer session, 1923; lecturer and teacher, Teacher Training Extension, Pa. State Coll., 1923-26. Mem. Pa. State Edn. Assn. (pres. higher edn. dept., 1933-34), N.E.A., Dickinson Library Guild (sec.-treas. since 1928), Nat. Institutional Teacher Placement Assn., Phi Beta Kappa (sec., Dickinson, Pa., chapter since 1921), Theta Chi, Phi Delta Kappa. Republican. Mason. Club: Kiwanis (Carlisle, Pa.). Author: Why I Am Compelled to Be An Idealist, 1914; Thomas Henry Burrowes and the Education Revival in Pennsylvania, 1917. Home: 412 W. South St. Office: Carlisle, Pa.

CARVER, George, univ. prof., author; b. Cincinnati, O., Dec. 19, 1888; s. Robert Dieuaide and Elizabeth Darby (McGraw) C.; student U. of Ala. and U. of Chicago; A.B., Miami U., 1916; m. Eva Schultz, July 23, 1919; 1 son, Robert Bradley. Instr. in English, Pa. State Coll., 1916-18; same, State U. of Ia., 1919-23, asso. in English, 1923-24; lecturer in English, U. of Pittsburgh, 1924-26, asst. prof. English, 1926-27, became asso. prof., 1927, now prof. English. Served with A.E.F., 1918-19. Author: The Catholic Tradition in English Literature, 1926; Points of Style, 1928; Essays and Essayists, 1929. Co-Author: Writing and Rewriting, 1923; Minimum Essentials of Good Writing, 1924. Co-Editor: Representative Catholic Essays, 1926; The Stream of English Literature, 1930; Periodical Essays of the Eighteenth Century, 1930. Address: University of Pittsburgh, Pittsburgh, Pa.

CARVIN, Frank Dana, coll. prof., engr.; b. Phila., Pa., Nov. 16, 1892; s. Frank and Minnie Dana (Johnson) C.; student Southern High Sch., Phila., 1908-11; B.S., M.E., U. of Pa., 1916; M.A., Columbia U., 1930; Ph.D., N.Y.U., 1938; m. Caroline Cathrine Snyder, Apr. 25, 1917. Mech. engr. elec. ry. constrn., Penns Grove, N.J., 1916-17; instr. mech. engring., U. of Pa., 1919-24; summer work in power plant operation, 1919-24; asst. prof. mech. engring., Poly. Inst. of Brooklyn, N.Y., 1924-34; prof. and head dept. mech. engring., Newark (N.J.) Coll. of Engring., since 1934; cons. engr., N.Y. license, since 1924. Served as sergt., Signal Corps, U.S. Army, 1917-19, also test work with Air Service. Mem. safety com., N.J. Dept. of Labor, since 1934. Mem. Am. Soc. M.E., Soc. for Promotion Engring. Edn., A.A.A.S., Tau Beta Phi, Sigma Tau. Republican. Home: 25 Manor Hill Rd., Summit, N.J. Office: 367 High St., Newark, N.J.

CARWILE, Preston Banks, asso. prof. of physics; b. Campbell Co., Va., Aug. 7, 1896; s. Tam Ora and Verna Beatrice (LeGrand) C.; A. B., Davidson (N.C.) Coll., 1920; A.M., U. of Va., Charlotteville, Va., 1924, Ph.D., 1927; m. Lois Corinne Ketcham, Sept. 4, 1923; children—Corine Shearer, Roger Leonard, Kenneth Baldwin. Test man Gen. Electric Co., Schenectady, N.Y., 1920-21; teacher of science and mathematics, North Wilkesboro (N.C.) High Sch., 1921-22; instr. in physics, U. of Va., Charlottesville, Va., 1922-23, teaching fellow, 1923-27; asst. prof. of physics, Lehigh U., Bethlehem, Pa., 1927-31, asso. prof. since 1931. Served in Inf., U.S. Army, with A.E.F. 6 months, 1918-19. Mem. Am. Phys. Soc., Am. Assn. Univ. Profs., Phi Beta Kappa, Sigma Xi (sec. Lehigh Chapter). Democrat. Presbyterian (elder). Home: 803 7th Av., Bethlehem, Pa.

CARY, Charles Reed, sales exec.; b. Baltimore, Md., Dec. 26, 1881; s. Charles Jackson and Sue B. (Reed) C.; prep. edn., Westtown (Pa.) Boarding Sch., 1896-99; B.S., Haverford (Pa.) Coll., 1902; S.B., Mass. Inst. Tech., 1904; m. Margaret Morris Reeve, Sept. 7, 1912; children—Barbara Lloyd, Stephen Grellet, Sarah Comfort. Salesman James G. Biddle, 1904-15; engr., Pa. R.R. East River Tunnels, 1905-08; with Leeds & Northrup Co., Phila., since 1908, v.p. in charge sales since 1922. Home: Ellet Lane, Mt. Airy. Office: 4901 Stenton Av., Philadelphia, Pa.

CARY, Dale Emerson, physician; b. Waynesburg, Pa., Dec. 26, 1880; s. Marcena Mitchner and Elizabeth (Baker) C.; student Waynesburg College; grad. S. W. State Teachers College, California, Pa., 1904; M.D. Jefferson Med. Coll., Phila., 1911; m. Florence Bard, May 10, 1914 (dec.); children—Kathryn Bard, Mary Elizabeth; m. 2d, Helen Landgraf, June 29, 1929; 1 dau., Alice Landgraf. Interne Lancaster (Pa.) Gen. Hosp., 1911-12, on med. staff since 1913, lecturer Sch. of Nursing, 1924-36; med. dir. Rossmere Sanatorium, Lancaster. Served as mem. dft. bd., U.S. Army, during World War. Serving as mayor of Lancaster for term 1938-42. Mem. bd. dirs. Rossmere Sanatorium, 1926-39. Mem. Lancaster City and Co. med. socs. (past pres. both). Republican. Lutheran. Home: 204 E. King St. Office: Municipal Bldg., Lancaster, Pa.

CARY, Lewis Robinson, educator; b. Topsham, Me., Sep. 1, 1880; s. Seth Franklin and Sarah (Robinson) C.; student Bowdoinham (Me.) High Sch., 1893-97; B.S., U. of Me., Orono, Me., 1901, M.S., 1902; Grad. student Johns Hopkins, 1903-05; Ph.D., Princeton U., 1909; unmarried. Asst. in biology, U. of Me., Orono, Me., 1901-03; biologist in charge of Gulf Biol. Sta. of Louisiana, Cameron, La., 1905-08; instr. of biology, Princeton U., 1909-16; asst. prof. since 1916; research asso., Carnegie Inst. of Washington expeditions to Samoa and Fiji, 1917-20. Fellow A.A.A.S. Republican. Address: 153 Jefferson Rd., Princeton, N.J.

CARY, Page, artist; b. Los Angeles, Calif., Aug. 29, 1904; d. Burdette Nelson and Margaret (Knight) C.; ed. Page Sch. for Girls, Los Angeles, Calif., 1913-17, Mary Baldwin Coll., Staunton, Va., 1921-24, Calif. Sch. of Art, Berkeley, 1924-25, Ecole des Beaux Arts, Paris, France, 1926-27, Art Students' League, New York City, 1929-30. Engaged as free lance artist in Washington, D.C. and New York City, 1928-32; asst. to D'Alton Valentine, illustrator, New York, 1932-34; free lance in Los Angeles, 1934-35, in Phila. since 1935; has exhibited in the larger cities; has painting in Contemporary Art Exhbn., N.Y. World's Fair. Won freize competition in New York, 1930, scholarship Cooper Union Art Sch., 1931-32; awarded various prizes and medals for art in schs. Mem. Professional Artists League, Soc. of Independent Artists. Republican. Episcopalian. Address: 260 S. 16th St., Philadelphia, Pa.

CASBARIAN, Harvey Tyndal, comptroller, U. of Md.; b. Prince Georges County, Md.; s. Boghas G. and Carrie Tyndal (Wilforg) C.; B.C.S., Southeastern Univ., Washington, D.C., 1925; m. Anna Louise Worley, June 2, 1924; children—Mary Louise, Harvey Tyndal. Bookkeeper War Finance Corpn., Washington, D.C., 1922-23; with U. of Md. since 1923, as budget accountant, 1923-28, cashier, 1928-34, comptroller since 1934, also treas. Agrl. Expt. Station since 1934. Trustee Southeastern U. C.P.A., Md., 1931. Mem. Am. Inst. Accountants, Md. Assn. C.P.A., Alumni Assn. U. of Md., Alumni Assn. Southeastern U. Democrat. Presbyterian. Club: College Park Rotary (past treas.). Home: 601 Joseph St. Office: University of Maryland, College Park, Md.

CASE, Andrew Wallace, college prof.; b. Tipton, Ind., July 19, 1898; s. LeSueur L. and Georgia (Deibert) C.; student Sch. of Fine and Applied Art, Pratt Inst., Brooklyn, N.Y., 1919-23; B.S., Pa. State Coll., 1928, A.M., 1930; m. Sara Evelyn Dietz, Aug. 23, 1924; 1 dau., Frances Evelyn. Supervisor of art edn., St. Clair (Pa.) Public Schools, 1923-25; teacher of art, Shippensburg (Pa.) State Teachers Coll., summer 1925; prof. of art, California (Pa.) State Teachers Coll., 1925-26; prof. of art, Pa. State Coll., since 1926; painter. Exhibited: N.Y. Water Color Club, Am. Water Color Soc., Tricker Galleries (N.Y.), Warwick Galleries (Phila.), Ind. Artists (Indianapolis), Cincinnati, Johnstown (Pa.), Pottsville (Pa.) Served in U.S. Navy during World War. Mem. Am. Fed. of Art, College Arts, Scarab, Alpha Pi Alpha, Pi Gamma Alpha. Republican. Clubs: University (State College, Pa.). Home: 826 W. Beaver Av., State College, Pa.

CASE, Clarence Edwards, judge; b. Jersey City, N.J., Sept. 24, 1877; s. Philip and Amanda V. (Edwards) C.; B.A., Rutgers Coll., New Brunswick, N.J ., 1900 (Phi Beta Kappa), M.A., 1903; LL.B., New York Law Sch., 1902; LL.D., Rutgers U., 1937; m. Anna Gist Rogers, Jan. 29, 1913 (died Nov. 28, 1922); children—Henrietta Rogers, Clarence Edwards, Philip; m. 2d, Mrs. Ruth Weldon Griggs, July 25, 1925. Entered office of Alvah A. Clark, Somerville, N.J., 1902; admitted as atty N.J. bar, 1903, counselor, 1907; mem. firm Clark & Case, 1906-10; clk. judiciary com. N.J. Senate, 1908-09; sec. to pres. N.J. Senate, 1909-10; judge of Somerset Co. Courts, 1910-13; resigned to resume practice. Member New Jersey Senate, 1918-29; acting governor of New Jersey, 1920; justice N.J. Supreme Court, 1929—. Trustee Rutgers Coll.; mem. Am., N.J. and Somerset Co. bar assns. Republican. Mem. Ref. Ch. in America. Mason, K.P. Clubs: University (New York); Raritan Valley Country. Home: Somerville, N.J.

CASE J(ames) Herbert, banker; b. Elizabeth, N.J., Aug. 20, 1872; s. Samuel Pyatt and Susan (Thorn) C.; ed. Lansley Sch., Elizabeth; m. Alice Needham, Sept. 28, 1898; children—Everett Needham, James H., Elizabeth Parker (Mrs. Hamilton Robinson). Successively sec., and vice-pres. Plainfield Trust Co., 1902-17; v.p. Farmers Loan & Trust Co., N.Y. City, 1912-17; dep. gov. Federal Reserve Bank, N.Y. City, 1917-1930, chmn. bd., 1930-36; partner R. W. Pressprich & Co., New York, since 1936. Trustee and chmn. finance com., Ministers and Missionaries Benefit Bd. of Northern Bapt. Conv. Trustee and chmn. com. on finance and investment, Elmira Coll.; mem. Chamber of Commerce State of N.Y.; trustee and treas. Community Chests and Councils, Inc.; chmn. I.R.T. 7 Per Cent Note Com.; mem. advisory council New York Chapter of Am. Inst. of Banking. Republican. Baptist. Clubs: Union League, Bond, Downtown Assn. (New York); Plainfield Country. Home: 1332 Evergreen Av., Plainfield, N.J. Office: 68 William St., New York, N. Y.

CASE-BLECHSCHMIDT, Dorothy, M.D.; b. Ithaca, Mich., Apr. 9, 1885; d. Marcus A. and Harriet (Helms) Case; prep. med., Battle Creek (Mich.) Coll., 1903; M.D., Women's Med. Coll. of Pa., Phila., Pa., 1907; post grad. work, Clinics—London, Berlin, Berne and Geneva during 1911; m. Dr. Jules Blechschmidt, Sept. 14, 1910; 1 dau., Helen Harriet. Asso. clinical prof. of gynecology, Women's Med. Coll. of Pa., Phila., 1916-22, asst. in gen. surgery to Dr. Deaver, 1922-24; asst. gynecologist, Woman's Hosp. of Phila., 1923-27; chief in gen. surgery, 1927-38, consulting surgeon since 1938. Chmn. of Pub. Health, Phila. Fed. of Women's Clubs and allied orgns.; mem. Bd. of Corporations of Woman's Med. Coll. of Pa. Fellow Am. Coll. Surgeons, A.M.A.; mem. Phila. Co., Pa. State med socs., Nat. Woman's Med. Assn. Republican. Lutheran. Clubs: One Hundred of Phila. (dir.), Contemporary, Phila. Music, Art Alliance, Women's Univ., Philomusian (Phila.); lectures on Cancer of the Breast, Cancer of the Uterus, Appendicitis, Duodenal Ulcer, Cholecystitis, Psychology of Drinking, The Liver's Budget, Women After 40, Backache in Women, Music and Medicine, Our Children. Home: 5125 Woodbine Av., "Wynnestay." Office: 255 S. 17th St., Philadelphia, Pa.

CASEY, Daniel Nulty, sec. Harrisburg Chamber of Commerce; b. Haverhill, Mass., May 2, 1888; s. Maurice F. and Mary J. (Nulty) C.;

grad. Haverhill (Mass.) High Sch., 1907; m. Helen M. Minnis, Jan. 31, 1923; children—Daniel J., James J. Bank clerk, 1907-09; reporter Haverhill (Mass.) Record, 1906-10; reporter and asst. editor Haverhill Evening Gazette, 1910-12; corr. Boston Post, Christian Science Monitor, United Press; advertising specialist and public relations counsellor; sec. Haverhill Chamber of Commerce, 1912-17; chief clerk Dist. Draft Bd., Lawrence, Mass., June-Aug. 1917; organization service sec. Pa. State Chamber of Commerce, 1919-21; sec. Harrisburg (Pa.) Chamber of Commerce of since Mar. 1, 1922. Served as sergt. Co. A, 302d Machine Gun Battalion, U.S. Army, student O.T.S., with A.E.F. 10 months, 1917-19; commd. capt. Quartermaster Reserve Corps, 1923, lt. col., 1938. Chmn. Harrisburg Welfare Campaign, 1932; mem. shelter com. Am. Red Cross during 1936 flood. Pres. New Eng. Commercial Secs. Assn., 1914; mem. Pa. Commercial Secs. Assn. (pres. 1923-24), Nat. Assn. Commercial Orgn. Secs. (dir. 1936-39). Republican. Roman Catholic. K.C. Public speaker (over 500 audiences) on organization subjects. Home: 25 N. 24th St., Camp Hill, Pa. Office: Market Sq. Bldg., Harrisburg, Pa.

CASEY, Frank I(gnatius), lawyer; b. Trenton, N.J., Jan. 5, 1890; s. John P. and Mary A. (Connelly) C.; A.B., St. Joseph's Coll., Phila., 1912; m. Marie Hurley, July 9, 1931; children—Frank I., Jr., Mary Ann. Employed with Am. Steel & Wire Co., Trenton, N.J., 1912-15; studied law in office of Martin P. Devlin, Trenton, N.J., 1915-18; admitted to N.J. bar as atty., 1918, as counselor, 1923; engaged in gen. practice of law at Trenton since 1918; pres. Anchor Chem. Co., Trenton, 1937, since 1939. Served as pvt. inf., U.S.A., 1918. Mem. Mercer Co. Bar. Assn. Democrat. Roman Catholic. Club: Catholic (Trenton). Home: 484 Greenwood Ave. Office: Broad St. Bank Bldg., Trenton, N.J.

CASEY, Helen Beatrice Niesley (Mrs. James Bernard Casey, Jr.); b. Boiling Springs, Pa., Nov. 8, 1889; d. George Brindle and Cora Ellen (Mountz) Niesley; grad. Phila. High Sch. for Girls, 1910; student Drexel Inst., Phila., 1911-15, Dickinson Coll. Sch. of Family Relations, one term; m. James Bernard Casey, Jr., May 27, 1922. Began as jr. auditor; installed accounting systems, Burroughs Co., Phila., private sec. J. J. Habermehl's Sons, Phila., 1920-24; active in welfare and patriotic orgns. Charter mem. Upper Darby Unit, Am. Legion Auxiliary (served as 1st v.p., sec., treas., historian, chaplain); now mem. Benjamin Franklin Unit, Phila. (served as pres., 1st v.p., membership chmn., welfare chmn.); Eastern chmn. on membership, Dept. of Pa. Auxiliary, 1931-35; Pa. chmn. on membership, 1935-36; Eastern vice-pres., 1936-37; pres. Am. Legion Auxiliary of Pa., 1938-39; mem. conv. com. on membership Am. Legion Auxiliary (nat.), 1936, conv. com. on rules, 1937, conv. com. on rehabilitation, 1938, nat. exec. committeewoman, 1939-40. Served as reconstruction aide, Regular Army, during World War. Mem. Eight and Forty, Drexel Inst. Alumni Assn. Republican. Presbyterian. Eastern Star, Oriental Shrine. Clubs: LuLu Temple Country (North Hills, Pa.). Home: Normandie Hotel, Philadelphia, Pa.

CASEY, John Francis, Jr., pres. Allegheny Equipment Corpn.; b. Pittsburgh, Pa., Mar. 23, 1899; s. John Francis and Mary Ethel (Lee) C.; ed. St. Paul's Cathedral Sch., Pittsburgh, 1908-13, Shady Side Acad., Pittsburgh, 1913-17, U. of Pitts., 1917-20; m. Marie Helen Daley, Jan. 21, 1923 (divorced Mar. 1, 1929); 1 dau., Marjorie Louise. Timekeeper, John F. Casey Co., 1915-17; engr. W. G. Wilkins Co., 1917-19, machinist, 1919-20; asst. sec. John F. Casey Co., 1921-23, sec. 1923, v.p. since 1934; sec.-treas. Railway Maintenance Co. since 1925; sec.-treas. Allegheny Equipment Corpn., 1925-35; pres. since 1935; sec. Leechgrip Co.; treas. Star Tiling Co.; sec. Caxton Book Shop; dir. New Castle Refractories Co., Swindell-Dressler Co. Served with 41st Heavy Arty. Replacements, C.A., U.S. Army, Fortress Monroe, Va., 1918. Republican. Roman Catholic. Clubs: Pittsburgh Athletic Assn., Duquesne, Longue Vue Country (Pittsburgh). Home: 718 Devonshire St. Address: Box 1888, Pittsburgh, Pa.

CASEY, William Joseph, banker; b. Baltimore, Md.,; s. Thomas J. and Margaret (D'Oyley) C.; ed. St. Vincents Parochial Sch., Calvert Hall Coll.; m. Mary Creswell Twiname, 1899 (died April 1934); m. 2d, Catherine Gwinnette Doughty, of Augusta, Ga., Oct. 1936. Vice-pres., mem. exec. com. and dir. Maryland Trust Co. and Consolidated Gas, Electric Light and Power Co.; dir. Baltimore Steam Packet Co., Provident Savings Bank. Chmn. Commn. on Governmental Efficiency and Economy, a fact finding and planning body in municipal and state govt.; also devised and directed plan sponsored by similar organization which reorganized administrative methods of Baltimore, 1923-27. Trustee of various civic enterprises. Home: 4405 Norwood Rd., Guilford. Office: Calvert and Redwood Sts., Baltimore, Md.

CASH, William Edmund, art editor; b. Brooklyn, N.Y., Apr. 8, 1907; s. William Edmund and Fannie Caroline (Stall) C.; student Polytechnic Prep. Country Day Sch., 1922-24, Columbia (night school), 1924-25, Grand Central Sch. of Art, 1926, Pa. Acad. of Fine Arts, 1927-28, Wilmington Acad. of Art, 1929-30; married. Asso. with John C. Winston Co., Phila., since 1932; acting pres. Vir. Pub. Co.; has exhibited his art work in New York, Phila. and Wilmington, Del. Awarded 1st prize for painting by Wilmington Soc. Fine Arts, 1930. Republican. Congregationalist. Writer of short stories and children's books. Editor of Better Living Mag. Edited God's Purpose, 1939; God's Message, 1937. Home: 1521 Spruce St. Office: 1010 Arch St., Philadelphia, Pa.

CASHMAN, Bender Z.; gynecologist St. Francis and Elizabeth Steel Magee hosps.; asso. prof. gynecology, U. of Pittsburgh. Address: 121 University Pl., Pittsburgh, Pa.

CASKIE, Marion Maxwell, interstate commerce commr.; b. Remington, Va., July 29, 1890; s. Dr. James Maxwell and Olivia (Rixey) C.; ed. pub. and pvt. schs., at Remington and Roanoke, Va., and Baltimore, Md.; student Fork Union (Va.) Mil. Acad., 1904-05, Piedmont Coll., Lynchburg, Va. (business course), 1905-06; m. Helen Elizabeth Suess, Dec. 4, 1912; children—Marion Maxwell, Nell Comer, James Kennon (dec.), Charles Dimmock (dec.), Warren Watts, Challen Ellis. Served in gen. offices Southern Ry., Washington, D.C., 1906-11; engaged in interstate commerce work, Washington, 1911-16, Atlanta, Ga., 1916-17; gen. mgr. transportation bur., Chamber of Commerce, Montgomery, Ala., 1917-30, also traffic mgr., Ala. Farm Bur. Federation, Ala. Cottonseed Crushers Assn., Golf Coast Citrus Exchange, Montgomery live stock and cotton exchanges, 1917-30; exec. sec. Southern Traffic League, 1920-30, also past pres. and chmn. exec. com.; executive various manufacturing plants, 1930-31; gen. mgr. Ala. State docks, Mobile, 1931-33; traffic asst. at Atlanta, Ga., to Federal Coordinator of Transportation, 1933-35; exec. Waterman Steamship Co., 1935; apptd. Interstate Commerce commr., Aug. 1935. Ala. dir. div. of transportation for Federal Food Adminstrn., World War. Former mem. U.S. Chamber Commerce, Miss. Valley Assn. (traffic com.), Nat. Industrial Traffic League, (exec. com., regional v.p.), Traffic Clubs of America, Southeast Shippers Advisory Bd. (vice chmn.), Assn. of Practitioners before Interstate Commerce Commn. Democrat. Episcopalian. Mason. Home: 6309 Beechwood Drive, Chevy Chase, Md.; Montgomery, Ala. Office: Interstate Commerce Commn. Bldg., Washington, D.C.

CASLER, Dewitt Bellinger; asso. in gynecology Johns Hopkins U.; asst. visiting gynecologist Johns Hopkins Hosp.; cons. gynecologist Hosp. for Women of Md., Union Memorial Hosp., Bon Secours Hosp. and Church. Home and Infirmary. Address: 13 W. Chase St., Baltimore, Md.

CASSATT, Robert Kelso, investment banker; b. Haverford, Pa., Sept. 28, 1873; s. Alexander J. and Lois (Buchanan) C.; student Haverford Sch., 1884-91, except for two years at Ecole Monge, Paris; A.B., Harvard, 1895; m. Minnie Fell, Jan. 22, 1900; children—Alexander Johnston, Anthony Drexel. Began as rodman, Pa. Ry., 1896; left railroad, 1899, to become eastern sales mgr. Keystone Coal and Coke Co., with offices in Phila., vice-pres. in charge eastern sales until 1916 resigned, 1916 to devote attention to affairs of Cassatt & Co., investment bankers and brokers, senior partner until 1937; now retired; dir. United Gas Improvement Co., Electric Storage Battery Co., Air Reduction Co., Mid-Continent Petroleum Co., Waldorf Astoria Co., Midland Valley Ry Co., Charles E. Hires Co., Western Saving Fund Soc., Barahona Sugar Corpn., Arcade Real Estate Co., Commd. maj. Quartermaster Corps, U.S. Army, 1918; transferred to Army War Coll. and later assigned to duty with Operations Div., Gen. Staff; hon. discharged, Dec. 1918. Republican. Episcopalian. Clubs: Philadelphia, Racquet (Phila.); Knickerbocker, Links (New York); Clambake (Newport). Home: Rosemont, Pa. Office: Commercial Trust Bldg., Philadelphia, Pa.

CASSELBERRY, Russel David, educator; b. Howard, Pa., Jan. 1, 1892; s. George Washington and Lula (Schenck) C.; grad. Williamsport (Pa.) High Sch., 1911; B.S., Pa. State Coll., 1915, M.S., 1922; m. Ethel Carrie Berry, Nov. 30, 1916; children—Elizabeth Dorothy, William Sheldon, Eleanore Beatrice, James Ellsworth. Began as lab. asst., Williamsport (Pa.) High Sch., 1915, science teacher, 1916-18; instr. zoology, Pa. State Coll., 1918-23, asst. prof., 1923-33, asso. prof. since 1933; dir. Mt. Nittany Bldg. & Loan Assn. Mem. Am. Assn. Univ. Profs., Nat. Geog. Soc. Republican. Methodist. Home: 306 S. Atherton St., State College, Pa.

CASSELMAN, Arthur Jay, physician; b. Camden, N.J., Mar. 14, 1888; s. William Siebert and Anna Cecilia (Wood) C.; M.D., U. of Pa. Med. Sch., 1911; Dr. P.H., U. of Pa. Sch. Hygiene and Pub. Health, 1915; m. Zula Mae Boyd, July 21, 1924; children—Catherine, Arthur Jay. Demonstrator clin. pathology and instr. serology, Phila. Polyclinic, 1913; asst. pathologist for serology, Phila. Gen. Hosp., 1913; in charge med. lab. work, A.W. War Hosp., Paignton, Eng., 1915-17; chief, Bur. Venereal Disease Control, N.J. State Dept. Health, Trenton, N.J., since 1919, title now changed to Tech. Consultant; dir. labs. of Camden Co. and City since 1920; pathologist Camden Co. Gen. Hosp.; actg. asst. surg., U.S. Pub. Health Service; in pvt. practice, treats only venereal diseases and diabetes. Served with Med. Corps U.S.A., 1918-19 with A.E.F. in France, disch. as capt. Mem. A.M.A., Am. Pub. Health Assn., Am. Soc. Clin. Pathology, N.J. Soc. Clinic. Pathology, Phila. Pathol. Sco., N.J. San. Assn., Camden Co. Med. Soc., N.J. Health Officers Assn. Republican. Home: 301 N. 2d St., Camden, N.J. Office: State House, Trenton, N.J.

CASSELMAN, Arthur Vale, church official; b. Minerva, O., July 20, 1874; s. Rev. Amos and Louisa Carrie (Leyde) C.; grad. Wichita (Kan.) Acad., 1892; A.B., Heidelberg Coll., 1895, D.D., 1923; B.D., Heidelberg Theol. Sem., 1898; m. Nima Hodsdon Drake, July 26, 1905; 1 dau., Louise Climena. Ordained ministry Ref. Ch. in U.S., 1898; pastor Grace Ch., Columbiana, O., 1898-1902; field sec. Bd. of Foreign Missions, Ref. Ch., 1902-05; pastor Calvary Ch., Reading, Pa., 1906-21; sec. of missionary edn., Bd. of Home and Foreign Missions, Ref. Ch., 1922-32; asso. sec. Bd. of Foreign Missions, 1932-33, sec. since Dec. 1933. Grad. Chaplain's Training Sch., Camp Taylor, Ky., 1918; successively chaplain Camp Hill, Newport News, Va., transport S.S. Lutitia, Base Hosp. No. 46, Landernau, France. Made world tour of missionary visitation and exploration, 1922-23; gen. dir. motion-picture photographic expdn. to Asia under auspices of Inter-church World Movement, 1919-20; ednl. deputation to Bagdad, 1926; visit to mission fields, China and Japan, 1935. Republican. Author: Making America Christian, 1931; The Winnebago Finds a Friend, 1932; Into All the World, 1934; The End of the Beginning, 1936. Home: 731 N. Fourth St., Reading, Pa. Office: Schaff Bldg., 1505 Race St., Philadelphia, Pa.

CASSIDY, H. Creighton, chief surgeon Lewistown Hosp. Address: 139 E. Market St., Lewistown, Pa.

CASSIDY, Lewis Cochran, prof. of law; b. Philadelphia, Pa., Oct. 29, 1898; s. H(ugh) Gilbert and Mary Dorothea (Fagan) C.; 9th generation in desc. from David Ogden who came with Penn on Welcome to Phila., 1682; A.B., Mt. St. Mary's Coll.; Emmitsburg, Md., 1919, A.M., 1921; grad. study, Harvard Law Sch., 1919-20, Pugsley scholar, 1929-30, S.J.D., 1930; LL.B., Georgetown U., 1922, LL.M., 1923, Ph.D. cum laude, 1923; Academie de Droit International de la Haye, 1931; Carnegie scholar, 1933; U. of Leiden, 1933; m. Clara L. McGrew, Sept. 14, 1929; children—Lewis C. 4th, Isabelle, Truman. Admitted to D.C. bar, 1922, Pa. bar, 1923, Mass. bar, 1937; to bar of Supreme Court of U.S., 1937; practiced in Phila., 1923-28 and since 1937; prof. law, Creighton U., Omaha, Neb., 1928-29, Boston Coll., 1929-30, Georgetown Univ., 1930-34; dean. Univ. of San Francisco Law Sch., 1934-36; faculty research fellow Harvard Law Sch., 1936-37; prof. of law, Cumberland U., Lebanon, Tenn., 1937-38; prof. of law Duquesne U., Pittsburgh, since 1938. Apptd. consul to Pittsburgh by Republic of Panama, 1938. Served as pvt. inf., U.S.A., 1918; now capt. U.S. Marine Corps Reserve. Del. at large Dem. Nat. Conv., 1924; candidate for Dem. nomination for U.S. senator, 1932. Mem. Am. Bar Assn., Am. Soc. Internat. Law, S.A.R., Gamma Eta Gamma, Pi Sigma Alpha; corr. mem. Ancien Institut Historique et Heraldique de France. Club: Harvard. Contbr. to New York U. Law Quarterly Review, Georgetown Law Jour., Miss. Law Review, Dickinson Law Review, Juridical Review (Scotland), Lahore (India) Law Coll. Journal. Address: 1023 Bluff St. Office: 331 4th Av., Pittsburgh, Pa.

CASTALLO, Mario A., surgeon; b. Providence, R.I., Sept. 28, 1903; s. Salvatore and Josephine (DiTomassi) C.; A.B., Holy Cross Coll., Worcester, Mass., 1925; M.D., Jefferson Med. Coll., Phila., 1929; m. Maria Roma, June 8, 1929; children—Maria Josephine, Mario A. Interne, St. Joseph's Hosp., Providence, R.I., 1929-30; asst. house surgeon New York Lying-In Hosp., 1930; resident obstetrician and gynecologist Sloane Hosp. for Women, 1931-32; visiting gynecologist, St. Joseph's Hosp., 1932-33; visiting obstetrician, Sofia Little Home, Providence, R.I., 1932-33; clin. asst. in obstetrics, Jefferson Hospital, Phila., 1933; assistant obstetrician, St. Joseph's Hospital, Phila., Pa., 1935; asst. demonstrator obstetrics, Jefferson Med. Coll., 1933-36, instr. obstetrics, 1936-37, demonstrator, 1937; chief of clinic venereal diseases complicating pregnancy, Jefferson Hosp., since 1937; mem. staff, Germantown Hosp., Am. Hosp. for Diseases of Stomach. Diplomate Nat. Bd. Med. Examiners; fellow Am. Coll. Surgeons, A.M.A., Coll. of Phys. of Phila.; mem. Pa. and Phila. Co. med. socs., Am. Congress on Obstetrics and Gynecology, Pan-Am. Med. Assn., Am. Assn. of History of Medicine, Phila. Obstet. Soc., Med. Club (Phila.), Jefferson Soc. for Clin. Investigation, Phi Rho Sigma. Republican. Roman Catholic. Clubs: Art (Phila.); Venetian (Chestnut Hill, Pa.). Contbr. med. journs. Home: 2126 Spruce St., Philadelphia, Pa.

CASTLE, Alfred Watkins, educator; b. Brecksville, O., June 24, 1885; s. Charles Darius and Elizabeth (Von Wanger) C.; A.B., New Lyme Inst., O., 1906; B.S., O. State U., 1910, A.M., same, 1911; grad. study, Columbia U., 1912-15; m. Abigail Glade Gladding, June 28, 1907; children—Loveen Gladding (Mrs. Hermus P. Albright), Alfred Watkins, Jr., Richard Gladding. Began as supt. schs., North Kingsville, O., 1906-09; prin. high sch., Columbus, O., 1910-16; asst. supt. schs., Cleveland, O., 1916-19; lecturer on methods, N.Y. State Dept. Edn., 1919-20; State Dir. Extension Edn., Pa., since 1920. Mem. N.E.A., Nat. Council Edn., Nat. Council on Naturalization and Citizenship, Nat. Commn. on Enrichment of Adult Life, Am. Assn. for Adult Edn., Phi Delta Kappa. Republican. Conglist. Mason. O.E.S. Home: Castle Crest, Mechanicsburg. Office: Dept. Pub. Instrn., Harrisburg, Pa.

CASTLE, Elizabeth M., headmistress; b. St. Charles, Ill., July 16, 1884; s. Henry N. and Marie (Lane) C.; student Norfolk (Va.) High Sch., 1899-1903; A.B., Wellesley Coll., 1907; student Columbia U., summer, 1916. Teacher St. Agness Sch., Albany, N.Y., 1907-08, Ogontz Sch., Ogontz, Pa., 1908-16, Dana's Hall, Wellesley, Mass., 1916-21; headmistress Roland Park Country Sch. since 1921. Mem. Am. Assn. Univ. Women, Head Mistresses Assn. of the East, Nat. Assn. Prins. of Sch. for Girls, Commn. of Secondary Schs. and Colls. of Eastern States and Md. Episcopalian. Club: College (Baltimore). Home: 102 Ridgewood Road, Baltimore, Md.

CASTO, Theodore Demetrius, operating dentist; b. Buckhannon, W.Va., Sept. 27, 1870; s. Benjamin S. and Elizabeth (Flint) C.; D.D.S., Phila. Dental Coll., 1895; m. Emma Walker, Dec. 23, 1897. School teacher, 1889-91; in practice of dentistry, Phila., since 1899; instr. in anesthetics, Phila. Post Grad. Sch., 1911-17; prof. of roentgenology, Phila. Dental Coll. since 1917; prof. of pedodontology, Temple U. Sch. of Dentistry, Phila., since 1932. Fellow Am. Coll. Dentists, Coll of Anesthetists; mem. Nat. Dental Assn., Pa. State Dental Soc., Acad. of Stomatology, A.M.A., (asso.), First Dist. Dental Soc., Phila. Mouth Hygiene Assn., Pa. Soc. Promotion of Dentistry for Children, Internat. Anesthesia Research Soc. Mason. Episcopalian. Home: 5134 Chester Av. Office: 1831 Chestnut St., Philadelphia, Pa.

CATER, Douglas Aymar, physician and surgeon; b. New York, N.Y., Aug. 26, 1869; s. Aymar and Mary (Leaycraft) C.; B.S., Mass. Inst. Tech., 1892; M.D., Coll. Phys. & Surgs. of Columbia U., 1896; m. Meriel W. Hutchins, June 29; 1899 (dec. 1933); children—Berkeley Aymar, Mary Reed (Mrs. Kenneth Fisk). Interne, N.Y. Post Grad. Hosp., 1897-99; engaged in gen. practice of medicine and surgery at East Orange, N.J. since 1899; attdg. surgeon, Orange Memorial Hosp., Orange, N.J., 1918-30. Fellow Am. Coll. Surgeons; mem. Essex Co. Med. Soc., Orange Mountain Med. Soc., Am. Congress of Physical Therapy. Republican. Episcopalian. Home: 57 S. Harrison St., East Orange, N.J.

CATHCART, Charles Sanderson, chemist; b. New Brunswick, N.J., Jan. 2, 1865; B.Sc., Rutgers, 1886, M.Sc., 1889. Asst. chemist to Austin & Wilber, chemists, 1886-89; asst. chemist N.J. Agrl. Coll. Expt. Sta., 1889-93; chief chemist Lister's Agrl. Chem. Works, Newark, N.J., 1893-1907; chief chemist N.J. Agrl. Expt. Sta., 1907—; state chemist, 1912—. Fellow A.A.A.S.; mem. Am. Chem. Soc. Home: New Brunswick, N.J.

CATHERWOOD, Cummins, partner Roberts, Fleitas and Catherwood; b. Haverford, Pa., Jan. 30, 1910; s. Daniel B. C. and Jessica (Davis) C.; student St. George's Sch., Newport, R.I., Pierce Business Sch., Phila., and U. of Pa.; m. Virginia Tucker Kent, April 24, 1935; 1 dau., Virginia Tucker. Asst. statistician Paine Webber & Co., Phila., 1931-33, Parrish & Co., Phila., 1933-34; partner Roberts, Fleitas and Catherwood, ins. brokers, Phila., since 1934; treas. and dir. Keystone Wood Preserving Co.; dir. Delaware Co. Nat. Bank, Fidelity Phila. Trust Co., Santa Maria Timber Co., Trustee Children's Hosp. of Phila.; dir. Southeastern Chapter, Pa. Am. Red Cross. Clubs: Racquet, Rittenhouse, Corinthian Yacht (Phila.); New York Yacht; Merion Cricket. Home: Darby and Paoli Rd., Bryn Mawr, Pa. Office: Fidelity Philadelphia Trust Bldg., Philadelphia, Pa.

CATLIN, Joseph Priestley, v.p. Wood Newspaper Machinery Corpn.; b. Northumberland, Pa., July 25, 1879; s. Hasket Derby and Hannah Taggart (Priestley) C.; student Mass. Inst. Tech., m. Esther Hooker Trowbridge, June 9, 1904; 1 son, Joseph Priestley. V.-p., treas. and dir. Wood Newspaper Machinery Corpn. since 1923; dir. Phelps Can Co. (Baltimore), Wood, Nathan & Virkus (New York). Home: Plainfield, N.J. Office: 501 5th Av., New York, N.Y.

CATLIN, Sheldon, insurance; b. Bridgeport, Conn., July 8, 1873; s. Lyman S. and Helen J., C.; student Yale U.; m. Elsie E. Kiefer, June 14, 1905. V.p. Insurance Co. of North America since 1916; also officer or dir. other insurance companies. Home: Radnor, Pa. Office: 1600 Arch St., Philadelphia, Pa.

CATO, Henry Stuart, lawyer; b. St. Albans, W.Va., Feb. 26, 1878; s. John Lane and Sarah Maury (Lasley) C.; student St. Albans Pub. Sch., intermittently, 1884-93; grad. W.Va. U. Law Sch., 1900; unmarried. Admitted to W.Va. and federal bars, 1900; in private practice, 1900-02; mem. law firm Linn, Byrne & Cato, 1902-06, Littlepage, Cato & Bledsoe, 1906-11, Cato & Bledsoe, 1911-17; circuit judge (apptd. by Gov. John J. Cornwell), 1917-18; again in private practice since 1918, specializing in trial work and appellate practice. Mem. City of Charleston and W.Va. State bar assn., Phi Kappa Psi (W.Va. Alpha Chapter). Democrat. Episcopalian. Home: 1021 Virginia St. Office: 610 Charleston Nat. Bank Bldg., Charleston, W.Va.

CATTANACH, Lachlan McArthur, surgeon; b. Taneytown, Md., Jan. 23, 1900; s. James and Maud Isabell (Scholl) C.; A.B., Johns Hopkins U., 1921, M.D., Med. Sch., 1925; m. Helen Gibby, April 6, 1929; children—Natalie Stuart, Jean McArthur. Interne, U. of Va. Hosp., Charlottesville, Va., 1925-27; surg. fellowship, Cleveland Clinic, 1927-28; chief resident, Beekman St. Hosp., New York, 1928-29; in practice gen. surgery asso. with Dr. H. B. Gibby, Wilkes-Barre, Pa., since 1929; clin. asst. surg., transfusion service, Wilkes-Barre Gen. Hosp. Served in R.O.T.C., 1917-21. Fellow Am. Coll. Surgeon;s mem. Am. Med. Assn., Pa. State and Lehigh Valley med. socs., John Hopkins Surg. Soc., Assn. Fellows of Cleveland Clinic, Luzerne Co. Med. Soc. (sec.), Alpha Tau Omega, Phi Chi. Republican. Presbyterian. Club: University of Wilkes-Barre (past pres.). Home: 96 S. Franklin St., Wilkes-Barre, Pa.

CATTELL, Jaques, editor; b. Garrison, N.Y., June 2, 1904; s. James McKeen and Josephine (Owen) C.; student Harvard U., 1920-21, U. of Ariz., 1921-23, Columbia U., 1926; m. Gwynneth Pease, Feb. 23, 1938. Student asst. to G. H. Parker, Harvard U., 1921; research asst. Desert Bot. Lab., Carnegie Inst., 1921-22; investigator Bermuda Biol. Station, summer 1921, Marine Biol. Lab., Woods Hole, Mass., summers 1921-23; student asst. to C. T. Voorhees, U. of Ariz., Tucson, Ariz., 1923; acting editor "Science," 1931 and 34; asso. editor Am. Men of Science, 1923-37, editor since 1937; editor Leaders in Education (a biog. directory) since 1939; sec. and treas. Science Press Printing Co., Lancaster, since 1927, v.p. since 1933; acting editor The American Naturalist, 1934-38, editor since 1938. Mem. A.A.A.S. (chmn. Lancaster br. since 1934), Pa. Acad. Science (v.p., 1937-39), Lancaster Chamber of Commerce, N.Y. State Fruit Testing Co-operative Assn., York Club of Printing House Craftsmen, Muehlenberg Bot. Soc. Democrat. Presbyterian. Clubs: Rotary (mem. speakers com., 1938), Hamilton, Lancaster Country (Lancaster, Pa.). Home 510 School Lane. Office: Science Press Printing Co., Lancaster, Pa.

CAUFFMAN, Stanley Hart, accountant, author; b. Phila., Pa., Nov. 1, 1880; s. Frank Guernsey and Sarah Byerly (Hart) C.; ed. by private tutors and Pa. Sch. of Industrial Art; m. Marion Smith Wartman, June 23, 1910; 1 son, Stanley Hart. Auditor and accountant since 1908; author since 1925; formerly violoncellist Phila. Orchestra, Cincinnati Orchestra, Manhattan Opera Co., New Orleans Opera Co., Boston English Opera Co.; also conductor. Dem. nominee for Congress, 6th Dist. of Pa., 1928; Dem. nominee for Pa. Legislature, 1932. Mem. Manuscript Music Soc., Musical Art Club, Soc. of Colonial Wars, Sons of the Revolution, Huguenot Soc., Pa. German Soc., Soc. of 1812, Colonial Soc., Wissahickon Valley Hist Soc., Founders of Newbury. Episcopalian. Author: (novels) At the Sign of the Silver Ship, 1925; The Ghost of Gallows Hill, 1926; The Wolf, the Cat and the Nightingale, 1928; The Sun Sets Red, 1930; The Adventures of Polydore, 1930; The Witchfinders, 1934; also short stories, poems and articles. Composer of light opera Old Gold. Lecturer on historical subjects. Home: 127 Rochelle Av., Wissahickon, Pa.

CAUM, Samuel LeRoy, pres. Bethlehem Nat. Bank; b. Altoona, Pa., May 22, 1882; s. Ezra and Annie (Arthur) C.; student Altoona (Pa.) High Sch., 1896-1900; M.E., Lehigh U., Bethlehem, Pa., 1904; m. Elizabeth Cope, Dec. 7, 1904. Began as draftsman, 1904; draftsman Bethlehem Steel Co., 1904-06, Edison Cement Co., Stewartsville, N.J., 1906-10, Thomas A. Edison Co., Orange, N.J., 1910-14; dir. The Bethlehem (Pa.) Nat. Bank, 1910-33, pres. and trust officer since 1934; sec. and dir. Equitable Bldg. and Loan Assn., Industrial Bldg. and Loan Assn., Bethlehem, Pa., South Bethlehem Bldg. and Loan Assn. Mem. Pa. Bldg. and Loan League (past pres.). Republican. Lutheran. Mason. (Blue Lodge, Chapter, Council, Commandry, Red Cross of Constantine, Consistory, Shriner). Club: Saucon Valley Country (Bethlehem, Pa.; mem. bd. govs.). Home: 1104 Prospect Av. Office: 26 E. 3d St., Bethlehem, Pa.

CAVALCANTE, Anthony, state senator; b. Vanderbilt, Pa., Feb. 6, 1897; s. Michael and Antoinetta (Tate) C.; student Bucknell Coll., Lewisburg, Pa., Pa. State Coll.; LL.B., Dickinson Law Sch. Carlisle, Pa.; m. Salome Diehl, Sept. 5, 1923; children—Anthony, William M. Admitted to Fayette Co. bar, 1924, and in practice at Uniontown, Pa., 1924-38; state senator since 1934; democratic candidate for Ho. of Reps., Pa., 1932. Served as corpl., Co. D., 110th Inf., 28th Div., U.S. Army with A.E.F., during World War. Mem. Vets. of Foreign Wars, Am. Legion, United Workers of America. Democrat. Mason, Moose, Eagle, Elk. Home: 88 Dawson Av. Office: 97 E. Main St., Uniontown, Pa.

CAVELTI, John Elmer, prof. chemistry; b. Stratford, Conn., June 8, 1896; s. John and Grace A. (Welsh) C.; B.S., Wesleyan U., 1918, M.S., same, 1920; Ph.D., Yale U., 1929; m. Catherine Carpenter, Dec. 27, 1920; children—Catherine Ruth, Miracyl Jane. Began as chemist, Remington Arms-U.M.C. Co., Bridgeport, Conn., 1918-19; asst. in chemistry, Wesleyan U., 1919-20, instr., 1920-24, asst. prof., 1924-29, asso. prof., 1929-36; research chemist, Goodyear Rubber Co., Middletown, Conn., 1921-36; prof. chemistry and head dept. chemistry, Allegheny Coll., Meadville, Pa., since 1936. Fellow Am. Inst. Chemists, A.A.A.S. Mem. Am. Chem. Soc., Pa. Chem. Soc., Phi Beta Kappa, Sigma Xi, Delta Sigma Rho, Sigma Chi. Dir. Meadville Y.M.C.A. Democrat. Methodist. Club: Green Mountain (Vermont). Home: 468 Chestnut St., Meadville, Pa.

CAVICCHIA, Peter Angelo, ex-congressman; b. in Italy, May 22, 1879; s. Dominic and Maria Josephine (Lombardi) C.; brought to the United States at age of nine, 1888; B.A., Am. Internat. College, Springfield, Mass., 1906; LL.D., 1929; LL.B., New York Univ., 1908; m. Annabella Auger, Dec. 15, 1909 (died 1936); children—Priscilla Josephine, Eugene Auger, Paul Gaetano. Admitted to N.J. bar, 1909, and began practice at Newark; mem. and counsel Unity Building & Loan Assn.; became dist. supervisor inheritance tax for Essex Co., 1917; mem. 72d Congress (1931-33), 9th N.J. Dist. reëlected to 73d and 74th Congresses (1933-37), 11th N.J. Dist. Pres. Newark Bd. of Edn., 1924-26; mem. Essex Co. Bar. Assn., Italian Hist. Soc. Chevalier Crown of Italy. Republican. Presbyn. Mason, Eagle, Moose. Club: Newark Athletic. Home: 81 Longfellow Av., Newark, N.J.

CAVINATO, Lawrence A(ugustus), lawyer; b. N.Y. City, Nov. 14, 1900; s. Stephen and Albina (Moglia) C.; ed. Cornell Univ., 1919-22; LL.B., Cornell U. Law Sch., 1925; unmarried. Admitted to N.Y. bar, 1927 and in practice of law, N.Y. City; admitted to N.J. bar as atty., 1929, counsellor, 1934; engaged in gen. practice of law at Fort Lee since 1930; apptd. N.J. Supreme Ct. commr., 1935; served as mem. N.J. Ho. of Assembly, 1931-36, Rep. Majority Leader of Ho., 1936. Mem. Bergen Co. Chamber of Commerce. Mem. Am. Bar Assn., N.J. State and Bergen Co. bar assns., Cornell Alumni Assn. Republican. Roman Catholic. Home: 1622 Centre Av. Office: 200 Main St., Fort Lee, N.J.

CAVINS, Lorimer Victor, educator; b. nr. Mattoon, Ill., May 21, 1880; s. Joseph and Malissa Elizabeth (Ferguson) C.; grad. Ill. State Normal U., 1903; A.B., U. of Ill., 1906; A.M., Harvard, 1910; Ph.D., U. of Chicago, 1924; m. Neva Julia Adams, Oct. 2, 1913; children—Lawrence Everrett (dec.), Helen Irene, Arnold (dec.), Marjorie Mae, Virginia Lee. Supt. schs., Hinckley, Ill., 1903-05; head of English dept., East St. Louis, Ill., 1906-09; Stevens Point Normal Sch., Wis., 1910-12; Joliet (Ill.) Twp. High Sch. and Jr. Coll., 1913-17; prof. edn., W.Va., U., 1919-25; became dir. ednl. research, State Dept. Edn., W.Va., 1925; owner of Harvard Plantation, Yazoo Valley, Miss. Pres. Ill. State English Assn., 1917; dir. Bur. Ednl. Research; dir. state survey of edn., W.Va.; chmn. bur. of research, state depts. edn., N.E.A.; tech. adviser edn. in govt. survey of Okla., by Brookings Instn., 1934; ednl. specialist Md. Youth Study by Am. Council on Education, 1936-37. Member Phi Delta Kappa. Republican. Methodist. Author: Financing Education in West Virginia, 1925; Organization, Administration and Finance (Vol. I, Survey of Edn. in W.Va.) and Education Achievement (Vol. II), 1928; Standardization of American Poetry for School Purposes, 1928. Now editor in chief Am. Educator Encyclopedia. Home: 1612 Virginia St., Charleston, W.Va.*

CAWTHRA, W. H.; mayor of Du Bois, present term expires 1940. Address: Du Bois, Pa.

CHADWICK, E. Wallace; mem. law firm Chadwick, Weeks, Curran & Ives. Address: Chester, Pa.

CHAFEY, James Holmes, pharmacist; b. Point Pleasant, N.J., Apr. 9, 1894; s. Holmes and Susan E. (Harker) C.; grad. Pt. Pleasant High Sch., 1911; Ph.C., Columbia, 1921; m. Nathalie Meyerholz, Oct. 20, 1922; children—David Holmes, James Henry, Rita. Began with D. H. Hills Drug Co., Bay Head, N.J., 1912; purchased the business, 1921, and since prop.; pres. Bay Head Nat. Bank, 1927-35; dir. Bay Head Bldg. & Loan Assn.; treas. Bay Head Improvement Assn. Mem. Sinking Fund Commn. of Ocean County, N.J., since 1932. Served in Chem. Warfare Service, U.S. Army, 1917-18. Mem. Sons Am. Revolution, Kappa Psi. Republican. Mason. Home: 638 Main St. Office: 530 Main St., Bay Head, N.J.

CHAFFEE, Carl Harrison, banker; b. Friendship, N.Y., Dec. 19, 1883; s. William Harrison and Lucy I. (Johnson) C.; ed. Norwich (N.Y.) High Sch.; m. Mabel L. King, Sept. 5, 1904; children—Marian Kay, Virginia Lucy (Mrs. William M. Gwynn), William Harrison, John Howard; m. 2d, Lela McGrath Nichols, Apr. 23, 1924. Stenographer N.Y., Ontario & Western Ry. Co., Norwich, N.Y., 1899-1901, N.Y.C. & H.R.R., New Durham, N.J., 1901-03; private sec. to law firm, New York, N.Y., 1903-11, to v.p. First Nat. Bank of Phila., 1911-17; asst. cashier First Nat. Bank, Phila., 1917-20, cashier, 1920-27, v.p. and cashier since 1927; pres. First Trust Co. of Phila. since 1925; dir. Mohican Holding Corpn., Phila. Dairy Products Co. Inc., Crystal Oil Refining Corpn., John J. Deery Co., Inc., John J. Deery Co., Ltd. Presbyterian. Clubs: Union League, Midday (Phila.); Phila. Country (Bala-Cynwyd, Pa.). Home: Swarthmore, Pa., Office: 1500 Walnut St., Philadelphia, Pa.

CHAFFEE, Maurice Albert; prof. univ. extension, Rutgers U. Address: Rutgers University, New Brunswick, N.J.

CHAFFEE, Orel N., cons. surgeon St. Vincent's Hosp. Address: 820 Sassafras St., Erie, Pa.

CHAFFINCH, James Roland, banker; b. Potter's Landing, Md., June 12, 1887; s. Tilghman F. and O. Janie (Calloway) C.; grad. Caroline High Sch., Denton, Md. 1905; LL.B., Dickinson Coll., Carlisle, Pa., 1909; m. Lenore Clark Greenley, Aug. 12, 1915; children—Ellen Lenore, James Roland, Anne Louise. In mercantile business and postmaster, Hobbs, Md., 1909-18; dir. Denton (Md.) Nat. Bank since 1913, exec. vice-pres., 1918-26, pres. since 1926. Mem. Caroline County Bd. of Edn., 1924-26. Vice-pres. Md. Bankers' Assn., 1939. Chm. Caroline Co. Welfare Bd. since 1935. Mem. Sigma Alpha Epsilon. Republican. Episcopalian (vestryman). Mason. Club: Denton Rotary. Home: Denton, Md.

CHALFANT, Charles Elliott, pumping machinery; b. Steubenville, O., Nov. 6, 1886; s. Frank and Anna (Driscoll) C.; student Mount Union Coll., Alliance, O.; m. Alice McCune, Apr. 18, 1916; children—Dana, Jeanne Louise. In employ Platt Iron Works at Dayton, O. and New York City; then sales mgr. Wagener Steam Pump Co., Canton, O.; later dist. mgr. Weinman Pump Mfg. Co., Pittsburgh; now pres. and gen. mgr. Weinman Pump and Supply Co. Mem. Sigma Nu. Republican. Presbyn. Rotarian. Home: 241 Jefferson Drive, Mt. Lebanon, Pa. Office: 210 Boul. of Allies, Pittsburgh, Pa.

CHALFANT, P(aul) Floyd, pub.; b. Fordyce, Pa., July 13, 1889; s. James Fletcher and Eliza Minerva (Reeves) C.; student Charleroi (Pa.) Pub. and High Sch., 1898-1906; m. Julia Elizabeth Settles, June 15, 1915; children—Dorothy Dell, Jean Kathryn, Paul Floyd, Jr. Began as newspaper boy, 1903; reporter Charleroi (Pa.) Mail, 1907-13, city editor, 1913-17; editor Beaver (Pa.) Daily Times, 1917-25; chief owner and pub. Waynesboro (Pa.) Record Herald since 1925; pres., gen. mgr. and editor Record Herald Pub. Co., Inc., newspaper pub. and printing. Mem. Ohio River & Lake Erie Canal Bd., 1924-25, Pa. Elections Commn., 1926. Mem. Waynesboro (Pa.) Chamber of Commerce (pres. 1936-37), Pa. Newspaper Pubs. Assn. (pres. 1937), Am. Newspaper Pubs. Assn. Republican. Methodist. Mason (K.T., Shriner), Odd Fellow. Clubs: Rotary (Waynesboro, Pa.); Nat. Press (Washington, D.C.,). Home: 118 Sunnyside. Office: care Record Herald, Waynesboro, Pa.

CHALFANT, Sidney A.; gynecologist Allegheny Gen., Elizabeth Steel Magee and Women's hosps., Pittsburgh; asst. prof. gynecology, U. of Pittsburgh. Address: 500 Penn Av., Pittsburgh, Pa.

CHALLIS, David Anderson, pres. Sewickley Valley Trust Co.; b. Sewickley, Pa., July 6, 1877; s. Daniel William and Mary Frances (Jones) C.; student Sewickley (Pa.) Pub. Schs. and High Sch., 1883-94, Duffs Business Coll., Pittsburgh, Pa., 1895-96; m. Flora Jackson, Jan. 17, 1901; children—Dorothy (Mrs. Eugene Biddle), David Anderson, Daniel Chester. Began as timekeeper, D. W. Challis & Sons, Inc., gen. contractors and building supplies, Sewickley, Pa., 1898-1920, pres. since 1920; treas. Asso. Pa. Constructors, Harrisburg, Pa., 1926-27, pres., 1930-31, now member bd. of advisors; associated Gen. Constructors, Washington, D.C.; pres. Sewickley Valley Trust Co., Sewickley (Pa.) since 1933. Vice-pres. and dir. Sewickley (Pa.) Pub. Schs. Republican. Mason (K.T., Shriner). Home: 735 Beaver St. Office: 400 Centennial Av., Sewickley, Pa.

CHALMERS, Henry, economist; b. New York, N.Y., June 28, 1892; s. Isidor C. and Sarah (Abrams) C.; A.B., Cornell U. 1914, A.M., 1914; Ph. D., Brookings Grad. Sch. of Economics, Washington, D.C., 1928; m. Sallie Kittner, Sept. 2, 1923; children—Judith Louise, David Mark. Asst. to export mgr. Bear Mill Mfg. Co., 1912-13; statistician N.Y. State Dept. of Health, 1914-18; spl. expert U.S. Tariff Commn., 1918-21; chief div. of foreign tariffs, Dept. of Commerce, since 1921. On special missions to Japan for investigation of industrial and competitive conditions, 1919-20, to Europe, for survey of post-war tariff situation, 1923. Mem. or expert on Am. delegation to Internat. Customs Conf., Geneva, 1923, World Econ. Conf., Geneva, 1927, Pan-Am. Conf. on Consular Procedure (sec.-gen.), Washington, 1927, Internat. Chamber of Commerce, Washington, 1931, 4th Pan-Am. Commercial Conf., Washington, 1931, Internat. Monetary and Econ. Conf., London, 1933. Served for short time as pvt. with 39th Inf., U.S.A., World War. Mem. Am. Econ. Assn., Am. Acad. Polit. and Social Science, Phi Beta Kappa, Tau Epsilon Phi. Mason. Club: Cosmos. Author: Japanese Cotton Industry and Trade, 1921; Euro-

CHAMBELLAN, Rene Paul, sculptor; b. West Hoboken, N.J.; s. Pierre and Louise (Finiel) C.; student New York U., 1912-14, Beaux Arts Inst. of Design, 1914-17, Ecole Julian, Paris, 1918-19; m. Suzanne Houilloire, Mar. 11, 1919; children—Rene, Suzanne, Madeleine. Archtl. modeler and sculptor since 1910; instructor in sculpture New York Univ.; sculpture work for Yale Univ., Northwestern Univ., Lafayette and Cornell colls., Rockefeller Center (New York), State office buildings (New York and Buffalo), Buffalo City Hall, Bushnell Memorial (Hartford, Conn.), Scottish Rite Temple (Scranton, Pa.), Radiator and News Bldgs. (N.Y. City), Worcester Memorial Auditorium (Worcester, Mass.), Chicago Tribune Bldg., Engineers Memorial (Louvain Clock Tower, Belgium), Court House (Nashville, Tenn.), State Bldg., Nashville, Tenn., large group for N.Y. World's Fair; mausoleums for Healy, Berret, C. D. Ryan, Medill McCormick. Awarded Sterling Memorial Plaque, also various medals. Served as sergt., 11th Inf., U.S.A., in France, 1917-19. Home: Grantwood, N.J. Office: 332 E. 39th St., New York, N.Y.

CHAMBERLAIN, George Agnew, novelist; b. (Am. parents residing abroad) Sao Paulo, Brazil, Mar. 15, 1879; s. George Whitehill and Mary (Annesley) C.; grad. Lawrenceville (N.J.) Sch., 1898; spl. course in English lit. and Romance langs., Princeton; unmarried. Apptd. deputy consul gen. at Rio de Janeiro, Brazil, Apr. 29, 1904; vice and deputy consul-gen., June 24, 1904; retired Dec. 1904; consul at Pernambuco, Brazil, 1906-09, at Lourenco Marques, May 31, 1909-July 1916; consul gen. at Mexico City, Mexico, May 12, 1917-Aug. 1, 1919, resigned. Spl. corr. Associated Press 3d Pan-Am. Conf., Rio de Janeiro, 1906. Republican. Presbyn. Clubs: Cannon (Princeton); Century, Coffee House, The Whist Club (New York). Author: Home, 1914; Through Stained Glass, 1915; John Bogardus, 1916; White Man, 1919; Not All the King's Horses, 1919; Is Mexico Worth Saying? 1920; Pigs to Market, 1920; Taxi! 1920; Cobweb, 1921; Rackhouse, 1922; African Shooting Among the Thongs, 1923; Lip Malvy's Wife, 1923; The Lantean on the Plow, 1924; The Great Van Suttart Mystery, 1925; Lost (play), 1926; Man Alone, 1926; No Ugly Ducklings, 1927; The Silver Cord, 1927; The Stranger at the Feast, 1928; The Taken Child, 1929; When Beggars Ride, 1930; River to the Sea, 1930; Night at Lost End, 1931; The Auction, 1932; Marriage for Revenue, 1933; Two on Safari, 1934; Under Pressure, 1936; In Defense of Mrs. Maxon, 1938; also various short stories. Contbr. mags. on social and econ. subjects of S. America. Home: Lloyd's Landing, Quinton, Salem Co., N.J.

CHAMBERLAIN, Wilbur; editor Orange Courier. Address: Orange, N.J.

CHAMBERLAIN, W(illiam) Edward, physician; b. Ann Arbor, Mich., Aug. 5, 1892; s. Nelson Hoyt and Mabel (Rahm) C.; grad. Oakland (Calif.) High Sch., 1909; B.S., U. of Calif., 1913, M.D., 1916; m. Genevieve L. Owen, June 22, 1915; children—Owen, Ann. Began as asst. in roentgenology, U. of Calif., Med. Sch., 1916; lit. j.g., U.S. Naval Reserve Force, 1917-21, with active duty as roentgenologist Mare Island Naval Hosp., Aug.-Dec., 1917, and U.S. Navy Base Hosp., Strathpeffer, Scotland, 1918-19; instr., U. of Calif. Med. Sch., 1919-20; roentgenologist in charge at Children's, St. Mary's and Hahnemann Hosps., San Francisco, Calif., 1919-20; asst. prof. of medicine, Stanford U. Med. Sch., 1920-23, asso. prof., 1923-26, prof. of medicine, 1926-30; prof. of radiology, Temple U. Med. Sch. since 1930; in private practice, specializing in radiology, Phila., since 1930; mem. bd. dirs. Asso. Hosp. Service of Phila. Mem. bd. dirs. Phila. Health Council and Tuberculosis Com. Fellow Am. Coll. Radiology (chmn. bd. chancellors), Am. Coll. Physicians, A.M.A., Coll. of Physicians of Phila.; mem. Pa. State Med. Soc., Phila. Co. Med. Soc. (chmn. com. on med. economics), Am. Roentgen Ray Soc., Radiol. Soc. N. America (standardization com.), Am. Radium Soc., Laennec Soc. of Phila., Calif. Acad. Medicine, Calif. Acad. Sciences, Am. Assn. Physics Teachers, Phila. Mus. of Art, Franklin Inst., Alpha Omega Alpha, Alpha Kappa Kappa. Republican. Presbyterian. Mason. Clubs: Bohemian (San Francisco); Phila. Country, Manufacturers and Bankers, Medical, Gyro (Phila.). Author of many scientific articles and monographs. Home: 269 W. Tulpehocken St. Office: 3401 N. Broad St., Philadelphia, Pa.

CHAMBERLIN, Ralph Ellsworth, forester; b. Palmerton, Pa., July 14, 1909; s. William Charles and Ella Amanda (Reed) C.; B.S. in Forestry, Pa. State Coll., 1935; unmarried. In employ New Jersey Zinc Co. of Pa., Palmerton, 1926-31; instr. forestry, Pa. State Coll., 1935; asst. dist. forester Michaux State Forest Dist., Fayetteville, Pa., 1935-36, dist. forester same, 1936-37; sr. silviculturist Pa. Dept. Forests & Waters, Harrisburg, Pa., since 1937. Mem. Am. Forestry Assn., Soc. Am. Foresters, Pa. Forestry Assn., Xi Sigmi Pi, Gamma Sigma Delta. Lutheran. Club: Palmerton Rod and Gun. Home: 485 Delaware Av., Palmerton, Pa. Office: Dept. of Forests & Waters, Harrisburg, Pa.

CHAMBERLIN, William Beaver, retired coal producer; b. Danville, Pa., Aug. 2, 1865; s. William Hayes and Elizabeth Berryhill (Beaver) C.; student Hill Sch., Pottstown, Pa., 1877-82, Columbia U., 1882-85; m. Alice Leslie Rea, Dec. 16, 1891; children—William Beaver, John Rea. Asst. treas. Kingston (Pa.) Coal Co., 1886-92, treas. 1892-1903, pres. 1903-35; now retired. Mem. Phi Upsilon, Loyal Legion. Republican. Club: Union League (Phila.). Home: Torresdale, Pa.

CHAMBERS, Arthur Douglas, chem. engr.; b. Woodstock, Ont., Can., May 4, 1870; s. James Douglas and Josephine Augusta (Mollins) C.; came to U.S., 1892, naturalized, 1921; student Woodstock (Can.) Coll., 1884-88; A.B., Toronto (Can.) U., 1892; Ph.D., Johns Hopkins U., Baltimore, Md., 1896; m. May Fleming, July 21, 1897; children—Ivan Fleming, Ira Douglas, Arthur Edwin. Chem. engr. Solar Refining Co., Lima, O., 1896-97; asst. supt. Ashburn (Mo.) works, E. I. du Pont de Nemours & Co., 1897-1905, supt. Ashburn works, 1905-07, supt. Louviers (Colo.) works, 1907-15; technical investigator development department, Wilmington, Del., 1915-17, mgr. production dyestuffs dept., 1917-31, mgr. dyestuffs div., organic chemicals dept., since 1931. Mem. Franklin Inst., Am. Chem. Soc., Am. Inst. Chem. Engrs. Episcopalian. Clubs: Wilmington, Wilmington Country, Wilmington Whist, University (Wilmington, Del.); Chemists' (New York). Home: 509 Lore Av. Office: 8410 Nemours Bldg., Wilmington, Del.

CHAMBERS, Bernard Barton, sch. prin.; b. Dameron, W.Va., Aug. 24, 1889; s. Joseph and Eva (Cook) C.; S.T., Marshall Coll. Prep. Sch., 1913; A.B., Marshall Coll. 1931; student W.Va. U., summers 1928, 35, 38, 39; m. Bessie Jane Miller, June 1, 1927; children—Erlin Keith, Elnora. Teacher Raleigh Co. Schs., 1908-28; county supt. schs., Raleigh Co., 1931-37; prin. Beckley Jr. High Sch., 1937-39. Served with A.E.F., May 1918-July 1919, serving in France 1 yr. Mem. W.Va. Edn. Assn. Square and Compass. Democrat. Methodist. Mason, Odd Fellow, Elk. Club: Lions. Address: Beckley, W.Va.

CHAMBERS, Charles E.; pres. First Nat. Bank of Roselle. Home: 260 E. Third Av., Roselle, N.J.

CHAMBERS, Chester C., lawyer; b. Pecks Mill, W.Va., Dec. 11, 1890; s. Leroy and Martha C.; grad. Marshall Coll., Huntington, W.Va., 1908-12; LL.B., Washington and Lee Univ. Law Coll., 1915; m. Ida Robinette, Aug. 23, 1917. Teaching in pub. schs., 1909-13; admitted to W.Va. bar, 1915, and engaged in gen. practice of law at Logan since 1915; recorder city of Logan, 1916-17, mayor, 1925-26, city atty., 1926-27; divorce commr., 1916; judge Circuit Ct., Logan Co., W.Va., since 1937. Served as 2d lt. Sanitary Corps, U.S.A., 1918-19, comdg. officer detachment Gen. Hosp., Ft. Bayard, N.M. Mem. Am. Bar. Assn., W.Va. Bar Assn. Democrat. Mem. M. E. Ch. South. Mason (32°, K.T. Shriner). Club: Rotary. Home: 405 Cole St. Address: Court House, Logan, W.Va.

CHAMBERS, D. B.; mem. law firm Daniel B. Chambers & Son. Address: Central Savings Bank Bldg., Baltimore, Md.

CHAMBERS, Francis S.; orthopedic surgeon St. Joseph's Hosp. Address: 446 N. Duke St., Lancaster, Pa.

CHAMBERS, Francis T., patent lawyer; b. Cincinnati, Mar. 3, 1855; s. Francis T. and Elizabeth Lea (Febiger) C.; Ph.B., Sheffield Scientific Sch. (Yale), 1875; studied law in office of William Henry Rawle; LL.B., U. of Pa., 1877; m. Nanette Schuyler Bolton, June 10, 1890 (died 1912); children—Katharine Schuyler Chambers Munoz, Mrs. Christine Chambers Gray, Francis T. Began practice, Phila., 1877; asso. with late George Harding, 1878-88; alone since 1888 in federal cts. throughout U.S. Mem. board of dirs. Franklin Inst. Republican. Episcopalian. Clubs: Philadelphia, Rittenhouse. Home: 1530 Pine St., Phila., and Bryn-Llonydd, Penllyn, Pa. Office: Stock Exchange Bldg., Philadelphia, Pa.

CHAMBERS, Franklin S.; pres. Joseph J. White, Inc.; officer or dir. many companies. Address: New Lisbon, N.J.

CHAMBERS, Orlando C., banking; b. Danville, W.Va., Dec. 3, 1878; s. Jacob and Carrie (Stollings) C.; student County Normal Sch., Madison, W.Va., 1892-95, Marshall Coll., Huntington, 1900-04, normal certificate, 1904; m. Gertrude Hunter, June 28, 1905; children—Livingston Hunter, Mary Elizabeth (Mrs. James Enoch Johnston). Engaged in teaching pub. schs., W.Va., 1895-1905; mgr. gen. store, Hernshaw, W.Va., 1905-06; asso. with Boone Nat. Bank since 1906, vice-pres. and dir. since 1906. Served as city recorder, Madison, W.Va., 1908-10. Trustee M. E. Ch., Madison, W.Va., since 1916. Republican. Methodist. Mason (Shriner), O.E.S. Club Walhovde Golf (Madison). Home: Jackson St. Office: Boone Nat. Bank, Madison, W.Va.

CHAMBERS, Thomas Rodney; associate in surgery, Johns Hopkins Univ.; asso. prof. surgery, Univ. of Md.; assistant visiting surgeon Johns Hopkins Hosp.; mem. staff Mercy Hosp., Union Memorial Hosp. and Church Home and Infirmary. Address: 18 W. Franklin St., Baltimore, Md.

CHAMBERS, Will Grant, college dean; b. Pleasant Unity, Westmoreland Co., Pa., Apr. 26, 1867; s. Joseph Harold and Susan Brinker (Jamison) C.; grad. Central State Normal Sch., Lock Haven, Pa., 1887; A.B., Lafayette Coll., 1894, A.M., 1897; grad. scholar, Clark U., 1897-98, University of Chicago, 1899-1901; LittD., Lafayette Coll., 1917; Sc.D., Gettysburg Coll., 1934; m. Claudia May Orcutt, July 19, 1894 (died Mar. 19, 1896); 1 dau., Mrs. Claudia Orcutt Miller; m. 2d, Sunshine Foulke, June 27, 1901. Teacher pub. schs., Mt. Pleasant, Pa., 1887-88; instr. Central State Normal Sch., 1888-90, 1892; prof. mathematics, Indiana Normal Sch., Pa., 1894-97, 1899, 1900; prof. psychology and edn., Moorhead (Minn.) State Normal Sch., 1901-04; prof. psychology and child study, Colo. State Normal Sch., 1904-09; prof. edn., 1909-21, dean Sch. of Edn., 1910-21, U. of Pittsburgh; dean Summer Session, Pa. State Coll., 1921-37, dean Sch. of Edn. same, 1923-37; retired 1937. Republican. Protestant. Fellow A.A.A.S.; mem. N.E.A. (pres. dept. of child study, 1909-10), Am. Psychological Assn., Soc. Coll. Teachers of Edn. (pres. 1916-17), Simplified Spelling Bd. (advisory council), Pa. State Educational Assn. (pres. 1920), Pa. Schoolmasters' Club, Nat. Soc. for Study of Edn.; chmn. Sect. V, 4th Internat. Congress on Home Edn. Dist. dir. War and Navy Depts. Commn. on Training Camp Activities, Honolulu, 1918-19. Mem. Theta Delta Chi, Phi Beta Kappa, Phi Delta Kappa, Phi Kappa Phi,

Kappi Phi Kappa (nat. pres. 1931-33), Kappa Delta Pi, Pi Gamma Mu. Contbr. to edl. mags. and revs. Home: 333 W. Park Av., State College, Pa.

CHAMPION, John B., clergyman, educator; b. Prince Edward Island, Can., June 18, 1868; s. James W. and Margaret J. (Brooks) C.; grad. Prince of Wales Coll., 1885; B.A., U. of New Brunswick, 1900; M.A., Acadia U., 1903; B.D., Colgate Div. Sch., 1903; Th.D., Eastern Bapt. Theol. Sem., 1928; m. Emma J. Dunbar, Sept. 16, 1891 (died May 7, 1932); children—Una May (wife of Dr. Stanton G. Nichols), Gladys Mabel (wife of Dr. W. H. Bueermann), William D., Ralph L., C. Belle (Mrs. W. Hutton Granville), John C., Elaine C. (Mrs. Maurice Reed Entwistle); m. 2d, Edith M. Webster, May 15, 1935; 2 sons, Benjamin W., David C. Came to U.S. 1900, naturalized, 1923. Ordained Bapt. ministry, 1893; pastor at Geneva, N.Y., Calvary Ch., Brantford, Ont., Roxborough, Pa., McMinnville, Ore., White Plains, N.Y., until 1925; prof. Christian doctrine, Eastern Bapt. Theol. Sem., Phila., since 1925. Author: The Living Atonement, 1910; (monograph) The Virgin's Son, 1924; More Than Atonement, 1927; Why Modernism Must Fail, 1932; Sovereignty and Grace, 1933; Personality and The Trinity, 1935; Inspiration Explains Itself, 1938. Home: 4012 Primrose Rd., Torresdale, Philadelphia, Pa.

CHAMPLIN, Carroll Dunham, prof. edn.; b. Chelsea, Mich., Oct. 22, 1887; s. Henry W. and Delia A. (Sherwood) C.; A.B., Haverford (Pa.) Coll., 1914, A.M., 1915; Ph.D., U. of Pittsburgh, 1925; m. Helen Coreene Karns, Sept. 1, 1919; 1 dau., Carolyn King. Teaching in pub. schs., Pa., 1906-10; teaching fellow Haverford Coll., 1914-15, asst. in English, 1915-16; instr. Education, U. of Pittsburgh, 1919-21; head dept. edn. and psychology, Calif. (Pa.) State Teachers Coll., 1921-26; prof. edn., Pa. State Coll. since 1926; exch. prof., U. of Puerto Rico, 1st semester, 1932-33; summers teaching at U. of Pittsburgh, 1920, East Stroudsburg (Pa.) Teachers Coll., 1921, Pa. State Coll., 1924, Cornell U., 1928, George Washington Univ., 1934 and 1938, University of Pennsylvania, 1936. Served in Army Y.M.C.A. during World War. Am. rep. at several European ednl. confs. Mem. N.E.A., Nat. Soc. Study of Edn., Am. Assn. Univ. Profs., World Federation of Edn. Assns., National Society College Teachers of Education, National Travel Club, Am. Assn. Sch. Adminstrs., Phi Delta Kappa, Phi Gamma Mu, Kappa Phi Kappa, Alpha Chi Rho. Republican. Presbyterian. Contbr. articles to ednl. jours. Home: 627 W. Fairmount Av., State College, Pa.

CHAMPLIN, Helen Karns (Mrs. Carroll D. C.), coll. instr. and lecturer psychology; b. Phila., Pa., Nov. 27, 1894; d. Sedgwick Bert and Susan Caroline (Keeler) Karns; ed. Bloomsburg (Pa.) State Teachers Coll., 1912-13, Wilkes-Barre (Pa.) Inst., 1913-15; A.B., Bryn Mawr Coll., 1919; A.M., U. of Pittsburgh, 1925; m. Carroll D. Champlin, Ph.D., September 1, 1919; 1 dau., Carolyn King. Instr. physics and history, Ellis Sch., Pittsburgh, 1919-21; training teacher, Southwestern Teachers Coll., California, Pa., 1921-22, prof. psychology and edn., 1922-26; instr. psychology, Pa. State Coll., State Coll., Pa., irregularly, 1926-38; extension lecturer in psychology, U. of Puerto Rico, Rio Piedras, P.R., 1932. Dir. Inst. Social Relations for Pa. State Fed. of Womens Clubs and Extension Div. of Pa. State Coll. Mem. Am. Assn. Univ. Women (Fellowship chmn. for Pa. and Del. since 1936), Phi Lambda Theta, Kappa Delta Pi and Psi Chi frats. Republican. Presbyterian. Contbr. articles in nat. mags.; co-author: Sportsmanlike Driving, 1938. Home: 627 W. Fairmount Av., State College, Pa.

CHANCE, Burton, M.D.; b. Phila. Pa., Jan. 30, 1868; s. Robert Chambers and Elizabeth Gale (Corson) C.; ed. Philadelphia schools; M.D., U. of Pa., 1893; m. Maria Scott Beale, Oct. 14, 1903; children—Maria Lewis, Helen Scott (Mrs. William Sellers II), Burton. Began med. practice in Phila., 1893; served in gen. hosps. and entered Wills Hosp. (eye); in practice of ophthalmology since 1896. Served as lt. M.C., U.S.A., 1917-19; col. Med. R.C. since 1919. Trustee Episcopal Acad. Fellow Am. Ophthal. Soc., Ophthal. Soc. United Kingdoms of Great Britain; mem. A.M.A., Pa. Med. Soc., Phila. Med. Soc. Democrat. Episcopalian (vestryman of St. Marks). Contbr. on ophthalmic medicine and history of medicine to various jours. Home: Mayfield House, Radnor, Pa. Office: 317 S. 15th St., Philadelphia, Pa.

CHANCE, Edwin Mickley, pres. United Engineers and Constructors, Inc.; b. Phila., Pa., Jan. 13, 1885; s. Henry Martyn and Lillie E. (Mickley) C.; grad. DeLancey Sch., 1903; B.S. in Chemistry, U. of Pa., 1907; m. Eleanor Kent, Jan. 11, 1909; children—Henry Martyn II, Britton. Assaying and mining in Nev., 1907-09; chemist and engr. Phila. & Reading Coal & Iron Co., Pottsville, Pa., 1909-13; cons. practice, Wilkes-Barre, 1913-17; engring. mgr. Day & Zimmerman Inc., Phila., 1919-25; v.p. Day & Zimmerman, Inc., 1925-28; pres. Day & Zimmerman Engring. & Constrn. Co., Inc., 1928; v.p. United Engrs. & Constructors, Inc., 1928-31, pres. since 1931; pres. Dwight P. Robinson & Co., Inc., United Engrs. & Constructors Co. of Mexico, United Engrs. & Constructors Co. of Argentine, Dwight P. Robinson & Co. of Brazil, U.G.I. Contracting Co. Served as capt. to lt. col. Ordnance Department, Chem. Warfare Service, U.S.A., in charge design, construction and operation of poison gas, shell filling plant, Edgewood Arsenal, 1917-18; with A.E.F., 1918. Trustee, mem. bd. of engring. edn., U. of Pa.; trustee and mem. exec. bd. U. of Pa.; mem. Bd. Grad. Edn. and Research, U. of Pa.; trustee Moore Sch. of Elec. Engring., U. of Pa. Mem. Acad. Nat. Science (Phila.), Franklin Inst., Army Ordnance Assn. Awarded Edward Longstreth Medal of Merit, Franklin Inst. Republican. Episcopalian. Clubs: Engineers, Midday, Racquet (Phila.); New York Yacht, Corinthian Yacht, Mantoloking Yacht, Annapolis Yacht, Cruising Club America, Gibson Island Club. Contbr. to tech. publs.; many chem. and metall. inventions. Home: Ocean Av., Mantoloking, N.J. Office: 1401 Arch St., Philadelphia, Pa.

CHANDLEE, Grover C., prof. of chemistry; b. Delta, Pa., Sept. 5, 1884; s. Samuel and Elizabeth Ann (Barton) C.; Ph.B., Franklin and Marshall Coll., 1907; M.S., Pa. State Coll., 1913; A.M., Columbia, 1922, Ph.D., 1925; unmarried. With Pa. State Coll. as instr. in chemistry, 1907-10, asso. prof., 1912-18, prof. and head of dept. of chemistry since 1922, acting dean of Grad. Sch., 1933-34; industrial chemist, 1910-11. Served as 1st lt., U.S. Army, 1918-19. Mem. Am. Chem. Soc., Phi Kappa Phi, Phi Lambda Upsilon, Phi Kappa Sigma, Alpha Chi Sigma. Club: Chemists (New York). Home: University Club, State College, Pa.

CHANDLER, Alfred N(oblit), economist, publicist; b. Wilmington, Del., Aug. 27, 1858; s. George and Sarah Rebecca (Cain) C.; ed. North East Classical Sem., North East, Md.; bachelor. Telegrapher, operating Phila.-Chicago quadruplex, until 1880; with Robert Glendinning & Co., stock brokers, Phila., 1880-93, making a study of economics and finance. An organizer, 1884, and pres., 1884-89, Henry George Club of Phila., 1st club of that name, and forerunner of others of the name in different parts of the world; organizer, 1887, and served as sec. and treas. Pa. Ballot Reform Assn. to secure legislation to enact Australian secret ballot, finally enacted in all the states in U.S.; mem. lecture staff of Wharton Sch. of Economics and Commerce, U. of Pa., 1890-93; engaged in promotion of pub. utilities, New York and Phila., from 1893. Assisted, 1894, in organizing cavalry co. which developed into the 2d Troop, Phila. City Cav.; a founder of Aero Club of America (N.Y. City), 1905, and the first member to obtain a balloon, the "Initial," in which made a number of ascensions; organizer, 1906, and served as pres. Aero Club of Phila.; pres. Automobile Club of Phila., 1906-08. Winner of many yachting prizes. Writer and lecturer on the Henry George Philosophy. Home: Roseville, Newark, N.J.

CHANDLER, Paul Gladstone, coll. pres.; b. Princeton, Ky., Nov. 7, 1889; s. Joseph Stroud and Elizabeth Ann (Pillow) C.; A.B., Ky. Wesleyan Coll., Winchester, 1914; A.M., Columbia, 1920, Ph.D., 1927; m. Kathleen Hicks, Sept. 6, 1927; children—Elizabeth Ann (dec.), John Paul. Teacher rural sch. and high sch., Ky., 1908-11; prin. Lindsay Wilson Training Sch., Columbia, Ky., 1914-17; head dept. edn., State Normal Coll., Kent, O., 1920-27, Teachers Coll., Millersville, Pa., 1927-37; pres. Clarion (Pa.) State Teachers Coll. since 1937. Mem. N.E.A., Kappa Delta Pi, Pi Delta Kappa, Phi Sigma Pi. Methodist. Mason (K.T., Shriner), Elk, Lion, Kiwanian. Address: Clarion, Pa.

CHANDLER, Paul V.; pres. Chandler & Canning, Inc., real estate. Address: 21 S. 12th St., Philadelphia, Pa.

CHANDLER, Percy Milton, corpn. official; b. Philadelphia, Feb. 6, 1873; s. John Walter and Almira (Taylor) C.; ed. Friends' Central Sch., Phila.; m. Emma B. Mendenhall, Oct. 20, 1897; m. 2d, Nancy Louise Krebs, Nov. 1, 1917; m. 3d, Marie Leonard Langtree, Oct. 7, 1926. Chmn. of bd. Nat. Food Products Co., U.S. Stores Corpn.; pres. and dir. P. M. Chandler & Co., Inc., Securities Corpn. Gen., Internat. Utilities Corpn., Brandywine Farms Corpn., Pennsbury Farms Corpn., Pennfar Realty Co., Gen. Water, Gas & Electric Co.; dir. Community Public Service Co., Dominion Gas & Electric Co., P. H. Butler Co., Phila. Dairy Products Co., Woodlawn Farm Dairy Co., Lehigh Coal & Navigation Co.; voting trustee 1500 Walnut St. Bldg. Corpn. Member numerous clubs. Mem. Soc. of Friends. Home: 280 Park Av., New York, N.Y. Office: 120 Broadway, New York, N.Y.; and 1500 Walnut St., Philadelphia, Pa.

CHANDLER, Swithin, diagnostician and surgeon; b. Centerville, Del., May 13, 1870; s. Philemma and Rachel M. (Austin) C.; grad. U. of Pa. Med. Sch., 1892; grad. study, Vienna, Berlin, Paris, and London, 1901-02; m. Elizabeth Dickinson, April 3, 1910; children—Elizabeth Dickinson (Mrs. Charles B. Sunderland), Swithin; m. 2d, Reba McClintock, Dec. 24, 1929. Began practice of medicine in Wilmington, Del., 1892; elected chief surgeon Delaware Hosp., 1892; pres. Baltimore & Ohio Ry. Surgeons, 1900-01; chief surgeon Garretson Hosp., Phila., Pa., 1902 to 1918; asso. prof. abdominal surgery, Temple U., Phila., 1918 to 1928; in pvt. practice at Phila. since 1908. Served as san. officer, Pa. N.G. on Mexican border, 1916; officer Med. Res. U.S.A. until transferred to Pa. Div. Mem. Am. Med. Assn., Phila. Co. Med. Soc., Medical Club (mem. bd. govs., 11 yrs.), Phys. Motor Club. Republican. Soc. of Friends. Mason. Club: Whitemarsh (Pa.) Valley Country. Devised several operations; discovered several patholog. and anatom. conditions publishing same in connection with over 100 articles in various prominent med. jours. Pres. Chandler Family Assn., represented by at least 26 states, which family comprises of several thousand living descendants (book pub. on same). Home: Strafford, Pa. Office: Central Medical Bldg., Philadelphia, Pa.

CHANDLER, William Henry, traffic mgr.; b. Greenville, Ala., Jan. 13, 1871; s. Charles Henry and Catherine (Flowers) C.; ed. pvt. schs.; m. Margaret Blight, Jan. 12, 1898; 1 son, Desmond Blight. Clk., wholesale grocery, 1887-90; chief rate clk., L.& N. R.R., Montgomery, Ala., 1890-92, C. of Ga. Ry., Savannah, Ga., 1892-95, Ocean S.S. Co., N.Y. City, 1895-97, at Savannah, 1897; industrial traffic mgr. for Francis H. Leggett & Co. and Seacoast Canning Co., N.Y. City, 1898-1908; New England freight agt. for A.B.& A.R.R. and Brunswick and Tex. City S.S. companies, Boston, Mass., 1908; industrial traffic mgr., Boston Chamber Commerce, 1909-12, and 1914-24, Merchants Assn. of New York, 1912-14; mgr. traffic bur., Merchants Assn. of New York since 1924; Eastern traffic asst. federal coördinator of transportation, 1933-35 (on furlough). Chmn. legislative com. Shippers Conf. of Greater New York; mem. exec. com. Nat. Industrial Traffic League, N.E. Traffic League; mem. Assn. Practitioners before Interstate Commerce Commn. (pres. 1934-35). Practitioner before U.S. Maritime Commn. Mem. N.E. rate com., U.S.R.R. Adminstrn., during federal control. Mason. Author: Express Service and Rates, 1912. Compiler: Merchants Parcel Post and Express Guide, 1914. Home: 344 N. Mountain Av., Upper Montclair, N.J. Office: 233 Broadway, New York, N.Y.

CHANDLESS, Ralph W.; mem. law firm Chandless, Weller & Selser. Address: Hackensack, N.J.

CHANEY, George Scott, civil engr.; b. Washington Co., Pa., April 16, 1878; s. George W. and Elizabeth J. (Scott) C.; ed. Washington and Jefferson Acad., 1894-96; A.B., Washington and Jefferson Coll., Washington, Pa., 1900; grad. student Cornell U., 1901; m. Edith Ann White, Oct. 27, 1904; children—Joseph Lutton (dec.), Jane Evelyn (Mrs. James Franklin Abell), Katherine Louise (Mrs. William Simeon Yard). Instr. engring., Washington & Jefferson Coll., 1900-02; borough engr., Washington, Pa., 1904-05; county engr., Washington Co., Pa., 1909-36, county surveyor, 1916-36; civil engr. Mfrs. Light & Heat Co., Pittsburgh, since 1937; dir. Carothers Dairy Co., sec.-treas. Allison Valley Coal Co. Served as pres. East Washington Borough Council since 1932. Republican. Club: Bassett (Washington, Pa.; charter mem.). Home: 477 E. Beau St., Washington, Pa.

CHANEY, Newcomb Kinney, research chemist; b. Northfield, Minn., April 27, 1883; s. Prof. Lucian West and Mary (Hill) C.; B.S., Carleton Coll., Northfield, 1904 (honors in philosophy and biology), M.S. in chemistry and physics, 1905; Rhodes scholar, Balliol Coll., Oxford U., 1907-10, B.A. in chemistry, 1910; Harrison fellow in chemistry, U. of Pa., 1910-11, Ph.D., 1911; m. Elsie Elizabeth Webb (Asso. Royal Coll. Music, London), July 19, 1911; children—Elizabeth Webb, David Webb. Trail building in Mont., working in lumber camps of Northwest, and traveling from Can. to Mexico, 1905-06; head football coach and instr. biology, Carleton Coll., 1906-07; in Germany, summer 1908; apptd. chemist, Nat. Carbon Co., 1911; investigator battery and electro-chem. problems; also inventor same lines; consulting chemist, Bur. of Mines, war gas investigations, May 1917-Aug. 1918; sect. chief, charcoal unit, defense chem. research div. of American University Expt. Station; consulting chemists, Chem. Warfare Service, U.S.A., August 1918-19; was a "dollar-a-year man" during World War; asst. dir. research and development labs., Nat. Carbon Co., 1919-21; dir. chem. research, carbon and battery divs., Union Carbide & Carbon Research Laboratories, Inc., Long Island City, N.Y., June 1921-May 1925; asst. dir. Research Labs., Nat. Carbon Co., Inc., 1925-35; asst. dir. of research United Gas Improvement Co., 1935-36, dir. of research since 1936. Inventor of processes for manufacture of "activated carbon,"—toxic gas absorbent employed exclusively by Am. Army during World War. This material has since achieved industrial importance in solvent and gasoline recovery systems, abatement of odors, etc.; basic patents granted in U.S. and Can.; also numerous U.S. and foreign patents relating to various carbon products, synthetic resins, processes for ultra-violet irradiation of foods, etc. Appointed, 1925, by sec. of war, consulting chemist Chemical Warfare Service, U.S. Army. Awarded Howard N. Potts gold medal of Franklin Inst. "for pioneer work in the field of carbon activation," 1939. Fellow Chem. Soc. (London), A.A.A.S.; mem. Am. Institute Chemical Engineers (dir.), Am. Chem. Soc. (council and chmn. Cleveland sect.), American Gas Assn., Am. Physical Soc., Inst. of Petroleum Engrs. (London), Phi Beta Kappa, Alembic Club (Oxford, Eng.). Conglist. Mason. Clubs: Engineers (Phila.); Chemists (New York); Oxford Union (Eng.). Contbr. tech. articles to Jour. Industrial and Engring. Chemistry, Jour. Am. Chem. Soc., Jour. Chem. Soc. (London), Trans. Am. Electrochem. Soc., Trans. Illuminating Engring. Society; Coöperating expert, Industrial Carbon, Vol. II, Internat. Critical Tables. Home. Possum Hollow Rd., Rose Valley, Moylan, Pa. Address: United Gas Improvement Co., 1401 Arch St., Philadelphia, Pa.

CHAPIN, Edward David, furniture mfr.; b. Milton, Pa., April 9, 1896; s. George Corry and Jennie Cooper (Hause) C.; student Pa. State Coll., 1913-16, Mass. Inst. Tech., 1918; m. Helen Dorothy Balliet, of Milton, Pa., June 30, 1921. Asso. with West Branch Novelty Co., mfrs. furniture, Milton, Pa., since 1916, successively time and cost clk., plant mgr., treas., and pres. and dir. of sales since 1924; dir. First Milton Nat. Bank, Milton Cemetery Co. Served as 2d class seaman to ensign A.S., U.S.N.R.F., 1917-19. Served as dir. Milton Pub. Sch. Dist., Milton Chamber of Commerce; pres. Y.M.C.A. Mem. Phi Gamma Delta. Republican. Presbyterian. Elk. Clubs: Manufacturers, Rotary (pres.), Otzinachson Country (Milton); Manufacturers and Bankers (Phila.). Home: 102 N. Front St. Office: care West Branch Novelty Co., Milton, Pa.

CHAPIN, Katherine Garrison (Mrs. Francis Biddle), writer, poet; b. Waterford, Conn., Sept. 4, 1890; d. Lindley Hoffman and Cornelia Garrison (Van Auken) Chapin; ed. Miss Eleanor Keller's Pvt. Sch., 1901-08, Miss Joanna Davidge Classes, New York, 1908-10; m. Francis Biddle, Apr. 27, 1918; 1 son, Edmund Randolph Biddle. Mem. Authors League, Poetry Soc. of America, League of Am. Writers, Art Alliance of Phila., Nat. Arts Club of N.Y. Democrat. Clubs: Cosmopolitan, Acorn (Phila.); Cosmopolitan (New York). Author: Outside of the World, 1930; Bright Marriner, 1933; Time Has No Shadow, 1936; Lament for the Stolen, 1938; contbr. verse to mags. Home: 3460 West School Lane, Germantown, Philadelphia, Pa.

CHAPLIN, James C., pres. Colonial Trust Co. Home: 245 Frederick Av., Sewickley, Pa. Office: 414 Wood St., Pittsburgh, Pa.

CHAPLINE, George F., v.p. Wright Aeronautical Corpn.; b. Lincoln, Neb., July 9, 1894; s. William Ridgely and Henrietta R. (Duncan) C.; grad. U.S. Naval Acad., 1916; post-grad. study, Mass. Inst. Tech. With Wright Aeronautical Corpn. since 1929, v.p. in charge of sales and dir. since 1934. Address: Paterson, N.J.

CHAPMAN, Charles H.; pres. Security Bank & Trust Co. Office: Kensington and Allegheny Avs., Philadelphia, Pa.

CHAPMAN, Charles Shepard, artist; b. Morristown, N.Y., June 2, 1879; s. Henry Augustus and Laura (Shepard) C.; ed. Pratt Inst. High Sch. 3 yrs.; Chase's Art Sch., New York, 1899; m. Adele Blanche Ahrens, May 16, 1911. Has exhibited at Nat. Acad. Fine Arts (New York), Carnegie Inst., Buffalo Acad. Fine Arts, Corcoran Gallery (Washington, D.C.), Art Inst. Chicago. Awarded Saltus gold medal, Nat. Acad., 1917, painting purchased by Met. Mus.; Carnegie prize. Nat. Acad., 1921; Shaw prize, and Turnbull prize, Salmagundi Club, also Vezin prize and Isador prize; 2d Altman prize, N.A.D., 1926. N.A., 1926. Republican. Episcopalian. Clubs: Salmagundi, Nat. Arts Club (New York). Home: 156 Sylvan Av., Leonia, N.J.

CHAPMAN, Ernest Theodore, supt. schs.; b. Greene Co., Pa., Apr. 21, 1888; s. Alvinzi B. and Alice Jane (Neighbor) C.; student Ashland (O.) Coll., 1908-11, diploma, 1911; B.S., U. of Pittsburgh, 1926; m. Ida M. Replogle, Oct. 25, 1912 (dec.); children—Eugene Replogle, Marian Jane. Employed as prin. grade schs., Greene and Washington Cos., Pa., 1908-16; elementary prin. pub. schs., New Kensington, Pa., 1922-24, supt. schs., New Kensington, Pa., since 1924. Mem. N.E.A., Am. Assn. of Sch. Adminstrs., Pa. State Edn. Assn. Republican. Methodist. Mason. Clubs: Kiwanis, Hill Crest Country (New Kensington, Pa.) Home: 240 Freeport Rd., New Kensington, Pa.

CHAPMAN, Everett, engr.; b. Detroit, Mich., May 9, 1901; s. Glenn L. and Amanda L., C.; B.S. in Elec. Engring., U. of Mich., Ann Arbor, Mich., 1923, M.S., 1924; m. Gloria Herriman, 1927; 1 son, Everett. Instr. in elec. engring., Purdue U., Lafayette, Ind., 1924-25; research and development Lincoln Electric Co., 1925-29; dir. research and development Lukenweld, Inc., 1929-35; pres. and dir. Lukenweld, Inc., welded steel construction, Coatesville, Pa., since 1935; dir. By Products Steel Corpn. Mem. Sigma Xi. Club: Nutcrackers (New York). Home: "Back Acres," Marshallton, Pa. Omce: Lukenweld, Inc., Coatesville, Pa.

CHAPMAN, Ira T., supt. schs.; b. Lima, O., June 26, 1874; s. John Henry and Eliza Ann (Berry) C.; A.B., Ohio Wesleyan U., 1903; A.B., A.M., Harvard, 1905; grad. student Clark U., Worcester, Mass., 1908-10, Columbia U., 1912-17; m. Bertha Agnes Law, June 11, 1906; 1 dau., Eleanore Willis (Mrs. Richard D. Gerould). Teacher rural schs., village high sch., 1892-1900; supt. Huntington (Mass.) Dist., 1905-07, Milbury Oxford Dist., 1907-12; supt. schs., Norwalk, Conn., 1912-17, New Brunswick, N.J., 1917-23, Elizabeth, N.J., since 1923. Trustee Elizabeth Pub. Library. Mem. N.E.A. (dept. superintendence), Horace Mann League, Nat. Soc. for Study of Edn., N.J. State Teachers Assn., N.J. Council of Edn., N.J. School-Masters' Club. Republican. Methodist. Mason. Clubs: Harvard of N.J., Scholia (Columbia U.), Kiwanis. Home: 30 Hillside Road. Address: 417 S. Broad St., Elizabeth, N.J.

CHAPMAN, James Wilkinson, Jr., lawyer; b. Chestertown, Kent Co., Md., Sept. 30, 1871; s. James Wilkinson and Mary Amanda (Webb) C.; A.B., Washington Coll., Chestertown, 1892, M.A.; Ph.D., Johns Hopkins, 1896; LL.B., U. of Md., 1897; m. Julia Clare Vannort, Nov. 11, 1903; children—Samuel Vannort, Mary Clare. Practiced in Baltimore since 1897; U.S. commr., 4th Jud. Circuit, 1936. Pres. Sch. Bd., Baltimore, 1915-20. Mem. Board of Visitors and Govs. of Washington Coll.; mem. bd. dirs. Y.M.C.A., Baltimore; mem. Bd. of Law Examiners of Md. Mem. Am. Bar Assn., (mem. of House of Dels.), Md. State Bar Assn., (sec.; pres., 1930-31), Baltimore City Bar Assn., Eastern Shore Soc. of Baltimore (pres. 1927-28). Democrat. Clubs: University, Johns Hopkins. Author: State Tax Commissions in the United States, 1897; also (address) Maryland Laid the Cornerstone of Our Federal Union, 1931. Home: 214 Northway, Guilford, Baltimore. Office: Mercantile Trust Bldg., Baltimore, Md.

CHAPMAN, Katharine Antoinette, M.D.; b. Washington, D.C., Apr. 25, 1899; d. Frank T. and Alice I. (Brundage) C.; grad. Friends High Sch., Washington, D.C., 1916; A.B., George Washington U., 1922, M.D., 1925; unmarried. Began gen. practice of medicine, 1926; asso. univ. physician, George Washington U., 1927-36; examining physician, Y.W.C.A., Washington, 1928-30. Mem. A.M.A., Med. Soc. of D.C., George Washington U. Med. Soc., Woman's Med. Soc. of Md., Montgomery Co. Med. Soc., Med. and Chirurg. Faculty of Md. Republican. Baptist. Address: 20 W. Baltimore St., Kensington, Md.

CHAPMAN, Ross McClure, M.D., psychiatrist; b. Belleville, N.Y., July 13, 1881; s. Eugene A. and Agnes (McClure) C.; grad. Union Acad., Belleville, 1898; student Syracuse U., 1898-1901; M.D., U. of Mich., 1905; m. Marion E. Clapp, Dec. 29, 1908; 1 dau., Mary Harris. Began practice at Watertown, N.Y., 1905; interne, Utica State Hosp., 1906-07; sr. asst. physician, Binghamton State Hosp., 1908-16; 1st asst., St. Elizabeth's Hosp., Washington, D.C., 1916-20, also instr. psychiatry, George Washington U., 1916-20; med. supt. Sheppard and Enoch Pratt Hosp. since 1920; asso. prof. psychiatry, U. of Md., 1920-23, prof. since 1923. Commd. maj. M.C., U.S.A., 1918; div. psychiatrist, 6th Div., with Army of Occupation in Germany, as asst. consulting neuro-psychiatrist. Mem. American Medical Association, Md. Med. Soc., Baltimore Co. Med. Soc., Southern Med. Assn., Am. Psychiatric Assn., Am. Psychopathol. Assn., Am. Psychoanalytic Assn., Nu Sigma Nu, Phi Kappa Psi. Republican. Presbyn. Mason. Clubs: Maryland (Baltimore); Army and Navy (Washington). Home: Towson, Md.

CHAPMAN, Walter Hopkins, lawyer; b. Phila., Pa., Sept. 13, 1892; s. Samuel Spencer and Elizabeth Ireton (McDonough) C.; student Wm. Penn Charter Sch., Phila., 1900-09, U. of Pa., Class of 1913; LL.B., Temple U., Phila., 1917; m. Frances Louise Omerly, Aug. 20, 1921. Admitted to Pa. bar, 1917; asst. in law firm Chapman & Chapman, Phila., 1919-21, partner since 1921; dir. National Plan, Inc., John B. Hendrickson, Inc., Joel Baily

Davis, Inc., East Smithfield Farms, Inc., The McKean Company, Inc., Murphy-Parker Company. Served as 1st lt., 47th Inf., 4th Div., U.S. Army, 1917-19. Mem. Fourth Div. Assn. of Pa., S.R., Soc. of Founders and Patriots of Pa., Mil. Order of the World War. Republican. Clubs: Union League, Phila. Cricket, Meridian (Phila.). Home: 8412 Navahoe St., Chestnut Hill, Pa. Office: 1500 Walnut St., Philadelphia, Pa.

CHAPPELL, Ralph Hubert, supt. div., U.S. Bur. Engraving and Printing; b. Morenci, Mich., July 3, 1871; s. James Nelson and Emma A. (Baldwin) C.; B.S., U.S. Naval Acad., 1894; m. Jane Catherine Biays, July 8, 1896 (died June 7, 1937); children—Hubert Biays, Kenneth Baldwin. Lt. (j.g.) U.S. Navy, 1899; served in Spanish-Am. War, 1898; hon. discharged Oct. 1900; with U.S. Treasury Dept. since 1900, except 1 yr. with Vets. Bur.; was supt. of div. Bur. of Engraving and Printing, Washington, D.C.; retired, July 31, 1939. Member Kensington Town Council, 6 years. Awarded West Indian campaign medal, Santiago medal. Member Am. Museum Nat. History, Naval Acad. Graduates Assn., Nat. Geog. Soc., Naval and Mil. Order Spanish-Am. War, Vets of Fgn. Wars, Washington Soc. Engrs., Assn. Govt. Bldg. Supts. Clubs: Sojourner's, Fellowship. Home: Kensington, Md. Office: U.S. Bureau of Engraving & Printing, Washington, D.C.

CHARLES, Christian Eugene, pres. judge; b. Manor Twp., Lancaster Co., Pa., June 8, 1880; s. Amos and Mary A. (Bowers) C.; student pub. schs.; A.B., Franklin and Marshall Coll., Lancaster, Pa., 1900; studied law in offices of Hon. David McMullen, Lancaster; m. Emily Weaver Girvin, June 26, 1913; 1 dau., Anna Mary. Prin. Bart Twp. High Sch., Lancaster Co., Pa., 1901-05; prof. mathematics, phys. and chem. science, Shippen Sch. for Girls, Lancaster, Pa., 1905-08; admitted to practice law in Pa. state and county cts., 1908, and since practiced at Lancaster; has specialized in work of Orphans' Ct. and allied subjects and devoted major efforts to practice before Orphans' Ct.; elected, 1937, and since 1938 pres. judge, Orphans' Ct., 2d Judicial Dist., Lancaster Co., Pa.; pres. Nat. Store Specialty Co., mfrs. automatic counter computing scales, Bareville, Pa., since 1922. Formerly dir. pub. schs., East Hempfield Twp., Lancaster Co., sec. bd., 1909-13. Mem. Lancaster Chamber of Commerce, Rotary Internat. Republican. Mason (Royal Arcanum), Elk. Clubs: Hamilton, Lancaster Country (Lancaster, Pa.). Home: 1024 Woods Av. Office: Court House, Lancaster, Pa.

CHARLES, Robert Simpson, civil engr.; b. Richmond, Ind., June 20, 1876; s. Samuel Henley and Margaret (Simpson) C.; A.B., Earlham Coll., 1898; A.B., U. of Pa., 1903; m. Marian White, Oct. 12, 1904 (dec. 1935); children—Robert Simpson, Jr., John Roy; m. 2d, Helen D. White, July 28, 1937. Employed in engring. depts. various r.r. and land cos., 1899-1917; chief field engr., Layne & Bowler Co., N.Y. City, 1917-22; chief engr. and vice-pres., Layne N.Y. Co 1922-36; pres. and dir. since 1936; pres. Internat. Water Co. since 1936; pres. Internat. Water Supply, Ltd.; dir. Compagnie Hydraulique Asie, Layne & Bowler, Inc.; pres. Internat. Water Co. of S.A. Mem. Am. Soc. Civil Engrs. Republican. Mem. Religious Soc. Friends. Clubs: University (Philadelphia); Rock Spring Country (West Orange). Home: 2 Cobane Terrace, West Orange, N.J. Office: 92 Liberty St., New York, N.Y.

CHARLES, Rollin Landis, prof. physics; b. Bethlehem, Pa., Nov. 26, 1885; s. Milton Zepp and Amanda Zern (Landis) C.; ed. East Stroudsberg (Pa.) State Teachers Coll., 1900-02; A.B., Lehigh U., Bethlehem, Pa., 1907, A.M., 1910; grad. student Columbia, summer 1912, U. of Pa., 1926-30; m. Mary E. Haslam, June 17, 1908 (died 1918); children—Donald Randolph, Priscilla Haslam, Barbara Lee; m. 2d, Madeline V. Bishop, Apr. 25, 1921; 1 son, Edgar Bishop. Began as teacher in country sch., 1902; asst. in physics, Lehigh U., Bethlehem, Pa., 1905-07, instr., 1907-12, asst. prof., 1912-19, asso. prof., 1919-22; prof. physics, Franklin and Marshall Coll., Lancaster, Pa., since 1922; prof. physics, Albright Coll., Reading, Pa., 1927-31; mem. firm Franklin and Charles pub. scientific and tech. books. Fellow A.A.A.S.; mem. Am. Phys. Soc., Math. Assn. of America, Am. Assn. of Physics Teachers, Pa. Assn. of Physics Teachers, Pa. Acad. of Scis., Philatelic Soc. of Lancaster Co., Phi Beta Kappa, Sigma Pi Sigma, Chi Phi. Republican. Presbyterian. Club: Kiwanis. Home: 510 Race Av., Lancaster, Pa.

CHARLESWORTH, James Clyde, univ. prof.; b. Westmoreland Co., Pa., May 21, 1900; s. James and Priscilla (Hawkins) C.; student Carnegie Inst. Tech., 1919-22; A.B., U. of Pittsburgh, 1926, A.M., 1927, Ph.D., 1933; student Harvard, 1928; m. Dorothy Louise Coy, Aug. 14, 1928; children—Roger Owen (dec.), Audrey Elaine, Sylvia Jean. Chief mech. draftsman, Miller Machinery Co., Pittsburgh, 1922-24; instr. govt. and polit. philosophy, U. of Pittsburgh, 1926-33, prof. polit. philosophy and supervisor of governmental service training since 1933. Mem. Am. Polit. Science Assn., Am. Assn. of Univ. Profs., Pi Sigma Alpha. Socialist. Episcopalian. Home: 1324 S. Negley Av. Office: U. of Pittsburgh, Pittsburgh, Pa.

CHARLTON, C. Coulter; sr. surgeon and chief of clinic Atlantic City Hosp.; cousultant in otorhinolaryngology Municipal Hosp. and Children's Seashore Home. Address: 124 S. Illinois Av., Atlantic City, N.J.

CHARTER, Lena Mabel, supervisor of home econs. edn.; b. West Union W.Va.; d. Andrew Judson and Helena Victoria (Williams) C.; student rural schs., Doddridge Co., W.Va., 1882-93; grad. Fairmont (W.Va.) Normal Sch. (now Fairmont State Teachers Coll.), 1899; B.Sc., W.Va. U., Morgantown, W.Va., 1912; A.M., Columbia U., 1917; student U. of Wis., Madison, Wis., 1914; unmarried. Teacher rural schs., Doddridge Co., W.Va., 1893-98; prin. two-room graded sch., Flint, Doddridge Co., W.Va., 1899-1900; teacher graded schs., Pennsboro, Sistersville, Morgantown, W.Va., 1901-06; teacher Ravenswood (W.Va.) High Sch., 1906-07, Cameron (W.Va.) High Sch., 1907-10; student asst. teacher, W.Va. U., Morgantown, W.Va., 1911-12; head dept. home econs., Glenville (W.Va.) Normal Sch. (now Glenville State Teachers Coll.), 1912-20, also teacher German and chemistry; head dept. home econs., North Tex. Normal Coll. (now N. Tex. Teachers Coll.), Denton, Tex., 1920-22; W.Va. state supervisor home econs. edn., Charleston, W.Va., since 1922. Mem. Am. Vocational Assn., Am. Home Econs. Assn., N.E.A., W.Va. Edn. Assn., Am. Assn. Univ. Women (Charleston Chapter), D.A.R. (Ravenswood, W.Va., Chapter). Methodist. Order of Eastern Star. Home: 900 Ashton St., Ravenswood, W.Va. Office: State Department of Education, Charleston, W.Va.

CHASE, Burr Linden, pub. text-books; b. Niagara Falls, N.Y., June 11, 1891; s. Adin Burr and Louise (Lindenbolt) C.; A.B., Harvard U., 1913; m. Helen J. Whitney, Oct. 25, 1917; children—Burr Linden, Jr., Whitney. Began as printer with Niagara Printing Co., Niagara Falls, N.Y., 1913-16; with Stanhope Press, Boston, Mass., 1916-18; asso. with Silver Burdett Co., publishers of text-books, New York, N.Y., since 1920; sec. and dir. since 1924. Served as lt. (j.g.) A.S., U.S.N., 1918-20. Mem. Am. Inst. Graphic Arts. Ind. Republican. Mason. Clubs: Golf (Madison); Harvard of New Jersey; Harvard (New York, N.Y.). Home: 365 Woodland Rd., Madison N.J. Office: 45 E. 17th St., New York, N.Y.

CHASE, Charles Thomas, insurance; b. Phila., Pa., Oct. 27, 1876; s. Howard Aquilla and Mary Elizabeth (Gibbs) C.; grad. William Penn Charter Sch., Phila., 1894; student U. of Pa., 1894-97; m. Josephine M. Bauer, Feb. 21, 1903 (now deceased); 1 son, Charles Thomas, Jr.; m. 2d, Josephine M. S. Lovatt, Aug. 21, 1920; 1 son, Walter Thomas. With Daniel J. Walsh Sons since 1898, v.p., sec. and dir. City Investment Co.; sec. of exec. com. and dir. Home Life Ins. Co. of America; dir. Glen Willow Ice Mfg. Co. Mem. U. of Pa. Gen. Alumni Soc. Republican. Presbyterian. Mason (K.T. Shriner). Clubs: Phila. Country, Bala Golf of Phila. (charter mem.). Home: 6 Hampton Terrace, Bala-Cynwyd, Pa. Office: 504 Walnut St., Philadelphia, Pa.

CHASE, Eugene Parker, coll. prof.; b. New Britain, Conn., Apr. 19, 1895; s. Charles Francis and Elizabeth Hance (Parker) C.; A.B., Dartmouth, 1916; Rhodes scholar from New Hampshire to Magdalen Coll., Oxford U., B.A., 1919; M.A., Harvard, 1921, Ph.D., 1924; m. Ann Frances Hastings, June 30, 1923; children—Elisabeth Huntingdon, Katharine Safford. Instr. in history, Mass. Inst. Tech., 1919-20; tutor Harvard, 1921-23; asst. prof. history and govt., Wesleyan U., Conn., 1923-26, U. of Vt., summer, 1926; asso. prof. govt., Lafayette Coll., 1926-29, prof. since Aug. 1929. Mem. Am. Polit. Science Assn., Am. Hist. Assn., Foreign Policy Assn., Am. Assn. Univ. Profs., Phi Beta Kappa (sec. Lafayette Chapter, 1929—), Theta Chi. Democrat. Episcopalian. Editor and translator of Barbé-Marbois's Our Revolutionary Forefathers, 1929. Author: Democratic Governments in Europe—England, 1938. Contbr. articles in various jours. Address: Lafayette College, Easton, Pa., also Shadowsmark, Hebron, Conn.

CHASE, Eugene Wheeler, oil refining; b. Warren, O., Mar. 26, 1880; s. Eugene Clayton and Lillian Louvisa (Wheeler) C.; ed. in public schs. of Warren, O.; m. Mabel Gibbony Confer, April 2, 1903; children—Mary Confer (Mrs. John B. Mitchell), Sarah Wheeler. Pres. Wolverine-Empire Refining Co., Oil City, Pa., since 1930; dir. Oil City Nat. Bank, Citizens Banking Co. Mason (K.T., 32°). Clubs: Wanango Country, Oil City Boat (Oil City, Pa.). Home: 113 Wyllis St. Address: Wolverine-Empire Refining Co., Oil City, Pa.

CHASE, James Mitchell, ex-congressman; b. Glen Richey, Pa., Dec. 19, 1891; s. John M. and Jane T. (Phillips) C.; grad. high sch., Clearfield, Pa., 1911; LL.B., Dickinson Sch. of Law, Carlisle, Pa., 1916; m. Elise Lake, Oct. 6, 1920; 1 son, Henry Hughes. Admitted to Pa. bar, 1919, and began practice at Clearfield; mem. 70th, 71st and 72nd Congresses (1927-33), 23d Pa. Dist. Served in U.S. Air Service, 1917-19. Comdr. Am. Legion, Dept. of Pa., 1924-25. Republican. Baptist. Home: Clearfield, Pa.

CHASE, Lawrence Seward, county supt. schs; b. Whitesville, N.Y., Apr. 26, 1885; s. Amos Lawrence and May (Crittenden) C.; B.S., Colgate U., 1909; A.M., Columbia U. Extension, 1916; m. Elsie Taylor, June 27, 1914; children—Thomas Taylor, Janet. Began as prin. high sch., Morrisville, N.Y., 1909-10; teacher pub. schs., Montclair, N.J., 1910-18; dir. evening and summer schs., 1917-25, prin. elementary sch., 1918-25; prin. Jr. High Sch. and elementary sch., Montclair, N.J., 1925-33; supt. schs. Essex Co., N.J., since 1933; extension lecturer, N.J. State Teachers Coll., Newark, since 1933; instr. Mass. State Summer Sch., Hyannis, Mass., 1927-30. Served as pres. Council Social Agencies, Montclair, N.J., 1924-26. Mem. bd. dirs. Essex Co. Vocational Schs., Essex Co. Employees Pension Fund. Mem. N.E.A., N.J. State Teachers Assn. (v.p. 1925-26), N.J. Elementary Sch. Prins. (pres. 1922-24), N.J. Council of Edn., Phi Kappa Psi. Awarded Fellowship Geneva Switzerland Sch. Internat. Relations, summer 1935. Republican. Conglist. Club: Schoolmasters of N.J. Home: 38 Godfrey Rd., Montclair, N.J. Office: Hall of Records, Newark, N.J.

CHASE, Philip Hartley, elec. engr.; b. Hanover, N.H., May 18, 1886; s. Frederick and Mary Fuller (Pomeroy) C.; A.B., Dartmouth Coll., Hanover, N.H., 1907; B.S. in E.E., Mass. Inst. Tech., 1909; M. in E.E., Harvard Grad. Sch. of Applied Sci., 1910; m. Theora Hill Williamson, Oct. 25, 1913. Asst. to supt. of distribution, Pub. Service Electric Co., Newark, N.J., 1910-12, asst. engr., 1912-17; chief elec. engr. American Rys. Co., Philadelphia, 1917-21; asst. engr. transmission and distribution The Phila. Electric Co., 1921-27; engr., 1928, chief engr. since 1928; dir. Southern Pa. Power Co., Public Investing Co. Mem. Am. Inst. Elec. Engrs., Illuminating Engring. Soc., Am. Soc. Mech. Engrs., Delta Kappa Epsilon. Republican.

Presbyterian. Clubs: Penn Athletic, Engineers, Philadelphia Country (Phila.). Home: P.O. Box 150, Bala-Cynwyd. Office: 1000 Chestnut St., Philadelphia, Pa.

CHASE, Walter D.; otorhinolaryngologist St. Luke's Hosp. Address: 230 E. Broad St., Bethlehem, Pa.

CHASE, William Clark, lawyer; b. Clearfield, Pa., Feb. 24, 1905; s. John Wallace and Lelia (Brown) C.; student Clearfield (Pa.) pub. schs., 1911-22; A.B., Pa. State Coll., 1926; LL.B. Dickinson Sch. of Law, Carlisle, Pa.; 1929; m. Julia Boardman Kerr, Nov. 3, 1934; children—Emily Kerr, William Clark. Amitted to Pa. bar, 1930, and since practiced at Clearfield, Pa. Apptd. asst. dist. atty. Clearfield Co., 1938. Mem. Pa. Bar Assn., Sigma Chi. Republican. Methodist. Elk, Eagle, Moose. Club: Clearfield Country (Clearfield, Pa.). Home: 309 Pennsylvania Av. Office: Keystone Bldg., Clearfield, Pa.

CHATTO, Byron Herbert, photographer; b. Surry, Me., July 14, 1881; s. Merrill Dodge and Julia Adel (Bowden) C.; B.S., in E.E., U. of Me., Orono, Me., 1905; m. Frances Maud Stevens, Sept. 4, 1909; 1 dau., Doris Evangeline. Sec. Pittsburgh Salon of Photography, 1926-32; elec. engr., Westinghouse Mfg. & Elec. Co., East Pittsburgh, Pa., 1911-30, chief photographer since 1931. Mem. Acad. of Science and Art of Pittsburgh (sec. since 1932), Photographic Soc. of America (sec. 1933-36, sec.-treas. and dir. since 1936), Triangle Photographers Assn. Republican. Unitarian. Club: Westinghouse (edn. com.; Pittsburgh). Contbr. to engring. and photographic jours. Editor, Jour. of the Photographic Soc. of America, 1935. Home: 1300 Milton Av., Pittsburgh, Pa. Office: Westinghouse Mfg. & Elec. Co., East Pittsburgh, Pa.

CHENAULT, Roy Lee, engineer; b. Glendale, Ky., Feb. 3, 1903; s. George M. and Alice (Van Metre) C.; B.A., in Physics, George Washington U., Washington, D.C., 1927; m. Annabelle Day, Sept. 12, 1931; children—Nancy Day, George Lee. With Nat. Bur. of Standards, Washington, D.C., successively at lab. apprentice, aid, lab. asst., asst. scientific aid, jr. physicist, 1920-27; industrial fellow, Mellon Inst., of Industrial Research, Pittsburgh, 1927-30; engr. Gulf Research and Development Co., Pittsburgh, since 1930. Mem. Am. Petroleum Inst., A.A.A.S., Phys. Soc. of Pittsburgh. Club: Employees of Gulf Research and Development Co. (Pittsburgh). Contbr. of tech. articles to engring. and scientific jours. Holds several patents on pumping apparatus, deep well pumps, etc. Home: Route 1, Verona, Pa. Office: Box 2038, Pittsburgh, Pa.

CHENEY, Edith, librarian; b. Washington, D.C., April 14, 1892; d. James William and Margaret (Staver) C.; A.B., George Washington U., Washington, D.C., 1914, A.M., 1915; B.S. in Library Sci., Drexel Inst. Library Sch., Phila., 1926. Asst. card div., Library of Congress, 1915-17; cataloguer, Dept. of State; Washington, D.C., 1917-21; cataloguer, Fed. Res. Bd. Library, Washington, D.C., 1921-25; librarian, Temple U., Phila., 1926-36, first asst. and head order dept., Sullivan Memorial Library, Temple, since 1936. Mem. Am. Library Assn. Republican. Episcopalian. Home: 1929 N. Broad St., Philadelphia, Pa.

CHENEY, Elliott Ward, physicist; b. Orange, Mass., Feb. 10, 1899; s. Henry William and Eva E. (DeWolf) C.; A.B., Dartmouth Coll., 1920; M.S., Brown U., 1925; Ph.D., Princeton U., 1929; m. Carleton Pratt, June 19, 1926; children—Carleton, Elliott Ward. Instr. physics, Syracuse U., 1920, Brown U., 1921-24; Charles A. Coffin Fellow, 1924-26; asso. prof. physics, Middleburg Coll., 1926-27; acting prof. physics, Gettysburg Coll., 1927-29, prof. and head of dept., 1929-34; physicist, Consumers' Research since 1934. Fellow A.A.A.S. Mem. Am. Phys. Soc., Am. Chem. Soc., Theta Chi, Sigma Xi, Kappa Phi Kappa. Republican. Universalist. Home: 71 Carleton Av., Washington, N.J.

CHENOWETH, Arthur Shamberger, supt. city schs.; b. Trinidad, Colo., July 10, 1884; s. Thomas B. and Esther Rebecca (Shamberger) C.;

A.B., U. of Colo., 1906; Rhodes Scholar, 1907-10; B.A., Oxford U., Eng., 1929, M.A., 1939; m. Mary Eliza North, Aug. 22, 1910; children—James North, Mary North, Esther North (Mrs. Don C. Balsley). Engaged in teaching Latin, Univ. Sch. for Boys, Chicago, Ill., 1910-11, high sch., Oak Park, Ill., 1911-14; head dept. Latin and Greek, high sch., Atlantic City, N.J., 1914-22, asst. prin., 1922-31, supt. schs. Atlantic City, N.J. since 1931. Served as pres. Atlantic City Rotary Club, 1934-35, Atlantic City Chamber of Commerce, 1935-37. Dir. Atlantic City Y.M.C.A., Boy Scouts, Pub. Library, Salvation Army, Community Chest, Chamber of Commerce. Mem. Am. Assn. Sch. Adminstrs., Nat. Edn. Assn., N.J. State, Atlantic County, Atlantic City edn. assns., Phi Beta Kappa. Republican. Odd Fellow. Home: 20 E. New Jersey Av., Somers Point. Office: 1809 Pacific Av., Atlantic City, N.J.

CHERRINGTON, George H.; b. Covington, Ky., Nov. 25, 1883; s. George H. and Alice Jane (Hood) C.; student Covington, Ky., and Cincinnati, O., pub. schs.; m. Ada Perrone, 1905. Pres. Brown & Zortman Machinery Co., Standard Machinists Supply Co. Home: 5851 Marlborough St. Office: 129 McKean St., Pittsbugh, Pa.

CHERRY, C. Waldo, clergyman; b. Pittsburgh, Pa., May 17, 1873; s. John D. and Katherine (Stebbins) C.; B.A., Princeton, 1894; B.D., Western Theol. Sem., Pittsburgh, 1897; D.D., U. of Rochester, 1921; LL.D.; Beaver College, Jenkintown, Pa., 1933; m. Sarah Ann Fleming, June 30, 1898; children—Walter F., Katherine F. (Mrs. J Harold Thomson), Ralph Waldo. Pastor Natrona (Pa.) Presbyn. Ch., 1897-1901, Parnassus, Pa., 1901-03, Second Prebyn. Ch., Troy, N.Y., 1903-14, Central Presbyn. Ch., Rochester, N.Y., 1914-22, Pine St. Presbyn. Ch., Harrisburg, Pa., since 1922. Chaplain Co. 23, N.Y.N.G., Troy, 1903-14; Y.M.C.A. chaplain, Camp Dix, Wrightstown, N.J., 1917. Trustee Gen. Assembly Presbyn. Ch. U.S.A.; mem. Bd. Foreign Missions, same. Republican. Mason (32°). Clubs: Kiwanis, Torch, Eclectic, Country (Harrisburg); Juniata (Mt. Union, Pa.). Home: 315 N. Front St., Harrisburg, Pa.

CHESLOCK, Louis, musician; b. London, Eng., Sept. 9, 1899; s. Jacob and Rebecca (Neumark) C.; brought to U.S., 1901, naturalized, 1913; Certificate Violin, Peabody Conservatory Mus., 1917, Certificate Harmony, 1919, Artist Diploma, 1921; m. Elise Brown Hanline, May 31, 1926; 1 son, Barry. Violinist, Baltimore Symphony Orchestra, 1916-37, guest condr., 1928, asst. concert master, 1932-37; instr. violin, Peabody Conservatory Music since 1917, instr. harmony since 1922. Awarded Peabody alumni prize in composition, 1921, Chicago Daily News prizes for compositions for piano, violin, violoncello and orchestra, 1923, 24; hon. mention Chicago Theatre symphonic contest, 1923; hon. mention New York Women's Symphony Orchestra contest, 1938. Wrote: Introductory Study on Violin Vibrato, 1931. Composer of symphonic, operatic and ensemble works; also compositions for violin, piano, voice, etc. Mem. Am. Musicological Soc. Home: 2318 Sulgrave Av., Baltimore, Md.

CHESNEY, Alan Mason, M.D., internist; b. Baltimore, Md., Jan. 17, 1888; s. Jesse Mason and Annie Mary (Atkinson) C.; student Baltimore City Coll., 1905; A.B., Johns Hopkins, 1908, M.D., 1912; m. Cora Ferguson Chambers, May 17, 1917; children—Joan, Alan Dukehart, Peter. Began practice at Baltimore, 1912; asst. in medicine, Johns Hopkins, 1913; asst. resident phys., Rockefeller Inst. Hosp., 1914-17; asso. in medicine, Washington U., 1919-21; asso. prof. medicine, Johns Hopkins since 1921, asst. dean Med. Sch., 1927-29, dean since 1929; mng. editor Medicine since 1923. Served as lt., advancing to maj., Med. Corps, U.S.A., 1917-19. Pres. Assn. of American Med. Colleges, 1937-38. Mem. Assn. Am. Physicians, Soc. for Clin. Investigation, Soc. Exptl. Pathology, Phi Beta Kappa, Alpha Omega Alpha, Phi Gamma Delta. Clubs: 16 W. Hamilton St., Deer Isle Yacht.

Author: Immunity in Syphilis, 1926. Home: 1419 Eutaw Pl., Baltimore, Md.

CHESNUT, William Calvin, judge; b. Baltimore, Md., June 27, 1873; s. Calvin and Elizabeth Maxwell (Mace) C.; A.B., Johns Hopkins, 1892; LL.B., U. of Md., 1894; m. Florence E. Carroll, Oct. 24, 1899; children—Mary Mace (Mrs. Malcolm W. Ford), Elizabeth Maxwell Carroll (Mrs. Wilson King Barnes). Admitted to Md. bar, 1894; asst. state's atty., Baltimore, 1896-99; practiced at Baltimore, 1899-1931; asso. later mem. firm Gans & Haman, 1899-1914; mem. Haman, Cook, Chesnut & Markell, 1914-30, Cook, Chesnut & Markell, 1930-31; U.S. dist. judge, Dist. of Md., since 1931. Mem. of faculty council and lecturer on federal procedure, U. of Md. Law Sch. Ex-pres. Roland Park Civic League; mem. bd. of trustees Roland Park Country Sch.; mem. bd. of regents U. of Md. Mem. Am., Md. State and Baltimore City bar assns., Phi Beta Kappa, Phi Gamma Delta. Republican. Episcopalian (vestryman St. David's Ch.). Clubs: University, Merchants, Baltimore Country. Home: 111 Ridgewood Rd., Roland Park, Baltimore, Md.

CHESNUTT, Nelson Alexander, musician; b. Phila., Pa., June 1, 1872; s. Frank Lewis and Kate (MacNichol) C.; ed. public schools, under pvt. tutors and spl. studies, U. of Pa.; studied music under masters; m. Elizabeth Clarke, March 12, 1896 (died Nov. 20, 1928); children—Nelson A., Marjorie Clarke (Mrs. Edmund G. S. Flannigan); m. 2d, Helen Mayhew, Aug. 8, 1930; 1 son, William Alexander. Began study of piano at age of 5; organist Westminster Presbyn. Ch., Phila., at 10, later accompanist for vocalists and violin in Phila. and other cities; organist and choirmaster various chs.; numerous appearances in oratorio and concert; dir. vocal dept. Combs Conservatory of Music, Philadelphia, 1912-34. Musical director Philadelphia Consistory A.A.S.R. Mem. Music Teachers' National Association, Musical Fund Society, St. Andrew's Society of Philadelphia. Republican. Methodist. Mason (33°); hon. mem. Supreme Council A.A. S.R. for Northern Jurisdiction. Clubs: Orpheus, Music, Art. Contbr. to the Etude and other musical jours. Home: 205 Long Lane, Upper Darby, Pa.

CHESTER, John Needels, civil and mech. engr.; b. Columbus, O., Sept. 24, 1864; s. Hubert and Melvina S. (Needels) C.; B.S., U. of Ill., 1891, M.S. and C.E., 1909, M.E., 1911. Began as field supt. Nat. Water Supply Co., 1891; constrn. engr. Am. Debenture Co., Chicago and New York, 1892-94; sales engr. Henry R. Worthington Co., New York, 1894-99; chief engr. Am. Water Works Electric Co., Pittsburgh, Pa., 1899-1906; gen. mgr. Epping-Carpenter Pump Co., Pittsburgh, 1906-11; founder and head of J. N. Chester, Engrs., since 1911; pres. Edgeworth Water Co., Fayette City Water Co., Jamestown Water Co. Mem. bd. dirs. U. of Ill. Foundation. Past pres. U. of Ill. Alumni Assn.; dir. Boys Club of Pittsburgh. Mem. Am. Soc. C.E. (past dir., past v.p.), Am. Soc. Mech. Engrs., Engrs. Soc. Western Pa. (past dir., past v.p., past pres.), Am. Water Works Assn., Am. Pub. Health Assn. Presbyn. Clubs: Duquesne; Caxton Book (Chicago). Inventor of apparatus for water filtration. Contbr. to tech. publs. Collector of rare books and manuscripts. Visited every continent, every state of the U.S., every province of Canada, and practically every European country many times. Home: 4200 Center Av. Office: Century Bldg., Pittsburgh, Pa.

CHESTERMAN, Francis John, telephone exec.; b. Taunton, Mass., Feb. 19, 1884; s. Frederick Willam and Mary (Bacon) C.; B.Sc., Mass. Inst. Tech., 1905; D.Eng., U. of Pittsburgh, 1929; m. Mary Healey, Oct. 2, 1907; children—Elizabeth Newell, John Frederick. With Am. Telephone & Telegraph Co., Boston, Mass., 1905-07; in engring. dept. New York Telephone Co., 1907-12, plant supt. Central Div., Syracuse, 1912-20; chief engr. Bell Telephone Co. of Pa. & Associated Cos., 1920-26; v.p. and gen. mgr. Western Area, Bell Telephone Co. of Pa. since 1926; dir. Industrial Finance & Investment Co., Strip Tin Plate Co., First Federal Savings & Loan Assn. of Pittsburgh. Episcopalian. Clubs:

Duquesne, University (Pittsburgh); Pike Run Country (Mt. Pleasant, Pa.). Home: 205 Lytton Av. Office: 416 7th Av., Pittsburgh, Pa.

CHESTON, J. Hamilton, savings banker; b. Chestnut Hill, Phila., Pa., Oct. 30, 1893; s. James and Caroline Calvert (Morris) C.; grad. Chestnut Hill Acad.; A.B., U. of Pa., 1915, LL.B., 1920; m. Cornelia Carter Leidy, Aug. 24, 1917. Admitted to Pa. bar, 1920, and began practice in Phila.; asst. gen. solicitor Norfolk Western Ry. Co., 1920-30, Pa. R.R. Co., 1930-33; v.p. and mgr. Phila. Saving Fund Soc. since 1933; dir. Tradesmen's Nat. Bank, B.&O. R.R., North Penn R.R. Co., Del. and Bound Brook R.R. Co., Trenton R.R. Co., Arcade Real Estate Co.; trustee Mutual Assurance Co. Served as 1st lt. 6th F.A., 1st Div., U.S. Army, with A.E.F., 1917-19. Mgr. Home of the Merciful Saviour for Crippled Children. Mem. Pa. Soc. of Sons of the Revolution, Order of Coif, Delta Phi. Republican. Episcopalian. Clubs: Phila., University, Barge (Phila.) Home: Penllyn, Pa. Office: 1212 Market St., Philadelphia, Pa.

CHESTON, James, 3d; v.p. and treas. Pa. Co. for Insurances on Lives and Granting Annuities. Home: 217 W. Mt. Airy Av., Mt. Airy. Office: 15th and Chestnut Sts., Philadelphia, Pa.

CHEW, Oswald, lawyer, trustee; b. Phila., May 24, 1880; s. Samuel and Mary Johnson (Brown) C.; student William Penn Charter Sch., Phila., 1893-95; grad. St. Paul's Sch., Concord, N.H., 1898; B.A., Harvard, 1903; studied law at Harvard and U. of Pa., 1903-05; m. Ada Knowlton, of West Upton, Mass., June 3, 1908. Admitted to Pa. bar, 1907, and practiced in Phila.; dir. and sec. Food Gardens Assn., Inc. (for the unemployed), Phila., 1932—; pres. Mfrs. Land & Improvement Co. since 1933; pres. Radnor Realty Co.; v.p. Gloucester Land Co. Attended Camp Plattsburg, N.Y., 1915-16; mem. Commn. for Relief in Belgium, 1916 (awarded Commn.'s medal); volunteer ambulance driver, France, 1916-17; with Am. Field Service in Argonne and Verdun sectors; civilian interpreter, G.H.Q., A.E.F., 1917; commd. lt. and assigned to liaison service, 1918; hon. disch., 1919; captain cavalry U.S. Army Reserves, 1928. Awarded Croix de Guerre (France), 1917, field service medal by French Ministry of War, 1919, Medaille Commemorative de la Grande Guerre, 1922, French Victory medal, 1924, Chevalier French Legion of Honor, 1925, promoted Officer same. Mem. Assn. Franco-Americaine (pres. since 1932), Alliance Francaise of Phila. (pres. 1925-35; v.p. Fed. Alliance Francaise for Eastern States), Am. Legion, Hist. Soc. Pa., Valley Forge Hist. Soc. Republican. Episcopalian. Clubs: Philadelphia, Automobile of Phila., Business Men's Art of Phila. (vice-pres. 1935-36); Wayne Art Centre (pres.); Kittansett Golf (Marion, Mass.); Harvard (New York). Editor: France, Courageous and Indomitable, 1925; Stroke of the Moment, 1926. Home: Radnor, Pa.; (summer) Marion, Mass. Office: Commercial Trust Bldg., Philadelphia, Pa.

CHEW, Robert Elmer, business exec.; b. Camden, N.J., May 26, 1895; s. Robert E. and Laura L. (Coreltto) C.; grad. Camden (N.J.) High Sch., 1913, Temple U., Phila., 1917; m. Carol Maurer, May 19, 1917; 1 dau., Jeanne M. Sec. and office mgr. Geo. T. Ladd Co., Pittsburgh, 1919-25, Ladd Water Tube Boiler Co., 1925-28; v.p., sec., dir., and gen. mgr. Ladd Equipment Co., Pittsburgh, since 1928; sec. and dir. Ladd Securities Corpn. Served as lt., 19th Engrs., U.S. Army, 1917-19. Republican. Clubs: Metropolitan, St. Clair Country (Pittsburgh). Home: 265 Cochran Rd. Office: 2408 First National Bank Bldg., Pittsburgh, Pa.

CHEW, Samuel Claggett, coll. prof.; b. Baltimore, Md., Aug. 31, 1888; s. Samuel C. and Agnes Robb (Marshall) C.; grad. Boys' Latin Sch., Baltimore Md., 1906; A.B., Johns Hopkins, 1909 (winner Tocqueville medal), Ph.D., 1913; m. Lucy Evans, Dec. 21, 1918. Master, Gilman Country Sch., Baltimore, Md., 1909-10; fellow Johns Hopkins, 1910-12; senior master, the Hotchkiss Sch., Salisbury, Conn., 1913-14; asso., 1914-16, asso. prof., 1916-20, prof. English lit., Bryn Mawr Coll., since 1920; spl. lecturer, Johns Hopkins, 1921, Univ. of Chicago, 1923, Western Reserve U., 1927-29. Democrat. Episcopalian. Author: The Dramas of Lord Byron, 1915; Thomas Hardy—Poet and Novelist, 1921, enlarged edit., 1928; Byron in England—His Fame and After-Fame, 1924; Swinburne, 1929; The Crescent and the Rose—Islam and England During the Renaissance, 1937. Editor: T. Nashe, The Unfortunate Traveller, 1926; Byron, Childe Harold's Pilgrimage and other Romantic Poems, 1936. Contbr. articles and reviews to periodicals. Home: Pennstone, Bryn Mawr, Pa.

CHEW, Tobias Otterbein, prof. psychology; b. Montpelier, O., May 28, 1885; s. Nathaniel Durbin and Margaret (Hiestand) C.; B.S., Adrian (Mich.) Coll., 1908, M.S., 1912; A.M., U. of Pittsburgh, 1928; grad. study, U. of Mich., U. of Chicago, U. of Pittsburgh; m. Muriel Brown, June 18, 1914; children—Elwin Fayette (dec.), John Carrollton. Began as teacher in pub. schs. of O.; prin. high schs. in Wis., Mich. and Fla.; supt. pub. schs. in Wis., Ill. and Fla.; prof. in teachers colls., Danville, Indianapolis and Muncie, Ind.; prof. psychology, State Teachers Coll., Indiana, Pa., since 1925. Served as lecturer for Y.M.C.A., 10 mos. overseas, during World War. Mem. N.E.A., Pa. State Edn. Assn., Coll. Profs. of Edn., Alpha Tau Omega, Phi Delta Kappa, Phi Alpha Zeta, Pi Gamma Mu. Republican. Presbyn. Club: College Faculty (Indiana, Pa.). Author: World's Fair Guide Book, 1933; Practical High School Speller, 1931; Practical Speller, 1938. Traveled in Europe and West Indies; philatelist, collector stamps of U.S., Russia, and China; contbr. articles to philat. mags. Home: 351 S. 13th St., Indiana, Pa.

CHEYNEY, Edward Potts, univ. prof.; b. Wallingford, Pa., Jan. 17, 1861; s. Waldron J. and Fannie (Potts) C.; A.B., U. of Pa., 1883, A.M., 1884, LL.D., 1911; traveled, 1884, 94, 1904-05, visiting German univs. and studying in British Mus.; m. Gertrude Squires, June 10, 1886. Now prof. history emeritus, U. of Pa. Author: Social Changes in England in the 16th Century, 1896; Social and Industrial History of England, 1901; Short History of England, 1904; European Background of American History, 1904; Readings in English History, 1908; History of England from the Defeat of the Armada to the Death of Elizabeth, 1913; Dawn of Modern Europe, 1936. Also monographs and rev. articles on hist. and economic subjects. Home: R.D. 3, Media, Pa.

CHEYNEY, (Edward) Ralph, poet, teacher, editor, critic; b. Phila., Pa., Mar. 14, 1896; s. Prof. Edward Potts and Gertrude Levis (Squires) C.; grad. DeLancey Sch. (now Episcopal Acad.), Phila., 1914; student U. of Pa., 1914-16, New York U., 1925-26; m. Louise Drew Cook (Weda Yap), 1918 (divorced 1927); 1 dau., Gertrude Louise; m. 2d, Lucia Trent, Jan. 22, 1927; children—Lucia, Ralph, Trent. Publicity dir. Cooperative League of America, 1917-20; lecturer and contbr. to magazines since 1916; with wife, editor and pub. Contemporary Verse, 1926-28; mng. editor Poetry World, 1931-35, Horizons, 1935; editor in chief Poetry Publishers, Phila., 1930-34; poetry editor Unity since 1928, Peace Digest since 1937, Frontier since 1938; cons. editor Verse Craft since 1928; asso. editor Nuggets since 1937; conductor of newspaper column Peeks and Peeks since 1936; proprietor of the Cheyney-Trent Home Study Course in Poetics, Dreamers' House (book sales and services). Poet laureate of Pa. (installed at Phila. Art Alliance 1934). Ednl. dir. Western Poetry League. Mem. Poetry Soc. of America, Western Poets' Congress (pres.). Winner many poetry prizes. Author: Touch and Go, 1926; Women in a Lean Age, 1931; (with Lucia Trent) Dreamers' House, 1933; More Power to Poets, 1934; Sierra Dreamers' House, 1935; Thank You, America, 1937. Editor of anthologies: Banners of Brotherhood, 1933; (with Jack Conroy) Unrest, 1929, 1930, 1931; (with Lucia Trent) Pilgrims to Parnassus, Early Harvest, 1931; Voices in the Dawn, 1930; Spring Chorale, America Arraigned, 1927; edited with introduction, Sonnets, 1939. Author of several brochures on business; also prefaces of many books. Home: Route 3, Beatty Rd., Media, Pa. Office: Dreamers' House, 923 E. Mountain St., Pasadena, Calif.

CHIDECKEL, Maurice, M. D., author; b. Sarkov, Russia, Oct. 1, 1880; brought to U.S., 1894; s. Samuel and Beulah (Swerdlin) C.; student Russian schs.; M.D. U. of Md. Coll. Physicians and Surgeons, Baltimore, 1908; m. Hanna Higger, June 10, 1905; children—Vivian Lottie (Mrs. Stanley Klein), Seymour Morton. Began gen. practice of medicine, 1909; mem. staff Sinai Hosp., W. Balti. Gen. Hosp. Mem. fraternal and med. orgns. Democrat. Jewish religion: Author: Letters of a Greenhorn (impressions of a newcomer), 1926; Sonya Babushka (novel of the Russians), 1928; Strictly Private, The Diary of a Medical Practitioner, 1929; Fakers, Old and New, a History of Cunning and Stupidity, 1931; Behind the Screen, The Daily Doings of a Busy Doctor, 1933; Female Sex Perversion, A Study in the psychology of the Aberrated Female, 1936; The Single, the Engaged and the Married, A Study in Marital Adjustment, 1937; Sleep, Your Life's One Third, 1939; Leaves from a Doctor's Diary, 1939; The Attainment of a Goal, and After, The Autobiography of an Ambition. On staff Roche Review, a med. monthly. Contbr. numerous periodicals, lay and medical. Home: 2225 Linden Av., Baltimore, Md.

CHIDESTER, John Young, editor; b. Williamsport, Pa., Sept. 3, 1881; s. Francis LeRoy and Georgetta (Schuck) C.; grad. high sch., Williamsport, 1900; m. Rachel Estella Neece, Oct. 2, 1902; children—Louis Oren, John Young. Began as reporter on Gazette and Bulletin, Williamsport, 1900, later with The Sun, Grit and as mng. editor of The News; became connected with Pittsburgh Press, 1913, mng. editor, 1922-24; editor 1924-29; became pub. Daily News Standard, Uniontown, Pa., 1933; now retired. Democrat. Presbyn. Mason (Shriner). Home: 312 Morgantown St., Uniontown, Pa.

CHIDSEY, Andrew Dwight, Jr., architect and engr.; b. Easton, Pa., Oct. 7, 1879; s. Andrew Dwight and Emily (McKeen) C.; C.E., Lafayette Coll, Easton, Pa., 1901; m. Mada Smith, June 26, 1907; children—Jane Louise, Andrew Dwight III. Began as engr. maintenance of way dept. Pa.R.R., 1901; asst. engr. in office chief engr., L.V.R.R.; resident engr. at Wilkes-Barre, Pa.; engr. Alpha Portland Cement Co.; in pvt. practice as engr. and architect, Easton, Pa., since 1910; pres. Fire Ins. Co. of Northampton Co., Easton, Pa., since 1931; dir. West Ward Bldg. Assn., Easton Cemetery. Served as capt., Q.M.C., U.S. Army, 1918-19; maj., O.R.C., since 1919. Mem. City Planning Commn., Easton, Pa., since 1914. Trustee Easton Pub. Library. Mem. Lehigh Valley Engrs. Soc., Northampton Hist. and Geneal. Soc. (past pres.), Phi Kappa Psi. Republican. Presbyterian. Home: 321 Pierce St. Office: 319 Pierce St., Easton, Pa.

CHIDSEY, Harold Russell, coll. prof.; b. Easton, Pa., June 1, 1887; s. Andrew Dwight and Emily Stewart (McKeen) C.; student Easton (Pa.) High Sch., 1900-05; A.B., Lafayette Coll., Easton, Pa., 1909; grad. Union Theol. Sem., New York City, 1912; Ph.D., Harvard, 1920; unmarried. Asst. and asso. prof. philosophy, Union Coll., Schenectady, N.Y., 1919-24; asst. prof. philosophy, Dartmouth Coll., Hanover, N.H., 1924-25; asso. prof. philosophy, Brown U., Providence, R.I., 1925-30; prof. and head dept. philosophy, Lafayette Coll., Easton, Pa., since 1930. Served as maj., 14th Inf., 19th Div., U.S. Army, during World War. Mem. Am. Philos. Assn., A.A.A.S., Brit. Inst. of Philos. Studies. Clubs: Harvard (New York); Seaside Park (N.J.) Yacht. Author reviews and articles in professional jours. Address: 1 W. Campus, Lafayette College, Easton, Pa.

CHIDSEY, Thomas McKeen, lawyer; b. Easton, Pa., Jan. 26, 1884; s. Andrew Dwight and Emily Stewart (McKeen) C.; A.B., Lafayette Coll., Easton, Pa., 1904; LL.B., U.of Pa. Law Sch., 1907; m. Ellen Lea, Nov. 14, 1913; children—Louise Lea, Ellen. Admitted to Pa. bar, 1907, and since in practice at Easton, Pa.; solicitor, Northampton (Pa.) Co., 1916-20, dist. atty., 1920-24; dir. Easton (Pa.) Trust Co., Hotel Easton, Fire Ins. Co. of Northampton Co.

Trustee Easton (Pa.) Y.W.C.A.; dir. Easton (Pa.) chapter Am. Red Cross. Republican. Presbyterian. Club: Northampton Co. Country (dir.; Easton, Pa.). Home: 107 E. Wayne Av. Office: Jones Bldg., Easton, Pa.

CHILD, Harry Charles, architect and consulting engr.; b. Franklindale, Pa., May 2, 1886; s. Charles Anthony and Aline (Newell) C.; grad. high sch., Monroeton, Pa., 1902, Susquehanna Collegiate Inst., Towanda, Pa., 1903; C.E., Rensselaer Poly. Inst., Troy, N.Y., 1907; m. Leona May Mingos, Oct. 1908 (died 1911); m. 2d, Elizabeth Decker, July 1912; 1 dau., Kathryn Aline (Mrs. Albert Scott Taylor). Draftsman, Am. Bridge Co., Elmira, N.Y., 1907-08; N.Y. State Water Supply Commissioner, Albany, N.Y., 1908-09; asst. engr., N.Y. State Pub. Service Commn., N.Y. City, 1909-12; county engineer N.Y. State Highway Commn., Elmira, N.Y., 1912-15; with Stone & Webster, Boston, Mass., 1916-18; instr. in reinforced concrete and structural mechanics, Northeastern U. Night Sch., Boston, Mass., 1917-18; pvt. practice as architect and consulting engr., Sayre, Pa., since 1918; architect of numerous important public and pvt. bldgs.; consulting engr. in many civic undertakings; has maintained offices at New York, N.Y., and Elmira, N.Y. Served as fortification draftsman, Engrs. Corps, U.S. Army, Fort Dupont, Del. 1908-09. Dir. Tioga Co. (N.Y.) Gen. Hosp. Mem. Am. Inst. of Architects, Am. Soc. C.E., Soc. of Am. Mill. Engrs. Republican. Presbyterian. Mason (Consistory; Shriner; Commandery), Elk. Home: 404 Lincoln St. Office: 501-503 S. Keystone Av., Sayre, Pa.

CHILDERS, Robert J.; ophthalmologist and otorhinolaryngologist Muhlenberg Hosp. Address: 604 Park Av., Plainfield, N.J.

CHILDS, Harwood Lawrence, univ. prof., author; b. Gray, Me., May 1, 1898; s. Herman Andrew and Frances Eudora (Whittermore) C.; student Tilton (N.H.) Sch., 1911-15, Harvard Law Sch., 1921-22; B.A., M.A., Dartmouth Coll., Hanover, N.H., 1921; Ph.D., U. of Chicago, 1928; m. Willa Whitson, June 28, 1922; children—Elizabeth Ann, Margaret Frances, Martha Louise. Instr. pub. speaking, Dartmouth Coll., Hanover, N.H., 1919-20, instr. economics, 1920-21; asst. prof. economics, Syracuse (N.Y.) U., 1922-24; asso. prof. govt., William and Mary Coll., Williamsburg, Va., 1925-28; prof. polit. science, Bucknell U., Lewisburg, Pa., 1928-31; asso. prof. politics, Princeton U., since 1931; Social Science Research Council fellow, Germany, 1931-32; Guggenheim fellow, Germany, 1937-38. Apprentice seaman, U.S. Navy, Oct.-Dec. 1918. Mem. Am. Polit. Science Assn., Am. Assn. Univ. Profs., Alpha Chi Rho. Baptist. Author: Labor and Capital in National Politics, 1930; A Reference Guide to the Study of Public Opinion, 1934; The Nazi Primer, 1938; articles in Am. Polit. Science Rev., Am. Jour. of Sociology, Atlantic Monthly, Harpers Mag., Annals of Am. Acad. Polit. and Social Science. Founder and managing editor The Public Opinion Quarterly, pub. by Sch. of Pub. and Internat. Affairs, Princeton U.; editor Pressure Groups and Propaganda, Vol. 179, Annals of Am. Acad. Polit. and Social Science, 1935; Propaganda and Dictatorships, Princeton U. Press, 1936. Home: 106 Broadmead. Office: 123 Dickinson Hall, Princeton, N.J.

CHILDS, Louis Moore, II, lawyer; b. Norristown, Pa., June 2, 1900; s. Louis Moore and Alice Grace (Hibbard) C.; grad. William Penn Charter Sch., Phila., 1918; grad. U.S. Naval Acad., Annapolis, Md., 1922; LL.B., U. of Pa., 1928; m. Margaret Lewarne Moon, Feb. 19, 1936; 1 son, Louis Moore, III. Admitted to Pa. bar, 1928, and became asso. with High, Dettra & Swartz, Norristown, Pa.; dir. v.p. and title officer Montgomery Trust Co.; dir. Norristown Water Co. Commd. ensign, U.S. Navy, 1922, and served in Navy, 1922-25. Mem. Phi Kappa Sigma. Republican. Presbyterian. Clubs: Union League (Phila.); Army and Navy (Washington, D.C.); Plymouth Country (Norristown, Pa.). Home: Burnside Ave. Office: 40 E. Airy St., Norristown, Pa.

CHILDS, Marquis William, journalist; b. Clinton, Ia., Mar. 17, 1903; s. William Henry and Lilian Malissa (Marquis) C.; A.B., U. of Wis., 1923; A.M., U. of Ia., 1925; m. Lué Prentiss, Aug. 26, 1926; children—Henry Prentiss, Malissa Marquis. With United Press, 1923 and 1925-26, St. Louis Post-Dispatch, since 1926. Mem. Kappa Sigma. Club: Washington Press. Author: Sweden—The Middle Way, 1936; They Hate Roosevelt, 1936; Washington Calling, 1937; This Is Democracy, 1938. Home: 501 Dorset Av., Chevy Chase, Md. Office: St. Louis Post-Dispatch Washington Bur., 1422 F St., Washington, D.C.

CHILDS, Randolph W., lawyer; b. San Francisco, Calif., Feb. 1, 1886; s. Walter C. and Edith W. (Smith) C.; student Yonkers High Sch., Yonkers, N.Y., 1898-1902; A.B., Acad. of the New Church, Bryn Athyn, 1905; LL.B. (cum laude), U. of Pa. (law dept.), 1908; m. Hazel Damon, June 23, 1917; children—Faith (Mrs. J. Douglas Halterman), Edith Walton, Beatrice W., Carol, Randolph Damon. Began practice June 1908 and practiced in New York City until 1914; practiced law in Phila. since 1914; mem. firm Adams, Childs, McKaig & Lukens since 1934; dep. ins. commr. of Commonwealth of Pa., 1920; asst. counsel Delaware River Bridge Joint Commn., 1920. Campaign manager, Bohlen, Philips and Dorrance Republican Campaign, 1930; chmn. Phila. Citizens Com., 1930. Cap., 109th Inf., A.E.F., 1918. Dir. Acad. of the New Church (Bryn Athyn), Bryn Athyn Church of the New Jerusalem. Mem. Phila., Pa., and Am. bar assns., Montgomery Co. (Pa.) Bar Assn., Phila. Bar Assn. (former mem. bd. of govs., sec.). Republican. Swedenborgian. Clubs: Union League, Lawyers (Phila.). Home: Bryn Athyn, Pa. Office: 700 Integrity Bldg., Philadelphia, Pa.

CHILDS, William St. Clair, lawyer; b. Pittsburgh, Pa., Nov. 4, 1890; s. Asa P. Jr. and Caroline D. (Corcoran) C.; Ph.B., Sheffield Scientific Sch., Yale, 1912; LL.B., U. of Pittsburgh Law Sch., 1916; m. Mary Lee Colby, June 2, 1927; children—William St. Clair, Richard Henry Lee. Admitted to Pa. bar, 1916, and since in practice at Pittsburgh; mem. of firm Sterrett, Acheson & Jones since 1916. Mem. Pittsburgh Assn. for Improvement of the Poor (bd. of dirs.), Athalia Daly Home (bd. of mgrs.). Republican. Episcopalian. Clubs: Pittsburgh, Pittsburgh Athletic, Harvard-Yale-Princeton (Pittsburgh). Home: 607 Shady Av. Office: 1927 Oliver Bldg., Pittsburgh, Pa.

CHILES, Harry Linden, osteopathic physician; b. Louisa, Va., July 1, 1867; s. Henry and Isabella Pottie (Hunter) C.; student Louisa Acad., 1884 to 1890; D.O., Am. Sch. of Osteopathy (pres. grad. class), 1901; m. Anna Clare, Dec. 20, 1894; children—Henry, Ellen Clare (Mrs. J. H. R. Pickett). Editor and pub. local newspaper and teacher pub. schs., 1887-90; business mgr. and editor Roanoke (Va.) Evening World, 1894-95; supt. Fanning Sch. for Girls, Nashville, Tenn., 1895-99; studied law and admitted to Va. bar, 1889; sec.-treas. Old Domonion Investment Co., Roanoke, Va., 1890-94; removed to Auburn, N.Y., 1901 and began practice of osteopathy; asso. editor Jour. of Osteopathy (1st osteopathic pub.), 1900-01; sec., exec. officer and editor Jour. of Am. Osteopathic Assn. and Osteopathic Mag., 1903-23. Mem. Am. Osteopathic Assn. (sec. since 1901), New Jersey State and Essex Co. osteopathic societies; N.Y. State Osteopathic Soc. (sec-trustee, 1902-04). Active in founding A. T. Still Research Inst. and Osteopathic Foundation, 1907. Author many addresses and professional articles; contbr. of "Osteopathy" in Reference Handbook of the Medical Sciences; and chapters in volume The Lengthening Shadow of Dr. A. T. Still, by Dr. A. G. Hildreth, 1938. Awarded Distinguished Service certificate by Am. Osteopathic Assn., 1929. Democrat. Disciple of Christ. Mason. Clubs: Atlas, Rotary (since 1916). Home: 58 Main St., Orange, N.J.

CHILTON, Thomas Hamilton, chem. engr.; b. Greenboro, Ala., Aug. 14, 1899; s. Claudius Lysias and Mabel Cecilia (Pierce) C.; student Univ. Sch., Montgomery, Ala., 1910-13, Lanier High Sch., Montgomery, Ala., 1914-15, U. of Ala., Tuscaloosa, Ala., 1915-16; Chem. E., Columbia U., 1922; m. Cherridah McLemore, June 29, 1926; children—Thomas McLemore, Daniel Tanner, Research chemist, F.J. Carman, New York, 1922-25; chem. engr., chem. dept., E. I. du Pont de Nemours & Co., Wilmington, Del., 1925-35, asst. div. head, tech. div., engring. dept., 1935-38, dir. tech. div. since 1938. Mem. Am. Chem. Soc., Am. Inst. Chem. Engrs. (dir., 1937-39), Sigma Xi, Phi Lambda Upsilon, Tau Beta Pi. Presbyterian. Club: du Pont Country (Wilmington, Del.). Home: 703 Seville Av., Villa Monterey. Office: du Pont Experimental Station, Wilmington, Del.

CHILTON, William Edwin, Jr., publisher; b. Charleston, W.Va., Dec. 2, 1893; s. William Edwin and Mary Louise (Tarr) C.; B.A., Yale, 1917; m. Louise Burt Schoonmaker, June 20, 1929 (died June 1928); children—William Edwin III, Mary Carroll. Pres. Daily Gazette Co. since 1922; mng. editor Charleston Gazette since 1924. Served as ensign naval aviation, World War; mem. Delta Kappa Epsilon. Democrat. Elk. Clubs: Nat. Press, Delta Kappa Epsilon, (New York); Kanawha Country. Home: Charleston, W.Va.

CHINARD, Gilbert, prof. French; b. Châtellerault, France, Oct. 17, 1881; s. Hilaire and Marie (Blanchard) C.; student Collège de Châtellerault, Lycée de Poitiers, Université de Bordeaux, Sorbonne; B.L., Poitiers, 1899, Licencié ès lettres, 1902; LL.D. from St. John's, 1934; m. Emma Blanchard, 1908; children—Lucienne Gilberte, Francis Pierre. Instructor in French, College of the City of New York, 1908, Brown Univ., 1908-12, Univ. of Chicago, summer 1912; asso. prof. and prof. of French, U. of Calif., 1912-19, Columbia, summer 1919; at Johns Hopkins, 1919-36, as prof. French and comparative lit.; became mem. Walter Hines Page Sch. Internat. Relations, 1925; at U. of Calif., 1936-37; Pyne prof. of French lit., Princeton, since 1937. Mem. Modern Lang. Assn. America, Am. Philos. Soc., Philol. Assn. Pacific Coast (pres. 1918), Société des Américanistes de Paris; correspondent mem. l'Institut Académie des Sciences Morales et Politiques; Lauréat de l'Académie Française, 1914. Author: L'Exotisme américain dans la littérature française, au XVI siècle, 1911; L'Amérique et le rêve exotique, 1913; L'Exotisme américain dans l'œuvre de Chateaubriand, 1918; La doctrine de l'Américanisme, 1919; Volney et l'Amérique; Les amitiés américaines de Madame d'Houdetot, 1923; Jefferson et les Idéologues, 1925; Les Réfugeiés Huguenots en Amérique, 1925; Destutt de Tracy, de l'Amour, 1926; Les Amitiés Françaises de Jefferson, 1927; The Literary Bible of Thomas Jefferson, 1928; Jefferson, the Apostle of Americanism, 1928. Editor: The Commonplace Book of Thomas Jefferson, 1926; The Letters of Jefferson and Du Pont de Nemours, 1931; Un Française en Virginia, Chateaubriand les Natchez, 1932; Honest John Adams, 1933; Diderot Supplément an Voyage de Bougainville, 1935; Le Voyage de Lapérouse en Alaska et sur les côtes de Californie, 1937; Origines historiques de la Doctrine de l'Tsolement aux Etats. Unis., 1937. Mem. Phi Beta Kappa. Officer de la Lègion d'Honneur. Home: 93 Mercer St., Princeton, N.J.

CHIPMAN, Charles; pres. Butterfly Hosiery Mills, Charles Chipman's Sons Co;. also officer or dir. many other companies. Home: R.F.D. 3, Easton, Pa.

CHIPMAN, John Sniffen, hosiery mfr.; b. Easton, Pa., June 20, 1899; s. William Evan and Harriet Louise (Sniffen) C.; student Lawrenceville (N.J.) Sch., 1912-17, Lafayette Coll. (Easton, Pa.), 1917-19; m. Emilie Bacon Michler, July 29, 1922; children—William Evan, Frank Louis. With Chipman Knitting Mills, Easton, Pa., since 1919, pres. since Feb. 10, 1932; v.p. Chas. Chipman's Sons Co., Inc., since 1931; also pres. Chipman Spinning Mills, Easton, Pa. Served in U.S.N., World War. Mem. Zeta Psi. Republican. Episcopalian. Mason (32°). Home: 625 Paxinosa Av. Address: Chipman Knitting Mills, Easton, Pa.

CHIPMAN, Ralph N., pres. Chipman Chem. Co., Inc.; b. Beverly, N.J., Feb. 14, 1886; s. Russell B. and Anna E. (Bechtel) C.; student

Penn. Charter Prep. Sch. and Phila. High Sch. Pres. Chipman Chem. Co., Inc. Home: 452 W. 8th St., Plainfield, N.J. Office: Bound Brook, N.J.

CHISOLM, James Julian, physician; b. Winchester, Ky., Dec. 24, 1889; s. Rev. James Julius and Mary Virginia (Tweed) C.; prep. edn. Natchez (Miss.) Inst., 1901-05, Lawrenceville (N.J.) Sch., 1905-07; A.B., Princeton U., 1911; M.D., Johns Hopkins, 1915; m. Eva Aslee Frierson; children—James Julian, Mary Frierson. House officer Johns Hopkins Hosp., 1915-18; physician, specializing in ear, nose and throat diseases, Baltimore, since 1918; instr. in clin. laryngology, Johns Hopkins U., 1919-20, asso. since 1920; mem. visiting staff Johns Hopkins Hosp., Church Home and Infirmary, Hosp. for Women of Md.; dispensary laryngologist Johns Hopkins Hosp. Served as 1st lt. Med. Corps, U.S. Army, 1918-19; with Evacuation Hosp. No. 30 and 4th San. Train, A.E.F., 10 months. Mem. bd. govs. Presbyn. Eye, Ear and Throat Hosp., Baltimore. Mem. A.M.A., Southern Med. Assn., Baltimore City Med. Soc., Phi Beta Kappa. Democrat. Presbyterian. Home: 4424 Underwood Rd. Office: 1114 St. Paul St., Baltimore, Md.

CHISOLM, Oliver Beirne, v.p. Colonial Trust Co.; b. Charleston, S.C., Nov. 23, 1897; s. William Gregg and Nancy (Miles) C.; student Porter Mil. Acad., Charleston, 1909-12; grad. Smith Sch., Charleston, 1914; student U. of the South, Sewanee, Tenn., 1915 and 1919-20; m. Loti Moultrie Ficken, June 19, 1924; children—Nancy Miles, Oliver Beirne, Loti Moultrie. Asst. to supt. United Dredging Co., New York, 1920-22; salesman E. P. Burton Lumber Co., Charleston, 1922-23; v.p. S.C. Loan & Trust Co., Charleston, 1923-26; broker, Baltimore, 1927-29; v.p. and investment counsel Colonial Trust Co., Baltimore, since 1930. Served with U.S. Naval Reserve, Mar. 1917-Nov. 1918. Episcopalian. Clubs: Maryland (Baltimore); Gibson Island (Md.). Home: 5223 Putney Way. Office: Colonial Trust Co., Baltimore, Md.

CHITWOOD, Oliver Perry, educator, author; b. Franklin Co., Va., Nov. 28, 1874; s. Henry Clay and Gillie Anne (Divers) C.; A.B., William and Mary Coll., 1899; Ph.D., John Hopkins Univ., 1905; LL.D., from William and Mary College, 1926; m. Agnes Cady, Dec. 17, 1910; children—Henry Cady, Elizabeth Anne. Librarian, William and Mary Coll., 1898-99; headmaster Richmond (Va.) Acad., 1902-03; fellow in history, Johns Hopkins, 1904-05; prof. history and economics, Mercer U., 1905-07; prof. history, W.Va. Univ. since 1907; instructor in history, Johns Hopkins, summer 1922; visiting prof. of history, Ohio State U., summer 1938. Mem. Am. Hist. Assn., Am. Assn. Univ. Profs., Southern Hist. Assn., Phi Beta Kappa. Author: Justice in Colonial Virginia, 1905; Syllabus of Roman History, 1913; The Immediate Causes of the Great War, 1917; A History of Colonial America, 1931; John Tyler, Champion of the Old South, 1939. Joint Author: Makers of American History, 1904. Also author of hist. articles. Democrat. Baptist. Home: Morgantown, W.Va.

CHORLTON, William Harper, univ. prof.; b. Phila, Pa., Feb. 10, 1882; s. William and Louise A. (Kay) C.; B.S. in C.E., U. of Pa., 1902, C.E., 1908; m. Bertha M. Cox, June 30, 1904; 1 dau., Elizabeth (Mrs. George Brobyn); m. 2d, Madeline Mitch, Sept. 3, 1925. Draftsman Am. Bridge Co., Phila. office, 1902-07, asst. engr., New York office, 1907-23; prof. structural engring., U. of Pa., since 1923. Mem. Am. Acad. Polit. and Social Science, Am. Soc. C.E. (dir. Phila. section, 1934; v.p., 1935-37; pres. 1937-38). Republican. Home: 943 Fillmore St. Office: U. of Pennsylvania, Philadelphia, Pa.

CHRISMAN, Lewis Herbert, prof. English lit.; b. Upper Uwchlan Twp., Chester Co., Pa., Aug. 21, 1883; s. John and Carrie (Bewley) C.; Ph.B., Dickinson Coll., 1908, A.M., 1909, Litt.D., 1920; studied University of Pa., University of Mich., University of Wisconsin; m. Elizabeth Lash, Aug. 5, 1914; children—Esther Elizabeth, Margaret Lucille. Prof. of English, Union College, Barbourville, Ky., 1908-10; prof. English lit., Baldwin-Wallace College, Berea, O., 1911-19, W.Va. Wesleyan College since 1919, also acting dean, 1925-26; prof. English lit., W.Va. University, summers 1922 and 23, lecturer extension dept., 1922-25; spl. lecturer, Drew Theol. Sem., 1922, 25; lecturer on preaching, Garrett Bibl. Inst., summer 1930; contbg. editor, Jour. of Edn.; staff writer for church school pubs. of Meth. Ch. Mem. Alpha Chi Rho, Phi Beta Kappa. Democrat. Methodist. Author: John Ruskin, Preacher, and Other Essays, 1921; The English of the Pulpit, 1926; The Message of the American Pulpit, 1930; Ten Minute Sermons, 1935. Editor: Selections from Speeches of Abraham Lincoln (with Dr. Leon C. Prince), 1912. Lecturer on lit. and general subjects. Home: Buckhannon, W.Va.

CHRIST, Clarence Clayton, pres. Gen. Pub. Utilities, Inc.; v.p. and dir. many pub. service companies. Home: 211 Oakridge St., Summit, N.J. Office: 744 Broad St., Newark, N.J.

CHRISTIAN, Benjamin Daniel, v.p. Crocker Wheeler Mfg. Co.; b. Noblesville, Ind., July 5, 1889; s. George and Luna (Loehr) C.; E.E., Purdue U.; m. Mary Fisher, July 16, 1914; children—Elizabeth, Mary Alice. With Crocker Wheeler Electric Mfg. Co. since 1914, v.p. since 1935. Home: 297 Park St., Montclair, N.J. Office: Ampere, N.J.

CHRISTIANSEN, Oscar A., business exec.; b. McKees Rocks, Pa., Sept. 18, 1896; s. Christian Munson and Wilhelmina (Engelbrecht) C.; grad. McKees Rocks (Pa.) High Sch., 1914; student Duff's Business Coll., Pittsburgh, 1914-16; m. Estella Mae Bair, Jan. 4, 1918; 1 son, Frank Leslie. Clk. Pressed Steel Car Co., McKees Rocks, Pa., 1916-17; bookkeeper First Nat. Bank, McKees Rocks, 1918-19; timekeeper Dravo Contracting Co., Pittsburgh, 1919-20; with Taylor-Wilson Mfg. Co. since 1920, beginning as timekeeper, sec. and treas. since 1933; treas. McKees Rocks Borough. Served in Air Service, U.S. Army, 1917-18. Mem. Am. Legion. Republican. Presbyterian. Clubs: Rotary, Social Civic (McKees Rocks, Pa.). Home: 334 Russellwood Av. Office: Taylor-Wilson Mfg. Co., McKees Rocks, Pa.

CHRISTIE, Alexander Graham, prof. mech. engring.; b. Manchester, Ont., Can., Nov. 19, 1880; s. Peter and Mary Honor (Graham) C.; prep. edn., high sch., Port Perry, Ont.; M.E., Sch. of Practical Science (U. of Toronto), 1901; m. Flora Brown, June 28, 1919; children—Peter Graham, Catherine Graham. Came to U.S., 1901, naturalized citizen, 1918. With Westinghouse Machine Co., East Pittsburgh, Pa., 1901-04; instr. mech. engring., Cornell U., 1904-05; with steam turbine dept., Allis-Chalmers Co., 1905-07; mech. engr. Western Can. Cement & Coal Co., 1907-09; asst. and asso. prof. steam and gas engring., U. of Wis., 1909-14; asso., later prof. mech. engring., Johns Hopkins, since 1914; cons. practice in America and Great Britain. Fellow Am. Soc. Mech. Engrs. (pres. 1938-39), Am. Gas Assn., Soc. for Promotion Engring. Edn., Nat. District Heating Assn., Sigma Xi, Tau Beta Pi, Omicron Delta Kappa, Pi Tau Sigma. Clubs: Engineers (New York); Engineers, Johns Hopkins (Baltimore). Author of Steam Turbine Sec. Sterling's Marine Engineer's Handbook, and Steam Turbine Sec. Kent's Mechanical Engineer's Handbook, also numerous scientific papers and articles. Home: 211 Tunbridge Road, Baltimore, Md.

CHRISTIE, Samuel A.; mem. law firm Christie & Christie. Address: Keystone, W.Va.

CHRISTIE, Sidney L.; mem. law firm Christie & Christie. Address: Keystone, W.Va.

CHRISTMAN, Charles E., pres. and treas. Federal Enameling & Stamping Co.; b. Ross Twp., Pa., Mar. 19, 1870; s. Dawalt and Maryann (Van Bushkirk) C.; ed. business coll.; m. Edna Mary Mae Dean, Oct. 20, 1926; children—Paul, Isabel, Virginia. Organized, 1892, and since pres. and treas. Federal Enameling and Stamping Co., Pittsburgh, Pa. Home: 25 Roycroft Av., Mt. Lebanon. Office: Federal Enameling and Stamping Co., Pittsburgh, Pa.

CHRISTMAN, Howard Lewis, publisher; b. Washington, Pa., July 11, 1880; s. William and Fanny (Morgan) C.; student Washington (Pa.) pub. schs. and business coll.; m. Bessie Linn, Mar. 25, 1903; 1 son, Thomas Linn. Dir. Observer Pub. Co., Washington, Pa., since 1903, now v.p. and business mgr. Pres. Washington Chamber of Commerce, 1935-39. Mem. Pa. Newspaper Pubs. Assn. Clubs: Rotary (Washington, Pa.; pres. 1923). Home: 445 Allison Av. Office: 122 S. Main St., Washington, Pa.

CHRISTMAN, Paul Snyder, supt. of schools; b. Weissport, Pa., July 3, 1896; s. David Oscar and Ella Mae (Snyder) C.; student Albright Coll. and Prep. Sch., Myerstown, Pa., 1913-17; B.S., Franklin and Marshall Coll., 1919, M.S., 1921; m. Mary Edna Runkle, Aug. 26, 1926. Teacher of science, High School, Schuylkill Haven, Pa., 1922-26, prin. of High Sch., 1926-31, supt. of schools since 1931; vice-pres. and dir. Conewago Mutual Fire Ins. Co., Lancaster, Pa. Served as private Chem. Warfare Service, U.S. Army, Aug. 1918-Jan. 1919. Pres. Schuylkill Haven Library Assn. Trustee Shannon Scholarships. Mem. N.E.A., Pa. State Edn. Assn. (pres. Supervising Prins. Sect.; mem. legislative com.; sec. Eastern Conv. Dist.), A.A.S.A., Am. Legion (past comdr. Baker Post; chmn. Americanism Com., 13th Dist. of Pa.), Alumni Assn. Franklin and Marshall Coll. (vice-pres. Northeastern dist.), Phi Sigma Kappa. Republican. Mem. Reformed Ch. Elk. Clubs: Reading Country; Rotary of Schuylkill Haven (past pres.), Schuylkill County Schoolmen's (past pres.). Home: 205 W. Main St. Office: Haven St., Schuylkill Haven, Pa.

CHRISTY, George Lewis, civil engr.; b. Germantown, Pa., Jan. 30, 1867; s. Archie and Martha (Crawshaw) C.; student pub. schs., East Des Moines, Ia.; B.C.E., Ia. State Coll., Ames, Ia., 1891, C.E., 1909; m. Laura Bowne, 1899 (died 1924); 1 dau., Jeanne. Began as draftsman, 1891; engring. dept., Edgmoor Bridge Works, 1892; engring. asst. D. W. Church, cons. engrs., Chicago, 1892-93; engring. asst. Lewison and Just, New York, 1893-96, chief engr., 1896-1903; chief engr. and vice-pres. Lewison & Co., 1903-14; chief engr. Pittsburgh Des Moines Steel Co. since 1914. Mem. Am. Soc. C.E., Am. Soc. for Testing Materials, A.A.A.S., Engring. Soc. of Western Pa. Republican. Presbyterian. Home: 5586 Pocusett St. Office: Neville Island, Pittsburgh, Pa.

CHRISTY, William Gaston, engineer; b. Jerseyville, Ill., Oct. 27, 1886; s. John and Cordelia (Gaston) C.; student Jerseyville (Ill.) pub. schs., 1891-98, high sch., 1898-1902, Shurtleff Coll., Alton, Ill., 1902-06; M.E., Cornell U., 1911; m. Lillian Marsh, Apr. 8, 1914; 1 dau., Marcia Elizabeth. Engr. Heine Safety Boiler Co., Phoenixville, Pa., 1911-12; asst. to Henry H. Humphrey, cons. engr., St. Louis, Mo., 1912-16; propr. William G. Christy Co., cons. engr. in sale heating and power plant equipment, St. Louis, Mo., 1916-18; supt. and field engr. St. Louis Boat and Engring. Co., 1920-23, in charge constrn. four large steel Mississippi towboats for govt.; v.p. and gen. mgr. Schubert-Christy Constrn. & Machinery Co., St. Louis, 1923-25, cons. engrs. in design, manufacture and installation cooling towers and power plants; exec. sec. Citizens Smoke Abatement League, St. Louis, 1925-28, in charge largest smoke abatement program in country, working with $250,000 subscription fund and supervising field force of 40 and comprehensive ednl. campaign; sales engr. Fire King Stoker Co., St. Louis, 1928-29; cons. engr. Bd. of Edn., St. Louis, 1930, in charge plans and specifications for power plant and equipment of Hadley Vocational Sch.; smoke abatement engr., Hudson Co., N.J., since 1930, drew up smoke ordinance and rules and regulations adopted 1931, in charge Smoke Regulation Dept. covering 12 municipalities in Hudson Co., ordinance, regulations and campaign considered one of most up-to-date in U.S. Served as production engr., Emergency Fleet Corpn., U.S. Shipping Bd., St. Louis Dist., 1918-20; promoted to dist. mgr., Supply Div., 1919; in charge production, inspection, transportation all supplies and equipment for ships in 12 state dist., and later in charge cancellation of contracts. Vice-pres. bd. of trustees, 1st Baptist Ch., Hoboken, N.J.; dir. and v.p. Jersey City Boys Club. Mem. Am. Soc. M.E. (sec. St. Louis Sects. 1922-24, chmn. 1925-26; sec. Fuels Div., 1928-29, 1931-34, mem. exec. com. since 1935, chmn. program com. 1936-38), Hudson Co. Soc. Professional Engrs. (v.p. since 1937), Nat. Soc. of Professional Engrs., Nat. Assn. of Power Engrs., N.J. Soc. of Professional Engrs., Nat. Smoke Prevention Assn., Cornell Soc. of Engrs., Phi Kappa Sigma. Baptist. Club: Rotary (Jersey City, N.J.; dir. since 1938 and v.p. since 1939). Home: 1 Kingswood Rd., Weehawken, N.J. Office: Court House, Jersey City, N.J.

CHROSTWAITE, Thomas Francis, lawyer and pub.; b. Ashley, Pa., Jan. 6, 1873; s. John and Mary (Bligh) C.; grad. Ashley (Pa.) High Sch., 1890, Bloomsburg (Pa.) Teacher's Coll., 1892; A.B., Harvard, 1898; m. May Hull, Sept. 16, 1905. Teacher country sch., Hanover Twp., Luzeme Co., Pa., 1892-95; supt. schs., Hanover, Pa., 1899-1905; admitted to York Co. (Pa.) bar, 1905, and since practiced at Hanover, Pa.; editor and proprietor Municipal Law Reporter, now in 30th vol., since 1909; editor and pub. The Borough Bulletin, official organ of Pa. Assn. of Boroughs, since 1912. Solicitor for municipalities of Pa. Founder, 1910, and since pres. Pa. Assn. of Boroughs. Roman Catholic. Author: Pa. Borough Law, 1936; Municipal Ordinances and Forms, 1931; Short articles, occasional addresses at instns. Address: Hanover, Pa.

CHRYSLER, Minton Asbury; prof. botany, Rutgers U. Address: Rutgers University, New Brunswick, N.J.

CHUBB, Charles Frisbie, banker; b. Grand Rapids, Mich., Jan. 6, 1877; s. Archibald Lamont and Mary Ann (McMechan) C.; Ph.B., U. of Mich., 1897; m. Mary Clare Carroll Albert, Nov. 27, 1917; children—Charles Frisbie, Jr., Nicholas Carroll, Talbot Albert. Clk., and later mem. firm George Bros., real estate brokers, 1898-1915; rep. in Pittsburgh of Henry C. Frick and Estate of H. C. Frick, 1915-36; pres. The Dollar Savings Bank since 1936; pres. St. Paul Coal Co. Dir. Sewickley (Pa.) Acad. Republican. Presbyn. Clubs: Duquesne (Pittsburgh); Allegheny Country, Edgeworth Country (Sewickley). Home: Hidden Brook Farm, Coraopolis, Pa. Office: The Dollar Savings Bank, Pittsburgh, Pa.

CHUBB, Hendon, insurance exec.; b. Brooklyn, N.Y., Mar. 19, 1874; s. Thomas Caldecot and Victoria C.; student Dearborn Morgan Sch., Orange, N.J., 1889-92, Yale, 1892-95; m. Alice M. Lee, 1898; children—Thomas C., Margaret C. (Mrs. J. Russell Parsons), Percy II. With Chubb and Son since 1895, mem. firm since 1899, sr. mem. since 1930; v.p. Federal Ins .Co., 1901-29, pres. since 1929; chmn. exec. committee U.S. Guarantee Co. since 1930; dir. Prudential Ins. Co., South Porto Rico Sugar Co., St. Joseph Lead Co.; trustee Central Hanover Bank and Trust Co. Chmn. adv. bd. U.S. Bur. War Risk Ins., 1914-18; dir. ins. U.S. Shipping Bd., 1917-19. Unitarian. Home: Llewellyn Park, Orange, N.J. Office: 90 John St., New York, N.Y.

CHUBB, Lewis Warrington, electrical engr.; b. Fort Yates, N.D., Oct. 22, 1882; s. Col. Charles St. John and Sarah L. (Eaton) C.; prep. high sch., Columbus, O.; M.E. in Elec. Engring., Ohio State University, 1905; Sc.D., Allegheny College, 1933; D.Sc., University of Pittsburgh, 1933; m. Mary Porter Everson, Mar. 28, 1910 (died 1919); children—Lewis Warrington, John Everson, Morris Wistar; m. 2d, Ora Lee (Dias) McGregor, of Pittsburgh, Pa., May 10, 1926; 1 dau., Vivian McGregor. With Westinghouse Elec. & Mfg. Co., 1905-30; engring. apprentice, 1905-06; in research and development magnetic materials, 1906-18, in charge research sect.; with elec. development sect., materials and process engring. dept., 1916-20; mgr. radio engring. dept., 1920-30; asst. v.p. in charge engring. RCA Victor Co., Camden, N.J., Jan.-June 1930; dir. Westinghouse Research Labs. since 1930. Mem. Am. Inst. E.E., Inst. Radio Engrs., Physical Soc., Illuminating Soc., A.A.A.S., Engring. Foundation, Sigma Xi, Tau Beta Pi. Republican. Episcopalian. Clubs: University, Edgewood Country. Awarded between 100 and 200 patents as result of elec., mech. and chem. researches; Lamme medal, Ohio State U., 1934. Contbr. many articles and papers. Home: 7021 Penn Av., Pittsburgh, Pa.

CHURCH, Alonzo, univ. prof.; b. Washington, D.C., June 14, 1903; s. Samuel Robbins and Mildred Hannah Letterman (Parker) C.; grad. Ridgefield (Conn.) Sch., 1920; A.B., Princeton U., 1924, Ph.D., 1927; m. Mary Julia Kuczinski, Aug. 25, 1925; children—Alonzo, Mary Ann, Mildred Warner. Instr. of mathematics, U. of Chicago Summer Sch., 1927; nat. research fellow in mathematics, Harvard, 1927-28, Göttingen, Germany, 1928-29, Amsterdam, Holland, 1929; asst. prof. mathematics, Princeton U., 1929-39, asso. prof. since Sept. 1939. Mem. A.A.A.S., Am. Math. Soc., Assn. for Symbolic Logic, Phi Beta Kappa. Presbyterian. Editor: Jour. of Symbolic Logic since 1936. Address: 30 Jefferson Rd., Princeton, N.J.

CHURCH, Charles Frederick, nutrition and pub. health; b. Deer Lodge, Mont., Oct. 7, 1902; s. Christian Rudolph and Anna (Grinig) Schurch; student Deer Lodge (Mont.) Central Sch., 1909-16, Powell Co. (Mont.) High Sch., 1916-20; B.S., Mont. State Coll., Bozeman, Mont., 1924; M.S., U. of Ill., Urbana, Ill., 1926; M.D., Harvard Med. Sch., 1931; spl. work in pub. health adminstrn., U. of Michigan, Ann Arbor, Mich., 1938-39; m. Helen Nichols, June 5, 1928; children—Charles Frederick, David Nichols. Chemist Ill. State Water Survey, Urbana, Ill., 1924-26; asst. in food chemistry, Columbia U., 1926; biochemist, Tailby-Nason Co., Boston, Mass., 1926-30; asso. in pathology, Harvard Med. Sch., 1928-31; research fellow in pediatrics, U. of Pa. Sch. of Medicine, 1931-34, asso. in pediatrics, 1934-38; dir. of research, Nutrition Fund (later Rockefeller Nutrition Fund), Phila., since 1935; consultant, U.S. Pub. Health Service, 1939. Fellow Am. Pub. Health Assn.; mem. Soc. for Pediatric Research, Phi Kappa Phi. Home: 4025 Huey Av., Drexel Hill, Pa. Office: 1740 Bainbridge St., Philadelphia, Pa.

CHURCH, Franklin Higby, physician and surgeon; b. Lyons Falls, N.Y., Dec. 6, 1880; s. Artemas Mayanard and Jessie (Van Wie) C.; A.B., Hamilton Coll., Clinton, N.Y., 1902, A.M., 1905; M.D., Johns Hopkins U. Med. Sch., 1906; m. Grace Teresa McGuire, Nov. 27, 1907. Interne Utica General Hosp., 1907; engaged in gen. practice of medicine and surgery at Utica, N.Y., 1907-12; physician to Amazonian Expdn. of Univ. Mus., Phila., Pa., 1912-13; in pvt. practice, Boonville, N.Y., 1914-18; surgeon Du Pont Smokeless Powder plant, Carney's Point, N.J., 1918-19; in pvt. practice at Salem, N.J., since 1920; chief clinician, Salem County S.D. Clinics since 1934; physician to Salem County Home. Mem. Am. Med. Assn., Am. Assn. of History of Medicine, N.J. State Med. Soc., Salem Co. Med. Soc., Delta Kappa Epsilon. Democrat. Presbyn. Contbr. many articles to med. journs. Home: 86 W. Broadway, Salem, N.J.

CHURCH, Helen Landers, educator; b. Afton, N.Y.; d. George Landers and Charlotte (McWhorter) C.; A.B., Mt. Holyoke Coll., South Hadley, Mass., 1914; A.M., Teachers Coll. of Columbia U., 1928; grad. student, Cornell U., Harvard U., summer sessions. Engaged in teaching in high schs. and pvt. schs. in various cities since 1914; prin. and dir. Stevens Sch., Germantown, Phila., since 1925. A founder and mem. Germantown Art League, Germantown Community Council (past pres.); past mem. bd. Y.W.C.A.; mem. Bd. of Better Streets for Germantown Campaign; mem. exec. com. Assn. for Restoring Historic Mansions; mem. edn. com., League of Women Voters. Mem. Progressive Edn. Assn., Phila. Assn. of Childhood Edn., Fgn. Policy Assn. Episcopalian. Clubs: Mt. Holyoke of Philadelphia, Art League of Germantown. Home: 215 W. Walnut Lane, Germantown. Office: 143 W. Walnut Lane, Germantown, Philadelphia, Pa.

CHURCH, Nathan William, physician; b. Morris Run, Pa., Apr. 8, 1869; s. Frank Elmer and Emily Elizabeth (Bogart) C.; student Mansfield State Coll., Mansfield, Pa., 1887-89; M.D., Jefferson Med. Coll., Phila., Pa., 1893; m. Maude Elene Bolt, June 21, 1893 (died 1936); children—Emily Elizabeth (Mrs. Harry H. Archer), Lillian Narcissus (Mrs. P. W. Perkins), Nathan DeWitte, Winton Henry, Frank Elmer; m. 2d, Jessie Van Dusen, Jan. 1, 1938. In practice of medicine at Ulysses, Pa., since 1893; pres. Grange Nat. Bank of Potter Co. since 1934. Mem. Potter Co. (Pa.) Med. Soc., Pa. State Med. Soc., A.M.A. Republican. Baptist. Mason (Blue Lodge, Chapter, Commandry, Consistory). Address: Ulysses, Pa.

CHURCH, Samuel Harden, president of the Carnegie Institute; b. Caldwell County, Mo., Jan. 24, 1858; s. William and Emily (Scott) C.; Litt.D., Western U. of Pa., 1895; A.M., Bethany, 1896, Yale, 1897; LL.D., U. of Pittsburgh, 1909; m. Bertha Jean Reinhart, Mar. 15, 1898. Was col. on staff Gov. Hoadly of Ohio, and presented with sword by gov. and staff for conduct in handling troops for suppression of riots in Cincinnati, 1884; Republican speaker in nat. campaigns in various parts of U.S. since 1896; del. Rep. Nat. Conv., 1904. Was superintendent transportation, then became vice-pres. of Pennsylvania Lines West of Pittsburgh; director Blaw-Knox Company. Pres. Carnegie Institute, Pittsburgh, Pa.; trustee Carnegie Corporation of New York. Mem. American Missions to Morocco, 1923. Officer Legion of Honor, France. Protestant. Clubs: Duquesne, Athletic, Pittsburgh Golf, Allegheny, University, Junta, Rolling Rock, Fox Chapel (Pittsburgh); Authors (New York); National Liberal (London); American (Paris). Author: Oliver Cromwell, a History, 1894; John Marmaduke, 1897; Beowulf (poem), 1901; Corporate History of the Pennsylvania Railroad Lines West of Pittsburgh, 15 vols., 1898-1920; Penruddock of the White Lambs, 1907; A Short History of Pittsburgh, 1908; The American Verdict on the War, 1915; Flames of Faith, 1924; The Liberal Party in America, 1931. Also plays, The Unknown Soldier, The Road Home. Contbr. to mags. Home: 4781 Wallingford St. Address: Carnegie Institute, Pittsburgh, Pa.

CHURCH, W. J.; pres. Kearny Nat. Bank. Address: Kearny, N.J.

CHURCH, Walter Harry, sch. supt.; b. Waynesburg, Pa., Sept. 14, 1894; s. Edward and Anna (Philips) C.; grad. Calif. (Pa.) Teachers Coll., 1917; A.B., Waynesburg (Pa.) Coll., 1919; M.A., Washington & Jefferson Coll., Washington, Pa., 1926; student U. of Pittsburgh, since 1934; m. Jessie Williamson, May, 1917; children—Joseph Richard, Margaret Corrine, Bird Louise. Teacher Greene Co. (Pa.) Schs., 1912-16; supervising prin., Claysville (Pa.) Schs., 1919-26; prin. McKees Rocks (Pa.) High Sch., 1926-36; supt. of schs., McKees Rocks, Pa., since 1936. Pres., Principals' and Teachers' Round Table for Wash. Co., 1923-24. McKees Rocks (Pa.) Chamber of Commerce, 1938-39; member Phi Delta Kappa Fraternity. Mason. Clubs: Lions (past pres.), Bemas (dir.; McKees Rocks, Pa.). Home: 205 Greydon Av. Office: Hamilton Sch., McKees Rocks, Pa.

CHURCHILL, George Morton, prof. history; b. Elmwood, Mass., Jan. 23, 1874; s. Warren Keen and Elizabeth Hervey (Josselyn) C.; A.B., Boston U., 1896; student Bridgewater (Mass.) State Normal Sch., 1896-97; A.M., George Washington U., 1909, Ph.D., 1914; m. Mary Josephine Solyom de Antalfa, Apr. 2, 1910; children—Elizabeth Sarah, Warren Solyom de Antalfa, Morton Vincent. Teacher, Lawrence Acad., Groton, Mass., 1897-98; law clk., Harris & Barker, Brockton, Mass., 1898-1904; cataloguer and classifier, in charge social and polit. science, Library of Congress, 1904-20; part-time instr. in history, George Washington U., 1908-13, asst. prof. part-time, 1914-20, full time, 1920-22, prof. since 1922. Chmn. East Bridgewater Sch. Com., 1899-1904. Mem. Am. Hist. Assn., Am. Assn. Univ. Profs., Phi Beta Kappa, Beta Theta Pi. Republican. Unitarian. Mason. Clubs: Cosmos, Federal Schoolmen. Editor: Library of Congress Classification Schedules H and S (social sciences and agriculture), 1910-20. Home: Bethesda, Md.

CHURCHILL, H(arry) V(an Osdall); chief chemist Aluminum Co. of America. Address: P. O. Box 772, New Kensington, Pa.

CHURCHILL, Herman R(ichard); prof. and head dept. histology and comparative odontology, U. of Pa. Address: 323 Shadeland Av., Drexel Hill, Pa.

CHURCHMAN, Vincent T., Jr.; sr. eye, ear, nose and throat dept. St. Francis Hosp.; mem. staff Mountain State and Kanawha Valley hosps. Address: 1034 Quarrier St., Charleston, W.Va.

CHUTE, Charles Lionel, exec. Nat. Probation Assn.; b. Saugus, Mass., Aug. 4, 1882; s. Rev. Edward L. and Julia Hawes (Cleaveland) C.; A.B., Oberlin Coll., 1904; A.M., Columbia, 1910; grad. New York Sch. Social Work, 1910; m. Audrey Smith Chute, Aug. 3, 1915; children—Eloise, Alfred Lionel. Special agent of the National Child Labor Com., N.Y. City, 1910-12; sec. Pa. Child Labor Assn., Phila., 1912-13; sec. N.Y. State Probation Commn., Albany, N.Y., 1913-21; exec. dir. Nat. Probation Assn., N.Y. City, since 1921. Mem. Am. Inst. of Criminal Law and Criminology, Am. Assn. of Social Workers, Am. Prison Assn. Mem. City Club (New York). Author of chapters in "Probation and Criminal Justice," "Social Work Year Book," and numerous reports and mag. articles. Home: Mountain Lakes, N.J. Office: 50 W. 50th St., New York, N.Y.

CIAMPAGLIA, Carlo, mural painter; b. in Italy, Mar. 8, 1891; s. Natale and Benelde (Delmonaco) C.; student Cooper Union, New York, diploma, 1917; Nat. Acad. of Design, New York, 1909-15; m. Annette Paltrinieri, Sept. 7, 1920 (now dec.). Came to U.S. 1891, naturalized, 1919. Began mural painting, 1924; made designs for Masonic Temple, Scranton, Pa.; ceiling of Chicago Tribune Bldg., Chicago, niches and ceilings for Slovak Girls Acad., Danville, Pa.; decorations for Court House, Sunbury, Pa., residence Frank Potter, Rome, N.Y.; decorations in mosaic for Fairmont Mausoleum, Newark, N.J., in title for Green Hill Farm swimming pool, Phila., Pa.; murals in residence of David Milton, New York, and for Tex. Centennial Expn., 1936, Dallas, Tex., in Administration, Transportation, Foods, Agriculture and Live Stock bldgs.; designed murals Foods Bldg., N.Y. Worlds Fair, 1939. Instr. in life class, Cooper Union Art Sch. 10 yrs.; at present teaching life drawing, Traphagen Sch. of Fashion, New York. Awarded Am. Acad. in Rome fellowship in painting. Asso. Nat. Acad. of Design; mem. Allied Artists of America, Alumni of Am. Acad. in Rome. Home: Middle Valley, N.J. Address: 245 W. 28th St., New York, N.Y.

CLAGETT, Thomas Holland, mining engr.; b. Berryville, Va., Nov. 21, 1875; s. William Branson and Rebekah Hickman (Hopewell) C.; student Berryville (Va.) private schs., 1882-93; B.S. in metallurgy, Lehigh U., Bethlehem, Pa., 1897; m. Sarah Christe Douty, June 19, 1912. Draftsman Qualey Chem. Co., Plymouth Meeting, Pa., 1897; draftsman and survey corps Selwyn M. Taylor, Mining Engr., Pittsburgh, 1898-99, chief draftsman, 1901-04, asst. engr., 1904-05; draftsman and transitman Mich. Coal Co. and Jamestown Coal & Transportation Co., Saginaw, Mich., 1899; draftsman James W. Ellsworth & Co., Ellsworth, Pa., 1899-1900, asst. engr., 1900-01; asst. engr. Pocahontas Coal & Coke Co., Bluefield, W. Va., 1905-08, chief engr., 1908-37, supt. and chief engr. since 1937; registered professional engr., W.Va. Mem. W.Va. Conservation Commn., since 1934; dir. Southern W.Va. Forest Fire Protective Assn.; mem. State Registration Bd. for Professional Engrs., 1933-34, Bluefield (W.Va.) Sanitary Bd., 1937-38. Mem. Bluefield (W.Va.) Chamber of Commerce (dir.; v.p.), Am. Inst. Mining and Metall. Engineers, W.Va. Coal Mining Institute, American Mining Congress. Democrat. Presbyterian (Ruling Elder). Clubs: Bluefield Country, Rotary (past pres.), Bluefield Auto, University (Bluefield, W.Va.). Home: 1425 Whitethorn St. Office: P. O. Box 617, Bluefield, W.Va.

CLAPP, Alfred Comstock, lawyer; b. New York, N.Y., June 8, 1903; s. Alfred Chapin and Anna (Roth) C.; Ph.B., U. of Vt., 1923; LL.B., Harvard U. Law Sch., 1927; m. Catharine Shotwell, June 11, 1932; children—Alfred Comstock, Jr., Edward Shotwell, John Wells. Began as clk. in office McCarter & English, Newark, N.J., 1927-30; asso. with Noble, Morgan & Scammell, New York, N.Y., 1930-32; admitted to N.J. bar as atty., 1929, as counsellor, 1936; engaged in gen. practice of law at Newark, N.J., since 1933, mem. firm Colyer & Clapp since 1937. Treas. Montclair Rep. Club; Rep. leader First Ward, Montclair. Pres. Montclair Family Welfare Soc. Sec. Brookside Sch., Montclair. Mem. Am. Bar Assn., N.J. State Bar Assn., Essex County Bar Assn., Phi Beta Kappa, Sigma Nu. Republican. Conglist. Club: Essex (Newark). Author: Wills and Administration in New Jersey (yr. pub.), 1937. Contbr. to law pubs. Home: 17 Wayside Pl., Montclair. Office: 744 Broad St., Newark, N.J.

CLAPP, Clyde Alvin, ophthalmologist; b. Chatham, O., May 29, 1880; s. Alvin Rice and Martha Maria (Talbot) C.; ed. pub. schs., Ohio, 1886-98; M.D., Baltimore Med. Coll., 1902; m. Lilian A. Dickason, June 25, 1905 (died 1914); children—Roger Alvin, Clyde Melville; m. 2d, Ellen L. Richardson, of St. Louis, Mo., Aug. 7, 1928. Began practice in Baltimore, 1902; specialized in ophthalmology since 1905; asso. prof. ophthalmology, Baltimore, Med. Coll., 1910-13; asso. in ophthalmology, U. of Md., 1913-20, asso. prof., 1920-22; demonstrator in ophthalmology, Johns Hopkins, 1922-23, asso. prof. since 1923; surgeon Baltimore Eye and Ear Hosp., 1918-36; ophthalmologist St. Vincent's Infant Asylum. Mem. A.M.A., Am. Ophthal. Soc., Am. Coll. Surgeons, Baltimore City Med. Soc., Ophthal. Soc. United Kingdom. Republican. Presbyn. Club: Baltimore Country. Author: Cataract-Etiology and Treatment, 1934. Contbr. tech. articles on original research. Home: 300 E. Cold Spring Lane. Office: 513 N. Charles St., Baltimore, Md.

CLAPP, Earle Hart, forester; b. North Rush, N.Y., Oct. 15, 1877; s. Edwin Perry and Ermina Jane (Hart) C.; student Geneseo (N.Y.) Normal Sch., Cornell U., 1902-03; A.B., U. of Mich., 1905, D.Sc., 1928; m. Helen Adele Roberts, Oct. 15, 1908; children—Stewart, Helen Ermina. Asst. in forest service, U.S. Dept. Agr., 1905, chief of office forest management, 1908, asso. dist. forester, 1909-12, forest insp., 1912-15, asst. forester in charge research, 1915,35, asso. chief of forest service since 1935; organized research br.; planned and helped obtain legislation to insure plan-wise development of research commensurate with nat. needs, resulting in 12 regional forest expt. stas. and further development of a nat. forest products lab. Fellow Soc. Am. Foresters (twice v.p.); mem. Soc. Forestry Finland (corr.), Sigma Xi. Clubs: Cosmos (Washington); U. of Mich. Union (Ann Arbor, Mich.). Author: National Program of Forest Research, 1926, Supervised report "A National Plan for American Forestry," 1933; "The Western Range, A Great but Neglected National Resource," 1936; also various other govt. reports. Contbr. to forestry jours. Home: 6802 Meadow Lane, Chevy Chase, Md. Office: South Bldg., Washington, D.C.

CLAPP, Edward A.; pres., treas. and dir. Pyrene Mfg. Co. Home: Montclair, N.J. Office: 560 Belmont Av., Newark, N.J.

CLAPPER, Raymond, newspaper corr.; b. Linn Co., Kan., May 30, 1892; s. John William and Julia (Crow) C.; grad. high sch., Kansas City, Kan., 1913; student U. of Kan., 1913-16; m. Olive Ewing, Mar. 31, 1913; children—Janet, William Raymond. Began as reporter Kansas City (Mo.) Star, 1916; with United Press Assns., 1916-33, in Chicago, Milwaukee, St. Paul, New York and Washington offices, night mgr. and chief polit. writer, Washington bur., 1923-28, mgr. Washington bur., 1929-33; spl. writer Washington Post, 1934-35; polit. commentator Scripps-Howard Newspapers since Jan. 1936. Dir. Nat. Press Bldg. Corpn. Mem. Sigma Delta Chi (hon. nat. pres., 1939). Clubs: Gridiron (pres. 1939), Overseas Writers, National Press, Congressional Country. Author: Racketeering in Washington. Home: 209 Primrose, Chevy Chase, Md. Office: 1013 13th St., Washington, D.C.

CLAPPER, Samuel Mott Duryea; chmn. bd. Gen. Refractories Co.; v.p. Cannon Mills, Inc.; treas. Ewing Thomas Corpn.; chmn. bd. Schlieter Jute Cordage Co.; dir. Central Pa. Nat. Bank, Delaware County Nat. Bank of Chester (Pa.), Fire Assn. of Phila., Reliance Ins. Co., Guaranty Co. of North America. Trustee Jefferson Med. Coll. and Hosp. Office: Real Estate Trust Bldg., Philadelphia, Pa.

CLARE, Robert David; pastor St. Mark's Luthern Ch. Address: 1900 St. Paul St., Baltimore, Md.

CLARK, Arthur, v.p. Edison-Splitdorf Corpn.; b. Montclair, N.J., Jan. 22, 1894; s. Allison Perrine and Katherine (Moran) C.; student Montclair High Sch. and Temple U.; m. Marjorie Courter, June 17, 1917; children—Arthur, Marjorie, William. V.p. and gen. mgr. Edison-Splitdorf Corpn. Address: West Orange, N.J.

CLARK, Charles Cleveland, statistician, meteorologist; b. Washington, D.C., Mar. 6, 1875; s. Ezra Wescote and Sylvia (Nodine) C.; student Columbian U.; LL.B., Phila. Law Sch. (Temple Coll.), 1899; LL.M., Columbia, 1900, C.C.L., 1901; m. Mary Duncan Swingle, July 12, 1905; children—Charles Cleveland, Robert Duncan, Mary Elizabeth, Anita. Asso. statistician in charge Bur. of Statistics, Dept. of Agr., Washington, D.C., 1906-08, also chmn. crop-reporting bd.; statistician Internat. Inst. Agr., Rome, Italy, 1909, 1910; chief clk. U.S. Dept. Agr., 1911-13; exec. asst. U.S. Weather Bur., 1913-14; asst. chief same, since 1915. Represented U.S. in organizing Internat. Inst. Agr., at Rome, Italy, 1908. Mem. bar States of Pa. and Wash. and of Washington, D.C. Mem. Am. Statis. Assn., Am. Meteorological Soc., Loyal Legion, Columbia Hist. Soc., Am. Forestry Assn., Inst. of Aeronautical Sciences. Clubs: University, Torch, Federal, Congressional Country (Washington, D.C.). Author various bulls., and monographs on statis. and crop reporting subjects. Home: 21 W. Irving St., Chevy Chase, Md.

CLARK, Charles Patton, ins. med. dir.; b. Vincennes, Ind., Dec. 2, 1879; s. Thomas Jefferson and Emma Rose (Jennings) C.; A.B., U. of Ind., Bloomington, Ind., 1901; M.D., Rush Med. Sch., U. of Chicago, 1904; m. Elizabeth Garfield Burnet, Sept. 18, 1907; children—Burnet Jennings, Charles Patton, Thomas Favill, Elizabeth Drusilla. Research asst., McCormick Inst. for Infectious Diseases, Chicago, Ill., 1906-08; pathologist, Maurice Porter Memorial Hosp., Chicago, Ill., 1908-11; adjunct attending physician, St. Luke's Hosp., Chicago, Ill., 1911-16; med. dir., Mutual Benefit Life Ins. Co., Newark, N.J., since 1916. Served as lt., M.C., U.S. Army, during World War. Mem. Assn. of Life Ins. Med. Dirs., Sigma Chi, Alpha Omega Alpha. Republican. Episcopalian. Club: City (New York). Author of numerous monographs on build and its influence on mortality and physiology research in laboratory technique. Home: 123 Beechwood Rd., Summit, N.J. Office: 300 Broadway, Newark, N.J.

CLARK, Donald George, vice-pres. Firth-Sterling Steel Co.; b. South Bend, Ind., 1884; s. Lucius and Rose (George) C.; m. Fanchon Gauthier, June 1, 1910; children—Robert MacDonald, Dorothy (Mrs. E. R. Coyle). With Firth-Sterling Steel Co. since 1903, dir. since 1928, v.p. since 1933. Am. Inst. M.E., Am. Soc. Machinists. Presbyterian. Clubs: Duquesne (Pittsburgh); Yacht (Annapolis, Md.). Home: 5033 Castleman St., Pittsburgh. Office: McKeesport, Pa.

CLARK, Dora Mae, coll. prof.; b. Derby, Vt., June 10, 1893; d. Ezra Warren and Isadore Mellissa (Aldrich) C.; A.B., Mount Holyoke Cll., South Hadley, Mass., 1915; A.M., Columbia U., 1916; Ph.D., Yale, 1924. Engaged as instr. history, Western Reserve U., Cleveland O., 1925; pro. Am. history and polit. science, Wilson Coll., Chambersburg, Pa., since 1925. Mem. Am. Hist. Assn., Am. Polit. Science Assn., Pa. Hist. Assn. Republican. Congregationalist. Clubs: Chambersburg Golf, Hershey Skating (Chambersburg, Pa.). Author: British Opinion and the American Revolution, 1930; contbr. chapter to Essays in Colonial History, articles to hist. jours., and Dictionary Am. Biography. Address: Wilson College, Chambersburg, Pa.

CLARK, Edward Ross, accountant; b. Matawan, N.J., Jan. 16, 1871; s. Thomas E. and Sarah E. (Ross) C.; student Glenwood Inst., Matawan, N.J., N.Y. Prep. Sch., U. of Pa.; m. Ada M. Warrin, June 25, 1911; children—Edward Ross, Gertrude Kimber, Janet D., Ada Maddock, William Warrin. Began as clk., 1892; now gen. auditor Glen Alden Coal Co., Scranton, Pa.; comptroller Lehigh & Wilkes-Barre Coal Co., Wilkes-Barre, Pa., auditor and dir. Honey Brook Water Co., Hazelton, Pa.; gen. auditor Del., Lackawanna & Western Coal Co., New York; dir. Burns Bros., New York. Democrat. Episcopalian. Odd Fellow. Home: 579 Charles St., Kingston, Pa. Office: 310 Jefferson Av., Scranton, Pa.; 120 Broadway, New York, N.Y.

CLARK, Edwin Milligan, dist. atty.; b. Leechburg, Pa., Aug. 25, 1902; s. Lewis Gibson and Ida May (Rankin) C.; A.B., Muskingum Coll., New Concord, O., 1924; LL.B., Duquesne U., Pittsburgh, 1932; grad. studies, U. of Mich., Ann Arbor, Mich., summer 1930; m. Dora Elizabeth Martin, Aug. 10, 1926; children—Katherine, Lois Margaret, Elizabeth May, Alexander Martin. Teacher mathematics, social studies, Indiana (Pa.) High Sch., 1924-25, teacher and athletic coach, 1929-30; prin., Harrisville (Pa.) Pub. Schs., 1926-29; practice of law at Indiana, Pa., since 1932; elected dist. atty., Indiana (Pa.) Co., 1936. Republican. United Presbyterian. Mason, County Grange. Clubs: Lions (Indiana, Pa.). Home: 523 S. 6th St. Office: Philadelphia St., Indiana, Pa.

CLARK, Eliot Round, prof. anatomy; b. Shelburne, Mass., Nov. 13, 1881; s. George Larkin and Emma Frances (Kimball) C.; A.B., Yale, 1903; M.D., Johns Hopkins, 1907; studied U. of Munich and U. of Cracow; m. Eleanor Acheson Linton, Mar. 21, 1911; 1 dau., Margaret Brownson. Instr. anatomy, 1907-10, asso., 1910-14, Johns Hopkins Med. Sch.; prof. anatomy, U. of Mo., 1914-22; prof. anatomy, U. of Ga., 1922-26, also asst. dean, Med. Dept., 1923-25; prof. anatomy and dir. dept. of anatomy, U. of Pa. since 1926. Contract surgeon U.S.A., Sept.-Nov., 1918. Fellow A.A.A.S.; mem. Am. Asso. Anatomists (sec.-treas. since 1938), Am. Assn. Physiologists, A.M.A., Coll. of Physicians of Phila., Physiol. Soc. of Phila., Sigma Xi, Phi Beta Kappa, Alpha Omega Alpha, Phi Kappa Epsilon, Phi Beta Pi. Trustee of Marine Biol. Lab., Woods Hole, Mass. Contbr. results of original researches to professional jours., chiefly growth and reactions of lymphatics, blood vessels, connective tissue cells, bone, and blood cells, new methods for miscroscopic study of cells and tissues in the living mammal. Home: 315 S. 41st St. Address: Univ. of Pa. School of Medicine, Philadelphia, Pa.

CLARK, Ernest Judson, life insurance; b. Newtonville, O., June 27, 1872; s. Benjamin Franklin and Sarah (Roudebush) C.; ed. Newtonville Public Sch., 1879-88, Nat. Normal U., Lebanon, O., 1888-90; m. Marie Breson de La Tour, Nov. 14, 1900; children—Aileen de La Tour (Mrs. Joseph M. Gazzam, Jr.), Alicia Gilmer (Mrs. John R. Howland), Ernest Judson, Jr. Agt. Mutual Benefit Life Ins. Co., Cincinnati, 1891-92, asst. agency supervisor for Ohio, 1892-94; with John Hancock Mutual Life Ins. Co. since June 1, 1894, as supt. of agts., Ohio and W.Va., 1894-97, state agt., Md. and D.C., since January 1, 1897. One of founders Am. Coll. Life Underwriters, sec., 1927, pres., 1928-34, chmn. of bd., 1934-38, life mem. of the board; former pres. for five years Baltimore Criminal Justice Commn.; receiver United Surety Co. of Baltimore, 1911-26. Mem. Nat. Assn. Life Underwriters (sec. 1904-06; chmn. exec. com. 1909; pres. 1913-14); Baltimore Life Underwriters Assn. (founder 1900), Sons of the Am. Revolution (past pres. Md. Soc.; past vice-pres. nat. soc.). Republican. Baptist. Clubs: Maryland, University, Baltimore Country, Merchants (Baltimore). Home: 211 Highfield Rd., Guilford, Baltimore, Md. Office: 1039-55 Calvert Bldg., Baltimore, Md.

CLARK, Franklin Jones, clergyman; b. Phila., Pa., Sept. 23, 1873; s. George A. and Hannah Lippincott (Jones) C.; student U. of Pa.; S.T.B., Phila. Div. Sch., 1906; m. Eleanor Newhall Moss, June 1912; children—Margaret Steel, Frank, John Arthur. Deacon and priest P.E. Ch., 1906; asst. Holy Trinity Ch., Phila., 1906-08; rector St. Barnabas Ch., Reading, Pa., 1908-11; sec. Bd. of Missions, P.E. Ch., 1911-19; sec. Nat. Council, P.E.Ch., since 1919; sec. House of Deputies of Gen. Conv., 1934. Republican. Home: 250 N. Mountain Av., Montclair, N.J. Office: 281 4th Av., New York, N.Y.

CLARK, Frederic Lewis, lawyer; b. Conshohocken, Pa., Jan. 6, 1878; s. Charles Heber and Clara (Lukens) C.; student Episcopal Acad., Phila., Pa., 1888-95; A.B., U. of Pa., 1899, LL.B., Law Sch., 1902; m. Elizabeth Warner, Oct. 10, 1908; children—Clara Lukens, William Warner, Arthur Wayne. Admitted to Pa. bar, 1902, and since practiced at Phila.; mem. firm Shields, Clark, Brown & McGown, Phila. Mem. Phila. Bar Assn., Pa. Bar Assn., Am. Bar Assn., Am. Law Inst. Republican. Episcopalian. Club: Union League (Phila.). Home: Wissahickon Av. and Stafford St. Office: 1900 Girard Trust Bldg., Phila., Pa.

CLARK, Friend Ebenezer, prof. chemistry; b. New Martinsville, W.Va., Aug. 21, 1876; s. Josephus and Lina (Russell) C.; B.S., W.Va. U., 1898; Ph.D., Johns Hopkins, 1902; studied U. of Chicago, U. of Berlin; m. Emma May Hanna, June 29, 1911; children—Josephus Browne, Samuel Friend. Instr. chemistry, W.Va. U., 1902-03, Pa. State Coll., 1903-05; prof. chemistry, Centre Coll., Ky., 1905-14; prof. chemistry, W.Va. U., since 1914, also head of dept. since 1919, chmn. Grad. Council since 1935. Fellow A.A.A.S., Chem. Soc. (London); mem. Am. Inst. Chemists, Am. Chem. Soc., Phi Kappa Psi, Phi Beta Kappa. Democrat. Presbyn. Mason. Home: Morgantown, W.Va.

CLARK, Harry E., physician; b. Oakdale, Pa., Jan. 7, 1862; s. William Herdman and Catherine (Fritz) C.; student Oakdale (Pa.) Acad., 1878-81; read medicine under preceptor, Dr. W. P. Taylor, 1882-85; student Starling Med., Columbus, O., 1885-86 (then Western Pa. Med. Coll.), U. of Pittsburgh, 1887-88; m. Margaret R. Douglass, Aug. 15, 1894; children—Margaret R., William H., Harriet E., Armede B., Reid G. Interne Allegheny Co. Home & Hosp., Woodville, Pa., 1886-87; resident physician Allegheny Co. Home, 1889-91; in practice at Sheraden, Pittsburgh, since Apr. 1891; pres. Sheraden Bank of Pittsburgh since its orgn., Aug. 1901. Health officer, Borough of Sheraden, 1894-99; Fellow A.M.A.; mem. Allegheny Co. Med. Soc. (charter mem. of branch), Pa. State Med. Soc. Address: 2919 Chartiers Av., Sheraden, Pittsburgh, Pa.

CLARK, Heath S.; pres. Rochester & Pittsburgh Coal Co.; also officer or dir. various other companies. Address: Indiana, Pa.

CLARK, Henry Alden, lawyer; b. Harbor Creek, Erie Co., Pa., Jan. 7, 1850; s. Chauncey G. and Emiline Elizabeth (Wheelock) C.; A.B., Harvard, 1874; m. Sophy G. McCreary, July 18, 1878; children—Sophy Annette, Henry McCreary. Teacher, 1869. Admitted to Mass. bar, 1878, and practiced at Fall River, Mass.; admitted to Pa. bar, 1884, and since in practice at Erie, Pa.; former owner Erie Gazette; part owner Erie Dispatch. Common councilman, Erie, 1888, city solicitor, 1896, 1897; state senator, 1910, 1912; mem. 65th Congress (1917-19), 25th Pa. dist.; judge orphans' ct., Erie, 1921 to —. Mem. Erie Co. Hist. Soc. (ex-pres.). Trustee Erie Acad. One of the founders, 1873, The Harvard Crimson; pub. with F. O. Vaille, The Harvard Book, with C. F. Richardson, The College Book. Address: 131 E. 6th St., Erie, Pa.

CLARK, Herbert Lincoln, broker; b. Germantown, Pa., Jan. 8, 1866; s. Edward W. and Mary T. (Sill) C.; student Harvard; m. Edith Hall, Jan. 9, 1895; 1 dau., Marys (Mrs. Woodward R. Tappen); m. 2d, Elizabeth Conway Bent, June 18, 1907; children—Eleanor Foster, Elizabeth Conway (Mrs. Arthur B. Sinkler). Has been a partner E. W. Clark & Co., brokers, Phila., Pa., since 1900; mem. bd. dirs. Bangor (Me.) Hydro-Electric Co. Mem. bd. govs. Phila. Stock Exchange since 1933. Pres. Nicetown Club for Boys and Girls, Phila.; v.p. Inter-Agency Council for Youth; mem. bd. mgrs. and vice-chmn. Grad. Hosp. of U. of Pa.; trustee Berean Manual Training & Industrial Sch., Phila. Clubs: Rittenhouse, Midday, Harvard, Germantown Cricket (Phila.). Home. Golf House Rd., Haverford, Pa. Office: 1531 Locust St., Philadelphia, Pa.

CLARK, Hubert Galbraith, newspaper editor; b. Rocky Mount, Va., Jan. 13, 1890; s. Rev. Peter Cunningham and Sarah (Horne) C.; A.B., Hampden-Sydney Coll., Hampden-Sydney, Va., 1911; m. Edna J. Wirgman, June 13, 1921. Began as reporter, Birmingham (Ala.) Ledger, 1912-14; reporter, Tribune-Herald, Rome, Ga., 1914-16; reporter, Times, Roanoke, Va., 1916-17; editor Welch (W.Va.) Daily News, 1922-27; editor and mgr. Williamson (W.Va.) Daily News since 1927. Served as 2d lt. F.A., U.S.A. during World War. Mem. county ct. (fiscal body) Mingo Co., W.Va., since 1939. Pres. Williamson Chamber of Commerce since 1936. Mem. city council, Williamson, 1933-39. Mem. W.Va. Publishers Assn., Theta Chi. Democrat. Presbyn. Mason. Clubs: Kiwanis (past pres.), Mingo County Country. Home: 344 W. 4th Av. Office: 25 Third Av., Williamson, W.Va.

CLARK, J. Harold; prof. pomology, Rutgers U. Address: 50 Nassau St., New Brunswick, N.J.

CLARK, Janet Howell (Mrs. Admont Halsey C.), coll. dean and prof.; b. Baltimore, Md., Jan. 1, 1889; d. William Henry and Anne Janet (Tucker) Howell; A.B., Bryn Mawr Coll., Bryn Mawr, Pa., 1910; Ph.D., Johns Hopkins U., 1913; m. Dr. Admont Halsey Clark, July 9, 1917; 1 dau., Anne Janet. Engaged as lecturer in physics, Bryn Mawr Coll., 1914-15; instr. in physics, Smith Coll., 1916-17; instr. and asst. prof. physiology, Johns Hopkins U., 1918-24, asso. prof., 1924-35; lecturer in physiology, Johns Hopkins U., and head Bryn Mawr Sch., Baltimore, Md., 1935-38; dean of coll. for women, and prof. gen. physiology, Univ. of Rochester, Rochester, N.Y., since 1938. Mem. A.A.A.S., Am. Phys. Soc., Am. Physiol. Soc., Optical Soc. of America. Episcopalian. Home: 112 St. Dunstan's Rd., Baltimore, Md. Address: Univ. of Rochester, Rochester, N.Y.

CLARK, Jefferson Hamer, physician; b. Phila., Pa., Dec. 10, 1890; s. J. H. and Amy Brush (Hamm) C.; A.B., Haverford (Pa.) Coll., 1911; M.D., Johns Hopkins Med. Sch., 1915; m. Aileen Dixon, Jan. 1, 1927; children—Mary A., Jefferson Hamer, Dixon Vethake. Interne Temple U. Hosp., Phila., 1915-16, asso. in lab., 1916-17, asso. dir. and dir., 1919-29; demonstrator and asso. in pathology, Temple U. Med. Sch., 1919-29; chief of labs., Phila. Gen. Hosp. since 1929; asso. in pathology, U. of Pa. Grad. Sch. of Medicine since 1930; chmn. Pneumonia Control Com. Dept. of Health since 1938; served on many coms. of state, city, and local groups. Served as lt., then capt., Med. Corps, U.S.A., with A.E.F. in France, 1917-19. Mem. Soc. Pathologists and Bacteriologists, Pathologic Soc. of Phila. (v.p. 1937-39), Am. Coll. Physicians, Clin. Pathologists, Coll of Physicians of Phila., S.A.R., Am. Legion. Republican. Presbyterian. Contbr. articles to med. jours. Home: 101 Maple Av., Wyncote, Pa. Office: 3701 N. Broad St., Philadelphia, Pa.

CLARK, John Balfour; pres. Clark Thread Co.; officer or dir. many companies. Home: Bedminster, N.J. Office: 260 Ogden Av., Newark, N.J.

CLARK, John Brittan, clergyman; b. Brooklyn, N.Y., Sept. 2, 1864; s. Richard P. and Maria (Charles) C.; A.B., Amherst, 1886 (Phi Beta Kappa); grad. Union Theol. Sem., 1889; D.D., Alma (Mich.) Coll., 1913; m. Irene Woodbridge, Feb. 16, 1892; children—Dorothy (dec.), Elisabeth Woodbridge (dec.), David Cartwright. Ordained Presbyn. ministry, 1889; pastor Pilgrim Chapel, Brooklyn, 1890-92, Lee Av. Congl. Ch., Brooklyn, 1892-98, then Westminster Presbyn. Ch., Detroit, later 1st Ch., Washington, D.C., then Erskine Memorial Ch., Tryon, N.C. Moderator of Synod of Baltimore, Congl. Conf. of Carolinas. Certified Braille transcriber. Author: Guide Posts Along the Way, 1926; The Challenging Christ, 1929; The Future Life, 1931;

Things That Trouble People. Home: Cumberland, Md.; (summer) Middlefield, Mass.; (winter) St. Augustine and Bradenton, Fla.

CLARK, Joseph F., banking and finance; b. Wildwood, N.J., May 7, 1900; s. Frank P. and Sarah D. (Murray)—C.; ed. public school and Wildwood High Sch., until 1918; student U. of Pa., Coll. and Wharton Sch., 1934; Grad. Sch. of Banking, Rutgers U., 1938; unmarried. Bank clerk, 1918-21; asst. treas., asst. mgr., auditor, W.&D.B. R.R., 1921-30; treas. and dir. Fidelity Trust Co., Wildwood, N.J., 1926-32; city treas. City of Wildwood since 1932; vice-pres. Seaboard Fidelity Co., finance, Phila. and Atlantic City, since 1935; public accounting, own practice, 1923-26; dir. and treas. City of Wildwood Bldg. & Loan Assn.; dir. Five Mile Beach Bldg. & Loan Assn. Vice-pres. Municipal Finance Officers Assn. of N.J. Roman Catholic. Clubs: Rotary (past pres.), Wildwood Golf. Home: 211 E. Young Av., Wildwood, N.J.

CLARK, Joseph Sill; mem. law firm Clark, Hebard & Spahr. Home: Church Road, Wayne, Pa. Office: 1500 Walnut St., Philadelphia, Pa.

CLARK, L. J.; v.p. and sec. Pa. Co. for Insurances on Lives and Granting Annuities. Office: 15th and Chestnut Sts., Philadelphia, Pa.

CLARK, Laurence, architect, artist; b. Germantown, Phila., Pa., Mar. 25, 1881; s. William James and Deborah Cornelia (Earley) C.; grad. Germantown (Pa.) Acad., 1899; B.S. in architecture, U. of Pa., 1903; student Ecole des Beaux Arts, Paris, 1903-04; m. Agnes Gendell, June 25, 1913. Archtl. draftsman for various firms in Phila., 1904-10; opened office for practice of architecture, Phila., 1910; architect for Rankin & Kellogg, Zantzinger, Borie & Medary, Ballinger Co., etc., Phila.; architect for City Planning Commn., 1933, 1934, 1935; registered Architect in Pa. Water color artist; exhibited in Water Color Show of Pa. Acad. Fine Arts, 1932, 1934, 1935; fellowship of Pa. Acad. Fine Arts, 1932-38; one man shows, Phila., 1933, Review Club Oak Lane, Phila., 1937; annual show Southwest Harbor, Me., since 1930, Temple U., 1939. Mem. Fellowship Pa. Acad. Fine Arts. Republican. Clubs: Phila. Sketch, Phila. Water Color. Address: 125 W. Penn St., Germantown, Philadelphia, Pa.

CLARK, Lawrence Edmund, prof. sociology and economics; b. Eureka, Ill., Oct. 14, 1893; s. Olynthus Burroughs and Lilly (Rowell) C.; A.B., Drake U., Des Moines, Ia., 1916; A.M., Ohio State U., Columbus, 1923; student Harvard, 1923-24; Ph.D., Columbia, 1930; grad. student Teachers Coll., Columbia, 1934-35; m. Gladys Rice, Jan. 31, 1931; 1 son, Lawrence Edmund. Taught at Ohio State U., U. of Calif., Wash. State Coll.; prof. of sociology and economics and head of dept., Bethany (W.Va.) Coll. since 1936. Served in U.S. Army in Hawaii and Camp Funston, Kan., 1917-19. Mem. Am. Sociol. Soc., Am. Econ. Assn., Am. Acad. Polit. and Social Science, Acad. Polit. Science (New York), W.Va. State Edn. Assn., Assn. of Higher Edn. of W.Va., Nat. Council Social Studies, Sons Am. Revolution, Phi Beta Kappa, Pi Gamma Mu. Conglist. Author: Central Banking under the Federal Reserve System, 1935. Lecturer on economic and social subjects. Address: Bethany, W.Va.

CLARK, LeR(oy) V(incent), explosives chemist, organic chemist; b. Harlansburgh, Pa., July 2, 1902; s. Martin Luther and Frances Augusta (Vincent) C.; B.S. in chem. engring., Grove City (Pa.) Coll., 1925; student W.Va. U., Morgantown, W.Va., 1925-26, McGill Univ., Montreal, 1926-27, U. of Pittsburgh, 1930-34; m. Winsome Nancy Robinson, July 20, 1933; 1 dau., Barbara Ann Robinson. Demonstrator, McGill U., Montreal, 1926-27; bacteriologist Borden Farm Products, Ltd., Montreal, Can., 1927; chemist Grasselli Powder Co., New Castle, Pa., 1927-28, E. I. du Pont de Nemours & Co., Gibbstown, N.J., 1928-29; special investigator Western Cartridge Co., East Alton, Ill., 1929-30; asst. physical chemist U.S. Bureau of Mines, 1930-34; fellow, Mellon Inst., U. of Pittsburgh, 1934-36; research explosives engr., dept. of explosives, Am. Cyanamid & Chem. Corpn., Latrobe, Pa., since 1936. Fellow Am. Inst. of Chemists, Am. Inst. Chem. Engrs., A.A.A.S.; mem. Am. Chem. Soc. Republican. Presbyterian. Holder patents on Explosives, Blasting Methods, Equipment. Author: Absorbents for Liquid Oxygen Explosives, 1932; contbr. tech. articles on high explosives, etc., to scientific jours. Home: 716 Spring St., Latrobe, Pa.

CLARK, Lindley Daniel, author; b. Carthage, Ind., June 26, 1862; s. Daniel and Mary Robinson (Hoag) C.; A.B., Earlham Coll., 1886; studied De Pauw U.; A.M., Maryville Coll., Tenn., 1890; U. of Mich., LL.B., Columbian (now George Washington) U., 1897, LL.M., 1898; m. Maria E. Young, Dec. 29, 1886; children—Edward Daniel, Lindley Hoag, Thomas W. Y.; m. 2d, Dora J. Bradshaw, of Franklin, Va., Dec. 1, 1898; 1 dau., Mary Mildred (Mrs. J. E. Raymond). With U.S. Dept. of Labor, 1893-1927; economist in charge of industrial and economic law, 1924-27; with U.S. Employees Compensation Commn. as deputy commr. on Longshoremen's and Harborworkers' Compensation, 1927-32. Minister Soc. of Friends (Quakers). Mem. Am. Assn. Labor Legislation, Pi Gamma Mu. Author: The Law of the Employment of Labor, 1911; (bulls.) Workmen's Compensation Legislation U.S., Can., 1919, 26; Minimum Wage Laws of the U.S., 1921; and numerous articles and bulls. U.S. Bur. of Labor and articles in cyclopedias and periodicals. Home: Sandy Spring, Md.

CLARK, Norman Emmett, lawyer; b. South Franklin Twp., Washington Co., Pa., Nov. 8, 1861; s. John Gaylord and Sarah Herron (Clokey) C.; A.B., Washington and Jefferson Coll., Washington, Pa., 1882; m. Sarah Hanna Flack, Nov. 9, 1892; children—John Gaylord, Norman Emmett, Mary Foster (Mrs. Robert A. Ferree; dec.). Admitted to Washington Co., Pa., bar, 1885, and since practiced under own name at Washington, Pa.; admitted to Superior Ct. of Pa., 1894, Supreme Ct. of Pa., 1890, U.S. Dist. Ct., 1900, U.S. Supreme Ct., 1934; counsel Baltimore & Ohio R.R. since 1893. Solicitor for Borough of East Washington, Pa., since 1893; pres. judge orphans ct., Washington Co., 1923. Mem. Washington Co. Bar Assn. (pres., 1904-06). Republican. United Presbyterian. Club: Bassett (Washington, Pa.). Home: 116 S. Wade Av. Office: Washington Trust Bldg., Washington, Pa.

CLARK, Percy Hamilton; mem. law firm Clark, Hebard & Spahr. Home: Cynwyd, Pa. Office: 1529 Walnut St., Philadelphia, Pa.

CLARK, Ralph A., sales mgr.; b. Meadville, Pa., June 15, 1901; s. David M. and Blanche (Cushman) C.; student pub. schs., Meadville, Pa., 1907-20; B.S., Allegheny Coll., Meadville, Pa., 1924; m. Sarah McQuiston, Apr. 10, 1926; children—David Jackson, Sara Ann. Office worker Duquesne Light Co., Pittsburgh, Pa., 1924-25; salesman J. T. Baker Chemical Co., Pittsburgh, Pa., 1925-26, mgr. New York sales office, 1926-27, sales mgr., Phillipsburg, N.J., since 1927, dir. since 1933; treas. and dir. Taylor Chemical Corpn., Phillipsburg, N.J., since 1933. Mem. Am. Chem. Soc., Delta Tau Delta, Alpha Chi Sigma. Republican. Presbyterian. Clubs: Chemists (New York); Rotary, Northampton Country (Easton, Pa.). Home: 379 Shawnee Drive, Easton, Pa. Office: J. T. Baker Chemical Co., Phillipsburg, N.J.

CLARK, Sydney Procter, investment banker; b. Chestnut Hill, Philadelphia, Pa., Mar. 31, 1891; s. Edward Walter and Lydia Jane (Newhall) C.; student Chestnut Hill Acad., Phila., 1901-05, Pomfret (Conn.) Sch., 1905-10; A.B., Harvard, 1914; m. Isabella Lee Mumford, May 26, 1928; 1 son—Sydney Procter. Began as clk. E. W. Clark & Co., investment bankers, Phila., 1916, partner, 1921; pres. and dir. Crystal Oil Refining Corpn. Served in U.S. Navy, World War, 1917-19; hon. discharged as lt. U.S.N. Trustee Pomfret Sch.; v.p., mgr. Pa. Hosp.; pres. Seamen's Church Inst. of Philadelphia. Awarded Navy Cross. Republican. Episcopalian. Clubs: Germantown Cricket, The Racquet, Penn Athletic, Harvard (Phila.); Harvard (New York). Home: R.F.D. 4, Norristown, Pa. Office: 1531 Locust St., Philadelphia, Pa.

CLARK, T. S.; mem. law firm Clark, Woodroe & Butts. Address: Charleston, W.Va.

CLARK, Taliaferro, med. dir.; b. The Plains, Fauquier Co., Va., May 14, 1867; s. Edwin Parsons and Judith Ann (Taliaferro) C.; A.B., Emory and Henry Coll., 1886; M.D., U. of Va., 1890; m. Margaret Wolforth, Oct. 7, 1897; children—Judith Madison, William T., David S., Charles E., Richard H., Fitzhugh T. Interne, Randall's Island Hosp., N.Y. City, 1890-92; in practice at Washington, D.C., 1892-97; asst. surgeon, U.S. Pub. Health Service, 1897-1902, passed asst. surgeon, 1902-12, surgeon, 1912-25, sr. surgeon, 1925-30, med. dir., 1930, asst. surgeon gen. and chief of Division of Venereal Diseases, 1930-33; retired. Dir. child hygiene investigation, 1915; director bureau sanitary service, Am. Red Cross, 1917-19; in supervisory charge U.S.P.H.S. activities—immigration, quarantine, etc., British Isles and continental Europe 1926-29. Mem. Internat. Sanitary Conf., Paris, 1926; del. to Internat. Conf. Tropical Medicine, Cairo, Egypt, 1928. Am. mem. Office Internat. d'Hygiène Publique; consultant in health, Julius Rosenwald Fund. Mem. Sigma Alpha Epsilon. Contbr. many health bulletins and other papers. Home: R.F.D. 2, Germantown, Md.*

CLARK, Thomas Winder Young, lawyer; b. Maryville, Tenn., Feb. 26, 1892; s. Lindley Daniel and Maria Elizabeth (Young) C.; student pub. schs., Washington, D.C., 1907-14; B.S., with honor, Earlham Coll., Richmond, Ind., 1914-18; LL.B., George Washington U., Washington, D.C., 1921; m. Aurie Marion Austin, Oct. 1, 1938. Examiner U.S. Patent Office, Washington, 1918-21; admitted to Dist. of Columbia bar, 1921, Md. bar, 1922; asso. firm Brown, Marshall, Brune & Parker, Baltimore, 1921-25; independent practice, Baltimore, Md., 1925-35; mem. firm Samuels & Clark, Baltimore, since 1935. Trustee, Miles White Beneficial Soc., Baltimore. Mem. Baltimore City Bar Assn., Am. Bar Assn., Am. Patent Law Assn., Phi Alpha Delta. Mem. Religious Soc. of Friends. Clubs: Engineers (Baltimore, Md.); Merchants. Home: 311 E. Lake Av. Office: 712 Keyser Bldg., Baltimore, Md.

CLARK, Walter Eli, ex-governor, journalist; b. Ashford, Conn., Jan. 7, 1869; s. Oren Andrus and Emily Jeannette (Jones) C.; grad. Conn. Normal Sch., New Britain, 1887; student Williston Sem., 1891; B.Ph., Wesleyan U., Conn., 1895; m. Lucy Harrison Norvell, June 15, 1898 (died 1928); m. 2d, Juliet Staunton Clay, Aug. 13, 1929. Reporter Hartford Post, 1895; telegraph editor Washington Times, 1895-96, also editor Purple and Gold (Chi Psi mag.); Washington corr. New York Commercial Advertiser, 1897; asst. to Washington corr. New York Sun, 1897-1909; Washington corr. Seattle Post-Intelligencer, 1900-09; New York Commercial and Toronto Globe, 1904-09; gov. of Alaska, Oct. 1, 1909-May 21, 1913; prospector and gold miner, Alaska, 1900. Editor and propr. Charleston (W.Va.) Daily Mail, since 1914. Republican. Presbyterian. Pres. Am. Rose Soc., 1928-29; mem. Chi Psi. Clubs: Metropolitan, Chevy Chase (Washington, D.C.); Edgewood, Kanawha (Charleston, W.Va.). Home: Charleston, W.Va.

CLARK, Walter Gordon, sch. supt.; b. Westfield, Pa., Apr. 14, 1890; s. William C. and Kate (Baker) C.; student Mansfield (Pa.) Normal Sch., 1906-09, U. of Pa., 1920-22; B.S., Bucknell U., Lewisburg, Pa., 1926; unmarried. Prin. Woolrich (Pa.) Grades School, 1909-10; prin., Clymer Twp. (Pa.) High Sch., Sabinsville, Pa., 1910-21; supervising prin. Westfield (Pa.) Borough Pub. Schs., 1921-34; asst. supt. Tioga Co. (Pa.) Schs., Wellsboro, Pa., 1934-36, supt. since 1936. Mem. Tioga Co. Children's Aid Soc. (dir.), Tioga Co. Tuberculosis Soc.), Am. Legion (Westfield, Pa.; past commdr.). Republican. Episcopalian. Mason (past Master Westfield, Pa., Lodge No. 477; past High Priest, Westfield Royal Arch; Tyagahton Commandery, K.T.; Coudersport, Pa., Consistory; Shriner, Irem Temple, Wilkes-Barre, Pa.). Club: Rotary (Wellsboro, Pa.). Home: Stevenson, Westfield, Pa. Office: County Bldg., Wellsboro, Pa.

CLARK, Walter Loane, lawyer; b. McKean Co., Pa., Oct. 27, 1878; s. Robert Yealdhall and Ella L. (Loane) C.; student Baltimore City Coll., LL.B., U. of Md. Sch. of Law, 1902; unmarried. Admitted to Md. bar, 1903; gen. counsel Md. Casualty Co., Baltimore, 1911-21; in gen. practice since 1921; formerly instr. in ins., Johns Hopkins U., now instr. in evidence, U. of Md. Sch. of Law. Pres. City Service Commn., Baltimore. Mem. Am. Law Inst., Am. Bar Assn., Md. State Bar Assn. (pres. 1930), Baltimore Bar Assn. (pres. 1935), Am. Judicature Soc. Democrat. Episcopalian. Clubs: University, Chesapeake, Merchants, Athletic (Baltimore); Annapolis Roads (nr. Annapolis). Home: St. Paul Apts. Office: 1914 Baltimore Trust Bldg., Baltimore, Md.

CLARK, William, judge; b. Newark, N.J., Feb. 1, 1891; s. J. William and Margaretta (Cameron) C.; grad. Newark Acad., 1904; grad. St. Mark's Sch., 1908; B.A., Harvard, 1911, M.A., 1912, LL.B., 1915; m. Marjorie Blair, Sept. 20, 1913; children—Anne, John William, Ledyard B. Admitted to N.J. bar, 1916, counsellor at law, 1920; mem. firm Lindabury Depue & Faulks, 1920-23; apptd. judge N.J. Court of Errors and Appeals, 1923; judge U.S. Dist. Court, N.J., 1925-38; judge U.S. Circuit Court of Appeals for the Third Circuit, since July 5, 1938. Entered First R.O.T.C., Ft. Meyer, Va., May 1917; commd. 2d lt., Aug. 1917, and assigned to 314th F.A.; 1st lt., Jan. 1918; capt. Sept. 1918; oversea service 1 yr.; silver star citation "for gallantry in action"; maj., F.A., O.R.C. Trustee N.J. Hist. Soc., N.J. Mus. Assn. Mem. Am., N.J. and Essex County bar assns., Assn. Bar City of New York, Am. Law Inst., Am. Soc. Internat. Law, Am. Acad. Polit. Science. Republican. Presbyn. Home: 117 Library Pl., Princeton, N.J. Address: Post Office Bldg., Newark, N.J.

CLARK, William Mansfield, physiol. chemistry; b. Tivoli, N.Y., Aug. 17, 1884; s. James Starr and Caroline S. (Hopson) C.; grad. Hotchkiss Sch., Lakeville, Conn., 1903; B.A., Williams Coll., 1907, M.A., 1908; hon. Sc.D. from same college, 1935; Ph.D., Johns Hopkins University, 1910; m. Rose Willard Goddard, Sept. 14, 1910; children—Harriet Allen, Miriam Goddard. Research chemist, dairy div. U.S. Dept. Agr., 1910-20; prof. chemistry, Hygiene Lab., U.S. Pub. Health Service, 1920-27; De Lamar prof. physiol. chemistry, Johns Hopkins, since 1927. Awarded William H. Nichols medal, 1936. Fellow A.A.A.S.; mem. Am. Chem. Soc., Soc. Am. Bacteriologists (pres. 1933), Am. Soc. Biological Chemists (pres. 1934-35), Nat. Acad. of Sciences, Gargoyle, Alpha Zeta Alpha, Phi Beta Kappa, Sigma Psi. Clubs: Hamilton Street, The Elkridge (Baltimore). Author: The Determination of Hydrogen Ions, 1920, 28; Studies on Oxidation-Reduction, 1928. Home: The Gardens Apt., 40th St. and Stony Run Lane, Baltimore, Md.

CLARKE, A. Vinton, textile mfr.; b. Phila., Pa.; s. James H. Clarke; student Friends Sch., Phila., Lawrenceville (N.J.) Sch., Princeton U.; m. Helen P. Galbraith; children—Hugh James, Elizabeth Jane, Gilbert Galbraith. Pres. Orinoka Mills, mfrs. of upholstery and drapery, Phila.; dir. Ninth Bank & Trust Co. Republican. Presbyterian. Clubs: Union League (Phila.); Huntington Valley Country (Abington, Pa.). Home: 825 Carpenter Lane. Office: Ruth and Somerset Sts., Philadelphia, Pa.

CLARKE, Carl Dame, medical art; b. Danville, Va., Apr. 25, 1904; s. Lawrence Carter and Katherine Wilson (Shelton) C.; ed. McGuire U. Sch., Richmond, Va., 1920-23, Yale Sch. of Fine Arts, 1923-25, Johns Hopkins Sch. of Medical Illustration, 1925-28, Md. Inst. of Art, 1925-32; hon. A.M., Am. Internat. Acad., 1938; Ph.D., Am. Internat. Acad., 1939; married Marjorie Jane Rowland, June 29, 1933; children—Mary Virginia Zollickoffer, James Marshall Rowland. Began as med. illustrator, 1925; dir. dept. of art, U. of Md., 1928-34, asso. in art as applied to medicine, 1934-37, asso. prof., same, since 1937. Mem. Biol. Photographic Assn. (mem. bd. dirs., former editor of Jour.). Mng. editor Bulletin, Sch. of Medicine, U. of Md. First lt. San. Reserves, U.S. Army. Episcopalian. Author: Molding and Casting, 1938; Illustration, Its Technic and Application to the Sciences, 1939. Contbr. many articles to tech. jours. Home: Font Hill, Malvern Av., Ruxton, Md. Address: University of Maryland, Baltimore, Md.

CLARKE, Charles M.; mem. law firm Clarke & Doolittle. Home: 509 Grove St. Office: Oliver Bldg., Pittsburgh, Pa.

CLARKE, Charles Walter, M.D., dir. Am. Social Hygiene Assn.; b. Seattle, Wash., June 27, 1887; s. Martin Hale and Eliza (Crane) C.; A.B., U. of Wash., 1912; student Harvard, 1913-14, A.M., 1923; M.B., Chir. B., Edinburgh U., 1928; m. Emily McChesney Van Order, June 29, 1915; children—Stephen Van Order, Charles Walter, Joan Lysbeth, Heather May. Field sec. Am. Social Hygiene Assn., 1914-17; resident Hull House, 1914-17; dir. health edn., League of Red Cross Societies, Switzerland, 1919-22; sec. Nat. Health Council, 1922-23; European sec. Am. Social Hygiene Assn., 1923-28; rep. sociol. sect., League of Nations, 1925; med. dir. Am. Social Hygiene Assn., 1928-35; asst. syphilologist N.Y. Skin and Cancer Hosp., 1930-35; dir. Bur. Social Hygiene, N.Y. Dept. of Health, 1935-37; exec. dir. Am. Social Hygiene Assn. since 1937; consultant on syphilis N.Y. Dept. Health since 1937, N.Y. Dept. Hosps. since 1936, U.S. Dept. Interior, Office Indian Affairs, since 1934; acting asst. surgeon U.S. Pub. Health Service since 1936; mem. com. on gonococcus and com. on intensive therapy of syphilis, N.Y. City Dept. Health; dir. Staten Island case-finding project, N.Y. City Dept. Health; research in syphilis surveys Phila., Washington, D.C., Los Angeles, New Orleans, San Francisco, New York City. Served as 1st lt., later capt., Sanitary Corps, U.S.A., with A.E.F., 1917-19. Awarded fellowship Harvard, 1913-14, Carl Schurz Foundation, 1935; medalist in clin-medicine Edinburgh, 1928. Licentiate Royal Coll. of Phys., Edinburgh; diplomate Nat. Bd. Med. Examiners, U.S.A. Vice-pres. and chmn. exec. com. Nat. Health Council. Fellow Am. Coll. Phys.; mem. A.M.A., N.Y. Co. and N.Y. State med. socs., Acad. of Medicine (N.Y. City), Am. Neisserian Med. Soc., Am. Pub. Health Assn., Phi Delta Kappa. Advisory editor Am. Jour. Syphilis; med. editor Jour. Social Hygiene; contbr. many articles on medicine and social hygiene to jours. Home: 62 Arlington Av., Caldwell, N.J. Office: 50 W. 50th St., New York, N.Y.

CLARKE, Charles W(arrington) E(arle), cons. engr.; b. Chicago, Ill., Jan. 23, 1882; s. John Robert and Izelia (Smith) C.; ed. Lewis Inst., Chicago; m. Lucy Sima, Dec. 27, 1900; 1 dau., Lucille V. Successively draughtsman Hawley Downdraft Furnace Co. (Chicago); draughtsman and engr. Armour & Co. (Chicago), Sargent & Lundy (Chicago); engr. elec. zone, N.Y.C.&H.R. Ry. (New York); mech. engr. Stone & Webster (Boston); power and consulting engr. Dwight P. Robinson & Co., Inc. (New York); consulting engr. United Engineers & Constructors, Inc. (Phila.), 1928-35, and since 1937; private practice as cons. engr., 1935-37; cons. engr. United Engrs. & Constructors, Inc., since 1937. Served as civilian engr. on constrn. project, World War, France. Fellow Am. Soc. M.E.; mem. Instn. Mech. Engrs. (London). Republican. Mason (32°, Shriner). Clubs: Engineers (New York and Philadelphia); Art (Phila.); Duquesne (Pittsburgh); North Hills Country. Home: 728 Clarendon Road, Penn Valley, Pa.

CLARKE, Eugene Caldwell, mech. engring.; b. Phila., Pa., May 5, 1894; s. Vincent A. and Eugenia C. (Caldwell) C.; grad. North East Manual Training Sch., 1911; m. Alberta E. Goodwin, June 4, 1919; children—Eugene Caldwell, M. Goodwin, Sam C. Engaged in engring. business since 1914; pres. and dir. Chambersburg (Pa.) Engineering Co. since 1931, Clarke-Harrison, Inc., since 1936. Served as 2d lt., A.S. Res., U.S. Army, during World War. Mem. Am. Soc. M. E., Am. Soc. Metals. Republican. Clubs: Union League, Engineers' (Phila.); Railway Machinery (New York). Home: 110 Norland Av., Chambersburg, Pa.

CLARKE, Francis Palmer, prof. of philosophy; b. Coal City, Ill., Nov. 29, 1895; s. Harrison and Mary Frances (Barnes) C.; A.B., U. of Colo., Boulder, 1920; A.M., U. of Neb., 1922; Ph.D., U. of Pa., 1928; unmarried. Asst. in psychology, U. of Colo., 1919-20; grad. asst. in philosophy, U. of Neb., 1920-22; with U. of Pa. since 1922, as Harrison fellow in philosophy, 1922-24, instr. in philosophy, 1924-29, asst. prof., 1929-37, asso. prof., 1937-39, prof. of philosophy since 1939. Served in Psychol. Service, U.S. Army, 1918-19. Mem. Am. Philos. Assn., Am. Cath. Philos. Assn., Medieval Acad. of America. Roman Catholic. Clubs: University (Phila.); Lenape, Le Coin d'Or. Address: College Hall., Univ. of Pennsylvania, Philadelphia, Pa.

CLARKE, Harold Vaughan, pres. H. Vaughan Clarke & Co.; b. Flint, Mich., May 4, 1891; s. James and Frances (Aldous) C.; student Toronto pub. and high schs. Pres. and dir. H. Vaughan Clarke & Co. since 1932. Address: 15th and Locust Sts., Philadelphia, Pa.

CLARKE, Marjorie Rowland, sculptor; b. Baltimore, Md., Jan. 10, 1908; d. James Marshall Hanna and Mary Virginia (Zollickoffer) Rowland; grad. Girls Latin Sch., Baltimore, 1925; A.B., Goucher Coll., 1929; student Md. Inst. of Art, 1929-30; grad. Rinehart Sch. of Sculpture, 1936; m. Carl Dame Clarke, June 29, 1933; children—Mary Virginia Zollickoffer, James Marshall Rowland. Exhibited sculpture at Baltimore Museum of Art, Enoch Pratt Free Library and Women's College Club (Baltimore), Md. Inst. of Art, Nat. Flower Show. Sculpture permanently at Frank C. Bressler Research Lab., Sch. of Medicine, U. of Md., Druid Ridge Cemetery, Baltimore. Awards: 1st prize life class, Md. Inst. Night Sch.; 2d prize, Rinehart traveling scholarship, 1934, 1st prize, 1935. Democrat. Methodist. Home: Font Hill, Malvern Av., Ruxton, Md.

CLARKE, Robert, clergyman; b. Drumagarner, Kilrea, Co. Derry, Ireland, July 15, 1872; came to U.S., 1889; s. William and Mary Ann (Clarke) C.; A.B., Geneva Coll., Beaver Falls, Pa., 1898, D.D., 1923; student Reformed Presbyterian Theological Seminary, 1898-1901, graduate student, Princeton Theological Seminary, 1906-07, B.D., 1907; M.A., Princeton U., 1918; m. Bernice Mehard Wilson, Sept. 9, 1903; children—Robert Morton, Edwin Cameron. Ordained Reformed Presbyn. ministry, 1902; pastor following churches First Reformed Presbyn. Ch., Chicago, Ill., 1901-1909; v.p. Geneva Coll. since 1909, also teacher of moral philosophy and coach of inter-collegiate debaters. Mem. Pa. Oral Examining Bd. for appointment of relief workers. Pres. Presbyn. Social Union, Pittsburg. Mem. Minister's Assn. (Beaver Falls, Pa.), Geneva Coll. Alumni Assn., Princeton Alumni Assn. of Western Pa. Clubs: Harvard-Yale-Princeton (Pittsburgh); Blackhawk Golf (Beaver Falls, Pa.). Home: 3207 College Av., Beaver Falls, Pa.

CLARKE, William Anderson, pres. W. A. Clarke Mortgage Co.; b. Elizabeth, N.J., Jan. 31, 1896; s. William A. and Anna (Black) C.; A.B., Swarthmore (Pa.) Coll., 1917; m. Eleanor Palmer Stabler, May 30, 1918; children—Cornelia Stabler, William Anderson, Mary Palmer. Pres. W. A. Clarke Mortgage Co., W. A. Clarke Co., Seaboard Agency, Inc., Phila., since 1930. Mem. Mortgage Bankers' Assn. of America (mem. bd. of govs. since 1931; mem. exec. com., 1938-39). Club: Union League (Phila.). Home: Rogers Lane, Wallingford, Pa. Office: 1614 Walnut St., Philadelphia, Pa.

CLARKE, William Hawes Crichton, lawyer; b. Washington, D.C., July 15, 1882; s. William James Patmore and Sarah (Richardson) C.; studied medicine and law George Washington U.; LL.D., Oglethorpe U., 1928; m. Elizabeth Macpherson Crichton, June 15,1905 (divorced 1932); children—Douglas Richardson Crichton, James Malcoln Crichton; m. 2d, Ruth McNamara Work, of New York, Dec. 28, 1937. Admitted to Patent Office Bar, 1902; Supreme Court and Court of Appeals of District of Columbia, 1906; Supreme Court of U.S., 1911; Supreme Court of N.Y., 1913; counsel Kellogg Co. (Battle Creek, Mich.), Iodent Chemical Co., Am. Booksellers Assn., Am. Fair Trade League, Alliance Against

Food Frauds, Panama-Pacific Expn. Co., etc.; partner of late Edward Bruce Moore, ex-commr. of patents under Presidents Roosevelt, Taft and Wilson, in firm of Moore & Clarke; ran for Congress, 5th Dist. N.J., 1918; resided in India, 1903-04. Radio commentator; chmn. Assn. for a World Constitutional Conv.; chmn. Air Services Memorial Com. Dir. Clergy League of America, Humane Soc. of N.Y. Mem. Am. Bar Assn., N.Y. Patent Law Assn., Assn. of Bar of City of N.Y., S.A.R., Soc. Colonial Wars, Huguenot Soc. of America. Contbr. to mags. Clubs: Nat. Republican, Town Hall, etc. Home: Mountain Lakes, N.J.; and 1170 5th Av., New York, N.Y. Office: Bar Bldg., 36 W. 44th Street, New York, N.Y.

CLARKEN, Joseph A.; attending ear, nose and throat surgeon and asso. brain surgeon St. James Hosp.; attending nose and throat surgeon St. Michael's Hosp.; asso. attending otologist Newark Eye & Ear Infirmary; asso. attending otorhinolaryngologist Presbyn. Hosp.; asso. visiting otologist Essex Co. Hosp. Address: 43 Lincoln Park, Newark, N.J.

CLARKSON, Edward R.; b. Pannal, England, Sept. 1, 1886; s. Robert William and E. M. (Rycroft) C.; student Liverpool Coll.; m. Eunice A. Tomlinson, Apr. 15, 1914; children—Margaret J., William R., Eleanor M., Nancy J. With Kaufman Dept. Stores since 1921, beginning as sec. and controller, now treas., dir. and controller. Home: 1316 Murray Av. Office: Fifth Av. and Smithfield St., Pittsburgh, Pa.

CLAUS, William, ry. official; b. Phila., Pa., Aug. 4, 1885; s. John Henry and Emilie (Albrecht) C.; student Temple Coll., Phila., 1900, Drexel Inst., Phila., 1901-02; studied civil engring. under private tutor, Marshall R. Pugh, Phila., 1905-11; m. Annie Davenport, Nov. 11, 1911; children—Amelia Ann, William Davenport. Civil engr. Pugh & Hubbard, 1905-11; draftsman Southern Pacific R.R. Co., Victoria, Tex., 1911-1913, Phila. Rapid Transit Co., 1913-14; successively valuation engr., engr. maintenance of way and gen. mgr. Cumberland & Pa. R.R. Co., Cumberland, Md., since 1914, now also dir. Mem. Am. Soc. C.E., Cumberland Chamber of Commerce (dir.). Republican. Lutheran. Clubs: Engineers, Kiwanis (Cumberland, Md.). Home: 48 Windsor Road. Office: 50 Baltimore St., Cumberland, Md.

CLAUSE, Robert L.; v.p., chmn. mfg. dept. and dir. Pittsburgh Plate Glass Co. Home: Sewickley, Pa. Office: Grant Bldg., Pittsburgh, Pa.

CLAUSEN, Bernard Chancellor, clergyman; b. Hoboken, N.J., Apr. 5, 1892; s. Bernard and Mary (Chancellor) C.; A.B., Colgate, 1915, A.M., 1916; Union Theol. Sem., 1915-17; D.D., Syracuse U., 1922; m. Mary Elizabeth Darnell, Aug. 5, 1918; children—Mary Carolyn, Barton Randolph, Susan Elizabeth. Ordained Bapt. ministry, 1917; asst. pastor, Mt. Vernon, N.Y., 1915-18, pastor Hamilton, N.Y., 1919-20, 1st Ch., Syracuse, 1920-33, 1st Ch. Pittsburgh, Pennsylvania, since 1933. Chaplain U.S. Navy, on board U.S.S. North Carolina, December 1917-June 1919. Mem. Phi Beta Kappa, Delta Sigma Rho. Author: Preach It Again, 1922; The Miracle of Me, 1923; Pen Portraits of the Twelve, 1924; The Door That Has No Key, 1924; The Technique of a Minister, 1925; Pen Portraits of the Prophets, 1926; Pen Pictures in the Upper Room, 1927; Pen Pictures on Calvary, 1928; Tested Programs for Special Days, 1928; The A.B.C. of the New Testament, 1935. Home: 4425 Schenley Farms Terrace, Pittsburgh, Pa.

CLAWSON, John L., pres. The Clawson Co.; b. Nov. 4, 1862; s. Dr. James E. and Mary E. (Lyne) C.; ed. private schools; m. Adele A. Eisenbrey, Nov. 26, 1889; 1 dau., Mrs. Benjamin R. Hoffman. Pres. The Clawson Co., Second and Third Sts. Passenger Ry. Co.; dir. Frankford and Southwest Ry. Co. Republican. Episcopalian. Club: Union League (Phila.). Home: The Barclay Hotel. Office: 240 Chestnut St., Philadelphia, Pa.

CLAWSON, John Wentworth, prof. of mathematics; b. St. John, N.B., Can., Nov. 26, 1881; s. Joshua and Eleanor Ann (Hall) C.; came to U.S. 1905, naturalized, 1927; B.A., Univ. of New Brunswick, 1901, M.A., 1905; B.A., Cambridge Univ., Eng., 1904; (hon.) Sc.D., Ursinus Coll., Collegeville, Pa., 1920; m. Isabelle Chipman Robertson, Aug. 18, 1909; children—John Wentworth, Alexander Robertson, Jean Robertson; m. 2d, Ruth Slotterer, Aug. 13, 1938. Asst. in physics, Ohio State U., Columbus, O., 1905-06; prof. mathematics, Ursinus Coll., Collegeville, Pa., since 1907. Fellow A.A.A.S.; mem. Am. Math. Soc., Math. Assn. of America. Democrat. Episcopalian. Address: Collegeville, Pa.

CLAY, Joseph V. F.; prof. and head dept. otolaryngology, Hahnemann Med. Coll.; otologist Hahnemann Hosp.; consultant Allentown State Hosp., Coatesville Hosp. Address: 1806 Pine St., Philadelphia, Pa.

CLAY, Thomas A.; visiting surgeon Paterson Gen. Hosp. Address: 351 Totowa Av., Paterson, N.J.

CLAYCOMB, David Lloyd, lawyer; b. Alum Bank, Pa., June 19, 1878; s. Thaddeus and Catherine (Ickes) C.; ed. Franklin and Marshall Acad., Lancaster, Pa.; LL.B., Dickinson Coll. Law Sch., Carlisle, Pa., 1903; m. Frances Willis, Aug. 22, 1912; children—Marcella Ruth, Frances June. Admitted to Pa. bar, 1903 and since engaged in gen. practice of law at Altoona, Pa.; served as mem. Pa. Ho. of Rep., 1913-15; asst. U.S. atty. for Western Dist. of Pa., 1933-36; admitted to practice before all Pa. cts. and U.S. Circuit and Dist. cts. Democrat. Evang. Reformed Ch. Mason (K.T., 32°, Shriner). Home 896 20th St., Altoona, Pa. Office: Harrisburg, Pa.

CLAYTON, Alexander Benjamin, artist, painter; b. Chevy Chase, Md., Mar. 16, 1906; s. Richard Bard and Grace (Thompson) C.; studied at E. V. Brown School, Chevy Chase; student Chevy Chase Elementary and Central High Sch., D.C., Corcoran Sch. of Art, 1924-28; Studied painting in Spain, 1928; unmarried. Artist and painter since 1929. Exhibited at one-man shows at Arts Club, Washington, D.C., Bronxville (N.Y.) Women's Club, Chevy Chase (Md.) Women's Club, Tricker Galleries, New York City; exhibited at Corcoran Biennial and Nat. Acad. Design; now painting mural for St. Marys (W. Va.) post office (commd. through competition U.S. Treasury Dept.). Award first prizes for still life, life and portrait, second prize, composition, Corcoran Sch. of Art, Washington; prize for "most outstanding work of art," Soc. Washington Artists, 1938. Treas. Soc. Washington Artists, 1937, 38, 39. Methodist. Address: Chevy Chase, Md.

CLAYTON, N. W.; chmn. bd. First Nat. Bank. Address: South River, N.J.

CLEARY, Frank L.; judge Circuit Court of N.J., term expires 1941. Address: Somerville, N.J.

CLEAVELAND, Allan, judge; b. Baltimore, Md., June 28, 1872; s. Amos Joseph and Mary Ellen (Jones) C.; student Baltimore City Coll., 1886-89; LL.B., U. of Md., Law Sch., Baltimore, Md., 1896; m. Mary Malcolm Keeling, June 16, 1918; children—Allan Malcolm, Mary Virginia (Mrs. William K. Norwood, Jr.). Admitted to Md. bar, 1896, and since engaged as individual in gen. practice of law at Baltimore; mem. House of Delegates, Md. Legislature, 1906; asst. city solicitor, 1922-25; chief judge Juvenile Ct. of Baltimore, 1935-39; dir. and atty. Peabody Heights Bldg. & Loan Assn., Prudent Permanent Bldg. & Loan Assn., both Baltimore, Md. Served as 1st sergt. 2d Regt., Md. Nat. Home Guards during World War. Dir. Md. Tuberculosis Assn. Mem. Am., Md. State bar assns., Bar Assn. City of Baltimore. Republican. Baptist. Mason; grand inspector Grand Lodge of Md.; past master Md. Lodge, 120; Royal Arch Chapter, 40; Council Royal and Select Masters; past comdr. Beauseant Commandery No. 8, K.T.; Chesapeake Consistory, Scottish Rite; past potentate A.A.O.N.M.S.; Tall Cedars; Royal Jesters; Vets. Assn.; G.S.B., Grand Com. mandery of Md. Clubs: Scimiter Luncheon, Baldric Luncheon. Home: 2124 Mt. Holly St. Office: Munsey Bldg., Baltimore, Md.

CLEAVELAND, Winfield Miller, church exec.; b. New Oxford, O., July 7, 1872; s. Edward Warner and Clara (Miller) C.; A.B., Miami U., Oxford, O., 1896, D.D., 1911; student Princeton Theol. Sem., 1896-99; A.M., Princeton U., 1899; m. Frances Long, Aug. 1, 1900 (died 1918); children—Frances Genevieve (Mrs. William James Hokman), Emily Alice; m. 2d, Elizabeth Eberly, March 21, 1921; 1 dau., Elizabeth Anne. Ordained to ministry of Presbyterian Ch. in U.S.A., Apr. 15, 1900; pastor Presbyn. Ch., Herington, Kan., 1899-1904, Third Ch., Topeka, Kan., 1904-08, Joplin, Mo., 1908-20; asso. sec. Bd. of Foreign Missions, Presbyn. Ch. U.S.A., St. Louis, Mo., 1920-24; exec. sec. Synod of Ill., 1924-28; exec. sec. Pa. Synod of Presbyn. Ch. U.S.A. since 1928. Moderator Synod of Mo., 1916; pres. State Christian Endeavor Union, Kan., 1906. Dir. Westminster Foundation of Pa. State Coll. Mem. Beta Theta Pi. Republican. Mason (32°), Rotarian. Home: 28 N. 20th St., Camp Hill, Pa. Office: Payne-Shoemaker Bldg., Harrisburg, Pa.

CLEAVES, Benjamin Franklin, public utility exec.; b. Addison, Me., June 28, 1885; s. Melvin L. and Gertrude Alice (Plummer) C.; prep. edn. Addison High Sch., and Maine Wesleyan Sem. Kents Hill); student Lowell Inst., Boston, Mass., 1909-11; m. Mabel N. Darlington, Feb. 24, 1916; children—Robert Darlington, Marjorie Corinne, Gertrude Angelyn. Electrical apprentice Westinghouse Electric & Mfg. Co., East Pittsburgh, 1903-04; elec. work Gen. Electric Co., Lynn, Mass., 1905-11; with Penn Central Light & Power Co., Altoona, Pa., since 1911, as engr. of tests, 1911-17, elec. engr., 1917-24, supt. elec. operations, 1924-27, vice-pres. since 1927; vice-pres. Pa. Edison Co.; vice-pres. and dir. Blair Engring. Supply Co. Mem. Am. Inst. Elec. Engrs., Edison Elec. Inst. Republican. Mem. Christ Reformed Ch. Mason (Shriner). Home: 112 Aldrich Av. Office: 1200 11th Av., Altoona, Pa.

CLEE, Frederick Raymond, clergyman; b. Worcester, Mass., Oct. 25, 1897; s. Frederick and Margaret (Kelley) C.; A.B., Clark U., Worcester, Mass., 1917; B.D., Union Theol. Sem. N.Y. City, 1922; B.D., Rutgers U., 1927; m. Ethel Stevens, Sept. 7, 1922; children—Robert Stevens, Jane Margaret. Ordained ministry Presbyn. Ch., 1922; minister Good Shepherd Presbyn. Ch., N.Y. City, 1922-27, Old Bergen Ch., Reformed Ch. in America, Jersey City, N.J. (founded 1660), since 1927; dir. Domestic Mission Bd., Reformed Ch. in America; pres. Gen. Synod of Reformed Ch. in America, 1936-37. Served in Am. Field Service with French Army, 1917, in U.S.A., with A.E.F., 1918. Pres. Kiwanis Club of Jersey City, 1939. Home: 797 Bergen Av., Jersey City, N.J.

CLEE, Lester Harrison, clergyman; b. Thompsonville, Conn., July 1, 1888; s. Frederick and Margaret (Kelley) C.; ed. Worcester (Mass.) High Sch., 1900-05; m. Katherine Steele, Aug. 9, 1911; 1 son, Gilbert Harrison. Boys' sec. Y.M.C.A., Quincy, Mass., 1908-11; sec. boys' work Y.M.C.A., Providence, R.I., 1911-15; dir. boys' work N.Y. City Sunday Sch. Assn., 1915-18; asst. minister West End Presbyn. Ch., N.Y. City, 1918-22; minister Baptist Ch., Rutherford, N.J., 1922-26, 2d Presbyn. Ch., Newark, since 1926; speaker House of Assembly, State of N.J., 1935; elected to N.J. Senate, 1936. Rep. candidate for gov. of N.J., 1937. Dist. gov. N.J. Lions' Clubs, 1923, 24, 25. Home: 294 Mt. Prospect Av., Newark, N.J.

CLEETON, Glen Uriel, univ. prof.; b. Green City, Mo., July 2, 1895; s. Zina Ambrose and Dora (Ransom) C.; B.S., Mo. State Teachers Coll., Kirksville, Mo., 1917; M.A., Univ. of Ia., Iowa City, Ia., 1923; m. Jenny Frances Terry, April 12, 1914; children—Frances, Glenna, Robert, Merle. Prin., Kinloch Park (Mo.) Schs., 1915-16; supt. Ellington (Mo.) Schs., 1917-18; supt., Hilton Twp. (Ia.) Schs., 1918-22; prof. of psychology, Carnegie Inst. Tech., 1923-26, head, dept. of industrial edn., 1926-35, prof. of graphic arts and head dept. of printing since 1935; consulting psychologist, Pittsburgh Rys. Co. since 1935. Fellow Am. Assn. of Applied Psychologists; mem. Am. Psychol. Assn., Am. Assn. of University Professors, Pittsburgh Personnel Assn., National Graphic Arts Edn. Guild, Phi Kappa Phi, Epsilon Pi Tau. Methodist. Mason. Contbr. numerous articles on psychological measurement and industrial selection to tech. jours. Asso. editor, Graphic Arts Education Magazine. Home: 1417 Morningside Av. Office: Carnegie Inst. of Technology, Pittsburgh, Pa.

CLELAND, Charles S., clergyman; b. Owatonna, Minn., Dec. 17, 1863; s. William J. and Judith A. (Wilson) C.; A.B., Monmouth (Ill.) Coll., 1887; grad. Xenia (Ohio) Theol. Sem., 1890; D.D., Cooper Coll., Sterling, Kan., 1906; m. Edith Elinor Collins, May 14, 1891; children—Ralph Erskine, David Collins, James Wallace, Helen. Ordained ministry U.P. Ch., 1890; pastor Le Claire Prairie, Ia., 1890-94, 2d Ch., Phila., 1894-1935, now pastor emeritus; recording sec. Bd. of Foreign Missions U.P. Ch. of N.A. since 1896. Was mem. War Time Com. of Inter Ch. Federation of Phila.; mem. Nat. Service Commn. U.P. Ch.; moderator, Gen. Assembly, U.P. Ch., 1932-33. Home: 802 N. 17th St., Philadelphia, Pa.

CLELAND, William Erskine, prof. mathematics; b. Chicago, Ill., Sept. 7, 1891; s. John Wilson and Elizabeth (Scott) C.; student U. of Pittsburgh, 1908-10, M.A., 1917; B.A., Westminster Coll., New Wilmington, Pa., 1913; Ph.D., Princeton U., 1923; m. Janet Crawford, June 30, 1926; children—Janet Barbara, Mary Elizabeth. Teacher pub. schs., 1913-16; prof. mathematics, Waynesburg (Pa.) Coll., 1917-18; instr. mathematics, U. of Pittsburgh, 1918-20, Princeton U., 1920-22; prof. mathematics, Geneva Coll., Beaver Falls, Pa., since 1923. Dir. Boys Industrial Home, Oakdale, Pa. Fellow A.A.A.S.; mem. Am. Math. Assn. Republican. United Presbyterian. Club: Rotary (Beaver Falls, Pa.). Home: 3021 Sixth Av., Beaver Falls, Pa.

CLEMEN, Rudolf Alexander, coll. prof.; b. Halifax, N.S., June 11, 1893; s. Leopold and Harriet Byron (Taylor) C.; A.B., Dalhousie U., 1913; M.A., Harvard, 1915, Ph.D., 1926; m. Margaret May Jones, Dec. 29, 1923; children—Arthur Taylor, Rudolf Alexander. Instr. history and economics, Purdue U., 1917-18, Northwestern U., 1918-21; sec. to pres. Northwestern U. 1918-19; asso. editor The National Provisioner, 1921-23; economist Ill. Merchants Trust Co., 1923-26; asso. dir. Armour & Co.'s Livestock Bur., 1926-30; asso. chief Social Science, Century of Progress Expn., 1930-32; pres. Whitman Coll., Walla Walla, Wash., 1934-36; lecturer economics and business, Univ. of Wash., 1936; prof. economics, Grad. Sch., Am. Univ. since 1937. Mem. Am. Econ. Assn., Am. Hist. Assn., Am. Polit. Science Assn., Am. Assn. Univ. Profs. Conglist. Clubs: Cosmos (Washington, D.C.); University (Evanston, Ill.). Author: American Livestock and Meat Industry, 1923; By Products in the Packing Industry, 1927. Editor of Century of Progress Series. Contbr. Ency. of Social Sciences and Dictionary of Am. Biography. Home: 127 Brookside Drive, Chevy Chase, Md. Office: Graduate School, American University, Washington, D.C.

CLEMENT, John Kay, army officer; b. Sunbury, Pa., Nov. 5, 1880; s. Gen. Charles Maxwell and Alice (Withington) C.; B.S., Trinity Coll., 1900; Ph.D., U. of Göettingen, Germany, 1904; m. Isabel Colvin, Oct. 1, 1906; children—Charles Maxwell, Elizabeth Colvin. Began as asst., Geophys. Lab., Carnegie Instn., Washington, D.C., 1904-07; asst. physicist, Technol. Branch, U.S. Geol. Survey, 1907-10; physicist, U.S. Bur. Mines, 1910-17; maj. Ordnance Dept., U.S.A., 1920, lt. col. since 1935. Served as musician and corpl. 12th regt. Pa. Inf., U.S. Vols., Spanish-Am. War, 1898; maj. 111th Inf. 1917-18; maj. Ordnance Res. U.S.A., 1918, lt. col. Ordnance Dept. 1919. Mem. Am. Chem. Soc., Washington Acad. Seis., Delta Psi. Episcopalian. Clubs: St. Anthony (New York); Army and Navy (Washington). Home: 169 Orange Rd., Montclair, N.J. Office: 90 Church St., New York, N.Y.

CLEMENT, John Stokes, pres. Sandura Co., Inc.; b. Whiteford, Md., Oct. 27, 1883; s. Samuel and Eliza G. (Stokes) C.; student pub. schs. and George Sch.; A.B., Swarthmore Coll., 1908; m. Ada C. Graham, Oct. 27, 1909. Gen. sales agent Waltona Works, Inc., 1920-24; pres. Sandura Co., Inc., successors, since 1924; dir. various other companies. Home: 301 Meetinghouse Road, Jenkintown, Pa. Office: 1428 S. Penn Square, Philadelphia, Pa.

CLEMENT, Lewis Mason, research engring.; b. Oakland, Calif., Jan. 25, 1892; s. Russell Montague and E. Eugenia (Freeman) C.; B.S. in E.E., U. of Calif., Berkeley, Calif., 1914; m. Vesta L. Lynde, Nov. 12, 1917; children—Virginia Mason, Lauré Jean. Employed as shift engr. Marconi Co., Honolulu, T.H., 1914-16; engr. Western Electric Co. and Bell Telephone Labs., 1916-25; chief engr. F. A. D'Andrea Co., 1925-28; v.p. and chief engr. Kolsler Radio, 1928-30; asst. mgr. radio dept., Westinghouse Electric & Mfg. Co., 1930-31; European chief engr., Internat. Telephone & Telegraph Co., 1931-35; v.p. in charge research and engring. RCA Mfg. Co., Camden, N.J., since 1935. Fellow Inst. of Radio Engrs., Radio Club of America; mem. Franklin Inst. Republican. Mason. Clubs: Penn Athletic (Phila.); Aronimick Golf (Newtown Square, Pa.). Connected with radio engring. and development in U.S. and abroad in operating, research, development and engring. fields since 1910, in amateur field since 1905. Home: 104 Kenilworth Apt., Alden Park, Philadelphia, Pa. Office: Camden, N.J.

CLEMENT, Martin Withington, ry. pres.; b. Sunbury, Pa., Dec. 5, 1881; s. Charles Maxwell and Alice Virginia (Withington) C.; B.S., Trinity Coll., Hartford, Conn., 1901; D.Sc., Dickinson Coll., Carlisle, Pa., 1935; LL.D., Lafayette College, Easton, Pa., 1936, Wesleyan U., Middletown, Conn., 1937, U. of Pa., 1937; m. Irene Harrison Higbee, April 14, 1910 (now deceased); children—Harrison H., Alice W., James H.; m. 2d, Elizabeth S. Wallace, Feb. 14, 1931. With Pa. R.R. since 1901, successively rodman, assistant supervisor, supervisor, div. engr., supt., supt. freight transportation, supt. passenger transportation, gen. supt., gen. mgr., asst. vice-pres. operation, until 1926, vice-pres. operation, 1926-35, dir. since 1929, pres. since 1935; pres. various and subsidiary cos. of Pa. R.R.; pres. Chicago Union Sta. Co., Washington Terminal Co. (alternating); dir. Western Union Telegraph Co., N.&W. Ry. and Subsidiaries, N.Y. Connecting Ry. Co., Richmond, Fredericksburg & Potomac R.R. Co., Ins. Co. of N. America and affiliates. Member board directors Association American Railroads; member board managers Girard Trust Company, Philadelphia Saving Fund Society, Hospital of Univ. of Pa.; trustee Trinity Coll. Mem. S.A.R., Soc. War of 1812, Baronial Order of Runnymede, Colonial Soc. of Pa., Neucomen Soc. Republican. Episcopalian (vestryman Ch. of the Redeemer, Bryn Mawr, Pa.). Clubs: Union League, Rittenhouse, Philadelphia (Phila.); Merion Cricket (Haverford, Pa.). Home: Rosemont, Pa. Office: Broad Street Station Bldg., Philadelphia, Pa.

CLEMENT, Ray Allan, high sch. prin.; b. Derry, N.H., June 17, 1887; s. Walter Smith and Martha Ann (Langmaid) C.; A.B., Bates Coll., Lewiston, Me., 1912; A.M., Columbia U., 1923; student Cornell U., 1913-14, N.Y. Univ., 1928-29; m. Gwendolyn A. Kent, Aug. 21, 1920; children—Martha Ann, Robert Herrick, Susan Noble. Instr. Latin and Greek, Pennington Sch., 1912-13; instr. German, Cascadilla Sch., 1913-14, The Hill Sch., 1914-15, high sch. Morristown, N.J., 1915-18; prin. high sch., Southbridge, Mass., 1918-22; prin. high sch., Cranford, N.J., since 1922. Mem. Nat. Edn. Assn., N.J. High Sch. Prins. Assn. (past pres.), N.J. State Teachers Assn., Phi Beta Kappa, Phi Delta Kappa. Republican. Presbyn. Mason. Club: Rotary of Cranford (past pres.), Cranford Dramatic. Home: 8 Hamilton Av., Cranford, N.J.

CLEMENTS, Guy Roger, coll. prof.; b. Ravenna, O., Mar. 5, 1885; s. Clifford Warren and Fannie (Gross) C.; A.B., Hiram Coll., Hiram, O., 1905; A.M., U. of Chicago, 1907; Ph.D., Harvard U., 1913; m. Mildred Morrison, June 27, 1911; 1 son, Guy Morrison. Instr. mathematics, Williams Coll., Williamstown, Mass., 1907-09, Harvard U., 1908-10; substitute prof. pure mathematics, U. of N.C., 1910-11; instr. mathematics, U. of Wis. 1911-17; instr. mathematics, U.S. Naval Acad., Annapolis, Md., 1917-19, asst. prof., 1919-20, asso. prof., 1920-27, prof. since 1927. Dir. Westminster Foundation for Annapolis. Mem. Am. Math. Soc., Math. Assn. of America, Soc. for Promotion Engring. Edn., Sigma Xi. Republican. Presbyn. Author: Problems in the Mathematical Theory of Investment, 1916. Co-author: (with L. T. Wilson), Theoretical and Applied Mechanics, 1935; (with L. T. Wilson), Manual of Mathematics and Mechanics, 1937. Contbr. to math. publs. Home: 7 Thompson St., Annapolis, Md.

CLEMENTS, Rex Stowers, minister; b. Ogdensburg, N.Y., Aug. 13, 1903; s. Henry G. and Anna (Stowers) C.; A.B., Colgate U., Hamilton, N.Y., 1926; B.D., Yale, 1929; Ph.D., Edinburgh U., 1931; m. Marian K. Hutchison, June 29, 1933; children—Richard Hutchison, Rex Stowers. Ordained to the ministry of Presbyn. Ch., 1929; asst. minister Fifth Av. Ch., New York, N.Y., 1931-32; minister Ch. of the Covenant, Boston, Mass., 1932-37; minister Bryn Mawr (Pa.) Presbyn. Ch. since May 1937. Dir. Haverford Coll.; trustee Beaver Coll. Mem. The Cleric, Sigma Nu, Phi Beta Kappa, Delta Sigma Rho. Clubs: Merion Cricket (Haverford, Pa.); Gulph Mills Golf. Address: Bryn Mawr, Pa.

CLEMMER, Leon; prof. clin. obstetrics, Hahnemann Med. Coll.; sr. obstetrician and clin. asst. in Out-Patient Dept., Hahnemann Hosp. Address: 250 S. 18th St., Philadelphia, Pa.

CLENDENIN, J.; editor Huntington Herald-Dispatch. Address: Huntington Pub. Co., Huntington, W.Va.

CLEPHANE, Walter Collins, lawyer; b. West Haven, Conn., July 17, 1867; s. Lewis and Annie M. (Collins) C.; LL.B., George Washington University, 1889, LL.M., 1890, LL.D. from the same university, 1932; m. Nellie Mathilda Walker, Jan. 20, 1896; children—Beatrice A., Douglas W., John W. Clk. in wholesale store, New York, 1884; stenographer, Pa. R.R. Co., 1885-87; court stenographer, Washington, D.C., 1887-89; in practice of law at Washington since 1889; mem. Clephane, Latimer & Hall; became prof. law, George Washington University, 1897, now emeritus; director and member executive committee National Savings & Trust Co.; dir. Va. Brick Co. Judge adv. U.S.A., 1918-20; col. judge adv., O.R.C., since 1924. Ex-pres. bd. trustees Industrial Home Sch., D.C. Mem. Am. and D.C. bar assns., Columbia Hist. Soc., Order of Coif, Phi Delta Phi. Republican. Presbyn. (pres. bd. of trustees New York Av. Presbyn. Ch.). Clubs: Cosmos (Washington); Chevy Chase (Md.). Author: Clephane on Organization and Management of Business Corpns., 1905; Clephane on Equity Pleading and Practice, 1926. Home: 6000 Connecticut Av., Chevy Chase, Md. Office: Investment Bldg., Washington, D.C.

CLERF, Louis H.; prof. laryngology and bronchoscopy, Jefferson Med. Coll.; bronchoscopist Jewish, St. Joseph's, Pennsylvania and Germantown hosps. Address: 1530 Locust St., and 128 S. 10th St., Philadelphia, Pa.

CLEVELAND, Arthur, prof. of English; b. Phila., Pa., Feb. 18, 1883; s. Samuel McCoskry and Julia (Conover) C.; grad. Wm. S. Blight Jr. Sch (private prep. sch.), Phila., 1900; A.B., U. of Pa., 1904, A.M., 1905, Ph.D., 1906; m. Alverta Killen, Apr. 26, 1916; children—Elaine Louise, Samuel Mortimer. Asst. in dept. of English, U. of Pa., 1908-09, instr. of English, 1909-10; independent literary and journalistic work, Phila., 1910-17, 1919-24; asst. prof. of English, Temple U., 1924-26; prof. of English since 1926. In Employment Service, Dept. of Labor, U.S.A., during World War. Mem. Am. Assn. Univ. Profs., Pa. State Edn. Assn., Phi Beta Kappa. Home: 205 Upland Rd., Merion, Pa. Office: Temple University, Philadelphia, Pa.

CLEVEN, Nels Andrew Nelson, prof. of history; b. Lake Mills, Ia., Dec. 21, 1874; s. Nels Grovum and Turina (Sanders) C.; Ph.B. and Ed.B., U. of Chicago, 1906; Ph.D., U. of Munich, 1913; also student U. of Berlin, U. of Paris, U. of Grenoble, U. of Bonn, U. of Calif., Columbia; m. Hilma A. Willd, June 8, 1912. Taught in pub. schs., 1894-1918; asst. prof. history and politics, U. of Ark., 1919-21; with U. of Pittsburgh since 1921, prof. of history since 1927; visiting prof. history, U. of W.Va., summer 1929, George Washington U., summer 1932. Current history asso. Current History Mag., 1928-29; research asso. in history in Bolivia for Carnegie Instn. of Washington, 1930-31. Research asst. Bur. of Research, War Trade Bd., Washington, 1918-19. Official del. of U. of Pittsburgh to Hist. Congress of Rio, 1922, to Bolivarian Congress of Panama, 1926, Congress of Hist. Sciences, Oslo, 1928, 7th Am. Scientific Congress, Mexico City, 1935. Founder Phi Alpha Theta (nat. hon. history fraternity), permanent hon. pres. Mem. Am. Hist. Assn., Hist. Assn. of Pa., Academia de Historia de Cuba, Academia de Historia de Venezuela, Academia de Artes y Sciencias de Cadiz, Hispanic Am. Hist. Conf., Inter-Am. Hist. Commn., Hispanic Soc. of America, Delta Sigma Pi, Delta Sigma Phi, Pi Gamma Mu, Square and Compass, Scabbard and Blade. Mason. Clubs: Hungry (Pittsburgh), Civic (Allegheny County). Translator: Simon Bolivar: An Introduction to a Study of His Political Ideals, 1930. Lecturer and writer. Author: Readings in Hispanic American History, 1927; The Political Organization of Bolivia, 1939. Home: 4303 Andover Terrace, Pittsburgh, Pa.

CLEVENGER, William M.; mem. law firm W. M. & T. R. Clevenger. Address: 17 S. Stenton Pl., Atlantic City, N.J.

CLEWELL, Clarence Edward; prof. elec. engring., dir. U. Placement Service and Student Aid Dept., U. of Pa. Address: U. of Pennsylvania, Philadelphia, Pa.

CLIFT, John William, newspaper pub.; b. Nyack, N.Y., Dec. 5, 1856; s. John A. and Margaret C.; ed. public schools of Morristown, N.J.; m. Mary H. Class, Oct. 30, 1878; 1 son, Fred W. Began in newspaper business, 1872; pub. Madison (N.J.) Eagle, 1883-94, Morristown (N.J.) Chronicle, 1894-96, Summit (N.J.) Herald, 1896-1939. Mem. N.J. Assembly, 1922-28. Sec. N.J. Press Assn., 1909-30. Address: 35 De Forest Av., Summit, N.J.

CLIMENHAGA, Asa W., coll. dean; b. Grantham, Pa., July 1, 1889; s. Peter Martin and Anna Elizabeth (Winger) C.; student John Fletcher Coll., University Park, Ia., 1910-12, Messiah Bible Coll., Grantham, Pa., 1912-16, U. of Pa., summer 1920, Columbia U., summer 1921, Wittenberg Coll., summers of 1937, 1938, 1939; A.B. Taylor U., Upland, Ind., 1919; M.A. in Religious Edn., 1923 and Ph.D., 1925, Potomac, Washington, D.C.; M.A. in Edn., Wittenberg Coll., Springfield, O., 1939; m. Anna Elizabeth Kipe, July 30, 1919. Ordained to ministry, Brethren in Christ Ch., 1915, field sec. in interest higher edn., 1916-18, dir. religious edn., 1920-36; instr. and dir. religious edn., Messiah Bible Coll., Grantham, Pa., 1925-28, dean and registrar since 1928; mem. ednl. commn., Internat. Council of Religious Edn., Chicago, 1932-36; instr. religious edn., summer training camps, Rhodes Grove and Mt. Olivet, Pa., 1933-36; dir. extension classes, Messiah Bible Coll., Grantham, Pa., 1925-39. Mem. Nat. Assn. Teachers of Speech, Am. Assn. Collegiate Registrars. Brethren in Christ. Speaker on variety of occasions to many different groups. Address: Grantham, Pa.

CLINCHY, Everett Ross, clergyman; b. N.Y. City, Dec. 16, 1896; s. James Hugh and Lydie (Stagg) C.; student Wesleyan U., Middletown, Conn., 1916-18; B.S., Lafayette Coll., Easton, Pa., 1920; grad. study, Union Theol. Sem., 1920-21, Yale Grad. Sch., 1922-23; M.A., Columbia, 1921; Ph.D. in Edn., Drew U., 1934, teaching fellow at same univ. since 1934; m. Winifred Marcena Mead, Sept. 21, 1918; children—Everett Ross, Eleanor Marcena, Barbara Rex. Ordained Presbyn. ministry, 1921; pastor Fairmount (N.J.) Presbyn. Ch., 1921-23, Ch. of Christ, Wesleyan U., Middletown, 1923-28; sec. Federal Council Chs. of Christ in America, 1928-33; dir. Nat. Conf. Christians and Jews since 1928. Originated "Seminar," confs. for study Catholic-Protestant-Jewish relations; directed Williamstown Inst. of Human Relations, summers 1935, 37, 39. Second lt. F.A., U.S.A., World War. Member American Sociological Society, American Academy Polit. Science, Alpha Delta Phi. Clubs: City (New York); Canoe Brook Country. Author: All in the Name of God, 1934. Contbr. to religious and ednl. publs. Home: 46 Prospect St., Madison, N.J. Office: 300 Fourth Av., New York, N.Y.

CLINE, Thomas L.; Graeff prof. of English, Gettysburg Coll. Address: 135 Carlisle St., Gettysburg, Pa.

CLINE, William Preston, clergyman; b. Lexington, N.C., Oct. 20, 1890; s. William Pinckney and Julia Catherine (Bost) C.; A.B., Lenojr Rhyne Coll., Hickory, N.C., 1906; A.B., U. of N.C., Chapel Hill, N.C., 1912; A.M., U. of S.C., Columbia, 1914; B.D., Luth. Theol. Sem., Columbia, S.C., 1915; (hon.) D.D., Lenoir Rhyne Coll., 1931; m. Eva Barbara Schirmacher, Nov. 2, 1918; children—William Edward, Eva Catherine, Carolyn Christine. Ordained to ministry Luth. Ch., 1915; pastor, Birmingham, Ala., 1915-18, 1919-23, Fairmont, W.Va. 1923-34; pastor, Trinity Luth. Ch., Charleston, W. Va., since 1934. Served as camp pastor, Camp Johnston, Fla., and Camp Jackson, S.C., 1918-19; chaplain with rank of maj., W.Va. N.G. since 1928. Chaplain W.Va. Ho. of Dels., 1939. Pres. Luth. Synod of W.Va., 1927-30, W.Va. Council of Chs. since 1938. Sec. Christian Edn., Luth. Synod of W.Va. since 1933. Mem. Charleston Area Council, Boy Scouts of America since 1937, chmn. com. on leadership training since 1938. Dir. Nat. Luth. Home for Aged, Washington, D.C., since 1931. Democrat. Lutheran. Club: Lions of Charleston. Home: 1596 Lee St., Charleston, W.Va.

CLINGER, William Floyd, oil producer; b. Warren Co., Pa., Apr. 1, 1891; s. John Burt and Cora M. (Archer) C.; B.S. in Economics, U. of Pa., 1914; m. Lella May Hunter, June 30, 1917; children—Dorothy Hunter, Elizabeth Hunter, William Floyd. Owner and pub. Tidioute News, 1915-16; editor, pub. and treas. Warren (Pa.) Evening Mirror, 1916-21; oil producer since 1922; v.p. and treas. Superior Refining Co.; dir. Warren Bank & Trust Co.; partner Clinger Oil & Gas Co.; v.p. and treas. Superior Oil Works. Pres. bd. dirs. Warren Sch. Dist. Mem. Pa. Grade Crude Oil Assn. (pres. 1938), Am. Petroleum Inst. (dir.), Pa. Sch. Dirs. Assn. (dir.), Kappa Sigma. Republican. Presbyterian. Clubs: Conewango (Warren, Pa.); Pennsylvania Soc. (New York). Home: 316 Conewango Av. Address: Warren, Pa.

CLINTON, James B.; mem. surg. staff Cook Hosp. Address: 320 Jefferson St., Fairmount, W.Va.

CLIPMAN, William Henry, asso. judge; b. Phila., Pa., Aug. 2, 1863; s. William H. and Rebecca (Duffy) C.; A.B., Bucknell U., Lewisburg, Pa., 1888, A.M., 1891; m. Anna E. Brown, June 27, 1889 (died 1935); children—Kathryn R. (Mrs. Gay), Margaret G. (Mrs. Wentzel), William H., Gertrude C. (Mrs. Wolfe). Ordained to ministry Presbyn. Ch., 1890; served pastorates at Brockway, Pa., Johnstown, Pa., Mifflinburg, Pa., and McAlisterville, Pa.; honorably retired, 1936; has served as commr. to both Synod and Gen. Assembly, and continues to supply vacant pulpits as time permits. Served in ambulance and ednl. work with U.S. Army in England and France, 1918-19. Elected asso. judge of 17th Judicial Dist. of Pa. for term 1936-42. Mem. Hist. Soc. of Pa., Patriotic Order Sons of America, Am. Legion. Republican. Presbyterian. Mason. Home: 50 Brown St., Lewisburg, Pa.

CLIPPINGER, Richard D., physician; b. Toledo, O., Aug. 21, 1870; s. Samuel and Lucinda Ann (Cookston) C.; A.B., Kenyon Coll., Gambier, O., 1895; M.D., U. of Mich. Med. Sch., 1902; m. Anna McElheney, June 5, 1908; children—Robert Samuel, Richard Frederick, Londa Ann. Interne U. of Mich. Hosp., 1901-02; engaged in practice at Vineland, N.J., since 1918, practice limited to diseases of the eye since 1920; sec. and treas. N.J. Dehydrating Co., Vineland, since 1936. Served as 1st lt. Med. Corps during World War. Mem. N.J. State Med. Soc., Cumberland County Med. Soc., Phi Beta Kappa. Baptist. Mason. Home: 220 S. West Av. Office: 606 Landis Av., Vineland, N.J.

CLOAK, Andrew Bert, pres. Freedom Nat. Bank; b. Cowansville, Pa., Sept. 26, 1878; s. Simon and Isabella (Helm) C.; student Grove City (Pa.) Coll., 1898-99; M.D., U. of Pittsburgh, 1904; m. Edna Bell Purdue, Aug. 9, 1905; children—Lilly Bell, Sara Mae. Mem. surg. staff Rochester (Pa.) Gen. Hosp. since 1906; mem. urol. staff Providence Hosp., Beaver Falls, Pa., since 1922, Beaver Valley (Pa.) Gen. Hosp. since 1923; chief of staff Rochester (Pa.) Gen. Hosp., 1914-29; pres. Freedom (Pa.) Nat. Bank since 1936. Republican. Protestant. Club: Beaver Valley (Pa.) Country. Home: 511 Third Av., Freedom, Pa. Office: 262 Connecticut Av., Rochester, Pa.

CLOAK, Frank V. C.; bishop Reformed Episcopal Ch. Address: 244 S. Melville St., Philadelphia, Pa.

CLOETINGH, Arthur Charles, dir. dramatics; b. Muskegon, Mich., Dec. 26, 1895; s. Peter Leonard and Janet (Berkel) C.; A.B., Hope Coll., Holland, Mich., 1916; M.A., U. of N.D., Grand Forks, N.D., 1917; m. Evelyn Keppel, Aug. 24, 1923 (died Oct. 18, 1928); 1 son, Arthur Keppel; m. 2d, Esther Holmes, Aug. 9, 1930; 1 dau., Jean Ellen. Prof. of speech, Adrian (Mich.) Coll., 1917-18; teacher of English, Mt. Vernon (O.) High Sch., 1918-19; dir. and prof. dramatics, Pa. State Coll., since 1919. Mem. Omicron Kappa Epsilon, Theta Alpha Phi (nat. sec.-treas. since 1929), Am. Ednl. Theater Assn., Nat. Theater Conf., Nat. Assn. of Teachers of Speech. Presbyterian. Address: 717 W. Foster Av., State College, Pa.

CLOONAN, John Joseph, clergyman; b. Hancock, N.Y., Mar. 24, 1881; s. Michael and Mary Martha (Warner) C.; grad. high sch., Hancock, 1895; student Niagara University, 1897-1900, St. Vincent's Sem., Germantown, Pa., 1900-02; S.T.B., Gregorian Univ., Rome, 1905; S.T.D., Univ. of Rome, 1925. LL.D. from Niagara U., 1927. Joined Congregation of the Mission, Lazarist Fathers, 1900; ordained priest R.C. Ch., 1904; prof. English, Niagara U., 1905-06; asst. rector Ch. of Immaculate Conception, Germantown, 1906-08; treas., later v.p., St. John's Coll., Brooklyn, N.Y., 1908-24; pres., 1925-31; also pres. St. John's Theol. Sem., Brooklyn, Sept. 1925-31; pastor St. Vincent's Ch., Germantown, Pa., 1931-33; treas. St. Joseph's Coll., Princeton, 1933-36; treas. Vincentian Mission House, Bangor, Pa., since 1936. Author: History of the Miraculous Medal, 1916. Address: Vincentian Mission House, Bangor, Pa,

CLOOS, Wilmot David, cement mfr.; b. Tioga Co., Pa., Aug. 13, 1888; s. Luther Newberry and Cora Lynn (Hazlett) C.; grad. Mansfield (Pa.) State Teachers Coll., 1907; C.E., Miss. State Coll., Starkville, Miss., 1909; m. Hedwig Elizabeth Brautigam, Apr. 7, 1931. Began as eng. clk., Am. Bridge Co., Ambridge, Pa., 1909; teacher of athletics and business, East Greenwich (R.I.) Acad. and Oswego (N.Y.) High Sch., 1910-11; chief clerk and accountant Western Electric Co., Boston, Mass. and New York, N.Y. 1911-14; accountant and traveling auditor, Underwood Typewriter Co., New York, 1914-15; sec.-treas. Lima (O.) Locomotive Works, 1915-18; v.p. and gen. mgr. Edison Cement Corpn., Metropolitan Cement Corpn., New York, since 1918; v.p. Thomas Edison, Inc., since 1927. Democrat. Methodist. Home: Route 1, Lake Ariel, Pa. Office: 444 Madison Av., New York, N.Y.

CLOSE, Ralph, elec. coil mfr.; b. Millersburg, O., Oct. 2, 1883; s. Harvey and Laura Inez (Parkinson) C.; student high sch. Millersburg, O., O. State U., Columbus, O., 1903-04, Bliss Business Coll., Columbus, O.; m. Sarah Harris, June, 1915; m. 2d, Ethel Lenore Wilhelm, Aug. 26, 1927; children—Ruth Inez, Ralph Winton, Lois Virginia. In employ Jeffrey Mfg. Co., Columbus, O., 1904-18; pres. Pa. Electric Coil Corpn., mfrs. electric coils, Pittsburgh, since 1918; pres. Close Distributing Co., wholesale elec. insulating materials, since 1921. Republican. United Presbyterian (trustee Beverly Heights Ch.). Club: Chartiers Heights Country (pres.). Home: 24 Lebanon Hills Drive, Mt. Lebanon, Pa. Office: 1301 Saw Mill Run Boul., Pittsburgh, Pa.

CLOTHIER, Isaac Hallowell, Jr., business exec.; b. Sharon Hill, Pa., Nov. 12, 1875; s. Isaac Hallowell and Mary Clapp (Jackson) C.; student Swarthmore (Pa.) Coll.; m. Melinda K. Annear, Jan. 7, 1903; children—Isaac Hollowell III, Mrs. Herman K. Grange. With Strawbridge & Clothier, Phila., since 1896, partner, 1903, v.p. since 1922; dir. Provident Mutual Life Ins. Co. Chmn. of bd. Williamson Free Sch. of Mech. Trades; trustee Swarthmore (Pa.) Coll.; dir. Grandom Inst. Clubs: Racquet (Phila.); Radnor Hunt, Gulph Mills. Home: Radnor, Pa. Office: 801 Market St., Philadelphia, Pa.

CLOTHIER, Morris Lewis, merchant; b. Phila., July 24, 1868; s. Isaac Hallowell and Mary Clapp (Jackson) C.; B.S., Swarthmore Coll., 1890; hon. A.M., U. of Pa., 1910; LL.D., Villa Nova, 1912, and Pa. Coll., 1919, Fafayette, 1920, Swarthmore, 1921, Ursinus, Franklin and Marshall, Washington colleges, 1923; Litt.D., Pa. Military Coll., Chester, Pa., 1926; L.H.D., Dickinson College, 1937; m. Lydia May Earnshaw, April 26, 1900. Entered employ of Strawbridge & Clothier, June 30, 1890, admitted to partnership, 1895, sr. and mng. partner since 1903. Dir. Phila. Nat. Bank, United Gas Improvement Co., Penn. Mut. Life Ins. Co., Lehigh Valley R.. Co., Girard Trust Co. Member Pa. Commn. to St. Louis Expn., 1904; Rep. presdtl. elector at large for Pa., 1908. Trustee U. of Pa. Mem. Phi Kappa Psi, Phi Beta Kappa; hon. mem. sr. soc. Book and Key. Mem. Soc. of Friends. Mason (33°). Clubs: Rittenhouse, University, Art, Union League, Racquet (Phila.); University (New York). Home: Villa Nova, Pa. Office: 801 Market St., Philadelphia, Pa.*

CLOTHIER, Robert Clarkson, univ. pres.; b. Phila., Jan. 8, 1885; s. Clarkson and Agnes (Evans) C.; Haverford Sch., 1894-1903; Litt. B., Princeton, 1908, LL.D., 1932; LL.D., U. of Pittsburgh and Tusculum Coll., 1932, Dickinson Coll., 1933, New York Univ., 1935; Litt.D., Temple U., 1934; m. Nathalie Wilson, June 24, 1916; children—Agnes Evans, Arthur Wilson, Robert C. With Curtis Pub. Co., Phila., 1910-17, employment mgr., 1916-17; v.p. The Scott Co., Phila., 1918-23; asst. headmaster Haverford Sch., 1923-29; dean of men, U. of Pittsburgh, 1929-32; pres. Rutgers U. since 1932. Mem. Com. on Classification of Personnel, Washington, and A.E.F., World War; commd. lt. col. Trustee Haverford Sch., Princeton Univ., Baldwin Sch. Ind. Republican. Mem. Dutch Ref. Ch. Clubs: Century Assn., University (New York and Phila.). Author: Personnel Management (with Walter Dill Scott), 1923. Home: 185 College Av. Address: Rutgers Univ., New Brunswick, N.J.

CLOTHIER, William Jackson, coal mcht.; b. Sharon Hill, Pa., Sept. 27, 1881; s. Isaac Hallowell and Mary Clapp (Jackson) C.; A.B., Harvard, 1904; m. Anita Porter, Feb. 21, 1906. Pres. Boone County Coal Corpn. Clubs: Harvard, Racquet, Merion Cricket (Phila.); Pickering Hunt; Harvard (New York). Home: Valley Forge, Pa. Office: 1608 Walnut St., Philadelphia, Pa.*

CLOUD, Albert W.; attending surgeon Englewood Hosp. Address: 109 E. Palisade St., Englewood, N.J.

CLOUD, Samuel P.; pres. First Nat. Bank. Address: West Chester, Pa.

CLOUD, William Woodward, capitalist; b. Baltimore; s. Daniel and Maria Louisa (Woodward) C.; Baltimore City Coll., and Poly. Inst.; Law Sch., U. of Md.; m. Frances Dashiell, June 7, 1899. Jr. clerk Md. Savings Bank, 1885, and advanced through various positions, becoming pres., 1908-11; organized, 1911, and pres. to 1917, State Bank of Md.; pres. Taxicab Co., Yellow Cab Co.; formerly dir. Equitable Trust Co., Calvert Mortgage Co. (Baltimore). Formerly pres. Nat. Assn. Taxicab Owners; formerly gen. chmn. Baltimore Safety Council. Chmn. Ednl. Commn. Nat. Conf. Street and Highway Safety; mem. transportation and communication com., U.S. Chamber of Commerce; mem. Gov's. Commn. for Revising Motor Vehicle Laws of Md.; chmn. advisory com. Convention and Visitors Bureau; v.p. and dir. Baltimore Assn. Commerce. Democrat. Episcopalian. Clubs: Maryland, Merchants, Baltimore Country, Automobile of Md. (dir.). Home: 3 Hillside Rd., Roland Park, Baltimore. Office: 508 E. Preston St., Baltimore, Md.

CLOUGH, Paul Wiswall, physician; b. Portage, Wis., Sept. 27, 1882; s. Willoughby G. and Elsena (Wiswall) C.; B.S., U. of Wis., 1903; M.D., Johns Hopkins, 1907; m. Mildred Clark (M.D.), Sept. 5, 1916; children—Paul Clark, Eleanor Wiswall. Interne Johns Hopkins Hosp., 1907-08, asst. resident physician, 1908-13, resident physician, 1913-16; physician-in-charge, diagnostic clinic, since 1928; asst. instr. and asso. in medicine, Johns Hopkins U., 1909-16, asso. prof. of medicine, 1916-19; asso. in medicine, since 1919; asso. prof. of medicine, U. of Md., since 1922; visiting physician Johns Hopkins Hosp., Baltimore City Hosps.; private practice as physician, Baltimore. Fellow Am. Coll. Physicians; mem. A.M.A., Am. Soc. Clin. Investigation, Assn. Am. Physicians, Phi Beta Kappa, Alpha Omega Alpha, Sigma Xi. Author: Diseases of Blood, 1929; Practical Bacteriology, Hæmatology, Animal Parasitology (with E. R. Stett and Mildred C. Clough), 1938. Asst. editor of Annals of Internal Medicine. Home: 24 E. Eager St., Baltimore, Md.

CLOUTING, Elmer Sherman, M.D.; b. Cape May Co., N.J., May 14, 1872; s. George and Sarah (Willets) C.; M.D., Jefferson Med. Coll., Phila., 1896; m. Mary Porter, 1897; children —Reading Bertron, Charles Henry, George Sherman. Began as pub. sch. prin., N.J., 1890; with physiol. lab., Jefferson Med. Coll., Phila., 1896-98, asst. in neurological dept., 1907-08; committing chief, Phila. Gen. Hosp., since 1907; neurologist, St. Luke's and Children's Hosp., Phila., since 1935; consultant neuro-psychiatrist, Kenwood Sanitorium, Phila., since 1935. Mem. Phila., County and Pa. med. socs.; A.M.A. Republican. Address: 6008 Greene St., Philadelphia, Pa.

CLOVIS, Elijah Ellsworth, M.D.; b. Hebron, W.Va., Aug. 27, 1879; s. Amos and Martha Jane (Fleming) C.; M.D., Coll. Phys. and Surg., Baltimore, Md., 1905; m. Clara May McKnight, Jan. 1, 1904; children—Mildred, Madeline. Began practice at Hebron, 1905; organizer, 1912, and supt. State Tuberculosis Sanitarium, Hopemont, W.Va., to 1924. Med. dir. and v.p. Conservative Life Ins. Co., Wheeling, W.Va.; med. dir. Grand View Sanitorium, Moundsville, W.Va., since 1925; supt. Ohio County Tuberculosis Sanatorium. Fellow Am. Coll. Physicians, Am. Coll. of Chest Physicians, A.M.A.; mem. W.Va. Med. Assn., Ohio County Med. Soc. Republican. Methodist. Scottish Rite Mason (Shriner). Home: 56 Greenwood Av., Pleasant Valley. Office: Conservative Life Bldg., Wheeling, W.Va.

CLOVIS, James Robert, univ. prof.; b. Mt. Morris, Pa., Mar. 11, 1899; s. Mathias Benson and Agnes Loretta (Morris) C.; student Mt. Morris (Pa.) High Sch., 1912-16, Waynesburg (Pa.) Coll., 1917-19; B.S.C., Temple U., Phila., 1923; M.Sc., N.Y.U., 1936; m. Mildred Geraldine Harner, May 5, 1923; 1 son, James Robert. Alumni sec., Temple U., Phila., 1923-25, grad. mgr. of athletics and alumni sec., 1925-27; asso. prof., univ. extension div., Rutgers U., New Brunswick, N.J., 1927-35, sec. in charge, Newark Div., Univ. Coll., and asso. prof. since 1935. Mem. Rutgers U. Honor Soc., Blue Key Honorary Fraternity, Delta Sigma Phi. Republican. Methodist. Clubs: Raritan Arsenal Officers' (Metuchen, N.J.); Faculty (Rutgers U.); Varsity Letter (Waynesburg Coll.). Home: 312 N. 3d Av., Highland Park, N.J. Office: 37 Lincoln Av., Newark, N.J.

CLUSS, O. C., pres. O. C. Cluss Lumber Co.; b. St. Louis, Mo., Sep. 2, 1889; s. Otto E. and Jennie (Neihaus) C.; grad. McKinley High Sch., St. Louis, Mo., 1905-09; m. Helen Shields, Oct. 3, 1914; children—John, Jane, Helen, Charles. Lumber production in Mo. and Va., 1909-12; Phila. Bond; mgr. Kendall Lumber Co., Pittsburgh, 1913-17; pres. and gen. mgr. O. C. Cluss Lumber Co., Uniontown, Pa., since 1917; sec.-treas. Romesberg Store Co., Uniontown, Pa., since 1933. Republican. Episcopalian. Mason (32°, Shriner, Syria Mosque, Pittsburgh); Elk. Club: Uniontown (Pa.) Country. Home: 15 Eggleston St. Office: Uniontown, Pa.

CLUTZ, Frank H(ollinger), prof. civil engring.; b. Newville, Pa., June 29, 1873; s. Jacob A. and Liberty (Hollinger) C.; A.B., Midland Coll., Atchison, Kan., 1892; Ph.D., Johns Hopkins U., 1897; grad. study, U. of Kan., 1899-1900, U. of Wis., 1902; m. Mary Sara Baker, Apr. 30, 1903; children—John Jacob, Paul Alexander. Prof. mathematics, Carthage (Ill.) Coll., 1898-99; in employ Union Pacific R.R., 1900-02; engaged in structural engring. work, 1902-18; prof. civil engring., Gettysburg (Pa.) Coll. since 1918. Mem. A.A.A.S., Am. Concrete Inst., Soc. for Promotion Engring. Edn., Beta Theta Pi. Republican. Lutheran. Home: 159 Broadway, Gettysburg, Pa.

CLYDE, Arthur Wesley, agrl. engr.; b. Osage, Ia., Mar. 30, 1891; s. Jefferson Fern and Harriet (Wedgewood) C.; student Osage (Ia.) High Sch., 1905-09, Cedar Valley Sem., Osage, Ia., 1909-10; B.S., Ia. State Coll., Ames, Ia., 1915, M.S., 1931; m. Nellie Ruth Moe, Jan. 2, 1917; children—Robert Arthur, Dean Jefferson, Ruth. Salesman Internat. Harvester Co., Ft. Dodge, Ia., 1915-18; engr. Portland Cement Assn., Chicago, Ill., 1918-20; teacher agrl. engring., Ia. State Coll., Ames, Ia., 1920-31; rescarch engr., Pa. State Coll., since 1931. Mem. Am. Soc. Agrl. Engrs., Sigma Xi, Tau Beta Pi, Phi Kappa Phi, Delta Sigma Rho. Methodist. Author or co-author about 30 articles and bulls. on phases of engring. in agr. Now devotes nearly full time to research in farm power and machinery; built first apparatus in U.S. for accurate testing of soil tillage tools. Address: 204 Woodland Drive, State College, Pa.

COAD, Joseph Allan, banker, farmer, legislator; b. Cherryfields, St. Mary's Co., Md., Feb. 19, 1884; s. Joseph Edwin and Mary Ann (Allan) C.; educated at home, 1892-1900; m. Clara Hyatt, Nov. 22, 1917. Began in automobile and real estate business, Leonardtown, Md., 1915; farmer St. Mary's Co., Md., since 1937; pres. County Trust Co. of Md., Baltimore, since 1920; dir. Eastern Shore Trust Co., Montgomery Mutual Fire Ins. Co. Mem. Md. Ho. of Reps. from St. Mary's Co., 1919-26; State Senator since 1926 (re-elected 1930, 1934), chmn. Senate Finance Com. since 1935, Dem. floor leader since 1935; chmn. State Tercentenary Commn. since 1934. Mem. Bd. of trustees St. Mary's Sem., St. Mary's City, Md. Mem. Md. Tobacco Growers Assn. Democrat. Roman Catholic. Home: Leonardtown, St. Mary's Co., Md. Office: 701 Mercantile Trust Bldg., Baltimore, Md.

COAD, Oral Sumner, coll. prof.; b. Mt. Pleasant, Ia., Dec. 27, 1887; s. Laurel Evans and Sarah (Baldwin) C.; A.B., Knox Coll., Galesburg, Ill., 1909; A.M., Columbia U., 1911, Ph.D., 1917; m. Lucy Virginia Fitzwater, Dec. 29, 1915; 1 son, John Fitzwater. Engaged as instr. English, Ohio Wesleyan U., Delaware, 1911-14, Columbia U., 1916-23; asst. prof. English, N.J. Coll. for Women, New Brunswick, N.J., 1923-26, asso. prof., 1926-27, prof. since 1927, head of dept. since 1927. Mem. Modern Lang. Assn., Theatre Library Assn., Phi Beta Kappa. Presbyn. Author: William Dunlap: A Study of His Life and Works and of His Place in Contemporary Culture, 1917. Co-author (with Edwin Mims, Jr.), The American Stage, 1929. Contbr. articles on Am. drama and literature to various publs. Home: House R, Douglass Campus, New Brunswick, N.J.

COADY, Charles P., Jr., mem. law firm Coady & Farley. Address: 10 South St., Baltimore, Md.

COAKLEY, Thomas Francis, clergyman; b. Pittsburgh, Pa., Feb. 20, 1880; s. Thomas Francis and Agnes (Quinn) C.; A.B., Duquesne U., Pittsburgh, 1903; S.T.D., Am. Coll., Rome, 1908. Stenographer and pvt. sec. various corpns. until 1901; ordained ministry R.C. Ch., 1908; sec. to bishop of Pittsburgh, 1908-17; builder and administrator of De Paul Inst., Pittsburgh, largest pvt. oral sch. for deaf, costing $1,250,-000.00; builder and rector Sacred Heart Ch. (cost $2,000,000.00), Pittsburgh, since 1923. Chaplain 47th Inf., 4th Div., regular U.S. Army, World War, in France and Germany; asst. sr. chaplain Army of Occupation, Germany. Mem. U.S. Govt. Regional Labor Board, and Federal Housing Commn. Am. corr. Civilta Cattolica, Rome. Charter mem. Liturgical Arts Soc. Republican. Clubs: University, Long Vue. Author: Spiritism, the Modern Satanism, 1920; and many brochures and articles on religious ednl., architectural and artistic subjects in Am. and European mags.; lecturer on architecture, stained glass and ecclesiastical symbolism. Winner of 1st prize ($300) in internat. essay contest on the "Oxford Movement." Home: 6202 Alder St., Pittsburgh, Pa.*

COALE, James Johnson, clergyman; b. Arch Spring, Pa., May 25, 1879; s. Rev. James Johnson and Arabela (Parker) C.; B.S., Princeton, 1901; grad. Union Theol. Sem., 1905; m. Neilie Ansley Johnson, July 15, 1908; children—Virginia Bonham, James Johnson, III, Ansley Johnson. Ordained Presbyn. ministry, 1905; asst. minister Rutgers Ch., New York, 1904-06; pastor White Sulphur Springs, Mont., 1906-08, Belden Av. Ch., Chicago, 1909-11, Lackawanna, N.Y., 1912-17; exec. sec. Presbyn. Federated Council, of Baltimore, Md., 1917-24; supt. Ch. Extension Com., Presbyn. Union, Presbytery of Cleveland, 1924-27; asso. pastor and dir. student work, First Ch., Annapolis, Md., 1928-32, pastor since 1932; mem. staff council Presbyn. Bd. Nat. Missions, New York, 1922-27. Mason. Chautauqua lecturer. Writer of articles on social and religious topics in Yale Rev. and other periodicals. Home: Annapolis, Md.

COAR, Stanley F.; in gen. practice of law since 1915. Office: Mears Bldg., Scranton, Pa.

COATES, George Morrison, surgeon; b. Phila., Pa., Mar 24, 1874; s. Joseph Hornor and Elizabeth Gardner (Potts) C.; A.B., U. of Pa., 1894, M.D., 1897; m. Mildred Aspinwall Hodge, 1910; children—Elizabeth Gardner, George Woolsey. Resident phys. St. Christopher's Hosp. for Children, Phila., 1897; asst. surgeon U.S. Navy, Spanish-Am. War, 1898; res. phys. Pa. Hosp., 1899-1901; otolaryngologist Pa. Instn. for Blind, 1903-14; laryngologist Phipps Inst. Tuberculosis, 1906-10; asso. in laryngology, 1906, prof. otology since 1908, Phila. Polyclinic and Coll. for Grads. in Medicine; surgeon to ear, nose and throat, Pa. Hosp.; prof. oto-rhinology, U. of Pa. Grad. Sch. of Medicine since 1917, also prof. otolaryngology undergrad. dept., since 1933; surgeon in charge dept. of otolaryngology, Abington Memorial Hosp.; otolaryngologist to Presbyn. Hosp., Grad. Hosp.; chief dept. otolaryngology Univ. Hosp.; cons. otolaryngologist St. Agnes, Germantown, Sharon (Conn.), Lawrenceville Sch. hosps., U.S. Vets. Bur. Served as 1st lt., maj., lt. col., N.G. Pa., 1900-16; maj. and lt. col., World War; chief of sect. surgery of the head, base hosp., Camp Sevier, S.C., and Camp Hancock, Ga.; comdg. officer Base Hosp. No. 56, Allerey, France; then in charge otolaryngology and pres. Reclassification Bd., Embarkation Camp, Bordeaux, France, and surgeon to troops U.S. Transport Sierra; hon. discharged, May 24, 1919; col. M.O.R.C., 1923. Fellow Am. Coll. Surgeons, Coll. Physicians of Phila. (chmn. ear, nose and throat sect., 1928-30), Am. Laryngol., Otol. and Rhinol. Soc. (v.p. 1925, pres. 1937), Am. Laryngol. Assn. (pres. 1933-34), Am. Otol. Soc., Amer. Acad. Ophthalmology and Otolaryngology (pres. 1938), Am. Assn. Immunologists; mem. A.M.A. (chmn. ear, nose and throat section, 1927), Assn. Military Surgeons of U.S., Pathol. Soc. Phila., Med. Soc. State of Pa. (chmn. ear, nose and throat sect., 1921), Phila. County Med. Soc., Phila. Laryngol. Soc. (ex-pres.), Clin. Congress Surgeons of America (chmn. ear, nose and throat sect., 1921, 27, 36), Zoöl. Soc. Phila., Mil. Order Fgn. Wars, Am. Legion. Republican. Episcopalian. Clubs: University, Medical, Univ. Barge, Physicians' Motor, Union League. Editor-in-chief Archives of Otolaryngology. Address: 1721 Pine St., Philadelphia, Pa.

COATES, George Washington, banker; b. Beaver Falls, Pa., Feb. 21, 1886; s. George Washington and Grace (Reeves) C.; student Geneva Coll., Beaver Falls, Pa., 1900-03; B.S., Pa. Mil. Coll., Chester, Pa., 1907; student U. of Pa., 1907-09; m. Laura Hartzel, Jan. 4, 1916; children—Dorothy Jane, Grace Reeves (dec.). Chemist Crucible Steel Co. of America, Pittsburgh, 1910-11; cost dept. Townsend & Co., Fallston, Pa., 1911-12; automobile salesman, 1912-14; with John T. Reeves & Co., private bankers, Beaver Falls, since 1914, v.p. and cashier since 1929; dir. Community Loan Co., Hartzel Furniture Co.; treas. and dir. Columbia Bldg. and Loan Co. Mem. Delta Tau Beta (Pa. Mil. Coll.). Republican. Presbyterian. Mason (32°, Shriner, K.T.). Home: 1205 8th Av. Office: 1217 7th Av., Beaver Falls, Pa.

COBAU, William Duffy, lawyer; b. Ellwood City, Pa., July 4, 1903; s. Charles Duffy and Nettie (Clark) C.; student New Castle (Pa.) High Sch., 1916-20, U. of Pa., 1920-21; A.B., Amherst (Mass.) Coll., 1924; LL.B., U. of Pittsburgh, 1928; m. Sarah Mildred Weinschenk, July 12, 1928; children—Charles Duffy, William Weinschenk, John Reed. Admitted to Pa. bar, 1928, and since practiced at New Castle, Pa.; mem. firm Braham, Cobau & Berry, New Castle, 1934-36, Cobau & Berry, New Castle, since 1936. City solicitor, New Castle, since 1936. Mem. Pa. Bar Assn., Order of Coif, Beta Theta Pi, Phi Delta Phi. Republican. Presbyterian. Home: 317 Rhodes Pl. Office: 204 Johnson Bldg., New Castle, Pa.

COBB, Ebenezer Baker, clergyman; b. Auburn, N.Y., Oct. 23, 1855; s. Ebenezer Baker and Eleanor Matilda (Brownell) C.; A.B., Hamilton Coll., 1875, D.D., 1895; m. Helen Mills Starr, Aug. 11, 1886. Ordained Presbyn. ministry, 1880; pastor, Ramapo, N.Y., 1880-86, Second Ch., Elizabeth, N.J., 1886-1925, pastor emeritus since 1925. Treas. since 1890, also pres. trustees since 1895, Synod of N.J.; mem. Bd. of Foreign Missions, Presbyn. Ch., since 1903; pres. bd. trustees Bloomfield (N.J.) Theol. Sem., Presbyn. Home for Aged (Belvidere, N.J.); mem. bd. of founders Nanking (China) Univ. Mem. Soc. Mayflower Descendants. Home: Elizabeth, N.J. *

COBB, Stanwood, educator, author; b. Newton, Mass., Nov. 6, 1881; s. Darius and Laura Maria (Lillie) C.; A.B., Dartmouth, 1903 (valedictorian); A.M., Harvard, 1910; m. Ida Nayan Whitlam, 1919. Teacher Nautical Prep. Sch., 1904; instr. in English and Latin, Robert Coll., Constantinople, Turkey, 1907-10; pvt. teaching, Washington, D.C., 1910-12; touring Europe, Sargent's Travel Sch. for Boys, 1912-13; traveling tutor, 1913-14; head of English dept. St. John's Coll., Annapolis, Md., 1914-15, Asheville (N.C.) Sch. for Boys, 1915-16; instr. English and history, U.S. Naval Acad., 1916-19; founder, 1919, and prin. Chevy Chase Country Day School, founder, and dir., Mast Cove Camp, 1926. Founder, 1919, and chairman exec. com. Progressive Edn. Assn. (pres. 1927-30), Washington Lit. Soc. Clubs: Washington Arts, Cosmos, Authors, Harvard. Author: The Real Turk, 1914; Ayesha of the Bosphorus, 1915; The Essential Mysticism, 1918; Simla, a Tale in Verse, 1919; The New Leaven, 1928; The Wisdom of Wu Ming Fu, 1931; The Genius Within You, 1932; Security for a Failing World, 1934; New Horizons for the Child, 1934; Patterns in Jade of Wu Ming Fu, 1935; Character—A Sequence in Spiritual Psychology, 1938. Co-editor: World Order, 1935—; contbr. numerous articles to mags. Home: 17 Grafton St., Chevy Chase, Md.

COBERLY, Levi Wade, govt. official; b. Elkins, W.Va., Jan. 29, 1888; s. Christopher Columbus and Louisa (Gainer) C.; prep. edn., public schools, Randolph Co., W.Va.; student Davis and Elkins Coll., Elkins, W.Va., 1906-08, W.Va. U., 1909; m. Edna Blanche Pfau, Sept. 12, 1917; children—Willa Jean, Mary Louise. Teacher public schools of Randolph County, W. Va., 1906-11; fire and life ins. business, Elkins, W.Va., 1911-17; shipping agent W.Va. Coal & Coke Co., Elkins, W.Va., 1917-18; treas. and dir. Keystone Mfg. Co., lumber mfg., Elkins, W.Va., 1918-33; staff officer to supervisor, U.S. Forest Service, Monongahela Nat. Forest, 1933-34; project mgr. Tygart Valley Homesteads, Elkins, W.Va., U.S. Subsistence Homesteads and U.S. Resettlement Adminstrn., 1934-37; regional industrial advisor, Farm Security Adminstrn., U.S. Dept. of Agr., since 1937; sec.-treas. Central W.Va. Fire Protective Assn. Mem. Bd. of Edn., Elkins, W.Va., 1929-30; mayor City of Elkins, 1933-35. Active mem. Elkins Y.M.C.A. since 1912. Democrat. Methodist. Mason (K.T., Shriner). Club: Elkins Rotary (since 1924). Home: 128 Earle St., Elkins, W.Va. Office: Faircloth Hall, Raleigh, N.C.

COBHAM, James L.; attending surgeon Christ Hosp.; instr. surgery N.Y. Med. Coll. Address: 78 Brinkerhoff St., Jersey City, N.J.

COBLENTZ, Emory Lorenzo, lawyer, corpn. exec.; b. nr. Middletown, Md., Nov. 5, 1869; s. Edward Livingston and Lucinda F. (Bechtol) C.; grad. high sch., Middletown, Md.; studied law in the office of Charles W. Ross, of Frederick, Md.; LL.D., Franklin and Marshall College, 1926; m. Amy A. Douh, Sept. 26, 1893 (died Feb. 4, 1904); children—Mrs. Ruth Swank, Mrs. Naomi Winston, Esther Douh (Mrs. Frank C. Englesing), Miriam A. (Mrs. John C. Saur); m. 2d, Mary V. Kefauver, May 15, 1906; children—Mary Virginia, Helen O. Practiced at Frederick since 1897; organized and was pres. Potomac Edison Co., Frederick, Md., until 1923, now mem. board and exec. com.; v.p. and dir. Economy Silo and Mfg. Co.; dir. Ox Fibre Brush Co., Potomac Light & Power Co. (Martinsburg, W.Va.), South Penn Power Co. (Waynesboro, Pa.), Northern Virginia Power Co. (Winchester, Va.). Mem. Md. State Senate (chmn. com. on edn. and com. on revaluation and assessments), term 1930-34; mem. State Bd. of Edn., Md., 1924-36. Mem. Bd. State Aid and Charities, Md., 1912-16; v.p., dir. and chmn. finance com. Hood College (Frederick, Md.). Mem. Md. legislature, 1920, and majority floor leader of House; chmn. and dir. Md. Dept. of Welfare, 1922-24. Mem. Board Home Missions, Evang. and Reformed Ch., since 1917. Democrat. Mason (K.T.), Elk. Home: Middletown, Md. Office: Frederick, Md.

COBLENTZ, Leslie Ninian, lawyer; b. Middletown, Md., Sept. 15, 1895; s. Calvin R. and Lizzie (Brandenburg) C.; A.B., Heidelberg Coll., Tiffin, O., 1917; ed. U. of Md. Law Sch., 1918-20; m. Mary Helen Wyand, June 28, 1922; children—Janet Louise, Frances Elaine, Betty Ann. Admitted to Md. bar, 1920 and since engaged in gen. practice of law at Frederick; served as mem. bd. edn. for Frederick Co., 1926-36, pres. bd. 7 yrs.; dir. Potomac Edison Co. Served as pvt. to sergt. inf., U.S.A., 1918 and O.T.C. F.A., Camp Meade and Camp Zachary Taylor. Mem. Am. Legion. Democrat. Evang. and Ref. Ch. Club: Kiwanis of Frederick (past pres.). Home: Middletown. Office: 29 Court St., Frederick, Md.

COBLENTZ, Richard G.; asso. in neurosurgery, U. of Md.; visiting surgeon Church Home and Infirmary and Bon Secours, St. Agnes, St. Joseph's, Union Memorial and West Baltimore Gen hosps.; consulting surgeon Sydenham, Baltimore City, Presbyn. Eye, Ear and Throat Charity and Baltimore Eye, Ear and Throat Charity hosps. Address: Charles and Read Sts., Baltimore, Md.

COBURN, Fred L.; judge Third Judicial Circuit of Md., term expires 1953. Address: Havre de Grace, Md.

COBURN, Frederick Ward, mfg. exec.; b. Lowell, Mass., Aug. 9, 1879; s. Frank Fordyce and Mary (Ward) C.; S.B., Mass. Inst. Tech., 1901; m. Edith Cheney, Oct. 5, 1903; children—Fordyce, Frederick Ward, Sally. Supt. of Bessemer Mill, Md. Steel Co., Sparrows Point, Md., 1904-07; asst. supt. Toledo (O.) Furnace Co.,

1908-12; supt. Ella Furnace Co., West Middlesex, Pa., 1912-14, Perry Iron Co., Erie, Pa., 1914-23; v.p., gen. mgr. and dir., E. & G. Brooke Iron Co., Birdsboro, Pa., since 1924. Republican. Episcopalian. Mason. Clubs: Raquet (Phila.); Reading (Pa.) Country. Home: 140 N. Spruce St. Office: Birdsboro, Pa.

COCHRAN, George G.; pres. Cochran Coal & Coke Co.; also officer or dir. many other companies. Address: Dawson, Pa.

COCHRAN, Harry Alvan, educator; b. Elk Co., Pa., June 25, 1890; s. Robert Francis and Elizabeth Ann (Berkey) C.; B.S., University of Pittsburgh, 1916; M.S., Temple University, 1924, Ed.D., 1930; LL.D., LaSalle College, 1936; m. Molly Anderson, July 16, 1919; children—Bryce Clark, Robert Anderson, William Cody. Teacher pub. and high schs., Pa., 1909-14, high sch., St. Louis, Mo., 1916-20; asst. prof. commercial edn., U. of Pittsburgh, 1920-21; prof. finance, Temple U., since 1921, dir. Summer Schs., since 1925, dean Sch. of Commerce, since 1934. Served in O.T.C., Fort Riley, Kan., 1917. Mem. Am. Economic Assn., N.E.A., Phi Delta Kappa, Delta Sigma Pi, Beta Gamma Sigma. Republican. Episcopalian. Mason (Shriner). Home: 318 Roberts Av., Glenside, Pa. Address: Temple Univ., Philadelphia, Pa.

COCHRAN, Henry Jessup, banking; b. Mendham, N.J., Apr. 8, 1879; s. Rev. I. W. and Annie (Carter) C.; A.B., Princeton, 1900; m. Nannette R. Pierce, Apr. 12, 1904; children—Katharine (Mrs. K. C. Chamberlain), Homer P., Henry J., Bradford. Statistician for the Am. Locomotive Co. of New York, 1901-07; with Suffern & Son, certified public accountants, 1907-10; partner Patterson & Cochran, accountants, New York, 1910-12; v.p. Astor Trust Co., 1912-17; v.p. Bankers Trust Co., 1917-29, president 1929-31, vice chmn. board, 1931-37, vice chmn. trust investment committee, 1937-38; pres. Franklin Savings Bank since 1938; dir. Am. Smelting & Refining Co., Bankers Safe Deposit Co., Home Life Ins. Co., Princeton Inn Co., Am. Enka Corpn., Nat. Biscuit Co. Life trustee Princeton. Mem. St. Andrew's Soc., Japan Soc. Republican. Presbyn. Clubs: University, Princeton, Union League, Down Town (New York); Nassau (Princeton); Lake Placid (N.Y.); Plainfield (N.J.) Country. Home: 1341 Prospect Av., Plainfield, N.J. Office: 656 8th Av., New York, N.Y.

COCHRAN, Jean Carter, author; b. Mendham, N.J., Nov. 24, 1876; d. Israel Williams and Anne (Carter) C.; ed. Misses Babbitt Sch., Mendham, 1884-85, St. Paul (Minn.) public school, 1885-86, Miss Mason's Private Sch., New York, 1887-90, Miss Hazeltine's Sch., Morristown, 1890-95, Miss Dana's Sem., 1895-96; unmarried. Began to write for publication, 1909. Author: Nanny's Mother, 1913; Rainbow in the Rain, 1912; Foreign Magic (missions), 1921; Church Street (about Mendham, N.J., where father was Presbyn. pastor), 1923; Bells of the Blue Pagoda (story of China), 1922. Contbr. poems to periodicals. Awarded 1st prize for play by N.J. Fed. Woman's Clubs, 3d prize for sketch. Presbyterian. Clubs: Monday Afternoon, Razorez, S.O.S. (Plainfield, N.J.); Authors League (New York); Federation of Woman's Clubs of N.J. Home: 1003 Park Av., Plainfield, N.J.

COCHRAN, Thomas Cunningham, former congressman; b. Sandy Creek Twp., Mercer Co., Pa., Nov. 30, 1877; s. Wilson Henry and Elizabeth Eve (Robinson) C.; high sch., Mercer, Pa., 1896; A.B., Westminster Coll., New Wilmington, Pa., 1901, LL.D., 1937; studied law in father's office; m. Olive Belle Pierson, Aug. 15, 1906; children—Wilson Henry, Charles Edward, Cornelia Elizabeth, Olive Amanda, Thomas Cunningham. Admitted to Pa. bar, 1903, and began practice at Mercer; dist. atty. Mercer Co., 1906-09; solicitor Mercer Co., 1920-27; mem. 70th to 73d Congresses (1927-35), 20th Pa. Dist. (nom. for 1st term by Rep., Dem., Socialist and Prohibition parties). Del. from U.S. Congress to Congs. of Interparliamentary Union, Paris, 1927, Berlin, 1928, Geneva, 1929, London, 1930, Istanbul (Constantinople), 1934. Trustee Westminster Coll. Mem. Am. Pa. and Mercer Co. bar assns., Sigma Phi Epsilon. Republican. United Presbyn. Clubs: Wanango Country, Greenville Country. Home: Mercer, Pa.

COCKS, Orrin Giddings, social service; b. Augusta, Mich., May 12, 1877; s. Charles Willets and Orpha Pelton (Ives) C.; A.B., Union U., 1898, D.D. from same, 1928; B.D., Union Theological Sem., 1901; post-grad. work, Columbia; m. Evelyn G. O'Loughlin, June 27, 1908; children—Orrin Giddings, Robert Stuart, Laura Wilder, Mary Ives. Ordained Presbyn. ministry, 1901; asst. pastor Central Ch., Brooklyn, 1901-02; pastor and asso. pastor, Sea and Land Ch., New York, 1902-08 (trustee 1908-21); service sec. New York Federation of Chs., 1908-14; advisory sec. Nat. Bd. of Review of Motion Pictures, 1914-22. Sec. Nat. Commn. for Better Films; 1917-22. War work with Commn. on Training Camp Activities and War Camp Community Service, 1917-18. Awarded Silver Beaver, Boy Scouts of America, 1937. Dir. Boy Scouts of America, Bd. of Edn. (South Orange, N.J.), 1st Presbyn. Ch., Wellsboro, Pa. Mem. Phi Beta Kappa, Kappa Alpha. Mason. Moderator Northumberland Presbytery, 1936. Lecturer. Author: The Social Evil and Methods of Treatment, 1911; Engagement and Marriage, 1912; also many pamphlets, pub. addresses on sex questions and motion pictures. Home: Wellsboro, Pa.

COE, Conway Peyton, U.S. commr. of patents; b. Dunkirk, Md., Oct. 21, 1897; s. Walker Peyton Conway and Ada Ball (Prigg) C.; A.B., Randolph-Macon Coll., 1918; LL.B., George Washington U., 1922; m. Anna Hopton Hart, June 2, 1920; children—Conway Peyton, Anna Hopton, Mildred Hart. Admitted to D.C. bar, 1923; asst. examiner U.S. patent office, 1918-23; practiced patent law, Akron, 1923-24, Washington, D.C., 1924-33; U.S. commr. of patents since 1933. Served in field arty., U.S.A., 1918. Chmn. Am. delegation to Conf. of Internat. Conv. for Protection of Industrial Property, London, 1934. Mem. Am. Bar Assn., Am. Patent Law Ann., Phi Delta Phi, Sigma Phi Epsilon, Tau Kappa Alpha. Democrat. Methodist. Club: Congressional (Washington). Home: 10 E. Kirke St., Chevy Chase, Md. Office: Patent Office, Washington, D.C.

COE, Ward Baldwin, lawyer; b. Bluffton, S.C., Dec. 2, 1868; s. Theodore H. and Sarah (Baldwin) C.; student Porter Acad., Charleston, S.C., 1880-85; A.B., Charleston Coll., 1890, A.M., 1892; LL.B., Columbian (now George Washington) U. Law Sch., 1892; m. Marguerite Almy Hall, Oct. 12, 1904; children—Marguerite Hall (A.B., Goucher), Ward Baldwin, Jr. (A.B., Princeton, LL.B., Harvard). Admitted Md. bar, 1892; annotator, "Coe's Alexander's British Statutes in Force in Maryland"; master-in-chancery since 1913. Mem. Baltimore and Md. bar assns. Home: Riderwood, Md. Office: 1205 Fidelity Bldg., Baltimore, Md.

COES, Harold Vinton, engineer, mfr.; b. Hyde Park, Mass., June 21, 1883; s. Zorester Bennet and Alice (Miller) C.; prep. edn., Northeastern Manual Training Sch., Phila.; B.S., in Mech. Engring., Mass. Inst. Tech., 1906; m. Agnes Wickfield Day, June 5, 1909; children—Kent Day, Harold Vinton. Mech. engr. Liquid Carbonic Co., Chicago, 1908-11; industrial engr. Lockwood Greene & Co., Chicago and Boston, 1911-14; v.p. and gen. mgr. Sentinel Mfg. Co., New Haven, Conn., 1914-16; industrial engr. Gunn, Richards & Co., engrs., New York, 1916-18, Ford, Bacon & Davis, 1918-24; v.p. and gen. mgr. Belden Mfg. Co., mfrs. elec. wire, cables, etc., Chicago, since 1924; mgr. industrial dept. Ford, Bacon & Davis, Inc., New York, 1928-39, partner since 1937; also exec. v.p. and dir. Vulcan Iron Works, Wilkes-Barre, Pa., 1934; past pres. United Engring. Trustees, Inc. Civilian asst. in operation and administration munition plants in U.S. and Can., World War. Chmn. finance com. Engrs. Nat. Hoover Com.; mem. advisory com. Coll. of Engring., New York U.; vice chmn. finance com. of the Internat. Management Congress. Mem. Am. Soc. M.E. (past v.p.), Soc. Advancement of Management, Am. Management Assn. (chmn. finance com. and dir.), Am. Engring. Council, Industrial Marketing Executives Assn., Am. Marketing Assn., Assn. Cons. Management Engrs. (past pres.); fellow Inst. of Management (past pres.). Republican. Unitarian. Clubs: Engineers, Downtown Athletic (New York). Author: Production Control (Alex. Hamilton Inst.). Asso. editor Handbook of Business Administration, also of Management's Handbook (Ronald Press). Home: 18 Braemore Rd., Upper Montclair, N.J. Office: 39 Broadway, New York, N.Y.

COFFEY, Aubrey Jackson, clergyman; b. Nash, Va., July 21, 1889; s. Benjamin F. and Elizabeth Matilda (Fitzgerald) C.; student Va. Commercial Coll., Lynchburg, 1911, Lynchburg (Va.) Christian Coll., 1913-18; m. Willie D. Akers, Oct. 11, 1920; children—Dorothy Elizabeth, Doris June. Ordained to ministry Christian Ch.; missionary for Va. Christian Missionary Soc., 1918-21; pastor Logan, W.Va., 1921-26, Huntington, W.Va., 1926-30, Montgomery, 1930-33; evangelistic work, 1934; pastor First Christian Ch., Logan, W.Va., since 1934; during pastorate, erected and financed bldg. of ch.; pres. Logan Dist. Christian Ch.; sec.-treas. Logan Ministerial Assn.; mem. bd. mgrs. United Christian Missionary Soc., Indianapolis, Ind. Democrat. Christian Ch. Mason. Home: 431 Main St., Logan, W.Va.

COFFMAN, Joe W., motion picture exec.; b. Clarksville, Ark., Sept. 18, 1895; s. Joseph W. and Susan (Tankersley) C.; B.Sc., Arkansas Cumberland Coll., Clarksville, Ark., 1915; student U. of Chicago, 1915-16; m. Eloise Johnston, June 5, 1919; children—Eloise, Joe W., Sarah Constance, Dorothy. Head science dept., Moultrie (Ga.) High Sch., 1916, prin., Anniston (Ala.) High Sch., 1920; head science dept., Ensley High Sch., Birmingham, Ala., 1921; supervisor visual edn., Atlanta (Ga.) Pub. Schs., 1922-23; v.p. and production mgr. Graphic Films Corpn., Atlanta, Ga., 1924; exec. Carpenter-Goldman Labs., New York, 1925-27, v.p., 1927-29; consultant Eastman Kodak Co. in teaching films project, 1927-29, spl. consultant on sound film technique, 1929-30; consultant on talking motion pictures Bell Telephone Labs., 1928-30; pres. Audio-Cinema, Inc. (successor to Carpenter-Goldman Labs.), New York, 1929-31; spl. consultant Paramount-Famous-Lasky Corpn., 1929; consultant to Soviet Govt., Russia, 1930-31; consultant on processing motion picture sound film Consolidated Film Industries, Inc., New York, 1928-32; dir., mem. exec. com. and production exec. since 1932, in latter connection mgr. world's largest motion picture labs., Fort Lee, N.J.; pres. and mgr. record production Columbia Phonograph Co., Inc., New York, Chicago, Hollywood, Bridgeport, Conn., 1935-38; mgr. record production Brunswick Record Corpn., 1935-38 and mgr. record production Am. Record Corpn., 1932-39 (sold to Columbia Broadcasting Corpn.); pres. and mgr. molded products plant Consolidated Molded Products Corpn., Scranton, Pa., since 1938, (all subsidiaries of Consolidated Film Industries, Inc.); consultant in motion picture engring. Republic Pictures Corpn., Hollywood, Calif., since 1935; pres. Metropolitan Royalties Corpn., Fortlee, N.J., since 1936; v.p. and dir. Cajo Co., Inc., New York, N.Y., since 1935. Served as 1st lt., Air Service, A.E.F., 1917-19. Licensed private pilot (Aircraft) 1939. Inventor and patentee of processes and equipment for animated drawing, sound recording, motion picture processing, and phonograph recording. Mem. Soc. of Motion Engrs. (chmn. papers com. 1929-31, editor "Transactions" 1929-31). Club: Oritani Field (Hackensack, N.J.). Produced and directed first sound picture grand opera, Pagliacci, 1930. Home: 332 Maple Hill Drive, Hackensack, N.J. Office: 1776 Broadway, New York, N.Y.

COGGESHALL, Murray H., investment banker; b. Homer, N.Y., May 16, 1873; s. Almon E. and Henen (Farmer) C.; student St. Albans (Ill.) Mil. Acad., 1890-93; B.S., Trinity Coll., Hartford, Conn., 1896; m. Janie Magor, May 28, 1904; children—Marian (Mrs. Lorraine Pitman), Murray H., John, Bayard. With Grinnell, Willis & Co., 1897-1905; mem. Coggeshall & Hicks since 1906; pres. Morristown Securities Co.; dir. Columbia Gas & Electric Co. Servel Corporation. Served in Spanish-Am. War. Decorated Serbian Red Cross, Serbian Order of St. Sava. Republican. Episcopalian. Clubs: University, Down Town (New York); Morristown, Morris County Golf. Home: Morristown, N.J. Office: 111 Broadway, New York, N.Y.

COGILL, Lida Stewart; prof. obstetrics, Woman's Coll.; sr. obstetrician Woman's Hosp.; obstetrician Woman's Coll. Hosp. Address 1831 Chestnut St., Philadelphia, Pa.

COHEN, A. B., gen. agt. life ins. co.; b. Birzai, Lithuania, Sept. 4, 1873; s. Reuben and Frumi Hinda (Wittert) C.; ed. Lithuanian Talmudical Acad.; came to U.S., 1892 and naturalized citizen, 1900; m. Ella Wittert, 1892 (now deceased); m. 2d, Dora Benyas, 1930. Settled first in New York removed to Scranton, Pa., and engaged in jewelry business, 1894-1914; mem. firm A. B. Cohen & Son, ins. agency, since 1914; gen. agt. for life ins .co. and pub. adjuster since 1926; in 1923, in celebration of his 50th birthday, a community testimonial was presented to him at a banquet in his honor. Served as assessor City of Scranton, 1909-14; organized play ground movement and vice-pres. Recreation Bd., City of Scranton. Organized and is pres. Scranton Good Will Com. Vice-pres. Scranton Chamber of Commerce. For many yrs. very active and prominent in welfare and religious work among Jews, locally and nationally. Served as vice-pres. United War Drive, 1917. An officer or dir. of all local Jewish charitable orgns. Nat. v.p. United Synagogues of America; nat. bd. mem. Am. Jewish Congress; corporate mem. Am. Jewish Com.; chmn. B'nai B'rith Wider Scope Com.; pres. Eastern Pa. United Synagogues; nat. bd. mem. Zionist Orgn. of America. Mason. Elk. Y.M.H.A. (mem. bd.). Home: 738 Clay. Office: Connell Bldg., Scranton, Pa.

COHEN, Abraham, med. consultant; b. Brooklyn, N.Y., Apr. 5, 1900; s. William and Mary (Wolfson) C.; A.B., U. of Me., Orono, Me., 1921; M.D., Jefferson Med. Coll., Phila., 1925; m. Lillian Davidow, May 6, 1936; 1 son, Richard William. Served interneship at Phila. Gen. Hosp., 1925-27, chief of arthritis clinic since 1927, asso. chief on med. service since 1930; mem. of faculty and chief of arthritis clinic, Jefferson Med. Coll., Phila., since 1929; consultant to welfare dept., Dept. of Pub. Safety, Phila., since 1930. Mem. A.M.A., Phila. Co., Pa. State med. socs., Internat. Soc. of Med. Hydrology (London, Eng.), Internat. Rheumatism Assn. (Brussels, Belgium). Jewish religion. Home: 426 Ellet St., Germantown. Office: 801 N. 5th St., Reading, Pa., and 2106 Spruce St., Philadelphia, Pa.

COHEN, Barnett, univ. prof.; b. Rogachev, Russia, Feb. 16, 1891; s. Louis and Rose (Goedelberg) C.; came to U.S., 1893, naturalized, 1902; B.S., Coll. of City of N.Y., 1911; M.S., Sheffield Scientific Sch., Yale, 1918, Ph.D., 1920; unmarried. Began as chemist and bacteriologist, Meriden, Conn., 1912; chemist and bacteriologist Health Dept., Savannah, Ga., 1915-16; asst. in biochemistry and pub. health, Yale, 1916-20; chemist Hygienic Lab., U.S. Pub. Health Service, Washington, D.C., 1920-28; asso. prof. physiol, chemistry, Johns Hopkins U., since 1928. Served as 2d lt., Chem. Warfare Service, U.S. Army, 1918. Mem. Am. Chem. Soc., Soc. Am. Bacteriologists (archivist since 1935), Md. Bacteriol. Soc. (pres. 1939), Am. Pub. Health Assn., Soc., Exptl. Biology and Medicine, Phi Beta Kappa, Sigma Xi. Club: Cosmos (Washington, D.C.). Editor Bacteriological Reviews since 1937. Address: 10 W. Read St., Baltimore, Md.

COHEN, Harry; v.p. Commercial Trust Co. Address: Wilmington, Del.

COHEN, Herman Bernard, physician; b. New York, N.Y., Jan. 18, 1891; s. Barnett and Dora (Resnick) C.; student Central High Sch., Phila., Pa., 1905-09; M.D., U. of Pa., 1913; m. Mildred Werthheimer, Oct. 14, 1914. Began as gen. practitioner, 1914; asst. to Dr. Eli Klopp, 1914-17; asst. to Dr. Eli Klopp, 1914-17; asst. to Dr. S. M. MacCuen Smith, 1914-26, asso., 1926-30; asst. to Dr. R. F. Ridpath, 1914-20, asso., 1920-34; attending chief Jewish Hosp., Phila., since 1934; asst., asso., asst. prof. to Dr. Ross H. Skillen, 1915-31, Dr. George M. Coates, Phila., since 1931. Served as examiner, later consultant, Draft Bd., during World War. Mem. Phila. Laryngol. Soc. (sec., 1926-34, pres., 1936-38), Zeta Beta Tau. Jewish religion (Rodeph Sholom Congregation). Club: Philmont (Pa.) Country. Home: 250 S. 17th St. Office: Room 1105, 255 S. 17th St., Philadelphia, Pa.

COHEN, Lee; rhinologist and aurist Sinai Hosp.; surgeon Baltimore Eye, Ear and Throat Charity Hosp. Address: Naylor's Lane, Pikesville, Md.

COHEN, Lester, writer; b. Chicago, Ill., Aug. 17, 1901; s. Hyman and Anna (Harchovsky) C.; student pub. schs. and high sch., U. of Chicago; m. Priscilla Pardridge, Jan. 3, 1920; 1 son, Peter Gray. Began in advertising and newspaper work; has followed profession of writing since 1926. Mem. Authors League of America, League of Am. Writers, Screen Writers Guild. Author: Sweepings, 1926; The Great Bear, 1927; Oscar Wilde, A Play, 1928 (with Hyman Cohen) Aaron Traum, 1930; Two Worlds, 1936; and many motion pictures, including Sweepings, Of Human Bondage, etc. Home: R.F.D. No. 2, Doylestown, Pa.

COHEN, Louis, consulting engr.; b. Kiev, Russia, Dec. 16, 1876; s. Abraham and Nattie (Resnik) C.; B.Sc., Armour Inst. Tech., 1901; student U. of Chicago, 1902; Ph.D., Columbia, 1905; m. Ethel Slavin, Jan. 3, 1904; 1 dau., Louise Slavin. With scientific staff, Bur. of Standards, Washington, 1905-09; with Elec. Signaling Co., 1909-12; cons. practice since 1913; prof. elec. engring., George Washington U., 1916-29; cons. engr., War Dept., 1920-24; lecturer Bur. of Standards, Washington, 1928—; U.S. del. Provisional Tech. Com. Internat. Conf. on Elec. Communication, Paris, France, 1921; mem. advisory tech. bd., Conf. on Limitation of Armament, Washington, 1921-22. Fellow A.A. A.S., Am. Inst. E.E., Am. Inst. Radio Engrs., Am. Physical Soc. Author: Formulœ and Tables for Calculation of Alternating Current Problems, 1913; Heaviside's Electrical Circuit Theory, 1928; also many papers in scientific and tech. jours. Inventor of many devices in radio and cable telegraphy. Home: 303 Roosevelt St., Bethesda, Md.

COHEN, Louis, lawyer; b. Mt. Carmel, Pa., Aug. 1, 1905; s. Nathan and Nahama (Dziewietycki) C.; A.B., Dickinson Coll., Carlisle, Pa., 1926; LL.B., Dickinson Law Sch., Carlisle, Pa., 1930; unmarried. Counsel for Personal Finance Co., Mt. Carmel, Pa., since 1932, for Frack Coal Co., New Mokin Coal Co., Mowry Coal Co., Mowry, Pa., since 1935; solicitor for Borough of Mt. Carmel (Pa.) since 1934, for Italian-Am. Bldg. & Loan Assn., Mt. Carmel, Pa., since 1936, for Progressive Bldg. & Loan Assn., Mt. Carmel, Pa., since 1937; spl. counsel for Miners and Laborers Bldg. & Loan Assn. since 1937. Dir. Italian-Am. Bldg. & Loan Assn., Standard Drug Store, Inc., Eveready Pen Corpn. Mem. Boy Scouts of America (sustaining mem.), Coop. Concert Assn., Red Cross, Phi Epsilon Pi. Republican. Jewish religion. Elk, Eagle, Moose. Clubs: Jewish Fellowship, Maysville Tennis, South End (Mt. Carmel, Pa.). Home: 314 S. Lemon St. Office: 49 S. Oak St., Mt. Carmel, Pa.

COHEN, Mortimer Joseph, rabbi; b. New York, N.Y., Mar. 1, 1894; s. Joseph and Rachael (Levine) C.; student N.Y. pub. schs., 1900-15; A.B., Coll. of the City of N.Y., 1919; grad. as rabbi, Jewish Theol. Sem. of America, 1923; Ph.D., Dropsie Coll., Phila., 1934; m. Helen Kalikman, June 28, 1925; children—Hedvah Ray, Lorna Lee. Began as rabbi, 1920; now rabbi Beth Sholom Congregation, Phila. Home: 1624 Lindley Av. Address: Broad and Courtland Sts., Philadelphia, Pa.

COHEN, Solomon Solis, M.D.; b. Phila., Sept. 1, 1857; s. Myer David and Judith Simiah (da Silva Solis) C.; A.B., Central High Sch., 1872, A.M., 1877; M.D., Jefferson Med. Coll., 1883, hon. Sc.D., 1933; hon. D.H.L., Jewish Theological Sem. of America, 1928; m. Emily Grace, d. David Hays da Silva Solis, 1884; children—D. Hays, Emily, Leon, Francis N. Lecturer clin. medicine, 1888-1902, prof. clin. medicine, 1902-27, emeritus since 1927, Jefferson Med. Coll.; prof. medicine and therapeutics, Philadelphia Polyclinic and Coll. for Graduates in Medicine, 1887-1902. Lecturer therapeutics, Dartmouth, 1890-92; phys. to Phila. General, Jefferson and Jewish hosps., 1887-1927, now consulting physician to these hospitals. Mem. publ. committee of Jewish Publication Soc. America, Oriental Club of Phila. Trustee United States Pharmacopœia since 1920. Fellow College Physicians, Phila., Am. Coll. Phys., A.A.A.S., A.M.A. (ex-chmn. therapeutics sect.); pres. Phila. Co. Med. Soc., 1898-99; recorder Assn. Am. Physicians, 1899-1913; hon. mem. Med. and Chirurg. Faculty of Md. and other med. socs. Del. 3d Zionist Congress, Basle, 1899; mem. Council Jewish Agency for Palestine, 1929—. Mem. Bd. of Edn. of Philadelphia. Club: Franklin Inn. Author: Therapeutics of Tuberculosis, 1891; Essentials of Medical Diagnosis (with A. A. Eshner), 1892-1900; Pharmacotherapeutics (with T. S. Githens), 1928; When Love Passed By and Other Verses, including Translations from Hebrew Poets of the Middle Ages, 1929. Editor and contbg. author: A System of Physiologic Therapeutics (11 vols.), 1901-05. Translator: Selections from (Hebrew) Poems of Moses ibn Ezra, 1933. Contbg. editor and contbr. various med., Jewish and general cyclopedias and periodicals. Home: 135 S. 17th St. Office: 1906 Walnut St., Philadelphia, Pa.

COHILL, Edmund Pendleton, fruit grower; b. Elmira, N.Y., Dec. 3, 1855; s. Andrew Arnold and Mary Jane (Mapes) C.; grad. Harrisburg (Pa.) Commercial Coll., 1874; m. Mary Ellen Rinehart, Oct. 23, 1876; children—Marie Agnes (dec.), Louise Elizabeth (dec.), Samuel Rinehart, Leo Aloysius, William Joseph (dec.), James Andrew, Marguerite Cecelia (dec.), Suella; m. 2d, Emma M. Glover, Boston, Sept. 4, 1923. Private secretary to George M. Ball, gen. mgr. Empire Transportation Co., Phila., 1875; cashier same co., Baltimore, 1876-77; began fruit culture, 1886, which grew into Tonoloway Orchard Co., having 980 acres in apples; was an organizer and pres. Hancock Bank, and organizer and v.p. First Nat. Bank; pres. and treas. Tonoloway Orchard Co.; v.p. Russell Creek Coal Co., Corona Orchard Co.; dir. Baltimore br. Federal Reserve Bank of Richmond since 1924. Dir. Am. Angora Goat Breeders' Assn.; v.p. Md. State Hort. Soc. (pres. 1905-06); mem. exec. com. Eastern Apple Growers' Assn., Am. Apple Congress; exec. bd. Nat. Apple Growers' Assn., 1917-18; pres. Md. Agrl. Soc., 1918—; pres. Md. State Farm Bur., 1923—; v.p. Nat. Pecan Groves Co.; mem. exec. com. Southern region, Am. Farm Bur. Fed., 1924-26, now dir. for Southern Region. Sch. commr. Washington Co., Md., 1900-12. Democrat. Home: Hancock, Md.

COHILL, Maurice Blanchard, life ins. salesman and exec.; b. Milton, Pa., Apr. 27, 1887; s. Haskins Glancey and Anna Lawson (Van Buskirk) C.; student U. of Pa., 1908-09; m. Florence Sayers Clarke (Vassar, 1916), Nov. 12, 1921; children—Florence Beverly, Maurice Blanchard, Jr., Nancy Clarke. With Am. Water Works & Guarantee Co., 1909-12; in real estate business, San Diego, Calif., 1912-14; asso. with Equitable Life Ins. Soc. of U.S. continuously since 1914, asst. mgr. Edward A. Woods Co., largest life insurance agency in the world, Pittsburgh, Pa.; was one of first 25 to receive degree C.L.U.; lecturer on life ins. in many of larger cities; mem. Group Millionaire Club. Served in U.S.N.R.F. from gunners mate to lt. (j.g.), 1917-19. Mem. Nat. Life Underwriters Assn., Million Dollar Round Table. Republican. United Presbyterian. Mason (K.T., 32°, Shriner). Club: Shannopin Country (Ben Avon Heights, Pa.). Home: 500 Walnut Rd., Ben Avon. Office: Frick Bldg., Pittsburgh, Pa.

COHN, Arthur, musician; b. Phila., Pa., Nov. 6, 1910; s. Bernard Max and Pauline (Weissblatt) C.; student Juilliard Grad. Sch., 1932-33, Combs Conservatory of Music, 1922-30; m. Flora May Singer, Aug. 24, 1930 (died 1934); m. 2d, Hilda Levy, Dec. 27, 1935. Organized Dorian String Quartet, 1928, Stringart Quartet, 1932; dir. of music in summer camps, 1931-33; co-founder of Chamber Orchestra of Phila., 1933; mem. of Civic Symphony Orchestra, 1934; dir. of chamber music (Symphony Club), 1934; administrator of music copying project of Free Library of Phila., since 1934; head of composition dept. of Center Music Sch., Bryn Mawr Conservatory, Wurlitzer Sch. of Music, Phila., and Trenton, since 1937. Mem. MacDowell Colony, Peterboro, N.H., 1938. Mem. Composers Alliance, Allied Members of the MacDowell Colony, Nat. Assn. Am. Composers Conductors, Phila. Music Center. Awarded fellowship in composition at Juilliard Sch., 1933. Conductor Center Symphony Orchestra; guest conductor of Civic Symphony of Phila.; lecturer; contbr. to Modern Music. Works have been played by Rochester Civic Symphony; Roth Quartet, Phila. Civic Symphony; Phila. Music Center Orchestra; Stringart Quartet, Federal Music Project. Home: 1329 Pine St., Philadelphia, Pa.

COHN, Charles Mittendorff, pub. utilities; b. Baltimore, Md., Apr. 25, 1873; s. Moritz Gustav and Emily Caroline (Stoll) C.; A.B., Loyola Coll., Baltimore, 1897, A.M., 1899; LL.B., U. of Md., 1897; unmarried. Began as jr. clerk Consolidated Gas Co., 1885; sec. Consolidated Gas Electric Light & Power Co., 1906-10, gen. mgr. in 1910, v.p. 1910-31, exec. v.p. since 1931; pres. Industrial Corpn. of Baltimore, Industrial Bldg. Co.; dir. and chmn. trust com. Fidelity Trust Co.; dir. Pa. Water & Power Co., Safe Harbor Water & Power Corpn. Democrat. Presbyn. Mason (33°). Clubs: Maryland, Baltimore Country. Home: 2941 N. Charles St. Office: Lexington Bldg., Baltimore, Md.

COHN, Joseph E.; mem. law firm S. & J. E. Cohn; officer, dir. or counsel many companies. Home: 25 Girard Pl. Office: 972 Broad St., Newark, N.J.

COHN, L(eopold) Clarence, surgeon; b. Baltimore, Md., Dec. 14, 1895; s. William and Carrie (Rosenfeld) C.; A.B., Johns Hopkins U., 1915, M.D., 1919; m. Blanche Frensdorf, Mar. 4, 1925; 1 son, L. Clarence. Began in practice of surgery 1921; asst. instr. and asso. in surgery, Johns Hopkins U., 1930-39; attending surgeon St. Agnes' Hosp., Baltimore. Fellow Am. Coll. Surgeons, A.M.A.; diplomate Am. Bd. Surgery; mem. Southern Med. Assn., Am. Assn. for Study Neoplastic Disease, Baltimore City Med. Soc., Med.-Chirurg. Faculty of Md. Mem. Jewish religion. Club: Johns Hopkins (Baltimore). Home: 5716 Oakshire Road. Office: 3301 N. Charles St., Baltimore, Md.

COHN, Morris Metz, lawyer; b. Paterson, N.J., June 1, 1893; s. Benjamin and Annie Linn (Levy) C.; LL.B., N.Y. Law Sch., 1913; m. Madelin Long, Dec. 5, 1923; children—Ann Linn, Joseph S. Admitted to N.J. bar, 1915, as atty. and since engaged in practice at Paterson, counselor at law, 1922; mem. State Bd. of Tax Appeals of State of N.J. since 1937. Served in F.A., U.S.A., during World War. Mem. Passaic Co. Bar Assn. (pres. 1938). Republican. Jewish religion. Mason. Jr. O.U.A.M. Clubs: Y.M.H.A., Y.M.C.A. (Paterson). Home: 410 18th Av. Office: 115 Market St., Paterson, N.J.

COHN, Saul; mem. law firm S. & J. E. Cohn; officer or dir. many companies. Home: 25 Milford Av., Newark, N.J.

COIT, Charles Wheeler, clergyman; b. Concord, N.H., Jan. 13, 1861; s. Henry Augustus and Mary Bowman (Wheeler) C.; student St. Paul's Sch., Concord, N.H., 1871-79; A.B., A.M., Trinity Coll., Hartford, Conn., 1882; B.D., Gen. Theol. Sem., New York, 1885; m. Virginia Kilgour Hickman, Oct. 8, 1907. Ordained to ministry of Episcopal Ch., 1885; rector St. Luke's Ch., Charlestown, N.H., 1885-88; asst. master, St. Paul's Sch., Concord, N.H., 1888-98; rector St. Luke's Ch., Baltimore, 1898-1907, St. Paul's Ch., Windsor, Vt., 1907-11; prof. New Testament Greek, Nashotah House, Nashotah, Wis., 1911-21; rector St. Mark's Ch., Hammonton, and St. Mark's Ch., Pleasantville, N.J., 1921-25; rector of Ladbroke, Warwickshire, Eng., 1925-27; rector St. John's Ch., Chews Landing, and Ch. of the Holy Spirit, Bellmawr, N.J., 1927-34; retired 1934. Mem. Soc. of the Royal Martyr, Memorial of Merit, Alpha Delta Phi, Phi Beta Kappa. Democrat. Mem. Confraternity of the Blessed Sacrament, Guild of All Souls. Editor of "School Sermons," by H. A. Coit, 1909; The Royal Martyr, 1925. Contbr. to Horae Scholasticae, Catholic Champion, Granite Monthly, New Hampshire Poets, etc. Home: 300 Essex Av., Narbeth, Pa.

COLBERT, Charles Francis, Jr., corpn. official; b. Pittsburgh, Pa., November 9, 1886; s. Charles Francis and Philomena (Dischner) C.; ed. Cathedral Sch. of Ill. and Shurtleff Coll., Alton, Ill.; m. Marie Louise Benford, Jan. 12, 1911 (died Jan. 13, 1931); children—Jane Elizabeth (Mrs. Walter F. Friday), Dorothy Benford (Mrs. Ralph H. Irwin), Richard Gary (ensign U.S.N.), Margaret Louise, Patricia Ann. Began in coal, coke, iron and alloys business at Pittsburgh, 1908; v.p. Pittsburgh Metallurgical Co.; pres. U.S. Fuel & Iron Co., Colbert Supply Co. Mem. Am. Iron and Steel Inst. Clubs: Duquesne, Pittsburgh Athletic, Longue Vue Country. Home: 724 S. Negley Av. Office: Henry W. Oliver Bldg., Pittsburgh, Pa.

COLBY, Everett, lawyer; Ph.B., Brown, 1897, hon. A.M.; m. Edith Hyde, June 30, 1903; children—Edith Hyde, Anne Gordon, Everett, Chas. L. (dec.). Mem. Barry, Wainwright, Thacher and Symmers. Mem. N.J. Bd. of Edn., 1902-04; mem. N.J. Gen. Assembly, 1903-05, Senate, 1906-09. Served as aide to gov. of N.J., 1903-04, and as adj. N.G. N.J. Progressive candidate for gov. of N.J., 1913; mem. Rep. Nat. Campaign Com., 1916; chmn. exec. com. League of Nations Non-Partisan Com. from organization to 1930; chmn. exec. com. Nat. World Court Com.; mem. N.J. Rep. State Com., 1934; pres. Council for Moderation. Served in U.S. Food Administration, 1917. Maj. O.R.C., 1918. Home: Llewellyn Park, W. Orange, N.J. Office: 72 Wall St., New York, N.Y.

COLDREN, Daries Dee-Wees, pres. Coldren Knitting Mills. Address: Schuylkill Haven, Pa.

COLDREN, Ira Burdette, lawyer; b. Uniontown, Pa., Mar. 11, 1902; s. Ira W. and Maggie E. (Newcomer) C.; ed. Pa. State Coll., 1918-20; Ph.G., U. of Pittsburgh Sch. of Pharmacy, 1922; A.B., Pa. State Coll., 1925; LL.B., U. of Pittsburgh Law Sch., 1929; m. Eleanor Clarke Lincoln, Oct. 19, 1922; children—Ira Burdette, Clarke Lincoln. Admitted to Pa. bar, 1929, and since engaged in gen. practice of law at Uniontown, Pa., asso. with firm Shelby, Hackney and Ray, 1929-36; mem. firm Shelby, Ray and Coldren, Uniontown, Pa., since 1936; dir. and counsel, Uniontown Thrift Corpn.; v.p. and dir. Fayette Appliance Co. Captain Inf.-Res., U.S. Army. Mem. American, Pennsylvania and Fayette Co. bar assns., Reserve Officers Assn. of the U.S. (past pres. Dept. of Pa.). Republican. Presbyterian. Mason (K.T., 32°). Club: Rotary (Uniontown, Pa.). Home: 120 Union St. Office: 607 Fayette Title & Trust Bldg., Uniontown, Pa.

COLE, Charles Walter, lawyer; b. Towson, Md., Mar. 17, 1899; s. William Purington and Ida Estelle (Stocksdale) C.; grad. Towson (Md.) High Sch., 1917; A.B., U. of Md., College Park, Md., 1921; LL.B., Harvard Law Sch., 1924; m. Elizabeth Stephenson Silver, Dec. 8, 1926; children—Elizabeth Silver, Anne Hopkins, Charles Walter. Admitted to practice in Md., 1925, in Fla., 1925; asso. with Hall and Johnson, attys.-at-law, Fort Lauderdale, Fla., 1925-27; in practice at Towson, Md., since 1927; dir. Mutual Fire Ins. Co. in Hartford Co., Md. Appt. mem. Commn. for Promotion of Uniformity of Legislation in the U.S., 1939. Served as 2d lt., U.S. Inf. Res. Mem. Am., Md. State bar assns., Baltimore County Bar Assn. (past pres.), Kiwanis Internat. (past dist. gov. of Capital dist.), Alumni Assn. of U. of Md. (pres.), Sigma Phi Sigma. Episcopalian (mem. Vestry, Trinity P.E. Ch., Towson, Md.). Mem. Odd Fellows Lodge, Kiwanis Club (Towson, Md.), Sons of Am. Revolution. Home: 602 E. Joppa Rd., Towson, Md. Office: Masonic Bldg., Towson, Md.

COLE, David L(awrence), lawyer; b. Paterson, N.J., May 1, 1902; s. Nathan Cohen and Ethel (Feldman) C.; B.S. cum laude, Harvard U., 1921; LL.B., Harvard U. Law Sch., 1924; m. Helen David, Oct. 8, 1925; children—Elizabeth, Morrill, Charles T. Admitted to N.Y. bar, 1925, and asso. with Coleman, Stern & Ellenwood, N.Y. City, 1924-26; admitted to N.J. bar as atty., 1926, as counselor, 1929; in practice in Paterson since 1926; mem. firm Cole & Morrill since 1931; dir. and counsel National Union Bank of America, Paterson, N.J., since 1937. Served as asso. counsel Silk Textile Code Authority during N.R.A. Pres. Shapiro Foundation. Dir. Paterson Y.M.H.A., Y.W.H.A., Community Chest. Mem. Am. Bar Assn., Harvard Law Club, N.J. Bar Assn., Passaic Co. Bar Assn. Republican. Jewish religion. Mason. Club: Preakness Hills Country of Wayne Twp. (pres.). Home: 15 Overlook Av. Office: 45 Church St., Paterson, N.J.

COLE, Delbert Elmer, banking; b. Leroy, W. Va., July 16, 1883; s. James A. and Allie C.; student Ravenswood Coll., Ravenswood, W.Va., 1899-1901; W.Va. Univ., 1902-05; m. Cora H. Hutchinson, Sept. 6, 1907; children—Juanita (Mrs. Walter J. Purdy), Robert H. Began as clk., 1906; now pres. Jackson County Bank, Ravenswood, W.Va.; vice-pres. Ravenswood News; dir. Ravenswood Cemetery Co. Served as lt. W.Va. N.G. Dir. Ravenswood Chamber of Commerce. Democrat. Baptist. Club: Lions (Ravenswood). Address: Ravenswood, W.Va.

COLE, Felix, foreign service officer; b. St. Louis, Mo., Oct. 12, 1887; s. Theodore Lee and Kate Dunn (Dewey) C.; student U. of Wis., 1905; A.B., Harvard, 1910; LL.B., George Washington U., 1928; m. T. Imshenetzkaya, Oct. 10, 1916; 1 dau., Marian; m. 2d, Marilla C. Cole (cousin), Sept. 22, 1928; children—Marilla Callender, Catherine Dewey. Reporter Boston Herald, 1911-13; in automobile business, St. Petersburg, Russia, 1913-14, publisher there, 1914-15; in U.S. foreign service since Jan. 1915; now consul gen., Algiers, Algeria. Mem. Order of Coif, Psi Upsilon, Phi Beta Kappa. Club: University (Washington, D.C.). Home: 9 Mountain Terrace, Montclair, N.J. Address: Dept. of State, Washington, D.C.

COLE, Henry Ernest; b. Sedgwick, Me., Mar. 16, 1877; s. Edward Clarence and Hattie Maria (Coombs) C.; grad. Cape Elizabeth High Sch., 1893; B.S. in elec. engring., U. of Me., 1902, grad. student, 1902-03; m. Augusta Helene Schumacher, of Portland, Me., Sept. 4, 1907; children—Helen Louise (Mrs. Ed. J. Chalfant), Harriet Christine (Mrs. William C. Lewis). Began as car checker on Me. Central R.R., 1893; contracting engr. Watts, Cole, 1903; with Harris Pump & Supply Co., Pittsburgh, 1904-37, vice-pres. and dir., 1911-25, pres. and dir., 1925-37; vice-pres. and sec. Pittsburgh Machine & Supply Co., 1935-38. Dir. Pittsburgh Chamber of Commerce; pres. Allegheny Co. Sabbath Sch. Assn.; vice-pres. Pa. State Sabbath Sch. Assn.; mem. bd. mgrs. Am. Baptist Publ. Soc.; dir. Pittsburgh Baptist Assn.; trustee Crozer Theol. Soc.; supt. East End Baptist Ch. Sunday Sch. 30 years. Mem. Phi Kappa Sigma. Mason (32°). Club: Rotary of Pittsburgh. Home: 6100 Stanton Av., Pittsburgh, Pa.

COLE, Irving Delbert, physician; b. Harrison Co., W.Va., July 21, 1881; s. Daniel and Elizabeth (Wolverton) C.; student W.Va. Univ., Morgantown, W.Va., 1903-04; M.D., U. of Md. Med. Sch., Baltimore, 1908; grad. study U. of Vienna, Austria, 1932-33; m. Regina France, July 21, 1908 (divorced); 1 dau., Jane Elizabeth (Mrs. John Roach Cook). Interne Baltimore Eye, Ear, Nose and Throat Hosp., 1908-09; engaged in practice of medicine, specializing in diseases of eye, ear, nose and throat, Clarksburg, W.Va., since 1915; pres. staff St. Marys Hosp., Clarksburg, W.Va., 1932; chief of staff St. Marys Eye, Ear, Nose and Throat Hosp. since 1936; mem. staff Union Prot. Hosp. since 1929. Fellow Am. Coll. Surgeons. Mem. W.Va. State Med. Soc. (council 1924-26), Harrison Co. Med. Soc. (pres. 1919), Sigma Phi Epsilon. Democrat. Baptist. Mason (32°, Shriner). Elk. Club: Kiwanis (Clarksburg). Home: Waldo Hotel. Office: Goff Bldg., Clarksburg, W.Va.

COLE, Lloyd G.; surgeon-in-chief Blossburg State Hosp. Address: Blossburg, Pa.

COLE, Norman Brown, physician; b. Newport, R.I., July 14, 1886; s. Charles Mowry and Ella Josephine (Brown) C.; grad. Rogers High Sch., Newport, R.I., 1904; A.B., Harvard, 1909, M.D., 1913; unmarried. Interne Boston City

Hosp., 1914-15, Providence (R.I.) Lying-In Hosp., 1917; 3d asst. supt. R.I. Hosp., Providence, 1915-17; asso. with Lewellys F. Barker, M.D., Baltimore, 1920-32; practice alone, Baltimore, since 1932; asst. visiting physician and instr. clinical medicine, Johns Hopkins Hosp. and Med. Sch. Served as lt., advancing to maj., Med. Corps, U.S. Army, 1917-20; served at Walter Reed Hosp., Washington, D.C., Camp Upton, N.Y. (on tuberculosis bd.), Ft. McHenry, Baltimore; disch. as maj., chief of Med. Service. Mem. exec. bds. Baltimore Area Council of Boy Scouts of America, Travelers Aid Soc. (Baltimore), Gen. German Orphan Home, Catonsville, Md.; mem. Bd. of School Commrs., Baltimore. Mem. A.M.A., Southern Med. Soc., Delta Upsilon. Republican. Baptist. Clubs: University, Caduceus, Grachur (Baltimore). Author: First Aid for Boys (with C. H. Ernst), 1917; Blood Pressure (with Lewellys F. Barker), 1924; Rheumatism, 1926; First Aid Merit Badge (pamphlet for Boy Scouts). Contbr. to med. jours. Home: The University Club. Office: 622 Medical Arts Bldg., Baltimore, Md.

COLE, Thomas P.; cons. surgeon Westmoreland Hosp. Address: 234 S. Pennsylvania Av., Greensburg, Pa.

COLE, Versa Viola, teaching and research; b. Constantine, Mich., Mar. 5, 1906; d. Ernest and Ida Elva (Babcock) Cole; A.B., Kalamazoo (Mich.) Coll., 1927, M.S., 1928; Ph.D., U. of Chicago, 1931, M.D., 1938; unmarried. Douglas Smith fellow in surgery, U. of Chicago, 1931-33; research asst. in medical and surg. research, Ohio State U., Columbus, O., 1933-35; asst. prof. of pharmacology, Woman's Med. Coll., Phila., 1935-38, asso. prof. of pharmacology since 1938. Mem. Alpha Epsilon Iota, Sigma Xi, Sigma Delta Epsilon. Clubs: Phila. Trail, Appalachian Mountain. Home: 2809 Queen Lane, Philadelphia, Pa.

COLE, William Harder, prof. of physiology and biochemistry; b. Cayuga, N.Y., June 23, 1892; s. Walter Wesley and Floretta Elmina (Groves) C.; grad. Ballston Spa (N.Y.) High Sch., 1910; A.B., Hamilton Coll., Clinton, N.Y., 1914; A.M., Harvard, 1916, Ph.D., 1921; m. Florence Augusta Hanagan, July 8, 1918. Instr. in zoölogy, Pa. State Coll., 1916-20; prof. of biology, Lake Forest (Ill.) Coll., 1921-24, Clark U., Worcester, Mass., 1924-28; prof. of physiology and biochemistry and head of dept., Rutgers U., since 1928. Served as private, advancing to sergt. 1st class, U.S. Army, 1917-19. Dir. Cold Spring Harbor Biol. Lab.; trustee and dir. Mt. Desert Island Biol. Lab., Salisbury Cove, Me. Mem. Am. Soc. Zoölogists, Am. Naturalist Soc., Soc. for Exptl. Biology and Medicine, A.A.A.S., N.Y. Acad. Sciences. Republican. Home: 59 Adelaide Av., New Brunswick, N.J.

COLE, William Purrington, Jr., congressman; b. Towson, Md., May 11, 1889; s. William Purrington and Ida Estelle (Stocksdale) C.; B.C.E., Md. Agrl. Coll. (now U. of Md.), 1910; studied Law Sch., U. of Md., 1911-12; m. Edith Moore Cole, June 27, 1918; 1 son, William Purrington III. Admitted to Md. bar, 1912; gen. practice at Towson since 1914; dir. Towson Nat. Bank. Commd. 1st lt. 316th Inf., 79th Div., U.S.A., Dec. 1917; in 3 battles in France; promoted capt. Feb. 1918. Member 70th and 72d to 75th Congresses (1927-29 and 1931-39), 2d Md. Dist. Mem. Am., Md. and Baltimore Co. bar assns., Phi Kappa Sigma. Democrat. Episcopalian. Home: Towson, Md., also Fork, Md.

COLEMAN, Bernard Simpson, pub. health; b. Stafford Springs, Conn., July 2, 1898; s. Samuel Jacob and Ida (Kaplan) C.; student Boston (Mass.) English High Sch., 1911-15; S.B., Mass. Inst. Tech., 1918; m. Evelyn Bernardine Bornstein, June 25, 1922; children—Kenneth George, Roger William. Began as pub. health and social worker, 1919; chemist and bacteriologist Montclair (N.J.) Water Co., 1919-24; industrial sec. N.J. Tuberculosis League, Newark, N.J., 1925-27; exec. sec. Hudson Co. Tuberculosis League, Jersey City, N.J., 1928-31; municipal relief dir. State of N.J. Emergency Relief Administrn., Paterson and Passaic, N.J., 1932-34; sec. tuberculosis com. N.Y. Tuberculosis and Health Assn., New York City, sec. Sanatorium Conf. of Met. N.Y., Clin. Sect. on Chronic Pulmonary Diseases since 1934; lecturer Presbyn. Hosp., Newark, N.J., since 1931; licensed pub. health officer, State of N.J. Served as pvt., U.S. Army, Oct.-Dec. 1918. Pres. Maple Av. Sch. Parent Teacher Assn., Newark, N.J., since 1937; bd. mem. Weequahic (N.J.) Sch. of Adult Edn. Dir. Shapiro Scholarship Foundation; mem. med. advisory bd. Nat. Jewish Hosp., Denver, Colo. Fellow Am. Pub. Health Assn. (sec. industrial hygiene sect., 1932-35); mem. Am. Assn. Social Workers, N.J. Health and Sanatorium Assn., Am. Hosp. Assn. (chmn. tuberculosis sect. 1938), Nat. Tuberculosis Assn. (chmn. advisory com. vocational rehabilitation 1937), N.J. Fed. of Y.M. & Y.W. H.A.'s (chmn. dept. phys. and health edn., 1928-37), Internat. Assn. of Thalasso Therapy (sec. Am. com. 1938), Assn. of Industrial Physicians and Surgeons of Northern N.J. (sec. 1926-35), Nat. Conf. of Tuberculosis Secs., Sigma Alpha Mu. Jewish religion. Club: M.I.T. of Northern N.J. (Newark, N.J.). Author numerous articles on tuberculosis, industrial hygiene, pub. health and rehabilitation; reviewer scientific books for Am. Jour. Pub. Health and other pubs. Home: 87 Vassar Av., Newark, N.J. Office: 386 Fourth Av., New York, N.Y.

COLEMAN, Harry Shipp, engineer; b. Colony, Kan., July 30, 1886; s. Charles Stephen and Emma Jane (Fisher) C.; student high sch., Garnett, Kan., 1901-05; B.S., U. of Kan., 1909, M.E., 1939; m. Amy Wolfe, April 15, 1914; children—Charles Wolfe, Carmie Jane. Began as draftsman A.T.&S.F. Ry., 1909, mech. dept., 1909-11; engr. Lukens Steel Co., 1917-18; asst. dir. Mellon Inst. of Industrial Research, Pittsburgh, since 1918; bus. mgr. U. of Pittsburgh, 1922-26. Chmn. Nat. Research Council's Com. on Lab. Constrn. Mem. Nat. Assn. of Purchasing Agents, Ednl. Buyers Assn., Am. Soc. M.E., Sigma Xi, Tau Beta Pi. Republican. Presbyterian. Clubs: University; Faculty, U. of Pittsburgh (Pittsburgh). Home: 604 S. Linden Av. Office: 4400 5th Av., Pittsburgh, Pa.

COLEMAN, James Emory, physician and surgeon; b. Ansted, W.Va., June 23, 1866; s. Seaton and Lydia (Skaggs) C.; M.D., Univ. of Ky. Med. Coll., Louisville, Ky., 1894; m. Blanche Malcolm, 1896 (died 1939); children—Kelley Sherrill, Conrad Durand, Imogene (widow of Benton S. Davenport). Became physician Gauley Mountain Coal Co., 1894; later surgeon Lowmoor Iron Co.; then propr. and surgeon Beckley (W. Va.) Hosp.; now propr. and surgeon Riverside Hosp., Gauley Bridge, W.Va. Fellow Am. Coll. Surgeons. Home: Fayetteville, W.Va. Office: Gauley Bridge, W.Va.

COLEMAN, John, theologian; b. Beaver Falls, Pa., Jan. 25, 1882; s. William J. and Elizabeth (George) Coleman; A.B., University of Pittsburgh, 1904; Ph.D., same university, 1934; A.M., U. of Wis., 1908; grad. Ref. Presbyn. Sem., Pittsburgh, 1907; D.D., Geneva Coll., Beaver Falls, 1926; m. Mary G. Willson, 1909; children—Anna M., Mary E., Lois Catharine (dec.), Eleanor W. Ordained ministry Ref. Presbyn. Ch., 1908; pastor New Concord, O., 1908-20, also prof. psychology and philosophy, Muskingum Coll., 1909-20; prof. religious edn., Geneva Coll., since 1920; also prof. systematic theology, Ref. Presbyn. Theol. Sem., since 1929. Mem. Acad. Polit. Science. Lecturer on Bible and current issues. Home: Beaver Falls, Pa.

COLEMAN, Joseph Gilbert, physician; b. Goshen, N.Y., Aug. 18, 1875; s. James Cash and Ann Elizabeth (Hulse) C.; M.D., Union U. Med. Dept., Albany, N.Y.; 1897; m. Sallie Price Armstrong, Oct. 18, 1900; 1 son, William Armstrong. Interne Marshall Infirmary, 1895-96; engaged in gen. practice of medicine at Hamburg, N.J. since 1900; vice-pres. Hardyston Nat. Bank, Hamburg, N.J., S.&M. Bldg. & Loan Assn., Newton, N.J. Served in active duty Med. Corps, U.S.A., 1917-19; now maj. Med. Res. Mem. bd. edn., Hamburg, N.J. Mem. A.M.A., N.J. State and Sussex Co. med. socs., Am. Legion. Republican. Presbyn. Mason (K.T., Shriner), O.E.S. Examiner for Prudential Ins. Co. for 40 yrs. Home: Orchard St., Hamburg, N.J.

COLEMAN, Ralph Pallen, illustrator; b. Phila., Pa., June 27, 1892; s. William Herr and Anna M. (Pauline) C.; student Central High Sch., Phila., 1907-10, Sch. of Industrial Art, Phila., 1910-13; m. Florence L. Haeberle, June 2, 1917; 1 son, Ralph Pallen. Began as illustrator, 1913; illustrator for Red Book Mag., Saturday Evening Post, Ladies' Home Jour., Liberty, Am. Mag., Cosmopolitan, Good Housekeeping, Pictorial Review, Collier's, This Week, Country Gentleman, McCall's, McLean's Magazine of Canada. Illustrated stories for Somerset Maughm, Rex Beach, Edison Marshall, Tom Gill, Ursula Parrot, Vingie Roe, Grace Livingston Hill, Temple Bailey, Dorothy Canfield, Sir Philip Gibbs, Ben Ames Williams, Eleanor Mercien, Peter B. Kyne, Chas. L. Clifford, Paul Gallico, J. P. McAvoy. Vice-pres. Baederwood, Inc. Served with Marine Camouflage Dept., World War. Mem. Huguenot Soc. of Pa. Presbyn. Home: Baederwood, Jenkintown, Pa. Studio: 232 Walnut St., Philadelphia, Pa.

COLEMAN, Susan McTighe, realtor; b. Bolton, Lancashire, England, Aug. 1, 1891; d. Thomas and Margaret (Bermingham) McTighe; student St. Peter and Paul's Convent Acad., Bolton, England, 1896-1908; m. Thomas P. Coleman, Sr., Aug. 17, 1909; children—Mary Agnes P., Margaret Mary, Kathleen Rosemary, Thomas Patrick, Theresa Bernadette, John Joseph. Came to U.S., 1913, naturalized, 1920. Began as real estate operator, 1921; sr. partner Susan and Agnes Coleman, realtors. First and only woman pres. Broadway Assn., Newark, N.J.; mem. Newark Real Estate Bd., N.J. Assn. Real Estate Boards, Nat. Assn. Real Estate Bds., Susan M. Coleman Dem. Assn., Inc., N.J. League of Women Voters, Catholic Daughters of America, Parent-Teacher's Assn. of Immaculate Conception Sch., Montclair, N.J. Chairlady Dem. Com., Newark's 8th Ward; mem. Essex Co. Dem. Com. in N.J. Club: Essex County Dem. Women; 8th Ward Women's Democratic (Newark). Address: 362 Summer Av., Newark, N.J.

COLEMAN, William Caldwell, judge; b. Louisville, Ky., Oct. 17, 1884; s. John and Susan (Norton) C.; A.B., Harvard, 1905; LL.B., Harvard Law Sch., 1909; m. Elizabeth Channing Brooke, May 26, 1917; children—William Caldwell, Robert Henry, Susan Norton, Elizabeth Brooke. Admitted to Md. bar, 1910, and practiced at Baltimore; instr. in negotiable instruments, U. of Md. Law Sch., 1914-17; secretary Maryland Educational Survey Commn., 1916; mem. firm Semmes, Bowen & Semmes, Baltimore, 1914-20; became mem. Coleman, Fell, Morgan & Brune, 1920; U.S. dist. judge Dist. of Md. since Apr. 1927. Rep. candidate for atty.-gen. of Md., 1923. Enlisted as pvt. F.A., U.S.A., July 1918; student Field Arty., C.O.T.S., Camp Taylor, Ky., Aug.-Dec. 1918; hon. discharged, Dec. 1918. Mem. Am. Bar Assn. (sec. 1924-25), Md. State Bar Assn., Baltimore City Bar Assn., Md. Historical Society. Episcopalian. Clubs: Maryland (Baltimore); Harvard (New York). Author: Memoirs of a Brother (with John Coleman, Jr.), 1920; Past Hours, 1937. Frequent contbr. articles on legal subjects to Harvard, Columbia and American law reviews, also contbr. to periodicals on travel and hunting. Home: Eccleston, Md. Address: Post Office Bldg., Baltimore, Md.

COLEMAN, William Harold, prof. English; b. Albert, New Brunswick, Can., Sept. 25, 1885; s. Dr. Henry Hicks and Adelia Eliza (Bray) C.; A.B., Acadia U., Wolfville, Nova Scotia, Can., 1906, A.M., 1909, Litt.D., 1930; A.M., Yale, 1910; student U. of Wis., 1918-19; student summers, U. of Va., 1920, Harvard, 1922, Cambridge U., England, 1931; m. Edna Matthews Wilcox, of Mystic, Conn., June 16, 1908; 1 son, Rowland Henry. Came to U.S., 1907, naturalized, 1934. Vice-prin., Mt. Allison Acad., Sackville, N.B., 1906-07; supervising prin., Broadway Schs., Mystic, Conn., 1907-09; head dept. of English, Drury High Sch., North Adams, Mass., 1910-14; instr. in English, Bates Coll., 1914-18, U. of Wis., 1918-19; prof. English, Furman U., 1919-24, Bucknell U. since 1924; mem. of faculty Broad Leaf Sch. of English, 1929. Mem. Modern Lang. Assn. America, Shakespeare Assn., Am. Nat. Council Teachers of English, Am. Assn. Univ. Profs., Facsimile Text Soc., Tau Kappa Alpha, Sigma Tau Delta, Sigma Alpha Epsilon. Republican. Baptist. Mason (Wolfville, N.S.). Clubs: Lions of Lewisburg (mem. bd. dirs. Internat. Assn. of Lions Clubs, 1936-38). Editor: Western World Literature (with H. W. Robbins), 1938. Editor of drama sect. of Good Reading. Contbr. to The Dalhousie Rev. and English Jour. Lecturer. Home: 133 S. 13th St., Lewisburg, Pa.

COLEMAN, William John, clergyman; b. Lisbon, N.Y., May 12, 1851; s. John and Mary (Glass) C.; A.B., Geneva Coll., 1875, A.M., 1890, D.D., 1901; D.D., Wheaton Coll., 1902; m. S. Elizabeth George, 1879; children—John, Paul, George Slater, William Carithers (killed in battle, France, 1918), Mary Slater. Ordained ministry Reformed Presbyn. Ch., 1879; pastor McKeesport, Pa., 1879-81; lecturer on nat. reform, 1881-86; pastor Utica, O., 1886-87; prof. polit. philosophy, Geneva Coll., 1887-92; pastor Allegheny Reformed Presbyn. Ch., Pittsburgh, Pa., 1892-1924. Moderator Ref. Presbyn. Synod, 1905; chmn. and lecturer witness com., Reformed Presbyn. Ch., since 1924; prof. pastoral theology, Reformed Presbyn. Sem., since 1928. Home: Millvale, R.R. 4, Pittsburgh, Pa.

COLEMAN, William Sidney, pharmacist; b. Lynchburg, Va., Aug. 28, 1902; s. George W. and Betty L. (Spencer) C.; Ph.G., Med. Coll. of Va., Richmond, 1925; m. Ethel E. Whitten, Apr. 6, 1926; children—William Spencer, John Whitten, Mary Carolyn. Employed as pharmacist Rose's Drug Store, Hinton, W.Va., 1925-28; mgr. Midland Drug Store, Rainelle, W.Va., 1928-31; in bus. on own acct. as propr. Coleman's Pharmacy, Lewisburg, W.Va., since 1931. Mem. W.Va. Pharm. Assn. (pres. 1938-39), Kappa Psi. Democrat. Presbyn. Mason. Club: Rotary of Lewisburg. Home: Frankford Rd. Office: Washington St., Lewisburg, W.Va.

COLEMAN-NORTON, Paul Robinson, prof. of classics; b. Reading, Pa., Feb. 28, 1898; s. James Edward and Fannie Milholland (Coleman) N.; grad. Reading (Pa.) High Sch., 1915; A.B., Princeton U., 1919, A.M., 1920; D.Phil., Oxford U. (England), 1923; m. Marion Jefferis Stephenson de Victor, Oct. 6, 1928. With Princeton U. since 1923, as instr. in classics, 1923-26, asst. prof., 1926-33, asso. prof. since 1933. Served as private U.S. Army, Oct.-Dec. 1918. Life mem. Am. Philol. Assn., Reading High Sch. Alumni Assn.; mem. Sterilization League of N.J., Royal Arcanum, Am. Whig Soc., Phi Beta Kappa. Republican. Episcopalian. Club: Princeton (Phila.). Author: Palladii Dialogus de Vita S. Joannis Chrysostomi, 1928. Contbr. to professional jours. Address: Princeton University, Princeton, N.J.

COLER, Carl Seymour, community relations mgr.; b. Huron, S.D., Apr. 2, 1889; s. Cyphrian Seymour and Bertha (Townsend) C.; M.E., Cornell U., 1911; M.S., U. of Pittsburgh, 1930; m. Irene Shoemaker, Feb. 9, 1924; children—Roderick, Martha, Donald. Dir., trades training, Westinghouse Electric & Mfg. Co., Pittsburgh, 1917-19, mgr. edn. dept., 1919-34, mgr. office employment and training, 1934-37, mgr. community relations since 1937; mgr. Westinghouse Tech. Night Sch., 1914-19, pres. since 1919. Mem. Pittsburgh Chamber of Commerce, Pittsburgh Personnel Assn. (pres., 1919-20, 1923-24), Pittsburgh Council on Adult Edn. (pres., 1937-38), Boy Scouts of America (mem. bd. of dirs. and in charge of older boy program, East Boroughs Council). Republican. Clubs: Rotary (dir., 1935-36), Westinghouse, Cornell of Western Pa. (Pittsburgh). Home: 565 Ardmore Boul., Wilkinsburg, Pa. Office: Braddock and Cable Avs., East Pittsburgh, Pa.

COLGAN, Howard Oliver, banker; b. Homestead, Pa., Apr. 29, 1886; s. James M. and Amelia A. (Tafel) C.; m. Garnett F. Colvin, June 23, 1910; children—Howard Oliver, Betty Jean, Ruth Amelia, Elma Louise. Began as messenger Union Steel Co., Donora, Pa.; then clerk Am. Steel & Wire Co., and Carnegie Steel Co.; became bookkeeper First Nat. Bank, Donora, 1907, later cashier; now vice-pres. and cashier Union Nat. Bank; partner Colgan and Binns, real estate and insurance; dir. Donora Lumber Co. Treas. Donora Borough Sch. Dist. Republican. Methodist. Address: Donora, Pa.

COLGATE, Robert B.; v.p. Colgate-Palmolive-Peet Co. Home: Lloyd Neck, Huntington, L.I., N.Y. Office: 105 Hudson St., Jersey City, N.J.

COLGATE, Russell; A.B., Yale U., 1896; m. Josephine B. Kirtland. Pres. Internat. Council of Religious Edn. Trustee Colgate Univ., Colgate-Rochester Divinity Sch., Rochester, N.Y. Dir. Colgate-Palmolive Peet Co. Home: West Orange, N.J. Office: 15 Exchange Pl., Jersey City, N.J.

COLGATE, S(amuel) Bayard; b. Orange, N.J., Apr. 5, 1898; s. Sidney Morse and Caroline Bayard (Dod) C.; student Hill Sch., Pottstown, Pa., 1914-17; A.B., Yale, 1922; m. Anne Burr, Oct. 4, 1924; 1 son, Austen. Began with Colgate & Co., 1921, continuing with successor Colgate-Palmolive-Peet Co., mem. exec. com., 1928-33, v.p., 1928-29, pres., 1933-38, chmn. bd. since 1938. Republican. Baptist. Clubs: Yale, City Midday, Explorers, Rock Spring, American Yacht. Home: Orange, N.J. Office: Jersey City, N.J.

COLIE, F. R.; mem. law firm Colie & Schenck. Office: 744 Broad St., Newark, N.J.

COLIN, Philip Gordon, research chemist; b. Baltimore, Md., Dec. 16, 1902; s. Alvin E. and Rose (Gordon) C.; student pub. schs., State of Wash., 1908-14, high schs., Tacoma, Wash., 1915-19; B.S. in Chem. E. (cum laude), U. of Wash., 1923, B.S. in E.E., 1925, Ph.D. (chem.), 1927; m. Alice Bertha von Pressentin, May 21, 1932; children—Phyllis Diane, Carol von Pressentin. Research asso. Rockefeller Inst. for Med. Research, New York, 1926-27; research chemist for Tide Water Associated Oil Co., Bayonne, N.J., 1927-30, supervisor research dept. since 1931. Mem. Am. Chem. Soc., Am. Soc. for Testing Materials, Soc. of Automotive Engrs., Sigma Xi, Tau Beta Pi, Phi Lambda Upsilon. Democrat. Home: 468 Hoyt Av., West New Brighton, Staten Island, N.Y. Office: care Tide Water Associated Oil Co., Bayonne, N.J.

COLKET, Edward Burton, ry. official; b. Philadelphia, Pa., Jan. 10, 1873; s. William Walker and Jane Frances (Hoxsie) C.; student Wm. Penn Charter Sch., Phila., 1883-89; B.S., U. of Pa., 1893, M.E., 1894; m. Bessie Lippincott, Feb. 12, 1918; 1 dau., Jane Hoxsie. Successively with Baldwin Locomotive Works, Standard Steel Works, Self Clinching Nail Works; pres. Phila. City Passenger Ry. Co. since 1908, dir. since 1906; also pres. Phila. & Darby Ry. Co., Chestnut Hill R.R. Co.; mgr. Phila., Germantown & Norristown R.R. Co. Mem. Welcome Soc. of Pa., Sons of Revolution. Republican. Presbyterian. Club: Auto (Phila.). Home: 5237 Wissahickon Av., Philadelphia, Pa.

COLL, Edward Brennan, banking; b. Pittsburgh, Pa., Oct. 7, 1874; s. John and Annie (Brennan) C.; ed. pvt. sch. and three-yr. academic course, Duquesne U., Pittsburgh; m. Lillian M. Thomas, Jan. 14, 1896. Began as messenger Farmers Deposit Nat. Bank, 1891; cashier Farmers Deposit Savings Bank, 1903-19, pres. 1919-28; vice-pres. Farmers Deposit Nat. Bank (merger) since 1928; vice-pres. and dir. Suburban Rapid Transit Street Ry. Co.; dir. Reliance Life Ins. Co. Trustee Pittsburgh Chapter Am. Inst. Banking. Chmn. protective com. Pa. Bankers Assn. Republican. Presbyn. Mason (32°, Shriner). Clubs: Bankers, Lions. Home: 143 Main Entrance Drive, Mt. Lebanon. Office: Farmers Deposit Nat. Bank, Pittsburgh, Pa.

COLLESTER, Donald Gavin, lawyer; b. Hamilton, N.Y., Sept. 24, 1905; s. Harry J. and Ina C.; B.S., Colgate U., Hamilton, N.Y., 1926; LL.B., N.J. Law Sch., N.J., 1930; m. Constance Backer, July 15, 1934. In employ Wheeling Steel Co., Steubenville, O., 1926-27; engaged in teaching, sci. and biology, high sch., Clifton, N.J., 1927-30; admitted to N.J. bar, 1931; asso. with John C. Barbour in gen. practice of law at Clifton, N.J., 1932-36, in practice alone since 1936; judge Clifton Dist. Ct. since 1937. Served as City Rep. Chmn., Clifton, N.J., 1934-37, Passaic Co. Young Rep. Chmn., 1933-36; State chmn. Young Reps. of N.J., 1936; mem. N.J. State Rep. Exec. Campaign Com. for Landon and Knox, 1936. Mem. Clifton Unit Passaic Co. Rep. League, and Young Reps. of N.J. Mem. Am., N.J. State, Clifton City bar assns., Passaic Co. Bar Assn. (treas. 1938-39), Lambda Chi Alpha, Delta Theta Pi. Republican. Mem. Reformed Ch. Mason. Kiwanis. Home: 161 Union Av. Office: Clifton Nat. Bank. Bldg., Clifton, N.J.

COLLETT, Armand Rene, chemistry; b. Hartford City, Ind., Feb. 3, 1895; s. August and Eugenie (Loriaux) C.; A.B., W.Va. U., 1918; Ph.D., Yale, 1923; m. Dorothy May Atwood, Aug. 7, 1922; children—Dorothy May, Armand Joseph, Florence Marie. Instr. in chemistry, Yale, 1923-24; with W.Va. U. since 1924, as instr., 1924-26, prof. of chemistry since 1939. Served as 2d lt., Coast Arty. Corps, U.S. Army, 1918. Mem. Am. Chem. Soc. A.A.A.S., Sigma Xi, Alpha Chi Sigma, Gamma Alpha, Phi Lambda Upsilon. Republican. Club: Kiwanis. Home: 806 Des Moines Av., Morgantown, W.Va.

COLLETTI, Ferdinando, physician; b. Montemiletto, Prov. Avellino, Italy, Feb. 8, 1871; s. Giovanni and Concetta (Tecce) C.; student common sch., gymnasium and lyceum; M.D., U. of Naples, Italy; came to U.S., 1900; m. Elizabeth K. Yocom, Mar. 16, 1910. Examining physician for English steamship co., 1899; in gen. practice of medicine, specializing in obstetrics, Reading, Pa., since 1900. Pres. of Italian Com. for Celebration of 175th Anniversary of City of Reading; pres. of Com. for Columbus Monument presented to City of Reading, Oct. 12, 1925; mem. com. to help German children after World War. Mem. Reading Tuberculosis Assn. (v.p. 1908-09), Reading Med. Assn. (became pres. 1908), Order of Italian Sons and Daughters of America (nat. v.p.), Berks Co. Med. Soc., Pa. State Med. Assn., A.M.A. Club: Italo-American Social of Order of Italian Sons and Daughters of America (Reading). Speaker in many meetings for cause of Allies during World War. Mem. many coms. to help those in distress after fires, earthquakes, floods. Active in movements for naturalization of Italians in U.S. Address: 15 N. 4th St., Reading, Pa.

COLLEY, Robert H.; with Atlantic Refining Co. since 1919, became asst. treas., 1926, treas. and dir., 1929, v.p. 1937, now pres. Address: 260 S. Broad St., Philadelphia, Pa.

COLLIER, Bryan Cheves, pres. Cement Gun Co.; b. Indian Spring, Ga., Mar. 19, 1870; s. Bryan A. and Adrienne V. (Cheves) C.; B. Engring., U. of Ga., Athens, Ga., 1890; m. Minnie Barrett Sprague, Mar. 12, 1895; children—Adrienne Virginia (Mrs. Fred. J. Thomas), Agnes Sprague (Mrs. Ray W. Short), Evelyn May (Mrs. Charles Hayward Roberts). Began as asst. to an engr., New York City, 1890; engr. in charge right bank Mo. River Survey, 1890-91; with engring. firm, New York City, 1891-96; asst. engr. Dept. Highways, New York City, in charge highway constrn. Bronx, 1896-1907; engr. in charge constrn. John C. Rodgers, contractors, New York City, on Madison Av. Bridge, Riverside Drive, etc., 1907-10; engr. in charge field operations Valhalla Dam, 1910-14; chief engr. and gen. mgr. Hassom Paving Co., 1913-14; engr. in charge field operations for contractor Broadway and 7th Av. subways, New York, 1914-15; since 1915 with Cement Gun Co., Allentown, Pa., mfrs. of cement gun, who also maintain a contracting organization in use of this machine, pres. since 1921; pres. Gunite & Cement Gun Contracts, Ltd. (Can.); dir. Cement Gun Co., Ltd. (London). Mem. Am. Soc. Civil Engrs., Sigma Alpha Epsilon (mem. bd. of Trustees, 1901-16). Clubs: Lehigh Country (Allentown, Pa.); New York Fraternity. Home: 123 S. West St. Address: Allentown, Pa.

COLLIER, William Edwin, minister; b. Timperley, Cheshire, England, June 30, 1902; s. Edwin Charles and Gertrude (Coulborn) C.; student Bromsgrove Sch., Worcestershire, Eng., 1915-20; B.A., Merton Coll., Oxford U., Eng., 1925, M.A., 1929; student Cuddesdon Theol. Coll., Eng., 1925-26; m. Laura Margaret Williams, Nov. 8, 1927; 1 son, David Edwin. Came to U.S. 1934. Curate Christ Church, Moss Side, Manchester, Eng., 1926-29; lecturer Bolton Parish Ch., Lancashire, Eng., 1929-30, senior curate Our Lady and St. Nicholas Ch., Liverpool, Eng., 1930-32; asst. minister Ethical Ch., London, Eng., 1933-34; dir. and leader Phila. Ethical Soc. since 1934. Trustee Southwark Neighborhood House, Phila.; sponsor Phila. Marriage Counsel. Mem. Wider Quaker Fellowship; listed on Am. Unitarian Assn. List of Affiliated Ministers; Phila. Sec. Fellowship of Faiths. Mem. The World Foundation, Foreign Policy Assn., Indian Rights Assn., Civil Liberties Union, Pa. Conf. Social Workers, Contemporary Club of Phila., The Oxford Soc. Home: 317 S. 46th St. Office: 1906 Rittenhouse Square, Philadelphia, Pa.

COLLINS, Alexander Tichenor, treas. Westmoreland County; b. Louisville, Ky., Mar. 28, 1873; s. Jeremiah B. and Caroline (Tichenor) C.; student Louisville (Ky.) pub. schs. and Ben C. Weaver Business Sch.; m. Irene Shupe, 1897; children—Oliver Shupe, Alexander Tichenor. Auditor and paymaster Louisville (Ky.) Traction Co., 1888-1904; mgr. O. P. Shupe Flour Mills, Mt. Pleasant, Pa., since 1904; v.p. Pa. Miller's Mutual Fire Ins. Co. since 1932; was sch. dir. and chief burgess Mt. Pleasant (Pa.) Borough; treas. Westmoreland Co., Pa., since 1936. Mem. Eastern Com., U.S. Food Administrn., during World War. Mem. Pa. Millers and Feed Dealers Assn. (pres. 1914); hon. mem. Pa. State Volunteer Firemen's Assn. Mason (32°). Home: 525 Ridgeway Av. Office: 2 N. Main St., Greensburg, Pa.

COLLINS, Arthur J., Jr.; mem. N.J. Bd. of Conservation and Development, term expires 1940. Address: Moorestown, N.J.

COLLINS, Charles Henry, lawyer; b. Phila., Pa., Jan. 23, 1891; s. Charles Joseph and Mary Ellen (Morris) C.; student grammar schs., Atlantic City, N.J., 1900-05, high sch., Atlantic City, 1906-10; LL.B., Georgetown U., Washington, D.C., 1922, LL.M., 1923; unmarried. Editor Somers Point (N.J.) Record, 1912-18, Towson (Md.) New Era, 1919; mem. Hist. Sec., Army War Coll., War Dept., Washington, D.C., since 1919; lawyer, Washington, since 1921; dir. Neptune Mortgage Co., Atlantic City, N.J. Served successively as pvt., corp., sergt., warrant officer, lt., U.S. Army, 1918-19. Pres. bd. of edn., Somers Point, N.J., 1917-19. Mem. Am. Bar Assn., Officers' Reserve Corps, U.S. Army, Am. Legion. Democrat. Roman Catholic. Home: Gateway Casino, Somers Point, N.J. Office: Army War College, War Dept., Washington, D.C.

COLLINS, Charles Wallace, lawyer; b. Gallion, Hale Co., Ala., Apr. 4, 1879; s. Robert Wood and Ann Bates (Allen) C.; B.S., Ala. Poly. Inst., Auburn, 1899; Ph.B., U. of Chicago, 1908, A.M., 1909; fellow Semitic languages, same, 1908-09; student govt. and economics, Harvard Univ., 1910-11; studied law under pvt. tuition, 1899-1901; m. Susan Steele Spencer, July 12, 1933. Admitted to Ala. bar, 1901, to Supreme Court of U.S., 1917; practiced in Birmingham, 1901-06; librarian Haskell Oriental Mus., University of Chicago, 1909-10; in charge economic section legislative reference service, Library of Congress, 1915-18, dir. same, 1918-20. Mem. Legal Advisory Bd. to Draft Bd., 1918; legal adviser to Senate and House select coms. to devise a budget plan, 1919-20; drafted Senate bill to establish a nat. budget system; advisory com. on econ. sci. to Federal Reclassification Commn., 1919-20; contributing editor Commercial and Financial Chronicle, New York, 1920-23; law librarian of Congress, 1920-21; gen. librarian U.S. Supreme Court, same; counsel of Bureau of the Budget, Treasury Department, 1921-23, dep. comptroller of the currency, and gen. counsel, 1923-25, 1st dep. comptroller same, 1925-27; counsel merger Bank of America and Bowery & East River Nat. Bank (New York), 1928, merger Blair & Co. and Bancamerica Corpn. (New York), 1929, Blair Nat. Bank and the Bank of America N.A. (New York), 1929, Bank of America (Los Angeles) and Bank of Italy Nat. Trust & Savings Assn. (San Francisco), 1930; Counsel Bank of America Nat. Trust & Savings Assn., 1927—, Trans-America Corpn., 1928—; drafted McFadden-Pepper national bank bill, 1924. Mem. Alpha Tau Omega. Clubs: National Press, Metropolitan. Author: The Fourteenth Amendment and the States, 1912; The National Budget System and American Finance, 1917; Plan for National Budget System (House Doc. 1006, 65th Congress), 1918; The British Budget System, 1920; Essential Elements of a National Budget System, 1920; Constitutional Aspects of the President's Veto of the Budget Bill, 1920; The Branch Banking Question, 1926; Rural Banking Reform, 1931; (brochure) Constitutional Power of Congress to Enforce a Single System of Commercial Banking. Compiler: Codification of Federal Statutes in Estimates, Appropriations and Reports, 1921. Contbr. on law, finance and banking. Spl. counsel Am. Bankers Assn., 1933. Home: Harmony Hall, Oxon Hill, Prince Georges Co., Md. Office: National Press Bldg., Washington, D.C.

COLLINS, Charles Walter, entomology; b. Harrington, Del., July 6, 1882; s. George Washington and Sarah Pauline (Tharp) C.; B.S. in Agr., Univ. of Del., 1905, M.Sc., 1913; m. Eva Narcissa Hone, June 4, 1909; 1 son, Byron Hone. Asst. Gipsy Moth Lab., Mass., 1907-09; agent and expert, entomologist, senior entomologist, U.S. Dept. of Agr., Bureau of Entomology and Plant Quarantine, since 1909; in charge Gipsy and brown-tail moth investigations in New England, 1928-35; in charge Forest Insect Lab., Morristown, N.J., investigating insect carriers of Dutch elm disease fungus, since 1935. Fellow Entomol. Soc. Am.; mem. Am. Assn. Econ. Entomologists (sec., 1924-30; bus. mgr. Jour. Econ. Entomology, 1925-31), Cambridge Entomol. Club (pres. 1932). Contbr. to professional jours. Home: 54 Georgian Road. Office: 8 Whippany Road, Morristown, N.J.

COLLINS, Clarence Eugene, physician; b. Laurel, Del., Jan. 16, 1872; s. Jacob A. and Julia J. (Hitch) C.; Ph.G., Nat. Inst. Pharmacy, Phila., 1894; D.D.S., U. of Md. Dental Sch., Baltimore, 1897; M.D., U. of Md. Med. Sch., Baltimore, Md., 1901; m. Dollie Ward, Dec. 27, 1898; 1 son, Clarence Creston. Engaged in gen. practice of medicine in Crisfield, Md., continuously since 1901; dir. health and sanitation of City of Crisfield continuously through change of polit. administrns. since 1910. Pres. Crisfield Chamber of Commerce. Mem. Med. and Chirurg. Soc., Somerset Med. Soc. Democrat. Methodist. Mem. K. of P., Owls. Home: The Hygeia. Office: 302 Main St., Crisfield, Md.

COLLINS, G. Rowland; prof. marketing, U. of Newark. Address: University of Newark, Newark, N.J.

COLLINS, Henry; pres. Columbia Casualty Co. Home: Knoll Road, Tenafly, N.J. Office: 1 Park Av., New York, N.Y.

COLLINS, Herman LeRoy, newspaper man; b. Hepburn, Pa.; s. John and Catherine (Hyde) C.; A.B., Lafayette (Pa.) Coll., 1887, A.M., 1891, Litt.D., 1914; m. Marion H., dau. of S. C. and E. Long, May 22, 1913; 1 son, Herman LeRoy. Formerly news editor, mng. editor and financial editor, Philadelphia Press; mem. editorial staff Philadelphia Public Ledger beginning 1913, writing over pen name of "Girard"; later editor and pres. Phila. Evening Telegraph; now on editorial staff Phila. Inquirer; also writing under name of "Girard." Newspaper and mag. corr., London, Eng., 1901. Mem. Delta Kappa Epsilon. Republican. Episcopalian. Clubs: Union League, Philadelphia Country. Home: Cynwyd, Pa. Office: Broad and Callowhill Sts., Philadelphia, Pa.

COLLINS, J. M.; pastor Atonement Memorial Ch. (Episcopal). Address: 4708 Kingsessing Av., Philadelphia, Pa.

COLLINS, John B., editor; b. Brockport, N.Y. Editor The Pittsburgh Catholic (weekly), official organ of Diocese of Pittsburgh, since 1933. Home: 4739 Friendship Av. Office: Magee Bldg., Pittsburgh, Pa.

COLLINS, Laurence M.; surgeon-in-chief N.J. State Hosp. Address: Greystone Park, N.J.

COLLINS, Philip Sheridan; b. Phila., Pa., Oct. 28, 1864; s. James C. and Lucinda B. (Copeland) C.; ed. pub. schs., Pierce Coll.; m. Anna M. Steffan, Nov. 14, 1894 (died Apr. 1, 1910); children—James S., Alan C.; m. 2d, Mary F. Schell, of N.Y. City, Oct. 20, 1913. Reporter on Pub. Ledger, Phila., 1886-90; with Curtis Pub. Co., 1890-1937, circulation mgr., 1892-1937, dir. since 1909, gen. business mgr., 1916-27, treas. and business mgr., 1927, v.p. and treas., 1928-37, retired Oct. 1, 1937, but continues as dir.; also dir. Castanea Paper Co., Tradesmen's Nat. Bank & Trust Co. Pres. Am. Foundation; v.p. Curtis Inst. of Music. Mem. Soc. Mayflower Descendants. Republican. Presbyn. Clubs: Penn Athletic, Philadelphia Print, Philobiblon (Philadelphia); Nat. Press, Congressional Country (Washington, D.C.); Huntingdon Valley Country. Home: Wyncote, Pa. Office: 744 Public Ledger Bldg., Philadelphia, Pa.

COLLITZ, Klara Hechtenberg, author; b. Rheydt (Rhineland); grad. Höhere Lehrerinnen-Bildungsanstalt, Neuwied am Rhein, 1881; studied Lausanne, 1882-83; U. of London, Eng., Latin and French philology, 1889-92; 1st class honors, Oxford U., 1895, U. of Chicago, 1897, U. of Bonn, 1898; Ph.D., U. of Heidelberg, 1901; post-grad. work Bryn Mawr Coll., 1904-07, Johns Hopkins U., 1908-11; m. Hermann Collitz (prof. Germanic philology), Aug. 13, 1904 (died May 13, 1935). Lecturer in French philology, Victoria Coll., Belfast, Ireland, 1895-96; in charge of Germanic philology, Smith Coll., Mass., 1897-99; lecturer in Germanic philology, for women students, Oxford U., 1901-04. Mem. Am. Philological Assn., Linguistic Society of America, Modern Language Association of America, Old Students' Association (Oxford, Eng.); Alumni Assn. Johns Hopkins U., Am. Assn. of Univ. Women, Oxford Soc., Goethe Soc., Congrès International pour les Sciences Phonétiques (Gand, Belgium). Clubs: College (Bryn Mawr Coll.); Johns Hopkins U. Women's Faculty; Author: Das Fremdwort bei Grimmelshausen, 1901; Der Briefstil im 17 Jahrhundert, 1903; Fremdwörterbuch des 17 Jahrhunderts, 1904; Verbs of Motion in Their Semantic Divergence, 1931. Compiler: Selections from Early German Literature, 1910; Selections from Classical German Literature, 1914; Index to Paul & Braune's Beiträge (vols. 1-50), 1926; also contbr. to philol. jours. Home: 1027 N. Calvert St., Baltimore, Md.

COLPITTS, Edwin Henry, electrical engr.; b. Point de Bute, N.B., Can., Jan. 19, 1872; s. James Wallace and Celia Eliza (Trueman) C.; A.B., Mt. Allison U., Sackville, N.B., 1893, hon. LL.D., 1926; A.B., Harvard, 1896, A.M., 1897; m. Annie Dove Penny, Aug. 17, 1899; 1 son, Donald Bethune. Came to U.S., 1895, naturalized citizen, 1920. Asst. in physics, Harvard, 1897-99; telephone engr. Am. Telephone & Telegraph Co., Boston, 1899-1907; research engr. Western Electric Co., New York, 1907-17, asst. chief engr., 1917-24; asst. v.p. dept. of development and research, Am. Telephone & Telegraph Co., 1924-34; v.p. Bell Telephone Laboratories, 1933-37; now retired. Iwadare lecturer, Japan, 1937. Served with U.S. Signal Corps on staff Gen. Edgar Russel, 1917-18. Fellow Am. Inst. E.E., Inst. Radio Engrs., Am. Physical Soc., Acoustical Soc. of America, A.A.A.S.; mem. Am. Chem. Soc., Harvard Engring. Soc. of New York, Telephone Pioneers of America. Republican. Presbyn. Club: Canoe Brook Country. Home: 309 Lawn Ridge Rd., Orange, N.J.

COLPITTS, Walter William, consulting engr.; b. Moncton, N.B., Can., Sept. 17, 1874; s. Henry Herbert and Lucy Anne (Bissett) C.; B.Sc., McGill U., Montreal, 1899 (valedictorian; winner Brit. Assn. medal), M.Sc., 1901, LL.D., 1921; m. Florence Rossington, Oct. 15, 1907; children—Lucy Anne, Jeremy Rossington. Came to U.S., 1901, naturalized citizen, 1921. Began as office boy to chief engr. of Intercolonial Ry., 1892; served as draftsman, rodman and instrumentman on r.r. surveys; chief clk. to Sir Thomas Shaughnessy, pres. Canadian Pacific Ry., 1899-1900; trans. to constrn. dept., 1900-1901; engaged in r.r. constru., irrigation and power projects in Southwestern States and Mexico, 1901-13; mem. firm Coverdale & Colpitts, cons. engrs., New York, since 1913; dir. P.M. Ry. Co., Pierce Petroleum Corpn., S.A.L.Ry., Darby Petroleum Co., Central Nat. Corpn., Carriers & General Corpn., Bullock Fund, Ltd., Loft, Inc., Certain-Teed Products Corpn., Budd Internat.

Corpn., Phoenix Securities Corpn., Edw. G. Budd Mfg. Co., The Celotex Corpn., The Autocar Co. Mem. Am. Inst. Cons. Engrs., Am. Soc. C.E., Am. Ry. Engring. Assn., Engring. Inst. of Can., Alpha Delta Phi. Republican. Methodist. Clubs: Lawyers, Canadian (ex-pres.), Recess, Economic (New York); Nassau, Pretty Brook, Tiger Inn (Princeton). Home: 75 Cleveland Lane, Princeton, N.J., (summer) Big Moose, N.Y. Office: 120 Wall St., New York, N.Y.

COLSTON, J(ohn) A(rchibald) Campbell, surgeon; b. Baltimore, Md., Oct. 30, 1886; s. Frederick Morgan and Clara (Campbell) C.; prep. edn., Lawrenceville (N.J.) Sch., 1901-04; Ph.B., Yale, 1907; M.D., Johns Hopkins, 1911; m. Harriet L. Zell, Nov. 9, 1922; children—Frederick Campbell, John Archibald Campbell. House officer Johns Hopkins Hosp., 1911-12, asst. resident surgeon, 1912-13; practice as surgeon, Baltimore, since 1914; asst. in urology, Johns Hopkins Med. Sch., 1913-17, instr., 1919-28, asso., 1928-33, asso. prof. of urology since 1933. Served as 1st lt., capt. and major, Med. Corps, U.S. Army, 1917-19; with B.E.F. as batt. med. officer, June-Nov. 1917; with A.E.F., 42d (Rainbow) Div. and Base Hosp. 18, Dec. 1917-Mar. 1919. Mem. A.M.A., Baltimore Med. Soc., Med. and Chirurg. Faculty of Md., Southern Med. Soc., Am. Urol. Assn. (past pres. Mid-Atlantic branch), Am. Assn. Genito Urinary Surgeons, Clin. Soc. Genito Urinary Surgeons, Société Internationale d'Urologie, Delta Psi, Phi Beta Kappa, Alpha Omega Alpha. Episcopalian. Clubs: Maryland, Elkridge, Pithotomy (Baltimore); George Blakiston Shoetree and Gun. Asso. editor, Jour. of Urology. Home: Woodbrook Lane, Woodbrook, Md. Office: 1201 N. Calvert St., Baltimore, Md.

COLT, Martha Cox (Mrs. Guy Alton Colt), artist and teacher; b. Harrisburg, Pa.; dau. of Daniel Walker and Matilda Eleanor (Galbraith) Cox; student Moore Inst. and Sch. of Design, Phila.; 1898-1902, N.Y. Sch. of Art, New York City, 1907, Pa. Acad. of Fine Arts, 1901-02, 1928, U. of Pa.; 1930; m. Guy Alton Colt, April 30, 1914. Engaged in teaching art, Seiler Sch., Harrisburg, Pa., 1908-14, pres. Manchester Shale Brick Co., Emmigsville, Pa., 1920-26; dir. Harrisburg Sch. of Art and Central Pa. Art Sch., 1930-34; Pa. State Supervisor Mus. Extension Projects, Works Progress Adminstrn. since 1935. Mem. Harrisburg Art Assn., Plastic Club of Phila. Democrat. Presbyn. Home: 406 Spring St. Office: 46 N. Cameron St., Harrisburg, Pa.

COLTON, Ethan Theodore, Y.M.C.A., worker; b. Palmyra, Jefferson Co., Wis., Nov. 22, 1872; s. of Henry T. and Jane (Congdon) C.; B.A., Dak. Wesleyan U., 1898; LL.D. from same univ., 1929; post-grad. work, Univ. of Chicago and Columbia U.; m. Caroline Quigg, Oct. 11, 1900; children—Ethan Theodore, Elizabeth G. (dec.), Marjorie Congdon. Teacher in Prep. Dept. Dak. Wesleyan U., 1898-99; student sec. State com. Ill. Y.M.C.A., 1899-1900; traveling sec., student dept., Internat. Com. Y.M.C. Assns., 1900-04; sec. foreign dept. same, 1904-15, asso. gen. sec., 1915-24. Apptd. chmn. Commn. on Survey and Occupation of Congress on Christian Work in Latin America, Panama, 1916. Organized the Y.M.C.A. service in Russia and Siberia, 1918, and relief for Russian intelligentsia, 1922-25; administrative sec., 1925-1926, of the Home Base and the Russia-Baltic Areas for the Foreign Com. of the Nat. Councils of Y.M.C. Assns. of U.S. and Can., exec. sec., Foreign Com., 1926-32. Mem. Internat. Com. of Y.M.C.A., Am. Sect. of Universal Christian Council for Life and Work; Nat. Geog. Soc.; Am. Acad. Polit. Science, Phi Kappa Phi. Methodist. Author of The XYZ of Communism and Four Patterns of Revolution. Home: Upper Montclair, N.J.

COLTON, Isadore Harry, lawyer; b. Boston, Mass., Nov. 26, 1897; s. Harry and Celia (Schwartz) C.; LL.B., N.J. Law Sch., Newark, N.J., 1918; m. Gertrude Spector, Feb. 21, 1922; children—Clarice Judith, Malcolm Adrian. Admitted to N.J. bar as atty., 1919, as counselor, 1922; engaged in gen. practice of law as individual at Newark, N.J. since 1919; served as NRA adminstr. for cleaning and dyeing trade under N.J. State Code, 1933 to 1935; served as commr. on State Trade Bd. for cleaning and dyeing trade. Served in U.S.N. during World War. Mem. Essex Co. Bar Assn. Democrat. Hebrew religion. Club: Athletic (Newark). Home: 316 Tichenor Av., South Orange. Office: 24 Branford Pl., Newark, N.J.

COLVER, Alice Ross (Mrs. Frederic B. Colver), writer; b. Plainfield, N.J., Aug. 28, 1892; d. Louis Runyon and Sarah Greenleaf (Wyckoff) Ross; A.B., Wellesley, 1913; studied Dr. Savage's Normal Sch. Phys. Edn.; m. Frederic Beecher Colver, Sept. 8, 1915; children—Frederic Ross, Jean, John Richard. Mem. Authors' League America, Am. Assn. Univ. Women, Assn. of Women for World Peace, Dramatists Guild, Zeta Alpha. Presbyn. Club: Pen and Brush. Author: Babs Series for Girls (4 vols.), 1917-20; Jeanne Series for Girls (4 vols.), 1920-24; (novels) Dear Pretender; If Dreams Come True; Under the Rainbow Sky; The Look Out Girl; The Dimmest Dream; The Redheaded Goddess, 1929; Hilltop House, 1930; Windymere, 1931; Modern Madonna, 1932; Passionate Puritan, 1933; Three Loves, 1934; Wild Song, I Have Been Little Too Long, 1935; Strangers at Sea, Substitute Lover, 1936; Only Let Me Live, One Year of Love, 1937; Adventure for a Song, 1938; If You Should Want to Write, 1939; Adventure on a Hilltop; also short stories and articles. Home: 54 Magnolia Av., Tenafly, N.J.

COLVIN, Charles H(erbert), engineer; b. Sterling, Mass., Mar. 4, 1893; s. Fred Herbert and Mary (Loring) C.; student Eastern Grammar Sch., East Orange, N.J., 1898-1906, high sch., East Orange, N.J., 1906-10; M.E., Stevens Inst. Tech., Hoboken, N.J., 1914; m. Bessie Davis, July 9, 1929; children—Elizabeth, David Loring, Roger Davis. Mechanic Curtiss Aeroplane and Motor Cos., Hammondsport, N.Y., 1913; engr., mgr. aircraft instrument dept. Sperry Gyroscope Co., Brooklyn, N.Y., 1914-19; pres. and gen. mgr. Pioneer Instrument Co., Brooklyn, N.Y., 1919-31; dir. Colvin Labs., Morristown, N.J., 1932-37; gen. mgr. Kollsman Instrument Co., Elmhurst, N.Y., since 1937. Asso. fellow Inst. of Aeronautical Sciences, Royal Aeronautical Soc.; mem. A.A.A.S., Soc. of Automotive Engrs., Am. Soc. M.E., Franklin Inst., Nat. Aeronautic Assn. Club: Aviation Country (Hicksville, L.I., N.Y.). Home: Egbert Hill, Morristown, N.J. Office: Kollsman Instrument Co., Elmhurst, N.Y.

COLVIN, Fred Herbert, editor emeritus, American Machinist; b. Sterling, Mass., Oct. 5, 1867; s. Henry F. and Harriet (Roper) C.; ed. pub. schs. and Spring Garden Inst., Phila., Pa.; m. Mary Kendall Loring, Mar. 3, 1890; children—Charles Herbert, Henry Fred, Roger Porter (dec.). Began as contbr. to American Machinist, 1886; editor Machinery, 1894-1907; editor American Machinist since 1907. Mem. Am. Soc. M.E., Franklin Inst., Soc. Automotive Engrs. Unitarian. Author: Machine Shop Arithmetic (with W. L. Cheney), 1895; (with F. A. Stanley) American Machinist Handbook (7 edits., over 275,000 copies sold), 1908; (with H. F. Colvin) Aircraft Handbook, 1917; (with F. A. Stanley) Machine Shop Operations (2 vols.), 1920; (with K. A. Juthe) Working of Steel, 1920; and many other books and booklets. Travels about 10,000 miles a year visiting shops. Home: Point Pleasant, N.J. Office: 330 W. 42d St., New York, N.Y.

COLVIN, William Henry, lawyer; b. South Brownsville, Pa., Apr. 17, 1885; s. Levi and Emma (Ewart) C.; grad. Mercersburg Acad., 1904, Princeton U., 1908; LL.B., U. of Pittsburgh Law Sch., 1911; m. Katharine Friel, Oct. 14, 1914; children—Katharine-Elizabeth, Dorothy Jane, William Henry, Ralph Minehart. Admitted to practice before bars of Allegheny Co., Supreme Ct. of Pa., Superior Ct. of Pa. and U.S. Dist. Ct. 1911; served in Naturalization Bur. for Western Dist. of Pa., 1915-18; pres. and treas. Colvin, Atwell & Co., 1918-27; returned to private practice of law, 1927; asst. dist. atty. of Allegheny Co. since 1929. Mason (32°, K.T.). Home: 332 S. Lang Av. Office: 302 Court House, and 1207 Law & Finance Bldg., Pittsburgh, Pa.

COLWELL, Alexander Hunter, M.D.; b. Pittsburgh, Pa., Oct. 16, 1887; s. William Wilson and Sarah Ellen (Hunter) C.; M.D., with 1st honors, U. of Pittsburgh, 1914; m. Nancy Ann Martin, Oct. 10, 1916; children—Alexander Hunter, Nancy Ann. Interne Western Pa. Hosp., 1914-15; Mellon fellow in med. research, 1915-16; asso. prof. medicine, U. of Pittsburgh, since 1934; mem. staff St. Francis, Magee and Presbyn. hosps. Chmn. Mayor's Advisory Com. on Municipal Hosps., 1934. Served with A.E.F. in France, World War; hon. disch. with rank of capt., 1919. Dir. Pa. Pub. Charities Assn. Bur. of Social Research. Mem. Am. Med. Assn., Med. Soc. State of Pa. (pres. 1935-36), Allegheny County Med. Soc. (pres. 1930-31), Soc. Biol. Research, Pittsburgh Acad. Medicine, Alpha Omega Alpha. Ind. Republican. Mem. United Presbyn. Ch. Mason. Club: University. Contbr. to professional jours. Home: 1437 Browning Rd. Office: 121 University Place, Pittsburgh, Pa.*

COLWELL, Robert Cameron, physicist; b. Fredericton, N.B., Can., Oct. 13, 1884; s. David Colwell and Mary (Cameron) C.; A.B., U. of N.B., 1904, A.M., 1908; A.B., Harvard, 1907; student U. of Chicago, 1908-10; Ph.D., Princeton U., 1918; student Cambridge U., England, 1923-24; m. Mary Dell Walker, Dec. 21, 1911. Prof. physics, Geneva Coll., Beaver Falls, Pa., 1907-23; prof. physics, West Va. U. since 1924; asst. commr. weights and measures, State of W.Va., since 1924. Mem. Am. Phys. Soc., Franklin Inst., Inst. Radio Engrs., A.A.A.S., Am. Math. Soc. Optical Soc. America, Acoustical Soc. America, Phi Delta Theta, Sigma Pi Sigma, Sigma Xi. Republican. Presbyterian. Clubs: Harvard of Western Pa.; Princeton of W.Va. Author of many articles on radio waves, spinning tops and gyroscopes, vibrating plates, velocity of sound to tech. jours. Home: 224 Park St., Morgantown, W.Va.

COLYER, Morrison C.; mem. law firm Colyer & Clapp. Address: 740 Broad St., Newark, N.J.

COMAN, (Francis) Dana, M.D., psychiatrist; b. N.Y., Oct. 31, 1895; s. Frederick Henry (D.D.) and Evelyn Maria (Dana) C.; A.M., Harvard, 1920; M.D., Johns Hopkins, 1924; unmarried. Inst. in anatomy, Johns Hopkins, 1924-27, asst. in surgery, 1927-30, instr. in psychiatry since 1931; physician Grenfell Mission, Labrador, 1923; surgeon Lakeside Hosp., Cleveland, O., 1925, Johns Hopkins Hosp., Baltimore, 1927-28; med. dir. Byrd Antarctic Expdn., 1928-30, Ellsworth Trans-antarctic Expdn., 1934-35; leader Coman Oceanographic Expdn. in survey of recent U.S. acquisitions in islands of equatorial Pacific; master Am. Yacht Kinkajou; dir. Dept. of Colloid Chemistry, Fla. Southern Coll.; nutritional dir. U.S. Antarctic Expdn., 1939. Dir. Colloidal Inst. (New York), Loomis (N.Y.) Sanatorium Andean Anthropol. Inst. (Ecuador); psychiatrist Johns Hopkins Hosp., since 1931. Served as pvt. inf., French Army, 1917-19; cited on Somme, Chemin des Dames and at Navarin Farm. Hon. fellow Los Angeles Acad. Medicine, New Zealand Alpine Club; fellow Am. Geog. Soc., A.M.A., A.A.A.S.; mem. Am. Assn. Anatomists, Med. and Chirurg. Faculty of State of Md., Md. Hist. Soc. Awarded Congressional Medal for service in Antarctic. Clubs: Baltimore, Johns Hopkins, Maryland (Baltimore); Bachelor's Cotillon (Washington); Explorers (New York). Corr. New York Times, 1928-30. Research in exptl. neurology, also med. and nutritional problems of polar and equatorial explorations and colloid chemistry in nutrition. Home: 710 N. Washington St. Office: Johns Hopkins Univ. Med. School, Baltimore, Maryland.

COMANDO, Harry N.; attending surgeon Newark Beth Israel and Newark City Hosps.; cons. surgeon Irvington Gen. Hosp. Address: 690 Clinton Av., Newark, N.J.

COMBS Hugh Dunlap, surety co. exec.; b. Yonkers, N.Y., Dec. 30, 1889; s. Franklin Pierce and Rosetta (Dunlap) C.; LL.B., St. Lawrence U. Law Sch., Brooklyn, N.Y., 1921; m. Edith Eskesen, Oct. 20, 1921; 1 dau., Edith Eskesen. Admitted to N.Y. bar, 1921 and employed as atty. in N.Y. office of United States Fidelity & Guaranty Co. of Baltimore, Md., 1921-26, supt. of claims, 1926-32, vice-pres.

in charge of claims, at home office, Baltimore, Md. since 1932; member bd. of dirs. The Foundation Company. Served as enlisted private to 2d lt. Q.M.C., U.S.A., 1917-19, with A.E.F. in France. Mem. Am. Bar Assn. (chmn. casualty ins. law com.), Md. and N.Y. bars, Am. Legion. Conglist. Clubs: Merchants, Casualty and Surety, Baltimore Country (Baltimore); Lake Hopatcong Country (N.J.). Home: 4304 Rugby Rd. Office: 26 S. Calvert St., Baltimore, Md.

COMEN, Louis M., lawyer; b. Bridgeport, Conn., June 25, 1895; student high sch., Bridgeport, Conn., 1909-12; B.C.S., N.Y. U., 1920; LL.B., N.J. Law Sch., Newark, N.J., 1924; m. Beatrice Levenson, Nov. 20, 1919; 1 son, Richard L. Began as C.P.A., Ohio, 1919; C.P.A. states of N.J., Ohio, Conn.; admitted to N.J. bar, 1924; mem. firm Levenson, Comen & Levenson, lawyers, Union City, N.J. Served in U.S. Navy, 1918-19; now lt., U.S.N.R. Trustee Hudson Co. (N.J.) Tuberculosis League, Am. Red Cross (North Hudson Chapter); pres. West N.Y. Bd. of Trade since 1934. Mem. Am. Bar Assn., N.J. Bar Assn., Hudson Co. Bar Assn. Mason (Scottish Rite; Shriner). Home: 5699 Boulevard, North Bergen, N.J. Office: Dispatch Bldg., Union City, N.J.

COMFORT, Howard, coll. prof.; b. Haverford, Pa., June 4, 1904; s. William Wistar and Mary Lawton (Fales) C.; A.B., Haverford (Pa.) Coll., 1924; A.M., Princeton U., 1927, Ph.D., 1932; m. Elizabeth P. Webb, June 3, 1931; children—William Wistar II, Laura Washburn. Engaged as instr. Latin, Haverford Sch., 1924-26, Taft Sch., 1927; fellowship in classics, Am. Acad. in Rome, 1927-29; asst. prof. Latin and Greek, Hamilton Coll., Clinton, N.Y., 1929-30; instr. Latin and Greek, Haverford (Pa.) Coll., 1932, asst. prof., 1932-38, asso. prof. since 1938; cons. in Prison Industries Reorgn. Adminstrn., 1936. Dir. Indian Rights Assn., Pa. Com. on Penal Affairs, Family Soc. Phila., Community Health and Civic Assn. Ardmore, Pa., Phila. and Suburban Town Meetings, Osborne Assn. Mem. Am. Philol. Assn., Archæol. Inst. of America (pres. Phila. Soc. since 1937), Classical Club Phila., Phila. Oriental Club, Classical Assn. Atlantic States; corr. mem. Archæologisches Inst. des Deutschen Reiches. Republican. Soc. of Friends. Contbr. articles to philol. and archæol. jours. Home: Haverford, Pa.

COMFORT, William Wistar, college pres.; b. Germantown, Pa., May 27, 1874; s. Howard and Susan Foulke (Wistar) C.; A.B., Haverford College, Pa., 1894; A.B., Harvard, 1895, A.M., 1896, Ph.D., 1902; Litt.D., U. of Pa., 1917; LL.D., U. of Md., 1918, Lake Forest U., 1925 m. Mary Lawton Fales, 1902. Instr. in Romance langs., Haverford Coll., 1897-98; travel and study in Europe, 1898-1901; instr. and asso. prof. Romance langs., Haverford, 1901-09; prof. Romance langs. and lits. and head of dept., Cornell U., 1909-17; pres. Haverford (Pa.) Coll. since June 1917. Mem. Modern Lang. Assn. America, Soc. of Friends. Author: French Prose Composition, 1908; The Choice of a College, 1925. Editor: Calderon's La Vide es sueño, 1904; Les Maitres de la critique litéraire au disneuvième siècle, 1909. Contbr. numerous articles in philol. and other jours. Home: Haverford, Pa.

COMPTON, Earl Victor, lawyer; b. Springview, Neb., April 18, 1894; s. Horatio Hope and Nellie Gertrude (Rowland) C.; LL.B., U. of Neb., Lincoln, Neb., 1915; m. Elizabeth Farr Cornelius, Sept. 29, 1923. Admitted to Pa. bar, 1922 and since engaged in gen. practice of law at Harrisburg, Pa. Served as 2d lt. A.S., U.S. Army, 1918; maj. Air. Corps Res., U.S. Army. Mem. Pa. Bar Assn., Am. Legion, Vets. Fgn. Wars. Republican. Episcopalian. Mason. Home: 2032 Chestnut St. Office: 503 Keystone Bldg., Harrisburg, Pa.

COMROE, Bernard I., physician; b. York, Pa., Oct. 22, 1906; s. Julius H. and Mollie (Levy) C.; A.B., U. of Pa., 1925, M.D., Med. Sch., 1929; m. Grace N. Miller, Jan. 1, 1934; 1 dau., Barbara Joan. Interne University Hosp., 1929-31, chief resident in medicine, 1931-33; Edward Bok Fellow in medicine, 1931-33; instr. in medicine, schs. of medicine and dentistry, U. of Pa. since 1933, ward phys. University Hosp., Phila. Certified as specialist in internal medicine by Am. Bd. Internal Medicine. Fellow Am. Coll. Phys., A.M.A., Phila. Coll. Physicians; mem. Phi Beta Kappa, Alpha Omega Alpha, Sigma Xi, Eta Sigma Sigma, Phi Delta Epsilon. Author numerous med. articles and several text books on med. and dental subjects. Home: 106 Beverly Rd., Overbrook Hills, Pa. Office: 1726 Pine St., Philadelphia, Pa.

COMSTOCK, Glen Moore, sales engring; b. Lincoln, Neb., Jan. 21, 1887; s. Charles E. and Julia L. (Daniels) C.; grad. West Denver (Colo.) High Sch., 1906; B.S., Sheffield Scientific Sch., Yale, 1912; m. Meredith E. Riddle, 1916; 1 son, Glen Moore. Constrn. engr. Riter, Conley Mfg. Co., Leetsdale, Pa., 1912-15; engr. Koppers Co., Pittsburgh, 1915-18; steam and hydraulic engr. Pittsburgh Crucible Steel Co., Midland, Pa., 1918-21; combustion engr. Jones & Laughlin Steel Corpn., Aliquippa, Pa., 1921-24; sales engr. Surface Combustion Co., Pittsburgh, 1924-25; sales, chief engr., sales mgr., v.p. Rush Machinery Co., Pittsburgh, 1925-32; since 1932 operating own business, Glen Moore Comstock, sales engring., Pittsburgh. Mem. Yale Engring. Soc., Am. Soc. Heating and Ventilating Engrs., Engrs. Soc. Western Pa., Nat. Assn. Power Engrs., Y.M.C.A. Republican. Presbyterian. Clubs: Harvard-Yale-Princeton (Pittsburgh). Home: 154 College Av., Beaver, Pa. Office: 604 Chamber of Commerce Bldg., Pittsburgh, Pa.

COMSTOCK, Louis Kossuth, electrical engr.; b. Kenosha, Wis., Jan. 8, 1865; s. Charles Henry and Mercy (Bronson) C.; Ph.B., U. of Mich., 1888; m. Anne Wilson, Sept. 12, 1902; 1 son, Thomas B. With North Am. Constrn. Co., Pittsburgh, Pa., 1888-91; in practice as constructing engr. on own account, Chicago, 1891-97; supt. constrn. for Western Electric Co., 1897-1900; elec. engr. with George A. Fuller Co., New York, 1900-04; organizer, 1904, L. K. Comstock & Co., pres., 1904-26, now chmn. bd.; v.p., mem. bd. mgrs. Montclair (N.J.) Savings Bk.; dir. United Cigar-Whelan Corpn. and v.p. and dir. 16 E. 52d St. Co.; v.p. and sec. 975 Park Av. Corpn. (dir.), Realty Mortgages Servicing Corpn., Commr. Town of Montclair, N.J. Has installed elec. and mech. equipments in many of the largest bldgs. and industrial plants in New York, Chicago, Canada, and other localities. Mem. War Industries Bd., 1918. President Merchants' Assn.; dir. Am. Arbitration Assn.; del. to 4th Congress Internat. Chamber of Commerce, Stockholm, 5th Congress, Amsterdam, and 6th Congress, Washington; del. to 5th Internat. Congress Bldg. and Pub. Works, London. Fellow. Am. Inst. E.E.; mem. Am. Soc. M.E., Acad. of Polit. Science, Pilgrims of U.S. Clubs: Engineers, Bankers, University (New York); Montclair Golf. Home: Montclair, N.J. Office: 233 Broadway, New York, N.Y.

CONARD, Charles Wilfred, lawyer; b. Phila., Pa., Jan. 15, 1872; s. Thomas P. and Rebecca S. (Baldwin) C.; LL.B., U. of Pa. Law Sch., 1893; m. Mary E. Ogden, May 5, 1902; 1 dau., Mary B. (Mrs. Daniel D. Test Jr.). Admitted to Pa. bar, 1893, and since engaged in gen. practice of law at Phila. and in Delaware County; mem. firm Conard and Middleton, Phila., since 1898; dir. and counsel Lansdowne Bldg. and Loan Assn.; dir. Struthers Dunn Co. Dir. Elwyn Training Sch. for Feeble Minded Children, Family Welfare Soc., Phila. and Delaware Co. bar assns. Republican. Soc. of Friends. Home: "The Knoll," Lansdowne. Office: 1416 S. Penn Sq., Philadelphia, Pa.

CONARD, William Roberts, gen. engring; b. Burlington, N.J., May 19, 1872; s. William and Julia Ann (Powell) C.; student pub. schs., Burlington, N.J., Trenton Bus. Coll., 1888; m. Carabelle Topping, June 20, 1895; children—Wilfred George, Robert Powell, Carabelle Augusta (Mrs. Robert H. Mitchell), Esther Laurie. Was stock and asst. shipping clk., 1889-92; asst. to pres. Pocket List of R.R. Officials, 1894-95; inspecting engr. since 1895, engaged in bus. on own acct., gen. engring., inspections and testing materials since 1897. Mem. bd. edn., Burlington, N.J., 1901-12 and 1922-38, pres., 1932-37. Served as postmaster of Burlington, N.J., 1924-29. Mem. Am. Soc. Civil Engrs., Am. Soc. Mech. Engrs., N.E. Water Works Assn., Am. Water Works Assn. Republican. Methodist. Mason. Odd Fellow. Jr. O.U.A.M. Club: Burlington County Country. Home: 1004 High St. Office: 321 High St., Burlington, N.J.

CONAWAY, Walt. P.; attending gynecologist Atlantic City Hosp. Address: 1723 Pacific Av., Atlantic City, N.J.

CONDON, Harry Ruth, wood preserving; b. Conshohocken, Pa., Nov. 19, 1887; s. Patrick and Anne Elizabeth (Ruth) C.; student U. of Pa., 1907; B.S. in Forestry, Pa. State Coll., 1913; m. Nell Elizabeth Warren, June 3, 1920; 1 son, Richard Warren (dec.). Employed as asst. forester Pa. R.R. Co., 1913-27, forester, 1927; v.p. and gen. mgr. Am. Mond Nickel Co., 1927-29; v.p. Century Wood Preserving Co., 1929-35; v.p. Wood Preserving Corpn., Pittsburgh, since 1935. Served as capt. Engr. Corps, U.S. Army, during World War; officer Commn. to Negotiate Peace, 1918-19. Mem. Soc. Am. Foresters, Am. Wood Preservers Assn. (past pres.), Am. Ry. Engrs. Assn., Alpha Gamma Rho. Republican. Presbyterian. Clubs: Union League (Phila.); Aronimink Golf (Newton Square, Pa.). Home: Morewood Gardens. Office: Koppers Bldg., Pittsburgh, Pa.

CONE, Sydney M.; consultant in orthopedic surgery Sinai Hosp. Address: Woodholm Av., Pikesville, Md.

CONFREY, (Joseph) Burton, author, educator; b. LaSalle, Ill., Feb. 1, 1898; s. John Joseph and Mary Virginia (Mullen) C.; Ph.B., U. of Chicago, 1918, A.M., 1920; Ph.D., Cath. U. of America, Washington, D.C., 1931; unmarried. Teacher U. of Notre Dame, 1920-29; dir. of ednl. studies, Mount Mercy Coll., Pittsburgh, since 1932. Served with Chem. Warfare Service, 1918-19. Hon. mem. Institut Historique et Heraldique de France. Mem. Pi Gamma Mu. Catholic. Author: Secularism in American Education, 1931; Faith and Youth, 1932; Travel Light, 1933; Social Studies, 1934; Catholic Action, 1935; Original Readings for Catholic Action, 1936; Sensory Training for Catholic Schools, 1938; Initiating Research in Catholic Schools, 1938; Educational and Vocational Supervision for Catholic Schools, 1939; Stenciled of God, 1939; Method in literature, 1939; Moral Mission of Literature, 1939. Editor and compiler. Readings for Catholic Action, 1937. Contbr. many articles to periodicals. Home: 1039 7th St., LaSalle, Ill. Address: 3333 5th Av., Pittsburgh, Pa.

CONGDON, Clement Hillman, editor; b. Harrisburg, Pa., July 25, 1868; s. Brig. Gen. James Adams (U.S.V.) and Caroline Walker (Bishop) C.; ed. by mother and at Hahnemann Med. Coll., Phila., 1 term; m. Naomi Julia Broadnax, Apr. 18, 1892 (she died June 14, 1934); 1 son, Clem Harris (U. S. Navy). Learned telegraphy at the age of 12; joined the staff of Philadelphia Record, 1889, specializing in real estate, labor, crime and finally politics; exposed robbery of the city by political machine; wrote politics and crime for Sunday Transcript 12 yrs., owner of paper since 1904, made exposé that resulted in Mann Act and "White Slave" crusade; pres. Nat. Investment Transcript Corpn. (pubs. financial paper), Camden, N.J. Owner Victory Farms and breeder of pure-bred Holstein cattle, Berkshire hogs, Percheron horses and German shepherd dogs. An organizer Com. of Seventy which created the City Party of Phila.; pres. Constitutional Liberty League; an organizer World's Christian Citizenship Conf., Phila., 1910, Portland, Ore., 1913; publicity dir. of first conv. Anti-Saloon League, Columbus, O., 1913, also Atlantic City, N.J., 1914. Formerly capt. Co. C, Capital City Cadets, Harrisburg. Mem. Holstein Friesian Assn. America, Am. Rose Soc. Am. Berkshire Assn., Am. Telegraphers' Hist. Assn., Md. Hist. Soc., Sons of Vets, Pi Gamma Mu. Republican. Episcopalian. Mason (32°). Clubs: Nat. Press (Washington); Clover, Dot and Dash, Pen and Pencil, Phila. Bridge Club. Has made extensive study of all conditions attending production and distribution of milk. Writing and publishing weekly in Sunday Transcript, "Political History of Pennsylvania"; chapters written backwards from 1935 to Penn in England, so that errors may be corrected before book is published. Home: St. James Hotel. Office: 1700 Sansom St., Philadelphia, Pa.*

CONGDON, Wray Hollowell, prof. edn. and dean; b. Bradford, Pa., July 29, 1892; LaFayette and Frances Anna (Kingsley) C.; A.B., Syracuse (N.Y) U., 1914, A.M. in English, 1915; A.M. in Edn., U. of Mich., Ann Arbor, Mich., 1923, Ph. D., 1929; m. Anna May Stuart, July 29, 1918; children—June Anna May, Ednagene, Vera Antoinette (dec.). Engaged as teacher English and head English Dept. Peking U., China, 1915-19; asst. prin. and head English Dept., Hui Wen Acad., Tientsin, China, 1919-21; teaching fellow, Sch. Edn. U. of Mich., 1921-23; supt. edn., Three Eastern Dists., M.E. Ch., N. China, 1923-25; prin. Hui Wen Acad., Changli, N. China, 1925-26; prin. Hui Wen Acad., Tientsin, N. China, 1926-28; instr. Sch. Edn., U. of Mich., 1928-29, asst. prof., summers 1930-34; univ. inspr. high schs., 1929-31, asst. dir. bur. cooperation with edn. instns., 1931-34; dir. admissions, Lehigh U., Bethlehem, Pa., 1934-38, dean of undergrads. and prof. edn. since 1938. Mem. bd. dirs. Family Welfare Assn. Mem. A.A.A.S., Nat. Assn. Deans and Advisers of Men, Phi Delta Kappa, Delta Upsilon. Episcopalian. Club: Rotary (Bethlehem, Pa.). Home: 1227 Lorain Av., Bethlehem, Pa.

CONGER, William Higgins, Jr., lawyer, banker; b. Phila., Pa., Jan. 2, 1880; s. William Higgins and Clara Louise (Brewer) C.; student Phila. pub. schs. and U.S. Naval Acad., class of 1899; married; children—Anthony Wayne, John Strong. Studying alone, passed State Board law examinations and admitted to Pa. bar, 1905; asst. trust officer West End Trust Co., Phila., 1905; trust officer Integrity Trust Co., 1924, v.p. since 1930; dir. Hornung Brewing Co., Phila. Republican. Episcopalian. Mason. Club: Lawyers (Phila.). Home: 4418 Spruce St. Office: Integrity Trust Co., Philadelphia, Pa.

CONKLIN, Edwin Grant, biologist; b. Waldo, O., Nov. 24, 1863; s. Dr. Abram V. and Maria (Hull) C.; S.B., Ohio Wesleyan U., 1885, A.B., 1886, A.M., 1889; Ph.D., Johns Hopkins, 1891; hon. ScD., U. of Pa., 1908, Ohio Wesleyan U., 1910, Yale U., 1930; LL.D., Western Reserve U., 1925; m. Belle, d. Rev. L. G. Adkinson, June 13, 1889; children—Paul, Mary, Isabel. Prof. biology, Ohio Wesleyan 1891-94; prof. zoölogy, Northwestern, 1894-96, U. of Pa., 1896-1908, Princeton U., 1908-33, emeritus. prof. zoölogy since 1933, spl. lecturer in biology. Trustee Woods Hole Laboratory since 1897; also trustee of Woods Hole Oceanographic Instn.; prest. Bermuda Biol. Station, 1926-36; mem. Nat. Acad. Sciences; fellow A.A.A.S. (pres. 1936), Am. Acad. Arts and Sciences; mem. Am. Soc. Zoölogists (pres. 1899), Assn. Am. Anatomists, Am. Soc. Naturalists (pres. 1912), Am. Philos. Soc. (sec. 1900-08, vice-pres. since 1932, exec. officer since 1936), Philadelphia Acad. Natural Sciences (vice pres. since 1901); mem. adv. bd. Wistar Inst.; pres. Science Service, fgn. mem. Royal Soc. of Edinburgh, Zoöl. Soc. of London, Soc. Belge de Biologie, Soc. Royale de Sci. Med. et Naturelle de Bruxelles, Königlich Böhmische Gesellschaft der Wissenschaften. Co-editor Biological Bulletin, Journal of Experimental Zoölogy, Genetics. Author: Heredity and Environment; Mechanism of Evolution; Direction of Human Evolution; Synopsis of General Morphology; Future of Evolution; Revolt Against Darwinism; Science and the Faith of the Modern; Embryology and Evolution; Problems of Development; Biology and Democracy; Freedom and Responsibility; and about 150 other works on heredity, development, education, etc. Home: 139 Broadmead, Princeton, N.J. Office: American Philosophical Soc., Independence Square, Philadelphia, Pa.

CONKLIN, Franklin, Jr., vice-pres. Flood & Conklin Co.; b. New York, N.Y., June 23, 1886; s. Franklin and Frances M. (Fullgraff) C.; ed. Newark Acad., Princeton U.; m. Marie Berrian Riker, Apr. 8, 1908; children—Franklin 3d, Eleanor Frances. With Flood & Conklin, varnish and lacquer mfrs., Newark, N.J., since 1904, beginning as stenopgrapher and clerk, became salesman, 1907, sales mgr., 1920, and vice-pres. and dir. since 1926; dir. Doehler Die Casting Co., N.J. Worsted Mills, Am. Ins. Co., N.J. Bell Telephone Co., Crocker-Wheeler Electric Mfg. Co. Mem. Citizens Advisory Finance Com. of Newark, 1932; first municipal dir. of Emergency Relief Administrn., 1933; dir. Welfare Fed. of Newark, 1925-27, 1931-33, v.p., 1931-2, Dir. Newark Y.M.C.A. (pres. 1934-38); pres. State Y.M.C.A., 1929-30; dir. and v.p. Newark Museum; dir. Newark Chamber of Commerce, v.p., 1931-32; trustee Univ. of Newark (pres. of bd.), Newark Acad., Protestant Foster Home, Bach Soc. of New Jersey (trustee and v.p.). Designated most outstanding citizen of Newark for 1937 by Advertising Club of Newark. Licensed airplane pilot since 1929. Presbyterian. Clubs: Essex, Carteret Book, Down Town, Wednesday (Newark); Essex County Country (West Orange); New England Club of the Oranges; Somerset Hills Country (Bernardsville, N.J.); Somerset Lake and Game (Far Hills, N.J.); Princeton (New York). Home: 767 Ridge St. Office: 136 Chestnut St., Newark, N.J.

CONKLIN, Lewis Roberts, lawyer; b. Monroe, N.Y., Oct. 10, 1874; s. George Rensselaer and Isabella (Roberts) C.; grad. Philips Acad., Exeter, N.H., 1892; A.B., Yale, 1896; LL.B. New York Law Sch., 1898; m. Grace Hanford Frisby, Aug. 22, 1906. Admitted to N.Y. and N.J. bar; clerk with Frederic G. Dow, attorney, 1898-1901; partner in law firm Dow & Conklin, 1901; alone as Dow & Conklin, 1902-06; partner Hamlin & Conklin, 1906-13; alone, 1913-20; partner in law firm Conklin & Montross since 1920; dir. and counsel Am. Hard Rubber Co.; pres. and dir. Bruce & Cook Land Corpn.; vice-pres. and dir. Diamond Expansion Bolt Co., Inc.; treas. and dir. Weitling-Henry-Dale Castings Corpn. Mem. Am. Bar Assn., N.Y. Bar Assn., N.J. State Bar Assn., New York City Bar Assn., Bergen Co., N.J., Bar Assn., Beta Theta Pi. Republican. Episcopalian. Club: Ridgewood Country. Home: 145 Monte Vista Av., Ridgewood, N.J. Office: 63 Wall St., New York, N.Y.; and 201 E. Ridgewood Av., Ridgewood, N.J.

CONKLING, Wallace Edmonds, clergyman; b. Beacon, N.Y., Oct. 25, 1896; s. Charles Edmonds and Susan May (Bright) C.; grad. Matteawan (N.Y.) High Sch., 1914; A.B., Williams Coll., Williamstown, Mass., 1918; S.T.B., Phila. Divinity Sch., 1921; B. Litt., Oxford Univ., England, 1922; student U. of Pa. Grad. Sch., 1922-23; m. Constance L. Sowby of Louth, Lincs., England, July 10, 1930, at Oxford, England; children—Mary Margaret Sowby, Julia Edmonds. Special instr. in Latin, U. of Pa., 1920-21; teaching fellow, Phila. Divinity Sch., 1922-23; ordained to ministry of Episcopal Ch., 1921; rector St. Lukes Ch. and Nativity Chapel, Germantown, Phila., since 1923; also rector St. John the Baptist Ch., Germantown, since 1935. Examining chaplain Diocese of Pa.; mem. Dept. of Christian Social Service, Forward Movement Commn., Clerical Salaries and Pension Commn.; dep. to Gen. Conv., 1934 and 1937 (chmn.). Served in Naval Overseas Transportation Service, U.S.N.R.F., 1918-19. Mem. Phi Beta Kappa. Author: True Values, 1931; Darkness and Light, 1931; The Queen Mother, 1932. Home: St. Luke's Rectory, 5411 Germantown Av., Philadelphia, Pa.

CONLEN, William J.; mem. law firm Conlen, La Brum & Beechwood. Office: Packard Bldg., Philadelphia, Pa.

CONLEY, Bernard; chancellor Diocese of Altoona, R. C. Ch. Address: 900 Fourth St., Altoona, Pa.

CONLEY, Brooks Lawson, engr. and mfr. electric motors; b. Grove, W.Va., Jan. 23, 1889; s. Melville and Gay (Snider) C.; B.S., U. of Wis., 1918, M.S., same, 1920, E.E., 1926. Engaged as instr. elec. engring., Case Sch. of Applied Sci., Cleveland, O., 1920-22; elec. engr. The Hoover Co., North Canton, O., 1922-27, Emerson Electric Mfg. Co., St. Louis, Mo., 1927-28, Holtzer-Cabot Electric Co., Boston, Mass., 1928-29; chief engr., Sunlight Electric Mfg. Co., Warren, O., 1929-33; vice-pres., treas. and dir., Kingston-Conley Electric Co., mfr. electric motors, North Plainfield, N.J. since 1934. Served as ensign, U.S.N.R.F., 1918-19. Mem. Am. Inst. Elec. Engrs. Republican. Unitarian. Mason (K.T., 32°, Shriner). Club: Carteret (Jersey City). Home: 60 Tillotson Rd., Fanwood, N.J. Office: 68 Brook Av., North Plainfield, N.J.

CONLEY, Clarence A., supervising principal; b. Mars, Pa., Dec. 26, 1894; s. Andrew T. and Florence L. (Kennedy) C.; grad. Mars High Sch., 1910; A.B., Grove City (Pa.) Coll., 1914; student U. of Mich., summer 1928, U. of Pittsburgh, summers 1928, 37; m. Ora J. Brunton, Mar. 28, 1918; children—Betty Florence (Mrs. Richard J. Marshall), Margaret Jane. Teacher Mars (Pa.) High Sch., 1914-16; prin. Freedom (Pa.) High Sch., 1916-18; asst. prin. Ambridge (Pa.) High Sch., 1918, prin. 1919-20; supervising prin. Mars Borough (Pa.) Schs., 1920-32, Clarion Borough (Pa.) Schs. since 1932. Served in U.S. Army, 1918. Mem. Clarion Boy Scout Com.; mem. Dist. 9 Com. Pa. Interscholastic Athletic Assn. Mem. N.E.A., Assn. School Adminstrs., Pa. State Assn., Clarion Co. Prins. Assn. (pres.), Phi Delta Kappa. Presbyterian (mem. Clarion Ch. session, supt. Sunday school). Mason. Club: Kiwanis (dir.). Home: 403 Wood St., Clarion, Pa.

CONLEY, Claude Sawtell, clergyman; b. McPheron, Pa., Sept. 13, 1901; s. Earnest Sylvester and Nancy (Fishel) C.; student Nyack (N.Y.) Inst., 1920-22; S.T.B., Western Theol. Sem., Pittsburgh, 1925, S.T.M., 1927; student U. of Pittsburgh, 1925-27, Univ. of Edinburgh, Scotland, 1929-30; m. Dorothy Frost, Sept. 19, 1929; children—John Calvin, Mary Louise and Robert George (twins), Dorothy Ann. Ordained to ministry of Presbyterian Ch., May 22, 1925; pastor Plum Creek (Pa.) Presbyn. Ch., 1925-29, Mercer (Pa.) Presbyn. Ch., 1930-38; pastor Presbyn. Ch., Dormont, Pa., since 1938. Home: 2859 Espy Av., Dormont, Pa.

CONLEY, George Thomas, Sr., physician; b. Louisa, Ky., June 30, 1881; s. John and Jenny (Huggins) C.; M.D., Louisville (Ky.) Med. Coll. and Hosp., 1908; student N.Y. Post Grad. Coll., 1919; m. Martha Vaughn, Oct. 24, 1911; children—George Thomas, Jr., Patrick Henry, Mary Margaret, Martha Vaughn. Engaged in gen. practice of medicine and surgery at Williamson, W.Va.; pres. Williamson Memorial Hosp. Fellow Am. Coll. Surgeons. Mem. Chamber of Commerce, Williamson, W.Va. Republican. Mason. Elk. Office: Williamson Memorial Hosp., Williamson, W.Va.

CONLEY, James Steinaker, lawyer; b. Kingwood, W.Va., June 12, 1905; s. William G. and Bertie I. (Martin) C.; grad. Charleston (W. Va.) High Sch., 1922; A.B., W.Va. U., 1926; LL.B., Harvard, 1929; m. Gertrude E. Laing, Nov. 27, 1929; children—James Laing, William G. III, Michael Slagle. Admitted to W.Va. bar, 1929, and practiced as mem. firm of Conley & Klostermeyer, Charleston, 1929-35; mem. firm Conley & Conley, 1935-36, Conley, Thompson & Neff since 1936; sec., dir. and mem. exec. com. Ice Sports, Inc.; sec. and dir. Jones Collieries, Inc. Mem. Charleston, W.Va., and Am. bar assns., Phi Beta Kappa, Phi Kappa Psi. Republican. Presbyterian. Club: Edgewood Country (Charleston). Home: 849 Edgewood Drive. Office: 1101 Union Bldg., Charleston, W.Va.

CONLEY, Philip Mallory, publisher; b. Charleston, W.Va., Nov. 30, 1887; s. George W. and Alice (Simpson) C.; B.S., W.Va. University, 1914; Litt.D., W.Va. Wesleyan Coll., 1936; m. Pearl Scott, Aug. 5, 1914. Teacher and supt. pub. schs. 8 yrs.; dir. welfare work The Consolidation Coal Co., Jenkins, Ky., 1919-21; editor-in-chief The W.Va. Encyclopedia, 1929; pres. and treas. W.Va. Pub. Co.; pres. Charleston Printing Co.; Commd. 2d lt. U.S.A., Sept. 13, 1918; chief of ednl. service Mil. Hosp., Markleton, Pa., and Camp Wadsworth, Spartanburg, S.C., 1918-19. Nat. vice comdr. Am. Legion, 1937-38. Decorated Chevalier Legion of Honor (France), 1937. Mem. Nat. Editorial Assn.,

Phi Beta Kappa. Republican. Methodist. Mason (K.T., 32°, K.C.C.H., Shriner). Rotarian. Author: Life in a West Virginia Coal Field (monograph), 1923; Little Stories About West Virginia (series of mag. articles); West Virginia Yesterday and Today (textbook), 1931; Beacon Lights of West Virginia History, 1939; also contbr. 24 articles on Mining Town Morale to Coal Review, 1922. Home: 5326 Kanawha Av. Office: 810 Virginia St., W., Charleston, W.Va.

CONLEY, William Gustavus, ex-gov.; b. Kingwood, W.Va., Jan. 8, 1866; s. Maj. William and Mary (Freeburn) C.; LL.B., W.Va. U., 1893, LL.D., 1929; m. Bertie Ison Martin, July 14, 1892; children—William G. (dec.), Marion (dec.), Lillian (Mrs. Vincent Legg), Donald Martin, James Stalnaker. Teacher, pub. schs., 1886-91; supt. schs., Preston Co., 1891-93; admitted to W.Va. bar, 1893, and began practice at Parsons; pros. atty., Tucker Co., 1896-1904; mem. city council, Parsons, 1897-99; mayor of Parsons, 1901-03; editor and part owner Parsons Advocate, 1896-1903; mem. city council, Kingwood, 1903-05, mayor of Kingwood, 1906-08; apptd. atty. gen., W.Va., 1908, to fill vacancy; elected to same office, 1908, for term 1909-13; mem. State Bd. of Edn., 1924-29; gov. of W. Va., Mar. 4, 1929, for term 1929-33. Hon. sec. Rep. Nat. Conv., 1896. Mem. advisory council U.S. Law Review; mem. nat. advisory bd. Nat. Thrift Com. Mem. Am., W.Va. State and Charleston bar assns., Internat. Law Assn., Am. Law Inst., Am. Judicature Soc., Am. Acad. Polit. and Social Science, Phi Beta Kappa, Pi Gamma Mu, Scabbard and Sword, Mountaineer (fraternity). Republican. Methodist. Mason (33°, Shriner), K.P., Odd Fellow. Rotarian. Clubs: Union League (Washington, D.C.); Masonic, The Variety (Pittsburgh); Edgewood Country, Greenbrier Golf and Tennis, Berkeley Aviation, Southern W.Va. Auto, Melbourne Country (Fla.). Home: 1565 Virginia St. Office: Union Bldg., Charleston, W.Va.

CONN, Charles F.; cement mfr.; b. Concord, N.H., Nov. 11, 1865; s. Granville P. and Helen M. (Sprague) C.; student Dartmouth Coll., m. Mabel S. Dwight, Nov. 7, 1889. Pres. Giant Portland Cement Co. since 1913. Home: Wayne, Pa. Office: 603 Pennsylvania Bldg., Philadelphia, Pa.

CONNELL, William Brown; prof. animal husbandry extension, Pa. State Coll. Address: State College, Pa.

CONNELL, William Henry, civil engr.; b. N.Y. City, Jan. 12, 1878; s. Edward J. and Emma Augusta (McGean) C.; ed. De La Salle Inst., New York; m. E. Nena Watters, Apr. 23, 1913. Civ. engring. work, various depts., N.Y. City, 1908-1912, including topog. surveys, water supply, highway and bridge dept. service, dept. commr. pub. works assisting boro pres. in reorganization of engring. depts., also built service test roadway and installed modern methods of highway maintenance and constrn.; chief engr. Bur. Highways and Street Cleaning, Phila., modernizing highway and street cleaning work and built service test rd., 1912-17; engring. executive with Day & Zimmerman, placing a number of large orgns. in the field for war work, 1917-19; spl. staff engr. Phila. Rapid Transit Co., 1919-23; chief exec., dept. sec. and engring. executive Pa. Dept. of Highways, in charge of constrn. and maintenance of state highway system, comprising 11,500 miles of rd., 1923-27; in consulting practice, 1927-29; executive director Regional Planning Federation of Philadelphia Tri-State Dist. since 1929; civil works adminstr. Phila. County, 1933-34; director local work division Federal Emergency Relief Adminstrn., Phila. County, 1934-35. Mem. Nat. Highway Research Council, Am. Roadbuilders Assn. (ex-pres.), Am. Assn. State Highway Officials, Am. Soc. C.E.; hon. mem. Street and Road Assn. of England. Clubs: Engineers, Racquet, Phila. Cricket. Home: 7900 Lincoln Drive, Chestnut Hill, Philadelphia, Pa.

CONNELLEY, Clifford Brown; b. Monongahela City, Pa., Mar. 26, 1863; s. George and Elizabeth (Brown), C.; Teachers College (Columbia); Western U. of Pa.; hon. M.A., Sc.D., Duequesne U., Pittsburgh; m. Katherine J. Seiferth Pulp, Jan. 12, 1889; children—Ella, Katherine. Practical experience with Robinson & Rea, Westinghouse Elc. & Mfg. Co.; asst. to John Haliburton, engr., Phila.; instr. Mech. Dept., and supt. shops, Western U. of Pa.; prin. Fifth Ward Manual Training Sch., Allegheny, Pa.; organized industrial work for City of Allegheny and was consulting supervisor Pittsburgh Industrial Schs.; dean Sch. of Applied Industries, Carnegie Institute of Technology; sec.-treas. Marine Mfg. & Supply Co.; dir. Allegheny Carnegie Free Library. Mem. Bd. of Edn. and City Council, Pittsburgh; trustee Duquesne U.; mem. Frick Ednl. Fund Commn.; pres. Fineview Bd. of Trade, Pittsburgh. Mem. Am. Sch. Peace League (pres. Pa. br., 1917-18), Mothers' Pension League of Allegheny Co. (advisory bd.), Allegheny Co. Council Boy Scouts of America; chmn of Selective Draft Bd., Allegheny Co. Republican. Methodist. Pres. manual traing dept. N.E.A., 1911-12; mem. Am. Soc. M.E. Engring. Soc. Western Pa., Soc. Promotion Industrial Edn., Soc. Promotion Engring. Edn., A.A.A.S., Am. Acad. Arts and Sciences, Pittsburgh Art Soc., Hist. Soc. Western Pa., Schoolmen's Club of Pittsburgh. Clubs: Americus, Republican, Press, Pittsburgh Athletic, Harrisburg, Duquesne, Rotary, University. Author of many papers on tech. and industrial edn. Home: 300 Marsonia St., N.S. Address: Carnegie Inst. Technology, Schenley Park, Pittsburgh, Pa.*

CONNELLY, John A.; asso. surgeon St. Francis Hosp.; visiting surgeon Trenton Municipal Hosp.; med. dir. and visiting surgeon N.J. State Prison Hosp. Address: 212 W. State St., Trenton, N.J.

CONNELLY, John Robert, univ. prof. b. Danville, Ill., Oct. 15, 1905; s. William Asbury and Una (Suffield) C.; M.S., U. of Ill., Urbana, Ill., 1929; M.A., Lehigh U., Bethlehem, Pa., 1934; m. Martha Alice Alvord, June 1, 1929; children—Joan, John Robert. Jr. mech. engr. Ill. Power and Light Corpn., Danville, Ill., 1927-28; spl. research asst., Engring Experiment Sta., U. of Ill., Urbana, Ill., 1928-29; instr. in mech. engring., Lehigh U., Bethlehem, Pa., 1929-35, asst. prof. of mech. engring, 1935-38, asso. prof. of industrial engring., since 1938. Republican. Author: Elementary Principles of Industrial Operations and Plants; papers read before Am. Soc. M.E., and articles to engring. jours. Home: 611 Norway Pl. Office: Lehigh U., Bethlehem, Pa.

CONNER, John Gilbert, mfg. millwork; b Berwick, Pa., Mar. 20, 1864; s. Samuel J. and Elmira (Fowler) C.; ed. Bloomsburg (Pa.) Teachers Coll., 1881-83; A.B., Lafayette Coll., 1887, A.M., same, 1889; m. Carrie Helen Sciple, June 25, 1889 (died 1920); m. 2d, Frances R. Dickey, June 25, 1924. Engaged as headmaster, West Nottingham Acad., Md., 1887-1902; pres. The Conner Millwork Co., Trenton, N.J., since 1902; vice-pres. H. M. Voorhees & Bro., dept. store, 1916-32; dir. Tenton Trust Co. since 1910. Served as treas., dir. and trustee Trenton Y.M.C.A. since 1911. Trustee Lafayette Coll., and West Nottingham Acad. Mem. Soc. Colonial Wars, S.R., Symposium of Trenton (pres), Delta Upsilon Franternity (trustee), Old Guard Soc. Palm Beach Golfers. Republi. Presbyn. (elder). Mason (32°). Clubs: Trenton, Cartaret. Home: 8 Belmont Circle. Office: Front & Stockton Sts., Trenton, N.J.

CONNETT, Eugene Virginius, 3d, book publisher; b. South Orange, N.J., Mar. 8, 1891; s. Eugene Virginius, J., and May (Brewer) C.; grad. St. Paul's Sch., Concord, N.H., 1908; Litt.B., Princeton U., 1912; m. Kathryn E. Underhill, Nov. 5, 1913; children—Elise Brewer, Eugene Virginius, IV. Asso. with E. V. Connett & Co., hat mfrs., Orange, N.J., 1912-25; vice-pres. James N. Johnson, printers, New York, since 1926; founded The Derrydale Press, pubs. of limited editions of sporting books and prints, 1927, pres. since 1927. Served as sergt. 1st class Chem. Warfare Service, U.S. Army, during World War. Trustee South Orange Pub. Library; vice pres., Trustees Sect. of N.J. Library Assn., 1937. Mem. N.J. Fish and Game Conservation League (pres. 1922-23), Publishers' Lunch Club of New York City (sec.-treas. 1938). Republican. Episcopalian. Clubs: Princeton (New York); Anglers of New York (pres. 1923-24); Brodhead Flyfishers (Analomink, Pa); Bellport Bay Yacht of Long Island (rear commodore 1936); Colonial (Princeton, N.J.). Author: Wing Shooting and Angling, 1924; Magic Hours, 1927; Fishing a Trout Stream, 1934; Feathered Game, From a Sporting Journal, 1929; Any Luck?, 1933; Random Casts, 1939. Contributor of many articles to leading magazines and newspapers. Mem. advisory bd. Sportsman Mag., 1927-37; asso. editor Country Life since 1937. Expert fly fisherman. Home: 170 Turrell Av., South Orange, N.J. Office: 127 E. 34th St., New York, N.Y.

CONNETT, Harold, leather mfr.; b. Washington, D.C. June 22, 1895; s. Albert Neumann and Theodora (Speir) C.; student Tonbridge Sch., Tonbridge, Eng., 1908-13; B.A., Cambridge U., Eng., 1916; grad. student Mass. Inst. Tech. 1916-17; m. Louise S. Hegeler, July 15, 1920; children—Harold, Theodora Speir, Hugh Hegeler, Albert Neumann III, Hartley Speir. Asso. with Connett, Burton & Co., exporters, 1920-24; asst. treas. Surpass Leather Co., Phila., 1924-27, gen. mgr. since 1927, pres. since 1935; vice-pres. Densten Hair and Felt Co., Booth & Co., Inc., Booth-American Shipping Corpn., Mersey & Hudson Wharfage Co. Served as capt. C.A., U.S. Army, with A.E.F., 1917-19. Mem. Tanners Council of America (chmn., also chmn. kid group since 1938), Delta Upsilon. Republican. Episcopalian. Clubs: Racquet (Phila); Merion Cricket (Aardmore, Pa.); Shinnecock Yacht (Quogue, N.Y.). Home: N. Rose Lane, Haverford, Pa. Office: 9th and Westmoreland Sts., Philadelphia, Pa.

CONNING, John Stuart, church official; b. Whithorn, Scotland, June 4, 1862; s. James and Marian (McKeand) C.; student Oberlin (O.) Coll. and U. of Toronto; B.D., Knox Coll., Toronto, 1890; D.D., St. John's Coll., Annapolis, Md., 1919; m. Margaret Alison, Jan. 1, 1890; children—Norman Elmer, Gordon Russell, Margaret Helen, John Keith Gardner. Came to U.S., 1897, naturalized citizen, 1918. Ordained ministry Presbn. Ch., U.S.A., 1890; pastor successively Caledonia, Ont., Can., Knox Ch., Walkerton, Ont., Reid Memorial, Walbrook and Westminster chs., Baltimore, Md., until 1919; pres. Presbyn. Training Sch., Baltimore, 1898-1919; sec. Bd. Nat. Missions Presbyn Ch., U.S.A., 1919-32. Mem. com. on Hebrews of Internat. Missionary Council and sec. joint department of Coöperating Boards, Home Missions Council. Author: Our Jewish Neighbors, 1928; Leila Adler, 1929; The Jew in the Modern World, 1931. Contbr. to Missionary Rev. of World, Internat. Missionary Rev., Presbyn. Mag., etc. Home: 1 Highland Terrace, Upper Montclair, N.J. Office: 156 Fifth Av., New York, N.Y.

CONNOLE, Joseph V.; mem. staff Mercy Hosp. Address: 14 W. Market St., Wilkes-Barre, Pa.

CONNOLLY, H. J., executive; b. Scranton, Pa., May 15, 1883; s. Daniel W. and Alma (Price) C.; A.B., Princeton U. 1906; m. Caroline Palmer Miller, Sept. 29, 1937. Began as lawyer, Scranton, Pa.; v.p. The Pittston Co., Scranton, Pa., 1933-38; v.p. and dir. Pa. Coal Co. since 1938; also v.p. Hillside Coal and Iron Co., Northwestern Mining and Exchange Co., New York, Susquehanna and Western Coal Co., the Blossburg Coal Co.; dir. Northwestern Mining and Exchange Co. Trustee Scranton Communty Chest. Clubs: Scranton, Princeton (New York). Mason. Home: Clarks Summit, Pa. Office: Scranton, Pa.

CONNOLLY, John J.; chief of staff and attending surgeon St. Mary's Hosp.; attending surgeon St. Michael's Hosp.; asst. attending surgeon Hosp. and Home for Crippled Children. Address: 212 W. Market St., Newark, N.J.

CONNOLLY, John R.; mem. law firm Connolly & Hueston. Address: 125 Broad St., Elizabeth, N.J.

CONNOLLY, T. Vincent; otolaryngologist St. Joseph Hosp.; cons. otolaryngologist City Hosp. Address: 56 Hamilton St., Paterson, N.J.

CONNOR, William L., sch. supt.; b. Troy, Ind., April 24, 1889; s. Samuel Kyler and Alice Neill (Purcell) C.; A.B., Ind. State Teachers Coll.; M.A., Columbia U., grad. work U. of Wis., Madison, Wis. and Western Reserve U., Cleveland, O.; m. Ernestine Stutsman, Aug. 16, 1915; children—William Harold, John Samuel. Successively teacher, principal and supt. of Troy (Ind.) schs., 1906-11; supt. of schs., Hymera, Ind., 1911-13; prin. Forest Park Sch., Crystal Falls, Mich., 1914-16; supt. of schs., Republic, Mich., 1916-20; prin., Longwood High Sch., Cleveland, O., 1920-23; chief of bur. of ednl. research Cleveland pub. schs., 1923-36; supt. of schs., Allentown, Pa., since 1937. Mem. tech. advisory com. Ohio State Teachers Assn. which prepared study on financing edn. in O., resulting in plan which was adopted by legislature; mem. com. of Pa. State Edn. Assn., which prepared study of sch. costs and financing edn. in Pa. Mem. Allentown (Pa.) Chamber of Commerce (mem. com. on pub. relations), Allentown Community Chest (chmn. civic div., 1937, 38), Family Welfare and Soc. for Chippled Children (mem. bd. control), Rotary Internat. Clubs: Rotary (Allentown, Pa.); Livingstone, Lehigh Country. Co-author: Health Workbook (with Riley and Wight); Dynamic Biology (with Baker and Mills); Dynamic Chemistry (with Biddle and Bush); Dynamic Physics (with Bower and Robinson). Author numerous articles and speeches pub. in professional mags. and yearbooks. Home: 47 S. 14th St. Office: 31 S. Penn St., Allentown, Pa.

CONNORS, Charles Henry, prof. ornamental horticulture; b. New Brunswick, N.J., July 2, 1884; s. William Henry and Martha Matilda (Steinert) C.; ed. Rutgers Coll., 1902-04, 1910-13, B.Sc., 1913; Ph.D., Rutgers U., 1928; m. Jennie Roberta Wark, Oct. 10, 1916; 1 dau., Roberta Elizabeth. Asst. in hort. investigation, N.J. Agrl. Expt. Sta., 1913-21, asso. in plant breeding, 1921-26, ornamental horticulturist and head dept. since 1926; instr. horticulture, Rutgers U., 1920-26, asst. prof. ornamental horticulture, 1926-28, asso. prof., 1928-31, prof. since 1931. Served as mem. Shade Tree Commn., Highland Park, N.J. Vice-pres. Middlesex (N.J.) Council Boy Scouts of America; awarded Silver Beaver of Boy Scouts. Fellow A.A.A.S. Mem. Am. Soc. for Hort. Sci., Am. Dahlia Soc., Dahlia Soc. N.J., Garden Club N.J., Soc. Am. Florists, N.Y. Florists Club, Pi Alpha Xi, Sigma Xi, Alpha Kappa Pi. Democrat. Mem. Reformed (Dutch) Ch. in America. Mason. Clubs: Kiwanis of New Brunswick (v.p.); Raritan Arsenal Officers' (Metuchen). Home: 115 N. Sixth Av., Highland Park, N.J.

CONNORS, Garrett A.; b. Youngstown, O., Feb. 18, 1889; s. Garrett and Mary (Scanlon) C.; student Youngsetown Coll.; m. Frances Quinn, Nov. 24, 1910 (now dec.); children—Norbert, Louise, Harry. V.p. Sharon Steel Corpn. Home: 1851 Selma Av., Youngstown, O. Office: S. Irvine Av., Sharon, Pa.

CONOVER, Elbert Moore, clergyman; b. Harrisonville, N.J., May 31, 1885; s. Samuel S. and Atlantic (Moore) C.; Dickinson Prep. Sch., Carlisle, Pa., 1902-04; Dickinson Coll., 1904; B.D., Theological Sem. Drew U., 1913; m. Ethel Holdcraft, June 23, 1908; children—Paul H., Theodore. Joined N.J. Conf. M.E. Ch., 1910; pastor Haleyville, Wall, Thorofare, Millville, all in N.J.; organizer inter-church work, 1916-17; pastor Wenonah, N.J., 1917-19; asst. sec. dept. of war emergency and reconstruction, M.E. Ch., 1919-20, exec. sec., 1920-24; dir. Bur. of Architecture M.E. Ch., 1924-34; sec. Assn. Depts. of Ch. Architecture since 1924; dir. Interdenominational Bur. of Architecture since 1934; sec. N. Am. Conf. on Ch. Architecture, 1932—; mem. com. on worship and religious arts and field dept., Federal Council Chs. of Christ; mem. com. on church school administration, International Council of Religious Education. Organizer Social Service Commn., N.J. Conf. M.E. Church (sec. 1914-36). Author: Building the House of God (required study of all candidates for ministry in M.E. Ch.), 1928, also monographs Building a Seven Day a Week Church, The Church School Building, Leadership in Church Building, Rebuilding Town and Country Church; chapter on religious architecture in The Church Looks Ahead; chapter on The Church Building in Church Attendance (18 chapters by Roger W. Babson and others). Contbr. to religious and archtl. jours. Lecturer on religious arts and church adminstrn. Home: 538 Westfield Av., Westfield, N.J. Office: 297 4th Av., New York, N.Y.

CONOVER, Elisha, Jr., univ. prof. emeritus; b. Harrisonville, N.J., Aug. 14, 1860; s. Elisha and Eliza (Van Meter) C.; student Harrisonville (N.J.) pub. schs., 1866-77, Pennington ,N.J.) Sem., 1878-79, Johns Hopkins U., 1887-88; A.B., Dickinson Coll., Carlisle, Pa., 1884, A.M., 1887; m. Fannie Lee Lingo, Dec. 27, 1888. Prin. Elmer (N.J.) pub. sch., 1881-82, Georgetown (Del.) Acad., 1884-86, Oxford (Md.) High Sch., 1886-87; teacher Latin and Greek, Wesley Collegiate Inst., Dover, Del., 1888-91, Montpelier (Vt.) Sem., 1891-95; prof. Latin and Greek, U. of Del., Newark, Del., 1895-1938, prof. emeritus since 1938. Mem. Am. Assn. Univ. Profs., Am. Classical League, Am. Philol. Assn., Classical Assn. of Atlantic States, Phi Kappa Psi, Phi Beta Kappa, Phi Kappa Phi. Republican. Episcopalian. Internat. Order Good Templars, Modern Woodmen of America. Home: 247 W. Main St., Newark, Del.

CONOVER, Julian Darst, mining engr. and geologist; b. Madison, Wis., Dec. 27, 1895; s. Frederic King and Grace (Clark) C.; B.S., U. of Wis., 1917, E.M., 1921; m. Josephine Taylor, May 28, 1928; children—Julian Darst, Frederic King, 2d, John Taylor. Engaged in geol. work and mine exam. for various interests in Alaska, Ida., Ariz., Lake Superior region, Mexico, S.America, 1915-23, including 1 yr. in charge operations Brazilian Iron & Steel Co. in Minas Geraes, Brazil, and 1 yr. instr. engring. geology, U. of Wis.; sec. Tri-State Zinc & Lead Ore Producers Assn., Miami, Okla., 1924-29; sec. Am. Zinc Inst., N.Y. City, 1929-34; sec. Am. Mining Congress, Washington, D.C., since 1935. Served as lt., capt. and maj. Field and Heavy Arty., U.S. Army, 1917-19. Mem. Am. Inst. Mining and Metall. Engrs., Am. Soc. for Testing Materials, Holland Soc. of New York, Beta Theta Pi, Phi Beta Kappa, Sigma Xi. Conglist. Mason (32°, Shriner). Clubs: University, Burning Tree, Nat. Press (Washington, D.C.); Kenwood Golf and Country (Chevy Chase, Md.); Mining, Military-Naval (New York). Pub. and editorial dir. Mining Congress Jour. Contbr. professional reports, articles, addresses to mags. Home: 105 Brookside Drive, Kenwood, Chevy Chase, Md. Office: Munsey Bldg., Washington, D.C.

CONRAD, William Y., banker; b. Norristown, Pa., June 4, 1871; s. Edwin and Annie) (Yerkes C.; student Norristown (Pa.) High Sch. and Pierce Business Sch.; m. Elizabeth H. West, Oct. 16, 1900; 1 son, William W. Began as office boy Central Nat. Bank (now Central-Penn Nat. Bank), v.p. and dir., 1888-1920; v.p. Irving Nat. Bank (now Irving Trust Co.), New York, 1920-26; v.p. and dir. West Phila. Title & Trust Co., 1927-29; v.p. Integrity Trust Co., 1929-33; organized present Union Nat. Bank of Reading (Pa.), 1934, exec. v.p., 1934-37, pres. since 1937 Clubs: Union League (Phila.); Berkshire Country, Wyomissing (Reading, Pa.). Home: Chester Rd., Devon, Pa. Office: 445 Penn St., Reading, Pa.

CONSTABLE, William Pepper, lawyer; b. Elkton, Md., March 27, 1882; s. Albert and Elizabeth (Groome) C.; grad. Cecil Co. High Sch., Elkton, Md., 1899; A.B., U. of Del., 1903; LL.B., U. of Md. Law Sch., 1906; m. Hyla Webb, Oct. 12, 1909; children—Alice Groome (Mrs. Richard W. D. Jewett), George Webb, William Pepper, James Cheston. Admitted to Md. bar, 1906; mem. law firm Constable & Alexander since 1937. Mem. Md. State Bar Assn., Bar Assn. of Baltimore City. Democrat. Episcopalian. Home: 4509 Roland Av. Office: 1000 Maryland Trust Bldg., Baltimore, Md.

CONSTANT, Frank Henry, civil engr.; b. Cincinnati, O., July 25, 1869; s. Henry and Catherine (Ange) Constant; grad. Woodward High Sch., Cincinnati, 1887; C.E., with highest distinction, Cincinnati U., 1891, Sc.D., 1915; Sc.D., Lafayette, 1915; m. Annette G. Woodbridge, June 19, 1901; 1 son, Frank Woodbridge. Asst. engr. King Bridge So., Cleveland, O., 1891-93; prin. asst. engr. Osborn Engring. Co., Cleveland, 1893-5; asst. prof. structural engring., 1895-97, prof., 1897-1914, U. of Minn.; prof. civ. engring. and head of dept., Princeton, 1914-37, prof. emeritus since 1937. Mem. Am. Soc. C.E., Soc. Promotion Engring. Edn., Phi Beta Kappa, Sigma Xi, Beta Kappa Pi. Club: Princeton (N.Y. City). Home: 57 Battle Rd., Princeton, N.J.

CONTY, Anthony J.; dir. and sr. attending surgeon eye, ear, nose and throat dept. North Hudson Hosp., Weehawken, N.J. Address: 318 48th St., Union City, N.J.

CONVERSE, John Williams, manufacturer; b. Phila., Pa., Mar. 30, 1879; s. John Heman and Elizabeth (Thompson) C.; student Haverford (Pa.) Sch., 1887-95, Lawrenceville (N.J.) Sch., 1895-96; A.B., Princeton U., 1900; m. Hiltrud Schierenberg Barlow, Jan. 8, 1909; 1 dau., Sonia; m. 2d, Bertha de P. Churchman, June 15, 1918; 1 son, John Heman. Began as clk. Baldwin Locomotive Works, Phila., 1900-12; spl. partner Cassatt & Co., bankers, Phila., 1912-34; with Baldwin Locomotive Works, Eddystone, Pa., since 1934, dir. since 1938; dir. Bryn Mawr Trust Co. Served as capt. and maj., 311th F.A., U.S. Army, during World War; served as lt. col. 107th F.A., 103d Cav., Nat. Guard of Pa. Trustee Drexel Inst. Tech. Mem. Ivy Club (Princeton U.). Republican. Presbyterian. Clubs: Philadelphia; Rabbit (Phila.); Gulph Mills Golf (Conshohocken, Pa.); Merion Cricket (Haverford, Pa.); Radnor Hunt (Edgemont, Pa.). Home: Rosemont, Pa. Office: Eddystone, Pa.

CONWAY, G. W.; editor New Castle News. Address: 29 N. Mercer St., New Castle, Pa.

CONWAY, Lester Hebburn, educator; b. Cleveland, O., May 21, 1890; s. William J. and Anna Crosco (Sidells) C.; student New Wilmington (Pa.) High Sch., 1903-05; B.S., Westminster Coll., New Wilmington, Pa., 1912; A.M., Columbia, 1930; grad. student U. of Pittsburgh, 1931-38; m. Louise Markham, July 31, 1919; 1 son, Lester Markham. Prin. of schools, Mt. Pleasant Twp., Washington Co., Pa., 1912-15; teacher, Sewickley (Pa.) High Sch., 1915-17; prin., Ambridge Jr.-Ser. High Sch., 1917-18; prin. High Sch., Mt. Pleasant Twp., Westmoreland Co., Pa., 1919; supt. of schools and prin. of High Sch., Sewickley, Pa., since 1919. V.p. Globe Printing Co., New Wilmington, Pa. Served in Aviation Service, U.S. Army, 1918. Mem. Pa. State Edn. Assn., A.A.S.A., NEA. Presbyterian. Home: 514 Grove St. Office: High School Bldg., Sewickley, Pa.

CONWAY, Thomas Jr., corporation official; b. Lansdowne, Pa., Aug. 30, 1882; s. Thomas and Anna Elizabeth (Keebler) C.; student Friends' Central Sch., Phila., 1898-1900, Wharton Sch. of Finance and Commerce, U. of Pa., 1900-04, U. of Pa. Grad. Sch., 1905-07; unmarried. Instr. in finance, Wharton Sch. of Finance and Commerce, 1905-08; asst. prof. of finance, U. of Pa., 1908-14, prof. of finance, 1914-29; gen. pub. utility consultant, 1916-29; pres. Thomas Conway Jr. Corpn. since 1924, The Conway Corpn. since 1926 (mgrs. of properties and receivership); chmn. of bd. Schuylkill Valley Lines, Inc.; pres. Phila. & Western Ry. Co., Transit Research Corpn., dir. Darby, Media & Chester St. Ry. Co.; co-receiver Cincinnati & Lake Erie R.. Co. Pres. and trustee Delaware Co. Hosp.; chmn. Hosp. Council of Phila.; dir. Regional Planning Federation for the Phila. Tri-State Dist. Mem. Am. Transit Assn, Phi Sigma Kappa, Beta Gamma Sigma. Republican. Club: Union League. Office: Fidelity-Phila. Trust Bldg., Philadelphia, Pa.

CONWELL, Walter Lewis; b. Covington, Ky., Jan. 25, 1877; s. Lewis A. and Fannie (Danby) C.; grad. Manual Training High Sch., Phila.; engring. dept., U. of Pa., 1894-98; m. Josephine Whetstone, Jan. 1901; m. 2d, Lillian P. Deubsmen, 1937. With Tennis Construction Co., ry. contractors, advancing to chief engr., 1898-1901; salesman Westinghouse Electric & Mfg. Co., 1901-11, pres. Transportation Utilities Co., ry. supplies, 1911-16; asst. to pres. Safety Car

Heating & Lighting Co. (Pintsch system), 1916-19, pres., 1919—; chmn. bd. Pintsch Compressing Co.; pres. Vapor Car Heating Co., Products Protection Co., Safety Refrigeration, Inc.; dir. Carrier Corpn., Seatrain Lines, Wilcolator Co. Mem. Am. Inst. E.E., Psi Upsilon. Clubs: Downtown Athletic (pres.), Engineers', Railroad, Psi Upsilon, Montclair Golf, Knoll, Rolling Rock; Chicago (Chicago), Cloud; Fairway Yacht; Terrace and Yeomans Hall (Charleston, S.C.). Home: 80 Lloyd Rd., Montclair, N.J. Office: 230 Park Av., New York, N.Y.*

CONYNGHAM, William Hillard, banking, mine operator; b. Wilkes-Barre, Pa., June 7, 1868; s. William Lord and Olivia (Hillard) C.; grad. Wilkes-Barre Acad., 1884; Ph.B., Yale, 1889; m. Mae Turner, 1897 (died 1902); m. 2d, Jessie Guthrie, 1918; children—William Lord 2d, George Guthrie, John Nesbitt 3d. Began in wholesale mines supply and hardware business, 1889; now pres. Eastern Pennsylvania Supply Co.; pres. First Nat. Bank of Wilkes-Barre; chmn. bd. dirs. Lehigh Valley Coal Co.; dir. Lehigh Valley Coal Corpn., and the Morris Run Coal Mining Co. Republican. Clubs: Westmoreland, North Mountain (Wilkes-Barre); Rittenhouse (Philadelphia); University (New York); Saddle and Sirloin (Chicago); Graduate (New Haven, Conn.); Bankers of America (New York City). Home: 130 S. Rim St. Office: 1232 Miners Bank Bldg., Wilkes-Barre, Pa.*

COOCH, Francis A.; v.p. and trust officer Equitable Trust Co. Address: 9th and Market Sts., Wilmington, Del.

COOK, Albert Samuel, educator; b. Greencastle, Pa., Jan. 12, 1873; s. Samuel Hassler and Nannie A. (Fahrney) C.; grad. Cumberland Valley State Normal Sch., Shippensburg, Pa., 1889; Gettysburg Coll., 1892-93; A.B., cum laude, Princeton, 1895, A.M., 1906; post grad. work 1 yr. in edn., Teachers Coll. (Columbia), 1904-08; Litt.D., Western Md. Coll., 1923, St. Johns Coll., Annapolis, Md., 1923; University of Maryland, 1924; LL.D., Gettysburg College, 1937; m. Helen J. Earnshaw, Dec. 27, 1898; children—Earnshaw, Catherine Norris, Albert S. Teacher in country sch., 1889-91; prin. Bel Air (Md.) Acad. and Graded Sch., 1895-98; prin. Franklin High Sch., Reisterstown, Md., 1898-1900; supt. Baltimore County Schools, 1900-20; supt. schools of Md., 1920—. Democrat. Episcopalian. Mem. N.E.A., Nat. Soc. for Study of Education, Ednl. Soc., Baltimore, Md., State Teachers' Assn. (pres. 1908), Pa. Beta, Phi Delta Theta, Maryland Club, Chesapeake Club (Baltimore). Home: Towson, Md.

COOK, Arthur Norton, univ. prof.; b. Hampton, N.Y., Nov. 21, 1896; s. William Hotchkiss and Jennie Louis (Norton) C.; B.S., Colgate U., 1919; A.M., U. of Pa., 1921, Ph.D., 1927; studied and taught at Princeton U., 1922-27; m. Barbara Rowine Raab, Sept. 16, 1922; children—Jane Louise, Mary Carolyn, Barbara Emily. Teacher Trenton Pub. High Sch., 1921-22; instr. Princeton U., 1922-26; asst. prof., 1926-27; asst. prof. Temple U., Phila., 1927-28, prof. history since 1928, chmn. dept. of history since 1935. Mem. Am. Hist. Assn., History Teachers Assn. of the Middle States, Am. Assn. of Univ. Profs., Pa. Hist. Soc., Foreign Policy Assn., Kappa Delta Rho. Baptist. Editor: Readings in Modern and Contemporary History, 1937. Home: 406 E. Wharton Rd., Glenside, Pa.

COOK, Edmund Dunham, real estate consultant; b. Trenton, N.J., May 5, 1902; s. Edmund Dunham and Margaret (Parsons) C.; student Model Sch., Trenton, N.J., 1909-14; ed. under private tutor, 1914-19; studied Lincoln Sch. of Teachers Coll., N.Y. City, 1919-21. Began as timekeeper of bldg. construction, 1921; successively automobile salesman, automobile agency exec. and construction exec.; engaged in home building and construction, 1923-29; engaged in real estate sub-dividing since 1923; treas. Real Estate Operating Co., 1932-38, managed 1500 properties for financial instns.; appraised properties in Mercer County, N.J.; qualified as expert appraiser before Condemnation Commn., Courts and co. and state tax bds.; treas. Westover Corpn., Holder Corpn.; dir. and mem. appraisal com. Realtors Bldg. & Loan Assn.; dir. Hamilton Rubber Mfg. Co., Acme Rubber Mfg. Co. Mem. Trenton and Mercer Co. Real Estate Board (ex-pres.), N.J. Assn. Real Estate Bds. (past sec. property management div.), Nat. Assn. Real Estate Bds., N.J. Chapter No. 1 of The Inst. of Real Estate Management of Nat. Assn. Real Estate Bds., Sons of Am. Revolution. Republican. Episcopalian. Mason. Clubs: Nassau (Princeton); Lions (Trenton). Author numerous articles on real estate subjects. Lecturer on real estate. Home: 148 Library Place. Office: 176 Nassau St., Princeton, N.J.

COOK, Ernest Fullerton, pharmaceutical chemist; b. Lionville, Pa., Feb. 1, 1879; s. Herman Sidney and Celia (Failor) C.; grad. high sch. Waynesboro, Pa., 1895; Pharm.D., Philadelphia College Pharmacy, 1900, Pharm.M., 1918; graduate study, University of Berne, Switzerland, 1926-27; M.Sc., Univ. of Michigan, 1937; m. Marguerite Shaffer, June 17, 1909; children—Ruth Ernestine, Bruce Shaffer, Theodore Failor, John Samuel (dec.). Teacher, Phila. Coll. Pharmacy and Sci., 1900—, prof. operative pharmacy, dir. pharm. labs., 1918—. Dir. U.S.N. Training Sch. for Pharmacists, 1917-18. Mem. com. of revision of Nat. Formulary, 1908; chmn. com. of revision of Pharmacopœia of U.S., 1920, 1930 mem. Internat. Commn. of Pharm. Experts. Awarded Remington medal, 1931. Member Am. Pa. and N.J. pharm. assns., Internat. Pharm. Federation. Republican. Presbyn. Co-Editor Remington's Practice of Pharmacy (8th edit.), 1936. Home: P.O. Box 163, Swarthmore, Pa.

COOK, Frank H., newspaper publisher; b. Athens, Pa., May 24, 1875; s. Elliott H. and Margaret (Kohensfarger) C.; student high sch.; m. Evelyn T. Hinton; children—Charles H., Marguerite E. Began in newspaper business, 1900; published a weekly until 1911; began publishing Athens Evening News, 1911; sold interest in both papers, 1918; mem. editorial dept., Evening Times, 1918-21, mgr. since 1921; pres. Sayre Printing Co., Inc., publishers of Evening Times; dir. Farmers Nat. Bank, Athens Bldg. Loan & Savings Assn. Clubs: Sayre, Rotary. Home: 302 S. Elmira Av., Athens, Pa. Office: 99 Packer Av., Sayre, Pa.

COOK, George Rea III, banker; b. Trenton, N.J., Dec. 24, 1903; s. Edmund Dunham and Margaret (Parsons) C.; student Pawling (N.Y.) Sch., 1919-22; B.S., Princeton U., 1926; m. Margaretta Roebling White, June 23, 1926; children—Margaret Allison, Constance Rea. Investment banker Graham Parsons & Co., Princeton, N.J., 1926-33, v.p. and dir. Princeton (N.J.) Bank & Trust Co. since 1933; treas. and dir. Princeton Inn Co. since 1935; dir. Acme Rubber Mfg. Co., Hamilton Rubber Mfg. Co., Union Mills Paper Mfg. Co., Universal Paper Bag Co., v.p. and trustee Princeton (N.J.) Hosp. since 1932. Mem. Colonial Club of Princeton U. Clubs: Nassau, Nassau Gun, Pretty Brook Tennis (Princeton, N.J.); Blooming Grove Hunting and Fishing (Pike County, Pa.). Home: "Greenacres." Office: 14 Nassau St., Princeton, N.J.

COOK, Graham, prof. chemistry; b. Yoakum, Tex., Oct. 28, 1900; s. John William and Winnie (Graham) C.; A.B., Baylor U., Waco, Tex., 1922; M.S., Vanderbilt U., Nashville, Tenn., 1924; Ph.D., Columbia U., 1928; m. Marcella Watkins, June 21, 1929; children—Robert Daniell, John Graham. Began as instr. chemistry, high sch., Lockhart, Tex., 1922-23; teaching Fellow in chemistry, Vanderbilt U., 1923-24; prof. chemistry, Hendrix Coll., Conway, Ark., 1924-25; asst. in chemistry, Columbia U., 1925-28, instr., 1928-29; prof. chemistry, Albright Coll., Reading, Pa., since 1929. Mem. Am. Chem. Soc., Reading Chemists Club, Acacia, Sigma Xi, Phi Lambda Upsilon. Baptist. Mason. Contbr. scientific articles to chem. mags. and jours. Home: 1607 N. 15th St., Reading, Pa.

COOK, Gustavus Wynne; pres. South Chester Tube Co.; also dir. various companies. Home: Wynnewood, Pa. Office: Chester, Pa.

COOK, John H.; pres. N.J. Gen. Security Co. Home: 207 Aycrigg Av., Passaic, N.J. Office: 72 McBride Av., Paterson, N.J.

COOK, Leslie Lambert, mgr. The Credit Bureau, Inc.; b. Monitor, Monroe County, W.Va., Apr. 19, 1895; s. Owen Hampton and Malinda Alcieona (Hoke) C.; ed. public schools of W.Va., 1902-12, Ripley (W.Va.) Normal Sch., 1913; grad. Fairmont (W.Va.) State Normal Sch., 1917; m. Belle Virginia Morton, June 14, 1930; children—Belvia Marilyn, Gloria Carolyn. Public sch. teacher, Monongalia County, W.Va., 1913-14, 1914-16, 1919-20; credit dept., building supply house, 1921-23; area supt. Bradstreets, commercial rating, 1923-26; mgr. The Credit Bureau, Inc., Elkins, W.Va., since 1927; pres. Financial Service Co. (small loans). Served in U.S. Marine Corps 1917-19. Sec. Mountain State Forest Festival, 1930-33; sec. Elkins Municipal Band Assn., 1932-35; chmn. Red Cross roll call, 1931. Dir. and recording sec. Elkins Y.M.C.A. Mem. Elkins Business Men's Assn. (sec. 1927-37), Monongahela Forestry Assn., (sec. 1929-31), Mountain State Forest Festival Assn. (mem. finance com.), Am. Legion (adjt., 2 yrs., comdr., 1 yr.). Republican. Mem. United Brethren Ch. Clubs: Rotary (sec. 2 years, pres. 1 year), Randolph Rod and Gun. Home: Crystal Springs Rd. Office: Y.M.C.A., Elkins, W.Va.

COOK, Lora Haines; b. Lloydsville, O.; d. Lewis Gregg and Sarah (Jones) Haines; ed. Pittsburgh Female Coll., N.E. Conservatory of Music and under pvt. tutors; LL.D., George Washington U., 1926; m. Anthony Wayne Cook, Sept. 15, 1892; 1 son, Anthony Wayne. Presidential commr. U.S. Commn. for celebration of 200th anniversary of birth of George Washington (exec. com.); mem. Greater, Pa. Council by apptmt. of gov. of Pa.; mem. Valley Forge Park Commn.; mem. bd. dirs. Thomas Jefferson Foundation and of Summer Polit. Inst., U. of Va.; 1st v.p. Nat. Wakefield Memorial Assn. State vice-regent Pa. D.A.R. 3 yrs., state regent 3 yrs.; v.p. gen. Nat. Soc. D.A.R. 3 yrs., pres. gen., 1923-26, now hon. pres. gen.; mem. Colonial Dames of America, Daughters of Colonial Wars of Mass., Daughters of Founders and Patriots of America, Americans of Armorial Ancestry, Columbian Women of George Washington U. Republican. Presbyn. Clubs: Twentieth Century (Pittsburgh); Chevy Chase, Nat. Women's Country Club (Washington, D.C.); Venango Country (Oil City, Pa.). Contbr. to newspapers and mags. Home: Cooksburg, Pa.*

COOK, Orator Fuller, Jr., botanist; b. Clyde, N.Y., May 28, 1867; s. Orator Fuller and Eliza (Hookway) C.; Ph.B., Syracuse University, 1890, hon. D.Sc. from the same university, 1930; m. Alice Carter, Oct. 11, 1892. In charge dept. biology, Syracuse U. 1890-91; made (1891-97) extended visits to Liberia for exploration and investigation as agt. N.Y. State Colonization Soc.; prof. natural sciences in Liberia Coll., 1891-97, pres. same, 1896-97; secured extensive collection of plants and animals now under investigation in U.S. Nat. Mus.; custodian and asst. curator U.S. Nat. Mus. since 1898. Spl. agt. in charge plant importation, U.S. Dept. of Agr., 1898-1900; in charge of investigation in tropical agr. same since July 1, 1900, visiting P.R., Guatemala, Mexico, Costa Rica, etc.; prof. botany, George Washington U., 1904. Author of various articles and reports on Liberia and Africa colonization, P.R., tropical agr., botany zoölogy, evolution, history of cultivated plants, especially on breeding, acclimatization, and cultural improvement of cotton and rubber plants, also on classification of palms and millipeds. As botanist representing U.S. Department Agr. with Bingham expdn. to Peru under auspices of Nat. Geog. Soc. and Yale U., Mar.-Sept. 1915, investigating plants used by the Incas; expdn. to Haiti summer of 1917 on agrl. exploration and study for improvement of agricultural conditions. Expdn. to China for study of agrl. conditions, summer of 1919; Carnegie Instn. expdn. to Central America to study ancient Maya civilization, 1922; expdns. to Haiti, Panama, Mexico, Colombia, and Ecuador, to investigate native cottons and sources of rubber, 1923-31; botanist in charge palm classification, Fairfield Botanic Garden, Coconut Grove, Fla., 1937. Home: Lanham, Md.*

COOK, Roy Bird, pharmacist; b. nr. Weston, W.Va., Apr. 1, 1886; s. David Bird and Dora

Elizabeth (Conrad) C.; desc. on paternal side of Peter Thomas Holl (Hull), from Holland to Phila., 1741, later Augusta Co., Va.: grad. high sch., Weston, 1904; m. Nelle Williams Camden, Aug. 23, 1907; children— Betty Keith, Eleanor Bird, Mary Randolph. With Keller-Cook Co., Huntington, W.Va., 1910-19; treas. Kreig, Wallace & McQuaide, chain stores, Charleston, W.Va., 1919-26; pres. Older-Cook Co. Associate editor Weston (W.Va.) Independent, also now pres. Independent Publishing Company. Mem. W.Va. State Bd. of Pharmacy, Nat. Board of Pharmacy, W.Va. Commn. on Historic and Scenic Markers. Pres. Nat. Assn. Bds. of Pharmacy, 1938-1939; v.p. W.Va. Newspaper Council, 1939. Mem. American Pharmaceutical Association (chmn. of House of Delegates 1935-36), W.Va. Pharmaceutical Assn. (pres. 1918-19), S.A.R., Va. Hist. Soc., etc. Republican. Methodist. Mason. Author: Family and Early Life of Stonewall Jackson, 1924-25; Lewis County (W.Va.) in the Civil War, 1924; Lewis County in the Spanish-American War, 1925; Washington's Western Lands, 1926; Rise of Organized Pharmacy in West Virginia, 1931; Annals of Fort Lee, 1931; Lewis County Journalists and Journalism, 1936; also author of various hist. brochures and pamphlets. Collector of West Virginian and Virginian Civil War documents. Mem. Charleston Com. for Celebration of 200th Anniversary of Birth of George Washington. Home: 1559 Lee St. Office: 923 Quarrier St., Charleston, W.Va.

COOK, Sidney Albert, prof. psychology; b. New Haven, Conn., July 2, 1892; s. Albert Stanburrough and Emily (Chamberlain) C.; A.B., Yale U., 1915; ed. Cornell U. 1915-16; A.M., Yale U., 1921; Ph.D., Columbia U., 1928; m. Alison Loomis Cook, Sept. 4, 1920; children— Paul 2d, James Carey, Andrew Beveridge, Philip Sidney. Engaged as instr. psychology, Rutgers Coll., 1922-26, asst. prof., 1926-28; asso. prof. psychology, N.J. Coll. for Women, Rutgers U., 1929-31, prof. psychology since 1931, head of dept. philosophy and psychology since 1929; psychologist, pub. sch. system, New Brunswick, N.J., 1922-32. Mem. Twp. Bd. Edn. since 1937. Served as ambulance driver, 2d lt., 1st lt., motor truck supply train, and A.S., U.S.A., 1917-19 with A.E.F. in France. Fellow A.A.A.S. Mem. Am. Psychol. Assn., N.Y. Acad. Sci., Sigma Xi, Phi Delta Kappa, Pi Gamma Mu, Psi Chi, Lambda Chi Alpha. Republican. Episcopalian. Home: Hillcrest, River Rd., New Brunswick, N.J.

COOK, Thomas W.; instr. surgery, U. of .Pa. Grad. Sch.; surgeon Sacred Heart Hosp.; visiting surgeon Grad. Hosp. of U. of Pa., Phila.; cons. surgeon Haff Hosp., Northampton. Address: 631 St. John St., Allentown, Pa.

COOK, Vernon, lawyer; b. Baltimore, Md., Feb. 4, 1870; s. Henry F. and Catherine E. (Jarboe) C.; A.B., Johns Hopkins U., 1890; LL.B., U. of Md. Law Sch., 1892; m. Jessie R. Kellinger, Feb. 2, 1898; children—Jessie M., Vernon, Jr. Admitted to Md. bar, 1892 and since engaged in gen. practice of law at Baltimore; mem. firm Gans & Haman, 1901-14, Cook, Chesnut & Markell, 1914-31, Cook & Markell since 1931; dir. Emerson Drug Co., Md. Glass Corpn., Citro Chem. Co., Independent Ice Co. Dir. Legal Aid Bur. Mem. Am., Md. and Baltimore bar assns. Republican. Club: University. Home: 4 E. Highland Rd. Office: First Nat. Bank Bldg., Baltimore, Md.

COOKE, Donald Ewin, author, illustrator; b. Phila., Pa., Aug. 5, 1916; s. Philip Warren and Halchen (Mohr) C.; grad. Germantown High Sch., Phila., 1935; art edn. Pa. Museum Sch. of Industrial Art, Phila., 1935-38; unmarried. Illustrator and commercial artist, Phila., since 1936; pres. Folio Club, co-operative book publishing organization, since 1937; art dir. Eldon Press since 1937; asso. editor of Arts in Philadelphia, pub. by Phila. Arts Publs., Inc. Mem. Phila. Water Color Club, Phila. Art Alliance. Awarded hon. mention at Internat. Bookplate Exhbn., Los Angeles, 1936. Illustrator: "Markheim" in R.L.S. (1st publ. of Folio Club), 1937; poems in Jack and Jill (Curtis publ.), 1938-39. Author and illustrator: Nutcracker of Nuremberg (juvenile book), 1938; Firebird, 1939. Home: 1962 W. 71st Av., Philadelphia, Pa.

COOKE, Hereward Lester, physicist; b. Montreal, Can., Mar. 26, 1879; s. Miles Woodifield and Clara Maude (Eager) C.; B.A., McGill, 1900, M.A., 1903; studied Emmanuel Coll., Cavendish Lab., Cambridge U., 1903-06; m. Olive Lois MacCallum, 1911; children—Margaret Priscilla, Hereward Lester. With Princeton U. since 1906, prof. physics, 1919—. Researches in radioactivity, thermionics, 1903-13; surveying with aeroplane photographs, 1919—; theatre acoustics, 1928—. Served as capt. Royal Engrs., B.E.F., in France, 1916-19. Mem. Am. Physical Soc., Acoustical Soc. America, Am. Soc. Photogrammetry, Société Française de Physique. Clubs: Princeton (New York); Nassau (Princeton). Home: Nassau Club, Princeton, N.J.

COOKE, James Francis, editor; b. Bay City, Mich., Nov. 14, 1875; s. George A. and Caroline B. (Johnson) C.; ed. under many teachers, America and Europe; hon. Mus. Doc., Ohio Northern U., 1919, Capitol U., 1927, Cincinnati Conservatory, 1929, U. of Pa., 1930; LL.D., Ohio Northern U., 1925, Ursinus Coll., 1927; L.H.D., Bethany Coll., 1931; Ed.D., Coll. of Emporia, 1938; LL.D., U. of Mich., 1938; m. Betsy Eleanor Beckwith (concert soprano), Apr. 12, 1899; 1 son, Francis Sherman. Teacher of piano and voice, organist and conductor, New York and Brooklyn, many yrs.; was asst. to Prof. Franklin W. Hooper at Brooklyn Inst. Arts and Sciences; visited numerous European musical conservatories and Am. college to study teaching systems; wrote regularly in German for European publs.; pub. speaker on humanistic, business and artistic subjects (addresses also in French, German and Italian); editor The Etude Music Magazine, Phila., since 1907. Pres. Theo. Presser Co., Phila., 1925-36, John Church Co., 1930-36, Oliver Ditson Co., Inc., 1931-36. Pres. Presser Foundation since 1918, Phila. Music Teachers' Assn., 1910-27, Writeabout Club, 1916, 17, Drama League of Phila., 1917. "Four Minute Man," 1917. Pres. Henry Labarre Jayne Memorial Fund. Mem. Franco-Am. Inst. of Science (vice-pres.), Societa pro Cultura Italiano. Clubs: Rotary, Art, Musical Art, Plays and Players, Art Alliance. Author: Standard History of Music, 1909; Mastering the Scales and Arpeggios, 1913; Great Pianists on Piano Playing, 1914; Musical Playlets for Children; Music Masters, Old and New; Great Singers on the Art of Singing, 1921; Great Men and Famous Musicians, 1925; Young Folks' Picture History of Music, 1925; Light, More Light, 1925; Musical Travelogues, 1934; Street of the Little Candles, 1937; numerous published poems, also short stories, a novel, songs (including "Ol'Car'lina"), many pianoforte pieces (including Sea Gardens), and plays (4 plays produced professionally). Decorated Chevalier Legion of Honor (France), 1930. Home: Llanberris Rd., Bala-Cynwyd, Pa. Office: 1712 Chestnut St., Philadelphia, Pa.

COOKE, Jay; b. Phila., Pa., Apr..2, 1897; s. Jay and Nina L. (Benson) C.; student St. Paul's Sch., Concord, N.H., 1910-15; A.B., Princeton, 1919; m. Mary F Glendinning, Apr. 24, 1924; children—Nina, Mary Ellen. Began as clk. Charles D. Barney and Co. (now Smith Barney & Co.), Phila., 1921, partner, Jan. 1, 1924-July 1, 1935, limited partner since July 1, 1935; dir. Am. Briquet Co. With R.O.T.C. Fort Niagara, 1917; 1st lt. inf., Aug. 1917; capt., Aug. 1918-June 1919; with A.E.F. July 1918-May 1919. Trustee Oncologic Hosp. (Philadelphia), Chestnut Hill Hosp., Pa. Sch. for the Deaf, Home of the Merciful Saviour, Pres. Republican Central Campaign Com. of Philadelphia. Republican. Episcopalian. Clubs: Rittenhouse, Racquet, Union League (Phila.); Sunnybrook Golf. Home: Stenton and New Sts., Chestnut Hill. Office: 1411 Chestnut St., Philadelphia, Pa.

COOKE, Merritt Todd Jr., pres. Pa. Joint Stock Land Bank; b. Norfolk, Va., Oct. 24, 1884; s. Merritt Todd and Mary Elizabeth (Dickson) C.; ed. Lawrenceville (N.J.) Sch., 1900-03; E.E., U. of Va., Charlottesville, Va., 1908; m. Beatrice Virginia Crawford, of Alexandria, Va., June 30, 1917; children—Merritt Todd III, Virginia Laurie, Elizabeth Aymar. In employ Gen. Electric Co., 1909-14; mem. firm Stuart, James & Cooke, cons. engrs., Charleston, W.Va., New York, N.Y., 1914-17; mem. firm Baer, Cooke & Co., engrs., 1919-25; mem. firm Brooke Stokes & Co., 1925-35; pres. Pa. Joint Stock Land Bank, Phila., since 1935. Served as 1st lt. engrs. to capt., U.S. Army, 1917-19, with A.E.F. in France. Democrat. Episcopalian. Home: 250 W. Hartwell Lane, Chestnut Hill. Office: 1520 Locust St., Philadelphia, Pa.

COOKE, Morris Llewellyn, consulting engr. in management; b. Carlisle, Pa., May 11, 1872; s. William Harvey (M.D.) and Elizabeth Richmond (Marsden) C.; M.E., Lehigh U., 1895; Sc.D. from same univ., 1922; m. Eleanor Bushnell Davis, June 16, 1900. Reporter on Phila. Press, Denver News and Evening Telegram (New York), 1890-94; served apprenticeship in Cramp's Shipyard, Phila., later journeyman machinist at Southwark Foundry; engr. for Acetylene Co., Washington, D.C., 1896-97; asst. engr. U.S. Navy during Spanish-Am. War; engaged in commercial orgn. work, 1899-1905; consulting engr., 1905-11; dir. Dept. Pub. Works, Phila., 1911-15; chmn. storage sect. War Industries Bd. of Council Nat. Defense and mem. Depot Bd. U.S. A., 1917; exec. asst. to chmn. U.S. Shipping Bd., 1918. Made study of collegiate administrative methods in U.S. and Can. for Carnegie Foundation, 1910; dir. Giant Power Survey Pa., 1923; chmn. Miss. Valley Com. of Pub. Works Administration, 1933; dir. water resources sect. of Nat. Resources Bd. and chmn. water planning com., 1934; adminstr. Rural Electrification Adminstrn., 1935-37; chmn. Great Plains Com., 1936-37. Mem. bd. of trustees of The Power Authority of State of N.Y., 1931. Fellow A.A. A.S., Am. Soc. Mech. Engrs. (council 1915); mem. Soc. for Promotion Engring. Edn., Taylor Soc. (pres. 1927), Franklin Inst., Delta Phi, Sigma Xi; hon. mem. Masaryk Acad. (Prague), Czech-Slovak Order of the White Lion. Democrat. Episcopalian. Clubs: University (Phila.); Engineers' (Phila., New York); Cosmos (Washington, D.C.). Author: Academic and Industrial Efficiency, 1910; Snapping Cords, 1915; Our Cities Awake, 1918. Editor: Public Utility Regulation, 1922; What Electricity Costs, 1933. Homes: St. Georges Rd., Chestnut Hill, Philadelphia, Pa., and New Hope, Pa.

COOLEY, Arthur Stoddard, coll. prof.; b. Northampton, Mass., Sept. 22, 1869; s. William Henry and Charlotte Cornelia (Stoddard) C; grad. Newton (Mass.) High Sch., 1887; A.B. (magna cum laude) Amherst (Mass.) Coll., 1891; A.M., Harvard, 1893, Ph.D., 1896; student Am. Sch. of Classical Studies, Athens, Greece, 1897-99; m. Elizabeth Leota Reat, April 15, 1910; 1 son, Samuel Theodotos (dec.). Instr. in languages, Park Coll., Parkville, Mo., 1891-92; instr. in Greek, Harvard and Radcliffe Colls., 1896-97; instr. in Greek and German, Fairmount Coll., Wichita, Kan., 1899-1900; master in Greek, Latin and German, Allen Sch., West Newton, Mass., 1901-03; acting prof. of Greek, Lehigh U., Bethlehem, Pa., 1912-13, instr. in French, same, 1914-15; prof. of French and Greek, Moravian Coll. for Women, Bethlehem, Pa., since 1915, registrar since 1926; conducted tours to Europe, 1902-14, 1921, 22; lecturer on classic lands since 1900. Sec. Bethlehem Com. of Near East Relief, 1918-31. Mem. Bach Choir since 1914. Mem. Am. Assn. Teachers of French, Classical League of Lehigh Valley, New England Soc. of Eastern Pa., Phi Beta Kappa, Theta Delta Chi; formerly mem. Am. Philol. Assn., Archeol. Inst. of America. Independent Republican. Congregationalist. Contbr. to professional jours. Home: 728 7th Av., Bethlehem, Pa.

COOLIDGE, George Greer, manufacturer; b. Plainfield, N.J., Jan. 25, 1885; s. Henry and Carrie Louise (Wright) C.; Ph.B., Yale U., 1904; m. Ethel Van Kirk Byram, Oct. 22, 1910; 1 dau., Elizabeth Coolidge Ebbert. With Lackawanna R.R. Shops, Scranton, Pa., 1904-06; Westinghouse Air Brake Co. Shops, Wilmerding, Pa., 1906-07; v.p. and dir. Harbison Walker Refractories Co., Pittsburgh, since 1933; dir. Fidelity Trust Co., Pittsburgh; trustee Dollar Savings Bank, Pittsburgh. Mem. Asso. Charities (past pres.), Community Fund (dir.), Family Soc. of Allegheny Co., Trustee U. of Pittsburgh; dir. Municipal Planning Assn., Child Guidance Clinic. Republican. Episcopalian. Home: 5440 Aylesboro Av. Office: Pittsburgh, Pa.

COOMBES, Ethel Russell, editor and pub.; b. Plainville, Ill.; d. Albert Alan and Sarah Ann (Haynes) Russell; ed. high schs., by spl. study and George Washington U.; m. David S. Coombes; children—David Russell, Edward Raymond. With American Mining Congress, 1913-37; organized national standardization movement to eliminate waste and promote efficiency and economy in mineral production, 1919; organized industrial cooperation div. Am. Mining Congress; editor The Mining Congress Jour., 1923-37; conv. and expn. mgr. annual meetings Am. Mining Congress, 1925-37; established Mechanization, the Magazine of Modern Coal, 1937, now editor and pub. Contbr. on industrial subjects. Home: 6304 Maple Av., Chevy Chase, Md.

COOMBS, James Norman, M.D.; b. Shirley, N.J., Dec. 30, 1894; s. William Alderman and Mary (Hinchman) C.; grad. Woodstown (N.J.) High Sch., 1912; M.D., Medico-Chirurg. Coll., Phila., 1916; m. Alma Mae Hinman, M.D., March 15, 1924; 1 dau., Eve Hinman. Began as physician, 1919, practiced limited to surgery since 1923; asso. prof. surgery and asso. surgeon, Temple U. Med. Sch. and Hosp., Phila. Served as capt. Med. Corps, U.S. Army, 1917-19. Fellow Am. Coll. Surgeons; mem. A.M.A., Pa. State Med. Soc., Phila. Co. Med. Soc., Am. Therapeutic Soc. Republican. Presbyterian. Clubs: Cynwyd (Cynwyd, Pa.); Medical (Phila). Home: 134 Rochelle Av. Office: 1603 Diamond St., Philadelphia, Pa.

COOMBS, S. D.; editor Police and Public Safety Reporter. Address: Somerville, N.J.

COON, Philip Leslie, professor of chemistry; b. Dane Co., Wis., Feb. 5, 1887; s. Dayton Benjamin and Mary Angeline (Potter) C.; grad. Milton Junction (Wis.) High Sch., 1904; A.B., Milton (Wis.) Coll., 1910; A.M., U. of Wis., Madison, Wis., 1915, Ph.D., 1932; m. Ethel Mildred Saunders, Aug. 9, 1917; children—James Laurence, Philip Leslie, Virginia Mary. Teacher of rural sch., Rock Co., Wis., 1904-05; teacher Edgerton (Wis.) High Sch., 1910-12; asst., Milton Coll., 1912-13; teacher in high schs., Lake Linden and Hancock, Mich., 1915-17; supervising prin., Barron, Wis., 1917-20; prof. of chemistry, Geneva Coll., Beaver Falls, Pa., since 1920. Mem. Am. Chem. Soc., Sigma Xi, Phi Lambda Upsilon. Republican. Mem. Seventh Day Baptist Ch. Mason. Home: 3417 7th Av., Beaver Falls, Pa.

COON, William Edwin, high school prin.; b. Hughesville, Pa., May 19, 1893; s. Orlo O. and Mame E. (Miller) C.; grad. Albion (Pa.) High Sch., 1910; A.B., Allegheny Coll., Meadville, Pa., 1914; student Pa. State Coll., summer 1916, U. of Chicago, summers 1921, 1923; M.Ed., U. of Pittsburgh, 1930; m. Lina Clancy Power, Aug. 20, 1919; 1 son, Richard Power. Teacher Conneautville High and Vocational Schs., 1914-18; teacher of science and mathematics, Ambridge (Pa.) High Sch., Jan.-June 1919; teacher of science, East High Sch., Erie, Pa., 1919-23, asst. prin., 1923-29; prin. Roosevelt Jr. High Sch., Erie, 1929-31; asst. prin. Strong Vincent High Sch., Erie, 1931-32; prin. Wilson Jr. High Sch., Erie, 1932-34; prin. Strong Vincent High Sch., Erie, since 1934. Served as pvt., Med. Corps, U.S Army, 1918-19; 1st lt., Chem. Warfare Reserve, 1924-29. Mem. exec. bd. Erie Co. Council, Boy Scouts of America. Mem. Erie Teachers Assn., Pa. State Edn. Assn., N.E.A., Erie Sect., Am. Chem. Soc., Am. Legion, A.A.A.S., Alpha Chi Rho, Phi Delta Kappa. Republican. Presbyterian. Mason (32°). Club: Lake Shore Golf (Erie, Pa.). Contbr. articles on bird life of Bird Lore. Home: 611 Cranberry St. Office: Strong Vincent High School, Erie, Pa.

COONEY, John R., insurance; b. 1890; chmn. bd. Girard Fire & Marine Ins. Co.; pres. Firemen's Ins. Co., Newark, and Mechanics Ins. Co.,

Phila. Home: Maplewood, N.J. Office: 10 Park Pl., Newark, N.J.

COONS, Albert, retail exec.; b. Du Bois, Pa., Nov. 11, 1890; s. Cosmar P. and Theresa (Schwarz) C.; student Central High Sch., Phila, 1905-08, Alexander Hamilton Inst., 1911; m. May Lisette Bochroch, Jan. 14, 1920; 1 son, Albert. Leather goods mfr. and jobber, Coons Bros., Phila., 1907-10; with Louis Samler, dept. store, Lebanon, Pa., 1910-18, gen. mgr., 1919-33, part owner, 1919-29; dir. mem. exec. com. and merchandise counsellor for 14 stores, Hahn Dept. Stores, New York, since 1933; dir. and v.p. in charge of 16 stores, Allied Stores Corpn., New York, since 1934; dir. Lebanon (Pa.) Co. Trust Co., No Mend Hosiery, Inc.; pres. Lebanon (Pa.) Industrial Bldgs., Inc. Served as sergeant 1st class, Base Hospital 68, A.E.F., May 1918-May 1919. Dir. Pa. Retailers Assn., American Red Cross (Lebanon County, Pa., Chapter), Good Samaritan Hosp., Lebanon Library Association, Lebanon, Pa. Republican. Jewish religion. Clubs: Lebanon Country, Kiwanis (Lebanon, Pa.). Home: 300 Hathaway Park, Lebanon, Pa. Office: 1440 Broadway, New York, N.Y.

COOP, Jesse James, coll. prof.; b. Peytonsburg, Ky., Sept. 2, 1902; s. Leander Jackson and Mary Emily (Watson) C.; A.B., Berea (Ky.) Coll., 1928; M.S., U. of Ky., 1930; student U. of Ind., summers 1931-35, Ph.D., 1936; m. Thelma Cecil Powers, Aug. 25, 1930. Instr. physics and chemistry, Murray State Teachers Coll., summer 1930; instr. physics and mathematics, Washington Coll., 1930-32, asst. prof. physics, 1932-35, on leave of absence, 1935-36, prof. physics and head dept. since 1936. Mem. Am. Assn. Univ. Profs., Am. Assn. Physics Teachers, Sigma Xi, Tau Kappa Alpha, Sigma Pi Sigma, Lambda Chi Alpha. Democrat. Mem. Christian Ch. Home: 206 W. Campus Av., Chestertown, Md.

COOPER, Alex S., librarian; b. Harrisburg, Pa., March 8, 1871; s. William L. and Annie (Zellers) C.; student pub. schs., Harrisburg, Pa. Bus. Coll.; m. E. Romaine Cowan, June 22, 1914; 1 dau., Jean Elizabeth. With various city and co. offices, 1891-1906; sec. Rep. City & Co. Com., 1892-1934; with Ins. Dept. of Pa., 1906-14; asst. librarian Senate of Pa., 1914-36; librarian Senate of Pa., 1936-37, since 1939. Mem. and pres. Bd. Prison Insprs. Dauphin Co., 1920-31; asst. to chmn. Rep. State Com., 1934-38. Republican. Presbyterian. Mason (32°, Shriner), Elk. Clubs: Zembo Luncheon, Republican (Harrisburg, Pa.). Home: 2148 Green St. Office: Senate Library, Harrisburg, Pa.

COOPER, Arthur Eugene, minister; b. Selinsgrove, Pa., June 23, 1872; s. John Landis and Emma Amelia (Hummel) C.; B.S., Missionary Inst., Selinsgrove, 1890; B.D., Susquehanna U., Selinsgrove, Pa., 1900, A.M., 1914; m. Carrie Elizabeth Ulsh, Nov. 15, 1894; children—Florence Anita (Mrs. W. Boyd Tobias), Robert Ulsh, John Andrew, Kathryn Lois (Mrs. James G. Morgan). Ordained minister, Lutheran Ch., 1900; pastor, Montgomery, Pa., 1900-06, Manheim, Pa., 1906-12, Jersey Shore, Pa., 1912-21, Middletown, Md., 1921-24, Rohrerstown and Ascension Ch., Lancaster, Pa., 1925-28, Landisville and Millersville, Pa., 1928-34; organized Zion Luth. Congregation, Landisville, 1909; dir. and sec. Clergymen's Co-operative Beneficial Assn., Lancaster, since 1924; dir., sec. and gen. mgr. Teachers Protective Union, Lancaster, Pa., since 1924. Pres. West Branch Conf., Susquehanna Synod, 1916-20, Frederick Co. (Md.) Sunday School Assn., 1923-24; sec. Susquehanna Synod, 1920-21; asst. sec., Gen. Synod, Akron, O., 1915, Chicago, 1917, merger meeting United Lutheran Ch., New York, 1918; mem. exec. com. Sunday School Assn., Lycoming Co., Pa., 1912-21, Lancaster Co., Pa., 1926-35. Club: Kiwanis Internat. (Lancaster, Pa.); Author: (poems) One Red Rose, 1907; (hymns) The Sign of the Cross and the Heart; Come to Me, Go to Mine; Pennsylvania for Christian Endeavor; The Entrusted Life; O Israel Hear; Kneeling at the Mercy Seat; His Holy Day; (proposed state song) Pennsylvania; The Sowing and the Reaping. Home: Landisville, Pa. Office: 116 N. Prince St., Lancaster, Pa.

COOPER, David Alexander, physician; b. Henderson, N.C., July 12, 1897; s. John Downey and Fannie Spottswood (Burwell)· C.; B.S., U. of N.C., 1919; M.D., U. of Pa. Med. Sch., 1921; m. Virginia Furey, June 1, 1931; children—Virginia Furey, Anne Spottswood. Interne, Presbyn. Hosp., Phila., 1921-23; asst. resident phys. Trudeau Sanatorium, Saranac Lake, N.Y., 1923-25; resident in medicine, U. of Pa. Hosp., 1925-26; clinic phys. Henry Phipps Inst., 1926-29; instr. in medicine, U. of Pa. Sch. of Medicine since 1926, asso. prof. medicine, Grad. Sch. of Medicine since 1933, asst. attending phys. U. of Pa. Hosp. since 1926; phys. Phila. Gen. Hosp. since 1933; phys. and chief of chest clinic, Pa. Hosp. Served with U.S.N.R.F., 1918. Fellow Am. Coll. Phys., A.M.A., Phila. Coll. Phys.; mem. Pa. and Phila. Co. med. socs., Am. Assn. Thoracic Surgeons, Am. Clin. and Climatol. Assn., Nat. Assn. of Tuberculosis, Am. Sanatorium Assn., S.R., Colonial Soc. of Pa., Order of Founders and Patriots of America, Sigma Xi, Delta Kappa Epsilon, Phi Chi. Club: Philadelphia Country. Contbr. articles to med. jours. Home: 1328 Medford Rd., Wynnewood, Pa. Office 1520 Spruce St., Philadelphia, Pa.

COOPER, Drury W., lawyer; b. New Brunswick, N.J., Aug. 7, 1872; s. Jacob and Mary D. (Linn) C.; A.B., Rutgers Coll., 1892; LL.B., New York Law Sch., 1894; m. Esther Stevenson Nicholas, 1898; children—Esther Nicholas, Drury W.. Mary Linn, Elizabeth W., Jacob, John N., Theodore W., Richard Lawlor. Admitted to N.Y. bar, 1894, and practiced since at N.Y. City, specializing in patent law; mem. firm Cooper, Kerr & Dunham; dir. Internat. Business Machines Co., Republic Steel Company. Mem. board of trustees Rutgers University. Mem. Am. Bar Assn., Am. Law Inst., N.Y. State Bar Assn., N.Y. County Lawyers Assn., New York Law Inst., Assn. Bar City New York, S.A.R., Phi Beta Kappa, Delta Phi. Republican. Conglist. Clubs: University, Bankers. Home: 30 Parkhurst Place, Montclair, N.J. Office: 233 Broadway, New York, N.Y.

COOPER, Howell C., consulting gas engr.; Address: 545 William Penn Way, Pittsburgh, Pa.

COOPER, Maurice Diehl, mining engr.; b. Buffalo, N.Y., April 5, 1887; s. John Hingston and Laura Louise (Diehl) C.; prep. edn. Central High Sch., Buffalo, N.Y., 1902-05; Phillips Acad., Andover, Mass., 1905-06; Ph.B., Yale, 1910, E.M., 1912; m. Marion Hazel Lewis, June 19, 1912; children—John Lewis, Maurice Diehl, Mary Laura. Mem. of engring. corps, Ellsworth (Pa.) Collieries Co., 1912-16; asst. supt. Ford Collieries Co., Curtisville, Pa., 1916-17; div. supt. Hillman Coal and Coke Co., Pittsburgh, since 1917; dir. General Water Co. Dir. Brownsville (Pa.) Gen. Hosp., Travelers Aid Soc.; vestryman, Ch. of the Ascension, Pittsburgh. Mem. Am. Inst. Mining and Metall. Engrs., Am. Mining Congress, Engring. Soc. of Western Pa., Coal Mining Inst. of America (pres. 1924). Theta Xi. Republican. Episcopalian. Club: Harvard-Yale-Princeton (Pittsburgh). Home: 5430 Aylesboro Av. Office: Grant Bldg., Pittsburgh, Pa.

COOPER, Richard Watson, educator; b. Cheswold, Kent County, Del., Dec. 22, 1866; s. Richard M. and Susan (Jefferson) C.; grad. (highest honors), Dickinson Sem., Williamsport, Pa., 1887; A.B., cum laude, Wesleyan U., Conn., 1890, D.D., 1909; Litt.D., Hamline U., 1909; m. Emma White, June 29, 1892; children—Richard White, Harry P., Hermann, Edwin J., William Paul, Dorothy. Librarian, Wesleyan U., 1890-91; head dept. of English, Wesleyan Acad., Wilbraham, Mass., 1891-99; prof. English lit., Hamline U., St. Paul, 1899-1909; Minn. state lecturer in English, 1901-04; lecturer in English drama, U. of Minn., 1906-07; pres. Upper Iowa U., 1909-16; exec. sec., Council of Ch. Bds. of Edn., 1916-17; sec. Assn. of Am. Colls., 1915-18; with A.E.F., France, Apr. 1918-Aug. 1919, mem. Ednl. Corps, registrar, A.E.F. Univ., Beaune, France; decorated Officier d'Académie (palms), May 1919; dir. Bur. of Edn., Service Citizens of Del., 1919-

27. Lecturer; clergyman. Mem. N.E.A., Progressive Edn. Assn., Psi Upsilon, etc. Mason (32°). Wrote: Better Attendance in Delaware Schools, 1922; (with Hermann Cooper) Negro School Attendance in Delaware, 1923; The One Teacher School—A Study in Attendance, 1925. Address: R.D. 3, Newark, Del.; (summer) Cable, Wis.

COOPER, Roy C., otolaryngologist Homeopathic Med. and Surg. Hosp., and Dispensary. Address: 510 S. Aiken Av., Pittsburgh, Pa.

COOPER, Stuart, corpn. official; b. Clayville, N.Y., July 31, 1887; s. Charles Frank and Emily Cornelia (Avery) C.; E.E., Syracuse U., 1914; m. Mary Greene Bailey, May 22, 1920. Asst. constrn. engr., later statistician and distribution engr., New York & Queens Electric Light & Power Co., 1914-17; distribution engr. Counties Gas & Electric Co., 1917-18; asst. to elec. engr. United Gas Improvement Co., 1918-19; v.p. and mgr. Charleston Consol. Ry. & Light Co., 1919-27; v.p. and mgr., later pres., S.C. Power Co., 1927-28; v.p. Phila. Electric Co., 1928-29; v.p. United Gas Improvement Co. since 1929; also v.p. subsidiary companies. Mem. Am. Inst. of Elec. Engrs., Tau Beta Pi, Delta Upsilon. Presbyterian. Club: Old York Rd. Country. Home: 54 W. Upsal St. Office: 1401 Arch St., Philadelphia, Pa.

COOPER, Thomas Yost, newspaperman; b. Del Rio, Tex., Apr. 22, 1884; s. Dr. Moses and Kate (Miller) C.; ed. high sch., Hanover, Pa., 1897-1900, Phillips Andover Acad., Andover, Mass., 1900-02; A.B., Harvard, 1905; unmarried. Asso. with Evening Sun, Hanover, Pa., since 1920, city editor since 1922; dir. Evening Sun Co. since 1936. Mem. Arcadian Social Club. Republican. Author: Wren's Nest and Other Poems, 1929; contbr. verse to mags. and jours. Home: Hanover, Pa.

COOPERMAN, Morris Bernard, physician; b. Russia, Sept. 15, 1884; s. Benjamin and Etta (Adelson) C.; brought to U.S., 1890, naturalized, 1905; M.D., Univ. of Pa., 1907; m. Rae Goldsmith, Apr. 7, 1914; children—Natalie, Lawrence Raphael. Physician and surgeon since 1907; asso. in orthopedic surgery, Grad. Sch., U. of Pa., since 1918; chief of orthopedic dept., Mt. Sinai and Northern Liberties Hosp., Phila. Mem. A.M.A. Pa. and Phila. Co. med. socs., Am. Acad. Orthopedic Surgeons. Address: 2017 Pine St., Philadelphia, Pa.

COOVER, Carson, surgeon; b. Harrisburg, Pa., Oct. 2, 1882; s. Frederic Welty and Elizabeth (Foerster) C.; A.B., Princeton, 1905; M.D., U. of Pa. Med. Sch., 1909; m. Ethel Parsons, May 10, 1915; children—Judith Parsons, Ruth Welty. Interne U. of Pa. Hosp., 1909-10; engaged in practice of medicine, specializing in surgery, at Harrisburg, Pa., since 1912; surgeon Surg. Dispensary, 1913 to 1919; attending surgeon Harrisburg Hosp. since 1920. Served as capt., Med. Corps, U.S. Army, 1917-19. Mem. Am., Pa. State and Dauphin Co. med. assns., Am. Legion, Phi Beta Kappa. Republican. Presbyterian. Club: Torch (Harrisburg, Pa.). Home: 206 Rutherford St., Paxtang, Pa. Office: 223 Pine St., Harrisburg, Pa.

COOVER, Melanchthon, theologian; b. Johnstown, Pa., Mar. 26, 1861; s. Jacob and Ann Margaret (Lindsay-Teeter) C.; A.B., Pa. Coll., 1887, A.M., 1890; grad. Luth. Theol. Sem., Gettysburg, Pa., 1890; D.D., Franklin and Marshall Coll., 1905; LL.D., Gettysburg Coll., 1923; m. Lucy May Moses, Sept. 3, 1891; children—Donald Bruce, Margaret (wife of Rev. Howard R. Gold). Ordained Luth. ministry, 1890; pastor St. Paul's Ch., Ardmore, Pa., 1890-1901, Christ Ch., Gettysburg, 1901-04; prof. English Bible and chaplain Gettysburg Coll., 1904-05; prof. N.T. exegesis and ecclesiastical history, Luth. Theol. Sem., Gettysburg, 1905-16, prof. N.T. lang., lit. and theology, 1916-26, emeritus. Mem. bd. Luth. Pub. Soc., Gen. Synod, 1908-15, of Am. Sect. Internat. S.S. Lesson Com., 1908-14. Mem. Soc. Bibl. Lit. and Exegesis, Phi Beta Kappa, Phi Gamma Delta. Author: Quest and Query (verse), 1923; (booklets) Tempted, Messiah, and Peter's Confession and Keys, 1909; also Liturgics of the Sunday School (in Ency. of S.S. and Religious Edn.). Home: Gettysburg, Pa.

COPE, Henry Norton, forester and dir. forest sch., b. Perkiomenville, Pa., Sept. 4, 1893; s. Henry Irwin Kulpc and Anna Maria (Johnson) C.; B.S., Pa. State Coll., 1915; m. Susan LaBurr Hoffman, April 9, 1919; 1 dau., Virginia Shearer. Began as forest guard, U.S. Forest Service, 1916, forest ranger, 1917; administrative asst. U.S. Forest Service, 1919-21, dep. forest supervisor, 1921-24, asst. forest supervisor, 1924-26, forest supervisor, 1926-29; resident dir. Pa. State Forest Sch., Mont Alto, Pa., since 1929. Served as pvt. 10th Engrs. Forestry, U.S. Army, 1917-19. Sr. mem. Soc. Am. Foresters; mem. Xi Sigma Pi. Republican. Lutheran. Home: Pa. State Forest Sch., Mont Alto, Pa.

COPE, Thomas Darlington, physicist and prof. physics; b. West Chester, Pa., Dec. 28, 1880; s. Jesse Kersey and Lucy (Ingram) C.; B.E., West Chester State Normal, 1897; A.B., U. of Pa., 1903; grad. study, Cornell U., summers 1904-05; Ph.D., U. of Pa., 1915; grad. study, U. of Berlin, Germany, 1912-13; m. Sophie E. Foell, Sept. 20, 1919. Engaged in teaching pub. schs. and acad., 1898-99 and 1903-06; instr. U. of Pa., 1906-12, fellow, 1912-13, asst. prof. physics, 1913-22, prof. physics since 1922. Served as lt., then capt. A.S., U.S.A., 1917-19; U.S.A.S. Res., 1919-29. Mem. A.A.A.S., Am. Phys. Soc., Am. Assn. Physics Teachers (sec.), Am. Assn. Univ. Profs., Franklin Inst. of Pa. (past mem. of bd.), Pa. Acad. Sci. (past pres.), Pa. Hist. Assn., Chester Co. Hist. Soc., Pa. Conf. Coll. Physics Teachers, Physics Club of Phila. (past pres.), Phila. Physics Colloquium (past chmn.), Societe Francaise de Physique, Gen. Alumni of U. of Pa. (past dir.), Phi Beta Kappa, Sigma Xi. Republican. Mem. Religious Soc. Friends. Clubs: Lenape, Trail (Philadelphia); Martins Dam (Wayne). Home: 239 Lenoir Av., Wayne, Pa.

COPE, William C., pres. Drake Sch.; b. Salem, O., July 23, 1887; s. James Sherman and Catherine Matilda (Norris) C.; student Spencerian Coll., Cleveland, O., 1909-10; grad, 1910; D.C.S., Milton Univ., Baltimore, Md., 1938; m. Eliza Mary Miller, May 21, 1917; 1 dau., Jane Miller. Engaged in teaching in pub. schs., Ohio, 1904-11; teacher commercial coll., Stamford, Conn., 1911-13; commercial teacher with Drake Schs. of N.J., Newark, N.J., 1913, successively prin., treas., sec., vice-pres., and pres. since 1925; pres. William C. Cope, Inc., real estate, investment and operating co., Newark, N.J., since 1935. Mem. Newark Y.M.C.A., Chamber of Commerce, Essex Co. Rep. Club. Mem. Bd. Conservation and Development of N.J. (since 1929), Crippled Children's Comn. of N.J. (since 1927), Del. & Raritan Comn. of N.J. (since 1936), Tri-State Sanitation Commn. (since 1936). Republican. Methodist. Mason (32°, Shriner). Clubs: Down Town, Rotary (past pres.), Athletic (Newark). Home: 425 Ridgewood Av., Glen Ridge. Office: 790 Broad St., Newark, N.J.

COPELAND, Dean Burns, banking; b. Athens, O., Aug. 17, 1899; s. Charles M. and Nettie (Courtright) C.; A.B. in Commerce, Ohio U., Athens, O., 1920; m. Gertrude Carol Smith, Oct. 11, 1922; children—Carol Louise (dec.), William Dean and Jean Ellen (twins.) Engaged in banking since 1921; credit mgr. Midland Bank, Cleveland, O., and successively v.p., sec. and dir., Ohio-Pa. Joint Stock Land Bank, Cleveland, O., v.p. and dir. New York Joint Stock Land Bank, Rochester, N.Y., v.p. Sheridan Trust and Savings Bank, Chicago, Ill., v.p. Citizens Nat. Bank, South Bend, Ind.; v.p. and dir. Braddock (Pa.) Nat. Bank; v.p. and dir. The Butler Co. Nat. Bank and Trust Co., Butler, Pa., since 1934; dir. Pittsburgh Water Heater Co., Am. Bantam Car. Co., Standard Motor Co. Served in O.T.S., Camp Grant, Ill., 1918. Mem. Beta Theta Pi. Republican. Methodist. Mason. Clubs: University (Pittsburgh); Butler Country (Butler, Pa.). Home: 430 N. Main St., Butler, Pa.

COPELAND, Joseph Frank, artist, craftsman, teacher; b. St. Louis, Mo., Feb. 21, 1872; s. Joseph Alfred and Hannah (Doughty) C.; ed. Buffalo Acad. of Art, 1890; ed. Phila. Mus. of Art, 1896-99; m. Eleanor Rogers, Sept. 9, 1903; children—George Rogers, Ralph Alden. Engaged as teacher of art, Phila. Mus. of Art since 1898, teacher of drawing, design and color, 1898-1904, in charge of course in interior design, 1904-34, this course was asso. with the Beaux Arts Inst. of Design, N.Y. City, 1916-34, teacher course water color painting since 1934; has followed profession as artist during entire career, painting, mural decoration and stained glass; devotes much time to archtl. photography, interior and exterior; traveled and painted extensively in Europe. Mem. Phila. Sketch Club (v.p.), Phila. Water Color Club (treas.), Miniature Camera Club of Phila., Order of Founders and Patriots of America. Republican. Episcopalian. Author of textbooks on water color painting, color and design. Lecturer on art in Phila., N.Y. City and other cities. Home: 472 Forrest Av., Drexel Hill, Pa.

COPELAND, Wilbur Fisk Detchon, printer and publisher; b. McConnellsville, N.Y., July 14, 1864; s. Anson Tuller and Minerva (Detchon) C.; ed. Poland Union Sem., Poland, O., 1878-79; A.B., O. Wesleyan U., 1889; m. Ella A. Griffiths, June 18, 1891; children—Jennie Margaret (dec.), Wilbur Griffiths (dec.), John Anson, Ellen Minerva (dec.), Rachel Griffiths (dec.), Otis Kelly (dec.), Agnes Wilburta (Mrs. Joseph B. Harold), Ellanore (Mrs. Benjamin Scheuble), Laura Winnington (Mrs. Alfred J. Bell), Warren Brady (dec.), Raymond Webster. Engaged as editor and printer, 1880-83; pvt. sec. to pres. O. Wesleyan U., 1884-88; mem. editorial staff, Funk & Wagnalls Co., N.Y. City, 1889-96; mfg. extension bookcases, Girard, Pa., 1896-98; with bd. edn. M.E. Ch., N.Y., 1898-1900; pres. and gen. organizer Straight Edge Industrial Settlement, N.Y., and Alpine, N.J., since 1899; sponsor for Copeland Family Scrapbook since 1930; pres. Sylvan Homes, Inc.; sponsor Copeland Family Nook; publisher pamphlets. Served as councilman and borough clk. Mem. M.E. Ch. Club: Alden Kindred of New York and Vicinity. Home: Alpine, N.J.

COPPEDGE, Mrs. Fern Isabel, artist; b. Decatur, Ill., July 28, 1888; d. John Leslie and Maria Ann (Dilling) Kuns; ed. McPherson (Kan.) Coll. and U. of Kan.; art edn., Art Students League of New York, Art Inst. Chicago and Pa. Acad. Fine Arts; m. Robert William Coppedge, Jan. 2, 1910. Landscape painter; rep. by "The Thaw," Detroit Inst. Art; "Winter on the Schuylkill," Pa. State Coll.; "Snow Covered Hills," Pa. Acad. Fine Arts; "From the Hilltop," Am. Embassy, Rio de Janeiro, Brazil; "Frozen Canal," Witte Mus., San Antonio, Tex.; "A Village on the Delaware," Thayer Mus., Lawrence, Kans., 1929; "The River's Bend," Bryn Mawr Club, Bryn Mawr, Pa.; "Passing Winter," Benjamin West Mus., Swarthmore, Pa., "The Delaware in Winter," Reading (Pa.) Mus., 1934; "Three Churches," hon. mention Nat. Assn. Women Painters and Sculptors, New York, 1933; "Jersey Village," gold medal Expn. of Women's Achievements, Phila., 1932; "Christmas Marketing," New Century Club, Phila. H. O. Dean prize artist of Kansas City (Mo.) and vicinity, 1917; E. Shield prize artist, same, 1918; hon. mention, Nat. Assn. Women Painters, 1922; 1st Plastic Club (Phila.) prize, 1924; silver medal, Kansas City, 1924. Fellow Pa. Acad. Fine Arts; mem. Nat. Assn. Women Painters, Art League New York, Art Alliance Philadelphia, Ten Philadelphia Painters, Plastic Club. Home: 4011 Baltimore Av., Philadelphia, Pa.

COPPOCK, Walter J., engineer, economist; b. nr. West Branch, Ia., Nov. 9, 1889; s. Joseph J. and Rebecca (Ellyson) C.; grad. Scattergood Boarding Sch., West Branch, Ia., 1906, Barnesville (O.) Boarding Sch., 1908, Westtown (Pa.) Boarding Sch., 1910; B.S. in mech. engring., State U. of Ia., Iowa City, Ia., 1920, M.E., 1936; A.M. in economics, U. of Pa., 1922; m. Luella Mae West, Mar. 6, 1912; children—Ethel Rebecca (Mrs. Clifford A. Woodbury Jr.), Mabel Emma (Mrs. Ian Garriques), Harold West, Esther Louise, Walter J. Teacher pvt. schs., 1910-12; farmer in Iowa, 1912-16, where he pioneered in farm tractor, 2-row cultivator, low voltage farm lighting; draftsman Baldwin Locomotive Works, 1920; instr. industry Wharton Sch., Phila., 1920-24; contracting business, 1924-28; research and selling Eastman, Dillon & Co., investment bankers, Phila., 1928-30, J. E. Rhodes & Sons, leather belting, Phila., 1930-32; research and development work Am. Pulley Co., Phila., 1934-36, cons. engr. since 1936; instr. industrial engring. Pa. State Coll. extension div. confs. in foreman training since 1936; registered professional engr. in Pa. Mem. Soc. Advancement Management, English Folk Dance and Song Soc. Quaker. Granted patent on tension control motor base. Home: Moylan, Pa. Office: Board of Education Bldg., 21st and Parkway, Philadelphia, Pa.

COPPOLINO, John Frank, physician; b. Phila., Pa., Dec. 22, 1897; s. Frank and Anna (Pergolizzi) C.; A.B., Central High Sch., Phila., 1916; student U. of Pa., 1916-18; M.D., Jefferson Med. Coll., Phila., 1922; m. Elizabeth M. Yensen, June 8, 1928; children—Josephine Elizabeth, Joan Marie, John Francis. In practice as physician, Phila., since 1923; asst. demonstrator of pediatrics, Jefferson Med. Coll., Phila., 1925-27, instr. in pediatrics, 1927-35, demonstrator of pediatrics, 1935-37, asso. in pediatrics since 1937; pediatrician to St. Joseph's and St. Agnes hospitals. Certified by Am. Bd. Pediatrics. Mem. Am. Acad. Pediatrics, Phila. Pediatric Soc., Phila. Co. Med. Soc., Phi Rho Sigma. Roman Catholic. Contbr. of several articles to med. jours. Address: 2028 S. 13th St., Philadelphia, Pa.

CORBIERE, Anthony Sylvain, prof. Romance langs.; b. Nice, France, Mar. 8, 1892; s. Jules Eugene and Catherine (Rondeu) C.; came to U.S., 1907, naturalized, 1918; ed. high sch., Tacoma, Wash., U. of Wash., Seattle, Wash., 1914-17; Ph.B., Muhlenberg Coll., Allentown, Pa., 1920; grad. study Columbia, 1920-21; A.M., U. of Pa., 1923, Ph.D., same, 1927; Jusserand Traveling Fellow, grad. study, Centro de Estudios Historicos, Madrid, 1925-26, Sorbonne, U. of Paris, summer 1926; m. Marie Elizabeth Hinkle, Aug. 15, 1922; children—Paul Francis, Catherine Marie. Began as teacher high sch., Belleville, N.J., 1920; instr. and head dept. Romance langs., Muhlenberg Coll., Allentown, Pa., 1921, asst. prof., 1923-26, prof. and head dept. since 1926. Served as pvt. to top sergt. Ambulance Corps and Med. Corps, U.S. Army, 1917-19. Mem. Nat. Fed. Mod. Lang. Teachers, Mod. Lang. Assn. of America, Am. Assn. Teachers of French (pres. Lehigh Valley Chapter, 1929-38; now v.p.), l'Alliance Francaise (v.p. Easton, Pa., Chapter since 1934), Pa. State Mod. Lang. Assn. (mem. council 1935-38), Am. Legion, Allentown Parent-Teachers Assn., Muhlenberg Sch. Parent-Teachers Assn. (treas. 1937-39), Phi Kappa Sigma, Sigma Delta Chi, Phi Sigma Iota (pres. Lambda Chapter). Lutheran. Club: Brookside Country (Macungie, Pa.). Author: Juan Eugenio Hartzenbusch and the French Theatre, 1927. Life sec. Class of 1920, Muhlenberg Coll.; nat. historian Phi Sigma Iota and editor Journal since 1929. Home: 814 N. 21st St., Allentown, Pa.

CORBIN, Arthur Shennen; pres. gen. counsel and dir. N.J. Mortgage & Title Co. Home: 230 Boulevard. Office: 15 Broadway, Passaic, N.J.

CORBIN, Horace Kellogg, banker; b. Elizabeth, N.J., Apr. 25, 1887; s. William H. and Clementine (Kellogg) C.; student Hill Sch., 1902-04; Litt.B., Princeton U., 1908; m. Hannah Stockton, May 25, 1912; children— Clementine S., Horace K., Robert S., William O., Hannah B. Engring. contractor, 1911-17; v.p. and dir. Fidelity Union Trust Co., Newark, N.J., since 1929; pres. and dir. Motor Finance Co., Newark, since 1921; dir. Bankers Indemnity Ins. Co., Middlesex Water Co., Weston Elec. Instrument Corpn., Am. Ins. Co., Foster Wheeler Corpn. Served as 1st lt. Q.M.C., U.S. Army, 1918-19. Home: Llewellyn Park, West Orange, N.J. Office: 755 Broad St., Newark, N.J.

CORCORAN, Sanford William, clergyman; b. Ontario, Can., Feb. 25, 1876; s. John Sanford and Ann Jane (Highfield) C.; A.B., Ohio Wesleyan U., 1904, D.D., 1924; S.T.B., Boston U. 1906, grad. student, 1906-07; m. Anne Kunes, July 1909; children—Sanford William, John. Came to U.S., 1898, naturalized, 1903. Asst. pastor Christ Ch., Pittsburgh, 1907-09; pastor Walton Ch., Pittsburgh, 1909-11, Ben Avon Ch., Pittsburgh, 1911-17, 1st M.E. Ch., Beaver, Pa., 1917-22; supt. Washington Dist., Pittsburgh Conf., 1922-24, Allegheny Dist., 1924-26; supt. M.E. Ch. Union, Pittsburgh, since 1926. Mem. Gen. Conf. M.E. Ch., 1928, 32, 36 (judiciary com. 1936 conf.), Bd. Edn. of M.E. Ch., 1928-36, 6th Ecumenical Methodist Conf., 1931, Pittsburgh Council of Churches of Christ (exec. com.), Pa. Council of Churches, Budget Com. of Community Fund of Pittsburgh, Fed. Council of Churches of Christ in America, 1928-32; mem. exec. com. Bd. of Home Missions and Ch. Extension of M.E. Ch.; mem. bd. Fed. of Social Agencies of Pittsburgh. Del. to Uniting Conf., 1939. Home: 3218 Latonia Av., Dormont. Office: Smithfield St. and 7th Av., Pittsburgh, Pa.

CORDES, Frank, chmn. bd. Blaw-Knox Co.; b. Lewistown, Pa., Oct. 7, 1870; s. Joseph R. and Martha Catherine (Fichthorn) C.; ed. pub. schs. of Pa.; m. Ethel T. Lomax, July 5, 1899; children—Catherine (Mrs. Arthur Kline), Margaret Hilda (Mrs. Howard S. Philips), Ethel Gertrude, Frances Christiana. Chemist Edgar Thompson Works, Carnegie Steel Co., Braddock, Pa., 1888-95; metallurgist, later mgr. roll foundries Lincoln Foundry Co. (later merged with United Engring. & Foundry Co.), 1895-1912; pres. Best Mfg. Co., Pittsburgh, 1913-14; pres. Hubbard Steel Foundry Co., East Chicago, Ind., 1914-19; mgr. plant Wheeling (W.Va.) Mold and Foundry Co., 1922-27; pres. Lewis Foundry and Machine Co., 1927-29; v.p. Blaw-Knox Co., Pittsburgh, 1929-36, pres., 1936-37, chmn. bd. since Feb. 5, 1937; also chmn. bd. Lewis Foundry and Machine Co., Blaw-Knox Construction Co., Blaw-Knox Internat. Corpn., Hoboken Land Co., Nat. Alloy Steel Co., Union Steel Casting Co., Pittsburgh Rolls Corpn., Groveland Land Co., A. W. French & Co. Holder of several patents on appliances used in steel industry. Mem. Am. Iron and Steel Inst. Republican. Mason. Clubs: Metropolitan, Longue Vue Country; Castalia (O.) Trout Fishing. Home: 211 Lytton Av., Pittsburgh, Pa.; also (summers) Catawba Cliffs, O. Office: Farmers Bank Bldg., Pittsburgh, Pa.

CORDIE, Cornell Heckart, chemist; b. Oil City, Pa., Nov. 18, 1886; s. Cornelius S. and Adeline Veronica (Fisher) C.; student Oil City (Pa.) High Sch., 1898-1902; B.S., Pa. State Coll., 1906; m. Edna Blair Mitchell, May 15, 1912. Chemist Emporium Powder Co., dynamite plant, Emporium, Pa., 1906-08; chemist U.S. Geol. Survey, Pittsburgh, 1908-09; chief chemist Pluto Powder Co., Ishpeming, Mich., and Keystone-National Powder Co., Emporium, Pa., 1909-15; chief chemist Howard Smokeless Powder Plant, Emporium, Pa., 1915-17; supt. smokeless powder plant Aetna Explosives Co., Emporium, 1917-18, gen. supt. four dynamite plants, 1919-21; asso. with Hercules Powder Co., Wilmington, in various capacities, since 1921, mgr. explosives development since 1934. Mem. Am. Inst. Chem. Engrs., Kappa Sigma. Republican. Clubs: Wilmington Country, Hercules Country (Wilmington, Del.). Home: 1100 Shallcross Av. Office: Hercules Powder Co., Wilmington, Del.

CORDRAY, Albert Thornton, prof. speech and dir. theatre; b. London, O., Sept. 7, 1901; s. Albert Thornton and Jennie Emma (Kennedy) C.; A.B., O. Univ., Athens, O., 1923; A.M., State U. of Ia., Iowa City, Ia., 1926, Ph.D., 1939; m. Mary E. Tener, June 5, 1926. Engaged as head prof. of speech and dir. of Little Theatre, Westminster Coll., New Wilmington, Pa., since 1928. Mem. Nat. Assn. Teachers of Speech, Am. Assn. Univ. Profs., Am. Ednl. Theatre Assn., Phi Kappa Tau. Republican. Episcopalian. Mason (Scottish Rite). Home: 218 Mercer St., New Wilmington, Pa.

CORE, Earl L(emley), univ. prof.; b. Core, W.Va., Jan. 20, 1902; s. Harry M. and Clara E. (Lemley) C.; A.B., W.Va. Univ., 1926, A.M., 1928; Ph. D., Columbia U., 1936; m. Freda B. Garrison, June 8, 1925; children—Clara Ruth, John Merle, Harry Michael. Began as teacher in rural schs., 1920 to 1923; instr. botany, W.Va. Univ., Morgantown, W.Va., 1926-33, asst. prof. botany and curator of the herbarium since 1933. Mem. A.A.A.S., Bot. Soc. America, Southern Appalachian Bot. Club (organizer 1936), Torrey Bot. Club, W.Va. Acad. Sci., N.Y. Bot. Garden (collaborator), Phi Beta Kappa. Republican. Christian Ch. Kiwanis. Author: Syllabus of the Spermatophyta; Chronicles of Core. Co-author (with P. D. Strausbaugh, Nelle Ammons), Common Seed Plants; (with P. D. Strausbaugh), Trees and Shrubs of West Virginia; Contbr. to Biological Abstracts. Editor of Castanea, monthly jour., since 1936. Home: Core, W.Va.

CORIELL, Louis Duncan, periodontist; b. Baltimore, Md., Mar. 25, 1878; s. Alvin and Mary Aurelia (Lawrence) C.; DD.S., Baltimore City Coll., U. of Md., 1899; m. Elizabeth Reid Johnson, Oct. 12, 1904. In practice as periodontist since 1899; lecturer Baltimore Coll. of Dental Surgery; visiting and cons. dental surgeon, Johns Hopkins Hosp. Fellow Am. Coll. of Dentists; mem. Am. Dental Assn., Am. Acad. Periodontology, Md. Acad. Sciences, Mayflower Soc., Soc. of Colonial Wars, Huguenot Soc., S.R., Delta Sigma Delta, Theta Nu Epsilon. Episcopalian. Clubs: University, Johns Hopkins Faculty, Elkridge Kennels (Baltimore). Contbr. to professional jours. Home: 205 Club Rd., Roland Park. Office: 111 W. Monument St., Baltimore, Md.

CORKRAN, Wilbur Sherman, engr., architect and developer; b. Crisfield, Md., May 1, 1888; s. Wilbur Fisk and Josephine (Fleming) C.; C.E., U. of Del., Newark, Del., 1910; student Northwestern U. Night Sch., Evanston, Ill., 1919-20; m. Louise Chambers, Aug. 18, 1918; engr. on powder mills and in Chilean nitrate fields, du Pont Co., 1910-14; adminstrn. and engring. work in oil exploration in S.A., Standard Oil Co. of N.Y., 1915-16; field engr. in charge Md., D.C. and Va., Portland Cement Assn., 1917; spl. rep. negotiating with Chinese Govt. for oil leases, Sinclair Oil Corpn., 1919-20; in business for self as engr. and constructor on railroad, tunnel, foundation water-proofing bldg. constrn., land development, New York City and Short Hills, N.J., 1921-33; exec. officer and engr., Mosquito Control Commn., Del., organizing and supervising project covering 45,000 acres marsh land and costing approximately $2,000,000, Kent and Sussex Counties, State of Del., since 1933; in practice at Rehoboth Beach, Del., as W.S. Corkran, engr., and architect, specializing on engring. structures, land development, archtl. work and bldg. constrn.; licensed professional engr. and land surveyor, N.J., licensed architect, N.J.; pres. and owner Henlopen Acres, Inc., Del. Served as pvt., sergt., lt., Del. N.G., 1906-11; 1st lt., capt., maj., Corps of Engrs., 1st Div., A.E.F., 1917-19; 1st U.S. Engrs. and sr. instr., Camp Humphries, Va., 1918-19; lt. col., Engrs. R.C., U.S. Army, since 1919. Mem. Am. Soc. C.E., Am. Inst. Architects, Phi Kappa Phi, Sigma Nu. Episcopalian. Mason (32°). Home: Rehoboth Beach, Del. Office: Lewes, Del.

CORN, David; dir. gynecology Hackensack (N.J.) Gen. Hosp. Address: 119 Park St., Ridgefield Park, N.J.

CORNBROOKS, Thomas Mullan, naval architect; b. Wilmington, Del., Oct. 26, 1876; s. William Henry and Elizabeth Ellis (Mullan) C.; grad. Wilmington High Sch., 1892; course in naval architecture with pvt. tutor; m. Harriet Boulden Walters, June 12, 1900; children—Charles W., Thomas E., William H., Harriet W., Elizabeth M. Apprenticeship with The Harlan and Hollingsworth Co., Wilmington, 1892-97; asst. chief draftsman with same co., 1897-98; naval architect Md. Steel Co., 1898-1912, chief engr., 1912-14; asst. mgr. Md. Shipbuilding Plant of Bethlehem Steel Co., 1914-17; became supt. contracts and sales, Bethlehem Shipbuilding Corpn., Ltd., 1917; pres. Merrill-Stevens Shipbuilding Corpn., Louisiana Shipbuilding Corpn., S. Jacksonville Realty Corpn., 1918-19; asst. mgr. New York Shipbuilding Corpn., 1919-21; asst. to sr. v.p. N.Y. Shipbuilding Corpn., 1921-24; pres. Camden (N.J.) Motors Co., Security Fuel Oil

Burner Corpn., Camden, 1924-25; director marine sales Pusey & Jones Corpn. Tech. agt. Isherwood System of Ship Constrn. Commr. Borough of Collingswood, 1925-29. Chairman standardization com. Bethlehem Steel and subsidiary cos.; chmn. advisory com. and dir. Camden Dealers' Used Car Exchange, 1925. Mem. and sec. freeboard com. U.S. Govt.; mem. sub-com. on electric spot welding of Council National Defense; mem. sub-com. on standard ships U.S. Govt.; mem. tech. com. Am. Bur. Shipping. Mem. Soc. Naval Architects and Marine Engrs., Instn. Naval Architects, London; asso. mem. Inst. Naval Engrs., Washington, D.C. Republican. Methodist. Mason. Home: 132 N. Highland Av., Springfield, Pa. Office: care Pusey & Jones Corpn., Wilmington, Del.

CORNELISON, Robert Wilson, chemist; b. Washington, Ill., July 30, 1869; s. Isaac A. and Agnes (Forsyth) C.; grad. Washington (Ill.) High Sch., 1886; B.S., U. of Ill., 1890; Sc.D., Harvard U., 1893; m. Alice Loughridge, April 17, 1906; children—Margaret Loughridge (Mrs. Burnham Bowden), Elizabeth Forsyth, Alice Roberta. Asst. in chemistry, U. of Ill., 1890-91; lecturer organic chemistry, Harvard Summer Sch., 1892; mgr. various textile mills, 1896 to 1915; research chemist E. R. Squibb & Sons, 1903-05; food and drug inspection chemist Bur. of Chemistry, U.S. Dept. of Agr., 1905-06; prin. owner and mgr. Peerless Color Co. since 1916; formerly dir. several textile and chem. mfg. cos. Chmn. Red Cross Chapter, Somerville, N.J., and Vicinity. Mem. Dutch Reformed Ch. Club: Chemists (N.Y. City). Home: 275 W. Summit St., Somerville, N.J. Office: 521-535 North Av., Plainfield, N.J.

CORNELL, Walter Stewart, physician; b. Phila., Pa., Jan. 3, 1877; s. Watson and Mary E. (Hurtt) C.; B.S., U. of Pa., 1897, M.D., U. of Pa. Med. Sch., 1901, Dr.P.H., 1922; m. Mabel Bremer Kuhn, June 21, 1922. Served as dir. med. inspection of pub. schs., Phila., Pa., since 1912; lecturer in anatomy, U. of Pa. Med. Sch., 1902-26; lecturer in hygiene, U. of Pa. Sch. of Edn. since 1919; asst. prof. Pub. Health and Preventive Medicine, Temple U. Med. Sch., Phila., since 1937. Served as maj., Med. Corps, U.S. Army, 1917-19; lt. col. then col. U.S.A. Med. Res. Corps, 1919-35. Chmn. Phila. Pub. Sch. Health Fund since 1920. Fellow Phila. Coll. Phys.; mem. A.M.A., Am. Pub. Health Assn., Pa. State and Phila. Co. med. socs., Northeast High Sch. (Phila.) Alumni Assn. (pres. 1898-1908), Phi Beta Kappa, Sigma Xi, Delta Tau Delta, Alpha Mu Pi Omega. Presbyterian. Mason. Club: Union League (Phila.). Author: Health and Medical Inspection of School Children, 1912; contbr. articles to med. jours. Home: 5939 Drexel Rd. Office: Board of Education Bldg., Parkway and 21st St., Philadelphia, Pa.

CORNELL, William Bouck, univ. prof.; b. Bouck's Island, Fultonham, Schoharie Co., N.Y., July 14, 1883; s. Charles Ezra and Katharine Lawyer (Bouck) C.; M.E., Cornell U., 1907; m. Emily Adelaide Lebengood, Nov. 19, 1913; 1 son, William Ezra. Instr. in engring., Cornell U., 1907-08; asst. to engr. in charge constrn. of hydro electric power developments in Ida. and Utah with Telluride Power Co.; underground cable engr. Am. Telephone & Telegraph Co.; sales engr. Niles-Bement-Pond Co.; sales engr. Acheson Graphite Co. and sec. and gen. mgr. of affiliated co.; production engr. Willys-Overland Co.; prof. management and chmn. dept. of management and industrial relations, New York University since 1921. Licensed cons. engr. State of N.Y. Mem. Am. Soc. Mech. Engrs., Inst. of Management, Am. Management Assn., Alpha Tau Omega, Alpha Kappa Psi, Theta Nu Epsilon, Delta Mu Delta, Sphinx Head, Beta Gamma Sigma. Republican. Episcopalian. Mason. Editor and compiler: The Development of American Industries—Their Economic Significance, 1932. Author: Office Administration (with G. S. Childs), 1924; Syllabus of Industrial Organization and Management, Principles and Practice, 1925; Fundamentals of Business Organization and Management, 1927; Industrial Organization and Management, 1928; Business Organization, 1930; Business Organization and Practice, 1936; Organization and Management in Industry and Business, 1936. Home: 197 Grove St., Montclair, N.J.

CORNFELD, Harry George, pharmacist; b. Phila., Pa., Oct. 6, 1899; s. Samuel and Sarah (Lackerman) C.; student Temple U., Phila., 1916-17, Ph.G., 1924; student U. of Pa., 1932; m. Eva Schachter, Sept. 5, 1927. Retail pharmacist, Collingdale, Pa., since 1926; instr. in pharmacy, history and mathematics, Temple U. Sch. of Pharmacy, Phila., since 1924, asst. dir. of pharmacy labs. since 1936; instr. in materia medica, Temple U. Sch. of Chiropody since 1926. Served as corpl., 111th Inf., U.S. Army, 1917-19. Elected Republican Co. Committeeman, Delaware Co., Pa., 1934, re-elected, 1936. Sch. dir., Collingdale, Pa., 1935-41; elected pres. Bd. of Edn., Collingdale, Pa., 1937, re-elected, 1938. Mem. Pa., Am. pharmaceutical assns., Pharmacy Alumni Assn. of Temple U. (sec. 1924-30; pres. 1933-35), General Alumni Assn. of Temple U. (mem. bd. of dirs.), Alpha Zeta Omega. Republican. Home: 905 Clifton Av. Office: 907 Clifton Av., Collingdale, Pa.

CORNISH, Hubert Ray, sch. prin., author; b. Milan, Mich., April 5, 1878; s. Demmon and Mary Catherine (Haner) C.; student State Normal Coll., Ysilanti, Mich., 1897-1901, U. of Mich., Ann Arbor, Mich., 1903-05; B.S., A.M., Columbia U., 1913; m. Clara Alice Alward, Aug. 7, 1907; children—Dorothy Ella (Mrs. Edwin Winters Bramhall), Mary Catherine, Alice Elizabeth. Supt. schs., Camden, Mich., 1901-03; prin. Washington Sch., Sault Ste. Marie, Mich., 1903-04, John Moore Sch., Saginaw, Mich., 1904-09; prin. schs., Paterson, N.J., since 1910; sec. Lakeview Mortgage Co., Paterson, N.J., since 1926. Mem. N.J. Council of Edn., N.J. Schoolmasters Club, N.E.A. Republican. Methodist. Chmn. Ednl. Rev. (N.J.) Editorial Com., 1927-31. Co-author: Founders of Freedom in America, 1922; History of United States for Schools, 1929; Our Constitution, 1928; Metropolitan New York, 1930. Author: New Jersey—A Story of Progress, 1932. Home: 365 E. 37th St., Paterson, N.J.

CORNISH, Samuel Davis; b. Valley Forge, Pa., June 9, 1865; s. Alexander and Mary (Callahan) C.; D.D.S., Pa. Coll. of Dental Surgery, Phila., 1898; m. Dr. Mary Rebecca Rauch, June 5, 1901 (died 1909); 1 son, Samuel Louis; m. 2d, Irene H. Sacks, June 23, 1915; children—Freeland Sacks, Evelyn Sacks. Pvt. practice of dentistry, Collegeville, Pa., 1898-1924, retired in 1924; organized Collegeville (Pa.) Flag & Mfg. Co., 1909, and since pres. Mem. Collegeville (Pa.) Fire Co. Mem. Collegeville (Pa.) Bd. of Health (sec., 1900-06 and 1914-28; councilman, 1906-08). Mem. Boy Scouts of America, U. of Pa. Alumni. Awarded replica of five millionth copy of Handbook for Boys in recognition of services to Boy Scouts of America. Republican. Reformed Ch. Mason. (Royal Arch, K.T., Lehigh Consistory, Scottish Rite, 32°, Shriner), Odd Fellow. Clubs: Camp Biff Hunting and Fishing, Twin Springs Hunting and Fishing (Pike Co., Pa.); Acacia (Warren Lodge, Collegeville, Pa.; pres. emeritus); Lions (Collegeville, Pa.; past pres.). Home: 334 Main St. Office: Main and Walnut Sts., Collegeville, Pa.

CORNWELL, John J., ex-governor; b. Ritchie Co., W.Va., July 11, 1867; s. Jacob H. and Mary E. (Taylor) C.; student Shepherd Coll., Shepherdstown, W.Va., 1888, and W.Va. Univ., Morgantown, 1889-90; LL.D., W.Va. Univ., Univ. of Md., University of Vermont; m. Edna Brady, June 30, 1891; children—John J. (dec.); Mrs. Eugene E. Ailes. Prin. owner The Hampshire Review since 1890, editor; lawyer; financed and built Hampshire Southern R.R. (40 miles long), pres. Bank of Romney; dir. Baltimore & Ohio Railroad Company; General counsel same since July 20, 1922. Delegate Dem. Nat. Conv., 1896, 1912, 24, 32; mem. W.Va. Senate, 1896-1906; Dem. nominee for gov. of W. Va., 1904; elected gov., term 1917-21 (only Dem. elected). Mason, Odd Fellow, Elk. Author: Knock About Notes, 1915; A Mountain Trail, 1939. Home: Romney, W.Va. Office: Baltimore & Ohio Bldg., Baltimore, Md.

CORNWELL, Martha Jackson, sculptor; b. West Chester, Pa., Jan. 29, 1869; d. Robert T. and Lydia Ann (Jackson) Cornwell; student Sch. of Design, Phila., 1888-91, Art Students' League, New York, 1891-94; worked with Augustus Saint Gaudens; studied in Paris; unmarried. Sculptor since 1895; made many portraits in bronze, plaster and terra cotta, portraits of children in bas-reliefs and statuettes. Works: Bronze portraits of Richard Henry Stoddard, Thomas Buchanan Read, Bayard Taylor, George Morris Philips, Robert Thompson Cornwell, Dr. Joseph T. Rothrock, and others; drink-fountain in bronze at West Chester, Pa. Exhibited at: New York, Phila., Chicago and San Francisco. Awards: George W. Child's gold medal, Phila., 1895. Mem. bd. dirs. West Chester Library Assn. Mem. Fellowship Pa. Acad. Fine Arts, Chester Co. Art Assn. Republican. Presbyterian. Club: West Chester Golf and Country. Address: Virginia Av., West Chester, Pa.

CORR, Patrick Joseph, lawyer; b. Pittsburgh, Pa., Jan. 27, 1901; s. Patrick James and Ellen (McFarren) C.; student St. Peters R.C. Sch., 1907-15, Latimer Jr. High Sch., 1915-16, Allegheny High Sch., 1916-19 (all Pittsburgh); B.S. of Economics, U. of Pittsburgh, 1923, LL.B., Law Sch., 1926; m. Elizabeth Dutney, April 27, 1927 (died 1936); children—Patricia Ann, William Dutney, Robert Joseph. Admitted to Pa. bar, 1926, and since in practice at Pittsburgh; head swimming coach, U. of Pittsburgh, 1923-39, took position while in law sch. Formerly asst. city solicitor. Mem. Delta Theta Phi. Democrat. Roman Catholic. K. of C. Clubs: Metropolitan (Pittsburgh); Highland Country. Home: 1813 Morrell St. Office: 613 Bakewell Bldg., Pittsburgh, Pa.

CORRADINI, Robert Everett, exec. sec. Foundation for Narcotics Research and Information, Alcohol Information Com.; b. Fabbrico, Reggio Emilia, Italy, Sept. 11, 1891; s. Angelo and Domenica (Tasca) C.; Evang. Sem., Zurich, Switzerland, 1900-05; Gewerbeschule, Zurich, 1905-09; Bibl. Sem., N.Y. City, 1911-14; m. Annie Walton, Feb. 8, 1915 (died in 1919); 1 son, Everett Wesley; m. 2d, Constance Kreuter, May 22, 1935; one daughter, Barbara Ines. Served as associate pastor of Summerfield, M.E. Church, Dobbs Ferry, N.Y., 1911-14; pastor Prospect Street M.E. Church, Paterson, N.J., 1914-16; asso. pastor Mott Av. M.E. Ch., N.Y. City, 1916-19; field sec. for foreign work, New York Anti-Saloon League, 1919-22; research sec. World League Against Alcoholism, 1923-31; exec. sec. The Alcohol Information Com. since 1927; trustee and exec. sec. Foundation for Narcotics Research and Information, Inc.; pres. and dir. Euthenics Products Corpn. Mem. N.G. N.Y. 1917-18. Mem. Am. Econ. Assn., Am. Statis. Assn., Am. Sociol. Soc., Am. Acad. Polit. and Social Science, Soc. Study of Inebriety, London. Awarded diploma for ednl. work, City of Santiga, Chile, 1922. Republican. Methodist. Author of "Narcotics and Youth Today." Contbr. on alcohol question. Home: 393 Woodland Road, Madison, N.J. *

CORRADO, Gaetano, corpn. official; b. Marrietta, O., Oct. 29, 1887; s. Cataldo and Marie Josephine C.; ed. pub. schs.; m. Angeline Bell, Sept. 25, 1913; children—Albert, Josephine, Gloria. Began in employ of Pittsburgh, McKeesport & Connellsville St. Ry. Co., later in gen. mdse. and banking business; in charge foreign dept. Colonial Nat. Bank of Connellsville, 1908-16; pres. and gen. mgr. Bell Coal & Coke Co., Corrado & Galiardi Constrn. Co.; pres. Penn-Yough Contracting Co., Bradford Coal Co., Faywest Coal Co. and 10 other coal cos.; chmn. bd. Vanderbilt Coal & Coke Co.; v.p. Yough-Connellsville Coal & Coke Co.; treas. Crawford Coal & Coke Co.; dir. Yough Brewing Co. Trustee Connellsville State Hosp. Republican. Catholic. Clubs: Keystone Athletic, Pleasant Valley Country. Home: 232 E. Fairview Av. Office: Second Nat. Bank Bldg., Connellsville, Pa.

CORRADO, Guy, coal producer; b. Marietta, O., Oct. 29, 1887; s. Cataldo and Marie Josephine (Palladino) C.; student pub. schs.; m. Angelina Bell, Sept. 25, 1913; children—Dr. Albert, Josephine, Gloria. Began in employ of

Pittsburgh, McKeesport & Connellsville Ry. Co.; dir. and mgr. fgn. dept. Colonial Nat. Bank; pres. Yukon Nat. Bank; gen. mgr. Bell Coal & Coke Co.; pres. Bradford (Pa.) Coal & Coke Co., Corrado, Schenck Coal Co., Connellsville, Pa., Corrado Coal & Coke Corpn., Connellsville, Pa., Faywest Coal Co., Vanderbilt Coal & Coke Co., Penn Yough Contracting Co., Corrado & Galiardi Constrn. Co.; v.p. Yough-Connellsville Coal & Coke Co.; treas. and gen. mgr. Crawford Coal & Coke Co. Awarded Cross of Chevalier from King of Italy for philanthropic services. Home: 232 E. Fairview Av., Connellsville, Pa.

CORRIGAN, James Aloysius, physician; b. Milnesville, Pa., July 6, 1881; s. Martin and Mary (Walker) C.; ed. Bloomsburg State Normal Sch., 1909-11; M.D., Jefferson Med. Coll., Phila., 1915; m. Anna Monahan, June 26, 1918; children—Mary Margaret, James Aloysius. Interne, Hazleton, Pa., 1915-16; in pvt. practice of medicine and surgery at Hazleton, Pa., since 1916; surgeon, Lehigh Valley R.R. Co. since 1923; mem. firm and supt., Corrigan Maternity Hosp.; sec. and dir. Hazle Drugs, Inc.; dir. Markle Banking & Trust Co. Served as med. examiner Luzerne Co. Exemption Bd. No. 11 during World War. Mem. A.M.A., Pa. State and Luzerne Co. med. socs., Alpha Omega Alpha. Democrat. Roman Catholic. K.C. Club: Valley Country (Hazleton, Pa.). Home: 330 W. Broad St., Hazleton, Pa.

CORRIN, Kenneth Matthew, M.D., psychiatry; b. Canon City, Colo., May 4, 1898; s. John Thomas and Ada Hanna (Shepard) C.; B.S., Colo. State Coll., Fort Collins, Colo., 1922; M.D., Jefferson Med. Coll., Phila., 1926; m. Mary Barr, June 1, 1929; children—Genevieve Katherine, Kenneth Matthew, Dana Shepard. Resident physician Phila. Gen. Hosp., 1926-28; resident psychiatrist Wernersville State Hosp., Pa., 1930-34, clin. dir. and asst. supt., 1934-37; private practice of neurology and psychiatry, Phila., since 1937; hosp. appointments at Phila. Gen., Jefferson and St. Agnes hosps.; instr. in psychiatry, Jefferson Med. Coll.; lecturer in psychiatry, Jefferson Sch. for Nurses. Served as 1st lt. Med. Corps, Pa. Nat. Guard, 1927-29. Diplomate Am. Bd. Neurology and Psychiatry; fellow Am. Psychiatric Assn., A.M.A.; mem. Assn. for Research in Nervous and Mental Disease, Nat. and Internat. League Against Epilepsy, Pa. Div. of Mental Hygiene, Phila. Neurological and Psychiatric Socs., Phila. Co. Med. Soc., West Phila. Med. Assn., Jefferson Soc. for Clin. Investigation, Jefferson Hosp. Republican. Presbyterian. Club: Medical (Phila.). Home: 334 N. Preston St. Office: 2025 Walnut St., Philadelphia, Pa.

CORRINGTON, Julian Dana, biologist; b. Hot Springs, Ark., Dec. 22, 1891; s. Joe W. and Jessie W. (Knox) C.; A.B., Cornell U., 1913; Ph. D., 1925; m. Veronica Elisabeth Flicke. children—Mariette, Paul. Asst. zoölogy, Cornell U., 1915-16, curator of Mus., 1916-17 and 1919-20; asst. prof. biology, U. of S.C., 1921-22, prof. zoölogy, 1922-26; asst. prof. zoölogy, Syracuse U., 1926-30; asso. prof. biology, Drew U., 1930-31; dir. ednl. service Frank A. Ward Foundation of Natural Science, U. of Rochester, 1931-36; prof. biology and head of dept., Washington Coll., since 1936. Traveled and studied in Europe, 1913-14; student at Woods Hole, Mass., 1925; mem. N.Y. State Bd. of Regents, biology com., 1929-31. Served as 2d lt., U.S.A., 1918. Fellow, A.A.A.S.; mem. N.Y. Micros. Soc., Sigma Xi, Phi Beta Kappa, Phi Delta Sigma, Scabbard and Blade. Founder and permanent sec. Am. Soc. Amateur Microscopists. Author: Adventures with the Microscope, 1934. Writer on morphology of shark arteries, herpetology, faunal studies, amateur microscopy. Contbr. to professional and general periodicals; contbg. editor Nature Magazine. Home: 118 Water St., Chestertown, Md.

CORSER, John B.; ophthalmologist Hahnemann Hosp.; cons. ophthalmologist Scranton State Hosp., Scranton, and Hillside. Home: Clark's Summit. Address: 345 Wyoming Av., Scranton, Pa.

CORSON, Fred Pierce, coll. pres.; b. Millville, N.J., Apr. 11, 1896; s. Jeremiah and Mary E. (Payne) C.; A.B., Dickinson Coll., Carlisle, Pa., 1917, A.M., 1920; B.D., Drew Univ., 1920; D.D., Dickinson, 1931, Syracuse, 1933; Litt.D., U. of Md., 1936; LL.D., Western Md. Coll., 1936, Allegheny Coll., 1936, Franklin and Marshall Coll., 1936, Gettysburg Coll. 1937, U. of Pa., 1937; m. Frances Beaman, Mar. 22, 1922; 1 son, Hampton Payne. Ordained M.E. ministry, 1920; pastor successively Jackson Hgts., N.Y., New Haven, Conn., Port Washington, N.Y., Simpson Ch., Brooklyn, until 1929; supt. Brooklyn S. Dist., N.Y. East Conf., 1930-34; pres. Dickinson Coll. since June 8 1934. Del. to Gen. Conf. M.E. Ch., 1932; mem. University Senate of M.E. Ch.; mem. Book Com., M.E. Ch.; mem. World Peace Commn., M.E. Ch.; mem. exec. com. Federal Council Chs. of Christ in America, 1932-36; mem. Governor's com. for Revision of the Constitution of State of Pa.; mem. advisory council for Inst. for Industrial Progress, advisory Bd. of Am. Inst. Ednl. Travel. Mem. Kappa Sigma, Phi Beta Kappa, Omicron Delta Kappa. Mason (Grand Chaplain Grand Lodge Pa.). Clubs: Rotary, University (Phila.), Carlisle Country. Author of "Dickinson College—An Interpretation of Function and Purpose," and "The Dilemma of the Liberated," "The Lure of the Expected," "The Obligation of the Church-Related College to the Future." Home: Carlisle, Pa.

CORSON, George C., judge; b. Plymouth Meeting, Pa., Sept. 9, 1889; s. George and Elizabeth (Cadwallader) C.; A.B., Swarthmore (Pa.) Coll.; LL.B., U. of Pa.; m. Jane Webb, May 12, 1934; 1 son, George C. Admitted to Pa. bar, 1914, and since in practice at Norristown; asst. dist. atty., Montgomery Co. (Pa.), 1920-29; judge 28th jud. dist. of Pa. since 1929. Served successively as pvt., sergt., 2d lt., 1st lt. with A.E.F. during World War; was with 90th Div., Motor Transport Service, U.S. Army of Occupation (Germany). Mem. Montgomery Co. (Pa.) Fish, Game and Forestry Assn. (v.p.), Netherlands Soc., Soc. of Founders and Patriots. Clubs: Old York Rd. Country, Tockwogh Yacht, Rotary (Norristown, Pa.). Author of court opinions pub. in dist. and co. law reports. Home: 130 Glenview Av., Wyncote, Pa. Office: Court House, Norristown, Pa.

CORT, John S.; mem. law firm Cort & Cort. Office: 707 Plaza Bldg., Pittsburgh, Pa.

CORT, William Walter, prof. helminthology; b. State Center, Ia., Apr. 28, 1887; s. William Carson and Mary (Smalley) C.; A.B., Colo., Coll., 1909; A.M., U. of Ill., 1911, fellow, 1913-14, Ph.D., 1914; m. Nellie Magruder Gleason, June 18, 1913; children—Helen Louise, Margaret Jean, Dorothy Anne. Asst. in zoölogy, U. of Ill., 1909-12; instr. in biology, Colo. Coll., 1912-13; prof. biology, Macalester Coll., St. Paul, Minn., 1914-16; asst. prof. zoölogy, U. of Calif., 1916-19; cons. helminthologist, Calif. State Bd. of Health, 1917-19; asso. prof. helminthology, Sch. Hygiene and Pub. Health, Johns Hopkins, 1919-25, prof. since 1925, head of dept. since 1927; visiting prof. parasitology, Peking (China) Union Med. Coll., 1923-24; mem. staff, U. of Mich. Biol. Sta., summer 1927. Chairman editorial committee Journal of Parasitology, 1932-37; editorial board American Journal Hygiene. Director commission Internat. Health Division, Rockefeller Foundation, for investigation of hookworm disease. Trinidad, B.W.I., May-Oct. 1921, Porto Rico, June-Sept., 1922, China, June 1923-Sept.1924, Panama, June-Sept. 1926; dir. 5 yr. program (1927-32) for study of ascariasis in children, Nat. Research Council and Am. Child Health Assn. Fellow A.A.A.S.; mem. Am. Soc. Parasitologists (sec. 1925-29, pres. 1930), Am. Soc. Tropical medicine, Am. Acad. Tropical Medicine (treas. 1934-37, v.p. 1938, pres. 1939), Am. Soc. Zoölogists, Am. Micros. Soc. (pres. 1937), Am. Soc. Naturalists, Phi Beta Kappa, Sigma Xi, Delta Omega, Gamma Alpha, Phi Delta Theta. Republican. Author: (with R. W. Hegner) Diagnosis of Protozoa and Worms Parasitic in Man, 1921; (with R. W. Hegner and F. M. Root) Outlines of Medical Zoölogy, 1923. Writer of many monographs and articles in Am. Jour. Hygiene and Jour. Parasitology, etc. Home: 5000 Norwood Av., Baltimore, Md.

CORWIN, Edward Samuel, college prof.; b. nr. Plymouth, Mich., Jan. 19, 1878; s. Frank Adelbert and Dora (Lyndon) C.; Ph.B., U. of Mich., 1900 (pres. of class), LL.D., 1925; Ph.D., University of Pa., 1905; Litt.D., Harvard University, 1936; m. Mildred Sutcliffe Smith, June 28, 1909. Instr. history, Brooklyn Poly., 1901-02; one of original group of preceptors called to Princeton U. by Woodrow Wilson, 1905; preceptor in history, politics and economics, 1905-11, prof. politics, 1911-18, McCormick prof. jurisprudence, 1918—, Princeton. Trustee Princeton Yenching Foundation. Mem. Am. Hist. Assn., Am. Polit. Science Assn. (president 1931), Phi Beta Kappa (University of Michigan), Institut International de Droit Public. Club: Nassau. Author: Part VI of Woodrow Wilson's Division and Reunion, 1909, 21; National Supremacy-Treaty-Power vs. State Power, 1913; The Doctrine of Judicial Review, 1914; French Policy and the American Alliance, 1916; The President's Control of Foreign Relations, 1917; John Marshall and the Constitution, 1919; The Constitution and What It Means Today, 1920, 6th edit., 1938; The President's Removal Power, 1927; The Democratic Dogma and Other Essays, 1930; The Twilight of the Supreme Court, 1934, 4th edit., 1937; The Commerce Power versus States Rights, 1936; Court Over Constitution, 1938. Joint Editor: The War Cyclopedia (pub. by Com. on Public Information), 1917. Contributor to Cyclo. Am. Govt., Dictionary Am. Biography, Ency. of the Social Sciences, and various periodicals. Editor Am. Polit. Science Series. Visiting prof. of polit. science at Yenching Univ., Peiping, China, and lecturer at Chinese instns. under auspices of Carnegie Endowment for Internat. Peace, 1928-29; Irvine lecturer School of Law, Cornell U., 1933; Storrs lecturer Sch. of Law, Yale U., 1934; Wood lecturer Hamilton Coll., 1936; guest of Harvard U. and contbr. to Tercentenary Conf. on Authority and the Individual, 1936; Schouler lecturer Johns Hopkins U., 1937; Bacon lecturer Boston U., 1937; Cutler lecturer U. of Rochester, 1937; adviser Pub. Works Adminstrn. on constitutional questions, 1935; spl. asst. to atty. gen. of U.S., 1936; consultant of atty. gen. of U.S. on constitutional questions, 1937. Home: 115 Prospect Av., Princeton, N.J.

CORWIN, Margaret Trumbull, college dean; b. Phila., Pa., Nov. 29, 1889; d. Robert Nelson and Margaret Wardell (Bacon) C.; A.B., Bryn Mawr Coll., 1912; hon. M.A., Yale, 1934; unmarried. Sec. Yale Press, 1912-17; exec. sec. woman's com. of Conn. Div. of Council of Nat. Defense, 1917-18; canteen worker Y.M.C.A. with A.E.F. in France, 1918; exec. sec. Grad. Sch., Yale U., 1918-34; dean of N.J. Coll. for Women since 1934. Dir. N. Atlantic sect., Am. Assn. Univ. Women, 1924-28. Mem. Phi Beta Kappa. Club: Cosmopolitan (New York). Home: 135 George St., New Brunswick, N.J.

CORY, Ernest Neal, entomologist; b. Alden, N.Y., Aug. 13, 1886; grad. Central High Sch., Washington, D. C., 1907; B.S., Md. Agrl. Coll. (U. of Md.), 1909, M.S., 1913; Ph.D., Am. Univ., Washington, D.C., 1926; m. Elizabeth C. Elder, Oct. 31, 1911; children—Ernest Neal, Jr., William Robert, Jean Marie. Asst. entomologist, Md. Dept. of Entomology and Zoology, 1909-11; instr. in entomology, U. of Md., 1911-12, asst. prof., 1912-13, asso. prof. of entomology and zoology, 1913-14; state entomologist of Md., teaching, research, extension work, U. of Md., since 1914. Sec. and business mgr. Am. Assn. Economic Entomologists; sec.-treas. Eastern Plant Bd.; sec.-treas. M Club and mem. Athletic Bd. of Univ. of Md.; vice-chmn. Nat. Shade Tree Conf. Mem. Entomol. Soc. America, Washington Entomol. Soc., Kappa Alpha, Phi Kappa Phi, Sigma Xi, Omicron Delta Kappa. Episcopalian. Mason. Club: Rotary Internat. Contbr. sect. on insects to Encyclopedia of Farming, 1914; author of bulletins and reports of Md. Expt. Sta.; contbr. articles to tech. jours Address: University of Maryland, College Park, Md.

COSGROVE, John C., banker, coal operator; b. Houtzdale, Pa., Apr. 28, 1886; s. Patrick B. and Zaidee M (Shoff) C.; prep. edn., St. Vincent's Coll.; grad. short course in mining,

Pa. State Coll., 1905; m. Florence M. Neff, July 7, 1909; children—Pat B., F. Elizabeth, Margaret L., John C. Organizer By-Products Coal & Coke Co., 1906, Hastings Coal & Coke Co., 1907, Grazier Coal Mining Co., 1913, and was gen. mgr. of each; organizer, 1911, and pres. Lenox Coal Co.; dir. Federal Reserve Bank of Phila., 1922-34; past pres. Johnstown Chamber of Commerce and Farmers Bank & Trust Co., Johnstown, Pa.; now chmn. bd. Franco Mining Corpn.; pres. Bituminous Coal Research, Inc., Sunnygrove Corpn., Robinswood Estate; dir. Hi-Grade Coal Co., Sootless Coal Co., The Lowman Corpn., Grazier Supply Co., Brugh Furniture Co., Hall's Motor Transit Co., Johnstown Finance and Loan Co., The Brown-Fayro Co., Black Top Equipment Co.; chmn. and mem. Com. of 10—Coal and Heat. Industries. Mem. A.I.M.E.—committee on Local Speakers; mem. Com. Coal Mine Ventilation of Am. Standards Assn.; mem. Am. Mining Congress; trustees Pa. State Coll.; chmn. Grounds and Bldgs. Com. of Pa. State Coll.; mem. of Pa. State Mining Soc.; mem. Johnstown Motor Club; mem. Mining Standardization Correlating Com. of Am. Standards Assn. Commodore on staff gov. of Ky. Mem. Phi Delta Theta, Pa. Soc. of N.Y. City. Mason (Shriner). Clubs: Bachelors (Johnstown); Bankers (New York); Sunnehanna Country. Home: 455 Orchard St. Office: Swank Bldg., Johnstown, Pa.

COSGROVE, Samuel A.; attending obstetrician Jersey City Med. Center; cons. obstetrician Christ Hosp., Bayonne Hosp. and Dispensary, North Hudson Hosp., Holy Name Hosp. and Monmouth Memorial Hosp.; med. dir. Margaret Hague Maternity Hosp. Address: 254 Union St., Jersey City, N.J.

COSTABILE, Vincent, physician; b. Naples, Italy, Dec. 5, 1900; s. Francesco and Rosie C.; came to U.S., 1927, naturalized, 1932; M.D. Royal Univ. of Naples, Italy, 1924; m. Lina Colantuono, Nov. 5, 1937; 1 son, Francis Vincent. Asst. 3d Med. Clinic of Royal Univ. of Naples, 1923-27; asst. 1st Med. Clinic of Naples, 1925-27; course of study on tubercular diseases, 1926; passed N.J. Med. Bd. Examiners, 1933, N.Y. Med. Bd. Examiners, 1938; mem. staff Hackensack Hosp., Columbus Hosp., Newark, West Hudson Hosp., Kearny, N.J., all since 1934. Mem. N.J. State Med. Soc., Bergen Co. Med. Soc.; Italian-Am. Citizen League of Bergen Co., East End Dem. Club, Lyndhurst. Elk. Contbr. 18 medical articles on various disease and scientific subjects to jours. Home: 150 Ridge Rd., Lyndhurst, N.J.

COSTAIN, Thomas Bertram, editor; b. Brantford, Ont., Can., May 8, 1885; s. John Herbert and Mary (Schultz) C.; ed. pub. schs. Brantford; m. Ida Randolph Spragge, Jan. 12, 1909; children—Mary Randolph, Ida Dorothy Phyllis (Mrs. Richard Carroll Hoke). Came to U.S., 1920, naturalized, 1935. Editor Guelph (Ont.) Daily Mercury, 1908-10, MacLean's Mag. (Toronto), 1910-20; asso. editor Saturday Evening Post, 1920-34; eastern editor Twentieth Century-Fox Film Corpn., 1934-35; editor American Cavalcade since 1935. Clubs: Players, Regency. Home: Bethayres, Pa. Office: Graybar Bldg., New York, N.Y.*

COSTELLO, James P.; in gen. practice of law since 1924; mayor of Hazleton, term expires 1942. Address: Hazleton, Pa.

COSTELLO, William F., physician; b. Binghamton, N.Y., Jan. 22, 1884; s. Frank P. and Elizabeth (McGowan) C.; M.D., U. of Buffalo Med. Sch., 1907; m. Mary Laughlin, June 16, 1914; children—John William, Elizabeth Ann. Interne, St. John's Hosp., L.I. City, N.Y., 1907-09; engaged in gen. practice of medicine and surgery at Dover, N.J. since 1909; attdg. surgeon, Dover Gen. Hosp.; dir. Dover Trust Co. Served as lt. Med. Corps, U.S.A. during World War. Pres. Bd. Health, Dover, N.J. Trustee Med. Soc. of N.J. Fellow Am. Coll. Surgs. Mem. Am. Med. Assn., N.J. State Med. Soc., Morris Co. Med. Soc. Roman Catholic. K.C. B.P.O.E. Clubs: Elks, K. of C. (Dover). Home: 55 W. Blackwell St., Dover, N.J.

COSTIKYAN, S. Kent, merchant; b. Marsovan, Asia Minor, Jan. 23, 1867; s. Simeon and Turvanda C.; student Colgate U., 1884-86; Dr. of Commercial law, Lincoln Memorial U., 1926; m. Mary Ransom Kent, Jan. 15, 1895; children—Kent Ransom, Alexandra Kent (Mrs. Theodore C. Jewett), Clarke Warren, Granger Kent. Came to U.S., 1884, naturalized, 1891. Organized firm of Costikyan Freres, importers, Rochester, N.Y., 1886; reorganized as Kent-Costikyan, Inc., N.Y., City, 1900, and pres. of same since 1900. Served as chmn. Montelair (N.J.) Com. for Near East Relief World War; maintained sch. for orphans and needy children at Marsovan, Asia Minor, 1900-15. Mem. Organization Com. of 100 of Chicago World's Fair, 1893; trustee Lincoln Memorial U., 1925-36. Decorated by Shah of Persia for promoting commercial relations between Persia and U.S., 1907. Ind. Republican. Conglist. Mason, Elk, Moose. Clubs: Nat. Republican (New York); Montclair Golf, Congressional Country. Home: 49 Melrose Place, Montclair, N.J., Office: 711 Fifth Av., New York, N.Y.

CÔTÉ, Joseph Lacasse Jr., pres. A. E. Troutman Co.; b. Crafton, Pa., June 1, 1889; s. Joseph Lacasse and Alma Atwood (O'Neal) C.; B.A., Yale, 1912; m. Isabel Barclay Jamison, June 21, 1919; children—Carolyn Jamison, Joseph Lacasse III, John Jamison, Edward Troutman. Pres. A.E. Troutman Co., dept. stores, Greensburg, Pa., since 1929; pres. Côté Realty Co., Greensburg, Pa., since 1929. Republican. Episcopalian. Clubs: Greensburg (Pa.) Country; Pike Run Country (Jones Mills, Pa.); Bay Head (N.J.) Yacht. Home: 350 N. Main St. Office: Main and 2d St., Greensburg, Pa.

COTTERMAN, Harold F., prof. agrl. edn., state supervisor vocational agr.; b. Farmersville, O., Oct. 22, 1887; s. Marcus Ward and Martha (Brubaker) C.; student Miami U. Prep. Sch., Oxford, O., 1909-10; student Ohio State U., Columbus, O., 1910-13, B.S.A., 1916; M.A., Columbia U. Teachers Coll., 1917; part-time student George Washington U., Washington, D.C., 1923-27; part-time student Am. U., Washington, 1927-30, Ph.D., 1930; m. Maggie May Yingling, June 13, 1914; children—Harold F., Martha Ann, Jean. Teacher rural schs., O., 1906-09; prof. agr. Ohio Northern U., Ada, O., 1913-15; prof. agrl. edn., Univ. of Md., since 1917, asst. dean Coll. of Agriculture since 1937; acting state supervisor agr., Md., 1918-23; state supervisor vocational agr., Md., since 1935. Mm. Am. Vocational Assn., N.E.A., Md. State Teachers Assn., Md. Vocational Edn. Assn., Land-Grant Coll. Assn. (sec. resident teaching sect. 1938-39), Kappa Alpha, Kappa Phi Kappa, Democrat. Episcopalian. Clubs: Prince George's County (Md.) Kiwanis (pres. 1939); Federal Schoolmen's (Washington, D.C.; v.p. 1939-40). Address: College Park, Md.

COTTLE, (John) Brooks, newspaper editor; b. Peniel, W.Va., Nov. 22, 1897; s. Charles Clinton and Flora Inez (Ferrell) C.; student W.Va. Univ., Morgantown, 1915-19; m. Elizabeth Ann Wayman, Sept. 11, 1921; children—Carolyn Kenney, Ann Brooks. Employed as news reporter on New Dominion, Morgantown, W.Va., 1918-19; city editor Morgantown Post, 1919-26; asso. editor New Dominion, 1926-28; editor Morgantown Post, Morgantown, W.Va. since 1928; exec. vice-pres. Wetzel Republican, Inc. Served in F.A., C.O.T.S., Camp Zachary Taylor, Ky., 1918. Served as mayor town of Suncrest, W.Va., 1937-38. Pres. Morgantown Chamber of Commerce, 1938-39. Mem. Am. Soc. Newspaper Editors, W.Va. State Newspaper Council (pres. 1934), Kappa Sigma. Republican. Presbyn. Asso. editor West Virginia University Alumni Quarterly since 1936. Address: The Morgantown Post, Court St., Morgantown, W.Va.

COTTON, Albertus; prof. orthopedic surgery and roentgenology, U. of Md.; orthopedist and roentgenologist Mercy Hosp.; roentgenologist Presbyn. Eye, Ear and Throat Charity Hosp.; attending orthopedic surgeon James Lawrence Kerman Hosp. and Industrial Sch. for Crippled Children. Address: 101 E. Preston St., Baltimore, Md.

COTTON, Jarvis Madison, clergyman; b. Kaufman, Tex., Oct. 26, 1899; s. Jarvis Prim and Eliza Yates (Chilton) C.; A.B., Maryville Coll., Maryville, Tenn., 1921; S.T.B., Western Theol. Sem., Pittsburgh, Pa., 1924; grad. study. U. of Chicago Divinity Sch., 1927; m. Elsie Elmore Dawson, June 11, 1924; children—Elsie Jean, Jarvis Dawson, Elmore Arter. Ordained to ministry Presbyn. Ch. U.S.A., 1924; pastor New Waterford, O. and Clarkson, O., 1922-27, Lisbon, O., 1927-33; pastor Waverly Presbyn. Ch., Pittsburgh, Pa. since 1933. Served as pvt. U.S.A., 1918. Mem. Am. Legion. Presbyn. U.S.A. Club: Kiwanis. Home: 308 East End Av., Pittsburgh, Pa.

COTTON, Robert William, surgeon; b. Centerville, Pa., May 26, 1877; s. William Gibson and Anna (Young) C.; M.D., U. of Pittsburgh Med. Sch., 1906; m. Elizabeth Rennie, Oct. 3, 1934. Employed at various work, 1898-1900; resident West Pa. Hosp., Pittsburgh, 1906-07; engaged in gen. practice of medicine, McKees Rocks, Pa., 1907-17; surgeon P.& L. E. R. R. Co. since 1920. Served as lt. Med. Corps, U.S.Army, 1917-18, capt., 1918-20, with A.E.F. in France. Mem. A.M.A., Assn. of Surgeons, N.Y. Central System. Republican. Presbyterian. Mason. Home: 1133 Pemberton St. N.S., Pittsburgh, Pa. Office: McKees Rocks, Pa.

COTTON, William Edwin, supt. expt. sta.; b. Oskaloosa, Ia., Sept. 17, 1866; s. George E. and Mary M. (Binns) C.; D.V.M., George Washington U., 1911; m. Grace E. Caskey, Sept. 20, 1898 (died Sept. 11, 1928); children—Cornelia Marie, Edwin Rowland, John Caskey. Asst. Bur. Animal Industry, U.S. Dept. Agr., 1893-94, expert asst., 1894-1910, asst. supt. expt. sta. (now Animal Disease Sta.), Beltsville, Md., 1910-28, supt. since 1928. Mem. Am. Vet. Med. Assn. (first v.p. 1933-34), Internat. Vet. Congress, U.S. Livestock Sanitary Assn.; fellow A.A.A.S. Presbyn. Contbr. repts. and bulls., U.S. Dept. Agr. Research in animal diseases, tuberculosis, infectious abortion, etc. Home: Beltsville, Md.*

COTTRELL, James Ewing, physician; b. Knoxville, Tenn., Nov. 10, 1898; s. Arthur Jefferson and Anne Lucy (Cooley) C.; grad. Knoxville (Tenn.) High Sch., 1916; student U. of Tenn., Knoxville, 1916-18; M.D., U. of Pa., 1922; m. Mary Elizabeth Murray, Aug. 31, 1929; children—James Ewing, David Chadwell. Resident physician Episcopal Hosp., Phila. 1922-24; resident in medicine, Hosp. of U. of Pa., 1924-25; in practice as physician, Phila., since 1925; asso. in medicine, U. of Pa.; asst. ward physician Hosp. of U. of Pa.; asso. physician Episcopal Hosp.; mem. courtesy staff in internal medicine Presbyterian Hosp. Served in S.A.T.C. 1918. Certified by Am. Bd. Internal Medicine. Fellow Am. Coll. Physicians, Coll. of Physicians of Phila., A.M.A.; mem. Phila. Co. Med. Soc., Pa. Med. Soc., Pathol. Soc. of Phila., Sigma Phi Epsilon, Phi Chi, Alpha Omega Alpha; hon. mem. Knox Co. (Tenn.) Med. Soc. Presbyterian. Home: 6100 W. Oxford St. Office: 2031 Locust St., Philadelphia, Pa.

COUGHLIN, Alfred G., M.D.; b. Belfast, N.Y., June 27, 1883; s. Andrew and Jane (Costello) C.; m. Margaret M. Haire, Aug. 16, 1905; children—Mary M., Alfred G., Jane Rita, John B. Engaged in gen. practice of medicine since 1905; health physician, Athens Borough, 1938; pres. Athens Nat. Bank, 1937-38, now dir.; dir. Athens Bldg. & Loan Assn. Address: 410 S. Elmira St., Athens, Pa.

COUGHTRY, Frank G.; pres. Orange Savings Bank. Address: Orange, N.J.

COULBOURN, George Cookman, M.D., surgeon; b. Marion Station, Md., Jan. 14, 1886; s. Thomas Lanyon and Sarah Elizabeth (Conner) C.; prep. edn. Wilmington Confer. Acad., 1902-06; M.D., U. of Md., 1910; m. Maud Estelle Miller, Nov. 18, 1925. Interne Univ. Hosp., Baltimore, 1910-12; practice of gen. surgery, obstetrics and gen. medicine, Marion Station, Md., since 1912; dir. Bank of Crisfield, Bank of Marion. Pres. Bd. of Edn., Somerset County, Md., 1920-36. Fellow Am. Coll. of Surgeons. Democrat. Methodist. Mason (32°). Address: Marion Station, Md.

COULT, Joseph; mem. law firm Coult, Satz & Tomlinson. Address: Military Park Bldg., Newark, N.J.

COULTER, James A., vice-pres. Colgate-Palmolive-Peet Co.; b. Oxford, O., May 27, 1882; s. Thomas William and Caroline (Cooper) C.; A.B., Miami U., Oxford, O., 1905; m. Pearl M. Smith, Nov. 4, 1907; 1 dau., Mary Louise (Mrs. Ben K. Murchison). With Procter & Gamble, 1905-23, as chemist, Ivorydale, O., 1905-06, dept. supervisor, 1906-13, asst. supt., Port Ivory, N.Y., 1913-20, supt., 1920-23; asst. gen. supt. Palmolive Co., Milwaukee, Wis., 1923-28; gen. supt. Palmolive-Peet Co., Milwaukee, Jan.-Aug. 1928; gen. supt. Colgate-Palmolive-Peet Co., Chicago, 1928-34, vice-pres. in charge of production and dir., Jersey City N.J., since Jan. 1, 1934; vice-pres. and dir. Kirkman & Son, Inc. Mem. Am. Museum Natural History; mem. Delta Kappa Epsilon. Republican. Mem. United Presbyn. Ch. Mason (Scottish Rite, Shriner). Club: Bankers of America (New York). Home: New Hope, Pa. Office: 105 Hudson St., Jersey City, N.J.

COULTER, Richard, lawyer, banking; b. Greensburg, Pa., Oct. 3, 1870; s. Richard and Emma (Welty) C.; A.B., Princeton, 1892; LL.D., Washington and Jefferson, 1938; m. Matilda V. Bowman, of Uniontown, Pa., July 29, 1913; 1 dau., Emma. Admitted to Pa. bar, 1894, and since engaged in gen. practice of law at Greensburg; pres. First Nat. Bank of Greensburg since 1907. Served as 2d lieut. 10th Pa. Inf., U.S.V., Spanish-Am. War; advanced through grades to col. 10th regt. Pa. N.G.; col. then brig. gen. U.S.A. Res. in World War. Home: Greensburg, Pa.

COUNCILL, Wilford A. H.; visiting urologist Md. Gen., St. Joseph's, South Baltimore Gen., University and Franklin Square hosps.; cons. urologist Provident Hosp. and Md. House of Correction. Address: 9 E. Mt. Royal Av., Baltimore, Md.

COUNTY, Albert John, retired ry. official; b. Dublin, Ireland, Aug. 1, 1871; s. Thomas and Katharine Stackpole (Smith) C.; B.S. in economics, U. of Pa., 1908; m. Hester Caven Fraley, Sept. 2, 1902; children—William F., John O. Clk., purchasing dept. Gt. Southern & Western Ry. Co., Ireland, 1885-90; clk. in secretary's dept. Pa. R.R., Phila., 1890-98, chief clk., 1898-1900; asst. to sec. of P.R.R. Co., 1900-01; asst. sec. P.R.R. Co. and important subsidiary cos., and Supt. Employes' Saving Fund, 1901-06; asst. to v.p., 1906-13, and 1913-16, was spl. asst. to pres. Pa.R.R. Co. and nearly all subsidiary cos. in Pa. System East of Pittsburgh; apptd. v.p. in charge of accounting, Pa. R.R. Co., March 8, 1916; apptd. v.p. in charge accounting and corporate work, Pa.R.R.Co., May 1, 1923, v.p. in charge of treasury and accounting depts. and corporate work, 1925, and v.p. in charge of finance and corporate relations, 1929-38, retired Dec. 1, 1938; also former pres. and dir. of most of branch lines of Pa.R.R.; dir. Norfolk & Western Ry., Phila. Nat. Bank. Reporter for N. Am. to Internat. Ry. Congress on Ry. Accounts and Statistics, 1910. Mem. Am. Acad. Polit. and Social Science. Clubs: Union League, St. David's Golf (Phila.); Economic, Bankers' (New York). Home: St. Davids, Pa.

COURTICE, Thomas R., clergyman; b. Dunbarton, Ont.; s. Andrew J. and Janet (Annan) C.; came to U.S., 1899, naturalized, 1918; A.B., O. Wesleyan U., 1905, later A.M.; B.D., Drew Theol. Sem. (hon.) D.D., Allegheny Coll., 1920; m. Nellie F. Pool, May 1, 1906; children—Irma Jean, Allyn James. Minister in Erie Conf. M.E. Ch., 1906-25; minister in Pittsburgh Conf. since 1925; minister First Ch., McKeesport, Pa., since 1931. Mem. Beta Theta Pi, Delta Sigma Rho. Republican. Methodist. Club. Kiwanis of McKeesport. Home: 1419 Carnegie Av., McKeesport, Pa.

COUSE, William J., pres. Asbury Park Nat. Bank & Trust Co. Address: Asbury Park, N.J.

COUSE, William Percy, artist; b. Farmingdale, N.J., Dec. 17, 1898; s. William James and Mary Elizabeth (Winsor) C.; ed. Art Students League of N.Y., 1919-21; ed. N.Y. Univ. Sch. of Edn., 1930-31; m. Elizabeth Hanson Mears, Sept. 20, 1924; children—Elizabeth Anne, Harriet Hodgson, Thomas Preston Mears. Engaged as illustrator for well known publs., 1922-29; with art dept. St. Ry. Adv. Co., 1929-31; worked with Rudolph Scheffler on murals for O. State Office Bldg.; executed mural for Fitkin Hosp., Neptune, N.J.; painter portraits and landscapes; art dir. Deal Conservatoire, Deal, N.J.; painting "Morris Brenner" one of ten selected to represent N.J. at 2d annual exhbn. Am. Art, Fine Arts Bldg., N.Y. City; painting "Evelyn" one of 25 selected to hang in N.J. State Bldg. at N.Y. World's Fair, 1939. Served with H.F.A., U.S.A., 1917-19, with A.E.F. Sec. Police Pension Fund, Borough of Interlaken, N.J. Mem. Police Pistol Team. Republican. Clubs: Monmouth Players (Deal); Apollo (Asbury Park); Salmagundi (New York). Home: 615 Grassmere Av., Interlaken via Asbury Park, N.J.

COUSENS, Theodore Wells, coll. prof.; b. Kennebunk, Me.; s. George Eliot and Sylvia (Wells) C.; grad. Kennebunk High Sch., 1918; student Philips Exeter Acad., Exeter, N.H., 1918-19; A.B., Bowdoin Coll., Brunswick, Me., 1923; LL.B., Harvard U. Law Sch., 1926, LL.M., 1929; m. Mildred Ferguson, June 29, 1929; 1 son, Theodore Wells. Admitted to Me. and Mass. bars, 1926; associated with George H. Brown in practice of law, Boston, 1926, Warren, Garfield, Whiteside & Lamson, Boston, 1926-29; instr. and research asst. in govt. and law, Lafayette Coll., Easton, Pa., 1929-32, asst. prof., 1932-37, asso. prof. since 1937. Mem. Am. Polit. Science Assn., Alpha Tau Omega. Democrat. Mason. Clubs: Faculty of Lafayette Coll. (Easton, Pa.). Writer of numerous articles in law reviews, mostly on constitutional questions. Home: 525 Cattell St., Easton, Pa.

COUSLEY, Stanley William, banker; b. New York, N.Y., Sept. 8, 1887; s. Andrew and Margaret (Matthews) C.; ed. pub. sch. and high sch., Phila., Pa.; m. Grace Brinser, May 16, 1925; children—Patricia Ann, Stanley W., Jr. Asso. with Fidelity-Phila. Trust Co., starting as clk., 1902, successively asst. sec., sec., asst. vice-pres., and vice-pres. since 1928; dir. Murphy Oil Co., Tacony-Palmyra Bridge Co., F. W. Tunnell & Co., Inc., Botfield Refractories Co. Served as 1st lt., 30th Div., A.E.F., 1917-19. Republican. Presbyterian. Clubs: Manufacturers and Bankers, Midday, Philadelphia Country, Merion Cricket (Phila.). Home: 267 Hathaway Lane, Wynnewood. Office: 135 S. Broad St., Philadelphia, Pa.

COVELL, William Edward Raab, army officer, engineer; b. Washington, D.C., Nov. 29, 1892; s. Luther W. and Lefa Ann (Ransome) C.; student Eastern High Sch. and Central High Sch., Washington, D.C., 1906-10; B.S., U.S. Mil. Acad., 1915; B.S. in C.E., Mass. Inst. of Tech., 1923; m. Vera Henshaw, July 18, 1917; 1 dau.—Beverly. Commd. 2d lt., Corps of Engrs., U.S. Army, June 12, 1915; dir. 1st Corps Engrs. Sch., asst. in operations sect. Gen. Staff, 1st Army, comdg. officer 2d Engr. Regt., 2d Div., A.E.F., 1918; asst. Chief of Staff, 2d Div., 1919; dist. engr. U.S. Engr. Office, Buffalo, N.Y., 1920-22; asst. engr. commr. Dist of Columbia, 1924-28; student Command and Gen. Staff Sch., Ft. Leavenworth, Kan., 1928-30; exec. officer, Ft. Belvoir, Va., 1930-33; asst. engr. of maintenance Panama Canal, 1933-36; dist. engr. U.S. Engr. Office, Pittsburgh, Pa., since 1936. Term mem. of the corpn., Mass. Inst. of Tech. Mem. Am. Soc. C.E., Soc. Am. Mil. Engrs. (pres. Pittsburgh Post). Mason. Club: M.I.T. of Western Pa. (Pittsburgh; pres.). Wrote and put into effect the "Washington Plan" for control of electric utilities, 1924-28. Home: Schenley Apts. Office: 925 New Federal Bldg., Pittsburgh, Pa.

COVER, Harry Ralph, lawyer and inventor; b. Carroll Co., Md., June 13, 1892; s. Harry Fisher and Dora May (Hiteshew) C.; A.B., Western Md. Coll., Westminster, Md., 1910; LL.B., Harvard Law Sch., 1913; m. Anna Saulsbury Fisher, Dec. 11, 1919; 1 son, Paul Fisher. Admitted to Md. bar, 1913; asso. with Bond, Robinson & Duffy, Baltimore, Md., 1913-15; mem. firm Smith & Cover, Baltimore, Md., 1915-17; engaged in individual practice at Westminster, Md., since 1930; admitted to practice before Supreme Court of U.S., 1917; pres. The United Company, engaged in development of inventions, machines and methods employed in canning industry, Westminster, Md., since 1914. Served as asst. sec. priorities com., War Industries Bd. during World War. Mem. Am. Bar Assn., Md. Bar Assn., Carroll Co. Bar Assn., Old Guard Soc. of Canning Industry. Inventor many machines and methods employed in canning industry; dir. tech. experts in development of such machines; writer tech. treatises on these subjects; machines mfd. by nationally known mfrs. Home: 26 Willis St. Office: Times Bldg., Westminster, Md.

COVERT, William Chalmers, clergyman; b. Franklin, Ind., Oct. 4, 1864; s. Albert Newton and Susan Elizabeth (Magill) C.; B.A., Hanover (Ind.) Coll., 1885, A.M., 1888; grad. Presbyn. Theol. Seminary, Chicago, 1888; D.D., Hanover, 1905, D.Litt., 1933; LL.D., Blackburn College, Carlinville, Ill., 1917; m. Alice Brown Hudson, May 14, 1890; children—Hudson, Katharine (Mrs. L. H. Nichols), Seward. Ordained Presbyn. ministry, St. Paul, Minn., Sept. 1888; pastor, St. Paul Park, 1888-92, Merriam Park Ch., St. Paul, 1892-1900, First Ch., Saginaw, Mich., 1900-05, 41st St. Ch., Chicago, 1905-12, First Presbyn. Ch., Chicago, 1913-24; gen. sec. Bd. of Christian Edn. of Presbyn. Ch. since 1924; mem. Federal Council Chs. of Christ in America; mem. exec. com. Council of Ch. Bds. of Edn. and of exec. com. World Alliance of Internat. Friendship Through the Chs. Dir. Presbyn. Theol. Sem.; trustee Hood Coll. for Women; vice-chmn. Save the Children Fund. Inc.; chmn. Nat. Protestant Com. on Scouting; moderator Gen. Assembly Presbyn. Ch., 1935. Guest prof. of homiletics, Western Theol. Sem. of Pittsburgh, 1939-40. Awarded Silver Buffalo award by Boy Scouts of America, 1939. Mem. Presbyn. Hist. Soc., Philadelphia Hymn Soc. (pres.), Hyman Soc. of America (v.p.), Phi Delta Theta. Author: Glory of the Pines; Wildwoods and Waterways, 1914; New Furrows in Old Fields; Religions in the Heart, 1926; Christ and Culture, 1930; Facing our Day, 1934; Handbook to the Hymnal, 1935; With Cross and Crown in Every Land (pageant), 1937. Home: 6445 Green St., Germantown, Philadelphia, Pa.

COWAN, Carl Bryant, real estate; b. Parkersburg, W.Va., Feb. 1. 1911; s. John Holliday and Lida Irene (Welch) C.; student Wheeling (W.Va.) High Sch., 1926-29, Peirce Sch. of Business Adminstrn., Phila., 1929-32; unmarried. Began as office boy with S. Buckman & Sons., Phila., 1931, later leasing broker and then salesman; mgr. apartment house, 1934-37 in real estate for himself since 1937; sr. partner of Cowan & Cowan; dir. Common Sense Bldg. & Loan Assn. Organizer and charter mem. of Jr. Bd. of Commerce, Phila., 1937, and since served as sec.; mem. Phila. Real Estate Bd. Republican. Christian Scientist. Home: 40 E. Tulpehocken St., Germantown, Philadelphia, Pa. Office: 424 Walnut St., Philadelphia, Pa.

COWDEN, William K.; mem. law firm Cowden & Cowden. Address: 901 Chesapeake & Ohio Bldg., Huntington, W.Va.

COWHERD, Joseph Kile, physician; b. Hinton, W.V., Dec. 24, 1887; s. Gabriel G. and Tootie (White) C.; M.D., Univ. Coll. of Medicine, Va., 1909; m. Grace G. Gantz, Nov. 15, 1911; 1 dau., Barbra Louise. Engaged in gen. practice of medicine at Cumberland, Md., specializing in obstetrics and pediatrics; chief obstet. staff Allegany Hosp. Sisters of Charity, Memorial Hosp., both of Cumberland; mem. com. on Maternal & Child Welfare State of Md. Served as 1st lt. to capt. Med. Corps, U.S.A., 1917-19, with A.E.F. Mem. Am. Med. Assn., Med. and Chirurg. Faculty of Md., Allegany-Garrett Co. Med. Soc., Am. Congress on Obstetrics and Gynecology, Phi Chi. Episcopalian. Elk. Club: Country (Cumberland). Home: 747 Washington St. Office: 41 Greene St., Cumberland, Md.

COWIN, Roy Burford, univ. prof.; b. Hubbard, O., Nov. 14, 1889; s. John James and Sarah Louisa (Burford) C.; A.B., U. of Mich., Ann Arbor, Mich., 1916; M.A., 1918; m. Mary

Elizabeth Pfeiffer, Aug. 22, 1918; children—Roy Burford, Paul Frederick. Instr. in accounting, U. of Mich., Ann Arbor, Mich., 1916-18; auditor of plant accounts, Mich. State Telephone Co., Detroit, 1917-18; instr. in accounting, Ia. State Univ., 1918-19; accountant Telephone and Telegraph Administrn., Washington, D.C., 1919; asso. prof. of accounting, U. of N.C., Chapel Hill, N.C., 1919-20; asso. prof. of accounting, Carnegie Inst. Tech., Pittsburgh, 1920-24; lecturer in accounting, U. of Pittsburgh, 1922-23; prof. of accounting, Lehigh U., Bethlehem, Pa., since 1924, head of dept. of accounting since 1936. Mem. Nat. Assn. of Cost Accountants (dir. Allentown, Pa., chapter), Am. Accounting Assn., Am. Econs. Assn., Phi Beta Kappa (treas. Lehigh U. chapter), Alpha Kappa Psi (councilor Alpha Sigma chapter). Republican. Home: 1124 N. New St. Office: Lehigh Univ., Bethlehem, Pa.

COWLES, David Otis, clergyman; b. Pleasanton, Ia., Jan. 1, 1880; s. Henry Austin and Rosanna (Woods) Cowles; student public schools of Decatur County, Ia., Grand River Christian Union Coll., Edinburg, Mo., 1896-98, Capital City Commercial Coll., Des Moines, Ia., 1898; A.B., Cornell Coll., Mt. Vernon, Ia., 1908; B.D., Drew Theol. Sem., 1911; grad. study, N.Y., Univ., Union Theol. Sem.; m. Hazel Blackmore Wright, June 12, 1912 (died 1933); children—Marjorie Lyle, Helen Blackmore, Kathleen Wright. Employed in offices various mercantile houses, 1900-04; ordained to ministry of the Meth. Church, 1911; member of Newark Annual Conference; served Park Ridge, N.J., 1910-12; Arcola, N.J., 1912-14, Summit Av., Jersey City, N.J., 1914-18, Verona, N.J., 1918-20, Summerfield, N.Y. City, 1920-23, Summit, N.J., 1923-26, Perth Amboy, N.J., 1926-34, Park Av., East Orange, N.J., since 1934; dir. and treas. N.J. Sunday League, Newark, N.J. Republican. Methodist. Clubs: Cornell College (New York); Clergy of the Oranges (Oranges, N.J.). Contbr. articles to ch. journs. and prayer to God's Minute (book). Home: 291 Grove St., East Orange, N.J.

COWLES, Rheinart Parker, prof. of zoölogy; b. Washington, Ia., Apr. 8, 1872; s. Oscar Parde and Olive Rood (Parker) C.; A.B., Stanford (Calif.) U., 1899; Ph.D., Johns Hopkins, 1904; m. Sara Cecilia McConville, Aug. 6, 1909 (dec.); children—Margaret Ola (wife of Dr. Wilson Shaffer), Janet Madeline. Asst. in zoölogy, Johns Hopgins, 1904-07, instr. in zoölogy, 1907-10; asso. prof. of zoölogy, U. of Philippines, 1911-15; prof., 1915-19; asso. prof. of zoölogy, Johns Hopkins, 1919-30, prof. since 1930. Mem. A.A.A.S., Soc. of Zoölogists, Soc. of Naturalists, Delta Upsilon, Phi Beta Kappa, Sigma Xi. Club: Johns Hopkins (Baltimore). Home: 3333 N. Charles St., Baltimore, Md.

COWPERTHWAIT, William Decon, banking; b. Medford, N.J., Apr. 13, 1867; s. Budd S. and Anna P. W. (Coles) C.; ed. Friends Central Sch., Phila., Pa., 1884-86, Coll. of Commerce, Phila., Pa., 1886-87; m. Mary E. Hollinshead, Mar. 2, 1892; children—Charles C. (dec.), Clinton H., William C., Thornton Budd (dec.). Engaged in farming 1892-1919, retired 1919; pres. Burlington Co. Nat. Bank, Medford, N.J., since 1932, dir. since 1907; treas. Burlington Co. Assn. for Ins.; sec. Medford Firemen's Relief Assn. Served as assessor Medford Twp., 1920-39. Treas. Medford Chamber of Commerce. Pioneer mem. Del. River Bridge Commn., Camden to Phila. Life mem. N.J. State Firemen's Assn.; exempt mem. Union Fire Co., Medford. Democrat. Mem. Religious Soc. Friends. Mason (32°, Shriner). Patron of Husbandry. Home: 34 N. Main St., Medford, N.J.

COX, Douglas Farley, marine insurance; b. N.Y. City, Jan. 28, 1867; s. James Farley and Maria (McIntosh) C.; student Columbia, 1886-87; m. Dora Andrews Harris, Nov. 21, 1905; 1 son, Douglas Farley. Pres. Appleton & Cox, Inc., since 1920; dir. Westchester Fire Insurance Company, Seaboard Fire & Marine Insurance Company, North River Insurance Company; trustee Seamen's Bank for Savings (New York). Mem. Nat. Bd. of Marine Underwriters (pres. 1912-15), Bd. of Underwriters (marine) of New York (pres. 1924-25), Am. Inst. Marine Underwriters (pres. 1926-27), Nat. Automobile Underwriters Conf. (pres. 1916-18). Mem. Delta Psi. Republican. Episcopalian. Clubs: St. Anthony, Down Town, India House: Home: Llewellyn Park, West Orange, N.J. Office: 111 John St., New York, N.Y.

COX, Edward H.; B.S., Earlham Coll., Richmond, Ind.; A.M., Harvard; Sc.D., U. of Geneva; prof. of chemistry, Swarthmore (Pa.) Coll. Home: 8 Whittier Place, Swarthmore, Pa.

COX, F.; mem. law firm Cox & Cox. Address: Morgantown, W.Va.

COX, Floyd Brooks, county supt schs.; b. Morgantown, W.Va., Nov. 4, 1895; s. William Isaac and Laura Helen (Courtney) C.; A.B., W.Va. Univ., Morgantown, 1918, A.M., 1922; m. Mary Adele Wallman, Jan. 6, 1917; children—Floyd Brooks, Charles William, Mary Ann. Engaged as prin. high sch., Point Pleasant, W.Va., 1918-21; instr. English, high sch., Fairmont, W.Va., 1922-23; engaged in real estate bus., 1923-29; instr. English, high sch., Kingwood, W.Va., 1929-30, Morgantown, W.Va., 1930-31; supt. schs., Monongalia Co., W.Va., Morgantown since 1931; chmn. Monongalia Valley Round Table, 1935-36; administr. Federal Forum Project, Monongalia Co., 1936-37; chmn. Nat. Council for Adult Civic Edn., 1937-39; mem. Yearbook Commn., Am. Assn. Sch. Administrs., 1939. Candidate W.Va. Legislature, 1924; Dem. city chmn., Morgantown, 1920-28; mem. Monongalia Co. Art Guild, Inc.; dir. Crippled Children Society; mem. World Congress on Education for Democracy, Columbia University, 1939. Mem. Nat. Edn. Assn., American Assn. Sch. Adminstrs., W.Va. Edn. Assn. Awarded medal for Merit of Italian Culture, 1935 (Italy). Democrat. Mem. M.E. Ch. Elk. Rotarian. Contbr. to ednl. mags. and to Yearbook of Am. Assn. Sch. Adminstrs. Home: 322 Beverly Av. Office: 263 Prairie Av., Morgantown, W.V.

COX, John Calvin, physician; b. Coal Creek, Va., Apr. 13, 1893; s. Calvin Jones and Violet (Perry) C.; student William and Mary Coll., Williamsburg, Va., 1914-15; M.D., U. of Va. Sch. of Medicine, Charlottesville, Va., 1919; m. Florence Becker, Apr. 23, 1926; children—John Calvin, Stephen Lee, Charles Spencer. Began as physician, Maplewood, N.J., 1919; health officer and police surgeon for 8 years; attending surgeon Orange Memorial Hosp.; mem. courtesy staff East Orange General Hosp., Presbyn., Beth Israel Hosps. Fellow Am. Coll. Surgeons; mem. Soc. of Surgeons of N.J., A.M.A., Essex Med. Soc., Orange Mtn. Med. Soc. Clubs: Maplewood (N.J.) Country; Baltusrol Golf (Springfield, N.J.). Home: 55 Woodland Rd., Maplewood, N.J.

COX, John Harrington, univ. prof.; b. in Ill., May 27, 1863; s. Isaac and Mary Ann (Harrington) C.; grad Ill. State Normal U., 1891; Ph.B., Brown, U., 1897; A.M., Harvard, 1900, Ph.D., 1923; Litt.D., O. Wesleyan U., 1923; m. Mrs. Annie (Bush) Long, June 28, 1904. Ednl. dir. Twenty-third St. Branch Y.M.C.A., New York, 1897-99; prof. English lang. and lit., U. of N.D., 1901-02; instr. in English philology, 1902-03, asso. prof., 1903-04, professor, 1904-34; emeritus professor since 1934, West Virginia University. Institute dir., writer, and pub. lecturer. Pres. and gen. editor West Virginia Folk-Lore Soc. Lecturer in U. of Chicago, summer, 1914, University of Mo., summer, 1922, U. of Southern Calif., 1927-29. Mem. Modern Lang. Assn. America, Am. Assn. Univ. Profs, American Dialect Soc., Am. Folk-Lore Soc., Poetry Soc. America, Shakespeare Soc. America, Am. Folk Song Soc., Phi Beta Kappa. Author: Literature in the Common Schools, 1908; Knighthood in Germ and Flower, 1910; A Chevalier of Old France, 1911; Folk Tales of East and West, 1912. Special sch. edits. of Beowulf, 1910; A Knight of Arthur's Court, 1910; Sir Gawain and the Green Knight (London), 1911; The Song of Roland, 1912; A Hero of Old France (London), 1913; Siegfried, 1915. Folk-Songs of the South, 1925; Mrs. Annie Bush Cox (a memorial), 1933; Mrs. Elizabeth Davis Richards (a memorial), 1937. Contbr. to mags. Baptist. Republican. Home: Morgantown, W.Va.

COX, John Lyman, mech. engr.; b. Phila., Pa., June 7, 1866; s. James Sitgreaves and Mary Fullerton (Hazard) C.; ed. Stevens Hgh. Sch., Hoboken, N.J., 1882-83; M.E., Stevens Inst. Tech., Hoboken, 1887; m. Evelyn Quintard Jackson, May 16, 1914 (dec.); children—James Sitgreaves, Evelyn Quintard, Mary Lyman. Asso. with Midvale Steel Co., Midvale Steel and Ordnance Co. and Midvale Co., Phila., Pa., continuously since entering employ, 1888; asst. supt. forge, supt. of forge, supt. of armor plant, tech. adviser of patent counsel, asst. supt., then supt. projectile dept., asst. to gen. supt., asst. to pres., now chief engr. since 1932; v.p. New Boston Land Co. Fellow A.A.A.S.; mem. American Soc. Mechanical Engineers, American Soc. for Metals, Am. Iron and Steel Inst., Newcomen Soc., U.S. Naval Inst., Franklin Inst., Am. Geog. Soc., Hist. Soc. Pa., Am. Mus. Natural History, Pa. Acad. Fine Arts, Mass. Soc. of Cincinnati, Soc. Colonial Wars of Pa. Republican. Episcopalian. Clubs: Wilderness (Phila.); Ardnamurchan (Nova Scotia). Home: 609 E. Gravers Lane, Chestnut Hill., Philadelphia, Pa.

COX, Norman Wade, clergyman; b. Climax, Ga., Oct. 28, 1888; s. Barclay Wade and Alice Louise (Brock) C.; B.A. Mercer, 1914, D.D., 1928; Th.M., Southern Bapt. Theol. Sem., Louisville, Ky., 1918; m. Osye Lee Matthews, Sept. 7, 1910; children—Graham Wade, Sara Margaret. Ordained ministry Southern Bapt. Ch., 1910; pastor successively First Ch., Barnesville, Ga., Portsmouth, Va., Savannah, Ga., and Meridian, Miss., until 1931; pastor First Ch., Mobile, 1931-32, Fifth Av. Ch., Huntington, W.Va., since 1932. Received 5561 accessions to chs. in 21 yrs. Mem. bd. trustees Shorter Coll. (Rome, Ga.), Southern Bapt. Theol. Sem., Southwestern Bapt. Theol. Sem. Mason (Shriner), Rotarian. Author: Why the Skepticism of Christian Youth?; Youth's Return to Faith, 1938. Contbr. many papers and articles on religious subjects; author of "A Daily Tryst with God," a daily devotional used as a syndicated newspaper feature; author of "Tramping Trails of Faith," a weekly editorial published in newspaper since 1932. Editor The Baptist Messenger since June 1936. Home: 1112 6th Av., Huntington, W.Va.

COX, Philip Wescott Lawrence, prof. edn.; b. Malden, Mass., July 25, 1883; s. Alfred Elmer and Annie Adelaide (Bell) C.; B.A., Harvard, 1906, M.A., 1920; Ph.D., Columbia, 1925; grad. student U. of N.H., 1907; m. Ruth Dillaway July 17, 1909; children—Philip Westcott Lawrence, Edward Dillaway, Nancy Ryder, Kenneth Faulkner (dec.). Asst. instr. in botany, Harvard, 1905; master Cloyne House Sch., Newport, R.I., 1905-06; market gardener Norfolk, Mass., 1906-08; master Allen Sch. for Boys, W. Newton, Mass., 1907-08; instr. in science and athletic coach high sch., Milton, Mass., 1908-10; supt. schs. and prin. high sch., Easton, Mass., 1910-13; supt. schs., Solvay, N.Y., 1913-16; instr. Harris Teachers Coll., St. Louis, Mo., 1916-17; prin. Blewett Jr. High Sch., 1917-20; headmaster Washington Sch. of N.Y., 1920-22; prin. high sch. dept. Lincoln Sch. of Teachers Coll., N.Y. City, 1922-23; prof. secondary edn., New York U. since 1923. Mem. National Education Assn. (ex-pres. dept. elementary edn.), Nat. Assn. Secondary Sch. Principals (ex-v.p.), National Soc. Coll. Teachers of Education (chmn. editorial com. 1937), Teachers' Ins and Annuity Assn. (nominating com., 1926-27), Kappa Sigma, Phi Delta Kappa, Kappa Delta Pi, Pi Gamma Mu. Supervisor of advisement 5th dist., Federal Bd. for Vocational Edn., 1918-19. Clubs: Harvard of N.J.; The Greeks (Maplewood). Author: Curriculum Adjustment in the Secondary School, 1925; Creative School Control, 1927; The Junior High School and Its Curriculum, 1929; Principles of Secondary Education (with F. E. Long) 1932; Administration and Supervision of the High School (with R. E. Langfitt), 1934; Guidance by the Classroom Teacher (with J. C. Duff), 1938. Editor: Junior High School Practices (with R. L. Lyman), 1925; The Clearing House.

Asso. editor Jour. Ednl. Sociology, The Educational Forum. Home: 24 Collinwood Rd., Maplewood, N.J. Office: Washington Square, E., New York, N.Y.

COX, Reavis, economist; b. Guadalajara, Mexico, Sept. 2, 1900; s. Jackson Berry and Julia (Barcus) C., citizens of U.S.; A.B., U. of Tex., Austin, Tex., 1921; Ph.D., Columbia U., 1932; m. Rachel LaVerne Dunaway, Feb. 18, 1928; 1 son, David Jackson. Engaged in newspaper work in various parts of U.S., 1921-25; mem. staff Journal of Commerce, 1926-31, market editor, 1927-31; instr. bus. administrn., Columbia U., 1931-35, asso. prof., 1935-38, prof. marketing since 1938; chmn. marketing dept. Wharton Sch. Finance & Commerce of U. of Pa. since 1935. Served in U.S. Army during World War. Mem. Am. Econ. Assn., Am. Marketing Assn., Am. Statis. Assn., Am. Acad. Polit. and Social Science. Presbyterian. Club: Lenape (Phila.). Author: Hedging Cotton, 1928; Competition in the American Tobacco Industry, 1932; The Marketing of Textiles, 1938. Co-author: The Sales Tax in the American States, 1934. Home: Ogden Av., Swarthmore. Address: U. of Pa., Philadelphia, Pa.

COX, William Henry Dickerson, lawyer; b. Denville, N.J., Apr. 8, 1898; s. Martin L. and Harriet J. (Dickerson) C.; student Princeton U., 1915-16; A.B., Columbia U., 1919; LL.B., Columbia U. Law Sch., 1921; m. J. Elizabeth Larter, June 28, 1924 (dec.); children—William H. D., Jr., J. Elizabeth L. Admitted to N.J. bar as atty., 1922, counselor, 1926; in gen. practice at Newark since 1926; trial atty. for Globe Indemnity Co., 1921-24; asso. with Edwards & Smith, 1924-26; mem. firm Cox and Walburg since 1926; dir. Larter & Sons, Inc. Served as dir. Social Service Bur., Newark, N.J. Mem. Essex County and Am. bar assns., Alpha Chi Rho (pres. 1938-39). Methodist. Club: Athletic (Newark). Home: 28 Northern Drive, Short Hills. Office: 60 Park Place, Newark, N.J.

COX, William W., surgeon Mountainside Hosp. Address: 79 S. Fullerton Av., Montclair, N.J.

COXSON, Harold Paul, physician; b. Moorestown, N.J., Feb. 16, 1903; s. Mark A. and Emily (Gill) C.; A.B., U. of Pa., 1925; M.D., Temple U. Med. Sch., Phila., Pa., 1927; unmarried. Interne, Cooper Hosp., Camden, N.J., 1929-30; engaged in gen. practice of medicine at Stratford, N.J., since 1929; nat. examiner Am. Red Cross; Camden County fire surgeon; propr. Ben Franklin Variety Store, Clementon, N.J., since 1935; sec. bd. dirs. Nat. Bank of Clementon; pres. Silver Lake Knitting Mills, Inc., Clementon, N.J.; dir. Stratford Bldg. & Loan Assn., Signal Hill Bldg. & Loan Assn. Mem. Council Borough of Stratford since 1930. Mem. Am. N.J. State, and Camden Co. med. assns., Alpha Pi Epsilon, Omega Upsilon Phi, Laurel Springs' Male Chorus, Camden County Male Choruses (pres.), Stratford Rep. Club (pres.). Republican. Baptist. Mason. Club: Woodcrest Country Club. Office: Laurel Ave., Stratford, N.J.

COYLE, George Lacy, v.p. and gen. mgr. Coyle & Richardson; b. Charleston, W.Va., Oct. 3, 1890; s. George Fayette and Nannie (Gordon) C.; student Charleston pub. sch., Fishburn Mil. Sch. and Washington & Lee U.; m. Lucy Claiborne Green, June 16, 1923. With Coyle & Richardson since 1910, beginning in receiving room, v.p. and gen. mgr. since 1922. Home: Bridge W. Office: Lee and Dickinson Sts., Charleston, W.Va.

COYLE, William Radford, ex-congressman; b. Washington, D.C., July 10, 1878; s. Randolph and Mary (Radford) C.; prep. edn., Western and Central high schs. and Corcoran Scientific Sch., Washington, D.C.; short course, Naval War Coll., 1900; Law Sch., U. of Pa., 1906; m. Jane Weston Dodson, Dec. 21, 1904; children—William Radford, Jane Weston. Field asst. U.S. Geol. Survey, 1896-99; with U.S. Marines, 1900-06, advancing to capt.; v.p. Weston Dodson & Co.; mem. 69th, 71st and 72d Congresses (1925-27, 1929-33), 30th Pa. Dist. Capt. N.G. Pa., 1913-14; capt. and maj. U.S. Marines, 1918; four-minute man; chmn. Red Cross Campaigns; etc.; now lt. colonel U.S. Marine Corps Reserve. Republican. Episcopalian. Mason. Home: 47 E. Church St. Office: Dodson Bldg., Bethlehem, Pa.

COZZENS, James Gould, author; b. Chicago, Aug. 19, 1903; s. Henry William and Bertha (Wood) C.; grad. Kent (Conn.) Sch., 1922; student Harvard, 1922-24; m. Bernice Baumgarten, Dec. 31, 1927. Author: Confusion, 1924; Michael Scarlett, 1925; Cockpit, 1928; The Son of Perdition, 1929; S.S. San Pedro, 1931; The Last Adam, 1933; Castaway, 1934; Men and Brethren, 1936; also articles in mags. Home: Lambertville, N.J. Address: Brandt & Brandt, 101 Park Av., New York, N.Y.

CRABBE, George William, supt. Maryland-Delaware Anti-Saloon League; b. Range Township, Madison Co., O., June 1, 1875; s. John William and Ellen (Minshall) C.; student De Pauw U. Greencastle, Ind., and Ohio Wesleyan U., Delaware, O.; hon. A.M., Western Md. Coll., 1921; m. Maude Foster, June 20, 1900. Became teacher, pub. schs., Ohio, 1892; clk., Courts of Madison Co., 1900-06; admitted to O. bar, 1906; atty., Ohio Anti-Saloon League, 1906-13; atty. and supt. W.Va. Anti-Saloon League, 1913-17; atty. and supt. .Md.-Del. Anti-Saloon League since 1917. Editor Md.-Del. edit. Am. Issue. Mem. Gen. Conf. M.E. Ch., 1924, 28, 32, 36; mem. Uniting Conf. of Meth. Churches; chmn. which wrote declaration of M.E. Ch. stand on liquor question, 1924 and 28; mem. World Service Commn., M.E. Ch. Republican. Odd Fellow. Club: Optimist. Home: 2901 Mt. Holly St. Office: American Bldg., Baltimore, Md.

CRADDOCK, Bantz Wooddell, lawyer; b. Glenville, W.Va., Nov. 22, 1887; s. Joe Nelson and Virgie (Wooddell) C.; grad. Glenville (W.Va.) State Normal, 1906; diploma of graduation, W.Va. U., Morgantown, W.Va., 1910; m. Hallie J. Whiting, Dec. 5, 1913; children—Bantz Whiting, Marjorie Estella, Samuel Nelson. Admitted to bar, 1910, and since practiced at Glenville, W.Va.; has been recorder and mayor, Glenville, W.Va.; prosecuting atty., Gilmer Co., W.Va., 1917-29 (3 terms); asst. U.S. dist. atty., Northern Dist. of W.Va., since 1936. Mem. W.Va. Bar Assn., U.S. Bar Assn., Sphinx, Phi Sigma Kappa. Democrat. Mason, K.P., Rose Croix, Maccabee, Order of Eastern Star. Club: Rotary (Glenville, W.Va.). Address: Glenville, W.Va.

CRAIG, Albert Burchfield, mfg. exec.; b. Pittsburgh, Pa., Oct. 1, 1891; s. George Liggett and Henrietta (Burchfield) C.; A.B., Princeton U., 1915; m. Elizabeth West Gibson, Jan. 8, 1918; children—Henrietta Burchfield, Mary Elizabeth, Albert Burchfield. Gen. mgr. Chartiers Oil Co., Pittsburgh, 1917-24, dir., v.p. and gen. mgr. since 1924; v.p. The Freedom Oil Works Co., Pittsburgh, since 1930; dir. Nat. Fireproofing Corpn., Brownsville Water Co., California Water Co., Dewar Oil Co. Trustee Valley Hosp., Sewickley, Pa. United Presbyterian (trustee First U.P. Ch., Sewickley, Pa.). Clubs: Edgeworth (Sewickley, Pa.); Harvard-Yale-Princeton (Pittsburgh). Home: Creek Drive, Edgeworth, Sewickley P. O., Pa. Office: 808 Columbia Bldg., Pittsburgh, Pa.

CRAIG, Earl Burrell, physician; b. Phila., Pa., Jan. 20, 1881; s. Robert J. and Rebecca (Stewart) C.; student pub. schs., Phila.; M.D., Hahnemann Med. Coll., Phila., 1906, Jefferson Med. Coll., 1908; hon. M.A., Hahnemann Medical College, 1939; studied at Univ. of Vienna, 1929-30; m. Florence Gruninger, Dec. 30, 1919. Began gen. practice, 1908; began specialization in field of gynecology, 1917, and entered gynecol. dept. of Hahnemann Med. Coll. as interne, senior prof. in charge of gynecology and senior surgeon in gynecology since 1934. Confirmed full lt. Med. Corps. U.S.N., World War. Fellow Am. Coll. Surgeons, Internat. Coll. of Surgeons (Geneva), A.M.A., Am. Inst. Homeopathy; mem. Pa. State Med. Assn., Pa. State Homeo. Med. Soc. Methodist. Club: Union League (Phila.). Home: 7620 Mountain Av., Elkins Park, Pa. Office: 269 S. 19th St., Philadelphia, Pa.

CRAIG, Earle McKee, pres. Freedom Oil Company; b. New Castle, Pa., March 4, 1894; s. Percy Linwood and Eleanor Temoy (McKee) C.; grad. Lawrenceville (N.J.) Sch., 1913; Ph.B., Yale, 1916; m. Margaret Peters, Oct. 23, 1919; children—Margueritte, Earle McKee. With Freedom (Pa.) Oil Works Co., 1917-39, pres., 1930-39, name changed to Freedom Oil Co. and pres. latter since 1939; dir. Beaver Trust Co., Chartiers Oil Co. Served in field arty., Central O.T.S., 1918. Trustee Am. University at Cairo, Geneva Coll. Republican. United Presbyterian. Clubs: Beaver Valley Country (Beaver Falls, Pa.); Harvard-Yale-Princeton (Pittsburgh). Home: "Linwood," Beaver, Pa. Office: Freedom, Pa.

CRAIG, Frank Ardary, physician; b. Phila., Pa., Sept. 28, 1876; s. John Fullerton and Susan K. (Bird) C.; ed. U. of Pa. Sch. Biology, 1893-94; M.D., U. of Pa. Med. Sch., 1898; grad. study, Vienna, 1902; m. Florence Porter Frishmuth, Nov. 2, 1916 (died 1935). Resident phys. St. Christopher's Hosp., 1898-99, Pa. Hosp., 1900-01; attdg. phys. Henry Phipps Inst. since 1904; vis. phys. White Haven Sanatorium, 1906-36; asst. instr. in medicine, Polyclinic Hosp.; phys. in charge, Tuberculosis Dispensary, Presbyn. Hosp.; instr. medicine, U. of Pa. Med. Sch., 1915-33; phys. in charge, Spl. Diagnostic Clinic, Henry Phipps Inst.; med. dir. White Haven San. since 1935; asst. prof. Clin. Medicine, U. of Pa. Med. Sch. since 1933; asso. in pulmonary diseases, U. of Pa. Grad. Sch. of Medicine since 1932; consultant tuberculosis, Presbyn. Hosp. since 1921; vis. phys. Tuberculosis Div., Phila. Gen. Hosp. since 1933; in gen. practice at Phila. since 1902. Served as mem. Tuberculosis Examining Bd., Camp Dix, during World War. Pres. Free Hosp. for Poor Consumptives, and White Haven Sanatorium Assn. since 1936; dir. Pa. Tuberculosis Soc., Phila. Health Council and Tuberculosis Com. Fellow Am. Coll. Phys.; mem. A.M.A., Nat. Tuberculosis Assn. (charter), Am. Clin. and Climatol. Assn., Am. Sanatorium Assn., Internat. Union against Tuberculosis, John Morgan Soc. Phila.; Phila Co. Med., Phila. Pathol., and Pediatric socs., Phi Delta Theta, Nu Sigma Nu. Republican. Presbyterian. Clubs: Union League, Philadelphia Country (Phila.). Author: Diseases of Middle Life, 2 vols., 1923; contbr. many papers to med. jours. Home: Rittenhouse Plaza, 19th and Walnut Sts. Office: Henry Phipps Inst., Philadelphia, Pa.

CRAIG, George Liggett; b. Pittsburgh, Pa., 1865; s. Joseph and Matilda (Staunton) C.; student pub. schs.; m. Henrietta Burchfield, Oct. 14, 1890. Dir. Chartiers Oil Co. since 1887, pres. since 1915. Home: 860 Thorn St., Sewickley, Pa. Office: 808 Columbia Bldg., Pittsburgh, Pa.

CRAIG, George Roth, lawyer; b. Mt. Lebanon, Pa., Sept. 6, 1901; s. Edward Armstrong and Kate Anna (Roth) C.; student Mercersburg (Pa.) Acad., 1919-20; A.B., Williams Coll., Williamstown, Mass., 1924; LL.B., Harvard U. Law Sch., 1927; m. Caroline Martha Long, Sept. 5, 1931; children—Caroline Long, Katherine Roth. Admitted to Pa. bar, 1927, and since engaged in gen. practice of law at Pittsburgh; mem. firm Shrum, Harrison and Craig since 1933; sec. and counsel Pa. Water Co.; dir. and counsel, First Nat. Bank, Wilkinsburg, Pa., Wilkinsburg Federal Savings and Loan Assn. Served as Burgess, Borough of Edgewood since 1938. Mem. East Boroughs Council, Boy Scouts of America. Mem. Am., Pa., and Allegheny County bar assns., Delta Upsilon. Republican. Presbyterian (trustee Edgewood Church). Mason. Clubs: Edgewood, Edgewood Country (Edgewood, Pa.). Home: 424 Elmer St., Edgewood. Office: 1508 Law and Finance Bldg., Pittsburgh, Pa.

CRAIG, Harry Raymond, v.p. Wilmington Trust Co. Address: Wilmington, Del.

CRAIG, J. Reed; mem. law firm Craig & Blass. Address: Erie, Pa.

CRAIG, Josiah Kirkwood, clergyman; b. Deepwater, Mo., Apr. 13, 1881; s. James Benjamin and Anna Barbara (Shoup) C.; ed. Simpson Coll., Indianola, Ia., 1904-07; Ph.B., Upper Ia. U., Fayette, Ia., 1909, (hon.) D.D., 1924; S.T.B., Boston U. Sch. of Theology, 1912,

M.R.E., Sch. Religious Edn., 1921; m. Gertrude Wells Clarke, June 18, 1912. Ordained to ministry M.E. Ch., 1914; served in various pastorates, 1907-19; supt. edn. and exec. sec. Minneapolis Council of Rel. Edn., 1922-27; gen. sec. and dir. leadership edn., Allegheny Co. (Pa.) S.S. Assn. since 1927; mem. N.H. Conf. of M.E. Ch.; mem. bd. Pittsburgh Dist. Dairy Council. Served as chaplain, 1st lt. later capt., U.S. Res. Nat. chaplain Sons of Union Vets. of Civil War; mem. ednl. commn. and exec. com. Internat. Council Religious Edn. Mem. Pa. Assn. Religious Edn. Republican. Methodist. Mason (K.T.). Clubs: Book, Pittsburgh Methodist (Pittsburgh). Home: 2716 Broadway, South Hills, Pittsburgh, Pa. Office: 239 Fourth Av., Pittsburgh, Pa.

CRAIG, Mark Rodgers, lawyer; b. Brookville, Pa., Mar. 5, 1873; s. Samuel Alfred and Nancy Priscilla (Rodgers) C.; B.S., Washington and Jefferson Coll., Washington, Pa., 1896; m. Elizabeth Dilworth Rodgers, Apr. 22, 1911; children—Nancy Scott Elizabeth Rodgers, Caroline Hjelm. Admitted to Pa. bar, 1899; title dept. Fidelity Title & Trust Co., 1899-1902; law dept. Pittsburgh Coal Co., 1902-04; title officer Potter Title & Trust Co., later Lawyers Title Co., 1904-37; v.p. and title officer Union-Fidelity Title Ins. Co. of Pittsburgh since 1937. Mem. Am. Bar Assn., Pa. Bar Assn., Allegheny Co. Bar Assn., Phi Kappa Psi. Republican. Presbyterian. Clubs: Duquesne (Pittsburgh); Allegheny Country (Sewickley, Pa.). Home: 44 Thorn St., Sewickley, Pa. Office: Magee Bldg., 336 4th Av., Pittsburgh, Pa.

CRAIG, Robert, engr., patent attorney; b. Galt, Ont., Canada, May 24, 1876; s. William and Jessie E. (Somerville) C.; grad. Grafton (N.D.) High Sch., 1891; student U. of N.D., 1891-94; M.E., U. of Minn., 1897; m. Carrie Swift, Apr. 27, 1903; children—William S. (dec.), Robert S., Richard A. Tester stationary and marine gas engines Pierce Engine Co. and Racine Hardware Co., Racine, Wis., 1897-98; installed gas engines in field C. D. Holbrook & Co. and Otto Gas Engine Co., Minneapolis, 1898-99; studied oil and gas engines in Europe, summer, 1900; mgr. gas engine dept. Fairbanks Morse & Co., St. Paul, 1900-03; with A. F. Chase & Co., gas engines and automobiles, Minneapolis, 1903-06; mfrs. agent of gas engines, automatic scales and developing small gas tractors, Minneapolis, 1906-11; gen. mgr. Power Equipment Co., Minneapolis, 1911-13; oxy-acetylene welding, mfg. automobile turntables, screw presses, portable cranes, selling scales, Los Angeles and San Francisco, 1913-18; developed automatic scale inventions, later becoming chief engr. scale div., Internat. Business Machines Corpn., Endicott, N.Y., and Dayton, O., 1918-23; cons. engr. specializing in patent causes, Dayton, 1924-25; patent atty. with Cooper, Kerr & Dunham, New York, since Jan. 1926. Mem. Am. Soc. Mech. Engrs., Nat. Scale Men's Assn., Franklin Inst., Soc. Automotive Engrs., Sigma Xi. Unitarian. Clubs: Canoe Brook Country (Summit, N.J.); Downtown Athletic (New York City); Dayton Engineering (Dayton, O.). Home: 41 Roosevelt Road, Maplewood, N.J. Office: Woolworth Bldg., New York, N.Y.

CRAIG, Samuel G., editor; b. on farm, DeKalb Co., Ill., June 1, 1874; s. Andrew and Elizabeth Moorhead (Swan) C.; Tarkio (Mo.) Coll.; A.B., Princeton, 1895, A.M., 1900; B.D., Princeton Theol. Sem., 1900; studied U. of Berlin, 1910-11; D.D., Southwestern Presbyn. U., 1923; D.D., Grove City Coll., 1923; m. Carrie Hays, Dec. 1, 1909; 1 son, Charles Hays. Ordained to ministry of the Presbyterian Church, 1900; pastor First Ch., Ebensburg, Pa., 1900-09, North Ch., Pittsburgh, 1912-15; joint editor the Presbyterian, 1915-18; v.dir. dept. of allied bodies (religious sect.) of Com. of Pub. Safety, Pa., 1918-19; contbg. editor The Presbyterian, 1919-24, editor, 1925-30; editor Christianity Today since 1930. Dir. Princeton Theol. Sem., 1925-29; mem. organizing com. Westminster Theol. Sem. in Phila. and trustee, 1929-36. Republican. Author: Jesus as He Was and Is, 1914, also articles in religious jours. Home: Princeton, N.J. Office: 525 Locust St., Philadelphia, Pa.

CRAIN, William Eldridge, physician, surgeon; b. Wrights Corners, Ont., Can., July 21, 1881; s. Levi and Maria (Dake) C.; prep. edn. Ottawa Collegiate Inst.; M.D., Toronto Univ.; m. Isabella McDey, Dec. 25, 1905; children—Ethel Mable Patricia (wife of Harry L. Sinexon, M.D.), Jessie Elizabeth (wife of Baxter A. Livengood, M.D.), Isabella Stuart (deceased), Dorothy Mary. Came to U.S., 1927, naturalized, 1933. Practiced as physician and surgeon, Crysler, Ont., 1904-16, Ottawa, Ont., 1917-27, Woodbury, N.J., since 1928. Mem. Coll. of Physicians and Surgeons, Toronto, Ont. (pres. 1918); mem. A.M.A., N.J. State Med. Soc., Pa. State Med. Soc., Gloucester County Med. Soc. (pres. 1938). Mayor, Finch, Ont., 3 years. Presbyterian. Mason (life mem. Consistory and Shrine, Can.). Club: Phila. Medical. Home: 12 E. Kings Highway, Mt. Ephraim, N.J. Office: 43 Curtis Av., Woodbury, N.J.

CRAINE, W. M. C.; chmn. bd. Altoona Trust Co. Home: 408 Howard Av. Office: 1130 Twelfth Av., Altoona, Pa.

CRAMBLET, Wilbur Haverfield, coll. pres.; b. Harrison Co., O., July 10, 1892; s. Thomas Ellsworth and Della Stella (Weaver) C.; B.Pd., Bethany (W.Va.) Coll., 1910, A.B., 1910, also A.M.; A.M., Yale, 1911, Ph.D., 1913; m. Mildred Margaret Barnacle, Aug. 12, 1914; children—Thomas Ellsworth, Wilbur Haverfield, Joan Anthony. Began as instr. mathematics, U. of Rochester, 1913; prof. mathematics, Phillips U., 1915-17; prof. mathematics, Bethany Coll., 1917-34, dean, 1918-20, treas. since 1919, sec. bd. trustees, 1929-32, pres. since 1934. Served in S.A.T.C., Plattsburg, 1918. Pres. Coll. Assn. Disciples of Christ since 1937. Fellow A.A.A.S.; mem. Am. Math. Soc., Alpha Sigma Phi (nat. pres. since 1936). Republican. Mem. Disciples of Christ Ch. Mason (33°), K.T. Author of sect. on mathematics in Century Book of Facts, 1924. Home: Bethany, W.Va.

CRAMPTON, George S., ophthalmologist; b. Rock Island, Ill., Mar. 10, 1874; s. Richard and Martha (Betty) C.; M.D., U. of Pa., 1898; m. Hazel Smedes, May 16, 1907. Practiced at Phila., Pa., since 1898; prof. ophthalmology, Grad. Sch. U. of Pa.; asso. opthalmologist to Pa. Hosp. Served as dir. Field Hosps., 28th Div., U.S.A., rank of lt. col., 1918-19. Fellow A.M.A., Coll., Phys. of Phila.; mem. Am. Ophthal. Soc., Illuminating Engring. Soc. (ex-nat. pres.), Franklin Inst. Republican. Episcopalian. Home-Office: 2031 Locust St., Philadelphia, Pa.

CRANE, Clifford Fred, ry. exec.; b. Columbus, O., July 13, 1880; s. Clifford Ely and Mary Dell (Reddy) C.; m. Isabel Haefeker, Nov. 14, 1912. Gen. traffic mgr. Rochester and Eastern Ry. Co., Canadaigua, N.Y., 1904-08; supt. Eastern Pa. Rys. Co., Pottsville, Pa., 1908-14, Wilkes-Barre (Pa.) Rys. Co., 1914-17; pres. Wadell Products Corpn., Georgetown, S.C., 1917-19; asst. to pres. Harrisburg (Pa.) Rys. Co., 1920-35, v.p. since 1935; dir. Transit Co. of Harrisburg, Personal Finance Co. Mem. Pa. State and Harrisburg chambers of commerce. Mason. Club: Rotary (Harrisburg, Pa.). Home: 2727 N. 2d St. Office: 12 S. Market Sq., Harrisburg, Pa.

CRANE, Esther; prof. edn. Goucher Coll. Address: Goucher Coll., Baltimore, Md.

CRANE, Frederick Lea, newspaper publisher; b. Elizabeth, N.J., Feb. 12, 1888; s. Augustus Stout and Minerva Carlisle (Lea) C.; M.E., Stevens Inst. Tech., 1910; m. Gwendolen Kershner, of Lincoln, Neb., Jan. 20, 1917; children—Dorothy Jean (dec.), Marian Lea, Robert Clark. Became cadet engr. Westinghouse Machine Co., 1910; later appraisal engr. West Penn Traction Co.; then statistician West Penn Power Co., and constrn. engr. United Gas Improvement Co.; with Elizabeth (N.J.) Daily Journal since 1920, now pres., pub. and editor; v.p. and mgr. Union County Savings Bank; dir. Elizabethport Banking Co., Winfield Scott Hotel; trustee Evergeen Cemetery. Dir. Elizabeth Y.M.C.A. (past pres.); dir. Community Chest. Mem. Am. Newspaper Pubs. Assn., Asso. Press, Tau Beta Pi. Republican. Presbyn. (ruling elder and clerk of session). Mason (32°), Elk. Clubs: Rotary, Suburban Golf (Elizabeth). Home: 815 Salem Av. Office: 297 N. Broad St., Elizabeth, N.J.

CRANE, Harley Lucius, horticulturist; b. Terra Alta, W.Va., Mar. 31, 1891; s. Dee and Annie (Foreman) C.; B.S. in Agr., W.Va. U., Morgantown, 1914, M.S. in Agr., 1918; student Cornell U., Ithaca, N.Y., 1921-22 and 1928-29, Ph.D., 1929; m. Fern Coburn, Aug. 30, 1912; children—Margaret Lucile (Mrs. Herman Wotring), Julian Coburn, Helen Louise. Asst. prof. horticulture, W.Va. U. and Agrl. Expt. Station, 1914-20, asso. prof., 1920-29; horticulturist U.S. Dept. Agr., Albany, Ga., 1929-35, prin. horticulturist, Beltsville, Md., since 1935, also in charge of nut production and disease investigations. Mem. W.Va. Nat. Guard, 1906-12; distinguished cadet, W.Va. U., 1914. Mem. Am. Soc. for Hort. Science, Northern Nut Growers Assn., Kappa Alpha, Sigma Xi. Democrat. Presbyn. Mason (past master), Lodge of Perfection. Home: 25 Pine St., Hyattsville, Md. Office: U.S. Horticultural Station, Beltsville, Md.

CRANE, Jasper Elliot, v.p. E. I. du Pont de Nemours & Co.; b. Newark, N.J., May 17, 1881; s. Edward Nichols and Cordelia (Matthews) C.; A.B., Princeton, 1901, M.S., 1904; student Mass. Inst. Tech., 1903-04; m. Olive E. Crew, Oct. 24, 1908; children—Olive Cordelia, Helen, Catherine. With E. I. du Pont de Nemours & Co. since 1915, v.p. since 1929; dir. Canadian Industries, Ltd., D. Van Nostrand Co. Chmn. Temporary Emergency Relief Commn. of Del., 1932-34; dir. Wilmington Y.M.C.A. Mem. Am. Chem. Soc., Am. Inst. Chem. Engrs., Soc. of Chem. Engrs. Republican. Presbyterian. Clubs: Wilmington, Wilmington Country (Wilmington); University, Princeton Chemists' (N.Y. City); City (London). Home: Westover Hills, Wilmington, Del. Office: Du Pont Bldg., Wilmington, Del.

CRANE, Judson Adams, prof. law; b. Shelburn, Mass., May 7, 1884; s. Alvin Millen and Sarah (Adams) C.; A.B., Brown U., 1905; LL.B., Harvard, 1909, S.J.D., 1915; m. Corinna V. Foljambe, June 28, 1911; 1 dau., Dorothy Oakes (Mrs. Donald E. Reid). In practice of law at Boston, Mass., 1909-11; prof. of law, Pei Yang University, Tientsin, China, 1911-14, George Washington U., 1915-17, U. of Pittsburgh since 1917, also sec. Law Sch. Faculty; visiting prof. law Univ. of Southern Calif., 1928-29. Trustee First Bapt. Ch. Mem. Am., Pa. and Allegheny County bar assns., Am. Law Inst., Beta Theta Pi, Phi Beta Kappa, Phi Delta Phi. Republican. Baptist. Mason. Clubs: Harvard-Yale-Princeton (Pittsburgh); University, Chartiers Heights Country; Plymouth (Mass.) Country. Author: Cases on Partnership (Crane and Magruder), 1923; Clark and Marshall Criminal Law, 3d edit.; Crane's Cases on Damages; Pennsylvania Annotations American Law Inst. Contracts Restatement; Crane on Partnership, 1937. Mem. bd. editors Pa. Bar Assn. Contbr. on law topics. Home: 5721 Stanton Av. Office: 1401 Cathedral of Learning, Pittsburgh, Pa.

CRANE, Norman Tompkins, M.D.; b. Mahopac, N.Y., Sept. 4, 1901; s. Samuel B. and Gertrude (Tompkins) C.; grad. Katonah High Sch., 1918; A.B., Dartmouth Coll., 1922; M.D., Columbia U., Coll. Physicians and Surgeons, 1925; m. Marian Bradley, Aug. 3, 1926; children—Shirley Ann, Joan Virginia. In gen. practice of medicine, Bound Brook, N.J., 1926-31; resident interne Babies Hosp., N.Y. City, 1932; pediatrician, Plainfield, N.J., since 1933; sr. attending pediatrician Muhlenburg Hosp., Somerset Hosp. Mem. A.M.A., N.J. State Med. Soc., Union Co. Med. Soc., Plainfield Med. Soc., Phi Gamma Delta, Alpha Kappa Kappa. Republican. Presbyn. Club: Twin Brooks Country. Home: 1025 Sleepy Hollow Lane. Office: 147 E. 7th St., Plainfield, N.J.

CRANE, Utley E.; judge Municipal Ct. of Phila. since 1913, present term expires 1944. Address: City Hall, Philadelphia, Pa.

CRANMER, Clyde William, city supt. schs.; b. Williamsport, Pa., Mar. 11, 1884; s. J. S. and Anna L. (Edwards) C.; Ph.B., Bucknell U., Lewisburg, Pa., 1910; M.Ed., U. of Pittsburgh, 1936; m. Maude E. Fry, Apr. 21, 1906; 1 son, Clyde E. Engaged in teaching pub. schs.

and high schs., 1902-12; teacher high sch., Franklin, Pa., 1912-16, prin., same, 1916-19; supt. schs., Kittanning, Pa., since 1919; instr., Clarion State Teachers Coll., summers 1922-27; instr., Indiana State Teachers Coll., summer 1928. Mem. Am. Assn. Sch. Adminstrs., Pa. State Edn. Assn., Armstrong County Sch. Men's Club, Lambda Chi Alpha, Phi Delta Kappa. Republican. Methodist. Mason (32°), Odd Fellow. Club: Rotary (Kittanning, Pa.). Home: 550 N. McKean St., Kittanning, Pa.

CRAVEN, Charles Edmiston, clergyman, teacher; b. Newark, N.J., Nov. 23, 1860; s. Rev. Elijah Richardson (D.D.) and Hannah Tingey (Sanderson) B.; A.B., Princeton, 1881, A.M., 1884; grad. Princeton Theol. Sem., 1886; D.D., U. of Pittsburgh, 1909; m. Anna Schenck McDougall, Dec. 28, 1886; children—Virginia Coryell (Mrs. R. M. Lupton), Sarah Landreth (Mrs. L. C. Eichner), Julia McDougall, James McDougall, Charles E. Teacher, Collegiate Inst., York, Pa., 1881-83; ordained Presbyn. ministry, 1886; pastor, Birmingham, Pa., 1886-88, Downingtown, Pa., 1889-94, Mattituck, N.Y., 1895-1913. Head master of the Craven Sch. for Boys, 1913-20. Stated clk. Presbytery of L.I., 1903-23; acting pastor, Westfield, N.J., 1920-21; pastor, South Presbyn. Ch., Montclair, 1922-27, retired. Republican. Mem. Draft Exemption Bd. for 3d div., Suffolk Co., N.Y., 1917-19. Author: Jesus and Children, 1896; History of Mattituck, L.I., 1907. One of translators of Metrical Version of the Psalms, used by United Presbyn. Ch., U.S.A. Edited new edit. of Dr. Epher Whitaker's History of Southold, L.I., with additions, 1931; (booklet, numbered edit.) Southold's Claim to Priority (oldest English speaking town in N.Y. state), 1933. Home: 29 Oxford St., Montclair, N.J.

CRAVEN, D. Stewart (Col.); pres. N.J. State Bd. of Edn. Address: Salem, N.J.

CRAVEN, Henry Thornton, writer, publicity agt., lecturer; b. Phila., Pa., Apr. 28, 1879; s. John Jacob Ridgway and Julia (Thornton) C.; student William Penn Charter Sch., Phila., 1890-96; B.S. in economics, U. of Pa., 1900; m. Elizabeth Dickes Geisler, Dec. 1, 1914. Reporter Phila. Record, 1901-03, drama, music and lit. editor, 1905; drama editor Phila. Pub. Ledger, 1905-09; drama and music editor Phila. N. Am., 1909-14; Sunday editor Phila. Press, 1915-17; editorial writer, drama and music editor Phila. Evening Ledger, 1917-26; fgn. editor and fgn. corr. Phila. Pub. Ledger, 1923-27; lit. editor, editorial writer, columnist, drama and music editor, Phila. Record, 1927-31; in charge publicity Metropolitan Opera, Phila., since 1931; editorial writer Phila. Evening Bulletin, summers 1937, 38, 39; drama lecturer, agt. for opera and other publicity since 1931. Mem. Zoöl. Soc. of Phila., Library Co. of Phila. Democrat. Clubs: Franklin Inn, University, Clover (Phila.). Contbr. to Pa. Verse, Tom Masson's Library of Wit and Humor, Life (humorous), Sat. Rev. of Lit., The Bookman, Nation's Business, Musical America, Boston Transcript, Phila. Forum Mag. Address: 321 S. 18th St., Philadelphia, Pa.

CRAWFORD, Arthur Burdick, veterinarian; b. Willard, Seneca Co., N.Y., Dec. 5, 1888; s. Samuel Lyons and Sarah Maria (Morrell) C.; grad. Ovid (N.Y.) High Sch., 1906; student Bryant and Stratton Commerce Sch., Boston, Mass., 1907; student George Washington U. Coll. Arts and Sciences, Washington, D.C., 1910-11, D.V.M., Sch. of Vet. Medicine, 1914; m. Maude Anna Carlisle, Sept. 25, 1924. Asst. veterinarian, U.S. Bureau Animal Industry, Washington, D.C., 1914-15; transferred to Virus-Serum Control, 1915-19; scientific asst. Expt. Station, U.S. Bureau Animal Industry, Bethesda, Md., 1919-37; sr. veterinarian and asst. dir. Animal Disease Station, Beltsville, Md., since 1937. Served as 2d lt. Vet. Corps, U.S. Army, 1918-19. Mem. Am. Vet. Med. Assn., Am. Bacteriological Soc., Nat. Assn. Bureau Animal Industry Employees. Episcopalian. Mason. Club: Kenwood Golf (Bethesda, Md.). Contbr. articles relative to tuberculosis to jours. Home: 6676 32d Pl., Washington, D.C. Office: Beltsville, Md.

CRAWFORD, Benjamin Franklin, clergyman; b. near London, Madison Co., O., May 12, 1887; s. Burton and Frances (Gillespie) C.; A.B., Ohio Wesleyan U., Delaware, O., 1906; S.T.B., Boston U., 1909; A.M., Denison U., Granville, O., 1919; Ph.D., U. of Pittsburgh, 1937; D.D., Waynesburg (Pa.) Coll., 1927; m. Achsah Mead, June 29, 1910; children—Arthur Mead, Achsah Ruth, Margaret Elizabeth. Teacher of rural school, Madison Co., O., 1903; ordained to ministry of M.E. Ch., 1909; asst. minister First M.E. Ch., Baltimore, 1909-12; pastor Third Av. M.E. Ch., Columbus, O., 1912-17, Granville, O., 1917-21; pastor Tarentum, Pa., 1921-25, Waynesburg, Pa., 1925-30, Perrysville Av. M.E. Ch., Pittsburgh, 1930-35, First M.E. Ch., Carnegie, Pa., since 1935. Pres. Ministerial Assn., Carnegie, Pa.; pres. Pittsburgh Methodist Preachers Meeting, 1935; del. to Gen. Conf. M.E. Ch., Columbus, O., 1936. Chmn. Council for Peace and Social Action, Pittsburgh, 1933-34, 1936-37; chmn. Emergency Peace Campaign of Pittsburgh and Allegheny Co., 1935-37; chmn. Brotherhood of Jews, Catholics and Protestants (local branch); mem. exec. com. Am. League for Peace and Democracy. Dir. Carnegie Church Press. Mem. Hymn Soc. of America, Y.M.C.A., Theol. Circle of Pittsburgh. Mason. Clubs: Pittsburgh Book, Hungry, Lions. Author: Religious Trends in a Century of Hymns, 1938; Changing Motivations of Religion, 1937; Our Changing Hymnology, 1938; Changing Conceptions of Religion, 1939; Theological Trends in Methodist Hymnody, 1939; Methodism in the Chartiers Country, 1939; Fascism—the New Barbarism, 1939. Contbr. to Methodist periodicals. Home: 415 Washington Av., Carnegie, Pa.

CRAWFORD, Daniel, Jr., pres. Hotel Philadelphian; b. Phila., Pa., May 5, 1905; s. Daniel, Jr., and Charlotte (Lembert) C.; student Peddie Inst.; m. Connie Lee, July 7, 1937; 1 son, Alan. Pres. and gen. mgr. Hotel Philadelphian since 1928. Chmn. hotel div. U. of Pa. Bicentennial Com.; chmn. Phila. Citizens Com. of 75th Anniversary of Battle of Gettysburg; Phila. rep. of nat. advisory com. of N.Y. World's Fair in 1939. Mem. Phila. Hotel Assn. (com. mem.), Convention and Tourist Com., Hotel Greeters of America (chmn. Phila. civic com.; life mem.; regional pres. and charter pres. of local charter 45), N.J. Hotel Assn., Am. Hotel Assn., Club Mgrs. Assn. of Phila., Chamber of Commerce, Hotel Sales Mgrs. Assn., Pa. State Hotel Assn. (mem. bd.). Clubs: Reciprocity, Boosters', The 100, Lions' (Phila.); Llanerch Country. Address: Hotel Philadelphian, Philadelphia, Pa.

CRAWFORD, David Bovaird, oil well supplies; b. Limavady, Ireland, June 9, 1872; s. Joseph and Eliza Jane (McLenaghan) C.; came to U.S., 1886, naturalized, 1896; student Nat. Sch., Limavady, 1876-86, pub. schs., Bradford, Pa., 1886-89; m. Annetta Duncan, 1893; children—Harold Duncan, Claude Wallace, Doris Margaret (Mrs. Hayward E. Clovis), Helen Elizabeth. In employ Bovaird & Seyfang, mfrs. oil well supplies, Bradford, Pa., 1889-92, in charge branch store, McDonald, Pa., 1892-95, gen. salesman in Pa., W.Va. and O., 1895-99; asso. with brother in orgn. Parkersburg (W.Va.) Sucker Rod Co., mfrs., 1899-1915; sec. and treas. Parkersburg Rig & Reel Co., mfrs. oil well equipment, 1913-35, pres. since 1935; also asso. with brothers as operators and producers oil in W.Va., Ill., Kan., Okla. and Tex., 1900-25. Served as pres. and dir. Parkersburg Y.M.C.A. for many yrs. Active in religious and welfare work. Republican. Presbyn. (deacon). Mason (K.T., 32°, Shriner). Elk. Club: Parkersburg Country. Home: 1358 Market St. Office: 620 Depot St., Parkersburg, W.Va.

CRAWFORD, Glenn Martin, clergyman; b. Crab Tree, Pa., Oct. 1, 1888; s. James K. and Sarah Jane (Torrence) C.; student McElvain Inst., New Lebanon, Pa., 1909-10, Carnegie Inst. of Tech., Pittsburgh, 1910-11; A.B., Grove City (Pa.) Coll., 1914, D.D., 1934; student Western Theol. Sem., Pittsburgh, 1914-17; m. Mabel Elizabeth Montgomery, July 3, 1917; children—Helen Elizabeth, Marybelle, Hugh Martin. Ordained to ministry of Presbyn. Ch., May 1917; pastor Crooked Creek Chs., Appleby Manor, Pa., 1917-21, Presbyn. Ch., West Alexander, Pa., 1921-26, First Presbyn. Ch., Jeanette, Pa., 1926-32, First Presbyn. Ch., Meadville, Pa., since 1932. Dir. Meadville Y.M.C.A.; dir. Ministerial Assn. of Meadville. Republican. Clubs: Kiwanis, Round Table (Meadville, Pa.). Home: 525 Chestnut St., Meadville, Pa.

CRAWFORD, Harry Jennings; b. Emlenton, Pa., Jan. 19, 1867; s. Samuel Washington and Jane C.; ed. Emlenton pub. sch., m. Elizabeth Hafala; children—Elizabeth Louise, Katherine Jane. Began as foreman South Penn Oil Co.; now pres. First Nat. Bank (Emlenton, Pa.), Citizen's Banking Co. (Oil City), Oil City National Bank, Quaker State Oil Refining Corpn., Pa. Fuel Supply Co., Emlenton Milling Co., Emlenton Water Company, etc. Trustee Grove City Coll. Republican; del. Rep. Nat. Conv., Chicago, 1932. Presbyn. Mason (33°). Home: Emlenton, Pa.

CRAWFORD, James Pyle Wickersham, coll. prof.; b. Lancaster, Pa., Feb. 19, 1882; s. James and Corinne (Wickersham) C.; A.B., U. of Pa., 1902, grad. work, 1902-04, Ph.D., 1906; univs. of Grenoble, Madrid and Freiburg, 1904-06; Litt.D., Franklin and Marshall, 1925; m. Florence May Wickersham, June 3, 1909; 1 dau., Harriet de B. Instr. Romance langs., U. of Pa., 1906, prof. since 1914. Commd. capt. U.S.A., June 1918 and assigned duty at Washington, D.C.; mil. attaché to Colombia, S.A., Jan.-July 1919; hon. discharged Aug. 1919; commd. maj. O.R.C., Nov. 1919. Mem. Modern Lang. Assn. America, Delta Tau Delta, Phi Beta Kappa, Am. Philos. Soc.; corr. mem. Hispanic Soc. America, Real Academia Hispano-Americana de Ciencias y Artes, Cadiz, Real Academia Española, Academia de Bellas Artes de Valladolid, Am. Acad. Arts and Sciences. Club: Franklin Inn (Phila.). Author: Life and Works of Suarez de Figueroa, 1907; Spanish Composition, 1910; Temas Españoles, 1922; Spanish Drama before Lope de Vega, 1923 (revised edit. 1937); Un viaje por España, 1931; Spanish Pastoral Drama, 1915; First Book in Spanish, 1919. Editor: Tragedia de Narciso, 1909. Editor of Modern Language Journal, 1920-24, Hispanic Review, since 1933. Contbr. on Spanish, Italian and French lits. to various modern lang. jours. Home: 4012 Pine St., Philadelphia, Pa.

CRAWFORD, James Stoner, lawyer; b. Arch Spring, Blair Co., Pa., May 24, 1872; s. John Armstrong and Elizabeth (Stoner) C.; grad. Blair Acad., Blairstown, N.J., 1891; A.B., Princeton U., 1895; LL.B., Pittsburgh Law Sch., 1897; m. Mae Wilson, June 16, 1903 (now deceased); children—James Wilson, Virginia Crawford (Mrs. Wallace M. Parker). Admitted to Pa. bar, 1898, and since practiced in Pittsburgh; mem. firm Patterson, Crawford, Arensberg and Dunn; sec. and dir. Molybdenum Corpn. of America; dir. United Engring. and Foundry Co., Allemannia Fire Ins. Co., Pa. Water Co., Pittsburgh Forge & Iron Co. Presbyterian. Clubs: Duquesne (Pittsburgh); Oakmont Country (Oakmont, Pa.). Home: 121 S. Lexington Av. Office: First National Bank Bldg., Pittsburgh, Pa.

CRAWFORD, John M(cLenaghan), chmn. bd. dirs., Parkersburg Rig and Reel Co.; b. Limavady, County Derry, Ireland, Oct. 16, 1867; s. Joseph and Eliza Jane (McLenaghan) C.; ed. schs. of Limavady, Ireland, and Bradford, Pa.; m. Elizabeth McAllister, Dec. 6, 1910; children—Emma Elizabeth (Mrs. B. F. Harris III), John McAllister. Came to U.S., 1883, naturalized, 1889. Shipping clk., Bradford, Pa., 1884-93; with William Forgie, Washington, Pa., 1893-97; founded Parkersburg (W.Va.) Rig and Reel Co., mfrs. oil field equipment, 1897, serving as sec.-treas., pres., and since Jan. 1933, chmn. bd.; pres. North Fork Oil Co. (Ill.), Okla. Producing & Refining Co., N.Y. Quartet Oil Co., Hillside Oil Co., Homaokla Oil Co. (Okla.). Mem. City Council, Parkersburg, 1900-01; col. governor's staff, W.Va., 1900-12; pres. Parkersburg Board of Commerce, 1920-24; dir. Chamber of Commerce of U.S., 1921-27; mem. W.Va. Tax Commn., 1926-27, State Bd. of Edn., 1933-35; dir. Am. Peace Soc.; v.p. Ohio Valley Improvement Assn.; trustee Asheville (N.C.) Sch. Episcopalian. Mason (33°, K.T.). Clubs: Bankers (N.Y. City); Tulsa, Southern Hills Country (Tulsa); Parkersburg Country. Home: 1019 Juliana St. Office: 620 Depot St., Parkersburg, W.Va.

CRAWFORD, Matthew Alexander, attorney; b. Clarion Co., Pa., May 7, 1904; s. John and Helen (Snedden) C.; B.S. in Econ., U. of Pa., 1928; LL.B., U. of Pittsburgh Law Sch., 1931; m. Sara Bowser, Mar. 28, 1929. Admitted to Pa. bar, 1931, and since engaged in gen. practice of law at Brookville, Pa.; mem. firm Brown and Crawford since 1932; asst. gen. counsel, The Pittsburgh & Shawmut R.R. Co.; asst. sec. Allegheny River Mining Co., The Pittsburgh & Shawmut Coal Co. Mem. Pa. Bar Assn., Jefferson Co. Bar Assn. (sec.), Order of the Coif, Kiwanis International (lt. gov.), Delta Theta Phi. Republican. Christian Ch. Mason. Home: 130 Pine St. Office: 293 Main St., Brookville, Pa.

CRAWFORD, Ralston, artist; b. St. Catharines, Ontario, Canada, Sept. 25, 1906; s. George Burson and Lucy (Colvin) C.; brought to U.S., 1910; student Otis Art Inst., Los Angeles, Jan.-June 1927, Pa. Acad. Fine Arts, Oct. 1927-May 1930, Barnes Foundation, Merion, Pa., 1928-30, Breckenridge Sch., East Gloucester, Mass., summers, 1928, 29, 30, Academies Scandinav and Colarrossi, Paris, 1932; m. Margaret Stone, Oct. 17, 1932; children—James Ralston, Robert Frederick. Began as cartoonist Walt Disney Studios, Mar. 1927; mural and easel painter since 1930. Exhibited Corcoran Gallery (Washington), Pa. Acad., The Water Colour, Oil Annuals, Chicago Art Inst., Internat. Water Color Show, Dallas Museum, San Francisco World's Fair, New York World's Fair (on jury for selection of paintings from Pa.), etc.; one-man exhbns., Md. Inst., Boyer Galleries, Phila., 1937, Phila. Art Alliance, 1938, Boyer Galleries, New York, 1939. Mem. Am. Artists Congress; fellow Tiffany Foundation. Democrat. Home: Chadds Ford, Pa.

CRAWFORD, Stanton Chapman, zoölogist, univ. dean; b. Steubenville, O., Oct. 30, 1897; s. George Moore and Minnie (Chapman) C.; grad. Wells High Sch., Steubenville, 1915; A.B., Bethany (W.Va.) Coll., 1918; A.M., U. of Cincinnati, 1921; Ph.D., U. of Pittsburgh (Pa.), 1926; student Lane Sem., Cincinnati, and Carnegie Inst. of Tech.; m. Mary Belle Parks, Mar. 23, 1920; children—Nancy Elizabeth, Mary Alice. Ordained Christian (Disciples) ministry, 1918; pastor Oakley-Hyde Park Ch., Cincinnati, 1918-21; prof. biology, Lynchburg (Va.) Coll., 1921-24; instr. in zoölogy, U. of Pittsburgh, 1924-26; prof. biology and dean Lynchburg Coll., 1926-27; head of Johnstown Center, U. of Pittsburgh, 1927-33, successively asst. prof., asso. prof. and prof. of zoölogy, dir. of high sch. relations, 1933-35, dean of the coll. since 1935. Mem. A.A.A.S., Am. Soc. of Zoölogists, Pa. Acad. Science, Sigma Xi, Omicron Delta Kappa, Sigma Nu. Republican. Presbyn. Club: University. Contbr. to zoöl. and ednl. jours. Home: D'Arlington Apts., Bayard at Neville, Pittsburgh, Pa.

CRAWFORD, William Rex, univ. prof.; b. Beaver, Pa., May 13, 1898; s. Harry H. and Lulu (Rex) C.; Central High School, Phila., 1913-14, Mt. Hermon (Mass.) School, 1914-15; A.B., U. of Pa., 1919, A.M., 1922, Ph.D., 1926; m. Dorothy Buckley, June 28, 1924; children—William Rex, John Charlton. With the U. of Pa. since 1919, as instr. in English, 1919-20, Romance langs., 1920-22, instr. in sociology, 1922-27, asst. prof., 1927-35, asso. prof. since 1935, chmn. dept. of sociology since 1934, chmn. social science faculty in Grad. Sch., 1936-38. Trustee Pa. Sch. of Social Work; mem. bd. dirs. Internat. Inst. Fellow Social Science Research Council, 1933-34; mem. Am. Sociol. Soc., Phi Beta Kappa (v.p. U. of Pa. Chapter), Pi Gamma Mu. Home: 51 E. Penn St., Philadelphia, Pa.

CRECCA, William D., asso. surgeon Newark City and of Isolation hosps.; attending surgeon Newark Memorial Hosp.; mem. courtesy staff Newark Beth Israel Hosp., Presbyn. Hosp. and Hosp. for Women and Children. Address: 111 Park Av., Newark, N.J.

CREESE, James, educator; b. Leetsdale, Pa., June 19, 1896; s. James and Nancy R. (Speer) C.; Litt.B., Princeton U., 1918, A.M., 1920; m. Margaret Villiers Morton, Nov. 16, 1925; children—James, Jr. (dec.), Elizabeth Kirkbride, Thomas Morton. Engaged as publs. mgr. Am.-Scandinavian Foundation, 1919, dir. of students, 1920, gen. sec., 1922-28; vice-pres. and treas., Stevens Inst. of Technology, Hoboken, N.J., since 1928. Served as lt. F.A., U.S.A., 1918. Trustee Am.-Scandinavian Foundation. Dec. Order of Vasa, Sweden. Democrat. Presbyn. Clubs: Century, Princeton (New York). Home: Castle Point, Hoboken, N.J.

CREIGHTON, Edward Bright, insurance exec.; b. Montoursville, Pa., June 17, 1866; s. Abraham Muthersbaugh and Elmira (Gray) C.; grad. Philipsburg (Pa.) High Sch.; student Dickinson Sem., Williamsport, Pa.; m. Sarah Emma Wren, June 21, 1888 (died 1917); m. 2d, Marcella Diemer, Feb. 11, 1920; children—Edward Bright (deceased), Gray Diemer. Began as gen. asst. with coal companies in Pa., 1884; variously employed in several commercial and insurance companies as clerk, branch mgr. and dist. mgr.; pres. Eureka Casualty Co. since 1915; pres. Atlas Storage Co., Eldredge Storage Co., Creighton and Broderick; partner Creighton & Co., investments. Republican. Clubs: Union League, Midday (Phila.). Home: "Graydieton," Media, Pa. Office: Chester Av. at 41st St., Philadelphia, Pa.

CREIGHTON, Henry Jermain Maude, coll. prof.; b. Dartmouth, N.S., Mar. 2, 1886; s. Henry Dolby and Helen (Robson) C.; student pub. schs., Dartmouth, N.S., 1890-1902; A.B., A.M., Dalhousie U., Halifax, N.S., 1907; M.Sc., U. of Birmingham, Eng., 1909; student Heidelberg U., Germany, 1909-10; D.Sc., Federal Polytechnic, Zurich, Switzerland, 1911; m. Jean H. Walker, June 21, 1916; children—Robert Hervey Jermain, Rosamond Jermain. Lecturer in phys. chemistry, Dalhousie U., Halifax, N.S., 1911; instr. chemistry, Swarthmore (Pa.) Coll., 1912, asst. prof., 1913-23, asso. prof., 1923-28, prof. and head dept. since 1928. Mem. A.A.A.S. (councillor since 1936), Am. Chem. Soc. (chmn. com. on theoretical electrochemistry, 1933-36, Weston Medal com., 1936-38, v.p., 1936-38, pres., 1939-40), Nat. Research Council (chmn. com. on electro-organic chemistry), Franklin Inst. (chmn. com. on sci. and arts, 1918, mem. Franklin Medal com. since 1922, chmn., 1933, 1938), Faraday Soc., Can. Inst. Chemistry, Maritime Chemists' Assn. (v.p., 1920); N.S. Inst. (councillor and editor "Trans." 1911), London Chem. Soc., Bunsen Gesellschaft, Am. Inst. Chemists, Sigma Xi. Awarded University Medal, 1906, Langstreth Medal, 1918, Potts medal, 1939. Mem. Perkin Medal Com. since 1939. Clubs: Dalhousie (New York); Halifax, Royal Nova Scotia Yacht Squadron (Halifax, N.S.). Author: "Principles of Electrochemistry," 1924, 1928, 1935. Home: 515 Elm Av. Office: Swarthmore Coll., Swarthmore, Pa.

CREIGHTON, William J.; v.p. and dir. Jones & Laughlin Steel Corpn. Home: 1216 Beechwood Boul. Office: Jones & Laughlin Bldg., Pittsburgb, Pa.

CREITZ, Charles Erwin, church official; b. Lynnport, Pa., Oct. 24, 1865; s. Alvin F. and Caroline (Oswald) C.; A.B., Franklin and Marshall Coll., Lancaster, Pa., 1889, D.D., 1910; grad. Eastern Theol. Sem., Lancaster, 1892; m. Wilhelmina Schafer, Aug. 30, 1900; children—George Alvin, Mary Louise. Ordained ministry Ref. Ch. in U.S., 1892; pastor Weissport, Pa., 1892-95, Huntingdon, Pa., 1895-99; field agent Board of Home Missions, 1899-1900; pastor St. Paul's Memorial Reformed Ch., Reading, Pa., 1900-37, retired. Pres. Bd. of Foreign Missions Ref. Ch. in U.S. since 1924; visited Japan and China, 1926. Democrat. Contbr. numerous articles to Ref. Ch. Rev. Home: 29 N. 3d St., Easton, Pa.

CRENSHAW, James Llewellyn, coll. prof.; b. Dermott, Ark., July 10, 1887; s. John Thompson and Anna (Crawford) C.; A.B., Centre Coll., Danville, Ky., 1907, M.A., 1908; Ph.D., Princeton U., 1911; m. Louise Ffrost Hodges,

June 30, 1923. Asst. chemist Geophysical Lab., Washington, D.C., 1910-15; asso. in physical chemistry, Bryn Mawr (Pa.) Coll., 1915-18, asso. prof., 1918-25, prof. of chemistry since 1925. Served as capt., C.W.S., and chief of chem. section, Hanlon Field, U.S. Army with A.E.F., 1917-19. Mem. Am., French and German Chem. Socs., Franklin Inst., A.A.A.S., Am. Electrochem. Soc., Sigma Xi. Presbyterian. Contbr. articles on mineral chemistry, electrochemistry, etc., to scientific jours. Home: 217 Roberts Rd. Office: Chemistry-Geology Bldg., Bryn Mawr, Pa.

CRESCENTE, Fred James, physician; b. Haskell, N.J., July 28, 1908; s. Nunzio James and Susan (Jordan) C.; student Haskell (N.J.) Grammar Sch., 1914-22, Montclair (N.J.) High Sch., 1922-26; B.S., Georgetown U., Washington, D.C., 1928, M.D., Med. Sch., 1932; m. Helene Miller, of Pittsburgh; children—Helene and Kathleen (twins). Interne, St. Joseph's Hosp., Paterson, N.J., 1932-33, clinical surgeon, 1938-39, mem. courtesy staff since 1933; resident, Polyclinic Post-Grad. Med. Sch. and Hosp., New York, 1933-34; clinical surgeon, Gen. Hosp., Paterson, N.J., 1937-38, mem. courtesy staff since 1934; mem. courtesy staff, Med. Arts Hosp., New York, since 1938; physician to N.J. State Athletic Commn. since 1937; licensed medicine & surgery N.J. State, 1933, New York State, 1938; specializing in radiology for treatment of cancer and goiter since 1938. Mem. Wanaque Boro (N.J.) Bd. of Health, 1932-34; mem.' Central Italian-Am. Republican League (past pres.; ex-chmn. exec. com.), Passaic Co. Republican League (physician); mem. New York Goiter Com. Fellow A.M.A.; mem. Passaic Co. Med. Soc. (mem. Cancer Com.), N.J. State Med. Soc., Georgetown Med. Alumni Assn. of N.J. (founder and first sec.), Washington Inst. of Medicine, Italian Nat. Circle (past mcm. Bd. of Govs.), Nat. Alumni Assn., Georgetown Alumni Assn., Montelair High Sch. Alumni Assn., Lambda Phi Mu, Alpha Alpha. Republican. Catholic. K.C. Author of numerous scientific med. papers on radiology. Home: 250 Washington Av., Hawthorne, N.J. Offices: 595 Madison Av., New York, N.Y., and 827 Madison Av., Paterson, N.J.

CRESKOFF, Jacob Joshua, cons. engr.; b. Belz, Russia, Mar. 30, 1900; s. Louis and Tillie (Lerner) C.; brought to U.S., 1905; student Southwark Sch., Phila., 1906-14, S. Phila. High Sch., 1914-18; grad. Gratz Coll., Phila., 1919, B.S. in C.E., Towne Scientific Sch. (U. of Pa.), 1922; m. Mildred Blumenthal, Mar. 16, 1935. Began work as structural engr., 1922, designing bridges and bldgs. at Phila.; designed St. Elizabeth's Hosp., Washington, D.C., veterans hosps. at Albuquerque, N.M., Biloxi, Miss., Togus, Me., Wichita, Kan., U.S. Mint Bldg., San Francisco; made investigation of Washington Monument for spalling and aseismic qualities; consultant to depts. of U.S. Govt. on design of earthquake-proof bldgs., and on recording and analysis of structural vibrations, including aeronautical structures; devised first practical dynamic system of aseismic design; method of distribution of wind and earthquake forces to walls and columns; method of using site vibrations as check on geol. findings; method of using periods of vibration of structures as guide to end fixities and to detect invisible damage. Served in Engrs. S.A.T.C., U.S. Army, 3 months, 1918. Mem. Nat. Soc. Professional Engrs., Franklin Inst., Seismol. Soc. America, Am. Legion, Am. Concrete Inst. Author: Dynamics of Earthquake Resistant Structures, 1934. Contbr. on engring. subjects. Home: 5720 Malvern Av., Philadelphia; also 1 University Place, New York, N.Y. Office: Girard Trust Bldg., Philadelphia, Pa.; 30 Rockefeller Plaza, New York, N.Y.

CRESSMAN, Henry Milton, county supt. schs.; b. Sellersville, Pa., Nov. 17, 1871; s. Henry S. and Sarah A. (Snyder) C.; ed. Sellersville pub. schs.; student Bethlehem Prep. Sch., 1890-91; B.A., Lehigh U., 1895, M.A., 1901; Pd.D., Muhlenberg Coll., 1916; m. Emma F. Jacoby, Aug. 21, 1895; children—Ruth (Mrs. Spurgeon Cross), Paul (dec.); m. 2d, Harriet A. Simpson, July 20, 1928. Teacher Springtown, Pa., 1887-88, Rock Hill Twp., 1888-90; prin. schs.,

Egg Harbor City, N.J., 1895-1904, supervising prin., 1904-09; county supt. of schs., Atlantic Co., since 1909; pres. Egg Harbor Commercial Bank, Egg Harbor Bldg. & Loan Assn.; dir. Chelsea Title & Guarantee Co.; first pres. Egg Harbor City Gas Co. (now part of Atlantic City Electric Co.), 1904. Chmn. local branch Am. Red cross since 1917. Mem. Am. Assn. Sch. Supts., N.E.A. (life), Council of Edn. Republican. Lutheran. Mason, Odd Fellow, Grange, Tall Cedars. Club: Egg Harbor City Kiwanis (Dist. Gov. N.J. Dist., Kiwanis Internat., 1932). Home: Egg Harbor City, N.J.

CRESSMAN, Paul LeRoy, educator; b. Springtown, Pa., Apr. 29, 1893; s. George Landis and Clara Arabella (Meyers) C.; grad. State Teachers Coll., Kutztown, Pa., 1912; B.S., U. of Pittsburgh, 1925; grad. work at Columbia; Ed.D., Pa. State Coll., 1934; m. Lenora Grace LeClaire, Lehighton, Pa., June 24, 1916; children—Claire Marie, Hazel Irene, Paul LeRoy. Grade teacher and elementary sch. prin., Lehighton, Pa., 1912-15; head industrial arts dept., State Normal Sch., Bloomsburg, Pa., 1915-18; head industrial arts dept., high sch., Uniontown, Pa., 1918-20, cabinet trade instr., Acad. High Sch., Erie, Pa., 1920-21; dir. vocational edn., Erie City Sch., Pa., 1921-24; supervisor and later dir. of industrial edn., State Dept. Pub. Instrn., Pa., 1924-34; asst. supt. pub. instrn., Lansing, Mich., 1934-36; dir. Bur. of Instrn., Dept. Pub. Instrn., Harrisburg, Pa., since 1936; instr. in summer school, U. of Pittsburgh, 1924-25, Pa. State Coll., 1928-35. Chmn. nat. com. creating Future Craftsmen of America. Mem. Nat. Conf. on Supervised Correspondence Study, Part-time Edn. Com. of the Am. Vocational Assn., Middle States Assn. Colleges and Secondary Schs., Private Business Schs. of Pa. (mem. accrediting com.), Kappa Phi Kappa, Iota Lambda Sigma, Phi Sigma Pi, N.E.A., Am. Voc. Assn., Pa. State Ednl. Assn., Pa. Branch Nat. Dept. Secondary Sch. Prins. Methodist. Author: Junior Mechanics Handbook, 1931, Junior Mechanics Ceremonial, 1931-33. Contbr. to Industrial Arts and Vocational Edn. Mag., Industrial Edn. Mag., Furniture Manufacturer and Artisan Mag., Jour. of the A.V.A. Home: 33 E. Main St., Mechanicsburg, Pa. Office: Dept. of Public Instruction, Harrisburg, Pa.

CRESSMAN, W.D.; editor Norristown Times Herald. Address: Markley and Ann Sts., Norristown, Pa.

CRESSWELL, Donaldson, banker; b. Phila., Pa., May 26, 1902; s. Robert and Elise Hill (Donaldson) C.; grad. St. Luke's Sch., Wayne, Pa., 1919; A.B., Princeton U., 1924; LL.B., U. of Pa., 1927; m. Elizabeth Potter Stewart, June 16, 1926; children—Elizabeth Sturgis Potter, Elise Donaldson, Audrey. Admitted to Pa. bar, 1928; law dept. Penn Mutual Life Ins. Co., 1928-33, asso. counsel, 1933-34; asst. to the pres. The Phila. Saving Fund Soc., 1934-38, vice-pres. since 1939. Mem. Corpn. for Relief of Widows and Children of Clergymen of Episcopal Ch. in Pa. Trustee Pa. Sch. for the Deaf. Republican. Episcopalian. Clubs: Philadelphia, Rabbit, Gulph Mills Golf (Phila.); Ivy (Princeton, N.J.). Home: Hillbrook Rd., Bryn Mawr, Pa. Office: 1212 Market St., Philadelphia, Pa.

CRET, Paul Philippe, architeet; b. Lyons, France, Oct. 23, 1876; s. Paul Adolphe and Anna Caroline (Durand) C.; ed. Lycée of Bourg, École des Beaux Arts, Lyons, École des Beaux Arts, Paris; architecte diplômé du gouvernement français, 1903 (Sc.D., 1913); m. Marguerite Lahalle, Aug. 1905. Prof. design, Univ. of Pa., 1903-37, prof. emeritus since 1937, now associate trustee. Paris prize, 1896, Rougevin prize, 1901, and grand medal of emulation, École des Beaux Arts, Paris, 1901; gold medal, Salon des Champs Elysées, Paris, 1903; medal of honor, Architectural League of New York; Philadelphia award (Bok prize), 1931; distinguished award Washington Soc. Architects; gold medalist of A.I.A.; gold medal Pan.-Am. Expn.; grand prize, Paris, 1937. Architect (with Albert Kelsey) of Pan-American Union (Washington, D.C.); Valley Forge memorial arch, Rittenhouse Square, Philadelphia; Indianapolis Pub. Library (with Zantzinger, Borie and Medary); Detroit Institute of Arts (with Zantzinger, Borie and Medary); Hartford County Bldg.; Folger Shakespeare Library (Washington); Hall of Science at Century of Progress Expn., Chicago, 1933; Federal Reserve Bank and Delaware River Bridge, Phila.; war memorials at Varennes, Fismes (France); memorials at Chateau Thierry, Bony, Waereghem and Gibraltar for Am. Battle Monuments Commn.; Central Heating Plant, Washington; new bldgs. U. of Tex.; Federal Res. Bd. Bldg., Washington; Calvert St. Bridge; new bldgs. U.S. Mil. Acad., West Point, N.Y. Nat. Academician; mem. Am. Philos. Soc., N.Y. Inst. Arts and Letters, Art Jury, City of Phila. Member Société architectes diplômés, Soc. Beaux Arts Architects, T-Square Club (hon. pres.); fellow A.I.A.; hon. corr. mem. Royal Inst. Brit. Architects. Trustee Phila. Museum. Consultant bd. of design N.Y. Expn., 1939. Served in French Army and with 1st Div., A.E.F., 1914-19. Officer Legion of Honor, and Croix de Guerre (France). Mem. Archtl. Commn., Chicago World's Fair Centennial Celebration, 1933; consulting architect Am. Battle Monuments Commn., also Brown Univ. and univs. of Tex. and Pa. and Wis. Clubs: Racquet, Art, Art Alliance (Philadelphia); Century (New York). Home: 516 Woodland Terrace. Office: Architects Bldg., Philadelphia, Pa.

CRETCHER, Leonard Harrison, chemist; b. DeGraff, O., July 25, 1888; s. Harry Donelly and Nancy (Black) C.; A.B., U. of Mich., 1912; Ph.D., Yale, 1916; m. Frances L. Hickok, July 10, 1920. Instr. U. of Tenn., 1913-14; fellow Rockefeller Inst. for Med. Research, 1916-18; chemist Nat. Aniline and Chem. Co., 1919-22; sr. fellow in pure research, Mellon Inst., 1922-26, head dept. research in pure chemistry since 1926, asst. dir. Inst. since 1931; lecturer chemistry, U. of Pittsburgh since 1924. Capt., C.W.S., U.S.A., World War. Fellow A.A.A.S.; mem. Am. Soc. Biol. Chemists, Am. Chem. Soc. (chmn. Pittsburgh sect. 1931), Sigma Xi, Phi Lambda Upsilon, Theta Chi. Clubs: U. of Pittsburgh Faculty, University. Contbr. many papers on scientific subjects. Mem. bd. editors Journal of Organic Chemistry. Home: Dithridge Apts., Pittsburgh, Pa.

CRIBBS, Charles Clair, clergyman; b. Clarksburg, Pa., Nov. 8, 1880; s. Armour P. and Martha Ella (Marshall) C.; grad. Elders Ridge Acad., Eldersridge, Pa., 1905; A.B., Grove City (Pa.) Coll., 1908, A.M., 1908, D.D., 1924; B.S.T., Western Theol. Sem., Pittsburgh, 1911; m. Cecil Augusta Stewart, June 7, 1911; children—Mary Elizabeth (Mrs. Ralph Dunbar Pyle), Marjorie Cecil, Mildred Josephine. Ordained to ministry of Presbyterian Ch., May 1911; pastor East Butler, Pa., 1911-13, Beechwoods Presbyn. Ch., Falls Creek, Pa., 1913-19, First Presbyn. Ch., Apollo, Pa., 1919-23, First Presbyn. Ch., Ingram, Pittsburgh, since 1923. Republican. Mason (K.T.). Home: 94 W. Prospect Av., Ingram, Pittsburgh, Pa.

CRICHTON, Andrew B., engring. and coal mining; b. Arnot, Pa., Mar. 4, 1882; s. William and Margaret (Nelson) C.; ed. pub. schs. and pvt. instrn.; m. Edith Masters, Jan. 8, 1910 (dec.); children—Andrew Beachly, Clarendon Nelson, Robert Masters, Mary Edith. Engaged as cons. mining engr., Johnstown, Pa., since 1904; pres. Johnstown Coal & Coke Co., mine operators and wholesale coal, since 1917; pres. Vindex Supply Co., Chaffee Railroad Co., The Manor Coal Co., Portage Fuel Co.; sec. and treas. Martin Realty Co. Mem. Pa. State Registration Bd. for Professional Engrs.; dir. and pres. Westmont Sch. Bd. two terms. Dir. Family Welfare Soc., Pa. State Chamber of Commerce; councillor (state and nat.) Johnstown Chamber of Commerce; dir. Conemaugh Valley Memorial Hosp. Mem. Am. Inst. Mining and Metall. Engrs., Tri-County Engring. Soc., Central Pa. Coal Producers Assn. (dir.), Eastern Bituminous Coal Assn. Republican. Presbyterian. Mason. Clubs: Bachelors, Sunnehanna. Home: 800 Luzerne St. Office: 1006 U.S. Nat. Bank Bldg., Johnstown, Pa.

CRICHTON, Walter Greig, coal operator; b. Philipsburg, Pa., June 30, 1888; s. William and Margret (Nelson) C.; student W.Va. Univ., 1908-11; m. Elizabeth Thomas, Oct. 15, 1912; children—Margret Catherine (Mrs. C. T. McHenry), Griffith Thomas, Walter Greig, Jr., Robert Andrew, Harry Nelson. Has followed profession as mining engr. since 1911; pres. Crichton Engineering Co., Charleston, W.Va., since 1915; engaged as coal operator since 1920, vice-pres. Johnstown Coal & Coke Co., Charleston, W.Va., since 1921; vice-pres. and dir. The Nat. Bank of Commerce of Charleston, W.Va., since 1927. Mem. Am. Inst. Mining Engrs., Sigma Phi Epsilon. Presbyn. Mason (Shriner). Club: Kanawha Country (Charleston). Home: 1626 Kanawha St. Office: Nat. Bank of Commerce Bldg., Charleston, W.Va.

CRICHTON, William Jr., coal mine operator; b. Gurnee, Tioga Co., Pa., Mar. 12, 1884; s. William and Margaret (Nelson) C.; ed. Peale (Pa.) Elementary Sch., 1890-95; m. Addaline Morrisey, Dec. 25, 1901; children—William Albert, Helen Mary. Began as mine furnace tender, Peale, Pa., 1896, and engaged in all phases of mining, 1896-1915; mfg. and wholesaling elec. machinery and supplies, Charleston, W.Va., 1915-23; engaged as mine mgr. with other connections on side since 1923; mgr. and dir. Johnstown Coal & Coke Co., bituminous coal mine operators, Pa., Md., W.Va., since 1916; v.p. and dir. Va. Electric, Inc., Charleston, W.Va., since 1936; dir. Nat. Bank of Commerce, Electric Home Appliance Co. Mem. Greenbrier Smokeless Coal Assn. (sec. since 1933), Nat. Coal Assn., W.Va. Coal Assn., Am. Mining Cong., W.Va. Coal Mining Inst. Mason. Home: 1594 Jackson St., Charleston, W.Va. Office: Crichton, W.Va.

CRIDLAND, Harry Clifford, clergyman; b. Dayton, O., Aug. 28, 1879; s. Thomas Harper and Cora A. (Joyce) G.; ed. Ohio State U., 1899-1900, Harvard, 1906-07; m. Grace Lenore Faust, Feb. 21, 1901; children—Josephine Lenore (Mrs. Paul K. Noel), Thanet Faust. Began as mech. draftsman, 1900; pastor Susquehanna Charge, Allegheny Conf., 1935-37; pastor Schum Memorial Ch., Altoona, Pa., since 1937; mem. Bd. Christian Edn., Bd. Adminstrn. U.B. Ch. at Dayton, O.; pres. U.B. Ministerium of Altoona. Republican. Mem. United Brethren in Christ. Home: 4126 Broad Av., Altoona, Pa.

CRISPIN, M(ordecai) Jackson, historian and banker; b. Berwick, Pa., May 13, 1875; s. Benjamin Franklin and Margaret (Jackson) C.; desc. Capt. and Rear Adm. William C. and Rebecca (Bradshaw) grand-daughter of Capt. Giles Penn, the grandfather of William Penn; A.B., Princeton University, 1896; m. Marie Brockway, June 7, 1900 (died 1907); 1 dau., Elizabeth Brockway (wife of Count Olivero Tripcovich of Trieste, Italy); m. 2d, Erma Marchant, Apr. 3, 1916 (div.); m. 3d, Andree Detrez, Sept. 23, 1931; 1 dau., Jacqueline Margaret. In employ First Nat. Bank, Berwick, Pa., 1896; with Jackson & Woodin Mfg. Co., Berwick, 1897-99, and successor Am. Car & Foundry Co., 1899-1901; gen. mgr. and treas. United States Metal & Mfg. Co., New York City, 1901-16; with New York City office Am. Car & Foundry Co. as dir. purchase of materials for mfg. arms for Allies during U.S. participation in World War, 1917-20; engaged in pvt. investments, 1920-29; dir. since 1903, pres. since 1909 of First Nat. Bank (in continuous operation since chartered, 1864), Berwick, Pa.; served as trustee Crispin Cemetery (pvt.) since 1924, inc. 1843 to care for 1-acre cemetery in City of Phila. provided for in will Capt. Thomas Holme, first surveyor gen. of Pa., buried there, 1695, and many Crispin descs. to 1863, surrounded by the City, 1928, by the Holme-Crispin Park; in research work on Crispin genealogy in Eng. and France, summers 1925-30; mem. com. and in direct charge research to compile and complete Falaise Roll of seigneurs of William the Conqueror, with offices in Paris, 1930-35; dec. Officer of the Acad. (France) for this work; later corrected and wrote the publ. the Roll, and dec. Chevalier of Legion of Honor (France); served as gen. chmn. Sesquicentennial Com., Berwick, Pa., and entertained mayor and ofcls. of Berwick-on-Tweed, Eng., 1936, and in honor of Berwick the Council of Berwick-on-Tweed named a street in that city, "Crispin Road," 1938; always active in local civic affairs; donated to Berwick

High Sch. the Crispin Memorial athletic field, 1929; donated ground for Berwick Hosp. and Nurses Home; Dept. Pa. of Am. Legion officially cited him for distinguished services, 1938. Mem. Soc. Colonial Wars, S.A.R., Patriotic Order Sons of America, Am. Soc. of French Legion of Honor. Awarded silver medal by Am. Car & Foundry Co. for services in World War. Republican (del. Nat. Rep. Conv. 1916). Episcopalian. Mason (32°). Clubs: Berwick Golf (pres. 1936-38); Valley Country (Hazleton, Pa.); Westmoreland (Wilkes-Barre); Racquet (Philadelphia); University, Bankers, Princeton (New York); American (Paris). Author, editor and compiler, Falaise Roll, 1938; author: Captain William Crispin; Crispin's of Kingston-on-Hull; Thomas Holme Tercentenary; author, hist. monographs pvtly. printed; contbr. many articles on history and genealogy to hist. publs. Home: Berwick, Pa.

CRISS, Nicholas R(ittenhouse), lawyer; b. Washington Co., Pa., Jan. 5, 1873; s. Rittenhouse and Eliza Jane (Stewart) C.; desc. of Rittenhouse family which settled in Phila., 1688; student Grove City (Pa.) Coll., 1898-99; LL.B., Western U. of Pa. (now U. of Pittsburgh), 1903; hon. LL.D., U. of Pittsburgh, 1929; m. Anna B. Scott, June 15, 1909; children—Catherine Jane (Mrs. J. Byron Jones), Nicholas Rittenhouse. Began as teacher, 1892-1900; admitted to Pa. bar, 1903, and since practiced in Pittsburgh; solicitor Sch. Dist. of Pittsburgh since 1933; solicitor and dir. Sheradan Bank, Sheradan Bldg. & Loan Assn. Served as govt. appeal agt., 4-min. speaker, etc., during World War. Mem. Pa. and Allegheny Co. bar assns. Independent Republican. Presbyterian. Mason. Club: Alcoma Golf (Pittsburgh). Home: 119 Yorkshire Rd. Office: 808 Law and Finance Bldg., Pittsburgh, Pa.

CRIST, Richard Harrison, artist; b. Cleveland, O., Nov. 1, 1909; s. Robert Way and Bertha (Widdecombe) C.; grad. Bedford (O.) High Sch., 1926; student Carnegie Inst. Tech., Fine Arts Coll., Pittsburgh, 1926-28, Art. Inst. of Chicago, 1928-32; m. Ida Szecskay, Feb. 23, 1938. Awarded Am. Traveling scholarship (painting trip to Mexico), 1931; painted in New York, N.Y., 1932-33, Mexico, 1935, 38, Europe, 1937; dir. Bessemer Gallery, Pittsburgh. Exhibited paintings Art Inst. Chicago, Carnegie Inst. (Pittsburgh), Art Center (New York), Cincinnati Mus. Art, Butler Inst. (Youngstown). Painted mural, Prospect High Sch., Pittsburgh. Awarded 1st prize, 1932, Ida Smith prize, 1934, Benedum prize, 1938, Art Soc. prize, 1936, Asso. Artists of Pittsburgh annual exbns. Mem. Delta Tau Delta. Address: 3431 Forbes St., Pittsburgh, Pa.

CRIST, Samuel Smith, editor and publisher; b. Columbia, Pa., June 19, 1898; s. William Edward and Ida Catherine (Smith) C.; grad. Columbia (Pa.) High Sch., 1917; student Mercersburg (Pa.) Acad., 1917-18, Franklin and Marshall Coll., Lancaster, Pa., 1918-20; m. Jeannette Pearl Bernard, May 4, 1920; children—Edward Nevin, Jeanne Bernard, Samuel Smith, Dorothy Kay. In newspaper business since 1920; editor and pub. of The Columbia (Pa.) News since 1935; dir. Columbia Coal & Ice Co. Mem. Delta Sigma Phi. Republican. Presbyterian. Elk, Eagle. Clubs: Rotary, Columbia Canoe, Susquehannock Boat. Home: 508 Chestnut St. Office: 326 Locust St., Columbia, Pa.

CRITCHFIELD, Margaret E., librarian; b. Johnstown, Pa., 1903; d. John B. and Estelle (McCaffrey) Critchfield; student Penn Hall Sch. for Girls, 1920-21; B.S., Skidmore Coll., Saratoga Springs, N.Y., 1925; M.A., New York U.; grad. study Columbia Pratt Inst. Library Sch., 1925-26, U. of Pa., 1938. Jr. asst., Annie Halenbake Ross Library, Lock Haven, Pa., 1917-21; asst. Pa. State Teachers Coll. Library, Lock Haven, Pa., summers 1921-26; librarian Conn. State Teachers Coll., Danbury, 1926-31, Lancaster (Pa.) Free Pub. Library since 1931; instr. in library science, Temple U., summer 1934. Mem. Am. Library Assn., Pa. Library Assn., D.A.R., Conn. Nonpartisan League of Nations Assn., B. and P. W. Club. Author: State Course of Study in Use of Books and Libraries to be Taught in Normal Schools of Conn.; contbr. book reviews to newspapers and mags. Lecturer on books for children, and contemporary literature. Address: Lancaster Free Public Library, Lancaster, Pa.

CROASDALE, Francis Egbert, newspaper editor; b. Atlantic City, N.J., Oct. 6, 1886; s. Charles Wilson and Anna Frances (Conover) C.; grad. high sch., Atlantic City, 1904; m. Helen Florence Thorne, June 14, 1916; children—Charles Wilson, Frances Ella, Patricia Helen, Richard Bowen. Began with Atlantic City Daily Press, Atlantic City, 1906; editor Atlantic City Daily Press, Atlantic City Evening Union, Atlantic City Sunday Press since 1919. Sec. to Speaker Carlton Godfrey of N.J. Ho. of Assembly, 1915, to Gov. Walter E. Edge, 1917-19; librarian N.J. State Library, 1919-24; mem. N.J. Pub. Library Commn. Mem. Associated Press, N.J. Press Assn., N.J. Correspondents' Club. Republican. Presbyn. Home: 6101 Ventnor Av., Ventnor City, N.J. Mediterranean and Virginia Av., Atlantic City, N.J.

CROCCO, Anthony Edward; b. Genoa, Italy, July 20, 1865; s. Bartholomew and Marguerite (Bruzzo) C.; brought to U.S., 1880; student Commercial High Sch., Genoa, 1876-80, night schs., N.Y. City, 1880-83; m. Carmela Sciutti, Sept. 28, 1888 (dec.); children—Margaret Irene (dec.), Edward Andrew, Albert Richard, Anita Veronica, Walter Cyril, Gladys Angela (dec.). Compositor, 1882-86; foreman composing room of newspaper, 1887-92; linotype operator and machine tender, 1893-97; asst. to circulation mgr. Progress, newspaper, 1897-1904, in charge circulation, 1904-09, asst. to editor and business mgr., 1909-11, business mgr., 1911-19; treas. and mgr. Colonial Food Product Corpn., 1919-21, and successors, The DeMartini Macaroni Co., Jersey City, 1921-23; gen. mgr. and treas. Tiber Pub. Corpn., 1924-32; organized Crocco-Vicenzi Co., Inc., 1933, resigned, 1935. Spl. work for Intelligence Dept., in Italy, during World War. Decorated Order of the Crown of Italy, 1930. Democrat. Catholic. Elk. Home: 166 Franklin Av., Ridgewood, N.J.

CROCKER, Walter James, veterinarian; b. Ada, Minn., Nov. 20, 1885; s. Walter Joseph and Helen (Wiley) C.; B.S.A., Utah Agrl. Coll., 1909; V.M.D., U. of Pa., 1911; m. Rosa Binder, Feb. 6, 1915; 1 dau., Helen Marie. Lecturer and instr., 1911-13, asst. prof. vet. pathology, 1913-14, asst. prof. vet. pathology and bacteriology, 1914-16, prof. vet. pathology since Apr. 1916, Vet. Sch. U. of Pa.; asst. dir. Wistar Inst. of Anatomy and Biology, U. of Pa., 1920-21; dist. mgr. J. Lee Nicholson Inst., 1921; gen. mgr. Globe Laboratories, 1922-24; dir. Globe Labs., Globe Livestock Co. and Cleo Ranch Co., 1923-25; clin. pathologist, Phila. Gen.Hosp., since 1925. Mem. Am., Pa. State and Keystone vet. med. socs., Phila. Pathol. Soc., Internat. Assn. Vet. Med. Museums, Dallas and Fort Worth Vet. Med. Assn., Tex. Vet. Med. Assn., Sigma Xi, Sigma Alpha, Alpha Psi. Republican. Episcopalian. Mason (33°, Shriner). Club: University. Author: Veterinary Post Mortem Technic, 1917. Translator: Mastitis of the Cow and Its Treatment (by Sven Wall), 1918. Contbr. numerous scientific articles on hematology; hemography in diagnosis, prognosis and treatment; hemography in the diagnosis of appendicitis; nonspecific immune-transfusion in the treatment of septicemia and typhoid fever. Home: 5909 Christian St., West Philadelphia, Pa.

CROCKETT, James M., associate judge; b. Pocomoke City, Md., Oct. 23, 1886; s. Charles W. and Mary E. (Brown) C.; grad. Pocomoke City High Sch., 1904; LL.B., U. of Md., 1911; m. Lelia J. Bounds, June 3, 1919; 1 dau., Mary Priscilla. Admitted to Md. bar, 1911, and practiced in Pocomoke City, 1911-34; judge 1st Judicial Circuit of Md. since 1934. Mem. Md. State Senate, 1928-30. Mem. Md. State Bar Assn. Democrat. Methodist. Mason. Address: Pocomoke City, Md.

CROCKETT, Joseph M.; mem. law firm Crockett & Tutwiler. Address: Welch, W.Va.

CROFOOT, George Emerson; prof. mech. engring., U. of Pa. Address: U. of Pennsylvania, Philadelphia, Pa.

CROKER, Maria Briscoe, poet, lecturer, historian; b. Charlotte Hall, Md.; d. Edward Tayloe and Sallie (Vaughan) Briscoe; diploma, State Teachers Coll., Baltimore, 1893; student St. Mary's Sem., St. Mary's County, Md., 1889-90; certificate of completion, U.S. Sch. of Writing, New York (correspondence), 1936-37; m. Edward Joseph Croker, Aug. 24, 1895 (died 1933); children—Edward Briscoe (dec.), Dorothy G. (Mrs. Charles Lewis Lea), Douglas Vaughan, John Hanson, Nanette Frances (Mrs. Randolph Fenton). Prin. High Sch., St. Marys Co., Md., 1907-08; teacher of English, Berlitz Sch., Baltimore, Md., 1913-14. Served on Governor Ritchie's Commn. for Md. Tercentenary, 1933-34. Mem. D.A.R. (state chmn. Md. Tercentenary, 1932-34); formerly mem. The Soc. of the Ark and the Dove of Md. (mem. of council); mem. Poetry Soc. of America, League of Am. Pen Women (nat. registrar and librarian, 1933-37). Awarded Poet's Parchment for Md. by Nat. Poetry Center of N.Y., 1937; 3d award for non-fiction by League of Am. Pen Women, 1936. Episcopalian. Club: Woman's Literary of Baltimore (Md.; past v.p.). Author: Vision and Verity, poems, 1926; Tales and Traditions of Old St. Mary's historical sketches, 1934; Land of the Singing Rivers, poems, 1934; poetry in numerous periodicals and newspapers, Governor's delegate to Congress of Am. Poets, New York City, 1936-38. Address: 2624 St. Paul St., Baltimore, Md.

CROLL, Edward Everett, newspaper editor; b. Womelsdorf, Pa., Jan. 15, 1881; s. Rev. Philip C. and Sarah A. (Greiss) C.; ed. Lebanon (Pa.) High Sch.; m. Margie Elizabeth Gustina Dengler, June 23, 1909; children—Gustina May, Sarah Rebecca (Mrs. Martin H. Cronlund), Philip Dengler, Edwina. Began as a printer, Lebanon, Pa., 1898; reporter, later city editor, Lebanon (Pa.) Report, 1900-02; corr. Harrisburg Patriot, Phila. Inquirer, 1902-04; with Phila. Ledger since 1910, successively as reporter, copy reader, night editor and asst. editor. Mem. Am. Soc. Newspaper Editors, Pa. German Soc. Republican. Lutheran. Clubs: Philadelphia Art Alliance, Down Town, Horse Shoe Trail (Phila.). Home: 264 Mather Rd., Jenkintown, Pa. Office: Public Ledger, Philadelphia, Pa.

CROLL, Morris William, univ. prof.; b. Gettysburg, Pa., Apr. 16, 1872; s. Luther Henry and Jane Crawford (Smyth) C.; A.B., Gettysburg (Pa.) Coll., 1889, hon. Litt.D., 1932; A.B., Harvard, 1894, A.M., 1895; Ph.D., U. of Pa., 1901; unmarried. Teacher, University Sch., Cleveland, O., 1895-99; asso. editor Lippincott Worcester Dictionary, 1901-05; instr. in English Literature, Princeton U., 1905-06, asst. prof., 1906-18, asso. prof., 1918-23, prof., 1923-32, prof. emeritus since 1932. Mem. Modern Lang. Assn. America, Am. Acad. Arts and Sciences. Democrat. Lutheran. Club: Princeton (New York). Editor: Lyly's Euphues (with H. L. Clemons), 1916. Contbr. articles on English prose style of 16th and 17th Centuries to professional jours. Home: 40 Bayard Lane, Princeton, N.J.

CROLL, Philip C., clergyman; b. nr. Kutztown, Pa., Oct. 2, 1852; s. John and Katharine (DeLong) C.; prep. edn. State Normal Sch., Kutztown; A.B., Pa. Coll., Gettysburg, Pa., 1876, A.M., 1879, D.D., 1904; grad. Theol. Sem., Gettysburg, 1879; m. Sallie A. Greiss, Mar. 11, 1880; children—Edward Everett, Rose Wentworth, Herbert Greiss, Aimee Katharine, Raymond Philip, Paul Revere, Alden Theodore, Hilda Marion. Ordained Luth. ministry, 1879; pastor Womelsdorf, Pa., 1879-82, Schuylkill Haven, Pa., 1882-92, Lebanon, Pa., 1892-1909, Beardstown, Ill., 1909-21. Mem. Pa. Bible Soc. (life), Pa. German Soc., Lebanon Co. (Pa.) Hist. Soc., Ill. State Hist. Soc., Berks Co. (Pa.) Hist. Soc. Author: The Golden Wedding Ring, 1887; Historic Landmarks of the Lebanon Valley, 1895; Annals of Womelsdorf, 1923; Talpehocken Bicentennial, 1923. Translator: Jewish Artisan Life (by Delitzsch), 1883; Jesus and Hillel (by same), 1884; Alli, or The Blessed are the Merciful (by Hoffman), 1886. Contbr. verse and articles to mags. Home: Womelsdorf, Pa.

CROLLY, John William, lawyer; b. Scranton, Pa., Nov. 3, 1889; s. John G. and Mary J.

(Scott) C.; student pub. schs., Scranton, Pa., 1896-1904, St. Thomas Coll., Scranton, 1904-08; LL.B., Catholic U. Law Sch., Washington, D.C., 1915; m. Helen L. Kehoe, Feb. 12, 1918; children—John William, Anne K. Admitted to D.C. bar, 1916, and practiced at Washington, D.C., 1916-21; admitted to Pa. bar, 1921, and practiced at Phila., 1921-35; now in practice at Scranton; sec.-treas. Clark & Scott Co., mfrs. tobacco, Scranton. Served as 1st lt., 1st Officers Training Camp, Madison Barracks, New York, 1917. Life mem. Lincoln Legion of Honor of Lincoln Memorial U.; mem. Am. Bar Assn., Lackawanna Co. Bar Assn., Am. Legion. Democrat. Catholic. Home: 449 Arthur Av. Office: 409-12 Lincoln Trust Bldg., Scranton, Pa.

CROMER, Clinton Otis, prof. crop production; b. Middletown, Ind., Feb. 2, 1881; s. Rush Henry and Emma Frances (Sayford) C.; B.S. in Agr., Purdue U., 1906; M.S. in Agr., U. of Wis., 1937; m. Abbie Eliza Henby, of Greenfield, Ind., Mar. 23, 1921; children—Ruth Frances, Ellen Muriel. Engaged as asst. agronomist, Purdue U., 1906-1914, asso. agronomist, 1914-20; prof. crop production, Pa. State Coll. since 1920, in charge of farm crop instruction since 1920; propr. of farm in Ind. operated on share basis. Mem. Am. Assn. of Agronomy, Delta Chi. Republican. Methodist. Home: 630 W. Fairmount Av., State College, Pa.

CROMIE, William James, physical instr.; b. New Castle, Pa., Oct. 27, 1875; s. Robert and Annie (Beck) C.; ed. pub. schs. and Y.M.C.A. and Harvard summer schs.; Sc.D., 1920; m. Erma Gertrude Apple, Aug. 4, 1898; 1 dau., Erma Kathryn. Phys. dir. Y.M.C.A., New Castle, Pa., 1896, Aurora, Ill., 1897-98, Easton, Pa., 1899-1902, Germantown, Phila., 1903-04, 1905-06; instr. in gymnastics, 1907-12, in physical edn., 1913-16, acting dir. phys. edn., 1915-16, asst. dir., 1919-25, asst. dir. and asst. prof. phys. edn. since 1925, U. of Pa.; also dir. summer sch. course in phys. edn., U. of Pa. Instr. R.O.T.C. in U. of Pa., 1917; attended Bayonet and P.T. Sch., Ottawa, Can., 1918; instr. Central Bayonet and Physical Training Sch., S.A.T.C., Princeton U.; athletic dir. Camp Eustis, Va., 1918; instr. U. of Pa. S.A.T.C. and Naval Unit. Mem. Am. Physical Edn. Soc., Soc. Physical Edn. in Colls., Phi Epsilon Kappa, Sigma Pi. Republican. Presbyn. Mason. Author: Keeping Physically Fit, 1915; Gymnastics in Education, 1925; Volley Ball in School and College, 1937; also series of 12 pamphlets on phys. exercises for promotion of health; 325 group contests for army, navy and school, 1918. Contbr. to Outlook, Saturday Evening Post, Woman's Home Companion, American Magazine, Pictorial Review, etc. Home: 5324 Reinhard St., West Philadelphia, Pa.

CROMWELL, Doris Duke; b. New York, N.Y., Nov. 22, 1912; d. James Buchanan and Nanaline (Holt) Duke; student Brearley Sch., New York City, 1922-28, Ferniata Sch., Aiken, S.C., 1928-29, in Paris, 1930; m. James H. R. Cromwell, Feb. 13, 1935. Mem. bd. Duke Endowment since 1933, Institutions and Agencies of N.J. since 1938. Protestant. Clubs: River, Colony (New York City). Home: Somerville, N.J.

CROOKS, Esther Josephine; prof. Spanish, Goucher Coll. Address: Goucher Coll., Baltimore, Md.

CROOKS, Ezra Breckenridge, univ. prof.; b. Clinton, Ky., Oct. 6, 1874; s. James David and Mary Elizabeth (Bugg) C.; B.A., Central Coll., Fayette, Mo., 1899; M.A., Vanderbilt, 1901; S.T.B., Harvard, 1908, M.A., 1909, Ph.D., 1910; m. Mary Elizabeth Groves, Sept. 10, 1902 (died 1906); m. 2d, Mary Lasher, Sept. 8, 1909; children—Anna Elizabeth, James Lasher. Editor St. Louis Christian Advocate, 1901; ednl. missionary M.E. Ch., S., Brazil, 1902-06; asst. in depts. philosophy and history, Harvard, 1910-11; asst. prof. philosophy, Northwestern U., 1911-13; head dept. philosophy and edn., Randolph-Macon Woman's Coll., Lynchburg, Va., 1913-22; head dept. philosophy and social sciences, U. of Del., since 1922; also editor Delaware Notes (yearly publ. by members of faculty U. of Del.). Dir. publicity U.S. Food Administration in Va., 1917-18; went to France under Y.M.C.A. and was with Portuguese Troops, British 5th Army. Fellow A.A.A.S.; mem. Am. Philos. Assn., Am. Sociol. Soc., N.E.A., Am. Assn. Univ. Profs., Sigma Alpha Epsilon, Phi Kappa Phi. Decorated officer Mil. Order of Christ (Portuguese); two citations from the field. Democrat. Methodist. Clubs: University (Newark); Lions (Lynchburg); Harvard (Wilmington); Torch Club of Del. Home: Newark, Del.

CROOKS, Forrest Corydon, artist and craftsman; b. Goshen, Ind., Oct. 1, 1893; s. Amos Delson and Alta (Oman) C.; A.B., Carnegie Inst. Tech., 1917; m. Irene Phelps, 1918; children—Forrest Corydon, Malcolm Phelps. Engaged as commercial artist since 1917; illustrator for most of the well known mags. of nat. circulation; cartoon draftsman on stained glass windows for Sotter Stained Glass studio; designer of hand looms; one loom design published in Country Gentleman has had nat. recognition; another loom of his design has been put on the market. Dir. George Sch. Mem. Guild of Free Lance Artists & Asso. Handweavers. Republican. Soc. of Friends. Contbr. articles on marionettes, looms and weaving to Country Gentleman. Home: Solebury, Pa.

CROOKS, (Alexander) Richard, tenor; b. Trenton, N.J.; s. Alexander Struthers and Elizabeth (Gore) C.; ed. high sch., Trenton; m. Mildred Wallace Pine, July 23, 1921; children—Patricia, Richard. Began as boy soprano soloist in ch.; made début as boy soprano with Mme. Schumann-Heink, Asbury Park, N.J., 1910; début as tenor with New York Symphony Orchestra, Walter Damrosch, condr., 1922; European concert tour, 1925; operatic début in Tosca, Hamburg (Germany) Opera, 1927; début Metropolitan Opera, New York, 1933; concert tour of Australia, New Zealand and Tasmania, 1936. Served as cadet flying officer, Air Service, U.S.A., World War. Methodist. Home: Sea Girt, N.J. Address: Columbia Concerts Corpn., 113 W. 57th St., New York, N.Y.

CROOKS, Thomas L. R.; chmn. bd., pres. and dir. Clinton Trust Co. Home: 619 Prospect St., Maplewood, N.J. Office: 505 Clinton Av., Newark, N.J.

CROSBY, Charles Noel, ex-congressman; b. Cherry Valley, O., Sept. 29, 1876; s. Hiram William and Fanny (Spellman) C.; student New Lyme (Ohio) Inst., 1889-93; B.S., Western Reserve U., 1896; student Allegheny Coll., 1896-97; m. Isabelle Fetterman, 1901; children—Fanny, Theodore, Jean, Penelope (Mrs. R. A. Donaldson), Virginia, Charles N., Ronald, John, Ann. Organizer, 1901, National Silo & Lumber Company (later merged into International Silo Company), pres. and gen. mgr., 1901-33; bought control of Bunday Lumber Co., 1927. Owner and operator of 2 farms in Pa. and Ohio. Mem. 73d to 75th Congresses (1933-39), 29th Pa. Dist. Mem. Linesville and Meadville Sch. Bds., 1920-29; pres. Meadville Chamber of Commerce, 1922-24. Mem. Beta Theta Pi. Democrat. Presbyn. Club: Iroquois. Home: Meadville, Pa.

CROSBY, Henry Lamar, prof. Greek; b. Menominee, Mich., May 17, 1880; s. William Henry and Stella Maria (Sexmith) C.; B.A., U. of Tex., 1901, M.A., 1902; A.M., Harvard, 1903, Ph.D., 1905; m. Olive Williams, July 6, 1910; children—Henry Lamar, Oliver Sexmith. Instr. Greek, U. of Pa., 1905-06; asst. prof. Greek, U. of Mo., 1906-09; preceptor in classics, Princeton, 1909-10; asst. prof. Greek, 1910-19, prof., 1919—, dir. summer session, 1918-25, dean of Graduate School, 1928-38, U. of Pa. Annual prof., 1926-27, dir. 1938-39, Am. Sch. of Classical Studies, Athens, Greece. Mem. Am. Philol. Assn., Classical Assn. Atlantic States, Archæol. Inst. America, Phi Beta Kappa, Phi Gamma Delta, Phi Mu Alpha. Episcopalian. Home: 4312 Osage Av., Philadelphia, Pa.

CROSKEY, John Welsh, ophthalmologist; b. Phila., Pa., Jan. 26, 1858; s. Henry and Ann (Dunnohew) C.; student Swarthmore Coll., 1886-87; M.D., Medico-Chirurg. Coll., Phila., 1889 (gold medalist); certificate of proficiency, Phila. Sch. of Anatomy, 1889; m. Elisabeth Estes Browning, Dec. 15, 1880; children—Henry B., Elisabeth B. (Mrs. L. E. Bailey), Marion L., John Welsh Croskey, Jr. (dec.). Chief asst. to surg. clinic, Medico-Chirurg. Coll., 1889, later lecturer on minor and operative surgery; asst. surgeon to Wills Hosp., 1891-97; surgeon same, 1897-1902; apptd. consulting ophthalmic surgeons to George Nugent Home for Baptists, 1899; ophthalmic surgeon to Phila. Gen. Hosp., apptd. 1900, cons. surgeon, apptd. 1925; also lecturer to Training Sch. for Nurses; ophthalmic surgeon to Samaritan Hosp., Annie M. Warner Hosp., 1902-05; professor ophthalmology, laryngology and otology, Temple Univ., 1902-05, etc. Sec. and mem. bd. of Penn Metal Co. of Pa. Acting asst. surgeon, U.S. Pub. Health Service. Formerly editor and owner Internat. Med. Mag., and editor Medico-Chirurg. Jour. Fellow Am. Acad. Ophthalmology and Oto-Laryngology, A.M.A.; mem. Med. Soc. State of Pa., Phila. County Med. Soc. (sec. bd. of censors), W. Phila. Med. Assn. (ex-pres.), Hist. Soc. Pa., Valley Forge Hist. Soc., Acad. Natural Science of Phila., Am. Med. Authors Assn., Colonial Soc. America, S.R., Gen. Alumni U. of Pa., Medical Alumni U. of Pa., Alumni Assn. Medico Chirurg. Coll. (ex-pres.), Navy League (life), St. George Soc., St. Andrews Soc., Dickens Fellowship. Republican. Mason. Clubs: Kiwanis, Paxon Hollow Golf, Overbrook Golf, Merion Cricket, Golfers Association of Medical Society State of Pa. (ex-pres.), Am. Med. Golfing, Penn Club (dir.), Penn (dir.). Author: Dictionary of Ophthalmic Terms, 1907; also History of Blockley; Anatomy and Physiology of the Eye and Its Appendages; Historical Catalogue of the St. Andrews Society. Home: 3325 Powelton Av., Philadelphia, Pa.

CROSKEY, Ralph Smith, lawyer; b. Phoenixville, Pa., Nov. 3, 1890; s. Knowles and Kathryn (Smith) C.; LL.B., U. of Pa. Law Sch., 1913; m. Lucile Mary Stothart, July 19, 1919; children—Ralph Smith, Marylu, Thomas Stothart. Admitted to Pa. bar, 1913, and since engaged in gen. practice of law at Phila.; mem. firm Edwards and Croskey since 1937. Enlisted as pvt. inf. Pa. N.G., 1908, and promoted regularly through grades to capt., 1910; served as capt. inf. Pa. N.G., U.S.A., on Mexican border, 1916-17; capt. inf., U.S.A., 1917-19, with 28th Div. A.E.F.; maj. inf., O.R.C., 1922, lt. col. since 1923. Mem. Am., Pa., and Phila. bar assns., Mil. Order of World War, Res. Officers Assn. of U.S., Soc. of 28th Div., A.E.F., Am. Legion, Colonial Soc. of Pa., St. Andrews Soc. Republican. Baptist. Mason. Clubs: University, Lawyers (Phila.); St. Davids Golf. Home: 5 Aldwyn Lane, Villa Nova, Pa. Office: 526 Stephen Girard Bldg., Philadelphia, Pa.

CROSLAND, Edward Samuel, physician and surgeon; b. Bethania, N.C., June 16, 1896; s. Rt. Rev. Edward Shober (Bishop of Moravian Ch.) and Caroline (Mickey) C.; student Franklin and Marshall Coll., Lancaster, Pa., 1916-18; M.D., U. of Pa. Med. Sch., 1922; grad. study, Post Grad. Med. Sch. & Hosp., New York City, 1929; m. Anna Lillian Meiskey, July 24, 1923; children—Anna Dorothy, Nancy Caroline, Cynthia Louise. Interne Misericordia Hosp., Phila., Pa., 1922-23; chief resident phys., St. Joseph's Hosp., Lancaster, Pa., 1923-24; engaged in gen. practice of medicine and surgery at Lancaster, Pa., since 1924; visiting surgeon, Rossmere Sanitarium, Lancaster Co. and St. Joseph's hosps., Lancaster, Pa., since 1930; dir. Home Bldg. & Loan Assn. Served in Med. Res. Corps and S.A.T.C., 1918. Mem.A.M.A., Pa. State, Lancaster City and Co. med. socs., Artisans Order of Mutual Protection, Omega Upsilon Phi, Phi Sigma Kappa. Republican. Moravian. Mason (32°). Home: 142 College Av. Office: 134 College Av., Lancaster, Pa.

CROSS, Charles Whitman, geologist; b. Amherst, Mass., Sept. 1, 1854; s. Rev. Moses Kimball and Maria (Mason) C.; B.S., Amherst, 1875; Ph.D., U. of Leipzig, 1880; D.Sc., Amherst, 1925; m. Virginia Stevens, Nov. 7, 1895; 1 son, Richard Stevens. Asst. geologist, U.S. Geol. Survey, 1880-88, geologist, 1888-1925; retired account of age limit. Chief sect. petrology, 1903-06. Mem. Nat. Acad. Sciences (treas. 1911-19), Geol. Soc. America (pres. 1918), Washington Acad. Sciences, Am. Philos. Soc.;

hon. corr. Acad. Nat. Sc. Phila., 1924; foreign mem. Geol. Soc. London. Mem. Nat. Research Council, 1918-22 (treas., 1918-19, vice chmn. division of geology and geography, 1918). Author of geol. reports and maps published by U.S. Geol. Survey, and of many papers in periodicals, on geol., petrographical or mineral subjects. Part Author: Quantitative Classification of Igneous Rocks, 1903. Engaged in rose cultivation and cross-breeding since retirement. Home: 101 E. Kirke St., Chevy Chase, Md.

CROSS, William Redmond, pres. New York Zoölogical Soc.; b. S. Orange, N.J., June 8, 1874; s. Richard James and Matilda (Redmond) C.; grad. Groton (Mass.) Sch., 1892; A.B., Yale, 1896; m. Julia Newbold, Apr. 13, 1913; children—Emily Redmond, Richard James, William Redmond, Thomas Newbold, Mary Newbold. Dir. Federal Ins. Co., Nat. Iron Bank, Gauley Mountain Coal Co. Trustee Groton Sch.; pres. Bernards Library Assn., Bernardsville, N.J. Mem. N.Y. Zool. Soc. (pres.), Am. Geog. Soc. (chmn. of council). Clubs: Yale, Brook, Knickerbocker, Downtown Assn. (New York); Somerset Hills Country (Bernardsville, N.J.). Keeper of maps, Yale U. Home: Bernardsville, N.J. Office: 90 Broad St., New York, N.Y.

CROSSFIELD, Henry Charles, physician; b. Lawrenceburg, Ky., Aug. 7, 1898; s. William H. and Mary B. (Cole) C.; A.B., Transylvania Coll., 1919; spl. course, U. of Ky., 1922; M.D., U. of Louisville Med. Coll., 1927; m. Marian Hentz, June 22, 1935; children—Marian, Harry, and Elaine. Interne N.Y. Post Grad. Hosp., 1927-29, res. phys., 1929; instr. in medicine, N.Y. Post Grad. Hosp. and Columbia U., 1929-37; asst. attdg. phys. Orange Memorial Hosp. since 1932, cardiologist since 1938. Fellow Am. Coll. Phys., Am. Med. Assn., Acad. of Medicine of Northern N.J. Mem. Book and Bones, Kappa Alpha, Alpha Kappa Kappa. Mem. Southern Christian Ch. Clubs: Orange Lawn Tennis (South Orange); Essex County Country (West Orange). Contbr. articles on heart disease and gastro-intestinal conditions. Home: 331 N. Ridgewood Rd., South Orange. Office: 144 Harrison St., East Orange, N.J.

CROSSLEY, George Corliss, pres. United Clay Mines Corpn.; b. Trenton, N.J., June 18, 1881; s. Joseph and Martha (Bullock) C.; student Model Sch., Trenton, N.J., 1887-99, Stewart Sch. of Business, Trenton, N.J., 1899-1900, Drexel Inst. of Tech., Phila., 1901-05; m. Mabel Brown, Jan. 2, 1908; 1 dau., Betty Brown. Founded and organized United Clay Mines Corpn., Trenton, N.J., 1905, and since pres.; pres. Prospect Nat. Bank, Trenton, N.J., since 1926; dir. Prospect Bldg. & Loan Assn. Served as private and sergt., N.J. N.G., 1910-13. Trustee Prospect Hill Sch., 1934-35. Mem. Ceramic Assn. of N.J. (pres.), Am. Inst. Mining Engrs., Y.M.C.A., Am. Inst. of Banking, Trenton (N.J.) Chamber of Commerce. Republican. Presbyterian (Elder First Presbyn. Ch., Trenton, N.J.). Clubs: Rotary (past pres.), Engineer's (gov. 1935-36); Trenton, N.J.); Bay Head Yacht (Bay Head, N.J.). Home: River Rd. Office: 101 Oakland St., Trenton, N.J.

CROSSLEY, Moses Leverock, chemist; b. of Am. parents at Saba, Dutch West Indies, July 3, 1884; s. John George Everet and Frances Antoinette (Johnson) C.; Ph.B., Brown U., 1909; Sc.M., 1910, Ph.D., 1911; m. Elsie Emeline McCausland, Jan. 1, 1914; 1 son, Evan McCausland. Instr. in chemistry, Brown U., 1909-11; asso. prof. chemistry, William Jewell Coll., Liberty, Mo., 1911-13; same, Wesleyan U., Middletown, Conn., 1913-18, head of dept., 1914-18; chief chemist, Calco Chem. Co., Bound Brook, N.J., 1918-36, resident dir. since 1936. Mem. Inst. of Chemists (pres. 1924-26 and 1934-36; also mem. bd. trustees), American Chem. Society, The Faraday Society, Society Chemical Industry, A.A.A.S., Society Arts and Science of New York, Chem. Society (London), Plainfield Art Assn., Sigma Xi, Sigma Nu. Republican. Episcopalian. Clubs: Chemists, Brown University (New York); East Chop Country. Collaborated in Chemistry in Industry, 1925; contbr. chapter to Nat. Research Council's Annual Survey of Am. Chemistry, 1930, 31. Research and discoveries in dyes and pharmaceuticals. Home: 734 Park Av., Plainfield, N.J. Office: Bound Brook, N.J.*

CROTHERS, Wesley G.; asso. surgeon Chester Hosp., chief of Orthopedic and Fracture Clinic. Address: 415 E. 9th St., Chester, Pa.

CROUCH, Richard Conger, investments; b. Titusville, Pa., May 2, 1904; s. Jesse Vernon and Viola Jane (Conger) C.; grad. Titusville High Sch., 1922; student Allegheny Coll., 1923-25; B.S., Columbia, 1927; m. Martha Mackey, Jan. 2, 1931; children—Janet Mackey, John Conger. Mem. staff of Haskins & Sells, New York, 1927-28; asst. treas. and sec. U.S. Shares Corpn., 1928-31; treas. and asst. to pres. Supervised Shares Corpn., 1931; mgr. Root, Clark, Buckner & Ballatine since 1931; dir. Plymouth Fund, Inc. Mem. Delta Tau Delta, Alpha Kappa Psi. Democrat. Club: Labor (New York). Home: 897 Ridgewood Rd., Millburn, N.J. Office: 31 Nassau St., New York, N.Y.

CROUCH, Robert Pyle, clergyman; b. Phila., Pa., July 6, 1895; s. James Washington and Emma (Schultz) C.; ed. Crozer Sem., Chester, Pa., 1920-24; grad. study, U. of Pa., 1925-26; m. Mary R. McGarvey, Oct. 12, 1914; 1 dau., Violet Mae. Ordained to ministry at Third Bapt. Ch., Phila., 1924; pastor, Point Pleasant Beach, N.J., 1924-28, Hamburg, N.J., 1928-37, Homecrest Bapt. Ch., Trenton, N.J., since 1938; asst. supervisor recreation div., E.R.A., Sussex Co., 1935-36; investigator, N.J. State Juvenile Delinquency Commn., 1937-38; investigator, Child Welfare Div., State of N.J. since 1938; parole officer, Central Parole Bd., N.J., since 1939; mem. bd. mgrs. N.J. Bapt. State Conv. Served as pvt. inf., U.S.A., 1917-18; naval aviation, U.S.N., 1918. Mem. Am. Legion. Republican. Baptist. Mason. Home: 320 Berwyn Av., Trenton, N.J. Office: 571 Jersey Av., Jersey City, N.J.

CROUSE, Charles C(yrus), physician; b. Stahlstown, Pa., Apr. 1, 1888; s. J. W. and Sara (Ober) C.; ed. Monessen (Pa.) High Sch., Grove City (Pa.) Coll.; M.D., U. of Pa. Med. Sch., 1915; m. Elizabeth Blackburn, Sept. 28, 1916; 1 dau., Dorothy Marie. Interne Mercy Hosp., Pittsburgh, Pa., 1915-16; surgeon in British Army; mem. surg. staff, Westmoreland Hosp. since 1922. Served as maj., Med. Corps, U.S. Army, during World War. Mem. bd. dirs. Boy Scouts of Westmoreland Co. Fellow Am. Coll. Surgeons; mem. A.M.A., Pa. State Med. Soc., Phi Rho Sigma, Order of Purple Heart. Republican. United Presbyterian. Mason, Rotarian. Club: Greensburg (Pa.) Westmoreland Country. Home: Delmont Rd. Office: Union Trust Bldg., Greensburg, Pa.

CROW, Arthur E.; mem. surg. staff Uniontown Hosp. Address: 42 W. Main St., Uniontown, Pa.

CROW, Charles Sumner, univ. prof.; b. Point Marion, Pa., Apr. 6, 1880; s. Bowen Ross and Eliza (Frankenberry) C.; A.B., W.Va. U., Morgantown, W.Va., 1906; M.A., Harvard, 1913; student Columbia U., 1912-13, 1917-18, Ph.D., 1924; m. Laura Baldwin, Aug. 25, 1917; children—Mary Elizabeth, Eleanor Louise, Charles Sumner. Began as teacher in W.Va. country sch., 1899; teacher of science, Mannington (W.Va.) High Sch., 1906-08; prin. and teacher of English, New Kensington (Pa.) High Sch., 1909-10; first asst. prin. and teacher of mathematics and edn., Glenville (W.Va.) State Normal Sch., 1910-12; asst. prof. of edn. and philosophy, W.Va. U., Morgantown, W.Va., 1913-17; asso. prof. of edn., Rutgers U., New Brunswick, N.J., 1918-26, prof. since 1926, Rutgers lecturer in courses for teachers at Am. Mus. of Natural History and Metropolitan Mus. of Art, New York, since 1922; visiting prof. U. of Pittsburgh, summers 1915, 1917, W.Va. U., 1921, 1930, U. of Vt., Burlington, Vt., 1924, U. of Tex., Austin, Tex., 1939. Mem. Mt. Holly Ednl. Survey Commn., 1918 (wrote sect. on pupil achievements). Mem. N.E.A. (life), N.J. State Ednl. Assn., Kappa Phi Kappa, Phi Delta Kappa, Kappa Delta Pi, Sigma Nu. Awarded D.A.R. prize in composition, 1903, Tax Commn. prize in composition, 1906. Republican. Presbyterian. Author: English Literature in the High Sch., 1924; Creative Education, 1937. Edited (with Dr. Charles H. Elliott) a series of bulletins on Projects in the Public Schools, 1921-22. Address: 259 Lawrence Av., New Brunswick, N.J.

CROW, William Josiah, mayor; b. Uniontown, Pa., Jan. 22, 1902; s. U.S. Senator William Evans and Ada (Curry) C.; student Uniontown (Pa.) Hign Sch., 1916-18, Pa. Mil. Coll., Chester, Pa., 1918-22; C.E., Dickinson Law Sch., Carlisle, Pa., 1925; m. Charlotte Sheafer, Oct. 5, 1923; children—Robert Hustead, Richard Sheafer. Admitted to Pa. bar, 1926, and since in practice at Uniontown, Pa.; parole officer, Uniontown, Pa., 1926-28, asst. dist. atty., 1928-32; elected mayor, Uniontown, Pa., 1938. Republican. Baptist. Moose, Elk, Eagle. Club: Uniontown (Pa.) Exchange. Home: 75 Highland Av. Office: 52 E. Main St., Uniontown, Pa.

CROWE, John Joseph, industrial research mgr.; b. Washington, D.C., Jan. 3, 1886; s. Peter and Honora (Noonan) C.; student pub. schs., Washington, D.C., 1893-1901, McKinley High Sch., Washington, 1901-05, George Washington U., 1905-11; m. Hazel May Hartnett, Aug. 8, 1917; 1 son, John Joseph (dec.). Apprentice, advancing to asso. physicist, Nat. Bur. of Standards, Washington, D.C., 1905-15; phys. metallurgist U.S. Navy, Boston, 1915-17, Phila. 1917-24; mgr. apparatus research and development dept. Air Reduction Co., Inc., Jersey City, N.J., since 1924; dir. course in metallurgy, Temple U., Phila., Pa., 1919-23. Mem. Am. Welding Soc. (pres. 1935-36, dir. since 1924), Compressed Gas Mfg. Assn. (pres. 1938-39, exec. bd. since 1939), Am. Soc. of Metals (dir. 1921-22; chmn. N.Y. chapter, 1932-33, Phila. Chapter, 1923-24), Am. Inst. M.E., Internat. Acetylene Assn., Am. Soc. for Testing Materials. Awarded John Turner Morehead Medal, 1937. Home: 715 Westfield Av., Westfield, N.J. Office: 181 Pacific Av., Jersey City, N.J.

CROWE, Montgomery Fletcher, insurance; b. Piermont, N.Y., Nov. 9, 1890; s. Charles H. and Jessie M. (Durkee) C.; student East Stroudsburg (Pa.) State Normal Sch., 1904-08, Lafayette Coll., Easton, Pa., 1909-11; m. Frances K. Wirth, June 1, 1918; 1 dau., Jessie D. Began as solicitor C. H. Crowe Co., Inc., East Stroudsburg, Pa., 1911, pres. since 1914; v.p. Stroudsburg Security Trust Co. since 1924; dir. Sun Printing Co. since 1925. Served as 2d lt., Co. C, 110th Inf., U.S. Army, 1917, 1st lt. and personnel adjutant, Camp Mills, L.I., N.Y., 1918-19. State senator 14th Dist. Pa. (Wayne, Pike, Monroe and Carbon Cos.) since 1938. Chmn. Monroe Co. Pub. Assistance Bd., dir. The General Hosp. Mem. Am. Legion, 40 & 8, Patriotic Order Sons of America. Republican. Episcopalian. Elk, Odd Fellow, Eagle. Clubs: Skytop (Pa.); Kiwanis (Stroudsburg, Pa.). Home: 210 Park Av., Stroudsburg, Pa. Office: 169 Washington St., East Stroudsburg, Pa.

CROWE, Samuel James, surgeon; b. Washington Co., Va., Apr. 16, 1883; s. Walter Andrew and Flora (Thompson) C.; student Emory Coll., Oxford, Ga., 1901-02; A.B., U. of Ga., 1904; M.D., Johns Hopkins, 1908; grad. study univs. of Freiburg, Berlin and Vienna, 1908-14; m. Susie Childs Barrow, June 1908; children—Samuel James, David Francis. Began practice at Baltimore, 1908; asst. in gen. surgery to Dr. William S. Halsted and Dr. Harvey Cushing at Johns Hopkins Hosp., 1908-12; dir. nose, throat and ear dept., Johns Hopkins U. and Hosp., since 1912. Mem. Med. Advisory Bd., Baltimore, 1916-18. Fellow Am. Coll. Surgeons, A.M.A.; president American Otological Society, 1934-35; mem. Phi Beta Kappa, Sigma Xi, Chi Phi. Presbyn. Club: Maryland. Contbr. to med. jours. Established research lab. for study of deafness, Johns Hopkins Hosp., 1924. Home: 4332 North Charles St. Office: Johns Hopkins Hosp., Baltimore, Md.

CROWELL, Daniel Van Buren, lawyer; b. Greensburg, Pa., June 21, 1901; s. Charles Calvin and Henrietta Mowry (Turney) C.; ed. Lawrenceville (N.J.) Sch., 1918-20; A.B., Yale,

1924; LL.B., U. of Pittsburgh Law Sch., 1927; m. Muriel M. Moran, Nov. 23, 1921; children—Daniel V., Henrietta M., Ann. Admitted to Pa. bar, 1927, and since engaged in gen. practice of law at Greensburg, Pa.; mem. firm Crowell and Whitehead since 1927. Active in local civic affairs. Mem. Westmoreland Law Assn., Pa. State Bar Assn., Zeta Psi, Delta Theta Phi. Republican. Episcopalian. Eagle, U.C.T., K.P. Club: William Penn. Home: 146 Kenneth St. Office: Bank and Trust Bldg., Greensburg, Pa.

CROWLEY, James A.; pres. Peoples Bank & Trust Co. Address: Passaic, N.J.

CROWNFIELD, Gertrude, author; b. Baltimore, Md.; d. Herman Frederic and Sophia Henrietta (Ring) C.; ed. pub. schs., under pvt. tutelage and course of nursing in New York Post-Grad. Hosp.; unmarried. Teacher primary grades, pvt. and pub. schs., Urbana, Ohio, and Marinette, Wis., 10 yrs.; sec. to nerve specialist, 1906-27. Author: The Little Tailor of the Winding Way, 1917; Princess White Flame, 1920; The Shadow Witch, 1922; The Blue Swordsman, 1924; Time in Rime, (and other juveniles), 1925; Alison Blair, 1927; The Feast of Noël, 1928; Joscelyn of the Forts, 1929; Freedom's Daughter, 1930; Heralds of the King, 1931; Katharine Gordon—Patriot, 1932; Mistress Margaret, 1933; Where Glory Waits, 1934; Traitor's Torch, 1935; Conquering Kitty, 1935; King's Pardon, 1937; The Decree, 1937; Strong Hearts and Bold, 1938. Address: care J. B. Lippincott Co., Washington Sq., Philadelphia, Pa.

CROWTHER, Ernest, certified pub. accountant; b. England, Feb. 28, 1873; s. Josiah and Emily (Farrar) C.; came to U.S. 1889 and naturalized citizen, 1896; student high and prep. schs. in England, Drexel Inst., Phila., 1889-93, Pa. State Coll., 1915; m. Viola E. McMaster, Dec. 7, 1891; 1 son, Clarence Raymond (dec.). Employed by others as certified pub. accountant, 1907-11; propr. firm Crowther & Co., Crafton, Pa., 1911-37, retired from active practice except for cons., 1937. Served as auditor Food Adminstrn. Western Pa. during World War. Chmn. of Bd., Pittsburgh Sch. of Accountancy. Mem. Am. Inst. of Accountants, Pa. Inst. of Certified Pub. Accountants. Republican. Episcopalian. Mason (K.T., 32°, Shriner). Home: Crafton, Pa.

CROWTHER, Gwynn, banker; b. Cockeysville, Md., May 28, 1882; s. John and Worthena (Hiss) C.; ed. Baltimore pub. schs.; m. Mabel L. Cox, Apr. 27, 1905; children—G. Kenneth, Mabel L., Gwynn. With Baltimore Commercial Bank since 1915, pres. since 1920. Home: Kurtz and Melanchton Avs., Lutherville, Md. Office: 26 South St., Baltimore, Md.

CROWTHER, Henry L.; lecturer on obstetrics, Hahnemann Med. Coll.; obstetrician Hahnemann Hosp.; asst. obstetrician and gynecologist Broad St. Hosp. Address: 255 S. 17th St., Philadelphia, Pa.

CROWTHER, Rae, educator and mfr. athletic devices; b. Rosemont, Pa., Dec. 11, 1902; s. Dr. S. A. and Grace (Barbara) C.; student Lafayette Coll., Easton, Pa., 1920-22; B.S., Colgate U., Hamilton, N.Y., 1924; m. Jean Vaughan, June 25, 1938. Engaged as asst. prof. phys. edn., U. of Pa. since 1938; inventor of Crowther Charger Blocker and Tackler a device for teaching football players and used by colls. and high schs.; pres. Rae Crowther, Inc. mfrs. and sales agts. of the Crowther device since 1933. Mem. Delta Upsilon. Republican. Presbyterian. Home: 50 Chews Landing Rd., Haddonfield, N.J. Office: 901 Harrison Bldg., Philadelphia, Pa.

CROXTON, Frederick Emory, asso. prof. statistics; b. Washington, D.C., May 23, 1899; s. Frederick C. and Mattie Mae (Stocks) C.; A.B., O. State U., 1920, A.M., same, 1921; Ph.D., Columbia U., 1926; m. Rosetta Ruth Harpster, Sept. 14, 1921; children—Frederick Emory, Jr., Rosetta Harpster II. Asst., then instr. econs. and statistics, O. State U., 1919-26; lecturer statistics, O. Wesleyan U., 1920-21; lecturer, then asst. prof. statistics, Columbia U., 1926 to 1937, asso. prof. since 1937; lecturer N.Y. Sch. of Social Work, 1930-32; dir. Div. Statistics, N.Y. State T.E.R.A., 1933-34. Served as 2d lt. inf., U.S.A., 1918-19. Fellow A.A.A.S.; mem. Am. Statis. Assn., Acad. Polit. Sci., Econometric Soc., Am. Sociol. Soc., Phi Beta Kappa, Beta Gamma Sigma, Phi Delta Kappa, Delta Chi. Methodist. Club: Columbia University Faculty (New York). Author: Corporation Contributions to Organized Community Welfare Services (with Pierce Williams), 1930; Exercises in Statistical Methods (with R. E. Chaddock), 1928; Practical Business Statistics (with D. J. Cowden), 1934; Exercises and Problems in Business Statistics (with D. J. Cowden), 1935; Workbook in Applied General Statistics, 1937; Applied General Statistics (with D. J. Cowden), 1939; also author or joint author of pamphlets and articles dealing with measurement of employment and unemployment, statistical and graphic methods. Home: 314 Crescent Av., Leonia, N.J.

CRUIKSHANK, Burleigh; pastor St. Paul Presbyn. Ch. Address: 50th and Baltimore Av., Philadelphia, Pa.

CRUM, Earl LeVerne, prof. classical langs.; b. Athens, Pa., May 13, 1891; s. Theodore and Eva Marsh (Munn) C.; A.B., St. John's Coll., Annapolis, Md., 1913; A.M., Johns Hopkins U., 1916; Ph.D., N.Y. Univ., 1924; m. Mary Lyle Smith, July 10, 1918; 1 dau., Mary Lyle. Instr. classical langs., U. of Rochester, 1916-18; asst. prof., N.Y. Univ., 1921-26, State U. of Ia., 1926-28; asso. prof. of Greek and Latin and head dept. of Greek, Lehigh U., Bethlehem, Pa., since 1928; dir. Foyer Retrouvé, Charvieu, France, 1918-20. Served as 1st lt. U.S.A., 1918-19, with A.E.F. in France. Mem. Am. Philol. Assn., Classical Assn. of Atlantic States, Modern Lang. Assn., Am. Assn. Univ. Profs., Archæol. Inst. America, Eta Sigma Phi. Republican. Methodist. Author: Index of Proper Names to Servius, 1928. Contbr. articles to classical jours. Home: 717 Seventh Av., Bethlehem, Pa.

CRUM, Ralph Walter, banker; b. Athens, Pa., Aug. 20, 1896; s. Theodore and Evangeline (Munn) C.; grad. Athens High Sch., 1914; A.B., St. John's Coll., U. of Md., Annapolis, 1917; m. Marion Jamison, Aug. 21, 1920; children—John Jamison, Marion Janet, Mary Abbe. Began as commandant and instr., Stanford (Conn.) Mil. Acad., 1917; teacher, Westfield (N.J.) High Sch., 1919; with Nat. Bank of Commerce, New York, 1920-25, Nat. City Co., San Francisco, 1925-26; investment securities, Los Angeles, 1927-31; with Passaic Nat. Bank & Trust Co. since 1932, vice-pres. since 1935. Served with Med. Corps, U.S. Army, 1918-19; disch. as sergt. 1st class. Mem. Pa. Soc., Passaic Co. Bankers Assn. (vice-pres.). Republican. Congregationalist. Home: 711 Valley Rd., Upper Montclair, N.J. Office: 657 Main Av., Passaic, N.J.

CRUM, Rolfe Pomeroy, clergyman, educator, author; b. Cleveland, O., Jan. 5, 1889; s. Xenophon Xerxes and Anna Marcia (Phelps) C.; A.B. magna cum laude, Adelbert Coll., Western Reserve U., 1911, D.D., 1930; A.M., Harvard, 1914; B.D. (cum laude), Episcopal Theol. Sch., Cambridge, Mass., 1914; student Cambridge Univ., Eng., 1931-32; unmarried. Ordained deacon, P.E. Ch., 1914, priest, 1915; curate Trinity Episcopal Ch., Buffalo, N.Y., 1914-16; rector St. Mark's Ch., Syracuse, N.Y., 1916-20; special preacher St. Paul's Cathedral, Boston, 1919; rector Trinity Ch., Tulsa, Okla., 1920-25, St. Mark's Ch., San Antonio, Tex., 1926-31, St. Andrew's Ch., Phila., 1932-36; chaplain on world cruise, 1936; pres. Neff Coll., Phila., since 1938. Served as chaplain Am. Red Cross, France, 1918-19. Pres. San Antonio Ministerial Alliance, 1926-27. Mem. Phi Beta Kappa. Republican. Mason (32°). Clubs: Union League, Penn Athletic (Phila.), 1932-36. Author: Some of Life's Mysteries Interpreted in the Light of the Present World Struggle, 1918; Help from the Hills, 1931; Education in England, 1932. Address: Neff College, Box 6362, Philadelphia, Pa.

CRUMLEY, Thomas Ralston, elec. engr.; b. Wayne, Pa., Sept. 20, 1879; s. David and Mary (Coleman) C.; B.S., Pa. State Coll., 1901; m. Nancy Bartlett, 1908. Constrn. engr., Hudson River Water Power Co., 1901-04; asst. supt. Phila. and Westchester Traction Co., 1904-08; elec. engr., Evansville & Ind. Ry. Co., 1908-15; chief engr. Gen. Engring. & Management Corpn., 1915-21, pres., 1921-27; v.p. Nat. Pub. Service Corpn., 1925-27; v.p. Jersey Central Power & Light Co., 1925-28, pres. and gen. mgr. since 1928. Mem. Am. Inst. E.E. Republican. Episcopalian. Mason. Club: Deal Golf. Home: Eatontown, N.J. Office: 501 Grand Av., Asbury Park, N.J.*

CRUMLISH, James C.; judge Ct. of Common Pleas since 1937, term expires 1948. Address: City Hall, Philadelphia, Pa.

CRUMP, Edward, Jr., constructing engr.; b. Lynchburg, Va., July 9, 1891; s. Edward and Alpha (Lee) C.; student George Washington U., Washington, D.C., 1910-11; grad. Carnegie Inst. Tech., 1915; m. Florence S. Shaw, Dec. 10, 1917; 1 son, Edward III. Employed as draftsman and inspr. on construction work in Va. and N.C., 1908-10, in Washington, D.C., 1910-11; on construction work while in coll., 1911-15; in practice constructing engring., 1915-17; in employ Mellon-Stuart Co., 1919-21; in engring. and constructing business for self since 1921, pres. and treas. Edward Crump, Jr. Inc., Pittsburgh, since 1930; propr. Schenley Arms Co.; mem. firm Crump and McQuillan; pres. and treas. Parkway Improvement Co., Schenley Arms Improvement Co. Served as 2d lt. then 1st lt., Inf., U.S. Army, 1917-19, with A.E.F. in France and Germany. Comdr. 35th dist. (Pa.) Am. Legion, past comdr. East Liberty Post, Allegheny Co. Com. Mem. Vets. Fgn. Wars, Mil. Order World War, The Sojourners, Allied War Vets. Soc. of Allegheny Co. (past comdr.), Sons Am. Revolution, Southern Soc. of N.Y., Hist. Soc. of Va., Hist. Soc. of Western Pa., Pittsburgh Builders Exchange, Alpha Tau Omega. Republican. Episcopalian. Mason (32°, Shriner). Clubs: Pittsburgh Athletic, Longue View Country (Pittsburgh). Home: 5468 Wilkins Av. Office: 4031 Bigelow Bldg., Pittsburgh, Pa.

CRUMP, James Irving, author, editor; b. Saugerties, N.Y., Dec. 7, 1887; s. William Russell and Emma F. (Peters) C.; ed. public and private schools, and at Erasmus Hall, Columbia University; m. Marguerite Duryea Whitney, of N.Y. City, Apr. 4, 1910; children—Marguerite Whitney, James Irving. Asso. editor Edison Monthly, 1912-14; editor, Boys' Life (Boy Scout mag.), 1918-23; mng. editor Pictorial Rev., May 1923-Aug. 1924; again mng. editor Boys' Life since 1935. Mem. Ulster Co. Soc. of N.Y., Omega Gamma Delta. Republican. Baptist. Clubs: Town Hall, Players. Author: Conscript 2989, 1918; Boys' Book of Firemen, 1919; Boys' Book of Policemen, 1920; Boys' Book of Mounted Police, 1921; Boys' Book of Railroads, 1922; Og, Son of Fire, 1922; Boys' Book of Forest Rangers, 1923; Boys' Book of Arctic Exploration, 1924; Og, Boy of Battle, 1925; Boys' Book of the U.S. Mails, 1926; Boys' Book of Airmen, 1927; Boys' Book of the Coast Guard, 1928; Mog, the Mound Builder, 1931; Boys' Book of Fisheries, 1932; "Making" the School Newspaper, 1933; Newsreel Hunters, 1933; (with Capt. C. D. Woodyatt), Creole Wench, 1933; also The Great War Series for Boys (5 vols.); Adventures in Birdland (5 vols.); Boy Scout Fire Fighters; Cloud Patrol Series (3 vols.); Boys' Book of Cowboys, 1934; Og, of the Cave People, 1935; Our Police, 1935; Our Airmen, 1936; Our G-Men, 1937; Our Firemen, 1938. Contbr. fiction to mags., also radio dramatizations and original stories for motion pictures. Home: Oradell, N.J.

CRUMRINE, Clarence Acklin, physician; b. Washington Co., Pa., July 28, 1896; s. Clyde Warren and Luceola (Acklin) C.; A.B., Washington—Jefferson Coll., 1917; M.D., Harvard, 1921; m. Grace Garard, Sept. 26, 1922; 1 dau., Eleanor Anne. Interne Roosevelt Hosp., New York, 1921-23; mem. staff Pa. Hosp., Washington, Pa., 1923; senior med. staff Washington (Pa.) Hosp. since 1924; practice limited to internal medicine. Mem. East Washington Sch. Bd., 1931-37. Mem. A.M.A., Washington County and Pa. State Med. socs. Presbyterian. Mason (32°, Shriner). Home: 151 Le

Moyne Av. Office: 6 S. Main St., Washington, Pa.

CRUMRINE, Ernest E.; pres. Washington Record Co.; sr. partner law firm Crumrine & Crumrine. Home: 500 E. Maiden St. Office: 75 S. Main St., Washington, Pa.

CRUMRINE, Lucius McKennan, lawyer; b. Washington, Pa., Jan. 21, 1890; s. Ernest Ethelbert and Gertrude (Magill) C.; student Washington & Jefferson Acad., 1904-08; A.B., Washington & Jefferson Coll., Washington, Pa., 1912; LL.B., U. of Pa. Law Sch., 1915; m. Elizabeth Ford, June 21, 1926; children—Patricia Jane, Lucius McKennan, David Ford. Admitted to Pa. bar, 1916, and since in practice at Washington, Pa.; partner, Crumrine & Crumrine, Washington, Pa., since 1916; dir. Washington (Pa.) Record Co. since 1920, pres. since 1939. Served as sergt. 1st class, Q.M.C. with Hdqrs., 28th Div., 1918-19; 2d lt., 1920, 1st lt., 1920-24, capt. 110th Inf., 1924-36, maj., 1936-37, lt. col., 1937, asst. chief of staff, 28th Div., Pa. N.G., since 1936. Mem. Washington Co., Pa. State bar assns., Am. Legion (40 & 8; dept. commdr. Pa. Am. Legion, 1925-26), Phi Kappa Psi. Republican. Presbyterian. Mason (Chapter, Council, Commandery, Consistory; Shriner, past potentate Syria Temple; Royal Order of Jesters). Clubs: Bassett, Rotary (Washington, Pa.); University (Pittsburgh). Home: Redstone Rd. Office: First Nat. Bank Bldg., Washington, Pa.

CRUMRINE, Norman Ross, physician; b. Washington Co., Pa., Dec. 22, 1893; s. William Madison and Viola May (Longdon) C.; M.E., Southwestern State Normal Sch., 1912; student U. of W.Va., Morgantown, W.Va., summer 1912; M.D., Jefferson Med. Coll., Phila., 1919; m. Elizabeth Seiple, of New Brighton, Pa., June 26, 1926; children—Norman Ross II, Richard Seiple, Gretchen. After usual interneships engaged in practice of medicine at Beaver, Pa. since 1923, specializing in diseases of eye, ear, nose and throat. Served in med. enlisted corps, S.A.T.C., 1918. Mem. Borough Council, Beaver, Pa. since 1937. Fellow Am. Coll. Surgeons, Am. Acad. Ophthalmology and Otolaryngology; mem. A.M.A., Pa. State and Beaver Co. med. socs., Pittsburgh Otol. Soc., Phi Chi. Republican. Presbyterian. Mason. Clubs: Fort McIntosh (Beaver, Pa.); Beaver Valley Country (Beaver Falls, Pa.). Home: 650 2d St. Office: 595 3d St., Beaver, Pa.

CRUTCHFIELD, James Stapleton; b. Goshen, Ky., July 3, 1874; s. Albert and Harriet (Mayo) C.; ed. pub. and high schs., Louisville, Ky.; m. Alice Pilkington, June 7, 1900; children—Margaret, Harriet, Catharine, James Stapleton, Albin Pilkington, George Wythe (dec.), Robert Woolfolk, Alice Pilkington, Grace Pilkington. Began in Fla. as buyer and seller of fruits and vegetables, 1892; moved to Pittsburgh, Pa., 1896, and established firm Crutchfield & Woolfolk, commn. mchts.; organizer, 1919, and pres. Am. Fruit Growers, Inc.; chmn. Union Fruit Auction Co.; pres. William Penn Trust Co.; dir. Wabash Ry. Co.; treas. Deerfield Groves Co.; pres. Pittsburgh Fruit & Produce Exchange. Served as vice administrator and mem. exec. council Federal Food Administration, 1917-18; vice dir. food supply dept. Com. of Pub. Safety of Pa.; dir. Pittsburgh Chamber of Commerce. Vice chmn. Economic Policy Com. Mem. Foreign Policy Assn. (Pittsburgh Br.). Trustee Western Theol. Sem., Grove City Coll., Y.M.C.A. of Pittsburgh, Pine Mountain Settlement Sch. Presbyn. Clubs: Duquesne (Pittsburgh); Whitehall (New York); Edgeworth (Sewickley, Pa.). Home: Beaver Road, Sewickley, Pa. Address 1400 Chamber of Commerce Bldg., Pittsburgh, Pa.

CRYDER, Donald Stevens, univ. prof.; b. Tyrone, Pa., Nov. 29, 1891; s. Mahlon and Mary (Cramer) C.; B.S., Pa. State College, 1920, M.S., 1923; M.S., Mass. Inst. Tech., 1929, D.Sc., 1930; m. Ruth V. Strom, June 17, 1933; children—Ralph Strom, Paul Maurice. Instr. chemistry, Pa. State Coll., 1920-23, asst. prof., 1923-29, asso. prof. chem. engring., 1929-35, prof. since 1935. Mem. Am. Chem. Soc., Am. Inst. Chem. Engrs., Phi Lambda Upsilon, Sigma Xi, Phi Kappa Phi, Sigma Tau. Mason.

Clubs: Acacia, University (State College, Pa.). Home: 602 E. Foster Av. Office: State College, Pa.

CRYDER, James W.; v.p. Crescent Pub. Service Co. Address: Delaware Trust Bldg., Wilmington, Del.

CUBBON, Walter E., county commr.; b. Pithole City, Pa., Nov. 12, 1872; s. John C. and Christian (Callister) C.; student common schs., Pithole City, Pa., 1878-90; m. Edith B. Wright, Jan. 8, 1901; children—Ethel I., Arthur W., Frank W., Emma L., John W., Florence E., Lucille A. Raised on farm; followed oil business from 1892 as contractor of building rig and drilling wells and producing oil to the present time; supervisor Cornplanter Twp. (Pa.) 1910-14, 1930-36, sch. dir., 1914-20; pres. Venango Co. Nat. Farm Loan Assn., Oil City, Pa., since 1919; appraiser, Home Owners Loan Assn., Venango Co., Pa., 1933-35; county commr., Venango Co., Pa., since 1935; dir. W. E. Cubbon Oil Co. Mem. Venango Co. Agrl. Assn. Democrat. Methodist. Nat. Grange. Has written several articles on good roads. Address: R.D. No. 1, Oil City, Pa.

CUDLIPP, William C.; mem. law firm Cudlipp & Cudlipp. Address: 921 Bergen Av., Jersey City, N.J.

CULBERTSON, Andrew Augustus, pres. Pa. Telephone Corpn.; b. Edinboro, Pa., Dec. 15, 1874; s. Charles Lewis and Martha (Proudfit) C.; student Edinboro pub. schs., 1881-90, Edinboro State Normal Sch., 1890-93; A.B., Allegheny Coll., Meadville, Pa., 1901; m. Annie Reeder, Jan. 15, 1908. Taught school 2 yrs.; entered utility field 1901, at first with transportation, power and light and since 1917 with telephone service; pres. Pa. Telephone Corpn., Erie, Pa., since 1917; pres. The Culbertson Co. Past pres. Erie Chamber of Commerce; trustee Edinboro Normal Sch. for 18 yrs.; trustee Allegheny Coll. since 1917; corporator Hamot Hosp., Erie. Mem. Phi Kappa Psi. Democrat. Presbyterian. Mason (32°, Shriner). Clubs: University (pres. 3 yrs), Culbertson Hills Golf and Country (pres.). Recipient Allegheny Coll. alumni award for eminent service to alma mater. Home: Edinboro, Pa. Office: 20 E. 10th St., Erie, Pa.

CULBERTSON, Leland James, lawyer; b. Meadville, Pa., July 26, 1887; s. James Leland and Elizabeth Richmond (Edmeston) C.; prep. edn. Meadville grade and high schs.; student Allegheny Coll., 1906-07, Rensselaer Poly. Inst., 1908-09; m. Miriam Shryock, May 26, 1928; 1 son, John S. Admitted to Crawford Co., Pa., Courts, 1915, later to U.S. Dist. Court, Superior Court of Pa., Supreme Courts of Pa. and U.S.; atty. and dir. Merchants Nat. Bank & Trust Co., Meadville. Served in U.S. Navy, 1918. Mem. Dem. State Committee for Crawford Co. Pres. Boy Scout Council Crawford Co. since 1937; mem. Gov. Earle's Pa. Commn. of Assistance and Relief; dir. Pub. Charities Assn. of Pa.; chmn. Asso. Charities of Meadville; dir. Spencer Hosp. Mem. Bar Assn. of Pa. Mason, Odd Fellow. Club: Kiwanis of Meadville (pres. 1937). Home: 286 Chestnut St. Address: Meadville, Pa.

CULBERTSON, Stuart Arthur, lawyer; b. Meadville, Pa., Apr. 16, 1896; s. James L. and Elizabeth Richmond (Edmeston) C.; student Meadville (Pa.) pub. schs.; grad. Meadville High Sch., 1915; LL.B., Dickinson Sch. of Law, Carlisle, Pa., 1924; unmarried. Admitted to Pa. bar, 1924, Pa. Supreme Ct., 1924, Pa. Superior Ct., 1928, U.S. Federal Ct., U.S. Supreme Ct., 1928; in practice under own name, Meadville, Pa., 1924-27 and since 1936; sec., atty. and dir. Farmers Merchants Bank of Linesville, Pa.; atty. all Am. Legion Posts, Crawford Co.; dist. atty. Crawford Co., Pa., 1927-31, (re-elected) 1931-36; borough solicitor Boroughs of Linesville and Cochranton, Pa.; atty. several sch. dists. and twps., Crawford Co., Pa. Lt. U.S. Naval Res. Mem. Crawford Co. Bar Assn., Meadville Chamber of Commerce, Nat. Aeronautics Assn., Delta Chi. Democrat. Christian Scientist. Mason (Shriner, Olympas Encampment, Coudersport Consistory), Odd Fellow. Clubs: Rotary, Round Table (Meadville, Pa.); Iroquois Boating and Fishing. Holds private pilot's license from Civil Aeronautic Authority, owns own plane and does considerable flying; sailed five yrs. on Great Lakes and holds Able Seaman's papers. Office: 349 Center St., Meadville, Pa.

CULBERTSON, William Smith, lawyer and farmer; born, Greensburg, Pa., Aug. 5, 1884; s. George and Jennie (Smith) C.; A.B., Coll. of Emporia, Kan., 1907, LL.D.; A.B., Yale U., 1908, Ph.D., 1911; special studies Universities of Leipzig and Berlin; LL.D., Georgetown U., 1931; m. Mary J. Hunter, of Pratt, Kan., Dec. 28, 1911; children—Junia Wilhelmina, Margaret Jane, Mary Josephine. Examiner for U.S. Tariff Bd., 1910-12 (prepared 1st vol. of its report on the wool tariff, entitled "Glossary on Schedule K"); practiced law in Washington, D.C., 1912-15; mem. McLanahan, Burton & Culbertson, 1914-15; rep. Federal Trade Commn. studying trade conditions and the tariffs in Brazil, Uruguay, Argentina, Chile, Peru and Panama, 1915-16; special counsel and mem. bd. of rev. of Federal Trade Commn., 1916-17; apptd. mem. U.S. Tariff Commn. by President Wilson, Mar. 1917, and re-apptd. by President Harding, Mar. 1921, for term of 12 years, designated as vice chmn. Jan. 15, 1922, resigned as member and vice chmn. May 17, 1925. E.E. and M.P. to Rumania, by appointment of President Coolidge, 1925-28; A.E. and P. to Chile, 1928-33; now in gen. practice law and in farming. Overseas sec. Y.M.C.A. 1918. Tech. adviser in charge economic questions for Am. del., Conf. on Limitation of Armament, 1921; round table leader Inst. of Politics, Williamstown, Mass., 1922, 1923, 1924; prof. and head dept. economics, also mem. exec. faculty, Sch. of Foreign Service, Georgetown U. Trustee Santiago Coll., Chile. Mem. Am. Bar Assn. (chmn. com. restatement of internat. law; mem. Council, Sect. of Internat. and Comparative Law), Federal Bar Assn., Pa. Bar Assn. (mem. com. on labor and industry), Franklin County Bar Association, Bar Association of District of Columbia, American Soc. Internat. Law, Am. Econ. Assn., Phi Beta Kappa, Phi Alpha Delta (nat. supreme justice 1934-1936), Delta Phi Epsilon (nat. pres. 1922), Rotary (Waynesboro, Pa.). Republican. Presbyterian (trustee Nat. Presbyn. Ch.). Clubs: Metropolitan, Burning Tree, Chevy Chase, National Press (Washington, D.C.). Author: Alexander Hamilton, an Essay, 1911; Commercial Policy in War Time and After, 1919; Raw Materials and Food Stuffs in the Commercial Policies of Nations, 1924; International Economic Policies—A survey of the Economics of Diplomacy, 1925; Reciprocity, A National Policy for Foreign Trade, 1937. Contributor to magazines. Home: "Charmian Manor," Charmian, Franklin Co., Pa. Office: Colorado Bldg., Washington, D.C.

CULIN, Walter A.; pres. Water Service Companies, Inc.; officer or dir. many pub. service companies. Home: Dellwood Drive, Madison, N.J. Office: 90 Broad St., New York, N.Y.

CULLEN, Thomas Stephen, surgeon; b. Bridgewater, Ontario, Nov. 20, 1868; s. Rev. Thomas and Mary (Greene) C.; ed. Collegiate Institute, Toronto; M.B., University of Toronto, 1890, also LL.D.; hon. D.Sc., Temple University. Specialist in abdominal surgery; now professor gynecology, Johns Hopkins University, and visiting gynecologist, Johns Hopkins Hospital. Honorary member La Societa Italiana Ostetricia Ginecologia, Rome; corresponding member Gesellschaft für Geburtshülfe, Leipzig; corr. mem. Gynecol. Soc. of München; hon. fellow Edinburgh Obstet. Soc.; pres. Southern Surg. and Gynecol. Assn., 1916; Med. and Chirurg. Faculty of Md., 1927. Trustee and pres. of Enoch Pratt Library, Baltimore; trustee American Medical Assn. Chmn. Chesapeake Bay Authority, Pub. Works Dist. 10. Author: Cancer of the Uterus, 1900; Adenomyoma des Uterus, Verlag von August Hirschwald, 1903; Adenomyoma of the Uterus, 1908; Myomata of the Uterus (with Howard A. Kelly), 1909; Embryology, Anatomy and Diseases of the Umbilicus Together with Diseases of the Urachus, 1916; Henry Mills Hurd, 1920; Early Medicine in Maryland, 1927; also wrote Accessory Lobes of the Liver for Archives of Surgery. Contbr. to med. jours. on gynecol., pathology and abdominal surgery. Editor of 2 vols. on gynecology, Lewis System of Surgery, 1928. Home: 20 E. Eager St., Baltimore, Md.

CULLEN, Victor Francis, physician; b. Williamsport, Md., Sept. 5, 1881; s. Martin Emmett and Margaret Eva (Cushna) C.; A.B., Rock Hill Coll., Ellicott City, Md., 1902; M.D., Johns Hopkins, 1906; m. Ethel C. Bell, May 1925; 1 dau., Jeanne Margaret. Resident physician St. Joseph's Hosp., Baltimore, 1906-08; supt. Md. Tuberculosis Sanatorium; gen. supt. Tuberculosis Sanatoria of Md. since 1918. Dir. Nat. Tuberculosis Assn. Fellow Am. Coll. Physicians; mem. Med. and Chirurg. Faculty of Md. (acting pres.). Decorated Knight of St. Gregory by Pope Pius XI. Democrat. Catholic. Club: Johns Hopkins (Baltimore). Address: State Sanatorium, Md.

CULLEY, David Ernest, prof. Hebrew and O. T. lit.; b. Washington Co., Pa., Nov. 11, 1877; s. Jesse Edgerton and Ella Rachel (McClurg) C.; student Grove City (Pa.) Coll., 1897-98; A.B., Washington and Jefferson Coll., 1901, D.D., 1926; B.D., Western Theol. Sem., Pittsburgh, Pa., 1904; grad. study U. of Leipzig, Germany, 1904-05, summers 1907-12, Ph.D., 1912; grad. study U. of Florence, Italy, summer 1910, U. of Chicago, summer 1916; m. Mary Helen Craig, November 20, 1914; 1 dau., Mary Katharine. Ordained ministry Presbyn. Ch., 1906; instr. in N.T. Greek, Western Theol. Sem., 1906-08, instr. in Hebrew, 1908-12, asst. prof. Hebrew, 1912-21, asso. prof. Hebrew and O.T. lit., 1921-24, prof. same since 1924; also prof. Bible, Pa. Coll. for Women, 1922-24. Mem. Soc. Bibl. Lit. and Exegesis, Am. Oriental Soc. Republican. Clubs: Circle, Agora, Cleric. Author: Konrad von Gelnhausen, sein Leben, seine Werke und seine Quellen, 1913; Hebrew-English Vocabulary to the Book of Genesis (with J. A. Kelso), 1917. Home: 57 Belvidere St., Crafton, Pittsburgh, Pa.

CULLIMORE, Allan Reginald, educator; b. Jacksonville, Ill., Mar. 2, 1884; s. Thomas McIntyre and Mary Pearce (Joy) C.; B.S. in C.E., Mass. Inst. Tech., 1907; m. Edith Van Alst, Mar. 25, 1912. Draughtsman Am. Bridge Co., 1906-08; asst. supt. of constrn. City of St. Louis, Mo., 1909-12; dean Coll. of Industrial Science, Toledo, O., 1912-16; dean of engring., Delaware Coll., 1916-19; dean Newark Coll. of Engring., 1919-27, pres. since 1927. Major Sanitary Corps, U.S. Army, 1918-19. Mem. Am. Chem. Soc., Am. Soc. of Mech. Engrs., Soc. for Promotion of Engring. Edn., N.J. Sanitary Assn., Beta Theta Pi, Phi Kappa Phi. Presbyn. Clubs: Newark Athletic, Down Town, Rotary, Torch. Home: 158 Garfield Pl., South Orange, N.J.

CULLINAN, T. W.; pres. Beneficial Saving Fund Soc. Address: 1200 Chestnut St., Philadelphia, Pa.

CULP, Cordie Jacob, clergyman; b. Wintersville, O., Sept. 8, 1872; s. Calvin Beattie and Martha Jane (Dance) C.; A.B., Richmond Coll., O., 1895; grad. Princeton Theol. Sem., 1900; A.M., Princeton U., 1902; Ph.D., N.Y. Univ., 1914; (hon.) D.D., Rutgers U., 1920; m. Florence Maud Burns, June 27, 1900. Ordained to ministry Presbyn. Ch., 1900; minister, Glen Moore, Pa., 1900-03, Bound Brook, N.J., 1903-18; minister, First Presbyn. Ch., New Brunswick, N.J., since 1918. Served as dir. religious work, Naval Res. Camp, 1917-18. Stated clk. Presbyn. Synod of N.J., since 1925; moderator of Synod, 1929-30. Mem. Bd. Edn. City of New Brunswick; dir. Young Men's Bldg. & Loan Assn., New Brunswick. Mem. Phi Beta Kappa. Charter mem., past. pres. New Brunswick Rotary Club; past dist. gov., 36th Dist., Rotary Internat. Republican. Presbyn. Home: 58 Bayard St., New Brunswick, N.J.

CULP, Earl J., sch. prin.; b. Kewanee, Ill., Apr. 25, 1901; s. Frank E. and Cora (Kearns) C.; A.B., Salem (W.Va.) Coll., 1924; student U. of Ill. and W.Va. U., 2 summers; M.Edn., U. of Pittsburgh, 1938; m. Lillian M. Collins, May 26, 1932; 1 dau., Phyllis. Teacher and athletic coach, Cairo (W.Va.) High Sch., 1920-24; supt. Harrisville Schs., 1925-29, prin. Harrisville High Sch., 1929-35, and since 1937; supt. Ritchie Co. (W.Va.) Schs., 1935-37. Mem. N.E.A., W.Va. S.E.A., Secondary Sch. Prins. Assn. Republican. Methodist. Mason (K.T., Shriner). Club: Lions. Address: Harrisville, W.Va.

CULP, John F.; cons. otolaryngologist Harrisburg Hosp.; cons. otologist Pa. State Hosp. Address: 224 Pine St., Harrisburg, Pa.

CULVER, Charles Meylert, judge; b. Tuscarora, Pa., Jan. 23, 1871; s. Meylert S. and Harriet E. (Wilson) C.; student pub. schs., Tuscarora and Laceyville, Pa., high schs., and Keystone Acad., Factoryville, Pa., 1891-93; m. Florence Louise Arnold, Nov. 14, 1900; 1 son, Romeyn Francis. Teacher Mathematics, English, History, pub. schs., Tuscarora, Pa., 1889-95; dist. atty., Bradford Co., Pa., 1912-16; pres. judge, 42d Jud. Dist. of Pa., since 1925. Republican. Methodist. Mason (32°), Odd Fellow. Club: Rotary, Masonic (Towanda, Pa.). Home: 302 Third St. Office: Court House, Main St., Towanda, Pa.

CULVER, Edward Peck, univ. prof.; b. Mt. Vernon, N.Y., Nov. 4, 1892; s. Stephen Berry and Georgiana (Peck) C.; student Stevens Inst. Tech., Hoboken, N.J., 1911; B.E., Union Coll., Schenectady, N.Y., 1915; unmarried. Engr. Albany Boat Corpn., Watervliet, N.Y., 1915; calculating engr. Am. Locomotive Co., Schenectady, N.Y. 1916-19; instr. mech. engring., Princeton U., 1919-23, asst. prof., 1923-29, asso. prof. mech. engring. since 1929. Served as 2d lt., Air Service, U.S. Army, 1918. Mem. Am. Soc. M.E., Soc. of Automotive Engrs., Soc. for Promotion Engring. Edn., Founders and Patriots of America, Sigma Xi, Psi Upsilon. Republican. Methodist. Mason (K.T.). Club: Engineers (Trenton, N.J.). Address: Graduate College, Princeton, N.J.

CULVER, Montgomery Morton, univ. prof.; b. McClure, O., Aug. 31, 1891; s. Walter Scott and Lovina (Beatty) C.; A.B., Defiance Coll.; M.A., Ohio State U.; Ph.D., U. of Pittsburgh; m. Kathryn May Harman, Apr. 6, 1918; children—Phyllis Jeanne, Montgomery Morton, Teacher, 1909-10, prin., 1910-13, 1919-20, supt., 1914-17, 1921-22; asst. in mathematics, Ohio State U., 1922-23; instr. in mathematics, U. of Pittsburgh, 1924-26, asst. prof., 1927-30, asso. prof., 1931-32, prof. since 1933. Served as sergt., Co. E, 329th Inf., U.S. Army, 1917-18; as sergt., 1st class, Q.M.C., with A.E.F., 1918-19. Mem. Am. Math. Soc., S.A.R. Mason. Home: 219 Lehigh St., Edgewood, Pa.

CUMBERLAND, William Wilson, economist; b. La Verne, Calif., Jan. 2, 1890; s. Julian Fee and Clara Euphemia (Higgins) C.; A.B., Occidental Coll., Los Angeles, Calif., 1912; A.M., Columbia, 1913; Ph.D., Princeton, 1916; D.D., Occidental Coll., 1937; m. Edith Griffith Osmond, Sept. 14, 1916; children—Mary Catherine, Julian Osmond, William Wilson, Helen. Was supt. Chrystie Street House, New York, 1914; instructor, assistant professor, associate professor and chief div. of research in agrl. economics, U. of Minn., 1916-19; leave of absence, 1917-19; research asso., U. of Calif. and Doheny Research Foundation, 1917-18; trade expert War Trade Bd., Washington, D.C., 1918; economic expert with Reparation and Financial commns., Am. Commn. to Negotiate Peace, Paris, France, 1919; financial expert Am. Mil. Mission to Armenia (Harbord Commn.), 1919; financial expert with U.S. High Commn., Am. Embassy, Constantinople, Turkey, 1919-20; asst. fgn. trade adviser and fgn. trade adviser, Dept. of State, Washington, D.C., 1920-21; financial commr. and supt. gen. of customs, Republic of Peru, 1921-23; gov. Reserve Bank of Peru, 1923-24; financial adviser, gen. receiver of Republic of Haiti, 1924-27; financial expert for Dept. of State, in Nicaragua, 1927-28; partner Wellington and Co., firm mem. New York Stock Exchange, since 1928; dir. St. Louis Southwestern R.R., Warren Foundry & Pipe Corpn. Economist with NRA, Washington, 1933. Am. del. to Conf. on German Long-Term Debts, Berlin, 1934. Mem. economic advisory com. Nat. Industrial Conf. Bd. and nat. assn. of mfrs. Dir. Am. Hosp., Istanbul, Turkey; mem. Am. Council of Inst. of Pacific Relations. Mem. Am. Science, Foreign Policy Assn., The Pilgrims, Am. Econ. Assn., Am. Statis. Assn. (pres. New York Chapter 1938-39), Phi Beta Kappa. Author: Coöperative Marketing, 1918; Nicaragua—An Economic and Financial Survey, 1928. Clubs: Cosmos (Washington, D.C.); Downtown Athletic (New York); Englewood (N.J.) Field. Home: 349 Booth Av., Englewood, N.J. Office: 120 Broadway, New York, N.Y.

CUMMINGS, Harold Neff, coll. prof.; b. Oxford, Me., Dec. 30, 1884; s. Charles Sumner and Carrie Alice (Neff) C.; student Edward Little High Sch., Auburn, Me., 1898-1902; A.B., Bates Coll., Lewiston, Me., 1906; student Harvard Summer Sch., 1906, 1908; S.B. in C.E., Mass. Inst. Tech., 1910; m. Katherine Austin Taaffe, June 11, 1912; 1 son, Charles Sumner II. Instr. science, Worcester (Mass.) Acad., 1906-08; gen. field and office work Buck and Sheldon, Inc., Hartford, Conn., 1910-11; prin. asst. engr. Great Northern Paper Co., Millinocket, Me., 1911-13; head civil engring. dept., Mechanics Inst., Rochester, N.Y., 1913-14; head mathematics dept. and asst. to prin. in administrn. work, English High Sch., Lynn, Mass., 1914-17; instr. mathematics, Wentworth Inst., Boston, Mass., 1917-18; hydraulic computation work for H. K. Barrows, cons. engr., Boston, 1918; asso. prof. civil engring., U. of Del., Newark, Del., pvt. practice as surveyor, 1918-20; prof. applied mathematics, Newark (N.J.) Coll. of Engring., 1920-27, prof. civil engring. since 1927, adminstr. in charge evening courses since 1927, supervisor evening sessions since 1938; mathematician for Edmund Halsey, civil engr. and surveyor, Newark, N.Y., 1920-27; licensed professional engr., N.J. Served successively as pvt., corp., sergt., Co. C, 1st Inf., N.G. State of Me., 1902-05. Trustee Belleville (N.J.) Community Service Bur. Fellow A.A.A.S., Am. Geog. Soc.; mem. Am. Soc. C.E., Soc. Am. Mil. Engrs., Soc. for Promotion Engring. Edn., Am. Assn. Univ. Profs., Phi Beta Kappa. Republican. Methodist. Author: (with Prof. Robert Widdop) Elementary Hydraulic Notes, 1935. Currently engaged in investigation of hydraulic coefficients as affected by mech. mixtures. Home: 30 Lloyd Pl., Belleville, N.J. Office: 367 High St., Newark, N.J.

CUMMINGS, Herbert Wesley, judge; b. Montandon, Pa., July 13, 1873; s. R. M. and Mary Elizabeth (Albright) C.; grad. high sch., Lewisburg, Pa.; read law in office of father; m. Margurette Edna Howell, Feb. 20, 1902 (dec.). Admitted to Pa. bar, 1897, and engaged in gen. practice of law at Sunbury, Pa., 1897-1935; mem. firm Cummings and Gubin, 1923-35; served as dist. atty., Northumberland Co., 1902-05, 1905-08; judge Northumberland Co. cts., 1912-22; served as mem. 68th Congress from 13th Dist. of Pa., 1923-24; elected and serving as judge Courts Northumberland Co. for term, 1936-46. Democrat. Home: 406 Market St., Sunbury, Pa.

CUMMINGS, James Howell, Jr., business exec.; b. Phila., Pa., May 1, 1895; s. James Howell and Annie (Richards) C.; grad. William Penn Charter Sch., Phila., 1914; A.B., Cornell U., 1918; m. Isabella Wanamaker, June 1921; children—Isabella Wanamaker, James Howell, 3d. With John B. Stetson Co., Phila., since 1919, v.p. and sec. since 1938. Served in Air Service, U.S. Navy, 1917-19; now lt. comdr. U.S.N. R.F. Republican. Presbyterian. Home: Buttonwood Farm, Berwyn, Chester Co., Pa. Office: 5th and Montgomery Av., Philadelphia, Pa.

CUMMINGS, Robert Augustus, cons. civil engr.; b. Fakenham, Norfolk, Eng., Aug. 28, 1866; s. Thomas Charles and Sarah (Brown) C.; came to U.S., 1887; ed. Greshams, Holt, Norfolk, Eng.; articled pupil to cons. engr., London, Eng., 1881-87; m. Mary Eloise Hood, Dec. 14, 1892; children—Robert Augustus, Jr., Eloise Hood (Mrs. Wm. Simpson). Employed as engr. with various cos. and r.r.s, 1887-93; engaged in gen. practice civil engring. and cons. engr., Phila., Pa., 1893-99; gen. practice civil engring. and cons. engr., Pittsburgh, Pa., since 1900; patented Cummings System of Reinforced Concrete; propr. Cummings Structural Concrete

Co., Electric Welding Co., Lehigh Valley Testing Co., Pittsburgh, Pa., 1903; mem. firm Robert A. Cummings & Associates. Mem. Am. Soc. Civil Engrs., Am. Ry. Engrs. Assn., Am. Soc. for Testing Materials, Inst. Civil Engrs. of Gt. Britain. Episcopalian. Contbr. many papers to socs. and articles to tech. journs. Home: 5911 Elgin Av., Pittsburgh, Pa. Office: 239 Fourth Av., Pittsburgh, Pa.

CUMMINS, Annie Blair Titman, life regent and organist, D.A.R.; b. Bridgeville, N.J., May 13, 1867; d. William Blair and Margaret Elizabeth (Roseberry) Titman; direct desc. Lodewick Titman, to America, 1730, John Blair, Col. Abram Van Campen, Adm. Jan Van Campen, Nicolace Dupuis; student Centenary Collegiate Inst., Hackettstown, N.J., 1888-90; m. Dr. George Wyckoff Cummins, June 14, 1890. Organist 1st Presbyn. Ch. School, Belvidere, N.J., 1893-1903; organist and chorister Methodist Ch., Belvidere, 1903-16. Supt. Jr. League work, Paterson (N.J.) Dist., 1910-17; steward Methodist Episcopal Ch., Belvidere, 1908-14; treas. Ladies Aid, of same, 1906-16; mem. exec. com. Belvidere Chapter of Am. Red Cross. Organizing regent Nat. Soc. of D.A.R., Belvidere, since 1931; organized Gen. William Maxwell Chapter, D.A.R., 1931, and since regent and organist. Mem. Nat. Assn. of Organists, Pa. Assn. of Organists, Am. Guild of Organists, Daus. of Colonial Wars of N.J., Daus. of the Am. Colonists, D.A.R., Huguenot Soc. of N.J., Huguenot Memorial Assn., Revolutionary Memorial Soc. of N.J., Blair Soc., Northampton Co. Hist. Soc., Sussex Co. Hist. Soc. (life), Warren Co. Hist. Soc. (charter), Woman's Branch of N.J. Hist. Soc., Am. McAll Assn. (pres. Belvidere Auxiliary). Democrat. Presbyterian. Star of the East Shrine, White Shrine of Jerusalem (Queen), Order of Eastern Star, (organist Warren Chapter 128), Order Pythian Sisters (organist Belvidere Temple 32; grand organist of Grand Temple, Order Pythian Sisters of N.J., 1935-38), Order of the Amaranth (Forest Ct. 44). Address: 202 Mansfield St., Belvidere, N.J.

CUMMINS, Charles Albert, consulting engr.; b. Baltimore, Md., Nov. 10, 1882; s. Robert Keys and Margaret (Paterson) C.; student Baltimore City Coll., 1897-99; B.S., St. Johns Coll., Annapolis, Md., 1903; m. Florence Elanore Stalfort, Nov. 29, 1903; children—Albert Stalfort, Florence Elanore (Mrs. Robert Grinstead Vaughan), John Robert. Instr. McDonogh (Md.) Sch., 1903-04; estimator and gen. supt. Charles L. Stockhausen Co., builders, Baltimore, 1904-11; organized Consol. Engring. Co., June 1, 1911, v.p. and gen. mgr., 1911-37, pres., 1937-38, retired, 1938; organized Cummins Constrn. Co., Jan. 10, 1938, with sons and nephew as officers, now serves as adviser, cons. engr. and chmn. of bd.; dir. Fidelity & Guaranty Fire Corpn. Mem. of bd. dirs. Assn. of Commerce of Baltimore, 1932-38. Dir. Kernan's Hosp. for Crippled Children. Formerly trustee St. John's Coll. and Roland Park Presbyn. Ch. Mem. Assn. of Gen. Contractors of America (former treas.), Am. Soc. C. E., Baltimore Engrs. Club, Bldg. Congress of Baltimore, Md. Acad. Sciences, Baltimore Real Estate Bd. Democrat. Presbyterian. Mason (Scottish Rite, Shriner), Elk. Clubs: University, Maryland Yacht (past commodore), Baltimore Country, Hillendale Country (Baltimore); Surf, Com. of 100 (Miami Beach, Fla.). Northern Residence: Ambassador Apts., Baltimore, Md. Home: Lagorce Island, Miami Beach, Fla. Office: 803 Cathedral St., Baltimore, Md.

CUNEO, Edmund Raymond, O.S.B., headmaster; b. St. Marys, Pa., Sept. 17, 1904; s. George Lewis and Cunecunda Helen (Jaeger) C.; A.B., St. Vincent Coll., Latrobe, Pa., 1926; Ph.D., St. Vincent Sem., 1931; M.S., U. of Notre Dame, 1934. Engaged as prof. bacteriology, St. Vincent Coll., Latrobe, Pa., continuously since 1926, asst. to dean of St. Vincent Coll., 1929-32, headmaster St. Vincent Coll. Prep. Sch. since 1932. Trustee St. Vincent Coll. Mem. Soc. Am. Bacteriologists, Nat. Edn. Assn. Dept. Secondary Sch. Prins. Republican. Roman Catholic. K.C. Home: St. Vincents Coll. Prep. Sch., Latrobe, Pa.

CUNLIFFE, Rex Barnard, educator; b. Chicago, Ill., Sept. 19, 1892; s. Cicero Martin and Cora (Barnard) C.; grad. Central High Sch., Detroit, 1911; student Detroit Coll. of Law, 1911-12; A.B., U. of Mich., 1916; student Universitee de Besancon, France, 1919; Ed. M., Harvard, 1925; m. Elizabeth Lamson, Dec. 26, 1938; foster son, Daniel Stackhouse. Teacher of history, Mt. Vernon (O.) High Sch., 1916-18; teacher of English and history, Neinas Intermediate Sch. and Central High Sch., Detroit, 1919-21; investigator vocational bureau, Detroit public schools, 1921-22; vocational adviser, Central High School of Detroit, 1922-23; director of vocational bureau, Coll. of City of Detroit, 1923-28, Southeast High Sch., Detroit, 1928-30; asst. prof. of edn., Rutgers U., 1930-35, asso. prof. since 1935. Served in Judge Adv. Gen. Dept., U.S. Army, 1918-19; attached to Post Sch., G.H.Q., Chaumont, France, 1918. Mem. N.J. Advisory Com. of Emergency Recovery Adminstrn. Mem. N.E.A., Guidance and Personnel Assn., Am. Assn. Univ. Profs., Phi Delta Kappa, Kappa Phi Kappa. Pres. Nat. Vocational Guidance Assn., 1939-40. Asso. editor of Occupations since 1938. Author of "Trends in Vocational Guidance," "Guidance Practice in New Jersey," etc., pub. in Studies in Edn., Rutgers U Contbr. to ednl. jours. Home: 2 Prescott St., Stelton, N.J. Office: Rutgers University, New Brunswick, N.J.

CUNNINGHAM, Jesse E. B.; judge Superior Ct. of Pa. since 1925, present term expires 1946. Address: 560 City Hall, Philadelphia, Pa.

CUNNINGHAM, John Horn, banking; b. Westminster, Md., Jan. 1, 1867; s. Wm. Amos and Mary Louisa (Horn) C.; A.B., Western Md. Coll., Westminster, Md., 1885; m. Mary Bruce Irwin, Sept. 12, 1893; 1 dau., Mary Louise. In employ Farmer's and Mechanics' Nat. Bank, Westminster, Md., continuously since 1885, clk. then teller, 1885-93, cashier since 1893; v.p. Times Printing Co.; surveyor of Port of Baltimore, Federal, 1924-33; former treas. Westminster Garage, Westminster Water Co.; former sec. and treas. Westminster Gas Light Co. and Winchester (Va.) Gas and Electric Light Co. Past pres. Md. State Firemens Assn., Westminster Fire Dept. Mem. bd. trustees Western Md. Coll., Westminster, Md. Republican. Lutheran. Masor (K.T.). Club: Forest and Stream. Home: 95 W Green St. Office: 187 E. Main St., Westminster, Md.

CUNNINGHAM, Joseph A., Pa. state official; b. Phila., Pa., Apr. 20, 1893; s. Michael J. and Margaret L. (Powers) C.; ed. St. Joseph's Coll., Phila., Pa.; m. Irene M. McCloskey, Nov. 29, 1916; children—Joseph A., Mary, Anne, William, Margaret. Asso. with Ford Motor Co., Phila., 1915-32; dir. Liquid Fuel Tax Div. of Pa., 1935-36; dep. sec. Property and Supplies of Pa., 1936-37; administrative asst. to Dir. of Gen. State Authority, Harrisburg, Pa., since 1938. Democrat. Roman Catholic. Home: 5126 N. Broad St., Philadelphia, Pa. Office: 112 N. 2d St., Harrisburg, Pa.

CUNNINGHAM, Samuel Kirkwood, investment banker; b. Indiana Co., Pa., Feb. 5, 1883; s. Robert Harvey and Sarah Jane (McQuaide) C.; A.B., Westminster Coll., New Wilmington, Pa., 1907; M.A., Cornell U., 1914; m. Mabel Bracher, Aug. 15, 1912; children—Eleanor Harriet, Kirkwood Bracher, Mabel Lucille. Teacher, Ernest, Indiana, Co., Pa., 1904; prin. of schs., New Wilmington, Pa., 1906; instr. science and mathematics, Butler (Pa.) High Sch., 1907-08, McKeesport (Pa.) High Sch., 1908-11, Pittsburgh High Sch., 1911-18; prin. evening schs., Pittsburgh, 1916; salesman and asst. mgr. New York investment banking firm, 1918-25; mem. investment banking firm, Pittsburgh, 1926-39; pres. S. K. Cunningham & Co., Inc., investment bankers, Pittsburgh; dir. and treas. Waverly Oil Works Co.; dir. M. F. Snyder Co. Trustee Westminster Coll., New Wilmington, Pa.; mem. advisory com. Salvation Army. Mem. Am. Investment Bankers Assn. Republican. United Presbyn. Mason. Club: Duquesne (Pittsburgh). Home: 1418 N. Highland Av. Office: Commonwealth Bldg., Pittsburgh, Pa.

CUPP, John E.; in practice of law since 1900; dir. various corpns. Address: Williamsport, Pa.

CUPPETT, David Earl, lawyer; b. Glade Farms, W.Va., Feb. 13, 1878; s. Alpheus and Elizabeth Ann (Harned) C.; LL.B., W.Va. Univ. Law Coll., Morgantown, W.Va., 1904; m. Vida Barnes, Dec. 26, 1905; children—Reardon Stewart, David Earl, Jr., Mary Elizabeth. Admitted to W.Va. bar, 1905 and engaged in gen. practice of law at Thomas, W.Va., since 1905; atty. city of Thomas since 1906, recorder, 1906-08, mayor, 1929-33; commr. sch. lands Tucker Co., 1906-14; served as mem. W.Va. Ho. of Dels., 1908-10 and 1918-20; counsel Miners & Merchants Bank, Thomas, W.Va., since 1914, dir. since 1914. Served as chmn. Four Minute Men Tucker Co. during World War. Chmn. Citizens Mil. Training Camps, Tucker Co., since 1928. Mem. W.Va. Bar Assn., Tucker Co. Bar Assn., Sigma Nu. Republican. Methodist. Mason. K.P. Club: Fairfax. Home: Brown St. Office: East Av., Thomas, W.Va.

CUPPIA, Jerome Chester, stock broker; b. Pelham Manor, N.Y., Sept. 29, 1890; s. Caesar Augustus and Josephine Clementine (Klugist) C.; student Columbia U. and St. Francis Xavier Coll., New York; m. Helen Raymond, June 22, 1918; children—Jerome Chester, Helen Ramona. Connected with Craig & Jenks and its successor, Jenks, Gwynne & Co., 1907-16; partner Robertson & Co., becoming mem. N.Y. Cotton Exchange, 1916; formed firm Cuppia & Robertson, 1920, J. C. Cuppia & Co., 1923; partner E. A. Pierce & Co. since 1927; pres. and dir. Gen. Reconstruction Corpn.; v.p. and dir. Fundamental Investors, Inc., Fundamental Group Corpn.; dir. Seaboard Metal Corpn.; vice-pres. Commodity Exchange, Inc.; mem. N.Y. Stock Exchange, N.Y. Curb Exchange, N.Y. Cotton Exchange, Dallas Cotton Exchange, Memphis Cotton Exchange. Served in U.S. Navy during World War. Dir. Beekman St. Hosp. Catholic. Clubs: Lambs, Metropolitan, India House, Stock Exchange Luncheon, Lotos (New York); Montclair Golf, Sea View Golf, Nassau of Princeton, Orange Lawn Tennis (New Jersey). Home: 62 Undercliff Rd., Montclair, N.J. Office: 40 Wall St., New York, N.Y.

CURD, Thomas Henry Shelton, judge; b. Howardsville, Va., Dec. 19, 1882; s. Joseph Howard and Julia Elizabeth (Dooley) C.; student Randolph-Macon Acad., Front Royal, Va., 1898-1900; B.A., U. of Va., 1905, LL.B., 1906; m. Grace Harman, Feb. 28, 1910; children—Howard Harman, John Chandler, Thomas Henry Shelton Admitted to bars of Va. and W.Va., 1906; associated with law firm Ritz & Litz, Welch, W.Va., 1907-08, Kegley & Curd, Wytheville Va., 1908-09, Anderson, Strother, Hughes & Curd, 1909-21, Strother, Sale, Curd & Tucker, 1921-29, Strother, Sale, Curd & St. Clair, 1929-32, Strother, Curd & Berry, 1932-36; judge 8th judicial circuit of W.Va., since 1937, term expiring 1944. Dem. presidential elector, 1924; chmn. Dem. exec. com., 1918-24; Dem. candidate for Congress, primary, 1926, State Senate, primary, 1934; del. to Dem. Nat. Conv., 1932. Chmn. 4-Minute Men, World War; chmn. Citizens Military Training Camp. Mem. State Commn. on Historic and Scenic Markers. Past Pres. Boy Scout Council for Southern W.Va. area. Mem. Am. Bar Assn., W.Va. Bar Assn. (past v.p.; past chmn. exec. com.), McDowell Co. Bar Assn., Welch Chamber of Commerce (past pres.), S.A.R. Democrat. Episcopalian. Clubs: McDowell Country, Welch Kiwanis (past pres.). Mason (Shriner). Address: Welch, W.Va.

CURLEY, Michael Joseph, archbishop; b. Golden Island, Athlone, Ireland, Oct. 12, 1879; s. Michael and Maria (Ward) C.; A.B., Royal U. of Ireland, 1909; B.D., Propaganda Theol. U., Rome, Italy, 1901, S.T.L., 1903. Ordained R.C. priest, 1904; missionary in Florida, 1904-14; apptd. bishop of St. Augustine by Pope Pius X, Apr. 2, 1914; consecrated June 30, 1914; apptd. archbishop of Baltimore to succeed Cardinal Gibbons, Aug. 1, 1921; installed in Baltimore, Nov. 30, 1921. Address: 408 N. Charles St., Baltimore, Md.

CURRAN, James; judge Ct. of Common Pleas, Schuylkill Co., since 1937, term expires 1948. Address: Pottsville, Pa.

CURRAN, Thomas Aidan, lawyer; b. Morton, Pa., Aug. 6, 1900; s. Joseph F. and Mary (Conway) C.; student Morton (Pa.) Pub. Schs., 1906-14, Swarthmore (Pa.) Pub. High Sch., 1914-18; LL.B., Temple U. Sch. of Law, Phila., 1926; m. Grace McClatchy, June 7, 1930; children—Mary Grace, Thomas Aidan, Robert Emmett. Admitted to Delaware Co. Bar, 1925, and since in practice at Chester, Pa.; mem. of firm Taylor, Chadwick & Weeks, 1926-37, Chadwick, Weeks, Curran & Ives, since 1938. Served in students army training corps, Swarthmore (Pa.) Coll., 1918. Mem. state legislature, First Dist., Delaware Co., Pa., 1939; solicitor, co. controller, Delaware Co., Pa., 1929-32. Mem. Delaware Co., Pa. bar assns. Republican. Catholic. Elk, K.C. Clubs: Chester (Chester, Pa.); Lawyers (Delaware Co., Pa.), Springhaven Golf. Home: 501 E. 21st St. Office: Delaware Co. Nat. Bank Bldg., Chester, Pa.

CURRAN, William; in gen. practice of law since 1909. Address: Calvert Bldg., Baltimore, Md.

CURRIE, Barton Wood, editor; b. N.Y. City, Mar. 8, 1878; s. Duncan D. H. and Mary Wood (Depew) C.; student Harvard, 1895, 96, New York Law Sch., 1897, 98; m. Florence Louise Abbott. Reporter for the New York Evening Sun, 1900-02; New York Times, 1902-03; reporter and rewriter, New York Evening World, 1903-12; asso. editor Country Gentleman, 1912-17, editor 1917-20; editor Ladies' Home Journal, Oct. 1920-Aug. 1928; editor World's Work, Aug. 1928-June 1929. Sent by New York World to Labrador, 1909, to meet Peary on his return from his last polar expdn., and wrote story presenting Peary's side in the Cook-Peary controversy; contbr. about 100 short stories and articles to mags. up to 1913. Chief yeoman U.S.N., Spanish-Am. War. Mem. Bibliog. Soc. of America, Am. Fed. of Arts. Episcopalian. Clubs: Harvard, Grolier (New York); Harvard, Franklin Inn (Philadelphia). Author: (with Augustin McHugh) Officer 666 (from play of same name), 1912; The Tractor, 1916; Fishers of Books, 1931; Booth Tarkington—a Bibliography, 1932. Home: Bala-Cynwyd, Pa.; (summer) Chatham, Mass.

CURRIE, D. Angus, pres. Erie Foundry Co.; b. Midland, Mich., Nov. 14, 1886; s. Dougald and Flora (MacDonald) C.; student high sch.; m. Anna M. Quinn, Apr. 29, 1911; children—James A., Mary F. Pres. Erie (Pa.) Foundry Co. since 1930, also treas. and gen. mgr.; dir. First Nat. Bank of Erie (Pa.). Mem. Mfrs. Assn. of Erie (dir.; past pres.), Nat. Assn. of Mfrs. (dir.). Home: 4618 Cherry St. Office: Erie, Pa.

CURRIE, Edward W., lawyer; b. New York City, Apr. 19, 1896; s. Edward J. and Mary (Kensing) C.; grad. Keyport (N.J.) High Sch., 1913, Perkiomen Sch., Pennsburg, Pa., 1914, U.S. Army Sch. Aeronautics at Mass. Inst. Tech., 1918; Litt.B., Princeton, 1918; J.D., N.Y.U. Law Sch., 1926; m. Myrtle Thompson, Mar. 4, 1916; 1 dau., Janet. Practice of law at Matawan, N.J., since 1926; asst. atty. gen. and counsel to Dept. of Agr. and Milk Control Bd. of State of N.J. since 1934. Served as 2d lt., U.S. Army Air Service, during World War. Mayor, Borough of Matawan (N.J.), since 1932. Mem. Monmouth Co., Am. bar assns. Democrat. Presbyterian. Clubs: Princeton (New York City); Forsgate Country (Jamesburg, N.J.). Home: 87 Broad St. Office: 123 Main St., Matawan, N.J.

CURRIE, Norman W.; sr. attending surgeon Muhlenberg Hosp.; mem. surg. staff Somerset Hosp. Address: 508 Central Av., Plainfield, N.J.

CURRIER, Arnold John, univ. prof.; b. Georgetown, N.Y., Dec. 8, 1892; s. Floyd and Lillian Emma (Priest) C.; A.B., Colgate U., Hamilton, N.Y., 1915; M.S., Pa. State Coll., 1921; Ph.D., Cornell U., 1923; m. Norma Ida Utter, Dec. 24, 1918; children—Arnold John, Warren Wadsworth, Carolyn Ida, Ellen Edna, Constance Ann (dec.). Instr. science, high sch., 1915-17; instr. chemistry, Pa. State Coll., 1919-23, asst. prof., 1924-31, asso. prof. chemistry since 1932. Served in Ordnance Dept., U.S. Army, assigned to General Chem. Co., 1917-18. Mem. Am. Chem. Soc., Phi Beta Kappa, Sigma Xi, Phi Lambda Upsilon, Alpha Chi Sigma, Kappa Delta Rho. Republican. Methodist. Home: 508 E. Foster Av., State College, Pa.

CURRIER, Richard Dudley, lawyer, educator; b. Bridgeport, Conn., Aug. 25, 1877; s. Levi Wheeler and Sarah Elizabeth (Ayer) C.; B.A., Yale, 1900; Boston U. Law Sch., 1900-01; LL.B., New York Law Sch., 1902; m. Adèle Josephine Ames, Oct. 20, 1909; children—Elizabeth Adèle (Mrs. Thomas Jefferson Morris), Ruth Prentice, Richard Dustin, Eleanor Ames (dec.). Began practice in N.Y. City, 1902; founder, 1908, and pres. New Jersey Law Sch., Newark, 1908-34, treas. since 1934; founder, 1930, and pres. Dana Coll., Newark, 1930-34, treas. 1934-36; organizer Seth Boyden Sch. of Business, 1930; founder with Dr. T. Lawrence Davis of Stoneleigh Coll., Rye, N.H., pres. since 1934; pres. Dorset Investment Corpn., 40 Rector St. Corpn., N.J. Law Sch. Press. Mem. Am. Bar Assn., Am. Soc. Internat. Law, Internat. Law Assn., Acad. Polit. Science, English-Speaking Union. Republican. Unitarian. Clubs: Essex (Newark); Dorset (Vt.) Field; Bankers (New York). Author: Cases on Torts (with Oscar M. Bate), 1914; Negotiable Instruments, 1922. Editor: Commercial Law, 1922. Home: 95 S. Mountain Av., Montclair, N.J. Address: Stoneleigh College, Rye, N.H.; also 225 Broadway, New York, N.Y.

CURRY, Charles Henry; pres. Kopp Glass, Inc.; officer or dir. many other companies. Home: R.D. 3, Coraopolis, Pa. Office: Swissvale, Pa.

CURRY, Edward T.; mem. law firm Curry & Purnell. Address: Camden, N.J.

CURRY, Glendon Elder, M.D.; b. McKeesport, Pa., June 28, 1869; s. Moses L. and Sarah (Nicholls) C.; grad. McKeesport High Sch., 1885; M.D., U. of Pa., 1892; m. Ariana Riddle, June 29, 1911; 1 son, Daniel Noble. Asst. chemist Nat. Tube Co., McKeesport, 1887-88; interne St. Josephs Hosp., Phila., 1892, Phila. Hosp., 1893; house surgeon Wills' Eye Hosp., Phila., 1894-95; asst. ophthalmic surgeon Mercy Hosp., Pittsburgh, 1896-1901; ophthalmic surgeon St. Francis' Hosp., 1898-1904, Western Pa. Hosp., 1901-12; cons. ophthalmic surgeon Western Pa. Hosp., Pittsburgh, since 1912. Fellow Am. Coll. Surgeons; mem. A.M.A., Pa. State Med. Soc., Allegheny County Med. Soc., Pittsburgh Acad. Medicine, Pittsburgh Ophthalmol. Soc., Am. Acad. Ophthalmology and Otolaryngology. Republican. Episcopalian. Mason. Clubs. Duquesne, University (Pittsburgh). Home: 1505 Denniston Av. Office: 1002 Westinghouse Bldg., Pittsburgh, Pa.

CURRY, Grant, lawyer; b. Pittsburgh, Pa., July 7, 1884; s. Henry Milo and Harriet Virginia (Girty) C.; student Shady Side Acad., Pittsburgh, 1902-04; M.E., U. of Pittsburgh, 1908, LL.B., 1911; m. Carolyn Irwin Hays, June 3, 1911; children—James McCutcheon, William Hays, Carolyn Hays, Kate Crossan, Crossan Hays, Grant, Virginia, David Milo. Admitted to Pa. bar, 1912; practice Pittsburgh, 1912-21; trust officer Colonial Trust Co., 1922-29; sec. and dir. Iron City Tool Works; dir. Kopp Glass, Inc. Served as 1st lt. Field Arty. Res. Corps, 1917-19, with A.E.F., 1918-19. Mem. Civil Service Commn. of Pittsburgh, 1934-35; trustee Tuberculosis League of Pittsburgh. Mem. Am. Bar Assn., Pa. Bar Assn., Allegheny Co. Bar Assn., Chi Psi. Republican. Clubs: Duquesne, Pittsburgh, University (Pittsburgh). Home: 814 Morewood Av. Office: 1419 Park Bldg., Pittsburgh, Pa.

CURRY, Haskell Brooks, univ. prof.; b. Millis, Mass., Sept. 12, 1900; s. Samuel Silas and Anna (Baright) C.; A.B. (cum laude), Harvard, 1920; grad. study Mass. Inst. Tech., 1920-22, Harvard Grad. Sch. Arts & Scis., 1922-27, A.M., 1924; Ph.D., U. of Göttingen, Germany, 1930; grad. student Inst. for Advanced Study, Princeton, 1938-39; m. Mary Virginia Wheatley, of Hurlock, Md., July 3, 1928; children—Anne Wright, Robert Wheatley. Began as lab. asst. to Prof. P. W. Bridgman, Harvard, 1922-23; instr. mathematics, Harvard, half-time, 1926-27; instr. mathematics, Princeton U., 1927-28; asst. prof. mathematics, Pa. State Coll., 1929-33, asso. prof. since 1933; fellow Nat. Research Council, U. of Chicago, 1931-32; mem. corpn. Curry Sch. of Expression, Boston, Mass. Served in S.A.T.C., 1918. Mem. orgn. com. and chmn. conf. on math. logic, Internat. Congress of Mathematicians, 1940. Fellow A.A.A.S.; mem. Am. Math. Soc., Am. Philos. Assn., Assn. for Symbolic Logic (past v.p., pres. 1938-40), Math. Assn. of America, Nuttall Ornithol. Club, Sigma Xi, Pi Mu Epsilon, Sigma Pi Sigma. Episcopalian. Home: 228 E. Prospect Av., State College, Pa.

CURRY, P(eter) H.; pres. South Penn Oil Co., Pittsburgh, Pa.*

CURRY, Robert Granville, lawyer; b. Staunton, Va., Apr. 9, 1890; s. Charles and Grace Elizabeth (Duncan) C.; grad. Staunton High Sch., 1907, B.A., U. of Va., 1911, LL.B., 1913; m. Elise Haile, Dec. 2, 1914; children—Tempe Haile, Elise Duncan. Admitted to Va. bar, 1913, and began practice in Norfolk, Va., 1913; atty. Interstate Commerce Commn., 1916-20; asst. chief Bureau of Inquiry, same, 1920-23, asst. chief counsel, 1923, 1st asst. chief counsel, 1924-26; mem. firm McChord, Curry & Dolan, Washington, D.C., 1929-34; judge Juvenile Court, Montgomery County, Md., 1931-35; practice of law as mem. firm Curry & Dolan, Washington, D.C., since 1934. Served in O.T. C., Fort Monroe, Va., Oct.-Nov. 1918. Mem. Am. Bar Assn., Dist. of Columbia Bar Assn., Assn. of Practitioners before the Interstate Commerce Commn. (former chmn. grievance com.; now chmn. D.C. com. on admissions to practice; also mem. bd. editors Practitioners Jour.), Delta Psi, Phi Beta Kappa, Raven Soc. Democrat. Clubs: Chevy Chase; Edgemore (Bethesda, Md.); Farmington Country (Charlottesville, Va.). Home: 405 Battery Lane, Bethesda, Md. Office: Southern Bldg., Washington, D.C.

CURRY, W. Lawrence, organist, coll. prof.; b. Parnassus, Pa., Mar. 19, 1906; s. Rev. William M. (D.D.) and Juliet (Titsworth) C.; A.B., U. of Pa., 1927; M.S.M., Union Theol. Sem., 1931; m. Mary Louise Hummel, Sept. 10, 1932; 1 son, Lawrence Hummel. Organist 9th Presbyn. Ch., Phila., Pa., 1923-25, First Presbyn. Ch., Camden, N.J., 1925-27; organist various chs., 1928-32; organist First Meth. Ch., Germantown, Pa., since 1932; professional accompanist Choral Art Soc., Phila., and other orgns.; instr. piano, organ and theory, U. of Pa. Sch. Edn., since 1931; head dept. music, Beaver Coll., Jenkintown, Pa., since 1934. Mem. Am. Guild of Organists, Phi Delta Kappa, Phi Beta Kappa. Republican. Presbyn. Composer of a number of various works pub. by well known mus. pub. houses. Home: 117 Greenwood Av., Jenkintown, Pa.

CURTIN, Eugene A.; attending surgeon, dept. otolaryngology Moses Taylor, Mercy and St. Joseph's Hosps. Address: 506 Spruce St., Scranton, Pa.

CURTIS, Charles Minot, judge; b. Newark, Del., Aug. 19, 1859; s. Frederick Augustus and Harriet L. (Hurd) C.; A.B., Delaware Coll., 1877; LL.B., Harvard, 1881; m. Phœbe George Bradford, Mar. 31, 1886; children—Frederick A., Stephen. Admitted to bar, 1883; practiced at Wilmington, Del.; city solicitor Wilmington, 1891-93; chancellor, and presiding judge Supreme Court of Del., 1909-21. V.p. Delaware Trust Co.; judge Juvenile Court since 1926. Republican. Mgr. Del. Industrial Sch. for Girls, Babies' Hosp.; trustee U. of Del.; trustee and chancellor of the P.E. Diocese of Del. Home: 2611 W. 16th St., Wilmington, Del.

CURTIS, Eugene Newton, prof. history; b. White Plains, N.Y., June 23, 1880; s. Newton Freeman and Gertrude I. (Preudhomme) C.; grad. Phillips Acad., Andover, Mass., 1897; B.A., Yale, 1901; B.D., Episcopal Theol. Sch., Cambridge, Mass., 1904; M.A., Harvard, 1904; studied U. of Paris, 1912-14, U. of Munich, 1914; Ph.D., Columbia, 1917; m. Blanche O'Neill; 1 son, Franklin O'Neill. Instr. in history, U. of Wis., 1915-17; asst. prof. history Goucher Coll., Baltimore, Md., 1917-19, asso. prof., 1919-20, prof. since 1920, also acting dean, 1919-21. Mem. Am. Hist. Assn., Md. History Teachers' Assn., Société d'Histoire de la Révolution de 1848, Société d'Histoire Moderne. Republican. Episcopalian. Author: The French Assembly of 1848 and American Constitutional Doctrines, 1918; Saint-Just, Colleague of Robespierre, 1935; also hist. articles in Am. and European mags. Home: 4323 Wickford Rd., Baltimore, Md.

CURTIS, George Bartlett, educator; b. Pittsfield, Mass., Aug. 3, 1893; s. Charles Newman and Lillian (Bartlett) C.; grad. Pittsford (Vt.) High Sch., 1911; A.B., Wesleyan U., Middletown, Conn., 1916; A.M., Columbia, 1923; student Univ. of Edinburgh, Scotland, spring 1919, Am. Inst. of Banking, New York, 1919-20, Univ. of Grenoble, France, summer 1923; m. Josephine Crocker, June 23, 1923; children—Robert Bartlett, Dorothy Judd. Asst. office mgr. World Book Co., Yonkers, N.Y., 1916-18; foreign collections corr. Guaranty Trust Co., New York City, 1919-20; asso. with Lehigh U., Bethlehem, Pa., since 1920, as asst. prof. of economics, 1920-26, asst. dean and asst. registrar, 1926-28, registrar and asso. dean, 1928-38, registrar and univ. editor since 1938, sec. of faculty since 1927. Served in Q.M.C., U.S. Army with A.E.F., 1918-19; with U.S. Army detachment in Brit. univs., 1919. Mem. Am. Economics Assn., Modern Lang. Assn. America, Shakespeare Assn. of America, Bacon Soc. (London), Eastern Assn. of Coll. Deans and Advisers of Men (exec. com. since 1936), Middle States Assn. of Collegiate Registrars (vice-pres. 1936, pres. 1938), S.A.R., Scabbard and Blade, Sigma Xi, Alpha Kappa Psi (chmn. nat. scholarship com. since 1936), Phi Beta Kappa. Republican. Methodist. Author: A Study in Elizabethan Typography, 1939; (jointly with Bradley Stoughton) The Control and Stabilization of College Enrollment, 1939; contbr. to Baconiana, Quarterly Jour. of Bacon Soc., Jour. Engring. Edn., The Churchman. Lecturer: The Greater Shakespeare; Shakespeare, Bacon and the Great Unknown, Elizabeth and Leicester, Francis Bacon's Typographical Cipher. Home: 516 Brodhead Av. Address: Lehigh University, Bethlehem, Pa.

CURTIS, Harvey Lincoln, physicist; b. Mason, Mich., Dec. 14, 1875; s. Wm. Howell and Sarah Bowen (Ormsby) C.; grad. Mason High Sch., 1893; Ph.B., U. of Mich., 1900, A.M., 1903, Ph.D., 1910; m. Anna Puffer, Aug. 26, 1903; children—Roger W., Howard J., Alvin G. (dec.), Norma L., Mildred A. Asst. in Physical Lab., U. of Mich., 1902-03; instr. physics, Mich. State Agrl. Coll., 1903-07; with Bur. of Standards, Washington, D.C., successively as asst. physicist, 1907-13, asso. physicist, 1913-18, physicist, 1918-24, sr. physicist, 1924-28, prin. physicist since 1928. Fellow Am. Physical Soc., A.A.A.S., Am. Inst. E.E. (chairman of Washington, D.C., section, 1935); mem. Washington Acad. Sciences, Washington Philos. Soc. (pres. 1931), Am. Soc. for Testing Materials, Am. Optical Soc., Phi Beta Kappa; mem. Internat. Electrical Congress, Paris, France, 1933. Methodist. Club: Cosmos. Author: Electrical Measurements; also scientific papers of Bur. of Standards and articles in tech. jours. Home: 6316 Delaware St., Chevy Chase, Md.

CURTIS, Lawrence, D.D.S., M.D.; asso. prof. maxillofacial surgery U. of Pa. Grad. Sch. and U. of Pa. Dental Sch.; asso. in maxillofacial surgery Grad. Hosp. of U. of Pa.; visiting oral surgeon Phila. Gen. and Delaware County Hosps.; asso. oral surgeon Presbyn. Hosp.; oral surgeon Bryn Mawr Hosp. Address: 255 S. 17th St., Philadelphia, Pa.

CURTIS, Leona, sculptor; b. Plainfield, N.J., Jan. 26, 1908; d. John E. and Catherine (Bishop) C.; ed. Art Students League under R. Laurent, 1930-34; studied with Jose de Creeft, sculptor, 1936-38, C. Scaravaglione, sculptor, 1935. Exhibited at Pa. Acad. Fine Arts, 1935; Salons of America, N.Y. City, 1936; rep. N.J. at Nat. Exhbn. of Am. Art., N.Y. City, 1937; N.J. Artists, Warren Hotel, Spring Lake, N.J., 1938; 14th annual exhbn. of N.Y. Soc. of Women Artists, 1939; executed bronze relief of Abraham Clark, signer of U.S. Constitution, for High Sch., Roselle, N.J. Awarded First Prize, N.J. State Exhbn., Montclair, 1935. Mem. Am. Artists Professional League, N.Y. Soc. of Women Artists, Art Students League. Republican. Presbyn. Home: 768 Woodland Av., Plainfield, N.J.

CURTIS, Melville Goss, mfr. pile fabrics; b. Olean, N.Y., Aug. 21, 1875; s. Rev. Henry M. (D.D.) and Evelyn Cramer (Goss) C.; student pub. schs., Flint, Mich., Cincinnati, O., Franklin Sch., Flint; A.B., Yale, 1897; m. Emma Warren, May 24, 1909; children—Evelyn Goss (Mrs. James Houston Young), Katherine Wilson (Mrs. Theodore H. Vetterlein, Jr.). Asso. with Collins & Aikman Corpn., mfrs. pile fabrics, Phila., since entering employ in 1897, successively employee, foreman, asst. supt., supt., asst. treas., treas., pres., and chmn. of bd. since 1929. Republican. Presbyterian. Clubs: Union League, Racquet, Yale, Philadelphia Country (Phila.); Merion Cricket (Haverford, Pa.); Pine Valley (N.J.) Golf; Fishers Island (N.Y.); Seaview (Absecon, N.J.). Home: Bala. Office: 51st and Parkside Av., Philadelphia, Pa.

CURTIS, Richard, banker; b. Williamstown, N.J., Nov. 11, 1895; s. John and Emma (Pierce) C.; student pub. schs.; Camden Commercial Coll., 1912; m. Ruth E. Haines, June 18, 1919; 1 son, William J. Began in secretarial capacity, W.J.&S. Ry., 1912; asst. chief accountant Cambria Steel Co., 1917-23; asst. comptroller Yellow Cab Co. of Pa., 1923-27; vice-pres. and dir. Yellow Cab Co., Camden, N.J., 1926-28; sec.-treas. and dir. Yellow Cab Co. of Atlantic City, N.J., 1927-28; comptroller Mitten Bank & Trust Co., Phila., 1928-31, treas. since 1931; vice-pres. Securities Realty Co. since 1932; dir. Mitten Bank & Trust Co., Securities Realty Co. Served as pvt., U.S. Army, during World War. Mem. Am. Legion. Republican. Mason (Haddonfield Lodge 130, Excelsior Consistory). Clubs: Manufacturers and Bankers (Phila.); Tavistock Country (Haddonfield, N.J.). Home: 164 Wayne Av., Haddonfield, N.J. Office: Market St. and W. City Hall Sq., Philadelphia, Pa.

CURTIS, Samuel Philip, pres. Tunnel & Mine Machinery Co.; b. Penn Yan, N.Y., Jan. 1, 1871; s. Perley Phillips and Eva (Hewins) C.; grad. Penn Yan (N.Y.) High Sch., 1889; M.E., Lehigh U., Bethlehem, Pa., 1896; m. Louise Sumner, Apr. 5, 1904 (died 1920); children—Barbara (Mrs. William Cornell Archbold), Marjorie (Mrs. Raymond Frederick Brayer), Roger Sumner, Christine; m. 2d, Mrs. Lenore Victor Giddings, Feb. 1, 1922 (divorced 1932). Cadet engr. Newark (N.J.) Gas Co., 1896-97, gen. foreman Front St. Works, 1897-99; constrn. engr. and mgr. N.Y. Suburban Gas & Electric Co., Mt. Vernon, N.Y., 1899-1900; with Am. Gas Co., Phila., 1900-27, successively as constrn. engr., chief engr., gen. supt., gen. mgr.; pres. Tunnel & Mine Machinery Co., Phila., since 1926. Mem. Soc. Gas Lighting of N.Y., Delta Phi. Republican. Episcopalian. Clubs: Union League, Corinthian Yacht, Philadelphia Country (Phila.). Home: Corinthian Yacht Club. Office: 112 S. 16th St., Philadelphia, Pa.

CURTIS, William Franklin, college pres.; b. nr. Souderton, Bucks Co., Pa., Feb. 12, 1873; s. William Henry and Elizabeth Seiple (Miller) C.; A.B., Franklin and Marshall Coll., Pa., 1898, LL.D., 1926; graduated Theological Seminary of the Reformed Church, Lancaster, Pa., 1901; Litt.D., Muhlenberg Coll., 1913; m. Anna Frances Denlinger, June 11, 1901. Ordained Ref. Ch. in U.S. ministry, 1901; pastor St. Paul's Ref. Ch., Kansas City, Mo., 1901-08; pres. Cedar Crest Coll. for Women, Allentown, Pa., since June 1, 1908. Republican. Mason (32°, Shriner). Address: Allentown, Pa.

CURTISS, Charles Dwight, highway engring.; b. Camden, Mich., Dec. 23, 1887; s. Manly Jackson and Addie E. (Alward) C.; prep. edn. Camden and Hillsdale High Schools, Mich.; B.S. in engring., Mich. State Coll., East Lansing, Mich., 1911; A.M., Columbia, 1915; C.E., Iowa State Coll., Ames, Ia., 1916; m. Dorothea Davis, July 18, 1919; children—Charles Dwight, Martha. Instr. civil engring., Mich. Agr. Coll., 1911-13; chief of party for state road surveys, Mich. State Highway Dept., June-Dec. 1913; with Continental Public Works Co., asphalt paving, New York, 1914; asst. engr. Ia. Highway Commn., 1915-17; testing engr. J. B. McCrary, Atlanta, Ga., May-Sept. 1917; asst. to chief, Bureau Public Roads, U.S. Dept. Agr., Washington, D.C., 1919-27, chief div. of control since 1927. Served as 1st lt., later capt., Corps of Engrs., U.S. Army, 1917-19; 16 months with A.E.F. Mem. Am. Soc. Civil Engrs., Am. Assn. of State Highway Officials. Mason (32°). Home: 10 W. Virgilia St., Chevy Chase, Md. Office: 515 14th St., N.W., Washington, D.C.

CURTISS, Elliott Jr., editor and author; b. Lansdowne, Pa., Aug. 7, 1904; s. Elliott and Caroline (Turner) C.; student Germantown (Pa.) Acad., 1916-22, Fishburne Mil. Sch., Waynesboro, Va., 1922-24, Wharton Sch., U. of Pa., 1924-28; m. Isabel Brooks Graves, Sept. 14, 1929. Began as writer, 1924; editor The Automobile Trade Journal, Phila., 1935-38; asso. editor Click, nat. picture mag., Phila., since 1938. Mem. S.A.R. Republican. Episcopalian. Club: Advertising Club of New York (New York City). Author: Slang on Wheels, vols. 1 and 2, 1937; contbr. Saturday Evening Post. Home: Ivyland, Bucks County, Pa. Office: 400 N. Broad St., Philadelphia, Pa.

CURTISS, William John, journalist and publicity; b. Rochester, N.Y., July 16, 1873; s. Jay Charles Dan and Francis Marion (Sheffer) C.; A.B., Cornell U., 1896; m. Mary Isabel Smith, of Freeport, L.I., N.Y., Apr. 24, 1897; 1 dau., Marion (m. Joseph G. Stanton, dec., m. 2d, Edwin L. Slocum). Asso. editor Cornell Daily Sun, 1895, editor in chief, 1896; reporter, later market editor, New York Commercial, 1898-1902; asst. city editor, N.Y. Journ. Commerce, later night editor same, 1903-06; N.Y. mgr. Commercial Telegram Bur., 1907-11; Am. financial corr. London Times, 1912-16, Am. bus. mgr. same, 1917-22; mem. Bradstreet's staff, 1917-32; in charge pub. utility news Wall St. Journ., 1922-26; publicity with G. L. Ohrstrom & Co., N.Y. City, 1926-31, 1934-38; asso. with Federal Water Service Corpn. since 1926, now full time statistical work for same since 1938. School trustee, South Orange, N.J., 1915. Mem. Quill and Dagger, Kappa Sigma. Awarded N.Y. State scholarship 4-yr. course at Cornell. Republican. Episcopalian. Home: 41 N. Fullerton Av., Montclair, N.J. Office: 90 Broad St., New York, N.Y.

CURTZE, Alban William, lawyer; b. Erie, Pa., May 24, 1901; s. Julius E. and Baroness Meta (von Hanxleden) C.; A.B., U. of Mich., Ann Arbor, Mich., 1923; student Harvard Law Sch., 1923-24; LL.B., Dickinson Law Sch., Carlisle, Pa., 1926; M.A., Dickinson Coll., 1926; m. Virginia Marie Shissler, July 14, 1931; 1 son, Edward William. Admitted to Supreme Court of Pa. bar, 1927, and since practiced at Erie, Pa.; mem. firm Brooks and Curtze, Erie, Pa., 1928-30, Brooks, Curtze and Silin, Erie, since 1930; v.p. Erie Abstract Title Co.; sec. Sterling Aluminum Co., Sterling Factories, Inc.; dir. Erie Iron and Supply Corpn., Sterling Seal Co., Erie Motors, Inc. Vice-pres. Erie Art Club. Mem. Erie Co. Hist. Soc. (treas. since 1937), Corpus Juris, Erie Co. Bar Assn., Pa. State Bar Assn., Am. Bar Assn., Am. Judicature Soc., Delta Chi. Republican. Evang. Reform Ch. Mason (Shriner, Grotto), Odd Fellow. Clubs: University, Shrine, Lions, Erie Tennis and Country (Erie, Pa.). Contbr. to various legal jours. Home: 438 Vermont Av. Office: Erie Trust Bldg., Erie, Pa.

CURTZE, Frederick F.; pres. Heisler Locomotive Works; also officer and dir. many other corpns. Home: 356 W. 6th St. Office: 16th and Hickory Sts., Erie, Pa.

CUSHMAN, Edward H.; in practice of law since 1920. Office: Fidelity-Philadelphia Trust Bldg., Philadelphia, Pa.

CUSHWA, David K. Sr., pres. Victor Cushwa Sons, Inc.; b. Williamsport, Md., Mar. 14, 1869; s. Victor and Mary A. (Kreigh) C.; student Rock Hill Coll., Ellicott City, Md., 1885-87; m. Nannie M. Taylor, Apr. 17, 1895; children—Chistie Ann (Mrs. Charles H. McEnerney), David K., Catherine E. Clk. Victor Cushwa Sons, Inc., Williamsport and Hagerstown, Md., 1887-39, pres. since 1930; pres. Washington & Berkley Bridge Co., Savings Bank, Williamsport, Md., since 1935; dir. Blue Ridge Ins. Co.; dir. Washington Co. (Md.) Welfare Assn. Democrat. Roman Catholic. Address: 129 E. Potomac St., Williamsport, Md.

CUSICK, Martin Edward, lawyer; b. Sharpsville, Pa., Nov. 1, 1902; s. Michael Glynn and Ellen (Walsh) C.; student Sharpsville (Pa.) Pub. Primary and High Schs., 1910-25; B.S., Duquesne U., Pittsburgh, 1928, LL.B., Law Sch., 1930; m. Margaret Brown, Aug. 11, 1934. Began as lawyer, 1930, and since in practice at Sharon, Pa.; mem. of firm, Service, McNeal & Cusick, Sharon, 1934-38, Service, McNeal, Cusick & Isenberg since 1938; v.p. and dir., Cambria Slag Co. Asst. counsel, Pa. Pub. Utilities Commn. June 1938-Jan. 1939. Mem. Democratic State Com. since 1934. Mem. Pa. Bar Assn., Sigma Nu Phi. Democrat. Roman Catholic. K.C., Elks, Eagles. Club: University (Sharon, Pa.). Home: 819 Mayfield Rd., Sharpsville, Pa. Office: 107 E. State St., Sharon, Pa.

CUSTER, Christopher R(amsey) C(aldwell), automobile mfr.; b. Phila., Pa., June 30, 1893; s. George and Kate (Ramsey) C.; ed. Camden Bus. Coll., 1908-09, U. of Pa., 1913-16; m. Carolyn Lynch, Apr. 3, 1918; children—Carolyn Lenore, Richard. Began career as accountant; auditor Cook Coal & Coke Co. and Short Line Coal Mining Co.; asst. to treas. Midvale Steel Co. and Worth Steel Co.; asso. with Autocar Co., Ardmore, Pa., since 1917, auditor, treas. Autocar Sales & Service Co., vice-pres. and comptroller Autocar Co. since 1933; treas. and dir. Autocar Sales & Service Co. of Mo.; asst. treas. Autocar Sales & Service Co. of Calif. Mem. Am. Acad. of Polit. and Social Sci., Controllers Inst. of America, Nat. Assn. of Cost Accountants. Republican. Presbyterian. Mason. Club: Presbyterian Social Union, Martins Dam (Wayne, Pa.). Home: 219 Avon Rd., Narberth. Office: The Autocar Co., Ardmore, Pa.

CUSTER, Ruhl L., high school prin.; b. Grafton, W.Va., May 23, 1902; s. Henry A. and Lilly Belle (Knotts) C.; grad. Grafton High Sch., 1920; A.B., W.Va. Wesleyan Coll., 1924 M.A., W.Va. U., 1930; student U. of Pittsburgh, 1939; m. Madge Fultineer, May 1, 1924; children—Delores Grace, Charlotte Marie. Teacher Clay County, W.Va., 1924-28; prin. Ripley (W.Va.) High Sch., 1928-32, Weirton (W.Va.) High Sch. since 1932. Mem. N.E.A., Secondary Sch. Prins. Assn. Methodist. Mason. Club: Weirton-Cove Kiwanis (past pres.). Home: 3534 Orchard St. Office: Virginia Av., Weirton, W.Va.

CUSTER-SHOEMAKER, Dacia, (Mrs. John A. Shoemaker), historian, author; b. Westerville, O., May 21, 1873; d. Isaac Newton and Mary Arbina (Fisher) Custer; student Westerville (O.) Public Schs., 1890; Ph.B., Otterbein Coll., Westerville, O., 1895; student Berlitz Sch. of Languages, Pittsburgh; m. John A. Shoemaker, Sept. 10, 1896 (died 1931). Music teacher, Crockett, Tex., 1895-97; violinist with Crockett (Tex.) Orchestra, 1895, Leach Evangelistic Party (Tex.), 1896, Gaddy Evangelistic Party, 1896; Columbus (O.) Euterpean Sextette, 1896, Pittsburgh Ladies Quartette, 1905; publicity writer, 1917-19; curator of Hanby Historic House Museum, Westerville, O., since 1937. Mem. Nat. League Am. Pen Women (past dir., past pres. for Western Pa.), Am. Assn. Univ. Women, Cleiorhetean Alumni Assn. (pres.), Ohio State Archæol. and Hist. Soc., Va. State Hist. Soc., Hanby Memorial Assn. of Ohio. Republican. Presbyterian. Clubs: Women's Press of Pittsburgh (past dir., past pres.); Civic (Edgewood, Pittsburgh); Otterbein Coll.; Tuesday Musical (Pittsburgh). Home: 120 Oakview Av., Pittsburgh, Pa. Address: Hanby Historic House Museum, Westerville, O.

CUSTIS, John Trevor, editor; b. Philadelphia, Pa., Dec. 17, 1875; s. Rev. John William and Henrietta Elizabeth (Sheldrake) C.; grad. Central High Sch., Phila., 1893; m. Mary C. Farrell, of Phila., Nov. 3, 1900. With the Philadelphia Inquirer since 1894, reporter until 1899, city editor, 1899-1908, mng. editor, 1908-33, editor since 1933. Republican. Episcopalian. Club: Union League. Author: The Public Schools of Philadelphia, 1897. Home: 7620 Lincoln Drive, Chestnut Hill. Office: Inquirer Bldg., Philadelphia, Pa.

CUTCHIN, Esther, pianist; b. Baltimore, Md., Sept. 26, 1896; d. John Randolph and Cora (Armiger) Cutchin; ed. high sch., Baltimore; grad., with honors, Peabody Conservatory of Music, Baltimore, 1914; m. Thomas Moss, 1917; 1 son, Thomas Randolph. Has appeared in concerts and lecture recitals in many states; repertoire includes Beethoven, Chopin, Bach, Brahms, etc.; specializes in Chopin programs. Methodist. Home: 3936 Norfolk Av., Baltimore, Md.*

CUTHBERT, Frank Edward, prof. music; b. Duquesne, Pa., Nov. 1, 1894; s. Edward Lippington and Margaret Ann (Moore) C.; grad. McKeesport (Pa.) High Sch., 1912; musical edn. under private instrs.; fellowship in voice, Juilliard Musical Sch., 1924-25; Mus.D., Waynesburg (Pa.) Coll., 1937; unmarried. Soloist First Presbyn. Ch., McKeesport, 1914-15, Shadyside Presbyn. Ch., Pittsburgh, 1916 and 1920-21; professional singer, bass-baritone, 1922; soloist St. Bartholomew's Episcopal Ch., N.Y. City, 1922-34, East Liberty Presbyn. Ch., Pittsburgh, since 1934, choir dir. since 1935; pioneer broadcaster KDKA, Pittsburgh; soloist WEAF-WJZ, Nat. Broadcasting Co., 1922-34; taught privately, N.Y. City, 1924-34; dir. W. Va. U. Music Sch. since 1934; many professional appearances in recitals, concerts, oratorios, etc.; 550 performances as "Dr. Engel" in Student Prince; co-starred with DeWolf Hopper, Eva Davenport and Ilsa Marvenga, 1925-26. Served with U.S.N.R.F. aboard U.S.S. Ariz., World War. Presbyn. Mason. Home: Hotel Morgan, Morgantown, W.Va.

CUTHBERT, Virginia I. (Mrs. Philip Clarkson Elliott), artist; b. West Newton, Pa., Aug. 27, 1908; d. Rev. Richard Bruce and Frances Irene (Cartwright) Cuthbert; student high schs., Washington, Pa. and Crafton, Pa., 1922-26; B.F.A., Syracuse (N.Y.) U. Coll. of Fine Arts, 1930; Augusta Hazard Fellow, Academie Colarossi, Acad. de la Grande Chaumiere, Paris, 1930-31; student with George Luks, New York, N.Y., 1932; grad. student U. of Pittsburgh Fine Arts Dept., 1932-35, Carnegie Inst. Tech. Fine Arts Dept., 1934-36; m. Philip Clarkson Elliott, June 8, 1935. Has shown in many leading exhbns. in various larger cities annually since 1931; rep. in permanent collections by paintings in Syracuse U. Coll. Fine Arts, Hundred Friends of Pittsburgh Art; mural Municipal Bldg., Mt. Lebanon, O.; awarded Carnegie Inst. prize, $250, 1934, Alumnæ Prize, $100, 1935, Art Soc., $100, 1937, First Asso. Artists, $150, 1938. Mem. bd. dirs. Asso. Artists of Pittsburgh, Gulf Galleries of Pittsburgh. Mem. Kappa Alpha Theta, Tau Sigma Delta. Methodist. Home: 360 S. Winbiddle St., Pittsburgh, Pa.

CUTLER, Bertram, corporation official; b. Staten Island, N.Y., Sept. 17, 1880; s. William Henry and Annie (Standring) C.; student Westerleigh Collegiate Inst., Westerleigh, S.I., 1895-1900, Packard Business College, New York, N.Y., 1900-02; m. Edith May Coyne, Oct. 9, 1905; 1 son, Bertram. Associated in confidential capacity with John D. Rockefeller, later John D. Rockefeller, Jr. since 1902; dir. N.Y.C.R.R., Chase Nat. Bank, Morristown Trust Co., Radio Corpn. of America, Merchants Fire Assurance Corpn., Colorado Fuel & Iron Corpn.; trustee Equitable Life Assurance Soc. Conglist. Clubs: Morris County Golf, Blooming Grove Hunting and Fishing. Home: New Vernon Rd., Greens Village, N.J. Office: 30 Rockefeller Plaza, New York, N.Y.

CUTLER, George Chalmers, banker; b. Brookline, Mass., May 8, 1891; s. George C. and Mary (Wilson) C.; A.B., Harvard U., 1913, LL.B., 1916; m. Susan Margaret Stackpole, July 5, 1916; children—George C., Diana, Mary, Susan Margaret. Pres. Safe Deposit & Trust Co., Baltimore, since 1935. Home: "Pen-y-bryn," Garrison, Md. Office: 13 South St., Baltimore, Md.

CUTLER, Jacob William, M.D.; b. Phila., Pa., Nov. 5, 1900; s. Louis and Florence (Reisman) C.; M.D., U. of Pa., 1925; m. Ethel Reisman, June 25, 1926; children—Harriet, Sandra. Engaged in private practice of medicine, specializing in pulmonary diseases since 1929; physician in charge Collapse Therapy Clinic, Henry Phipps Inst., since 1929; instr. pulmonary diseases, Grad. Sch. of Medicine, U. of Pa. since 1931; med. dir. Wawa Chest Inst. since 1939. Mem. County, State and Am. med. socs., Phila. Pathol. Soc., Nat. Tuberculosis Assn., Am. Troudeau Soc., Am. Acad. Tuberculosis Physicians. Writer numerous articles on med. subjects with special reference to pulmonary tuberculosis. Address: 2107 Spruce St., Philadelphia, Pa.

CUTLIP, James E., lawyer; b. Cedar Creek, W.Va., Nov. 23, 1864; s. Wilson and Lucinda S. (Berry) C.; student pub. schs., Braxton Co., and W.Va. Univ., married Dec. 22, 1886 (wife dec.); m. 2d Maude Lambert, Mar. 28, 1898; children—Rebecca W. (Mrs. John H. Atkin), James Eldredge, Richard L., Katherine (Mrs. B. J. Gross), Clarence Edward, Jean Lorentz (Mrs. Edward Olham Berry), Thomas Morrison. Admitted to W.Va. bar; engaged in gen. practice of law at Sutton, W.Va.; served as prosecuting atty. Braxton Co.; served as state pardon atty., 1917-19. Address: Sutton, W.Va.

CUTTING, Charles Suydam, naturalist; b. New York, N.Y., Jan. 17, 1889; s. Robert Fulton and Helen (Suydam) C.; prep. edn. Groton Sch., 1903-09; A.B., Harvard, 1912; m. Helen McMahon, of New York, 1932. Trustee Robert F. Cutting Estate since 1913; field work on expdns. to Central Asia for Am. Museum Natural History, Field Museum of Natural History, Chicago, Pitt River Museum of Oxford, Eng. Trustee Am. Museum Natural History, New York Zool. Soc., Hon. fellow Field Museum of Natural History, Chicago. Served as 1st lt., U.S. Army, during World War; with A.E.F. in France, 15 months. Decorated Croix Noire (French). Mem. Bombay Natural History Soc., Royal Geog. Soc., Central Asia Soc. (all Brit.); Himmalyan Club. Republican. Episcopalian. Clubs: Knickerbocker, Brook, Racquet (New York). Author of a series of articles pub. by Am. Museum Natural History. Home: Gladstone, N.J. Office: 20 Pine St., New York, N.Y.

CUTTS, Henry Eastman, chemist; b. York, Me., Sept. 21, 1867; s. Eastman and Louisa (Eastman) C.; prep. edn. public schools, Portland, Me.; A.B., Bowdoin Coll., Brunswick, Me., 1891, A.M., 1892; m. Mary Louise Smith, Apr. 29, 1908; children—Richard Walter, Elizabeth Eastman, Mary Louise. Asst. in chemistry, Bowdoin Coll., 1891-92; chemist Stillwell & Gladding, 1892-97, Cudahy Packing Co., 1897, Nat. Lead Co., 1898-1905; vice-president and treas. Stillwell & Gladding, analytical and consulting chemists, New York, since 1905. Mem. Am. Chem. Soc., Soc. Chem. Industry, Am. Oil Chemists Soc., Am. Soc. Testing Materials, Assn. Cons. Chemists and Chem. Engrs., Psi Upsilon, Phi Beta Kappa. Republican. Home: 16 Grand View Terrace, Tenafly, N.J. Office: 130 Cedar St., New York, N.Y.

CYR, Howard Mason, research physical chemist; b. Somerville, Mass., July 11, 1896; s. Frank Broche and May (Mason) C.; B.S., Mass. Inst. of Tech., 1918; m. Elsie Shippy, Sept. 19, 1921; 1 son, Howard Mason. Chem. engr. U.S. Bureau Mines, 1918-19; with N.J. Zinc Co. since 1919, chief fundamental zinc oxide pigment sect. of research div., Palmerton, Pa., since 1926. Served in Chem. Warfare Service, U.S. Army, 1918-19. Mem. Am. Chem. Soc. (chmn. Lehigh Valley Sect. 1938-39), Lehigh Valley Engrs. Soc., Pa. Chem. Soc. (gov.). Baptist. Contbr. articles on research in zinc to jours. Home: Residence Park, Palmerton, Pa. Office: New Jersey Zinc Co. Research Laboratory, Palmerton, Pa.

CZARNIECKI, Myron James, v.p. A. M. Byers Co.; b. Pittsburgh, Pa., Mar. 11, 1892; s. Frank H. and Emma (Wettach) C.; student pub. schs.; m. Alma Eastin, Oct. 8, 1935; children—Myron James, Esther Louise. With A. M. Byers Co. since 1919, Chicago dist., mgr., 1919-20, N.Y. dist. mgr., 1920-25, asst. gen. mgr. of sales, 1925-30, gen. mgr. of sales, 1930-34, v.p. in charge of sales since 1934. Home:

South Drive, Fox Chapel Manor, Aspinwall, Pa. Office: Clark Bldg., Pittsburgh, Pa.

D

DADISMAN, Andrew Jackson, prof. of economics; b. Grafton, W.Va., Feb. 5, 1881; s. Newton and Lucetta (Williamson) D.; student Fairmont (W.Va.) State Normal Sch., 1906-08; B.S.A., W.Va. Univ., 1914; M.S.A., Cornell, 1914, Ph.D., 1924; student U. of Wis. (semester) 1916; m. Iona Smith, June 14, 1919. Teacher in rural schools, Taylor County, W.Va., 1901-04; prin. of Pruntytown (W.Va.) Sch., 1905-07, Thoburn Sch., 1908-09, prin. ward sch., Grafton, W.Va., 1909-11; with U.S. Dept. of Agr., 1914-16; with W.Va. U. since 1916, as asso. prof. and head dept. farm economics, 1916-24, prof. and head dept., 1924-33, prof. of economics since 1933, dir. of summer session since 1929. Served as farm help specialist, W.Va., Ky., Tenn., during World War. Mem. Am. Econ. Assn., Am. Assn. Univ. Profs., W.Va. Acad. Science, W.Va. State Edn. Assn. Phi Beta Kappa, Pi Gamma Mu, Kappa Sigma. Baptist. Odd Fellow. Home: 305 Beverly Av., Morgantown, W.Va.

DAGGETT, Edwin Hugh, M.D., orthopedist; b. Giles Co., Tenn., July 29, 1897; s. Ulysses Grant and Nettie (Thompson) D.; grad. Jones High Sch., Lynnville, Tenn., 1914; M.D., U. of Tenn., Memphis, 1927; grad. student U. of Iowa, 1936-37; m. Letitia Gray, Dec. 23, 1920. Gen. practice, Bogalusa, La., 1928-30; resident physician Muhlenberg Hosp., Plainfield, N.J., 1930-31; gen. practice, Plainfield, 1931-36, practice limited to orthopedics since 1937; orthopedics surgeon Muhlenberg Hosp. Mem. Plainfield Med. Soc., Union Co. Med. Soc., N.J. State Med. Soc., A.M.A., Med. Soc. of Northern N.J. Presbyterian. Home: 734 Park Av. Office: 916 Park Av., Plainfield, N.J.

DAGGETT, Parker Hayward, prof. elec. engring.; b. Boston, Mass., Apr. 5, 1885; s. Gilbert Alden and Elizabeth Jane (Hayward) D.; prep. edn. English High Sch., Boston. and Phillips Exeter Acad.; S.B., Harvard, 1910 as of 1907; m. Esther Jarvis, Jan. 17, 1910; children —Parker Hayward, Mary Elizabeth, Emma Jarvis, William Bosworth, Jane Alden, Jonathon Hayward (dec.), Thomas Randolph. Asst. in elec. engring., Harvard, 1908-09; engr. toll traffic dept., Am. Telephone & Telegraph Co., 1909-10; asso. prof. elec. engring., 1910-13; prof. and head of dept. 1913-29, U. of N.C., also acting dean Sch. of Applied Science, 1915-16; dean Coll. of Engring., Rutgers U., New Brunswick, N.J., since July 1, 1929. Acting dist. ednl. dir. 4th Dist., S.A.T.C., Oct. 1918-Jan. 1919; mem. N.C. State Bd. Registration Engrs., 1921-29, sec. 1925-29; sec. Council of State Bds. of Engring. Examiners, 1922-23, pres., 1925-26; mem. Engrs., Council for Professional Development, 1933; chmn. regional com. in charge of accrediting of engring. schools in Ohio, Ind., Ill., Ia., Minn., Wis., Mich. since 1933. Mem. Soc. for Promotion Engring. Edn. (council 1921-24, vice-pres. 1935-36), N.C. Soc. of Engrs. (pres. 1929), Phi Beta Kappa, Tau Beta Pi, Sigma Xi, Kappa Gamma Chi; asso. Am. Inst. E.E. Home: New Brunswick, N.J.

DAHLE, Chester Distad, coll. prof.; b. Cheney, Wash., Jan. 3, 1896; s. Nels Knute and Julia (Distad) D.; B.S., U. of Minn., Minneapolis, Minn., 1919, M.S., 1921, Ph.D., 1936; m. Agnes Haedecke, Sept. 6, 1922; 1 son, Robert David. Asst. in dairying, U. of Minn., Minneapolis, Minn., 1919-20, instr., 1920-22, asst. prof., 1922-24; asso. prof. dairy mfg., Pa. State Coll., 1924-29, prof. since 1929; v.p. Centre Theater Corpn. Served with A.E.F., air service, 375 and 135th Aero Squadrons, Mar. 1918-May 1919. Mem. Am. Dairy Science Assn., Pa. Milk Sanitarians, Rotary Internat., Delta Tau Delta, Alpha Zeta, Gamma Sigma Delta, Sigma Xi. Lutheran. Clubs: Rotary, Centre Hills Country (State College). Author: Book on Ice Cream Manufacturing; several extension and reseach bulls. pertaining to dairy mfg. research; also (with others) many scientific papers in same field. Lecturer on dairy mfg. subjects at many univ. dairy short courses. Tech. editor Ice Cream Field; abstract editor of ice cream subjects for Journal of Dairy Science. Home: 628 Locust Lane, State College, Pa.

DAHLGREN, Ulric, prof. biology; b. Brooklyn, N.Y., Dec. 27, 1870; s. Charles Bunker and Augusta (Smith) D.; State Model Sch., Trenton, N.J., 1883-85; grad. Mt. Pleasant Mil. Acad., Ossining, N.Y., 1890; A.B., Princeton, 1894, M.S., 1896; m. Emillie Elizabeth Kuprion, Sept. 3, 1896. Instr., 1896, prof. biology, 1911-39, prof. emeritus since 1939, Princeton U. Asst. dir. Marine Biol. Lab., Woods Hole, Mass., 1899; trustee Harpswell (Me.) Biol. Lab., 1912-16; dir. Mount Desert Island Biol. Lab., Bar Harbor, 1921, pres. of Corpn. since 1937. Pres. Princeton (N.J.) Bd. of Health. Fellow A.A.A.S., Phila. Acad. Sciences; mem. Am. Soc. Zoölogists, Am. Soc. Naturalists, Am. Philos. Soc., N.J. Soc. of the Cincinnati, N.J. Soc. S.R., Loyal Legion, Sons Colonial Wars. Club: Princeton (Phila.). Author: Principles of Animal Histology (with W. A. Kepner), 1908. Wrote series on Production of Light by Organisms (Jour. of Franklin Inst.), 1915; also zoöl. memoirs in German and Am. jours., mostly on production of light and electricity by animals. Home: 7 Evelyn Place, Princeton, N.J.

DAILEY, Elmer M.; pres. Middle Atlantic Baseball League, Pa. State Assn. (baseball). Address: Butler, Pa.

DAKER, Jess Oliver, mfg. electric signs; b. Pittsburgh, Pa., Jan. 6, 1886; s. Duncan and Elizabeth (Morgan) D.; ed. pub. sch. and high sch., Pittsburgh; m. Alverda Lockhart, June 21, 1910; children—Jean Elizabeth, Jack Lockhart, Helen Joan. Employed as salesman, later dist. mgr., Federal Electric Co.; propr. Flexlume Sales Co. of Pa., Neon sign and lighting devices, since 1920; dir. Flexlume Corpn. of Buffalo, N.Y. Presbyn. Mason. Home: 26 Midway Rd. Office: 718 E. Carson St., Pittsburgh, Pa.

DALAND, Elliot, engineer; b. Brookline, Mass., Jan. 3, 1886; s. Tucker and Emily Jane (Elliot) D.; A.B., Harvard U., 1909; aeronautical engring., Mass. Inst. Tech., 1918; m. Katharine Maynadier Browne, Oct. 26, 1910; children—Peter, Judith, Benjamin. Machinist, Sullivan Machinery Co., Clairmont, N.H., 1910-11, Am. Gas Tool Co., Chicago, Ill., 1911-16, Eastern Brass and Ingot Co., Waterbury, Conn., 1916-17; engr. on analysis, Standard Aero Corpn., Elizabeth, N.J., 1918-19, Curtis Airplane and Motor Co., Garden City, N.Y., 1919-20; v.p. and engr. Huff Daland & Co., Ogdensburg, N.Y., 1920-27; v.p. and spl. engr. Keystone Aircraft Corpn., Bristol, Pa., 1927-30; asst. chief engr. Kellett Autogiro Co., Phila., 1930-32; exptl. engr. Pa. Aircraft Syndicate, Philadelphia, 1933, chief engr., 1935-39; now with Platt-Le Page Aircraft Company. Mem. Inst. of Aeronautical Sciences, Soc. of Automotive Engrs. Club: Harvard (Phila.). Author of several articles on Rotary Wing Aircraft; speaker before Am. Soc. of M. E. Home: Crestmont Farms, Torresdale, Pa. Office: 1118 Real Estate Trust Bldg., Philadelphia, Pa.

DALE, Frederick Allport; col. Med. Corps, U.S. Army, retired. Address: 100 W. University Parkway, Baltimore, Md..

DALY, Edwin King; b. Bridgeport, Conn., Nov. 15, 1896; s. Michael J. and Elizabeth (King) D.; student Fordham U.; m. Alice F. Ryan, June 5, 1924. Pres. Horn & Hardart Co. since 1936; exec. v.p. Horn & Hardart Baking Co. since 1930. Home: The Kenilworth, School Lane and Wissahickon Av., Germantown, Philadelphia, Pa. Office: 600 W. 50th St., New York, N.Y., and 208 S. Warnock St., Philadelphia, Pa.

DALY, J(ohn) Burrwood, congressman; b. Philadelphia; A.B., La Salle Coll., Philadelphia, also A.M. and LL.D.; LL.B., U. of Pa. Admitted to Pa. bar and practiced in Phila.; asst. city solicitor 12 yrs.; mem. faculty La Salle Coll.; mem. 74th to 76th Congresses (1935-41), 4th Pa. Dist. Democrat. Home: 3232 W. Penn St. Office: Real Estate Trust Bldg., Philadelphia, Pa.

DALY, Thomas Augustine, writer; b. Phila., May 28, 1871; s. John Anthony and Anne Victoria (Duckett) D.; ed. pub. schs., Villanova Coll., Pa., Fordham U. to close of sophomore yr., 1889; hon. M.A., Fordham U., 1901, Litt.D., same, 1910; LL.D., Notre Dame U., 1917; LL.D., Boston Coll., 1921; m. Nannie Barrett, of Philadelphia, June 24, 1896; children— Leonard Barrett, John Anthony, Thomas Augustine, Ann Elizabeth, Stephen Barrett, Brenda Rutledge (dec.), Frederic Rutledge, Frances Joan. Clerk, 1889-91, reporter and editorial writer, 1891-98, Phila. Record; gen. mgr. Catholic Standard and Times, Phila., 1898-1915; asso. editor Evening Ledger, Phila., 1915-18; asso. dir. Philadelphia Record, 1918-29; columnist, Phila. Evening Bulletin, since 1929. Lecturer since 1905. Author: Canzoni, 1906; Carmina, 1909; Madrigali, 1912; Little Polly's Pomes, 1913; Songs of Wedlock, 1916; McAroni Ballads, 1919; Herself and the Houseful (prose), 1924; A Little Book of American Humorous Verse (anthology), 1926; The House of Dooner (with Christopher Morley, prose); McAroni Medleys, 1931; Selected Poems of T. A. Daly, 1936. Compiler: The Wissahickon, 1922. Home: 4937 Rubicam Rd., Germantown, Pa. Office: Bulletin Bldg., Philadelphia, Pa.

DALZELL, George Walton, lawyer; b. Waddington, N.Y., Oct. 10, 1877; s. Charles Nathaniel and Annie Margaret (Dodds) D.; LL.B., Columbian (now George Washington) U., 1897, LL.M., 1898; unmarried. Admitted to Dist. of Columbia bar, 1898, and began practice in Washington, D.C.; mem. firm Hayden & Dalzell, Washington, D.C.; lecturer on maritime law, Georgetown U. Sch. of Foreign Service. Episcopalian. Co-author: The Law of the Sea, 1921. Home: 5 W. Irving St., Chevy Chase, Md. Office: 1653 Pennsylvania Av., Washington, D.C.

DALZELL, Robert Duff, lawyer; b. Hawkins Station, Allegheny Co., Pa., Aug. 27, 1882; s. John and Mary Louise (Duff) D.; student University Sch., Washington, D.C., 1895-1901; A.B., Yale, 1905; LL.B., George Washington U., Washington, D.C., 1909; m. Alice McFarlane, Aug. 14, 1915; children—Robert Duff, William Sage II (dec.), Kathleen Alden. Admitted to Pa. bar, 1910, and in practice at Pittsburgh since; employee Dalzell, Fisher and Hawkins; successively partner, Dalzell, Fisher and Dalzell, Dalzell, Dalzell and McFall; now mem. Dalzell, McFall and Pringle, Pittsburgh. Mem. Am. Bar Assn., Internat. Assn. of Ins. Counsel, Pa. State Bar Assn., Allegheny Co. Bar Assn., Pittsburgh Law Club, Psi Upsilon, Phi Delta Phi. Presbyterian. Clubs: Duquesne, University, Oakmont Country (Pittsburgh). Home: 1419 Browning Rd. Office: 450 Fourth Av., Pittsburgh, Pa.

DAMBACH, John, univ. prof.; b. Hayes Center, Neb., June 12, 1894; s. George and Mary (Able) D.; B.A., Reed Coll., Portland, Oregon, 1919; Ph.D., Columbia U., 1937; m. Beulah Dayton, Nov. 6, 1920; 1 dau., Gretchen. Instr. of phys. edn., Columbia U., 1919-20; asst. prof. of phys. edn., Peabody Coll., Nashville, Tenn., 1920-21, Columbia U. summer sessions, 1919-27; dir. dept. of phys. edn., Toledo (O.) Bd. of Edn., 1924-26; prof. of phys. edn., U. of Pittsburgh, since 1927, Am. Phys. Edn. Assn., Coll. Dirs. Assn., Pa. State Phys. Edn. Assn. Republican. Lutheran. Home: E. Waldheim Rd., Fox Chapel, Pa. Office: Univ. of Pittsburgh, Pittsburgh, Pa.

DAMBACH, L. Earl, retail lumber mcht.; b. Zelienople, Pa., May 1, 1891; s. Henry William and Sarah Jeanette (Zeigler) D.; student high schs., Ellwood City, Pa., and Youngstown, O., Westminster Coll., New Wilmington, Pa., 1910-12, Carnegie Inst. Tech., 1913-15; m. Leah Morrison, Sept. 20, 1916; children— Charlotte Ruth, Lois Jean. Employed as cost clk. Am. Bridge Co., Ambridge, Pa., 1913-16; sec. Zeigler Lumber Co., retail lumber mchts., Duquesne, Pa., 1916-27, treas. and mgr. since 1927. Mem. Duquesne Business Men's Assn. (sec., once yr.; pres., four yrs.; dir., eight yrs.). Republican. Presbyterian. Mason (32°, Shriner). Home: 816 Richford St. Office: 90 N. First St., Duquesne, Pa.

DANA, Charles Anderson, mfr.; b. Apr. 25, 1881; s. Charles and Laura (Parkin) D.; A.B., Columbia, 1902, A.M., 1904; m. Agnes Ladson; children—Charles A., Agnes L. Pres. and gen. mgr. Spicer Mfg. Corpn.; pres. and trustee Corralitos Co.; dir. Empire Trust Co., Mfrs. Trust Co., Equitable Office Bldg. Corpn. (all of New York), Commerce Guardian Bank (Toledo, O.), Fisk Rubber Corpn., Foundation Co. (foreign), Kelsey-Hayes Wheel Co., Birfield Industries, Ltd. (London), Hardy Spicer Co., Ltd. (Birmingham, Eng.). Clubs: University, Union, Down Town, Essex Fox Hounds. Home: "Brookwood," Bernardsville, N.J. Office: 60 John St., New York, N.Y.

DANBY, H. Gregg; pres. Union Nat. Bank. Home: Chadds Ford, Pa. Address: 8th and Market Sts., Wilmington, Del.

DANDY, Walter E(dward), M.D., surgeon; b. Sedalia, Mo., Apr. 6, 1886; s. John and Rachel D.; A.B., U. of Mo., 1907, LL.D., 1928; M.D., Johns Hopkins, 1910, A.M., 1911; m. Sadie Martin, Oct. 1, 1924; children—Walter E., Mary Ellen, Kathleen Louise, Margaret Martin. Began practice, Baltimore; now prof. neurol. surgery, in charge surgery of nervous system, Johns Hopkins. Mem. Am. Surgery. Assn., Am. Neurol. Association, Southern Surgical Association, Phi Beta Kappa, Sigma Xi. Contbr. numerous articles to surgical and neurological journals. Introduced new operative procedure for tumor of the brain and neuralgias and other disturbances of cranial nerves; introduced ventriculography, ventricular estimation and cerebral pneumography, for diagnosis and localizing of tumors of the brain and intracranial lesions. Home: 3904 Juniper Rd. Office: Johns Hopkins Hosp., Baltimore, Md.

DANE, Charles, physician and surgeon; b. Yarmouth, N.S., Can., Feb. 8, 1886; s. William Henry and Lois Annette D.; came to U.S., 1897; naturalized, 1917; A.B., Harvard U., 1907; M.D., Harvard U. Med. Sch., 1910; m. Madeline L. Noyes, Dec. 21, 1936; 1 dau., Lois Madeline. Interne Orange Memorial Hosp., 1910-11; in gen. practice of medicine and surgery at South Orange, N.J., since 1911; attending surgeon Orange Memorial Hosp., Orange, N.J. Served as 1st lt., capt. and maj. Med. Corps, U.S.A., 1917-19, with A.E.F. in France; now lt. col. Med. Res. Pres. Bd. of Health, South Orange, N.J. Fellow Am. Coll. Surgeons; mem. Am., N.J. State, and Essex Co. med. assns., Orange Practitioners (past pres.), Orange Mountain Med. Soc. Republican. Episcopalian. Mason. Clubs: Essex County Country (West Orange); Harvard of New Jersey. Home: 410 West End Rd. Office: 61 Scotland Rd., South Orange, N.J.

DANFORTH, Irving Wilckens, pres. Danforth Co.; b. Cleveland, O., Nov. 25, 1894; s. John Howard and Kate (Ingersoll) D.; ed. pub. schs., Cleveland, O.; m. Elizabeth Mary Nicola, Apr. 12, 1921; children—Robert Nicola, Richard William. With Gabriel Mfg. Co., mfrs. of Gabriel Snubbers, 1919-30; salesman, 1919-25; sales mgr., 1925-30; pres. Danforth Co., Distributor of Westinghouse Refrigerator and other Westinghouse Products since 1930. Served in Air Service, U.S. Army during World War. Pres. Pa. Golf Assn., 1938. Republican. Presbyterian. Clubs: Duquesne, Fox Chapel, Oakmont, Pittsburgh Athletic (Pittsburgh); Mayfield (Cleveland). Home: 212 Tennyson Av. Office: 5820 Centre Av., Pittsburgh, Pa.

DANIEL, Channing Williams, investment counsel; b. Richmond, Va., Mar. 18, 1890; s. James Robertson Vivian and Hallie (Williams) D.; student McGuire's Univ. Sch., Richmond, Va., 1898-1905, Episcopal High Sch., Alexandria, Va., 1905-08; A.B., U. of Va., Charlottesville, Va., 1912; m. Katharine Verner, Nov. 25, 1916; children—Channing Williams, Helen Randolph, Peter Vivian, William Verner. Began as sch. teacher, 1911; asso. Robt. W. Daniel & Co., bankers and brokers, Phila., 1913-17; organized own firm Daniel & Co., investment securities, Phila., 1919, merged with Martin & Co., Inc., investment counsel, Phila., 1932, now v.p. Served in R.O.T.C., 1917; commd. 1st lt. F.A., U.S. Army, and served with 4th Div., A.E.F.; wounded Oct. 1918, returned to U.S. and hon. disch., 1919; capt. F.A. Res. Corps. Mem. Delta Phi. Episcopalian. Clubs: Racquet, St. Elmo, Virginia. Home: St. David's, Pa. Office: Packard Bldg., Philadelphia, Pa.

DANIEL, Todd, lawyer; b. New Orleans, La., June 29, 1891; s. Selden Brooke and Eliza (Todd) D.; grad. Emerson Inst., Washington, D.C., 1909; LL.B., George Washington U. Law Dept., 1913; m. Rose Lucy Bennett, June 19, 1928; children—Mary Todd, Robert Todd, Sally Ward. Began as messenger Library of Congress, Washington, D.C., 1908; spl. agt. bur. investigation, U.S. Dept. Justice, Washington, D.C., 1913; admitted to bar D.C., 1914; div. supt. Phila. Div., U.S. Dept. Justice, 1917; spl. asst. to U.S. Atty. Eastern Dist. Pa., 1918; admitted to Pa. bar, 1920 and since engaged in gen. practice of law at Phila.; counsel Workmen's Compensation Bd. Pa., Phila. region, 1923-31; Pa. atty. in Dept. Justice for liquidation of closed banks, 1931-34; registration commr., 1934-35; civil service commr., 1938; v.p. and Phila. counsel, Keystone Automobile Club, Keystone Automobile Club Casualty Co. Mem. Order of the Coif, Sigma Chi, Phi Delta Phi. Democrat. Mason (32°). Home: 5940 Overbrook Av. Office: 1420 Walnut St., Philadelphia, Pa.

DANIELS, Frank E., pres. Curwensville State Bank; b. Clearfield, Pa., Apr. 7, 1885; s. Harry and Eliza (Shaffer) D.; student pub. schs.; student course Westinghouse Electric Co.; m. Cora Phelps, Apr. 28, 1907. Chief electrician Jamison Coal Co., Greensburg, Pa., 1908-17; owner Greensburg Baking Co., 1917-21, Stewart Baking Co., 1921-25, Quality Bakery & Quality Market, 1925-30, Sanitary Milk Co. since 1930; pres. and dir. Curwensville (Pa.) State Bank. Mason (32°), Odd Fellow, K.P. Home: 227 State St. Office: State St., Curwensville, Pa.

DANN, Alexander William, business exec.; b. Downsville, N.Y., Nov. 1, 1885; s. Matthew and Margaret Comrie (Montgomery) D.; C.E., Cornell U., 1907; m. Ella E. Berry, Nov. 27, 1916; children—Dorothy E., Alexander William. With Dravo Corpn., Pittsburgh, since 1913, exec. v.p. since 1934; dir. and pres. Charleroi Supply Co., Eastern Ohio Sand and Supply Co., Inland Rivers Wharf Co., Southern Transfer Co., Standard Builders Supply Co., Union Barge Line Corpn.; dir. Dravo Doyle Co., Cumberland River Sand Co. Asso. mem. Am. Soc. Civil Engrs.; mem. Engrs. Soc. Western Pa., Sigma Nu. Republican. Presbyterian. Clubs: Duquesne, Shannopin Country, Montour Heights Country (Pittsburgh). Home: 1207 A Beaver Rd., Sewickley, Pa. Office: 300 Penn Av., Pittsburgh, Pa.

DANNEHOWER, William Franklin, judge; b. Norristown, Pa., July 28, 1890; s. William F. and Bessie (McCarter) D.; grad. Norristown (Pa.) High Sch., 1908; Ph.B., Lafayette Coll., Easton, Pa., 1912; LL.B., Yale Law Sch., 1915; m. Le Edda S. Dressler, July 18, 1928; children—William F., 3d, Le Edda, James Cheston. Admitted to Montgomery Co. (Pa.) bar, 1915; in gen. practice of law, 1915-17 and 1921-33; elected judge Common Pleas Ct., 38th Jud. Dist., Nov. 7, 1933, for term expiring 1943. Served with Pa. Hosp. and Mobile Hosp. No. 8, World War; with Am. Red Cross in France, Germany, Russia and Turkey, 1917-21. Dir. Sacred Heart Hosp., Norristown, Pa. Mem. S.A.R., Am. Legion, Vets. of Foreign Wars, Phi Kappa Psi, Phi Delta Phi. Republican. Lutheran. Mason (Lehigh Consistory), Elk, Moose. Clubs: Plymouth Country, Rotary (Norristown, Pa.). Home: 1549 DeKalb St. Office: Court House, Norristown, Pa.

DANNENBERG, Arthur Mansbach, physician; b. Phila., Pa., Jan. 7, 1891; s. Gerson and Hannah (Mansbach) D.; M.D., U. of Pa. Med. Sch., 1913; m. Marion Loeb, Aug. 21, 1922; children—Arthur Milton, James Loeb. Engaged in practice of medicine at Phila. since 1913. Served as capt., Med. Corps, U.S. Army, 1917-19. Fellow Am. Med. Assn., Phila. Coll. Physicians, Am. Acad. Pediatrics. Republican. Jewish religion. Club: Country (Rydal, Pa.). Home: 135 S. 17th St. Office: 235 S. 15th St., Philadelphia, Pa.

DANTON, J(oseph) Periam, librarian; b. Palo Alto, Calif., July 5, 1908; s. George Henry and Annina (Periam) D.; ed. U. of Leipzig (Germany), 1925-26; A.B. magna cum laude, Oberlin (O.) Coll., 1928; B.S., Columbia, 1929; A.M., Williams Coll., Williamstown, Mass., 1930; Ph.D., U. of Chicago, 1935 (Carnegie Fellow, 1933-35); m. Emily Van Dorn Miller, Nov. 29, 1933. Asst. in reading room, N.Y. Pub. Library, 1928, supervisor of stacks, 1928-29; reference asst., Williams Coll. Library, Williamstown, Mass., 1929-30; with A.L.A., 1930-33; librarian and asso. prof. bibliography, Colby Coll., Waterville, Me., 1935-36; librarian and asst. prof. bibliography, Temple U., Phila., since 1936; National Library Consultant, U.S. Works Progress Administration, 1937 (leave of absence). Mem. A.L.A. (on various coms. since 1934), Assn. Coll. and Ref. Libraries (treas. since 1938), Pa. Library Assn., Am. Assn. Univ. Profs., Bibliog. Soc. of America, Sigma Alpha Epsilon, Phi Kappa Pi. Democrat. Club: Williams (New York). Compiler (with others); Library Literature 1921-1932, (pub.) 1934; translator sects. on German libraries in Popular Libraries of the World, 1933. Contbr. to ednl. and book revs. jours. Home: 7801 Winston Rd., Chestnut Hill, Pa. Office: Sullivan Memorial Library, Philadelphia, Pa.

DANTZIG, Tobias, univ. prof.; b. Shavli, Russia, Feb. 19, 1884; s. Samuel and Augusta (Demont) D.; student High Sch., Shavli, Russia, 1892-96, Sch. of Commerce, Lodz, Russia (now Poland), 1897-1901; Licencié'es Sciences, Sorbonne, Paris, France, 1906-09; Ph.D., U. of Ind., Bloomington, 1916; m. Anna G. Ourisson, 1908; children—George Bernard, Henry Poincare. Came to U.S., 1910, naturalized, 1917. Began as mathematician, 1906; instr. mathematics, Indiana U., Bloomington, Ind., 1914-17; mathematician, U.S. War Dept., 1917-18; instr. mathematics, Columbia U., 1918-19, Johns Hopkins U., 1919-21; consulting mathematician for S. K. F. industries and other corpns., 1921-26; prof. mathematics, U. of Md., Baltimore, since 1926, head of dept. since 1936. Mem. Am. Math. Soc. Author: Number, The Language of Science, 1st edit., 1930, 2d edit., 1936, 3d edit., 1939, also British French and Russian edits.; Aspects of Science, 1938, French edit., 1939; The Story of Geometry, 1939; contbr. tech. and math. articles to various periodicals. Home: 26 Hyatt Av., Hyattsville, Md. Office: University of Maryland, College Park, Md.

DANTZSCHER, Walter Frederick, coll. publicity dir.; b. Brooklyn, N.Y., Aug. 13, 1905; s. Frederick Otto and Emma Catherine (Otterstedt) D.; A.B., Columbia U., 1925; m. Janice Mary Gilliams, Oct. 21, 1926 (div.); children—Dorothy Ann, Walter Frederick, Jr.; m. 2d, Ann(a) Mae Dietz, July 18, 1934; children—David Dietz, Stephen Douglas. Asso. in various capacities with Gilliams Service, 1925-34, also serving as syndicate writer for 12 met. newspapers and later with large adv. agencies; publicity dir., coll. editor, Pa. State Coll. since 1934; pres. Gilrubin Corpn. Mem. Am. Coll. Publicity Assn., Phi Beta Kappa. Awarded Van Amringe Math. Prize, Columbia Univ. Lutheran. Home: 21 Orlando Apts., State College, Pa.

DARBAKER, L(easure) K(line), univ. prof.; b. Pittsburgh, Pa., Jan. 13, 1879; s. Rev. Dr. Henry D. and Agness Jane (Kline) D.; studied Grove City (Pa.) Coll., Ohio Northern U., Ada, O., U. of Pittsburgh and U. of Berlin, Germany; specialized study U. of Edenburg, Scotland; m. Susan B. King, Aug. 15, 1915. Asso. with U. of Pittsburgh since 1906, successively as quizz master, associate prof. of botany and materia medica, and prof. of pharmacognosy and bacteriology; dir. and cons. microscopist Pittsburgh Testing Labs. and consultant in microscopy to Am. Bur. of Inspection and Tests. Mem. Com. Materia Medica Bds. of Pharmacy Dist. 2 (N.F. Color Com.). Fellow A.A.A.S.; chmn. sects. of various scientific assns. and mem. various coms.; mem. Pa. Pharm. Assn. (chmn. com. on biology and pharmacognosy several times), Naturalist Soc. of Western Pa. (past pres.), Nat. Plant Science Seminar, Pa. Acad. of Science (pres.), Am. Pharm. Assn., Pittsburgh Acad. of Science and Art, A.M.A., Nat. Geog. Soc., Sullivant Moss Soc., Am. Soc. Bacteriologists, Am. Bot. Soc., Plant Physiol. Soc., Plant Pathol. Soc., Natural Mus., Collembolæ Biol. Soc., Am. Forestry Assn., Am. Micros. Soc., Kappa Psi (grand historian), Phi Sigma. Mason. Author many articles on plant physiology, pathology, bacteriology, hematology, urinology, and plant histology; also manuals of histological pharmacognosy, microbiology, microscopy, botany and biology. Home: 424 Franklin Av., Wilkinsburg, Pa. Office: 1431 Boul. Allies, Pittsburgh, Pa.

DARBY, Arleigh Lee, univ. prof.; b. Bruceton, W.Va., May 4, 1878; s. James Ezra and Elizabeth (Humbert) D.; A.B., Waynesburg Coll., 1899, A.M., 1907, Litt.D., 1927; A.B., U. of Chicago, 1906; studied Université de Grenoble, France, 1904; unmarried. Prof. languages, Waynesburg Coll., 1900-10; with W.Va. U. since 1910, now prof. Romance languages, teaching French and Italian, also pre-medical class adviser, head resident Men's Residence Halls; prof. languages, Miami U., summer 1908, Notre Dame U., summer 1926. Served with Italian Army, 18 mos., World War. Awarded medal, Italian Govt., 1918; awarded medal Italian Govt. for service rendered Italian edn. and culture in U.S., 1933. Trustee Waynesburg Coll., Alderson Broaddus Coll. Mem. Phi Beta Kappa, Sigma Chi. Baptist. Address: Morgantown, W.Va.

DARLING, Benjamin James, lawyer; b. Hoboken, N.J., June 14, 1879; s. Henry Isaac and Martha Jane (Dowden) D.; ed. bus. and prep. schs., 1896-99; LL.B., N.Y. Univ. Law Sch., 1901; m. Marcella Foster, Oct. 19, 1908; children—Marcella Foster (Mrs. Edward H. Heyd), Elizabeth Dowden (Mrs. Clifford C. Hantke), Martha Susan. Admitted to N.J. bar as atty., 1901, as counsellor, 1904; engaged in gen. practice of law at Jersey City, N.J., since 1902; pres. Darling Realty Corpn.; sec. Fulton Theatre Co.; dir. Stuyvesant Bldg. & Loan Assn., Home Bldg. & Loan Assn. Served as govt. appeal agt. to dft. bd., 1918. Mem. N.J. Bar Assn., Hudson Co. Bar Assn., N.J. State Seniors Golf Assn. Republican. Episcopalian (vestryman). Mason (32°, Shriner). Clubs: Lions (Jersey City); Forest Hill Field (Bloomfield). Home: 91 Glenwood Av. Office: 921 Bergen Av., Jersey City, N.J.

DARLING, Chester Arthur, prof. biology; b. Leon, N.Y., Oct. 4, 1880; s. Charles D. and Dora R. (Laing) D.; A.B., Albion (Mich.) Coll., 1904, A.M., 1906; Ph.D., Columbia, 1909; m. Madge Williams, of Raymond, O., Aug. 5, 1908; 1 son, Richard W. Prof. biology, Defiance (Ohio) Coll., 1904-06; asst. in botany, 1906-08, tutor, 1908-10, instr., 1910-13, Columbia; prof. biology and head dept. of biology, Allegheny Coll., Pa., since 1913. Fellow A.A.A.S.; mem. Bot. Soc. America, Am. Pub. Health Assn., Am. Genetic Assn., Soc. of Am. Bacteriologist, Sigma Xi, Delta Sigma Rho, Phi Gamma Delta, Phi Beta Kappa. Club: Round Table. Author: Handbook of the Wild and Cultivated Flowering Plants, 1912; Spring Flowers, 1913; etc. Home: Meadville, Pa.

DARLING, Ira A., hosp. supt.; b. Wolcott, Vt., March 9, 1888; s. Elial G. and Ella (Hodgdon) D.; M.D., U. of Vt., Burlington, 1911; m. Jennie L. McGill, Dec. 5, 1914; 1 dau., Ella N. Interne Lynn (Mass.) Hosp., 1911-12; asst. physician Warren (Pa.) State Hosp., 1912-17 and 1919-32, supt., 1933-35; supt. Springfield State Hosp., Sykesville, Md., since 1936. Served as 1st lt. Medical Corps, U.S. Army, with Base Hosp. 89, A.E.F., 1918-19. Fellow Am. Coll. Physicians; mem. Warren Co. Med. Soc., Pa. State Med. Soc., A.M.A., Baltimore Co. Med. Soc. (affiliate), Pittsburgh, Buffalo and Baltimore Neuropsychiatric socs., Nat. Soc. for Mental Hygiene, Am. Psychiatric Assn., Am. Legion (chief cornplanter Post 130, Warren, Pa.). Clubs: Rotary (Westminster, Md.); Oriole Archers (Baltimore). Author numerous articles on psychiatric subjects. Home: North Warren, Pa. Office: Sykesville, Md.

DARLINGTON, Hart, fire ins. co. exec.; b. Muscoda, Wis., Nov. 26, 1875; s. Charles Howard and Louise (Hart) D.; ed. high sch., Morristown, Tenn., and Washington Coll., Tenn.; m. Sept. 17, 1898; 1 son, Horace. Began as clk. ins. office, 1893; asst. mgr. Phoenix Assurance Co., 1913-21; U.S. Mgr., Norwich Union Fire Ins. Co., New York, N.Y.; pres. and dir. Norwich Union Indemnity Co., Eagle Fire Ins. Co. of N.Y. Republican. Methodist. Mason (K.T.). Clubs: Country (Maplewood); Lawyers, Drug and Chemical (New York). Home: 28 Woodland Rd., Maplewood, N.J. Office: 75 Maiden Lane, New York, N.Y.

DARLINGTON, Isabel, lawyer; b. Phila., Pa., June 22, 1865; d. Smedley and Mary Edwards (Baker) Darlington; graduate Darlington Sem., West Chester, Pa., 1880; B.S., Wellesley (Mass.) Coll., 1886; LL.B. (cum laude), U. of Pa., 1897; unmarried. Admitted to Chester Co. (Pa.) bar, 1897, Superior Ct. of Pa., 1902, Supreme Ct. of Pa., 1905; mem. firm Thomas & Butler, West Chester, Pa., 1899-1928; receiver Parkesburg (Pa.) Nat. Bank, 1924-26. Mem. Chester Co. Hist. Soc. (v.p. since 1936), Wellesley Coll. Alumnæ Assn., U. of Pa. Alumnæ Assn. Republican. Christian Scientist. Clubs: Wellesley (Phila.); Women's Republican Club of Chester Co. (West Chester, Pa.). Home: Faunbrook. Office: 16 E. Market St., West Chester, Pa.

DARMS, John Martin George (originally D'Arms), ch. official; b. Philadelphia, Pa., July 24, 1873; s. Lorenz and Ursula von (Arduseer) D.; A.B., Mission House Coll., Plymouth, Wis., 1892; D.D., 1912; grad. Theol. Sem. of same instn., 1895; post-grad. study Columbia U. and Teachers Coll., 1923; m. Charlotte von Tacky, of Titusville, Pa., May 2, 1900; 1 son, Edward Francis. Ordained ministry Ref. Ch. in U.S., 1895; organized ch. in Buffalo, N.Y., with 4 members and continued as pastor 16 yrs. (now nearly 1,000 members); pastor Emanuel Ch., Rochester, 3 yrs.; Salem Ch., Allentown, Pa., 1914-23 ($300,000 ch. erected); pres. Mission House Coll. and Sem., also prof. comparative religion and religious edn., 1923-30; asst. exec. sec. of exec. com. Reformed Ch. in U.S. since 1930; executive sec. Reformed Churchmen's League, 1933; exec. sec. Churchman's Brotherhood since 1937; pastor Hope Evangelical and Reformed Ch., Phila., Pa. President of the Northwestern Philadelphia Ministerium; formerly v.p. United Stewardship Council of North America and Canada; member Board of Foreign Missions of Reformed Church, Council Federation of Churches in U.S.A., Alliance of Presbyterian and Reformed Churches, National Service Commn. Trustee Huping Coll., Hunan, China, Central China Coll., Wuchang. Active in war work at Camp Meade (Cape May, N.J.) and Camp Allentown, Pa. Republican. Rotarian. Author: On the Threshold of the Christian Ministry, 1912; Manual of Christian Stewardship, 1915; With Christ Through Lent, 1927. Wrote adult lessons for 10½ yrs.; also editor of Christian Forum (monthly) and asso. editor The Churchman's Brotherhood and Men's Dept. of Outlook of Missions. Home: 331 Farwood Rd., Carroll Park, West Park P.O. Office: 1505 Race St., Philadelphia, Pa.

DARRAH, Leon C.; chief of obstetrical service Reading Hosp. Address: 300 N. Fifth St., Reading, Pa.

DARRIN, Marc de Lepine, chem. engr.; b. Elmira, N.Y., Jan. 11, 1891; s. Dr. Charles Bennett and Caroline (de Lepine) D.; B.S. in chemistry, U. of Wash., Seattle, Wash., 1912, M.S. in chem. engring., 1913; m. Kathleen Sullivan, June 22, 1915. Chemist in Forest Products, U.S. Forest Products Lab., Seattle, Wash., 1914-16; in charge of research div. Koppers Co., and mgr. Koppers Products Co., Pittsburgh, 1916-22; with Sterling Varnish Co., 1922-23; with F. N. Burt Co., Ltd., Buffalo, N.Y., and paper finishing fellowship, Mellon Inst., Pittsburgh, 1923-34; senior industrial fellow, Mellon Inst., 1934-36; with Mutual Chem. Co. of America and chromium fellowship, Mellon Inst., Pittsburgh, since 1936. Mem. Am. Chem. Soc., Am. Inst. Chemists, Pi Kappa Alpha, Sigma Xi, Tau Beta Pi, Phi Lambda Upsilon. Club: University (Pittsburgh and Baltimore); Chemists' (New York). Home: 301 Wingate Rd. Office: Mutual Chemical Co of America, Baltimore, Md.

DARROW, George Potter, congressman; b. Waterford, Conn., Feb. 4, 1859; s. Edmund and Elizabeth (Potter) D.; A.B., Alfred U., 1880, LL.D., 1922; m. Sarah Johnson, of Athens, Pa., Feb. 8, 1887 (died Sept. 18, 1888); m. 2d, Elizabeth Shore, of Phila., Pa., Sept. 16, 1897. Mem. bd. mgrs. Mut. Fire Ins. Co., Germantown, Phila.; pres. 22d sectional Sch. Bd., Phila., 3 yrs.; mem. Common Council, Phila., 1910-15; mem. 64th to 74th Congresses (1915-37) and 76th Congress (1939-41), 6th and 7th Pa. Dists. Republican. Baptist. Club: Union League. Home: 5625 Germantown Av., Philadelphia, Pa.

DARTON, Nelson Horatio, geologist; b. at Brooklyn, Dec. 17, 1865; s. William and Caroline M. (Thayer) D.; common sch. edn.; D.Sc., U. of Ariz., 1922; m. Alice Weldon Wasserbach, 1903. Chemist in N.Y., 1882-86; geologist, U.S. Geol. Survey, 1886-1910 and 1913-36 (retired); geologist, Bur. Mines, 1910-13. Inventor of a sugar process; researches in tannic acid and water analysis, etc. Lectured at various colleges. Fellow Geol. Soc. America (ex-v.p.), A.A.A.S.; memb. Washington Acad. Sciences (former vice-pres.), Geol. Soc. Washington (former pres.), Soc. Economic Geologists, Mining and Metallurgical Soc., Am. Inst. Mining and Metall. Engrs., Soc. Linn de Lyons, Inst. Français, Pi Gamma Mu, Soc. Géol. de France, Assn. Am. Geographers, Internat. Geol. Congress, Soc. Fine Arts, Wyo. Valley Geol. Soc., Am. Geophysical Union, Archæol. Soc., Federal Bd. of Surveys and Maps, Italy-America Soc., Alliance Française (v.p.), Spanish Atheneum (expres.), Instituto de las Españas; hon. mem. Am. Assn. of Petroleum Geologists; mem. sub-com. Nat. Council. Awarded Daly gold medal, Am. Geog. Soc., 1929. Wrote: The Story of the Grand Canyon; Geologic Guide to Santa Fe Railroad; Geologic Guide to Southern Pacific Railroad; Geology of Great Plains, Black Hills, Bighorn Mountains; Geology Dist. Columbia region; Geologic maps Great Plains, Grand Canyon, S.D., Neb., Ariz., N.M., Lower Calif. and Tex.; many folios U.S. Geol. Survey, etc. Contributor on geol. subjects; geol. maps and reports on many districts, topog. maps; many articles in Ency. Americana. Explored ruins of the temple of Cuicuilco, Mexico, for Nat. Geog. Soc. and oil geology of Lower Calif., Santo Domingo, Eastern Cuba and Central Venezuela. Clubs: Cosmos, Inquirendo. Home: 6969 Brookeville Rd., Chevy Chase, Md. Office: U.S. Geological Survey, Washington, D.C.

DARTT, Henry H.; pres. and gen. mgr. Scranton Transit Co. Home: Dalton, Pa. Office: 234 Lackawanna Av., Scranton, Pa.

D'ASCENZO, Nicola, artist; b. Torricella, Peligna, Italy, Sept. 25, 1871; s. Giacinto and Mary Joseph (Italiana) D'A.; came to U.S., 1882; ed. Pennsylvania Academy Fine Arts, Philadelphia, Pa., Pa. Mus. and Sch. Industrial Art, New York Sch. of Design, Scuola Libera, Rome, Italy; m. Myrtle Goodwin, of Philadelphia, June 12, 1894; 1 son, Nicola Goodwin. Proprietor. The D'Ascenzo Studios, makers of stained glass, murals, mosaics, Phila. Prin. works: historical windows, Washington Memorial Chapel, Valley Forge, Pa.; clerestory windows, Mercersburg (Pa.) Acad.; chapel windows Georgetown Prep. Sch., Garrett Park, Md.; windows Folger-Shakespeare Library of Washington, D.C.; windows and Stations of the Cross, Ch. of the Holy Child, Phila.; great west window, Princeton Univ. Chapel; also windows for Riverside Bapt. Ch. (New York), St. James P.E. Ch. (Bristol, Pa.), Unitarian Ch. (Phila.), and Fidelity Phila. Bldg. (Phila.); window in Chapel of the Holy Spirit, Nat. Cathedral, Washington, D.C.; clerestory and aisle windows in Labour Bay, Cathedral of St. John the Divine, N.Y. City. Awarded gold metal, Archtl. League of New York, 1925; gold medal, T-square Club, 1897-98; gold medal Alumni Assn. of Pennsylvania Mus. and Sch. of Industrial Art; medalist Columbian Exp. Mem. Archtl. League New York, Soc. Mural Decorators; hon. mem. Am. Inst. Architects. Former Sec. State Art Jury, Pa.

Home: 425 W. Price St. Office: 1604 Summer St., Philadelphia, Pa.

DASHIELL, Philip Thornton; v.p. The Phila. Gas Works Co.; b. Annapolis, Md., Feb. 9, 1879; s. Julius Matthias and Mary Thorton (Voss) D.; student St. John's Coll. Annapolis, Md., and St. Paul's Sch., Concord, N.H.; Ph.B., Yale Scientific Sch.; m. Alice Dorey Paschall, Apr. 19, 1904; children—Alice Thornton, Virginia Paschall. Began as cadet engr. United Gas Improvement Co., 1899, asst. supt. Pt. Breeze Works, Phila., Pa., 1902-04, asst. engr. of works, Phila., 1913-28; asst engr. Essex Div., Pub. Service Corpn. of N.J., 1904-13; engr. of works Phila. Gas Works Co., 1928-33, v.p. in charge production since 1933, dir. since 1938. Active in Welfare Fed. and United Campaign charities, Phila. Mem. Phila. Chamber of Commerce, Am. Gas Assn., The Franklin Inst., Yale Engring Assn., Newcomen Soc. of America. Awarded Beal Medal by Am. Gas Assn. for best paper of year, 1931; Walton Clark Medal for contbn. to advancement of gas industry, 1932. Clubs: Yale, University, Midday (Phila.). Author several tech. articles. Home: (winter) Drake Hotel, Phila. (summer) Glenmoore, R.D. 1, Pa. Office: 1401 Arch St., Philadelphia.

DAUGHENBAUGH, Paul Jones, research biochemist; b. Thomas, W.Va., Nov. 15, 1898; s. James Monroe and Ellen (Moran) D.; B.A., West Virginia U., 1924; student U. of Chicago, 1922-23; M.S., West Virginia U., 1927; Ph.D., Rutgers U., 1930; student Yale U., 1930-33; m. Jane E. Stevens, July 8, 1933; 1 son, Peter Scott. Soils technician, W.Va. Agrl. Expt. Sta., 1924-25; jr. agrl. chemist W.Va. Agrl. Expt. Station, 1926; jr. state chemist W.Va. Dept. Agr., 1927; asst. biochemist J.&J. Research Bur., Rutgers U., 1927-30; research biochemist Sharp & Dohme Research Labs., 1933-36; asst. dir. tech. div. Sharp & Dohme, Inc., since 1936; nat. research council fellow in biol. sciences, Yale U., 1930-32, A. Homer Smith fellow, 1932-33. Served as private, U.S. Inf., 1918. Fellow Am. Inst. of Chemists; mem. A.A.A.S., Am. Chem. Soc., Soc. for Study of Internal Secretions, Franklin Inst., Phi Beta Kappa, Phi Lambda Upsilon, Sigma Xi, Sigma Chi. Home: Wrightstown, Pa.

DAUGHERTY, Carroll Roop, economist; b. Annville, Pa., Dec. 3, 1900; s. Benjamin Franklin and Della Frances (Roop) D.; A.B., Lebanon Valley Coll., Annville, Pa., 1921; A.M., U. of Pa., 1924, Ph.D., 1927; m. Miriam Craiglow, June 21, 1928; children—James Carroll, David Henry. Instr. in English, Mercersburg (Pa.) Acad., 1921-23; instr. in geography, Wharton Sch., U. of Pa., 1925-28; prof. of economics, U. of Ala., 1928-31; prof. of economics, U. of Pittsburgh, since 1931; research economist on labor conditions in the iron and steel industry under the NRA for Bureau of Business Research, U. of Pittsburgh, 1934-35; principal economist for labor productivity studies, U.S. Bureau of Labor Statistics, 1936; chief economist, wage and hour div., U.S. Dept. of Labor, since 1938. Mem. Am. Econ. Assn., Am. Statis. Assn., Am. Assn. for Labor Legislation, Am. Assn. for Social Security, Am Civil Liberties Union, Am. Assn. University Profs., Artus (hon. economics fraternity), Alpha Sigma Phi. Democrat. Author: Labor Problems in Am. Industry, 1933, Labor Under the NRA, 1934; co-author: Man and His World, 1932; Economic Principles and Problems, 1936; Economics of Iron and Steel Industry, 1937. Home: 5505 Beverly Pl. Office: U. of Pittsburgh, Pittsburgh, Pa.

DAUGHERTY, Harry Kerr, lawyer; b. Mercer Co., Pa., Dec. 28, 1868; s. William Watson and Mary (Kerr) D.; ed. Grove City Coll.; m. Mabel A. Gould, of Washington, D. C., and Pa., Sept. 6, 1899; children—Mrs. Helen Gould Murray, Haywood H. Admitted to bar, 1895; 1st lt. 15th Pa. Regt., Spanish-Am. War; mustered out at Athens, Ga., Jan. 31, 1899; mem. Pa. Ho. of Rep., 1901, 1903; apptd. asst. atty. for defense of claims before Spanish Treaty Claims Commn., Wash., spent 6 mos. in investigation and taking testimony in Cuba, 1906; mem. Spanish Treaty Claims Commn., Washington, 1907-12. Arbitrator in controversy bet. N.Y. Central and Nickel Plate rys. and Brotherhood of Telegraphers. Del. Rep. Nat. Conv., 1916, 20. Borough solicitor Grove City Borough, 1913-26; dep. atty. gen. of Pa., 1917-20; asst. solicitor of U.S. Treasury since 1926. Methodist. Home: Grove City, Pa.

DAUGHERTY, John Fenton, univ. prof.; b. Baltimore, Md., Aug. 16, 1897; s. Richard Bassett and Edith Page (Krozer) D.; student Franklin High Sch., Reisterstown, Md., 1912-16; student Dickinson Coll., Carlisle, Pa., 1916-18, 1919-21, A.B., 1921; A.M., U. of N. C., Chapel Hill, N. C., 1925, Ph.D., 1930; m. Edna May Henry, Dec. 27, 1921; children—Mary Elizabeth, Dorothy Page. Instr. physics, U. of N. C., 1921-26; acting head dept. of physics, U. of The South, Sewanee, Tenn., 1926-27, head of dept., 1927-29; acting head dept. of physics, U. of Del., Newark, Del., 1929-30; prof. physics and head of dept. since 1930. Served in U.S.N.R.F., 1918-19. Mem. Am. Phys. Soc., Am. Assn. Univ. Profs, Phi Kappa Psi, Sigma Xi. Episcopalian. Mason (Summit Lodge 497). Address: 42 E. Delaware Ave., Newark, Del.

DAUGHERTY, Martin Marion, economist; b. San Antonio, Tex., Dec 8, 1894; s. William and Josephine (Powell) d.; B.S., Tex. A. and M. Coll., 1916, M.S., 1925; A.M., Harvard, 1930; m. Kate Lee Henley, June 23, 1919. Asst. prof. of economics, A. and M. Coll., College Station, Tex., 1919-26, with U. of Del. since 1927, asst. agrl. economist, 1927-28, research. prof. since 1928; asst. economist, Coordinator of Transportation, Washington, D.C., 1936; consulting economist, Del. Tax Commn., Wilmington, Del., 1937, 39; dir. Southside Development Corpn. Served as 1st lt., Air Service, U.S. Army, 1917-19. Mem. Am. Econ. Assn., Acad. of Polit. and Social Sciences, Am. Farm Econ. Assn. Episcopalian. Mason. Clubs: Torch (Wilmington, Del.); Harvard of Delaware. Home: 208 Orchard Rd., Newark, Del.

DAUME, Edward Frederick, real estate appraiser; b. Wheeling, W.Va., June 14, 1858; s. Frederick and Friederika (Rager) D.; ed. pub. schs., Jefferson and Belmont Co., O., 1863-73; m. Harriet Angeline Schillinger, Feb. 3, 1887 (died, 1910); children—Harriet Anna, Robert Edward. Active as real estate salesman, Pittsburgh, Pa., 1886-1905; asso. with Commonwealth Real Estate Co. as salesman, counsellor and appraiser since 1905. Mem. Nat. Tax. Assn., Am. Acad. Social and Polit. Science, Nat. Assn. of Real Estate Boards, Pa. Real Estate Assn., Hist. Soc. of Western Pa. Republican. Lutheran. Home: 339 West Penn Place. Office: 312 Fourth Av., Pittsburgh, Pa.

DAVEY, Wheeler P(edlar), physics and chemistry; b. Cleveland, O., Mar. 19, 1886; s. Thomas George and Myra Eliza (Christian) D.; A.B., Western Reserve U., 1906; M.S., Pa. State Coll., 1911; grad. study U. of Chicago summers 1909, 10, 11; Huntingdon fellow, Cornell U., 1912-13, Ph.D., 1914; m. Laura L. Gunn, of Jacksonville, Ill., Aug. 28, 1912; children—Myra Ellen, George Thomas, Ruth Barton, Mary Louise. Teacher of physics and chemistry, Central Inst., Cleveland, 1906-08; high sch., Mansfield, O., 1908-09; instr. in physics, Pa. State Coll., 1909-11; asst. in physics, Cornell U., 1911-12, instr. in physics, 1913-14; research physicist research lab. Gen. Electric Co., Schenectady, N.Y., 1914-26; prof. physical chemistry and prof. industrial research, Pa. State Coll., 1926-31; research prof. physics and chemistry since 1931; consultant Radiological Research Inst. since 1931. Chmn: Schenectady (N.Y.) Civil Serv. Commn., 1916-17. Lecturer on X-rays and crystal structure, Union U., 1920-26; lecturer in physics dept., Graduate School, Pennsylvania State Coll., summers 1922, 23, 24; lecturer on crystal structure, U. of Mich., summer 1925; Thurston lecturer, Am. Soc. M.E., 1928. Mem. elect. insulation com. Nat. Research Council since 1928, chmn. physics sub-com. since 1935. Mem. optics sub-com., Chicago Century of Progress Expn.; mem. Am. Inst. Physics Council on Applied Physics, 1935. Mem. editorial bd. Jour. of Chemical Physics, 1933. Fellow Am. Phys. Soc., A.A.A.S., Inst of Physics (London); mem. governing bd. Am. Inst. of Physics, 1931-33 and since 1937; mem. Am. Chem Soc., Optical Soc. America, Am. Inst. Mining and Metall. Engrs., Soc. for Chem. Industry (Great Britain), Iron and Steel Inst. (Great Britain), Am. Soc. for Metals, Soc. of Rheology (pres. 1930-33); also asso. editor, 1933-36, editor since 1936), Sigma Xi, Phi Lamda Upsilon, Sigma Pi Sigma, Alpha Pi Mu, Acacia. Republican. Presbyn. Mason. Contbr. to Fairbanks' Laboratory Investigation of Ores, 1928. Author: A Study of Crystal Structure, 1934; also articles on X-rays and crystal structure. Home: 423 W. Park Av., State College, Pa.

DAVID, Abraham Joseph, lawyer; b. Elizabeth, N.J., Aug. 21, 1876; s. Joseph and Caroline (Stern) D.; LL.B., N.Y. Law Sch., N.Y. City, 1896; m. Anna Kampner, Apr. 4, 1909; children—Jane Carol (Mrs. Aaron W. Lewin), Betty Theresa (Mrs. Philip Manne), Anne Jane. Admitted to N.J. bar as atty, 1898, as counselor, 1909; engaged in practice of law at Elizabeth since 1898; served as judge Elizabeth Dist. Ct., 1914-19; prosecutor of the pleas, Union Co., since 1923; vice-pres. Better Land Realty Co. Past pres. Elizabeth Chamber of Commerce. Hon pres. Y.M.H.A. and Y.W. H.A., Elizabeth, N.J. Hon. mem. Theta Alpha Phi, Phi Epsilon Pi. Democrat. Jewish religion. Mason. B.P.O.E. Clubs: Suburban Golf (Union). Home: 408 Chestnut St., Roselle. Office: 1143 E. Jersey St., Elizabeth, N.J.

DAVID, Charles Wendell, prof. European history; b. Onarga, Ill., Mar. 20, 1885; s. Charles and Alvira (Harper) D.; ed. Northwestern U., 1905-08; B.A., Oxford U., Eng., 1911; A.M., U. of Wis., 1912; Ph.D., Harvard U., 1918; m. Mary Virginia Martin, Sept. 11, 1918 (died 1936); m. 2d, Margaret Florence Simpson, May 27, 1939. Teaching Fellow, U. of Wis., 1911-13; instr. history, U. of Wash., Seattle, 1915-18; asso. prof. European history, Bryn Mawr Coll., 1918-27, prof. since 1927; chmn. bd. dirs. Union Library Catalogue of the Phila. Met. Area. Mem. Am. Hist. Assn., Mediaeval Acad. of America, Am. Assn. Univ. Profs., Am. Assn. Rhodes Scholars, Hist. Soc. of Pa., Royal Hist. Soc. of Great Britain, Phi Delta Theta. Rhodes Scholar at Oxford from Ill., 1908-11. Republican. Methodist. Author: Robert Curthose Duke of Normandy, 1920; De Expugnatione Lyxbonensi (The Conquest of Lisbon), 1936. Home: 13 Arthur Rd., Rosemont, Pa. Office: Bryn Mawr College, Bryn Mawr, Pa.

DAVID, William M.; v.p. Pa. Co. for Insurance on Lives and Granting Annuities. Home: 42 W. School Lane, Germantown. Office: 15th and Chestnut Sts., Philadelphia, Pa.

DAVIDSON, Adeline T., librarian; b. Huntington, N.Y.; B.L., Smith Coll., 1902; ed. Library Sch. N.Y. Pub. Library, 1922-23. Engaged in teaching in prep. and high schs., Stamford, Conn., Norfolk, Va., Morristown, N.J., 1902-12; librarian, pub. library, Duluth, Minn., 1923-26; librarian, Free Pub. Library, East Orange, N.J., since 1926. Mem. Am. Library Assn., N.J. Library Assn., Chamber of Commerce of the Oranges and Maplewood, Business and Professional Woman's Club of the Oranges, College Club of the Oranges, Smith College Club of the Oranges. Republican. Episcopalian. Home: 9 Summit St., East Orange, N.J.

DAVIDSON, Arthur Julius, physician, orthopedic surgeon; b. Philadelphia, Pa., Mar. 20, 1886; s. Charles C. and Florence (Stern) D.; student Phila. pub. schs. and William Penn Charter Sch., Phila.; M.D., Jefferson Med. Coll. Phila., 1907; m. Julia Brown, June 26, 1914; 1 dau., Dorothy Ruth. Began as physician, 1907; clin. prof. of orthopedic surgery, Jefferson Med. Coll., Phila.; orthopedic surgeon, Jefferson Hosp., Phila.; orthopedic surgeon to many other hosps. Lt. comdr., U.S.N.R. Fellow Am. Coll. Surgeons, Am. Acad. Orthopedic Surgeons; diplomate, Am. Bd. of Orthopedic Surgery; mem. Phila. Co. Med. Soc., Pa. State Med. Soc., A.M.A., Phila Med. Club, Phila. Orthopedic Club. Republican. Mason, Elk. Author numerous original articles on orthopedic subjects in med. jours. Home: 1901 Walnut St. Office: N.E. Corner 20th and Chestnut Sts., Philadelphia, Pa.

DAVIDSON, Edwin Lee, manufacturer; b. Parkersburg, W.Va., Nov. 3, 1863; s. Fred E. and Virginia (Mitchell) D.; ed. pvt. sch.; m. Nettie R. Johnson, June 9, 1887; 1 dau., Dorothy Burdette (dec.). President and general manager The Parkersburg Mill Co.; vice-pres. Community Savings & Loan; dir. Parkersburg Corrugated Box Co. Chmn. Liberty Loan and Am. Red Cross drives, World War. Ex-pres. Y.M.C.A., Parkersburg, Parkersburg Bd. of Commerce. Democrat. Methodist. Home: 1331 Market St. Office: 430 Third St., Parkersburg, W.Va.

DAVIDSON, Hobart Oakes, mech. engr.; b. Herkimer, N.Y., Nov. 28, 1891; s. Rev. William C. and Helen (Oakes) D.; B.S., Colgate U., 1913; B.S., Mass. Inst. Tech., 1920; m. Augusta Moulton, Nov. 25, 1920; children— Amy Jane, Hobart William. Engaged in teaching, 1913-17; engr. Ralston Purina Co., St. Louis, Mo., 1920-21; research work, Nat. Refrigerator Co., 1921-23; asso. with Am. Viscose Corpn. since 1923; asst. to chief engr. at Marcus Hook, Pa., 1923-25; chief engr. at Lewiston, Pa., 1925-28; chief engr. plant, Meadville, Pa., 1928-38; chief engr. Am. Viscose Corpn., Marcus Hook, Pa., since 1939. Served as chmn. Crawford Co. Chapter Am. Red Cross. Dir. Meadville Chamber of Commerce, Meadville Y.M.C.A., Spencer Hosp. Mem. Am. Soc. M.E., Beta Theta Pi, Phi Beta Kappa. Republican. Methodist (trustee Stone M.E. Ch.). Clubs: Rotary, Literary Union, Round Table (Meadville, Pa.). Home: Guernsey Rd., Swarthmore, Pa. Office: Del. Trust Bldg., Wilmington, Del.

DAVIDSON, Max David, rabbi; b. Newark, N.J., Mar. 8, 1899; s. Charles and Bessie (Stern) D.; A.B., N.Y. Univ., 1919; ed. Columbia U., 1919-20; Rabbi, Jewish Theol. Sem. of America, 1922; A.M., Rutgers U., 1930; m. Margaret Kussy of Newark, N.J., Jan. 30, 1927; children—Judith, Doris. Served as rabbi, Asbury Park, N.J., 1922-28; rabbi, Temple Beth Mordecai, Perth Amboy, N.J., since 1928; pres. United Synagogue of N.J. since 1937. Chaplain, Rahway Reformatory, Jamesburg Home for Boys. Past pres. Rabbinical Assn. of N.J. Jewish religion. Mason. Elk. Golden Chain (past grand patron). Author: Take Thou My Vow, 1927; The Golden Chain, 4th edit., 1939. Contbr. articles on Am. history and on the theatre. Dramatic critic Asbury Park Press since 1925. Home: 118 State St. Office: 224 High St., Perth Amboy, N.J.

DAVIES, Arthur W.; pastor Hazlewood Presbyn. Ch. Address: 245 Johnston Av., Pittsburgh, Pa.

DAVIES, Earl Claudius Hamilton, prof. of phys. chemistry; b. Delaware, O., Jan. 13, 1889; s. Matthew and Sarah (Hamilton) D.; A.B., Ohio Wesleyan U., Delaware, O., 1910, A.M., 1911; PhD. magna cum laude, U. of Chicago, 1917; m. Vivian Hobart, June 2, 1917; children—Evelyn Vivian, Marie Gwendolyn, Dorothy Frances. Chemistry asst., Ohio Wesleyan U., 1908-10, instr. of chemistry, later asst. prof., 1910-15; chemistry asst. U. of Chicago, 10 quarters during 1912-17; instr. of phys. chemistry, Washington U., St. Louis, 1917-18; head of chemistry dept., Butler U., Indianapolis, Ind., 1918-20; asso. prof. of phys. chemistry, W.Va. U., 1920-31, prof. since 1931. Fellow A.A.A.S.; mem. Am. Chem. Soc. (charter mem. northern W.Va. Sect., v. chmn. 1927, chmn. 1928, councilor 1929, sec.-treas. 1934), W.Va. Acad. Science (charter mem., chmn. Chemistry Sect. 1st 2 yrs. and 1930), Phi Eta, Phi Lambda Upsilon, Sigma Xi. Republican. Methodist. Mason (32°, Shriner). Author: Physical Chemistry Pre-medical Students, 1927; Fundamentals of Physical Chemistry, 1932. Contbr. of 28 articles to professional jours. Home: 321 Richwood Av., Morgantown, W.Va.

DAVIES, George Russell, ins. agency; b. Pittsburgh, Pa.; s. David S. and Sarah (Davies) D.; ed. pub. schs. and grad. Central High Sch., Pittsburgh. Engaged in ins. and pres. Pa. Ins. Agency, Inc., Pittsburgh, since 1912. Republican. Presbyterian. Mason (32°, Shriner). Clubs: Pittsburgh Athletic Assn., Oakmont Country (Pittsburgh). Home: 4201 5th Av. Office: 239 4th Av., Pittsburgh, Pa.

DAVIES, Thomas Russell, engineer; b. Clifford, Pa., Jan. 27, 1887; s. Frank A. and Christine A. (Russell) D.; M.E., Lehigh U., Bethlehem, Pa., 1911; m. Carolyn Read, May 19, 1923. Engr. Lackawanna Steel Co., Buffalo, N.Y., 1911, Fairbanks Valve Co., Binghamton, N.Y., 1912; engr. W. R. Grace & Co., Chile, S.A., 1913-16, engr., New York, 1917, 1920-21; partner Davies & Bertschy, Brooklyn, N.Y., 1922-23; pres. and dir. Davies Nitrate Co., Inc., mfrs. nitrates, Brooklyn, Croton Chem. Corpn., chem. mfrs., Brooklyn, since 1923. Served as capt., Ordnance Dept., U.S. Army, 1918-19. Mem. Tau Beta Pi, Sigma Phi Epsilon. Republican. Presbyterian. Mason (Shriner). Home: 3 Grant Av., East Orange, N.J. Office: 59 Commerce St., Brooklyn, N.Y.

DAVIES, Tom; football coach, U. of Scranton. Address: Scranton, Pa.

DAVIS, Alan Benjamin, music dir.; b. Johnstown, Pa., July 21, 1885; s. Owen and Sarah (Gettings) D.; artist diploma in music, Indianapolis Conservatory of Music, 1916; m. Eleanor Elissa Mentch, May 25, 1912; children—Richard Alan, Harvy Owen, John Elmer, Charlotte Eleanor, Sarah Louise and Carolyn Hope (twins). Began as concert singer and voice teacher, 1910; fellowship (voice teacher) Indianapolis Cons. of Music, 1913; founded Johnstown (Pa.) Coll. of Music, 1916, dir., 1916-20; private voice teacher, Pittsburgh, 1920-24; soloist radio station KDKA, 1921, dir. ch. music, Pittsburgh, 1920-24; dir. music 1st Presbyn. Ch. and soloist teacher, Johnstown, Pa., 1924-28; prof. music, head dept. and dir. Cons. of Music, Westminster Coll., New Wilmington, since 1928; music critic Johnstown (Pa.) Tribune, 1925-28; lecturer (music) County Teachers Inst., guest conductor music festivals, etc.; special guest conductor Midwestern Div. State High School Chorus, Zelienople, Pa., 1938; special guest conductor All Grade School Chorus, Aliquippa, Pa., 1939. Mem. Pa. State Edn. Assn. Republican. Presbyn. Mason, K.P. Home: 146 Waugh Av., New Wilmington, Pa.

DAVIS, Andrew Jay, ins. exec.; b. Pittsburgh, Pa., Sept. 13, 1887; s. Wilmer M. and Julia B. (Minehart) D.; B.S., Maple Inst., Concordville, Pa.; LL.B., U. of Pa.; m. Anne Pennock Bishop, Oct. 10, 1911; children—J. Bishop, Andrew Jay. Lawyer, Provident Mutual Life Ins. Co., Phila., 1912-18, asst. gen. counsel, 1918, gen. counsel, 1918-23, v.p. and gen. counsel, 1923-31, v.p. and dir. since 1931. Mem. Law Assn. of Phila., Assn. of Life Ins. Counsel, Order of the Coif. Clubs: Union League (Phila.); Aronimink Golf. Home: Drexel Park, Drexel Hill P.O., Pa. Office: N.W. Corner 46th and Market Sts., Philadelphia, Pa.

DAVIS, Arthur George, orthopedic surgeon; b. Sebringville, Ontario, Can., Mar. 3, 1887; s. George and Catherine (Ney) D.; came to U.S., 1896; naturalized, 1901; Ph.B., U. of Buffalo (N.Y.), 1907, M.D., 1913; post-grad. work, Harvard Med. Sch., 1922; m. Helen Kopcinski, Mar. 6, 1933; children—Helen, Janet, Arthur, Susan. Chief orthopedic surgeon, Hamot Hosp., Erie, Pa. since 1924, Shrine Hosp., Erie, Pa., since 1927; surgeon-in-chief Crippled Children, North Western, Pa., since 1936; Social Security of Northwestern Pa. Served as lt., U.S. Army M.C. with A.E.F., 1917-18. Episcopalian. Mason (Shriner). Author various articles on spinal fracture and other orthopedic subjects. Home: R.F.D. 3, Erie, Pa. Office: 716 Sassafras St., Erie, Pa.

DAVIS, Arthur Lorenzo, coll. prof.; b. Pulteney, N.Y., June 30, 1897; s. Loren Arthur and Julia (Smith) D.; A.B., Ohio Wesleyan U., Delaware, O., 1924; A.M., U. of Wis., Madison, Wis., 1926, Ph. D., 1932; grad. study univs. of Munich and Cologne, Germany, 1930-31; m. Kaethe Anne Weber, Apr. 7, 1922. Instr. German, Ohio Wesleyan Univ., Delaware, O., 1924-28, asst. prof. German, 1928-33; prof. German and head modern lang. dept., Washington Coll., Chestertown, Md., since 1933. Served with U.S. Army of Occupation, Germany, 1919-22; with Inter-Allied Rhineland High Commn., Coblenz, Germany, 1922-23. Mem. Modern Lang. Assn. America, Am. Assn. German Teachers, Am. Assn. Univ. Profs., Phi Beta Kappa. Methodist. Contbr. literary and critical articles to various publs. Home: 102 Mt. Vernon St., Chestertown, Md.

DAVIS, Arthur Vining, officer corpns.; b. Sharon, Mass., May 30, 1867; s. Perley B. and Mary Frances (Vining) D.; A.B., Amherst, 1888; m. Elizabeth Hawkins, Mar. 1912. Chmn. bd. Aluminum Co., of America; dir. Mellon Nat. Bank (Pittsburgh), Union Trust Co. of Pittsburgh, Pennsylvania Water & Power Co., Niagara Hudson Power Corpn. Mem. Psi Upsilon. Republican. Episcopalian. Clubs: Pittsburgh, Duquesne; Metropolitan (New York). Address: 801 Gulf Bldg., Pittsburgh, Pa.*

DAVIS, Austin Waters, banker; b. Phila., Pa., Jan. 23, 1883; s. Charles K. and Jeannette (Allison) D.; student Central High Sch., Phila., Am. Inst. of Banking; m. Ethel M. Bell, June 17, 1916. Mgr. collection dept. First Nat. Bank of Phila., 1900-26, asst. cashier and trust officer since 1926; v.p. and sec. First Trust Co. of Phila.; dir. Pacific Bldg. & Loan Assn. Club: Overbrook Golf. Home: 1101 N. 63d St. Office: 315 Chestnut St., Philadelphia, Pa.

DAVIS, Benjamin Woodhull, supt. city schs.; b. Coram, L.I., N.Y., Sept. 26, 1898; s. E. Everett and Margaret (Steen) D.; B.S., Wesleyan Univ., Middletown, Conn., 1919; A.M., Columbia U., 1927; m. Irma W. Nelson, Mar. 26, 1921; 1 son, Sherman Woodhull. Engaged as teacher mathematics, Matawan, N.J., 1920-22, Plainfield, N.J., 1922-29, principal Junior-Senior High Sch., Princeton, N.J., 1929-32; supt. schs., Princeton, N.J., since 1932. Pres. Princeton Y.M.C.A. since 1933. Mem. N.J. Schoolmasters Club. Methodist (trustee M.E. Ch.). Club: Springdale Golf. Home: 10 Patten Av., Princeton, N.J.

DAVIS, Carl Henry, obstetrician, gynecologist; b. Halsey, Linn Co., Ore., Aug. 6, 1883; s. Henry Clinton and Clara Bell (Penland) D.; A.B., U. of Ore., 1905; S.B., U. of Chicago, 1906; M.D., Rush Med. Coll., Chicago, 1909; m. Elizabeth Greene, d. late Horace A. J. Upham, Sept. 6, 1919; children—Horace Upham, Henry Clinton, John Upham, Mary Upham. Interne and resident Presbyn. Hosp., Chicago, 1909-10 and 1912-13; asst. to med. dir. N.W. Life Ins. Co., Milwaukee, 1911; asst. and instr. obstetrics and gynecology, Rush Med. Coll. and Central Free Dispensary, Chicago, 1913-19, asst. clinical professor of same, 1929-30; clin. prof. and dir. dept. obstetrics and gynecology, Marquette U. Med. Sch., Milwaukee, since 1930; assistant and later associate attending obstetrician and gynecologist, Presbyn. Hosp., Chicago, 1914-19; attending obstetrician and gynecologist to Columbia and Milwaukee Co. hosps., 1919-36; now gynecologist to Deleware Hosp. and obstetrician and gynecologist to St. Francis Hosp., Wilmington. First lt. Med. R.C., 1916 and 1917; capt. Aug. 3, 1918; maj., Oct. 29, 1918; active duty as instr., etc., M.O.T.C., Ft. Riley, Kan.; hon. discharged, Jan. 2, 1919. Fellow A.M.A. (sec. sect. obstetrics, gynecology and abdominal surgery, 1920-28, chmn. 1928-29), Am. Coll. Surgeons (mem. bd. of govs.), 1929; mem. New Castle County Med. Soc., Delaware State Medical Society, The Obstetrical Society of Philadelphia, Milwaukee Acad. Medicine (pres. 1926), Chicago Gynecol. Soc. (pres. 1929), Am. Gynecol. Soc., Alpha Kappa Kappa. Methodist. Clubs: University, Milwaukee Country. Author: Painless Childbirth, Eutocia and Nitrous Oxid-Oxygen Analgesia (2d edit.), 1916. Contbr. Ency. Americana and to med. jours. Editor and contbr. to Davis' Gynecology and Obstetrics (3 loose leaf vols.), 1933. Home: 1100 Blackshire Rd. Office: Medical Arts Bldg., Wilmington, Del.*

DAVIS, Chester Morrison, clergyman; b. Sturgis, Ky., Nov. 3, 1891; s. Charles Medcalf and Josephine Caroline (Eberley) D.; student Sturgis (Ky.) High Sch., 1906-10; A.B., Lincoln Coll. of James Millikin U., Lincoln, Ill., 1914, M.A., 1919; B.D., McCormick Theol. Sem. (now Presbyterian Theol. Sem., Chicago), 1919; D.D. (hon.), Coll. of the Ozarks, Clarksville, Ark.,

1936; m. Elisabeth Logan, March 14, 1922; children—Anne Logan, Josephine Caroline. Pastor 1st Presbyn. Ch., Warren, Ill., 1917, Immanuel Presbyn. Ch., Chicago, 1919-22, 1st Presbyn. Ch., Rahway, N.J., since 1922; v.p. Citizens Bldg. & Loan Assn., Rahway, N.J., since 1932. Chmn. Synod's Permanent Com. of Program and Field Activities since 1934 (5 yr. term); pres. Rahway Fed. of Churches, 1939; leader Fellowship Club of Rahway (N.J.) Y.M.C.A. since 1937. Mem. at large Nat. Social Science Honor Soc. Honored by Moderatorship of Elizabeth Presbytery, 1924. Club: Kiwanis (Rahway, N.J.; sec. since 1925). Address: 552 Union St., Rahway, N.J.

DAVIS, Clarence Ernest, lawyer; b. Blacklick Twp., Pa., July 28, 1887; s. John and Mary R. D.; student Indiana (Pa.) State Teachers Coll., 1904-08; LL.B., U. of Pa., 1912; m. Martha Cowles, June 20, 1917; children—Mary Martha, Clarence Cowles, Phyllis Ann, Larry Lee. Admitted to Cambria Co. and Pa. bars, 1912, and since practiced under own name at Ebensburg, Pa.; pres. Summit Pub. Co. since 1916; treas. Cresson Pub. Co., Asst. dist. atty. Cambria Co., Pa., 1918-32. Dir. Ebensburg Y.M.C.A., Lloyd Cemetery Assn. Mem. Pa. State Bar Assn., Cambria Co. Bar Assn., Acacia. Republican. Presbyterian. Mason, Moose, Elk. Clubs: Kiwanis, Esquire, Ebensburg Country (Ebensburg, Pa.). Home: 419 Horner St. Office: Trust Co. Bldg., Ebensburg, Pa.

DAVIS, Daniel Elias, engineer; b. Columbus, O., June 15, 1886; s. Stephen S. and Elizabeth (Morgan) D.; C.E., Ohio State U., Columbus, O., 1908; M.S., U. of Wis., Madison, Wis., 1912; m. Adele Cochran, June 4, 1921; children—Daniel Elias, Stephen Cochran. Asst. city engr., Alliance, O., 1910-11; fellowship, Wis. Railroad Commn., 1912-13; asst. engr. Chester & Fleming, Pittsburgh, 1913-17; mem. of firm The Chester Engrs., sanitary and hydraulic engrs., Pittsburgh, since 1919; dir. Edgeworth Water Co., Jamestown Water Co., Fayette City Water Co. Served as 1st lt. and capt., U.S. Army, 1917-19; constructing q.m. and utilities officer, Camp Hancock, Georgia, 1918-19. Asso. water consultant, National Resources Bd., 1936. Mem. Y.M.C.A. (pres., Sewickley, Pa., 1934-39); Am. Soc. C.E. (dir. Pittsburgh section); Pa. Soc. of Professional Engrs. (former dir. Pittsburgh section). Republican. Presbyterian. Clubs: Edgeworth (Sewickley, Pa.); Civic (Pittsburgh). Home: Glen Osborne, Sewickley, Pa. Office: 1050 Century Bldg., Pittsburgh, Pa.

DAVIS, Daniel Louis, rabbi; b. Baltimore, Md., Aug. 22, 1903; s. Isaac and Fannie D.; grad. Baltimore City Coll., 1919; A.B., Johns Hopkins U., 1923; Rabbi, Hebrew Union Coll., 1926; grad. study, U. of Chicago, U. of Mich.; m. Sonia Kochman, June 23, 1926; 1 son, Baruch J. Rabbi of Cong. Beth-El, Hammond, Ind., 1926-27; rabbi Cong. Shaarai Shomayim, Lancaster, Pa., since 1927. Treas. Hebrew Union Coll. Alumni Assn. Jewish religion. Home: 1019 Woods Av., Lancaster, Pa.

DAVIS, David M., physician; b. Buffalo, N.Y., July 23, 1886; B.S., Princeton, 1907; M.D., Johns Hopkins U. Med. Sch., 1911; married. Asst. and asso. in urology, Johns Hopkins, 1914-24; asst. prof. urol. surgery, U. of Rochester, 1924-28; urologist, Phoenix, Ariz., and visiting urologist, Desert Sanitorium, Tucson, Ariz., 1930-35; prof. genito-urinary surgery, Jefferson Med. College, since 1935; attending genito-urinary surgeon, Jefferson Med. Coll. Hosp. Served as lt., capt. and maj., Med. O.R.C., 1917-19 (2 yrs. service in France). Awarded certificate Am. B^d of Urology. Fellow Coll. Phys. of Phila.; mem. Am. Med. Assn., Am. Urol. Assn., Am. Assn. Genito-Urinary Surgeons, Halsted Club, Alpha Omega Alpha, Phi Beta Kappa. Contributor 61 books and articles in scientific jours. Home: 215 Cheswold Lane, Haverford, Pa. Office: 255 S. 17th St., Philadelpia, Pa.

DAVIS, David Roy, prof. mathematics; b. Clarkshill, Ind., April 30, 1893; s. David Moss and Carrie L. (Whipple) D.; A.B., Ind. Univ., 1917, A.M., same, 1923; Ph.D., Univ. of Chicago, 1927; m. Vera May Brooke, May 29, 1920. Engaged as teacher elementary and secondary schs., 4 yrs., prin. high sch., Ind., 2 yrs.; head dept. mathematics and sci., high sch., Granite City, Ill., 1920-24; asst. prof. mathematics, U. of Ore., Eugene, Ore., 1926-31; prof. mathematics, State Teachers Coll., Upper Montclair, N.J., since 1931. Mem. Am. Math. Soc., Am. Math. Assn., A.A.A.S., Sigma Xi, Phi Beta Kappa. Ind. Republican. Methodist. Mason. Club: Lake Mohawk Country (Sparta, N.J.). Author: Introductory College Mathematics, 1935. Contbr. research papers on calculus of variations. Lecturer on teaching and on popular phases of mathematics. Home: 43 College Av., Upper Montclair, N.J.

DAVIS, E. Asbury, merchant; b. Somerset Co., Md., Aug. 24, 1870; s. Francis A. and Sallie (Long) D.; Baltimore City Coll., 1885; m. Jennie Conradt, Oct. 20, 1892; children—Francis A., Allan C., Hamilton C., Clara A., Virginia. Partner F. A. Davis & Sons, cigar mfrs.; pres., Washington Tobacco Co., U.S. Fidelity & Guarantee Co.; v.p. Old Dominion Tobacco Co. Home: 305 Somerset Rd. Office: 119 S. Howard St., Baltimore, Md.

DAVIS, Earle Clifton, supervising prin. of schools; b. Glen Hope, Pa., April 18, 1896; s. Walter Blake and Ellen (Copenhaver) D.; grad. Bigler Twp. High Sch., Madera, Pa., 1915; grad. State Normal School, Lock Haven, Pa., 1918; B.S., New York U., 1926; M. Ed., U. of Pittsburgh, 1933; student summers, Syracuse U., 1921, U. of Me., 1932, Pa. State Coll., 1938; m. Anna Mary Nelson, Dec. 18, 1920; 1 dau., Beverly Ann. Teaching prin., Oswayo, Pa., 1919-21; prin., Tidioute, Pa., 1921-27; supervising prin., North East Borough and Twp. Schs., Pa., since 1927. Served in U.S. Navy, 1918-19. Mem. N.E.A., Pa. State Edn. Assn., Alumni Assn. U. of Pittsburgh (Pittsburgh), Alumni Assn. New York U. (New York), Am. Legion, Phi Delta Kappa. Republican. Presbyterian. Mason (32°). Club: Service. Home: 51 N. Lake St. Office: Joint High School Bldg., North East, Pa.

DAVIS, Edward LeRoy, lawyer; b. Orange, N.J., Nov. 19, 1884; s. Michael E. and Malvina (Faivre) D.; grad. Orange (N.J.) High Sch., 1902; LL.B., Columbia, 1905; unmarried. Admitted to N.J. bar, 1907, and since practiced in Orange; mem. firm Howe & Davis; judge Police Court, Orange, 1927-35. Served in U.S. Army, Oct. 1917-March 1919. Pres. Children's Aid and Protective Soc. of Oranges and Maplewood, 11 years; dir. Children's Aid Soc. of Newark, 10 years; trustee Orange Free Library; pres. Chamber of Commerce and Civics of Oranges and Maplewood. Mem. Glee Club of Oranges, Am. Bar Assn., Essex Co. (N.J.) Bar Assn. Democrat. Roman Catholic. Home: 147 Cleveland St. Office: 282 Main St., Orange, N.J.

DAVIS, Edwin Bell, univ. prof.; b. Lawrence, Mass., June 13, 1866; s. Bryan Bell and Amelia (Lockwood) D.; grad. Manchester (N.H.) High Sch., 1885; B.L., Dartmouth Coll., 1889; student Ecole des Hautes Etudes, Paris, 1894-95, Sorbonne, 1894-95, U. of Rome, 1910-11 and 1922-23, also summer schs. in Paris and Grenoble, France; A.M., Rutgers U., 1916; m. Elizabeth Stetson Norris, June 16, 1892; children—Donald Edwin, Elizabeth Kidder. Teacher New Brunswick (N.J.) High Sch., 1889-90, Salt Lake Acad., 1890-91; tutor N.H. State Coll., 1891-95; tutor Dartmouth Coll., 1892-93; instr. Rutgers Coll. (now Rutgers U.), 1895-1901, asso. prof., 1901-04, prof. Romance langs. since 1904, now also chmn. dept. of Romance langs. Mem. 10th Inf. O.T.C., Plattsburgh, N.Y., 1916. Awarded Palmes Académiques (French), 1913; medal (Rutgers), 1938. Mem. Modern Lang. Assn. America, Am. Assn. Teachers of French, Am. Assn. Teachers of Italian, Assn. Modern Lang. Teachers of Middle States (ex-pres., ex-v.p.), N.J. Modern Lang. Teachers' Assn. (1st pres.), L'Assan Phonétique Internationale, Phi Beta Kappa, Delta Kappa Epsilon. Independent Republican. Mem. Reformed Ch. in America. Contbr. to The Nation, Modern Language Jour., Italica, Maître Phonétique. Home: 35 Huntington St., New Brunswick, N.J.

DAVIS, Elwood Craig, prof. physical edn. and athletics, Pa. State Coll., also mem. council on research. Address: State College, Pa.

DAVIS, Francis Asbury, business exec.; b. Baltimore, Md., July 25, 1893; s. E. Asbury and Virginia (Conradt) D.; student Boys Latin Sch., Baltimore, 1902-10; A.B., Johns Hopkins U., 1914; m. Antoinette Biggs, Oct. 10, 1916; children—Dorothy Land, Antoinette Biggs, Margaret Conradt, Francis Asbury. Mem. firm F. A. Davis & Sons, hotel supplies, Baltimore; dir. Nat. Marine Bank, Provident Savings Bank. Chmn. advisory com. Dept. of Pub. Welfare, Baltimore, since 1937. Trustee U. of Richmond, Va.; pres. Baltimore Y.M.C.A., 1935-37. Mem. Delta Upsilon. Democrat. Baptist. Clubs: Johns Hopkins Faculty, Merchants (Baltimore, Md.). Home: 304 Somerset Rd. Office: 119 S. Howard St., Baltimore, Md.

DAVIS, Francis B.; vice-chancellor N.J. Court of Chancery. Address: Camden, N.J.

DAVIS, Frank Garfield, prof. edn.; b. Saginaw, Mich., Aug. 16, 1884; s. Levi Herbert and Iris Ramona (Winegarden) D.; student Clarion (Pa.) State Normal Sch., 1901-03, Kans. Wesleyan University, 1905-06; Ph.B., summa cum laude, Bucknell University, 1911; M.A., Columbia, 1924; Ph.D., New York U., 1930; m. Bess Estelle Carnall, of Ft. Smith, Ark., Feb. 6, 1915; children—Carol Lee, Margaret Louise, Frank Alan. Teacher rural schs., 1902-03; prin. grade schs., 1903-05; and 1906-08; supt. schs., Valdez, Alaska, 1911-17, Auburn, Wash., 1917-18; prin. jr. high sch., Cleveland, O., 1918-24; prof. edn. and head of dept., Bucknell U., since 1924, dir. Demonstration Sch. since 1925, also dir. Summer Sch. and extension work, 1935—. Mem. N.E.A., Pa. State Edn. Assn. (pres. 1927 and 1934; sec.-treas., coll. teachers of edn. sect.; chmn. commn. on professional ethics), Nat. Dept. Secondary Sch. Prins. (mem. planning com.; chmn. research com.; regional coordinator Pa. Branch), Assn. Liberal Arts Colls. of Pa. for Advancement of Teaching (sec.-treas.), Am. Assn. Univ. Profs., Phi Delta Kappa, Kappa Phi Kappa. Baptist. Mason. Author: Guidance for Youth (with wife), 1928, new edit., 1937; A Course in Supervised Teaching, 1933. Contbr. to professional publs. Home: Lewisburg, Pa.

DAVIS, Fred Wallace, lawyer; b. South Gibson, Pa., Jan. 29, 1897; s. Earl L. and Jessie (Warren) D.; LL.B., Dickinson Coll. Law Sch., Carlisle, Pa., 1922; m. Jeannette Kistler Pelton, Oct. 22, 1927. Engaged as prin. pub. schs. 1916-18; admitted to Pa. bar, 1924 and since engaged in gen. practice of law at East Stroudsburg, Pa.; mem. firm Brittain and Davis, 1926-32, continued alone since 1932; dir. and counsel Keystone Bldg. & Loan Assn., East Stroudsburg; solicitor and dir. East Stroudsburg Nat. Bank; sec. and counsel East Stroudsburg Sewerage Co. Mem. Pa. Ho. of Rep., 1929-30; spl. dep. atty. gen. of Pa., 1931-35; solicitor for Borough East Stroudsburg, and East Stroudsburg Sch. Dist. Mem. Monroe-Pike Bar Assn., Phi Kappa Sigma. Republican. Methodist. Mason, Elk. Home: 39 N. Courtland St. Office: 50 Washington St., East Stroudsburg, Pa.

DAVIS, George Earl, prof. physics.; b. Warsaw, Ind., Dec. 29, 1889; s. William Edmund and Ada Justine (Parker) D.; A.B., Ind. Univ., 1914; Fellow Rice Inst., 1919-20; M.S., Ia. State Coll., 1922; Ph.D., U. of Minn., 1929; m. Theresa J. R. McClure, May 8, 1915. Engaged as instr. physics, chemistry and mathematics, high sch., 1914-18; instr. later asst. prof. physics, Ia. State Coll., 1920-27; Mayo Foundation Fellow in Biophysics, U. of Minn., 1927-29; head dept. biophysics, Desert Sanatorium and Inst. Research, Tucson, Ariz., 1929-32; research assoc. and fellow, Ia. State Coll., 1933-34; research for Iowa State Planning Bd., 1934-36; asst. prof. physics, Duquesne U., 1936-37, asso. prof., 1937-39, prof. and head of dept. since 1939. Mem. A.A.A.S., Am. Phys. Soc., Assn. Physics Teachers of Western Pa. and Environs, Am. Assn. Univ. Profs., Ia. Acad. Sci., Sigma Xi, Phi Kappa Phi. Democrat. Baptist. Contbr. papers to sci. socs. and articles to tech. jours. Home: 1412 Gardner St., Pittsburgh, Pa.

DAVIS, George Garrett, lawyer; b. Wheeling, W.Va., Jan. 4, 1890; s. William Festus and Alice Eleanor (Shaffer) D.; LL.B., W.Va. Univ. Law Coll., 1913; m. Helene Ann Juergens, Aug. 18, 1917; children—William Ernest, Theresa Eleanor. Admitted to W.Va. bar, 1913; engaged in gen. practice of law at Sutton, W.Va., 1913-16, at Logan, W.Va., 1916-17, in practice at Sutton since 1919; mem. firm Hines & Davis since 1931; served as mayor of Sutton, W.Va. two terms, 1921-23; mem. Workmen's Compensation Appeal Bd. of W.Va. since 1935. Served as 1st lt., U.S.A., 1917-19. Mem. Am. Legion, Vets. Fgn. Wars of U.S., Kappa Alpha. Republican. Methodist. Mason. Home: Main St. Office: Fox Bldg., Sutton, W.Va.

DAVIS, George Thompson Brown, author; b. nr. Staunton, Ill., July 4, 1873; s. Rev. James Scott and Elizabeth Amelia (Rogers) D.; B.A., Lake Forest (Ill.) University, 1894; grad. McCormick Theological Seminary, 1898; m. Rose Helen Fox, Nov. 20, 1934. Assistant editor Ram's Horn, 1894-1901; manager Davis Literary Syndicate, 1901-04; evangelist, 1904—. Internat. sec. Pocket Testament League, 1912-24; condr. of various campaigns to distribute the New Testament. Presbyterian. Author: D.L. Moody—The Man and His Mission, 1899; Metlakahtla, 1903; When Christ Was Here, 1904; Torrey and Alexander, 1905; Twice Around the World with Alexander, 1907; Korea for Christ, 1910; The Pocket Testament League Around the World, 1910; Winning the World with the Bible, 1912; China's Christian Army, 1925; Adventures in Soul-Winning, 1929; Fulfilled Prophecies that Prove the Bible, 1931; Caleb Maccabee, 1934; Rebuilding Palestine According to Prophecy, 1935; Seeing Prophecy Fulfilled in Palestine, 1937. Conducted Pocket Testament League evangelistic campaign British and Am. mil. camps, 1914-19; made tour of world to promote world-wide Bible revival, 1921-25; conducted campaign to distribute one million Testaments in China, 1925-28; conducted one million testaments campaign for Latin America, 1928-31, also for students in the U.S. and Canada, 1931-34; campaign for quarter million Testaments for people of Philippine Islands, 1934-37. Home: 2012 W. Tioga St. Address: 1505 Race St., Philadelphia, Pa.

DAVIS, Harvey Grandville, pres. Charleston Milling Co.; b. Norfolk, Va., Feb. 20, 1885; s. Samuel and Jane (Tabb) D.; ed. pub. schs.; m. Agnes Ronan, June 19, 1913; children—Helen, Harvey G., Jane, John, Jean, George. Pres. and gen. mgr. Charleston Milling Co. since 1922. Home: Oakwood Drive. Office: Morris St., Charleston, W.Va.

DAVIS, Harvey Nathaniel, mech. engineer; b. Providence, R.I., June 6, 1881; s. Nathaniel French and Lydia Martin (Bellows) D.; A.B., Brown U., 1901, A.M., 1902; A.M., Harvard, 1903, Ph.D., 1906; Sc.D., Brown University, 1928, Northeastern Univ., 1938; LL.D., Rutgers, 1928; D.Eng., New York U., 1936, Rose Poly. Inst., 1938; m. Suzanne C. Haskell, June 28, 1911 (died Jan. 1, 1919); children—Susanne, Louisa Frederica; m. 2d, Alice M. Rohde, Sept. 20, 1920 (died Aug. 22, 1933); children—Marian, Nathaniel; m. 3d, Helen Clarkson Miller, Feb. 8, 1935. Instr. mathematics, Brown Univ., 1901-02; inst. physics, 1904-10, assistant prof., 1910-19, prof. mech. engring., 1919-28, Harvard Univ.; pres. Stevens Institute of Technology since 1928. Engr. in turbine dept., Gen. Electric Co., 1917-18; aeronautical mech. engr., Air Service, 1918-22; cons. eng. U.S. Bur. of Mines, 1921-25, Franklin Ry. Supply Co., 1920-27, Air Reduction Co., 1922-25. Regent Smithsonian Instn., 1938-44; mem. Bd. of Visitors to U.S. Naval Acad., 1939, Fellow Am. Soc. Mech. Engrs. (pres. 1937-38), Am. Acad. Arts and Sciences; Am. Physical Soc., A.A.A.S. (mem. council); mem. Am. Math. Soc. (life), Franklin Inst. (hon.), Soc. for Promotion of Engring. Edn. (mem. council), Am. Philos. Soc., Washington Acad. Science, Phi Beta Kappa, Sigma Xi, Tau Beta Pi, Delta Pi. Congregationalist. Clubs: Cosmos (Washington); Brown Univ. (president 1935), Harvard, Century (New York). Author: (with L. S. Marks) Steam Tables and Diagrams, 1908; (with N. Henry Black) Practical Physics for High Schools, 1913, Elementary Practical Physics, 1938. Home: Hoxie House, Castle Pt., Hoboken, N.J.

DAVIS, Helen Clarkson Miller (Mrs. Harvey Nathaniel Davis), educator, lecturer, writer; b. Roselle, N.J.; d. Charles Dexter and Julia (Hope) Miller; ed. pvt. schs., St. Timothy's Sch., Catonsville, Md.; grad. kindergartner; spl. student in history; m. Harvey N. Davis (pres. Stevens Inst. Tech.), Feb. 8, 1935. Served as teacher in private schs.; mem. bd. dirs. Miss Spence's Sch., Inc. (now The Spence Sch.), N.Y. City, 1914-18, asso. prin., 1924-29, headmistress, trustee, 1929-32. Organizer and dir. Training Sch. for Women War Workers, Y.M.C.A., New York, 1918; dir. personnel and chief of Women's Bur. Y.M.C.A., Paris, 1919; Metropolitan sec. Y.W.C.A., City of New York, 1920-24. Mem. Nat. Com. on Prisons and Prison Labor, 1916-19. Mem. Presbyn. Bd. of Foreign Missions, 1914-32; mem. bd. dirs. and chmn. nat. ednl. com. League of Nations Assn.; apptd. alternate mem. Sub-Com. Experts for Instrn. of Youth, League of Nations, 1931; mem. internat. com. World Alliance for Friendship Through the Chs.; mem. Am. Council Inst. of Pacific Relations; trustee Internat. House, N.Y. City. Fellow Am. Geog. Soc.; mem. Soc. Mayflower Descendants. Democrat. Presbyn. Author of articles and research studies in regard to the Near East. Home: Hoxie House, Castle Point, Hoboken, N.J.

DAVIS, Henry; mem. finance com. and dir. U.S. Rubber Co. Address: du Pont Bldg., Wilmington, Del.

DAVIS, Hoagland Cook; instr. clin. laryngology, Johns Hopkins U.; asst dispensary laryngologist Johns Hopkins Hosp.; attending oculist, aurist and laryngologist Sydenham Hosp.; mem. staff Hosp. for Women of Md., Union Memorial and Bon Secours hosps., Church Home and Infirmary; cons. laryngologist Children's Hosp. Sch. Address: 405 N. Charles St., Baltimore, Md.

DAVIS, Holmes A.; pres. H. A. Davis & Co., McKeesport Coal & Coke Co., Washington Gas Coal Co. Home: 5537 Fifth Av. Office: Keystone Bldg., Pittsburgh, Pa.

DAVIS, Horace Nichols, lawyer; b. Clark's Green, Pa., Feb. 14, 1883; s. Nathaniel Sheldon and Mary (Nichols) D.; ed. Scranton (Pa.) Business Coll., 1900-01, West Chester (Pa.) Normal Sch., 1901-05; A.M., Temple U., Phila., 1917, LL.B., Law Sch., 1915; m. Emma Townsend, Jan. 22, 1910 (died 1929); children—Henrietta Thornton (Mrs. Marvin McEuen), Horace Nichols, Mary Townsend; m. 2d, Mary King, Dec. 26, 1930. Engaged in teaching at various pub. schs. in Pa., 1905-10; teacher pub. schs., Phila., 1910-17; admitted to Pa. bar, 1917, and since in gen. practice of law at Bristol, Pa.; asso. with Howard I. James; sec. and dir. Bristol Bldg. Assn., Harriman Bldg. Assn., Croyden Bldg. Assn.; dir. and counsel Union Bldg. and Loan Co., Fidelity Bldg. Assn. Mem. Bucks Co. Bar Assn. Republican. Soc. of Friends. Mason, Odd Fellow, Elk. Home: 323 Otter St. Office: 205 Radcliffe St., Bristol, Pa.

DAVIS, Howard Atlee, judge; b. Phila., Pa., Feb. 12, 1862; s. Thomas and Anne M. (Ferguson) D.; student Central High Sch., Phila., 1876-79; B.L., U. of Pa., 1883; m. Laura Mabel Mann, Oct. 31, 1898. Apptd. asst. city solicitor, Phila., 1886-1902; asso. judge of Ct. of Common Pleas No. 3, 1st Jud. Dist., 1910-11, elected to full term, 1911, re-elected, 1921, 1931; apptd. president judge, 1932. Served as lt. col. and a.d.c. on the staff of Gov. Hastings, 1896-99; maj. and judge advocate, 1st Brig., Pa. N.G., 1907-11. Elected to Select Council, 1908; presidential elector (Pres. Wm. Howard Taft), 1908. Republican. Clubs: Phila. Country, Union League (Phila.). Home: The Kenilworth, Alden Park. Office: City Hall, Philadelphia, Pa.

DAVIS, Howard B. F.; surgeon Chester County Hosp., West Chester, Pa. Address: 106 W. Lancaster Av., Downingtown, Pa.

DAVIS, Howard Clarke, musician; b. Lynn, Mass., May 4, 1881; s. Charles E. and Elizabeth (Clarke); D.; prep. edn., Vt. Mil. Acad., Saxtons River; student Colgate, 1899-1900; spl. student Boston U., 1913-14; B.Mus., Cincinnati Conservatory, 1930; Mus.D., Chicago Conservatory, 1931; M.A., from the University of Pittsburgh, 1933; m. Ottilie Czerny, Sept. 30, 1922. Formerly voice teacher, Lawrence, Chelsea, Boston, Yonkers, N.Y., and N.Y. City; choral condr., Lawrence, Chelsea, Andover, Malden, Newburyport, Watertown, Boston, 1905-17, Yonkers and Fredonia, N. Y., since 1917; dir. Sch. of Music, Chelsea, 1913-17, Yonkers, 1917-21; head of dept. music, State Normal Sch., Fredonia, 1924-31; prof. voice and head of sch. music dept., Villa Maria Coll., Erie, Pa., since 1931; v.p. Chicago Conservatory; dir. extension work, Nat. Acad. Music, N.Y. City, 1921-24. Founder, 1925, since dir. Western N.Y. Music Festival (6 days). Mem. Music Supervisors Nat. Conf., Music Teachers Nat. Assn., Eastern Music Supervisors Assn. (founder). Republican. Mason. Co-Author: University Course of Music Study (10 vols.). Contbr. to The Musician (formerly asso. editor). Home: 342 W. 9th St., Erie, Pa.*

DAVIS, Howard Lee, vocational dir.; b. Cincinnati, O., Sept. 23, 1877; s. William Henry and Mary Elizabeth (Sargent) D.; student pub. schs., Cincinnati, O., 1883-91, Philips Andover Acad., Andover, Mass., 1891-92, Taft Sch., Watertown, Conn., 1892-95; Ph.B., Yale, 1899; m. Ione Tefft Hatch, Oct. 1, 1902 (divorced 1936); children—Mary Sargent (Mrs. Daniel B. Conger), Alma Ruth, Ione Tefft (Mrs. Robert Trent Jones). Began as asst. to office boy Lukenheimer Brass Co., Cincinnati, O., 1895; asst. engr., Eastchester Electric Co., Mt. Vernon, N.Y., 1899-1900; superintendent of Hudson River Gas and Electric Co., Tarrytown, N. Y., 1900-04; sales engr., S. Edward Eaton & Co., New York, 1904-06; engr. outside plant, New York Telephone Co., 1906-25, dir. tech. employment and training, 1925-38; vocational dir. Poly. Inst. of Brooklyn, N.Y., since 1939. Mem. Soc. for Promotion Engring. Edn., Engrs. Council for Professional Development, Eastern Coll. Personnel Officers, Yale Engring. Assn., N.Y. Adult Edn. Council, Am. Management Assn. Republican. Episcopalian. Club: Montclair (N.J.) Dramatic. Author: The Young Man in Business, 1931; Preparation for Seeking Employment, 1937. Lecturer at Cornell U., Mass. Inst. Tech., Rensselear Poly. Inst., Lafayette Coll., Lehigh U., Columbia U., Union Coll., Yale, Swarthmore Coll., U. of Me., etc. Home: 92 Watchung Av., Upper Montclair, N.J. Office: 99 Livingston St., Brooklyn, N.Y.

DAVIS, Hugh H.; pres. Monongahela Tube Co. Home: 327 Broad St., Sewickley, Pa. Office: 321 Third Av., Pittsburgh, Pa.

DAVIS, Innis Cocke (Mrs), archivist; b. Low Moor, Va., Sept. 15, 1883; d. William Joseph and Charmian (Hambrick) Cocke; student pub. and private schs of W.Va.; grad. Marshall Coll., Huntington, 1900; m. Thomas B. Davis, June 1905 (died Feb. 1935). Began as teacher pub. schs., Huntington, W.Va., 1901; appt. chief of Crippled Children's Div., State of W.Va., Feb. 1935; resigned to accept apptmt. as state archivist, June 1935. Trustee Gen. Federation of Women's Clubs; past state pres. and fed. dir. W. Va. Federation of Women's Clubs; mem. D.A.R., United Daughters of the Confederacy. Democrat. Baptist. Clubs: Charleston Woman's; Logan Woman's; Business and Professional Women's. Home: 1264 Franklin Av. Office: State Capitol, Charleston, W.Va.

DAVIS, Irene M.; registrar Johns Hopkins U. Address: Johns Hopkins University, Baltimore, Md.

DAVIS, J. Warren, judge; b. Elizabeth City, N.C., Mar. 14, 1867; s. John S. and Emmie Virginia (Sawyer) D.; B.A., Bucknell U., Lewisburg, Pa., 1896, A.M., 1904, LL.D., 1919; B.D., Crozier Theol. Sem., Chester, Pa., 1899; studied U. of Chicago, 1900-01, U. of Leipzig, 3 semesters, 1902-03; LL.B., U. of Pa., 1906; J.U.D., Lebanon Valley Coll., Annville, Pa., 1927; m. Marguerite N. Gay, June 14, 1913. Began practice in Phila., 1907; removed to

Salem, N.J., 1913; practiced with bro. James M., as Davis & Davis, Camden, N.J. Mem. N.J. Senate, 1912-13 (majority leader, 1913; introducer and sponsor for progressive administration measures in legislature in the administration of Gov. Wilson, 1913); resigned from senate, June 12, 1913. U.S. atty. for Dist. of N.J., 1913-16; judge U.S. Dist. Court, Dist. of N.J., 1916-20; judge U.S. Circuit Court of Appeals, 3d Circuit, since 1920. Democrat. Baptist. Mem. Kappa Sigma. Mason: Home: Lawrenceville, N.J.

DAVIS, James Elmer, coll. prof; b. Barneveld, Wis., Apr. 22, 1887; s. David J. and Sarah (Williams) D.; grad. State Normal Sch., Platteville, Wis., 1907; A.B., U. of Wis., Madison, Wis., 1912, A.M., 1913; m. Frances Walker, Aug. 25, 1920; children—David James, Frank Llewellyn, John Henry. Teacher in pub. sch., Barneveld, Wis., 1904-09, Wolsey, S.D., 1909-10; instr., later asst. prof. mathematics, Pa. State Coll., 1913-17; instr. mathematics, U. of Wis., Madison, Wis., 1919-22; asst. prof. mathematics, U. of Ark., Fayetteville, Ark., 1922-23; asst. prof. mathematics, Drexel Inst. Phila., 1923-25, asso. prof. mathematics since 1926; asso. prof. engring extension, Pa. State Coll., 1925-26. Served as 2d lt., 1st lt., capt., 313th Inf., U.S. Army, with A.E.F., 1917-19; comdt. Am. detachment, U. of Toulouse, France, 1919; successively capt., maj., lt. col., col., Inf. Res. since 1920; comdg. officer, 313th Inf. Res. since 1937. Mem. Math. Assn. of America, Am. Legion, Mil. Order of Foreign Wars of U.S., Acacia, Scabbard and Blade, Phi Beta Kappa, Gamma Alpha. Awarded scholarship, U. of Wis., 1912-13. Republican. Presbyterian. Mason, Sojourner. Home: 37 Amherst Av., Swarthmore, Pa. Office: 32d and Chestnut Sts., Philadelphia, Pa.

DAVIS, James John, senator; b. Tredegar, South Wales, Oct. 27, 1873; s. David James and Esther Ford (Nicholls) D.; ed. pub. sch. until 11, later business course, 4 mos.; LL.D., Bucknell, Pa. Mil. Acad., U. of Pittsburgh, Drake U., St. Bonaventure's Sem.; m. Jean Rodenbaugh, of Pittsburgh, Nov. 26, 1914; children—James, Jane, Jean, Joan, Jewel. Came to U.S. with parents, 1881; began as puddler's asst. in iron works at Sharon, Pa., later in Pittsburgh, at 11; was a puddler at 16; moved to Elwood, Ind., 1893, and worked in steel and tin plate mills; city clk. Elwood, 1898-1902; recorder Madison Co., Ind., 1903-07; dir. gen. Loyal Order of Moose, 1906— (membership increased from 247 to over 600,000); sec. of labor, by apptmt. of President Harding, Mar. 5, 1921, and continued under Presidents Coolidge and Hoover until Dec. 9, 1930; elected U.S. senator from Pa. to fill vacancy, for term expiring 1933, re-elected for terms 1933-1939, 1939-45. Founder Mooseheart Home and Sch.; chmn. Mooseheart govs., also Home for Old Folks, Moosehaven, Florida. Mem. Amalgamated Assn. Iron, Steel and Tin Workers of America. Mem. Veterans of Foreign Wars, Spanish Am. War Veterans. Mason. Odd Fellow, K. P., Elk., etc. Clubs: Duquesne, Pittsburgh; Press, Chevy Chase (Washington, D. C.). Home: Pittsburgh, Pa.; 3012 Massachusetts Av., Washington, D. C.

DAVIS, James Rankin, lawyer; b. Wilmington, Del., Sept. 2, 1890; s. Thomas and Clara (Springer) D.; student Wilmington Friends Sch., 1898-1907; B.A., U. of Del., Newark, Del., 1911; student Yale Law Sch., 1911-13; m. Lenore Stayton Holt, Feb. 9, 1920; 1 dau., Virginia. Admitted to Delaware bar, 1914; referee in bankruptcy, 1920-23; in practice at Wilmington, Del., since 1914. Mem. New Castle Co. Bar Assn. (pres.), Del. Bar Assn. (1st v.p.), Am. Bar Assn., Book and Gavel, Phi Alpha Delta. Presbyterian. Mason. Clubs: Wilmington (Del.) Country; West Chester Golf and Country. Home: 714 Coverdale Rd. Office: 810-12 Equitable Bldg., Wilmington, Del.

DAVIS, John Alexander, Jr., supt. of schools; b. Elizabeth, W.Va., Feb. 26, 1904; s. John Alexander and Corilla Ann (Gilmore) D.; A.B., Marshall Coll.; B.S. and M.S., Ohio U.; A.M. and Ph.D., U. of Mich.; m. Jean Manchester, Feb. 22, 1930; 1 son, John Alexander, III. Successively prin. Jr. High Sch. and grades, Powhatan, W.Va., teacher Charleston (W.Va.) High Sch., instr. Marshall Coll., prin. Central Jr. High Sch., Parkersburg, W.Va., fellow U. of Mich., now supt. of schools, Parkersburg, W.Va. Mem. Am. Assn. Sch. Adminstrs., Ninety Six Club, Alpha Sigma Phi, Pi Gamma Mu, Kappa Delta Pi. Republican. Episcopalian. Club: Lions. Home: 902 Dickle Av. Office: 725 Green St., Parkersburg, W.Va.

DAVIS, John Staige, surgeon; b. Norfolk, Va., Jan. 15, 1872; s. William Blackford and Mary Jane Kentie (Howland) D.; student Episcopal High Sch. of Va., Alexandria, Va., 1887-88, St. Paul's Sch., Garden City, N.Y., 1888-92; Ph.B., Yale, 1895, M.A. (hon.), 1925; M.D., Johns Hopkins Med. Sch., 1899; m. Kathleen Gordon Bowdoin, Oct. 26, 1907; children—Kathleen Staige (Mrs. Charles E. Scarlett Jr.), Dr. William Bowdoin, Howland Staige. Began as surgeon, Baltimore, 1899; asso. prof. surgery, Johns Hopkins U., since 1923; visiting plastic surgeon Johns Hopkins Hosp., Union Memorial Hosp., Hosp. for Women of Md., Children's Hosp. Sch., Baltimore. Served as capt., M.C., U.S. Army, 1917-19. Fellow Am. Coll. Surgeons; mem. Am. Surg. Assn., Am. Bd. Surgery, Am. Bd. Plastic Surgery, Southern Surg. Assn., Am. Assn. Traumatic Surgery, Interurban Surg. Soc., Surg. Research Soc. Democrat. Episcopalian. Clubs: Maryland, Elkridge Kennels (Baltimore); Yale (New York City). Home: 215 Wendover Rd. Office: 701 Cathedral St., Baltimore, Md.

DAVIS, John T.; pres. Davis Colliery Co.; officer or dir. several companies. Address: Elkins, W.Va.

DAVIS, John Warren, coll. pres.; b. Milledgeville, Ga., Feb. 11, 1888; s. Robert Marion and Katie (Mann) D.; A.B., Morehouse Coll., Atlanta, Ga., 1911, A.M., 1920; studied U. of Chicago, 1911-13; D.Litt., State College, Orangeburg, S.C., 1931; m. Bessie Rucker, Aug. 24, 1916 (deceased); children—Constance Rucker, Dorothy Long; m. 2d, Ethel McGhee, September 2, 1932; one daughter, Caroline Florence. Was teacher at Morehouse College, Atlanta, Ga., 1911-15, registrar, 1914-17; exec. sec. 12th Street branch, Y.M.C.A., Washington, D.C., 1917-19; pres. W.Va. State College since 1919. Mem. President Hoover's Organization on Unemployment Relief, Nat. Advisory Com. on Edn. of Negroes; mem. Nat. Land Grant Coll. Survey Staff, 1928, Nat. Advisory Com. on Edn., 1929; mem. Commn. on Instns. of Higher Edn. of North Central Assn. of Colleges, 1936-40. Mem. N.E.A., Nat. Assn. Teachers in Colored Schools (pres. 1928), Sigma Pi Phi. Granted Harmon Award in Edn., 1926. Republican. Baptist. Home: Institute, W.Va.

DAVIS, John Warren; vice chmn. and acting chmn. bd. trustees Bucknell U. Address: Lewisburg, Pa.

DAVIS, Jonathan R., banking; b. Danville, Pa., July 22, 1864; s. John J. and Ann (Rogers) D.; ed. Wyoming Sem., Kingston, Pa.; m. Mollie Coggswell, Oct. 10, 1894; children—John Allen, Albert Gordon, Helen Coggswell, Elizabeth Armina. Engaged in business of ins. and real estate, 1906; sheriff Luzerne Co., 1905-08; assessor Luzerne Co., 1911-15; pres. Wilkes-Barre Deposit & Savings Bank, 1918-35; pres. Mount Greenwood Cemetery Assn. since 1912; pres. Luzerne Co. Institutional Dist. since 1938; dir. First Nat. Bank, Kingston, Pa., Roger Foundry & Machine Co., Finch Mfg. Co. of Scranton. Served as Rep. Co. Chmn., 1906-10. Republican. Presbyterian. Mason (K.T., 32°, Shriner). Home: 145 S. Maple Av., Kingston, Pa. Office: Deposit & Savings Bank Bldg., Wilkes-Barre, Pa.

DAVIS, J(oseph) Lawrence, lawyer; b. Phila., Pa., Feb. 3, 1905; s. James T. and Martha U. (Waldman) D.; A.B., U. of Pa., 1925, LL.B., Law Sch., 1928; m. Madge F. Wise, Sept. 2, 1933. Admitted to Pa. bar, 1928, and since in gen. practice of law at Bangor, Pa.; mem. firm Woodley and Davis since 1930; asst. dist. atty. for Northampton Co. since 1936; dir. Citizens Bank of Wind Gap, Slate Belt Bldg. and Loan Assn. Dir. Bangor Sch. Bd., Young Rep. Club, Northampton Motor Club. Mem. Pa. and Northampton Co. bar assns., Patriotic Order Sons of America, Theta Xi, Phi Delta Phi. Republican. Episcopalian. Mason, Elk, Jr. Order United Am. Mechanics. Club: Pomfret (Easton, Pa.). Home: 232 Broadway. Office: Bowers Bldg., Bangor, Pa.

DAVIS, Nelson Fithian, biologist; b. Seeley, Cumberland Co., N.J., Aug. 10, 1872; s. George D. and Frances (Moore) D.; Sc.B., Bucknell U., Lewisburg, Pa., 1895, Sc.M., 1896, Sc.D., 1903; student Marine Biol. Lab., Cold Spring Harbor, L.I., N.Y., summers, 1895-96; m. Nellie Taylor, 1899 (died 1904); children—Nelson Fithian, Frances Moore; m. 2d, Ella Marion Briggs, 1905 (died 1936); m. 3d, Jessie Alma Palmer, 1937. With biol. dept. Bucknell U. since 1898, prof. biology and head of dept. since 1910; instr. biology, Marine Biol. Lab., Cold Spring Harbor, summers, 1898-1903; in charge zoölogy, U. of Vt., Summer Sch., 1914. Mem. Soc. Am. Naturalists, Bot. Soc. America, Acad. Natural Sciences, Sigma Chi. Republican. Presbyn. Mason. Club: Triton (fish and game). Author of check list of birds of Lewisburg, Pa., and bulletins on apple-tree tent caterpillar, chestnut culture, etc. Home: Lewisburg, Pa.

DAVIS, Nelson P.; mem. surg. staff Mercy Hosp. Address: 435 Fifth Av., Pittsburgh, Pa.

DAVIS, Paul A., 3d, architect; b. Philadelphia, Pa., June 18, 1872; s. Paul A. and Henrietta Scull (Duy) D.; grad. William Penn Charter Sch., Phila., 1890; B.S., U. of Pa., 1894; diplômé, École des Beaux Arts, Paris, 1900; m. Frances Ward Smillie of Washington, D.C., Mar. 18, 1903; children—Elizabeth Smillie (Mrs. Edwin Frain Nimmo), Paul A., 4th, David Richard. Began practice at Philadelphia, 1900, Principal works: University of West Virginia Buildings; High Sch. and Jr. High Sch., Camden, N.J.; Am. Bank & Trust Co., Holmesburg Trust Co., 9th Bank & Trust Co. and Presbyn. Ministers' Fund Life Ins. bldgs., Phila.; Overbrook Presbyn. Ch.; Cheltenham High Sch., Elkins Park, Pa., etc. Fellow Am. Inst. Architects (dir. 1926-29; pres. Phila. chapter); mem. Société des Beaux Arts, Société des Architectes Diplômés, Acad. Fine Arts, Pa. Clubs: Union League, Egypt Mills Club. Home: 6412 Church Rd., Overbrook Philadelphia. Office: Architects Bldg., Philadelphia, Pa.

DAVIS, Paul B(ell), research chemist; b. West Liberty, O., Aug. 15, 1889; s. Paul S. and Roe (Garwood) D.; A.B., Roanoke Coll., Salem, Va., 1908, A.M., 1909; Ph.D., Johns Hopkins U., Baltimore, 1912; unmarried. Asst. in chemistry, Johns Hopkins U., 1913, instr. 1914-16, asso. in chemistry, 1916-19; research chemist Davison Chem. Corpn. since 1919. Mem. A.A.A.S., Am. Chem. Soc., Gamma Alpha. Democrat. Lutheran. Club: Johns Hopkins (Baltimore). Home: 1404 Mt. Royal Av. Office: Davison Chem. Corpn., Baltimore, Md.

DAVIS, Richard S., pres. Denman & Davis; b. Jersey City, N.J., Mar. 29, 1896; s. William Edwin and Annie (Jeffery) D.; ed. Hasbrouck Inst., Jersey City, N.J., 1909-10, Blair Acad., Blairstown, N.J., 1911-13; m. Gladys Meyer, June 21, 1917; children—Richard Stoliker, Cynthia Lee. Began as mail clerk, Manning, Maxwell & Moore, Inc., New York, 1914; asso. with Denman & Davis, steel mfrs., North Bergen, N.J., since 1915, successively as asst. sec. 1920-23, sec., 1923-31, treas., 1931-36, pres. and treas. since 1936. Dir. North Bergen (N.J.) Industrial Terminal. Republican. Methodist. Mason (Scottish Rite). Clubs: Ridgewood (N.J.) Country; Overlook (Summit, N.J.); Mink Pond (Pike Co., Pa.); Shawnee Country (Delaware, Pa.). Home: Palisade-on-Hudson, N.J. Office: Denman & Davis, North Bergen, N.J.

DAVIS, Robert C.; surgeon Conemaugh Valley Memorial Hosp. and B.&O. R.R. Address: 218 Franklin St., Johnstown, Pa.

DAVIS, Roland Parker, civil engr.; b. Beverly, Mass., Aug. 2, 1884; s. Parker Steven and Julia Etta (Andrews) D.; B.S., Mass. Inst. Tech., 1906; M.C.E., Cornell U., 1908, Ph.D., 1914; m. Bessie Belle Strentzsch, June 16, 1910. Draftsman Am. Bridge Co., 1906-07;

instr. civil engring., Cornell U., 1908-11; engr. with Eastern Bridge & Structural Co., summer 1908, Am. Bridge Co. summer 1910; asso. prof. W.Va. U., 1911-12, prof. head dept. structural and hydraulic engring. since 1912, asst. dean Coll. of Engring, 1930-32, dean, 1932—; bridge engr., W.Va. State Road Commn., 1914-19, now consulting engr. same; div. engr. Camp Eustis, 1918. Mem. Am. Soc. C.E. (dir.), Am. Ry. Engring. Assn. (com. on iron and steel structures), Am. Soc. for Testing Materials, Sigma Xi, Tau Beta Pi. Republican. Clubs: Faculty, Kiwanis. Author: Foundations of Bridges and Buildings (with H. S. Jacoby), 1914, 25; Timber Design and Construction (with H. S. Jacoby), 1929; asso. editor Architects' and Builders' Handbook, 1931, General Engineering Handbook, 1931. Home: Morgantown, W.Va.

DAVIS, Roy Tasco, diplomatic service, educator; b. Ewing, Missouri, June 24, 1889; s. John Albert and Bessie (White) D.; A.B., LaGrange (Mo.) Coll., 1908; Ph.B., Brown U., 1910; m. Loyce Enloe, Aug. 16, 1913; children—Roy T., Mercedes. Statistician Mo. Bur. Census and Labor, 1911; clk. to commn. that built Mo. State Capitol, 1912, 13; sec. and business mgr. Stephens Coll., Columbia, Mo., 1914-21; del. Rep. Nat. Conv., 1920; E.E. and M.P. to Republic of Guatemala, 1921-22, Republic of Costa Rica, 1922-29, Republic of Panama, 1930-33; chmn. Honduran-Guatemalan Boundary Commn., 1928; del. of U.S. govt. to North Am. Radio Conf., Mexico City, 1933; asst. to pres. and dir. of pub. relations, Stephens Coll., Columbia, Mo., 1933-37; apptd. mem. Inter-American Commn. of Inquiry, 1938; pres. Nat. Park College (formerly Nat. Park Sem.), Forest Glen, Md., since July 1, 1937. Address: National Park College, Forest Glen, Md.

DAVIS, Russell Stewart, clothing mcht.; b. Cambridge, Md., Oct. 13, 1894; s. William R. and Mary C. (Hubbard) D.; student pub. schs. and high sch., Dorchester Co., Md.; m. Edith M. Vanfure, June 26, 1920; children—Russell Stewart, Jr., Robert Barton. In employ Stevens, Smith & Co., retail clothing mchts., Cambridge, Md., as clk., 1911-16, mem. firm, 1916-29, propr. since 1929; dir. County Trust Co. since 1933. Served as seaman, then chief storekeeper, then asst. paymaster, U.S.N.R.F., 1917-19. Asso. mem. Unemployment Compensation Bd. of Md.. since 1936. Dir. Cambridge-Md. Hosp. Mem. Bus. Men's Assn., Am. Legion. Democrat. Methodist. Mason (K.T., 14°, O.E.S.). Clubs: Rotary, Yacht, Country (Cambridge). Home: 137 Mill St. Office: 23 Race St., Cambridge, Md.

DAVIS, Samuel Griffith, Jr.; prof. anesthetics, U. of Md.; visiting anesthetist University, Mercy, Union Memorial, Bon Secours, South Baltimore Gen. hosps. and Church Home and Infirmary; cons. anesthetist St. Joseph's, West Baltimore Gen. and Hebrew hosps.; mem. staff Hosp. for Women of Md. Address: 220 Chancery Road, Baltimore, Md.

DAVIS, Shelby Cullom, economist, author; b. Peoria, Ill., April 1, 1909; s. George Henry and Julia Mabel (Cullom) D.; student Lawrenceville (N.J.) Sch., 1924-26; A.B., Princeton U., 1930; A.M., Columbia, 1931; Dr. Polit. Sci., U. of Geneva, Switzerland, 1934; m. Kathryn Edith Wasserman, of Germantown, Pa., Jan. 4, 1932; children—Shelby Moore Cullom, Diana Cullom. Special foreign corr., also asso. with Columbia Broadcasting Co., Geneva, 1932-34; economist Investment Corpn. of Phila., 1934-37; treas. Delaware Fund, Inc., since 1937; dir. Erie Nat. Bank; v.p. and sec. Wilmington Chem. Co., Trustee Nat. Ednl. Film Foundation, Inc.; dir. Phila. Theatre; mem. exec. com. Alumni Council Lawrenceville Sch. Mem. Am. Statis. Assn., Am. Econ. Assn., Pa. Soc. S.R. Republican. Presbyn. Clubs: University, Penn Athletic, Princeton (Phila.); Princeton, Bankers (New York); Charter (Princeton). Author: Reservoirs of Men, 1934; The French War Machine, 1937; The Investment Decisions of Industry, 1939. Contbr. to Events (mag.), London Financial Times. Home: Haverford, Pa. Office: 225 S. 15th St., Philadelphia, Pa.

DAVIS, Staige, lawyer; b. Albemarle Co., Va., May 15, 1877; s. Rev. Dabney Carr Terrell and Mary Baynham (Anderson) D.; student private sch., 1886-92, Episcopal High Sch., Alexandria, Va., 1892-95; LL.B., U. of Va., 1903; m. Evelyn G. Purcell, April 24, 1929; children—Mary Bolling, Theodosia Staige. Admitted to Charleston (W.Va.) bar, 1903; mem. law firm Davis & Painter since 1922. Formerly pres. Bar Assn. of City of Charleston. Mem. Phi Delta Phi. Democrat. Episcopalian. Home: 912 Ridgemont Road. Office: 710 Charleston Nat. Bank Bldg., Charleston, W.Va.

DAVIS, T. Carroll; asst. prof. rhinolaryngology, Temple U.; chief nose and throat clinic Temple U. Hosp. Address: 3128 N. Broad St., Philadelphia, Pa.

DAVIS, T. Edward; football coach, Salem Coll. Address: Salem Coll., Salem, W.Va.

DAVIS, Warren Beagle, otorhinolaryngologist and maxillo-facial surgeon; b. Nicholasville, Ky., Sept. 6, 1881; s. Luther Ambrose and Mary (Donohue) D.; student Ky U. (now Transylvania U.), Lexington, Ky., 1898-1900 and 1904-05, Jefferson Med. Coll., Phila., 1906-10, M.D., 1910; Corinna Borden Keen Research Fellow, U. of Berlin, Germany, 1912; (hon.) D.Sc., Georgetown (Ky.) Coll., 1938; m. Ada Springer, June 4, 1913; children—Warren Springer, John Wallace, James Leslie II, Richard Coleman. After interneship in Jefferson Med. Coll. Hosp. engaged in pvt. practice in Phila. continuously since 1913; asso. with Jefferson Med. Coll. since 1913, clin. prof. oral surgery since 1934 and maxillofacial surgeon to Jefferson Hosp. since 1934, in charge of dept. maxillofacial surgery since 1936; cons. maxillofacial surgeon to Kensington Hosp. for Women since 1932. Served as mem. Med. Adv. Bd. of War Dept. for Pa., 1918-19; capt., Med. Corps, U.S.A., 1918-19; instr. maxillo-facial surgery, Med. Officers Training Camp, Ft. Oglethorpe, Ga., 1918. Fellow Am. Coll. Surgs., Coll. of Phys., Phila., Acad. of Surgery, Phila., Am. Acad. Ophthalmology and Otolaryngology; mem. A.M.A., Am. Assn. Oral and Plastic Surgs. (mem. bd. trustees), Soc. Plastic and Reconstructive Surgery (mem. bd. and past pres.), Assn. Mil. Surgs., Am. Assn. Anatomists, Am. Bd. of Otolaryngology, Pa. State and Phila. med. socs., Pi Kappa Alpha, Phi Alpha Sigma. Honored by award of gold medal at Phila. Scientific Exhibit, A.M.A., 1931. Republican. Baptist. Clubs: Union League (Phila.); Philadelphia Country (Bala, Pa.). Contbr. many papers to med. jours. Home: 2425 N. 59th St. Office: 135 S. 18th St., Philadelphia, Pa.

DAVIS, William Chalmers, supervising prin. schs.; b. Winthrop, N.Y., Jan. 26, 1874; s. Samuel Wilder and Harriett (Miller) D.; student State Normal Sch., Potsdam, N.Y., 1892-95, U. of Mich., 1898-99; A.B., Harvard U., 1904; student Columbia U. summers and extension courses; m. Effie Estelle Clark, Dec. 27, 1902; children—Roland Clark, Harriett Marion (Clarence H. Sergent), William Chalmers, Jr. Prin. villege sch., Massena, N.Y., 1895-98, Norwood, N.Y., 1899-1902; prin. high sch., Nutley, N.J., 1904-12, Cobleskill, N.Y., 1912-16, Easton, Pa., 1916-24; supervising prin. schs., Haddon Heights, N.J., since 1924. Trustee Pub. Library, Haddon Heights, N.J. Mem. Nat. Edn. Assn., N.J. State Edn. Assn., County Edn. Assn. Republican. Presbyn. Home: 24 First Av., Haddon Heights, N.J.

DAVIS, William Herman, mfr. brush handles; b. Kane, Pa., Sept. 29, 1867; s. Joshua and Hannah (Howells) D.; student Eastman Business Coll., Poughkeepsie, N.Y., 1886, Allegheny Coll., Meadville, Pa., 1886-88; m. Maud L. Long, Oct. 14, 1896 (died 1914); children—Elizabeth (dec.), Ruth (dec.), Dorothea (dec., former wife of Lawrence K. Frank), Joshua A.; m. 2d, Ida M. Speck, June 17, 1916. Began as bank clk., 1886-88; treas. and dir. Holgate Brothers Co., mfrs. brush handles since 1888; chmn. bd. dirs. Kane Bank and Trust Co.; dir. Kane Mfg. Co. Served as mem. Borough Sch. Bd. for 12 yrs. Mem. Pa. Soc. of New York, Phi Gamma Delta. Republican. Congregationalist. Mason (K.T., 32°, Shriner). Clubs: Country (Kane, Pa.); Phi Gamma Delta (New York City). Home: 98 Clay St., Kane, Pa.

DAVIS, William Howe, lawyer; b. Orange, N.J., March 8, 1904; s. Judge Thomas A. and Mary Adele (Jacobs) D.; student Carteret Acad., Orange, N.J., 1916-17, Seton Hall Prep. Sch. and Seton Hall Coll., South Orange, N.J., 1917-25; LL.B., N.J. Law Sch., Newark, N.J., 1928; m. Ruth Bayley Shanley, June 3, 1937. Admitted to N.J. bar, 1928, and since practiced at Orange, N.J.; mem. firm Howe & Davis, lawyers, Orange, N.J., since 1928; v.p. since 1936 and dir. Orange First Nat. Bank since 1933. Mem. advisory bd. and counsel Salvation Army, Orange, N.J. Mem. Chamber of Commerce (v.p. 1936-37; pres. 1938; dir.), Essex Co. Bar Assn. (mem. membership com.), Am. Bar Assn. Democrat. Catholic. Club: Essex County Country (West Orange, N.J.) Home: 313 Highland Av. Office: National Bank Bldg., Orange, N.J.

DAVIS, William Potter, Jr., lawyer; b. Wilmington, Del., July 24, 1876; s. William Potter and Mary Clarke (Draper) D.; A.B. and A.M., Princeton U.; LL.B., U. of Pa.; m. Alice M. Mowbray, June 2, 1908; children—William Potter, III, Richard Holland, Robert Draper, Virginia Mary. In gen. practice of law at Phila. before Federal and State cts., acting as receiver or trustee by apptmt. Federal Ct. in some 50 estates, 1900-17; dir. Commercial Banking Corpn., Asso. dir. Four Minute Men, Phila., and mem. numerous coms. on Council for Nat. Defense, World War. Mem. Am. Bar Assn., Pa. State Bar Assn. Clubs: Union League, Philadelphia Country (Philadelphia). Home: Polo Road, Bryn Mawr, Pa. Office: 650 Real Estate Trust Bldg., Philadelphia, Pa.

DAVISON, George Stewart, civil engr.; b. Pittsburgh, Pa., Sept. 21, 1856; s. Edward and Isabel (Kennedy) D.; prep. edn., high sch., Pittsburgh; C.E., Rensselaer Poly. Inst., 1878; D.Sc., U. of Pittsburgh, 1926; Dr. Engring., Rensselaer, 1926; m. Clara Elizabeth Lape, of Troy, N.Y., May 19, 1881; 1 son, Allen Stewart. Began with engring. dept. Pa. Lines West, 1878; with U.S. Engring. Corps, 1879; with engring. dept. A..T.& S.F.Ry. and Pa. Lines West, 1880-82; chief engr. Pittsburgh, Chartiers & Youghiogheny R.R., 1882, gen. supt., 1883-90; mem. firm Wilkins & Davison, 1890-1900; gen. mgr. Monongehela and Pittsburgh and Birmingham Ry. Lines, Pittsburgh, 1900-02; president Pa. Water Co. since 1902; asst. to pres. subsidiary cos. of Gulf Oil Corpn., 1905-11. In 1911 became pres. Gulf Refining Co. and other subsidiaries of Gulf Oil Corpn., resigned, 1929; since 1914 president Allen S. Davison Company; pres. Green Bag Cement Company of West Va.; chmn. bd. Pittsburgh Coke & Iron Company, Pittsburgh & Ohio Valley R.R., Green Bag Cement Company of Pennsylvania, Allegheny River Limestone Co.; dir. Bellefield Co., Schenley Hotel Co.; v.p. and trustee Homewood Cemetery. Dir. Pittsburgh Chamber of Commerce; pres. Flood Commn. of Pittsburgh. Trustee Rensselaer Poly. Inst.; v.p. and dir. West Penn Hosp., Pittsburgh; mem. Bd. of Industrial Preparedness, 1916, Com. of Public Safety of Pa., oil sub-com. Nat. Council of Defense and Nat. Petroleum War Service Commn., World War. Mem. Am. Soc. C.E. (past pres.), Am. Inst. Consulting Engrs., Engrs. Soc. of Western Pa. (past pres.), Am. Soc. Mil. Engrs., Delta Phi. Republican. Presbyn. Clubs: Pittsburgh Athletic, Duquesne (Pittsburgh). Home: Pittsburgh Athletic Assn. Office: Oliver Bldg., Pittsburgh, Pa.

DAVISON, Joseph H(omer), supt. of schools; b. West Newton, O., Oct. 16, 1894; s. John and Clara (Hay) D.; grad. Lima (O.) High Sch., 1912; B.S., Ohio State U., Columbus, O., 1925, A.M., 1938; m. Dorothea Richards, Nov. 5, 1917; 1 dau., Dorothea Richards. Began as steel worker, 1917; teacher elementary grade, Elida, O., 1921-22; prin. and supt., Cridersville, O., 1922-24; supt. of schools, Waldo, O., 1925-26; head dept. social science, Lima, O., 1925-26; prin. Lima High Sch., 1926-38; supt. schools, Ashland, Pa., since 1938. Mem. N.E. A., Pa. State Edn. Assn., Am. Assn. Sch. Adminstrs., Beta Theta Pi. Phi Delta Kappa. Republican. Lutheran. Mason, Elk. Clubs: Rotary

(Lima, O.; hon. life mem.); Kiwanis (Ashland, Pa.). Address: Ashland, Pa.

DAVISON, Watson R(owe), judge court of common pleas; b. Greencastle, Pa., Oct. 15, 1870; s. William H. and Florence S. (Rowe) D.; ed. Greencastle and Antrim Twp. public schools, 1876-88, Chambersburg (Pa.) Acad., 1888-89; m. Anna Mary Clippinger, Dec. 6, 1898; children—Florence S. (deceased), Elizabeth S. (Mrs. John R. Lashley, Jr.), Mary C. (Mrs. Guy E. Elden, Jr.), Jane Watson (Mrs. Carl L. Fisher), Katrina H., Watson Rowe, Charles H. Learned printing trade and was foreman and editor Greencastle Press, 1889-93; admitted to Pa. bar, 1893, and began practice in 1893; judge Court of Common Pleas, Franklin County, Pa., since 1926. Trustee Wilson Coll., Chambersburg, Pa., Dickinson Sch. of Law, Carlisle, Pa. Republican. Presbyterian. Mason (K.T.), Odd Fellow. Home: 1208 Edgar Av. Office: Court House, Chambersburg, Pa.

DAVISON, William Richardson, lawyer; b. Greencastle, Pa., Mar. 31, 1876; s. Joseph Robinson and Laura Virgina (Wampler) D.; ed. Chambersburg (Pa.) Acad., 1892-94; A.B., Lafayette Coll., Easton, Pa., 1898, A.M., 1901; m. Frances Winger, Apr. 30, 1902. Admitted to Pa. bar, 1900, and since engaged in gen. practice of law at Greencastle, Pa.; editor Greencastle Press, 1907-12; dir. First Nat. Bank, Greencastle Packing Co. Mem. Pa. State Bar Assn., Pa. Scotch Irish Soc., Kittochtinny Hist. Soc., Theta Delta Chi. Republican. Presbyterian. Mason. Club: Country (Chambersburg, Pa.). Home: 501 E. Baltimore St. Office: Franklin Bldg., Greencastle, Pa.

DAVISSON, Clinton Joseph, physicist; b. Bloomington, Ill., Oct. 22, 1881; s. Joseph and Mary (Calvert) D.; B.S., U. of Chicago, 1908; Ph.D., Princeton Univ., 1911; D.Sc. (hon.), Purdue Univ., 1937, Princeton, 1938; m. Charlotte Sara Richardson, Aug. 4, 1911; children—Clinton Owen Calvert, James Willans, Elizabeth Mary Dixon, Richard Joseph. Instr. in physics, Carnegie Inst. Tech., 1911-17; mem. tech. staff Bell Telephone labs. (formerly engring. dept. Western Electric Co.) since 1917; mem. editorial bd. Physical Review. Mem. National Research Council. Fellow A.A.A.S. (chmn. sect. B 1933), Am. Phys. Soc., Optical Soc. America; mem. Nat. Acad. Sciences, Am. Philos. Soc., Am. Acad. Arts and Sciences, Franklin Inst., Am. Inst., Phi Beta Kappa. Awarded Comstock prize ($2,300), Nat. Acad. Sciences, 1928, for "most important research in electricity, magnetism and radiant energy made in N.A., during the past 5 years"; Elliot Cresson medal, 1931; Hughes medal, Royal Soc. London, 1935; Nobel prize for physics, 1937. Discoverer (with Dr. L. H. Germer) of diffraction of electrons by crystals, 1927. Republican. Contbr. on scientific subjects. Home: Short Hills, N.J. Office: 463 West St., New York, N.Y.

DAVISSON, George I.; mem. law firm Davisson & Kurtz. Address: Weston, W.Va.

DAVY, Ralph. clergyman; b. Marengo, O., Jan. 2, 1871; s. Ezra Joseph and Olive Ann (Wilson) D.; student high sch., Marengo, O., 1888-89, Ohio Normal U., Ada, O., 1891-93, Houghton (N.Y.) Coll., 1909-12; A.B., Ohio Wesleyan U., Delaware, O., 1913; B.D., Drew Theol. Sem., Madison, N.J., 1915; m. Josephine Cronk, June 23, 1896; children—Ralph Bruce, Bernice Louise (Mrs. Zophar Edward DeGraw). Teacher pub. schs., Morrow and Columbiana Cos., O., 1889-95; teacher dept. mathematics and history, Houghton Wesleyan Methodist Sem., Houghton, N.Y., 1895-1900; prin. pub. sch., Fillmore, N.Y., 1900-01; ordained to ministry Wesleyan Methodist Ch. of America, 1899, and pastor Fillmore, N.Y., Fargo, Morrow Co., O., Haskinville, Steuben Co., N.Y., 1899-1909; received into the Presbyterian Ch. of U.S.A., 1913, and pastor, Succasunna, N.J., 1913-28, exec. sec. Presbytery of Morris and Orange, N.J. since 1928, in charge of nat. missions or aid receiving chs. of Presbytery. Chmn. Morris Co. (N.J.) Council of Christian Edn. since 1936; mem. exec. com. Morris Co. Council of Chs. Mem. Morris Ministerial Assn. Republican. Presbyterian. Address: 32 Burnham Rd., Morris Plains, N.J.

DAWKINS, George Evans, clergyman; b. Pittsburgh, Pa., Sept. 19, 1887; s. Thomas and Rachel (Evans) D.; A.B., Muskingum Coll., New Concord, O., 1916, D.D., 1935; student Rochester Theol. Sem., 1916-19; m. Leila M. Garwin, Sept. 6, 1916; children—George Evans, John Parrish. Messenger boy Western Union and Postal Telegraph Co., Vandergrift, Pa., 1901-02; freight cashier Pa. R.R., Vandergrift, 1902-03, ticket seller, 1903-11; ordained to ministry Baptist Ch., 1919; minister, Royal Oak, Mich., 1919-25, Muscatine, Ia., 1925-28, Jackson, Mich., 1928-31; minister, Leddie Memorial Ch., Newark, N.J., since 1931. Mem. evangelistic com. Federal Council of Churches. Home: 195 Elmwood Av., Newark, N.J.

DAWLEY, Clarence A., mech. engr., mfr.; b. Friendsville, Pa., Dec. 23 1879; s. Stephen A. and Frances Emma (Horton) D.; grad. Cook Acad., Montour Falls, N.Y., 1900; M.E., Cornell U., 1904; m. Helen Louise Rildgway, Oct. 10, 1907; children—Roger Ridgway, Helen Ridgway, Mary Frances, Webster, Nancy Elizabeth. Engr. of tests Ingersoll Rand Co., 1904-08; cons. engr., New York, 1908-15; organized N.J. Meter Co., mfrs. flow meters and compressed air specialties, Plainfield, N.J., 1915, and since propr. and chief engr. Mem. Am. Soc. Mech. Engrs. (past chmn. Plainfield sect.), Cornell Soc. of Mech. Engrs. (past pres.), Sigma Xi. Republican. Baptist. Clubs: Engineers (Plainfield; past pres.); Cornell (Plainfield; past pres.). Mng. editor Sibley Jour. of Engring. Granted patents for air compressors, rock drills, flow meters, separators, etc. Home: 1234 Watching Av. Office: New Jersey Meter Co., 120 Waynewood Park, Plainfield, N.J.

DAWSON, Coningsby (William), author; b. High Wycombe, Buckinghamshire, Eng., Feb. 26, 1883; s. Dr. William James and Jane (Powell) D., grad. honor history schs., Merton Coll. (Oxford U.), Eng., 1905; m. Helen, d. Peter Campbell, 1918. Came to America, 1905; spl. work for English newspapers on Canadian affairs; at Taunton, Mass., 1906-10; lit. adviser to George H. Doran Pub. Co., New York, 1910-13. Joined the Canadian 1st Div. at the front as lt. F.A., 1916, and served till end of the World War; lectured in U.S. 1 month, 1917, after having been wounded; made study of Am. mil. preparedness in France under British Ministry of Information, winter 1918; rejoined the Canadians spring of 1918 and was wounded in Sept.; lectured in U.S. under the British Mission Nov. and Dec. 1918; returned to Eng. to make study of European reconstruction problems; lectured in every state of the Union on the results of the war, 1919-20; at request of Herbert Hoover visited stricken areas of Central and Eastern Europe and reported thereon. Fellow Royal Geog. Soc. Author: The Worker and Other Poems, 1906; The House of the Weeping Woman, 1908; Murder Point, 1910; The Road to Avalon, 1911; The Garden Without Walls, 1913; Florence on a Certain Night (poems), 1914; The Raft, 1914; Slaves of Freedom, 1916; The Seventh Christmas, 1917; Carry On, 1917; The Glory of the Trenches, 1918; Out to Win, 1918; Living Bayonets, 1919; The Test of Scarlet, 1919; The Little House, 1920; It Might Have Happened to You, 1921; The Kingdom Round the Corner, 1921; The Vanishing Point, 1922; The Coast of Folly, 1924; Old Youth, 1925; When Is Always?, 1927; Pilgrims of the Impossible, 1928; The Unknown Soldier, 1929; When Father Christmas Was Late, 1929; Fugitives from Passion, 1929; The Auctioning of Mary Angel, 1930; A Path to Paradise, 1932; The Moon Through Glass, 1934; Inspiration Valley, 1935. Co-editor: (with father) The Readers' Library, 1908. Home: 533 Mt. Prospect Av., Newark, N.J.

DAWSON, Daniel Boone, lawyer, mayor; b. Sissonville, W.Va., Sept. 12, 1897; s. Daniel S. and Lillie (Aultz) D.; grad. Charleston High Sch., Charleston, W.Va., 1917; LL.B., Washington and Lee U. Law sch., 1921; m. Elizabeth Brown, Dec. 24, 1923; 1 dau., Anne Kathryn. Admitted to W.Va. bar, 1921, and since engaged in gen. practice of law at Charleston; became judge Municipal Ct., 1931; mayor of Charleston since 1935, reelected for term, 1939-43. Mem. W.Va. League of Municipalities (past pres.), Tri-State Flood Control (exec. com.), Boy Scout Council, Am. Legion, Phi Alpha Delta. Republican. Baptist. Elk. Moose. Clubs: Automobile (dir.), Lions, Pioneer (Charleston). Home: 1030 Columbia Boul. Office: City Hall, Charleston, W.Va.

DAWSON, Edward, clergyman; b. Walden, N.Y., Oct. 10, 1871; s. Joseph Thomas and Sarah Catherine (McKinney) D.; A.B., Rutgers, 1898, M.A., 1901, D.D., 1924; studied New Brunswick Theol. Sem., 1898-01; D.D., Central Coll., Ia., 1924; m. Sadie Estelle Voorhees, Apr. 30, 1902; 1 dau., Edna Voorhees. Ordained ministry Protestant Ref. Ch., 1901; pastor Ref. Ch., Union City, N.J., 1901-12; organized First Ref. Ch., W. Hoboken, N.J., 1912; pastor Old First Protestant Ref. Ch., of Acquackanok, Passaic, N.J., since 1912, pres. Gen. Synod. Ref. Ch. in America, 1932-34; pres. Bd. Fgn. Missions, 1932-35, pres. since 1935. Mem. Ministerial Assn., Passaic, N.J. (pres.), Chi Psi, Alpha Rho. Clubs: Clerical, Alpha Sigma (New York); Rotary (Passaic, N.J.). Home: 127 Passaic Av., Passaic, N.J.

DAWSON, H(enry) Donald, coll. prof.; b. Haskins, O., Jan. 7, 1895; s. John H. and Julia (Browne) D.; grad. Bowling Green (O.) High Sch., 1912; B.S., Denison U., 1916; M.S., Ohio State U., Columbus, 1930; student Bowling Green State U. and Ohio State U., summers; m. Edith Deming Dawson, June 15, 1916; children—Donald, Janet Ione. Works chemist Canadian Explosives, Ltd., 1916-17; asst. cordite supt. and supt. Nobel Plant, Imperial Munitions Bd., 1917-19; chief chemist Beloeil Works, Canadian Explosives, 1919-21; supt. schs. Haskins and Monclova, O., 1922-27; grad. asst. in chemistry, Ohio State U., 1928-30; prof. chemistry, Bethany Coll., Bethany, W.Va., since 1930. Mem. A.A.A.S., Am. Chem. Soc., W.Va. Acad. Science, Lambda Chi Alpha. Republican. Mason. Address: Bethany, W.Va.

DAWSON, Thomas Lawrence, lawyer; b. Rockville, Md., Sept. 15, 1892; s. Thomas and Mary A. (Peter) D.; LL.B., Georgetown U. Law Sch., Washington, D.C., 1914; m. Anne Frazier Davidson, Apr. 17, 1922; children—Thomas Frazier (dec.), Mary Anne, Frazier Peter. Admitted to Md. bar, 1915, and engaged in gen. practice of law at Rockville, Md., as mem. firm with father, Dawson & Dawson, 1915-24; served as state's atty. Montgomery Co., 1920-24; in pvt. practice since 1924; served as sec. of state of Md., 1935-36. Served as 2d lt., Inf., U.S. Army, 1917-19; instr. C.O.T.C., Camp Lee, 1918. Mem. Am. Bar. Assn., Md. State Bar Assn., Montgomery Co. Bar Assn. Republican. Episcopalian. Mason. Home: 100 Forest Av. Office: Farmers BankTrust Co. Bldg., Rockville, Md.

DAWSON, Walter Wyatt, lawyer; b. Mt. Lake Park, Md., Mar. 28, 1894; s. Charles Fillmore and Helena J. (Soelter) D.; grad. Oakland (Md.) High Sch., 1912; student Cumberland U., Lebanon, Tenn. 1927-28; m. Lulu Belle Friend, Oct. 5, 1915; 1 son, Walter Edwin. Clk. First Nat. Bank, Oakland, Md., 1912-16, asst. cashier, 1916-22, cashier, 1922-27; admitted to Md. bar, 1930; with E. R. Jones, atty., Oakland, Md., 1927-37; mem. law firm Jones & Dawson, Oakland, 1930-37; pvt. practice, Oakland, since 1938. State's atty. for Garrett County, 1930-34; pres. Garrett County Bd. of Edn. since 1937; treas. Oakland Vol. Fire Dept.; committeeman Boy Scouts. Mem. Garrett County Bar Assn. (pres. since 1936). Republican. Methodist. Mason (Scottish Rite, Shriner), K.P., Odd Fellow. Club: Rotary (Oakland, Md.; past pres.). Home: 64 Alder St. Office: First Nat. Bank Bldg., Oakland, Md.

DAWSON, William Mercer Owens, II, editorial writer; b. Charleston, W.Va., Sept. 2, 1912; s. William Mercer Owens and Maude (Brown) D.; student Culver (Ind.) Mil. Acad., 1926-31; B.A., Williams Coll., Williamstown, Mass., 1935; m. Virginia Meade Noyes, Mar. 10, 1938. Reporter and asst. news editor Orlando (Fla.) Morning Sentinel, Feb. 1936-Apr. 1937; editorial writer Charleston Daily Mail since Apr. 1937. First lt., F.A., U.S. Army Res. Mem. Charleston Chapter of Am. Business Club, Beta Theta Pi (v.p. Zeta Chapter). Republican. Was asst. mgr. varsity soccer team and mgr. intramural sports. Home: 1635 Franklin Av. Address: Charleston Daily Mail, Charleston, W.Va.

DAY, Arthur Louis, physicist; b. Brookfield, Mass., Oct. 30, 1869; s. Daniel P. and Fannie M. (Hobbs) D.; A.B., Yale, 1892, Ph.D., 1894; Sc.D., Groningen, 1914, Columbia, 1915, Princeton, 1918, Univ. of Pa., 1938; m. 2d, Ruth Sarah Easling, March 27, 1933. Was instructor in physics at Yale University, 1894-97; member scientific staff Physikalisch-Technische, Reichanstalt, Charlottenburg, Germany, 1897-1900; physical geologist, U.S. Geol. Survey, 1900-06; dir. Geophysical Lab., Carnegie Instn. of Washington, 1907-36, retired. V.p. Corning Glass Works, 1919—. Mem. Nat. Acad. Sciences (home sec. 1913-18, v.p. 1933—); fellow Am. Acad. Arts and Sciences; mem. Washington Acad. Sciences (pres. 1924), Geological Society of America (pres. 1938), American Physical Society, American Chem. Soc., Geol. and Philos. socs. Washington, Am. Philos. Socs., Franklin Inst.; foreign mem. Acad. dei Lincei (Rome), Turin Acad., Geol. Soc. London, Norwegian Acad. Sci., U.S.S.R. Acad. Sci. Awarded John Scott medal, 1923; Roozeboom Medal, Royal Acad. Sci., Amsterdam, 1939. Clubs: University (New York); Cosmos of Washington (pres. 1933). Home: 1565 Old Georgetown Rd., Bethesda, Md.

DAY, Cyrus Lawrence, univ. prof., author; b. New York, N.Y., Dec. 2, 1900; s. William Scofield and Emily Hoe (Lawrence) D.; student Phillips Exeter Acad., Exeter, N.H., 1916-18; S.B., Harvard, 1923; Ph.D., 1930; A.M., Columbia, 1925; m. Camilla Downing, Sept. 1, 1935; 1 son, Benjamin Downing. Instr., U. of Tex., Austin, Tex., 1925-26; asst. prof. English, U. of Del., Newark, Del., 1931-37; asso. prof. since 1937. Mem. Modern Lang. Assn., Am. Assn. Univ. Profs., Brooklyn Inst. of Arts and Sciences. Awarded Sheldon Travelling Fellowship (Harvard) 1930. Republican. Author: The Songs of John Dryden, 1932; The Songs of Thomas D'Urfey, 1933; Sailors' Knots, 1935; articles in professional jours. Address: 175 W. Main St., Newark, Del.

DAY, Ewing Wilber, M.D.; b. Deerfield, O., Nov. 1, 1862; s. Edgar M. and Frances (Reed) D.; A.B., Allegheny Coll., Meadville, Pa., 1884, A.M., 1886; M.D., Georgetown U., 1889; m. Annie A. Mosier, of Meadeville, Pa., July 23, 1890; children—Edgar Mortimer (dec.), Ewing W., Kenneth Mosier, Percival Eaton, Mrs. Elizabeth Autrey (dec.). Practiced in Pittsburgh, Pa., 1889-1935 (retired); emeritus prof. otology of the U. of Pittsburgh; member of the Collegium Oto-Rhino-Laryngologicum. Mem. A.M.A., Pa. State Med. Soc., Am. Laryngol., Rhinol. and Otol. Soc. (pres.), Am. Otol. Soc. (pres.), Allegheny County Med. Soc. (pres.), Pittsburgh Acad. Medicine (pres.). Episcopalian. Lt. col. Med. R.C., 1917. Club: University. Home: 616 Commercial St., Provincetown, Mass. Office: 121 University Pl., Pittsburgh, Pa.

DAY, Gardiner Mumford, clergyman; b. New Brighton, Staten Island, N.Y., Feb. 22, 1900; s. Nathaniel Briggs and Mary (Copelin) D.; A.B., Yale, 1922; student Union Theol. Sem. and Columbia U., 1923-25, A.M., Columbia, 1925; B.D., Episcopal Theol. Sch., 1926; m. Katharine P. Bennett, Apr. 2, 1932. Instr. English, Dartmouth Coll., Hanover, N.H., 1922-23; instr. philosophy, Columbia U. Extension Dept., 1923-25; actg. minister Ch. of the Good Shepherd, Boston, Mass., 1925-26; ordained to ministry P.E. Ch., deacon and priest; asst. minister Trinity Ch., Boston, 1926-29; rector St. John's Ch., Williamstown, Mass., 1929-36; rector St. Stephen's Ch., Wilkes-Barre, Pa., since 1936. Served in S.A.T.C., Yale, 1918. Mem. bd. dirs. United Charities of Wilkes-Barre, Osterhout Pub. Library, Children's Service Center; chmn. Council of Social Agencies of Wilkes-Barre. Mem. S.R., Zeta Psi. Republican. Episcopalian. Club: University. Home: 49 S. Franklin St., Wilkes-Barre, Pa.

DAY, John Henry, clergyman; b. Norfolk, Va., Sept. 5, 1883; s. John Henry and Martha E. (Fitchett) D.; LL.B., Washington and Lee U. Law Sch., Lexington, Va., 1904; B.D. Crozer Theol. Sem., Chester, Pa., 1914, M.Th., 1915; (hon.) D.D., Washington and Lee Univ., 1923; m. Jessie May Newland, May 9, 1908; children—Jessie Bird (Mrs. John Sanders Morris), William Newland, John Henry, Newland Edward. Admitted to Va. bar, 1904 and engaged in gen. practice of law at Norfolk, Va., 1904-11; ordained to ministry Bapt. Ch., 1911; ad interim minister, Frederick, Md., 1913; minister, Ridley Park, Pa., 1914-16, Yonkers, N.Y., 1916-22, Memorial Bapt. Ch., Phila., 1922-26; minister Seventh Bapt. Ch., Baltimore, since 1926. Served as religious work dir. Y.M.C.A., Camp Dix, 1918. Trustee Crozer Theol. Sem., Chester, Pa. Mem. Kappa Alpha (Southern). Baptist. Mason. Club: Inter-Church (Baltimore). Home: 2734 St. Paul St. Office: care Seventh Baptist Church, North Ave. and St. Paul St., Baltimore, Md.

DAY, Joseph Paul, real estate; b. New York, N.Y., Sept. 22, 1873; s. John W. and Catherine A. (Hayes) D.; ed. pub. schs.; m. Pauline M. Pope, June 1, 1898; children—Joseph P., Bernard Pope, Charles Pope, Pauline Pope, Laura Pope, Fairfield Pope. Entered real estate and ins. bus. at 21; negotiated, 1898, what is said to be the largest accident policy ever written covering ins. against accidents resulting from change of motive power on 3d Av. surface ry.; sold at auction, 1910, the 3d Av. R.R. which brought $26,000,000, etc.; active in negotiating many large purchases of real estate at pvt. sale; sold for U.S. Shipping Bd. Emergency Fleet Corpn. 6 war villages, involving over $6,000,000; also more than $100,000,000 real estate in United States and Canada, in 1922; sold at Auction over $1,500,000 real estate holdings of closed nat. banks, 1937. Pres. Real Estate Auctioneers' Assn., N.Y.; pres. Indian Point, Inc., Gramercy Co., Castle Hill Estates, Inc., Joseph P. Day, Inc.; dir. R. H. Macy & Co., Consolidated Edison Co., Fifth Av. Hosp., Nat. Horse Show Assn., Westchester Fire Insurance Co., Metropolitan Life Ins. Co., Union Carbide & Carbon Co., Phoenix Indemnity Co., Imperial Assurance Co.; trustee Union Dime Savings Bank. Chmn. Interstate Sanitation Commn. Trustee Mount Prospect Sch., Gramercy Park (pres.). Was one of organizers American Relief Com. in London, Eng., at outbreak of European War, to bring Americans back to U.S. Mem. Real Estate Bd. of New York (pres. 2 terms, honorary governor), Chambers of Commerce of N.Y. and N.J., Geneal. Soc. Clubs: Bankers', Metropolitan, New York Yacht, Lake Placid. Home: 34 Gramercy Park, N.Y. City (country) Short Hills, N.J. Office: 67 Liberty St., New York, N.Y.

DAY, Kenneth Mosier, physician; b. Pittsburgh, Pa., Apr. 8, 1896; s. Ewing Wilbur and Annie (Mosier) D.; A.B., Princeton U., 1917; M.D., Johns Hopkins, 1921; m. Ruth Elizabeth Piper, Oct. 9, 1935; 1 dau., Elizabeth Anne. Interne St. Francis Hosp., Pittsburgh, 1921-22; resident, Mass. Eye and Ear Infirmary, Boston, 1923-24; in pvt. med. practice, Pittsburgh, since 1924; instr. in otology, U. of Pittsburgh, 1925-30; asst. prof. since 1930. Served in M.R.C., S.A.T.C., 1917-18. Dir. Am. Soc. for the Hard of Hearing. Mem. Pittsburgh Acad. Med., A.M.A., Am. Otol. Soc., Am. Acad. Ophthalmology and Otolaryngology, Am. Laryngol., Rhinol. and Otol. Soc. (treas. since 1937). Republican. Episcopalian. Clubs: University, Alcoma Country, Stanton Heights Golf (Pittsburgh). Home: 905 Maryland Av. Office: 121 University Pl., Pittsburgh, Pa.

DAY, Sarah J., poetic writer; b. Cincinnati, O., Nov. 5, 1860; d. Timothy Crane and Mary J. (Johnson) D.; grad. Packer Collegiate Inst., Brooklyn, N.Y., 1879. Author: Mayflowers to Mistletoe (verse), 1900; Fresh Fields and Legends Old and New, 1909; Wayfares and Wings, 1924; The Man on a Hilltop (biography), 1931. Won prize, Brooklyn Inst. Arts and Sciences, for poem, Battle of Long Island, 1913. Many poems have been set to music. Home: 81 Woodland St., Englewood, N.J.

DAYHOFF, Harry Oscar, state athletic commr.; b. Gettysburg, Pa., May 25, 1896; s. James Willard and Minnie Alice D.; A.B., Bucknell U., Lewisburg, Pa., 1923; m. Marion Sprow, July 31, 1926; 1 dau., Harriet Marie. Professional football player Frankford Yellow Jackets (now Phila. Eagles), 1923-27; in clothing business, Harrisburg, 1927-32; Ford Automobile Agency, 1932-37; Pa. State athletic commr., Harrisburg, since 1937. Served in U.S. Naval Air Service during World War. Mem. Vets. Fgn. Wars, Am. Legion, Royal Fire Co. of Harrisburg, Eastern League of New York City, Barn & Key Soc., Sigma Chi. Republican. Zion Lutheran. Elk. Clubs: Republican (Harrisburg); Inter-Collegiate Football Officials (Phila.). Home: 1838½ Derry St. Office: Capitol Hill, Harrisburg, Pa.

DAYTON, Arthur Spencer, lawyer; b. Philippi, W.Va., May 6, 1887; s. Alston Gordon and Lummie (Sinsel) D.; A.B., W.Va. U., Morgantown, W.Va., 1907, LL.B., 1908; M.A., Yale, 1909; m. Ruth Woods, June 14, 1916. Admitted to W.Va. bar, 1908; practiced at Philippi, W.Va., 1909-23; practiced at Charleston, W.Va., since 1923; mem. firm Blue, Dayton & Campbell, Charleston, since 1926. Approved for 1st lt., Army Service Corps, U.S. Army, during World War. Mem. State Library Commn. of W.Va., Kanawha Co. Pub. Library Bd., Charleston. Mem. Am. Bar Assn., W.Va. State Bar Assn., City of Charleston Bar Assn., Phi Beta Kappa, Delta Tau Delta, Phi Alpha Delta. Republican. Presbyterian. Clubs: Edgewood Country (Charleston, W.Va.); Yale (New York City); Duquesne, University, Stanton Heights Golf (Pittsburgh, Pa.). Author various legal articles. Home: 915 Edgewood Drive. Office: Security Bldg., Charleston, W.Va.

DEAHL, Jasper Newton, univ. prof.; b. Kasson, Barbour Co., Va. (now W.Va.), Apr. 19, 1859; s. Henry and Katharine (Kline) D.; student Fairmont (W.Va.) State Normal Sch., W.Va. U., Morgantown; diploma, Peabody Normal Sch., Nashville, Tenn., 1888; A.B., U. of Nashville, 1889; A.B., Harvard, 1893; A.M., Columbia, 1899, Ph.D., 1906; U. of Pa., summer 1913; m. Mary Anderson, Aug. 1, 1901, children—Martha Kline, Henry George. Teacher and prin. pub. schs., 8 yrs.; prin. West Liberty (W.Va.) State Normal Sch., 1893-98; prof. edn. W.Va. U., 1901—, also dean Coll. of Edn. Prof. edn., summer schs., U. of Tex., U. of Pittsburgh, Rutgers Coll. Mem. State Bd. of Edn., W.Va., 1908-19, State Book Commn., 1912-17; mem. Soc. Coll. Teachers of Edn., Nat. Soc. Study Edn., N.E.A., W.Va. State Teachers' Assn. (ex-pres.), Phi Beta Kappa. Democrat. Presbyn. Mason (K.T.). Home: Morgantown, W.Va.

DEAL, Erastus Charles, officer public utility cos.; b. Gainesville, Ga., Nov. 15, 1876; s. Columbus Lafayette and Mary Olivia (Stringer) D.; grad. high sch., 1893; student business sch., Brockton, Mass.; m. Carrie Wahl, of Baltimore, Md., Mar. 5, 1902; children—Louis Lafayette, Erastus Charles. With Ga. Electric Light Co. (now Ga. Ry. and Power Co.), Atlanta, 1895-98; operating and constrn. work, Stone and Webster, pub. utility operators, 1899-1904; with Public Service Corpn. of N.J., as chief engr. Bergen County Gas and Electric Co. and supervisor corpn.'s properties in Central N.J., 1904-09; gen. mgr. Public Service Co. of N.C., 1909-11; with J.G. White & Co., as v.p. and gen. mgr. Augusta Aiken Ry. and Electric Corpn. and Ga. Carolina Power Co., 1911-14; simultaneously, 1914-17, pres. Yadkin Constrn. Co., v.p. and gen. mgr. N.C. Public Service Co., Salisbury-Spencer Ry. Co., Carolina & Yadkin R.R. Co., Delaware County Power Co., Henry County Light & Power Co., Tacoma Water Co., Interstate Public Service Co., Galena Water Co.; chief engr. W. N. Coler & Co.; gen. mgr. Trinidad Electric, Transmission, Ry. & Gas Co., Springfield Gas & Electric Co. and Springfield Traction Co., 1917-22; with Electric Bond and Share Co., as v.p. and gen. mgr. Campania Cubana de Electricidad and 12 subsidiary cos., and Phoenix Utility Co.,

1922-24; on staff of pres. Federal Light and Traction Co., 1924-26; spl. supervisor Nat. Public Service Corpn., 1926-27; now pres. Scranton-Springbrook Water Service Co. and many other water service companies; dir. N.Y. Water Service Co., Utilities Operators Co., New York, Sterling Hotel Co., Wilkes-Barre, Pa. Engaged in elec. constrn. work, Key West, Spanish-Am. War, mgr. elec. power utility, Colo. coal fields, World War. Mem. Nat. Electric Light Assn. (ex-pres. southeastern sect.); ex-pres. Ga. Pub. Utility Assn.; ex-vice-pres. Mo. Assn. Public Utilities. Clubs: Bankers, New York Press, Luncheon Club of Wall Street. Home: 92 W. River St. Office: 30 N. Franklin St., Wilkes-Barre, Pa.

DEAN, Ernest Woodward, chemist; b. Taunton, Mass., Sept. 28, 1888; s. Everett King and Annie Janette (Woodward) D.; A.B., Clark U., Worcester, Mass., 1908; A.M., Yale, 1912, Ph.D., 1914; m. Gladys Campbell Moyer, Oct. 20, 1915; children—Raymond Moyer, Margaret Woodward, Constance Campbell, Walter Craig. Instr. in chemistry, Hobart Coll., Geneva, N.Y., 1908-11; lab. asst., Yale, 1911-14; petroleum chemist U.S. Bureau of Mines, Pittsburgh, Pa., 1914-22; dir. standard inspection lab. Standard Oil Development Co. (subsidiary of Standard Oil of N.J.) since 1922. Mem. Am. Chem. Soc., Am. Soc. Testing Materials, Inst. of Petroleum (Great Britain), Internat. Soc. Testing Materials, Sigma Xi. Republican. Presbyterian. Club: Echo Lake Country (Westfield, N.J.). Home: 140 Stanmore Place, Westfield, N.J. Office: 26 Broadway, New York, N.Y.

DEAN, Willis Leonard, educator; b. Waverly, Pa., Feb. 5, 1857; s. Nelson and Clarissa (Searle) D.; grad. Wyoming Sem., 1873; hon. A.M. Dickinson Coll., 1890; m. Mary Goodwin, June 20, 1878 (died July 14, 1933); children—Searle Goodwin (dec.), Marjorie (Mrs. George W. Carey). Began as teacher, Lowell's Commercial Coll., Binghamton, N.Y., 1873; teacher, Wyoming Sem., Kingston, Pa., 1875-1882; prin. Dean Sch. of Business, Wyoming Sem. since 1882. Republican. Methodist. Home: Kingston, Pa.

DEANE, Philip Bernard, land development; b. Middleboro, Mass., Aug. 16, 1889; s. Leonidas and Anna Davis (Pratt) D.; B.S., Haverford (Pa.) Coll., 1911; m. E. Louise Spahr, Apr. 10, 1920. Employed as fgn. salesman with H. K. Mulford Co., 1911-13, overseas, 1913-19; gen. mgr. Smythfield Export Co., Madrid, Spain, 1919-20; export sales mgr., York Safe and Lock Co., 1920-24, gen. sales mgr., 1924-37; v.p., gen. mgr. Wyndham Hills Corpn. since 1938; dir. York Trust Co.; v.p. and dir. Central Market Co. Served as pres. York Chamber of Commerce; dir. Community Concert Assn.; trustee Y.W.C.A. Republican. Episcopalian. Mason, Rotarian. Clubs: Rotary, Lafayette, Country (York, Pa.; pres.); Circumnavigators (New York); Haverford (Phila.) Home: "The Fairways," Wyndham Hills. Office: Central Nat. Bank Bldg., York, Pa.

DEANS, William, chief engr. I-T-E Circuit Breaker Co.; b. Astoria, L.I., N.Y., Aug. 11, 1891; s. William and Ida (Saarke) D.; M.E., Cornell U., 1913; m. Frances Miriam Winfield, Nov. 14, 1914; children—Robert D., Rosalie V. Design and development engr. Star Electric Co., Binghamton, N.Y., 1913-14; mem. faculty of elec. engring., Cornell U., Ithaca, N.Y., 1914-17; mem. personal staff Thomas A. Edison, West Orange, N.J., 1917-18; chief engr., later gen. mgr. Sundh Electric Co., Newark, N.J., 1918-33; chief engr, I-T-E Circuit Breaker Co., Phila., since 1933. Fellow Am. Inst. Elec. Engrs. Mason (Scottish Rite, Shriner). Writer numerous tech. articles. Home: Claremont Road, Ridgewood, N.J. Office: 19th and Hamilton St., Philadelphia, Pa.

DEAR, Joseph Albert, judge, pub.; b. Jersey City, N.J., Nov. 28, 1871; s. Joseph Albert and Katharine Augusta (Barbour) D.; grad. Hasbrouck Inst., Jersey City, 1889; A.B., Princeton, 1893; m. Julia Allene Reid, Oct. 21, 1897; children—Joseph Albert, Bertha Allene (dec.), Helen. Began as reporter Jersey Journal, Jersey City, N.J., 1893, editor and pub. since 1908; pres. Evening Journal Assn.; apptd. judge N.J.

Court of Errors and Appeals, 3 terms, 1926-44. Trustee and treas. Jersey City Free Pub. Library. Mem. Princeton U. Grad. Council, Princeton Alumni Assn. of Paterson, Passaic and Ridgewood. Republican. Presbyn. Clubs: Carteret, Arcola Country, Ridgewood Country; Princeton (New York). Home: 325 Heights Rd., Ridgewood, N.J. Address: Jersey Journal, Journal Sq., Jersey City, N.J.

DEARDORFF, Merle Henry, banking; b. Waynesboro, Pa., Aug. 5, 1890; s. Aaron Henry and Sarah Harriet (Breidenthal) D.; Ph.B., Dickinson Coll., Carlisle, Pa., 1911, A.M., 1913; grad. student Sorbonne, Paris, 1918-19, Rutgers U. Grad Sch. of Banking, New Brunswick, N.J., 1935-38; m. Mary Elizabeth Taylor, June 10, 1919; children—Julia Harriet, Mary Elizabeth, David Henry. Employed as teacher in pub. schs., 1911-16; asst. comdt. St. Johns Mil. Sch., Manlius, N.Y., 1917; supervising prin. schs. Reynoldsville, Pa., 1919-22; supt. schs., Warren, Pa., 1922-26; instr. various State Teachers Colls., 1922-26; with Warren Bank and Trust Co. since 1927, v.p. and dir. since 1934. Served in U.S. Army with A.E.F., 1918-19. Trustee Edinboro State Teachers Coll., 1931-32. Mem. Pa. Hist. Soc., German Folk Lore Soc. of Pa., Phi Delta Theta. Republican. Presbyterian. Club: Conewango. Home: 15 Jackson Av., Warren, Pa.

DEARING, Arthur Herbert, chief surg, service U.S. Naval Hosp.; comdr. Med. Corps, U.S. Navy. Address: U.S. Naval Hosp., Annapolis, Md.

DEAROLF, Walter S., casualty ins. exec.; b. Reading, Pa., Aug. 6, 1884; s. Howard and Sallie (Matz) D.; ed. pub. sch. and high sch., Reading, Pa., 1898-1902; m. Jennie M. Neff, June 18, 1910; children—Kenneth N., Scott N. Began as accountant Pa. R.R., 1902-05; with Montello Brick Co., 1905-07; asso. with Am. Casualty Co., Reading, Pa., since 1907, sec. since 1934; treas. Acco Realty Company. Republican. Lutheran. Home: 71 Park Rd., Wyomissing Hills, West Lawn. Office: 607 Washington St., Reading, Pa.

DEARTH, Walter Alfred, physician; b. Brownsville, Pa., April 2, 1881; s. Orlando P. and Luella (Higginbotham) D.; B.S., Washington and Jefferson Coll., Washington, Pa., 1903; M.D., U. of Pa. Med. Sch., 1908; m. Augusta Rahn Hean, Aug. 10, 1918; children—Walter Alfred, William Hean. Engaged in practice of medicine and surgery at Pittsburgh since 1908; surgeon Allegheny General Hosp.; adjunct surgeon St. Margaret's Hosp.; cons. surgeon Valley Hosp., Sewickley, Pa.; chief surgeon National Tube Co. Served as lt. col., Med. Corps, U.S. Army, chief surgeon Evacuation Hosp. No. 20, during World War. Mem. Allegheny Co. Med. Soc., Pittsburgh Acad. of Medicine, Phi Kappa Sigma, Phi Alpha Sigma. Republican. Presbyterian. Clubs: Duquesne, University, Allegheny Country (Pittsburgh). Home: 5867 Marlborough Av. Office: 7048 Jenkins Arcade, Pittsburgh, Pa.

DEASY, John Francis, ry. official; b. Hammorton, Pa., March 25, 1882; s. Daniel J. and Mary (Ford) D.; ed. Philadelphia Textile Sch. and Brown Prep. Sch. (law study 4 yrs.); m. Lillian C. Kershaw, June 29, 1912; children—Scott (dec.), John Kershaw. Began as telegraph operator with Pa. R.R., 1901, clk. and operator, Pa. R.R., 1903-05, clerical work, yards and stas., 1905-07, acting extra agt., Amboy Div., 1908-10, acting terminal and shipping agt.; Amboy Div., 1910-12, extra and supervising agt., Trenton Div., 1912-17, asst. freight claim agt., 1917-18, supt. stas. and transfers, Lines E. of Pittsburgh, 1918-20, asst. chief freight transportation, 1920-27, chief, 1927-28, asst. v.p. of operation, 1928-31, regional vice-pres. Central Region, 1931-33, v.p. in charge operation since 1933; officer or dir. Waynesburg & Washington R.R. Co., Baltimore & Eastern R.R. Co., Fruit Growers Express Co., Grand Rapids & Ind. Ry. Co., Keystone Container Car Co., L.I. R.R. Co., N.Y. Connecting R.R., N.Y., Phila. & Norfolk R.R. Ferry Co., Northern Central Ry. Co., Pennsylvania Greyhound Lines, Inc., Peoples

Rapid Transit Co., Inc., Virginia Ferry Corpn., Washington Terminal Co., Pennsylvania-Reading Seashore Lines, Phila. & Camden Ferry Co., Phila., Baltimore & Washington R.R. Co., P., C., C. & St.L. R.R. Co., Pittsburgh, Ft. Wayne & Chicago Ry., Pittsburgh, Youngstown & Ashtabula Ry., W. Jersey & Seashore R.R. Co. Republican. Presbyn. Mason. Clubs: Pittsburgh, Duquesne (Pittsburgh); Union League, Racquet (Philadelphia); Merion Cricket (Haverford, Pa.); Rolling Rock (Ligonier, Pa.). Home: Minden Way and Berwind Rd., Wynnewood, Pa. Office: Broad St. Station Bldg., Philadelphia, Pa. *

DEATON, John Leroy, clergyman; b. Sellwood, S.C., June 12, 1894; s. Willis Alexander and Margaret Pauline (Miller) D.; A.B., Lenoir Rhyne Coll., 1915, D.D., 1935; B.D., Lutheran Theol. Sem., 1918; m. Isabelle Blanche Berger, Aug. 22, 1928; children—Lewis Crosley, Hugo Leroy, Barbara Jane. Pastor Atonement Luth. Ch., Wyomissing, Pa., 1918-24, Luth. Ch. of Advocation, Phila., 1924-34, Christ Luth. Ch., Baltimore, since 1934. Dir. Luth. Inner Mission Soc., Baltimore; mem. Bd. of Edn., United Luth. Ch. Home: 520 Old Orchard Rd., Baltimore, Md.

DEBEVOISE, Thomas (McElrath), lawyer; b. N.Y. City, April 2, 1874; s. George W. and Kaatherine Price (McElrath) D.; A.B., Yale, 1895; LL.B., New York Law Sch., 1897; m. Anne Farnam Whitney, Dec. 6, 1898; children—Eli Whitney, Katherine Price. Admitted to N.Y. bar, 1897, and began practice at N.Y. City; dir. Debevoise Co., Springler Van Beuren Estates, Inc., and other corporations. Mem. American, N.Y. State, New York Co. bar assns., Assn. Bar City of New York, Alpha Delta Phi. Republican. Episcopalian. Clubs: Yale, University, Century, Down Town, Union, Rockefeller Center Lunch (New York); Morristown, Morris County Golf. Home: Green Village, N.J. Office: 30 Rockefeller Plaza, New York, N.Y.

DE BLASIO, James, mfr. fireworks; b. Benevento, Italy, May 12, 1889; s. Sabatino and Carmela. DeB.; ed. grade sch., Benevento, Italy; m. Irene Lizza, May 15, 1910; children —Fiore (dec.), Harry (dec.), Silvio, Dante, Gene. Came to U.S.A. 1906, naturalized, 1914. Apprentice in fireworks factory, Italy, 1905; pyrotechnician, Rochester, N.Y., 1911; organized Continental Fireworks Mfg. Co., mfrs. commercial and exhibition fireworks, Dunbar, Pa., 1911, and has seen it grow from 1 building on 1 acre of land to 38 buildings and 234 acres; now supt. and pres. Hon. mem. Vol. Firemen; mem. Bd. of Trade, Sons of Italy in America. Catholic, Elk. Home: 56 Railroad St. Address: 15 Railroad St., Dunbar, Pa.

DE BLOIS, Austen Kennedy, educator; b. Wolfville, N.S., Dec. 17, 1866; s. Dr. Stephen W. and Mary S. (Fitch) D.; Horton Academy, 1881; in Europe, 1885; grad. Acadia Coll., N.S., 1886; A.M., Brown, 1888, Ph.D., 1889, D.D., 1914; student Newton (Mass.) Theol. Instn., 1889; U. of Berlin, 1890; U. of Leipzig, Germany, 1891; LL.D., Franklin Coll., 1897; D.D., Acadia U., 1925; m. Erminie A. Day, of Sheffield, N.B., June 25, 1890; children —Stephen George, Cedric (dec.), Mary Ailsa, Charles Austen, Laurier St. John, Erminie Stanhope. V. prin. Union Baptist Sem., St. Martins, N.B., 1892, prin. 1892-94; pres. Shurtleff Coll., Alton, Ill., 1894-99; traveled in Europe and Africa, 1900-01; pastor First Bapt. Ch., Elgin, 1899-1902, First Bapt. Ch., Chicago, 1902-11, First Bapt. Ch., Boston, 1911-26; editor The Watchman-Examiner, New York, 1926-1928; president Eastern Baptist Theol. Seminary, 1926-36; president emeritus since 1936. Lecturer psychology of religion, Newton Theology Institution, 1913-17, philosophy of religion, 1914-15; annual course on pastoral experience, Colgate, 1915. Trustee, Shurtleff Coll., West China Union U. Div. Sch. U. of Chicago, Newton Theol. Instn., Gordon Coll.; pres. N.E. Acadia Alumni Assn.; pres. Chicago Bapt. Orphanage, 1900-11, Home for Missionaries' Children, Morgan Park, Ill., 1909-11; mem. bd. of mgrs. Am. Bapt. Fgn. Mission Soc.; mem. laymen's commn. to the Orient, making around the world tour of Christian missions, 1907; pres.

Bapt. Council of Greater Boston, 1915-16, Northern Bapt. Edn. Soc., since 1917. Evang. Alliance of Greater Boston, 1918; chaplain Canadian Club, 1917-23; v.p. Am. Brit. Federation, 1917; mem. Brit. Recruiting Mission of N.E., 1917-18; mem. bd. mgrs. Am. Bapt. Home Mission Soc. since 1922; chmn. Nationwide Home Mission Centenary Campaign, 1930-32. Mem. Delta Upsilon, Phi Beta Kappa. Mason. Clubs: Classical, Canadian, Penn Athletic. Author: Bible Study in American Colleges, 1899; The Pioneer School, 1900; Imperialism and Democracy, 1901; History of the First Baptist Church in Boston, 1665-1915, 1916; Life of John Mason Pec, Prophet of the Prairies, 1917; The Message of Wisdom; Studies in the Book of Proverbs, 1920; Some Problems of the Modern Minister, 1928; John Bunyan, the Man, 1928; Fighters for Freedom, 1929; Evangelism in the New Age, 1933; The Church of Today—and Tomorrow, 1934; The Making of Ministers, 1936. Editor: The Evangelical Faith, 1931. Editor The Christian Review since 1931. Home: 2652 Lenape Rd., West Park, Philadelphia. Office: 1814 South Rittenhouse Sq., Philadelphia, Pa. *

DeCAMP, Joseph Edgar, prof. psychology; b. Desha, Ark., Feb. 19, 1887; s. Edgar Farra and Emelie Ann (Smith) DeC.; B.S., Arkansas Coll., Batesville, Ark., 1905; A.M., U. of Mich., Ann Arbor, Mich., 1912, Ph.D. 1914; student U. of Ill., Urbana, Ill., 1914-15, U. of Chicago, summer 1915; m. Margaret Taylor Parker, June 6, 1923 (dec.); m. 2d, Anna Doretta Miller, May 28, 1932; children—Mary Anne (dec.), Joseph Edgar. Teacher pub. schs. of Ark., 1903-05; asst. in psychology, U. of Mich., Ann Arbor, Mich., 1912-13 and summer, 1914, U. of Ill., Urbana, Ill., 1914-15; instr psychology, U. of Calif., Berkeley, Calif., 1915-16 and summer, 1916, Stanford (Calif.) U., 1916-19; asst. prof. psychology, Pa. State Coll., 1919-21, asso. prof., 1921-23, prof. since 1923. Served as pvt. in psychol. work at Camp Kearney, U.S. Army, 7 mos., 1918. Mem. Am. Psychol. Assn., Am. Assn. Univ. Profs., Nat. Soc. Coll. Teachers of Edn., Sigma Xi, Phi Delta Kappa, Psi Chi, Kappa Delta Pi, Phi Sigma Iota. Democrat. Home: 629 W. Park Av., State College, Pa.

DECHANT, Miles Boyer, architect; b. Reading, Pa., Jan. 10, 1890; s. William Henry and Rebecca Cathrine (Hagman) D.; grad. Reading (Pa.) High Sch., 1910; B.S. in architecture, U. of Pa., 1915; student A.E.F. Art Training Center, France, Feb.-July 1919; m. Sarah Light Garvin, Feb. 11, 1921; children—William Garvin, Donald Hagman; m. 2d, Dorothy Marie Kachline, June 22, 1935; 1 son, Miles Kachline. Started practice of architecture as archtl. draftsman, 1915; asso. with father and brother in firm of William H. Dechant & Sons, Reading, Pa., since 1915; designed Berks Co. Court House, also schools and residences. Awards: Arthur Spayd Brooke gold medal for archtl. design, 1915; Harbeson medal for design of archtl. ornament, 1915; winner House Beautiful Small House Competition for Remodeled Houses, 1938, hon. mention, 1928, 1930. Artist: water colors exhibited at Pa. Acad. Fine Arts, Reading Pub. Art Gallery, Art Inst. of Chicago, Wilmington Soc. Fine Arts, Staten Island Soc. Fine Arts. Mem. Am. Inst. of Architects, Pa. Assn. of Architects. Reformed Ch. Home: 250 Friedensburg Rd. Office: 526 Franklin St., Reading, Pa.

de CHARMS, George, bishop; b. Denver, Colo., Aug. 24, 1889; s. Richard and Harriet (Jung) de C.; ed. Acad. New Ch., 1904-08, Pa. State Coll., 1908-10; B.Th., Theol. Sch., Bryn Athyn, Pa., 1914; m. Fidelia Asplundh, May 10, 1915; children (adopted)—Aurelle, Charles. Minister to Advent Soc., Phila., Pa. 1914-15, pastor 1915-16; asst. pastor Bryn Athyn (Pa.) Soc., 1916-36; ordained Bishop, 1928; asst. bishop of Gen. Ch. 1930; dean of coll. Acad. of New Ch., 1928, vice-pres., 1930-36, pres. Acad. New Ch. since 1936; bishop of the Gen. Ch. of the New Jerusalem since 1937; pastor ex officio Bryn Athyn Ch. Republican. Swedenborgian. Home: Bryn Athyn, Pa.

DECHERT, Philip, lawyer; b. Phila., Pa., June 16, 1906; s. Henry Taylor and Virginia Louise (Howard) D.; student Wm. Penn Charter Sch., Phila., 1913-23; A.B., U. of Pa., 1927, LL.B., 1930; m. Anne Lewis Ross, Feb. 21, 1936; 1 dau., Frances Eliot. Admitted to Pa. bar, 1930; asso. Hepburn & Norris, Phila., 1930-36, partner since 1936; asst. counsel NRA, 1934. Mem. First Troop Phila. City Cav., 19— to 19—. Vice-pres. Community Fund of Phila., dir. Babies Hosp. of Phila. Mem. Phila., Pa. State, Am. bar assns., Juristic Soc., Delta Psi. Episcopalian. Clubs: Rittenhouse, Sunnybrook Golf, St. Anthony (Phila.); Whitemarsh Hunt (Whitemarsh, Pa.); St. Anthony (New York). Home: Germantown Pike, Chestnut Hill. Office: 1500 Walnut St., Philadelphia, Pa.

DECHERT, Robert, lawyer; b. Philadelphia, Pa., Nov. 29, 1895; s. Henry Taylor and Virginia Louise (Howard) D.; grad. Lawrenceville (N.J.) Sch., 1912; A.B., U. of Pa., 1916, LL.B., 1921; U.S. Army student, St. John's Coll., Oxford U., Eng., 1919; m. Helen Hope Wilson, of Villa Nova, Pa., May 24, 1922; children—Peter, Helen Hope, Marian Godey. Admitted to Pa. bar, 1921, and began practice at Philadelphia; associated with Hepburn, Dechert & Norris, 1921-27; mem. faculty U. of Pa. Law Sch. since 1923; v.p. and counsel Penn Mut. Life Ins. Co., 1927-30, counsel since 1930; mem. firm Dechert and Bok, now Dechert, Smith and Clark, since 1930; mem. bd. dirs. Fidelity-Philadelphia Trust Co. Trustee U. of Pa. Was 2d lt., inf., later 1st lt. and capt., U.S.A., World War, in 6 major engagements; awarded D.S.C., for gallantry in action, Le-Charmel, France, July 23-25, 1918. Pres. Community Council of Phila. (1930-1937); vice chmn. Phila. Unemployment Relief Com., 1930-32, v.p. Pa. Sch. for Social Work; vice-pres., Y.M.C.A. of Phila.; trustee Community Fund of Phila.; mem. Pa. State Board of Law Examiners. Mem. Am. Pa. and Phila. bar assns., S.R., Phi Beta Kappa, Delta Psi. Order of Coif. Republican. Episcopalian. Clubs: Rittenhouse, Gulph Mills. Home: Gulph Mills (Bridgeport P.O.), Pa. Office: Packard Bldg., Philadelphia, Pa.

DECK, Luther J.; prof. mathematics, Muhlenberg Coll. Address: 232 N. 15th St., Allentown, Pa.

DECK, Roy, physician; b. Hauto, Pa., July 16, 1890; s. Louis and Annie (Short) D.; Pharm.D., Phila. Coll. of Pharmacy, 1910; M.D., Jefferson Med. Coll., Phila., 1914; m. Mabel Rice, Feb. 6, 1923; 1 son, Roy. After usual internships engaged in practice of medicine, Lancaster, since 1920; laryngologist, St. Josephs Hosp., Lancaster, and Rossmere Sanatorium. Served as 1st lt., Med. Corps, U.S.A. during World War. Fellow Am. Coll. Surgeons; mem. Lancaster Co. Med. Soc., Pa. Med. Soc., A.M.A. Republican. Lutheran. Mason, Elk. Club: Hamilton (Lancaster, Pa.). Home: 243 N. Duke St., Lancaster, Pa.

DECKER, Alonzo G.; v.p., gen. mgr. and dir. Black & Decker Mfg. Co. Address: Towson, Md.

DECKER, Harry Ryerson, surgeon; b. Jackson, Mich., Feb. 26, 1883; s. Josiah and Mary Adelaide (Ryerson) D.; A.B., Princeton, 1903; M.D., Columbia U. Sch. of Medicine, 1907; m. Marian Shuman, June 8, 1922; children—Richard Ryerson, Anne Shuman, Roger Bradford. After usual internships engaged in pvt. practice of medicine specializing in surgery at Pittsburgh; visiting surgeon Presbyn. Hosp., Tuberculosis League Hosp.; cons. surgeon Vets. Hosp.; asst. prof. surgery, U. of Pittsburgh Med. Dept. Served as maj., Med. Corps, U.S. Army, 1918-19. Fellow Am. Coll. Surgeons, Am. Assn. for Thoracic Surgery; mem. A.M.A., Pa. and Allegheny Co. med socs., Biol. Soc. U. of Pittsburgh, Pittsburgh Acad. of Medicine, Pittsburgh Surg. Soc. Republican. Presbyterian. Clubs: Harvard-Yale-Princeton, Stanton Heights Golf (Pittsburgh). Home: 6309 Bartlett St. Office: 923 Westinghouse Bldg., Pittsburgh, Pa.

DECKER, Josef Ben, manufacturer; b. Düsseldorf, Germany, Apr. 4, 1888; s. Josef Ben and Maria (Keller) D.; student Gymnasium, Germany, 1900-09, Inst. of Tech., Germany, 1910-13; m. Gertrude Willis, June 20, 1919; children—Mary Ann, Josef Benedict. Came to U.S., 1914, naturalized, 1919. Began as chemist, 1916; pres. Victory Sparkler & Specialty Co., Elkton, Md., 1919-31; pres. Victory Fireworks & Specialty Co., Elkton, Md., 1932-33; exec. vice-pres. Triumph Explosive, Inc., Elkton, Md., since 1933. Catholic. Clubs: University, Delaware Turf (Wilmington, Del.); Wellwood (Charleston, Md.); Manhattan (New York City). Home: Hill Top Farm. Office: Triumph Explosives, Inc., Elkton, Md.

DECKER, Oliver John, lawyer; b. Armstrong Twp., Lycoming Co., Pa., Feb. 2, 1879; s. John Christian and Julia R. (Fausel) D.; grad. Bucknell Acad., 1895; A.B., Bucknell U., Lewisburg, Pa., 1899; attended U. of Pa. Law Dept., Class of 1902; (hon.) LL.D., Susquehanna U., Selinsgrove, Pa., 1926; m. Eleanor Dawson, Sept. 4, 1912; 1 son, John Christian III. Admitted to Pa. bar, 1902, and since engaged in gen. practice of law at Williamsport, Pa.; dir. Bank of South Williamsport. Mem. Bd. Trustees, Bucknell U. since 1919, sec. of bd. since 1920; pres. Williamsport Community Concert Association, 1924-29; Associate Lutheran Brotherhoods of Lycoming Co. (1923), General Alumni Association Bucknell University (1917-18); president Lycoming Historical Society since 1939, Pa. Folk Lore Society; member Pa. Soc. of N.Y. Fellow Am. Acad. of Polit. Sci., Am. Geog. Soc. Mem. Am., Pa., and Lycoming Co. (pres. 1928) bar assns., Pa. Hist. Soc., Kappa Sigma (nat. pres. 1931-33; nat. historian since 1937). Republican. Lutheran. Mason (K.T., 32°). Clubs: University (past pres.), Lions (past pres.), Ross, Williamsport Country, Haleeka Country (Williamsport, Pa.) Author: History of Bucknell Chapter of Kappa Sigma, 1911. Home: 121 W. Southern Av., South Williamsport, Pa. Office: 120 W. Fourth St., Williamsport, Pa.

DECKER, Philip H.; eye, ear, nose and throat service Williamsport Hosp. Address: 748 Vallamont Drive, Williamsport, Pa.

DEEMER, Bert, coal business; b. Mauch Chunk, Pa., Sept. 2, 1876; son of Henry G. and Martha J. (Walker) D.; grad Mauch Chunk High Sch., 1892; m. Harriet Watson McCormick, 1906; children—Ethel Irene (Mrs. William S. Pattison), Robert Walker. Stenographer Mill Creek Coal Co., 1894-1902; with Pa. R.R., 1902-20, succesively as sec. to supt. of passenger transportation, sec. to passenger traffic mgr. and statistician passenger dept.; sec. and treas. Boone County Coal Co., Phila., since 1920. Republican. Presbyterian. Mason. Home: 5216 N. Warnock St. Office: 1608 Walnut St., Philadelphia, Pa.

DEEMER, William Russell, banker; b. Milford, N.J., June 6, 1867; s. Elias and Henrietta (Hunt) D.; student Lawrenceville (N.J.) Sch., 1884-87; A.B., Princeton U., 1891, M.A. (hon.), 1893; m. Sara January Grundy, Dec. 19, 1901; children—William Russell, Mary Elizabeth (Mrs. Lawrence D. Willison Jr.), John January Grundy. Admitted to Pa. bar, 1893, Supreme Ct. of Pa., 1896, U.S. Supreme Ct., 1907; pres. Williamsport (Pa.) Nat. Bank, 1918-38, chm. bd. of dirs. since 1938. Mem. Univ. Cottage Club (Princeton U.). Republican. Presbyterian (pres. bd. of trustees, Covenant Central Presbyn. Ch.). Clubs: Ross (Williamsport, Pa.); Princeton (New York). Home: 870 W. Fourth St. Office: 329 Pine St., Williamsport, Pa.

DEER, Roy Burton, clergyman; b. Harbor Beach, Mich., Dec. 16, 1891; s. John Jacob and Margaret Ann (Crecine) D.; Ph.B., Denison U., Granville, O., 1915, D.D., 1938; B.D., Rochester Theol. Sem., 1919; m. Emilie Spencer, of Granville, O., Sept. 14, 1915; children—Gordon Spencer, Margaret Emily, Donald Spencer. Ordained ministry, Bapt. Ch., Feb. 7, 1919; pastor Maple St. Ch., Buffalo, N.Y., 1919-21, First Ch., Terre Haute, Ind., 1921-29, First Ch., Lansing, Mich. 1930-36; exec. sec. Pa. Bapt. Conv. since 1936. Pres. Bapt. Young People's Union, Buffalo, N.Y., 1920-21; mem. bd. promotion and exec. com. Ind. Bapt. Conv., 1921-29, chmn. dept. evangelism, 1922-29; mem.

bd. mgrs. Mich. Bapt. Conv., 1931-32 and 1935-36; chmn. Centennial Com. on Evang., Mich. Bapt. Conv., 1934-36; mem. Headquarters Com. Mich. Anti-Saloon League, 1935-36; mem. com. on Conf. with Gen. Baptists, Northern Bapt. Conv., 1929-32; pres. Lansing Council Religious Edn. until 1936. Republican. Baptist. Author: Evangelism for the Whole Church. Contbr. to religious jours. Home: 508 Berkley Rd., Narberth, Pa. Address: 1703 Chestnut St., Philadelphia, Pa.

DEFANDORF, Francis Marion, physicist; b. Garrett Park, Md., Apr. 18, 1897; s. Jason Fremont and Harriet (Holmes) D.; B.E., Johns Hopkins U., 1920; A.M., Harvard U., 1923; Ph.D., Johns Hopkins U., 1927; m. Marion Phillips, Mar. 29, 1932; children—May, Edward Holmes. Engaged as lab. apprentice, Nat. Bur. of Standards, Washington, D.C., 1917, advanced through various positions, physicist since 1930; research work in high voltage measurements. Served in S.A.T.C. and R.O.T.C., 1917-18. Mem. Am. Inst. Elec. Engrs., American Phys. Soc., Philos. Soc. of Washington, Washington Acad. Scis., Phi Gamma Delta, Sigma Xi. Home: 205 W. Bradley Lane, Chevy Chase, Md.

DE GRAW, John, lawyer; b. Morris Co., N.J., July 29, 1877; s. John and Mary (Hiler) DeG.; student N.Y. Law Sch., 1904-06; m. Helen E. Marsh, Mar. 29, 1907; 1 son, John Burr. Admitted to N.J. bar as atty., 1907, as counselor, 1911; engaged in gen. practice of law at Newark, N.J., since 1907; mem. firm DeGraw & Murray, Newark, N.J. since 1930; pres. and counsel Jersey Central Realty Co., Newark, N.J., since 1936. Mayor of Belleville, N.J., 1925-26. Trustee Silver Lake Community House, Newark, N.J. Republican. Methodist. Mason. Club: Wednesday (Newark). Home: Montague, N.J. Office: Raymond-Commerce Bldg., Newark, N.J.

DEISON, Edward B.; pres. Empire Nat. Bank. Address: Clarksburg, W.Va.

DEITRICK, George Albert, M.D.; b. Mt. Carmel, Pa., Oct. 5, 1887; s. Samuel and Margaret Jane (Manney) D.; student Gettysburg Coll.; M.D., U. of Pa.; m. Eva C. Seebold, Dec. 4, 1912; children—Emma C., Margaret Jane, George Albert, Samuel Charles. Engaged in gen. practice of medicine and surgery, Sunbury, Pa., since 1911; surgeon Mary M. Packer Hosp., Sunbury, Pa.; treas. Rea & Derick, Inc.; dir. Consumers Discount Co. Formerly mem. Pa. State Senate, 27th Dist. Served as capt. U.S. Med. Corps, 1917-19. Fellow Am. Coll. Surgeons; mem. A.M.A., Pa. State Med. Assn. Northumberland Co. Med. Soc., Am. Legion, Patriotic Order Sons of America, Sigma Alpha Epsilon, Alpha Kappa Kappa, Delta Delta Delta. Club: Temple. Home: 242 Arch St. Office: 28 N. Third St., Sunbury, Pa.

DE JUHASZ, Kalman John, coll. prof.; b. Csap, Hungary, Feb. 4, 1893; s. Kalman John and Mary (Bleha) DeJ.; M.E. (summa cum laude), U. of Engineering Sciences, Budapest, Hungary, 1914; came to U.S., 1927, naturalized, 1936; m. Bergliot Synnove Strand, Aug. 29, 1929; children—Peter Kalman, Sari Bergliot, Karin Marianne. Asst. and asso. prof. of heat engring., U. of Engring. Sciences, Budapest, Hungary, 1914-23; chief engr. Lehmann & Michels, mfrs. of engring. instruments, Hamburg, Germany, 1923-24; research consultant on racing engines, Fabbricca Italiana Automobili, Torino, Italy, and Officine Meccaniche, Brescia, Italy, 1924-25; instrument designer for spl. devices, Gamma Ltd., Budapest, Hungary, 1926; with Ministry of Industry, Budapest, Hungary, 1926-27; instr. in mech. engring., U. of Minnesota, Minneapolis, Minn., 1927-28; asst. and asso. prof. of engring. research, Pa. State College since 1928. Mem. Am. Soc. M.E., Franklin Inst., A.A.A.S., Sigma Xi. Awarded Silver Medal of Soc. of Hungarian Engrs. and Architects, 1921, Rudolph Diesel Award of Am. Soc. M.E., 1931, Gold Medal of Franklin Inst., 1939. Republican. Calvinist. Author of books and numerous articles on engring. instruments and Diesel engring. Holds several patents on engine indicators, measuring instruments, carburetor, fuel pump. Home: 730 N. Atherton.

Office: Pennsylvania State College, State College, Pa.

DE KNIGHT, Edward William, pres. Hydrex Asphalt Products Corpn.; b. Washington, D.C., June 17, 1865; s. William Francis and Rose Hannah (Pettibone) DeK.; LL.B., Georgetown U., Washington, D.C., 1893, LL.M., 1893; m. Daisy Johnson, about 1895, divorced); 1 dau., Dorothy Dawn (Mrs. Graham); m. 2d, Alice Grogan (died April 4, 1934); children—Edward W., Patricia Alice, Jacquelin (dec.). Admitted to bar, 1893, and practiced Washington, D.C. Dept. mgr. Johns Mfg. Co., New York, 1901; N.Y. mgr. Bird & Son, East Walpole, Mass., 1903; pres. Hydrex Asphalt Products Co., Passaic, N.J., and New York since 1904. Presbyterian. Home: Passaic, N.J.; Wilmington, Del. Office: Hydrex Asphalt Products Corpn., Passaic, N.J.

DE LAND, Clyde Osmer, artist; b. Union City, Pa., Dec. 27, 1872; s. Theodore D. and Nancy F. (Howard) D.; U. of Rochester, 1891-92; grad. Drexel Inst., Phila., 1898; studied Pyle Sch. of Illustration, Phila.; unmarried. Teacher of music and concert pianist, 1889-94; art editor Sotheran's Mag., Phila., 1896; artist and illustrator since 1897. Mem. Alpha Zeta, Delta Upsilon, Historical Society of Pennsylvania (Phila.). Has furnished many important illustrations to leading weeklies and mags., especially on subjects of Am. history. Paintings: First Am. Flag (property of the City of Somerville, Mass.); Balboa—Discoverer of the Pacific; Inauguration of Washington; First Shot of 1812; in U.S. Nat. Mus.—The First Steamboat, The First Automobile, The First Street Railway; in Carpenters' Hall, Phila.—(painting) The First Continental Congress. Books illustrated: The Count's Snuff-Box (Rivers), 1898; Cinderella (Crockett), 1901; Barnaby Lee (John Bennett), 1902; A Forest Hearth (Major), 1903; Mr. Kris Kringle (Weir Mitchell), 1904; Captain Blood (Sabatini), 1923; Nicholas Rowntree (Kauffman), 1924; The Carolinian (Sabatini), 1925. Lecturer (with stereopticon) on "Drama of American History." Home and Studio: 19 N. 50th St., Philadelphia, Pa.

DE LANEY, Lewis Edwin, supt. of schools; b. Sayre, Pa., July 17, 1878; s. Wesley H. and Sarah Isabella (Lamont) DeL.; grad. Sayre High Sch., 1897; B.S., Wesleyan U., Middletown, Conn., 1902; grad. student Columbia and Pa. State Coll.; m. Margaret Griswold, July 19, 1907; children—Margaret Louise (Mrs. Richard Johnston), William Wesley, Edwin Griswold, George Frederick. Asso. with public schools of Sayre, Pa., since 1902, as teacher of science, High Sch., 1902-08, supervising prin., 1908-18, supt., 1918-33, science teacher, 1934-38, supt. of schools since 1938; dir. Sayre Bldg. & Loan Assn. Mem. Pa. State Edn. Assn., N.E.A., Am. Assn. Sch. Administrs., Sigma Chi. Republican. Methodist. Mason, Odd Fellow. Club: Acacia (Sayre, Pa.). Address: Sayre, Pa.

DELANEY, William E., Jr., chief of surg. service Williamsport Hosp.; surgeon-in-charge Devitts Camp, Allenwood, Pa. Address: 416 Pine St., Williamsport, Pa.

DELANY, Joseph Reynolds Kerr, railroad official; b. Phila., Pa., Dec. 2, 1872; s. Henry St. Clare and Johannah (Houck) D.; student evenings Drexel Inst., Phila., 1893-94, U. of Pa. Sch. of Accounts and Finance, 1904-06; m. Caroline Trautwein, July 21, 1906. Began as office boy, 1888; in employ Francis I. Gowen, lawyer; clk. Choctaw, Okla. & Gulf Ry. Co.; clk. Girard Trust Co., Phila.; sec. and asst. treas. Midland Valley R.R. Co.; sec., treas., and dir. Sebastian County Coal and Mining Co. Republican. Protestant. Home: 2936 Girard Av. Office: 135 S. 5th St., Philadelphia, Pa.

DELAPLAINE, Edward Schley, judge; b. Frederick, Md., Oct. 6, 1893; s. William T. and Fannie (Birely) D.; B.A., Washington and Lee U., Lexington, Va., 1913; student Washington and Lee U. Law Sch., 1913-14, U. of Md. Law Sch., Baltimore, 1914-15. Admitted to Md. bar, 1915, and since engaged in gen. practice of law at Frederick, Md.; served as mem. Md. Ho. of Dels., 1916-18; city atty. Frederick, 1919-22; codified Frederick City

Code, 1920; admitted to practice before the Supreme Ct. of the U.S., 1932; U.S. conciliation commr., 1934-38; county atty., Frederick Co., 1935-38; chief judge 6th jud. circuit and judge Ct. of Appeals of Md. since 1938. Mem. state councils sect. Council of Nat. Defense, Washington, 1918; chmn. Frederick Co. Com. European Relief Council, 1921; sec. Frederick Co. Chapter Am. Red Cross, 1921-38; treas. Frederick Chapter Wakefield Nat. Memorial Foundation, 1926-27. Mem. Md. Tercentenary Commn., 1927-34; pres. Roger Brooke Taney Home, Inc., since 1929; treas. Roger Brooke Taney Nat. Memorial Foundation since 1933. Trustee C. Burr Artz Library of Frederick since 1935. Mem. Am., Md. State bar assns., Am. Judicature Soc., S.A.R. (pres. Sergt. Lawrence Everhart Chapter, 1926-28), Md. Hist. Soc., Star-Spangled Banner Flag House Assn. (life), Phi Beta Kappa, Delta Sigma Rho. Republican. Episcopalian. Author: Roger B. Taney: His Career as a Lawyer, 1918; The Life of Thomas Johnson, 1927; Francis Scott Key, Life and Times, 1937. Contbr. to Dictionary of American Biography, and Dictionary of American History. Home: 308 Upper College Terrace, Frederick, Md. Office: Court House, and 25 Court St., Frederick, Md.; Court of Appeals Bldg., Annapolis, Md.

DELAPLAINE, Robert Edmonston, publisher; b. Frederick, Md., Apr. 19, 1885; s. William T. and Fannie (Birely) D.; student Frederick Pub. Sch., 1890-98, Frederick High Sch., 1898-1901; m. Ruth Millinix, Nov. 19, 1913. Employed by Farmers and Mechanics Nat. Bank, 1901, resigning as bookkeeper, 1909; actively engaged in newspaper work since 1909; assumed management Frederick News-Post, Apr. 19, 1909; sec. and treas. Great Southern Printing & Mfg. Co.; v.p. and dir. Farmers & Mechanics Nat. Bank; dir. Walkersville Bank, Frederick County Products, Mutual Insurance Co., Potomac Edison Co., Domestic Bldg. Assn. Mem. bd. visitors Md. State Sch. for the Deaf; member bd. of trustees Frederick City Hosp. Republican. Episcopalian (vestryman). Mason (Past High Priest Enoch Chapter No. 23, R.A.M.; treas. Enoch Council No. 10; Past Eminent Commander Jacques de Molay Commandery No. 4, K.T.; Shriner). Club: Catoctin Country. Home: 310 Upper College Terrace, Frederick, Md.; (summer) Braddock Heights, Md. Office: care News-Post, Court St., Frederick, Md.

DELAPLAINE, William Theodore, editor and pub.; b. Frederick, Md., Jan. 22, 1891; s. William Theodore and Fannie (Birely) D.; A.B., Washington and Lee U., Lexington, Va., 1909, student law sch., 1909-10; m. Janie H. Quynn, Nov. 15, 1916; children—William Theodore 3d, Eleanor Frances (dec.). Joined editorial staff, 1910, Frederick (Md.) Daily News, started by father, 1883, and with bro. assumed management; acquired Frederick Evening Post, morning daily, 1916; pub. both newspapers and operate commercial printing dept. all under corporate name The Great Southern Printing and Mfg. Co.; serves as mgr. and asst. sec.-treas.; mem. firm and mgr. Quynn Orchards, growers and packers apples and peaches, near Frederick, Md.; pres. Fidelity Bldg. & Loan Assn.; sec. Frederick County Products, Inc.; sec. Kiwanis Club, Frederick, Md., 1922-29, pres., 1929; v.p. Community Chest, Inc., Frederick, Md., 1938-39. Independent Republican. Episcopalian. Clubs: Catoctin Country. Home: 317 Dill Av. Office Care of News-Post, Court St., Frederick, Md.

DE LAUTER, Henry Kieffer, lawyer; b. Middletown, Md., Jan. 23, 1878; s. Daniel T. and Martha DeL.; student elementary schs., 1884-91, high sch., 1891-95; Wolfe's Business Coll., 1895-96; also U. of Md. and Sprague's Corr. Sch. of Law; unmarried. Teacher pub. schs., 1897-1907; admitted to Md. bar, 1907; dir. and counsel Peoples Nat. Bank, Frederick, Md. Counsel to Burgess and Council of Myersville, Md. Mem. com. on Christian Edn., Potomac Synod of Evang. and Reformed Ch. Mem. Am. Bar Assn., Local Bar Assn. Democrat. Mem. Evang. and Reformed Ch. K.P. Home: Braddock Heights, Md. Office: Frederick, Md.

DELBRIDGE, Thomas Gerard, chemist; b. Batavia, N.Y., Feb. 20, 1884; s. Walter and

Mary E. (Mogridge) D.; grad. Batavia (N.Y.) Union Sch., 1899; A.B., Union Coll., Schenectady, N.Y., 1903; Ph.D., Cornell U., 1907; m. Belle E. Warner, Dec. 26, 1904; children—Doreen Maie (Mrs. Karl E. Gerlach), Sheila Claire (Mrs. Matthew B. Miller). Asst. instr. in chemistry, Cornell U., 1906-09; with Atlantic Refining Co., Phila., since 1909, as works chemist, 1909-14; asst. supt., 1914-18; chief chemist, 1918-22; asst. plant mgr., 1923-24; mgr. research and development dept., Phila., since 1924. Mem. Am. Chem. Soc., Am. Soc. Testing Materials (pres. 1938-39), Am. Petroleum Inst., Franklin Inst. Republican. Home: 836 Wilde Av., Drexel Hill, Pa. Office: 260 S. Broad St., Philadelphia, Pa.

DELCHAMPS, Harold John, elec. engring.; b. Mobile, Ala., Apr. 16, 1892; s. Willie Boyle and Mary (Black) D.; ed. Mobile Mil. Inst., 1907-10, Washington & Lee U., Lexington, Va., 1910-12; B.E., Union Coll., Schenectady, N.Y., 1915; m. Winifred Peckham Brown, Sept. 6, 1917; children—Harold John, Jr., Thomas Brown, Winifred Forbes. Asso. with engring. dept., Western Electric Co. and the successor of that dept., Bell Telephone Labs., continuously since 1919, exec. asst., Bell Telephone Labs., 1928-36, specifications engr. since 1936; professional engr., State of N.Y. since 1931. Served with U.S.N.R.F. during World War. Mem. Bd. Edn., Mountain Lakes, N.J., since 1935, pres. since 1937. Mem. Am. Inst. Elec. Engrs., N.Y. Acad. of Sciences, Chi Psi. Clubs: Mountain Lakes (Mountain Lakes); Morris County Engineers (Morristown). Home: 99 Pocono Rd., Mountain Lakes, N.J. Office: 463 West St., New York, N.Y.

de LEEUW, Adele Louise, author; b. Hamilton, O., Aug. 12, 1899; d. Adolph Lodewyk and Katherine (Bender) deL.; grad. Hartridge Sch. for Girls, Plainfield, N.J., 1918. Has followed profession as author since 1924; traveled extensively abroad and in Dutch East Indies; lecturer on travel and literary subjects since 1932. Dir. Pen and Brush Club, N.Y. City, 1938-41. Mem. Author's League of America, Poetry Soc. America, Plainfield Art Assn. Republican. Club: Monday Afternoon (Plainfield). Author: Berries of the Bittersweet (verse), 1924; The Flavor of Holland, 1928; Rika, 1932; Island Adventure, 1934; Year of Promise, 1936; A Place for Herself, 1937; Life Invited Me (verse), 1936; Doll Cottage (for pub. 1939). Co-author (with Cateau de Leeuw), Anim Runs Away, 1938. Contbr. stories, verse, gen. articles, travel articles to met. newspapers and mags. of nat. circulation, and to mags. in Eng. Home: 1024 Park Av., Plainfield, N.J.

de LEO de LAGUNA, Grace Mead Andrus, coll. prof.; b. East Berlin, Conn., Sept. 28, 1878; d. Wallace R. and Annis (Mead) Andrus; student Tacoma (Wash.) Pub. Schs., 1889-96; A.B., Cornell U., 1903, Ph.D., 1906; m. Theodore de Leo de Laguna, Sept. 9, 1905 (died 1930); children—Frederica Annis, Wallace. Reader in philosophy, Bryn Mawr (Pa.) Coll., 1907-08, asso. in philosophy, 1911-16, asso. prof. philosophy, 1916-29, professor since 1929. Mem. Am. Philos. Assn., (v.p. 1932; Eastern Div.), Am. Assn. Univ. Profs., Am. Assn. Univ. Women, Phi Beta Kappa. Democrat. Club: Fullerton (Phila.). Author: Speech: Its Function and Development, 1927; co-author (with Theodore de Leo de Leguna): Dogmatism and Evolution; articles in philos. and psychol. jours. Home: 221 Roberts Rd. Office: Bryn Mawr Coll., Bryn Mawr, Pa.

DELK, Edwin Heyl, clergyman; b. Norfolk, Va., Aug. 15, 1859; s. Edwin Holoman and Margaret (Esher) D.; desc. Roger Delk, of Va., 1647; M.A., Central High Sch., Phila., Pa., 1880; D.D., Luth. Theol. Sem., Gettysburg, Pa., 1901; m. Ella Buehler, of Gettysburg, Pa., 1884; m. 2d, Adeline Grim Miller, of Phila., Jan. 19, 1905. Ordained Luth. ministry, 1882; pastor Schoharie, N.Y., 1882-85, Hagerstown, Md., 1885-1902, St. Matthew's Ch., Phila., 1902-29; lecturer on theology, Temple U. Pres. Phila. Federation of Chs., 1910-14; trustee Luth. Theol. Sem., Luth. Deaconess' Motherhouse. Mem. Acad. Polit. and Social Science. Republican. Club: Union League. Author: Three Vital Problems, 1909; The Need of a Re-Statement of Theology, 1911; Life of Charles S. Albert, D.D., 1912. Home: 39 W. Phil-Ellena St., Philadelphia, Pa. *

DELLA CIOPPA, Thomas Edmund, clergyman; b. Villa Volturno, Italy, Aug. 8, 1876; s. Gaetano and Carmela Natale della Cioppa; student Collegio Attanasio, Naples, 1889-91, Collegio Telesino (Benevento), 1891-95; Seminario Metrapolitana, Capua, 1895-1900 (Ph.D., S.T. D.); m. Neila H. Gill, April 20, 1911; children—Hector Edmund, Guido Gill, Constance Neila, Thomas Bridges, Marius Noel, Lawrence Clifton; m. 2d, Delores Priori, Jan. 6, 1932. Came to U.S., 1907, naturalized, 1919. Ordained to ministry of R. C. Ch., 1900; received into ministry of Episcopal Ch., 1909; rector of St. Nicholas of Falchi (Archdiocese of Capua), 1900-07; teacher of Latin and history, Biblical Sem., New York, 1907-08; rector Ch. of L'Emmanuello, Phila., 1908-29; vicar of L'Emmanuello (St. Elizabeth's Ch.), Phila., since 1929. Home: 1606 Mifflin St., Philadelphia, Pa.

DELLINGER, John Howard, physicist; b. Cleveland, O., July 3, 1886; s. John Pfohle and Catherine (Clark) D.: Western Reserve U., Cleveland, 1903-07; A.B., George Washington U., 1908; Ph.D., from Princeton, 1913; D.Sc., George Washington University, 1932; m. Carol Van Benschoten, Oct. 11, 1909. Instr. physics, Western Reserve U., 1907-07; physicist. Nat. Bur. of Standards, since 1907; chief of Radio Sect. since 1918; chief engr. Federal Radio Commission, 1928-29; chief of radio sect. of research div., Aeronautics br., Dept. of Commerce, 1926-34. Del. Conf. of Interallied Tech. Com. on Radio Communication, Paris, 1921; mem. tech. staff Conf. on Limitation of Armament, Washington, D.C., 1921; tech. adviser Internat. Radio Conf., 1927; U.S. del. Internat. Tech. Cons. Com. on Radio Communications, The Hague, 1929, Copenhagen, 1931, and chmn. U.S. delegation, Lisbon, 1934, and Bucharest, 1937; rep. at Internat. Electrotechnical Commn., Italy, 1927, and Scandinavia, 1930; tech. adviser Internat. Telecommunication Conf., Madrid, 1932. Fellow Inst. Radio Engrs. (v.p. 1924; pres. 1925); mem. Am. Geophys. Union (sect. terrestrial magnetism and electricity), Internat. Scientific Radio Union (v.p.), Washington Acad. Sciences, Am. Engring. Standards Com. (sectional committees on electrical units and radio), Associazione Italiana di Aerotecnica (hon.), Alpha Tau Omega, Phi Beta Kappa. Mem. Unitarian Church. Arthur: (with others) The Principles Underlying Radio Communication (govt. publ.), 1918; Radio Instruments and Measurements (govt. publ.), 1918; Radio Handbook (with L. E. Whittemore), 1922; also many articles and treatises on radio and elec. topics. Home: 618 Pickwick Lane, Chevy Chase, Md.

DELLINGER, Martin C., pres. K-D Mfg. Co.; b. Lancaster, Pa., May 13, 1895; s. A. M. and Elizabeth (Cope) D.; student high sch., 1911-13; m. Inez Estelle Knox, July 20, 1933; 1 son, Michael Alan. Dept. foreman A. M. Dellinger Co., Lancaster, Pa., 1915-18, v.p. and dir. since 1937; junior partner K-D Mfg. Co., Lancaster, Pa., 1918-34, pres. since incorporation, 1934; treas. and dir. D.M.D., Inc.; treas. Gabani Co., Inc., Baltimore, Md. (a Md. corpn.); dir. Howett Labs., all Pa. corpns. in Lancaster, Pa. Mem. Lancaster Co. Branch of Pa. Assn. for the Blind (sec. since 1927). Elk. Club: Lions' (Lancaster, Pa.). Home: 900 Grand View Boul. Office: 526 N. Plum St., Lancaster, Pa.

DELLPLAIN, Morse, pres. Am. Street Illuminating Co.; b. New Orleans, La., Sept. 17, 1880; s. Frank X. and Mary (Ryckman) D.; student Genesee Wesleyan Sem., Lima, N.Y., 1898-1901, Syracuse (N.Y.) U., 1901-03; m. Grace Perry, Feb. 28, 1910. Salesman-engr. Westinghouse Electric Mfg. Co., 1903-09; power engr., Syracuse Lighting Co., 1909-18; v.p. and gen. mgr. Northern Ind. Pub. Service Co., later pres., 1918-34; pres. and dir. Am. Street Illuminating Co., Phila., since 1934; dir. and v.p. Welsbach Street Illuminating Co.; pres. and dir. Kitson Co. Mem. Am. Inst. Elec. Engrs., Am. Soc. Mech. Engrs., Illuminating Engring. Soc. Republican. Baptist. Mason (K.T., Shriner). Clubs: Midday, Merion Cricket (Phila); Ill. Athtletic (Chicago); Engineers (New York). Home: 305 Airdale Rd., Rosemont, Pa. Office: 1500 Walnut St., Philadelphia, Pa.

Del MANZO, Milton Carl Edward, educator; b. Milwaukee, Wis., Dec. 29, 1889; s. Ernest and Bertha (Bachmann) Del M.; U. of Dubuque (Ia.), 1909-13; B.A., State U. of Ia., 1915, M.A., 1921, Ph.D., 1924; m. Mildred R. Dewees, Aug. 28, 1916; children—Donald Dewees, Jessie Elizabeth. Teacher, high sch., Dallas Center, Ia., 1916-18, supt. schs., 1918-20; same, West Branch, Ia., 1920-21; prin. University Schs., State U. of Ia., 1922-24; prof. edn. U. of Kan., and supt schs., Lawrence, 1924-25; asso. Internat. Inst., 1925-32, asso. director since 1932; asst. prof. edn., Teachers Coll., Columbia, 1927, prof. since 1928, provost since 1929. Dir. Parents' Mag. Mem. N.E.A., Coll. Teachers of Edn., Phi Delta Kappa, Kappa Delta Pi. Author: The Financing of Education in Iowa (with others), 1924; Public School Bonding in Iowa, 1926. Contbr. on edn. Home: 501 W. 120th St., New York, N.Y.; and York Road, New Hope, Pa.

DeLONG, Berton Henry, metallurgist; b. Taylor, N.Y., Aug. 16, 1885; s. Willis H. and Bertha (Brown) D.; A.B., Cornell U., 1909; m. Nellie E. Bean, Aug. 16, 1911; children—William B., Charles B. (dec.), Margaret E., Allen R.; m. 2d., Irene M. Boyer, June 16, 1925. Chemist, The Stanley Works, New Britain, Conn., 1909-10; metallurgist, The Carpenter Steel Co., Reading, Pa., 1911-19, chief metallurgist since 1919; dir. Reading, (Pa.) Savings & Loan Assn. Mem. Iron and Steel Inst. of Great Britain, A.A.A.S., Am. Soc. of Testing Materials, Am. Soc. for Metals, Soc. of Automotive Engrs. Republican. Methodist. Elk. Club: Reading (Pa.) Country. Home: 33 Howard St., West Lawn, Pa. Office: 101 W. Bern St., Reading, Pa.

DeLONG, Calvin Martin, clergyman; b. Topton, Berks Co., Pa., July 7, 1876; s. Joseph S. and Mary H. (Yoder) DeL.; B.S., Keystone State Normal Sch., Kutztown, Pa., 1897; A.B., Franklin and Marshall Coll., Lancaster, Pa., 1900 D.D., 1933; student Theol. Sem. of Reformed Ch. in U.S., Lancaster, Pa., 1900-03, U. of Chicago Divinity Sch., summer 1901; m. Bessie Mae Bauscher, May 5, 1906; 1 dau., Betty Emma Mary. Teacher pub. sch., Lehigh and Berks Cos., Pa., 1894-96; teacher of Latin, Franklin and Marshall Acad., Lancaster, Pa., 1901-02; supply pastor St. Stephens Reformed Ch., Reading, Pa., summer 1902; ordained to ministry of New Goshenhoppen Reformed Ch., 1903, and since then pastor, East Greenville, Pa.; teacher, Perkiomen Sch., Pennsburg, Pa., spring 1916; prin. East Greenville High Sch., 1918-19. Treas. Goshenhoppen Classis of Reformed Church since 1927; pres. Eastern Synod of Reformed Church, 1939. During World War served as four-minute man, mem. Liberty Loan Com., and chmn. War Chest Com. for East Greenville. Trustee Perkiomen Sch. for Boys; mem. Home Mission Bd. of Reformed Ch. Mem. Pa. German Soc., Phi Beta Kappa. Republican. Home: 310 Third St., East Greenville, Pa.

DE LONG, Irwin Hoch, Orientalist; b. near Bower's, Pa., May 11, 1873; s. Adam B. and Caroline (Hoch) D.; Keystone State Normal Sch., Pa., 1889-91; Muhlenberg Coll., Pa., 1894-95; A.B., Franklin and Marshall Coll., 1898, A.M., 1901, D.D., 1928; grad. Theol. Sem. of Ref. Ch. in U.S., 1901; instr. Latin and Roman history, Perkiomen Sem., a., 1901-02; D.B., U. of Chicago, 1902; Thayer fellow Am. Sch. for Oriental Study and Research in Palestine, Jerusalem, 1902-03; studied univs. of Berlin and Strassburg, Germany, 6 semesters; Ph.D., Strassburg, 1905; U. of Chicago, summer quarter, 1906; m. Mary R. Meister, of Lancaster, Pa., Oct. 10, 1907; children—Margaret Eleanor (Mrs. William G. Carrington), Dorothy Meister, Emilie Meister, May Meister. Has traveled extensively in Palestine, trans-Jordanic countries, Egypt, Asia Minor, Greece and Constantinople, 1902-03, in Europe, 1897, 1903-06; ordained ministry Ref. Ch. in U.S., 1909; instr. O.T. science, 1906-09, prof. Hebrew and O.T.

science, 1909—dean, 1921—, librarian, 1909-22, Theol. Sem. Ref. Ch. in U.S. Mason (32°). President, Classis of East Pennsylvania, 1921-22. Mem. Soc. Bibl. Lit. and Exegesis, Am. Oriental Soc., Deutsche Morgenländische Gesellschaft, Vorderasiatisch-Aegyptische Gesellschaft, Die Deutsche Orient-Gesellschaft, Zentralstelle für Deutsche Personen und Familiengeschichte, Pa. German Soc. Author: Die hebraeische Praepositioneר ב, 1905; Early Occurrences of the Family Name De Long in Europe and in America, 1924; Descendants of Otto Henrich Wilhelm Brinkman, 1925; Pennsylvania Gravestone Inscriptions, 1925; The Lineage of Malcolm Metzger Parker from Johamies Delang, 1926; Pioneer Palatine Pilgrims, 1928; My Ancestors, 1930; An Early Nineteenth Century Constitution of a Union Church, 1931; An Early Eighteenth Century Reformed Church—a Contribution to Church and Family History, 1934. Home: Lancaster, Pa.

DE LONG, Roy Allen, lawyer; b. Northumberland, Pa., June 24, 1888; s. George A. and Emma (Jane) De L.; B.S., Bucknell U., Lewisburg, Pa., 1911, A.M., 1921, Ph.B., 1912; LL.B., Temple U. Law Sch., Phila., 1920; m. Marion Myers, Mar. 10, 1923; children—Marion Myers, Eleanor Estella, George David. Engaged as head dept. music, Berry Schs., Rome, Ga., 1914-15; instr. bus. law and mathematics, High Sch., Danville, Pa., 1915-16; head history dept., Pa. Mil. Coll., Chester, Pa., 1916-18, Irving Sch., Tarrytown, N.Y., 1918-19, Harrisburg Acad., Harrisburg, Pa., 1920-21; head bus. law dept., Phila. Bus. Coll. and instr. law, Temple U. Law Sch., 1921-23; admitted to Pa. bar, 1921; served as U.S. Atty. Prohibition Unit, at Phila., 1923-26; in gen. practice of law at Phila. since 1926, asso. with D. J. Myers, Phila., since 1926. Mem. Kappa Delta Phi. Republican. Lutheran. Mason (K.T., 32°) Grotto, Odd Fellows. Club: Lambskin. Contbr. articles to mags. Home: 109 S. 37th St. Office: 4304 Walnut St., Philadelphia, Pa.

DE LONG, Vaughn Russell, supt. of schs.; b. Corning, O., Jan. 24, 1903; s. George Washington and Addie (Moore) D.; grad. Dresden (O.) High Sch., 1918; A.B., Ohio Wesleyan U., Delaware, O., 1923; A.M., Ohio State U., Columbus, O., 1929; student New York U., 1937; m. Doris Britt, July 3, 1922; children—Merrill Britt, Lynnette (dec.). Teacher chemistry, High Sch., Ashland, Ky., 1923-26, prin. of elementary sch., Ellwood City, Pa., 1929-32, supt. of schs., 1932-38; supt. of schs., Oil City, Pa., since 1938. Mem. N.E.A., Pa. State Edn. Assn., Am. Assn. Sch. Adminstrs. Republican. Methodist. Club: Oil City Kiwanis. Contbr. articles on ednl. subjects to mags. Home: 101 Bissell Av. Office: Spring St., Oil City, Pa.

DE LONG, Warren Benner, counselor on tax problems; b. Allentown, Pa., July 8, 1883; s. Alfred and Sarah Elizabeth (Benner) De L.; ed. Peirce Bus. Coll., Temple U. (Phila.); m. Myrtle May Salter, Phila., Pa., June 30, 1914; 1 dau., Marie Louise. Engaged as instr. in pub. schs., Lehigh Co., Pa., 1899; in real estate business on own acct., 1906, securities brokerage until 1916; founded Tax Audit Co., counselor on tax problems, Phila., and propr. since 1917. Mem. Pa. Acad. of Fine Arts. Republican. Mason (K T., 32°, Shriner). Clubs: Union League, Penn Athletic, Philadelphia Country (Phila.); Congressional Country (Washington, D.C.). Ardent horse lover and fancier of saddle horses for show and pleasure purposes. Home: Beechwood Park, Ardmore. Office: Packard Bldg., Philadelphia, Pa.

DE LORENZO, William, lawyer; b. Serino, Italy, Dec. 28, 1886; s. Alessio and Maria C. (De Feo) DeL.; came to U.S., 1899, naturalized, 1903; student Columbia, 1907; LL.B. with honor, N.Y. Law Sch., 1909; m. Aida M. Pavignano, Oct. 6, 1927; children—William, Jr., Gioia Beatrice, Cornelius Alexis. Engaged in teaching at night pub. sch., 1907-12. Admitted to N.J. bar as atty., 1909, as counselor, 1912; admitted to Calif. bar, 1926; admitted to practice before Supreme Ct. of the U.S., 1932; mem. firm De Lorenzo & Garofalo; mem. N.J. Ho. of Assembly, 1922-24; counsel Health Bd., Hackensack, 1922-24; recorder City of Hackensack, 1924-26; dir. and atty. Rochelle Park Bank, Citizens Bldg. & Loan Assn., All-America Investment Co.; counsel Rural Bldg. & Loan Assn. Trustee North Jersey Rapid Transit Co. Mem. Am., N.J. State, Bergen Co. bar assns. Republican. Roman Catholic. Odd Fellow. Clubs: Kiwanis, Elks. Home: 87 Summit Av. Office: 15 Main St., Hackensack, N.J.

DEMAREE, David Ralph, investment banker; b. Newport, Pa., July 27, 1892; s. Benjamin Franklin and Margaret Jane (Stambaugh) D.; grad. Harrisburg (Pa.) Acad., 1912; A.B., Princeton U., 1916; m. Jane Catherine Baughman, Feb. 6, 1926. Bond salesman Phila. office Nat. City Bank, 1916-17; accountant Federal Shipbuilding Co., Newark, N.J., 1920-21; salesman Tide Water Oil Co., Reading, Pa., 1921-26; pres. Blue Seal Oil Co., Reading, 1926-31; special rep. Socony Oil Co., Pittsburgh, 1931-33; v.p. K. W. Todd Co., investment bankers, Pittsburgh, since 1933; pres. and chmn. of bd. Carnegie Metals Co., Pittsburgh, since 1934; v.p. and dir. Pa. Housing Co., Jeanette Glass Co.; pres. and dir. Carnegie-Bote Mining Co., Mexico. Served in 1st O.T.C., Ft. Niagara, May-Aug. 1917; commd. 2d lt. Q.M.C., U.S. Army, 1917, 1st lt.; 1919; with A.E.F., Feb. 1918-Sept. 1919. Mem. Dial Lodge Club, Princeton U. Republican. Episcopalian. Mason. Clubs: Longue Vue Country (Pittsburgh); Iron City Fishing (Georgian Bay, Ont.). Home: Morewood Gardens. Office: 2212 Oliver Bldg., Pittsburgh, Pa.

DEMAREST, Charles Sidney, research engr.; b. Baldwin, Mich., Aug. 15, 1886; s. Sidney Bryant and Georgianna (Reed) D.; E.E., U. of Minn., 1911; m. Ethel West, June 26, 1915; children—Paul West, Ruth. Engaged as engr. in engring. dept., Am. Telephone & Telegraph Company, New York City, 1911-19, engineer, dept. development and research, 1919-34; switching research engr., Bell Telephone Labs., N.Y. City, since 1934; has had responsible charge of important tech. developments for telephone systems, principally in long distance field; awarded a number of patents in this field. Fellow Am. Inst. Elec. Engrs. Mem. Am. Phys. Soc., Inst. Radio Engrs., Theta Xi. Republican. Presbyn. Home: 192 Unadilla Rd., Ridgewood, N.J. Office: 463 West St., New York, N.Y.

DEMAREST, William Henry Steele, clergyman, educator; b. Hudson, N.Y., May 12, 1863; s. David D. and Catherine L (Nevius) D.; A.B., Rutgers, 1883, A.M., 1886; grad. New Brunswick (N.J) Theol. Sem., 1888; D.D., Rutgers, 1901, New Brunswick Univ., 1916; LL.D., Columbia Univ., 1910, Union Coll., Schenectady, N.Y., 1911, U. of Pittsburgh, 1912; unmarried. Ordained Ref. Ch. in Am. ministry, 1888; pastor Walden, N.Y., 1888-97, Catskill, N.Y., 1897-1901; prof. ch. history, New Brunswick Theol. Sem., 1901-06; president Rutgers College, 1905-24; president New Brunswick Theological Seminary, 1925-35, emeritus since 1935. Member Holland Soc., Huguenot Soc., Phi Beta Kappa, Delta Phi. Author: History of Rutgers College. Compiler: New Brunswick (1680-1930), 1932. Club: University (New York). Home: New Brunswick, N.J.

de MERLIER, Franz, artist; b. Ghent, Belgium, Oct. 28, 1878; s. Edouard and Elizabeth (Van Troostenberghe) deM.; student art schs. Bruges, Ghent and Bruxelles, Belgium, 1884-1900; came to U.S., 1900, naturalized, 1939; m. Elisa Thevenot, Nov. 26, 1910; children—Edouard, Josephine (Mrs. Paul Randolph White). Lithographic artist and painter since 1894; worked in Bruges, Ghent and Brussels, Belgium, 1894-1900; newspaper artist at Louisville, Ky., 1900-01, at Cincinnati, O., 1901-02, Phila., Pa., 1902-14; newspaper artist, Phila., 1914-32; painter murals and country and farm subjects; Pocopson, Pa., since 1932; represented by decors of Lititz Community Theatre, Claridge Hotel, Atlantic City, West Allegheny Theatre, Great Northern Theatre, Phila., decors in foyer of new auditorium West Chester Pub. Schs. Mem. Am. Federation of Arts, Chester Co. Art Assn., Wilmington Soc. of Fine Arts, Cercle Labeur of Brussels. Awarded hon. mention and purchase for permanent collection, Wilmington Soc. Fine Arts, 1935; first prize, Chester Co. Art Assn., 1937; first award and purchase, West Chester, Pa., 1939. Roman Catholic. Club: Pen and Pencil (Phila.). Home: Pocopson, Pa. Office: 925 N. Darien St., Philadelphia, Pa.

DEMMLER, Oscar William, music educator; b. Pittsburgh, Pa., Feb. 25, 1892; s. Edward W. and Minnie A. (Mayer) D.; ed. Columbia Coll., 1917-18, Pittsburgh Mus. Inst., 1915-21; Mus. B., U. of Pittsburgh, 1933; A.M., Carnegie Inst. Tech., 1937; unmarried. Began as pvt. music teacher, 1911-13; organist Trinity Luth. Ch., Pittsburgh, 1913; teacher music Fifth Av. High Sch., 1913; spl. supervisor instrum. music in schs. of Pittsburgh since 1937; prof. music edn., Duquesne U. Grad. Sch., since 1938. Served as pvt. inf., U.S.A., 1918-19, with A.E.F. in France. Treas. Music Teachers Nat. Assn. since 1927. Home: 217 Dalzell Av., Ben Avon, Pittsburgh, Pa. Office: 341 Bellefield Av., Pittsburgh, Pa.

DEMMY, Maurice Clinton, supervising prin. of schs.; b. Bainbridge, Lancaster Co., Pa., Sept. 1, 1888; s. Christian C. and Mary (Ruthrauff) D.; grad. Bainbridge (Pa.) High Sch., 1907; grad. Millersville (Pa.) Teachers Coll., 1911; B.S., Valparaiso (Ind.) U., 1914; A.B., Lebanon Valley Coll., Annville, Pa., 1927; A.M., Columbia, 1932; m. Aurora Phalm, Dec. 23, 1916; 1 dau., Arlyne Phalm. Began as teacher, Bainbridge, Pa., 1907; teacher, Bainbridge (Pa.) High Sch., 1911-13, Manheim, Pa., 1914-15; grade school prin., Enhaut, Pa., 1916-18; supervising prin., Schaefferstown, Pa., 1918-22, Morrisville, Pa., 1922, Lititz, Pa., since 1922. Dir. Library Assn.; pres. Lancaster Co. (Pa.) Forensic and Music League. Republican. Mason (32°, Shriner). Clubs: Rotary (past pres.), Chamber of Commerce (v.p.). Home: 234 S. Spruce St. Office: Orange and Cedar St., Lititz, Pa.

de MOLL, Carl, architect, engineer; b. Philadelphia, Pa.; s. Charles G. and Josephine (Bower) de M.; m. Mary Hitchner, Oct. 21, 1916; children—Charlotte, John David, Louis. Mem. of firm, The Ballinger Co., architects and engrs.; registered engr. N.Y., Pa., Va.; registered architect N.Y., N.J., Pa., D.C., Va., W.Va. Mem. A.I.A., Am. Soc. C.E. Mason. Clubs: Sketch, Art, Engineers (Phila.). Home: 221 Park Av., Swarthmore, Pa. Office: 105 S. 12th St., Philadelphia, Pa.

DEMPWOLF, Frederick Greiman, architect; b. York, Pa., June 29, 1885; s. John Augustus and Sarah Anna (Greiman) D.; student York County Acad., York Collegiate Inst., Mass. Inst. Tech., Ecole des Beaux Arts (Paris); m. Mary Keesey Stair, Oct. 20, 1927; children—Sarah Helen, Mary Stair. Designer Marshall & Fox, Chicago, architects, 1911-13, Hewitt & Bottomley, New York, architects, 1913-14; returned to York, 1914, becoming associated with father in gen. practice of architecture, operating under own name since death of father, 1926; dir. York Trust Co., York Chem. Works, Pittsburgh Glatfelter Co. (Spring Grove). Served as 1st lt., later cap., U.S. Army, 1917-19. Trustee York Collegiate Inst.; v.p. Children's Home of York. Mem. York Engring. Soc. Mason. Clubs: Country, Rotary, Lafayette (York). Home: 904 S. George St. Office: Cassat Bldg., York, Pa.

DeMUTH, Peter Joseph, ex-congressman; b. Pittsburgh, Pa., Jan. 1, 1892; s. John and Barbara (Dietrich) De M.,; B.S. in civil engring., Carnegie Inst. Tech., 1914; m. Elizabeth Quirk, of Pittsburgh, Oct. 30, 1928; children—Joan Mary, Peter James and Barbara Kathryn. Mem. 75th Congress (1937-39), 30th Pa. Dist. Served as engring. ensign, U.S.N., during World War. Mem. North Side Chamber of Commerce, Am. Legion, Alpha Tau Omega. Democrat. Catholic. K.C., Eagle. Home: 930 Davis Av., Pittsburgh, Pa.

DENDE, John, editor, publisher; b. Serock, Poland, Jan. 23, 1885; s. Jacob and Apolonja (Skalska) D.; student Pultusk Coll., Poland; m. Marie Borowska, Nov. 15, 1914; children—Edmund, Edward, Henry, Richard, Raymond, Wanda, Eleonore. Came to U.S., 1911, naturalized, 1917. Conducted bakery, 1912-28; purchased Republika (published by Ignacy Haduck, Wilkes-Barre), 1918, removed same to Scranton; purchased Gornik Pensylwanski, 1920; combined both newspapers and changed name to Republika-Gornik Pensylwanski (Republic Pennsylvania Miner) and so continues. Mem. board of dirs. St. Stanislas Polish Orphanage, Nanticoke, Pa. Member Scranton Chamber of Commerce, Polish Nat. Alliance, Polish Roman Catholic Union, Polish Union of America, Polish Falcons Alliance (hon. pres. 15th dist.), Polish Am. Soc. of Lackawanna Co. (v.p.), Polish Veterans Assn. (hon. pres.), Polish Am. Polit. Federation of Lackawanna Co. (founder, pres.). Club: Polish American Citizens Political. Address: 409 Cedar Av., Scranton, Pa.

DENGLER, Calvin Franklin, educator; b. Coplay R.F.D. 1, Pa., Jan. 13, 1891; s. Charles and Jane Amanda (Heintzelman) D.; student Keystone State Normal, Kutztown, Pa., 1912-14; B.S., Muhlenberg Coll., Allentown, Pa., 1925; A.M., Teachers Coll., Columbia U., 1930; grad. student Rutgers U., New Brunswick, N.J., summer and extension, 1936-39; m. Lottie May Gruver, June 23, 1916; children—Merritt Gruver, Marjorie Eleanor. Engaged in teaching, rural schs., Pa., 1908-12; prin., Gouldsboro, Pa., 1914-16; teacher, high sch., Emaus, Pa., 1916-17; supervising prin., pub. schs., Bath, Pa., 1917-18, Shickshinny, Pa., 1918-26 and 1928-29; asst. county supt., Luzerne Co. Pa., 1926-28; supervising prin., Palmyra, N.J., 1930-36; supervising prin. schs., Carteret, N.J. since 1936. Mem. N.E.A., Am. Assn. Sch., Administrs., N.J. Edn. Assn., Progressive Edn. Assn., Nat. Soc. Study of Edn., N.J. Shoolmasters Club (Newark), Phi Delta Kappa. Lutheran. Home: 514 Rahway Av., Woodbridge. Office: High School Bldg., Washington Av., Carteret, N.J.

DENGLER, Robert Ewing, prof. classical langs., Pa. State Coll. Address: State College, Pa.

DENIG, Fred, engineer; b. LaPorte, Colo., Dec. 20, 1896; s. George Jacob and Gertrude (Baum) D.; Chem. E., Rensselaer Poly. Inst., Troy, N.Y., 1919, M.S., 1921; m. Anne Roslyn Branagan, Feb. 12, 1924. Asst. to chief technologist H. L. Doherty & Co., New York City, 1919-20; chem. engr. The Koppers Constrn. Co., 1921-29, gen. supt., 1930-31, v.p., research div., 1934-36; supt. Phila. Coke Co. 1929-30; v.p. The Koppers Research Corpn., 1931-34; v.p. engring. and constrn. div., Koppers Co., Pittsburgh, since 1936. Clubs: Pittsburgh Field, University (Pittsburgh). Author of numerous articles on gas purification, etc., to engring. jours. Home: 4601 Bayard St. Office: Koppers Bldg., Pittsburgh, Pa.

DENISE, Garret Augustus, banker; b. Tennent, Manalapan Twp., Monmouth Co., N.J., Apr. 27, 1876; s. Sidney and Sarah Jane (Van Derveer) D.; ed. public schools, Freehold, N.J., and vicinity; unmarried. Began as clerk in D. V. Perrine's store, 1890; with Central Nat. Bank of Freehold, N.J., since Mar. 14, 1901, beginning as bookkeeper, became cashier, 1906, dir., 1916, pres. trust officer and dir. since 1922; executor-trustee of several estates. Mem. Monmouth Co. Hist. Assn. (trustee, chmn. finance com., treas.), Monmouth Co. Bankers Assn. (pres. 1920-21), N.J. Bankers Assn. (pres. 1936-37). Mem. Second Reformed Ch. Mem. Holland Soc. of N.Y. Home: 18 E. Main St. Office: Central National Bank, Freehold, N.J.

DENMAN, David Nelson, mem. Pa. State Ho. of Rep.; b. Greensburg, Pa., May 20, 1895; s. Everett Nelson and Mary English (Kuhns) D.; A.B., Washington & Jefferson Coll., Washington, Pa., 1917; student U. of Pittsburgh Sch. of Edn., 1923, Law Sch., 1919-21; m. Mary Catherine Thompson (atty.), June 30, 1924; children—David Nelson III, Richard Everett. Teacher, Greensburg (Pa.) High Sch., 1919-22, Latrobe (Pa.) High Sch., 1922-26; admitted to practice before Pa. Supreme Court, 1923, U.S. Dist. Court, 1927, Pa. Superior Court, 1931, U.S. Supreme Court, 1937, and in practice at Latrobe, Pa., since 1926; mem. Pa. State Ho. of Rep. since 1939. Served in U.S. Army Air Service during World War. Mem. Westmoreland Co. Bar Assn., Am. Legion, Kappa Sigma, Delta Theta Phi. Republican. Presbyterian. Home: 720 Walnut St. Office: 308 Main St., Latrobe, Pa.

DENMAN, Mary Thompson (Mrs. David Nelson D.), lawyer; b. Pittsburgh, Pa., June 1, 1899; d. Frank Leslie and Mary Elizabeth (Love) Thompson; A.B., U. of Pittsburgh, 1920; LL.B., U. of Pittsburgh Law Sch., 1922; m. David Nelson Denman, June 30, 1924; children—David Nelson III, Richard Everett. Admitted to Pa. bar, 1922, Pa. Supreme Ct., 1922, U.S. Dist. Ct., 1927, Pa. Superior Ct., 1931, U.S. Supreme Ct. 1937; asso. with title dept. Potter Title and Trust Co., Pittsburgh, 1922-24; engaged in gen. practice of law at Latrobe since 1924; served as mem. Pa. Ho. of Rep., 1931-32; made study and compilation for Pa. Dept. Welfare of all poor laws ever enacted by Pa. Legislature, 1934. Mem. bd. dels. Pa. Fed. of Merit System; mem. bd. dirs. Taxpayers Forum of Pa. Mem. Nat. Fed. Business and Professional Women's Club (nat. chmn. of legislation), Internat. Fed. Business and Professional Women's Club (mem. legislative com.), Business and Professional Women's Club of Latrobe, Mortarboard, Delta Delta Delta, Phi Delta Delta. Republican. Presbyn. Club: Women's of Latrobe. Home: 720 Walnut St. Office: Realty Bldg., Latrobe, Pa.

DENMEAD, Garner Wood, v.p. New Amsterdam Casualty Co. Home: 4214 Wickford Road, Roland Park. Office: 227 St. Paul St., Baltimore, Md.

DENNEY, John DeWitt, M.D.; b. Columbia, Pa., July 27, 1892; s. DeWitt Clinton and Clara (Patton) D.; grad. Columbia (Pa.) High Sch., 1909; A.B., Cornell U., 1913, A.M., 1915; M.D., U. of Pa., 1919; post grad. work in surgery, Cook County Hosp., Chicago, Ill.; m. Anne Libhart, 1920; 1 son, John DeWitt. Surgeon since 1920; now gen. surgery at Columbia (Pa.) Hosp.; dir. Columbia Trust Co., Keeley Stove Co., Mt. Bethel Cemetery Co. Served as sergt. Med. Corps, U.S. Army, with A.E.F., 1917-18. Dir. Bd. of Edn., Columbia; mem. standing com. Episcopal Diocese of Harrisburg. Mem. A.M.A., Pa. State Med. Soc., Lancaster Co. Med. Soc., Med. Club of Phila. Episcopalian. Mason, Elk, Lions. Author of papers read before Pa. med. socs. Home: 32 S. 2d St. Office: 30 S. 2d St., Columbia, Pa.

DENNEY, Oswald Evans, officer U. S. Pub. Health Service; b. Smyrna, Del., July 21, 1885; s. Robert and Henrietta (Holding) D.; M.D., U. of Pa., 1913; D.T.M., U. of Philippines, 1915; m. Bertha Oliva Harris, Oct. 27, 1920; children—Robert Harris, Philip Holding, Oswald Evans, Mary Elizabeth Anne. Resident physician at Philippine General Hospital, 1913-14, San Lazaro Hospital, Manila, 1914-15; resident physician and later chief, Culion Leper Colony, P.I., 1915-19; exec. officer 4th dist. U.S. Pub. Health Service, 1919-20; med. officer in charge Nat. Leprosarium, Carville, La., 1921-35; chief quarantine officer Panama Canal Zone since 1936. Fellow Am. Coll. Physicians; mem. A.M.A., Am. Soc. Tropical Medicine, Assn. Mil. Surgeons of U.S., Internat. Leprosy Assn., Am. Legion, Phi Chi, Sigma Xi. Democrat, Presbyn. Clubs: Marine Hospital Golf (Carville), Fort Amador Golf. Author numerous papers on tropical medicine, particularly on Asiatic cholera and leprosy. Home: Smyrna, Del. Address: Balboa Heights, Canal Zone.

DENNEY, William du Hamel, ex-governor; b. Dover, Del., March 31, 1873; s. William and Anna (du Hamel) D.; ed. Wesleyan Collegiate Inst., Dover; m. Alice Godwin, Oct. 27, 1917; children—Anna, Alice Godwin. Formerly in fire ins. business; dir. Farmers Bank. Mem. Del. Ho. of Rep., 1904-06 (speaker); del. Rep. Nat. Convs., 1908, 24, 28; mem. Rep. State Com. since 1920, chmn., 1926-27; gov. of Del., term 1921-25; chmn. Rep. State Conv., 1924-26. Mem. Am. Legion. Episcopalian. Mason. Home: Dover, Del.

DENNIS, Charles James, lumber and building; b. Bradford, Pa., Feb. 16, 1886; s. William Henry and Margaret (Andrew) D.; student Bradford (Pa.) High Sch., 1901-04; m. Alta Weller, Jan. 28, 1918; 1 dau., Jane Loraine. Began as office clerk, 1904; since 1904 with Tuna Mfg. Co., lumber yard, planing mill, building contractors, Bradford, pres. and gen. mgr. since 1933. Dir. Bradford Library Assn. Republican. Baptist. Mason, Elk. Home: 24 Sanford St. Office: 70 Mechanic St., Bradford, Pa.

DENNIS, George Palmer, editor, propr. newspaper; b. Ventura, Calif., May 9, 1877; s. Frank Bowdoin and Fanny (Walton) D.; ed. high sch. and bus. coll., Ventura, Calif., grad. 1897; m. May Sexsmith, 1907; children—Dorothy May, Edward Philip, Marjorie Sexsmith, Kathryn Sexsmith, Elizabeth Sexsmith, Walton Palmer, George Foster. Began as newspaper reporter, corr. met. papers and Asso. Press, Ventura, Calif., 1897-1903; rep. Ventura Co. at World's Fair, St. Louis, 1904, Portland, Ore., Expn., 1905; various positions in Calif. to 1912; editor, pub., and propr. Hightstown Gazette weekly newspaper, printing and publishing, Hightstown corr. met. newspapers, Hightstown, N.J. since 1912. Served as sec. Bd. Edn., Hightstown, N.J., 1918-29; borough clk., Borough of Hightstown since 1918. Republican. Presbyn. Home: 248 Stockton St. Office: Gazette Bldg., Hightstown, N.J.

DENNIS, George R., Jr., mem. law firm Dennis & Haller. Address: Frederick, Md.

DENNIS, Paul Gill, clergyman; b. Newark, N.J., Aug. 25, 1887; s. Charles A. and Julia B. (Vansant) D.; A.B., Wesleyan U., Conn., 1910; B.D., Drew Theol. Sem., Madison, N.J., 1913; grad. student Columbia U., 1912-13; D.D., Wesleyan U., 1935; m. Effie M. Ditmars, April 8, 1913 (dec.); children—Robert Paul, Frank Ditmars; m. 2d, Mrs. A. Lorene Newman, May 10, 1928. Joined Newark Conf., M.E. Ch., 1913; pastor, Alpine, N.J., 1913-14; Cranford, 1915-17, Hackensack, 1918-22, Belleville, 1923-27, East Orange, 1928-30; dist. supt., Paterson Dist., 1931-38; pastor First M.E. Ch., Plainfield, N.J. since 1939; pres. State Council of Chs. since 1937; vice-pres. State Council Religious Edn. since 1938; mem. exec. com. Federal Council Chs. of Christ in America. Trustee Drew Univ., Madison, N.J. Mem. Delta Kappa Epsilon. Home: 610 Central Av., Plainfield, N.J.

DENNIS, Samuel K., judge; b. Worcester, Md., Sept. 28, 1874; s. Samuel K. and Sally Handy (Crisfield) D.; prep. edn., Blair Acad., Blairstown, N.J.; LL.B., U. of Md., 1903; LL.D., Washington Coll., Chesterton, Md., 1931; Litt.D., Loyola Coll., Baltimore, 1938; m. Helen Gordon Moore, June 1, 1911. Sec. to gov. of Md., 1900-04; practiced in Baltimore since 1904. Mem. Ho. of Dels., 1904; U.S. atty. Dist. of Md., 1915-20; chief judge, Supreme Bench of Baltimore since Sept. 1928; prof. equity jurisprudence, U. of Baltimore Law Sch.; dir. Eutaw Savings Bank. Was dir., sec., sec.-treas. and pres. Md. Tuberculosis Sanatorium for 23 yrs. Democrat. Presbyn. Mem. Am., Md. State (pres.), and Baltimore bar assns., Md. Hist. Soc. (v.p.). Club: Maryland. Home: 100 Ridgewood Rd., Roland Park, Md. Address: Court House, Baltimore, Md.

DENNIS, William Varney, prof. rural sociology; b. Dover, N.H., Sept. 21, 1879; s. William Brown and Leah Helen (Goodwin) D.; A.B., Haverford (Pa.) Coll., 1902; ed. U. of Pa. Grad. Sch., 1912-14; m. Louise Martha Haines, Dec. 25, 1902; children—Elizabeth Comfort (Mrs. William Carl Calhoun), William Varney, Harlan Goodwin (dec.), Joseph Henry II. Began as teacher, athletic coach, Friends' Acad., Moorestown, N.J., 1902-10; head English Dept., athletic coach, Friends' Select Sch., Phila., 1910-19; dir. vocational sch., supervisor twp. schs., Spring Mills, Pa., 1919-21; asst. prof. then prof. rural sociology Pa. State Coll. since 1921. Mem. Am. Assn. Univ. Profs., Rural Sociology Soc., Kappa Delta Pi, Alpha Tau Alpha, Pi Gamma Mu, Gamma Sigma Delta, Alpha Zeta. Republican. Methodist. Home: 50 Glenland Apts., State College, Pa.

DENNISON, Boyd Coe, prof. of elec. engring.; b. Hanibal, N.Y., Sept. 9, 1881; s. William and Emma (Coe) D.; grad. Binghamton (N.Y.) High Sch., 1900; M.E., Cornell U., 1904,

M.M.E., 1910; m. Ada Miriam Pease, July 26, 1910; children—Boyd Coe, Richard Wheeler, Marcia Pease (dec.). Engr. Gen. Electric Co., Schenectady, N.Y., 1904-05; instr. in elec. engring., Cornell U., 1905-10; with Carnegie Inst. of Tech., Pittsburgh, since 1910, successively as instr., asst. prof., asso. prof., and since 1928 prof. of elec. engring.; elec. consultant of Morris Knowles Co., Inc., engrs. Mem. Am. Inst. Elec. Engrs., Soc. for Promotion of Engring. Edn., Am. Assn. Univ. Profs., Phi Kappa Psi, Alpha Phi Omega, Sigma Xi, Tau Beta Pi, Eta Kappa Nu. Republican. Christian Ch. (vice-pres. East End Ch.). Author: Electrical Problems (with H. H. Norris), 1910; Experimental Electrical Engineering (with V. Karapetoff), 1933 and 1939; Electrical Laboratory Experiments, 1936. Home: 1005 Lancaster St. Office: Carnegie Institute of Technology, Pittsburgh, Pa.

DeNOON, Anna L(aura), coll. prof.; b. Ravenswood, W.Va., Dec. 6, 1887; d. John W. and Laura (Hoyt) DeN.; A.B., Marietta Coll., Marietta, O., 1909; A.M., Columbia U., 1930. Instr. mathematics, Marshall Coll., Huntington, W.Va., 1909-20, asso. prof., 1920-39, prof. mathematics since 1939. Mem. Nat. Council of Mathematicians, Am. Assn. Univ. Women, Phi Beta Kappa, Chi Beta Phi. Democrat. Episcopalian. Club: Woman's of Huntington. Home: 843 12th Av., Huntington, W.Va.

DENT, Herbert Warder, judge; b. Grafton, W.Va., April 16, 1880; s. Marmaduke H. and Mary (Warder) D.; A.B., West Va. Univ., Morgantown, 1904; LL.B., W.Va., Univ. Law Coll., 1905; m. Mary M. Welch, Oct. 25, 1924; 1 dau., Mary Virginia. Admitted to W.Va. bar, 1905 and engaged in gen. practice of law at Grafton since 1905, served as judge 19th Jud. Circuit of W.Va. since 1932. Served as 2d lt. inf., U.S.A., during World War. Mem. W.Va. Bar Assn., Kappa Alpha, Delta Chi, Am. Legion. Democrat. Presbyn. Club: Grafton Country. Home: 804 W. Main St., Grafton, W.Va.

DENTON, David William, executive; b. Cadoxton, S.Wales, Sept. 11, 1875; s. James Thomas and Eliza (Thomas) D.; student Grade Sch., Waunerlwydd, Wales, 1881-87, Gowerton Intermediate Sch., Gowerton, 1888-92; came to U.S., 1894, naturalized, 1899; m. Florence Courtney, July 29, 1894; children—Gertrude Mary (Mrs. Elias Frederick Mengel), James Courtney. Began as worker, Rochester (Pa.) Tumbler Co., glass factory, 1894-95, selector, 1895-97, glazer, 1897-1900; foreman of finishing dept., H. C. Fry Glass Co., Rochester, Pa., 1900-02, gen. supt. of dept., 1902-10, asst. to v.p. in charge of sales, 1910-24; pres. Rochester (Pa.) Bldg. & Loan Assn. since 1937; 1st v.p. and dir. Rochester (Pa.) Thrift Corpn. since 1927; 1st v.p. and dir. Penn-Beaver Hotel, Rochester, Pa., since 1926; sec.-treas. and director Beaver Falls Thrift Corpn. since 1935. Treas. Beaver Co., Pa., 1924-28, pres. Rochester (Pa.) Borough Council, 1908-12; mem. Beaver Falls (Pa.) Bd. of Trade since 1937. Dir. Rochester (Pa.) Gen. Hosp., mem. adv. bd. Salvation Army, Rochester, Pa. Republican. Baptist (pres. bd. of govs., First Baptist Ch., Rochester, Pa.). Mason (Rochester, Pa., Lodge 229, Pittsburgh Consistory, New Castle, Pa., Consistory, 32°). Home: Denton Plan, Rochester, Pa. Office: Federal Title & Trust Co., Beaver Falls, Pa.

DENWORTH, Hugh Frederick, banker; b. Williamsport, Pa., Dec. 12, 1891; s. James B. and Mary E. (Friedel) D.; grad. West Chester (Pa.) State Normal Sch., 1911; A.B., Swarthmore (Pa.) Coll., 1916; M.A., U. of Pa., 1918; m. Verna Slade, Jan. 2, 1920; 1 dau., Dorothy Slade. Dep. Federal Food Administrator of Phila. under Jay Cooke, 1917-19; dir. of sales and advertising, Crane Ice Cream Co., Phila., 1919-22; asst. to pres., Bank of North America, Phila., 1922-23, asst. treas., 1923-28; v.p. United Security Life Ins. & Trust Co. of Pa., Phila., 1928, pres., 1929-31; pres. United Security Trust Co., Phila., 1929-31; acting mgr. Phila. Loan Agency, Reconstruction Finance Corpn., 1933-34; v.p. Land Title Bank & Trust Co., Phila., since 1934; v.p. and dir. Bldg. Operation Holding Co., Title Holding Co.; sec. and mem. bd. of dirs. Cranberry Co., Medford, N.J.; mem. bd. dirs. Quaker City Federal Savings & Loan Assn. Mem. bd. of trustees, Phila. Yearly Meeting of Friends; mem. bd. of mgrs., Swarthmore (Pa.) Coll. Republican. Soc. of Friends. Mason (West Chester, Pa., lodge). Clubs: Union League (Phila.); Rolling Green Golf (Media, Pa.). Home: 211 Elm Av., Swarthmore, Pa. Office: Broad and Chestnut Sts., Philadelphia, Pa.

DENWORTH, Katharine Mary, educator; b. Williamsport, Pa.; d. James Buchanan and Mary Elizabeth (Friedel) D.; A.B., Swarthmore (Pa.) Coll., 1914, Joshua Lippincott fellow, 1924-25; A.M., Columbia, 1921, Ph.D., 1927; unmarried. Instr. State Normal Sch., West Chester, 1914-16; co-prin. Friends High Sch., Moorestown, N.J., 1916-18, prin., 1918-20; headmistress Stevens Sch., Germantown, Phila, Pa., 1920-25; president Bradford (Mass.) Junior Coll. since 1927. Pres. Am. Assn. of Junior Colls., 1937-38, vice pres., 1936-37; pres. N.E. Junior Coll. Council, 1934-36. Mem. Phi Beta Kappa, Kappa Delta Pi, Mortar Board, College Club of Boston, Am. Assn. University Women (dir. Boston Br., 1930-32), Haverhill Women's Club, Soc. for Study of Edn., Nat. Assn. of Prins. of Schools for Girls, Dept. of Secondary Sch. Prins., School Administrators, New England Assn. of Colls. and Secondary Schs., A.A.A.S. Research on effect of length of school attendance on mental and ednl. ages, pub. in yearbook of Nat. Soc. for Study of Edn., 1928. Protestant. Home: Swarthmore, Pa. Address: Bradford, Mass.

DENWORTH, Raymond Keenan, lawyer; b. Williamsport, Pa., Apr. 13, 1887; s. James B. and Mary E. (Friedel) D.; A.B., Swarthmore (Pa.) Coll., 1911; LL.B., U. of Pa. Law Sch., 1917; m. Hilda Lang, Dec. 27, 1926; children—Mary Elizabeth, Hilda Lang, Raymond Keenan, Jr., Ann Berlinger. Admitted to Pa. bar, 1917; engaged in gen. practice of law at Philadelphia; asso. with firm Drinker, Biddle and Reath since 1921. Served as maj., Ordnance Dept., U.S. Army, during World War. Mem. Am., Pa., and Phila. bar assns., Phi Kappa Psi, Delta Sigma Rho, Phi Delta Phi, Order of Coif. Republican. Mem. M.E. Ch. Mason. Clubs: Union League of Philadelphia, Lawyers, Constitutional. Home: 301 Elm Av., Swarthmore, Pa. Office: 1429 Walnut St., Philadelphia, Pa.

De PIERRO, M. Salvador, lawyer; b. Freeland, Pa., Apr. 4, 1886; s. Frank and Anna (Bush) De P.; grad. Freeland (Pa.) High Sch.; student Bucknell U., Lewisburgh, Pa., 1910-12; LL.B., U. of Pa., 1914; m. Frances Thomas, Nov. 22, 1917; children—Dorothy Ann, Frank Thomas, Salvatore (dec.), Lucille; m. 2d, Kate Briehof, Nov. 22, 1926. Admitted to Pa. bar, 1915, and since practiced in Freeland; solicitor borough council and borough and township schools since 1917; 1st asst. dist. atty., 1922-29; special dep. atty. gen., 1935-38; dir. and solicitor Citizens Bank of Freeland, Freeland Bldg and Loan Assn., Conyngham Nat. Bank, Conyngham Water Works. Former trustee Hazleton State Hosp. Republican. Roman Catholic. Elk, Eagle. Club: Kiwanis (Hazleton, Pa.). Home: 934 Washington St. Office: 536 Center St., Freeland, Pa.

DEPP, Walter Mark, clergyman; b. Punxsutawney, Pa., Nov. 13, 1893; s. Philip Bush and Anna Louisa (Neff) D.; grad. Punxsutawney High Sch., 1911; A.B., Allegheny Coll., Meadville, Pa., 1916; D.D., 1931; S.T.B., Boston U. Sch. of Theology, 1918; m. Ethel Beatrice Foskett, of Worcester, Mass., May 15, 1917; children—William Fraser, Philip Mark, Doris Mae, Beatrice Louise. Ordained to ministry M.E. Ch., 1916; successively pastor St. Paul's Ch., Sykesville, Md., Rognel Heights Ch., Baltimore, Market St. Ch., Winchester, Va., Towson, Md., Calvary Ch., Washington, D.C., St. Mark's Ch., Baltimore, Md., Christ Ch., Pittsburgh, Pa., since 1936. Served as chaplain U.S. Army during World War. Trustee Baxter Sem. Mem. Delta Sigma Rho. Mason. Clubs: Criterion, Quiz, Theological Circle (Pittsburgh). Home: 311 S. Graham St., Pittsburgh, Pa.

DEPPELER, John Howard, mech. engring.; b. New York, N.Y., Feb. 19, 1885; s. John Jacob and Ada (Bouquet) D.; M.E., Stevens Inst. Tech., 1906; m. Minnie Hartwig, Oct. 9, 1909; 1 son, John Howard, Jr. Employed as engr. N.Y.C.&H.R. R.R. Co., 1906-08; engaged in bus. as J. H. Deppeler Co., 1908-12; chief engr. and works mgr., Metal & Thermit Corpn., mfrs. welding apparatus and supplies, New York, N.Y., since 1912; sec. Am. Murex Co. Mem. Am. Welding Soc. (past pres., dir. and mem. exec. com.), Am. Soc. Mech. Engrs., Phi Sigma Kappa. Republican. Clubs: Carteret (Jersey City); Country (Arcola); Machinery (New York). Home: 825 Boul. East, Weehawken, N.J. Office: 120 Broadway, New York, N.Y.

DEPTA, Michael, M.D.; instr. U. of Pittsburgh; mem. staff Pittsburgh Hosp.; asso. mem. staff Presbyn. and St. Francis Hosps. Address: 500 Penn Av., Pittsburgh, Pa.

DERBY, Harry L., corpn. official; b. Afton, N.Y., July 3, 1882; pres. Am. Cyanamid and Chemical Corpn., Ariz. Chem. Co.; v.p. and dir. Am. Cyanamid Co., Southern Alkali Corporation; director National Mfrs. Assn.; chmn. exec. com. Manufacturing Chemists Assn. Home: 47 Porter Pl., Montclair, N.J. Office: 30 Rockefeller Plaza, New York, N.Y.

de REGT, Albert Chester, univ. prof.; b. Clinton, N.Y., Nov. 24, 1877; s. Cornelis and Sarah J. (Nelson) de R.; A.B., Hamilton Coll., Clinton, N.Y., 1900, A.M., 1904; m. Madge VanDeventer McDowell, June 14, 1905 (dec.). Employed with U.S. Geol. Survey, 1900-01; with N.J. State Geol. Survey, and chemist, 1901-03; consultant to Franklin Furnace and Mines Co., 1901-08; instr. chemistry, Rutgers Coll., New Brunswick, N.J., 1902-06, asso. prof. chemistry, since 1906. Mem. Nat. Geog. Soc., Emerson Literary Soc., New Brunswick Hist. Soc., Phi Beta Kappa, Phi Lambda Upsilon. Republican. Dutch Ref. Ch. Mason. Home: 37 Huntington St., New Brunswick, N.J.

DEREUME, Raymond John, consul; b. Jumet, Belgium, June 5, 1889; s. Auguste and Agnes (Frere) D.; student Jumet (Belgium) High Sch., Jumet, Belgium, 1900-04, University Coll., London, Eng., 1914-16; m. Amelia Eva Derr, Oct. 24, 1936; 1 son, August. Hon. consul for Belgium at Pittsburgh since 1929; owner and mgr. Raymond Dereume, export-import firm, Punxsutawney, Pa., since 1922. Served as pvt., U.S. Army, during World War. Treas. St. Vincent De Paul Conference, Punxsutawney, Pa. Mem. Consular Assn. (Pittsburgh), Am. Legion. Roman Catholic (trustee S.S. Cosmos and Damian R.C. Ch., Punxsutawney, Pa.). Home: 420 E. Mahoning St., Punxsutawney, Pa. Office: 705 Grant St., Pittsburgh, Pa.; Spirit Bldg., Punxsutawney, Pa.

DERICK, Clarence George, chemist; b. Sutton, Quebec, Can., Oct. 29, 1883; s. Wesley Talmage and Emma Delia (Ryan) D.; S.B., Worcester Poly. Inst., 1906; M.S., U. of Ill., 1909, Ph.D., 1910; m. Edith Lillian Blowe, Aug. 27, 1907; children—Clarence George, Kenneth Earl, William Blowe, Edith Dawne, Hazel Gertrude (dec.), Lincoln, Goldie L., June Phyllis. Research asst. to Prof. Moore, Mass. Inst. Tech., 1906-07, to Prof. W. A. Noyes, U. of Ill., 1907-08; asst. in organic chemistry, 1908-10, asso., 1910-13, asst. prof., 1913-16, U. of Ill., dir. of research, Schœllkopf Aniline & Chem. Co., Inc., Buffalo, N.Y., 1916-17, Nat. Aniline & Chem. Co., Buffalo, 1917-21; v.p. By-Products Steel Corpn., Buffalo, 1924-25; pres. Derick Laboratories, Inc., Buffalo, since 1925; cons. practice. Consulting chemist Bureau of Mines, at Edwood Arsenal br., Buffalo, during World War, in charge research on mustard gas. Mem. Nat. Research Council, 1919-22. Fellow A.A.A.S., Am. Inst. of Chemists; mem. Am. Chem. Soc., Sigma Xi, Phi Lambda Upsilon. Republican. Contbr. upon organization of chemical research; articles dealing with chemistry in organic and physical fields; patents in dye and zinc salts fields. Home: Sewaren, N.J.*

DERICKSON, Samuel Hoffman, prof. biology; b. Perry Co., Pa., Apr. 9, 1879; s. Henry Benner and Lizzie Naomi (Hoffman) D.; student Lebanon Valley Acad., 1897-98; B.S. Lebanon Valley Coll., 1902, M.S., also hon. D.Sc., 1925;

student Johns Hopkins U., 1903 and 1910; also student biol. labs., Cold Spring Harbor, N.Y. and Bermuda Islands; m. Jennie Vallerchamp, of Harrisburg, Pa., June 28, 1905; children—George Vallerchamp, Mary Elizabeth (dec.). Actg. prof. biology, Lebanon Valley Coll., 1903, prof. since 1907, actg. pres., 1912, treas. and trustee since 1918. Fellow A.A.A.S.; mem. Bot. Soc. of America, Am. Fern Soc., Pa. Acad. Science (pres.), Am. Soc. Zoölogists (asso.). Republican. Mem. United Brethren Ch. Mason (past master). Home: 473 E. Main St., Annville, Pa.

DE RIVAS, Damaso, bacteriologist; b. Dira, Granada, Nicaragua, Dec. 11, 1874; s. Mauricio and Carmen (Aleman) deR.; student Nat. Inst. of Nicaragua and Guatemala; B.S. in biology, U. of Pa. Med. Sch., 1899, M.S., 1908, Ph.D., 1910; m. Rosa Reinish, 1904; children—Carlos Theodore, Ana Rosa, Maria Luisa. Co-worker, Pasteur Inst., Paris, France, 1899-1900; asst. Koch Inst., 1900-02; bacteriologist filtration bur., Phila., 1904-06; with Pa. State Dept. of Health, 1907-10; asst. dir. dept. of comparative pathology, Sch. of Tropical Medicine, since 1910, asst. prof. of parasitology since 1917; prof. Grad. Sch. of Medicine since 1922; pathologist, Friends Hosp., Frankford, Pa., since 1916; with Skin and Cancer Hosp., Phila., since 1922, Pan-Am. Hosp., New York, 1927, Pa. Dept. of Health since 1933. Mem. Malaria and Tropical Diseases Commn., Italy, 1900-02; pres. Nicaragua delegation Pan-Am. Scientific Congress, Washington, D.C., 1906-07; Pa. del. Internat. Congress of Tuberculosis, Washington, D.C., 1908; Quinto Congreso de Medicina Nacional, Cuba, 1921; Nicaragua del. and hon. pres. Congreso Medico Latino-Americano, Havana, 1922; Nicaragua del. Pan-Am. Med. Congress, Havana, 1928-29; U. of Pa. del. to Mexico, 1931. Mem. A.M.A., Soc. of Parasitology, Soc. of Tropical Medicine, Pathological Soc. of Phila., Societe de Pathologie exotique, Paris (correspondent) Coll. of Physicians of Phila. Author: Textbook on Human Parasitology, 1930; Clinical Parasitology and Tropical Medicine, 1935; also various articles on bacteriology, pathology, etc. Mem. of scientific excursion for study of tropical diseases of Africa and the organization of schs. of tropical medicine and parasitology in Europe, 1922. Originator of the inter-intestinal thermal therapy method for treatment of parasitic and other infections of the intestines. Home: 106 Plumstead Av., Lansdowne, Pa. Office: 1831-3 Chestnut St., Philadelphia, Pa.

DERMITT, H. Marie, exec. sec. Civic Club of Allegheny Co.; b. Pittsburgh; parents Edward H. and Katherine (Goldthorpe) D.; ed. Bishop Bowman Inst. (P.E.). Engaged as exec. sec. Civic Club of Allegheny Co., Pa., at Pittsburgh, Pa.; has acted as sec. for a number of important civic movements and orgns.; apptd. by Sec. Stimson as U.S. Rep. to Internat. Congress on Housing and Town Planning in Rome, 1929; mem. Pres. Hoover's Conf. on Home Bldg. and Home Ownership, 1931; initiated Nat. Stephen C. Foster Day. Served as vice chmn. Allegheny Co. Council of Nat. Defense during World War. Dir. Am. Planning and Civic Assn.; sec. Nat. Assn. Civic Secs. Republican. Episcopalian. Home: 5724 Darlington Rd. Office: Hotel William Penn, Pittsburgh, Pa.

DeROY, Mayer S.; demonstrator Dept. of Orthopedic Surgery, U. of Pittsburgh; asso. mem. orthopedic staff Falk Clinic; mem. orthopedic staff St. Francis Hosp.; asso. orthopedist Presbyn. and Montefiore Hosp. Address: 519 Liberty Av., Pittsburgh, Pa.

DERR, Amnon Immanuel, railroad official; b. Cumberland, Md., Mar. 15, 1885; s. Clarence Victor and Emma Myrtie (Flury) D.; grad. Allegheny High Sch., Cumberland, Md., 1903; student Mountain State Business Coll., 1903-04; m. Helen L. King, Sept. 2, 1908; children—Clarence King, Virginia Lee. Began as stenographer with B.&O. R.R., 1904; sec. to gen. mgr. Morgantown & Kingwood R.R. Co.; auditor, traffic mgr., and gen. mgr., Morgantown & Wheeling Ry., Morgantown, W.Va.; asso. with Pittsburgh & W.Va. Ry. Co., Pittsburgh, Pa., since 1924, as asst. to vice-pres., asst. to pres., sec. and treas., then vice-pres. and sec. since 1938; sec., treas., and dir. Acme Coal Cleaning Co. Republican. Presbyn. Mason (K.T., 32°, Shriner). Clubs: Traffic, Railway, Traffic and Transportation. Home: 2723 Espy Av., Dormont. Office: Wabash Bldg., Pittsburgh, Pa.

DERR, Ralph Becker, chemist; b. Milton, Pa., Aug. 15, 1895; s. Charles L. and Dora M. (Becker) D.; B.S. in Chem. Engring., Bucknell U., Lewisburg, Pa., 1917; m. Sarah A. Hester, Oct. 11, 1919; children—Dorothy Wilhelmina, Ralph Becker. At Laurel Hill (L.I., N.Y.) Research Labs., Gen. Chem. Co., 1917-21, works chemist in charge insecticide research, Baltimore, Md., 1921-24, in charge insecticide research, Laurel Hill, L.I., N.Y., 1924-26; asst. chief chem. development div. Aluminum Research Labs., Aluminum Co. of America, New Kensington, Pa., 1926-29, chief since 1929. Mem. Visiting Engrs. Advisory Com., Bucknell U. Mem. Am. Chem. Soc., Am. Inst. Chem. Engrs., Phi Kappa Psi. Presbyn. (elder First Presbyn. Ch., Oakmont, Pa.), Mason (Consistory, Shriner). Club: Hill Crest Country. Author of numerous articles on aluminum, its uses, and new aluminum products, etc. Holder more than 20 patents on new alumina products, insecticides, thermal insulation, water purification, aluminum solders and fluxes, Zeus cigarete holder, production of absolute alcohol. Home: 534 Tenth St., Oakmont, Pa. Office: Aluminum Research Laboratories, New Kensington, Pa.

DERRICK, William Harrison, supervising prin. of schs.; b. Grampian, Pa., Nov. 15, 1888; s. James Calvin and Viola Jennie (Rowles) D.; student Penn Twp. High Sch., Grampian, Pa., 1906-08; A.B., Pa. State Coll., 1929, M. Edn., 1934; m. Cartha McCracken, Dec. 16, 1914. Teacher of grade sch., Grampian, Pa., 1908-14, Portage, Pa., 1915-17; teacher and prin. of Portage High Sch., 1918-33; supervising prin. of schools, Portage, since 1934. Auditor of Portage Borough, 1918-30. Mem. Supervising Prins. of Cambria Co. (pres. 1936-37), Kappa Phi Kappa. Republican. United Brethren Ch. Mason (32°, Shriner). Club: Acacia (Williamsport, Pa.). Home: 506 Prospect St., Portage, Pa.

DERSHUCK, J. R.; editor and pub. Plain Speaker and Standard Sentinel. Address: 23 N. Wyoming St., Hazleton, Pa.

DERY, D(esiderius) George, silk mfr.; b. Baja, Austria; s. Maxmilian G. and Joan (Latinov) D.; grad. Vienna Textile Acad., 1884; A.B., St. Mary's Acad., Vienna, 1885; m. Helen Meszaros, of Moov, November 21, 1891 (dec.); children—Joan (dec.), George M., Charles F., Helen. Came to America, 1887; supt. silk mills in New York, 1888-92; began mfg. in own name, at Paterson, N.J., 1892; built silk mill in Pa., at Catasauqua, 1897; owner of 42 factories in N.J., Pa., Mass. and Va.; retired 1936. Mem. Silk Assn. America (dir.), Nat. Assn. Mfrs., A.A.A.S., Met. Mus. Art. Republican. Lutheran. Mem. Chamber Commerce U.S.A. Clubs: Republican, Manhattan, Aldine, Engineers', Army and Navy (New York); Manufacturers' (Philadelphia); Hamilton (Paterson, N.J.); etc. Author: Under the Big Dipper, 1916; Jean Kressley, 1919. Home: Catasauqua, Pa.

DESCHLER, Lewis, parliamentarian; b. Chillicothe, O., Mar. 3, 1905; s. Joseph Anthony and Lilian Louise (Lewis) D.; Miami U., Oxford, O., 1922-25, George Washington U., 1925; M.P.L., J.D., National U., 1932; m. Virginia Agnes Cole, Jan. 18, 1931; children—Lewis II, Joan Mari. Admitted to D.C. bar in 1934, U.S. Supreme Court, 1937. Apptd. messenger at speakers table, U.S. Ho. of Rep., Dec., 1925; apptd. asst. parliamentarian U.S. Ho. of Rep., Jan. 1927, parliamentarian since Jan. 1928. Served as asst. sec. Am. Group of Interparliamentary Union Con., London, July 1930. Mem. Delta Tau Delta. Editor: House Rules and Manual, 1929, 31, 34, 37, 39. Home: Chillicothe, O.; (winter) Bethesda, Md. Address: Speakers Rooms, House of Rep., Washington, D.C.

de SCHWEINITZ, Paul, bishop Moravian Ch.; b. Salem, N.C., Mar. 16, 1863; s. Robert de and Marie Louise von (Tschirschky) S.; A.B., Moravian Coll. and Theol. Sem., Bethelehem, Pa., 1882, B.D., 1884 (D.D., 1907); studied U. of Halle, Germany, 1885-86; m. Mary C. Daniel, Bethlehem, Pa., Jan. 27, 1887; children—Karl, Mrs. Helena Couch, Dorothea, Mrs. Louise Darrow. Ordained Moravian ministry, 1886; home missionary, Northfield, Minn., 1886-90; pastor Nazareth, Pa., 1890-98; sec. of Missions of Moravian Ch. in America, 1898-1930. Treas. governing bd. Northern Province Moravian Ch., v.p. Bd. Ch. Extension, treas. Soc. of U.B. for Propagating the Gospel among the Heathen, treas., trustee Moravian Coll. and Theol. Sem., all 1893-1935; advisory trustee Moravian Sem. and Coll. for Women, 1898-1930; treas. of three Moravian Corporations, 1898-1937; treasurer of Moravian Missions, 1898-1937. Consecrated a bishop Moravian Church, Mar. 14, 1937. Trustee St. Luke's Hospital (Bethlehem, Pa.), since 1915. Vice-pres. Moravian Hist. Soc.; pres. Huguenot Soc., Pa., 1927-29; a founder Pa. German Soc. (pres. 1919-20). Del. World's Missionary Conf., New York, 1900, Missionary Conf., Edinburgh, Scotland, 1910; pres. Fgn. Missions Conf. of N.A., 1917-18; chmn. exec. bd. Fgn. Missions Conf. of N.A., 1920-22; mem. Internat. Missionary Council, 1920-28. Dir. Lehigh Valley Nat. Bank, Bethlehem, Pa., 1916; mem. bd. mgrs. Farmers' Fire Ins. Co. of Upper and Lower Saucon Townships since 1922, pres. since 1930; also dir. sundry local corpns. Hon. mem. Phi Beta Kappa (Beta of Pa., Lehigh U.; pres., 1929-30). Mem. numerous interdenominational coms. and commns. Republican. Clubs: Wingolf, Rotory, Torch. Home: Bethlehem, Pa.

DETJEN, Louis Reinhold, univ. prof.; b. Algoma, Wis., Feb. 27, 1884; s. Hermann and Bertha (Radünz) D.; student pvt. and pub. schs., Algoma, Wis., 1890-1905; B.S. (in agr.), U. of Wis., Madison, Wis., 1909; M.S., N.C. State Coll., Raleigh, N.C., 1911; m. Edith Marian Lefavour, Aug. 28, 1917; children—Lois Marion, Edson Reinhold. Instr. and asst. in horticulture, N.C. State Coll., Raleigh, N.C., 1909-20; asso. prof. and asso. horticulturist, U. of Del., Newark, Del., 1920-28, prof. of horticulture since 1928. Fellow A.A.A.S., Am. Soc. Hort. Science; mem. Nat. Geographic Soc., Am. Genetic Assn., Phi Kappa Phi, Alpha Zeta. Presbyterian. Mason. Clubs: Univ. of Del. Faculty, Newark Garden (Newark, Del.). Author numerous papers on hort. subjects. Address: Old Oak Rd., Newark, Del.

DETLEFSEN, John A., physiology, genetics; b. Norwich, Conn., Sept. 12, 1883; s. George Detlef and Augusta (Nadolny) D.; Cambridge Latin Sch., 1898-1902; A.B., Dartmouth, 1908; A.M., Harvard, 1910, S.D., 1912; m. Ruth Sarah Atwell, of Evanston, Ill., June 18, 1914; children—John Detlef, Ruth Henrietta. Austin teaching fellow in zoölogy, Harvard, 1908-12; asst. prof. genetics, 1912-18, asso. prof., 1918-19, prof., 1919-22, U. of Ill.; prof. genetics, Wistar Inst. Anatomy, Phila., 1922-25; in charge sect. on mouth hygiene, Phila. Hosp. and Health Survey. Director Police School of Eastern Pa., 1935. Associate editor in chief Biological Abstracts, 1925. Mem. White House Conference on Child Health and Protection. Fellow A.A.A.S.; mem. Am. Soc. Zoölogists, Am. Soc. Naturalists, Am. Genetic Assn., Internat. Assn. Dental Research, Philadelphia Mouth Hygiene Assn. (exec. dir. since 1928), Ky. Acad. Sciences (hon.), Phi Beta Kappa, Sigma Xi, Phi Gamma Delta. Chevalier Order of Danneborg. Author: Studies on Cavy Species Cross, 1914. Contbr. to Our Present Knowledge of Heredity, 1926; also contbr. on heredity, species crosses, physiology, med. and dental biometry and etiology. Home: Swarthmore, Pa.

DETWEILER, George H., lawyer; b. Schuylkill Haven, Pa., June 25, 1883; s. Peter Christman and Luzetta Rebecca (Horn) D.; prep. edn. Temple Sch., Phila., 1903-05; LL.B., Temple U., 1907-11; m. Eleanore Gambel Middleton, of Phila., Jan. 25, 1908; children—Sylvia Eleanore, Robert Aaron. Clerk of P.&R. Ry., Reading, Pa., 1901-02, Phila., 1903, stenographer Pullman Co., Phila., 1903-13; admitted to Pa. bar, 1912; in practice, Phila., since Feb. 10, 1913. Mem. Am. Bar Assn., Pa. Bar Assn., Phila. Bar Assn., Internat. Assn. Insurance Counsel, Gen.

Alumni of Temple U. (1st v.p.). Republican. Methodist. Mason (K.T.; Dist. Dep. Grand Master, Pa.). Clubs: Union League, Lawyers, Cavest (Phila.). Home: 550 Riverview Rd., Swarthmore, Pa. Office: Lewis Tower, Philadelphia, Pa.

DETWILER, W. Frank; chmn. bd. Allegheny-Ludlum Steel Corpn. Address: Brackenridge, Pa.

DE VAULT, Samuel H., prof. agrl. economics; b. Jonesboro, Tenn., July 1, 1889; s. Fred W. and Laura (Martin) DeV.; A.B., Carson-Newman Coll., 1912, A.M., U. of N.C., 1915; student U. of Mo., 1916-17; Ph.D., Mass. State Coll., 1931; m. Nell C. Milton, Sept. 5, 1917. Prin. Conkling High Sch., Telford, Tenn., 1912-14; investigator in food products, U.S. Dept. Agr., 1918; special agt., Bureau of Census, 1919-22; specialist in transportation, U.S. Dept. Agr., June-Aug., 1922; asst. prof. of agrl. economics, U. of Md., 1922-25, prof. and head of dept. agrl. economics since 1926; special investigator in econ. studies, U.S. Chamber of Commerce, 1923; chmn. special advisory com., Census of Agr., since 1939; vice-pres. 1st Md. Bldg. & Loan Assn.; dir. Industrial Loan Co., Hyattsville, Md. Served with 89th San. Corps, U.S. Army, Camp Meade, Md., 1918-19. Mem. Nat. Assn. Marketing Officials, Am. Farm Econ. Assn., Am. Assn. Univ. Profs., Grange, Am. Farm Bureau, Pi Gamma Mu, Alpha Gamma Rho. Democrat. Baptist. Co-author: Vol. VI, 1920 Census Reports on Agr.; author of many agrl. Bulletins. Home: 200 University Drive, Hyattsville, Md. Office: Univ. of Maryland, College Park, Md.

DEVENS, Henry Fairbanks; chmn. bd. Oliver Iron & Steel Corpn. Home: 417 Park Av. Office: 1001 Muriel St., Pittsburgh, Pa.

DEVEREUX, Robert Trafford, physician; b. Phila., Pa., Aug. 17, 1881; s. Arthur Trafford and Betsy (Blyton) D.; Ph.G., Temple U., Phila., 1905, M.D., 1909; student Grad. Sch. of Medicine, U. of Pa., 1929-30; m. Blanche E. Salfingere, 1914 (divorced 1931); children—Mary Helena (wife of J. Clifford Scott, M.D.), Robert Trafford (dec.); m. 2d, Dorothea A. Kern, June 25, 1932. Resident physician, Temple U. Hosp., 1909-10, Phila. Gen. Hosp., 1910-11; physician-in-charge Home for Consumptives, Chestnut Hill, Pa., 1911-13; instr. in medicine, Temple U., 1913-17; pediatrician Chester Hosp., 1926-30, Chester County Hosp. since 1932. Served successively as 1st lt., capt., major Med. Corps, U.S. Army, with A.E.F. 16 months, participating in St. Mihiel and Meuse-Argonne, 1917-19. Fellow Am. Acad. Pediatrics; mem. A.M.A., Pa. Med. Soc., Chester Co. Med. Soc., Phila. Pediatric Soc., Phi Chi. Republican. Presbyterian. Mason. Address: 124 S. High St., West Chester, Pa.

DEVILBISS, Wilbur, educator; b. Johnsville, Md., Jan. 15, 1904; s. David M. and Ida Belle (Etzler) D.; A.B., Western Md. Coll., Westminster, Md., 1925; A.M., U. of Md., Baltimore, 1935; m. Bernice B. Ryan, Aug. 29, 1927. Teacher of science, high sch., 1925-32; prin. Brunswick (Md.) High Sch. since 1932; teacher of science, Middletown, Md., 1926-1931, Frederick, Md., 1931-1932. Republican. Reformed Ch. Mason. Club: Rotary (Brunswick, Md.). Home: Brunswick, Md.

DE VISME, Alice Williamson, prof. of French; b. Paris, France, Sept. 26, 1882; d. Edouard and Jenny (Tattet) de Visme; student Sorbonne, Paris, 1899-1904; m. Hiram Parker Williamson (known professionally as Henri Pierre Williamson de Visme, 1906, (died 1926); children—Rene de Visme Williamson, Eric de Visme Williamson. Founder with husband, Ecole du Chateau de Soisy-sous Etiolles (Seine-et-Oise), 1913, dir. 1913-19; co-dir. French Summer Sch., Middlebury, Vt., 1920; co-founder, Ecole Champlain, Ferrisburg, Vt., 1923; co-founder, French Inst., Pa. State Coll., 1924, co-dir., 1924-26; co-founder, Middlebury Coll. French House and dir., 1920-24; dir. Middlebury Coll. Chateau House since 1928; instr. Middlebury French Summer Sch. since 1921; asso. prof. of French lang. and lit., N.J. Coll. for Women, since 1927, founder French House and dir., 1928-35, head French dept., 1927-32. Mem. N.J. Modern Lang. Teachers Assn., Am. Soc. Teachers of French, Am. Assn. of Univ. Profs., Alliance Française de New Brunswick (pres. 1927-35, vice-pres. since 1935). Decorated Officier d'Académie (Palmes Académiques) 1931; Chevalier du Nichan-Iftikahr. Presbyterian. Home: 12 Suydam St., New Brunswick, N.J.

DE VITIS, Michael Angelo, teacher, author; b. Walls, Allegheny Co., Pa., Feb. 15, 1890; s. Anthony and Elizabeth (Martone) D.; grad. Union High Sch., Turtle Creek, Pa., 1907; A.B., Allegheny Coll., 1910; A.M., Washington U., 1914; m. Julia Margaret Sterrett, of Erie, Pa., June 27, 1911; 1 son, James S. Instr. Latin, Spanish and German, Kemper Mil. Sch., Boonville, Mo., 1910-11; instr. Spanish, Montclair (N.J.) Acad., 1911-12; head dept. French and German, El Paso (Tex.) High Sch., 1912-13; teaching fellow in Spanish, Washington U., 1913-14; instr. Spanish, Soldan High Sch., St. Louis, Mo., 1914-16; instr. Spanish and Portuguese, Bryan St. High Sch., Dallas, Tex., 1916-17; instr. Spanish and French, Fifth Ave. High Sch., Pittsburgh, Pa., 1917-24; asst. prof. Romance langs., U. of Pittsburgh, since 1924, asso. prof. of modern languages since 1927. Teacher of languages in summer schs. of Culver Mil. Acad., 1912, 14, 16; instr. Spanish, French and Italian, Coll. of Industrial Arts, Denton, Tex., summer 1917; lecturer and radio commentator on Italian and Hispanic culture and on world literature. Life member Am. Assn. Teachers of Spanish, Pa. Modern Lang. Association, Sigma Kappa Phi, Phi Beta Kappa; hon. mem. Royal Spanish-Am. Acad. Arts and Scs., 1920; corr. mem. Inst. d'Etudes Europeénnes et Mondiales. Knight-Commander (Comendador, con placa) Royal Order Isabella the Catholic, 1923. Author: A Spanish Grammar, 1915; A Spanish Reader, 1917; Brief Spanish Grammar, 1922. Editor: Valera's Pájaro Verde, 1918; Pérez Escrich's Fortuna and Tony, 1922; Parnaso Paraguayo, 1925, and Tesoro del Parnaso Hispano-Americano, 1927 (Maucci's Series of Parnasos Americanos, Barcelona), 1925. Co-Editor: Cervantes' El Cautivo (with Dorothy Torreyson), 1929; Easy Modern Spanish Lyrics (with same), 1930; Garcia Gutiérrez' El Trovador (with H. H. Vaughan), 1930; (with Dorothy Torreyson) Valera's Pepita Jimenez, 1934. Co-Author: (with Dorothy Torreyson) Tales of Spanish America, 1933. Editor: Short Spanish Stories, 1933. Home: 1311 La Clair Av., Swissvale, Pa.

DEVITT, William, physician; b. Manayunk, Phila., Pa., Sept. 18, 1874; s. William and Katherine (Blakeley) D.; ed. Bucknell U., Lewisburg, Pa., 1894-97; M.D., Medico-Chirurg. Coll., Phila., 1902; (hon.) D.Sc., Bucknell U., 1929; m. Laura Longacre, 1902 (died 1933); children—William, Helen (Mrs. Kenneth Butler); m. 2d, Lida Wendle, June, 1934. Engaged in gen. practice of medicine at Manayunk, Phila., Pa., 1902-20; founder Devitt's Camp, Allenwood, Pa., 1912 and phys. in charge since 1922. Fellow Am. Coll. Physicians; mem. Am. Bd. Internal Medicine, Am. Coll. Chest Physicians (past pres.), Internat. and Nat. Tuberculosis socs., Pa. Tuberculosis Assn. (pres.), Am., Pa. and Lycoming Co. med. assns. Republican. Baptist. Mason. Home: Devitt's Camp, Allenwood, Pa.

DEVLIN, Thomas Francis, M.D.; b. at Phila., Pa., Jan. 20, 1869; s. Thomas and Helen (Sanford) D.; A.B., LaSalle Coll., Phila., 1887; student Georgetown U., 1887-88; M.D., U. of Pa., 1891, post grad., 1891-92; m. Stella Hill, of Phila., May 29, 1905; children—Thomas Francis, John Joseph. Physician, Phila., since 1892; asso. with St. Mary's Hosp.; staff mem. Misericordia Hosp., Archbishop Ryan Memorial for Deaf-mutes; pediatrist; pioneer in endocrinology as applied to children. Dir. and partner with wife, Marydell Sch. for physically and mentally retarded children. Republican. Catholic. Home: Manor Av., Langhorne, Pa.

DEVOE, William Beck, lawyer; b. N.Y. City, Sept. 6, 1884; s. Charles and Anne Elizabeth (Beck) D.; A.B., Columbia, 1906; LL.B., New York Law Sch., 1908; m. Edith Guy Taylor, Oct. 6, 1908; 1 son, Alan Taylor. Admitted to N.Y. bar, 1908, to U.S. Supreme Court bar, 1924; law clk. in office Geo. D. Beattys, 1908-11; asst. to Abram I. Elkus, 1911-13; partner of Carl L. Schurz, 1913-24; gen. counsel Hamburg-Am. Line since 1924; counsel for German shipping companies in internat. arbitration U.S. and Germany to settle war claims, 1928-30; sec. and dir. Oceanic Service Corpn., N.J. Machine Corpn., Palm Fechteler & Co.; sec. and dir. United Am. Lines; dir. Domestic Fuel Corpn., UFA Films, Inc.; trustee estate of Carl L. Schurz. Mem. Am. Bar Assn., New York Law Inst., Am. Soc. Internat. Law, Delta Tau Delta Fraternity. Republican. Conglist. Club: Lawyers'. Author: Corporation Almanac, 1919; Where and How, a Manual of Corporate Procedure (8th edit.), 1928. Home: 356 N. Mountain Av., Montclair, N.J. and Meadowview, South Egremont, Mass. Office: 165 Broadway, New York, N.Y.

DE WALT, Horace Edward, surgeon; b. Sioux City, Ia., June 7, 1896; s. John Edward and Miriam Tealie (Underwood) DeW.; ed. Morningside Coll., Sioux City, Ia., 1914-16; M.D., U. of Pa. Med. Sch., 1920; grad. student U. of Vienna, and Royal Hungarian U. of Budapest, 1925-26; m. Ella May Langley, Sept. 27, 1926; children—John Edward, Peter Langley. Interne Allegheny Gen. Hosp., Pittsburgn, 1920-21, asst. surgeon, 1921-28, asso. surgeon since 1928. Called active from Med. Enlisted Res. Corps, U.S. Army, 1918. Fellow Am. Coll. Surgeons; mem. A.M.A., Med. Soc. State of Pa., Allegheny Co. Med. Soc., Pittsburgh Surg. Soc., Pittsburgh Acad. of Medicine, Ptolemy, Phi Rho Sigma. Republican. Mason (32°, Shriner). Clubs: University (Pittsburgh); St. Clair Country (Mt. Lebanon, Pa.). Home: 626 Osage Rd., Mt. Lebanon, Pa. Office: 7048 Jenkins Arcade, Pittsburgh, Pa.

DEWEES, Lovett, physician; b. Westtown, Pa., Jan. 17, 1880; s. Watson Wood and Sarah Lovett (Brown) D.; A.B., Haverford (Pa.) Coll., 1901; M.D., U. of Pa., 1907; m. Margaret Dakin, 1917 (died 1925); 1 son, Robert Lovett; m. 2d, Edith Hilles, 1931; children—Allen Hilles, Nancy Hilles. Interne, Germantown Hosp., Phila., 1907-08, Pa. Hosp., Phila., 1908-10; interne Bryn Mawr (Pa.) Hosp., 1911, asst. physician, out-patient dept., 1917-24, attending physician, house med. service, 1924-30, consulting physician since 1930. Chmn. Haverford Twp. (Pa.) Bd. of Health, 1913-26, Maternal Health Centre Com. of Phila. since 1928, Visiting Nurse Com., 1926-30. Mem. Montgomery Co. Med. Soc. (sec., Main Line Branch, 1917-30, pres. 1930-32), Phila. Coll. of Physicians. Republican. Soc. of Friends. Clubs: Medical, United Bowman (Phila.); Merion (Pa.) Cricket. Author med. articles to Jour. A.M.A. Home: Sweetwater Farms, Glen Mills, Pa. Office: Times Medical Bldg., Ardmore, Pa.

DEWEY, Ralph S(mith), sch. supt.; b. Ripley, N.Y., Jan. 20, 1894; s. Alonzo B. and Anna Rosina (Smith) D.; B.S., Allegheny Coll., Meadville, Pa., 1917, M.S., 1919; M.A., Columbia U. Teachers Coll., 1927; m. Winifred Lena Post, Aug. 1, 1923; children—Rosemay, Edward. Asst. chemist, Akron (O.) City Water Works, 1918; teacher of Science, Kane (Pa.) High Sch., 1919-20, prin., 1920-21; supervising prin. of pub. schs., Kane, Pa., 1921-24, supt. of schs., 1924-26; supt. of schs., Corry, Pa., since 1926. Served as pvt., 1st class, U.S. Army S.C., 1918-19. Mem. Sigma Alpha Epsilon, Alpha Chi Sigma. Methodist. Clubs: Golden Rule, Rotary, Corry Country (Corry, Pa.). Home: 55 East Frederick St. Office: Library Bldg., Corry, Pa.

DEWING, Henry Bronson, educator; b. Westminster, Conn., Mar. 2, 1882; s. Stephen and Eva Victoria (Lincoln) D.; B.A., U. of Calif., 1903, M.A., 1905; Ph.D., Yale University, 1908; L.H.D. from Bowdoin College, 1928; m. Eunice Dewing, 1910; children—Charles Edward, Elizabeth Ogden, Henry Lincoln (dec.), Stephen Bronson. Teacher of classics, high sch., Berkeley, Calif., 1904-06; instr. in Greek, Yale, 1907-08, in classics, Princeton, 1908-10; prof. Latin and dean Robert Coll., Constantinople, Turkey, 1910-16; asst. prof. classics, Princeton, 1916-18; sec. and commr. Am. Red Cross Mission to Greece, 1918-20; asst. prof. classics, Princeton, 1920-22; asso. prof. ancient langs., U. of Tex., 1922-23; prof. Greek, Bowdoin

Coll., 1923-28; pres. Athens (Greece) Coll., 1927-31; visiting prof. ancient and modern langs., Colorado Coll., 1932-35; visiting prof. Latin, U. of N.C., 1935-36. Mem. Abracadabra, Phi Beta Kappa. Presented medal of Military Merit and Cross of the Savior, by Greece, 1920. Address: 15½ Chambers St., Princeton, N.J.

DE WITT, George Ashley, editor; b. Appleton, Wis., Oct. 22, 1893; s. William George and Nan Frances (Philpot) D.; ed. pub. schs., Fond du Lac, Wis.; m. Ilma Henrietta Spaar, June 21, 1916; children—George Ashley, Clinton William. Began as reporter, Fond du Lac, 1909; city editor Milwaukee (Wis.) Free Press, 1911-12, mng. editor, 1912-14; successively telegraph editor, city editor, day mng. editor, Chicago Herald and Examiner, 1915-34, mng. editor, 1934 and 1935; mng. editor Washington (D.C.) Herald, 1936-39; mng. editor Washington Times-Herald since Feb. 1, 1939. Clubs: Congressional Country, National Press. Home: 402 Fairfax Rd., Bethesda, Md. Office: Washington Times-Herald, Washington, D.C.

DE WITT, Irvin A., lawyer; b. Fishers Ferry, Pa., Apr. 2, 1870; s. Anson P. and Delilah E. (Moore) D.; grad. Bloomsburg (Pa.) State Normal Sch., 1893; M.E. (summa cum laude), Bucknell U., Lewisburg, Pa., 1900; student Columbian U. Law Sch., Washington, D.C., 1900-01; m. Fannie M. Yocum, Dec. 27, 1900; children—Iva (Mrs. Voris B. Hall), Hilda B. Mem. of faculty, Bloomsburg (Pa.) State Normal Sch., 1893-96; admitted to bar of Northumberland Co. (Pa.), 1901, to practice before Pa. Supreme Ct., 1902; prin. of schs., Herndon, Pa., 1901-05; pvt. practice of law at Sunbury, Pa., since 1905; Justice of the Peace, Sunbury, Pa., 1909-16; auditor, apptd. by the court, to distribute estate of James C. Packer, 1922-25; pres. and dir. Westside Cemetery Co.; v.p. and dir. Consumer Discount Co.; sec.-treas. and dir. Sunbury Mausoleum Co.; solicitor and director, Sunbury Mutual Fire Ins. Co., Sunbury Milk Products Co. Del. to World's Sunday Sch. Conv., Washington, D.C., 1910, Oslo, Norway, 1936. Home: 1046 E. Chestnut St. Office: Bittner Bldg., Sunbury, Pa.

DeWITT, John Dalton, lawyer, real estate; b. Dunkirk, O., Aug. 12, 1871; s. Charles Franklin and Angeline (Harris) DeW.; graduate MacDonald Inst. of Law, Cincinnati, O., 1893-96; m. Anna E. Moore, Mar. 18, 1896; 1 son, Dalton Granger. Engaged in teaching in rural schs. of Ohio, 1889-90; admitted to Ohio bar and engaged in practice at Cincinnati, asso. with well-known law firms, 1896-1905, in practice alone, 1905-10; moved to Nutley, N.J., 1910 and engaged in practice of law in N.Y. City, 1910-18; engaged in real estate business as vice-pres. Wood, Dolson Co., 1918-23; pres. DeWitt, Smith & DeWitt, real estate financing, N.Y. City, since 1923; treas. No. 1 W. 39th St. Corpn. since 1934; pres. Western Mica Corpn., Moncton, New Brunswick, since 1914. Served as mem. Bd. Edn., Nutley, N.J., since 1933, pres., 1935-39. Pres. Asso. Bds. of Edn. of Essex Co., N.J., 1939. Mem. Real Estate Board of New York City and N.Y. State, Real Estate Board (Newark, N.J.), Ohio Soc. of N.Y. City. Republican. Conglist. Mason. Home: 308 Kingsland Rd., Nutley, N.J. Office: 22 W. 48th St., New York, N.Y.

DE WITT, John Phillips, food mcht.; b. Wyoming, Pa., Feb. 15, 1893; s. Ira and Dora (Phillips) De W.; student Wyoming Sem., Kingston, Pa., 1909-13, Wyoming Coll. of Bus., 1914, Wharton Sch. Extension, U. of Pa., 1915; m. Elisabeth Jones Howell, Nov. 7, 1916; 1 son, John Phillips. Engaged in business as food mcht. since 1916, propr. De Witt's Market, Wyoming, Pa., since 1915; dir. First Nat. Bank, Wyoming, Pa., Franklin Thrift & Loan Co., Pittston, Pa. Served as pres. Wyoming Business Men's Club, 1931-32; dir. Pittston Hosp. Mem. Pittston (Pa.) Chamber of Commerce. Mem. Kappa Delta Pi Frat. Republican. Presbyterian. Mason (K.T., Shriner). Clubs: Craftsmens, Irem Temple Country. Home: 535 Wyoming Av., Wyoming, Pa.; Dallas, Pa. Office: 17 W. 8th St., Wyoming, Pa.

de YOUNG, Bertram Isaac, lawyer; b. Phila., Pa., Feb. 20, 1877; s. Charles Z. and Fannie S. (Schwartz) de Y.; student William Penn Charter Sch., Phila., 1890-95; LL.B., U. of Pa., 1900; m. Rosa Stein, June 10, 1901; 1 dau., Elizabeth (Mrs. Sylvan Levin). Admitted to Pa. bar, 1900, and since in practice at Phila. under own name; dir. Union Bank & Trust Co. Asst. U.S. dist. atty., Phila., 1924-27; chief legal adviser U.S. Prohibition Dept. for N.J., Del. and Eastern Pa., 1927. Mem. Am. Bar Assn., Pa. Bar Assn. Republican. Jewish religion. Mason, Royal Arcanum. Club: Pa. Athletic, Lawyers (Phila.). Home: 2122 Delancey Pl. Office: 1700 Bankers Securities Bldg., Philadelphia, Pa.

DIAMENT, George Elmer, banker, canner; b. Chesapeake City, Md., Feb. 28, 1874; s. John Elmer and Cora (Cleaver) D.; student West Jersey Acad., Bridgeton, N.J., 1890-93, U. of Pa., 1893-94; unmarried. With John E. Diament Co., canners, since 1894, becoming sec. and treas., 1904; dir. Cumberland Nat. Bank of Bridgeton, 1906-23, v.p., 1923-32, pres. since 1932. Mem. twp. com. and treas. Twp. of Lawrence, Cumberland Co., N.J., since 1916. Republican. Presbyterian. Club: Cohanzick Country (Bridgeton). Home: Cedarville, N.J. Office: Cumberland Nat. Bank, Bridgeton, N.J.

DIAMOND, Herbert Maynard, prof. economics; b. Dansville, N.Y., May 21, 1892; s. Frank J. and Mary (Brua) D.; B.A., Yale, 1914, Ph.D., 1917; m. Margaret Lake, Dec. 28, 1915; children—Maynard Lake, Jack Lake. Instr. in social science, Goucher Coll., 1917-18; chief clk., later supt. New Haven office U.S. Employment Service, U.S. Dept. Labor, 1918-19; asst. sec. and legislative research worker Conn. Child Welfare Commn., 1919-20; asst. prof. economics and asst. dir. Wall St. Div. New York U., 1920-25; prof. economics and dean of Sch. of Business Administration, U. of Md., 1925-26; asso. prof. New York U., 1926-27; prof. economics, Lehigh, since 1927, also head of dept. of economics and sociology since 1936; mem. staff Pa. State Coll., summers 1929-31. Mem. Com. on Economical Accord, American Sociological Soc., Am. Econ. Assn., Am. Assn. for Labor Legislation, Am. Acad. Polit. and Social Science, Phi Beta Kappa, Delta Sigma Pi. Conglist. Author: Religion and the Commonweal, 1928; also monographs, Street Trading Among Connecticut Children, The Legal Handling of Juvenile Offenders in Connecticut. Editor and reviser of Ettinger and Golieb's Credits and Collections, 1927. Contbr. to Scientific Monthly, Survey, Am. Jour. of Sociology, Am. Federationist, American Econ. Review, Labor Legislation Review. Home: 801 W. Broad St., Bethlehem, Pa.

DIAMOND, Norman Harry, rabbi; b. Buffalo, N.Y., Nov. 1, 1905; s. Morris and Nelly (White) D.; grad. Hutchinson Central High Sch., 1923; A.B., U. of Cincinnati, 1932; rabbi Hebrew Union Coll., 1935; unmarried. Student rabbi, Buffalo, N.Y., Sandusky, O., and Anderson, Ind.; rabbi Temple Israel, New Castle, Pa., since 1935. Chaplain Citizens Mil. Training Camp, Ft. Niagara, summer 1931. Mem. Central Conf. Am. Rabbis, Zionist Orgn., Salvation Army (mem. New Castle bd.), New Castle Ministerial Assn., B'nai B'rith (v.p. New Castle Chapter). Reform Jewish religion. Address: 301 Boyles Av., New Castle, Pa.

DICE, J(ustus) Howard, librarian; b. Pittsburgh, Pa., May 6, 1887; s. Justus and Anna J. C. (Freese) D.; A.B., U. of Pittsburgh, 1911, B.L.S., N.Y. State Library Sch., 1913; m. Helen Frost, of Pittsburgh, June 23, 1920; children—Stanley Frost, Katherine Dalbey. Began as asst. librarian Mt. Washington br., Carnegie Pub. Library, Pittsburgh, 1913; asst. reference librarian Ohio State U. Library, 1914-15; asst. librarian Ohio State Library, 1915-16; state library organizer, Ohio Bd. Library Commrs., 1916-18; asst. dir. Libraries U.S. Army, 1919-20, dir. 1920; dir. libraries and asst. prof. of bibliography, U. of Pittsburgh since 1920. Served in U.S.A. with A.E.F., 1918-19. Mem. Am. and Pa. library assns., Bibliog. Soc. of America, Pittsburgh Library Club (pres. 1927-29). Methodist. Mason. Clubs. Hungry, Faculty. Home: 6510 Bartlett St., Pittsburgh, Pa.

DICK, George Alexander, dean; b. Cheapside, Ont., Can., Nov. 29, 1877; s. John and Jennie (Young) D.; came to U.S., 1880, parents Am. citizens; prep. edn. Port Allegany Public Schools; V.M.D., U. of Pa. Sch. of Vet. Medicine, 1904; B.S. in animal husbandry, Ia. State Coll., Ames, Ia., 1919; m. Cornelia Eugenie Colony, Sept. 5, 1905; 1 son, John Mandeville. Veterinarian, Kane, Pa., 1904-16; with Sch. of Vet. Medicine, U. of Pa. since 1917, dean since 1931, dir. of operations, Sch. of Animal Pathology, since 1937. Mem. Am. Vet. Med. Assn., U.S. Live Stock Sanitary Assn. Home: 234 Sagamore Rd., Upper Darby, Pa. Office: 39th and Woodland Av., Philadelphia, Pa.

DICKE, Henry Frederick, transportation exec.; b. Wabash, Ind., Jan. 11, 1881; s. Diedrick and Wilhelmina (Klepper) D.; ed. pub. and parochial schs., Ft. Wayne, Ind., 1887-98, Internat. Business Coll., 1898-1900; m. Louise Emily Traub, Aug. 20, 1913; children—Harold Paul, Richard MacLane, Harriet Louise. Cashier and bookkeeper Ft. Wayne Traction Co., 1901-04; auditor and office mgr. Ohio & Ind. Construction Co., Ft. Wayne, 1904-06; supt. of transportation Ft. Wayne, Van Wert & Lima Traction Co., 1906, Ohio Electric Ry. Co., Lima, O., 1907-11; gen. mgr. Ida. Traction Co., Boise, Ida., 1911-17; Utah Light and Traction Co., Salt Lake, 1917-25; v.p. Lehigh Valley Transit Co., electric railway and bus line, Allentown, Pa., 1925-36, pres. since 1936; pres. and dir. Lehigh Valley Transportation Co., Easton Transit Co., Valley Rys. Co., Valley Transportation Co., Central Park Amusement Co., Allentown Bridge Co.; v.p. and dir. East Pa. Transportation Co. Republican. Episcopalian. Mason (32°). Club: Lehigh Country (Allentown). Home: 2643 Livingston St. Office: Lehigh Valley Transit Co., Allentown, Pa.

DICKERSON, Edwin Trundle, judge; b. Dickerson, Md., Nov. 26, 1878; s. William Hempstone and Elizabeth (Trundle) D.; A.B., Univ. of Md., College Park, Md., 1898, A.M., 1903; grad. student Johns Hopkins U., 1898-99; LL.B., U. of Md. Law Sch., Baltimore, 1902; unmarried. Admitted to Md. bar, 1902 and engaged in gen. practice of law at Baltimore; asso. with uncle W. Burns Trundle and mem. firm Trundle & Dickerson, 1902-14, mem. firm with Harry W. Nice, 1919-34, when Mr. Nice was elected gov. of Md.; prof. law, Baltimore Law School, 1907-13 and its successor by merger, University of Md. Law School since 1913; prof. law, Am. Inst. Banking, Baltimore, 1907-24 and its successor, Johns Hopkins University, 1924-28; conducted classes for grads. of law schs. preparing for state bar examinations, 1902-18; apptd. to Supreme Bench of Baltimore City, 1936, and in Nov. 1938 elected for 15-yr. term; mem. jud. council of Md. for study of law and to make recommendations to Gen. Assembly, 1937-41. Mem. S.A.R., St. Andrews Soc., Hibernian Soc., German Soc. Episcopalian. Mason. Odd Fellow. Elk. Moose. Home: 3004 Garrison Boul. Office: Court House, Baltimore, Md.

DICKERSON, Roy E(rnest), petroleum geologist; b. Monticello, Ill., Aug. 8, 1877; s. Meritt Michael and Martha D.; B.S., U. of Calif., 1900, M.S., 1910, Ph.D., 1914; m. Delle Howard, July 14, 1904. Engaged in teaching and prin. high schs. in Calif., 1900-18; asst. curator paleontology, Calif. Acad. Sci., 1914-17, curator, 1917-19, hon. curator since 1919; geologist and geol. supt. Standard Oil Co. of Calif., 1918-26; geologist and chief geologist, foreign dept., Atlantic Refining Co., Phila., Pa., since 1926. Fellow A.A.A.S., Paleontol. Soc., Am. Geog. Soc., Geol. Soc. America. Mem. Phila. Acad. Natural Sci., Calif. Acad. Sci., Sigma Xi. Republican. Club: Explorers. Contbr. monographs on stratigraphy and paleontology of Pacific states, Philippines, Cuba and Caribbean countries and others. Office: 260 S. Broad St., Philadelphia, Pa.

DICKEY, Charles Denston, banker; A.B., Yale, 1916; m. Catherine D. Colt. Partner J. P. Morgan & Co., New York, and Drexel & Co., Phila., resident in Phila.; dir. Sharp & Dohme, Inc., Stonega Coke & Coal Co., Beaver Coal Corpn., Gen. Steel Castings Corpn., Phila. Contributionship for the Insurance of Houses from Loss by Fire, Lumbermen's Ins. Co., Va. Coal &

Iron Co.; mem. bd. of mgrs. Western Saving Fund Soc. of Phila. Servd in U.S. Navy, World War. Clubs: Philadelphia (Phila.); University, Yale (New York); The Links. Home: Chestnut Hill, Philadelphia, Pa. Office: 15th and Walnut Sts., Philadelphia, Pa.

DICKEY, Charles Emmet, educator; b. Brothersvalley Twp., Somerset Co., Pa., Sept. 24, 1871; s. Ephraim F. and Josephine (Carns) D.; grad. California (Pa.) State Normal Sch., 1891; A.B., U. of Pittsburgh, 1919; post-grad. work, Columbia and Harvard universities; LL.D., University of Pittsburgh, 1932; m. Della M. Boyer, of Elk Lick, Pa., June 10, 1896; children—Paul Hamilton, Lloyd Emmet, Josephine S., Harriet Katherine. Teacher rural schs., high sch., normal sch.; supervising principal Avalon, Pa., 12 yrs., Elk Lick, 2 yrs.; asst. county supt. schs., Allegheny Co., Pa., 1907-22, county supt. since 1922; pres. Ohio Valley Building & Loan Assn. Mem. bd. dirs. Pa. Safety Council World War. Trustee Thomas Patton Instn. for Boys; chmn. Pa. State Commn. for Studying Instns. for Blind and Deaf. Mem. N.E.A., Pa. State Ednl. Assn. (pres. 1926), Am. Acad. Polit. and Social Science, Phi Delta Kappa. Republican. Presbyn. Mason (33°). Clubs: Lions, Butler Country. Home: 1365 Sheridan Av. Office: County Office Bldg., Pittsburgh, Pa.

DICKEY, Edward Thompson, radio engring.; b. Oxford, Pa., Nov. 16, 1896; s. G. Renie and Ella (Thompson) D.; B.S., Coll. of City of N.Y., 1918; unmarried. Began as lab. asst., Research Dept., Marconi Wireless Telegraph Co. of America, 1918, later Tech. and Test Dept. Radio Corpn. of America; with engring. dept. RCA Mfg. Co., Camden, N.J., since 1929, now in charge publs., engring, socs. contact. Fellow Radio Club of America. Mem. Inst. Radio Engrs. Republican. Persbyn. Clubs: Electronic (Camden); Talo (Philadelphia). Home: 4632 Walnut St., Philadelphia, Pa. Office: RCA Mfg. Co., Inc., Camden, N.J.

DICKEY, Elmer L.; mem. surg. staff Oil City Gen. Hosp. Address: 102 Seneca St., Oil City, Pa.

DICKEY, Samuel, lecturer classical and N.T. Greek; b. Oxford, Pa., Nov. 27, 1872; s. Samuel and Jennie (Rutherford) D.; A.B., Princeton U., 1894, A.M., 1896; grad. Princeton Theol. Sem., 1897; grad. student Univs. of Berlin, Marburg, and Erlangen, Germany, 1897-99; m. Louise Parke Atherton, of Wilkes Barre, Pa., Feb. 26, 1908; children—Parke Atherton, John Miller, Louise Atherton, Thomas Atherton. Engaged as prof. classical and Hellenistic Greek, Lincoln U., Pa., 1899-1903; adjunct prof. N.T. lit. and exegesis, McCormick Theol. Sem. (now Presbyn. Theol. Sem.), Chicago, Ill., 1903-05, prof., 1905-23; lecturer in edn., Lincoln U., Pa., 1931-35, lecturer in classical and N.T. Greek since 1935; dir. Nat. Bank of Oxford, Pa. (vice-pres., 1935). Mem. Bd. Pub. Assistance for Chester Co., Pa., 1936-39. Mem. Presbytery of Chicago. Democrat. Presbyterian. Author: The Constructive Revolution of Jesus, 1924; contbr. to Outline of Christianity, 1926, Studies in Early Christianity, 1928, and various theol. revs. Home: Runnymede Orchards, Oxford, Pa.

DICKIE, J. Roy, mem. law firm Dickie, Robinson & McCamey. Office: Grant Bldg., Pittsburgh, Pa.

DICKINSON, C(linton) Roy, publisher, writer; b Newark, N.J., Mar. 14, 1888; s. Philemon Olin and Anna Elizabeth (Van Riper) D.; grad. Newark Acad., 1905; Litt.D., Princeton, 1909; m. Marjorie S. Bostick, Feb. 15, 1916; children—Philemon, Katharine Bostick, Clinton Roy, Jr. With Cosmopolitan Mag., 1910-15, Puck, 1915-16, New York Times, 1916, Frank Presbrey Co., advertising agts., 1916-17; asso. editor Printers' Ink and Printers' Ink Monthly, 1919-33; president Printers' Ink Publishing Co. since 1933. First lieutenant and later captain and major, office of chief of staff, U.S.A., World War; lt. col. O.R.C. Mem. President Harding's Unemployment Conf. (with Samuel Gompers signed minority report against cut in wages). Mem. Nat. Publishers Assn. (dir.), Associated Business Papers, Inc. (treas. and dir.). Republican. Methodist. Clubs: Princeton, Dutch Treat, Advertising, Players, Essex County Country. Contbr. short stories to Harper's, Scribner's, Ladies' Home Journal, American Legion Monthly, Elks Magazine, etc., articles to Printers' Ink, etc.; included in O'Brien's Best Short Stories of the Year, 1918, 26 and 28. Author: Wages and Wealth, 1931; The Cowards Never Started, 1933. Home: 32 Chelsea Pl., East Orange, N.J. Office: 185 Madison Av., New York, N.Y.

DICKINSON, Edmund Charles, prof. law; b. Menomonie, Wis., Oct. 13, 1881; s. Edmund Carey and Mary M. (Reppeto) D.; A.B., Earlham Coll., Richmond, Ind., 1903; J.D., U. of Mich., 1911; m. Emily Wiechardt, June 17, 1914; children—Mary Althea, Emily Claire, Elizabeth Ann, Dorothy Jean. Prof. law, U. of Fla., 1911-13, U. of Ala., 1913-20, Vanderbilt, 1920-21, W.Va. U. since 1921; visiting prof. law, U. of Mich., summers 1920 and 1921, Cornell, summer 1929. Mem. W.Va. Bar Assn., Am. Assn. Univ. Profs.; Phi Kappa Phi, Phi Alpha Delta, Order of the Coif. Republican. Rotarian. Club: The Hermitage. Author: West Virginia Annotations to Restatement of Conflict of Laws. Contbr. to W.Va. Law Quarterly, Mich. Law Review, Ill. Law Review. Home: 317 Simpson St., Morgantown, W.Va.

DICKINSON, Everett H.; surgeon Broad St. Hosp.; asso. surgeon Hahnemann, St. Luke's and Children's hosps.; asst. neurol. surgeon Phila. Gen. Hosp.; instr. in surgery and surg. pathology, Hahnemann Med. Coll. Address: 250 S. 18th St., Philadelphia, Pa.

DICKINSON, John, lawyer; b. Greensboro, Md., February 24, 1894; s. Willard and Caroline (Schnauffer) D.; A.B., Johns Hopkins, 1913; A.M., Princeton, 1915, Gordon Macdonald fellow, 1915-16, Charlotte Elizabeth Procter fellow, 1916-17, Ph.D., 1919; LL.B., Harvard, 1921; LL.D., Tusculum Coll., 1929, Dickinson Coll., Carlisle, Pa., 1934. Lecturer on hist., Amherst Coll., 1919; tutor in div. hist., govt. and economics, Harvard, 1919-21; clk., law office John C. Hammond, Northampton, Mass., summers 1920, 21; law clk., McAdoo, Cotton & Franklin, N.Y. City, 1921-22; in practice with Hon. William G. McAdoo, Los Angeles, Calif., 1922-25; lecturer on govt., Harvard and Radcliffe Coll., 1924-27; asst. prof. politics, Princeton, 1927-29; prof. law, U. of Pa., since 1929; asst. sec. of Commerce, 1933-35; chairman U.S. Central Statistical Board, 1934-35; asst. U.S. Atty. General, 1935-37; gen. solicitor Pa. R.R. since 1937. Economist, U.S. War Trade Bd., 1917; 1st lt., U.S.A., attached to Gen. Staff, 1918. Economist and editor Governor's Advisory Commn. on cloak and suit industry of N.Y. City, 1925. Fellow Am. Acad. Arts and Sciences; mem. Social Science Research Council, Am. Polit. Science Assn., Am. Law Inst., Am. Bar Assn. (com. on commerce), Am. Statis. Assn., Am. Soc. Internat. Law, Institut Internat. de Philosophie du Droit et de Sociologie Juridique (Paris), Phi Beta Kappa. Democrat. Episcopalian. Clubs: Princeton, Lenape, University, Contemporary (Philadelphia); Princeton, Century (New York); Metropolitan, National Press (Washington, D.C.); Jefferson Island. Author: The Building of an Army, 1922; Administrative Justice and the Supremacy of Law, 1927; Hold Fast the Middle Way, 1935. Co-author: Report on the Cloak and Suit Industry of New York City, 1925. Editor and translator: The Statesman's Book of John Salisbury, 1927. Contbr. to Am. Polit. Science Rev., Polit. Science Quarterly, Speculum, Am. Jour. Internat. Law, Dictionary Am. Biography, etc. Home: "Crosiadore," Trappe, Md. Address: Broad St. Station Bldg., Philadelphia, Pa.

DICKINSON, John Lewis, banker; b. Malden, W.Va., Jan. 26, 1870; s. John Quincy and Mary Dickinson (Lewis) D.; ed. Kanawha Mil. Inst., Charleston, W.Va., Va. Mil. Inst., Lexington, and Eastman Bus. Coll., Poughkeepsie, N.Y.; m. Maude Hubbard, Feb. 8, 1899; children—Mary Lewis, Anastasia Hubbard (Mrs. Andrew A. Payne), Nelle Carmichael (Mrs. Ray Marshall Evans), Dorcas Laidley, Rebecca Gray. Began with J. Q. Dickinson Salt Works, Malden; began banking business as runner, 1890, later bookkeeper, teller, v.p., pres. Kanawha Valley Bank; pres. Central Trust Co., Dickinson Co., Quincy Dairy Co., Southern Land Co., The Buffalo Bank, Quincy Coal Co. Presbyn. Mason. Clubs: Rotary, Edgewood Country, Kanawha Country. Home: South Hills, Charleston. Office: Kanawha Valley Bank, Charleston, W.Va.

DICKINSON, Neville Sawrey, elec. engring.; b. Nashua, Fla., Jan. 19, 1890; s. John Morris and Margaret Jane (Tompson) D.; ed. Stetson Univ., DeLand, Fla., 1907-10; B.E., Union Coll., Schenectady, N.Y., 1913, E.E., 1915; m. Hilda Evelyn Feldman, Apr. 30, 1921. Draftsman and student engr., General Electric Co., 1912-15; in charge elec. dept., Newark Tech. Sch., 1915-18; cons. elec. adviser, Nairn Linoleum Co., Kearny, N.J., 1917-25; with firm nr. N.Y. city, mfg. and installing elevator equipment, 1918-23; with firm mfg. elec. controlling apparatus, 1923-26; mem. firm Motor Sales and Engring. Co., constrn. and engring., Newark, N.J., since 1926. Mem. Am. Inst. Elec. Engrs., Sigma Xi, Rotary Club. Licensed Professional Engineer, State of N.J. Ind. Democrat. Protestant. Home: 507 Richmond Av., Maplewood. Office: 84 13th Av., Newark, N.J.

DICKINSON, Oliver Booth, judge; b. Dayton, O., Sept. 25, 1857; s. Edmund W. (D.D.) and Caroline A. (Atkinson) D.; matriculated Bucknell U., Pa., class of 1877, A.M., 1903, LL.D., 1919; m. H. Evelyn Sines, of Chester, Pa., Oct. 2, 1881. Admitted to Pa. bar, 1878, and practiced in Chester; del. to Dem. Co., State and Nat. convs.; judge U.S. Dist. Court, Eastern Dist. of Pa., by appmt. of President Wilson since May 4, 1914. Trustee Pa. Mil. Coll., Y.W.C.A. of Chester, Pa., Crozer Theol. Sem., J. Lewis Crozer Home and Hosp., A. O. Deshong Memorial. Mem. American, Pa. and Delaware County bar associations, Delaware County Hist. Soc., Del. Co. Inst. Science, Phila. Acad. Fine Arts, Ohio Soc., Phila., Sigma Chi. Democrat. Baptist. Club: Penn. Home: Chester, Pa. Office: Federal Bldg., Philadelphia, Pa.

DICKSON, Conway Wing, lawyer; b. Berwick, Pa., Aug. 14, 1885; s. Sterling W. and Lillian E. (Baucher) D.; ed. Lawrenceville (N.J.) Prep. Sch., 1903-04; A.B., Yale, 1908; LL.B., U. of Pa. Law Sch., 1910; m. Gertrude A. Finck, May 7, 1927. Admitted to Pa. bar, 1910, and since engaged in gen. practice of law at Berwick. Served as Govt. Appeal Agt. during World War; chmn. Liberty Loan drive for Columbia and Montour Cos. Pres. and dir. Berwick Chamber of Commerce, Berwick Community Chest; pres. Columbia-Montour Council Boy Scouts; served for 25 yrs. either as sec., treas. or pres. Berwick Hosp.; pres. Cooperative Concert Assn. Mem. Columbia Co. Bar Assn., Wilkes-Barre Law and Library Assn., Patriotic Order Sons of America, Zeta Psi. Democrat. Methodist. Odd Fellow, Knights of Malta. Club: Berwick Rotary (past pres.). Home: 1011 East Front St. Office: Berwick Savings & Trust Co. Bldg., Berwick, Pa.

DICKSON, Halsey Edwin, elec. engring.; b. Newark, N.J., June 19, 1899; s. Charles Augustus and Adelaide (Huff) D.; B.S. in Engring., Lafayette Coll., 1925; m. Mildred Lee Kline, Sept. 24, 1930; children—Carol Lee, Virginia Ann. Inspr. and investigator, Metropolitan Edison Co. at Easton, Pa., 1925, at Reading, Pa., 1925; with customer relations, N.J. Power & Light Co., asst. to dist. mgr., Netcong, N.J., 1926; div. lighting dir., Met. Edison Co., Easton, Pa., 1927-38, div. sales mgr., Reading Pa., since 1938; designer and originator of many unique, decorative and utilitarian lighting installations which have been published in journs. of U.S., Gt. Britain and France; designer bridge lighting for Easton, Pa.-Phillipsburg, N.J., Bridge, known as "world's most brilliant bridge" lighted by largest series st. lamps made. Served in Tank Corps U.S.A., 1919. Active in civic affairs in Easton, Pa., and Phillipsburg, N.J. Mem. Illuminating Engring. Soc., Am. Inst. Elec. Engrs., Alpha Chi Rho, Am. Legion, Nat. Rifle Assn., U.S. Revolver Assn., Reading Chamber of Commerce, Y.M.C.A. Republican. Presbyn. Mason, B.P.O.E. Clubs: Warren Co. Rod & Gun; Nat. Exchange, Wyomissing (Reading);

Green Valley Country (Sinking Spring, Pa.). Home: 1227 N. 13th St. Office: 412 Washington St., Reading, Pa.

DICKSON, Harold Edward, asso. prof. fine arts; b. Sharon, Pa., July 18, 1900; s. William E. and Blanche (Young) D.; B.S., Pa. State Coll., 1922; student Harvard, 1922-23, 1926-27, A.M., 1927, grad. study, 1935-36; m. Eleanor Brassington, June 21, 1927; children—Lois Jane, Eleanor Rae. Asso. with Pa. State Coll. continuously since beginning as instr., 1923, asso. prof. fine arts since 1930. Mem. Am. Assn. Univ. Profs., Coll. Art Assn., Scarab, Delta Sigma Phi. Mason. Home: 206 Harstwick Av., State College, Pa.

DICKSON, John McCrea, surgeon; b. Hunterstown, Pa., Jan. 22, 1889; s. Dr. John Russell and Margaret Rebecca (McCrea) D.; grad. Gettysburg (Pa.) Acad., 1904; A.B., Gettysburg (Pa.) Coll., 1908, M.A., 1924, Sc.D., 1932; M.D., U. of Pa. Med. Dept., 1912; m. Marion Elizabeth Ball, Nov. 1, 1916; 1 son, Harrison McCrea. Asso. surgeon Chambersburg (Pa.) Hosp., 1916-19; chief surgeon, Annie M. Warner Hosp., Gettysburg, Pa., since 1919. Trustee Gettysburg (Pa.) Coll. since 1932. Fellow Am. Coll. Surgeons, A.M.A., Phila. Coll. of Physicians; mem. Adams Co., Pa. State med. socs., Harrisburg Acad. of Medicine, Sigma Chi, Sigma Xi. Presbyterian. Mason (32°), Elk. Home: 55 W. Broadway. Office: 103 W. Middle St., Gettysburg, Pa.

DICKSON, R. R.; pres. Milbourn Co.; v.p. and dir. Benedum-Trees Oil Co.; also officer or dir. several other companies. Office: Benedum-Trees Bldg., Pittsburgh, Pa.

DICKSON, Reid Stuart, denominational sec.; b. Hoboken, N.J., Jan. 26, 1885; s. James Stuart and Mary Agnes (Campbell) D.; A.B., U. of Pa., 1906; grad. of Princeton Theological Seminary, 1910; D.D., Missouri Valley College, Marshall, Mo., 1932, Grove City (Pa.) College, 1932; m. Margaret Tooker, May 12, 1910; children—Sarah Tooker, Carol Campbell. Ordained Presbyn. ministry, 1910; pastor New Providence, N.J., 1910-14, Lewistown, Pa., 1915-23; western sec. Bd. of Pensions, Presbyn. Ch., 1923-25, asso. sec., 1925-37, gen. sec. since Oct. 1, 1937. Gen. Sec. Y.M.C.A. and athletic dir. Maryville (Tenn.) Coll., 1906-07. Dir. religious work, Y.M.C.A. in France and Germany, 1917-19. Mem. St. Andrews Soc. of Phila., Kappa Alpha. Democrat. Clubs: University, Midday (Phila.); University of Pa. (New York). Home: University Club. Office: Witherspoon Bldg., Philadelphia, Pa.

DICKSON, Thomas Sinclair, clergyman; b. Phila., Pa., June 1, 1888; s. James Stuart and Mary Agnes (Campbell) D.; grad. Blight's School, Phila., 1905; A.B., U. of Pa., 1909; student Theol. Sem., Princeton, N.J., 1909-12; D.D., Tennant Coll., Phila., 1935; m. Barbara Stone Root, 1914; children—Mary Elizabeth, James Stuart, Douglas Root, Frances Caroline. Ordained to ministry of Presbyterian Ch., 1912; pastor Ridgeview Ch., West Orange, N.J., 1912-14; asst. pastor Immanuel Ch., Milwaukee, Wis., 1914-16; pastor Presbyn. Ch., Juniata, Pa., 1916-20; asso. pastor First Presbyn. Ch., Johnstown, Pa., 1920-23, First Ch., New Kensington, Pa., 1923-28, First Ch., Warren, Pa., 1928-37; pastor First Presbyn. Ch., York, Pa., since 1937. Served as camp sec., Y.M.C.A., during World War. Mem. advisory bd. Beaver Coll., Jenkintown, Pa.; trustee York (Pa.) Collegiate Inst. Mem. Kappa Alpha. Club: Rotary (York, Pa.). Home: 7 N. Queen St., York, Pa.

di DOMENICA, Angelo, clergyman; b. Schiavi d'Abruzzo, Italy, Mar. 29, 1872; s. Domenico and Gabriela (Falasca) di D.; student elementary sch., Italy; private tutoring in America; B.D., Yale Div. Sch., 1910; D.D., Denison U., 1937, Bucknell U., 1938; m. Emilia Prior, Dec. 5, 1900 (died Mar. 6, 1912); m. 2d, Mary A. Traver, May 27, 1914; children—Sylvia Ada, Edna, Eleanor. Came to U.S., 1892, naturalized, 1903. Missionary among Italians, Newark, N.J., 1896-1903, New Haven, Conn., Feb. 1, 1903-May 31, 1914, Phila., Pa., since June 1, 1914; instr. at the Bapt. Inst. for Christian Workers. Trustee Internat. Bapt. Sem., East Orange, N.J. One of organizers Italian Baptist Assn. of America, 1898. Republican. Mason. Author: Italian Helper for Christian Workers, 1912; graded lessons in English for Italians, 1922; also many tracts, booklets and pamphlets in English and Italian. Compiler bi-lingual hymnal for Italian Chs. in America. Editor-in-chief Bapt. Bi-Lingual weekly paper, L'Aurora, about 25 yrs. Home: 1414 Castle Av., Philadelphia, Pa.

DIEBEL, Alfred H.; gynecologist and obstetrician Northeastern Hosp. Address: 996 Pratt St., Philadelphia, Pa.

DIEFENBACH, Carl Michael, educator; b. Ebenezer, N.Y., Mar. 27, 1895; s. Michael and Mary (Schneckenburger) D.; student North Central Coll., Naperville, Ill., 1915-17; A.B., cum laude, Syracuse (N.Y.) U., 1919; M.A., Am. U., Washington, D.C., 1926; grad. student Columbia U., 1922-26, Yale, 1926-31, New York U., 1931, U. of Pa., 1939; m. Myrtle May Jones, June 28, 1920; 1 son, Edward Albert. Teacher grade sch., East Seneca, N.Y., 1913-15, Parsons Coll., Fairfield, Ia., 1919-22, West Orange (N.J.) High Sch., 1922-24, 1925-26; editor Chevy Chase (Md.) News, 1924-25; prin. Jefferson Jr. High, Meriden, Conn., 1926-31; supt. of schs. and high sch. prin., Putnam, Conn., 1931-38; supervising prin., Collingswood, N.J., since 1939. Dir. Meriden (Conn.) Y.M.C.A., 1929-31; chmn. Putnam (Conn.) Tercentenary Com., 1937, Annual Red Cross Drive, Meriden, Conn., 1928. Mem. West Orange Teachers Assn. (pres. 1925-26), Meriden Teachers Assn. (pres. 1929-30), Conn. State Teachers Assn. (past dir.), Eastern Conn. Schoolmen (pres. 1938), N.E.A., Pi Kappa Delta, Theta Alpha. Received White Memorial Oratorical Award, 1919. Congregationalist. Clubs: Kiwanis (Meriden, Conn.; past pres.); Rotary (Putnam, Conn.; past pres.). Ivy orator, Class of 1919, Syracuse U. Home: 1024 Stokes Av. Office: Collingswood High Sch., Collingswood, N.J.

DIEFENDERFER, Alpha Albert, univ. prof.; b. Jenner Cross Roads, Pa., Apr. 23, 1881; s. Moses Henry and Salome Heart (Allshouse) D.; B.S. in Chem., Lehigh U., Bethlehem, Pa., 1902, M.S., 1908; student Kaiser Wilhelm U., Berlin, Germany, 1927-28; m. E. Olive Girvin, Dec. 25, 1906. Asst. in chemistry, Lehigh U., Bethlehem, Pa., 1902-03, instr., 1903-05, instr. in qualitative analysis, assaying and industrial chemistry, 1905-07, instr. in qualitative analysis and assaying, 1907-11, asst. prof., 1911-20, asso. prof., 1920-28, prof. since 1929. Mem. Bd. of Health, Bethlehem, Pa., 1914-18; mem. Sch. Bd., Bethlehem, Pa., 1919-21. Mem. Bd. of Mgrs., Bethany Orphans Home, Womelsdorf, Pa. Fellow A.A.A.S.; mem. Am. Chem. Soc. Democrat. Home: 725 W. Broad St. Office: Lehigh Univ., Bethlehem, Pa.

DIEFENDORF, Adelbert, univ. prof.; b. Newark, N.J., May 19, 1891; s. Adelbert and Alice (Sexton) D.; B.S. in C.E. and C.E., Ohio Northern U., Ada, O.; m. Mary V. Frame, Apr. 28, 1913; children—John Stuart, Randall A. Cons. engr., New York, City, 1911-21; instr., U. of Illinois, Urbana, Ill., 1921-24; asst. prof., S.D. Sch. of Mines, Rapid City, S.D., 1924-27; prof. and head civil engring. dept., U. of N.M., Albuquerque, N.M., 1927-30; prof. civil engring., U. of Pittsburgh, since 1930. Mem. Am. Road Builders Assn. (v.p. since 1935), Am. Soc. C.E. Episcopalian. Home: 9 Dunmoyle Pl. Office: 306 State Hall, Pittsburgh, Pa.

DIEFFENBACH, Rudolph, land valuation engr.; b. Westminster, Md., Dec. 25, 1884; s. Ferdinand Albert and Jeannette Rix (Frankforter) D.; student Baltimore (Md.) City Coll., 1901-05; B.F., Biltmore (N.C.) Forest Sch., 1908; m. Anne Louise Molitor, Oct. 17, 1922; children—Karl Christian, Albert Woodson, Rudolph Jacob, Ann, Philip and Paul (twins). Began as junior forester, United States Forest Service, 1908, detailed to western U.S. on land classification and forest boundary surveys; dep. forest supervisor, Nev. Nat. Forest, 1910-12; organizer and dir. cadastral surveys of nat. forests in White, Ozark and Appalachian mts., 1912-20; in charge examination and appraisal land for nat. forests in eastern U.S., 1920-24; forest and land valuation engr. since 1924, sr. land valuation engr. since 1929; in charge acquisition Upper Miss. River Wild Life and Fish Refuge and Bear River Migratory Bird Refuge, 1925; organizer and dir. appraisal and acquisition of land for nation-wide system of wild life refuges since 1929; sec. Migratory Bird Conservation Commn. since 1930. Senior mem. Soc. Am. Foresters; mem. Am. Forestry Assn. Unitarian. Mason. Author of tech. handbooks on surveys, examination and valuation of lands, etc., pub. by Dept. of Agr.

DIEGEL, Leo, golf professional; b. Detroit, Mich., Apr. 27, 1899. Began as caddie, Detroit, 1910; formerly with Detroit Country Club, Lake Shore Country Club, Chicago, Lockmoor Country Club, Detroit, at New Orleans and Agua Caliente; now golf professional at Philmont (Pa.) Country Club; won Professional Golf Assn. Championship, 1929; member Ryder Cup Team, 1927, 1929, 1931, 1933, setting record in singles with 65, in doubles (Espinosa partner) with 66, 1929; winner many open and professional championships; pvt. instr. for 10 yrs. Ranked leading professional, 1928-29; ranked in 1st 10 continuously since 1919. Address: care Philmont Country Club, Philmont, Pa.

DIEHL, Charles F.; chmn. bd. Life Ins. Co. of America. Address: 109 E. Redwood St., Baltimore, Md.

DIEHL, Jacob, clergyman and educator; b. at Greencastle, Pa., Feb. 20, 1884; s. John Luther and Martha Ellen (Kuhn) Diehl; A.B., Gettysburg (Pa.) College, 1903; student at Gettysburg Theological Seminary, 1907, Leipzig University, 1908-09 and 1914; m. Sara Matilda Klapp, of Lock Haven, Pa., Apr. 22, 1914; children—Dorothea Prieson, Sara Matilda, William Adolph, Marian Louise. Ordained ministry Luth. Ch., 1910; pastor St. John's Luth. Ch., Lock Haven, Pa., 1909-15, Trinity Luth. Ch., Carthage, Ill., 1915-22; prof. religious edn., Carthage Coll., 1920-22; pastor Trinity Luth. Ch., Selinsgrove, Pa., 1924-29; acting pres., Susquehanna U., 1927-28; pres. Carthage Coll., 1929-33. Dir. Luth. Mutual Life Ins. Co.; spl. rep. Presbyn. Ministers' Fund for life ins. Served as chaplain, 1st lt., U.S.A., Camp Custer, Battle Creek, Mich., Feb. 1918-Jan. 1919. Mem. A.A.A.S., Alpha Tau Omega, Pi Gamma Mu, Phi Beta Kappa. Republican. Mason. Home: Lock Haven, Pa.

DIEKE, Gerhard Heinrich, physicist; b. Rheda, Germany, Aug. 20, 1901; s. Gerard and Bertha (Fischer) D.; student U. of Leiden, Holland, 1920-25; Ph.D., U. of Calif., 1926; student Calif. Inst. Tech., 1926-27, Inst. of Physical Chem. Research, Tokyo, Japan, 1927-28; m. Sally Fairfax Harrison, June 8, 1938. Research fellow Nat. Research Council, 1926-27; research asso. Inst. Physical Chem. Research, Tokyo, 1927-28; conservator and privaat docent, U. of Groningan, Holland, 1928-30; associate Johns Hopkins U., 1930-31, asso. prof. physics, 1931-39, prof. physics since 1939. Home: 609 Somerset Road, Baltimore, Md.

DIELMAN, Louis Henry, librarian; b. New Windsor, Md., Jan. 16, 1864; s. Louis and Theodora (Müller) D.; A.B., New Windsor Coll., 1884; student Md. Coll. of Pharmacy; Ph.G., Phila. Coll. Pharmacy, 1885; m. Anna Good Barkdoll, Oct. 8, 1890. Cataloguer Md. State Library, 1900-04; asst. librarian Enoch Pratt Free Library, Baltimore, 1904-11; exec. sec. Peabody Inst., Baltimore, since 1912, librarian since 1927. Mem. Am. Hist. Assn., Md. Hist. Soc. Democrat. Editor and Compiler: British Invasion of Maryland, 1913. Editor of Md. Hist. Mag. (Vols. 4-32), 1909-37. Home: 1514 Park Av. Address: Peabody Institute, Baltimore, Md.

DIEMAND, John A.; exec. v.p. Indemnity Ins. Co. of North America. Address: 1600 Arch St., Philadelphia, Pa.

DIENER, Louis, M.D., surgeon; b. Culpeper, Va., Jan. 18, 1892; s. Samuel and Pauline (Schloss) D.; grad. Culpeper High Sch., Culpeper, Va., 1909; M.D., University of Maryland, 1915; m. Lillian Goodman, Aug. 6, 1929; children—Royce, Edgar J. In gen. practice med. and surgery since 1915; mem. staff Union Memorial, Baltimore Eye, Ear, Nose and Throat,

Sinai, Sydenham and Mercy hosps. Served as capt., Med. Corps, 112th Machine Gun Batt., World War; 1 yr. overseas. Awarded Distinguished Service Cross. Mem. Am. Bd. Otolaryngology, A.M.A., Southern Med. Assn., Med. and Surg. Faculty of Md., Baltimore City Med. Soc., Phi Delta Epsilon. Democrat. Jewish religion. Mason. Clubs: Phoenix, Suburban (Baltimore). Home: Biltmore Apts. Office: 2449 Eutaw Place, Baltimore, Md.

DIEROLF, Claude Octavius, clergyman; b. Lancaster, Pa., July 20, 1892; s. Edwin and Orella Nora (Groff) D.; grad. Boy's High Sch., 1910; A.B., Franklin and Marshall Coll., Lancaster, Pa., 1914; student Luth. Theol. Sem., 1914-17; B.D., Internat. Christian Bible Coll., Minneapolis, Minn. (corr. course), 1919; S.T.D., Oskaloosa (Ia.) Coll., 1920; m. Clara Hiller Bohn, June 27, 1917; children—Clara Orella, Claude Edwin, Harold Earle. Ordained to ministry of Lutheran Ch., 1917; pastor Zion Luth. Ch., Leacock, Pa., 1917-23, St. John's Luth. Ch., Shiremanstown, Pa., 1923-28, pastor Bethlehem Luth. Ch., Phila., since 1928. Home: 3008 Diamond St., Philadelphia, Pa.

DIETER, Clarence Dewey, prof. of biology; b. Pittsburgh, Pa., July 19, 1898; s. Christian and Elizabeth (Bender) D.; grad. Allegheny (Pa.) High Sch., 1917; B.S., U. of Pittsburgh, 1922, Ph.D., 1934; M.S., Washington and Jefferson Coll., Washington, Pa., 1924; student U. of Chicago, summers 1924-28, Marine Biol. Lab. summers 1933, 1935; m. Nola May Dieter, June 9, 1928. Instr. biology, Washington & Jefferson College, Washington, Pa., 1924-34, prof. of biology since 1934. Mem. Theta Kappa Nu, Sigma Xi, Phi Sigma. Republican. Home: 103 Dewey Av., Washington, Pa.

DIETRICH, Daniel W.; pres. Food Industries, Inc., Luden's, Inc. Home: 6906 Lincoln Drive, Philadelphia, Pa. Office: Delaware Trust Bldg., Wilmington, Del.

DIETRICH, Harvey Oscar, supt. of schools; b. Berks Co., Pa., May 6, 1881; s. Jonathan P. and Ellamanda Esther (Raubenhold) D.; student Keystone State Normal Sch., Kutztown, Pa., 1897-1900; A.B. (magna cum laude), Bucknell U., Lewisburg, Pa., 1906, A.M., 1909; Ed.D., Webster Coll., Webster Groves, Mo., 1933; also student at U. of Pa., Columbia, New York U., Temple U.; m. Eva Deibert, Dec. 1906 (died 1929); children—Stanley Benjamin, Dorothy Ruth, Florence Rose; m. 2d, Edith Remmlein, Aug. 1931. Teacher in rural school, Berks Co., Pa., 1900-04; prin. Fleetwood (Pa.) High Sch., 1906-10; cost accounting, 1910-12; supervising prin., Curwensville, Pa., 1912-16; supt. of schools, Kane, Pa., 1916-22, Norristown, Pa., since 1922; prof. of edn., summers, U. of Ark., Fayetteville, Ark., 1918, U. of Okla., Norman, Okla., 1918, State Teachers Coll., La., 1918, Normal Sch., Gunnison, Colo., 1918, Normal Sch., Edinboro, Pa., 1917-18. Selected by Nat. War Council to serve as ednl. dir. with A.E.F. in France, 1918. Mem. Governor's Ednl. Cost Survey; merit counselor Boy Scouts. Mem. N.E.A. (mem. legislative commn.), Am. Assn. Sch. Adminstrs., Pa. State Edn. Assn., Am. Acad. Polit. and Social Science, Nat. Youth Radio Conf., Am. Geog. Soc., Progressive Edn. Assn., Am. Assn. Adult Edn., Council of 100 of Y.M.C.A., Community Chest (mem. exec. council), Phi Delta Kappa, Pi Gamma Mu. Mason. Club: Lions. Author: many school bulletins on school administration. Home: 1532 Powell St. Address: Norristown, Pa.

DIETZ, Alvin Francis, clergyman; b. Pen Argyl, Pa., Dec. 14, 1888; s. Joseph Jacob and Sarah Matilda (Eckert) D.; A.B., Franklin and Marshall Coll., 1916; B.D., Eastern Theol. Sem., 1919; m. Florence Sophia Uhler, Aug. 6, 1918; 1 son, Roderic Alvin. Ordained to ministry Evang. and Reformed Ch., 1919; minister, Numidia, Pa., 1919-22; minister Salem Reformed Ch., Shamokin, Pa., since 1922; dir. Heitzman Safety Blasting Plug Corpn., Shamokin, Pa.; dir. and treas. Heitzman Sales Corpn., Shamokin, Pa., and Washington, D.C. Served as sec. Y.M.C.A. and S.A.T.C., 1918-19. Trustee Phœbe Old Folks Home, Allentown, Pa. Mem. Sigma Pi. Republican. Mem. Evang. & Reformed Ch. Club: Kiwanis (Shamokin). Established the first Unified Ch. Worship and Educational System in the Evang. and Reformed Ch. denomination, 1929. Home: 1310 W. Pine St., Shamokin, Pa.

DIETZ, William H.; dir. of athletics and football coach, Albright Coll., Reading, Pa. Address: 2548 Cumberland Av., Mt. Penn, Reading, Pa.

DIEZ, Max, coll. prof.; b. Heidenheim, Germany, Apr. 21, 1887; s. August and Anna (Haller) D.; came to U.S., 1889, naturalized 1910; student St. Louis pub. schs., 1893-1905; A.B., M.A., Washington U., St. Louis, Mo., 1910; student U. of Wis., Madison, Wis., 1910-11; Ph.D., U. of Texas, Austin, Tex., 1916; m. Martha Meysenburg, June 17, 1917; 1 dau., Bettina (dec.). Instr. German, Washington U., St. Louis, 1911-15; asso. prof., U. of Texas, 1915-18; translator, Armour & Co., Chicago, 1919-21; prof. German, Centre Coll., Danville, Ky., 1921-25, Bryn Mawr Coll., Bryn Mawr, Pa., since 1925. Served as pvt., U.S. Army, 1918. Dir. and sec. The German Junior Year, Inc. Mem. Am. Assn. of Teachers of German, Am. Assn. Univ. Profs., Goethe Soc., Carl Schurz Foundation, Phi Beta Kappa, Omicron Delta Kappa. Author: The Nibelungenlied, edited for American Students, 1931; Introduction to German, 1934; numerous articles in professional jours. Address: Bryn Mawr College, Bryn Mawr, Pa.

DIFFENDERFER, George M., clergyman; b. East Petersburg, Lancaster Co., Pa., Jan. 5, 1869; s. Emanuel G. and Frances L. (Knier) D.; A.B., Gettysburg (Pa.) Coll., 1893, A.M., 1896, D.D., 1911; grad. Luth. Theol. Sem., Gettysburg, 1896; attended lectures in philosophy, U. of Berlin, 1910; m. Laura A. Diehl, of Gettysburg, June 30, 1896; children—Isabel Romayne (Mrs. John Russell Yates), George M. Ordained Luth. ministry, 1896; pastor St. Paul's Ch., Newport, Pa., 1896-1900, First Ch., Carlisle, 1900-14 (built ch., $130,000, and hosp., $125,000), Luther Place Memorial Ch., Washington, D.C., 1919-1930. Lecturer on Comparative Religions, Dickinson Coll., 1910-11, Washington Sch. of Religious Edn., 1922-24, on Evolution of North American Indian, Oberammergau, God's Garden of Wonders. Chaplain U.S. Industrial Indian Sch., Carlisle, 1900-10; executive secretary ministerial relief, Luth. Ch., 1914-17; member Pennsylvania Relief Board; chaplain at Newport News, Va., 1917-18; maj., chaplain O.R.C., U.S.A. Pres. Washington Federation of Chs., 1922-23; trustee Tressler Orphanage (v.p. since 1924); trustee Standard Woman's Coll. since 1923; mem. Com. on Army and Navy Chaplains, Washington Com. of Federal Council Chs. of Christ; trustee United Christian Endeavor Soc. Grand Chaplain Pa. A.F. and A.M., 1924-25; K.P. Republican. Editor of Army Chaplain, 1934-36. Home: 2 N. Hanover St., Carlisle, Pa.*

DIFFENDERFFER, Charles H.; partner Diffenderffer & Co. Mem. New York and Phila. stock exchanges. Home: Wynnewood, Pa. Office: 123 Broad St., Philadelphia, Pa.

DIFFENDORFER, Ralph Eugene; b. Hayesville, O., Aug. 15, 1879; s. Frank and Addie L. (Arnold) D.; A.B., Ohio Wesleyan U., 1902 (Phi Beta Kappa); B.D., Drew Theol. Sem., 1907; studied Union Theol. Sem., 1913-14; D.D., Ohio Wesleyan, 1925; m. M. Edna Saylor, Nov. 4, 1903. Asst. sec. Epworth League, 1902-04; sec. Missionary Edn. Movement U.S. and Can., 1904-16; ednl. sec. Bd. Home Missions and Ch. Extension and Bd. of Foreign Missions, M.E. Ch., 1916-17; asso. sec. Centenary Commn., Bd. of Home Missions and Ch. Extension, M.E. Ch., 1918; dir. of Home Missions Survey, Interchurch World Movement, 1919-20; sec. dept. of edn., com. on conservation and advance, M.E. Ch., Chicago, Ill., 1920-24; corr. sec. Bd. of Foreign Missions, M.E. Ch., since 1924. Del. 1st Internat. Conf. on Missionary Edn., Lunteren, Holland, 1911; del. to Gen. Conf. M.E. Ch., 1928, 32, 36, Rock River Annual Conference; del. to Internat. Missionary Council, Jerusalem, 1928; del. to Life and Work Council, Oxford, Eng., 1937; mem. Exec. Com. and Inter-racial Commn. of Federal Council Chs.; mem. Foreign Mission Conference of North America; chairman Com. on Coöperation in Latin America; mem. Philippine Islands Council of Am. Mission Boards; pres. Bd. of Founders Nanking Theol. Sem.; mem. Com. of International Missionary Council. Trustee Santiago (Chile) Coll., Colegio Ward (Buenos Aires), Univ. of Nanking; pres. Associated Boards for Christian Colleges in China. Mem. Methodist Fed. for Social Service, Phi Beta Kappa, Pi Gamma Mu, Theta Phi. Author: Child Life in Mission Lands, 1904; Junior Studies in the Life of Christ, 1904; A Modern Disciple of Jesus Christ—David Livingstone, 1913; Thy Kingdom Come, 1914; Missionary Education in Home and School, 1917; The Church and the Community, 1920; China-Japan?, 1937. Editor: The World Service of the Methodist Episcopal Church, 1923. Home: 8 Academy Rd., Madison, N.J. Office: 150 Fifth Av., New York, N.Y.

DI GENOVA, John; pres. Banca D'Italia & Trust Co. Home: 7238 Bradford Road, Upper Darby, Pa. Office: 727 S. Seventh St., Philadelphia, Pa.

DILKS, Walter Howard, Jr., lawyer; b. Philadelphia, Pa., Oct. 29, 1902; s. Walter H. and Clara L. (Durfor) D.; A.B., Princeton U., 1924; LL.B., Harvard Law Sch., 1927; unmarried. Admitted to Phila. bar, 1927; associated with law firm Duane, Morris & Heckscher, Philadelphia, 1927-30; in private practice since 1930; pres. and dir. Southwestern Market Co. Mem. Phila. County Bd. Law Examiners, Am. Bar Assn., Pa. Bar Assn., Philadelphia Bar Assn., Juristic Soc., Harvard Law Sch. Assn. of Philadelphia, Lawyers' Club (corr. sec.). Republican. Episcopalian. Clubs: Union League, Penn Athletic (mem. bd. govs.), Philadelphia Country (Philadelphia). Home: 8201 St. Martins Lane, Chestnut Hill. Office: 123 S. Broad St., Philadelphia, Pa.

DILL, George Clayton, elec. engring.; b. Lucas Co., O., Sept. 24, 1884; s. George Adam and Alice (Holloway) D.; ed. Northern Ind. Normal Sch., 1901-02; B.S. in E.E., Purdue U., Lafayette, Ind., 1909; unmarried. Employed in engring. and constrn. work, with various firms, 1900-11; asso. with Westinghouse Electric & Mfg. Co., East Pittsburgh, Pa., continuously since 1911; in charge application, design and mfg. lightning arresters of all kinds, designed and had charge of mfg. the Boulder Dam lightning arresters, the largest and highest arresters ever built; work has taken him to some fgn. countries; connected with electrification of many rys. in U.S. and abroad; expert in the protection of elec. systems against lightning, high voltage and high frequency disturbances. Mem. Am. Inst. E. E., L'Association Phonoïque Internationale, Internat. Lang. Assn. of Great Britain. Awarded insignia Colonial Order of The Crown and the Sovereign, Colonial Order, Americans of Royal Descent. Democrat. Student fgn. langs. and interested in an internat. lang. Office: Care Westinghouse Electric & Mfg. Co., East Pittsburgh, Pa.

DILLEN, John H.; pres. Altoona Trust Co. Home: 115 Aldrich Av., Llyswen. Office: 1130 12th Av., Altoona, Pa.

DILLER, Mary Black, portrait painter; b. Lancaster, Pa.; d. William Frey and Lida (Schofield) D.; student Carnegie Inst., 1919-20, Pa. Acad. of Fine Arts, 1920-21, Art Students League, 1921-22, Students Assn. of Drawing and Painting, 1922-23, Metropolitan Art Sch., 1922-23; unmarried. Art teacher, Shippen Sch. for Girls, Lancaster, Pa., since 1927; painter of portraits, landscapes, murals; poet. Awards: portrait prize, Iris Club, Lancaster, 1925; hon. mention for landscape, Ogunquit (Me.) Art Center, 1938; Studio Club Award, New York, 1923. Represented in permanent collections: "The Blue Pool," Albany Inst. of Art; "Piazza of Laurelton Hall," Tiffany Foundation Collection, Oyster Bay, N.Y. Lancaster County chmn., Am. Artists Professional League, 1936-1937; state dir. Am. Art Week since 1938. Mem. Lancaster County Art Assn. (pres. and founder), Am. Artists Professional League (New York), Independent Artists Assn. (New York), Am. Fed. Arts (Washington, D.C.), Art Students League of

N.Y. Episcopalian. Contbg. art editor Every Child's Mag.; contbr. to "Poetry" to "Town and Country," "Etude," "Forestry," etc. Illustrator of children's books; art critic, columnist, and feature writer, Sunday News, Lancaster, Pa., and "Arts in Phila.," Phila., Pa. Home: 48 Cottage Av., Lancaster, Pa.

DILLER, Theodore, M.D.; b. Lancaster, Pa., Aug. 25, 1863; s. of George J. and Mary (Kreider) D.; parochial and high schs.; M.D., U. of Pa., 1886; m. Rebecca Chambers Craig, of Allegheny, Pa., Sept. 8, 1899 (died 1908); children—Theodore Craig, George E., Winifred (Mrs. A. C. Mann). Practiced at Lancaster and Danville, Pa., 1886-90, Pittsburgh, 1890—. Republican. Episcopalian. Mem. A.M.A., Am. Neurol. Assn., Pittsburgh Neurol. Soc., Pittsburgh Acad. Medicine. Clubs: Duquesne, University. Author: Franklin's Contribution to Medicine, 1911; Washington in Western Pennsylvania, 1916; Pioneer Medicine in Western Pennsylvania, 1927. Home: 6861 Penn Av. Office: Westinghouse Bldg., Pittsburgh, Pa.

DILLINGER, Gregg Arthur, physician; b. Greensboro, Pa., July 21, 1871; s. L. B. and Anna M. (Evans) D.; student Waynesboro Coll.; M.D., U. of Pa. Med. Dept., 1894; m. Mary R Lynn, Nov. 9, 1897; 1 dau., Nancy. Port physician, Port of Galveston, Tex., 1898-1901; in pvt. practice at Pittsburgh, Pa., since 1904. Served as lt.-col., Med. Corps, 28th Div., A.E.F., during World War. Mem. Pittsburgh City Council, 1914-18. Author: Electro-Coagulation of Tonsils; several articles on same subject. Home: 705 S. Linden Av. Office: 1021 Empire Bldg., Pittsburgh, Pa.

DILLINGER, Harvey Eugene, lawyer; b. Dillingersville, Pa., Sept. 21, 1881; s. Charles Allen and Emma Catherine (Frederick) D.; student Perkiomen Sch. for Boys, Pennsburg, Pa., 1901-04, Keystone State Teachers Coll., Kutztown, Pa., 1904-06; LL.B., Valparaiso (Ind.) U., 1908-10; m. Bertha Velle Sparks, July 12, 1916; children—Kathleen Vivian, Harvey Eugene, James Allen, Frances Jane. Began as pub. sch. teacher, Pa. and N.J., 1902; admitted to W.Va. bar, 1912; in practice at Richwood, 1912-36, at Charleston, W.Va., since 1936; with State Tax Dept., Charleston, since 1936. Mayor, Richwood, 1916-17, city mgr., 1932-34; asst. prosecuting atty., Nicholas County, W.Va., 1924-28; chief gasoline tax dept. of W.Va., Charleston, since 1936. Democrat. Lutheran. Mason. Address: 123 Monongalia St., Charleston, W.Va.

DILLON, Charles W.; sr. mem. firm Dillon, Mahon & White; officer or dir. several companies. Address: Fayetteville, W.Va.

DILLON, Edward Saunders, physician; b. Woodbury, N.J., Mar. 21, 1890; s. Edward and Mary (Saunders) D.; grad. William Penn Charter Sch., Phila., 1907; A.B., Princeton U., 1911; M.D., Harvard, 1916; m. Eugenia Vansant, May 26, 1923; children—Edward Vansant, John Saunders, Eugenia Epting, Richard Snowdon, Charles William Larue. Interne Pa. Hosp., 1917-18; in practice as physician, Phila., since 1923; asst. prof. of metabolic diseases, U. of Pa., Grad. Sch. of Medicine since 1932; chief of metabolic div., Phila. Gen. Hosp.; asso. physician Pa. Hosp.; asst. med. dir. Penn Mutual Life Ins. Co. Served as capt. Royal Army Med. Corps, Brit. Expeditionary Force, 1916; capt., Med. Corps, U.S. Army, with A.E.F., 1918-19. Fellow Am. Coll. of Physicians, Coll. of Physicians of Phila., A.M.A. Republican. Presbyterian. Club: Princeton (Phila.). Home: Penn Valley, Pa. Office: 2016 DeLancey St., Philadelphia, Pa.

DILLON, Howard William, sales engr.; b. Altoona, Pa., Mar. 19, 1890; s. Stewart James and Carrie May (Sickles) D.; ed. South Amboy (N.J.) Pub. Sch., 1902-06, Peddie Inst., Hightstown, N.J., 1906-10; m. Cecil Waters, Mar. 1, 1911; 1 son, Darwin Walters. Apprentice machinist Pa. R.R. Co., Phila., Pa., 1909-13, draftsman, 1913-17, shop inspector, 1917-19, buyer and inspector, 1919-22; securities salesman, Campbell, Stenzel & Peterson, New York City, 1922-23; purchasing agt., Federated Engrs. Development Corpn., New York City, 1923-24, factory mgr., 1924-25; sales engr., Buckeye Portable Tool Co., New York City, 1925-26, Chicago Pneumatic Tool Co., Phila., 1926-28, Gold Car Heating & Lighting Co., New York City, 1928-35, Paxton-Mitchell Co., Omaha, Neb., since 1935. Pres. South Amboy (N.J.) Bd. of Edu. Pres. South Amboy (N.J.) Chapter Am. Red Cross. Dir. South Amboy (N.J.) Hosp. Bd. Mem. Am. Soc. M.E. Republican. Methodist. Jr. O.U.A.M., K.P., Artisans Order ot Mutual Protection. Clubs: New York R.R. (New York); Pittsburgh (Pa.) R.R. Home: 312 Main St., South Amboy, N.J. Office: Paxton-Mitchell Co., Omaha, Neb.

DILLON, Samuel M.; pres. Wilmington Sash & Door Co. Home: 1114 Berkley Road. Office: Front and Madison Sts., Wilmington, Del.

DILLON, Walter Stanley, newspaper editor; b. Reading, Pa., Feb. 23, 1893; s. William Henry and Margaret Amanda (McKinney) D.; grad. Reading (Pa.) High Sch., 1911; m. Irene Catharine Leas, of Reading, Pa., Jan. 28, 1929. Reporter successively on Reading (Pa.) Times, Reading (Pa.) Telegram, Reading (Pa.) Eagle, 1912-26; asst. city editor, Reading (Pa.) Eagle, 1926-33, city editor, 1933-34, mng. editor since 1934. Home: 216 Amherst Av., Lincoln Park, Pa. Office: 30 N. 4th St., Reading, Pa.

DILSER, F. Harry; editor Pottstown Herald. Address: 146 King St., Pottstown, Pa.

DIMMITT, Luther Mason, writer and educational research; b. Kansas City, Mo., Sept. 27, 1889; s. Frederick Robert and Martha (Mason) D.; U. of Mo., 1911-12; A.B., Westminster Coll., Fulton, Mo., 1920; Th.M. Princeton Theol. Sem., 1922; A.M., U. of Tex., 1924; grad. study, U. of Pa., 1927, Columbia, 1926-28; m. Mary Robnett, Apr. 22, 1922; children—Margaret Anne, Mary Frances. Salesman, wholesale drugs, 1909-11; student sec. Y.M.C.A., Ore. State Agrl. Coll., 1920-21; sec. Presbyn. Com. of Christian Edn., Louisville, Ky., 1921-22; student pastor, University of Tex., 1922-24, instructor in educational psychology, same university, 1924-26; assistant editor Young People's Publications, Bd. of Christian Edn., Presbyn. Ch. in U.S.A., 1926-27; asst. prof. edn., Duke U., 1928-30, mem. faculty Summer Sch.; gen. dir. dept. ednl. research, Bd. of Christian Edn., Presbyn. Ch. in U.S.A., since 1930; dir. Department of Student Aid since 1937. Mem. American Acad. Polit. and Social Science, Am. Assn. Adult Edn., Internat. Council Religious Edn. (Young People's Professional Advisory Sect. and Research Advisory Sect.), Gen. Edn. Board Fellowship, N.E.A., Am. Assn. Univ. Profs., Delta Tau Delta, Phi Delta Kappa, Kappa Delta Pi, Appalachian Mountain Club. Home: 7 Swarthmore Pl., Swarthmore, Pa. Office: 814 Witherspoon Bldg., Philadelphia, Pa.

DINES, Lloyd Lyne, univ. prof.; b. Shelbyville, Mo., Mar. 29, 1885; s. Henry Bascom and Martha Lyne (Duncan) D.; A.B., Northwestern U., Evanston, Ill., 1906, A.M., 1907; Ph.D., U. of Chicago, 1911; unmarried. Instr., Columbia U., 1911-13; asso. prof. mathematics, U. of Arizona, Tucson, Ariz., 1913-14; asst. prof. mathematics, U. of Saskatchewan, Can., 1914-19, prof., 1919-33, dean, 1930-33; prof. and head dept. of mathematics, Carnegie Inst. Tech., since 1933. Mem. Am. Math. Soc., Math. Assn. of America, A.A.A.S., Royal Soc. of Can., Societe Mathematique de France, Cricolo Matematico di Palermo, Phi Beta Kappa, Sigma Xi. Club: Riverside Country (Saskatoon, Can.). Author many articles for math. jours. and speeches before math. orgns. Home: 120 Ruskin Av. Office: Carnegie Institute of Technology, Pittsburgh, Pa.

DINSMORE, Carlos Millson, church official; b. nr. St. Marys, Ont., Can., Jan. 28, 1875; s. Andrew and Mary B. (Millson) D.; brought to U.S., 1881; A.B., Kalamazoo (Mich.) Coll., 1900; B.D., U. of Chicago, 1907; D.D., Franklin (Ind.) Coll., 1920; m. Bertha Irwin Buschman, Aug. 26, 1903; children—Dorothy Irwin (Mrs. Raymond E. Blackwell), Margaret Millson (Mrs. H. A. Lynes), William James, Bertha Elizabeth. Ordained Bapt. ministry, 1902; pastor Ocoya and Harvey, Ill., until 1907, Anderson, Ind., 1907-14, Evansville, 1914-15; gen. supt. Ind. Bapt. Conv., 1915-31; sec. Am. Bapt. Home Mission Soc. since 1931. Republican. Home: 1119 E. Laurelton Parkway, West Englewood, N.J. Office: 23 E. 26th St., New York, N.Y.

DINTENFASS, Henry, physician; b. Tarnow, Austria, Apr. 2, 1885; s. Jacob and Miriam (Rosenfeld) D.; brought to U.S. when 3 months old; student Central High Sch., Phila., 1888-1901; M.D., U. of Pa., 1905; U. of Vienna, 1907-08; m. Lillian Beck, Mar. 29, 1932; 1 dau., Miriam. Asso. prof. of otology, Grad. Sch. of Medicine, U. of Pa.; otological staff, Hosp. of the Grad Sch. of Medicine; chief otolaryngologist Skin and Cancer Hospital; also consulting otolaryngologist Northeastern Home, Downtown Jewish Orphans Home, Homewood, and Jewish Seaside Home (Atlantic City, N.J.). Fellow American College of Surgeons, American Bd. of Otolaryngology, Am. Coll. Laryngology, Otology, and Rhinology, Coll. of Physicians of Phila.; mem. Phila. Laryngol. Soc., Phila. Co. Med. Soc. (chmn. 1938, Southeast Branch), Pathological Soc., Med. Club, Phi Delta Upsilon. Hebrew. Club: Philmont (Pa.) Country. Devised paracentesis knife, 1922; has collection of motion pictures showing all operative procedures on ear, nose and throat; author of many articles on ear, nose and throat diseases, operations and treatment. Home: Lenox Apt. Office: 1305 Spruce St., Philadelphia, Pa.

DIPPEL, Adelbert Louis, obstetrician; b. La Grange, Tex., July 10, 1901; s. Albert Julius and Amelia Christine (Kuhn) D.; student Blinn Memorial Coll., Brenham, Tex., 1919-20; A.B., U. of Tex., Austin, 1924, A.M., 1924; M.D., U. of Tex. Med. Sch., Galveston, 1928; m. Ann Rebecca Bond, June 1, 1933; 1 dau., Patricia Ann. Interne Hermann Hosp., Houston, Tex., 1928-29, Presbyn. Hosp., Chicago, 1929-30, Johns Hopkins Hosp., Baltimore, 1931-35; asst. in pathology, Johns Hopkins U. Med. Sch., 1930-31; in practice, Baltimore, since 1935; instr. in obstetrics, Johns Hopkins U. Med. Sch., 1934-37, asso. in obstetrics since 1937. Certified by Am. Bd. Obstetrics and Gynecology. Fellow Am. Coll. Surgeons, A.M.A.; mem. Med. and Chirurg. Faculty of Md., Theta Kappa Psi. Home: 300 E. 30th St., Baltimore, Md.

DIPPELL, Victor William, prof. German; b. Huntington, Ind., Feb. 17, 1874; s. P. H. and Martha (Merman) D.; A.B., U. of Pa., 1895, Ph.D., 1899; (hon.) LL.D., Franklin & Marshall Coll., Lancaster, Pa., 1935; m. Marion Fox, Apr. 3, 1902. Began as instr. Temple Coll., Phila., 1897-98; minister St. John's Reformed Ch. Lebanon, Pa., 1901-10; prof. German, Franklin and Marshall Coll., Lancaster, Pa., since 1910; dir. Educators Beneficial Assn., Health and Accident Ins. for Teachers, Lancaster, Pa. Served on Mil. Intelligence div. U.S. Army. Dir. Stevens Industrial Sch. Mem. Assn. of Teachers of German, Modern Lang. Assn., Phi Beta Kappa, Phi Kappa Sigma. Republican. Evang. and Reformed Ch. Mason, Odd Fellow. Clubs: University (dir.), Kiwanis, (Lancaster, Pa.) Lebanon Co. Golf (Lebanon, Pa.). Author: History of Red Cross (Lancaster Branch) in World War; Register of Officers and Nurses of Lancaster Co. in World War. Formerly editorial writer for Lancaster New Era. Home: 520 President Av., Lancaster, Pa.

DISQUE, Robert Conrad, educator; b. Burlington, Ia., Mar. 14, 1883; s. Frederick Jacob and Marie Louisa (Holstein) D.; B.L., U. of Wis., 1903, B.S. in E.E., 1908; grad. study, U. of Pa., 1925-31; m. Laura Maud Crafts, of Manchester, N.H., June 14, 1921; children—Sarah Marie, Robert Otis, Helen Cushman. Teacher high sch., Burlington, Ia., 1903-05; engr., Milwaukee Electric & Ry. Co., 1908; instr. in elec. engring., U. of Wis., 1908-17; prof. elec. engring., Drexel Inst., Philadelphia, Pa., 1919-24, academic dean since 1924, dean of the faculty, 1932. Served as 1st lt. Air Service, U.S.A., 1917, capt., 1918; maj. U.S. Res., 1918-24. Dir. Sch. Dist. of Swarthmore. Mem. Am. Inst. E.E., Soc. for Promotion Engring. Edn., Phi Beta Kappa, Sigma Xi, Tau Beta Pi, Alpha Sigma Phi, Eta Kappa Nu, Phi Kappa Phi.

Democrat. Mason. Home: 918 Strath Haven Av., Swarthmore, Pa.*

DISSINGER, Chester Becker, sch. supt.; b. Dauphin, Pa., May 3, 1898; s. S. Neitz and Minerva Lindley (Ennis) D.; student State Teachers Coll., Kutztown, Pa., 1915-17; B.S., U. of Pittsburgh, 1932; M.A., New York U., 1935; LL.D., Hahnemann Med. Coll., Phila., 1938; m. Blanche Cross, Sept. 20, 1923. Teacher Milford (Pa.) High Sch., 1917, asst. prin., 1918; prin., Union Twp. (Pa.) Consolidated Sch., Schuylkill Co., 1919-20; asst. prin., Milford (Pa.) Schs., 1920-22; supt. Pike Co. (Pa.) Schs. since 1922. Served as pvt. Chem. Warfare Service, U.S. Army, 1918. Member Pa. State Edn. Assn., Nat. Edn. Assn., Am. Assn. Sch. Adminstrs., Phi Delta Kappa, Pi Gamma Mu, Kappa Phi Kappa. Democrat. Mason, Lions. Home: 507 Broad St. Office: Court House, Milford, Pa.

DISSTON, Henry; pres. Henry Disston & Sons. Home: Bellevue-Stratford Hotel. Office: Unroh & Milner Sts., Tacony, Philadelphia, Pa.

DISTLER, Theodore August, coll. dean; b. Brooklyn, N.Y., Nov. 22, 1898; s. Ernst Frederick and Marie (Kossman) D.; student Stevens Sch., N.J., 1914-18, Brown U., Providence, R.I., 1918-19; B.S., N.Y. Univ., 1922, M.A., 1932; m. Alice Boxold, of Brooklyn, N.Y., June 30, 1923; children—Theodore Alden, Paul Antonie. Mem. faculty N.Y. Univ., 1922-25, asst. in pub. speaking, 1924-25, instr. pub. speaking and sec. com. on admissions, 1925-26, sec. same and asst. dir. student welfare, 1926-28, sec. same and dir. student welfare, 1928-29; dir. student personnel, 1929-34, instr. in personnel administrn., summer 1932, grand marshal, 1929-34; dean of Lafayette Coll., Easton, Pa., since 1934. Now maj. Ordnance Res., U.S. Army. Mem. Eastern Assn. Coll. Deans and Advisers of Men (sec.-treas. 1929-33, pres. 1933-34, mem. exec. com. since 1934), Eastern Coll. Personnel Officers Assn., Soc. for Promotion Engring. Edn., Nat. Vocational Guidance Assn., Nat. Assn. Deans and Advisers of Men, Am. Coll. Personnel Assn., Scabbard and Blade, Phi Beta Kappa, Zeta Psi, Phi Delta Kappa, Tau Kappa Alpha. Presbyn. Clubs: Rotary (dir. 1935-36, pres. 1936-37), Faculty clubs of New York U. and Lafayette Coll., Northampton Country (all Easton, Pa.); Faculty, Zeta Psi (New York). Home: Dean's House. Office: Pardee Hall, Easton, Pa.

DITHRICH, W. Heber, judge; b. Pittsburgh, Pa., Oct. 25, 1886; s. William J. and Ellen J. (Welsh) D.; A.B., Washington and Jefferson Coll., Washington, Pa., 1909; LL.B., U. of Pittsburgh Law Sch., 1912; m. Lois Wood, Nov. 2, 1918; 1 son, Charles Wood. Admitted to Pa. bar, 1912, and since engaged in gen. practice of law at Pittsburgh; served as mem. Pa. Ho. of Rep., 1916-21; asst. U.S. Atty., 1921-24; solicitor Allegheny Co., 1924-30; apptd. judge Ct. of Common Pleas, 1930, elected for ten-yr. term, 1931; dir. Coraopolis Trust Co. Served as 1st lt. Cav., U.S. Army, on Mexican border and in World War. Trustee Mercersburg Acad., Family Soc. of Allegheny Co., Valley Hosp., Sewickley. Mem. Pa. State and Allegheny Co. bar assns., Phi Delta Theta, Phi Delta Phi. Republican. Episcopalian. Clubs: Duquesne (Pittsburgh); Hunt (Sewickley, Pa.). Home: Richwood, Coraopolis, Pa. Office: City-County Bldg., Pittsburgh, Pa.

DITTER, J. William, congressman; b. Philadelphia, Pa., Sept. 5, 1888; s. George and Elizabeth (Weissgerber) D.; LL.B., Temple U. Law Sch., 1913; m. Mabel Sylvester Bearné, of Phila., Sept. 2, 1913; children—Mabel Bearné, John William. Prof. history and commerce, Phila. high schs., 1912-25; admitted to Pa. bar, 1913; in practice since 1925; now mem. firm Ditter and Menges; mem. 73d to 76th Congress (1933-41), 17th Pa. Dist. Trustee Burd Rogers Memorial Home. Mem. Pa. and Montgomery bar assns. Republican. Protestant. Mason, Moose. Club: Rotary. Home: Tennis Av. Office: Old Nat. Bank Bldg., Ambler, Pa.

DITTMAR, Charles Frederick, lawyer; b. Freehold, N.J., Dec. 12, 1888; s. Adolph C. and Pauline S. (Graeber) D.; grad. Freehold High Sch., 1905; LL.B., N.Y. Law Sch., 1912; student Bordeaux (France) U., 1918; m. Margaret Arabella Ehrlen, July 17, 1938. Admitted to N.J. bar, 1913, counsellor at law, 1916; mem. firm C. F. & J. E. Dittmar, attys. at law, Freehold, N.J., since 1916. Continuously except for War period and a time thereafter in Arizona on account of health. Served in U.S. Army, 1917-19. Private, capt. Mem. Am. Bar Assn., N.J. State Bar Assn., Monmouth Co. Bar Assn., Am. Legion. Episcopalian. Home: 128 W. Main St. Office: 11 South St., Freehold, N.J.

DIVELY, G. Nevin, lawyer; b. Claysburg, Pa., Nov. 29, 1895; s. Benjamin F. and Generva (Claar) D.; ed. Millersville (Pa.) Teachers Coll., 1913-17; LL.B., Dickinson Coll. Sch. of Law, Carlisle, Pa., 1922; m. Esther Hower, June 7, 1921. Began as teacher high sch., Altoona, Pa., 1922-26; admitted to Pa. bar, 1926 and engaged in gen. practice of law at Altoona, Pa., since 1926; solicitor for important local corpns. Served as hosp. sergt. Med. Corps, U.S.A., 1918-19. Mem. Bd. Viewers Blair Co. since 1932. Mem. Pa. and Blair Co. (bd. govs.) bar assns., Woolsack, Travelers Club, Am. Legion, Am. Legion Home Assn, Beta Theta Pi. Republican. Reformed Ch. Mason (32°, Shriner). Clubs: Jaffa Shrine, Y.M.C.A. (Altoona, Pa.); Acadia (Williamsport, Pa.). Home: 105 Aldrich Av. Office: 1321 11th Av., Altoona, Pa.

DIVELY, M. Augustus, sch. supt.; b. Sproul, Pa., Oct. 17, 1872; s. George M. and Margaret A. (Dell) D.; student Lock Haven (Pa.) Teachers Coll., Pa. State Coll., U. of Pittsburgh, Harvard U., Columbia U.; m. Mattie A. Dodson, Sept. 9, 1898; children—George S., Clyde A., Mrs. Jennie Gardner. Country sch. teacher, Greenfield Twp., Pa., 1892-1902; prin. Graysport Borough Sch., Pa., 1902-06, Miller Sch., Altoona, Pa., 1906-20; supervising prin., Miller and Garfield schs., Altoona, 1920-24; supt. Logan Twp. (Pa.) schs., 1924-31; asst. supt., Blair Co., Pa., 1931-33, supt. since 1933, having been re-elected, 1938, for term ending 1942; teacher summer normal schs., 1898-1906; instr. for Am. Banking Assn. and adult night classes, Altoona, Pa.; also engeged in state highway constrn. and banking. Mem. Pa. State Edn. Assn., N.E.A. Mason (K.T., Shriner). Author: numerous articles and addresses on ednl., scientific, social, hist., and religious subjects. Home: 108 Logan Av., Altoona, Pa. Office: Court House, Hollidaysburg, Pa.

DIVEN, John, M.D.; b. Anderson, Ind., Oct. 2, 1883; s. William S. and Laura M. (McConnell)• D.; student pub. schs., Anderson, Ind., 1890-99, pvt. sch., Strassbourg, Alsace, Germany, 1900-02; A.B., Ind. U., Bloomington, Ind., 1904; M.D., Med. Sch., U. of Pa., 1912; unmarried. Engaged in practice of medicine, specializing in diseases of infants and children, since 1912. Mem. Phila. Co. Med. Soc., Pa. State Med. Soc., A.M.A., Phi Kappa Psi, Nu Sigma Nu. Home: Green Hill Farms, Overbrook. Office: 326 S. 19th St., Philadelphia, Pa.

DIX, Edgar Hutton, Jr., metallurgist; b. Baltimore, Md., Aug. 11, 1892; s. Edgar Hutton and Margaret Jane Grey (Chesley) D.; student Baltimore Poly. Inst., 1907-11; M.E., Cornell U., 1914, M.M.E., 1916; m. Mary Opie Tabb, Oct. 15, 1919. Instr. engring. materials and materials testing, Cornell U., 1914-16; in employ mfg. concerns, 1916-18; asst. engr. of tests, Lynite Labs. Aluminum Castings Co., Cleveland, O., 1919-20; chief, metals branch, material sect., engring, div., A.S., U.S.A., Dayton, O., 1920-23; metallurgist in charge New Kensington Metall. Div., Aluminum Research Labs., Aluminum Co. of America, New Kensington, Pa., 1923-30, chief metallurgist since 1930. Served as chief, testing dept., gen. labs., Bur. of Aircraft Production, U.S. Army, Pittsburgh, 1918-19. Mem. Am. Soc. for Testing Materials, Am. Inst. Mining and Metall. Engrs., Am. Soc. for Metals, Soc. of Automotive Engrs., British Inst. of Metals, Nat. Advisory Com. for Aeronautics (mem. materials com.), Sigma Xi. Republican. Presbyterian. Clubs: Hillcrest County (New Kensington, Pa.); University (Pittsburgh). Home: 834 Tenth St., Oakmont. Office: P.O. Box 772, New Kensington, Pa.

DIX, William Frederick, life ins.; b. Newark, N.J., Nov. 18, 1867; s. John Edwin and Mary Fisher (Joy) D.; student Princeton, 1889; m. Mary Alice Tennille, June 2, 1900; children—Tennille Dix, Alison Joy, Norman B. World tour, 1890-92; literary editor The Churchman, 1894; editor The Home Journal, New York, name changed to Town and Country, 1900-06; sec. Mut. Life Ins. Co. of New York, May, 1906-33. Trustee Adelphi Coll., Brooklyn, 1913; chmn. bd. trustees Carnegie Fund. Mem. Soc. Colonial Wars (gov. 1910-12; dep. gov. gen. 1913, N.J. Soc.), Soc. Founders and Patriots (gov. N.J. Soc., 1918-21; sec. gen. of Gen. Ct., 1920-22); formerly chmn. Bd. Internat. Hospitality of N.Y., chmn. exec. com. Nat. Security League and treas. and trustee Carteret Acad. (Orange, N.J.). Capt. E. Orange (N.J.) Rifles; col. New York Police Reserve. Consul gen. of Montenegro in New York, 1918-21, in charge of Legation, 1920-21. Decorated by King Nicholas with Grand Cross of the Order of Danilo I, in recognition of services for Montenegro. Clubs: Authors (former treas.), Princeton (New York); Westhampton Country (L.I.), Orange Lawn Tennis, Rock Spring Country. Author: The Face in the Girandole; The Lost Princess; Daphne of the Forest; (in collaboration) Man and the Two Worlds. Home: South Orange, N.J.; and Westhampton Beach, L.I., N.Y.

DIXON, Charles Francis, engineer, b. Newburgh, N.Y., May 3, 1877; s. Charles A. and Kathryn Ann (Harris) D.; student Newburgh (N.Y. High Sch., 1890-92, Acad., 1892-94; m. Jessie Fraser Lamb, June 20, 1900; children—Marion B. Minard, Janet K. Mainwaring. Asst. supt. Wright Steam Engine Works, Newburgh, N.Y., 1898-1900; chief draftsman Am. Stoker Co., New York, 1900-03; partner Mangelsderff, Dixon and Brower, New York, 1903-05; supervising engr. and dir. C. E. Hewitt Co., New York, 1905-08, Smith, Meeker Co., New York, 1908-10; power engr. The New England Engring Co., Waterbury, Conn., 1910-14; asst. constrn. engr. Interboro Rapid Transit Co., New York, 1914-15; supt. river station Buffalo (N.Y.) Gen. Electric Co., 1915-17; power and supervising engr. Westinghouse, Church, Kerr Co., which merged with Dwight P. Robinson Co., 1920, which merged with United Engrs. and Constructors, Phila., 1928, since 1917. Mem. Am. Soc., M.E. Republican. Mason (Hudson River Lodge, Newburgh, N.Y.; Long Beach Consistory, Calif.; Al Malaikah Temple, Los Angeles, Calif.). Home: Brookside Av., St. Davids, Pa. Office: 1401 Arch St., Philadelphia, Pa.

DIXON, Frank Haigh, educator; b. Winona, Minn., Oct. 8, 1869; s. Alfred C. and Caroline A. D.; Ph.B., U. of Mich., 1892, Ph.D., 1895; m. Alice L. Tucker, Apr. 17,1900; children—William Tucker, Caroline Moorhouse, Roger Coit. Asst. polit. economy, 1892-95, instr. history, 1896-97; asst. prof. polit. economy, 1897-98, U. of Mich.; asst. prof. economics, 1898-1903, prof. 1903-19, Dartmouth Coll.; prof. economics, Princeton Univ., 1919-38, prof. emeritus since 1938. Sec. Amos Tuck Sch. of Administration and Finance, Dartmouth, 1900-04; expert for Interstate Commerce Commn., 1907-08, Nat. Waterways Commn., 1909; chief statistician, Bur. of Ry. Economics, 1910-18; spl. expert U.S. Shipping Bd., 1918. Mem. exec. com. N.H. Com. on Pub. Safety, 1917-18. Mem. Am. Economic Assn. (vice-pres. 1927), Am. Assn. University Profs. Club: Princeton (New York). Author: State Railroad Control, 1896; A Traffic History of the Mississippi, 1909; (joint author) War Administration of Railways in United States and Great Britain, 1918; Railroads and Government, Their Relations in the United States, 1922. Joint Author: Stabilization of Business, 1923; Facing the Facts, 1932. Contbr. to mags. Home: 101 Broadmead, Princeton, N.J.

DIXON, James, banker; b. nr. Easton, Md., May 4, 1873; s. Robert Bartlett and Sarah Amanda (Amoss) D.; student Friends Sch., Easton, Md., 1879-89, Swarthmore (Pa.) Coll., 1889-91; m. Elizabeth Thomas Wright, Apr. 30, 1912; 1 son, Robert Bartlett. Pres. Easton Nat. Bank of Md. since 1918; pres. Robert B. Dixon & Co., Inc., Easton, Md., since 1921;

dir. Baltimore Branch Federal Reserve Bank. Republican. Mem. Soc. of Friends. Club: Chesapeake Bay Yacht. Address: Easton, Md.

DIXON, John Edward, pres. Lima Locomotive Works; b. Milwaukee, Wis., Sept. 11, 1877; s. Fred J. and Harriett M. (Buck) D.; B.S. in mech. engring., U. of Wis.; m. Elizabeth Sherman, Oct. 5, 1905 (died Aug. 14, 1927); children—John Sherman, Dorothy (Mrs. John G. Watson); m. 2d, Helen C. Windle, Nov. 18, 1937; children—William W. Windle, Joy Windle. Began with Brooks Locomotive Works, Dunkirk, N.Y., 1900, successively asst. foreman, foreman, draftsman, traveling engr., chief inspector, 1900-04; asso. with N.Y. Am. Locomotive Co., 1904; asst. mgr., later mgr., Atlantic Equipment Co. (branch of Am. Locomotive Co.) to 1907; salesman, later asst. mgr. sales, Am. Locomotive Co., 1907-16; with Lima Locomotive Works, Inc., since 1916, as v.p., 1916-39, pres. and dir. since 1939; dir. Franklin Ry. Supply Co., Combustion Engring. Co., Inc. Home: 295 Harrison St., East Orange, N.J. Office: 60 E. 42d St., New York, N.Y.

DIXON, John W.; surgeon Pittsburgh Hosp. Address: 901 Wood St., Wilkinsburg, Pa.

DIXON, Mary Quincy Allen (Mrs. George Dallas Dixon), writer; b. Phila., Pa., Mar. 30, 1859; d. William H. (LL.D.) and Mary F. (Quincy) Allen; father served as pres. Dickinson Coll., State Coll., Pa., and Girard Coll.; desc. Edmund Quincy, from England to Boston, 1628; ed. pvt. schs. and corr. courses; m. George Dallas Dixon (formerly v.p. Pa. R.R.), Nov. 26, 1879; children—George Mifflin Dallas, II, Honora Allen, Mary F. Quincy. Mem. Soc. Mayflower Descendants (dep. gov. gen., Pa.), Dames of the Magna Charta, Colonial Dames of America, D.A.R., Society of New England Women, League Am. Pen Women (v.p. Pa. br.), Phila. Art Alliance, Republican Women of Pa. Clubs: Plays and Players of Phila. (charter mem. and v.p.), Acorn. Author: (three-act plays) The Bootleggers' Landing, and The Iron Grip; (one-act plays) Among the Pines, Which Turn?, and The Other Body; also book and lyrics of a musical comedy, The Marriage Tax. Contbr. verse and short stories. Home: Chateau Crillon, 19th and Locust Sts., Philadelphia, Pa.

DIXON, Russell Winfield, banker; b. Penn Twp., Butler Co., Pa., Jan. 19, 1880; s. Winfield Scott and Annie (Balph) D.; student West Sunbury Academy, Slippery Rock State Normal School; m. Gaynelle McAnallen, June 1920. Paymaster Am. Tin Plate Co., 1901-02; dep. county treas., Butler Co., Pa., 1902-03; cashier Farmers Nat. Bank, Butler, Pa., 1903-27; v.p. Butler County Nat. Bank & Trust Co., Butler, Pa., 1927-33, v.p. and trust officer since 1934; conservator Oil City (Pa.) Nat. Bank, 1933-34. Methodist (mem. 1st M.E. Ch., Butler). Clubs: Butler (Pa.) Country. Home: 246 W. Penn St. Address: The Butler County National Bank and Trust Co., Butler, Pa.

DOAK, Frank F., banker; b. Pittsburgh, Pa., Aug. 10, 1888; s. William and Mary (Neillie) D.; ed. pub. sch. and high sch. to 1905; m. Meta Waltenberger, of Louisville, Ky., July 22, 1914; 1 son, Frank E. Began as clk. LaBelle Plant of Crucible Steel Co., 1905-09; asso. with Fidelity Trust Co., Pittsburgh, continuously since 1909, asst. sec., 1915-34, v.p. since 1934; dir. McCann & Co. Republican. United Presbyterian. Clubs: Longue Vue, Pittsburgh Athletic, Metropolitan, Highland Country (Pittsburgh); Pendennis (Louisville, Ky.). Home: 501 Edgerton Pl. Office: 341 4th Av., Pittsburgh, Pa.

DOAN, Francis Janney, prof. dairy mfg.; b. Phila., Pa., Sept. 20, 1896; s. James Irwin and Elisabeth Torbert (Janney) D.; student Pa. State Coll., 1915-18, B.S., 1922, M.S., 1928; student U. of Md., 1922-25; m. Josephine Cornelia Bentley, Aug. 28, 1923 (dec.); children —David Bentley, Cynthia Janney; m. 2d, Lucy Adell Jennison, Aug. 23, 1930; 1 dau., Marilyn Almah. Began as plant chemist, Nestles Food Co., 1919, dist. chemist, mid-west div., Chicago, 1921-22; chemist and bacteriologist, Waddington Condensed Milk Co., N.Y. City, 1922; instr. dairy chemistry, U. of Md., 1922-25; asst. prof. dairy mfg., Pa. State Coll., 1925-28, asso. prof., 1928-33, prof. dairy mfg. since 1933. Served as pvt., Inf. U.S.Army, 1918. Mem. Am. Dairy Science Assn., Sigma Xi, Gamma Sigma Delta, Theta Chi. Republican. Presbyterian. Club: University (State College, Pa.). Contbr. professional and tech. papers and bulls. on dairy chemistry and dairy tech. Home: 711 Holmes St., State College, Pa.

DOAN, Gilbert Everett, physical chemist; b. Lansdale, Pa., Jan. 16, 1897; s. William E. and Agnes Sibbald (McKinlay) D.; Chem. E., Lehigh U. (Mercur scholar), 1919; Ph.D., U. of Berlin, Germany, 1927; m. Alice Curtis Olney, of Charleston, S.C., Nov. 23, 1929; children—Gilbert Everett, Julia Alice Curtis, Agnes Sibbald. Metallographist, U.S. Naval Expt. Sta., Annapolis, 1919-20; dir. research Una Welding Co., Cleveland, 1920-24; spl. mission to Germany, 1922-23; prof. metallurgy, Lehigh U., since 1926; consultant U.S. Naval Research Lab., 1929; consultant General Electric Co., 1929, Roller Smith Co., 1929, Union Carbide & Carbon Co., 1934; dir. Engring. Foundation Welding Research, 1930; guest lecturer Franklin Inst., 1932. Inventor of welding processes, and circuit breakers. Commended by President Hoover for work in discovery of radiographic testing by gamma rays from radium, 1929. Fellow A.A.A.S.; mem. Sigma Xi and many scientific and tech. socs., Omicron Delta Kappa, Delta Upsilon. Club: Saucon Valley Country. Author: The Principals of Physical Metallurgy, 1935. Joint-Author: The Principles of Metallurgy, 1933, also many tech. and scientific papers. Contbr. to "The American Scholar." Home: R. 2, Bethlehem, Pa.

DOANE, Joseph Chapman, M.D.; b. Tioga, Pa., Nov. 3, 1884; s. Joseph Chapman and Myra (Horton) D.; grad. Mansfield (Pa.) State Teachers Coll., 1903; M.D., Medico-Chirurg. Coll. of Phila., 1912; m. Lelah Sterling, Brooklyn, Pa., Dec. 30, 1914. Teacher, high sch., St. Marys, Pa., 1903-06; chief resident physician, Presbyn. Hosp., Phila., Pa., 1912-13; asst. surgeon and asst. supt. Pa. State Hosp., Shamokin, 1914; chief resident physician, Phila. Gen. Hosp., 1914-19, med. dir. and supt., 1920-28; also supt. bureau of hosps., Phila. Dept. Pub. Health, 1920-28; asso. prof. medicine, grad. sch., U. of Pa., since 1920; med. dir. Jewish Hosp., Phila., since 1928; prof. of clin. medicine, Temple U. Med. School of Phila.; editor Modern Hospital Mag. V.p. Phila. Co. Prison Bd.; mem. Phila. Bd. Health. Fellow A.M.A., Am. Coll. Physicians, Phila. Coll. Physicians; mem. Am. Hosp. Assn. (ex-pres.), Pa. State Hosp. Assn. (ex-pres.), Phila. Hosp. Assn. (ex-pres.), Phila. Co. Med. Soc., Phi Rho Sigma. Republican. Mason. Club: Medical. Contbr. to Modern Hospital, Med. Clinics of N. America, etc., and med. textbooks. Home: 617 W. Hortter St. Office: 269 S. 19th St., Philadelphia, Pa.

DOBBS, Edward Clarence, dental educator; b. Holyoke, Mass., May 8, 1903; s. Scott Edward and Mary (Lafabre) D.; D.D.S., U. of Md., Baltimore, 1929; Interne Church Home and Infirmary Hosp., 1929-30; Rockefeller fellow U. of Rochester (N.Y.) Med. Sch., 1930-32; unmarried. Head dept. of pharmacology and therapeutics, Dental Sch., U. of Md., Baltimore, since 1932. Mem. Am. Dental Assn., U. of Md. Biol. Soc., Gorgas Odontological Soc., A.A.A.S. Internat. Assn. Dental Research, Xi Psi Phi, Omicron Kappa Upsilon, Sigma Xi. Congregationalist. Contbr. research articles to Jour. Am. Dental Assn., etc. Home: 3603 Hicks Av. Office: Dental School, University of Maryland, Baltimore, Md.

DOBBS, Joseph, bldg. contractor; b. Far Hills, N.J., Aug. 30, 1878; s. Francis and Anna Eliza (Crampton) D.; student Mine Brook Sch., Far Hills, N.J., 1883-95; diploma for complete archtl. course, Internat. Corr. Sch., 1907; m. Lizzie Anna Nuse, Nov. 19, 1903; children—Clarence Ellsworth, Marjorie Elna (Mrs. Ray Saunders Taylor), Harold Joseph, Evelyn (Mrs. Alan Hynd), Vera (Mrs. Charles Herbert Lighthipe), Wilma. Began as carpenter, Bernardsville, N.J., 1894; began own contracting business, 1909, incorporated as Joseph Dobbs, Inc., bldg. contractor specializing in residence work, Bernardsville, N.J., 1925, pres. since 1925; founded Bernards Builders' Supply Co., Inc., Bernardsville, N.J., 1928, and since pres.; v.p. B. & B. Sales Corpn. since 1932; dir. Bernardsville Nat. Bank. Served as 1st lt., N.J. Militia Res., 1917-19. Commr. pub. safety, Bernardsville, N.J., 1931-33, mem. Borough Council, 1924-33, v.p. Bd. of Health since 1936, fire chief Bernardsville Fire Co., 1915-17. Mem. Eastern Assn. of Fire Chiefs. Republican. Presbyterian (elder Liberty Corner, N.J., Presbyn. Ch.). Mem. Order United Am. Mechanics (North Star Council 222). Mason; life mem. A.A.S.R. (32°) Valley of Trenton; mem. Odo de St. Amand Commandery, No. 12, K.T., State of N.J.; mem. Salaam Temple, A.A.O.N.M.S., Newark, N.J.; mem. Madison Chapter No. 27, Grand Royal Arch Chapter of N.J. (Morristown); mem. Congdon Lodge No. 201 F. and A. M., Bernardsville, N.J., Blue Lodge. Club: Bernardsville (N.J.) Rotary (first pres., 1927-28). Home: 56 Mt. Airy Rd. Office: Bernardsville, N.J.

DOBSON, Edgar F.; v.p. and dir. New Amsterdam Casualty Co. Address: 227 St. Paul St., Baltimore, Md.

DOBSON, Frank M.; football coach, U. of Md. Address: University of Maryland, College Park, Md.

DODD, Francis Joseph, clergyman; b. Brooklyn, N.Y., Apr. 8, 1888; s. James and Elizabeth (Hughes) D.; prep. edn., St. Johns Coll. Prep., Brooklyn; A.B., St. Johns Coll., 1908, A.M., 1910; grad. study St. Vincent's Sem., Germantown, Phila., Pa., 1910-12; Ph.D., De-Paul U., 1920. Ordained priest R.C. Ch., 1912; prof. in science dept. St. Johns Coll. High Sch. Dept., 1913-14; prof. chemistry, Niagara U., 1914-17, prof. philosophy, 1919; dir. of seminarians, Sem. of Our Lady of Angels, Niagara U., 1920-27; pres. Niagara U., 1927-29; dir. Sisters of Charity, Eastern Prov. of U.S., 1929—; Chaplain, rank of 1st lt., U.S.A., Camp Merritt, N.J., 1918-19. Mem. Am. Catholic Philos. Assn.; honorary corr. mem. Institut Littéraire et Artistique de France. Address: Emmitsburg, Md.

DODD, Howard Saunier, lawyer; b. Glen Ridge, N.J., Feb. 15, 1886; s. Lewis K. and Susan A. (Hanna) D.; A.B., Williams Coll., 1909; LL.B., N.Y. Law Sch., 1911; LL.M, New Jersey Law Sch., 1912; m. Angie M. Crowell, June 4, 1914; children—Beatrice, L. Kellsey 2d, Howard S., Jr. Admitted to N.J. bar as atty., 1912, as counsellor, 1915; engaged in gen. practice of law at Montclair since 1928; sr. mem. firm, Boyd and Dodd since 1931; serve. as police magistrate, Glen Ridge, N.J., 1915-21; register of deeds and mortgages of Essex Co., 1920-30; dir. and counsel, Bloomfield Bank & Trust Co., Essex Title Guaranty & Trust Co., Glen Ridge Bldg. & Loan Assn.; trustee and counsel, Davella Mills Foundation. Mem. Am. Judicature Soc., Am., N.J. State and Essex Co. bar assns. Republican. Presbyn. Club: Yacht (Groton Long Point, Conn.). Home: 133 Forest Av., Glen Ridge. Office: 483 Bloomfield Av., Montclair, N.J.

DODD, William Earle, physician and surgeon; b. Berkeley Co., W.Va., July 28, 1893; s. David Henry and Mary Virginia (Shaffer) D.; ed. Pa. Coll., Gettysburg, Pa., 1914-16; M.D., U. of Pa. Med. Sch., 1920; m. Mabel White, Apr. 25, 1923; children—William Earle, Jr., Robert White. After internship, engaged as industrial surgeon and gen. practitioner since 1923; asst. in coal mine practice, 1923; industrial surgeon in charge of practice at Rossiter mine under co.'s chief surg. with limited amt. gen. country practice, 1923-29; in gen. practice, Martinsburg, W. Va., 1929-30; in gen. practice and gen. surgeon, Beach Haven, N.J., since 1930; served with rescue squad underground in mine explosion disaster, Clymer, Pa., 1925; treated survivors U.S.N. dirigible J-3 which crashed in searching for survivors of airship "Akron," 1933; cooperated with staff of Point Pleasant Hosp. in treatment survivors burning S.S. Morro Castle, 1934; treated survivors A.S. Hindenburg, burned at

Lakehurst, N.J., 1937. Served as pvt. Med. Res. Corps, U.S.A., 1917; corpl. S.A.T.C., 1917-19. Fellow Am. Coll. Surgs. Sec. Ocean Co. Med. Soc. Republican. Methodist. Club: Little Egg Harbor Yacht of Beach Haven, N.J. (fleet surgeon). Home: Ocean St. and Bay Av., Beach Haven, N.J.

DODDS, Gideon Stanhope, univ. prof.; b. Westmoreland Co., Pa., July 11, 1880; s. John Cannon and Letty Margaret (Dodds) D.; B.A., U. of Colo., Boulder, Colo., 1904, M.A., 1905; Ph.D., U. of Pa., 1910; m. Mildred Boland, July 5, 1921. Instr. biology, U. of Colo., Boulder, Colo., 1905-08; Harrison fellow, U. of Pa., 1908-10; instr. biology, St. Louis (Mo.) U. Sch. of Medicine, 1910-11; asst. prof. zoology, U. of Mo., Columbia, Mo., 1911-18; instr., Marine Biol. Lab., Woods Hole, Mass., summers 1909-11, 1918, Colo. Mountain Lab., Tolland, Colo., summers 1912-17; asst. prof. histology and embryology, W.Va. U. Sch. of Medicine, Morgantown, W.Va., 1918-20, asso. prof., 1920-25, prof. histology and embryology since 1925. Mem. A.A.A.S., Am. Soc. Zoologists, Am. Assn. Anatomists, W.Va. Acad. of Science, Sigma Xi. Presbyterian. Author: (text-book): Essentials of Human Embryology, 1929; numerous papers in tech. jours. on animal ecology, embryology, histology. Address: 829 Price St., Morgantown, W.Va.

DODDS, Harold Willis, pres. Princeton U.; b. Utica, Pa., June 28, 1889; s. Samuel and Alice (Dunn) D.; A.B., Grove City (Pa.) College, 1909, A.M., Princeton Univ., 1914; Ph.D., Univ. of Pa., 1917; LL.D., Grove City Coll. 1931, Yale, Dickinson, American Univ., Rutgers, New York Univ., Harvard and Williams, 1934, Cincinnati, 1935, U. of Pa., 1936, Dartmouth, 1937, Purdue, 1938; Litt.D., Columbia, 1934, Hahnemann Med. Coll., 1937; Dr. Humane Letters, Hobart Coll., 1936; Dr. Humanities, Wooster, 1938; m. Margaret Murray, Dec. 25, 1917. Instr. in economics, Purdue U., 1914-16; asst. prof. polit. science, Western Reserve U., 1919-20; sec. Nat. Municipal League, 1920-28; editor Nat. Municipal Review, 1920-33; prof. politics, Princeton, since 1927; pres. Princeton U. since June 1933. Exec. sec. U.S. Food Adminstrn., Pa., 1917-19. Comdr. Order of King Leopold, 1937. Electoral adviser to Govt. of Nicaragua, 1922-24; tech. adviser to pres. Tacna-Arica Plebiscitary Commn., 1925-26; chief adviser to pres. Nat. Bd. Elections of Nicaragua, 1928; dir. Prudential Ins. Co.; dir. Council on Foreign Relations. Mem. bd. Rockefeller Foundations and Brookings Inst. Trustee Carnegie Foundation for Advancement of Teaching, 1935; mem. and trustee, Gen. Edn. Bd., 1937. Mem. Phi Beta Kappa, Am. Philos. Soc. Republican. Presbyn. Clubs: Century, University, Princeton (New York); Nassau (Princeton). Wrote numerous articles, surveys and reports in polit. science. Home: "Prospect," Princeton, N.J.

DODDS, John Harper, civil engr.; b. Lonaconing, Md., Oct. 12, 1893; s. Joseph and Elizabeth (Harper) D.; C.E., U. of Pittsburgh, 1916; m. Catherine Marie Deimling, Apr. 28, 1932. Draftsman B. & L. E. R.R. Co., Greenville, Pa., 1916-17, structural detailer, 1919-20; resident engr., Am. City Engring. Co., Pittsburgh, Pa., 1920-22, office engr., 1924-25; field engr. U.S. Engr. Office, Pittsburgh, 1922-24, since 1925 successively field engr., supt. of constrn., overseer, asso. engr., and senior civil engr.; registered professional engr., Pa. Served with 305th Ammunition Train, U.S. Army, 1917-19. Mem. Allegheny Co. (Pa.) U.S. Govt. Employees Federal Credit Union (v.p. since 1937), Transportation Research Commn. of City of Pittsburgh, Am. Legion. Republican. Mason (Shriner, Syria Temple). Clubs: Propeller, Port (Pittsburgh). Home: 485 Parkview Drive, Mt. Lebanon, Pa. Office: 919 Federal Bldg., Pittsburgh, Pa.

DODDS, Robert J., lawyer; b. Allegheny Co., Pa., Oct. 20, 1877; s. Joseph Spratt and Sarah Jane (Wallace) D.; LL.B., U. of Pittsburgh, 1903; m. Agnes J. Raw, of Southport, Eng., Feb. 14, 1914. Began practice at Pittsburgh, 1903; mem. firm Reed, Smith, Shaw & McClay;

served as U.S. atty., Western Dist. of Pa., by apptmt. of U.S. Court, May 1920. Trustee Am. Univ., Cairo, Egypt. United Presbyn. Clubs: Duquesne, University, Longue Vue Country, Pittsburgh Country. Home: 1452 N. Highland Av. Office: Union Trust Bldg., Pittsburgh, Pa.*

DODDS, William Paul; mem. staff Elizabeth Steel Magee Hosp.; asso. prof. obstetrics, U. of Pittsburgh. Address: 121 University Pl., Pittsburgh, Pa.

DODGE, Arthur Byron; pres., treas. and dir. Dodge Cork Co. Home: 306 E. Orange St., Lancaster, Pa.

DODGE, Kern, cons. engr.; b. Chicago, Ill., July 20, 1880; s. James Mapes and Josephine (Kern) D.; grad. Germantown Acad., Phila., 1899, Drexel Inst., 1901; m. Helen Peterson Greene, Nov. 16, 1904; children—Dorothy (Mrs. John F. Whelihan Jr., now dec.), Donald, Jane (Mrs. J. Allen Barnett Jr.), Robert Mapes. Mem. firm Dodge and Day, const. engrs., 1901-12, private consulting practice, Phila., since 1912; pres. Dodge Brower & Company, Inc., Phila., until 1939; treas. Hosiery Patents, Inc.; dir. Link-Belt Co. Served in Naval Intelligence work during World War. Mem. bd. of mgrs. Moore Inst. of Art, Science and Industry; trustee Germantown Acad.; pres. Air Defense League. Mem. Am. Soc. M.E., Am. Inst. E.E., Franklin Inst., N.Y. Elec. Soc. Republican. Unitarian. Clubs: Union League, Keystone Automobile (dir.), Engineers (Phila.); Seaview Golf (Absecon, N.J.); Aero of Pennsylvania (pres.). Home: 425 W. Clapier St., Germantown. Office: Lewis Tower Bldg., Philadelphia, Pa.

DODGE, M(arcellus) Hartley, mfr.; b. 1883; s. Norman W. D. and g.s. of Marcellus Hartley, founder Remington Arms Co.; A.B., Columbia, 1903; m. Geraldine R., d. William Rockefeller, Apr. 18, 1907. Chmn. bd. Remington Arms Co. Inc.; mem. bd. mgrs. D.L.&W. R.R. Co. Trustee Columbia U. since 1907. Clubs: River, Columbia, Down Town, Racquet and Tennis, Morris County Golf. Home: Madison, N.J. Office: 350 5th Av., New York, N.Y.

DODGEN, Lily M., librarian; b. Cassville, Ga.; d. George Newton and Rosina (Milholland) Dodgen; graduate State Normal Sch., Athens, Ga.; student U. of Chicago, 1908-10; grad. Pratt Sch. of Library Science, Brooklyn, N.Y., 1912; B.S., Teachers Coll., Columbia U., 1930, M.A., dept. of English and Comparative Lit., Columbia, 1936; unmarried. Asst. N.Y. Pub. Library, 1912; head of children's dept., Savannah (Ga.) Pub. Library, 1913-19, dir. of training class, 1916-19; organizer S.A.L. Ry. Libraries, 1920; reference librarian Tampa (Fla.) Pub. Library, 1920-21; librarian State Teachers Coll., Trenton, N.J., since 1921. Mem. N.J., Am. library assns. Home: 435 Bellevue Av. Office: State Teachers Coll., Trenton, N.J.

DODRILL, Draco; city mgr. of Clarksburg. Address: Clarksburg, W.Va.

DODSON, Alan Craig; pres. Weston, Dodge & Co. Home: 724 Delaware Av. Office: 528 N. New St., Bethlehem, Pa.

DODWORTH, James Russell Jr., mining engr.; b. Allegheny, Pa., Feb. 16, 1900; s. James Russell and Elizabeth (Kenah) D.; E.M., U. of Pittsburgh, 1922; m. Dorothy Thompson, Apr. 26, 1928; children—Dorothy Laura, James Russell III, Russell Thompson. Mining engr., Pittsburgh, Pa., since 1922; pres. Callinan-McKay Exploration Ltd., Ontario, Can., since 1932; v.p. and dir. Night Hawk Peninsular Mines Ltd., Ontario, Can., Porcupine Peninsular Gold Mines Ltd., Ontario, since 1933. Mem. Am. Inst. Mining and Metall. Engrs. Republican. Episcopalian. Home: 1620 Beechwood Boul. Office: 323 Fourth Av., Pittsburgh, Pa.

DODWORTH, Paul Kenah, merchant; b. Pittsburgh, Pa., July 23, 1902; s. James Russell and Elizabeth (Kenah) D.; B.S., U. of Pittsburgh, 1927; m. Jean Pitcairn Daub, Apr. 11, 1929; children—Catherine Elizabeth, Paul Kenah. Life ins. underwriter, Equitable Life Co. of N.Y., Pittsburgh, 1926-35; sec. and dir. Night Hawk Peninsular Mines Ltd., Callinan McKay Exploration Co., Ltd.; dir. Porcupine Peninsular Gold Mines Ltd., Schenley Mines Ltd. Republican.

Episcopalian. Home: 600 Forest Av., Bellevue, Pa. Office: 323 4th Av., Pittsburgh, Pa.

DOE, Charles L., banking; b. Elizabeth, N.J., June 1, 1882; s. Thomas A. and Clara G. (Harris) D.; C.E., Princeton U., 1903; m. Edna Osborne, Mar. 25, 1911; children—Katharine, Charles L., Jr. Began as draftsman Am. Bridge Co., 1903; asst. engr. Interborough Rapid Transit Co., 1905-06; v.p. Am. Concrete Steel Co., 1914-18; v.p. and gen. mgr. Charles R. Hedden Co., 1918-22; pres. Doe-Wathey Co., 1922-30, Charles L. Doe & Co., 1930-32; v.p., trust officer and dir. Glen Ridge Trust Co. since 1932; spare time devoted to dairy farming since 1938. Served in cav., N.J.N.G., 5 yrs. Mem. council, Glen Ridge, N.J., 2 terms, mayor, 2 terms. Past dir. Newark Chamber of Commerce; formerly trustee Newark Univ. Independent Republican. Conglist. Home: 45 Church St., Montclair, N.J.; also R.F.D. Long Valley, N.J. Office: Glen Ridge Trust Co., Glen Ridge, N.J.

DOERING, Alois H., supervising engr.; b. Burlington, Ia., Dec. 21, 1886; s. John and Madeline (Fey) D.; m. Marie C. Muench, June 7, 1916; 1 son, John Ward. Successively draftsman, estimater, designer, chief draftsman, operating engr., asst. gen. mgr. and chief engr. until 1914; chief engr. and asst. gen. mgr. Riverside Bridge Co., Wheeling, W.Va., 1914-24; engaged in private contracting business, 1924-26; mng. engr. Forest City Steel Co., 1926-28; contracting engr. Pittsburgh Bridge & Iron Works, 1928-33; chief supervising engr. City of Pittsburgh since 1933. Served in advisory capacity with Emergency Fleet Corpn., World War. Mem. Am. Soc. Civil Engrs., Engrs. Soc. of Western Pa. Elk. Club: Kiwanis. Home: 307 Fiske St. Office: 419 City-County Bldg., Pittsburgh, Pa.

DOERSAM, Charles Henry, teacher, musician, concert organist; b. Scranton, Pa., Sept. 29, 1878; s Philip and Elizabeth (Schlager) D.; ed. Scranton High Sch.; studied piano under August Spanuth (N.Y. City) and Karl Beving (Leipzig), organ under Samuel P. Warren (N.Y. City) and Wallace Goodrich (Boston), theory under Cantor Gustav Schreck (Leipzig), counterpoint and composition under Geo. W. Chadwick; received highest honors New England Conservatory of Music, 1909 (made mem. faculty); m. Mary Davenport, June 20, 1916; children—Philip Davenport, Charles Henry. Mem. faculty and head organ dept., Columbia U., since 1920, in charge chapel choir, summer sessions, since 1933; with theatre orchestra, conducting Gilbert & Sullivan operas, 1901-03; condr. Scranton Symphony Orchestra, 3 yrs.; accompanist for many nationally known artists; director and organist First and Second Presbyn. Chs., Scranton, First M.E. Ch., Wilkes-Barre, also chs. in Carbondale, Pa., Wellesley, Dorchester and Boston, Mass., Rye, N.Y., Park Av. Synagogue and Rutgers Presbyn. Ch., N.Y. City. Has given many organ recitals throughout U.S. Warden Am. Guild Organists since 1933, dean Northeastern Pa. Chapter. sec. New England Chapter. Fellow Am. Guild Organists. Mem. Pi Kappa Lambda. Presbyn. Clubs: Sinfonia (Boston); Men's Faculty (Columbia U.); St. Wilfrid (N.Y. City). Composer church anthems, songs and chamber music. Home: 7 Buckingham Road, Palisade, N.J.

DOGGETT, Leonard Allison, prof. elec. engring.; b. Boston, Mass., Nov. 10, 1888; s. Frederick Fobes and Mary Chipman (DeWolf) D.; ed. Boston Latin Sch., 1899-1905; A.B., magna cum laude in engring., Harvard U., 1908; M.E.E., Harvard U. Sch. Applied Sci., 1910; E.E., Pa. State Coll., 1930; m. Alice W. Gantt, Aug. 21, 1916 (dec.); 1 dau., Alice DeWolf; m. 2d, Elizabeth A. Creelman, Dec. 23, 1920; children—Frederick Fobes, 2d, Leonard A., Jr. (dec.), Margaret Clyde. Engaged as asst. at Harvard, 1909-10, inst., 1910-13; prof. elec. engring. and physics, Post Grad. Sch. of U.S. Naval Acad., 1913-23; prof. elec. engring., Pa. State Coll. since 1923. Served with Battle Fleet U.S.N. on bd. U.S.S. Arizona, summer 1918. Fellow A.I.E.E.; past mem. Am. Soc. Naval Engrs.; mem. Soc. for Promotion Engring. Edn., Centre Co. Engrs. (pres. 1934-35), Harvard Engring. Soc., Am. Assn. Univ. Profs., member

National Council (1937-1939), Navy Athletic Assn., Tau Beta Pi, Sigma Xi, Eta Kappa Nu, Kappa Delta Rho. Democrat. Episcopalian. Clubs: University of Annapolis and State Coll. Author: (with others) Naval Electricians' Text Book, Vol. I, edit., 1915; Alternating Current Analysis, 1933; An Outline of Public Utilities, 1938. Contbr. many papers before sci. socs. and articles to elec. publs. Home: 357 E. Prospect Av., State College, Pa.

DOHAN, Edith Hall (Mrs. Joseph M.D.), archæologist; b. New Haven, Conn., Dec. 31, 1877; d. Ely R. and Mary Jane (Smith) Hall; A.B., Smith Coll., Northampton, Mass., 1899; grad. student Am. Sch. of Classical Studies, Athens, Greece, 1903-05; grad. student Bryn Mawr (Pa.) Coll., 1901-03, 1905-07, Ph.D., 1908; m. Joseph M. Dohan, May 12, 1915 (died 1933); children—David Hayward Warrington, Katharine Elizabeth (Mrs. Denys Lionel Page). Instr. Mt. Holyoke Coll., South Hadley, Mass., 1908-12; curator University Mus., Phila., 1912-15; lecturer Bryn Mawr (Pa.) Coll., 1924-25, 1930-31; curator, University Mus., Phila., since 1931. Mem. Archæol. Inst. of America, Phi Beta Kappa; corr. mem. German Archæol. Inst. Congregationalist. Home: Darling, Pa.

DOHERTY, Robert Ernest, coll. pres.; b. Clay City, Ill., Jan. 22, 1885; s. Anthony and Clara (Sauther) D.; B.S., U. of Ill., 1909; M.S., Union Coll., Schenectady, N.Y., 1921; hon. M.A., Yale, 1931; m. Pearl Edna Mills, of Sherodsville, O., June 20, 1911; children—Robert Ernest, Vera Maud, James Anthony. With Gen. Elec. Co., Schenectady, 1909-31, test engr., 1909-10, designing engr., 1910-18, asst. to Dr. C. P. Steinmetz, 1918-23, cons. engr., 1923-31; prof. elec. engring., Yale, since 1931, dean of Sch. of Engring., Yale, 1933-36; pres. Carnegie Inst. Technology, Pittsburgh, since 1936; mayor of Scotia, N.Y., 1922; mem. Bd. of Edn., 1925-29. Mem. Am. Inst. E.E., Soc. for Promotion Elec. Engring., Sigma Xi, Tau Beta Pi, Eta Kappa Nu, Theta Delta Chi. Conglist. Clubs: Graduates, Duquesne, University, Pittsburgh Athletic. Author: Mathematics of Modern Engineering (with E. G. Keller), 1936. Contbr. tech. articles. Home: 1085 Devon Rd. Address: Carnegie Inst. of Technology, Pittsburgh, Pa.

DOHERTY, T. A.; in private practice of law since 1895. Address: Susquehanna, Pa.

DOHME, Alfred Robert Louis, chemist; b. Baltimore, Md., Feb. 15, 1867; s. Charles E. and Ida (Schultz) D.; A.B., Johns Hopkins, 1886, Ph.D., 1889; post-grad. courses in chemistry, geology and mineralogy; U. of Berlin, lab. of Fresenius, Wiesbaden, and U. of Strassburg, 1889-91, U. of Paris, 1905; m. Emma D. Blumner, Feb. 15, 1893 (now deceased); m. 2d, Paula Carl, Nov. 22, 1909. In bus. as mfg. chemist, 1891-1929; pres. Sharp & Dohme, 1911-29. Instr. pharmacy, Johns Hopkins, 1901-12; sec. Nat. Com. of Revision of Pharmacopœia of U.S. for 1900-10 at decennial conv., Washington, 1900, and mem. Com. of Revision, 1900-30. Pres. Md. Pharm. Assn., 1899-1900, Am. Pharm. Assn., 1918, Baltimore Drug Exchange, 1916-18; trustee Walters Art Gallery, Gilman Country Sch. for Boys; mem. bd. dirs. Sharp & Dohme, Fidelity Trust Co.; pres. City Wide Congress, Baltimore, 1911-21; v.p. Baltimore Mus. of Art, The Lyric Co. Clubs: University, Maryland, Chesapeake, Elkridge Kennels, Baltimore Country. Home: 5204 Roland Av. Office: 702 Baltimore Life Bldg., Baltimore, Md.

DOLAN, Albert Harold, clergyman; b. Fond du Lac, Wis.; s. Andrew W. and Anna (Conley) D.; ed. St. Lucy's Acad., Syracuse, N.Y., 1906-09, Niagara Univ., 1910-11, North American Coll., Rome, Italy, 1911-13, St. Augustine's Sem., Toronto, Can., 1913-18. Mem. Carmelite Order since 1918; ordained priest Roman Cath. Ch., 1919; prefect of discipline, Mt. Carmel Coll., Chicago, 1919-23; nat. dir. Soc. of the Little Flower, Chicago, 1923-31, Eastern dir., Englewood, N.J., since 1931; nat. dir. Carmelite Press and editor The Sword (Carmelite quarterly). Author: The Life of the Little Flower, Living Sisters of the Little Flower, The Little Flower's Mother, Letters of the Little Flower's Mother, Where the Little Flower Seems Nearest, Our Sister is in Heaven, An Hour with the Little Flower, Volumes I and III, Scapular Facts, Collected Little Flower Works, A Modern Messenger of Purity, St. Therese Returns, Enjoy the Mass, All the Answers, Saint Thomas More, The Little Flower's Conquest of the World, Our Lady's Easter, A Miniature of Mary, Mother, I Belong to Thee, Mobilize for Christ, Roses Fall Where Rivers Meet, Carmelite Life, Who Can Be a Carmelite Nun?, You Can Be a Carmelite Sister, In the Valley of St. Therese, The Gateway to Peace. Address: 55 Demarest Av., Englewood, N.J.

DOLE, Esther Mohr, prof. of history; b. Chicago, Ill., Apr. 24, 1883; d. Edward Kern and Alice Hall (Eldredge) Mohr; grad. Ill. State Normal U., Normal, Ill., 1903; A.B., U. of Ill., 1906; A.M., U. of Wis., 1910, Ph.D., 1926; student Harvard, summers 1929, 31; m. Arthur L. Dole, June 26, 1912 (died 1919); children—Alice Emily, Charles Edward. Teacher high schools of Genoa, Ill., 1903-05, Pontiac Twp., Ill., 1906-09; teacher, La Crosse (Wis.) Teachers Coll., 1911-12; teacher of history Cottey Coll., Nevada, Mo., 1920-22; dean Flat River (Mo.) Jr. Coll., 1922-24; prof. of history, Washington Coll., Chestertown, Md., since 1926, dean of women, 1932-34, associate dean of women since 1934; summer school teacher at Cape Girardeau (Mo.) Teachers Coll., 1924, Alfred (N.Y.) U., 1927-39. Mem. Am. Hist. Soc., Md. Hist. Soc., D.A.R. (state historian Md. 1937-40), Phi Gamma Mu, Zeta Tau Alpha. Republican. Methodist. Club: Women's Literary (Chestertown). Home: 117 Water St., Chestertown, Md.

DOLFINGER, Henry; chmn. bd. Abbotts Dairies. Inc. Home: Merion, Pa. Office: 3043 Chestnut St., Philadelphia, Pa.

D'OLIER, Franklin, insurance; b. Burlington, N.J., Apr. 28, 1877; s. William and Annie (Woolman) D.; A.B., Princeton, 1898; m. Helen Kitchen, Nov. 11, 1903. Pres. and treas. Franklin D'Olier & Co., Inc., founded by father, 1869, until 1926; pres. Prudential Ins. Co.; dir. Howard Savings Instn. of Newark, National Biscuit Co., Pa. R.R., Morristown (New Jersey) Trust Company. Trustee Princeton U. Commd. capt. U.S.A., Apr. 1917; arrived in France, July 1917; organized salvage service of A.E.F.; hon. discharged as lt. col. Gen. Staff, Apr. 1919. Awarded D.S.M. (U.S.); Comdr. Legion of Honor (France). Elected first nat. comdr. Am. Legion, Nov. 12, 1919. Episcopalian. Clubs: Princeton (Phila.); University, Princeton, Lawyers (New York); Morristown, Morris County Golf, Essex. Mem. Soc. Colonial Wars. Home: Morristown, N.J. Office: Prudential Insurance Co., Newark, N.J.

DOLL, Albert M.; pres. Lovell Mfg. Co. Home: 516 W. 7th St., Erie, Pa.

DOLL, Edgar Arnold, psychologist; b. Cleveland, O., May 2, 1889; s. Arnold and Katherine (Radermacher) D.; A.B., Cornell U., 1912; Pd.M., N.Y. Univ., 1916; Ph.D., Princeton, 1920; m. Agnes Martz, June 30, 1914 (now dec.); children—Eugene Edgar, Bruce; m. 2d, S. Geraldine Longwell (Ph.D., Cornell, 1937), of Sayre, Pa., Dec. 28, 1938. Instr. exptl. psychology, U. of Wis., 1912-13; instr. ednl. psychology, Cornell, summers 1912-13; research and clin. psychologist, Training Sch. at Vineland, 1912-17; spl. lecturer, N.Y. Univ., 1915-16; lecturer ednl. and abnormal psychology summers at U. of Mont., 1914, N.Y. Univ., 1915, 16, U. of Calif., 1917, Cleveland Sch. of Edn., 1920, Northwestern U., 1924; chief state psychologist of N.J., 1920-23; asst. prof. clin. psychology, Ohio State U., 1923-25; research consultant to N.J. State Dept. Instns. and Agencies since 1925; mem. bd. mgrs. N.J. State Reformatory at Rahway since 1929; asso. editor Training Sch. Bull. since 1925, Jour. Ednl. Research, 1932-37, Jour. Exptl. Edn., 1932-37, Jour. Juvenile Research, 1932-37, Jour. Consultants Psychology, 1937. Served as 1st lt. sanitary corps, U.S.A., assigned to Psychol. Examining Bd., 1917-18. Trustee Training Sch. at Vineland, 1921-25; mem. White House Conf. on Child Health and Protection; commr. of juries, Cumberland Co., N.J., since 1935; chmn.-sec. Adv. Council on Research, Mooseheart, Ill., 1929. Fellow A.A.A.S., Am. Orthopsychiatric Assn.; mem. Am. Psychol. Assn., Am. Prison Assn., Am. Pub. Welfare Assn., Am. Assn. on Mental Deficiency, Assn. Consulting Psychologists, Am. Ethnological Soc., Internat. Council for Exceptional Children, Nat. Conf. Juvenile Agencies, Soc. for Research in Child Development, Nat. Soc. for Study of Edn., Psychometric Soc., Taylor Soc., Royal Medico-Psychological Assn. (hon.). Rotary (hon.). Author: Anthropometry, 1916; The Growth of Intelligence, 1921; Clinical Studies in Feeblemindedness, 1927; Mental Deficiency Due to Birth Injuries (with W. M. Phelps and R. T. Melcher), 1932. Editor: Twenty-five Years, 1932. Home: East Chestnut Av. Address: Dept. of Research Training Sch., Vineland, N.J.

DOLLIVER, Alan Kemp, finance exec.; b. Baltimore, Md., Oct. 24, 1898; s. Park K. and Alice C. (Lofgren) D.; student Baltimore (Md.) Pub. Schs., 1904-12, Poly. Inst., Baltimore, Md., 1912-14, U. of Md. Law Sch., Baltimore, Md., 1915-18, Industrial Lenders Tech. Inst., New York, 1925-26; m. Sara B. Sinnott, July 5, 1919; children—Alan Kemp (dec.), Mary Ann (dec.), Brian Alan. Adjuster Central Loan & Finance Co., Baltimore, Md., 1915-18; branch office mgr. Beneficial Loan Soc., 1919-22; with Beneficial Management Corpn., New York, 1922-32, successively as field supt., auditor, field supervisor, gen. supervisor; v.p. Family Finance Corpn., New York, since 1933; exec. v.p. and dir. Security Bankers Management Corpn., Wilmington, Del., since 1936; exec. v.p. and dir. Community Investment & Loan Corpn., Mutual Loan & Thrift Corpn.; dir. Family Loan Soc. Mem. Am. Legion. Awarded Order of the Purple Heart. Independent Republican. Episcopalian. Home: Bellevue, Del. Office: 200 W. 9th St., Wilmington, Del.

DOLLIVER, Charles Marvin, lawyer; b. South Somerville, N.J., Jan. 10, 1878; s. Garret Quick and Kate Sutphen (Van Zandt) D.; LL.B., N.Y. Univ. Law Sch., 1902; m. Alberta Elizabeth Reiber, June 27, 1906; children—Florence Alberta (Mrs. John L. Owen, Jr.), Charles M., Jr. Admitted to N.J. bar as atty., 1903, as counselor, 1906, spl. master in chancery, 1911; engaged in gen. practice of law at Plainfield, N.J., since 1903; mem. firm Dolliver & Feaster since 1927; judge police ct. Borough of North Plainfield, 1907-12, and later for 1½ years; borough clk., 1912-14, corpn. counsel North Plainfield since 1935; dir. and counsel Mid-City Trust Co., Union Bldg. & Loan Assn., Plainfield Bldg. & Loan Assn.; counsel Dunellen Bldg. & Loan Assn. Served as 1st lt. Home Defense Corps, North Plainfield during World War. Past pres. North Plainfield East End Civic Assn. Mem. N.J. State and Somerset Co. bar assns., Plainfield Bar Assn. (past pres.), S.A.R. Republican. Mem. Ref. Ch. Mason. Club: Lions of Plainfield (past pres.). Home: 130 DeLacy Av., North Plainfield. Office: 400 Park Av., Plainfield, N.J.

DOLMAN, John, Jr., prof. English; b. Philadelphia, Pa., May 21, 1888; s. John and Christine Harriet Melanie (Nickinson) D.; grad. Central Manual Training High Sch., Philadelphia, 1906; B.S., U. of Pa., 1910, A.M., 1913; m. Ethel Louise Schatte, of Philadelphia, Sept. 2, 1912 (died Apr. 26, 1937); children—Barbara Caroline, John Phillips, Robert Effingham, Geoffrey. Reader in English, U. of Pa., 1910-11, instr. in English, 1911-20, asst. prof. English, 1920-27, prof. since 1927, dir. Summer Sch. since 1925. Editor Quarterly Jour. of Speech, 1923-26. Mem. Nat. Assn. Teachers of Speech (pres. 1930), Eastern Pub. Speaking Conf. (pres. 1922), Nat. Assn. of Summer School Directors (pres. 1932), Nat. Theatre Conf., Am. Iris Soc. Clubs: Players' (Swarthmore); Art Alliance (Philadelphia). Author: A Handbook of Public Speaking, 1922; The Art of Play Production, 1928; Gogol's Inspector-General (adaptation, 1937); sundry articles on speech and drama. Home: Swarthmore, Pa.

DOMVILLE, Paul Compton Kellock, artist, prof. of drawing; b. Hamilton, Ont., Can., June

16, 1893; s. Frederic James and Elizabeth Adele (Barr) D.; student Hamilton (Ont.) Collegiate Inst., 1905-08, Hamilton Art Sch., 1908-10; B.S. in Architecture, U. of Pa., 1920; student Pa. Acad. of Fine Arts, 1922; m. Mary Whelan Farr, Aug. 22, 1927; 1 son, Peter Dudley. Came to U.S., 1922, naturalized, 1939. Began as architect, 1909; registered architect, asso. with Gordon Hutton, Hamilton, Ont., Can., 1920-22; mural painter, Phila., since 1922; instr. in drawing, Sch. of Fine Arts, U. of Pa., 1922-25, asst. prof., 1925-38, asso. prof. and chmn. dept. of drawing and painting since 1938; instr. of interior decoration, Phila. Sch. of Design for Women, 1922-38, head of dept., 1925-38; instr. of drawing, Moore Inst., Phila., since 1938. Murals: Upjohn Memorial, St. Luke's Ch., Germantown; City Nat. Bank, Phila.; Mutual Trust Co., Phila.; Seamens Ch. Inst., Phila.; Uptown Theatre, Phila.; others in public and private bldgs. Served with Royal Naval Canadian Vol. Res., 1917-19. Mem. Nat. Soc. Mural Painters, Archtl. League of N.Y., Phila. Water Color Club, Tau Sigma Delta. Episcopalian. Clubs: Phila. Art Alliance, British Officers (Phila.); Woodstock (N.Y.) Country; Royal Hamilton (Ont.) Yacht. Home: 2407 Pine St. Studio: 2037 Moravian St., Philadelphia, Pa.

DONAHOE, Thomas A.; mem. law firm Donahoe & Helriegel. Office: Mears Bldg., Scranton, Pa.

DONAHUE, Frank Rogers; mem. law firm Donahue, Irwin, Merritt & Gest. Office: Packard Bldg., Philadelphia, Pa.

DONALDSON, Holland H.; surgeon Mercy Hosp.; prof. clin. surgery, U. of Pittsburgh. Address: Mercy Hosp., Pittsburgh, Pa.

DONALDSON, John A.; owner Donaldson Paper Co.; officer or dir. many companies. Home: 1925 N. Front St. Office: 113 N. Second St., Harrisburg, Pa.

DONALDSON, John C.; prof. anatomy, U. of Pittsburgh. Home: 1633 Beechwood Boul., Pittsburgh, Pa.

DONALDSON, John Speer, orthopaedic surgeon; b. Bellevue, Pa., May 14, 1905; s. John Speer and Isla Flora (Rodgers) D.; B.S., Harvard, 1927, M.D., Med. Sch.; 1931; m. Cornelia Adams, July 20, 1931. Mem. dispensary staff, Allegheny Gen. Hosp., Pittsburgh, 1932-34, asst. staff since 1934; chief surgeon Pa. State Hosp. for Crippled Children, 1936-38; on sr. staff, Presbyn. and Childrens hosps., Pittsburgh, and asso. staff Magee Hosp., Pittsburgh, since 1938. Fellow Am. Coll. Surgeons, Acad. Orthopedic Surgeons; mem. Am. Med. Assn., Pa. State Med. Soc. Republican. Presbyterian. Clubs: Harvard of Western Pa., University (Pittsburgh). Home: 223 Gladstone Rd. Office: 121 University Place, Pittsburgh, Pa.

DONALDSON, Walter Foster, physician; b. Bridgeville, Pa., Sept. 13, 1873; s. John Boyce and Elizabeth (Foster) D.; grad. Canonsburg (Pa.) High Sch., 1889; student Jefferson Acad., 1889-91; M.D., Northwestern U., 1898; m. Nan Swearingen, of Ingram, Pa., June 19, 1913; children—Walter Foster, Sarah (Mrs. Robert R. Stoll), Joseph Van Swearingen, John Boyce, Nancy Elizabeth, William Paul. Asst. on staff Western Pa. Hosp., 1902-08; mem. staff South Side Hosp., 1906-12; asst. on staff Presbyn. Hosp. since 1912; instr. in medicine, U. of Pittsburgh, 1921-34; med. dir. Standard Life Ins. Co. of America since 1919. Dir. Allegheny Co. Med. Soc. since 1921 (pres. 1923); sec. Med. Soc. State of Pa. since 1918 (pres. 1917); mem. Commn. on Grad. Med. Edn. of Advisory Board for Med. Specialties; chmn. health com. Pittsburgh Chamber of Commerce. Fellow A.M.A. (mem. judicial council since 1931, mem. council on med. edn. and hosps., 1924-1931), Pittsburgh Acad. of Medicine, Am. Coll. of Physicians; mem. Nu Sigma Nu. Republican. Presbyn. Mason. Editor of Pittsburgh Med. Bull.; contbr. to Pa. Med. Journal. Home: 4724 Bayard St. Office: 500 Penn Av., Pittsburgh, Pa.*

DONATO, Giuseppe, sculptor; b. Maida, Province of Catanzaro (Magna Grecia), Mar. 14, 1881; s. Antonio and Teresa Maria (Bilotta) D.; came to America, 1892; grad. Phila. Pub. Industrial Art Sch., 1897; studied under Charles Grafly, Pa. Acad. Fine Arts, 1897-03; drawing under Wm. M. Chase, Thomas P. Anshuts, Hughes H. Breckenridge; anatomy under Dr. George McClellan; studied modeling and architecture, Pa. Mus. Industrial Art; entered École des Beaux Arts, Paris, 1903; studied Acad. Julian under Angelbert, Acad. Colorossi, Paris, under Messieurs Gouquiet and Roland; pvt. student under Auguste Rodin; m. Emily Ciliberti, of Phila., Apr. 1906; children—Anthony, Joseph G., Beatrice, Teresa Cecilia. Awarded city scholarship, Phila. Pub. Industrial Art Sch., 1897; Stewardson sculpture prize, Pa. Acad. Fine Arts, 1900; Emily Cresson European traveling scholarship for 1903-05; diploma, Acad. Colorossi, 1904. Represented in Pa. Acad. Fine Arts; Reservoir Park, Harrisburg, Pa.; monument to Christopher Columbus, Easton, Pa. Works: Dawn, Dance of Eternal Spring; "Fawn"; Age of Eternal Inspiration; The Hand of Immortality; portraits of Mussolini, John H. Converse, Adam Tindell, Robert B. Mantell, Alexander Berkovitz, John W. Stockwell, Albert Francine, etc. Exhibited Grand Salon, Paris; Acad. Fine Arts and Art Club, Phila.; Art Inst., Chicago; Nat. Acad. of Design, New York; Nat. Sculpture Soc. Exhbn., Baltimore, San Francisco Expn., etc. Member Fellowship Pa. Acad. Fine Arts, Nat. Sculpture Soc., Internat. Soc. Arts and Letters, Am. Art Assn., Paris, Am. Federation Fine Arts, Architectural League New York; hon. mem. Société Académique Historie Internationale (Paris), Internat. Mark Twain Society; apptd. Am. corr. Internat Soc. Arts and Letters, Paris, France; sculptor mem. Art Jury, City of Phila. Home: 1512 S. 9th St. Studio: 700 S. Washington Sq., Philadelphia, Pa.*

DONELSON, Earl Tomlinson, artist; b. Scranton, Pa., July 19, 1908; s. Eric and Lavinia Blackfan (Tomlinson) D.; ed. Trenton Sch. Industrial Arts, 1917-18, Pa. Acad. Fine Arts, 1925-31; m. Edna Carr Keedy, June 11, 1930; children—Edna Carlotta (dec.), Edward Keedy (dec.). Has followed profession as artist since 1930; instr. art, Trenton Sch. Industrial Arts, 1931; pvt. classes in landscape and portraiture since 1932; commercial art for advertising, free lance in fine art painting; exhibited N.J. State Museum, Nat. Academy Design, Montclair Art Museum, Penna. Acad. Fine Arts, Va. Museum Fine Arts, Phila. Museum Art, Chicago Art Inst., Baltimore Museum of Art, Newark Art Club; represented permanently in Phila. Museum of Art, N.J. State Museum, Nat. Federation of Women's Clubs, Orange, N.J., and in pvt. collections, Dr. J. F. Pessel, Dr. Henry M. Rowan, etc. Mem. Fellowship Pa. Acad. Fine Arts. Awarded First Cresson Travelling European Scholarship, 1929, Second Cresson Scholarship, 1930, both Pa. Acad. Fine Arts; Hon. Mention and Prize $100, Chas. Toppan Competition, 1930, 2d Prize $200, same, 1931; Grand Prize (oil), N.J. Gallery, Newark, 1937. Republican. Baptist. Club: Chess (Trenton). Home: 44 Edgemere Av., Trenton, N.J.

DONEY, Paul Herbert, prof. of English; b. Columbus, O., July 10, 1900; s. Carl Gregg and Jennie Anna (Evans) D.; A.B., Willamette U., Salem, Ore., 1920; A.B., Wesleyan U., 1921; S.T.B., Boston U. Sch. of Theology, 1925; A.M., Harvard U., 1926, Ph.D., 1928; m. Lucy Minerva Holt, July 5, 1924; children—Jean Marie, Hugh Holt, John Marvin. Asso. prof. of English, Dickinson Coll., 1928-29, Thomas Beaver prof. of English lit. and head dept. of English since 1929; visiting prof. of English, Willamette U., summer 1929. Served in Central Inf. O.T.C., 1918. Mem. Mod. Lang. Assn. America, Phi Beta Kappa, Beta Theta Pi, Omicron Delta Kappa. Methodist. Club: Rotary (Carlisle, Pa.). Home: 503 W. South St., Carlisle, Pa.

DONEY, Willis F.; pres. First Nat. Bank. Address: Duquesne, Pa.

DONGES, Ralph Waldo Emerson, judge; b. Donaldson, Pa., May 5, 1875; s. John W. (M.D.) and Rose (Renaud) D.; grad. Rugby Acad., Phila., Pa., 1892; m. Lillian L. Mosebach, Oct. 1, 1921. Admitted to N.J. bar, 1897; counsellor at law since 1900; pres. Pub. Utilities Commn. of N.J., 1913-18; judge Circuit Ct. of N.J., 1920-30; asso. justice Supreme Ct. of N.J., since 1930. Served as lt. col., U.S.A., 1918-19. Mem. Am., N.J. State and Camden Co. bar assns. Democrat. Episcopalian. Mason. Moose. Home: Broadway cor. Cooper St. Address: Court House, Camden, N.J.

DONIGER, Simon, social worker; b. Russia, Nov. 19, 1896; s. Morris and Mira (Jalkut) D.; came to U.S., 1911, naturalized, 1918; A.B., N.Y. University, 1935, A.M., 1936, Ph.D., 1938; m. Rose Eisen, 1927; 1 son, David; m. 2d, Irma Robin, 1935; 1 dau., Ann Frances. Employed as social worker, Jewish Bd. of Guardians, 1926-28, supervisor of case work and asst. exec. sec. Big Brother Dept., 1928; exec. dir., Jewish Child Guidance Bur., Newark, N.J., since 1928; mem. exec. com. N.J. Chapter, Am. Assn. Social Workers; mem. governor's com. on health and welfare; chmn. div. on individual and family welfare, Nat. Conf. Jewish Social Welfare. Jewish religion. Home: 161 Prospect St., East Orange, N.J. Office: 118 Clinton Av., Newark, N.J.

DONLEY, Edward Gregg, lawyer; b. Mount Morris, Pa., Mar. 23, 1878; s. David Lemley and Louisa (Evans) D.; LL.B., W.Va. Univ. Law Sch., 1899; m. Eleanor Tucker, July 25, 1900; 1 son, Robert Tucker. Admitted to W. Va. bar, 1899 and since engaged in gen. practice of law at Morgantown; mem. firm Donley & Hatfield since 1899; served as mayor of Morgantown, W.Va., three terms, 1910-12, 1924-25; pres. First Nat. Bank since 1935, Athens Bldg. & Loan Assn. since 1910, United Federal Bldg. & Loan Assn. since 1937, Consolidated Oil & Gas Co. since 1933, all of Morgantown, W.Va. Mem. Am. Bar Assn., W.Va. Bar Assn., Monongalia County Bar Assn., Phi Sigma Kappa. Jeffersonian Democrat. Methodist. Home: 238 Kirk St. Office: 174 Chancery Row, Morgantown, W.Va.

DONLEY, Robert T.; mem. law firm Donley & Hatfield. Address: Morgantown, W.Va.

DONN, Edward Wilton, Jr., architect; b. Washington, D.C., Apr. 2, 1868; s. Edward W. and Laura (Gardner) D.; B.S., Mass. Inst. Tech., 1891; student Cornell U., 1892; traveled in Europe; unmarried. Chief designer in office of architect of the treasury, Washington, 1900-03; mem. Wood, Donn & Deming, Washington, 1903-12, Donn & Deming, 1912-24, Edward W. Donn, Jr., since 1924; dir. Northern Market Co. Architect for restoration and rehabilitation of "Wakefield," birthplace of George Washington. President Board Examiners and Registrars of Architects, D.C. Fellow A.I.A. (dir. also chmn. bd. of examiners); mem. Arch. Inst. America, Am. Fed. Arts, Washington Soc. Fine Arts, Zeta Psi. Episcopalian. Mason. Clubs: Metropolitan, Arts (dir.), Chevy Chase, Racquet (Washington); City (New York). Home: 10 E. Bradley Lane, Chevy Chase, Md. Office: 1920 K St., N.W., Washington, D.C.

DONNALLY, H. R.; pres. Iron & Glass Dollar Savings Bank of Birmingham. Office: 1112-14-16 Carson St., Pittsburgh, Pa.

DONNELL, Harold Eugene, penologist; b. Mt. Desert, Me., Nov. 10, 1887; s. Orrin A. and Laura A. (Gilley) D.; student Harvard U., 1907-08, Colby Coll., Waterville, Me., 1908-09, U. of Md. Law Sch., Baltimore, 1925-26; m. Mildred L. Ayer, Mar. 28, 1912 (divorced); children—Doris A. (Mrs. John A. Vickery), Jean M.; m. 2d Ruth E. Meeth, June 14, 1934; 1 son, Harold E., Jr. Engaged as prin. high sch. and supt. schs. in Me., 1909-14; dep. sec. State of Me., 1914-16; asst. supt. Sockanossett Sch. for Boys, Howard, R.I., 1916-18; administrative officer U.S. Naval Prison, Portsmouth, N.H., 1918-20; supt. Reformatory for Men, South Windham, Me., 1920-24; supt. Md. Training Sch. for Boys, Loch Raven, Md., 1924-30; supt. Md. Prisons, Baltimore, Md., since 1930; chmn. Md. Welfare Survey Com., 1929-31. Served as lt. (j.g.) U.S.N., 1918-21. Mem. Am. Prison Assn. (v.p.), Osborne Assn. (dir.), Prisoner's Aid Soc. (dir.), Salvation Army of Baltimore (dir.), Mental Hygiene Soc. (1932-35 dir.), Md. Parole Bd., Prison Labor

Authority (v.p., 1933-36), Delta Kappa Epsilon. Democrat. Baptist. Mason (32°, Shriner). Odd Fellow. Home: 505 Overbrook Rd. Office: Union Trust Bldg., Baltimore, Md.

DONNELLY, Marcus Edwin, lawyer; b. Jersey City, N.J., June 29, 1900; s. Thomas Marcus and Philenia (Crockett) D.; student N.Y. Univ., 1919-20, Fordham Univ. Law School, 1920-23; m. Hedwig Dreimuller, Sept. 1, 1928. Admitted to N.J. bar as atty., 1923; engaged in gen. practice of law at Jersey City since 1923. Served as pvt. inf., U.S.A., 1918. Sec. Hudson Co. Mosquito Extermination Commn. since 1937. Mem. Hudson Co. Bar Assn., Past Masters Masonic Assn. of Hudson Co., Am. Legion. Democrat. Mem. Dutch Ref. Ch. Mason, Foresters of America, Eagle, Elk. Home: 5 31st St., North Bergen. Office: 591 Summit Av., Jersey City, N.J.

DONOGHUE, Daniel C.; mem. law firm Donoghue & Gibbons. Address: Fidelity-Philadelphia Trust Bldg., Philadelphia, Pa.

DONOHO, Edmond Sheppard, educator; b. Baltimore, Md., Sept. 19, 1891; s. Thomas Winfield and Cecelia Genevieve (Sheppard) D.; A.B., Johns Hopkins, 1914; student U. of Md. Law Sch., 1914-16; m. Ellen Dickinson Thomas, June 17, 1922; children—Ellen Dickinson, Cynthia. Security salesman P. H. Goodwin & Co., 1914-16; v.p. Strayer Coll. Baltimore and Washington, 1917-23, pres. since 1924; pres. Strayer Coll. of Accountancy, Washington, since 1929. Mem. Baltimore Emergency Re-employment Com., N.R.A., 1933. Served as capt., A.E.F., World War; lt. col., U.S.R.; apptd. civilian aide to Sec. of War Dern for Md., 1933. Awarded div. citation, Silver Star, "for gallantry in action." Mem. Nat. Assn. Accredited Commercial Schs., Eastern Commercial Teachers Assn. (bd. govs. 1929-32), Pub. Sch. Assn. of Baltimore, Md., Vocational Guidance Assn., Reserve Officers Assn. (mem. exec. com. for Md.), Mil. Order of Foreign Wars, Am. Legion. Democrat. Episcopalian. Clubs: Bachelors, Cotillion, Maryland, University, Gibson Island, Baltimore Country. Home: 1706 Park Av. Office: 18 N. Charles St., Baltimore, Md.

DONOHUE, Francis Michael, banker; b. New Brunswick, N.J., Mar. 12, 1900; s. Francis Michael and Elizabeth Van Vorhees (Butler) D.; student Lawrenceville (N.J.) Sch., 1914-17; Litt.B., Princeton U., 1921; m. Mary Marvel, Apr. 20, 1929; 1 son, Francis Michael III. With Andrews Mill Co., worsted mfrs., 1921-25; v.p. Wilmington (Del.) Trust Co. since 1932; pres. Estate of Samuel Bancroft Jr., Inc.; dir. Del.-N.J. Ferry Co., Wilson Line, Inc. Club: Wilmington (Del.) Country. Home: Greenville, Del. Office: Wilmington Trust Co., Wilmington, Del.

DONOVAN, Edward Francis, editor, writer, lexicographer; b. Kingston, Ont., Can.; s. Peter and Catharine (Kelly) D.; came to U.S. as a child; LL.B., John B. Stetson University, DeLand, Fla.; m. Elizabeth Snowdon, Nov. 16, 1904. Admitted to Fla. bar, 1916, to practice in U.S. courts, 1916; mem. editorial staff, Standard Bible Dictionary, 1908-09; editor Unabridged New Standard Dictionary, 1909-14; wrote and revised legal articles for Ency. Americana, 1917-18, 1926-27; editor Practical Standard Dictionary, 1920-23; style editor and head of transcription and proofreading depts. in the New York editorial offices of the Ency. Britannica (14th edit.), Nov. 1927-Aug. 1929; editor and orthoepist Weedon's Modern Encyclopedia, 1930-31; editor Funk & Wagnalls' New Standard Encyclopedia, Sept.-Nov. 1931; revised legal articles Nelson's Encyclopedia, 1934; asso. editor Unabridged Standard Dictionary, 1937 and 1938 edits., New College Standard Dictionary, 1938. Mem. Phi Alpha Delta. Home: 1288 Longfellow Av., West Englewood, N.J.

DONOVAN, William Murray, physician; b. Scranton, Pa., Mar. 15, 1893; s. Cornelius C. and Margaret (Murray) D.; ed. St. Thomas Coll., Scranton, Pa., 1907-10, Pa. State Coll., 1910-12; M.D., U. of Pa. Med. Sch. 1916; m. Kathryn King, May 9, 1918; children—Cornelius, Murray, Robert, Paul. Resident phys., U. of Pa. Hosp., 1916-17, chief resident phys.,

same, 1917-18; instr. medicine, U. of Wis., 1919-22; in pvt. practice of medicine at Scranton, Pa., specializing in internal medicine, since 1918; chief in medicine Scranton State Hosp. and Mercy Hosp., Scranton; consultant in medicine Mater Misericordiae Hosp., Scranton; heart and chest specialist, U.S. Veterans Adminstrn. since 1923. Served as 1st lt. Med. Corps, U.S. Army, 1918-19. Diplomate of Am. Bd. of Internal Medicine; fellow Am. Coll. Physicians, Am. Med. Assn., Radiol. Soc. of America; mem. Phi Chi. Democrat. Roman Catholic. Home: 302 Pittston Av. Office: 442 Orchard St., Scranton, Pa.

DOOLITTLE, Harold; v.p. Koppers Co.; officer or dir. many companies. Home: 433 Glen Arden Drive. Office: Grant St. and Seventh Av., Pittsburgh, Pa.

DOOLITTLE, Lewis Joseph, lawyer specializing in patent cases; b. Plantsville, Conn., Dec. 9, 1868; s. Joseph Rodney and Cornelia (Paddock) D.; m. Mary Randall, 1898; children—Gerald Joseph, Ethel Cornelia (dec.), Eleanor Randall (Mrs. David J. Shauffler). Became engr. Mather Electric Co., 1893; later pres. and dir. Manhattan Switchboard Co., N.Y. Switchboard Co., New York; in practice law, New York, since 1902, specializing in patent cases. Mem. Sigma Alpha Epsilon. Congregationalist. Mason, Elk. Home: Maplewood, N.J. Office: 256 Broadway, New York, N.Y.

DOONER, Emilie Zeckwer, (Mrs. Richard T. D.), artist; b. Phila., Pa., Aug. 31, 1877; d. Richard and Marie T. (d'Invilliers) Zeckwer; student Acad. Fine Arts, Phila.; studied in Paris, France, 1901-02; pupil of Thos. Anshutz, Cecilia Beaux, Chas. Grafly, Hugh Breckenridge; abroad, under Simon, Menard-Cottet; student Alfred (N.Y.) U.; m. Richard T. Dooner, Apr. 22, 1914. Has followed profession as artist since 1905; since 1933 working in ceramics; exhibited in Paris Salon, 1904, Acad. Fine Arts, Phila., Corcoran Art Gallery, Cincinnati Mus. Art; exhibitor in Nat. Ceramic Exhbns., Syracuse, N.Y., and in Paris Exposition, 1937. Mem. Phila. Art Alliance, Phila. Print Club. Fellowship of Pa. Acad. Fine Arts. Home: Merion, Pa. Studio: 1724 Chestnut St., Philadelphia, Pa.

DOONER, Richard T(homas), photographer; b. Phila., Pa., May 19, 1878; s. Thomas H. and Margaret (McCunney) D.; ed. LaSalle Coll., Pa. Acad. Fine Arts, Pa. Mus. & Sch. of Industrial Art; m. Emilie Zeckwer, Apr. 22, 1914. Began as staff artist and news photographer, 1896; propr. studio, Phila., Pa., since 1900; medals for excellence of work received from Budapest, Dresden, London, Middle Atlantic States Exhbn., National, Paris, Pittsburgh, Buffalo, New York City; specially created medal awarded by the Royal Soc. of Gt. Britain. Mem. Fellowship of Pa. Acad. of Fine Arts. Roman Catholic. Clubs: Rotary, Print, Art Directors, Penn Athletic. Home: 523 Kenilworth Rd., Merion, Pa. Studio: 1724 Chestnut St., Philadelphia, Pa.

DORASAVAGE, William Charles, physician and surgeon; b. Shenandoah, Pa., Oct. 1, 1893; s. Charles and Elizabeth (Kravitas) D.; grad. Shenandoah High Sch., 1913; student Jefferson Med. Coll. (pre-med.), Phila., 1913-14, M.D., 1918; M.Sc., U. of Pa., 1924; m. Mary Unaitas, June 5, 1916; children—Mary Elizabeth, William Joseph, John Bernard, Margaret Anne, Agnes Helene. Interne Phila. Gen. Hosp., 1918-19; in practice of medicine and surgery, Pottsville, Pa., since 1930; mem. of staffs of A. C. Milliken Hosp. and Lemos B. Warne Hosp. Fellow Am. Coll. Surgeons; mem. Schuylkill Co. Med. Soc. Alpha Omega Alpha, Beta Kappa Psi. Republican. Roman Catholic. Eagle. Address: 700 Mahantongo St., Pottsville, Pa.

DORAU, Herbert Benjamin, economist; b. Calumet, Wis., May 9, 1897; s. Rev. John Paul and Louise (Franzke) D.; grad. high sch., Jefferson, Wis.; B.A., Lawrence Coll., Appleton, Wis., 1919; M.A., U. of Wis., 1920, Ph.D., 1928; m. Esther Elizabeth Hilberts, Feb. 2, 1922; children—Jean Tii, John Hilberts (dec.), Joan Elizabeth, Jane Louise. Asst. instr. economics, U. of Wis., 1920-23; research instr.,

Inst. for Economic Research, Northwestern, 1923-24, research asso., 1925-29, asst. dir., 1930-31; also asst. prof. economics, Northwestern U. Sch. of Commerce, 1925-28, asso. prof. since 1928; economist (on leave of absence from Northwestern U.), August Belmont & Co., 1929-33; asso. prof. economics, New York University, 1933-35, prof. economics since 1936 and chmn. dept. of pub. utilities since 1937; lecturer on public service corporations, New York University, 1930-33; cons. on business economics. Mem. President's Conf. on Home Building and Home Ownership, 1931. Mem. Am. Econ. Assn., Am. Statis. Assn., Phi Beta Kappa, Phi Kappa Alpha. Republican. Presbyn. Mason. Author: Real Estate Merchandising (with A. G. Hinman), 1926; Urban Land Economics, 1928; Municipal Ownership in the Electric Light and Power Industry, 1929; Materials for the Study of Public Utility Economics, 1930; Economic Principles and Problems (with others), 1932, rev. edit., 1936; Some Economic Considerations Bearing on the Place and Significance of the Holding Company, 1935; (with others) Economic Planning, 1937. Contbr. to Journal of Land and Public Utility Economics. Home: 268 Mountain Av., Ridgewood, N.J. Office: 236 Wooster St., New York, N.Y.

DORETY, Sister Helen Angela, prof. botany; b. Kaolin, S.C.; d. James Nicholas and Ellen (McCallion) Dorety; A.B., Coll. Saint Elizabeth, Convent, N.J., 1903; grad. study, Columbia U., 1905, Yale U., summer 1906; Ph.D., summa cum laude, U. of Chicago, 1908. Teacher Latin and English, Cheverus High Sch., Boston, Mass.; prof. botany and head of dept. botany, Coll. Saint Elizabeth, Convent, N.J., since 1908, lecturer in anthropology since 1914 and art since 1920; first woman to receive summa cum laude in botany, U. of Chicago; first nun in U.S. to receive degree Ph.D.; founder and moderator of Sodality of Saint Elizabeth. Fellow A.A.A.S. since 1910. Mem. Bot. Soc. America, Phi Beta Kappa since 1908, Sigma Xi since 1908. Roman Catholic. Author: Botany Course for College Sophomores, 1927; Character Formation, 1914; A Guide to the Shakespeare Garden, 1930. Contbr. articles to journs. Home: Convent St. Elizabeth, Convent, N.J.

DORMAN, George Ramsey; pres. Stevenson & Foster. Home: Club Drive. Office: 421 Seventh Av., Pittsburgh, Pa.

DORN, Forest D.; pres. Forest Oil Co.; officer or dir. numerous corpns. Home: 116 Congress St., Bradford, Pa.

DORR, John Henry, supt. of schools; b. Sharon, Pa., Nov. 23, 1889; s. Jacob and Elizabeth (Bohlender) D.; grad. Grove City (Pa.) High Sch., 1907; A.B., Grove City (Pa.) Coll., 1915; student Columbia U., 1922; A.M., U. of Pittsburgh, 1933; m. Iloe S. Eakin, Mar. 25, 1915; children—John Charles, Paul Eakin, Clyde Ellis. Prin. of grade schs., Petrolia, Pa., 1909-10; prin. of grades and high sch., Eau Claire, Pa., 1915-18; supt. of schs., Midland, Pa., 1918-21, Ludlow, Pa., 1921-22, Monongahela, Pa., since 1922. Served in Co. M, 16th Regt., Pa. N.G., 1906-09. Dir. Washington Co. Chapter Monongahela Red Cross, Washington Co. Tuberculosis Assn. Mem. Pa. State Edn. Assn., Pi Gamma Mu, Phi Delta Kappa. Republican. Presbyterian. Mason (32°, Shriner). Clubs: Rotary, Monongahela Valley Country (Monongahela, Pa.). Address: 801 Howard St., Monongahela, Pa.

DORRANCE, Anne, writer; b. Kingston Twp., Luzerne Co., June 26, 1873; d. Benjamin and Ruth Woodhull (Strong) Dorrance; grad. Wyoming Sem., Kingston, Pa., 1891; B.A., Vassar Coll., 1895; unmarried. Began as office asst. for father, Benjamin Dorrance, rose grower, Dorrancetown, Pa., 1896, partner, 1904-18. Mem. Dorranceton and combined Dorrance-Kingston Sch. Bds., 1911-22, 1927-35, pres. 12 terms. Pres. Wyoming Commemorative Assn. since 1922. Mem. exec. com. Pa. State Rep. Com., 1928-30. Trustee Wyoming Valley Homeopathic Hosp., Wilkes-Barre. Episcopalian. Author: Gardening in the Greenhouse, 1935; Fragrance in the Garden, 1936. Contbr. ednl. and gardening articles to magazines; also articles on local history. Home: Wild Ledges, Dallas, Luzerne County, Pa.

DORRANCE, Arthur Calbraith, pres. Campbell Soup Co.; b. Bristol, Pa., June 21, 1893; s. John and Eleanor Gillingham (Thompson) D.; prep. edn., Episcopal Acad., Philadelphia; B.S., Mass. Inst. Tech., 1914; m. Elsie Allan Ross, Feb. 7, 1918; children—Arthur Calbraith, David Ross. Associated with canning industry since 1914; pres. The Franco-American Food Co. since 1921; asst. gen. mgr. Campbell Soup Co., 1923-28, gen. mgr. since 1928, pres. since 1930; dir. Federal Reserve Bank, Philadelphia, 1928-31, Phila. Nat. Bank, 1932-35; mem. of bd. mgrs. Girard Trust Co.; dir. Lehigh Valley R.R. Co., West Jersey & Seashore R.R. Co., Baltimore & Eastern R.R. Co., Port Reading R.R. Co., Guaranty Trust Co. of New York, Bell Telephone Co. of Pa.; trustee Penn Mutual Life Ins. Co. Served as 1st lt., later capt. arty., U.S.A., World War; maj. Reserve Corps. Term mem. corpn. Mass. Inst. Tech. Mem. Am. Legion, Sigma Alpha Epsilon. Republican. Episcopalian. Clubs: Technology, Rittenhouse, Racquet (Philadelphia); Merion Cricket; Gulph Mills Golf; Fishers Island (N.Y.). Home: "Leahurst," Ardmore, Pa. Office: Campbell Soup Co., Camden, N.J.

DORRANCE, Charles, v.p. Consolidation Coal Co.; b. Meadville, Pa., Mar. 12, 1883; s. James Ford and Elizabeth Wilson (Dick) D.; student Wyoming Sem., Kingston, Pa., and Yale U.; Engr. of Mines, Lehigh U. 1907; m. Florence Waring, Feb. 25, 1921; 1 dau., Mary Waring. V.p. in charge of operations Consolidation Coal Co., Inc. Address: Watson Bldg., Fairmont, W.Va.

DORRANCE, Frances, librarian; b. Wilkes-Barre, Pa., June 30, 1877; d. Benjamin and Ruth Woodhull (Strong) Dorrance; student Wyoming Sem., Kingston, Pa., 1892-96, Marine Biological Lab., Wood's Hole, Mass., 1900, 1902, Columbia U., 1912, U. of Berlin (Germany), 1910-11, 1914; A.B., Vassar Coll., Poughkeepsie, N.Y., 1900; B.L.S., N.Y. (N.Y.) Library Sch., 1918; unmarried. Head of lending dept., Trenton (N.J.) Pub. Library, 1918-19; head of lending dept. Osterhout Free Library, Wilkes-Barre, Pa., 1919-22; dir. Wyoming Historical & Geological Soc., Wilkes Barre, Pa., 1922-38; librarian, The Hoyt Library, Kingston, Pa., since 1938. Mem. of the Pa. Hist. Commn., 1927-36. Dir. The Hoyt Library, Kingston, Pa., 1927-34, 1935-38. Mem. of council, Pa. Hist. Assn., 1932-38; v.p. Pa. Library Assn., 1927; mem. Phi Beta Kappa. Republican. Presbyterian. Translated from the German: Sorauer, Manual of Plant Diseases, Vol. 1; Kuster, Pathological Plant Anatomy; Brefeld and Falck, Smut Diseases in Grain. Edited: Vols. 18-22, Proceedings and Collections of the Wyoming Historical and Geological Society, Wilkes-Barre, Pa. Home: 111 Park Pl. Office: The Hoyt Library, Kingston, Pa.

DORRANCE, George Morris, M.D., surgeon; b. Bristol, Bucks Co., Pa., Apr. 24, 1877; s. John and Eleanor Gillingham (Thompson) D.; prep. edn., Peekskill Mil. Acad., Ossining, N.Y.; M.D., U. of Pa., 1900; m. Emily Fox, of Torresdale, Pa., Nov. 10, 1921; children—George Morris, Emily Fox. Practiced in Phila. since 1900; prof. surgery Women's Med. Coll. of Pa., 1923-24; prof. maxillo-facial surgery, Thomas Evans Inst., U. of Pa.; surgeon in chief Am. Oncologic Hosp.; surgeon St. Agnes Hosp.; cons. surgeon Sacred Heart Hosp., Allentown, Pa.; chmn. bd. Campbell Soup Co.; dir. Atlantic City R.R. of N.J. Served overseas as maj. Med. Reserve Corps, U.S.A. Fellow Am. Coll. Surgeons, Coll. Physicians of Phila.; mem. A.M.A., Pa. State Med. Soc., Phila. County Med. Soc., Pathol. Soc., Phila. Acad. Surgery. Republican. Episcopalian. Clubs: Racquet, Medical, Physicians' Motor, Phila. Country. Home: 2218 Delancey St. Office: 2101 Spruce St., Philadelphia, Pa.

DORRANCE, Gordon, publisher, author; b. Camden, N.Y., June 14, 1890; s. Daniel James and Edith Lillian (Turner) D.; prep. edn., Manlius (N.Y.) School; Forest Engineer, Biltmore (N.C.) Forest Sch., 1913, supplementary work at Technische Hochschule, Darmstadt, Germany; studied Grad. Sch., U. of Pa., 1919-20; m. Émile Berthe deVaulte, of New York, N.Y., Sept. 12, 1922. With State Bd. of Forestry, Md., 1913-17; pres. and chmn. bd. Dorrance & Co., Inc., since 1920. Served as lt. engrs., U.S.A., in France, Feb. 1918-Apr. 1919; capt., staff specialist, Reserves, 1925, maj., 1930. Mem. Pa. State Forest Commn., 1936-38. Mem. Pa. Forestry Assn., Pa. Soc. Mayflower Descendants (capt. 1934-35; mem. bd. 1936-38), Am. Legion, S.R. Decorated Comdr. Order of the Phœnix, Manlius School, 1930. Presbyterian. Mason. Clubs: Army and Navy (dir.), United Service Club (mem. bd. dirs.). Author: The Story of the Forest (13th edit.), 1916; Broken Shackles (novel) 1920. Editor: The Pocket Chesterfield, 1920; Contemporary Poets, An Anthology of Fifty, 1927. Contbr. New York Evening Post, Scientific American, Popular Science Monthly, London Times Imperial Trade Supplement, New York Times Annalist, Magazine of Wall St., etc. Home: Alden Park Manor. Office: Drexel Bldg., Philadelphia, Pa.

DORRANCE, Harold James, osteopathic physician; b. Jefferson Co., O., June 21, 1877; s. William Gilmore and Harriet (Saltzman) D.; desc. of French Huguenot family, Dorrance, which settled in central Pa.; student Salienville (O.) High Sch., Atlantic Sch. of Osteopathy, Buffalo, N.Y.; D.O., Am. Sch. of Osteopathy, Kirksville, Mo., 1906; m. Maie LaSalle Sebben, Jan. 21, 1906; children—Harriet LaSalle (Mrs. David Marshall Humphreys), Eloise Foster (Mrs. Brewster Reed Randolph). Began practice as osteopathic physician, Pittsburgh, 1906, retired June 1934; member Pennsylvania State Board Osteopathic Examiners, 1926-38; former dir. Brown Dorrance Electric Co., Syntron Electric Co. Mem. Am. Osteopathic Assn., Pa. Osteopathic Assn., Theta Psi. Republican. Episcopalian. Mason. Clubs: Pittsburgh Athletic, Automobile (Pittsburgh); Foxburg Country (Foxburg, Pa.); Sea Spray (Palm Beach, Fla.). Inventor of several mechanical devices used in physical therapy. Home: (winter) Palm Beach, Fla.; (summer) Wianno, Cape Cod, Mass.; (permanent) 632-42 Duquesne Way, Pittsburgh, Pa.

DORRANCE, Roy Gilbert, wholesale elec. appliances; b. Jefferson Co., O., Sept. 11, 1886; s. William Gilmore and Harriet (Saltzman) D.; student pub. sch. and high sch.; m. Olive M. Loeffler, June 30, 1913; children—Dr. Roy Gilbert, Jr., Jean Yvette, John William, Mary Christine, Nancy Lou. Employed as ins. salesman, 1906-10; entered retail and wholesale appliance business, 1910, pres. Brown-Dorrance Electric Co., wholesale elec. and gas appliances, Pittsburgh; dir. Syntron Co. Republican. Presbyterian. Clubs: Highland Country (Pittsburgh); Madison (O.) Golf and Country. Home: 1930 Wightman St. Office: 632 Duquesne Way, Pittsburgh, Pa.

DORSEY, Frank Joseph Gerard, ex-congressman; b. Phila., Pa., Apr. 26, 1891; s. John Henry and Ellen Catherine (Maher) D.; B.S., U. of Pa., 1917; m. Cecelia Mae Alphonsene Ward, of Frankford, Phila., Apr. 14, 1920; 1 dau., Cecelia Marie. Assayer, Keystone Watch Case Co., 1908-13; asst. in finance, Wharton Evening Sch. (U. of Pa.), 1916-17; with Henry Disston & Sons, Inc., saw, steel file mfrs., 1919-34; mem. 74th and 75th Congresses (1935-39), 5th Pennsylvania District; dir. Northeast Nat. Bank, 41st Ward Bldg. & Loan Assn. Enlisted as pvt. in U.S. Army, June 1917; hon. disch. as lt. Apr. 1919. Mem. Sesqui-Centennial Constitution Commn. Mem. Am. Legion, Sigma Nu, Beta Gamma Sigma. Democrat. Mem. Knights of Columbus. Clubs: Frankford-Torresdale Country, Philopatrian Lit. Inst. (Phila.). Home: 7021 Torresdale Av., Tacony, Philadelphia, Pa.

DORSEY, John Lanahan, physician; b. Baltimore, Md., Dec. 14, 1893; s. John R. and Lillian (Hooper) D.; A.B., Johns Hopkins, 1914, M.D., 1918; m. Gertrude Allen Dixon, Jan. 31, 1924; children—Gertrude Dixon, Deborah Dixon. Interne Johns Hopkins Hosp., Baltimore, 1919-22; practice as physician, Baltimore, since 1923. Served as capt. Med. Corps, U.S. Army, 1918. Fellow Am. Coll. Physicians; mem. A.M.A. Home: 1015 St. George's Rd. Office: 1129 St. Paul St., Baltimore, Md.

DOTSON, Beril Alphonsio, banking and ins.; b. Waverly, W.Va., Dec. 20, 1889; s. William C. and Fannie O. (Houser) D.; student Marietta, (O.) Acad., 1905-07; A.B., Marietta Coll., Marietta, O., 1911; m. Frances Lucille Stanley, June 1, 1916; children—John Stanley, Martha E. Has been asso. with First Nat. Bank, St. Marys, W.Va., continuously since 1912, successively teller, asst. cashier, cashier, now vice-pres. and dir.; propr. ins. agency at St. Marys, W.Va. Served as mem. W.Va. Ho. of Reps., 1935-37. Pres. Chamber of Commerce, St. Marys. Organizer and first pres. Kiwanis Club of St. Marys; lt. gov. Kiwanis W.Va. Dist. Mem. Alpha Tau Omega. Democrat. Methodist. Mason (K.T., Shriner). Maccabee. Home: 810 Dewey Av. Office: First Nat. Bank, St. Marys, W.Va.

DOTTERER, Ray Harbaugh, clergyman, prof. philosophy; b. Merwin, Pa., Aug. 4, 1880; s. John and Mary Catherine (Meyer) D.; grad. Central State Normal Sch., Lock Haven, Pa., 1902; Ph.B., Franklin and Marshall Coll., Lancaster, Pa., 1906; grad. Theol. Sem., Lancaster, Pa., 1909; A.M., Johns Hopkins U., 1916, Ph.D., 1917; m. Mabel Resh, Oct. 25, 1910 (died 1939); children—John Emanuel, Anna Mary (Mrs. Selwyn Edwards). Ordained to ministry Reformed Ch., U.S.A., 1909; pastor Rockwood, Pa., 1909-12, Trinity Ch., Baltimore, Md., 1913-18, State College, Pa., 1918-20; successively, instr., asst. prof., asso. prof. philosophy and psychology, Pa. State Coll., 1918-26; prof. psychology, Franklin and Marshall Coll., Lancaster, Pa., 1926-30; prof. philosophy, Pa. State Coll. since 1930, head of dept. since 1938. Mem. A.A.A.S., Am. Assn. Univ. Profs., Am. Philos. Assn., Assn. for Symbolic Logic, Phi Beta Kappa, Phi Kappa Phi, Pi Gamma Mu, Lambda Chi Alpha. Awarded Phi Eta Sigma medal, 1932. Democrat. Evang. and Ref. Ch. Author: Beginners' Logic, 1922; Philosophy by Way of the Sciences, 1929; contbr. to scientific and philos. journs. Home: 825 W. Foster Av., State College, Pa.

DOTY, Robert Wesley, clergyman; b. Jefferson, Md., Aug. 23, 1876; s. Abner Deloss and Emily Jane (Porter) D.; student Frederick (Md.) Acad., 1893-94, Gettysburg Coll., Acad., 1894-95; A.B., Gettysburg (Pa.) Coll., 1899, A.M., 1902; B.D., Gettysburg Sem., 1902; D.D., Geneva Coll., Beaver Falls, Pa., 1923; m. Mary Alice Roelkey, Aug. 14, 1902; 1 dau., Louise R. Ordained to ministry of Lutheran Ch., 1902; pastor Salem Charge, Westminster, Md., 1902-12, Christ Luth. Ch., Cambridge, O., 1912-18, Grace Luth. Ch., Rochester, Pa., 1918-28, Grace Luth. Ch., Butler, Pa., since 1928. Sec. Middle Conf. of Md. Synod, 1904, East Ohio Synod, 1914; del. to Gen. Synod that merged with Gen. Council and formed the United Luth. Ch. in America, 1918; del. to conv. of United Luth. Ch. from Pittsburgh Synod, 1922, 1926, 1930. Dir. and sec. of bd. Orphans' Home, Zeleinopli, Pa.; dir. Butler Y.M.C.A. Mem. Sigma Alpha Epsilon. Mason, Odd Fellow. Clubs: Rotary (Rochester, Pa.); Kiwanis of Butler (pres. 1938). Home: 227 New Castle St., Butler, Pa.

DOTY, Robert Wilson, state banking official; b. Mifflintown, Pa., July 30, 1889; s. Ezra Chalmers and Anna Margaret (Wilson) D.; ed. public schools, Mifflingtown, Pa., 1895-1905, pvt. acad. Lewistown, Pa., 1905-09; m. Lillian Estella Potteiger, Jan. 21, 1925. Teller and bookkeeper First Nat. Bank, Mifflintown, Pa., 1909-12, asst. cashier, 1912-17; asst. to gen. auditor U.S. Housing Corpn., Washington, D.C., 1917-19; asst. nat. bank examiner, Cleveland, O., 1919-21, nat. bank examiner, 1921-24, senior examiner, 1924-25, chief examiner, 1925-31, Dept. of Banking of Pa.; first dep. sec. of banking, Commonwealth of Pa., Harrisburg, Pa., since 1931; sec. of Banking, Commn. of Pa., Harrisburg, since Jan. 17, 1939. Republican. Presbyterian. Mason. Home: 2601 Derry St. Office: Dept. of Banking, Harrisburg, Pa.

DOTY, William Shaw, lawyer; b. Bellevue, Pa., Oct. 29, 1892; James Cloyd and Margaret

M. (Shaw) D.; student San Diego (Calif.) High Sch., 1906-10; Monmouth (Ill.) Coll., 1910-11; A.B., Princeton, 1915; Pittsburgh Law Sch., 1915-17; m. Elisabeth Lawrence, July 11, 1917; children—Margaret Lawrence (dec.), Elisabeth Jane, Juliet Helen (dec.), James Cloyd. Admitted to Pa. bar, 1918, and practiced at Pittsburgh since 1918; associate Sterrett and Acheson, Pittsburgh, 1919-23; individual practice, 1924; partner Doty and Thornton since 1925. Air service, U.S. Army, Jan.-Dec. 1918. Chmn. Allegheny Co. Bd. of Assistance, 1938. Mem. Allegheny Co., Pa., Am. bar. assns., Phi Delta Phi, Am. Legion. United Presbyterian. Home: 118 Irwin Av., Ben Avon, Pa. Office: 210 Jones Law Bldg., Pittsburgh, Pa.

DOUBMAN, John Russell, asso. prof. marketing, author; b. Phila., Pa., Sept. 27, 1894; s. John M. and Alice G. (Keller) D.; B.S. in econs., U. of Pa., 1917; LL.B., U. of Pa. Law Sch., 1920; A.M., U. of Pa. Grad. Sch., 1923, Ph.D., 1925; m. Martha Gibbons, May 1, 1933. Engaged in teaching at U. of Pa. since 1917; asso. prof. of marketing, Wharton Sch. of U. of Pa. since 1926; asst. dir. Dept. of Liquidation, Banking Dept. of Pa., 1935-39. Served on Govt. Code Authority, NRA, Wallpaper Industry, Washington, D.C., 1933-35. Mem. Am. Marketing Soc., Acacia, Delta Sigma Rho, Delta Sigma Pi. Methodist. Mason (32°), I.O.O.F. Author: Fundamentals of Sales Management; Sales Management Today; Retail Merchandising; etc. Home: 6214 Wayne Av., Philadelphia, Pa.

DOUGALL, John B.; supt. of schools at Summit. Address: Board of Education, Summit, N.J.

DOUGAN, James E(dward), educator; b. Prince Edward Island, Can., Nov. 6, 1880; s. William T. and Elizabeth A. (Lear) D.; brought to U.S., 1883, naturalized, 1890; student summer courses, Harvard U., 1908, Mass. Inst. Tech., 1909, Cornell U. 1910, Columbia U., 1927, N.Y. Univ., 1925; m. Frances T. Vail, Aug. 19, 1907. Instr. manual training, Piqua, O., 1907-10; prin. Boys Vocational Sch., Newark, N.J., 1910-20; asst. supt. schs., Newark, N.J., since 1920. Served in 8th U.S. Cav. in Cuba in Spanish-Am. War. Mem. Am. Assn. Sch. Adminstrs., N.J. Ednl. Assn., N.J. Schoolmasters Club, Schoolmen's Club of Newark, Vets. Fgn. Wars, Spanish-Am. War Vets. Clubs: Athletic (Newark); Crestmont Golf (West Orange); Country (Lake Mohawk). Home: 16 Elizabeth St., Caldwell. Office: Board of Edn., Newark, N.J.

DOUGHERTY, Denis J., cardinal; was ed. St. Charles Sem., Overbrook, Pa.; became first Am. bishop of Nueva Segovia, P.I., 1903, bishop of Jaro, P.I., 1908, of Buffalo, 1915; archbishop See of Philadelphia and Province of Pa., July 1918; Cardinal, Mar. 1921. Address: 1723 Race St., Philadelphia, Pa.

DOUGHERTY, George; pres., treas. and dir. Morgantown Glass Works, Morgan Hotel Corpn. and Hotel Equipment Corpn. Home: Riverview Drive. Office: Fifth St., Morgantown, W.Va.

DOUGHERTY, Gregg, univ. prof.; b. Steubenville, O., Nov. 14, 1892; s. William Armstrong and Sallie (Gregg) D.; student Steubenville (O.) pub. schs., 1900-10, Philips Exeter Acad., Exeter, N.H., 1910-13; B.S., Princeton U., 1917, M.A., Ph.D., 1921; m. Grace Ely Bassett, Dec. 18, 1924; children—James Gregg, Robert Ely. Instr. of chemistry, Princeton U., 1921-24, asst. prof., 1924-29, asso. prof. since 1929. Served as 1st lt., Chem. Warfare Service, U.S. Army, 1917-18. Trustee Princeton Country Day Sch. Mem. Phi Beta Kappa, Sigma Xi. Republican. Presbyterian. Clubs: Princeton, Chemists (New York); University Cottage, Pretty Brook Tennis (Princeton, N.J.). Address: 95 Library Pl., Princeton, N.J.

DOUGHERTY, Joseph F.; surgeon Fitzgerald-Mercy Hosp., Darby, Pa.; asst. surgeon Misericordia Hosp., Phila. Address: 7199 Radbourne Road, Upper Darby, Pa.

DOUGHTON, Isaac, coll. dean; b. Abernant, Wales, Oct. 26, 1881; s. Morgan and Rachel (Evans) D.; brought to U.S., 1883, naturalized, 1886; A.B., Harvard, 1906; A.M., U. of Pa., 1922, Ph.D., same, 1925; m. Margaret John, Nov. 23, 1907 (died 1917); children—Allan Isaac, Margaret Ruth, Anna Elizabeth (Mrs. Harold Schanbacher); m. 2d, Elizabeth John, July 3, 1923; children—Betty Jane, Morgan John, Richard Edmund. Teacher high sch., Phoenixville, Pa., 1906-10, prin., 1910-13, supt. schs., 1913-24; head dept. edn., State Teachers Coll., Mansfield, Pa., 1924-38, dean of instrn. since 1938. Mem. N.E.A., Pa. State Edn. Assn., A.A.A.S., Nat. Soc. Coll. Teachers of Edn., Nat. Soc. for Study of Edn. Republican. Baptist. Mason. Author: Preparing for the World's Work, 1922; Modern Public Education; Its Philosophy and Background, 1935. Home: Mansfield, Pa.

DOUGHTY, Howard Ewing, pres. and gen. mgr. Lorenson-Matthews Mfg. Co.; b. Phila., Pa., Aug. 1, 1891; s. John and Grace (Hirst) D.; student high sch., Phila., 1905-08, Internat. Corr. Schs., 1907-09; m. Alida Hay, June 30, 1914; children—Leona, John, Franklin. Draftsman Link Belt Co., Phila., Pa., 1910-12; chief clk. Gifford-Wood, Hudson, N.Y., 1912-26; pres. and gen. mgr. Lorenson-Matthews Mfg. Co., steel fabricators, Dickson City, Pa., since 1928. Mem. Scranton (Pa.) Chamber of Commerce. Republican. Mason. Clubs: Kiwanis (Scranton, Pa.); Abington Men's (Clarks Summit, Pa., pres.). Home: 211 Grove Av., Clarks Summit, Pa. Office: Dickson City, Pa.

DOUGLAS, George William, editor; b. Liberty, Sullivan Co., N.Y., Apr. 8, 1863; s. Rev. Samuel J. and Annie Suthers (Jackson) D.; A.B., Colgate U., 1888, A.M., 1891, Litt.D., 1915; m. Gertrude Douglas Greenwood, of Meadville, Pa., Dec. 4, 1895; children—Mrs. John M. Compton, Gertrude Wellesley. Asso. with brothers in publishing amateur paper in Springfield Center, N.Y., 1872-6; reporter Brooklyn Citizen, 1888-91; law reporter Brooklyn Daily Eagle, 1891; Albany legislative corps, same, 1892, asso. editor and editorial writer on Eagle, 1892-1902; asso. editor Youth's Companion, 1902-14; asso. editor Phila. Public Ledger, 1914-15; asso. editor Evening Public Ledger, 1915-34, lit. editor, 1917-24. Mem. Phi Beta Kappa, Delta Upsilon; mem. Pa. Hist. Soc. Alumni trustee Colgate U.; 1896-1937. Author: The Many-Sided Roosevelt; The American Book of Days; also various short stories and spl. articles on pub. topics. Home: 3926 Locust St. Office: Evening Public Ledger, Philadelphia, Pa.*

DOUGLAS, Robert S., banking; b. Newark, N.J., July 27, 1880; s. William James and Margaret (Stewart) D.; grad. Newark High Sch. 1897; m. Mary Hitchcock, Apr. 22, 1913; children—Margaret Stewart (Mrs. Erik B. J. Roos), Mary Hitchcock, William James. Began as runner with Nat. State Bank, Newark, N.J., 1898; with Union County Trust Co., Elizabeth, N.J., since Sept. 1, 1903, successively floater, asst. sec. and asst. treas., treas., asst. trust officer, vice-pres.; vice-pres. and trust officer since 1938. Ind. Republican. Presbyterian. Mason. Home: 58 Summit Road. Office: 142 Broad St., Elizabeth, N.J.

DOUGLAS, William Orville, associate justice, Supreme Court of U.S.; b. Maine, Minn., Oct. 16, 1898; s. William and Julia Bickford (Fiske) D.; A.B., Whitman Coll., Walla Walla, Wash., 1920; hon. LL.D., 1938; LL.B., Columbia, 1925; hon. A.M., Yale, 1932; children—Mildred M. Riddle, Aug. 16, 1923; children—Mildred Riddle, William. Instr. high sch., Yakima, Wash., 1920-22; editor Columbia Law Review, 1924-25; with law firm in N.Y. City, 1925-27; admitted to N.Y. bar, 1926; lecturer in law, Columbia, 1925-27, asst. prof. law, 1927-28, Yale, 1928-29; asso. prof. law, Yale, 1929-31, prof., 1931-32, Sterling prof., 1932-39; on leave of absence, 1936-39; bankruptcy studies, Yale Inst. Human Relations, 1929-32; collaborator with U.S. Dept. Commerce in bankruptcy studies, 1929-32; sec. to Com. on the Study of Business of Federal Courts, Nat. Commn. on Law Observance and Enforcement, 1930-32; dir. protective com. study, Securities and Exchange Commn., Washington, D.C., 1934-36; mem. Securities and Exchange Commn., 1936-39, chmn., 1937-39; nominated by Pres. Roosevelt as associate justice Supreme Court, Mar. 20, 1939; confirmed by the Senate, April 4, 1939; sworn in April 17, 1939. Served as pvt. U.S. Army, fall of 1918. Mem. Am. Bar Assn., Beta Theta Pi, Phi Alpha Delta, Delta Sigma Rho, Phi Beta Kappa. Democrat. Presbyn. Mason. Clubs: Mory's Assn., New Haven, Conn.; Yale (New York); Manor Country, Cosmos (Washington). Contbr. articles to law jours. Home: Eastern Av., Silver Spring, Md. Office: 1 First St., N.E., Washington, D.C.

DOUGLASS, Alfred Eugene, pres. Fuller Co.; b. Allentown, Pa., Jan. 16, 1888; s. William Merton and Helen Louise (Billings) D.; student Mercersburg (Pa.) Acad., 1904-06; m. Jean Melicent Ellis, Dec. 7, 1907; children—Alfred Eugene, Donald Stoughton, Elizabeth Laurene. Supt. Allentown (Pa.) Portland Cement Co., 1912-18; mgr. crushing dept. Fuller-Lehigh Co., Fullerton, Pa., 1918-25; v.p. and gen. mgr. Fuller Co., machinery mfrs., Catasauqua, Pa. 1926-29, pres. since 1929; dir. Allentown Portland Cement Co., Valley Forge Cement Co., Nat. Bank of Catasauqua, Pa. Mem. Nat. Assn. of Mfrs. Pa. State Chamber of Commerce, Am. Soc. M.E., Lehigh Valley Engrs. Club. Episcopalian. Elks (Lodge 130). Clubs: Catasauqua; Livingston, Lehigh Country (Allentown, Pa.). Home: Pine and American Sts. Office: 128 Bridge St., Catasauqua, Pa.

DOUGLASS, Earl Leroy, clergyman; b. McKeesport, Pa., Aug. 22, 1888; s. Elisha Pearis and Elvira (Weddle) D.; grad. Mercersburg Acad., 1909; A.B., Princeton, 1913; grad. Union Theol. Sem., 1916, post. grad. work, 1923-25; D.D., Tusculum Coll., 1931, Wooster Coll., 1936; m. Lois Haler, Sept. 4, 1913; children—Elisha Pearis, Dorothy Lois. Ordained Presbyn. ministry, 1917; pastor First Ch., Tonawanda., Pa., 1917-23, First Ch., Poughkeepsie, N.Y., 1923-31, Summit Ch., Germantown, Phila., since 1931; mem. bd. dirs. McKeesport Tin Plate Co. Mem. exec. com. World Alliance for Internat. Friendship through the Churches; mem. bd. Foundation for Narcotics Research and Information. Trustee Wooster Coll., Silver Bay Assn., Mercersburg Acad. (pres. bd.), Lincoln Univ., Westminster Choir School (Princeton, N.J.). Mason. Clubs: Adelphoi, Union League, University (Phila.); Clergy (New York). Author: Prohibition and Common Sense, 1931; The Faith We Live By, 1937. Editor of Snowden Sunday School Lessons. Syndicates daily article "Strength for the Day" in 25 newspapers. Home: 6745 Greene St., Mt. Airy, Philadelphia, Pa.

DOUGLASS, H(arlan) Paul, clergyman; b. Osage, Ia., Jan. 4, 1871; s. Truman Orville and Maria (Greene) D.; A.B., Ia. Coll., 1891, A.M., 1896; grad. Chicago and Andover Theol. sems., 1894; Williams fellowship, Harvard; courses U. of Chicago, Columbia and New York Sch. of Philanthropy; D.D., Drury Coll., 1905; m. Rena Sherman, June 25, 1895; 1 dau., Dorothea (Mrs. William A. Leech, Jr.). Ordained Congl. ministry, 1894; pastor, Manson, Ia., 1894-95, Ames, 1896-1900, Springfield, Mo., 1900-06; instr. in psychology, 1900-04, prof. philosophy, 1905-06, Drury Coll.; supt. of edn., Am. Missionary Assn., in charge of 75 schs. for negroes and mountaineers in the South, 1906-10; corr. sec., Am. Missionary Assn., 1910-18; with A.E.F. in France as Y.M.C.A. sec. and mem. of Army Ednl. Corps, 1918-19; mgr. agrl. labor br. Interchurch World Movement, 1919-20. Research dir., Inst. of Social and Religious Research, 1921-33; dir. China Survey of Laymen's Foreign Missions Inquiry, 1930-34, Commn. of Appraisal of American Unitarian Assn., 1934-35; sec. Commn. to Study Christian Unity, Federal Council of Churches of Christ in American, since 1937; editor of Christendom since 1938. Mem. Phi Beta Kappa. Author: Christian Reconstruction in the South, 1909; The New Home Missions, 1916; The Little Town, 1919; The St. Louis Church Survey, 1924; The Suburban Trend, 1925; How Shall Country Youth Be Served? 1926; The Church in the Changing City, 1927; How to Study the City Church, 1928; Church Comity, 1929; City's Church, 1929; Protestant Coöperation in American Cities, 1930; Church Unity Movements in the United States, 1934: A

Decade of Objective Progress in Church Unity. Home: Upper Montclair, N.J. Office: 297 Fourth Av., New York, N.Y.

DOUGLASS, Herbert W., banker; b. New Brighton, Pa., Jan. 22, 1882; s. George D. and Ellen (Wilde) D.; grad. New Brighton (Pa.) High Sch., 1900; m. Ida B. Harris, Sept. 1, 1905; children—Helen Elizabeth (Mrs. Justus D. Duve), Herbert W. With Beaver County Trust Co., since 1900 (except 1 yr. as asst. sec. and treas. Rochester, Pa. Trust Co.), now exec. v.p. and dir.; pres. and dir. Beaver County Ins. Agency, Inc.; treas. and mem. bd. mgrs. Grove Cemetery. Dir. New Brighton Sch. Dist. about 20 yrs.; trustee Beaver Valley Y.M. C.A. Republican. Episcopalian (senior warden). Mason. Clubs: Beaver Valley Country (Beaver Falls, Pa.); Brighton, Community (New Brighton, Pa.). Home: 408 15th St. Address: Beaver County Trust Co., New Brighton, Pa.

DOUGLASS, Louis Harriman; prof. of obstetrics, U. of Md.; chief obstetrical clinic and out-patient dept. U. of Md. Hosp.; visiting obstetrician Woman's and Bon Secours hosps.; obstetrician in chief Baltimore City Hosps. and Provident Hosp. and Free Dispensary. Address: 101 W. Read St., Baltimore, Md.

DOUGLASS, Mabel Smith, coll. dean; b. Jersey City, N.J., Feb. 11, 1877; d. James Weaver and Wilhelmine Joanne (Midlige) Smith; grad. high sch., Jersey City; A.B., Columbia, 1899; Litt.D., Rutgers U., 1924; m. William Shipman Douglass, Apr. 14, 1903; children—Edith Shipman, William Shipman (deceased). Teacher, public schools, N.Y. City, 1899-1902; administrative dean N.J. Coll. for Women, Rutgers U., since founded, 1918. Mem. N.J. State Bd. of Edn. Mem. Am. Assn. Univ. Women, Phi Beta Kappa. Awarded Columbia Univ. medal, 1931. Protestant. Clubs: College (New Brunswick); College (Jersey City). Home: New Brunswick, N.J.*

DOUTHETT, Walter Richard, sch. supt.; b. Allegheny Co., Pa., Jan. 9, 1886; s. Lemuel and Margaret (Graham) D.; student Slippery Rock (Pa.) State Normal Sch., 1907; A.B., Ursinus Coll., Collegeville, Pa., 1912; A.M., U. of Pa., 1923; m. Margaret Moser, June 20, 1913; children—Elsie, Elwood, Bertha, Dorothy; m. 2d, Hannah Matthews, Nov. 25, 1929; 1 dau., Patricia. Teacher ungraded rural sch., Allegheny Co., Pa., 1903-04, 1905-06; principal, College Hill Elementary Sch., Beaver Falls, Pa., 1907-08; head history dept., Bloomfield (N.J.) High Sch., 1912-15; asst. principal, Radnor High Sch., Wayne, Pa., 1915-19; principal, Darby (Pa.) High Sch., 1919-23; supt. of schs., Darby, Pa., since 1923. Dir. Ursinus Coll., Family Welfare Soc., East Delaware Co., Pa. Mem. Phila. Suburban Supts. Assn. (pres. 1938-39), Pa. Dist. Supts. Assn. (pres. 1938-39), Pa. State Teachers Assn. (mem. exec. council, 1937-39), Eastern Assn. of Intercollegiate Football Officials. Club: Pennsylvania Schoolmen's (past pres.). Home: 606 Pine St. Office: 7th and Spruce Sts., Darby, Pa.

DOUTRICH, Isaac H., ex-congressman; b. Dauphin Co., Pa., Dec. 19, 1871; s. Eli and Caroline D.; grad. Keystone State Normal Sch., Kutztown, Pa.; m. Lena Erb (died June 1933). Mem. 70th to 74th Congresses (1927-37), 19th Pa. Dist. Republican. Address: Harrisburg, Pa.

DOUTY, Daniel Ellis, pres. tech. service co.; b. Omro, Wis., Apr. 3, 1872; s. Daniel Ellis and Martha Ann (Shears) D.; B.S., U. of Wash., Seattle, 1892; fellow Clark U., Worcester, Mass., 1898-1901; spl. study Cornell U., 1900, 1903; m. Madeleine Quackenbush, Sept. 27, 1913. Tutor and instr. physics, Univ. of Wash., Seattle, 1895-98; supervisor of sciences, high schs., Seattle, Wash., 1901-03; asst. and asso. physicist, Nat. Bur. Standards, Washington, D.C., 1903-13; vice-pres. and gen. mgr., United States Testing Co., Inc., N.Y. City, 1913-34, pres. at Hoboken, N.J., since 1934, a commercial lab. orgn. furnishing phys., chem. and engring. tech. service in research, testing, inspection and consulting to industry. Served in Wash. N.G.; lt. U.S.N.R.F. (CC). Trustee and treas. China Inst. in America. Dir. U.S. Inst. for Textile Research. Mem. Am. Soc. for Testing Materials, Council Am. Standards Assn., Am. Council of Commercial Labs. (sec.). Awarded Cavaliere dell' Ordine della Corona d'Italia. Republican. Unitarian. Clubs: Knickerbocker Country (Englewood); Manhattan, National Arts, National Republican (New York); Cosmos (Washington). Home: 232 Lydecker St., Englewood. Office: 1415 Park Av., Hoboken, N.J.

DOUTY, Nicholas, tenor singer; b. Phila., Pa., Apr. 14, 1870; s. Henry Browne and Helen Matilda (Barber) D.; studied singing with Aline Osgood, William Castle in U.S., Alberto Randegger, London, Guiseppe Sbriglia, Paris; hon. Mus.D., George Washington Univ., 1919; Philadelphia Musical Academy, 1929; m. Frieda Shloss of Philadelphia, Mar. 4, 1894; children—Nicholas (dec.), Alfred, Blanche. Known as singer of Bach's music; soloist, in Bach performances in New York, Chicago, Boston, Phila., Pittsburgh, Milwaukee, Montclair Bach Festival, etc.; soloist every festival Bethlehem Bach Choir for 25 years, and of many choral socs. and orchestras; also conductor. Club: Pegasus (pres.). Author: What the Vocal Student Should Know; also many articles in mags. Composer of numerous published songs, part songs, etc. Editor of Oratorio Repertoire (4 vols.). Translator song, opera and oratorio texts from European langs. Home: 331 Harrison Av., Elkins Park, Pa. Studio: 1712 Chestnut St., Philadelphia, Pa.*

DOUW, John dePeyster, retired banker; b. Albany, N.Y., Aug. 18, 1873; s. Volckert Petrus and Ella Brooks (Gould) D.; student Albany (N.Y.) Boys Acad., 1880-84, Brookville (Md.) Acad., 1885-87, Columbian Prep., Washington, D.C., 1887-89, Naval Acad. Prep. Sch., Annapolis, Md., 1889-91, N.Y. Nautical Sch., 1891-94; m. Harriet Rooker Tate, Oct. 20, 1896 (died 1919); children—Julia Agnes (Mrs. Walter C. Holt), Helen Louise (Mrs. Alfred H. Richards), Volckert Petrus; m. 2d, Anne M. Olyphant, Jan. 1921. Began in merchant marine, 1894; mcht., N.Y., San Francisco, 1894-96; city engr. Mil. Dept. State of Md., Annapolis & Baltimore, Md., 1906-18; U.S. property and disbursing officer for Maryland, supt. State of Md. Rifle Range, Saunders Range, Md., 1911-18; asst. adj. gen. of Md., 1912-15; pres. Annapolis (Md.) Commercial Credits, 1920-24, County Trust Co. of Annapolis, 1933-37; dir. Annapolis and Eastport Bldg. Assn. Served as pvt. to lt. col. Md. N.G., 1904-28, as maj., U.S. Army, during World War; served as ensign, U.S. Navy, Spanish-Am. War. Alderman, Annapolis, 1899-1901; mayor, Annapolis, 1903-05; county commr., Anne Arundel Co., Md., 1905-07. Mem. Am. Legion, Mil. Order Fgn. Wars. Democrat. Episcopalian. Mason (life). Clubs: Army-Navy (Washington, D.C.); Annapolitan (Annapolis, Md.); Propeller of U.S. Port of Annapolis. Address: 23 Southgate Av., Annapolis, Md.

DOVEY, Clayton Cresswell, coal operator, banker; b. Shenandoah, Pa., 1882; s. John C. and Mary (Faust) D.; m. Alice Reynolds, 1907; children—Mrs. Eleanor Veigle, John, Clayton, II. Pres. Cambria Fuel Co., First Nat. Savings & Loan Assn., Cambria Store Co.; sec.-treas. Wilmore Fuel Co., Shade Realty & Equipment Co., Wilmore Store Co.; dir. United States Nat. Bank, Johnstown, Pa. Mason. Clubs: Bachelor (Johnstown, Pa.); Sunnehanna Country, North Fork Country; Miami-Baltimore Year Round (Miami, Fla.). Home: 345 Luzerne St., Johnstown, Pa.; and 1006 S. Greenway Drive, Coral Gables, Fla. Office: Federal Savings & Loan Blg., Johnstown, Pa.

DOWN, Sidney George, first v.p. Westinghouse Air Brake Co.; b. Swansea, Wales, Jan. 1, 1876; s. Richard and Annie (Button) D.; student Detroit Engring. Sch.; m. Elnora N. Edwards, of Greensboro, N.C., April 29, 1907. First v.p. and dir. Westinghouse Air Brake Co. since 1923; pres. and dir. Am. Brake Co., Westinghouse Pacific Coast Brake Co.; v.p. Wilmerding Corpn.; exec. v.p. and dir. Bendix-Westinghouse Automotive Air Brake Co.; v.p. and dir. Westinghouse Air Brake Home Bldg. Co.; dir. Bendix Aviation Corpn., Union Switch & Signal Co., Cleveland Pneumatic Tool Co. Mem. Pan-Am. Soc., Japan Soc., Engrs. Soc. of Western Pa. Clubs: Duquesne, Longue Vue, Pittsburgh Athletic (Pittsburgh); Engineers, Bankers (N.Y. City); Chicago, Union League (Chicago). Home: 204 Hawthorne St., Edgewood, Pittsburgh, Pa. Office: Westinghouse Air Brake Co., Wilmerding, Pa.

DOWNING, Charles Thompson, lawyer; b. Wharton, N.J., Sept. 6, 1890; s. John and Esther Ann (Firstbrook) D.; student pub. schs. and high sch., 1904-08; m. Natalie B. Wardell, Oct. 12, 1920; 1 son, Robert L. Studied law in office of John C. Losey; admitted to N.J. bar as atty., 1914, as counselor, 1930; engaged in gen. practice of law at Newton since 1914; mem. firm Morris, Downing & Sherred since 1917; atty. for Borough of Stanhope and Sandyston Township; prosecutor Sussex Co., 1933-39; served as mem. N.J. Ho. of Assembly, 1932-33; vice-pres. New Jersey Properties Co.; dir. Newton Bldg. & Loan Assn. Served at Camp Dix, N.J. during World War. Mem. N.J. State Bar Assn., Sussex County Bar Assn. Democrat. Methodist. Mason, Tall Cedars of Lebanon, Elk. Home: 9 Halsted St. Office: 30 Park Pl., Newton, N.J.

DOWNS, Charles B.; in gen. practice of law since 1900. Office: Pennsylvania Bldg., Philadelphia, Pa.

DOWNS, William Findlay, pub. utility exec.; b. Dover, Del., July 11, 1887; s. Dr. Presley Spruance and Elizabeth (Brown) D.; g.s. Charles Brown, mem. Congress; gt.g.s. Francis Shunk, gov. of Pa.; gt.gt.g.s. William Findlay, gov. Pa. and U.S. senator; grad. Mercersburg (Pa.) Acad., Lafayette Coll., Easton, Pa., and Mass. Inst. Tech.; m. Minnie C. Litchfield, of Brookline, Mass., May 28, 1913; children—Anna Elizabeth, Marjory Litchfield, Nancy Irwin Shunk. Began as forestry surveyor, U.S. Engring. Survey Corps, 1909, in charge of corps, 1909-10; cadet engr., United Gas Improvement Co., Philadelphia, Pa., 1910-12; asst. engr., J. G. White Engring. Corpn., 1912-14; valuation engr., New York Telephone Co., 1914-15; asst. engr., Pub. Service Commn., Pa., 1915-18; report engr., Day & Zimmermann, Inc., Philadelphia, 1919-21, dir., 1921-37; v.p., 1927-29, pres. since 1929; pres. Day & Zimmermann Securities Corpn.; dir. Red Star Lines, Interborough Rapid Transit Co. (New York), Victor Lynn Transportation Co., Davidson Transfer & Storage Co., Phila. and Western Ry. Co., Am. States Utilities Corpn., Scranton Spring Brook Water Service Co., Federal Water Service Corpn., Lukens Steel Co. Mem. Bd. of Pub. Edn., Sch. Dist. of Phila. Mem. Am. Soc. M.E., Franklin Inst., Delta Kappa Epsilon. Democrat. Presbyn. Clubs: Racquet, Bankers, Cruising, Corinthian Yacht, Eastern Yacht, Gibson Island Yacht. Home: 422 W. Mermaid Lane, Chestnut Hill, Pa. Office: Packard Bldg., Philadelphia, Pa.

DOWNS, William Smith, consulting engr.; b. Martinsburg, W.Va., Mar. 15, 1883; s. Joseph Allen and Janet Caroline (Evans) D.; student Martinsburg (W.Va.) pub. schs., 1889-99; B.S. in C.E., W.Va. U., 1906, C.E., 1915; m. Nellie Jane Albright, June 22, 1910; children—William Richard, James Albright, Jane. Topographer Com. for Study Railroads, Bolivia, S.A., 1904-05; chief draftsman Morgantown & Kingwood R.R., 1906-08; resident engr. and later engr. in charge Hydro Electric Co. of W.Va. (State Line development), 1909-15; chief engr. Monongalia Co. Highway Dept., 1916-19; division engr. W.Va. State Road Commn., 1919-29; private practice as consulting engr. since 1929; prof. ry. and highway engring., W.Va. U., since 1932. Mem. Am. Soc. Civil Engrs., W.Va. Soc. Professional Engrs. (dir.), Soc. for Promotion Engring. Edn., Am. Road Builders Assn. (dir. ednl. div.), Beta Theta Pi. Republican. Presbyn. Clubs: Morgantown Engineers, Morgantown Rotary. Contbr. to tech. mags., tech. socs., etc. Home: 204 Euclid Av., Morgantown, W.Va.

DOXSEE, Carll Whitman, prof. English lit.; b. Bay Shore, L.I., N.Y., Sept. 26, 1887; s. Wm. F. G. and Mary Emily (Sprague) D.; A.B., Wesleyan Univ., 1909, A.M., same, 1910; Ph.D., Princeton, 1916; m. Effie Blydenburgh, Aug. 12, 1914. Began as instr. English, Morningside Coll. (Ia.), 1910; instr., U. of Kan., 1913-14; prof. English, Grove City Coll., 1914-

20; prof. English lit. and head dept. English, Pa. Coll. for Women, Pittsburgh, Pa., since 1920. Mem. Am. Philos. Assn., Modern Lang. Assn., Phi Beta Kappa. Democrat. Episcopalian. Clubs: The Quiz, Author's (Pittsburgh). Contbr. articles to encyc. Home: 1139 Murray Hill Av., Pittsburgh, Pa.

DOYLE, Bartley J., pres. Keystone Pub. Co. Home: The Warwick. Office: Real Estate Trust Bldg., Philadelphia, Pa.

DOYLE, Henry Grattan, university dean; b. Somerville, Mass., Sept. 22, 1889; s. Edward W. and Mary (Ring) D.; A.B., Harvard, 1911, A.M., 1912; m. Marion Wade Sharkey (A.B., Radcliffe), Sept. 15, 1917; children—Henry Grattan, Marion Wade, Robert Carr. Instr. Romance langs., Harvard, 1913-16; instr. Romance langs., 1916-18, asst. prof., 1918-21, prof. since 1921, dean of men, 1927-29, dean lower div., 1929-30, dean jr. coll., 1930-34, dean Columbian Coll. since 1934, George Washington U. Lecturer in French philology, Johns Hopkins, 1926-27, 1931-32 and 1934; visiting prof. of methodology, Middlebury Coll., 1939. Mem. Harvard Council on Hispano-Am. Studies. Mng. editor Modern Lang. Jour., 1934-38; asso. editor Hispania; in charge Spanish, summers, Cornell, 1920, 23. Decorated, Order of Merit (Ecuador), 1938. Mem. Am. Council on Edn., Am. Assn. Teachers of Italian, Mediæval Acad. of America, American Assn. of Teachers of Spanish, Eastern Assn. Coll. Deans and Advisers of Men, Nat. Dante Com., Washington Dante Com., Dante Soc. Cambridge, Mass., Internat. Phonetic Assn., Am. Dialect Soc., Am. Folklore Soc., Modern Lang. Assn. America, Am. Assn. Univ. Profs., Literary Soc. (Washington, D.C.), Pi Delta Epsilon, Omicron Delta Kappa, Phi Beta Kappa, Federal Schoolmen's Club, Modern Humanities Research Assn. (Eng.); fellow A.A. A.S.; corr. member Hispanic Soc. America. Clubs: Harvard (Boston and New York); Cosmos (Washington, D.C.). Author: Spanish Studies in the United States, 1926; A Tentative Bibliography of the Belles-Lettres of Panama, 1934; A Bibliography of Rubén Darío, 1935; A Tentative Bibliography of the Belles-Lettres of Central America, 1935; George Ticknor, 1937; (also with G. Rivera) En España, 1921; (with C. K. Jones and A. Cabrillo y Vázquez) Trozos escogidos, 1931. Translator: On the Slopes of Calvary (from the Italian), 1918; Catecismo cívico de los derechos y deberes de ciudadanos americanos, Washington, 1923. Home: 5500 33d St., Chevy Chase, D.C. Address: George Washington Univ., Washington, D.C.

DOYLE, Marion Wade (Mrs. Henry Grattan Doyle); b. Cambridge, Mass., Oct. 30, 1894; d. John F. and Joanna T. (Phelan) Sharkey; prep. edn., Cambridge Latin Sch.; A.B., with distinction in Romance Langs., Radcliffe Coll., 1914; m. Henry Grattan Doyle, Sept. 15, 1917; children—Henry Grattan, Marion Wade, Robert Carr. V.p. Nat. League of Women Voters, 1932-34. Pres. Bd. of Edn., D.C., since 1935; v.p. D.C. Bur. of Rehabilitation, dir. Child Guidance Clinic, Social Hygiene Soc., Family Service Assn., Visiting Nursing Assn., D.C. Congress of Parents and Teachers, Self-Help Exchange. Member Nat. League of Women Voters, Am. Civic Assn., Am. Assn. Univ. Women, Radcliffe Coll. Alumnae Assn., Columbian Women of George Washington Univ. (ex-pres.), Chevy Chase Citizens' Assn. Clubs: Radcliffe Club of Washington (ex-pres.), Twentieth Century, Monday Evening. Lecturer. Contbr. to ednl. jours. Home: 5500 33d St., Chevy Chase, D.C. Office: Board of Education, Washington, D.C.

DOYLE, Michael Francis, lawyer; mem. Permanent Court of Internat. Arbitration; b. Phila.; s. John J. and Mary (Hughes) D.; LL.B., University of Pa., 1897, post-graduate work, 1897-99; LL.D., Villanova (Pa.) College, 1935; m. Nancy O'Donoghue, 1917. In gen. practice, including internat. law. Mem. White House Conf. on dependent children; mem. Citizens' Relief Com., Comprehensive Plans Com., Phila.; spl. agt. Dept. of State, 1915, to care for American citizens in Europe at beginning of the war; actg. counsellor Am. Legation, Switzerland, Am. Embassy, Vienna, 1915; counsel for Sir Roger Casement, on trial for treason, London, 1916. Spl. asst. chief of ordnance, War Dept., 1917-18; secured nearly million pledges of loyalty from employes of shipyards and munition plants during war; counsel Delaware River Shipbuilders' Council, 1918-21; Am. counsel for Irish Republican Movement, 1921; counsel for Eamon De Valera, Mrs. Terrence McSwiney, Donald O'Callaghan, Lord Mayor of Cork and other Irish revolutionary leaders in various courts and state and other depts. nat. govt., 1920-22; adviser Irish Free State Com. in drafting Nat. Constn., 1922; counsel Rayti-San Domingo before State Dept., 1922. Chmn. Am. Com., Geneva, since 1923; dir. League of Nations Association. Apptd. by Pres. Roosevelt Plenipotentiary del. representing U.S. at Inter-Am. Conf. for Maintenance of Peace, Buenos Aires, 1936; signatory 8 treaties on behalf of U.S. Govt. with 20 Am. Republics, 1936; hon. mem. Bar of Buenos Aires, Argentine, 1936; mem. exec. com. Federal Constitution Celebration, Philadelphia, 1937; apptd. mem. Permanent Court of Internat. Arbitration at the Hague, 1938; v.p. Cath. Assn. Internat. Peace. Dem. Presdl. elector, 1928, 32; chmn. Dem. Presdl. electors, inauguration of Pres. Roosevelt, 1933. Mem. Am., Pa. Federal, and Phila. bar assns., Phila. Law Acad., Soc. Internat. Law, Am. Acad. Polit. and Social Science, Pontifical Tiberian Acad. (Rome); one of founders Nat. Conf. Catholic Charities; hon. chmn. Cercle Catholique de Genève; dir. Catholic Missionary Soc., dir. League of Nations Assn. U.S. Decorated Knight Comdr. Order of Holy Sepulchre, 1929; Grand Cross Order of Holy Sepulchre, 1931; pres. Order of Holy Sepulchre (Am. Council), 1932; Chevalier Legion of Honor (France); Knight Comdr. Order of Merit, 1st Class (Bulgaria); Officer Legion of Honor (France), 1937; Comdr. Order of Honor and Merit (Haiti), 1937; Knight Comdr. Order of Merit Juan Pablo Duarte (Dominican Republic). Clubs: Penn, Contemporary, Lawyers, International of Geneva (dir.), etc. Home: 1900 S. Rittenhouse Sq. Office: Girard Trust Bldg., Philadelphia, Pa.

DOYLE, Thomas L., sr. surgeon Hahnemann Hosp.; cons. surgeon Broad St. Hosp.; asso. prof. surgery and lecturer in gen. and plastic surgery, Hahnemann Med. Coll. Address: 230 S. 19th St., Philadelphia, Pa.

DOZIER, Herbert Lawrence, biologist; b. Wilmington, N.C., June 24, 1895; s. Leonidas Byrd and Susan Annie (Gibson) D.; B.S., U. of S.C., Columbia, S.C., 1915; M.S., U. of Fla., Gainesville, Fla., 1917; Ph.D., Ohio State U., Columbus, O., 1922; student L'Université de Clermont-Ferrand, France, 1919; m. May Marion Keating, Dec. 26, 1923; children—Herbert Lawrence, Byrd Keating, Catherine Ann, May Marion. Field asst. U.S. Bureau of Entomology, 1915; asst. entomologist State Plant Bd., Miss., 1920-21; entomologist in charge New Orleans Sta., U.S. Bureau Entomology, 1922-23; entomologist Gulf Coast Citrus Exchange, Mobile, Ala., 1923-24; chief entomologist Insular Expt. Sta., Puerto Rico, 1924-25; entomologist Expt. Sta., Del., 1925-29; head dept. zoology and entomology, Ecole Central, Port-au-Prince, Haiti, 1929-31; asst. state dir. mosquito control, Civil Works Adminstrn., La., 1934; asso. entomologist U.S. Bureau of Entomology and Plant Quarantine, Mayaguez, Puerto Rico, 1935-36; research entomologist La. Dept. Agr., 1936-37; dir. U.S. Fur Animal Field Sta., Blackwater Refuge, U.S. Bureau Biol. Survey, Cambridge, Md., since 1937. Served as 1st class pvt., U.S. Army, France, 1918-19. Mem. Gamma Alpha, Phi Sigma, Sigma Xi. Democrat. Methodist. Mason (32°, Shriner). Home: 203 Oakley St., Cambridge, Md.

DRACH, John George Peter, clergyman; b. Greenport, L.I., N.Y., Sept. 3, 1873; s. John Peter and Pauline (Simon) D.; student Wagner Coll., Staten Island, N.Y., 1888-92, Luth. Theol. Sem., Phila., 1892-95; (hon.) D.D., Muhlenberg Coll., Allentown, Pa., 1918; m. Marie Douglas Sterr, Oct. 19, 1899; children—Ruth Dorothy (Mrs. S. Louis Cornish), Katharine Amelia (Mrs. John A. Blair), John Douglas, Robert Welden, Howard Sterr (dec.). Ordained to ministry Luth. Ch., 1895; asst. pastor, Reading, Pa., 1895-97; pastor St. Stephen's Luth. Ch., Phila., Pa., 1897-1905; gen. sec. bd. fgn. missions of United Luth. Ch., Baltimore, Md., since 1905; mem. various bds. and coms. in Ministerium of Pa.; mem. Luth. Fgn. Missions Conf., Fgn. Missions Conf. of N.A. Lutheran. Author: The Telugu Mission in India, (pub.) 1914; Forces in Foreign Missions, 1925; Seeing Things in the Far East, 1926; The Voice of Jesus, 1936; The Words of the Law, 1911; Luther's Catechism for the Blind, 1900. Editor: The Foreign Missionary since 1908. Contbr. to Luth. journs. and publs. Home: 2511 N. Calvert St. Office: 18 E. Mt. Vernon Place, Baltimore, Md.

DRAKE, Charles L.; chmn. bd. and pres. First Stroudsburg Nat. Bank. Address: Stroudsburg, Pa.

DRAKE, J(ames) Frank, mfr.; b. Pittsfield, N.H., Sept. 1, 1880; s. Nathaniel Seavey and Mary A. R. (Green) D.; prep. edn., Kimball Union Acad., Meriden, N.H.; A.B., Dartmouth, 1902; Master Commercial Science, Amos Tuck Sch. (Dartmouth), 1903; m. Mildred Augusta Chase, of Plymouth, N.H., July 25, 1907; children—Ruth Elliott, Virginia, James Frank, Constance Chase. Sec. Bd. of Trade, Springfield, Mass., 1903-08; sec. Phelps Pub. Co., Springfield, 1908-14, treas. and dir., 1914-18; asst. to pres. Gulf Oil Corpn., Pittsburgh, Pa., 1919-23; pres. Standard Steel Car Co. and subsidiary companies, 1923-30; chmn. bd. Pullman, Inc., Mar. 1930-Apr. 1931; pres. Gulf Oil Corporation since Apr. 1931; also pres. Gulf Refining Company, Standard Securities Corporation, Osgood Bradley Securities Co., Standard Car Finance Co.; chmn. bd. Mexican Gulf Oil Co., Western Gulf Oil Co., Venezuela Gulf Oil Co., Gulf Exploration Co., Am. Internat. Fuel & Petroleum Co., Gulf Research and Development Corpn.; vice-pres. Pittsburgh Equitable Meter Co., United Petroleum Securities Corpn., dir. Belgium Gulf Oil Co., Allgemeine Europaische Transportmittel Atkiengesellschaft (Zurich, Switzerland), Pullman Inc., Pullman Co., American Rolling Mill Co. Mem. Common Council, Springfield, 1908-12, pres. 1910-12. Commnd. maj. Ordnance Dept., U.S.A., June 1918; served as comdg. officer finance div. Pittsburgh Dist.; lt. col. Mar. 25, 1919; hon. discharged, June 3, 1919. Mem. Am. Philatelic Soc., S.A.R., Soc. Colonial Wars, Order of Founders and Patriots of America, Am. Legion, Mil. Order World War, Theta Delta Chi. Republican. Episcopalian. Clubs: University, Duquesne, Pittsburgh Golf, Fox Chapel Golf (Pittsburgh); Rolling Rock (Ligonier, Pa.); Cosmos, Congressional Country (Washington); Allegheny Country (Sewickley, Pa.); University, Recess (New York); Chicago; Embassy (London); Union Interalliée, Travellers (Paris). Home: 5210 Pembroke Pl. Office: Gulf Bldg., Pittsburgh, Pa.

DRAKE, Quaesita Cromwell; prof. chemistry, U. of Del. Address: University of Delaware, Newark, Del.

DRANT, Patricia (Hart), dermatologist; b. Grenola, Kan., Jan. 27, 1895; d. James Lafayette and Nora Coombs (Demmitt) Hart; B.S., U. of Kan., 1917; M.D., Univ. of Pa., 1920; grad. student dermatology, U. of Pa. Graduate Hosp., Phila., 1921-22; St. Louis Hosp., Paris, 1924-25, Vienna, 1925, Budapest, 1925; m. Reginald Drant, of New York, N.Y., Sept. 1, 1920 (divorced); m. 2d, William Warren Rhodes, executive DuPont Company, Wilmington, Del., Aug. 18, 1934. Dermatologist M.E. Ch. Hosp. (Phila.), Phila. Gen. Hosp., Woman's Hosp. (Phila.). Diplomate of Am. Bd. Dermatology and Syphilology. Mem. Am. Med. Assn., Phila. Dermatol. Assn., Phila. County Med. Soc., Alpha Omicron Pi. Clubs: Art Alliance, Plays and Players. Contbr. to Ency. on Medicine and professional mags. Home: "Rhodesia," Westtown, Pa. Office: Medical Arts Bldg., Philadelphia, Pa.

DRAPER, John William, philologist; b. Hastings-on-Hudson, N.Y., July 23, 1893; s. Daniel and Ann Maury (Ludlow) D.; A.B., New York U., 1914, A.M., 1915; A.M., Harvard, 1918, Ph.D., 1920; m. Lulu Clay, June

6, 1919; children—Daniel Clay, John William Christopher, Charles Ludlow. Instr. in English, New York U., 1916-17, U. of Minn., 1920-21; lecturer English lit., Bryn Mawr Coll., 1921-22; asso. prof. of English, U. of Me., 1922-24, prof. 1924-29; prof. English, U. of W.Va., since 1929. Visiting prof. Harvard Summer Sch., 1925-30, U. of Ia., summer 1929, Duke U., 1939; fellow Guggenheim Foundation for research in Eng., 1927-28. Mem. Modern Lang. Assn. America, Modern Humanities Research Assn., Am. Assn. Univ. Profs., Phi Kappa Phi, Phi Beta Kappa; pres. Andiron Club New York, editor-in-chief of The Colonnade, 1913-17, 1921-25. Democrat. Episcopalian. Clubs: Authors' (London); XX Club (Morgantown). Author: Poems, 1913; Exotics, 1915; William Lyndon Wright, A Memoir, 1923; William Mason, A Study in Eighteenth Century Culture, 1924; The Funeral Elergy and the Rise of English Romanticism, 1929; Eighteenth Century English Æsthetics, a Bibliography, 1931; The Hamlet of Shakespeare's Audience, 1938. Editor: Bragg's Formal Eclogue in the Eighteenth Century, 1926; Davis's Stephen Duck, 1927; A Century of Broadside Elegies, 1928. Extensive contbr. to philol. journals. Editor of W.Va. Phil. Bull., 1937. Home: Morgantown, W.Va.

DRASHER, Clark L.; partner J. H. Brooks & Co. Home: 714 W. Diamond Av., Hazelton, Pa. Office: Brooks Bldg., Scranton, Pa.

DRAYTON, John W.; v.p. Insurance Co. of North America; dir. numerous cos. Home: Penllyn, Pa. Office: 1600 Arch St., Philadelphia, Pa.

DREIFUS, Charles; chmn. bd. Charles Dreifus Co.; chmn. finance com. Blaw-Knox Co. Home: 5563 Northumberland Ave. Office: Oliver Bldg., Pittsburgh, Pa.

DRENNEN, William James, supervising prin. schs.; b. Fairmount, Pa., Feb. 14, 1902; s. Harry James and Winona (Shoemaker) D.; grad. Millersville State Normal Sch., 1921; B.S., Franklin and Marshall Coll., 1925; A.M., U. of Pa., 1934; m. Loraine Musselman, June 30, 1927; children—Winona Jane, Robert James. Engaged as teacher, then asst. prin. high sch., 1921-22; prin. high sch., Peach Bottom, Pa., 1922-24; supervising prin., North Coventry Dist. Schs., S. Pottstown, Pa., 1925-30; supervising prin. pub. schs., Narberth, Pa., since 1930; active in Boy Scout work at Narberth. Mem. Nat. Edn. Assn., Pa. State Edn. Assn., Phila. Suburban Prins. Assn., Sigma Pi. Republican. Presbyn. (deacon). Clubs: Bala-Cynwyd-Narberth Ro*ary (Narberth); U. of Pa. Alumni Club (Philadelphia). Home: 417 Grove Place, Narberth, Pa.

DRESDEN, Arnold, mathematician; b. Amsterdam, Netherlands, Nov. 23, 1882; s. Mark and Anna (Meyerson) D.; U. of Amsterdam, 1901-03; S.M., U. of Chicago, 1906, Ph.D., 1909; m. Louise Schwendener June 12, 1907; 1 son, Mark Kenyon. Came to U.S., 1903, naturalized citizen, 1912. Teacher of mathematics, University High Sch., Chicago, 1906-09; instr. mathematics, 1909-12, asst. prof., 1912-21, asso. prof., 1921-27, U. of Wis.; prof. mathematics, Swarthmore Coll., 1927—. Service with A.R.C. in France, Sept. 1918-June 1919. Fellow A.A.A.S.; mem. Math. Assn. America (pres. 1933-35), Am. Math. Soc., Académie de Macon, France, Société Mathématique de France, Deutsch Mathematiker Vereinigung. Author: Plane Trigonometry, 1921; Solid Analytical Geometry and Determinants, 1930; An Invitation to Mathematics, 1936. Home: 606 Elm Av., Swarthmore, Pa.

DREW, Ira Walton, congressman; b. Hardwick, Vt., Aug. 31, 1878; s. John Herring and Fannie A. (Walton) D.; student Hardwick Acad.; D.O., Phila. Coll. of Osteopathy, 1911, LL.D., 1937; m. Margaret Spencer, Oct. 28, 1911; children—John Walton, Hubert Spencer. Learned printing trade, becoming journeyman, 1899; reporter Burlington (Vt.) Free Press, 1899; reporter and news editor, Boston, 1906-08; began practice osteopathy, Phila., 1911; prof. diseases of children, Phila. Coll. of Osteopathy for 20 yrs.; mem. 75th Congress (1937-39), 7th Pa. Dist. Mem. Am. Osteopathic Assn., Pa. Osteopathic Soc., Iota Tau Sigma. Democrat. Episcopalian. Mason, Elk. Club: Elks (Phila.). Address: 5304 Wayne Av., Philadelphia, Pa.

DREW, James Byron, judge; b. Pittsburgh, Pa., Apr. 27, 1877; s. John and Martha (Rorke) D.; student U. of Mich., 1896-97; A.M., LL.B., Columbia Univ., 1900; m. Mary Black Snyder July 12, 1918; children—Stanley T., Rhoda, John, Barbara. Admitted to N.Y. bar 1900, Pa. bar, 1902; in practice at Pittsburgh, 1902-06; city solicitor, Pittsburgh, 1906-11; judge County Court, 1912-18; judge Common Pleas Court, 1918-29; judge Superior Court of Pa., 1930; justice Supreme Court of Pa. since 1931. Capt. U.S.A., World War. Republican. Catholic. Clubs: Everglades (Palm Beach); Union Interalliée (Paris); Duquesne, Allegheny Country. Home: 625 Morewood Av. Address: City-County Bldg., Pittsburgh, Pa.

DREW, Thomas Bradford, chem. engr.; b. Medford, Mass., Feb. 9, 1902; s. Henry Jay Washburn and Henrietta Cook (Cole) D.; B.S., Mass. Inst. Tech., 1923, M.S., 1924; m. Alice Wait, June 9, 1930; children—Mary, Emilie. Instr. chemistry and chem. engring., Drexel Inst., Phila., Pa., 1925-28; instr. thermodynamics and chem. engring. and research asso., Dept. of Chem. Engring., Mass. Inst. Tech., 1929-34; chem. engr., E. I. duPont de Nemours & Co., Wilmington, Del., since 1934; lecturer in chem. engring., Columbia U., since 1937. Mem. Mass. Soc. of the Cincinnati, Am. Chem. Soc., Am. Inst. Chem. Engrs., Am. Soc. M.E. (chmn. heat transfer professional group, 1938-39), Army Ordnance Asso., Soc. of Rheology, Boy Scouts of America (local troop committeeman). William H. Walker Award, Am. Inst. Chem. Engrs., 1937. Ind. Democrat. Unitarian. Club: Lions (Kennett Sq., Pa.). Author and co-author numerous articles on heat transmission, mass transfer, etc. Home: Locust Lane, Kennett Sq., Pa. Office: duPont Experimental Station, Wilmington, Del.

DREXEL, George W. Childs; b. Philadelphia, July 1868; s. Anthony Joseph D., banker and philanthropist; ed. pvt. schs. and by tutors; m. Mary S. Irick Nov. 18, 1891. Succeeded George W. Childs as editor and pub. the Public Ledger; sold paper and retired, 1903. Home: "Wootton," Bryn Mawr, Pa. Office: 350 Drexel Bldg., Philadelphia, Pa.

DREYER, Ashley Eliot, mcht. sheets and metal products; b. Glendale, Mo., Oct. 30, 1880; s. Rudolf Henry and Sally Lewis (Coleman) D.; student pub. sch., high sch. and business coll., St. Louis, Mo., 1888-98; m. Mary Jane Balson, June 12, 1906; 1 dau., Marion Eliot (Mrs. John W. Macdowell Jr.). Engaged as auditor James Stewart & Co., contractors, 1903-12; v.p. Perritt Iron & Roofing Co., Pittsburgh, 1912-20; pres. and dir. Dreyer Metal Products Co., sheet metal and metal products, Pittsburgh, since 1920. Served as non-commd. officer, 6th Cav., U.S. Army, in China and Philippines, 1900-03. Senior vice comdr., Maj. Wm. H. Davis Camp 98, Dept. of Pa. Republican. Presbyterian. Mason (32°, Shriner). Club: Pittsburgh Athletic. Home: 7115 Card Lane. Office: 5607 Butler St., Pittsburgh, Pa.

DREYFUSS, Leonard, advertising; b. Brooklyn, N.Y., Nov. 6, 1886; s. Henry and Fanny (Young) D.; ed. pub. schs. and high schs., Brooklyn, N.Y., and Pratt Inst.; m. Alice Ransom Feb. 24, 1934. Salesman, later vice-pres. John Matthews Co., 1905-09; as N.Y. mgr. and sales mgr. Charles C. Hires Co., Phila., Pa., 1909-14; sales mgr., then vice-pres. Newark Sign Co., Newark, N.J., 1914-20; vice-pres. United Advertising Corpn., Newark, N.J., 1920-23, pres. since 1923; founded United Adv. Agency, 1923, and now chmn. bd.; pres. and dir. Am. Outdoor Adv. Service, Long Branch, N.J., Consolidated Adv. Corpn., Trenton, N.J., Canterbury Realty Co., Essex Trading Corpn., both of Newark, N.J., Federal Adv. Corpn., Paterson, N.J., Lehigh Adv. Co., Allentown, Pa.; mem. exec. com. and dir. Outdoor Advertising Inc., N.Y. City; dir. West Side Trust Co., Newark, N.J., Sussex Fire Ins. Co.; dir. Outdoor Adv. Assn. of America; vice chmn. advisory com. of Dept. Pub. Information, N.Y. World's Fair 1939, Inc. Mem. of Governor's Street and Highway Safety Commn., N.J. Clubs: Downtown, Athletic, Advertising (Newark); Uptown, Advertising, Terrace, N.Y. World's Fair (New York); Sands Point Bath (Long Island); Crestmont Country (West Orange); Mountain Ridge Country (Caldwell, N.J.); Fairway Yacht Club (N.Y.). Home: Essex Fells. Office: 354 Park Av., Newark, N.J.; and 60 E. 42d St., New York, N.Y.

DRINKER, Henry Sandwith, lawyer; b. Phila., Pa., Sept. 15, 1880; s. Henry S. and Aimee Ernesta (Beaux) D.; student Haverford Sch., 1892-96; A.B., Haverford Coll., 1900, Harvard, 1901; student Harvard Law Sch., 1902-03; LL.B., U. of Pa., 1904; m. Sophie Lewis Hutchinson May 16, 1911; children Henry Sandwith, Cecelia, Ernesta, Pemberton H. Admitted to Pa. bar, 1904, asso. firm Dickson, McCouch & Glasgow, later Dickson, Beitler & McCouch; admitted to partnership, 1917; sr. mem. firm Drinker, Biddle & Reath since 1932. Asso. trustee U. of Pa.; mgr. Phila. Savings Fund Soc.; v.p. Pa. Acad. of Fine Arts, Settlement Music Sch. Mem. Phi Beta Kappa. Republican. Presbyn. Clubs: Philadelphia (Phila.); Century (New York). Author: The Interstate Commerce Act, 1908; The Chamber Music of Johannes Brahms, 1933. Home: 249 Merion Rd., Merion, Pa. Office: 1429 Walnut St., Philadelphia, Pa.

DRISCOLL, Denis J., chmn. Pa. Pub. Utility Commn.; b. N. Lawrence, N.Y., Mar. 27, 1871; ed. Lawrenceville Acad. and State Normal and Training Sch., Potsdam, N.Y., studied law pvtly.; m. Elizabeth Biglan of St. Marys, Pa.; 2 daughters. Principal St. Mary's High Sch., 4 yrs.; admitted to Pa. bar, 1898, and since practiced in St. Marys; sr. partner Driscoll, Gregory & Coppolo; U.S. atty. for Western Dist. of Pa., 1920-21; mem. 74th Congress (1935-37), 20th Pa. Dist. Mar. 30, 1937, apptd. mem. Pa. Public Utility Commn. by Gov. Earle for 10 yrs. (chairman). Served as 2d lt. in 16th Pa. Inf. under Gen. Miles in Puerto Rico, Spanish-Am. War; mem. Pa. N.G. 3 yrs. Pres. St. Marys Sch. Bd., 25 yrs. Mem. Am., Pa. State and Elk County bar assns., United Spanish War Vets., Vets. of Foreign Wars, Am. Lawyers Guild. Del. to Nat. Dem. Convs., 1916, 20, 24, 28; chmn. Dem. State Com., 1905, mem. 23 yrs. Home: St. Marys, Pa. Office: North Office Bldg., Harrisburg, Pa.

DRITTLER, Max Wolfgang, pianist, teacher, lecturer; b. Birmingham, Eng., May 10, 1891; s. Frederick and Fanny (Edwards) D.; brought to U.S., 1903, naturalized, 1919; grad. high sch., Boonton, N.J., 1909; studied piano under Frederick Drittler, Leopold Wolfsohn, Leopold Godowsky, Sina Lichtmann, theory and composition under Rubin Goldmark; unmarried. Engaged in teaching piano since 1912; appeared in piano recitals in N.Y. City and other eastern cities since 1922; soloist with N.J. Symphony Orchestra; mem. faculty, Master Inst. of Roerich Mus., N.Y. City, 12 yrs.; lecture recitals on symphonic music, 1936-38; artist over four leading radio stations. Served in arty., U.S.A., 1917-19, with A.E.F. in France. Home: 307 Church St., Boonton, N.J.

DRIVER, Leeotis Lincoln, educator; b. Stony Creek Tp., Randolph Co., Ind., Feb. 22, 1867; s. Joab and Mary Ellen (Burres) D.; grad. Central Normal Coll., Danville, Ind., 1883; A.B., Ind. U., 1919; A.M., Earlham Coll., Richmond, Ind., 1919; LL.D., Wabash Coll., Crawfordsville, Ind., 1921; m. Carrie Ann Wood, of Randolph Co., Ind., Apr. 15, 1886; children—Clarence William, Herschel Wood, Mary (dec.), Agnes Juanita. Teacher, elementary schs., Randolph Co., 1883-87, high sch., Winchester, Ind., 1895-1907; prin. high sch., Winchester, 1900-07; supt. schs., Randolph Co., 1907-20; dir. Bur. Rural Edn., in charge sch. consolidation, Dept. Pub. Instrn., Pa., 1920-27; dir. Bur. Rural Service same, 1927-31, dir. Div. Rural Schs. 1931-1937. Mem. N.E.A. and Dept. Superintendence of same (one of organizers of rural div.), Pa. State Ednl. Assn. (pres. rural sch. sect. 1926-27), Ind. State Teachers Assn., Phi Delta Kappa; pres. Nat. Assn. Rural Sch.

Supervisors and Inspectors, 1915-17; pres. Indiana County Supts. Assn., 1917. Republican. Methodist. Mason (32°, Shriner). Clubs: Indiana School Masters, Torch, Eslectic. Author: History of Randolph County, Indiana, 1914; also many articles on rural sch. consolidation. Home: 1700 N. 2d St., Harrisburg, Pa.

DROZESKI, Edward H., physician; b. Erie, Pa., Mar. 27, 1880; s. Julius R. and Fredericka C. (Kolb) D.; M.D., U. of Buffalo (N.Y.), 1903; grad. study, Paris, Vienna, Berlin, 1924; m. Blanche Whitehill, Apr. 29, 1920. House surgeon Buffalo (N.Y.) Gen. Hosp., 1903-04; in pvt. practice at Erie, Pa., since 1905; med. examiner Police Civil Service Commn., Erie, Pa., 1918-24; chief Pa. Genito-Urinary Clinic, Erie, 1918-24. Served as acting med. officer, Co. G, Pa. N.G., 1918-24. Mem. Erie Co. Med. Soc., Pa. Med. Soc., A.M.A. Republican. Episcopalian. Mason (32°, Shriner, Zem Zem Temple); Elk. Club: Shrine (Erie, Pa.). Address: 117 E. 6th St., Erie, Pa.

DRUCK, Samuel, real estate brokerage; b. Scranton, Pa., Jan. 1, 1897; s. Rev. Nathan Barnum and Martha (Leebert) D.; student pub. sch. and Tech. High Sch., Scranton, Pa.; unmarried. Engaged in advertising business, newspaper and pub.; propr. real estate business at Scranton, Pa., since 1926. Served at O.T.C., Camp Lee, Va. during World War. Former dir. pub. safety, Scranton, Pa., and civil service commr.; chmn. publicity Rep. Com.; former vice-chmn. Rep. Com., Lackawanna Co. Dir. Jewish Home of Friendless, Y.M.H.A., B.P.O.E.; an incorporator Scranton Community Chest; past pres. Pa. Fed. Y.M.H.A. and Y.W.H.A.; former mem. exec. com. Jewish Welfare Bd. of U.S.; mem. state exec. com. Pa. Rep. War Vets; chmn. exec. com. Pa. Rep. War Vets of Lackawanna Co. Mem. Jewish War Vets (sr. vice comdr. local post). Republican. Jewish religion. Mason (32°, Shriner), Elk, Eagle. Clubs: Elks, Masons, Eagles, Purple, Am. Legion. Home: 402 N. Webster Av. Office: Davidow Bldg., Scranton, Pa.

DRUKKER, Dow Henry, publisher; b. Holland, Feb. 7, 1872; s. Henry and Winifred (Terpsma) D.; came to U.S., 1872, naturalized, 1893; student Pub. and Pvt. Schs., Grand Rapids, Mich., 1878-86, pvt. instruction, 1886-92; m. Helena Denhonwer, 1893; children—Winifred, Nella (Mrs. Eugene F. Steketee), Marion (Mrs. Amos N. Prescott), Helena (dec.), Dow Henry, Richard, Louise (Mrs. Ralph Prescott), Virginia. Began in credit dept., Spring Dry Goods Co., Grand Rapids, Mich., 1892; with Union Bldg. & Constrn. Co., Passaic, N.J., since 1897, now pres.; acquired Passaic (N.J.) Herald, 1917, treas. and pub.; 1917-31; acquired Passaic (N.J.) News, 1925, treas. and pub., 1925-31; merged both papers into Passaic (N.J.) Herald News, 1931, and since treas. and pub.; pres. Hobart Trust Co., 1926-30; chmn. of bd., Peoples Bank & Trust Co., 1930-33; pres. Union Bldg. & Investment Co., Pompton Crushed Stone Co.; dir. Ramapo Finishing Co., Passaic Transit Co. Dir., Bd. of Freeholders, Passaic Co. (N.J.), 1906-12. Mem. Bd. of Govs., Passaic (N.J.) Gen. Hosp. Republican. Dutch Reformed Ch. Club: Upper Montclair Country (Clifton, N.J.). Home: 202 Lafayette Av. Office: Main Av., Passaic, N.J.

DRUKKER, Dow Henry, Jr., publisher Herald-News. Address: 140 Prospect St., Passaic, N.J.

DRUSHEL, J. Andrew, educator; b. Mt. Hope, O., Nov. 24, 1872; s. Henry and Catherine (Rowe) D.; A.B., Nat. Normal U., Lebanon, O., 1895, A.M., 1897; A.B., Yale, 1905; Ph.D., New York U., 1927; m. Hortense Wilson, Aug. 26, 1897. Teacher in Ohio pub. schs., 1890-92; instr. in mathematics, Nat. Normal U., 1893-95; in biology and geology, E. Tex. Normal Coll., Commerce, Tex., 1895-98; prin. pub. schs., Frankfort, O., 1898-1900; prof. geology and biology. Nat. Normal U. 1900-04; instr. teacher training courses, elementary science and mathematics, Harris Teachers Coll., St. Louis, 1905-24; asst. prof. of the teaching of mathematics, New York U., 1924-26, asso. prof., 1926-28, prof. education since 1928. Mem. A. A.A.S., N.E.A., Central Assn. of Science and Mathematics Teachers, Am. Nature Study Soc.

(pres. 1920-21), Am. Museum of Natural History, Torrey Bot. Club, Vt. Bot. Club, St. Louis Acad. Science, Sigma Xi, Phi Delta Kappa, Rho. Mason. Author: Arithmetical Essentials, 1922, 1923 (with J. W. Withers) Junior High School Mathematical Essentials, 1924. Home: 209 Edgewood Av., Westfield, N.J. Office: 32 Washington Place, New York, N.Y.

DRYDEN, Raymond Curtis, flour and feed mfr.; b. Pocomoke, Md., May 3, 1882; s. William Tubman and Lydia (Cannon) D.; student Rehoboth (Md.) Acad., 1887-1905; grad. Beacoms Business Coll., Wilmington, Del., 1906; m. Helen Grace Beauchamp, Nov. 26, 1916; children—Raymond Curtis, Grace. Engaged as canner, partner firm Johnson & Dreyden, 1912-17; owner Eagle Mills, mfrs. flour and poultry feeds, Pocomoke, Md., since 1915; v.p. and dir. Citizens Nat. Bank, Pocomoke, Md. Trustee Pocomoke High Sch. Del. Internat. Rotary Convs., Dallas, Tex., 1928, San Francisco, Calif., 1938. Republican. Presbyterian. Club: Pocomoke Rotary (ex-pres.). Home: 805 Market St. Office: Maple St., Pocomoke, Md.

DUANE, Howard, lawyer; b. Wilmington, Del., Oct. 23, 1902; s. Franklin and Catharine Neillson (Carpender) D.; prep. edn., Gilman Country Sch., Baltimore, Md., 1912-1919, St. George's Sch., Newport, R.I., 1919-20; A.B., Princeton U., 1924; LL.B., U. of Pa., 1927; m. Suzanne Voss du Vivier, Mar. 5, 1931; children—Catharine Franklin, Mary Neilson, Edwina Elder. Admitted to Del. and Penna. bars, 1927; asso. with Marvel, Morford, Ward & Logan, Wilmington, Del., 1927-30; practiced alone, 1931, partner in firm of Keedy & Duane, 1932-34; practice of law, alone, Wilmington, since 1934; dir., asst. sec.-treas. Chestnut Securities Co. Mem. Am., Del. State and New Castle County bar assns., Delta Phi. Democrat. Episcopalian. Club: Princeton Charter (Princeton). Home: 1515 W. 14th St. Office: 811 Industrial Trust Bldg., Wilmington, Del.

DUANE, Morris, lawyer; b. Phila., Pa., Mar. 20, 1901; s. Russell and Mary (Morris) D.; ed. Episcopal Acad., Phila., St. George's Sch., Newport, R.I.; A.B., Harvard, 1923; student U. of Pa. Law Sch., 1923-25; LL.B., Stetson U. Law Sch., 1927; m. Maud S. Harrison, June 11, 1927; children—Margaretta Sergeant Large, Russell II. Admitted to Pa. bar, 1927, and since engaged in gen. practice of law at Phila.; asso. with firm Duane, Morris & Heckscher since 1927, mem. firm since 1931; examiner Pa. State Bd. Law Examiners, 1929-34; sec. Com. of Censors, Phila. Bar Assn., 1928-29, chmn. com., 1939; dir. Theodore Presser Co., publishers, John Faulkner Arndt & Co., advertising. Trustee Presser Foundation, Vol. Defender Assn., Episcopal Acad., Sandlot Sports Assn.; mem. Com. of Seventy; mem. exec. bd. Salvation Army; chmn. intercollegiate com. U.S. Lawn Tennis Assn., 1928-33. Mem. Delta Psi. Independent Republican. Episcopalian. Clubs: Harvard, Philadelphia, Gulph Mills Golf, Fly Club. Author: The New Deal in Court, 1934; contbr. articles to legal jours. Home: Wakefield Rd., Rosemont, Pa. Office: 1617 Land Title Bldg., Philadelphia, Pa.

DUBELL, Charles B.; pastor St. Simeon's Ch. Address: 2650 N. Ninth St., Philadelphia, Pa.

DuBOIS, Charles Gilbert, retired business man; b. New York City, Mar. 22, 1870; s. William H. and Anne Eliza (Gilbert) D.; grad. high sch., Randolph, Vt., 1887; A.B., Dartmouth, 1891 (specializing last 2 yrs. in physics and economics), A.M., 1923; m. Sue Sanford, June 6, 1901; children—William Sanford, Susan. Began with Western Electric Co., at New York, 1891, at Chicago, 1897, became sec. and supervisor branch houses of the co., 1902-07; comptroller Am. Telephone & Telegraph Co., 1907-18 (on leave of absence war period, as comptroller Am. Red Cross, Washington, 1917-18); v.p., 1918-19, pres. 1919-26, chmn. bd., 1926-27, Western Electric Co.; dir. New York Ins. Co., Bankers & Shippers Insurance Co. of New York, Pacific Fire Ins. Co., N.Y. Trustee Dartmouth Coll., 1923-33. Club: University. Home: 70 Lydecker St., Englewood, N.J.

DU BOIS, John Ezekiel Jr., mfr. gas meters; b. Du Bois, Pa., Aug. 13, 1898; s. John Ezekiel and Willie (Gamble) D.; student Fay Sch., Southborough, Mass., 1910-12, St. George's Sch., Newport, R.I., 1912-18, Harvard, 1920-23, Columbia U. Business Sch., 1925. Unmarried. Employed as foreman in lumber camp, 1923, supt. logging camp, office mgr.; pres. Westwood Lumber Co., Wheeler, Ore., 1926-30; pres. Du Bois (Pa.) Iron Works, 1930-36; adminstr. John E. Du Bois Estate, lumber milling and real estate, since 1934; treas. Pittsburgh-Du Bois Co., mfr. gas meters since 1936. Republican. Episcopalian. Club: Harvard (New York). Home: Du Bois, Pa.

DUBOIS, John Latta, lawyer; b. Doylestown, Pa., Jan. 30, 1873; s. John Latta and Emma M. (Rex) D.; student Doylestown (Pa.) pub. sch., 1879-88, Doylestown Sem., 1888-90, William Penn Charter Sch., Phila., Pa., 1890-93; unmarried. Admitted to Bucks Co. bar, 1896, Supreme and Superior Cts. of Pa., 1900, Dist. Ct. of the U.S., 1898; gen. practice of law, trial cases in civil and criminal ets., equity cases at Doylestown, Pa., since 1896. Republican. Presbyterian. Home: 40 E. Court St., Doylestown, Pa.

DU BOIS, William F., gen. practice of law since 1899; pres. First Nat. Bank of Coudersport. Address: Coudersport, Pa.

DUCKETT, Thomas Howard, lawyer; b. Bowie, Md., July 28, 1880; s. Marion and Gabriella Augusta (Du Val) D.; LL.B., George Washington U., Washington, D.C., 1902; m. Josephine Dent, July 18, 1905; children—Thomas Howard, Helen Louise (wife of R. R. Waller, U.S.N.), Josephine (wife of Thos. Jeter, U.S.N.), Richard B. Admitted to bar, 1902, in practice, Washington, since 1905; president Prince Georges Bank & Trust Co.; chmn. bd. and gen. counsel Suburban Nat. Bank of Silver Spring, Md. Served with 1st D.C. Vols. in Cuba during Spanish-Am. War. Chmn. Washington Suburban San. Commn.; commr. Md. Nat. Capital Park and Planning Commn. Mem. Am. Bar Assn., Md: Bar Assn. (past pres.), Kappa Sigma. Democrat. Episcopalian. Clubs: University (past pres.); Burning Tree, Manor. Home: 57 Franklin St., Hyattsville, Md. Office: 812 Tower Bldg., Washington, D.C.

DUCKWORTH, George Eckel, univ. prof.; b. Little York, N.J., Feb. 13, 1903; s. Edwin James and Eva (Eckel) D.; student elementary sch., Little York, N.J., 1908-16, high sch., Clinton, N.J., 1916-20; A.B., Princeton U., 1924, A.M., 1926, Ph.D., 1931; m. Dorothy Elwood Atkin, July 8, 1929; children—Dorothy Ann, Thomas Atkin. Instr. classics, U. of Neb., Lincoln, Neb., 1926-28; part-time instr. classics, Princeton U., 1924-25, instr., 1929-30, asst. prof. classics since 1930. Trustee Rider Coll., Trenton, N.J., Mem. Am. Assn. Univ. Profs., Am. Philol. Assn., Classical Assn. of Middle Atlantic States, Phi Beta Kappa. Republican. Presbyterian. Author: Foreshadowing and Suspense in the Epics of Homer, Apollonius and Vergil, 1933; numerous articles and reviews in Am. Jour. Philology, Classical Philology, Classical Weekly, Transactions Am. Philol. Assn. Address: 25 Haslet Av., Princeton, N.J.

DUDLEY, Adolphus Mansfield, elec. engring.; b. Cincinnati, O., Feb. 14, 1877; s. Adolphus Spring and Elizabeth Phipps (Mansfield) D.; B.S., U. of Mich., Ann Arbor, Mich., 1902, E.E., 1931, hon. D. Eng., 1939; M.S., U. of Pittsburgh, 1933; m. Lila McGaughan, Oct. 10, 1906; 1 son, Winston Mansfield. Asso. with Westinghouse Electric & Mfg. Co. continuously since 1904, control design engr., 1904, motor design engr., 1905, commercial engr., 1906, section engr., 1907-20, engring. mgr., 1920-26, supervisor of development, 1926-35, marine engr., 1935-38, engring. rep. in patent dept. since 1938. Fellow Am. Inst. Elec. Engrs.; mem. Soc. for Promotion Engring. Edn., Pa. Soc. Order of Founders and Patriots of America, Tau Beta Pi, Sigma Tau. Republican. Presbyn. Clubs: Agora (Pittsburgh); Westinghouse (Wilkinsburg). Author: Connecting Induction Motors, 1920; Induction Motor Practice, 1928.

Contbr. to Ency. Britannica, 1928. Home: Oakmont. Office: East Pittsburgh, Pa.

DUDLEY, Edward, Jr., golf professional; b. Brunswick, Ga., Feb. 10, 1902; s. Edward Bishop and Ethel (Bunkley) D.; ed. Glynn County High Sch., 1914-16, Belmont Abbey Coll., 1915-18, Ga. Tech., 1918-19; m. Ruth Johnson, June 6, 1922; children—Ruth Elizabeth, Janice Tamora. Golf professional, Miami (Fla.) Country Club, 1920, Joplin (Mo.) Country Club, 1922-24, Oklahoma City Country Club, 1925-26, Hollywood (Calif.) Country Club, 1927-28, Concord Country Club, Wilmington, Del., 1929-33, Phila. Country Club since 1933. Mem. Professional Golfers Assn. of America, vice-pres. 1939, pres. Phila. Sect. since 1934, chmn. Nat. Tournament Com. since 1936. Won Western Open Championship, 1931, Pa. Open and Phila. Open Championship, 1932, Shawnee (Pa.) Open Championship, 1936, many other open and professional championships; mem. Ryder Cup Team, 1929-31, 1937. Home: 20 Overbrook Parkway. Address: Philadelphia Country Club, Philadelphia, Pa.

DUDLEY, Wray, elec. engr. Nat. Tube Co. Office: Frick Bldg., Pittsburgh, Pa.

DUER, John Van Buren; chief elec. engr. Pa. R.R. Co. Home: Narberth, Pa. Office: Broad St. Station Bldg., Philadelphia, Pa.

DUFF, James Henderson, lawyer; b. Mansfield, Pa., Jan. 21, 1883; s. Joseph Miller and Margaret (Morgan) D.; A.B., Princeton, 1904; student U. of Pa. Law Sch., 1904-06; LL.B., U. of Pittsburgh Law Sch., 1907; m. Jean Taylor, Oct. 26, 1909; 1 son, John Taylor (dec.). Admitted to Pa. bar, 1907, and since in gen. practice of law at Pittsburgh continuously; mem. firm Duff, Scott and Smith since 1925; dir. Carnegie Nat. Bank, Superior Steel Co. Served as Nat. Elector for Pa., 1912; del. Rep. Nat. Convs. 1932 and 1936. Trustee Carnegie Library, Carnegie, Pa. Republican. Presbyterian. Mason, Elk. Club: Duquesne (Pittsburgh). Home: Washington Av., Carnegie. Office: Grant Bldg., Pittsburgh, Pa.

DUFF, John Taylor, Jr., lawyer; b. Pittsburgh, Pa., Nov. 18, 1882; s. John Taylor and Margaret Anna (Kahl) D.; LL.B., U. of Pittsburgh Law Sch., 1908; m. Katherine O'Neil, Jan. 22, 1913; children—John Miller, William Robert, Richard O'Neil. Admitted to Pa. bar, 1908, and since engaged in gen. practice of law at Pittsburgh; prof. law, Univ. of Pittsburgh Law Sch. since 1909; dep. atty. gen. of Pa., 1938-39; spl. counsel to Pub. Utility Commn. Pa., since 1939. Served as mem. N.G. Res. of Pa., 1917-20. Mem. Pa. State Bar Assn., Allegheny Co. Bar Assn., Order of the Coif, Phi Delta Phi. Club: University. Home: 1435 Denniston Av. Office: Grand Bldg., Pittsburgh, Pa.

DUFF, Samuel Eckeberger, cons. engr.; b. Pittsburgh, Pa., Nov. 1, 1867; s. Col. Levi Bird and Harriet Howard (Nixon) D.; A.B., Western U. of Pa. (now U. of Pittsburgh), 1886, A.M., 1889; m. Agnes Graham Eccles, Jan. 23, 1890; children—Levi Bird III, Catharine (Mrs. Edmund Carnwath Dalzell). Leveller Oregon Pacific Ry., Malheur Canyon, Ore., 1886-87; transitman, Northern Pacific Ry., Tacoma, Wash., 1887, Northern Pacific Terminal Co., Portland, Ore., 1887, C. O. Bean, city engr., Tacoma, Wash., 1888; engr. in charge 12 miles constrn., Ore. Ry. & Navigation Co., Wallula, Ore., 1888; engr. in charge 13 miles constrn., Wash. & Ida. Ry., Rockford, Wash., 1888; asst. engr. Northern Pacific Terminal Co., Portland, Ore., 1889-91, 1892, chief engr. and purchasing agt., 1893-94; engr. Portland (Ore.) Birdge & Bldg. Co., 1891-92; supt. constrn. (including Grand Central Sta., Portland, Ore.), Van Brunt & Howe, architects, Kansas City, Mo., 1892-93; estimating engr., Riter-Conley Mfg. Co., Pittsburgh, Pa., 1896-1901, mgr. works, 1901-08; pvt. practice as cons. engr. continuously since 1908. Mem. Engrs. Soc. of Western Pa. (dir. 1911-13, v.p. 1914-15, pres. 1916), Loyal Legion (Commandery of Pa.). Liberal Republican. Mason (Bellevue Lodge 530, worshipful master and rep. to Grand Lodge). Author numerous contributions to proceedings of Engr.'s Soc. of Western Pa. and various tech. publs.; addresses before univs., chs., pub. schs., and social groups. Home: 7215 McCurdy Pl., Ben Avon. Office: 712 Magee Bldg., Pittsburgh, Pa.

DUFF, William Henry, II; pres. P. Duff & Sons, Inc., Corundite Refractories, Inc. Address: 5819 Howe St., Pittsburgh, Pa.

DUFF, William McGill, life insurance; b. Pittsburgh, Pa., Feb. 2, 1878; s. James Alexander and Charlotte (McGill) D.; grad. Allegheny High Sch., Pittsburgh, 1895; m. May Prenter, of Pittsburgh, July 19, 1919; children—Charlotte, Letitia. Began as messenger Edward A. Woods Co.; gen. agt. for Equitable Life Assurance Soc., 1895, advancing through various positions to v.p., 1925, pres. since 1927; dir. Colonial Trust Co. Trustee Westminster Coll., New Wilmington, Pa.; v.p. Am. Coll. of Life Underwriters (degree C.L.U.); mem. Pittsburgh Life underwriters (ex-pres., treas., dir.). Mem. S.R., Sigma Phi Epsilon. Republican. Presbyn. Mason. Clubs: Pittsburgh Athletic, Insurance, Duquesne, Edgeworth, Bankers of America; The Clan Chattan Assn. (Scotland); Shannopin Country. Home: (winter) 144 Ridge Av., Ben Avon, Pa.; (summer) Jacks Run Rd., Ross Township, Bellevue, Pa. Office: 200 Frick Bldg., Pittsburgh, Pa.

DUFFY, Charles Edward, lawyer; b. Salisbury, Md., July 7, 1902; s. Charles Edward and Emma Aline (Twilley) D.; grad. Wicomico High Sch., Salisbury, Md., 1919; student Dickinson Coll., Carlisle, Pa., 1919-20; A.B., Washington Coll., Chestertown, Md., 1924; LL.B., Temple U., 1929; m. Florence Maybelle Stidham, June 14, 1928. Admitted to Del. bar, 1929, and began general practice of law with firm Hastings, Stockly & Morris, Wilmington, partner of firm in 1931; now partner in firm Hastings, Stockly, Duffy & Layton; engaged in gen. practice of law, specializing in corporation law and in corporate reorganizations; atty. for Trustees of the Poor, 1932-33; apptd. dep. atty. gen. for New Castle County, 1933; chief dep. atty. gen. of Del., 1937-39. Mem. Bd. of Trustees of Mt. Pleasant Sch. Mem. New Castle County Bar Assn., Del. State Bar Assn., Am. Bar Assn., Phi Delta Theta. Republican. Methodist. Mason (32°, Shriner). Clubs: Lions, Wilmington Country, Shrine (Wilmington, Del.). Home: R.D. 3, Carrcroft, Wilmington, Del. Office: 400 Industrial Trust Bldg., Wilmington, Del.

DUFFY, Edmund, cartoonist; b. Jersey City, N.J., March 1, 1899; s. John Joseph and Anna (Hughes) D.; educated in the Art Students' League, New York, 1914-19, and continued art studies in Paris; m. Anne Rector, Nov. 26, 1924; 1 daughter, Sara Anne. Contributor illustrations and sketches, 1918-23, to Scribner's, Century, Colliers, Elks' Magazine, New York Tribune, New York Evening Post and Brooklyn Daily Eagle; polit. cartoonist New York Leader, 1923; polit. cartoonist Baltimore Sun since 1924. Winner Pulitzer prize for cartoons, 1930, 33. Clubs: The Players (New York); Maryland. Contbr. of cartoons to Nation, Saturday Evening Post, Colliers. Home: 901 Cathedral St. Address: The Sun, Baltimore, Md.

DUFFY, Edward, lawyer; b. Baltimore, Md., Feb. 11, 1867; s. Edward and Emma C. (McMillan) D.; A.B., Johns Hopkins U., 1887; LL.B., U. of Md. Law Sch., Baltimore, Md., 1889; m. Chloe Tyler Sams, Jan. 25, 1898; children—Mary Tyler (Mrs. Seth Barton French), Elizabeth Carter (wife of Lt. Col. John Kennard, U.S.A.), Frances Munford. Admitted to Md. Bar, 1889, and since in gen. practice of law at Baltimore. Mem. Am. Bar Assn., Baltimore City Bar Assn. Republican. Club: University (Baltimore). Home: 138 W. Lanvale St. Office: Mercantile Trust Bldg., Baltimore, Md.

DUFFY, James T., Jr., pres. Read Machinery Co.; b. Marietta, Pa., Dec. 10, 1895; s. Col. James and Mary (Malone) D.; B.S., Dartmouth Coll., Hanover, N. H.; m. Margaret Gaul, Sept. 8, 1921; children—James III, Margaret, Sheila, Patricia, Sarah, John. With Ingersoll-Rand Co., Phillipsburg, N.J., 1919-21; became supt. Thompson Products Co., Detroit, Mich., 1921, later gen. supt.; gen. mgr. Nice Ball Bearing Co., Phila., 1928-31; pvt. practice as consulting engr., Phila., 1931-34; v.p. and gen. mgr. Read Machinery Co., York, Pa., 1934-35, pres. since 1935. Served as lt. j.g., U.S. Destroyer Flotilla, U.S. Navy, at Brest, France, 1918-19. Home: R.D. No. 3. Office: 900-50 Richland Av., York, Pa.

DUFFY, John, ry. official; b. Memphis, Tenn.; s. John J. and Jennie (Barry) D.; A.B., Christian Brothers Coll., Memphis, Tenn.; post grad. study Catholic U. of America; m. Anne Beauvais; 3 children. Entered newspaper work with Memphis Scimitar; later on editorial staff of other Memphis newspapers, Chicago Tribune and New York World; writer and speaker for League for Promotion of a Sound Banking System during campaign which culminated in enactment of Federal Reserve Law; was in advertising dept. Lehigh Valley R.R., asst. to federal mgr., 1918-19, asst. to pres., 1919-29, v.p. since 1929; dir. Wyoming Valley Water Supply Co., Bay Shore Connecting Ry., Lehigh & N.Y. R.R. Co., Lehigh Valley Harbor Terminal Ry. Co., Lehigh Valley Ry. Co, Lehigh Valley R.R. Co. of N.J., Pa. & N.Y. Canal & R.R. Co., Wyo. Transportation Co., Owasco River R.R., Nat. Storage Co. Dir. Am.-Russian Chamber of Commerce. Home: 103 Trenton Av., Point Pleasant, N.J. Office: 143 Liberty St., New York, N.Y.

DUGAN, Raymond Smith, prof. astronomy; b. Montague, Mass., May 30, 1878; s. Jeremiah Welby and Mary Evelyn (Smith) D.; B.A., Amherst, 1899, M.A., 1902; Ph.D., Heidelberg, 1905; m. Annette Rumford Odiorne, July 28, 1909; children—Kenneth Langdon, Hannah Priscilla. Instr. mathematics and astronomy and acting dir. obs., Syrian Protestant Coll., Beirut, Syria, 1899-1902; asst. Astrophys. Obs., Heidelberg, 1902-04; instr. astronomy, 1905-08, asst. prof., 1908-20, prof. since 1920, Princeton; exchange prof. Lowell Obs., 1929; acting dir. Princeton U. Obs., 1929-30. Mem. Lick Obs. eclipse expdn. to Spain, 1905. Fellow A.A.A.S.; mem. Am. Astron. Soc. (sec. 1927-36), Am. Philos. Soc., Internat. Astron. Union (sec. Am. sect. 1927-36), Phi Beta Kappa. Republican. Presbyn. Co-Author: Astronomy. Specializes in study of eclipsing variables. Home: 16 Prospect Av., Princeton, N.J.

DUGDALE, Horace Kirkus, advertising exec.; b. Baltimore, Md., Nov. 24, 1890; s. Horace Cleveland and Edith Mary (Kirkus) D.; student Adams Sch., Washington, D.C., 1897-1905; m. Margaret Dashiell Lindale, Feb. 18, 1911; children—Horace Kirkus, William Morris. Retail sales clk. Sanders & Stayman, Washington, D.C., 1905-08; publishing exec., Washington, D.C., 1908-15; advertising writer, Washington, D.C., 1915-19; advertising agency accountant exec., Baltimore, Md., 1919-25; v.p. and treas. Van Sant, Dugdale & Co., Inc., advertising agts., Baltimore, Md., since 1925; lecturer advertising and marketing, U. of Md. Sch. of Commerce, 1922-23; dir. Anchor Post Fence Co., The Manhattan Co. Mem. bd. mgrs. Md. Children's Aid Soc. Mem. Baltimore Assn. of Commerce (chmn. publicity since 1936), Am. Assn. Advertising Agencies (vice-chmn. Atlantic Council since 1938). Republican. Christian Scientist. St. George's Soc. (Baltimore). Clubs: Rotary, Merchants, Baltimore Country (Baltimore, Md.). Home: 218 Longwood Rd. Office: Court Square Bldg., Baltimore, Md.

DUGGAN, Frank Loughney, pres. Consol. Ice Co.; b. Pittsburgh, Pa., Jan. 10, 1885; s. Michael Joseph and Louise (Dunn) D.; ed. parochial and pub. schs., Pittsburgh; m. Blanche Margaret Kane, Nov. 29, 1911; children—Frank Loughney, Mary Louise (Mrs. William C. Kouns), Jack Kane, Robert Ward. Since 1900 with Consol. Ice Co., ice and distilled water, successively as clerk, gen. mgr., and pres. since 1935; pres. Diamond Ice Co., Consol. Storage Co. Pres. Pittsburgh Chamber of Commerce, 1938; mem. Pittsburgh City Council since 1933; pres. Western Pa. Safety Council, 1928-31; organizer and chmn. Better Traffic Com. of City of Pittsburgh. Trustee Central Catholic High Sch., St. Paul Orphanage, Western Pa. Hist. Soc. Western States Penitentiary (trustee under 4 govs.). Past pres. Eastern States Ice Assn.; dir. Nat. Assn. Ice Industries; past pres. and

DUKE, Charles Clarke, pres. Provident Savings Bank of Baltimore; b. Royal Oak, Md., Sept. 4, 1882; s. James O'Connor and Emily Jane (Benson) D.; student St. Michael's (Md.) High Sch., 1890-1900, Johns Hopkins U. Night Sch., 1916-18; unmarried. Began as messenger Mfrs. Nat. Bank, Baltimore, 1901; clk. in gen. store, Royal Oak, Md., 1900; treas. Provident Savings Bank of Baltimore, 1919-23, v.p. and treas., 1923-24, exec. v.p. and treas., 1924-26, pres. since 1926; mem. trust com. and real estate com. Baltimore Nat. Bank since 1935; dir. Md. Title Co., State Mutual Bldg. & Loan Assn., Mortgage Guarantee Co. Pres. trustee Kelso Home for Orphan Girls of M.E. Ch.; trustee Dickinson Coll., Carlisle, Pa., Baltimore Annual Conf. of M.E. Ch., ednl. fund of Baltimore Conf., Thomas Wilson Fuel Saving Soc.; trustee and recording steward Walbrook M.E. Ch., Inc.; mem. exec. com. Md. Gen. Hosp., City Missionary and Ch. Extension Soc. of M.E. Ch.; mem. council Boy Scouts of Am. (Md); mem. bd. dirs. Am. Red Cross. Mem. S.A.R. (mem. bd. govs. since 1939), Soc. of Colonial Wars. Democrat. Methodist. Mason (York Rite, Scottish Rite, Shriner, Tall Cedars). Clubs: University, Kiwanis, Chesapeake(Baltimore, Md.); Bankers (New York). Home: 101 W. Monument St. Office: Howard and Saratoga Sts, Baltimore, Md.

DUKE, Charles Wesley, writer; b. Tyrone, Pa., Apr. 17, 1885; s. George Washington and Mary Ann (Stratiff) D.; grad. high sch., Jersey Shore, Pa., 1903; Dickinson Sem., Williamsport, Pa., 1905; student Ohio Wesleyan U.; m. Edith May Butler, Oct. 21, 1910; children—Charles W., Mary Louise, Suzanne Virginia. City editor Daily Herald, Jersey Shore, Pa., 1905; reporter Sun, later Gazette & Bulletin, Williamsport, 1906, Phila. North American, 1907; with Phila. Evening Times, 1908-12; reporter, editor and feature writer Philadelphia Public Ledger, 1912-22; Sunday editor Phila. Public Ledger, 1922-34; with Watkins Syndicate, Phila., 1935; contbr. to various mags., newspaper syndicates and radio. Mem. Sigma Chi. Mason. Home: Upper Darby, Pa.; and Cape May, N.J. Office: Upper Darby, Pa.

DUKE, Nathaniel, ry. official; b. Prince Frederick, Md., May 29, 1863; s. James and Maria Helen (Parran) D.; grammar sch. edn.; m. Jennie Wilce Wadleigh, Dec. 1, 1897. Clerk B.&O. R.R., 1881-85; with C.B.&Q. R.R., 1885-92, G.N.R.R., 1892-94 and 1896, Elgin, Joliet & Eastern Ry., 1894-96; gen. Western agt. Nickel Plate Fast Freight Line, Chicago, 1896-98; commercial agt. West Shore R.R., New Haven, Conn., 1898-1901; N.E. agt. L.V. R.R., 1902; with D.L.&W.R.R. since 1902, v.p. in charge traffic, 1929-35, v.p. retired since 1935; dir. Harlem Transfer Co., Morris & Essex Extension R.R. Co., N.Y., L.&W. Ry. Co., Oswego & Syracuse R.R. Co., Syracuse, Binghamton & New York R.R. Co., Utica, Chenango & Susquehanna Valley Ry. Co., Sussex R.R. Co., Newark & Bloomfield R.R. Co., Erie & Central New York R.R. Co. Regional dir. of traffic U.S. Food Administrn., 1918-20. Episcopalian. Mason. Elk. Clubs: Bankers, Traffic, Essex County Country, National Freight Traffic Golf Assn. Home: 41 Yale Terrace, West Orange, N.J. Office: 140 Cedar St., New York, N.Y.

DUKE, Roy F., banking; b. Jersey City, N.J., Feb. 5, 1895; s. Louis F. and Augusta T. (Mann) D.; ed. high sch., Poughkeepsie, N.Y., Eastman Bus. Coll., Poughkeepsie, N.Y.; m. Florence F. Lee, Jan. 19, 1922; children—Roy, Alan. Began as credit man Irving Nat. Bank, N.Y. City, 1914-17; mgr. credit dept. Fidelity Union Trust Co., Newark, N.J. 1923-26, asst. treas., 1926-27, treas., 1927-29, asst. vice-pres., 1929-36, vice-pres. since 1936; dir. Tung-Sol Lamp Works, Newark, N.J. Served as 2d lt. inf., U.S.A. during World War. Mem. adv. bd. Newark Univ. Mem. Nat. Assn. Credit Men, Robert Morris Assos. Republican. Methodist. Mason: Clubs: Essex, Downtown, Athletic (Newark); Golf (East Orange). Home: 36 Madison Av., East Orange. Office: 755 Broad St., Newark, N.J.

DULLES, Heatly C.; partner Wurts, Dulles & Co. Mem. N.Y. Stock Exchange. Home: Villa Nova, Pa. Office: 1416 Chestnut St., Philadelphia, Pa.

DUMBAULD, George L., v.p., treas. and dir. Blaw-Knox Co.; also treas. numerous other companies. Address: P.O. Box 1198, Pittsburgh, Pa.

DUMBAULD, Horatio Snyder, judge; b. Saltlick Twp., Fayette Co., Pa., May 15, 1869; s. George Adams and Elizabeth (Snyder) D.; B.S., Mount Union Coll., Alliance, O., 1895; m. Lissa Grace MacBurney, June 9, 1903; 1 son, Edward. Teacher pub. schs. at various times, 1884-98; admitted to Pa. bar, 1899, and began practice at Uniontown; mem. Pa. Ho. of Rep., 1899-1901; U.S. atty. Western dist., Pa., 1933-36; judge of Court of Common Pleas, Fayette County, Pennsylvania, since January 1936. Member Democratic Central Com., Fayette County several campaigns; del. Dem. Nat. convs., 1916 and 1932. Mem. Pa. and Fayette Co. bar assns., Sigma Nu. Democrat. Presbyn. Mason (Shriner) Elk. Club Triangle. Home: 44 S. Mt. Vernon Av., Uniontown, Pa. Office: Uniontown, Pa.*

DU MEZ, Andrew Grover, univ. dean; b. Horicon, Wis., Apr. 26, 1885; s. Andrew Alexander and Anna (Meister) DuM.; student graded schs. 1891-97, high sch., Cashton, Wis., 1897-1900; Ph.G., U. of Wis., Madison, Wis., 1904, B.S., 1907, M.S., 1910, Ph.D., 1917; m. Mary Elizabeth Fields, June 9, 1912. Instr. pharm. chemistry, U. of Wis., Madison, Wis., 1905-10; prof. chemistry, Pacific U., Forest Grove, Ore., 1910-11; asst. prof. chemistry, Okla. Agrl. and Mech. Coll., Stillwater, Okla., 1911-12; dir. Sch. of Pharmacy, U. of Philippines, Manila, P.I., 1912-16; Hollister Fellow, U. of Wis., 1916-17; asso. pharmacologist Hygienic Lab., U.S. Pub. Health Service, Washington, D.C., 1917-26; dean Sch. of Pharmacy, U. of Md., Baltimore, since 1926. Mem. com. to revise pharmacy and drug laws of Philippine Islands, 1914; investigated schs. and colls. of pharmacy, Philippine Islands, 1915; mem. and sec. spl. com. to investigate narcotic traffic in U.S., 1918-19; mem. of Revision Com. of Pharmacopœia of U.S. since 1920, chmn. sub-com. on nomenclature, 1920-30, vice-chmn. of com. since 1930; official del. of U.S. Govt. to Second Conf. on Unification of Standards for Potent Remedies, Brussels, Belgium, Sept. 1925; sec-treas. Am. Council on Pharm. Edn. since 1932. Mem. Wis. Acad. of Science, Arts and Letters, Am. Pharm. Assn. (pres. 1939-40; chmn. scientific sect. 1920-21, mem. council since 1920, sec. council 1920-23), Am. Chem. Soc., Am. Assn. of Colls. of Pharmacy (pres. 1928-29), Am. Pub. Health Assn., Md. Pharm. Assn., Sigma Xi, Rho Chi, Phi Delta Chi, Kappa Psi. Fellow A.A.A.S. Congregationalist. Mason (Temple Noyes Lodge 32, Washington, D.C.). Club: Kiwanis (Baltimore). Author: Quantitative Pharmaceutical Chemistry (with Glenn L. Jenkins), 1930; editor Year Book of the American Pharmaceutical Association, 1921-35, Pharmaceutical Abstracts since 1935; also bulletins and numerous scientific articles in U.S. Pub. Health Reports, Philippine Jour. of Science, Jour. A.M.A., Am. Jour. of Pharmacy, Jour. of Am. Pharm. Assn., Jour. of Chem. Edn., etc. Home: Garden Apts., 40th St. and Stoney Run Lane. Office: 32 S. Greene St., Baltimore, Md.

DU MONT, Francis Meyer, prof. Romance languages, Pa. State Coll. Address: State College, Pa.

DUMONT, Frederick Theodore Frelinghuysen, foreign service officer; b. Phillipsburg, N.J., Mar. 17, 1869; s. John Finley and Anna K. (Kline) D.; C.E., Lafayette, 1889, M.S., 1895; m. Mary, d. Dr. N. B. Wolfe of Lancaster Co., Pa., and Cincinnati, Ohio, May 16, 1900. Engineer, 1889-1900; founder and dir of trust companies, 1901-04; cons. engr. for mining companies in Canada, Mexico, and United States, 1901-03, 1905-10; appointed consul at Guadeloupe, W.I., Aug. 19, 1911; consul at Madrid, Spain, 1912-14, Florence, Italy, 1914-19, Dublin, Ireland, 1919-22, Frankfort-on-Main, Germany, 1923, consul gen., Frankfort, 1923-26; apptd. to Am. Foreign Service, 1924; chief of consular commercial office, Dept. of State, Washington, D.C., 1926-29; consul gen., Habana, Cuba, 1929-34, retired. Rep. of Department of State in conferences of Nat. Foreign Trade Council at Charleston, S.C., 1926, Detroit, Mich., 1927, Houston, Tex., 1928, Baltimore, Md., 1929. Del. of U.S. and chmn. Pan-Am. Commn. for the standardization and simplification of consular invoice procedure, Washington, 1927. Specialist in foreign economic and commercial matters. Mem. N.J. Hist. Soc., Am. Soc. Internat. Law, Internat. Law Assn. (London), Academy of Polit. Science (New York), Delta Upsilon Fraternity. Presbyterian. Republican. Club: Biscayne Bay Yacht (Miama, Fla.). Author: Inland Waterways from New York to Key West, 1912, and numerous commercial and economic reports. Home: "The Anchorage," Ronks, Lancaster Co., Pa.

DUMONT, Paul Emile, prof. Sanskrit and Indology; b. Brussels, Aug. 27, 1879; s. Constant and Hermine (De Vos) D.; U. of Brussels, 1897-99; Ph.D., University of Bologna, 1903; m. Marie Marguerite Howard, Dec. 27, 1937. Chargé de cours, University of Brussels, 1924-29; visiting lecturer in Indology, Johns Hopkins, 1929, prof. Sanskrit and Indology since 1931. Mem. Am. Oriental Soc., Linguistic Soc. America, Société Belge des Etudes orientales, Provincial Utrechsch Genootschap van Kunsten en Wetenschappen. Decorated Chevalier Order of Leopold (Belgium). Author: Histoire de Nala, 1923; L'Asvamedha, 1927; L'Illuminé, 1933; L'Isvaragita, 1934; L'Agnihotra, 1939. Home: 3919 Cloverhill Rd., Baltimore, Md.

DUMPER, Arthur, clergyman; b. England, July 7, 1872; s. Walter and Jane (Lewis) D.; came to U.S., 1873, naturalized, 1893; student Cleveland (O.) pub. schs., 1879-90; B.A., Kenyon Coll., Gambier, O., 1895, D.D., 1921; B.D., Bexley Hall, Gambier, O., 1900; m. Grace Chamberlain Sargent, June 2, 1903; children—Arthur Sargent, Robert Sargent. Began as tutor to Franklin D. Roosevelt, Hyde Park, N.Y., 1896; master, St. Paul's Sch., Concord, N.H., 1897-98; asst. minister Trinity Cathedral, Cleveland, O., 1900-03; rector St. Paul's Ch., Norwalk, O., 1903-10, Christ Ch., Dayton, O., 1910-17; dean Trinity Cathedral Ch., Newark, N.J., since 1918. Pres. standing com., Diocese of Newark since 1938. Trustee Hosp. of St. Barnabas, Newark, N.J., Social Service Bur., Newark. Mem. Beta Theta Pi, Phi Beta Kappa. Episcopalian. Clubs: Kappa Chi (East Orange, N.J.); The Club (N.Y. City). Home: 510 Mt. Prospect Av. Office: 24 Rector St., Newark, N.J.

DUMPER, Arthur Sargent, real estate, insurance; b. Norwalk, O., Mar. 28, 1904; s. Arthur and Grace (Sargent) D.; prep. edn. St. Paul's Sch., Concord, N.H., 1918-22; A.B., Princeton Coll., 1926; m. Gertrude Hebbard, Dec. 28, 1928; 1 dau., Joan Hebbard. Salesman Internat. Business Machines Corpn., Washington, D.C., 1926-28; asst. sec. Fidelity Union Title & Mortgage Co., Newark, N.J., 1928-33; pres. Sargent Dumper, Inc., real estate and ins., Newark, since 1933. Trustee Prospect Hill Country Day Sch., Newark Y.M.C.A., Florence Crittenton League. Mem. bd. of govs. Real Estate Bd., Newark; mem. Inst. Property Management of Nat. Assn. Real Estate Bds. Episcopalian. Clubs: Essex, Exchange (Newark). Home: 375 Mt. Prospect Av. Office: 30 Clinton St., Newark, N.J.

DUNAWAY, John Allder, economist; b. Stockton, Mo., Oct. 10, 1886; s. William I. and Lucy J. (Allder) D.; A.B., Park Coll., Parkville, Mo., 1910, A.M., 1912; m. Mary C. Ferguson, July 20, 1916 (died July 10, 1917); m. 2d, Rosa Shayeb, Aug. 22, 1920; children—Allder, William, Sylvia. Prof. economics, Kang Coll., Bristol, Tenn., 1912-13; grad. student and instr. in industry, Wharton Sch., U. of Pa., 1914-16; chautauqua lecturer, 1916-18; treas. Near East Relief, Aleppo Dist., Syria, 1919; chautauqua lecturer, 1920; asst. chief, later chief research div., Bur. Foreign and Domestic

Commerce, Washington, D.C., 1921-22; statistician Am. Finance Commn. to Persia, 1922-28; economist dairy sect. Agrl. Adjustment Administration, 1933-35; supervisor revenues Republic of Liberia since 1935, financial adviser since 1938. Mem. Phi Eta. Democrat. Presbyn. Mason. Club: Monrovia. Home: Maplewood, N.J. Address: Monrovia, Liberia, Africa.

DUNAWAY, Wayland Fuller, prof. of Am. history; b. Kilmarnock, Va., May 22, 1875; s. Wayland Fuller and Roberta Jane (Pinckard) D.; A.B., U. of Richmond (Va.), 1894; student Crozer Theol. Sem., Chester, Pa., 1898- 1901, B.D., 1917, Th.M., 1918; A.M., U. of Chicago, 1917; Ph.D., Columbia, 1923; m. Mary Warren May, Apr. 27, 1911; children—Wayland Fuller, Mary May, Anne Warren. Prin. Woodville (Va.) Classical Sch., 1894-95, Southside Acad., Chase City, Va., 1895-97; prof. of Latin and mathematics, Averett Coll., Danville, Va., 1897-98; pastor of Baptist Churches in Va. and W.Va., 1901-16; asst. prof. of history, Pa. State Coll., 1920-22, asso. prof., 1922-26, prof. Am. history since 1926. Mem. Am. Hist. Assn., Hist. Soc. of Pa., Pa. Hist. Assn., Western Pa. Hist. Soc., Sons of Am. Revolution, Phi Beta Kappa, Pi Gamma Mu. Democrat. Baptist. Clubs: Centre Hills Country (State Coll., Pa.); Pa. State College Literary (faculty club, Pa. State Coll.). Author: History of the James River and Kanawha Company, 1922; A History of Pennsylvania, 1935. Given grant-in-aid by Hist. Soc. Pa. for The Scotch-Irish of Pennsylvania (monograph); conbr. hist. articles to Va. Law Register, Pa. Mag. of History and Biography, etc. Address: State College, Pa.

DUNBAR, James Crawford, real estate and building; b. Pittsburgh, Pa., Sept. 11, 1899; s. Edwin W. and Mary Daisy (Dunbar) D.; B.S., U. of Pittsburgh, 1923; m. Anna Lois Siebert, May 5, 1928; children—James Crawford, Jr., Audrey Gay, Robert Edwin. Employed in various lines of work while attending sch. and coll.; became real estate salesman, 1923 and ins. agt., 1924; mem. firm Trilli & Dunbar, home builders, Pittsburgh, 1924; sec. and treas. Trilli & Dunbar Co., Pittsburgh, since 1928; mem. firm Reliable Plumbing & Heating Co. since 1929, Acme Real Estate Co. since 1930; dir. First Federal Savings & Loan Assn. Mem. Alumni Assn. of U. of Pittsburgh, Sigma Pi. Republican. Presbyterian. Mason (Milnor Lodge 286). Club: Rotary (Pittsburgh). Home: 253 Arden Rd., Mt. Lebanon, Pa. Office: 763 Washington Road, Mt. Lebanon, Pittsburgh, Pa.

DUNBAR, Paul Brown, asst. chief Food and Drug Administrn.; b. Lebanon, Pa., May 29, 1882; s. William Henry and Jennie (Chamberlain) D.; Baltimore City Coll., 1897-1902; B.S., Gettysburg Coll., 1904, hon. Sc.D., 1937; Ph.D., Johns Hopkins, 1907; m. Alice L. Davison, Sept. 7, 1910; children—Lucy, Emilie (Mrs. Stanley E. True), Jane C. Chemist U.S. Bur. of Chemistry, Dept. of Agr., Washington, D.C., 1907-25; asst. chief Bur. of Chemistry, 1925-27; asst. chief Food & Drug. Adminstrn., Washington, D.C. since its orgn., 1927. Trustee Gettysburg Coll. Mem. Am. Chem. Soc., Assn. Official Agrl. Chemists, Phi Delta Theta, Phi Beta Kappa. Home: 311 Cumberland Av., Somerset, Chevy Chase, Md. Office: Food & Drug Adminstration, Washington, D.C.

DUNCAN, Alexander Edward, commercial banker; b. nr. Louisville, Ky., May 27, 1878; s. John Thomas and Ida (Smith) D.; ed. Louisville Male High Sch.; m. Flora Ross, Apr. 11, 1900 (died June 20, 1936); 1 dau., Elizabeth Duncan Yaggy. Began as clerk at Louisville, Ky., 1896; member Ross & Duncan, Crestwood, Ky., 1900-02; spl. and gen. agt. Ocean Accident & Guaranty Corpn., Cincinnnati, 1903-06; gen. agt. at Baltimore for Am. Credit-Indemnity Co., 1907-09; organized, 1910, and pres. until 1912, Manufacturers' Finance Co., of Baltimore, Md. Organized, 1912, and president Commercial Credit Company, Baltimore, chmn. bd. since June 1916; mem. Robert Garrett & Sons, investments, 18 mos., 1916-17; reorganized Humphreys Mfg. Co., Mansfield, O., 1917, and since chmn. bd.; chmn. bd. Am. Credit Indemnity Co. of N.Y. (St. Louis), May Oil Burner Corpn. (Baltimore);

dir. Textile Banking Co., Inc., Edmund Wright Ginsberg Corpn. (New York), Savings Bank of Baltimore, Safe Deposit & Trust Co. of Baltimore. Gen. chmn. Y.M.C.A. War Work compaign (Baltimore), 1917, and for United War Work campaign, 1918. Mem. advisory bd. Hosp. for Women of Md.; dir. Children's Hosp. School and Home for Incurables. Republican. Episcopalian. Clubs: Bachelors Cotillon, Maryland, Elkridge, Merchants, Chesapeake, University, Baltimore Country (Baltimore); Bankers, Cloud, Manhattan (New York); Westbrook Country (Mansfield, O.). Home: "Cedarwood," 4604 N. Charles St. Office: First Nat. Bank Bldg., Baltimore, Md.

DUNCAN, Charles Miguel, educator; b. Panama City, Panama, Sept. 29, 1877; s. Bazil Brawner and Maria (Guillen-Arosemena) D.; prep. edn., Worrall Hall, Peekskill, N.Y., 1888-90, and New York Mil. Acad., Cornwall, N.Y., 1890-94; stud. Cornell U., 1894-96; asst. engr. Panama Canal, summer 1895-96; m. Katharine Taylor Neafie, June 6, 1914; children—Katharine Maria, Charles Miguel, Thomas Hazard Perry, Bazil Brawner. Teacher Cayuga Lake Military Academy, and New York Military Academy, 1896-97, Worrall Hall Mil. Acad., 1897-98, prin. and owner of latter, 1898-1900; v. prin. Glenwood Inst., Matawan, N.J., 1900-01; founder, 1901, and since prin. Freehold Mil. Sch.; pres. Times Pub. Co., Panama City. Regtl. adj. Spanish-Am. War. Pres. Civic Assn., Sea Girt, N.J.; trustee St. Mary's Sch. of Girls, Burlington, N.J. Mem. Headmasters' Club, Assn. Mil. Colls. and Schs. Republican. Episcopalian; dep. Gen. Conv., 1928, 31, 34, 37. Mason. Clubs: Old Colony, Nat. Travel, Union League, Army and Navy. Address: Freehold Military School, Freehold, N.J.

DUNCAN, David Christie, coll. prof.; b. Churchville, N.Y., July 30, 1889; s. James and Margaret (Christie) D.; A.B., U. of Mich., Ann Arbor, Mich., 1911, A.M., 1913, Ph.D., 1924; m. Mildred Webb, Aug. 28, 1913; children—Gordon Webb, Donald Christie. Instr. physics, Purdue U., Lafayette, Ind., 1911-18; prof. physics, Pa. State Coll., since 1918. Mem. A.A.A.S., Am. Assn. Physics Teachers, Soc. for Promotion of Engring. Edn., Sigma Xi, Phi Kappa Phi. Home: 149 W. Fairmont Av. Address: Pa. State Coll., State College, Pa.

DUNCAN, Garfield George, M.D.; b. Johnston's Corners, Ont., Can., Aug. 2, 1901; s. Samuel and Matilda (Mansfield) D.; grad. Kemptville (Ont.) High Sch., 1918; M.D., C.M., McGill U., Montreal, 1923; post-grad. work Physiatric Inst., Morristown, N.J., 1924-26; m. Dorothea E. Waterman, of Carp, Ont., Sept. 3, 1927; children—Theodore Garfield, Barbara Nancy, Peter Waterman. Began as interne, Hamilton (Ont.) Gen. Hosp., 1923; practiced in Philadelphia since 1926; demonstrator clinical medicine, Jefferson Med. Coll., Phila., 1927-34, asso. in medicine, 1934-37, asst. prof. medicine since 1937; chief clin, asst. diabetic clinic Jefferson Hospital since 1937; mem. staff Pa. Hosp. since 1927, chief med. service 1937, chief metabolic clinic since 1932. Fellow Coll. of Physicians, Phila. Episcopalian. Mason. Author: Diabetes Mellitus and Obesity, 1935. Contbr. to med. pubs. Home: 7040 Limekiln Pike. Office: 1930 Chestnut St., Philadelphia, Pa.

DUNCAN, Harry A.; gynecologist and obstetrician Phila. Gen. Hosp.; asst. gynecologist Temple U. Hosp.; asso. prof., Temple U. Address: 1420 W. Erie Av., Philadelphia, Pa.

DUNCAN, Ralph Winfred; prof. physics, U. of Pa. Home: 247 Green Av., Lansdowne, Pa.

DUNFORD, Edward Bradstreet, lawyer; b. Manchester, Va., Dec. 26, 1890; s. Frank Bernard and Edith May (Manahan) D.; grad. high sch., Manchester, 1909; student Va. Mechanics Inst., Richmond, 1909-11; LL.B., Richmond Coll., 1915; LL.D., Otterbein College, Westerville, O., 1934; m. Laura Bear, Apr. 6, 1917; 1 dau., Edith Bear. Admitted to Va. bar, 1915, and began practice at Richmond; chief clk. and atty. for commr. of prohibition of Va., 1917-21; asst. atty. Anti-Saloon League of America, 1921-27, atty. since 1927; sec. Nat. Temperance and Prohibition Council. Served with Va.

N.G. on Mexican border, 1916-17. Mem. Sigma Phi Epsilon, Delta Theta Phi. Democrat. Methodist. Home: 206 Washington Av., Riverdale, Md. Office: 131 B St. S.E., Washington. D.C.

DUNHAM, Frederic G(ibbons), lawyer; b. Buffalo, N.Y., Mar. 22, 1878; s. John C. and Abby Louise (Gibbons) D.; A.B., Cornell U., 1902; LL.B., A.M., Columbia, 1905; m. Caroline L. Allen, Apr. 10, 1909; children—Anna Louise, Elizabeth (Mrs. William M. Aurelius). Admitted to N.Y. bar,. 1904; law clk., 1904; mem. law firm Finegan & Dunham, 1905-09; chief Liquidation Bur., N.Y. State Ins. Dept., 1909-16; atty. Assn. of Life Ins. Pres., 1916-27; asst. gen. counsel Metropolitan Life Ins. Co., 1927-36; gen. counsel since 1936. Served as capt. and admiralty claims officer U.S.A., with A.E.F., 1918-19; maj. Judge Advocate Gen. Dept. (Res.), 1920-35. Mem. Am. Bar Assn., Assn. of Bar of City of N.Y., N.Y. Co. Lawyers Assn. Home: 450 Beverly Rd., Ridgewood, N.J. Office: 1 Madison Av., New York, N.Y.

DUNHAM, Henry Bristol, physician; b. Abington, Mass., Jan. 31, 1872; s. Henry and Ella (Bristol) D.; Ph.G., Mass. Coll. Pharmacy, Boston, 1893; M.D., Tufts Coll. Med. Sch., Boston, 1894; m. Agnes Traynor, Mar. 29, 1924; children—Nancy A., Arthur H. Resident at Mass. State Sanitorium, Rutland, Mass., 1899-1907; resident, State Sanatorium, Glen Gardner, N.J., 1907-18; supt. Essex County Sanatoria, Verona and Soho, 1919-23; chief of Bur. of Tuberculosis, N.J. State Dept. Health, 1924-25; resident, Camden County Tuberculosis Sanatorium, Grenloch, N.J., since 1926. Founder Nat. Tuberculosis Assn.; life member Am. San. Assn. Mason. Home: Clifton Av., Blackwood, N.J.

DUNHAM, James Henry, clergyman, educator; b. Bedminster, N.J., July 31, 1870; s. Sering P. and Anna L. (Bergen) D.; A.B., Princeton, 1891, A.M., 1894; grad. Princeton Theol. Sem., 1895; studied U. of Berlin, Germany, 1895-96; Ph.D., U. of Pa., 1913; LL.D., Franklin & Marshall Coll., 1923; m. Mary McMullin Barrows, of Mt. Holly, N.J., June 10, 1904; 1 son, Barrows. Ordained Presbyn. ministry, 1896; pastor 1st Ch., Mt. Holly, 1896-1912; teacher, Haverford (Pa.) Sch., 1914-15; prof. ethics, 1914-15; prof. philosophy and dean Coll. Liberal Arts and Sciences since 1915, Temple U., Phila. Served as moderator Presbytery, 1902; commr. Gen. Assembly, 1905. Mem. Am. Philos. Assn., A.A.A.S., Archæological Inst. America, Am. Acad. Polit. and Social Science, Am. Assn. Univ. Profs., Medieval Acad. of America, Pa. Acad. Fine Arts, Hist. Soc. of Pa., Societas Spinozana, Sons of the Revolution, Order of Founders and Patriots (chaplain-gen. 1938-40), Phi Beta Kappa. Club: University. Author: Freedom and Purpose—The Psychology of Spinoza, 1916; John Fourteen, 1917; Principles of Ethics, 1929. Home: Hamilton Court, Philadelphia, Pa.

DUNHAM, Russell H.; chmn. bd. and pres. Hercules Powder Co. Office: Delaware Trade Bldg., Wilmington, Del.

DUNKELBERGER, George Franklin, coll. prof.; b. Kreamer, Pa., July 21, 1879; s. Daniel and Sarah (Maurer) D.; A.B., Susquehanna U., 1908; A.M., U. of Pittsburgh, 1919; Ph.D., New York U., 1927; m. Dilla Maurer, June 10, 1905. Teacher rural schs., Pa., 1896-1903; supervising prin. pub. schs., Perry and Dauphin counties, Pa., 1908-16; prof. edn., Calif. (Pa.) State Normal, 1916-21, Waynesburg (Pa.) Coll., 1921-25; instr. in edn., New York U. 1925-26; prof. edn. Susquehanna U., since 1926, formerly dean coll. Mem. N.E.A., Nat. Soc. for Study of Edn., Pa. State Edn. Assn., Phi Delta Kappa, Pi Gamma Mu. Democrat. Mem. Reformed Ch. Contbr. to Pa. School Jour., N.E.A. Jour., Jour. Ednl. Sociology, Jour. Gen. Psychology. Home: Selinsgrove, Pa.

DUNKERLEY, Charles Arthur, ins. and real estate; b. Pittsburgh, Pa., Oct. 10, 1887; s. William Henry and Mary Elizabeth (Lenor) D.; student pub. sch. and Butcher's Bus. Coll.; m. Mary Catherine McDonald McLean, May 30, 1906; children—Ruth Elizabeth, Jean Beaumont,

DUNKLE — Lois Mae. Employed as bookkeeper in r.r. office, Pittsburgh, 1903-11; engaged in grocery bus., 1911-28, in retail shoe bus., 1915-22; in ins. and real estate bus. since 1928; former dir. Federal Title & Trust Co., Beaver Falls, Pa., Beaver Falls Community Loan Assn.; pres. Beaver Falls Cemetery Co. since 1923. Served as pres. Bd. Edn., Beaver Falls, 1932-35, and mem. since 1927. Mem. Beaver Falls Bd. of Trade; former mem. Chamber of Commerce; through Rotary Club served as chmn. Chippled Children Program, and made first survey that led to Crippled Children's work in Pa. Republican. Methodist. Club: Rotary (Beaver Falls, Pa.; past pres.). Home: 315 Fourteenth St., Beaver Falls, Pa.

DUNKLE, John Lee, college pres.; b. Deer Run, W.Va., November 4, 1884; s. Newman Greenberry and Genina Margaret (Dahmer) D.; grad. Shepherd Coll. State Normal Sch., Shepherdstown, W.Va., 1907; B.S., W.Va. U., 1912; M.A., Columbia, 1917; m. Mary Henrietta Taylor, Apr. 19, 1919; children—Dorothy Lee, John Lee. Teacher, elementary schs., Pendleton Co., W.Va., 1899; prin. high sch., La Follette, Tenn., 1907-08; supervisor schs., Edray Dist., Marlinton, W.Va., 1909-10; prin. high sch., Keyser, W.Va., 1912-14; supervisor town schs., Port Deposit, Md., 1914-16; dir. teacher training, Md. State Normal Sch., Towson, 1917-23; prin. Md. State Normal Sch., Frostburg, 1923-35; pres. Md. State Teachers Coll., Frostburg, since 1935. Mem. Dept. Superintendents, N.E.A., Am. Assn. Teachers Colls., Nat. Soc. for Study Edn., Phi Delta Kappa. Democrat. Episcopalian. Mason. Rotarian. Home: Frostburg, Md.

DUNLAP, Emma Wysor (Mrs. Robert F. Dunlap); b. Newbern, Va., Aug. 16, 1880; d. Joseph Claude and Jennie May (Gardner) Wysor; grad. music Randolph Macon Woman's Coll., Lynchburg, Va., 1902; m. Robert F. Dunlap, Nov. 17, 1904; children—May Lucile (Mrs. Lawrence N. Seldomridge), Emma (Mrs. Jess C. Wise). Mem. Hinton Civic League. Active in work Presbyn. Ch. of U.S., sec. Woman's Adv. Com., 1922, pres. Greenbrier Presbyterial Auxiliary, 1919-20, pres. Synodical Auxiliary, 1920-24, clk. Com. of Woman's Work, 1930-31; mem. Gen. Assembly exec. com. of religious edn. and pub. Mem. D.A.R., U.D.C., W.Va. Fed. Women's Clubs (pres. 1932-33). Democrat. Presbyterian. Club: Wednesday of Hinton (one of founders, pres. 1907 and 1931). Writer religious booklets and leaflets. Contbr. articles to ch. papers. Editor, Democratic Daily, 1920. Home: 101 Ballengee St., Hinton, W.Va.

DUNLOP, Walter Scott., clergyman; b. at Ayrshire, Scotland, Feb. 23, 1878; s. Walter and Margaret (Kennedy) D.; came to U. S., 1901, naturalized, 1920; A.B., Waynesburg (Pa.) Coll., 1908, D.D., 1929; B.D., Crozer Theol. Sem., Chester, Pa., 1911; studied U. of Pa., 1910-11; m. Elsie Rae Wolf, Aug. 19, 1908; children—Walter Scott, Bonnie St. Clair, Margaret Jean, Jack Grenfell. Ordained Bapt. ministry, 1911; pastor chs. in Pa., Washington, D.C., and W.Va. until 1929; pres. Alderson (W.Va.) Jr. Coll., 1929-32; pres. Alderson-Broaddus Coll., 1932-36; became pastor North Baptist Ch., Camden, N.J., 1936. V-p. Am. Bapt. Publication Soc.; mem. bd. W.Va. Bapt. State Conv. Republican. Mason. Home: Camden, N.J.*

DUNMIRE, Glenn Dewitt, surgeon; b. Duquesne, Pa., Oct. 14, 1893; s. Addison J. and Amanda (Lowstetter) D.; grad. Duquesne (Pa.) High Sch., 1912; A.B., U. of Pittsburgh, 1916, M.D., 1921; m. Bessie Botkin, Sept. 20, 1922; children—Lester Addison, Glenn Dewitt. Interne Western Pa. Hosp., 1921-22; asst., associate, now chief surg. staff, West Penn Hospital, Pittsburgh. Served as pvt., Med. Res. Corps. Fellow Am. Coll. Surgeons; mem. Pa. State Med. Soc., Allegheny Co. Med. Soc., Nu Sigma Nu, Alpha Omega Alpha. Republican. Presbyterian. Mason (Shriner, K.T.). Club: Pittsburgh Athletic Assn. Home: 2794 Beechwood Boul. Office: Western Pa. Hosp., Pittsburgh, Pa.

DUNN, David, pastor St. Johns Reformed Ch. Address: 226 Woodbine St., Harrisburg, Pa.

DUNN, Edward K., investment banker; b. Baltimore, Md., June 15, 1899; s. Charles Irwin and Emily Oliver (Shiff) D.; student Gilman Country Sch., Baltimore, 1911-18; B.S., Princeton U., 1922; m. Anne Butler, Nov. 24, 1931; children—Anne Butler, Edward K. Began as clk. Merchants Nat. Bank, Baltimore; partner Robert Garrett & Sons, investment bankers, Baltimore since 1929; pres. Park Crescent Hotel Co., New York; v.p. and dir. Nat. Food Products Corpn., Petroleum Bldg. Inc., Midland, Tex., dir. D. Pender Grocery Co., Southern Grocery Co. Served in Air Force, U.S. Navy, during World War. Trustee Gilman Country Sch., Baltimore; treas. Family Welfare Assn. of Baltimore, Legal Aid Assn. of Baltimore. Mem. Ivy Club (Princeton). Democrat. Episcopalian. Clubs: Merchants, Eldridge Kennels (Baltimore, Md.). Home: W. Bellona Av. Office: Garrett Bldg., Baltimore, Md.

DUNN, Emmett Reid, David Scull prof. biology, Haverford Coll. Address: Haverford, Pa.

DUNN, F(rederick) Eldred, organist and teacher; b. Phila., Pa., July 14, 1904; s. Frederick T. Jr., and Nina M. (Van Fossen) D.; studied piano, organ and theory with Frederick Maxson; voice with F. E. Edmunds and Mildred Faas-Korndoeffer, Phila.; unmarried. Organist M.E. Ch., Hopewell, Pa., 1923-26; organist and dir. music, Fifth Bapt. Ch., Phila., Pa., 1926-37; organist and dir. music, Olney Bapt. Ch., Phila., since 1937; instr. organ, Eastern Univ., Phila., 1929-30; mem. Phila. Light Opera Co., 1932-33, Paramount Opera Co., 1933-34. Colleague Am. Guild of Organists; mem. Am. Organ Players Club, Pa. Assn. Organists, Phila. Music Teachers Assn. Home: Wallingford Apts., 39th & Chestnut Sts., Philadelphia, Pa.

DUNN, H. Stewart, lawyer; b. Pittsburgh, Pa., April 20, 1892; s. Thomas A. and Bella A. D.; B.S., U. of Pa., 1913, student Law Sch., 1912-13; LL.B., Duquesne U. Law Sch., Pittsburgh, 1915, (hon.) LL.M., 1922; m. Marie Galvin, June 16, 1921; children—Thomas A. II, Elizabeth G., H. Stewart, Jr., James Galvin, John. Admitted to Pa. bar, 1915, and since engaged in gen. practice of law at Pittsburgh; admitted to Pa. Supreme and Superior cts. and to U. S. courts; Asst. City Solicitor for Pittsburgh, 1922-29; spl. counsel Pa. Pub. Utility Commn. Served as lt., 83d F.A., U.S. Army, with A.E.F., 1917-19. Mem. Am. Legion (county comdr. Allegheny Co., 1935, Dept. J.A., Pa., 1937), Kappa Alpha. Democrat. Roman Catholic. K.C. Clubs: Pittsburgh Athletic, Stanton Heights Golf (dir. and sec.). Home: 315 S. Atlantic Av. Office: 1108 Commonwealth Bldg., Pittsburgh, Pa.

DUNN, Herbert L., ins. co. exec.; b. Baltimore, Md., Feb. 14, 1894; s. James Thomas and Catherine (Sheridan) D.; student Calvert Hall Coll., Baltimore, 1903-10; m. Dorothea Mary Zerhusen, Oct. 3, 1922; 1 dau., Dorothea Barbara. In employ Edward J. Reilly & Co., Baltimore, 1910-11; asso. with Fidelity & Deposit Co., fidelity and surety bonds, Baltimore, continuously since 1911, v.p. since 1934. Club: Merchants (Baltimore). Home: 3927 Edmondson Av. Office: Charles & Lexington Sts., Baltimore, Md.

DUNN, Matthew A., congressman; b. Braddock, Pa., Aug. 15, 1886; ed. pub. schs., Pittsburgh and Meyersdale, Pa., and schs. for blind, Pittsburgh and Phila., after loss of sight at age of 20. Agt. Birmingham Fire Ins. Co., since 1920; mem. Pa. Ho. of Rep. 1926-32; mem. 73d to 76th Congresses (1933-41), 34th Pa. Dist. Home: Mount Oliver, Pa.

DUNN, Raymond Hauger, surgeon b. Staunton, Va., Dec. 9, 1886; s. Raymond Thomas and Anna Rebecca (Smales) D.; M.D., Med. Coll. of Va. Richmond, Va., 1910; m. Janet Thorne Alexander, Oct. 9, 1913; children—Betty Jane (Mrs. T. D. Staples), Mary Ann (Mrs. Keith A. Dunlap), Janet Alexander, Ida June, Nancy Ellen. Resident surgeon Chesapeake and Ohio Hosp., Huntington, W.Va., 1910-12; later chief surgeon for Pond Creek Coal Co., Stone, Ky.; then resident surgeon McMillan Hosp., Charleston, W.Va.,; purchased small hosp. in South Charleston, W.Va., built present two bldgs., 1918, and operate as Dunn Hosp., South Charleston, W.Va., of which is surgeon in charge and owner; surgeon for C.& O. R. R. Co., Greyhound Bus Lines, Evans Div. of Nat. Lead Co., Trojan Steel Co., Barium Reduction Corpn., Westvaco Chlorine Products Corpn.; physician and surgeon, U.S. Naval Ordnance Plant, South Charleston; registered to practice medicine in Va., Ky, W. Va. Pres. bd. edn., Loudon Dist., South Charleston, W.Va., 1922-27; mem. Kanawha Bridge Com. which built Patrick St. Bridge, Charleston, and purchased Kanawha City Bridge, which reconditioned, saving citizens $250,000 from estimated cost. Fellow Am. Coll. Surgeons; mem. Kanawha Co. Med. Soc. (ex-pres.), W.Va. State Med. Assn. (ex-v.p.), A.M.A., W.Va. Hosp. Assn., W.Va. Industrial Surgeons Assn., Phi Beta Pi. Democrat. Presbyterian. (deacon 1st Presbyn. Ch., South Charleston, W.Va., and one of its seven organizers). Mason (32°). Club: Kanawha Country (South Charleston, W.Va.). Home: 335 5th Av. Office: Corner C & 5th Av., South Charleston, W.Va.

DUNN, Thomas Phillips, lawyer; b. Erie, Pa., Oct. 26, 1896; s. Ira Jesse and Adda (Phillips) D.; student Grove House Sch., London, Eng., 1910, Haverford (Pa.) Coll., 1915-17; B.S., U. of Chicago, 1919; LL.B., Harvard Law Sch., 1922; m. Elizabeth Reimers, April 23, 1938. Admitted to Pa. bar, 1922, and since practiced at Erie, Pa. City atty., Erie, Pa., 1927-32; chmn. com. on unauthorized practice of law, Erie Co. since 1932. Mem. Am. Bar Assn., Pa. Bar Assn., Erie Co. Bar Assn. Republican. Club: Erie (Erie, Pa.). Home: Harbourcreek, Pa. Office: 1115 Erie Trust Bldg., Erie, Pa.

DUNN, Wilbur Linley, city engr.; b. Fayette, Co., Pa., March 31, 1875; s. Samuel Watson and Mary Ellen (Stoner) D.; student South Western Teacher's Coll., California, Pa., 1897; m. Leora Hazen, Sept. 30, 1903; children—John Hackney, Catherine (dec.), Mary. Teacher pub. schs., Uniontown, Pa., 1894-1900; asso. with pvt. engring. firm, Gans & Dunn., Uniontown, Pa., 1901-10; mem. Pa. Dept. of Highways, Uniontown, Pa., 1911-13; road and bridge engr., Fayette Co., Pa., 1913-17; city engr., Uniontown, Pa., since 1917. Trustee and treas. Redstone Presbytery. Mem. Y.M.C.A. Republican. Presbyterian (ruling elder). Mason (chaplain; past officer Union Royal Arch Chapter, Uniontown Commandery; K.T.). Home: 87 Lincoln St. Office: City Hall, Uniontown, Pa.

DUNNE, Edward F., lawyer, executive; b. Chicago, Ill., Nov. 26, 1887; s. E. F. and Elizabeth J. (Kelly) D.; prep. edn. high schs. of Oak Park and Chicago, Ill., 1901-05; LL.B., U. of Mich., 1909; m. Rosina M. Powers, April 17, 1912; children—Edward F., Harry P., Rosemary, Richard A., Gerald J., William, Dorothy, Josephine, Marie. Admitted to Ill. bar, 1909, and practiced in Chicago, 1909-19; sec. and asst. counsel 4-one Box Machine Makers, New York and Rockaway, N.J., 1919-20, sec. and gen. counsel since 1929; mem. firm Blair, Curtis & Dunne, patent attorneys, New York, 1929-37; sec. and gen. counsel Stapling Machines Co., Rockaway since 1937; sec., dir. and gen. counsel Wirebounds Patents Co. Trustee All Souls Hosp., Morristown, N.J. Mem. Chicago Bar Assn., Bar Assn. of City of New York, Patent Bar Assn. of New York City, Assn. of Practitioners before the Interstate Commerce Commn., Phi Kappa Psi. Democrat. Roman Catholic. Club: Morristown Field (Morristown, N.J.). Home: Convent, N.J. Office: Rockaway, N.J.

DUNNELLS, Clifford George, structural engr.; b. Pittsburgh, Pa., July 8, 1875; s. Charles Clifford and Susan Emma (Christy) D.; student Pittsburgh Central High Sch., 1889-93, U. of Pittsburgh, 1893-94; C.E., Lehigh U., Bethlehem, Pa., 1897; m. Inez Mullian; children—Clifford George, Dorothy Rene, Elizabeth Cora, Mary Susan, Margaret Ellen. Draftsman Pittsburgh Bridge Co., 1897-1900; designing engr. Am. Bridge Co., Pittsburgh, 1900-10; mem. of faculty Carnegie Inst. Tech. since 1910, now prof. civil engring., mem. firm Hunting Davis & Dunnells, Pittsburgh, engrs. since 1925. Mem. Y.M.C.A. (mem. com. of management, Allegheny Branch; pres. com. of management, Carnegie Tech.; mem. state com.), Am. Soc. C.E., Engring. Soc. of Western Pa., Delta Upsilon. Republican. Episcopalian. Mason (McKinley Lodge 318, Pa. Consistory, Syria Temple). Club: Church (Diocese of Pittsburgh; pres.). Home: 141 Riverview Av. Office: 1150 Century Bldg., Pittsburgh, Pa.

DUNNING, Henry Armitt Brown, mfg. pharmacist; b. Denton, Md., Oct. 24, 1877; s. Charles Alexander and Ella M. (Redden) D.; Ph.G., Maryland Coll. of Pharmacy, 1897, Pharm.M., 1925, grad. work at Johns Hopkins U. and Johns Hopkins Hosp.; hon. M. Pharm., Phila. Coll. Pharmacy and Science, 1925, Pharm.D., U. of Maryland; m. Beatrice Fitzgerald, Oct. 24, 1901 (died 1906); children—James H. Fitzgerald, Catherine Ellen (Mrs. H. Charles Kersten); m. 2d, Ethel Adams, of Baltimore, 1908; children—Henry Armitt Brown, Charles Alexander. With Hynson, Westcott & Co., Mfg. pharmacists, Baltimore, since 1894, purchased part ownership in 1901, pres. Hyonson, Westcott & Dunning, Inc., since 1930; formerly asso. prof. of chemistry, U. of Md. Trustee Maryland Acad. of Sciences, Home for Incurables; v.p. Friends of Library, Johns Hopkins U. Served with 4th U.S. Vols. in Cuba, Spanish Am. War. Donated organic chemistry lab. to U. of Md.; established 1st scholarships in pharmacy in the U.S.; subscriber to Nat. fellowship movement Johns Hopkins U. Awarded Remington honor medal, 1925. Apptd. 1st Capt. by Pres. Wilson of 1st U.S. Life Saving Corps. Pres. Am. Pharm. Assn., Md. Pharm. Assn. (former pres.); chmn. bldg. plans com. and Prize Essay com. Am. Inst. of Pharmacy. Mem. Am. Inst. of Chemists, Inc., Am. Chem. Soc. (chmn. of various coms.), Rho Chi, St. George's Soc., U.S. Seniors Golf Assn. Clubs: Engineers, Elkridge (Baltimore); Lake Placid (N.Y.); Baltimore Country, Hillendale Golf. Home: 4215 Greenway. Office: Charles & Chase Sts., Baltimore, Md.

DUNNING, J. H. Fitzgerald, chem. exec.; b. Baltimore, Md., Aug. 26, 1902; s. H. A. Brown and Beatrice Garelle (Fitzgerald) D.; student Baltimore (Md.) City Coll., 1916-20; A.B., Ph.D., Johns Hopkins U., Baltimore; m. Frances McPherson, March 27, 1926; children—J. H. Fitzgerald, Betty Carey. Research chemist, Hynson, Westcott & Dunning, Inc., Baltimore, Md., 1925-30, dir. chem. research, 1930-33, sales mgr., 1933, sec.-treas. since 1933; treas. Chase Realty Corpn.; sec. Morton Realty Co. Mem. A.A.A.S., Am. Pharm. Assn., Am. Inst. Chemistry, Am. Chem. Soc., Sigma Xi, Phi Gamma Delta, Pi Delta Epsilon, Omicron Delta Kappa. Clubs: Baltimore Country, Johns Hopkins (Baltimore, Md.). Home: 107 Churchwarden's Rd. Office: Charles and Chase Sts., Baltimore, Md.

DUNNINGTON, Virginius G.; pres. Mfrs. Finance Co., Mfrs. Mortgage Co. Home: 2803 St. Paul St. Office: Baltimore Trust Bldg., Baltimore, Md.

DUNSFORD, Jan R.; chmn. bd. Union Steel Casting Co. Home: 310 Quaker Road, Edgeworth, Pa. Office: 62d and Butler Sts., Pittsburgh, Pa.

DUNSMORE, John Ward, artist; b. nr. Oxford, O., Feb. 29, 1856; s. Joseph Pollock and Margaret Annette (Ward) D.; ed. U. of Cincinnati; studied art with Thomas Couture, Paris; married. Dir. Detroit Mus. of Art, 1888-90, Detroit Sch. of Arts, 1890-94. Specializes in historical subjects. Exhibited in U.S., Eng., and France. Represented in Nat. Acad. Design, New York Hist. Soc. and Salmagundi Club, New York; Cincinnati Mus. Art and Ohio Mechanics Inst., Cincinnati; Lasell Sem., Auburndale, Mass.; entire room in Wagnall's Memorial Library, Lithopolis, O.; 30 hist. paintings of Am. Revolution in gallery of S. R. at Fraunces Tavern and 11 in offices of Title Guarantee & Trust Co., New York. Medal for "Macbeth," Boston, 1881; Evans prize for "The Music Room," Salmagundi Club, 1914. A.N.A.; pres. Cincinnati Art Club, 1898-1901; mem. Am. Water Color Soc. (pres.), Am. Fine Arts Soc. (pres.), Am. Artists Professional League, New York Water Color Club, N.Y. State Hist. Assn., Cincinnati Art Club (hon.), Salmagundi Club (v.p. 1924-25), S.R., etc. Cannoneer Vet. Corps Artillery, N.Y., and did field service on Aqueduct, 1917; member 9th C.A.C., 1918; maj. with regular army in charge Red Cross activities, U.S. Gen. Hosp. No. 5, and U.S. Gen. Hosp. No. 41 until end of 1920. Home: Hoboken, N.J. Studio: 96 Fifth Av., New York, N.Y.

DUNTON, William Rush, Jr., M.D., psychiatrist; b. Philadelphia, Pa., July 24, 1868; s. Jacob and Annie Gordon (Gemmill) D.; grad. Germantown (Pa.) Acad., 1885; B.S., Haverford (Pa.) Coll., 1889, M.A., 1890; M.D., U. of Pa., 1893; m. Edna Drusilla Hogan, July 1, 1897; children—Helen McClean (Mrs. Edward Albert Furst), William Rush III, Henry Hurd. Interne Germantown, Children's, University, German and Johns Hopkins hosps., 1893-95; asst. physician, Sheppard and Enoch Pratt Hosp., Towson, Md., 1895-1924, research asst., 1924-25; instr. in psychiatry, Johns Hopkins, since 1903; dispensary psychiatrist, Johns Hopkins Hosp., since 1903; med. dir. Harlem Lodge, 1924-39. Mem. Med. Advisory Bd. No. 2 (Md.), World War. Fellow A.M.A.; mem. Am. Psychiatric Assn., American Occupational Therapy Association (mem. board of managers), Maryland Occupational Therapy Association, Md. Psychiatric Soc., Med. and Chirurg., Faculty of Md., Haverford and Johns Hopkins alumni assns., Soc. Colonial Wars, Sons of Revolution, Sons of the American Revolution, and Phi Beta Kappa Fraternity. Democrat. Episcopalian. Club: University. Author: Occupation Therapy, 1915; Reconstruction Therapy, 1919; Prescribing Occupational Therapy, 1928. Editor: Occupational Therapy and Rehabilitation. Asso. editor Am. Jour. of Psychiatry. Address: 33 N. Symington Rd., Catonsville, Md.

DU PONT, A. Felix, v.p. E. I. duPont de Nemours & Co.; b. Wilmington, Del., Apr. 14, 1879; s. Francis G. and Elise (Simons) duP.; student U. of Pa.; m. Mary Richard Chichester, Apr. 9, 1902; m. 2d, Ann Burton DeArmond, Sept. 3, 1937. V.p. and dir. E. I. duPont de Nemours & Co. since 1916. Address: Wilmington, Del.

DU PONT, Alfred Victor, architect; b. Wilmington, Del., Mar. 17, 1900; s. Alfred Irénée and Bessie (Gardner) duP.; student Lawrenceville (N.J.) Sch., 1914-18, Yale, 1920-21, Ecole des Beaux Arts, Paris, France, 1928-30; m. Marcella Miller, Aug. 8, 1924. Chemist and chem. engr. E. I. duPont de Nemours & Co., Wilmington, Del., 1922-27; chem. engr. duPont Rayon Co., Buffalo, N.Y., 1927-28; partner Masséna & duPont, architects, Wilmington, Del., since 1930; sec. and treas. Masséna & duPont, Inc., since 1932. Served as pvt., U.S. Marine Corps, 1918-19. Mem. Am. Inst. Architects (Del. chapter), Archtl. League (N.Y.), Soc. of Beaux Arts Architects. Republican. Episcopalian. Clubs: Wilmington, Wilmington Country, Vicmead Hunt (Wilmington, Del.); Yale (New York). Home: "Calmar," Greenville, Del. Office: 704 Delaware Av., Wilmington, Del.

DU PONT, E. Paul, pres. Indian Motocycle Co.; b. Montchanin, Del., Apr. 24, 1887; s. Francis G. and Elise Wigfall (Simons) duP.; B.S., U. of Pa., 1909; m. Jean Kane Foulke, June 9, 1910; children—E. Paul, Francis George, Stephen, Benjamin Bonneau, R. Jacques Turgot, Alexis Irénée. Pres. Indian Motocycle Co. since 1930. Home: Montchanin, Del.

DU PONT, Ernest; pres. U.S.F. Powder Co.; dir. several companies. Home: Kennett Pike. Office: Delaware Trust Bldg., Wilmington, Del.

DU PONT, Francis V., v.p. Equitable Trust Co. of Wilmington; b. Johnstown, Pa., 1894; s. Thomas Coleman and Alice duP.; grad. Mass. Inst. Tech., 1917; student U.S. Mil. Sch. of Aeronautics, Boston; m. Katherine Clark, June 16, 1917 (divorced 1931); m. 2d, Janet M. Gram, 1932. V.p. Equitable Trust Co. of Wilmington since 1931. Office: Equitable Office Bldg., Wilmington, Del.

DU PONT, Irénée, officer E. I. duPont de Nemours & Co. b. nr. Wilmington, Del., Dec. 21, 1876; s. Lammot and Mary (Belin) duP.; B.S. in Chem. Engring., Mass. Inst. Tech., 1897, M.S., 1898; m. Irene Sophie du Pont, Feb. 1900; children—Irene Sophie (Mrs. Ernest N. May), Margaretta L. (Mrs. Crawford H. Greenewalt), Constance S. (Mrs. Colgate W. Darden Jr.), Eleanor F. (Mrs. Philip G. Rust), Doris Elise (dec. 1930), Mariana (Mrs. Henry H. Silliman), Octavia M., Lucile E. (Mrs. Robert B. Flint), Irénée. Pres. E. I. duPont de Nemours & Co., 1919-26, vice chmn. bd. since 1926; v.p. Christiana Securities Co.; dir. General Motors Corpn. One of founders Am. Liberty League. Home: Granogue, Del. Office: DuPont Bldg., Wilmington, Del.

DU PONT, Lammot; b. Wilmington, Del., Oct. 12, 1880; s. Lammot and Mary (Belin) duP.; B.S., Mass. Inst. Tech., 1901; m. 4th Margaret A. Flett, Nov. 24, 1933. Formerly chmn. bd. General Motors Corpn., now dir.; pres. E. I. duPont de Nemours & Co.; dir. Gen. Motors Acceptance Corpn., Wilmington Trust Co. Mem. Am. Chem. Soc. Clubs: Metropolitan (New York); Union League (Philadelphia); Wilmington. Address: DuPont Bldg., Wilmington, Del.

DU PONT, Pierre Samuel, mfr.; b. Wilmington, Del., Jan. 15, 1870; s. Lammot and Mary (Belin) duP.; prep. edn. Penn Charter Sch., Phila., Pa., Mass. Inst. Tech., class of 1890; m. Alice Belin, Oct. 6, 1915. Chmn. bd. E. I. duPont de Nemours & Co., explosives and chemicals; dir. Gen. Motors Corpn., Pa. R.R. Co., Wilmington Trust Co.; apptd. liquor commr. of Del., 1933, term of 5 yrs. Mem. Corpn. Mass. Inst. Tech., Am. Philos. Soc., Phi Kappa Sigma. Clubs: Wilmington, City (Wilmington); Metropolitan (New York). Home: Wilmington, Del.

DU PONT, William, Jr.; pres. Delaware Trust Co. Address: Wilmington, Del.

DURAND, Frank, banking; b. Asbury Park, N.J., Mar. 9, 1895; s. Frank and Florence (Bates) D.; ed. Rutgers U., 1913-15; m. Florence Campbell, Feb. 10, 1923; children—Frank III, Priscilla Campbell, Mary Elizabeth. Engaged as real estate and ins. broker, 1919-33; vice-pres. First Nat. Bank of Spring Lake, N.J. since 1933. Served as ensign, U.S.N., 1917-19. Served as mayor Borough of Sea Girt, N.J, 1926-31; mem. N.J. Ho. of Assembly from Monmouth Co., 1930-31; mem. N.J. Senate from Monmouth Co., 1933-38; pres. N.J. Senate and actg. gov., 1937. Mem. Beta Theta Pi. Republican. Presbyn. Mason. Club: Carteret (Trenton). Home: Sea Girt. Office: First Nat. Bank, Spring Lake, N.J.

DURANT, Frederick Clark, Jr., telephone official; b. New York, N.Y., Nov. 7, 1879; s. Frederick Clark and Clara Elizabeth (Harrison) D.; student Colorado Coll., 1898-99, Mass. Inst. Tech., 1899-1903; m. Cornelia Allen Howel, of Little Rock, Ark., Jan. 10, 1912; children—Elizabeth (Mrs. Robert C. Sullivan), Frederick Clark III. Was in investment banking business and with Day & Zimmermann, Inc., engrs., Phila. Now pres. Keystone Telephone Co., Phila., Camden & Atlantic Telephone Co.; vice-pres. of Telephone Securities, Inc.; dir. Cuban-Am. Manganese Corpn., Telephone Securities, Inc., Camden & Atlantic Telephone Co. Mem. Phi Gamma Delta. Clubs: Rittenhouse, Midday. Home: 1901 Walnut St. Office: 135 S. 2d St., Philadelphia, Pa.

DURBIN, Joseph William II, sales promotion; b. Williamstown, Pa., Feb. 2, 1898; s. William Joseph and Elizabeth A. (Chester) D.; ed. Mercersburg (Pa.) Acad., 1915-16; A.B., Princeton U., 1921; m. Elsie Marie Chenoweth, Mar. 17, 1931; 1 dau., Joan Calvert. Employed in sales promotion dept., U.S. Rubber Products, Inc., New York, N.Y., 1921-23, Milwaukee, Wis., 1923-27; mgr. Durbin-Mellon Hosiery Co., Williamstown, Pa., 1927-32, engaged in retail bus., 1933-36; chief clk. U.S. Rubber Products, Inc., New Orleans, La., 1936-37, with sales promotion dept. at Baltimore, Md., since 1937; dir. Williams Valley Bank, Williamstown, Pa. Served as sergt. field signal batln., 8th Div., U.S.A., 1917-19. Chm. Welfare Drive, Williamstown, Pa., 1936; treas. Williamstown Red Cross, 1932-36, Merchants Assn. of Dauphin Co. Comdr. Am. Legion, Williamstown, Pa., 1927-29. Republican. Methodist. Mason (K.T., Shriner). Clubs: American Legion (Williamstown, Pa.; Princeton Terrace (Princeton, N.J.); Roads (Annapolis, Md.). Home: 704 Brookwood Rd. Office: U.S. Rubber Products, Inc., 429 S. Charles St., Baltimore, Md.

DURHAM, Fred Stranahan, manufacturer; b. Williamsport, Pa., July 2, 1884; s. Joseph Edward and Nellie Rebecca (Stranahan) D.; A.B., Princeton U., 1906; m. Christine Witherspoon Bryden, Apr. 29, 1916; 1 son, Fred Stranahan. Spl. agt. Penn. Mutual Life Ins. Co., Phila., Pa., 1906-07; v.p. and treas. Bonney Forge & Tool Works, Allentown, Pa., mfrs. automotive tools, pipe fittings, spl drop forgings, 1907-33, pres. since 1933; v.p. and dir. Nassau Products; dir. Allentown Nat. Bank, Pa. Power & Light Co. Republican. Presbyterian. Mason. Clubs: Livingston, Lehigh Country (Allentown, Pa.); Skytop (Pa.) Lodge. Home: 3d and Pine Streets, Catasauqua, Pa. Office: Allentown, Pa.

DURHAM, Hannah Margaret (Mrs. J. Edward Durham, Jr.), mem. Nat. Rep. Program Com.; b. Allentown, Pa., Dec. 12, 1891; d. Edward M. and Kate R. (Anewalt) Young; ed. Baldwin Sch., Bryn Mawr, Pa., 1910, Miss Hill's Sch., Paris, France, 1911; m. J. Edward Durham, Jr., Feb. 25, 1913. Served as vice chmn. Lehigh Co. Rep. Com., 1920-24; vice chmn. Rep. State Com., 1924-26; officer Pa. Council of Rep. Women since 1923; mem. exec. com. Lehigh Co. Rep. Com. since 1920, exec. com. Rep. State Com. since 1924; mem. Nat. Rep. Program Com. since 1938; served as alternate del. at large to Rep. Nat. Convs., 1924, 1928, 1932, 1936. Mem. Allentown Red Cross, and Community Chest. Republican. Presbyn. Club: Woman's of Allentown (pres. 1929-30). Home: 45 S. 16th St., Allentown, Pa.

DURHAM, Joseph Edward, Jr., mfg. forgings and tools; b. Williamsport, Pa., Aug. 23, 1882; s. Joseph Edward and Nellie Rebecca (Stranahan) D.; Bordentown Mil. Inst., 1901-02; A.B., Princeton, 1906; m. Hannah Margaret Young, Feb. 25, 1913. Began as sec. Bonney Forge and Tool Works, mfrs. wrenches, tools, drop forgings, weldings, Allentown, Pa., 1907, vice-pres. since 1910; pres. Nassau Products Co. Trustee Allentown State Hosp. Charter mem. Honorary First Defenders; mem. Am. Soc. Mech. Engrs., S.R., Scotch Irish Soc., Newcomen Society, Pa. Soc. Sons of Revolution, Bethlehem Bach Choir. Republican. Presbyn. Mason. Clubs: Livingston, Lehigh Country. Home: 45 S. 16th St. Office: Bonney Forge & Tool Works, Allentown, Pa.

DURIG, William Eugene, bldg. materials mcht.; b. New Martinsville, W.Va., Dec. 19, 1896; s. John Jay and Rosa (Schultz) D.; student Marshall Coll., Huntington, W.Va., 1911-12, W.Va. Univ., 1917, Carnegie Inst. Tech., 1917; m. Minnie Riggenbach, Apr. 23, 1919; children—Mary Eloise, Wanda Ruth. Engaged in teaching in rural schs. also farming and writing life ins., 1912-19; salesman for grocery co., 1920; asso. with E. F. Phillips Lumber Co., lumber and bldg. materials dealer and contractor, New Martinsville, W.Va. since entering its employ as shipping clk., 1921, gen. mgr. since 1930, pres. and dir. since 1931; v.p. W.Va. Title & Trust Co. since 1931; also engaged in farming. Served in A.S., U.S.A. as sergt., 1919. Mem. Chamber of Commerce. Pres. Kiwanis Club. Democrat. Baptist. Odd Fellow. Home: 735 Fifth St. Office: 178 Commercial St., New Martinsville, W.Va.

DUSHAM, Edward Henry, prof. of entomology; b. Amesbury, Mass., Sept. 1, 1887; s. Peter and Catherine (Murphy) D.; A.B., Dartmouth Coll., Hanover, N.H., 1910; student Iowa State Coll., Ames, 1910-12; M.S., Pa. State Coll., 1915; Ph.D., Cornell U., 1924; m. Mary E. Atkinson, Oct. 1, 1912; 1 dau., Sara Catherine (Mrs. James O. Beveridge). Grad. asst in zoölogy, Ia. State Coll., 1910-12; instr. in zoölogy, Pa. State Coll., 1913-15, asst. prof., 1915; grad. asst. in biology, Cornell U., 1916, instr. in natural history, 1917; prof. of entomology and head of dept. of zoölogy and entomology, Pa. State Coll. since 1918. Mem. A.A.A.S., Pa. Acad. Science, Am. Assn. Univ. Profs., Entomol. Soc. America, Am. Assn. Econ. Entomology, Sigma Xi, Gamma Sigma Delta, Sigma Phi Epsilon. Home: 607 N. Burrows St., State College, Pa.

DUSTMAN, Robert Barclay, univ. prof.; b. Youngstown, O., Jan. 9, 1892; s. George S. and Christina (Barclay) D.; student, country schs., Mahoning Co., O., 1898-1908, Rayen High Sch., Youngstown, O., 1908-10; B.S. in Agr., Ohio State U., Columbus, 1915; M.S., U. of Chicago, 1923, Ph.D., 1924; m. Gay Zinn, July 27, 1917; children—Robert Barclay, Mary Jean. Teacher, high sch., Shinnston, W.Va., 1915-16; extension agronomist, W.Va. U., 1916-19; extension prof. soils, Ohio State U., 1919-22; asst. prof. agrl. chemistry, W.Va. U., 1924-26, asso. prof., 1926-30, prof. since 1930; agrl. chemist W.Va. Expt. Station since 1930. Mem. A.A.A.S., Am. Chem. Soc., Am. Soc. Plant Physiologists, Sigma Xi, Phi Lambda Upsilon, Alpha Zeta. Lutheran. Home: 108 Cornell Av., Morgantown, W.Va.

DUTCHER, Edward Merriam, retired shoe mfr.; b. Newton, N.J., Feb. 17, 1875; s. William Lewis and Hortense (Couse) D.; ed. Newton (N.J.) High Sch., Phillips Andover Acad., Newark (N.J.) Business Coll.; m. Mary Lucy Pierce, Oct. 21, 1903; children—Adelaide Pierce, Hortense Couse (Mrs. Mario Lucci), Mary Pierce (wife of Dr. Dorset LaRue Spurgeon). Associated with H. W. Merriam Shoe Co., Newton, N.J., 1894-1925, working in all depts. to learn business, supt. of factory 3 years, became vice-pres. at death of father, pres. of firm, 1908, and later treas.; dir. Sussex & Merchants Nat. Bank, Newton, N.J. Fuel adminstr. for Sussex and Warren Counties during World War; chmn. town com. of Newton, N.J., 5 years; dir. of old age assistance, 3 years; chmn. Rep. Co. Com., 2 years. Trustee Dennis Library Assn.; trustee Presbyterian Ch., Newton. Mem. Omega Nu Iota. Republican. Clubs: Sussex County Country, Newton Tennis. Home: 35 Linwood Av., Newton, N.J.

DUTCHER, Raymond Adams, biochemist; b. Raymond, S.D., Mar. 28, 1886; s. Paul and Susie (Adams) D.; B.S., S.D. State Coll., 1907, M.S., 1910; M.A., U. of Missouri, 1912; grad. study U. of Illinois and U. of Minnesota; D.Sc., Univ. of Puerto Rico, 1936; m. Mary Marguerite Wright, of De Smet, S.D., Sept. 14, 1912; children—Adams Wright, Rachel Mary. Instr. S.D. State Coll., 1907-10, U. of Mo., 1910-12, U. of Ill., 1912-13; asst. prof. Ore. State Coll., 1913-17; asst and asso. prof. agrl. biochemistry (nutrition), U. of Minn., 1917-21; head of dept. agrl. and biol. chemistry, Pa. State Coll., State Coll., Pa., since 1921. Oberlaender fellow Carl Schurz Foundation (Germany), 1934. Served as capt., food and nutrition div., Sanitary Corps, U.S.A., Camp Meade, Md., 1918. Mem. Land Grant Coll. Advisory Com. on Vitamin Research; mem. White House Conf. on Child Health and Protection; mem. Research Advisory Com. of Farm Chemurgie Council, 1935. Fellow A.A.A.S.; mem. Am. Inst. Nutrition, Am. Chem. Soc. (chmn. biochem. div.), Soc. for Exptl. Biology and Medicine Am. Soc. Biol. Chemists (chmn. vitamin terminology com.), Pa. Acad. Science, Brit. Biochem. Soc., Sigma Xi, Gamma Sigma Delta, Alpha Zeta, Phi Lambda Upsilon, Alpha Chi Sigma, Theta Chi, Acacia, Phi Kappa Phi. Republican. Presbyn. Mason. Clubs: University, Centre Hills Country (State College); Chemists (New York). Co-Author: Chemistry in Agriculture, 1926; Introduction to Agricultural Biochemistry (with D. E. Haley), 1931. Home: 254 E. Hamilton Av., State College, Pa.

DUTTON, Charles Judson, clergyman, writer; b. Fall River, Mass., Aug. 22, 1888; s. Rev. John George and Esther (Kippax) D.; student Albany (N.Y.) Law Sch., 1905-07, LL.B., 1907; studied Brown U., 1909-10; theol. dept. Defiance (O.) Coll., 1910-11; m. Laura E. Meigs, of Albany, Apr. 16, 1910; 1 son, Odard Charles. Admitted to R.I. bar, 19 0; ordained ministry, 1910; pastor Little Compton, R.I., 1913-14, Congl. Ch., Rensselaer, N.Y., 1914-17, All Souls' Unitarian Ch., Troy, N.Y., 1917-21, 1st Unitarian Ch., Erie, Pa., 1921-29, Unitarian Ch., Des Moines, Ia., 1929-34; now agt. Pa. Dept. Justice, Bd. Pardons and Parole; state historian of Pa., 1937. Asst. prof. English, Rensselaer Polytechnic, 1918. Y.M.C.A. war sec., Humphries, Va., 1917-18. Mem. British Soc. Authors, Composers and Dramatists. Mason, Elk. Clubs: University, Liberal, Writers, Pa. Society of Engrs. Author: The Underwood Mystery, 1921; Out of the Darkness, 1922; The Shadow on the Glass, 1923; The House by the Road, 1924; The Second Bullet, 1925; The Crooked Cross, 1926; Flying Clues, 1927; The Clutching Hand, 1928; Streaked with Crimson, 1929; The Shadow of Evil, 1930; Murder in a Library, 1931; The Samaritans of Molokai (biography), 1932; Poison Unknown, 1932; The Circle of Death, 1933; Black Fog, Founder of an Empire (biography), 1934; Oliver Hazard Perry (biography), 1935; Murder in a Lighthouse, 1936. Writer of column, "World We Live In," Albany Sunday Telegram, 1916-28; also many short stories in Am. and British mags. Home: 958 W. 9th St., Erie, Pa.

DUTTON, George Elliott, coll. dean; b. Seaford, Del., Dec. 16, 1881; s. James E. and Mary R. (Elliott) D.; A.B., Del. Coll., now U. of Del., 1904; grad. student Johns Hopkins U., 1905-08; A.M., Harvard U., 1911; m. Elsie Smith, Apr. 6, 1912; 1 son, George Elliott. Instr. English, U. of Mo., 1908-10; instr. English, U. of Del., Newark, Del., 1911-13, asst. prof., 1913-17, asso. prof., 1917-18, prof. English since 1918, dean Del. Coll. since 1923. Mem. Assn. Deans of Land Grant Colls., Nat. Assn. Deans and Advisers, Nat. Assn. Coll. Registrars, Sons of Del. of Phila. Ind. Democrat. Presbyterian. Co-author (with W. O. Sypherd), Outline of Survey Course in English Literature; Specimens of English Compositions; English Composition for College Freshmen. Contbr. to sch. journals. Home: 183 W. Main St., Newark, Del.

DUTTON, Lewis Richard, banker; b. Millbourn, Chester Co., Pa., Aug. 2, 1873; s. Richard and Mary Louise (Green) D.; student Friends Select Sch., West Chester, Pa., 1892-94, State Normal Sch., West Chester, 1894-96, Temple U., Phila., 1900-01; m. Elsie Jones, Dec. 6, 1913; children—Barbara Roberts (Mrs. John P. Moorhouse), Marjory H. (Mrs. Herbert L. Badger Jr.), Sara Pauline. Supt. Gas Co. of West Chester, 1896-98; supt. Jenkintown & Cheltenham Gas Co., 1898-1900, supt. and pres. 1906-10; div. mgr. Phila. Suburban Gas & Electric Co., 1910-25; pres. Jenkintown (Pa.) Bank & Trust Co. since 1925. Trustee Abington Memorial Hosp., Baptist Home, Phila., and Baptist Camp Federation, Phila. Served as Y.M.C.A. war work sec., Camp Dix, N.J., 1918. Republican. Club: Union League (Phila.). Home: 201 Washington Lane. Address: York Rd. and West Av., Jenkintown, Pa.

DUY, Albert William, lawyer; b. Chicago, Ill., June 13, 1868; s. Judge George C. and Lucy Kinney (Gookins) D.; student high sch. and mil. acad.; m. Pauline Elizabeth Kester, June 4, 1891; children—Albert William, Josephine (Mrs. F. S. Hutchison). Admitted to Pa. bar, 1898, Pa. Supreme Ct., 1902, United States Ct., 1902, Pa. Superior Ct., 1903; in practice at Bloomsburg; dir. First Nat. Bank (Bloomsburg), North Branch Bus Co. Referee in bankruptcy, U.S. Dist. Ct., Western Dist. of Pa., 1900-03; dist. atty. Columbia Co. (Pa.), 1902-05 (only Rep. ever elected to that position in co.); chmn. Columbia Co. Rep. Com., 1905-10. Senior warden St. Paul's Episcopal Ch., Bloomsburg; chancellor of diocese of Harrisburg, Pa., P.E. Ch. since 1928. Episcopalian. Mason. Elk. Clubs: Rotary, Craftsmen, Bloomsburg Country (pres. and gov.), Irem Temple Country (Bloomsburg, Pa.). Home: 152 W. 4th St. Office: First National Bank Bldg., Bloomsburg, Pa.

DWIER, W. Kirkland; v.p. Phila. Bd. of Trade. Address: Garden Court Apts., Philadelphia, Pa.

DWYER, Frank P., physician and surgeon; b. Renovo, Pa., Dec. 3, 1882; s. Michael and Mary Liddy (Nagle) D.; grad. Renovo (Pa.) High

Sch., 1899; M.D., Jefferson Med. Sch., Phila., 1906; m. Mary Howell, July 29, 1914; children—James Richard, Frank Philip, Constance Marie. Interne St. Mary's Hosp., Hoboken, N.J., 1906-07; physician and surgeon, Renovo, Pa., since Sept. 1907; pres. Renovo Bd. of Health; vice-pres. Citizens Bank, Renovo. Pres. Renovo Sch. Bd., Renovo Bd. of Health; former chief burgess of Renovo; trustee Renovo Hosp. Served as fuel administrator for Clinton Co. during World War. Fellow A.M.A; mem. Clinton Co. Med. Soc. (past pres.), Pa. Med. Soc. Phi Rho Sigma. Republican. Roman Catholic. Home: 600 Huron Av. Office: 165 6th St., Renovo, Pa.

DWYER, Vincent Courtney, mail advertising; b. Norwalk, Conn., Dec. 29, 1876; s. Patrick Henry and Katherine (Shea) D.; A.B., St. Bonaventure Coll., Allegheny, N.Y., 1899; grad. student Paris, France, 1891, U. of Pittsburgh Econ. Sch., 1910; (hon.) Master of Letters, St. Bonaventure Coll., 1936; m. Mary W. Heidenkamp, Dec. 29, 1915; children—Vincent Courtney, Jr., James C. (dec.), Joseph Heidenkamp, Mary Louise, Jack Harrington. Employed as salesman, 1905-07; organized Tanki Mail Advertising Service, Pittsburgh, and propr. and mgr. since 1907; propr. Office Machines Co. since 1915; organized Pittsburgh-Hooven Co, 1917; propr. and mgr. V. C. Dwyer & Co., advertising, since 1919. Mem. Chamber of Commerce. Mem. Mail Adv. Service Assn., Nat. Lithographers Assn., Pittsburgh Adv. Club, Asso. Artists of Pittsburgh, Philatelic Soc. of Pittsburgh. Republican. Roman Catholic. Home: 1606 Murray Av. Office: 319 Fifth Ave., Pittsburgh, Pa.

DYCHE, Howard Edward, prof. elec. engring.; b. Spring Valley, O., Jan. 19, 1884; s. Samuel Edward (M.D.) and Flora Alice (Carey) D.; grad. high sch., Spring Valley, 1901; M.E. in E.E., Ohio State U., 1906; m. Edith Mae Guy, of Pittsburgh, Pa., Feb. 2, 1910; 1 son, Howard Edward. Engr., ry. dept. Westinghouse Electric & Mfg. Co., 1906-11; prof. elec. engring., Westinghouse Tech. School, Pittsburgh, 1909-11; instr. in mathematics and physics, U. of Pittsburgh, 1911, instr. in elec. engring., 1912-14, asst. prof. elec. engring., 1914-17, asso. prof., 1917-19, prof. and head of dept. since 1919; cons. engr.; registered professional engr., Commonwealth of Pa. Asst. dir. war training, U. of Pittsburgh, 1918. Mem. Am. Inst. E.E. (past chmn. Pittsburgh, sect.), Soc. Promotion Engring. Edn., Sigma Xi, Sigma Tau, Eta Kappa Nu. Lutheran. Mason (32°), Odd Fellow. Clubs: University, Faculty. Home: 317 South Av., Wilkinsburg, Pa., and Spring Valley, O. Address: University of Pittsburgh, Pittsburgh, Pa.

DYE, William Seddinger, Jr., college prof.; b. Philadelphia, July 9, 1880; s. William Seddinger and Cherry A. Eliza (Callahan) D.; grad. Central High Sch., Phila., 1899; student Dickinson Coll., 1901-02; A.B., U. of Pa., 1905, Ph.D., 1915; A.M., Pa. State Coll., 1908; m. Bertha Ross Bill, of Phila., Dec. 28, 1910; 1 son, Wm. S. Harrison; fellow English, U. of Pa., 1912-14; with Pa. State Coll., 1907—, prof. English lang. and lit., 1920—, head of dept. since 1926. Mem. Modern Lang. Assn. of America, Pa. Hist. Soc., Phi Kappa Phi, Acacia Fraternity (nat. pres. 1922-29). Episcopalian. Mason. Author: Father Penn (pageant), 1914; Melodrama in England (1800-1840), 1915; Expository Writing, 1920. Home: 327 S. Atherton St., State College, Pa.

DYER, Charlotte Leavitt (Mrs. George Bell Dyer), mag. editor; b. New York, N.Y., Feb. 16, 1906; d. Charles Wellford and Clara Gordon (White) Leavitt; ed. Scarborough Sch., 1917-19, Rosemary Hall, 1920-22, Wykeham Rise, 1923-25, U. of N.M., summer 1928; A.B., Barnard Coll., 1931; m. George (Bell) Dyer, June 26, 1930. Instr. in anthropology, Barnard Coll., 1930-31; made field trips to Kutenai Indians, Brit. Columbia, 1929 and 1931; since 1932 mgr. Diabase Farm, registered Aberdeen-Angus cattle and Chester White hogs, Bucks Co., Pa.; one of founders Farmers Digest and asst. editor since 1937; instr. Sch. of Horticulture, Ambler, Pa., 1937-38. Episcopalian. Club: Art Alliance of Philadelphia. Home: Diabase Farm, New Hope, Pa.

DYER, Dorothy Tunell (Mrs. John Ruskin D.), dean of women; b. Minneapolis, Minn., Dec. 11, 1895; d. George Henry and Jennie Winifield (Ayers) Tunell; student U. of Minn., Minneapolis, Minn., 1914-15, A.M. in Psychology, 1935; student Stout Inst., 1915-16; B.S. in Home Economics, Ohio State University, 1918; m. John Ruskin Dyer, July 29, 1920 (died 1933); children—Jean Elizabeth, John Ruskin, George Craig. With War Work Council of Y.W. C.A., 1918-19; traveling student sec. for Y.W. C.A. North Central Area, 1919-20; grad. asst. U. of Minn., Minneapolis, Minn., 1934-35; asst. jr. dean, Coll. Arts & Scis., O. State U., Columbus, O., 1936-37; asst. prof. psychology and dean of women, Bucknell U., Lewisburg, Pa., since 1937. Mem. Nat. Assn. Deans of Women, Pa. Assn. Deans of Women, Vocational Guidance Assn., Hazen Conf. Group, Am. Assn. Univ. Women, Mortar Board, Phi Upsilon Omicron. Methodist. Club: Civic (Lewisburg, Pa.). Home: 9 Walker St., Lewisburg, Pa.

DYER, Frank Lewis, mechanical and electrical expert and inventor; b. at Washington, August 2, 1870; s. George Washington and Kate (Huntress) D.; ed. pub. schs., and Columbian (now George Washington) U. Law Sch.; m. Annie Augusta Wadsworth, 1892; children—John Wadsworth, Frank Wadsworth; m. 2d, Isabelle Dawson Archer, 1924. Practiced patent law,' Washington, 1892-97, New York, 1897-1903; gen. counsel for Edison interests, 1903-08; exec. officer T. A. Edison's industrial corpns., 1908-1912; pres. Gen. Film Co., 1912-14; treas. Condensite Co. of America, 1910-20; officer and dir. numerous corpns.; has secured over 100 patents in various arts, including talking books for the blind; practicing since 1914 as mech. and elec. expert. Asso. mem. Am. Soc. Mech. Engrs.; mem. Am. Geog. Soc., N.Y. Southern Soc. Democrat. Mason. Clubs: Engineers', Rockefeller Center Lunch (New York); Sea View Golf Club (Absecon, N.J.); Congressional Country (Washington, D.C.). Author: Edison—His Life and Inventions (with T. Commerford Martin), 1910-29. Home: 24 N. Cornwall Av., Ventnor, N.J.

DYER, George (Bell), writer; b. Washington, D.C., Apr. 12, 1903; s. George Palmer and Dorothy (Bell) D.; prep. edn, Oahu Coll. (Honolulu), Maury High Sch. (Norfolk, Va.), Phillips Acad. (Andover, Mass.); Ph.B., Yale, 1925; m. Charlotte Leavitt (asst. editor Farmers Digest), of Hartsdale, N.Y., June 26, 1930. Insurance salesman, 1926; reporter San Francisco Examiner, 1929-30; free lance writer since 1930. Mem. Authors' League of America, Nat. Rifle Assn., Zeta Psi. Club: The Players (New York). Author: The Three-Cornered Wound, 1931; The Five Fragments, 1932; A Storm is Rising, 1934; The Catalyst Club, 1936; The Long Death, 1937; Adriana, 1939. Home: Diabase Farm, New Hope, Pa., and Silverado, Calistoga, Calif.

DYER, John H., supt. schs.; b. Scranton, Pa., Aug. 29, 1894; s. Stephen T. and Margaret A. (Jones) D.; A.B., Lafayette Coll., 1916; M.A., Columbia, 1921; Ph.D., U. of Pa., 1927; m. Florence E. Morgan, of Scranton, June 17, 1924; 1 dau., Marjorie M. Began as teacher in pub. schs. of Scranton, 1916, supt. of schs. since 1929. Research chemist Chem. Warfare Service, World War. Mem. N.E.A., Phi Beta Kappa. Conglist. Kiwanian. Wrote thesis, An Analysis of Objectives in the Teaching of Physics. Home: 1416 Jackson St. Office: Administration Bldg., Scranton, Pa.

DYER, Luther Lee, lawyer; b. Bolair, W.Va., Feb. 9, 1880; s. Cyrus Newman and Sarah Ann (Dodrill) D.; diploma Mountain State Bus. Coll., Parkersburg, W.Va., 1904; student W.Va. Univ. Law Sch., Morgantown, W.Va., 1907-08; m. Elizabeth Chidester Billingsley, Oct. 4, 1913. Engaged in teaching in country and town schs., 1900-08; admitted to W.Va. bar, 1908 and since engaged in gen. practice of law at Webster Springs; mem. firm Dyer & Dyer since 1923. Served as chmn. home service dept. of Webster Co. Chapter Am. Red Cross during World War. Democrat. Methodist. Mason. Home: Union St. Office: Court Square, Webster Springs, W.Va.

DYER, William Elmer Seibert, cons. engr. and architect; b. Phila., Pa., Dec. 5, 1880; s. Paris P. and Florence D.; m. Bertha M. Faber; children—Margaret F., William Elmer Seibert, Elizabeth S. Cons. engr. and architect, Phila., since 1908; designing and constrn. of power plants, factories and equipment of plants; specializes on equipment high efficiency power plants; designed power plant for pressure said to be highest in America; served on Fair Practice Commn. of Am. Boiler Mfrs. Assn. Mem. Am. Soc. Mech. Engrs., Engrs. Club of Phila., S.A.R. Clubs: Penn Athletic, Art, Seaview Golf, Whitemarsh Golf, Elk River, Larchmont Yacht, Philadelphia Yacht, Delaware River Yacht, Pennsylvania Barge. Home: Old York Rd., Noble, Pa. Office: Land Title Bldg., Philadelphia, Pa.

DYSON, John Milnes, physician; b. Hazleton, Pa., Apr. 7, 1903; s. John Rose and Mary (Lauderbach) D.; ed. Lawrenceville (N.J.) Sch., 1919-21; A.B., Princeton, 1925; M.D., U. of Pa. Med. Sch., 1929; grad. study, Harvard Med. Sch., 1935; unmarried. Interne Phila. Gen. Hosp., 1929-31; in gen. practice of medicine at Hazleton, Pa., since 1931, practice now limited to internal medicine; phys. Hazleton State Hosp. since 1931; acting roentgenologist Hazleton State Hosp. since 1931; surgeon Lehigh Valley R.R. since 1938; chief of med. service and lecturer Sch. of Nursing, Hazleton State Hosp. Diplomate, Nat. Bd. Med. Examiners; fellow Am. Coll. Physicians, A.M.A.; mem. Am. Heart Soc., Pa., Luzerne Co., Lehigh Valley med socs., Zeta Psi, Nu Sigma Nu. Republican. Presbyterian. Clubs: Valley Country (Hazleton, Pa.); Cloister Inn (Princeton, N.J.). Home: 309 W. Diamond Av. Office: Hazleton State Hosp., Hazleton, Pa.

E

EABY, Charles Willis, dist. atty.; b. Paradise, Pa., May 7, 1876; s. Jacob M. and Catherine E.; student Millersville (Pa.) Normal Sch.; m. Elizabeth M. Merritt, Oct. 10, 1911; children—Charles Willis, Josephine E. Admitted to Lancaster Co. (Pa.) bar, 1899, Supreme Court of Pa., 1902, Superior Court of Pa., 1905; appointed U.S. commr. by U.S. Dist. Court for Eastern Dist. of Pa., 1905; asst. dist. atty., Lancaster Co., 1912-16; dist. atty. since 1935, serving four-yr. term. Became pres. Young Reps. of Lancaster; solicitor of Lancaster Automobile Club; dir. Lancaster Osteopathic Hosp. Assn.; mem. of advisory bd. Salvation Army. Mem. Pa. Motor Fed. (chmn. laws and legislative com.). Republican. Elk (Past Exalted Ruler Lancaster Lodge 134). Club: Kiwanis of Lancaster (past pres.). Home: 1253 Wheatland Av. Office: 56 N. Duke St., Lancaster, Pa.

EAGER, Auville, investment banking; b. Rome, Italy, Oct. 12, 1889; s. John Howard and Olive May (Board) E., citizens of U.S.; student U. of Ga., Athens, Ga., 1910-12; m. Clara H. Murray, June 2, 1917; children—Auville, Jr., Clare Murray, Joan, June, John Howard III. Began as bank employee, 1916; mgr. new business dept., Mercantile Trust Co., Baltimore, 1916-18; v.p. Fidelity Securities Corpn., 1918-21; mem. N.Y. Stock Exchange firm of Mackubin Legg & Co., Baltimore, since 1921; pres. and dir. Nat. Union Co.; dir. Nat. Bondholders Corpn., Houston Natural Gas Corpn., James River Bridge Corpn., Union Series Eye Corpn., Nat. Union Mortgage Corpn. Mem. Sigma Alpha Epsilon. Democrat. Episcopalian. Clubs: Elkridge, Chesapeake (Baltimore). Home: Woodbrook. Office: 222 E. Redwood St., Baltimore, Md.

EAGLETON, Wells Phillips, surgeon; b. Brooklyn, N.Y., Sept. 18, 1865; s. Thomas Aston Proud and Mary Emma (Phillips) E.; Polytechnic Inst., Brooklyn; M.D., Coll. Phys. and Surg. (Columbia), 1888; m. Florence Peshine Riggs, May 24, 1913. Practiced at Newark since 1890; med. dir. bd. trustees Newark Eye and

Ear Infirmary; chief div. of head surgery, Newark City Hosp.; consulting cranial surgeon St. Barnabas, St. Michael's, Memorial, Presbyn., and Beth Israel hosps. (Newark), Mountain Side Hosp. (Montclair), Muhlenberg Hosp. (Plainfield), All Souls Hosp. (Morristown, N.J.), Irvington General Hospital, Orange Memorial Hospital, Elizabeth General Hosp., West Hudson Hosp. of Kearny (all N.J.); cons. ophthalmologist and otologist Women's & Children's Hosp., Newark, Hosp. & Home for Crippled Children, Newark, Morristown (N.J.) Memorial Hosp.; member of consulting staff of Essex County Hospital, Overbrook, N.J., div. cranial surgery, Essex County Isolation Hosp., Soho; former trustee Federal Trust Co. Vol. U.S.A., April 10, 1917; served as chief of surgery of the head Base Hosp., Camp Dix, until after signing of Armistice; col. Officers' Reserve Corps, M.D. President Newark Council of Social Agencies, trustee Welfare Federation of Newark, Newark Museum. Mem. A.M.A. (house of delegates), N.J. State Med. Soc. (pres. 1923-24 and chmn. welfare com.), Am. Otol. Soc. (pres. 1921), N.Y. Otol. Soc. (pres. 1929), Browning Soc. of N.Y., Am. Acad. Ophthalmology and Otolaryngology (pres. 1934-35), Nat. Med. Acad. Rio de Janeiro (hon.); hon. mem. Sociedad Otorinoloargingologica (Madrilena, Spain); trustee American College of Surgeons; former N.J. rep. on the Med. Adv. Bd. of the Veterans' Bur.; formerly mem. N.J. Com. for the Blind. Clubs: Essex, Essex County Country. Author: Brain Abscess—Its Surgical Pathology and Operative Treatment, 1922; Cavernous Sinus, 1925; Thromboses (both translater into French), 1925; also numerous published speeches and monographs. Home: 212 Elwood Av. Office: 15 Lombardy St., Newark, N.J.

EAKIN, Frank, educator; b. Emlenton, Pa., Dec. 24, 1885; s. James Alexander and Sarah Margaret (Perry) E.; A.B., magna cum laude, Grove City Coll., 1910; grad. Western Theol. Sem., Pittsburgh, 1913, B.D., 1915; studied U. of Marburg, 1914, U. of Glasgow, 1914-15; Ph.D., magna cum laude, U. of Chicago, 1922; m. Mabel Mechlin, June 12, 1913; children—Lloyd Russell, Paul Mechlin, Frank, Eleanor Josephine; m. 2d, Mildred Olivia Moody, March 28, 1931. Teacher of history, North Washington (Pa.) Institute, 1908-09; ordained Presbyn. ministry, 1913; pastor Glenfield and Haysville, Pa., 1913-14; instr. N.T. Greek, Western Theol. Sem., 1915-23, asso. prof. N.T. dept., 1923-25, prof. ecclesiastical history and history of doctrine, 1925-27, also librarian, 1919-27; lecturer in N.T., Hartford Theol. Sem., 1927-28; visiting prof., U. of Chicago Div. Sch., summer 1930, editorial adviser to religious dept. of Macmillan Co., New York, 1928-31; pres. Item Pub. and Printing Co., Millburn, N.J., 1932-33; prof. history, Essex County Junior Coll., Newark, N.J., 1933-35; engaged in freelance literary and ednl. work since 1935. Mem. bd. dirs. N.J. Consumers' Cooperative, Inc. Author: Getting Acquainted with The New Testament, 1927; Revaluing Scripture, 1928. Contbr. to religious and ednl. publs. Home: 15 Oak Hill Rd., Short Hills, N.J.

EAKIN, Mildred Olivia Moody (Mrs. Frank Eakin), religious edn.; b. Wilson, N.Y., March 28, 1890; d. Alfred James and Mary Evelyn (Pettit) Moody; grad. Wilson Acad., 1906; A.B., Syracuse U., 1910; A.M., New York Univ., 1934; post-grad. study, Syracuse U. and U. of Chicago, Drew U. and New York U.; m. Frank Eakin, March 28, 1931. Teacher high sch., Wilson, 1910-16; dir. children's activities, W.C.T.U., 1916-19, asso. nat. dir., 1919; dir. elementary edn. for 7 states, Bd. of Edn., M.E. Ch., 1919-21, supt. dept. of elementary edn., at central office, Chicago, 1921-32; teaching fellow religious edn., Drew Univ., 1932-34, instr. religious edn. since 1934, dir. demonstration sch. in religious edn. dept. since 1937. Mem. Religious Edn. Assn., Child Study Assn. of America, Internat. Council Religious Edn. (Children's Professional Advisory Sect.), Alpha Chi Omega. Author: Tales of Golden Deeds (with Teacher's Manual), 1923; Kindergarten Course for Daily Vacation Schools, 1925; Teaching Junior Boys and Girls, 1934; A Junior Teacher's Guide on Negro Americans (co-author), 1936; Exploring Our Neighborhood (with pupil's books, Under the Church Flag and In Anybody's Town), 1936. Contbr. to religious and ednl. publs., etc. Home: 15 Oak Hill Rd., Short Hills, N.J.

EALY, Charles H(odge), lawyer; b. Schellsburg, Pa., Jan. 25, 1884; s. Taylor F. and Mary (Ramsey) E.; A.B., Bucknell U., 1904, A.M., 1905; LL.B., U. of Pittsburgh Law Sch., 1908; m. Edna May Pritts, June 16, 1914; children—Mary Ellen, Ruth Rea, Edna May. Admitted to Pa. bar, 1908, and since engaged in gen. practice of law at Somerset; admitted to practice., all Pa. courts, U.S. Dist Courts and before the Supreme Court of U.S.; mem. firm Uhl & Ealy, now Uhl, Ealy & Uhl; served as solicitor Somerset Co., 1916-19; mem. Pa. Senate since 1926. Mem. Am., Pa. State, and Somerset Co. bar assns., Sigma Chi. Republican. Presbyn. Home: 517 W. Main St. Office: Schell Bldg., Somerset, Pa.

EARHART, Will, music edn.; b. Franklin, O., April 1, 1871; s. Martin Washington and Hanna Jane (Corwin) E.; ed. pub. schs.; mus. edn. pvtly.; Mus.D., U. of Pittsburgh, 1920; m. Birdelle M. Darling, Dec. 29, 1897; 1 son, William Corwin. Supervisor music pub. schs., Greenville, O., 1896-98, Richmond, Ind., 1898-1912 (condr. festival chorus and symphony orchestra); dir. music pub. schs., Pittsburgh, Pa., since 1912; lecturer in music, Sch. of Edn., U. of Pittsburgh, 1913-18, prof., 1918-21; lecturer Carnegie Inst. Tech., Pittsburgh, 1916-18 and since 1921. Mem. Pittsburgh Municipal Band Concert Com., 1925-30, Nat. Advisory Com. of Federal Music Project under Works Progress Adminstrn., 1935-36. Mem. Mus. Educators Nat. Conf. (ex-pres.), Mus. Teachers Nat. Assn., N.E.A. (dept. superintendent), Progressive Edn. Assn., Phi Mu Alpha, Phi Delta Kappa. Republican. Clubs: Musicians, Univ. Civic, Authors. Author: The Eloquent Baton, 1931; Music to the Listening Ear, 1932; The Meaning and Teaching of Music, 1935; Choral Technics, 1937; also several bulls. Co-editor mus. instrn. books. Contbr. to mus. jours. Home: 215 Lothrop St. Office: 341 Bellefield Av., Pittsburgh, Pa.

EARLE, Beatrice Lowndes, educator; b. Newport, R.I., June 5, 1895; d. William Henry and Emma (Bradfield) Lowndes; student high sch., Mt. Vernon, N.Y., 1910 to 1914; B.A., Barnard Coll., N.Y., 1917; M.A., Columbia U., 1918; m. Edward Mead Earle, Feb. 11, 1919; 1 dau., Rosamond. Registrar, New Sch. for Social Research, New York, 1919 to 21; teacher history, Katharine Gibbs Sch., New York, 1921-25; asst. to dean, Barnard Coll., New York, 1929-31; headmistress, Miss Fine's Sch., Princeton, N.J., 1934-36. Trustee and v.p. bd. Miss Fine's Sch. since 1936. Mem. Phi Beta Kappa. Democrat. Club: Cosmopolitan (New York). Address: 57 Cleveland Lane, Princeton, N.J.

EARLE, Edgar P., pres., treas. and dir. Earle Gear & Machine Co.; also dir. many other companies. Home: Mantoloking, N.J. Office: 4707 Stenton Av., Philadelphia, Pa.

EARLE, Edward Mead, prof. history; b. N.Y. City, May 20, 1894; s. Stephen King and Helen Martha (Hart) E.; B.S., with highest honors, Columbia, 1917, M.A.,.1918, Ph.D., 1923; m. Beatrice Lowndes, Feb. 11, 1919; 1 dau., Rosamond. Served as 2d lt. and 1st lt. F.A. and A.S., U.S.A., 1917-19, World War. With Nat. City Bank, New York, 1919-20; lecturer in history, Columbia, 1920-23, asst. prof., 1923-26, asso. prof. since 1926; prof. Sch. of Economics and Politics, Inst. for Advanced Study, Princeton, N.J., since 1934. Representative International Opium Commn., Turkey and Greece, 1924. Lecturer Inst. of Politics, Williamstown, Mass., 1923, Army War Coll., 1924-27, Army Industrial Coll., 1927. Vice chmn. Foreign Policy Assn., 1924-27; ednl. dir. New York Chapter Am. Inst. Banking, 1921-27; mem. Am. Hist. Assn., Am. Soc. Internat. Law, Acad. Polit. Science, Council on Foreign Relations, Phi Beta Kappa, Alpha Delta Phi. Specialist in Near Eastern affairs and in Am. foreign relations. Club: Century (New York). Author: An Outline of Modern History, 1921; Turkey, The Great Powers, and Bagdad Railway (winner of George Louis Beer prize for best work of year on European diplomacy), 1923; also contbr. articles in Polit. Sci. Quarterly, Foreign Affairs, Am. Hist. Review, etc. Edited and wrote introduction to sesquicentennial edition of the Federalist, 1937. Home: 57 Cleveland Lane. Address: Institute for Advanced Study, Princeton, N.J.

EARLE, George Howard, former governor; b. Devon, Pa., Dec. 5, 1890; s. George Howard and Catherine Hansell (French) E.; grad. Delancey Sch., Phila.; student Harvard, 1909-11; LL.B., Temple U., Phila.; L.H.D., Waynesburg (Pa.) Coll., D.C.L., Susquehanna U., Selinsgrove, Pa., and LL.D., La Salle Coll., Phila. (all 1935)); m. Huberta Potter, Jan. 20, 1916; children—George Howard, Hubert, Lawrence, Ralph. Asso. with father in sugar industry, Phila.; later engaged in various business enterprises in Chicago; after World War founded Flamingo Sugar Mills, Phila.; occupied with various business activities until apptd. E.E. and M.P. to Austria, 1933; resigned, 1934, to become Dem. candidate for gov. State of Pa.; elected 1st Dem. gov. of Pa. in 44 yrs. for term, 1935-39. Enlisted as pvt. 2d Pa. Inf., 1916; served as 2d lt. on Mexican Border; enlisted in U.S. Navy, 1917, as lt. (j.g.), became comdr. U.S.S. Victor, submarine chaser; awarded Navy Cross for service thereon. Trustee U. of Pa., U. of Pittsburgh. State Coll. of Pa. Mem. Tall Cedars of Lebanon, Soc. Friendly Sons of St. Patrick. Episcopalian. Mason (Shriner), Elk. Clubs: Racquet, Harvard, Penn Athletic (Phila.); Merion Cricket (Haverford); Whitmarsh (Pa.) Valley Country; Leash (New York). Home: Grays Lane, Haverford, Pa. Office: State Capitol, Harrisburg, Pa.

EARLE, Murray, mfr. gears and machines; b. Bethlehem, Pa., Mar. 6, 1892; s. Edgar Pardee and Harriette W. (Murray) E.; grad. P.E. Acad., Phila., Pa., 1912; student U. of Pa., 1913-15; grad. Army Pursuit Sch., Gerstner Field, La., 1918; m. Isabel M. Yost, Mar. 30, 1918; children—Jane (Mrs. Britton Chance), James Morris, Harriette, Constance. Began career as machinist apprentice, 1915; asso. with The Earle Gear & Machine Co., mfr. gears and machines, Phila., Pa., since 1919, dir., asst. sec. and treas. since 1920; dir. Eastern Tenn. & Western N.C. R.R., E.T. and W.N.C. Motor Transportation Co., Linville River R.R. Co., Cranberry Furnace Co. Served as pvt., sergt., 1st lt., capt., maj., A.S., U.S.A., Nat. Army and Res. Mem. Borough Council, Mantoloking, N.J. Mem. Zeta Psi. Episcopalian. Home: Bay Av., Mantoloking, N.J. Office: 4707 Stenton Av., Philadelphia, Pa.

EARLE, Ralph; pres. Pa. Warehousing & Safe Deposit Co.; also officer or dir. many other companies. Home: 113 S. Third St., Philadelphia, Pa.

EARLE, Swepson, hydrographic engr.; b. Queen Anne Co., Md., Aug. 3, 1879; s. William Brundige and Louisa (Stubbs) E.; ed. high sch. and business coll.; engring. course, U. of Va.; m. Mabel Streett, June 4, 1902 (dec.); children—Juliet Gover Streett, Louise Shepherd, Elizabeth Swepson. With U.S. Coast and Geod. Survey, 1899-1903; Office of U.S. Lighthouse Bd., Washington, D.C., 1903-06; hydrographic engr. Md. Shell Fish Commn., 1906-16; made oyster survey of Md. waters, 1906-12; chief engr. Conservation Commn., 1916-17, now commr. Conservation Dept. of Md. Yeoman, U.S.N., at 18; ensign, U.S.N.R.F., Apr. 1, 1917; comdr. U.S.S. McLane; range officer Naval Proving Grounds, Dahlgren, Va.; constructed range for big navy guns on Lower Potomac River; promoted lt. (j.g.) and sr. lt. during World War, and placed on inactive list, July 1, 1919. Ex-pres. Nat. Assn. Fisheries Commrs.; mem. S.R., Mil. Order World War. Democrat. Episcopalian. Clubs: Engineers', Elkridge Kennels (Baltimore). Author: Maryland's Colonial Eastern Shore (with P. G. Skirven), 1916; The Chesapeake Bay Country, 1923, 24, 3d edit., 1929; also Md. Supplement to Frye-Atwood Geography. Inventor of continuous sounding machine for measuring depth of water, also the Amphibious Tank. Home: 4202 Roland Av., Baltimore, Md.*

EARLEY, Albert, supervisor of schs.; b. Clayton, N.J., Jan. 29, 1890; s. Charles and Isabella (Henry) E.; student Trenton (N.J.) Normal Sch.; B.S., Dickinson Coll., Carlisle, Pa., extension work and summer courses at Columbia U., New York U., Cornell U., U. of Mich., U. of Wis., U. of Del.; m. Elsie Phillips; children—Linnaeus Kepler, Trudeau. Sch. prin., Hopewell, N.J., high sch. prin., North Plainfield, N.J.; supt. schs., Leonia, N.J.; now supervisor of schs., Del. State Bd. of Edn., Georgetown, Del. Served as mem. draft bd., war conservation speaker and three-minute speaker, during World War. Dir. Del. Safety Council. Mem. Franklin Inst., Am. Mus. Natural History, Japan Soc., N.E.A., Travel Club. Presbyterian. Mason (Royal Arch), Jr. Order United Am. Mechanics, Odd Fellow. Club: Georgetown (Del.) Kiwanis (sec. since 19—; mem. internat. com. on publicity). Author: Geography of Del. (revised), 19—; numerous articles in various mags. Speaker at Silver Jubilee Meeting Nat. Safety Council and over radio. Has traveled widely in America, Orient, Europe, West Indies and South America. Address: Court House, Georgetown, Del.

EARNEST, William Hoffer, lawyer; b. Jonestown, Pa., Apr. 3, 1875; s. Napoleon Desh and Mary (Hoffer) E.; A.B., Lafayette Coll., Easton, Pa., 1897, A.M., 1900; m. Estelle Penney, Apr. 30, 1900; children—Ernest Penney, Joel Gates. Admitted to Pa. bar, 1900 and since in gen. practice of law at Harrisburg; co. solicitor of Dauphin Co., 1920-24; mem. Pa. Senate, 1924-32; vice-pres. Hershey Estates, Hershey, Pa.; dir. Hershey Nat. Bank, Hershey Trust Co. Served as chmn. Legal Advisory Bd., 2d Div., Dauphin Co. 1917. Mem. Bd. Law Examiners of Dauphin Co. since 1920. Mem. Bd. Mgrs. Hershey Industrial Sch. Mem. Pa. Bar Assn., Dauphin Co. Bar Assn. (pres. 1928), Delta Kappa Epsilon. Republican. Lutheran. Mason (32°, Shriner). Home: 311 N. Front St. Office: 310 Bergner Bldg., Harrisburg, Pa.

EARP, Edwin Lee, sociologist; b. Illchester, Md., Oct. 26, 1867; s. Israel S. and Rachel Melcena (Barnette) E.; A.B., Dickinson Coll., Pa., 1895; A.M., New York U., 1897; B.D., Drew Theol. Sem., 1898; Berlin, 1898-99; Ph.D., Leipzig, 1901; m. Lina Gibb Pearsall, May 1, 1901; children—Ruth, James Pearsall. Ordained M.E. ministry, 1900; pastor Newark and Plainfield, N.J., 1900-04; prof. sociology, Syracuse U., 1904-09, Drew Theol. Sem., 1909-38, retired, June 1938. Mem. Am. Sociol. Soc., National Civic Federation, Phi Delta Theta, Pi Gamma Mu, Phi Beta Kappa; mem. Nat. Council Y.M.C.A.; terms 1924-30; pres. World's Conf. on Town and Country Work of World's Com. Y.M.C.A., Dassel, Germany, 1930; hon. chmn. Morris County Y.M.C.A.; hon. trustee Madison Public Library. Mem. Madison Rotary Club. Author: Die Relative Vollständigkeit und Hinlänglichkeit der Entwicklungs-Ethik und der Christlichen Ethik, 1901; Social Aspects of Religious Institutions, 1908; The Social Engineer, 1911; The Rural Church Movement, 1914; A Community Study, 1917; The Rural Church Serving the Community, 1918; Rural Social Organization, 1921; Biblical Backgrounds for Our Rural Message, 1922. Contbr. chapter to Socialized Church, 1909. Home: Basking Ridge, N.J.

EASLEY, David Milton, Circuit Court judge; b. Pearisburg, Va., Mar. 10, 1875; s. John White and Minerva Boyd (Pack) E.; ed. public schools of Giles County, Va., 1881-86, Pearisburg Acad., 1886-91; LL.B., U. of W.Va., 1900; m. Maude Ella Oliver, Oct. 16, 1907; 1 dau., Evelyn Oliver. Admitted to W.Va. bar, 1900, and practiced in Bluefield, 1900-36; city atty., 1924-29; judge Circuit Court, 9th Judicial Circuit of W.Va., since 1937. Pres. Mercer County Bd. of Edn., 1934-37; trustee Bluefield Coll. Mem. Mercer County Bar Assn. (former pres.), W.Va. Bar Assn., Phi Sigma Kappa. Democrat. Baptist. Mason. Clubs: The Virginias Senior Golf Assn., Bluefield Country. Home: 301 Russell St. Office: 618 Law & Commerce Bldg., Bluefield, W.Va.

EASLEY, Frank S.; pres. Bluefield Coal & Coke Co.; officer or dir. many companies. Address: Bluefield, W.Va.

EASLEY, George Albert, mining engr.; b. Harwood, Mo., Aug. 28, 1884; s. Stephen and Frances Virginia (Gibbons) E.; ed. Mo. State Coll., 1902-04; B.S., U. of Mo., 1909, M.E., 1912; hon. D.Engr., U. of Mo., 1938; m. Lura Whitfield, Oct. 2, 1912; children—Virginia (dec.), Nita, Nancy (Mrs. John Larkin), George A., Jr. Employed as supt. Pan American Tin Co., 1909-11; gen. mgr. Olla de Oro Gold Mining Co., 1911-14; mem. firm Easley and Inslee, mining engrs., La Paz, Bolivia, since 1914; vice-pres. and treas., Internat. Mining Corpn., New York. Mem. Am. Inst. of Mining Engrs., Am. Mining and Metall. Soc., Kappa Alpha, Tau Beta Pi. Republican. Episcopalian. Clubs: Morris Co. Golf, Morristown, Mining. Home: Loautaka Road, Morristown, N.J. Office: 630 5th Av., New York, N.Y.

EAST, Clyde Harold, newspaper editor; b. White Sulphur Springs, W.Va., Apr. 7, 1899; s. Benjamin A. and Belle (Campbell) E.; m. Pearl Sayre, Jan. 1, 1918; children—Mary Frances (Mrs. James Franklin Grandin), Clyde Harold. Editor Charleston (W.Va.) Gazette. Methodist. Democrat. Mem. Elks, Modern Woodmen, Cinten. Home: South Charleston, W.Va. Office: Charleston Gazette, Charleston, W.Va.

EASTELL, Richard T.; pres. and treas. Washington Oil Co. Home: 601 Pitcairn Pl. Office: Vandergrift Bldg., Pittsburgh, Pa.

EASTER, James Miller, chmn. bd. Daniel Miller Co.; b. Baltimore, Md., Aug. 17, 1864; s. James W. and Margaret Elizabeth (Miller) E.; student Md. Agrl. Coll. (now U. of Md.), 2 yrs.; m. Henrietta N. Toel, Feb. 3, 1887. With Daniel Miller Co., wholesale dry goods, since 1880; partner, 1897-99; sec., 1899-1909; treas., 1909-12; v.p., 1912-14; pres., 1914-32; chmn. bd. since 1932; treas. since 1935. Home: Owings Mills, Baltimore Co., Md. Office: 32 Hopkins Place, Baltimore, Md.

EASTERLY, George Roberts, college dean; b. Topeka, Kan., Aug. 13, 1901; s. George A. and Eleanor (Rittenhouse) E.; A.B., U. of Kan., 1923; M.B.A., Harvard U., 1925; m. Helen Westwater, Dec. 18, 1929. Asst. prof., U. of Ark., 1925-26; teaching fellow in Marketing, Northwestern U., 1926-27; instr. of Marketing, U. of Pittsburgh, 1927-29; prof. of Marketing, U. of Newark, Newark, N.J., since 1929; dean Sch. Bus. Adminstrn. since 1936. Mem. Nat. Assn. Cost Accountants, Am. Marketing Assn., Phi Kappa Psi, Delta Sigma Pi, Phi Beta Kappa. Republican. Presbyn. Clubs: Lions, Torch (Newark). Home: Short Hills, N.J.

EASTMAN, Albert Sherman, university prof.; b. Charlotte, Vt., Jan. 24, 1882; s. Frank Leslie and Lillie Louisa (Sherman) E.; B.S., U. of Vt., Burlington, Vt., 1905, M.S., 1911; Ph.D., Princeton U., 1916; m. Katrina Lord, June 29, 1910. Instr. chemistry, Union Coll., Schenectady, N.Y., 1906-12; grad. asst., instr., fellow in chemistry, Princeton U., 1912-16; asst. prof. chemistry, U. of the South, Sewanee, Tenn., 1916-17; research chemist Hercules Powder Co., Wilmington, Del., 1917-19, Calco Chem. Co., Bound Brook, N.J., 1919-22; prof. chemistry since 1922 and dept. chairman since 1926, U. of Del., Newark. Mem. Am. Chem. Soc., Am. Assn. Univ. Profs., Soc. for Promotion Engring. Edn., Phi Kappa Phi, Kappa Alpha. Author articles on chem. subjects in tech. jours. and before tech. socs. Address: University of Delaware, Newark, Del.

EASTMAN, Nicholson Joseph, M.D.; b. Crawfordsville, Ind., Jan. 20, 1895; s. Thomas Barker and Ota Beale (Nicholson) E.; A.B., Yale U., 1916; M.D., Indiana U. Sch. of Medicine, 1921; m. Lo Retta Bernice Rutz, July 7, 1925; children—Elizabeth, Thomas Barker. Instr. obstetrics, Indiana U. Sch. of Medicine, 1922-24; asso. in obstetrics and gynecology, Peiping Union Med. Coll., 1924-28; instr. and asso. in obstetrics, Johns Hopkins U., 1928-33; prof. obstetrics and gynecology, Peiping Union Med. Coll., 1933-35; obstetrician-in-chief, Johns Hopkins Hosp., since 1935. Mem. Am. Gynecol. Soc., Am. Assn. Obstetricians, Gynecologists and Abdominal Surgeons, A.M.A., Soc. Exptl. Biology and Medicine, Sigma Xi. Republican. Methodist. Home: 111 Witherspoon Road. Office: Johns Hopkins Hospital, Baltimore, Md.

EASTWOOD, Sidney Kingman, engring. accountant; b. Owego Tioga Co., N.Y., Dec. 5, 1890; s. Charles Kirk and Helen Elizabeth (Kingman) E.; student Owego (N.Y.) Free Acad., 1906-09; M.E., Cornell U., 1913; studied U. of Pittsburgh, 1933-37; m. Mary Elma Lay, Nov. 19, 1917 (died Nov. 1918); 1 dau., Elizabeth Lay. Draftsman Day & Zimmerman, Phila., 1913-14, Lay & Eastwood, contractors, Owego, N.Y., 1914-16; clk., 1916-32, erecting dept. accountant Am. Bridge Co., Pittsburgh. Mem. Am. Soc. Mammalogists, Pa. Acad. Science, Am. Numismatic Assn., Am. Numismatic Society (N.Y.), Western Pa. Numismatic Soc. (v.p. 1938)), Engrs. Soc. of Western Pa., Torrey Bot. Club, Bot. Soc. of Western Pa., Pittsburgh Acad. Science and Art, S.A.R., Cornell Alumni Assn. of Western Pa., Sullivant Moss Soc., Phi Sigma. Republican. Episcopalian. Clubs: University, Pittsburgh Architectural (Pittsburgh). Contbr. to biol. jours. Lecturer on biol. and natural history subjects. Home: 301 S. Winebiddle Av. Office: 1625 Frick Bldg., Pittsburgh, Pa.

EATON, Alice Rhea, librarian; b. Venango Co., Pa.; d. Morris M. and Flora C. (McCrea) E.; ed. pub. sch., pvt. tutors, and High Sch., Titusville, Pa.; certificate Drexel Inst. Library Sch., 1908. Employed as asst. Buffalo Pub. Library, Buffalo, N.Y., 1908-09; cataloguer State Library of Pa., Harrisburg, 1909-10; first asst. Utica Pub. Library, Utica, N.Y., 1910-13; librarian Harrisburg Pub. Library, Harrisburg, Pa., since 1913. Lecturer Johns Hopkins, summer, 1927, 1931. Mem. Am. Library Assn., Pa. Library Assn. (pres. 1927). Republican. Mem. M.E. Church. Clubs: Civic, Art. Address: Harrisburg Pub. Library, Harrisburg, Pa.

EATON, Charles Aubrey, congressman; b. Nova Scotia, Can., Mar. 29, 1868; s. Stephen and Mary D. (Parker) E.; B.A., Acadia U., N.S., 1890, M.A., 1893; grad. Newton Theol. Instn., Mass., 1893; M.A., McMaster U., Toronto, Ont., 1896; (D.D., Baylor U., 1899, Acadia, 1907; LL.D., McMaster, 1916); m. Winifred Parlin, June 26, 1895; children—Marion Aubrey, Margaret Evelyn, Frances Winifred, Charles Aubrey, Mary Rose, Catharine Starr. Ordained Bapt. ministry, 1893; pastor First Ch., Natick, Mass., 1893-95, Bloor St. Ch., Toronto, 1895-1901, Euclid Av. Ch., Cleveland, 1901-09, Madison Av. Ch., New York, 1909-19; editor Leslie's Weekly, 1919-20. Expert in industrial relations. Sociol. editor Toronto Globe, 1896-1901; asso. editor Westminster, Toronto, 1899-1901; spl. Canadian corr. New York Tribune and Boston Transcript, 1897-1901; spl. corr. London Times. Head of nat. service sect. U.S. Shipping Bd. Emergency Fleet Corpn., Nov. 1917-Jan. 1919, head industrial relations dept. Nat. Lamp Works, Gen. Electric Co. Editor of Light, 1923—. Mem. 69th to 72d Congresses (1925-33), 4th N.J. Dist., and 73d to 76th Congresses (1933-41), 5th N.J. Dist. Home: Plainfield, N.J.

EATON, Charles C.; mem. law firm Eaton & Eaton. Office: Ariel Bldg., Erie, Pa.

EATON, George Outhit, orthopedic surgeon; b. Truro, N.S., Can., June 21, 1901; s. Dr. Foster Fitch and Laura (Margeson) E.; student Colchester Acad., Truro, N.S., 1915-18, Acadia U., Wolfville, N.S., 1918-19, Dalhousie U., Halifax, N.S., 1919-20; M.D., C.M., McGill U., Montreal, 1925; m. Catherine Elizabeth Johnson, Apr. 28, 1934; children—William Foster, David Rupert. Came to U.S., 1926, naturalized, 1935. Interne Royal Victoria Hosp., Montreal, 1925-26; resident Bon Secours Hosp., Baltimore, 1926-28; asst. resident Union Memorial Hosp., Baltimore, 1928-29, Cincinnati Gen. Hosp., 1929-31; in practice of orthopedic surgery, Baltimore, since 1931; mem. of firm Drs. Bennett & Johnson, Baltimore; on visiting staffs of Johns Hopkins, Children's, Union Memorial, Bon Secours, Provident hosps. and Church Home and Infirmary, Hosp. for Women of Md. Fellow A.M.A.; mem. Am. Acad. Orthopedic Surgeons. Democrat. Baptist. Clubs: University, Johns

Hopkins (Baltimore). Home: 3813 Fenchurch Rd. Office: 4 E. Madison St., Baltimore, Md.

EATON, Harry Burton, constrn. mgr.; b. Wilmington, Del., Dec. 11, 1884; s. George Reeves and Jennie (Windal) E.; student Wilmington High Sch., 1890-1902; Temple U. Law Sch., Phila., 1900-07; engring. by correspondence and at U. of Pa., 1905-08; m. Lydia Emma Talley, Jan. 7, 1911; children—Dorothy (Mrs. E. Leigh Johnson), Harry Burton, Ann Windal. Began as jr. engr., Am. Car and Foundry Co., 1909; contractor, Wilmington, Del., 1909-11; constrn. supt. E. I. duPont de Nemours & Co., Wilmington, 1911-12, head of estimating and order sect., 1912-20, asst. mgr. constr. div., 1920-28, mgr. constrn. div. since 1928. Loaned by duPont Co. to War Dept. in early part World War. Pres. Bd. of Pub. Edn., Wilmington, Del. Mem. Tau Beta Pi (Del. Coll. 1939). Mason. Clubs: Kiwanis, Wilmington Country, DuPont Country (Wilmington, Del.). Home: 2310 Boulevard. Office: DuPont Bldg., Wilmington, Del.

EATON, Herbert Nelson, hydraulic engr.; b. Auburn, Mass., Nov. 4, 1892; s. Arthur Adelbert and Mary Ellen (Hilton) E.; grad. Rindge Manual Training High Sch., Cambridge, Mass., 1911; A.B., Worcester (Mass.) Poly. Inst., 1916; A.M., Johns Hopkins, 1923; student Technische Hochschule, Karlsruhe, Germany, 1927-28, Charlottenburg, Germany, 1928; m. Mary Isabelle Mason, Nov. 28, 1917; children—Herbert Nelson, Janet Ann, Arthur Mason. Instr. in civil engring., Worcester (Mass.) Poly. Inst., 1916-17; engr. Nat. Bureau of Standards, Washington, D.C., 1918-26; engr. W.A. Baum Co., New York, 1926-27; John R. Freeman traveling scholar in hydraulics, 1927-28; hydraulic engr. Nat. Bureau of Standards since 1928; dir. Nat. Hydraulic Lab. Served as pvt., later 1st class sergt., Signal Corps, Sect. of Aerial Photography, U.S. Army, 1917-18. Mem. Am. Soc. M.E., A.A.A.S., Am. Geophys. Union, Washington Soc. of Engrs., Sigma Xi, Tau Beta Pi, Lambda Chi Alpha. Presbyterian. Author: Aircraft Instruments, 1926. Home: 3 E. Inverness Driveway, Chevy Chase, Md. Office: Nat. Bureau of Standards, Washington, D.C.

EATON, Paul Burns, prof. of mech. engring.; b. Scranton, Pa., May 31, 1888; s. Herbert H. and Minnie (Burns) E.; M.E., Cornell U., 1911; m. Hannah Wilkins, Sept. 9, 1925; 1 son, John Paul. Engr. Allis-Chalmers Mfg. Co., Scranton, Pa., 1911-12, Canadian Tap & Die Co., Galt, Ont., 1912-13, Dominion Bridge Co., Lachine, P.Q., 1913; instr. Sibley Coll., Cornell U., 1911-14; head dept. of mech. engring., Chinese Govt. Engring. Coll., Tangshan, China, 1915-18; engr. U.S. Shipping Bd., Emergency Fleet Corpn., Baltimore, Md., 1918-20; instr. Carnegie Inst. Tech., 1919; instr. mech. engring. and machine design, Cornell U., 1920-23; prof. of mech. engring., Pa. State Coll., 1924; head dept. of mech. engring., Lafayette Coll., since 1932. Mem. Am. Soc. Mech. Engrs. (speaker of local sects.), Am. Assn. Univ. Profs., Soc. for Promotion Engring. Edn., Theta Xi, Pi Tau Sigma, Tau Beta Pi, Engineers' Club of Lehigh Valley (pres. 1937), Kiwanis Club. Decorated Chia Ho for distinguished service by Chinese govt., 1918. Author: Machine Design, 1926. Home: 719 Cattell St., Easton, Pa.

EAVENSON, Howard Nicholas, mining engr.; b. July 15, 1873; s. Alben Taylor and Susan (Bean) E.; Public and Friends' Central School, Phila., Pa.; B.S., Swarthmore Coll., 1892, C.E. 1895; Dr. Engring. Univ. of Pittsburgh, 1928; m. Ada J. Daugherty, Sept. 20, 1898. Engring. work in Va., N.J., and with U.S. Lake Survey, 1892-97; with H. C. Frick Coke Co., and Allied cos. as div. engr., asst. chief engr., chief engr., Uniontown, Pa., 1897-1902; chief engr. U.S. Coal and Coke Co., Gary, W.Va., 1902-20; consulting engr. since 1920, now head firm Eavenson, Alford & Auchmuty; pres. and dir. Clover Splint Coal Co., vice-pres. and dir. Boone County Coal Corpn., Appalachian Coals, Inc., West Va. Coal & Coke Corpn., Pittsburgh Coal Co. Mem. Am. Soc. C.E., Am. Inst. Mining and Metall. Engrs., pres. (1934), Am. Soc. Testing Materials, Delta Upsilon, Tau Beta Pi. Republican. Mem. Society of Friends. Clubs: University, Duquesne. Author: Coal Through the Ages; The Pittsburgh Coal Bed—Its Early History and Development. Home: 4411 Bayard St. Office: Koppers Bldg., Pittsburgh, Pa.

EBELING, Herman Louis, emeritus prof. of Greek; b. Catonsville, Md., May 10, 1857; s. George Wilhelm and Marie (Keidel) E.; prep. edn., Overlea Home Sch. (for boys), Catonsville, Md.; A.B., Johns Hopkins, 1882, Ph.D., 1891; student Univ. of Berlin, Germany, 1894-95; also at U. of Bonn and U. of Gottigen, 1895; m. Emma Sophia Stakeman, Dec. 21, 1896; children—Karl Wilhelm, Elsa Stakeman. Clerk in leaf tobacco business, 1873-77; teacher Overlea Home sch., Catonsville, Md., 1877-79; instr. in Greek and Latin, German Theol. Sem., Bloomfield, N.J., 1882-86; prof. of Greek, Miami (O.) U., 1891-99; acting prof. of Greek, Haverford (Pa.) Coll., 1901-02, acting prof. of Latin, 1902-03; asst. prof. of Greek and Latin, Hamilton Coll., Clinton, N.Y., 1903-11; prof. of Greek and asst. in Latin, Goucher Coll., 1911-33, prof. emeritus of Greek since 1933; taught in pvt. schools between coll. positions; also pvt. tutor to boys. University scholar Johns Hopkins, 1889, fellow in Greek, 1890-91. Home: 329 Hawthorn Rd., Baltimore, Md.

EBELING, Karl Wilhelm, physician; b. Oxford, O., Oct. 28, 1897; s. Herman Louis and Emma S. (Stakeman) E.; A.B., Johns Hopkins U., 1919; M.D., Johns Hopkins U. Med. Sch., 1923; m. Elizabeth W. Sharp, June 25, 1923; children—Alice Ellen, Elizabeth Ann. Interne, Brooklyn (N.Y.) State Hosp., 1923-24, Phila. Gen. Hosp., 1924-25; resident, St. Christophers Hosp., Phila., 1925-26; asst. chief resident; Phila. Hosp. for Contagious Diseases, 1926-27. Engaged in gen. practice of medicine at Baltimore since 1927, specializing in pediatrics since 1927; mem. med. staff, St. Agnes, Bon Secours, Union Memorial hosps., all of Baltimore. Served in S.A.T.C., 1918. Licentiate Am. Bd. Pediatrics. Fellow Am. Acad. Pediatries, Am. Med. Assn.; mem. Med. and Chirurg. Soc. of Md., Baltimore City Med. Soc., Phi Beta Kappa. Republican. Lutheran. Home: 5200 Tilbury Way. Office: Medical Arts Bldg., Baltimore, Md.

EBERHARD, William N.; pres. F. Hersch Hardware Co.; mem. exec. com. Allentown Nat. Bank. Home: 1527 Turner St. Office: 825 Hamilton St., Allentown, Pa.

EBERHARDT, Fred L., machinery mfr.; b. Newark, N.J., Feb. 27, 1868; s. Ulrich and Emeline Taylor (Hudson) E.; ed. grammar and private school, Newark, and Newark Tech. Sch.; m. Martha Lou Boals, Oct. 16, 1895; children—Ruth Boals, Frederick Gordon, Eleanor Hudson. Began as gen. machine apprentice, 1881; with Gould & Eberhardt, mfrs. of machine tools, shaping machines, automatic gear cutting machines, Newark, N.J., since 1901; pres. and gen. mgr. since 1927; advisory dir. Fidelity Union Trust Co. Vice-pres. bd. of trustees Newark Tech. Sch. and Newark Coll. of Engring. Republican. Methodist. Mason (K.T., Shriner). Club: Newark Athletic. Home: 629 Prospect St., Maplewood, N.J., Office: 433 Fabyan Place, Newark, N.J.

EBERHARTER, Herman Peter, congressman; b. Pittsburgh, Pa., April 29, 1892; s. Jacob and Louisa (Ramer) E.; LL.B., Duquesne U., 1925; m. Emma A. Naughton, Jan. 13, 1934; 1 son, Herman Peter. Admitted to Pa. bar, 1925, and practiced since in Pittsburgh. Mem. Pa. Ho. of Rep., 1935-36; mem. 75th and 76th Congress (1937-41), 32d Pa. Dist. Served as pvt. 20th Inf., U.S.A., World War; capt., O.R.C. Mem. Allegheny Co. Bar Assn. Democrat. Catholic. Home: 3408 Parkview Av. Office: 1306 Berger Bldg., Pittsburgh, Pa.

EBERLEIN, Harold Donaldson, author; b. Columbia, Pa.; ed. Episcopal Acad., Philadelphia, Pa.; B.A., U. of Pa. Author: Colonial Homes of Philadelphia and Its Neighborhood (with H. M. Lippincott), 1912; The Practical Book of Period Furniture (with Abbot McClure), 1914; The Architecture of Colonial America, 1915; The Practical Book of American Antiques with Abbot McClure), 1916; The Practical Book of Interior Decoration (with Abbot McClure and E. S. Holloway), 1919; Villas of Florence and Tuscany, 1920; Architectural Details of Florence and Tuscany (with Oliver Reagan), 1922; Manor Houses and Historic Homes of the Hudson Valley, 1924; The Smaller English House of the Later Renaissance (with A. E. Richardson, F.S.A.), 1925; The Practical Book of Chinaware (with Roger Wearne Ramsdell), 1925; The English Inn Past and Present (with A. E. Richardson, F.S.A.), 1925; Small Manor Houses and Farmsteads in France (with Roger Wearne Ramsdell), 1926; The Smaller Houses and Gardens of Versailles (with Leigh French, Jr.), 1926; The Practical Book of Italian, Spanish and Portuguese Furniture (with Roger Wearne Ramsdell), 1927; Manor Houses and Historic Homes of Long Island and Staten Island, 1928; Little Known England, 1930; Down the Tiber and Up to Rome (with Goeffrey Marks and Frank Wallis), 1930; The Rabelaisian Princess (A biography of the sister-in-law to Louis XIV), 1931; Remodelling and Adapting the Small House (with D. G. Tarpley), 1933; The Practical Book of Garden Structure and Design (with Cortlandt Van Dyke Hubbard), 1937; Colonial Interiors, With Federal and Greek Revival (with Cortlandt Van Dyke Hubbard), 1937. Address: 2125 Locust St., Philadelphia, Pa.; and Royal Societies Club, St. James's St., London, England.

EBERLY, Isaac C.; pres. and treas. Hosiery Mills, Inc. Address: Lancaster Av. and Noble St., Reading, Pa.

EBERT, Charles E., transportation official; b. Bucyrus, O., June 18, 1894; s. Charles M. and Margaret Elizabeth E.; student Bucyrus pub. schs. and Columbus high schs.; m. Celia Little, Aug. 30, 1918. V.p. of finance Phila. Rapid Transit Co. since 1931. Home: 223 Hamilton Road, Merion, Pa. Office: Mitten Bldg., Philadelphia, Pa.

EBREY, Glen O(gle); chief chemist Pennzoil Co. Address: Oil City, Pa.

EBY, Frank Hobart, univ. prof.; b. Lancaster Co., Pa., Aug. 12, 1896; s. Phares E. and Salinda (Hershey) E.; Ph.G., Temple U. Sch. of Pharmacy, 1919, Pharm.D., 1921; m. Dorothy M. Keller, July 28, 1921; 1 son, Frank Hobart, Jr. Began as apprentice pharmacist, 1912; instr. botany and pharmacognosy, Temple U., 1919-27, asst. professor, 1927-29, prof. since 1929; cons. pharmacognocist since 1935. Served as pharmacist's mate, U.S.N., 1917-18. Boy Scout officer since 1926. Mem. Am. Pharm. Assn. (pres. Phila. branch 1935), Pa. Pharm. Assn., Pa. Acad. Sci., Am. Assn. Univ. Profs., Am. Legion, Blue Key, Kappa Psi. Republican. Presbyn. Mason. Home: 109 Fairview Rd., Springfield, Pa.

ECHOLS, Angus B., dir. E. I. du Pont de Nemours & Co. since 1927, v.p. in charge of finances since 1930. Office: du Pont Bldg., Wilmington, Del.

ECHOLS, Charles Patton, army officer; b. Huntsville, Ala., Sept. 6, 1867; s. William Holding and Mary Beirne (Patton) E.; grad. U.S. Mil. Acad., 1891; unmarried. Commd. additional 2d lt. engrs., June 12, 1891; 2d lt., Oct. 4, 1894; 1st lt., Jan. 6, 1896; in command of A Co. U.S. Engrs. in 3d expdn. to Philippines in War with Spain, 1898; asso. prof. mathematics, U.S. Mil. Acad., Nov. 1898, prof. since 1904; on detached service visiting foreign schools, July 1905-June 1906; lt. col., 1904; col., 1914; observer with Allied Armies in France, July-Sept. 1918; retired from active service Sept. 1931. Fellow A.A.A.S.; mem. Math. Assn. America, U. of Va. Alumni Assn., Soc. Carabao. Clubs: Century, New York Southern Society, Army and Navy (Washington). Home: 46 Lydecker St., Englewood, N.J.

ECHOLS, Leonard Sidney, ex-congressman; b. Madison, W.Va., Oct. 30, 1871; s. George A. and Cartha Grace (Atkins) E.; grad. Commercial Coll. of Ky. U., Lexington, Ky., 1894, Concord Normal Sch., Athens, W.Va., 1898; LL.B., Southern Normal U., Huntingdon, Tenn.,

ECK, Lee, sch. administr.; b. Lebanon Co., Pa., May 11, 1904; s. Eugene Allison and Mary Lovinia (Weigley) E.; ed. State Teachers Coll., Kutztown, Pa., 1920-22; A.B., Albright Coll. 1926; M.S., Lebanon Valley Coll., 1931; grad. study, Pa. State Coll., 1934, N.Y. Univ., 1936; m. Mary Elizabeth Gecks, of St. Louis, Mo., June 29, 1926. Employed as prin. pub. schs., Tullytown, Pa., 1922-23; teacher pub. schs., Richland, 1923-26, supervising prin. pub. and high schs. since 1926. Served as mem. council Richland Borough, 1929-37; treas. borough, 1929-31, pres., 1936-37; Dist. chmn. Court of Honor, Boy Scouts of America. Dir. Palmyra-Lebanon Co. Auto Club, Inc. Mem. Am. Assn. Sch. Adminstrs., Pa. State Edn. Assn. Mem. Reformed Ch. Mason (K.T., Shriner), Pythian. Traveled in Europe and N.A.; lecturer, motion picture travelogues. Home: Richland, Pa.

ECKELMANN, Luis Enrique, chemist, tech. exec.; b. Ponce, Puerto Rico, May 17, 1895; s. Luis B. and Herminia Fournier (del Toro) E.; B.Sc., Brooklyn Poly. Inst., 1916; unmarried. Began career as chemist, 1916; mgr. Metal Finishing Div., Pyrene Mfg. Co., Newark, N.J. since 1920; consultant, Otis Elevator Co., Parker Rust Proof Co., Detroit, Mich., Pyrene Co. Ltd., England; dir. Udylite Corpn., Detroit, Mich.; vice-pres. and dir. Bright Nickel Corpn., Detroit, Mich. Mem. Am. Inst. Chem. Engrs., Am. Electrochem. Soc., Pi Kappa Phi. Republican. Roman Catholic. Club: Chemists (New York). Home: 65 Montague St., Brooklyn, N.Y. Office: 560 Belmont Av., Newark, N.J.

ECKELS, John Perry, lawyer; b. Cambridge Springs, Pa.; s. Clark D. and Mary Ann (Perry) E.; student Cambridge Springs (Pa.) High Sch.; LL.B., De Paul U., 1913; m. Leah Crandall, June 16, 1915; 1 son, John Crandall. Admitted to bar, 1913, and since practiced in Crawford Co., Pa. Mem. Pa. Ho. of Rep., 1937-38, and re-elected for 1938-39. Mem. Pa. State Bar Assn., Crawford Co. Bar Assn., Phi Alpha Delta. Awarded 2d senior prize, De Paul U. Law Sch. Republican. Methodist Episcopalian. Mason. Clubs: Iroquois, Meadville Country (Meadville, Pa.). Home: R.D. 1, Conneaut Lake, Pa. Office: 353 Center St., Meadville, Pa.

ECKERT, Charles R., ex-congressman; b. Pittsburgh, Pa., Jan. 20, 1868; ed. Piersols Acad. and Geneva Coll., Beaver Falls, Pa.; studied law pvtly. Admitted to Pa. bar, 1894, and since practiced at Beaver; mem. 74th and 75th Congress (1935-39), 26th Pa. Dist. Democrat. Home: Beaver, Pa.*

ECKERT, Clyde J., lumber wholesaler; b. Ridgway, Pa., Sept. 5, 1887; s. George and Kate (Walker) E.; students Canisius Coll., Buffalo, N.Y., Villa Nova, Phila.; m. Daisy M. Spence, Oct. 7, 1907; 1 son, Donald Thomas; m. 2nd, Marguerite Riehl, Mar. 27, 1927. In employ Carnegie Mill and Lumber Co., Carnegie, Pa., 1911-12; salesman American Lumber and Mfg. Co., Pittsburgh, 1912-13; salesman, later vice pres. Acorn Lumber Co., Pittsburgh, 1913-38. Republican. Roman Catholic. Clubs: Erie, Kahkwa (Erie, Pa.); Cleveland Country (Cleveland, O.). Home: 944 W. 9th St., Erie, Pa.

ECKERT, Frank Earl, oil and gas operator; b. Ridgway, Pa.; Dec. 18, 1894; s. Henry and Carrie (Fox) E.; Petroleum Engr., U. of Pittsburgh, 1919; m. Ruth Anna Ross, Sept. 10, 1923; 1 son, Frank Earl. Engr. and geologist for Ralph E. Davis, Pittsburgh, 1921-26; mgr. Hanley & Bird, Bradford, Pa., since 1926; pres. Lawsonham Oil & Gas Co. since 1932. Mem. Am. Petroleum Inst. (chmn. Eastern Div. 1938); Am. Assn. Petroleum Geologists, Am. Gas Assn. Clubs: Bradford, Pennhills Country. Home: 666 E. Main St. Office: 28 Kennedy St., Bradford, Pa.

ECKERT, William Henry, lawyer; b. Pittsburgh, Pa., Mar. 27, 1900; s. William G. and Matilda (Nickel) E.; B.S., U. of Pittsburgh Sch. of Econs., 1921; LL.B., U. of Pittsburgh Sch. of Law, 1924; m. Josephine B. Gibson, July 13, 1934; children—Josephine G., Dorothy L. Admitted to Pa. bar, 1924 and since engaged in gen. practice of law at Pittsburgh; mem. firm Smith, Buchanan and Ingersoll since 1930; instr. law, U. of Pittsburgh Law Sch. since 1924, prof. of law since 1929; dir. Crafton Nat. Bank. Mem. Crafton Borough Sch. Bd., Zoning Appeal Bd. Dir. Gumbert Industrial Sch. for Girls. Mem. Am., Pa., and Allegheny County bar assns. Republican. United Presbyn. Mason (K.T.). Clubs: Metropolitan, Chartiers Heights Country. Home: 99 Union Av., Crafton. Office: 1025 Union Trust Bldg., Pittsburgh, Pa.

ECKFELDT, Howard, prof. of mining engring.; b. Conshohocken, Pa., Oct. 17, 1873; s. Jacob B. and Jeannette Rose (Latch) E.; grad. Conshohocken (Pa.) High Sch., 1891; B.S. in metallurgy, Lehigh U., Bethlehem, Pa., 1895; E.M., 1896; m. Catalina Trousselle, Oct. 3, 1898; children—Jacob T., Emily C. (Mrs. Omar V. Greene), Jeannette M. (Mrs. Harcourt Black). Mining engr. Mazapil Copper Co., Mexico, 1896-1900; instr. mining engring., Lehigh U., Bethlehem, Pa., 1900-02, asst. prof., 1902-04, prof. and head of dept. since 1904 (absent on leave for engring. work in Mexico, 1910-11); dir. Wissamaking Corpn., real estate, Bethlehem. Chmn. 1st (1938) and 2d (1939) Annual Anthracite Conf. of Lehigh U. Served as instr. S.A.T.C. Lehigh U., during World War. Mem. Am. Inst. Mining and Metall. Engrs., Soc. for Promotion Engring. Edn., Sigma Xi, Tau Beta Pi, Alpha Tau Omega. Republican. Presbyterian. Club: Engineers of Lehigh Valley (Bethlehem, Pa.). Home: 438 Seneca St., Bethlehem, Pa.

ECKHARDT, Engelhardt August, physicist; b. Cedarburg, Wis., Aug. 11, 1888; s. Henry J. T. and Dorothea (Ammermann) E.; B.S., U. of Pa., 1908, Ph.D., 1912; Harrison research fellow, Göttingen, Germany, 1912-13; m. Eliza Reed Hunt, July 31, 1916; children—Douglas Lohr, Robert Hunt, David Carol. Instr., later asst. prof. physics, U. of Pa.; 1908-17; asst. to sr. physicist, Nat. Bur. Standards, Washington, D.C., 1917-25; asst. chief research dept. Marland Oil Co., 1925-28 inclusive; asst. dir. Gulf Research Development Co., 1929—. Lecturer in geology, U. of Pittsburgh, June 1917 to close of war. Mil. research, Bur. of Standards, June 1917 to close of war. Fellow A.A.A.S., Am. Phys. Soc., Physical Soc. (London); Acoustical Society of America; member Washington Acad. Sciences, Chamber of Commerce Pittsburgh, Am. Petroleum Inst., Seismol. Soc. of America, Am. Assn. of Petroleum Geologists, Soc. of Petroleum Geophysicists, Franklin Inst., Am. Geophys. Union, Am. Inst. Mining and Metall. Engrs., Deutsche Geophysikalische Gesellschaft, Phi Beta Kappa, Sigma Xi. Club: University (Pittsburgh). Developed methods and apparatus for sound measurements, ranging by sound and radio, longitude determinations by radio, projectile chronographs, other ballistic research instruments and gravity and seismograph instruments for geophysical exploration. Contbr. to building and auditorium accoustics and geophysics. Home: 1520 Shady Av., Pittsburgh, Pa.

ECKHARDT, Henry P.; pastor St. Andrews Evang. Lutheran Ch. Home: 318 Morewood Av., Pittsburgh, Pa.

ECKLES, Robert Arthur, architect; b. New Castle, Pa., Mar. 8, 1898; s. William George and Nina (Henderson) E.; student Amherst (Mass.) Coll., 1916-18; A.B. in architecture, Mass. Inst. Tech., 1921; m. Margaret Gallinger, June 1, 1922; children—Eleanor, William George II. Asso. with W. G. Eckles Co., architects, New Castle, Pa. since 1921, mem. firm since 1923; dir. Dollar Savings Bldg. & Loan Assn. Served in U.S.A. during World War; mem. Officers Res. Mem. bd. New Castle Community Chest; trustee New Castle Y.W.C.A., Almira Home; dir. Jameson Memorial Hosp. Mem. Am. Inst. Architects, Delta Upsilon. Republican. United Presbyterian. Mason (32°). Club: Rotary (past pres.), New Castle Field (New Castle, Pa.). Home: 501 Winter Av. Office: Lawrence Savings & Trust Bldg., New Castle, Pa.

EDDY, Henry Stephens, artist; b. Rahway, N.J., Dec. 31, 1878; s. Charles and Edith Harriet (Stephens) E.; student Art Students League, New York; pupil of Volk, Cox, Twachtman, Alphonse Mucha, George Elmer Browne; m. Catherine Day Cleveland, April 17, 1901; 1 dau., Catherine Edith (Mrs. Norman laCour Olsen). Represented in collections of Milwaukee (Wis.) Art Inst., Reid Memorial Library, Passaic, N.J., Arnot Art Gallery, Elmira, N.Y., Lotus Club, N.Y. City, etc. Mem. Artists Fellowship, Artists Fund Soc., Provincetown, Mass.) Art Assn., Guild Am. Painters, Allied Artists of America, Westfield (N.J.) Art Assn. (trustee), Am. Artists Museums, Plainfield Art Assn., Philadelphia Art Alliance, Am. Fed. Arts, The Art Centre of the Oranges, New Haven Paint and Clay Club. Clubs: Salmagundi, Lions, Nantucket Yacht. Home: Springfield Rd., Westfield, N.J.

EDDY, Milton Walker, coll. prof.; b. Calcutta, India, Dec. 6, 1884; s. Thomas Barton and Sarah (Walker) E.; B.S., Northwestern U., 1910, M.S., 1912; Ph.D., U. of Pa., 1928; m. Rebecca West Reiley, Dec. 27, 1911; children—Lois Barton, Frances Du Val, Jeanette Hulet. Instr. zoology, Pa. State Coll., 1910-11, head of dept., 1912-18; asst. chief engr. Atlas Powder Co., 1918; associated with U.S.P.H.S., 1920-21; prof. biology and head of dept., Dickinson Coll., since 1921; visiting prof. U. of Pa., summer, 1931. Mason. Writer various articles on respiration, blood rhythm and hair classification. Home: 249 W. Louther St., Carlisle, Pa.

EDDY, William Woodbridge, prof. of history; b. New Rochelle, N.Y., Feb. 23, 1889; s. Robert Condit and Cora (Barker) E.; A.B., Princeton, 1911; A.M., Harvard, 1916; unmarried. Teacher, Am. Univ. of Beirut, 1911-13; instr. history and politics, Princeton, 1919-20; instr. of history, U. of Wash., 1920-23; instr. of history, Lafayette Coll., Easton, Pa., 1923-31, asso. prof. since 1931. Served in Coast Arty., U.S. Army, 1918. Mem. Am. Hist. Assn., Am. Assn. Univ. Profs. Democrat. Presbyterian. Clubs: Princeton (New York); Faculty (Easton). Contbr. to Jour. Modern History. Home: 401 High St., Easton, Pa.

EDELMAN, Samuel, pub. relations counsel; b. Phila., Pa., Feb. 12, 1885; s. Jacob and Reba (Leiken) E.; ed. at Central High School, Philadelphia, and United States Mil. Academy; m. Etta Krasa, July 1, 1917; children—Reba Irwell, Elizabeth Sonia. Entered Am. Consular Service, 1909, and successively stationed at Constantinople, Turkey, 1909-12; Jerusalem, Palestine, 1912-15, Aleppo, Syria, 1915-16, Damascus, Syria, 1916-17, Geneva, Switzerland, 1917-19; resigned, 1919; v.p. Charles J. Webb Fgn. Corpn., Phila., Pa., 1919-21, bond broker, 1921-31; receiver Northern Central Trust Co., Manheim Trust Co., Phila., Pa., 1931-35; consultant to banks in capacity pub. relations counsel, Phila., since 1935. Intelligence duty, U.S. Army and State Dept. in Switzerland and War Zone, during World War; now maj., Mil. Intelligence Dept., U.S. Army R.C., Pres. Alliance Israelite Universelle, Phila. Branch. Mem. Omega Pi Alpha. Republican. Jewish religion. Address: 911 N. 64th St., Philadelphia, Pa.

EDER, Charles E., pastor Grace Episcopal Ch. Address: 224 E. Gowen Av., Mt. Airy, Philadelphia, Pa.

EDGCOMB, Ervin Roberts, lumber wholesaler and importer; b. Knoxville, Pa., Feb. 27, 1898; s. Alfred E. and Ada (Roberts) E.; B.S. in Econs., U. of Pa., 1920; m. Ruth Evelyn Blackwell, June 19, 1937. Began as sec. to father, 1920-22; sec. and purchasing agt. Insular Lumber Co., Phila., Pa., 1922-33, sec. and sales mgr., 1933-36; sec. and treas. John A. Hunter Hardwood Corpn., importers tropical hardwoods, New York City, since 1938; sec., treas. and dir. Embreeville Timber Co. Mem. Lambda Chi Alpha. Republican. Methodist.

EDGE, James B. D.; v.p. and dir. E. I. du Pont de Nemours & Co. Home: Kennett Square. Office: du Pont Bldg., Wilmington, Del.

EDGE, Walter Evans, diplomat; b. Phila., Nov. 20, 1873; s. William and Mary (Evans) E.; ed. pub. schs.; m. Lady Lee Phillips, June 10, 1907 (died July 14, 1915); m. 2d, Camilla Loyall Ashe Sewall, Bath, Me., Dec. 9, 1922. Began as printer's "devil" on Atlantic Review, Atlantic City, N.J.; later established a nat. and internat. adv. agency; was propr. Atlantic City Daily Press, and Atlantic City Evening Union, also identified with banking and other lines of business. Journal clk., N.J. Senate, 1897-99; sec. of senate, 1901-04; Rep. presidential elector, 1904; delegate at large Rep. Nat. Conv., Chicago, 1920 and 32, Cleveland, 1924 and 36, Kansas City, Mo., 1928; member N.J. Assembly, 1910 (Rep. leader), Senate, 2 terms, 1911-16 (Rep. leader 1912, pres. 1915); was chmn. economy and efficiency commn. and a leader in securing passage of workmen's compensation bill, state budget system bill and central purchasing bureau bill; elected gov. of N.J. for term 1917-20; resigned, 1919, to take seat in U.S. Senate, term 1919-25, re-elected for term, 1925-31, resigned, A. E. and P. to France, 1929-1933. With Secretary of Treasury Mellon negotiated Franco-Am. Accord of July 6, 1931. Served as lieut. Co. F, 4th New Jersey Vol. Infantry, Spanish-Am. War; later capt. Co. L, 3d Regt. N.J.N.G.; mem. staffs of Govs. Murphy and Stokes; was lt. col. and chief ordnance dept., staff of Maj. Gen. C. Edward Murray, N.J.N.G. Episcopalian. Clubs: Union League (Phila.); Brook, Union League (New York). Home: Ventnor, N.J.*

EDGECOMBE, Arthur Clarence, prof. civil engring.; b. St. John, N.B., Can., Oct. 7, 1896; s. Arthur Clarence and Mabel (Estey) E.; came to U.S., 1919, naturalized, 1931; M.Sc. in C.E., U. of N.B., Can., 1919; M.Sc. in C.E., U. of Pittsburgh, 1931; m. Carolyn M. Brown, June 1, 1921; chidren—David Allison, Carolyn Allison. Employed as resident engr., Highway Dept. State of Del., 1919-21; prof. civil engring. and head dept. of engring., Geneva Coll., Beaver Falls, Pa. since 1921. Served with C.E.F. during World War. Mem. Bd. of Trade, Beaver Falls, Pa. Mem. Soc. for Promotion Engring. Edn. Republican. Episcopalian. Club: Beaver Valley Country (Beaver Falls, Pa.). Home: 3201 6th Av., Beaver Falls, Pa.

EDGERLY, Beatrice, artist, writer; b. Washington, D.C.; d. Webster and Edna Reid (Boyts) Edgerly; student Gunston Hall, Washington, D.C., 1906-10, Sch. of Industrial Art, Trenton, N.J., 1910, Corcoran Gallery Sch., Washington, D.C., 1911-16, Pa. Acad. of Fine Arts, Phila., 1916-20; m. J. Havard Macpherson, Oct. 28, 1922; children—John Havard, Donald Edgerly. Illustrating and ink drawings for books and mags. since 1925. Exhibited: Corcoran Gallery, Washington, D.C.; Pa. Acad. of Fine Arts, Phila.; Nat. Acad., New York, etc. Awarded Cooper Prize for oil painting, Nat. Assn. of Women Painters and Sculptors Exhbn., New York, 1937; prize for oil painting and hon. mention, Tucson Fine Arts Assn., Tucson, Ariz., 1938. Mem. Nat. Assn. of Women Painters and Sculptors, Phila. Art Alliance, Pa. Acad. of Fine Arts (Fellow), Mystic (Conn.) Art Assn., Am. Artists Professional League. Address: Bushkill, Pike Co., Pa.

EDGETT, Eugene Albert, lawyer; b. Baltimore, Md., Sept. 28, 1897; s. Albert Roswell and Ada Mai (Maloy) E.; A.B., Johns Hopkins U., 1917; LL.B., U. of Md. Law Sch., Baltimore, 1920; m. Priscilla Ann Streett, Jan. 4, 1921; children—Sophia Priscilla, Eugene Albert, William Maloy, Ann Streett. Admitted to Md. bar, 1919, and since in gen. practice of law at Baltimore; asst. state's atty. of Baltimore City, 1923-26, asst. city solicitor, Baltimore, 1931. Served as 2d lt. F.A., U.S. Army during World War. Mem. Md. Bar Assn., Baltimore City Bar Assn., Phi Kappa Sigma. Democrat. Episcopalian. Club: University (Baltimore). Home: 4301 Keswick Rd. Office: Central Savings Bank Bldg., Baltimore, Md.

EDISON, Charles, asst. sec. U.S. Navy; b. Llewellyn Park, West Orange, N.J., Aug. 3, 1890; s. Thomas Alva and Mina (Miller) E.; prep. edn., Carteret Acad. (Orange, N.J.), Hotchkiss Sch. (Lakeville, Conn.); Mass. Inst. Tech., 1909-13; m. Carolyn Hawkins, Mar. 27, 1918. Apptd. asst. sec. U.S. Navy by President Roosevelt. Pres. and dir. Thomas A. Edison, Inc., including Edison Storage Battery Supply Co., Edison Cement Corpn., Ediphone Corpn., Thomas A. Edison of Canada, Ltd.; dir. Thomas A. Edison, Ltd., London. Trustee Newark Museum. During World War directed manufacture of war materials and was chmn. West Orange Liberty Loan Organization. Mem. Delta Psi. Clubs: Essex County Country, Rock Spring Country; Army Navy Country (Arlington, Va.); Metropolitan, 1925 F Street (Washington, D.C.); Alumni Assn. of Mass. Inst. of Tech. (Cambridge, Mass.); St. Anthony, Boston and Essex (Newark, N.J.). Home: Llewellyn Park, West Orange, N.J. Office: West Orange, N.J.

EDISON, Theodore M(iller), research engr.; b. West Orange, N.J., July 10, 1898; s. Thomas Alva and Mina (Miller) E.; B.S., Mass. Inst. Tech., 1923; m. Ann(a) M. Osterhout, April 25, 1925. Employed in various positions with Thomas A. Edison, Inc., West Orange, N.J. since 1924; research engr. and pres. Calibron Products, Inc., West Orange, N.J., since 1931. Clubs: Orange Camera, Rock Spring (West Orange). Home: West Orange, N.J.

EDMISTON, Andrew, congressman; b. Weston, W.Va., Nov. 13, 1892; s. Matthew and Ella Blair (Jackson) E.; ed. Friends Select School, Washington, D.C., 1900-08, Ky. Mil. Inst. Lyndon, Ky., 1908-12; student U. of W.Va., 1912-14; m. Merle Williams, Apr. 21, 1920; 1 dau., Ann Bland. Began as a farmer, 1915; editor Weston (W.Va.) Democrat, since 1920; mayor of Weston, 1924-26; state chairman Democratic Executive Committee, 1928-32; member 73d to 76th Congresses (1933-41), 3d West Virginia District; sec. and treas. C. A. Borchet Glass Co.; dir. Weston Nat. Bank. Served as 2d lt. U.S.A., with A.E.F. Awarded D.S.C. and Order of Purple Heart. Mem. Am. Legion, Vets. of Foreign wars. Democrat. Episcopalian. Mason, Moose. Home: Weston, W.Va.

EDMONDS, Franklin Spencer, lawyer; b. Phila., Mar. 28, 1874; s. Henry R. and Catharine Ann (Huntzinger) E.; A.B., Central High Sch., Phila., 1891, A.M., 1896; Ph.B., U. of Pa., 1893, LL.B., 1903; Andrew D. White fellow, Cornell, 1894-95; LL.D., Juniata Coll., 1929, Ursinus Coll., 1932; m. Elise Julia, d. Hon. Abraham M. and Julia L. Beitler, Dec. 6, 1909. Asst. sec. Am. Soc. for Extension of University Teaching, 1893-94; instr. history, 1895-97, asst. prof. polit. science, 1897-1902, prof. polit. science, 1902-04, hon. lecturer in polit. science since 1904, Central High Sch., Phila.; prof. law, Swarthmore (Pa.) Coll., 1904-10; in practice of law, Phila., 1904—; mem. law firm Edmonds, Obermayer & Rebmann. Solicitor for Pa. Museum of Art. Editor The Teacher, 1898-1901. Candidate for Select Council on City Party ticket, 1905; receiver of taxes, 1907; chmn. City Com. of City Party, 1905; mem. Lincoln Party State Com., 1905, 1906; chmn. 2 City Party co. convs. Mem. Bd. Pub. Edn., Phila., 1906-11; chmn. citizens' campaign com. of Washington party (Progressive), 1912; mem. Pa. House of Reps., 1921, 23 and 1925; chmn. Pa. Tax Commn., 1924-27; pres. Nat. Tax Assn., 1932-33; mem. State Senate, from Montgomery Co., since 1938. Republican. Pres. Ednl. Club of Phila., 1900-03, Phila. Teachers' Assn., 1903-05; mem. Am. Econ. Assn., Am. Hist. Assn., Am. Polit. Science Assn., Am. Acad. Polit. and Social Science, Am. Bar Assn., Hist. Soc. of Pa., Am. Statistical Assn., Beta Theta Pi and Phi Delta Phi frats. Clubs: Art, Union League, City, Franklin Inn, Lawyers, Schoolmen's, Church. Author: Century's Progress in Education (pamphlet), 1899; History of Central High School of Philadelphia, 1838-1902, 1902; Life of Ulysses S. Grant (Am. Crisis Biographies); Reciprocity in State Inheritance Taxation (pamphlet). Organizer, and head of Savoie leave area, France, 1918; head of soldiers' leave dept. and of legal dept., Y.M.C.A., A.E.F., 1918-19. Home: Whitemarsh, Montgomery Co., Pa. Office: 111 S. 15th St., Philadelphia, Pa.

EDMONDS, George Washington, ex-congressman; b. Pottsville, Pa., February 22, 1864; s. Henry R. and Catherine Ann (Huntzinger) E.; Central High Sch., Phila.; Ph.G., Phila. Coll. of Pharmacy, 1885; m. Julia H. Riley, June 14, 1899. In retail drug business until 1887; an organizer of Black Diamond Coal Co., 1887; subsequently partner in coal firms of George Warner (later Warner, Shuster & Co.), G. W. Edmonds & Co., 1892, until merged with George B. Newton Coal Co. in 1912; mem. firm Edmonds & Heidler, wholesale coal and lumber, 1925-36; dir. George B. Newton Coal Co. Mgr. Port of Philadelphia Ocean Traffic Bureau, 1927-32. Mem. Common Council, Philadelphia, 3 terms of two yrs. each; mem. 63d to 68th and 73d Congresses (1913-25 and 1933-35), 4th Pa. Dist. Progressive Republican. Episcopalian. Mason. Home: 1520 Spruce St., Philadelphia, Pa.

EDMONDSON, David Edward, life ins.; b. Danville, Pa., Feb. 6, 1887; s. George D. and Anna A. (Rees) E.; student pub. sch. and high sch., Danville, Pa.; m. Elmira Foust, June 12, 1907; children—Anna Jean (Mrs. James J. Durkin), Carol Mary. Engaged in life ins. business since 1908; agt., 1908-24, then dir. and mgr. branch office Phila. Life Ins. Co.; dir. Danville Nat. Bank. Served as pres. Danville Sch. Bd., 18 yrs.; sec. Danville State Hosp. Bd. Gov. 177th dist., Rotary International. Lutheran. Rotarian. Home: 102 E. Market St. Office: 129 Mill St., Danville, Pa.

EDMUNDS, Albert Joseph, librarian; b. Tottenham, Middlesex, Eng., Nov. 21, 1857; s. Thomas and Rebecca (Hallat) E.; ed. Friends' Sch., Croydon, and Flounders Inst., Ackworth; matriculated U. of London, 1877; pvt. student of N.T., under James Rendel Harris (hon. A.M., U. of Pa., 1907); fellow U. of Pa., 1914; unmarried. Sec. to T. W. Backhouse, astronomer, 1879-83; emigrated to U.S., 1885; asst. librarian, Haverford Coll., 1887-89; classifier Phila. Library, 1889-90; cataloguer Hist. Soc. of Pa., 1891-1936. Prepared Catalogue Sunderland (Eng.) Library, 1881-84. Author: English and American Poems, 1888; Songs of Asia Sung in America, 1896; Marvelous Birth of the Buddhas, 1899; Hymns of the Faith (Dhammapada), 1902; Buddhist and Christian Gospels, 1902, 3d edit., Tokyo, 1905, 4th edit. Phila., 1908-09, with postscripts, 1912, 14, 21, 26, 28, 35, 37, 38; Italian transl., Palermo, 1913; Buddhist Bibliography, 1903; Buddhist Texts in John, 1906, 2d edit., 1911; Fairmount Park and Other Poems, 1906; A Dialogue Between Two Saviors, 5th edit., 1931; Lucy Edmunds (1859-1935) in The Two Worlds, 1935; Leaves from the Gospel of Mark, 1936; Christianity Reconstructed (an old-age book on cards, 1921-38). Contbr. to jours. on subjects of comparative religion. Home: 213 Ryers Av., Cheltenham, Pa.

EDMUNDS, Page; prof. traumatic surgery, U. of Md.; visiting surgeon University Hosp.; consulting and gen. surgeon B.&O.R.R. Co. Address: University Hosp., Baltimore, Md.

EDMUNDSON, George L., pres. Hunter-Edmundson-Striffler Co.; offices or dir. various companies. Home: 902 Huey St. Office: 600 Market St., McKeesport, Pa.

EDREHI, Isaac Chalom, rabbi; b. Agadir, Morocco, Feb. 2, 1898; s. Chalom and Zohra (Ibghi) E.; ed. Ecole d L'Alliance Israélite Universelle, Mogador, Morocco, 1908-12; Sepharadic Minister, Jewish Theol. Sem. of America, New York, N.Y. 1927. Came to U.S., 1920, naturalized, 1925. Served as interpreter of Hebrew, Arabic, French, English and Spanish langs. to late Sultan of Morocco, Mulay Hafid, Tangier, Morocco, 1914-18; supt. and paymaster of civilian labor for Q.M.A., dist. of Paris, France, 1918-20, disbursed five million francs for U.S.

Govt. without loss; asso. minister Spanish and Portugese Synagogue, Phila., Pa., since Sept. 1927. Author: Moreh Rabbah, an index of all Biblical verses in the Midrash Rabbah and Tanhumah, including the five Meghillot (in preparation); The Wit of Babylon (collection of all sayings found in the Talmud and Midrash with the authors' names and translated into English); Rabbinical Preaching by Parable (series of sermons based on parables found in Midrash). Sole relative in U.S. of Dr. Isaac Edrehi, the Spanish Jew, of Longfellow's "Tales of a Wayside Inn." Mem. Am. Acad. for Jewish Research, Am. Acad. Polit. and Social Science. Home: 2343 N. Park Av., Philadelphia, Pa.

EDRIS, Warren P., financial and insurance investigations; b. Reading, Pa., Mar. 26, 1886; s. Peter W. and Ida A. (Small) E.; grad. Reading High Sch., 1902; m. Emma Belle Hart Kelvie, 1911; children—Robert B., Helen J., Warren P., Lucile C. Began as newspaper reporter on Brooklyn Daily Eagle, 1903; in insurance business with Norwich Union Ins. Co., 1905-08; pres. Edris Service Corpn., financial and ins. investigations, since 1914. Served in Intelligence Dept., Res. Corps, for 6 months during World War. Mem. Rep. Com. for Mountain Lakes, N.J., 1921-30. Helped organize borough govt. and Fire and Police Depts. of Mountain Lakes, 1926, and served as chief of Fire Dept., 1924-28. Mason. Clubs: Rockaway River Country, Masonic. Home: Mountain Lakes, N.J. Office: 51 Madison St., New York, N.Y.

EDROP, Arthur Norman, artist and writer; b. Birmingham, Eng.; s. George Thomas and Annie (Lane) E.; ed. Pratt Inst. and Adelphi Art Classes and Brooklyn Art Sch., pupil of Whittaker and Boston, all Brooklyn, N.Y.; m. Edith Bellzora Macartney, June 9, 1909; children—Arthur Macartney, Edith Marjorie (Mrs. Robert Cooper Morris II). Employed as staff artist on newspapers, Brooklyn Daily Eagle, Newark Sunday Call, Phila. Evening Bulletin, Evening Telegraph (cartoons), New York Sunday Tribune; worked for advtg. agencies, and cons. art dir.; planning, designing, and illustrating advertisements; illustrator for leading mags. including Ladies Home Journal, Saturday Evening Post, Colliers and others; now engaged in writing and illustrating. Served on Dept. Pictorial Publicity under Charles Dana Gibson during World War. Chmn. Wayne Com. for Civic Progress. Vice-pres. and dir. Wayne Art Center (charter mem.). Mem. Soc. Illustrators. Republican. Episcopalian. Writer radio plays and articles. Writer and lecturer on uniforms and costumes. Home: Radnor Inn, Radnor, Pa. Studio: 700 S. Washington Square, Philadelphia, Pa.

EDWARDS, A. L.; deputy atty. gen. of Pa. Home: Osceola Mills, Pa. Office: care Dept. of State, Harrisburg, Pa.

EDWARDS, Bateman; prof. Romance languages and head of dept., Lehigh U. Address: Lehigh U., Bethlehem, Pa.

EDWARDS, (F.) Boyd, clergyman, educator; b. Lisle, N.Y., May 5, 1876; s. Mortimer Burr and Harriett Louise (Boyd) E.; grad. Phillips Acad., Andover, Mass., 1896; B.A. Williams Coll., 1900, D.D., 1920; Union Theol. Sem., 1902-04; S.T.D., Univ. of Pa., 1925; LL.D. Franklin and Marshall Coll., 1931; m. Frances McCarroll (A.B., Smith Coll., 1903), May 24, 1904. Ordained Congl. ministry, 1904; asst. pastor Tompkins Av. Ch., Brooklyn, 1904; asso. pastor South Ch., Brooklyn, 1905-10; pastor same, 1908-10; pastor Hillside Ch., Orange, N.J., 1910-22; headmaster and trustee The Hill Sch., Pottstown, Pa., 1922-28; headmaster Mercersburg Acad. since 1928; trustee Mt. Holyoke Coll., 1920-37, Williams Coll., 1923-28. Mem. student div. Nat. Council Y.M.C.A.; chmn. Nat. Prep. Sch. Com. of Nat. Y.M.C.A. Mem. Nat. Headmasters' Assn., Assn. Schs., Colls. and Sems. of Ref. Ch. in U.S. (v.p.), Phila. Headmasters' Assn., Zeta Psi. Clubs: Century, Zeta Psi (New York). Author: Have Faith in Youth; Boys Will Be Men. Editor: Mr. Rolfe of the Hill; Prayers in the Hill School Chapel; Religion in the Preparatory Schools (co-editor). Home: Mercersburg, Pa.

EDWARDS, Carolyn Hodgdon (Mrs. Llewellyn N. Edwards); b. Tremont, Me.; d. Matthew Snowman and Alice (Alden) Hodgdon; A.B., U. of Maine, 1906; grad. student U. of Toronto, 1913-15; m. Llewellyn N. Edwards, July 2, 1911. Teacher of Greek, Livermore Falls (Me.) High Sch., 1906-11. Mem. Daughters of Founders and Patriots of America; organizer and 1st pres. Me. Chapter, 1927; nat. councillor, 1933-34; nat. corr. sec., 1934-37; nat. pres. since 1937. Mem. Daughters of Colonial Wars (nat. 3rd vice-pres. 1935-38), U.S. Daughters of 1812 (credential chmn. 1932-37), D.A.R. (regent Koussinoc Chapter, Augusta, Me., 1927-28), Phi Kappa Phi. Unitarian. Eastern Star. Organizing mem. Augusta College Club, Am. Women's Club (Toronto). Home: Glen Echo, Md. Office: 1828 I St., N.W., Washington, D.C.

EDWARDS, Charles R.; prof. clin. surgery, U. of Md.; chief out-patient surg. service and visiting surgeon University Hosp.; visiting surgeon Church Home and Infirmary and Union Memorial Hosp. Address: 101 W. Read St., Baltimore, Md.

EDWARDS, Edward Tudor, v.p. and gen. mgr. Latrobe Electric Steel Co.; b. Sheffield, Eng., June 28, 1877; s. Edward and Sara Ann (Tudor) E.; B.S. in M.E., U. of Pittsburgh; m. Dora Belle Bailey, 1908 (died 1919); children—Marion Elizabeth Zink, Dorothy Louise Klingensmith; m. 2d, Eleanor Culbertson Sterling, Mar. 31, 1921; children—Eleanor Jane, Kathryn Ann, Edward Tudor. Draftsman U.S. Steel Corpn., 1903-04; engr. Firth Sterling Steel Co., 1904-10; pres. Vanadium Alloys Steel Co., 1910-15; v.p. and gen. mgr. Latrobe Electric Steel Co., Latrobe, Pa., since 1915, now also dir.; dir. Vulcan Mould and Iron Co., First Nat. Bank of Latrobe. Dir. Latrobe Hosp. Assn. Mason (K.T.; Shriner), Elk. Clubs: Duquesne, Pittsburgh Athletic (Pittsburgh); Engineers (New York); Latrobe (Pa.) Country. Home: 437 Main St. Office: 2626 Ligonier St., Latrobe, Pa.

EDWARDS, Eugene (Red); football coach, St. Vincent Coll., Latrobe, Pa. Address: Latrobe, Pa.

EDWARDS, George J., Jr.; mem. law firm Edwards & Croskey. Address: Stephen Girard Bldg., Philadelphia, Pa.

EDWARDS, Henry Boyd; rector Ch. of the Ascension since 1926. Home: D'Arlington Apts., Pittsburgh, Pa.

EDWARDS, Lester Richard, manufacturer; b. LaCrosse, Wis., Aug. 10, 1890; s. Julius Augustus and Olive Content (Spicer) E.; grad. Elkhorn (Wis.) High Sch., 1908; M.E., Lewis Inst., Chicago, Ill., 1912; m. Caroline Katherine Steckhahn, Sept. 1, 1915; children—Jean Olive, Betty Lou, Charlotte Helen, Joyce Lillian. With Aeroshade Co., Waukesha, Wis., 1912-18, advancing from salesman to sales mgr.; with P. Hohenadel Canning Co., Janesville, Wis., 1919-21; pres. and gen. mgr. Garden Canning Co., Fairview Farms Co., Evansville, Wis., 1921-25; sec. and treas. Kieckhefer Container Co., Milwaukee, Wis., Eddy Paper Corpn., Chicago, and Quick Service Box Co., Chicago and New York, 1925-35; pres. and gen. mgr. Northeastern Container Corpn., Bradford, Pa., since 1935; partner Highway Stations, Bradford; dir. Columbus Foods Corpn. Served in U.S. Navy, 1918-19, disch. as ensign. Dir. Bradford Chamber of Commerce. Mem. Daedalian (Lewis Inst.). Republican. Presbyterian. Mason (K.T., 32°, Shriner). Clubs: Bradford, Rotary (pres. 1939-40), Country, Pennhills (Bradford). Home: 61 School St. Address: Box 217, Bradford, Pa.

EDWARDS, Levi Arthur, lawyer; b. Mason Co., W. Va., July 16, 1884; s. Charles S. and Jennet A. (Roush) E.; student Marshall Coll., Huntington, W. Va., 1904-06, W. Va. Univ., Morgantown, W. Va., 1909-11; m. Carrie C. White, Nov. 28, 1912; children—Lewis Arthur, Charles Edward. Engaged as teacher rural schs. then high sch. and sch. supervisor, 1908-20; admitted to W. Va. bar, 1911; engaged in gen. practice of law at Charleston since 1921; local. atty. Federal Land Bank of Batlimore since 1930; served as mem. W. Va. Ho. of Dels., 1925; sec., treas. and atty. Kanawha Co. Nat. Farm Loan Assn. since 1930; dir. St. Albans Bldg. & Loan Assn. Mem. W. Va. Bar Assn., Charleston Bar Assn. Republican. Southern Presbyn. Mason. Club: Rotary of St. Albans. Home: 1313 Oakland Av., St. Albans. Office: Security Bldg., Charleston, W. Va.

EDWARDS, Monte, surgeon; b. Kingston-on-Thames, England, Feb. 20, 1896; s. John Warden and Eliza (Vining) E.; ed. Tiffin Sch., Kingston - on - Thames, Eng., 1906-12, St. Thomas's Hosp. Med. Sch., London, Eng., 1912-17; Licentiate Royal Coll. Physicians, London; Mem. Royal Coll. Surgeons of England; m. Constance Gilchrist, June 6, 1925; children—Valerie, John Gilchrist. Came to U.S., 1923, naturalized, 1933. House surgeon St. Thomas Hosp., Eng., 1917; Lieut. and Capt. R.A.M.C. 1917 to 1920; resident med. officer King Edward Memorial Hosp., London, 1920 to 1921; ship's surgeon Royal Mail Steam Packet Co., 1921 to 1923; surgical interne and resident surgeon Univ. Hosp., Baltimore, 1923 to 1925; asso. prof. of surgery and lecturer in surgical anatomy, U. of Md., since 1935; visiting proctologist University and Baltimore City Hosps. Fellow Am. Coll. Surgeons, A.M.A.; mem. Baltimore Med. Soc. Home: 404 Marlow Rd., Guilford. Office: Medical Arts Bldg., Baltimore, Md.

EDWARDS, Ogden Matthias, Jr., M.D.; b. Pittsburgh, Pa., Dec. 23, 1869; s. Ogden M. and Sara (Herron) E.; B.S., Princeton, 1893; M.D., Coll. Phys. and Surg. (Columbia), 1896;. m. Lela Harkness, Nov. 28, 1898; children—Martha Harkness (Mrs. John M. Lazear), Lela Harkness (Mrs. Harry Cook), Harkness, Katherine Harkness (Mrs. H. Willis Nichols, Jr.). Began practice in Pittsburgh, Pa., 1898; professor of pediatrics, 1909-17, actg. dean, 1917-19, Sch. of Medicine University of Pittsburgh; retired from practice, 1917. Trustee Shady Side Acad., University of Pittsburgh. Presbyn. Clubs: Fox Chapel Golf, Pittsburgh, Duquesne, University, Pittsburgh Golf, Allegheny Country (Pittsburgh); Metropolitan, New York Yacht, University, Union League, Nat. Golf Links (New York). Home: 5607 Fifth Av. Office: Commonwealth Bldg., Pittsburgh, Pa.

EDWARDS, Paul Kenneth, univ. prof.; b. Oskaloosa, Ia., Oct. 26, 1898; s. David Morton and Della (Russell) E.; student Penn Coll., Oskaloosa, Ia., 1917-18; A.B., Earlham Coll., Richmond, Ind., 1920; M.B.A., Harvard Grad. Sch. of Bus. Adminstrn., 1922, D.C.S., 1936; m. Mary Carroll, May 29, 1926; children—Patricia Ann, David Carroll. Engaged as prof. econs., Ursinus Coll., Collegeville, Pa., 1922-23; with Harvard Bur. Bus. Research, 1923-24; asst. prof. commerce, U. of Va., 1924; asst. to gen. sales mgr. Crosley Radio Corpn., 1925; with Daniel Starch in sales research in N.Y., 1926; sales research Simmons Co., N.Y., 1926-28; prof. econs., Fisk Univ., 1928-34; dir. Sales Promotion in Negro Markets for Rumford Co., 1932-37; prof. marketing and chmn. dept., U. of Newark, Newark, N.J., since 1937. Served with Am. Red Cross, France, 1918. Mem. Am. Marketing Assn., Delta Sigma Pi. Mem. Religious Soc. Friends. Club: Newark Athletic (Newark). Home: 3 Winthrop Pl., Maplewood. Office: 40 Rector St., Newark, N.J.

EDWARDS, Rowland Hill, surgeon; b. King William Court House, Va., Apr. 27, 1897; s. John Hooper and Maude R. (Lewis) E.; teachers certificate, William & Mary Coll., 1917; M.D., Med. Coll. of Va., 1923; m. Margaret Hess Hay, Oct. 15, 1936. Interne Med. Coll. of Va., 1923-24; resident surgeon, same, 1924-26; chief surgeon Galax Hosp. and Clinic, 1926-28; founder Park View Hosp., Houston, 1928-29; surgeon Raleigh Gen. Hosp., Beckley, W. Va., 1929-30; chief surgeon Stevens Clinic Hosp., Welch, W. Va., since 1930; asst. surgeon Norfolk & Western Ry. since 1934; spl. examiner for W. Va. State Compensation Commn. since 1938; cons. surgeon Bluefield Sanitarium, Bluefield, W. Va., and Richlands Clinic, Richlands, Va. Fellow Am. Coll. Surgeons, Internat. Coll. of Surgeons (Geneva); mem. A.M.A.,

McDowell Co. Med. Soc. (pres. 1937), W. Va. Med. Soc. (pres. surg. sect. 1937), Southern Surgical Assn. Republican. Club: Gary Country. Home: Welch, W. Va.

EDWARDS, Vere Buckingham, pres. Dravo Corpn.; b. Glenburn, Pa., Jan. 17, 1890; s. James Ellsworth and Jennie (Buckingham) E.; C.E., Lehigh U., 1912; m. Edith Hitchcock, Nov. 15, 1915; children—Virginia (wife of Dr. James Stewart), Ruth, Marion, Alan, Carol; successively engr., chief engr., gen. mgr. and vice-pres., Dravo Corpn., Pittsburgh, Pa., pres. since Jan. 1, 1937, also dir.; dir. Union Barge Line Corpn. Dir. Ohio Valley Hosp. (McKees Rock, Pa.), Valley Hosp. (Sewickley, Pa.). Mem. Soc. Naval Architects and Marine Engrs. Republican. Presbyn. Mason. Clubs: Montour Heights Country (Coraopolis); Duquesne (Pittsburgh). Home: R.F.D. Coraopolis. Office: Neville Island, Pittsburgh, Pa.

EDWARDS, Walter Herbert, railroad official; b. Wilmington, Del., Jan. 29, 1890; s. Walter Roland and Margaret Marshall (Earle) E.; B.S. in C.E., Bucknell U., 1913; grad. student Harvard U., 1913; m. Hazel Taylor Merryman, Oct. 8, 1917. Began with Engring Corps, Construction Dept., B.&O. R.R., 1909 and furloughed to attend Bucknell U. and later, Harvard; again with B.&O. R.R., 1913-26 in various engring. capacities and cost engr., 1926-30; gen. supt. Lehigh and New England R.R., 1930-38, vice-pres. and gen. mgr. since Jan. 1, 1939; dir. Union Bank and Trust Co., The Bethlehem Globe Pub. Co., Inc. Served as dir. Bethlehem Chamber of Commerce, 1933-38. Trustee St. Luke's Hosp. Mem. Am. Ry. Engring. Assn., Am. Assn. R.R. Supts. Delta Sigma. Republican. Baptist. Mason. Rotarian. Clubs: Bethlehem, Saucon Valley Country (Bethlehem); Old Company's (Lansford); Penn Athletic (Phila.); New York Railroad, Railroad and Machinery (New York). Home: 826 Tioga Av. Office: Anthracite Bldg., Bethlehem, Pa.

EDWARDS, William (Henry) Grimm, forester, prof. of lumbering; b. Beaver Falls, Pa., Mar. 13, 1888; s. John and Margaret Elizabeth (Stinson) E.; prep. edn. Geneva Coll. Prep. Dept., 1903-06; B.S., Geneva Coll., 1910; B.S., Dept. of Forestry, Pa. State Coll., 1914, M.S., Dept. of Botany, Pa. State Coll., 1915; M.S., Div. of Forestry, U. of Calif., 1925; m. Carolyn Reed Buckhout, July 14, 1919; children—Margaret Elizabeth, Mary Harkness. Clerk in furniture store, Beaver Falls, Pa., 1910-12; asst. in forestry and botany, Pa. State Coll., 1914-16, instr., 1916-17, asst. prof. of forestry, 1919-22, asso. prof., 1922-24, prof. of lumbering since 1924; lecturer, div. of forestry, U. of Calif., Jan.-June, 1925. Served with 10th Engrs., U.S. Army, 1917-19; commd. 2d lt., 20th Engrs. (Forestry), Nov. 1918; now 2d lt. Engr. Reserve. Mem. Soc. of Am. Foresters, Am. Forestry Assn., Pa. Forestry Assn., Reserve Officers Assn. Republican. Presbyterian. Mason. Home: 503 W. Fairmount Av., State College, Pa.

EELLS, Walter Crosby, educator; b. Mason Co., Wash., Mar. 6, 1886; s. Myron and Sarah (Crosby) E.; A.B., Whitman Coll., 1908, Sc.D., 1938; A.M., U. of Chicago, 1911; Ph.D., Stanford, 1927; m. Natalie Esther Soules, Jan. 1, 1912; children—Kenneth Walter, Frances Natalie, Donald Cushing. Teacher, high sch., Wash., 1908-10; prof. mathematics, Whitworth Coll., Tacoma, Wash., 1911-13; instr. mathematics and mechanics, U.S. Naval Acad., 1913-16; instr. surveying, Harvard, summer 1916; prof. applied methematics and sec. alumni assn., Whitman Coll., 1916-27; asso. prof. edn., Stanford, 1927-31, prof. edn., 1931-38; coördinator of Coöperative Study of Secondary School Standards, Washington, D.C., 1935-39; exec. sec., Am. Assn. of Junior Coll., Washington, D.C., since 1938. Mem. N.E.A., Am. Ednl. Research Assn., Am. Assn. Univ. Profs., Nat. Soc. for Study of Edn., Phi Delta Kappa, Phi Beta Kappa, Sigma Xi, Delta Sigma Rho. Republican. Conglist. Author: (with J. B. Sears, et al) Sacramento School Survey, 1928; (with N. Ricciardi et al) Junior College Survey of Siskiyou County, 1929; Bibliography on Junior Colleges, 1930; The Junior College, 1931; Salary and Cost Study of Fresno Schools, 1932; (with E. P. Cubberley) Introduction to the Study of Education, 1933; Teachers Salaries and the Cost of Living, 1933; (with J. B. Sears, et al) Tracy Union High School Survey, 1935; (with H. D. Anderson) Alaska Natives—A Survey of Their Sociological and Educational Status, 1935; Surveys of American High Education, 1937; Educational Temperatures, 1938; (with others), How to Evaluate a Secondary School, 1938; and Evaluative Criteria, 1938. Contbr. articles to numerous statistical and ednl. jours. Editor of Whitman Alumnus, 1917-27, also of Junior College Jour. since 1930. Home: 5702 York Lane, Bethesda, Md. Address: 744 Jackson Place, Washington, D.C.

EFFING, Gerald H.; pres. Farmers Bank & Trust Co. Address: Lancaster, Pa.

EGAN, Charles M.; vice chancellor Chancery Court of N.J. Address: Jersey City, N.J.

EGAN, John P.; judge Ct. of Common Pleas since 1931, present term expires 1942. Address: Pittsburgh, Pa.

EGBERT, Lester Darling, ins. broker; b. Jersey City, N.J., Mar. 4, 1892; s. James Chidester and Emma Gross (Pennington) E.; student Irving Sch., New York, N.Y.; 1908-10; A.B., Columbia U., 1914; m. Beatrice Valerie Cook, May 14, 1921; children—John Pennington, Richard Cook. With Fidelity & Casualty Co., New York, 1914-16; asso. with Brown Crosby & Co., Inc., ins. brokers, New York, N.Y., since 1916, sec. and dir. since 1923; treas. and dir. Empire Underwriting Co., New York, since 1927. Served as 1st lt., 22d Aero Squadron, A.E.F. during World War. Mem. Assn. of Alumni of Columbia Coll. (v.p. since 1937), Columbia Alumni Fed. (dir.), Zeta Psi (trustee since 1936). Awarded Conspicuous Columbia Alumni Service Medal, 1937, World War Conspicuous Service Metal of N.Y. State, 1919. Republican. Episcopalian. Clubs: Downtown Assn., Columbia University (New York); Rock Spring Country (West Orange, N.J.); Manasquan River Golf (Brielle, N.J.; trustee since 1938); Bay Head (N.J.) Yacht. Home: 7 Marion Rd., Montclair, N.J. Address: 96 Wall St., New York, N.Y.

EGBERT, Seneca, M.D.; b. Petroleum Centre, Pa., Feb. 17, 1863; s. Albert G. and Eliza (Phipps) E.; A.B., Princeton, 1884, A.M., 1887; M.D., U. of Pa., 1888, Dr. P.H., 1921; m. Nancy McClellan Bredin, Sept. 26, 1888; children—Victor Egbert, Mrs. Catherine Bredin Sparks. Lecturer on hygiene at U. of Pa., 1890-92, at P.E. Ch. Training Sch., 1891-1931; prof. hygiene, 1893-1916, dean, 1898-1916, Medico-Chirurg. College; prof. of hygiene, Temple Coll., 1896-99; Univ. of Pa. Med. Sch., 1916-31, emeritus prof. since 1932. Major Medical O.R.C., 1917-18. Mem. Phila. Co. Med. Soc., Pa. State Med. Soc., A.M.A., Am. Pub. Health Assn., Am. Sch. Hygiene Assn., Am. Social Hygiene Assn., A.A.A.S., Phi Kappa Psi, Phi Rho Sigma, Sigma Xi. Author: A Manual of Hygiene and Sanitation, 1898, 8th edit., 1926; Personal Hygiene for Nurses, 1930. Contbr. to scientific jours. Address: 200 E. Beech Tree Lane, Wayne, Pa.

EGGERS, Clifford Robinson, mfr. paints; b. Pittsburgh, Pa., Feb. 18, 1885; s. William and Susan Elizabeth (McFerrin) E.; student pub. schs., Millvale, Pa.; m. Stella E. Haug, Oct. 2, 1907; children—Mildred Elizabeth (widow of Frank Hale), Helen Marie (Mrs. B. Franklin Howard). Employed by others in various capacities, 1901-11; asso. with James B. Sipe and Co., mfrs. paints, varnishes, and lacquers, Pittsburgh, Pa., since 1911, sec. and dir. 1915-36, and vice-pres., treas., dir., and chmn. exec. com. since 1936; dir. Millvale Bldg. and Loan Assn. Republican. United Presbyterian. Mason. Maccabee. Home: 280 Summit Av., Beltzhoover. Office: Post Office Box 8010 South Hills Branch, Pittsburgh, Pa.

EGGLESTON, Charles Fellows, lawyer; b. Brooklyn, N.Y., Jan. 8, 1868; s. Asahel Coe and Isabella Victoria (Dare) E.; student Wilbraham Acad., Mass., 1883-86; A.B., Wesleyan U., Middletown, Conn., 1890; LL.B., U. of Pa., 1893; m. Mary E. Lovett, June 4, 1896; children—Elisabeth Dare, Miriam Lovett (Mrs. William Stanley Kite), Catherine Coe (Mrs. Howard W. Newnam), Virginia Alden (Mrs. Robert Handel Morgan). Admitted to Pa. bar, 1893, and since in civil law practice in Phila.; pres. Phila Suburbs Co.; dir. Darby Bldg. & Loan Assn. Dir. Bd. of Home Missions of M.E. Ch.; lay del. to Gen. Conf. M.E. Ch., 1924, 1928, 1932, 1936, 1939. Republican. Mason. Home: 19 N. Scott Av., Glenolden, Pa. Office: 1701 Arch St., Philadelphia, Pa.

EGLIN, James Milton, research physicist; b. Berea, O., May 12, 1901; s. James William and Rosa (Gardner) E.; A.B., Oberlin (O.) Coll., 1919; Ph. D., U. of Chicago, 1922; m. Margaret Hedwig Proche, June 26, 1926; 1 son, James Milton. Research physicist, Western Electric Co., Bell Telephone Labs., since 1922. Fellow Am. Phys. Soc. Author: (articles) Viscosity and Slip of Carbon Dioxide, and the Law of Fall of an Oil Drop at Low Pressures, 1923; (monograph) D.C. Amplifier for Measuring Small Currents, 1929. Home: 53 Emerson Rd., Glen Rock, N.J. Office: 463 West St., New York, N.Y.

EGNER, Arthur Frederick, lawyer; b. Newark, N.J., Sept. 20, 1882; s. Henry W. and Emily S. (Nasher) E.; A.B., Columbia, 1903, A.M., 1905; LL.B., N.Y. Law Sch., 1905; m. Adele B. Gifford, June 21, 1923; children—Mary Gifford, Emily Nasher. Admitted to bar, 1905; mem. McCarter, English & Egner since 1912; v.p. and dir. Kresge Dept. Stores, Inc., chmn. bd. and counsel N.J. Realty Title Ins. Co. and N.J. Realty Co. since 1937; counsel and dir. Art Metal Works, Inc., N.J. Worsted Mills; dir. Lincoln Nat. Bank, Eagle Fire Ins. Co. Employee, Gen. Staff, U.S. Army, 1918. Mem. City Planning Commn., Newark, 1912-14. President Newark Mus. Assn., Hosp. and Home for Crippled Children (Newark); v.p. of trustees Newark U. Mem. Essex Co. Bar Assn. (pres. 1924-25). Received award of Advertising Club of Newark, 1938. Democrat. Lutheran. Clubs: Grolier (New York); Essex (Newark, N. J.); Carmel Country. Home: 406 Centre St., South Orange, N.J. Office: 13 Commerce St., Newark, N.J.

EHLERS, Henry Edward, cons. engineer; b. Philadelphia, Pa., Jan. 25, 1879; S. Peter and Helen (Collins) E.; B.S. in M.E., U. of Pa., 1900; m. Eliza Estelle Bradley, July 18, 1907; children—Peter, Henry Edward, Harriet Elizabeth. With New York Ship Bldg. Co., 1900-02, Am. Hawaiian Steamship Co., 1902-03; instr. in mech. engring., U. of Pa., 1903-06, asst. prof., 1906-11, prof., 1911-15; asst. chief engr. Pub. Service Commn. of Pa., 1914-24; dir. city transit, City of Phila., 1924-28; v.p. Day & Zimmermann, cons. engrs., since 1928. Mem. Am. Soc. M.E. (ex-pres. Phila. Sect.), Am. Soc. C.E.; ex-pres. Engrs. Soc. of Pa. Republican. Episcopalian. Club: Engineers (pres. 1932-33). Home: 508 W. Mt. Airy Av. Office: Packard Bldg., Philadelphia, Pa.

EHNES, Morris Wellington, clergyman; b. Dashwood, Ont., Can., Mar. 3, 1873; s. August G. and Mary (Haist) E.; came to U.S., 1891; A.B., Ohio Wesleyan U., Delaware, O., 1898; spl. work, Columbia, 1907-08; m. Belle Gates, Aug. 22, 1898; children—Margaret Gates (Mrs. Wm. R. Canner), Bayard Freeman, Elizabeth Ruth (Mrs. Frederick G. Welsh), Robert Morris, Helen Belle (Mrs. Henry E. Gammerstorf). Missionary to Rhodesia, 1898-1901; gen. sec. Coll. Y.M.C.A., Delaware, O., 1902-04; asst. gen. sec. Student Volunteer Movement for Fgn. Missions, 1904-05; editorial sec. Missionary Edn. Movement and editor missionary text books, 1905-16; exec. sec. Ohio Wesleyan U., 1916-19; asst. treas. Methodist Centenary movement, 1919-20, treas. Com. on Conservation and Advance of M.E. Ch., 1920-24; treas. Bd. of Foreign Missions M.E. Ch. since 1924; mem. bd. mgrs. Missionary Edn. Movement; pres. Nanking Realty Corpn., New York; mem. bd. trustees Santiago Coll., Santiago, Chile, Ward Coll., Buenos Aires, Argentina; treas. Wendell Foundation, New York. Mem. Phi Beta Kappa, Phi Gamma Delta. Republican. Mason. Home:

196 Park Av., Leonia, N.J. Office: 150 Fifth Av., New York, N.Y.

EHRENFELD, Frederick, prof. of geology and mineralogy; b. Washington Co., Pa., Jan. 8, 1872; s. Charles Lewis and Helen (Hatch) E.; A.B., Wittenberg Coll., Ohio, 1893; Ph.D., U. of Pa., 1898; m. Alice Stockton Allen, 1910. Instr. chemistry and physics, York (Pa.) Collegiate Inst., 1893-94; instr. geology and mineralogy, U. of Pa., 1897-1906, asst. prof. and prof., 1906-23, head of dept. since 1917. Mem. Pa. State Geol. Survey Commn., 1917-19. Mem. Franklin Inst., Phila. Acad. Natural Sciences, Seismological Soc. of America, Sigma Xi. Author: Minerals of Pennsylvania. Contbr. to tech. jours. Home: 3804 Locust St., Philadelphia, Pa.

EHRHART, Oliver Tillman, clergyman; b. Lancaster Co., Pa., Oct. 8, 1881; s. George Z. and Elizabeth S. (Tillman) E.; ed. Millersville State Teachers Coll., 1899-1902, Pa. Business Coll., summers 1904-06; A.B., Lebanon Valley Coll., 1911; (hon.) D.D., Lebanon Valley Coll., 1928; m. Edna E. Yarkers, June 28, 1916; children—Carl Y., Jane Y. Ordained to ministry Ch.U. Brethren in Christ, 1910; served Lebanon, Hebron Charge, Lebanon, Pa., 1910-20, Covenant Ch., Lancaster, Pa., since 1920; sec. E. Pa. Conf. of Ch.U. Brethren in Christ since 1927; mem. Bd. Fgn. Missions; mem. Bd. Christian Work in Santo Domingo. Trustee Lebanon Valley Coll. Republican. Mem. Ch.U. Brethren in Christ. Home: 937 W. Walnut St., Lancaster, Pa.

EHRHART, Victor Hugo; pres. Jamestown Paint & Varnish Co.; dir. many other cos. Address: Jamestown, Pa.

EIBECK, John, fraternal insurance; b. Germany, Apr. 1, 1879; s. Andrew and Eva (Werner) E.; brought to U.S. 1883, naturalized 1888; ed. public and private schools of Pittsburgh; m. Anna Feidt, Apr. 10, 1907; children —Irma, Alice (wife of Herbert B. Crumbaker, D.D.S.), Anna Mae, John, Ruth. Pres. Catholic Knights of St. George, fraternal insurance order, since 1932. Home: 329 S. Home Av., Avalon. Office: 14 Wabash St., Pittsburgh, Pa.

EICHELBERGER, Percy Samuel, high sch. prin.; b. York Springs, Pa., Mar. 2, 1894; s. Benjamin F. and Sallie (Foulk) E.; grad. Shippensburg Teachers Coll., 1913, Perkiomen Sch. for Boys, 1916; A.B., Gettysburg Coll., Gettysburg, Pa., 1921; student Columbia U., 1925-26; A.M., U. of Pa., 1929; m. Dora Schneider, June 30, 1924; children—Raymond Foulk, Gerald Stover. Engaged in teaching pub. schs., Lisburn, Pa., 1913-15; instr. Perkiomen Prep. Sch., Pennsburg, Pa., 1915-17; vice prin. and head history dept., high sch., Amityville, N.Y., 1921-23; prin. jr. and sr. high sch., Patchogue, N.Y., 1923-27; prin. sr. high sch., Collingswood, N.J. since 1927. Served as pvt. inf. to 2d lt., U.S.A. with A.E.F., 1917-19, in six major offensives, wounded twice; in U.S.A. Res., 1920-25. Life mem. Nat. Edn. Assn.; mem. Camden County Teachers Assn. (past pres.), Am. Legion (past comdr. Gettysburg, Pa., post), Alpha Tau Omega. Republican. Protestant. Mason. Clubs: Woodcrest Country, Indian Head Fish and Gun, Hidden Lake Swimming, Square. Home: 11 E. Linden Av., Collingswood, N.J.

EICHENAUER, John Benjamin, lawyer; b. Pittsburgh, Pa., Aug. 24, 1872; s. John and Mary Ann (Steffen) E.; A.B., Washington and Jefferson Coll., 1896; student Harvard Law Sch., 1899-1901; LL.D., Monmouth (Ill.) Coll., 1929; m. Mary Jane McKinney (died Dec. 17, 1932). Admitted to Pa. bar, 1902, and began practice at Pittsburgh; asst. city solicitor, 1909-13; mem. firm Rose & Eichenauer since 1917; Pres. bd. trustees The United Presbyterian; pres. Bd. of Am. Missions of United Presbyn. Ch.; trustee Westminster Coll., New Wilmington, Pa.; Knoxville (Tenn.) Coll.; mem. Lake Erie & Ohio River Canal Bd. of Pa.; mem. Bd. of Law Examiners, Allegheny Co., 1930-34. Mem. Am. Law Inst., Am., Pa. State and Allegheny Co. bar assns., Delta Tau Delta. Republican. Presbyn. Clubs: Duquesne, Harvard of Western Pa. (Pittsburgh). Drafted direct primary election law of Pa., 1913. Home: Schenley Apts., 5th Av. Office: Oliver Bldg., Pittsburgh, Pa.

EICHER, Alex, Jr.; mem. law firm Eicher & Eicher. Address: Greensburg, Pa.

EICHER, C. Ward; mem. law firm Eicher & Eicher. Address: Greensburg, Pa.

EICHER, Charles Grant, physician; b. Somerset Co., Pa., Sept. 24, 1870; s. John Kern and Martha (Cunningham) E.; student Teacher's Training Sch., Confluence, Pa., 1888-89; M.D., U. of Pittsburgh Med. Dept., 1897; m. Nancy Tannehill, June 28, 1913; children—Virginia, Mary Margaret (Mrs. Delmont D. Barbor), Alice Agnes. Interne Western Pa. Hosp., 1897-98; contract surgeon, U.S.A., 1898-1901, capt. and asst. surgeon, U.S. Vols., 1901-1903; in pvt. practice, McKees Rocks, Pa., 1903-17, and since 1918; dir. Bank of McKees Rocks. Served as capt. then maj. Med. Res. Corps, 1917-18. Mem. Allegheny Co., Pa. State and Am. Med. Assn. Phi Rho Sigma. Republican. Methodist. Mason (Royal Arch, 32°, Shriner). Clubs: Bemas (McKees Rocks); Chartiers Heights (Crafton). Home: 10 Midway Rd., Mt. Lebanon. Office: 604 Chartiers Av., McKees Rocks, Pa.

EICHER, HuBert Clark, dir. Bur. of Sch. Bldgs.; b. Mt. Pleasant, Westmoreland Co. Pa., Sept. 23, 1886; s. Thomas Clark and Mary Ellen (Crayton) E.; B.Sc., Ohio Northern U., 1909, M.Sc., 1916, D.Sc., 1923; A.B., U. of Pittsburgh, 1917; grad. work, Columbia U., 1921; m. Ada Pearl Barnhart, Sept. 2, 1929. Prin., later supt. schs., Westmoreland Co., Pa., 1910-16; dir. sch. architecture and asst. exec. sec. Pa. State Bd. of Edn., 1916-19; dir. Bur. of Sch. Bldgs., Dept. of Pub. Instrn., Harrisburg since 1919; instr. U. of Pittsburgh and Pa. State Coll., summer sessions; has made sch. surveys throughout U.S., Canada, Mexico, Cuba, British Isles and Continental Europe. State dir. Pa. Soc. Professional Engrs. Mem. N.E.A., Pa. State Edn. Assn., Phi Delta Kappa, Theta Nu Epsilon; hon. mem. Am. Inst. Architects; past pres. Nat. Council on School House Construction; past regional dir. Nat. Council on Sch. Bldg. Problems. Republican. Methodist. Mason (K.T., 32°, Shriner). Clubs: University, Rotary (Harrisburg). Author: America School Architecture, 1925. Contbr. to various publs. Home: 207 N. 30th St. Office: State Capitol, Harrisburg, Pa.

EICHLEAY, Roy Oliver, pres. Pittsburgh Thermoline Co.; b. Pittsburgh, Pa., Nov. 27, 1888; s. John, Jr., and Margaret (Pollitt) E.; ed. high sch., Pittsburgh.; C.E., Rensselaer Poly. Inst.; m. Marion Helen Maple, June 17, 1914; 1 son, William. Employed as designer and estimator, John Eichleay Jr. Co., 1913-25, vice-pres. in charge machinery and real estate, 1925-30, sec. and treas., 1930-35; pres. Pittsburgh Thermoline Co., compressed gases, cutting and welding apparatus, Pittsburgh, Pa. since 19—; pres. Anchor Land Co. Republican. Home: 2717 Grenmore Av., Dormont, Pa. Office: 14 S. 19th St., Pittsburgh, Pa.

EICHLER, George A., supt. of schools; b. Laury's, Pa., Mar. 6, 1892; s. Augustus and Mary (Auer) E.; A.B., Muhlenberg Coll., 1914; M.A., Pa. State Coll., 1928, Ed.D., 1934; m. Edna Bellman, June 9, 1921; children—Mary Jane, Emma Louise, George Robert. Teacher North Whitehall Twp., 1908-10; teacher and prin. Mauch Chunk High Sch., 1914-17; prin. Palmerton High Sch., 1919-20; supervising prin. Pine Grove Borough Schs., 1922-28, Porter Twp. schs., 1928-30; supt. schs., Northampton, since 1930. Served in U.S. Army, World War, 1917-19. V.p. Brotherhood Ministerium of Pa.; dist. chmn. Whitehall Dist., Boy Scouts of America. Past Cmdr. Am. Legion. Democrat. Lutheran. Mason (32°). Club: Rotary (expres.). Contbr. educational mags. Home: 320 E. 20th St. Office: 18th and Lincoln Av., Northampton, Pa.

EICHLER, George M., lawyer; b. Hoboken, N.J., Dec. 20, 1896; s. Morris and Julia (Greenwald) E.; LL.B., N.Y. Univ., 1917; m. Sally Jacobs, Sept. 8, 1935; 1 son, Peter M. Admitted to N.J. bar as atty., 1919, as counsellor, 1922; engaged in gen. practice of law at Jersey City, N.J., since 1920; served as asst. atty. gen. of N.J., 1929-34; gen. counsel N.J. Motor Bus Assn., Inc., since 1935; Rep. nominee for U.S. Ho. of Reps., 1926-28; Rep. nominee for N.J. Senate, 1934. Served in air service, U.S.A., 1917-19. Mem. Hudson Co. Bar Assn., Am. Legion. Republican. Jewish religion. Home: 787 Boul. East, Weehawken, N.J. Office: 26 Journal Sq., Jersey City, N.J.

EICHNER, Laurits Christian, mech. engring., craftsman; b. Struer, Denmark, Mar. 7, 1894; came to U.S. 1922, naturalized, 1930; M.E., Maskinteknicum, Odense, Denmark, 1917; m. Sarah Craven, Mar. 30, 1925. Employed in various engring. positions in Denmark and Norway, 1917-21; machinist, Pardee Steel Corpn., Perth Amboy, N.J., 1922-23; engr. Westinghouse Electric & Mfg. Co., East Pittsburgh, Pa., 1923-24, Solvay Process Co., Detroit, Mich., 1924-25, Horni Signal Co., Newark, N.J., 1925-26; in charge engring. dept., Lovell Dressel Co., Arlington, N.J., 1926-31; craftsman with workshop at Bloomfield, N.J., since 1931, worker in silver, bronze and pewter; spl. work in reproductions of antique timekeeping devices and instruments; instr. in metal work, Crafts Students League, N.Y. City and Cedar Grove, N.J. Awarded Diplome de Medaille d'Or, Exposition Internationale des Arts et des Techniques, Paris, 1937. Pres. N.Y. Soc. of Craftsmen. Received George Blumenthal Award, N.Y. Soc. of Craftsmen, 1939; Master Craftsman, Boston Soc. Arts and Crafts, and also, Arts and Crafts Guild, Phila. Lutheran. Home: 271 Franklin St., Bloomfield, N.J.

EIDMANN, Frank Lewis, prof. mech. engring.; b. Kingston, N.Y., Dec. 20, 1887; s. John Frederick and Susanna (Reinmuth) E.; prep. edn. Stevens Prep. Sch., Hoboken, N.J., 1902-05; M.E., Stevens Inst. of Tech., 1909; m. Ethel Irene Fischbeck, 1924; 1 son, John Frank. Began as instr., Stevens Inst. Tech., 1909; with engring. dept. Olds Gas Power Co. and Seager Engine Works, Lansing, Mich., 1909-13; instr. in gas engines, Y.M.C.A. Evening Sch., Lansing, 1910-13; instr. in mech. engring., Rensselaer Poly. Inst., Troy, N.Y., 1913-15; instr. in gas engines, Albany (N.Y.) Evening Schs., 1914-15; engr. for developing mfg. processes, Am. LaFrance Fire Engine Co., Elmira, N.Y., 1915-16; plant engr. Heald Machine Co., Worcester, Mass., 1916-17; factory mgr. and chief engr. Cowan Truck Co., Holyoke, Mass., 1917-18, 1919-20; travel around the world, 1921-22; cons. engr. Barrett-Cravens Co., Chicago, and Revolvator Co., Jersey City, N.J., 1922-23; asso. prof. of machine design and industrial practice, Princeton U., 1923-30; prof. mech. engring., Columbia, since 1930; dir. research lab., Gen. Time Instruments Corpn., New York, since 1931. Served as lt. j.g., U.S. Naval Aviation, 1918-19. Mem. Am. Soc. Mech. Engrs., Am. Soc. for Metals, Soc. for Promotion Engring. Edn., Princeton Engring. Assn., Brit. Horological Inst., Am. Assn. Univ. Profts., Tau Beta Pi, Sigma Xi. Republican. Presbyterian. Clubs: Columbia University (New York); Men's Faculty (Columbia U.). Author: Economic Control of Engineering and Manufacturing, 1931. Editor: Aircraft Engine Manual, 1919. Contbr. to engring. publs., granted 14 patents on materials handling machinery. Home: 15 Princeton Av., Princeton, N.J. Office: Columbia University, New York, N.Y.

EIESLAND, John (Arndt), mathematician; b. Ny Hellesund, nr. Christianssand, Norway, Jan. 27, 1867; s. Andreas and Angnete (Abrahamsen) E.; Normal Sch. and Gymnasium, Christianssand; Ph.B., U. of S.Dak., 1891; Ph.D., Johns Hopkins, 1898; Johns Hopkins Scholar, 1897-98; m. Clara Jane Snyder, Sept. 15, 1904. Came to U.S., 1888; teacher Lutheran Acad., Albert Lea, Minn., 1891-92; prof. mathematics, Thiel Coll., Greenville, Pa., 1895-1903; instr. mathematics, U.S. Naval Acad., 1903-07; prof. mathematics and head of dept., W.Va. U., 1907-38, prof. emeritus since 1938. Sec. W.Va. Acad. Science, 1905-06, pres., 1906-07. Fellow A.A.A.S.; mem. Am. Math. Soc., Math. Assn. America, Circolo Matematico di Palermo (Italy), Deutsche Mathematiker

Vereinigung, Phi Beta Kappa. Democrat. Lutheran. Author: Advanced Algebra for Technical Schools and Colleges, 1910; also numerous memoirs in math. jours. on differential geometry, differential equations, and geometry of n-dimensional space. Home: Morgantown, W. Va.

EIKENBERRY, William Lewis, college prof.; b. Waterloo, Ia., July 12, 1871; s. William E. H. and Susan (Berkley) E.; student Mt. Morris (Ill.) Acad. and Coll., 1889-92; B.S., U. of Mich., 1894; studied U. of Chicago; m. Florence Shaw, June 30, 1903; 1 son, Robert S. Prof. sciences, Mt. Morris Coll., 1894-1901; instr. botany, Central High Sch., St. Louis, Mo., 1903-04; head dept. of botany, McKinley High Sch., St. Louis, 1904-09; instr. botany, University High Sch., U. of Chicago, 1909-16; asst. prof. edn., 1916-19, asso. prof., 1919-22, U. of Kan.; prof. and head dept. of science, State Teachers Coll., E. Stroudsburg, Pa., 1922-29; head of Science Dept., State Teachers Coll., Trenton, N.J., 1929—. Lecturer and instructor on gen. science methods. Fellow Am. Assn. Advancement Science; mem. Am. Bot. Soc., Assn. for Research in Science Teaching (pres. 1928-30), Central Assn. Science and Math. Teachers, Sigma Xi, Phi Delta Kappa. Republican. Mem. Ch. of the Brethren. Author: Problems in Botany, 1919; The Teaching of General Science, 1922. Co-Author: Elements of General Science, 1914 (with O. W. Caldwell), 3d edit., 1926; Laboratory Manual of General Science (with same), 1914; Laboratory Problems in General Science (with same), 1924; Educational Biology (with R. A. Waldron), 1929. Home: 1730 Riverside Drive, Trenton, N.J.

EILENBERGER, William Bush, lawyer; b. Middle Smithfield Twp., Monroe Co., Pa., Oct. 3, 1867; s. John Michaels and Catharine Vandermark (Bush) E.; student Kutztown State Normal Sch., 1887-89, Nat. Normal U., Lebanon, O., 1889-90; m. Clara Rhodes, Mar. 23, 1893; 1 dau., Kathryn Burdine (Mrs. H. C. Edwards). Deputy treas. Monroe Co., 1894-97; admitted to Monroe Co. bar, Sept. 1894; mem. law firm Eilenberger & Huffman, 1897-1938 (terminated by death of Harvey Huffman), Eilenberger & Edwards since 1938; atty. Monroe Co. Nat. Bank, 1902-04; local atty. Erie R.R. Co. since 1904, East Stroudsburg Nat. Bank since 1904, Stroudsburg Trust Co.; 1922-33, D.,L.&W.R.R. Co. since 1936; licensed as agent for Fidelity & Deposit Co. of Md. since 1898; pres. Wilkes-Barre & Eastern R.R. since 1937; dir. Erie & Wyoming Valley R.R. Co., Buffalo, Bradford & Pittsburgh R.R. Co., Jefferson R.R. Co., West Claron R.R. Co., Tioga R.R. Co. Mem. Monroe County Bar Assn., Pa. Bar Assn. Ind. Democrat. Mason, Patriotic Order Sons of America. Home: Club Court. Office: 2 N. Seventh St., Stroudsburg, Pa.

EINARSSON, Stefán, univ. prof.; b. Iceland, June 9, 1897; s. Einar Gunnlaugsson and Margrét Jónsdóttir; came to U.S., 1927; B.A., Coll., Reykjavík; M.A., Univ. of Iceland, 1923; grad. student U. of Helsingfors, Finland, 1924-25; Ph.D., Univ. of Oslo, Norway, 1927; m. Margarethe Schwarzenberg, Aug. 26, 1925. Research fellow Johns Hopkins U., 1927; instr. in English philology, Johns Hopkins U., 1928-32, asso., 1932-36, asso. prof. since 1936. Mem. Modern Lang. Assn. of America, Linguistic Soc. of America, Icelandic Nat. League of Winnipeg, Icelandic Literary Soc., Icelandic Soc. of Sciences. Club: Johns Hopkins (Baltimore). Author: Contributions to the Phonetics of the Icelandic Language, 1927; A Specimen of Southern Icelandic Speech, 1931; Life of Eiríkur Magnússon, 1933. Contbr. many articles to American, Icelandic and European learned jours. Cooperating editor, Journal of English and Germanic Philology since 1939. Home: 2827 Forest View Av., Baltimore, Md.

EINSTEIN, Albert, theoretical physicist; b. Ulm a.d. Donau, Germany, Mar. 14, 1879; s. Hermann and Pauline (Koch) E.; ed. Luitpold Gymnasium (Munich), Aargauer Kantonsschule (Aarau, Switzerland), Technische Hochschule, Zürich; Dr. honoris causa, Geneva, Oxford, Cambridge, Manchester, Princeton, Paris, Madrid, Rostock, Buenos Aires, Zürich, Yeshiva, Harvard, London, Brussels; m. Mileva Marec, 1901; children—Albert, Eduard; m. 2d, Elsa Einstein, 1917 (died 1936). Professor at Universität Zürich, Deutsche University (Prague), Technische Hochschule (Zürich), Preuss. Akademie d. Wissenschaft (Berlin); came to United States, 1933; appointed for life as mem. of Inst. for Advanced Study, Princeton, N.J., 1933; discoverer and exponent of the theory of relativity. Awarded Nobel prize, 1922; Franklin Inst. medal, 1935. Member Institut de France. Author: Meaning of Relativity, 1923; Sidelights on Relativity, 1923; Investigation on the Theory of the Brownian Movement, 1926; About Zionism, 1931; (with others) Living Philosophies, 1931; Builders of the Universe, 1932; On the Method of Theoretical Physics, 1933; (with Sigmund Freud) Why War?, 1933; The World as I See It, 1934; also brochures and articles in mags. Home: 112 Mercer St., Princeton, N.J.

EINSTEIN, Jacob R.; sr. partner Einstein & Campbell; pres. Merchants Nat. Bank. Home: 413 N. McKean St. Office: 245 Market St., Kittanning, Pa.

EISAMAN, Howard Glover; chmn. Pa. State Milk Control Commn. Home: East Springfield, Pa. Address: 2350 Green St., Harrisburg, Pa.

EISELE, Richard O.; pastor Birmingham Congl. Ch. Home: 128 Madeline St., Pittsburgh, Pa.

EISENBERG, Harry O., supt. of schools; b. Phila., Pa., Dec. 29, 1901; s. Andrew Shoch and Leonora (Stocher) E.; A.B., Temple U., 1923, M.S. in edn., 1931; grad. student Lehigh U.; m. Elizabeth Bente, July 11, 1923; 1 son, William David. Teacher of Latin and German, Northeast High Sch., Phila., 1922-23; teacher, Girard Coll., summer 1925; teacher Latin and German and coach of wrestling, Perkiomen Sch. 1925-29; prin. Bangor (Pa.) High Sch., 1929-38; supt. of schools, Bangor Sch. Dist., since 1938. Chmn. Mayor's Com. for Unemployment Census; dir. Bangor Merchants' Assn.; pres. Bangor Welfare Bureau; chmn. Tuberculosis Seals Sales; dir. Bangor Pub. Library; dir. Eastern Northampton Co. Tuberculosis and Health Soc.; mem. bd. dirs. Easton Hosp. Mem. N.E.A., Pa. State Edn. Assn. (mem. Dist. XI com.), A.A. A.S., Phi Delta Kappa. Awarded Faculty medal for outstanding senior, Temple U., 1923. Republican. Baptist. Mason. Club: Kiwanis of Bangor (vice-pres.). Author: Comparative Study of Resident and Non-resident Pupils, 1931; The Pupils' Characteristics of a Good Teacher, 1938; also short stories and poems. Historian for the Slate Centennial. Home: 323 Broadway. Office: 4th and Broadway, Bangor, Pa.

EISENBERG, J(ohn) Linwood, educator; b. East Coentry, Chester Co., Pa., Apr. 7, 1877; s. John Y. and Mary A. (Isett) E.; B.E., Juanita Coll., 1895; A.B., Ursinus Coll., 1906, A.M., 1908; Ph.D., U. of Pa., 1913; LL.D., Grove City Coll., 1928; m. Emma H. Johnson, 1905; 1 dau., Margaretta H. Teacher and prin. schs. until 1905; prof. edn., Ursinus Coll., 1910-11; supervising prin., Royersford, Pa., 1905-12; head dept. edn., West Chester (Pa.) State Normal Sch., 1912-14; supt. schs., Chester, Pa., 1914-17; prin. Slippery Rock (Pa.) State Teachers Coll., 1917-29, pres. 1929-34; prof. psychology, Cumberland Valley State Teachers Coll., since 1934, chmn. dept. of edn. and chmn. program com. Mem. N.E.A., Academy Polit. Science (Phila.), Pi Gamma Mu, Phi Sigma Pi, Phi Delta Kappa. Methodist. Mason, Odd Fellow, Rotarian. Joint Author: Happy Hour Readers. Home: Shippensburg, Pa.

EISENHART, Jacob C., pres. J. C. Eisenhart Wall Paper Co.; b. York, Pa., June 14, 1878; s. Charles A. and Emma (Pfahler) E.; student York pub. schs.; m. Rosa Bott, Oct. 1, 1902. With York Card & Paper Co. (since merged with United Wall Paper Factory, Inc.) 1895-1937, becoming dir.; purchased E. R. Haffelfinger Co., Hanover, Pa., 1937; pres. J. C. Eisenhart Wall Paper Co., Royal Wall Paper Co.; dir. York Nat. Bank & Trust Co. Pres. Wall Paper Inst. since 1938. Mason (Shriner). Clubs: Lafayette, York Country, Shrine (York). Home: Sunnyhill, R.D.1, York, Pa. Office: Pine St., Hanover, Pa.

EISENHART, Luther Pfahler, university dean; b. York, Pa., Jan. 13, 1876; s. Charles Augustus and Emma Catherine (Pfahler) E.; A.B., Gettysburg Coll., 1896; Ph.D., Johns Hopkins, 1900; hon. Sc.D., Gettysburg Coll., 1921, LL.D., 1926; hon. Sc.D., Columbia, 1931, U. of Pa., 1933, Lehigh, 1935; m. Anna Maria Dandridge Mitchell, Aug. 17, 1908 (she died Mar. 20, 1913); 1 son, Churchill; m. 2d, Katharine Riely Schmidt, June 1, 1918; children—Anna Small, Katharine Riely. Instr. preparatory dept., Gettysburg Coll., 1896-97; instr. mathematics, 1900-05, asst. prof., 1905-09, prof. since 1909 and dean of the faculty, 1925-33, dean of the graduate school since 1933, Princeton University. Editor Annals of Mathematics; editor Trans. of Am. Math. Society, 1917-23. Trustee Pa. Coll. 1907-14; pres. Association of Am. Colleges, 1930; chmn. div. of physical sciences, Nat. Research Council, since 1937. Decorated Officer Order Crown of Belgium, 1937. Episcopalian. Mem. Am. Math. Soc. (pres. 1931-32), Am. Philos. Soc., A.A.A.S. (v.p. and chairman Sect. A, 1916-17), Société Mathématique de France, Phi Kappa Psi, Phi Beta Kappa, Nat. Acad. Science. Clubs: Nassau (Princeton, N.J.); Princeton, Century (New York City). Author: Differential Geometry of Curves and Surfaces, 1909; Transformations of Surfaces, 1923; Riemannian Geometry, 1925; Non-Riemannian Geometry, 1927; Continuous Groups of Transformations, 1933; Coordinate Geometry, 1939; also a number of papers dealing with mathematics. Home: Wyman House, Princeton, N.J.

EISENHART, William S.; v.p. and treas. York Telephone & Telegraph Co. Address: 105 W. Market St., York, Pa.

EISENHART, Willis Wolf, supt. schs.; b. Abbottstown, Pa., May 29, 1877; s. John Franklin and Katherine M. (Wolf) E.; grad. Shippensburg State Teachers Coll., 1897; A.M., U. of Pa., 1921, B.S., 1917; m. Ella B. Good, Aug. 11, 1904. Supervising prin. schs., Morrisdale, Pa., 1903-15, Clarion, 1917-20; supt. schs., Tyrone, Pa., since 1921. Life mem. N.E.A., Pa. State Edn. Assn. (pres. Central Conv. Dist. 1934-35); mem. Am. Assn. Sch. Adminstrs., Nat. Soc. for Study of Edn., Tyrone Pub. Health Assn., Phi Beta Kappa (charter mem. Tau Chapter). Republican. Lutheran. Mason (K.T., Shriner). Author: Art Education, 1937; How a College Education Should Influence Teaching, 1935; Pennsylvania Germans in the History of the Commonwealth (pamphlet); also numerous addresses. Address: 1111 Lincoln Av., Tyrone, Pa.

EISENHAUER, John Henry, educator; b. Lewisburg, Pa., Aug. 13, 1882; s. Uriah Abraham and Lucy Ann (Grove) E.; student Lewisburg High Sch., 1897-99, Bucknell Acad., 1899-1900; A.B., Bucknell U., 1905; A.M., Columbia, 1922; hon. Ped.D., Franklin and Marshall Coll., 1934; m. Eve Alverna Dershem, June 12, 1906; children—Josephine Louise (Mrs. Glennville Good), John Henry. Teacher rural school, Kelly Twp., Union Co., Pa., 1902-04, teacher in high schools, Scottsdale, Pa., 1905-07, McKeesport, Pa., 1907-17, Pittsburgh, 1917-18; prin. Jr. High Sch., McKeesport, 1918-20; supervising prin., Beaver, Pa., 1920-23; prin. Reading (Pa.) High Sch., 1923-28; asso. prof. of edn., of extension div. and summer session, Bucknell U., 1928-34; dir. Bucknell U. Jr. Coll., 1933-36; prin. Sr. High Sch., Reading, Pa., since 1936. Mem. Gen. Council of Gen. Synod of Evang. and Reformed Ch. in U.S. Mem. N.E.A., Pa. State Edn. Assn., Dept. of Secondary Sch. Prins. of N.E.A., Delta Sigma, Kappa Phi Kappa, Phi Delta Kappa. Republican. Clubs: Kiwanis (past pres. Reading Club); past lt. gov.; chmn. vocational guidance com. Pa.). Home: 1529 Linden St. Office: Senior High School Bldg., Reading, Pa.

EISNER, Mortimer, lawyer; b. Newark, N.J., Jan. 12, 1895; s. Henry and Henrietta (Lindeman) E.; A.B., Amherst Coll., 1917; LL.B., Columbia U. Law Sch., 1921; m. Jeannette Goldsmith, Feb. 1926; children—Gretchen, Joan, Henry. Began as law student and clk. in office, Frank J. Hogan, Washington, D.C., 1921-24;

admitted to D.C. and N.J. bars; now engaged in gen. practice of law at Newark; prof. law, Law Sch. U. of Newark and predecessor since 1927; N.J. corr. for office Frank J. Hogan, Washington, D.C. Served as ensign and chief petty officer, U.S.N. Res. Mem. Am. Bar Assn., Essex Co. Bar Assn., Delta Sigma Rho. Clubs: Athletic (Newark); Amherst (New York). Home: 585 High St. Office: 24 Branford Pl., Newark, N.J.

EKAITIS, George Leo, athletic coach; b. Donora, Pa., July 15, 1906; s. George Joseph and Annette (Pollack) E.; grad. Donora (Pa.) High Sch., 1923; B.S., Western Md. Coll., Westminster, Md., 1931; m. Elsie Louise Herman, July 28, 1929 (died 1931); 1 dau., June Louise; m. 2d, Fredericia Lyles Moessner, Sept. 6, 1938. Asst. football and head lacrosse coach, Washington Coll., Chestertown, Md., 1931, instr. of phys. edn., 1931-36, head football coach since 1932, head track coach since 1935, asst. prof. of phys. edn. since 1936. Served in R.O.T.C., 1927-31, maj.; 2d lt. O.R.C., 1931-36. Hon. fire chief Kennedyville, Md. Mem. Am. Football Coaches Assn., Alpha Gamma Tau. Republican. Catholic. Club: Chester River Yacht and Country (Chestertown, Md.). Home: Kennedyville, Md. Office: Washington College, Chestertown, Md.

EKIN, John Jamison, ry. official; b. Whitestown, Pa., June 8, 1873; s. Robert Findley and Mary Jane (Brenneman) E.; grad. Ellwood City (Pa.) High Sch., 1895; m. Estelle Huntley, June 8, 1903; children—John Jamison, Kenneth Huntley, Robert Lee, Charles William. Warehouseman and yardman Pittsburgh & Western R.R. Co. (now B.&O. R.R.), Ellwood City, 1895-96, clerk, Mar. 1896-Aug. 1896, clerk accounting dept., Pittsburgh, 1896-1901, chief clerk accounting dept., Pittsburgh, 1901-02, bookkeeper, 1902-03; chief clerk to auditor subsidiary lines, B.&O. R.R. Co., Baltimore, 1903-08; auditor Washington Terminal Co., Washington, D.C., 1908-13; gen. accountant B.&O. R.R. Co., Baltimore, 1913-15, gen. auditor, 1915-18; federal auditor Allegheny Region, U.S. R.R. Adminstrn., Baltimore, 1918-20; comptroller B.&O. R.R. Co., Baltimore, 1920-36, v.p. and comptroller since 1936; comptroller Alton R.R. Co. since 1931. Pres. Ry. Accounting Officers Assn., 1922. Republican. Presbyterian. Clubs: Chesapeake, Maryland (Baltimore). Home: Charles and Boyce Avs., Towson, Md. Office: 906 B.&O. Bldg., Baltimore, Md.

ELBIN, Paul Nowell, educator; b. Cameron, W.Va., Apr. 21, 1905; s. Harry and Nellie (Nowell) E.; student Fairmont (W.Va.) State Teachers Coll., 1923-25; A.B., Ohio State U., 1926; A.M., Teachers Coll., Columbia, 1928, Ph.D., 1932; m. Helen Elizabeth Pierce, of Cameron, W.V., Sept. 3, 1929. Teacher Cameron High Sch., 1926-27; with West Liberty State Teachers Coll. since 1928, as head dept. of English and speech and chaplain, 1928-35, pres. since 1935; ordained to ministry of M.E. Ch., 1934. Author: The Improvement of College Worship, 1932. Address: West Liberty, W.Va.

ELDER, Alexander Harold, lawyer; b. Moncton, New Brunswick, Can., Oct. 8, 1883; s. Alexander and Julia Ann (MacArthur) E.; entered U.S., 1892, naturalized; A.B., Harvard U., 1907; LL.B., Harvard Law Sch., 1910; m. Wilhelmina Erdmann, July 8, 1927; 1 dau., Ida. Admitted to Mass. bar, 1909, bar of U.S. Supreme Court, 1917; engaged in practice at Boston in 1910; served as atty., then chief, bur. of prosecution, Interstate Commerce Commn., Washington, D.C., 1911-17; asst. gen. counsel, The C.R.R. Co. of N.J., N.Y. City, 1917-23, gen. solicitor, N.Y. City since 1923; dir. Edroyal Corpn., N.Y. City, since 1928. Served as councilman, Borough of Glen Ridge, N.J., 1935-39. Trustee Canadian Soc. of N.Y.; dir. N.J. Taxpayers Assn. Mem. Am. Bar Assn., The Pilgrims Soc. of the U.S. Republican. Presbyterian. Clubs: Country (Glen Ridge); Harvard of New Jersey. Home: 13 Ferncliff Terrace, Glen Ridge, N.J. Office: 143 Liberty St., New York, N.Y.

ELDER, Walter Thomas, adult edn. dir.; b. North Braddock, Pa., Jan. 30, 1893; s. Argyle Warreston and Edith (Ellenberger) E.; grad.

Dayton (Pa.) Normal Sch., 1909; A.B. (1st honors), Pa. State Coll., 1916; student U. of London, Eng., 1919; M.Sc., New York U., 1934; m. Helen Aline Conaghan, Oct. 30, 1916; children—Elizabeth Anne, Walter Thomas. Mathematics prof. and athletic coach, Renovo (Pa.) High Sch., 1916; instr. and asst. prof., engring. extension div., Pa. State Coll., 1919-25; became asso. prof. Rutgers U., New Brunswick, N.J., 1926, now prof.; asst. dir. Univ. Coll. Served as corpl., Co. I, 320th Inf., 80th (Blue Ridge) Div., U.S. Army, 1917-19, wounded at Nantillois, France, 1919. Mem. Am. Legion (New Brunswick, N.J.), Vets. of Fgn. Wars (State Coll., Pa.), Pi Kappa Alpha, Phi Kappa Phi, Eta Mu Pi. Independent Republican. Methodist. Clubs: Kiwanis (New Brunswick, N.J.); Raritan Arsenal Officers (Metuchen, N.J.). Advisor to Univ. Coll. Honor Soc. and Kappa Upsilon Fraternity, Rutgers U. Home: 205 N. 2d Av., Highland Park, N.J. Office: Rutgers U., New Brunswick, N.J.

ELDERKIN, George Wicker, educator, editor; b. Chicago, Ill., Oct. 5, 1879; s. Noble Strong and Lena (Wicker) E.; A.B., Dartmouth, 1902; Ph.D., Johns Hopkins, 1906; studied Am. Sch. of Classical Studies, Athens, Greece, 1906-10; m. Kate D. McKnight, May 3, 1924; children—George Wicker, John Denny, Janet Sage. With Princeton since 1910, asso. prof. art and archæology, 1921-1928, professor since 1928; editor in chief Am. Jour. of Archæology, 1924-31. First lieut. Army Ambulance Service, U.S.A., 1917-19. Mem. Archæol. Inst. America, Psi Upsilon; mem. German Archæol. Inst. Author: Problems in Periclean Building, 1912; Kantharos —Studies in Dionysiac and Kindred Cult, 1924. Home: Princeton, N.J.

ELDREDGE, Laurence Howard, coll. prof., lawyer; b. Cold Springs, N.J., Mar. 18, 1902; s. Irvin Howard and Marie Louise (Benton) E.; student Cape May (N.J.) High Sch., 1916-20; B.S., Lafayette Coll., Easton, Pa., 1924; LL.B., U. of Pa., 1927; m. Helen Biddle Gans, Sept. 30, 1926; children—Mary Harriet, Deborah, Helen Louise. Admitted to Phila. bar, 1927, Supreme Ct. of Pa., 1928, U.S. Supreme Ct., 1933; asso. with firm Montgomery & McCracken (formerly Roberts & Montgomery), Phila., Pa., 1927-38; prof. law, Temple U. Sch. of Law, Phila., 1928-33; asso. in law, U. of Pa., 1933-34, 1937-38, prof. law since 1938. Speaker for United Campaign, 1936, 1937, 1938 and for various other causes. Trustee Protestant Episcopal Hosp., Phila.; dir. and mem. exec. com. Phila. Art Alliance. Mem. com. on Torts Am. Law Inst. since 1932, mem. since 1936. Mem. Am., Pa. State and Phila. bar assns., Am. Acad. Polit. and Social Science, Am. Mus. Natural History (asso.), Franklin Inst. (asso.), Pa. Soc. Mayflower Descendants (gov., 1935-37), S.R., Colonial Soc. of Pa., Soc. of Colonial Wars in Commonwealth of Pa., Order of Founders and Patriots, Juristic Soc., Phi Beta Kappa, Pi Delta Epsilon, Delta Upsilon, Delta Theta Phi. Republican. Episcopalian. Clubs: Union League, Franklin Inn, Lawyers (Philadelphia). Author: Pa. Annotations to Restatement of the Law of Torts, 1938; contbr. articles to legal jours., syndicated newspaper articles; editor Pa. Bar Assn. Quarterly since 1938; asst. to State Reporter since 1937. Home: Green Valley Road, Bryn Mawr, Pa. Office: 3400 Chestnut St., Philadelphia, Pa.

ELDRIDGE, Francis Reed, commercial expert; b. Haddonfield, N.J., May 28, 1889; s. Francis Reed and Viola (League) E.; grad. Baltimore City Coll., 1908; student George Washington U. (non-grad.); m. Kathleen Sanzo, Nov. 16, 1912; children—Francis Reed, Karin Monica, Richard Adams, Patricia Darling. Student interpreter, Am. Embassy, Tokio, Japan, 1909-11; asst. sec. and treas. Nipponophone Co., Ltd., Japan, 1911-14; with Swift & Co., packers, Columbia and Augusta, Ga., 1914-18; chief Far Eastern Div. of Bur. Foreign and Domestic Commerce, under Dept. of Commerce, since 1918; asst. registrar, later registrar, China Trade Act Cos., since 1922; v.p. Asiatic Selling Co., Ltd., 1926-27; New York commercial agent, Dept. of Commerce, 1927; executive v.p. Am. Mfrs. Export Assn.,

1930. Professor of foreign trade, New York Univ. Sch. of Commerce, 1930; now chief of Commercial Intelligence Div., U.S. Dept. of Commerce, Washington, D.C. Maj. O.R.C., Military Intelligence Division, General Staff, U.S.A. Member American Economic Assn. Episcopalian. Mason. Author: Trading with Asia, 1921; Oriental Trade Methods, 1923; Financing Export Shipments, 1929; Advertising and Selling Abroad, 1930; Dangerous Thoughts on the Orient, 1933; Export and Import Practice, 1938. Home: 810 Garfield St., Bethesda, Md. Address: U.S. Dept. of Commerce, Washington, D.C.

ELGIN, Joseph Clifton, prof. chem. engring.; b. Nashville, Tenn., Feb. 11, 1904; s. John Clifton and Elizabeth (Vogely) E.; Ch.E., U. of Va., 1924, M.S., same, 1926; Ph.D., Princeton U., 1929; m. Anne Marjorie Wilkins, Sept. 18, 1929; children—Alice Ball, Sarah Elizabeth, Joseph Clifton, Jr. Fellow in chemistry, U. of Va., 1924-25, Du Pont Fellow, 1925-26, actg. asst. prof. chemistry, 1926-27; Du Pont Fellow, Princeton U., 1927-28, Procter Fellow, 1928-29; instr. chem. engring., Princeton U., 1929-31, asst. prof., 1931-35, asso. prof., 1935-39, prof. since 1939, chmn. dept. chem. engring. since 1936; control chemist, Johns Manville Corpn., summer 1925; research fellow Am. Petroleum Inst., Princeton, 1929-31; licensed engr. state of N.J.; consultant in chemistry and chem. engring. Mem. Am. Inst. Chem. Engrs., Am. Chem. Soc., Am. Inst. Mining & Metall. Engrs., Soc. for Promotion Engring. Edn., Army Ordnance Assn., Princeton Engring. Assn., Sigma Phi, Epsilon, Alpha Chi Sigma, Tau Beta Pi, Sigma Xi, The Raven Soc. Demogrrat. Episcopalian (vestryman Trinity Ch.). Contbr. many tech. and sci. articles to mags. and journs. Home: 10 College Rd. Office: Frick Chemistry Laboratory, Princeton University, Princeton, N.J.

ELGIN, William Worcester, physician; b. Cincinnati, O., Apr. 26, 1905; s. William Jackson and Lula (Worcester) E.; grad. Richlands (Va.) High Sch., 1922; A.B., Washington and Lee U., Lexington, Va., 1925; student U. of Va., 1923-25; M.D., Johns Hopkins, 1929; m. Elizabeth Jane Knight, Aug. 2, 1930. Interne Church Home and Infirmary, Baltimore, 1929-30; mem. staff Sheppard and Enoch Pratt Hosp., Towson, Md., since 1930, now sr. physician; specialist in psychiatry. Certified in psychiatry by Am. Bd. Psychiatry and Neurology, 1939. Mem. Baltimore City Med. Soc., Med. and Chirurg. Faculty of Md., A.M.A., Southern Med. Assn., Am. Psychiatric Assn., A.A.A.S., Mental Hygiene Soc., Am. Psychopathol. Assn., Phi Beta Kappa, Phi Beta Pi. Democrat. Club: Am. Power Squadron (Baltimore). Address: Towson, Md.

ELIASBERG, Louis Edward, pres. Finance Co. of America at Baltimore; b. Selma, Ala., Feb. 12, 1896; s. Adolph and Hortense R. (Schwartz) E.; student Baltimore City Coll.; spl. student, U. of Pa.; m. Hortense M. Kahn, June 1, 1927. Pres. Finance Co. of America at Baltimore since 1919. Home: 3320 Bancroft Road. Office: Munsey Bldg., Baltimore, Md.

ELIASON, Eldridge L.; surgeon Hosp. of U. of Pa., Gen. and Presbyn. hosps.; prof. surgery, U. of Pa.; prof. clin. surgery Pa. Grad. Sch. Address: 326 S. 19th St., Philadelphia, Pa.

ELIASON, James Bayard, treas. E. I. du Pont de Nemours & Co.; b. Middletown, Del., July 20, 1885; s. James D. and Laura (McIntire) E.; student high sch. and business coll.; m. Gertrude Lindale, Oct. 25, 1911. Treas. E. I. du Pont de Nemours & Co. since June 1, 1930. Home: 606 Edgehill Road, Westover Hills. Office: du Pont Bldg., Wilmington, Del.

ELK, Benjamin Raymond, mfg. chemist; b. New York, N.Y., Oct. 11, 1897; s. Samuel and Luba (Gordon) E.; ed. Coll. of City of N.Y., 1914; Ph.B., Sheffield Sci. Sch. of Yale U., 1920; m. Janet R. Cohen, Oct. 26, 1930; children —Frances, Seymour. Employed as lab. chemist, United Piece Dye Works, Lodi, N.J., 1915-16; chemist, mgr. plant-dept., Central Dyestuff & Chem. Co., Newark, N.J., 1916-17; gen. mgr.

B. R. Elk & Co., Inc., mfg. chemists, Garfield, N.J., 1920-32, pres. and gen. mgr. since 1932; dir. Spray-All Mfg. Co. Served in U.S.A., 1918. Dir. and sec. Beth Israel Hosp., Passaic, N.J., 1930-36. Mem. Phi Alpha. Republican. Jewish religion. Mason. B.P.O.E. Home: 357 Van Houten Av. Office: 195 Palisade Av., Garfield, N.J.

ELKAN, Henri, musician and publisher; b. Antwerp, Belgium, Nov. 23, 1897; s. Sem and Clara (Blitz) E.; came to U.S., 1920, naturalized, 1938; ed. Antwerp Conservatorium, Amsterdam Conservatorium; m. Tanis Cohen, Sept. 9, 1921; 1 dau., Louise. Pres. and founder Elkan-Vogel Co., Inc., music publishers, Phila., Pa., since 1925; conductor Phila. Grand Opera Co., 1926; conductor Phila. Ballet since 1927; conductor Steel Pier Grand Opera Co. since 1930. Home: 2310 Pine St. Office: 1716 Sansom St., Philadelphia, Pa.

ELKIN, Cortlandt Whitehead Wilson, M.D.; b. Smicksburg, Pa., Mar. 26, 1885; s. Francis and Mary Ann (McCausland) E.; A.B., Allegheny Coll., Meadville, Pa., 1909; M.D., Johns Hopkins U., Baltimore, 1913; m. Pauline M. Lewis, June 16, 1925. Interne Allegheny Gen. Hosp., Pittsburgh, 1913-14, asst. pathologist, 1914-15, asst. in medicine, 1915-17, mem. asso. staff, 1919-25, mem. attending staff since 1925. Served as 1st lt. and capt., M.C., U.S. Army, 1917-19. Fellow A.M.A.; mem. Pittsburgh Acad. of Medicine (librarian since 1934), Hist. Soc. of Western Pa. (sec. since 1935), Pa. Med. Soc. (sec. med. section, 1937, chmn., 1938), Allegheny Co. Med. Soc. Mason (Ionic Lodge 525 of Pa.). Author article on history of Indiana Co., Pa. Contbr. to med. jours. Home: 474 S. Braddock Av. Office: 121 University Place, Pittsburgh, Pa.

ELKIN, Curtis E(dison), banker; b. Porter, Pa., June 13, 1887; s. James H. and Mary Ella (Oberlin) E.; ed. State Teachers Coll., Indiana, Pa.; m. Helen M. Steving, Feb. 6, 1912; 1 dau., Helen Elizabeth (Mrs. R. Gerald Mcwrey). Private sec. to Congressman J. N. Langham, 1911-12; clerk Pa. R.R. Co., Indiana, Pa., 1913-14; teller and sec. First Nat. Bank, Glen Campbell, Pa., 1915-17; prin. commercial dept., State Teachers Coll., Indiana, Pa., 1918-19; pres. Rossiter (Pa.) State Bank (now Homer City State Bank), 1920-39; pres. Elderton State Bank since 1920; sec. and treas. Indiana Construction Co. since 1925; dir. Homer City State Bank, Elderton State Bank. Republican. Methodist. Mason (Shriner). Address: 442 S. Seventh St., Indiana, Pa.

ELKINS, Davis, ex-senator; b. Washington, D.C., Jan. 24, 1876; s. U.S. Senator Stephen B. and Hallie (Davis) E.; student Harvard University; m. Mary Reagan; children—Hallie Katherine, Davis, Maureen. Left college, 1898, to enlist as pvt. 1st W.Va. Vol. Inf., at beginning of Spanish-Am. War; commd. 1st lt. and later served as capt. on staff of Brig. Gen. Theodore Schwan, in Cuba and Porto Rico; assumed charge of business interests of father, upon leaving army; apptd. by Gov. Glasscock of W.Va. to U.S. Senate to fill vacancy caused by death of father, serving Jan. 9-Jan. 31, 1911. Commd. maj. U.S.A., Dec. 27, 1917, and served as adj. 13th Inf. Brigade, 7th Div., in Tex. and France; hon. discharged, Dec. 27, 1918, after being elected in absence to U.S. Senate for term 1919-25. Republican. Clubs: The Links, Racquet and Tennis (New York); Deepdale Golf. Home: Morgantown, W.Va.; 2029 Connecticut Av., Washington, D.C.

ELKINS, William McIntire, investment banking; b. Phila., Pa., Sept. 3, 1882; s. George W. and Stella (McIntire) E.; grad. St. Marks Sch., 1901; student Harvard, 1901-05; m. Elizabeth Wolcott Tuckerman, June 10, 1905; children—William L., Elizabeth W., Bayard T. Began in investment banking business at Phila., 1906; mem. firm Elkins, Morris & Co. since 1911; vice-president Land Title Building Corporation; dir. Land Title Bank & Trust Co., Vulcanite Portland Cement Co.; trustee Penn Mutual Life Ins. Co. Lieut. U.S.N.R.F., 1917-19. Vice-pres. Pa. Mus. and Sch. of Industrial Art; trustee St. Mark's Sch.; dir. Phila. Free Library. Republican. Episcopalian. Clubs: Philadelphia, Pine Valley, Sunny Brook, Farmers', Whitemarsh Country. Home: Chestnut Hill, Pa. Office: Land Title Bldg., Philadelphia, Pa.

ELKINTON, J. Passmore, corpn. official; b. Moylan, Pa., Jan. 18, 1887; s. Joseph and Sarah (West) E.; student Westtown (Pa.) Sch., 1899-1904; A.B., Haverford (Pa.) Coll., 1904; m. Mary Bucknell; children—J. Russell, Rebecca (Mrs. Robert S. Schoonmaker, Jr.), David Cope; m. 2d, Anna Griscom, Nov. 5, 1931. Began as clerk Phila. Quartz Co., 1908; now v.p. and dir. Phila. Quartz Co.; sec. National Silicates, Ltd., Toronto, Can. Dir. Am. Friends Service Com. Mem. Society of Friends. Club: Down Town (Phila.). Home: Moylan, Pa. Office: 121 S. Third St., Philadelphia, Pa.

ELKINTON, Thomas William, pres. Philadelphia Quartz Co.; b. Philadelphia, Pa., Aug. 22, 1892; s. William T. and Eleanor (Rhoads) E.; ed. Westtown Sch.; B.S., Haverford Coll., 1914; m. Elizabeth West Roberts, May 10, 1916; children—Dorothy, Thomas, Herbert R. Associated with Philadelphia Quartz Co. since 1914, becoming works mgr., 1919, dir. since 1919, v.p., 1921, pres. since 1930. Mem. bd. mgrs. Corpn. of Haverford Coll., 1935. Mem. Franklin Inst. Soc. of Friends. Home: 45 E. Maple Av., Moorestown, N.J. Office: 121 S. Third St., Philadelphia, Pa.

ELLENBOGEN, Henry, judge, ex-congressman; b. Vienna, Austria, Apr. 3, 1900; s. Samson and Rose (Franzos) E.; LL.B., Duquesne U. Law Sch., 1924; m. Rae Savage, Dec. 18, 1927; 1 dau., Naomi Ruth. In practice of law, Pittsburgh, since 1926; mem. 73d to 75th Congresses (1933-38), 33d Pa. Dist.; judge Court of Common Pleas of Allegheny County since Jan. 3, 1938. Home: 5711 Pocusset St. Office: City-County Bldg., Pittsburgh, Pa.

ELLENSTEIN, Meyer C.; mayor of Newark for term ending 1941. Address: Newark, N.J.

ELLERHUSEN, Florence Cooney, painter; b. Norwood, Ont., Can.; d. John Ward and Mary Ann (O'Callahan) Cooney; studied art at Art Inst. Chicago, Art Students' League (New York); pupil of William M. Chase, William H. Vanderpoel, George Elmer Brown and George Luks; m. Ulric H. Ellerhusen, sculptor, Jan. 19, 1921. Exhibited at Art Inst. Chicago, Nat. Acad. Design, Allied Artists America, New York Water Color Club, Am. Water Color Soc., Baltimore Water Color Soc., Newport Art Assn., Montclair Art Assn. Mem. Nat. Assn. Women Painters and Sculptors, Allied Artists of America, Pen and Brush Club. Democrat. Catholic. Home: Towaco, N.J.

ELLERHUSEN, Ulric Henry, sculptor; b. Waren, Mecklenburg, Germany, Apr. 7, 1879; s. Henry Christopher and Mary (Quapp) E.; grad. high sch., Leipzig, 1892; studied at Art Inst. Chicago, Art Students' League, and Cooper Union, New York, also with Karl Bitter; m. Florence Cooney (portrait and landscape painter), Jan. 19, 1921. Came to U.S., 1894, naturalized citizen, 1900. Exhibited at Nat. Acad. Design, Architects' League, Allied Artists America, Union League Club (New York), Pa. Acad. Fine Arts (Phila.), Carnegie Inst. (Pittsburgh), Corcoran Art Galleries (Washington, D.C.), San Francisco Expn., Blackstone Galleries (Buffalo, N.Y.), St. Louis Art League (winner of design of St. Louis Art League); etc. Prin. works: "Meditation," and "Maidens Bearing Garlands," also figures of "Conception" and "Contemplation," Palace of Fine Arts, San Francisco Expn.; Schwab memorial fountain, Yale Univ.; Diana panel at "Greystone," N.Y. estate of Samuel Untermeyer; rowing trophy for U.S. Navy; war hero medals for Pa. R.R. Co.; Peace monument, Elmwood Park, N.J.; communion rail, "The Life of Christ," Ch. of St. Gregory, New York; "St. Michael," St. Mary's Coll., Notre Dame, Ind.; "History of Religion," 21 statues, Chapel, U. of Chicago; statues and symbolical decorations main entrance, Ch. of the Heavenly Rest, N.Y. City; exterior stone sculpture, Oriental Inst., U. of Chicago; friezes, La. State Capitol; colossal reliefs, Electrical Bldg., Century of Progress, Chicago; "First Permanent Settlement of the Old Northwest" monument, Harrodsburg, Ky.; frieze, Post Office, Columbus, O.; "Lewis and Clark" and "The Road to Oregon," friezes, Kansas City (Mo.) City Hall; "The Oregon Pioneer," figure for the new State Capitol, Salem, Oregon. Awarded gold medal for sculpture, Architectural League of New York, 1929, Allied Artists of America, 1934. Member National Sculpture Soc. (sec.), Archtl. League N.Y. (v.p.), Allied Artists America; hon. mem. Beaux Arts Inst. Design, Salmagundi Club; Nat. Academician. Instr. in sculpture, Beaux Arts Inst. 8 yrs. Lutheran. Home: Towaco, N.J. Studio: 101 Park Av., New York, N.Y.; also Towaco, N.J.*

ELLEY, Harold Walter, chemist; b. Madison, Neb., May 16, 1891; s. Walter Christopher and Emeline (Seeley Field) E.; B.S., U. of Neb., Lincoln, Neb., 1912, M.A., 1913; Ph.D., Cornell U., 1916; m. Sarah Palmer Caswell, Sept. 26, 1916; children—Carolyn Palmer, Elizabeth Caswell. Research chemist, Eastern Lab., E. I. du Pont de Nemours & Co., Wilmington, Del., 1916-17, div. head Eastern Lab., 1917-19, asst. mgr. organic div., chem. dept., 1919-21, div. head Jackson Lab., 1921-26, asso. dir. Jackson Lab., 1926-29, chem. dir. organic chemicals dept. 1929-33, since 1938. Mem. Am. Chem. Soc., Am. Inst. Chem. Engrs., Franklin Inst., Sigma Xi, Alpha Chi Sigma, Gamma Alpha. Presbyterian. Clubs: Wilmington Country, du Pont Country (Wilmington, Del.). Home: 716 Greenhill. Office: Nemours Bldg., Wilmington, Del.

ELLICOTT, Valcoulon LeMoyne, physician; b. Lake Roland, Md., Nov. 15, 1893; s. Charles Ellis and Madeleine (LeMoyne) E.; student Princeton U., 1911-13; B.S., Mass. Inst. Tech., 1916; M.D., Johns Hopkins U. Med. Sch., 1920; Dr.P.H., Johns Hopkins U. Sch. Hygiene and Pub. Health, 1921; m. Mary Purnell Gould, Apr. 5, 1926; children—John Valcoulon LeMoyne, Grace Joycelin, Clarendon Gould. Engaged as epidemiologist, N.Y. State Dept. of Health, Albany, N.Y., 1922-23; epidemiologist, Baltimore Health Dept., 1923-32; county health officer, Montgomery Co., Md. since 1932. Enlisted in Med. Res. Corps during World War later transferred to S.A.T.C. Fellow Am. Pub. Health Assn.; mem. A.M.A., Southern Med. Assn., Phi Kappa Psi, Phi Chi. Democrat. Episcopalian. Clubs: Rotary (Rockville); Wednesday (Baltimore); Edgemoor (Bethesda, Md.). Home: 6818 Glenbrook Rd., Bethesda, Md. Office: Court House, Rockville, Md.

ELLIOTT, Charles Herbert, commr. of education; b. Normal, Ill., Aug. 2, 1878; s. David Spangler and Emily Alberta (Muilberger) E.; B.S., McKendree College, 1907; A.M., Columbia University, 1908, fellow in education, 1909-10, Ph.D., 1914; LL.D., John Marshall College of Law, 1933; Litt.D., Rutgers University, 1937; m. Helen Peters, Aug. 24, 1912; children—Mary Peters, Kathryn Helen. Teacher, prin. and supt. pub. schs., 1899-1906, 1908-09; instr., Southern Ill. Normal Sch., 1910-13; prof. edn. and dir. training sch., N.C. State Coll. for Women, 1914-15; prof. edn. and head of dept., Rutgers, 1915-23, dean of Sch. of Edn., 1923-27, dir. Summer Session, 1915-27, dir. extension courses, 1916-27; commr. of edn. State of N.J., since 1927; sec. N.J. State Bd. of Edn. since 1927. Mem. and sec. Ednl. Survey Commn. of N.J., 1927-31; mem. N.J. State Bd. of Regents (sec., 1929-30), N.J. State Pub. Library Commn., N.J. State Commn. for Rehabilitation of Handicapped Persons, N.J. Conf. on Child Health and Protection (exec. com. since 1931), N.J. Washington Bi-Centennial Com.; mem. White House Conf. on Child Health and Protection (sub com. on spl. classes), 1929-30; mem. N.J. Sch. Survey Commn., 1932-34; one of organizers N.J. State High Sch. Conf. in 1918 (mem. gen. conf. com. 10 yrs.); chmn. sub-com. on state activities Child Edn. Sect., Nat. Safety Council, since 1936; hon. mem. N.J. United States Constitution Commn. since 1936. Trustee Rutgers U. Mem. N.E.A. and Dept. Superintendence same, Am. Inst., Ednl. Research Assn., Am. Acad. Polit. and Social Science, Nat. Soc. Coll. Teachers of Edn., Nat. Soc. for Study of Edn., N.J. Council of Edn. (chmn. com. on pedagogics, 1920-25), N.J. State Teachers Assn., N.J. Science Teachers' Assn., N.J. Schoolmasters Club, N.Y. Schoolmasters Club, Phi Beta Kappa, Sigma Xi, Phi Delta Kappa; fellow A.A.A.S. Presbyn. Club: Newark Athletic. Home: 330 Lincoln Av., New Brunswick, N.J. Office: State House, Trenton, N.J.

ELLIOTT, Foster Floyd, agrl. economist; b. Eubank, Ky., Jan. 3, 1895; s. Simon Thomas and Mary Belle (Floyd) E.; grad. Berea (Ky.) Acad., 1914; B.S. in Agr., U. of Ky., 1919; M.S. in economics, U. of Ill., 1920; student Harvard, 1922-23; Ph.D., U. of Wis., 1926; m. Florence Esther Street, Apr. 12, 1926; children—James Robert, Elizabeth Belle, Mary Lou. Extension economist, U. of Ill., 1920-22; statistician Nat. Milk Producers' Fed., 1925; statistician and economist, Bureau Agrl. Economics, U.S. Dept. of Agr., 1925-30; agrl. expert, Bureau of Census, U.S. Dept. of Commerce, 1930-32; agrl. economist, Bureau of Agrl. Economics, U.S. Dept. of Agr., 1933-34; chief production planning sect., Program Planning Div., A.A.A., 1934-36, dir. Program Planning Div. since 1936; mem. Am. Farm Econ. Assn., Alpha Zeta, Sigma Xi. Presbyn. Mason. Author of govt. bulletins and monograph, Types of Farming in the U.S. Contbr. to scientific jours. Home: 121 Hasketh St., Chevy Chase, Md. Office: Dept. of Agriculture, Washington, D.C.

ELLIOTT, George Warren, gen. sec. Philadelphia Chamber of Commerce; b. Philadelphia, Pa., Oct. 23, 1884; s. William and Rebecca (Hemphill) E.; grad. Central High Sch. of Phila.; student U. of Pa. Law Sch., 1907-08; m. Laura Martin Thiess, June 6, 1916; children—George Warren, Douglas Hemphill, Marie Elizabeth. With Phila. Inquirer, 1905-08, Fidelity & Aetna Ins. Cos., 1908-11; asst. fire marshal, Phila., 1911-12, fire marshal, 1912-24; asst. dir. pub. safety, Phila., 1924-26, dir. 1926-28; asst. gen. sec. Phila. Chamber of Commerce, 1928-29, gen. sec. since 1929. Pres. Boy Council of Phila.; v.p. Crime Prevention Assn. of Phila.; mem. bd. mgrs. Central High Sch. Alumni Assn.; dir. Big Brothers Assn., Nat. Fire Protection Assn. (pres.), Nat. Fire Waste Council; mem. exec. com. Nat. Safety Council; v.p. Army Ordnance Assn. Republican. Methodist (pres. bd. trustees Calvary Ch.). Mason. Clubs: Penn Athletic (bd. govs.), Lambskin, Union League, Rotary, Maskenoza Fishing, Ocean City Yacht. Home: 6400 Sherwood Rd. Office: 1129 Walnut St., Philadelphia, Pa.

ELLIOTT, Grace Young (wife of Dr. John Wesley Elliott), teacher and home maker; b. Millers Mills, N.Y., June 5, 1887; d. Israel I. and Martha Jane (Hadley) Young; Ph.B., Syracuse U., 1910, spl. student, Cons. of Music, Rochester, N.Y., 1913-15; m. Dr. John Wesley Elliott, Sept. 25, 1916; children—Grace Elizabeth, Martha Jeffress, John Young. Engaged as teacher in pub. and high schs. in N.Y., 1905-15; volunteer instr. English to Italians in Phila. and vicinity since 1916; student counselor Eastern Pa. Baptists; mem. bd. Bapt. Womens Mission Soc. of Pa., Bapt. Union of Phila. and Vicinity, Womens Interdenominational Union, Pa. Cong. of Parents and Teachers. Pres. Glenside W.C.T.U. Mem. Womens Missionary Soc., Womens Union, Alpha Chi Omega, Eta Pi Upsilon, Pandaisia (orgn. ministers' wives), Grange. Republican. Baptist. Address: Alderson-Broaddus College, Philippi, W.Va.

ELLIOTT, John Wesley, clergyman; b. South Boston, Va., Aug. 19, 1891; s. John Wesley and Sallie Henry (Jeffress) E.; A.B., U. of Richmond, 1913; B.D., Colgate, 1916; M.A., U. of Chicago, 1917; D.D., Kalamazoo Coll., 1935, U. of Richmond, 1936; m. Grace Aline Young, Sept. 25, 1916; children—Grace Elizabeth, Martha Jeffress, John Young. Ordained ministry Bapt. Ch., 1917; pastor First Bapt. Ch., Canton, N.Y., 1917-18; acting pastor Haddonfield, N.J., 1918-19; pastor Central Bapt. Ch., Wayne, Pa., 1919-23; gen. sec. Edn. Bd. Pa. Bapt. Gen. Conv., 1923-25; dir. social edn., Am. Bapt. Publ. Soc., 1925-33, sec. of Christian Edn., 1933-39; pres. Alderson-Broaddus College since 1939. Mem. various coms. Northern Bapt. Conv., Internat. Council of Religious Edn., Federal Council Chs. of Christ in America, Pa. Council of Christian Edn., Pa. Council of Chs., World's Sunday Sch. Assn. and many other orgns. working for social betterment. Mem. Am. Acad. Polit. and Social Science, Phi Delta Theta. Democrat. Address: Alderson-Broaddus College, Philippi, W.Va.

ELLIOTT, William John, church official; b. Grundy Co., Ia., Sept. 11, 1878; s. George B. and Susan (Weedon) E.; student Cornell Acad., Mount Vernon, Ia., 1899-1901; A.B., Cornell Coll., 1904; LL.D., Dakota Wesleyan U., 1936; m. Emma Cora Bruett, Oct. 10, 1906; children—George Bruett, Orlo John, Duane William (dec.). Bookkeeper and asst. cashier Hubbard (Ia.) State Bank, 1896-99; bookkeeper, auditor and asst. cashier Cedar Rapids (Ia.) Savings Bank, 1904-16, cashier and dir., 1916-19; sec. and mgr. Cedar Rapids Clearing House Assn., 1908-19; nat. treas. Bd. of Home Missions and Church Extension of M.E. Ch. since 1919; treas. and dir. Robert Morris Hotel Co., Phila.; vice-pres. and dir. 22d and Arch St., Inc., Phila.; mem. and treas. Nat. Bureau of Goodwill Industries of M.E. Ch. Del. to Gen. Conf. M.E. Ch., 1916; del. Uniting Conf. of Meth. Churches, Kansas City, Mo., 1939. Trustee Cornell Coll., Mount Vernon, Ia., 1914-19; trustee and treas. Lansdowne (Pa) Meth. Ch. Mem. Phi Beta Kappa. Republican. Mason. Home: 204 Wayne Av., Lansdowne, Pa. Office: 1701 Arch St., Philadelphia, Pa.

ELLIS, Carleton, S.A.R., chemist; b. Keene, N.H., Sept. 20, 1876; s. Marcus and Catharine (Goodnow) E.; B.Sc., Mass. Inst. Tech., 1900; m. Birdella M. Wood, Nov. 28, 1901. Instr. Mass. Inst. Tech., 1900-02; has worked extensively in field of edible oils, fats, waxes, synthetic resins, paints, varnishes, petroleum products, and gasoline mfr.; has taken out many patents; dir. Ellis-Foster Co. Charter mem. Inventors' Guild; mem. Am. Chem. Soc., Am. Inst. Chem. Engrs., Soc. Chem. Industry; fellow Chem. Soc. (British); pres. N.J. Chem. Soc., 1918-21; mem. Sons Am. Revolution. Gold medal for inventions at Jamestown Exposition, 1907; Edward Longstreth medal, Franklin Institute, 1916. Author: Hydrogenation of Organic Substances, 3d edit., 1930; Synthetic Resins and Their Plastics, 1923; 2d edit., 1935; Chemistry of Petroleum Derivatives, 1934; Vol. 2, 1937; Soilless Growth of Plants, 1938; and many papers in tech. jours. Co-Author: Gasoline and Other Motor Fuels; The Vital Factors of Foods; Ultra Violet Light; Chemistry of Printing Inks, etc. Home: 143 Gates Av., Montclair, N.J.; (summer) "Seal Rock," Hyannis Port, Mass.; (winter) Nassau, Bahama Islands. Laboratory: 92-98 Greenwood Av., Montclair, N.J.

ELLIS, Charles Calvert, clergyman, educator; b. Washington, D.C., July 21, 1874; s. Henry Jennings and Kate Calvert (Kane) E.; B.E., Juniata Coll., Huntingdon, Pa., 1890, A.B., 1898; A.M., Ill. Wesleyan U., 1903, Ph.D., 1904; Ph.D., U. of Pa., 1907; studied Princeton, 1919-20, Harvard, summer 1922; B.D., Temple U., 1920; D.D., Juniata, 1925; m. Emma Susan Nice, Dec. 25, 1902; children—Calvert Nice, John Dwight. Teacher pub. schs., 1890-94; prof. English, Juniata Coll., 1898-99, 1900-01; head dept. edn., 1907-30, v.p., 1917-30, pres. since 1930; asso. pastor First Brethren Ch., Phila., 1899-1900, pastor, 1919-21; lyceum lecturer, 1908-13. Asso. Victoria Inst. (Gt. Britain). Mem. N.E.A., Pa. State Ednl. Assn., Nat. Soc. for Study of Edn., Soc. Coll. Teachers of Edn., English-Speaking Union; mem. Pa. Commn. for Study of Ednl. Problems, 1931-35; moderator Church of Brethren Nat. Conv., 1935; pres. Assn. of Coll. Presidents of Pa., 1936; pres. Gen. Edn. Board of Church of Brethren. Rotarian. Author: Lancasterian Schools in Philadelphia (thesis), 1907; Studies in Doctrine and Devotion (Part III), 1919; The Religion of Religious Psychology, 1922, 28; The Christian Way of Life, 1924. Frequent speaker at commencements and summer confs.; author of This Week's Teaching Principle in S.S. Times, 1919-30. Home: 1830 Mifflin St., Huntingdon, Pa.

ELLIS, Francis A., dermatologist; b. Baltimore, Md., Oct. 3, 1899; s. John H. and Katherine Odella (Adams) E.; A.B., Johns Hopkins U., 1921; M.D., U. of Md. Med. Sch., 1925; post grad. study in dermatology, U. of Pa., 1927-28; m. Marguerite C. Bautz. Began in gen. practice of medicine, 1926, dermatology, 1928; mem. staff Mercy Hosp., Univ. of Md. Hosp. Mem. S.A.T.C., 1918; commd. lt. Nat. Guard, 1932, capt., 1935. Diplomate Board of Dermatology; mem. A.M.A., Baltimore-Washington Dermatol. Assn. Catholic. Home: 10 W. Read St. Office: 104 W. Madison St., Baltimore, Md.

ELLIS, Furey, insurance broker; b. Phila., Pa., May 14, 1890; s. Peter and Theresa (Grossa) E.; ed. St. Veronica's Parochial Sch., Phila.; m. Mary A. Kelly, June 25, 1929. In insurance business since 1912; pres. Furey Ellis, Inc., Phila. Served with 304th Ammunition Train, U.S. Army, with A.E.F., during World War. Del. Rep. Nat. Conv., 1932. Mem. Phila. County Bd. of Prison Inspectors; vice-pres. Prisoners' Family Welfare Assn.; mem. bd. mgrs. Catholic Childrens Bureau; trustee Fitzgerald Mercy Hosp.; dir. St. Francis Industrial Sch. for Boys, St. John's Orphan Asylum, Catholic Protectory (for boys), Phoenixville. Apptd. Ky. Colonel by Gov. Ruby Lafoon, Apr. 15, 1935. Comdr. Order of the Crown of Italy; Private Chamberlain of the Cape and Sword to His Holiness Pope Pius XII; Medaglia D'Argento by King of Italy; Verdun Medal (U.S.). Mem. 304th Ammunition Train Assn. (past pres.), Am. Legion (past post comdr.), Catholic Philopatrian Lit. Inst. of Phila., Circolo Dante Alighieri (past pres.), Vet. of Foreign Wars. Republican. Catholic. K. of C. (4°), Elk (past sec. to grand exhalted ruler). Clubs: Penn Athletic, Friendly Sons of St. Patrick, City Business (past pres.), Poor Richard (Phila.); Whitemarsh Country (Whitemarsh, Pa.); Manufacturers Golf and Country. Home: 1701 Locust St. Office: 708 Widener Bldg., Philadelphia, Pa.

ELLIS, Mell Brantley, investment brokerage; b. Due West, S.C., Feb. 17, 1882; s. Melvin Brantley and Lily (Easler) E.; ed. pub. schs., Due West, S.C., and U. of Pa. Wharton Sch. of Commerce; m. Mary Ann Clayton, Aug. 5, 1909. Engaged in investment brokerage business since 1915, mem. firm Cadbury, Ellis and Co., Phila., Pa., since 1920. Trustee Burd Sch. Republican. Episcopalian (vestryman St. Stephen's Ch., Phila.). Mason. Clubs: Orpheus, Bond. Home: 115 Argyle Rd., Ardmore. Office: 1420 Walnut St., Philadelphia, Pa.

ELLIS, William John; b. Muncy, Pa., Nov. 18, 1892; s. Rev. John R. and Annie (Thomas) E.; A.B., Hobart Coll., 1914, M.A., 1914, LL.D., 1929; grad. study, Columbia, 1914-17; Ph.D., Rutgers, 1928; m. Marie Law, June 30, 1917; children—Janet Lee, Mary Ellen, John. Teacher, Morse Sch., Englewood, N.J., 1914-17; asst. in classification work, Dept. Instns. and Agencies, N.J., 1919-21, dir. div. of classifications and edn., 1921, commr. of dept. since 1926; secretary N.J., Social Security Commn. and of N.J. Crime Commn.; mem. N.J. Police Radio. Served as 1st lt. infantry, U.S.A., 1917-19. Mem. President's White House Conf. (chmn. com. on physically handicapped), 1928-29; mem. New Jersey State Rehabilitation Commn.; United States del. to Am. Prison Congress, Prague, 1929; N.J. del. to First Internat. Conf. on Mental Hygiene; mem. advisory council N.J. State Emergency Relief Adminstrn.; mem. Advisory Com. on Prisons, Probation and Parole (of which Dr. Hastings H. Hart was chmn.), apptd. by the Wickersham Com on Law Enforcement and Observance; mem. N.J. Juvenile Delinquency Commn.; past pres. N.J. Hosp. Assn., N.J. Conf. of Social Work; mem. N.J. Commn. on Inter-state Coöperation; chmn. Interstate Commn. on Social Security of State Govts.; mem. bd. The Osborne Assn.; chmn. Nat. Com. to Survey Juvenile Instns.; pres. N.J. Tuberculosis League; chmn. com. on preparation for parole, Nat. Parole Conf. called by President Roosevelt and Atty. Gen. Frank Murphy, April 1939; mem. N.J. Unemployment Relief Commn., 1939; rep. of N.J. White House Conf. on Children, 1939; mem. exec. com. Nat. Com. on Mental Hygiene. Trustee Hobart Coll., Vineland Training Sch. Hon. fellow Am. Coll. Hosp. Adminstrs.; mem. Am. Pub. Welfare Assn. (past pres.), Am. Prison Congress, Nat. Conf. for Social Work, Phi Beta

Kappa. Presbyn. Kiwanian. Author of many articles and reports on crime. Home: Station A, Trenton. Office: State Office Bldg., Trenton, N.J.

ELLIS, William T., M.D., surgeon; b. Masonville, Ky., Sept. 12, 1880; s. J. W. (M.D.) and Elizabeth (Whipp) E.; A.B., Washington and Lee U.; M.D., U. of Pa.; m. Mary O'Donnell, 1911. In gen. practice of medicine; surgeon St. Joseph Hosp., 1908-25, Stetson Hosp. since 1921; division surgeon Dept. Pub. Safety, Philadelphia, since 1911. Served as capt. Med. Corps, U.S. Army, World War. Mem. A.M.A., Pa. State Med. Soc., Philadelphia Co. Med. Soc. Artisan. Clubs: Physicians Motor, Keystone Motor. Home: 1115 Lindley Av. Office: Hardt Bldg., Broad and Columbia Av., Philadelphia, Pa.

ELLIS, William Thomas, writer; b. Allegheny, Pa., Oct. 25, 1873; s. Charles H. and Mary E. (Davis) E.; pub. sch. edn.; (LL.D., Davidson Coll., 1913); m. Margaret H. McKinnon, Oct. 3, 1899; children—Franklin Courtney, Mackinnon, Margaret Amelia. On staff Phila. dailies till 1894; editor the Internat. Christian Endeavor Organ, 1894-97; editor Forward, Presbyn. weekly, 1897-1902; on editorial staff Phila. dailies; toured the world investigating social, religious and polit. conditions for syndicate of Am. newspapers, 1906-07, 1910-11; toured Chinese famine field, winter of 1906-07, and by his writings raised more than million dollars for relief; at his suggestion, in personal interview, President Theodore Roosevelt invited Chinese students to America and had government allocate part of Indemnity Fund for their support; interviewed Dalai Lama; travel in Russia, 1917; war correspondent Russian, Persian, Caucasus, Roumanian and French fronts, 1917-18; the only correspondent present at the first all-American action of the War, Battle of Apresmont; special correspondent of New York Herald and asosciated newspapers in Balkans, Turkey, Egypt, 1919; represented Chicago Daily News and associated newspapers at Conf. on Limitation of Armament, Washington, 1921-22; in Near East for Saturday Evening Post and other mags., 1923. Made complete tour of Bible lands, identifying real site of Kadeshbarnea in Mid-Sinai, 1925-26, revisited Sinai, Akabah and Petra, 1930; in Palestine and Near East for Herald-Tribune, 1938. Has lectured and addressed many conventions, especially of churchmen, in all parts of country; several seasons on Chautauqua circuits; writer of S.S. lessons in syndicate of newspapers since 1897; candidate for Congress, 1922. Sec. commn. on Christian publicity Men and Religion Cong., New York, 1912, and edited and largely wrote its vol., The Church and the Press. Author: Men and Missions; Billy Sunday—the Man and His Message; Advertising the Church; Bible Lands Today, 1927. Contributor to magazines; newspaper columnist. Clubs: Art (Phila.); Cosmos, Nat. Press, Overseas Writers (Washington). Staff contributor to The Christian Herald; author of "Religion Day by Day," syndicated daily newspaper feature, Originator of Nat. Recognition Day for Sunday Sch. Teachers. Home: (winter) Swarthmore, Pa.; (summer) Lyndhurst, Ont.

ELLMAKER, Lee, publisher and editor; b. Lancaster, Pa., Aug. 7, 1896; s. Alfred and Mary (Hess) E.; ed. West. Phila. High Sch., 1910-14; m. Myrtle Wolf, Sept. 15, 1921; children—Lee, Jr., William. Employed as newspaper reporter, 1913-15; pvt. sec. to Hon. William S. Vare, 1915-18; v.p. Nat. City Bur., Washington, D.C., 1918-25, corr. for Internat. News Service, 1919-23; organized and pub. Phila. Daily News, 1926-38; pub. Liberty and others publs. for Macfadden Publications, 1927-31; pub. Pictorial Review, 1931-33; pub. Woman's World since 1932, Teck Publications since 1930; pres. Excello, Woman's World and Pictorial Review Pattern Cos., 1931-35; pres. Philadelphia Daily News, Inc., Woman's World Pub. Co. In radio service, U.S.N., 1918. Republican. Mason. Home: Haddonfield, N.J. Address: Daily News, Philadelphia, Pa.

ELLSBERG, Edward, engr., author; b. New Haven, Conn., Nov. 21, 1891; s. Joseph and Edna (Lavine) E.; student U. of Colo., 1910, Eng. D., 1929; B.S., U.S. Naval Acad., 1914, grad. sch. same, 1916; M.S., Mass. Inst. Tech., 1920; m. Lucy Knowlton Buck, June 1, 1918; 1 dau., Mary Phillips. Served with U.S.N. until 1926, advancing through grades to lt. comd.; salvage officer, raising U.S. Submarine S-51 from sea bottom, 1926 (awarded D.S.M.); also salvage officer, initial operations on S-4, 1927; promoted to comd., Special Act of Congress, for work on S-51 and S-4, 1929; comdr., U.S.N.R. Chief engr. Tide Water Oil Co., 1926-35, now cons. engr. Mem. Westfield School Bd. since 1935. Mem. N.J. Soc. Professional Engrs., Am. Petroleum Inst., Naval Inst., Am. Polar Soc. Awarded campaign badges, World War and Mexican Campaign. Clubs: Army and Navy (Washington); Military-Naval (New York); Explorer's; The Adventure Soc. Author: Salvage Operations on S-51, 1927; On the Bottom, Literary Guild selection (also Brit., Danish, Argentine and Spanish editions), 1929; Thirty Fathoms Deep, 1930; Pigboat (also British and Danish edits., prod. as film Hell Below), 1931; Ocean Gold, 1935; Spanish Ingots, 1936; Hell on Ice (Book-of-the-Month Club selection Feb. 1938), 1938; Men Under The Sea, 1939. Contributor Scientific American, Marine Engineering, Collier's, World's Work, Saturday Evening Post. Inventor of under water torch for cutting steel; designed system used by U.S.N. for salvaging submarines; inventor of improved method in fields of dehydrating and dewaxing lubricating oils and in cracking crude oil for anti-knock gasoline. Lecturer on world affairs, neutrality and disarmament. Home: 714 Hanford Pl., Westfield, N.J.

ELLSON, John Vernon, Jr.; chief of service, obstetrics and gynecology Delaware Co. Hosp.; obstetrician and gynecologist Phila. Lying-In Hosp. of Pa. Hosp. Address: 255 S. 17th St., Philadelphia, Pa.

ELMEN, Gustaf Waldemar, elec. engr.; b. Stockholm, Sweden, Dec. 22, 1876; s. Claes Julius and Josephine (Ericson) E.; B.S., U. of Neb., 1902, M.A., 1904, D. Eng., 1932; m. Ruth M. Halvorsen, 1907; children—James Frederick, Richard Spencer, Paul Halvorsen; came to U.S., 1893, naturalized, 1915. Fellow in physics, U. of Neb., 1902-04; elec. engr. for Gen. Electric Co., 1904-06, for Western Electric Co., 1906-25, for Bell Telephone labs. since 1925. Fellow Am. Inst. E.E. Mem. Sigma Xi. Awarded John Scott medal by City of Philadelphia, 1927, Elliott Cresson medal by Franklin Inst., Phila., 1928. Republican. Inventor magnetic materials used in elec. communications. Author of papers on magnetic properties of alloys. Home: 104 High St., Leonia, N.J. Office: 463 West St., New York, N.Y.

ELMER, Manuel Conrad, sociologist; b. Monroe, Wis., Dec. 5, 1886; s. John and Anne (Denier) E.; S.B., Northwestern Coll., Naperville, Ill., 1911; A.M., U. of Ill., 1912; Ph.D., U. of Chicago, 1914; m. June Maud Ashley, Sept. 3, 1914; children—Anne-June, Patricia Ashley, Glaister Ashley. Prof. sociology and economics, Fargo (N.D.) Coll., 1914-16; asso. prof. sociology and dir. sociol. surveys, U. of Kan., 1916-19; asso. prof. sociology and social work, U. of Minn., 1919-26; prof. sociology and head of dept., U. of Pittsburgh, since 1926, and dir. graduate div. social work, 1932-38. Mem. Am. Sociol. Soc., Kappa Delta Pi, Pi Gamma Mu, Delta Sigma Phi. Presbyn. Author: Social Survey of Urban Communities, 1914; Social Statistics, 1926; Technique of Social Surveys, 1927; Family Adjustment, 1932; Social Research, 1938; General Sociology (with Verne Wright), 1938; also many monographs, among them—A City Within a City, Women and Industry, Women in Church and Secretarial Work, Juvenile Delinquency, etc. Home: 427 Elmer Av., Edgewood, Pittsburgh, Pa.

ELMER, Robert Potter, physician; b. Bridgeton, N.J., Mar. 15, 1877; s. Macomb Kean and Laura (Molten) E.; B.S., Princeton, 1899; M.D., U. of Pa. Med. Sch., 1902; m. Mary Cogswell, May 1, 1906; children—Elizabeth, Laura Moulton, Robert Potter, Jonathan. After usual interneships engaged in gen. practice of medicine at Wayne, Pa., since 1902. Mem. Montgomery Co. Med. Assn. (pres.), Phi Kappa Sigma, Phi Alpha Sigma. Held championship in archery of U.S. for 8 different yrs.; mem. Club of United Bowmen of Phila. (founded 1828). Republican. Presbyn. Club: Schuylkill Valley Medical (Norristown). Author: American Archery, 1917; Archery, 1925, rewritten and enlarged, 1932, 3rd printing 1939. Contbr. on archery to Encyc. Britannica; spl. editor on archery for Webster's Dictionary. Author (under name Dr. T. Hudson Christopher): Unmarried Minds, 1937. Home: 120 Audubon Av., Wayne, Pa.

ELMER, Walter Gray, physician; b. Trenton, N.J., Oct. 3, 1872; s. Dr. William and Alice (Gray) E.; student State Normal, Trenton, N.J., 1890; B.S., Princeton U., 1894; M.D., U. of Pa., 1897. Resident physician Presbyn. Hosp., Phila., 1897-99; now prof. of orthopedics, Grad. Sch. of Medicine, U. of Pa.; prof. orthopedic surgery, Woman's Med. Coll. of Pa.; visiting orthopedic surgeon, Grad. Hosp. of U. of Pa., Hosp. of Woman's Med. Coll., Phila. Gen. Hosp. Served as capt. Med. Sect. Officers Reserve Corps, U.S. Army, Dec. 21, 1917 to Dec. 1937. Fellow Coll. of Physicians of Phila., Phila. Acad. Surgery, Am. Coll. Surgeons, Am. Acad. Orthopedic Surgeons; mem. Phila. Pediatric Soc., Phila. Orthopedic Club, Phila. Co. Med. Soc., Pa. Med. Soc., A.M.A., Pa. Hist. Soc., Pa. Soc. Sons of Revolution. Presbyterian. Clubs: Corinthian Yacht, University (Phila.); Tiger Inn (Princeton U.). Home: 1801 Pine St., Philadelphia, Pa.

ELMES, Frank Corkins, lawyer; b. Berwick, Pa., Oct. 1, 1906; s. William Edward and Mary Lillian (Corkins) E.; A.B., Lafayette Coll., Easton, Pa., 1928; LL.B., Dickinson Sch. of Law, Carlisle, Pa., 1931. Admitted to Pa. bar, 1931, U.S. Dist. Court for Middle Dist. of Pa., 1932; practice in Berwick since 1931; dir. and sec. of bd. First Nat. Bank of Berwick; dir. Berwick Bldg. & Loan Assn. Trustee Berwick Y.M.C.A. Dir. Berwick Chamber of Commerce. Mem. Am. Bar Assn., Pa. State Bar Assn., Columbia and Montour Counties Bar Assn. Republican. Presbyterian. Mason (32°), Elk. Clubs: Acacia, Kiwanis (pres. 1938), Berwick Golf (pres. 1939). Home: 314 E. Front St. Office: First Nat. Bank Bldg., Berwick, Pa.

ELMORE, Carl Hopkins, clergyman; b. Maryville, Tenn., May 13, 1878; s. Edgar Alonzo and Edith Miriam (Bartlett) E.; A.B., Maryville Coll., (Tenn.), 1898; A.B., Princeton U., 1900; ed. Union Theol. Sem., 1903-06, New Coll., Edinburgh, Scotland, 1907, Marburg U., Germany, 1907, U. of Berlin, Germany, 1913; m. Amelia Josephine Burr, Nov. 19, 1921. Ordained to ministry Presbyn. Ch., 1906; pastor Congl. Ch., Briarcliff Manor, N.Y., 1908-20; pastor, First Presbyn. Ch., Englewood, N.J., since 1920. Served as religious dir. Rainbow Div. Y.M.C.A. in France, 1917-18. Mem. Phi Beta Kappa. Republican. Presbyn. Club: Princeton (New York). Author: The Inexhaustible Christ, 1935. Home: 150 E. Palisade Av., Englewood, N.J.

ELSASSER, Theodore Herman, M.D.; b. Union City, N.J., Dec. 19, 1899; s. Adolph Otto and Mary (Klein) E.; student New York U. (premedic), 1919-20, M.D., 1924, post grad. surg. course, 1927-30; m. Elise Valentine Zibetti, of Jersey City, N.J., Mar. 17, 1924; children—Elise Theodora, Mary Ellen, Elaine Dolores. Interne North Hudson Hosp., Weehawken, N.J., 1924-25; instr. in surgery, New York U., Coll. of Medicine, since 1928; asso. gynecologist, North Hudson Hosp., Weehawken; asst. attending surgeon, Christ Hosp., Jersey City, N.J.; asso. with Prof. George B. Wallace, dept. of pharmacology, New York U., in cancer research since 1930. Served in R.O.T.C., 1919. Mem. Clin. and Post Grad. Surg. Soc. of New York U., A.M.A., Hudson City and North Hudson Physicians Soc., Phi Alpha Sigma. Mason. Protestant. Contbr. to med. jours. Home: 906 Park Av., North Bergen, N.J. Office: New York Univ. College of Medicine, New York, N.Y.

ELSE, Frank Lester, college prof.; b. Conyngham, Luz Co., Pa., Dec. 18, 1896; s. John Frank and Anna (Hander) E.; B.S., U. of Del., 1923; student Ohio State U., summer 1925; Ph.D., U. of Pa., 1932; m. Myrtle Reynolds, Dec. 26, 1927; children—Joan, Frank Robert,

Barbara Gail. Teacher, Martinsburg (Pa.) High Sch., 1923-24; salesman Am. Agr. Chem. Co., 1924-25; instr. in zoölogy, U. of Pa., 1925-29; asst. prof. of physiology, Med. Sch., U. of Okla., 1929-30; instr. in biology, Temple U., 1930-34; asso. prof. of histology and embryology, Dental Sch., Temple U., since 1934. Served as private Med. Detachment, 318th Inf., 80th Div., U.S. Army, with A.E.F., Apr.-Sept. 1918; casual Sept. 12, 1918-Jan. 1919. Mem. A.A.A.S., Am. Assn. Univ. Profs., Vets. of Foreign Wars, Am. Legion, Phi Kappa Tau, Sigma Xi. Baptist. Mason. Home: 33 Shawnee Rd., Ardmore, Pa. Office: Temple University, Philadelphia, Pa.

ELSON, Henry William, historian, lecturer; b. Muskingum Co., Ohio, Mar. 29, 1857; s. Jacob and Clara (Swingle) E.; A.B., Thiel Coll., Pa., 1886, A.M., 1889; grad. Lutheran Theol. Sem., Phila., 1889; spl. student U. of Pa., 1895-96; Litt.D., Newberry Coll., 1906; m. Hannah E. Smith, 1889 (died 1895); children—Delma Viola, Harold Altair, Winfred Paul; m. 2d, Ida S. MacMullan, 1898; 1 son, Henry William (dec.). Pastor St. John's Evang. Luth. Ch., Kittanning, Pa., 1889-93, St. Stephens, Phila., 1893-95; resigned the ministry and became writer and lecturer of Univ. Extension Soc. of Phila.; prof. history and economics, Ohio U., 1905-16; pres. Thiel Coll., Greenville, Pa., 1916-21; lecturer on history New York Univ. since 1927. Mem. Ohio Constl. Conv., 1912; author of the proposal to enable three-fourths of a jury to render a verdict. Pres. Ohio Valley Hist. Assn., 1914-15. Del. Dem. Nat. Conv., St. Louis, 1916. Author: Side Lights on American History, 2 vols., 1899, 1900 (republished, 1928); Historical Biographies for Children—Andrew Jackson, U.S. Grant, Daniel Boone and Frances Willard, 1899; How to Teach History, 1901; Star-Gazer's Hand-Book, 1902; History of the United States, 1904 (enlarged and republished in 1926 and translated into the French language, 1927, into the Spanish, 1932); History of the United States (5 vols.), 1906; A Guide to American History, 1909; Guide to English History, 1911; Modern Times, and the Living Past, 1921; United States—Its Past and Present, 1925; Through the Years with Our Constitution, 1937; Juvenile Biography of La Fayette, 1937. Wrote nearly 4 vols. of Review of Reviews' "Photographic History of the Civil War," 1911. Home: 1314 Watchung Av., Plainfield, N.J.

ELSWICK, Walter Murrey, lawyer; b. Richlands, Va., May 9, 1899; S. Buena Vista and Lovice (Reed) E.; student Richlands (Va.) High Sch., 1915-19; B.S., U. of Va., 1923, LL.B., 1926; m. Maria Tiffany St. Clair, Jan. 6, 1934. Worked on father's farm until 17, in coal mines, 1917-19, and worked way through sch. and univ.; admitted to Va. bar, 1925, W.Va. bar, 1926; in private practice, Hinton, W.Va., since 1929; pres. B. & G. Realty Co., Hinton, W.Va., since 1938; v.p. and dir. Meadows Furniture Co., Hinton, since 1937; dir. Willow Wood Land Co. Commr. in Chancery, Summers County, 1931-38, divorce commr., 1932-38; commr. of accounts and city atty., Hinton, W.Va., since 1936. Mem. Summers County Bar Assn., W.Va. State Bar Assn. Awarded Thomas F. Ryan Scholarship, U. of Va., 1921, 1922. Mem. bd. of govs. W.Va. Municipal Attorney's Conf., 1938-39. Democrat. Club: Willow-Wood Country (Hinton, W.Va.). Owner of tract of land on Greenbrier River containing 1047 acres on which has developed lodge. Home: 107 Ballengee St. Office: Ewart-Miller Bldg., Hinton, W.Va.

ELTONHEAD, Frank, art dir.; b. Philadelphia, Pa., Oct. 17, 1902; s. Benjamin Franklin and Charlotte (Entwistle) E.; ed. Pa. Museum and Sch. of Industrial Art, Phila., 1919-23; m. Lillias Taylor Egolf, Dec. 10, 1924. Free-lance illustrator, 1923; on advertising staff La France Textile Industries, 1924; free-lanced, 1925-29; art dir. advertising dept. Curtis Pub. Co., Phila., 1929-32; art dir. Ladies Home Journal since 1932. Home: Hatboro, Pa. Address: Curtis Publishing Co., Philadelphia, Pa.

ELVERSON, Howard Wayne, pottery mfr.; b. New Brighton, Pa., Mar. 18, 1875; s. Thomas A. and Katherine (Sherwood) E.; grad. New Brighton High Sch., 1892; student mech. engring., Western U. of Pa., Pittsburgh, 1892-94; m. Carrie Thomas, Mar. 23, 1899; 1 son, Thomas Wayne. Began learning pottery business while student in high sch. and continued to 1898; field engr. bridge construction, 1898-1900; mfr. railway equipment, 1900-28; returned to W. H. Elverson Pottery Co., Inc., 1933, v.p., treas. since 1933. Republican. Methodist. Mason (K.T., 32°, Shriner). Home: Bellevue, Pa. Address: New Brighton, Pa.

ELVERSON, Lew, football coach; B.S., U. of Pa. Football coach and asst. in phys. edn. for men, Swarthmore (Pa.) Coll. Address: Swarthmore, Pa.

ELWOOD, Robert Arthur, preacher, lecturer; b. Newburgh, N.Y., Nov. 27, 1873; s. James and Mary Eggleson (Hoy) E.; student Cedarville (O.) Coll., 1894-95; Ref. Presbyn. Sem., Phila., 1895-96; Princeton Theol. Sem., 1896-97 (non-grad.); m. Eva Madden, Feb. 22, 1900; children—Russell M. and 4 not living. Began as office boy with F. Middleton & Co., Phila., later with John Wanamaker; entered evangelistic work, 1897; ordained Presbyn. ministry, 1899; pastor Absecon, N.J., until 1901, Olivet Ch., Wilmington, Del., 1901-05, 1st Ch., Leavenworth, Kan., 1905-08; founder, 1909, and since pastor Boardwalk Ch., Atlantic City, N.J.; only ch. of its kind in the world: "no members, no officers, no choir and no collection plates." Served two enlistments in Pa. N.G.; corpl. 6th Pa. Vols., Spanish-Am. War, 1898; Y.M.C.A. worker early part of World War; grad. Chaplains' Sch., Camp Taylor, Louisville, Ky., 1918; acting chaplain 157th F.A., 82d Div., Camp Gordon, Ga., 1918; chaplain O.R.C., U.S.A. Mem. Presbytery of West Jersey, Presbyn. Ch. in U.S.A.; mem. Hotel Greeters of America; nat. chaplain Nat. Restaurant Assn., 1928-30; chaplain N.J. Exempt Firemen's Assn. since 1931. Mem. United Spanish War Vets. (chaplain in chief 1911, 18), Jr. Order United Am. Mechanics. Odd Fellow. Kiwanian. Author: Meditations, 1900; Model Conditions of Life, 1904; He Is Coming, 1907; Travel Talks, 1915. Contbr. to mags. Home: "Rest-Haven," Absecon, N.J.

ELY, Sumner Boyer, educator; b. Watertown, N.Y., Nov. 5, 1869; s. Frederick Gustavus and Matilda Caroline (Boyer) E.; S.B., Mass. Inst. Tech., 1892; m. Mary Rodman Updike, Jan. 25, 1899; children—Esther Stockton, Frederick Sumner. Asst. supt. Pressed Steel Car Co., McKees Rocks, Pa., 1900; chief engr. Am. Sheet Steel Co., Pittsburgh, 1901; chief engr. Am. Sheet & Tin Plate Co., Pittsburgh, 1903-06; v.p. Chester B. Albree Iron Works, Pittsburgh, 1906-16; prof. commercial engring., Carnegie Inst. Tech., since 1920; consulting engr. Pa. Giant Power Survey, 1923-24. Sec. Internat. Conf. on Bituminous Coal held under the auspices of Carnegie Inst. Tech., Pittsburgh, 1926, 28. Ex-pres. Univ. Extension Soc., Pittsburgh; mem. Am. Soc. Mech. Engrs., Engrs.' Soc. Western Pa., A.A.A.S., Soc. for Promotion Engring. Edn., Pittsburgh Art Soc., etc. Presbyn. Home: 5122 Pembroke Pl., Pittsburgh, Pa.

ELY, William Harvey Johnson, lawyer; b. Rutherford, N.J., Sept. 18, 1891; s. Addison Ely and Emily (Johnson) E.; student Rutherford (N.J.) High Sch., 1904-08, U. of Mich., Ann Arbor, Mich., 1908-10, 1911-12, N.Y.U. Law Sch., 1910-11, 1912-13; m. Mary Rogers, Apr. 30, 1917; children—William Harvey Johnson, Joseph L., Edward C., Mary, Elizabeth. Admitted as N.J. bar atty., 1915, as N.J. bar counsellor, 1918; judge, Bergen Co. Dist. Ct., 1924-29; Supreme Ct. commr. since 1933; spl. master in chancery since 1928; mem. firm Ely and Ely, lawyers, Rutherford, N.J., since 1922; dir. Rutherford Nat. Bank; adminstr. Works Progress Adminstrn. for N.J., 1935-38. Served as lieut., N.J.N.G., during World War. Councilman, Rutherford, N.J., 1926-32; N.J. State Senator, 1932-35; candidate for U.S. Senate, 1938; pres. Jefferson Dem. Club since 1918. Mem. Alpha Delta Phi, Phi Delta Phi. Democrat. Presbyterian. Elk. Clubs: Down Town (Newark, N.J.); Arcola Country (Arcola, N.J.); Ridgewood Country (Ridgewood, N.J.). Home: 171 Montrose Av. Office: 10 Ames Av., Rutherford, N.J.

ELY, William Newbold, Jr., advertising and publishing exec.; b. Chestnut Hill, Pa., June 3, 1896; s. William Newbold and Lillie (Cairns) E.; student Chestnut Hill (Pa.) Acad., 1904-13; A.B., Yale, 1917; m. Elizabeth Taylor, June 2, 1923; children—Roland, Clinton Newbold, Donald. Clk. Nat. Bank of Commerce, New York, 1919-21; dept. mgr. Brown Bros. & Co., Phila., 1921-23; with George W. Edwards & Co., Phila., 1923-25; v.p. Fisher, Wilson & Co., 1925-29; v.p. William Jenkins Advertising Co., Bridgeport, Pa., since 1930; editor Judge Mag., 1933; partner Dougherty, Corkran & Co., Philadelphia, since 1932; asso. editor Country Life & The Sportsman. Served as 2d lt., F.A., U.S. Army, 1917-19. Trustee Univ. Vet. Hospital, University of Pennsylvania. Member Alpha Delta Phi. Republican. Clubs: Penllyn, 1st City Troop (Phila.); Yale. Home: Ambler, Pa. Office: Bridgeport, Pa.

EMBERY, Frank; chief of ear, nose and throat service Frankford Hosp. Address: 4801 Penn St., Philadelphia, Pa.

EMBERY, Joseph R.; mem. law firm Embery, Outterson & Fuges. Address: Oxford Bank Bldg., Philadelphia, Pa.

EMBREE, Harland Caleb, scientist; b. Linn Co., Ia., Aug. 8, 1890; s. Ezra Ben and Annie Wilhelmina (Engle) E.; student Iowa State Coll., Ames, Ia., 1914-16; A.B., Cornell Coll., Mt. Vernon, Ia., 1919; M.S., U. of Chicago, 1924, grad. student 1925-26; m. Neva Dumond, Dec. 26, 1921; children—Harland Dumond, Edwin Louis. Instr. in physics and chemistry, Monmouth (Ill.) Coll., 1920-23, asso. prof., 1923-24; asst. prof. of chemistry, La. State Normal Coll., Natchitoches, La., 1924-25; senior chemist Coroner's Chem. Lab., Chicago, 1926-27; head chemistry dept., Youngstown (O.) Jr. Coll., 1927-30; head chemistry dept., Flint (Mich.) Jr. Coll., 1930-35; prof. of science, U. of Baltimore, since 1938. Served as 2d lt., 68th F.A., U.S. Army, 1918-19. Mem. A.A.A.S., Am. Chem. Soc., Sigma Xi. Methodist. Home: 5605 Fernpark, Baltimore, Md.

EMBREE, William Dean, lawyer; b. Humboldt, Kansas; s. of William N. and Laura (Fee) Embree; B.L., Berea (Ky.) College, 1899; LL.D., 1933; A.B., Yale U., 1902, LL.B., 1905 (Townsend oratorical prize), A.M., Italian lang. and lit., 1910; m. Etta Parsons, Mar. 9, 1912; children—Catherine, William Dean. Admitted to bar, Conn., 1905, N.Y., 1906; asst. dist. atty. N.Y. City, 1906-17; an organizer Voluntary Defenders Com. for Criminal Courts, 1917, and its chief counsel until 1920; now mem. Milbank, Tweed, Hope & Webb; dir. Manhattan Railway Co.; director Legal Aid Society of New York. Was in charge state-wide graft investigation, 1914; conducted prosecution of criminal charges involving charity orgns. of City of New York, 1916; apptd. mem. bd. mgrs. N.Y. State Reformatory for women, 1920; apptd. spl. dep. atty. gen. to prosecute election frauds, 1922. Trustee Berea (Ky.) Coll.; dir. Katy Ferguson Home for Colored Girls; dir. Soc. for Italian Immigrants; pres. bd. trustees Tenafly (N.J.) Free Pub. Library; pres. Tenafly Community Chest. Lt. col. Remount Div. O.R.C., U.S.A. Mem. Am. and N.Y. State bar assns., Assn. Bar City of N.Y., New York County Lawyers' Assn. (vice-pres. and dir.). Mem. New York County Republican Com. Conglist. Clubs: Yale, Bankers, Broad Street, Downtown Athletic, Oraworth Polo, Knickerbocker Country, Aldecress, Englewood Field. Home: Tenafly, New Jersey. Office: 15 Broad St., New York, N.Y.

EMERSON, Edith, artist, lecturer; b. Oxford, O.; d. Alfred and Alice Louisa (Edwards) E.; ed. Art Inst., Chicago, Ill., Pa. Acad. Fine Arts, Phila., and abroad. Has executed murals, paintings and stained glass for pub. bldgs.; paintings in exhbns., Chicago, New York City, Washington, D.C., Phila., Pa., etc., and in traveling exhibits of Am. Federation of Arts; illustrator for books and mags. including oriental subjects for Asia Mag., also posters, bookplates, portraits, and decorative pen drawings illustrating The Song of Roland, 1938; traveled and studied in Japan,

Mexico, India, Morocco, and 7 European countries. Mem. Nat. Soc. Mural Painters, Am. Soc. Bookplate Designers, Fellowship Pa. Acad. Fine Arts, Phila. Water Color Club, Phila. Art Alliance. Awarded two Cresson traveling scholarships, Pa. Acad. Fine Arts, 1914-15; 2d Toppan prize, 1915; Fellowship prize, 1919; Bryn Mawr May Day poster prize. Home and Studio: Lower Cogslea St. George's Rd., Mt. Airy, Philadelphia, Pa.

EMERSON, Linn, M.D., oculist; b. McDonough, N.Y., Sept. 4, 1873; s. Herbert and Amelia (Puffer) E.; prep. edn. Oxford (N.Y.) Acad.; M.D., Jefferson Med. Coll., Phila., 1897; m. Daisy V. Brewster, 1898 (died 1913); children—Gerald Brewster, Dorothy Brewster; m. 2d, Marie D. S. Franklin, of New Windsor, Md., 1914; children—Marie Franklin, Barbara Jane. Began practice, Orange, N.J., 1901; attending oculist, Manhattan Eye, Ear and Throat Hosp. (New York), 1901-18, Orange Memorial Hosp., Dover Gen. Hosp., N.J. Orthopedic Hosp., Orphans' Home and House of the Good Shepherd (Orange), Arthur Home for Blind Babies (Summit), Essex County Tuberculosis Sanatorium (Verona); lecturer on diseases of eye, ear, nose and throat; Orange Training Sch. for Nurses. Fellow Am. Coll. Surgeons; mem. Am. Laryngol., Rhinol. and Otol. Soc., Am. Acad. Ophthalmology and Oto-Laryngology, Soc. Surgeons State of N.J., A.M.A., Med. Soc. of N.J., N.Y. Acad. Medicine, Alumni Assn. Jefferson Med. Coll. Methodist. Royal Arch Mason. Author: Michael Emerson and Some of His Descendants, 1912; also about 50 monographs and papers on med. topics. Home: 303 Park Av., Orange, N.J. Office: Metropolitan Bldg., Orange, N.J.

EMERY, Chester Alexander, travel agent; b. Apollo, Pa., May 9, 1900; s. Warren Alexander and Nellie (Guffey) E.; student Pittsburgh elementary schs., 1906-14, Fifth Av. High Sch., Pittsburgh, 1914-18, Carnegie Inst. Tech., 1920-24; m. Ruth McDavid, July 11, 1925; children—Suzanne, Jane. Gen. agent French Line, fgn. travel, New York, N.Y., 1924-25, sales, Cleveland (O.) office, 1925-26, asst. gen. agt., 1926-30, gen. agt., Pittsburgh office, since 1930; rep. French Govt. Tourist Bur., French Nat. R.Rs., Pittsburgh, since 1936; gen. agt. Air-France, Pittsburgh, since 1937. Served as private, O.T.C., U.S. Army, Camp Gordon, 1918; 2d lt., F.A. Res., 1920-35. Mem. Theta Xi. Republican. Presbyterian. Mason (Pa. Consistory, Syria Shrine, Islam Grotto). Club: South Hills Country (Pittsburgh). Home: 727 Osage Rd., Mt. Lebanon. Office: Gulf Bldg., 705 Grant St., Pittsburgh, Pa.

EMERY, James Augustan, lawyer; b. Detroit, Mich., Mar. 29, 1876; s. Augustan Havens and Mary (Harrington) E.; student St. Ignatius Coll., San Francisco, Calif.; A.B., Santa Clara (Calif.) U., 1896; attended Hastings Coll. of Law (U. of Calif.), 1898; m. Emily Aloise Hartrick, Jan. 30, 1903; children—Mary Aloise, Letitia Alexia, Alice Suzzane. Admitted to Calif. bar, 1903, and began practice at San Francisco; counsel Health Bd., San Francisco, 1903-04, Citizens' Industrial Assn. America, 1905-08; gen. counsel Nat. Assn. Mfrs., 1910, Nat. Founders' Assn., 1920; assisted in orgn. Nat. Industrial Conf. Bd., 1916; assisted in orgn. of War Labor Bd., 1917; adviser Employer Group of 1st Internat. Labor Conf., Washington, D.C., 1919, has actively participated in presentation of industrial questions in litigation and legislation; factor in transition of Am. industry from system of employers' liability to workmen's compensation. Roman Catholic. Clubs: Chevy Chase (Washington, D.C.); and Bohemian (San Francisco). Author: Accident Prevention and Relief (with F. C. Schwedtman), 1911; Workmen's Compensation in the States (legal phase), 1917. Home: Chevy Chase, Md. Office: Investment Bldg., Washington, D.C.

EMERY, R. Edson; pres. Jessop Steel Co. Home: King Edward Apts., Pittsburgh, Pa. Office: Washington, Pa.

EMHARDT, William Chauncey, clergyman; b. Phila., Pa., Jan. 29, 1874; s. Charles Stokes and Anne Catharine (Burk) E.; grad. Episcopal Acad., Phila., 1890; B.A., U. of Pa., 1894; post-grad. work U. of Pa., Columbia; student Phila. Div. Sch., 1895, S.T.D., 1931; grad. Gen. Theol. Sem., 1897; Ph.D., U. of Kan., 1898; m. Anne Lindsey Haines, Oct. 25, 1900; children—Anne Catharine, Elisabeth Montgomery (dec.). Deacon, 1897, priest, 1898, P.E. Ch.; missionary Western Kan., Indian Ty. and Okla., 1897-98; curate St. Luke's Ch., Germantown, Pa., 1898-1902; rector Ch. of Ascension, Gloucester City, N.J., and St. Luke's Ch., Newton, Pa., until 1919; in charge Country Centre Mission, Bucks Co., Pa., 1911-19; sec. Commn. for Ch. work among Immigrants, Diocese of Pa., 1910-19, Province of Washington, 1917-24, etc.; then field dir. foreign born work, Nat. Council P.E. Ch.; counselor on ecclesiastical relations, P.E. Ch.; vicar of Pro-Cathedral of Saint Mary, Philadelphia, since 1936; spl. chaplain Lambeth Conference, London, 1930; negotiated recognition of Anglican ordinations, Constantinople, 1922; trustee Near East Relief, etc.; chmn. Commn. on Correlation of Chs. in Near East; chmn. Am. Com. of Russian Theol. Sem., Paris; chmn. Am. Com. on Greek Centenary (1830-1930); chmn. Hill School, Athens, 1929-35; chmn. com. on Christian Approach to the Jew; mem. Federal Council Chs. Made hon. archpriest in Constantinople, 1922. Knight Comdr. Order of S. Saviour, Order of Holy Sepulchre. Mem. Am. Acad. Social and Polit. Science, Am. Schs. of Archæology, Am. Soc. Church History, Sons of the American Revolution, Colonial Soc. of Pa. Clubs: Clergy (New York); Penn Athletic (Philadelphia). Author: Oldest Christian People, 1926; Eastern Church in the Western World (with others), 1928; Religion in Soviet Russia, 1929; (monograph) The Anglican Communion and Reunion, 1931. Home: Longport, N.J. Address: 602 S. Broad St., Philadelphia, Pa.

EMIG, William Harrison, asso. prof. biology; b. Coulterville, Ill., Dec. 21, 1888; s. Christian and Amelia (Spindler) E.; ed. Smith Acad., St. Louis, Mo., 1905-07; A.B., Washington U., 1911, Ph.D., same, 1915; m. Katherine E. Ervin, Dec. 30, 1916; 1 dau., Katherine Elizabeth. Instr. biology, U. of Okla., 1914-16; instr. biology, U. of Pittsburgh, 1916-17, asst. prof. botany, 1917-26, asso. prof. botany, 1926-37, asso. prof. biology since 1937. Fellow A.A.A.S.; mem. Bot. Soc. of America, Sigma Xi, Phi Beta Kappa, Phi Sigma. Protestant. Club: Faculty of University of Pittsburgh. Home: 4605 Fifth Av., Pittsburgh, Pa.

EMLEN, John Thompson, architect and social work; b. Philadelphia, Pa., Dec. 28, 1878; s. James and Susan Trotter (Thompson) E.; A.B., Haverford Coll., 1900; B.S. in Architecture, U. of Pa., 1904; m. Mary Carpenter Jones, Mar. 6, 1906; children—Susan Thompson (Mrs. William Guild Taussig), John Thompson, Mary Carpenter, Woodruff Jones. Employed as architect with Cope and Stewardson, 1900-02; actively interested in social work since 1904; mem. bd. dirs. Germantown Savings Fund; mem. bd. dirs. and trustee Richard Humphries Foundation, Emlen Inst.; mem. bd. dirs. White Williams Foundation, Pub. Edn. Assn., Armstrong Assn. of Phila.; trustee Community Fund; mem. exec. com. Council of Social Agencies; chmn. Interagency Council for Youth, Wissahickon Boys Club. Mem. Sigma Xi. Republican. Mem. Religious Soc. of Friends. Club: University. Home: 36 W. School Lane. Office: 1638 Land Title Bldg., Philadelphia, Pa.

EMMERICH, Mary Ashburton Pew (Mrs.); b. Staten Island, N.Y., Mar. 24, 1864; d. William Park and Caroline (Dix) Pew; ed. private schools, Hazleton (Pa.) High Sch. and special course at Wellesley Coll., for one year; m. Louis Oscar Emmerich, Sept. 16, 1891 (died Sept. 23, 1922); children—Franz T., Rudolf (deceased). Began as organist, Presbyterian Ch., Hazleton, 1880; chorus dir. and music teacher until marriage, 1891; active in civic affairs; pres. Hazleton Civic Club several years; planned and developed Roosevelt Park, Hazleton, 1919-22; traveled extensively, 1922-38; lived in Paris, France, 10 years; traveled in South America, S.E. and N. Africa, and spent 2 years in travel in Japan, China, Java, Bali and other countries of the Orient; painted (under name of Mary Ashburton) while in Paris (pictures exhibited in Salon d'Antonine, 1931). Mem. Nat. Soc. Colonial Dames. Episcopalian. Club: Arts (Washington, D.C.). Home: Hazleton, Pa.

EMMET, Herman LeRoy, works mgr. Gen. Electric Co.; b. New Rochelle, N.Y., Sept. 26, 1889; s. Robert Temple and Helena Van Cortlandt (Phelps) E.; M.A., Yale U., 1912; m. Helen Dunscomb Auerbach, June 22, 1912; children—Lydia Field, Katharine Hone, Anna Page, Herman LeRoy, Helena Van Cortlandt. With Gen. Electric Co. since 1912, production mgr. Schenectady works, 1920-29, works mgr. Erie works since 1929; dir. First Nat. Bank of Erie, Lawrence Park Nat. Bank. Dir. Erie County Community Chest, Hamot Hosp., Pa. Assn. for the Blind, Child-Parent Bureau. Republican. Episcopalian. Clubs: University, Yale (New York); University, Erie, Erie Tennis and Country (Erie, Pa.); Lawrence Park (Pa.) Golf; Kahkwa-Tobique Salmon, Chagrin Valley Hunt (Cleveland, O.). Home: 446 W. 6th St. Office: East Lake Road, Erie, Pa.

EMMETT, Paul Hugh, chemist; b. Portland, Ore., Sept. 22, 1900; s. John Hugh and Vina (Hutchens) E.; B.S. in chem. engring., Ore. State Coll., 1922; Ph.D., Calif. Inst. Tech., 1925; m. Lela Jones, July 24, 1930. Instr. in chemistry, Ore. State Coll., 1925-26; research in catalysis, Fixed Nitrogen Research Lab., U.S. Dept. Agr., Washington, D.C., with final rank of sr. chemist, 1926-37; lecturer on catalysis, George Washington U., alternate yrs., 1927-36; prof. chem. and gas engring., Johns Hopkins U., since 1937; consultant U.S. Dept. Agr. since 1937. Mem. Am. Chem. Soc., Sigma Xi, Sigma Tau, Delta Sigma Rho, Phi Kappa Phi, Phi Kappa Tau. Club: Engineers (Baltimore). Contbr. articles on results of research in catalysis, adsorption, nitrogen fixation to scientific jours. Asso. editor of Jour. of Phys. Chemistry, 1938-39. Home: 39th and Canterbury Rd., Baltimore, Md.

EMMONS, Peter Kenneth, clergyman; b. Monmouth Junction, N.J., May 9, 1892; s. Peter Dénise and Emma Catherine (Kennedy) E.; A.B., Princeton University, 1912; graduate Princeton Theological Seminary, 1915; D.D., Washington & Jefferson College, 1937, Grove City College, 1937; m. Helen Augusta West, May 19, 1915; children—Roberta West, Doris Elizabeth, Mary Alice, Helen Patricia. Ordained ministry Presbyn. Ch., 1915; pastor, Bridge St. Presbyn. Ch., Catasauqua, Pa., 1915-16, First Presbyn. Ch., Stroudsburg, Pa., 1916-19, First Presbyn. Ch., Trenton, N.J., 1919-27, Westminster Presbyn. Ch., Scranton, Pa., since 1927. Served with Y.M.C.A., World War. Trustee Princeton Theological Seminary. Mem. Presbyn. Bd. Foreign Missions. Mem. Scranton Chamber Commerce (dir.), Rotary Internat. (former gov. 36th Dist.). Ind. Republican. Mason (32°, Shriner); chaplain Grand Lodge Pa. F.&A.M.). Clubs: Irem Temple Country, Elmhurst Country. Home: 816 Olive St., Scranton, Pa.

EMRICH, John Oscar, librarian; b. Allegheny, Pa., Aug. 6, 1881; s. Conrad and Margaret Sophia (Haseman) E.; student pub. schs. and pvt. tutoring; m. Ida Blanche Oakley, Feb. 20, 1908; children—Margaret Blanche (Mrs. Randall Edward Widrig), Oscar William. In law book business to 1907; librarian Allegheny Co. Law Library, Pittsburgh, Pa., since 1907. Served as mem. legal advisory bd. North Side Dist., Pittsburgh, during World War. Mem. Am. Assn. Law Librarians, Spl. Librarians Assn. Republican. Presbyterian. Mason (32°, Shriner). Author article on cataloguing in Law Library Jour., 1915; editor Voter's Guide, Digest of Election Laws in Pa., since 1920 (annual pub.). Home: 48 Perry View Av., N.S. Office: City-County Bldg., Pittsburgh, Pa.

ENCK, Schuyler Colfax, clergyman; b. Hopeland, Pa., July 3, 1868; s. David S. and Sarah (Yost) E.; B.S., Lebanon Valley Coll., Annville, Pa., 1891, A.M., 1906; B.D., Bonebreak Theol. Sem., Dayton, O., 1893; (hon.) D.D., Lebanon Valley Coll., 1910; m. Elizabeth S. Seltzer, July 20, 1893; children—Ruth Elizabeth (Mrs. Ralph L. Engle), Miriam Yost (Mrs. Robert MacFarland), Paul Seltzer, Schuyler Colfax. Served as student pastor, various chs.,

1889-93; ordained to ministry Ch. of the United Brethren in Christ and pastor, Manheim, 1893-98, Columbia, 1898-1912, Second Ch., Phila., 1912-17; conf. supt. since 1917; trustee Lebanon Valley Coll., Bonebreak Theol. Sem., Quincy U.B. Orphanage and Home; mem. bd. adminstrs., Pub. House, Dayton, O., Conf. Ch. Extension and Home Missionary Soc.; pres. Mt. Gretna Bible Conf.; mem. Commn. of Ch. merger between U.B. and Evang. chs.; editor Conference Herald. Republican. Ch. of United Brethren in Christ. Home: 704 N. 16th St., Harrisburg, Pa.

ENDEAN, M. P.; editor New Kensington Dispatch. Address: New Kensington, Pa.

ENDERS, Martin Luther, clergyman; b. Richmond, Ind., Feb. 11, 1878; s. George W. and Phoebe (Miller) E.; A.B., Gettysburg (Pa.) Coll., 1899, A.M., 1902, D.D. (hon.), 1924; B.D., Gettysburg Theol. Sem., 1902; m. Grace Hubner, Oct. 7, 1902; children—Grace Hubner, Mary Phoebe (Mrs. G. H. Willis), Martin Luther, John George. Ordained to ministry Luth. Ch., 1902; minister, Catonsville, Md., 1901-10, Cumberland, Md., 1910-25; minister First English Evang. Luth. Ch., Baltimore, since 1925. Trustee Tressler Orphans Home, Loysville, 1924. Mem. Phrenna Lit. Soc. of Gettysburg Coll. Republican. Lutheran. Mason (K.T.). Home: Charles and 39th Sts., Baltimore, Md.

ENDERS, Robert Ambrose, banker; b. Enders, Pa., Feb. 12, 1871; s. Isaiah T. and Mary Ellen (Bowman) E.; ed. pub. schs.; m. Gertrude Cooper Bender, May 4, 1905 (died 1910); children—Robert Cooper, Eril Elizabeth, Gertrude Dorothy; m. 2d, Marie Lyle Baillie, Oct. 11, 1927. Succeeded his father in the grocery business in 1897, and continued until 1911; pres. Sixth St. Bank, Harrisburg, 1912-16, Camp Curtin Trust Co., successors, since 1916. Finance commr. of Harrisburg, 1937. Chmn. Camp Curtin Memorial Commn., which erected a memorial to Gov. Curtin, 1922, Italian Park Commn., Harrisburg; mem. bd. dirs. Polyclinic Hosp.; formerly pres. Polyclinic Nurses Home Assn.; dir. Central Y.M.C.A., Harrisburg, pres. of bd., 1927-35; pres. Enders Family Memorial Assn. until 1937. Former pres. Harrisburg Bd. of Edn.; former dir. Harrisburg Chamber of Commerce. Republican. Mem. United Brethren Ch. (Sunday Sch. supt., 1906-36). Home: 2011 N. 3d St. Office: 2100 N. 6th St., and City Hall, Harrisburg, Pa.

ENDERS, Robert Kendall, biologist; b. Essex, Ia., Sept. 22, 1899; s. Emanuel Allen and Frances (Seibert) E.; student Wooster Coll., 1918, 21, 23; A.B., U. of Mich., 1925, Ph.D., 1927; m. Abbie Crandell, Aug. 29, 1923; children—Abbie Gertrude, Allen Coffin. Asst. prof. biology, Union Coll., Schenectady, N.Y., 1927-28; prof. and head dept. of biology, Missouri Valley Coll., Marshall, Mo., 1928-30; mammalogist, Ohio Conservation Commn., 1930; fellow Nat. Research Council, 1930-32; asst. prof. of biology, Swarthmore (Pa.) Coll., 1932-38, asso. prof. since 1938; biologist U.S. Dept. Agr. since 1938; research assoc., Academy of Natural Sciences since 1938. Served in U.S. Army, 1918-19. Mem. Am. Assn. Anatomists, Soc. of Zoölogists, A.A.A.S., Am. Assn. Univ. Profs., Am. Soc. Mammalogists (sec. 1933-38), Wild Life Soc., Sigma Xi, Gamma Alpha, Phi Sigma. Presbyterian. Home: Cedar Lane and College Av., Swarthmore, Pa.

ENDSLEY, Andrew Doak, supt. pub. schs.; b. Coshocton Co., O., May 16, 1875; s. John Q. and Isabel (Elliott) E.; ed. Wooster Coll. Prep. Dept., 1893-94; Ph.B., Coll. of Wooster (O.), 1898; grad. study, summer schs. and extension courses, Columbia, U. of Pittsburgh, Pa. State Coll.; m. Daisy Gray, 1904 (died 1907); 1 son, Robert Gray; m. 2d, Elva Lardin, of Tarentum, Pa., 1912; 1 dau., Jane. Engaged in teaching high sch., Coshocton, O., 1899-1900; prin. high sch., Tarentum, Pa., 1900-03, supervising prin. schs., 1903-05, supt. pub. schs., Tarentum, Pa., since 1905. Dir. Allegheny Valley Y.M.C.A. Mem. N.E.A., Pa. State Edn. Assn., Am. Assn. Sch. Adminstrs., Phi Delta Kappa. Presbyn. Mason. Home: Tarentum, Pa.

ENDSLEY, James William, coal operator; b. Somerfield, Pa., Sept. 15, 1857; s. William and Julianne (Watson) E.; ed. pub. schs. and normal schs. of Pa.; m. Mary Hagans Connelly, May 8, 1880; children—Edna M. (dec. wife of L. E. White), Gilbert F., Mary (Mrs. A. R. Springer). Engaged in retail business as mem. firm William Endsley & Son, 1878; in lumber mfg., 1880-1905; engaged in coal mining operations since 1905; pres. Listonburg Coal Co., Yough Coal Co., Somerfield Coal Co. Served as mem. Pa. Ho. of Rep., 1805-07; mem. Pa. Senate, 1911-17. Republican. Home: Somerfield, Pa.

ENDSLEY, Louis Eugene, cons. engr.; b. Richmond, Ind., Sept. 9, 1879; s. Stephen G. and Eliza Catherine (Beeson) E.; grad. Richmond High Sch., 1898; B.S., Purdue U., 1901, M.E., 1903; m. Mary Alice Barcus, June 7, 1904; children—Edith Alice (Mrs. Robert Martin Fleming), Louis Eugene. Instr. Locomotive Lab., Purdue U., 1901-05, asso. prof. ry. mech. engring., 1905-11, prof., 1911-14; same, U. of Pittsburgh, 1914-22, lecturer since 1922; cons. engr. Am. Steel Foundries, 1910-21, Union Draft Gear Co., 1917-29, Grip Nut Co., 1919-24, Waugh Draft Gear Co., 1922-25, Detroit Steel Products Co., 1923-28, Pittsburgh Annealing Box Co., 1926-37, Verona Tool Works, 1928-33, Fort Pitt Malleable Iron Co. since 1917, Frost Ry. Supply Co. since 1922, Gulick-Henderson Co. since 1923, Edgewater Steel Co. since 1926, Locomotive Economizer since 1927, Fairbanks-Morse Co. since 1932. Mem. Am. Soc. Mech. Engrs., Soc. for Promotion Engring. Edn., Engring. Soc. of Western Pa., Am. Assn. of Railroads (Mech. Sect.), Western Railway Club, Pittsburgh Railway Club, Phi Kappa Psi, Sigma Xi, Tau Beta Pi, Sigma Tau. Republican. Baptist. Mason. Licensed professional engr. in states of Pa. and N.Y. Home: 516 East End Av. Office: 524 Fourth Av., Pittsburgh, Pa.

ENGARD, Charles I., sec. of welfare; b. Mt. Airy, Pa., May 28, 1895; s. Abram and Martha J. (Sibel) E.; ed. Philadelphia pub. schs. and Northeast High Sch.; m. Reeda May Wartman, Apr. 7, 1920. Upon leaving high sch. took position in a bank, later with an automobile concern; apptd. deputy receiver in State banking dept., Oct. 21, 1931, having charge of 32 closed banks in Philadelphia dist., resigned, 1938; apptd. mem. State Veterans' Commn., 1931, later elected chmn., resigning, 1938; sec. of welfare, Pa., since Jan. 11, 1938. Served in both army and navy air service, World War, 1917-19.* Mem. Am. Legion (held various offices; Dept. Comdr. of Pa. 1931; comdr. Henry H. Houston, 2d, Post No. 3, 3 yrs.); Forty and Eight (Grand Chef de gare 1924). Mason. Clubs: Whitemarsh Valley Country, Penn Athletic (Philadelphia). Home: 430 E. Durham St., Mt. Airy, Pa. Office: Dept. of Welfare, Harrisburg, Pa.

ENGEL, Gilson Colby, surgeon; b. Baltimore, Md., Aug. 25, 1898; s. William Henry and Anna May (Metcalfe) E.; student Baltimore City Coll., 1913-17; A.B., Johns Hopkins U., 1922; M.D., Harvard, 1926; m. Doris Gherky, Dec. 22, 1923. Resident physician Lankenau Hosp., Phila., 1926-28; asst. surgeon Germantown Hosp. since 1929; demonstrator in anatomy, Jefferson Med. Coll., 1928-29; with Grad. Sch. of Medicine, U. of Pa., since 1929, as asst. instr. in surgery, 1929-31, instr., 1931-35, asso., 1935-37, asst. prof. since 1937; asst. surgeon Lankenau Hosp. since 1931, Children's Hosp. of Mary J. Drexel Home since 1929. Served as Q.M., 1st class, U.S. Navy, on U.S.S. Massachusetts, 1917-19. Diplomate Am. Bd. of Surgery; fellow Am. Coll. Surgeons, Phila. Coll. Surgeons, Phila. Acad. Surgery, A.M.A.; mem. Phila. Co. Med. Soc., Phila. Pathol. Soc., Phila. Pediatrics Soc., Eastern Surg. Club, Kappa Alpha (Southern), Omicron Delta Kappa, Nu Sigma Nu. Republican. Lutheran. Clubs: Aesculapian (Boston, Mass.); Union League (Phila.). Co-inventor of Engel-May 2-plane direction finder for nailing fractures of the femur. Contbr. of several articles on surgery to med. jours. Home: 700 W. Mt. Airy Av. Office: 1914 Pine St., Philadelphia, Pa.

ENGELDER, Carl John; prof. chemistry, U. of Pittsburgh Address: U. of Pittsburgh, Pittsburgh, Pa.

ENGELS, William Henry, research chemist; b. Karlsruhe, Germany, May 25, 1885; came to U.S., 1911, naturalized, 1924; Diplomingenieur, Tech. Hochschule, Karlsruhe, 1908, Dr. Ingenieur, same, 1911; m. Anna Estelle Lorance, Mar. 4, 1914; 1 dau., Eileen Hope. Employed as plant chemist, Merck & Co., mfg. chemists, Rahway, N.J., 1911-18, dir. applied research, 1918-36, asso. dir. research and development since 1936. Mem. Am. Chem. Soc. Clubs: Rotary (Rahway); Colonia Country (Colonia); Chemists (New York). Home: 265 E. Lincoln Av., Rahway, N.J.

ENGH, Harry M.; v.p. Pa. Telephone Corpn.; also pres. several telephone companies. Home: Edinboro, Pa. Office: 20 E. Tenth St., Erie, Pa.

ENGLAND, Charles Walter, prof. of dairy manufacturing; b. Rising Sun, Md., Dec. 5, 1899; s. Charles Clifford and Nettie May (Clark) E.; grad. Calvert Agr. High Sch., Rising Sun, Md., 1917; student U. of Del., Newark, Del., autumn 1918; B.S., University of Md., 1923; M.S., Cornell University, 1931, Ph.D., 1933; m. Alma Estelle Lease, Apr. 2, 1925; children —Carmen Louise (dec.), Nancy Ann. Chemist and bacteriologist Simpsons Dairy, Inc., Frederick, Md., 1923-29; operated The England Labs., Frederick, Md., 1929-30; bacteriologist Inlet Farms Dairy, Ithaca, N.Y., 1931-32; with University of Md. since 1933, successively instr. asst. prof., asso. prof., now prof. dairy mfg. since 1938; pres. West Mar Creamery Co., Elkins, W.Va. Served in S.A.T.C., U. of Del., 1918. Mem. Dairy Technology Soc. of Md.-D.C. (sec.-treas. since 1939), Am. Dairy Science Assn., Alpha Gamma Rho, Sigma Xi. Democrat. Methodist. Mason (Council of York Rite, Lodge of Perfection of Scottish Rite). Author of scientific papers and bulletins on dairy mfg. Home: 111 Rush Rd., University Park, Md. Office: Univ. of Maryland, College Park, Md.

ENGLAND, Herbert Kingsbury, clergyman; b. Peoria, Ill., Mar. 22, 1878; s. Elias B. and Mary Emma (Chickering) E.; A.B., Princeton U., 1900; ed. Auburn Theol. Sem., N.Y., 1901-04; (hon.) D.D., Coll. of the Ozarks, 1929; m. Ella D. Brungate, Apr. 4, 1905; children— Elizabeth Lawrence, Herbert K., Jr. Ordained to ministry Presbyn. Ch., 1904; minister, Elizabeth, N.J., 1904 to 1907; minister, City Park Branch, First Presbyn. Ch., Brooklyn, N.Y., 1907-11; pastor, First Presbyn. Ch., Roselle, N.J., since 1911; stated clk. of Presbytery of Elizabeth since 1921. Presbyn. Mason. Rotarian. Home: 117 W. 5th Av., Roselle, N.J.

ENGLAND, Welch; mem. staff Camden-Clark Memorial and St. Joseph's Hosps. Address: 717 Market St., Parkersburg, W.Va.

ENGLANDER, Samuel; mem. law firm Englander & Englander. Address: 1222 Spruce St., Philadelphia, Pa.

ENGLAR, George Monroe, real estate reorgn.; b. New Windsor, Md., July 10, 1891; s. George P. B. and Mary Susan (Nusbaum) E.; student New Windsor Coll., Md., 1903-05; A.B. (summa cum laude), Western Md. Coll., Westminster, Md., 1910; m. Elizabeth Downey Walker, Aug. 29, 1921; children—Elizabeth Walker, George Monroe. Employed as teller Farmers & Mechanics Bank, Westminster, Md., 1910-12; chief dep. commr. motor vehicles, Md., 1912-20; treas., later v.p. Title Guarantee & Trust Co., Baltimore, 1921-33; pres. Property Management, Inc., Baltimore, since 1934; voting trustee, v.p. and dir. 1088 Park Ave., Inc., New York City. Served as 1st lt. F.A., U.S. Army, 1917-18. Mem. finance com. Bryn Mawr Sch., Baltimore; treas. Emmanuel P.E. Ch., Baltimore, since 1924. Republican. Episcopalian. Club: Gibson Island. Home: Roland Park Apts. Office: 1020 St. Paul St., Baltimore, Md.

ENGLE, Benjamin (Homer), banker, real estate; b. Harrisburg, Pa., Oct. 11, 1894; s. Benjamin H. and Emma F. (Hershey) E.; prep. edn., Harrisburg (Pa.) High Sch.; B.S., Pa. State Coll., 1916; m. Ruth Bennett, June 4,

1919; children—Robert Homer, Walter Malcolm, Marian Ruth. County Farm Bureau agt., 1916-19; vocational supervisor, Dauphin Co., Pa., 1919-23; chief appraiser Federal Land Bank, 1923-27; reviewing appraiser Farm Loan Bd., 1927-29; sec. Md.-Va. Joint Stock Land Bank, Baltimore, 1929-38; organized Md.-Va. Realty Corpn., Baltimore, to liquidate assets of Land Bank and do brokerage business, 1938, and since pres.; treas. Meadow Brook Farms. Served in U.S. Army, 1918. Pres. Bd. of Edn. of Baltimore County. Mem. Phi Sigma Kappa. Republican. Presbyterian. Mason. Clubs: Optimist Internat., Hillendale Country, Rodgers Forge Country (Baltimore). Farm specialist; owns and operates farms in Md. and Va. Home: 510 Park Av., Towson, Md. Office: Munsey Bldg., Baltimore, Md.

ENGLE, John Raymond; b. Palmyra, Pa., Mar. 13, 1885; s. Samuel F. and Agnes (Balsbaugh) E.; A.B., Yale, 1906; LL.B., U. of Va., 1908; 'LL.D., Lebanon Valley Coll., 1925; m. Nelle Moyer, Sept. 3, 1908; children—Mary Elizabeth, Eleanor Caroline. Began law practice at Huntington, W.Va., 1908, Lebanon, Pa., 1910; treas. E. Pa. Conf. of Ch. of United Brethren in Christ, 1916; mem. bd. administration, U. B. Ch., 1917; trustee Lebanon Valley Coll., 1917, chmn. endowment campaign, 1924; chmn. finance com. and pres. bd. trustees, 1929, acting pres., 1932; pres. Palmyra Improvement Co.; solicitor and dir. Valley Trust Co. Pres. Palmyra Bd. of Edn., 1929. Trustee Bonebrake Theol. Sem., Dayton, O. Mem. Delta Chi. Republican. Mason. Clubs: Pennsylvanians, Pennsylvania German Society. Home: 622 N. Lincoln St. Office: Valley Trust Co. Bldg., Palmyra, Pa.

ENGLERTH, Louis D.; surgeon Frankford, Phila. Gen. and St. Joseph's Hosps. and Girard Coll.; cons. surgeon Friends Hosp., Phila., and Grandview Hosp., Sellersville; asst. demonstrator clin. surgery, Jefferson Med. Coll. Address: 1710 Locust St., Philadelphia, Pa.

ENGLISH, Ada Jeannette, (Mrs. Philip M. English), librarian; b. Washington, N.J., June 11, 1889; d. Walter B. and Bertha Gertrude (Opdyke) Cox; ed. N.J. State Normal Sch., Newark, 1921-22, N.Y. Univ., 1924-25; B.S., Rutgers U., 1927, A.M., same, 1930; B.S., Columbia U. Library Sch., 1932; m. Philip M. English, Apr. 24, 1907 (dec.); 1 son, Wilton Opdyke. Employed as gen. asst., Bayonne, N.J. Pub. Library, 1920-21; librarian N.J. Coll. for Women Library since 1923; organizer N.J. Coll. for Women Library Sch., 1927 and dir. 1927-28; chmn. scholarship examining com. N.J. Library Assn., 1930-33. Mem. Am. Assn. Univ. Profs., Am. Library Assn., Coll. and Reference Assn., Spl. Libraries Assn., N.J. Library Assn., Rutgers U. Sch. of Edn. Alumni Assn., Columbia U. Sch. of Library Service Alumni Assn. (regional chmn. for N.J. and Pa., 1938-39). Democrat. Protestant. Club: Zonta of New Brunswick (pres. 1935-38). Contbr. many articles to various periodicals. Home: 248 Livingston Av., New Brunswick, N.J.

ENGLISH, Charles Henry, lawyer; b. Erie, Pa., Oct. 30, 1883; s. Michael Martin and Maria (Sheridan) E.; LL.B., Georgetown U., 1905, LL.M., 1906, LL.D., 1935; m. Mary O'Brien, June 16, 1910 (died Oct. 8, 1928); children—Richard O'Brien, John William, Mary Patricia; m. 2d, Aline Walker Warfel, of Erie, Pa., Nov. 23, 1929. Admitted to Pa. bar, 1907, and since practiced in Erie; mem. firm English, Quinn, Leemhuis & Tayntor; v.p. and dir. Erie Rys. Co., Erie Coach Co.; dir. Gen. Telephone Corp., Union Bank of Erie, Times Pub. Co., Griffin Mfg. Co.; city solicitor of Erie, 1912-16; mem. Pa. Commn. on Constl. Amendment and Revision, 1919; mem. State Law Revision Commn., 1922; chmn. com. on municipalities in Constl. Conv., 1920; apptd. by Supreme Court of Pa. on com. of 5 on Revision of Rules of Practice, 1922; mem. State Bd. of Law Examiners since 1925, chmn. since 1930. Mem. Erie Chamber of Commerce (pres. 1919); 1st pres. Erie Community Chest, 1918; trustee and treas. St. Vincent's Hosp. Mem. Am. Bar Assn. (mem. council on legal edn. since 1935), Pa. Bar Assn. (pres. since 1937), Am. Law Inst., Am. Judicature Soc., Delta Chi. Republican.

Roman Catholic. K.C. Clubs: Erie, Kahkwa (Erie). Contbr. legal articles to jours. Home: 2050 South Shore Drive. Office: Erie Trust Bldg., Erie, Pa.

ENGLISH, Charles Reid, automobile dealer, mayor; b. Englishtown, N.J., May 18, 1886; s. John Perrine and Anna (Reid) E.; student pub. schs., N.J. Mil. Acad., Freehold, N.J., 1901-05; m. Ethel Mount, June 29, 1910; children—Charles Donald, Mary Elizabeth. Bank clk., 1905-08; treas. and mgr. W. E. Mount Co., gen. mdse., 1908-22; treas. and mgr. Mount English Co., gen. sales and service agency Ford and Lincoln automobiles, Red Bank, N.J., since 1922; chmn. bd. dirs. Merchants Trust Co., Red Bank, N.J.; v.p. W. E. Mount & Sons, Inc., New Brunswick, N.J.; dir. and mem. finance com. Mainstay Bldg. & Loan Assn., Red Bank, N.J. Mayor of Red Bank, N.J., since 1930. Mem. bd. mgrs. N.J. State Hosp., Marlboro, N.J.; dir. Riverview Hosp., Red Bank, N.J. Republican. Presbyterian. Mason, Odd Fellow. Club: Lions (Red Bank, N.J.; pres.). Home: 224 Maple Av. Office: 90 Monmouth St., Red Bank, N.J.

ENGLISH, Conover, lawyer; b. Elizabeth, N.J., Jan. 1, 1877; s. Nicholas C. J. and Ella J. (Hall) E.; desc. English family settlers Englishtown, N.J., about 1700; A.B., Princeton U., 1899; LL.B., N.Y. Law Sch., 1902; m. Sara Elizabeth Jones, Germantown, Pa., June 25, 1908; children—Woodruff Jones, Nicholas Conover. Began as law clk., 1900-02; admitted to N.J. bar as atty., 1902, as counsellor, 1905; master in chancery and spl. master in chancery; mem. firm McCarter & English, Newark, N.J. since 1906; dir. First Nat. Bank, Summit, N.J., A. H. Bull Steamship Co., New York, N.Y., Jersey Mortgage Co., Elizabeth, N.J. Trustee The Pingry Sch., Elizabeth, N.J., State Y.M. C.A. Mem. Am. Judicature Soc., Am., N.J. State, Essex Co. bar assns., N.J. Hist. Soc. Republican. Presbyn. Club: Essex (Newark). Home: Summit. Office: 11 Commerce St., Newark, N.J.

ENGLISH E(ugene) Schuyler, editor; b. New York, N.Y., Oct. 12, 1899; s. Eugene Montgomery and Clara (Stoiber) E.; grad. Phillips Acad., Andover, Mass., 1918; student Princeton U., 1918-20; Litt.D., Wheaton (Ill.) Coll., 1939; m. Eva Linde Schultz, Mar. 2, 1937. Sec. Sterling Pure Food Co., Phila., 1920-21; asst. purchasing agt., Curtis Pub. Co., 1922-31; pres. Am. Bible Conf. Assn., Inc., since 1930; mng. editor Revelation, magazine, 1931-39; mem. faculty, Phila. Sch. of the Bible, since 1935, pres., 1936-39; asso. editor Our Hope, magazine, since 1939; trustee China Inland Mission, Inc., D. M. Stearns Missionary Fund, Inc., Nat. Radio and Missionary Fellowship, Inc. Served as private, U.S. Army, Sept.-Dec. 1918. Mem. Cottage Club (Princeton), Kappa Omega Alpha. Author: Studies in the Gospel According to Matthew, 1935; By Life and By Death, 1938. Contbr. to Revelation, Our Hope, etc. Home: Chateau Crillon, Rittenhouse Square, Philadelphia. Office: 1831 Chestnut St., Philadelphia, Pa.

ENGLISH, James Henry, prof. Romance langs.; b. Armagh, Ire., Sept. 10, 1886; s. John and Ellen (Kew) E.; came to U.S., 1889, naturalized, 1904; A.B., Dartmouth Coll., 1912; grad. study, U. of Dijon, France, 1911-12; Ph.D., Columbia U., 1926; grad. study, Centro de Estudios, Madrid, Spain, 1927; m. Sarah Conover, July 12, 1922; 1 dau., Elizabeth Conover. Instr. Romance langs., Lafayette Coll., 1912-13, Rutgers Prep. Sch., 1913-16, Choate Sch., 1916-19, Columbia U. Extension, 1919-24; asst. prof. Spanish, N.Y. Univ., 1924-30; prof. Romance langs., Lincoln Memorial Univ., 1930-31; prof. Romance langs., Grove City Coll. since 1931. Mem. Modern Lang. Assn. of America, Am. Assn. Univ. Profs. Republican. Presbyn. Home: 405 Woodland Av., Grove City, Pa.

ENGLISH, John Theodore, physician; b. Elizabeth, N.J., Nov. 6, 1881; s. Theodore Cowan and Sarah (Boyle) E.; Ph.B., Lafayette Coll., Easton, Pa., 1905; M.D., Coll. Phys. and Surgs. of Columbia U., 1909; m. Cora Johnson, June 4, 1913 (dec.); 1 son, John Theodore, Jr.; m. 2d, Helen Kemter, July 16, 1936. Engaged in gen.

practice of medicine and surgery at Irvington, N.J. Served as capt. inf. U.S.A., 1917-19. Fellow Am. Coll. Surgeons; mem. Am., State and Co. med. assns., Sigma Chi, Am. Legion, Vets. of Fgn. Wars. Republican. Presbyn. Mason, Jr. O.U.A.M. Home: 110 Yale Av., Irvington, N.J.

ENGLISH, Kenneth Joseph, lawyer, mayor; b. Pittston, Pa., Dec. 27, 1899; s. Thomas Francis and Frances Teresa (Webber) E.; grad. elementary and high sch., Pittston, Pa., 1918; LL.B., Georgetown U. Law Sch., Washington, D.C., 1922; m. Mary Frances Burke, Nov. 16, 1938. Admitted to Luzerne Co. bar, 1925, and since practiced individually at Pittston. Enlisted U.S. Army, Oct., hon. disch., Dec. 1918. Elected mayor of Pittston, Nov. 1937, for 4 yr. term. Dir. Pittston Hosp. Mem. Luzerne Co. Law and Library Assn. Democrat. Roman Catholic. Club: Fox Hill Country (Pittston, Pa.). Home: 171 William St. Office: Dime Bank Bldg., Pittston, Pa.

ENGLISH, Oliver Spurgeon, psychiatrist; b. Presque Isle, Me., Sept. 27, 1901; s. George Wesley and Annie Louise (Hemphill) E.; student U. of Me., 1918-20; M.D., Jefferson Med. Coll., Phila., 1924; m. Ellen Mary Brown, Feb. 28, 1933; children—Wesley John, Oliver Spurgeon. Resident physician Jefferson Med. Coll., 1924-27; interne Boston Psychopathic Hosp., 1927-28; resident neurological div., Montefiore Hosp., New York, 1928-29; Commonwealth fellow in psychiatry, Harvard, 1929-32; instr. in psychiatry, Harvard Med. Sch., 1929-32; volunteer asst. in psychiatry, Charite Hosp., Berlin, Germany, 1931-32; clin. prof. of psychiatry, Temple U. Med. Sch., 1933-38, prof. since 1938; physician to psychopathic dept., Phila. Gen. Hosp. since 1933. Trustee Pennhurst Sch. since 1937. Mem. A.M.A., Am. Psychiat. Assn., Phila. Co. Med. Soc., Phila. Psychiat. Soc., Phi Gamma Delta, Nu Sigma Nu. Home: 3925 Henry Av. Office: 255 S. 17th St., Philadelphia, Pa.

ENGLUND, A. Helmer, exec. v.p. Electric Service Supplies Co.; b. East Gothland, Sweden, June 10, 1867; brought to U.S., 1880; ed. high sch. and Bryant & Stratton Business Coll.; studied commercial law; m. Luella Hoge, Nov. 1, 1898; 1 dau., Mrs. Helen Silliman. Cashier Bryant & Stratton Business Coll. 1884-85, Poole Bros., printers, 1886-88; field accountant Sprague Electric Ry. & Motor Co., on construction of electric rys., 1889-91; sec.-treas. Electric Merchandise Co., Chicago, 1891-92; organized Internat. Register Co., 1892, sec.-treas. and mgr., until 1895; formed partnership Mayer & Englund, 1895, later sec.-treas. Mayer & Englund Co. until 1906 when company merged into Electric Service Supplies Co., since exec. v.p. Mem. Am. Transit Assn. (former mem. exec. com.), Nat. Electrical Mfrs. Assn. Republican. Presbyterian. Mason. Clubs: Union League, Phila. Country, Overbrook Farms (v.p. and dir.), Overbrook Golf (Philadelphia); Electrical Manufacturers (New York). Home: 6401 Church Road, Overbrook. Office: 17th and Cambria Sts., Philadelphia, Pa.

ENGLUND, Carl Robert, radio engr.; b. Sioux City, Ia., Nov. 13, 1884; s. Carl Hinrick and Emma (Roman) E.; B.S., U. of S.D., Vermillion, S.D., 1909; student U. of Chicago, 1910-12, U. of Mich., Ann Arbor, Mich., 1913-14; m. Ethel Isabel Groat, June 13, 1913; children—Carl Robert, Jane Isabel. Chemist S.D. Food and Drug Commn., Vermillion, S.D., 1910-11; teacher Belle Fourche (S.D.) High Sch., 1911; prof. physics and geology, Western Md. Coll., Westminster, Md., 1912-13; radio engr. Western Electric Co., New York, 1914-25; mem. tech. staff Bell Telephone Labs., New York, since 1925. Fellow Inst. Radio Engrs.; mem. Am. Phys. Soc., Phi Beta Kappa, Sigma Xi. Republican. Address: Holmdel, N.J.

ENNIS, Joseph (Burroughs), v.p. Am. Locomotive Co.; b. Wortendyke, N.J., May 29, 1879; s. William C. and Kate E. (Burroughs) E.; grad. high sch., Paterson, N.J., 1895; m. Lillian R. Jersey, Dec. 14, 1903; 1 dau., Ruth L. Draftsman, Rogers Locomotive Works, 1895-99; leading draftsman, Schenectady (N.Y.) Locomotive Works, 1899-1900, Rogers Locomotive Works, 1900-01, Cooke Works of Am. Locomotive Co.,

1901-02; in mech. engr.'s office of Am. Locomotive Co., N.Y. City, 1902-05, asst. to mech. engr., 1906-08, designing and estimating engr., 1908-12, chief mech. engr., 1912-17, v.p. of engring., dir. Am. Locomotive Co. since 1917; dir. Federation Bank & Trust Co. of New York. Mem. Am. Soc. M.E., Am. Soc. Steel Treaters. Methodist. Clubs: Engineers, Railroad, New York Railroad, Mohawk; North Jersey Country; Metropolitan (New York). Home: 9 Pope Rd., Paterson, N.J. Office: 30 Church St., New York, N.Y.

ENNIS, William Duane, engineer; b. in Bergen County, N.J., January 6, 1877; s. William C. and Kate E. (Burroughs) E.; M.E., Stevens Inst. Tech., 1897, Dr. Engring., 1934; m. Margaret Schuyler, Dec. 28, 1898. Mech. engr. with Walworth Co., Boston, 1898-1900; engr. on staff John D. Rockefeller, in various companies, including Am. Linseed Co., 1900-05; engr. Am. Locomotive Co., 1905-07: served as prof. mech. engring., Poly. Inst. of Brooklyn, Columbia U., U.S. Naval Acad. Consultant in mech. engring. and specialist in industrial management. Commd. maj. U.S.R. and on active duty, Ordnance Dept., Washington. and Watervliet Arsenal, N.Y., 1917-18; dir. of research, Tech. Advisory Corpn., New York; Alexander Crombie Humphreys prof. of economics of engring., Stevens Inst. Tech. Fellow A.A.A.S., Royal Econ. Soc.; mem. Am. Soc. M.E. (treas.), Am. Economics Assn., Nat. Municipal League, Am. Management Assn., Am. Soc. Civil Engrs., Tau Beta Pi. Club: Engineers (New York). Author: Linseed Oil, 1909; Applied Thermodynamics, 1910; Vapors for Heat Engines, 1912; Flying Machines To-Day, 1911; Works Management, 1911; Thermodynamics Abridged, 1920. Home: Wyckoff, N.J.

ENRIGHT, John Joseph, research chemist; b. New Haven, Conn., Mar. 1, 1896; s. Thomas and Mary (Dinneen) E.; Ph.B., Sheffield Sci. Sch. of Yale U., 1917; ed. Army Med. Sch., Washington, D.C., 1918; M.S., Yale Grad. Sch., 1920, Ph.D., 1923; m. Gertrude Molloy, Aug. 24, 1920; children—Gertrude, John, Martha, Thomas. Engaged as chief of lab., Vets. Bur., West Haven, Conn., 1919-26; in charge Diagnostic Center Lab., Vets. Bur., Washington, D.C., 1926; research chemist and bacteriologist, on tooth decay, health beverages, and baker's yeast, Mellon Inst., Pittsburgh, Pa., since 1926. Served in Med. and San. Corps, U.S.A. during World War. Mem. Am. Chem. Soc., Soc. Am. Bacteriologists, Internat. Assn. for Dental Research, Am. Assn. of Cereal Chemists. Roman Catholic. Club: Chemists (Pittsburgh). Home: 6600 Dalzell Place, Pittsburgh, Pa.

ENSLIN, Morton Scott, prof. N.T. lit. and exegesis; b. Somerville, Mass., Mar. 8, 1897; s. Theodore Vernon and Ada Eudora (Scott) E.; A.B., Harvard, 1919, Th.D., 1924; B.D., Newton Theol. Instn., 1922; m. Ruth May Tuttle, June 21, 1922; children—Theodore Vernon, II, Priscilla. Prof. N.T. lit. and exegesis and head of dept., Crozer Theol. Sem., Chester, Pa., since 1924. Lecturer in textual criticism, Phila. Div. Sch., 1924-25; lecturer in patristics, Grad. Sch., U. of Pa., since 1926; visiting prof., Chicago Theol. Sem., summer 1929. Ensign U.S. N.R.F., 1918-22; active duty, 1918-19. Mem. mng. com. Am. Sch. of Classical Studies, Athens. Mem. American Theological Soc. (treas. since 1927), Soc. Biblical Literature and Exegesis, American Oriental Soc., Philadelphia Oriental Club (pres. 1938-39), Pi Gamma Mu. Republican. Baptist. Mason (K.T., Shriner). Clubs: Wranglers, Photozetetics. Author: The Ethics of Paul, 1930; (with K. Lake and others) Six Collations of New Testament Manuscripts, 1933; Christian Beginnings, 1938. Translator: God, the Eternal Torment of Man (from the French of Marc Boegner), 1931. Contbr. to Crozer Quarterly, Jour. of Bibl. Lit., Harvard Theol. Rev. Home: 4 Seminary Av., Chester, Pa.; (summer) Dennis Port, Mass.

EPPINGER, John Gottlieb, orgn.; b. Quincy, Ill., July 20, 1893; s. George Charles and Louise (Fuehrhoff) E.; grad. Quincy (Ill.) High Sch., 1911; A.B., U. of Ill., 1916; m. Cornelia Maria Luther, Aug. 1, 1917; children—Alvene Louise, George Charles. Advertising mgr. Jos. Kuhn & Co., Champaign, Ill., 1916-18; bookkeeper, later mgr., Harris-Dillavon & Co., Champaign, Ill., 1919-24; mgr. coal dept., Twin City Ice & Cold Storage Co., Champaign, Ill., 1924-25; sec. Chambersburg (Pa.) Chamber of Commerce since Jan. 1926; sec. Chambersburg Motor Club, Franklin Co. Credit Exchange; business mgr. and editor Chambersburg Motorist; sec. Chambersburg Industries, Community Progress Corpn. Served in U.S. Naval Aux. Res. Sch., Chicago, 1918. Mem. secretariat 2d Pan-Am. Financial Conf., Washington, D.C., 1920. Mem. Nat. Assn. Commercial Orgn. Secs., Pa. Commercial Secs. Assn. (pres. 1930), Corda Fratres Assn. of Cosmopolitan Clubs, Am. Legion, Beta Gamma Sigma. Republican. Presbyterian. Mason, Elk. Club: Rotary (sec.). Home: 601 E. King St. Office: 54 Lincoln Way, W., Chambersburg, Pa.

EPSTEIN, Jacob, merchant, philanthropist; b. Tauroggen, Lithuania, Dec. 28, 1864; s. Isaac and Jennie E.; m. Lena Weinberg. Pres. Am. Gen. Corpn., Ethmar Realty Co.; v.p. Industrial Corpn. of Baltimore. Founded and built at his own expense The Mt. Pleasant Sanitorium, 1907, donated building and grounds for original Hebrew Home for Incurables, also donated a building to Eudowood Tuberculosis Sanitorium (non-sectarian)—all Baltimore, Md.; presented the Baltimore Mus. of Art with a heroic bronze figure "The Thinker" by Rodin, 1930; his collection of paintings, particularly of old masters, is internationally known. Past mem. Bd. of Supervisors of City Charities, Pub. Improvement Commn. of Baltimore. Dir. Baltimore Mus. of Art, Palestine Foundation Fund, Eudowood Tuberculosis Sanitorium, Asso. Jewish Charities, Am. Jewish Relief Com., Am. Red Cross (Baltimore chapter); del. rep. the country at large and sustaining mem. Am. Jewish Com. Clubs: Phoenix (Baltimore); Suburban of Baltimore County. Home: 7200 Park Heights Av. Office: Baltimore Trust Bldg., Baltimore, Md.

ERB, Elmer Ellsworth, lawyer; b. Hockersville, Pa., Aug. 12, 1882; s. Will C. and Lavina (Hocker) E.; A.B., Lebanon Valley Coll., 1905; LL.B., U. of Mich., 1911; m. Jean B. Leitzel, June 7, 1922. Asst. prin. Hershey-Derry Twp. pub. schs., 1906-08, prin., 1911-12; prin. Lebanon Valley Normal Sch., 1908; chief deputy prothonotary, chief deputy clerk, Dauphin Co. Ct. of Quarter Sessions, and deputy naturalization clerk, 1914-18; solicitor Hummelstown Borough, Derry Twp., 1918-20, Dauphin Co. Poor Directors, 1920-30; dir. of corpns., Pa. Dept. of State, 1934-35; now in private practice of law. Mem. Dauphin County Bar Assn. (ex-pres.). Republican. Mem. Reformed Ch. Mason (32°, Shriner), Royal Arcanum, Patriotic Order Sons of America. Clubs: Harrisburg Hunters' and Anglers' Assn. (pres.), Pa. Rifle and Pistol Assn., Lions, Shrine. Home: 4211 Derry St. (Lawntown), Harrisburg, R.D. 1, Pa. Office: 219 Walnut St., Harrisburg, Pa.

ERB, John Warren, composer, prof. music, conductor; b. Massillon, O., Apr. 17, 1885; s. John Samuel and Ida (Steele) E.; grad. high sch., Massillon, O., 1900; ed. Scharwenka Conservatory, Berlin, Germany, 1904-07; hon. Mus. D., Washington and Jefferson Coll., 1930; unmarried. Has followed profession of music since 1908; orchestra conductor; prof. music and dir. music dept., Lafayette Coll. since 1928; dir. instrumental music, Sch. of Edn., N.Y. Univ. since 1920; composer choral and symphonic orchestra music. Mem. Assn. Am. Composers and Conductors, Phi Mu Alpha. Republican. Mem. Christian Ch. Mason. Club: The Bohemians (New York). Address: 43 Fifth Av., New York, N.Y.; Lafayette College, Easton, Pa.

ERB, Russell Casper, teaching, research; b. Bethlehem, Pa., Feb. 22, 1899; s. Rev. William Harvey and Mary Andora (Fryer) E.; grad. Bethlehem (Pa.) High Sch., 1916; B.S., Lafayette Coll., Easton, Pa., 1921; student Lehigh U., 1921-22, U. of Pa., 1922-24; M.S., Temple U., 1927; m. Catherine Victoria Humble, June 28, 1921; children—Ida Ethylene, Catherine Andora. Chemist's asst., 1916-17; instr. of science, Conshohocken (Pa.) High Sch., 1921-23, head of science dept., 1923-25; asst. prof. of chemistry, Phila. Coll. of Osteopathy, Phila., 1925-28, prof. of toxicology and asso. dean since 1928; mem. of staff Osteopathic Hosp. of Phila. since 1928. Served in S.A.T.C., 1918-19. Founder Conshohocken Art League. Fellow Am. Inst. of Chemists (asso. editor The Chemist); mem. Am. Chem. Soc. (editor Phila., Del. and S. Jersey sect. bulletin). Republican. Mem. Reformed Ch. Mem. editorial bd. Jour. Am. Osteopathic Assn.; abstractor for Chem. Abstracts. Author: Chemical Tests, 1927; Physiological Chemistry, 1929; Poisoning the Public, 1938. Originator and investigator of new electrical device for gastric study in humans. Home: 1006 Maple St., Conshohocken, Pa. Office: 48th and Spruce Sts., Philadelphia, Pa.

ERDLY, Calvin Victor, supt. city schs.; b. Selinsgrove, Pa., May 5, 1896; s. Lewis Jefferson and Sallie (Kantz) E.; B.S., Susquehanna U., 1920; M.S., Pa. State Coll., 1930; m. Alma E. Peterson, June 14, 1922; children—Ralph P., Elinor M. Engaged in teaching pub. schs., 1920-21; supervising prin. pub. schs., Philipsburg, Pa., 1921-25; supt. pub. schs., Hollidaysburg, Pa., 1925-33, Hanover, Pa., 1933-38; supt. pub. schs., Lewistown, Pa., since 1938. Served in Ambulance Service, U.S.A., 1917-19, non-commd. officer attached to French Army. Awarded Croix de Guerre, citation for spl. service (France). Active in Tuberculosis Soc. Has held offices and com. memberships in edn. assns. Mem. N.E.A., Pa. State Edn. Assn., Kappa Phi Kappa, Pi Gamma Mu, Am. Legion. Republican. Methodist. Mason. Clubs: Kiwanis, Craftsman's. Home: 445 S. Main St., Lewistown, Pa.

ERDMAN, Charles Rosenbury, theologian; b. Fayetteville, N.Y., July 20, 1866; s. William Jacob and Henrietta (Rosenbury) E.; A.B., Princeton, 1886, D.D., 1925; grad. Princeton Theol. Sem., 1891; D.D., U. of Wooster, 1912; LL.D., Davidson Coll., 1924; m. Estelle Pardee, June 1, 1892; children—Calvin Pardee, Mrs. Henry Lewis, Charles R., Mrs. Francis Grover Cleveland. Ordained to Presbyn. ministry, 1891; pastor Overbrook (Pa.) Ch., 1891-97, 1st Ch., Germantown, 1897-1906; prof. practical theology, Princeton Theol. Sem., 1906-36, prof. emeritus since 1936; moderator Gen. Assembly of Presbyn. Ch., U.S.A., 1925; moderator Presbytery of New Brunswick, 1925; pastor First Presbyn. Ch., Princeton, N.J., 1924-34. Mem. Presbyn. Bd. Foreign Missions, 1906—; del. Presbyn. Gen. Assembly, 1906, 15, 24, 25, 26, World's Missionary Conf., Edinburgh, 1910, Nat. Christian Council, Shanghai, 1922; elected pres. Presbyn. Bd. of Foreign Missions, 1926. Republican. Author: Coming to the Communion, 1912; Gospel of John, an Exposition, 1916; The Gospel of Mark, an Exposition, 1917; The General Epistles, 1918; The Acts, 1919; Matthew, 1920; Luke, 1921; Within the Gateways of the Far East, 1922; The Return of Christ, 1922; Pastoral Epistles, 1923; The Lord We Love, 1924; The Work of the Pastor, 1924; Romans, 1925; The Spirit of Christ, 1926; The Life of D. L. Moody, 1927; First Corinthians, 1928; Second Corinthians, 1929; The Epistle of Paul to the Galatians, 1930; The Epistle of Paul to the Ephesians, 1931; The Epistle of Paul to the Philippians, 1932; The Epistle to the Hebrews, 1933; The Epistles of Paul to the Thessalonians. 1934; The Revelation of John, 1936. Home: 20 Library Pl., Princeton, N.J.

ERDMAN, Wilton A.; mem. law firm Erdman & Williams. Address: Stroudsburg, Pa.

ERLER, Eugene W(illiam), physician; b. Newark, N.J., Oct. 19, 1882; s. Edward E. and Mary (Silbereysen) E.; A.B., Rutgers U., 1903; M.D., Coll. of Physicians and Surgeons of Columbia U., 1907; m. Lillian I. Vliet, Sept. 15, 1909; 1 son, Robert Eugene. Interne Bellevue Hosp., 1907-09. Engaged in gen. practice of medicine at South Orange, N.J., since 1936; visiting obstetrician Presbyn. Hosp., Newark, N.J. Mem. Acad. of Medicine of Northern N.J., N.J. State Med. Soc., Essex Co. Med. Soc., Soc. of Surgeons of N.J., Doctors' Club, Practitioners' Club. Delta Upsilon. Presbyn. Mason. Club: Baltusrol Golf. Home: 360 Irving Av., South Orange, N.J.

ERNST, James Emmanuel, prof. English; b. Centerport, Pa., Oct. 17, 1893; s. Charles Klopp and Ida Priscilla (Phillips) E.; grad. Kutztown (Pa.) Teachers Coll., 1913; A.B., Muhlenberg Coll., Allentown, Pa., 1917; grad. Mt. Airy Theol. Sem., Phila., 1922, B.D., 1925; A.M., U. of Pa., 1922; Ph.D., U. of Wash., 1926; unmarried. Head English dept., Jamestown (N.D.) Coll., 1922-24; asso. in English, U. of Wash., 1925-26; instr. in English, U. of Ill., 1926-27, asso. in English, 1927-29; extension lecturer in Am. history, Western Md. Coll., Westminster, Md., 1932-33; prof. English, Potomac State Sch. of U. of W.Va., Keyser, W.Va., 1931-33, head of dept., 1937-38; prof. English, Woodrow Wilson Coll., Chicago, Ill., since 1938. Served as sergt. 316th Inf., 79th Div., U.S. Army, 1917-19; with A.E.F. Awarded fellowship in English, U. of Wash., 1924-25; John Simon Guggenheim Research fellowship, libraries of England, 1929-30. Mem. Modern Lang. Assn. America, Am. Assn. Univ. Profs., Pa. German Folklore Soc., Vets. Assn. of 316th Inf., Pi Kappa Delta. Lutheran. Author: The Political Thought of Roger Williams, 1929; Literary Studies for Rhetoric Classes (with Jefferson, Landis and Secord), 1929, revised edit., 1932; Roger Williams—New England Firebrand (biography), 1932; Models of Structure and Style (with Jefferson, Landis and Secord), 1933. Contbr. to learned jours. Home: Mohrsville, Pa.; also Keyser, W.Va.

ERRIGO, Joseph A., lawyer; b. Phila., Pa., Dec. 2, 1903; s. Joseph and Michelina (Tavani) E.; A.B., U. of Pa., 1925; student U. of Pa. Law Sch., 1925-28; m. Catherine E. Martin, Feb. 21, 1938. In employ Federal Res. Bank, Phila., 1926; teacher history and mathematics, pub. schs., Phila., 1927-29; admitted to Del. bar, 1929, and since in gen. practice of law at Wilmington; sec. and treas. Diamond State Brewery, Inc. Served as dir. Del. Chapter Am. Red Cross; mem. exec. bd. Cath. Athletic Council; chmn. Cath. Action of Del. Hon. mem. Vets. Fgn. Wars; mem. Am., Del. State and New Castle Co. bar assns., Sons of Italy, Dem. League, Alpha Phi Delta. Democrat. Roman Catholic. K.C., Holy Name Soc. (pres.). Clubs: University, Unital, Chain (Wilmington); Lions. Home: Marshallton, Del. Office: Equitable Bldg., Wilmington, Del.

ERSKINE, Archibald Mortimer, chemist; b. New York, N.Y., Aug. 2, 1892; s. Archibald Campbell and Sara Jeannie (Mortimer) E.; B.Chem., Cornell U., 1914, Ph.D., 1921; m. Mabel Gingell Baldwin, July 20, 1918; children —Kenneth Mortimer, Donald Baldwin, Richard. Chemist S.S. White Dental Mfg. Co., Staten Island, N.Y., 1914-15; asst. and instr., Cornell U., 1915-18; research chemist. E. I. du Pont de Nemours & Co., 1918-21, asst. research dir. Krebs Pigments Dept., Newark, N.J., since 1928; asst. prof., Smith Coll., Northampton, Mass., 1921-22; prof. chemistry, Hamilton Coll., Clinton, N.Y., 1922-28. Served as 2d lt., Chem. Warfare Service, U.S. Army, June-Dec. 1918. Mem. Alpha Chi Sigma, Gamma Alpha, Phi Beta Kappa, Sigma Xi, Tau Beta Pi. Republican. Presbyterian. Home: 115 Watchung Av., Chatham, N.J. Office: 256 Vanderpool St., Newark, N.J.

ERSKINE, Bernard G.; pres. and dir. Hygrade Sylvania Corpn. Address: Emporium, Pa.

ERSKINE, Laurie York, author, educator; b. Kirkcudbright, Scotland, June 23, 1894; s. Wallace and Ada Margery (Bonney) E.; father an actor; brought to United States, 1901; ed. Choir Sch. of Cathedral of St. John the Divine, New York City; m. Doreene Joyce Pullinger, Aug. 1936. Formerly with National City Co., Detroit, Mich.; began writing stories for boys, 1921; editorial writer, Detroit News, 1921-22; one of 4 organizers of Solebury Sch. for Boys, New Hope, Pa., 1925. Served as 1st lt. British Royal Flying Corps, 1916-18, World War. Author: Renfrew of the Royal Mounted (for boys), 1922; The River Trail, 1923; The Laughing Rider, 1924; The Confidence Man, 1925; Valor, 1925; The Coming of Cosgrave, 1926; After School, 1927; Renfrew Rides Again (for boys), 1927; Renfrew Rides the Skies, 1928; Fine Fellows, 1929; Comrades of the Clouds, 1930; Renfrew Rides North, 1931; Renfrew's Long Trail, 1933; Renfrew Rides the Range, 1934; Renfrew in the Valley of Vanished Men, 1936; also plays for boys, The Boy Who Went, A Christmas Escape, Three Cans of Beans, and numerous short stories. Also author of radio drama "Renfrew of the Mounted." Home: The Solebury School, New Hope, Pa.

ERSNER, Matthew Shayne, physician and surgeon; b. Russia, July 23, 1890; s. Israel and Minnie (Shayne) E.; brought to U.S. 1900 and naturalized citizen; M.D., Temple U. Med. Sch., Phila., 1912; m. Sadie Rosenfield, July 24, 1923; children—Matthew Shayne, Lenore. Interne Samaritan Hosp., 1912-13; now asso. otologist, Grad. Hosp.; chief otologist, Temple U. Hosp.; otolaryngologist, Mt. Sinai Hosp.; asso. prof. otology, Grad. Sch. Medicine U. of Pa. since 1921; prof. otology, Temple U. Med. Sch. since 1929; cons. otolaryngologist to many hosps. Served as 1st lieut. Med. Corps, U.S.A., 1918. Fellow Am. Coll. Surgs., Am. Bd. Otolaryngology; mem. A.M.A., Pan-Am., Pa. State and Phila. Co. med. socs., Am. Acad. Ophthalmology and Otolaryngology, Am. Otol., Rhinol. and Laryngol. Soc., Phila. Laryngol. Soc., Am. Med. Authors' Assn., Phil Delta Epsilon, Alpha Omega, Blue Key. Jewish religion. Mason. B'nai B'rith. Clubs: Locust, Philmont Country. Address: 1915 Spruce St., Philadelphia, Pa.

ERVIN, Carl Edgar, M.D.; b. Troutmans, N.C., Apr. 7, 1891; s. James Franklin and Susan (Collins) E.; A.B., U. of N.C., 1915; M.D., U. of Pa., 1918; m. Marjorie Read, Sept. 23, 1926; children—Nancy Read, James Franklin. Began practice of medicine, 1918; became chief med. dept. Geisinger Memorial Hosp., 1921; since engaged in pvt. practice internal medicine. Served as lt., U.S. Navy Med. Corps, 1918-20. Pres. Montour Med. Soc., 1925-26; chmn. med. sects. Pa. State Med. Soc., 1934. Mem. Sigma Psi. Democrat. Presbyterian. Mason. Author: Diabetes and Arteriosclerosis, 1936; Diagnosis and Treatment of Undulant Fever, 1937; Diagnosis of Hyperthyroidism Masquerading as Heart Disease (with Robert F. Dickey), 1938; etc. Home: Locust Knolls, R.D. 1, Camp Hill, Pa. Office: 902 Payne-Shoemaker Bldg., Harrisburg, Pa.

ERVIN, James S.; pres. Mackintosh-Hemphill Co.; dir. many other companies. Home: 360 Jefferson Drive, Mt. Lebanon, Pa. Office: Ninth and Bingham Sts., Pittsburgh, Pa.

ERVIN, Spencer, executive; b. Phila., Pa., Feb. 9, 1886; s. Spencer and Katharine Albright (Mudge) E.; student The DeLancey Sch., Phila., 1895-98, St. Mark's Sch., Southborough, Mass., 1898-1904; A.B. cum laude, Harvard, 1907, LL.B., Harvard Law Sch., 1910; m. Harriet Virginia Rodman, Sept. 9, 1916 (died 1918); m. 2d Miriam Williams Roberts, Apr. 22, 1922; children—Miriam, Katharine Mudge, Louise Spencer, Virginia, Ellen Williams, Spencer. Admitted to Pa. bar, 1910, practiced at Phila., 1910-18, 1919-28; since then engaged in writing and administration. V.p. exec. council, Episcopal Diocese of Pa., dir. Public Charities Assn. of Pa., pres. Family Society of Phila. Mem. Am., Pa., and Phila. bar assns., Phi Beta Kappa. Republican. Episcopalian. Clubs: Philadelphia (Phila.); Fly Club (Harvard). Author: The Law of Building and Use Restrictions in Pennsylvania, 1928; The Magistrates' Courts of Phila., 1931; Henry Ford vs. Truman H. Newberry: The Famous Senate Election Contest, 1935. Address: Bala-Cynwyd, Pa. Office: 202 S. 19th St., Philadelphia, Pa.

ESCHER, Franklin, banker; b. New York, June 19, 1881; s. Henry and Louise (Fasmacht) E.; student Yale, 1902; m. Mildred B. Gleason, Oct. 19, 1909. Began editorial work in New York, 1900; editor Investment Magazine, 1910-13, finance editor of Harper's Weekly, 1908-13; now mem. firm of Dresser & Escher, bankers, New York. Author: Elements of Foreign Exchange, 1910; Practical Investing, 1913; Foreign Exchange Explained, 1917; Modern Foreign Exchange, 1933. Home: Englewood, N.J. Office: 111 Broadway, New York, N.Y.

ESCUE, Henry Merritt, physician; b. Kanawha County, W.Va., Sept. 25, 1903; s. Edgar and Florence Maria (Moore) E.; student Eastern State Teachers Coll., Richmond, Ky., 1922-24, New River State Coll., Montgomery, W.Va., 1925-28; M.D., Med. Coll. of Va., Richmond, 1932; m. Mrs. Mabel Johnson, Dec. 8, 1935; 1 son, Henry Merritt. Interne, Roanoke (Va.) Hosp., 1932-33, practiced medicine, Rainelle, W.Va., July-Dec. 1933; practice, St. Albans, W.Va., since Dec. 1933. Elected mayor of St. Albans, 1937, re-elected 1939. Mem. Am., State and Kanawha County med. assns. Methodist. Democrat. Mason. Home: 139 Lee St. Office: 366 Main St., St. Albans, W.Va.

ESENWINE, William A., banker; b. Lock Haven, Pa., May 6, 1876; s. George W. and Barbara R. (Spring) E.; ed. pub. schs.; m. Eva Elmira Kahl, Aug. 23, 1900. Associated with implement business, 1896-1921; bookkeeper Furst Bros., 1921-23; cashier Mill Hall State Bank, 1923-25, pres. since 1928, now also dir.; partner Krape & Esenwine since 1927. Dir. Cedar Hill Cemetery Assn., Cedar Springs, Pa. Republican. Lutheran. Elk, Odd Fellow, Sons of America, Knights of the Golden Eagle. Home: Salona, Pa. Office: Main St., Mill Hall, Pa.

ESHBACH, Ovid Wallace, elec. engring.; b. Pennsburg, Pa., Apr. 13, 1893; s. Horace W. and Lena (Hill) E.; ed. Perkiomen Sch., 1908-11; E.E., Lehigh U., 1915, M.S., same, 1920; m. Clara E. Ortt, Oct. 4, 1919; children—John Robert, Frances Elinor. Engring. asst., U.S. Naval Engring. Expt. Sta., Annapolis, Md., 1915-16; instr. elec. engring., Lehigh U., 1916-17, asst. prof., 1922; asst. engr., Bell Telephone Co. of Pa., 1923-25; spl. asst. Personnel Dept. Am. Telephone & Telegraph Co., New York City since 1925. Served as 2d lt. Signal Corps, U.S.A., 1917-18; instr. Radio Sch. for Officer Candidates, 1919. Pres. bd. trustees, Perkiomen Sch., Pennsburg, Pa. Mem. Soc. for Promotion Engring. Edn. (mem. council, 1936-39), Am. Inst. Elec. Engrs., Am. Legion, Glenside War Memorial Assn., Eta Kappa Nu, Sigma Xi. Republican. Reformed Ch. Clubs: Glenside Tennis, Seven O'Klockers. Author: Handbook of Engineering Fundamentals, 1936. Dir. of ednl. surveys in N.Y. City Industrial Area, 1932-33. Home: 243 Brookdale Av., Glenside, Pa. Office: 195 Broadway, New York, N.Y.

ESHELMAN, Fayette Clinton, M.D.; b. Franklin, Pa., July 4, 1890; s. Uriah H. and Malinda (Carrier) E.; B.S., M.S., Bucknell U., 1913; M.D., Jefferson Med. Coll., 1917; studied U. of Pa. Post-Grad. Sch. of Medicine, 1920-21, New York Post-Grad. Med. Coll., 1920-21; m. Bess Boyer Schell, Apr. 21, 1919; 1 dau., Marilyn Jane. Began gen. practice of medicine, 1919. Pres. Hazelton Branch Luzerne Co. Med. Soc., 1936, dir. since 1937, pres. of bd., 1939. Mem. Am. and Pa. State Med. assns., Pa. and New Eng. Hist. and Genealogy Socs. Republican. Methodist. Mason (Scottish Rite, Bloomsburg, Pa.; Shriner, Irem Temple, Wilkes-Barre, Pa.; Franklin Commandery No. 44, K.T., Franklin, Pa.). Clubs: Shrine Country (Dallas, Pa.); Craftsmans, Valley Country (Hazelton, Pa.). Home: 712 W. Diamond Av. Office: 402 Traders Bank Bldg., Hazelton, Pa.

ESHERICK, Wharton, artist, sculptor, furniture designer. Address: Paoli, Pa.*

ESHNER, Augustus Adolph, M.D.; b. Memphis, Tenn., Nov. 17, 1862; s. James and Jane E.; A.B., Central High Sch., Phila., 1879, A.M., 1884; M.D., Jefferson Med. Coll., 1888; m. Julia Friedberger, 1904; children—Mrs. Annette E. Dalsimer Mrs. Juliet E. Nathanson. Resident physician Philadelphia Hosp., 1888-89; registrar neurology department same, 1891-96; chief clin. asst. outpatient med. dept., Jefferson Med. Coll. Hosp., 1892; prof. clin. medicine, Phila. Polyclinic, 1895-1918; phys. Phila. Hosp., 1896-1914; asst. phys. Orthopædic Hosp. and Infirmary for Nervous Diseases, 1900-17; visiting physician Hosp. for Diseases of the Lungs, 1901-02; consulting physician Mercy Hosp. since 1910. Asst. editor Medical News, 1891-95, Phila. Med. Journal, 1898-99; asso. editor Pennsylvania Medical Journal, 1904-22. Commd. 1st lt. Med. R.C., 1917. Fellow Coll. Physicians of

Phila., A.A.A.S.; mem. Phila. Co. Med. Soc. (chmn. dirs. 1904-05), Pa. State Med. Soc., A.M.A., Pathol. Soc. Phila., Northern Med. Assn., Science League America, Franklin Inst. Pa., Pa. Mus. and Sch. Industrial Art, Pa. Acad. Fine Arts, Hist. Soc. Pa., Phila. Zoöl. Soc., Academy Natural Sciences of Phila., Valley Forge Historical Society, Associated Alumni Central High Sch. of Phila, Fairmount Park Art Assn., Jewish Publ. Soc. of America. Club: Physicians Motor. Author: Essentials of Diagnosis (with Dr. Solomon Solis Cohen), 1892, 2d edit., 1900; Hand-Book of Fevers, 1895. Asst. editor: American Text-book of Applied Therapeutics, edited by Dr. James C. Wilson, 1896. Transl. and edited: Atlas and Methods of Clinical Investigation (Dr. Christfried Jakob), 1898; Elements of Clinical Bacteriology (Dr. Ernest Levy and Dr. Felix Klemperer), 1900; A Textbook of the Practice of Medicine (Dr. Hermann Eichhorst), 1900. Collaborator on Annual of the Universal Med. Sciences, 1890-95; Sajous' Annual and Cyclo, of Practical Medicine, 1899; Cyclo. of Practical Medicine and Surgery, 1900; System of Physiologic Therapeutics, 1902-03; Reference Handbook of the Medical Sciences, 1903; A Textbook of Human Physiology (L. Landois), 1904. Has written many med. monographs and articles in med. jours., etc. Editor: Trans. Phila. County Med. Soc., 1896, 97; Phila. General Hospital Reports, Vol. IX, 1913. Address: 1019 Spruce St., Philadelphia, Pa.

ESSICK, Charles Rhein, lens mfr.; b. Reading, Pa., Feb. 17, 1883; s. William Wallace and Susan (Rhein) E.; A.B., Yale, 1905; M.D., Johns Hopkins Med. Sch., 1909; (hon.) D.Sc., Albright Coll., Reading, Pa., 1936; m. Alice L. Weed, June 1, 1916. Asst. in anatomy, Johns Hopkins Med. Sch., 1909-10, instr. and asso. in anatomy, 1910-14; mgr. lens grinding plant, Pa. Optical Co., Reading, Pa., 1915-30, propr. since 1930. Served as capt. Med. Corps, U.S.A., 1917-19. Mem. A.A.A.S., Am. Assn. Anatomists, Am. Assn. Chemists, Am. Ceramic Soc., Nu Sigma Nu. Republican. Clubs: Wyomissing, Berkshire Country, University (Reading); West Hamilton Street (Baltimore, Md.). Home: 700 Centre Av. Office: 234 S. 8th St., Reading, Pa.

ESSIG, Norman Sturges, doctor dental surgery; b. Phila., Pa., Nov. 6, 1869; s. Charles James and Mary Augusta (Sturges) E.; D.D.S., U. of Pa. Dental Sch., 1889; m. Mercy Richards, June 3, 1896; children—Charles James, Jos. Richards; m. 2d, Margaret Calder Emack, Jan. 7, 1928. Engaged in practice of dentistry at Phila., Pa., since 1889; lecturer on prosthetic dentistry, U. of Pa., 1894-1901; prof. prosthetic dentistry, Temple U. Dental Coll. since 1917; asso. with development dept. S. S. White Dental Mfg. Co., Phila., Pa., for 5 yrs. Taught reduction of jaw fractures in course for officers going overseas in course organized by Gen. Gorgas at U. of Pa. during World War. Pres. Acad. of Stomatology, 1923-24. Fellow Am. Coll. Dentists; mem. Blue Key, Delta Upsilon, Psi Omega, Kappa Kappa Omicron, Kappa Epsilon. Republican. Episcopalian. Clubs: Penn Athletic (charter mem.), Manufacturers and Bankers (Phila.). Author: Dental Science Primer on Prosthetic Dentistry, 1937. Contbr. to The Essig and later the Turner edits. of American Textbook on Prosthetic Dentistry and many articles to dental jours. Home: 1700 Locust St., Philadelphia, Pa.

ESTABROOK, Edward Lewis, petroleum engineer; b. Brandon, S.D., May 10, 1885; s. Lewis Mitchell and Mary Maud (Cornwall) E.; Wis. Sch. of Mines, Platteville, 1907-08; E.M., U. of Pittsburgh, 1911; Lehigh U., Bethlehem, Pa., 1911-12; m. Florence Anna Mattick, May 15, 1916; children—Mary Abbott, Georgiana Mattick (dec.). Instr. geol. dept., Lehigh U., 1911-13; instr. Wis. Sch. of Mines, 1913-14; geologist Standard Oil Co. of N.Y. (China), 1914-16, Wis. Zinc Co., 1916-17, Johnson & Huntley. (U.S and S.A.), 1917-18, Midwest Refining Co., 1918-20; petroleum engr. Midwest Refining Co., 1920-25, Pan-Am. Petroleum and Transport Co., 1925-32, Standard Oil Co. of N.J., since 1932; dir. European Gas and Electric Co. Mem. Am. Inst. of Mining and Metall. Engrs., Am. Assn. of Petroleum Geologists. Club: Orange Lawn Tennis (South Orange, N.J.). Author of articles on engring. subjects. Home: 25 Luddington Rd., West Orange, N.J. Office: 30 Rockefeller Plaza, New York, N.Y.*

ESTEP, Harry Allison, ex-congressman; b. Pittsburgh, Pa., Feb. 1, 1884; s. James E. and Isabella S. (Kaye) E.; prep. edn., high sch., Marion, Ind.; student Purdue U., Lafayette, Ind.; LL.B., U. of Pittsburgh, 1913; m. Blanche Alward, of Canton, O., Aug. 10, 1918. Admitted to Pa. bar, 1914; mem. 70th to 72d Congresses (1927-33), 35th Pa. Dist. Home: 410 Bailey Av. Office: Law and Finance Bldg., Pittsburgh, Pa.

ESTEP, Thomas Gemmill, Jr.; prof. mech. engring. Carnegie Inst. Tech. Address: Schenley Park, Pittsburgh, Pa.

ESTERLY, Charles J., ex-congressman; b. Reading, Pa., Feb. 8, 1888; s. Herman A. and Louisa G. (Zable) E.; ed. pub. schs.; m. Beulah S. Deem, Feb. 14, 1912; children—Henry Hermon, Richard Harding; m. 2d, Willa R. Nicely, June 23, 1934. Connected with Metropolitan Electric Company, Reading, 1906-16; with Berkshire Knitting Mills, 1916-32; breeder Ayrshire cattle and Berkshire hogs. Trustee Keystone State Teachers Coll., Kutztown, Pa. Resides at Sally Ann Furance Manor dating back to 1791 where ten plate colonial stoves were made. An organizer Reading Fair Association; director Reading Baseball and Athletic Association. Del. Rep. Nat. Conv., Chicago, 1920; mem. Rep. State Com., Pa., 1923-24; mem. 69th and 71st Congresses (1925-27 and 1929-31), 14th Pa. Dist. Former dist. chmn. Rep. County Com., Berks Co., Pa. Pres. Pa. State Soc. of Washington. Lutheran. Mason. Clubs: Wyomissing (Reading); Town Hall, City, New York Advertising (New York); Penn Athletic (Phila.). Home: Sally Ann Furnace, Pa. Address: Reading, Pa.*

ESTERLY, John E., insurance; b. Exeter Twp., Berks Co., Pa., Aug. 9, 1894; s. John S. and Sallie B. E.; student Keystone State Normal Sch. (now Kutztown State Teachers Coll.), 1910-13; B.S., Pa. State Coll., 1920; m. Della S. Nein, Feb. 4, 1929; children—Joann Natalie, John Roosevelt. Began as metall. engr., 1920; teacher science Mohnton High Sch.; teacher mathematics Kutztown High Sch., later Reading Jr. High Sch.; served as deputy sheriff, chief deputy sheriff and acting sheriff, Berks County, also as indictment clerk Dist. Attys. office, and chief clerk Bd. of Berks Co. Commrs., pres. Mt. Penn Assurance Exchange; v.p. Mt. Penn Fire Co. Pres. Berks Co. Sunday Sch. Assn. Mem. Berks Co. Firemans Assn., Pa. Magistration Assn., Reading Fair Boosters Assn., Phi Kappa Psi. Democrat. Lutheran. Mason (32°), Modern Woodman of America. Club: Penn State, Berks Co. Home: 2223 Dengler St., Mt. Penn, Reading, Pa.

ESTERMANN, Immanuel, univ. prof.; b. Hamburg, Germany, Mar. 31, 1900; s. Arieh Leo and Rahel (Brenner) E.; student Univs. of Giessen, Berlin, Freiburg and Hamburg, Germany, 1918-21; D.Sc.; m. Rose Chwolles, May 18, 1923; children—Hannah, Eva Frances. Came to U.S. 1933, naturalized, 1939. Asst. in physics, U. of Rostock, 1921-22; lecturer in physics, U. of Hamburg, 1922-28, privatdozent in physics and physical chemistry, 1928-33; research fellow, Rockefeller Foundation, U. of Calif., 1931-32; asso. prof. of physics, Carnegie Inst. Tech., Pittsburgh, since Oct. 1933. Mem. Am. Phys. Soc., A.A.A.S., Pittsburgh Phys. Soc., Sigma Xi. Home: 5416 Beacon St., Pittsburgh, Pa.

ESTERSON, Albert A., mfr. rubber heels and soles; b. Baltimore, Md., Dec. 4, 1890; s. Joseph and Rebecca (Esterson) E.; student Baltimore pub. schs., 1896-1904; m. Mollie B. Beskin, Nov. 18, 1914; 1 son, Lorman Lee. Mfr. neckwear, 1908-15; sec. and treas. Holtite Mfg. Co., Inc., mfrs. rubber heels and soles, Baltimore, since 1915; pres. Cats Paw Rubber Co., Foster Rubber Co., Holtite Rubber Co. of Canada, Ltd., Shipley Heights Development Co. Dir. Hebrew Home for Aged and Infirm. Mason, Elk. Clubs: Civitan, Woodholme Country (Baltimore). Home: 3239 Powhatan Av. Office: Warner & Ostend Sts., Baltimore, Md.

ESTES, William Lawrence, surgeon; b. on plantation nr. Brownsville, Tenn., Nov. 28, 1855; s. Albert Monroe and Marcia Burton Owen E.; ed. Bethel Coll., Ky., 1872-74; M.D., U. of Va., 1877; M.D., Univ. Med. Coll. (New York U.), 1878; (hon. A.M., Bethel Coll., 1893); Sc.D., Lehigh University, Bethlehem, Pa., 1934; m. Jeanne Wynne, Oct. 5, 1881 (died Nov. 1903). Emeritus surgeon in chief, St. Luke's Hosp., Bethlehem, Pa.; lecturer on physiology and hygiene, Lehigh U., 1883-1923; chief surgeon, Lehigh Valley R.R., 1886-1904. Mem. A.M.A., Pa. State Med. Soc.; fellow Internat. Surg. Assn., Am. Surg. Assn., N.Y. Acad. Medicine, Am. Coll. Surgeons; asso. fellow Coll. Physicians Phila.; hon. mem. Assn. Industrial Surgeons of America. Baptist. Club: Medical (Phila.). Author: Treatment of Fractures, 1900. Contbr. chapter on surgery of accidents in Keen's System of Surgery. Office: Union Bank Bldg., Bethlehem, Pa.●

ESTES, William Lawrence, Jr., surgeon; b. Bethlehem, Pa., Mar. 1, 1885; s. William Lawrence and Jeanne Williams (Wynne) E.; studied Moravian Parochial Sch., Lehigh U., Bethlehem, Pa., and Johns Hopkins U., Baltimore; m. Anne Greble, June 11, 1913. Interne Johns Hopkins Hosp., Baltimore, 1909-10; asst. at Mayo Clinic, 1910-12; adj. surgeon, St. Luke's Hosp., Bethlehem, 1912-28, asso. chief surgeon, 1929-30, chief surgeon since 1930; med. adviser Lehigh U., 1912-23; mem. Fountain Hill (Pa.) Health Bd., 1919-24. Served as lt., capt. and maj., Mobile Operating Unit No. 1, A.E.F., 1918-19. Fellow Am. Coll. Surgeons; mem. Pa. State Med. Soc. (chmn. surg. sect. 1923), Med. Soc. of Pa. (mem. cancer commn. since 1934), Northampton Co. Med. Soc., Phila. Path. Soc., A.M.A., Lehigh Valley Med. Assn., N.Y. and New England Ry. Surgeons, Alumni Assn. of Mayo Clinic and Mayo Foundation, Acad. of Polit. Sciences, Am. Surg. Soc., Southern Surg. Soc., Surg. Research Soc., N.Y. Acad. of Medicine, Am. Geog. Soc., Visiting Nurses Assn. (dir.), Am. Legion, Phi Beta Kappa, Sigma Xi, Alpha Omega Alpha. Clubs: Rotary (Bethlehem); Saucon Valley Country. Writer articles on abdominal surgery, fracture treatment, ovarian implantation, etc., also numerous other articles on med. subjects. Home: R.F.D. 4. Office: Union Bank and Trust Co. Bldg., Bethlehem, Pa.

ETCHISON, Bates, dentist; b. Montgomery Co., Md., Aug. 26, 1883; s. Joseph Melvin and Martha Jane (Clagett) E.; student Eaton and Brunett Coll., Baltimore, 1900-01; D.D.S., U. of Md., Baltimore, 1905; m. Helen Starr Myers, June 3, 1916. In practice of dentistry at Gaithersburg, Md., since 1905; dir. First Nat. Bank of Gaithersburg, Md., since 1918; pres. since 1935; treas. and dir. Gaithersburg Realty Co., Inc. Mem. S. Md. Dental Soc., Psi Omega. Democrat. Methodist. Mason (Shriner), K.P. Club: Manor (Montgomery Co., Md.). Address: 107 Russel Av., Gaithersburg, Md.

ETTER, Harry Blaine, physician; b. Williamson, Pa., Mar. 13, 1884; s. Henry Milton and Columbia (Kline) E.; student Chambersburg (Pa.) Acad., 1899-1902, Pa. State Coll., 1902-03; M.D., New York U., 1907; student Army Med. Sch., Washington, D.C., 1909-10; post grad. course Eye and Ear Infirmary, New York, 1921; m. Helen Augusta Stough, Nov. 26, 1914; children—Harry Stough, Robert Milton. Interne Bellevue Hosp., New York, 1907-09; 1st lt. Med. Reserve Corps, U.S. Army, 1909-10, 1st lt. Med. Corps, U.S. Army (active duty), 1910-13; practice of medicine and surgery, Shippensburg, Pa., 1913-21; practice of specialty of eye, ear, nose and throat, Shippensburg, Pa., since 1921; mem. of staff Chambersburg (Pa.) Hosp.; physician to State Teachers Coll., Shippensburg. Fellow A.M.A.; mem. Pa. Med. Soc., Cumberland Co. Med. Soc., Omega Upsilon Phi. Republican. Lutheran. Mason (K.T.). Home: 27 N. Washington St. Office: 9 N. Penn St., Shippensburg, Pa.

ETTING, Emlen, artist; b. Merion, Pa., Aug. 24, 1905; s. Emlen Pope and Florence (Lucas)

ETTINGER   263   **EVANS**

E.; ed. St. Georges at Newport and Harvard Coll.; student of Andre Lhote, Paris; m. Gloria Braggiotti, June 20, 1938. Artist since 1924. Exhibited at: Dallas (Tex.) Museum, Worcester (Mass.) Museum, Phila. Museum, Corcoran Gallery (Washington, D.C.), San Francisco World's Fair, N.Y. World's Fair; one-man shows in Paris, New York, Phila. Represented in Whitney Mus. of Am. Art, Pa. Acad. Fine Arts, and private collections. Episcopalian. Club: Phila. Art Alliance. Home: Haverford, Pa. Studio: 10 S. 18th St., Philadelphia, Pa.

ETTINGER, Amos Aschbach, educator; b. Allentown, Pa., May 24, 1901; s. George Taylor and Emma (Aschbach) E.; A.B., Muhlenberg Coll., Allentown, Pa., 1921; A.M., U. of Pa., 1923, grad. student, 1923-24; D.Phil., Oxford U. England, 1930; Litt. D., Oglethorpe U., 1933; m. Kathryn Mae Gable, Apr. 30, 1938. Asst. in history, U. of Pa., 1922-23; instr. history, Lafayette Coll., 1924-26, Yale, 1930-31; hist. research, Brit. Mus., Pub. Record Office (London), Bodleian Library (Oxford), 1932, 33, 34, in America, 1931-36; acting asso. prof. history, Lehigh U., 1936-37, asso. prof. since 1937; Georgia Bi-Centennial lecturer, Oglethorpe U., 1933. Awarded Beit prize in colonial history, Oxford U., 1929; Alexander medal, Royal Hist. Soc., London, 1930; John H. Dunning prize, Am. Hist. Assn., 1933. Fellow Royal Hist. Soc. (London), Am. Geog. Soc., mem. A.A.A.S., Am. Assn. Univ. Profs., Am. Hist. Assn., Hist. Soc. of Pa., Pa. Hist. Assn., Am. Acad. of Polit. and Social Science, Brasenose Coll. (Oxford), Lehigh Co. Hist. Soc., Phi Alpha Theta, Phi Kappa Tau. Club: Torch of the Lehigh Valley. Author: The Mission to Spain of Pierre Soulè, 1853-55, 1932; James Edward Oglethorpe, Imperial Idealist, 1936. Contbr. to Dictionary of American Biography and hist. jours. in England and U.S. Home: 1011 Highland Av. Address: Coppee Hall, Lehigh Univ., Bethlehem, Pa.

ETTINGER, George Taylor, college dean; b. Allentown, Pa., Nov. 8, 1860; s. Amos and Susan (Laudenschläger) E.; A.B., Muhlenberg Coll., Allentown, 1880, A.M., 1883, Litt.D., 1920, LL.D., 1937; Ph.D., New York U., 1891; m. Emma C., d. Gustavus A. Aschbach, Aug. 17, 1899; 1 son, Amos Aschbach. Teacher Muhlenberg Coll. since 1880; now dean emeritus and prof. Latin emeritus. Was lit. editor Allentown Morning Call; teacher and dean Pa. Chautauqua, 9 yrs.; mem. bd. sch. dirs., Allentown, 15 yrs. (ex-sec., ex-pres.); mem. bd. prison inspectors Lehigh Co., Pa., 12 yrs. (ex-sec.); first and only pres. Allentown Library Assn. since 1912; ex-pres. trustees' sect. Pa. State Lib. Assn.; mem. A.L.A. many yrs.; many yrs. alumni editor Muhlenberg Weekly. Ex-pres. Lehigh Valley Classical League, 1924-25. Often del. conf., to ministerium of Pa. and to Gen. Council Lutheran Ch. N. America; dir. Luth. Theol. Sem., Phila., 1924-33. Mem. Am. Hist. Assn., Hist. Soc. Pa., Lehigh Co. Hist. Soc. (ex-pres.), Am. Philol. Assn., Pa. German Soc. (ex-pres.), Pa. Soc. New York, Nat. Inst. Social Sciences, Am. Assn. Univ. Profs., Archæol. Inst. America, S.R., Phi Beta Kappa, Phi Gamma Delta, Omicron Delta Kappa, Eta Sigma Phi; fellow Am. Geog. Soc.; ex-pres. Alumni Assn. Muhlenberg Coll. Clubs: Contemporary, Schoolmen's, Lions, Rotary (Allentown). Republican. Lutheran. Author various papers and addresses. Home: 1114 Hamilton St., Allentown, Pa.

ETZKORN, Leo Rudolph, librarian; b. Rockport, Ind., July 2, 1897; s. Rudolph and Mary (Brehl) E.; A.B., Whitman Coll., Walla Walla, Wash., 1921; B.L.S., N.Y. State Library Sch., Albany, N.Y., 1925; m. Helen Hinman Martin, Aug. 20, 1927; children—Helen Harriet, Christine Marie. Employed in various depts. N.Y. State Library, 1923-25; head industrial dept., pub. library, Youngstown, O., 1925-26; librarian, pub. library, Cambridge, Mass., 1926-29, Fall River, Mass., 1929-31; librarian, Free Pub. Library, Paterson, N.J., since 1931. Served in O.T.S., U.S.N.R.F., Seattle, Wash., 1918; war camp library, Camp Lewis, Wash., 1917-18, 1919. Dir. Family Welfare Soc.; trustee Paterson Community Forum. Mem. Am. Library Assn. (mem. bd. on salaries, staff and tenure), N.J. Library Assn., Adv. Council North Jersey Adult Edn. Center, Phi Delta Theta, Phi Beta Kappa. Roman Catholic. Clubs: Rotary, Manuscript, Camera (Paterson). Home: 44 13th Av. Office: 250 Broadway, Paterson, N.J.

EUBANK, Weaver K.; pastor Ninth Presbyn. Ch. Home: 842 S. 57th St., Philadelphia, Pa.

EULER, Ralph Stapleton, banker; b. Howell, Mich., June 10, 1888; s. Frederick C. and Ella (Stapleton) E.; student Howell pub. schs., 1895-1905, U. of Mich., 1906-08; m. Bertha Bragg Grey, June 1911. Began in investment securities, 1911; mgr. investment dept. Colonial Trust Co., Pittsburgh, 1913-18; with Federal Reserve Bank, Cleveland, O., 1917-18; with The Union Trust Co. of Pittsburgh since 1918, v.p. since 1920; dir. Pullman-Standard Car Mfg. Co., Pullman-Standard Car Export Corpn., Union Fidelity Title Ins. Co., Tube City Collieries, Inc., Fort Pitt Steel Casting Co., Elliott Co., Am. Fruit Growers Inc. (mem. exec. com.), Standard Steel Spring Co. Republican. Clubs: Duquesne, Oakmont Country (Pittsburgh); Detroit (Detroit); Chicago (Chicago); Edgeworth (Edgeworth, Pa.). Home: 538 Irwin Drive, Sewickley, Pa. Office: Union Trust Bldg., Pittsburgh, Pa.

EUSTACE, Bartholomew Joseph, bishop; b. New York, N.Y., Oct. 9, 1887; s. Bartholomew A. and Elizabeth (Nolan) E.; ed. St. Francis Xavier Coll., New York, 1902-10, St. Joseph's Sem., Yonkers, N.Y., 1910-11, North Am. Coll., Rome, Italy, 1911-15. Ordained priest Roman Catholic Ch., in Rome, Nov. 1, 1914; asst. Ch. of Blessed Sacrament, New Rochelle, N.Y., 1915-16; prof. philosophy, St. Joseph's Sem., Yonkers, 1916-37; rector Ch. of Blessed Sacrament, New Rochelle, Sept. 1937-Mar. 1938; named bishop of Camden, N.J., Dec. 16, 1937, installed, May 4, 1938. Home: 500 Browning Rd., West Collingswood, N.J. Address: 721 Market St., Camden, N.J.

EVANS, Anna L.; prof. chemistry and head dept. chemistry and physics, Pa. Coll. for Women. Address: Pennsylvania College for Women, Pittsburgh, Pa.

EVANS, Cadwallader, Jr., gen. mgr. Hudson Coal Co.; b. Pittsburgh, Pa., Sept. 21, 1880; s. Cadwallader and Margaret Brown (Oliver) E.; M.E., Lehigh U.; m. Myra Haldeman Thornburg, Jan. 11, 1911; children—Kathleen, Cadwallader, III. Gen. mgr. Hudson Coal Co., Scranton, since 1925. Home: Waverly, Pa. Office: 421 Wyoming Av., Scranton, Pa.

EVANS, Charles; prof. German, Temple U. Address: Broad St. and Montgomery Av., Philadelphia, Pa.

EVANS, Charles Conner, judge, banker; b. Berwick, Pa., Jan. 10, 1858; s. Francis and Jane E.; ed. Bloomsburg State Normal Sch. and Lafayette Coll.; m. Annie Sloan, Feb. 23, 1888; children—Morris Sloan, Charles Clark; m. 2d, Elizabeth Mears, Oct. 24, 1928. Pres. and dir. Berwick Nat. Bank since organization, 1902; pres. judge 26th Pa. Judicial Dist., 1906-38. Mason. Club: Berwick Rotary. Address: 211 W. Second St., Berwick, Pa.

EVANS, D. Bargar, lawyer; b. Moundsville, Va. (now W.Va.), Dec. 18, 1859; s. Walter and Susannah (Francis) E.; ed. Moundsville (W. Va.) pub. schs., Waynesburg (Pa.) Coll.; read law in office of J. Alexander Ewing, Moundsville; m. Mary Estelle Myers, Sept. 11, 1890; children—Virginia Bargar, Laurence Myers. Admitted to W.Va. bar, after examination by judges of Supreme Ct. of Appeals, 1883; mem. law firm Evans & Evans, Moundsville, W.Va., since 1930. Mem. N.G. of W.Va., 1877. Mem. council, City of Moundsville, W.Va. Mem. W.Va. State Bar Assn., Marshall Co. Bar Assn. Republican. Methodist. Elk (Moundsville Lodge 282). Home: 1018 Tomlinson Av. Office: Mercantile Bank Bldg., Moundsville, W.Va.

EVANS, Edward Wyatt, lawyer; b. Phila., Pa., Jan. 31, 1882; s. Jonathan and Rachel Reeve (Cope) E.; A.B., Haverford Coll., 1902; A.B., Harvard, 1903; LL.B., U. of Pa. Law Sch., 1907; m. Jacqueline Pascal Morris, Sept. 15, 1911; children—Ernest Mervyn, Francis Cope, Katharine Wistar, Elizabeth Morris (dec.), Christopher, Jacqueline Pascal. Admitted to Pa. bar, 1907, and engaged in gen. practice of law at Phila.; asso. with firms Innes and Williams and Williams and Sinkler, 1907-12; asst. counsel, Bell Telephone Co. of Pa., 1912-15; sec. Fellowship of Reconciliation, 1915-18; sec. Friends' Social Order Com., Phila., 1918-25; asst. prof. Internat. Law, U. of Pa., 1932-33; engaged in study and writing in internat. affairs, 1933-38; sec. Yearly Meeting of The Religious Soc. of Friends of Phila. and Vicinity since 1938. Mem. and sec. Bd. Mgrs. The Corpn. of Haverford Coll.; mem. bd. mgrs. Pendle Hill Sch. for Grad. Study; dir. White-Williams Foundation (retired 1939), Am. Friends Service Com. Mem. Am. Soc. Internat. Law, Phi Beta Kappa. Mem. Religious Soc. Friends. Home: Awbury, Chew St., Germantown, Philadelphia, Pa. Office: 304 Arch St., Philadelphia, Pa.

EVANS, George Heberton, Jr., univ. prof.; b. Baltimore, Md., Jan. 20, 1900; s. George Heberton and Mary Virginia Crawford (Sherlock) E.; student Elementary Sch. of Md. State Normal Sch., Baltimore, Md., 1905-08, Jefferson Sch. for Boys, Baltimore, Md., 1908-16; A.B., Johns Hopkins U., Baltimore, Md., 1920, Ph.D., 1925; m. Elinor Virdin, Nov. 26, 1924; children—George Heberton III, Richard Virdin, Ellen. Instr. in polit. economy, Johns Hopkins U., Baltimore, Md., 1924-27, asso., 1927-35, asso. prof. since 1935. Served in S.A.T.C., 1918. Mem. Nat. Bur. of Econ. Research (research asso., 1939-40), Am. Econ. Assn., Am. Statis. Assn., Am. Assn. Univ. Profs., Phi Beta Kappa, Beta Theta Pi. Episcopalian. Clubs: 14 W. Hamilton St., Johns Hopkins (Baltimore, Md.). Author: British Corporation Finance 1775-1850: A Study of Preference Shares, 1936; articles in econ. jours. Address: 5734 Pimlico Rd., Baltimore, Md.

EVANS, Harold, lawyer; b. Phila., Pa., Oct. 26, 1886; s. Jonathan and Rachel R. (Cope) E.; A.B., Haverford Coll., 1907; LL.B., U. of Pa. Law Sch., 1910; m. Sylvia Hathaway, May 1, 1914; children—Sylvia H. (Mrs. Joseph H. Taylor), Margaret, Nathaniel H., Faith, Thomas, Anna. Admitted to Pa. bar, 1910, and since engaged in gen. practice of law at Phila.; mem. firm MacCoy, Brittain, Evans and Lewis since 1934; dir. Mine Hill and Schuylkill Haven R.R. Served as mem. Pa. Pub. Service Commn., 1925-26; chmn. Phila. Co. Relief Bd., 1936-37; trustee Community Fund of Phila. Overseer William Penn Charter Sch., vice chmn. Am. Friends Service Com. Mem. Am., Pa., and Phila. bar assns., Am. Law Inst., Phi Beta Kappa. Democrat. Mem. Religious Soc. of Friends. Club: University. Home: Awbury, Germantown. Office: 1000 Provident Trust Bldg., Philadelphia, Pa.

EVANS, Harold Glenn, casualty co. exec.; b. Armstrong Co., Pa., Jan. 27, 1906; s. George Monroe and Annie Rebecca (Foster) E.; Ed. Culver Mil. Acad., 1920-23, Gettysburg Coll., 1923-25, DePauw U., 1925-26; m. Mary Jo Springer, Sept. 28, 1929; children—George Monroe II, Catherine Hughes, Nancy Crittenden. Began with Travelers Ins. Co.; served as chief of Div. of Cos., Pa. Ins. Dept., 1933 to 1936; asso. with American Casualty Co., Reading, Pa., since 1936, pres. and dir. since 1936; mem. bd. dirs. Union Nat. Bank (Reading, Pa.). Trustee Welfare Assn., Homeopathic Hosp., Reading, Pa. Mem. Pa. Soc. of New York City, Phi Kappa Psi. Republican. Presbyn. Clubs: Wyomissing, Lions, Berkshire Country (Reading). Home: 4 Wyomissing Hills Boul., West Lawn, Pa. Office: 607 Washington St., Reading, Pa.

EVANS, Henry Brown, univ. prof.; b. Dayton, O., July 2, 1871; s. Lewis Girdler and Frances Eliza (Brown) E.; M.E., Lehigh U., 1893; Ph.D., U. of Pa., 1901; m. Helen Elizabeth Mendenhall, 1912 (dec.). Instr. mathematics and astronomy, Lehigh U., Bethlehem, Pa., 1894-95, U. of Pa., 1895-1901; asst. U.S. Nautical Almanac, 1901-04, piece work computer, 1904-20; asst. prof. mathematics, U. of Pa., 1904-11, prof. since 1911; dean, Towne Scientific Sch., 1918-19, chmn. dept. of mathematics since 1933. Mem. Am. Math. Soc.; Am. Astron. Soc.; Math. Assn. of America; A.A.A.S. Author (textbooks): Analytic Geometry and Plane and Spherical Trigonometry (with Prof. E. S. Crawley). Home: 88 Merbrook Lane, Merion, Pa.

EVANS, J. Ray, retail lumber and builders supplies; b. Carmichaels, Pa., July 10, 1879; s. Brice and Sarah (Clawson) E.; ed. pub. schs., Carmichaels, Pa.; m. Alice Giles, June 28, 1922. Successively clk., merchant, theatre mgr. and propr.; engaged as mcht., 1900; pres. Donora Lbr. Co. since 1934. Republican. Presbyn. Mason. Elk. Club: Monongahela Country. Home: 644 McKean Av. Office: 232 Meldon Av., Donora, Pa.

EVANS, James Carmichael, coll. adminstr.; b. Gallatin, Tenn., July 1, 1900; s. James Royal and Lillie (Carmichael) E.; A.B., Roger Williams U., Nashville, Tenn., 1921; B.S. in E.E., Mass. Inst. Tech., 1925, M.S. in E.E., 1926; m. Rosaline McGoodwin, Aug. 30, 1928. Elec. engr. and constructor, Miami, Fla., 1926-28; teacher Booker T. Washington High Sch., Miami, 1927; instr. electricity and mathematics, W.Va. State Coll., 1928-29, prof. mech. industries and dir. trade and tech. div. since 1929, administrative asst. to pres. since 1937. Instr., S.A.T.C., 1918. Mem. Am. Inst. E.E., Inst. Radio Engrs., Nat. Tech. Assn. (exec. sec. since 1931); Am. Teachers Assn. (chmn. Industrial Arts Sec. since 1930), W.Va. State Teachers Assn. (chmn. Vocational sect. since 1931). Received Harmon Award in Science, Harmon Foundation, 1926, on basis of tech. elec. research. Baptist. Clubs: Adelphian (Miami, Fla.); Business and Professional Men's (Charleston, W.Va.). Home: Institute, W.Va.

EVANS, John Brooke, lawyer; b. Pottstown, Pa., Nov. 16, 1872; s. Jesse Worth and Ellie Gordon (Reifsnyder) E.; grad. Pottstown High Sch., 1890; student The Hill School, 1892-93; LL.B., U. of Pa., 1896; m. Mabel Senior, Oct. 28, 1903; 1 dau., Helen E. Palmer. Admitted to Pa. bar, 1896, and since in practice in Pottstown; solicitor Pottstown Sch. Dist., 1905-35; borough solicitor, 1899-1907; asst. dist. atty., Montgomery Co., Pa., 1908-12; asst. treas. of U.S. at Phila., 1915-21; acting postmaster, Pottstown, 1935-36; dir. Pottstown Gas & Water Co. Mem. Montgomery Co. Bar Assn. (vicepres.). Democrat. Mem. Reformed Ch. Home: 125 N. Hanover St. Office: Exchange Bldg., Pottstown, Pa.

EVANS, John Clarence, prof. business adminstrn.; b. Scranton, Pa., May 21, 1891; s. Moses David and Rachel E.; B.Sc., in Econs., U. of Pa., 1925, A.M., 1932; m. Augusta Caroline Rodemann, Jan 7, 1920; children—John Rodman, Philip Warren. Employed as office sec. Y.M.C.A., Scranton, Pa., Toledo, O., and Ithaca, N.Y., 1909-13; ry. accountant, Lackawanna Ry., Scranton, Pa., 1914-18; instr. business adminstrn., U. of Pa. Wharton Sch., 1925-32; prof. business adminstrn., Albright Coll., Reading, Pa., since 1932. Served as corpl. inf., U.S.A., 1918-21, with A.E.F.; awarded Purple Heart. Chmn. Finance Com. of Borough Council, Ridley Park, Pa., 1925-29. Candidate for Congress. Rep. ticket, 1938. Served as impartial chmn. Keystone Hosiery Mfrs. Assn. and Branch 10 of Am. Fed. of Hosiery Workers. Mem. Hosiery Industry Com., Wages and Hours Div., U.S. Dept. of Labor. Mem. Am. Accounting Assn., Pi Gamma Mu, Kappa Alpha Phi, Am. Legion, Vets. Fgn. Wars. Republican. Presbyn. Club: Reading Hungry. Home: 1420 Linden St., Reading, Pa.

EVANS, John Fairhurst, lawyer; b. Paterson, N.J., Aug. 10, 1891; s. John William and Emily Ann (Wadsworth) E.; student N.Y. Univ., 1910-11; A.B. cum laude, Harvard U., 1914; LL.B., Columbia U. Law Sch., 1916; m. Mayrose Waterman, Sept. 9, 1918; 1 son, John Fairhurst, Jr. Admitted to N.J. bar as atty., 1916, as counselor, 1919; engaged in gen. practice of law at Paterson since 1916; mem. firm Evans, Smith & Evans since 1925; served as judge recorder's ct., Paterson, 1925-27; dir. code authority rayon and silk dyeing and printing industry, 1934; dir. and counsel, Haledon Nat. Bank, Haledon, N.J., Fair Lawn-Radburn Trust Co., Financial Bldg. & Loan Assn., Paterson, Richmond Piece Dye Works, Richmond, Va., Great Eastern Stores, Paterson, N.J. Served as 1st lt. F.A., U.S.A., 1917-18. Trustee Paterson Y.M.C.A. Mem. Am. Bar Assn., Psi Upsilon. Republican. Baptist. Mason. Clubs: Hamilton (Paterson); North Jersey Country (Wayne); Harvard (New York). Home: 178 Vreeland Av. Office: 5 Colt St., Paterson, N.J.

EVANS, John Henry, lawyer, banker; b. Tarentum, Pa.; s. John H. and Catharine E.; ed. Duquesne U. and Duquesne U. Sch. of Law, Pittsburgh, Pa.; m. Catherine C. Gatens, Feb. 8, 1915; children—John Henry, Albert J., Claudia C., Betty E. Admitted to Pa. bar, 1917; engaged in banking and trust business at Pittsburgh and Sharon, Pa., since 1917; asso. with Union Trust Co., Pittsburgh, Pa.; vice-pres., trust officer and dir. McDowell Nat. Bank. Sharon, Pa., since 1927; dir. Youngstown Terminal Bldg. Co., Youngstown, O. Mem. Pa. Bar Assn., Mercer Co. Bar Assn., Pa. Bankers Assn. (pres. Trust Company Sect.). Republican. Catholic. Home: 1180 Griswold St. Office: McDowell Nat. Bank, Sharon, Pa.

EVANS, John J.; chmn. bd. Armstrong Cork Co. Home: 1063 Wheatland Av., Lancaster, Pa.

EVANS, Louis Hadley, clergyman; b. Goshen, Ind., May 31, 1897; s. William and Laura (Torgerson) E.; A.B., Occidental Coll., Los Angeles, 1918; B.D., McCormick Theol. Sem., Chicago, 1922; D.D., Washington & Jefferson Coll., 1932, Jamestown Coll., 1932; m. Marie M. Egley, Dec. 22, 1922; children—Lauralil, Louis H., Mary Eileen, William Oren. Ordained Presbyn. ministry, 1922; pastor First Ch., Westhope, N.D., 1922-25, Calvary Presbyn. Ch., Wilmington, Calif., 1925-28, First Ch., Pomona, Calif., 1928-31, Third Ch., Pittsburgh, since 1931. Mem. Bd. of Foreign Missions, Presbyn. Ch. of the U.S.A., 1935, mem. Bd. of Nat. Missions since 1936. Dir. Passavant Memorial Home (Rochester, Pa.), Pittsburgh Assn. for Improvement of the Poor, Western Theol. Sem.; mem. bd. advisors Nat. Recreational Assn.; mem. Pittsburgh advisory bd. Internat. Soc. Christian Endeavor. Clubs: Cleric, Longue Vue Country. Home: 1085 Shady Av. Office: Fifth Av. at S. Negley, Pittsburgh, Pa.

EVANS, Owen David, supt. Mech. Sch., Girard Coll.; b. Youngstown, O., Nov. 20, 1876; s. Roger and Elizabeth (Jones) E.; grad. Rayen High Sch., Youngstown, O., 1895; A.B., Harvard, 1900, A.M., 1901; m. Annie L. Jackson, June 26, 1901; children—Roger Jackson, David Wendell, Barbara Anne, Janet Elizabeth (Mrs. Oliver C. Lyon Jr.), Owen Daniel, Alan Somers. Teacher, Nichols Sch., Buffalo, N.Y., 1900-05; teacher, Rindge Manual Training Sch., Cambridge, Mass., 1905; teacher and prin. Boston Pub. Schs., 1905-20; dir. of continuation schs., Pa. State Dept. Pub. Instrn., 1920-24; Contbr. Nat. Transportation Inst., Washington, D.C., 1924; asso. on adult edn. survey Carnegie Corpn. of New York, 1925; with Girard Coll., Phila., since 1925, supt. Mech. Sch. since 1925; has given teacher training courses for state depts. of Mass., N.Y., N.J., and at Pa. State Coll., U. of Pa., Columbia U. Teachers Coll., U. of Pittsburgh. Mem. Bd. Sch. Dirs., Ridley Park, Pa. Mem. N.E.A., Am. Vocational Assn., Adult Edn. Assn., Pa. Hist. Soc., Phi Beta Kappa, Delta Upsilon. Republican. Presbyterian. Mason (32°). Contbr. to vocational edn. mags. and to Encyclopædia Britannica; author "Educational Opportunities for Young Workers" and courses of study for continuation schs. Home: 107 W. Ridley Av., Ridley Park, Pa. Office: Girard College, Philadelphia, Pa.

EVANS, Powell; pres. Schuylkill Transportation Co. Home: Grays Lane, Haverford, Pa. Office: Mahoney City, Pa.

EVANS, Raymond Louis, surgeon; b. Cincinnati, O., Feb. 2, 1905; s. Lester and Emma (Doepke) E.; B.S., U. of Cincinnati, 1924; M.D., U. of Cincinnati Med. Coll., 1928; M.Sc. in Surgery, U. of Cin. Pa. Grad. Sch. of Medicine, 1931; unmarried. Interne U.S. Marine Hosp., New Orleans, La., 1928-29; asso. surg., Warsaw N.Y. Hosp., 1933-35; asso. surgeon Guthrie Clinic, Sayre, Pa., since 1935. Certified by Am. Board of Surgery. Fellow American College Surgeons; mem. A.M.A., Pa. Med. Soc., Delta Tau Delta, Nu Sigma Nu. Home: Cincinnati, O. Office: Guthrie Clinic, Sayre, Pa.

EVANS, Robert David, engr.; b. Springwater, Wis., Oct. 14, 1892; s. David R. and Sarah J. (Ellis) E.; B.S. in E.E., U. of Okla., 1914; m. Ruth Carrington Lane, Sept. 22, 1917; children—Marjorie, Nancy Ruth. With Westinghouse Electric & Mfg. Co. since 1914, gen. engr., 1916-31, mgr. transmission engring., 1931-34, central station engr., 1934-38, cons. transmission engr. since 1938. Mem. Am. Inst. Elec. Engrs. (mem. tech. coms.). Author: Symmetrical Components (with C. F. Wagner), 1933; also (with others) numerous tech. papers and articles on power transmission, system stability and elec. transients. Home: 1125 Milton Av., Pittsburgh, Pa. Office: Westinghouse Electric & Mfg. Co., East Pittsburgh, Pa.

EVANS, Roy S., pres. Am. Bantam Car Co.; b. Bartow, Ga., Oct. 17, 1900; s. Samuel and Eva (Jordan) E.; ed. Ga. Inst. Tech.; unmarried. Associated with automobile industry since 1920; distributor and dealer under name of Evans Motors, 1919-37; pres. Am. Bantam Car Co. since 1937, also dir.; dir. Am. Finance & Motors Co., Evans Operations, Inc., Evans Motors, Advance Corpn. (all of Atlanta), R.S. Evans Motors (Miami, Tampa and Jacksonville, Fla.). Methodist. Clubs: Pittsburgh Athletic Assn., Capitol City Country (Atlanta); Tampa (Fla.) Yacht. Home: Schenley Apts., Pittsburgh, Pa. Office: Butler, Pa.

EVANS, Rulison, v.p. and gen. mgr. Scranton Spring Brook Water Service Co.; b. Wilkes-Barre, Pa., July 16, 1894; s. John Lloyd and Anna Esther (MacDonald) E.; ed. Wilkes-Barre schs. and Wharton Sch. of Finance (U. of Pa.); m. Marion Louise Bowkley, Apr. 4, 1923; 1 son, Robert R. With Scranton Spring Brook Water Service Co. since 1911, chief clerk, later paymaster, 1923-27, asst. to v.p., 1927-29, gen. mgr. since 1929, v.p. since 1933; v.p. Pa. Water Service Co. Mem. Wilkes-Barre Chamber of Commerce, Am. Legion. Republican. Protestant. Mason, Kiwanian. Clubs: Iren Temple Country, Fox Hill Country, Westmoreland, Franklin (Wilkes-Barre). Home: 77 E. Walnut St., Kingston, Pa. Office: 30 N. Franklin St., Wilkes-Barre, Pa.

EVANS, Samuel J., pres. Tri City Traction Co.; b. Middle Creek, Pa., Dec. 21, 1869; s. John B. and Sara Ann (Williams) E.; student pub. schs.; m. Ada Pearl Cawley, Nov. 18, 1896; children—Sara Ann, Ineze, Samuel J. Organized 1920 and since pres. and gen. mgr. Tri City Traction Co. Home: 218 Center St. Office: 1448 Main St., Princeton, W.Va.

EVANS, Silliman, chmn. bd. Md. Casualty Co.; b. Joshua, Tex., Apr. 2, 1894; s. Columbus Asbury and Alice (Silliman) E.; studied Polytechnic Coll. (now Southern Methodist U.), Fort Worth, 1911-13; m. Lucille McCrea, Nov. 22, 1924; children—Silliman, Amon C. Began as newspaper reporter, 1913; reporter, mem. staff and Washington corr., Ft. Worth Star-Telegram, 1913-26; v.p. Tex. Air Transport until 1928, Southern Air Transport until 1929, Am. Airways, Inc., until 1932; 4th asst. postmaster gen., 1933-34; resigned to accept presidency Maryland Casualty Co., Baltimore, now chmn. bd.; pres. and pub. Nashville Tennessean. Democrat. Clubs: Forth Worth, Glen Garden (Fort Worth); National Press (Washington); Baltimore Country, Elkridge, Maryland, Merchants (Baltimore). Address: 40th and Keswick Rd., Baltimore, Md.

EVANS, Thomas; pres. and gen. mgr. Merchant & Evans Co.; officer or dir. many companies. Office: 2035 Washington Av., Philadelphia, Pa.

EVANS, William A(ugustus) D(arling), pres. Gen. Electric Vapor Lamp Co.; b. New York, N.Y., Feb. 3, 1881; s. Frank Overton and Henrietta (Darling) E.; student Barnard Sch. for Boys, New York, 1895-99, Columbia U., 1899-1903; m. Margaret Isabel Sharkey, Nov. 20, 1906; children—William Augustus, Margaret

Darling (Mrs. John S. Ferry). Engr. Cooper Hewitt Electric Co. (Gen. Electric Vapor Lamp Co. since 1930), Hoboken, N.J., 1903-19, v.p., 1919, pres. since June 1919; mem. bd. mgrs. Hoboken Bank for Savings. Mem. N.J. State Chamber of Commerce (dir.), Hoboken Chamber of Commerce, Nat. Electric Mfrs. Assn., Nat. Assn. of Mfrs., Illuminating Engring. Soc., Delta Kappa Epsilon. Republican. Episcopalian. Clubs: Columbia Univ., St. David's Soc., Electrical Manufacturers (New York); Canoe Brook Country (Summit, N.J.). Home: 100 Whittredge Rd., Summit, N.J. Office: 410 Eighth St., Hoboken, N.J.

EVANS, Williams B.; surgeon and gynecologist Chester Hosp.; asso. gynecologist Fitzgerald-Mercy Hosp., Darby, Pa. Address: 320 E. Broad St., Chester, Pa.

EVANS, William D.; gen. counsel Jones & Laughlin Steel Corpn. Home: 714 Amberson Av. Office: Oliver Bldg., Pittsburgh, Pa.

EVANS, William Raymond, realtor; b. Upper Darby Twp., Pa., Dec. 3, 1887; s. William B. and Florence (Worley) E.; ed. Lansdowne (Pa.) High Sch. and Drexel Inst., Phila.; m. Ella A. Payne, Nov. 15, 1921; 1 son, William Raymond. Sec. and mgr. Upper Darby (Pa.) Bldg. & Loan Assn. since 1908; real estate officer Lansdowne (Pa.) Bank & Trust Co., 1916-24, v.p., 1924-32; sec. Drexel Hill Title & Trust Co., 1922-32; pres. Delaware Co. League Bldg. & Loan Assn., 1936; dir. Quaker City Federal Saving & Loan Assn. Pres. Yeadon Borough Council, 1918-35; pres. Delaware Co. Real Estate Bd., 1925; gov. Philadelphia Real Estate Bd., 1936. Mem. Pa. Real Estate Assn. (dir. 1938); Delaware Co. Parks Assn. Republican. Presbyterian. Mason (32°, Past Master George W. Bartram Lodge 298). Clubs: Union League, Rolling Green Golf, Skytop, Lansdowne Golf. Home: 653 Church Lane, Yeadon, Pa. Office: 19 N. Lansdowne Av., Lansdowne, Pa.

EVANS, William Wadsworth, lawyer; b. Paterson, N.J., Oct. 5, 1886; s. John W. and Emily Amelia (Wadsworth) E.; student pub. schs., Paterson, N.J.; LL.B., N.Y. Law Sch., 1908; married; children—Barbara, William Wadsworth. Admitted to N.Y. bar, 1909, N.J. bar, 1911; senior mem. firm Evans, Smith & Evans, Paterson, N.J. Has been mem. N.J. Assembly, majority leader, 1923, speaker of house, 1924; now mem. Judicial Council of N.J. Mem. Am. Bar Assn. (formerly mem. house of dels., and mem. com. on bar orgn. activities), N.J. State Bar Assn. (pres. 1936-37), Passaic Co. Bar Assn. (former mem. character and fitness com.). Club: Hamilton (Paterson, N.J.; pres. 1938, 1939). Home: 396 E. 30th St. Office: 5 Colt St., Paterson, N.J.

EVERARD, Joshua Grover, supt. schs.; b. Wapwallopen, Pa., May 9, 1894; s. Francis E. and Mary Ellen (Grover) E.; Ph.B., Lafayette Coll., 1917; Ed.M., Pa. State Coll., 1935; m. Grace Marian Young, Nov. 26, 1919; 1 dau., Mary Jane. Supt. schs., Huntingdon, Pa., since 1934. Home: 531 Penn St. Office: 723 Portland Av., Huntingdon, Pa.

EVERETT, Edith Mary, educator; b. Burke, N.Y., Dec. 23, 1880; d. Oliver and Anna (McKenzie) E.; B.L., Smith Coll., 1903; Pd.B., N.Y. State Coll. for Teachers, 1905; A.M., Columbia U. Extension, 1919. Engaged as instr. English, high schs. in N.Y., 1905-21; mem. faculty Pa. Sch. Social Work of U. of Pa. since 1921; asso. dir. White-Williams Foundation, Phila., 1922-31, dir. since 1931; lecturer in edn., Swarthmore Coll., 1923-36; instr. Mental Hygiene Extension Course, Phila. Normal Sch., 1930-37. Mem. Am. Assn. Social Workers, Progressive Edn. Assn., Nat. Edn. Assn., Am. Assn. Visiting Teachers, Am. Assn. Univ. Women. Presbyterian. Clubs: Women's University, Art Alliance (Philadelphia). Home: Flourtown, Pa. Office: Administration Bldg., Board of Public Education, 21st St. and Parkway, Philadelphia, Pa.

EVERETT, Harold Arthur, mech. engr.; b. Manchester, N.H., March 17, 1880; s. Arthur Gordon and Emma F. (Campbell) E.; B.S., Mass. Inst. Tech., 1902; M.E., Pa. State Coll., 1924; m. Alice DeSilva, Sept. 1908; children—Elizabeth, Ruth. Outside machinist, estimator and computer Fore River S. & E. Bldg. Co., Quincy, Mass., 1902-03, New York Shipbuilding Co., Camden, N.J., 1903-04; asso. prof. naval architecture, Mass. Inst. Tech., 1904-15; prof. marine engring., Post-Grad., U.S. Naval Acad., 1915-18; chief engr. and naval architect Union Shipbuilding Co., Baltimore, 1918-22; asso. prof. mech. engring., Pa. State Coll., 1922-24, prof. thermodynamics, 1924-31, head mech. engring. dept. since 1931; voting machine expert, Allegheny Co., Pa. Mem. Soc. Naval Architecture and Marine Engring., Am. Soc. Mech. Engrs., Soc. Automotive Engrs., Soc. of Aero Sciences, Soc. Promotion Engring. Edn., Sigma Xi, Phi Kappa Phi, Sigma Tau, Pi Tau Sigma. Republican. Presbyterian. Clubs: University, Triangle. Author: Thermodynamics, 1937; also numerous papers on engring. subjects. Home: 262 E. Hamilton Av., State College, Pa.

EVERETT, Hermon David, pres. and gen. mgr. Smokeless Fuel Co.; officer or dir. many companies. Home: 1632 Kanawha St., Charleston, W.Va.

EVERETT, Houston Spencer, M.D., gynecologist; b. Richmond Co., N.C., June 27, 1900; s. Arey Covington and Ella (Spencer) E.; grad. Rockingham (N.C.) High Sch., 1916; A.B., U. of N.C., 1920, A.M., 1921; M.D.,, Johns Hopkins, 1925; m. Excie Robertson, Oct. 1, 1932; children—Excie Witcher, Houston Spencer. Interne Johns Hopkins Hosp., 1925-26, asst. in gynecology, 1926-29, resident in gynecology, 1929-31, visiting gynecologist since 1931; instr. in gynecology, Johns Hopkins U., since 1929. Fellow A.M.A., Southern Med. Assn.; mem. Med. and Chirurg. Faculty of Md., Baltimore City Med. Soc., Pi Kappa Alpha, Nu Sigma Nu, Phi Beta Kappa, Alpha Omega Alpha, Sigma Psi. Democrat. Presbyterian. Mason. Club: Johns Hopkins U. Faculty. Contbr. numerous articles to med. jours. Home: 108 Longwood Rd. Office: 11 E. Chase St., Baltimore, Md.

EVERITT, Frank Bateman, clergyman; b. Stroudsburg, Pa., March 8, 1866; s. Benjamin Smith and Helen C. (Bateman) E.; A.B., Princeton U., 1886, A.M., same, 1889; Th.B., Princeton Theol. Sem., 1890; m. Sara Helena Van Dyke, Sept. 11, 1895; children—Kenneth Van Dyke, Helen Gladys (wife of Rev. J. Clyde Foose), James Donald. Ordained to Presbyn. ministry, 1890; home missionary, Kansas City, Mo., 1890-91; chapel minister and pastor, East Trenton, N.J., 1891-1900; supt. young people's work, 63d St. Mission Fifth Av. Presbyn. Church, N.Y. City, 1900-03; pastor, New Park, Pa., 1903-11; Allentown, Pa., 1911-15; Lewisburg, Pa., 1916-29, Cranbury, N.J., 1929-37, stated supply, Farmingdale, N.J., 1937-39, retired, hon. mem. State Christian Endeavor Com. First sec. and treas. N.J. State Christian Endeavor Union, 1886-90, a vice-pres., first evangelistic supt. and officer, 1890-1900, mem. and hon. mem. State Christian Endeavor Com. since 1929. Independent Republican. Presbyn. Home: Rehoboth Beach, Del.

EVERY, William Franklin, lawyer; b. Mulberry, Pa., June 26, 1905; s. Gaines O'B. and Lota M. (Hicks) E.; student Baltimore (Md) City Coll., 1920-23; LL.B., U. of Md., Baltimore, Md., 1926; m. Hilda Dale Willis, June 1, 1932; children—Patricia Dale, William Franklin III. Practice of law at Baltimore, Md., since 1926; instr. in law, U. of Baltimore (Md.) since 1927. Mem. Md. State Senate, 1934 to 1937; mem. Interstate Commn. on Crime, 1937 to 1939. Mem. Baltimore City Bar Assn. (mem. Com. to Study Plan to Reorganize Am. Bar Assn.; Entertainment Com.; Ethics Com.), Am. Bar Assn. (mem. State Council, 1935 to 1397; mem. Md. Legislative Com., 1935 to 1937; mem. Com. of Judicial Selection and Tenure, 1937 to 1938), Delta Theta Phi. Democrat. Baptist. Author of several legal articles and papers. Delegate to 1935 Dem. Nat. Conv., Phila. Radio commentator: Attorney to the Board of Examiners of Public Accountants of Maryland, 1939. Home: 815 E. 33th St. Office: 1134 Baltimore Trust Bldg., Baltimore, Md.

EVES, William, III., educator; b. Wilmington, Del., Oct. 11, 1889; s. Hiram Pyle and Mary Kirk (Horner) E.; ed. Friends Sch.; B.S., Princeton U., 1911, E.E., 1913; student U. of Pa. Grad. Sch. of Edn.; m. Julia Downman Thom, Oct. 16, 1915; children—Benjamin Miller, Mary Elizabeth, Rebecca Thomas. Works engr. Am. Vulcanized Fibre Co., Wilmington, Del., 1913-20; instr. mathematics and head dept., George Sch., 1921-26, dean, 1926-38, vice-prin. in charge enrollments, scholarships, publicity and administrn. since 1938. Mem. Am. Friends Service Com. since 1921, chmn. foreign service sect. and dir. since 1924, Com. on Spain since 1937; mem. Am. Com. for Christian German Refugees since 1936. Dir. Pendle Hill (Quaker grad. centre for religious study), Wallingford, Pa., since 1930; mem. Carl Schurz Memorial Foundation. Mem. N.E.A., Progressive Edn. Assn., Foreign Policy Assn., Phi Beta Kappa. Ind. Republican. Mem. Soc. of Friends. Club: Princeton (Philadelphia). Author: Electrical Resistance of Vulcanized Fibre, 1913; Electrical Properties of Vulcanized Fibre, 1917. Address: George School, Bucks Co., Pa.

EWALD, Louis, artist; b. Minneapolis, Minn., Dec. 19, 1891; s. Leo and Isabelle (Gardiner) E.; student Pa. Museum and Sch. of Industrial Art, Phila., 1912-16; m. Evelyn Brain, Oct. 21, 1921; children—John Louis, Thomas Morris. Began as artist, decorative work on Bryn Athyn Cathedral, 1916; later with art dept. N. W. Ayer Advertising Agency; now free lance artist engaging in miscellaneous work, advertising layouts and illustrations, lettering, illustrations for med. books, portraits and murals; principally interested in ecclesiastical paintings, color schemes and decorations. Prin. work in McGraw Hill Publs.; med. drawings appear in Dr. P. B. Blands "Gynecology" and "Obstetrics," pub. by F. A. Davis. Represented by murals and ecclesiastic work in several homes in vicinity of Phila., Muhlenberg Coll., Allentown, Pa., about 12 chs. in or near Phila. Served in Med. Dept., U.S. Army, June 1918-Mar. 1919. Mem. Art Alliance, Phila. Episcopalian. Home: Box 52, Bryn Athyn, Pa. Office: 1430 S. Penn Sq., Philadelphia, Pa.

EWAN, Stacy Newcomb, Jr., supt. schs.; b. Millville, N.J., May 13, 1900; s. Stacy N. and Eleanor (Jenkins) E.; B.S., Haverford (Pa.) Coll., 1921; A.M., U. of Pa., 1933, Ph.D., 1935; m. Marian E. Young, Dec. 21, 1927. Teacher science, Millville (N.J.) High Sch., 1922; head science dept., Jenkintown (Pa.) High Sch., 1923-26, Lansdowne (Pa.) High Sch., 1926-30, prin. of latter, 1930-34, supt. schs., Lansdowne, since 1934. Served as lt., U.S. Naval Reserve. Mem. N.E.A., Am. Assn. Sch. Adminstrs., Pa. State Edn. Assn., Home and Sch. Assn. of Lansdowne (v.p.), Phila. Suburban Supts. Assn. (ex-pres.), Am. Legion (chmn. Americanization com.), Phi Delta Kappa. Republican. Presbyterian. Clubs: Union Athletic Assn. (ex-pres., dir.), Rotary, Neighbors (Lansdowne, Pa.). Writer numerous articles on edn. Home: 216 Wayne Av. Office: Essex and Green Avs., Lansdowne, Pa.

EWERS, John Ray, clergyman; b. West Unity, O., Nov. 9, 1877; s. Edwin Patterson and Harriet Jane (Bostater) E.; B.S., Fayette (Ohio) Normal Coll., 1895; A.B., Hiram (O.) Coll., 1899; B.D., U. of Chicago, 1905; D.D., U. of Pittsburgh, 1926; m. Mary Alice Canfield, Sept. 21, 1899 (she died July 21, 1935); children—Edwin Patterson (M.D.), John Canfield; m. 2d, Laura La Croix, Oct. 1, 1936. Ordained to ministry of the Christian Church 1899; pastor Buffalo, N.Y., 1899-1900, Bowling Green, O., 1900-03; Chicago, Ill., 1903-05; Youngstown, O., 1905-09, East End Christian Ch., Pittsburgh, Pa., since 1909. Trustee Christian Union Quarterly, Disciples Divinity House of U. of Chicago, Campbell Inst. of Chicago; dir. Pittsburgh Housing Commn. Mem. Philosophical Soc. of Pittsburgh. Mason (32°). Clubs: Quiz, Fellowship Circle, Longue Vue. Contbr. articles on religious subjects to books and jours. Regular corr. of Christian Century; an editor The Twentieth Century Quarterly. Home: The Ruskin Apts., Pittsburgh, Pa.

EWING, Jack Sweetser, investment banking; b. Brooklandville, Md., Apr. 9, 1901; s. George Washington and Betty (Sherley) E.; student Hotchkiss Sch., Lakeville, Conn., 1918-21;

A.B., Yale, 1925; m. Carolyn Brooks Gibson, June 4, 1927; children—Jack Sweetser (dec.), Edward Gibson, Jacklyn. Began as clk. in bank, then salesman securities, 1926; with Farmers Loan & Trust Co., N.Y. City, 1925-26; with J. A. W. Iglehart & Co., Baltimore, 1926-30; with Field, Glore & Co., 1931-35; with W. E. Hutton & Co., Baltimore, since 1935; dir. Gathmann Engring. Co., Title Guarantee & Trust Co. Dir. and treas. Home for Incurables of Baltimore. Mem. Delta Kappa Epsilon. Democrat. Episcopalian. Clubs: Racquet (Baltimore); Green Spring Valley Hunt. Home: Lutherville, Md. Office: First Nat. Bank Bldg., Baltimore, Md.

EWING, John Minor, pres. Dobbs Co.; b. Columbus, O., Apr. 24, 1901; s. Jacob Otto and Delia Frances (Deitz) E.; ed. high sch. and Ky. Mil. Inst.; m. Nancy Jean Ramsey, May 10, 1930. Employed by Fawcett Publications, 1921-22; became associated with Cannon Valley Milling Co., Minn., 1922, asst. sales mgr., 1924, v.p., 1925-29; pres. Dobbs Co. since organization, 1931. While pres. United Medicine Mfrs. of America, 1932-35, assisted in having passed new and better laws on cleaner advertising and protection of public in foods, drugs and cosmetics. Mem. Nat. Code Authority for Package Medicine Industry (elected by entire industry), 1934-35. Donor Minor Ewing Progress Award (awarded annually by Ky. Mil. Inst.). Mem. New York Bd. of Trade, Legislative Com. of Proprietary Assn.; dir. Ligonier Valley Bd. of Trade, 3 yrs.; formerly dir. Inst. of Medicine Mfrs. Mem. United Presbyn. Ch. Clubs: William Penn, Ligonier Country; Greensburg Advertising (dir. 1937-39, pres. 1939-40). Delivered speech before Conv. of United Medicine Mfrs. of America, 1934. Home: Ligonier, Pa.

EWING, Joseph Neff, lawyer; b. Uniontown, Pa., July 4, 1890; s. Samuel Evans and Fannie Badger (Neff) E.; grad. Haverford (Pa.) Sch., 1908; A.B., Princeton U., 1912; LL.B., U. of Pa., 1915; m. Anne Ashton, Nov. 29, 1924; children—Joseph Neff, Anne Ashton, Thomas Ashton, Samuel Evans, 3d. Admitted to Pa. bar, 1915, and since in practice at Phila.; mem. firm Saul, Ewing, Remick & Saul; dir. Baldwin Locomotive Works. Served with 1st Troop, Phila. City Cavalry, Pa. Nat. Guard, 1915-17, including 6 months' service on Mexican Border; successively lt. of cav., capt. inf., and maj. field arty., U.S. Army, 1917-19. Pres. and chmn. of bd. Haverford Sch.; dir. Bryn Mawr Hosp. Mem. Phila., Chester County, Pa. State and Am. bar assns. Republican. Presbyterian. Clubs: Princeton, University (Phila.). Home: Valley Forge, Pa. Office: 2301 Packard Bldg., Philadelphia, Pa.

EWING, Lucy Elizabeth Lee, writer; b. Phila., Pa.; d. Rev. Charles Henry and Charlotte Elizabeth (Page) Ewing; named for Gen. Robert E. Lee, cousin of her mother; ed. pvt. tutors. Author: Dr. John Ewing and Some of His Noted Connections (biography of author's great grandfather), 2 edits., 1924, 1930; George Frederic Watts; Sandro Botticelli; Matthew Arnold. Contbr. essays and articles to mags. Home: 1130 Spruce St., Philadelphia, Pa.

EWING, Warren Walter, univ. prof.; b. Winterset, Ia., Nov. 4, 1889; s. Frederick Walter and Effie Jane (Tarbell) E.; B.S., Parsons Coll., Fairfield, Ia., 1912; M.S., U. of Chicago, 1918, Ph.D., 1920; m. Adah Shawver, July 25, 1929; 1 dau., Sally. Teacher and mgr. Mission High Sch., Fatehgarh, India, 1912-15; warrant officer British Army in East Africa, 1916; teacher, Marshalltown (Ia.) High Sch., 1916-17; asst. prof., Lehigh U., 1920-28, asso. prof., 1928-37, prof. since 1937. Served as sergeant Chem. Warfare Service, Edgewood Arsenal, 1918. Mem. A.A.A.S., Am. Chem. Soc. (chmn. Lehigh Valley Sect. 1933-34), Sigma Xi, Phi Kappa Phi. Writer articles on photochemistry, surface tension, adsorption, calorimetry and phase equilibria. Home: 106 W. Langhorn Av., R.D. 2, Bethlehem, Pa.

EXLEY, Gordon R., dir. City Transit, Phila.; b. Bernice, Pa., May 20, 1893; s. Henry Charles and Mertie (Potter) E.; student mech. and structural engineering, Franklin Inst., and other technical schs.; m. Anna Marie Gallagher, Aug. 30, 1913; children—Dolores, Earle, Anna, Ruth, Gordon, Albert (dec.), Pearl, Norma, Gerard. Engr. on structural and mech. design and squad engr. Link Belt Co., Specialty Engring. Co., E.G. Budd Co., Barrett Co., Phila. Rapid Transit Co., 1912-24; engr. in charge constrn. Gulf Refining Co., Girard Point, Phila., 1925-26; designer heavy concrete structures U.G.I. Contracting Co., 1926-28; chief engr. in charge steel structures, chmn. material standardization and welding coms., instr. advanced engring. design, Gen. Electric Co., 1928-35; cons. engr. to City Council and Controller, Phila. (prepared revaluation of property of Phila. Rapid Transit Co. which later presented as evidence in reorgn. of co.), 1935; dir. City Transit Dept., Phila., since 1936; mem. mayor's cabinet; registered professional engr. in Pa.; became councilman Borough of Yeadon, Pa., 1932, later dir. pub. safety. Pres. Yeadon Civic Assn., 1930-35; mem. Am. Soc. M.E. Engring. author and lecturer; wrote "Classification and Physical Tests of Welded Plate Joints." Composed musical composition "If I were an Artist." Home: 200 E. Cliveden St. Office: City Hall Annex, Philadelphia, Pa.

EXTON, William Gustav, M.D.; b. Savannah, Ga., Feb. 25, 1876; s. Gustav and Rosalie (Unger) E.; M.D., Coll. Phys. and Surg. (Columbia), 1896; house phys. Mount Sinai Hosp., N.Y. City, 1896-99; post grad. and research work, Pathol. Inst., Vienna, also in London and aris, 1906-07; m. Florence Phillips, Sept. 20, 1905; children—William, Manning Mason, John Marshall. Practiced, N.Y. City, 1901-06; spl. practice and research in urology-metabolism, 1907-16; dir. laboratories Prudential Ins. Co., Newark, N.J., since 1914, planned and directed longevity service since 1917. Mem. A.M.A., Med. Soc. State of N.Y., New York County Med. Soc., Am. Pub. Health Assn., Am. Urol. Assn., Am. Soc. Clinical Pathologists (pres.), Assn. Life Ins. Med. Dirs., Optical Society of America, Am. Assn. Advancement of Science, Am. Chem. Soc. Inventor of gastroscope, 1906; urological table, 1907; immiscible balance, 1915; protein tests, 1918; turbidimeter, 1918; euscope, 1920; spectroscopic method of colorimetry, 1921; scopometer, 1924; junior scopometer, 1927; quantitative microscopy, 1928; photoelectric scopometer, 1929; a new test for sugar tolerance, 1930; new methods for identifying the various sugars that occur in urine, 1932; new method for measuring the number, diameters, volume, and hemoglobin content of red blood cells, 1933; the one-hour-two-dose dextrose tolerance test, 1934; incidence of sugars and reducing substances other than glucose in 1000 consecutive cases, 1934; instrument and method for measuring size of sub-microscopic particles photo-electrically by transmitted light and Tyndall beam, 1934; fibrinogen as an index of disease and its clinical determination by photo-electric scopometry, 1935—; partition of blood fats, 1936; one hour renal condition test, 1937; colorimetric determination of oxygen in blood, 1938. Author: The Prudential Urinalysis System, 1934. Contbr. on preclinical medicine, longevity, clinical pathology, etc. Awards Ward Burdick memorial medal, Am. Soc. Clin. Pathologist; N.Y. State and N.J. State Med. socs. and others. Home: Flofields, Millbrook, N.Y.; also 135 Central Park W., New York, N.Y. Office: Prudential Ins. Bldg., Newark, N.J.

EYERLY, Paul R.; editor Bloomsburg Press. Address: Bloomsburg, Pa.

EYMAN, Elmer Vail, psychiatrist; b. Madison, Wis., Feb. 13, 1885; s. Franklin Pierce and Thirza Alice (Prickett) E.; A.B., U. of Wis., M.D., Rush Med. Coll. (U. of Chicago); m. Euretta Sheldon, May 5, 1915; 1 dau., Alice Frances. Asst. physician Massillon (O.) State Hosp., 1911, Yankton (S.D.) State Hosp., 1912-17; senior asst. physician dept. for mental and nervous diseases, Pa. Hosp., Phila., 1919-30, chief-of-service since 1930; dir. Mental Hygiene Survey of Tex., Nat. Com. for Mental Hygiene, 1924; psychiatrist Juvenile Court Wilmington, Del., 1925-30; cons. in psychiatry, assigned to Federal Courts, U.S. P. H. S., 1937-38; asst. prof. psychiatry, U. of Pa. Grad. Sch. of Medicine since 1936; certified as phychiatrist by Am. Bd. of Neurology and Psychiatry, 1936. Served as 1st lt., M.C., U.S.A., 1918. Fellow Am. Psychiatric Assn., A.M.A.; mem. Pa. Pub. Charities Assn. (mem. mental hygiene com.), Phila. Psychiatric Soc., Phila. Neurol. Soc., Alpha Omega Alpha. Home: 613 Ferne Av., Drexel Hill. Office: 4401 Market St., Philadelphia, Pa.

EYMAN, William G., chief gynecol. service South Side Hosp. Address: 529 Liberty Av., Pittsburgh, Pa.

EYRE, Louisa, sculptor; b. Newport, R. I., Jan. 16, 1872; d. Wilson and Louisa Lincoln (Lear) Eyre; art. edn. Pa. Acad. of the Fine Arts, Art Students' League (New York); studied under Augustus St. Gaudens; studied in Paris in pvt. studio. Began as asst. in one of studios of Augustus St. Gaudens, New York, 1895-96; sculptor, New York, beginning 1897; sculptor, Phila., since 1904. General character of work: portrait reliefs, busts, decorative work for buildings, garden reliefs, figures and reliefs of children. Works: bronze, fountain, figure "Pan"; (tablets) Gen. George Sykes, Memorial Hall, West Point, N.Y.; Hon. John A. Kasson, Des Moines, Ia.; Maj. Gen. Hugh Lenox Scott, Washington (D.C.) Cathedral; (shield decorations) U. of Pa.; (medals): J. G. Holland, Charles E. Dana gold medal for water color award Pa. Acad. Fine Arts. Studios: 1003 Spruce St., Philadelphia, Pa.

EYRE, Wilson, architect; b. Florence, Italy, Oct. 30, 1858; s. Wilson and Louisa (Lear) E.; ed. in Italy until 1869, Newport, R. I., 1869-72, Lenoxville, Can., 1872-74; and, 1875, Woburn to prepare for inst.; Mass. Inst. Technology, 1876; unmarried. With James P. Sims, architect, 1876-81; since then in independent practice. Has built many bldgs. in Phila. and New York, also several bldgs. for Newcomb Memorial Coll., New Orleans; the Detroit Club, Detroit, etc. A.N.A., 1910; mem. A.I.A., Am. Social Science Assn. Address: 1003 Spruce St., Philadelphia, Pa.

EYSMANS, Julien L., ry. official; b. Brussels, Belgium, Mar. 18, 1874; s. Charles P. and Josephine E.; brought to U.S., 1875; ed. pub. schs., Baltimore, Md.; m. Mary Emory, June 6, 1903; children—Julien L., Thomas Lane Emory. Began as messenger, office of div. freight agt., Pa. R.R., Baltimore, 1891; various clerical positions, same r.r., until 1896; freight solicitor Anchor Line, 1896-98; soliciting agt. same, Baltimore, 1898-1900; freight solicitor, Star Union Line, Reading, Pa., 1900-02, Baltimore, 1903-04; eastern supt. same r.r., N.Y. City, 1904-05; gen. freight agt. Cumberland Valley R.R., 1906-11; with Pa. R.R. since 1911, div. freight agt., Pittsburgh, 1911-12, asst. gen. freight agt., 1912-16, gen. freight agt., 1916-20, traffic mgr. Eastern Region, Pa. System, 1920-23, traffic mgr. Central Region, 1923-24, asst. gen. traffic mgr., 1924, gen. traffic mgr., 1925, became v.p. 1925, and v.p. and asst. to pres., 1933. Republican. Episcopalian. Clubs: Racquet, Philadelphia, Duquesne; Cloud, Traffic (New York); Rolling Rock; Traffic (Chicago). Home: 1924 Panama St., Philadelphia, Pa.

EYSTER, William Henry, botanist; b. Fishers Ferry, Pa., July 13, 1889; s. Henry and Alice (Star) E.; A.B., Bucknell U., 1914, A.M., 1915; Ph.D., Cornell U., 1920; grad. study Harvard, 1923, U. of Berlin, 1928, Botanisches Institut, Erlangen, Germany, 1928; m. Elmira Snyder, June 18, 1914; children—William Henry, Paul Morris, Helen Elizabeth. Asst. prof. botany, U. of Mo., 1920-24; prof. U. of Me., 1924-27; fellow John Simon Guggenheim Memorial Foundation for Study Abroad, 1927-28; prof. botany, Bucknell U., since 1928; genetic adviser W. Atlee Burpee Co., Philadelphia. Fellow A.A.A.S.; mem. Am. Bot. Soc., German Bot. Soc., Am Optical Soc., Am. Genetic Soc., Am. Soc. of Plant Physiologists, Am. Soc. Naturalists, Phi Gamma Delta. Author: College Botany, 1931; Genetics of Zea Mays, 1934. Contbr. to Genetics, Am. Jour. Botany, Zeitschrift für abstamungslehre und Verebungs wissenschaft, etc. Home: 130 S. 13th St., Lewisburg, Pa.

EZEKIEL, Mordecai Joseph Brill, economist; b. Richmond, Va., May 10, 1899; s. Jacob Levy and Rachel (Brill) E.; B.S., U. of Md., 1918; M.S., U. of Minn., 1924; Ph.D., Robert Brookings Grad. Sch. of Economics and Govt., Washington, D.C., 1926; m. Lucille Finsterwald, Dec., 24, 1927; children—Donald Finsterwald, Jonathan. Statistical asst. in agr., U.S. Census Bur., 1919-22; with div. farm management, U.S. Dept. Agr., 1922-30; asst. chief economist Federal Farm Bd., 1930-33; economic adviser to the sec. of agr. since Mar. 1933. Visiting prof. U. of Minn., spring 1926, Cornell U., summer 1927. Awarded Guggenheim Fellowship for Economic Study, 1930. Developed quantitative methods of analyzing data; discovered new method of curvilinear multiple correlation; pioneered in methods of price forecasting for farm products; assisted in formulating plans for farm relief and in drafting Agrl. Adjustment Act. Served as 2d lt. inf., U.S.A., World War. Fellow Am. Statis. Assn.; mem. Am. Farm Economic Assn., Am. Econ. Assn., fellow Econometric Soc. Mem. Jewish Ref. Ch. Author: Methods of Correlation Analysis, 1930; $2,500 a Year—from Scarcity to Abundance, 1936; Jobs for All, 1939. Contbr. articles to jours. of statis. and economic socs. Home: Bethesda, Md. Office: Department of Agriculture, Washington, D.C.

EZICKSON, William J., physician; b. Phila., Pa., Mar. 26, 1892; s. Samuel and Cecelia (Kahn) E.; A.B., Central High Sch., 1910; M.D., Medico-Chirurg. Coll., 1915; grad. study, U. of Pa. Post-Grad. Sch. of Medicine, 1920-21; m. Bessie Davis, Oct. 4, 1923; children—Robert D., Phoebe Jane, S. David. Interne St. Joseph's Hosp., Phila., 1915-17; in pvt. practice in Phila. since 1919; cons. urologist, U.S. Vets. Adminstrn., 1919-34; asst. urologist, Pa. Hosp.; chief urologist, St. Joseph's Hosp.; urologist, courtesy staff, St. Luke's, Methodist, and Bryn Mawr hosps.; instr. urology, U. of Pa. Post Grad. Sch. of Medicine since 1938. Served as lieut. then capt. Med. Corps, U.S.A., 1917-18, maj., 1919 (youngest maj. in Med. Corps, U.S.A.) assigned to staff Surg. Gen. U.S.A. to establish Div. of Phys. Rehabilitation for Disabled. Mem. A.M.A., Am. Urol. Assn., Phi Delta Epsilon. Mason. Home: 108 S. Narberth Av., Narberth, Pa. Office: 2100 Walnut St., Philadelphia, Pa.

F

FABEL, Harry E., mgr. Community Loan Co.; b. Lock Haven, Pa., Oct. 1, 1868; s. Michael and Elizabeth (Sorgen) F.; student high sch.; m. Nancy E. Maum, Sept. 3, 1889 (dec). Entered jewelry business, 1884, becoming proprietor of own concern, Meadville, Pa., 1897, business sold, 1924; mgr. Community Loan Co., Meadville, Pa., since 1925; treas. Meadville Housing Corpn. since 1913, now also dir.; dir. Meadville Bldg. and Loan Assn., Crawford County Trust Co. Pres. Meadville Sch. Bd. since 1937. Mason (32°). Clubs: Meadville Country, Iroquois Boating and Fishing (Meadville). Home: 460 Chestnut St. Office: 895 Market St., Meadville, Pa.

FACKENTHAL, Benjamin Franklin, Jr., iron mfr.; b. Doylestown, Pa., June 2, 1851; s. Benjamin Franklin and Catharine (Dennis) F.; ed. public schs., and special course in chemistry and metallurgy, Lafayette College, 1874-75; hon. A.M., from the same college in 1897, ScD., 1911, and LL.D., 1929; m. Sarah J. Riegel, July 15, 1875 (died 1925). With Durham Iron Works, of Cooper & Hewitt, 1866-92, becoming supt. works and mines, 1876-92; also gen. mgr. Cooper & Hewitt's blast furnaces and mines, Ringwood and Pequest, N.J., and Riegelsville, Pa., 1879-92; pres. Thomas Iron Co., 1893-1913; pres. Ironton R.R. Co., 1893-1914; pres. Clymer Power Co., 1905-26; pres. Taylor, Stiles & Co., knife works, 1926-37; v.p. and chmn. exec. com. Easton Trust Co., 1893-1938; dir. Lehigh Portland Cement Co. Receiver Consolidated Lake Superior Company, Sault Ste. Marie, 1902-03. Trustee Franklin and Marshall Coll. since 1899, pres. bd. since 1915; endowed chair biology and geology, 1910, and erected Fackenthal Labs., 1929, for chem. biol. depts., also indoor swimming pool, 1930, and a library, 1937. Mem. Washington Crossing Park Commn., 1922-24. Member British Iron and Steel Institute, Am. Iron and Steel Inst., Am. Inst. Mining and Metall. Engrs., Am. Soc. Testing Materials, Lake Superior Mining Inst., Pa. Soc. in New York. Hist. Soc. Pa., Bucks Co. Hist. Soc. (pres.), Northampton County Hist. Soc., Lancaster Co. Hist. Soc., Moravin Hist. Soc., Pa. German Soc., Sons of Rev., Soc. War of 1812. Republican. Mason. Address: Riegelsville, Pa.

FACKLER, Charles Lewis, physician; b. East Berlin, Pa., Aug. 1, 1894; s. Lewis H. (M.D.) and Catherine (Spangler) F.; ed. Staunton Mil. Acad., 1910-11, Franklin and Marshall Coll., 1911-12; M.D., Jefferson Med. Coll., 1916; grad. study, U. of Vienna, 1932; m. Harriet Stone, of Baltimore, Md., Nov. 14, 1917; 1 dau., Jean Brinton. Interne Union Prot. Infirmary, Baltimore, Md., 1916-17; resident phys., Baltimore Eye & Ear Hosp., 1922-24; mem. staff York Hosp., York, Pa. since 1924; mem. dispensary staff, Baltimore Eye & Ear Hosp. since 1925; specializing in diseases of eye, ear, nose, and throat, York, Pa. since 1924; pres. York Optical Co. Served as lt. Med. Corps, U.S.N., 1917-18; lt. comdr. Med. Corps, Fleet Res. U.S.N., 1922-38. Diplomate Am. Bd. Otolaryngology & Am. Bd. Ophthalmology. Fellow Am. Acad. Ophthalmology and Otolaryngology. Mem. Am., Pa. State, York Co. med. assns., York Med. Club (pres.), Chi Phi, Phi Chi. Episcopalian (Vestryman). Clubs: Rotary, Country. Home: Country Club Rd. Office: 11 E. Market St., York, Pa.

FADDIS, Charles I., congressman; b. Loudenville, O., June 13, 1890; s. Samuel C. and Edna (Moredock) F.; student Waynesburg (Pa.) Coll., 1909-11; B.S., Pa. State Coll., 1915; grad. Gen. Staff and Command Sch., Ft. Leavenworth, Kans., 1930; m. Jane Morris, Dec. 1, 1917; children—William George, James M., Edna G., Laura Lucille. In gen. contracting business, Waynesburg, Pa., 1919-26; broker of oil and gas properties since 1926. Served as pvt. Pa. Inf., Mexican border, 1916; capt. and lt. col., inf., U.S.A., World War; in major offensives and occupation of Germany; with O.R.C. since 1924; commd. col., 1930. Citation by Gen. Pershing; awarded Purple Heart. Mem. 73d to 76th Congresses (1933-41), 25th Pa. Dist. Mem. Am. Legion, Vets. of Foreign Wars, Elks. Democrat. Home: 395 Park Av., Waynesburg, Pa.

FADUM, Ernest Frederick, lawyer; b. Baltimore, Md., Jan. 4, 1889; s. Ernest William and Anna E. (Sieck) F.; LL.B., Baltimore U. Sch. of Law (now U. of Md.), 1908; m. Welka Bauer, May 3, 1913. Admitted to Md. bar, 1910, and since in gen. practice of law at Baltimore; employed as underwriter, spl. agt., atty., etc., for various bonding cos. locally and in N.Y. City, also in pvt. law practice; asst. city solicitor defending damage suits for the city and specializing in zoning, 1927-36; in pvt. practice since 1936; pres. Geo. Brehm Perpetual Bldg. & Loan Assn., Baltimore, since 1936; lecturer on municipal law, Mt. Vernon Law Sch., since 1938. Served on legal adv. bd. during World War. Served on various civic bds. from time to time; Republican candidate for state's atty. for Baltimore City, 1930. Mem. Am., Md. State, Baltimore City bar assns., Ancient and Honorable Mechanical Co. of Baltimore. Republican. Lutheran. Home: 1929 E. 30th St. Office: Hearst Tower, Baltimore, Md.

FAGAN, Arthur; editor Jersey Observer. Address: Jersey Publishing Co., Hoboken, N.J.

FAGAN, Frank Nelson, prof. pomology; b. Richmond, Ind., Sept. 29, 1888; s. Joseph Atwood and Mary Anne (Kitson) F.; B.Sc., O. State U., Columbus, O., 1910; student Mass. State Coll., Amherst, Mass., 1917-18; m. Etta Wingate Jones, Apr. 25, 1912; children—Anne Bourne (Mrs. Fred V. Grau), Frank Nelson. Employed as ranch mgr., E. H. Everett Ranch, Port O'Connor, Tex., 1910; asst. inspr. Nursery and Orchard Div., State Dept. Agr., Columbus, O., summers 1907-09 and 1911-12; asst. prof. Horticulture, Pa. State Coll. and Agr. Expt. Sta., 1912-19; prof. Pomology, Pa. State Coll. since 1919; dir. Buffalo Valley Fruit Farms, Inc. Served as chmn. Shade Tree Commn. of State College, Pa., 1924-29. Mem. A.A.A.S., Soc. for Advance Hort. Sci., Alpha Gamma Rho. Republican. Episcopalian. Mason. Home: Locust Lane, State College, Pa.

FAGAN, Patrick T., union pres.; b. Crab Tree, Pa., July 27, 1888; s. Thomas and Helen (Furrie) F.; m. Ida Bernarding, Oct. 17, 1912; children—Gerald B., Charles J., Thomas Leo, Patrick Michael, William James, Philip Regis, Joseph. Mem. and sec. Local Union 2363, United Mine Workers of America, Mollenauer, Pa., 1917; del. Cleveland (O.) Conv., 1919; mem. scale com., 1919, that negotiated contract that went into effect, Apr. 1, 1920; v.p. Dist. No. 5 United Mine Workers of America, 1920-22, pres. since 1922; acting pres. and in charge of strike, 1922; pres. Pittsburgh Central Labor Union, 1931-37. Mem. Gov. Earle's Com. on Pub. Assistance and Relief; mem. Federal Labor Bd. for Allegheny Co., N.R.A.; mem. Pa. Labor Relations Bd. since 1937. K.C., Holy Name Soc., Ancient Order of Hibernians, Elk, Eagle. Home: 822 Woodbourne Av. Office: 1208 Commonwealth Bldg., Pittsburgh, Pa.

FAGIN, Nathan Bryllion, educator, author; b. Russia, June 15, 1892; brought to U.S., 1900; s. Nathan and Matilda (Eisenstadt) F.; student New York City pub. schs., 1900-08; A.B., George Washington U., Washington, D.C., 1923, A.M., 1924; Ph.D., Johns Hopkins U., 1931; m. Mary Berke, June 4, 1918. Clk. Bur. of Chemistry, Dept. of Agr., Washington, D.C., 1916-21; instr. English, U. of Md., Baltimore, 1923-24, asst. prof., 1924-25; prof. English, U. of Baltimore, 1926-31; instr. English, Johns Hopkins U., 1929-32, asso. in English and dir. Playshop since 1932. Mem. Modern Lang. Assn., Am. Assn. Univ. Profs., Tudor and Stuart Club. Author: Short Story Writing: An Art or a Trade?, 1923; Of Love and Other Trifles, 1925; The Phenomenon of Sherwood Anderson, 1927; Wm. Bartram: Interpreter of the American Landscape, 1933; America Through the Short Story, 1936. Home: 2514 Talbot Road, Baltimore, Md.

FAHNESTOCK, (James) Murray, magazine editor; b. Pittsburgh, Pa., Dec. 16, 1885; s. Thomas Howe and Mary Herron (Thompson) F.; student Carnegie Inst. Tech., 1906-09, U. of Pittsburgh, 1912-13; m. Hazel Margaret Alberts, June 6, 1925; children—Lois Kay, Jean Howe. Draftsman engring. dept. Crucible Steel Co., Pittsburgh, 1909-12; tech. editor Motor Cycling, Chicago, 1912-13; asst. service mgr. Pittsburgh Branch, Ford Motor Co., 1913-14; free lance writer for magazines, Motor, Motor Age, etc., 1914-18; tech. editor Ford Field (mag.), Pittsburgh, 1918-29, editor since 1929; spl. writer Ford Motor Co., Dearborn, Mich., 1932-33; tech. editor Ford Power Age, 1924-28. Lecturer to automotive mechanics, teacher elec. engring., U. of Pittsburgh, teacher army mechanics, Carnegie Inst. Tech., during World War. Mem. Soc. of Automotive Engrs. (chmn. Pittsburgh sect., 1933). Republican. United Presbyterian. Club: Pittsburgh Figure Skating (Pittsburgh). Author: Know the Ford, 1928; The Model A Ford, 1930; Secrets of Ford Engineering, 1929; The Service Handbook, 1934; L'Auto Ford Modele A (in French), 1929; lecturer on automobile engring. before civic and ednl. groups. Address: 524 S. Murtland Av., Pittsburgh, Pa.

FAHRNEY, Henry Laurence, M.D.; b. Frederick, Md., Apr. 18, 1902; s. Henry Peter and Bessie Amelia (Yourtee) F.; grad. Frederick High Sch., 1919; B.S., Juniata Coll., Huntingdon, Pa., 1922; M.D., Jefferson Med. Coll., Phila., 1926; m. Gladys M. Murray, June 25, 1931; children—David Laurence, Peter Martin. Interne Md. Gen. Hosp., Baltimore, 1926-27; chief resident physician St. Joseph's Hosp., Baltimore, 1927-28; in gen. practice of medicine since 1928; active mem. staff Frederick City Hosp. since 1928. Mem. Frederick Co. Med. Soc. (sec. 1939), A.M.A., Omega Upsilon Phi. Republican. Methodist. Elk. Home: 516 Fairview Av. Office: 17 E. Second St., Frederick, Md.

FAIR, Frederick, pres. Oil City Transit Co.; b. Oil City, Pa., Dec. 8, 1871; s. Henry H.

and Francis (Gilder) F.; ed. Oil City High Sch.; m. Ellen Stephenson, Oct. 15, 1903. With Oil City Trust Co. since 1887, pres. since 1926, now also dir.; dir. Venango Oil & Land Co., Cario Oil Co., O'Day Oil Co., Citizens Savings & Loan Assn., United Hardware & Supply Co., McCoy Natural Gas Co., Tionesta Gas Co., Wolverine-Empire Refining Co. Clubs: Wanango Country, Oil City Boat. Home: 121 W. Third St. Office: 56 Seneca St., Oil City, Pa.

FAIR, James Hollyday Stone, clergyman, educator; b. Baltimore, Md., Aug. 4, 1886; s. Very Rev. Campbell and Mary Whitely (Stone) F.; grad. high sch., Omaha, Neb., 1903; prep. edn., St. Paul's Sch., Concord, N.H., 1904, Mackenzie Sch., Dobbs Ferry, N.Y., 1905; student Yale, 1907-08, Gen. Theol. Sem., New York, N.Y., 1911-12; m. Rosalie Bard Moran, Aug. 5, 1919; 1 son, James H. S. Deacon, 1914, Priest, 1915, P.E. Ch.; vicar St. John's Chapel, Bernardsville, N.J., 1914-17, 1919-20; headmaster St. Bernard's Sch., Gladstone, N.J., 1919; chaplain St. George's Sch., Newport, R.I., 1921-24; headmaster, pres. and treas. Somerset Hills since 1924. Served as pvt., later sergt. and 2d lt. U.S.A., World War. Republican. Club: Yale (New York). Home: Far Hills, N.J.

FAIR, Marvin Luke, prof. transportation and economics; b. Cameron, W.Va., Aug. 19, 1897; s. Franklin H. and Mary Virginia (Mason) F.; grad. State Coll., W. Liberty, W.Va., 1916; A.B., Ohio, 1923; M.A., Ohio State U., 1926; College Teacher's Scholar Harvard U., 1930; Ph.D., Ohio State U., 1930; m. Rachel Johnson, June 14, 1924; children—Mary Elizabeth, Harlan Wirt. Engaged in teaching high sch. and as prin. high schs., 1916-23; asst. prof. history and econs., Hilldale Coll., Mich., 1924-26; instr. business orgn., Ohio State U., 1926-30; asst. prof. transportation, Temple U., Phila., Pa., 1930-32, prof. transportation and econs. since 1932; also research dir., Great Lakes and Inland Waters Survey, Federal Communications Commn. since 1937. Mem. exec. com. Suburban Civic Assn.; mem. advisory com. Port of Phila. Mem. Am. Econ. Assn., Tau Kappa Alpha, Theta Chi, Kappa Delta Pi, Pi Gamma Mu, Beta Gamma Sigma. Republican. Mem. Reformed Ch. Contbr. articles to econ. jours. Home: 329 Jenkintown Rd., Elkins Park, Pa.

FAIRBANK, Herbert Sinclair, highway engineer; b. Baltimore, Md., Sept. 16, 1888; s. Charles Alexander and Sarah Sherwood (Sinclair) F.; prep. edn. Baltimore Poly. Inst., 1903-07; C.E., Cornell U., 1910; unmarried. Civil engr. student U.S. Bureau of Mines, Sept.-Nov. 1910; with U.S. Office Pub. Roads since 1910, as civil engr. student, 1910-11, asst. then speaker on Good Roads Trains operated over railways of South and West, 1912-13, object lesson road building, highway research, etc., 1911-17, editor "Public Roads," mag., 1920-27, chief div. of information, 1927, chmn. Research Com., Bureau of Pub. Roads, 1927, dir. of Statewide highway planning surveys, U.S. Bur. of Public Roads (now Public Roads Administration) in co-operation with highway depts. of 46 states since 1935. Aide to sec.-gen. 6th Internat. Road Congress, Washington, D.C., 1930; mem. Permanent Internat. Com. of Permanent Internat. Assn. of Road Congresses; del. U.S. Govt. to 7th Internat. Road Congress, Munich, 1934. Served as 1st lt. later capt. Chem. Warfare Service, U.S. Army, 1918-19. Mem. Am. Assn. State Highway Officials, Tau Beta Pi. Presbyterian. Home: 2041 E. 32d St., Baltimore, Md. Office: Willard Bldg., Washington, D.C.

FAIRBANKS, Benjamin; pres. United States Savings Bank. Address: Newark, N.J.

FAIRCHILD, Mildred, asso. prof. social economy; b. Tabor, Ia., Apr. 30, 1894; d. James Thome and Emma Louise (Dickinson) F.; A.B., Oberlin Coll., 1916, A.M., same, 1925; Ph.D., Bryn Mawr Coll., 1929. Engaged as instr., Fisk U., 1916-18; with Playground and Recreation Assn. of America, 1920-22; campaign field organizer Oberlin Coll., 1923; fellow social economy and social research, Bryn Mawr Coll., 1925-27, research asst. grad. dept., 1927-28; student London (Eng.) Sch. Econs., 1928-29; research fellow in U.S.S.R., of Am. Russian Inst., 1929-30; asso. in social economy and social research, Bryn Mawr Coll., 1930-34, asso. prof. since 1934. Served in War Camp Community Service, 1918-20. Mem. bd. dirs. Pa. Pub. Edn. and Child Labor Assn., Pa. Com. on Penal Affairs of Pub. Charities Assn. of Pa. Mem. state exec. com. Pa. Merit System League, State Adv. Council on Unemployment Compensation and Employment Service. Mem. Am. Econs. Assn., Am. Sociol. Soc., Am. Assn. Univ. Women, Am. Assn. Univ. Profs., Am. Federation of Teachers, Phi Beta Kappa. Club: Women's University (Philadelphia). Co-author (with Susan M. Kingsbury), Factory, Family and Woman in Soviet Russia, 1935. Contbr. articles and surveys. Home: 219 Roberts Rd., Bryn Mawr, Pa.

FAIRFIELD, Erle, univ. prof.; b. Cleveland, O., June 14, 1892; s. Howard Parker and Kate Frances (Coffin) F.; A.B., Dartmouth Coll., 1914; A.M., Harvard U., 1915; post-grad. study, Harvard, 1917-18; m. Editha Cora Smith, Aug. 23, 1919; children—Barbara, Doris. Instr. German, U. of Pittsburgh, 1915-17; registrar and head German dept., Morristown (N.J.) Sch., 1918-20; prof. modern langs., U. of Pittsburgh, since 1920. Mem. Modern Lang. Assn. America, Pittsburgh Modern Lang. Assn. (pres. 1938-39), Pa. State Modern Lang. Assn., Sigma Kappa Phi. Republican. Unitarian. Co-author: A German Science Reader, 1934. Home: 1023 East End Av., Wilkinsburg, Pa.

FAIRING, John Walker, physician; b. Glasgow, Scotland, June 13, 1872; s. Henry and Catherine (Paterson) F.; prep. edn. Free Ch. Normal Training Sch., Glasgow, Scotland; B.M.C., U. of Md., 1898; student New York Post Grad. Sch., 1898, U. of Pa. Grad. Sch. of Bronchoscopy, 1922; m. Lora Lewis, Jan. 9, 1901; children—Lora (Mrs. Eugene Arter Myers), Robert Lewis. Came to U.S., 1888, naturalized, 1920. In gen. prectice of medicine, Springfield, Mass., 1901-09; at Bartholemew's Clinic, New York, 1909; resident house surgeon Manhattan Eye, Ear and Throat Hosp., New York, 1910-12; engaged in special eye, ear and throat practice, Greensburg, Pa., since 1912; on eye, ear and throat service Westmoreland Hosp. since 1912. Patron Nat. Red Cross. Fellow Am. Coll. Surgeons, Am. Acad. of Ophthalmology and Otolaryngology; certified by Am. Bd. for Ophthalmic Examinations and Am. Bd. of Otolaryngology; mem. Westmoreland Co. Med. Soc., Greensburg Acad. of Medicine, Pa. Med. Soc., A.M.A., Pa. Governing Com. of Gorgas Memorial Inst. Presbyterian. Mason (K.T., 32°, Shriner), Elk. Clubs: Kiwanis (past pres.), Hannastown Golf. Author: Some Disease Conditions of the Nose and Throat, 1930; Focal Infection in the Pathogenesis of Ocular Pathology, 1934. Home: 126 Westmoreland Av. Office: 122 N. Main St., Greensburg, Pa.

FAIRLESS, Benjamin F., pres. U.S. Steel Corpn.; b. Pigeon Run, O., 1890; grad. Ohio Northern U., 1912; formerly pres. of Carnegie-Illinois Steel Corpn., Carnegie Land Corpn., Conneaut Land Co., Bessemer Electric Power Co., Sharon Coke Co.; now pres. and dir. of U.S. steel Corpn. of N.J. and U.S. Steel Corpn. of Del. Mason, Elk, Moose. Home: Schenley Apts., Pittsburgh, Pa.; and New York, N.Y. Office: U.S. Steel Corpn., New York, N.Y., and Pittsburgh, Pa.

FAKE, Guy Leverne, judge; b. Cobleskill, N.Y., Nov. 15, 1879; LL.B., New York U. Law Sch., 1904; m. Grace Elizabeth Mucklow, children—Leverne M., Elwood B. Admitted to N.J. bar and began practice at Rutherford; mem. N.J. Gen. Assembly, 1907-08; judge, Dist. Court, 2d Jud. Dist. of Bergen Co., N.J., 1909-24; Supreme Court commr., 1926; judge, U.S. Dist. Court, N.J. Dist., since 1929. Mem. S.A.R.; hon. mem. Jr. Order United Am. Mechanics. Presbyn. Mason, Elk. Address: U.S. District Court, Newark, N.J.

FALCK, Frederick McQuhae, railroad official; b. Atlanta, Ga., July 5, 1874; s. William and Mary Bradford (McQuhae) F.; student pub. schs. and Free Acad., Elmira, N.Y., Cornell U., 1892-94; m. Theresa J. McGovern, Apr. 29, 1903 (dec.); children—Mary Theresa (Mrs. G. Harrison Frazier), Catherine (Mrs. J. Nevin Schroeder Jr.), Frederick William. Began as mining engr. for coal operator, 1895; connected with Reading Co. continuously since 1898, beginning as asst. supervisor at Shamokin, Pa., successively supervisor, division engr., asst. supt., supt., asst. gen. mgr., gen. mgr., and asst. v.p. Reading Co. and Central R.R. of N.J. since 1936; dir. twelve subsidiary R.R. Cos. Mem. Mil. Order of the Loyal Legion. Republican. Presbyterian. Clubs: Racquet, Philadelphia Cricket (Phila.); Pine Valley Golf (Clementon, N.J.); Seaview Golf (Absecon, N.J.). Home: Lincoln Drive and Springfield Av. Office: Reading Terminal, Philadelphia, Pa.

FALES, David, Jr., Hill prof. of English Bible and ethics, Rutgers U. Address New Brunswick, N.J.

FALION, William Marcus, oil exec.; b. Rahway, N.J., Jan. 16, 1885; s. William Marcus and Viola (Mott) F.; student Rahway (N.J.) Pub. and High Sch., 1890-1901; m. Iola Savacool, Oct. 30, 1908; children—Madeleine Louise (Mrs. Clyde VanKirke Beard), William Marcus III. Began as messenger, Dick Bros. and Co., New York, 1901, mgr., 1910-15; cashier S.B. Chapin & Co., New York, 1916-19; both firms members New York Stock Exchange; asst. treas. Guaranty Trust Co., New York, 1919-34; sec.-treas. Columbia Oil & Gasoline Corpn., Wilmington, Del., since 1937; sec.-asst. treas. The Ohio Fuel Supply Co., The Preston Oil Co., Union Gasoline & Oil Corpn., Viking Distributing Co., Virginian Gasoline & Oil Co. (all of Charleston, W.Va.) since 1937. Com. work, Village of Garden City, N.Y., 1927-36. Cathedral of Incarnation, Garden City, 1927-36. Republican. Divine Science. Mason (Montauk Lodge 286, Brooklyn, N.Y.). Club: Wilmington (Del.) Whist. Home: Denbigh Hall, 1305 N. Broom St. Office: 822 Delaware Trust Bldg., Wilmington, Del.

FALK, Isidore Sydney, bacteriologist, public health and medical economist; b. Brooklyn, N.Y., Sept. 30, 1899; s. Samsin and Rose (Stolzberg) Falk; graduate Brooklyn Boys High School, 1915, spl. student Sheffield Scientific Sch., Yale, 1915-17, Ph.B., 1920; Ph.D., Yale, 1923; m. Ruth Hill, March 18, 1925; children—Sydney Westervelt, Stephen Ackley. Asst., dept. pub. health, Yale, 1915-21, instr., 1921-23; asst. prof. hygiene and bacteriology, U. of Chicago, 1923-26, asso. prof., 1926-29, prof., 1929; also dir. surveys, Chicago Dept. Health, 1925-27; asso. dir. Com. on Costs of Medical Care, 1929-33; research asso. Milbank Memorial Fund, 1933-36; now chief of health studies, and asst. dir Bureau Research and Statistics, Social Security Board, Washington, D.C. Fellow Am. Pub. Health Assn., A.A.A.S.; mem. Soc. Am. Bacteriologists, Assn. Am. Immunologists, Soc. Experimental Biology and Medicine, Am. Acad. Polit. Sciences, Am. Statistical Assn. Author: Principles of Vital Statistics, 1923; Organized Medical Service at Fort Benning, Ga., 1932; Present Trends in Health Insurance, 1935; Compulsory Health Insurance, 1935; Security Against Sickness, 1936; Health, Sickness and Social Security, 1936; Cash and Medical Benefits in Health Insurance, 1936; Health Insurance and the Doctor, 1936. Co-Author: Laboratory Outlines in Bacteriology and Immunology (with J. F. Norton), 1926; Community Medical Service in Roanoke Rapids, North Carolina (with D. M. Griswold and H. I. Spicer), 1932; The Incidence of Illness and the Receipt and Costs of Medical Care Among Representative Families (with M. C. Klem and N. Sinai), 1933; The Costs of Medical Care (with C. R. Rorem and M. D. Ring), 1933; Health Indices—A Study of Objective Indices of Health in Relation to Environment and Sanitation (with K. Stouman), 1936. Co-editor and contbr. to The Newer Knowledge of Bacteriology and Immunology, 1928. Research in eugenics of infant welfare, electrical determination and theory of microbic virulence, microbic cause of influenza, economics of med. care and pub. health, social insurance. Home: 41 W. Kirke St., Chevy Chase, Md. Office: Social Security Board, Washington, D.C.

FALK, Leon, Jr., treas. Falk & Co.; b. Pittsburgh, Pa., Sept. 23, 1901; s. Leon and Fanny

(Edel) F.; student Phillips Exeter Acad., Exeter, N.H., 1918-20; B.S., Yale, 1924; m. Katharine Sonneborn, June 24, 1926; children—Ellen, Sara, Sigo, David. Treas. Falk & Co., mfrs. greases and oils, Pittsburgh, since 1926; pres. and dir. Pittsburgh Waste Co., Webster Hall Hotel, Tunnel Street Garage; dir. Falk & Co., Ruskin Corp., Bedford Feed Co. Trustee U. of Pittsburgh. Mem. Pi Lambda Phi. Republican. Reformed Jewish religion. Clubs: Westmoreland Country (Pittsburgh); Concordia, Harvard-Yale-Princeton. Home: 1200 Bennington Av. Office: 1900 Farmers Bank Bldg., Pittsburgh, Pa.

FALK, Louis Austin, meat packer; b. Poland, Nov. 7, 1895; s. Rubin and Ida (Lewin) F.; came to U.S., 1906, naturalized, 1906; LL.B., Hamilton Coll. of Law, Chicago, Ill., 1923; m. Bessie Fineberg, Oct. 10, 1920; children—Lucille Hope, Doris Evelyn. With Union Packing Co., chain of meat stores, Jersey City, N.J., since 1921, half owner and sec.-treas. since 1922; sec.-treas. Bergen Market Co., Jersey City since 1922; v.p. Own Your Home Bldg. & Loan Assn., Jersey City, N.J., since 1925; v.p. Hamilton Coll. of Commerce, Jersey City, N.J., since 1938. Served as pvt. 89th Mil. Police Co., U.S. Army, with A.E.F., 1918-19. Mem. and sec. N.J.-U.S. Constrn. Commn., 1935-38. V.p. and chmn. finance com. Hebrew Home for Orphans and Aged of Hudson Co. since 1934; dir. Y.M. H.A., Jersey City; pres. Congregational Emanuel, Jersey City, 1932-34. Mem. Jersey City Chamber of Commerce, N.J. Chamber of Commerce. Mem. Am. Legion (past comdr. Albert L. Quinn Post 52), Jewish War Vets. of U.S. (past comdr. Jersey City Post 10), Vets. of Fgn. Wars, Jewish Theol. Sem. of America, Am. Museum. Natural History, Jewish Publ. Soc. America. Mason. (Bethel Lodge 207; Scottish Rite 32, Jersey City; Shriner, Salaam Temple). Editor-in-chief The Jewish Veteran, 1937-38. Home: 107 Kensington Av. Office: 2d and Provost Sts., Jersey City, N.J.

FALK, Maurice; b. Pittsburgh, Pa., Dec. 15, 1866; s. Charles and Sarah (Sanders) F.; ed. pub. schs., Pittsburgh; m. Laura Klinordlinger, 1888 (died Dec. 21, 1928); m. 2d, Mrs. Selma K. Wertheimer, Sept. 25, 1930. In clothing business until 1893; organizer, 1893, with brother, Leon Falk, of Duquesne Reduction Co., merged, 1924, with Federated Metals Corpn., of which is vice-pres.; treas. Pittsburgh Waste Co.; dir. Nat. Steel Corpn., Edgewater Steel Co., Blaw-Knox Co., Farmers Deposit Nat. Bank, Farmers Deposit Savings Bank, Farmers Deposit Trust Co., Reliance Life Ins. Co. Dir. Fed. Jewish Philanthropies, Montefiore Hosp., Pittsburgh Y.M.H.A., Pittsburgh Y.W.H.A. Republican. Jewish religion. Clubs: Concordia (dir.), Hundred, Westmoreland Country. With brother, Leon Falk, donor of Falk Clinic to U. of Pittsburgh, designed to treat 750 daily free patients; established The Maurice and Laura Falk Foundation ($10,000,000 foundation for religious, charitable and ednl. purposes). Home: Hotel Schenley. Office: Farmers Bank Bldg., Pittsburgh, Pa.

FALKNER, Roland Post, statistician; b. Bridgeport, Conn., April 14, 1866; s. Rev. John B. and Helen (Butler) F.; Ph.B., U. of Pa., 1885; studied economics at Berlin, Leipzig and Halle-on-Saale, Ph.D., Halle, 1888; m. Agnes I. Hamilton April 14, 1898; children—Charles Hamilton (dec.), Elizabeth Helen (Mrs. Harold F. Schmehl), Helen Butler (Mrs. William H. Sargeant), Francis Howard (capt. U.S.A.). Instr. in accounting and statistics, Wharton School of Finance and Economy, Univ. of Pa., 1888-91; associate prof. statistics, 1981-1900; chief div. of documents, Library of Congress, 1900-04; commr. of edn., Porto Rico, 1904-07; statistician in charge of sch. inquiries for U.S. Immigration Commn., 1908-11; assistant director U.S. Census, 1911-12; mem. Joint Land Commn., U.S. and Panama, 1913; editor, 1915-23, dir. of research, 1923-26, Alexander Hamilton Inst., New York; research staff Nat. Industrial Conf. Bd. since 1926. Statistician, U.S. Senate Com. of Finance, 1891; sec. U.S. delegation Internat. Monetary Conf., 1892, and sec. of conf.; chmn. U.S. commn. to Republic of Liberia, 1909. Mem. Am. Econ. Assn., Am. Statis. Assn., Am. Acad. Polit. and Social Science (v.p. 1896-98), Internat. Statis. Inst. Translator The History, Theory and Technique of Statistics, by August Meitben, 1891. Editor, Annals Am. Acad. of Polit. and Social Science, 1890-1900; Report of Statistician on Wholesale Prices and Wages, Aldrich Report, 1892. Contbd. essays on statis., econ. and ednl. subjects to econ., statis. and other jours. Home: East Orange, N.J. Office: 247 Park Av., New York, N.Y.

FALL, Gilbert Haven, educator; b. Somersworth, N.H., March 27, 1883; s. John Albert and Susan (Lord) F.; grad. Somersworth High Sch., 1901; A.B., Dartmouth, 1905; hon. M.A., U. of Pa., 1931; m. Ethel May Bernier, June 1910 (died 1936); 1 son, Gilbert Haven; m. 2d, Florence Huff Candor, June 1938. Teacher of science, high sch., Bellows Falls, Vt., 1905-06; with Chestnut Hill Acad. since 1906, as teacher of history, registrar, asst. to headmaster, and as headmaster, 1930-36, head department social studies since 1936. Member Progressive Edn. Soc., Headmasters' Assn. of Phila. Dist., Headmasters' Assn. Country Day Schs., Chi Phi. Republican. Episcopalian. Mason. Home: 500 W. Willow Grove Av., Chestnut Hill, Pa.

FALLS, Laurence Edward, insurance; b. West Point, Mass., March 10, 1890; s. Walter Lee and Hettie L. (Wise) F.; ed. pub. and high schs., Milwaukee and Cleveland; m. Amy C. Horr, April 21, 1917; children—Laurence H., Esther H. (deceased), Norton H. Began as insurance clerk and examiner, Western Reserve Insurance Company of Cleveland, Ohio, 1907-1913, auditor and dept. mgr., 1913-15, local and gen. agt., 1915-23, spl. agent, Newark, 1923, supt. of agencies, 1924-26, asst. sec., 1926-27, v.p. since 1927, now also dir.; v.p. and dir. Columbia Fire Ins. Co. (Dayton), Dixie Fire Ins. Co. (Greensboro, N.C.), Bankers Indemnity Ins. Co. (Newark); dir. U.S. Protection & Indemnity Agency, Inc. (N.Y.City). Former lecturer Cleveland Sch. Tech. and Columbia U. V.P. U.S. Fire Cos. Conf., N.Y. City; v.p. and dir. Nat. Automobile Underwriters Assn.; dir. Newark Chamber of Commerce, 1935-38. Fellow Insurance Inst. America (pres. and dir.). Republican. Methodist. Clubs: Essex (Newark); Essex County Country (West Orange); Maplewood (Maplewood); Shongum (Dover, N.J.); Gyro (Cleveland); Drug and Chemical (N.Y.City); Skytop (Skytop, Pa.); Dartmouth College (N.Y. City). Writer many articles on insurance and handbook on use and occupancy, leasehold and rents ins. Home: 14 Euclid Av., Maplewood, N.J. Office: 15 Washington St., Newark, N.J.

FALLS, William Franklin, univ. prof.; b. Augusta, Ga., Feb. 11, 1900; s. William Grier and Lillie Ida (Weir) F.; A.B., U. of N.C., Chapel Hill, N.C., 1922; A.M., Vanderbilt U., Nashville, Tenn., 1928; Ph.D., Univ. of Pa., 1932; grad. study, Toulouse, Paris, France, and Heidelberg, Germany, 1924-25, 1929-30; m. Elizabeth Westbrook McGowen, Dec. 29, 1926; 1 son, William Franklin. Prof. French, high sch., Wilmington, N.C., 1923-24; instr. French, U. of Pa., 1928-32; asst. prof. French, U. of Md., College Park, Baltimore, 1932-34, asso. prof., 1934-35, prof. since 1935. Served in S.A.T.C., 1918. Mem. Modern Lang. Assn. of America, Am. Assn. Teachers of French, Am. Assn. Univ. Profs., Pi Kappa Phi. Home: 62 Wine Av., Hyattsville, Md.

FANKHAUSER, Gerhard, associate prof. biology; b. Burgdorf, Switzerland, Mar. 11, 1901; s. Max and Anna (Hermann) F.; came to U.S., 1929, naturalized, 1939; student Univ. of Geneva, 1919-20, Univ. of Zürich, 1920-21; Ph.D., Univ. of Berne, 1924; m. Erna Koestler, Aug. 28, 1931; 1 son, David Andreas. Instr. zoölogy, U. of Berne, 1925-29; Rockefeller Foundation Fellow, U. of Chicago, 1929-30, Yale U., 1930-31; asst. prof. biology, Princeton U., 1931-39, asso. prof. since 1939. Mem. A.A.A.S., Am. Soc. Zoölogists, Am. Assn. Anatomists, Genetics Soc. America, Swiss Soc. Naturalists, Swiss Soc. Zoölogists, Sigma Xi. Mem. Swiss Reformed Church. Home: 205 Moore St., Princeton, N.J.

FARAGE, D. James, lawyer; b.. June 9, 1909; s. John and Mary A. (Dangels) F.; A.B., U. of Pa., 1930; LL.B. (cum laude), U. of Pa. Law Sch., 1933; m. Lillian Irene Randenbush, of Phila., Pa., Sept. 21, 1933; 1 dau., Joan Irene. Admitted to Pa. bar, 1933, and since engaged in gen. practice of law; asso. with George Hart, Phila., 1933-34; asst. to Prof. Francis H. Bohlen, reporter for Am. Law Inst., on restatement of torts, 1933-35; prof. law, Dickinson Law Sch., Carlisle, Pa., since 1934. Mem. Nat. Lawyers Guild, Pa. Bar Assn., Order of the Coif. Club: Country (Carlisle, Pa.) Annotator, Restatement of Restitutions for Pa.; contbr. to law revs. Home: 121 Parker St., Carlisle, Pa.

FARAGHER, Helen Mary, social worker; b. Buffalo, N.Y.; d. John and Ella (Biggins) F.; ed. Mt. St. Joseph Acad., Buffalo; A.B., Seton Hill Coll., Greensburg, Pa., 1927; M.A., U. of Pittsburgh, 1938; studied Nat. Catholic Social Service Sch., Washington, D.C., 1 yr. Successively case worker for family agency, medical social worker in Pittsburgh Hosp., supervisor family dept., Catholic Charities, Pittsburgh, and case supervisor children's dept.; child welfare consultant Ind. State Dept. of Pub. Welfare, Children's Div., since Oct. 1, 1938. Served on Oral Examining Bd., Pa. Dept. of Public Assistance, Feb. 1938; mem. Ind. Conf. on Social Work, Pa. Conf. on Social Work, Nat. Conf. of Catholic Charities. Pres. Seton Hill Coll. Alumnae Assn., 2 yrs., now v.p. Mem. Pittsburgh Chapter of Am. Assn. Univ. Women, Am. Assn. Social Workers, Am. Pub. Welfare Assn. Club: University Catholic (Pittsburgh). Home: Lebanon Hall, Pittsburgh, Pa. Office: 141 S. Meridian St., Indianapolis, Ind.

FARAGHER, Paul Vance, metallurgist; b. Sabetha, Kan., June 17, 1888; s. Henry William and Delphine (Davis) F.; A.B., U. of Kan., Laurence, Kan., 1910; Ph.D., Mass. Inst. Tech., 1912; grad. study, U. of Calif., Berkeley, Calif., 1912-13; m. Ida Keeley June 4, 1915; children—Vance Monroe, Martha Jean. Asst. prof. chemistry, U. of Kan., Laurence, Kan., 1913-17, asso. prof., 1918; Fellow Mellon Inst. Industrial Research, 1918-19; chief chem. development div., Research Bur., Aluminum Co. of America, Pittsburgh, 1919-21, metallurgist since 1922. Served as consultant to U.S. Bur. of Mines in helium gas development, 1917-18. Mem. Phi Beta Kappa, Sigma Xi. Republican. Home: 314 Sixth St., Oakmont, Pa. Office: 801 Gulf Bldg., Pittsburgh, Pa.

FARAGHER, Warren Fred, research chemist; b. Sabetha, Kan., Apr. 25, 1884; s. William Henry and Delphine A. (Davis) F.; grad. high sch., Sabetha, 1901; A.B., U. of Kan., 1905, Ph.D., 1910; m. Nina May Poole, of Corning, Kan., June 23, 1909; children—Robert Vance, William Arthur. Instr. chemistry, 1905-07; industrial research fellow, 1907-09, U. of Kan.; research chemist, Alden Speare's Sons Co., Boston, 1909-18; sr. fellow Mellon Inst., Pittsburgh, Pa., 1918-23; asst. dir. same, 1923-26; prof. and head dept. of petroleum refining, Sch. of Mines, U. of Pittsburgh, 1922-26; in charge research and investigation Universal Oil Products Co. of Chicago, 1926-31. Assistant Chief Research Laboratory of Vacuum Oil Co., Paulsboro, N.J., 1931. Dir. research, Houdry Process Corpn. (holding company of Catalytic Development Co.) since 1931. Mem. Am. Chem. Soc., Am. Soc. for Testing Materials, Am. Petroleum Inst., German Chem. Soc., French Soc., Chem. Industry, English Petroleum Inst., Kansas Acad. Science, Phi Beta Kappa, Sigma Xi, Phi Lambda Upsilon, Sigma Gamma Epsilon, Alpha Chi Sigma. Republican. Methodist. Contributor to Manual of Industrial Chemistry, 1909, and Handbook of Chemical Engineering, 1922. Home: 316 S. Chester Rd., Swarthmore, Pa. Office: 1608 Walnut St., Philadelphia, Pa.

FARDELMANN, John Henry, Jr., mech. engineering; b. Jersey City, N.J., Feb. 9, 1895; s. John Henry and Meta Catharine (Freese) F.; M.E., Stevens Inst. Tech., 1916; m. Katharine Quinn Whitney, Aug. 14, 1918; children—Dorothy Helen, John William. Employed as asst. engr. and field engr., Internat. Paper Co., 1916-17; engr. estimating and sci. depts., Federal Shipbuilding Co., 1919-21; mech. engr. in charge of estimating, drafting and supervision of erection, M. H. Treadwell Co., New York, N.Y., since 1922. Served as designer mobile gun carriage sect. Ordnance Branch War Dept., 1917-18. Licensed as professional engr. in N.Y. and N.J. Mem. Am. Soc. Mech. Engrs. Mem. Reformed Ch. Mason. Club: Masonic (Jersey City). Home: 217 Alexander Av., Montclair, N.J. Office: 140 Cedar St., New York, N.Y.

FARGO, Lee Kendall, asso. in urology, U. of Md. and Mercy Hosp.; visiting urologist South Baltimore Gen. and Mercy hosps.; cons. urologist Veterans Administrn. Hosp. Address: 1800 N. Charles St., Baltimore, Md.

FARIS, Paul Patton, editor, writer; b. Clinton, Ill., June 14, 1877; s. Rev. Wm. Wallace (D.D.) and Isabella Hardy (Thomson) F.; grad. Pittsburgh Academy, 1894; student Rollins Coll., Winter Park, Fla.; A.B., Park Coll., 1901, Litt.D., 1937; grad. McCormick Theol. Sem. (now Presbyn. Theol. Sem.), Chicago, 1905; m. Mary Helena Alexander, May 24, 1905; children —Eunice Thomson (Mrs. Alexander Cowie), Mary Alexander and Margaret Wallace (twins, both dec.), Rosemary Alexa. Formerly printer and teacher; ordained Presbyn. ministry, 1905; sent as missionary to China, 1905; prin. McPherson Acad. for Boys, Ichowfu, 1907-14; literary editor The Continent, Chicago, 1914-26; editor Fleming H. Revell Co., New York, 1926-29; editor-in-chief of Presbyterian Banner, Pittsburgh, 1932-34; Publicity dir. Presbyterian Ch., U.S.A., 1934—. Regional dir. Internat. Y.M.C.A. in France, 1918-19. Mem. Race Relations Publicity Com. of Federal Council of Chs. Author: Builders of the Church, 1922; The Child in His World (with Gertrude Hutton), 1923; Modern Builders of the Church, 1924; Adventures in Money Raising (with Cornelius M. Steffens), 1930; also many articles in Dictionary of American Biography. Contbr. to religious periodicals. Editor of Presbyn. Pastors' News, 1934-35; editor Presbyn. Plan Book, Gen. Assembly Daily News; mem. editorial bd. Monday Morning mag. Republican. Club: Manufacturers' and Bankers' (Phila.). Home: Buck Inn, Old Buck Lane, Haverford, Pa. Office: 518 Witherspoon Bldg., Philadelphia, Pa.

FARLEY, Arthur James, univ. prof.; b. Waltham, Mass., Sept. 2, 1885; s. Frederick W. and M. Wheatie (MacDonald) F.; B.S., Mass. Agrl. Coll., Amherst, 1908; m. Edith Blish McLaury, June 3, 1914 (dec.); children—Margaret W. (Mrs. Henry F. Skelton), Charles McLaury. Asst. horticulturist, N.J. Expt. Sta., New Brunswick, N.J., 1908-12, asso. horticulturist in extension, 1912-14, actg. horticulturist, 1919-21, asso. in horticulture, 1926-28, extension horticulturist (pomology) since 1928; instr. horticulture, Rutgers U., New Brunswick, N.J., 1914-16, asst. prof., 1916-18, asso. prof., 1918-26, prof. pomology since 1926. Sec.-treas. N.J. State Hort. Soc., N.J. Peach Council, Inc.; treas. N.J. Fruit Inst. Mem. Am. Soc. for Hort. Science. Presbyn. Home: 49 Nichol Av., New Brunswick, N.J.

FARLEY, Eugene Shedden, educator; b. Phoenixville, Pa., Sept. 29, 1899; s. Robert and Sarah Aubrey (Shoemaker) F.; B.S., Pa. State Coll., 1921; A.M., U. of Pa., 1926; Ph.D. same, 1933; m. Eleanor Ethel Coates, Aug. 24, 1921; children—Ethel Shoemaker, Robert Coates, Eugene Shedden, Jr. Engaged in teaching, Germantown Acad., 1922-25; instr. U. of Pa., 1927-29; dir. research, Bd. of Edn., Newark, N. J., 1929-36; dir. Bucknell U. Jr. Coll. since 1936. Served in S.A.T.C., 1918. Dir. Wilkes-Barre Y.M.C.A., Recreational Assn. Mem. Phi Delta Theta, Phi Delta Kappa, Kappa Phi Kappa. Republican. Mem. Religious Soc. Friends. Club. Kiwanis. Home: 78 W. Northampton St., Wilkes-Barre, Pa.

FARLEY, Frederic Henry Morton Stanley, artist; b. at sea, July 4, 1895; s. Henry Farley (born de la Rochefoucauld) and Charlotte Bennett (Shipley) F.; student Knapp's Inst., 1904-12, Columbia U. 1913-14, U. of Pa., 1920-21; B.S. Sorbonne, Paris, 1922; also student Jefferson Med. Coll., Md. Inst. of Design, Pa. Acad. of Fine Arts, Academie Julien, Paris; studied under Timothy Cole, Howard Pyle, Joseph Pennell, Leon Kroll, Augustus Johns, Bernard B. de Monvel; m. Aileen Beverly Bates, sculptress and writer, Apr. 16, 1928. Represented by permanently owned works in Baltimore Mus. of Art, Metropolitan Mus. of Art, Princeton U., British Mus. (London), Nat. Library (Paris). Works include portraits of Pres. Woodrow Wilson, the pres. emeritus of Johns Hopkins and four deans, former Gov. Albert C. Ritchie of Md., Mr. Moriz Rosenthal, Field Marshal Sir Douglas Haig and many others in the musical, theatrical and educational world. Hon. mention, Paris, for his drypoint work "The Squall," 1934. Flight comdr. Royal Flying Corps (British), 1914-15; wounded in action and hon. disch., Dec. 24, 1915. Episcopalian. Author: A History of the United States Frigate Constellation; Catalog of Works and Life of David Edwin, Engraver. Home: 136 W. Read St., Baltimore, Md.

FARLEY, Richard Blossom, artist; b. Poultney, Vt., Oct. 24, 1876; s. Dickinson Harvey and Freberne Lucia (Blossom) F.; ed. N.J. State Model Sch., Trenton, N.J., studied art at Pa. Acad. Fine Arts, Phila.; awarded traveling scholarship and studied in Europe under Whistler and at Beaux Arts, Paris; m. Abigail Rosenthal, June 17, 1914 (died 1926); children—Richard Blossom, Abigail Freberne. Has specialized in portraits and in painting sand, sea and sky. Awards: Fellowship prize, Pa. Acad. Fine Arts, 1912; gold medal, Phila. Art. Club, 1913; silver medal, San Francisco Expn., 1915; Fourth Clark prize, Corcoran Gallery, Washington, D. C., 1914. Represented in Corcoran Gallery by "Fog"; in Pa. Acad. by "Morning Mists." Mural paintings in Phila. Art Alliance, N.J. State Teachers Coll., Am. Theosophical Soc. (Wheaton, Ill.), South Phila. High Sch. for Girls. Marine camoufleur, stationed at N.Y. City and Norfolk, Va., World War. Fellowship Pa. Acad. Fine Arts; mem. Phila. Sketch Club, Art Alliance, Phila. Protestant. Home: "Sarobia," Eddington, Pa. Studio: 1828 S. Rittenhouse Sq., Philadelphia, Pa.

FARMER, Clarence R., M.D., surgeon; b. Elm City, N.C., Oct. 16, 1886; s. John Lawrence and Laura Ann (Brinkley) F.; student U. of N.C., 1903-07; M.D., Jefferson Med. Coll., 1909; m. Laura Wohlsen, Jan. 17, 1911; children—John Lawrence, Thomas Wohlsen, Mary Catharine, Clarence Richard. Practiced at Lancaster since 1911; consulting surgeon of Lancaster Gen. Hosp.; mem. surg. staff Rossmere Sanatorium. Fellow Am. Coll. Surgeons; mem. A.M.A., Pa. and Lancaster Co. med. socs. Democrat. Lutheran. Home: 1022 Buchanan Av. Office: 573 W. Lemon St., Lancaster, Pa.

FARMER, Vincent, surgeon; b. Ottawa, Can., Nov. 12, 1899; s. John Peter and Hannah (Murphy) F.; student Vankleek Collegiate Inst., Ontario, Can., 1900-14; M.D., C.M. McGill U., Montreal, Quebec, Can., 1920; m. Augustine Lynch, May 1932; children—Vincent, Stuart. Came to U.S. 1921, naturalized, 1925; physician Ottawa (Can.) Gen. Hosp., 1920-21; Bellevue Hosp., New York, 1921-23; asst. surgeon U.S. Pub. Health Marine Hosp. 21, New York, 1923-24; attending surgeon Hackensack (N.J.) Hosp. since 1928. Fellow Am. Coll. Surgeons. Roman Catholic. Club: Arcola Country. Author several med. articles. Address: 288 State St., Hackensack, N. J.

FARMER, Walter David, physician and surgeon; b. Butte City, Mont., Dec. 22, 1900; s. David Thomas and Jane (Bickerton) F.; M.D., C.M., McGill Univ., Montreal, 1919, L.M.C.C., 1926; m. Mabel Armstrong, July 4, 1922 (divorced); children—Osler, Millicent and Walter, Jr. (twins); m. 2d, Mildred Farlee, June 27, 1931; 1 son, Keith Morrow. Resident physician and surgeon Mercer Hosp., Trenton, N.J., 1926-27; began practice in Allentown, N.J., 1927, and mem. staff Mercer Hosp., 1927-33, on courtesy staff since 1933; founded pvt. hosp. in Allentown, 1933, established new enlarged hosp., 1937, under name Dr. Farmers' Pvt. Hosp., practicing surgery, medicine and obstetrics, dir. propr. and chief of staff. Served in C.O.T.C. at McGill U. Pres. bd. health, Allentown, N.J. since 1929. Mem. Mercer Co. Med. Soc. Republican. Episcopalian. Mason (32°, Shriner).

Clubs: Lions (Allentown); Forsgates Country (Jamesburg). Home: 123 Main St. Office: 28 Main St., Allentown, N.J.

FARMER, William Robertson, teacher; b. New York, July 19, 1867; s. Samuel Farmer and Jeannette (Macduff) F.; A.B., Washington and Jefferson Coll., Pa., 1892; grad. Western Theol. Sem., Pittsburgh, 1895; post-grad., U. of Marburg, Germany, 1906; m. Joy H. Chain, Sept. 24, 1895; m. 2d, Mrs. Alice Brown Morrison, Mar. 13, 1930. Ordained Presbyn. ministry, 1895; pastor 1st Ch., St. Paul, Minn., 1895-96, Edgewood Ch., Pittsburgh, Pa., 1896-1907; asst. prof. N.T. lit. and exegesis, 1907-11, prof., 1911-18, prof. practical theology since 1919, Western Theol. Sem. Home: Alder Court Apts., Pittsburgh, Pa.

FARNAM, George Oscar, banker; b. Lumberton, N.J., Nov. 25, 1882; s. George and Elizabeth Jane (Lippincott) F.; student grammar sch., Lumberton, N.J., 1887-93, Trenton, N.J., 1893, Port Jervis, N.Y., 1893-95, acad., Port Jervis, N.Y., 1895, high sch., Bridgeton, N.J., 1895-96, Asbury Park, N.J., 1896-97, Trenton, N.J., 1897-98; unmarried. Clk. Anchor Pottery, Trenton, N.J., 1898-1905; cashier Del. and Atlantic Telephone & Telegraph Co., Trenton, N.J., 1905-06; shipping clk. Whitehead Bros. Rubber Co., Trenton, N.J., 1906-08; clk. First Nat. Bank of Bordentown, N.J., 1908-12, teller, 1917-24, cashier since 1924, trust officer since 1923, sec. since 1924; clk. Hamilton Rubber Mfg. Co., Trenton, N.J., 1912-17; treas. Manor Realty Co. No. 2, Bordentown, N.J., since 1923. Sec. Union Rep. League of Mercer Co. (formerly The Rep. Club, Trenton), 1916-25, treas. since 1929. Mem. Sons of the Revolution, Sons and Daughters of the Pilgrims, Soc. of Mayflower Descendants. Republican. Mason (Tall Cedars; Scottish Rite; Shriner), Odd Fellow. Club: Yapewi Aquatic. Home: 718 Riverside Av., Trenton, N.J. Office: First National Bank, Bordentown, N.J.

FARNHAM, George Wright; b. Putneyville, N.Y., July 28, 1892; s. Henry Philip and Frances (Wright) F.; Ph.B., Yale U., 1916; m. Hazel C. Durfee, Aug. 20, 1917; 1 son, Roger Durfee. Held position of senior engn. Elbert Clarke Co., 1916-17; asst. treas. Kellogg Mfg. Co., 1919-20; production mgr. McClellan Refrigerating Co., 1920-21; mgr. ednl. dept. McGraw-Hill Book Co., 1922-33; mgr. coll. dept. Internat. Textbook Co. since 1933. Mem. N.E.A., Am. Soc. Mech. Engrs., Soc. for Promotion Engring. Edn. Served as capt. U.S. Coast Arty. Corps, A.E.F., 1917-19; now major Coast Arty. Reserves. Republican. Christian Scientist. Clubs: Yale (New York); Graduate (New Haven, Conn.). Home: 302 Stone Av., Clarks Summit, Pa. Office: 1001 Wyoming Av., Scranton, Pa.

FARNHAM, Robert, chief engr.; b. Washington, D.C., Dec. 19, 1877; s. Robert and Emma Jane (Lowry) F.; student Columbian (now George Washington) U., 1894-95; C.E., Lehigh U., 1899; m. Gertrude Hanley, Nov. 22, 1911; 1 son, Robert. Asst., engr. corps, engring. dept., D.C., 1899-1902; with J. H. Gray & Co., N.Y. City, 1902-03; with Pa. R.R. Co. since 1903, transitman, engr. corps, Mar.-Aug. 1903, asst. engr. constrn., in charge constrn. work, Washington, D.C., 1903-10, asst. engr. office of engr. bridges and bldgs., 1910-13, asst. to engr. bridges and bldgs, 1913-16, asst. engr. bridges and bldgs, 1916-23, engr. same, 1923-27, chief engr., Philadelphia improvements, 1927-37, asst. chief engr. Eastern Region of Pa. R.R. since Sept. 1937. Mem. Am. Soc. C.E. (dir. 1924-26), Am. Ry. Engring. Assn., Am. Soc. Testing Materials, Sigma Chi. Republican. Episcopalian. Clubs: Engineers, Pennsylvania Golf. Home: 7126 Cresheim Rd., Mount Airy. Office: Broad St. Station, Philadelphia, Pa.

FARNSWORTH, Floyd Forney, M.D.; b. Buckhannon, W. Va., Apr. 2, 1869; s. Frank L. and Martha (Currence) F.; B.Pd., Union Coll., 1897; student U. of the South, 1901-03; M.D., Md. Medical Coll., 1904; D.O., Phila. Optical Coll., 1922; m. Lasora Martin, Sept. 26, 1890; children—French Marion, Lief Ericson, Ora Gail, Dorsey Artemus. Teacher country sch., 1887-98; prin. Thomas (W.Va.) Graded Sch., 1898-99,

Parsons (W.Va.) High Sch., 1899-1900, Buckhannon (W.Va.) Graded Sch., 1900-02, Buckhannon High Sch., 1902-03; in gen. practice of medicine since 1904; health officer, Milton, W. Va., since 1930; passed asst. surgeon U. S. Pub. Health Service; formerly v.p. Milton Nat. Bank, now dir. its successor, Bank of Milton. Mem. W.Va. State Legislature, 1913; mayor of Milton, 1925-26. Served as major Med. Corps, World War. Republican. Methodist. Mason. Club: Lions. Address: Milton, W. Va.

FARNSWORTH, Philo Taylor, research engr.; b. Beaver, Utah, Aug. 19, 1906; s. Louis Edwin and Serena (Bastian) F.; student Rigby (Ia.) High Sch., 1922-23, Brigham Young U., 1923-26; m. Elma Gardner, May 27, 1926; children—Philo Taylor; Kenneth Gardner (dec.), Russell Seymour. Engaged in television research work with Crocker Research Labs., later Television Labs., Inc., Farnsworth Television, Inc., since 1926; pres. Farnsworth Television, Inc., of Pa., v.p. in charge of research, Farnsworth Television, Inc., San Francisco. Fellow Royal Soc. of Arts (London), A.A.A.S.; mem. Nat. Radio Inst. (dir.), Mass. Television Inst. (dir.), Franklin Inst., Inst. Radio Engrs., Soc. Motion Picture Engrs., Television Soc. of London. Awarded Brigham Young Alumnus Award, 1937; hon. mention Eta Kappa Nu citation. Mem. Ch. of Latter Day Saints (Mormon). Club: Philadelphia Cricket. Home: 524 Gresheim Valley Rd. Office: 127 E. Mermaid Lane, Philadelphia, Pa.

FARNY, George Wimbor, cons. engr.; b. Rostoff on Don, Russia, Mar. 21, 1872; s. Gregory and Eugenia Farny; came to U.S., 1895, naturalized, 1908; ed. schs. and colls., Russia, Belgium, Germany, France; B.S. and E.M., Mich. Coll. of Mines, Houghton, Mich., 1899; m. Sylvia Wurlitzer, Feb. 18, 1896; children—Eugene R., Cyril, Alice (Mrs. Richard Carver Wood). Employed as engr., Laidlaw, Dunn & Gordon Co., 1896-98, Internat. Steam Pump Co., 1900-02; cons. engr. and gen. mgr. Worthington Pump Co., Ltd., 1902-17; chief engr. E. Tillmans Co., 1904-10, Paul Boeckel, Ltd., 1905-12; cons. engr. City of Nicolaeff, Russia Water Works, 1910-12; pres. and treas., Jireh Food Co., Inc., 1917-36; retired from active work, 1919. Served as maj. Engrs. Corps, U.S.A.R. with A.E.F. in Russia and France. Trustee N.Y. Mus. of Sci. and Industry. Mem. Am. Soc. Mech. Engrs., Am. Inst. Mining & Metall. Engrs., Soc. Am. Mil. Engrs., Morris Co. Engrs. Club, Am. Soc. Planning Ofcls., Am. Legion, Nat. Co. Rds. Planning Commn. (chmn.), Nat. Highways Assn. (v.p.), Am. Rd. Bldrs. Assn. (pres. Planning Div.), N.J. State Planning Bd., N.J. Parks & Recreation Assn. (pres.), Morris Co. Planning Bd. (chmn.), Morris Co. Assn. (pres.). Republican. Unitarian. Clubs: Mining, Chemists (New York); Shongum (Dover, N.J.) Home: Craftsman Farms. Address: Box F, Morris Plains, N.J.

FARQUHAR, Allan, fire ins. exec.; b. Sandy Spring, Md., Nov. 23, 1853; s. William Henry and Margaret (Briggs) F.; student pub. schs., 1862-71; m. Charlotte Harris Pleasants, Jan. 15, 1880 (dec.); children—Marion (Mrs. Ronald Van Auken Mills), Ethel (Mrs. Richard Bentley Thomas), Arthur Douglas; m. 2d, Mrs. Alice Councilman Cockey, Aug. 14, 1924. Engaged in farming with father, 1862-78; sec. Savings Instn., Sandy Spring, Md., 1878-95; asst. sec. Mutual Fire Ins. Co. of Montgomery Co., Md., 1889-95, sec. and treas. since 1895; charter mem. and dir. First Nat. Bank, Sandy Spring, since 1900. Served as mem. Montgomery Co. Ct. House Commn., 1890; mem. Jamestown Expn. Commn., 1907. Dir. and v.p. Montgomery Co. Gen. Hosp. Mem. Home Interest Soc. Mem. Grange, Patrons of Husbandry since 1874. Soc. of Friends. Club: Montgomery Farmers. Has attended 19 presdl. inaugurations, traveling from Sandy Spring to Washington. Home: Sandy Spring, Md.

FARQUHAR, Francis, manufacturer; b. York, Pa., Oct. 13, 1868; s. Arthur Briggs and Elizabeth (Jessop) F.; student York (Pa.) Collegiate Inst., 1879-85; Ph.B., Yale, 1888; m. Charlotte Gibson, Nov. 16, 1998 (died 1932); children—Arthur F. (dec.), Robert F. (dec.), Charlotte Elizabeth (Mrs. Donald G. Wing). Admitted to N.Y. bar, 1890, and practiced at New York, 1890-99; with A.B. Farquhar Co., Ltd., York, Pa., since 1899, sec-treas. since 1908, also pres. since 1925. Trustee York (Pa.) Collegiate Inst., dir. York (Pa.) Hosp., chmn. York Co. Chapter Am. Red Cross. Mem. A.A.A.S., Am. Soc. M.E., Yale Library Assn. Address: York, Pa.

FARQUHAR, Harold B.; editor Globe-Times. Address: Bethlehem, Pa.

FARQUHAR, Thomas Lippincott, insurance; b. Phila., Pa., Dec. 22, 1875; s. Benjamin Hallowell and Martha D. (Lippincott) F.; ed. pub. schs. and York (Pa.) Collegiate Inst.; m. Mary E. Chapman, June 6, 1905; 1 dau., Ellenor Hallowell. Began in ins. business with Spring Garden Ins. Co., 1893; pres. Newark (N.J.) Fire Ins. Co., 1925-30, retired. Protestant. Home: 7 Woodland Rd., Maplewood, N.J.

FARR, Clifford Bailey, M.D.; b. Landis Twp., N.J., Apr. 17, 1872; s. Lincoln Dow and Hannah (Bailey) F.; A.B., Haverford, 1894, A.M., 1909; M.D., U. of Pa., 1898; m. Katharine Elliott, Nov. 22, 1904; children—Robert Lincoln, Frank Winslow Elliott, James Bailey, Anne Bailey (Mrs. John Foot). Began practice at Phila., 1901; mem. teaching staff of med. dept. U. of Pa., 1901-19, advancing to prof. in Grad. Sch.; phys. or asst. to various hosps.; with med. research dept. B. F. Goodrich Co., Akron, O., 1920-22; dir. labs., dept. mental and nervous diseases, Pa. Hosp., 1922-37. Served as lieut., capt. and maj. Med. Corps, U.S.A., June 1917-Jan. 1919; with A.E.F. in France 1 yr. Fellow A.M.A.; mem. Pathol. Soc. of Phila., Am. Psychiatric Soc., Coll. Physicians Phila., Phi Beta Kappa. Republican. Episcopalian. Author: Outlines of Internal Medicine, 5th edit., 1929. Contbr. to Da Costa's Handbook of Med. Treatment, and Craig's Diseases of Middle Life. Home: Bryn Mawr, Pa. Office: 111 N. 49th St., Philadelphia, Pa.

FARR, Edward B., judge; b. Mehoopany, Pa., Mar. 30, 1876; s. Jonathan and Alice (Robinson) Farr; educated Mansfield (Pa.) State Normal School, Pa. State College and University of Pa. Law School; m. Sara Morris, July 2, 1902; children—Morris DeWolfe, Robert Edward, John Burns, Josephine, Samuel Wister. Admitted to bar, 1903; postmaster, Tunkhannock, Pa., 1906-14; dist. atty. Wyoming Co., Pa., 1915-24, co. solicitor, 1928-36; elected president judge, 44th Pa. Judicial Dist., Jan. 1, 1936, for 10-year term; dir. Citizens' Nat. Bank of Tunkhannock, Scranton (Pa.) Lackawanna Trust Co. Chmn. Speakers Bur. for Wyoming Co., during World War. Trustee Mansfield State Normal Sch., 1905-09, Pittston (Pa.) Hosp. since 1936. Mem. Am. and Pa. bar assns. Republican. Presbyterian. Clubs: Scranton Country, Iram Temple Country. Home: 41 Wyoming Av., Tunkhannock, Pa.

FARR, Irving Lord, physician; b. Pierrepont Manor, N.Y., Mar. 7, 1872; s. Mortimer Ives and Henrietta Rose (Lord) F.; B.Pd., Syracuse U., 1901; M.D., N.Y. Homeo. Med. Coll. & Flower Hosp., 1911; m. Elizabeth N. Coons, June 28, 1905. Employed successively as clk., bookkeeper, expressman, sch. prin., 1896-1905; interne Flower and Metropolitan Hosp., N.Y. City, 1910-11; engaged in practice of medicine in Brooklyn, 1911-18, at Montclair, N.J., since 1913; chief of staff Montclair Community Hosp. since 1937. Served as 1st lt. N.J. regulars, 1915-16. Chmn. med. com. Welfare Bd., Montclair, N.J. Mem. Am. Anesthetic Soc., Am., N.J. State, and Co. med. assns. Republican. Episcopalian. Home: 214 Walnut St., Montclair, N.J.

FARR, Walter John, surgeon; b. Hoboken, N.J., Oct. 27, 1901; s. John Clark and Jane (Clark) F.; A.B., Cornell U., 1922; M.D., Cornell U. Med. Sch., 1925; m. Dorothy Strickland, June 9, 1928; children—Sibyl Clark, Dorothy Strickland, Walter John, Jr. Interne Sloane Hosp. for Women, New York, 1926-27; practiced gen. medicine and surgery with father, John Clark Farr, in Hoboken, N.J., 1927-31 at the Farr Sanitorium; in practice of medicine specializing in surgery at Teaneck, N.J. since 1931; dir. dept. gen. surgery, Hasbrouck Heights Hosp., Hasbrouck Heights, N.J. since 1935; assisted in organizing Baby Keep Well Stations in Teaneck. Mem. mayor's com. on parks and playgrounds; past pres. Teaneck Kiwanis Club. Mem. A.M.A., N.J. Med. Soc., Bergen County Med. Soc., Sigma Pi, Nu Sigma Nu. Ind. Republican. Mason, Elk. Clubs: Teaneck Kiwanis, Oritani Field. Home: 288 Griggs Av., Teaneck, N.J.

FARRAND, Wilson, head master, emeritus; b. Newark, N.J., Sept. 22, 1862; s. Samuel Ashbel and Louise (Wilson) F.; grad. Newark Acad., 1878; A.B., Princeton, 1886, A.M., 1889; hon. A.M., Columbia, 1907; L.H.D., Hamilton Coll., 1918; Litt.D., Princeton Univ. 1935; L.H.D., Rutgers University, 1936; m. Margaret Washburne Walker, Nov. 23, 1889; children—Margaret L. Katharine (dec.), Dorothy W. Asst. editor Scribner's Magazine, 1886-87; master, 1887-89, asso. head master, 1889-1901, head master, 1901-35, emeritus, 1935, Newark (N.J.) Acad. Mem. of College Entrance Examination Board since 1900, Schoolmasters' Assn. of New York (president, 1895-96), Middle States Assn. Colls. and Prep. Schs. (pres. 1902), Head Masters' Assn. of U.S. (pres., 1911), N.E. Soc. of Orange (pres., 1906-08); pres. Princeton Alumni Federation of N.J., 1909-11. Alumni trustee Princeton U., 1909-19, life trustee and clerk bd., 1919—; mem. Commn. on Higher Institutions, Middle States Assn. Presbyn. Clubs: University, Century, Princeton (New York); Nassau (Princeton). Editor: Carlyle's "Essay on Burns," 1896; Tennyson's "Princess," 1898. Has written many papers and delivered many addresses on edni. topics, especially coll. entrance requirements and relation of sch. and coll. Address: Princeton, N.J.

FARRELL, Charles LeRoy, banker; b. Bristol, Ind., Nov. 14, 1874; s. John W. and Mary Josephine (Maffitt) F.; student Transylvania U., Ky.; m. Nellie May Richards, Oct. 12, 1898. Began as bookkeeper State Bank of Ind., Indianapolis, 1894; asst. cashier Capitol Nat. Bank, Indianapolis, 1898-1903; v.p. Ft. Dearborn Nat. Bank, Chicago, 1903-06; v.p. Irving Nat. Bank, New York, 1906-09; pres. Essex County Nat. Bank, Newark, N.J., 1909-18, when the bank consolidated with the Nat. Newark Banking Co., forming the Nat. Newark & Essex Banking Co., of which is pres.; also pres. Newark & Essex Securities Corpn.; dir. Am. Ins. Co., Howard Savings Instn., Mut. Benefit Life Ins. Co. (all of Newark). Treas. Trustee of State Assn. Y.M. C.A.'s of N.J.; pres. Babies Hosp.; trustee Marcus L. Ward Home, Newark. Mem. Am. Bankers' Assn. (exec. council, 1903-06); sec. Ind. Bankers' Assn., 1899-1903. Republican. Methodist. Clubs: Union League, Bankers (N.Y. City); Essex County Country (gov.), Essex, Down Town, Bond (Newark, N.J.). Home: 624 Clifton Av. Office: National Newark & Essex Banking Co., Newark, N.J.

FARRELL, John Joseph, professional golfer; b. White Plains, N.Y., Apr. 1, 1901; s. James C. and Katherine (Breen) F.; ed. public schs. of Tuckahoe, N.J., and Waverly (N.J.) High Sch.; m. Catherine T. Hush, Nov. 24, 1931; children—John Joseph, James Charles, William Henry. Began as caddie, 1910, later caddie master and golf club maker, Siwanoy Country Club, Mt. Vernon, N.Y.; professional, Baltusrol Golf Club, Short Hills, N.J., since 1934. Nat. Open Champion, 1928; N.J. Open Champion, 1936. Roman Catholic. Mem. K.C. Home: 19 Stoneleigh Park, Westfield, N.J. Office: Baltusrol Golf Club, Short Hills, N.J.

FARRELL, John T(hompson) Jr., physician; b. Providence, R.I., Oct. 7, 1897; s. John T. and Louise Allen (Smith) F.; B.S., Hobart Coll., Geneva, N.Y., 1918; M.D., Jefferson Medical Coll., Phila., 1922; m. Miriam Ott, Aug. 17, 1926. Interne, R.I. Hosp., Providence, R.I., 1922-24; asst. roentgenologist, Jefferson Hosp., Phila., 1930-38; asst. prof. roentgenology, Jefferson Med. Coll.; roentgenologist, White Haven Sanatorium, White Haven, Pa. Fellow Am. Coll. Phys., Phila. Coll. Phys.; mem. A.M.A., Pa. State and Phila. Co. med. socs., Radiol. Soc. of N.A. (v.p. 1934), Am. Roentgen Ray Soc., Laennec Soc. (pres. 1938), Phila. Roentgen Ray Soc. (pres. 1930), Theta Delta Chi, Nu Sigma

FARRELL, **Thomas Francis**, judge; b. Sugar Notch, Pa., Nov. 30, 1874; s. Michael and Bridget (McGroarty) F.; student pub. schs.; m. Catherine McGrane, July 16, 1901; children—Mary Catherine, Margaret, Ann, Thomas Francis, Joseph P., Michael J. Judge of Court of Common Pleas of Luzerne Co., 11th Judicial Dist. of Pa. since Jan. 2, 1938, serving 10-yr. term; spl. counsel Reconstrn. Finance Corpn., 1935, 36 and 37; dir. First Nat. Bank of Ashley, Pa. Del. to Dem. Nat. Conv., New York, 1924; chmn. Pa. Delegation, Dem. Nat. Conv., Houston, Tex. 1928. Trustee Junior Coll. of Bucknell U., Bloomsburg State Teachers Coll. Home: 85 W. Union St. Office: Court House, N. River St., Wilkes-Barre, Pa.

FARREN, **Oran Bearl**, school prin.; b. Arvilla, W.Va., June 1, 1910; s. Bearl B. and Mary Edna (Wagner) F.; A.B., Marietta (O.) Coll., 1931; A.M., Southern Meth. U., Dallas, Tex., 1932; grad. student Ohio State U., 1932-33, Ohio U., 1936, W.Va. U., summers 1937, 38; m. Marjorie Bergen, Aug. 21, 1935; 1 dau., Judith Marianna. Teacher, St. Marys (W.Va.) High Sch., 1933-35; school supt., Pleasants County, W.Va., 1935-37; prin. St. Marys Graded Sch. since 1937. Boy Scout dir., St. Marys several years. Held Arnold fellowship in govt., Southern Meth. U. Mem. Kappa Alpha. Republican. Presbyterian. Home: 915 2d St., St. Marys, W.Va.

FARWELL, **Hermon Waldo**, univ. prof.; b. Keene, N.H., Dec. 29, 1879; s. Calvin Waldo and Ella Jane (Gilbert) F.; student Keene (N.H.) High Sch., 1893-98; A.B., Dartmouth Coll., Hanover, N.H., 1902, A.M., 1906; student Columbia U., 1906-10; m. Elizabeth Whitcomb, Aug. 21, 1909; children—Fred Whitcomb, Alice (Mrs. Charles F. McCann), Hermon Waldo. Teacher mathematics and science, Hanover (N. H.) High Sch., 1902-03; Weymouth (Mass.) High Sch., 1903-04; instr. physics, Dartmouth Coll., Hanover, N.H., 1904-06; asst. in physics, Columbia U., 1906-09, tutor, 1909-11, instr., 1911-17, asst. prof., 1917-23, asso. prof., 1923-29, prof. physics since 1929. Served as instr., U.S. Army Sch. of Photography, 1917-18; also engaged in research on war problems. Fellow Am. Phys. Soc., A.A.A.S.; mem. Optical Soc. of America, Am. Assn. Physics Teachers, Phi Gamma Delta, Phi Beta Kappa, Sigma Xi. Republican. Presbyterian. Club: Men's Faculty (Columbia U.). Author and co-author several physics text books; author objective tests in physics; contbr. numerous papers pub. in scientific jours. Home: 130 Woodridge Pl., Leonia, N.J.

FASSETT, **Harvey Learn**, high sch. prin.; b. Scottsville, Pa., Oct. 6, 1867; s. James Gary and Sarah (Learn) F.; Ph.B., Bucknell U., Lewisburg, Pa., 1894, M.S., 1899; student Cornell U., 1899-1900; student Teachers Coll. of Columbia U., 1926-28; m. Bertha Woodruff, June 30, 1903; children—Alda Woodruff (dec.), Helen Woodruff (wife of Harold J. Muendel, M.D.), Sarah Lois (wife of Albert D. Angell), James Woodruff. Instr. mathematics and chemistry, Peddie Inst., Hightstown, N.J., 1894-99; chmn. dept. mathematics, high sch., Troy, N.Y., 1902-07; instr. mathematics, Barringer High Sch., Newark, N.J., 1907-10, East Side High Sch., 1910-13; chmn. dept. mathematics, South Side High Sch., Newark, N.J., 1913-33; instr. of mathematics, Mt. Pleasant Mil. Acad., Ossining, N.Y., 1900-02, Newark Jr. Coll. 1916-19; prin. South Side High Sch. Annex, Newark, N.J., 1925-33; prin. South Side High Sch. summer sch., 1919-29; prin. Barringer Evening High Sch., 1933-38. Mem. bd. edn., Newark, N.J., since 1938. Mem. High Sch. Men's Assn., Newark, Secondary Sch. Prins. Assn. N.J. Democrat. Presbyn. Mason. Clubs: Wednesday (Newark, N.J.). Home: 554 Highland Av., Newark, N.J.; and Bellport, N.Y.

FAST, **Gustave**, consulting engr.; b. Sweden, May 18, 1884; s. Johan P. and Maria Charlotta (Swenson) F.; ed. Chalmers Tech. Coll., Goteborg, Sweden, 1900-04, City and Guild Tech. Coll., London, England, 1904-06; m. Ganna Kjaergaard-Nielsen, Aug. 23, 1929; 1 son, Jon Gustave Viking. Came to U.S., 1910, naturalized, 1924. Mech. engr. Gwynne's, Ltd., London, Eng., 1906-07, Atlas Iron Works, Birmingham, Eng., 1908-09, Swedish State Ry., 1909-10, Worthington Pump & Machinery Co., Harrison, N.J., 1910-12, Crown Cork & Seal Co., Baltimore, 1912-15, Poole Engine & Machine Co., Baltimore, 1915-25, Bartlett Hayward Co., Baltimore since 1919, pres. Gustave Fast Engring. Co., Annapolis, since 1931; pres. The Fast Bearing Co., Baltimore, since 1936; cons. engr. Koppers Co., Baltimore, since 1919. Fellow Am. Soc. Mech. Engrs. Awarded John Price Wetherill medal by Franklin Inst. for "discovery and invention in the physical sciences," 1929. Club: Cosmos (Washington, D.C.). Home: Lindamoor-on-Severn, Annapolis, Md. Office: 200 Scott St., Baltimore, Md.

FAST, **Louis Arba**, lawyer; b. Newark, N.J., Nov. 5, 1893; s. Max and Anna (Kurtz) F.; student Grammar Schs., Newark, N.J., 1899-1907, Barringer High Sch., Newark, N.J., 1907-11; LL.B., New York Law Sch., 1913; m. Selma Jennis, April 11, 1918; children—Erwin Joseph, Phyllis Joan. Began as lawyer, 1914, and since in practice at Newark, N.J.; mem. of firm Fast & Fast, Newark, since 1920; solicitor Lawyers Title Guaranty Co., 1928-31. Pres. Newark (N.J.) Tax Bd., 1925-29, asst. corpn. counselor, 1929-33. Mem. Theta Alpha Phi (hon.). Republican. Hebrew religion. Home: 59 Baldwin Av. Office: 60 Park Place, Newark, N.J.

FAUNCE, **Benjamin Franklin**, mech. engr.; b. Norway, Me., Dec. 18, 1878; s. Franklin W. and Phoebe Maria (Shackley) F.; grad. Norway (Me.) High Sch., 1896; M.E., U. of Me., 1900; m. Emily Davies, Oct. 16, 1902 (died 1935); children—Benjamin Franklin, David D., John H.; m. 2d, Bertha Edwards, Feb. 24, 1937. Began as mech. engr., 1901; chief inspector Cambria Steel Co., 1902-03; designer elec. equipment Westinghouse Electric and Mfg. Co., 1904; asst. engr. Edgar Thompson Works, Carnegie Steel Co., 1905-06; asst. engr. Carnegie Steel Co., 1907-12; supt. Homestead Steel Works, 1913-19, Midvale Steel Co., 1920-23, Bethlehem Steel Co., 1923-28; chmn. bd. and sec. Brown-Fayro Co. since 1928. Served in Spanish-Am. War, 1898. Republican. Methodist. Mason (K.T., Shriner). Club: Sunnehanna Country. Home: 105 Fayette St. Office: 940 Ash St., Johnstown, Pa.

FAUSET, **Joseph Hartman**, broker; b. Braddock, Pa., April 9, 1896; s. William and Anna (Hartman) F.; ed. Wilkinsburg High Sch. and U. of Pittsburgh; m. Mary Wrenshall, Oct. 31, 1923. Partner Singer, Deane & Scribner, brokers and investment bankers; v.p. and dir. Pa. Bradford Co.; dir. Monongahela Incline Plane Co. Served in U.S. Army, with A.E.F., 1917-19. Republican. Clubs: Duquesne, University. Home: Woodville, Pa. Office: Union Trust Bldg., Pittsburgh, Pa.

FAUSOLD, **Samuel**, coll. pres.; b. Mt. Pleasant, Pa., Jan. 21, 1888; s. Martin Luther and Ada (Hays) F.; A.B., Gettysburg Coll., 1910; Ph.D., U. of Pittsburgh, 1934; m. Edna Breegle, Aug. 1, 1912; children—Samuel, George, Patricia, Martin, Alice. Prin. East Huntington Twp. High Sch., 1910-14, Irwin Schs. and Norwin High Sch., 1914-22; supt. schs., Ambridge, 1922-30, Monessen, 1930-35; Pa. state deputy supt. of pub. instrn., 1935-36; pres. Indiana (Pa.) State Teachers Coll. since 1936. Mem. Phi Beta Kappa. Democrat. Lutheran. Club: Rotary. Home: Indiana, Pa.

FAUST, **J(acob) Frank**, high school prin.; b. Mowersville, Pa., Aug. 21, 1890; s. Jacob A. and Jennie S. (Hoch) F.; grad. Shippensburg (Pa.) State Teachers Coll., 1911; B.S., Susquehanna U., Selinsgrove, Pa., 1915, Pd.D. hon., 1938; A.M., Columbia, 1928; Ed.D., Pa. State Coll., 1935; m. Catherine Richter Schoch, Aug. 24, 1921 (dec.); m. 2d, Margaret McDowell, Dec. 23, 1932. Teacher in rural schools, Franklin Co., Pa., 1907-10; asst. prin. and teacher of mathematics and science, Acad. of Susquehanna U., 1912-15; teacher and head of biology dept., Johnstown (Pa.) High Sch., 1915-18; teacher of science and mathematics, Peabody High Sch., Pittsburgh, 1918-20; prin. Chambersburg (Pa.) High Sch. since 1922; sec. Lemoyne Trust Co., 1911; sales rep. Fisher Scientific Co., Pittsburgh, 1920-22. Served in Air Service, U.S. Army, July 1918-Feb. 1919. Mem. N.E.A. (mem. supporting com. of Nat. Policies Commn., 1938; vice chmn. com. to cooperate with Am. Legion 1938), Pa. State Edn. Assn. (pres. 1938; past pres. Southern Conv. Dist.; chmn. com. to make school costs survey, 1938; state del. to N.E.A., 1924, 31, 32, 36, 38, 39), Nat. Assn. Secondary Sch. Prins., Franklin Co. Edn. Assn. (past pres.), Kittochtinny Hist. Soc., Am. Legion (past comdr. Chambersburg Post), Forty and Eight (past corr.), Phi Sigma Pi, Kappa Phi Kappa, Phi Delta Kappa. Republican. Member United Brethren Church. Mason; member Harrisburg Consistory (32°). Clubs: Rotary (pres. 1939), Republican, Republican Men of Pa. (mem. state exec. com.), Chambersburg Golf, Chambersburg Men's Commercial (past pres.). Author: Experience Units in Biology (with George R. Biecher), 1938; A Study of Certain General Control Officers and Certain Gen. Control Practices of Fourth Class School Districts of Pa., 1935; contbr. many articles to ednl. jours. Home: 524 Montgomery Av. Office: High School, Chambersburg, Pa.

FAWCETT, **Ivan**, physician; b. Salem, O., Jan. 31, 1889; s. John Mervin and Nancy L. (Barber) F.; M.D., U. of Pa. Med. Sch., 1910; m. Florence York, Aug. 2, 1916; children—Ivan York, John Everett, Raphael Alan. Interne Phila. Gen. Hosp., 1910-11; engaged in practice of medicine at Wheeling, W.Va., since 1913, specializing in diseases of eye, ear, nose and throat. Dir. Wheeling Y.M.C.A. Mem. Nat. Council Boy Scouts of America. Awarded Silver Beaver of Boy Scouts. Trustee Oglebay Inst. (pres.), Linsley Inst., Wheeling, W.Va. Fellow Am. Coll. Surgeons, Am. Med. Assn. (mem. of house of dels.), sr. fellow Am. Acad. Ophthalmology and Otolaryngology; mem. W.Va. State Med. Soc., Pittsburgh Otol. Soc., Phila. Laryngol. Soc. (hon. life), Nu Sigma Nu. Presbyn. Mason (32°, Shriner). Clubs: Rotary, Schwinn Study, Twilight, Drama Reading (Wheeling). Home: 3 Orchard Terrace, Woodsdale, Wheeling, W.Va. Office: 75 12th St., Wheeling, W.Va.

FAWCETT, **William Hagan**, banking; b. Pittsburgh, Pa., Mar. 4, 1883; s. James T. and Marian (Love) F.; ed. pub. schs. of Pittsburgh; m. Laura C. Kelly, Oct. 31, 1904; children—James T. III, William Hagan, Jack Kelly. Engaged as asst. cashier Peoples Nat. Bank, Pittsburgh, Pa., 1920-21; asst. cashier, First Nat. Bank, Pittsburgh, 1921-33, v.p. since 1933. Mem. Banking Studies Com., Am. Bankers Assn. 1936; chmn. Group 8, Pa. Bankers Assn., 1938; treas. Western Pa. Div., Nat. Safety Council, 1938-39; treas. Pa. Bankers Assn., 1939-40. Republican. Methodist. Clubs: Pittsburgh Athletic, Duquesne, Pittsburgh Field, St. Clair Country, Bankers (pres. 1934), Metropolitan (Pittsburgh). Home: 26 Mt. Lebanon Boul., South Hills Station, Pittsburgh. Office: Fifth Av. and Wood St., Pittsburgh, Pa.

FAWLEY, **James Linwood**, engr. and contractor; b. Phila., Pa., July 25, 1883; s. Benjamin and Sarah (Wilde) F.; A.B., Yale, 1906, A.M., 1907; m. Edna Jones, May 17, 1916; children—James Linwood, John Jones. Began as draftsman, 1901, with Am. Bridge Co., Phila., Milliken Bros., New York, N.Y.; structural engr. F. M. Andrews & Co., New York, Phila. Rapid Transit Co.; structural engr. and v.p. George F. Pawling & Co., Phila.; engaged in business on own acct. as engr. and contractor since 1921, inc. as J. L. Fawley, Inc., 1929, and since pres. and treas.; pres. Newportville Land & Improvement Co.; mem. firm tri-County Appraisal Co. Mem. bd. trustees Lovett Memorial Library. Mem. Am. Soc. C.E., Sigma Xi, Phi Beta Kappa. Independent Democrat. Episcopalian. Mason (K.T., Shriner). Club: Penn Athletic (Phila.). Home: 7113 Chew St. Office: 2121 Walnut St., Philadelphia, Pa.

FAY, Frank L., retired ry. car. mfr.; b. Cleveland, O., July 18, 1869; ed. pub. schs., Cleveland, O.; hon. D. Bus. Adminstrn., Thiel. Coll., 1937; married. In employ Western Union Telegraph Co., Cleveland, O., 1884-88; employed as r.r. telegraph operator, station agt., car accountant, 1888-1910; pres. Greenville Steel Car Co., mfrs., Greenville, Pa. 1910-38. Served as mem. Pa. Senate, 1926-34. Pres. Greenville Pub. Library. Pres. bd. trustees Greenville Hosp. Trustee Thiel Coll. Republican. Presbyn. Mason. Rotarian. Clubs: Duquesne (Pittsburgh); Bankers of America, Union League (New York); Congressional Country (Washington, D.C.). Home: Greenville, Pa.

FEASER, George W(ashington), supt. of schools; b. Dauphin, Pa., Jan. 24, 1901; s. Elmer S. and Sarah E. (Duncan) F.; A.B., Elizabethtown Coll., 1928; A.M., Columbia U., 1934; m. Mary Crisswell, June 6, 1920. Teacher rural schs., Dauphin Co., Pa., 1918-23; teacher and prin. grade schs., Middletown, 1923-29; teacher mathematics Middletown High Sch., 1929-30, prin., 1930-34; supt. schs., Middletown, since 1934. Mem. N.E.A., Pa. State Edn. Assn., Am. Assn. of Sch. Adminstrs. Republican. Presbyterian. Odd Fellow. Knight of Malta (Past Comdr.), Knight of Golden Eagle (Past Chief). Club: Kiwanis. Home: 235 Spruce St. Office: High School Bldg., Middletown, Pa.

FEATHER, Harry Edgar, surgeon; b. Latrobe, Pa., Mar. 2, 1902; s. Curtis William and Gertrude Elizabeth (Campbell) F.; M.D., U. of Pittsburgh, 1926; m. Katherine Roth Emmerling, Dec. 18, 1928; children—Nancy Emmerling, Donald Edgar. Began as surgeon, 1926; instr. surgery U. of Pittsburgh Med. Sch. Reserve med officer U.S. Army. Fellow Am. Coll. Surgeons; mem. A.M.A., Pa. State Med. Assn., Pittsburgh Acad. of Medicine, Pittsburgh Surg. Soc., Allegheny Co. Med. Soc. Republican. Mason (Shriner). Clubs: University, Pittsburgh Athletic Assn. (Pittsburgh); Wildwood Country. Home: 1428 Greystone Dr. Office: 535 Medical Arts Bldg., Pittsburgh, Pa.

FEATHERSTON, Daniel Francis, surgeon; b. New York, N.Y., June 10, 1896; s. Daniel F. and Mary (Fitzgerald) F.; B.S., Dartmouth Coll., 1919; M.D., N.Y. Univ. Med. Sch. and Bellevue Hosp., 1922; m. Norma O'Connor, 1924; children—Daniel Francis, Jr., Ann. Engaged in practice of medicine at Asbury Park, N.J., and specializing in surgery; asst. surgeon Monmouth Memorial Hosp., Long Branch, N.J.; visiting surgeon Fitkin Memorial Hosp., Neptune, N.J.; cons. orthopedist Riverview Hosp., Red Bank, N.J.; dir. Seacoast Trust Co., Asbury Park, N.J. Fellow Am. Coll. Surgeons; mem. Am. Med. Assn., N.J. State Med. Soc., Monmouth Co. Med. Soc. (sec.). Roman Catholic. Home: 506 Fourth Av., Asbury Park, N.J.

FEDIGAN, Edward John, pres. E. J. Fedigan, Inc.; b. Pittsburgh, Pa., July 22, 1893; s. James Edward and Anna (Kearney) F.; ed. Epiphany Sch., St. Mary's Coll., Duquesne U., Pittsburgh; m. Eleanor Elford, Jan. 17, 1915; children—Eleanor, Betty, Edward, James E. Richard. Played professional baseball and football, 2 yrs.; sec. to sheriff of Allegheny Co. 1 yr.; later sec. to treas. Pittsburgh Construction Company; founded, 1914, and since president E. J. Fedigan, Inc., Pittsburgh. Elk. Clubs: Metropolitan, Teutania Maennerschor, Duquesne University Assn. (Pittsburgh). Home: 6433 Monitor St. Office: B. & O. Stores, N.S., Pittsburgh, Pa.

FEE, George Erskine, sch. supervisor; b. Stafford, Kan., Feb. 14, 1889; s. James Andrew and Amanda Isabelle (Cook) F.; grad. Stafford (Kan.) High Sch., 1911; B.S., Geneva Coll., Beaver Falls, Pa., 1916; studied U. of Pittsburgh, 1927-30; m. Ann Graham, July 14, 1929; children—James Graham, George Thomas, John Samuel. School teacher and coach, Beaver (Pa.) High Sch., 1916-17; employed in efficiency dept. Am. Bridge Co., 1917-18; teacher and athletic coach, Monongahela (Pa.) High Sch., 1919-20, Tarentum (Pa.) High Sch., 1920-22; supervising prin. of schs., Belle Vernon, Pa., since 1922. Entered U. S. Army, June 1918; hon. disch. as 2d lt., Feb. 1919. Reformed Presbyn. Mason. Home: Belle Vernon, Pa.

FEICK, Harry William, banker; b. Pittsburgh, Pa., Feb. 10, 1887; s. John Charles and Anna (Workmaster) F.; student pub. schs., Avalon, Pa.; m. Pearl Harger, July 19, 1912; children—Harry William, Donald Harger, Nancy Jane, Herman David. With Avalon Bank since 1905, beginning as bookkeeper, v.p. since 1929; v.p. and dir. Ohio Valley Bldg. & Loan Assn. Dir. Suburban Gen. Hosp. Republican. Mem. Reformed Ch. Mason (32°, Shriner). Clubs: Bankers (Pittsburgh); Butler Country (Avalon, Pa.). Home: 231 S. Home Av. Office: 600 California Av., Avalon, Pa.

FEIRER, William A(nthony), M.D.; b. Roselle Park, N.J., Jan. 18, 1900; s. Frank and Mary A. (Salzman) F.; B.S., Rutgers U., New Brunswick, N.J., 1922; D.Sc., Johns Hopkins U., 1925, M.D., 1930; m. Jeanne L. Corrington, Feb. 10, 1932. Began practice of medicine, 1930; asso. prof. bacteriology, Johns Hopkins U., 1923-30; staff physician Johns Hopkins Hosp., 1932-34; med. dir. Sharp & Dohme, Phila., since 1936. Mem. A.M.A., Am. Pub. Health Assn., Soc. Am. Bacteriologists, Sigma Xi, Alpha Omega Alpha. Republican. Author: Hexylresorcinal as a General Antiseptic; Wound Infections: Intestinal Flora; Drug Fastness and Rotation; etc. Home: 719 E. Dorset St. Office: 640 N. Broad St., Philadelphia, Pa.

FEISE, (Karl Richard Wilhelm) Ernst, prof. German; b. Braunschweig, Germany, June 8, 1884; s. Johannes and Auguste (Witzell) F.; Gymnasium, Braunschweig, 1893-1902; studied U. of Berlin, 1902-03, U. of München, 1903-05, U. of Leipzig, 1905-08, Ph. D.; m. Dorothy Flint Findlay, Sept. 6, 1910; children—Richard Ernst, Frederik Findlay, Dorelen. Came to U.S., 1908, naturalized citizen, 1931. Successively instr., asst. prof. and asso. prof. German, University of Wis., 1908-17; oberlehrer, Colegio Aleman, Mexico City, 1920-24; insp. English, Mexican pub. schs., 1923-24; asst. prof. German, Ohio State U., 1924-27; asso. prof. German, Johns Hopkins, 1927-28, prof. since 1928. Dir. Middlebury Coll. Sch. of German, Bristol, Vt., since 1931. Mem. Modern Lang. Assn. America, Am. Assn. of Univ. Profs., Am. Assn. Teachers of German (pres. 1939), Phi Beta Kappa. Club: Germania. Editor: Die Leiden des jungen Werthers (by Goethe), 1914; Hermann and Dorothea (by same), 1916. Co-Editor: Einsame Menschen (by Hauptmann), 1930; Gateway Books (gen. editor). Contbr. articles and revs. to periodicals. Home: 401 Rosebank Av., Baltimore, Md.

FELDMEYER, George T., dentist; b. Annapolis, Md., Oct. 28, 1859; s. Gotlieb and Dorothea (Oberry) F.; student pub. and pvt. schs., Annapolis, Md., 1866-76; D.D.S., U. of Md., Baltimore, 1888; m. Emma Nice Buch, of Phila., Apr. 26, 1899; 1 dau., Emma Nice. In practice at Annapolis, Md., since 1888; pres. Workingmen's Bldg. & Loan Assn., Annapolis, dir. Annapolis Dairy Products Co. Mem. Md. State Dental Assn. (pres., 1912-13; mem. bd. of govs.). Democrat. Methodist (treas., steward, mem. finance com., sec. Men's Bible Class, chorister, mem. choir Calvary Methodist Ch., Annapolis). Mason. Clubs: Triangle (Annapolis, Md.); Harris Hayden (hon. mem.; Baltimore). Address: 2 Southgate Av., Annapolis, Md.

FELIX, Anthony G., v.p. The Pa. Co. for Insurances on Lives and Granting Annuities; b. Philadelphia County, Pa., Jan. 25, 1885. Clubs: Philadelphia Country, Racquet, Union League (Phila.). Home: 343 Brookway Av., Merion, Pa. Office: Packard Bldg., Philadelphia, Pa.

FELIX, Otto Francis; b. Pittsburgh, Pa., June 18, 1862; s. Charles Francis and Mary (Ilg) F.; ed. pub. schs. and Iron City Business Coll.; m. Annie E. McCullough, June 29, 1892; children—Francis Chester, Gladys M. (Mrs. W. H. Herrick), Kenneth A., Fantine E. (Mrs. W. F. Healey), Romaine A. (Mrs. Eugene Lilly), Paul G., John D. Began as bookkeeper, 1878; organized, 1883, and sec. and treas. Pittsburgh Supply Co., 1883-1913; organized 1890, and sec. and treas. Equitable Meter Co., 1890-1927; one of organizers of Nat. Electric Products Co., 1908, and asso. same, 1908-28; retired from active business, 1928; dir. Pittsburgh Equitable Meter Co., Allegheny Trust Co., Real Estate Co. of Pittsburgh. Republican. Catholic. Clubs: Duquesne, Pittsburgh Athletic (Pittsburgh). Home: 204 Tennyson Av. Office: 307 4th Av., Pittsburgh, Pa.

FELL, Edgar Tremlett; mem. law firm Fell & Hartman. Address: Calvert Bldg., Baltimore, Md.

FELL, Frank J., Jr., ry. official; b. Philadelphia, Pa., July 29, 1878; s. Francis J. and Harriet (Markward) F.; student Temple U., Phila., Pa.; m. Cordelia Bromer, Apr. 12, 1911; children—William F., Mary B. Began with Pa. R.R. as clk. accounting dept., 1896, statistician, 1909-15, chief statistician, 1915-17, gen. accountant, 1917-18, asst. comptroller, 1918-25, dep. comptroller, 1925-27, comptroller, 1927; now v.p. and comptroller Pa. R.R., L.I.R.R., and affiliated lines; dir. Pa. R.R. Co., Central Penn. Nat. Bank (Phila.). Republican. Episcopalian. Mason (32°). Clubs: Union League, Kiwanis. Home: Phoenixville, Pa. Office: Broad St. Station Bldg., Philadelphia, Pa.

FELLER, Alexander, lawyer, author, lecturer; b. New Brunswick, N.J., Jan. 21, 1904; s. Meyer and Mary (Peshkin) F.; Litt.B., Rutgers U., 1924; LL.B., Columbia U. Law Sch., 1927; A.M., Columbia U. Grad. Sch., 1927; m. Freda Kaminsky, Feb. 17, 1933; children—Mark Richard, Paul Edward. Admitted to N.J. bar as atty., 1928, and engaged in pvt. practice Newark, and adv. counsel to Trust Dept., New Jersey Nat. Bank & Trust Co., 1928-29; mem. firm Feller & Feller, New Brunswick and Newark, 1930-35; mem. firm Schenck & Feller, New Brunswick, 1935-36; in practice alone at New Brunswick and Newark since 1936; lecturer on N.J. Pleading and Practice, Columbia U., since 1931; lecturer on govt., Rutgers U., summer 1926; asso. with Prof. R. R. B. Powell of Columbia U. in revising and codifying N.J. Real Property Statutes under supervision of Legislative Com. Mem. Am. and Middlesex County bar assns., Phi Epsilon Pi, Alpha Gamma Phi, Upsilon Lambda Phi. Democrat. Jewish religion. Club: Raritan Photographic (New Brunswick). Trustee Rutgers U. Fund Council. Co-author: How to Deal with Organized Labor, 1937; How to Operate Under the Wage-Hour Law, 1938. Asso. editor Current Legal Thought, 1934-36. Home: 225 Harrison Av., Highland Park. Office: 77 Paterson St., New Brunswick, also 744 Broad St., Newark, N.J.

FELLNER, Felix Joseph, prof. history; b. Rotthalmuenster, Bavaria, Nov. 24, 1874; s. Joseph and Emerentia (Wenig) F.; came to U.S., 1893, naturalized 1899; A.M., St. Vincent Coll., 1895; ed. St. Vincent Sem., 1896-1901; (hon.) LL.D., St. Vincent Coll., 1934. Ordained priest R.C. Ch., 1901; prof. history, St. Vincent Coll., Latrobe, Pa., since 1904. Mem. Cath. Hist. Assn., Hist. Soc. Western Pa. Democrat. Roman Catholic. Author: St. Vincenz Gemeinde und Erzabtei, 1905. Contbr. articles to hist. mags. and journs. Home: St. Vincent Archabbey, Latrobe, Pa.

FELS, Samuel S., mfr.; b. Yanceyville, N.C., Feb. 16, 1860; s. Lazarus and Susannah F.; student high school, Philadelphia, Pa., 2 yrs.; LL.D., University of Pennsylvania, June, 1937; m. Jennie May, May 15, 1890. Partner Fels & Co., soap mfrs., 1881 until incorpn., 1914, since pres.; pres. Paschall Oxygen Co. Trustee Wistar Inst., Franklin Inst. Author: This Changing World, 1933. Home: 39th and Walnut St. Office: 73d and Woodland Av., Philadelphia, Pa.

FELTON, Holden S.; in gen. practice of law since 1914; now referee in bankruptcy. Address: Frederick, Md.

FENE, William J., mining engr.; b. Huntington, Ark., Mar. 18, 1891; s. William and Ella (Marks) F.; student U. of Ark., and Okla. Sch. of Mines; m. Wilhelmina Planthaber, Dec. 29, 1928; children—W. Richard, Kim M. Assayer, ore buyer and development of zinc mines in North Arkansas, 1915-18; state highway engr., Ark., 1919-20; mining engr. U.S. Bur. of Mines, Pittsburgh, since 1921. Mem. Coal

Mining Inst. of America, Mine Rescue Assn. of America. Mason. Writer numerous articles pub. by U.S. Bur. of Mines on mining accidents, coal mine explosions, accident prevention and protection for miners, accident causes, accident prevention devices, etc. Home: 811 Virginia Av. Office: 4800 Forbes St., Pittsburgh, Pa.

FENERTY, Clare Gerald, ex-congressman; b. Philadelphia; A.B. and J.D., St. Joseph's Coll., Phila.; LL.B., U. of Pa.; LL.D., Loyola Coll., Baltimore; studied Hahnemann Med. Coll. and U.S. Naval War Coll.; m. Miriam Elizabeth Loughran, 1934; 1 dau. Admitted to Pennsylvania bar and practiced in Philadelphia; mem. law faculty Wharton School, Univ. of Pa., 5 yrs.; mem. Bd. Phila. Law Examiners since 1926; asst. dist. atty., 1928-35; mem. 74th Congress (1935-37), 3d Pa. Dist. Served with U.S. Navy, A.E.F., 1917-18; now sr. lt. U.S. Naval Res. Republican. Home: 2618 Thompson St. Office: Land Title Bldg., Philadelphia, Pa.

FENHAGEN, George Corner, architect; b. Baltimore, Md., Dec. 7, 1884; s. Charles Denny and Jane (Corner) F.; student U. of Pa., 1903-05, Am. Acad. in Rome, Italy, 1906-07; m. Mildred Thurston Pierce, Sept. 10, 1911 (died 1919); children—George Corner, Jr., J. Pierce; m. 2d, Helen Weston, Oct. 14, 1921 (died 1926); 1 son, F. Weston; m. 3d, Mary Ford Pringle, June 30, 1929; 1 dau., Christina Wood. In employ Pell & Corbett, N.Y. City, 1905-06, 1907-10; asst. cons. architect, Philippine govt., 1911-14, const. architect, 1914-16; mem. firm Sill, Buckler & Fenhagen, architects, Baltimore, Md., 1916-21, Buckler & Fenhagen since 1921; asst. prof. design, U. of Pa., 1923. Mem. Md. Bd. for Registration of Architects. Mem. council Md. Hist. Soc. Fellow Am. Inst. Architects (past pres. Baltimore Chapter). Mem. Alumni Soc. Am. Acad. in Rome. Awarded Alumni travelling fellowship U. of Pa., 1906. Democrat. Club: 14 W. Hamilton St. (Baltimore); Philippine (New York). Home: 916 St. Paul St. Office: 325 N. Charles St., Baltimore, Md.

FENHAGEN, James Corner, banker; b. Baltimore, Md., Aug. 10, 1875; s. Charles D. and Jane Dungan (Corner) F.; student Friends' Sch., Baltimore; m. Marion G. Stansbury, Sept. 12, 1899. Clk. and officer Mchts. Nat. Bank., Baltimore, 1892-1905; v.p. and cashier Md. Nat. Bank, Baltimore, 1905-11; partner Robert Garrett & Sons, Baltimore, 1911-31; chmn. trust com., Baltimore Trust Co., 1932-33; chmn. exec. com. Baltimore Nat. Bank since 1933; also dir.; mem. exec. and finance coms. and dir. Commercial Credit Co., Baltimore; mem. exec. com. and dir. Md. Casualty Co., Baltimore; dir. A. S. Abell Co. (pubs. Baltimore Sun), Md. Drydock Co., Consolidation Coal Co. Mem. exec. and finance coms. Community Fund of Baltimore, Inc. Republican. Presbyterian. Clubs: Maryland, Elkridge, Chesapeake (Baltimore, Md.). Home: 2 Wyndhurst Av. Office: care Baltimore Nat. Bank, Baltimore, Md.

FENIAS, Edward, lawyer; b. Brooklyn, N.Y., Aug. 9, 1898; s. Edward and Julia (Krauss) F.; student U. of Mich., 1916-19; student N.Y. Univ., 1919-22; m. Miriam Germanus, Nov. 25, 1936. Engaged in practice of law at Newark; instr. philosophy and ethics, N.J. Inst. for Social Research; instr. Citizens Union Inst. for Polit. Research; pres. N.J. Inst. for Social Research; sec. Newark Oxwelding Corpn. Chmn. Newark Citizens Union. Mem. Essex Co. Bar Assn., Phi Sigma Delta. Home: 25 Hansbury Av. Office: 60 Park Place, Newark, N.J.

FENLON, John F., univ. pres.; b. Chicago, Ill., June 23, 1873; s. Thomas and Mary (O'Keeffe) F.; student St. Ignatius Coll., Chicago, 1891; A.B., St. Mary's Sem., Baltimore, 1895, A.M., 1896; D.D., Angelico U., Rome, Italy, 1900; hon. grad. study Johns Hopkins, 1894-96, Sapienza U., Rome, 1898-1900. Ordained priest R.C. Ch., 1896; curate Holy Name Cathedral, Chicago, 1896-98; prof. Holy Scriptures, St. Joseph Sem., Yonkers, N.Y., 1901-04, St. Mary's Sem., Baltimore, 1904-19; pres. St. Austin's Coll., Washington, D.C., 1904-11; pres. Divinity Coll., Cath. U. of America, Washington, 1911-24; pres. Sulpician Sem., Washington, 1924-25; pres. St. Mary's Sem. and Univ., Baltimore, since 1925; provincial of Sulpicians in U.S. since 1925. Secretary Nat. Cath. War Council, 1917-22. Sec. Nat. Cath. Welfare Conf., 1919-26. Contbr. to Johns Hopkins Journal, and other reviews. Address: St. Mary's Seminary, Roland Park, Baltimore, Md.

FENN, Don Frank, clergyman; b. Wichita, Kan., Dec. 31, 1890; s. Frank and Belle (Edwards) F.; B.D., Nashotah House (Wis.), 1915, D.D., 1931; m. Addie Kelly, Nov., 1916 (died Aug., 1929); 1 son, Don Perry; m. 2d, Cleos Lepha Rockwell, Apr. 16, 1932; 1 dau., Janet Rockwell, Deacon, 1914, priest, P.E., Ch., 1915; rector Calvary Ch., Golden, Colo., 1915-17; rector Christ Ch., Canon City, Colo.; vicar St. Alban's Ch., Florence, Colo., and chaplain Colo. State Penitentiary, 1917-22; rector Gethsemane Ch., Minneapolis, Minn., 1922-31, Ch. of St. Michael and All Angel's Ch., Baltimore, Md. since 1931; mem. faculty various summer confs.; mem. faculty Md. Diocesan Ch. Mission for Help; chmn. coms. Apportionments and Canons and mem. Commn. on City Mission for Diocese of Md.; 1st v.p. Nat. Ch. Mission of Help (mem. of exec. com.); mem. Standing Com. of Diocese of Md.; dep. to Gen. Convs., 1919, 25, 28, 37; mem. bd. trustees Ch. Home and Infirmary; mem. bd. dirs. Council of Social Agencies in Baltimore; mem. bd. dirs. Family Welfare Assn. of Baltimore; pres. Maryland Clericus; mem. social clerics dept., Diocese of Md. Trustee Hannah More Acad., Reisterstown, Md., Nashotah House. Democrat. Mason. Club: Optimist of Baltimore (chaplain). Author: Parish Administration. Contbr. articles to ch. publs. Home: 4210 Wickford Rd. Office: 20th and St. Paul Sts., Baltimore, Md.

FENNER, Clarence Norman, geologist; b. nr. Paterson, N.J., July 19, 1870; s. William Griff and Elmina Jane (Carpenter) F.; E.M., Sch. of Mines (Columbia), 1892, A.M., Columbia, 1909, Ph.D., 1910; unmarried. Mining and economic geol. work in U.S., Can., Mexico, Central and S. America, 1892-1907; petrologist Geophys. Lab., Carnegie Instn., Washington, D.C., 1910-37, research asso., 1937-Feb. 1938, engaged on researches in application of physics and chemistry to geology, retired, Feb. 1938; expd. of N.Y. Academy Sciences on geolog. reconnaissance of Porto Rico, 1914; researches on optical glass for mil. purposes under War Industries Bd. (in charge one of prin. plants), 1917-1918; geologist Nat. Geog. expdn. to Valley of 10,000 Smokes, Alaska, 1919; leader of 2d expdn. sent by Geophys. Lab. to same locality, 1923; rep. of Geol. Soc. America on Nat. Research Council, 1925-28 (mem. exec. com. div. geology and geography, 1926-28). Fellow Geol. Soc. America, Am. Phys. Soc., A.A.A.S.; mem. Am. Inst. Mining and Metall. Engrs., Wash. Acad. Sciences, N.Y. Acad. Sciences, Am. Geophysical Union (chmn. sect. of volcanology, 1933-35), Geol. Soc. of Washington (pres. 1933); foreign corr. Geol. of London. Writer of many scientific papers, especially on geol. and volcanological subjects. Club: Cosmos. Home: 64 Broad St., Clifton, N.J.

FENNING, Karl, lawyer, b. Washington, D.C., Mar. 30, 1881; s. James A. and Annie R. (Dey) F.; grad. Central High Sch., Washington, D.C.; A.B., Trinity Coll., Conn., 1903, A.M.; LL.B., Nat. U., Washington, D.C., 1904; M.P.L., Columbian (now George Washington) U.; m. Hazel M. O'Neil, June 7, 1917. Mem. bar, D.C., N.Y. and Ohio; practiced at Washington, D.C., 1904-06 and 1925—, N.Y. City, 1906-11, Cleveland, 1911-21; asst. commr. of patents, by apptmt. of Pres. Harding, 1921-25; prof. patent law, Georgetown U. since 1923; spl. asst. to atty. gen. of U.S., 1925-28; editor U.S. Patents Quar. since 1929. Chmn. Nat. Com. on Patent Legislation, 10 yrs.; chmn. legislative committee of National Council of Patent Law Association; mem. advisory council Com. on Patents, U.S. House of Repr. Mem. Am. Bar Assn., Friends Law Library of Congress (sec.), Am. Patent Law Assn., Am. Acad. Air Law, Internat. Assn. for Protection of Industrial Property (vice-pres. Am. group), Phi Gamma Delta; an organizer Cleveland Patent Law Assn. Republican. Presbyn. Clubs: Cosmos, Chevy Chase (Washington, D.C.); Phi Gamma Delta (New York). Co-author of first circulars giving general information as to patents and trade marks issued by U.S. Patent Office. Contbr. numerous articles on copyrights, patents, trade marks and the Patent Office. Home: 5863 Chevy Chase Parkway, Chevy Chase, D.C.; and Hazelfen, Gaithersburg, Md. Address: National Press Bldg., Washington, D.C.

FENNO, George Francis, sales engr.; b. New York, N.Y., Aug. 12, 1884; s. George N. and Ida (Tuthill) F.; B.S., Coll. of City of N.Y., 1903; M.E., Cornell U., 1906; m. Ada Vaughan, Apr. 20, 1910. Test engr. Bell Telephone Co., 1906-07; insurance insp. Middle States Inspection Bureau, 1907-09; partner George H. Gibson Co., 1909-13; sales mgr. Richardson-Phenix Co., 1913-17; vice-pres. Kissick Fenno Co., Phila., 1919-32; pres. Fenno-Fischer Co., manufacturer's rep., since 1932. Served as capt. Air Service, U.S. Army, 1917-19. Mem. Am. Inst. Elec. Engrs. Republican. Methodist. Clubs: Engineers, Rolling Green Golf, Cornell, Ben Franklin (Phila.). Home: 309 Swarthmore Av., Swarthmore, Pa. Office: 935 S. 53rd St., Philadelphia, Pa.

FENTON, Beatrice, sculptor; b. Philadelphia, Pa., July 12, 1887; d. Thomas Hanover (M.D.) and Lizzie Spear (Remak) F.; ed. under governesses; art study, Sch. Industrial Art, Phila., 1903-04, Pa. Acad. Fine Arts, 1904-11; 2 Cresson European scholarships, 1909 and 10; unmarried. Prin. works: Seaweed Fountain, Fairmount Park, Phila.; Fairy Fountain, Wister Woods, Phila.; bronze memorial tablet to Charles M. Schmitz, Acad. Music, Phila.; Eyre gold medal design, Phila. Water Color Club; Nereid Fountain and Boy and Starfish Fountain, private estates; bust of Peter Moran, bust of Thomas H. Fenton and statuette of John F. Huneker Philadelphia Art Club; bust of William Penn, Penn Club, Philadelphia; bust of Marjorie D. Martinet, Martinet Sch. of Art, Baltimore; bust of I. P. Strittmater, M.D., Phila.; "Wood-Music," Danby Park, Wilmington, Del.; gate-post figures, Children's Hosp., Philadelphia; bust of Felix E. Schelling, Univ. of Pa.; garden sculpture, "Bacchanale" and "Leaping Dolphin Fountain"; Turner Memorial tablet, Johns Hopkins Univ.; Ariel sun-dial, Shakespeare Garden U. of Pa. Mem. National Association Women Painters and Sculptors, National Sculpture Society, Fellowship of Pennsylvania Academy Fine Arts. Winner of McClellan anatomy prize, 1907; Edmund Stewardson prize for sculpture, 1908 (both at Pa. Acad. Fine Arts); hon. mention, Panama-Pacific Internat. Expn., 1915, Plastic Club, 1916; George D. Widener memorial gold medal, Pa. Acad. Fine Arts, 1922; Fellowship of Pa. Acad. Fine Arts prize, 1922; silver medal, Plastic Club, 1922; bronze medal, Sesquicentennial Internat. Expn., Phila., 1926. Club: Art Alliance. Home: 621 Westview St., Mt. Airy, Phila. Studio: 1824 Cherry St., Philadelphia, Pa.

FENTRESS, Helena (Trafford) Devereux (Mrs. James Fentress), educator; b. Phila., Pa.; d. Arthur Trafford and Betsy (Blyton) Devereux; ed. Phila. Normal Sch., Temple U. and U. of Pa; m. James Fentress. Formerly teacher in primary sch., Phila., and Phila. Normal Sch.; founder, 1912, and since dir. Devereux Tutoring Schs., also Devereux Farm Sch. and Devereux Pines Camps in Maine. Mem. bd. dirs. Juvenile Protective Assn., Mental Hygiene Soc. of Ill. Mem. P.E.O. Sisterhood. Congregationalist. Clubs: Chicago Woman's; Winnetka Woman's, Winnetka Questors. Home: Old Lancaster Road, Devon, Pa.

FENWICK, Charles Ghequiere, political scientist; b. Baltimore, Md., May 26, 1880; s. Henry Martin and Gay (Tiernan) F.; A.B., Loyola Coll., Baltimore, 1907; Ph.D., Johns Hopkins, 1912; unmarried. Law clk. div. of internat. law, Carnegie Endowment for Internat. Peace, 1911-14; lecturer on internat. law, Washington Coll. of Law, 1912-14; asso. in polit. science, 1914-15, asso. prof., 1915-18, prof., 1918—, Bryn Mawr Coll. U.S. del. to Inter-Am. Conf. for Maintenance of Peace, Buenos Aires, 1936; del. to 8th Internat. Conf. of Am. States, Lima, 1938. Mem. Am. Polit. Science Assn., Am. Soc.

Internat. Law, American Academy Political and Social Science, International Law Association. Associate editor Internat. Law Journal. Catholic. Author: The Neutrality Laws of the United States (Carnegie Endowment for Internat. Peace), 1913; Political Systems in Transition, 1920; (with W. W. Willoughby) Types of Restricted Sovereignty and of Colonial Autonomy (Govt. Printing Office), 1919; International Law, 1924, 1934; Cases on International Law, 1935; Cases on Constitutional Law, 1938. Translator of Vattel's Droit des Gens, 1914; Schucking's Der Staatenverband der Haager Konferenzen, and also of Wehberg's Das Problem eines internationalen Staatengerichtshofes, 1915. Home: Bryn Mawr, Pa.

FERGUSON, Arthur Wesley, supt. schs.; b. Phila., Pa., Apr. 20, 1890; s. Rev. William A. and Carrie L. (Lake) F.; B.S., U. of Pa., 1912, Ph.D., 1924; A.M., Lafayette Coll., Easton, Pa., 1920; m. Mary Leila Wells, Dec. 27, 1915; 1 son, William Wells. Engaged as prin. pub. schs. and teacher high schs., 1912-21; supt. schs., Swarthmore, Pa., 1923-30; supt. schs., York, Pa. since 1930; lecturer, Swarthmore Coll., 1924-30; visiting prof., U. of Pa. summer sch., 1926, 1927, 1937, Pa. State Coll., 1925, U. of Pittsburgh, 1928. Mem. Nat. and Pa. State edn. assns., Am. Assn. Sch. Adminstrs., Phi Delta Kappa, Pa. Schoolmen's Club. Republican. Presbyn. Mason. Clubs: Lafayette, Rotary (York, Pa.). Home: 500 Roosevelt Av., York, Pa.

FERGUSON, Charles Walker, judge; b. Wayne, W.Va., Dec. 30, 1892; s. Lucian B. and Fannie P. (Ferguson) F.; student Oak View Acad., Wayne, W.Va., 1900-08, Marshall Coll., Huntington, W.Va., 1908-12; LL.B., U. of Mich., Ann Arbor, Mich., 1915; m. Shirley Burgess, Nov. 29, 1919; children—Charles Walker III, Dorothy. Admitted to bar, 1915; prosecuting atty., Wayne Co., W.Va., 1917-29 (3 terms); judge, 24th Judicial Circuit, W.Va., since 1929 (in 2d term). Served as 2d lt., F.A., U.S. Army, during World War. Trustee Morris Harvey Coll., Charleston, W.Va. Mem. W.Va. State Bar Assn., Delta Chi. Democrat. Methodist. Mason. Address: Wayne, W.Va.

FERGUSON, Daniel LeRoy, Jr., educator; b. Salem, Va., April 7, 1891; s. Daniel LeRoy and Sara Elizabeth (Eddens) F.; student Raymond City Elementary Sch., Putnam Co., W.Va., 1897-1900; Garnet Elementary Sch., Charleston, 1900-05, Garnet High Sch., 1905-06; grad. W.Va. Colored Inst., Institute, W.Va., 1909, studied summers, 1910-12; B.S. in Agr., Ohio State U. (class orator, and Varsity "O"), 1916, M.S., 1917, post-grad. study, summers, 1928, 29; m. Katherine Watson Stewart, Jan. 2, 1918; children—Jane Elizabeth, Daniel LeRoy, Katherine Lyndall, Stewart Alexander, Warne Leon, Joseph Tobias, Raynina Hope. Successively bootblack, water-boy in boarding house, bell boy, farmer, teacher, high sch. teacher, college teacher, dean of coll., W.Va. Collegiate Inst.; coll. teacher, W.Va. State Coll., W.Va. U., 1919, extension agent, 1922-23, asso. prof. and head dept. sociology, and chmn. social studies div., W.Va., State Coll., since 1934; mem. exec. bd. Ferguson Hotel; dir. W.Va. Four "H" Park Assn. Entered U.S. Army, Oct. 30, 1917, as private, transferred to Officers' Machine Gun Training Sch., Camp Hancock, Ga., grad. with honors, commd. 2d lt., served as capt., comding. 84th Machine Gun Co. Del. to State Republican Conv., 1932 and 1936; supervisor Kanawha County Housing Survey of 1349 households. Mem. Nat. Com. on Parent Edn.; chmn. State Com. on Parent Edn.; chmn. Child Welfare Com.; pres. W.Va. Safety Organization for Negroes; pres. Community League; chmn. Recreational Council, Institute, W.Va. Mem. W.Va. State Teachers Assn. (mem. legislative com. and chmn. health and safety div.), W.Va. Athletic Union (pres. 1932-34), Am. Legion, W.Va. Federated Social Agencies (v.p.), Am. Legion, Am. Acad. Polit. and Social Science, Southern Sociol. Soc., Assn. for Study Negro Life and History, Alpha Phi Alpha, Pi Gamma Mu. Republican. Baptist. Mason (32°, Shriner). Clubs: Charleston Professional Men's; El Cubo Civic (Institute, W. Va.). Home: Institute, W.Va.

FERGUSON, James W(alter), physician; b. Jeannette, Pa., Jan. 26, 1886; s. Samuel and Margaret (Busch) F.; ed. Grove City Coll., 1905-07; M.D., U. of Pittsburgh Med. Sch., 1911; m. Sara B. Trout, July 8, 1911; children—James, Margaret. Field surgeon West Moreland Coal Co., 1911-13, Pittsburgh Coal Co., 1913-22, Pittsburgh & L.E. R.R., 1914-18; U. of Mich. X-Ray Dept., 1924; demonstrator in roentgenology, U. of Pittsburgh Free Dispensary, 1926-34; instr. roentgenology, U. of Pittsbugh Falk Clinic since 1934; engaged in practice of medicine in Pittsburgh since 1926, specializing in radiology since 1922. Mem. A.M.A., Allegheny Co. Med. Soc., Pa. Med. Soc., Diplomate Am. Board of Radiology. Republican. Presbyterian. Mason (K.T., 32°, Shriner). Home: 338 S. Linden Av. Office: 500 Penn Av., Pittsburgh, Pa.

FERGUSON, John Berton, civil engr.; b. Woburn, Mass., Jan. 8, 1877; s. John and Annette Elizabeth (Teare) F.; prep. edn. pub. schs., Woburn, Mass.; B.S. in civil engring., Mass. Inst. Tech., 1899; m. Beulah Lippincott Darby, Sept. 21, 1904; 1 son, John Berton. Began as asst. div. engr. C.B.& Q. R.R., June 1899, asst. and div. engr., 1899-1902; transit man and asst. supervisor Pa. R.R., 1902-06; roadway engr. Ohio Electric Ry., 1906-09; sr. partner J. B. Ferguson & Co., engrs., Hagerstown, Md., 1909-20, propr., 1920-39; city engr. Hagerstown, Md., 1914-27; chief engr. Hagerstown Sewer. Commn., 1916-25; Washington County surveyor, 1916-30; supervising engr. Camp Eustis, Balloon Observers Sch. and Camp Morrison to Yorktown Road Projects, Va., constrn. Div. War Dept., 1918-20; mgr. of Hagerstown Homes Corpn., 1920; dir. Western Md. Ry. Co. Vice-pres. and sec. Washington Co. Free Library; trustee Washington Co. Museum Fine Arts; pres. Washington Co. Council Boy Scouts America, 1927-38; pres. Hagerstown Chamber of Commerce, 1930-39; mem. Md. Geol. and Econ. Survey Commn., 1923-33; mem. Md. Commn. N.Y. World's Fair. Mem. Am. Soc. C.E. Awarded Silver Beaver Award, Boy Scouts of America, 1938. Ind. Republican. Clubs: Rotary, Antietam Archers (Hagerstown, Md.). Contbr. articles to mags. and newspapers. Home: 518 Brown Av. Office: 312 W. Washington St., Hagerstown, Md.

FERGUSON, John Maxwell, univ. professor; b. Chicago, Ill., April 3, 1890; s. Franklin La Du and Margaret Jeannette (Maxwell) F.; A.B., Harvard, 1908; A.M., Columbia, 1911, Ph.D., 1927; Jur. Dr., Leipzig Univ., Germany, 1912; unmarried. Instr. in economics, Vassar Coll., 1915-17; asst. prof. of economics, U. of Kan., 1918-20; asst. prof. of economics, U. of Pittsburgh, 1927-37, asso. prof. since 1937. Served with U.S. Army, 1917-19. Mem. Am. Econ. Assn., Am. Assn. Univ. Profs., Order of Artus, Phi Kappa Psi. Republican. Congregationalist. Clubs: Harvard (New York); Harvard of Western Pa.; Authors (Pittsburgh). Author: Das Deutsche Eisenbahnsystem, 1912; Social Workers Handbook, 1913; State Regulation of Railroads in the South, 1916; Landmarks of Economic Thought, 1938. Home: Hotel Fairfax. Office: Univ. of Pittsburgh, Pittsburgh, Pa.

FERGUSON, John William, corpn. official; b. Tiffin, O., Dec. 19, 1857; s. Peter and Jeanette (Bixby) F.; prep. edn. pub. schs. and high sch., New Haven, Conn.; m. Jennie Beam Cooke, May 25, 1892; children—John William (dec.), Arthur Donald, Jean B. (Mrs. L. L. Buck). Began engring. career with Lehigh & Wilkes-Barre Coal Co., 1875; with Boston & N.Y. Air Line R.R., 1875-77; in engring. dept. N.Y., Lake Erie & Western R.R., through grades to asst. chief engr., 1878-91; entered business for self in engring. and bldg. constrn., 1892; pres. John W. Ferguson Co., Inc., since 1895; also hon. pres. Mfrs. Assn. of N.J. and Affiliates, Alexander Hamilton Hotel Corpn.; v.p. Cedar Lawn Cemetery Co.; dir. Paterson Nat. Bank. Mem. Nat. Industrial Conf. Bd., Am. Soc. of Mech. Engrs., Gen. Soc. of Mechanics and Tradesmen of N.Y., Am. Soc. of Civil Engrs., S.A.R. Clubs: Engineers (New York); Hamilton (Paterson); Arcola Country. Home: 421 12th Av. Office: 152 Market St., Paterson, N.J.

FERGUSON, Lewis Kraeer, surgeon; b. Caledonia, N.Y., April 29, 1897; s. Huber and Caroline (Kraeer) F.; A.B., Westminster Coll., 1918; M.D., U. of Pa. Med. Sch., 1923; m. Elizabeth Gardiner, Sept. 26, 1926; children—Jean Gardiner, Carolyn Kraeer. Began practice of medicine, 1925; asso. in surgery, U. of Pa., 1931-38, asst. prof. since 1938; asst. surgeon, U. of P. Hosp., 1929-37, surgeon since 1937; surgeon, Phila. Gen. Hosp. Fellow Am. Coll. Surgeons; mem. Phila. Acad. of Surgeons, John Morgan Soc.; Assn. Asso. mem. Am. Gastro-enterological Assn. United Presbyterian. Club: Philadelphia Country. Author: Surgical Nursing (with Dr. E. L. Eliason and Elizabeth Keller Lewis), 1929; also numerous med. articles. Translator: Operative Gynecology (from German, by Peham and Amreich), 1934. Home: McClenaghan Mill Road, Penn Valley, Narberth P.O., Pa. Office: 133 S. 36th St., Philadelphia, Pa.

FERGUSON, Melville Foster, editor, author; b. Phila., Pa., Sept. 8, 1874; s. John L. and Emma Josephine (Ball) F.; A.B., Central High Sch., Phila., 1893; m. Margaret Evelyn Stein, June 28, 1899; children—Dorothy Elizabeth, Marjorie Josephine (wife of Dr. Horace R. Blank), Katharine Murray. Began as reporter with Phila. Record, May 30, 1896, editorial writer, 1903-23, mng. editor, 1923-25, editor, 1926-28; editorial writer Evening Bulletin, 1929-37, chief of editorial page since 1937. Presbyn. Author: Motor Camping on Western Trails, 1925. Home: 139 E. Durham St., Philadelphia, Pa.

FERGUSON, Nancy Maybin, artist; b. Phila., Pa.; d. George Sloan and Margaret (Maybin) F.; ed. Girls High Sch., Phila., Phila. Sch. Design for Women, Pa. Acad. Fine Arts. Work has been exhibited in Carnegie Inst. (N.Y.), Acad. of Design (Phila.), Phila. Acad. of Fine Arts, Corcoran Biennial (Washington, D.C.), Buffalo, Detroit, Milwaukee, Boston, California, Texas and Paris Salon; represented in Phila. Acad. of Fine Arts, Reading Mus. and other collections. Did Red Cross work with disabled soldiers and their families after World War. Mem. Fellowship of Pa. Acad. of Fine Arts, Phila. Sch. of Design Alumnæ, Provincetown Art Assn., Phila. Art Alliance. Awarded Phila. Sch. of Design European Fellowship; Pa. Acad. Fine Arts European Fellowship; 1st and 2d Tappan Prizes, Pa. Acad. Fine Arts; hon. mention, Nat. Assn. Women Painters and Sculptors, N.Y., gold medal, Men's Sketch Club, Phila.; Fellowship of Pa. Acad. of Fine Arts First Prize; prize from Gimbel's Store, Phila., for being selected by Art Jury as best woman painter in Phila. and vicinity. Republican. Episcopalian. Home: 53 W. Tulpeho Green St., Germantown, Philadelphia, Pa.; (summer home), Provincetown, Cape Cod, Mass.

FERGUSON, Smith Farley, chmn. bd. Gen. Time Instruments Corpn.; b. Essex, N.Y., Sept. 8, 1872; s. Everard D. and Marion A. (Farley) F.; Ph.B., Yale, 1894; m. Margaret C. Florence, June 8, 1918. With Ludlow Valve Mfg. Co., Troy, N.Y., 1894-1903; pres. Mackenzie, Quarrier & Ferguson, Inc., engrs. and contrs., New York, 1903-14; mem. Hill & Ferguson, cons. engrs., New York, 1914-22; dir. and active in management Seth Thomas Clock Co. since 1925; v.p. Gen. Time Instruments Corpn., 1931-36, chmn. bd. dirs. since 1936; dir. Stromberg Time Corpn. Dir. N.Y. Assn. for the Blind. Mem. Clock Mfrs. Association of America (now pres.), Delta Phi. Republican. Episcopalian. Clubs: University, Yale, Merchants (New York); Short Hills (Short Hills, N.J.); Graduates (New Haven, Conn.) Home: Stewart Rd., Short Hills, N.J. Office: 109 Lafayette St., New York, N.Y.

FERGUSON, Walter Dewey, asso. prof. English; b. Fairville, Pa., Dec. 8, 1897; s. Charles Philip and Jessie (Black) F.; ed. West Chester Normal Sch., 1915-17; A.B., U. of Pa., 1921, A.M., same, 1924, Ph.D., same, 1932; m. Mary Minshall, June 17, 1922; children—Russell Myers, Ellen Louise, Mary Alice. Began as teacher in pub. sch., 1917; prin. pub. schs., Morton, Pa., 1918-19; instr. English, Ga. Sch. Tech., Atlanta, 1921-23; asst. instr., U. of Pa., 1923-25; instr. English, Temple U., Phila., Pa.,

1925-33, asst. prof., 1933-36, asso. prof. since 1936. Served as cadet officer heavy arty., Fortress Monroe, 1918. Mem. Philomathean Soc. (U. of Pa.). Republican. United Presbyn. Home: 8244 Brookside Rd., Elkins Park, Philadelphia, Pa.

FERGUSON, William Hugh, artist; b. Reading, Pa., Sept. 8, 1905; s. Hugh and May (Deppen) F.; studied Pa. Acad. of Fine Arts and in Europe (2 European scholarships); unmarried. Artist, painter, since 1926. Exhibited: one-man show, Gimble Modern Art Gallery, 1937; Penn Acad. Annual, 1937, 38; Chicago Internat. Water Color, 1938, 39; one-man show, Art Alliance and Valentine Gallery, New York, 1938. Home: 1335 Perkiomen Av., Reading, Pa.

FERNALD, Ernest Mercer, coll. prof.; b. New York, N. Y., Oct. 7, 1893; s. Frederik A. and Natalie (Richmond) F.; M.E., Cornell U., 1915, M.M.E., 1925; m. Mrs. Matilda Bates Atkinson, Oct. 15, 1928. Asst. mech. engr. Remington Arms Co., 1915-17; asst. engr. of tests Washington Navy Yard, 1917-23; instr. exptl. engring., Cornell U., 1923-27; asst. prof. mech. engring., Lafayette Coll., 1927-31, asso. prof., 1931-35, prof. since 1935; registered professional engr. in Pa. Mem. Am. Soc. Mech. Engrs., Soc. for Promotion Engring. Edn., Am. Assn. Univ. Profs., Am. Museum Natural Science. Episcopalian. Club: Faculty. Author: Elements of Thermodynamics, 1930, 2d edit., 1938; also various tech. articles. Home: 215 W. Lafayette St., Easton, Pa.

FERNALD, Henry Barker; b. McConnelsville, O., Jan. 9, 1878; s. James Champlin and Nettie (Barker) F.; A.B., New York U., 1901; C.P.A., 1909; m. Emma Woolley, Nov. 21, 1907; children—Henry Barker, Elizabeth. Went to Philippines as teacher pub. schs., 1901, and became dep. div. supt. schs., Isabella Province, later dep. provincial treas.; returned to U.S., 1906; entered employ Suffern & Son, C.P.A., and was admitted to firm, 1909; organized, 1914, firm of Loomis, Suffern & Fernald, of which is now sr. partner. Apptd., 1917, by Gov. Edge, as his spl. asst. in charge preparation of newly established N.J. State Budget, and continued under Govs. Edwards and Silzer. Member of Council, New York U.; mem. com. on federal finance Chamber of Commerce of U.S.; vice chmn. Commn. on fiscal questions, International Chamber of Commerce; has served on taxation coms. of Am. Inst. Mining Engrs., and Mining and Metall. Soc. America, Am. Mining Congress, etc.; known as an authority on mining taxation. Mem. N.J. Militia Reserve, 1917-18. Mem. Am. Inst. Accountants, N.Y. State Soc. C.P.A.'s, N.J. Soc. C.P.A.'s (pres. 1931-33), Nat. Assn. Cost Accountants, Ohio Soc., Accountants Club America, Alumni Fed. of New York Univ. (pres. 1935-37), S.A.R., Zeta Psi, Phi Beta Kappa; asso. mem. Am. Inst. Mining and Metall. Engrs. Republican. Baptist. Clubs: Down Town (Newark); Bankers, Lotos, Mining, University, Zeta Psi, Philippine Club of New York; Metropolitan, University (Washington, D.C.); Montclair Athletic, Upper Montclair Country. Contbr. articles on accounting and tax subjects. Home: 145 Lorraine Av., Upper Montclair, N.J. Office: 80 Broad St., New York, N.Y.

FERNBERGER, Samuel Weiller, prof. psychology; b. Phila., Pa., June 4, 1887; s. Henry and Julia (Weiller) F.; B.S., U. of Pa., 1908, A.M., 1909, Ph.D., same, 1912; m. Eve Wallerstein, July 12, 1922; children—Edward, John Marshall. Asst. in psychology, U. of Pa., 1908-10, instr., 1910-12; instr. psychology, Clark U., 1912-15, asst. prof., 1915-20; asst. prof. psychology, U. of Pa., 1920-27, prof. since 1927; lecturer, Curtis Inst. of Music, 1926-28. Served as 2d lieut. then 1st lieut. inf., U.S.A., 1917-19. Dec. with Croix de Guerre (France). Fellow A.A.A.S.; mem. Am. Psychol. Assn. (treas. 1922-24, sec. 1926-28), Soc. Exptl. Psychologists (sec. since 1928), Nat. Inst. Psychology (pres. since 1936), Eastern Psychol. Assn. (pres. 1936), Sigma Xi. Democrat. Reformed Jewish religion. Mason. Clubs: Lenape, British Officers (Philadelphia); Brodheads Forest and Stream (Analomink, Pa.). Author: Elementary General Psychology, 1936. Contbr. monographs and articles to psychol. journs. Editor: The Psychological Bulletin, 1918-30, Journal of Experimental Psychology since 1930; co-operating editor, American Journal of Psychology since 1925. Home: 6314 Wissahickon Av., Philadelphia, Pa.

FERNLEY, George Adamson, dir. of trade organizations; b. Phila., Pa., June 13, 1891; s. T. James and Harriet (Adamson) F.; B.S. in economics, Wharton Sch. of Commerce and Finance, U. of Pa., 1912; student Law Sch. of U. of Pa., 1912-14; m. Mildred Bougher, Mar. 15, 1916; children—Lois Adamson, T. James II, Robert Clute, Joan Adamson. Sec. Metal Branch of Nat. Wholesale Hardware Assn., 1912-39; sec.-treas. Nat. Wholesale Hardware Assn., 1926-39; advisory sec. Nat. Supply and Machinery Distributors Assn., 1923-39; sec. Am. Brush Mfrs. Assn., 1921-39; sec. Nat. Wholesale Jewelers Assn., 1923-39; sec.-treas. Hardware Merchants' and Mfrs. Assn., Phila., since 1926; dir. North Bros. Mfg. Co. Served as capt. Ordnance Dept., U.S. Army, 1917-18. Mem. Kappa Sigma. Republican. Episcopalian. Clubs: Union League, Phila. Cricket, Down Town (Phila.). Home: Crefeld Farm, Plymouth Meeting, Pa. Office: 505 Arch St., Philadelphia, Pa.

FERREE, Clarence Errol, psychologist; b. Sidney, O., Mar. 11, 1877; s. Jeremiah Dixon and Arvesta (Line) F.; B.S. and A.M., Ohio Wesleyan U., 1900, M.S., 1901; Sage fellow in psychology, Cornell U., 1902-03, Ph.D., 1909; D.Sc. Ohio Wesleyan U., 1939; m. Gertrude Rand, Sept. 28, 1918. Assistant in psychology, Cornell U., 1903-05, 1906-07; instr. in physics and psychology, U. of Ariz., 1905-06; lecturer in exptl. psychology, 1907-09, asso., 1909-12, asso. prof., 1912-17, prof., 1917-28, dir. Psychol. Lab., 1912-28, Bryn Mawr Coll.; dir. Research Lab. Physiol. Optics, and resident lecturer in ophthalmology, 1928-32, prof. physiol. optics and dir. Research Lab. Physiol. Optics, 1932-36, Wilmer Ophthal. Inst., Johns Hopkins Med. Sch.; dir. Research Lab. Physiol. Optics, Baltimore, since 1936. Fellow A.A.A.S.; mem. Am. Psychol. Assn., Illuminating Engring. Soc., Optical Soc. Amer., Franklin Inst., Phi Gamma Delta, Sigma Xi, P.B.K. (hon.). Apptd. mem. Engr. Reserve Corps Com., May 1917. Inventor (with G. Rand) various lighting appliances, apparatus for measuring the speed of accommodation and convergence of the eye, apparatus for testing visual acuity and the light and color sense, perimeter, pupilometer, central-vision scotometer and other optical and ophthalmic instruments. Author: Radiometric Apparatus for Use in Psychological and Physiological Optics, Studies in Physiol. Optics, 2 vols., (with G. Rand), 1934. Editor and author: Studies in Psychology, 3 vols., 1916, 1922, 1925. Contbr. more than 250 articles in scientific, technical and ophthalmol. journals on lighting in its relation to the eye, hygiene of the eye, methods and apparatus for refracting the eye, etc. Contbr. (with same) of apparatus and research, air service of army and lookout and signal service of navy. Contbr. Fourth Internat. Congress Sch. Hygiene, 1913, Internat. Congress of Ophthalmology, 1922, English-speaking Congress of Ophthalmology, London, 1926, Joint Discussion on Vision, The Physical and Optical Societies, London, 1932. Member committee of 4 on standards of field taking in study of eye diseases, Internat. Congress of Ophthalmology, 1922, Nat. Research Council's Com. on Industrial Lighting, 1924, Inter Soc. Com. on Color, 1931. Granted several patents on illuminating devices and optical instruments. Home: 2609 Poplar Drive, Baltimore. Address: Research Laboratory of Physiological Optics, Baltimore, Md.

FERRELL, Harrison Herbert, coll. dean; b. Chicago, Ill., Aug. 28, 1900; s. Harrison Herbert and Susanna H. (Reed) F.; B.S., Northwestern U., Evanston, Ill., 1924, M.A., 1925, Ph.D., 1928; m. Emily Miriam Grazia Bell, Sept. 15, 1929. Prof. of German, W.Va. State Coll., Institute, W.Va., since 1928, acting dean, 1930-32, asst. dean, 1932-33, acting registrar, 1934-35, registrar, 1935-37, dean since 1937. Served in S.A.T.C., 1918. Mem. Modern Language Assn. of America, Am. Teachers' Assn., W.Va. Foreign Language Assn. (sec.), Nat. Assn. of Negro Musicians, Kappa Alpha Psi. Research fellow in Germanic philology, Northwestern U., 1924-27; winner of violin scholarship, Nat. Assn. of Negro Musicians, 1926. Baptist. Concert violinist since 1915; founded Ferrell Symphony Orchestra, Chicago, 1920, conductor, 1920-30, 1934-35. Address: Institute, W.Va.

FERRIS, Edythe, artist; b. Riverton, N.J., June 21, 1897; d. Julius Roscoe and Cora May (Styles) Fisher; grad. Palmyra (N.J.) High Sch., 1916; student Phila. Sch. of Design for Women, 1916-21; m. Raymond Henry Ferris, Oct. 26, 1918; 1 son, Clifford Duras. Artist in oil, water color, gouache, pen and ink. Exhibited in Phila., New York, Boston, Washington since 1920; one-man shows in Phila., 1924, 1932, 1935, 1938, Boston, 1930, Hollins College, Va., 1939. Awards: gold medal, Gimbels, 1932; life painting award, Phila. Sch. of Design for Women, 1920, fellowship, 1919, 1920; hon. mention Nat. Assn. Women Painters and Sculptors, 1935. Taught and supervised art, Clifton Heights, Pa., 1924-28, Media (Pa.) Friends Select Sch., 1925-28; museum research, study and travel, Europe, 1928-29; dir. Craft Studio, Central Y.W.C.A., 1934-38; instr. in arts and crafts Fletcher Farm, Vt., summers 1934, 35, 36. Head crafts dept., Bryn Mawr (Pa.) Art Center, since 1938. Lectures on Color, Design, Crafts in Edn., Women in Art. Mem. Am. Water Color Soc., Nat. Assn. Women Painters and Sculptors, Am. Artists Professional League, Studio Guild. Home: 3724 Locust St., Philadelphia, Pa.

FERRIS, Seymour Washington, chemist; b. Hunter, N.Y., Feb. 22, 1900; s. George Fletcher and Nancy Avery (Beach) F.; B. Chemistry, Cornell U., 1922; m. Lucretia Gertrude Davis, Apr. 10, 1925; children—Marjorie Ruth, Gilbert Nelson. Began as instr. mathematics, high sch., Camden, N.J., 1922; research chemist, Atlantic Refining Co., Phila., Pa., 1923-36, chief chemist since 1936. Mem. Am. Chem. Soc., Franklin Inst., Am. Petroleum Inst., Soc. Chem. Industry, Eng. Republican. Clubs: Cornell, Hamilton (Philadelphia). Home: 124 E. Providence Rd., Alden, Delaware Co., Pa. Office: 3144 Passyunk Av., Philadelphia, Pa.

FERRIS, Walter Rockwood, clergyman; b. N.Y. City, Jan. 22, 1869; s. Frank A. and Mary A. (Cape) F.; student Coll. of N.J. (Princeton), 1894; Auburn Theol. Sem., 1894-95; B.D., Union Theol. Sem., 1897; B.D., State Bd. of Regents, N.Y., 1897; D.D., Syracuse, 1912; m. Eugenie Viola Hill, Nov. 24, 1896; children—Mrs. Henry A. Horstman, Walter Rockwood, Frank Arthur 2d, Muriel. Ordained Presbyn. ministry, 1897; pastor Bay Ridge Ch., Brooklyn, N.Y., 1897-1902, 1st Ch., Middletown, N.Y., 1902-08, Park Central Ch., Syracuse, 1908-28 (emeritus). Moderator N.Y. Synod, 1914; del. Aberdeen (Scotland) World Congress, 1913. Democrat. Mason. Home: "By-Peachblossom," Easton, Md.

FERRY, Leland F., judge Criminal Dist. Court of N.J. Address: Teaneck, N.J.

FESPERMAN, Harvey Augustus, clergyman; b. Rowan County, N.C., Oct. 11, 1892; s. Boydep A. and Lottie (Holshouser) F.; prep. edn. Crescent (N.C.) Acad., 1905-09; A.B., Catawba Coll., Salisbury, N.C., 1914, D.D., 1938; student Central Theol. Sem., 1914-15; m. Mary Naomi Peeler, May 22, 1916; children—Mary Brown, Lottie Sue, Betty Grey, Katherine Naomi. Ordained to ministry Evang. and Reformed Ch., Apr. 1916; pastor South Fork Charge, Catawba County, N.C., 1916-21; pastor First Reformed Ch., Greensboro, N.C., 1921-30, Christ's Reformed Ch., Hagerstown, Md., since 1930. Trustee Hood Coll., Frederick, Md.; mem. Bd. of Visitors Theol. Sem., Lancaster, Pa.; mem. Commn. on Higher Edn. of Evang. and Reformed Ch.; mem. advisory bd. Salvation Army, Hagerstown, Md.; mem. Washington Co. Bd. of Health, Hagerstown Jr. Order United American Mechanics. Club: Lions (Hagerstown, Md., past pres.). Home: 52 Broadway, Hagerstown, Md.

FETHEROLF, Fred Abram Philip, physician; b. Litzenberg, Lehigh Co., Pa., Dec. 7, 1880; s. Abraham Philip and Susan F.; B.S. and hon.

M.S., Muhlenberg Coll.; M.D., U. of Pa., 1902; post grad. work in Berlin and Vienna, 1903; m. Mary Irma Sieger, 1909; 1 son, Fred Abraham. In practice of medicine, Allentown, Pa.; staff surgeon Sacred Heart Hosp. since 1916, sec. surg. dept. since 1919; surgeon Allentown Gen. Hosp. since 1924. Fellow Am. Coll. Surgeons; mem. A.M.A., Pa. Med. Soc., Lehigh Co. Med. Soc., Alpha Tau Omega. Republican. Lutheran. Mason (32°). Clubs: Livingston, Lehigh Country (Allentown). Home: 2803 Chew St. Office: 941 Hamilton St., Allentown, Pa.

FETROW, Ward Willard, agrl. economist; b. Haddam, Kan., Nov. 3, 1893; s. George S. and Rachel B. (Thornburg) F.; grad. Washington (Kan.) High Sch., 1911; student Baker U., Baldwin, Kan., 1913-14; B.S., Kansas State Coll., 1920; Ph. D., U. of Wis., 1924; m. Cora W. Rafter, Aug. 30, 1922; children—George Morris, Ward Willard. Public sch. teacher, Kan., 1911-15; farm cost accountant, Jackson Co., Kan., 1920-21; asst. in agrl. economics, U. of Wis., 1922-24; teacher agrl. economics, Kan. State Agrl. Coll., summers, 1923, 24; in charge teaching and research in marketing, Okla. Agrl. and Mech. Coll., 1924-28; research in cotton demand, div. of cotton marketing, Bur. Agrl. Economics, U.S. Dept. of Agriculture, Washington, D.C., 1928-31; in charge cotton sect., Federal Farm Bd., 1931-33, same in coöp. div., Farm Credit Administration, 1933-34, chief research economist coöp. div. since 1934. Served in U.S. Army, June 1917 to May 1919. Mem. Am. Farm Economic Assn., Acacia, Alpha Zeta, Gamma Sigma Delta, Phi Kappa Delta. Methodist. Mason. Author of several agricultural bulletins; contributor professional articles to magazines. Home: 13 Drummond Av., Chevy Chase, Md. Office: 1300 E. St., Washington, D.C.

FETTER, Elwood Merrill, prothonotary, clerk of courts; b. Cowan, Union Co., Pa., Aug. 15, 1902; s. Aaron and Alice Jane (Duck) F.; grad. Mifflinburg (Pa.) High Sch., 1918; student Susquehanna U., Selinsgrove, Pa., 1918-20; m. Ruel Emily Rogers, May 29, 1922; children—Richard Elwood, Roger William, Mary Jane, Robert Aaron. Chief paymaster Lewisburg (Pa.) Chair Co., 1920-27; county auditor, Union Co., Pa., 1927-29; elected prothonotary and clerk of courts, Union Co., 1929, for term 1930-34, reelected without opposition for terms, 1934-38, 1938-42. Served in Pa. Nat. Guard, 1920-23. Mem. Pa. Safety Council, 1937, 38; mem. Constl. Commemoration Com., 1938; mem. Union Co. Rep. Com., 1928-30. Mem. Pa. State Prothonotary and Clerk of Courts Assn. (pres. 1936-37), Nat. County Officers Assn. (dir.), Lewisburg Business Men's Assn., Union County Business Council (sec.), William Cameron Engine Co. (Lewisburg). Republican. Evang. Ch. Mem. Patriotic Order Sons of America (past pres., past co. sec.), Royal Arcanum (past regent), Odd Fellows (past noble grand, past chief), Elk, Moose. Club: Lewisburg. Home: 235 N. Front St. Office: Court House, Lewisburg, Pa.

FETTER, Frank Albert, univ. prof.; b. Peru, Ind., Mar. 8, 1863; s. Henry G. and Ellen (Cole) F.; A.B., Ind. U., 1891; Ph.M., Cornell, 1892; post-grad. studies at The Sorbonne and École de Droit, Paris, 1892-93, and Halle, 1893-94, Ph.D., 1894; LL.D., Colgate, 1909, Occidental, 1930, Indiana University, 1934; m. Martha Whitson, July 16, 1896; children—Frank Whitson, Ellen Cole, Theodore Henry. Bookseller, Peru, Ind., 1883-90; winner Interstate Oratorical Contest, Des Moines, Ia., 1891; instr. polit. economy, Cornell, 1894-95; prof. Ind. U., 1895-98, Leland Stanford Jr. U., 1898-1900; prof. polit. economy and finance, 1901-10, economics and distribution, 1910-1911, Cornell U.; prof. polit. economy, Princeton, 1911-31, prof. emeritus since 1931, chmn. dept. of economics and social instns., 1911-22; visiting prof. Harvard, 1906-07, Columbia, 1912-13, The Claremont Colleges, 1928-29, U. of Illinois, 1934-36; lecturer at various times at Johns Hopkins, U. of Chicago, Northwestern U. Commissioner New York State Board Charities, 1910-11; gen. mgr. Nat. War Camp Community Service, 1918-19; mem. bd. mgrs. N.J. State Home for Boys, 1918-28; pres. N.J. Conf. for Social Welfare, 1919; vice-pres. Princeton Bd. of Edn., 1923-28; economic adviser to the Asso. States opposing Pittsburgh-Plus., 1923; special expert on the basing-point practice, for the Fed. Trade Commn., 1938-39. Secretary-treasurer American Economic Association, 1901-1906 (president 1912). Member Am. Philos. Soc., Am. Acad. Arts and Sciences, Beta Gamma Sigma, Phi Kappa Psi, Phi Beta Kappa, Delta Sigma Rho. Author: The Principles of Economics, 1904; Economic Principles, 1915; Modern Economic Problems, 1916, 22; The Masquerade of Monopoly, 1931; also many articles, monographs, etc., on econ. subjects. Editor: Source Book in Economics, 1912. Home: 168 Prospect Av., Princeton, N.J.

FETTER, Frank Whitson, economist; b. San Francisco, Calif., May 22, 1899; s. Frank Albert and Martha (Whitson) F.; A.B., Swarthmore Coll., 1920; A.M., Princeton, 1922, Ph.D., 1926; A.M., Harvard, 1924; m. Elizabeth Garrett Pollard, Jan. 14, 1929; children—Robert Pollard, Thomas Whitson. Instr. in economics, Princeton U., 1924-25 and 1927-28, asst. prof., 1928-34; associate prof. economics, Haverford Coll., 1934-36, prof. since 1936. Mem. of Am. Commn. of Financial Advisers to governments of Chile (1925), Poland (1926), Ecuador (1926-27), Bolivia (1927), China (1929); mem. commn. on Cuban affairs of Foreign Policy Association (1934); editorial writer St. Louis Post-Dispatch, 1930-34. Guggenheim fellow, 1937-38. Decorated Knight Order Polonia Restituta (Poland), 1927; Order of Merit First Class (Ecuador), 1927. Member American Economic Assn., Academia de Ciencias Economicas (Chile), Phi Beta Kappa. Author: Monetary Inflation in Chile, 1931. Co-Author: Facing The Facts, 1932; Problems of The New Cuba, 1935. Contbr. articles on economics. Home: Waterloo Rd., Berwyn, Pa.

FETTERHOOF, Chester D(aniel) judge; b. Spruce Creek, Pa., Jan. 20, 1885; s. Daniel and Susan (Chamberlain) F.; ed. pub. schs. and Juniata Coll. LL.B., Dickinson Sch. of Law, 1910; m. Anna Huston, Oct. 15, 1913; 1 dau., Helen Elizabeth. Admitted to Huntington County, Pa., bar 1911; dist. atty., Huntingdon, Pa., 1915-27; solicitor County of Huntingdon, 1928-35; president judge Ct. of Common Pleas of Huntingdon Co. since 1936; dir. First Nat. Bank of Huntingdon, Basalt Trap Rock Co. Republican county chmn., 1921-23. Lutheran. Mason (K.T., Shriner), Odd Fellow, K.P., Kiwanian. Home: 701 Warm Springs Av. Office: 324 Penn St., Huntingdon, Pa.

FETTERMAN, Henry Herbert, owner H. H. Fetterman Co.; b. Allentown, Pa., Apr. 24, 1883; s. Hiram J. and Emma K. (Oswald) F.; ed. pub. schs.; m. Lillie M. Harter, June 25, 1912; 1 son, Henry Harter. Began as office boy with R. G. Dun & Co., 1895; advancing to chief clerk; with L. L. Anewalt Co., 1900-20; organized, 1920, and since owner H. H. Fetterman Co.; pres. Allentown Home Buyers & Bldg. Loan Assn., since 1937; dir. Liberty Bank & Trust Co. Democrat. Lutheran. Home: 2608 Tilghman St. Office: 245 N. Seventh St., Allentown, Pa.

FETTINGER, Theodore Sheridan, pres. United Advertising Agency; b. Altoona, Pa., Mar. 28, 1865; s. Henry and Catherine (Nixdorf) F.; student Altoona (Pa.) Pub. Schs., 1875-83; m. Rosetta Keithley, Apr. 25, 1890; children—Edwin Forrest, Beatrice Eugenie (Mrs. A. Clyde Hamilton). Began as clerk in stationery store, Altoona, Pa., 1880; with Harrisburg, Pa. Telegram, Altoona Graphic-News, 1885-95, successively as correspondent, columnist, editor, publisher; advertising dir., Wm. F. Gable & Co., Altoona, Pa., W. V. Snyder & Co. and Hahne & Co., Newark, N.J., 1895-1915; pres. and dir. United Advertising Agency, Newark, N.J., since 1915. Newark (N.J.) city tax commr., 1913-1924. Mem. Pa. Soc. of N.J. Episcopalian. Elk. Clubs: Newark Athletic (pres. 1934-37; sec., 1937-39), Rotary, Advertising Men's (Newark, N.J.). Established first Eastern airmail terminal field at Newark; instrumental in bringing about adoption of Commn. Gov. in Newark; established Saturday half-holidays for dept. stores. Home: 893 S. 17th St. Office: 744 Broad St., Newark, N.J.

FETZER, Karl McAtee, telephone engr.; b. Reidsville, N.C., Oct. 11, 1891; s. Charles Harrison and Mary (Williams) F.; student Reidsville (N.C.) pub. schs., 1899-1909; B.S. in E.E., N.C. State Coll. of Agr. and Engring., Raleigh, N.C., 1914; m. Pattie Wray Womack, Apr. 7, 1917; children—Charles Harrison, William Womack. With Gen. Ry. Signal Co., Rochester, N.Y., 1914-20; with telephone engring. dept. Western Electric Co., New York, 1920-25, dept. became Bell Telephone Labs., 1925, and since with latter, supervising engr. since 1923. Mem. Am. Inst. E.E., Kappa Sigma. Presbyterian. Home: 180 E. Pierrepont Av., Rutherford, N.J. Office: 463 West St., New York, N.Y.

FEY, Harold Edward, editor, clergyman; b. Elwood, Ind., Oct. 10, 1898; s. Edward Henry and Eva (Gant) F.; A.B., Cotner Coll., Lincoln, Neb., 1922; B.D., Yale Div. Sch., 1927; m. Golda Conwell, July 20, 1922; children—Russell Conwell, Gordon Edward, Constance Ann. Ordained to ministry, Disciples of Christ, 1924; univ. pastor First Christian Ch., Lincoln, 1925-26; pastor First Ch., Hasting, Neb., 1927-29; prof. sociology, Union Theol. Sem., Manila, P.I., 1929-31; editor World Cal. Internat. Mag. of Disciples of Christ, 1932-35; editor Fellowship since 1935; exec. sec. Fellowship of Reconciliation, since 1935. Enlisted U.S.A., 1918. Del. from P.I. to confs. of Inst. of Pacific Relations, 1929 and 1931. Mem. Nat. Peace Conf. Ednl. chmn. Leonia Co-operative Assn. Mem. Central Christian Ch., N.Y. Author: World Peace and Christian Missions. Cntbr. to religious mags. Home: 142 Highwood Av., Leonia, N.J. Office: 2929 Broadway, New York, N.Y.

FICHMAN, Meyer Edward, social worker; b. New York, N.Y., Mar. 29, 1904; s. David M. and Dora (Isserman) F.; grad. New Britain High Sch., 1920; B.S., New York U., 1924; student Cornell, summer 1923; m. Sylvia Kornblith, June 13, 1927; children—Lionel Lazarus, Marshal Paul. Boys' worker Baltimore Jewish Ednl. Alliance, 1924; asso. dir. Washington Jewish Community Center, 1924-27; exec. dir. Y.M.H.A., Hartford, Conn., 1927-29, Stamford (Conn.) Jewish Center, 1929-36, Jewish Community Center, Harrisburg, Pa., since 1936, United Jewish Community, Harrisburg, since 1936. Mem. Pa. exec. com. United Palestine Appeal. Mem. Nat. Assn. Jewish Center Workers (treas., chmn. Palestine com.), Pa. State Assn. for Adult Edn. (mem. exec. com.), Nat. Conf. Jewish Social Welfare, Group Work Assn., Alpha Lambda Phi. Contbr. articles to jours. Home: 54 Taylor Boul. Office: 1110 N. 3d St., Harrisburg, Pa.

FICKES, Edwin Stanton; b. Steubenville, O., Nov. 3, 1872; s. George Jackson and Mary Akin F.; C.E., Rensselaer Poly. Inst., 1894; m. Marguerite Knapp Webb, Apr. 10, 1909; children—Harriet Webb, George Jackson, Charles Webb. Began as civil engr. with Wilkins & Davison, Pittsburgh, 1894; with F. S. Pearson, New York, 1898-99; with Pittsburgh Reduction Co. (now Alumnium Co. of America) since 1899, sr. v.p., since 1931; dir. Aluminum Co. of America. Mem. Metall. Adv. Bd. Carnegie Inst. Trustee Resselear Alumni Assn. Fellow Am. Geog. Soc.; mem. Am. Soc. C.E., Am. Inst. Mining & Metall. Engrs., A.A.A.S., Sigma Xi. Episcopalian. Clubs: Junta, Duquesne (Pittsburgh); Engineers, University (New York); Caxton (Chicago). Home; Spruce Point Annapolis Royal, Nova Scotia, Canada. Office: 2014 Gulf Bldg., Pittsburgh, Pa.

FIDES, Sister Mary; see Shepperson, Isabel.

FIELD, Carter, newspaper man; b. Baltimore, Md., Dec. 19, 1885; s. Charles Carter, Jr., and Mary Virginia (Lane) F.; student Baltimore City Coll., 1905; studied Johns Hopkins; m. Janet Weart Fickenscher, Apr. 21, 1910. Reporter Baltimore American, 1908-09, Baltimore Sun, 1909-10; telegraph editor Norfolk Landmark, 1910, also spl. writer Baltimore Sun; editor and mgr. Cumberland Press, 1912-13; U.S. Senate corr. United Press, 1913; Washington corr. New York Tribune (now New York Herald Tribune), Apr. 2, 1915-June 1, 1929; became

Washington corr. Bell Syndicate, 1929; now spl. writer for McGraw Hill publications. Mem. Troop A, Md. N.G., 1906-07. Republican. Clubs: Nat. Press, Gridiron, Metropolitan, Overseas Writers, Columbia Country. Home: Columbia Country Club, Chevy Chase, Md. Office: National Press Bldg., Washington, D.C.

FIELD, Frank L(ongstreet), physician; b. Bayonne, N.J., Mar. 7, 1870; s. Jacob T. and Mary (Minifie) F.; student Columbia U., 1886-89; M.D., N.Y. Univ., 1893; m. Belle Hammond, Jan. 26, 1898; children—Mary Evelyn (Mrs. John F. R. Staats), Fred H. L. Surgeon for Pacific Mail S.S. Co., 1893-94; engaged in gen. practice of medicine at Far Hills, N.J. since 1896, served as coroner, 1900-03, 1904-07; sch. physician since 1919. Served as 1st lt., later Capt. Med. Corps, U.S.A., 1917-20; with A.E.F. in France. Mem. Am. Med. Assn., N.J. State Med. Soc., Somerset Co. Med. Soc., Alumni Assn. N.Y. Univ., Assn. Am. Mil. Surgeons, Vets. Fgn. Wars. Republican. Ref. Ch. Mason. Odd Fellow. Home: Far Hills, N.J.

FIELD, Isaac S., publisher; b. Baltimore, Md., Nov. 20, 1860; s. Abiathar William and Penelope Jane (Healey) F.; ed. pub. schs. and City Coll., Baltimore; m. Rose Ellen Parsons, Dec. 21, 1881 (now dec.); children—A. William, Mrs. Rose Ellen Wood, Mrs. Marie Field Jones (deceased). Became v.p. Mfrs.' Record (weekly), 1882, now retired; dir. and mem. exec. com. Real Estate Trust Co., Baltimore. Pres. Bd. Sch. Commrs., Baltimore, for 6 yrs.; asso. judge of The Orphans Court of Baltimore City; pres. Montrose Sch. for Girls (state instn. for delinquents); pres. Md. Soc. to Protect Children from Cruelty and Immorality; pres. Children's Fresh Air Soc. Inc., of Baltimore; dir. West Baltimore Gen. Hosp.; mem. bd. China's Children Fund, Inc. Mem. Med. Com. Nat. Golden Rule Foundation. Mem. advisory council Salvation Army; mem. Civitan Club; dir. Free Summer Excursions for the Poor. Republican. Baptist. Mason (32°, K.T., Shriner). Mem. Md. advisory council Yenching U., Peiping, China. Home: 3801 Juniper Rd., Guilford, Baltimore, Md.

FIELD, Richard Stockton, govt. official; b. Pocahontas, Miss., June 9, 1890; s. Dr. Robert and Belle (Daniel) F.; grad. U.S. Naval Acad., 1907-11; student U.S. Naval War Coll., 1935-36; m. Mildred Fearn, Oct. 15, 1913; children—Richard Stockton, Fearn. Commd. ensign U.S. Navy, 1912, and advanced through the grades to comdr., 1931, retired Sept. 1, 1937; dir. Bureau of Marine Inspection and Navigation, U.S. Dept. of Commerce, Washington, D.C., since 1937. Decorated Victory, Haitian, Mexican, Nicaraguan campaign medals (U.S.). Commendatore of Order of Crown of Italy. Episcopalian. Club: Chevy Chase (Washington, D.C.) Home: Redland Rd., Norbeck, Rockville, Md. Office: Dept. of Commerce, Washington, D.C.

FIELD, William Jefferson, banker; b. Jersey City, N.J., Oct. 9, 1873; s. George Hobson and Mary C. (McWilliams) F.; ed. high sch., Jersey City; spl. student New York U. Law Sch.; m. Hazel Stephens Clarke, Apr. 14, 1903; 1 son, Richard Clarke. With Hanover Nat. Bank, N.Y. City, 1890-1900; with Commercial Trust Co. of N.J., Jersey City, 1900—, pres. 1924—; v.p. Registrar & Transfer Co. of N.J., Registrar & Transfer Co. of N.Y. Treas. Jersey City chapter Am. Red Cross, World War. Mem. Bd. of Finance, Jersey City, 1910-13. Mem. Am. Bankers Assn. (exec. council 1903-06); N.J. Bankers Assn. (pres. 1928-29; sec. 1903-28). Republican. Club: Carteret (Jersey City); Baltusrol Golf (Short Hills, N.J.); Sankaty Head Golf (Siasconset, Mass.). Home: 142 Gifford Av. Office: 15 Exchange Pl., Jersey City, N.J.

FIELDER, James Fairman, ex-governor; b. Jersey City, N.J., Feb. 26, 1867; s. George B. and Eleanor A. (Brinkerhoff) F.; ed. Selleck's Sch., Norwalk; studied law with William Brinkerhoff, Jersey City; LL.B., Columbia Law Sch., 1887; LL.D., Rutgers, 1914, Columbia, 1929; m. Mabel C. Miller, June 4, 1895. Practiced law. Mem. N.J. Ho. of Assembly, 1903, 1904, State Senate, 1907-13 (pres. of Senate, 1912-13); as pres. of Senate succeeded Woodrow Wilson to governorship of N.J., for unexpired term, March 1913-Jan. 19, 1914; resigned as senator Oct. 28, 1913, thus creating vacancy in office of governor; in Nov. 1913, elected gov. for term, 1914-17; apptd. v. chancellor N.J. Court of Chancery, Dec. 1, 1919. Democrat. Conglist. Mem. Hudson Co. Bar Assn. Home: 139 Gates Av., Montclair, N.J. Office: 1 Exchange Pl., Jersey City, N.J.

FIELDING, Mantle, architect; b. N.Y. City, Sept. 20, 1865; s. Mantle and Anna M. (Stone) F.; grad. Germantown Acad., 1883; student Boston Sch. of Tech., 1 yr.; m. Amy Reeve Williams, 1898; children—Richard M., Frances. Practiced at Phila. since 1889; architect of Page Memorial Chapel, Oswego, N.Y.; Terry Office Building, Roanoke, Va.; also many residences. Mem. Philadelphia Acad. Fine Arts, Walpole Soc., Pa. Historical Soc. Republican. Episcopalian. Club: Art Club of Philadelphia. Author: Life and Works of David Edwin, Engraver (3d vol. in Stauffer's Am. Engravers), 1917; Life and Works of Thomas Sully (with Edward Biddle), 1922; Gilbert Stuart and His Portraits of Washington, 1923; Dictionary of American Painters, Sculptors and Engravers; Life Portraits of George Washington and Their Replicas by Mantle Fielding (with John Hill Morgan). Home: 330 W. Springfield Av., Chestnut Hill, Philadelphia, Pa. Office: 225 S. 6th St., Philadelphia, Pa.

FIELDING, William John, author, editor; b. Wharton, N.J., April 10, 1886; s. William and Mary (Mitchell) F.; ed. public schools; m. Elizabeth C. Veale, June 20, 1910 (now dec.); children—Elsie (dec.), John Carbis; m. 2d, Margaret L. Cameron, June 21, 1929. Editor Newark Leader, 1915-18; lt. editor New Jersey Leader, 1919-22; editor Know Thyself, 1923-24; dramatic editor Golden Rule Mag., 1925-27; Sketch Book Magazine since 1927. Mem. A.A.A.S., Am. Social Hygiene Assn., Am. Birth Control League, Soc. for Constructive Birth Control and Racial Progress (London), Freethinkers of America (honorary vice-pres.), Author's League of America, Pi Gamma Mu; hon. corr. mem. Institut Litteraire et Artistique de France. Author: Pebbles from Parnassus, 1917; Sanity in Sex, 1920 (Japanese ed., 1921); Psychoanalysis—the Key to Human Behavior, 1921; The Puzzle of Personality, 1922; The Caveman Within Us, 1922; Health and Self-Mastery Through Psycho-Analysis and Autosuggestion, 1923; Autosuggestion—How It Works, 1923; Rejuvenation, 1924; Rational Sex Series, 13 vols., 1924-25; Teeth and Mouth Hygiene (collaboration), 1925; Dual and Multiple Personalities, 1925; The Cause and Nature of Genius, 1926; Sex and the Love Life, 1927 (20th large printing 1938); Woman—the Eternal Primitive, 1927; Woman—the Criminal, 1928; Woman—the Warrior, 1928; Unconscious Love Elements in Psycho-Analysis, 1929; How the Sun's Rays Give Health, 1930; The Marvels and Oddities of Sunlight, 1930; Boccaccio—Lover and Chronicler of Love, 1930; The Art of Love, 1931; Love and the Sex Emotions, 1932; Sex in Civilization (synposia), 1929; The Shackles of the Supernatural, 1937. Contbr. to anthologies of poetry: Principal Poets of the World (London), 1938; The World's Fair Anthology, 1939; The Poetry Digest Annual Anthology of Verse, 1939; The Paebar Anthology of Verse, 1939; Eros, an Anthology of Love Poems, 1939. Home: 248 N. 4th St., Newark, N.J. Office: 401 Fifth Av., New York, N.Y.

FIESER, James Lewis, pub. service adminstrn.; b. Ravenna, O., Oct. 8, 1883; s. Sebastian and Martha (Doerflinger) F.; grad. high sch., Alexandria, Ind., 1903; Ind. U., 1903-04, 1905-06; U. of Wis., summer, 1909; m. Mary Elizabeth Bailey, Feb. 20, 1935; children—Elizabeth Ann (by 1st marriage), James Lewis. Teacher in schools of Alexandria, Ind., 1904-05; financial agt. of Charity Orgn. Soc., Indianapolis, Ind., 1906; with pub. schs., Indianapolis, 1907-12; supt. Asso. Charities, Columbus, O., 1912-17; mgr. Social Service Bur., Chamber of Commerce, Columbus, Feb.-Sept. 1917; with Am. Nat. Red Cross, Washington, D.C., since 1917, respectively, as dir. of Civilian Relief, Lake Div., Cleveland, asso. dir. gen. Civilian Relief, asst. gen. mgr. and acting gen. mgr., Washington, D.C., mgr. Southwestern Div., St. Louis; v.-chmn. in charge domestic operations, Washington, D.C., since May 15, 1922. Directed flood relief work, Columbus, 1913; in association with Herbert Hoover, directed flood relief work, Miss. Valley Floods, 1927; directed drouth relief operation for Am. Red Cross, 1930-31, conversion of govt. surplus wheat and cotton into food and clothing for needy under act of 1932, establishment first aid stations and prevention of accidents, 1935-37; directed flood relief work, 1936, and Ohio Valley floods, 1937. Red Cross rep. Nat. Social Work Council. Decorated by German Red Cross and Cuban Red Cross. Pres. Indianapolis Social Workers Club, 1909; mem. Ohio State Council Defense, 1917-18; pres. Ohio State Conf. Social Work, 1918; sec.-treas. Ind. Child Labor Com., 1907-12, Ohio Child Welfare League, 1914-16, Columbus (Ohio) Central Philanthropic Council, 1912-17; sec. Columbus Chapter of Am. Red Cross, 1917; mem. bd. dirs. Nat. Tuberculosis Assn. since 1932; rep. Ohio Inst. of Pub. Efficiency, 1916-17. Mem. Nat. Health Council, Nat. Fire Prevention Bd. of Chamber of Commerce of U.S., Nat. Conf. Social Work. Unitarian. Mason. Maccabee. Clubs: Cosmos, Edgemoor. Home: 5009 Edgemoor Lane, Bethesda, Md. Address: Am. Nat. Red Cross, Washington, D.C.

FIFE, Joseph Paull; A.B., Stanford U., 1896; LL.B., Harvard, 1900. In practice of law at Pittsburgh; chmn. bd. McKeesport Tin Plate Corpn. Office: Frick Bldg., Pittsburgh, Pa.

FILBERT, B. Ludwig Spang, motor freight; b. Philadelphia, Sept. 3, 1890; s. Richard Yates and Margaret (DeRonde) F.; grad. Delancey Sch., 1909; m. Florence Thelenberg, Oct. 19, 1912. Engaged in street paving and contracting, 1909-16; started first motor freight line between Phila. and New York City, 1916, now pres. L. S. Filbert, Inc.; dir. Fox Chase Bank & Trust Co. (founded 1898 by Richard Yates F.), 1917-31; mem. exec. bd. Express Owners Assn., New York, N.Y.; dir. Pa. Motor Truck Assn. Republican. Mem. M.E. Ch. (treas. Cynwyd M.E. Ch.). Mason (32°, Shriner). Club: Union League of Phila. Home: 119 Cynwyd Rd., Bala-Cynwyd. Office: 3647 Ludlow St., Philadelphia, Pa.

FILE, William H.; mem. law firm File, File & Scherer. Address: Beckley, W.Va.

FILER, Enoch Crawford, lawyer; b. Grove City, Pa., March 17, 1897; s. Enoch L. and Mary (Crawford) F.; student pub. and high chs., Greenville, Pa., 1903-15; A.B., Allegheny Coll., Meadville, Pa., 1919; LL.B., Harvard, 1921; m. Margarita McIntosh Burns, Dec. 28, 1921; children—Mary Jane, Elizabeth and Margarita (twins). Admitted to Pa. bar, 1921, and since practiced in Erie, Pa.; pres. Erie Malleable Iron Co. since July 27, 1936; dir. The Marine Nat. Bank of Erie, Penn Union Electric Co., Erie Window Glass Co., Erie Cemetery. Served with U.S. Army, Camp Jackson, S.C., 1918-19. U.S. Commr., apptd. by judges of U.S. Ct. of Western Dist. of Pa., 1924-35. Mem. Chapter Cathedral of St. Paul (Episcopal) Ch., Am. Bar Assn., Pa. Bar Assn. (regional dir., 1937-38; mem. bar integration com., 1936-37, legal aid com., 1936-37), Erie Co. Bar Assn., Phi Kappa Psi. Republican. Episcopalian. Mason (Consistory, Shriner). Clubs: Erie, Kahkwa, Shrine (Erie, Pa.). Home: 555 W. 6th St. Office: 1005 Ariel Bldg., Erie, Pa.

FILES, Ellery K(napton), pres. Lea Fabrics, Inc.; b. Eagle, Neb., Oct. 13, 1888; s. Moses and Lillian (Knapton) F.; B.Sc., Neb. Wesleyan U., Lincoln, Neb., 1908; A.M., U. of Neb., Lincoln, 1910; m. Fay Myers, June 1917. Engr. of tests, City of Cincinnati, 1912-17; chem. engr. and works mgr. Duratex Corpn., Newark, N.J., 1920-29; v.p. and gen. mgr. Lea Fabrics, Inc., Newark, N.J., 1929-34, pres. and gen. mgr. since 1934; treas. and dir. Rubber Associates, Inc., New York, since 1938. Served as capt., Corps of Engrs., U.S. Army, 1918-19; maj., Chem. Warfare Service Res. Corps since 1920. Mem. Sigma Xi, Phi Kappa Phi. Republican. Methodist. Clubs: Newark

FILLION, Ferdinand, teacher and violinist; b. Holyoke, Mass., Jan. 29, 1892; s. Arthur and Ella (Demary) F.; ed. public schools, So. Hadley Falls, Mass.; musical edn. Inst. of Musical Art, New York, 1910-12 and private study with Eugene Ysaye; m. Fern Goltré, 1916 (divorced 1930); 1 son, Paul Raoul; m. 2d, Helene Kremer, April 9, 1938. Violinist since 1912, conductor since 1918; founded and conducted Pittsburgh String Orchestra, Fillion Quintet, Fillion Quartet; as violinist has given concerts in Can., New England States, Pa., the South and Detroit, Niagara Falls, Buffalo, etc.; soloist with Toronto Symphony, 1922; head of violin dept., Toronto Conservatory, 1920-25; established Fillion Studios, school of music, drama, dancing, art, languages, Pittsburgh, 1925, and since dir. Republican. Presbyterian. Address: 5321 Fifth Av., Pittsburgh, Pa.

FILMER, Robert Sterling, entomologist; b. Stratford, Conn., May 23, 1902; s. Sterling and Nettie Almy (Strickland) F.; B.S., Conn. State Coll., 1926; M.S., Rutgers Univ., 1930; m. Lillian E. Arrants, Dec. 26, 1929. Engaged as field supervisor, Corn Borer Project, U.S. Dept. Agr., 1926-27; jr. entomologist, Bur. Entomology, U.S. Dept. Agr., Washington, D.C., 1927-29; research fellow, Nicotine Fellowship, Rutgers U., 1929-31, instr. entomology, 1931-36, asst. prof., 1936-39; asso. entomologist, N.J. Expt. Sta., New Brunswick, N.J. since 1931. Served in R.O.T.C., 1922-24. Mem. Am. Assn. Econ. Entomologists, Am. Entomol. Soc., N.J. Beekeepers Assn., Essex Co., Beekeepers Assn., Alpha Gamma Rho, Sigma Xi. Dutch Reformed Ch. Clubs: Rutgers (New Brunswick); Mid Jersey Field Dog (Plainfield). Home: Plainfield Av., Stelton, N.J. Office: N.J. Experiment Sta., New Brunswick, N.J.

FINAN, Joseph B., editor, pub.; b. Cumberland, M.D., June 10, 1869; s. James and Anne (McDonough) F.; ed. Carroll Hall Acad., Cumberland; m. Clara Helen Doerner, June 12, 1895; children—Rev. Gerald J., Anna Irene, Mary Josephine. Editor and gen. mgr. Cumberland Times since 1918; pres. Times & Alleganian Co. Democrat. Catholic. Rotarian. Home: 527 Washington St. Office: 7 S. Mechanic St., Cumberland, Md.

FINCH, Francis Eldon, mfg. process machinery; b. Marquette, Mich., July 23, 1889; s. Robert B. and Elbertie (Dixon) F.; M.E., Cornell U., 1912; m. Dorothy Corwin, Sept. 21, 1916 (div.); children—Mary Sibley, Francis Eldon, Jr. Corwin; m. 2d, Katharine Finch, Feb. 14, 1931. Began as mech. engr., 1912; asso. with Ruggles-Coles Engring. Co. in various capacities to vice-pres. then pres., 1913-23, absorbed by Hardinge Co., Inc., mfrs. process machinery, and sec. and dir. since 1923; sec. and dir. Steacy-Schmidt Mfg. Co. Mem. Psi Upsilon. Presbyterian. Clubs: Lafayette (York); Cornell (New York). Contbr. articles on dryers and drying to tech. press and engring. handbooks. Home: 804 S. George St. Office: 240 Arch St., York, Pa.

FINCH, George Augustus; b. Washington, D.C., Sept. 22, 1884; s. James D. and Emma B. (Fitnam) F.; LL.B., Georgetown U., 1907; m J. Mae Wright, 1905; children—Eleanor Harrison, Augusta Emma (Mrs. Gerald J. Davis), David Wright (dec.), Mary Roberta (Mrs. E. Orville Johnson), George Augustus, Beatrice Anne. Clk. War Dept., 1905; law clk., Dept. of State, 1906-11, sec. Am. Commn. to Liberia, 1909; expert on internat. questions, War Industries Bd., 1918; asst. tech. adviser Am. Commn. to Negotiate Peace, 1919; secretary board editors American Journal International Law, and asst. sec. Am. Soc. Internat. Law, 1909-24, mag. editor and sec. since 1924; asst. sec. and asst. dir. Div. Internal. Law, Carnegie Endowment for Internat. Peace, since 1911; del. of the Endowment to 2d Pan Am. Scientific Congress, Washington, 1915-16, to 3d Pan Am. Scientific Congress, Lima, Peru, 1924-25; rep. of Endowment to the Orient, 1929; prof. of internat. law, Washington Coll. of Law, 1931-34; prof. internat. law, summer session, U. of Mich., 1932-38; prof. internat. law, Acad. Internat. Law, The Hague, 1935; mem. advisory com. research in internat. law, Harvard Law Sch., since 1928. Asst. sec. gen. Am. Inst. of Internat. Law since 1927. Mem. bar of D.C., Am. Soc. Internat. Law. Author: Sources of Modern Internat. Law. Clubs: Cosmos, Columbia Country. Home: 100 Virgilia St., Chevy Chase, Md. Office: 700 Jackson Pl. N.W., Washington, D.C.

FINCH, John Wellington, geologist, engineer; b. Lebanon, N.Y., Nov. 3, 1873; s. DeLoss S. and Mary Elizabeth (Lillibridge) F.; A.B., Colgate, 1897, A.M., 1898; fellow U. of Chicago, 1898-99, D.Sc., 1913; LL.D., U. of Ala., 1936; m. Ethel Ione Woods, 1901; children—Ione Lillibridge (Mrs. George M. Nye), Nancy Allen. Instr. in geology and physics, Colgate, 1898, in geology, U. of Chicago, 1899; state geologist of Colo., 1901-02; consulting engr. at various times for Guggenheim Exploration Co., Venture Corpn. (London, Eng.), Amalgamated and Anaconda copper cos., Hayden, Stone & Co., J. P. Morgan & Co., William Boyce Thompson, Newmont Corpn., etc., v.p. and gen. mgr. N.Y. Orient Mines Co., 1916-22; dir. Anglo-Am. Corpn. of S. Africa, 1921-22. Exploration in China, Siam and India, 1916-20, Africa, 1921, Turkey and Near East, 1922; v.p. Yunnan Ming Hsing Mining Co., Ltd., since 1920. Industrial adviser to gov. of Yunnan, China, 1922-25. Prof. economic geology, Colo. Sch. of Mines, 1926-30; dean of Sch. of Mines, U. of Ida., 1930-34. Dir. Ida. State Bur. of Mines and Geology, 1930-34; dir. U.S. Bur. of Mines since 1934; mem. Assn. of State Geologists, 1930-34, Fellow Geol. Soc. of America; mem. Northwest Sci. Assn., Am. Inst. Mining and Metall. Engrs., Soc. Economic Geologists, Am. Assn. Petroleum Geologists, Colo. Scientific Soc. (pres. 1929-30), Sigma Xi, Sigma Gamma Epsilon, Sigma Tau, Delta Kappa Epsilon. Author of various scientific articles. Home: Chevy Chase, Md.

FINCK, Furman Joseph, artist; b. Chester, Pa., Oct. 10, 1900; s. Harry August and Caroline (Smith) F.; student Chester High Sch., 1915-19, Industrial Art Sch., 1919-20; Cresson traveling scholarship, Acad. of fine Arts, 1920-24; studied École de Paris, 1924; m. Mildred Price Smith, 1938. Instr. art, Country Day Sch. of Temple U., since 1927, Tyle Sch. of Fine Arts, Temple U., 1935-39, Fieldston Sch., N.Y. City, 1929-30, Birch Wathan Sch., 1930-31; lecturer and radio speaker. Paintings in One Man Exhbns., MacBeth Galleries, N.Y. City, 1938; one-man exhibit, Carlan Galleries, Philadelphia; exhibited in many important exhibitions of painting; represented in many private collections. Mem. Commn. on Art, Gen. Edn. Bd.; mem. advisory group of the edn. program, Modern Museum. Mem. Am. Artists Congress (N.Y. branch), Conn. Acad. Fine Arts, Philadelphia Academy Fellowship. Author: (monograph) History of Art; (articles) The Meaning of Art in Education. Home: 6416 N. 8th St., Philadelphia, Pa. Office: 356 W. 22d St., New York, N.Y.

FINDLEY, Alvin Irwin, editor; b. Monmouth, Ill., June 29, 1859; s. Samuel and Mary Ann (Hardie) F.; Buchtel Coll., Akron, O., 1875-77; B.A., Wooster, 1881, M.A., 1886; m. Belle Holloway, May 28, 1884. City editor Akron Daily Beacon, 1877-79; staff Chicago Interior, 1881, Phila. Press, 1882; editor Akron Daily Beacon, 1883-90; spl. corr., Akron, 1890-92; editor Iron Trade Rev. Cleveland, and v.p. Iron Trade Rev. Co., 1892-1905; editor Iron Age, 1905-10; editor-in-chief, 1910-30, now editor emeritus; dir. Iron Age Pub. Co.; v.p. Montclair Nat. Bank, 1922-24, and dir. 1922-35. Vice-pres. Am. Foundrymen's Assn., 1902-03; trustee Biblical Sem. in N.Y., 1907-35; v.p. Nat. Fgn. Trade Conv., 1920. Mem. Am. Iron and Steel Inst., Iron and Steel Inst. (Brit.), Am. Acad. Polit. and Social Science, Phi Beta Kappa, Phi Kappa Psi; first pres. Nat. Conf. Bus. Paper Editors, 1919-20. Contbr. many articles in mags. and newspapers on tech. and econ. problems in iron and steel industry. Home: 31 Parkway, Montclair, N.J.; (winter) 115 7th Ave., N.E. St. Petersburg, Fla. Office: 239 W. 39th St., New York, N.Y.

FINDLEY, Frank DeWitt, clergyman; b. North Side Pittsburgh, Pa., Sept. 20, 1869; s. Rev. Wm. Abel and Margaret (Gordon) F.; A.B., Monmouth Coll., Monmouth, Ill., 1893, A.M., same, 1895; B.D., Pittsburgh Theol. Sem., 1896; hon. D.D., Westminster Coll., New Wilmington, Pa., 1929; m. Mary Abigail Robb, Sept. 16, 1896; children—Margaret Katherine, Elizabeth (Mrs. R. C. Eadie), Jeannette (Mrs. J. Ernest Miller). Ordained to ministry United Presbyn. Ch., 1896; pastor Mansfield, O., 1897-1904, Wellsville, O., 1904-08, First Ch., Portland, Ore., 1908-16, Turtle Creek, Pa., 1916-32, McConnellsburg, since 1932. Served as Y.M.C.A. speaker during World War. Served as sec. exec. com. State Anti-Saloon League of Ore., 1912-16; moderator Synod of Pittsburgh, 1923-24; sec. Gen. Assembly Commn. for Consolidating Bds. of the Ch., 1930. Trustee Gen. Assembly U. Presbyn. Ch., 1930-32, mem. bd. adminstrn. since 1934. Republican. United Presbyn. Home: McConnellsburg, Pa.

FINK, A. J., financier, art collector; b. Baltimore, Md., Sept. 19, 1890; ed. pub. schs, Baltimore; married. Chmn. of bd. Southern Hotel Companies, Pa. Glass Sand Corpn., Consol. Feldspar Corpn., Chairman of Board, Everel Propeller Corpn.; mem. board of dirs. McCrory Stores Corporation, Pa. Pulverizing Co., Feldspar Mines Corpn., N.Y. Feldspar Co., Baltimore Commercial Bank. Mem. Baltimore Finance Commn., Baltimore City Planning Commn.; mem. Baltimore Zoning Commn., 1923-26. Mem. Nimrods of America, Baltimore Assn. Commerce. Clubs: Lions, Advertising, Chesapeake, Suburban, Phoenix, Woodmont, Rod and Gun, Oriole Gun, Bankers Club of America. Home: South Rd., Mt. Washington. Office: Southern Hotel Bldg., Baltimore, Md.

FINK, Clarence Henry, paint and varnish mfg.; b. Pittsburgh, Pa., Aug. 3, 1890; s. Meyer and Amelia (Crone) F.; ed. Central High Sch., Pittsburg, Pa., 1904-08; m. Ruth Klein, Sept. 5, 1922; children—Suzanne Ruth, Nancy Carol. Asso. with Pittsburgh Testing Lab., 1908-15; with Sterling Varnish Co., Haysville, Pa., since 1915, pres. since 1927; pres. Industrial Paint Co. Trustee Emma Farm Assn., Harmony, Pa. Jewish religion. Mason. Clubs: Concordia (Pittsburgh); Westmoreland Country (Verone, Pa.). Home: 1273 Bellerock St., Pittsburgh. Office: Haysville, Pa.

FINK, Cornelius Winfield, coll. prof.; b. Irville, O., Nov. 10, 1893; s. Rodolphus M. and Susanna (Hursey) F.; ed. A.B., Muskingum Coll., 1914; A.M., Ohio State U., 1924; m. Oneta M. Compher, Dec. 24, 1916; children—Esper Winfield, Elizabeth Mildred, Phylis Eileen. Newspaper reporter and city editor Coshocton (O.) Tribune, 1915-17; city editor Zanesville (O.) Times Recorder, 1917-19; social science teacher Dresden (O.) High Sch., 1920-22; instr. economics, O. State U., 1922-24; asst. prof. economics, Ohio U., 1924-26, asso. prof., 1926-30; asso. prof. economics and polit. science, Dickinson Coll., since 1930. Mem. Am. Acad. Polit. and Social Science, Am. Economic Assn., Tau Kappa Alpha. Republican. Methodist. Mason. Contbr. Ohio Social Science Journal. Home: 359 W. High St., Carlisle, Pa.

FINK, Scott, lawyer; b. Irwin, Pa., Aug. 18, 1887; s. George W. and Agnes J. (Bowman) F.; student Irwin (Pa.) High Sch., 1902-05, Kiskiminetas Springs Sch., Saltsburg, Pa. 1905-06; A.B., Amherst (Mass.) Coll., 1910; LL.B., Harvard, 1913; m. Lera Mae Johnson, June 15, 1920; children—David, Jerry. Admitted to Pa. bar, 1913, and since practiced in Greensburg, Pa.; dir. Barclay-Westmoreland Trust Co., Greensburg, Irwin (Pa.) Savings and Trust Co., 1st Nat. Bank of Export, 1st Federal Savings & Loan of Irwin. Served in U.S.N.R., 1918. Mem. Delta Kappa Epsilon. Democrat. Presbyterian. Mason, Elk. Club: Greensburg Country. Home: Route 3, Irwin, Pa. Office: Coulter Bldg., Greensburg, Pa.

FINK, William LaVilla, research metallurgist; b. Fairmount, Ind., Sept. 14, 1896; s. James Otto and Vella E. (Lindsey) F.; B.S.E., U. of Mich., 1921, M.S.E., same, 1923, Ph.D., 1926; m. Laura F. French, July 14, 1926; children—

Lucie French, Joanna Roslyn. Asso. with Research Labs. of Aluminum Co. of America, Cleveland, O., and New Kensington, Pa., since 1925, asst. to head Metall. Div. and in charge fundamental research and corrosion investigations since 1930. Mem. Am. Chem. Soc., Am. Soc. for Metals, Am. Inst. Mining and Metall. Engrs., Brit. Inst. Metals, Tau Beta Pi, Phi Lambda Upsilon, Sigma Xi, Gamma Alpha. Republican. Presbyn. Contbr. a number of articles on metallurgy and corrosion of aluminum alloys. Home: 531 Pennsylvania Av., Oakmont, Pa.

FINKE, George William, surgeon; b. Hoboken, N. J., Aug. 25, 1882; s. John H.D. and Mary (Mellor) F.; M.D., N.Y. Univ. & Bellevue Hosp. Med. Coll., 1906; m. Ella Bennitt, Aug. 14, 1918. Engaged in gen. practice of medicine at Hackensack, N.J. since 1907, specializing in surgery since 1911; chief surg. div., Hackensack Hosp. since 1927; dir. surgery, Bergen Pines Hosp., Oradell, N.J. since 1935. Served in Med. Corps, U.S.A., 1918. Fellow Am. Coll. Surgeons; mem. Am. Med. Assn., Surgical Club of Hackensack (pres.), N.Y. Univ. Alumni Assn. Protestant. Mason. Clubs: Pioneer Masonic, American Legion (Hackensack). Home: 237 State St. Office: Hackensack Hosp., Hackensack, N.J.

FINKELSTEIN, Isaac Bernard, wholesale hardware exec.; b. New York, N.Y., Mar. 27, 1884; s. David and Esther (Baer) F.; student pub. schs., Wilmington, Del., spl. courses U. of Pa.; m. Clara Statnekoo, 1905; 1 son, Arthur. Began as stock boy in retail store, 1897; became v.p. Del. Notion Co., 1920; v.p. and treas. Del. Hardware Co., wholesale hardware, iron and steel, Wilmington, Del., since 1922; dir. Mutual Bldg. & Loan Assn. Chmn. Mayor's Com. for Stabilization of Employment, 1931-32, Del. Festival of the Arts Com., 1935-39; pres. Del. Safety Council, 1932-33, now dir. Pres. Wilmington Chamber of Commerce, 1932, 33, 34, Social Workers' Club, 1934-38; has also been pres. Arden Club, Social Service Club, Del. State Conf. for Social Work, Y.M. and Y.W.H.A.; dir. Del. Anti-Tuberculosis Soc., Prisoners' Aid Soc., Wilmington Soc. of the Fine Arts, Consumers League, Jewish Fed. of Del., Jewish Welfare Soc. (ex-pres.); mem. Del. Advisory Bd. of Nat. Youth Adminstrn.; del. from Del. to Pres. Hoover's White House Conf. on Child Health and Protection. Mem. Wilmington Civic Assn. (pres.), Taxpayer's Research League (pres.), Am. Civic Assn., Am. Acad. Polit. and Social Science, U.S. Chamber of Commerce, Wilmington Housing Assn., Drama League, Hist. Soc. of Del., Archaeol. Soc. of Del., Jewish Publ. Soc., Del. Citizens' Association. Member B'nai B'rith (member Del. Chapter). Club: Kiwanis (Wilmington, Del.). Home: 1618 Franklin St. Office: Delaware Hardware Co., Wilmington, Del.

FINKLER, Rita Sapiro (formerly Mrs. Samuel Jacob Finkler), physician; b. Kherson, Russia, Nov. 1, 1888; d. Wolf and Sara (Hopner) S.; came to U.S., 1910, naturalized, 1913; law degree, U. of St. Petersburg, Russia, 1909; M.D., Womans Med. Coll., Phila., 1915; m. Samuel Jacob Finkler, July 6, 1913 (div.); 1 dau., Sylvia Pauline. Interne, Phila. Polyclinic Hosp., 1915-16; in charge of a health center, Phila., 1916-18; adjunct on pediatric staff, Beth Israel Hosp., Newark, N.J., 1919-27, adjunct on gynecol. staff, same, 1927-37, asso. in pathology in charge dept. biology, 1933-37, chief of endocrine clinic, asso. in gynecology, 1934-39, chief of dept. endocrinology since 1939. Served as chmn. Refugee Com., Am. Med. Woman's Assn.; mem. N.J. State Refugee Co-ordinating Com. Med. Am. Med. Assn., N.J. State Med. Soc., Acad. Medicine, Assn. for Study Internal Secretions, Congress on Obstetrics and Gynecology, Am. Med. Woman's Assn. (regional dir.), First Ladies Robert Treat Orgn., Pioneer Woman Orgn. Del. to Congress Internat. Woman Med. Orgns. Award for Sci. Exhibit at N.J. State Med. Soc. Annual Meeting, 1938. Mem. Labor Party. Jewish Religion. Mem. Hadassah. Club: Y.W.H.A. (Newark). Contbr. about 17 publs. to med. lit. Home: 35 Leslie St., Newark, N.J.

FINLEY, Charles William, biologist; b. Cooks Mills, Ill., Aug. 10, 1880; s. Thomas Putnam and Martha Elizabeth (Covert) F.; diploma State Normal Sch., Charleston, Ill., 1908; B.S., U. of Chicago, 1910, M.S., 1911; Ph.D., Columbia, 1926; m. Sylvia Fears Finley, Aug. 8, 1906; children—Charles Otis, Eleanor Eliza. Teacher rural schs., Ill., 1902-07; head of biol. dept., State Normal Sch., Macomb, Ill., 1912-17, Lincoln Sch. of Teachers Coll., Columbia, 1917-22, and prin. high sch. div. of same, 1922-27; dean of instrn. State Teachers Coll., Montclair, N.J., since 1927. Fellow A.A.A.S.; mem. N.E.A., N.J. State Teachers Assn., Ill. Acad. Science, Am. Assn. Univ. Props., N.J. Schoolmasters' Club, Phi Delta Kappa, Sigma Xi, Kappa Delta Pi (hon.). Republican. Baptist. Mason, K.P. Author: Biology in the Public Press (with Otis W. Caldwell), 1923; Biology in the Secondary Schools and the Training of Biology Teachers, 1926. Contbr. to mgs. Home: 50 Aubrey Rd., Montclair, N.J.

FINLON, Frank T., editor Free Press. Address: Braddock, Pa.

FINN, Albert Edward, clergyman, retired; b. Todmordon, Yorkshire, Eng., May 21, 1868; s. Josiah and Mary James (Lockwood) F.; came to U.S., 1872, naturalized, 1900; student Bucknell Acad., 1887-90; A.B., Bucknell U., Lewisburg, Pa., 1894; student Crozer Theol. Sem., 1894-97; (hon.) D.D., Geneva Coll., Beaver Falls, Pa., 1915; m. Cora Reiff Perry, Dec. 14, 1898 (dec.); 1 son, William Albert; m. 2d, Mrs. Bertha Perry Rogers, Aug. 4, 1921; step-children—Carolyn Gladys (dec.), Dr. Samuel Perry Rogers, Rev. William Raymond Rogers. Ordained to ministry Bapt. Ch., 1897; pastor Cherryville, N.J., 1897-1903, Plainfield, N. J., 1904-09, Rochester, Pa., 1909-18, Newburgh, N.Y., 1918-29, Frankford, Phila., Pa., 1929-34, retired 1934; exec. sec. North Phila. Assn. Bapt. Chs., 1935-38. Served in Pa.N.G. while in coll. Mem. bd. mgrs. Bapt. Hist. Soc. Mem. Phi Gamma Delta. Republican. Baptist. Mason, Rotarian. Now engaged in writing short poems which are syndicated in weekly newspapers in Pa. towns. Home: 110 Linden Av., Hatboro, Pa.

FINNEY, George Gross, surgeon; b. Baltimore, Md., Dec. 15, 1899; s. John Miller Turpin and Mary Elizabeth (Gross) F.; prep. edn. Gilman Country Sch., Baltimore, 1908-17; A.B., Princeton U., 1921; M.D., Johns Hopkins, 1925; m. Josephine Lurman Stewart, Sept. 20, 1924; children—George Gross, Katherine Latimer, Redmond Conyngham Stewart, Jervis Spencer. Asst. resident surgeon Johns Hopkins Hosp., 1926-29, resident surgeon, 1929-30; practice of surgery, Baltimore, since 1930; now asso. in surgery Johns Hopkins U.; mem. surgical staffs of Johns Hopkins, Union Memorial hosps., Hosp. for Women of Md., Church Home and Infirmary Hosps. of Baltimore. Served as instr. S.A.T.C., Rutgers Coll., New Brunswick, N.J., Sept.-Dec. 1918; disch. as 1st lt. Inf., U.S. Army. Trustee Gilman Country Sch., Baltimore. Mem. Bd. of Correction, State of Md.; mem. bd. of dirs. Henry Watson Childrens Aid Soc., Baltimore, Boys' Clubs of Am., James Lawrence Kernan Hosp. for Crippled Children. Mem. Medico-Chirurg. Faculty of Md., A.M.A., Southern Surgical Assn.; associate member Am. Assn. Thoracic Surgery. Democrat. Presbyterian. Clubs: Maryland, Green Spring Valley Hunt (Baltimore). Home: Eccleston, Md. Office: 2947 St. Paul St., Baltimore, Md.

FINNEY, John Miller Train, surgeon; b. Baltimore, Md., July 26, 1894; s. John Miller Turpin and Mary Elizabeth (Gross) F.; prep. edn. Hill Sch., Pottstown, Pa., 1908-11; B.S., Princeton U., 1915; M.D., Johns Hopkins, 1919; m. Virginia Lee Milton, Feb. 4, 1922; children—John Miller Turpin III, William Hammond Milton, Daniel Gross (dec.), Virginia Lee, Mary Ann, Alexander Miller. Successively interne, asst. resident, resident surgeon Union Memorial Hosp., Baltimore, 1919-23; in pvt. practice, Baltimore, since 1923; successively asst., instr., asso. in surgery Johns Hopkins U., med. dept., since 1925. Served in Base Hosp. No. 18, U.S. Army, with A.E.F. in France, 1917-19. Chmn. Health and Safety Commn., Baltimore Area Council; mem. Nat. Council Boy Scouts America. Fellow Am. Coll. Surgeons; mem. A.M.A., Southern Med. Assn., Am. Surgical Assn., Southern Surgical Assn., Am. Bd. of Surgery, Southern Soc. of Clin. Surgeons, Eastern Surg. Assn., etc. Democrat. Presbyterian (elder). Clubs: L'Hirondelle (Ruxton, Md.); Cedar Point. Home: Ruxton, Md. Office: 2947 St. Paul St., Baltimore, Md.

FINNEY, John Miller Turpin, surgeon; b. June 20, 1863; s. Ebenezer D. and Annie L. (Parker) F.; A.B., Princeton, 1884; M. D., Harvard, 1889, LL.D., 1937; LL.D., Tulane U., New Orleans, 1935; m. Mary E. Gross, Apr. 20, 1892; children—John Miller Train, Eben Dickey, George Gross, Mary Elizabeth. In practice at Baltimore since 1889; prof. surgery emeritus, Johns Hopkins. Fellow Am. Surg. Assn. (ex-pres.), Am. Coll. Surgeons (ex-pres.), Southern Surg. and Gynecol. Assn. Brig. gen., Med. R.C. U.S.A.; chief consultant in surgery A.E.F. Decorated D.S.M. (U.S.); Comdr. de l'Ordre de la Couronne (Belgian); Officier de la Légion d'Honeur (French). Club: Maryland. Home: 200 Goodwood Gardens, Roland Park. Office: 2947 St. Paul St., Baltimore. Md.

FINNEY, Theodore Mitchell, music educator; b. Fayette, Ia., Mar. 14, 1902; s. Ross Lee and Caroline (Mitchell) F.; A.B., U. of Minn., 1924; study Conservatoire Americaine, Fontainebleau, France, summer 1926, U. of Berlin and Stern Conservatory, Berlin, Germany, 1927-28; Litt.M., U. of Pittsburgh, 1938; m. Myrle Greeley, Aug. 1, 1925. Mem. Minneapolis Symphony Orchestra, 1923-25; asst. dir. instrumental music, pub. schs. Council Bluffs, Ia., 1925; mem. faculty music dept. Carleton Coll., Northfield, Minn., 1925-32; mem. faculty Smith Coll. Summer Sch. of Music, Northampton, Mass., 1930-38; dir. music, pub. schs. Council Bluffs, Ia., 1933-36; dir. music activities, asso. prof. music appreciation, U. of Pittsburgh since 1936. Mem. Music Teachers Nat. Assn., Am. Musicol. Soc., Music Educators Nat. Conf., Pa. German Soc., Phi Mu Alpha. Congregationalist. Author: A History of Music, 1935. Edited and composed many musical works, pub., 1932-35. Editor Bulletin of Music Teachers Nat. Assn. Home: 426 Elmer St., Edgewood, Pittsburgh, Pa.

FINNEY, William Parker, b. near Nachez, Miss., Sept. 9, 1861; s. Ebenezer Dickey and Annie Louise (Parker) F.; A.B., Princeton, 1883, A.M., 1886; grad. Princeton Theol. Sem., 1886; D.D., Cumberland (Tenn.) U., 1910; m. Pamela Richardson, Oct. 5, 1887 (died 1889); m. 2d, Katherine Richardson, Oct. 5, 1897 (died 1907); m. 3d, Eleanor Hoopes, June 11, 1910. Ordained Presbyn. ministry, 1886; pastor Cream Ridge and New Egypt, N.J., 1886-92, Moorestown, N.J., 1892-1910; prof. English, Lincoln U., Chester Co., Pa., 1910-26; gen. sec. Presbyn. Hist. Society, Philadelphia, 1926-33. Mem. Soc. of Cincinnati of Pa. (hon. pres.), Order of Founders and Patriots of America. Home: Wood-Norton Apt., 6347 Wayne Av., Philadelphia, Pa.

FIREMAN, Peter, chemist; b. Lipovetz, Russia, Apr. 4, 1863; grad. Gymnasium Charkov, Russia, 1881; came to U.S., 1882; studied at U. of Odessa, Königsberg, Zürich and Berne, Ph.D., Berne, 1893. Asst. in chemistry, 1892, 94, instr., 1894-98, asst. prof., 1898-1901, Columbian (now George Washington) U.; prof. chemistry Mo. Sch. of Mines, 1901-02; chem. geologist, U.S. Nat. Mus., 1901; in charge Chem. Research Lab., Alexandria, Va., 1904-06; mfg. chemist since 1906; pres. Magnetic Pigment Co. since 1911. Address: Lambertville, N.J.

FIROR, Whitmer Bennett, M.D., roentgenologist; b. Scranton, Pa., Apr. 23, 1902; s. Rev. Marion L. and Anna Percival (Achey) F.; grad. Thurmont (Md.) High Sch., 1919; A.B., Johns Hopkins, 1923, M.D., 1927, post grad. study in roentgenology, 1927-28; m. Mildred Isabelle Carley, Aug. 25, 1928; 1 son, Whitmer Bennett. Fellow Trudeau Sanatorium, Saranac Lake, N.Y., July-Sept. 1927; house officer Henry Ford Hosp., Detroit, 1928-29; jr. instr. in roentgenology U. of Mich. Hosp., Ann Arbor, 1929-30; practice of roentgenology as jr. asso. with Dr. Charles A. Waters, Baltimore, since 1930; assistant in roentgenology, Johns Hopkins University and Hospital; assistant visiting roentgenologist Union Memorial Hosp., Hospital

FIRTH — for Women of Md., Sheppard Pratt Hosp. Commd. 1st lt., Med. Reserve Corps, U.S. Army. Diplomate in radiology, Am. Bd. Radiology. Mem. Baltimore City Med. Soc., A.M.A., Am. Roentgen Ray Soc. Democrat. Clubs: University, Johns Hopkins (Baltimore). Asso. editor Year Book of Radiology. Home: 4 St. Dunstan's Garth. Office: 1100 N. Charles St., Baltimore, Md.

FIRTH, Norman Charles, editor; b. Westfield, Mass., Sept. 30, 1895; s. Charles and Henrietta (Humphreville) F.; B.S. in E.E., Worcester Poly. Inst., 1920; grad. study New York U.; m. Mary Parker, Sept. 10, 1921; children—Louise, Elizabeth. Editorial work with A. W. Shaw Co. and McGraw-Hill Pub. Co., Inc., 1920-32; editor of "System," 1928-35; vice-pres. of Management Publs., Inc., 1932-35; eastern editor American Business, 1935-36; cons. editor McGraw-Hill Practical Business Manuals; mng. editor and business mgr. Dun's Review since 1936. With W. H. Leffingwell conducted Nat. Office Ratio Survey, 1930. Entered U.S. Army, Sept. 1917; commd. 2d lt. engrs., Aug. 1918; hon. discharged, July 1919. Mem. Alpha Tau Omega. Republican. Episcopalian. Author: Check Your Office at These 333 Points. Contbr. to mags. Home: 35 Roosevelt Rd. Maplewood, N.J. Office: 290 Broadway, New York, N.Y.

FISCHELIS, Robert Phillip, pharmaceutical chemist; b. Phila., Pa., Aug. 16, 1891; s. Philipp and Ernestine (Kempt) F.; Ph.G., Medico-Chirurgical Coll. of Phila., 1911, Ph.C, 1912; Pharm.D., 1913; B.Sc. in Chemistry, Temple U., 1812; Pharm. M., Phila. Coll. of Pharmacy, 1918; spl. courses U. of Pa., 1916-18; hon. Pharm. D., Conn. Coll. of Pharmacy, 1934; m. Juanita Celestine Deer, Feb. 24, 1919. Instr. in pharmacy and organic chemistry, Medico-Chirurgical Coll., Phila., 1912-14, spl. lecturer, 1914-17; asso. editor Druggists Circular, 1914-16; chemist H. K. Mulford Co., Phila., 1916-19; spl. lecturer Phila. Coll. of Pharmacy, since 1917; consulting pharmacist and chemist since 1919; mng. editor news edition, Industrial and Engineering Chemistry, 1922-27; dean and prof. of pharmacy, N.J. Coll. of Pharmacy, 1921-25; exec. sec. and chief chemist Bd. of Pharmacy of State of N.J. since 1926; coöperating state official Food and Drug Administration, U.S. Dept. of Agr., since 1926; mem. research staff Com. on Costs of Medical Care, 1929-33; founder Pa. Pharmacist, editor, 1916-19; founder N.J. Jour. of Pharmacy, editor, 1927-30 and since 1935. Served as sergt. 1st class in Chem. Warfare Service, U.S.A., 1918. Mem. Governor's Sch. Survey Commn., N.J., 1932-33, N.J. Social Security Commn., 1935-36, Nat. Health Conf., 1938, N.J. Health and Welfare Conf., 1939. Mem. Nat. Drug Trade Conf., Conf. of Allied Med. Professions of N.J. (chmn. 1935, and since 38) Mem. Am. Pharm. Assn. (v.p. 1933-34, pres. 1934-35, mem. council 1923-26 and since 1933, sec. council 1923-25), Am. Chem. Soc., A.M.A., Nat. Assn. Bds. of Pharmacy (v.p. 1931-34), Am. Assn. Colls. of Pharmacy (v.p. 1924-25), A.A.A.S., Am. Public Health Assn., Am. Acad. Polit. and Social Science, Nat. Pharm. Syllabus Com., Drug Trade Bur. of Pub. Information (editor 1920-32), Pa. Pharm. Assn. (sec. 1916-19, pres. 1919-20), N.J. Pharm. Assn. (v.p. 1923-25, sec. 1926-29, trustee since 1935, dir. Research Bureau since 1937), N.H. Pharm. Assn. (hon.), Trenton Hist. Soc., Am. Legion, Kappa Psi, Beta Phi Sigma, Phi Lambda Upsilon. Episcopalian. Clubs: Rotary, Chemists (N.Y. City). Collaborator (with 38 others) Remington's Practice of Pharmacy, 7th edition, 1926. Co-Author: (with C. Rufus Rorem) Costs of Medicines, 1932; (with H. V. Arny) Principles of Pharmacy, 4th edition, 1937. Editor: New Jersey Formulary since 1935; Basic Material for a Pharmaceutical Curriculum, 1927. Contbr. to Jour. Am. Pharm. Assn., N.J. Jour. of Pharmacy and other pharm. and scientific jours.; author of moograph on medical materials industry in Vol. X, Encyclopedia of the Social Sciences. Author of monograph on drug control in Nelson's Loose Leaf Medicine, Vol. VII. Home: 640 W. State St. Office: 28 W. State St., Trenton, N.J.

FISCHER, Carl Castle, pediatrician; b. Phila., Pa., Oct. 13, 1902; s. John A. and Millie (Leupold) F.; B.S., Princeton U., 1924; M.D., Hahnemann Med. Coll. and Hosp., Phila., 1928; grad. study, N.Y. Post-Grad. Med. Sch., Washington U. Med. Sch.; (hon.) A.M., Hahnemann Med. Coll. and Hosp., 1938; m. Mae A. Charles, Mar. 7, 1931; children—Elaine Lois, Charles Thomas. Interne Hahnemann Hosp., Phila., 1928-29, since then, asst., instr., demonstrator, and now asso. in pediatrics, Hahnemann Med. Coll. and Hosp.; visiting pediatrician to Hahnemann, Broad Street, St. Lukes, and Childrens hosps.; cons. pediatrician to Pottstown (Pa.) Homeopathic Hosp. and Allentown (Pa.) State Hosp. Mem. Phila. Council, Boy Scouts of America. Fellow Am. Acad. of Pediatrics, Am. Coll. Phys.; mem. Phi Alpha Gamma. Republican. Presbyterian. Clubs: Kiwanis, Princeton (Phila.); Gateway, Princeton Univ. Triangle (Princeton, N.J.). Home: 409 Glen Echo Rd. Office: Germantown Professional Bldg., Philadelphia, Pa.

FISCHER, Emil Eisenhardt, clergyman, educator; b. Phila., Pa., July 14, 1882; s. Christian G. and Emily (Eisenhardt) F.; A.B., Rutgers, 1904, A.M., 1907; grad. Lutheran Theol. Seminary, Phila., 1907; D.D., Muhlenberg College, 1920; D.D., Rutgers University, 1933; m. Anita Emily Lins, June 19, 1912; children—Theodore Lins, Jean. Ordained Luth. ministry, 1907; pastor Holy Trinity Ch., Brooklyn, 1907-13; instr. in Hebrew, Lutheran Theol. Sem., Phila., 1910-13; pastor Christ Ch., Allentown, Pa., 1913-20; prof. systematic theology, Luth. Theol. Sem., Phila., since 1920. Mem. Board of Foreign Missions of United Lutheran Ch.; mem. Am. sect. of Universal Christian Council for Life and Work. Mem. Am. Acad. of Polit. and Social Science, Delta Upsilon. Republican. Author: Social Problems—The Christian Solution, 1927. Contbr. to "Leaders of Lutheran Reformation," 1917, "New Testament Commentary," 1936, and to The Lutheran (mag.); co-editor of Lutheran Church Quarterly. Home: 7322 Boyer St., Philadelphia, Pa.

FISCHER, John William, editor; b. Macksburg, O., Oct. 20, 1876; s. John and Margaret (Collins) F.; m. Dollie Koenig, 1904. With Parkersburg Sentinel since 1896, editor since 1919; dir. Parkersburg Sentinel Co. Democrat. Elk. Home: 130 Seventh St., Parkersburg, W. Va.

FISH, Harry Spaulding, surgeon; b. Waverly, N.Y., March 26, 1880; s. George Warren and Anna Dana (Parsons) F.; pre-medical course, Cornell U., 1899; M.D., U. of Pa., 1903; m. Ruth Mary Esser, March 26, 1910; 1 dau., Harriet Parsons (Mrs. Henry I. Shaw). Interne Robert Packer Hosp., Sayre, Pa., 1903-04, asst. surgeon, 1905-08; visiting surgeon Peoples Co-operative Hosp., Sayre, 1910-30; mem. Lehigh Valley R.R. surg. corps since 1904; visiting surgeon Tioga Co. Gen. Hosp. since 1930; surgeon Northern Pa. Power Co.; pres. South Waverly (Pa.) Water Co. Dir. Sayre Borough Sch. Dist., 1915-29. First Pres. Gen. Sullivan Council, Boy Scouts of America; pres. local exec. bd. and mem. state exec. bd. Y.M.C.A. Dist. gov. 35th Rotary dist., 1923-24; chmn. Rotary International Conv. Com., 1924-25; dir. Rotary International., 1925-26, vice-chmn. finance com. 1927-28. Mem. Bradford Co. Med. Soc. Pa. Med. Soc. (past pres.), New York and New England Ry. Surgeons. Republican. Presbyterian. Mason, Elk, Moose. Clubs: Sayre Rotary, Shepard Hills Country. Home: 710 W. Lockhart So. Office: 113 W. Lockhart St., Sayre, Pa.; also Waverly, N.Y.

FISHER, Charles A., banker; b. Union City, Pa., Sept. 9, 1875; s. Samuel J. and Caroline (Stranahan) F.; ed. Pittsburgh High Sch.; m. Ritchie Newell, Oct. 20, 1897 (now dec.); children—Howard R., Henry C., Charles N. Bookkeeper, Oliver Wire Co., 1894-98; with Jones & Laughlin Steel Corpn., Pittsburgh, 1898-1928, advancing from bookkeeper to pres.; pres. Pitt. Nat. Bank, Pittsburgh, since 1933. Vice-pres. Pittsburgh Park and Playground Soc.; Bd. of Edn., Pittsburgh. Clubs: Duquesne (Pittsburgh); Ross Mountain Park (New Florence, Pa.). Home: 5139 Westminster Pl. Office: Pitt Nat. Bank, Pittsburgh, Pa.

FISHER, Charles F., mem. surg. staff St. Mary's Hosp.; visiting surgeon St. Joseph's Hosp., Buckhannon, W.Va., also Gen. and Weston City hosps., Weston, W.Va. Address: 321 W. Main St., Clarksburg, W.Va.

FISHER, Clarence Conrad, clergyman; b. Beaver County, Pa., Feb. 27, 1887; s. Dan and Ada (Bentel) F.; prep. edn. Ellwood City (Pa.) High Sch., 1902-05, Beaver Coll. Prep. Sch., 1906-07; A.B., Allegheny Coll., Meadeville, Pa., 1911; B.D., Drew U., Madison, N.J., 1916; D.D., Waynesburg (Pa.) Coll., 1934; m. Mildred Deyo, 1920; children—Ruth Ina, Dan Deyo. Ordained to ministry Meth. Ch., 1913; pastor College Hill M.E. Ch., Beaver Falls, Pa., 1916-18, First M.E. Ch., Meyersdale, Pa., 1919-25, Brushton M.E. Ch., Pittsburgh, 1925-28, First M.E. Ch., Waynesburg, Pa., 1929-36; pastor Dormont Meth. Ch., Pittsburgh, since 1937. Served as chaplain, U.S. Army, 1918-19. Mem. bd. of mgrs. M.E. Hosp. and Home for Aged, Pittsburgh. Mason. Home: 2973 Mattern Av., Pittsburgh, Pa.

FISHER, Frank, Jr.; v.p. U.S. Fidelity & Guaranty Co. Home: 526 Orkney Road, Govanstown, Md. Office: Calvert and Redwood Sts., Baltimore, Md.

FISHER, Frank Palmer, clergyman; b. nr. Milesburg, Pa., Aug. 15, 1880; s. James John and Margaret (Glossner) F.; student Gettysburg (Pa.) Coll. Acad., 1903-04, A.B., 1908, A.M., 1911; study Luth. Theol. Sem., Gettysburg, Pa., 1908-11; (hon.) D.D., Thiel Coll., Greenville, Pa., 1937; m. Mary Edith Buck, Oct. 26, 1911; 1 son, Frank Palmer. Engaged in teaching pub. schs., 1902-03; ordained to ministry Luth. Ch., 1911; pastor Petersburg, Pa., 1911-13, Altoona, Pa., 1913-22; pastor Bethel Luth. Ch., Pittsburgh, Pa., since 1922; mem. Synodical Bd. Home Missions; del. to Nat. Convs., 1918, 1922, 1936, 1938; Ch. Synodical Com. to raise $107,000; Ch. Synodical Com. on Ministerial Education; conference sec. and president; mem. bd. mgrs. Luth. Inner Mission Society. Mem. exec. com. Ministerial Union of Allegheny Co.; pres. Manchester Ministerial Assn.; mem. of Nat. Geog. Soc. Republican. Lutheran. Odd Fellow. Club: K.D.K. Literary. Editor The Lutheran Monthly, ofcl. organ Pittsburgh Synod. Home: 1323 Liverpool St., Pittsburgh, Pa.

FISHER, George Curtis, clergyman; b. East Liverpool, O., Feb. 21, 1873; s. Richardson and Ellen Margaret (Thompson) F.; A.B., Coll. of Wooster (O.), 1900; B.D., Western Theol. Sem., 1903; S.T.B., Princeton Theol. Sem., 1904; (hon.) D.D., Wooster Coll., 1921; unmarried. Ordained to ministry Presbyn. Ch., 1904; pastor Mt. Pleasant, Pa., 1904-08, Latrobe, Pa., 1908-21; pastor Highland Presbyn. Ch., Pittsburgh, Pa., since 1921. Pres. Bd. trustees Western Theol. Sem., and Johnson C. Smith Univ., Charlotte, N.C. Republican. Presbyterian. Home: 5919 Wellesley Av., Pittsburgh, Pa.

FISHER, Gordon, mfr. welded tubular products; b. Swissvale, Pa., Nov. 2, 1874; s. Rev. Samuel J. (D.D.) and Annie (Shreve) F.; B.A., Princeton, 1895; LL.B., New York Law Sch., 1897; m. Matilda C. Milligan, July 6, 1901; children—Gordon, John M. Began practice with Dalzell, Scott and Gordon, Pittsburgh, 1898, admitted to firm, 1906, under title of Dalzell, Fisher & Dalzell, and continued to practice until 1929; pres. Spang, Chalfant & Co., Inc., mfrs. seamless and welded tubular products, 1927-30, chmn. bd. since Sept. 15, 1930; director First National Bank (Etna, Pa.); trustee Thaw Coke Trust. Formerly lecturer on med. law, University of Pittsburgh. Republican. Presbyterian. Mason (32°, Shriner). Clubs: Duquesne, Pittsburgh, Pittsburgh Athletic, Pittsburgh Golf, Fox Chapel Golf, Longue Vue. Home: 4 Colonial Place. Office: Grant Bldg., Pittsburgh, Pa.

FISHER, Grant Eugene, clergyman; b. East Brook, Pa., Oct. 30, 1865; s. Thomas George and Mary (Burns) F.; student Westminster Coll., New Wilmington, Pa., 1884-86; A.B., Grove City (Pa.) Coll., 1891, (hon.) A.M., 1896, (hon.) D.D., 1906; m. Carroll Loupe,

June 18, 1896. Ordained to ministry Presbyn. Ch. U.S.A., 1896; pastor, Fairview, W.Va., 1896-1900, West Alexander, Pa., 1900-09, Dundee Ch., Omaha, Neb., 1909-15; pastor Turtle Creek, Pa., 1915-1932; commr. to Gen. Assembly of Presbyn. Ch. U.S.A., Denver, Colo., 1909, St. Louis, Mo., 1919, Grand Rapids, Mich., 1924. Republican. Presbyterian. Author: Outline Studies Book of Acts, 1911; Commentary on Esther; contbr. articles to religious and secular jours. Wrote several sacred solos, among them, "By the Rivers." Home: 926 Adams St., New Castle, Pa.

FISHER, Henry, physician; b. Phila., Pa., Sept. 19, 1856; s. Jacob and Susan Frost (Harmer) F.; Ph.G., Phila. Coll. Pharmacy and Sci., 1877; M.D., Medico-Chirurg. Coll., Phila., 1883; (hon.) Pharm.D., Temple U., Phila., 1910; unmarried. Engaged as pharmacist in Phila., 1877-83; engaged in practice medicine and teaching in Phila. continuously since 1883; asst. prof. materia medica and pharmacy, Medico-Chirurg. Coll., Phila., 1884-1900, prof. materia medica and botany, Pharmacy Dept., 1900-06; prof. pharmacology, Pharmacy Dept. Temple U., Phila., 1907-35, emeritus prof. materia medica and pharmacology since 1935 and lecturer on pharm. ethics. Served in Sr. Med. Corps during World War. Mem. Phila. City Councils and Sch. Bd. (sectional). Pres. North Branch Y.M.C.A., Phila., 1912-20; now pres. bd. of council, Penn Asylum. Mem. Pa. State and Phila. Co. med. socs., Phi Rho Sigma, Zeta Phi. Republican. Methodist. Mason (K.T., 32°, Shriner). Club: N.E. Medical. Home: 1129 Dyre St., Philadelphia, Pa.

FISHER, Isaac Calvin, clergyman; b. Marion Twp., Berks Co., Pa., Oct. 16, 1867; s. Benneville and Eliza (Miller) F.; A.B., Ursinus Coll., 1889, A.M., same, 1893; grad. Ursinus Sch. Theology, 1891; (hon.) D.D., Ursinus Coll., 1908; m. Eva S. Kehl, of Boyertown, Pa., Nov. 4, 1891; 1 dau., Ada M. Ordained to ministry Reformed Ch. in U.S., 1891; pastor East Vincent-Pikeland Reformed Charge, nr. Phoenixville, Pa., 1891-92; pastor, St. Mark's Reformed Ch., Lebanon, Pa., 1892-1932, pastor emeritus since 1932; served as pres. Lebanon Classis, 1899 and since 1938; pres. Eastern Synod Reformed Ch. in U.S., 1920-21; mem. Bd. Home Missions, 1908-26; vice-pres. Pa. Christian Endeavor Union, 1904. Mem. and pres. Lebanon Co. Emergency Relief Bd., 1936-39; mem. bd. dirs. Lebanon Co. Childrens Aid Soc. since 1937; gen. sec. Pa. Chantauqua, Mt. Gretna, 1896-98. Dir. Ursinus Coll., Collegeville, Pa., since 1905. Reformed Ch. in U.S. Home: 135 S. Tenth St., Lebanon, Pa.

FISHER, J. Wilmer, lawyer; b. Reading, Pa., June 18, 1870; s. Henry J. and Mary C. (Keever) F.; student pub. schs., Reading, Pa.; LL.B., Dickinson Sch. of Law, Carlisle, Pa., 1896; unmarried. Began career as civil engr., 1886; admitted to Pa. bar, 1896, and since engaged in gen. practice of law at Reading; admitted to bars of Pa. Superior and Supreme cts. and U.S. Circuit and Dist. cts.; mem. bd. dirs. and gen. counsel trust dept., Berks County Trust Co., Reading. Treas. Rep. Co. Com., Rep. Candidate Dist. Atty. of Berks Co., 1901, Rep. Candidate for Congress, Berks-Lehigh Dist., 1906 and 1918. Pres. bd. trustees, Reading Pub. Library; trustee Muhlenberg Coll., Dickinson Sch. of Law, Reading Musical Foundation. Mem. Am., Pa., Berks Co. bar assns., Delta Chi. Republican. Lutheran. Mason (K.T., 32°). Clubs: Wyomissing, University, Temple, Torch, Hungry, Bean, Northeastern Republican League. Home: 130 N. 8th St. Office: 29 N. 6th St., Reading, Pa.

FISHER, Jake, judge; b. Flatwoods, W.Va., May 26, 1871; s. Benjamin Franklin and Margaret (Sutton) F.; student Glenville (W.Va.) State Normal Sch., 1888-89; B.S., Nat. Normal U., Lebanon, O., 1892; student law Washington and Lee U., Lexington, Va., 1892-93; m. Ella Corbett, Aug. 3, 1897; children—Frank Corbett, Mary Jake (Mrs. Raymond E. Freed), Virginia (Mrs. R. E. Bierer), Barbara. Admitted to bar, 1893; mem. W.Va. House of Delegates, 1898-1900, W.Va. State Senate, 1904-12; judge W.Va. Circuit Ct. since 1912; mem. W.Va. Judicial Council. Democrat. Methodist. Address: Sutton, W.Va.

FISHER, John S., lawyer, ex-gov.; b. South Mahoning Twp., Indiana Co., Pa., May 25, 1867; s. Samuel Royer and Mariah (McGaughey) F.; grad. Indiana State Normal Sch. of Pa., 1886; LL.D., Lafayette, Franklin and Marshall, Westminster and Juniata colls., U. of Pa., Pa. Mil. Coll. and Temple Univ.; m. Hapsie Miller, Oct. 11, 1893; children—Robert M., Mrs. Mary F. Brown. Admitted to Pa. bar, 1893, and practiced at Indiana as mem. Cunningham & Fisher until assuming duties as gov.; now chmn. bd. Nat. Union Fire Ins. Co.; dir. Forbes Nat. Bank (Pittsburgh), Savings & Trust Co. (Indiana, Pa.). Mem. Pa. State Senate, 1901-09; chairman Capitol Investigating Commn. which exposed the frauds in connection with furnishing of State Capitol at Harrisburg; apptd. state commr. of banking, 1919; also mem. Commn. on Constitutional Amendment and Revision, Pa.; del. Rep. Nat. Conv., Chicago, 1916, at large, Kansas City, Mo., 1928, Cleveland, 1936; gov. of Pa., term 1927-30, retiring from all business connections and trusteeships while in office. Mem. Pittsburgh Chamber Commerce (dir.), Am. and Pa. bar assns., Pa. Soc. Sons of Am. Revolution (pres.). United Presbyn. Clubs: Union League (Phila.); Harrisburg (Harrisburg, Pa.); Cosmopolitan (Indiana, Pa.); Duquesne (Pittsburgh). Home: Indiana, Pa.

FISHER, John Ward, educator; b. Cumberland Valley, Pa., Oct. 20, 1888; s. John Thomas and Nancy (Growden) F.; grad. Gettysburg (Pa.) Acad., 1910; A.B., Gettysburg Coll., 1914; graduate student at Columbia Univ., 1921-22; A.M., Univ. of Md., 1934; m. Naomi Goulding Shipley, May 20, 1918; children—John Ward (dec.), Edna Evelyn, Grace Charlotte. Began as rural sch. teacher, Bedford Co., Pa., 1906; teacher Dickinson Sem., Williamsport, Pa., 1914-16, Troy Conf. Acad., Poultney, Vt., 1916-17, Wilbraham (Mass.) Acad., 1919-21, Newark (N.J.) Acad., 1921-22, Allegany High Sch., Cumberland, Md., 1922-25, Boonsboro (Md.) High Sch., 1925-26, Hagerstown (Md.) High Sch., 1926-27; prin. Bruce High Sch., Westernport, Md., since 1927. Served 2d lt., 87th Div., 312th Trench Mortar Batt., U.S. Army, during World War; now maj. 622d Coast Arty. Reserve. Mem. Reserve Officers Assn., Coast Arty. Assn., N.E.A., Phi Sigma Kappa, Kappa Phi Kappa. Republican. Methodist. Club: Rotary Internat. (Piedmont, W.Va.). Home: 164 River Rd., Westernport, Md.

FISHER, Mahlon Leonard, author; b. Williamsport, Pa., July 20, 1874; s. John Stires and Mary Elizabeth (Jamison) F.; ed. high sch. and pvtly. Studied architecture in various offices, and in practice many years. Founder, 1917, and editor The Sonnet; asso. editor The Golden Galleon, Kansas City, Mo., since 1924. Mem. Poetry Soc. America. Author: Sonnets—A First Series, 1917; Lyrics Between the Years, 1928; (verse) River's Gift, 1928. Contbr. verse to mags. Extensively represented in various anthologies. Home: Williamsport, Pa.

FISHER, Ralph F., lawyer; b. York, Pa., Nov. 3, 1901; s. Henry F. and Amelia (Carls) F.; LL.B., Dickinson Sch. of Law, Carlisle, Pa.; m. Katherine J. Rohrbaugh, Apr. 7, 1926; 1 dau., Katherine Jane. Admitted to Pa. Supreme Ct. bar, 1924, and established private practice at York, Pa., 1924; sr. mem. law firm Fisher, Ports & May since 1937; dir. Central Nat. Bank & Trust Co. Dist. atty., York Co., Pa., 1930-34. Mem. York Co. and Pa. bar assns. Republican. United Brethren. Clubs: Lafayette, University, Rotary, Country (York, Pa.). Home: 137 Peyton Road. Office: 103 E. Market St., York, Pa.

FISHER, Robert Miller, lawyer; b. Indiana, Pa., Sept. 5, 1894; s. John S. and Hapsie (Miller) F.; student Indiana Normal Sch., 1909-11, Kiskiminetas Springs Sch., 1911-13; A.B., Amherst Coll., 1917, Harvard Law Sch., 1918-21; m. Gladys Washburn, June 22, 1925; children—Mary Washburn, John Stuchell, II. Admitted to Pa. Supreme Ct. bar, 1922; since in gen. practice of law; mem. law firm Fisher & Ruddock since 1931; dir. Savings & Trust Co. of Indiana (Pa.), Indiana Thrift Corpn., Stewart R.R. Co., Shenango Valley R.R., Beech Creek Extension R.R. Co., Clearfield Supply Co., Musser Forests, Inc. Dir. Indiana County Hosp. Mem. Am. Bar Assn., Pa. State Bar Assn., Indiana County (Pa.) Bar Assn., Phi Kappa Psi. Republican. Presbyn. Clubs: Cosmopolitan, Kiwanis (Indiana, Pa.); Amherst (New York). Home: 220 N. Sixth St. Office: Savings & Trust Co. Bldg., Indiana, Pa.

FISHER, Samuel Jay; mem. law firm Fisher & Fisher. Address: Union Trust Bldg., Baltimore, Md.

FISHER, William Alexander, surgeon; b. Baltimore, Md., Apr. 26, 1874; s. William Alexander and Louise (Este) F.; grad. St. Paul's Sch., Concord, N.H., 1892; A.B., Princeton U., 1896; M.D., Johns Hopkins, 1900; m. Anne Courtenay Baylor, Oct. 17, 1906; children—Ellen Bruce (wife of Dr. John Earle Bordley), Elizabeth Gault, William Alexander. Interne Johns Hopkins Hosp., 1900-01; asst. resident and resident Union Memorial Hosp., 1901-03; asst. visiting surgeon Johns Hopkins Hosp., Baltimore, since 1924; now visiting surgeon Union Memorial Hosp., Church Home and Infirmary, Hosp. for Women of Md.; asso. in surgery, Johns Hopkins U. since 1920. Served as lt. col., Med. Corps, U.S. Army, with A.E.F., during World War. Decorated D.S.M. Trustee Gilman Country Sch. for Boys. Fellow Am. Coll. of Surgeons; mem. Am. Surg. Assn., A.M.A., Soc. Clin. Surgery, Interurban Surgery Soc., Med. and Chirurg. Faculty of Md. Democrat. Episcopalian. Clubs: Maryland (Baltimore); University Cottage (Princeton, N.J.). Home: 20 Blythewood Rd. Office: 715 Park Av., Baltimore, Md.

FISHER, William Henry, corpn. official; b. Chambersburg, Pa., Jan. 24, 1873; s. Henry and Elizabeth F.; student pub. schs. and high sch.; m. Mary Florence Wood, of Chambersburg, Pa., Nov. 15, 1899. Asso. with T. B. Wood's Sons Co., mfrs., Chambersburg, Pa., continuously since entering employ as clk., 1891, sec., sales mgr. and dir. when co. was inc., 1906-28, vice-pres. and dir. since 1928; vice-pres. and dir. Nat. Bank of Chambersburg, Cumberland Valley Transit Co.; pres. and dir. Chambersburg Industries, Inc. Trustee Theol. Sem. of Reformed Ch. Dir. Hoffman Orphanage, Pa. State Soc. for Crippled Children. Dir. Power Transmission Council, Chambersburg Chamber of Commerce; nat. counselor U.S. Chamber of Commerce. Mem. Pa. State Chamber of Commerce, Chambersburg Commercial Club, Kittochtinny Hist. Soc. Republican. Mem. Evang. Reformed Ch. Mason (K.T., Shriner). Club: Rotary (dir., past pres.). Home: 301 Philadelphia Av., Chambersburg, Pa.

FISHLER, Franklin; editor Ridgewood News. Address: Ridgewood, N.J.

FISKE, Charles, P.E. bishop; b. New Brunswick, N.J., Mar. 16, 1868; s. William H. and Mary Elizabeth (Houghton) F.; A.B., St. Stephen's Coll., Annandale, N.Y., 1893, D.D., 1912; B.D., Gen. Theol. Sem., 1896, also S.T.D.; LL.D., Syracuse U., 1916, Litt.D., 1930; D.D., Hamilton Coll., 1921; L.H.D., Hobart Coll., 1926; m. Bessie Curlett Crampton, 1901. Deacon, 1896, priest, 1897, P.E. Ch.; asso. missionary Trenton, N.J., 1896-97; rector Westfield, N.J., 1897-1900; asst. Mt. Calvary Ch., Baltimore, 1900-01; rector Ch. of the Transfiguration, Philadelphia, 1901-02, Somerville, N.J., 1902-08, St. John's Ch., Norristown, Pa., 1908-10, St. Michael and All Angels, Baltimore, 1910-15; consecrated bishop coadjutor of Central N.Y., 1915, bishop, 1923. Declined election as bishop coadjutor of Dallas, 1913; retired, May 1936; since then spl. lecturer at Coll. of Preachers, Washington, at Phila. Divinity Sch., etc.; asso. editor of the Living Church, Milwaukee; special preacher at various colleges and city parishes. Author: The Perils of Respectability; The Experiment of Faith; Back to Christ; The Faith by Which We Live; Sacrifice and Service; The Religion of the Incarnation; The Christ We Know; The Confessions of a Puzzled Parson, 1928; Calvary Today, 1929; The Real Jesus (with Prof. B. S. Easton), 1929;

From Skepticism to Faith, 1934. Contbr. to mags., also to various collections of essays and special articles. Address: 3405 Greenway, Baltimore, Md.

FISS, Ira Thomas, banker; b. Shamokin Dam, Pa., Nov. 7, 1888; s. R. C. and Utica (Gemberling) F.; student Bucknell Acad. and Susquehanna U.; m. Anna Amanda Hottenstein, Dec. 14, 1916. Operator of contracting firm since 1910; pres. Snyder County State Bank. First burgess of Shamokin Dam, 2 terms; mem. Pa. Ho. of Reps. Scout master, Boy Scouts of America, 1912-20. Dist. pres. Patriotic Order Sons of America. Republican. Mason (32°), Grange. Club: Snyder County Republican. Address: Shamokin Dam, Pa.

FISTER, H. Ray, partner Stoehr & Fister; b. Orangeville, Pa., Dec. 16, 1879; s. Ranslo and Caroline (Stiner) F.; student pub. schs. and business coll.; m. Jessie MacLeod, May 21, 1938. Employed by P. B. Finley Dept. Store, 1901-02; bookeeper, later office mgr., J. Scott Inglis Carpet Store, partner to 1906; partner Stoehr, Fister & Jennings, 1906-12, Stoehr & Fister, successors, since 1912; dir. Third Nat. Bank & Trust Co. Clubs: Rotary, Scranton, Scranton Country (Scranton); Mens (Benton); Gatneau Rod and Gun (Quebec, Canada). Mason. Home: R.D. 1, Dalton, Pa. Office: 200 Adams Av., Scranton, Pa.

FITCH, Edgar Kaaz, mfr. cotton textiles; b. Baltimore, Md., Aug. 21, 1892; s. Alfred and Emma (Kaaz) F.; student Bryant & Stratton Bus. Coll., Baltimore, 1905-06, Md. Inst., 1906-10; B.S., Washington Coll., Chestertown, Md., 1914; grad. study Johns Hopkins U., 1914-17; m. Thelma Buffington, Sept. 21, 1918; 1 dau., Lee. Employed as auditor, Standard Oil Co. of N.J., New York City, 1917-19; with Haskins & Sells, accountants, Baltimore, 1919; asso. with Mount Vernon—Woodberry Mills, Inc., mfrs. cotton textiles, Baltimore, since 1919, accountant, 1919-26, asst. sec., 1926-33, treas. since 1933; sec., treas. and dir. Tallassee Falls Mfg. Co., Tallassee, Ala., since 1933; asst. sec., asst. treas. and dir. Columbia (S.C.) Mills Co., since 1933. Served on spl. com. Baltimore Emergency Relief Commn., 1936; citizens com., Dept. Pub. Welfare, 1939. Democrat. Episcopalian. Club: Mt. Washington (Md.). Home: 1706 South Rd., Mt. Washington, Md. Office: Mercantile Trust Bldg., Baltimore, Md.

FITCH, William Kountz, pres. Dravo Doyle Co.; b. Rockford, Ill., Nov. 2, 1889; s. William H. and Katherine (Kountz) F.; A.B., Yale, 1910; M.E., U. of Wis., Madison, Wis., 1913; unmarried. Began as salesman Dravo Doyle Co., Pittsburgh; 1913, mgr. Indianapolis (Ind.) office, 1915, mgr. Cleveland (O.) office, 1920, vice-pres. 1925-34, pres. since 1934; vice-pres. and dir. Dravo Corpn.; dir. Dravo Doyle Co., Trilok Co., Am. Tubular Elevator Co., Standard Builders Supply Co. Served as 1st lt., Ordnance Dept., U.S. Army, 1917-18, capt. Coast Arty. Res. Corps, 1918-28, mem. Troop A, 107th Cavalry, Ohio N.G., Cleveland, 1925-26. Mem. Psi Upsilon, Tau Beta Pi. Republican. Episcopalian. Clubs: University, Duquesne, Pittsburgh, Harvard-Yale-Princeton, Allegheny Country, Fox Chapel Golf (Pittsburgh); University (Cleveland); Yale (New York). Home: University Club. Office: 300 Penn Av., Pittsburgh, Pa.

FITE, Warner, college prof.; b. Philadelphia, Mar. 5, 1867; s. George and Sallie Gibbs (Liddle F.; A.B., Haverford (Pa.) Coll., 1889; Phila. Div. Sch., 1889-90; post-grad. student, univs. of Pa., 1890-91, Berlin, 1891-92, Munich, 1892-93, Pa., 1893-94, Ph.D., 1894; m. Esther Wallace Sturges, June 29, 1901 (died Oct. 2, 1916); children—Charles S., George L., Mary D., Franklin K.; m. 2d, Florence Odell, of Chicago, Oct. 10, 1930. Instr. philosophy, 1894-96, and dean of faculty, 1895-97, Williams Coll.; docent, asst., and instr. psychology, U. of Chicago, 1897-1903; instr. philosophy, U. of Tex., 1903-06; jr. prof. philosophy, 1906-08, prof. 1908-15, Ind. U., Bloomington; Stuart prof. ethics, 1915-35, professor emeritus since 1935, Princeton University. Lecturer in philosophy, Harvard Univ., 1911-12; acting prof. philosophy, Leland Stanford Jr. U., fall semester, 1913. Mem. Am. Philos. Assn., Phi Beta Kappa. Author: Introductory Study of Ethics, 1903; Individualism, 1911; Moral Philosophy—the Critical View of Life, 1925; The Living Mind, 1930; The Platonic Legend, 1934. Translator: Mist ("Niebla"), by Miguel de Unamuno, 1928. Contbr. to mags. Home: Hopewell, N.J.

FITERMAN, Morris, physician; b. Philadelphia, Pa., May 14, 1901; s. Manuel and Sophia (Davidman) F.; ed. Dartmouth Coll., 1920-24; M.D., Hahnemann Med. Coll., Phila., 1928; unmarried. Interne St. Luke's and Children hosps., Phila., 1928-29; engaged in practice medicine, Phila., since 1929; lecturer medicine, Hahnemann Med. Coll. and Hosp. since 1929; med. inspr. Bur. Health, Phila., since 1931. Mem. Am. Inst. Homeopathy, Pa. State Med. Soc., Phila. Homeopathic Med. Soc., Phi Lambda Kappa. Jewish religion. Club: Dartmouth Alumni (Phila.). Home: 6152 Spruce St., Philadelphia, Pa.

FITHIAN, J(osiah) Herbert, ins. agency; b. Bridgeton, N.J., Jan. 21, 1893; s. Howard W. and Jennie (Hosford) F.; ed. pub. sch. and high sch., Bridgeton, N.J., Penn Charter High Sch., Phila., 1912-15; m. Laura A. Mayer, Dec. 16, 1921; children—J. Herbert, Jr., Sarah Allen. Mem. firm H. W. Fithian & Son, 1915-18; surveyor Seabrook Farms, Bridgeton, N.J., 1920; foreman of maintenance N.J. State Highway Dept., 1920-25; vice-pres. Protection Service Co., ins. agts. and brokers, Bridgeton, N.J., since 1925; dir. Bridgeton Gas Light Co., Cohanzick Bldg. & Loan Assn. Served in Med. Detachment F.A., U.S.A., 1918-19. Republican. Presbyn. Mason. Home: 19 Franklin Drive, Bridgeton, N.J. Office: 26 S. Laurel St., Bridgeton, N.J.

FITZGERALD, Rufus Henry, educator; b. Pelham, N.C., November 22, 1890; s. James Obadiah and Mary Reese (Shelton) F.; B.A., Guilford (N.C.) Coll., 1911; M.A., U. of Tenn., 1919; m. Damie Mildred Cornell, June 11, 1914; children—Helen Cornell, Damie Mildred. General sec. Y.M.C.A., Miss. Agrl. and Mech. Coll., 1911-12, U. of Tenn., 1912-16; athletic coach and dir., U. of Tenn., 1917-19; gen. sec. Y.M.C.A., State U. of Ia., 1919-23, dir. Ia. Memorial Union Corpn. of State U. of Ia., 1923-38; dir. student service, 1925-38; dir. and prof. Sch. of Fine Arts, head dept. history and appreciation of fine arts, State U. of Ia., 1929-38; provost U. of Pittsburgh since 1938. Trustee Ia. Sch. of Religion; chmn. Fine Arts Commn. of Am. Assn. of Colls.; dir. The Art Soc. of Pittsburgh. Mem. Sigma Chi, Phi Kappa Phi (hon.). Presbyn. Clubs: Rotary, University (Pittsburgh); University Faculty. Home: 4303 Parkman Av. Address: University of Pittsburgh, Pittsburgh, Pa.

FITZGERALD, Thomas, street ry. exec.; b. Baltimore, Md., May 30, 1878; s. Thomas and Fanny (Kettlewell) F.; A.B., Johns Hopkins, 1898; m. Laura Unger, Dec. 5, 1899; children—Elizabeth K. (Mrs. Francis P. Browning, deceased), Thomas, Frances K. (Mrs. Lynford A. Keating). General superintendent Norfolk, Portsmouth & Newport News Company, 1902-03; gen. mgr. Lexington Ry. Co., 1903-05; purchasing agt. and asst. to v.p. Cincinnati Traction Co., 1905-07; asst. gen. mgr. same and Ohio Traction Co., 1907-13, gen. mgr. both cos., 1913-17; cons. electric ry. engr., Pittsburgh, Pa., 1920-24; gen. mgr. Pittsburgh Rys. Co., 1924-25; v.p. Pittsburgh Rys. Co. and Pittsburgh Motor Coach Co., also dir. 37 subsidiaries, 1925-38; trustee and gen. mgr. 1938; dir. Pittsburgh Rys. Co., Pittsburgh Motor Coach Co. Maj., inf., U.S.R., 1917; maj., inf., U.S.A., 1918, lieutenant colonel, 1918-19. Member Am. Transit Assn., Am. Inst. Elec. Engrs., Soc. Am. Mil. Engrs., Engring. Soc. Western Pa., Vets. of Foreign Wars, Am. Legion, Kappa Alpha. Mason (K.T., Shriner). Clubs: Duquesne, University, Traffic, Railway, Fellows, Rotary, Pittsburgh Atheltic Assn., Longue Vue. Home: 5216 5th Av. Office: 435 6th Av., Pittsburgh, Pa.

FITZHUGH, Percy Keese (pseudonym Hugh Lloyd), author; b. Brooklyn, N.Y., Sept. 7, 1876; s. William Wyvill and Mary (Keese) F.; educated public schools and at the Pratt Institute, Brooklyn; m. Harriet Lloyd LePorte, July 13, 1900; children—Lawrence Stetson Millicent Alden (dec.). Author: The Golden Rod Story-Book, 1906; The Colonial Series (6 vols.), 1907; The Story of a Fight, 1907; The Galleon Treasure, 1908; King Time, 1908; Along the Mohawk Trail, 1912; For Uncle Sam, Boss, 1913; In the Path of La Salle, 1914; Tom Slade, Boy Scout of the Moving Pictures, 1915; Uncle Sam's Outdoor Magic, 1916; Tom Slade at Temple Camp, 1916; Tom Slade on the River, 1917; The Boys' Book of Scouts, 1917; The History of the United States from Appomattox to Germany, 1918; Tom Slade with the Colors, 1918; Tom Slade with the Boys Over There, 1918; Tom Slade on a Transport, 1918; Tom Slade, Motorcycle Dispatch Bearer, 1918; Tom Slade with the Flying Corps, 1919; Roy Blakeley, Scout, series (5 vols.), 1918; The Winning of the Golden Cross, 1920; Bobby Cullen on the Mississippi, 1920; Tom Slade Back Home, 1920; Tom Slade, Scout Master, 1920; Tom Slade, Scout Hero; Tom Slade on Mystery Trail; Roy Blakeley's Motor Caravan; Roy Blakeley—Lost, Strayed or Stolen; Tom Slade at Black Lake, 1921; Roy Blakeley at the Haunted Camp; Roy Blakeley's Bee Line Hike; Roy Blakeley's Funny Bone Hike; Pee-wee Harris, 1922; Pee-wee Harris on the Trail, 1922; Pee-wee Harris in Camp, 1922; Pee-wee Harris in Luck, 1922; Pee-wee Harris Adrift, 1922; Tom Slade's Double Dare, 1923; Pee-wee Harris, F.O.B. Bridgeboro, 1923; Tom Slade on Overlook Mountain, 1924; Pee-wee Harris, Clean-up Worker, 1924; Roy Blakeley on the Tangled Trail, 1924; Westy Martin, 1924; Westy Martin in the Yellowstone, 1924; Tom Slade at Bear Mountain, 1924; Pee-wee Harris As Good as His Word, 1925; Roy Blakeley On the Mohawk Trail, 1925; Westy Martin in the Rockies, 1925; Tom Slade Forest Ranger, 1926; Roy Blakeley's Elastic Hike, 1926; Pee-wee Harris Mayor for a Day, 1926; Tom Slade in the North Woods, 1927; Roy Blakeley's Roundabout Hike, 1927; Pee-wee Harris and the Sunken Treasure, 1927; Hervey Willetts, 1927; Tom Slade at Shadow Isle, 1928; Pee-wee Harris on the Briny Deep, 1928; Roy Blakeley's Happy-go-lucky Hike, 1928; Westy Martin in the Purple Sage, 1928; Skinny McCord, 1928; Tom Slade in Haunted Cavern, 1929; Roy Blakeley's Go As You Please Hike, 1929; Pee-wee Harris in Darkest Africa, 1929. Westy Martin on Old Indian Trail, 1929; Wigwag Weigand, 1929; Spiffy Henshaw, 1929; Westy Martin in the Sierras, The Parachute Jumper, Pee-wee Turns Detective, Roy Blakeley up in the Air, Mark Gilmore—all 1930; The Hermit of Gordon's Creek, Kidnapped in the Jungle, The Copperhead Trail Mystery, The Mysterious Arab, The Smuggler's Secret—all 1931; Out West with Westy Martin, 1933; Adventures of Holman Barcley, 1934; Skippy Dare Stories, 3 vols., 1935; The Concise Biographical Dictionary, 1935. Editor Every Girl's Library (10 vols.), 1909. Co-editor Lossing's History of the United States. Contbr. to mags. Home: Oradell, N.J. Address: care Grosset & Dunlap, Publishers, 1140 Broadway, New York, N.Y.

FITZ-HUGH, Thomas, Jr., physician; b. Baltimore, Md., Dec. 1, 1894; s. Thomas and Katharine (Lefevre) F.; grad. Jefferson Sch. for Boys, Charlottesville, Va., 1912; A.B., U. of Va., 1915, A.M., 1917; M.D., U. of Pa., 1921; m. Anne Mary Will, May 30, 1925; 1 dau., Mary Ann Harrison. Interne U. of Pa. Hosp., 1921-23; practicing physician in Phila. since 1923; instr. in medicine, U. of Pa. Sch. of Medicine, 1923-30, asso. 1930-33, asst. prof. clin. medicine since 1933; chief of hematologic clinic, U. of Pa. Hosp., since 1929. Served as private Med. Corps, U.S. Army, with Base Hosp. No. 41, A.E.F. in St. Denis, France, 1917-19. Fellow Am. Coll. Physicians, Coll. of Physicians of Phila., A.M.A.; mem. Am. Soc. Clin. Investigation, Assn. of American Physicians, Delta Psi, Phi Beta Kappa, Alpha Omega Alpha and Sigma Xi fraternities. Republican since 1934. Episcopalian. Clubs: Philadelphia Country, St. Anthony (Phila.). Contbr. to med. jours., articles on diseases of the blood and blood forming organs. Home: 336 Penn Rd., Wynnewood. Office: 2016 De Lancey Place, Philadelphia, Pa.

FITZMAURICE, Edmond J., bishop; b. Tarbert, County Kerry, Ireland, June 24, 1881; s. William and Joan (Costello) F.; student St. Brendan's Coll., Killarney, Ireland, Coll. St. Trond, Belgium; grad. North Am. Coll., Rome, Italy, 1904. Came to U.S., 1904, naturalized, 1910. Ordained priest, R.C. Ch., 1904; asst. rector Annunciation Ch., Philadelphia, Pa., 1904-06; prof. theology, St. Charles' Sem., Overbrook, Phila., 1906-14; chancellor Archdiocese of Phila., 1914-20; rector St. Charles' Sem., 1920-25; bishop of Diocese of Wilmington, Del., since 1925. Home: 1301 Delaware Av., Wilmington, Del.*

FITZPATRICK, Clarke J., v.p., sec. and dir. U.S. Fidelity & Guaranty Co. Home: 18 Seminole Av., Catonsville, Md. Office: Calvert & Redwood Sts., Baltimore, Md.

FITZPATRICK, Helena Way, artist; b. Cape May Court House, N.J., Aug. 10, 1889; d. Julius and Ella (Corson) Way; grad. Bucknell Inst., Lewisburg, Pa., 1909; grad. Phila. Sch. of Design for Women, 1912; B.F.A., Moore Inst. and School of Design, Phila., 1938; m. William Edgar Fitzpatrick, Nov. 13, 1921; 1 son, Julius Way. Art dir., Bucknell U., Lewisburg, Pa., 1913-17; art teacher, Cape May (N.J.) High Sch., 1918-20; art dir., State Teachers Coll., Millersville, Pa., 1920-21; docent, Phila. Museum of Art, since 1934; has had private studio for several years. Exhibited: Plastic Club, Circulating Exhibitions, Cape May Co. (N.J.) Art League, Moore Inst. Sch. of Design, Montclair (N.J.) Mus., Special Show for N.J. Artists; one man Show Carnegie Library, Lewisburg, Pa. Mem. Bucknell Alumnæ, Sch. of Design Alumnæ, D.A.R., Am. Artists and Professional League, C.E.A. (Pan Hellenic Sorority) Bucknell U., Cape May Co. Art League, Pi Phi. Club: Plastic (Phila.). Home: 443 E. Washington Lane. Office: Philadelphia Museum of Art, Philadelphia, Pa.

FITZPATRICK, Herbert, lawyer; b. Washington, Va., May 19, 1872; s. Rev. James Bailey (D.D.) and Elizabeth Augusta (Dear) F.; A.B., Washington and Lee U., 1892, LL.B., 1893, LL.D., 1927; LL.D., Marshall Coll., Huntington, W.Va., 1929; LL.D., Bethany College, Bethany, W.Va., 1939; unmarried. Admitted to W.Va. Bar, 1895, and began practice at Huntington; asst. pros. atty., Cabell Co., W.Va., 1904; city solicitor, Huntington, 1906; mem. firm Fitzpatrick, Brown & Davis; counsel Western Union Telegraph Co., Adams Express Co., C.&O. Ry. Co., Chesapeake & Potomac Telephone Co., Am Car & Foundry Co., Columbia Gas & Electric Co., Huntington Water Co.; v.p. and gen. counsel, C.&O. Ry. Co., 1923-35; now vice-pres.-law, C.&O. Ry. Co., Pere Marquette Ry. Co. N.Y.,C.&St.L. R.R. Co. (Nickel Plate Road); chmn. bd. C.&O. Ry. Co. since 1937; vice-pres., law and corporate relations, Mo. Pacific R.R. Co., Tex. & Pacific Ry. Co., Internat.-Great Northern R.R. Co., Gulf Coast Lines, 1930-37; dir. C.&O. Ry. Co., Pere Marquette Ry. Co. N.Y.C.&St.L. R.R. Co., First Huntington Nat. Bank, Cravens-Green Co., Sharlow Coal Gas Co., and other corpns. Mem. Capitol Commn., W.Va. since 1921; mem. Dem. Nat. Com., W.Va., 1928-36. Trustee Washington and Lee Univ. since 1931. Mem. Am., W.Va., and Cabell County bar assns., Am. Law Inst., Phi Delta Theta, Theta Nu Epsilon, Phi Beta Kappa. Episcopalian. Clubs: Guyandot, Guyan Country, Rotary of Huntington (pres. 1917); Edgewood Country (Charleston, W.Va.), Metropolitan (Washington, D.C.). Home: Huntington, W.Va. Office: Terminal Tower, Cleveland, O.

FITZPATRICK, John Joseph, editor; b. Boston, Mass., Sept. 24, 1886; s. Louis Joseph and Margaret (Sullivan) F.; ed. pub. schs.; m. Mary J. Mulroy, Oct. 23, 1909; children—John Joseph, Paul William. Identified with newspaper business since 1908; news editor Boston American, 1922-26; mng. editor Boston Advertiser, 1926-27, Washington Times, 1928-29, Boston American, 1929-30; again mng. editor Washington Times, 1931-37; editor Miami Tribune, 1937; now mng. editor Phila. Inquirer. Club: National Press. Home: 826 Harper Av., Drexel Hill, Pa.

Office: Philadelphia Inquirer, Broad St., Philadelphia, Pa.

FLACK, Horace Edgar, city official; b. Rutherfordton, N.C., May 14, 1879; s. Millard Benton and Alice Jane (Kilpatrick) F.; A.B., A.M., Wake Forest Coll., 1901, LL.D., 1933; Ph.D., Johns Hopkins, 1906; LL.B., U. of Md., 1912; m. Edith Henning, Oct. 12, 1909; 1 dau., Mary Alice. Director Dept. of Legislative Reference, Baltimore, Jan. 1, 1907 (first dept. of the kind for cities established in U.S.). Sec. New Charter Revision Com., Baltimore, 1909-10; sec. City-Wide Congress of Baltimore, 1910-13; sec. Charter Bd., 1917-18, sec. Baltimore Special Tax Commn., 1923, Charter Revision Commn., 1925-27; sec. Tax Survey Commn. Md., 1931-33. Mem. Am. Polit. Science Assn., Phi Beta Kappa. Democrat. Clubs: University, Chesapeake, Johns Hopkins. Author: Spanish-American Diplomatic Relations Preceding the War of 1898, 1906; The Adoption of the Fourteenth Amendment, 1908. Editor of "Notes on Current Leglisation" of the Am. Polit. Science Review, 1910-14, and (with Hon. Theodore Marburg) of Taft Papers on League of Nations, 1920; Baltimore City Charter, 1927; Baltimore City Code, 1927; Code of Public Local Laws of Maryland, 1930; 1935 Supplement to Code of Public General Laws of Maryland; Baltimore City Charter and Public Local Laws, 1938. Contbr. to Cyclopedia of Am. Govt. Baptist. Home: 1808 Dixon Rd., Mt. Washington. Office: City Hall, Baltimore, Md.

FLAGG, Herbert Judson, civil engring.; b. Avon, Wash., Nov. 3, 1888; s. Alfred Eugene and Lola Jane (Jenkins) F.; B.S. in C.E., U. of Wash., 1912; grad. study, N.Y. Univ., 1936-38; m. Helen Gray, Sept. 30, 1922; children—John Graylen, Alice Janet. Registered professional engr., Wash., N.Y., N.J. Asst. engr. and chief engr. pub. service commn., Wash., 1915-24; staff engr. Federal Light & Traction Co., N.Y. City, 1924-37; chief engr. Bd. of Pub. Utility Commrs. of N.J. since 1937. Served as 1st lt. then capt. C.A., U.S.A., 1917-19; maj. C.A. Res. and Auxiliary Res. Mem. Am. Soc. Civil Engrs., Am. Assn. Engrs., Psi Upsilon. Presbyn. Mason, Elk. Home: 146 Melrose Pl., Ridgewood. Office: 1060 Broad St., Newark, N.J.

FLAHERTY, E. P.; treas. Baltimore Sun. Address: Sun Bldg., Baltimore, Md.

FLANNERY, J. Harold, congressman; b. Pittston, Pa., Apr. 19, 1898; s. John T. Flannery; grad. Wyoming Sem., Kingston, Pa.; LL.B., Dickinson Sch. of Law, Carlisle, Pa.; m. Anne Allen, Oct. 29, 1929; 1 son, J. Harold. Admitted to Pa. bar, 1921, and began practice at Pittston, Pa.; solicitor Pittston City, 1926-30; asst. dist. atty. Luzerne Co., 1932-36; mem. 75th and 76th Congresses (1937-41), 12th Pa. Dist. Served in U.S.A., 1918-19. Mem. Luzerne County (Pa.) Bar Assn. Democrat. Home: 906 Susquehanna Av., West Pittston, Pa.

FLANNERY, John Rogers, mfr.; b. Pittsburgh, Pa., Nov. 3, 1879; s. James Joseph and Harriet (Rogers) F.; A.B., Mt. St. Mary's Coll., Emmitsburg, Md., 1899, A.M., 1902, LL.D., 1916; LL.B., U. of Pittsburgh, 1902; m. Adelaide Naomi Friday, Oct. 24, 1907; children—John Rogers, Adelaide Elizabeth, Hilda Adelaide. Admitted to Pa. bar, 1902; investigating rubber and mineral concessions, Nicaragua, 1903; began in bolt mfg., 1904, vanadium metals mfg., 1909; pres. Flannery Bolt Co., Am. Vanadium Co., Vanadium Metals Company, Flannery Manufacturing Co.; v.p. Montour & Lake Erie Coal Co., also pres. Pittsburgh Dry Stencil Co. Dir. service and supplies, Am. Red Cross, May-Oct. 1917; asst. to chmn. U.S. Shipping Bd., dir. housing, Oct. 1917-May 1918; dir. ry. equipment and supplies, War Industries Bd., May-Nov. 1918; lt. col. ordnance, U.S.A., 1918. Pres. Mercy Hosp.; trustee Duquesne U., DePaul Inst., St. Barnabas Free Home, St. Paul's Orphan Asylum. Republican. Catholic. Clubs: Pittsburgh Athletic Assn.; Congressional (Washington). Home: 1544 Beechwood Boul. Office: Flannery Bldg., Pittsburgh, Pa.

FLECK, Harvey Kauffman; asso. prof. ophthalmology, U. of Md.; visiting ophthalmologist and otologist St. Agnes Hosp.; surgeon Baltimore Eye, Ear and Throat Charity Hosp.; cons. ophthalmologist Mt. Hope Retreat. Address: 513 Cathedral St., Baltimore, Md.

FLECK, Wilbur H., educator; b. Tyrone, Pa., Feb. 4, 1874; s. Abram L. and Martha (Cryder) F.; prep. edn., Grove City Acad. and Gettysburg Acad. until 1898; B.A., Gettysburg Coll., 1902; M.A., U. of Pa., 1909; LL.D., Lafayette Coll., Easton, Pa., 1934; m. Evelyn Heine, June 14, 1905. Vice-prin. Hazelton (Pa.) High Sch., 1902-07; teacher Latin, William S. Blight Sch. and De Lancey Sch., Phila., 1907-11; with Wyoming Sem., Kingston, Pa., since 1911, successively as teacher, dean, and since Apr. 1936, pres. and teacher of psychology and Bible. Served as mem. The Sheridan Troop, N.G. Pa. Mem. bd. dirs. Wyoming Valley Chamber Commerce, Nesbitt West Side Hospital, Kislyn Sch. for Boys. Mem. Phi Beta Kappa. Mason. Methodist. Kiwanian. Address: Wyoming Seminary, Kingston, Pa.*

FLEISCHMANN, Edwin M., pres. distilling corpn.; b. Baltimore, Md., Mar. 8, 1892; s. Ernst and Lillie (Gottschalk) F.; student Baltimore City Coll., 1905-09, Johns Hopkins U., 1909-11; m. Marcelle Strauss, June 5, 1916; children—Mary Louise, Betty. Began as salesman, 1911; sec. and dir. Maryland Distilling Co., 1913-20; v.p. Standard Brewery, Inc., 1917-22; pres. May Oil Burner Corpn., 1923-33; pres. Calvert Distilling Co., 1933-38, Maryland Distillery, Inc., 1933-38; pres. E. M. Fleischmann Distilling Corpn. since 1938; mem. voting trust com. May Oil Burner Corpn. Dir. Baltimore Assn. of Commerce, Baltimore Safety Council. Clubs: Phoenix, Suburban, Chesapeake (Baltimore). Home: 2214 Rogers Av., Baltimore, Md. Office: Lansdowne, Md.

FLEISHER, Alexander, federal official; b. Phila., Pa., Apr. 27, 1889; s. Louis Fleisher and Ida Gerhard (Foreman) F.; B.A., U. of Pa., 1908, Ph.D., 1915; M.A., U. of Wisconsin, 1911; m. Corinne Glaser Myers, Oct. 1, 1929. With Metropolitan Life Ins. Co., New York, 1914-26 (asst. sec., 1919-26); asst. mgr. I. Magnin & Co., San Francisco, Calif., 1927-29; managing dir. Phila. Child Health Soc., 1930-35; consultant Nat. Resources Bd., Harrisburg, Pa., 1934-36; with Social Security Bd., Phila., 1936-39, Railroad Retirement Bd. since 1939. Mem. Pa. State Planning Bd. since 1935; mem. Gov's. Commn. on Occupational Diseases, 1933-37. Fellow Am. Pub. Health Assn.; mem. Am. Assn. Social Workers. Author: Newsboys of Milwaukee, 1912; Human Factor in Industry, 1920; Railroad Labor Management, 1924; numerous reports and articles in tech. mags. Home: Churchville, Pa. Office: Railroad Retirement Board, New York, N.Y.

FLEISHER, Louis Morton, lawyer and camp dir.; b. Cape May, N.J., June 23, 1884; s. Penrose and Amanda (Dannenbaum) F.; B.S., U. of Pa., 1904; LL.B., U. of Pa. Law Sch., 1907; m. Olga Markova, Feb. 12, 1923. Admitted to Pa. bar, 1907, and engaged in gen. practice of law at Phila., 1907-25; trust officer Peoples Trust Co., 1909-11; mem. firm Sundheim, Folz & Fleisher, 1911-19; organized Camp Kennebec, 1907, mng. dir. Kennebec Camps, Belgrade, Me., since 1907. Served in French Foyer du Soldat, 1917-18; 2d lieut. U.S.A., 1918-19; 1st lieut. U.S.A. Res., 1919-25. Vice-pres. Phila. Council Boy Scouts; honored by award Silver Beaver. Dir. Oakland Country Day Sch., 1914-17. Mem. Philomathian Soc. State champion foil and saber fencing, 1904-12; capt. U. of Pa. fencing teams, 1903-07; capt. U.S.A. fencing teams, Pershing Stadium games, Paris, 1919. Past pres. Camp Dirs. Assn. of America. Clubs: Fencers, Studio, American Legion. Contbr. articles on organized camping to mags. Home: Mayfair House, Germantown. Office: 404 Sansom St., Philadelphia, Pa.

FLEISHER, Samuel S., retired mfr., philanthropist; b. Phila., Pa., 1872; s. Simon B. and Cecilia (Hoffheimer) F.; student Wharton Sch. of Finance (University of Pa.), class of 1892. Was v.p. S. B. & B. W. Fleisher, Inc., mfrs. worsted yarn. Dir. Jewish Foster Home and Orphan Asylum, 1903-15, now hon. dir.; trustee Baron de Hirsch Fund of America, 1903-

32; chmn. Baron de Hirsch Fund Agricultural School, 1908-20, Woodbine Community Center, 1926-32; mem. National Conf. on Care of Dependent Children, 1909; v.p. Juvenile Protective Assn., 1909-13; mem. exec. com. Phila. Vice Commn., 1913; dir. Court Aid Soc., 1913-18; v.p. Ellis Coll. for Fatherless Girls, 1919-23; hon. v.p. Phila. Art Alliance, Nat. Plant, Fruit and Flower Guild; mem. Pa. Council for Edn., 1925-1933; v.p. Phila. Playgrounds Assn.; dir. S.E. Pa. Chapter Am. Red Cross, Jewish Welfare Soc., Phila., Emergency Aid Soc. Pa., Nat. Economic League, also advisory com. Pa. League of Women Voters, and hon. com. Scholastic Awards of Pa. (art div.); hon. pres. Asso. Amateur Art Clubs of America, Phila.; founded Phila. Sch. Art League; mem. Phila. Commn. for Beautification of Metropolitan Area, 1925-32; chmn. bd. trustees Pa. State Home for Training in Speech of Deaf Children, 1932-33. Mem. Phila. Advisory Com. of Housing for the Federal Emergency Administration of Pub. Works since 1934; mem. bd. trustees Neighborhood Centre and of Reform Congregation of Keneseth Israel; sponsor Foreign Policy Assn., 1926-33; one of the founders and charter members Phila. Sch. Occupational Therapy; dir. Sesqui-Centennial Expn., 1926; chmn. Mayor's Com. on Child Welfare and Recreation, 1929; mem. Regional Planning Com., 1928-32; mem. Phila. Zoning Com., 1929-32, Greater Pa. Council, 1931-33, Com. for Employment Artists under Pub. Works Art Project, 1933-34; mem. advisory bd. Housing Com. of Phila. Assn. of Settlements; mem. bd. dirs. Nat. Com. on Enrichment Adult Life, 1931-34; sponsor Nat. Theater Movement; mem. Nat. Recreation Congress; elected trustee Philadelphia Award, 1935; mem. advisory com. Acad. of National Sciences; apptd. by Mayor Wilson as mem. Philadelphia Recreation Commn., 1936; apptd. commr. of Fairmount Park, 1936; chmn. Recreation Com. Fairmount Park Commn.; mem. gen. advisory council Nat. Assn. for Art Edn., 1936; apptd. by Gov. Earle mem. Pa. Constitution Commemoration Com., 1937; mem. bd. dirs. Crime Prevention Assn. since 1936; official Norfolk Museum of Arts and Sciences since 1934. Honorary member American Inst. Architects; hon. Knight Am. Order Round Table; mem. Am. Federation of Arts, Art Alliance, Art Teachers' Assn., Hist. Soc. Pa., Fairmount Park Art Assn., Pa. Acad. Fine Arts, Regional Planning Federation of Phila., Y.M. Hebrew Assn., Y.W. Hebrew Assn., Gen. Alumni Soc. Mason. Clubs: T-Square (hon.), Pa. Athletic, City, Manufacturers', Business Men's Art Club of Phila. (a founder and dir.), Men's Temple, Penn Club, Art Alliance. Received, 1923, the Phila. Award (gold medal and $10,000) conferred each yr. upon the citizen "advancing the best and largest interest of Philadelphia." Founder and sole supporter of Graphic Sketch Club (free, non-sectarian art school, 2,200 students). Mem. Phila. Zoning Commn. Home: 2220 Green St. Office: 1616 Walnut St., Philadelphia, Pa.

FLEMING, Alenson Robert (Len Fleming), specialist in song construction; b. Delmar Twp., Tioga Co., Pa., Apr. 23, 1884; s. Lester Monroe and Susan Merib (Spencer) F.; student Syracuse U., 1902-06, Inst. of Musical Art, New York, 1908-09; m. Mabel Deans, Aug. 10, 1927. Began as music arranger, 1911; song specialist and authority on song construction, serving the music trades and professions since 1915. Republican. Mason. Home: 1 Cortland St., Wellsboro, Pa.

FLEMING, Allison Sweeney, lawyer, wholesale mcht.; b. Fairmont, W.Va., Jan. 28, 1878; s. Thomas Walter and Annie Eliza (Sweeney) F.; student Colo. Coll.; A.B., Yale U., 1902; LL.B., W.Va. Univ. Law Sch., 1903; unmarried. Admitted to W.Va. bar, 1903, and engaged in gen. practice of law at Fairmont, 1903-17, retired from practice, 1917; prop. Fairmont Auto Supply Co., not inc., wholesale auto supplies, Fairmont, W.Va.; also propr. and operator several business blocks in Fairmont, W.Va.; pres. First Nat. Bank in Fairmont; pres. Independent Distributor Co., Peoples Bldg. Co. Pres. Community Chest of Fairmont, Marion County Crippled Children's Soc. Mem. Phi Kappa Psi. Republican. Methodist. Club: Field (Fairmont). Home: Edgemont, W.Va. Office: 117 Fairmont Av., Fairmont, W.Va.

FLEMING, Brooks, Jr., coal mining exec.; b. Fairmont, W.Va., July 10, 1882; s. Aretus B. and Caroline (Watson) F.; student Pa. Mil. Coll. (Chester, Pa.), Princeton (N.J.) Prep. Sch., Princeton U., W.Va. U. Law Sch. (Morgantown); m. Ry Boggess, June 7, 1910; children—Carolina Fleming (Mrs. Richard C. Moore), Virginia, Ida Watson, Sara (dec.). Began as laborer with Consolidation Coal Co., Fairmont, W.Va., 1905, and successively foreman, supt., asst. div. mgr., asst. gen. mgr., asst. to pres. and dir. of allied operations, now dir. employees service; pres. and dir. South Side Land Co. (Fairmont, W.Va.), Fairmont Land & Bldg. Corpn., Watson Coal Co. (Fairmont), Ohley Coal Co. (Fairmont); sec. and dir. Fairmont Grain & Milling Co.; dir. Greater Fairmont Investment Co., Watson Co., Fairmont Development Co., Fairmont Bldg. & Investment Co., Stevenson Co., Dull Mercantile Co., Fairmont Supply Co., Monongah Service Co. Dir. of distribution of bituminous coal for Northern W.Va., during World War. Dir. Cook Hosp. (Fairmont); mem. advisory council W.Va. Dept. of Unemployment Compensation; pres. W.Va. Univ. Stadium Corpn. Mem. Cannon Club (Princeton), Phi Kappa Psi. Democrat. Episcopalian. Elk (Lodge 294, Fairmont). Clubs: Fairmont (W. Va.) Field; Virginias Seniors Golf Assn. (White Sulphur Springs, W.Va.). Home: Country Club Rd. Office: Watson Bldg., Fairmont, W.Va.

FLEMING, Charles LeRoy, physician; b. Middletown, Pa., Dec. 7, 1884; s. Charles and Catherine (Miller) F.; A.B., Dickinson Coll., Carlisle, Pa., 1903; M.D., Hahnemann Med. Coll., Phila., Pa., 1906; grad. study U. of Pa. Med. Sch., 1906-07, Univ. of Vienna, Austria, 1909; m. Florence Adele Thorpe, June 16, 1910 (died 1938); 1 son, Charles LeRoy, Jr. Interne Childrens Homeo. Hosp., Phila., 1907-08; engaged in practice of medicine at Penn's Grove, N.J., since 1910. Mem. bd. dirs. Penn's Grove National Bank. Served as member draft bd. and mem. county med. examining bd. during World War. Trustee Masonic Lodge. Dir. Penn's Grove Y.M.C.A. Mem. Am. Med. Assn., N.J. Med. Soc., Salem Co. Med. Soc. (twice past pres.), Pa. Med. Soc., Phila. Pediatric Soc. Republican. Presbyn. Mason (33°), Odd Fellow. Club: Du Pont of Penn's Grove, N.J. Home: 42 W. Main St., Penn's Grove, N.J.

FLEMING, Eric, cons. engr. and architect; b. New York, N.Y., Jan. 1, 1897; s. Roderick Michael and Mary Briggitta (Farrel) F.; student Rutgers U., 1916-20, B.Sc. in C.E., 1920, C.E., 1923; student Nat. Acad. Design, N.Y. City, 1922-24, Columbia U., 1927; m. Margareta Lucille Pendleton, July 9, 1933. Licensed professional engr. and land surveyor, N.J., 1923; registered architect, N.J., 1926; in capacity as municipal engr., 1916-20; as architect and structural engr. since 1920; in pvt. practice and employed by New Brunswick, N.J., N.Y. & N.J. Bridge & Tunnel Commissioners, Port of New York Authority; Guilbert & Betelle, Schneider & Werther, J. H. & W. C. Ely, Newark, N.J.; Electric Bond & Share Co., William Whitehill, Nat. Biscuit Co., Equity Constrn. Co., Kohn & Butler, Watson Engring. Co., The Austin Co., Ambursen Dam Co., Voorhees Gmelin & Walker, Henry Manley, Norman Bel-Geddes, W. J. Barney Constrn. Co., H. K. Ferguson Co., Linde Air Products Co., New York; National Park Service, Washington, D.C.; work includes many large projects throughout U.S., including Inland Terminal, N.Y., Holland Tunnel bldgs., and bldgs. for N.Y. World's Fair, 1939; dir. design personnel Gen. Motors "Futurama" at N.Y. World's Fair; chief engr. $25,000,000 govt. constrn. program. Served as sergeant infantry, U.S.A., 1918. Past dir. New Brunswick Jr. Chamber of Commerce. Mem. Am. Soc. Civil Engrs., Soc. Am. Mil. Engrs., Am. Civic & Planning Assn., N.J. State Soc. Professional Engrs. and Land Surveyors, Middlesex Co. Chapter Licensed Professional Engrs. (dir.), Nat. Geographic Soc., Am. Legion. Republican. Mem. Christian Ch. B.P.O.E. Responsible for use of architectural and engring. subjects on U.S. postage stamps since 1932. Home: 209 Townsend St., New Brunswick, N.J.

FLEMING, John Adam, magnetician, geo-physicist; b. Cincinnati, Ohio, January 28, 1877; s. Americus V. and Catherine B. (Ritzmann) F.; B.S., University of Cincinnati, 1899, D.Sc., 1933; D.Sc., Dartmouth College, 1934; m. Henrietta C. B. Ratjen, June 17, 1903 (died Mar. 26, 1912); 1 dau., Margaret Catherine; m. 2d, Carolyn Ratjen, Oct. 30, 1913. Aid, 1899-1903, asst., 1903, magnetic observer, 1904-10, U.S. Coast and Geod. Survey; chief magnetician of dept. of terrestrial magnetism, Carnegie Instn., Washington, 1904— , chief observatory division, 1915-18, chief magnetic survey div., 1919-21, asst. dir. 1922-29, acting dir., 1929-34, dir., 1935—. Trustee of Woods Hole Oceanographic Inst. since 1930. Pres. Assn. Terrestrial Magnetism and Electricity of Internat. Union Geodesy and Physics, 1930-39; mem. Internat. Commn. Terrestrial Magnetism and Atmospheric Electricity since 1930; mem. since 1931 of Internat. Commn. for Polar Year, 1932-33; mem. exec. council International Council of Scientific Unions since 1937; acting chmn. Am. sect. Aeroarctic, 1929-33; del. from Nat. Research Council to Stockholm Assembly, 1930, Lisbon Assembly, 1933, Edinburgh Assembly, 1936, of Internat. Union Geodesy and Physics. Fellow A.A. A.S., Washington Acad. Sciences, Am. Physical Soc., Am. Geog. Soc.; mem. Nat. Acad Sciences, Am. Geophysical Union (gen. sec. since 1925), Seismol. Soc. of America, Md. Acad. Science, Philos. Soc. Washington (sec. 1913-16, pres. 1925), Sigma Xi; hon. mem. State Russian Geog. Soc.; cor. mem. Michelsen Inst. of Science and Intellectual Freedom. Republican. Presbyn. Club: Cosmos. Editor and Co-Author: Scientific Results of the Ziegler Polar Expedition of 1903-1905, 1908. Co-author of vols. II to VII, Researches of Dept. of Terrestrial Magnetism, Carnegie Instn., Washington, 1915, 17, 21, 25, 27, 37. Editor of Journal Terrestrial Magnetism and Atmospheric Electricity since 1927. Contributor numerous articles and reviews on terrestrial magnetism. Home: 8 Drummond Av., Chevy Chase, Md. Office: 5241 Broad Branch Rd. N.W., Washington, D.C.

FLEMING, Len; see Fleming, Alenson Robert.

FLEMING, Mervin Robert, clergyman; b. New Chester, Pa., Apr. 13, 1883; s. Charles W. and Mary F.; A.B., Lebanon Valley Coll., Annville, Pa., 1910; (hon.) D.D., 1924; B.D., Bonebrake Theol. Sem., Dayton, O., 1913; m. Estella R. Rexroth, June 29, 1909. Served as student pastor during 9 yrs. sch. work; ordained to ministry U.B. Ch. and pastor Salem Ch., Baltimore, Md., 1913-16; pastor Red Lion (Pa.) U.B. Ch., since 1916. Trustee Lebanon Valley Coll., bd. and exec. com. U. B. Orphanage and Home, Quincy, Pa.; adv. mem. trustee bd. U. B. Sem., Dayton, O. Mem. Bd. Adminstrn. U. B. Ch., Gen. Bd. Christian Edn., Pa. Conf. Bd. Christian Edn., Philokosmian Lit. Soc. Republican. U. B. Ch. Mason (32°, Shriner). Club: Lions of Red Lion (charter mem.). Author: A Confession of Faith for the Average Christian, 1916; Heavenly Reunion, 1924; Twenty Years of History, 1926. Home: 123 W. Broadway, Red Lion, Pa.

FLEMING, Montgomery Ward, lawyer; b. Bellefonte, Pa., Aug. 23, 1884; s. Wilson Isaac and Bella Priscilla (Ward) F.; student Bellefonte (Pa.) High Sch., 1895-99, Bellefonte Acad., 1899-1901; A.B., Haverford (Pa.) Coll., 1905; student U. of Pa., 1905-07; LL.B., U. of Pittsburgh, 1908; m. Winifred M. Donaldson, Oct. 24, 1908; children—John Montgomery, Mary Isabel, Winifred Maud. Admitted to Allegheny Co. bar, 1908, and since practiced in Philipsburg and Bellefonte, Pa.; mem. firm Fleming & Litke, Bellefonte, Pa. Referee in bankruptcy, Centre Co., Pa., 1915-28; judge Ct. of Common Pleas, Bellefonte, Pa., 1928-38; mem. Rep. Co. Com., 1911-28. Dist. gov. Rotary Internat., 1925-26; mem. Am. Bar Assn., Pa. Bar Assn. Republican. Methodist. Mason (K.T., Royal Arch, Consistory), Elk, Moose, Red Man. Clubs: Rotary (Phillipsburg, Pa.; pres. 1922-24); Rotary (Bellefonte, Pa.; pres.

since 1938). Home: Linn and Armor Sts. Office: 3 S. Spring St., Bellefonte, Pa.

FLEMING, Paul; see Gemmill, Paul Fleming.

FLEMING, Wallace B., college pres.; b. Cambridge, O., Nov. 22, 1872; s. William A. and Mary A. (Glenn) F.; A.B., Muskingum Coll., New Concord, O., 1894, A.M., 1897, D.D., 1912; B.D., Drew Theol. Sem., 1897; Ph.D., Columbia, 1914; m. Bertha G. Baldwin, Apr. 3, 1897 (died Oct. 20, 1931); children—Paul, Bertha Jane; m. 2d, Helen Wilson, of Baldwin, Kan., Dec. 16, 1932. Ordained M.E. ministry, 1897; pastor N. Paterson, N.J., 1897-99, Bayonne, 1899-1904, Maplewood, 1904-11; prof. Hebrew and Greek, Drew Theol. Sem., Madison, N.J., 1911-15; pres. W.Va. Wesleyan Coll., Buckhannon, W.Va., 1915-22; pres. Baker Univ., 1922-36; pres. emeritus since 1936; v.p. W.Va. Wesleyan Coll., 1937—. Mason. Author: History of the City Tyre, 1915; Guide Posts to Life Work, 1923. Home: Buckhannon, W.Va.*

FLETCHER, Arthur, editor of publications; b. Phila., Pa., Feb. 20, 1909; s. William and Justine Arnold (Fitzpatrick) F.; grad. Upper Darby High Sch., Delaware Co., Pa., 1926; B.S. in Edn., U. of Pa., 1931, A.M. in Economics, 1932; student Geneva Sch. of Internat. Studies, summers 1930-32, U.S. Office of Edn. Radio Workshop, summer 1936; m. Vivian Roegner, Nov. 21, 1936. Travel abroad as student, teacher, writer, 1932-34; asst. editor N.J. Educational Review, 1934, editor, 1935-39; visiting instr., Montclair (N.J.) State Teachers Coll., 1938-39; editor of publications, Newark Bd. of Edn., since Sept. 1, 1939. Home: 45 N. Fullerton Av., Montclair, N.J. Address: Board of Education, 31 Green St., Newark, N.J.

FLETCHER, Charles William, pres. Titeflex Metal Hose Co.; b. Brookfield, Mo., July 1, 1874; s. Charles Vinton and Minnie (Merriam) F.; student Atchison (Kan.) Pub. Schs., 1885-90, Latin Sch., Atchison, Kan., 1890-93; B.S., U. of Kan., Lawrence, Kan., 1897; m. Catharine Westinghouse, Sept. 12, 1906 (divorced); 1 son, Herman Westinghouse. Began as elec. engr., Atchison Power & Light, 1897; engrs. asst. Gen. Electric Co., Schenectady, N.Y., 1897-1906; student and engr. Morse Chain Co., Ithaca, 1906-10; engr. and asst. mgr. Walter Motor Truck Co., New York, 1910-16; treas. Titeflex Metal Hose Co., Newark, N.J., 1916-22, pres. since 1922; pres. Fisco, Inc., investments, Newark, N.J., since 1931; dir. Clinton Trust Co. Mem. Soc. Elec. Engrs., Soc. Automotive Engrs., Phi Gamma Delta. Presbyterian. Clubs: Metropolitan, New York Athletic (New York); Knollwood Country (White Plains, N.Y.); Timuquana Golf (Jacksonville, Fla.); St. Bernard Fish & Game (St. Alexis des Monts, Can.); Beaverkill (N.Y.) Trout. Home: 1855 Elizabeth Pl., Jacksonville, Fla. Office: 500 Frelinghuysen Av., Newark, N.J.

FLETCHER, Stevenson Whitcomb, horticulturist; b. Littleton, Mass., Sept. 10, 1875; s. Charles Kimball and Anna (Holton) F.; B.Sc., Mass. Agrl. Coll., 1896; M.S., Cornell, 1898, Ph.D., 1900; m. Margaret Rolston, June 28, 1905; children—Robert Holton, Richard Rolston, Stevenson Whitcomb, Peter Whitcomb, John Emmett, Margaret, Emmett Hine. Prof. horticulture and horticulturist, Expt. Sta. of Wash. Agrl. Coll., Pullman, 1900-02; same, W.Va. U., 1902-03; asst. prof. extension teaching in agr., Cornell U., 1903-05; prof. horticulture, Mich. Agrl. Coll., 1905-08; dir. Va. Agrl. Expt. Sta., 1908-16; prof. horticulture, Pennsylvania State College, since 1917, also vice dean and director research since 1927. Member Phi Kappa Phi (Massachusetts Agricultural College), Alpha Gamma Rho, Alpha Zeta, Sigma Xi. Republican. Baptist. Author: How to Make a Fruit Garden, 1906; Soils—How to Handle and Improve Them, 1907; Strawberry Growing, 1917; The Strawberry in North America, 1917; A History of Fruit Growing in Pennsylvania, 1933. Home: State College, Pa.

FLEXNER, Abraham, educator; b. Louisville, Ky., Nov. 13, 1866; s. Morris and Esther (Abraham) F.; A.B., Johns Hopkins, 1886; A.M., Harvard, 1906; University of Berlin, 1906-07; LL.D., Western Reserve University, 1914; LL.D. from Swarthmore College, 1934; M.D., honoris causa, U. of Berlin, 1929; M.D., honoris causa, U. of Brussels, 1930; LL.D., New York U., 1936; Litt.D., U. of Ia., 1936; m. Anne Laziere Crawford, June 23, 1898; children—Jean Atherton (Mrs. Paul Lewinson), Eleanor. Began teaching, Louisville High Sch., 1886; expert, Carnegie Foundation for Advancement of Teaching, New York, 1908-12; asst. sec., 1913-17, sec., 1917-25, dir. div. of studies and med. edn., 1925-28, Gen. Edn. Bd.; dir. Institute for Advanced Study since 1930. Comdr. Legion of Honor (France), 1926. Rhodes memorial lectureship, Oxford, Eng., 1927-28, also the Taylorian lectureship, Oxford, 1928; lecturer Fondation Universitaire, Belgium, 1929. Trustee William Holland Wilmer Foundation since 1931; also trustee of High Fields, Inc., since 1933. Fellow A.A.A.S.; mem. Kaiserlich Leopold Deutsche Akademie der Naturforscher. Author: The American College, 1908; Medical Education in the United States and Canada, 1910; Medical Education in Europe, 1912; Prostitution in Europe, 1913; A Modern School, 1916; A Modern College, 1923; Medical Education, A Comparative Study, 1925; Do Americans Really Value Education?, 1927; Universities—American, English, German, 1930; also ednl. papers. Home: Princeton, N.J.; and 150 E. 72d St., New York, N.Y. Address: 20 Nassau St., Princeton, N.J.

FLEXNER, Anne Crawford (Mrs. Abraham Flexner), playwright; b. Georgetown, Ky., June 27, 1874; d. Louis G. and Susan (Farnum) Crawford; A.B., Vassar Coll., 1895; m. Abraham Flexner, June 23, 1898; children—Jean Atherton (Mrs. Paul Lewinson), Eleanor. Mem. Soc. Am. Dramatists (dir.). Club: Cosmopolitan. Author: (plays) Miranda of the Balcony, 1901; Mrs. Wiggs of the Cabbage Patch, 1903; A Lucky Star, 1909; The Marriage Game, 1913; The Blue Pearl, 1918; All Souls Eve, 1919; also (book) Aged 26, 1936; and (book) The Marriage Game, 1916. Home: 150 E. 72d St., New York, N.Y.; and Princeton, N.J.

FLIGHT, John William, coll. prof.; b. Cleveland, O., Dec. 12, 1890; s. Klaas J. and Minnie (Barge) F.; grad. Cleveland High Sch., 1909; A.B., Hope Coll., Holland, Mich., 1914; B.D., Hartford U. Theol. Seminary, 1917, Ph.D., 1921; student Strâsbourg U. (France) and U. of Paris, 1919-20; A.M., Yale, 1929; m. Marjory Lois Strong, May 17, 1924; children—David Strong, Lois Abigail, John William, Jr. Ordained to ministry of Congregational Ch., 1918; minister Bunker Hill Ch., Waterbury, Conn., 1918-19, First Ch., Winsted, Conn., 1921-27, Gilbert Memorial Ch., Georgetown, Conn., 1927-29; instr., Yale, 1927-29; prof. of biblical lit., Haverford Coll., since 1929. Mem. Am. Assn. Univ. Profs., Oriental Club of Phila., Nat. Assn. Bibl. Instrs., Soc. of Bibl. Lit. and Exegesis (sec.), Phi Beta Kappa. Mason. Asso. editor Jour. of Bible and Religion since 1933. Home: 753 College Av., Haverford, Pa.

FLINN, Alexander Rex, contractor; b. Pittsburgh, Pa., Feb. 5, 1885; s. William and Nancy (Galbraith) F.; student Shady Side Acad. Pittsburgh, Hotchkiss Sch. Lakeville, Conn. and Yale U.; m. Eleanor Bradley, Nov. 6, 1915; children—William II, Mary Louise. Treas. Duquesne Lumber Co., Pittsburgh, 1911-24, pres. since 1924; pres. Booth & Flinn Co., Pittsburgh, since 1929. Republican. Episcopalian. Clubs: Duquesne, Rolling Rock, Pittsburgh Golf, Fox Chapel Golf, Allegheny Country (Pittsburgh). Home: 5558 Aylesboro Av. Office: 1942 Forbes St., Pittsburgh, Pa.

FLINT, Homer Abial, church exec. sec.; b. Northfield, Vt., Mar. 21, 1875; s. John Hackett and Phoebe Helen (Andrews) F.; student Dartmouth Coll., Hanover, N.H., 1891-92; A.B., St. Stephen's Coll., 1897, A.M., 1900; B.D., Gen. Theol. Sem., 1900; A.M., N.Y.U., 1900; Ph.D., U. of Pittsburgh (then Western U. of Pa.), 1906; m. Theodora May Plumley, Nov. 14, 1900; children—Frank Plumley, Phoebe Helen Miller. Ordained deacon P.E. Ch., 1900, priest, 1900; curate Calvary Parish, Pittsburgh, in charge St. Philip's Chapel, 1900-01; asst. Christ Ch., Pittsburgh, 1901-03; archdeacon of Pittsburgh, 1903-07; rector Christ Ch., Montpelier, Vt., 1907-15; rector Ch. of Nativity, Crafton, Pa., 1916-18; rector St. Peter's Ch., Pittsburgh, 1918-20; exec. sec. and treas. Diocese of Pittsburgh since 1920. Deputy to Gen Conv. Episcopal Ch., 1922, 25, 28, 34, 37. Mem. Trinity Cathedral Chapter, Pittsburgh, 1928-29. Chaplain Varietes Club, Pittsburgh. Mem. Theta Delta Chi. Mason (33°). Clubs: Duquesne (Pittsburgh); Lake Mansfield (Vt.). Home: 58 Bradford Av., Crafton, Pa. Office: 325 Oliver Av., Pittsburgh, Pa.

FLITCROFT, William, physician; b. Paterson, N.J., Feb. 27, 1862; s. John and Rebecca (Smith) F.; student Shortlidge Acad., Media, Pa., Centenary Coll. Inst., Hackettstown, N.J.; M.D., Columbia, 1890; m. Elizabeth Ehret, Oct. 27, 1892 (died Feb. 13, 1904); children—John Ehret, Dorothy E.; m. 2d Mrs. Emmons T. Fullerton, June 3, 1935. Engaged in gen. practice of medicine, Paterson, N.J., since 1890; at present not active in practice; consulting physician to Paterson Gen. Hosp. since 1929; mem. bd. edn., Paterson, N.J., since 1900. Mem. A.M.A., Passaic County Dist. Med. Soc. (past pres.). Republican. Baptist. Home: 691 14th Av., Paterson. Office: 510 River St., Paterson, N.J.

FLOCK, Herman Frederick William, pres. Flock Brewing Co.; b. Williamsport, Pa., Mar. 15, 1870; s. Henry Jacob and Eva Barbara (Metzger) F.; ed. high sch.; m. Lillian May Bloom, Dec. 12, 1894; children—Herman F. W., Barbara Belle Waddell, J. Fred, George Edward. Pianist in orchestra, 9 yrs.; with Flock Brewing Co., Williamsport, Pa., since 1890, beginning as bookkeeper, pres. and gen. mgr. since 1905; dir. Susquehanna Trust & Safe Deposit Co. (now West Branch Bank & Trust Co.). Dir. Williamsport Hosp. Democrat. Lutheran. Mason (32°), Elk (life). Club: Larrys Creek Fish and Game (dir.). Home: 266 Lincoln Av. Office: 601-625 Franklin St., Williamsport, Pa.

FLOERSHEIM, Berthold, piping engring. and contracting; b. Pittsburgh, Pa., Sept. 17, 1875; s. Samuel and Pauline F.; student pub. and high sch., Pittsburgh, Pa.; unmarried. Began career as cash boy for Rosenbaum Co. Dept. Store; bill clk., Haworth and Dewhurst, wholesale grocers; with Paragon Mfg. Co., ladies shirt waists, Fort Wayne, Ind.; v.p. and gen. mgr. sales, Best Mfg. Co., Pittsburgh, Pa.; founder B. Floersheim & Co., Inc., piping engrs. and contractors, Pittsburgh, Pa., and pres. since 1916; dir. Oil Industries, Inc., of Tex. One of founders Pittsburgh Skin and Cancer Foundation; co-organizer Pittsburgh Symphony Orchestra. Republican. Jewish religion. Mason. Club: Westmoreland Country. Home: 5837 Bartlett St. Office: Farmers Bank Bldg., Pittsburgh, Pa.

FLOOD, Gerald F.; judge Court of Common Pleas. Home: 2317 N. 50th St., Phila., Pa.

FLOOD, Henry, Jr., cons. engr.; b. Elmira, N.Y., Feb. 9, 1887; s. Henry and Ella Louise (Seeley) F.; grad. Elmira Acad., 1904; grad. Wertz Sch., Annapolis, Md., 1905; M.E., Cornell U., 1909; m. Iona Grace Sandford, Apr. 6, 1912; 1 dau., Iona Sandford. Chief engr. Central Hudson Gas & Electric Co., 1909-17; mech. engr. Am. Smelting & Refining Co., 1917-19; associated in practice with Dr. John Price Jackson, New York, 1920; engrs. sec. U.S. Superpower Survey, 1920-21; partner Murray and Flood, cons. engrs., New York; pres. and dir. Murray and Flood, Inc.; chmn. of bd. Biflex Pistons, Inc.; exec. v.p. Lanova Corpn.; sec. and dir. Howell & Co.; dir. Ozonite Corpn. Fellow Am. Inst. E.E.; mem. Am. Soc. M.E., Phi Gamma Delta; asso. mem. Soc. Automotive Engrs. Episcopalian. Club: Engineers. Home: Rahway, N.J. Office: 7 Dey St., New York, N.Y.

FLORCYK, Edward Martin, designing engr., inventor; b. Yonkers, N.Y., Aug. 30, 1896; s. Martin and Marie (Maleska) F.; ed. Saunders Tech. Sch., Yonkers, N.Y., 1911-15, Muhlenberg Coll., 1922-26, U. of Pa. Extension, 1922-25, Columbia U. Sch. of Edn., 1925-26, Ordnance Officers Schs., U.S. Govt. Arsenals; m. Ann Elizabeth Lux; children—Edwin Arthur, William Edward. Designer and engr., instr. in high schs., organizer engring. and vocational courses, 1920-26; chief designing engr., inventor, mem. bd. dirs., Stapling Machines Co., Rockaway, N.J., 1929-38; asso. with Ordnance Dept. in tech. branches

FLORY

since 1923; asso. with Rutgers U. Engring. Extension Sch., 1928-34. Served in U.S. Army, World War; now maj. Res. Corps. Co. chmn. Citizens Mil. Training Camps Assn. Spl. staff officer Hdqrs. 3d Mil. Area. Mem. advisory bd. Catholic Youth Orgn., Paterson (N.J.) Diocese; mem. exec. bd. Boy Scouts America, Morris-Sussex Arch., N.J. Mem. Am. Soc. Mech. Engrs., Army Ordnance Assn., Reserve Officers Assn., Am. Legion, Forty and Eight. Republican. Roman Catholic. Clubs: Officers of Army and Navy (New York); Republican Veterans of Morris Co., N.J. Writer of spl. texts and sch. manuals. Inventor many mechanisms and devices now in commercial use. Home: 46 Rockaway Av., Rockaway, N.J.

FLORY, Clyde Reuben, physician; b. Martin's Creek, Pa., Feb. 14, 1892; s. John Henry and Eliza (Seipel) F.; B.Pd., East Stroudsburg State Teachers Coll., 1913; A.B., Lehigh U., 1920; M.D., U. of Mich. Med. Sch., 1926; grad. study Harvard U. Med. Sch., 1930 and 1936; m. Miriam Wagner Hummel, June 14, 1927; children—Lucille Elizabeth, Clyde R., Jr. Engaged in teaching, pub. and high schs., 1913-15; instr. biology, Lehigh U., 1920-21; asst. surgeon Grand View Hosp., Sellersville, Pa., since 1927; in gen. practice of medicine since 1927, specializing in gen. surgery since 1936. Enlisted U.S.N., 1917, on competitive examination apptd. to Officers' Material Sch., Hampton Rds., Va., and commd. ensign (line), 1918; in command sub-chaser 219 and asst. navigator transport U.S.S. Powhatan. Dir. Grand View Hosp., Nurses Training Sch. Mem. Am., Pa. State, Lehigh Valley, Bucks Co. med. assns., Pa. German Soc., S.R., S.A.R., Pi Upsilon Rho, Alpha Epsilon Mu, Kappa Kappa Psi. Lutheran. Mason (K.T., Shriner). Clubs: Shrine of Bucks Co.; Penn Manor Sportsmans (Morrisville). Lecturer on health and med. subjects. Home: 27 Temple Av., Sellersville, Pa.

FLOSDORF, Earl William, scientist and educator; b. Phila., Pa., Jan. 27, 1904; m. William Frederick and Emily (Erny) F.; student Northeast High Sch., Phila., 1919-21; B.S., Wesleyan U., Middletown, Conn., 1925, M.A., 1926; A.M., Princeton U., 1928, Ph.D., 1929; B.S. (cum laude), Nat. Research Fellow in Medicine; m. Esther Wells, Aug. 7, 1930; children—James William, David Wells. Instr. chemistry and physics, Princeton (N.J.) High Sch., 1926-28; chem. consultant since 1927; instr. chemistry, Haverford (Pa.) Coll., 1929-32; research asso., dept. of bacteriology, U. of Pa., 1932-35, asso., 1935-36, asst. prof. since 1936. Mem. A.A.A.S., Am. Chem. Soc., Soc. Am. Bacteriologists, Am. Pub. Health Assn., Sigma Chi, Sigma Xi. Presbyn. Author: Qualitative Analysis of Inorganic Materials, 1938; Semimicro Qualitative Analysis, 1939; contbr. to scientific jours. Home: 305 Lincoln Av., Lansdowne, Pa.

FLOUNDERS, Charles Lare, partner Miller-Flounders Dairy; b. Linwood, Delaware Co., Pa., Feb. 17, 1896; s. Alfred Eugene and Sarah (Halsey) F.; student pub. schs. and business coll.; m. Sara Taylor, May 9, 1917; children—Sara, Marguerite. Began career in dairy business assuming father's business, 1917; formed partnership with Howard A. Miller, Miller-Flounders Dairy, Chester, Pa., 1925; dir. First Nat. Bank, Chester Merchants and Mechanics Bldg. and Loan Assn. Pres. Chester Dist. Boy Scouts of America, 1937-38; v.p. Delaware Co. (Pa.) Welfare Council, 1937; pres. Youth Council of Chester and Vicinity, 1936-37; mem. Boys' Work Com. of Y.M.C.A. Mem. Chester and Delaware Co. Milk Dealers Assn. (pres. 4 terms), Pa. Assn. of Milk Dealers (dir.), Interstate Dairy Council (dir.), Chester Boys' Club (dir.). Clubs: Rotary (pres. 1937-38), Chester (dir.), Springhaven Country (Chester). Home: 39 Elkinton Av. Office: Concord Rd. and Engle St., Chester, Pa.

FLOURNOY, Harry Lightfoot, newspaper associate editor; b. Romney, W.Va., Mar. 5, 1878; s. S. L. and Frances A. (White) F.; ed. Romney and Charleston schools, W.Va. Univ.; unmarried. Law clerk Flournoy, Price & Smith; later auditor City of Charleston; also served as dep. collector Internal Revenue Dept.; with Charleston (W.Va.) Gazette since 1918, successively as reporter, city editor, asso. mng. editor; sec.-treas. Superior Realty Co. Presbyterian. Elk. Address: Charleston Gazette, Charleston, W.Va.

FLOURNOY, Patrick Wood, wholesale hardware; b. Charlotte C.H., Va., Dec. 10, 1873; s. Nicholas Edmunds and Kate (Wood) F.; student pub. sch. and high sch., Charlotte C.H., Va.; m. Grace Hathaway, June 3, 1916; one son, Patrick Wood, Jr. Began work as hardware clk., 1892; asso. with Charleston Hardware Co., wholesale hardware and mine supplies, Charleston, W.Va., since 1900, pres. since 1908; vice-pres. Kanawha Banking & Trust Co., Charleston, W.Va., since 1930. Republican. Episcopalian. Mason (K.T., Shriner). Clubs: Edgewood Country, Kanawha Country. Home: 1604 Virginia St. Office: 1124 Smith St., Charleston, W.Va.

FLYNN, Bernard Joseph, lawyer; b. Baltimore, Md., Feb. 10, 1888; s. Bernard and Mary (McGann) F.; student Calvert Hall Coll., Baltimore, 1901-05, U. of Md., 1908; m. Teresa Margaret Berger, Aug. 31, 1937. Admitted to Md. bar, 1908, and since practiced in Baltimore; asso. justice Traffic Court, 1922-24; sec. Supervisors of Elections, 1925-34; U.S. atty. for Md. since 1934. Served as sec. K. of C. activities, Camp Meade, Md., 1917-20. Mem. Am. Bar Assn., Md. Bar Assn., Bar Assn. of Baltimore, Barristers Club, Am.-Irish Soc., Hibernian Soc. Democrat. Roman Catholic. K. of C. Club: Knight of Columbus (Baltimore). Home: 3515 Newland Rd. Office: 508 Post Office Bldg., Baltimore, Md.

FLYNN, Clarence Edward, educator; b. Riverton, W.Va., June 21, 1890; s. Miles and Della (Whitecotton) F.; grad. Shepherd State Teachers Coll., Shepherdstown, W.Va., and Davis and Elkins Coll., Elkins, W.Va.; m. Edith Arbogast, Sept. 9, 1914; children—Evelyn (Mrs. Homer Sutton), Ruth. Employed as prin. schs., Greenbank, W.Va., 1916, West Grafton, 1917-20, Durbin, 1922-27; county supt. schs., Pocahontas Co., 1927-37; state supervisor under A.A.A. program. Chairman of Pocahontas Red Cross, 1929-34, now chairman disaster relief. County and state dir. W.Va. Tuberculosis and Health Assn. Mem. W.Va. State Edn. Assn. (exec. com.), Greenbrier Valley Round Table (past pres.), Central W.Va. Supts. Assn. (past pres.). Republican. Methodist. K.P. Modern Woodmen. Moose. Home: Arbovale, W.Va. Office: Marlinton, W.Va.

FLYNN, John P.; pres. Reno Oil Co.; officer or dir. many companies. Address: Sistersville, W.Va.

FOCARINO, Vincent Charles, pub. weekly newspaper; b. New York, N.Y., Jan. 11, 1901; s. Joseph and Carmela (Viscardi) F.; grad. high sch. Hasbrouck Heights, 1919; m. Jule Fasso, Apr. 3, 1932; children—Joseph, Ronald. Employed in real estate and ins. office, then with accounting firm; reporter on Passaic Daily News, 1923-25; engaged in pub. Lodi Bulletin and News-Letter, weekly newspaper, Lodi, N.J., since 1925; vice-pres. Lodi Trust Co.; mgr. Vince's Sweet Shoppe, ice cream parlor, confectionery and stationery store, Lodi, N.J. Served three yrs. on Lodi Bd. Edn. Roman Catholic. Club: Rotary of Lodi (vice-pres.). Home: 136 Grove St. Office: 483 Passaic Av., Lodi, N.J.

FOELSCH, Charles, clergyman; b. Ottumwa, Ia., Mar. 31, 1891; s. Henry and Caroline (Wagner) F.; A.B., Wartburg Coll., Clinton, Ia., 1909; grad. work, Chicago Lutheran Sem., 1915; Ph.D., U. of Pittsburgh, 1924; D.D. (hon.), Newberry (S.C.) Coll., 1934; m. Pauline Gray, May 4, 1920; children—Carolyn, Barry, Donald. Began as clergyman, Pittsburgh, Pa., 1915; Supt. Passavant Hosp., Pittsburgh, 1916-20; pastor Calvary Ch., Wilkinsburg, Pa., 1920-27, St. Andrews Ch., Charleston, S.C., 1927-34, Zion Ch., Sunbury, Pa., since 1934; instr. of pub. speaking, Susquehanna U., Selinsgrove, since 1937; lecturer on sermon delivery, Gettysburg Theol. Sem. since 1938. Pres. Charleston (S.C.) Free Library, 1930, Charleston (S.C.) Community Chest, 1930-34; v.p. Sunbury (Pa.) Pub. Library; trustee bd. of social missions of United Lutheran Ch., Charleston (S.C.) Free Library. Lutheran. Address: 29 S. 5th St., Sunbury, Pa.

FOERDERER, Percival Edward, pres. Robert H. Foerderer Estate, Inc.; b. Phila., Pa., Oct. 25, 1884; s. Robert Hermann and Caroline (Fischer) F.; student Cheltenham Mil. Acad., 1896-98; William Penn Charter Sch., 1898-1902; U. of Pa., 1903; m. Ethel Tillyer Brown, June 1, 1910; children—Mignon Estabrook, Florence Rappelyé, Shirley Avril. Associated with Robert H. Foerderer, Inc. (mfrs. of Vici kid) since 1903, as asst. supt., 1903-06, vice-pres., 1906-07, dir. since 1907, pres. and gen. mgr. since 1908; dir. Robert H. Foerderer, Inc., Robert H. Foerderer Estate, Inc., U.S. Leather Co., Pa. Forge Corpn., Fairmount Park Transit Co.; also dir. various other industrial and pub. utility cos. since 1912. During World War served as vice chmn. storage com., Council of Nat. Defense, 1917-18; mem. War Industries Bd., Requirements Div., 1918; vice chmn. Employment Management Div. and chief of Priorities Sect., 4th Regional War Industries Bd., 1918. Served various terms as dir. Tanners' Council of America, vice chmn., 1932-34, chmn., 1934-36; chmn. Code Authority for Leather Industry under NRA, 1935-36. Mem. Phila. Chamber of Commerce (dir. 1921-24; mem. com. on foreign trade, 1919; chmn. municipal affairs com., 1920; chmn. Delaware River Bridge com., 1921; mem. industrial relations com., 1921-25). Mem. special committee, Chamber of Commerce of the United States, Washington, D.C. Vice-pres. and trustee Foundation of Research Laboratory of Tanners' Council; trustee Jefferson Med. Coll. and Hosp. of Phila., Med. Research Foundation at Frankford, Phila.; hon. pres. Delta Kappa Epsilon Assn. of Phila.; mem. Hist. Soc. of Pa., Numismatic and Antiquarian Soc. of Phila. Clubs: Union League, Gulph Mills Golf, Philadelphia Country, Merion Cricket, Radnor Hunt, Racquet. Home: La Ronda, Bryn Mawr, Pa. Office: 123 S. Broad St., Philadelphia, Pa.

FOERING, Howard A., corpn. exec.; b. Locust Valley, Pa., Nov. 24, 1867; s. William F. and Julia (Jacoby) F.; ed. Lehigh U.; m. Elizabeth Hartzell, June 17, 1903 (died 1905); m. 2d, Helen Wilbur, Nov. 24, 1908; children—Louise, Howard A., Adda C., June W. Asst. prin. Ulrichs Prep. Sch., Bethlehem, Pa., 1890-97; head master Bethlehem Prep. Sch., 1897-1914; pres. Bethlehem Trust Co., 1914-21, Bethlehem Bldg. & Loan Co., 1919-34, Minsi Trail Bridge Co. since 1921, Melrose Land Co. since 1921, Gem Oil Co. since 1924; formerly dir. Lehigh Valley Transit Co., Easton Transit Co., Easton Consolidated Transit Co. Republican. Episcopalian. Clubs: Bethlehem, Saucon Valley Country. Author: Work in Trigonometry, 1908. Home: 828 W. Broad St. Office: Bethlehem Trust Bldg., Bethlehem, Pa.

FOERSTER, Robert Franz, economist; b. Pittsburgh, Pa., July 8, 1883; s. Adolph Martin and Henrietta Margaret (Reineman) F.; A.B., Harvard, 1905 as of 1906, Ph.D., 1909, studied Harvard, Berlin and Paris; m. Lilian Hillyer, d. Theobald Smith, June 5, 1916; children—Lilian Egleston, Margaret Dorothea. Instr., 1909-13, asst. prof. social ethics, 1913-21, Harvard; prof. economics and dir. industrial relations sect., Princeton, 1922-26. Director Social Research Council, Boston, 1911-13; chmn. commn. on support of dependent children of widows, Mass., by apptmt. of Gov. Foss, 1912; mem. spl. com. of Boston Chamber of Commerce on Social Insurance, 1916-17; mem. Am. Management Assn. Com. on Personnel Administration, 1925—. Mem. Am. Economic Assn., Am. Statis. Assn. Author: The Italian Emigration of Our Times, 1919; also (report to Secretary of Labor) The Racial Problems Involved in Immigration from Latin America and the West Indies to the United States, 1925; Employee Stock Ownership in the United States (in collaboration), 1926. Contbr. to economic jours. Address: 75 Olden Lane, Princeton, N.J.

FOGEL, Edwin Miller, educator; b. Fogelsville, Pa., May 29, 1874; s. Rev. Dr. Edwin J.

and Jennie E. (Miller) F.; A.B., Ursinus Coll., Collegeville, Pa., 1894; student Johns Hopkins, 1894-96; Ph.D., U. of Pa., 1907; unmarried. Editor German-American Annals, 1914-17; business mgr. Americana Germanica Press since 1914; asst. prof. German, U. of Pa., 1925-28. V.p. Fogelsville Nat. Bank. Mem. Anthrop. Soc. of Phila. (pres.), German-American Hist. Soc. (exsec.), Acacia. Mem. bd. of directors of Ursinus College, 1930; one of organizers Pa. German Folk-Lore Soc., dir. and treas., 1935—. Clubs: Lenape (treas.), Livingston. Author: Beliefs and Superstitions of Pennsylvania Germans, 1914; Proverbs of the Pennsylvania Germans, 1929; The Pennsylvania Germans in Peace and War, 1933; also wrote History of St. John's Reformed Church. Contbr. to German American Annals, Jour. English and Germanic Philology, Handwörterouch des Deutschen Volkstums (Leipzig). Home: Fogelsville, Pa.

FOGG, John Milton, botanist; b. Phila., Pa., Nov. 8, 1898; s. John Milton and Grace (Kirby) F.; B.S., U. of Pa., 1925; Ph.D., Harvard, 1929; m. Helen Biggs, June 27, 1930; children—Sonia, Felicia. Instr. of botany, U. of Pa., 1925-32, asst. prof. of botany since 1932; curator of Herbarium, U. of Pa. since 1922. Served in S.A.T.C., Sept.-Dec. 1918. Fellow A.A.A.S.; mem. Phila. Botanical Club (pres.), Pa. Acad. Science, Bot. Soc. Pa., Bot. Soc. of America, Torrey Bot. Club, New Eng. Bot. Club, Lenape Club (U. of Pa.), Phi Beta Kappa, Sigma Xi. Contbr. many articles on flora of eastern North America to jours.; engaged in preparation of Flora of Pa. Home: 131 W. Phil-Ellena St., Philadelphia, Pa.

FOKKER, Anthony H(erman) G(erard), airplane designer and mfr.; b. of Dutch parents, Kediri, Dutch East Indies, Apr. 6, 1890; ed. Haarlem, Holland); m. Viola Lawrence, Feb. 8, 1929 (died 1929). Began flying, 1911; head of important aircraft concerns in Germany during World War; came to U.S., 1922. Former pres. Fokker Aircraft Corpn. of America. Mem. Netherland Benevolent Soc. Clubs: Netherland, N.Y. Athletic, Columbia Yacht. Home: Alpine, N.J. Office: 330 Highland Av., Clifton, N.J.; also Nyack, N.Y.*

FOLEY, Charles Joseph; surgeon Havre de Grace Hosp.; chief cons. surgeon Veterans Adminstrn. Hosp., Perry Point, Md. Address: 327 S. Union Av., Havre de Grace, Md.

FOLEY, Gerald Thomas, lawyer; b. Newark, N.J., Apr. 21, 1903; s. Thomas Henry and Mary (Grey) F.; LL.B., N.J. Law Sch., 1925; m. Ann Marie Bennett, July 22, 1931; children —Gerald Thomas, Jr., Sheila, David. Admitted to N.J. bar as atty., 1926; asso. with Pub. Service Corpn. as trial atty., 1926-27; asso. with firm Coult & Satz, 1927-30 and Coult, Satz & Tomlinson, 1930-37; mem. firm Foley & Francis since 1937; town counsel, West Orange, N.J.; dir. Midtown Warehouse Co., N.Y. City. Mem. Internat. Bar Ins. Counsel, Am. Bar Assn., N.J. Bar Assn., Essex Co. Bar Assn., Delta Theta Phi. Democrat. Roman Catholic. Home: 152 Mitchell St., West Orange, N.J. Office: 11 Commerce St., Newark, N.J.

FOLEY, Michael Aloysius, lawyer; b. Phila., Pa., Feb. 8, 1899; s. William Paul and Catherine Theresa (Kelly) F.; student Frankford High Sch., Phila., 1912-15, Central High Sch., 1915-16; LL.B., Temple U., 1920; m. Eileen Mercedes Flick, Nov. 27, 1933. Admitted to Pa. bar, Feb. 16, 1920; asso. in practice with Wm. E. McCall, Jr., Phila., 1920-22; opened own law office, 1922; asst. dist. atty., 1924-28; mem. firm Graham, Garagoso & Foley, Phila., 1925-32; own practice in gen. law, Phila., since 1932; trial counsel for Indemnity Ins. Co. of N.A. Served on special com. apptd. by courts, 1934, to investigate connection between attorneys and organized crime; mem. County Bd. of Law Examiners for Phila. County. Mem. Pa. Bar Assn., Phila. Bar Assn. (mem. com. on criminal justice and law enforcement), Lawyers Club of Phila., Phila. Whist Assn. (pres. 1938-39), Phila. Suburban Bridge League (pres. since 1933). Republican. Roman Catholic. Clubs: Union League, Penn Athletic (Phila.). Home: 1832 Delancey Pl. Office: 1806 Girard Trust Bldg., Philadelphia, Pa.

FOLGER, Oliver Hayward, engineer; b. Buffalo, N.Y., Jan. 24, 1886; s. George W. and Lucy G. (Miller) F.; student Masten Park High Sch., Buffalo, N.Y., 1900-04, U. of Pa., 1904-08; m. Elsie Stocton Moon, Jan. 1, 1913; children—Oliver Hayward, Edith Virginia. Began as gas engr., Passaic, N.J. 1908; supt. gas dept., Public Service Electric & Gas Co., Passaic, N.J., 1908-17, Newark, N.J., 1917-22; div. engr. gas dept., Bergen div., Pub. Service Electric & Gas Co., Hackensack, N.J., since 1922; dir. Hackensack (N.J.) Mutual Bldg. & Loan Assn. Trustee Maywood Bd. of Edn. Mem. N.J., Am. gas assns., N.J. Professional Engrs., Scalp and Blade. Republican. Presbyterian. Mason (Royal Arcanum). Club: Hackensack (N.J.) Rotary (past pres.). Home: 21 E. Magnolia Av., Maywood, N.J. Office: Public Service Electric & Gas Co., Hackensack, N.J.

FOLINSBEE, John Fulton, landscape painter; b. Buffalo, N.Y., Mar. 14, 1892; s. Harrison Davis and Louise (Mauger) F.; ed. Gunnery Sch., Washington, Conn.; studied Art Students' League (New York), Woodstock Sch. of Art, Ulster Co., N.Y.; pupil of John Carlson, F. V. Du Mond and Birge Harrison; m. Ruth Baldwin, 1914; children—Elizabeth, Joan Baldwin. Third Hallgarten prize, N.A.D. 1916; 2d Hallgarten prize, 1917; Richard S. Greenough prize, Newport, R.I. 1917; hon. mention Art Inst. Chicago, 1918, Conn. Acad. Fine Arts, 1919; Isador prize, Salmagundi Club, 1920; Carnegie prize, N.A.D., 1921; J. Francis Murphy prize, 1921; 3d William A. Clark prize, and Corcoran bronze medal, 1921; 3d prize Nat. Arts Club, 1922; hon. mention, Phila. Art Club, 1922; 1st Hallgarten prize, N.A.D., 1923; Phila. Sketch Club medal, 1923; Charles Noel Flagg prize, Conn. Acad. Fine Arts, 1924; Phila. Art Club Purchase prize, 1924; Plimpton prize, Salmagundi Club, 1924; Gedney Bunce prize, Conn. Acad. Fine Arts, 1925; Frank A. Thompson prize, Salmagundi Club, 1926; bronze medal, Sesquicentennial Internat. Expn., 1926; U. Francis Murphy prize, N.A.D., 1926; Vezin prize, Salmagundi Club, 1930; Jennie Sesnan gold medal, Pennsylvania Acad. Fine Arts, 1931; 2d Altman prize, N.A.D., 1936. Represented in Corcoran Gallery (Washington, D.C.), Syracuse Mus., Nat. Arts Club, Grand Rapids Art Assn., Phila. Art Club, R.I. Sch. of Design, Reading (Pa.) Mus., Mus. Fine Arts (Houston, Tex.), Pa. Academy of Fine Arts. Mem. Conn. Acad. Arts, A.N.A., 1919, N.A., 1928. Clubs: Nat. Arts, Century (New York). Home: New Hope, Pa.

FOLLIS, Richard H., Sr., asso. prof. surgery Johns Hopkins U.; asst. visiting surgeon Johns Hopkins Hosp.; cons. surgeon Johns Hopkins Hosp. Dispensary; surgeon Hosp. for Women of Md. Address: 30 Whitefield Road, Baltimore, Md.

FOLLMER, Frederick Voris, lawyer; b. Milton, Pa., Dec. 13, 1885; s. Dr. John Samuel and Elizabeth B. (Voris) F.; A.B., Bucknell U., Lewisburg, Pa., 1906; LL.B., Harvard, 1909; m. Ella Brown, May 30, 1921; 1 dau., Mary Elizabeth. Admitted to Pa. bar, 1910, practicing in Milton; asst. dist. atty. Northumberland County, 1911-14; apptd. U.S. atty. for Middle Dist. Pa., May 1935; dir. and solicitor Milton Trust & Safe Deposit Co., Bldg. & Loan Assn. of Milton; solicitor Borough of Watsontown; gen. counsel Milton Mfg. Co., also dir. Dir. and trustee Methodist Home for Aged, Central Pa. Conf.; dir. Milton Y.M.C.A. Democrat. Methodist (trustee). Mason (32°). Clubs: Rotary (past pres.), Manufacturers (dir.). Home: 635 E. Broadway. Office: Odd Fellows' Bldg., Milton, Pa.

FOLWELL, Amory Prescott, civil engr.; b. Kingston, N.Y., Jan. 15, 1865; s. Rev. G. W. and Mary P. F.; A.B., Brown U., 1885; studied civil engring., at Mass. Inst. Tech.; Sc.D., Lafayette Coll., Easton, Pa., 1907; m. Helen P. Peck, Dec. 4, 1894. Engaged in practice as cons. municipal engr.; asso. prof. municipal engring., 1896-1904, prof., 1904-06, Lafayette Coll.; editor Municipal Journal and Engineer (now Public Works) since 1906. Mem. New England Water Works Association, American Water Works Association, American Society C.E., Beta Theta Pi, Sigma Xi; ex-pres. Am. Soc. Municipal Improvements. Contbr. to engring. jours. Author: Sewerage, 1897, 11th edit., 1935; Water Supply Engineering, 1900, 3d edit., 1917; Municipal Engineering Practice, 1916; Practical Street Construction, 1916. Home: Montclair, N.J. Office: 310 E. 45th St., New York, N.Y.

FOLWELL, William Hazelton, textile mfr.; b. Phila., Pa., Dec. 5, 1876; s. William H. and Mary R. (Pearsol) F.; student U. of Pa., 1895, Ecole Nationale des Beaux Arts, France, 1896, Bradford Tech. Coll., Eng., 1897-98; m. Miriam E. Neff, Mar. 30, 1904; children—Miriam, Elizabeth. Began as apprentice in textile mill; v.p. Folwell Bros. & Co., 1900-30, pres. since 1930. Pres. Mfrs. Assn. Casualty Ins. Co., Pa. Mfrs. Assn. Fire Ins. Co.; dir. Fidelity Mutual Life Ins. Co., Girard Life Ins. Co. Republican. Theosophist. Clubs: Manufacturers, Bankers, Phila. Country. Home: 251 Linden Lane, Merion, Pa. Office: 250 W. Cambria St., Philadelphia, Pa.

FOLZ, Stanley, lawyer; b. Phila., Pa., Sept. 22, 1878; s. Leon H. and Alice (Rhine) F.; A.B., U. of Pa., 1900; LL.B., U. of Pa. Law Sch., 1903; m. Blanche G. Marks, Dec. 11, 1916 (dec.). Fellow Dept. of Law of U. of Pa., 1903-05; admitted to Pa. bar, 1903 and since engaged in gen. practice law at Phila.; asso. with father, 1903-16; mem. firm Sundheim, Folz and Fleisher, Phila., since 1916 and successor Sundheim, Folz and Sundheim. Served as mem., sec., and atty. for Draft Bd. No. 7 during World War. Past pres. Community Health Center. Mem. Am., Pa., and Phila. bar assns., Phi Beta Kappa. Republican. Jewish religion. Clubs: Locust, Lawyers (Phila.); Country (Philmont, Pa.). Home: Chateau Crillon. Office: Bankers Securities Bldg., Philadelphia, Pa.

FONTAINE, Edgar Clarke, educator; b. Pocomoke City, Md., Oct. 12, 1882; s. Edgar and Alice C. (Julian) F.; A.B., St. John's Coll., Annapolis, Md., 1903, A.M., 1911; A.M. Teachers Coll. of Columbia U., 1925; (hon.) Litt.D., Washington Coll., Chestertown, Md., 1935; m. Mary Hearse Stevenson, Aug. 26, 1914 (dec.); children—Edgar Clarke, Elizabeth (Mrs. Robert B. Harrison); m. 2d, Elba R. White, Apr. 15, 1937. Vice-prin., Pocomoke City (Md.) High Sch., 1903-05, princ., 1905-17; teacher Gilman Co. Sch., Roland Park, Md., 1917-18; sr. master Stuyesant Sch., Warrenton, Va., 1918-19; prin. Allegany High Sch., Cumberland, Md., 1919-21; state supervisor of Md. high schs., Baltimore, since 1921. Mem. Am. Assn. Sch. Adminstrs., Md. State Teachers Assn. Democrat. Presbyterian. Mason. Club: Chester River Yacht and Country (Chestertown, Md.). Author: Ways to Better Teaching in the Secondary School, 1929; The Teaching of the Social Studies, 1926; Maryland High School Standards, 1934; The Teaching of Oral and Written Expression, 1939; contbr. many articles to ednl. jours. Home: 114 Front St., Chestertown, Md. Office: Lexington Bldg., Baltimore, Md.

FOOTE, Mark, newspaper corr.; b. Battle Creek, Mich., July 21, 1882; s. Dr. Lewis Adelbert and Adella (Inman) F.; student St. John's Coll., Annapolis, Md.; A.B., U. of Mich., 1903; m. Mildred E. Gove, Aug. 4, 1918; children— Grace, Barbara, Jeanne. Editorial staff System Magazine, Chicago, 1903-04; with Grand Rapids (Mich.) Press, 1905-13; Washington corr. Booth Newspaper Syndicate since 1913; one of 20 Am. newspaper men who went to Manila in 1935 as guests of Philippine govt. to witness setting up of new Philippine Commonwealth and inauguration of Manuel L. Quezon as pres.; traveled in Japan and China, writing series of newspaper articles on conditions in Far East. Member American Institute Archæology, American Academy Political and Social Science, Mich. State Soc., Sigma Delta Chi. Unitarian. Mason. Clubs: Gridiron, Nat. Press (ex-pres.), Overseas Writers, Columbia Country, Univ. of Michigan (pres. 1932). Home: 3211 Northampton St. N.W., Chevy Chase, D.C. Office: Colorado Bldg., Washington, D.C.

FOOTE, Paul D(arwin), physicist; b. Andover, O., Mar. 27, 1888; s. Howard Spencer and Abbie Lottie (Tourgee) F.; A.B., Western Reserve U., 1909; A.M., U. of Neb., 1911; Ph.D., U. of Minn., 1917; m. Berenice C. Foote, Feb. 3, 1913; children—Mrs. C. Jane Halliwell, William Spencer. Began as assistant physicist United States Bureau Standards, Washington, D.C., 1911, senior physicist, 1924-27; now executive vice-president Gulf Research & Development Co., Pittsburgh, Pa.; lecturer, University of Pittsburgh. Senior fellow Mellon Inst. of Industrial Research, 1927-29; fellow Am. Physical Soc. (president 1933), A.A.A.S.; mem. Optical Soc. America, Am. Philos. Soc., Am. Petroleum Inst., Washington Acad. Sciences (v.p., 1936), Inst. Petroleum Technology, Am. Inst. Mining and Metallurgical Engineers, Am. Geophysical Union, Pittsburgh Chamber Commerce, Phi Beta Kappa, Sigma Xi, Sigma Pi Sigma. Club: University. Author: Pyrometric Practice (with others), 1921; (with Fred Loomis Mohler) The Origin of Spectra, 1922; (with others) Physics in Industry, 1937. Editor in chief Jour. Optical Soc. America Rev. of Scientific Instruments, 1921-32; asso. editor Jour. Franklin Inst. Inventor Harrison-Foote Heatmeter, F. & F. optical pyrometer. Contbr. to various tech. jours. in radiation, atomic structure, capillarity, oil recovery, etc. Home: 6317 Darlington Rd. Office: Gulf Research & Development Co., Pittsburgh, Pa.

FOOTE, Percy Wright, retired naval officer; b. North Willsboro, N.C., Aug. 13, 1879; s. James Henry and Susan (Hunt) F.; grad. U.S. Naval Acad., 1901, U.S. Naval War Coll., 1929; m. Genevieve Clary, Oct. 1, 1910; children—Lt. Thomas Clary, U.S.A., Diana Harrison. Commd. ensign, U.S.N., 1901, and promoted through grades to capt. comdg. receiving station, Phila. Navy Yard; retired June, 1936, with rank of rear-adm. in recognition of distinguished service in combat with the enemy World War. Comd. U.S.S. President Lincoln in engagement with German submarine U-90, 1918; served as aide to sec. of the Navy, 1918-21; comd. forces from U.S.S. Baltimore during Chinese uprising, Shanghai, 1905. Decorated by Order of the Crown of King Albert of Belgium, 1919; also decorated D.S.M. Commr. Pa. Motor Police Force since July 29, 1937. Democrat. Episcopalian. Mason. Clubs: Army and Navy (Washington); New York Yacht. Home: Riverview Manor Apts. Office: Capitol Bldg., Harrisburg, Pa.

FOOTNER, Hulbert, author; b. Hamilton, Can., Apr. 2, 1879; s. Harold John and Frances Christine (Mills) F.; ed. evening high sch., New York; m. 1916, Gladys, d. Dr. W. H. Marsh; children—Mary Ann, Phoebe, Jane, Geoffrey. In newspaper work, New York, 1905, Calgary, Alberta, Can., 1906. Club: Players (New York). Author: Two on the Trail, 1911; New Rivers of the North, 1912; Jack Chanty, 1913; The Sealed Valley, 1914; The Fur Bringers, 1917; The Huntress, 1917; The Fugitive Sleuth; Thieves' Wit, 1918; The Substitute Millionaire, 1919; The Owl Taxi, 1921; Country Love, 1922; The Deaves Affair, 1922; Ramshackle House, 1923; Officer!, 1924; The Wild Bird, 1925; The Under-Dogs, 1925; Antennae, 1926; Queen of Clubs, 1927; Cap'n Sue, 1928; The Doctor Who Held Hands, 1929; The Mystery of the Folded Paper, 1930; Easy to Kill, 1931; Dead Man's Hat, 1932; The Ring of Eyes, 1933; Dangerous Cargo, 1934; Scarred Jungle, 1935; The Murder of a Bad Man, 1936; Dark Ships, 1937; New York—City of Cities, 1937; More Than Bread, 1938; Charles' Gift, 1939; also Shirley Kaye, comedy, prod. Hudson Theatre, New York, Dec. 25, 1916. Contbr. stories to mags. Home: Charles' Gift, Lusby, Md.

FORAKER, Forest Almos; prof. of mathematics, U. of Pittsburgh. Address: 1313 Macon Av., Pittsburgh, Pa.

FORBES, B(ertie) C(harles), writer, pub.; b. New Deer, Aberdeenshire, Scotland, May 14, 1880; s. Robert and Agnes (Moir) F.; ed. University Coll., Dundee, Scotland, night schools; Litt.D., University of Southern Calif., 1935; m. Adelaide Stevenson, Apr. 20, 1915; children—Bruce Charles, Malcolm Stevenson, Gordon Buchan, Wallace Federate. Learned shorthand at 13; printer's devil at 14; reporter on Dundee Courier at 17; sub-editor and editorial writer at 19; went to S. Africa, 1901; assisted in founding Rand Daily Mail, Johannesburg; came to New York, 1904, and started as reporter Jour. of Commerce, later financial editor same and editorial writer Financial and Commercial Chronicle; business and financial editor New York American, 1912-16; resigned to found Forbes Mag. (semi-monthly), of which is editor and pub.; writer of syndicated daily column. Naturalized citizen of U.S., 1917. Mem. Acad. Polit. Science, Met. Mus. Art, St. Andrews Soc., Burns Soc., Inst. of Journalists (London). Mem. Bd. of Edn., Englewood. Presbyn. Clubs: Knickerbocker Country (Englewood, N.J.). Author: Finance, Business and the Business of Life, 1915; Men Who Are Making America, 1917; Keys to Success, 1919; Forbes Epigrams, 1922; Men Who Are Making the West, 1923; Automotive Giants of America, 1925; How to Get the Most Out of Business, 1927; Self Helps, 1933; Tax Tyrannies, 1936; The Salesman's Diary, 1937. Home: Fountain Rd., Englewood, N.J. Office: 120 Fifth Av., New York, N.Y.

FORBES, Ernest Browning, physiology; nutrition; b. Normal, Ill., Nov. 3, 1876; s. Stephen Alfred and Clara Shaw (Gaston) F.; B.S. in science, U. of Ill., 1897, B.S. in agr., 1902; Ph.D., U. of Mo., 1908; m. Lydia M. Mather, Aug. 18, 1903; children—Lydia Frances, Winifred Mather, Stephen Alfred, II, Rosemary, Richard Mather. Zoöl. asst., Ill. Biol. Sta., 1894-96; asst. to state entomologist of Minn., 1897-98; zoöl. asst., Ill. State Lab. Natural History, 1899; actg. state entomologist of Minn., 1901; asst. animal husbandry, Ill. Agrl. Expt. Sta., 1901-02; instr. in animal husbandry, U. of Ill., 1902-03; asst. prof. animal husbandry, U. of Mo., 1903-07; chief Dept. Nutrition, Ohio Agr. Expt. Sta., 1907-20. Maj. Sanitary Corps U.S.A., 1918-19. Specialist in nutrition, United Chem. and Organic Products Co., 1921, Inst. of Am. Meat Packers, 1922; dir. Inst. of Animal Nutrition and prof. animal nutrition, Pa. State Coll. since 1922. Fellow A.A.A.S.; mem. Am. Chem. Soc., Am. Physiol. Soc., Am. Soc. Animal Production (pres. 1914, 15), Am. Inst. of Nutrition, Delta Tau Delta, Sigma Xi, Alpha Zeta, Phi Lambda Upsilon, Gamma Sigma Delta. Republican. Unitarian. Author: Phosphorus Compounds in Animal Metabolism (with M. Helen Keith), 1914; also numerous reports of research on energy, protein and mineral metabolism. Home: State College, Pa.

FORD, Adelbert, psychologist; b. Cadillac, Mich., Apr. 23, 1890; s. Dexter R. and Mary A. (Seymour) F.; A.B., U. of Mich., 1920, A.M., 1923, Ph.D., 1926; m. Helen Nickerson, Sept. 22, 1919; children—Mary Gail, Richard Nickerson, Helen Sumner. Instr. psychology, Drake U., 1920-21; instr. psychology, U. of Mich., 1921-26, asst. prof., 1926-31; prof. psychology and head dept., Lehigh U., since 1931. Asso. mem. Am. Psychological Assn.; mem. Phi Beta Kappa, Sigma Xi, Phi Sigma, Alpha Sigma Phi. Author: A Scientific Approach to Labor Problems, 1931; Group Experiments in Elementary Psychology, 1931; also various scientific articles. Home: 1408 W. Broad St., Bethlehem, Pa.

FORD, Charles A(lfred), psychologist; b. Columbus, O., Jan. 19, 1901; s. Charles and Florence (Kendal) F.; B.S., Ohio State U., 1923, M.A., 1926, Ph. D., 1930; m. Marion Lingo, Feb. 3, 1923; children—Charles Douglass, Robert Stanley. With. Am. Rolling Mills Co. in employment dept., 1923-24; prin. Antwerp (O.) High Sch., 1924-25; supt. schs. Brown Twp., Miami Co., O., 1925-27; dir. of research State Bur. of Juvenile Research, Columbus, O., 1927-29; with Temple U. since 1929, as prof. of psychology since 1929, head of dept. since 1937, dir. Evening Coll. of Liberal Arts and Evening Extension Div. since 1935, administrative asst. to pres. since 1936. Served with S.A.T.C., 1918. Mem. Am. Psychol. Assn., Am. Assn. Applied Psychology, Pa. Assn. Clin. Psychology, Am. Assoc. of Univ. Profs., Alpha Psi Delta, Phi Delta Kappa, Scabbard and Blade. Mason. Club: Manufacturers and Bankers (Phila.). Home: 9 W. Tulpehocken St., Philadelphia, Pa.

FORD, L(loyd) Stanley, lawyer; b. East Cleveland, O., Jan. 23, 1905; s. Frank Pierce and Alta (Hibbard) F.; student Oberlin Bus. Coll., 1923-24; LL.B., Ohio Northern U. Law Sch., Ada, O., 1927; m. Agnes Steenland, Aug. 11, 1926; children—Janet C., F. Peter, Lewis S., Richard Q., Ruth Ellen. Admitted to N.J. bar as atty., 1929, as counselor, master in chancery, 1932; spl. master in chancery, supreme ct. commr., 1938; admitted to various federal cts.; admitted to practice before Supreme Ct. of U.S., 1933; mem. of Richenaker & Ford, 1929-34; in practice as individual, Hackensack, N.J., since 1934; dir. various local corpns. Former trustee Bergen Co. Jr. Coll. Mem. Am. Bar Assn. (house of dels.), N.J. State Bar Assn. (trustee), Conf. Co. Bar Assns. N.J. (sec.), N.J. Lawyers and Bankers Conf. Com. (sec.), Bergen Co. Bar Assn. (sec.), Lawyers Club Bergen Co. (past pres.), Phi Mu Delta, Theta Alpha Sigma, Delta Theta Phi. Republican. Mem. Plymouth Brethren Ch. Home: Leonia, N.J. Office: 210 Main St., Hackensack, N.J.

FORD, O(rfa) Rex, univ. prof.; b. Clover Dale, W.Va., May 1, 1893; s. Albert Colwell and Amanda M. (Carder) F.; B.S., Salem Coll., Salem, W.Va., 1915; A.M., W.Va. Univ., 1923; grad. student Cornell U., 1924-26, 1930-31, Ph.D., 1931; m. Ethel Bassel, Mar. 14, 1919 (dec.); 1 dau., Mary Esther (dec.); m. 2d Eleanor Mayo Barnett, Aug. 28, 1937. Engaged as prin. high sch., Jane Lew, W.Va., 1915-17; chemist Nat. Carbon Co., Clarksburg, W.Va., 1917-19; instr. physics, W.Va. Univ., 1920-23; instr. physics, Cornell U., 1924-26; prof. physics, W.Va. Univ., since 1926. Mem. A.A. A.S., Am. Phys. Soc., Sigma Xi, Sigma Pi Sigma. Baptist. Home: Evansdale Addition. Address: Martin Hall, Morgantown, W.Va.

FORD, Thomas Henry, supt. of schools; b. Mt. Carmel, Pa., Mar. 12, 1894; s. Edwin and Frances Jane (Lugg) F.; Ph.B., Dickinson Coll., Carlisle, Pa., 1914; A.M., U. of Pa., 1925; hon. Litt.D., Albright Coll., Reading, Pa., 1936; m. Marie Elizabeth Van Reed, 1924. Teacher high sch. Sag Harbor, N.Y., 1914-15, Minersville, Pa., 1915-17; teacher and prin. high sch., Glastonbury, Conn., 1917-21; with Pub. Schs. of Reading, Pa., since 1921, as teacher high sch., 1921-25, prin. and dir. Evening High Sch., 1924-33; prin. Junior High Sch., 1925-28, dir. of research, 1928-30, asst. supt. of schools, 1930-33, supt. of schools since 1933. Mem. bd. dirs. Reading Hosp., Visiting Nurse Assn., Reading Tuberculosis Assn., Reading Y.M.C.A.; past pres. Berks Co. Guidance Inst. Mem. N.E.A., Am. Assn. Sch. Adminstrs., Pa. State Edn. Assn., Pa. and Nat. Secondary School Prins., Phi Delta Kappa, Theta Chi. Mason. Clubs: Rotary (past pres.), Torch, Pennsylvania Schoolmen's. Home: 1415 Rose Virginia Rd. Office: 8th and Washington Sts., Reading, Pa.

FORD, William Webber, bacteriologist; b. Norwalk, Ohio, December 15, 1871; s. James B. and Cornelia (Cook) F.; A.B., Western Reserve U., 1893; M.D., Johns Hopkins, 1898; fellow, McGill U., 1899-1901, Rockefeller Inst., New York, 1901-02; D.P.H., McGill U., 1902; m. Charlotte Manning. Instr. bacteriology, 1903-05, asso., 1905-06, asso. prof. hygiene and bacteriology and lecturer on legal medicine, 1906-16, Johns Hopkins Medical School; prof. bacteriology, School of Hygiene and Pub. Health and lecturer on hygiene, Medical Sch. Johns Hopkins U., 1917-37. Mem. A.M.A. Clubs: Maryland, Baltimore Country. Home: Woodbrook, Md. Address: 10 Otis Place, Boston, Mass.

FORKER, John Norman, corpn. official; b. Mercer, Pa., Nov. 25, 1885; s. George Campbell and Caroline Belle (Moon) F.; B.S., Pa. State Coll., 1907; m. Mary Katharine Fencil, Oct. 9, 1915; children—Robert Fencil, Helen Louise. Engr. with steel corpns. 1907-15; engr. with Koppers Co., Pittsburgh, Pa., 1915-25; v.p. Am. Tar Products Co., 1925-31; pres. Koppers Products Co. since 1931; vice-pres. and dir. Koppers Co. since 1936; pres. White Tar Co. of N.J.,

Inc., dir. Wood Preserving Corpn. Mem. Phi Kappa Phi. Republican. Episcopalian. Clubs: Duquesne (Pittsburgh); Union League (New York); Oakmont Country. Home: 5833 Howe St. Office: Koppers Bldg., Pittsburgh, Pa.

FORMAN, Alexander Hardie, univ. prof.; b. Grafton, W.Va., June 12, 1883; s. Alexander and Lucy Ellen (Payne) F.; B.S. in M.E., W.Va. Univ., 1906, E.E., 1908; M.M.E., Cornell U., 1909; Ph.D., Cornell U., 1912; m. Clara Mott Corbin, Sept. 1, 1914; 1 son, Alexander Hardie. Employed in research div. engring. dept. Westinghouse Electric & Mfg. Co., East Pittsburgh, Pa., 1906-07; asst. in physics, Cornell U., 1909-10, instr., 1910-13; asst. prof. exptl. and elec. engring., W.Va. Univ., Morgantown, W.Va., 1913-16, prof. elec. engring. since 1916, head dept. elec. engring. since 1916. Mem. Am. Inst. Elec. Engrs., Am. Phys. Soc., Soc. for Promotion Engring. Edn., Professional Engrs. Soc. of W.Va., W.Va. Acad. Science, W.Va. Univ. Scientific Soc., Pi Kappa Alpha, Tau Beta Pi, Sigma Xi. Republican. Presbyn. Mason (32°, Shriner). Club: West Va. Univ. Faculty. Home: 233 Morris St., Morgantown, W.Va.

FORMAN, Max Leon, rabbi; b. Albany, N.Y., Mar. 6, 1909; s. Isaac and Celia (Bernstein) F.; student West Phila. High Sch., 1923-26; A.B., U. of Pa., 1926; rabbi, Jewish Theol. Sem. of America, New York, 1934; m. Diana Slavin, July 4, 1933; 1 dau., Gayl. Spiritual leader Congregation B'rith Achim, Petersburg, Va., 1934-36; rabbi Congregation Adath Zion, Phila., 1936-38; rabbi Congregation Beth Judah of Logan, Phila., since 1938. Founder Petersburg (Va.) Round Table of Jews and Christians. Charter mem. Petersburg (Va.) Peace Council; mem. Rabbinical Assembly, Bd. of Jewish Ministers, Zionist Organizaiton of America, Zelosophic Soc. (U. of Pa.). Conservative Judaist. B'nai B'rith, B'rith Achim, B'rith Chaim. Author many articles, weekly column in Anglo-Jewish newspapers and mags. Home: 5056 N. 8th St. Address: 4820-22 N. 11th St., Philadelphia, Pa.

FORMAN, Phillip, judge; b. N.Y. City, Nov. 30, 1895; s. Morris and Tilly (Peters) F.; LL.B., Temple University, 1919; m. Pearl Edith Karlberg, April 12, 1937. Admitted to New Jersey bar, 1917, and began practice at Trenton; member firm Forman & Levy. Asst. U.S. atty., Dist. N.J., 1923-28, U.S. atty., 1928-32; judge U.S. District Court, N.J., since 1932. Served as chief petty officer, U.S.N., World War; maj., O.R.C.; lt. col., judge adv. gen.'s dept. N.J. N.G. Dir. McKinley Memorial Hosp.; mem. bd. mgrs. N.J. State Hosp., Trenton. Comdr. dept. of N.J., Am. Legion, 1923-24. Mem. Am., N.J. State and Mercer Co. bar assns. Republican. Hebrew religion. Home: 611 W. State St. Office: Federal Bldg., Trenton, N.J.

FORNANCE, Joseph Knox, lawyer; b. Norristown, Pa., Sept. 16, 1882; s. Joseph and Ellen (Knox) F.; grad. Swarthmore (Pa.) Prep. Sch., 1900; A.B., Princeton, 1904; LL.B., U. of Pa., 1907; m. Ruth Dodson Ryder, Apr. 5, 1930. Admitted to practice of law in cts. of Montgomery and Phila. Cos., Supreme and Superior cts. of Pa., U.S. Dist. Ct. for Eastern Dist. of Pa., Supreme Ct. of U.S.; practice of law Norristown, Pa., 1907-16 and since 1931; asst. appraiser U.S. Customs Service, Phila., 1913-16. Served as pay clerk U.S. Navy, 1910; 2d lt., 1st lt., capt. and maj. Field Arty., U.S. Army, 1917-20 (with A.E.F. at St. Mihiel and Meuse-Argonne, 1918-19); mem. Am. Armistice Commn., 1918-19; capt. U.S. Regular Army, 1920-31 (resigned). Alternate del. Dem. Nat. Conv., 1912; presidential elector from Pa., 1936. Gen. chmn. Community Chest Campaign, Norristown, 1938-39, trustee since 1938. Trustee Aged Woman's Home of Montgomery Co.; sec. of bd. trustees Norristown State Hosp. Mem. Pa. State Bar Assn., Montgomery Co. Bar Assn. (pres.), State Soc. of the Cincinnati of Pa. (sec.), Pa. Soc. Sons of Revolution, Colonial Soc. of Pa., Hist. Soc. of Montgomery Co., Phi Delta Phi. Decorated Brit. Mil. Cross. Presbyterian. Mason. Club: Plymouth Country (Norristown). Address: 325 Swede St., Norristown, Pa.

FORRER, Charles D.; mem. law firm Marshall & Forrer; officer or dir. several companies. Address: Parkersburg, W.Va.

FORREST, Earle Robert, author; b. Washington, Pa., June 29, 1883; s. Joshua Rhodes and Mary Belle (Boyle) F.; B.S., Washington and Jefferson Coll., Washington, Pa., 1908; post grad. student in forestry, U. of Mich., 1908-09; m. Margaret Bingham, June 29, 1909; 1 dau., Margaret Isobel. Was a cowboy on ranches in Colo. and Ariz.; civil engr., 1910-13; forest ranger Deerlodge Forest, Mont., 1913-14; newspaper feature writer since 1914. Mem. Cooper Ornithol. Club of Calif., Quivira Soc., Sigma Phi Epsilon. Awarded Hazzard gold medal in natural history, Washington and Jefferson Coll., 1906-08. Republican. Mason. Author: History of Washington County Pa., 1926; Missions and Pueblos of the Old Southwest (containing 46 original photos of Indian life), 1929; (with J. E. Milnor) California Joe, Noted Scout and Indian Fighter (with an account of Custer's last fight), 1935; Arizona's Dark and Bloody Ground, 1936; Wicked Dodge (early history of Dodge City, Kan., and Tex. cattle trade of 1870's and 1880's), 1938. Contbr. serials and hist. articles to mags. since 1918. Home: 205 N. Main St., Washington, Pa.

FORREST, Henry Ogley, chem. engring.; b. Lawrence, Mass., Dec. 9, 1897; s. Thomas and Annie Elizabeth (Ogley) F.; B.S., Mass. Inst. Tech., 1920, M.S., same, 1921; m. Ann E. Feather, June 24, 1922; children—Henry Ogley, Jr., Robert Arthur. Instr. chem. engring., Mass. Inst. Tech., 1921-22, research asso., 1922-27, asst. prof. chem. engring. and asst. dir. Research Lab., 1927, dir. Research Lab. Applied Chemistry, 1927-31, asso. prof. chem. engring., 1929-31; chem. engr., M. W. Kellogg Co., N.Y. City since 1931. Mem. Am. Chem. Soc., Am. Inst. Chem. Engring., Amer. Petroleum Inst. Conglist. Mason. Home: 586 Ramapo Rd., Teaneck, N.J. Office: 225 Broadway, New York, N.Y.

FORREY, Harry N., wholesale dairying; b. Lancaster Co., Pa., Oct. 24, 1873; s. John and Mary (Newcomer) F.; ed. pub. schs., New Town, Pa., 1879-89; diploma Lancaster Business Coll., 1893; m. Elizabeth R. Keller, Jan. 18, 1898; 1 dau., Margaret K. Employed as bookkeeper, 1893-98; formed partnership with E. L. Garber and mem. firm Emigsville Creamery Co., Emigsville, Pa., 1898, later expanded and inc. York Sanitary Milk Co., York, Pa., and Lancaster Sanitary Milk Co., Lancaster, Pa., merged later as Pennsylvania Dairies, Inc., of which is vice-pres., dir. and mgr.; dir. First Nat. Bank. Propr. two farms, one rented on shares, other stocked and farming himself. Pres. Good Rds. Assn., 1918, Kiwanis Club, 1925. Pres. Milk Dealers Assn. to 1932. Republican. Mason (32°, Shriner). Elk. Clubs: Temple and Shrine. Home: 1414 E. Market St. Office: North George St. and Hamilton Av., York, Pa.

FORSHT, Ruth, lawyer; b. Juniata, Pa., Nov. 12, 1894; d. Samuel I. and Annie (Bailey) F.; student Zeth's Bus. Coll., Altoona, Pa.; B.S., U. of Pittsburgh Sch. Bus. Adminstrn., 1924, LL.B., Law Sch., 1927. Began as sch. teacher; asso. with Pa. R.R. Co.; in various exec. positions, 14 yrs.; admitted to Pa. bar, 1927, and since in practice of law in Altoona and Pittsburgh; served in Atty. Gen. office, State of Pa., 1931-35. State chmn. Professional & Bus. Women of Pa. Council Rep. Women, 1939. Regional chmn. Dist. III, Zonta Internat., 1937-38. Mem. Pa. State Bar Assn., Mortar Board, Am. Assn. Univ. Women, League of Women Voters, Pittsburgh. Phi Chi Theta, Phi Delta Delta. Republican. Presbyterian. Clubs: Zonta, Business and Professional Women's, Woman's City (Pittsburgh). Contbr. Articles to women's mags. and newspapers. Home: Royal Yorke Apts. Office: 2911 Grant Bldg., Pittsburgh, Pa.

FORSTALL, Alfred Edmond, cons. engr.; b. New Orleans, La., May 23, 1864; s. Theobald and Annie (Walton) F.; M.E., Lehigh U., Bethlehem, Pa., 1883, spl. course in chemistry, 1883-84; m. Alice Norcross Dunn, Aug. 25, 1892 (died 1938); children—Theobald, Alfred Edmond (dec.), Stuart, Walton Clark, Alice (dec.). Insp. constrn. Chicago Gas Light & Coke, 1885-87, mgr. North Sta., 1887-89, asst. engr. in charge mfr., 1889-90; gen. supt. Newark (N.J.) Gas Light Co., 1891-97; gen. mgr. Montclair (N.J.) Gas & Water Co., 1897-98; cons. engr. in pub. utility matters, Montclair, N.J., since 1899. Served as mem. Nat. Com. on Gas & Electric, 1917-18. Sec. of trustees Gas Ednl. Fund, 1897,1920. Mem. Am. Inst. Cons. Engrs., Am. Gas Assn., Am. Soc. M.E., Soc. of Gas Lighting, N.J. Gas Assn., Am. Gas Light Assn. (sec.-treas. 1896-1904), Am. Gas Inst. (pres. 1916-18). Independent Rep. Episcopalian (mem. finance and advisory bd., Diocese of Newark). Author: (and in charge publ.) Catechism of Central Station Gas Engineering in the U.S., 1909; Subsection on Illuminating Gas, Kent's Mech. Engrs. Handbook, 1923; lesson books on mfr., distribution and utilization of gas for Internat. Text Book Co.; various papers for gas assns. and periodicals, 1890-1938. Club: Lehigh University (New York). Address: 5 Champlain Terrace, Montclair, N.J.

FORSTALL, Walton, retired engr.; b. New Orleans, La., Feb. 11, 1870; s. Theobald and Annie (Walton) F.; E.E., Lehigh U., Bethlehem, Pa., 1891; m. Ednah Logan, Oct. 29, 1895; children—Anne Logan, Edward Logan, Charles Fletcher, Walton; m. 2d, Nina D. Jones, June 26, 1931. Resident engr. for erection natural gas pumping station, Columbus Construction Co., Greentown, Ind., 1891-93; engr. of mains East River Gas Co., New York, 1893-95; supt. Lockport (N.Y.) Gas & Electric Light Co., 1895-98; asst. engr. distribution Phila. Gas Works of United Gas Improvement Co., 1898-1918, engr. of distribution, 1918-27; engr. of distribution Phila. Gas Works Co., 1928-32, v.p. in charge of distribution, 1932-36; retired, 1936. Vice-pres. and mem. bd. mgrs. Franklin Inst.; mem. exec. bd. Valley Forge Council, Boy Scouts of America. Presbyterian (sec. bd. trustees Bryn Mawr Ch.). Author: A Manual of Gas Distribution, 1920. Club: University (Phila.). Home: Ithan Av., Rosemont, Pa.

FORSTER, William Hays, pres. Hays Mfg. Co.; b. Erie, Pa., Jan. 28, 1872; s. Edwin Sumner and Mary Eunice (Hays) F.; student Erie Acad., 1878-87, Erie High Sch., 1887-89, Tufts (Mass.) Coll., 1894-96 (B.Sc. engring.); m. Susan B. Lamberton, Jan. 2, 1907; 1 son, William Hays. Apprentice mech. engr., Erie City Iron Works, 1889-94; with Hays Mfg. Co. since 1896, pres. since 1900; dir. Marine Nat. Bank, Erie. Pres. Hamont Hosp., 1915-17, Erie Asso. Charities, 1909-11. Mem. Delta Upsilon. Episcopalian. Clubs: Erie, Kahkwa (Erie). Home: 323 W. 6th St. Office: 801 W. 12th St., Erie, Pa.

FORSYTHE, William Henry, judge; b. Sykesville, Md., May 16, 1874; s. William Henry and Arabella Crawford (Welling) F.; A.B., Western Md. Coll., 1894, A.M., 1896; student Johns Hopkins, 1894-95; LL.B., U. of Md., 1897; m. Mell Adella Osborne, Nov. 23, 1903; 1 dau., Kathryn Winchester (Mrs. Middleton Pope Barrow). Admitted to Md. bar, 1897; in law practice from 1897; appointed asso. judge 5th Judicial Circuit of Md., Dec. 23, 1907, elected, Nov. 2, 1909, appointed, same, Nov. 2, 1924, again elected, Nov. 6, 1926. Chmn. Draft Bd., 1916-18; mem. Md. Gen. Assembly, 1902-04. Democrat. Methodist. Mason. Home: Sykesville, Md. Office: Ellicott City, Md.

FORT, Leslie Runyon, pres. Interstate Printing Corpn.; b. Newark, N.J., Sept. 17, 1883; s. John Franklin and Charlotte Elizabeth (Stainsby) F.; student pvt. schs., East Orange, N.J., 1890-97, Stevens Prep. Sch., Hoboken, N.J., 1897-1901, Amherst (Mass.) Coll., 1901-03; m. Helen W. Osmun, Oct. 10, 1906; children—Margaret (Mrs. Robert E. Royes), John Franklin II, Osmun. Began as reporter, N.J. shore resorts, 1902; pub. Lakewood (N.J.) Times and Journal, 1905-12; sec. to gov., 1908-10; pub. Plainfield (N.J.) Daily Press, 1912-17; pres. Luminite Corpn., Newark, N.J., 1922-39, Interstate Printing Corpn., Plainfield, N.J., since 1931. Served as capt., Adjutant General Dept., during World War. Mem. city council, Plainfield, N.J., 1918. Pres. Plainfield (N.J.) Y.M.C.A., since 1935; treas. and vice-pres. Community Chest since 1932. Mem. Plainfield

Chamber of Commerce (pres. 1937-38), Chi Psi. Republican. Presbyterian. Club: Rotary (Plainfield, N.J.; pres. 1936-37). Home: 945 Cedarbrook Rd. Office: 400 Watchung Av., Plainfield, N.J.

FORT, Tomlinson, prof. mathematics; b. Albany, Ga., Dec. 17, 1886; s. John Porter and Lulah Hay (Ellis) F.; A.B., U. of Ga., 1906, A.M., 1909; A.M., Harvard, 1910, Ph.D., 1912; studied at Univ. of Göttingen and Univ. of Paris, 1912-13; m. Madeline Kean Scott, July 7, 1931. Instructor mathematics, U. of Ga., 1907-09, Harvard, 1910-11, U. of Mich., 1913-14; asst. prof. mathematics, U. of Mich., 1914-17; prof. mathematics, U. of Ala., 1917-24, also head of dept.; prof. mathematics and head of dept., Hunter Coll., New York, 1924-27; prof. mathematics and head of dept., Lehigh U. since 1927, dean of Grad. Sch. since 1938; visiting prof., U. of Pa., summer 1933. Mem. Math. Assn. America, Am. Math. Soc., A.A.A.S., Phi Beta Kappa, Sigma Xi, Pi Mu Epsilon. Author: Infinite Series, 1930; A Vacation in Africa, 1931; Analytic Geometry (with J. W. Young and F. M. Morgan), 1936. Writer of numerous tech. math. papers. Address: Lehigh University, Bethlehem, Pa.

FORTENBAUGH, Robert, prof. of history; b. Harrisburg, Pa., July 17, 1892; s. James Penrose and Mary Jeannette (Zimmerman) F.; student Harrisburg (Pa.) High Sch., 1906-09; A.B., Gettysburg Coll., 1913; grad. Lutheran Theol. Sem., Gettysburg, Pa., 1916; A.M., Syracuse U., 1920; Ph.D., U. of Pa., 1926; m. Lena Schweinberger, Aug. 16, 1921; children—Robert Behrend, Ruth Emma, Ann Elizabeth. Ordained to ministry of Lutheran Ch., 1916; pastor Ch. of the Atonement, Syracuse, N.Y., 1916-23; instr., later asst. prof. of history and sociology, Syracuse U., 1918-23; acting prof. of history, Gettysburg Coll., 1923-26, Adeline Sager prof. of history since 1923; mem. of faculty, summers, Bucknell U., Pa. State Coll., Syracuse U. Mem. Am. Hist. Assn., Am. Soc. Ch. History (asst. sec. since 1937), Pa. Hist. Assn., Central Pa. Synod of United Luth. Ch. in Am., Alpha Tau Omega, Phi Beta Kappa, Phi Kappa Phi, Kappa Phi Kappa. Republican. Contbr. of hist. articles to jours. Lecturer and special preacher. Home: 150 Broadway, Gettysburg, Pa.

FORTESCUE, Horace, banking; b. Phila., Pa., Sept. 20, 1873; s. Walter Scott and Maria Chase (Grey) F.; ed. pvt. schs. Phila. and vicinity; m. Irene Archambault, Oct. 2, 1899; 1 son, Frank Archambault. Began as clk. in commercial office, 1890-93; asso. with The Philadelphia Nat. Bank continuously since entering their employ as jr. clk., 1893, asst. cashier, 1904-15, cashier, 1915-19, vice-pres. since 1915. Republican. Episcopalian (vestryman and rector's warden, Grace Ch., Mount Airy). Clubs: Church Club (gov.), Art. Home: 387 E. Gowen Av. Office: 421 Chestnut St., Philadelphia, Pa.

FOSA, Joseph William, univ. prof.; b. Spadafora, Sicily, Italy, July 6, 1892; s. Domenico and Flavia (Scattareggia) F.; came to U.S., 1894, naturalized, 1918; A.B., Wesleyan U., Middletown, Conn., 1915, A.M., 1916; student Yale Grad. Sch., 1928-29, Columbia U. Grad. Sch., summer 1932; m. Genevieve Catherine Rau, Sept. 9, 1920; children—Elizabeth Joan, Joyce Ann. Instr. French and Spanish, Marietta (O.) Coll., 1916-17; instr. French, Spanish and Italian, U. of Pittsburgh, 1917-18; master in French and Spanish, head coach football, basketball and track, Kingsley Prep. Sch., Essex Falls, N.J., 1919-20; asst. prof. Romance langs. and literatures, Pa. State Coll., 1920-27; asso. prof. since 1927. Served in O.T.S., Camp Devens, Mass., 1918-19. Mem. Phi Sigma Iota. Democrat. Author: Italian Studies in Yale University, 1929; contbr. to mags. and to Athletics at Wesleyan. Home: 704 W. Fairmount Av., State College, Pa.

FOSNOT, Walter, newspaper publisher; b. Lewistown, Pa., Oct. 22, 1879; s. Henry Jacob and Harriet Jane (Walker) F.; pub. schs. Lewistown, Pa., 1887-95; m. Mary Grace Russell, Apr. 23, 1907; 1 dau., Mary Grace (dec.). Began as printer with Democrat & Sentinel, weekly, Lewistown, Pa., 1895, changed to semiweekly, 1898, and daily since 1903; mem. firm H. J. Fosnot & Son, 1900-20; pres. and bus. mgr. Sentinel Co., Lewistown, Pa., since 1920, publishers, job printers, mfrs. office supplies; pres. and dir. Russell Nat. Bank, Lewistown Housing and Development Co.; vice-pres. and dir. Lewistown Ice & Storage Co. Trustee Lewistown Y.M.C.A. Presbyterian. Mason. Odd Fellow. Home: 17 E. 3d St., Lewistown, Pa.

FOSS, Feodore Feodorovich, mining and metall. engr.; b. Odessa, Russia, Dec. 29, 1874; s. Feodore A. and Olga A. (Mansfield) F.; grad. Classical Gymnasium, St. Petersburg, 1893; entered through competitive exam. (60 out of 1,000) Imperial Mining Inst. and grad. M.E., cum eximia laude, 1898; m. Zenaida M. Magula, Apr. 28, 1899. Came to U.S., 1917, naturalized citizen, 1926. Asst. prof. metallurgy, Mining Inst. of St. Petersburg, 1900-02; as chief engr., later mng. dir. Lyssva Mining Dist., developed iron and steel industry there by introduction of manufacture of tin plate, galvanized sheet iron, holloware, etc.; developed platinum mining of same district to output of nearly 2 tons per yr.; tinplate produced in the plants under his management was only resource for canning food for Russian armies; during World War built new plants employing 15,000 men to supply Russian armies with shells, fuses, powder boxes, soldiers' canteens and trench instruments; awarded hon. degree in engring. by Imperial Russian Govt.; former pres. and dir. Lyssva Mining Dist., Inc., Russia, Urals, vice chairman board Verch-Issetsk Mining Dist., director Bogoslovsk Mining Dist., col. Russian Mining Corps; came to U.S., 1917, as chmn. industrial commn. to study Am. methods of developing natural resources; severed connection with Russia on account of Bolshevik upheaval; now dir. research and metallurgy, Wheeling Steel Corpn. Mem. Am. Inst. Mining and Metall. Engrs., Am. Soc. M.E., Am. Soc. for Metals, Am. Soc. for Testing Materials, Am. Electro-Chem. Soc., Am. Iron and Steel Inst., Am. Chem. Soc., Royal Soc. of Arts (England), British Iron and Steel Inst., Inst. of Metals (England), Am. Economic Soc., Am. Acad. Polit. Science, Am. Geog. Soc., Soc. Am. Mil. Engrs., Army Ordnance Assn., Am. Ceramic Soc., Verein Deutscher Ingenieure, Verein Deutscher Eisenhüttenleute. Republican. Unitarian. Home: Emerson Road, Woodsdale, Wheeling, W.Va. Office: Wheeling Steel Corpn. Bldg., Wheeling, W.Va.

FOSS, George Ernest, commercial sec.; b. Pittsfield, N.H., Mar. 10, 1873; s. Horace Melvin and Abigail Hannah (Green) F.; A.B., Dartmouth, 1897; m. Martha Longfellow Brown, June 28, 1899 (died July 19, 1936); 1 son, Bradbury Poor; m. 2d, Olive Anderson Sipe, of Latrobe, Pa., May 25, 1938. Principal grammar and high schs., N.H., 1897-1901, jr. high schs., Springfield, Mass., 1901-14; gen. sec. Springfield Chamber of Commerce, 1914-19, Pa. State Chamber of Commerce since 1919. Dollar-a-year man in Ordnance Dept., Western Mass. Dist., Jan. 11, 1918-Mar. 24, 1919. Mem. Charter Revision Commn., Springfield, 1912-13. Mem. Harrisburg Chamber of Commerce, National Association of State Chamber of Commerce Officials, Nat. Assn. Commercial Orgn. Secs. (ex-pres.), Dartmouth Alumni Assn., Phi Kappa Psi. Republican. Presbyterian. Clubs: Dartmouth of Central Pa. (ex-pres.), Rotary of Harrisburg (ex-pres.), Harrisburg Country. Home: 1915 N. Front St. Office: State Chamber of Commerce Bldg., Harrisburg, Pa.

FOSS, Harold Leighton, surgeon; b. Malden, Mass., Feb. 14, 1883; s. Eliphalet J. and Louise W. (Sanborn) F.; student biology, Mass. Inst. Tech., 1903-05; M.D., Jefferson Med. Coll., Philadelphia, Pa., 1909; Sc.D., Bucknell University, Lewisburg, Pa., 1933; grad. study, Univ. of Pa., 1912-13; student Berlin and Vienna, 1914; m. Isabel Grier Polk, June 22, 1917; children—Elizabeth Polk, Barbara Polk. Resident physician Phila. Gen. Hosp., 1909-10; surgeon in chief Fairhaven Hosp., Candle, Alaska, 1911-12; asst. surgeon Mayo Clinic, Rochester, Minn., 1913-15; surgeon in chief and chief of staff Geisinger Memorial Hosp., Danville, Pa. since 1915; surgeon to Pa. R.R. and D.L.&W. R.R.; cons. surgeon Pa. State Hosp. for Insane, Danville; dir. First Nat. Bank (Danville) Scranton-Lackawanna Trust Co., Scranton. Fellow Am. Coll. Surgeons; mem. A.M.A., American Surgical Association, Southern Surgical Association, Pa. Med. Soc., Am. Hosp. Assn., Am. Assn. for Study of Goiter, Assn. Ex-Resident Physicians of Mayo Clinic (pres. 1917-19), Nu Sigma Nu, Alpha Omega Alpha. Republican. Presbyn. Mason (K.T.). Clubs: Gibson Island Yacht; Madison Beach, Milton Country. Home: Danville, Pa.

FOSS, Wilson P(erkins), Jr., chmn. bd. New York Trap Rock Corpn.; b. Haverstraw, N.Y., Dec. 17, 1890; s. Wilson P. and Anna (De Baun) F.; student Hill Sch., Pottstown, Pa., 1906-10; Ph.B., Sheffield Scientific Sch. (Yale), 1913; m. Mary Burns, Dec. 7, 1924; children—Wilson III, Hugh H., Mary. Salesman, New York Trap Rock Co., 1914-16; pres. Haverstraw Crushed Stone Co., 1916-17; with Tex. Oil Co. in Spain, 1919-20; v.p. Parish-Watson & Co. (works of art) since 1920; with New York Trap Rock Corpn. since 1930, now chmn. bd.; chmn. bd. Core Joint Concrete Pipe Co. since 1930; pres. Kohl Realty Corpn.; v.p. Carbonate of Lime Corpn. Served as capt. inf., overseas 17 months on spl. duty with Mil. Intelligence Div., U.S.A., World War. Presbyn. Mason (32°). Clubs: Union, Yale, St. Anthony, Pine Valley, Rockland Country; Triton Fish and Game Club (Quebec, Can.). Home: 155 E. 72d St., New York, N.Y.; also Centreville, Md. Office: 230 Park Av., New York, N.Y.

FOSTER, Alexander, Jr., v.p. Warner Co.; b. Phila., Pa., Dec. 20, 1884; s. Alexander and E. Jane (Nicholson) F.; C.E., U. of Pa.; m. Marion Stockton, June 10, 1912; children—Sara Stockton, Eliza Jane. Road surveyor, South Jersey, 1908; engr. in charge concrete design William Steele & Sons Co., 1909-21; pres. West Jersey Sand & Supply Corpn., 1921-27; v.p. Charles Warner Co., 1927-31; v.p. and dir. Warner Co. since 1931; pres. and dir. Kings Farms Co., King Supply Co.; dir. Am. Lime & Stone Co., Kensington Nat. Bank. Home: 123 Township Line, Jenkintown, Pa. Office: 219 N. Broad St., Philadelphia, Pa.

FOSTER, Laurence, anthropologist; b. Pensacola, Fla., Feb. 3, 1903; s. Frank Lee and Pearl (Hill) F.; A.B., Lincoln U., 1926, S.T.B., 1929; Ph.D., U. of Pa., 1931; m. Ella Mae Gibson, June 30, 1936; 1 dau., Yvonne Camille. Univ. scholar, U. of Pa., 1927-29; teacher history, Stowe Teachers Coll., St. Louis, Mo., 1929-32; prof. of history and edn., Lincoln U., Chester Co., Pa.; also research asso., U. of Pa. Museum, since 1933; gen. editor Huxley Publishers, N.Y. City, since 1935; guest lecturer, Museo Nacional de Mexico, 1930; spl. rep. of Pan-Am. Union, Washington, D.C., to Mexico, 1930. Field research in Canada, Mexico, and Guatemala, under grant from Columbia U., spring and summer of 1929; grant in aid fellow, Nat. Research Council, 1931-32. Fellow to Council, Am. Anthrop. Assn.; fellow Am. Folk-Lore Soc.; mem. A.A.A.S., Internat. Acad. of Phys. Anthropology (mem. exec. com.), Orthological Inst., Los Peros, Mexico (Hon.). Republican. Presbyterian. Clubs: U. of Pa., Scribes (N.Y. City). Author: The Functions of a Graduate School in a Democratic Society, 1936; Statistics for Anthropometrists, 1938. Editor: History of Civilization Series. Home: Lincoln University, Chester Co., Pa.

FOSTER, Lloyd Ellis, clergyman; b. at Mt. Pleasant, Ia., May 20, 1894; s. Charles and Arminda (Brown) F.; A.B., U. of Neb., 1916, B.D., Garrett Bib. Inst., 1918; A.M., U. of Chicago, 1925; (hon.) D.D., Syracuse U., 1931; m. Agnes A. Hyatt, Sept. 22, 1915; children—Marian Lucile, Sidney Charles. Ordained to ministry Meth. Ch., 1918; minister, Palatine, Ill., 1916-18, Lake Bluff, Ill., 1919-20, Lincoln, Neb., 1920-23; dir. Wesley Foundation, U. of Pa., 1923-28; minister, Syracuse, N.Y., 1928-35; minister, Calvary Ch., East Orange, N.J., since 1935; broadcasts over NBC under auspices Federal Council of Chs. of Christ in America. Republican. Methodist. Clubs: Kappa Chi, Monday (New York). Home: 109 Woodland Av. Office: 400 Main St., East Orange, N.J.

FOSTER, Major Bronson, economist; b. Robertsville, Tenn., Jan. 6, 1892; s. Joshua Burnsides and Sarah Ann (Du Pee) F.; grad. Chilhowee Inst., Seymour, Tenn., 1907; A.B., Carson-Neuman Coll., Jefferson City, Tenn., 1910, A.M., 1911; studied, Cornell U., 1911-13; m. Helen Margaret Vertner, Oct. 12, 1918; 1 dau., Marjorie Helen. Teacher pub. schs., Tenn., 1907; instr. in physics, Carson-Neuman Coll., 1909-10; prin. Watauga Acad., Butler, Tenn., 1910-11; fellow in polit. economy, Cornell U., 1912-13; asst. to dean, and instr. in economics New York U. Sch. of Commerce, Accounts and Finance, 1913-15; asst. prof. economics and sec. Sch. of Commerce, Accounts and Finance, 1915-18; asst. to chmn. bd. dirs. Federal Reserve Bank of New York, 1918-19; automobile distributor, 1919-20; v.p. 13 Astor Pl., Inc., 1921-24; administrative officer Alexander Hamilton Inst. (N.J.), 1920-29, now president; also president Alexander Hamilton Institute, Ltd. (Canada); prof. banking and finance and chmn. dept. New York U. since 1923. Mem. Am. Economic Association, American Academy Polit. and Social Science, Economic Club of New York, Royal Economic Society (London), Delta Mu Delta, Theta Nu Epsilon. Republican. Baptist. Mason (32°, Shriner); mem. Eleusis Fraternity. Clubs: Lawyers, Lotos (N.Y. City). Author: Banking, 1917. Co-author: Money and Banking, 1936. Editor: Modern Business Series, Business Conditions Service. Home: Cheltenham, Pa. Address: 13 Astor Pl., New York, N.Y.

FOSTER, Ronald Martin, mathematician; b. Brooklyn, N.Y., Oct. 3, 1896; s. Frederick Langdon and Emily Jane (Martin) F.; B.S., Harvard U., 1917; m. Annabel Conover, Apr. 12, 1924; children—Ronald Martin, Jr., Hubert Conover, Theodore Dean, Alan Stuart. Asst. in mathematics, Harvard U. 1916-17, instr., 1921-22; employed in engring. dept., Am. Telephone & Telegraph Co., 1917-19, dept. development and research, 1919-21, 1922-34; with research dept., Bell Telephone Labs. since 1934. Mem. A.A.A.S., Am. Math. Soc., Assn. for Symbolic Logic, Inst. Math. Statistics, Math. Assn. of America, Edinburgh Math. Soc., London Math. Soc., Phi Beta Kappa. Republican. Methodist. Co-author (with George A. Campbell) of monograph, Fourier Integrals for Practical Applications, 1931. Contbr. articles to tech. jours. Home: 122 E. Dudley Av., Westfield, N.J. Office: 463 West St., New York, N.Y.

FOSTER, Sadie Levy (Mrs. Solomon F.); b. Cincinnati, O., Aug. 14, 1875; d. Joseph and Theresa (Epstein) Levy; ed. pub. schs. and U. of Cincinnati, many summer coll. courses; m. Rabbi Solomon Foster, June 22, 1904. Engaged as head worker at Columbia Council Sch., Pittsburgh, Pa., making it a settlement later named Irene Kaufman Settlement, 1900-03. Trustee N.J. Normal Sch. for Jewish Teachers. Pres. Women's Assn. of Temple B'nai Jeshurum, 10 yrs.; pres. Jewish Sisterhood of Newark, N.J., later named Jewish Day Nursery and Neighborhood House, 15 yrs. Founder N.J. Fed. of Temple Sisterhoods, Jewish Day Nursery and Neighborhood House, Paterson Sect. Council of Jewish Women, also Elizabeth and Newark sects. Mem. U. Order True Sisters. Awarded Gold Medal for Meritorious Service, Temple B'nai Jeshurum, 1934. Republican. Jewish religion. Clubs: Contemporary (Newark); College Women's of Essex County. Home: 90 Treacy Av., Newark, N.J.

FOSTER, Solomon, rabbi; b. Americus, Ga., Feb. 15, 1878; s. Meyer Benjamin and Henrietta (Cohen) F.; A.B., Univ. of Cincinnati, 1901; Rabbi, Hebrew Union Coll., Cincinnati, 1902; m. Sadie Levy, of Cincinnati, O., June 22, 1904. Served as rabbi Cong. B'nai Jeshurum, Newark, N.J., continuously since 1902, asso. rabbi, 1902-05, rabbi in full charge cong. and religious sch. since 1905, organized Men's Club, Women's Assn., Jr. and Sr. Alumni Assn., organized N.J. Assn. of Rabbis, 1910, built the new temple, 1915, organized N.J. Normal Sch. for Jewish Teachers, 1926; mem. bd., Newark Red Cross, Newark Univ., Newark Mus., Salvation Army Newark Div., N.J. Normal Sch. for Jewish Teachers. Served as welfare worker auspices Jewish Welfare Bd. in Camp Dix, Camp Vail and Fort Hamilton, 1917-18. Dir. Y.M.H.A., Y.W.H.A. of Newark. Past pres. Alumni Assn. Hebrew Union Coll. Served as grand chaplain Grand Lodge Masons of N.J., 4 terms. Republican. Jewish religion. Mason. Clubs: Progress, Newark Athletic (Newark); Mt. Ridge Country (Caldwell, N.J.). Home: 90 Treacy Av. Office: 783 High St., Newark, N.J.

FOSTER, Thomas J., structural engr.; b. Jacksonville, Ill., Feb. 23, 1867; s. Asbury Milton and Mary Louisa (Larimore) F.; student pub. schs., Los Angeles, Calif., 1880-87; C.E., Rensselaer Poly. Inst., Troy, N.Y., 1892; m. Mary Lydia May, June 22, 1892; children —May (dec.), Larimore (dec.). Draftsman Purdy & Henderson, Chicago, Ill., 1892-94; draftsman Harris Archtl. Iron Works, Chicago, 1894-95; engr. South Halsted St. Iron Works, Chicago, 1895-97; engr., W. G. Triest, N.Y. City, contractor, 1897-98; mem. Foster and Greene, cons. engrs., New York, 1899-1902; organized Nat. Bridge Works, New York, 1902, starting new type of business by combining steel warehouse with fabricating plant for quick delivery structural steel, specializing in theater and other difficult constrns., first to sell "steel lumber" and "junior beams" and designed first self-supporting "curtain wall" constrn. for 12 story bldgs., pres., 1902-17, chmn. bd., 1917-35, sold co. to Jones & Laughlin Steel Corpn., 1935; dir. Citizens First Nat. Bank & Trust Co. Finance commr., Ridgewood, N.J., 1919-23, mem. Shade Tree and Park Coms., 1909-12. Pres. Larry Foster Foundation since 1926, Y.M. C.A., 1909-11; chmn. joint com. Y.W. & Y.M.C.A., 1933-34; chmn. bd. trustees Centenary Junior Coll. (Hackettstown, N.J.), 1931-34, Methodist Ch. since 1930; trustee Northfield Schs., East Northfield, Mass., since 1927; former trustee Pub. Library, Ridgewood, N.J., Sch. of Related Arts and Sciences, Utica, N.Y.; mem. Nat. Hi-Y Com. Former mem. Fed. Mens Club (pres. 1910-13), Am. Soc. C.E., Archtl. Iron Workers (dir. and treas.), Iron League (dir.), Am. Steel Warehouse Assn., Am. Iron and Steel Inst., Am. Inst. of Steel Constrn. (dir. and treas.), Rensselaer Soc. of Civil Engrs., Bldg. Congress. Republican. Methodist. Clubs: Engineers (former mem.), Building Trades (New York); Ridgewood Country (dir., sec., chmn. bldg. com., 1927-1930; Ridgewood, N.J.). Compiler: Larry—Thoughts of Youth, 1930 (among first six best-sellers in non-fiction, 1931; 15 eds., over 80,000 copies); author numerous articles on steel, steel constrn., steel houses, etc., industrial practices and conditions, etc., in trade jours. and periodicals. Address: 206 Prospect St., Ridgewood, N.J.

FOSTER, Thomas V.; pres. First Nat. Bank of Foster; partner various gas companies. Address: Spencer, W.Va.

FOSTER, Warren Dunham, patent lawyer and editor; b. at Geneseo, Ill., Nov. 13, 1886; s. William Horton and Edith (Dunham) Foster; educated University School, Chicago, and University of Chicago; m. Willie Curtis, Aug. 31, 1908; children—Elizabeth, William. Mem. editorial staff Chicago Daily Journal, 1905-06; reader in English, U. of Chicago, 1907; instr. in English, Ia. State Coll., 1908-09; with The Youth's Companion, 1909-16, dept. editor, 1912-16; pres. Community Motion Picture Service and chmn. Community Service, Ltd., of Great Britain, furnishing practically all pictures used in army and navy camps of Am. and allied armies and navies, in America and throughout the world, through Y.M.C.A., K. of C., and other welfare and governmental agencies, 1917-21; pres. Community Internat. Corpn., Kinatome Patents Corpn., Camera Patents Corpn. and related cos.; chmn. Kinema Patents, Ltd., of London; operator large farms in Middle West, growing certified seeds; member Mass. Homestead Commn., 1910-20. Mem. Delta Upsilon; fellow Royal Geog. Soc., Soc. of Motion Picture Engrs. Methodist. Clubs: City (New York); Cosmos (Washington). Author: (with Elmer C. Adams) Heroines of Modern Progress, 1912. Editor: Heroines of Modern Religion; Heroines of the Modern Stage; Debating for Boys; etc.; inventor various photographic and projection apparatus; joint inventor of ultra-violet system of sound motion pictures; granted about 100 patents. Home: "Seven Chimneys," Washington Twp., Bergen Co. (post office, Westwood), N.J. Office: Ridgewood, N.J.; also 42 Theobald's Road, W.C.2, London, Eng.

FOSTER, William Edward; b. Thomaston, Me., Sept. 26, 1864; s. Benjamin T. and Susan (Harrington) F.; ed. pub. schs.; m. Rebecca Clarendon, June 19, 1900; children—Madeleine (Mrs. Charles H. Conklin), Jane (dec.). Began as office boy Am. Sugar Refining Co., N.Y. City, 1883, auditor, 1901-11, comptroller, 1911-13, treas., 1913-20, v.p. 1920-25, pres., 1925-29, vice-chmn. bd. since 1929; dir. Hackensack Trust Co., Preferred-Havana Tobacco Co., M.E. Clarendon Sons Co. Chmn. Liberty Loan and Am. Red Cross drives, Hackensack, World War. Gov. Hackensack Hosp., Hackensack Y.M.C.A.; mem. Hackensack Sinking Fund Commn. Mem. New York Chamber Commerce. Mem. Bd. of Foreign Missions and Board of Direction, Dutch Ref. Ch. in America. Republican. Clubs: Crescent Athletic (Brooklyn); Hackensack Golf, Arcola Country, Oritani Field. Home: 336 Prospect Av., Hackensack, N.J. Office: 120 Wall St., New York, N.Y.

FOUILHOUX, Jacques Andre, architect; b. Paris, France, Sept. 27, 1879; s. Jean Baptiste and Leonie Gasparine (d'Etcheverry) F.; B.A., B.S., Ph.B., Sorbonne, Paris, 1898; C.E., M.E., Ecole Centrale des Arts et Manufactures, Paris, 1901; m. Jean Butler Clark, July 8, 1908; 1 dau., Anita Clark. Came to U.S., 1904, naturalized, 1913. With Baltimore Ferro Concrete Co., 1904-07; mem. firm Whitehouse & Fouilhoux, architects, Portland, Ore., 1908-17; architect, office of Albert Kann, Detroit, 1919; asso. with Raymond M. Hood, architect, New York, 1920-34; mem. firm Hood & Fouilhoux, 1927-34; mem. firm W. K. Harrison & J. A. Fouilhoux since 1935. Works: News Building, New York City (asso. with Raymond M. Hood and John Mead Howells); McGraw-Hill Bldg., New York City (asso. with Raymond Hood); addition to Am. Radiator Bldg., New York City; one of 3 firms of architects of Rockefeller Center, New York; Theme Bldg., New York World's Fair (asso. with Wallace K. Harrison). Treas. and trustee Beaux Arts Inst. of Design; mem. advisory council Art Schs. of Cooper Union; visiting critic Schs. of Architecture, Columbia and Princeton; sec. and trustee French Benevolent Soc. and French Hosp.; mem. bd. mgrs. N.Y. Cath. Protectory; mem. bd. trustees St. Vincent de Paul Inst. Served as capt. and maj. F.A., U.S. Army, 1917-19; in battles of St. Mihiel and Meuse-Argonne. Mem. Am. Inst. Architects, Archtl. League of N.Y., Am. Soc. Civil Engrs., N.Y. State Chamber of Commerce. Democrat. Roman Catholic. Clubs: Baltusrol Golf, Short Hills (Short Hills, N.J.); University, Centre Assn., Rockefeller Center Luncheon (New York). Home: Short Hills, N.J. Office: 45 Rockefeller Plaza, New York, N.Y.

FOULK, Paul Levi, clergyman; b. Littlestown, Pa., Dec. 31, 1896; s. Levi Ulrich and Ella Marie (Rudisill) F.; A.B., Gettysburg (Pa.) Coll., 1922, A.M., 1925; student Luth. Sem., 1922-25; m. Mary Louella Bower, June 26, 1923; 1 dau., Dorothy Bower. Began as teacher rural schs., 1915-17; ordained to ministry Luth. Ch., 1925; pastor, Martinsburg, W.Va., 1922-25 and Rossville, Pa., 1924, Clarksburg, W.Va., 1925-29; pastor Trinity Ch., Altoona, Pa., since 1929. Served as machinist mate, U.S.N., 1918-19 in fgn. service; U.S.N. Res., 1918-21. Sec. W.Va. Synod, 1928-29; mem. mediation com. Central Synod of Pa., 1938-39. Mem. Vets. Fgn. Wars (state chaplain for W. Va., 1927-29, nat. chaplain, 1935-36, ofcl. mem. Good Will Delegation to Japan, 1936), Tau Kappa Alpha. Republican. United Lutheran. Mason. I.O.O.F. Editor West Virginia Lutheran, 1927-29; editor and pub. Clarksburg Christian, 1926-29; editor Allegheny Synod Bulletin, 1937-38. Co-author: (with P. S. Eichelberger) Adams County in the World War, 1921; author: They Twain Shall Be One, 1934; The Golden Anniversary, 1937; contbr. to religious publs. Home: 606 5th Av., Juniata, Altoona, Pa.

FOULK, William Henry, lawyer; b. Wilmington, Del., Aug. 22, 1897; s. Charles Henry and

May Amelia (Blake) F.; B.A., U. of Del., Newark, Del., 1921; LL.B., U. of Va., Charlottesville, Va., 1923; m. Mildred Jones Clifton, Jan. 30, 1932; children—William Henry, Gerald Clifton, Richard Warren. Admitted to practice of law in Del., 1923; in practice at Wilmington, Del., since 1923; dep. atty. gen. in charge of taxes, State of Del., 1929-33; spl. counsel, State Tax Dept., Del., 1934-37; atty. Del. Liquor Commn., 1933-38; mem. firm Satterthwaite & Foulk, Wilmington, Del., since 1928. Mem. Am., Del. State bar assns., Am. Legion. Republican. Baptist. Mason. Clubs: University, Young Men's Repub. (Wilmington, Del.). Home: Centreville, Del. Office: du Pont Bldg., Wilmington, Del.

FOULKE, Roland Roberts, lawyer; b. Phila., Pa., May 10, 1874; s. J. Roberts and Emma (Bullock) F.; LL.B., U. of Pa., 1897; m. Ellen R. Griffith, June 6, 1900. Admitted to Pa. bar, 1897, and since practiced in Phila. Republican. Episcopalian. Author: Rule Against Perpetuities in Pa., 1909; Treatise on Price Act, 1914; Treatise on International Law, 1919. Contbr. articles to law jours. Home: 125 Edgewood Rd., Ardmore, Pa. Office: 400 Chestnut St., Philadelphia, Pa.

FOULKE, Thomas Albert, lawyer; b. Moorestown, N.J., Sept. 25, 1893; s. Joseph Thomas and Laura Lydia (Lippincott) F.; grad. George School (Pa.), 1912; A.B., U. of Pa., 1916; LL.B., Temple U., 1921; m. Eliza Moore Ambler, June 1, 1923; 1 dau., Anne. Admitted to Pa. bar, 1921, and since practiced in Ambler; mem. firm Foulke, Foulke & Duffy; solicitor and trust officer Ambler Trust Co.; solicitor Ambler Bldg. & Loan Assn, Community Bldg. Assn. of Ambler, Peoples Building and Loan Assn. of North Wales. Pres. Ambler Pub. Library since 1934. Mem. Montgomery Bar Assn. (pres. 1938), Pa. Bar Assn., Am. Bar Assn. Republican. Mem. Soc. of Friends. Home: Hague Mill Rd. Office: 201 Knight Bldg., Ambler, Pa.

FOULKE, Willing Bayard, metallurgical engring.; b. Bala Farm, West Chester, Pa., Mar. 31, 1898; s. George Rhyfedd and Jean Duval Leiper (Kane) F.; ed. St. Lukes Sch., Wayne, Pa., 1912-14, Marionfield, Samarcand, N.C., 1914-15, U. of Pa., 1916; m. Elisabeth Innes Bennett, Oct. 10, 1925; children—Willing Bayard, Elisabeth Bennett, Richard Flaidd. Bond salesman, 1921; machinists apprentice, 1922; quarry supervisor Va. Alberene Corpn., Schuyler, Va., 1923; sales engr., Wagner Electric Corpn., St. Louis, Mo., 1923-25; own business of selling paint and varnish, 1925-27; security salesman, Baker Young & Co., Phila., 1927-29; v.p. and sales mgr. Treiber Diesel Engrs. Corpn., New York Ship Building Corpn., Camden, N.J., 1929-30; v.p. and gen. mgr. Delaware Chem. Engring. Co., Wilmington, 1930-34; dir. minerals separation div. E. I. du Pont de Nemours & Co. since 1934. Served with 1st Pa. Cav., 103d Engrs. and 103d Trench Mortar Batt., U.S. Army, 1917-19; with A.E.F.; wounded in action; disch. as 1st duty sergt. Decorated Victory medal with 5 bars. Hon. mem. 1st Troop Phila. City Cav. Mem. Am. Inst. Mining and Metall. Engrs., Phi Kappa Sigma. Republican. Episcopalian. Developed sink and float method of recovering coal and minerals from waste piles and run of mine material. Home: Bowling Green, Media, Pa. Office: E. I. du Pont de Nemours & Co., Wilmington, Del.

FOULKES, William Hiram, clergyman; b. Quincy, Mich., June 26, 1877; s. Rev. William and Harriet A. (Johnson) F.; A.B., Coll. of Emporia, Kan., 1897, A.M., 1901, D.D., 1907, LL.D., 1915; grad. McCormick Theol. Sem., Chicago, 1901; fellow New Coll., Edinburgh, 1901-02; D.D., Whitworth Coll., Wash., and Lenox Coll., Ia., 1907; m. Catherine E. Lamb, Jan. 21, 1898; children—Frederick Richard, Paul Bergen, William Robertson, Mrs. Catherine Price. Ordained Presbyterian ministry, 1901; pastor, Elmira, Ill., 1901-04, Clinton, Ia., 1904-07, First Ch., Portland, Ore., 1907-11, Rutgers Ch., New York, Apr. 1911-13; gen. sec. Ministerial Relief and Sustentation of the Presbyn. Ch. in U.S.A., 1913-18; gen. sec. New Era Movement of Presbyn. Ch. of U.S.A., 1918-24; pastor Old Stone (First) Ch., Cleveland, Ohio, 1924-26; pastor Old First (Presbyn.) Ch., Newark, N.J., since 1926. Chmn. finance com., Internat. Soc. Christian Endeavor, trustee since 1918, v.p. since 1925. Mem. Bd. Foreign Missions Presbyn. Ch., U.S.A.; chmn. Com. on Coöperation in Near East; mem. bd. Bloomfield (N.J.) Theol. Sem.; trustee Am. Coll. of Sofia, Bulgaria; chmn. exec. com Work In Europe; trustee Am. Waldensian Soc., Presbyterian Hospital in Newark. Mem. Sons of Am. Revolution, St. David's Soc. (N.Y. City), Portland Chamber Commerce (life). Del. World's Missionary Conf., Edinburgh, 1910; mem. Council of Chs. Holding Ref. Faith; chmn. Nat. Preaching Mission, 1936-37; Moderator 149th Gen. Assembly of Presbyn. Ch. in U.S.A., 1937. Author: Living Bread from the Fourth Gospel, 1914; Sunset by the Lakeside, 1917; Youth—Ways to Life, 1927; Homespun, along Friendly Road, 1936. Contbr. to religious press; condr. "Homespun," Nat. Broadcasting Co., 1934-37. Home: 583 Mt. Prospect Av., Newark, N.J.

FOURNIER, Louis Francis, newspaper pub.; b. Paterson, N.J., June 5, 1889; m. Rose M. Vincent, June 1915; children—Mary, Louise. Mgr. and editor Bergen Herald, East Paterson, N.J., Nat. Auto Racing News, Paterson. Republican. Catholic. Club: St. Leo's R.C. Ch. Holy Name Society (East Paterson, N.J.; pres.). Home: 24 Grove St. Office: 26 Grove St., East Paterson, N.J.

FOUST, Leslie Alexander, registrar and college prof.; b. Bolivar, Pa., Feb. 5, 1895; s. Frederick and Elizabeth (Muir) F.; B.S., Washington and Jefferson Coll., 1922, M.S., same, 1924; Ph.D., U. of Pittsburgh, 1937; m. Dorothy Park, Dec. 24, 1921; children—Carolyn Elizabeth, Lois Margaretta, Dorothy Park. Teacher in pub. schs., 1912-13 and 1914-15; prin. schs., Webster, Pa., 1915-18; administrative sec. Washington and Jefferson Coll., 1922-26, registrar since 1926, also asst. prof. polit. sci. since 1937. Served as corpl. inf., U.S.A., 1918-19, with A.E.F. and Army of Occupation. Mem. Am. Assn. Coll. Registrars, Lambda Chi Alpha, Pi Sigma Alpha, Delta Sigma Rho. Republican. Mem. Christian Ch. Mason. Home: 411 Wilson Av., Washington, Pa.

FOUST, Madeleine Skelly (Mrs. Raymond King F.), dean sch. of drama; b. Pittsburgh, Pa., May 9, 1904; d. Charles Joseph and Juliet (Purcell) Skelly; A.B., Seton Hill Coll., 1924; A.M., Duquesne U., 1928; student Am. Acad. Dramatic Art, 1925, Pa. State Coll., 1932; m. Raymond King Foust, Dec. 8, 1928. Actress, Keystone Repertory, Harry Schwartz Stock Co., East End Stock Co., 1925-27; dir. Newman Players, 1927-28; instr. drama, Seton Hill Coll., Parochial High Schs. of Pittsburgh, also Recreation Bur. City of Pittsburgh, 1927-32; actress Stage Guild, Twentieth Century Players (designer), Civic Playhouse (dir., stage mgr.), 1932-33; press agt. Kilbuck Theatre, 1934-35, dir. same, 1936-37; dean Sch. of Drama, Duquesne U. since 1936; mem. bd. dirs. Pittsburgh Playhouse. Mem. Am. Assn. Univ. Profs., Am. Assn. Univ. Women, Assn. Teachers of Speech, Am. Edn. Theatre Assn., Nat. Theatre Conf. Republican. Roman Catholic. Clubs: Congress Women's (Pittsburgh); Studio Club (New York). Home: 3887 Bigelow Boul., Pittsburgh, Pa.

FOWLE, Lester Perham, physician; b. South Sudbury, Mass., Dec. 15, 1898; s. Wm. E. and Alice (Perkins) F.; ed. Bucknell U., 1916-18; M.D., U. of Pa., Med. Sch., 1923; m. Marguerite Hartman, June 25, 1925; children—Genevieve, Louise Hartman, Alice Amelia. Interne Geisinger Memorial Hosp., Danville, Pa., 1923-25; engaged in gen. practice of medicine at Lewisburg, Pa., since 1925; med. dir. Student Health Service, Bucknell U. since 1927; asst. prof. anatomy, Bucknell U. since 1933; engaged also in painting in Oil, exhibited at New York City, State College, Pa., San Francisco. Mem. Am. Med. Assn., Soc. of Investigative Dermatology, Am. Phys. Art Assn., Central Pa. Art Club. Republican. Presbyn. Mason. Home: Lewisburg, Pa.

FOWLER, Burton Philander, educator; b. South Butler, N.Y., June 19, 1887; s. Marcus S. and Charlotte E. (Winegar) F.; A.B., Syracuse U., 1907; A.M., Columbia, 1925; m. Mertie M. Dense, Aug. 6, 1913; children—Charlotte Ellen (dec.), Mary Melissa. Biology teacher, Syracuse (N.Y.) High Sch., 1907; prin. Oneida High Sch., 1908-13, Dunkirk High Sch., 1913-16, Milton (Mass.) High Sch., 1916-18, Central High Sch., Cleveland, 1918-23; head master Tower Hill Sch., Wilmington, Del., since 1923. Mem. directing com. Sch. and Coll. Relations Commn.; mem. Nat. Committee for Mental Hygiene, Education Council of Julius Rosenwald Fund; director Del. chapter Am. Red Cross; dir. Children's Bur. of Del.; mem. advisory bd. Safety Edn. Mag.; pres. Del. Citizens Assn.; dir. Del. Safety Council; trustee Wilmington Inst. Free Library, Sarah Lawrence Coll. Mem. N.E.A., Progressive Edn. Assn. (past pres.; mem. advisory bd.), American Council of Education (problems and plan com.), Headmasters and Secondary School Principals' Assn., Psi Upsilon, Phi Delta Kappa. Republican. Presbyterian. Editor: (with Henry W. Holmes) The Path of Learning, 1926; Growth in English, 1935. Advisory editor School Management. Contbr. ednl. articles to mags.; lecturer on ednl. subjects. Address: Tower Hill School, Wilmington, Del.

FOWLER, Laurence Hall, architect; b. Baltimore Co., Md., Sept. 5, 1876; s. David and Mary (Brinkley) F.; A.B., Johns Hopkins, 1898; B.S. in architecture, Columbia, 1902; studied École des Beaux Arts, Paris; m. Mary Josephs, January 1926. Practiced at Baltimore since 1906; architect of Calvert Sch. and the War Memorial, Baltimore, Maryland Hall of Records, Annapolis, and many pvt. residences. Fellow Am. Inst. Architects: mem. Friends of Art (dir.), Baltimore Mus. Art (dir.), Delta Phi. Democrat. Episcopalian. Home: 10 W. Highfield Rd. Office: 347 N. Charles St., Baltimore, Md.

FOWLER, William Henry, engring. exec.; b. San Antonio, Tex., Dec. 1, 1890; s. Harry L. and Bertha (Schleuning) F.; A.B., U. of Tex., Austin, Tex., 1912; C.E., U. of Wis., Madison, Wis., 1916; m. Violet Lee Baker, June 17, 1919; children—William Henry (dec.), Robert Asa, Virginia Lee. With Dravo Contracting Co. since 1916, successively as field engr., 1916-17, asst. supt. of constrn., 1917-18, engr. on costs, 1918-20, asst. to pres., 1920-25, dir. since 1926, sec., 1925-34, vice-pres. since 1934; vice-pres. and dir. Dravo Corpn. (successor Dravo-controlled corpns.) since 1930; vice-pres. and dir. Fullerton-Portsmouth Bridge Co., Portsmouth, O.; dir. Eastern Ohio Sand & Supply Co., Cumberland River Sand Co., Dravo-Doyle Co. Vice chmn. heavy engring. and railroad contractors div. Asso. Gen. Contractors of America, 1935, chmn. 1936. Mem. Gamma Alpha, Delta Upsilon, Phi Beta Kappa, Tau Beta Pi. Republican. Presbyterian. Mason. Clubs: Edgeworth (Sewickley, Pa.); Dixie (Madison, Wis.). Home: Osborne Lane, Sewickley, Pa. Office: Dravo Bldg., 300 Penn Av., Pittsburgh, Pa.

FOX, Fred Lee, judge; b. Braxton Co., W.Va., Oct. 24, 1876; s. Camden and Caroline (McMorrow) F.; LL.B., W.Va. Univ., 1899; m. Annie Lee Frame, June 27, 1900; children—Gordon Byrne, John Holt, George McMorrow, Agnes Jane, Rebecca Ellen (Mrs. Charles A. Duffield, Jr.), Anna Jean (Mrs. J. Fleet Greene). Admitted to W.Va. bar, 1899, and practiced in Sutton until 1933; mem. State Senate, 1912-20; state tax commr. 1933-36; judge Supreme Court since 1937. Mem. Am. and State bar assns. Democrat. Presbyterian. Mason. Home: 206 Ruffner Av. Address: State Capitol, Charleston, W.Va.

FOX, H(amilton) P(hilips), clergyman; b. Washington, D.C., Mar. 13, 1889; s. William T. and Gertrude (Hamilton) F.; ed. Taylor U., Upland, Ind., 1907-08; William and Mary Coll., 1908-10; Syracuse U., 1910-12; studied Johns Hopkins and New Coll. (Oxford); m. Louise Savage, Sept. 18, 1913; children—William Wescott, Hamilton Philips. Ordained ministry M.E. Ch., 1910; successively pastor Newport and Cleveland, N.Y., Baltimore, Hamline Ch., Washington, D.C., Asbury Ch., Salisbury, Md., until 1926, and First Ch., Lincoln, Neb., 1926-32,

St. Paul's Ch., Ocean Grove, N.J., 1932-37, Ashbury Church, Salisbury, Maryland, since 1937. Won Taylor scholarship for poetry, William and Mary Coll., also medal for oratory, same coll. Trustee various religious and benevolent boards. Mem. Theta Chi Beta, Theta Phi. Democrat. Mason, Odd Fellow. Traveled extensively in Europe, Asia and Africa. Lecturer. Author of various mag. articles. Home: 602 N. Division St., Salisbury, Md.

FOX, Henry, biologist; b. Germantown, Pa., Feb. 18, 1875; s. William and Elizabeth Ellen (Saylor) F.; B.S. in Biology, U. of Pa., 1899, M.A., 1903, Ph.D., 1905; m. Adelaide Townsend Godfrey, June 27, 1906; 1 dau., Emily Elizabeth (Mrs. George Alfred Clark). Instructor biology, University of Wisconsin, 1902-03; prof. biology, Temple U., Phila., 1903-05; instr. natural science, Manual Training High Sch., Phila., 1905-07; prof. biology, Ursinus Coll., 1907-12; field investigator U.S. Bur. of Entomology, 1912-18; prof. biology, Mercer U., Macon, Ga., 1918-24; asso. entomologist (Japanese Beetle project), U.S. Bur. Entomology, 1925-36; teaching fellow New York Univ. since 1936. Fellow A.A.A.S.; mem. Am. Entomol. Soc., Phila. Acad. Natural Science, New York Entom. Soc., Sigma Xi; pres. Ga. Soc. Biologists, 1929; sec. Ga. Acad. Sciences, 1922-24. Contbr. on professional topics. Address: Cape May Court House, N.J.

FOX, Herbert, pathologist; b. Atlantic City, N.J., June 3, 1880; s. Samuel Tucker and Hannah Ray (Freas) F.; A.B., Central High Sch., Phila., 1897; M.D., Med. Dept., U. of Pa., 1901; studied U. of Vienna; m. Emma Louise Gaskill, Nov. 9, 1904 (she died Nov. 16, 1933); children—Margaret, John Freas (deceased), Samuel Tucker. Vol. asso. in William Pepper Clin. Lab., 1903-06; pathologist to Rush Hosp., since 1904; pathologist to Phila. Zoöl. Soc., since 1906; chief of Labs., Pa. Dept. of Health, 1906-11; dir. William Pepper Lab. of Clinical Medicine, Hosp. U. of Pa., since 1911; pathologist to the Children's Hosp., 1915-26; prof. comparative pathology, Univ. of Pa. since 1927. Member College of Physicians, American Philosophical Society, Academy of Natural Sciences, County Med. Society, Pathol. Society (all of Phila.), A.M.A., Am. Assn. Pathologists and Bacteriologists; fellow A.A.A.S. Served as chief cantonment lab., Camp Zachary Taylor, Ky., 1917-19; maj., M.C.U.S.A. Republican. Author: Elementary Bacteriology and Protozoölogy, 1912, 5th edit., 1931; Text Book of Pathology (with Alfred Stengel), 8th edit., 1927; Disease in Captive Wild Mammals and Birds, 1923. Home: Hamilton Court, 39th and Chestnut Sts., Philadelphia, Pa.

FOX, J. Francke; surgeon Bluefield Sanitarium and Norfolk & Western Ry.; cons. surgeon Stevens Clinic Hosp., Welch, W.Va., and Clinch Valley Clinic, Richlands, Va. Address: Bluefield Sanitarium, Bluefield, W.Va.

FOX, John Edgar; judge Court of Common Pleas. Address: Harrisburg, Pa.

FOX, John Herbert, engr.; b. Lucas, O., Sept. 20, 1870; s. Herman and Sarah A. (Mowers) F.; student Greentown Acad., Perryville, O., 1885-88, Wittenberg Coll., Springfield, O., 1889-91; M.E., Ohio State U., 1897, grad. student 1897-98; unmarried. Teacher in pub. schools, Ohio, 1888-89, 1891-92; teacher Y.M.C.A. Training Sch., Springfield, Mass., 1895-96; mech. engr. Brown Hoisting Machinery Co., Cleveland, O., 1898-1905; consulting engr. in firm of Frazier, Fox & Spencer (later Frazier & Fox), Cleveland, 1905-10; with Pittsburgh Plate Glass Co. since 1910, as chief engr. 1910-22, exec. engr., 1922-36, tech. advisor to pres. since 1936; consulting engr. for Pittsburgh Valve & Fittings Co. Served as advisory engr. to U.S. Shipping Bd. and Ordnance Dept. during World War. Mem. Am. Soc. Mech. Engrs., Engr. Soc. Western Pa., Soc. Am. Mil. Engrs., A.A.A.S., Beta Theta Pi, Tau Beta Pi. Republican. Presbyterian. Mason. Clubs: Duquesne, University, Oakmont Country (Pittsburgh). Home: (summer) University Club, Pittsburgh, Pa.; (winter) St. Petersburg, Fla. Address: 2000 Grant Bldg., Pittsburgh, Pa.

FOX, John Lawrence, lawyer; b. Baltimore Co., Md., Mar. 16, 1879; s. William Obington and Martha Elizabeth (Burton) F.; LL.B., U. of Md., Baltimore, 1908; m. Mary Katharine Garland (D.A.R.), Nov. 24, 1910; children—Martha Katharine (Mrs. Norman A. Jones), John Brockenbrough, May Christian. Admitted to bar, 1909, and in gen. practice at Baltimore, 1909-18; war risk ins. work, U.S. Shipping Bd., 1918-21; law lecturer Y.M.C.A. Law Sch., Baltimore, 1921-22; gen. practice, New York City, 1922-25; asso. with James W. Bowers in law practice, Baltimore, 1909-33; pvt. practice, Baltimore and New York, since 1933. Mem. Am. Bar Assn., Baltimore City Bar Assn., Md. Hist. Soc. Home: 2222 N. Calvert St. Office: Calvert Bldg., Baltimore, Md.

FOX, John Pierce, municipal consultant; b. Boston, Nov. 5, 1872; s. George William and Mary Susannah (Poor) F.; A.B., Harvard University, 1894; m. Esther Taber, Nov. 11, 1908; 1 dau., Katherine T.; m. 2d, Grace Newton Wallace, Aug. 2, 1927; children—Georgia W., John W. Investigated transit conditions in American and in Europeon cities, for the Merchants' Association, the City Club, and the Rapid Transit R.R. Commn. of New York, and other orgns., cos. and cities, 1899-1908; sanitary expert for Met. Sewerage Commn., New York, 1908, 1909, and for N.Y. City in Passaic Valley Sewer case, 1912; investigated Pittsburgh transit conditions, 1908-09; transit expert to City of Pittsburgh, 1909-11; investigated N.Y. City hosp. bldgs., 1912; reported on transit problems of Montreal, Can., 1912, Brookline, Mass., 1914, Reading, Pa., 1916, Springfield, Mass., 1917; transit expert and consultant on city planning to Bd. of Estimate and Apportionment, New York, 1914-18; with Pub. Utilities Commn., Washington, 1918; transit expert, City of Reading, Pa., 1918-19, City of New York, 1919; consultant on zoning to Newton, Fall River, Norwood, Wellesley, Dedham, Winchester, Arlington, Salem, Malden, Weston, Plymouth, Canton, Beacon Hill Assn. (Boston), Maplewood, N.J., Northport, L.I., Keene and Laconia, N.H., North Smithfield, R.I., and to the restoration of Williamsburg, Va., since 1928. Exec. sec., Murray Hill Assn., New York, since 1914. Mem. Am. Transit Assn., A.A.A.S., Am. Assn. Variable Star Observers, Am. Acad. Polit. and Social Science, Am. Meteorol. Soc., Citizens' Housing Council of N.Y. Club: City. Contbr. to tech. jours. of U.S. and Europe. Home: 440 Richmond Av., Maplewood, N.J. Address: City Club, 55 W. 44th St., New York, N.Y.*

FOX, Robert T(homas), lawyer; b. Derry Twp., Dauphin Co., Pa., Aug. 30, 1883; s. James G. and Emma Brightbill (Strickler) F.; grad. Dowingtown (Pa.) High Sch., 1901; Ph.B., Lafayette Coll., Easton, Pa., 1905; LL.B., U. of Pa., 1908; m. Lillie Sophia Walton, Nov. 17, 1914; children—Robert Thomas, Caroline Goehmann. Admitted to Pa. bar, 1911, and since practiced in Harrisburg; search clerk Legislative Reference Bur., Harrisburg, Jan.-July 1911; asst. dist. atty. Dauphin Co., 1912-24, dist. atty., 1924-32; gen. practice law since 1932; mem. firm Caldwell, Fox & Stoner; dir. Farmers Bank of Hummelstown. Mem. Alpha Chi Rho. Republican. Lutheran. Elk, Moose, Royal Arcanum. Club: University, Kiwanis (Harrisburg). Home: Hummelstown, Pa. Office: 23 S. 3d St., Harrisburg, Pa.

FOX, Will S., pres. Fox Knapp Mfg. Co.; b. Reading, Pa., Oct. 1, 1874; s. Adam G. and Sarah (Staller) F.; student business coll.; m. Anna Boothroyd, Dec. 11, 1902. Pres. Fox Knapp Mfg. Co., New York, since 1926, now also dir.; dir. Schuylkill Trust Co., Pottsville, Pa., Pine Grove (Pa.) Nat. Bank & Trust Co., Pine Grove and Cressonia Telephone Co. Chmn. dist. council, Boy Scouts of America. Mason. Clubs: Square, Schuylkill Country. Home: 164 Main St., Pine Grove, Pa. Office: 230 Fifth Av., New York, N.Y.

FOX, William Joseph, librarian; b. Phila., Nov. 21, 1872; s. Benjamin F. and Elizabeth (Quirk) F.; ed. pub. schs., Phila.; m. Margaret Muldoon, Apr. 27, 1897; 1 son, Edward Nolan; m. 2d, Louise P. Hellyer, June 22, 1904. Asst. librarian Academy Nat. Sciences of Philadelphia, 1888-1933, librarian, 1933—, editor publs., 1921-38. Original investigator in entomology. Mem. Acad. Natural Sciences, Philadelphia, Zoöl. Society Philadelphia, Pa. Library Club, Special Libraries Council Phila. Address: Academy of Natural Sciences, Philadelphia, Pa.

FRACK, William Arthur, lawyer; b. Bushkill Twp., Northampton Co., Pa., Nov. 8, 1896; s. James and Emma (Miller) F.; student Nazareth High Sch., Nazareth, Pa., 1911-13, Perkiomen Sch., Pennsburg, Pa., 1913-14; Ph.B., Lafayette Coll., Easton, Pa., 1919, M.A., 1921; LL.B., Harvard Law Sch., 1925; m. Edna Rafetto, Oct. 17, 1927; 1 son, William Arthur. Sch. teacher, Hanover Twp., Pa., 1914-15, Penn Argyl, Pa., 1919-20; admitted to bars of Northampton County, Pa., Supreme Court, 1925, and since practiced at Easton Pa.; mem. firm Chidsey, Maxwell and Frack, Easton, Pa., since 1928; dir. and trust officer Lafayette Trust Co. Served as sergeant, U.S. Army, during World War. First asst. dist. atty. Northampton Co., Pa., 1932-36, dist. atty. since 1936. Dir. Visiting Nurses Assn. Mem. Northampton Court Bar Assn. (pres. 1939), Am. Legion, Pa. Soc., Acacia, Phi Beta Kappa. Republican. Lutheran. Mason, Elk, Odd Fellow, Patriotic Order Sons of America. Clubs: Rotary, Pomfret, Northampton Country, (Easton, Pa.). Home: 117 W. Wayne Av. Office: Jones Bldg., Easton, Pa.

FRADKIN, Elvira Kush (Mrs. L. Henry Fradkin); b. Aug. 22, 1891; d. Gustave and Rose (Reichert) Kush; A.B., Vassar Coll., 1913; A.M., Columbia, 1914; m. Dr. L. Henry Fradkin, June 1, 1916; children—Rosalind Foster, Noel Morris (dec.), Philip Lawrence. Founder Montclair Internat. Relations Council, 1923; state chmn. Dept. of Internat. Coöperation of N.J. League of Women Voters, 1927-33, vice-pres., 1933-38; chmn. N.J. Council on Internat. Relations, 1933-36, hon. pres. since 1936; mem. delegation of 4 women to Disarmament Conf., Geneva, Switzerland, representing all U.S. women's organizations and presenting petitions signed by over a million Am. women, 1932; mem. Nat. Peace Conf., Coll. Women's Club of Montclair (pres. 1936—), Nat. Defense Com. of Nat. Peace Conf. since 1937; trustee N.J. League of Nations Assn., Agnes Wilson Osborne World Friendship Fund; dir. N.J. Com. on Cause and Cure of War; asst. dir. Montclair Emergency Relief, 1933. Ind. Democrat. Unitarian. Clubs: Cosmopolitan (founder and hon. pres.), College Women's (pres. 1936-38), Golf (Montclair); Town Hall (New York). Author: Chemical Warfare—Its Possibilities and Probabilities, 1929; Air Menace and the Answer, 1934. Home: 36 Lloyd Rd., Montclair, N.J.

FRAIM, Samuel Reuben, pres. E. T. Fraim Lock Co.; b. Lancaster, Pa., June 29, 1881; s. Edward T. and Arabella (Fairer) F.; student Mercersburg (Pa.) Acad., 1898-99; M.E., Lehigh U., 1903; m. Mary G. Metzger, Jan. 19, 1904; children—Samuel E., Edward T. With E. T. Fraim Lock Co. since 1903, beginning as mech. engr., pres. since 1921; dir. Conestoga Nat. Bank. Mem. Am. Soc. Mech. Engrs. Republican. Mason (32°, Shriner). Clubs: Hamilton, Lancaster Country (Lancaster). Home: Wilson Drive. Office: 237 Park Av., Lancaster, Pa.

FRAME, Grace Martin, artist, teacher; b. Morgantown, W.Va., Feb. 11, 1903; d. Joseph Wesley and Anna (McClure) Martin; student Pa. Acad. Fine Arts, Phila., 1922-23; pvt. study under Blanche Lazzell, Provincetown, Mass., 1929-30, under Roy Hilton, Carnegie Inst. Tech., 1937; A.B., W.Va. Univ., Morgantown, W.Va., 1928, grad. study, 1939; m. Wilbur Conan Frame, June 15, 1929; 1 dau., Lucie Anne. Teacher, Kanawha Coll., Charleston, W.Va., 1933-34; art instr., Mason Coll. of Music and Fine Arts, Charleston, W.Va., since 1934; exhibited: Brooklyn (N.Y.) Mus., Phila. Print Club, traveling exhbns. of Am. Fed. of Art, numerous other nat. galleries. Mem. City Art Commn., Charleston, W.Va. Mem. Allied Artists Assn. of Charleston (pres., 1933-35), Am. Artists Professional League, Southern Printmakers, Wichita Art Assn., Provincetown Art Assn. Print judged one of Fifty Best Prints in U.S. and

Can., 1933, by Print Makers Soc. of Calif. Republican. Episcopalian. Lecturer before clubs, ednl. assns. Address: 1900 McClung St., Charleston, W.Va.

FRAME, Nat T(erry), agricultural extension; b. Depauville, Jefferson Co., N.Y., Feb. 25, 1877; s. S. W. (M.D.) and Harriet (Terry) F.; A.B., Colgate, 1899, D.Sc., 1928; m. Grace Boomer; children—Luke W., Robert N., S. William. Formerly pub. sch. teacher and prin.; engaged as orchardist and farmer in W.Va.; county agrl. agt., Louisville, Ky., 1912-13; dir. agrl. extension W.Va. U., 1919-33; ednl. supervisor Civilian Conservation Corps, Fort Hayes, Columbus, Ohio, 1934-37; dir. Oglebay Inst., Wheeling, W.Va., since 1937. Originator West Virginia Community Score Cards; organized "4-H" clubs for country boys and girls; chairman West Virginia Beautification Conference, 1925-27; sec. Am. Country Life Assn., 1920-28; vice chmn. and sec. W.Va. Conservation Commn., 1925-29; pres. Nat. Coöp. Extension Workers Assn., 1930-31; v.p. and pres. Am. Country Life Assn., 1933-34. Hon. col. staff of Gov. Hatfield. Mem. Phi Kappa Psi. Republican. Kiwanian; chmn. agrl. com. Kiwanis Internat., 1925-26; gov. W.Va. Kiwanis Dist., 1928. Wrote bulls., Focussing on the Country Community; Helping the Country Community Lift Itself by Its Own Bootstraps; also numerous pamphlets and articles on rural life. Home: Oglebay Park, Wheeling, W.Va.*

FRAME, Col. Thomas Clayton, lawyer; b. Camden, Kent Co., Del., Aug. 10, 1871; s. Dr. Thomas Clayton and Mary Elizabeth (Layton) F.; student Wesley Collegiate Inst., Dover, Del., 1886-89; B.A., U. of Del., Newark, Del., 1891; m. Adella Cann Clayton, Nov. 24, 1897; children—Clara Clayton (formerly Mrs. G. Hale Harrison, now Mrs. Oliver Farrow), Jeannette Clayton. Admitted to Del. bar, 1894, and in pvt. practice at Dover, Del., since 1894. Appointed Aide-de-Camp on staff of Gov. Richard Cann McMullen of Del., 1937. Appointed Labor Commr., 1916, chmn. Labor Commn. of Del. since 1938. Trustee U. of Del. Mem. Am. Bar Assn., Del. State Bar Assn. (treas. since 1923), Soc. of Colonial Wars in State of Del. (charter), Del. Soc. of Sons of Am. Revolution. Democrat. Episcopalian. Clubs: Episcopal Church of Delaware (Wilmington, Del.; pres. 1932-33); Wilmington (Wilmington, Del.); Mapledale Country (Dover, Del.). Address: 34 The Green, Dover, Del.

FRAMPTON, James Villard, lawyer; b. Strattanville, Pa., July 24, 1883; s. B. Hayes and Nellie M. (Mohney) F.; Ph.B., Bucknell U., 1903; studied law in law office; m. Lavinia Magee, Oct. 19, 1910; 1 son, William. Admitted to Pa. bar, 1907, and since practiced in Oil City; mem. firm Speer, Frampton & Courtney, 1919-26, Frampton & Courtney since 1926; gen. practice in county courts, state appellate and federal courts; dir. and mem. investment com. of trust dept. Oil City Nat. Bank; vice-pres. and dir. Charles N. Hough Mfg. Co.; dir. Henry I. Beers Corpn., New England Terminal Co. Dir. Grandview Instn.; chmn. bd. dirs. Venango Co. Branch of Pa. Assn. for the Blind. Mem. Pa. State Bar Assn. (mem. com. on taxation), Am. Judicature Soc., Sigma Chi. Republican. Mason (K.T., 32°, Shriner). Clubs: Wanango, Lions (Oil City). Home: W. 3d St. Office: Quaker State Bldg., Oil City, Pa.

FRANCE, Jacob, lawyer, business exec.; b. Baltimore, Md., July 5, 1882; s. Jacob and Ida Jane (Cullimore) F.; LL.B., U. of Md., 1903; m. Annita Applegarth, Feb. 11, 1914. Admitted to Md. bar, 1903, and practiced since at Baltimore; pres. Mid-Continent Petroleum Corpn.; chmn. bd., dir. and mem. exec. com. Equitable Trust Co.; dir. Commercial Nat. Bank & Trust Co. of New York, Savings Bank of Baltimore. Republican. Presbyn. Clubs: Maryland, Baltimore. Home: Pikesville, Baltimore. Office: Calvert Bldg., Baltimore, Md.

FRANCE, Mary Adele, educator; b. Chestertown, Md., Feb. 17, 1880; d. Thomas Dashiell and Emma Price (deCorse) F.; grad. Washington Coll. Prep. Sch., Chestertown, Md., 1896; B.A. Washington Coll., 1900, M.A., 1902; M.A., Teachers Coll. (Columbia), 1923. Teacher in own pvt. sch., 1901-07; teacher science and mathematics, St. Mary's Sem., Md., 1909-13; teacher science and mathematics, Bristol Sch., Washington, D.C., 1913-14, St. Mary's Sem., 1917-18; supervisor elementary schs., Kent Co., Md., 1918-20, Shelby Co., Tenn., 1920-22; prin. St. Mary's Sem., 1923-37, name changed to St. Mary's Female Sem.-Junior Coll., 1937, pres. since 1937. Mem. Am. Assn. Univ. Women, Am. Assn. Sch. Adminstrs. of Jr. Coll. Council of Middle States, Assn. Deans of Women and Advisers of Girls, N.E.A., Teachers College Alumni, D.A.R. Ind. Democrat. Episcopalian. Home: St. Mary's City, Md.*

FRANCIS, James Draper, pres. Island Creek Coal Co.; b. Pikeville, Ky., Feb. 25, 1884; s. David L. and Kate (Dean) F.; student Pikeville (Ky.) Coll. and Centre Coll., Danville, Ky.; LL.B., U. of Va., 1908; m. Permele Crawford Elliott, 1910. Began practice of law, 1908; atty. Island Creek Coal Co., 1911-18, gen. counsel and v.p., 1918-34, pres. since 1934; pres. Pond Creek Pocahontas Co., Mallory Coal Co. Home: 250 Ridgewood Road. Office: Robson-Prichard Bldg., Huntington, W.Va.

FRANCIS, Richard S(tandish), building construction; b. Phila., Pa., July 1, 1880; s. William Allen and Mary (Winterbottom) F.; student Irving Inst., 1891-94, Montclair (N.J.) High Sch., 1894-97; B.S., Harvard, 1902; m. Louise Buffum Congdon, May 9, 1908; children—Richard Standish, William Allen. Engaged in bldg. constrn. since 1902, beginning as estimator; vice-pres. and dir. George A. Fuller Co. since 1922. Republican. Clubs: Franklin Inn, Harvard (Phila.); Merion Cricket (Haverford). Author: Samuel Lyle, Criminologist, 1920; Ghosts, 1921; Ben Thorpe, 1921; Golf—Its Rules and Decisions, 1937, revised edit., 1939. Contbr. short stories to publs. Home: Haverford, Pa. Office: 12 S. 12th St., Philadelphia, Pa.

FRANCIS, Thomas, supt. of schools; b. Forest City, Pa., June 8, 1888; s. William and Liza (Little) F.; B.S., Pa. State Coll., 1928; M.A., Columbia U., 1933; m. Tranie Sterner, 1913; children—Thomas S., Mrs. William E. Chalfant. Prin. Turbotville High Sch., 1908-09; supervising prin. Delaware Twp. and Dewart (Pa.) pub. schs., 1909-13; prin. Audubon Sch. Scranton, 1913-26; supervisor evening grade schs., Scranton, 1917-26; county supt. schs., Lackawanna Co., Pa., since 1926. Dir. Am. Red Cross of Scranton, Visiting Nurse Assn. of Scranton. Mem. Pa. State Edn. Assn. (pres. 1938-39; pres. Northeastern Dist. 1938-39; ex-pres. Graded and Supervising Prins. Depts.), Bloomsburg Alumni Assn., Phi Delta Kappa, Phi Gamma Mu, Kappa Phi Kappa. Methodist. Mason. Club: Rotary (ex-pres.). Wrote several articles on ednl. subjects. Home: 1707 Pine St. Office: Court House, Scranton, Pa.

FRANCIS, Vida Hunt, illustrator, educator; b. Philadelphia, Pa.; d. Harry C. and Annie I. (Hunt) F.; B.Litt., Smith Coll., Mass., 1892; unmarried. Gen. sec. Assn. Collegiate Alumnæ. Chmn. bd. "Hillside," a prep. sch. for girls, Norwalk, Conn.; treas., Am. Sch. for Girls, Damascus, Syria; v.p. Woman's Med. Coll. of Pa.; trustee Pa. League of Women Voters; pres. Permanent Emergency Aid of Germantown. Mem. Am. Acad. Polit. and Social Science, Smith Coll. Alumnæ Assn. Mem bd. Business Women's Christian League, English-Speaking Union, Philadelphia Elections Assn., Foreign Policy Assn. Clubs: Smith College (Phila. and N.Y. City); Woman's University (Phila.); Appalachian Mountain, Touring de France. Illustrator: Bible of Amiens, 1904; Cathedrals and Cloisters of the South of France, 2 vols., 1906; Cathedrals and Cloisters of Midland France, 2 vols., 1908; Cathedrals and Cloisters of Isle de France, 2 vols., 1910; Cathedrals and Cloisters of Northern France, 2 vols., 1914. Home: 1531 Greene St., Philadelphia, Pa.

FRANCK, Harry Alverson, author; b. Munger, Mich., June 29, 1881; s. Charles Adolph and Lillie E. (Wilsey) F.; A.B., U. of Mich., 1903; post-grad. studies, Harvard, Columbia and abroad; m. Rachel Whitehill Latta, June 28, 1919; 5 children. Teacher of French, Central High School, Detroit, 1903-04; traveled around the world, 1904-05; master modern languages, Bellefonte, Pa., 1906, Browning School, New York, 1906-08; head of modern language department, Technical High School, Springfield, Mass., 1908-11; traveling in Central and South America, 1911-15, West Indies, 1919-20, Far East, 1922-24, Near East, 1927, Europe, 1929-31, 1933-34, U.S.S.R., 1934, Mexico, 1936, Hawaii, 1936-37; air tour of Caribbean, 1937; tour in Alaska, 1938. Commd. lt. N.A., and with A.E.F. in France, 1917-19. Author: A Vagabond Journey Around the World, 1910; Four Months Afoot in Spain, 1911; Zone Policeman 88, 1913; Tramping Through Mexico, Guatemala and Honduras, 1916; Vagabonding Down the Andes, 1917; Vagabonding Through Changing Germany, 1919; Roaming Through the West Indies, 1920; Working North from Patagonia, 1921; Wandering in Northern China, 1923; Glimpses of Japan and Formosa, 1924; Roving Through Southern China, 1925; East of Siam, 1926; The Fringe of the Moslem World, 1928; I Discover Greece, 1929; A Scandinavian Summer, 1930; Marco Polo, Junior, 1930; Footloose in the British Isles, 1932; A Vagabond in Sovietland, 1935; Trailing Cortez through Mexico, 1935; Roaming in Hawaii, 1937; Sky Roaming Above Two Continents, 1938; Series Geographical School Readers; Travels in Many Lands. Address: New Hope, Pa.

FRANK, Eli, judge; b. Baltimore, Md., Feb. 8, 1874; s. Moses and Isabella (Cohen) F.; A.B., Johns Hopkins, 1894; LL.B., U. of Md., 1896; m. Rena Ambach, Dec. 8, 1897; children—Margaret R. (Mrs. Bertram M. Friedman), Eli, Isabel (Mrs. Sydney M. Cone, Jr.). Admitted to Maryland bar, 1896, and began practice at Baltimore; professor law, University of Md., since 1904; judge, Supreme Bench, Baltimore, since 1922. Chmn. commn. to revise laws affecting crimes and punishment, Md. Former pres. Associated Jewish Charities of Baltimore, Hebrew Hosp. of Baltimore City; former vice-pres. Enoch Pratt Free Library; former mem. Board of School Commrs., Baltimore; member executive com. Am. Jewish Com.; non-zionist mem. Jewish Agency for Palestine. Trustee Johns Hopkins U. Mem. Am. Bar Assn., Am. Law Inst., Md. State Bar Assn., Bar Assn. Baltimore City (former pres.), Phi Beta Kappa. Democrat. Jewish religion. Clubs: Suburban, University, Chesapeake. Author: Title to Real and Leasehold Estates, 1912. Home: 2007 Sulgrave Av. Address: Court House, Baltimore, Md.

FRANK, Eli, Jr., lawyer; b. Baltimore, Md., Aug. 29, 1902; s. Eli and Rena (Ambach) F.; student Park Sch., 1912-18; A.B., Johns Hopkins U., 1922; LL.B., Harvard U., 1925; m. Amy Heilbronner, May 7, 1928; children—Marcia, Victoria. Admitted to bar, 1925; associated with law firm Emory, Beewkes, Skeen & Oppenheimer, 1925-34; chief counsel of customs, U.S., Washington, D.C., 1934-36; asst. gen. counsel, Treasury Dept., Washington, 1936; mem. law firm Lauchheimer & Lauchheimer since 1936. Trustee Park Sch. Mem. Am. Bar Assn., Md. State Bar Assn., Baltimore City Bar Assn. Democrat. Jewish religion. Clubs: University, Phoenix, Suburban, Chesapeake (Baltimore). Home: 2407 Rogers Av. Office: 111 N. Charles St., Baltimore, Md.

FRANK, Fritz John, publisher; b. Emporium, Pa., Sept. 9, 1871; s. Joseph Warren and Eliza (Campbell) F.; A.B., Rollins Coll., Winter Park, Fla., 1896; m. Anna Raynor Bush, Mar. 11, 1909. Advertising mgr. Mines and Minerals (mag.), 1898-1907; pres. Savage Safety Brake Co., 1907-09; pres. Iron Age Pub. Co.; exec. v.p. Chilton Co.; dir. Robbins Pub. Co.; dir. Savage Arms Co., U.P.C. Realty Co. Trustee Rollins Coll. Clubs: Engineers, Machinery (governor). Home: Madison, N.J. Office: 239 W. 39th St., New York, N.Y.

FRANK, Grace (Mrs. Tenney F.), prof. Romance philology; b. New Haven, Conn., June 28, 1886; d. Murray Charles and Frances Mayer; A.B., U. of Chicago, 1907; ed. Bryn Mawr Coll., and univs. Göttingen and Berlin, 1908-11; m. Prof. Tenney Frank, 1907. Lecturer in Romance philology, Bryn Mawr Coll., 1926-27, asso. prof., 1927-33, prof. since 1933; visiting prof. Romance philology, Johns Hopkins U., 1934-36. Mem. Mediaeval Acad., Modern Lang. Assn., Phi Beta Kappa. Author: La Passion du Palatinus, 1922; Le Miracle de Theophile, 1925; Le Livre de la Passion, 1930; La Passion d'Autun, 1934; Proverbes en Rimes, 1937. Translator, Sudermann's Roses, 1909. Adv. editor, Modern Language Notes; mem. editorial com. Modern Lang. Assn. Contbr. articles. Home: 110 Elmhurst Rd., Baltimore, Md. Office: Bryn Mawr College, Bryn Mawr, Pa.

FRANK, Morris, physician; b. Minsk, Russia, Oct. 30, 1886; s. Hyman and Sarah (Levitas) F.; brought to U.S., 1890, naturalized, 1914; M.D., Cornell U. Med Coll., 1909; unmarried. Interne Bayonne Hosp., 1909-10; engaged in gen. practice of medicine at Bayonne, N.J., since 1910, specializing in orthopedics since 1915; attdg. phys., Bayonne Hosp. since 1917; instr. orthopedic surgery, Post Grad. Hosp., N.Y. City, 1918-29, attdg. orthopedist, Bayonne Hosp. since 1927, Margaret Hague Maternity Hosp. since 1931. Served as 1st lt. Med. Corps, U.S.A., during World War. Orthopedic specialist for city of Bayonne. Mem. Am. Med. Assn., N.J. State Med. Soc., Hudson Co. Med. Soc., Bayonne Med. Soc. Jewish religion. Mason (32°). Home: 920 Av. C., Bayonne, N.J.

FRANK, William Klee, corpn. official; b. Pittsburgh, Pa., Apr. 27, 1890; s. Isaac William and Tinnie (Klee) F.; student Pittsburgh pub. schs., 1890-1903, Shady Side Acad., 1903-07; M.E., Cornell U., 1911; m. Florence Kingsbacher, Dec. 14, 1914; children—Thomas William, James Allen, Margaret. Began as chemist, July 1911; with Damascus Bronze Co., 1911-27; with Copperweld Steel Co. since 1927, now chmn. bd. and vice-pres.; pres. and dir. Amalgamated Realty Co.; dir. United Engineering and Foundry Co., Apollo Steel Co. Mem. Engrs. Soc. of Western Pa., Tau Kappa Epsilon. Republican. Jewish religion. Mason. Clubs: Concordia (Pittsburgh); Westmoreland Country (Verona, Pa.); Cornell (New York). Home: 5535 Aylesboro Av. Office: Farmers Bank Bldg., Pittsburgh, Pa.

FRANKEL, Emil, statistician; b. Vienna, Austria, Aug. 20, 1886; s. Joseph and Rosalia (Gassner) F.; came to U.S., 1905; grad. New York Sch. of Social Work; m. Elsbeth Winkel, Sept. 2, 1924; 1 dau., Harriet Leona. Spl. agt. N.Y. State Factory Investigating Commn., 1912-14; resident Univ. Settlement, N.Y. City, 1912-14; statis. expert Bur. Labor Statistics, U.S. Dept. Labor, 1915-20; advisor to President's Industrial Commn., 1919; student of European labor conditions, 1921-23; statistician Pa. State Welfare Dept., 1924-27; dir. of statistics and research, N.J. State Dept. Instns. and Agencies since Aug. 1927. Mem. Am. Assn. Social Workers, Am. Statis. Assn., Am. Prison Assn., Nat. Conf. of Social Work, Federal Social Security Bd., Am. Pub. Welfare Assn., N.J. Welfare Council, N.J. Hosp. Assn., N.J. Tuberculosis League, N.J. Health and San. Assn. Mem. the President's Conference on Child Health and Protection, 1930, N.J. Health and Welfare Conf.; statistical consultant of Interstate Commn. on Crime. Author: Labor Turnover in Industry (with P. F. Brissenden), 1923; Poor Relief in Pennsylvania, 1925; (also monographs) County and State Welfare Work in New Jersey; The Care and Treatment of Nervous and Mental Patients in General Hospitals (with T. B. Kidner), Institutional Education and Training for Community Release. Contbr. Jour. of Polit. Economy, Social Service Review, etc. Address: Dept. Institutions and Agencies, Trenton, N.J.

FRANKENFIELD, Clyde Simon, supervising prin. of schools; b. Passer, Bucks Co., Pa., Dec. 2, 1887; s. William B. and Mary Jane (Hammel) F.; student Springfield Twp. High Sch., Bucks Co., Pa., 1903-05, Keystone Normal Sch., Kutztown, Pa., 1906-08; Ph.B., Muhlenberg Coll., Allentown, Pa., 1912-17; A.M., Columbia, 1921; m. Marie Bogh Faulkner, June 29, 1922; children—Elizabeth Marie, Bruce Austin. Teacher in rural school, Bucks Co., Pa., 1905-06; teacher in Northampton (Pa.) High Sch., 1908-15; prin., 1915-22; supt. of schools, Northampton, 1922-30; supervising prin. of schools, Catasauqua, Pa., since 1930. Served in O.T.C., Camp Lee, Va., Apr.-Dec., 1918. Mem. N.E.A., Pa. State Edn. Assn., Kappa Phi Kappa. Republican. Presbyterian. Mason. Clubs: Rotary of Catasauqua. Home: 309 E. 19th St., Northampton, Pa. Office: High School, Catasauqua, Pa.

FRANKLIN, Curtis, investment banker; b. Washington, Conn., Oct. 20, 1891; s. William Suddards and Hattie (Titus) F.; student The Gunnery Sch., Washington, Conn., 1905-07, Bethlehem (Pa.) Prep. Sch., 1907-08, Lehigh U., Bethlehem, Pa., 1908-10, Harvard, 1920; Ph.B., Yale, 1913; m. Evelyn Horst, of Columbus, O., 1921 (died 1923); m. 2d, Roberta Saunders, May 24, 1937; children—Betsey Fenn, Curtis. Began as messenger Pa. R.R. Co., 1913, asst. foreign freight agent, 1913-14; asst. sec. The N.Y. Trust Co., 1921-25; treas. and dir. British Type Investors, Inc., Jersey City, N.J., since 1925, Allied Internat. Investing Corpn., Jersey City, N.J., since 1937, Automatic Products Corpn., Jersey City, N.J., since 1938; dir. The Permutit Co., Majestic Radio & Television Co., The Spun Steel Corpn. Served as capt., 28th London Regt., Gordon Highlanders, Brit. Army, during World War; mem. Am. Relief Adminstrn., 1919-20. Mem. Mountain Lakes (N.J.) Borough Council, 1933-36. Mem. Camp Com. Y.M.C.A. of N.Y. Mem. Phi Delta Theta, Phi Beta Kappa. Republican. Episcopalian. Clubs: Yale, Bankers (New York); Graduates (New Haven, Conn.). Home: 131 Kenilworth Rd., Mountain Lakes, N.J. Office: 15 Exchange Pl., Jersey City, N.J.

FRANKLIN, James Henry, clergyman, educator; b. Pamplin, Va., May 13, 1872; s. Samuel R. and Mary J. (Burruss) F.; Richmond Coll., Va.: Th.M., Southern Bapt. Theol. Sem., 1898; D.D., University of Denver, 1909, Brown Univ., 1922; LL.D., University of Richmond, 1925; m. Augusta Terry, Nov. 15, 1900. Ordained Bapt. ministry, 1896; pastor Leadville, Colo., 1898-1901, Cripple Creek, 1901-04; dist. sec. Am. Bapt. Home Mission Soc., 1904-06; pastor 1st Ch., Colorado Springs, Colo., 1906-12; fgn. sec., Am. Bapt. Foreign Mission Soc., 1912-34; president of Crozer Theol. Seminary, Chester, Pa., since 1934. Pres. Northern Bapt. Conv., 1935-36. Mem. Internat. Missionary Council, 1921-34; mem. Com. of Direction, Dept. of Internat. Justice and Good Will, Federal Council of Chs. of Christ in America. Decorated Legion of Honor (France). Mem. Phi Beta Kappa, Kappa Alpha. Author: In the Track of the Storm; The Never Failing Light. Address: Crozer Theological Seminary, Chester, Pa.

FRANKLIN, Neil Starr, elec. engr., pub. utility exec.; b. Guilford, Vt., Mar. 23, 1885; s. James Henry and Emma Mary (Franklin) F.; second cousin to Calvin Coolidge; B.S. in E.E., U. of N.H., 1906; m. Ruth Pauline Morse (desc. S. F. B. Morse), Apr. 21, 1914; children—Paul Morse, Kenneth Starr. Began as testing engr., Westinghouse Electric & Mfg. Co., East Pittsburgh, Pa., 1906-08, sales engr., Phila., 1908-13; dist. mgr., Pa. Power & Light Co., Allentown, Pa., 1913-19, Conn. Light & Power Co., New Britain, Conn., 1919-21; gen. power sales engr., Henry L. Doherty Co., 1921-26; asst. to operating vice-pres. Utilities Power & Light Corpn., N.Y. and Chicago, 1927-31; chmn. Economy Com., LaClede Gas Light Co., St. Louis, Mo., 1932; pvt. cons. engr., Asbury Park, N.J. since 1932; exec. engr., mem. exec. bd., N.J. Waterways; mem. Atlantic Deeper Waterways Assn. Served mil. training 4 yrs. sr. capt. batln. U. of N.H. Mem. Kappa Sigma. Republican. Baptist. Mason. Active as state leader in N.J. Ship Canal. Conceived and promoted the Nat. Broadcasting Co., July 1926. Home: Belmar. Office: Asbury Park, N.J.

FRANKLIN, Walter Simonds, ry. official; b. Ashland, Md., May 24, 1884; s. Walter Simonds and Mary Campbell (Small) F.; A.B., Harvard, 1906; m. Cassandra Morris Small, Dec. 6, 1919; children—William Buel II, Cassandra Small. Began with Pa. R.R., 1906, advanced through various positions to asst. gen. freight agent; became v.p. Am. Trading Co., New York, 1919, later pres.; reëntered service of Pa. R.R., 1928, apptd. gen. agt. at Detroit, 1928, gen. supt. Northwestern div., 1929, asst. to v.p. in charge operation, 1931; pres. Detroit, Toledo & Ironton R.R. Co., 1929-31; became pres. Wabash Ry. Co., 1931, receiver, 1931-33; receiver Ann Arbor R.R. Co., 1931-33; v.p. Pa. R.R. Co. since Oct. 1933; dir. Pa. R.R. Co., Norfolk & Western Ry. Co., Bell Telephone Co. of Pa., Ry. Express Agency, Inc., Pa. Greyhound Lines; trustee Western Savings Fund Soc.; mem. bd. mgrs. Girard Trust Co., Phila. Capt., later maj. and lt. col., Transportation Corps, U.S.A., during World War. Awarded D.S.M. (U.S.); Chevalier Legion of Honor (France); Distinguished Service Order (Gt. Britain). Presbyn. Clubs: University, Harvard, Recess (New York); Gulph Mills Golf, Racquet, Merion Cricket, Philadelphia, Harvard, Mill Dam (Phila.). Home: Ardmore, Pa. Office: Broad St. Station Bldg., Philadelphia, Pa.

FRANTZ, Jacob Paul, physician; b. Lancaster, Pa., July 18, 1885; s. Andrew Frick and Susan Herr (Bausman) F.; grad. Franklin and Marshall Acad., 1902; Ph.B., Franklin and Marshall Coll., Lancaster, Pa., 1906; M.D., U. of Pa., 1910; m. Mary Hay Graff, 1912; children—Jacob Paul, John Graff, Mary Louise, Martha Graff, Susan Bausman. Interne St. Christophers, Lying-in Charity, St. Joseph hospitals, Phila., 1910-12; gen. practice of medicine, Phila., 1912-17; specialized in internal medicine and tuberculosis, Clearfield, Pa., since 1917; clinic chief State Dept. of Health, tuberculosis div., 1913-39; staff Clearfield Hosp., 1918-39. Served on Selective Service Bd., Clearfield, Pa., 1918; 1st lt. Md. Corps, U.S. Army, 1918. Pres. Clearfield Bd. of Health, 1928-38; mem. Borough Council since 1938. Dir Clearfield Y.M.C.A.; pres. and dir. Clearfield Co. Tuberculosis Soc. Fellow Am. Coll. Chest Physicians (gov. for Pa.); mem. A.M.A., Pa. State Med. Soc. (mem. tuberculosis com.), Clearfield Co. Med. Soc., Am. Acad. Tuberculosis Physicians, Pa. R.R. Surgeons Assn., Am. Health Assn., Phi Kappa Psi. Republican. Lutheran. Mason (32°), Elk. Contbr. many articles on tuberculosis to med. jours. Home: 213 N. 2d St., Clearfield, Pa.

FRANTZ, Oswin Stricker, clergyman, educator; b. Trumbauersville, Pa., Dec. 14, 1880; s. Alfred Singmaster and Sarah Jane (Stricker) F.; grad. Perkiomen Sem. Pennsburg, Pa., 1902; A.B., Franklin and Marshall Coll., 1905, D.D., 1925; grad. Theol. Sem. Ref. Ch. in U.S., Lancaster, Pa., 1908; B.D., Union Theol. Sem., New York, 1922; m. Alice Brubaker, Oct. 7, 1908; children—Harold Melvin, Clair Gordon, Miriam Elizabeth, Robert Oswin. Ordained ministry Ref. Ch. in U.S., 1908; pastor Memorial Ch., Easton, Pa., 1908-12, Christ Ch., Altoona, Pa., 1912-21; prof. N.T. science, Theol. Sem. Ref. Ch., Lancaster, since 1922. Mem. Bd. Visitors, Theol. Sem. Ref. Ch. Mem. Phi Beta Kappa, Sigma Pi, Cliosophic Soc., Lancaster. Democrat. Mason. Rotarian. Home: 527 W. James St., Lancaster, Pa.

FRANTZ, Samuel Gibson, engineer; b. Duluth, Minn., Mar. 15, 1897; s. Alfred J. and Mary Katherine (Gibson) F.; student Edinburgh (Scotland) Acad., 1907-09, Lawrenceville (N.J.) Sch., 1910-14; C. E., Princeton U., 1919, M.S. 1923; student Ecole Superieure d'Elecricité, Paris, France, 1923-24; m. Sarah Wistar Morton, Apr. 18, 1921; children—Katherine Macdonald, Margaret Wistar, Sarah Wistar Morton. Engr. Crossett (Ark.) Lumber Co., 1921-22; chief engr. Ashley Drew & Northern Ry. Co., Crossett, Ark., 1921-22; asst. engr. E. L. Phillips Co., New York, 1923; head pvt. contracting business, Princeton, N.J., 1925-27; cons. engr., New York, since 1927; formed S. G. Frantz Co., engrs., designers and builders magnetic separation equipment, New York, 1936, and since in practice. Served with Am. Ambulance Service with French Army, Mar.-Nov. 1917, as 2d lt. aeronautics, U.S. Air Service, 1917-19. Mem. N.Y. and N.J. Smoke Abatement Bd.; justice of peace, Princeton (N.J.) Borough since 1939. Mem. Am. Ceramic Soc., Phi Beta Kappa, Sigma Xi. Democrat. Presbyterian. Mason. Home: 28 Hibben Rd., Princeton, N.J. Office: 161 Grand St., New York, N.Y.

FRANZHEIM, Edward Bates, architect; b. Wheeling, W.Va., July 20, 1866; s. George William and Mary Ann (Hornung) F.; ed. Linsly Inst., Wheeling, Chauncey Hall, Boston, also private tutors and European travel; m. Mai Burnedetta Whitty, Nov. 1, 1905. Studied architecture with John Sturgis, Boston; now architect at Wheeling, W.Va. Mem. Am. Inst. of Architects; mem. W.Va. State Bd. of Architects. Episcopalian. Mason (K.T., 32°, Shriner), Elk. Clubs: Fort Henry, Elks, Jesters (Wheeling); Lambs (New York). Home: Howard Place. Office: Chapline St., Wheeling, W.Va.

FRARY, Francis Cowles, chemist; b. Minneapolis, Minn., July 9, 1884; s. Francis Lee and Jeanette (Cowles) F.; A.C., U. of Minn., 1905; M.S., 1906, Ph.D., 1912; studied U. of Berlin 1 yr.; m. Alice Hall Wingate, June 12, 1908; children—Faith Margaret, John Loveland. Instr. in chemistry, U. of Minn., 1905-11, asst. prof., 1911-15; research chemist, Oldbury Electrochem. Co., Niagara Falls, N.Y., 1915-18; capt. Ordnance O.R.C. and maj., Chem. Warfare Service U.S.A., 1918 (Edgewood Arsenal); dir. of research, Aluminum Co. of America, New Kensington, Pa., since Dec. 15, 1918. Mem. Am. Chem. Soc., The Electrochem. Soc. (past pres.), Am. Inst. Mining and Metall. Engrs., Am. Inst. Chem. Engrs., Inst. of Metals, Alpha Chi Sigma. Republican. Presbyterian. Author: Laboratory Manual of Glassblowing, 1914; (with J. D. Edwards and Zay Jeffries) The Aluminum Industry (2 vols.). Home: 1218 Hulton Rd., Oakmont, Pa.

FRASER, Albert Gray, social worker; b. Pictou Co., Nova Scotia, Can., Dec. 1, 1877; s. Alexander and Christena F.; ed. Pictou Acad., 1895-97, 1898-99, New York Sch. of Social Work, 1915-16; m. Martha C. McInnes, Feb. 25, 1913; 1 son, Donald Gray. Came to U.S., 1900, naturalized, 1908. School teacher, Nova Scotia, 1897-1900; industrial insurance agt., 1900-08; worker children's instns., 1908-15; extension service New Eng. Home for Little Wanderers, Boston, Mass., 1916-19; supt. N. E. Kurnhattin Homes, Westminster, Vt., 1919-21; agt. New Eng. Home for Little Wanderers, Bridgeport, Conn., 1922; exec. sec. Travelers Aid Soc., Phila., 1922-25; supt. dept. of released prisoners, Pa. Prison Soc., Phila., 1925-31; exec. sec. Pa. Prison Soc. since 1931. Commr. Upper Darby Twp., 1926-27; pres. Bd. of Health, Upper Darby, Pa., 1927-30; pres. Upper Darby Free Pub. Library, 1928-33; dir. Upper Darby Sch. Dist. since 1933, vice-pres. since 1937; mem. Phila. Com. on Public Affairs. Mem. Am. Assn. Social Workers. Democrat. Presbyterian. Editor of Prison Jour. (publ. Pa. Prison Soc.). Home: 170 Overhill Rd., Upper Darby, Pa. Office: 311 S. Juniper St., Philadelphia, Pa.

FRASER, Donald McCoy, associate prof. of geology; b. Pueblo, Colo., June 1, 1903; s. Edwin Mungo and Maud (McCoy) F.; student Ore. State Coll., 1920-21, Stanford U., 1921-22; A.B., U. of Ore., 1925, A.M., 1926; Ph.D., Columbia, 1932; m. Marjorie Emma Rowell, Aug. 16, 1923; 1 dau., Phyllis Jean. Teaching fellow, U. of Ore., 1925-26; instr., Occidental Coll., 1926-28; fellow, Columbia U., 1928-29; asst. prof., Dana Coll., Newark, N.J., 1929-31; teacher, Hunter Coll., New York, summer 1929; co-operating geologist, Calif. State Mining Bureau, summer 1930; geologist Reploge Iron Mines, N.J., 1929-30; with Lehigh U. since 1930, as instr., 1930-33, asst. prof., 1933-38, assoc. prof. since 1939; co-operating geologist, Topographic and Geologic Survey, Pa., since 1936. Fellow A.A.A.S., Am. Mineral. Soc.; mem. Soc. Econ. Geologists, Am. Geophysical Union, Pa. Acad. Science, Sigma Xi, Theta Xi. Contbr. of articles on petrology and economic geol. to professional jours. Home: 220 W. Langhorne Av., Bethlehem, Pa.

FRASER, Herbert Freeman, coll. prof.; b. Mansfield, O., Mar. 3, 1890; s. Alexander and Maria (Milne) F.; grad. Phillips Acad., Andover, Mass., 1908; M.A., U. of Aberdeen, Scotland, 1915; m. Mabel Heald Ward, Aug. 31, 1918; children—Sarah Jean, Herbert Ward. Agent Fraser Granite Co., Aberdeen, Scotland, 1912-15, mgr. same, Mansfield, O., 1915-18; instr. Phillips Acad., 1919-26; asso. prof. economics, Swarthmore Coll., 1926-29, prof. since 1929. Served in Gas Defense Service, U.S. Army, 1918-19. Spl. advisor Consumers Advisory Bd., N.R.A., Washington, D.C., summer, 1933; head economic analyst U.S. Dept. of State, Washington, 1934-35. Mem. com. of management, George Sch., since 1931. Fellow Royal Economic Soc.; mem. Am. Econ. Assn. Republican. Mem. Soc. of Friends. Clubs: Franklin Inn (Phila.); Rotary (Swarthmore). Author: Foreign Trade and World Politics, 1926; The Economic Foundations of Peace, 1931 (revised edit. 1935); Great Britain and the Gold Standard, 1933. Home: Sherwood Lane, Wallingford, Pa.

FRASER, James Wallace, clergyman; b. Las Vegas, N.M., Mar. 26, 1889; s. James and Ella (McFarlan) F.; A.B., New Windsor Coll. (later Blue Ridge Coll.), New Windsor, Md., June 7, 1909, hon. D.D., 1921; student Princeton (N.J.) Theol. Sem., 1910-12; S.T.D., Western Theol. Sem., Pittsburgh, 1914; m. Mary Dee Stuchul, Aug. 23, 1917; children—Betsy Jean, James Wallace III. Began as teacher of english and history, New Windsor Coll., 1912; licensed by Presbytery of Baltimore (Md.), 1912; ordained by Presbytery of Kittanning (Pa.), 1914; pastor, Plumville, Pa., 1914-19, Ellicott City, Md., 1919-20, Ebenezer, Pa., and Clarksburg, Pa., 1920-24, Girard, Pa., 1924-26, New Bethlehem, Pa., since 1926. Dean, New Bethlehem (Pa.) Sch. of Religion since 1929. Mem. Internat. Council of Religious Edn., Pa. Lord's Day Alliance (v.p.). Mission work in Grassy Lake, Alberta, 1910; rep. Seventh World Sabbath Sch. Convention, Zurich, Switzerland, 1913; one of 29 representing the Presbyn. Ch. in United Christian Adult Movement (Lake Geneva); commr. to 148th Gen. Assembly of Presbyn. Ch. of U.S.A., Syracuse, N.Y., 1936; editor of Centennial History of Clarion Prebytery. Presbyterian. Mason. Odd Fellow. Address: New Bethlehem, Pa.

FRASER, John Falconer, clergyman; b. Edinburgh, Scotland, Sept. 27, 1875; s. John and Margaret (Falconer) F.; Brandon (Can.) Coll., 1899-1902; Southern Bapt. Theol. Sem., 1905-08; U. of Chicago, 1909-10; D.D., Franklin (Ind.) Coll., 1917; m. Mina Rowe, Sept. 12, 1906; 1 son, Donald. Ordained ministry Bapt. Ch., 1905; pastor Muncie, Ind., 1913-20, Louisville, Ky., 1920-26, Central Bapt. Ch., N.Y. City, 1926-33, University Bapt. Church, Baltimore, Oct., 1933—. Pres. Ind. Bapt. Conv., 1917-20; pres. Southern N.Y. Bapt. Assn., 1927-28; pres. N.Y. Ministers Conf.; chmn. evangelism com. N.Y. City Bapt. Mission Soc. Trustee Bibl. Sem. in New York. Clubs: Quill, Clergy. Contbr. to Watchman Examiner, The Baptist. Lecturer on sociol. and patriotic topics. Author of "Visions and Allusions in the Apocalypse." Home: 3607 Kimble Rd., Ednor Gardens, Baltimore, Md.

FRASURE, Carl Maynard, univ. prof.; b. Oakland, O., Jan. 15, 1903; s. Nelson W. and Minnie (Valentine) F.; A.B., O. State Univ., Columbus, O., 1924, A.M., 1925, Ph.D., 1928; student asst. George Washington Univ., Washington, D.C., 1925-26, U. of Chicago, summers 1925-26; grad. student Cambridge U., Eng., 1929-30; m. Louise Durham, Dec. 26, 1930; 1 son, C. Maynard. Teaching asst., George Washington U., 1925-26; instr. polit. sci. and history, W.Va. Univ., Morgantown, W.Va., 1927-29, asst. prof. polit. sci., 1930-35, asso. prof. since 1935, actg. head dept. polit. sci. since 1935, asst. dean, Coll. Arts and Sciences since 1935. Mem. Am. Polit. Sci. Assn., Am. Assn. Univ. Profs., Kappa Delta Rho. Democrat. Club: Kiwanis of Morgantown. Contbr. articles on internat. relations. Home: 505 Beverly Av., Morgantown, W.Va.

FRAZER, John, chemist; b. of Am. parents, Paris, France, Feb. 5, 1882; s. Persifor and Isabella Nevins (Whelen) Frazer; B.S. in chemistry, University of Pa., 1903, A.M., from same univ., 1904, Ph.D., 1907; m. Mary Foxley, d. Oswald Tilgham, June 9, 1915. Instr. chemistry, 1904-06 and 1907-08, asst. prof., 1908-18 and 1919-21, prof., 1921-33, dean of Towne Scientific Sch., 1912-18 and 1919-28, sec. bd. of deans, 1921-22, chmn. faculty policy com., 1920-21, Univ. of Pa.; Am. exchange prof. of applied science to French universities, 1922-23; rep. of U. of Pa. on College Entrance Exam. Bd., 1912-21; sec. com. on science and the arts, Franklin Inst., Phila., since 1936. Active mem. 1st Troop, Phila. City Cav., 1903-16, hon. roll, 1921; commd. capt. Chem. Warfare Service, U.S.A., Aug. 9, 1918; trained in France and detailed as asst. gas officer, 1st A.C., and later with 78th and 6th divs. in Argonne, A.E.F., and at Hdqrs. C.W.S., at Tours, France; hon. discharged Jan. 10, 1919; lt. col. O.R.C., C.W.S., U.S.A., 1924-29. Fellow, life mem. A.A.A.S.; mem. Am. Chem. Society, Franklin Institute, Historical Society of Pa., Société de Chimie Industrielle (Paris), Soc. War of 1812, Loyal Legion, Delta Psi, Sigma Xi, Phi Beta Kappa. Republican. Clubs: University, Mask and Wig (Philadelphia); St. Anthony (New York). Home: 8015 Navajo St., Chestnut Hill. Office: Franklin Inst., Philadelphia, Pa.

FRAZER, John G., lawyer; b. Mansfield, Pa., July 19, 1880; s. Robert S. and Loretta (Gilfillan) F.; A.B., Princeton, 1901; LL.B., U. of Pittsburgh, 1904; m. Katharine Reed, Apr. 24, 1911; children—Katharine (Mrs. George D. Lockhart), John G. Admitted to Pennsylvania bar, 1904; member firm of Reed, Smith, Shaw and McClay; dir. Am. Fruit Growers Inc., Farmers Deposit Nat. Bank, Reliance Life Ins. Co., Pennsylvania Water Company, Bessemer & Lake Erie Railroad Company, Union R.R. Co., Consolidated Ice Co. Trustee Carnegie Inst.; Carnegie Inst. of Tech., U. of Pittsburgh, Shady Side Acad.; dir. Western Pa. Hosp.; mem. Carnegie Hero Fund Commn. Mem. Am. Pa. and Allegheny County bar assns. Republican. Presbyterian. Clubs: Princeton (New York City); Duquesne, University, Harvard-Yale-Princeton, Pittsburgh Golf, Fox Chapel Golf (Pittsburgh). Home: 720 Amberson Av. Office: Union Trust Bldg., Pittsburgh, Pa.

FRAZER, Joseph Christie Whitney, prof. chemistry; b. Lexington, Ky., Oct. 30, 1875; s. Joseph George and Mary Jane (Filson) F.; B.S., Ky. State U., 1897, M.S., 1898; Ph.D., Johns Hopkins, 1901; Sc.D., Kenyon Coll., 1926; m. Grace Carvill, Sept. 16, 1903; children—Joseph Hugh, Grace Carvill, Jean Cameron (dec.), Jeanne Henry. Asst. and asso. in chemistry, Johns Hopkins, 1901-07; chemist, U.S. Bur. of Mines, 1907-11; prof. chemistry since 1911, chmn. dept. of chemistry, 1916-36, B.N. Baker prof. since 1921, Johns Hopkins. Fgn. mem. Soc. of Arts and Sciences, Utrecht; mem. Kappa Alpha, Phi Beta Kappa, Tau Beta Pi (hon.). Democrat. Presbyn. Research work on osmotic pressure and vapor tension of solutions, catalysis and the chem. behavior of surfaces. Home: 5607 Roxbury Pl., Mt. Washington, Baltimore, Md.

FRAZER, Spaulding, lawyer; b. Brooklyn, N.Y., Oct. 7, 1881; s. David R. and Rose (Thompson) F.; student Newark (N.J.) Acad., 1891-97; B.S., Princeton, 1901, A.M., 1904; LL.B., N.Y. Law Sch., 1904; m. Olive Lord Hollister, Oct. 24, 1906; m. 2d, Anne Bunner Ingham, of New London, Conn., June 23, 1928. Admitted to N.Y. and N.J. bars, 1904; in pvt. practice, 1904-07; mem. firm Riker & Riker, Newark, N.J., 1907-18, Frazer & Trimble, 1926-31, Frazer, Stoffer & Jacobs since 1934; corpn. counsel City of Newark, 1915-17; has also served as counsel on numerous N.J. coms. and commns.; asso. counsel Port of N.Y. Authority (transit div.), 1928; dean Sch. of Law, U. of Newark, also trustee Univ. Mem. Am., N.J. Essex Co. bar assns., American Judicature Soc., Newark Music Festival Assn. (ex-pres.). Republican. Clubs: Essex, Downtown, Carteret. Home: Hardscrabble Rd., Bernardsville, N.J. Office: 744 Broad St., Newark, N.J.

FRAZIER, Chauncey Earl, pres. Frazier-Simplex, Inc.; b. Butler, Pa., Mar. 9, 1879; s. Thomas A. and Hallie (Bickett) F.; m. Mary E. Gibson; children—John Earl, Helen M. Chauncey T., Gladys E., Dorothy O. Chief engr. Gee Electric Co., 1903-09, Hazel Atlas Glass Co., Wheeling, W.Wa., 1909-19; now pres. Frazier-Simplex, Inc., engrs. to glass industry, Washington, Pa. Mem. Professional Engrs. Soc.; fellow Am. Ceramic Soc. Mason (32°; Shriner, Syria Temple; Royal Order of Jesters). Clubs: Washington (Pa.) Golf and Country. Home: 417

E. Beau St. Office: 436 E. Beau St., Washington, Pa.

FREAR, Frank A., county supt. of schools; b. Lake Winola, Pa., Mar. 28, 1878; s. Asa H. and Angeline (Stevens) F.; grad. Tunkhannock (Pa.) High Sch., 1899; Ph.B., Lafayette Coll., Easton, Pa., 1904, A.M., 1924; m. Elizabeth Smith, June 14, 1906; children—Edgar Paul, Betty J. Teacher rural sch., 1899-1900; teacher graded schs., Bloomsburg, Pa., 1906-10; supervising prin., Catawissa, Pa., 1910-18, Pine Grove, Pa., 1922, East Mauch Chunk, Pa., 1924, Montrose, Pa., 1924-34; co. supt. of schs., Susquehanna Co., Pa., since 1934. Pres. Susquehanna Co. Hist. Soc. and Free Library Assn. Mem. Pa. State Edn. Assn., N.E.A. Republican. Presbyterian. Mason. Club: Men's Community (Montrose, Pa.). Home: 35 S. Maine St., Montrose, Pa.

FREDERICK, Halsey Augustus, telephone engring.; b. Essex, N.Y., Oct. 27, 1887; s. Augustus and Sarah Elizabeth (Telford) F.; B.S., Princeton U., 1910, E.E., same, 1912; m. Celina Blanche Bouquet, Apr. 16, 1913; children—Elizabeth Maxime (Mrs. Peter B. Robinson), Halsey Augustus, Ulric Bouquet. Employed as telephone engr., Western Electric Co., Inc., 1912-24; transmission instruments dir. with Bell Telephone Labs., Inc., New York, N.Y., 1925-35, electro-mechanical dir. since 1935; working on problems of transmission instruments, recording and reproduction of sound, 1912-35, on development of electromech. apparatus since 1935. Served on council, Mountain Lakes, N.J., 1929-32, pres. council, 1930-32; mayor of Mountain Lakes since 1933. Fellow Am. Inst. Elec. Engrs. Mem. A.A.A.S., Am. Phys. Soc., Acous. Soc. America. Republican. Conglist. Home: 166 Laurel Hill Rd., Mountain Lakes, N.J. Office: 463 West St., New York, N.Y.

FREDMAN, Samuel, rabbi; b. Grodno, Russia, March 7, 1886; s. Robert and Cippy (Kohen) F.; brought to U.S., 1888, naturalized citizen; A.B., Johns Hopkins U., 1909; Rabbi, Jewish Theological Seminary, 1913; grad. study, Columbia, U. of Pa.; fellow Dropsie College, Phila.; m. Bessie Stashower, Nov. 29, 1923; children—Judith, David. Called to Congregation Beth El, Phila., rabbi there since 1913. Served as chaplain U.S. Army during World War. Dir. Rabbinic Assembly, United Synagogue, Associated Talmud Torahs; former pres. Phila. Branch Jewish Ministers; vice pres. Phila. Branch of Jewish Theol. Sem. Mem. Zionist Organization, Acad. of Jewish Research, Johns Hopkins Alumni, B'nai Brith, Conf. Jews and Christians, Judaic Union. Home: 6046 Washington Av. Office: 135 S. 58th St., Philadelphia, Pa.

FREED, Cecil Forest, surgeon; b. Parkersburg, W.Va., Nov. 30, 1893; s. William R. and Mary Margaret (Williams) F.; M.D., U. of Pa., 1920; M.S. in Surgery, U. of Minn., Minneapolis, Minn., 1925; studied Mayo Foundation; m. Florence Hannah Evans, Jan. 22, 1916; children—William Malcolm, Betty Frances, Mary Kathryn. Began practice of medicine, 1921; practiced surgery, Reading, Pa., since 1927; chief surgeon Reading Hosp. since 1929. Mem. Pa. State Med. Soc., A.M.A., Am. Coll. Surgeons. Ch. of Christ. Clubs: Rotary, Torch, Berkshire Country (Reading, Pa.). Home and Office: 336 N. Fifth St., Reading, Pa.

FREEDMAN, Abraham L., lawyer; b. Trenton, N.J., Nov. 19, 1904; s. Louis and Anna (Goldman) F.; LL.B., Temple U., Phila., 1926; m. Jane G. Sunstein, Jan. 23, 1939. Admitted to Pa. bar, 1926; prof. law of domestic relations, Temple U., Phila., since 1931; mem. law firm Wolf, Block, Schorr & Solis Cohen, Phila.; gen. counsel Phila. Housing Authority. Mem. Am. Bar Assn., Phila. Bar Assn., Lawyers Club, Law Acad. of Phila. (pres. 1928-30); hon. mem. Lambda Sigma Kappa, Tau Epsilon Rho. Author: Law of Marriage and Divorce in Pa. (2 vols.); various articles in law reviews. Home: 910 E. Haines St. Office: 1204 Packard Bldg., Philadelphia, Pa.

FREEHOF, Solomon B., rabbi; b. London, Eng., Aug. 8, 1892; s. Isaac and Golda (Blonstein) F.; brought to America in 1904; grad. Baltimore City Coll., 1909; A.B., U. of Cincinnati, 1914; rabbi, Hebrew Union Coll., Cincinnati, 1915, D.D., 1920; m. Lillian Simon, Oct. 29, 1934. Prof. in rabbinics and liturgy, Hebrew Union Coll., Cincinnati, 1915-23; rabbi, K.A.M. Temple, Chicago, 1924-34; rabbi, Rodef Shalom Temple, Pittsburgh since 1934. First lt. chaplain, U.S. Army in France, World War. Author: "Stormers of Heaven," 1931; "The Psalms" (a Commentary), 1938. Home: 120 Ruskin Av., Pittsburgh, Pa.

FREEMAN, Allen Weir, sanitarian; b. Lynchburg, Va., Jan. 7, 1881; s. Walker Burford and Bettie Allen (Hamner) F.; student Richmond (Va.) Coll., 1895-1900, B.S., 1899; M.D., Johns Hopkins, 1905; m. Julia Griffin Brown, June 30, 1906; children—Bettie Charter (Mrs. Cuthbert Rogerson), Margaret Brown (Mrs. L. A. Poole, Jr.). Interne Newark (N.J.) City Hosp., 1905-06; demonstrator in physiology, Med. Coll. of Va., 1906-07; med. insp. Richmond Health Dept., 1907-08; asst. commr. of health, Va., 1908-15; state dir. Rockefeller Hookworm Commission. for Va. 1910-14; epidemiologist U.S. P.H.S., 1915-17; state commr. of health, Ohio, 1917-21; with Johns Hopkins U. since 1921, as res. lecturer pub. health administration, School of Hygiene and Pub. Health, 1921-23, prof., 1923—, dean, 1934-37. Commd. maj. Med. Corps U.S.A., 1918; was epidemiologist to bd. for investigation of pneumonia in Army camps, Camp Funston, Kan., and Camp Pike, Ark.; now maj. Med. O.R.C. Spl. mem. Rockefeller Foundation, 1926; lecturer, U. of Rio de Janeiro, Brazil, 1926. Fellow Am. Pub. Health Assn.; Am. Acad. Pub. Health; Mem. American Med. Assn., Medical Soc. of Va., Phi Gamma Delta, Sigma Xi, Phi Beta Kappa, Delta Omega (nat. pres. 1932). Democrat. Episcopalian. Clubs: 14 West Hamilton Street, Johns Hopkins (Baltimore). Contbr. numerous articles pertaining to epidemiology and pub. health administration. Home: 3952 Cloverhill Road. Office: 615 N. Wolfe St., Baltimore, Md.

FREEMAN, Charles, prof. of chemistry; b. Espyville, Pa., Oct. 16, 1864; s. Joseph Hampton and Julia Anne (Wildrick) F.; A.B., Allegheny Coll., Meadville, Pa., 1891, Ph.D., 1896; student Johns Hopkins U., 1893-94; LL.D., Westminster Coll., New Wilmington, Pa., 1929; m. Mary Nevada Miller, July 12, 1911 (died 1937). Prof. chemistry, Westminster Coll., New Wilmington, Pa., since 1894. Fellow A.A.A.S.; mem. Am. Chem. Soc., Sigma Alpha Epsilon, Phi Beta Kappa. United Presbyterian. Mason (32°). Home: New Wilmington, Pa.

FREEMAN, Edgar W., trust officer; b. Detroit, Mich., July 12, 1891; Walter H. and Ada (Fox) Freeman; student Philipps Acad., Andover, Mass., 1907-08; A.B., Yale, 1912; LL.B., Harvard, 1915; m. Alice Winton Murray, Oct. 21, 1922; children—Katharine Murray, Ailsa Fox, Murray Fox, Priscilla Alden. Admitted to N.Y. bar, 1915; asso. with Cadwalader, Wickersham & Taft, New York, 1915-22; asst. counsel Federal Reserve Bd., Washington, D.C., 1922-25; trust officer Corn Exchange Nat. Bank & Trust Co., Phila., 1926-29, v.p. and trust officer since 1929; dir. Keystone Automobile Club, Roberts Filter Mfg. Co., Casanave Supply Co.; v.p. and dir. Rider-Wilkinson, Inc. Served as 1st lt. F.A., U.S. Army, with A.E.F., 1917-19. Dir. Merion Civic Assn.; dir. Merion Community Assn. Mem. Delta Kappa Epsilon. Republican. Presbyterian. Home: Merion, Pa. Office: 1510 Chestnut St., Philadelphia, Pa.

FREEMAN, Elmer Burkitt, physician; b. Mattoon, Ill., Feb. 5, 1875; s. Joseph Biglow and Mary Jane (Moore) F.; B.S., Austin Coll., Effingham, Ill., 1896; M.D., Baltimore Med. Coll., 1900; m. Rosa May Weeks, Aug. 29, 1903. Resident physician Md. Gen. Hosp., Baltimore, 1900-01, visiting physician, 1901-17, physician in chief since 1917; gastro-enterologist St. Agnes Hosp. since 1910; dispensary physician, gastrointestinal dept., Johns Hopkins Hosp. since 1912, asst. visiting physician since 1929; visiting physician Bon Secours Hosp., 1917-38, chief gastro-enterologist since 1938; visiting physician, Church Home and Infirmary since 1929; mem. asso. staff Union Memorial Hosp., 1936-38, mem. active staff since 1938; instr. of clinical medicine, Baltimore Med. Coll., 1901-04, asso. prof., 1904-10, prof. of therapeutics, 1910-14; asso. prof. clinical medicine, U. of Md., 1913-14, lecturer in medicine since 1935; asst. in clin. medicine, Johns Hopkins U., 1916-22, instr., 1922-29, asso. in clinical medicine since 1929. Served as mem. Med. Advisory Bd. No. 4, Md., during World War. Mem. bd. govs. Md. Tuberculosis Assn., Inc. Fellow Am. Coll. Physicians, Nat. Soc. for Advancement of Gastroenterology, Premier Congress Internat. de Gastroenterlogie; mem. Am. Gastro-enterol. Assn., A.M.A., Med. and Chirurg. Faculty of Md., Baltimore City Med. Soc., Southern Med. Assn. (sec. Sect. on Gastro-enterology 1930-31, chmn. 1932), Md. Hist. Soc., Sons Am. Revolution, Phi Chi; hon. mem. Minn. State Med. Soc. Episcopalian. Mason. Clubs: University (Baltimore); Gibson Island; Maryland Jockey. Address: 807 Cathedral St., Baltimore, Md.

FREEMAN, Forster Weeks, lawyer; b. Jersey City, N. J., Sept. 27, 1870; s. George Titus and Ann Marie (Potter) F.; ed. N.Y. Law Sch., 1893-94; grad. study various courses; m. Minnie Louise Long, June 8, 1898; children—Forster Weeks, Jr., George Steven. Employed as rancher, farmer, and clk. in Neb., 1882-89; clk. in grocery, truck driver, and studied law, Paterson, N.J., 1889-94; admitted to N.J. bar as atty., 1894, as counsellor, 1897; engaged in gen. practice of law at Paterson since 1894; master in chancery, 1897; judge Second Dist. Ct., Paterson, 1929-31; judge First Judicial Criminal Dist. Ct., 1931-36; now mem. State Water Policy Commn. of N.J. Vice pres. and dir. Swedenborg Foundation N.Y. City; pres. bd. of home and fgn. missions of Gen. Conv. of Ch. of New Jerusalem in U.S.A. Republican. Mem. New Ch. (Swedenborgian). Rotarian. Home: 26 Hamilton St. Office: 26 Hamilton St., Paterson, N.J.

FREEMAN, Forster Weeks, Jr., lawyer; b. Paterson, N.J., July 14, 1899; s. Forster W. and Minnie L. (Lang) F.; student N.Y. Univ., 1918; LL.B., N.Y. Univ. Law Sch., 1921; m. Esther Blackwood, Oct. 28, 1922; children—E. Gwendolyn, Forster W. 3d. Admitted to N.J. bar as atty, 1921, as counselor, 1926; engaged in gen. practice of law at Paterson. Mem. N.J. State Bar Assn. (trustee), Passaic Co. Bar Assn. (pres. 1937). Home: 430 E. 28th St. Office: 26 Hamilton St., Paterson, N.J.

FREEMAN, Jonathan W., corpn. official; b. Troy, N.Y., Nov. 8, 1883; s. George H. and Elizabeth (Ferris) F.; grad. Lawrenceville (N.J.) Sch., 1901; Ph.B., Yale, 1904; m. S. Adele Shaw, Nov. 27, 1924; 1 son, Jonathan W. Vice pres. and dir. Pittsburgh Tube Co., mfrs. standard butt welded pipe and cold drawn tubing. Served as capt. engrs., U.S. Army with A.E.F., 8 months, 1917-18. Home: 5023 Castleman St. Office: Vandergrift Bldg., Pittsburgh, Pa.

FREEMAN, Norman Easton, surgeon; b. Cape May, N.J., July 22, 1903; s. Walter J. and Corinne (Keen) F.; grad. St. Paul's Sch., Concord, N.H., 1920; A.B., Yale, 1924, M.D., 1928; m. Charlotte Elizabeth Hume, June 7, 1930; children—David Norman, Nancy Scott, Corinne Keen. Interne U. of Pa. Hosp., Phila., 1928-30; med. fellow Nat. Research Council, dept. of physiology, Harvard Med. Sch., 1930-32; asst. resident surgeon Mass. Gen. Hosp., 1932-34, resident surgeon 1935, Dalton research fellow in surgery since 1936; J. William White asst. prof. of surgical research, U. of Pa. Med. Sch. since 1936. Fellow Am. Coll. Surgeons, Phila. Acad. surgery, Phila. Coll. of Physicians, A.M.A., Am. Soc. for Clin. Investigation, Am. Physiol. Soc.; mem. Pa. Soc. for Protection of Scientific Research (sec. of exec. com.), Am. Heart Assn. (sec.-treas. sect. for study of peripheral circulation), Alpha Omega Alpha, Sigma Xi. Home: 320 Hathaway Lane, Wynnewood, Pa. Office: Univ. of Pennsylvania Medical School, Philadelphia, Pa.

FREEMAN, Richard Dingnell, physician and surgeon; b. Dublin, Ireland, Sept. 7, 1866; s. William and Anna (Breakey) F.; student Rathmines Sch., Dublin, 1880-84; B.A., Trinity Coll., Dublin U., 1888; B.M., 1890, M.D., 1891; came to U.S., 1892, naturalized, 1936;

m. Adrienne Adam, Aug. 31, 1927; children—Margaret Martin, Katherine Berg, Eileen Sisco, Richard Deane. Surgeon S.S. Alaska, 1891-92; attending surgeon Orange (N.J.) Memorial Hosp., 1894-1932, chief of staff since 1925; attending surgeon Orange Orphan Home since 1910, Seton Hall. Coll., South Orange, N.J., since 1904. Fellow Am. Coll. Surgeons; mem. A.M.A.; past pres. Soc. of Surgeons of N.J. Awarded Silver Beaver of Boy Scouts of America, 1930. Republican. Episcopalian. Mason. Clubs: British Schools and University, Hosp al Graduates (New York). Address: 103 Scotland Rd., South Orange, N.J.

FREIHOFER, Stanley Herbert, bakery executive; b. Phila., Pa., Jan. 15, 1894; s. William and Anna (Ihrig) F.; student Penn Charter Sch., Phila., to 1913; grad. Wharton Sch., U. of Pa., 1917; m. Hazel Parsells, Sept. 19, 1921; children—Stanley Herbert, Richard Charles, Charlotte Ann. Began as jr. exec. Freihofer Baking Co., Philadelphia, 1919, sec., 1932-39, v.p. since 1939; sec. Wm. Freihofer Baking Co., 1932-36, v.p. and gen. mgr.; 1936-39, pres. and gen. mgr. since 1939. Served as lieut. jr. grade, U.S. Navy, during World War. Mem. Penn Chapter Alumni Soc., Am. Legion (Merion Post), Sphinx Sr. Soc. (U. of Pa.), Delta Tau Delta. Lutheran. Mason (La Lodge 380, Lu Lu Temple), Mary Commandery 36. Clubs: Phila Country, Penn Athletic, Undine Barge (Phila.). Home: 415 Montgomery Av., Merion, Pa. Office: 20th St. and Indiana Av., Philadelphia, Pa.

FRELINGHUYSEN, Joseph Sherman, insurance; b. Raritan, N.J., Mar. 12, 1869; s. Frederick I. and Victoria (Sherman) F.; M.A., Rutgers University; m. Emily Brewster, Nov. 29, 1905; children—Victoria (Mrs. John Grenville Bates, Jr.), Emily (Mrs. Henry Edward Bilkey), Joseph Sherman. Began as insurance underwriter, 1885; pres. and dir. Stuyvesant Ins. Co., J. S. Frelinghuysen Corpn., Raritan Valley Farms, Inc., R. V. F. Inn, Inc.; dir. Pilot Re-Insurance Co. Mem. N.J. State Senate, 2 terms, 1905-11 (pres. 1909 and 1910); acting gov., 1909; pres. State Bd. of Agr., 1911-28; pres. State Bd. of Edn., 1911-17; mem. U.S. Senate, 1917-23; chmn. Am. Delegation, Internat. Conf. on Shore Pollution, 1925. Served as 2d lt., N.Y. Vol. Cavalry, Spanish-Am. War. Republican. Mem. Dutch Reformed Ch. Mason (32°). Clubs: Union, Somerset Hills Country. Home: "Brookwood," Far Hills, N.J. Office: 111 William St., New York, N.Y.

FRENCH, Clifford Woodworth, clergyman; b. Albany, N.Y., Apr. 15, 1884; s. Harvey John and Mary (Nichols) F.; graduate Trinity Sch., N.Y. City, 1908 (valedictorian); S.T.B., Gen. Theol. Sem. of P.E. Ch., 1911; m. Louise Hazel Dorman, June 14, 1911; children—William Owen, John Woodworth. Private sec. to rector St. Andrew's P.E. Ch., Yonkers, N.Y., 1905-08; ordained deacon P.E. Ch., 1911, priest, 1912; vicar St. Luke's Ch., Chatham, N.Y., 1911-12; curate Trinity Ch., Mt. Vernon, N.Y., 1912-15; rector St. Gabriel's Ch., Hollis, N.Y., 1915-29; rector Trinity Ch.; Steelton, Pa., and vicar missions at Middletown, Elizabethtown and Harrisburg, 1930-32; chaplain and sec. to bishop of Harrisburg, canon St. Stephen's Cathedral, Harrisburg. Chmn. dept. of publicity, Diocese of Harrisburg since 1932. Diocesan corr. P.E. Church periodicals. Editor of The Harrisburg Churchman. Home: 213 S. Front St., Harrisburg, Pa.

FRENCH, James Hansell; born at Philadelphia, Pa., July 30, 1885; s. Samuel H., Jr., and Sara E. (Barker) F.; ed. Delancey Sch.; m. Jeanne Rosset, June 6, 1923; children—Samuel, IV, Jeanne Rosset, Mary Catherine, Huberta Hansell. Associated with Samuel H. French Paint Co., 1904-20, v.p., 1928-35; dist. mgr. Edison Cement Corpn., Orange, N.J., 1921-35; sec. of agriculture, Commonwealth of Pa., 1935-39. Home: Twin Meadows Farm, Collegeville, Pa. Office: State Capitol, Harrisburgh, Pa.

FRENCH, John Calvin, educator; b. Monmouth, Ill., Jan. 21, 1875; s. Jonathan and Elizabeth Lydia (Sprout) F.; A.B., Johns Hopkins, 1899, Ph.D., 1905; studied Harvard,

1899-1900; m. Jennie E. Beck, Apr. 8, 1901 (died 1914); children—Ruth Helen A.; m. 2d, Anna S. Sievers, Apr. 4, 1917. With Johns Hopkins U. since 1900, instr. in English, 1904-09, associate, 1909-14, asso. prof., 1914-25, prof., 1925-27, librarian since 1927. Mem. American Library Assn., American Assn. Univ. Profs., Phi Beta Kappa, Omicron Delta Kappa. Phi Gamma Delta. Founder and 1st pres. Edgar Allan Poe Soc. of Baltimore; mem. advisory bd. Poe Shrine. Clubs: Johns Hopkins, Tudor and Stuart. Author: The Problem of the Prologs to Chaucer's Legend, 1905; The Speech for Special Occasions (with others), 1911; Writing, 1924; English in Business (with others), 1925; College Writing (with others), 1932; Practice Work in College English (with others), 1934. Home: 416 Cedarcroft Rd. Address: Johns Hopkins University, Baltimore, Md.

FRENCH, Walter Bernard, banking; b. Jersey City, N.J., Dec. 15, 1897; s. Henry and Frances (Kruse) F.; grad. pub. schs., Jersey City, N.J., 1904-12; ed. N.Y. Prep Sch., 1919-21, grad.; ed. Am. Inst. of Banking, 1921-24, grad.; ed. Grad. Sch. Banking Rutgers U., 1935-37, grad.; student N.Y. Univ. Extension; m. Esther Schunsberg, Sept. 4, 1920; children—Donald, Elaine. Employed as clk. First Nat. Bank, Jersey City, N.J., 1913-17; teller Nat. City Bank, New York City, 1919-23; cashier Merchants Nat. Bank, Jersey City, N.J., 1924-26; asst. to pres. Hudson Co. Nat. Bank, 1927-28; vice-pres. Trust Co. of New Jersey, Jersey City, since 1928. Served in U.S. Marine Corps, 1918-19, with 2d Div. A.E.F. in France. Trustee Hudson Co., N.J., chapter Am. Inst. of Banking. Conglist. Clubs: Spring Meadow, The Knoll. Home: 552 Lotus Rd., Ridgewood, N.J.

FRENCH, William Cullen, univ. prof.; b. Weston, Tex., Mar. 18, 1883; s. John Wesley and Eliza (Webb) F.; student Grayson Coll., Whiteright, Tex., 1898-1902. A.B., U. of Okla., 1907; A.M., U. of Chicago, 1923; Ph.D., New York U., 1929; m. Susie Lawrence, June, 1907; children—John Lawrence, William Culler, Helen (Mrs. C. J. Walsh); m. 2d, Marline Ray, May 1920; 1 son, Robert Bruce. Teacher country sch., 1902-03; supt. schs., Wynnewood, Okla., 1904-06, 1907-10; same, Wagoner, Okla., 1910-13; prof. edn., Central State Teachers Coll., Edmond, Okla., 1913-14; supt. schs. Lawton, Okla., 1914-17, Drumright, Okla., 1917-22, 1924-27; instr. in edn., New York U., 1927-29; prof. edn., George Washington U., since 1929. Mem. N.E.A. Awarded Gen. Edn. Bd. fellowship, 1923. Democrat. Presbyn. Club: Cosmos (Washington). Author: Breed-French Speller (with F. S. Breed), 1927; Child Story Readers (with F. N. Freeman, Grace Storm and Eleanor M. Johnson), 1927. Editor: Self Directing Series of Workbooks, 1925-32: Home: Gaithersburg, Md.

FRESCOLN, Leonard Davis, surgeon; b. Philadelphia, Pa., Mar. 25, 1878; s. George and Mary (Lovett) F.; A.B., U. of Pa., 1900, M.D., 1904; post-grad. work, Besançon, France; m. Elizabeth Keller, Sept. 3, 1922. Acting chief resident physician Phila. Gen. Hosp., 1906-12; chief resident physician Episcopal Hosp., 1912; Phila. police surgeon, 1913; physician U.S. Indian Service, 1913-14; med. expert U.S. Veterans' Bur., 1919-22; instr. physical edn. and orthopædic surgery, U. of Pa., since 1930; asst. chief orthopaedic service Phila. Gen. Hosp. since 1933. Surgeon, U.S. Army, 109th Inf., 1914-18. V.p. Friendly Farmers (Chester Co., Pa.); mem. Bd. of Edn., Meth. Ch.; City Mission Bd.; mem. bd. Am. S.S. Union. Fellow Am. Coll. Orthopædic Surgeons; mem. A.M.A., Pa. Med. Assn., Phila. Co. Med. Assn., Alpha Chi Rho. Republican. Club: Art Alliance (Phila.) Author: Gleanings From World Travel, 1928; Mustard Gas Burns (Jour. of A.M.A.). Address: 222 S. 46th St., Philadelphia, Pa.

FRETZ, Floyd C., supt. schs.; b. Lumberville, Pa., Apr. 11, 1893; s. Samuel and Elizabeth (Morris) F.; ed. West Chester State Teachers Coll.; B.S., U. of Pa., 1927, A.M., 1930; m. Mildred Buchanan, June 24, 1925; 1 dau., Jeanne B. Teacher rural schs., Bristol Twp., Pa., 1910-13; prin. Malvern High Sch., 1916-18; asst. to supt., Chester Co., Pa., 1918-24; supervising prin. Unionville Consolidated Schs., 1924-31, Downingtown Schs., 1931-36; supt. schs., Bradford, since 1936. Dir. Bradford Community Chest, Bradford Carnegie Library. Mem. N.E.A., Nat. Soc. for Study of Edn., Am. Assn. Sch. Administrs., Pa. State Edn. Assn., Progressive Edn. Assn., Pa. Schoolmen's Club, Bradford Teachers Assn. Kappa Phi Kappa, Phi Delta Kappa. Republican. Presbyn. Mason. Clubs: Rotary, Pennhills Country. Home: 95 Mechanic St., Bradford, Pa.

FRETZ, Franklin Kline, clergyman, educator; b. Line Lexington, Pa., Apr. 6, 1876; s. Henry Landis and Wilhelmina (Kline) F.; A.B., Muhlenberg Coll., Allentown, Pa., 1897, D.D., 1921; grad. Luth. Theol. Sem., Mt. Airy, Phila., 1900, A.M., same yr.; Ph.D., U. of Pa., 1911; m. Cora Weikel, Nov. 7, 1900; 1 dau., Barbara Catherine. Ordained Luth. ministry, 1900; pastor St. John's Ch., Easton., Pa., since 1912; organized psychol. clinic, Temple U., Phila., 1911; prof. research dept. of theology, Temple U., since 1909; prof. sociology, Temple U., Sch. of Theology, since 1910. Chaplain City of Easton, by apptmt. of mayor, 1916-20. Dir. Phila. Sem. Ministerium of Pa.; mem. Bd. of Edn. and Bd. of Inner Missions, United Luth. Ch. in America; pres. Com. of the Revision of the Constitution of the Ministerium of Pa.; trustee Easton Pub. Library. Mem. Pa. German Soc. (pres.), Northampton Co. Geneal. and Hist. Soc. (pres.). Republican. Kiwanian. Author: The Furnished Room Problem in Philadelphia, 1911; The Family, 1924. Home: 330 Ferry St., Easton, Pa.*

FRETZ, John Edgar, physician; b. Doylestown, Pa., Nov. 29, 1873; s. Philip H. and Wilhelmina (Johnston) F.; prep. edn. Doylestown (Pa.) Pvt. Sem.; A.B., Lafayette Coll., Easton, Pa., 1933, A.M., 1937; M.D., U. of Pa., 1897; m. Frances J. Rodenbough, Dec. 7, 1904; 1 dau., Emily Wilhelmina. Practiced as physician, Easton, Pa., since 1900; formerly physician to Easton Hosp., Carter Junior Republic, Easton; former physician to Lafayette Coll. and lecturer of hygiene; now mem. staff Easton Tuberculosis Soc.; physician to Easton Children's Home since 1900. Served as contract surgeon, Camp Lafayette, during World War. Dir. Easton Children's Home. Fellow Am. Coll. Physicians, Coll. of Physicians of Phila., A.M.A.; mem. Lehigh Valley Med. Soc., Northampton Co. Med. Soc., Easton Tuberculosis Soc. (v.p.), Pa. State Med. Soc., Am. Soc. Colonial Wars, Sons of Revolution, Soc. War of 1812, Pa.-German Soc., Colonial Soc. of Pa., Huguenots Soc., Bucks Co. Hist. Soc., Northampton Co. Hist. Soc., Phi Gamma Delta. Republican. Presbyterian (elder). Club: Northampton County Country. Home: "Hill Crest." Office: 114 N. 3d St., Easton, Pa.

FRETZ, William Fox, clothing mfr., banker; b. Bedminster, Pa., July 1, 1870; s. Amos and Catharine (Fox) F.; ed. Peirce Business Sch., Phila.; m. Carrie Mills, Mar. 18, 1895; children—Helen LeWorthy, Lulu Brunner, Kathryn Miller, A. Water. Mfr. of clothing under name A. Fretz & Son and successors A. Fretz's Sons, Wm. F. Fretz and Wm. F. Fretz & Son, Doylestown, Pa., since 1891; v.p. and dir. Doylestown Nat. Bank & Trust Co., 1903-29, pres. since 1929; breeder of Guernsey cattle since 1904. Republican. Presbyterian. Mason (32°). Club: Doylestown Kiwanis (pres. 1927). Home: Pipersville, Pa. Office: Doylestown, Pa.

FREVERT, Harry Louis, pres. The Midvale Co.; b. Dayton, O., June 21, 1881; s. George Louis and Bertha (Prass) F.; A.B., Harvard, 1905, Ph.D., 1908; m. Josephine Bate, Sept. 1, 1913. Asst. in chemistry, Harvard, 1903-04, Austin teaching fellow in phys. chemistry, 1904-05, instr. in phys. chemistry, 1905-09; chemist, later chief chemist, Midvale Steel Co., 1909-13, Supt. armor and ordnance, 1913-21; gen. supt. Midvale Steel & Ordnance Co., 1921-23; dir. and vice-pres. in charge operations The Midvale Co., 1923-31, pres. since 1931; dir. Baldwin Locomotive Works. Mem. Metall. Advisory Bd., U.S. Army, and mem. advisory bd. Phila. Ordnance Dist., U.S. Army. Mem. advisory bd. to Sch. of Mines and Metallurgy, Pa. State Coll.; mem. advisory com. John Scott Medal and Award, Bd. of City Trusts, Phila. Mem. Newcomen Soc., Am. Iron and Steel Inst., Chem. Inst., Mining and Metall. Engrs. Clubs: Germantown Cricket, Harvard, Pohoqualine Fish Assn. (Phila.). Home: 435 E. Mt. Airy Av. Office: Nicetown, Philadelphia, Pa.

FREW, William, broker; b. Pittsburgh, Pa., Nov. 24, 1881; s. William Nimick and Emily (Berry) F.; prep. edn. St. Paul's Sch., Concord, N.H.; A.B., Yale, 1903; LL.B., U. of Pittsburgh, 1906; m. Margaretta Park, 1909; children—Emily B. (Mrs. Henry Oliver Jr.), Margaretta Park (Mrs. Theodore H. Conderman II). Admitted to Pa. bar, 1906, and practiced in Pittsburgh, 1906-17; with Union Trust Co., 1919-22; mem. firm Hill, Wright & Frew, 1922-32; partner Moore, Leonard & Lynch, mems. N.Y. Stock Exchange since 1932; trustee and v.p. Dollar Savings Bank, Pittsburgh. Served as lt., later capt., Air Service, U.S. Army, 1917-19. Asst. dist. atty., Pittsburgh, 1906-09. Trustee Carnegie Inst., Pittsburgh. Republican. Presbyterian. Clubs: Duquesne, Pittsburgh Golf, Fox Chapel Golf (Pittsburgh); Yale (New York). Home: 1055 Devon Rd. Office: Union Trust Co., Pittsburgh, Pa.

FREY, Alexander Hamilton, prof. law; b. Long Island City, N.Y., June 2, 1898; s. Walter Guernsey and Susan Baker (Hamilton) F.; student Columbia, 1915-17, A.M., 1920; A.B., Yale, 1919, LL.B., 1921, J.S.D., 1925; student Oxford U., 1921-23; m. Alice Field Hubbard, Feb. 2, 1930; children—Alicia, Alexander Hamilton, Charles. Admitted to practice, Conn., 1921, N.Y., 1922, Pa., 1934; with Simpson, Thacher & Bartlett, N.Y. City, 1923-24; asst. to reporter and special adviser Restatement of Business Assns., 1925-32; asst. prof. Yale Sch. of Law, 1926-30; visiting prof., Columbia U. Law School, summer 1929, U. of Pa. Law Sch., 1930-31, Duke U. Sch. of Law, 1931-32; prof. U. of Pa. Law Sch. since 1932. Fellowships from Carnegie Endowment for Internat. Peace, 1921-23, Social Science Research Council, 1928-29. Served as seaman, U.S.N., Oct.-Dec. 1918. Chmn. Philadelphia Good Neighbor League, 1936, Phila. Civil Liberties Com. since 1936. Mem. Am. Bar Assn., Assn. Bar of City of N.Y., Nat. Lawyers Guild (exec. bd.), Pa. Bar Assn., Am. Law Inst. (adviser, Restatement of Security), The Juristic Society (Phila.), Order of Coif, Delta Upsilon. Democrat. Presbyterian. Clubs: University, Lenape (Phila.). Author: Frey's Cases and Statutes on Business Associations, 1935; articles on legal and other periodicals. Home: Radnor, Pa. Address: U. of Pa. Law Sch., Philadelphia, Pa.

FREY, Herbert Oswin, banker; b. Phila., Pa., Jan. 22, 1891; s. Conrad and Elizabeth (Schmitt) F.; ed. Girard Coll., Phila., 1900-07; B.D. Temple U., Phila., 1914; m. Bessie Rotan, Aug. 11, 1913; children—Dorothy Bessie, Edwin Herbert. Began as stenographer and clk. with The Pa. Co. for Ins. on Lives and Granting of Annuities, Phila., 1907-17; ordained to ministry Bapt. Ch., 1915; pastor Glen Run Ch., 1917-19, 34th St. Bapt. Ch., 1920-28; asst. real estate officer, The Pa. Co. for Ins. on Lives and Granting Annuities, 1927-32, real estate officer, 1932-37, vice-pres. in charge of real estate since 1937; pres. and dir., Elkins Court Corpn.; dir. Property Service, Inc., Shelburne Hotel Co. Trustee Baptist Home of Phila. Vice-pres. Phila. Real Estate Bd.; Pres. Phila. Mortgage Bankers Assn. Republican. Baptist: Home: 510 Murdoch Rd., Mt. Airy, Philadelphia, Pa.

FREY, John Walter, M.D.; b. Pittsburgh, Pa., Jan. 7, 1892; s. John and Hedwig (Feibelman) F.; grad. high sch., Avalon, 1909; B.S., U. of Pittsburgh, 1913, M.D., 1916; grad. study, Johns Hopkins, 1921; m. Annette Hirsch, Dec. 18, 1919; children—John Walter, William Arthur, Margaret Ann. Interne Allegheny Gen. Hosp., 1916-17; resident Children's Hosp., 1917; instr. in U. of Pittsburgh, 1919-22; asst. in clin. diagnosis, St. Francis Hosp., 1922-23; research work Mellon Inst., 1928, 30, 32; mem. visiting staff Children's Hosp.; specializes in pediatrics. Served as capt. Med. R.C., World War, 1917-19, Base Hosp. 114, Beau Desert, France, 1918-19. Fellow A.M.A.; mem. Allegheny County Med. Soc., Phi Rho Sigma. Republican. Mason (Shriner). Club: Oakland Lions (pres. 1937). Contbr. to mags. Home: 4330 Center Av. Office: Schenley Apartments, Pittsburgh, Pa.

FREY, Oliver W., ex-congressman; b. Bucks Co., Pa., Sept. 7, 1890; A.B., Coll. of William and Mary, Williamsburg, Va., 1915; LL.B., U. of Pa., 1920; m. Jessie M. Straub, June 28, 1928. Admitted to Pa. bar, 1920, and since practiced in Allentown; elected to 73d Congress, Nov. 7, 1933, and reëlected to 74th and 75th Congresses (1935-39), 9th Pa. Dist. Served as commd. officer U.S. Army, 1917-19. Democrat. Home: Allentown, Pa.*

FREY, Victor Max, cons. engr.; b. York, Pa., Mar. 16, 1886; s. Victor K. and Flora (Baker) F.; A.B., Johns Hopkins, 1906; B.S. in Mining Engring., Mass. Inst. Tech., 1908; m. Mary Cathryn Snively, Nov. 29, 1911; children—John Philip, Mary Elizabeth, William Snively. Gen. supt. of operations J. E. Baker Co., York, Pa., 1912-28; pres. and gen. mgr. Central Heating Co., Hanover, Pa., since 1931; cons. engr. to numerous firms quarrying limestone, etc.; pres. and treas. Virginia Lime Sales Co., Supreme Supply Co.; gen. mgr. E. Bair Gitt Trust Estate. Home: 507 N. Beaver St. Office: 25 N. George St., York, Pa.

FREYGANG, Walter Henry, mfg. exec.; b. New York, N.Y., Dec. 19, 1890; s. George and Theresa (Vance) F.; student Hoboken (N.J.) Acad., 1900-08; M.E. Stevens Inst., Hoboken, N.J., 1912; m. Marie Antoinette Neumann, June 15, 1918; 1 son, Walter Henry. Supt. mains and service East River Gas Co., New York, 1912-16; v.p. and dir. Walter Kiddie & Co., Inc., high pressure gas specialties, New York and Bloomfield, N.J., since 1916; v.p. and dir. Walter Kidde Sales Co. since 1936, Bloomfield Tool Corpn. since 1934. Mem. Tau Beta Pi. Clubs: Railroad-Machinery (New York); Essex Fells (N.J.) Country. Home: Old Chester Rd., Essex Fells, N.J. Offices: 140 Cedar St., New York, N.Y.; 60 West St., Bloomfield, N.J.

FRICK, Ezra, pres. Frick Co., Inc.; b. Ringgold, Md., Jan. 12, 1856; s. George and Fredericka (Oppenlander) F.; ed. Chambersburg Acad.; m. Kate Mehaffey, Feb. 26, 1885; 1 dau., Frederica. Machinist's apprentice, 4 yrs., becoming refrigeration engr.; with Frick & Co. (now Frick Co., Inc.), Waynesboro, Pa., since 1875, gen. clk. in office, 1878-85, sec., 1885-1906, gen. mgr., 1897-1924, pres. and dir. since 1924; pres. and dir. Citizen's Nat. Bank & Trust Co.; dir. Landis Tool Co. Charter mem. Am. Soc. Refrigeration Engrs. (pres. 1918). Home: 403 Clayton Av. Office: W. Main St., Waynesboro, Pa.

FRICK, John Arthur, pres. Allentown-Bethlehem Gas Co.; b. York, Pa., Sept. 6, 1880; s. John Jacob and Mary Louise (Myers) F.; student York (Pa.) Collegiate Inst., 1892-97; M.E., Lehigh U., Bethlehem, Pa., 1903; m. Ruth Evelyn Linderman, Jan. 29, 1908; children—Mary Norris (Mrs. Hollis Stratton French), John Arthur, Robert Packer Linderman, Ruth Sayre. Cadet engr. Phila. Gas Works, 1903-06; with Consumers Gas Co., Reading, Pa., 1906-08, Savannah (Ga.) Gas Co., 1908-09; supt. Allentown Gas Co., 1909-13; with Allentown-Bethlehem Gas Co., Allentown, Pa., since 1913, gen. mgr., 1913-25, v.p., 1925-27, pres. since 1927; dir. Jefferson Coal Co., Brown-Borhek Co., Allentown Airport Corpn. Trustee St. Luke's Hosp., Bethlehem. Mem. Soc. of Gas Lighting, Newcomen Soc., Am. Gas Assn., Pa. Gas Assn., Chi Psi. Republican. Episcopalian (junior warden). Mason. Clubs: Livingston, Lehigh Country (Allentown); Sancon Valley Country, Bethlehem, University (Bethlehem); Catasauqua (Catasauqua, Pa.); Saw Creek Hunting and Fishing Assn. (Marshalls Creek, Pa.); Engineers Club of the Lehigh Valley. Home: Salisbury House. Office: 516 Hamilton St., Allentown, Pa.

FRIED, Hiram; mem. staff Church Home and Infirmary. Address: 101 W. Read St., Baltimore, Md.

FRIEDENWALD, Edgar Bar, pediatrician; b. Baltimore, Md., Nov. 20, 1879; s. Aaron (M.D.) and Bertha (Bamberger) F.; Baltimore City Coll., 1893-96; Marston's Univ. Sch., Baltimore, 1896-97; Md. Coll. Pharmacy, 1897-99; M.D., Coll. Phys. and Surg. (now U. of Md.) 1903; grad. study, Johns Hopkins, 1905-06, U. of Berlin, 1909-10; m. Bettie Freundlich, May 23, 1908; 1 son, Aaron. Surgeon at mines, Cabin Creek, W.Va., 1903-05; in gen. practice of medicine, Charleston, W.Va., 1906-09; pediatrician, Baltimore, Md., since 1910; asst. in pediatrics, U. of Md., 1910-11, asso., 1911-15, clin. prof., 1915-27, prof. clin. pediatrics since 1927; pediatrician Mercy and Sinai hosps.; consultant in pediatrics, Eye, Ear and Throat Charity Hosp. Served as 1st lt. Med. R.C., U.S.A., 1911-17, capt., 1917, maj., 1918; active service on Mexican Border, 1916, World War, 1917-19, overseas, 1918. Dir. Jewish Children's Soc. Fellow American Medical Assn.; mem. Southern Med. Assn., Med. and Chirurg. Faculty of Md., Assn. Mil. Surgeons U.S., Baltimore City Med. Soc., Phi Beta Pi. Democrat. Mason. Club: University. Contbr. on pediatrics. Home and Office: 1616 Linden Av., Baltimore, Md.

FRIEDENWALD, Harry, ophthalmologist; b. Baltimore, Sept. 21, 1864; s. Dr. Aaron and Bertha (Bamberger) F.; Baltimore City Coll., 1879-81; A.B., Johns Hopkins, 1884; M.D., Coll. of Phys. and Surg., Baltimore, 1886; D.H.L. from Jewish Institute of Religion, New York, 1932; D.Sc., University of Md., 1932; post-grad. work univ. of Berlin and Vienna; m. Bertha Stein, June 28, 1892. Resident phys. City Hosp. of Baltimore, 1886-87; asst. at Prof. Hirschberg's Augenheilanstalt, Berlin, 1887-89; asso. prof. ophthalmology and otology, 1894-1902, prof., 1902-1929, now emeritus, College Physicians and Surgeons, Baltimore (now Univ. of Md.); ophthalmic surgeon, Baltimore Eye, Ear and Throat Charity Hosp. and Mercy, Sinai, Union Protestant Infirmary and Woman's hospitals. Dir. Jewish Theol. Sem. America; gov. Dropsie Coll., Phila. Fellow A.A.A.S., Am. Coll. Surgeons; mem. A.M.A., Am. Ophthal. Soc. (pres. 1936-37), Am. Otological Soc., Ophthalmological Congress of Oxford, Ophthal. Soc. of the United Kingdom, Med. and Chirurg. Faculty of Md., Phi Beta Kappa. Clubs: University (Baltimore). Author: Life, Letters and Addresses of Aaron Friedenwald, 1906. Office: 1212 Eutaw Pl., Baltimore, Md.

FRIEDENWALD, Jonas Stein, ophthalmologist; b. Baltimore, Md., June 1, 1897; s. Harry and Bertha (Stein) F.; A.B., Johns Hopkins, 1916, M.D., 1920; A.M., Harvard, 1922; m. Marie Louise Sherwin, Apr. 19, 1925. Instr. ophthalmic pathology, Johns Hopkins, 1923-29, asso. in clin. ophthalmology, 1929-31, asso. prof since 1931; asst. visiting ophthalmologist, Johns Hopkins Hosp., 1929-31, visiting ophthalmologist since 1931; opthalmic surgeon, Baltimore Eye and Ear, Union Memorial, Women's Sinai and Provident hosps. Fellow Am. Coll. Surgeons; mem. A.M.A., Am. Ophthal. Soc., Am. Optical Soc., Am. Acad. Ophthalmology and Otolaryngology, Am. Assn. Clin. investigation, Ophthal. Soc. United Kingdom. Awarded Lucien Howe medal for research in ophthalmology by A.M. A., 1935. Jewish religion. Club: University. Author: Pathology of the Eye, 1929. Contbr. to professional jours. Address: 1212 Eutaw Pl., Baltimore, Md.

FRIEDENWALD, Julius, M.D.; b. Baltimore, Dec. 20, 1866; s. Dr. Aaron and Bertha (Bamberger) F.; A.B., Johns Hopkins, 1887; M.D., Coll. Phys. and Surg. (now U. of Md.), Baltimore, 1890; student Berlin, Vienna, Paris, London, 1891-1893; hon. A.M., Loyola Coll., Baltimore, 1898; m. Esther Lee Rohr, Oct. 24, 1900. Practicing medicine in Baltimore since 1890. Prof. emeritus gastro-enterology, U. of Md. Sch. of Medicine and Coll. Phys. and Surg., Baltimore; visiting gastro-enterologist to Mercy Hosp.; consultant in digestive diseases to Union Memorial Hosp., Ch. Home and Infirmary, Sinai and Woman's hosps.; advisor Am. Board Internal Medicine. Trustee Inst. for Advanced Study, Princeton, N.J. Fellow A.M.A. (chmn sect. on gastro-enterology, 1930), Am. Coll. Physicians; mem. Assn. Am. Physicians, Am. Gastro-

Enterol. Assn. (pres. 1908-10), Am. Therapeutic Soc., Southern Medical Assn., Am. Assn. of History of Medicine, Med. and Chirurgical Faculty of Maryland, Baltimore Med. Soc. (pres. 1933), Phi Beta Kappa, Phi Lambda Kappa (medalist 1930). Clubs: University, Johns Hopkins, Research. Author: Guide to Clinical Laboratory Diagnosis (with Drs. Beck and Knapp), edits., 1901-04; Diet in Health and Disease (with Dr. John Ruhrah), 6 edits., 1905-25; Dietetics for Nurses (with same), 5 edits., 1905-24; Clinics on Secondary Gastro-intestinal Disorders, 1938 (with Drs. Theodore and Samuel Morrison), Advisory editor in gastro-enterology, Tice's Practice of Medicine. Contbr. many articles in various med. jours. Address: 1013 N. Charles St., Baltimore, Md.

FRIEDLAND, Jacob, lawyer; b. New York, N.Y., Sept. 5, 1901; s. Joseph and Yetta (Starobin) F.; LL.B., N.Y. Law Sch., N.Y. City, 1926; m. Miriam Rose, Feb. 28, 1934; 1 son, Joel David. Admitted to N.J. bar as atty., 1928; engaged in gen. practice of law at Jersey City since 1928; specialized in representing labor unions and is gen. counsel for more than fifty trade unions; elected mem. N.J. Ho. of Assembly, 1939. Mem. Hudson County Bar Assn., Jersey City Community Center. Democrat. Hebrew religion. K. of P. Mem. 11th Ward Democratic Club, Jersey City. Home: 110 Palisades Av. Office: 591 Summit Av., Jersey City, N.J.

FRIEDMAN, Harry, lawyer; b. Lewiston, Me., Feb. 4, 1883; s. Faibel and Fannie (Goodman) F.; student Grafton (W.Va.) High Sch., 1899-1901; LL.B., W.Va. Univ. Law Sch., 1906; m. Florence Greensfelder, Jan. 17, 1923; children—Stanley E., Miriam F. Admitted to W.Va. bar, 1906, and since engaged in gen. practice of law at Grafton; civil and chancery practice in circuit cts. also in W.Va. Supreme Ct. and in Federal Dist. Ct.; Dem. nominee for prosecuting atty., 1916 also 1932; now chmn. Taylor Co. Dem. Com.; sec. and atty. Mutual Bdg. & Loan Assn.; dir. Parrish Realty Co.; now serving as gen. receiver of Circuit Ct. of Taylor Co. Mem. Sigma Nu. Democrat. Mason (32°). Elk. Moose. Home: 506 Maple Av. Office: 59 W. Main St., Grafton, W.Va.

FRIEDMAN, Theodore, rabbi; b. Stamford, Conn., Jan. 5, 1908; s. Harry and Anna (Kapit) F.; A.B., Coll. of City of N.Y., 1928; Rabbi, Jewish Theol. Sem., 1931; A.M., Columbia U., 1931; m. Ruth Braunhut, Dec. 27, 1931; children—Hillel Ira, Naomi Vita. Rabbi Temple Beth El, North Bergen, N.J., since 1931. Dir. Hebrew Home for Orphaned and Aged. Mem. Rabbinical Assembly of America. Mem. bd. govs. Nat. Young Judea. Home: 988 Park Av., North Bergen, N.J.

FRIEDRICH, F. A.; editor The Call. Address: 33 Church St., Paterson, N.J.

FRIES, Irvin A., M.D.; b. Reading, Pa., May 4, 1861; s. Joseph A. and Amelia (Greth) F.; B.A., Stewart Acad., Reading, Pa.; M.D. Jefferson Med. Coll., 1891; m. Jennie Whiteside, Aug. 3, 1882. Engaged in gen. practice of medicine since 1892; mem. otolaryngology staff, Jefferson Hosp., 1893-98. Served as capt. Med. Corps, U.S. Army, Spanish-Am. and World wars. Fellow Am. Coll. Physicians and Surgeons, Phila. Co. Med. Soc.; mem. A.M.A. Republican. Catholic. Clubs: Manufacturers, Medical. Home: Providence Road, Wallingford, Va. Office: 1534 Pine St., Philadelphia, Pa.

FRIESELL, H. Edmund, dental educator; b. Pittsburgh, Nov. 10, 1873; s. Jacob and Margaret J. (McClaren) F.; D.D.S., Pa. College Dental Surgery, 1895; B.S., U. of Pittsburgh, 1911; LL.D., Marquette University, 1919; D.Sc., University of Pittsburgh, 1930; m. Esther J. Hutchison, Aug. 1898; children—Dorothy Marion, Charles Edmund, Aimee Elizabeth. Prof. operative dentistry, and dean Sch. Dentistry, U. of Pittsburgh, since Oct. 1903; prof. operative dentistry and dental pathology, Western Reserve University, Cleveland, 1906-17. Assistant editor The Journal of Dental Research. Mem. Nat. Board of Dental Examiners, Commission on Survey of the Dental Curriculum; ex-pres. National Association Dental Faculties, Dental Council of Pa., Am. Institute Dental Teachers, Pa. State Dental Soc.; hon. mem. Northern Ohio, Ohio State and R.I. State dental socs; pres. Nat. Dental Assn., 1920-21; pres. Am. Assn. of Dental Schs.; 1st v.p. Seventh Internat. Dental Congress; pres. Omicron Kappa Upsilon; fellow Am. Coll. of Dentists (pres.), Am. Acad. Dental Surgeons; advisory fellow Mellon Inst. Industrial Research; mem. Ill. State, Chicago, Pittsburgh, and Lake Erie dental socs., Odontol. Soc. Western Pa., A.M.A., Dental Ednl. Council America, Internat. Assn. Dental Research, Fed. Dentaire Internationale, Psi Omega (supreme grand master), Delta Tau Delta, Omicron Delta Kappa, Scabbard & Blade. Mason (32°). Republican. United Presbyn. Clubs: University, Pittsburgh Athletic Assn.; Chemists (New York). Extensive contbr. on dental subjects; also writer on history; pub. speaker. Home: Murrysville, Pa. Address: University of Pittsburgh, Pittsburgh, Pa.

FRINK, Orrin, Jr., prof. of mathematics; b. Brooklyn, N.Y., May 31, 1901; s. Orrin and Elizabeth Blauvelt (Romeyn) F.; grad. Boys' High Sch., Brooklyn, N.Y., 1918; A.B., Columbia U., 1922, A.M., 1923, Ph.D., 1926; student U. of Chicago, 1926-27, Princeton U., 1927-28; m. Aline Huke, June 3, 1931; children—Orrin, Peter Hill. Instr. of mathematics, Princeton U., 1925-26; Nat. Research fellow in mathematics, U. of Chicago, 1926-27, Princeton, 1927-28; asst. prof. of mathematics, Pa. State Coll., 1928-29, asso. prof., 1929-33, prof. since 1933. Mem. Am. Math. Soc., Math. Assn. of America, A.A.A.S., Soc. for Symbolic Logic, Phi Beta Kappa, Sigma Xi, Pi Mu Epsilon, Sigma Pi Sigma. Congregationalist. Contbr. articles to tech. math. jours. Home: Sunset Rd., State College, Pa.

FRISHMUTH, Harriet Whitney, sculptor; b. Phila., Pa., Sept. 17, 1880; d. Frank B. and Louise Otto (Berens) F.; studied art in Paris, France, under Rodin and Injalbert, in Berlin under Prof. Cuno Von Euchtritz, Art Students League, New York, under Borglum and McNeil, and was awarded the St. Gaudens 1st prize. Exhibited at Nat. Acad. Design, Architectural League, Nat. Assn. Women Painters and Sculptors, Acad. Fine Arts (Phila.), San Francisco Expn., Salon, Paris. Awarded Helen Foster Barnet prize; Nat. Arts Club prize, 1921; Watrous gold medal, Nat. Acad., 1922; Julia A. Shaw memorial prize, Nat. Acad., 1923; Joan of Arc silver medal, Nat. Assn. of Women Painters and Sculptors, 1924, sketch exhibition for speed; hon. mention, San Francisco Expn., 1928; Garden Club of America gold medal, 1929; Irving T. Bush prize, Grand Central Art Gallery, 1928. Prin. works: "Joy of the Waters," fountain, Mus. of Fine Arts, Dayton, O.; memorial sundial, Englewood, N.J.; "Slavonic Dance," Met. Mus., New York: "Vine," Metropolitan Mus.; "Play Days," Dallas (Tex.) Mus.; Morton memorial, Windsorville, Conn. N.A., 1929; portrait bust of President Woodrow Wilson, for Capitol at Richmond, Va. Designed medals for New York Acad. Medicine and Garden Club of America (Fenwick medal). Mem. Nat. Acad. of Design, Nat. Assn. Women Painters and Sculptors, Nat. Sculpture Soc., Allied Artists America, League Am. Artists, Art Alliance America, Archtl. League of N.Y. Republican. Episcopalian. Address: Swiss Cottage, Lancaster Av. and City Line, Overbook, Philadelphia, Pa.

FRITSCH, Joseph Laux, civil engr.; b. Cincinnati, O., Jan. 15, 1873; s. Francis and Clara (Roessler) F.; student St. Xavier Coll., Cincinnati, O., 1886-89; A.B., Xavier University, Cincinnati, O., 1893; B.S., U. of Cincinnati (O.), 1897; m. Mary Gertrude Ward, Oct. 16, 1907; children—Mary Elizabeth, Anna Claire (Mrs. Edward T. Fitch), Dorothy Jane. Began as draftsman Commr's. of Cincinnati (O.) Water Works, 1898-1902; bridge engr. Pittsburgh McKeesport & Connellsville Ry., Connellsville, Pa., 1902-03, chief engr., 1903-04; chief engr. West Penn Rys. Co., Pittsburgh, 1904-29, chief engr. and v.p. since 1929; v.p. and dir. Steubenville Bridge Co., Allegheny Valley St. Rys., Kittaning & Leechburg Rys. Co., Steubenville, Wellsburg & Weirton Rys. Co. Mem. Am. Transit Assn. Republican. Catholic. K.C. Home: 87 S. Linwood Av., Crafton, Pa. Office: 14 Wood St., Pittsburgh, Pa.

FRITSCH, Robert Roland, clergyman and coll. prof.; b. Allentown, Pa., Sept. 10, 1879; s. John G. and Sarah Y. (Moyer) F.; A.B., Muhlenberg Coll., Allentown, Pa., 1900, A.M., 1903; Ph.B., Ill. Wesleyan U., Bloomington, Ill., 1904, A.M., 1908; grad. study U. of Pa. Post Grad. German Seminar Course, 1910-13; (hon.) D.D., Wittenberg Coll., Springfield, O., 1929; m. Carrie M. Fehr, June 30, 1904; children—Dorothy Anna (wife of Rev. Roland G. Bortz), Rev.-prof. Charles Theodore. Engaged in teaching, high sch., Allentown, Pa., 1900-07; mem. faculty Muhlenberg Coll., Allentown, continuously since 1907, prof. German, Bible and Greek; ordained to ministry Luth. Ch., 1915; teacher at Bible Confs. in 12 states; made three trips for study in Europe and Bib. Lands, 1927, 1928, 1930. Mem. Nat. Assn. Bib. Instrs., Am. Assn. Univ. Profs., Pa. Luth. Ministerium, Lehigh Valley Classical League. Lutheran. Club: Rotary (Allentown; chaplain). Home: 2220 Chew St., Allentown, Pa.

FRITZ, F. Herman, supt. of schs.; b. Bloomsburg, Pa., 1883; s. Andrew L. and Eudora (Evans) F.; A.B. and A.M., Bucknell U. Ed.M., Harvard; m. Marjorie Ladd, 1920; children—F. Herman, Charles Ladd. Prin. grammar school, Wilkes-Barre, Pa., 1909-14; dean Pennington Sch. for Boys, 1914-16; supervisor of English, Springfield, Mass., 1916-25; supt. of schs., Ashley, Pa., 1925-28, Pottstown, Pa., 1928-34, Chester, Pa., since 1934. Mem. bd. dirs. Chester Y.M.C.A.; mem. Youth Council, Chester. Mem. N.E.A., Nat. Soc. for Study of Curriculum, Delaware County Hist. Soc. Presbyterian (mem. session First Presbyn. Ch.). Rotarian. Home: 201 E. Avon Rd. Office: Larkin Bldg., Chester, Pa.

FRIZZELL, John Henry, prof. pub. speaking; b. Easthampton, Mass., Oct. 10, 1881; s. Rufus Allen and Annie Maria (Strangford) F.; A.B., Amherst (Mass.) Coll., 1902; A.M., Pa. State Coll., 1912; grad. study, U. of Pa., 1914-15; m. May Newell Reynolds, June 20, 1906; children—Marjorie Elinor (Mrs. Richard Rolston Fletcher), John Strangford, Rensselaer Reynolds, Barbara May. Instr. rhetoric and oratory, Pa. State Coll., 1902-08; asst. prof. English, then asso. prof., Pa. State Coll., 1912-20; prin. High Sch. for Boys, Reading, Pa., 1920-23; field sec., Brotherhood of St. Andrew (P.E.Ch.), 1923-26; asso. prof. pub. speaking, Pa. State Coll., 1926-30, prof. pub. speaking and head dept. since 1930, chaplain of Coll. since 1928. Served as Four Minute Man, Com. on Pub. Information, U.S. Govt., 1917-18. Mem. Nat. Assn. Teachers of Speech, Eastern Pub. Speaking Conf. (charter mem.), Am. Assn. Univ. Profs., Phi Kappa Psi. Republican. Episcopalian. Odd Fellow. Author: Notes on Public Speaking, 1905; The Chapel Prayer Book, 1939. Only living mem. of the Pa. Debating League (1903), now Debating Assn. of Pa.; an organizer of Speech Round Table of Pa. State Edn. Assn. Home: 226 Highland Av., State College, Pa.

FROBISHER, Martin Jr., bacteriologist; b. New York, N.Y., Jan. 17, 1896; s. Martin and Charlotte Augusta (Biggam) F.; student Franklin Sch., Englewood, N.J., 1912-16, Cornell U., 1916-20; B.S., Johns Hopkins, 1922, D.Sc., 1925; m. Amy Westervelt Willis, June 3, 1922. Began as scientific aid, U.S. Dept. of Agr., Washington, D.C., 1921; asst. bacteriologist Md. State Health Dept., 1922-24; chief Bureau of Chemistry, Baltimore City Health Dept., 1924-25; asso. in bacteriology, Johns Hopkins Med. Sch., 1925-28; special mem. Internat. Health Div., Rockefeller Foundation, 1928-32; dir. of labs. Eastern Health Dist., Johns Hopkins U., 1932-38; senior bacteriologist U.S. Pub. Health Service, 1936, consultant, 1937. Served in Motor Transport and Med. Corps, U.S. Army, 1917-19. Fellow Am. Pub. Health Assn., A.A.A.S.; mem. Am. Soc. Bacteriologists, Soc. Exptl. Biol. and Medicine, Soc. of Hygiene (past sec. Johns Hopkins), Nat. Orgn. for Pub. Health Nursing, Sigma Xi, Gamma Alpha, Delta Omega (past. sec.), Sigma Phi Epsilon. Author: Fundamentals of Bacteriology, 1937; Bacteriology for Nurses (with M. E. Morse); contbr. numerous scientific papers to med. jours. Mng. editor of Am. Jour. of Hygiene. Home: 5806 Kipling Ct. Office: 615 N. Wolfe St., Baltimore, Md.

FROCHT, Max Mark, prof. of mechanics; b. Warsaw, Russia-Poland, June 3, 1894; s. Meyer Loeb and Eva (Egerwald) F.; came to U.S., 1912, naturalized, 1922; B.S. in M.E., U. of Mich., 1922, Ph.D. ,1931; M.S., U. of Pittsburgh, 1926; m. Dora Lipkin, Oct. 1918. Designer and research asst. with various automobile companies, 1912-16, 1918-19; instr. Carnegie Inst. Tech., 1922-26, asst. prof., 1926-31, asso. prof. since 1931. Served as private U.S. Army during World War. Mem. Am. Assn. Univ. Profs., A.A.A.S., Soc. Promotion Engring. Edn., Am. Soc. Mech. Engrs., Phys. Soc. of Pittsburgh. Author: Strength of Materials (with N. C. Riggs); 1938. Contbr. articles on researches in photoelasticity and strength of materials to professional jours. Home: 6659 Northumberland, Pittsburgh, Pa.

FROHLING, Edward Adam, banking; b. Phila., Pa., May 1, 1887; s. Valentine and Elizabeth (Mater) F.; ed. pub. schs., Princeton, N.J., Rider-Moore & Stewart, Trenton, N.J., 1903-05, Am. Inst. Banking, 1932-36; m. Agnes O'Dendhal, Aug. 26, 1920; children—Edward Sebastine, Marie Theresa, Elizabeth Mercier, Lucille Helene, Agnes Marion, John B. Manning, Lucien O'Dendhal. Asso. with First Nat. Bank, Princeton, N.J. since 1905, vice pres. since 1937; served as mem. bd. health Borough of Princeton since 1927. Republican. Roman Catholic. Club: Lions of Princeton. Home: 12 Stockton St. Office: 90 Nassau St., Princeton, N.J.

FROHMAN, Philip Hubert, architect; b. N.Y. City, Nov. 16, 1887; s. Gustave and Marie (Hubert) F.; ed. Throop Poly. Inst., Pasadena, Calif., 1899-1903; Throop Coll. of Engring. (now Calif. Inst. Tech.), specializing in art, architectural engring. and civ. engring., 1903-07; m. Olivia Avery, July 15, 1922; children—Mary Satterlee, Alice Patricia. Began practice as architect at Pasadena, Calif., 1908; mem. firm Frohman & Martin, 1909-17; opened office in Boston, 1919; mem. firm of Frohman, Robb & Little, 1920-34; in practice alone since January, 1934; opened office in Washington, D.C., 1924, continuing association with former partners in Boston and Calif. on certain projects; specializes in church architecture; firm architects for National Episcopal Cathedral, Washington, Maryland Cathedral, Baltimore, Trinity Coll. Chapel, Hartford, Conn., and other monumental chs.; cons. architect Kent Sch. Chapel, Nat. Joint Commn. on Ch. Architecture of P.E.Ch., also various chs.; cons. architect for several cathedral projects. Enlisted in U.S. Army, 1917; assigned to Ordnance Constrn. Sect. and Supply Div.; designed bldgs. at Rock Island Arsenal and Aberdeen Proving Grounds; in charge architectural div. of Aberdeen Proving Grounds; discharged Feb. 6, 1919. Mem. Am. Inst. Architects, also Washington Chapter of same, Nat. Cathedral Assn., Nat. Child Labor Com., Knights of the Ch., Liturgical Art Society, The Restorers of Mount Carmel in Maryland. Republican. Catholic. Clubs: Boston Art; Cosmos (Washington); Gibson Island Club, Gibson Island Yacht Squadron. Specialist in structural engring. as applied to cathedrals, etc. Regarded as an authority on Romanesque and Gothic architecture, stained glass, and also on design and voicing of ch. organs and in field of science of musical sounds. Inventor electric organs and various apparatus for elec. reproduction of mus. sounds. Writer on ecclesiastical art and architecture. Home: 3121 Cleveland Av., Washington, D.C.; (summer) Gibson Island, Md. Office: Washington Cathedral. Offices: Mount St. Alban, Washington, D.C.

FROLICH, Per K(eyser), chemist; b. Kristiansand, Norway, June 29, 1899; s. Johan Keyser and Beate (Corneliussen) F.; came to U.S., 1922, naturalized, 1929; B.S., Norway Inst. Tech., 1921; M.S., Mass. Inst. Tech., 1923, D.Sc., 1925; m. Astrid Fronsdal, Mar. 7, 1927; children—Elizabeth Ann K., Astrid K. Asst. in chemistry, Norway Inst. Tech., 1919-20; instr. chemistry and physics, Kristiansand Business Coll., 1921-22; Am.-Scandinavian fellow to U.S., 1922-23; research asst., Mass. Inst. Tech. 1923-25, research asso., 1925-27, asst. prof. chem. engring., 1927-29, asso. prof., 1929, also asst. dir. research labs. of applied chemistry, 1927-29; research chemist, Standard Oil Development Co., Elizabeth, N.J., 1929-31, asst. dir. research labs., 1931-33, dir., 1933-35, chief chemist, 1935-36, dir. chem. labs. since 1936. Served in inf. Norwegian Army, 1922. Mem. Am. Chem. Soc., Am. Inst. Chem. Engrs., Am. Soc. Automotive Engrs., Soc. Chem. Industry (Brit.), Chem. Soc. (Brit.), Deutsche Chemische Gesellschaft. Awarded Grasselli medal, 1930. Club: Chemists (New York). Asso. editor Chemical Reviews, 1935. Home: 930 Mountainview Circle, Westfield, N.J. Address: P.O. Box 243, Elizabeth, N.J.

FRONEFIELD, Joseph M., real estate broker; b. Phoenixville, Pa., Oct. 30, 1861; s. Joseph M. and Eliza A. (Rogers) F.; ed. Phila. Coll. of Pharmacy and Science; m. Lizzie M. Pugh, June 16, 1886; children—Frances (Mrs. Winfield W. Crawford), Joseph M. III, Edward H. Pugh. In retail drug business, Wayne, Pa., 1883-1910; in real estate business Wayne, Pa., since 1910, doing business as J. M. Fronefield, Realtor. Mem. Phila. Real Estate Bd. Democrat. Baptist. Mason. Home: 225 Audubon Av. Office: 103 W. Lancaster Av. (Lincoln Highway), Wayne, Pa.

FROST, Ellis Mills, physician; b. Pittsburgh, Pa., July 3, 1883; s. Albert Ellis and Mary Addie (Dalbey) F.; ed. U. of Pittsburgh Pre-Med., 1902-03, U. of Pittsburgh Med. Sch., 1903-05; M.D., U. of Pa. Med. Sch., 1907; m. Alice Real Bell, 1910; children—Mary Elizabeth, Robert Ellis, Richard Bell (dec.). Interne Mercy Hosp., Pittsburgh, 1907-08; entered pvt. practice of medicine, 1908, and specialized in internal medicine; asso. with U. of Pittsburgh Sch. of Medicine since 1909, with Dept. Anatomy, 1909-15, in Dept. Medicine since 1915, now asst. prof. medicine; connected with Mercy Hosp. since 1909, mem. sr. med. staff since 1927. Fellow Am. Coll. Phys. Mem. Am. Med. Assn., Rhi Rho Sigma. Methodist. Mason (32°). Home: 1376 Sheridan Av. Office: 4715 Fifth Av., Pittsburgh, Pa.

FROST, Frank Raymond, pres. Superior Steel Corpn.; b. Meadville, Pa., June 17, 1883; s. Benjamin Franklin and Margaret (Phanco) F.; B.S., Allegheny Coll., Meadville, Pa., 1905; m. Amy Lusk, May 6, 1905; children—Amy Lucille (Mrs. James D. Clokey, Jr.), Frances Elizabeth (Mrs. Roscoe L. Potter). Transit man and asst. engr. Southern Ry. Co., 1905-07; supt. and asst. engr. Hales Bar Dam, Guild, Tenn., 1907-10; gen. supt. Ft. Orange Constrn. Co., Waterford, N.Y., 1910-11; with Pittsburgh Hickson Co., Butler, Pa., 1911-17, successively as asst. supt., supt. and purchasing agt., and asst. to pres.; with Superior Steel Corpn. since 1917, successively as salesman, asst. mgr. sales, gen. mgr. sales, vice pres. and gen. mgr. sales, dir. of company and since 1921 pres. Dir. Am. Iron and Steel Inst.; trustee Allegheny Coll. Mem. Sigma Alpha Epsilon. Republican. Presbyterian. Mason. Clubs: Duquesne, Pittsburgh Athletic, Longue Vue Country, Pittsburgh Field, University (Pittsburgh); Detroit Athletic; Chicago Athletic; Union League (Phila.); Cloud, Bankers (New York). Home: 1060 Morewood Ave. Office: 3112 Grant Bldg., Pittsburgh, Pa.

FROST, Inglis Folger, physician; b. Attica, N.Y., June 6, 1886; s. Henry Weston and Abigail (Ellinwood) F.; student Norristown (Pa.) High Sch., 1902-04, Germantown Acad., Phila., 1904-05, Toronto (Can.) U., 1905-07; M.D., Yale Med. Sch., 1912; m. Barbara Brewster, July 28, 1915; children—Barbara Ellinwood, Marie Brewster; m. 2d, Elizabeth Baker, 1931. Began as physician, 1914, and since in practice at Morristown, N.J. Served as lieut. 1st India Med. Service, British Army, 1916-18. Fellow Am. Coll. Surgeons, A.M.A., N.J., Morris Co. med. socs., Soc. of Surgeons of N.J., Am. Bd. of Obstetrics and Gynecology; mem. N.Y. Obstetrical Soc., Alpha Delta Phi. Republican. Presbyterian. Clubs: Alpha Delta Phi (New York); Somerset Hills Golf (Bernardsville, N.J.). Home: Lushan Farm, Chester, N.J. Office: 181 South St., Morristown, N.J.; 930 Park Av., New York, N.Y.

FROST, Stuart Ward, prof. econ. entomology; b. Tarrytown, N.Y., Dec. 4, 1891; s. Homer R. and Josephine Francis (Carpenter) F.; B.S., Cornell U., 1915, Ph.D., 1928; m. Helen M. Middaugh, 1925; 1 son, Stuart Homer. Has been associated with Pa. State Coll. since 1918, dept. zoology and entomology since 1918, prof. econ. entomology since 1930. Mem. A.A.A.S., Am. Soc. Econ. Entomologists, The Entomol. Soc. of America, Société Linnéene de Lyon, Soc. for Pa. Archaeology, Sigma Xi, Pi Gamma Mu. Presbyterian. Author: Ancient Artizans, the Wonders of the Insect World, 1936. Co-author (with J. G. Needham), Leaf-mining Insects, 1928; more than 150 tech. papers on zoöl. and entomol. papers. Home: 465 E. Foster Av., State College, Pa.

FRY, George Arthur, clergyman; b. Orwigsburg, Pa., June 23, 1878; s. Aaron and Sallie (Rickson) F.; student Orwigsburg (Pa.) Public Schs., 1884-96; B.D., Temple U., Phila., 1908; student Luth. Theol. Sem., Gettysburg, Pa., 1908-09; D.D., Susquehanna U., Selinsgrove, Pa., 1922; m. Elva Gertrude Bair, June 7, 1911; 1 dau., Elizabeth Bair. Ordained to ministry of Evang. Lutheran Ch., 1908; pastor St. John's Luth. Ch., Maytown, Pa., 1908-13; pastor St. Luke's Luth. Ch., North Side, Pittsburgh, since 1913. Pres. Pittsburgh Synod of Evang. Luth. Ch., 1919; mem. bd. of dirs. Luth. Inner Mission Soc. of Pittsburgh, 15 years; former pres. Union Ministerial Assn. of Pittsburgh; former pres. Central Conf. of Pittsburgh Synod; dir. Sabbath Assn. of Western Pa.; chmn. examining com. Pittsburgh Synod; pres. Intersynodical Com. on Luth. Student Work. Mem. bd. dirs. Thiel Coll., Greenville, Pa., for 9 years. Address: 2630 Perryville Av., Pittsburgh, Pa.

FRY, Guy Edgar, art director; b. Milton, Pa., Aug. 5, 1903; s. William Howard and Sally Gertrude (Mauger) F.; grad. Milton (Pa.) High Sch., 1921; student Sch. of Industrial Art, Phila., 1922-26; m. Emma Hulbert, Apr. 28, 1927; children—Patricia Hulbirt, Karel Ann. Illustrator of books and magazines, 1927-32; producer of art for advertising, 1932-37; dir. of art in advertising for Jerome B. Gray & Co., Phila., since 1937. Illustrator: Christmas Everywhere, 1931; Thirteen Ghostly Yarns, 1932. Designer of covers for House Beautiful, St. Nicholas, Nature. Awarded 1st prize in water color group at Chester Co. Art. Show, 1933, 1934. Clubs: Phila. Sketch, Art Directors, (Phila.), Chester County Art Assn. Home: Thornton, Pa. Office: 12 S. 12th St., Philadelphia, Pa.

FRY, Howard Massey, coll. prof.; b. Drifton, Luzerne Co., Pa., Oct. 2, 1889; s. William Bickley and Sarah Catherine (Massey) F.; student Mining and Mech. Inst., Freeland, Pa., 1903-07; E.E., Lehigh U., Bethlehem, Pa., 1910, M.S., 1915; m. Edith Louise Marsteller, Nov. 23, 1911 (died 1930); 1 dau., Helen Louise (Mrs. Charles E. Frick Jr.); m. 2d, Anna Augusta Veith, Mar. 6, 1931. Instr. physics, Lehigh U., Bethlehem, Pa., 1910-15, asst. prof., 1915-18, asso. prof., 1918-25; asso. prof. physics and electricity, Franklin and Marshall Coll., 1925-35, prof. since 1935. Civilian dir. Telegraph Sch., Camp Capper, Lehigh U., 1918. Fellow A.A.A.S. (treas. Lancaster, Pa., branch since 1935); mem. Pa. Conf. Coll. Physics Teachers (mem. exec. com.), Pa. Acad. Science (mem. membership com.), Am. Inst. E.E., Am. Physics Soc., Soc. for Promotion Engring. Edn., Am. Assn. Physics Teachers, Alpha Tau Omega, Tau Beta Pi, Sigma Pi Sigma, Alpha Delta Sigma. Republican. Episcopalian. Author: Laboratory Manual of Physics, 1924. Home: 509 State St., Lancaster, Pa.

FRY, Morton Harrison, banker; b. Ephrata, Pa., Jan. 27, 1888; s. Jacob Martin and Margaret (Ruth) F.; prep. edn., high sch., Ephrata, and Franklin and Marshall Acad., Lancaster, Pa.; A.B., Princeton, 1909; m. Julia Gladys Angell, June 22, 1909; children—Morton Allan Harrison, George Thomas Clark. Partner Scholle Bros., bankers, N.Y. City, since 1923; pres. Overseas Securities Co.; dir. Ala. Great Southern R.R., Tubize Chatillon Corpn., The Equity Corpn., Overseas Securities Co., Inc. Mem. Am. Acad. Polit. Science, Phi Beta Kappa. Democrat. Clubs: University, Princeton,

FRY, Thornton Carle, mathematician; b. Findlay, O., Jan. 7, 1892; s. William Watson and Elizabeth Hanna (Dingle) F.; A.B., Findlay, (O.) Coll., 1912; A.M., U. of Wis., 1913, Ph.D., 1920; m. Alma Schumacher, 1912 (died 1924); 1 dau., Dinah Elizabeth; m. 2d, Jessie L. Smith, of Brooklyn, N.Y., 1925. Instr. mathematics, U. of Wis., 1912-16; mathematician, Western Electric Co., 1916-24; Bell Telephone labs. since 1924; lecturer elec. engring., Mass. Inst. Tech., 1927; lecturer mathematics, Princeton, 1929-30. Fellow American Physical Society, A.A.A.S., Institute of Math. Statistics; mem. Am. Math. Soc., Math. Assn. of America, Am. Astron Soc., Soc. for Promotion Engring. Edn., Econometric Soc., Nat. Research Council, Sigma Xi. Author: Elementary Differential Equations, 1929; Probability and Its Engineering Uses, 1928. Contbr. tech. articles. Home: 91 Maple St., Wyoming, N.J. Office: 463 West St., New York, N.Y.

FRY, William Clinton, Jr., cons. engr.; b. Pottstown, Pa., Jan. 17, 1889; s. William Clinton and Valeria A. (Hanley) F.; C.E., Lehigh U., 1913; M.A., Columbia U., 1915; m. Anna A. Kassur, July 20, 1921; 1 son, Lester Paul. Instr. civil engring., Brooklyn Poly. Inst., 1913-16; asst. county engr., Berks Co., Pa., 1916-18; chief engr. Whittaker & Diehl, contractors, 1919-21; prin. asst. engr. on designing and construction of $4,500,000 Victory bridge, Perth Amboy, N.J., 1921-26; asst. engr. Port of New York Authority, 1926-29; engr. design and construction $2,900,000 Columbia-Wrightsville Bridge, 1929-31; county engr., Berks Co., Pa., 1932-36; in private practice as cons. engr. since 1937. Served as private, Aviation Corps, U.S. Army, 1 yr., World War. Mem. Am. Soc. C.E., Pa. Soc. Professional Engrs. Democrat. Lutheran. Address: Reiffton, Pa.

FRYE, Edwin Gibson, clergyman and editor; b. West Unity O., Mar. 6, 1876; s. Jacob Albert and Ellen (Gibson) F.; ed. Alma Coll., 1894-96; (hon.) D.D., Western Union Coll., Le Mars, Ia., 1927; m. Mildred A. Schalow, Dec. 12, 1900; children—Neil S. (dec.), Eloise Gibson (Mrs. Joseph W. Leverenx). Licensed as preacher Evang. Ch., 1895, ordained deacon, 1898, ordained elder, 1900; served charges in Mich. Conf. continuously, 1896-1915, when elected dist. supt. Detroit Dist.; asst. editor Evangelical Messenger, Harrisburg, Pa., 1915-19; editor since 1919; mem. Joint Commn. on Ch. Federations and Union when Evang. Assn. and U. Evang. Ch. merged, 1922; mem. Gen. Confs. Evang. Assn. and since merger of Evang Ch., 1915-38; officer and mem. many important coms. Mem. Bd. Trustees Pa. Anti-Saloon League; hon. v.p. Anti-Saloon League of America. Republican. Mem. Evang. Ch. Home: 2721 4th St., Harrisburg, Pa. Office: Third & Reily Sts., Harrisburg, Pa.

FRYER, Eugénie Mary, author; b. Phila., Pa., Sept. 17, 1879; d. Greville E. and Elizabeth P. (Frost) F.; grad. the Misses Hayward's Sch.; certificate eclectic courses, Drexel Inst., Phila.; studied Grad. Sch., U. of Pa., 1914, 15; unmarried. Contbr. stories, essays, travel and biog. sketches, etc., to magazines since 1900. Librarian Sch. of Industrial Art., Phila. Mem. Phila. Art Alliance. Republican. Episcopalian. Clubs: Automobile (Phila.); American Women's (London); Contemporary. Author: The Hills-Towns of France, 1917; A Book of Boyhoods, 1920; Unending Quest (poems), 1932. Home: 1906 Sansom St., Philadelphia, Pa.

FRYER, Jane Eayre (Mrs. John Gayton Fryer), author; b. Phila., Pa.; d. Mortimer Haines and Isabella (Van de Veer) Eayre; grad. Northfield (Mass.) Sem., 1896; spl. courses in domestic art and domestic science; special course in normal classes, U. of Pa.; m. Rev. John Gayton Fryer, of Providence, R.I., Jan. 1902. Teacher Latin and English, Mt. Holly (N.J.) Mil. Acad., 1897-98; supervisor domestic sc. and art, Jacob Tome Inst., Port Deposit, Md., 1899-1902. Baptist. Mem. Northfield Alumni Assn.; hon. mem. Women's Club of Merchantville, N. J. Author: The Mary Frances Cook Book, 1912; The Mary Frances Sewing Book, 1913; The Mary Frances Housekeeper, 1914; The Mary Frances Garden Book, 1915; The Mary Frances First Aid Book, 1916; The Mary Frances Knitting and Crocheting Book, 1918; Young American Readers (civic), 1918-1919; The Mary Frances Story Book, 1921; Mrs. Fryer's Loose Leaf Cook Book, 1923; The Bible Story Book for Boys and Girls, 1924; Young American Civic Readers (with others), 1938. Home: 9 Alexander Av., Merchantville, N.J.

FRYLING, George Richard, manufacturer; b. St. Marys, Pa., Mar. 24, 1901; s. George Percy and Emma Elisabeth (Spratt) F.; student Mercersburg (Pa.) Acad., 1917-18, Rensselaer Poly. Inst., Troy, N.Y., 1918-23; m. Florence K. McCauley, Sept. 22, 1927; children—Florence Elizabeth, George Percy II, Richard McCauley, Mary Patricia. Salesman Speer Carbon Co., St. Marys, Pa., 1923-26; v.p. and gen. mgr. Elk Graphite Milling Co., St. Marys, 1926-32; v.p. Erie (Pa.) Resistor Corpn. since 1928; v.p. Erie Resistor of Can.; financial dir. Erie Resistor, Ltd., London, Eng. Mem. Theta Chi. Republican. Episcopalian. Club: Kahkwa Country (Erie, Pa.). Home: 406 Seminole Drive. Office: 644 W. 12th St., Erie, Pa.

FUCHS, Walter, chemist, prof. fuel technology; b. Vienna, Austria, June 8, 1891; s. Adolf and Anna (Fischer) F.; came to U.S., 1934, naturalized citizen, 1939; Ph.D., Vienna Univ., 1914; m. Frieda Weinstock, Mar. 16, 1936. Engaged in profession as chemist since 1919; privat dozent, Technische Hochschule, Brunn, Czechoslovakia, 1919-26; head dept. Kaiser Wilhelm Inst. for Coal Research, Mulheim-Ruhr, 1927-31; prof. industrial chemistry, Aachen Univ., 1931-33; research prof. Rutgers U., New Brunswick, N.Y., 1934-35; prof. fuel technology, Pa. State Coll. since 1935. Served as lt. Austrian Army, 1914-18. Mem. Am. Inst. Mining Engrs., Am. Chem. Soc., Tech. Assn. Paper and Pulp Industry, Am. Gas Assn., Sigma Xi. Home: 440 W. Foster Av., State College, Pa.

FUCHS, William W., chem. engring.; b. Stamford, Conn., Sept. 2, 1895; s. M. Joseph and Margaret (Eiden) F.; B.S., in Chemistry, Worcester Poly. Inst. 1918; grad. study, Cooper Union, 1930-32; m. Anna M. C. Weissenborn, Oct. 25, 1922; 1 son, William Christian. Employed as analyt. chemist on high explosives, U.S. Ammonium Nitrate Plant, Perryville, Md., 1918-19; plant chemist, John Carle & Sons, Stamford, Conn., 1919; analytical chemist, Mallinckrodt Chem. Works, St. Louis, Mo., 1919-20, in charge analyt. lab., same co., Jersey City, N.J., 1920-22. head of mfg. dept. since 1922. Mem. Am. Chem. Soc., Am. Inst. Chem. Engrs. Lutheran. Home: 79 Wilson St., Brooklyn, N.Y. Office: 223 West Side Av., Jersey City, N.J.

FUELLHART, William Clarke, sales mgr.; b. Endeavor, Pa., June 10, 1903; s. William O. and Florence R. (Clarke) F.; student Kiski Prep. Sch. and Princeton U.; m. Katharine M. Marsh, June 16, 1928; children—William Clarke, Joseph Marsh, James Ingraham, David Clark. Redwood sales mgr.˙ Wheeler & Dusenbury, Endeavor, Pa., since 1930; v.p., and dir. G. A. Stiles Coal Co., Endeavor, Pa., since Dec. 1936; pres. and dir. Oil City (Pa.) Sand and Gravel Co. since Jan. 1937, Seneca Lumber & Supply Co., Warren, Pa., since orgn., Aug. 1937; dir. Mayburg (Pa.) Supply Co., Hickory Bridge Co. (Endeavor), Forest County Nat. Bank (Tionesta). Dir. Tidioute (Pa.) Sch. Bd. Presbyn. (trustee Tidioute Ch.) Mason. Clubs: Titusville (Pa.) Country; Cannon (Princeton, N.J.). Home: 9 Scott St., Tidioute, Pa. Office: Care Wheeler & Dusenbury, Endeavor, Pa.

FUHLBRUEGGE, Edward; prof. of history and dir. div. of social sciences, U. of Newark. Address: Newark, N.J.

FULD, Leonhard Felix, lawyer; b. New York, Aug. 12, 1883; s. Bernhard and Helene (Schwab) F.; A.B., Columbia, 1903, A.M., 1904, LL.B., 1905, LL.M., 1906, Ph.D., 1909; Dipl. (hon.) Am. Acad. Phys. Edn., 1913; unmarried. In practice since 1905. Editor for Carnegie Instn., Washington, of Sabin's Dictionary Am. Bibliography, 1905-07; examiner for Municipal Civ. Service Commn., New York, 1907-14, asst. chief examiner 1914-19; expert U.S. Bur. Edn., 1915-19; examiner, civilian personnel, U.S. War Dept., 1917-19; editor of "Corpus Jurist," 1919-21; ednl. dir. Henry L. Doherty & Co., 1919-23; now dir. Medical Center, Jersey City, N.J. Mem. Phi Beta Kappa, Civil Service Reform Assn. Author: Police Administration, 1909; Kings College Alumni, 1911; Service Instruction (bull.), 1915; Opportunities in Civil Service, 1917; Securities Salesmanship, 1919; Pulse of Organization, 1920; Thrift Encouragement, 1921; Student Nurses Health Record Book, 1938. Home: 8 Baldwin Av. Office: Medical Center, Jersey City, N.J.

FULLER, Caroline Macomber, novelist; b. Bangor, Me., Sept. 10, 1873; d. Henry D. and Julia (Muzzy) F.; B.Litt., Smith Coll., 1895; unmarried. Author: Across the Campus, 1899; The Old Songs (play) 1903; The Alley Cat's Kitten, 1904; The Flight of Puss Pandora, 1906; Brunhilde's Paying Guest (novel), 1907; The Bramble Bush (novel), 1911; Kitten Whiskers, 1927. Contbr. of song-poems to The Magic of Song, 1934, The World of Music, 1936; contbr. "Her Christmas Gift" to Christmas Plays for Women, 1936; contbr. poems to mags. Home: Lakewood, N.J.

FULLER, Earl William, physician; b. Utica, N.Y., July 3, 1885; s. Earl D. and Mary Louise (Heath) F.; M.D., Albany Med. Coll., Albany, N.Y., 1908; m. Lilian Anna Elwood, Nov. 26, 1914; 1 dau., Lilian Louise. Interne Albany Hosp., Albany, N. Y., 1908-09; in pvt. practice of medicine at Utica, N.Y., 1909-10; physician, Rome State Sch., Rome, N.Y., 1910-21; psychiatrist, N.Y. State Commn. for Feebleminded, 1921-24; supt. Pennhurst State Sch., Pennhurst, Pa., 1924-28; dir. Northern N.J. Mental Hygiene Clinics, N.J. State Hosp., Greystone Park, N.J., since 1929. Mem. A.M.A., Am. Psychiatric Assn., Am. Assn. on Mental Deficiency, Assn. for Research in Nervous and Mental Diseases, Nat. Com. for Mental Hygiene, N.Y. Soc. for Clin. Psychiatry, Am. Mus. Natural History. Presbyn. Mason. Elk. Home: 8 Mill Rd., Morris Plains, N.J.

FULLER, Edward, newspaper man; b. Syracuse, N.Y., June 30, 1860; s. George and Mary (Griffiths) F.; A.B., Harvard, 1882; m. Anne Devens Robinson, July 3, 1885. Editorial writer, Boston Advertiser, 1883-85; dramatic critic Boston Post, 1885-91; editorial writer and lit. editor, 1891-1906; leading editorial writer in charge of editorial page, 1906-14. Providence Journal; editorial writer on Phila. Public Ledger, 1914-19; asso. editor, Phila. Inquirer, 1919-36, retired in 1936. Author: Fellow Travelers, 1886; The Dramatic Year, 1888; The Complaining Millions of Men, 1893; John Malcolm, 1902. Plays: Fetters; The Invaders; The Price of Silence. Contbr. to mags. Home: 318 S. 10th St., Philadelphia, Pa.*

FULLER, Edward Laton, pres. international Salt Co.; b. Scranton, Pa., Nov. 23, 1904; s. Mortimer Bartine and Kathryn I. (Steell) F.; student Lawrenceville (N.J.) Sch., 1920-25, Princeton, 1925-27; m. Laura Rice Green, Aug. 28, 1929; children—Kathryn Emelene, Susanne Steell, Edward Laton III. With Internat. Salt Co. since 1927, v.p., 1929-31, pres. since 1931; pres. Avery Salt Co., Genesee & Wyoming R.R. Co., Empire Limestone Company, Detroit Rock Salt Co., Retsof Mining Co.; dir. First Nat. Bank, Scranton Lackawanna Trust Co., Scranton Life Ins. Co., Sprague Henwood Co. Republican. Presbyn. (trustee Westminster Ch.). Clubs: Kiwanis, Abington, Hills Hunt, Scranton Country (Scranton); Union League, Princeton (New York); Cap and Gown (Princeton); Waverly Country (Waverly, Pa.). Home: Dalton, Pa. Office: Scranton, Pa.

FULLER, Merton Otis, asso. prof.; b. Belleville, N.Y., Apr. 13, 1885; s. Fred and Melva (Tanner) F.; C.E., Syracuse U., 1910; M.S., Lehigh U., 1933; m. Ethel Osborn, Aug. 9, 1911. Asst. to P. C. Nugent on design and construction of Hydraulic Lab., Syracuse U., 1910; asst. in civil engring., Purdue U., 1910-12; instr. civil engring., Lehigh U., 1912-17, asst. prof., 1917-22, asso. prof. since 1922; employed by various businesses and governmental interests for several summers. Mem. Am. Soc. C.E. (sec. Lehigh Sect.), Soc. for Promotion Engring. Edn., Lambda Chi Alpha. Republican. Presbyterian. Club: Engineers of Lehigh Valley (sec.). Wrote numerous articles on engring. subjects. Home: 1340 Madison Av., Bethlehem, Pa.

FULLER, Ralph Briggs, cartoonist and artist; b. Capac, Mich., Mar. 9, 1890; s. Arthur E. and Louise (Briggs) F.; grad. high sch., Richmond, Mich., 1908; ed. Chicago Acad. Fine Arts; m. Alexa Baillie, Dec. 31, 1914; children—Robert Arthur, Elizabeth Alexa. Has followed profession as cartoonist since 1906; began selling drawings to mags. while in high sch.; mem. of art staff Chicago Daily News, 1909-11; free lance since 1919; has exhibited water colors, N.Y. Water Color Club, Am. Water Color Soc., Pa. Acad. Fine Arts, Salmagundi Club; drawings have appeared in all leading mags. of nat. circulation including Curtis Publs.; now doing daily comic strip, "Oaky Doaks" for Asso. Press. Republican. Presbyn. Home: 170 Ames Av., Leonia, N.J.

FULLER, Walter Deane, publishing; b. Corning, Ia., June 5, 1882; s. Walter and Nellie Elizabeth (Deane) F.; ed. Norwich (Conn.) Acad., and tech. evening and corr. schs.; m. Mae Schaeffer, Nov. 6, 1931; children by previous marriage—Elizabeth, Jane, Walter. Bank clerk, 1899; salesman for Butterick Pub. Co., 1904-05; office mgr. Crowell Pub. Co., 1906, S.S. McClure Co., 1906-08; with Curtis Pub. Co. since 1908, advancing through various positions to pres., 1934; dir. First Nat. Bank (Phila.), Castanea Paper Co. (New York); trustee Penn Mut. Ins. Co. Chmn. Planning Commn., Lower Merion Twp., Montgomery Co., Pa.; pres. Penn Valley Assn.; dir. Nat. Mfrs. Assn. Mem. Am. Soc. Mech. Engrs. Republican. Episcopalian. Mason. Clubs: Union League, Bala Golf (Phila.); Poor Richard; Seaside Yacht (N.J.). Home: Penn Valley, Pa. Address: Curtis Publishing Co., Philadelphia, Pa.

FULMER, Clarence A., educator; b. Blooming Glen, Pa., Nov. 28, 1896; s. John M. and Mary J. (Anglemoyer) F.; A.B., Goshen (Ind.) Coll., 1922; M.A., U. of Pa., 1927; student extension courses, Columbia U., 1932; m. Mary Eunice Guth, June, 1925; 1 son, Richard James. Teacher, Hilltown Twp., Bucks Co., Pa., 1915-19; vice-prin., Collegeville (Pa.) High Sch., 1922-25; mem. history dept., Wilmington (Del.) High Sch., 1925-32, dean of boys, 1932-35, prin. since 1935. Mem. Del. State Edn. Assn. (pres. 1939), Social Service Club of Wilmington (v.p. 1939). Methodist. Club: Kiwanis (Wilmington, Del.). Home: 514 W. 25th St. Office: Delaware Av. and Monroe St., Wilmington, Del.

FULPER, William Hill, Jr., real estate; b. Flemington, N.J., Apr. 6, 1909; s. William Hill and Marietta (Pearce) F.; ed. Gilman Sch., Baltimore, 1923-26. Peace Inst., New York, 1926-27, Hun School of Princeton, 1927-29, Princeton U., 1929-31; m. Agnes Foran Shields, Apr. 22, 1936; 1 dau., Agnes Shields. With Bell Telephone Co., 1931; later sec. treas. Fulper Pottery Co., now pres. William H. Fulper, Inc., real estate brokers; pres. Allied Realty Appraisal Co. Mem. Trenton-Mercer Bd. of Realtors, Nat. Real Estate Bd.; jr. mem. Am. Inst. Real Estate Appraisers. Republican. Protestant. Clubs: Trenton; Princeton (New York). Home: Washington Crossing, Pa. Office: 1 W. State St., Trenton, N.J.

FULTON, Chester Alan, pres. Southern Phosphate Corpn.; b. Brooklyn, N.Y., Dec. 18, 1883; s. Charles Alexander and Anne (McGuiness) F.; grad. Yonkers (N.Y.) High Sch., 1902; E.M., Columbia U. Sch. of Mines, 1906; m. Ethel B. Pagan, Jan. 20, 1909; children—John Charles, Bette. Began as assayer Standard Smelting Co., Rapid City, S.D., 1906; shift boss in cyanide plant, Guanajuato, Mexico, 1907; mine supt. Guanajuato M. & M. Co., 1908-12; engring. work, Mexico, Central America, U.S., 1912-14; supt. Lo. Increible Mine, Venezuela, 1914-16; mineral exploration, Cuba, 1916-18; mgr. Davison Sulphur Co., Cuba, 1918-21; cons. engr. Davison Chem. Co., Baltimore, 1921-28; pres. and dir. Southern Phosphate Corpn., Baltimore, since 1929; dir. Davison Chem. Corpn. Dir. Am. Inst. Mining and Metall. Engrs.; mem. Theta Delta Chi. Independent Democrat. Episcopalian. Mason. Clubs: Maryland, Baltimore Country, Merchants, Cheasapeake (Baltimore); Mining, Chemists, Columbia University (New York City). Home: 302 Somerset Road. Office: 3106 Baltimore Trust Bldg., Baltimore, Md.

FULTON, Clarence Edward, ceramic engr.; b. New Brunswick, N.J., Jan. 22, 1889; s. George E. and Mary Elizabeth (Hall) F.; B.Sc., Rutgers U., New Brunswick, N.J., 1911; ceramic fellow, U. of Ill., Urbana, Ill., 1911-12; m. Minnie Hazel Wilmurt, Dec. 30, 1914; children—Ruth Augusta, Theodore Ramsay. Employed as research worker in Research Dept., Pittsburgh Plate Glass Co., Creighton, Pa., 1912-16, chief ceramic engr. since 1916, in gen. charge of refractory development and uses; granted several patents covering new methods of making clay pots used in melting glass; pres. Allegheny Gasoline & Oil Co., Inc. Dir. and trustee Tarentum Y.M.C.A.; pres. bd. trustees First Presbyn. Ch. Fellow Am. Ceramic Soc.; mem. Inst. Ceramic Engrs., Am. Soc. For Testing Materials, Kappa Sigma. Republican. Presbyterian. Clubs: Kiwanis (past pres.), Brackenridge Heights Country (Tarentum, Pa.). Home: 1024 Carlisle St., Tarentum, Pa. Office: Pittsburgh Plate Glass Co., Creighton, Pa.

FULTON, Dorothy, artist and teacher; b. Uniontown, Pa.; d. Elwood Donaldson and Lucy (Ulery) F.; ed. Beechwood Sch., Jenkintown, Pa., 1914-16 Pa. Acad. Fine Arts, 1917-22, U. of Southern Calif., summer 1928, U. of Calif., Los Angeles Branch, 1928; B.F.A., U. of Pa., 1936. Has followed profession as artist since 1922; teacher of art, Swarthmore Prep. Sch. for Boys, 1922-24; teacher of art and other subjects, jr. high sch. Fort Meyers, Fla., 1924-26; Teacher of Art Memorial Jr. H. S. Tampa, Fla., 1927-28; teacher art, evening high sch., Los Angeles, 1928-30, Immaculate Heart Coll., Los Angeles, 1929-30; head of Design Dept. Washburn Coll., Topeka, Kan., 1930-33; head of art dept. Linden Hall Jr. Coll., Lititz, Pa., since 1936; exhibited paintings in professional exhibits since 1923, in all important cities; represented permanently by oil portrait in Mulvane Art Mus., Topeka, Kan.; awarded first hon. mention, Tampa Art Inst., 1927; several one-man exhbns. in important galleries. Mem. Fellowship Pa. Acad. of Fine Arts, Lancaster Art Assn. Presbyn. Home: Bokeelia, Fla. Office: Linden Hall, Lititz, Pa.

FULTON, James Grove, lawyer; b. Pittsburgh, Pa., Mar. 1, 1903; s. James Ernest and Emilie Blake (Fetterman) F.; A.B., Pa. State Coll., 1924; LL.B., Harvard, 1927; unmarried. Admitted to Pa. bar, 1928. and since practiced in Pittsburgh; asso. with firm Alter, Wright & Barron; dir., vice-pres. and sec. Brubaker Paper Company since 1928. Sec. and mem. exec. board Pittsburgh Playhouse. Chmn. Dormont Borough Rep. com. since 1935; commr. Young Republicans of Allegheny Co., 1936, 37, 38; nominated unanimously for Rep. nomination senator, 45th district, Pa., 1939. Mem. Phi Delta Theta. Republican. United Presbyterian. Clubs: Duquesne, Metropolitan, St. Clair Country (sec. 1933-36, pres. 1936), Harvard of Western Pa., (sec. 1935-38; v.p. 1939), Harvard-Yale-Princeton (dir. 1936-37; Pittsburgh, Pa.). Home: 2850 Espy Av. Office: 2200 First Nat. Bank Bldg., Pittsburgh, Pa.

FULTON, John Charles, phosphate mining; b. Guanajuato, Mexico, Nov. 2, 1909; s. Chester Alan and Ethel Belle (Pagan) F.; came to U.S., 1921, naturalized, 1930; student Lawrenceville (N.J.) Sch., 1923-25, Woodberry Forest Sch., 1925-27, Yale, 1927-29; m. Helen Evelyn Price, Mar. 13, 1936; 1 son, Frank Alan. In employ Baltimore Copeland Refrigeration, Inc., 1928-30; with Cities Service Co., 1930-31; with Shell Union Oil Co., 1931-33; with Southern Phosphate Corpn., mining and selling phosphate rock, Baltimore, since 1933, treas. since 1935; dir. Standard Wholesale Phosphate and Acid Works. Mem. bd. dirs. Keystone Automobile Club of Md. Democrat. Clubs: Racquet (treas.), Chesapeake, Merchants, Baltimore Country (Baltimore). Home: Brooklandville, Md. Office: Baltimore Trust Bldg., Baltimore, Md.

FULTON, William Stewart, surgeon; M.D., Ohio Med. U., Columbus, O., 1898. Practiced at Wheeling, W.Va., since 1898; now mem. surg. staff Ohio Valley Gen. Hosp.; cons. surgeon Wheeling Hosp.; visiting surgeon Reynolds Memorial Hosp., Glendale, W.Va.; mem. surg. staff Barnesville (Ohio) Gen. Hosp.; founder and dir. Wheeling Clinic. Mem. W.Va. Advisory Bd. of Pub. Assistance, Gov. Am. Coll. Surgeons; mem. A.M.A., W.Va. State Med. Assn. (pres.). Mason (32°, Shriner). Clubs: Wheeling Country, Cedar Rocks Country, Fort Henry (Wheeling, W.Va.); Explorers (N.Y. City). Home: Echo Point. Office: 58 16th St., Wheeling, W.Va.

FUNK, Nevin Elwell, elec. and mach. engr.; b. Bloomsburg, Pa., Nov. 4, 1883; s. Nevin Ursinus and Mary Louise (Elwell) F.; grad. Bloomsburg State Normal Sch., 1901; E.E., Lehigh U., Bethlehem, Pa., 1905; m. Mary Stevens MacNair, Dec. 27, 1906; children—Jean Ferguson, Henry Elwell. Apprentice Westinghouse Electric & Mfg. Co., East Pittsburgh, 1905-06; subforeman N.Y. Central R.R., Berwick, July-Sept. 1906; asst. prof. elec. machine design and mathematics and charge lab., Ga. Sch. Tech., Atlanta, 1906-07; sales mgr. Sterling Switchboard Co., Camden, N.J., 1912-13; with Phila. Electric Co. since 1907 (except 1912-14) as asst. foreman station elec. constrn. dept., 1907-09, asst. supt. Schuylkill Sta., 1909-12, asst. engr. transmission and distribution dept., 1914, combustion engr. Schuylkill Stations 1 and 2, 1914-15, asst. to operating engr., 1915-17, supt. Schuylkill Sta., Feb.-Aug. 1917, asst. operating engr., 1917-18, operating engr., 1918-26, asst. chief engr., 1926-28, chief engr., Feb.-June 1928, asst. gen. mgr., 1928-29, v.p. in charge engring. since Aug. 28, 1929; v.p. and dir. Deepwater Light and Power Co., Susquehanna Electric Co., Phila. Electric Power Co., Phila. Hydro-Electric Co., Phila. Steam Co., Susquehanna Power Co., v.p. Electric Realty Corpn., Susquehanna Utilities Co. Mem. Phila. Bd. of Trade, U.S. Chamber of Commerce, Pa. Chamber of Commerce, Phila. Chamber of Commerce (mem. regional and city planning com.). Mem. Am. Soc. M.E., Am. Inst. Elec. Engrs., Assn. of Edison Illuminating Cos., Edison Electric Inst., Kappa Sigma, Sigma Xi. Awarded bronze medal, Internat. Jury of Awards, Sesqui-Centennial, 1926. Republican. Clubs: Engineers (past pres.; mem. bd. dirs.), Union League, University, Phila. Country, Rotary, Lehigh University (Phila.). Home: 1520 Spruce St. Office: 1000 Chestnut St., Philadelphia, Pa.

FUNK, Wilfred John, publisher; b. Brooklyn, Mar. 20, 1883; s. Isaac Kauffman and Helen Gertrude (Thompson) F.; Litt.B., Princeton, 1909; Litt.D., Oglethorpe U., 1932; m. Eleanor McNeal Hawkins, July 29, 1915; children—Wilfred John, Peter Van Keuren, Eleanor Joan. Connected with Funk & Wagnalls Co., pubs., since 1909, secretary, 1912, vice-pres., 1914-25, pres. since 1925; editor in chief Literary Digest, 1936-37; pres. and directing editor Your Life Magazine since 1938, Your Personality Magazine and Your Health Magazine since 1939. Independent Democrat. Episcopalian. Clubs: Princeton, Authors, Players, Illustrators (New York); Montclair Golf, Shinnecock Golf, National Golf; Meadow (Southampton, L.I.). Author: Manhattans, Bronxes and Queens (verse), 1931; Light Lines and Dears (verse), 1933; So You Think It's New (prose), 1937; It Might Be Verse (verse), 1938; When the Merry-Go-Round Breaks Down (prose), 1938. Home: 16 Erwin Park Rd., Montclair, N.J. Office: 354 4th Av., New York, N.Y.

FUNKHOUSER, Elmer Newton, slate mfr.; b. Cherry Run, W.Va., Jan. 26, 1891; s. Newton E. and Mary E. (Lowman) F.; student Shenandoah Inst., Dayton, Va., 1906-10; A.B., Otterbein Coll., Westerville, O., 1913; m. Nelle E. Spielman, Jan. 1, 1916; children—Elmer Newton, Richard Nelson, Robert Brane. Partner, with brother R. J. Funkhouser, the R. J. Funkhouser

& Co., Inc., 1928, and since v.p. and treas.; entered slate business, 1918, incorporating The Funkhouser Co., 1929, since v.p. and treas.; pres. Home Builders Subdividers & Loan Assn., Hagerstown, Md. Trustee Shenandoah Coll., Dayton, Va., Otterbein Coll., Westerville, O., and Lebanon Valley Coll., Annville, Pa.; v.p. Hagerstown Y.M.C.A. Democrat. United Brethren. Mason (Royal Arch, K.T., Shriner). Clubs: Hagerstown Rotary, Fountain Head Country (Hagerstown, Md.). Home: 603 N. Potomac St. Office: 138 W. Washington St., Hagerstown, Md.

FUREY, Francis James, clergyman, coll. pres.; b. Summit Hill, Pa., Feb. 22, 1905; s. John Francis and Anna (O'Donnell) F.; student public and parochial schools, Coaldale, Pa., 1916-20, St. Charles' Sem., Overbrook, Pa., 1920-24; Ph.D., Seminario Romano Maggiore, Rome, Italy, 1926, S.T.D., 1930. Ordained priest Roman Catholic Ch., Rome, 1930; sec. to Cardinal Dougherty, archbishop of Phila., 1930-36; pres. Immaculata Coll., Immaculata, Pa., since 1936. Vice-pres. bd. of trustees Immaculata Coll. Mem. Am. Cath. Hist. Assn., Assn. Coll. Pres. of Pa., Assn. of Am. Colls. Club: Penn Athletic (Phila.). Address: Immaculata, Pa.

FURLONG, Thomas Francis, Jr., surgeon; b. Milwaukee, Wis., Sept. 26, 1900; s. Thomas Francis and Jane (Whitcomb) F.; grad. Marquette Acad., Milwaukee, Wis., 1919; A.B., U. of Wis., Madison, Wis., 1926, M.D., 1930; M.S. in medicine, U. of Pa., Grad. Sch. of Medicine, 1934; m. Ada Frances Hardt, Jan. 30, 1932; children—Barbara Jane, Nancy Liscom. Resident physician Grad. Hosp., U. of Pa., 1930-32, chief resident physician in otorhinolaryngology, 1932-34; in practice as surgeon, specializing in ear, nose and throat, Ardmore, Pa., since 1934; head of dept. of otolaryngology, Pa. Sch. for Deaf, since 1934; asst. otolaryngologist Out-Patient Dept., Bryn Mawr Hosp., 1934-38, senior asst. attending otolaryngologist since 1938; courtesy staff of Episcopal Hosp. and Chestnut Hill Hosp., Phila.; asst. otolaryngologist to Grad. Hosp. of U. of Pa.; instr. in otorhinology, Grad. Sch. of Medicine, U. of Pa. Served as ambulance driver Am. Field Service, U.S. Army, 1918. Diplomate Am. Bd. Otolaryngology; fellow Am. Acad. Ophthalmology and Otolaryngology, A.M.A.; mem. Pa. State Med. Soc., Phila. Co. Med. Soc., Main Line Branch of Montgomery Co. Med. Soc., Phila. Laryngol. Soc., Coll. of Physicians of Phila., Pa. Soc. of Sons of the Revolution, Chi Psi, Nu Sigma Nu. Republican. Roman Catholic. Club: Merion Cricket and Golf (Haverford, Pa.). Home: 156 Shawnee Rd., Merion Golf Manor. Office: Times Medical Bldg., Ardmore, Pa.

FURMAN, Franklin De Ronde, educator; b. Ridgely, Md., Aug. 30, 1870; s. John Lewis and Adelia Catherine (De Ronde) F.; grad. Hasbrouck Inst., Jersey City, 1888; M.E. Stevens Inst. Tech., Hoboken, N.J., 1893; m. Minnie Adelaide Thompson, Nov. 3, 1894. Successively instr., asst. prof. and prof. mechanism and machine design and dean for junior class, Stevens Institute of Technology, since 1893, dean of coll. since 1928. Conducted course for Steam Engring. Sch., U.S. Navy, during World War. Trustee Stevens-Hoboken Acad. since 1929. Mem. Am. Soc. Mech. Engrs., Newcomen Society, Society Promotion Engineering Education; fellow A.A.A.S. (chmn nat. com. on standardization of drawings and drafting room practice). Editor: Stevens Institute Indicator, 1897-1902. Author: Valves and Valve Gears for Steam Engines, 1903, Steam Turbines added, 1911; History of the Stevens Family of Engineers; History of Stevens Institute of Technology; Biographies of Alumni of Stevens Institute, 1905; Career of Graduates in Mechanical Engineering, 1908; Cams for Automatic Machinery, 1911; Questions and Problems in Machine Design, 1912; Valves and Valve Gears for Gas, Gasoline and Oil Engines, 1915; Questions in Engineering Drawing, 1919; Cams, Elementary and Advanced, 1921; Planetary Gearing, 1924; Mechanism, 1929; also ednl. notes on mech. subjects and tech. articles to engring. magazines. Home: Castle Point, Hoboken, N.J.

FURMAN, N(athaniel) Howell, prof. of chemistry; b. Lawrenceville, N.J., June 22, 1892; s. Nathaniel Higgins and Caroline (Howell) F.; B.S., Princeton, 1913, A.M., 1915, Ph.D., 1917; m. Hannah S(covel) Hendrickson, Aug. 23, 1919; children—Carolyn Louise, Richard Howell. Instr. in chemistry, Stanford U., 1917-19; with Princeton U. since 1919, as asst. prof. of chemistry, 1919-27, asso. prof., 1927-37, prof. of chemistry since 1937. Chmn. J. T. Baker Fellowship award in analytical chemistry since 1930. Served as civilian chemist U.S. Navy, Phila., 3 months, 1916; Chem. Warfare Service, U.S. Army, 3 months at research, Am. Univ., Washington, D.C., 1918. Fellow Am. Inst. Chemists, A.A.A.S.; mem. Am. Chem. Soc. (chmn. phys. and inorganic chemistry div. 1935), Electrochem. Soc., Am. Assn. Univ. Profs., Phi Beta Kappa, Sigma Chi. Charlotte Elizabeth Procter fellow, 1916. Republican. Presbyterian. Club: Cloister Inn (Princeton). Author: Elementary Quantitative Analysis (with H. H. Willard), 1935. Translator: Indicators, 1926; Volumetric Analysis, 1928; Potentiometric Titrations (with I. M. Kolthoff), 1931. Contbr. to Taylor's Physical Chemistry; Annual Survey of American Chemistry; Newer Volumetric Methods. Editor-in-chief Scott's Standard Methods of Chemical Analysis, 2 vols., 1939. Asso. editor of Industrial Engring. Chem. Analytical Edition. Contbr. about 50 papers to scientific jours. Address: Princeton University, Princeton, N.J.

FURMAN, Roy E., gen. contractor; b. Davistown, Pa., Apr. 6, 1901; s. James L. and Luna B. (Evans) F.; grad. Mt. Morris High Sch.; A.B., Waynesburg Coll., 1922; m. Mary Helen Ross, Oct. 6, 1922; 1 dau., Mary L. Asst. mathematics instr., sr. year, Waynesburg Coll.; gen. contractor since 1924. Dem. State committeeman, 1928-32. Mem. Pa. Ho. of Reps. since 1932; chmn. Highway Com., 1935; acting majority floor leader, 1935; elected speaker spl. session, May 1936, succeeding late Wilson C. Sarig, re-elected 1937. Address: Waynesburg, Pa.

FURST, George, lawyer; b. New York, N.Y., May 11, 1891; s. Samuel and Mary (Flaumenhaft) F.; LL.B., N.J. Law Sch., Newark, 1910; LL.M., N.Y. Univ. Law Sch., 1911; unmarried. Admitted to N.J. bar as atty., 1912, as counsellor, 1915; engaged in gen. practice of law at Newark since 1912; mem. firm Furst & Furst since 1915. Chmn. social service dept. Beth Israel Hosp.; vice-pres. Temple B'nai Abraham; pres. Social Center of B'nai Abraham. Trustee Beth Israel Hosp., Newark, Temple B'nai Abraham of Newark. Mem. Am., Federal, N.J. State, Essex Co. and N.Y. County bar assns., Am. Judicature Soc., Commercial Law League of America. Jewish religion. Clubs: Jumping Brook Country (vice-pres.), Down Town, Progress (Newark). Home: 52 Baldwin Av. Office: 60 Park Pl., Newark, N.J.

FUSSELL, Robert, banker; b. Media, Pa., Jan. 21, 1875; s. Henry Moore and May (Townsend) F.; grad. Friends Central Sch., Phila., 1893; unmarried. Clerk Strawbridge & Clothier, 1895-96; with First Nat. Bank of Media since 1896, as clerk 1896-1907, cashier, 1907-25, pres. since 1925; pres. Second Media Loan & Savings Assn.; dir. Delaware-Montgomery Counties Co. for Guaranteeing Mortgages. V.p. Delaware Co. Chamber of Commerce; treas. Sch. Dist. of Media; v.p. Elwyn Training Sch.; dir. Media Free Library; dir. Community Center (welfare). Republican. Soc. of Friends. Clubs: Union League (Phila.); Chester (Chester, Pa.); Media, Media Swimming and Rowing (Media, Pa.). Home: 24 E. Jefferson St. Office: First Nat. Bank, Media, Pa.

G

GABBERT, Mont Robertson, prof. philosophy; b. Casey Creek, Ky., Aug. 29, 1889; s. Zachary Taylor and Agatha (Robertson) G.; prep. edn., Lindsay Wilson Training Sch., Columbia, Ky.; A.B., Transylvania Coll., Lexington, Ky., 1915, A.M., 1916; Ph.D., U. of Chicago, 1921; m. Myra Anna Love, Sept. 7, 1921; 1 dau., Eleanor Frances (dec.). Ordained ministry Disciples of Christ Ch., 1911; pastor Junction City (Ky.) Christian Ch., 1913-16; served with Y.M.C.A. Chicago, July 1917-Sept. 1918; prof. psychology and edn., Hiram (O.) Coll., 1918-20; asst. prof. philosophy, U. of Pittsburgh, 1921-24, prof. since 1924, head of dept. since 1926. Mem. Am. Philos. Assn., Southern Assn., Philosophy and Psychology, British Inst. of Philosophy, A.A.A.S., Am. Econ. Assn., Pa. Acad. Science, Am. Assn. Univ. Profs. (pres. 1933-35), Sigma Xi. Mason. Clubs: Faculty (pres. 1933—), Quiz, Philosophy. Contbr. chapter to Religion and the Modern Mind, 1929. Home: 520 S. Murtland Av., Pittsburgh, Pa.

GABEL, Arthur Bertram, educator; b. Mt. Joy, Pa., Apr. 26, 1890; s. Clayton Grant and Annie Augusta (Hoffer) G.; A.B., Franklin & Marshall Coll., Lancaster, Pa., 1910; student Worcester (Mass.) Poly. Inst., 1912-13; M.A., Columbia U., 1917; spl. cours École Supérieure d'Électricité and Sorbonne, Paris, 1919; D.D.S., U. of Pa. Dental Sch., 1925; m. Lenore Dorsey, Sept. 9, 1923; 1 dau., Ann Dorsey (dec.). Began as teacher science; teacher physics, chemistry and biology, Alfred (N.Y.) Acad., 1910-11, physics, chemistry and mathematics, Princeton Prep. Sch., 1914-16; asst. in physics, Columbia U., 1916-17; sales-engr. D. Lupton's Sons Co., 1919-21; Edwin T. Darby prof. of operative dentistry, U. of Pa. Dental Sch., since 1933. Served as 1st lt. Signal Corps, 2 yrs., World War (19 mos. in France). Mem. A.A.A.S., Am. Dental Assn., Phila. Co. Med. Assn., Psi Omega, Eta Sigma Sigma, Omicron Kappa Upsilon (hon.). Mason (32°). Home: 228 Upland Road, Merion, Pa.

GABRIELSON, Guy George, lawyer; b. Sioux Rapids, Ia., May 22, 1891; s. Frank August and Ida (Jansen) G.; B.A., U. of Ia., 1914; LL.B., Harvard Law Sch., 1917; LL.D., Upsala Coll., 1932; m. Cora M. Speer, Feb. 5, 1918; children—Guy George, Nance Lou. Admitted to N.J. bar, 1919, and since in private practice, N.J.; also practice in N.Y. City since 1931; pres. and dir. Sall Mountain Co., Nicolet Asbestos Mines, Ltd.; dir. Hightstown Rug. Co., Stumpp & Walter Co. Mem. N.J. Ho. of Assembly, 1926-30, majority leader, 1928, speaker, 1929. Served as 2d lt., Air Service, Aircraft Production, during World War. Pres. and trustee Carteret Sch. for Boys. Mem. N.J. State Bar Assn., N.Y. County Lawyers Assn., Am. Legion, S.A.R. Republican. Methodist. Mason. Clubs: Bankers, Harvard (New York); Essex (Newark); Somerset Hills Country (Bernardsville). Home: Bernardsville, N.J. Office: 70 Pine St., New York, N.Y.

GADSDEN, Philip Henry, pub. utility exec.; b. Charleston, S.C., Oct. 4, 1867; s. Christopher Schulz and Florida I. (Morrall) G.; student Porter Mil. Acad., Charleston, 1880-84; A.B., U. of S.C., 1888, LL.D., 1918; m. Sallie Pelzer Inglesby, Apr. 19, 1895 (died July 22, 1900); children—Philip Henry, Lavinia Inglesby (Mrs. Douglas M. Dimond); m. 2d Estelle Blanche White, June 17, 1910; children—Henry White, Margaret Eleanor, Charles Christopher. Admitted to S.C. bar, 1890, and practiced at Charleston, mem. firm Mordecai & Gadsden, 1890-1907; vice-pres. Charleston Consol. Ry. & Lighting Co., 1900-03, pres., 1903-26; v.p. Charleston Light & Water Co., 1907-17; v.p. United Gas Improvement Co. since 1919; dir. Fidelity Mut. Life Ins. Co. Mem. S.C. Ho. of Rep., 1893-98; mem. Federal Electric Rys. Commn., 1919. Chmn. war bd. Am. Electric Ry. Assn. and chmn. Nat. Com. on Pub. Utility Conditions, World War; chief Phila. Dist. Ordnance Office, War Dept. Pres. Southern Gas Association, 1922, and Eastern States Gas Conference, 1923. Mem. bd. trustees Edison Electrical Inst. (chmn. Com. of Utility Executives); mem. Am. Gas Assn., Am. Electric Ry. Assn. (pres. 1921), Am. Acad. Polit. and Social Science, U.S. Chamber Commerce (dir. 1921-29), Pa. State Chamber Commerce (dir.), Phila. Chamber Commerce (pres. 1926-35), Army Ordnance Assn. (pres. Phila. post), Kappa Alpha. Democrat. Episcopalian. Mason (Shriner), K.P. Clubs: Engineers, Midday, Rittenhouse, Philadelphia Country (Philadelphia); Congressional Country, Metropolitan (Washington); City Midday (New York). Home: 6420 Drexel Rd. Office: 1401 Arch St., Philadelphia, Pa.

GAG, Wanda, artist, author; b. New Ulm, Minn., Mar. 11, 1893; d. Anton and Lissi

(Biebl) G., studied St. Paul Art Sch., 1913-14, Minneapolis Art Sch., 1915-17, Art Students League, N.Y., 1917-18. Permanently represented at Met. Mus. of Art, New York Pub. Library, Newark Mus., Art. Inst. Chicago, Wadsworth Athenaeum, British Mus., South Kensington Mus., Bibliotheque Nationale, Paris, Kupferstich Kabinett, Berlin, Whitney Mus. of Am. Art, Boston Mus. of Fine Arts, Mus. of Fine Arts of Houston; exhibited in Am. Printmakers show, 1927-36. Awarded 1st prize Phila. Lithograph show, 1930. Mem. Am. Artists Congress, League of Am. Writers. Translator and illustrator of Tales from Grimm, 1936; Snow White and the Seven Dwarfs, 1938. Author and illustrator: Millions of Cats, 1928; Snippy and Snappy, 1931; The Funny Thing, 1929; The A.B.C. Bunny, 1933; Gone is Gone, 1935. Home: Milford, N.J.

GAGE, Albert Henry, clergyman; b. Worcester, N.Y., Aug. 8, 1878; s. Edgar Van Ess and Malissa C. (Turck) G.; A.B., Colgate, 1902, A.M., 1906, D.D., 1923, also B.D. from same college, 1936; graduate Hamilton Theological Seminary, 1905; m. Fanny Vail, author, Aug. 15, 1906; children—Ralph Vail, Carolyn Virginia. Ordained Bapt. ministry, 1905; pastor 1st Ch., St. Johnsbury, Vt., 1905-09, 1st Ch., Bridgeton, N.J., 1909-12; asst. sec. Am. Bapt. Foreign Mission Soc., Boston, 1913; pastor Garfield Park Ch., Chicago, 1913-17; dir. religious edn., Bapt. Exec. Council, Chicago, 1917-23; acting pastor North Shore Ch., Chicago, Sept. 1, 1923-May 1, 1924; pastor First Bapt. Ch., Brattleboro, Vt., Oct. 1, 1924-Sept. 1, 1927; pastor First Bapt. Ch., Scranton, Pa., Sept. 1, 1927-Nov. 1, 1929, First Bapt. Ch., Wakefield, Mass., 1929-35; pastor at large, special work for chs. and pastors, 1935-37; interim pastor Mt. Lebanon Ch., Pittsburgh, since Sept. 1937. Former mem. Exec. Com. and Com. on Ministry, Northern Baptist Conv.; sec. Ministers Council of Northern Bapt. Conv.; member Bd. of Mgrs. of Bapt. Home and Orphanage of Western Pa.; mem. bd. of dirs. Pittsburgh Bapt. Assn.; mem. com. on evangelism, Pa. Bapt. Conv. Mem. Beta Theta Pi, Phi Beta Kappa. Republican. Mason. Club: Kiwanis. Author: How to Conduct a Church Vacation School, 1921; Evangelism of Youth, 1922; Stories for Young Americans, 1923. Joint compiler of Living Hymns, 1923; (with Mrs. Gage) Stories of Jesus, 1925; A Bigger Better Sunday School, 1927; The House of Friendship, 1929; Increasing Church Attendance, 1938. Home: Brattleboro, Vt. Address: Mt. Lebanon Baptist Church, Pittsburgh, Pa.

GAGE, Hy (Harry), cartoonist and writer; b. Hartford, Conn., Apr. 13, 1878; s. Frank and Nancy (Hare) G.; B.Sc., U. of Neb., Lincoln, Neb., 1898; student Pratt Inst. of Art, Brooklyn, N.Y., 1898-99, Acad. of Fine Arts, Phila.; m. Florence Whiteside, Apr. 14, 1903. Began as cartoonist, Phila. Press, 1899; cartoonist, Phila. North American, Phila. Bulletin, Country Gentleman; free lance cartoonist, contbr. Saturday Evening Post, New Yorker, Colliers, Magazine of Wall Street (regularly for 13 yrs.) and others; painter mag. covers in oil and water colors; worked on murals under Wm. Tefft Schwarz. Contbr. and illustrator more than 100 short stories mostly on outdoor life. Home: 2103 Chestnut St., Philadelphia, Pa.

GAGEBY, Frank Augustus, clergyman; b. Marion, Ia., Jan. 26, 1878; s. James Allen and Mary (Cooper) G.; grad. Tama (Ia.) High Sch.; A.B., Western Coll. (now Coe Coll.), Ia., 1903; student McCormick Theol. Sem., 1903-06; D.D., Parsons Coll., Fairfield, Ia.; m. Carolyn Baldwin, Jan. 7, 1900; 1 son, Paul (M.D.). Ordained to ministry of Presbyterian Ch., May 1906; pastor Bethel Presbyn. Ch., West Union, Ia. 1906-08, Union Presbyn. Ch., Fort Madison, Ia., 1908-14, First Presbyn. Ch., Washington, Ia., 1914-18, St. Paul's Union Ch., Chicago, 1918-27, Austin Manor Presbyn. Ch., Chicago, 1927-28; gen. sec. Synod of Ill., 1928-32; pastor First Presbyn. Ch., Crafton, Pa., since 1932. Home: 27 N. Emily St., Crafton, Pa.

GAINES, Joseph Holt, ex-congressman; b. D.C., Sept. 3, 1864; s. Theophilus and Ariadne (Stockton) G.; taken by parents to Fayette Co., W.Va., 1867; prep. edn. W.Va. U.; A.B., Princeton, 1886; m. Marjorie Lewis Gentry, Nov. 23, 1898. Admitted to bar, 1887; U.S. dist. atty. for W.Va., 1897-1901; mem. 57th to 61st Congresses (1901-11), 3d W.Va. Dist.; Republican. Defeated for 62d Congress; asst. to gen. counsel U.S. Shipping Bd., 1921-22. Chmn. W.Va. Rep. State Com., 1916; del. at large to Rep. Nat. Conv., Chicago, 1920. Home: 1116 Kanawha St., Charleston, W.Va.

GAINES, Ludwell Ebersole, lawyer; b. Fayetteville, W.Va., Mar. 9, 1893; s. Ludwell Graham and Martha (Ebersole) G.; grad. Lawrenceville (N.J.) Sch., 1912; Litt.B., Princeton U., 1916; m. Betty Chilton, Jan. 31, 1925; children—Martha, Ludwell Ebersole, George Chilton, Ludwell Graham, Stanley Noyes. Admitted to practice before state courts of W.Va., Federal courts of W.Va., U.S. Bd. of Tax Appeals, Interstate Commerce Commn. and Supreme Court of U.S.; pres., dir. and chmn. exec. com. The New River Co.; v.p. and dir. Amherst Coal Co., Amherst Fuel Co., Logan County Coal Corpn., Buffalo Creek Coal & Coke Co., Star Coal & Coke Co. Mayor of Fayetteville, 7 yrs. Served as officer in U.S. Naval Flying Corps, 1917-19. Mem. grad. council Lawrenceville Sch. Mem. Am. Bar Assn., W.Va. Bar Assn., Fayette Co. Bar Assn., University Cottage Club. Republican. Presbyn. Club: Rotary (hon.). Address: Fayetteville, W.Va.

GALANTI, Marinus Charles, high sch. prin.; b. Lodi, N.J., Oct. 25, 1903; s. Paul and Rosalie (Martinico) G.; Ph.B., Brown Univ., Providence, R.I., 1927; A.M., Teachers Coll. of Columbia U., 1933; m. Silvia Guarino, Feb. 17, 1927; children—Silvia, Frances, Garry. Engaged in teaching, Columbus Sch., Lodi, N.J., 1927-31; vice prin. high sch., Teaneck, N.J., 1931-34; prin. Lodi High Sch., Lodi, N.J., since 1934. Mem. Am. Assn. Sch. Adminstrs., Secondary Schs. Prins. Assn., N.J. State Teachers Assn., Bergen Co. Schoolmen's Club, Kappa Alpha Phi. Episcopalian. Mason. Club: Rotary of Lodi. Home: Grove St., Lodi, N.J.

GALBALLY, Edward J(oseph), publisher; b. Carlisle, Eng., Sept. 17, 1872; s. Thomas and Jane Ann (McGrath) G.; student St. Edmund's Coll., Douai, France, 1884-87; B.A., St. Cuthbert's Coll., Ushaw, Durham, Eng., 1893; (hon.) LL.D., St. Joseph's Coll., Phila., 1920; m. Anna Regina Costello, May 6, 1911; children—Thomas Aloysius, Edward Joseph, James Francis, Vincent Joseph, Joseph Edward, Mary Patricia, Philip Richard, John Joseph. Came to U.S. 1893, naturalized 1900. Began as sec. to publisher, 1893; asst. editor The Ecclesiastical Review, Phila., 1896-1903, asso. editor, 1903-04, mng. editor since 1904, publisher since 1905; owner of printing house The Dolphin Press since 1922; owner Wickersham Printing Co., Lancaster, Pa.; mem. bd. mgrs. Beneficial Saving Fund Soc., Phila. Mem. Catholic Philopatrian Inst., Marquette Soc. of N.Y., Geneal. Soc., Cath. Alumni Sodality, Am. Cath. Hist. Soc. (trustee; pres.). K.C. Home: 120 E. Cliveden Av. Office: 1722 Arch St., Philadelphia, Pa.

GALBRAITH, Wilbur F(loyd), lawyer; b. Coal Center, Pa., Aug. 12, 1891; s. Alexander W. and Oella (Bedall) G; student South Western State Normal, 1905-09, U. of N.C., 1909-10; A.B., Allegheny Coll., 1913; LL.B., U. of Pittsburgh, 1916. Admitted to Pa. bar, 1916, and since practiced in Pittsburgh; served as asst. city solicitor, water assessor and sec. to mayor. Served as private Air Service, U.S. Army, 1918. Mem. Allegheny Co., Pa. State and Am. bar assns., Sigma Alpha Epsilon. Ind. Democrat. Home: Coal Center, Pa. Office: St. Nicholas Bldg., Pittsburgh, Pa.

GALBREATH, Robert Ferguson, clergyman; educator; b. Cabot, Pa., Oct. 7, 1884; s. Henry Albert and Flora (Ferguson) G.; A.B., Westminster Coll., 1907, D.D., 1924; grad. Pittsburgh Theol. Sem., 1910; m. Eva Smiley, Sept. 9, 1909; children—Robert Ferguson, Dale Smiley, John Henry, Mary Louise, Ruth Elisabeth. Ordained United Presbyn. ministry, 1910; pastor Romeo, Colo. 1910-12, Woodlawn, Pa., 1912-15, North Side Ch., Pittsburgh, 1915-20, Bellevue (Pa.) Ch., 1920-32; pres. Westminster Coll. since 1932. Served with Y.M.C.A. at the front in France, 1918. Rotarian. Address: Westminster College, New Wilmington, Pa.

GALIARDI, Philip, owner Corrado & Galiardi Construction Co.; b. Aurano, Italy, Nov. 1, 1881; s. Rimonti and Rose (Caretti) G.; ed. common schs.; m. Rose Gagliardi, June 14, 1905; children—Loretta, Madeline, Raymond. Began in coal business, 1917; mgr. and dir. Vanderbilt Coal & Coke Co. since 1928; sec.-treas. and dir. Faywest Coal & Coke Co. (operating 3 mines) since 1935; owner Corrado & Galiardi Construction Co. since 1919. Chmn. Community Fund Campaign, 1938; pres. Connellsville Hosp. Assn. which erected $400,000 modern hosp. V.p. Connellsville Bd. of Trade; mem. Western Pa. Contractors Assn., Sons of Italy. Republican. Catholic. Club: Pleasant Valley Country. Home: 201 W. Cedar Av. Office: 802 Second Nat. Bank Bldg., Connellsville, Pa.

GALLAGER, Herbert Van Buren, banker; b. New York, N.Y., Oct. 7, 1887; s. James Young and Therese (Van Buren) G.; prep. edn., Delancey Sch., Phila., 1905-07; student Haverford (Pa.) Coll., 1911, U. of Pa., 1911-12; m. Emilie Melvin Moore, June 9, 1915. Elec. engr. and salesman with Cutter Elec. Co., 1912-13; draftsman Walker Electric Co., 1913; bond trader and partner with Reilly Brock & Co., 1913-25; partner and exec. Yarnall & Co. (banking) since 1925. Commr. Lower Merion Twp., Montgomery Co., Pa. Republican. Presbyterian. Clubs: Union League, Penn Athletic (Phila.). Home: Little Lane, Haverford, Pa. Office: 1528 Walnut St., Philadelphia, Pa.

GALLAGHER, Edward J., Jr., pres. E. J. Gallagher Realty Co.; officer or dir. many companies. Home: 3900 N. Charles St. Office: 3501-3505 Ednor Road, Baltimore, Md.

GALLAGHER, Katharine Jeanne; instr. history, Goucher Coll., 1915-17, asst. prof., 1917-19, asso. prof., 1919-20, prof. since 1920. Address: Goucher College, Baltimore, Md.

GALLAGHER, Sister Miriam, educator and writer; b. Hazleton, Pa., Aug. 9, 1886; d. Hugh and Bridget (Boner) G.; A.B., Creighton U., Omaha, Neb., 1921; A.M., U. of Notre Dame, Ind., 1927; candidate for Ph.D., Cath. Univ., Washington, D.C., 1937-39. Engaged in teaching, high schs., Pa., 1906-15, high schs., Ia., 1915-21, again in Pa., 1921-27; prof. English, Coll. Misericordia, Dallas, Pa., 1927-37, librarian, 1928-38. Mem. Nat. Council English Teachers, Writers Guild, Catholic Poetry Soc. of America, Cath. Bibliography Com. of Cath. Library Assn. Awarded Scholarship at Cath. Univ., 1937-39. Democrat. Roman Catholic. Contbr. verse and essays to leading Cath. mags.; contbr. articles to ednl. mags. Faculty adviser Litany, 1928, 1930, 1933. Home: College Misericordia, Dallas, Pa.

GALLAGHER, Ralph P., educator; b. St. Johns, Mich., Feb. 23, 1902; s. Patrick Lewis and Ida Mae (Ellis) G.; student Hill Dist. Sch., Clinton Co., Mich., 1907-15, Fowler (Mich.) High Sch., 1915-19, Harvard, summer 1929; state certificate, Mich. State Normal Coll., Ypsilanti, Mich., 1920; B.S., Teachers Coll., Columbia U., 1933, M.A., 1939; m. Natalie Elizabeth Forcheimer, of New Orleans, La., July 29, 1933; children—Patrick Ximenes, Ralph P. Science teacher, Almont (Mich.) High Sch., 1920-23; supt. of schs., Hadley, Mich., 1923-25; teacher and supervisor Elizabeth (N.J.) Schs. since 1925; summer sch. instr., Tulane U., New Orleans, La., 1930, 31, 32; instr. (parttime), Fordham U., New York, since 1934. Mem. N.E.A., Pi Kappa Delta, Alpha Tau Delta, Phi Delta Kappa. Author: Courses in Careers, 1930; The Intelligent Job Seeker's Guide Book, 1939; contbr. to Basic Units in Vocational Guidance, 1931; chmn. N.J. Secondary Sch. Teachers Assn's. com. on guidance, 1936-37, 1937-38, to publish Guidance Service Standards for Secondary Schools, 1937, A Discussion Outline in Guidance, 1938. Home: 577 N. Broad St. Office: Jefferson Annex, Elizabeth, N.J.

GALLAHER, Sarah McCune, educator; born at New Washington, Pa., June 8, 1864; d. George Washington and Elizabeth Amanda (Hallesen) Gallagher; student State Normal School, Indiana, Pa., 1883-84, 1887-88; Ph.B., Cornell

U., 1895; student Univs. of Oxford (Eng.), Sorbonne, Berlin, 1900-01; A.M., U. of Pa., 1902. Teacher in public schools of Pa., 1880-83, 1884-87; teacher, State Normal Sch., Indiana, Pa., 1888-93, 1895-96; co-prin. private school, Birmingham, Pa., 1896-1900, 1902-04; mem. editorial staff University Publ. Co., New York, 1904-07; established private boarding school for children, Ebensburg, Pa., 1907, and since then owner and prin. Mem. Pa. Assembly, 1923-25. Mem. bd. trustees Mothers' Assistance Fund, 1917-35. Mem. Am. Hist. Assn., Am. Assn. Univ. Women. Awarded Bennett fellowship in Am. History by U. of Pa., 1901. Republican. Methodist. Address: Ebensburg, Pa.

GALLO, Anthony James, lawyer; b. Montchanin, Del., Oct. 31, 1900; s. Michael and Julia (Riccio) G.; student Wilmington (Del.) High Sch., 1915-19; B.S., U. of Del., Newark, Del., 1923; LL.B., George Washington U., Washington, D.C., 1928; student Nat. U., Washington, D.C., 1928-29; unmarried. Admitted to Del. and New Castle County bar, 1929, and since in pvt. practice at Wilmington, Del. Asst. city solicitor, Wilmington, Del., 1931-33; sec. New Castle Co. (Del.) Rep. Exec. Com. since 1933. Mem. Del. Bar Assn., New Castle Co. Bar Assn., Phi Beta Gamma. Republican. Catholic. Elk (Wilmington Lodge), Siracusa Lodge (Wilmington, Del., hon. pres. since 1937). Club: Unital (Wilmington, Del.). Home: 718 Madison St. Office: 316 Industrial Trust Bldg., Wilmington, Del.

GALLOWAY, Charles William, railway official; b. Baltimore, Md., Dec. 11, 1868; s. Charles Barton and Susan Jane (Smith) G.; ed. pub. schs.; m. Margaret B. Leiritz, Nov. 10, 1890; 1 dau., Mrs. Marguerite Jane Dickey. Began as messenger telegraph dept., B.&O. R.R. Co., 1883; clk., stenographer, etc., same rd., until 1897; trainmaster Baltimore div., 1897-99, asst. supt. main line, 1st div., 1899-1901; supt. Cumberland div., 1901-03, Baltimore div., 1903-06; supt. transportation, at Baltimore, 1906-10, all with B.&O. R.R. Co.; gen. supt. transportation, same rd. and B.&O.S.W. R.R., July-Sept. 1910; gen. supt. B.&O.S.W. R.R. Co., at Cincinnati, O., 1910-12; gen. mgr. B.&O. R.R., 1912-16; v.p. and gen. mgr. B.&O.S.W. R.R. and B.&O. R.R. Western Lines, 1916-18; federal mgr. U.S. R.R. Administration, over B.&O. Western Lines, Dayton & Union R.R. and Dayton Union Ry., 1918-19, and of B.&O. Eastern Lines, Coal & Coke R.R., Morgantown & Kingwood R.R., Western Md. Ry., Cumberland Valley R.R. and Cumberland & Pa. R.R., 1919-20, and B.&O. System, S.I. Rapid Transit Ry., and Baltimore & New York, Coal & Coke, Morgantown & Kingwood, Dayton Union and Dayton & Union Railroads, Jan. 15-Mar. 1, 1920; v.p. operation and maintenance, B.&O. System, Baltimore, since 1920. Mem. Nat. Econ. League. Clubs Maryland Traffic, Engineers, Baltimore Country, Rolling Road Golf (Baltimore); Queen City (Cincinnati); Duquesne (Pittsburgh); Saddle and Sirloin (Chicago); Railroad Machinery, New York Railroad, Railway Guild (New York). Home: Old Frederick Rd. and Charing Cross. Office: B.&O. R.R. Co., Baltimore, Md.

GALLUP, George Horace, public opinion statistician; b. in Jefferson, Iowa, November 18, 1901; s. of George Henry and Nettie (Davenport) Gallup; B.A., State University of Iowa, Iowa City, 1923, M.A., 1925, Ph.D., 1928; m. Ophelia Smith Miller, Dec. 27, 1925; children—Alec Miller, George Horace, Jr. Head dept. of journalism, Drake U., 1929-31; prof. journalism and advertising, Northwestern U., 1931-32; dir. of research Young & Rubican Advertising Agency, N.Y., since 1932; prof. Pulitzer Sch. of Journalism, Columbia U., since 1935; pres. Market Research Council, 1934, 35; treas. Coöperative Analysis of Broadcasting since 1934. Made editorial surveys of many newspapers, and editorial and advertising surveys of Liberty, Saturday Evening Post, Lit. Digest and Colliers', 1931. Mem. Am. Assn. Advertising Agencies (research com.), Am. Marketing Soc., Sigma Alpha Epsilon, Sigma Delta Chi; asso. mem. Am. Psychol. Assn. Founder of Am. Institute of Pub. Opinion, 1935, dir. since 1935; founder of British Inst. of Pub. Opinion, 1936; founder Quill and Scroll (internat. hon. soc. for high school journalists). Originator of method to measure comparative interest of readers in news features and advertising in newspapers and mags., also a method for measuring radio audiences of individual radio programs. Episcopalian. Author: A New Technique for Measuring Reader Interest; also numerous articles on public opinion. Home: The Great Rd., Princeton, N.J.

GALLUP, Wallace Lester, clergyman; b. Hingham, Mass., Dec. 14, 1891; s. Stephen Paine and Flora (Reed) G.; A.B., Brown U., 1915, A.M., same, 1916, Ph.D., same, 1922; study, Union Theol. Sem., N.Y. City, 1920-21; m. Edna Ketcham, Aug. 31, 1921; children—Edith Winifred, Howard Frederick. Engaged as minister, Bapt. Ch., Manton, R.I., 1913-17; ordained to ministry Baptist Ch., 1915; asst. minister, Faith Presbyn. Ch., N.Y. City, 1917-18; minister, Greene Av. Presbyn. Ch., Brooklyn, N.Y., 1919-23; asst. prof. Bible, Conn. Coll., New London, Conn., 1923-28; minister, Valley Stream, N.Y., 1928-33; minister, Weequahic Presbyn. Ch., Newark, N.J., since 1933. Served as 1st lt., chaplain, inf., U.S.A., with A.E.F., 1917-19; capt. chaplain, U.S.A. Res., retired. Awarded Chaplain's Medal, A.E.F. Ribbon, Two Stars. Democrat. Presbyn. U.S.A. Mason. Home: 290 Meeker Av., Newark, N.J.

GALLUP, William Dennison, lawyer; b. Smethport, Pa., June 7, 1903; s. Fred D. and Margaret Mary (McKean) G.; grad. Smethport (Pa.) Public Schools, 1921; student Milford (Conn.) Sch., 1921-22; Ph.B., Yale, 1926, LL.B. 1934; m. Harriet Welles Robbins, Dec. 8, 1934; 1 dau., Margaret Robbins. Salesman Hanley Co., Inc., New York, 1926-31; admitted to Pa. bar, 1934, and began practice as partner in firm Gallup, Potter & Gallup, Smethport and Bradford, Pa. Pres. Family Welfare Soc., Bradford, v.p. and dir. Bd. of Commerce, Bradford. Mem. Am., Pa. State and McKean Co. bar assns. Republican. Episcopalian. Mason. Clubs: Kiwanis, Bradford, Pennhills (Bradford, Pa.); Yale (New York). Home: 44 Abbot Rd. Office: Hooker-Fulton Bldg., Bradford, Pa.

GALPIN, Sidney Longman, geologist, hydrologist; b. Jefferson, O., Oct. 29, 1886; s. Alfred F. and Mary (Slaughter) G.; grad. Jefferson (O.) High Sch., 1903; A.B., Western Reserve U., Cleveland, O., 1907; A.M., Cornell U., 1910, Ph.D., 1912; m. Julia Yeend, Dec. 31, 1912; children—Sidney Stewart, Mary Elizabeth. Grad. asst. in geology, Cornell U., 1907-10, instr. in geology and mineralogy, 1910-12; junior geologist U.S. Geol. Survey, 1910; asst. state geologist Ga. Geol. Survey, 1912-14; asst. prof. of geology, Ia. State Coll., 1914-17, asso. prof., 1919-27; cons. geologist, 1917-19; prof. of geology, W.Va. U., 1927-33; consultant Nat. Resources Com., 1934-38; hydrologist Agrl. Expt. Sta., W. Va., since 1938. Mem. Geol. Soc. America, Am. Assn. Petroleum Geologists, Am. Ceramic Soc., W.Va. Acad. Science, Sigma Xi, Phi Gamma Delta, Phi Lambda Upsilon, Sigma Gamma Epsilon, Gamma Alpha. Congregationalist. Home: 424 Clark St. Office: Agricultural Experiment Station, Morgantown, W.Va.

GALVIN, Thomas K.; asso. in gynecology, U. of Md.; gynecologist and obstetrician Mercy Hosp., St. Joseph's Hosp. and Hosp. for Women of Md.; attending obstetrician Union Memorial Hosp. Address: 1129 N. Calvert St., Baltimore, Md.

GAMBLE, Cary Breckinridge Jr., physician; b. Tallahassee, Fla., Oct. 13, 1863; s. Cary Breckinridge and Eduarda (Shaw) G.; A.B., Princeton U., 1885, A.M., 1887; M.D., U. of Md. Med. Sch., Baltimore, 1887; licentiate Univ. of Berlin, Univ. of Vienna, 1887, 1888; m. Vera Jenness, Dec. 10, 1896; children—Eduarda Jenness (widow Charles H. Boehm), Cary Breckinridge III. Served in out-patient dept. Johns Hopkins Hosp., 1889-96; physician in chief St. Joseph's Hosp., Baltimore, 1896-1904; prof. clin. medicine, Coll. Phys. & Surgs., Baltimore, and U. of Md., 1904-25; med. referee for Md., Mutual Life Ins. Co. of N.Y. since 1894; engaged in gen. practice of medicine at Baltimore since 1891; former mem. bd. med. examiners State of Md., bd. of supervisors of City Charities; on visiting staffs, Hosp. for Women of Md., Mercy, Union Memorial hosps. Served as maj., Med. Corps, U.S. Army, 1917-19; cardiovascular expert Camp Meade, 1917-18; sr. med. officer and comdr. base hosp. with A.E.F. in France. Mem. A.M.A., Baltimore City Med. Soc. Independent Democrat. Episcopalian. Club: Maryland (Baltimore). Home: 3908 N. Charles St., Baltimore, Md.

GAMBLE, Guy Paden, dentist; b. Mercer Co., Pa., June 10, 1879; s. Charles W. and Maria (Paden) G.; grad. McKeesport High Sch., 1896; D.D.S., Western U. of Pa. (now U. of Pittsburgh), 1900; m. Lucille Richey, Oct. 10, 1914; children—Guy Paden, Amy Verna (Mrs. Louis Lannan), Gene. Practiced as dental surgeon, McKeesport, since 1900; dir. Peoples City Bank. Dir. McKeesport Chamber of Commerce; dir. and treas. McKeesport Jour., 1927-30. Club: Youghiogheny Country (dir.). Home: 1407 Library St. Office: Peoples Bank Bld., McKeesport, Pa.

GAMBLE, John Taylor, prof. biology; b. Moline, Ill., Apr. 29, 1900; s. John Alexander and Kathryn Cushman (Taylor) G.; B.S., Thiel Coll., Greenville, Pa., 1925; M.S., U. of Pittsburgh, 1927, Ph.D., same, 1931; grad. study, U. of Mich. Biol. Sta., Cheboygan, Mich., summer 1931; m. Lydia Katharine Rissell, June 18, 1926; children—Winifred Louise, Kathryn Taylor. Instr. biology and chemistry, Thiel Coll., Greenville, Pa., 1925-26, 1928-30, asst. prof. biology, 1930-31, prof. biology since 1931; grad. asst. in zoölogy, U. of Pittsburgh, 1926-28. Served as pvt. U.S. Army, 1918; served in U.S.N., 1920-21. Mem. Entomol. Soc. of America, Pa. State Edn. Assn., Am. Assn. Univ. Profs., Phi Sigma, Beta Beta Beta, Delta Sigma Phi. Republican. Lutheran. Home: 308 Clinton St., Greenville, Pa.

GAMBLE, Robert Bruce, M.D., surgeon; b. Mosiertown, Pa., June 28, 1871; s. William J. and Helen (Beebee) G.; A.B., Allegheny Coll., Meadville, Pa., 1893, A.M., 1896; M.D., U. of Buffalo Med. Dept., 1896; m. Nella M. White, July 5, 1900. House surgeon, City Hosp., Rochester, N.Y., 1896-97; settled in Meadville, Pa., 1897; surgeon City Hosp.; dir. First Nat. Bank, Meadville. Capt. 15th Pa. Vol. Inf., Spanish-Am. War, later lt. col. 16th Inf., N.G. Pa.; lt. col. of the 112th Inf., 1917; with A.E.F., 15 months. Chevalier Legion of Honor (France). Trustee Allegheny College. Fellow Am. Coll. of Surgeons; mem. Pa. Med. Assn., Crawford Co. Med. Soc., Sigma Alpha Epsilon. Republican. Episcopalian. Mason (32°). Clubs: University, Meadville Country, Rotary, Iroquois Boating and Fishing. Home and Office: 917 Diamond Sq., Meadville, Pa.

GAMBLE, Samuel Cooper, clergyman; b. Jamestown, Pa., Oct. 13, 1878; s. Hugh M. and Ellen P. (Dickey) G.; A.B., Westminster Coll., 1901, D.D., 1924; B.Th., Pittsburgh Sem., 1904; m. Anna Boyd, July 24, 1906; children—Rev. William B., Lillian W. Ordained United Presbyn. ministry, 1904; pastor Martins Ferry, O., 1904-09, Second Ch., New Castle, Pa., 1909-14, First Ch., Philadelphia, 1914-18, Second Ch., Butler, Pa., since 1919. Treas. and dir. Butler Co. Memorial Hosp. since 1932; dir. Salvation Army since 1921, Pittsburgh Xenia Sem. Republican. Club: Butler Rotary (hon. mem.; ex-pres.). Author: Letters of Benedicite, 1931; Voices from the Past, 1936; Home Spun Homilies (series of 85 weekly articles); Monday Musings (series of articles). Asso. editor The United Presbyterian. Home: 550 Third St., Butler, Pa.

GAMBLE, William Dickey, sch. supt.; b. Jamestown, Pa., Apr. 9, 1873; s. Hugh M. and Ellen (Dickey) G.; ed Jamestown pub. schs. and Jamestown Sem.; A.B., Westminster Coll., 1896, A.M., 1901, Ph.D., 1930; m. Mabel McMichael, Aug. 5, 1903; children—Mary Eleanor, Hugh M., William Paul. Teacher, Ingleside Acad., McDonald, Pa., 1896-98, Mission Coll., Norfolk, Va., 1899-1902; prin. pub. schs., Jamestown, Pa., 1902-10, High Sch., Sharon, Pa., 1910-13; supt. schs., Sharon, since 1913; dir. Valley Savings & Loan Assn. Trustee Westminster Coll.; pres. bd. dirs. Christian H. Buhl

GAMBRILL, Hosp.; pres. Salvation Army Advisory Bd. Mem. N.E.A. (life), Pa. State Edn. Assn.; charter mem. Sharon Chamber of Commerce. Republican. United Presbyterian. Wrote: A Code for Americans. Contbr. ednl. pubs. Lectured before Rotary and other service clubs, ednl. and religious orgns. Home: 198 Cedar Av. Office: High School Bldg., Sharon, Pa.

GAMBRILL, James H., Jr.; pres., treas. and dir. Dietrich & Gambrill, Inc.; officer or dir. many companies. Address: Frederick, Md.

GANEY, J. Cullen, U.S. dist. atty.; b. Phillipsburg, N.J., Apr. 22, 1899; s. Thomas and Catherine (Cullen) Ganey; A.B., Lehigh U., 1920; LL.B., Harvard, 1923; m. Evelyn Gorman, Nov. 19, 1933; 1 dau., Jean Mary. Admitted to Pa. bar, 1923, and practiced in Bethlehem, Pa.; U.S. dist. atty. for Eastern Distr., Pa., since 1937. Mem. Pa. State Bar Assn. Democrat. Home: 1866 Cloverleaf St. Office: Union Bank Bldg., Bethlehem, Pa.

GANNETT, Farley, pres. Gannett, Eastman & Fleming, Inc.; b. Washington, D.C., May 6, 1880; s. Henry and Mary (Chace) G.; student Mass. Inst. Tech., Boston; m. Janet R. Sanders, June 14, 1905; children—Muriel S., Jane E. and Alice C. Chief engr. Water Supply Commn. of Pa., 1905-15; pres. Gannett, Eastman & Fleming, Inc., engring. and public utilities, since 1915. Home: 2841 N. 2d St. Office: 600 N. 2d St., Harrisburg, Pa.

GANNON, John Mark, bishop; b. Erie, Pa., June 12, 1877; s. Thomas Patrick and Julia (Dunlavey) G.; A.B., St. Bonaventure's Coll., Allegany, N.Y., 1899; S.T.B., Catholic U., Washington, D.C., 1900, S.T.L., 1901; D.D. and D.C.L., Appolinare U., Rome, Italy, 1903; spl. studies, U. of Munich, 1902; LL.D., Duquesne University, 1914, Notre Dame U., 1927, St. Bonaventure's Coll., 1933, St. Vincent's Coll., 1935. Pastor St. Anthony's Ch., Cambridge Springs, Pa., 1904-15, St. Bridget's Ch., Meadville, later St. Andrew's Ch., Erie; consecrated auxiliary bishop of Erie, Feb. 6, 1918, bishop of Erie, Dec. 15, 1920. Supt. Catholic edn. Diocese of Erie, 1911-19; Episcopal. chmn. Cath. Press Assn., Nat. Cath. Welfare Conf., Washington, D.C., also episcopal chmn. Mexican Affairs and mem. administrative bd., same. Home: 205 W. 9th St., Erie, Pa.

GANS, Hilary Wall, lawyer; b. Towson, Md., Sept. 21, 1898; s. Edgar Hilary and Elizabeth Virginia (Wall) G.; grad. Boys Latin Sch., Baltimore, 1914; A.B., Georgetown U., Washington, D.C., 1918; LL.B., U. of Md., 1921; m. Mary Rosalie O'Donovan, June 2, 1928; children—Mary Rosalie, Anne Jenkins, Hilary Wall, Elizabeth Virginia. Admitted to Md. bar, 1921, and became asso. with Cook & Markell, Baltimore; partner in law firm Brune, Parker, Carey & Gans, (now Brown & Brune) since 1927; asst. states atty., Baltimore, 1923-28; 1st asst. atty. gen. for Md., 1935-38. Served as ensign, Air Service, U.S. Navy, during World War. Dir. Asso. Hosp. Service of Baltimore, Inc. Mem. Phi Kappa Sigma. Democrat. Catholic. Clubs: Elkridge Kennels, Racquet (Baltimore). Home: 116 Ridgewood Rd. Office: 1904 First National Bank Bldg., Baltimore, Md.

GANT, Charles Henry, harbor commr.; b. Neptune Twp., N.J., Sep. 24, 1892; s. Henry P. and Bertha (Megill) G.; B.S., Rutgers U., New Brunswick, N.J., 1914, C.E. (hon.) 1923; m. Enid Roys, Oct. 14, 1917; children— Charles Henry, Richard Roys. In shop course Am. Bridge Co., Ambridge, Pa., 1914-15; borough engr. and clerk, Bradley Beach, N.J., 1915; field engr. Hercules Powder Co., Parlin, N.J., 1915-17; sec. Bd. of Harbor Commrs., Wilmington, Del., since 1919, mgr. since 1923. Served as 2d lt., F Co., 101st Engrs., U. S. Army, A.E.F., 1917-18, 1st lt., 1918-19; capt. Engrs. R.C., 1921-31. Sec. Del. Waterfront Commn.; mem. Interstate Commn. on Del. River Basin. Dir. Children's Bur., Peoples Settlement, Wilmington, Del.; pres. Delmarva Council, Boy Scouts of America. Mem. Am. Assn. of Port Authorities (past pres.), Pi Kappa Alpha, Tau Beta Pi, Theta Nu Epsilon. Episcopalian. Mason. Clubs: Rotary (past pres.), Wilmington Whist (sec.), Del. Motor (dir.), Wilmington (Wilmington, Del.); Yankee Div. (Boston, Mass.). Home: 1410 Woodlawn Av. Office: Marine Terminal, Wilmington, Del.

GANTERT, Frank A.; pres. Fidelity & Guaranty Fire Corpn.; dir. several companies. Home: 212 Goodale Road. Office: 301 Water St., Baltimore, Md.

GARARD, Ira Dufresne, prof. of chemistry; b. Dunkard, Pa., March 19, 1888; s. Charles Alexander and Margaret (Herrington) G.; grad. South Western State Normal Sch., California, Pa., 1908; B.S., Grove City (Pa.) Coll., 1911; Ph.D., Columbia, 1918; m. Mabel Baldwin, Sept. 20, 1919. Began as teacher, 1904; teacher Coraopolis (Pa.) High Sch., 1908-09, Grove City (Pa.) High Sch., 1911-14, Carnegie Tech., 1917-18; asso. prof. chemistry, N.J. Coll. for Women, 1919-22, prof. since 1922; dir. Provident Bldg. & Loan Assn. Mem. Am. Chem. Soc., Am. Inst. of Chemists, A.A.A.S., Assn. Official Agrl. Chemists, Phi Beta Kappa, Sigma Xi. Club: Lawrence Brook Country (New Brunswick, N.J.). Home: 119 Livingston Av., New Brunswick, N.J.

GARBER, Daniel, painter; b. N. Manchester, Ind., April 11, 1880; s. Daniel and Elisabeth (Blickenstaff) G.; grad. high sch., N. Manchester, art studies, Cincinnati Art Acad. and Pa. Acad. Fine Arts; m. Mary Franklin, June 21, 1901; children—Tanis, John Franklin. Mem. faculty, Pa. Acad. Fine Arts since 1909. 1st Hallgarten prize, Nat. Acad. Design, 1909; hon. mention, Carnegie Inst., 1910; 4th Clark prize and hon. mention, Corcoran Gallery Art, Washington, 1910; hon. mention Art Club of Phila., 1910, bronze medal, Internat. Expn., Buenos Aires, 1910; Walter Lippincott prize, Pa. Acad., 1911; Potter Palmer gold medal and 1st prize $1,000, Art Inst. Chicago, 1911; awarded $1,500 and Corcoran silver medal for painting "Wilderness," 1912; gold medal, San Francisco Expn., 1915; 2d Altman prize, N.A.D., 1915; Shaw prize, Salmagundi Club, 1916; H. S. Morris prize, Newport (R.I.) Art Assn.; 1st Altman prize for figure painting, N.A.D., 1917; Edward Stotesbury prize, Pa. Acad. Fine Arts, 1918; Temple medal, Pa. Acad., 1919; $2,000 and 1st Clark prize, Corcoran Gallery of Art, Washington, 1921; 1st Altman prize for landscape, N.A.D., 1922; gold medal, Art Club of Phila., 1923; Carnegie prize, N.A.D., 1923; 3d prize Internat. Exhibit Carnegie Inst., 1924; gold medal, Sesquicentennial Expn., Phila., 1926; 1st Altman prize for landscape painting, awarded 2d time, 1927; gold medal of honor, Pa. Acad. Fine Arts, 1928; Sesnan medal in landscape, Pa. Acad. Fine Arts, 1937. Represented in permanent collections of City Art Mus., St. Louis; Corcoran Gallery of Art, Washington, D.C.; U. of Mo., Columbia; Mary Ann Brown Memorial, Providence, R.I.; Art Inst. Chicago; Carnegie Inst., Pittsburgh; Nat. Arts Club, New York, Mus. of Arts and Science, Los Angeles; Pa. Acad of Fine Arts; Nat. Gallery of Art, Washington, D.C.; Duncan Philips Memorial Collection, Washington, D.C.; Wilstach Collection, Memorial Hall, Phila.; Mt. Holyoke College; Albright Gallery, Buffalo; University Club, Phila.; John Herron Art Inst., Indianapolis; Metropolitan Mus. of Art, New York; Reading (Pa.) Mus.; Hackley Mus., Muskegon, Mich., N.A. Clubs: Art (Phila.); Nat. Arts, Salmagundi (New York). Address: Lumberville, Bucks Co., Pa.

GARBER, Eli L., pres. Penn Dairies, Inc.; b. Florin, Pa., Feb. 11, 1864; s. Christian S. and Anna Z. (Lindimuth) G.; ed. pub. schs.; m. Mary N. Forrey, Nov. 11, 1886; children— J. Forrey, Erla, Gertrude, Mary, Clarence F. (dec.). Mgr. and part owner butter-making plan, 1890-96; independent dairy operator, 1896-1920; pres. York Sanitary Milk Co., 1920-29, company merged with Lancaster Sanitary Milk Co. and changed name to Penn Dairies, Inc., of which is pres.; owner Garber, Peters & Jacoby Co.; dir. Farmers' Nat. Bank, Lititz, Pa. Club: Rotary. Home: 22 N. Broad St., Lititz, Pa. Office: 572 N. Queen St., Lancaster, Pa.

GARBER, Ralph John, dir. of research; b. Apr. 24, 1890; s. John and Lena (Oswald) G.; grad. Gibson City (Ill.) High Sch., 1908; B.S., Coll. of Agr., U. of Ill., Urbana, Ill., 1912; M.S., Coll. of Agr., U. of Minn., Minneapolis, Minn., 1917, grad. student, 1916-17, Ph.D., 1922; m. Mildred Evelyn Fitschen, July 19, 1917; children—John Douglas, Joy Marie. On farm in central Ill., June 1912-Aug. 1913; instr. Morgan (Minn.) High Sch., 1913-15; Monticello (Minn.) High Sch., 1915-16; asst. prof. of agronomy, U. of Minn., 1917-20; asso. prof., prof. and head of dept. of agronomy and genetics, Coll. of Agri., W.Va. Univ., 1920-; dir. U.S. Regional Pasture Research Lab., State College, Pa., since 1936. Fellow A.A.A.S. (mem. council), Am. Soc. Agronomy (pres. 1938-39); mem. Am. Genetic Assn., Genetics Soc. of America, Am. Soc. Naturalists, Sigma Xi, Alpha Zeta, Gamma Sigma Delta, Acacia. Presbyterian. Club: Centre Hills Country. Author: Breeding Crop Plants with (H. K. Hayes), 1921, revised edit., 1927; many scientific articles and bulletins; mem. advisory editorial com. of Jour. of Am. Soc. of Agronomy. Home: 613 West Park Av., State College, Pa. Office: U.S. Regional Pasture Research Laboratory, State College, Pa.

GARDEN, George Alan; mem. law firm Handlan, Garden & Matthews. Office: 1226 Chapline St., Wheeling, W.Va.

GARDNER, Ashton, lawyer; b. Hollidaysburg, Pa., June 18, 1894; s. Harry Ashton and Julia (Over) G.; student Martinsburg, (W.Va.) High Sch., 1910-12, U. of Pa., 1913-17; m. Jennie Ruth Dively, Jan. 25, 1930. Admitted to Blair Co. (Pa.) bar, 1924, and since practiced in Hollidaysburg, Pa.; sec.-treas. McLanahan & Stone Corpn., Hollidaysburg, Pa., since 1926; dir. Duncansville Lime & Stone Co. Mem. Hollidaysburg Borough Council, 1924-28. Mem. Blair Co. Bar Assn. Republican. Presbyterian. Mason (Juniata Lodge 282). Home: 701 Penn St. Office: 418 Allegheny St., Hollidaysburg, Pa.

GARDNER, Frank Duane, agronomist; b. Gilman, Ill., Nov. 19, 1864; s. Isaac James and Invern (Bennett) G.; B.S., U. of Ill. Coll. of Agr., 1891; grad. student, George Washington U., 1895-96; m. Ellen P. Crum, June 6, 1894; children—Matthias Bennett, Frank Easter, Reina Elisa. Agriculturist, U. of Ill., 1891-95; soil expert, U.S. Dept. Agr., 1895-1901; dir. Porto Rico Agrl. Expt. Sta., 1901-04; in charge of soil management investigations, U.S. Dept. Agr., 1904-08; prof. of agronomy, Pa. State College and Experiment Station, 1908-37, now prof. of agronomy, emeritus. Propr. of Pleasant View Farms. Mem. Am. Soc. Agronomy (pres. N.E. sect. 1932-33), American Farm Economics Assn., American Association Univ. Profs., Pa. State Edn. Assn., Gamma Sigma Delta. Republican. Presbyn. Club: University (State College, Pa.). Author: Successful Farming, 1916; Soils and Soil Management, 1918; Farm Crops, Their Cultivation and Management, 1918. Contbr. to Rural Pennsylvania, also to The Book of Rural Life; writer many bulls. on soil and crop investigations. Home: State College, Pa.

GARDNER, Henry Alfred, chemist; b. Pawtucket, R.I., Oct. 12, 1882; s. Walter S. and Ellen (Muir) G.; grad. Pawtucket High School; studied Brown University, 1902; U. of Pa., 1903; D.Sc., Lehigh University; m. Laura Paul, Oct. 12, 1910; children—Henry A., Paul Norris. Dir. Scientific Section of Am. Paint and Varnish Assn.; pres. and director Institute of Paint and Varnish Research, Washington, D.C.; chemist at large Small Arms Div., Ordnance Dept., U.S.A.; lt. U.S. N.R.F.; chmn. Sub-com. Fabrics and Protectives, Nat. Advisory Com. for Aeronautics. Fellow American Institute of Chemists; mem. American Chemical Soc., Soc. Chem. Industry, Am. Electrochem. Soc., Am. Soc. Testing Materials, British Oil and Color Chem. Assn., Verein Deutscher Chemiker, Col. Dir. les Matieres Grasses. Republican. Baptist. Clubs: Chemists (New York), Cosmos, Columbia Country, Chevy Chase. Home: 27 W. Kirk St., Chevy Chase, Md.

GARDNER, Horace John, writer and radio commentator; b. Grenloch, N.J., Nov. 9, 1895;

s. John Walker and Anna Amanda (Myers) G.; grad. Woodbury High Sch., New Jersey, 1913; student U. of Pa., 1915; m. Mildred Rainier, Mar. 22, 1919. Suburban newspaper editor, Grenloch, N.J., 1914-15; writing for newspapers and mags. since 1919; conducted "The Literary Parade" on radio, 1935-37; head spl. service dept., J. B. Lippincott Co., Phila., Pa., since 1930. Presbyterian. Club: Fifth Estate (New York). Author: Games and Stunts for All Occasions, 1935; The Year 'Round Party Book, 1936; Courtesy Book, 1937; Both Sides of the Microphone, 1938; The Book of Original Plays and How to Give Them, 1938; Happy Birthday to You!, 1939; several radio features. Home: Grenloch, N.J. Office: 227 S. 6th St., Phila., Pa.

GARDNER, Irvine C(lifton), physicist; b. Idaville, Ind., Sept. 19, 1889; s. James W. and Sarah J. G.; A.B., DePauw Univ., Greencastle, Ind., 1910; A.M., Harvard U., 1912, Ph.D., 1915; D.Sc., DePauw Univ., 1939; m. Merriel Maslin, June 30, 1927. Asst. and instr. at Harvard Univ., 1915-17; civilian in Ordnance Dept., U.S.A., optical engr. on development fire control apparatus, 1917-22; physicist at Nat. Bur. of Standards, chief of optical instruments sect. since 1922; rep. Nat. Bur. Standards on Nat. Geographic Soc.-Nat. Bur. Standards Eclipse Expdn. and photographed solar corona in color, Asiatic Russia, 1936; rep. Nat. Bur. Standards on Nat. Geographic Soc.-U.S.N. Eclipse Expdn. and photographed solar corona, Canton Island, in South Pacific, 1937. Mem. A.A.A.S., Am. Phys. Soc., Optical Soc. America, Am. Soc. Photogrammetry, Wash. Acad. Scis., Wash. Philos. Soc., Sigma Xi, Phi Beta Kappa, Delta Kappa Epsilon. Contbr. to professional jours. Home: 12 Shepherd St., Chevy Chase, Md.

GARDNER, Paul, manufacturer; b. Phila., Pa., Feb. 27, 1900; s. Walter and Anna (Brunish) G.; student Strasburg High Sch., 1914-17; m. Anna Miriam Herr, Jan. 1, 1935; children—Paul, Eugene. Began as partner Eddy-Gardner Service, Paradise, Pa., 1922-24; partner DeWalt Products Co., Leola, Pa., 1924-28; pres. DeWalt Products Corp., Lancaster, Pa., since 1928; dir. Economy Rock Bit Corp., Motors, Inc. Mem. Code Authority Woodworking Machinery Mfrs. during N.R.A. Clubs: Hamilton, Lancaster Country (Lancaster, Pa.). Home: 1103 Helen Av. Office: Box 149, Lancaster, Pa.

GARDNER, Theodore Roosevelt, lawyer, U.S. Commr.; b. Allentown, Pa., Aug. 14, 1904; s. C. Forrest and Mary (Snyder) G.; Ph.B., Muhlenberg Coll., 1928; LL.B., U. of Pa. Law Sch., 1931; m. Margaret Knoll, Mar. 3, 1928; 1 son, Theodore Roosevelt. Admitted to bar of Pa. Supreme Ct., 1931; apptd. U.S. Commr., 1931, reapptd., 1935; v.p. and dir. Lyons Textile Print Corpn. Rep. candidate for Congress, 1934, 36; elected solicitor Sch. Dist. of Borough of Emmaus, 1938. Served in U.S. Navy, 1920-22; hon. discharged, 1922. Dist. chmn. Boy Scouts of America; mem. exec. bd. Lehigh County Council. Dir. and solicitor Emmaus Chamber of Commerce. Republican. Mem. Protestant Reformed Ch. Elk (past exalted ruler). Clubs: Elks, Rotary. Home: 401 N. Second St., Emmaus, Pa. Office: 467 Linden St., Allentown, Pa.

GARDNER, Wallace John, bishop; b. Buffalo, N.Y., July 25, 1883; s. Frederick A. and Sarah Jane (McConnell) G.; A.B., St. Stephen's Coll., Annandale, N.Y., 1906, A.M., 1906, hon. D.D.; student Gen. Theol. Sem., N.Y. City, 1908-11, S.T.D., 1937; unmarried. Taught private schs., 1906-08; ordained deacon P.E. Ch., 1911, priest, 1912; chaplain schs. Garden City, 1911-19; rector St. Paul's Ch., Flatbush, Brooklyn, N.Y., 1919-33; vicar Chapel of Intercession, N.Y. City, 1933-36; bishop coadjutor Diocese of N.J., 1936-37; bishop of N.J. since Nov. 1, 1937. Trustee Gen. Theol. Sem. Mem. Sigma Alpha Epsilon. Club: Canadian (N.Y. City). Home: 15 S. Overbrook Av. Office: 814 Berkeley Av., Trenton, N.J.

GARDNER, Walter, artist; b. Liverpool, England, May 7, 1902; s. Herman G. and Lily (Cuddy) G.; elementary edn. in England; student Pa. Acad. of Fine Arts, 1921-25; m. Emilie Roland, Nov. 1, 1937. Exhibited at Whitney Mus., New York; Corcoran Gallery, Washington, D.C.; Chicago Art Inst.; Detroit Inst. of Art; Pa. Acad. Awards: Cresson Traveling scholarship, 1924; purchase prize, Wanamaker Regional Art Exhibit, 1934; fellowship prize, Pa. Acad., 1938. Murals: post offices at Honesdale, Pa., Phila. (Station O), Berne, Ind. Home: 32 E. Logan St., Germantown, Philadelphia, Pa.

GARDNER, Walter Pennett, banker; b. Jersey City, N.J., May 27, 1869; s. Edward Charles and Content Wilkinson (Scobey) G.; hon. LL.D., Lafayette Coll., 1933; m. Rebecca C. Horstmann, Oct. 7, 1896; 1 son, Arthur. In banking business since 1888; with N.J. Title Guarantee & Trust Co., 1912-39, as dir., 1912-39, sr. v.p., 1914-35, pres., 1935-39; judge N.J. Ct. of Errors and Appeals, 1915-25. N.J. commr., Panama-Pacific Expn., 1913-15; chmn. Jersey City Liberty Loan Com. World War. Decorated Chevalier Legion of Honor (France), 1934. Mem. Am. Friends of Lafayette, Soc. of Friends of de Grasse, N.J. Hist. Soc., Hudson Co. (N.J.) Hist. Soc. Clubs: Princeton (New York); Carteret (Jersey City, N.J.). Home: 122 Gifford Av., Jersey City, N.J.

GARDNER, William Sisson, gynecologist; b. Athens Co., Ohio, Sept. 23, 1861; s. Wilson and Emma Charlotte (Brown) G.; grad. Nelsonville (O.) High Sch., 1878; M.D., Coll. Phys. & Surgs., Baltimore, 1885; m. Mary A. Maslin, Dec. 29, 1897; children—William Maslin, Wilson Carville, Helen. Practiced, Baltimore, since 1885; now prof. emeritus gynecology, Univ. of Md. Sch. of Medicine and Coll. Phys. and Surg. Fellow Am. Coll. Surgeons; mem. Med. and Chirurg. Faculty of Md., A.M.A. Methodist. Author: Text Book of Gynecology, 1912. Address: 1025 N. Calvert St., Baltimore, Md.

GAREY, Enoch Barton, educator; b. Tuckahoe Neck, Md., Aug. 7, 1883; s. Robert J. and Vashti (Saulsbury) G.; A.B., St. John's Coll., Annapolis, Md., 1903, LL.D., 1933; grad. U.S. Mil. Acad., 1908; LL.D., Washington (Md.) Coll., 1923; m. Alice Brewer Ross, Dec. 31, 1914; children—Enoch Barton, Albert Ross (dec.), Arthur Ellis, Wilson Saulsbury, Alice Ross, Stewart Towers, Barbara Lyden. Commd. 2d lt. inf., Feb. 1908; promoted through grades to maj. regular army, July 1920; maj. A.E.F., Jan.-Sept. 1917, promoted to lt. col., Sept. 1918, "for meritorious conduct under fire"; comdr. 18th Machine Gun Batt. in France; resigned July 1923 to become pres. St. John's Coll., Annapolis, pres. emeritus since 1929; pres. The Garey Sch., Aberdeen, Md., 1933-36. Citation and D.S.C. (U.S.); Croix de Guerre (French). Mem. Omicron Delta Kappa, Phi Sigma Kappa. Republican. Presbyterian. Clubs: Johns Hopkins, University (Baltimore). Co-Author: Plattsburg Manual, 1917; Junior Plattsburg Manual, 1918; Guide-Book to France and Its Battlefields, 1920; R.O.T.C. Manuals and numerous other mil. textbooks. Home: (summer) near Oakland, Md.; (winter) 3400 Devon Rd., Coconut Grove, Fla.

GARIS, Howard Roger, author; b. Binghamton, N.Y., Apr. 25, 1873; s. Simeon H. and Ellen A. (Kimball) Garis; academic education; m. Lilian C. McNamara, Apr. 26, 1900; children—Roger Carroll, Cleo Fausta (Mrs. John J. Clancy). Reporter and special writer for the Evening News, Newark, N.J., since 1896. Mem. Authors' League of America, Reptile Study Soc., Nat. Press Club. Catholic. Author: With Force and Arms, 1902; Uncle Wiggily series, 35 vols.; Curlytops series, 10 vols.; Daddy series, 10 vols.; Rick and Ruddy series, 5 vols.; Two Wild Cherries series, 5 vols.; Tom Cardiff's Circus; Tam of the Fire Cave; Tuftoo the Clown; The Buddy series, 10 vols.; Chad of Knob Hill; Rocket Riders series, 4 vols.; Teddy series, 4 vols.; other books for children, more than 200, since 1902. Inventor Uncle Wiggily game, Jack and Jill game, Mary and John game, Moving Picture game, Bedtime game. Home: 103 Evergreen Pl., East Orange, N.J. Office: Newark Evening News, Newark, N.J.

GARIS, Lilian C. (Mrs. Howard R. Garis), author; b. Cleveland, O.; d. Edward J. and Winifred (Noon) McNamara; studied in private schools and academies and Columbia U.; m. Howard Roger Garis, Apr. 26, 1900; children—Roger Carroll, Cleo Fausta (Mrs. John J. Clancy). Began writing verse for newspapers, 1890; in charge Woman's Work, Newark (N.J.) Evening News, 1895-1900. Originator movement for playgrounds, Newark; active in pub. affairs, woman suffrage, war work, etc.; councillor Girl Scouts of America. Catholic. Author: Two Little Girls, 1901; followed by many girls' books in series, under various pen names; also (under own name) Girl Scout Series (5 vols.); Gloria Books (2 vols.); Joan Books (2 vols.); Make Believe Books (4 vols.); Nancy Brandon (2 vols.); Mystery series; Melody Lane series, etc. Home: 103 Evergreen Pl., East Orange, N.J.

GARLACH, Elsie Anna, educator; b. Gettysburg, Pa., Dec. 10, 1887; d. J. William and Sarah Frances (Rasche) G.; B.A., Gettysburg Coll., 1907, M.A. (majoring in English), 1916; M.A. (majoring in French), Columbia U., 1924; student Sorbonne, U. of Paris, summers, 1922 and 36; unmarried. Teacher of French, Richford (Vt.) High Sch., 1907-08, Tarboro (N.C.) Acad., 1908-09, Cathedral Sch. for Girls, Orlando, Fla., 1909-11, Irving Coll., Mechanicsburg, Pa., 1911-15, Lyons (N.Y.) High Sch., 1916-18, Gettysburg (Pa.) High Sch., 1918-21; prof. French, Albright Coll., Reading, Pa., since 1921. Formerly ednl. advisor University Forum, Reading, Pa. Received badge of thanks from Girl Scouts. Mem. Nat. Advisory Cabinet. Sigma Tau Delta. Republican. Lutheran. Eastern Star. Clubs: French (Reading, Pa.); Woman's (Myerstown, Pa.). Home: 56 Chambersburg St., Gettysburg, Pa.

GARLAND, Fred Miller, ry. exec.; b. Crestline, O., 1887; s. Charles W. and Argall M. (Miller) G.; ed. Allegheny High Sch., Pittsburgh, French Sch. of Langs., Pittsburgh, U. of Pittsburgh (night sch.); m. Sarah Hutchinson, Apr. 5, 1917; 1 dau., Jean. Began as clk. transportation and engring. dept. Pa. R.R.; with Pressed Steel Car Co., Pittsburgh, from 1905, successively rate clk., chief clk. traffic dept., asst. gen. freight agent, asst. traffic mgr., traffic mgr. and gen. traffic mgr.; traffic mgr. Huntington and Broad Top Mountain R.R. Co., 1926-33; traffic mgr. Lincoln Gas Coal Co.; treas., Pittsburgh, Allegheny & McKees Rocks R.R., 1911-23, v.p., 1924-36, pres. since 1936; v.p. Chicago & Calumet River R.R. Co., 1924-36, pres. since 1936. Mem. Acad. Science and Art of Pittsburgh (v.p. astron. sect.). Clubs: Traffic (Pittsburgh); Highland Country. Contbr. articles to Scientific Am., Popular Astronomy and other scientific mags. Home: 1006 David Av. Office: 2515 Grant Bldg., Pittsburgh, Pa.

GARLAND, Robert, mfr.; b. North Ireland, Sept. 27, 1862; s. Robert and Eliza Jane (Atwell) G.; ed. pub. schs.; came to U.S., 1876; m. Alice Noble Bailey, Apr. 12, 1888; children—Robert (dec.), Alice Gertrude (Mrs. Roy H. McKnight). Began as clk., Oliver Iron & Steel Co., Pittsburgh, 1876, gen. sales mgr., 1886-90; began as mfr., 1890; president Garland Mfg. Co., mfrs. electric conduits, Pittsburgh, since 1898. Chmn. War Resources Com., Western Pa. and W.Va., World War. Mem. City Council, Pittsburgh, 1911-30. Trustee Carnegie Inst., Grove City (Pa.) Coll. Republican. Episcopalian. Mason (K.T., Shriner). Clubs: University, Duquesne, Pittsburgh Athletic. Wrote: History of the Scotch Irish in Western Pennsylvania; Ten Years of Daylight Saving, from the Pittsburgh Standpoint. Home: 1428 Inverness Av. Office: Grant Bldg., Pittsburgh, Pa.

GARMAN, Harry F., surgeon; b. Barnesboro, Pa., Jan. 19, 1888; s. Daniel A. and Rachel Ann (Bracken) G.; ed. Pittsburgh Acad., 1908-10; M.D., U. of Pittsburgh Med. Sch., 1914; m. Velma E. Montgomery, Sept. 27, 1921. Interne, St. Johns Gen. Hosp., 1914-15, med. asst. at Sagamore, Pa., 1915-16; engaged in gen. practice of medicine and surgery at Spangler, Pa., 1916-17 and since 1919; asst. in gen. surgery, Spangler Hosp., 1919-31, chief gen. surgeon since 1929, chief orthopedic surgeon since 1932; mem. firm Drs. H. F. Garman and S. L. Earley since 1932; vice pres. Farmers and Merchants Bank, Cherry Tree, Pa., 1930-38, pres. since 1938. Served as capt. Med. Corps, U.S.A.,

1917-19, with A.E.F. in France. Mem. Pa. State and Cambria Co. med. socs., Am. Legion, Phi Beta Pi. Republican. Presbyn. Mason (32°, Shriner). Club: Merit. Home: R.F.D. 2, Barnesboro, Pa. Office: 1100 Philadelphia Av., Barnesboro, Pa.

GARNER, James Bert, chemical engr.; b. Lebanon, Ind., Sept. 2, 1870; s. James Washington and Orrah Jane (Shepard) G.; B.Sc., Wabash Coll., Crawfordsville, Ind., 1893, M.Sc., 1895; Ph.D., magna cum laude, from the University of Chicago, 1897; m. Glenna May Green, Dec. 31, 1900 (died Dec. 7, 1918); children—Mrs. Lura Faulkenburg, Mrs. Marjorie Schmeltz, James Herbert, Mrs. Eleanor Shannon, Mrs. Mildred Lose, Mason Gemil, Jean Hale, Harry F., Glenna Green, Ruth Miller; m. 2d, Margaret Martin, June 30, 1923 (died Sept. 19, 1932); 1 son, William Jenkins; m. 3d, Sarah Elizabeth Harrold, May 12, 1934; 1 dau., Sarah Elizabeth. Teacher chemistry, Bradley Polytechnic Institute, and Wabash Coll., 1897-1914; fellow and prof. Mellon Inst. (Univ. of Pittsburgh), since 1914; dir. natural gas investigations same, since 1915; dir. Utility Survey Commn. of Greater Pittsburgh; former dir. research gas, oil and coal for Hope and Peoples Natural Gas Cos., subsidiaries of Standard Oil Co. of N.J. Inventor of gas mask Apr. 1915, making use of absorbent qualities of activated carbon. Mask was adopted by the British Govt. and U.S. Army in the World War. Fellow A.A.A.S.; mem. Am. Chem. Soc., Natural Gas Assn. of America, Phi Delta Theta, Phi Beta Kappa, Alpha Chi Sigma, Phi Sigma, Sigma Psi. Mem. United Presbyn. Ch. Mason (32°). Home: 54 Lebanon Hills Drive, Mt. Lebanon, Pittsburgh, Pa.

GARNETT, Leslie Coombs, ex-asst. atty. gen. U.S.; b. Mathews, Va., Dec. 15, 1876; s. G. Taylor and Ellen Douglas (Browne) G.; Randolph-Macon Coll.; LL.B., Georgetown U., 1899, LL.M., 1900; m. Clara E. Tinsley, Apr. 25, 1905; 1 son, George Tinsley. Began practice at Mathews, 1900; Dem. presdl. elector 1st Va. Dist., 1904; commonwealth's atty., Mathews, 1904-12; asst. atty. gen. of Va., 1916-17; atty. Dept. of Justice, Washington, D.C., 1917-19; counsel for Tex. Pacific Coal & Oil Co., Thurber, Tex., and New York, 1919-20; asst. atty. gen. in charge of Pub. Lands Div., Dept. of Justice, 1920-21; formerly U.S. dist. atty. for D.C.; now chancellor Nat. Univ. Law Sch. Mem. bar Supreme Court of U.S., of Va., Tex., and D.C. Mem. Phi Kappa Sigma. Mason. Clubs: Metropolitan, Chevy Chase. Home: 21 E. Melrose St., Chevy Chase, Md. Office: Tower Bldg., Washington, D.C.

GARRETSON, Cornelius David, pres. Electric Hose & Rubber Co.; b. York, Pa., Feb. 12, 1882; s. Cornelius R. and Sallie V. (Ginter) G.; student Girard Coll., Phila.; m. Katherine B. Miller, Feb. 17, 1904. With Electric Hose & Rubber Co. since 1904, beginning as asst. treas. and sales mgr., pres. since 1923. Home: 304 Hawthorne Drive, Brandywine Hills, Wilmington. Office: 12th and Dure Sts., Wilmington, Del.

GARRETSON, Leland Beekman, lawyer; b. Jersey City, N.J., Aug. 16, 1880; s. Abram Quick and Josephine (Boker) G.; A.B., Princeton U., 1903; ed. Columbia U. Law Sch., 1903-06; unmarried. Admitted to N.Y. bar, 1906; with Philbin, Beekman & Menken, 1906-07; with Joline, Larkin & Rathbone, N.Y. City, 1907-15; mem. firm Garretson & Maurice, 1915-21; practiced alone in N.Y. City, 1921-27; admitted to N.J. bar as atty., 1909, as counsellor, 1922; engaged in practice of law in Morristown, N.J. since 1930; mgr. Morris Co. Savings Bank, Morristown, N.J.; dir. Nat. Iron Bank, Morristown. Served as mem. Essex Troop, N.J.N.G., 1914-17; capt. cav. O.R.C., 1917; maj. inf., U.S.A., 1918, with A.E.F., 1918-19, Somme, St. Mihiel, Meuse-Argonne offensives. Dir. Morristown Memorial Hosp., Morristown Library. Mem. Am., N.J. State, Morris Co. bar assns. Democrat. Episcopalian. Clubs: Morristown (Morristown); Morris County Golf (Convent). Home: Blue Mill Rd. Office: First Nat. Bank Bldg., Morristown, N.J.

GARRETT, Arthur S(ellers), pres. Am. Water Softener Co.; b. Garrettford (now Drexel Hill), Pa., Nov. 24, 1873; s. George Sellers and Mary West (Maris) G.; grad. Westtown Sch., Pa., 1892; M.E., Cornell U., 1897; m. Hannah Worrall Ogden, June 1, 1906; children—George Sellers, Margaret Ogden, Charles Spencer (dec.), Mary Frances, Elizabeth Maris. In cons. engrs. office, 1897-1902; one of incorporators Am. Water Softener Co., 1902, pres. since 1907. Mem. Bd. Edn., Upper Darby Twp., 21 yrs., pres. 14 yrs.; retired from Board, Dec. 1937. Dir. Elwyn (Pa.) Training Sch., pres. since 1930, mem. of Bd. since 1908. Republican. Mem. Soc. of Friends. Home: Drexel Hill, Pa. Office: 4th and Lehigh Av., Philadelphia, Pa.

GARRETT, Erwin Clarkson, author; b. Germantown, Phila., Pa., Mar. 28, 1879; s. George L. and Sophia Cooper (Gray) G.; descendant of early Colonial Pa. and N.Y. ancestry; father, captain Union Army, Civil War; g.g. grandfather, Capt. John Garrett, Revolutionary War; B.S., U. of Pa., 1906; unmarried. Served as pvt., cos. L and G, 23d U.S. Inf. and Troop I, 5th U.S. Cav., in Philippine Insurrection, 1899-1902. Made trip around world, including Central Borneo, the home of the head hunting Dyaks, and crossed the Emperor's closed, "sacred," red bridge at Nikko, Japan, 1908. Went to France, Aug. 1917, as civilian, at own expense, so as to insure "front line" service in the World War, enlisted in Paris, Sept. 1, 1917, and on Sept. 8, became private Co. G, 16th United States Inf., 1st Div., A.E.F., serving until 1919 (wounded at Soissons, in 2d Battle of the Marne, July 18, 1918). Received Order of the Purple Heart and citation from 1st Div. hdqrs. and his regt. and div. were awarded the fourragère from French Govt. Mem. Rittenhouse Astronomical Soc., Hist. Soc. of Pa., Colonial Soc. of Pa., Soc. of Colonial Wars (Pa.), Sons of Revolution, Military Order Loyal Legion of U.S. (Pa.), Soc. of First Div. A.E.F. (v.p. nat. soc.), Soc. of Descendants of Continental Congress (v.p.), Plantagenet Soc. (recorder). Author: Army Ballads and Other Verses, 1916; Trench Ballads and Other Verses, 1919; Jenghiz Khan and Other Verses, 1924; Io Triumphe and Other Verses, 1928. Contbr. army verse since 1904. Lecturer on astronomy. Address: 431 W. Stafford St., Germantown, Philadelphia, Pa.

GARRETT, Garet (christened Edward Peter Garrett), writer; b. at Pana, Ill., Feb. 19, 1878; s. Charles J. and Alice Loretta (Conrad) G.; ed. pub. schs. Financial writer New York Sun, 1903-05, New York Times, 1906-07, Wall Street Journal, 1907-08, Evening Post, 1909-12; editor New York Times Annalist, 1912-14; asst. editor New York Tribune, 1916-19. Clubs: Salmagundi (N.Y.); The Family (San Francisco). Author: Where the Money Grows, 1911; The Blue Wound, 1920; The Driver, 1921; The Cinder Buggy, 1922; Satan's Bushel, 1923; Ouroboros, 1925; Harangue, 1927; The American Omen, 1929; The Bubble that Broke the World, 1932; also various economic and polit. essays. Home: Tuckahoe, N.J.

GARRETT, Harold Michael, lawyer; b. Bridgeport, W.Va., Sept. 27, 1897; s. Edmund F. and Fannie D. (Late) G.; A.B., W.Va., Univ., 1918; LL.B., W.Va. Univ. Law Sch., Morgantown, W.Va., 1920; m. Margaret Martha Hoyt., Apr. 14, 1924; children—Edmund Hoyt, Betty Late. Admitted to W.Va. bar, 1920 and since engaged in gen. practice of law at Clarksburg; since 1924 has been retained by oil and gas interests in W.Va.; engaged in gen. practice with special attention to oil and gas litigation; asso. with Kemble White and Anthony F. McCue; mem. Harrison Co. Bd. Edn. since 1938. In Coast Artillery Corps and 41st Railway Artillery, U.S.A. during World War. Mem. W.Va., Am. and Harrison County bar assns., Order of Coif, Phi Delta Phi. Democrat. Baptist. Mason. Elk. Home: Bridgeport. Office: Hope Natural Gas Co. Bldg., 445 W. Main St., Clarksburg, W.Va.

GARRETT, John Work, diplomat; b. Baltimore, May 19, 1872; s. T(homas) Harrison and Alice Dickinson (Whitridge) G.; B.S., Princeton, 1895, LL.D., 1922; LL.D., St. John's Coll., Annapolis, 1934; m. Alice Warder, Dec. 24, 1908. Partner in banking firm of Robert Garrett & Sons, Baltimore, 1896-1934 (firm founded by great-grandfather). Sec. Am. Legation at the Hague, 1901-03, to the Netherlands and Luxemburg, 1903-05; 2d sec. Am. Embassy at Berlin, 1905-08; 1st sec. Am. Embassy at Rome, 1908-11; E.E. and M.P. to Venezuela, Dec. 15, 1910-Nov. 1911, to Argentina, 1911-14; special agent Dept. of State to assist Am. ambassador, Paris, Aug. 6, 1914-Aug. 23, 1917; in charge of German and Austro-Hungarian civilian prisoners of war, etc., 1914-17; rep. at Bordeaux of the Am. Embassy at Paris, Sept. 3-Dec. 9, 1914; E.E. and M.P. to The Netherlands and Luxemburg, Aug. 23, 1917-August 1919; A.E. and P. to Italy, 1929-33. Was delegate to fifth and seventh National Irrigation Congresses, 1896, 98; sec. Am.-Russian sealing arbitration, The Hague, 1902; sec. Arbitral Tribunal in Venezuela preferential treatment case, The Hague, 1903-04; del. Hosp. Ship Conf., The Hague, 1904, and signed the Hosp. Ship Convention, Dec. 21, 1904. At request of the French Government inspected camps of French prisoners in Germany, 1916; chmn. spl. diplomatic mission to negotiate treaty regarding prisoners of war with Germany; jointly negotiated and signed such treaty at Berne, Nov. 11, 1918; sec. gen. Conf. on Limitation of Armaments, Washington, 1921-22. Mem. Am. Soc. Internat. Law, Archæol. Inst. America, English Speak. Union, Am. Forestry Assn., Council on Foreign Relations, Am. Geog. Soc., Am. Numismatic Soc., Am. Acad. Polit. and Social Science. Delegate at large from Md. to Republican National Conv., Chicago, 1920, Cleveland, 1924. Clubs: Metropolitan (Washington); Century, Princeton, Grolier, N.Y. Yacht (New York); Maryland, Elkridge Kennels, Merchants', Bachelors' Cotillon (Baltimore). Home: "Evergreen," 4545 N. Charles St., Baltimore, Md.

GARRETT, Robert, banker; b. Baltimore Co., Md., June 24, 1875; s. T(homas) Harrison and Alice Dickinson (Whitridge) G.; B.S., Princeton, 1897; m. Katharine Barker Johnson, May 1, 1907; children—Harrison, Johnson, Katharine Barker, Alice Whitridge, Ella Brock Johnson, Barbara Close, John Work, II. Partner banking firm Robert Garrett & Sons; dir. Provident Savings Bank, Safe Deposit & Trust Co., B. & O. R.R., Gathmann Engring. Co., Roland Park Co., etc. Trustee Princeton U.; mem. bd. Calvert Sch. (Baltimore); mem. Internat. Com. Y.M.C.A.; pres. Playground Athletic League, Baltimore; v.p. Nat. Recreation Assn. America. Presbyn. Clubs: Maryland, etc. (Baltimore); Princeton, Grolier (New York). Home: Charles St. Av., Roland Park. Office: Garrett Bldg., Baltimore, Md.

GARREY, George Henry, mining geologist and engr.; b. Reedsville, Wis., June 29, 1875; s. John Eugene and Harriet (Anderson) G.; B.S., U. of Chicago, 1900, M.S., in Geology, 1902; E.M., Mich. Coll. of Mines, 1904; unmarried. Economic geologist with U.S. Geol. Survey, 1904-06; asst. chief geologist Am. Smelting & Refining Co., Am. Smelters Securities Co. and allied Guggenheim interests, 1906-08; mem. Spurr & Cox, Inc., 1908-11; partner J. E. Spurr in gen. consulting business, 1911; again with Am. Smelting & Refining Co., etc., as chief geologist, 1911-14; cons. practice, 1914-15; in charge exploration dept. Tonopah Belmont Development Co., 1915-23; cons. mining geologist and engr. since 1923. Mem. Mining and Metall. Sec. America, Soc. Economic Geologists, Am. Inst. Mining and Metall. Engrs., Geol. Soc. Washington, Phi Delta Theta, Sigma Rho, Alpha Nu. Republican. Mason. Club: Engineers (Phila.). Author or co-author various professional papers, many repts. and bulls. of U.S. Geol. Survey, etc. Home: 1555 Sherman St., Denver, Colo. Office: Bullitt Bldg., Philadelphia, Pa.; and Hobart Bldg., San Francisco, Calif.

GARRISON, F(rank) Lynwood, mining engr.; b. Phila., Jan. 12, 1862; s. David Rea and Maria Morgan (Pleiss) G.; ed. Rittenhouse and Rugby acads., Phila.; B.S., U. of Pa., mining and civ. engring. metallurgy, chemistry and geology, 1883; Royal School of Mines of London, England, 1884-85; m. Adele Mary Dwight, Nov. 21, 1894 (died Sept. 1929); children—Dwight, Elizabeth D., Laura D.; m. 2d, Mrs. Edith Brinton McKenna, Oct. 17, 1931. Was in Russia investigating methods of making iron during years,

1887-88; commr. Paris Expn., 1889; practiced profession U.S., Alaska and Canada, 1890-99, in China, 1900; chief engr. Empire Lumber and Mining Co., Johnson Co., Tenn., 1902-04; in cons. practice S. America, S. Africa and U.S., since 1904. Mem. Soc. Economic Geologists, Am. Inst. Mining and Metall. Engrs., Franklin Inst. (mem. bd. mgrs.), Acad. Natural Sciences Phila., Instn. Mining and Metallurgy (London), Newcomen Soc., Zeta Psi. Chmn. Nat. Manganese Commn., 1917. Mason. Clubs: Union League, Contemporary. Author: Kerl's Assaying, 1889; also many tech. papers. Home: 1019 Clinton St., Philadelphia, Pa.

GARRISON, Samuel Frederick, lawyer; b. Bordentown, N.J., Oct. 15, 1879; s. Samuel and Hannah Gary (Mershon) G.; student Bordentown Mil. Inst., 1893-97, grad., 1897; m. Agnes Welling Howell, Apr. 18, 1906 (dec.); 1 son, Samuel Frederick, Jr. Engaged in bus. as propr. gen. store, Bordentown, N.J., 1896-1901, also cranberry grower, 1896-1927; studied law in office of Linton Satterthwait; admitted to N.J. bar as atty., 1901, as counselor, 1904; engaged in gen. practice of law at Bordentown, N.J., since 1901; served as city commr. of Bordentown, 1913-21, mayor, 1917-21; vice-pres., dir. and gen. counsel First Nat. Bank of Bordentown; dir. and solicitor Peoples Bldg. & Loan Assn. Mem. Burlington Co. Bar Assn. Republican. Episcopalian. Mason. Home: 329 Farnsworth Av. Office: 327 Farnsworth Av., Bordentown, N.J.

GARTMAN, George Edward, pres. Edgemont Paper Co.; b. York, Pa., May 16, 1897; s. George E. and Mary R. (Harmon) G.; ed. pub. schs.; m. Edna Margaret Wisotzkey, Mar. 31, 1934. Pres. Edgemont Paper Co. since 1937. Republican. Mem. Reformed Ch. Home: 271 N. Hartley St. Office: Louck's Mill Road, York, Pa.

GARVER, Francis Marion, coll. prof.; b. on farm near Cleone, Ill., Sept. 29, 1875; s. Abraham Jerome and Nancy Melinda (Morrell) G.; grad. Ind. State Normal Sch., Terre Haute, 1900; A.B., Ind. Univ., 1906; A.M., Columbia, 1912; Ph.D., U. of Pa., 1920; m. Della Viola Hisey, Aug. 18, 1903; 1 dau., Margaret Elizabeth. Prin. schs. Ogden, Ill., 1900-01; prin. high sch., Brazil, Ind., 1901-05, Gallipolis, O., 1906-07, Ithaca, N.Y., 1907-08, Binghamton, 1908-13; supt. schs., Leonia, N.J., 1913-17; head master Oak Lane Country Day Sch., 1917-21; prof. elementary edn., U. of N.Dak., 1921-23; asst. prof. elementary edn., U. of Pa., 1923-26, prof. edn. since 1926; participated in school surveys at East Manch Chunk, Harrisburg, Wyomissing, Bethlehem, Phila., etc. Mem. N.E.A., Nat. Soc. Coll. Teachers of Edn., Nat. Soc. for Study of Edn., Supervisors and Directors of Instrn., Am. Ednl. Research Assn., Phi Delta Kappa. Democrat. Presbyn. Mason. Author and editor of a series of language art books for schools. Home: Ivyland, Pa.

GARVER, Ivan Edison, manufacturer; b. Roaring Spring, Pa., Oct. 18, 1887; s. Abraham Lincoln and Ella (Bare) G.; student Dickinson Sem., Williamsport, Pa., 1902-05, Phillips Acad., Andover, Mass., 1905-06, Harvard, 1906-07; unmarried. Began as employee Roaring Spring Blank Book Co., Roaring Spring, Pa., 1907-10, sec., 1910-20, gen. mgr., 1920-33, pres. since 1933; pres. D.M. Bare Paper Co., Roaring Spring Bank; dir. Hollidaysburg (Pa.) Trust Co., Pa. Mfg. Asso. Casualty Ins. Co. Served in U.S. Army during World War. Delegate to 1936 Republican Conv. from 23d Pa. Dist. V.p. Roaring Spring (Pa.) Sch. Bd. Pres. Nason Hosp., Roaring Spring, Pa., dir. Dickinson Sem., Williamsport, Pa. Mem. Kappa Sigma. Republican. Methodist Episcopalian. Mason (Jaffa Temple, A.A.O.N.M.S., Altoona, Pa.). Clubs: Harvard (New York); Union League (Phila.); Duquesne (Pittsburgh); Maryland Yacht (Baltimore, Md.); Sea View Golf (Atlantic City). Home: 715 Spang St. Office: 740 Spang St., Roaring Spring, Pa.

GARY, E(dward) Stanley, cotton mfr.; b. Alberton, Howard Co., Md., July 26, 1862; s. James Albert and Lavinea W. (Corrie) G.; ed. Friends' elementary and high sch., Baltimore; m. Mary Ragan Macgill, Sept. 30, 1885. Pres. James S. Gary & Son. Inc.; dir. Chesapeake Steamship Co., Hopkins Pl. Savings Bank, Md. Hosp. for Consumptives. Was a mem. Emergency Com. after fire of 1904; mem. State Bd. of Edn., Commn. for Improvement of R.R. Service; mem. com. for securing silver service for U.S.S. Maryland, and many other civic orgns. Ex-pres. Bd. of Trade, Merchants & Mfrs.' Assn., Baltimore. Ex-pres. McDonogh Sch. Republican. Episcopalian. Clubs: Maryland, Merchants'. Home: Catonsville, Baltimore Co., Md. Office: American Bldg., Baltimore, Md.

GARY, James Albert Jr., mfr. cotton duck; b. Baltimore, Md., Jan. 19, 1887; s. Edward Stanley and Mary Ragan (Macgill) G.; student Boys' Latin Sch., Baltimore, 1897-1906; B.S., Harvard, 1910; m. Ann Franklin Keyser, Oct. 4, 1919; children—Caroline Fischer, Ann Franklin, James Albert III. With James S. Gary & Son, Inc., Baltimore, since 1910, beginning as clk., v.p. and dir. since 1921; dir. First Nat. Bank of Baltimore, Savings Bank of Baltimore, Calvert Bldg. & Construction Co. Served in U.S. Navy during World War, on U.S.S. "Missouri," U.S.S. "Margaret" (part time in command), U.C.G. "Yamacraw." Trustee and v.p. Enoch Pratt Free Library; mem. bd. and v.p. Md. Training Sch. for Boys. Mem. Am. Legion (former state comdr.), Forty and Eight. Republican. Episcopalian (vestryman Ch. of The Redeemer). Clubs: Merchants (mem. bd. and sec.), Harvard (Baltimore); Harvard (New York). Home: 318 Overhill Road. Office: 204 American Bldg., Baltimore, Md.

GASCOYNE, William J.; pres. Gascoyne & Co.; dir. several companies. Home: 2741 N. Charles St. Office: 27 S. Gay St., Baltimore, Md.

GASKILL, Burton A., lawyer; b. May's Landing, N.J., Oct. 9, 1889; s. Edmund C. and Hester M.; grad. May's Landing High Sch., 1907; LL.B., U. of Tenn., 1910; m. Irene Gordon, May 31, 1911; children—Gordon, Mary Hester, Isabel (Mrs. Lacon Hubert Carlock, Jr.). Admitted to N.J. bar, 1912, and since practiced in Atlantic City; mem. firm Gaskill & Rosenberg. Served as pres. Bd. of Edn., Hamilton Twp. Mem. Phi Kappa Phi. Republican. Mason (Shriner). Odd Fellow (grand sire). Club: Morris Guards (Atlantic City). Home: May's Landing, N.J. Office: Atlantic City, N.J.

GASKILL, Joseph Franklin, sales mgr. Philadelphia Electric Co.; b. Philadelphia, Jan. 31, 1889; s. Nathan B. and Emma S. (Wilson) G.; B.S., Swarthmore Coll., 1910, E.E., 1919; m. Marion E. Cook, Sept. 29, 1923; children—Marion C., Joseph F., Sally P. With Parsons Pulp & Lumber Co., Laneville, W.Va., 1912-13; with Gen. Electric Co., 1913-15; with Westinghouse Electric & Mfg. Co., 1916-17; with Philadelphia Electric Co. since 1919, becoming sales mgr., 1936. Served as lt., later capt., Ordnance Dept., A.E.F., 1917-19. Received A.E.F. citation. Mem. Am. Inst. E.E., Pa. Electric Assn., Edison Electric Inst., Phi Kappa Psi. Republican. Mem. Soc. of Friends. Clubs: Union League, Philadelphia Country, Welcome Society. Home: 104 Tenby Road, Llanerch, Pa. Office: 1000 Chestnut St., Philadelphia, Pa.

GASKILL, Thomas Logan, lawyer, referee in bankruptcy; b. nr. Pemberton, N.J., July 6, 1874; s. (Judge) Joseph H. and Ella S. (Logan) G.; grad. Peddie Sch., Hightstown, N.J., 1892; A.B., Princeton, 1896; ed. U. of Pa. Law Sch., 1897 to 1899, unmarried. Studied law in office of father, judge Ct. Common Pleas, Burlington Co.; admitted to N.J. bar, as atty., 1899, counsellor, 1903; admitted to practice U.S. Dist. Ct., 1903; engaged in gen. practice, 1899-1930; master in chancery, 1899; N.J. Supreme Ct. commr., 1915; referee in bankruptcy for Dist. Ct. of the U.S., Dist. of N.J., Camden, N.J. since 1922. Served in N.J. Militia, 1899-1904. Mem. N.J. Bar Assn., Burlington Co. Hist. Soc., Am. Numismatic Assn. Republican. Episcopalian. Mason. Club: Union League (Philadelphia). Home: Hotel Walt Whitman. Office: 401 Market St., Camden, N.J.

GASSAWAY, Frederic Gerrish, chamber of commerce mgr.; b. Portland, Me., June 24, 1888; s. Dr. James Morsell and Susan (Ramsey) G.; student schs. of San Francisco and Berkeley, Calif., 1898-1905, Tulane U., New Orleans, La., 1921-22, Northwestern U., Evanston, Ill., summers 1926-36; m. Lillian Garic, Oct. 26, 1914; children Frederic Gerrish, Mary Eleanor. Began as cow hand, Northern Calif., 1905; clk., chief clk., Mfrs. Ry., St. Louis, Mo., 1906-09; salesman Meyer Bros. Wholesale Drug Co., St. Louis, Mo., 1909-12; fruit agt. Tex.-Pacific Ry., New Orleans, La., 1912-16; sales mgr. Interstate Land Co., New Orleans, La., 1912-16; industrial mgr. Assn. of Commerce, New Orleans, 1920-21; sec. Chamber of Commerce, Newport News, Va., 1921-22; pres. Southern Advertising Agency, Baltimore, Md., Phila. and New York, 1922-24; mgr. Chamber of Commerce, Wilmington, Del., since 1924. Served as pvt. to 2d lt., 141st F.A., U.S. Army, Mexican Border, 1916, as pvt. to maj., 3d F.A., A.E.F., 1916-19. Sec. Del. River Crossing Commn., 1938-39; Del. state dir., N.R.A., 1932-33; asso. state dir., Federal Housing Administration, 1933-35; sec. Del. Industrial Recovery Survey Commission, 1932-34; Wilmington City Charter Commn., 1928-30; chmn. Wilmington Centennial Commn., 1932; vice chmn. (Del.) N.Y. World's Fair Commn. 1938-39. Mem. Nat. Assn. Commcl. Orgn. Secs. (pres. 1931-32), Del.-Md.-Va. Eastern Shore Assn. (v.p. at large since 1926), Am. Automobile Assn., Del. Motor Assn., Am. Legion, Vets Fgn. Wars, S.A.R. Episcopalian. Mason (La. Lodge 102), Elk (New Orleans Lodge 30). Clubs: Rotary (pres. 1939-40), Wilmington, Exchange, Advertising, Wilmington Country, Concord Country (Wilmington, Del.). Home: Cragmere, Del. Office: 400 Mullin Bldg., Wilmington, Del.

GASSAWAY, Louis Dorsey, banking; b. Annapolis, Md., Dec. 14, 1862; s. Louis Gardner and Marian Bradford (Dorsey) G.; A.B., St. John's Coll., Annapolis, Md., 1881; m. Mary Brooke Iglehart, Oct. 15, 1891 (dec.). Engaged in banking since 1881; asso. with Farmers Nat. Bank, Annapolis, Md., since 1881, now chmn. bd. Mem. Soc. of the Cincinnati, Soc. of Colonial Wars. Democrat. Episcopalian. Mason. Clubs: South River, Annapolis Yacht. Home: Hotel Maryland, Annapolis, Md.

GASTON, John Montgomery; b. E. Liverpool, O., Sept. 12, 1868; s. George and Rachel G.; student Wooster U., D.D., 1918; B.A., Princeton, 1892, M.A., 1895; S.T.D., Princeton Theol. Sem., 1895; LL.D., Johnson C. Smith U., Charlotte, N.C., 1925; m. Harriet Cramp, Dec. 31, 1895 (died Nov. 5, 1922); children—Mrs. Marion Gaston Ballard, John Montgomery; m. 2d, Eva A. Montgomery, of Phila., Dec. 5, 1925. Ordained Presbyn. ministry, 1895; pastor chs. at Pittsburgh, Pa., 1895-1911; gen. sec. and treas. Bd. of Missions for Freedmen of Presbyn. Ch. of U.S.A., 1911—; sec. Unit of Work for Colored People. Pres. bd. dirs. Presbyn. Book Store, Pittsburgh; gen. sec. and treas. Johnson C. Smith, Charlotte, N.C., 1938. Mem. Phi Delta Theta. Republican. Home: 305 Pasadena Drive, Aspinwall, Pa. Office: 510 Bessemer Bldg., Pittsburgh, Pa.

GATES, Caleb Frank, college pres.; b. Chicago, Oct. 18, 1857; s. Caleb Foote and Mary Eliza (Hutchins) G.; A.B., Beloit (Wis.) Coll., 1877; grad. Chicago Theol. Sem., 1881; D.D., Knox Coll., 1897; LL.D., Edinburgh U., 1899; same degree from Beloit College, 1927; m. Mary Ellen Moore, May 31, 1883; children—Edward Caleb (dec.), Herbert Frank, Moore, Elizabeth Davidson (dec.), Caleb Frank. Ordained Congregational ministry, 1881; missionary A.B.C.F.M., Mardin, Turkey in Asia, 1881-94; pres. Euphrates Coll., Harpoot, Turkey, 1894-1902; pres. Robert Coll., Constantinople, 1903-32. Chmn. Near East Relief Commn. in Constantinople, 1917-19. Mem. Nat. Inst. of Social Science, Acad. of Polit. Science. Decorated Knight Comdr. George I. (Greece), Knight Comdr. Alexander (Bulgaria). Author: A Christian Business Man, 1893; also (article) "Caliphate in The Modern Moslem World." Address: Box 217, Princeton, N.J.

GATES, Charles Bernard, property mgr. and investment mgr.; b. Charleston, W.Va., May 27th, 1890; s. Charles Amos and Clara Lorena (Cole) G.; student Charleston (W.Va.) pub. schs., 1895-1906, Culver (Ind.) Mil. Acad., 1906-10, Washington & Lee U., Lexington,

Va., 1910-11; m. Harriet Hostetter, Nov. 15, 1919; children—Charles Bernard, Philip Custer. Became mem. firm C. A. Gates & Son, 1910; sec. and treas. Kanawha Groves Co., Charleston, since 1915; dir. Charleston Nat. Bank. Served as 1st lt., F.A., U.S. Army, 1917-18. Formerly pres. Charleston Chamber of Commerce. Mem. Delta Tau Delta. Republican. Presbyterian. Mason (Shriner). Clubs: Rotary, Edgewood Country (Charleston, W.Va.). Home: 1307 Virginia St. Office: 108½ Capitol St., Charleston, W.Va.

GATES, Theodore J(ay), prof. of English composition; b. Vestaburg, Mich., Nov. 21, 1893; s. Thurman Jay and Mary (Spencer) G.; A.B., Alma Coll. (Mich.), 1915; A.M., Pa. State Coll., 1921; student U. of Ill., summer 1920; grad. study, U. of Mich., 1926-28; m. Leota Dee Brown, June 14, 1917; children—Marshall Jay, Morris Brown (dec.), Thurman John. Began as teacher in high sch., Amboy, Ill., 1915-16; asso. with Pa. State Coll. since 1916, as instr. of English, 1916-21, asst. prof., 1921-23, asso. prof., 1923-30, prof. English composition since 1930, head of dept. since 1936. Republican. Presbyterian. Home: 510 E. Fairmount Av., State College, Pa.

GATES, Thomas Sovereign, university pres.; b. Germantown, Phila., Pa., Mar. 21, 1873; s. Jabez and Isabel (Sovereign) G.; Ph.B., U. of Pa., 1893; LL.B., 1896; LL.D., Villa Nova Coll., 1923, Allegheny College, 1928, U. of Pa., Lafayette Coll., Haverford Coll., Dickinson, Coll., Lehigh Univ., 1931, New York Univ., 1932, Univ. of Pittsburgh, Temple Univ., 1933, Harvard Univ., 1936; m. Emma Barton Brewster Waller. Admitted to Pa. Bar, 1896; assistant in law office of John G. Johnson, of Philadelphia, 1895-1906; trust officer, 1906-10, v.p. and trust officer, 1910-12, v.p., 1912, The Pennsylvania Co. for Insurance on Lives and Granting Annuities; pres. Phila. Trust Co., 1912-18; partner Drexel & Co., 1918-30, J. P. Morgan & Co., 1921-30; pres. Univ. of Pennsylvania since 1930; dir. Pa. R.R. Co. (chmn. finance comm.), Phila., Baltimore and Washington R.R. Co., Pittsburgh, Fort Wayne and Chicago Ry. Co., Pittsburgh, Cincinnati. Chicago and St. Louis Ry. Co., Pa. Co., United Gas Improvement Co.; pres. and dir. Beaver Coal Corpn.; trustee Penn Mutual Life Ins. Co.; mgr. Phila. Saving Fund Soc. Treas. Bethesda Children's Christian Home, Church Soc. for College Work; chmn. bd. Phila. Orchestra Assn.; pres. Union Library Catalogue (Phila.); dir. Pa. Acad. of the Fine Arts; trustee Univ. of Pa., Thomas W. Evans Dental Museum and Inst. Society (pres.), Moore Sch. of Elec. Engring. (chmn.), Acad. of Natural Sciences of Phila., Divinity Sch. of P.E. Ch. in Phila., Internat. Cancer Research Foundation, Phila. Commercial Museum, Exhibition and Convention Halls; manager The Morris Arboretum (pres.), The University Museum (Phila.), Leamy Home; commr. Valley Forge Park; councillor Hist. Soc. of Pa. Mem. Am. Philos. Soc., Am. Acad. of Polit. and Social Science, Washington (D.C.), Cathedral Council, Newcomen Soc., Wistar Assn., Phi Beta Kappa, Phi Kappa Sigma. Episcopalian. Clubs: Rittenhouse, Philadelphia, University (Phila. and New York), Art Alliance, Bank Club of London, Boca Raton (Florida), Contemporary, Legal, Lenape, Mask and Wig, Midday, Penn Athletic, Philadelphia Cricket, Print, Racquet, Sunnybrook Golf, Seaview Golf, U. of Penna. in New York City, Union League. Home: Rex and Seminole Avs., Chestnut Hill, Philadelphia. Office: University of Pennsylvania, Philadelphia, Pa.

GATESON, Daniel Wilmot, clergyman; b. Brooklyn, N.Y., July 14, 1884; s. Daniel Thompson and Augusta Virginia (Smith) G.; B.A., Trinity Coll., Conn., 1906; grad. Gen. Theol. Sem., N.Y., 1909; studied Columbia, 1918-20; M.A., Lehigh, 1925; D.D., Hahnemann Med. Coll. and Hospital, 1936; m. Marian Anne Blackstone, July 1, 1912; children—Marianne Augusta, Constance Blackstone, Elizabeth Wilmot, Gloria. Deacon and priest, P.E. Ch., 1909; rector St. Paul's Ch., Georgetown, Del., 1909-12; vicar St. Thomas Chapel, N.Y. City, 1912-17; rector Trinity Ch., Williamsport, Pa., 1917-22; dean Pro-Cathedral of the Nativity, Bethlehem, Pa., 1922-31, also chaplain Lehigh U.; rector Ch. of the Savior, Phila., since 1931. Mem. Delta Kappa Epsilon. Club: Union League. Widely known as lecturer and speaker on religious, hist. and social subjects, also at baccalaureate exercises; preacher and instr. at ch. conferences, especially on "Devotional Life," "Religious Healing," etc. Home: 3725 Chestnut St., Philadelphia, Pa.

GATLEY, H(oward) Prescott, lawyer; b. Washington, D.C., Mar. 23, 1875; s. William Albert and Mary Greenleaf (Goodrich) G.; LL.B., George Washington U., 1895, LL.M., 1896; m. Maybelle Hermann, Dec. 17, 1902; children—Helen H., H. Prescott. Resigned as asst. clk. Supreme Court of D.C., 1900; practiced in Washington, 1900-34; pres. and dir. Nat. Savings and Trust Co.; also dir. Washington Gas Light Co., Washington Suburban Gas Co., Washington Gas Light Co. of Montgomery County (Md.), Alexandria (Va.) Gas Co., Rosslyn (Va.) Gas Co., Arcade Co. (Washington, D.C.). Mem. Am. Bar Assn., Bar Assn. District of Columbia (ex-pres.), Phi Delta Phi. Republican. Presbyn. Clubs: Metropolitan, Lawyers' (ex-pres.), Chevy Chase (pres.). Home: Chevy Chase, Md. Office: care Nat. Savings & Trust Co., Washington, D.C.

GAUGER, Alfred William, chem. engineer; b. St. Paul, Minn., July 31, 1892; s. Augustus F. and Albertine O. (Nitschke) G.; A.B., U. of Minn., 1914; fellow, Princeton, 1919-20, A.M., 1920, Charlotte Elizabeth Procter fellow, 1921-22, Ph.D., 1922; Nat. Research Council fellow in chemistry, U. of Calif., 1922-24; m. Margaret Baxter Carnegie, July 22, 1922; children—Marcia Carnegie, Mary Jane Carnegie. Chemist Great Western Sugar Co., Sterling, Colo., 1914-15; jr. chemist U.S. Bur. Mines, Pittsburgh, Pa., 1915-17; research asso., Am. Sheet & Tin Plate Co., Pittsburgh, 1920-21; chem. engr. and mgr. Burnham Chem. Co., Westend, Calif., 1924-25; research chemist R. & H. Chem. Co., Perth Amboy, N.J., 1926; dir. div. mines and mining experiments, U. of N.D., 1926-31; prof. fuel technology and dir. research, Sch. of Mineral Industries, Pa. State Coll., since 1931. Served as 1st lt., later capt. Chem. Warfare Service, U.S.A., 1917-19, 19 mos. overseas; organized 1st sch. for gas defense, Fort Sill, Okla., Aug. 1917; dir. Army Gas Sch. and gas officer 90th Div., A.E.F.; awarded citation by comdg. gen.; mem. War Damages Bd., Am. Peace Mission. Mem. Nat. Coal Bd. of Arbitration, 1935. Mem. Am. Inst., Chem. Engrs., Am. Chem. Soc. (sec. Pittsburgh sect. 1917; chmn. gas and fuel div. 1933, Central Pa. sect., 1935), Am. Ceramic Soc., Am. Soc. for Testing Materials, Am. Inst. Mining and Metall. Engrs., Sigma Xi, Sigma Tau, Phi Lambda Upsilon, Alpha Chi Sigma. Contbr. tech. articles on fuel technology, catalysis, absorption, inflammability of gases, etc. Inventor and patentee of several processes for extraction of salts from natural salines. Home: Baum Boul., State Coll., Pa.

GAUGLER, Jos. P., color and textile consultant; b. Paterson, N.J., Mar. 17, 1896; s. Franz F. and Kathrine (Vesper) G.; student Paterson pub. and high schs., 1902-12, Phillips Private Sch., 1912-14, Ecole du Saumur, France, 1917, also tutors and summer schs.; m. Marion Montgomery Trimble, June 23, 1921; 1 dau., Gloria Lillian. With Frank A. McBride Construction Company, 1916; textile buyer for Sears Roebuck & Company, New York and Chicago, 1916-22; later manager Slater Div., Clarence Whitman Sons, Inc.; pres. and treas. Fiatelle, Inc. (originally a Whitman subsidiary); treas. Ridgewood Art Assn. Served as exec. officer and capt. of batteries F and E, 103d F.A. Regt., 20 months overseas; asst. operation officer 51st F.A. Brigade; also 4 months in U.S. Cited for destruction of enemy battery on June 25, 1917, while in command 155m.m. Roving Gun, 103d F.A. Awards: Dennison 1st prize for Water Colors, Ridgewood Art Exhibit, 1935; Montclair Art Mus. 1st award for water colors, N.J. State Exhibit, 1936; Ridgewood Art Assn. award for portraiture, 1939. Home: Sheridan Terrace, Ridgewood, N.J. Office: 320 Broadway, N.Y.

GAUL, Harriet Avery, author; b. Youngstown, O., June 25, 1886; d. Rev. Frederick Burt and Ione (Lester) Avery; student Hathaway Brown Sch., Cleveland, 1901-05, Smith Coll., 1905-06; m. Harvey B. Gaul, June 13, 1908; children— James Harvey, Ione (Mrs. Hudson D. Walker). Began as contbr. to newspaper syndicates, 1906; free lance writer of fiction and spl. articles to newspaper supplements; asst. editor of books, music, theatre to Harvey B. Gaul on Pittsburgh Post Gazette, 1928-35; lecturer on lit. and travel; travel advisor Thos. Cook & Son, Pittsburgh, 1937. Author: Five Nights at the Five Pines, 1922; Who'll Take Papa (3-act comedy), 1934. Contbr. of spl. articles to women's mags. and of short stories to fiction mags. Wrote lyrics for songs by Harvey B. Gaul. Democrat. Episcopalian. Clubs: Women's Press, Author's (Pittsburgh). Home: 12 Dunmoyle Pl., Pittsburgh. Pa.

GAUL, Harvey B., organist, composer; b. N.Y. City, 1881; s. James Harvey and Louise (Bartlett) G.; studied with George F. Lejeune (New York) Alfred R. Gaul (Birmingham, Eng.), Dr. Armes (Durham, Eng.), Schola Cantorium and Paris Conservatory with Guilmant, Widor, Decaux and D'Indy; with Mons. Rella of Sistine Chapel Choir and Mons. Rienzi of St. Peter's (Rome); hon. Dr. Mus., University of Pittsburgh, 1933; m. Harriette Avery, a writer, June 13, 1908; children—James Harvey and Ione Avery (Mrs. Hudson D. Walker). Associate organist, Saint John's Chapel, New York City, 1899; organist Emmanuel Church, Cleveland, 1901-09, Calvary Church, Pittsburgh, since 1910. Formerly mem. faculty, University of Pittsburgh, Carnegie Institute Technology, Washington and Jefferson Univ.; conductor Singers Club, Cleveland, O., 1924-26, Pittsburgh Apollo Male Chorus, 1925-30, Pittsburgh Chamber of Commerce Chorus, 1925-29; conductor of Y.M.& W.H.A. Choral Soc. since 1925; conductor Civic String Orchestra since 1936; member faculty Fillion Studio of Music, 1931—; music critic Pittsburgh Post-Gazette, 1914-34, editor of music, art, drama and book dept., 1919-34, feature editor Mus. Forecast, 1934—. Mem. Am. Guild Organists, Musicians' Club. Episcopalian. Composer cantatas, anthems, part-songs, solos, organ and orchestral works; first prize, "Water Lilies," Tuesday Mus. Club, Chicago; "Madrigal," Chicago Madrigal Clubs; "Ode to Vulcan." Pittsburgh Male Chorus; "Euridice," Federated Clubs, etc.; Mendelssohn Club prize, Phila.; Strawbridge & Clothier's prize, Phila.; first prize for woodwinds ensemble "John Brashear Sings in the Night," by Pittsburgh Art Soc., 1936. Lecturer on mus. subjects. Home: 12 Dunmoyle Pl., Pittsburgh, Pa.

GAUM, Carl Gilbert, prof. engring. extension; b. Saginaw, Mich., Jan. 13, 1884; s. Gilbert and Ottilie C. (Roethke) G.; B.Sc., Ala. Poly. Inst., 1908, M.E., same, 1909; unmarried. Instr. in machine design, Ala. Poly. Inst., 1909-13, also asst. coach football and track teams; instr. mech. engring., Pa. State Coll., 1913-14, instr. engring. extension, same, 1914-17; asst. prof. engring. extension, Pa. State Coll., then asso. prof. and prof., same, 1920-30; prof. Univ. Extension Div., Rutgers U., New Brunswick, N.J., since 1930. Served as ensign, U.S.N.R.F., 1917-20. Fellow A.A.A.S. Mem. Am. Soc. Mech. Engrs., Am. Con. Assn., Am. Acad. Polit. and Social Sci., Acad. Polit. Sci., Soc. for Promotion Engring. Edn., Adult Edn. Assn., New Brunswick Sci. Soc., American Legion. Democrat. Ch. of Disciples of Christ. Author: Personal Efficiency, 1928; Report Writing (with H. E. Graves), 1929. Editor of Engineering Extension News, 1920-30. Editor, extension texts in variety of engring. subjects. Contbr. to management and exec. training mags. Home: 605 S. 2d Av., New Brunswick, N.J.

GAUNT, Harold Garfield, clergyman; b. Gilford, Mich., Mar. 10, 1882; s. John George and Evalyn Cornelia (Crittenden) G.; student Vassar (Mich.) High Sch., 1898-1901; A.B., Alma (Mich.) Coll., 1906; M.A., Princeton U., 1908; student Princeton Theol. Sem., 1906-09; D.D., Davis and Elkins Coll., Elkins, W.Va., 1926; m. Susie Lou Hawes, June 9, 1910; children—Margaret Philna (Mrs. Clarence W. Lynch), Virginia Lou, Richard Hawes. Ordained minister

Presbyn. Ch., 1909; minister 1st Presbyn. Ch., Wheaton, Minn., 1909-12, 2d Presbyn. Ch., East Liverpool, O., 1912-16, 1st Presbyn. Ch., Moundsville, W.Va., 1916-25, Olivet Presbyn. Ch., Atlantic City, N.J., since 1925; chaplain W.Va., State Penitentiary, Moundsville, W.Va., 1919-24. Served as chaplain, U.S. Army, Camp Taylor, Louisville, Ky., Camp Johnson, Jacksonville, Fla., during World War; capt.-chaplain, O.R.C., since 1919. Mem. Mil. Order of World War. Democrat. Presbyterian. Mason (32°, Shriner). Address: 18 S. Jackson Av., Atlantic City, N.J.

GAUSS, Christian, univ. dean; b. Ann Arbor, Mich., Feb. 2, 1878; s. Christian and Katherine (Bischoff) G.; A.B., U. of Mich., 1898, A.M., 1899, LL.D., 1933; Litt.D., Washington, 1914; L.H.D., Lehigh, 1928; m. Alice Hussey, June 15, 1902; children—Katherine, Dante Christian, Natalie, Hildegarde. Instructor Romance langs., U. of Mich., 1899-1901; Lehigh U., 1901-03; asst. prof. Modern langs., Lehigh U., 1903-05; ast. prof. Romance langs., 1905-07, prof. modern langs. since 1907, chmn. department, 1913-36, dean of the College since 1925, Princeton. Non-resident lecturer on Ropes Foundation for Comparative Lit., U. of Cincinnati, 1913; grad. lecturer, New York U., 1915-16; lecturer, Columbia U. Inst. Arts and Sciences. Lit. editor Princeton Alumni Weekly, 1914-20, asso. editor Journal of Education, mem. editorial bd. The American Scholar. Trustee Princeton U. Press, Teachers Ins. and Annuity Assn. Decorated Knight of Legion of Honor of French Republic, 1935. Mem. Kappa Sigma, Phi Beta Kappa (senator); Pres. Dante League America, 1918-20. Clubs: Princeton (N.Y.), Century, Nassau. Translator: Ferrero's The Women of the Cæsars; (with Alice Gauss) Bainville's History of France, 1925. Editor: Selections from J. J. Rousseau, 1914; Democracy Today, An American Interpretation, 1917; Flaubert's Madame Bovary, 1930. Author: The German Emperor, 1915; Through College on Nothing a Year, 1915; Why We Went to War, 1918; Life in College, 1930; A Primer for Tomorrow, 1934. Home: Princeton, N.J.

GAY, Frank Roy; prof. classics and comparative literature, Bethany Coll. Address: Bethany College, Bethany, W.Va.

GAY, Hiram Burton, v.p. Electric Storage Battery Co.; b. Cambridge, N.Y., Aug. 18, 1871; s. Joseph William and Anna (Smith) G.; ed. Cornell U.; m. Louise Allan Mayo, Apr. 30, 1903; children—Louise Gay Moore, Hiram Burton, Jr. Salesman Westinghouse Electric & Mfg. Co., 1895-1901; with Electric Storage Battery Co. since 1901; successively salesman, branch manager and gen. sales mgr., v.p. and dir. since 1926; dir. Chloride Elec. Storage Co., London, Exide Batteries of Canada, Ltd., Toronto. Republican. Baptist. Club: Merion Cricket. Home: Laurel Lane, Haverford, Pa. Office: Allegheny Av. and 19th St., Philadelphia, Pa.

GAY, Leslie Newton, physician; b. Shamokin, Pa., Nov. 7, 1892; s. Harry S. and Sarah J. (Batdorff) G.; Ph.B., Lafayette Coll., Easton, Pa., 1913; M.D., Johns Hopkins, 1917; m. Julia Adele Griffith, June 4, 1919; 1 son, Leslie Newton. Physician since 1917; dir. Asthma-Hay Fever Clinic, Johns Hopkins Hosp. since 1920; asso. in medicine, Johns Hopkins U., since 1936; visiting physician to Johns Hopkins Hosp., Women's Hosp. of Md., Church Home and Infirmary. Served as lt., Med. Corps, U.S. Army, 1917-18. Mem. A.M.A., Soc. for Study of Asthma and Allied Conditions (past pres.), Southern Med. Soc., Am. Assn. Immunologists. Ind. Republican. Presbyterian. Clubs: Maryland, Elkridge (Baltimore); Gibson Island (Md.). Contbr. articles to professional jours. Home: Hollins Av. near Lake Av. Office: 1114 St. Paul St., Baltimore, Md.

GAY, Walter Arthur, Jr., lawyer; b. Dawson, Ga., May 30, 1904; s. Walter A. and Anna (Josey) G.; A.B., U. of Pa., 1926, LL.B., 1929; unmarried. Professor of philosophy, Wilberforce U., 1929-31; admitted to Pa. bar, 1930; asst. U.S. atty., Phila., since 1935. Mem. Omega Psi Phi. Home: 532 N. 58th St. Office: 400 Custom House Bldg., Philadelphia, Pa.

GAYLORD, Franklin Augustus, retired Y.M.C.A. official; b. Glenwood near Yonkers, N.Y., May 1, 1856; s. Gen. Augustus and Martha (Champlin) G.; A.B., Yale, 1876; grad. Union Theological Seminary, 1881; studied at Collège de France, Paris, 1883; m. Mary Louise Robinson, Sept. 10, 1891. General secretary Y.M.C.A., Paris, France, 1887-93; ordained Presbyn. ministry, Oct. 1, 1894; transferred to Manhattan Congl. Assn., 1895; pastor Trinity Congregational Church, New York, 1895-99; gen. sec. Russian Y.M.C.A., St. Petersburg, 1899-1911; dir. Russian Soc. for Moral and Physical Development of Young Men, 1911-18. Sec. Am. Hosp. for wounded Russian soldiers, 1916; sec. Internat. Com. Y.M.C.A., 1918-19; trustee Jas. Stokes Soc. for forwarding work of Y.M.C.A. 1920; representative at Odessa, Russia, of Internat. Com. Y.M.C.A., 1919-20, also at Constantinople and in Egypt; lectured in U.S.; again in Europe, at Berlin, Warsaw, Belgrade, Sophia, Constantinople; returned to New York, Nov. 1921; was sent to Washington, D.C., to invite delegates to Conf. on Disarmament to lecture in U.S. Chevalier Order St. Anne, Russia, 1902; presented to Czar, 1907, 1911; Chevalier, Order St. Stanislaus, 1916, Chevalier Russian Red Cross, 1920. Mem. Congl. Association of Ministers of New York City since 1895; member The Hymn Society of America, Delta Kappa Epsilon, Phi Beta Kappa. Clubs: Yale, Town Hall, Clergy (New York); Graduate (New Haven); Authors (London). Author: The Builders of the Atoll and other poems. Translator into English verse of various Russian poems. Home: 47 Englewood Av., W. Englewood, N.J.

GAZZAM, Joseph M. Jr., lawyer; b. Phila., Pa., Jan. 8, 1895; s. Joseph M. and Nellie (Andrews) G.; prep. edn., St. Paul's Sch., Concord, N.H., 1908-13; A.B., Harvard, 1917; LL.B., U. of Pa., 1921; m. Aileen de LaTour Clark, Apr. 14, 1928; 1 son, Joseph M. III. Admitted to Pa. bar, 1921, and since practiced in Phila.; asst. city solicitor, 1924-26; dep. atty. gen. of Pa., 1935-39; prof. of mortgages and legal ethics, Phila. Coll. of Law; dir. Peale, Peacock & Kerr; dir. Am. Gold Dredging Co. Served as 1st lt. 302d Inf., 76th Div., U.S. Army, and in aerial observation for field arty., during World War. Dir. Keeler Home. Mem. Am. Legion, Mil. Order - Loyal Legion, Delta Phi, Phi Delta Phi. Episcopalian. Clubs: Harvard, Phila. Cricket (Phila.). Home: 7820 Roanoke St. Office: 1324-30 Lincoln-Liberty Bldg., Phila., Pa.

GEARHART, Ephraim Maclay, clergyman; b. Sunbury, Pa., Dec. 25, 1880; s. Robert Harris and Mary (Cornman) G.; A.B., Susquehanna U., 1903, grad. theol. dept. same, 1906, A.M., 1906, D.D., 1920; m. Minnie Louise Kline, Dec. 19, 1905; 1 son, Ephraim Maclay; m. 2d, Bessie Alice Leonard, July 8, 1911; children—Robert Paul, Gordon Cornman. Ordained Luth. ministry, 1906; pastor Trinity Ch., Sunbury, 1904-11, Bethany Ch., Montoursville, Pa., 1911-16, Zion Ch., Indiana, Pa., 1916-22, Luther Memorial Ch., Erie, Pa., 1922—. State supt. prison work, Pa. State C.E. Union, 1909-11. Physical dir. for Y.M.C.A. at U.S. Naval Air Sta., U.S. Navy Yard, Pensacola, Fla., World War. Scout master 15 yrs.; mem. Nat. Commn. Boy Scouts America, 1919—. Chmn. com. on ministerial edn. of Pittsburgh Synod United Lutheran Church America. Director Erie Chamber Commerce, 1923-32; dir. Erie Y.M.C.A. Mem. Pennsylvania State Hist. Commn., 1924-30; mem. Commn. to Commemorate the Battle of Lake Erie. Mem. Am. Philatelic Soc., Pi Gamma Mu fraternity; corr. member Académie Latine, Arts, Sciences and Belles Lettres, Paris, Accademia Internazionale di Lettere e Scienze, Naples. Mem. bd. trustees Thiel Coll.; trustee Edinboro Teachers Coll., 1924-26. Awarded Second Class Order of Red Cross of Japan, also title of "The Silver Bearer," by Nat. Com. Boy Scouts America. Republican. Mason (K.T., 32°, Shriner). Clubs: Kiwanis (Erie); Collectors (New York). Lecturer on Indian Mythology; has made field research in Am. archæology and history in Susquehanna Valley, Pa. Author: Skalalatoot Stories, 1922. Home: 444 Kahkura Boul., Erie, Pennsylvania.

GEARHART, Ethan Allen, judge; b. Allentown, Pa., Apr. 11, 1896; s. Dr. Ethan Allen and Mary (Gregory) G.; student Allentown (Pa.) High Sch., 1911-15, Allentown Prep. Sch., 1915-16; LL.B., Dickinson Sch. of Law, Carlisle, Pa., 1922; m. Marcella Geissenhainer, Jan. 1, 1923; children—Mark, Ethan Allen, III. Admitted to Lehigh County bar, 1922, and practiced at Allentown, Pa., 1928-32; dist. atty., Allentown, Pa., 1928-32; pres. judge Orphans' Court, Lehigh County, Pa., since 1932 (yr. of its creation by legislature). Served as private, 4th Regt., U.S. Army, Mexican Border ,1916-17, sergt., 1st class, Camp Hancock, during World War. Mem. Lehigh County Bar Assn., Pa. Bar Assn., Am. Legion, Delta Chi. Democrat. Reformed Ch. Mason, Elk, Odd Fellow. Home: 3102 Turner St. Office: 457 Hamilton St., Allentown, Pa.

GEARHART, Robert Harris, Jr., clergyman; b. Sunbury, Pa., Oct. 7, 1885; s. Robert Harris and Mary (Cornman) G.; A.B., Gettysburg (Pa.) Coll., 1910, (hon.) D.D., 1933; student Gettysburg Sem., 1910-13, U. of Pa. Grad. Sch., 1916-24; m. Harriet S. Davies, June 15, 1914. Ordained to ministry U. Luth. Ch. in America, 1913; pastor, St. Matthew's Ch., Mansfield, O., 1913-15, Grace Ch., Phila., Pa., 1915-22, with leave of absence, 1918-19; Luth. Campus Pastor, Met. Dist. of Phila. since 1922. Served as chaplain, then sr. chaplain 78th Div., then sr. chaplain 2d Army Area, U.S.A., 1918-19 with A.E.F. Nat. pres. Assn. Ch. Workers in State Univs., 1927-30. Mem. Acacia. Awarded two citations for Exceptionally Conspicuous and Meritorious Services. Lutheran. Mason. Author: Jesus, the Unique, 1929; Perennial Problems, 1933; Finding the Way, 1935; contbr. articles to mags. and jours. Home: 231 S. 39th St. Office: 3601 Locust St., Philadelphia, Pa.

GEARY, Alexander Brooke, lawyer; b. Wallingford, Pa., Nov. 24, 1870; s. George W. and Susannah (Armstrong) G.; ed. pub. schs.; studied law under Hon. Oliver B. Dickinson; m. Eleanor J. Wilson, May 10, 1902; children—Eleanor, Alexander Brooke. Admitted to Del. Co. (Pa.) bar, 1894; since in gen. practice of law at Chester, Pa.; mem. Superior and Supreme cts. of Pa., Philadelphia cts., U.S. Courts in Philadelphia; pres. and dir. Marcus Hook (Pa.) Nat. Bank since 1920; sec. and dir. Delaware County Bldg. Assn.; solicitor Keystone Bldg. & Loan Assn., Delaware County Trust Co., etc.; county solicitor, 1 yr. Federal fuel adminstr. for Delaware Co. and counsel Federal Food Adminstrn., during World War. Sch. dir., Wallingford, Pa., 1900-02. Mem. Fed. Commn. for Celebration of Delaware Valley Tercentenary of Settlement of Swedes and Finns. Solicitor and dir. Community Welfare Soc.; dir. & treas. Helen Kat Furness Free Library, Wallingford; mem. Wallingford Red Cross, League of Nat. Assns., Inc. (Pa. branch). Mem. Lawyers' Guild of U.S. and Pa., Pa. state and Delaware Co. bar assns., Pa. Hist. Soc., Delaware Co. Hist. Soc., Delaware Co. Inst. of Science, Nat. Geog. Soc. Democrat. Mason, Odd Fellow, Concord Grange. Clubs: Penn, Manufacturers' and Bankers' (Phila.). Author: Legal Lore of Delaware County, Pa., 1910; Legal Reminiscences of the Bench and Bar of Delaware County, 1912. Owner, editor and pub. Weekly Reporter (legal jour. of Delaware Co.), Delaware Co. Reports. Home: Possum Hollow Road, Wallingford, Pa. Office: 515 Welsh St., Chester, Pa.

GEARY, Theodore Carlton, physician and surgeon; b. Zerbe, Pa., July 19, 1900; s. Albert Edward and Catharine (Diener) G.; grad. High School, Minersville, Pa., 1918; B.S., Hahnemann Coll. of Science, Phila., 1923; M.D. Hahnemann Med. Coll., 1924; post grad. student U. of Vienna, 1936. Physician, Phila., since 1925; instr. in surgery, Hahnemann Med. Coll., Phila., since 1927, lecturer since 1928; asso. surgeon Hahnemann Hosp., Broad St. Hosp., Phila., Fitzgerald Mercy Hosp., Darby, Pa. Served in S.A.T.C., 1918. Fellow Am. Coll. Surgeons, A.M.A.; mem. Eastern Delaware Co. Med. Club, Delaware Co. Med. Soc., Pa. State Med. Soc., Germantown Med. Soc., Phila. Homeop. Med. Soc., Pa. Homeop. Med. Soc., Am. Inst. Homeopathy, Phi Alpha Gamma. Republican. Clubs: Medical, Medical Tower (Phila.). Home: 25 W. Plumstead Av., Lansdowne, Pa. Office: 255 S. 17th St., Philadelphia, Pa.

GEARY, W. B.; pres. The Diamond, Inc., Daniel Boone Hotel, Geary Securities Co., Geary Realty Co. Address: 315 Capitol St., Charleston, W.Va.

GEBERT, Herbert George, prof. of education; b. Tamaqua, Pa., May 11, 1900; s. George and Amanda (Henning) G.; A.B., Muhlenberg Coll., Allentown, Pa., 1922; A.M., U. of Chicago, 1926; student New York U., summer 1930; Ph.D., U. of Pittsburgh, 1937; m. Lucy Johnstone, 1926; 1 son, Herbert G. With Thiel Coll., Greenville, Pa., since 1922, as instr., 1922-26, asst. prof. of edn., 1926-37, prof. since 1937, registrar since 1927, sec. of faculty since 1927. Treas. Greenville Consumers Co-operative Assn. Served in S.A.T.C., 1918; C.M.T.C., 1919. Mem. N.E.A., Pa. State Edn. Assn., Am. Assn. Univ. Profs, Am. Assn. Coll. Teachers of Edn., Am. Assn. Coll. Registrars, Alpha Tau Omega. Democrat. Lutheran. Home: 15 Ridgeway Av., Greenville, Pa.

GEBHARDT, Homer, banking; b. Glenwood, W.Va., Apr. 9, 1894; s. Anthony Joseph and Nora Mae (Baumgardner) G.; grad. Huntington (W.Va.) High Sch.; student Marshall Coll., Huntington, W.Va., 1 year; unmarried. Asso. with First Nat. Bank (later First Huntington Nat. Bank), Huntington, W.Va., since 1915, vice-pres., dir. and trust officer since 1928; sec. and dir. First Huntington Nat. Co.; pres. and dir. Blue Jay Mfg. Co.; sec., treas. and dir. Huntington-Ohio Bridge Co.; treas. and dir. C. W. Watts Investment Co.; vice-pres., sec. and dir. J. L. Caldwell Co.; dir. Ohio Valley Bus Co., Hagen Ratcliffe Co.; all corpns. are at Huntington, W.Va. Served as pvt. inf. U.S.A., during World War. Dir. W.Va. Chamber of Commerce; sec. W.Va. Bankers Assn.; pres. Huntington Community Chest, 1939. Republican. Presbyn. Clubs: Guyan Country, Gypsy (Huntington). Home: 801 Park Hills. Office: First Huntington Nat. Bank, Huntington, W.Va.

GEBHARDT, Neil Harrison, mcht. fuels; b. Erie, Pa., Apr. 4, 1896; s. Gustave John and Ada (Potter) G.; ed. U. of Chicago, 1915-17; m. Helen Humphrey, June 26, 1924; children —Neil Humphrey, Lois Janet. Asso. with G. J. Gebhardt Coal & Coke Co., retail mcht. fuels at Erie, Pa., since starting as salesman, 1919, pres. since 1931. Served as enlisted pvt. Ordnance Dept., U.S.A., promoted regularly through grades to 1st lieut., 1917-19. Mem. Sigma Alpha Epsilon. Republican. Baptist. Club: Lions. Home: 437 Crescent Drive. Office: 1426 Chestnut St., Erie, Pa.

GEBHARDT, William Reading, lawyer; b. Clinton, N.J., Mar. 28, 1895; s. William Cavanaugh and Evelina Evans (Reading) G.; student Clinton pub. schs., 1900-12, Lafayette Coll., 1912-14; LL.B., New York Law Sch., 1917; m. Edna Mahan, Aug. 15, 1935. Admitted to N.J. bar, 1919; mem. law firm William C. Gebhardt & Son, 1920-29, Gebhardt & Gebhardt since 1929; v.p. First Nat. Bank of Clinton; pres. and treas. Bituvert Corpn. Mem. Clinton Bd. of Edn. Served in U.S. Naval Reserve Force, 1918-19. Mem. Nat. Bd. of Y.M.C.A.; chmn. exec. com. N.J. Y.M.C.A.; chmn. co. com. Hunterdon Co. Y.M.C.A. Mem. Am. Bar Assn., N.J. Bar Assn., Hunterdon Co. Bar Assn., Warren Co. Bar Assn., Delta Theta Phi. Democrat. Presbyn. Mason, Odd Fellow, K.P. Address: Clinton, N.J.

GECHTOFF, Leonid, artist; b. Odessa, Russia, Apr. 15, 1883; s. Ilia and Sonia (Teplitzkai) G.; ed. School of Art, Odessa, 1895-1905; France, Italy, Germany; m. Ethel D. Freeman, May 1919; children—Sonia, Anna. Came to U.S., 1921, naturalized, 1933. Artist since 1909. Exhibited: one-man show, Sketch Club, Phila., 1938; annual exhbns. of Sketch Club, Phila., 1938, 39; Cornish Art Sch., Seattle, Wash., 1921; Graphic Sketch Club, Phila., 1923; Trenton (N.J.) Fair, 1925; Art Alliance, New York, 1933; Plastic Club, 1933. Represented in permanent collection of paintings at White House, Hall of Justice (Washington, D.C.), Edward Bok's collection, Dr. Stanley P. Reimann's collection. Served in the arty. of Serbian and Russian armies, 1914-17; decorated with Military Cross of St. George of Imperial Russia, 1917. Mem. Art Alliance and Sketch Club, Phila. Home: 1408 Spruce St., Philadelphia, Pa.

GEE, Howard James, b. at Chicago, Ill., Nov. 23, 1884; s. William Stanley and Katharine Belle (James) G.; grad. South Side Acad., Chicago, 1903; A.B., Princeton, 1907; m. Myrtle Garrison Bates, 1925. Editor ednl. pubis. of Hinds, Hayden & Eldridge, Inc., 1917-26; v.p. W. L. Thomas & Co., investment securities, 1926—. Republican. Presbyterian. Clubs: Mendelssohn Glee Club, Princeton, Rotary (New York). Author: Methods of Church School Administration, 1920. Contbr. to religious mags.; writer of short stories. Home: 111 S. Mountain Av., Montclair, N.J. Office: 551 5th Av., New York, N.Y.

GEEGAN, James G., coal operator; b. Pittsburgh, Pa., Dec. 27, 1872; s. James and Susan E. (McNish) G.; student Pittsburgh pub. schs. and Pittsburgh Central High Sch. (1888-90); m. Cera Woodford, Nov. 1, 1899; 1 dau., Sylvia Woodford. Began as errand boy, 1890; mgr. Saw Mill Run Coal Co., 1894-99; gen. office mgr. Clyde Coal Co., 1900-05, gen. mgr.; 1905-29, sec., 1910-24, sec. and treas., 1924-29; sec. and treas. Chartiers Creek Coal Co., 1929-39, receiver, 1929-33; sec. and treas. Chartiers Supply Co. since 1934; pres. Neale Oil & Gas Co.; executor James Neale Estate; trustee Clyde Coal Co. Republican. Episcopalian. Home: 5633 Elgin Av., Pittsburgh, Pa. Office: 218 E. Pike St., Canonsburg, Pa.

GEHMAN, Henry Snyder, Orientalist, clergyman; b. Ephrata Twp., Lancaster Co., Pa., June 1, 1888; s. Christian Eberly and Amanda Minerva (Snyder) G.; A.B., Franklin and Marshall Coll., 1909 (1st honors), A.M., 1911; Ph.D., U. of Pa., 1913; student Dropsie Coll., 1921-26; S.T.B., Div. Sch. of P.E. Ch., Phila., 1926, S.T.D., 1927; student Divinity Sch., U. of Chicago, summer 1922; m. Bertha W. Lausch, Aug. 30, 1917; children—Amanda Elizabeth, Henry Nevin. Teacher rural sch. and prin. high school, Pa., 2 yrs.; successively univ. scholar and Harrison fellow in classics, Harrison fellow and Harrison research fellow in Indo-European philology, 1910-14, all Univ. of Pa.; asst. in Latin, Univ. of Pa., 1913-Jan. 1914; teacher Latin and Greek, Hill Sch., Pottstown, Pa., Jan.-June 1914; research work in Latin, Greek and Sanskrit, U. of Pa., 1914-15; teacher modern langs., South Phila. High Sch. for Boys, 1915-1929; instr. in Semitic langs., Princeton U., 1929-35, lecturer in Semitic langs., June 1935; instr. in New Testament Greek, Princeton Theol. Sem., 1930-31, acting prof. Old Testament, 1931-34, prof. Old Testament lit. since 1934. Ordained ministry Reformed Church in U.S., 1917; organized Tabor Ref. Ch., Phila., and pastor, July 1917-Feb. 1921; univ. research fellow, 1920-29; asst. in Sanskrit, U. of Pa., 1920-21; mem. of faculty, Winona Lake Sch. of Theology, summers since 1937; asso. mem. Am. Schs. of Oriental Research since 1937. Lecturer of Biblical subjects at various conferences. Mem. Am. Oriental Soc., Soc. Bibl. Lit. and Exegesis, Canadian Soc. of Bibl. Studies, Linguistic Soc. America, Phi Beta Kappa, Phila. Classical Club, Phila. Oriental Club (pres. 1929-30). Republican. Author: The Interpreters of Foreign Langs. Among the Ancients, 1914; The Sahidic and Bohairic Versions of The Book of Daniel, 1927; Some Present-Day Values of Old Testament Studies, 1934; The John H. Scheide Biblical Papyri—Ezekiel (with A. C. Johnson and E. H. Kase). Special editor of etymologies for 2d edit. of Webster's New International Dictionary. Contbg. editor Am. Jour. of Archæology. Contbr. to periodicals. Home: 60 Stockton Street, Princeton, N.J.

GEIGER, Marlin George, chem. mfg.; b. Harrisburg, Pa., Nov. 15, 1897; s. John Albert and Laura Margaret (Stouffer) G.; B.S., Pa. State Coll., State Coll., Pa., 1921; m. Marie J. Owens, Aug. 29, 1925; children—Marlin George, Jr., William Thom. Asso. with Westvaco Chlorine Products Corpn., chem. mfrs., South Charleston, W.Va., since 1921, chem. engr., 1921-26, asst. mgr., 1926-28, resident mgr. since 1928, dir. of corpn. since 1939; dir. McAlpin Oil Co., Charleston, W.Va., 1937. Served in S.A.T.C. during World War. Mem. Am. Chem. Soc., Alpha Chi Sigma, Phi Lambda Upsilon. Republican. Baptist. Mason. Sigma Tau. Clubs: Kanawha Country, Revellers (Charleston); Black Knight Country (Beckley). Home: 6 Roller Road, Charleston, W.Va. Office: MacCorkle Av., South Charleston, W.Va.

GEISINGER, Arch L(ee), manufacturer; b. Medina Co., O., Aug. 1, 1891; s. John M. and Eva Caroline (Buchanan) G.; grad. Medina (O.) High Sch., 1910; M.E., Ohio State U., 1914; m. Mary Lillian Fisher, Oct. 25, 1916; children—Robert Willis, Thomas Richard. Draftsman Phila. Quartz Co., Phila., 1914-20; chief engr. Standard Silicate Co., Cincinnati, 1920-25; gen. mgr. and vice-pres. Lockport (N.Y.) Chem. Co., 1925-30; div. mgr. Standard Silicate Div. Diamond Alkali Co., Pittsburgh, since 1930; pres. Standard Silicate Corpn., Lockport, N.Y. Republican. Methodist. Mason. Club: Chartiers Heights Country (Crafton, Pa.). Home: Priscilla Lane, Carnegie, Pa. Office: Oliver Bldg., Pittsburgh, Pa.

GELLERT, Nathan Henry, pub. utility exec.; b. Baltimore, Md., Sept. 7, 1889; s. Horace and Minna (Goldman) G.; B.A., Yale, 1910; Ph.B., Sheffield Scientific Sch. (Yale), 1915, C.E., 1916; m. Edna Louise Smith, June 18, 1912; children—Nathan Henry, Eleanor Louise, Helen Elizabeth, Edward Bradford. Cadet engr. Am. Gas Co., 1910-11; chief engr. Pub. Service Constrn. Co., 1912-14; v.p. several gas cos., 1916-20; cons. engr. and v.p. Atlantic Gas Co., 1920-30, became pres., 1930; pres. Nat. Pub. Utilities Corpn. and subsidiaries since 1930; pres. Great Lakes Utilities Co.; dir. Bearings Co. of America. Vice-chmn. Manufactured Gas Industry Code Com.; asso. mem. Am. Soc. C.E.; mem. Am. Soc. Mech. Engrs., Am. Gas Association, Sigma Xi. Chmn. personnel com. of executive bd. Valley Forge Council Boy Scouts America. Republican. Episcopalian. Clubs: University, Yale (New York); Delaware River Yacht Club. Designer and builder of 1st elec. blast furnace gas cleaners in U.S. Author of many tech. papers. Home: Trellande, Meadowbrook, Pa. Office: Packard Bldg., Philadelphia, Pa.

GELSTHARP, Frederick, chemist; b. Gateshead-on-Tyne, England, Jan. 12, 1877; s. Charles and Ann Isabella (Milburn) G.; student School of Science and Art, Heaton, Eng., 1889-92, Rutherford's Coll., Newcastle-on-Tyne, Eng., 1892-95, Manchester Univ. of Technology, Eng., 1895-97; m. Lily Norris, Feb. 2, 1916; 1 dau., Mildred. Came to U.S., 1907, naturalized, 1923. Chemist C. J. Schofield, Ltd., mfg. chemists, England, 1897-1901; Chemist Union Plate Glass Co., St. Helens, Eng., 1901-03, asst. supt. and later supt., 1903-07; chief chemist 1907, and dir. of glass research Pittsburgh Plate Glass Co. since 1923. Fellow Am. Ceramics Soc., Am. Chem. Soc., Electrochem. Soc., Am. Soc. for Testing Materials. Republican. Episcopalian. Club: Chemists (New York). Home: 1134 Park St., Tarentum, Pa. Office: Research Laboratory, Creighton, Pa.

GEMMILL, Benjamin McKee, clergyman; b. New Park, Pa., Oct. 24, 1866; s. John Brown and Agnes Mary (Workman) G.; A.B., Lafayette Coll., 1889, D.D., 1922; McCormick Theol. Sem., 1889-90; grad. Princeton Theol. Sem., 1892; Ph.D., Blue Ridge Coll., New Windsor, Md., 1895; m. Clara Marie Genso, June 1, 1898; children—Charlotte Eleanor, Chalmers Laughlin, Kenneth Wilfred, Janet Muriel. Ordained Presbyn. ministry, 1892; pastor Anacortes, Wash., 1892-93, 1st Ch., Cresson, Pa., 1893-1905; asst. pres. Kendall Coll., Muskogee, Ind. Ty., 1905; connected with The Presbyterian, Phila., 1905-06; pastor Hartsville, Pa., since 1908; also professor of Bible and philosophy, Beaver College for Women, Jenkintown, Pa. Stated clerk, Synod of Pennsylvania, permanent clerk 17 years; member Permanent Judicial Com. of Gen. Assembly Presbyn. Ch. in U.S.A.; moderator Philadelphia North Presbytery; secretary of The Curran Foundation. Mem. Phi Beta Kappa Fraternity, Delta Upsilon. Democrat. Author: Manual of Parliamentary Practice for Church Courts; Manual of Synod of Pennsylvania; (brochure) The Judicial Decisions of the General Assembly of 1925; Faith for a Bewildered World; Psychology of the Will of God; The Problems of Youth; also many religious tracts. Home: Hartsville, Pa.

GEMMILL, Charles Wesley, supervising prin. schs.; b. York Co., Pa., June 25, 1892; s. Wesley Street and Amanda (Sprenkle) G.; A.B., Lebanon Valley Coll., Annville, Pa., 1918; A.M., Columbia U., 1925; m. Mildred Kuntelman, Aug. 15, 1925; children—June Marie, Nancy Louise, Mary Ann. Prin. high sch., Enola, Pa., 1919-27; supervising prin., New Cumberland, Pa., since 1927. Served in Air Service, U.S. Army, 1918-19. Mem. Am. Assn. Sch. Adminstrs. Republican. Methodist. Mason (32°, Shriner), Rotarian. Home: 521 Haldeman Av., New Cumberland, Pa.

GEMMILL, Paul Fleming, university prof.; b. Muddy Creek Forks, York Co., Pa., May 30, 1889; s. William James and Sue Mary (Jamison) G.; prep. edn., York County Acad.; A.B., Swarthmore Coll., 1917; Ph.D., U. of Pa., 1925; m. Jane Pancoast Brown, Mar. 29, 1920; children—Robert Fleming, Jean McAllister. Began as cashier McClellan & Gotwalt Co., York, Pa., 1902; stenographer York Printing Co., 1905-08; asst. sec. Y.M.C.A., York, 1908-09; pub. entertainer ("magician"), 1909-11, also summers 1911-17; with U. of Pa. since 1919, successively instr. in industry, 1919-21, asst. prof. economics, 1922-28, prof. economics since 1928, chmn. grad. group in economics since 1938. Entertainer in France, under direction of Nat. War Council, 1918; pvt. Gas Defense Div. of Chem. Warfare Service, Aug. 1918-Jan. 1919. Mem. Kappa Sigma, Phi Beta Kappa, Delta Sigma Rho, Pi Gamma Mu. Author: Collective Bargaining by Actors, 1926; Present-Day Labor Relations, 1929; Fundamentals of Economics (also issued under title "The Economics of American Business"), 1930, revised and enlarged, 1935, 3d edit. rev., 1939; (with others) An Economics Question Book, 1931; (with others) Contemporary Economic Problems, 1932; (with R. H. Blodgett) Economics: Principles and Problems, 2 vols., 1937; (with R. H. Blodgett) Current Economic Problems, 1939. Contbr. to mags. and scientific journals. Has appeared as pub. entertainer (as "Paul Fleming, the Magician") for many yrs. Home: 406 Thayer Road, Swarthmore, Pa.

GENTER, Albert Legrand, chem. and san. engring.; b. Breckenridge, Colo., June 23, 1881; s. Edward William and Minnie Emilie (Gray) G.; Diplomingenieur, Royal Technische Hochschule, Berlin-Charlottenburg, Germany, 1904; m. Lillie Richards, Apr. 25, 1905. In employ General Engring. Co., 1906; chief designer Kelly Filter Press Co., Salt Lake City, Utah, 1906-11, European rep. same, 1911-14; chief engr., Kelly Filter Press Co. and United Filters Corpn., 1915-20; pres. Genter Thickner Co., Salt Lake City, Utah, 1920-26; engr. with Bartlett Hayward Co., Baltimore, Md., 1927-31; engaged in pvt. research in san. engring. since 1931, discoverer, propr. and consultant re Sludge Elutriation Process since 1932; inventor processes and apparatus for sludge treatment and disposal. Mem. A.A.A.S., Am. Chem. Soc., Md.-Del. Water & Sewage Works Assn. Club: Timpanogos (Salt Lake City). Home: Wyman Park Apts., Baltimore, Md.

GEORGE, Charles Albert, librarian; b. New York, Oct. 11, 1867; s. Charles Timmons and Mary Louisa (Huff) G.; grad. Peddie Inst., Hightstown, N.J., 1893; A.B., Princeton, 1897, A.M., 1899; m. Mary Leslie Guion, Aug. 9, 1900; 1 dau., Julia Guion. Asst. to librarian and chief of catalogue dept., Princeton U. Library, 1898-1909; librarian, Pub. Library, Elizabeth, N.J., Nov. 17, 1909—. Mem. A.L.A., N.J. Library Assn. (pres. 1908-09), N.J. Hist. Soc., Union Co. Hist. Soc., Alpha Phi. Address: Public Library, Elizabeth, N.J.

GEORGE, Forney Philip, M.D., surgeon; b. Middletown, Pa., Jan. 22, 1904; s. Henry William and Katherine (Forney) G.; student Middletown High Sch., 1918-21; B.S., Pa. State Coll., 1925; M.D., Jefferson Med. Coll., 1928; student Grad. Sch. of Medicine, U. of Vienna, 1930-31; unmarried. Began practice medicine and surgery, 1928; asst. to Dr. G. L. Dailey, Harrisburg, Pa., 1928-29; asso. mem. staff Harrisburg Hosp., 1931-36; surgeon, eye, ear, nose and throat, Harrisburg Hosp. since 1936; chief surgeon, eye, ear, nose and throat, Carlisle Hosp. since 1935. Mem. R.O.T.C., 1921-28, 1st lt., 1928-33. Fellow Am. Coll. Surgeons; mem. A.M.A., Am. Bd. Otolaryngology, Am. Acad. Ophthalmology and Otolaryngology, Pa. State Med. Soc., Dauphin Co. Med. Soc., Harrisburg Acad. Medicine, Deutsches Ophthalmologische Gesellschaft, Ophthalmol. Soc. of the United Kingdom, Phi Mu Alpha, Alpha Pi Mu, Delta Sigma Chi, Alpha Kappa Kappa. Republican. Presbyn. Mason (32°, Shriner), Knight of Malta, Royal Arcanum, Jr. Order United Am. Mechanics. Clubs: Harrisburg (Pa.) Country; Carlisle (Pa.) Country. Office: 31 S. Front St., Harrisburg, Pa.; and 118 S. Hanover St., Carlisle, Pa.

GEORGE, Henry William, physician; b. Wilkes-Barre, Pa., May 27, 1878; s. Herman Nicholas and Magdalena (Bornmann) G.; grad. Muhlenberg Acad., 1894, Muhlenberg Coll., Allentown, Pa., 1897; M.D., Jefferson Med. Coll., Phila., 1901; grad. study, U. of Pa. Grad. Sch. Medicine, 1915, U. of Vienna, Austria, 1927, 1929, 1931; m. Katharine W. Forney, June 25, 1901; children—Dorothy (Mrs. James Earle Miller), Forney P. (M.D.), Helen (Mrs. Charles R. Foster), Mary (Mrs. Harold Harrisson). Engaged in practice of medicine and surgery at Middletown, Pa., since 1901, specializing in ophthalmology since 1918; surgeon Pa. R.R. Co. continuously since 1904; ophthalmologist, Pa. State Home of I.O.O.F., and Jednota Orphan Home, both Middletown, Pa.; vice-pres. Citizens Bank & Trust Co. Served as med. examiner U.S. Marine Corps during World War; now Vol. Med. Res. U.S. Med. Examiner for C.C.C. camp admission. Pres. Middletown Pub. Sch. Dist.; served as commr. to gen. assembly Presbyn. Ch. of U.S.A. Fellow Am. Acad. Ophthalmology and Otolaryngology; Am. Bd. of Ophthalmology; mem. Ophthal. Soc. Heidelberg, Germany, Ophthal. Soc. United Kingdom, London, Am. Med. Assn., Vienna, Harrisburg Acad. Medicine (pres. bd. dirs.). Republican. Presbyterian (elder). Mason, Odd Fellow, Knight of Malta. Home: 19 N. Union St., Middletown, Pa.

GEORGE, Homer (Clayton), merchant and banker; b. Summerhill, Pa., Jan. 8, 1883; s. Nicholas S. and Mary (Paul) G.; ed. pub. sch. and high sch., South Fork, Pa.; m. Elizabeth Brennan, July 8, 1904; children—Mary Kathleen, Homer Clayton. Mem. firm of George Bros., hardware, furniture and funeral dirs., South Fork, Pa., since 1900, gen. mgr. since 1908; pres. Union Deposit Bank since 1917; dir. South Fork Water Co. Served as mem. Internat. Y.M.C.A., 8 mos. in Italy, during World War. Served as co. commr. Cambria Co., 1923-29, sheriff, 1929-33. Pres. Sheriff's Assn. of Pa., 1933, now trustee; trustee Pittsburgh Conf. Evang. Ch. Republican. Evang. Ch. Mason (K.T., 32°, Shriner), Odd Fellow, Knight of Malta. Club: Johnstown Motor (dir.). Home: 521 Main St. Office: 313 Main St., South Fork, Pa.

GEORGE, Howard, mcht. sporting goods; b. Phila., Pa., Nov. 2, 1869; s. William and Sarah A. (Fox) G.; ed. Northeast Grammar Sch., 1880-84; m. Mary E. Pritchard, June 25, 1892; children—Lillian E. (dec.), Howard B., Marion V. (Mrs. Raymond T. Bohn), Sarah A. (dec.). Employed with Edw. K. Tryon, Jr. & Co., Phila., 1886-93; engaged in business on own acct. as dealer in sporting goods, Phila., since 1893; was one of organizers and dir. Oxford Bank of Frankford until merged with Corn Exchange Nat. Bank of Phila. Mem. Guild of Photographic Dealers of Phila. Republican. Mason. Club: Torresdale-Frankford Country (Torresdale, Pa.). Home: 1307 Wakeling St. Office: 4359 Frankford Av., Philadelphia, Pa.

GEORGE, John J., univ. prof.; b. Latta, S.C., Sept. 1, 1897; s. John J. and Anne (Rogers) G.; A.B., Washington and Lee Univ., Lexington, Va., 1920; A.M., U. of Chicago, 1922; grad. student, U. of Wis., 1924-25; Ph.D., U. of Mich., 1928; m. Marie Dodd, June 4, 1925; children—John Warren, Margaret (dec.), Martha Lydia. Engaged as instr., Clemson Coll., S.C., 1919-20; instr. Baylor U., Waco, Tex., 1920-21; asst. prof. of govt., Denison U., Granville, O., 1922-24; asst. prof. govt., U. of Ky., 1925-27; instr. govt., U. of Mich., 1927-28; prof. of history and govt. Converse Coll., Spartanburg, S.C., 1928-29; asst. prof. govt., Rutgers U., New Brunswick, N.J., 1929-33, asso. prof. since 1933. Served as 2d lt. Inf., O.R.C., U.S.A., 1918-25. Mem. Metropolitan Polit. Science Assn., Am. Civil Liberties Union. Liberal Democrat. Baptist. Author: Motor Carrier Regulation in the United States, 1929. Contbr. to professional journs. Lecturer. Home: Colonial Gardens, New Brunswick, N.J.

GEORGE, Walter L., coal operator; b. South Bend, Pa., Dec. 30, 1864; s. Samuel and Mary (Lellers) G.; m. Edna Lydie, Oct. 22, 1902; 1 son, Samuel N. Pres. First Nat. Bank, Apollo, Pa., since 1901; mgr. George & Jameson Coal Co. since 1926; sec.-treas. West Pa. Land Co. since 1928; pres. West Pa. Coal Mining Co. since 1932. Home: 309 First St. Office: Warren Av., Apollo, Pa.

GEORGE, William Dickson, real estate; b. Washington Co., Pa., Dec. 15, 1869; s. John L. and Elizabeth (Shaw) G.; grad. Allegheny High Sch., 1887; m. Eleanore Willard, 1903; children—William Dickson, Rebekah W., Elizabeth, Eleanore W. Partner George Bros., real estate, Pittsburgh, since 1895; pres. Edwards, George & Co., insurance, Pittsburgh, since 1905; dir. First Nat. Bank at Pittsburgh; dir. Peoples-Pittsburgh Trust Co.; treas. Sewickley Valley Land Co.; pres. and dir. Atlantic Land Co.; receiver Pittsburgh Rys., 1919-24; trustee Pittsburgh Rys. and Pittsburgh Motor Coach Co. Served as food adminstr. Allegheny Co. during World War. Mem. bd. of govs. Dixmont Hosp. Presbyterian. Clubs: Duquesne (Pittsburgh); Sewickley (Pa.) Country; Beaumaris Yacht (Can.). Home: Beaver and Nevin St., Sewickley, Pa. Office: 307 4th Av., Pittsburgh, Pa.

GEPPERT, William L., editor and pub.; b. Cincinnati, O., Sept. 18, 1882; s. William and Nettie (Kilmartin) Geppert; student W.Va. U., 1907-10; m. Ruth Henking, Apr. 5, 1911; children—William Henking, Ruth Dionis. Began as reporter Gallipolis (O.) Daily Journal, 1898; editor in chief Clarksburg (W.Va.) Daily Telegram, 1901-34; now editor and gen mgr. Cumberland (Md.) News. Admitted to W.Va. bar, 1911. Mem. W.Va. State Council Journalism. Republican. Episcopalian. Clubs: Rotary, Cumberland Country. Contbr. to various newspapers and mags. Home: 328 Cumberland St. Office: Times-News Bldg., 5-7 S. Mechanic St., Cumberland, Md.

GERAGHTY, William Russel, instr. surgery, U. of Md.; visiting surgeon St. Joseph's Hosp. Address: 2225 St. Paul St., Baltimore, Md.

GERBERICH, Albert Horwell, prof. modern langs.; b. Williamstown, Pa., Feb. 23, 1898; s. Albert Henry and Martha Eleanor (Horwell) G.; A.B., Dickinson Coll., 1918; A.M., U. of Pa., 1926; Ph.D., Johns Hopkins U., 1932; m. Gisela Margit Heim-Zimanyi, June 21, 1934. Served as vice consul in charge consulate, Puerto Cortes, Honduras, 1919-22; consul at Bremerhaven, Germany, 1922-24; consul at Maracaibo, Venezuela, 1924-25; resigned from fgn. service, 1925; instr. Spanish, high sch. West Phila., Pa., 1925-26; head Latin dept., high sch., Coatesville, Pa., 1926-28; prof. Spanish and German, Dickinson Coll. since 1928. Served as radio-electrician, U.S.N., 1918-19. Mem. Kappa Sigma, Phi Beta Kappa. Mem. Am. Fgn. Service Assn., Washington, D.C. Republican. Methodist. Mason (K.T.). Author: The Gerberich (Genealogy) History (1613-1925), 1925; The Brenneman History (1477-1938), 1938. Research including Luther and the English Bible, 1933. Contbr. articles, pamphlets, in field of genealogy. Home: 36 W. Pomfret St., Carlisle, Pa.

GERBERICH, Enos S., pres. Gerberich-Payne Shoe Co.; b. East Hanover Twp., Lebanon Co., Pa., Jan. 2, 1870; s. Joseph and Elizabeth

(Snoke) G.; student pub. schs., Lebanon Valley Coll. (Annville, Pa.); m. Mary Elizabeth Early, Dec. 18, 1890; children—Clyde E., Grant D., W. Harold (dec.). Owner retail shoe stores, 1896-1908; treas. and dir. Kreider Shoe Co., Middletown, Pa., 1909-15; sec. and dir. A. S. Kreider Co., Middletown, Pa., 1915-18; founder, 1919, and since pres. Gerberich-Payne Shoe Co., Mt. Joy, Pa.; pres. First Nat. Bank & Trust Co., Mt. Joy, Pa., since 1933. Trustee Lutheran Theol. Sem., Gettysburg, Pa., since 1921; mem. deaconess bd. United Luth. Ch. in America, since 1932; gen. supt. Sunday Sch., Zion Luth. Ch., Harrisburg, Pa., since 1931. Mem. Nat. Boot and Shoe Mfrs. Assn. (dir. 1931-37, now treas.). Lutheran. Home: 2403 North Front, Harrisburg, Pa. Office: Mount Joy, Pa.

GERHEIM, Mearl Frederick, high school prin.; b. Leechburg, Pa., Dec. 23, 1905; s. Philip Henry and LuEmma (Brothers) G.; grad. Bell Twp. High Sch., Salina, Pa., 1925; A.B., Pa. State Coll., 1930, A.M., 1931; student U. of Pittsburgh, 1933; unmarried. Elementary school teacher, Armstrong Co., Pa., 1925-26; grad. asst. in history dept., Pa. State Coll., 1930-31; English teacher, Bell Twp. High Sch., Salina, Pa., 1931-32, prin. since 1932. Mem. N.E.A., Dept. of Secondary Sch. Prin. N.E.A., Am. Assn. Sch. Adminstrs., Pa. State Edn. Assn., Kappa Phi Kappa; jr. mem. Am. Assn. Univ. Profs. Republican. Mem. Reformed Ch. Elk. Home: 55 Whitesell St., Salina, Pa.

GERICKE, Oscar Carl, pres. Domestic Coke Corpn.; b. Cleveland, O., Aug. 12, 1891; s. John F. and Jennie L. (Warnicke) G.; student Cleveland grade and high schs.; B.S. in Chem. Engring., Case Sch. of Applied Science, Cleveland, 1914; m. Millie Yonkers, Apr. 10, 1917. Began as chemist Cleveland Furnace Co., 1913; with East Ohio Gas Co., 1914-18; with Domestic Coke Corpn. since 1918, as resident engr., 1918-20, supt., 1921-33, v.p., 1933-39, pres. since Mar. 1939. Presbyterian. Home: 428 Benoni Av. Office: Domestic Coke Corpn., Fairmont, W.Va.

GERMAN, Arthur R.; pres. Baltimore Life Insurance Co. Home: 5215 St. Albans Way. Office: Charles and Saratoga Sts., Baltimore, Md.

GERMUTH, Frederick George, chemist; b. Baltimore, Md., Apr. 6, 1891; s. Ferdinand J. H. and Magdalena (Schlickenmaier) G.; student City Coll., Baltimore, 1907-08, Blue Ridge Coll., New Windsor, Md., 1908-10, Johns Hopkins, 1910-14, 1921-23, University of Maryland, 1929-30; Sc.D., University of Maryland, 1937; m. Anna Elizabeth Brown, May 18, 1910; children—Viola Anna, Gordon Henry, Bertha May, Laura Marie, Ruth Elizabeth, Frederick G. In tin-testing div. Crown Cork & Seal Co., Baltimore, 1916-18; chemist, Wilson Martin Co., 1918-20, Bur. Water Supply, Baltimore, 1921-25; research chemist, Baltimore Bur. Standards since 1925; research consultant McCormick & Co., Inc., 1933—; consulting chemist; consultant to Sheppard-Enoch Pratt Hosp., Towson, Md.; discoverer of method for determination of phenylethylmalonylurea and related barbiturates and ureides in cerebrospinal fluid, blood serum and urine; researcher in the effects of drug administration upon urinary pigment formation, in the rate of conversion of certain acid salts into their normal compounds, and the effects of temperature and dilution on the system, in the catalytic effect of certain metals and their oxides upon the oxidation of carbon monoxide to carbon dioxide in the automative engine, in evolution of hydrogen sulfide from sinapis alba and sinapis nigra and methods of elimination, in improved method for estimating volatile oils in spices. Fellow Chemical Society (London); member Am. Chemistry Soc., A.A.A.S., Am. Internat. Acad. (awarded double wreath 1930), Maryland Acad. of Sciences, Soc. of Hygiene of Johns Hopkins U. Republican. Member Ref. Church. Contbr. to Jour. Am. Chem. Soc., Jour. Industrial and Engring. Chemistry, Jour. Am. Water Works Assn., The Analyst, Indian Med. Gazette, etc. Abstractor for Chem. Abstracts and Biol. Abstracts. Co-discoverer with Dr. Clifford Mitchell of new reagent for detection of uranium and other metallic elements. Home: 6 Second Av., Halethorpe, Md. Office: Municipal Office Bldg., Baltimore, Md.

GERNERD, Fred B(enjamin), ex-congressman; b Allentown, Pa., Nov. 22, 1879; s. C. W. B. and Ellen V. (Schmoyer) G.; A.B., Franklin and Marshall Coll., 1901; A.M., Columbia, 1903, LL.B., 1904; m. May G. M. Klein, Feb. 18, 1915; children—David Klein, Margaret Ellen. Began practice at Buffalo, N.Y., 1904; dist. atty. Lehigh Co., Pa., 1908-12; mem. Rep. State Conv., Pa., 1912-20; mem. 67th Congress (1921-23), 13th Pa. Dist. Del. to Rep. Nat. Conv., Kansas City, 1928. Republican. Reformed Ch. Trustee Franklin and Marshall College, Cedar Crest College; pres. Allentown Hosp. Assn.; hon. pres. Allentown Council Boy Scouts of America, John Hay Republican Assn. Mem. Am., Pa. and Lehigh County bar assns., Sigma Chi. Club: Union League (Phila.). Home: 1519 Hamilton St. Office: 502 Hamilton St., Allentown, Pa.

GEROULD, Gordon Hall, teacher; b. Goffstown, N.H., Oct. 4, 1877; s. Rev. Samuel Lankton and Laura Etta (Thayer) G.; B.A., Dartmouth, 1899; B. Litt., Oxford U., 1901; m. Katharine Fullerton, June 9, 1910; children—Christopher, Sylvia. Reader in English, 1901-02, asso. English philology, 1902-05, Bryn Mawr Coll.; assistant professor English, 1905-16, prof. English since 1916, Princeton. Fellow of Mediæval Academy of America. Author: The North English Homily Collection, 1902; Sir Guy of Warwick, 1905; The Grateful Dead, the History of a Folk-Story, 1908; Saints' Legends, 1916; Peter Sanders, Retired (novel), 1917; Youth in Harley (novel), 1920; Filibuster, 1924; A Midsummer Mystery (novel), 1925. The Ballad of Tradition, 1932; How to Read Fiction, 1937. Editor; Selected Essays of Fielding, 1905; (with Charles Gayly, Jr.), Contemporary Short Stories, 1927; Poems of James Thomson, 1927; Mediæval Literature, Sixteenth Century (2 vols. in Nelson's English Readings), 1929. Translator: Beowulf and Sir Gawain, 1933. Contbr. to philol. publs. and mags. Capt. U.S.A., 1918. Home: Princeton, N.J.

GEROULD, Katharine Fullerton, writer; b. Brockton, Mass., Feb. 6, 1879; d. Bradford Morton (D.D.) and Julia M. (Ball) Fullerton; A.B., Radcliffe Coll., 1900, A.M., 1901; m. Gordon Hall Gerould, June 9, 1910; children—Christopher, Sylvia. Reader in English, Bryn Mawr Coll., 1901-10, on leave of absence in England and France, 1908-09. Author: Vain Oblations, 1914; The Great Tradition, 1915; Hawaii, Scenes and Impressions, 1916; A Change of Air, 1917; Modes and Morals (essays), 1919; Lost Valley, 1922; Valiant Dust, 1922; Conquistador, 1923; The Aristocratic West, 1925; The Light That Never Was, 1931; Ringside Seats, 1937. Winner of prize for best story in the Century's competition for coll. grads., 1900; contbr. stories, essays and verse to mags. Home: Princeton, N.J.

GERSON, Felix Napoleon, editor and author; b. Philadelphia, Oct. 18, 1862; s. Aaron and Eva (Goldsmith) G.; ed. Central High Sch., Philadelphia; studied civil engring.; m. Emily Goldsmith, 1892 (died 1917); children—Mrs. Cecelia G. Reinheimer, Dorothy G.; m. 2d, Emma Brylawski, 1936. Corr. for various papers; mng. editor Chicago Israelite, 1890-91; mgr., 1891-1908, mng. editor since 1908, pres. since 1919, Jewish Exponent. Staff writer for Philadelphia Public Ledger, 1895-1916; contbr. prose and verse to various publs. Mem. publ. com., Jewish Publ. Soc. America. Clubs: Franklin Inn, Philmont, Art Alliance, Judæans, Pharisees. Author: Some Verses (collection of his poems). Translations of hist. and dramatic works. Home: The Sprucemont, 16th and Spruce Sts., Philadelphia, Pa.

GERWIG, George William; b. Paris, O., Jan. 18, 1867; s. Charles W. and Henrietta (Taylor) G.; B.A., U. of Neb., 1889, M.A., 1891; Ph.D., Western U. of Pa. (now U. of Pittsburgh), 1904; m. Margaret McGrew, June 4, 1896 (died 1901); children—Percy McGrew, Margaret Darsie. Began 1892, as sec. Bd. of Edn., Allegheny, Pa. (now North Side, Pittsburgh), and continued as sec. Bd. of Edn., Pittsburgh, until 1929; pres. Percy Pub. Co.; in charge U.S. Census, Pittsburgh Dist., 1910; trustee H. C. Frick Ednl. Commn. (sec. and treas. since 1926); trustee Chautauqua Institution; director State Child Welfare Association, Inc. Mem. Phi Delta Theta. Republican. Mem. Christian (Disciples) Ch. Author: Art of the Short Story, 1909; Schools With a Perfect Score, 1918; Washington, the Young Leader, 1923; Chautauqua, An Appreciation, 1924; The Declaration of Independence for Young Americans, 1926; Templed Hills, 1929; Shakespeare's Ideals of Womanhood, 1929; Character, 1930; Emotion, 1931; Guideposts to Character, 1932; Jesus: A Sister's Memories, 1934. Home: 1121 Davis Av., N.S. Office: Union Trust Bldg., Pittsburgh, Pa.

GESCHICKTER, Charles Freeborn, pathologist; b. Washington, D.C., Jan. 8, 1901; s. Leon and Rose (Zirkin) G.; B.A., George Washington U., 1920, M.A., 1922; M.D., Johns Hopkins Med. Sch., 1927; m. Mildred A. Clark, May 21, 1937; children—Charles, Edmund Harrison. Resident in medicine Baltimore City Hosp., 1927-28; fellow in surgery, Mayo Clinic, 1928-29; asso. in surgery, Johns Hopkins Med. Sch. since 1938; dir. Surgical Pathol. Lab., 1929-39. Past pres. Am. Assn. for Study Neoplastic Diseases. Clubs: Johns Hopkins, Homewood (Baltimore). Mem. editorial bd. The Review of Tumor Therapy; mem. com. publication of jour. "Surgery." Home: 100 E. Gittings Av. Office: Johns Hopkins Hospital, Baltimore, Md.

GEST, Margaret Ralston, artist; b. Phila., Pa., July 27, 1900; d. John Marshall and Emily Judson (Baugh) G.; ed. Agnes Irwin Sch., 1912-18, Pa. Mus. and Sch. Industrial Art, 1920-24, Pa. Acad. Fine Arts, 1924-28. Has followed profession as artist at Phila. since 1929; exhbns. at Pa. Acad. Fine Arts, Phila., Pa., Nat. Acad. Design, New York City; represented in collections of Pa. Acad Fine Arts, Phila. Water Color Club. Dir. Settlement Music Sch., Phila. Mem. Fellowship Pa. Acad. Fine Arts, Art Alliance, Contemporary Club, Plastic Club, Phila. Water Color Club. Awarded two Cresson Travelling scholarships at Pa. Acad. Fine Arts. Presbyterian. Home: Overbrook, Phila. Studio: 34 S. 17th St., Philadelphia, Pa.

GETHOEFER, Louis Henry, pres. Peoples-Pittsburgh Trust Co.; b. Sept. 20, 1866; s. George and Emelie (Rudolf) G.; ed. pub. schs. Employed by Bank of Buffalo (N.Y.), 1890-93, City Bank of Buffalo, 1893-1901, Marine Bank of Buffalo, 1901-03, v.p., 1903; cashier Columbia Bank of Buffalo, 1903-13; v.p. Bankers Trust Co. of Buffalo, 1913-16; pres. and dir. Pittsburgh Trust Co., 1916-29; v.p. and dir. Peoples-Pittsburgh Trust Co., 1929-31, pres. and dir. since 1931; pres. and dir. Nufer Cedar Co.; dir. Mercantile Bridge Co., Pittsburgh Terminal Warehouse & Transfer Co. Pres. and dir. Passavant Hosp. of Pittsburgh. Mason (32°, K.T., Scottish Rite). Clubs: Duquesne, Pittsburgh Athletic Assn., Metropolitan, Pittsburgh Field, Oakmont Country. Home: Schenley Apts. Office: Fourth Av. and Wood St., Pittsburgh, Pa.

GETSON, Philip, neurologist and editor; b. Russia, Oct. 15, 1884; s. Abraham and Frieda (Katz) G.; prep. edn. Gymnasium, Russia; M.D., Temple U., Phila., 1914; m. Ada Soboloff, July 5, 1914; children—Maurice, Frances. Interne Northwestern Gen. Hosp., 1914-15; med. inspr. Phila. Pub. Schs., 1915-17; neurologist to Skin and Cancer Hosp., Phila.; adj. neurologist Mt. Sinai Hosp., Phila.; editor Am. Physician, 1917-26; former asso. editor Med. Mentor (official organ of Am. Med. Editors and Authors Assn.). Mem. Phila. Co. and Pa. State Med. Socs., A.M.A., Phila. Neurol. Soc. Republican. Jewish religion. Mem. Krakauer Lodge, Phila. Author of short stories, a novelette and many articles on med. and philos. topics. Address: 2611 N. 29th St., Philadelphia, Pa.

GETTY, Frank Dales, clergyman; b. Pittsburgh, Pa., Feb. 23, 1890; s. Frank (D.D.) and Mary Elizabeth (Stewart) G.; A.B., Boys Central High Sch., Phila., 1908; ed. Phila. Sch. Pedagogy, 1908-10, courses U. of Pa.; D.D., Maryville Coll., Maryville, Tenn., 1936; m. Helen E. McKinney, May 3, 1922; children—

Richard Frank, Helen Meredith. Engaged in teaching, pub. schs., Phila., 1910-11; sec. service dept. Y.M.C.A., Phila., 1911-15; gen. sec. Y.M.C.A., Carbondale, Pa., 1915-18; asso. dir. Young Peoples Work, Bd. Christian Edn., Presbyn. Ch. U.S.A., 1919-27, dir. same since 1927; ordained to ministry Presbyn. Ch. U.S.A., 1927; mem. adminstrn. com. United Christian Youth Movement U.S.A.; mem. ednl. commn., and com. religious edn. of youth, Internat. Council of Religious Edn.; mem. Protestant Com. on Scouting, Boy Scouts of America. Trustee Internat. Soc. Christian Endeavor. Republican. Home: 7433 Devon St. Office: Witherspoon Bldg., Philadelphia, Pa.

GETTY, George Allen, pres. Brookville Bank & Trust Co.; b. Numedia, Pa., June 2, 1888; s. George W. and Matilda (Hoffman) G.; student common sch. and Bloomsburg (Pa.) State Normal Sch.; m. Cleo C. Shultz, Jan. 29, 1908; 1 dau., Ethel (Mrs. Ditty). Worked in car shops, Berwick, Pa.; later clk. in office Haines, Jones and Cadberry, Norristown, Pa.; became bookkeeper Benedictine Stores, St. Benedict, Pa., 1910, later asst. mgr.; mgr. and partner Peoples Supply Co., Summerville, Gordontown and Sligo, Pa., 1914-25; pres. and partner Orchard Coal Co., 1917-27; pres. Union Nat. Bank, Summerville, Pa., 1921-27, cashier, 1927-36, now dir.; in 1925 instrumental in having Hanley Co. of Bradford, Pa., locate brick plant at Summerville, which is now most modern in U.S.; pres. Brookville (Pa.) Bank & Trust Co. since 1936; pres. Thrift Plan Corpn. of Brookville; dir. Clarion County Thrift Plan, Inc., Lake Erie, Franklin and Clarion R.R. Co. Methodist (mem. First Ch., Summerville, Pa.). Mason (Shriner), Club: Brookville (Pa.) Community. Home: Summerville, Pa. Office: 256 Main St., Brookville, Pa.

GEYELIN, Antony Laussat, estate planning counselor; b. Villa Nova, Pa., Oct. 17, 1888; s. Henry Laussat and Alice Reed (Rawle) G.; ed. Coll. de St. Gregoire, Tours, France, 1901-02; grad. Haverford Sch., Haverford, Pa., 1905; A.B., U. of Pa., 1909; m. Marie Windrim Flagg, Apr. 23, 1912; children—Elisabeth Flagg (Mrs. Noel Sissons), Alice Reed Rawle (Mrs. Edward Wagg); m. 2d, Mary-Virginia Allen, June 14, 1933. In employ Pa. R.R. Co., 1909-15; fgn. trade dept. Nat. City Bank, New York, N.Y.; sales mgr. Stanley G. Flagg & Co., 1915-17; traffic exec. British Ministry of Shipping, New York; sr. mem. firm Geyelin, Morss and Frey; pres. and dir. Geyelin & Co., Inc., since 1919; chmn. Geyelin & Frink, Inc. since 1931; vice-pres. and dir. Wilson Air Conditioning Corpn. since 1938; dir. Philadelphia Bourse. Served as major engrs., exec. officer to Gen. Mgr. Transportation Corps; chief R.T.O., A.E.F.; pres. Examining Board of Engineer Corps. Member Constitution Commemoration Com., Citizens com. of Y.M.C.A. Pres. Macaulay Club of Sun Life of Canada. Mem. Million Dollar Round Table of Nat. Assn. Life Underwriters, Phi Kappa Sigma. Republican. Episcopalian. Clubs: Racquet; University of Pa. Varsity; Penn Athletic. Home: "Hardwicke," Villa Nova, Pa. Office: 1616 Walnut St., Philadelphia, Pa.

GHENT, Pierre Mowell, civil engring. town planning; b. Baltimore, Md., Apr. 27, 1903; s. Charles Maurice and Sarah Elizabeth (Hawkins) G.; grad. Baltimore Poly. Inst., 1920; course Alexander Hamilton Inst., 1923-25; B.E., Johns Hopkins U., 1923; A.M. (Nat. Resources Planning), Am. Univ., Washington, D.C., 1939; m. Helen V. Mork, Nov. 27, 1936. Employed as jr. engr. various cos., 1923-26; res. engr. constrn. Bethlehem Steel Corpn., Sparrows Point, Md., 1926-27; design engr. Western Md. Ry., Hagerstown, Md., 1927-30; design engr. Westchester Co. (N.Y.) Park Commn., 1930-32; tech. adviser Civil Works Adminstrn. Aberdeen Proving Grounds, Md., 1933-34; with Asso. Engrs., Inc., Washington, D.C., 1934-36; town planner, Greendale, Wis., 1936-37; architect-town planner, Site Planning Sect., U.S. Housing Authority, Washington, D.C. since 1938. Mem. Am. Soc. Planning Officials, Nat. Assn. Housing Officials, Md. Assn. Engrs., Alpha Chi Rho, Johns Hopkins Alumni Club of Washington (treas.). Democrat. Episcopalian. Club: Johns Hopkins (Baltimore). Home: 6017 Sycamore Rd., Govans, Baltimore, Md. Office: North Interior Bldg., Washington, D.C.

GHERARDI, Bancroft; b. San Francisco, Calif., Apr. 6, 1873; s. Bancroft (rear adm. U.S.N.) and Anna Talbot (Rockwell) G.; B.Sc., Poly. Inst. Brooklyn, 1891, Dr. Engring. from same institute, 1933; M.E., Cornell University, 1893, M.M.E., 1894; m. Mary Hornblower Butler, June 15, 1898. Began as engr. asst., New York Telephone Co., 1895; traffic engr. same, 1900; chief engr. New York and New Jersey Telephone Co., 1901-06; asst. chief engr. New York Telephone Co., and New York and N.J. Telephone Co., 1906-07; equipment engr. Am. Telephone & Telegraph Co., 1907-09, engr. of plant same, 1909-18; acting chief engr. same co., 1918-19, chief engr., 1919-20, v.p. and chief eng., 1920-38, retired May 1, 1938. Ex-pres. Am. Inst. of Electrical Engrs.; mem. Nat. Acad. Sciences, Chi Psi, Sigma Xi. Trustee Cornell U. Republican. Episcopalian. Clubs: University, Railroad-Machinery (New York). Awarded Edison Medal, 1932, "for contributions to the art of telephone engineering and the development of electrical communication." Home: Short Hills, N.J.

GHEZZI, Victor, golf professional; b. New Jersey. Professional at Deal (N.J.) Golf Club; won Los Angeles Open Championship, 1935, North and South Open Championship, 1938; winner several other tournaments. Address: Deal Golf Club, Deal, N.J.

GHINGHER, J. J.; pres. National Central Bank. Address: Baltimore and Holliday Sts., Baltimore, Md.

GIACOMANTONIO, Archimedes Aristides Michael, sculptor; b. Jersey City, N.J., Jan. 17, 1906; s. Gaetano and Rosina (Fanelli) G.; student pub. schs. Jersey City, Leonardo Da Vinci Art Sch., N.Y. City; grad. Royal Acad. of Art, Rome, Italy, 1929; studied privately with Onorio Ruotolo and Vincenzo Gemito; m. Muriel Rose Ruoff, Aug. 10, 1935. Principal works: "Mediterranean Flower," original terra cotta in Museum Mussolini, Rome; "Grandma," Royal Palace, King of Italy; bust of Vincenzo Gemito, Home of Mussolini; bust of Prince George of Bavaria; and Torso of Boy, Royal Palace, Bavaria; Janet Gaynor and "Russian Eyes," Museum of Jersey City; "The Railsplitter," Lincoln High Sch., Jersey City; bust of Gov. A. Harry Moore, Moore Sch. for Crippled Children; bust of Gov. Harold G. Hoffman, State House, Trenton, N.J.; bust of Dean Mabel Smith Douglass, N.J. State Coll. for Women, New Brunswick, N.J.; heroic size bronze "Guarding Patrolman," Bay View Cemetery, Jersey City; heroic size bronze Christopher Columbus, Columbus Park, Hoboken, N.J.; Thomas M. Donnelly Memorial, West New York, N.J. (erected by Foresters of America). Awarded first prize 6th Annual N.J. State Exhbn., Montclair Mus., 1936. Trustee Mus. of Jersey City, Internat. Inst. Jersey City. Catholic. Kiwanian. Home: 288 Sherman Av., Jersey City, N.J.

GIARTH, David I., physician; b. Bedford, Pa., Nov. 11, 1859; s. Andrew J. and Mahala (Morris) G.; M.D., Jefferson Med. Coll., Phila., 1889; m. Ida Montgomery, Jan. 20, 1902; 1 dau., Mary M. Mem. of staff, Armstrong Co. Hosp., Kittanning, Pa., since 1906. Eye Hosp., Pittsburgh, since 1912. Mem. Armstrong Co. Med. Soc. (pres., 1921-22). Republican. Methodist. Mem. Maccabees, Elks. Club: Jefferson Alumnus. Home: 701 4th Av., Ford City, Pa. Office: Weylman Bldg., Kittanning, Pa.

GIBBLE, Phares Brubaker, clergyman; b. Rapho Twp., Lancaster Co., Pa., June 3, 1888; s. Abram S. and Annie Longenecker (Brubaker) G.; student Elizabethtown (Pa.) Coll., and Lebanon Valley Acad., Annville, Pa., 1910-12; A.B., Lebanon Valley Coll., 1915, A.M., 1927, D.D., 1929; B.D., Bonebrake Theol. Sem., Dayton, O., 1918; m. Pearl Beatrice Sherk, June 15, 1910; children—Alfred Tennyson, Velma Leona, Grant Wilbur, Beatrice Mary, Phares Bernard. Teacher in public schools, 1906-10; ordained to ministry United Brethren Ch., 1918; pastor Otterbein Ch., Baltimore, Md. (Philip William Otterbein, founder of United Brethren, pastor in this church, 1774-1813), 1918-23; pastor First Ch., Palmyra, Pa., since 1923; Trustee Lebanon Valley Coll. since 1922. Pres. and dir. bd. of edn. East Pa. Annual Conf., United Brethren in Christ. Mem. Pa. Sabbath Sch. Assn. (mem. adult work com.), Adult Dept. Christian Edn., State Council of Chs., Pa. German Soc., Lebanon Co. Hist. Soc. Republican. Mason, Patriotic Order Sons of America. Club: Lions. Author: One Hundred and Seventy-five Years of Palmyra, History, Historian and genealogist. Home: 36 N. College St., Palmyra, Pa.

GIBBON, John Heysham, surgeon; b. Charlotte, N.C., Mar. 16, 1871; s. Robert (M.D.) and Mary Amelia (Rogers) G.; prep. edn. Macon Sch., Charlotte; M.D., Jefferson Med. Coll., Phila., 1891; m. Marjorie G. Young, Sept. 2, 1901; children—Marjorie Young, John H., Samuel Young, Robert. Prof. surgery and clin. surgery, Jefferson Med. Coll., 1907-31 (emeritus); consulting surgeon Pa., Jefferson Med. and Bryn Mawr hosps. Surgeon U.S. Volunteer Engineers, Spanish-Am. War, 1898; col. M.C. U.S.A. and consultant in surgery to A.E.F., World War. Fellow and ex-pres. Am. Surgical Assn., Coll. Physicians of Phila., Phila. Acad. Surgery; mem. A.M.A., Med. Soc. State of Pa., Phila. Pediatric Soc., Nat. Soc. Study and Prevention Tuberculosis, etc. Contbr. to Reference Hand-Book of Medical Sciences, Keen's System of Surgery, also many articles to surg. jours. Address: 1608 Spruce St., Philadelphia, Pa.

GIBBONS, George Rison, aluminum mfr.; b. Bartow Co., Ga., July 18, 1879; s. John Rison and Annie America (Felton) G.; prep. edn., Piedmont Inst., Rockmart, Ga., 1894-97; A.B., Emory Coll. (now Univ.), 1900; m. Helen L. Maxfield, July 12, 1919; children—George Rison, Maxfield Scott, Felton Lewis. With Aluminum Co. of America since 1901, sec. since 1910, v.p. since 1911, sr. v.p. since 1931, also a dir.; pres., v.p. or dir. associated and subsidiary cos. Trustee Emory U. Mem. Delta Tau Delta. Republican. Methodist. Clubs: Duquesne, University, Oakmont Country, Fox Chapel Country, Rolling Rock. Home: 5455 Dunmoyle St. Office: Gulf Bldg., Pittsburgh, Pa.

GIBBONS, Helen Davenport (Mrs. Herbert Adams Gibbons), author; b. Phila., Pa., Dec. 2, 1882; d. Clement M. and Emily Eckert (Myers) Brown; Bryn Mawr Coll., 1902-05; Simmons Coll., 1906-07; m. New York, Rev. Herbert Adams Gibbons, June 3, 1908; children—Christine Este, Lloyd Irving, Mimi, Hope Delarue. Mem. bd. mgrs. Student Hostel, Paris, extensive traveler. Founder of French relief orgn., "Sauvons les Bébés." Y.M.C.A. lecturer with A.E.F., 1917-18; corr. Century Mag., Peace Conf., 1919; lecturer Chautauqua Summer Assembly, 1920; in Middle West and Calif. for Near East colleges, 1925; Albert Kahn around the world traveling fellow, 1929-30. Mem. Am. Legion Auxiliary, St. Nazaire Assn.; del. Paris Conv. same, 1927. Hostess, Byrd transoceanic flight crew, in France, 1927. Presbyn. Clubs: Present Day (Princeton); Bryn Mawr, Town Hall (New York); American Women's, Autour du Monde (Paris). Author: The Red Rugs of Tarsus, 1917; Les Turcs ont Passés Là!, 1918; A Little Gray Home in France, 1919; Paris Vistas, 1919; Four Little Pilgrims, 1926. Translator: Donnay's Lysistrata, 1919; Chauvelot's Parvati, 1920; Séché's Radiant Story of Jesus, 1927. Contbr. to Century, Harper's, Pictorial Rev., Cosmopolitan and other mags. Home: Princeton, N.J.*

GIBBONS, Paul Wellington, publishing; b. Phila., Pa., Aug. 17, 1885; s. George W. and Elizabeth (Morris) G.; ed. St. Joseph's Coll., 1899-1903; m. Agnes Falls, June 8, 1904; children—Paul W., Jr. (dec.), King W., Roy G. Engaged in printing and pub. since starting as apprentice in father's establishment, 1903; treas. Geo. W. Gibbons & Sons, 4 yrs.; pres. Rotary Pub. Co., 2 yrs.; pres. Paul Gibbons, Inc., since 1914; pres. Sport Pub. Co. since 1918; adv. dir. Pennac Monthly Mag.; dir. Bankers Nat. Life Ins. Co. Served as vice-pres. Boy Council of Phila. for 5 terms. Past pres. Phila. Boosters Assn. An incorporator and first pres. Penn Athletic Club. Dir. U.S. Lawn Tennis Assn., mem. Davis Cup Com. since 1926, mem. nat. exec. com. since 1918, finance and advisory com. since 1925. Pres. Phila. Tennis Assn. since 1914; pres. Middle States Tennis Assn., 1926, 30, 39. Founder and first pres. Optimist Service Club, dist. gov. Optimist Internat. for 5 yrs.; vice-pres. Optimist Internat., 1926, 27, 28; vice-pres. Phila. Boosters Assn.; pres. Sportsmens Civic League. Honored by Phila. award for having done most for sports in 1936. Democrat. Roman Catholic. Clubs: Penn Athletic, West Side Tennis, Whitemarsh Valley Country (Philadelphia); Y.M.C.A. (Germantown and New York); Moorestown Field. Home: 4613 Cedar Av. Office: Penn Athletic Club, Rittenhouse Square, Philadelphia, Pa.

GIBBONS, Walter Bernard, lawyer; b. Coatesville, Pa., Dec. 19, 1894; s. Patrick Henry and Mary (Bowen) G.; grad. Woodward High Sch., Cincinnati, O., 1912; LL.B., Temple U., Phila., 1916; m. Helen Mercedes Eustace, Dec. 26, 1918; 1 son, Walter Bernard. Admitted to Pa. bar, 1916, and since practiced in Phila.; asso. with Frank R. Savidge, 1912-1916, Wilson & McAdams, 1916-21; sr. partner Gibbons & Whitaker, 1921-30; mem. firm Donogue, Gibbons & Donoghue, 1930-31; individual practice, 1931-1937; partner Donoghue & Gibbons since 1937. Served as ensign U.S. Navy during World War. Pres. Angora Terrace Improvement Assn.; solicitor Neighborhood Club of Bala-Cynwyd; chmn. bd. Phila. Co. House of Detention, Voluntary Defenders Assn. Mem. Am. Bar Assn., Pa. Bar Assn. (mem. exec. com.), Phila. Bar Assn. (mem. bd. govs.), Alumni Law Sch. Temple U. (pres.). Republican. Roman Catholic. Clubs: Penn Athletic, Lawyers, Caveat (Phila.). Home: 35 Penarth Rd., Bala-Cynwyd, Pa. Office: 123 S. Broad St., Philadelphia, Pa.

GIBBONS, Willis Alexander, chemist; b. Long Island City, N.Y., Nov. 1, 1888; s. Samuel George Naylor and Mary Garland (Graham) G.; B.A., M.A., Wesleyan U., Middletown, Conn., 1910; student Cornell U., 1910-12, Ph.D., 1916; spl. student Columbia U., 1913-14; m. Stella Louise Hopewell, June 21, 1913; children—Virginia Graham, Dorothy Hopewell. Research chemist U.S. Rubber Co., New Brunswick, N.J., 1912-17, 1919-22, in charge research dept., gen. labs., 1922-27, dir. gen. labs., 1928, mgr. development dept., 1929, dir. development, 1930-38, dir. gen. development div. since 1939; dir. Dispersions Process, Inc. Served as 1st lt., Coast Arty. Res. Corps, capt., Inf., U.S. Army, 1917, capt., ordnance, 1918; chief loading sect., Washington, D.C., asst. mil. attache, Am. Embassy, London, 1917-18; hon. disch., 1919. Fellow A.A.A.S.; Am. Inst. Chemists, London Chem. Soc., Inst. of Rubber Industry; mem. Am. Chem. Soc. (mem. exec. com. rubber div.), Am. Phys. Soc., Deutschen Kautschuk Gesellshaft, Soc. Chem. Industry, Soc. Rheology, Phi Beta Kappa, Alpha Delta Phi. Republican. Episcopalian. Clubs: Passaic City (Passaic, N.J.); Upper Montclair Country (Montclair, N.J.). Inventor number of processes relating to vulcanization of rubber, applications of latex, mfr. of rubber thread, etc. Home: 357 Park St., Montclair, N.J. Office: General Laboratories, U.S. Rubber Co., 1 Market St., Passaic, N.J.

GIBBS, Alfred T., pres. First Nat. Bank and Trust Co. of Montclair; b. England, Sept. 29, 1885; s. Frederick William and Mary (Holloway) G.; came to U.S. as infant, 1887, naturalized; student Montclair (N.J.) High Sch., 1898 to 1902; m. May Isabel Etzel, 1911; 1 dau., Marjorie Carolyn (Mrs. John H. Day). Bank clk. Bank of Montclair, N.J., 1904-09; helped organize First Nat. Bank & Trust Co., Montclair, 1909, asst. cashier, 1909-11, cashier, 1911-23, vice-pres., 1923-32, pres. since 1932; pres. Upper Montclair Bldg. & Loan Assn. since 1920. Pres. Montclair Sinking Fund Commn. since 1937; trustee Boy Scouts of America (Eagle Rock Chapter). Mem. Upper Montclair Rep. Club. Republican. Episcopalian. Pres. Rotary Club of Montclair, N.J. Home: 54 Glenwood Rd. Office: First National Bank & Trust Co., Montclair, N.J.

GIBBS, Ferry Lee, clergyman, church exec.; b. Alamance Co., N.C., Nov. 25, 1901; s. Henry Ellis and Ida (Gerringer) G.; A.B., Elon (N.C.) Coll., 1925, A.M., 1926; B.D., Westminster Theol. Sem., 1928; spl. student Duke U., 1930-31; m. Margaret Estelle Wilson, Sept. 18, 1929; children—Kathryn Beatrice, Wilson Lee. Ordained to ministry of M.P. Ch., Nov. 1925; pastor Liberty and Siler City Chs., N.C., 1925-27; asst. sec. Bd. of Young People's Work, Meth. Protestant Ch., 1927-28, asso. sec., 1928-32; exec. sec. Bd. of Christian Edn., Dept. of Religious Edn., Meth. Protestant Ch. since 1932. Trustee Internat. Soc. Christian Endeavor. Mem. Internat. Council of Religious Edn. (mem. exec. com., mem. com. on leadership edn.); mem. Allegheny County Council of Christian Edn. (chmn. com. on edn.). Mem. Pi Gamma Mu, Alpha Pi Delta. Democrat. Clubs: Kiwanis, South Hills (Pittsburgh). Home: 3322 Eastmont Av. Office: 3269 W. Liberty Av., Pittsburgh, Pa.

GIBBS, George, author, illustrator; b. New Orleans, Mar. 8, 1870; s. Benjamin Franklin and Elizabeth Beatrice (Kellogg) G.; U.S. Naval Acad., 1886-88; studied art, Corcoran Sch. of Art and Art Students' League, Washington; m. Maud Stovell Harrison, Apr. 24, 1901; children—George Fort, Theodore Harrison, Sarah Stovell. Progressive. Episcopalian. Clubs: Art, Franklin Inn, Pegasus, Merion Cricket, Rittenhouse (Phila.). Author and Illustrator: Pike and Cutlass, 1900; In Search of Mademoiselle, 1901; The Love of Monsieur, 1905; The Medusa Emerald, 1907; Tony's Wife, 1909; The Bolted Door, 1911; The Forbidden Way, 1911; The Maker of Opportunities, 1912; The Silent Battle, 1913; Madcap, 1913; The Flaming Sword, 1914; The Yellow Dove, 1915; Paradise Garden, 1916; The Secret Witness, 1917; The Golden Bough, 1918; The Black Stone, 1919; The Splendid Outcast, 1920; The Vagrant Duke, 1921; Youth Triumphant, 1921; The House of Mohun, 1922; Fires of Ambition, 1923; Sack Cloth and Scarlet, 1924; Mad Marriage, 1925; How to Stay Married, 1925; The Up Grade, 1927; The Joyous Conspirator, 1927; The Castle Rock Mystery, 1927; The Shores of Romance, 1928; The Isle of Illusion, 1929; The Fire Within, 1930; Old Philadelphia, 1931; Foul Weather, 1932; Honor Among Women, 1933; The Yellow Diamond, 1934; Out of the Dark, 1935; The Vanishing Idol, 1936; Hunted, 1937; The Road to Bagdad, 1938; also American Sea Fights (a portfolio of colored drawings), 1903. Address: Rosemont, Pa.

GIBBS, Harrison, sculptor; b. Rosemont, Pa., Sept. 24, 1908; s. George and Maud Stovell (Harrison) G.; student Montgomery Sch., Wynewood, Pa., 1929, U. of Pa., 1932, Pa. Acad. of Fine Arts, 1934, Am. Acad. in Rome, 1936-38; married Maurine Wade Montgomery. Instr. sculpture, Cornell U. Mem. Zeta Psi. Winner, Prix de Rome, 1936. Episcopal. Home: Rosemont, Pa. Address: Dept. of Fine Arts, Cornell U., Ithaca, N.Y.

GIBBS, Raymond B., gen. sec. Scranton Chamber of Commerce; b. Clarkston, Mich., Oct. 29, 1883; s. William Henry and Phoebe (Millard) G.; ed. Clarkston High Sch.; commercial and spl. courses, Ferris Inst., Big Rapids, Mich.; B.S., Colgate U., 1910; m. Elizabeth Anderson, June 30, 1915; children—William A., Klare M., Elizabeth B. Teacher Oak Hill Rural Sch., 1902-03; instr. commercial subjects, Warsaw (Ind.) High Sch., 1904-05; clk. Nat. Foundrymen's Assn., Detroit, summer, 1905; head commercial dept. South Jersey Inst., Bridgeton, 1905-06; in office of Pullman Co., Detroit, summer, 1906; clk. and stenographer Div. Freight Agent's office, Wabash R.R., Detroit, summer, 1907; clk. Ford Motor Car Co., summer, 1908, Welded Steel Barrel Corpn. (subsidiary Berry Bros.), Detroit, summer, 1909, Fletcher Hardware Co., summer, 1910; in accounting dept. Standard Oil Co., summer, 1911; spl. work Hayes Mfg. Co., summer, 1912; head commercial dept., Tome Sch. for Boys, Port Deposit, Md., 1910-13; associated with City Mgr. Campaign, Sandusky and Dayton, O., summer, 1913; sec. Olean (N.Y.) Chamber of Commerce, 1913-16, Lockport (N.Y.) Chamber of Commerce, 1916-19; mgr. Kansas City (Kan.) Chamber of Commerce, 1919-25; sec.-treas., 1923-24, vice-pres., 1924-25, pres., 1925-26, Nat. Assn. of Commercial Organization Secs.; gen. sec. Scranton (Pa.) Chamber of Commerce since 1925. Campaign mgr. for liberty loans, Am. Red Cross, Y.M.C.A., war chest, food conservation, war savings stamps and all other war work in Lockport, N.Y., and vicinity during World War. Pres. Northeastern Pa. Alumni Assn. of Colgate U., 1927-30; dir. Colgate Univ. Alumni Corpn., 1927-30; mem. Assn. Advertising Clubs of the World, Phi Kappa Psi, Phi Beta Kappa. Republican. Presbyterian. Mason (32°, Scottish Rite), Elk. Charter mem. Lockport (N.Y.) Rotary Club; mem. Rotary clubs of Kansas City (Kan.) and Scranton (Pa.). Home: 606 Harrison Av. Office: Chamber of Commerce Bldg., Scranton, Pa.

GIBSON, Alva Jason, sch. adminstrn.; b. Corley, W.Va., Sept. 1, 1888; s. George Rhea and Elvira (Wheeler) G.; A.B., W.Va. Univ., Morgantown, 1916; A.M., Columbia U., 1920; m. Flora Lewis, Sept. 1, 1915; children—Robert Lewis, Martha Virginia, Mary Eleanor. Began as teacher of sci., high sch., Grafton, W.Va., 1914-16; prin. high sch., Williamstown, W.Va., 1916-17, supt. schs., 1917-18; prin. high sch., Elkins, W.Va., 1918-23; prin. E. Fairmont high sch., Fairmont, W.Va., 1923-29; supt. E. Fairmont Schools, 1929-33; state supervisor high schs., Dept. Edn., Charleston, W.Va., since 1933; instr. Fairmont State Teachers Coll., Fairmont, W.Va., summers 1923-33. Mem. N.E.A., Am. Assn. Sch. Adminstrs., Nat. Assn. State High Sch. Supervisors and Dirs., Nat. Assn. Secondary Sch. Prins., W.Va. Assn. Secondary Prins. (pres. 1925-26), W.Va. State Edn. Assn., W.Va. High Sch. Athletic Assn. (sec. 1918-23), Bd. Pub. Library, Fairmont, W.Va., Kappa Delta Pi. Democrat. Methodist. Mason. Home: 1567-A Lee St. Office: State Dept. of Edn., State Capitol, Charleston, W.Va.

GIBSON, David C., v.p. Md. Casualty Co. Home: 106 W. Melrose Av. Office: 701 W. 40th St., Baltimore, Md.

GIBSON, George Gordon, physician; b. London, Ont., Feb. 19, 1901; s. George and Margaret (McMurphy) G.; came to U.S., 1925, naturalized, 1929; ed. London Collegiate Inst., 1914-19; M.D., U. of Western Ont. Med. Sch., 1925; m. Mary E. Wilkey, Nov. 27, 1927; children—Mary Janet, George Wilkey, William Giffin. Interne Pittsburgh Hosp., 1925-26; engaged in gen. practice of medicine at Wilkinsburg, Pa., since 1926. Fellow Am. Coll. Physicians, A.M.A.; mem. Pa. Med. Soc., Alpha Kappa Kappa. Republican. Presbyterian. Home: 449 Maple Av., Edgewood, Pa. Office: 1017 Center St., Wilkinsburg, Pa.

GIBSON, George Herbert, cons. engr.; b. Wayne Co., Mich., Mar. 29, 1876; s. George and Catherine (Speyrer) G.; student Waterford (Mich.) Dist. Sch., 1882-89, Northville (Mich.) Pub. and High Sch., 1889-94; B.S. in E.E., U. of Mich., Ann Arbor, Mich., 1899; m. Anna Jackson, Dec. 25, 1901; children—George, Luis, Augustus, Mary Elizabeth. Began as workman Westinghouse Shops, Pittsburgh, Pa., 1899; asst. editor Engring. News, New York, 1899-1901; editor Westinghouse Companies' Pub. Dept., Pittsburgh, 1901-03; advertising mgr. B. F. Sturtevant Co., Boston, Mass., 1903; dir. publicity Internat. Steam Pump Co., New York, 1903-05; proprietor and senior partner George H. Gibson Co., tech. and industrial advertising and tech. and commercial development of products, New York, since 1905. Mem. Am. Soc. M.E. Clubs: Germantown Cricket (Phila., Pa.); U.S. Power Squadrons, Inc., New York; Northport (N.Y.) Yacht. Author: Finding and Stopping Waste in Modern Boiler Rooms, 1917, 21, 27, 28; numerous articles and papers on engring. subjects. Inventor and patentee numerous patents on heaters, softeners, filters, meters, combustion control system, etc. Home: 110 Montclair Av., Montclair, N.J. Office: 100 Gold St., New York, N.Y.

GIBSON, James Edgar, author, builder; b. Williamsport, Pa., May 1, 1875; s. William and Mary Alice (Otto) G.; ed. private and pub. schs. and grad. Wharton Sch. of Finance and Economy, U. of Pa., 1896; m. Eleanor Landell Fox, of Phila., Oct. 10, 1906. Salesman of bldg. supplies, 1897-99; supt. of constrn. Keystone Fireproofing Co., Phila., 1899-1901, v.p., 1901-03, pres., 1903-17; pres. Metropolitan Fireproofing Co., New York, 1908-17; treas. and gen. mgr. Victoria Gypsum Mining & Mfg. Co., Can., 1908-17; gen. mgr. Keystone Plaster Co., Chester, Pa., 1908-17; sec. and treas. Price Engine Co., Phila., 1917-24; concrete specialist engaged in polychrome concrete work, concrete roof constrn. since 1924; an asst. to chief of ordnance, U.S. Army, Middle Div., 1917-18; sec. U.S. Army Claims Bd., Middle Div., 1918-22. Republican. Episcopalian. Author: Dr. Bodo Otto and the Medical Background of the American Revolution, 1937. Contbr. to hist. jours.; also chapter "Captured Medical Men and Hospitals of the American Revolution" to the Annals of Medical History, 1938. Home: 500 W. Chelton Av. Office: Land Title Bldg., Philadelphia, Pa.

GIBSON, Kasson Stanford, physicist; b. Afton, N.Y., Jan. 7, 1890; s. Stanford Jay and Gertrude Justine (Sage) G.; grad. Norwich (N.Y.) High Sch., 1908; A.B., Cornell U., 1912, Ph.D., 1916; m. Mildred Lovett Brown, July 12, 1917; 1 son, Gilbert Lewis. Asst. instr. and instr. in physics, Cornell U., 1912-16; with Nat. Bureau of Standards since 1916, successively as asst. physicist, asso. physicist, physicist, sr. physicist, and since 1936 prin. physicist, and since 1933 chief of colorimetry and spectrophotometry sect. Fellow A.A.A.S., Am. Phys. Soc.; mem. Optical Soc. of America (dir. since 1935; vice-pres., 1937-39; pres. since 1939; rep. in div. of phys. sciences, Nat. Research Council since 1939; asso. editor of Journal since 1928), Illuminating Engring. Soc., Washington Acad. of Sciences, Philos. Soc. of Washington, Phi Beta Kappa, Sigma Xi; asso. mem. Am. Oil Chemists Soc. Received Journal Award of Soc. Motion Picture Engrs., 1937. Ind. Republican. Baptist. Author of 35 papers on spectrophotometry, colorimetry, photometry, etc. Home: 417 Cumberland Av., Chevy Chase, Md. Office: National Bureau of Standards, Washington, D.C.

GIBSON, Philip Pendleton, lawyer; b. Jefferson Co., W.Va., June 29, 1890; s. John Shackelford and Ilicia (Davis) G.; student Marshall Coll., Huntington, W.Va., 1904-09; B.A., Washington & Lee U., Lexington, Va., 1913, LL.B., 1915; m. Morrell Sanford Jones, Sept. 10, 1929; children—Anne Morrell, Philip Pendleton. Admitted to W.Va. bar, 1916; engaged in practice of law, Huntington, since 1916; atty. City of Huntington, 1925-28; mem. law firm Marcum & Gibson; spl. counsel City of Huntington for Flood Control, 1939. Mem. W.Va. State Bd. of Edn. since 1935, present term expires 1943; counsel for state banking commr. and receivers in liquidation of closed banks. Mem. Am. Bar Assn., W.Va. Bar Assn., Cabell Co. Bar Assn. (pres. 1935-36), Pi Kappa Alpha, Phi Delta Phi, Omicron Delta Kappa. Democrat. Episcopalian. Clubs: Guyan Country, Associated Executive, National (Huntington, W.Va.); Democratic of America (Washington, D.C.). Home: 1517 Sixth Av. Office: First Huntington Nat. Bank Bldg., Huntington, W.Va.

GIBSON, Robert Johnston, mcht. books; b. Beaver, Pa., Feb. 4, 1868; s. John Glenn and Margery Jane (McGeorge) G.; student pub. schs. Bellevue, Pa. and Emsworth Acad., 1874-86; m. Florence Walker, Aug. 9, 1904; children—Richard Walker, Marjorie Glenn. Employed as clk. Presbyn. Book Store, Pittsburgh, 1886-1902; mgr., Phila. Presbyn. Book Store, 1902-06; supt. Presbyn. Book Store, Pittsburgh, Pa., since 1906. Mem. bd. trustees, Presbyn. Hosp., Pittsburgh, Johnston C. Smith Univ., Charlotte, N.C., Pikeville Coll., Pikeville, Ky.; chmn. Bd. of Pensions, Presbytery of Pittsburgh; mem. bd. dirs. Allegheny Co. S.S. Assn.; clk. of Session and mem. Official Bd., First Presbyn. Ch., Pittsburgh. Republican. Presbyterian. Home: 454 Teece Av., Bellevue, Pa. Office: 6th Av. and Wood St., Pittsburgh, Pa.

GIBSON, Robert Wesson, clergyman; b. Ryegate, Vt., Jan. 3, 1897; s. Martin H. and Mary (Clark) G.; prep. edn. St. Johnsburg (Vt.) Acad., 1910-14; A.B., Muskingum Coll., New Concord, 1918; student Pittsburgh Theol. Sem., 1919-21; D.D., Westminster Coll., 1934; m. Helen Mitchell, June 16, 1921; children—Joan Mitchell, Robert Wesson. Ordained to ministry of United Presbyn. Ch., 1921; pastor, Springdale, Pa., 1921-29, Beverly Heights U.P. Ch., Mt. Lebanon, Pa., 1929-35, Third U.P. Ch., Pittsburgh, since 1935. During World War was student Sch. Mil. Aeronautics, Ohio State U.; served in aviation branch, U.S. Army, Jan. 1918-Jan. 1919. Chmn. Home Mission Com., U.P. Ch., since 1935; mem. bd. trustees Muskingum Coll. since 1933; mem. U.P. Bd. of Publ. and Bible Sch. Work since 1935; chmn. commn. on evangelism, Pittsburgh Council of Churches; mem. bd. Oakdale Industrial Home for Boys since 1936. Mem. Am. Legion, Tau Kappa Alpha. Republican. Clubs: Theological Circle, Alpha Tau Epsilon. Home: 2227 Beechwood Boul., Pittsburgh, Pa.

GIBSON, William Herbert, cons. engr.; b. Tunnelton, W.Va., July 15, 1877; s. Ashbel F. and Elizabeth (Brown) G.; B.S. in civil engring., U. of W.Va., 1903; m. Louise L. Hubbard, Jan. 12, 1916; 1 dau., Jean. Engaged in electric railroad work, W.Va., 1902-03, mining work in Western Pa., 1904; associated with Walter Loring Webb in design of reinforced concrete and railroad surveys, 1905-09; cons. engr., designing and superintending structural work and foundations for architects since 1909. Principal works: 17 bldgs., Princeton U.; 5 bldgs., Yale U.; 4 bldg., Wellesley Coll.; 9 bldgs., U. of Del.; 18 bldgs., Pa. State Coll.; bldg., Hahnemann Hosp.; 5 bldgs., Concordia Sem.; 5 lbdgs., Hotel Dennis, Atlantic City, N.J.; several pub. schs., Atlantic City, N.J.; Hill Creek Housing, Philadelphia. Mem. Am. Soc. C.E., Am. Concrete Inst., Am. Welding Soc. Protestant. Coauthor: Concrete Design and Construction, 1939. Home:. 2258 N. 53d St. Office: Architects' Bldg., Philadelphia, Pa.

GIDDENS, Paul Henry, coll. prof.; b. Bellflower, Mo., Feb. 1, 1903; s. Jackson and Bertha (Patterson) G.; diploma Winterset (Ia.) High Sch., 1920; A.B., Simpson Coll., Indianola, Ia., 1924; A.M., Harvard, 1926; Ph.D., State U. of Ia., Iowa City, Ia., 1930; m. Marie Jeanette Robins, Mar. 17, 1927; 1 son, Jackson Alfred. Instr. history, U. of Kan., Lawrence, Kans., 1926; instr. history and govt., Ia. State Coll., Ames, Ia., 1926-28; asst. prof. hist., Ore. State Coll., Corvallis, Ore., 1930-31; instr. hist., State U. of Ia., Iowa City, Ia., summer 1929, 1930, 1931; asst. prof. hist. and govt., Allegheny Coll., Meadville, Pa., 1931-37, asso. prof., 1937-38, prof. since 1938. Mem. Am. Hist. Assn., Mississippi Valley Hist. Assn., Pa. Hist. Assn., Alpha Tau Omega, Pi Kappa Delta, Pi Gamma Mu. Republican. Methodist. Author: The Birth of the Oil Industry, 1938; contbr. hist. articles to hist., biog., govt. and legal jours. Home: 365 Park Av. Office: Allegheny Coll., Meadville, Pa.

GIDEON, Henry Joseph, dir. compulsory edn.; b. Phila., Pa., Feb. 12, 1875; s. Henry Edward and Rose (Robbins) G.; ed. Phila. Sch. of Pedagogy, 1893-94; B.S., Temple U., 1909; grad. study, U. of Pa., 1909-10, Cornell U., summers 1932, 1937-38; (hon.) LL.D., St. Joseph's Coll., Phila., 1936; m. Nina Marie Mitchell, June 30, 1928. Engaged in teaching, Thomas Potter Sch., Phila., 1894-1900; prin. evening sch., Germantown, 1899; supervising prin., Sheridan Sch., Phila., 1900-11; dir. bur. (now div.) of compulsory edn., a div. of Dept. of Superintendence of Phila. Pub. Schs. since 1911. Served as mem. Phila. Sch. Mobilization Com. and Boys Working Res. during World War. Trustee Pub. Edn. and Child Labor Assn. of Pa., The Elliot House for Boys, Am. Red Cross Southeastern Chapter. Mem. N.E.A., Nat. Assn. Sch. Adminstrs., Nat. League to Promote Sch. Attendance (v.p.), Phila. Teachers Assn., Phila. Council Boy Scouts of America. Chmn. Schs. Com. United Campaign, 1937-39. Republican. Episcopalian. Mason. Clubs: Manufacturers and Bankers, Schoolmens (past pres.), Kiwanis of Philadelphia (pres.). Home: 215 E. Sedgwick St., Philadelphia, Pa. Office: 21st & Parkway, Philadelphia, Pa.

GIESECKE, Albert Anthony, educator; b. Phila., Nov. 30, 1883; s. Albert and Catherine Elizabeth G.; B.S. in Economics, Central High Sch., Phila., 1902; same, U. of Pa., 1904; Univs. of Berlin, Paris and Lausanne, 1905, 1906; Ph.D., Cornell, U., 1908; m. Esther Matto, Jan. 19, 1914; children—Esther Catherine, Albert Anthony. Instr. political science, Cornell U., 1906-08, U. of Pa., 1908-09; prof. commercial geography and economics, Central High Sch., Phila., 1908-09; apptd. spl. expert in commercial edn. for govt. of Peru, 1909; pres. U. of Cuzco, Peru, Feb. 1910-23; dir. exams. and courses of study for elementary, secondary and normal schs. of Peru, 1923; dir. general of pub. edn., Peru, 1924-30; tech. adviser to minister of education since 1930; apptd. by President of Peru mem. Peruvian delegation of Plebiscitary Commn. of Tacna-Arica, 1925; collaborated with Kemmerer Financial Commn. to Peru, Jan.-Apr. 1931. Mem. 3d Pan-Am. Scientific Congress, Lima, 1924; pres. educational sect. of VI Pan-Am. Child Welfare Congress, Lima, 1930; asst. sec. U.S. Delegation to Inter-Am. Aeronautic Conf., Lima, 1937; sec., U.S. Delegation to VIII Internat. Conf. of Am. States, Lima, 1938; dir. of Conservation of Ancient Ruins at Pachacamac and Cajamarquilla, 1938; mem. bd. Instituto Cultural Peruano, norteamericano, 1938. Mem. Am. Econ. Assn., Am. Acad. Polit. and Social Science, Am. Anthropol. Soc., Sociedad Geografica de Lima, Centro Geografico del Cuzco, Sociedad de Anticuarios del Cuzco, Club Internacional de Tiro al Blanco (Cuzco); mem. Sociedad de Beneficencia Pública del Cuzco, Touring Club Peruano; corr. mem. Hispanic Soc. of America; hon. life mem. Archæol. Soc. of N.M.; pres. com. for erection statue of first Inca Emperor, Manco Capacc; dir. Instituto de Educación, San Marcos U., Lima, 1931-32; mem. exec. council Latin-Am. Inst. for Race and Cultural Studies, 1935. (U. of Pa. Mus. present headquarters.) Discovered remains of prehistoric animals and archæol. remains in Dept. of Cuzco. Served as mem. and mayor City Council of Cuzco; hon. pres. Instituto Histórico del Cuzco; pres. Centro de Labor Industrial, etc. Clubs: Nacional, Terrazas (both of Lima). Author: Municipal Civics; The Commercial Policy of the U.S. before 1789; also numerous articles; spl. investigator for the Carnegie Institution; collaborator U.S. Census Bur., 1906. Mem. editorial staff Annals of Am. Acad. Polit. and Social Sciences; editor Guía General del Sur del Peru. Home: 4515 Pine St., West Philadelphia, Pa. Address: Calle General Suarez 174, Miraflores, Peru.

GIESKE, Alfred W.; pres. Baltimore Oil Engine Co.; dir. several companies. Home: Catonsville, Md. Office: Munsey Bldg., Baltimore, Md.

GIFT, Foster U.; pastor and dir. instrn. Lutheran Deaconess Motherhouse and Training Sch. Home: 1901 Thomas Av. Study: 2500 W. North Av., Baltimore, Md.

GIGLIO, Alphonsus Salvatore Vincent, physician; b. New York, N.Y., Jan. 5, 1896; s. Vincenzo and Giovanna (Freschia) G.; student Columbia U., 1915-17, Coll. Phys. & Surgs. of Columbia U., 1917-19; M.D., Tulane U. Med. Coll., New Orleans, La., 1921; m. Rose Marinello, Dec. 26, 1927; children—Alphonsus S.V., Jr., Bernice. Interne Alexian Bros. Hosp., Elizabeth, N.J., 1921-22; commr. bd. health, Elizabeth, N.J., 1935-38, asst. city physician since 1938. Pres. Members Bldg. & Loan Assn. Foreman grand jury, Union Co., 1936. Served in U.S.A. during World War. Fellow Am. Med. Assn.; mem. N.J. Med. Soc., Union Co. Med. Soc., Alpha Phi Delta, Mu Alpha Mu. Mem. Grand Jurors Assn. Union Co., Italian-Am. Civic League Union Co., Italian-Am. Democratic League of Union County (v.p.); hon. mem. N.J. State P.B.A. Democrat. Mason (32°); master Mayflower Lodge. Clubs: Square (pres.), Elks, Eagles, American Legion (Elizabeth). Home: 626 Elizabeth Av., Elizabeth, N.J.

GILBERT, Ernest Marvin, engr.; b. Wilton, Conn., Apr. 11, 1874; s. George K. and Elizabeth (Marvin) G.; M.E., Cornell U., 1896; m. Alice R. Robertson, 1910. With Am. Stoker Co., Dayton, O., 1896-99; gen. supt. Am. Stoker Co., London, Eng., 1899-1907; chief eng. Leadville (Colo.) Light & Power Co., 1907-

09; chief engr. and asst. mgr. Colo. Power Co., 1909-14; cons. engr. Bonbright & Co., Waterbury, Conn., 1914-16; vice-pres., dir. and chief engr. W. S. Barstow & Co., Reading, Pa., 1916-30, pres. and chief engr., 1930-33; pres. and chief engr. E. M. Gilbert & Co. (successor to W. S. Barstow & Co.), Reading, since 1933; vice-pres. and dir. The Utility Management Corpn., New York; dir. Lexington Water Power Co., Berks County Trust Co. Pres. Berks Co. Chapter Am. Red Cross; dir. Reading Hosp. Clubs: Berkshire Country, Wyomissing (Reading, Pa.). Home: 404 Lynn Av., Wyomissing, Pa. Office: 412 Washington St., Reading, Pa.

GILBERT, Frank Albert, coll. prof.; b. Exeter, N.H., Mar. 22, 1900; s. Frank Albert and Nellie Rowell (Welch) G.; B.S., Mass. State Coll., 1922; M.A., Harvard U., 1925, Ph.D., 1927; m. Eleanor Hitchens Marshall, Aug. 13, 1929; children—Carter Rowell, Robert Frank, William Marshall. Began as plant pathologist, Mass. State Dept. Agr., 1923; asst. prof. of botany, Marshall Coll., 1927-28, asso. prof., 1928-29, prof. of botany since 1929. Mem. Harvard U. Bot. Expdn. to Newfoundland and Labrador, 1925. Served as private, S.A.T.C., 1918; 1st lt., Cavalry Organized Reserves. Mem. A.A.A.S., Bot. Soc. America, Mycol. Soc. America, Southern Appalachian Bot. Club (pres.), Lambda Chi Alpha, Gamma Alpha, Chi Beta Phi, New England Bot. Club. Congregationalist. Mason. Home: 15 Roland Park Drive, Huntington, W.Va.

GILBERT, Henderson, transportation; b. Harrisburg, Pa., Sept. 13, 1880; s. Spencer C. and Harriet (Henderson) G.; grad. Harrisburg Acad., 1896, St. Paul's Sch., Concord, N.H., 1898; Ph.B., Sheffield Sci. Sch., Yale, 1901; m. Sarah Wister Boas, 1905; children—Harriet Henderson (Mrs. J. W. McPherson III), Henry Boas, Sarah. Engaged in mill supply business, 1901-29; pres. Harrisburg Rys. Co. since 1930; dir. Bell Telephone Co. of Pa.; v.p. Harrisburg Hotel Co.; dir. Penn Harris Hotel Co. Dir. Harrisburg Pub. Library, -Harrisburg Hosp., Sylvan Heights Orphans' Home. Mem. Am. Transit Assn. (vice chmn. bus div.), Book and Snake Soc. (Yale), Sigma Xi Fraternity. Presbyterian. Mason. Clubs: Union League (Phila.); Tourilli Rod and Gun (Quebec). Home: 1600 N. 2d St. Office: 12 S. 2d St., Harrisburg, Pa.

GILBERT, John, corpn. official; b. Phila., Pa., Oct. 6, 1880; s. Samuel Hatfield and Georgeine (Stoddart) G.; student Cheltenham Mil. Acad., 1889-96, U. of Pa., 1896-1900; m. Maude Mary Rowland, June 4, 1902; children —Samuel Hatfield, John and Rowland (deceased). Dir. Ames Shovel & Tool Co., sec., treas. and dir. East Broad Top R.R. & Coal Co.; vice-pres. Shenandoah Land Co.; trustee Estate of John Gilbert (dec.), West Va. Lands; pres. Lawrence Fuels, Inc., and Gilberton Fuels, Inc. Vice-pres. and trustee Abington Memorial Hosp. Chief statistician, dir. of Pa., U.S. Fuel Adminstrn., World War. Mem. Zeta Psi. Republican. Episcopalian. Clubs: Union League, Eagles Mere Golf, Huntingdon Valley Country. Home: Rydal, Pa. Office: 1421 Chestnut St., Philadelphia, Pa.

GILBERT, Keller Hughes, lawyer; b. Pottstown, Pa., Nov. 27, 1892; s. Lyman B. and Mary J. (Hughes) G.; student prep. schs. Pottstown and Phila., Pa.; LL.B., Temple U. Law Sch., Phila., 1919; grad. Carnegie Inst. Effective Speaking, 1938; m. Ethel Dorothy Clayton, Jan. 12, 1931. Pvt. sec. to Pa. Supreme Ct. Justice, 1914-18; admitted to Pa. bar, 1919, since engaged in gen. practice of law at Phila.; law clk. Orphans' Ct. of Phila. Co., 1919-25; dep. atty. gen. of Pa., 1927-35. Served in U.S. Navy, 1918-19. Mem. 46th Ward (Phila.) Rep. Exec. Com. Mem. Phila. Bar Assn., Law Acad. of Phila., Temple U. Alumni Assn., Speakers' Forum of Phila., Am. Legion, Artisans Order of Mutual Protection. Methodist. Author: Pennsylvania Inheritance Taxation, 1934. Lecturer and writer on law subjects. Home: 5112 Hazel Av. Office: 1304 Lincoln-Liberty Bldg., Philadelphia, Pa.

GILBERT, Richard H(enry), lawyer; b. Emporium, Pa., Mar. 26, 1885; s. Richard H. and Julia (Lau) G.; Ph.B., Syracuse U., 1908; A.M., Dickinson College, 1911; LL.B., Dickinson Law School, 1911; m. Missoura Wolfgang, Sept. 25, 1912; children—Jane Louise, Julia Ann. Admitted to Pa. bar, 1911, and since engaged in gen. practice of law at Tyrone; served as dist. atty. Blair Co., 1928-36. Served in 1st Pa. Cav. on Mexican border, 1916. Mem. Pa. State Bar Assn., Sigma Chi. Republican. Methodist. Mason (32°, Shriner). Club: Kiwanis of Tyrone, Pa. Home: 907 Jefferson Av. Office: Municipal Bldg., Tyrone, Pa.

GILBERT, Ross Kirby, editor; b. Chambersburg, Pa., Apr. 17, 1881; s. Harry S. and Kate Marshall (Kirby) G.; student Chambersburg (Pa.) Acad., 1898-1901; B.S., Gettysburg (Pa.) Coll., 1905; unmarried. Reporter Public Opinion, daily newspaper, Chambersburg, Pa., 1905-11, editor since 1911. Home: 250 E. Queen St. Office: 33 Lincoln Way West, Chambersburg, Pa.

GILBERT, William Marshall, prof. home missions; b. Monmouth, Ill., Aug. 24, 1879; s. Abram V. T. and Maria M. (Gaylord) G.; A.B., Cornell Coll., Mt. Vernon, Ia., 1904, D.D., 1920; S.T.B., Boston U. Sch. of Theology, 1909; m. Harriet Harmon Herrick, Dec. 31, 1908; children—Harmon, George, Harriet. Ordained deacon, 1906, elder, 1908, M.E. Ch.; entered Central Ill. Conf., 1904; pastor Fairview, Ill., 1904-05, Peoria, 1905-06, Cliftondale, Mass., 1909-13; Morgan Memorial Ch., Boston, 1913-18, First Ch., 1918-21; dir. Bur. of Foreign Speaking Work, Bd. of Home Missions and Ch. Extension, 1921-23; prof. home missions and dir. of field supervision, Drew U., since 1923. Mem. Home Missions Council; sec. Commn. of Foreign Language Work of the Gen. Conf. M.E. Ch., 1920-24. Republican. Club: Rotary; dist. gov. 36th Dist., Rotary Internat., 1935-36. Editor: Social Pioneering, 1928. Home: Drew Forest, Madison, N.J.

GILBERTSON, Catherine Peebles, writer; b. Washington, D.C., Aug. 14, 1890; d. Collin and Mary (Robertson) Peebles; student Washington (D.C.) pub. schs., 1897-1908; B.A., Wellesley (Mass.) Coll., 1912; m. Henry Stimson Gilbertson, June 30, 1920. Writer mag. articles, biography, etc., since 1929. Republican. Episcopalian. Author: Harriet Beecher Stowe, 1937; contbr. biog., etc., articles to mags. Address: Lansford, Pa.

GILBRETH, Lillian Moller, consulting engr.; b. Oakland, Calif., May 24, 1878; d. William and Annie (Delger) Moller; B.Litt., U. of Calif., 1900, M.Litt., 1902; Ph.D., Brown, 1915, Sc.D., 1931; M. Engring., U. of Mich., 1928; Dr. Engring., Rutgers College, 1929; Sc.D., Russell Sage College, 1931; LL.D., University of California, 1933; m. Frank Bunker Gilbreth, October 19, 1904; children—Anne Moller (Mrs. Robert E. Barney), Mary Elizabeth (dec.), Ernestine Moller (Mrs. Charles E. Carey), Martha Bunker, Frank Bunker, William Moller, Lillian Moller (Mrs. Donald D. Johnson), Frederick Moller, Daniel Bunker, John Moller, Robert Moller, Jane Moller. Pres. Gilbreth, Inc., consulting engrs. in management; dir. courses in motion study and the one best way to do work; Professor of Management, Purdue Univ., 1935—. Mem. President's Emergency Com. for Employment, President's Organization on Unemployment Relief. Mem. New Jersey State Board of Regents, 1929-33. Mem. Am. Management Assn., Institute of Management, Society for the Advancement of Management, Academy Masaryk, American Psychological Association, Soc. of Mechanical Engineers, Inst. for Scientific Management of Poland, Phi Beta Kappa. Author: Psychology of Management, 1912; also, with husband, Time Study, Fatigue Study, 1916, Applied Motion Study, 1917, Motion Study for the Handicapped, 1919; The Home Maker and Her Job, 1927; Living With Our Children, 1928; and papers on edn., management, psychology and re-edn. of the crippled soldiers; contbr. article on Scientific Management in New Internat. Ency. Hon. mem. Soc. Industrial Engineers. Home: 68 Eagle Rock Way, Montclair, N.J.; also The Shoe, Nantucket, Mass.

GILDEA, James Hilary, ex-congressman; b. Coaldale, Pa., Oct. 21, 1890; s. Dennis Carr and Marjorie (Rodgers) G.; ed. pub. schs.; m. Genevieve Gallagher, Nov. 10, 1915; children— Marjorie, James, Kathleen, Robert, John (dec.), Daniel. Began as apprentice printer's trade, 1905; editor and pub. Coaldale Observer (Dem. weekly) since 1910; chmn. Coaldale Relief Soc. and Panther Valley Miners' Equalization Com.; mem. 74th and 75th Congresses (1935-39), 13th Pa. Dist. Awarded D.S.C. of Am. Legion for community service and service to the Legion. Catholic. Home: Coaldale, Pa.

GILDERSLEEVE, Nelson Burroughs, clergyman, rector; b. Brooklyn, N.Y., Sept. 14, 1888; s. Joseph and Anna Louise (Wills) G.; student Pub. Sch. No. 11, Brooklyn, N.Y., 1895-1903, Poly. Prep. Sch., Brooklyn, 1903-07, Poly. Inst., Brooklyn, 1907-08; A.B., Columbia U., 1911, A.M., 1914; student Gen. Theol. Sem., New York, 1918-20; m. Willetta Douglas Courter, June 18, 1919 (died 1938)—children Nelson Burroughs, Mary-Elizabeth. Teacher, Irving Sch. for Boys, New York, 1915-18, head Eng. and Latin Depts., 1916-22; ordained deacon Protestant Episcopal Ch., 1919; in charge St. Simon's Ch., Brooklyn, N.Y., 1919-20; ordained priest, 1920; head Latin and Eng. Depts. Irving Sch., Tarrytown, N.Y., 1920-22; asst. to dean St. Luke's Cathedral, Portland, Me., 1922-24; rector St. Michael's Ch., Auburn, Me., 1924-28, St. Jude's Ch., Brooklyn, N.Y., 1928-30, St. Agnes Episcopal Ch., East Orange, N.J., since 1930. Pres., chaplain House of the Good Shepherd, Orange, N.J., since 1933. Republican. Episcopalian. Mason (Solomons Lodge 196, Tarrytown, N.Y.; Royal Arch, Orient Chapter 138, Brooklyn, N.Y.; Damascus Commandery 58, K.T., Brooklyn.) Address: 304 Central Av., East Orange, N.J.

GILES, Raymond Coleman, investments; b. Pittsburgh, Pa., May 11, 1890; s. Edwin S. and Ella Blanche (Wilson) G.; ed. high sch.; m. Janet Liddell Whyte, Aug. 18, 1920; .children— Janet Lavinia, Sara Ann. Employed by U.S. Nat. Bank, Portland, Ore., 1910-14, Columbia Nat. Bank, Pittsburgh, 1914-17; partner S. M. Vockel & Co., investment bankers, 1920-29; owner R. C. Giles & Co., investments, since 1929. Township commr., Mt. Lebanon, Pa. Chmn. Community Com. Boy Scouts of America. Republican. United Presbyn. (supt. ch. sch.); elder Beverley Heights U.P. Ch.). Mason (32°). Club: Brighton Community. Home: 49 Ordale Boul., Mt. Lebanon, Pa. Office: 229 Fourth Av., Pittsburgh, Pa.

GILKYSON, Hamilton Henry, Jr., fire ins. co. exec.; b. Phoenixville, Pa., Nov. 4, 1882; s. Hamilton H. and Eleanor (Trego) G.; ed. George Sch., 1897-1901, Swarthmore Coll., 1901-04; m. Phoebe Hunter, June 27, 1912; children— Grace Whitaker, Hamilton H. 3d, Eliza Neal, Martha Kersey. Began as mem. firm Gilkyson Bros., ins. agts., Phoenixville, Pa., 1904; asso. with Mutual Fire Ins. Co. of Chester Co., Coatesville, Pa., since 1907, dir. since 1907, v.p. and exec. mgr., 1923-39, pres. since 1939; dir. Farmers & Mechanics Nat. Bank, Phoenixville, since 1910; dir. Phoenixville Pub. Co., The Daily Republican, since 1916, pres. since 1932. Served as pres. Pa. State Assn. Mutual Fire Ins. Cos., 1935-36; pres. Eastern Federation Mutual Fire Insurance Companies. Mem. Phi Kappa Psi. Clubs: Art Alliance (Phila.); Pickering Hunt (Phoenixville, Pa.). Home: Mont Clare, Montgomery Co., Pa. Office: Coatesville, Pa.; also Phoenixville, Pa.

GILKYSON, Phoebe Hunter, writer; b. Mont Clare, Pa., Apr. 3, 1891; d. Charles Field and Grace (Thompson) Hunter; prep. edn. Frances Stiteler Sch., Phoenixville, Pa., 1900-05; A.B., Hollins (Va.) Coll., 1909; student Acad. of the Fine Arts, Phila., 1910-11; m. Hamilton Henry Gilkyson, Jr., June 27, 1912; children—Grace Whitaker, Hamilton Henry, 3d, Eliza Neal, Martha Kersey. Writer of short stories which have appeared in McClures Mag., Woman's Home Companion, Pictorial Review, Harpers Monthly since 1922; book reviewer for Phila. newspapers since 1918. Dir. Phoenixville Hosp., Agnes Irwin Sch., Wynnewood, Pa. Mem. Womens Ad-

GILL, Arthur Bruce, orthopedic surgeon; b. Greensburg, Pa., Dec. 12, 1876; s. John Duff and Agnes Brown (Gemmell) G.; A.B., Muskingum Coll., New Concord, O., 1896, hon D.Sc., 1938; M.D., U. of Pa., 1905; m. Mabel Woodrow, Aug. 3, 1936. Prof. orthopedic surgery U. of Pa., since 1920; chief surgeon Widener Sch. for Crippled Children since 1920; orthopedic surgeon Presbyn. Hosp. since 1915 and Orthopædic Hosp. since 1918; mem. Am. Acad. of Orthopædic Surgery (pres. since), Am. Orthopædic Assn., A.M.A., Phila. Acad. of Surgery, Coll. of Physicians of Phila., Société Internationale de Chirurgie Orthopedique. Club: Merion Cricket (Haverford, Pa.); Franklin Inn. Home: Merion, Pa. Office: 1930 Chestnut St., Philadelphia, Pa.

GILL, Elizabeth, prin. pvt. sch. for girls; b. Mexico, Mo., Feb. 20, 1879; d. Thomas McElderry and Mary Anderson (Brooks) G.; ed. U. of Mo., summers, 1903-09; A.B. in Edn., Colo. State Teachers Coll., 1914; ed. Wash. U., St. Louis, 1927-28; A.M., Teachers Coll. of Columbia U., 1929. Engaged in teaching English and mathematics, high sch., Mexico, Mo., 1900-14; teacher mathematics and asso. prin., Miss Evans Sch., St. Louis, Mo., 1914-34; founder, pres. and head, Miss Gill's Sch. in the Mendham Hills, Mendham, N.J., since 1934. Mem. Nat. Council Mathematics Teachers, Nat. Assn. Prins. of Schs. for Girls. Conglist. Club: Women's University (New York). Home: Mendham, N.J.

GILL, James Presley, metallurgist; b. Montgomery City, Mo., Jan. 21, 1896; s. James William and Julia (Kirn) G.; B.S., U. of Mo. Rolla Sch. of Mines, 1918, M.S. in Metall. Engring., 1919; grad. study Columbia U. Sch. of Mines, 1918-20; m. Clarice Powell, July 14, 1922; children—James Powell, Mary Julia. Began as metallurgist Anaconda Copper Co., 1918; chief metallurgist, Vanadium Alloys Steel Co. since 1920, Anchor Drawn Steel Co. since 1925, and Colonial Steel Co. since 1928. Served as councilman Borough of Latrobe, Pa. Trustee and v.p. Am. Soc. for Metals (pres. elect). Mem. Am. Inst. Mining & Metall. Engrs., Am. Soc. for Testing Materials, Am. Electrochem. Soc., British Inst. of Metals, Am. Standards Ass., Am. Iron & Steel Inst., British Iron & Steel Inst., Tau Beta Pi, Pi Kappa Alpha, Theta Xi. Republican. Presbyterian. Mason (K.T., 32°, Shriner). Clubs: Country (Latrobe, Pa.); University (Pittsburgh). Author: Tool Steels, 1934; contbr. over 35 articles on metall. subjects; has delivered over 200 different lectures on metall. subjects. Home: 850 Weldon St. Office: Vanadium-Alloys Steel Co., Latrobe, Pa.

GILL, John David, economist; b. Phila., Pa., Dec. 11, 1889; s. Thomas and Anna Scott (Kennedy) G.; grad. Central Manual Training High Sch., Phila., 1907; B.S. in chem. engring., U. of Pa., 1911; m. Martha Arstaken Ritchie, Feb. 5, 1914; children—John David, Martin Scott Davey, Martha Joan. Teacher chemistry and physics, Pa. Mil. Coll., Chester, Pa., 1911-12; with Atlantic Refining Co., Phila., since 1912, successively as research engr., refinery supt., personnel mgr., and since 1928 economist, dir. since 1931. Mem. Franklin Inst., Royal Econ. Soc., Am. Econ. Assn., Am. Statistical Assn., Am. Sociol. Soc. Presbyterian. Club: University (Phila.). Home: 307 Bryn Mawr Av., Bala-Cynwyd, Pa. Office: 260 S. Broad St., Philadelphia, Pa.

GILL, John Goodner, coll. dean; b. Trenton, N.J., Feb. 22, 1905; s. John Edward and Nellie May (Goodner) G.; grad. Woodberry Forest (Va.) Sch., 1925; student Washington & Lee U., Lexington, Va., 1925-26, Lafayette Coll., Easton, Pa., 1928-29, Columbia U., summers 1936, 1937, Rutgers U., New Brunswick, N.J., 1936; B.B.A. (hon.), Rider Coll., Trenton, N.J., 1934; m. Verna Leonora Lindert, Mar. 25, 1933; children—Verna Lindert, John Edward II. Teller Phila. (Pa.) Nat. Bank, 1927-28; grad. mgr. athletics, Rider Coll., Trenton, N.J., 1929-31, placement dir., 1931-34, dean since 1934; dir. Trenton Banking Co. Mem. Mayor's Citizens Com., Trenton, N.J.; pres. of bd. Trenton Chapter of Salvation Army; dir. Trenton Chapter of Am. Red Cross (past roll call chmn.), Trenton Community Chest, The City Rescue Mission; trustee Rider Coll. Mem. N.J. Crippled Children's Commn., Trenton Chamber of Commerce (dir.), Eastern Commercial Teachers Assn., N.E.A., Delta Upsilon (Lafayette Chapter). Mason (Tall Cedars of Lebanon; Scottish Rite; Shriner, Crescent Temple), Elk, Moose. Republican. Presbyterian. Clubs: Kiwanis (pres. 1938), Carteret, Trenton Country (Trenton, N.J.); Advertising (New York). Home: 831 W. State St. Office: Rider College, Trenton, N.J.

GILL, Richard Dulany, physician; b. Bloomfield, Va., Feb. 17, 1899; s. John Love and Sue V. (Leith) G.; M.D., Univ. of Va. Med. Sch., 1923; m. Frances E. Walling, June 25, 1932; children—Sue Leith, Sally Stribling. Interne University Hosp., University, Va., 1923-25; urologist, Wheeling Clinic since 1927. Fellow Am. Coll. Surgeons; mem. Am. Urol. Assn., Southern Med. Assn., W.Va. Med. Soc., A.M.A., Am. Neisserian Soc., Phi Chi. Democrat. Episcopalian. Mason. Club: Ft. Henry (Wheeling). Home: Howard Place, Wheeling, W.Va.

GILL, Robert Joshua, lawyer; b. Baltimore, Md., June 22, 1889; s. John Montgomery and Emma C. (Yingling) G.; A.B., Western Md. Coll., Westminster Md., 1910; LL.B., Univ. of Va. Law Coll., Charlottesville, Va., 1913; unmarried. Admitted to Md. bar, 1914 and since engaged in gen. practice of law at Baltimore; mem. firm Barroll & Gill, 1914-17; mem. firm Gill, Greene & Waters since 1919, sole partner since 1934; dir. Finance Company of Baltimore. Served as lt. col. on staff Rainbow Div., 1917-19, with A.E.F. in France; awarded Croix de Guerre with Palm (France). Trustee Western Md. Coll., Westminster, Md. Mem. Phi Beta Kappa, Phi Kappa Psi. Democrat. Methodist. Clubs: Maryland, Hillendale Golf (Baltimore). Home: 7100 Wardman Rd. Office: Baltimore Trust Bldg., Baltimore, Md.

GILL, Wilson Lindsley, educator; b. Columbus, O., Sept. 12, 1851; s. John Loriman and Mary Smith (Waters) G.; 8th generation from Gov. Wm. Bradford; mem. 1st kindergarten class in America, taught by Caroline Frankenberg, Froebel's first kindergarten teacher; Dartmouth Coll.; Sheffield Scientific Sch. (Yale); LL.B., Yale Law Sch. (pres. of class), 1874; postgraduate study social and polit. sciences, Yale; m. Florence Lydia Henry, 1882 (dec.); 1 son, Bradford; m. 2d, Abbie McClennen, Mar. 1895; children—Mary Allis Patience (Mrs. William Calvin Stamm), Constance (Mrs. Ray Wilbert Strong). Gen. mgr. Gill Car & Car Wheel Works, Columbus, 1874-84, also of various mercantile and mfg. concerns; editor "Our Country" (mag.) 1895-1901; projector and engr. tunnel under 42d St. New York and East River. Was gen. supervisor moral and civic training, Island of Cuba, during 1st Am. occupation, to introduce method he had successful applied in New York City public schools, 1897; United States supervisor at large of Indian schools, Department of Interior, charged especially to organize each Govt. Indian Sch. as a democracy for moral and civic training. President American Patriotic League, Mount Airy, Phila.; dir. Nat. Soc. for Improving Methods of Sch. Discipline in Great Britain and Ireland. Originator and architect of Children's Bldg., Chicago World's Fair, 1893, and St. Louis later. Mem. nat. advisory com. of 100, Jamestown Tercentenary World's Fair. Pres. since 1908 of Children's Internat. State, founded by commrs. from govts. of Sweden, Germany, Argentine and Japan, for promotion of efficient citizenship and internat. friendship. Recipient Elliott Cresson gold medal, Franklin Inst., for originating the School Republic method of moral and civic training; wrote constitutions of the two national societies of the Sons and Daughters of American Revolution. Presbyterian. Author: City Problems, 1897; Gill System of Moral and Civic Training, 1900; The School Republic, 1903; The Boys' and Girls' Republic, 1913; Civic Practices for Boys and Girls, 1913; A New Citizenship, 1913; American Citizenship in the Schools, 1920; The Third Act of the American Revolution, 1921; Youths' Commonwealth, 1923; Children and the Constitution, 1928; Manual of the School Republic, 1932; also writer of monographs on social topics. Secured enactment of law in Mass., 1917, requiring training in the duties of citizenship in all pub. schs., the 1st of its kind in U.S.; ednl. dir. Constitutional League America, 1920—; organized all pub. schs. in Washington, D.C., as Sch. Republics, 1925, and Madison, Wis., 1931. For ednl. purpose induced the Govt. to put names under portraits on paper money and postage stamps, and for health and good roads, to remove import duty from asphalt. Mem. Psi Upsilon. Home: 501 W. Mt. Pleasant Av., Mt. Airy, Philadelphia, Pa.

GILLESPIE, James Edward, European history; b. Au Sable Forks, N.Y., Apr. 2, 1887; s. Henry Easton and Lucy Helen (Stickney) G.; A.B., Cornell U., 1909; M.A., Harvard, 1910; Ph.D., Columbia, 1920; unmarried. Prof. history and social science, Goshen (Ind.) Coll., 1913-14; prof. history, Windom Inst., Montevideo, Minn., 1916-17; adj. prof. history and social science, Macalester Coll., St. Paul, Minn., 1917-18; prof. history, Bellevue (Neb.) Coll., 1918-19; instr. in modern European and English history, U. of Ill., 1919-22; prof. modern European history, Pa. State Coll., since 1922. Mem. Am. Hist. Assn., Foreign Policy Assn., Am. Assn. University Professors, Pi Gamma Mu, Phi Kappa Phi. Republican. Presbyn. Author: The Influence of Overseas Expansion on England, 1920; A History of Europe (1500-1815) 1928; A History of Geographical Discovery (1400-1800), 1933. Home: 231 E. Park Av., State College, Pa.

GILLESPIE, Mary Edith, dean of women, dir. conservatory of music; b. Uniontown, Ind.; reared by James E. and Melvina (Ammons) Gillespie; ed. Oberlin Conservatory of Music, 1915-16; B.S. Columbia U. Teachers Coll., 1926, A.M., same, 1934. Began as teacher rural schs. in Ind., 1913-15; music supervisor, Scottsburg, Ind., 1916-18, Braddock, Pa., 1918-19; head music dept. Womens Coll., U. of Del., Newark, Del., 1925-30; dir. conservatory of music, Lebanon Valley Coll., Annville, Pa., since 1930, dean of women since 1927. Trustee Lebanon Valley Coll. Mem. Music Educators Nat. Conf., Am. Assn. Univ. Women, Pa. State Edn. Assn., Harmonia Circle, Psi Iota Xi. Republican. Presbyn. Home: Seymour, Ind. Office: Lebanon Valley College, Annville, Pa.

GILLESPIE, Stanley Alexander, real estate; b. Greenville, Pa., June 20, 1883; s. Eugene Pierce and Ella (Davidson) G.; grad. Greenville High Sch., 1901; student Thiel Coll., Greenville, 1901; m. Bess Anthony, Oct. 20, 1909; children—Nancy Jane, Eugene Pierce. Sec. and treas. People Electric Light, Heat and Power Co., 1901-04; pres. and dir. Valley Land Co.; dir. Pa. Power Co. Trustee Greenville Pub. Library, Shenango Valley Cemetery, Greenville Hosp., Passavant Memorial Home for Epileptics, Thiel Coll. Mem. Pa. Real Estate Advisory Bd., Pa. Real Estate Assn. (v.p.), Pa. Soc. of New York, Delta Sigma Phi. Democrat. Lutheran. Home: 5 Chambers Av. Office: 54 Clinton St., Greenville, Pa.

GILLESPIE, William, mathematician; b. Hamilton, Ont., Can., Nov. 1870; s. George Hamilton and Elizabeth Agnes G.; B.A., Toronto U., 1893; Ph.D., U. of Chicago, 1900; unmarried. Teacher of mathematics, Princeton U., since 1897, prof. since 1905. Presbyn. Address: Graduate College, Princeton, N.J.

GILLET, Joseph Eugene, prof. Spanish; b. Hasselt, Belgium, Aug. 14, 1888; s. Léopold and Hélène (Uytterschout) G.; ed. Royal Athenaeum, Hasselt; Ph.D., U. of Liège, 1910; studied univs. of Paris, Leyden, Munich and Berlin; m. Myrtle Margaret Mann, 1915. Came to U.S., 1913, naturalized, 1918. Asst. lecturer French, U. of Edinburgh, 1910-11; instr. German, U. of Wis., 1913-15; asso. in comparative literature and Romance langs., U. of Ill., 1915-18; asst. prof. Romance langs., U. of Minn., 1921-24; asso. prof. Spanish, Bryn Mawr Coll., 1924-29, prof. since 1929; visiting prof. Spanish, U. of Chicago, summers 1923, 1929, Princeton U., 1st semester, 1928-29, 1929-30. Served in U.S. Army, 1918-19. Mem. Am. Assn. Univ. Profs. (pres. Bryn Mawr Coll. chapter), Modern Lang. Assn. America (monograph com. and com. on research activities), Hispanic Soc. America, Academia de Bellas Artes, Valladolid. Author: Molière en Angleterre (1660-70), Paris, 1910; Micael de Carvajal, Tragedia Josephina, Princeton and Paris, 1932; also other editions of 16th century Spanish plays. Translator Dr. C. Snouck Hurgronje, The Holy War "Made in Germany," New York and London, 1915. Contbr. numerous articles and reviews in European and Am. periodicals on Spanish and Spanish-Am. lit. and linguistics. Associate editor: The Hispanic Review. Home: 227 N. Roberts Road, Bryn Mawr, Pa.

GILLET, Stanley Adrian, editor religious publications; b. West Union, Iowa, Jan. 12, 1897; s. Eugene Herman and Lizzie M. (Grimes) G.; A.B., Des Moines (Ia.) U., 1920; Th.M., Southern Bap. Theol. Sem., 1923; m. Mary Lu Capps, June 2, 1920; children—Robert Stanley, Dorothy Evelyn, Barbara Winnifred. Ordained to ministry of Baptist Ch., 1919; student pastor, Milan, Ind., 1921-23; pastor Winterset, Ia., 1923-25, Caldwell, Ida., 1925-27; dir. Christian edn., Am. Bapt. Publ. Soc., in Ida., 1925-29, in Northern Calif. and Nev., 1929-34; editor of young people's publs., Am. Bapt. Publ. Soc., Phila., since Sept. 1934. Active duty as aviation machinist, 1st class, U.S. Naval Reserve Force, July-Dec., 1918; hon. disch., Sept. 1921. Mason. Club: Heilikrinites (Phila.). Home: 137 Walnut St., Jenkintown, Pa. Office: 1701-1703 Chestnut St., Philadelphia, Pa.

GILLETTE, Ninde Troy, physician; b. Harlansburg, Pa., July 7, 1887; s. John Cookson and Sara Catherine (Burns) G.; ed. Slippery Rock State Normal Sch., 1904-06, Coll. Phys. & Surgs., Baltimore, Md., 1908-09; M.D., U. of Pittsburgh Med. Sch., 1914; m. Berenice Patterson, Dec. 29, 1907; children—Berenice Ninde (Mrs. Wright W. Hilyard), Robertte Troy (Mrs. E. H. Harmon), Mary Elizabeth. Employed as civil engr., 1906-07; interne St. Johns Hosp., Pittsburgh, 1914-15; in gen. practice medicine and surgery at Corry, Pa., since 1916. Fellow Am. Coll. Surgeons; mem. Erie Co. Med. Soc., Phi Beta Pi. Republican. Methodist. Mason. Home: 109 E. Smith St., Office: 8 Park Place, Corry, Pa.

GILLIAM, Marion Williams, elec. engr.; b. Buckingham Co., Va., Apr. 30, 1890; s. William Edward and Margaret (Daniel) G.; B.S. in E.E., Va. Poly. Inst., Blacksburg, Va., 1913; m. Mary Barber, June 14, 1918; children—David Marshall, Margaret Daniel, Robert Leigh, Marion Williams. Repairman Appalachian Power Co., 1913-14, supt. meter dept., 1914-15, foreman Coalwood div., 1915-16; v.p. and dist. mgr. W.Va. Engring. Co. since 1916; v.p. United Light & Power Co., and Iaeger Water Works, Iaeger, W.Va.; v.p. Union Power Co., and Mullens Water Works, Mullens, W.Va.; v.p. Kimball (W.Va.) Light & Water Co., War (W. Va.) Light & Water Co., Black Diamond Power Co. (Sophia and Chattaroy, W.Va.). Served as lt., U.S. Marine Corps, 1918. Mem. W.Va. State Com. of Y.M.C.A. Mem. Am. Legion (comdr. 1922), Tau Beta Pi. Democrat. Presbyterian. Club: Kiwanis of Williamson (pres. 1933). Home: 6 First St. South. Office: Cinderella Bldg., Williamson, W.Va.

GILLINGHAM, Clinton Hancock, coll. president; b. Phila., Pa., Sept. 29, 1877; s. Jonathan and Henrietta (Smith) G.; B.A., Maryville (Tenn.) Coll., 1905, M.A., 1907, D.D., 1919; student Princeton Theol. Sem., 1905-06; B.D., Presbyn. Theol. Sem. of Ky., 1908; spl. studies in Palestine, Jerusalem, 1923; m. Nancy Virginia Gardner, Nov. 2, 1903 (now deceased); children—George Gardner, Mrs. Alice Armitage McDowell, Samuel Wilson, Mary (Mrs. J. M. Padgette) and Jonathan (twins), Edward Clinton; m. 2d, Helen Lewis, of Middletown, O., July 14, 1935. Ordained Presbyterian ministry, September 29, 1907; junior sec. Y.M.C.A., Philadelphia, Pa., 1890-93; clk. and accountant Pa. R.R. Co., 1893-1901; with Maryville Coll., 1907-29, regstrar, 1907-26, prof. O.T. history and lit., 1907-11, prof. English Bible and head of dept. of Bible and religious edn., 1911-29; pres. Tennent Coll. of Christian Education since 1929. Served as major infantry 4th Tennessee Regiment, 1918-19; reserve officer Tennessee N.G., 1919-29. Mem. bd. dirs. Presbyn. Theol. Sem. of Ky., 1923-32; pres. bd. trustees Tennent Coll. of Christian Edn.; sec.-treas. Tenn. Coll. Assn., 1924-29. Mem. Religious Edn. Assn., N.E.A. Club: Kiwanis (past pres.). Home: Glenside, Pa. Address: Tennent College of Christian Education, 6063 Drexel Rd., Overbrook, Philadelphia, Pa.

GILLINGHAM, Harrold Edgar, insurance, numismatist; b. Hainesport, N.J., Aug. 25, 1864; s. Frank Clemens and Tacy Shoemaker (Morris) G.; student pvt. schs. and Germantown (Pa.) Acad.; m. Louise Hance Long, of Phila., Feb. 9, 1891; 1 dau., Edith Harrold (Mrs. Lansing Colton Holden Jr.). Began as ins. agt. and mgr. for dist., 1888; local agt. for several fire ins. companies and later mgr. of suburban dept. for Providence Washington Ins. Co. and Birmingham Fire Ins. Co.; combined offices with Robt. M. Coyle & Co., 1915; mgr. Saving Fund Soc. of Germantown; v.p. Mine Hill & Schuylkill Haven R.R., 13th and 15th Sts. Passenger Ry. Co.; dir. Green and Coats Sts. Passenger Ry. Co., Germantown Passenger Ry. Co., Phila. and Grays Ferry Passenger Ry. Co. Vice-pres. Hist. Soc. of Pa., Numismatic and Antiquarian Soc. of Phila.; treas. Am. Numismatic Soc. of N.Y., Welcome Soc. of Pa.; pres. Geneol. Soc. of Pa.; dir. Phila. Soc. for Preservation of Landmarks. Awarded Huntington medal of honor by Am. Numismatic Soc., N.Y., 1931. Republican. Episcopalian. Club: Down Town (Phila.). Author: French Orders and Decorations, 1922; Italian Orders and Medals of Honour, 1923; Spanish Orders of Chivalry, 1926; Decorations and Medals of the French Colonies, 1928; South American Decorations and War Medals, 1932; Ephemeral Decorations, 1935 (all pub. by Am. Numismatic Soc.); Marine Insurance in Phila., 1721-1800; Indian Ornaments made by Philadelphia Silversmiths, 1936; Fire Marks of American Fire Insurance Companies, 1914; contbr. articles on hist. matters and Phila. craftsmen to Pa. Mag. of History and Biography, and articles on antiques to The Antiquarian and to Antiques, etc. Home: 432 W. Price St., Germantown. Office: 423 Walnut St., Philadelphia, Pa.

GILLIS, Alexander James; clin. prof. urology, U. of Md.; urologist Mercy Hosp. Address: 20 E. Preston St., Baltimore, Md.

GILLMORE, Quincy Adams, army officer; b. West Point, N.Y., Jan. 12, 1881; s. Quincy O'Mahr and Margaret (Van Kleeck) G.; prep. edn., Mohegan Lake (N.Y.) Sch. and Preston Sch., Washington, D.C.; student Colo. Sch. Mines, 1898-1900; grad. U.S. Mil. Acad., 1904; m. Frances West Hemley, Nov. 16, 1904; children—Quincy A., Frances West, Frederick Hemsley. Commd. 2d lt., Arty., U.S.A., 1904, col., F.A., 1917, brig. gen., N.J. N.G., 1922, maj. gen., 1924; comdg. gen. N.J.N.G. and 44th Div. (N.Y. and N.J. troops), 1924-32, resigned. Comd. 112th F.A., A.E.F., 1917-19. Mem. Huguenot Soc., Soc. Colonial Wars, Loyal Legion. Awarded Distinguished Service Medal, State of N.J. Republican. Episcopalian. Clubs: Rittenhouse, Racquet (Philadelphia, Pa.); Union, Racquet and Tennis, Turf and Field, Deepdale. Home: Rumson, N.J.; 840 Park Av., New York, N.Y.

GILMAN, Charles, civil engring.; b. Cambridge, Mass., May 2, 1882; graduate Rindge Manual Training School, Cambridge, Mass., 1899; B.S. in C.E., magna cum laude, Harvard U., 1904; m. Alva Howe Story, June 26, 1909 (died Mar. 17, 1934); children—Karl Quincy, Roger Howe; m. 2d, Marion Smith Carter, July 20, 1935. Engaged in engring. and concrete constrn. work, 1904-12; with Massey Concrete Products Corpn., N.Y. City since 1912, in capacities of Eastern engr., Eastern mgr. and vice-pres., 1919-37, 1st v.p. and gen. mgr. since May 1937; pioneered use of reinforced concrete culvert pipe, cribbing and piling. Served with Engring. Adv. Com. of N.J. State League of Municipalities, 1934; chmn. joint commn. for constrn. viaduct over Greenbrook between city of Plainfield and North Plainfield, N.J.; sec. bd. appeals city of Plainfield. Trustee Plainfield Humane Soc. Mem. Am. Soc. Civil Engrs. (past dir.), Am. Soc. for Testing Materials, Plainfield Engrs. Club (past pres.), Harvard Engring. Soc. (past pres.), Am. Concrete Inst. Licensed professional engr. in N.J. and N.Y. Republican. Presbyterian. Clubs: Plainfield Country; Harvard, Railroad-Machinery (New York); Illinois Atheltic (Chicago). Home: 954 Kensington Av., Plainfield, N.J. Office: 50 Church St., New York, N.Y.

GILMAN, James Bruce, clergyman; b. Lowell, Mass., Jan. 23, 1878; s. James Bradbury and Catharine (Whitney) G.; A.B., Brown U., 1900; B.D., Newton Theol. Sem., 1903; S.T.M., New Brunswick Theol. Sem., 1929; S.T.D., Bib. Sem. in N.Y., 1932; m. Essa Mabel Starkweather, July 21, 1908; children—Katherine Anne, Dorothy Edith. Ordained to ministry Bapt. Ch., 1903; pastor, Pittsfield, Mass., 1903-09, Nashua, N.H., 1909-21; pastor, First Bapt. Ch., New Brunswick, N.J., since 1921; served as pres. N.Y. City Bapt. Ministers' Conf., 1937. Trustee Internat. Bapt. Sem., East Orange, N.J. Republican. Baptist. Home: 255 Handy St., New Brunswick, N.J.

GILMAN, Robert Louis, physician; b. Dubuque, Ia., Nov. 27, 1896; s. Louis Paschal and Avis Eleanor (Mann) G.; student State Normal Sch., Oshkosh, Wis., 1914-16; B.Sc., U. of Wis., Madison, Wis., 1920; M.D., U. of Pa. Med. Sch., 1922, M.Sc., Grad. Sch., 1928; m. Marie Victoria Detzel, July 31, 1923; 1 dau., Marion Thornton. Interne U. of Wis. Gen. Hosp., Madison, Wis., 1922-23; engaged in gen. practice of medicine, Ashland, Wis., 1923-26; grad. student and asst. prof. dermatology, U. of Pa. Med. Sch., 1926-30; asst. prof. dermatology, Womens Med. Coll., 1930-35; asst. prof. syphilology, U. of Pa. Grad. Sch. of Medicine, 1934-37, asso. prof. since 1938; engaged in pvt. practice at Phila. since 1930; dermatologist, Student Health Service, U. of Pa. Served as sergt. Med. Corps, U.S. Army, 1917-19, with A.E.F. in France; lieut. comdr., U.S.N.R. Fellow Coll. of Phys. of Phila.; mem. Am. Dermatol. Assn., Sigma Xi, Phi Delta Theta. Episcopalian. Club: Philobiblon (Phila.). Home: Moylan-Rose Valley, Pa. Office: 1930 Chestnut St., Philadelphia, Pa.

GILMER, Albert Hatton, prof. speech and drama; b. Loraine, Ill., Dec. 31, 1878; s. Park Hatton and Elizabeth (Riggs) G.; B.S., Knox Coll., 1900, A.M., same, 1911; study, U. of Chicago, summer 1905; grad. student, U. of Munich, Germany, 1908-09; grad. student, Harvard U., 1912-14; grad. student, Oxford, Eng., summer 1925, Univ. of London, 1934; (hon.) Litt.D., Knox Coll., 1936; m. Mabel Bishop, June 25, 1910. Engaged in teaching pub. schs. in Ill. and Detroit, Mich., 1900-1908; instr. English, Bates Coll., Lewiston, Me., 1909-10; instr., then prof. English and later of dramatic literature, Tufts Coll., Medford, Mass., 1910-28; prof. speech and dramatic art, Lafayette Coll., Easton, Pa., since 1928. Mem. Am. Assn. Univ. Profs., Nat. Assn. Teachers of Speech, Phi Beta Kappa, Beta Theta Pi. Hon. Officer French Acad. of Edn., awarded "Palms" as speaker rep. of Lafayette Coll. and Am. Friends of Lafayette at 100th anniversary memorial celebration of death Gen. Lafayette, 1934. Republican. Author (plays): The Edge of the World, 1912; Old John Brown, 1913; A Wake or a Wedding, 1936. Writer and dir. pageants. Home: 923 Fairfield Av., Easton, Pa.

GILMORE, Edward Robert, research engr.; b. Keene, N.H., Nov. 11, 1897; s. Charles E. and Agnes Edith (Bowker) G.; M.E., Rensselaer Poly. Inst., 1920; m. Clessie Jackson, June 10, 1922. Leakage engr. Empire Cos., Bartlesville, Okla., 1920-23; supt. gas distribution Western Distributing Co., Duncan, Okla., 1923-24; engr. and supt. Gas Service Co., Topeka, Kan., 1924-36; research engr. Pittsburgh Equitable Meter Co. since 1936. Inventor and mfr. Gilmore gas stethoscope. Republican. Christian. Contbr. Gas Age Record. Home: 413 N. Homewood Av. Office: Pittsburgh Equitable Meter Co., Pittsburgh, Pa.

GILPIN, Sherman Fletcher, physician; b. La Anna, Pa., Dec. 14, 1871; s. William Ritner and Elizabeth (Wallace) G.; M.E., State Teachers Coll., Mansfield, Pa., 1891; M.D., Jefferson Med. Coll., 1896; m. Emily Reeve Hefft, Apr. 28, 1900; 1 son, Sherman Fulmer. Interne Phila. Gen. Hosp., 1896-98, asst. chief resident phys., 1898-1900; on neurologic staff, Jefferson Med. Hosp., 1899-1933, asso. prof. nervous and mental diseases when resigned, 1933; asst. visiting neurologist Phila. Gen. Hosp. until 1918, visiting psychiatrist, 1920-35, committing examiner of insane since 1935. Home: Fort Washington, Pa. Office: 432 N. 52d St., Philadelphia, Pa.

GILROY, Helen Turnbull, prof. physics; b. Phila., Pa., May 9, 1887; d. Louis K. and Laura C. (Bailey) G.; A.B., Bryn Mawr (Pa.) Coll., 1909, A.M., 1912; grad. study, U. of Chicago, 1915-17; Ph.D., Cornell U., 1931. Engaged as instr. physics, Mount Holyoke Coll., South Hudley, Mass., 1912-14; demonstrator physics, Bryn Mawr Coll., 1914-15; instr. physics, Vassar Coll., Poughkeepsie, N.Y., 1917-20, asst. prof., 1921-24; asst. prof. physics, Lingnan U., Canton, China, 1924-27, asso. prof., 1931-34; prof. physics, Beaver Coll., Jenkintown, Pa., since 1937. Fellow A.A.A.S.; mem. Am. Phys. Soc., Am. Assn. Physics Teachers, Sigma Xi, Sigma Delta Epsilon, Phi Tau Phi, Pi Lambda Theta. Presbyterian. Home: Rydal Rd., Noble, Jenkintown P.O., Pa.

GILSON, C. Albert; pres. Farmers & Mechanics Nat. Bank. Address: Frederick, Md.

GILSON, James Franklin, real estate; b. Pittsburgh, Pa., May 6, 1893; s. Clarence Townsend and Ida May (Hysong) G.; ed. Allegheny High Sch., Pittsburgh, 1908-12, U. of Pittsburgh, 1912-14; unmarried. Began as clk. in real estate office, Pittsburgh, 1915; asso. with Freehold Real Estate Co., sub-divs., sales, management appraisals, ins. and mortgage financing, Pittsburgh, since 1915, vice-pres. since 1938; asst. sec. and treas. St. Clair Land Co. Served in Inf., U.S. Army, 1917, in motor corps, 1918-19. Mem. Pittsburgh Chamber of Commerce. Mem. Nat. Assn. Real Estate Bds., Pa. State Real Estate Assn. (v.p.), Pittsburgh Real Estate Bd. (pres. 1936), Bldg. Owners & Mgrs. Assn. of Pittsburgh. Awarded title Certified Property Manager, 1938. Republican. Methodist. Mason (32°, Shriner). Home: 1436 W. North Av. Office: 311 Fourth Av., Pittsburgh, Pa.

GILTINAN, David Murray, pres. Eskew, Smith & Cannon; b. St. Paul, Minn., Dec. 18, 1892; s. George M. and Mary F. (Donnelly) G.; B.S., U. of Minn., 1915, M.E., 1916; m. Elsie Quarrier Smith, Sept. 3, 1921; children—David M., Jr., Alexander S., Ethelind A. Employed as metall. engr. and asst. dir. research, Midvale Steel Co., Phila., Pa., 1916-17; asst. supt. ordnance heat treatment, U.S. Naval Ordnance Plant, South Charleston, W.Va., 1919-21; asso. with Eskew, Smith & Cannon, wholesale distributors gen. merchandise, Charleston, W.Va., since 1921, pres. since 1925; dir. George Washington Life Ins. Co., Kanawha Banking & Trust Co., Kanawha Land Co., Kanawha Drug Co., Charleston Transit Co., all of Charleston, W.Va.; v.p. and dir. W.Va. Airways, Inc. Served as lt. (j.g.) U.S.N.R.F., 1918-19. Mem. W.Va. State Bd. Aeronautics since 1933; mem. Sportsman Pilots Assn. of U.S.; dir. Charleston Community Fund. Mem. Delta Upsilon, Theta Tau, Tau Beta Pi. Democrat. Clubs: Edgewood Country, Boat (Charleston). Home: 1223 Virginia St. Office: Brooks & Wilson Sts., Charleston, W.Va.

GIMBEL, Ellis A., merchant; b. Vincennes, Ind., 1865; chmn. bd. and v.p. Gimbel Bros.; pres. Ninth Ward Realty Co., Gimbel Bros. Bank & Trust Co.; chmn. bd. Pa. Broadcasting Co. Home: 1900 Locust St. Office: care Gimbel Bros., Market and 9th Sts., Philadelphia, Pa.

GINGERY, Don, ex-congressman; b. Woodland, Pa., Feb. 19, 1884; s. Dorsey J. and Ada Mary (Albert) G.; student Ohio and Northern U., 1900-01; m. Anna Leavy, 1912; children—Donald E., Sarah L., Mary Louise, Hugh Albert. Began as civil engr., 1903; in hardware and mine supplies business, 1902-34; with Logan-Gregg Hardware Co., Pittsburgh; mem. Pa. legislature, 1915-16; mem. 74th and 75th Congresses (1935-39), 23d Pa. Dist. Was Clearfield Co. chmn. Dem. Com. and mem. Dem. State Com. and State Exec. Com. Formerly capt. Pa. N.G. Democrat. Methodist. Mem. Eagles, Moose. Home: Clearfield, Pa.*

GINGRICH, Christian C., pres. Valley Trust Co.; b. Lawn, Pa., Dec. 25, 1866; s. Christian and Susan (Bachman) G.; student pub. schs., Lawn, 1872-84; m. Minnie Risser, Feb. 18, 1888; children—Christian R., Almeda Gruber. Shipper of beef cattle, 1892-1932, cattle breeder since 1932; charter mem. bd. of dirs., Valley Trust Co., Palmyra, Pa., since 1903, pres. since 1916; dir. Capitol City Milk Producers Assn. Mem. Lebanon Co. Supervisors' Assn. (pres.), Pa. State Assn. of Township Supervisors (mem. exec. com.). Republican. Mem. United Brethren Ch. Mason (32°). Home: Lawn, Pa. Office: Valley Trust Co., Palmyra, Pa.

GINGRICH, Christian Risser, lawyer and coll. prof.; b. Lawn, Pa., Oct. 12, 1891; s. Christian Christmas and Minnie (Hoffer) G.; A.B., Franklin and Marshall Coll., Lancaster, Pa., 1911; LL.B., U. of Pa. Law Sch., 1916; m. Velma Mabel Stauffer, May 22, 1913; children—June Stauffer (Mrs. David Yake), Velma Stauffer (Mrs. George Bow), Christian A. Admitted to Pa. bar, 1916, and since engaged in gen. practice of law at Lebanon and Annville, Pa.; lecturer and prof. social sciences, Lebanon Valley Coll., Annville, Pa., since 1916; dir. Kingsley & Brown, Inc., Palmyra Automobile Club; solicitor Annville Twp. Sch. Dist. Served in S.A.T.C., 1918. Trustee Lebanon Valley Coll. Mem. Lebanon Co. Bar Assn., Chi Phi, Lebanon Co. Firemen's Assn. Republican. United Brethren Ch. Mason, Red Man. Clubs: Royal Men's, Pleasant Hill Gun (Lebanon, Pa.). Home: 36 College Av., Annville, Pa.

GINGRICH, Felix Wilbur, prof. Greek and Bible; b. Annville, Pa., Sept. 27, 1901; s. Felix Moyer and Minnie (Shiffer) G.; A.B., Lafayette Coll., Easton, Pa., 1923; student U. of Pa., 1923-26; A.M., U. of Chicago, 1927, Ph.D., 1932; m. Lola Engel, Mar. 28, 1929; children—John Wilbur, Barbara Helen Adeline. Began as asst. prof. Latin and German, Schuylkill Coll., Reading, Pa., 1923-26; prof. Greek and Bible, Schuylkill Coll. and Albright Coll., Reading, Pa., since 1927. Mem. Soc. Bib. Lit. and Exegesis, Nat. Assn. Bib. Instrs., Classical Assn. Atlantic States, Am. Assn. Univ. Profs., Phi Beta Kappa, Zeta Omega Epsilon. Republican. Evang. Ch. Author: Paul's Ethical Vocabulary, 1932; contbr. articles to mags. Home: 1629 N. 11th St., Reading, Pa.

GINSBERG, Louis, poet; b. Newark, N.J., Oct. 1, 1896; s. Pinkus and Rebecca (Schechtman) G.; student Barringer High Sch., Newark, N.J., 1910-14; B.A., Rutgers U., New Brunswick, N.J., 1918; M.A., Columbia U., 1924; m. Naomi Levey, 1919; children—Eugene Brooks, Allen Irwin. Teacher English, Woodbine (N.J.) High Sch., 1918-20, Central High Sch., Paterson, N.J., since 1921. Mem. Paterson Y.M.H.A. (mem. lecture com.), Poetry Soc. of America, Catholic Poetry Soc., Chaucer Guild (Paterson, N.J.). Awarded: Circle Poetry Prize, 1929; B'nai Brith Prize in Poetry; Contemporary Verse Lyric Poetry Prize, 1930; Stratford Monthly $100 Poetry Prize, 1932. Club: M.S. (Paterson, N.J.). Author (books of poems): The Attic of the Past, 1921; The Everlasting Minute and Other Poems, 1937; poems in The American Mercury, The Forum, Saturday Rev. of Lit., The Commonweal, Poetry, The New Statesman, G.K.'s Weekly, The Christian Century, The Lyric, The Modern Monthly, Frontier and Midland; poems included in Untermeyer's Modern Am. and Brit. Poetry, Modern Am. Poetry; Rittenhouse Third Little Book of Modern Verse; Clark and Garrison Poems of Peace; Moult's Best Poems of 1935 and 1936; Hill's Twentieth Century Love Poems; book rev. editor Newark Ledger, 1921; sometime lecturer on poetry, Newark Adult Sch., N.J. Adult Sch. Home: 288 Graham Av. Address: P.O. Box 1533, Paterson, N.J.

GINTER, Robert McNiel; b. Delmont, Pa., Apr. 14, 1877; s. Gideon and Emily (Lose) G.; Indiana (Pa.) Normal Sch., Wooster (O.) U.; m. Marguerite E. Sellers, Oct. 5, 1909. Learned printer's trade on Indiana Times; reporter, telegraph editor, Sunday editor, night editor and mng. editor Pittsburgh Gazette-Times, and Washington corr. for paper, 1911-27, except 3 yrs. as mng. editor. Vice chmn. State Aeronautics Commn. by apptmt. of Gov. John S. Fisher, until July 31, 1931. Republican. Presbyn. Mason. Club: Gridiron (Washington, D.C.). Home: 525 Roslyn Place, Pittsburgh, Pa.

GINTHER, Mrs. Pemberton, artist and author; b. Philadelphia, Pa.; d. David and Mary Esther (Shapley) Ginther; studied Sch. of Design (Phila.), Pa. Acad. Fine Arts; m. Willis A. Heyler, Sept. 25, 1915. Painter of landscapes and figures; has exhibited at Pa. Acad. Fine Arts, Art Club (Phila.), etc.; also pvt. exhbns. of oil, water color and charcoal; designed stained glass windows: "Peter and John at the Tomb," St. John's P.E. Ch., Suffolk, Va.; "John on Patmos," Ch. of the Restoration, Phila.; etc. Presbyn. Author: Miss Pat Series (9 vols.), 1915; Beth Anne Series (4 vols.), 1915; Betsy Hale Series (4 vols.); Hilda of Grey Cot Series (4 vols.), 1922-25; The Secret Stair, 1928; The Jade Necklace, 1929; The Thirteenth Spoon, 1930; Through the Wilderness. Illustrates own books. Awarded Federation 1st prize for 1-act play, "One of Those Things." Mem. Fellowship Pa. Acad. Fine Arts. Clubs: Plastic, Art Alliance, Salon Music, Odds and Ends (pres.), Doylestown Nature (art chmn.), Doylestown V.I.A. (art chmn.), Colonial (pres.). Home: Gable End, Old York Road, Buckingham, Pa.

GIPSON, Lawrence Henry, historian; b. at Greeley, Colo., Dec. 7, 1880; s. Albert Eugene and Lina Maria (West) G.; A.B., U. of Ida., 1903; Rhodes scholar from Ida. to Oxford U., Eng., 1904; B.A. with honors in history, 1907; Farnham fellow Yale, 1910-11; U. of Chicago, summers, 1912-16; Bulkley fellow, Yale, 1917-18, Ph.D., 1918; m. Jeannette Reed, Oct. 8, 1909. Asst. in history, U. of Ida., 1903-04; prof. history, Coll. of Ida., 1907-10; prof. history, 1911-17, prof. history and polit. science, 1918-24, Wabash Coll.; prof. history and govt. and head of dept., Lehigh U. since 1924. Visiting prof. history summers, Indiana U., 1922, Pa. State Coll., 1923, U. of Pa., 1931. Fellow Royal Historical Society; member American Assn. Univ. Profs., Foreign Policy Assn., Am., Miss. Valley and Pa. (council) hist. assns., Am. Polit. Science Assn., Hist. Soc. of Pa., Archæol. Inst., Phi Beta Kappa; hon. corr. mem. Institut Historique et Heraldique de France. Justin Winsor prize in Am. history, 1922. Conglist. Author: The Historical Monograph, 1918; Jared Ingersoll—A Study of American Loyalism in Relation to British Colonial Government, 1920; Studies in Connecticut Colonial Taxation, 1931; The British Empire before the American Revolution, Vols., Great Britain and Ireland, The Southern Plantations, The Northern Plantations, 1936; The Moravian White River Indian Mission, 1938. Contbr. the portion relating to U.S., to "The Expansion of the Anglo-Saxon Nations," London, 1920; also various hist. articles in jours. and revs. Home: 836 Delaware Av., Bethlehem, Pa.

GIRDWOOD, John, physician; b. Barbados, B.W.I., Apr. 10, 1871; s. James and Margaret (Price) G.; came to U.S., 1875, naturalized upon reaching majority; student Pub. Schs., Baltimore, Md., 1877-87, Baltimore (Md.) City Coll., 1884-85, Baltimore (Md.) Poly., 1886-87; M.D., U. of Md., Baltimore, Md., 1894; post-grad. work, Johns Hopkins U., Baltimore, Md., 1900-04; m. Sallie Peyton Burton, Oct. 10, 1900. Practice of medicine at Baltimore, Md., since 1894; med. examiner, Vets. Bur., Washington and Baltimore, 1920-25; med. examiner City Service Commn., Baltimore, Md., 1920-39. Served with Am. Red Cross, France and Montenegro, during World War; Rockefeller Foundation, France, 1918-20. Mem. A.M.A., Baltimore City Med. Soc., Med. and Chirurg. Faculty of Md. Democrat. Episcopalian. Address: 2806 St. Paul St., Baltimore, Md.

GISH, Oliver Holmes, physicist; b. Abilene, Kan., Sept. 7, 1883; s. John Engle and Fannie

Rider (Herr) G.; prep. edn. secondary schools of Dickinson Co., Kan.; B.S., Kan. State Coll., Manhattan, 1908; A.M., U. of Neb., 1913; grad. student Univ. of Göttingen, Germany, 1913-14, U. of Chicago, summers, 1915, 16, 17; m. Edna Miller, June 9, 1915; children—Eleanor Elizabeth, Lois Eileen, Helen Pauline, Donald Miller. Teacher of physics and mathematics, Maryville (Kan.) High Sch., 1908-09; observer U.S. Weather Bureau, Lincoln, Neb., 1909-10; research observer, Mt. Weather Observatory, Bluemont, Va., 1910; grad. asst. dept. of physics, U. of Neb., 1911-13, instr. in mathematics, 1914-16, instr. in physics, 1916-18; research engr. Westinghouse Electric & Mfg. Co., East Pittsburgh, Pa., 1918-22; asso. physicist dept. terrestrial magnetism, Carnegie Instn. of Washington, 1922-27, physicist, 1927-28, chief sect. of terrestrial electricity since 1928, asst. dir. since 1933. Mem. A.A.A.S., Am. Phys. Soc., Am. Geophys. Union, Am. Meteorol. Soc., Am. Seismol. Soc., Philos. Soc. of Washington, Washington Acad. of Sciences, Sigma Xi. Unitarian. Home: 315 Essex Av., Chevy Chase, Md. Office: 5241 Broad Branch Rd., Washington, D.C.

GISH, Warren Froebel, high school prin.; b. Marietta, Pa., Oct. 6, 1894; s. Eli Nissley and Lizzie A. (Gingrich) G.; grad. Millersville Model High Sch., 1913; student Millersville State Normal Sch., 1913-16; A.B., Franklin and Marshall Coll., 1921; A.M., Columbia, 1929; student Univ. of Berlin, Germany, summer 1930; m. Reba Mae Townsley, June 30, 1924; 1 son, Warren Froebel (deceased). Teacher in rural school near Shocks Mills, Lancaster Co., Pa. (father had taught in same school), 1916-18; prin. Salisbury Twp. High Sch., 1921-24; prin. Wellsburg (W.Va.) High Sch., 1924-25; teacher of German, Reading (Pa.) Senior High Sch. since 1925; prin. Reading Standard Evening High Sch. since 1927. Served as private Med. Corps, U.S. Army, Camp Hancock, Ga., 1918-19. Awarded Wyomissing Foundation scholarship for study in Germany, 1930. Mem. N.E.A., Pa. State Edn. Assn., Reading Teachers Assn., Lambda Chi Alpha. Club: Athenaeum (Reading High Sch.). Home: Carsonia and Melrose Avs., Stony Creek Mills, Pa.

GITHENS, Thomas Stotesbury, physician, med. research; b. Phila., Pa., July 29, 1878; s. William H. H. (M.D.) and Adele (Stotesbury) G.; student U. of Pa. Biol. Sch., 1892-94; M.D., U. of Pa. Med. Sch., 1899; grad. study U. of Strassburg, Germany, 1903-04; m. Louise Seyfert, Oct. 14, 1920. Engaged in pvt. practice of medicine at Phila., 1900-09; with Rockefeller Inst., New York, N.Y., 1910-19; in med. research, asso. with Mulford Labs. of Sharp & Dohme, Glenolden, Pa., since 1919. Served as capt., Med. Corps, U.S. Army, during World War. Mem. Coll. of Phys., Phila., Am. Physiol. Soc., Soc. for Exptl. Biology and Medicine. Republican. Episcopalian. Home: The Cambridge, Germantown, Phila. Office: Sharp & Dohme, Glenolden, Pa.

GITT, Josiah William, editor and publisher; b. Hanover, Pa., Mar. 28, 1884; s. Clinton J. and Emma (Koplin) G.; A.B., Franklin and Marshall Coll., Lancaster, Pa., 1904; m. Elizabeth Moul, June 12, 1913; children—Charles M., Eleanor C., Marian L., Susan E. Admitted to Pa. bar, 1908, and engaged in gen. practice of law at York, Pa., 1908-15; editor and publisher The Gazette and Daily, York Gazette Co. since 1915; dir. Hanover Wire Cloth Co., Hanover, Pa., York Ice Machinery Corpn. Democrat. Reformed Ch. Home: R.F.D. No. 3, Hanover, Pa. Office: 31 E. King St., York, Pa.

GITTINGS, J(ohn) Claxton, pediatrist; b. Pa., May 23, 1874; s. J. B. Howard and Katherine Scott (Claxton) G.; M.D., U. of Pa., 1895; m. Katherine Colhoun, Sept. 23, 1903. William H. Bennett prof. pediatrics, U. of Pa. Sch. of Medicine. Mem. A.M.A., Am. Pediatric Soc. (emeritus); fellow Coll. of Physicians, Phila. Republican. Episcopalian. Clubs: St. Elmo, South River Club (Md.). Home: The Delmar-Morris, Germantown, Philadelphia. Address: University Hospital, 36th and Spruce Sts., Philadelhia, Pa.

GIVEN, Walter May, clergyman; b. Sutton, W.Va., July 11, 1879; s. Reynolds and Virginia (McMorrow) G.; student Morris Harvey Coll., Barboursville (now Charleston), W.Va., 1899-1901, D.D., 1925; m. Leonore Wilson, Nov. 19, 1903; children—Walter May, Virginia (Mrs. K. K. Hood), Leonore (Mrs. T. F. Wilshire). Ordained to ministry Meth. Ch., 1903; pastor in W.Va. at Enterprise, 1901-02, Grays Flat, 1902-04, Davis, 1904-06, Barboursville, 1906-08, New Martinsville, 1908-10; presiding elder, Charleston Dist., Charleston, W.Va., 1910-14; pastor, Ashland, Ky., 1914-16, Clendenin, W.Va., 1916-23; presiding elder, Ashland Dist., Ashland, Ky., 1923-24; pastor Humphreys Memorial Ch., Charleston, W.Va., 1924-27, Fairmont, W.Va., 1927-31, Beckley, W.Va., 1931-33, Humphreys Memorial Ch., Charleston, W.Va., 1933-35; dist. supt. Charleston Dist., Charleston, W.Va., since 1935. Del. of Western Va. Conf. to Gen. Conf., 1930, 38; mem. Uniting Conf. of Meth. Ch., Kansas City, Mo., 1939. Trustee and sec. exec. com. Morris Harvey Coll.; pres. bd. W.Va. Anti-Saloon League. Mason (32°, K.C.C.H.). Club: Kiwanis. Home: 1556 Dixie St., Charleston, W.Va.

GLADFELTER, Millard Elwood, registrar Temple U.; b. York Co., Pa., Jan. 16, 1900; s. Phillip and Ida Jane (Shearer) G.; A.B., Gettysburg (Pa.) Coll., 1925; A.M., U. of Wis., 1930; post-grad. work U. of Pa., 1935; m. Martha Louise Gaut, Dec. 28, 1931; children—Phillip Elmore, Bruce Gaut. Began as teacher rural schs. of Pa., 1918; prin. and teacher history, West York High Sch., 1925-28; supv. prin., West York Schs., 1928-30; dir. Temple U., Jr.-Sr. High Sch., 1930-31; registrar, Temple U., Phila., since 1931. Mem. scholarship com., Phila. Council Boy Scouts of America; mem. Mayor's Scholarship Com. of Phila. Mem. N.E.A., Am. Assn. Collegiate Registrars (exec. com.), Pa. State Edn. Assn., Pa. Dept. of Secondary Sch. Prins., Phila. Suburban Prins. Assn., Alumni Assn. of Gettysburg Coll. (mem. exec. com.), Phi Delta Theta, Kappa Phi Kappa, Phi Delta Kappa, Phi Beta Kappa. Lutheran. Mason. Club: Kiwanis (Phila.). Editor, Journal Am. Assn. Collegiate Registrars. Home: 5419 Westford Road. Address: Temple University, Philadelphia, Pa.

GLAHN, Albert Thomas, corpn. management; b. Forty Fort, Pa., Feb. 13, 1893; s. Adam and Charlotte (Rothhaar) G.; ed. Forty Fort High Sch. and Wyoming Sem.; m. Irma Wilhelmina Gollus, Nov. 18, 1916. Clerk Mahoney & Co., grocery store, 1910-12, Lehigh Valley Coal Co., 1912-23; with Andrew J. Sordoni and successor, Sordoni Constrn. Co., since 1923; pres. and dir. Commonwealth Telephone Co., Luzerne Telephone Co., Bradford County Telephone Co., Harvey's Lake Light Co., Pub. Service of Pa., Inc.; vice-pres. and dir. Montrose Inn, Inc., Jermyn Hotel Co., Johnson Engring. & Mfg. Co., Sterling Hotel Co., Sordoni Constrn. Co. (all foregoing owned by State Senator Andrew J. Sordoni); dir. and sec. Forty Fort State Bank; vice-pres. and treas. Arlington Hotel, Binghamton, N.Y. Republican. Presbyterian (sec. Forty Fort Presbyn. Ch.). Mason, Moose, Patriotic Order Sons of America. Club: Shrine (Dallas, Pa.). Home: 1735 Wyoming Av. Office: 45 Owen St., Forty Fort, Pa.

GLAHN, Mark Martin, corpn. official; b. Forty Fort, Pa., Aug. 1, 1895; s. Adam and Charlotte (Rothhaar) G.; grad. Forty Fort High Sch., 1913; student Wyoming Sem. (Wyoming Coll. of Business), Kingston, Pa., 1913-14; m. Helen DePew, June 28, 1920; 1 dau., Shirley Jane. Clerk to cashier Nat. Biscuit Co., 1914-16; payroll clerk and paymaster Lehigh and Wilkes-Barre Coal Co., 1918-23; with Andrew J. Sordoni and Sordoni Constrn. Co. since 1923, office mgr. to 1937, sec. and treas. since 1937; sec., treas. and dir. Commonwealth Telephone Co., Luzerne Telephone Co., Bradford County Telephone Co., Harvey's Lake Light Co., Johnson Engring. & Mfg. Co., Public Service of Pa., Montrose Inn, Inc., Jermyn Hotel Co., Sterling Hotel Co. Served as 2d lt., Field Arty., U.S. Army, 1917-19. Mem. Nat. Assn. Cost Accountants (past pres. local chapter). Republican. Methodist. Mason (Shriner). Club: Shrine Country. Home: 27 Poplar St., Kingston, Pa. Office: 45 Owen St., Forty Fort, Pa.

GLASNER, Samuel, rabbi; b. Phila., Pa., June 19, 1912; s. Max and Louisa (Faerber) G.; grad. South Phila. High Sch. for Boys, 1928; A.B., U. of Pa., 1931; grad. Gratz Coll., Phila., 1931; B.H.L., Hebrew Union Coll., 1933, rabbi, 1936; m. Jennie Solomon, July 9, 1933; 1 dau., Antoinette Joy. Rabbi Temple Israel, Uniontown, Pa., since 1936. Pres. Uniontown Community Forum; dir. Family Guidance Council; chmn. Uniontown Co-ordinating Com.; hon. chmn. United Jewish Appeal of Uniontown; cultural chmn. Zionist District of Uniontown. Mem. Central Conf. Am. Rabbis (mem. com. on marriage, family and home), Hebrew Union Coll. Alumni Assn. Reform Jewish religion. B'nai B'rith. Club: Adelphi (Uniontown, Pa.). Contbr. to Jewish Education, The Synagogue, The Am. Hebrew, Opinion, etc. Home: 51 E. Fayette St., Uniontown, Pa.

GLASS, Alexander, corpn. official; b. July 24, 1859; s. Andrew and Harriet (Harris) G.; student pub. schs.; m. Sarah R. Whitaker, Dec. 10, 1885. Chmn. bd. Wheeling Steel Corpn. Home: Wheeling, W.Va.

GLASS, Leopold, C., judge Municipal Court of Phila. Address: Rittenhouse Plaza, Philadelphia, Pa.

GLASSER, Norman Louis, sch. supt.; b. Marion Center, Pa., May 13, 1883; s. John F. and Laura A. (Boucher) G.; A.B., Grove City Coll., 1909, A.M., U. of Pittsburgh, 1913; m. Ora B. Gorman; children—Louise G., Harriet R., Virginia. Prin. Waynesburg High Sch., 1907-12, Carnegie High Sch., 1913-26; supt. Carnegie pub. schs. since 1926. Mem. advisory com. Allegheny Co. Jr. Red Cross. Mem. N.E.A., Am. Assn. Sch. Adminstrs., Pa. State Edn. Assn., Allegheny Co. Principals' Round Table, Allegheny Co. Supts. Assn. Presbyn. (elder 1st Ch.). Club: Carnegie Rotary. Writer of various speeches. Home: 637 Beechwood Av. Office: Broadway and Roberts Av., Carnegie, Pa.

GLATFELTER, Philip Hollinger, paper mfg.; b. Spring Grove, Pa., Mar. 30, 1889; s. William Lincoln and Katherine (Hollinger) G.; grad. Hill Sch., 1910; m. Cassandra McClellan, June 1, 1911; children—Elizabeth G. (Mrs. William M. Eyster), Philip H. III, William L. II, Theodore McC., George H. In employ York Mfg. Co., 1910-14, elected treas. 1914; vice-pres. P. H. Glatfelter Co., paper mfrs., 1908-14, resigned as vice-pres. then sec.-treas., 1914-30, pres. since 1930; pres. Hanover Wire Cloth Co.; dir. York Ice Machinery Corpn., Western Md. Ry. Co., Pa. Mfrs. Assn. Fire Ins. Co., Pa. Mfrs. Assn. Casualty Ins. Co., Spring Grove Nat. Bank. Served as 1st lieut. O.R.C., 1917, capt. 1919, with A.E.F., 1918-19. Mem. Tech. Assn. of Pulp and Paper Industry. Republican. Lutheran. Mason (32°). Clubs: Lafayette, Country (York); Union League (New York); Yacht (Annapolis). Address: Spring Grove, Pa.

GLAUNER, George Lease, univ. prof.; b. Cardington, O., July 16, 1895; s. John William and Nell (McKeown) G.; A.B., Otterbein Coll., 1919; A.M., Syracuse U., 1923; Ph.D., Ohio State U., 1935; m. Marcia-Mae Horton, July 18, 1926; 1 son, John Horton. Admitted to Ohio bar, 1921; practiced law, Newark, O., 1921-22; prof. history and polit. science, W.Va. Wesleyan Coll., 1923-29; prof. history W.Va. Wesleyan Coll., since 1929; prof. history, U. of Me., summers, 1932, 33. Mem. Am. Soc. Ch. History, Pi Kappa Delta. Republican. Methodist. Mason. Club: Lions (Buckhannon, W.Va.). Home: 46 College Av., Buckhannon, W.Va.

GLAZEBROOK, Francis H(enny), physician and surgeon; b. Baltimore, Md., Mar. 7, 1877; s. Otis A. and Virginia C. K. (Smith) G.; ed. Trinity Coll., Hartford, 1895-97, Columbian Med. Coll., Washington, D.C., 1897-98; M.D., Cornell U. Med. Sch., 1900; m. Grace Squire, June 3, 1902 (dec.); children—Janet G. (Mrs. George Barker, Jr.), G. Truxtun, Virginia C. K., Francis H., Jr., Grace (dec.); m. 2d, Josephine Long Billings, June 5, 1937. Engaged in gen. practice of medicine and surgery, Morristown, N.J., 1902-12, practice limited to surgery and gynecology since 1912; mem. dir. N.Y. Stock Exchange, 1928-39; gen. practice since 1939. Served in 7th Regt., N.Y., and Essex Troop,

N.J., both N.G. Assigned by Govt. as surgeon to Morristown Memorial Hosp. during World War. Fellow Am. Coll. Surgeons, Am. Assn. Industrial Phys. and Surgeons; mem. Am. Med. Assn., Soc. Surgeons of N.J., Acad. Medicine of N.Y., Alpha Delta Phi. Republican. Episcopalian. Mason. Club: Morristown (N.J.). Home: 37 Ogden Pl., Morristown, N.J. Office: 111 Broadway, New York, N.Y.

GLEASON, Rutherford Erwin, prof. of mathematics, Temple U. Home: 2022 N. Park Av., Philadelphia, Pa.

GLENDENING, John, fire ins. exec.; b. Phila., Pa., July 5, 1894; s. John Franklin and Emilie B. (Young) G.; grad. Northeast High Sch., Phila., 1910; m. Amanda Hutchins, 1935. With Franklin Fire Ins. Co. since 1910, beginning as office boy, v.p. since 1938; treas. and dir. Fire Ins. Patrol of Phila. Served as yeoman 1st class, 4th Naval Dist. (naval intelligence), 1918. Dir. Fire Ins. Soc. of Phila.; past pres. Ins. Soc. of Phila. Presbyterian. Mason (Shriner). Clubs: Penn Athletic, Down Town (Phila.); Whitemarsh Valley Country. Home: Mayfair House, Germantown. Office: 421 Walnut St., Philadelphia, Pa

GLENN, Alfred Thomas Jr., lawyer; b. Atlantic City, N.J., Nov. 24, 1899; s. Alfred T. and Florence M. (Willits) G.; student Atlantic City (N.J.) High Sch., 1914-18; student U. of Pa. and Dickinson Law Sch., Carlisle, Pa.; m. Jane Browning, Sept. 15, 1923. Admitted to N.J. bar, 1922, as counsellor-at-law, 1925; mem. Glenn & Glenn, lawyers, Atlantic City, N.J., since 1927; trust officer and solicitor Ventnor City Nat. Bank since 1935; solicitor and dir. Seashore Bldg. & Loan Assn. since 1935; dir. South Jersey Title Co., Chelsea Title Co., Equitable Bldg. & Loan Assn., Chelsea Bldg. & Loan Assn. Supreme Ct. Commr., N.J., since 1926; spl. master in chancery since 1935. Dir. Y.M.C.A., Social Service Bur., Atlantic City; trustee Ventnor Community Ch.; judge advocate, Post 2, Am. Legion, Atlantic City. Mem. Atlantic City Chamber of Commerce (counsel), Am., N.J. State and Atlantic Co. Bar assns., Sigma Xi, Phi Delta Sigma (grand master, 1920-21). Republican. Presbyterian. Mason (Trinity Lodge), Elk. Clubs: Kiwanis, Country, Morris Guards, Tuna, Absecon Island Yacht (Atlantic City). Home: 106 S. Quincy Av., Margate City, N.J. Office: 538 Guarantee Trust Bldg., Atlantic City, N.J.

GLENN, Earl Rouse, coll. prof.; b. Vevay, Ind., June 12, 1887; s. James Drummond and Jennie (Culbertson) G.; A.B., with honors, Ind. U., 1913; student U. of Chicago, summer 1916; A.M., Columbia, 1928, grad. student, 1918-28; m. Mary Elizabeth Easley, June 21, 1914; children—Jean, Alfred Hill, Rosemary. Teacher of high school physics, Brookville, Ind., 1909-10, Bloomington, Ind., 1911-13, Gary, Ind., 1913-15; teacher physics, Harrison Tech. High Sch., Chicago, 1915-17; asst. in jr. coll. physics, U. of Chicago, summer 1916; ednl. research in science edn., Lincoln Sch., Teachers Coll., Columbia, 1917-28; instr. dept. natural science, Teachers Coll., Columbia, 1920-28; prof. physics and head of science dept., N.J. State Teachers Coll., Montclair, since 1928. Fellow A.A.A.S.; mem. Am. Physical Soc., Am. Chem. Soc., Ednl. Research Assn., Ind. Acad. Science, N.E.A., Am. Science Teachers Assn. (a founder), N.Y. Chemistry Teachers Club (past pres.), Nat. Assn. for Research in Science Teaching (a founder), Nat. Council on Elementary Science, Am. Nature Study Soc., Phi Beta Kappa, Phi Delta Kappa. Methodist. Author: Elements of General Science; Laboratory Problems (with O. W. Caldwell, W. L. Eikenbery), 1920, 1924; Bibliography of Science Teaching in Secondary Schools, 1925; Instructional Tests in Physics (with E. S. Osbourn), 1930; Instructional Tests in Chemistry (with L. E. Welton), 1930; Instructional Tests in General Science (with B. G. Gruenberg), 1932, 1939. Contbr. many articles to ednl. jours. Home: Upper Montclair, N.J. Address: State Teachers College, Montclair, N.J.

GLENN, Herbert Ross, physician; b. Lemont, Pa., Aug. 5, 1902; s. George and Mary Etta (Ross) G.; B.S., Pa. State Coll., 1924; M.D., Jefferson Med. Coll., 1927; m. Norma Prudence Eves, May 27, 1926; 1 son, Herbert Ross, Jr. Resident phys., Presbyn. Hosp., Phila., 1927-29; engaged in gen. practice of medicine, State College, Pa., since 1929; mem. surg. staff Centre County Hosp., Bellefonte, Pa., since 1934; fire surgeon Alpha Fire Co. Served as officer Med. Corps, U.S.N. Res. since 1937. Mem. Am., Pa. State, and Centre Co. med. assns., Phi Kappa Tau, Alpha Kappa Kappa. Republican. Presbyn. Clubs: Centre Hills Country (State College); Spruce Creek (Franklinville). Home: 219 S. Patterson St. Office: 322 W. College Av., State College, Pa.

GLENN, John Gray, coll. prof.; b. Gettysburg, Pa., Sept. 21, 1896; s. George Meek and Ellura Susannah (Gray) G.; ed. Dickinson Sem., 1911-14; A.B., Wesleyan U., Middletown, Conn., 1918, A.M., 1920; Ph.D., Princeton, 1932; m. Hazel Collier, Sept. 1, 1925; children—John Gray, Jr., Doris Collier, William Collier. Instr. mathematics, Culver (Md.) Mil. Acad., summer, 1918; instr. Latin and mathematics, Mercersburg (Pa.) Acad., 1918-19; instr. Greek, Dickinson Sem., 1920-21; instr. Latin, Poly. Prep. Country Day Sch., Brooklyn, N.Y., 1921-24; prof. Latin, Gettysburg (Pa.) Coll. since 1925; coach of tennis, Gettysburg Coll. since 1925. Mem. Am. Philol. Assn., Classical Assn. of Atlantic States, Am. Assn. Univ. Profs., Am. Classical League, Phi Beta Kappa, Eta Sigma Phi, Kappa Phi Kappa, Tau Kappa Epsilon. Democrat. Methodist. Mason. Contbr. articles to classical jours. Home: 29 E. Lincoln Av., Gettysburg, Pa.

GLENN, Marshall, athletics coach, phys. edn.; b. Elkins, W.Va., Apr. 22, 1908; s. Albert Hudson and Sara Ella (Wolf) G.; grad. Elkins (W.Va.) High Sch., 1926; B.S. in agr., W.Va. U., 1930; M.D. Rush Med. Sch., U. of Chicago, 1938; m. Helen Deffenbaugh, Aug. 22, 1929; children—Walter Marshall, Mary Ann. Backfield coach, W.Va., U., 1930-31, basketball coach, 1933-38, freshman football coach, 1934-37, head football coach since 1937, in phys. edn. since 1933; athletics coach, Martinsburg (W.Va.) High Sch., 1931-33. Commd. 2d lt. Inf., O.R.C. Mem. A.M.A., Am. Assn. Intercollegiate Football Coaches, Sigma Phi Epsilon. Methodist. Elk. Selected on first team All-Am. Athlete Union Basketball Team, 1931; 2d All-Am. Basketball Team by Coll. Humor, 1928; hon. mention quarterback, 1928. Address: West Virginia Univ., Morgantown, W.Va.

GLENN, Oliver Edmunds, educator, author; b. Moorefield, Ind., Oct. 3, 1878; s. James Drummond and Jane Harvey (Culbertson) G.; A.B., Ind. U., 1902, A.M., 1903; Ph.D., U. of Pa., 1905; m. Alice Thomas Kinnard, Aug. 18, 1903; children—William James, Robert Culbertson. Instr. U. of Ind., 1902-03; acting prof. mathematics, Drury Coll., Springfield, Mo., 1905-06; instr. in mathematics, 1906-10, asst. prof., 1910-14, prof., 1914-30, U. of Pa. Mem. Am. Math. Soc. (councilor 1914-17), Ind. Acad. of Science, Sigma Xi, Kappa Sigma. Fellow A.A.A.S., 1906-27. Author: A Treatise on the Theory of Invariants, 1915; The Mechanics of the Stability of a Central Orbit, 1933; The Sources of Error (essays), 1933; contbr. since 1905 numerous memoirs in math. and other scientific jours.; also scientific biography in Poggendorff Biographical Dictionary of the Exact Sciences (Leipzig). Home: 127 McKinley Av., Lansdowne, Pa.

GLINTENKAMP, Hendrik, artist; b. Augusta, N.J., Sept. 10, 1887; s. Hendrik and Sophie (Dietz) G.; ed. by pvt. tutors; student Nat. Acad. of Design, 1903-06; studied under Robert Henri, 1906-08; m. Helena Ruth Gibbs, 1916; m. 2d, Fann Rosenthal, 1930; 1 son, Hendrik. Artist, painter, sculptor, wood engraver, etcher, illustrator and teacher since 1908; instr. Hoboken (N.J.) Art Club, 1912-17; cartoonist on staff Hudson Dispatch, 1912; instr. in drawing and mem. bd. of control Am. Artists Sch., New York. Mem. exec. bd. and chmn. nat. exhbn. com. of Am. Artists Congress, 1938. Represented by wood block, Victoria and Albert Mus. (London); Birobijan, U.S.S.R.; wood block and bookplates in print collection and also reproductions in circulating picture collection, New York Pub. Library; wood cuts, Newark Pub. Library, Metropolitan Mus. of Art (N.Y. City); Cleveland (O.) Mus.; Baltimore Mus. and private collections; also represented in exhbns. at Pa. Acad. of Fine Arts, Am. Water Color Soc., New York Water Color Club, Salon of Am. Artists, Whitney Studio Club, Phila. Print Club, McDowell Club (New York), Peoples Art Guild, Am. Salon of Humorists, British Soc. of Painters (London), Syracuse (N.Y.) Mus., N.J. State Mus., N.C. State Art Assn., New York U. and many others. Represented in 50 prints of the year, Inst. of Graphic Arts. Asst. sec.-mem. exec. Bd. and Council of The Artists' Conf. of the Americas, since 1939. Mem. Am. Artists Congress, Artists Union, Teachers' Union. Author: A Wanderer in Woodcuts, 1932; also illustrator of books and mags. Home: Sparta, N.J. Studio: 19 E. 16th St., New York, N.Y.

GLOVER, David Livingston, lawyer; b. Hartleton, Pa., Dec. 17, 1866; s. Robert V. and Helen Caroline (Pellman) G.; student Blairstown (N.J.) Acad., State Normal Sch., Bloomsburg, Pa., 1884-86; A.B. and A.M., Lafayette Coll., Easton, Pa., 1890; m. Minnie Gertrude Kurtz, June 12, 1900 (died 1903); 1 dau., Louise Kurtz (Mrs. Raymond R. Goehring); m. 2d, Susan Elizabeth Kurtz, Apr. 12, 1911. Admitted to Pa. bar, 1893, and since practiced in Mifflinburg, Pa.; dist. atty. Union Co., 1896-1908; solicitor for Borough of Mifflinburg, 1905-20; partner Kurtz & Son, mfrs. of overalls, Mifflinburg, Pa.; pres. Mifflinburg Bank & Trust Co.; treas. Mifflinburg Body Co.; pres. Mifflinburg Cemetery Co.; mgr. of farm in Buffalo Valley for 30 yrs. Served as county chmn. of Union County banks for 4th Liberty and Victory loans, mem. legal advisory bd., counsel for food adminstr., pres. Community War Chest. Trustee Presbyn. Home of Central Pa. since 1928; trustee Bloomsburg State Teachers Coll., Alumni Assn. of Lafayette Coll. Mem. Am. Bar Assn., Pa. State Bar Assn., Union County Bar Assn., Delta Upsilon. Republican. Presbyterian. Mason. Club: Masonic (Mifflinburg, Pa.). Home: 411 Walnut St. Office: 324 Chestnut St., Mifflinburg, Pa.

GLOVER, Robert Hall, clergyman; b. Leeds Quebec, Can., Oct. 17, 1871; s. Thomas and Jennie (Hall) G.; ed. Collegiate Inst. and U. of Toronto; grad. New York Missionary Training Coll., 1893; M.D., Univ. Med. Coll. (New York U.), 1894; m. Caroline Robbins Prentice, Nov. 20, 1902; children—Bernard Prentice (dec.), Florence Jennie, Marjorie Evelyn, Robert Prentice. Missionary in China under Christian and Missionary Alliance, 1894-1913; ordained to Christian ministry, 1896; founded Bible Training Sch., Wuchow, 1900, and Blackstone Bible Inst., Wuchang, 1905; deputational sec. Christian and Missionary Alliance, 1911-13; foreign sec. same, 1913-21; dir. Missionary Course, Moody Bible Inst., Chicago, 1921-26; asst. home dir. China Inland Mission, 1926-29, home dir. since 1930. Visited Christian missions in many parts of world. Fellow Royal Geog. Soc. Author: Ebenezer—A Record of Divine Deliverances in China, 1905; The Progress of World-Wide Missions, 1924; also many magazine articles on travel and missions. Home: 5516 Morris St. Office: 237 W. School Lane, Germantown, Philadelphia, Pa.

GLUCK, Arthur, stock broker; b. Brooklyn, N.Y., July 29, 1898; s. Leopold and Regina (Klein) G.; student Eastern Dist. High Sch., Brooklyn, 1911-12, Y.M.C.A., Wilmerding, Pa., 1912-16, U. of Pittsburgh (Night Sch.), 1916-22; m. Hulda Hartung, June 17, 1926; children—Ruth Regina, Ronald Charles. Began in newspaper office, 1912; with Westinghouse Air Brake Co., Wilmerding, 1913-16; with R. W. Evans & Co., bond house, 1916-31; with H. G. Hetzel & Co., stock brokers, Pittsburgh, 1931-33; since 1933 senior partner Gluck, Hetzel & Co., stock brokers, mem. Pittsburgh Stock Exchange; chmn. of bd., v.p. and dir. Herzog Products Co. Scout commr., Castle Shannon, Pa., 11 yrs. Republican. Mem. Meth. Protestant Ch. (steward). Home: 951 Castle Shannon Boul., Castle Shannon, Pa. Office: 1502 Arrott Bldg., Pittsburgh, Pa.

GLUCKMAN, Isaac Edward, physician; b. New York, N.Y., July 12, 1882; s. Saul and Miriam G. (Klein) G.; M.D., Long Island Med. Coll. & Hosp., 1905; m. Mignonette Kaiser, May 23, 1905; children—Dr. Saul Kaiser, Suzanne K. Specialist in diseases of chest, Newark, N.J., since 1905; supt. Newark Tuberculosis Sanatorium, 1907-09; mem. and v.p. bd. mgrs., State Sanatorium, Glen Gardner, 1917-28; pres. cons. and adv. staff Essex Mountain Sanatorium since 1926; vis. phys. Deborah Sanatorium since 1925; courtesy cons. tuberculosis, Beth Israel Hosp.; on staff of number hosps. Dir. N.J. Tuberculosis Assn., Essex Co. Tuberculosis Assn. Mem. Am., N.J. State and Essex Co. med. assns., Zeta Beta Tau. Jewish religion. Mason. Elk. K.P. (past grand tribunal). Address: 78 Johnson Av., Newark, N.J.

GNICHTEL, Frederick W., lawyer; b. Newark, N.J., June 20, 1860; s. Frederick and Amalia (Lightloff) G.; student pub. schs., 1865-74; m. Caroline Stevenson, Aug. 15, 1888; 1 dau., Julia Stevenson (Mrs. Andrew B. Hammitt). Began as official court reporter, 1881; admitted to N.J. bar, 1893, and since practiced at Trenton, N.J.; chmn. finance com. of City of Trenton, 1902; mayor of Trenton, 1906; became judge of Ct. of Common Pleas, 1909; advisory master of Ct. of Chancery, 1916; mem. of bd. of pub. utilities, State of N.J., 1923; mem. state bd. of bar examiners since 1929; dir. and v.p. Del. & Bound Brook R.R. Trustee N.J. Hist. Soc. Republican. Presbyterian. Mason (Ashlar Lodge 76), Odd Fellow (Trenton Lodge). Club: Trenton (Trenton, N.J.). Home: 909 W. State St. Office: Broad St. Bank Bldg., Trenton, N.J.

GOCKE, William Thomas, physician and surgeon; b. Tunnelton, W.Va., Dec. 4, 1889; s. Thomas William and Mary Frances (Kessler) G.; A.B., Rock Hill Coll., Ellicott, Md., 1907; M.D., Coll. Phys. and Surgeons, Baltimore, 1911; m. Clara Agnes Boyle, May 31, 1912; children—Mary Frances (wife of Dr. Donald H. Lough), John Thomas. Interne Mercy Hosp., Baltimore, 1910-11; engaged in gen. practice of medicine and surgery at Clarksburg, W.Va., since 1911; practicing as mem. firm, Drs. Gocke, Gocke & Lough since 1929; mem. staffs St. Marys Hosp., Union Protestant Hosp. Mem. Am. Med. Assn., W.Va. State Med. Assn., Harrison Co. Med. Assn. Democrat. Roman Catholic. Elk, K. of C. Club: Kiwanis of Clarksburg. Home: 349 Buckhannon Av. Office: Gore Hotel Bldg., Clarksburg, W.Va.

GODCHARLES, Frederic Antes, librarian, historian; b. Northumberland, Pa., June 3, 1872; s. Charles Aiken and Elizabeth (Burkenbine) G.; grad. high sch., Milton, 1888; E.E., Lafayette Coll., Easton, Pa., 1893; Litt.D. from Susquehanna University, 1928; m. Mary Walls Barber, June 15, 1904. Elec. engr., city hall, Phila., Pa., 1893-95; pres. F. A. Godcharles Co., Milton Nail Works, 1895-1914; editor and pub. The Miltonian and Milton Morning Bulletin, 1910-26; dir. Pa. State Library and Museum, 1927-31. Mem. Pa. N.G., 1893-98; served with same, Spanish-Am. War, mem. staff Brig. Gen. J.P.S. Gobin; regimental insp. of rifle practice, rank of capt., 1900-10; capt. ordnance, on staff Maj. Gen. Leonard Wood, World War. Mem. Pa. Gen. Assembly, 1900 Pa. Senate, 1904, 08; dep. sec. Commonwealth of Pa., 1915-23. Mem. A.L.A., Pa. Federation Hist. Socs. (past. pres.), Pa. Hist. Soc., Northumberland County Hist. Soc. (pres.), First Soc. New York, Pa. Hist. Association (director), Eastern States Archæol. Fed. (pres.), Pa. Soc. Archæology (past pres. and editor), Pa. Folk-Lore Soc. (v.p.), Huguenot Society, Pa. German Soc. (dir.), Mil. Order Foreign Wars, Sons of Union Vets. of Civil War (past state comdr.), S.A.R., Am. Legion, Newcomen Soc. of Great Britian, Phi Kappa Psi. Republican. Presbyn. Mason (33°). Clubs: Manufacturers, Rotary (ex-pres.), Acacia (Williamsport); Union League (Phila.); Explorers (New York); Tilghman Island (Md.). Author: Freemasonry in Northumberland and Snyder Counties, 1911; Daily Stories of Pennsylvania, 1924 and 1927; Pennsylvanians Past and Present, 1926; also Daily Stories of New York. Editor Encyclopedia of Pennsylvania Biographies; Pennsylvania, Political, Governmental, Military and Civil; also writer of syndicate hist. articles. Expert marksman. Home: Milton, Pa.

GODDARD, Eunice Rathbone, coll. prof.; b. New London, Conn., Sept. 22, 1881; d. George Willard and Mary Adeline (Thomas) G.; A.B., Mount Holyoke Coll., South Hadley, Mass., 1903; A.M., Columbia U., 1907; grad. study Radcliffe Coll., Cambridge, Mass., 1911-12; study Univs. of Leipzig, Munich, Geneva, 1906-07, 1912-14; Ph.D., Johns Hopkins U., 1925. Engaged in teaching, pub. schs., Springfield, Mass., 1903-04, 1905-06; instr. German, Mt. Holyoke Coll., South Hadley, Mass., 1909-11; instr. German and French, Bryn Mawr (Pa.) Sch., 1916-24; instr. French, Goucher Coll., Baltimore, 1924-25, asst. prof., 1925-28, asso. prof., 1929-33, prof. French since 1933. Mem. Modern Lang. Assn., Am. Assn. Teachers of French, Assn. Modern Lang. Teachers, Am. Assn. Univ. Women, Phi Beta Kappa. Democrat. Club: College (Baltimore). Co-author: (with A. G. Bovée), Deuxième Année de Français, 1926, D'Artagnan, 1933; (with J. Rosselet), Introduction à Molière, 1936; contbr. articles and reviews to lang. jours. Home: Calvert Court Apts., Baltimore, Md.

GODDARD, Harold Clarke, college prof.; b. Worcester, Mass., Aug. 13, 1878; s. Lucius P. and Mary A. (Clarke) G.; A.B., Amherst, 1900; A.M., Columbia, 1903, Ph.D., 1908; m. Fanny Whiting Reed, July 31, 1906; children—Eleanor, Margaret. Instr. mathematics, Amherst Coll., 1900-02; instr. English lit., 1904-06, asst. prof., 1906-09, Northwestern U.; prof. English, Swarthmore Coll. since 1909. Author: Studies in New England Transcendentalism, 1908; Morale, 1919; W. H. Hudson—Bird-Man, 1928. Home: Swarthmore, Pa.

GODFREY, Edward, civil engring.; b. Pittsburgh, Pa., Mar. 7, 1871; s. James and Eliza Belle (Ferguson) G.; C.E., U. of Pittsburgh, 1893; m. Kittie Clyde Marks, Sept. 12, 1894 (dec.); 1 son, Norman Forward. Began as draftsman with G. W. G. Ferris & Co., 1889, merged with Robert W. Hunt Co. and continuously in their employ since; instr. engring., Western U. of Pa. (now U. of Pittsburgh), 1900-02. Mem. Am. Soc. Civil Engrs., Author's Club of Pittsburgh. Democrat. Presbyn. (clk. session Point Breeze Presbyn. Ch.). Author: Godfrey's Tables, 1905; Steel Designing, 1913; Engineering Failures and Their Lessons, 1924; Underpinning Science, 1928. Contbr. more than 100 articles on engring. and astronomy; regular contbr. to Popular Astronomy. Has given many programs on radio. Home: 630 Kirtland St. Office: Professional Bldg., Pittsburgh, Pa.

GODSHALK, Clarence Allison, manufacturer; b. Phila., Pa., May 2, 1881; s. Edward Hocksworth and Elizabeth (Downs) G.; grad. William Penn Charter Sch., Phila., 1899; student, U. of Pa., 1903; m. Jane Lee Bond, Oct. 14, 1911; children—James Bond, Robert, Elizabeth Lee. Started with Godshalk Co., textile mfrs., 1901, v.p., 1902-04; v.p. Keystone Motor Car Co., 1904-12, A. H. Fox Gun Co., 1913-30; dir. United Security Life Ins. and Trust Co., 1928-32; pres. Fox Co., 1925-37; pres. Fox Products Co. since 1931. Mem. Phi Delta Theta. Republican. Clubs: Union League, Phila. Country (Phila.); Merion Cricket (Haverford). Home: 139 Valley Rd., Ardmore, Pa. Office: 4720 N. 18th St., Philadelphia, Pa.

GODSHALL, Wilson Leon, prof. of polit. science and history; b. Lansdale, Pa., Apr. 26, 1895; s. Wilson Hackman and Blanche (Rosenberger) G.; grad. South Phila. High Sch., 1914; B.S., U. of Pa., 1919, A.M., 1920, Ph.D., 1923; Teachers Coll., Columbia Univ., 1934; m. Annetta Howard Metcalf, Sept. 8, 1920. Instr. in polit. science and anthropology, U. of Pa., 1919-23; prof. and head of dept. of polit. science, Union Coll., 1923-30; visiting prof., U. of Wash., 1928, U. of Pa., 1929, 31, Potsdam State Normal Sch., 1926, 1927, St. John's Univ. (Shanghai), 1925, 31, Lingnan Univ. (Canton), 1932, U. of Philippines, 1932, Pa. State Coll., 1935-38, U. of Me., 1939; prof. of polit. science and history and head of dept., Dickinson Jr. Coll., Williamsport, Pa., 1934-39, Lehigh University, Bethlehem, Pa., since 1939. Served as chief quartermaster, U.S.N. R.F., 1917-21; active duty, 1917-19. Conf. round table leader, Inst. Internat. Relations, Seattle, 1928; round table leader, conf. on World Interdependence, Buffalo, N.Y., 1934. Mem. Am. Polit. Science Assn., Am. Acad. Polit. and Social Science, Am. Soc. Internat. Law, Philippine Acad. Social Science, Chinese Social and Polit. Science Assn., Am. Assn. Univ. Profs., Am. Council of Inst. of Pacific Relations, Sons Am. Revolution, Lambda Chi Alpha, Tau Kappa Alpha, Pi Gamma Mu. Awarded Penfield Traveling Scholarship in Internat. Law and Diplomacy by U. of Pa., 1924-25, 1931-32; Carnegie Endowment Summer Session Fellowship in Internat. Law, 1937. Republican. Episcopalian. Mason. Author: International Aspects of the Shantung Question, 1923; Tsingtau Under Three Flags, 1929; American Foreign Policy; Formulation and Practice, 1937; Map Studies in European History, 1939. Lecturer for Rotary Inst. of Internat. Understanding since 1938. Address: Lehigh University, Bethlehem, Pa.

GOELLER, Jacob, M.D., born in N.J., Dec. 24, 1899; s. Marx and Esther Leah (Gottlieb) G.; student South Side High Sch., Newark, N.J., 1912-15; B.A., Coll. City of N.Y., 1918; M.D., Cornell U. Med. Coll., N.Y. City, 1922; unmarried. Interne Newark City Hosp., 1922-24, resident anesthetist, 1924-25; dir. anesthesia dept. Newark City Hosp. since 1938, Newark Memorial Hosp. since 1930; consulting anesthetist Hosp. for Women and Children and St. Barnabas Hosp., Newark, N.J., also Overlook Hosp., Summit, N.J.; visiting physician, genito urinary service, Irvington Gen. Hosp. Served as 1st lt., Med. Reserve Corps. Fellow Am. Soc. Anesthetists, Internat. Coll. Anesthetists, A.M.A.; mem. N.Y. Soc. Anesthetists, Internat. Anesthesia Research Soc., Acad. Medicine of Northern N.J., Essex Co. Med. Soc., Essex Co. Pathol. and Anatom. Soc., Physicians Club of Essex County, Post Grad. Fraternity Assn. of Regional Anesthesia, Irvington Physicians Assn. Republican. Jewish Religion. Home: 1165 Clinton Av., Irvington, N.J.

GOETZ, A(lphonso) John, supt. of schools; b. Dayton, O., June 24, 1896; s. Charles R. and Mary (Hand) G.; B.A. in edn., U. of Dayton, 1916; S.T.B. and Ph.D., U. of Fribourg, Switzerland; m. Catherine M. Fisher, June 11, 1928 (now deceased); children—John and twins, Charles and Daniel. Asst. high school prin., Detroit, Mich., 1918; supervisor of studies, U. of Dayton Normal Sch., 1920-22; exchange prof. of edn., Coll. of St. Michels, Univ. of Fribourg, Switzerland, 1922-25; psychological consultant, Dayton, O., 1926; teacher sociology, economics, education, Xavier U., Cincinnati, 1927-28; prof. of edn., Duquesne U., Pittsburgh, 1928-36; instr. sociology and economics, Pa. State Extension, Pittsburgh, 1930-32; supervising prin. S. Fayette Twp. Schools, 1936-38; supt. of schools, Monessen, Pa., since 1938. Mem. N.E.A., Pa. State Edn. Assn., Chamber of Commerce, Small Business Men's Assn., Cultural Soc. of Western Pa. Lecturer on education. Home: 34 Aliquippa Av. Office: High School Bldg., Monessen, Pa.

GOETZENBERGER, Ralph Leon, v.p. Brown Instrument Co.; b. Minneapolis, Minn., Dec. 4, 1891; s. Edward and Emma (Gatzman) G.; B.Sc., U. of Minn., 1913, E.E., 1914; m. Edna Cooper, 1921; children—Louise, Ralph, Edward. Engr. Gen. Electric Co., Schenectady, N.Y., 1914-17; development engr. Leeds & Northrup Co., Philadelphia, 1926-28; mgr. industrial regulator dept., Minneapolis-Honeywell Regulator Co., 1928-36; v.p. and dir. Brown Instrument Co., Philadelphia, since 1936. Major Ordnance Dept., U.S. Army, 1917-21, cons. engr., same, 1921-26. Mem. A.A.A.S., Am. Inst. E.E., Am. Soc. Mech. Engrs., Am. Gas Assn., Am. Soc. for Metals, Am. Marketing Assn., Franklin Inst., Psi Upsilon, Theta Tau. Republican. Episcopalian. Clubs: Cedarbrook Country, Germantown Cricket. Writer many tech. articles. Home: 1704 Hillcrest Road, Chestnut Hill. Office: Wayne and Robert Avs., Philadelphia, Pa.

GOFF, William R.; mem. staff Parkersburg City Hosp. Address: 304 Fifth St., Parkersburg, W.Va.

GOHEN, Charles Marsh, banker; b. Aurora, Ind., Sept. 18, 1875; s. James Alfred and Malvina Fenton (Marsh) G.; ed. pub. schs., Huntington, W.Va.; m. Mary Elizabeth Emmons, June 14, 1906. Began with Commercial Bank, Huntington, 1890; pres. 1st Huntington Nat. Bank since 1924; v.p. Fesenmeier Packing Co.; dir. Chesapeake & Potomac Telephone Co. County chmn. War Savings Com., Cabell Co., W.Va. Democrat. Episcopalian. Clubs: Guyandot, Guyan Country. Home: 1515 5th Av. Office: 1st Huntington Nat. Bank, Huntington, W.Va.

GOLD, John Steiner, asso. prof. mathematics; b. Turbotville, Pa., Nov. 24, 1898; s. Horace and Julia Ann (Steiner) G.; B.Sc., Bucknell U., 1918, A.M., same, 1921; grad. study U. of Chicago, summers, and 1929-30; m. Sybil Marie Ulrich, Sept. 1, 1921; children—David Horace, William Donald, Anna May. Engaged as teacher in high schs., 1918-20; instr. mathematics, Bucknell U., 1920-27, asst. prof. mathematics and astronomy, 1927-34, asso. prof. since 1934. Mem. Math. Assn. of America, Sigma Xi, Pi Mu Epsilon (nat. sec. since 1927), Theta Upsilon Omega. Republican. German Reformed Ch. Club: Simga Xi of Bucknell University. Home: Lewisburg, Pa.

GOLDBACH, Leo John; asso. prof. ophthalmology, Johns Hopkins U.; ophthalmologist St. Joseph's Hosp.; ophthalmologist-in-charge Hopkins Dispensary; visiting ophthalmologist Johns Hopkins Hosp. and Md. Sch. for Blind. Address: 6 E. Eager St., Baltimore, Md.

GOLDBACHER, Lawrence, physician; b. Phila., Pa., Dec. 4, 1890; s. Raphel and Mary (Alkus) G.; M.D., Jefferson Med. Coll., 1920; m. Selma Gerson, Dec. 4, 1923; children—Lawrence R., Ruth. After usual internships engaged in gen. practice of medicine at Phila. since 1920; practice now limited to proctology and herniology; chief dept. proctology, Women's Homeopathic Hosp.; cons. proctologist, U.S. Naval Hosp., Phila., and Underwood Hosp., Woodbury, N.J. Lieut. comdr., U.S.N.R.F., Med. Corps during World War. Mem. Am. Med. Assn., Pa. State and Phila. Co. med. socs. Jewish religion. Author: Hemorrhoids, the Injection Treatment, and Pruritus Ani, 1930; Rectal Diseases in Office Practice, 1933; The Injection Treatment of Hernia and Hydrocele, 1938. Home: 5737 Ogontz Av. Office: 3701 N. Broad St., Philadelphia, Pa.

GOLDBERGER, Henry Robert, rabbi; b. Hungary, Oct. 5, 1899; s. Rabbi Leo Jehudah and Ethel (Saphier) G.; A.B., Coll. of City of New York, 1921; Rabbi, Rabbinical Coll. of America, 1922; m. Goldie Leah Turnansky, Apr. 16, 1923; children—Daniel, Sonia Ruth. Rabbi at Steubenville, O., 1922-24, Erie, Pa., 1924-27, Beth Jacob Synagogue, New Kensington, Pa., 1927-34; rabbi Agudath Achim Synagogue, Altoona, Pa., since 1934. Former chmn. Red Cross Chapter, New Kensington, Pa. Mem. council Altoona Boy Scout Chapter, Adv. Bd. Girl Scouts. Mem. Zionist Orgn. of America (administrative bd.). Republican. Mem. Jewish religion, conservative. B.P.O.E., B'nai B'rith. Club: Elks. Home: 2318 Broad Av. Office: 17th St. and 14th Av., Altoona, Pa.

GOLDEN, Benjamin I.; surgeon-in-charge Davis Memorial Hosp. Address: Elkins, W.Va.

GOLDEN, Charles Otis, artist; b. Newlon, W.Va., Feb. 3, 1899; s. William Ellsworth and Charlotte E. (Smalridge) G.; student Corcoran Sch. of Art, Washington, D.C., 1916-19, Pa. Acad. of Fine Arts, Phila., 1919-21; unmarried. Illustrator of books and magazines, 1922-28; on staff Phila. Public Ledger, 1927; artist specializing in water color portraits since 1928. Exhibited at: Pa. Acad., Corcoran Gallery, Nat. Acad. of N.Y., Art Inst. of Chicago, Mystic, Conn., etc. Awarded cash prize for best portrait, Tucson (Ariz.) Fine Arts Exhibit, 1938. Mem. Phila. Sketch Club, Phila. Water Color Club, Washington, D.C., Water Color Club, Mystic (Conn.) Art Assn., Am. Artists Professional League of New York. Address: Bushkill, Pike Co., Pa.

GOLDENBERG, John Brooks, shoe mfr.; b. Philadelphia, Pa., Nov. 28, 1892; s. Morris and Eva (Brooks) G.; student Wharton Sch., U. of Pa., 1910-13; m. Sadye Strauss, Oct. 22, 1922; children—Zelma S., E. Joel. Began as accountant, 1913; formed Brooks Shoe Mfg. Co., 1914, now owner. Treas. Y.M.H.A., Y.W.H.A. (Philadelphia); dir. Board of Jewish Edn. (Philadelphia); v.p. Beth El Congregation. Sec. Boot and Shoe Mfrs. Assn. Home: 206 N. Bowman Av., Merion, Pa. Office: Swanson & Ritner Sts., Philadelphia, Pa.

GOLDENWEISER, Emanuel Alexander, economist; b. Kiev, Russia, July 31, 1883; s. Alexander S. and Sofia (Munstein) G.; grad. First Kiev Gymnasium, 1902; A.B., Columbia, 1903; A.M., Cornell U., 1905, Ph.D., 1907; m. Pearl Allen, Dec. 1916; children—Margaret Ellen, John Alexander. Came to U.S., 1902, naturalized citizen, 1907. Spl. investigator U.S. Immigration Commn., 1907-10; spl. agt. U.S. Census, 1910-14; statistician, Office of Farm Management, Dept. of Agr., 1914-19; asst. statistician Federal Reserve Bd., 1919-24, asst. dir. Div. of Research and Statistics, 1925, dir. 1926—; economist, Federal Open Market Com. since 1936; tech. adviser U.S. Bituminous Coal Commission, 1920. Fellow of American Statistical Association; member American Economic Assn. Club: Cosmos. Author: Immigrants in Cities (Vols. 26 and 27 of Repts. Immigration Commn.), 1909; (with L. E. Truesdell) Farm Tenancy in the United States (U.S. Census), 1924; Federal Reserve System in Operation, 1925; also articles in economic jours. Home: 5914 Cedar Parkway, Chevy Chase, Md. Address: Board of Governors of Federal Reserve System, Washington, D.C.

GOLDER, Benjamin M., ex-congressman; b. Vineland, N.J., Dec. 23, 1891; ed. pub. schs., Phila.; LL.B., U. of Pa., 1913. Admitted to Pa. bar, 1913, and began practice at Phila.; ensign Naval Aviation Service, World War; mem. 69th to 72d Congresses (1925-33), 4th Pa. Dist. Republican. Home: 2011 N. 33d St. Office: 1622 Chestnut St., Philadelphia, Pa.

GOLDER, Marjory Steuart, coll. dean; b. Washington, D.C., Apr. 15, 1892; d. Alexander S. and Linda (Hogue) Steuart; grad. Western High Sch., Washington, D.C., 1909; A.B., Northwestern U., 1914; A.M., Columbia, 1921; grad. student Radcliffe Coll., 1923-25; m. Harold Golder, June 17, 1925 (died August 3, 1934); children—John Steuart, Sarah Nourse. Teacher of English, El Paso (Tex.) Sch. for Girls, 1914-16; sec. Red Cross Hdqrs., Washington, D.C., 1916-17; with War Dept., Washington, D.C., 1917-20; instr. in English, Lawrence Coll., Appleton, Wis., 1921-23; registrar, American U., Washington, D.C., 1935-38; dean Women's Coll., U. of Del., since 1938. Mem. Modern Lang. Assn., Nat. Assn. Deans of Women, Am. Assn. Univ. Women, Chi Omega, Phi Beta Kappa. Episcopalian. Home: Newark, Del.

GOLDMAN, David H., pres. Rosa Goldman Co.; b. Pittsburgh, Pa., June 13, 1871; s. Henry D. and Rachel (Friedman) G.; ed. high sch. and mercantile coll.; m. Rita Kohn, July 25, 1926; children—Henry, Foster, Robert. Pres. Rosa Goldman Co. since 1917; dir. United Housing Corpn. since 1925. Dir. Gusky Orphanage, 1920-30, trustee since 1930. Pres. Retail Credit Assn. of Pittsburgh, 1932-34, pres. regional div., same, 1934; nat. dir. Nat. Retail Credit Assn., 1935-36; permanent dir. Retail Credit Assn. of Pittsburgh. Address: 1522 Denniston Av., Pittsburgh, Pa.

GOLDMANN, Sidney, lawyer; b. Trenton, N.J., Nov. 28, 1903; s. Samuel and Stella (Reich) G.; B.S., Harvard U., 1924; LL.B., Harvard U. Law Sch., 1927; m. Beatrice Corosh, Nov. 20, 1938. Admitted to N.J. bar as atty. 1928, counsellor, 1933; admitted to practice before Supreme Ct. of the U.S., 1937; engaged in gen. practice of law at Trenton, N.J., since 1929; city atty. of Trenton, N.J., 1935-39. Pres. Jewish Fed. of Trenton; pres. Community Council of Trenton; vice-pres. Y.M.H.A. Community Home; sec. Trenton Hist. Soc.; mem. exec. com. Trenton Symphony Assn. Mem. Am. Bar Assn.,

Mercer Co. Bar Assn., Alpha Mu Sigma. Jewish religion. Home: 860 Stuyvesant Av. Office: 410 Wallach Bldg., Trenton, N.J.

GOLDSBOROUGH, Felix Vincent, Sr., pres. Records & Goldsborough; b. Baltimore, Md., Nov. 1, 1882; s. Henry Paul and Helena Augustus (McManus) G.; student private sch., Calvert Hall Coll. and Bryant & Stratton Business Coll.; m. Melvina Shinkle Eaton, Aug. 9, 1902. Entered father's business Records & Goldsborough, liquor industry, 1898, supt., 1904-06, head of rectification, 1906-09, eastern sales rep., 1909-11, gen. mgr., 1911-15, pres., 1915-20 and since 1933. Home: 607 Somerset Road, Roland Park. Office: 117-119 W. Lombard St., Baltimore, Md.

GOLDSBOROUGH, Phillips Lee, director Federal Deposit Insurance Corporation; b. Cambridge, Maryland, August 6, 1865; s. M. Worthington and Nettie M. (Jones) G.; educated in private and pub. schs. of Md.; studied law in office of Daniel M. Henry, Jr., and admitted to Md. bar, 1886; LL.D., Univ. of Pa., Univ. of Md., Washington College, and St. John's College; m. Mary Ellen Showell, 1893 (now deceased); children—Phillips Lee, Brice W., II. Practiced, Dorchester Co.; elected state's attorney, 1891, and reëlected, 1895; comptroller of Md., 1898-1900; apptd. collector internal revenue, District of Md., by President McKinley, and twice reapptd. by Presidents Roosevelt and Taft; gov. of Md., term Jan. 1912-Jan. 1916; mem. U.S. Senate, term 1929-35. Mem. bd. dirs. Federal Deposit Insurance Corpn. since Apr. 29, 1935. Republican. Episcopalian. Home: Tudor Arms Apts., University Parkway, Baltimore, Md. Office: National Press Bldg., Washington, D.C.

GOLDSBOROUGH, T(homas) Alan, congressman; b. Greensboro, Md., Sept. 16, 1877; s. Washington E. and Martha P. (Laird) G.; A.B., Washington Coll., 1899, LL.D., 1935; LL.B., U. of Md., 1901; m. Laura Hall, June 16, 1909 (died 1930); children—Martha Winder, Thomas Alan, Eliza Hall, George Hall. Began practice at Denton, Md., 1901; state's atty. Caroline Co., Md., 1904-08; mem. 67th to 76th Congresses (1921-41), 1st Md. Dist. Democrat. Episcopalian. Home: Denton, Md.

GOLDSMITH, Clifford, writer; b. East Aurora, N.Y., Mar. 29, 1899; s. Charles and Edith (Henshaw) G.; grad. Moses Brown Sch., Providence, R.I., 1917; student U. of Pa., 1917-18, Am. Acad. Dramatic Art, New York, N.Y., 1918-19; m. Kathryn Allen, Dec. 26, 1933; children—Peter, Thayer, Charles Barclay. Employed as actor on stage, 1919-22; engaged in pub. speaking and advertising, 1922-37; now writing for weekly radio broadcasts. Presbyn. Club: Franklin Inn (Philadelphia). Author: What A Life (play) produced at Biltmore Theatre, New York, N.Y., 1938. Home: Westtown, Pa.

GOLDSMITH, Harry, physician; b. Kovna, Russia, Nov. 22, 1889; s. Louis and Celia (Davis) G.; came to U.S., 1894, naturalized, 1910; student elementary and grammar schs., Baltimore, 1896-1905, Baltimore City Coll., 1905-09; M.D., U. of Md., Baltimore, 1913; m. Charlotte Goldstein, Aug. 20, 1916; 1 son, Jewett. Interne Baltimore City Hosp., 1913-14; gen. practice of medicine at Baltimore, 1914-17; physician in chief and dir. psychopathic div., Baltimore City Hosp., 1917-35; prt. practice of neuro-psychiatry at Baltimore since 1935. Lt. comdr., Nav. Res. Corps, since 1935. Mem. Am. Psychiatric Assn., Baltimore City Med. Soc., Md. Acad. of Medicine and Surgery. Mason (Scottish Rite). Home: 4029 Cold Spring Lane. Office: Medical Arts Bldg., Baltimore, Md.

GOLDSMITH, Lester M., engr.; b. Pottsville, Pa., July 1, 1893; s. George Jay and Sara (Rohrheimer) G.; ed. Drexel Inst. Technology; m. Florence Frankel, June 26, 1921; children—George Jay, Richard Lester, John Charles. Research engr. Perpetual Fuse Co., 1914; jr. engr. (temporary) United Gas Improvement Co., 1914-15; inspector gas engring., Dept. of Pub. Works, Phila., 1915-16; mech. draftsman Atlantic Refining Co., 1916, research engr., 1917-19, engr. of tests and supt. mech. lab., 1919-

23, tech. asst. to pres., 1923-24, cons. engr., 1924-37, mgr. engring. and construction dept., 1934-37, chief engr. since 1937; chief engr. Keystone Pipe Line Co., Buffalo Pipe Line Corpn.; v.p., dir. and chief engr. Atlantic Pipe Line Co.; dir. Atlantic Oil Shipping Co. Mem. Am. Inst. Elec. Engrs., Am. Petroleum Inst., Am. Soc. Mech. Engrs., Am. Welding Soc., Am. Soc. Naval Engrs., Soc. Automotive Engrs., Soc. Naval Architects and Marine Engrs., Amateur Cinema League. Club: Engineers (Philadelphia). Writer numerous papers on engring. subjects. Registered engr. Pa., N.Y. and Tex. Holder various patents. Home: 1012 W. Upsal St., Germantown. Office: 260 S. Broad St., Philadelphia, Pa.

GOLDSMITH, Malcolm, merchant; b. Braddock, Pa., Apr. 26, 1888; s. Louis J. and Hannah (Katz) G.; student Braddock Pub. Sch., 1894-1902, Braddock High Sch., 1902-06; B.S., U. of Pa., 1910, LL.B., Law Sch., 1912, accounting, 1918; m. Mildred Baer, Apr. 10, 1917; children—Joel, Kenneth. Admitted to Pa. bar, 1912; mem. law firm Weil and Thorp, Pittsburgh, 1912-19; partner Katz and Goldsmith (The Famous), Braddock, since 1919; v.p. and treas. The Famous Co., dept. store, McKeesport, Pa., since 1922; pres. Braddock Dry Goods Co., Yale Trading Stamp Co., Braddock; dir. DuBois Brewing Co., DuBois, Pa., 1st Nat. Bank, Braddock. Ensign, U.S. Navy, June 1917-Dec. 1918. Trustee Irene Kaufmann Settlement, Carnegie Library (Braddock), East Boros Council of Boy Scouts; pres. Braddock Gen. Hosp. Mem. Order of Coif (U. of Pa.). Jewish religion. Club: Concordia (Pittsburgh). Home: 5444 Albemarle St., Pittsburgh, Pa. Office: Braddock, Pa.

GOLDSMITH, Maurice F(rank), M.D.; b. Pittsburgh, Pa., July 18, 1885; s. Bernard M. and Sophie (Blum) G.; A.B., Bucknell U., 1906, A.M., 1910; M.D., U. of Pittsburgh, 1909; m. Laura K. Schulz, Aug. 14, 1914; children—Eleanor, William, Gretchen; adopted children—Patricia Castle, Ann Castle. Interne Montefiore Hosp., Pittsburgh, 1909-10; engaged in practice of medicine at Pittsburgh since 1910; roentgenologist Montefiore Hosp. since 1913. Jewish religion. Mason. Home: 5700 Bartlett St. Office: 3459 Fifth Av., Pittsburgh, Pa.

GOLDSTEIN, Albert Elias, surgeon; b. New York, N.Y., Mar. 8, 1887; s. Joseph and Sarah (Rosenberg) G.; grad. Boardman Manual Training High Sch., New Haven, Conn., 1905; student Yale Scientific Sch., 1906-07; M.D., Coll. of Physicians and Surgeons, Baltimore, Md., 1912; m. Elsie May Martin, Dec. 3, 1914; children—Albert E., Martin J., Robert B., William O. In gen. practice medicine, Baltimore, 1914-19, practice limited to genito-urinary surgery since 1919; cons. urologist Mt. Pleasant Hosp., Baltimore; chief dept. genito-urinary surgery, Sinai Hosp., Baltimore; also mem. med. exec. com.; med. dir. Hebrew Home for Aged and Infirm; asso. in pathology, U. of Md. Served as examining urologist in Mercy Hosp. during World War. Fellow Am. Coll. Surgeons; mem. Am. Bd. Urology, A.M.A., Am. Urol. Assn., Southern Med. Soc., Phi Delta Epsilon. Democrat. Jewish religion. Clubs: Suburban, Phoenix (Baltimore). Contbr. many articles to med. jours. and books. Home: 2807 Allendale Rd. Office: Medical Arts Bldg., Baltimore, Md.

GOLDSTEIN, Hyman I(saac), physician; b. Baltimore, Md., Nov. 2, 1887; s. Solomon Joseph and Rosa (Zuckerman) G.; M.D., U. of Pa. Med. Sch., 1909; post grad. student U. of Vienna, Austria, 1929; m. Dorothy Wessel, Sept. 24, 1924; children—Joan, Alice, L. Marshall. Formerly mem. staffs of Phila. Gen., Northwestern Gen. and Mt. Sinai (Phila.) Hosps.; consulting physician to Deborah Sanatorium, Brown's Mills, N.J., Bellview Hosp.; in practice at Camden, N.J., since 1909, specializing in diagnosis, internal medicine and gastroenterology since 1910. Fellow A.M.A., Nat. Gastroenterol. Assn.; mem. A.A.A.S., Assn. for Study Internal Secretions, Am. Assn. of History of Medicine, Med. Soc. of N.J. (sec. Gastroenterologic Sect., 1938-39, chmn. of sect., 1939-40), Am. Heart Assn., Northern Med. Assn. of Phila. (pres.), N.J. Gastroenterol. Soc., Camden Co. Med. Soc., Med. Club of Phila., Phila. Pediatric Soc., Internat. Soc. Gastroenterology, Internat. Therapeutic Union. Corr. mem. Italian Soc. Gastroenterology, Hungarian Dermatologic Assn. Asso. Am. Coll. Phys. Made trips to European clinics, 1929, 31, 32, 35, 37, and attended internat. med. congresses in various countries of Europe. Mem. editorial bd. The Review of Gastroenterology. Contbr. many articles to med. jours. Democrat. Jewish religion. Home: 1425 Broadway, Camden, N.J. Offices: 1715 Spruce St., Philadelphia, Pa.; 1425 Broadway, Camden, N.J.

GOLDSTEIN, William Kaufman, lawyer, referee in bankruptcy; b. Canton, Pa., Aug. 12, 1903; s. Jacob Philip and Jennie Esther (Kaufman) G.; student Canton (Pa.) High Sch., 1917-21, U. of Pa., 1921-22; LL.B., Dickinson Sch. of Law, Carlisle, Pa., 1925; A.B., St. Thomas U. (now U. of Scranton), Scranton, Pa., 1927; unmarried. Admitted to Lackawanna County, Pa., bar, 1928, and since practiced at Scranton, Pa.; asso. with Philip V. Mattes, county solicitor, Scranton, since 1928. Asst. U.S. atty. for middle dist. of Pa., 1930-32; U.S. referee in bankruptcy, Scranton, Pa., since 1936. Mem. Lackawanna Bar Assn., Nat. Assn. of Referees in Bankruptcy (mem. ethics com.). Phi Epsilon Pi. Republican. Jewish religion. Home: 749 N. Webster Av. Office: 705 Mears Bldg., Scranton, Pa.

GOLDSWORTHY, George W., Jr., bank note engraving and printing; b. Chicago, Ill., May 24, 1905; s. George Walter and Katherine Elizabeth (Sherman) G.; grad. Arnold Sch., Pittsburgh, Pa., 1923; B.S., Bowdoin Coll., Brunswick, Me., 1927; m. Sarah Margaret Feltyberger, Jan. 4, 1930. With Republic Bank Note Co. since Aug. 1, 1927, successively as estimator, advertising and commercial sales mgr., asst. to pres., 1927-34, dir. since 1933, v.p. and gen. mgr. since 1934. Mem. Beta Theta Pi. Republican. Methodist. Mason. Club: Pittsburgh Athletic. Home: 6430 Bartlett St. Office: 3113 Forbes St., Pittsburgh, Pa.

GOLLMAR, Frank Irvin, lawyer; b. Pittsburgh, Pa., Oct. 25, 1885; s. Gottlieb and Adeline (Geye) G.; ed. Baldwin-Wallace Coll., 1906-09; Pittsburgh Law Sch., 1909-12; U. of Pittsburgh, 1909 to 1912; m. Selma Josephson, June 10, 1920. Admitted to Pa. bar, 1913 and since engaged in gen practice of law at Pittsburgh; mem. firm Mulvihill, Gollmar and Herrington since 1938; served as asst. county solicitor, Allegheny Co.; asst. city solicitor, Pittsburgh; dep. atty. gen. of Pa.; judge Common Pleas Ct. of Allegheny Co., 1926-28; sheriff Allegheny Co., 1931-38. Served as mem. Met. Commn. of Allegheny Co. Chmn. Allegheny Co., Gov. Pinchot's 1930 Campaign. Vice-pres. Zoar Home, Allison Park, Pa. Mem. Allegheny Co. Bar Assn. Republican. Protestant. Mason (K.T., Shriner), Moose. Clubs: Kiwanis, Business Mens (Pittsburgh). Home: 158 Highland Av., West View, Pa. Office: Law and Finance Bldg., Pittsburgh, Pa.

GOLOMB, Elhanan Hirsh, rabbi, coll. prof.; b. Stravenick, Wilno, Russia, Jan. 6, 1887; s. Rabbi Judah Leib and Sarah (Jacobsohn) G.; A.B. (cum laude), Amherst (Mass.) Coll., 1918; A.M., U. of Pa., 1920; Ph.D., Dropsie Coll., Phila., 1922; Rabbi, Jewish Theol. Sem. of America, 1926; m. Minnie Nadel, Apr. 24, 1922; children—Edna Rebecca, Solomon Wolf. Instr. Talmud, Mishna and Bible, Baltimore Hebrew Coll., since 1926. Served in R.O.T.C., Amherst, 1916-18. Mem. Zionist Dist. Bd. of Baltimore, Md. Mem. Rabbinical Assembly of Jewish Theol. Sem. of America, Am. Acad. for Jewish Research, Amherst Coll. Alumni Assn., Dropsie Coll. Alumni Assn. (past pres.). Democrat. Jewish religion. Author: Judah Ben Solomon Companton and his Arbaah Kinyanim, 1930; contbr. book revs. to Jewish Quarterly Review. Home: 2448 Lakeview Av. Office: 1201 Eutaw Pl., Baltimore, Md.

GOLZ, Walter, dir. music; b. Camden, N.J., Sept. 20, 1881; s. Julius and Alphonsine (Bigot) G.; grad., Phila. Mus. Acad., 1898-1902, Cologne Conservatory, Germany, 1902-06; m. Effie Leland, Apr. 5, 1914; children—Anne Leland, John Leland. Engaged as professional musician since 1906; teacher piano and theory, Chicago Mus. Coll., 1906-10; teacher piano, Phil. Mus. Acad., 1910-19; dir. music, Coker Coll., S.C., 1919-21; dir. music, Columbia Coll., 1921-29; dir. music, Wilson Coll., Chambersburg, Pa., since 1929; composer many numbers for piano pub. by leading music pubs. Home: 1506 Philadelphia Av., Chambersburg, Pa.

GOOD, John Daniel, clergyman; b. Harrisonburg, Va., Jan. 29, 1885; s. Daniel H. and Lydia (Shank) G.; student Shenandoah (Jr.) Coll., 1907-10; A.B., Otterbein Coll., Westerville, O., 1913, D.D., 1928; student Columbia, summer, 1913; m. Rachel Virginia Seneff, June 24, 1914; children—Lora Kathryn, John Daniel, Ray David, Martha Virginia. Social and religious sec. Y.M.C.A., Poughkeepsie, N.Y., 1913-14; ordained to ministry of Ch. of United Brethren in Christ (Allengheny Conf.), 1918; pastor, Scottdale, Pa., 1926-27, Greensburg, Pa., 1927-31, Altoona, Pa., 1931-37, McKeesport, Pa., since 1937. Del. to Gen. Conf. of United Brethren Ch., 1925, 29, 37; mem. Bd. of Administration since 1933; mem. Bd. of Home Missions and Ch. Erection since 1925; pres. Conf. Christian Endeavor, 1922-26, sec. and treas. 1927-29; pres. Conf. Bd. of Edn. since 1936; dean of Bible Conf., since 1936. Republican. Home: 1911 Beaver Av., McKeesport, Pa.

GOOD, Oscar Ellis, banker; b. Progress, Pa., December 23, 1871; s. John and Elizabeth (Sheesley) G.; student Harrisburg Acad. 1888-90; A.B., Lebanon Valley Coll., Annville, Pa., 1894, A.M., 1895; m. Jessie M. Haverstick, Aug. 26, 1897 (deceased); 1 dau., Mary Elizabeth (Mrs. Vernon W. Hoerner); m. 2d, Catharine P. Mumma, May 5, 1938. Instr. Lebanon Valley Coll., 1894-96, Spring Mills (Pa.) Acad., spring 1897; asso. with father in market gardening, 1899-1917; teacher in pub. schs., Dauphin Co., Pa., 1897-1907; prin. Penbrook Schs., 1907-16; teacher Latin and mathematics, Susquehanna Twp. High Sch., 1916-20; pres. Penbrook Trust Co. since 1920. Mem. bd. dirs. Pub. Schs., Susquehanna Twp., Dauphin Co., 1923-37. Connected with the superintendency of Grace United Brethren S.S. since 1896, as asst. supt. 1 yr., supt. adult dept. 35 yrs., gen. supt. since 1932; rep. his church in Gen. Conf., Akron, O., 1933, and Chambersburg, Pa., 1937. Served as mem. fire companies of Progress and Penbrook, Pa. Mem. Patriotic Order Sons of America (treas. local camp since orgn. 1925). Republican. Mem. Ch. of United Brethren in Christ. Clubs: Republican (Pembrook); Motor (Harrisburg). Home: 3405 Jonestown Rd., Progress, Pa. Office: Penbrook, Harrisburg, Pa.

GOODALE, Stephen Lincoln, univ. prof.; b. Saco, Me., Aug. 31, 1875; s. Benjamin Nourse and Ella Adelaide Augusta (Scammon) G.; A.B., Colorado Coll., Colorado Springs, 1899, A.M., 1909, hon. D.Sc., 1921; E.M., Colo. Sch. of Mines, Golden, 1904; studied Harvard Summer Sch., 1910; m. Nelle Priscilla Sater, May 22, 1906; children—Priscilla Harriet, Prudence Nourse, Stephen Lincoln. Spent summers, 1901-04, working in mines of Colo.; asst. in chemistry, Colorado Coll., 1901-02; at Camp Bird Mine, Ouray, Colo., 1904-06; assayer Annie Laurie Mine, Utah, summer, 1906; independent professional work, Lander Co., Nev., 1906-08; asst. supt. Bristol Consolidated Mining & Smelting Co., nr. Pioche, Nev., 1908-09; head dept. of metallurgy, Sch. of Mines, U. of Pittsburgh, 1909—; professional engr. in mining and metallurgy. Mining engring. work, Newfoundland, summer of 1911. Presbyn. Mem. A.A.A.S., Am. Inst. Mining Engrs., 1904, Am. Electrochem. Soc., Engrs.' Soc. Western Pa., American Soc. for Metals, Sigma Gamma Epsilon (U. of Pittsburgh), Sigma Tau. Commd. capt., Ordnance O.R.C., Sept. 20, 1917; hon. discharged, Sept. 3, 1919; maj. O.R.C. Club: Authors. Author: Chronology of Iron and Steel, 1920. Contbr. to scientific mags. Home: 1156 Murrayhill Av., Squirrel Hill, Pittsburgh, Pa.

GOODALL, Charles Edward, clergyman; b. Drighlington, Yorkshire, Eng., May 25, 1876; s. Thomas and Hannah (Ayer) G.; brought by parents to U.S. at early age; grad. South Jersey

Inst., Bridgeton, N.J., 1898; Ph.B., ucknell U., 1902, M.A., 1904, D.D., 1922; B.D., Crozer Theol. Sem., Chester, Pa., 1905; grad. study, Oxford U., 1905-06; m. Sara Mickel, June 19, 1907. Ordained ministry Bapt. Ch., 1906; student pastor Westmont, N.J., 1902-04; asso. pastor Linden Bapt. Ch., Camden, N.J., 1906-07; pastor Huntingdon, Pa., 1907-09, First Bapt. Ch., Roselle, N.J., 1909-22; exec. sec. N.J. Bapt. Conv. since 1922. Trustee Internat. Bapt. Sem., Crozer Theol. Sem. Mem. Phi Gamma Delta, Theta Delta Tau. Republican. Mason. Clubs: Newark Athletic, Locust Grove Golf, Roselle Golf. Editor N.J. Bapt. Bulletin. Home: 119 6th Av. W., Roselle, N.J. Office: 158 Washington St., Newark, N.J.

GOODALL, Herbert Whittaker, banker; b. Philadelphia, Pa., Jan. 1, 1884; s. Frank B. and Elizabeth (Hartley) G.; ed. pub. schs.; m. Ruth Ferguson Dorr, June 5, 1909; children—Herbert Whittaker, Robert Dorr, Patricia. Began as broker's clk., Isaac Starr, Jr., & Co., 1898; with The Pennsylvania Co., 1903-11, asst. treas., 1909-11; partner Evan Randolph & Co., 1911-14; mem. Goodall, Wistar & Co., 1914-18; v.p. Guarantee Trust & Safe Deposit Co., 1918-26, pres., 1926-28; pres. Tradesmen's Nat. Bank & Trust Co. since 1928; pres. Chelten Corpn., Chelten Title Company; dir. Pennroad Corpn., Cranberry Coal & Iron Co., Patterson Oil Terminals, Incorporated, Commonwealth Title Co., Roane County Oil Co., Davison Chemical Corpn. Treas. and dir. Glen Mills (Pa.) Schs.; mem. Sinking Fund Commn., City of Phila.; mem. bd. of mgrs. Christ Church Hosp. Episcopalian (vestryman of Christ Ch.). Clubs: Union League, Racquet, Penn Athletic, Philadelphia Cricket, Pine Valley Golf. Home: 8315 Seminole Av., Chestnut Hill, Philadelphia. Office: 1420 Walnut St., Philadelphia, Pa.

GOODELL, Edwin Burpee, lawyer, retired; b. Rockville, Conn., May 7, 1851; s. Francis and Sophia Louisa (Burpee) G.; A.B., Yale, 1877; LL.B., Yale U. Law Sch., 1880; m. Annette Cotton Doremus, Oct. 26, 1881; children—Philip, Francis, Florence, Edwin Burpee, Jr. Admitted to Conn. bar, 1881; removed to N.Y. City, 1882; admitted to N.Y. bar, 1882 and N.J. bar, 1883 and since engaged in gen. practice of law at Montclair; counsel to Bd. Pub. Health, Montclair, 1894-1910; town atty., 1902-06; served as pres. Montclair Savings Bank, 1915-35, retired, 1935, now mem. bd. mgrs. of same. Trustee School District No. 9 of Essex Co., N.J., 1884-94; mem. Bd. Edn., Town of Montclair, 1894-1902, pres. bd., 1897-1902. Awarded DeForest Prize Medal by Yale Univ., 1877; awarded John A. Porter Prize by Yale Univ., 1880. Republican. Club: Yale of New York City (charter mem.). Home: 176 Walnut St., Montclair, N.J.

GOODELL, William Newport, artist; b. Germantown, Phila., Pa., Aug. 16, 1908; s. Edward Prime and Mary (Newport) G.; grad. Germantown Friends Sch., 1926; student U. of Pa., 1927-28, Pa. Acad. of Fine Arts, Chester Springs, 1929-39; unmarried. Artist (painter) since 1930; teacher of art and handicraft, Germantown Friends Sch., Phila., since 1933. Exhibited since 1930 at Pa. Acad. Fine Arts, Nat. Acad. (N.Y.), Corcoran Biennial (Washington, D.C.), Art Inst. of Chicago, Golden Gate Internat. Exposition, and others. Awards: 1st Hallgarten prize for painting, Nat. Acad., New York, 1933. Home: 5339 Knox St. Studio: 5269 Germantown Av., Philadelphia, Pa.

GOODKIND, Morris, bridge engr.; b. N.Y. City, May 24, 1888; s. Nathan and Anna (Baidatch) G.; A.B., Columbia U., 1908; C.E., Columbia U. Engring. Sch., 1910; m. Dorothy Feller, Nov. 30, 1914; children—Herbert, Donald R. Employed in various engring. positions and as structural designer, N.Y. City, 1910-19; bridge engr., Mercer Co., N.J., 1919-22; gen. supervisor of bridges, N.J. State Highway Dept., 1922-25, bridge engr. since 1925; also in pvt. practice as cons. engr. Mem. Am. Soc. Civil Engrs., Am. Soc. for Testing Materials, Am. Assn. State Highway Officials, Nat. Soc. Professional Engrs., N.J. Soc. Professional Engrs., Engrs. Club Middlesex Co., Engrs. Club of Trenton. Awarded Phebe Hobson Fowler prize for design Raritan River Bridge by Am. Soc. Civil Engrs., 1930; first and second prizes by Am. Inst. Steel Constrn., 1933; second prize by Am. Inst. Steel Constrn., 1938. Democrat. Jewish religion. Mason. Home: 10 Llewellyn Pl., New Brunswick, N.J. Office: State House Annex, Trenton, N.J.

GOODLING, Cletus Leroy, dean farm sch.; b. Loganville, Pa., Jan. 4, 1885; s. David B. and Emeline (Sprenkel) G.; B.Sc., Pa. State Coll., 1907; M.Sc., Pa. State Coll., 1909; m. May Narcissus Park, June 17, 1908; children—Emily May (Mrs. Reuben Yoselson), Catherine Elizabeth. Engaged as asst. in dairy husbandry, Pa. State Coll., 1907-09; supt. Pa. State Coll. farms, 1909-12, asst. prof. agronomy in charge of farms, 1912-14, prof. agronomy in charge of farms, 1914-27; dean of National Farm Sch., Farm School, Pa. since 1927. Mem. Alpha Zeta (past pres. Alumni chapter). Republican. Mem. Reformed Ch. Mason (K.T., 32°). Woodman. Clubs: Kiwanis, Country (Doylestown). Home: Farm School, Pa.

GOODLOE, Don Speed Smith, educator; b. Lowell, Ky., June 2, 1878; s. Don and Amanda (Reed) G.; student Berea Coll., Ky., until 1899; grad. Meadville (Pa.) Theol. Sch., 1906; A.B., Allegheny Coll., Meadville, 1906; m. Fannie Lee Carey, of Knoxville, Tenn., June 9, 1899; children—Don Burrowes, Wallis Anderson, Reid Carey. Teacher and prin. Normal Dept., Greenville (Tenn.) Coll., 1899-1903; teacher, and in business, Danville, Ky., 1906-1910; vice prin. Manassas Industrial Sch., 1910-1911; prin. State Normal Sch. No. 3 of Md., 1911-21; engaged in lit. work since 1921. Mem. Am. Acad. Polit. and Social Science. Mason. Home: Bowie, Md.

GOODLOE, Jane F.; instr. German, Goucher Coll., 1923-27, asst. prof., 1927-30, asso. prof., 1930-37, prof. since 1937. Address: Goucher College, Baltimore, Md.

GOODMAN, Alexander, lawyer; b. Baltimore, Md., Aug. 30, 1902; s. Israel and Theresa (Fax) G.; LL.B., Univ. of Md. Law Sch., Baltimore, 1922; unmarried. Admitted to Md. bar, 1922, and since in gen. practice of law at Baltimore; admitted to practice before Supreme Ct. of U.S., 1925; mem. firm Goodman and Glick, Baltimore, since 1930; police magistrate at large for Baltimore since 1923; mem. Md. Ho. of Dels., 1931-35; lecturer in commercial law U. of Baltimore, 1933-35; declined appointment as federal judge of Virgin Islands, 1930; resident dir. Baron de Hirsch Fund, Woodbine, N.J., 1928-29. Mem. Baltimore Bar Assn., Phi Alpha, Phi Delta Tau. Jewish religion. Brith Sholom. Home: 2349 Eutaw Pl. Office: Court Square Bldg., Baltimore, Md.

GOODMAN, Horace L., surgeon-in-charge Greenbrier Valley Hosp. Address: Ronceverte, W.Va.

GOODMAN, Morris Harold, dermatologist, syphilologist; b. Baltimore, Md., Jan. 3, 1900; s. Israel and Theresa (Fax) G.; grad. Baltimore primary schs., 1914; student High Sch. and Baltimore City Coll., 1914-17; A.B., Johns Hopkins U., 1920; M.D., Johns Hopkins Med. Sch., 1924; m. Gertrude Harris, Feb. 5, 1928; children—Nelson Gates, Marion Adelaide. Resident house officer Johns Hopkins Hosp., 1924-25; training in dermatology and syphilology, 1925-28, since in active practice of same; instr. dermatology and dispensary dermatologist, Johns Hopkins U., since 1929; asso. in dermatology and syphilis, U. of Md. and Sinai Hosp., Baltimore; dermatologist Robert Garrett Child Hosp.; health officer, Baltimore City Health Dept., 1929-31. Served in S.A.T.C., during World War; hon. disch., Dec. 10, 1918. Mem. A.M.A., Baltimore-Washington Dermatol. Soc. (v.p.), Baltimore City Med. Soc. (v.p.), Atlantic Dermatol. Conf., Phi Delta Epsilon, Phi Alpha. Jewish religion. Mason (Carria 45). Clubs: Medical Research of Baltimore (pres.). Author: Number of articles in the field of dermatology. Home: 2442 Eutaw Pl. Office: 401-402 Medical Arts Bldg., Baltimore, Md.

GOODMAN, Nathan Gerson, historian, journalist; b. Phila., Pa., Jan. 9, 1899; s. Louis Jacob and Bertha (Bamberger) G.; A.B., U. of Pa., 1920, A.M., 1922, Ph.D., 1924; research and travel in Europe, 1923, 25, 28; m. Julia Nusbaum, Dec. 25, 1924; 1 dau., Susan. Instr. in English history, U. of Pa., 1920-22, modern European history, 1922-23, English constl. history, 1924; research work in British archives, 1923; European travel, 1925, 1928. Contbr. historical articles to newspapers and magazines since 1924, including sketches of noted Americans who flourished to 1850; lit. editor Atlantic City Press; regular contbr. to various newspapers; publishers' reader. Mem. of Pub. Com. of Jewish Publ. Soc. of America. Mem. Am. Hist. Soc., Hist. Soc. of Pa. Germantown Hist. Soc. Author: Diplomatic Relations Between England and Spain (1597-1603), 1925; Benjamin Rush, Physician and Citizen (1746-1813), a Biography, 1934; Benjamin Franklin's Own Story, 1937. Compiler: One Hundred Books Chosen by Prominent Americans, 1931, and other reading lists. Editor: The Ingenious Dr. Franklin, 1931; The Autobiography of Benjamin Franklin and Selections from His Other Writings, 1932. Editor: Profile of Genius: Poor Richard Pamphlets (Franklin Inst.), 1938. Home: 301 W. School House Lane, Germantown, Phila., Pa.

GOODNOW, Frank Johnson, univ. pres.; b. Brooklyn, Jan. 18, 1859; s. Abel F. and Jane M. (Root) G.; A.B., Amherst, 1879, A.M., 1887; LL.B., Columbia, 1882; studied École Libre des Sciences Politiques, Paris, and U. of Berlin; LL.D., Amherst, 1897, Columbia, 1904, Harvard, 1909, Brown, 1914, Princeton, 1917, Johns Hopkins, 1930; J.D., U. of Louvain, 1927; m. Elizabeth Lyall, June 2, 1886. Instr. history and lecturer administrative law of U.S., 1883-87, adj. prof. same, 1887-91, prof. administrative law, 1891-1903, Eaton prof. administrative law and municipal science, 1903, acting dean of polit. science, 1906-07, Columbia. Legal adviser to Chinese Govt., Mar. 13, 1913-14; pres. Johns Hopkins U., 1914-29, emeritus. Author: Comparative Administrative Law, 1893; Municipal Home Rule, 1895; Municipal Problems, 1897; Politics and Administration, 1900; City Government in the United States, 1904; Principles of the Administrative Law of the United States, 1905; Municipal Government, 1910; Social Reform and the Constitution, 1911; Principles of Constitutional Government, 1916. Editor: Selected Cases on the Law of Taxation, 1905; Selected Cases on Government and Administration, 1906; Selected Cases on the Law of Officers, 1906; Principles of Constitutional Government, 1916; China, an Analysis, 1926. Mem. Chi Psi, etc.; fellow Am. Acad. Arts and Sciences. Clubs: Century, University (New York); University, Maryland. Address: Johns Hopkins Univ., Baltimore, Md.

GOODRICH, Charles Francis, engr.; b. Manchester, N. H., Nov. 7, 1881; s. John Allen and Amoretta Jane (Sweatt) G.; ed. Manchester pub. schs. and Dartmouth Coll.; B.S., Thayer Sch. of Civil Engring., 1905, C.E., 1906; hon. Dr. Engring., Dartmouth Coll., 1939; m. Ruth Wheeler Drake, Sept. 14, 1907; children—Elizabeth J. (Mrs. Stanley V. Malek), Robert A. With Am. Bridge Co. since 1906, draftsman, Trenton plant, 1906-10, designer and estimator, New York office, 1910-19, asst. to chief engr., 1919-33, asst. chief engr., 1933-35, chief engr. since 1935. Mem. Am. Soc. Civil Engrs., Am. Inst. of Steel Construction, Am. Soc. for Testing Materials, Engrs. Soc. of Western Pa., Thayer Soc. Engrs.; asso. mem. Am. Welding Soc. Republican. Protestant. Club: Metropolitan (Pittsburgh). Home: 101 Lawncroft Av., Mt. Lebanon, Pa. Office: Frick Bldg., Pittsburgh, Pa.

GOODRICH, Donald Wells, head master; b. Brooklyn, N.Y., Jan. 20, 1898; s. Charles Howard and Matilda Antoinette (Brant) G.; A.B., Williams Coll., 1919; A.M., Harvard, 1920; grad. student Columbia, 1923, 24; m. Violet Elizabeth Walser, June 24, 1922; children—Donald Wells, Charles Howard, Alice Jacqueline. Master in English, Hoosac (N.Y.) Sch., 1921, Lawrenceville (N.J.) School, 1921-23; head master Great Neck (L.I.) Prep. Sch., 1923-28; sr. master lower sch., Tamalpais Sch., San Rafael, Calif., 1928-32; head master Calvert Primary Sch., Baltimore, since 1932. Served in

S.A.T.C., Williams Coll., 1918. Mem. private Sch. Assn. of Baltimore (pres. 1937-38), Ednl. Records Bur. (N.Y.), Country Day School Headmasters' Assn., Phi Beta Kappa. Presbyterian. Clubs: L'Hirondelle (Ruxton, Md.); 12:30 (Baltimore). Author: Beginners Course in Arithmetic, 1935; Second Course in Arithmetic, 1936; Kindergarten at Home (with Marguerite Bradley), 1937. Home: 3807 Juniper Rd. Address: Calvert Sch., Tuscany Rd., Baltimore, Md.

GOODRICH, Edgar Jennings, lawyer; b. Anoka, Minn., Nov. 15, 1896; s. George Herbert and Mary Anne (Funk) G.; spl. course for Am. soldiers, U. of Nancy, France, 1919; LL.B., State U. of Ia., 1922; m. Beulah E. Lenfest, Sept. 30, 1922; children—George Herbert, Mary Alice, Charles Lenfest. Admitted to bar Ia. and Minn., 1922, W.Va., 1923, to District of Columbia bar, 1935; assistant county attorney, Anoka County, Minn., 1922-23; removed to Charleston, W.Va., 1923, and associated in practice with Price, Smith & Spilman, specialized in federal and state taxation; apptd. mem. U.S. Bd. of Tax Appeals, 1931; re-entered law practice, charge Washington, D.C., office Guggenheimer & Untermeyer of New York, 1935. Served with 3d Minn. Inf. on Mexican border, 1916; with 1st Officers Training Camp, Ft. Snelling, Minn., 1917; duty with troops, 34th Div., later staff duty; in France with 59th Field Arty. Brigade; assigned to Air Service as arty. observer 1st Aero Squadron, and served in Army of Occupation; commd. 1st lt. Mem. Am. Bar Assn. (com. on federal taxation, 1936-37), W.Va. Bar Assn., Phi Kappa Psi. Republican. Congregationalist. Mason. Clubs: Metropolitan (Washington). Contbr. numerous articles on taxation. Home: Charleston, W.Va.; Rehoboth Beach, Del. Office: Investment Bldg., Washington, D.C.; and 30 Pine St., New York, N.Y.

GOODRICH, Herbert F., prof. and dean law; b. Anoka, Minn., July 29, 1889; s. George Herbert and Mary Ann (Funk) G.; A.B., Carleton Coll., Minn., 1911; LL.B., Harvard Univ., 1914; LL.D., University of Pennsylvania, 1929; m. Edith Eastman (now dec.); children—Elizabeth Whitney, Charlotte Anne; m. 2d, Natalie E. Murphy, Aug. 1, 1927. Instructor in law, 1914-15, assistant professor, 1915-19, professor, 1919-21, acting dean College of Law, 1921-22, State University of Iowa; prof. law, U. of Mich., 1922-29; dean and prof. of law, U. of Pa., since 1929, v.p. since 1931. Chmn. Phila. County Relief Bd., 1935-36, Pa. Com. on Relief and Assistance, 1936. Pres. Assn. of Am. Law Schs., 1931; mem. Am., Pa. State, Phila. and Mich. bar assns., Am. Philos. Soc., Am. Law Institute (adviser professional relations); Harvard Law Sch. Assn. in Phila. (pres. since 1938), Phi Betta Kappa, Delta Sigma Rho, Phi Alpha Delta, Alpha Sigma Phi, Order of the Coif. Democrat. Mason. Clubs: University, Lenape, Franklin Inn, Contemporary (pres. 1932-33). Editor Mich. State Bar Jour., 1924-27. Author: Goodrich on the Conflict of Laws, 1927, 2d edit., 1938; also chapter on torts in Ballentine's Problems in Law, 1927, 2d edit., 1937; and articles in legal and other periodicals. Home: 7701 Cresheim Rd., Chestnut Hill., Philadelphia, Pa.

GOODSPEED, Arthur Willis, physicist; b. at Hopkinton, N.H., Aug. 8, 1860; s. Obed and Helen B. (Morse) G.; A.B. Harvard Univ., 1884; Ph.D., U. of Pa., 1889; m. Annie H. Bailey, June 24, 1896; children—Frederick Long, Willis Bailey, Helen Gertrude; m. 2d, Ethel W. Mitchell, Aug. 19, 1913; 1 son, Arthur Willis. Assistant in physics, 1884-85, instr., 1885-89, asst. prof., 1889-1904, prof. physics, 1904-31, now emeritus, U. of Pa. Mem. Jury Awards, Nat. Export Expn., 1899. Fellow A.A.A.S.; mem. Am. Röntgen Ray Soc. (pres. 1902-03), Royal Soc. Arts, Am. Philos. Soc. (sec. 1900-35, editor publs.), Am. Phys. Soc., N.H. Antiq. Soc. (v.p. 1901-14, pres. 1914—), Société francaise de Physique. Mem. Jury of Awards, Sesquicentennial, Phila., 1926. Has written numerous articles on Röntgen Rays and other scientific subjects. Home: 4623 Sansom St., Philadelphia, Pa.

GOODWIN, Russell B., lawyer; b. Wheeling, W.Va., Jan. 5, 1893; s. James T. and Jennie (Bryan) G.; A.B., Washington and Jefferson Coll., Washington, Pa., 1915; LL.B., Washington and Lee Univ. Law Coll., 1918; m. Helen N. Marsh, June 20, 1915; children—Virginia F., Thomas A., Helen Louise, Jane B., Russell B., Jr., Andrew J. Admitted to W.Va. bar, 1918, and since engaged in gen. practice of law at Wheeling; mem. firm Hall, Goodwin & Paul; served as mem. Council City of Wheeling. Mem. Am. Bar Assn., W.Va. State Bar Assn., Ohio Co. Bar Assn. Democrat. Presbyterian. Mason. Elk. K.P. Club: Country (Wheeling). Home: 32 Maple Av. Office: Board of Trade Bldg., Wheeling, W.Va.

GOODWIN, Thomas Campbell, physician; b. Richmond, Va., Sept. 17, 1901; s. Robert Archer and Harriet M. (Butts) G.; B.S. and M.D., Univ. of Va.; M.D., Johns Hopkins U. Med. Sch., 1927; m. Mary Stewart Hooke, Feb. 1, 1938; 1 dau., Jane Stewart. Instr. pediatrics, Johns Hopkins U. Med. Sch., 1930-33; asso. in pediatrics, Cornell U. Med. Sch., 1933-35; asso. in pediatrics, Johns Hopkins Med. Sch. since 1935; asso. prof. pediatrics, U. of Md. Med. Sch. since 1936; pediatrician in chief Baltimore City Hosp. since 1935; in practice at Baltimore, Md., specializing in pediatrics since 1935. Mem. A.M.A., Baltimore City Med. Soc., Soc. for Pediatric Research, Phi Sigma Kappa, Phi Beta Kappa. Democrat. Episcopalian. Home: 104 W. University Parkway. Office: 16 E. Biddle St., Baltimore, Md.

GOODWIN, William Nelson, Jr., electrical engr.; b. Phila., Oct. 10, 1876; s. William Nelson and Annie Reese (Shaw) G.; B.S., Elec. and Mech. Engring. Dept., U. of Pa., 1897, E.E., 1908; married; 1 son, Nelson Werner. With F. G. Thorn, civil engr., Brooklyn, 1897-98; designer Pa. Iron Works Co., Phila., several mos., 1898; with Weston Elec. Instrument Co. since July 1898, in charge Standardizing Lab., 1903-06, since chief engr. and dir. research. Fellow Am. Inst. E.E., A.A.A.S.; mem. Am. Phys. Soc., Inst. Radio Engrs., Am. Soc. for Testing Materials. Home: 30 Scheerer Av. Office: Weston Electrical Instrument Co., Newark, N.J.*

GOODYKOONTZ, Wells, ex-congressman; b. Newbern, Pulaski Co., Va., June 3, 1872; s. William M. and Lucinda K. (Woolwine) G.; ed. Oxford (Va.) Acad.; studied law under Judge Z. T. Dobyns, of Floyd C.H., Va., and at Washington and Lee U.; m. Irene Hooper, Dec. 22, 1898. Practiced at Williamson, W.Va., since 1894; mem. firm of Goodykoontz & Slaven; mem. W. Virginia Ho. of Delegates, 1911-12, Senate, 1914-18 (Rep. floor leader, 1915-16, pres. of Senate, 1917-18); the only one of the presidents of W.Va. Senate concerning whose rulings no appeal was ever taken; mem. 66th to 67th Congresses (1919-23), 5th W.Va. Dist. Pres. Nat. Bank of Commerce, Williamson. Mem. Am. Bar Assn., W.Va. Bar Assn. (pres. 1917-18); chmn. com. of lawyers that directed W.Va. bar in assisting registrants in connection with draft and in aiding soldiers, sailors and their families. Apptd. 1926, by President Coolidge, commr. from W.Va. to Sesquicentennial, Phila.; also apptd., same yr., by gov. of W.Va., mem. State Tax Commn. Mason. Home: Williamson, W.Va.

GORDON, Alfred, neurologist; b. Paris, France, Nov. 2, 1874; s. Michael and Esther G.; M.D., U. of Paris, 1895; m. Victorine Lyon, July 20, 1898. Came to America, 1896; asso. in nervous and mental diseases, Jefferson Med. Coll., Phila., 1899-1908; examiner of the insane, Phila. Gen. Hosp., 1904-08; has served as neurologist Mt. Sinai, Northwestern Gen., and Douglas Memorial hosps. Mem. A.M.A., Am. Neurol. Assn., Coll. Physicians of Phila., Phila. Neurol. and Pathol. socs., Omega Upsilon Phi (Rho Chapter). Author: Diseases of the Nervous System, 1908. Address: 19th and Locust Sts., Philadelphia, Pa.

GORDON, Benjamin Lee, ophthalmologist; b. Lithuania, July 5, 1875; s. Abraham B. and Sarah (Skub) G.; brought to U.S., 1886, naturalized, 1890; ed. N.Y. City Coll., 1888-91; M.D., Jefferson Med. Coll., 1896; grad. study in Vienna, Austria, 1909-10; m. Dorothy Cohen, June 7, 1900; children—Judith (Mrs. Edward I. Baker), Cyrus Herzl, Norman Ezra, Maurice Bear. Engaged as instr. obstetrics, Jefferson Med. Coll. of Phila. and Polyclinic Hosp., 1897-1901; asso. ophthalmologist, St. Agnes Hosp., 1908-16; ophthalmologist, Lebanon Hosp., 1906-12; on staff U. of Pa. Grad. Sch. Medicine, 1929-39; ophthalmologist, Atlantic Shores Hosp., Somers Point, N.J., since 1934, med. examiner Nat. Bur. of Air, Dept. of Commerce, since 1936; practiced in Phila., 1896-1930; practiced in Atlantic City, N.J., since 1930. Certified by Am. Bd. Ophthalmology. Mem. Am. and Atlantic Co. med. assns., Acad. Ophthalmology and Otolaryngology. Enlisted in Keegan's Brigade in Spanish-Am. War. Served as mem. Med. Adv. Bd. and mem. Vol. Med. Corps during World War. Mem. Jewish War Vets. of America. Democrat. Jewish religion. I.O.B.S. Clubs: Hebrew Circle (Atlantic City); Dorshe Doath Soc. (Philadelphia). Author: New Judea, 1919. Contbr. articles to med. journs., and Archives of Ophthalmology. One of the founders of Zionist Orgn. of America and Am. Jewish Cong. Home: 7203 Atlantic Av. Office: 1616 Pacific Av., Atlantic City, N.J.

GORDON, Burgess L., physician; b. Spokane, Wash., Apr. 10, 1892; s. Burgess Lee and Raphaeleta (Simpson) G.; A.B., Gongaza U., 1912; ed. Harvard U., 1913-15, St. Louis Sch. of Medicine, 1915-17; M.D., Jefferson Med. Coll., 1919; unmarried. Interne Jefferson Hosp., Phila., 1919-22; resident physician, Peter Bent Brigham Hosp., Boston, 1921-25; mem. staff Jefferson Med. Coll. and Hosp., the Pa. Hosp., and White Haven Sanatorium; mem. bd. dirs. White Haven Sanatorium, Frederick Douglass Hosp., Phila., Pa. Fellow Am. Coll. Physicians; mem. Am. Soc. Clin. Investigation, Assn. Am. Physicians. Clubs: University, Penn Athletic, Harvard (Phila.). Home: University Club. Office: 1832 Spruce St., Philadelphia, Pa.

GORDON, Clarence McCheyne, physicist; b. Fannettsburg, Pa., Apr. 14, 1870; s. Rev. Jeremiah Smith and Margaret Beatty (Kyle) G.; A.B., Princeton, 1891, A.M., 1893; Ph.D., Göttingen, 1897; m. Amie Baker Lanier, July 17, 1909; 1 dau., Margaret Lanier. Math. fellow Princeton, 1891-92; instr. physics, Williams Coll., 1893-95; instr. physical chemistry, Harvard, 1897-98; prof. physics, Centre Coll., Ky., 1898-1909, Lafayette Coll. since 1909. Optical engr., Wollensak Optical Co., Rochester, N.Y., 1918-19; elec. engr. Western Elec. Co., New York, 1920; prof. physics, Temple U., summer 1923, Muhlenberg Coll., summer 1924, 27. Fellow A.A.A.S., Am. Physical Soc. Republican. Presbyn. Author: Experiments in General Physics, 1922; also articles in Physical Rev., Jour. Am. Chem. Soc., etc. Address: College Campus, Easton, Pa.

GORDON, Douglas Huntly, lawyer; b. Baltimore, Md., Apr. 22, 1902; s. Douglas Huntly and Elizabeth Southall (Clarke) G.; student Gilman Country Sch., Baltimore, 1914-21; A.B., Harvard, 1926; grad. student Harvard Law Sch., 1926-28, LL.B., 1928; LL.D. (hon.), U. of Md., Baltimore, 1932; m. Winifred Macmillan Claude, June 2, 1934. Admitted to Md. bar, 1929, and in gen. practice of law at Baltimore, 1929-31 and since 1934; pres. St. Johns Coll., Annapolis, Md., 1931-34; asst. U.S. atty., Md. dist. since 1934; mem. firm Brune & Gordon, Baltimore, since 1935; mem. Md. Ho. of Dels., 1930-34. Mem. mayor of Baltimore's com. on city plan, 1937-39. Pres. Municipal Art Soc.; trustee Gilman Country Sch., Baltimore, Baltimore Mus. Art, Peabody Inst. of City of Baltimore. Mem. Am. Bar Assn., Baltimore City Bar Assn. (Bill of Rights conf.), Md. Hist. Soc. (mem. of council), Phi Beta Kappa. Democrat. Episcopalian. Clubs: Harvard of Md. (pres. 1937-39), University, (Baltimore; mem. bd. govs.). Home: 100 E. Chase St. Office: First Nat. Bank Bldg., Baltimore, Md.

GORDON, Franklin Hall, vice-pres. Lukens Steel Co.; b. Coatesville, Pa., May 27, 1878; s. William T. and Mary Pennock (Hall) G.; grad. Coatesville High Sch., 1895; m. Lillian Moore, June 5, 1902. Vice-pres. Lukens Steel Co., dir. Lukenweld, Inc., By-Products Steel

Corpn.; dir. and mem. exec. com. Home Bldg. & Loan Assn. Dir. Coatesville Chamber of Commerce; trustee and treas. Coatesville Presbyn. Ch. Clubs: Union League (Phila.); Railroad-Machinery, Bankers (New York). Home: 558 E. Lincoln Highway. Office: S. 1st Av., Coatesville, Pa.

GORDON, Irwin Leslie, publicity executive, journalist, author; b. Lowell, Mass., Oct. 24, 1888; s. Rev. John (D.D.) and Caroline A. (Irvin) G.; father dean emeritus Theol. Dept., Temple U.; spl. course Temple U. Joined editorial staff Phila. Pub. Ledger, 1909; an editor Evening Public Ledger from its foundation, 1914 to 1921; was head Dept. of Journalism, Temple U.; publicity mgr. Reading R.R.; mem. pub. relations com. Assn. of Am. Railroads. Enlisted as chief petty officer U.S.N.R.F., Dec. 13, 1917; commd. ensign, Apr. 20, 1918. Fellow Royal Geog. Soc. (London). Republican. Author: The Log of the Ark (with A. J. Frueh), 1915; What Allah Wills, 1917. Home: Bywood, Pa. Office: Reading Terminal, Philadelphia, Pa.

GORDON, John Kyle, M.D.; b. Fannettsburg, Pa., Aug. 6, 1877; s. Rev. J. Smith and Margaret B. (Kyle) G.; student Mercersburg Acad., 1894-95; A.B., Princeton U., 1899; M.D., U. of Pa., 1904; m. Eleanor Wharton Wood, Mar. 20, 1909 (died 1919); children—John Kyle, Jr.; Louis Chancellor (M.D.); m. 2d, Alice Hibberd Childs, Oct. 18, 1926. Began gen. practice of medicine, 1904; mem. med. staff Chambersburg Hosp. Mem. A.M.A., Pa. State Med. Soc., Franklin Co. Med. Soc. Republican. Presbyn. Clubs: Chambersburg Golf. Address: 253 N. Main St., Chambersburg, Pa.

GORDON, Joseph Berkeley, physician; b. Richmond, Va., July 22, 1901; s. Joseph Henry and Ada (Ogilvie) G.; ed. Univ. of Richmond, Va., 1919-22; M.D., Med. Coll. of Va., 1926; m. Isabel Richardson, Sept. 1, 1927; children—Richard Berkeley, Jane Stowell. Served in Med. Corps, U.S.N., 1926-29; res. phys. State Home for Boys, Jamesburg, N.J., 1929-30; med. dir. N.J. State Hosp., Marlboro, N.J. since 1930; attdg. psychiatrist Monmouth Memorial Hosp., Long Branch, N.J., Fitkin Memorial Hosp., Asbury Park, N.J., Riverview Hosp., Red Bank, N.J. Served as sergt. inf., Va. N.G., 1921-25; lt. (j.g.) Med. Corps, U.S.N., 1926-29. 1st lieut. (M.C.) N.J.N.G., 1931-32 (183rd Med. Regt.). Mem. Am. Psychiatric Assn., N.J. Health and San. Assn., Med. Soc. of N.J., Monmouth Co. Med. Soc., N.J. Hosp. Assn., N.J. Neuropsychiatric Assn., Phi Chi. Mason (32°, Shriner). Rotarian. Editorial consultant Nat. Conf. of Juvenile Agencies. Home: N.J. State Hosp., Marlboro, N.J.

GORDON, Maude Willis, b. Erie, Pa., July 15, 1882; d. Richard B. and Clara Augusta (Melhorn) Willis; grad. Central High Sch., Erie, 1901; student U. of Mich., 1902-04; m. Spencer R. Gordon, 1913 (divorced Oct. 6, 1938); 1 dau., Ruth Willis. Deputy county treas., Erie Co., Pa., 1904-05; dep. clerk of courts, Erie, Pa., 1905-13; life ins. and annuity underwriter since June 1937. Pres. Coll. Women's Club, Erie, 1910-11; pres. Woman's Club of Erie, 1931-34; dir., 1934-37; dir. State Fed. of Pa. Women, 1932-36, chmn. dept. of social welfare, 1933-36, gen. chmn. 40th annual conv., 1935; dir. Erie Co. Fed. Women's Clubs, 1933-37; dir. Erie Y.W.C.A., 1935-37; dir. Erie Social Hygiene Assn., 1932-35; dir. Asso. Charities of Erie, 1918-26. Episcopalian. Clubs: College Women's, Woman's (Erie). Collector-appraiser of antiques. Home: 925 Plum St. Office: Erie Trust Bldg., Erie, Pa.

GORDON, Myron Boyd, aviation exec.; b. Slippery Rock, Pa., Jan. 17, 1892; s. Samuel Myron and Mary (Espy) G.; M.E., U. of Cincinnati, 1916; student Sch. of Mil. Aeronautics, Admiralty Compases Observatory, Slough, Eng., 1918; m. Catherine Rote, Sept. 1, 1924 (died June 9, 1934); 1 son, Robert Boyd. Patent work Westinghouse Machine Co. (later Westinghouse Electric & Mfg. Co.), 1916-19; industrial engring., financial investigations, reorganizations, etc., 1920-24; comptroller Seth-Thomas Clock Co., 1924-25; asst. comptroller Internat. Combustion Engring. Corpn. and comptroller to subsidiaries, sec. Heine Boiler Co., sec. and treas. Combustion Engring. Corpn., 1925-29; with Wright Aeronautical Corpn., Paterson, N.J., since 1929, as sec. and treas., 1929-30, treas., 1930-35, v.p. and asst. gen. mgr., 1933-35, v.p. and gen. mgr. since 1935; dir. Caldwell Wright Airport, Inc., Paterson Nat. Bank. Served as 2d lt., U.S. Army, 1918. Mem. Am. Soc. Mech. Engrs., Nat. Assn. Cost Accountants, Inst. of Aeronautical Sciences, Tau Beta Pi. Licensed professional engr., State of N.Y. Clubs: Larchmont Yacht (Larchmont, N. Y.); Engineers (New York); Hamilton (Paterson, N.J.); Army and Navy (Washington, D.C.). Home: 57 Watchung Av., Montclair, N.J. Office: 132 Beckwith Av., Paterson, N.J.

GORDON, Ralph Thompson, pump mfg.; b. Newburgh, N.Y., May 7, 1894; s. Joseph Bogart and Margaret (Thompson) G.; grad. Webb Inst. of Naval Architecture and Marine Engring., New York, N.Y., 1915; grad study, Brooklyn Poly. Inst., 1919-20; m. Grace A. Hamilton, Jan. 25, 1921; children—Ralph Thompson, Jr., Joan Hamilton. Began as jr. naval architect, Brooklyn Navy Yd., 1915; test engr., Alberger Pump & Condenser Co., 1915-17, sales engr., N.Y. City, 1917-23; N.Y. Dist. Mgr., Dean Bros. Co., pump mfrs., N.Y. City 1923; dir. Mahwah (N. J.) Bldg. & Loan Assn. Mem. Am. Soc. of Naval Architects & Marine Engrs., Am. Soc. Mech. Engrs. Republican. Episcopalian. Mason. Clubs: Downtown Athletic (New York); Hoovenkopf Country, Suffern, N.Y. (mem. bd. govs.). Home: Armour Rd., Mahwah, N.J. Office: 92 Liberty St., New York, N.Y.

GORDON, Seth (Edwin), game exec.; b. Richfield, Pa., Apr. 2, 1890; s. G.B.M. and Caroline (Wocheley) G.; student common schs. of Pa., New Bloomfield (Pa.) Acad., 1907-08; finished full course Pa. Business Coll., Lancaster, Pa., 1911; m. Dora Belle Silverthorn, Jan. 29, 1910; children—Seth Edwin, Phyllis Rowena. Teacher common and graded schs., Pa., 1907-11; clerical work Pa. Steel Co., 1911-13; employed by Pa. Game Commn., Harrisburg, 1913-19, administrative head, 1919-26, exec. dir. since 1936; conservation dir. Izaak Walton League of America, Chicago, Ill., 1926-31; pres. Am. Game Assn., Washington, D.C., 1931-36. Mem. Internat. Assn. of Game, Fish and Conservation Commrs. (v.p.), Am. Fisheries Soc. (sec.-treas.), Nat. Com. on Wildlife Legislation (sec.-treas.) Am. Wildlife Inst. (founder and since trustee), Am. Game Assn. (dir.), Nat. Rifle Assn. (dir.), Am. Forestry Assn. (ex-v.p.), Izaak Walton League of America. Republican. Lutheran. Clubs: Cosmos (Washington, D.C.); Camp Fire of America (New York City; hon. mem. conservation com.). Writer and lecturer on conservation subjects, especially wildlife restoration and management; consultant on conservation adminstrn., legislation. Home: 2001 Market St. Office: State Capitol, Harrisburg, Pa.

GORDY, Urie Lee, supt. schs.; b. nr. Sharptown, Md., September 20, 1872; s. J. J. M. and Rebecca E. (Wheatley) G.; student Washington Coll., Chestertown, Md., 1894; m. Helen L. Weaver, July 2, 1902; children—Edward L., Margaret D.; m. 2d, Jessie R. Null, July 3, 1935. Teacher village sch., Sharptown, Md., 1894-96; master Cary Collegiate Sem., Oakfield, N.Y., 1896-97; teacher Shamokin (Pa.) High Sch., 1897-1900; prin. Danville (Pa.) High Sch., 1900-01; supt. Danville pub. schs., 1901-07; supervising prin. Mt. Pleasant (Pa.) pub. schs., 1907-17; dist. supt. pub. schs., Chambersburg, Pa., since 1917. Episcopalian. Mason. Home: Nelson Hall Apts., Chambersburg, Pa.

GORDY, William Sidney, Jr., banker; b. Salisbury, Md., Dec. 21, 1873; s. William Sidney and Virginia (Brewington) G.; student pub. schs. of Wicomico Co., Md.; m. Mary Clara White, Nov. 14, 1901. With Salisbury Nat. Bank since 1896, becoming pres., 1932; comptroller State of Md. since 1921. Home: W. William St. Office: Salisbury Nat. Bank, Salisbury, Md.

GORE, Howard Mason, ex-governor; b. at Clarksburg, West Virginia, October 12, 1887; s. Solomon D. and Marietta Payne (Rogers) G.; B.A., W.Va. U., 1900; m. Roxilene Corder Bailey, Sept. 30, 1906 (died 1907). Largely engaged in agriculture and live stock raising, also in hotel, banking and mercantile business; mem. State Bd. of Edn., W.Va., 1920-25; asst. sec. agr., Washington, D.C., 1923-24; sec. of agr., Nov. 1924-Mar. 1925; gov. of W.Va., term 1925-29; comr. of agriculture, W.Va., 1931-33; W.Va. administr. Farm to Market Roads Administrn. Served as assistant food administrator, W.Va., and mem. Council of Defense, World War. Pres. of West Va. Livestock Assn., 1912-16; pres. West Va. Hereford Breeders Assn., 1918-21; was mem. of Com. of Fifteen of Am. Farm Bur. Federation; mem. first bd. dirs. Nat. Producers Livestock Coöperative Assn.; life mem. Internat. Livestock Expn.; a founder and patron of boys' and girls' organization work; pres. W. Va. Farm Bur. Coöperative Assn.; dir. Producers Coöperative Live Stock Assn.; chmn. Drouth Relief Com. of W.Va. Mem. Phi Sigma Kappa, Phi Beta Kappa. Republican. Baptist. Mason. Odd Fellow, Elk, Moose, K.P. Club: Cosmos (Washington). Home: Clarksburg, W.Va.*

GORE, John Kinsey, actuary; b. Newark, N. J., Feb. 3, 1864; s. George W. and Mary L. (Kinsey) G.; A.B., Columbia U., 1883, A.M., 1886; received the Univ. medal from Columbia, 1932; m. Jeannette Littell, Feb. 16, 1898. Teacher and prin. Woodbridge Sch., New York, 1884-92; clk. actuarial dept., 1892-94; mathematician, 1894-95, asst. actuary, 1895-97, became actuary, Mar. 1897, dir., 1907, v.p., 1912, now retired, Prudential Ins. Co. of America; dir. Nat. State Bank of Newark. Inventor of a system of tabulating machines. Fellow Actuarial Soc. America (pres. 1908-10); mem. N.E. Soc. of Orange (pres. 1912-13). Mem. Newark Bd. of Edn., 1895-96. Republican. Clubs: Phi Gamma Delta, Columbia U. (New York). Writer scientific papers pub. in trans. of Actuarial Soc. of America, Internat. Congress of Actuaries, and "A World War Against Disease," pub. by Assn. Life Ins. Presidents, 1927. Home: 69 High St., Orange, N.J.

GORESLINE, Harry E(dward), bacteriologist; b. Gardner, Kan., Aug. 13, 1898; s. Truman Dennis and Jessie Pearl (Mossman) G.; B.S. in Chem. Engring., Ore. State Coll., Corvallis, 1926, M.S., Bacteriology, Ia. State Coll., Ames, Ia., 1928, Ph.D. same, 1931; m. Mary Lucille Duncan, Sept. 15, 1920. Employed as jr. bacteriologist, Ia. Engring. Expt. Sta., Ames, Ia., 1927-30; asso. bacteriologist Bur. Chemistry and Soils, U.S. Dept. Agr., Washington, D.C., 1930-36, bacteriologist, 1936-37, sr. bacteriologist since 1937, in charge Microbiology Sect. of Food Research Div. including field stas. at Geneva, N.Y. and Raleigh, N.C. Del. to 6th Internat. Chem. Congress, Budapest, Hungary, 1939. Mem. A.A.A.S., Am. Chem. Soc., Soc. of Am. Bacteriologists, Am. Pub. Health Assn., Assn. of Official Agrl. Chemists, Inst. of Food Technology, Sigma Xi, Phi Lambda Upsilon. Republican. Methodist. Home: 7909 Chicago Av., Silver Spring, Md.

GORHAM, Donald R., prof. Christian edn.; b. Kalamazoo, Mich., May 23, 1903; s. Adelbert Leroy and Emma Louise (Rogers) G.; certificate Western State Teachers Coll., 1923; B.Th., Colgate U., 1926, M.A., 1927; D.R.E., Eastern Bapt. Theol. Sem., 1929; university scholar U. of Pa., 1929-30, Ph.D., 1934; m. Elizabeth Ann Young, June 23, 1926. Ordained ministry Bapt. Ch., 1926; apptd. acting prof. Christian edn., Eastern Bapt. Theol. Sem., 1930, prof. and dir. Sch. of Christian Edn. since 1931; interim editor Young People's publs. for Am. Bapt. Publ. Soc. summer 1934; mem. bd. Phila. Council of Christian Edn. since 1934; mem. bd. Bapt. Union of Phila. and Vicinity since 1936; chmn. Professional Planning Com. for Vacation Schools for neglected areas of Pa., 1936-37; dir. Bapt. Boys Camps in Pa., Unami, 1931, Corbly, 1937. Mem. Phi Delta Kappa. Republican. Author: The Status of Protestant Weekday Church Schools, 1934. Editor: Contributions to Christian Education. Home: 1918 Ringgold Place. Address: 1808-16 S. Rittenhouse Sq., Philadelphia, Pa.

GORHAM, Robert Charles, educator; b. Smith Center, Kan., Apr. 11, 1893; s. Charles and Anna (Van Fleet) G.; A.B., Neb. Wesleyan U.,

1917; E.E., Cornell U., 1924; m. Margaret McKeown, Apr. 30, 1920; children—Marjorie Ann, Ina Mae, James Robert. Rural schoolmaster, Neb., 1912-13; asst. in physics lab., Neb. Wesleyan U., 1915-17; tester Westinghouse Elec. & Mfg. Co., 1917; electrician U.S. Navy, 1918-19; farm mgr., Franklin, Neb., 1919-20; physics asst., U. of Okla., 1920-21; instr. elec. engring., Cornell U., 1921-24; designer synchronous machines, power engring. dept., Westinghouse Electric & Mfg. Co., summer, 1923; spl. tester United Electric Light & Power Co., New York, 1924-25; instr. elec. engring., U. of Pittsburgh, 1925-27, asst. prof., 1927-36, asso. prof. since 1936. Licensed professional engr., Pa., since 1936; consulting practice includes development of domestic fuse and central power station studies. Mem. Am. Inst. Elec. Engrs., Inst. Radio Engrs., Soc. for Promotion Engring. Edn., Sigma Tau, Eta Kappa Nu, Beta Delta. Methodist. Club: Faculty. Author: "Power Economics" for engring. students. Home: 1247 Trevanion St., Pittsburgh, Pa.

GORMAN, Lawrence Clifton, clergyman, educator; b. New York, N.Y., Sept. 28, 1898; s. Lawrence Patrick and Anna Teresa (Nagle) G.; A.B., Fordham U., N.Y. City, 1920; A.M., Boston Coll., 1926; Ph.D., Gregorian Univ., Rome, Italy, 1938. Joined Soc. of Jesus (Jesuit) at New York City, Sept. 28, 1920; ordained Priest R.C. Ch., 1932; asst. prof. chemistry, Georgetown U., Washington, D.C., 1926-29, acting dean Coll. Arts and Scis., 1934, prof. organic chemistry and head chemistry dept., 1934-35; v.p. and dean of studies, Loyola Coll., Baltimore, since 1936. Trustee Loyola Coll., Baltimore, Md. Mem. A.A.A.S., Am. Council of Edn., Am. Assn. of Colls., Eastern Assn. Coll. Deans and Advisers of Men, Jesuit Ednl. Assn., Nat. Catholic Edn. Assn. Roman Catholic. Home: 4501 N. Charles St., Baltimore, Md.

GORRELL, John Joseph Neville, editor and vice consul; b. Glasgow, Mo., Oct. 3, 1889; s. William Louis and Mary (Neville) G.; A.B., Pritchett Coll., 1909; B.S., U. of Mo., 1910; Ph.D., Oxford (Eng.), 1913; D.Sc., U. of Gottingen, 1914; hon. Litt. D., U. of Lisbon, Portugal; m. Catherine Charleton, Nov. 12, 1919; 1 dau., Mary Catherine. Employed as chemist Lackawanna Steel Co., Buffalo, N.Y.; chief chemist, Pressed Steel Car Co., Pittsburgh, Pa.; now editor Catholic Observer and Sunday Observer; also vice consul of Latvia at Pittsburgh for Western Pa. and W.Va. Served in C.W.S., U.S.A. during World War. Incorporator and trustee Mount Mercy College, Pittsburgh. Pres. Consular Assn. of Pittsburgh. Has received many decorations from European countries. Roman Catholic. K.C. Home: 246 Pinecastle Av. Office: 208 Third Av., Pittsburgh, Pa.

GOSS, Albert S., federal land bank commr.; b. at Rochester, N.Y., October 14, 1882; s. John W. and Flora M. (Alling) G.; ed. high sch. and business coll., Portland, Ore.; m. Minnie E. Hand, Dec. 21, 1907; children—Ruth Dorothy, Warren Hand, Betty Jane. Began as bookkeeper, 1901, later connected with cereal and flour milling, general store, telephone business, and farming; actively identified with Grange affairs, 1920-33; master Washington State Grange, 1922-33; land bank commr., Farm Credit Administration, since 1933. Chmn. exec. com. Nat. Grange, 1924-33. Presbyn. Mem. Woodmen of World. Home: 6119 Brookeville Rd., Chevy Chase, Md. Office: Farm Credit Administration, Washington, D.C.

GOSSLING, John Howard, lawyer; b. Phila., Pa., Apr. 6, 1895; s. Harry J. and Ella Love (Haines) G.; studied law in office of Joseph R. Embery, 1912-18; LL.B., Temple U., 1918; m. Elsie S. Smith, Jan. 31, 1923; children—Marjorie Waddington, Joan Haines, Patricia Ann. Began as bank clerk Corn Exchange National Bank, 1912; admitted to Phila. bar, 1918; associated with Allen M. Stearne (now judge of Orphans Ct. of Phila. Co.), 1919-27; partner law firm Moore, Gossling & Panfil since 1927; dir. La France Industries, H. B. Newton Co., Alpha Bldg. & Loan Assn., Prudential Holding Co., La France Textiles, Ltd., Pendleton Mfg. Co. Served as sergeant, U.S. Med. Corps, World War. Dir. Northeast Boys Club. Mem. Am. Bar Assn., Pa. Bar Assn., Phila. Bar Assn. Republican. Episcopalian. Clubs: Union League, Torresdale-Frankford Country, Meridian (Phila.). Home: 1027 Allengrove St. Office: 603 Stephen Girard Bldg., Philadelphia, Pa.

GOTSHALL, Roy J., banking; b. Shamokin, Pa., Mar. 16, 1893; s. Adam J. and Matilda G.; ed. high sch., Lancaster, Pa., 1909-12, U. of Pa., 1913-14; m. Grace C. Steen, Apr. 21, 1919; 1 son, Roy Jordan. Has engaged in profession of banking since 1913; asso. with City Nat. Bank, Phila., Pa., since 1929, vice-pres. since 1929. Served with U.S. Army, 1917-19. Republican. Presbyn. Mason. (Shriner). Club: Springhaven of Wallingford (treas.). Home: 11 Bailey Rd., Lansdowne, Pa. Office: 6500 Woodland Av., Philadelphia, Pa.

GOTT, Ernest Fred, surgeon Kanawha Valley Hosp. Address: 1014 Virginia St. East, Charleston, W.Va.

GOTT, Estep Tillard, vice-pres. Dravo Corpn.; b. West River, Anne Arundel Co., Md., Oct. 9, 1883; s. Edwin and Elizabeth (Hays) G.; student St. John's Coll. Prep., Annapolis, Md., 1896, pub. and private schs., Baltimore, 1896-1902; C.E., Lehigh U., 1906; m. Frances Pinkney Gordon, Apr. 28, 1913; 1 dau., Frances Pinkney. With Dravo Corpn., gen. contracting, since 1906, beginning as field engr. and time keeper, vice-pres. and dir. since 1917, also gen. mgr. tunnel dept. of the contracting div. Mem. Am. Soc. Civil Engrs., Engrs. Soc. Western Pa., Coal Mining Inst., Chi Phi. Ind. Democrat. Episcopalian. Clubs: University, Civic (Pittsburgh); Edgeworth (Sewickley); Montour Heights Country (Coraopolis, Pa.); Cove (West River, Md.). Home: 1306 Beaver Rd., Sewickley, Pa. Office: Neville Island Branch, Pittsburgh, Pa.

GOTTLIEB, Albert Samuel, architect; b. Portchester, N.Y., July 8, 1870; s. Samuel and Julia (Rothschild) G.; student Mass. Inst. Tech., 1887-92, Ecole des Beaux Arts, Paris, France, 1896-1900; m. Catherine Mary Welch, June 19, 1920. Draftsman with McKim, Mead & White, New York City, 1892-96; individual practice as architect, New York City, 1900-34, Harrington, Del., since 1934; designed Greenville Branch Pub. Library and addition to Main Library, Jersey City, N.J., Temple B'nai Jeshurun, Newark, N.J. Mem. A.I.A., Soc. of Beaux Arts Architects. Jewish religion. Clubs: Rotary (Harrington, Del.); Bohemians, N.Y. Musicians (New York City). Address: Harrington, Del.

GOTTLIEB, Maxim B., instr. of fine arts; b. Grodzisk, Poland, May 5, 1903; s. Benjamin W. and Bessie (Potechin) G.; student Graphic Sketch Club, 1920-24, Pa. Acad. of Fine Arts, 1924-28, Grand Chambier, Paris, France, 1928-29; m. Kathryn McGarrity, Aug. 30, 1933; 1 son, Brian Michael. Came to U.S., 1920, naturalized, 1928. Teacher of fine arts and lecturer Graphic Sketch Club, Phila., since 1929; also teacher at private schools. Address: 5044 Golf Rd., Philadelphia, Pa.

GOTTLIEB, Moritz Melvin, prin. M. M. Gottlieb Associates; b. Washington, D.C., July 19, 1893; s. Max and Mathilda (Augenstein) G.; m. Anita R. Goldstein, Jan. 7, 1917; children —Richard Melvin, David Abraham. Sales agent Lanston Monotype Machine Co., 1907-14; western sales mgr. Napier Saw Works, Springfield, Pa., 1914-19; v.p. Woodstock Mfg. Co., 1919-25; pres. Carrib Mfg. Corpn., 1919-25; sales mgr. H. C. Cohn Co., 1919-25; v.p. and dir. sales L. F. Grammes & Sons, Inc., Allentown, Pa., 1925-38; prin. M. M. Gottlieb Associates since 1938. Chmn. finance com. and dir. Jewish Community Center; zone chmn. Joint Distribution Com.; zone chmn. United Palestine Appeal; past pres. and mem. exec. com. Pa.-Middle Atlantic Federation of Y.M.H.A. and Y.W.H.A.; chmn. Camp Com. Federation; officer or dir. various philanthropic and civic orgns. Mason (32°), Elk, B'nai B'rith (trustee). Clubs: Berkleigh Country (v.p., chmn. finance com.); Lehigh Valley Shrine. Home: 218 N. 17th St. Office: Dime Bldg., Allentown, Pa.

GOTTLIEB, Solomon, supervisor manual training; b. Brooklyn, N.Y., Jan. 14, 1894; s. Joseph and Annie (Rosenfeld) G.; M.E., Stevens Inst. Tech., 1915; m. Elsie Stiner, Jan. 14, 1917; children—Alexander, Beatrice, Adele. Engaged in gen. practice as mech. engr., 1915-22; instr. of mathematics and science, high sch., 1922-29; supervisor manual training, pub. schs., Hoboken, N.J., since 1929. Served as mem. local adv. bd. during World War. Past pres. Industrial Arts Assn. of Hudson Co. Democrat. Jewish religion. B.P.O.E. Home: 1209 Washington St. Office: 506 Park Av., Hoboken, N.J.

GOTTSCHALL, Andrew William, clergyman; b. Adamstown, Pa., Jan. 23, 1892; s. Andrew Mussellman and Emma (Bollman) G.; student Adamstown (Pa.) Pub. Sch., 1898-1908, Perkiomen Sch. for Boys, Pennsburg, Pa., 1909-12, George Washington U., Washington, D.C., 1912-15; m. Erma Hackett, June 20, 1916; children—Dorothy Laura, Esther Grace, Andrew William, Francis Elizabeth, Everett Edward Morris. Pastor, Strauss Memorial Christian Ch., Washington, D.C., 1912-14, Ch. of Christ, Lancaster, Pa., 1914-19, Calhoun St. Christian Ch., Baltimore, Md., 1919-22; sec., Christian Missionary Soc. for Md., Del. and D.C., 1922-23; pastor, 25th St. Christian Ch., Baltimore, Md., 1923-26, First Christian Ch., Baltimore, Md., 1926-39; nat. capitol and southern area sec., Nat. Conf. of Christians and Jews, Washington, D.C., since 1935. Trustee, Lynchburg (Va.) Coll.; trustee, Md. Bible Soc. Christian Ch. Mason. Middle Atlantic Area Sec., Religious Edn. Assn.; dir. Md. Council of Chs. Lecturer before colls., univs. and state teachers colls. Home: 4921 Chevy Chase Boul., Chevy Chase, Md. Office: 721 Southern Bldg., Washington, D.C.

GOTWALS, John Elmer, physician; b. Yerkes, Pa., Oct. 17, 1882; s. John Grater and Lydiah H. (Detwiler) G.; grad. West Chester State Teachers Coll., 1902, B.Ped., 1907; M.D., U. of Pa., 1911; m. Margaret Methven, Nov. 27, 1913 (died Feb. 11, 1938); children—William Methven, Russell Lauer, John Grater, James Elmer. School teacher, 1902-06; resident physician Dionville Miners Hosp., 1911-13; in gen. practice of medicine, Phoenixville, Pa., since 1914; on surgical staff Phoenixville Hosp. since 1916, radiologist, 1915-28. Served as capt. Med. Corps, U.S. Army, at Camp Gordon, Ga., during World War. Trustee Phoenixville Hosp.; dir. Chester Co. Council Boy Scouts of America. Mem. A.M.A., Pa. State Med. Soc., Montgomery Co. Med. Soc. (trustee), Phila. Med. Club. Republican. Presbyterian. Mason. Odd Fellow. Clubs: Rotary (Phoenixville); Schuylkill Valley Medical. Address: 500 Gay St., Phoenixville, Pa.

GOUGH, John Francis, lawyer; b. Jersey City, N.J., Feb. 20, 1880; s. John Ambrose and Catharine (Mathews) G.; A.B. cum laude, Harvard U., 1902; m. Lucie M. Harney, Apr. 10, 1909 (dec.); children—John, Helen; m. 2d Elizabeth A. Kelly, Sept. 20, 1916. Studied law in law office, 1902-05; admitted to N.J. bar as atty., 1905, as counselor, 1908; supreme ct. commr., 1914; admitted to practice before the Supreme Ct. of the U.S., 1927; served as sec. Com. on Character and Fitness of Candidates from Hudson Co. for admission to bar since 1923. Mem. Hudson Co. Bar Assn. (pres. 1919-20). Honored as Officier d'Académie, 1934 (France). Democrat. Roman Catholic. Club: Harvard (New York). Translator, Letters of Baron de Vioménil on Polish Affairs, 1771-72, 1935; Life of Baron de Vioménil by Count Roger de Montmort, 1935. Author: St. Mary's in Jersey City, 1938. Home: 91 Bentley Av. Office: 26 Journal Sq., Jersey City, N.J.

GOULD, Arthur Benjamin, coll. prof.; b. Lewis Co., W.Va., Nov. 7, 1901; s. Percy Benjamin and Iva Dell (Cooper) G.; B.S., W.Va. Wesleyan Coll., Buckhannon, W.Va., 1923; M.S., Cornell U. 1926, Ph.D., 1935; unmarried. Engaged as instr. science, W.Va. Wesleyan Summer Sch., 1924-26; teacher gen. sci., high sch., Elkins, W.Va., 1924-25; prof. chemistry, Salem (W.Va.) Coll., since 1926. Mem. A.A.A.S., Am. Chem. Soc., Am. Inst. Chemists, W.Va. Acad. Science. Republican. Presbyn. Home: R.F.D. No. 3, Buckhannon, W.Va. Office: 99 W. High St., Salem, W.Va.

GOULD, Arthur Morgan, farmer, banker; b. French Creek, W.Va., Jan. 23, 1853; s. Benjamin and Eliza (Morgan) G.; ed. grammar schs.; m. Louise Sexton, Nov. 21, 1889. Engaged in farming since 1867; pres. Adrian Buckhannon Bank (formerly Bank of Adrian) since 1919. Republican. Presbyterian. Home: Adrian, W.Va. Office: Buckhannon, W.Va.

GOULD, Beatrice Blackmar, co-editor Ladies' Home Journal; b. Emmetsburg, Ia.; d. Harry E. and Mary Kathleen (Fluke) Blackmar; B.A., State U. of Ia.; M.S., Columbia U. Sch. of Journalism; m. Charles Bruce Gould; 1 dau., Sesaly. Newspaper reporter, writer and woman's editor N.Y. Sunday World, 1926-29; writer for mags., 1929-35; editor (with husband) Ladies' Home Journal since July 1, 1935. Mem. Kappa Kappa Gamma, Theta Sigma Phi. Club: Cosmopolitan (New York and Phila.). Author: (with husband) Man's Estate and The Terrible Turk (plays), 1927 and 1934. Contbr. to Saturday Evening Post, Cosmopolitan and other mags. Home: Hopewell, N.J. Address: Curtis Publishing Co., Philadelphia, Pa.

GOULD, Charles Bruce, co-editor Ladies' Home Journal; b. Luana, Iowa, July 28, 1898; s. Wilbur Samuel and Edna Earle (Davidson) G.; student Grinnell (Iowa) College, one year, 1917-18; B.A., State University of Iowa, 1922; grad. study Columbia Univ., 1923-24; m. Beatrice Blackmar, Oct. 4, 1923; 1 dau., Sesaly. Reporter Des Moines (Ia.) Tribune, 1922, New York Sun, 1923-24; reporter New York Evening Post, 1924-27, lit. editor, 1927-28, aviation editor, 1928-31; dramatic critic Wall Street News, 1927-30; asso. editor Saturday Evening Post, 1934-35. Became editor (with wife) Ladies' Home Journal, 1935. Served as ensign U.S.N.R.F. Flying Corps, 1918-19. Mem. Sigma Delta Chi, Kappa Sigma. Clubs: Players, Dutch Treat, Rittenhouse. Author: Sky Larking, 1929; Flying Dutchman, 1931; plays (with wife) Man's Estate, 1929, The Terrible Turk, 1931; movies, Reunion, 1936. Contbr. fiction to Saturday Evening Post, Cosmopolitan, Liberty, etc. Home: Hopewell, N.J. Address: Ladies' Home Journal, Philadelphia, Pa.

GOULD, Clarendon Ivan Theodore, banking; b. Oshawa, Ont., Nov. 10, 1862; s. John T. and Adelaide (Cronk) G.; came to U.S., 1887, naturalized, 1892; B.A., Victoria U. (now U. of Toronto) Can., 1884; m. Grace Purnell, June 7, 1893; children—Mary Purnell (wife of Dr. V. L. Ellicott), Theodore, Purnell, Franklin P. Engaged in practice of law at Baltimore, 1887-1902; pres. Central Trust Co. of Md., 1902-06; pres. Mutual Loan Co. (now Public Bank) Baltimore, 1912-16, dir. since 1912, hon v.p. since 1912. Pres. bd. election supervisors, 1914; police commr., 1915-16; judge state industrial accident comn., 1919. Pres. and trustee Patterson Memorial Assn. since 1894. Republican. Episcopalian (vestryman St. Paul's since 1912, registrar of parish since 1924). Club: Maryland (Baltimore). Home: 713 Park Av. Office: 15 E. Fayette St., Baltimore, Md.

GOULD, Frank, publisher; b. Baltimore, Md., June 18, 1873; s. John Robert and Amelia (Mege) G.; student Baltimore City Coll., 1885-88; m. Elma Halstead, Nov. 14, 1894; 1 dau., Minnie (Mrs. William Martz Beury). Began as office boy, Manufacturers Record Pub. Co., pubs. Manufacturers Record, Blue Book of Southern Progress, 1888, successively bookkeeper, traveling salesman, sec. and v.p. until 1929; pres., editor and prin. owner since 1930; chmn. Fleet-McGinley, Inc., printers, pubs., since 1926; dir. Baltimore Commercial Bank; dir. Md. Certificate Corpn. Mem. Am. Iron and Steel Inst. Baptist. Club: Merchants. Home: Towson, Md. Office: Commerce and Water Sts., Baltimore, Md.

GOULD, George, univ. prof.; b. East Palestine, O., Sept. 30, 1898; s. George and Isabell (Atchison) G.; B.S., Grove City Coll., 1920; Ph.D., U. of Pittsburgh, 1929; m. Kathryn B. Hosack, June 30, 1922; 1 dau., Kay. Teacher history, Grove City (Pa.) High Sch., 1920-23, Homestead (Pa.) High Sch., 1923-24, prin. of latter, 1924-29; asst. prof. edn., U. of Pittsburgh, 1929-31, asso. prof. edn. and dir. student teaching 1931-39, prof. edn., 1939. Mem. N.E.A., Pa. State Edn. Assn., Nat. Soc. for Study of Edn., Dept. of Secondary Sch. Prins.,

Phi Delta Kappa. Presbyn. Mason. Home: 33 Lakemont Drive, Mt. Lebanon, Pa.

GOULD, Justinus, lawyer; b. Germany, Aug. 12, 1901; s. Dr. Conrad and Regina Rebecca (Popper) G.; brought to U.S. at age of 1 yr.; grad. Baltimore Poly. Inst. (certificate of honor), 1921; student Johns Hopkins U., 1921-23, 1928-29, 1931; LL.B., U. of Md., 1927; S.J.D., Nat. Univ., 1934; unmarried. Admitted to Md. bar, 1927; admitted to practice before U.S. Dist. Court, 1928, U.S. Circuit Court of Appeals, 1930; practiced in Baltimore since 1927. Dem. Candidate for House of Dels. of Md., 1930; mem. Md. Dem. State Conv., 1932. Mem. Am. Bar Assn., Bar Assn. of Baltimore, Am. Judicature Soc., Md. Hist. Soc., Theta Nu Pi (chancellor 1934), Citizens Civic League (pres.), Young Peoples Dem. League (bd. govs.). Clubs: United 4th Dist. Democratic (vice-pres.), Albert C. Ritchie Civic (chmn. civic com.), Tuesday (chmn. civic com.), Sovereign Democratic, Concord. Author: The Law of Pleading in Criminal Cases, 1937. Contbr. articles to law jours. and newspapers; speaker at bar luncheon club. Home: 2108 Eutaw Place. Office: Hearst Tower Bldg., Baltimore, Md.

GOULD, Laura Stedman (Mrs. George M. Gould), author; b. New York, Feb. 18, 1881; d. Frederick Stuart and Ellen (Douglas) Stedman; g.d. Edmund Clarence Stedman; ed. Miss Brackett's Sch., New York; m. Dr. George Milbry Gould, Oct. 3, 1917 (died Aug. 8, 1922). Lit. asst. to E. C. Stedman, 1898-1908; and to George M. Gould, M.D. 1906-22; literary executor to both. Author: Bibliography of Lafcadio Hearn, 1908. Asso. editor of Stedman's Complete Poems, 1908; Life and Letters of Edmund Clarence Stedman, 1910; Genius and Other Essays (by E. C. Stedman), 1911; Mrs. Kinney's Italian Reminiscences, 1913. Life mem. Am. Mus. Natural History. Contbr. to mags. Home: 215 Atlantic City, N.J.*

GOULD, Ralph Ronald, pres. Pittsburgh Vitreous Enameling Co.; b. Midway, Pa., May 30, 1898; s. John H. and Linnie B. (Cool) G.; ed. Pittsburgh pub. schs.; m. Katherine J. Wenning, Sept. 7, 1920; children—Patricia W., John W. With Pittsburgh Vitreous Enameling Co. since 1925, pres. since 1927, also dir. Presbyterian. Home: 3217 Faronia St. Office: 745 Oliffe St., Corliss Station, Pittsburgh, Pa.

GOULD, William Drum, coll. prof.; b. Philadelphia, Pa., Aug. 8, 1897; s. William H. G. and E. Myrtle (Drum) G.; B.A., Wesleyan U., 1919; B.D., Garrett Biblical Inst., 1922; Ph.D., Boston U., 1929; m. Evelyn Davenport, Sept. 26, 1922; 1 son, William Harold. Prof. history, Ia. Wesleyan Coll.. 1929-33, coll. dean and prof. history and polit. science, 1933-37; asso. prof. history and polit. science, Dickinson Coll., since 1937. Mem. Am. Hist. Assn., Pa. Hist. Assn., Alpha Chi Rho, Phi Beta Kappa. Republican. Methodist. Mason. Contbr. Miss. Valley Hist. Review. Home: 121 W. Pomfret St., Carlisle, Pa.

GOULDEN, Harold DeWitt, cosmetics; b. Bridgeport, Conn., Sept. 28, 1900; s. Louis DeWitt and Hattie Heaton (Bennett) G.; student Franklin St. Grammar Sch., Stamford, Conn., 1906-14, Stamford (Conn.) High Sch., 1914-18; B.Sc., Rutgers U., New Brunswick, N.J., 1923; m. Mary Elizabeth Williams, June 23, 1926. Research chemist Howe Rubber Co., New Brunswick, N.J., 1923-24, E. R. Squibb & Sons, New Brunswick, 1924-27; instr. biological sciences, N.J. Coll. of Pharmacy, Rutgers U., Newark, N.J., 1927-31; dir. labs. Health Products Corpn., Newark, 1927-31; research fellow N.J. Coll. of Pharmacy, Newark, 1931-32; dir. chem. research Mennen Co., Newark, 1933-35; gen. mgr. and chief chemist Jacqueline Cochran Cosmetics, Roselle, N.J., since 1935. Fellow A.A.A.S., Am. Pharm. Assn.; Scabbard and Blade, Phi Lambda Upsilon, Kappa Psi, Kappa Sigma. Republican. Dutch Reformed. Home: 57 Cobane Terrace, West Orange, N.J. Office: 1203 Chandler Av., Roselle, N.J.

GOURLEY, W. Clyde, realtor; b. Woodbury, N.J., June 23, 1895; s. Walter and Annie (Yetter) G.; student Singerly Pub. Sch., Phila., Peirce Business Sch., Phila.; m. Dorothy I. Darrah, Sept. 13, 1919; children—Roberta, Walter Clyde, John, Jane. Became real estate rent collector for Thomas A. McCorkel & Co., Atlantic City, N.J., 1910; removed to Willow Grove, Pa., and entered partnership with Wm. P. Albrecht; firm incorporated as Albrecht & Gourley, 1924, and changed to W. Clyde Gourley Inc., 1930; pres. Overlook Hills Bldg. & Loan Assn.; v.p. Montgomery County Real Estate Bd. Republican. Presbyn. Mem. Phila. Real Estate Bd. Club: Jenkintown (Pa.) Rotary. Home: 22 Edgely Av., Glenside, Pa. Office: York and Welsh Roads, Willow Grove, Pa.

GOW, J(ames) Steele, foundation exec.; b. Pittsburgh, Jan. 3, 1895; s. Harry Campbell and Elizabeth Gray (Steele) G.; ed. Pittsburgh Academy, 1909-12; A.B., cum laude, U. of Pittsburgh, 1916, LL.D., 1938; Ed.M., Harvard, 1927; m. Hazel Evelyn Steele, May 10, 1917; children—James Steele, Don Wallace, Robert Campbell. With U. of Pittsburgh since 1916, successively head dept. of pub. relations, until 1918, financial sec., 1918-20, asst. to pres., 1920-24, exec. sec. of the Univ., 1924-29, dean of administration, 1929; exec. dir. Falk Foundation, Pittsburgh, since 1930. Austin fellow in edn., Harvard, 1924-25; lecturer on edn. sociology, U. of Pittsburgh, since 1925. Instr. O.T.S., U.S.A., 1918; sec. Bd. of Hospitalization for War Vets. (U.S. Treasury Dept.), 1920. Mem. research com. President Hoover's Conf. on Home Bldg. and Home Ownership; mem. bd. trustees Falk Med. Clinic, Children's Service Bureau; mem. advisory bd. Allegheny County Juvenile Court. Mem. Nat. Com. for Mental Hygiene, Council on Foreign Affairs, Sigma Alpha Epsilon, Omicron Delta Kappa, Pi Tau Alpha. Republican. Baptist. Mason. Clubs: Harvard of Western Pa., Longue Vue. Home: 222 Gladstone Rd. Office: Farmers Bank Bldg., Pittsburgh, Pa.

GOWEN, James Emmet, banker; b. Phila., Apr. 22, 1895; s. Francis Innes and Alice (Robinson) G.; grad. St. Paul's Sch., Concord, N.H., 1913; A.B., Princeton U., 1917, LL.B., U. of Pa., 1921; m. Sally Drexel Henry, June 25, 1925; children—Francis Innes, Howard Henry. Admitted to Pa. bar, 1921; legal dept., Pa. R.R. Co., Phila., 1921-30; v.p. Phila. Saving Fund Soc., 1930-33; pres. Western Saving Fund, Phila., 1933-39; pres. and mem. bd. mgrs. Girard Trust Co. since 1939; mem. bd. mgrs. Western Saving Fund Soc.; dir. Penn Mutual Life Ins. Co., Ins. Co. of N.A., Indemnity Ins. Co. of N.A., Alliance Ins. Co., Phila. Fire & Marine Ins. Co., United Firemen's Ins. Co., Muskogee Co. Served as ensign, U.S. Navy, during World War. Trustee Drexel Inst. Tech. Democrat. Episcopalian. Clubs: Philadelphia, Rabbit, Sunnybrook (Phila.). Home: Chestnut Hill, Philadelphia. Office: Girard Trust Co., Philadelphia, Pa.

GRABACH, John R., artist and teacher; b. Greenfield, Mass., 1900; s. John R. and Genouefa (Asam) G.; student Art Students League, New York; unmarried. Instr. Newark (N.J.) Sch. of Fine and Industrial Art since 1929. Exhibited: Art Institute of Chicago; Vanderpoel Art Assn., Chicago; John Herron Art Inst., Indianapolis, Ind.; Philadelphia Art Alliance; Biro-Bidjan, Russia. Awarded: Peabody Prize, Art Inst. of Chicago, 1926; Sesnan Gold Medal, Pa. Acad. of Fine Arts, 1927; Preston Harrison Prize, Los Angeles Mus., Calif., 1931; The Corcoran Silver Medal, Corcoran Gallery of Art, Washington, D.C., 1932. Address: 915 Sanford Av., Irvington, N.J.

GRABER, Henry, M.D.; b. Steinsville, Pa., June 10, 1880; s. Dr. James D. and Emma E. (Keeler) G.; student Royersford (Pa.) High Sch., 1894-98; A.B., Ursinus Coll., Collegeville, Pa., 1903; M.D., Johns Hopkins U., Baltimore, Md., 1907; m. Arvilla Whiteman, June 10, 1911; children—Jeanne Bernice, Martha Whiteman, Margaret Jane. Began as physician, 1907; interne Presbyn. Hosp., Phila., 1907-09, chief resident physician, 1909-10; practiced at Royersford, Pa., since 1910; dir. Nat. Bank of Royersford, Pa. Pres. and sch.

bd. dir. Royersford (Pa.) Sch. Dist. Mem. Montgomery Co. Med. Soc. (pres. 1939). Fellow A.M.A. Republican. Mem. Reformed Ch. Mason (Royersford, Pa., 585). Address: 454 Walnut St., Royersford, Pa.

GRACE, Eugene Gifford, steel mfr.; b. Goshen, N.J., Aug. 27, 1876; s. John W. and Rebecca (Morris) G.; E.E., Lehigh University, 1899, D. Engring, same University, 1927; m. Marion Brown, June 12, 1902; children—Emmeline Marion, Charles Brown, Eugene Gifford. With Bethlehem Steel Co. since June 29, 1899, beginning in charge of an electric crane; supt. yards and transportation, 1902-05; gen. supt. Juraga Iron Co. (subsidiary co.), 1905-06; gen. supt. Bethlehem Steel Co., 1906-08; elected gen. mgr. same, and mem. bd. dirs., 1908; apptd. v.p. and gen. mgr., Bethlehem Steel Co., and elected dir. Bethlehem Steel Corpn., 1911; pres. Bethlehem Steel Co. since Apr. 1, 1913; pres. Bethlehem Steel Corpn. since Feb. 17, 1916; pres. Bethlehem Shipbuilding Corpn. since Oct. 30, 1917. Active during war period in supplying cannon, ammunition, armor plate and ships to War and Navy Depts. Trustee Lehigh U., St. Luke's Hosp. (Bethlehem). Mem. Am. Iron and Steel Inst. (dir.), Iron and Steel Inst. of Great Britain, Am. Inst. Mining and Metall. Engrs., Soc. Arts and Sciences (New York). Presbyn. Clubs: Metropolitan, Bankers of America (New York); Maryland (Baltimore); etc. Recreation golf; won Hay cup, 1917, in Northampton County Country Club Tournament; won the cup, 1919, in the Shawnee Fall Tournament; won Saucon Valley Country Club championship, 1928. Home: 12th and Prospect Avs., Bethlehem, Pa. Address: Bethlehem Steel Corpn., New York, N.Y.

GRACE, John Francis, mech. engring.; b. Liverpool, Eng., Dec. 17, 1880; s. Richard Raleigh and Mary Anne (Fitzpatrick) G.; brought to U.S., 1884, naturalized, 1891; ed. pub. schs. and high sch., Brooklyn, N.Y.; m. Adele Marie Hague, apr. 26, 1913; children—Adele Marie (Mrs. Walter Russell Lane), Marion Louise, Richard Hague, Jeanette Rita. In employ Worthington Pump and Machinery Corpn. and predecessors, Harrison, N.J., continuously since 1897, successively machinist, tool maker, tester, draftsman, designing mech. engr. and inventor; awarded forty patents upon condensers, pumps and meters. Mem. Am. Soc. Mech. Engrs. since 1915. Independent Democrat. Roman Catholic. Home: 24 Alpine Pl., Arlington. Office: Harrison, N. J.

GRACIE, William Anderson; mem. staff Memorial Hosp.; visiting surgeon Allegany Hosp. of Sisters of Charity, Cumberland, Md., Miners Hosp., Frostburg, Md., and Somerset Community Hosp., Somerset, Md. Address: 122 S. Centre St., Cumberland, Md.

GRAF, Julius E., mech. engr.; b. Pittsburgh, Pa., Aug. 23, 1891; s. Henry and Elizabeth (Theis) G.; ed. Caton Tech. Sch. and (nights) Carnegie Inst. Tech.; m. Mabelle Bliss, Oct. 2, 1912; children—Florence E., Norman T. Began as shipping clerk Graham Nut & Bolt Co., 1908; engring. draftsman, chief engr. Am. Sheet & Tin Plate Co., 1911-36; asst. chief engr. Carnegie-Illinois Steel Corpn., 1936-39; vice-pres. Treadwell Engring. Co. since 1939. Mem. Am. Soc. M.E., Am. Iron & Steel Inst., Engrs. Soc. of Western Pa. Republican. Methodist. Club: Duquesne (Pittsburgh). Home: 1019 Hamilton Av., Avalon, Pa. Office: 2113 Farmers Bank Bldg., Pittsburgh, Pa.

GRAFF, F. Malcolm, banker; b. Blairsville, Pa., May 1, 1899; s. Frank M. and Anna P. Graff; grad. Lafayette Coll., 1922; m. Julia Westman, Oct. 24, 1925; 1 son, F. Malcolm. Clerk in coal company office, 1922-26; gen. mgr. Westmoreland Mining Co., 1926-28; v.p. Blairsville Savings & Trust Co., 1928-36, pres. since 1936; pres. Westmoreland Mining Co.; v.p. Braeburn Alloy Steel Corpn. Republican. Episcopalian. Clubs: Art, Union League (Philadelphia). Home: 286 S. Walnut St. Office: 1 Market St., Blairsville, Pa.

GRAFF, George Washington, life insurance; b. York, Pa., Dec. 23, 1894; s. Charles W. and Emma J. (Diehl) G.; B.S., Pa. State Coll., 1916, C.E., same, 1921; C.L.U., Am. Coll. Life Underwriters, 1938; m. Ethel M. Harner, May 11, 1918; children—Vivian Winifred, George Harner. Began as water works chemist and bacteriologist, 1916; field engr. Pitometer Co., New York, 1917; field engr. Simplex Valve & Meter Co., 1920; production engr., Martin Perry Corpn., 1921-25; splty. salesman, 1925-26; engaged in underwriting life ins. since 1927. Served in arty. O.T.S., 1918. Mem. Nat., Pa. State, and York Life underwriters assns., Nat. Assn. Chartered Life Underwriters, Am. Legion, Phi Kappa Phi. Republican. Episcopalian. Mason (32°). Home: 318 Reinecke Pl. Office: 15 E. Market St., York, Pa.

GRAFF, Richard Morris, manufacturer; b. Worthington, Pa., June 30, 1900; s. John Francis and Carrie Louise (Brown) G.; student Blair Acad., Blairstown, N.J., 1915-19; E.M., Lehigh U., Bethlehem, Pa., 1923; m. Elizabeth W. Mayers, Sept. 10, 1930. Began as engr. Graff Kittanning Clay Products Co., Worthington, Pa., 1924-25, gen. mgr., 1925-29, pres. since 1929; partner Craigsville Supply Co.; dir. and sec. Peter Graff & Co., Inc. Mem. Chi Psi. Republican. Lutheran. Mason (32°), Elk, Odd Fellow. Club: Kittanning (Pa.) Country. Address: Worthington, Pa.

GRAFLY, Dorothy, writer; b. of Am. parents, Paris, France, July 29, 1896; d. Charles and Frances (Sekeles) G.; brought to U.S. in infancy; B.A., Wellesley, 1918; grad. work under Prof. George P. Baker, of Harvard, 1918-19. Art critic Phila. North American, 1920-25; art editor and editorial and feature writer same, 1925; art editor Public Ledger, Phila., 1925-34; art critic Evening Public Ledger, 1934; art editor Phila. Record since Oct. 1934; special correspondent Christian Science Monitor; Phila. correspondent Am. Mag. of Art to 1928; mem. advisory board "Prints"; curator of collections, Drexel Inst., Phila., since 1934; lecturer on art, Temple Univ., 1938-39. Member Art Alliance (Phila.), Alumnæ assn. of Wellesley Coll., 47 Club (Harvard), Pi Gamma Mu. Clubs: Contemporary, Art Alliance, New Century Guild (Phila.), The Durant (Boston); Phila. Altrusa (charter mem.; pres. 1930-32), Nat. Travel, Nat. Geographic. Wrote and produced Masque of Night; Masque of Life; The Phœnix; Metamorphosis; Images—all prod. Gloucester, Mass., 1914-20; winner prize for one-act play, Plays and Players' Club, Phila., 1921. Author: History of the Philadelphia Print Club, 1929; also series of articles dealing with living European sculptors. Contbr. Dictionary of American Biography; Encyclopedia Britannica and to mags. Lecturer on art. One of 6 Am. critics invited by Chicago Art Inst. to broadcast over nat. hook-up at opening of 1934 Century of Progress Expn. Art Exhbn. Home: 131 N. 20th St., Philadelphia, Pa.; (summer) Lanesville, Mass.

GRAHAM, Albert D.; chmn. bd. First Nat. Bank of Baltimore. Home: Lutherville, Md. Address: Light and Redwood Sts., Baltimore, Md.

GRAHAM, Arthur Kenneth, cons. engr.; b. Philadelphia, Pa., Dec. 25, 1896; s. Clarence Moore and Mary Virginia (Fox) G.; B.S. in Chem. Engring., U. of Pa., 1919, M.S., 1924. Chem. E., 1923, Ph.D., 1927; m. Marion Braungard, Sept. 8, 1931; 1 son, Arthur Hughes. With Scovill Mfg. Co., Waterbury, Conn., 1919-20, Welsbach Co., Gloucester, N.J., 1920-21; instr. chemistry, U. of Pa., 1921-26; chem. engr. Hanson Van Winkle Munning Co., Matawan, N.J., 1926-28; instr. chem. engring., U. of Pa., 1928-34, asst. prof., 1934-37; consultant A. Kenneth Graham & Associates since 1937. Mem. Am. Chem. Soc., Am. Electro-Platers Soc., Am. Inst. Chem. Engrs., Electrochem. Soc. (mgr. 1935-38, v.p. 1938-40); Electrodepositors Tech. Soc. (British); Assn. of Consulting Chemists and Chem. Engrs. (dir. 1937-40); Philadelphia Inst. Chemists and Chem. Engrs. (pres. 1938-39); Sigma Xi, Sigma Tau, Alpha Chi Sigma, Delta Sigma Phi. Democrat. Baptist. Club: Chemists. Writer numerous articles on electrodeposition of metals, structure of electrodeposits, etc. Awarded patent on zinc anode composition. Home: 632 E. Wadsworth St., Philadelphia, Pa. Office: Medical Arts Bldg., Jenkintown, Pa.

GRAHAM, Ben George, supt. schools; b. East Moravia, Pa., May 18, 1880; s. Benjamin and Caroline (Palmer) G.; A.B., Westminster Coll., Pa., 1904, A.M., 1908, Sc.D., 1924; M.A., Univ. of Pittsburgh, 1925, LL.D., 1932; LL.D., Juniata College, 1934; m. Zelma Burroughs, June 7, 1908; children—Ben G., Burns, Betty, Harriet Inez, John Muir, David, Paul, Ella Ruth. Teacher, Lawrence Co., Pa., 1900-03, high sch., McKeesport, Pa., 1903-07; prin. high sch., Greensburg, Pa., 1907-09; teacher of chemistry, Central High Sch., Pittsburgh, 1909-16; prin. Latimer Jr. High Sch., Pittsburgh, 1916-19; supt. schs., New Castle, Pa., 1919-26; asso. supt. schs., Pittsburgh, 1926-27, first asso. supt., 1927-30, supt. since 1930. Mem. N.E.A., Am. Assn. of Sch. Adminstrs., Pa. State Edn. Assn., Phi Delta Kappa, Omicron Delta Kappa. Republican. United Presbyn. Mason. Clubs: University, Rotary (Pittsburgh); Alcoma Country. Contbr. to ednl. periodicals. Home: 5614 Woodmont St. Office: 341 Bellefield Av., Pittsburgh, Pa.

GRAHAM, Edwin Eldon, pediatrist; b. Phila., Pa., Feb. 28, 1864; s. Archibald Hunter (M.D.) and Eliza J. (Sampson) G.; Harvard, 1882-84; M.D., Jefferson Med. Coll., 1887; interne, Phila. Hosp., 1887-88; studied, Göttingen, Berlin and Munich, 1888-89; m. Lorraine Goodrich, Jan. 2, 1893. Prof. diseases of children, Jefferson Med. Coll., since 1899; pediatrist, Phila. Hosp., 1903-18. Mem. A.M.A., Med. Soc. State of Pa., Am. Pediatric Soc., Phila. Pediatric Soc. Presbyn. Clubs: Rittenhouse, Merion Cricket, Mill Dam. Address: 1713 Spruce St., Philadelphia, Pa.

GRAHAM, Frank Dunstone, economist; b. of Am. parents, Halifax, N.S., Jan. 1, 1890; s. George and Jessie (Woodill) G.; B.A., Dalhousie U., 1913, LL.B., 1915; A.M., Harvard, 1917, Ph.D., 1920; m. Mary Louise Power, Sept. 14, 1920; children—Frank Dunstan, Hugh, John. Instr. in economics, Rutgers Coll., 1917-20; with R.O.T.C., 1917-19; asst. prof. economics, Dartmouth, 1920-21; with Princeton U. since 1921, asst. prof. economics, until 1925, asso. prof., 1925-30, prof. since 1930. Sec. Am. Commn. Financial Advisers to Poland, 1926; economic adviser to Business Men's Commn. on Agr., 1927; Guggenheim fellow, Germany, 1927-28; economic adviser, Federal Farm Bd., 1930-31; prof. of internat. economics, Institut Universitaire de Hautes Etudes Internationales, Geneva, Switzerland, 1931-32; mem. of the Commission on Cuban Affairs, 1934; Oberlaender Trust fellow, 1936, Knight Order of Polonia Restituta. Mem. American Economic Association, American Assn. for Labor Legislation, Am. Assn. Univ. Profs. Unitarian. Club: Princeton (New York). Author: Exchange, Prices and Production in Hyper-Inflation, Germany (1920-23), 1930; The Abolition of Unemployment, 1932; Protective Tariffs, 1934; Money (with C. H. Seaver), 1936; Banking (with C. H. Seaver), 1937; also writer on agriculture, money, finance and internat. trade. Home: 214 Western Way, Princeton, N.J.

GRAHAM, John Charles, lawyer; b. Butler, Pa., Oct. 8, 1868; s. Walter Lowry and Margaret Ann (Zimmerman) G.; student Lafayette Coll., 1890-91; m. Lovey Ayres, Dec. 6, 1894 (dec.); children—Elizabeth D. Walter (dec.), John C., Margaret Louise; m. 2d, Elizabeth Wilson, July 3, 1913. Newsboy, 1879-87; admitted to Butler County, Pa., bar, 1894, to all other cts. of Pa., 1906; atty. at various times for banking instns.; now serves as counsel for all large circuses showing in Pa.; organizer and since pres. Allegheny Foundry & Machine Co.; operator of Graham mines. Served in N.G. Pa., 10 yrs., retiring as adjutant. Apptd. by Gov. Brumbaugh of Pa. to First League of Nations Congress in New York, presided over by former President Taft. Decorated by Albert-King of Belgium for War Work, 1922. Vice Butler Bd. of Trade, 1900-06. Mem. Pa. Soc. of N.Y., Phi Gamma Delta. Mason (K.T., Shriner), Odd Fellow. Republican. Presbyterian. Clubs: Bankers (New York), Pittsburgh Athletic. Author: Historical Recollection of

Butler (65 years ago); also various articles for newspapers. Home: 230 N. McKean St. Office: Graham Bldg., Butler, Pa.

GRAHAM, John Howard, chemist; b. Phila., Pa., Dec. 29, 1880; s. Jonathan Wesley and Anna Elizabeth (Mifflin) G.; A.B., Central High Sch., 1898; B.S., U. of Pa., 1902, A.M., same, 1927; m. Lillian Mae Cogswell, June 19, 1906; children—Marguerite Rae (Mrs. Robert G. Wetmore), Dorothy Cogswell (Mrs. David C. Miller), Ruth Eleanor (Mrs. Herbert S. Simons), Lois Adele, Janet Mae. Began as chief chemist, Spanish-American Iron Co., Daiquiri, Cuba, 1902; teacher chemistry, Central High Sch., Phila., also Drexel, Central, Frankford, Mastbaum, and Germantown evening schs. and Central High Summer Sch., 1903-30; chemist, Smith, Kline, French Co., Henry K. Wampole Co.; consultant Central Ry. Signal Co. Prof. and head of dept., of organic chemistry and physics, Temple U. Pharmacy Sch. since 1926. Trustee, Phila. Sect. Am. Chem. Soc.; trustee Philadelphia North Presbytery. Mem. Am. Chem. Soc., Am. Pharm. Assn., Pa. Bee Assn., Sigma Xi. Republican. Presbyn. Mason (32°, Shriner). Home: 7 Cliveden Av., Glenside, Montgomery, Co., Pa. Office: 1808 Spring Garden St., Philadelphia, Pa.

GRAHAM, Kelley, banking; b. Austin, Tex., Jan. 3, 1889; s. Lucien and Katherine Elizabeth (Field) G.; grad. Ogden Coll., Bowling Green, Ky., 1907; student U. of Va.; m. Valerie Atherton, Oct. 14, 1914; children—John MacDougall Atherton, Mary Goodenow. Began with 1st Nat. Bank, Louisville, 1908; vice-pres. Irving Nat. Bank (now Irving Trust Co.) N.Y. City, 1919-23; pres. 1st Nat. Bank, Jersey City, N.J., since 1925; pres., dir. Hoboken Land & Improvement Co., Hoboken Dock Co., Hoboken R.R., Warehouse & Steamship Connecting Co.; dir. Hackensack Water Co., Spring Valley Water Co. Trustee Stevens-Hoboken Acad., Indian Mountain Sch., Lakeville, Conn.; dir. N.J. State Chamber of Commerce, Jersey City Chamber of Commerce, Hoboken Chamber of Commerce. Mem. Soc. Colonial Wars, Pilgrims Soc., St. Nicholas Soc. of New York. Episcopalian. Clubs: Carteret (Jersey City); Church, Union, City Midday, Racquet & Tennis (New York); Metropolitan (Washington). Home: 1021 Park Av., New York, N.Y. Office: 1 Exchange Place, Jersey City, N.J.

GRAHAM, Louis Edward, lawyer; b. New Castle, Lawrence Co., Pa., Aug. 4, 1880; s. Lewis and Elizabeth (Carter) G.; prep. edn., high sch., Beaver, Pa.; A.B., Washington and Jefferson Coll., 1901; unmarried. Admitted to Pa. bar, 1906 and began practice at Beaver, Pa.; deputy sheriff Beaver County, 1903-06; dist. atty. Beaver County, 1912-24; spl. dep. atty. gen. of Pa., 1924-26; chief legal advisor 6th Federal Prohibition Dist., 1926-29; U.S. atty. Western Dist. of Pa., Nov. 7, 1929-Sept. 1, 1933; now in practice at Beaver, Pa.; spl. asst. to the Attorney Gen. of U.S., 1934-35. Mem. 76th Congress (1939-41), 26th Dist. of Pa. Republican. Methodist. Mason. Odd Fellow, K.P. Home: 328 East End Av., Beaver, Pa.

GRAHAM, Robert Xavier, prof. journalism; b. Moosic, Pa., Mar. 26, 1901; s. James and Catherine (Drexel) G.; A.B., Colgate U., 1925; A.M., U. of Wis., 1933; grad. study U. of Pittsburgh, 1935-36; m. Eleanor Kathryn Warner, Nov. 21, 1931. Engaged as instr., asst. prof., then prof. English and journalism, Westminster Coll., 1925-35, also dir. of publicity, 1926-35, track and cross country coach, 1932-35, asst. athletic dir., 1933-35, editor Westminster Alumni News, 1933-35; prof. journalism and dir. publicity, U. of Pittsburgh since 1935; served in various capacities on papers and mags., 1919-35. Mem. Am. Coll. Publicity Assn. (nat. editor 1934-38, nat. pres. 1938-39), Assn. Coll. Teachers of Journalism, Kappa Delta Rho, Pi Delta Epsilon, Tau Gamma Delta, Gorgon's Head, Druids, Omicron Delta Kappa. Vet. Scout, Boy Scouts of America. Republican. Presbyn. Club: Faculty. Home: 2333 McNary Boul., Blackridge Estates, Wilkinsburg, Pa.

GRAHAM, William Clinton, high sch. prin.; b. North East, Md., Feb. 7, 1907; s. William C. and Ada (Robinson) G.; A.B., Univ. of Md., 1927; student Univ. of Md. summers 1929-32, and 36; m. Bessie Baliff, July 16, 1930; children—Isabelle Kennedy (adopted), William Jacob. Engaged in teaching, high sch., North East, Md., 1927-31; prin. high sch., Deal Island, Md., 1931-38; prin. high sch., Rising Sun, Md. since 1938. Mem. N.E.A., Cecil County Teachers Assn., Md. State Teachers Assn. Democrat. Methodist. Mem. O.U.A.M. Clubs: Lions. Home: Cherry St., Rising Sun, Md.

GRAINGER, Isaac Bates, pres. Montclair Trust Co.; b. Wilmington, N.C., Jan. 15, 1895; s. John Victor and Katie (Reston) G.; student Woodberry Forest (Va.) Sch., 1909-13, Princeton U., 1913-15; m. Catherine Garrett, Aug. 4, 1917; children—Isaac Bates, William Garrett, John Victor, III. Began as banker, Murchison Nat. Bank, Wilmington, N.C., 1915; asst. cashier and v.p. Murchison Nat. Bank, Wilmington, N.C., 1919-29; exec. v.p. N.C. Bank & Trust Co., Greensboro, N.C., 1929-33, conservator, 1933-34; pres. Montclair (N.J.) Trust Co. since 1934. Served as capt., Inf., U.S. Army, during World War. Mem. Acad. Polit. Science, New York Chamber of Commerce, Metropolitan Golf Assn. (exec. com.), Tiger Inn (Princeton U.). Independent Republican. Episcopalian. Clubs: Montclair Golf, Rotary (Montclair, N.J.); Princeton, Economic (New York). Home: 3 S. Mountain Terrace. Office: 475 Bloomfield Av., Montclair, N.J.

GRAMLEY, Dale Hartzler, asso. prof. journalism; b. Loganville, Pa., Sept. 23, 1905; s. Andrew Daniel and Ada Laura (Meals) G.; A.B., Albright Coll., 1926; M.S., Columbia, 1929; m. Caroline Lois Illick, Dec. 27, 1929; children—Hugh Andrew, William Eugene, Dale Illick. Employed as reporter, copyreader, asst. editor York (Pa.) Dispatch, 1926-28; copydesk, N.Y. Journal of Commerce, 1929; instr. in journalism, 1929-33, Lehigh U., asst. prof., 1933-35, asso. prof. since 1935, dir. courses in journalism since 1931, University News Editor since 1936, actg. dir. Lehigh summer session, 1938-39. Served as pub. dir. Bethlehem Community Chest. Trustee Albright Coll. and Evang. Sch. of Theology, Reading, Pa. Mem. Am. Assn. Univ. Profs., Am. Assn. Teachers of Journalism, Intercoll. Newspaper Assn. of Middle Atlantic States (exec. treas.), Pa. Hist. Soc., Lehigh U. Scholastic Press Conf. (dir.), Tau Kappa Alpha, Pi Delta Epsilon, Pi Gamma Mu, Kappa Upsilon Phi. Republican. Evang. Ch. Home: 34 W. Church St., Bethlehem, Pa.

GRAMMER, Carl Eckhardt, clergyman; b. Smyrna, Del., Nov. 11, 1858; s. Julius Eckhardt (D.D.) and Elizabeth Anne (Sparrow) G.; A.B., Johns Hopkins University, 1880; grad. P.E. Theological Sem. in Va., 1884; S.T.D., Trinity Coll., Conn., 1895; m. Mary W. Page, July 3, 1889; children—Mrs. Elizabeth Torrey, Mary Page, Mrs. Dorothy Croyder. Deacon, 1884, priest, 1885, P.E. Ch.; rector Hancock, Md., 1884-87, Ch. of the Epiphany, Walnut Hills, Cincinnati, O., 1887; prof. ch. history, P.E. Theol. Sem. in Va., 1887-98; rector Christ Ch., Norfolk, Va., 1898-1905, St. Stephen's Ch., Phila., Pa., 1905-36, rector emeritus, 1937; deputy to Gen. Conv. P.E. Ch., 1895, 1901, 04, 07, 10, editor P.E. Review (now defunct), 1890-98; pres. Inter Church Federation of Philadelphia, 1918-20, president Evangelical Educational Society; emeritus pres. Bd. of Sweet Brial Coll., Va. Member Phi Beta Kappa, Beta Theta Pi. Mason. Clubs: Union League (Phila.); Old Guard (Summit, N.J.). Author of Bohlen lectures for 1928, entitled Things That Remain, etc., and of numerous pamphlets on religious and humanitarian topics, also mag. articles and a history of St. Stephen's Club. Contbg. editor Chronicle. Home: 6 Valley View Av., Summit, N.J.

GRANOWITZ, Abram Maurice, rabbi; b. Pittsburgh, Pa., Jan. 10, 1909; s. Samuel Philip and Sarah Hannah (Goldman) G.; A.B., U. of Pittsburgh, 1929; teacher's certificate, Hebrew Inst. of Pittsburgh, 1929; Rabbi and M.H.L., Jewish Inst. of Religion, New York, N.Y., 1933; m. Rose Vera Block, June 6, 1931. Has served as rabbi Beth Zion Temple, Johnstown, Pa. since 1933. Mem. Oral Examining Bd. Pa. Dept. Pub. Assistance. Active in Community Chest, Red Cross and gen. community affairs; dir. Family Welfare Soc. of Johnstown, Pa. Mem. nat. administrative com. Zionist Orgn. of America, Central Conf. American Rabbis, Alumni Assn. Jewish Inst. of Religion; mem. nat. exec. com. Am. Jewish Congress. Mem. exec. com. Johnstown Peace Council. Club: World Affairs. Home: 628 Napoleon St. Office: 416 Vine St., Johnstown, Pa.

GRANT, Catharine Harley, artist; b. Pittsburgh, Pa., Jan. 27, 1897; d. Horace Ellison and Kate Harley (Blackstock) G.; grad. Thurston Prep. Sch., 1914; ed. Vassar Coll., 1914-16; grad. Pa. Acad. Fine Arts, 1921; student U. of Pa. Sch. Fine Arts, 1933-35. Engaged in profession as artist since 1922, specializing as figure, portrait and landscape painter in both oil and water color; exhibited at Pa. Acad. Fine Arts, Phila., Art Club, Phila., State Mus., Harrisburg, Scranton (Pa.) Mus., Mus. Art, Baltimore, Md., Art Mus., Cincinnati; represented in permanent collections of U. of Pa., Central High Sch., Phila., Pa. Sch. of Social Work, and also pvt. collections; teacher of art, Holman Sch., Ardmore, Pa., 1921-25, pub. schs. Del. Co., 1930-33; dir. Harrisburg Art. Assn. since 1937. Awarded Cresson Traveling Scholarship, Pa. Acad. Fine Arts. Home: 500 E. Willow Grove Av., Philadelphia, Pa. Studio: 500 Race St., Harrisburg, Pa.

GRANT, William Henry, brick mfr.; b. Circleville, O., Oct. 8, 1888; s. William Vernor and Eleanor Virginia (van Swearingen) G.; student grade schs., Jackson Twp., Pickaway Co., O., 1896-1900, Circleville (O.) grade sch., 1900-02, High Sch., 1902-06; Ceramic Engr., Ohio State U., Columbus, O., 1912; m. Lura D. Miller, Dec. 11, 1916; children—Eleanor Virginia, Mary Elizabeth Ceramic engr., Elk Fire Brick Co., St. Mary's, Pa., 1913-16, sales and order dept., 1916-29; sales mgr., Kane Brick & Tile Co., mfrs. of clay products, St. Mary's, Pa., 1929-38, gen. mgr., sec. and treas. since 1938; dir. and v.p. St. Mary's (Pa.) Savings & Loan Assn. Served as sergeant Ohio Nat. Guard, 1912-14. V.p. and treas. St. Mary's (Pa.) Sch. Bd., 1934-36; dir. St. Mary's Community Chest (pres. 1935-36). Mem. Am. Ceramic Soc., Phi Kappa Psi. Republican. Presbyterian. Mason (32°, St. Mary's Temple Club). Home: 470 Chestnut St. Office: Dimitri Bldg., St. Marys, Pa.

GRANT, William Thomas, merchant; b. Stevensville, Pa., June 27, 1876; s. William T. and Amanda Louise (Bird) G.; ed. high sch., Malden, Mass.; m. Lena Blanche Brownell, Oct. 5, 1907; children—Helen (Mrs. E. Vernon Biddle, Jr.), Marian (Mrs. John R. Henry); m. 2d, Beth Bradshaw, September 3, 1930; 1 child, Shirley. Founder, 1906, now chairman of the board W. T. Grant Company, chain of department stores. Mem. American Acad. Political Science, 250 Associates of Harvard Business Sch., N.E. Historic Geneal. Soc. Clubs: Wilmington Country (Wilmington, Del.); Everglades, Bath & Tennis (Palm Beach, Fla.); Woods Hole Golf (Mass.); Town Hall, Knollwood, New York Yacht (New York). Home: Ashland, Del. Office: 707 Market St., Wilmington, Del.

GRAPER, Elmer D(iedrich), univ. prof.; b. Princeton, Ind., June 24, 1885; s. August D. and Alvina (Luhring) G.; A.B., North Central Coll., Naperville, Ill., 1911; Ph.D., Columbia U., 1921; m. Ada Leffler, Sept. 2, 1913; children—Marian Louise, Nancy Loanne. Instr. history and govt., Bradley Poly. Inst., Peoria, Ill., 1911-16; instr. govt., Columbia U., 1919-23; asst. prof. polit. science, U. of Pittsburgh, 1923-24, asso. prof., 1924-25, prof. since 1925, head dept. since 1930. Chmn. Police Research Commn., City of Pittsburgh, 1934-36; mem. Gov.'s Com. on Constl. Revision, 1935; mem. Allegheny Co. Bd. for Assessment and Revision of Taxes, 1936-37. Author: American Police Administration, 1921; also articles in various publs. Home: 215 Elm St., Edgewood. Address: University of Pittsburgh, Pittsburgh, Pa.

GRAPIN, Camille, coll. prof.; b. Savigny-Les-Beaune, France, Aug. 4, 1886; s. Etienne and Anastasie (Goby) G.; student Ecole Nationale Supérieure des Beaux-Arts de Paris; unmarried.

Apptd. architecte des Batiments Civils et des Palais Nationaux, 1921; employed various offices in Milan, Italy, and Paris; became chief of design faculty for Dept. of Architecture, Carnegie Inst. Tech., 1923, now prof. architecture. Awarded: Muller-Schoenee Prize, Grande Médaille d'Emulation, Prix Jean-Leclere, The Prix Labarre, Prix Chenavard, Prix Abel Blouet, Prix Stillman, Prix St. Agnan Boucher, Prix Roux by Ecole Nationale des Beaux-Arts de Paris; Fondation Detors and Fonation Chaplain by Société Centrale des Architectes Français; travelling scholarship on sketches by magazine, l'Architecte, 1913; mention with "encouragement spécial" at Salon des Artistes Français, 1921; Deuxieme Grand Prix de Rome of The French Institute, 1920. Mem. Société des Artistes Français. Has travelled by airplane to Mexico, Guatemala and Russia. Painter of water-colors. Home: Henry St., Pittsburgh, Pa.

GRASSELLI, Thomas Saxton, mfr.; b. Cleveland, O., Nov. 14, 1874; s. Caesar A. and Johanna (Ireland) G.; ed. Mt. Saint Mary's Coll., Emmitsburg, Md.; m. Emilie Smith, May 29, 1899; children—Caesar A. II, Thomas Fries, Harry Williams. Engaged in chem. mfg., since 1893; pres. The Grasselli Chemical Co., 1916-36, when co. became div. of E. I. duPont de Nemours & Co., v.p. and dir. latter co. Captain 1st Ohio Vol. Cav., Spanish-Am. War, 1898, later capt. q.m. dept. Mem. Ohio Soc. of New York, Cleveland Chamber Commerce. Republican. Catholic. Clubs: Union, Chagrin Valley Hunt, Kirtland Country, The Country (Cleveland); Vicmead Hunt, Wilmington Club, Wilmington Country (Wilmington); Chemists (New York). Home: 2775 S. Park Boul., Shaker Heights, Cleveland. Office: DuPont Bldg., Wilmington, Del.

GRAVATT, William Loyall, bishop; b. Port Royal, Va., Dec. 15, 1858; s. Dr. John James and Mary Eliza (Smith) G.; ed. Blacksburg Mil. Coll.; grad. Va. Theol. Sem., 1884; D.D., Washington and Lee U., 1904, U. of the South, 1907; m. Sidney S. Peyton, Oct. 13, 1887; children—Thomas Peyton (dec.), William Loyall, Anne Cary, Mary Elizabeth. Deacon, 1884, priest, 1885, P.E. Ch.; asst. rector St. Paul's, Richmond, Va., 1885-87; rector St. Peter's Norfolk, Va., 1887-93, Zion Ch., Charles Town, W.Va., 1893-99; elected, July 26, 1899, consecrated, Nov. 10, 1899, coadjutor bishop of W.Va., and bishop of W.Va., 1916. Home: 1583 Virginia St., Charleston, W.Va.

GRAVELL, James Harvey, pres. Am. Chem. Paint Co.; b. Phila., Pa., Oct. 12, 1880; s. Thomas and Ella E. (Davis) G.; student Phila. pub. schs.; ScD., Pa. Mil. Coll.; m. C. Marguerite Riehl, Oct. 14, 1911. Engr. on electric welding, Elwood Ivins Tube Works, 1898-1900, Am. Tube and Stamping Co., 1900-08; laboratorian of electric devices, Phila. Electric Co., 1908-10; engr. on electric welding Hale & Kilburn, 1910-14; pres. and dir. Am. Chem. Paint Co., Ambler, Pa., since orgn., 1914; pres. Delaware River Ferry Co. since 1929; dir. Ambler Nat. Bank, Grabar Corpn. Mem. Acad. of Natural Sciences, Franklin Inst., Am. Chem. Soc., Am. Inst. E.E., Am. Soc. for Metals, Nat. Industrial Conf. Bd. Mason. Clubs: Union League, Engineers (Phila.); Rotary (Ambler); Delaware River Yacht; Huntington Valley Country. Author: Cause and Cure of Depressions; Fair Trade Practice; How Long Is a Week? Address: Ambler, Pa.

GRAVES, Arthur Roselle, steel designer; b. Citra, Fla., Dec. 4, 1895; s. George Stevens and Sarah Roselia (Root) G.; ed. Rensselaer Poly. Inst.; m. Irma Zimmermann, July 14, 1928; children—Edith Margaret, George Martin, Ruth Anna. Transitman Central R.R. of N.J., Wilkes-Barre, Pa., 1919; draftsman Bethlehem Steel Co., 1919-20, shop inspector, 1920, resident engr., Hauto, Pa., 1920-21, estimator and designer, 1921-31, sr. designer since 1931. Supervised structural design of Presbyn. Eye and Ear Hosp., Pittsburgh; Continuous Strip Mill, Lackawanna, N.Y., and Sparrows Point, Md.; also wire mill extensions, Sparrows Point, Md. Mem. Am. Soc. C.E. Republican. Baptist. Mason, Odd Fellow. Home: 551 E. Goepp St. Office: 701 E. Third St., Bethlehem, Pa.

GRAVES, Charles Coakley, Jr., M.D., psychiatrist; b. Richmond, Va., Jan. 16, 1901; s. Charles Coakley and Lilly Grayson (Eaton) G.; A.B., U. of Iowa, 1922; B.D., Episcopal Theol. Sch., 1925; M.D., Med. Coll. of Va., 1929; grad. student Harvard, 1922-25; m. Charlotte West, Jan. 1924; children—Charles Coakley III, Thomas West, Charlotte Taylor. Ordained to ministry of Episcopal Ch., 1925; rector St. John's Ch., West Point, Va., 1925-29; interne in medicine, surgery, obstetrics, pediatrics and psychiatry, St. Elizabeths Hosp., Washington, D.C., 1929-31; senior resident State Hosp., Marlboro, N.J., since 1931. Mem. Bd. of Edn., Marlboro. Mem. Am. Psychiatric Assn., N.J. State Med. Soc., N.J. Neuro-Psychiatric Assn., Phi Beta Pi. Club: Rotary (pres. 1938-39). Address: State Hospital, Marlboro, N.J.

GRAVES, Harold F(rank), prof. English composition; b. South Royalton, Vt., Mar. 12, 1898; s. Frank Kilburn and Eva (Wyman) G.; B.S., Wesleyan U., 1921; A.M., Pa. State Coll., 1924, Ph.D., same, 1934; m. Mildred E. Joyce, June 20, 1923; 1 son, John Wyman. Engaged as instr. English, Pa. State Coll., 1922-25, asst. prof., 1925-30, asso. prof. English composition, 1930-36, prof. since 1936. Mem. Am. Assn. Univ. Profs., Delta Upsilon, Phi Kappa Phi. Author: Argument, 1938. Co-author: Art of Argument (with C. B. Spotts), 1927; Report Writing (with C. G. Gaum), 1929; Types of Persuasion (with J. S. Bowman), 1938. Home: 437 E. Fairmount Av., State College, Pa.

GRAVES, Harold Theodore, Jr., banking; b. Jamestown, N.D., Nov. 26, 1904; s. Harold Theodore and Lenna (Ford) G.; ed. Jamestown Coll., 1921-22; B.S. in Econs., U. of Pa., 1927; m. Mary Gertrude Burke, Oct. 24, 1932; 1 son, Harold Theodore III. Began with Guaranty Co. of N.Y. City, 1927; with First of Boston Corpn., N.Y. City, 1928-34; mem. firm Gordon, Graves & Co., mem. N.Y. Stock Exchange, N.Y. City, 1934-36; vice-pres. Summit Trust Co., Summit, N.J., since 1937. Presbyn. Home: 29 Whittredge Rd. Office: Summit Trust Co., Summit, N.J.

GRAVES, W(illiam) Brooke, prof. polit. science; b. Charlottesville, Va., May 4, 1899; s. William Clayton and Lina Elizabeth (Barber) G.; A.B., Cornell U., 1921; M.A., U. of Pa., 1923, Ph.D., 1936; m. Hazel Wallace, Aug. 31, 1922; 1 son, Wallace Barbour. Asst. in Am. history, Cornell U., 1920-21; instr. in polit. science, U. of Pa., 1921-23; instr. economics and polit. science, Temple U., 1923-25, prof. polit. science and head department since 1925; visiting professor Swarthmore Coll., 1936-37, Duke University, summer sessions, 1925; Temple Univ., 1926-36; University of Texas, 1937. Research consultant, Joint Legislative Com. on Finances of Pa., 1933; chmn. Phila. Conf. on Govt., 1933-35; chmn. com. on research, Commonwealth Club of Pa.; mem. com. on research and information, Interstate Commn. on Delaware River Basin; mem. com. on legislation, Pa. Economic League. Served in R.O.T.C. and S.A.T.C., 1917-19. Mem. Am. Polit. Science Assn., Am. Hist. Assn., Governmental Research Assn., Am. Acad. Polit. and Social Science, Nat. Municipal League, Am. Assn. Univ. Profs. (mem. council 1935-37), Pi Gamma Mu. Mason. Clubs: University, Contemporary (Philadelphia). Author: Readings in Public Opinion, 1928; Uniform State Action, 1934; (with others) A Survey of the Government of Pennsylvania, 1934; American State Government, 1936. Editor: Our State Legislators (The Annals, Jan. 1938). Contbr. numerous articles in professional jours. Home: 48 Whitemarsh Road, Merion Golf Heights, Ardmore, Pa.

GRAVES, William Sidney, army officer; b. Mt. Calm, Tex., Mar. 27, 1865; s. Andrew C. and Evelyn (Bennett) G.; grad. U.S. Mil. Acad., 1889; m. Katherine Boyd, Feb. 9, 1891; children—Sidney C., Dorothy (wife of Wm. R. Orton, U.S.A.). Commd. 2d lt. 7th Inf., June 12, 1889; promoted through grades to maj. gen. July 11, 1925. Instr. small arms practice, Dept. of Columbia, 1897-99; also acting judge advocate, 1898-99; same, Dept. of Colo., 1899; ordered to P.I., 1899, participating in various campaigns; received thanks of Gen. J. F. Bell for gallantry in action against insurgents at Caloocan, Dec. 31, 1901; again in P.I., 1904-06; at San Francisco, Apr.-May 1906, after earthquake; duty Gen. Staff, 1909-11; sec. Gen. Staff Corps, Jan. 1911-July 1912, and Sept. 3, 1914-Feb. 6, 1918; comdr. A.E.F. in Siberia, 1918-20; comdr. Ft. William McKinley, P.I., Apr.-Oct. 1920, 1st Brigade of 1st Div., Dec. 1920-Apr. 1, 1925; comdr. 1st Div., Apr. 1-July 10, 1925; comdr. 6th Corps Area, Chicago, July 11, 1925-Oct. 26, 1926; comdr. Panama Canal Div., Dec. 14, 1926-Oct. 1, 1927; comdr. Panama Canal Dept., Oct. 1, 1927; retired, 1928. Awarded D.S.M., 1919; Order of Rising Sun, 2d Class, Japan; Order of the Wen Hu (Striped Tiger), China; War Cross, Czechoslovakia; Comd. Order of Crown of Italy. Clubs: Army and Navy (Washington and Manila). Home: Shrewsbury, N.J. Address: War Dept., Washington, D.C.

GRAY, Arthur Wellington, physicist and metallurgist; b. Brooklyn, N.Y., Feb. 19, 1875; s. John Hatfield and Cornelia Ludlow (Dolbear) G.; A.B., U. of Calif., Berkeley, 1896; Ph.D., cum laude, U. of Berlin, Germany, 1904; m. Alma Marie Nelson, July 17, 1899 (died Sept. 15, 1899); m. 2d Susie Perkins Atkinson, June 28, 1908; 1 son, John Wellington (dec.). Lecture asst. in physics, U. of Calif., 1897-99; teaching science and mathematics, San Francisco and Merced, Calif., 1900-02; research asst. to dir. Cryogenic Lab., U. of Leyden, Holland, 1904-05; Whiting Research instr. physics, U. of Calif., 1905-09; chief thermal expansivity sect., Nat. Bur. Standards, Washington, D.C., 1909-16; dir. phys. research, L. D. Caulk Co., Milford, Del., 1916-25; physicist, Calco Chem. Co., Bound Brook, N.J., 1925-28; vice-pres. and dir. research, Dielectric Products, Inc., Newport, Del., 1928; asso. dir. research, Brown Instrument Co., Phila., 1929-30; cons. physicist and metallurgist, Dental Mfg. Dept., Baker & Co., Inc., Newark, N.J., 1932-37; cons. physicist and metallurgist, Westfield, N.J., since 1937. Fellow Am. Phys. Soc., A.A.A.S., Royal Soc. of Arts (London). Mem. Optical Soc. America, Am. Inst. Mining & Metall. Engrs., Am. Soc. for Testing Materials, Inst. Metals Gt. Britain, Sigma Xi. Mem. Mathematics, Physics and Chemistry Club, Westfield. Home: 512 Colonial Av., Westfield, N.J.

GRAY, Bernard Elbert, civil engr.; b. Andover, Mass., Oct. 13, 1888; s. Walter Edward and Florence May (Joy) G.; grad. Medford (Mass.) High Sch., 1907; B.S., Tufts Coll., Mass., 1911, hon. C.E., 1935; m. Violet Powell Noland, Sept. 3, 1921. Resident engr. Mass. Highway Commn., 1911-16, asst. div. engr., 1916-17; engr. economist U.S. Bureau Pub. Roads, 1917, sr. highway engr., 1919-21; div. engr. W.Va. Highway Commn., 1921-28; chief of maintenance, 1929-30; highway engr. Asphalt Inst., 1930-34, chief engr. since 1934. Served as lieut., orientation officer, 38th Arty., Coast Arty. Corps, U.S. Army, 1918-19; lt. col. 325th Engrs., U.S. Reserve, since 1939. Mem. Governor's Commn., which wrote basic road law of W.Va., 1920-21. Associate of Asphalt Paving Technologists; mem. Highway Research Bd., Internat. Road Congress, Am. Legion (past comdr. Keyser Post). Republican. Presbyterian. Mason (Shriner). Club: Keyser Rotary (past pres.). Author: Asphalt Pocket Reference for Highway Engineers (with Prevost Hubbard), 1937. Contbr. over 300 articles on highway constrn. to mags.; author of formula for design flexible pavements. Home: Keyser, W.Va. Office: 801 2d Av., New York, N.Y.

GRAY, Charles Mickel, physician; b. Millville, N.J., Aug. 26, 1879; s. William Lee and Mary Ann (Jones) G.; student pub schs., Bridgeton, N.J., 1888-97, South Jersey Inst., Bridgeton, 1897-99; M.D., U. of Ill. Med. Sch., Chicago, 1904; m. Myrtle M. Dickey, June 27, 1906; 1 dau., Kathryn Lee. Began as physician, 1904; now in practice at Vineland, N.J.; sr. med. officer Newcomb Hosp.; pres. Wiegand Glass Co., mfrs. scientific glassware, Vineland, N.J., since 1927. Mem. N.J. State Med. Assn., A.M.A., Alpha Kappa Kappa.

Republican. Address: 6th and Grape Sts., Vineland, N.J.

GRAY, David J., educator; b. Scranton, Pa., Aug. 28, 1893; s. William and Margaret (Davis) G.; ed. Scranton Business Coll.; married Miss Edith Reese, Dec. 2, 1922; children—Arline, David. Began as accountant Internat. Corr. Schs., 1911; controller Internat. Ednl. Pub. Co. (Internat. Corr. Schs. in foreign countries) since 1919, v.p. since 1928, dir. since 1929; pres., controller and dir. Internat. Corr. Schs. of Latin America since 1937; dir. Internat. Corr. Schs., Ltd. (London), Internat. Corr. Schs. of Buenos Aires (Argentine). Roll call chmn. Am. Red Cross, 1938. Pres. and dir. Scranton Chapter of Nat. Assn. Cost Accountants. Delivered speech: "20,000 Miles Around the Pan-American Airways." Home: 1412 Oram St. Office: 1000 Wyoming Av., Scranton, Pa.

GRAY, Edith Stearns (wife of Capt. George Alphonso G., pioneer aviator), writer; b. Richmond, Va.; d. Franklin II and Emily Somers (Palmer) Stearns; student Mary Baldwin Sem., Staunton, Va., Miss Jennie Ellett's Sch., Richmond, Va.; grad. Stuart's Sch., Washington, D.C., 1907; m. Capt. George Alphonso Gray, June 4, 1913; children—George Alphonso, Newcombe Stearns, Jacquelyn Stearns. Made first flight of woman passenger over Adirondack Mts., Oct. 5, 1912; first flight of woman as passenger from Va. soil at Culpeper, Va., Dec. 7, 1912, both flights with Capt. Gray, in Wright Model B., 35 h.p. machine. Mem. Women's Nat. and Internat. Aeronautical Assns., Nat. Woman's Party, League of Am. Pen Women, D.A.R., Alumnae of Mary Baldwin. Episcopalian. Club: Woman's (Chevy Chase, Md.). Author: (pen name "Jack" Stearns Gray) Up, a story of aviation. Home: 5 W. Leland St., Chevy Chase, Md.

GRAY, Edward Winthrop, writer, pub.; b. Jersey City, N.J., Aug. 18, 1870; s. Edward and Elizabeth (Beggs) G.; ed. pub. schs.; m. Altha R. Hay, Sept. 29, 1898; children—Altha R., Julia B. (dec.), Elizabeth. Reported New York Herald, 1894, New York World, 1894-96; owner and pub. Summit (N.J.) Herald, 1897-98; city editor and mng. editor, Newark Daily Advertiser, 1898-1902; pres. and gen. mgr. Newark Daily Advertiser Pub. Co., 1902-04; sec. to Gov. Edward C. Stokes, 1904-07; organizer, 1909, Commercial Casualty Ins. Co. of Newark. Mem. 64th and 65th Congresses (1915-19), 8th N.J. Dist.; candidate for Republican nomination for U.S. Senate, on antiprohibition platform, 1918, 28. Appointed by Gov. Murphy commissioner to investigate tenement house conditions, 1902; mem. Bd. Tenement House Supervision of N.J., 8 yrs.; sec. Rep. State Com. of N.J., 1908-13. Clubs: Union, Newark Athletic (1st pres. and 1st hon. mem.). Home: 141 Wakeman Av. Office: 16 Park Pl., Newark, N.J.*

GRAY, Howard Lowell, lumberman; b. Ironton, O., Jan. 13, 1885; s. D. B. and M. Jennie (Raine) G.; grad. Ironton High Sch., 1902; m. Helen M. Bishop, June 17, 1908 (died 1932); children—Howard Robert, John Gray, Virginia, Elma Jean; m. 2d, Nellie E. Clower, Aug. 16, 1933; children—Mary Lowell, Charles David, Ruth Ellen. Employed by Fearon Lumber Co., Ironton, O., 1902-10, becoming head sawyer and later mill supt.; with Meadow River Lumber Co., hard woods, Rainelle, W.Va. since 1910, beginning as head band-saw filer, became mill supt., 1911, asst. gen. mgr., 1918, gen. mgr., 1936, now dir., vice-pres. and gen. mgr.; dir. and vice pres. Bank of Rainelle; dir. Meadow River Coal & Land Co. Republican. Methodist. Address: Rainelle, W.Va.

GRAY, James H., lawyer; b. Pittsburgh, Pa., Aug. 20, 1872; s. Joseph H. and Mary McJunkin (Kuhn) G.; ed. pub. schs., Pittsburgh; m. Anna E. Dunlap, June 15, 1899; 1 son., James Dunlap. Admitted to Pa. bar, 1895, and since practiced in Pittsburgh; partner James H. Gray and James D. Gray; judge Court of Common Pleas, Allegheny Co., 1926-37; dir. Parkersburg Iron & Steel Co. Mem. advisory com. on community councils of Fed. of Social Agencies, Pittsburgh. Trustee Western Pa. Sch. for the Deaf. Mem. Allegheny County, Pa. and Am. bar assns. Republican. Presbyterian. Mason (Shriner). Mem. Civic Club of Allegheny Co. Home: 5516 Aylesboro Av. Office: Law and Finance Bldg., Pittsburgh, Pa.

GRAY, Jessie, educator; b. London, Eng., June 2, 1876; d. Alfred and Sarah Jane (Percy) Gray; came to U.S., 1881; grad. Phila. Normal Sch., 1896; student U. of Pa., 1922-24, Temple U., 1925-26, Columbia, 1928; hon. A.M., U. of Pa., 1935; unmarried. Classroom teacher elementary sch., Phila., 1896-1914; training teacher Thaddeus Stevens practice dept., Phila., Normal Sch., since 1914. Mem. N.E.A., state dir., 1925, v.p., 1930-31, pres. 1933-34, 1st v.p., 1934-35, mem. legislative com., 1921-36, mem. tenure com., 1929-32; del. to World Fed. of Edn. at Edinburgh, 1925, Toronto, 1927, Dublin, 1933; mem. Pa. State Edn. Assn., pres. 1925-26, mem. legislative com., 1921-38, mem. welfare com., 1929-38, chmn. com. on management of teachers home; mem. Phila. Teachers Assn., pres. 1928-31, 34-35; mem. Women's Legislative Council of Pa., v.p., 1927-35, pres. 1935-38; mem. Women's Sesquicentennial com., chmn. First Brick House, High St., 1926; mem. Mayor Wilson's Constl. Celebration Com., 1938; mem. Gov. Earle's Com. to Supervise Civil Service Exam., 1937. Mem. League of Women Voters (chmn. edn. com. 1935-38), Phila. Normal Sch. Alumni (pres. 1927-31), Business and Professional Women's Club (chmn. edn. com. 1937-38). Episcopalian. Clubs: Temple University Women's; Am. Rocky Mt. Alpine; Frankford Country (capt. hockey team). Contbr. articles to jours. Home: 1210 Fillmore St., Philadelphia, Pa.

GRAY, John Basil, Jr., lawyer; b. Prince Frederick, Md., Mar. 23, 1894; s. John Brown and Kate Laveille (Dorsey) G.; B.S., U. of Md. College Park, Baltimore, 1914; student U. of Md. Law Sch., 1916; m. Aimee Atlee Truan, June 8, 1918; children—John Basil III, Frank Truan, Sue Atlee, Sara Dorsey. Admitted to Md. bar, 1916, and since in gen. practice of law at Prince Frederick, Md.; spl. asst. atty. gen. of Md. and counsel to Md. State Rds. Commn., 1932-35; mem. Md. Waterfront Commn., 1929-36; treas. Bay Side Realty Co.; sec. Kenwood Beach, Inc., since 1934. Served as batln. sergt. maj., U.S.A., 1918-19. Dir. Calvert Co. Hosp., Prince Frederick, Md. Mem. Am. Bar Assn., Md. State Bar Assn. Kappa Alpha. Democrat. Episcopalian. Club: Solomons Island Yacht. Address: Prince Frederick, Md.

GRAY, John Clifford, coll. prof.; b. Arlington, Mass., Aug. 5, 1884; s. John and Annie Maria (Hill) G.; A.B., Harvard, 1908; A.M., Dartmouth Coll., Hanover, N.H., 1912; m. Odilee G. Burnham, Aug. 24, 1910; children—Edward Edgecomb, Joseph Burnham, John Frederick, George Ellis, Martha Elizabeth. Instr. chemistry, St. John's Coll., Annapolis, Md., 1913-16; with U.S. Naval Acad., Annapolis, Md., since 1916, instr. physics and chemistry, 1916-19, prof. chemistry since 1938. Mem. Am. Chem. Soc., Soc. for Promotion Engring. Edn., Naval Inst. Clubs: Officers, Harvard (Annapolis, Md.). Home: 141 Monticello Av., Annapolis, Md.

GRAY, John Stanley, psychologist; b. Freeport, O., Nov. 8, 1894; s. Thomas Andrew and Elizabeth Catherine (Johnston) G.; A.B., Muskingum Coll., 1920; A.M., U. of Mich., 1924; Ph.D., Ohio State U., 1929; m. Gunbrog Berglund, June 18, 1923; children—Mary Catherine, John Stanley, Olga Ruth. Teacher Zanesville (O.) High School, 1920-21; prof. of speech, Gustavus Adolphus Coll., St. Peter, Minn., 1921-23; instr. of English, U. of Minn., 1924-25; asst. prof. of English, U. of Ore., 1925-27; asst. prof. of psychology, U. of Pittsburgh, since 1930; dir. Psychological Research Labs., Inc. Served with U.S. Army, 1917-18. Mem. Am. Psychol. Assn. A.A.A.S., Am. Assn. Applied Psychology. Author: Communicative Speaking, 1928; Psychological Foundations of Education, 1935; Introduction to Human Psychology, 1936. Contbr. many articles to professional jours. Home: Wilkinsburg, Pa. Office: Univ. of Pittsburgh, Pittsburgh, Pa.

GRAY, Joseph, ex-congressman; b. Spangler, Pa.; s. Joseph A. and Margaret (Hipps) G.; m. Elizabeth Glass, July 7, 1905. Admitted to Pa. bar; mem. 74th and 75th Congresses (1935-39), 27th Pa. Dist. Served U.S.A., Spanish-Am. War. Mem. Vets. of Fgn. Wars. Democrat. Home: Spangler, Pa. Office: Barnesboro, Pa.*

GRAY, Joseph Rex, real estate; b. Pittsburgh, Pa., June 8, 1885; s. Joseph H. and Mary (Kuhn) G.; student Pittsburgh High Sch., 1899-1902; m. Edith Milliken, June 2, 1914; children—Joseph Milliken, Robert Kuhn. Bank clerk Colonial Trust Co., 1902-08; sec., treas. Kelly-Wood Real Estate Co., real estate and ins., 1908-25, pres. since 1925. Republican. Presbyterian. Club: Longue Vue Country (Pittsburgh). Home: 203 S. Linden Av. Office: 6001 Center Av., Pittsburgh, Pa.

GRAY, Lewis Cecil, economist; b. Liberty, Mo., Dec. 2, 1881; s. Lewis Pressley and Elizabeth (Chambliss) G.; B.A., William Jewell Coll., Liberty, 1900; M.A., 1903; student Univ. of Chicago, summers 1907-08; Ph.D., U. of Wis., 1911; LL.D., William Jewell College, 1927; m. Pearl B. Patterson, 1905; children—Mrs. Marceline E. Eder, Emily Belle, Lois Cecilia, John Lewis. Prof. history and economics, Okla. Agrl. and Mech. Coll., 1905-08; instr. economics, U. of Wis., 1910-13; prof. economics, U. of Saskatchewan, 1913-15; prof. rural economics, George Peabody Coll. for Teachers, Nashville, Tenn., 1915-19; became economist in charge div of land economics, U.S. Bur. Agrl. Economics, Apr. 1919, now asst. chief of Bureau; asst. adminstr. Resettlement Administration, Dec. 1935. Spl. agt. Bur. of Census, 1911; in charge price fixing div., U.S. Food Administration, State of Tenn., 1918; chmn. special com. on land utilization apptd. by Sec. of Agriculture; dir. of land use section, Nat. Resources Com.; member President Roosevelt's Great Plains Com. and executive secretary President's Farm Tenancy Committee. Mem. Am. Economic Assn., Am. Farm Economic Assn. Represented U.S. Dept. Agr. at meeting of Internat. Inst. Agr., Rome, 1922, 28. Democrat. Christian Scientist. Club: Cosmos. Author: An Introduction to Agricultural Economics; History of Agriculture in the Southern United States to 1860; also numerous articles and bulls. Home: 119 Wooten Av., Chevy Chase, Md. Address: 3048 South Bldg., Washington, D.C.

GRAY, William Robert, banker; b. Pamplin, Va., Mar. 11, 1872; s. George Edwin and Rhoda Holland (Anderson) G.; ed. pub. sch., of Appomattox Co., Va., and Shenandoah Business Coll., Reliance, Va.; m. Mary Hanes, Nov. 24, 1897; children—William James (dec.), Robert Hanes. Began as' mcht., Mount Hope, W.Va., 1899; became v.p. Bank of Mount Hope, W.Va. 1926, chmn. of bd. since 1931, dir. since 1902; v.p. Long Branch Coal Co., Mount Hope, 1911-26; pres., gen. mgr. and treas. Pemberton Fuel Co., Mount Hope, 1916-26; v.p. Princewick Coal Co., Mount Hope, 1917-26; v.p. and dir. Fayette Smokeless Fuel Co., Mount Hope, 1917-27, Sugar Creek Coal Company, 1921-32; v.p. and treas. Mount Hope (W.Va. Bldg. Co. since 1920; v.p. New River Hotel Co. since 1930. Pres. Mount Hope Chamber of Commerce since 1936. Democrat. Methodist. Mason (K.T., Shriner). Clubs: White Oak Country (Mt. Hope, W.Va.); Virginia Seniors (White Sulphur Springs, W.Va.). Home: 828 Main St. Office: Main St., Mount Hope, W.Va.

GREBE, Melvin Henry, builder, developer; b. Fort Washington, Pa., Jan. 18, 1897; s. Harry Conrad and Ida May (Espenship) G.; ed. public schools of Phila.; m. Mabel Lillian Marple, Mar. 9, 1921; children—Melvin Henry, Joanne, Edythe. Architect, contractor and builder since 1917; treas. Grebar Corpn. Served in U.S. Naval Reserve Force, 1918-19, in aviation school and regular service. Mem. Bd. of Trade, United Business Men's Assn.; Am. Legion. Republican. Episcopalian. Mason (K.T., Shriner). Home: 6802 Crittenden St. Office: 5 E. Highland Av., Philadelphia, Pa.

GRECE, Philip William, judge Dist. Court of N.J. Address: Jersey City, N.J.

GREEN, Charles Henry, exposition director; b. Albion, Mich., Apr. 17, 1867; s. Henry S. and Mary E. (Ketcham) G.; ed. Homer Acad., Mich.; registered chemist in Mich.; m. Ada May Kerhaghan, July 16, 1890 (died Oct. 16, 1917); children—Lloyd Francis, Harold Clement; m. 2d, Adele Wright Drummond, of Brooklyn, Nov. 26, 1920; 1 dau., Marilynn Adele. Advertising and sales mgr. Shredded Wheat Co., Niagara Falls, N.Y., 1900-02; in expn. work as mng. dir. or pres. of over 50 trade expns., 1903-13; chief of Dept. of Mfrs. and Varied Industries, Panama-Pacific Internat. Expn., San Francisco, 1913-15; U.S. commr. to Japan and China in interest of same; mem. Superior Jury Internat. Jury of Award. Panama P.I. Expn., 1915. Managing dir. Nat. Music Show, Internat. Silk Expn., Internat. Fur Expn., Architectural and Allied Arts Expn., Internat. Fabric Expn.; del. representing Architectural League of N.Y. to Paris Decorative and Industrial Arts Expn., 1925. Tech. advisor N.J. Commn. to New York World's Fair 1939; mem. Bd. of Adjustment (zoning), Ridgewood, N.J. Veteran Co. A, 4th Regt. Mich. N.G. Received Chia Ho decoration from Pres. of China, 1916; Gold Medal of Honor, Architectural League of N.Y., 1925. Republican. Episcopalian. Home: 389 Spring Av., Ridgewood, N.J. Office: 127 W. 43d St., New York, N.Y.

GREEN, Clyde Chapman, supt. schs.; b. Kittanning, Pa., June 4, 1877; s. James R and Sara Jane (Morrison) G.; ed. Slippery Rock State Normal Sch., Grove City Coll. and Columbia U.; m. Edith Nesbit, Aug. 27, 1902; children—Dorothy Lucile, Lois Edith, James Reid. Began as teacher in rural and urban schs.; Prin. Irwin (Pa.) High Sch., 1902-05; supervising prin., Irwin schs., 1905-06; supt. schs., New Brighton, Pa., 1906-11, Beaver Falls, Pa., 1911-18; prin. Clarion State Normal Sch., 1918-26; supt. schs., New Castle, Pa., since 1926. Served in U.S. Army during Spanish-Am. War. Mem. Associated Charities, Am. Red. Cross. Mem. Chamber of Commerce, United Spanish War Vets. (past comdr.). Republican. Presbyterian (elder). Mason (32°; past master). Clubs: New Castle Field, New Castle Rotary (pres.). Delivered addresses before N.E.A., Pa. State Edn. and other ednl. meetings. Contbr. to ednl. jours. Home: 111 Sheridan Av. Office: 116 East St., New Castle, Pa.

GREEN, Florence Topping, artist, insurance; b. London, Eng.; d. John James and Hannah Elizabeth (Green) Topping; parents U.S. citizens; grad. Long Branch (N.J.) High Sch., 1893, Woman's Art Sch., Cooper Union, New York, 1899; studied art under R. S. Gifford and John Carlson at Woodstock, Summer School, Nat. Acad. of Design; m. Howard Green, 1899; children—Howard Francis, Florence Marjorie (wife of Murvale T. Farrar, U.S.N.), Elizabeth Topping (Mrs. William George Daub). Artist since 1896; pres. H. W. Green & Bro. (real estate and ins.) since death of husband, 1935. Represented by miniature of Buzzie Dall in White House, Washington, D.C.; oil paintings in state collections of Kan., Wis., Ariz., Ohio, Ill., Va., N.J.; Research Club, Atlantic City, N.J.; Monmouth Memorial Training Sch.; Long Branch (N.J.) High Sch.; Long Branch Woman's Club. Recent paintings: portraits of Princess Elizabeth and Princess Margaret Rose, London, 1937; portrait of Elizabeth Daub, accepted by New York jury for exhibition in Contemporary Art Building, World's Fair, New York, 1939. Awards: Medal, Newark Art Club, 1934; special hon. mention, Montclair Art Museum, 1938. Nat. chmn. arts and crafts, Gen. Fed. Women's Clubs, 1924-28, chmn. nat. art. div., 1928-32; chmn. nat. women's div., Am. Artists Professional League since 1932, chmn. Nat. Am. Art Week, from 1935, mem. nat. advisory bd.; v.p. Internat. Art Congress, del. to Prague, 1928, Vienna, 1935, official del. (apptd. by President Roosevelt), Paris, 1937. Vice-pres. Long Branch Pub. Library. Mem. Asbury Park (N.J.) Soc. Fine Arts. Republican. Episcopalian. Clubs: Pen and Brush (New York); Woman's (Long Branch). Lecturer; author of booklets, First Aid in Art, Art in the Community; also many magazine articles. Editor of Women's Page of Art Digest. Home: 104 Franklin Av. Office: 176 Broadway, Long Branch, N.J.

GREEN, Francis Harvey, educator; b. Booth's Corner, Delaware Co., Pa., May 19, 1861; s. Sharpless and Mary (Booth) G.; ed. West Chester (Pa.) State Normal Sch., Amherst Call., Harvard U.; A.M., Dickinson Coll., 1893; Litt.D., Temple U., 1909; LL.D., Juniata Coll., Huntingdon, Pa., 1931; m. Gertrude (Langdon) Heritage, Sept. 12, 1911. Prof. English, Juniata Coll., Huntingdon, Pa., 1884-88; head Dept. English, West Chester (Pa.) Normal Sch., 1888-1920; headmaster Pennington Sch., 1921—. Pres. Y.M.C.A. of West Chester Normal Sch.; dir. West Chester Y.M.C.A. Mem. Transatlantic Soc. (Phila.), Dickens' Fellowship (Chester, Pa.), Chester Co. Hist. Soc. (pres.), Am. Asiatic Assn.,, Pa. State Teachers' Assn., N.E.A. Clubs: Harvard (Phila.); Pittsburgh Traffic; British Empire (Providence, R.I.); Ancient and Hon. Mech. Assn. of Baltimore. Republican. Methodist. Mason. Author: Notes on Rhetoric, 1909; Desirable Degrees, 1922; also verse and prose in mags. Compiler: Quotations from Great Authors, 1912; What They Say Day by Day, 1916; What Others Say Each Passing Day, 1920. Lecturer on lit., ednl. and moral subjects. Home: "Lowellden," Pennington, N.J.*

GREEN, G. Edward, pres. Ellis Coal Co.; b. Pittsburgh, Pa., May 15, 1885; s. Anthony and Jennie (Sweeney) G.; m. Clara G. McCaffrey, June 8, 1911; children—Mrs. Marjorie G. Shoemaker, G. Edward. Pres. and dir. Ellis Coal Co., Pittsburgh, since 1928, Ellis Barging Co. since 1931. Sec. Rep. State Com. of Pa., 1936-37, chmn., 1937-38. Dir. Pittsburgh Athletic Assn. Republican. K.C. Clubs: Duquesne, Pittsburgh Athletic, Pittsburgh Field (Pittsburgh). Home: 251 Maple Av., Edgewood. Office: Law and Finance Bldg., Pittsburgh, Pa.

GREEN, George Rex., univ. prof.; b. Glen Hope, Pa., June 29, 1884; s. Abraham Keagy and Emma Jane (Rex) G.; student Dickinson Coll., 1904-05; A.B., U. of Mich., 1907-11; M.S., Pa. State Coll., 1915; student Cornell U., 1924, U. of Pa., 1927-29; m. Edith Newton, Apr. 16, 1913; children—George Rex, Betty Irene. Public sch. teacher, at Irvona, Pa., 1903-04; asst. state forester of Ohio, 1911-12; asst. prof. of forestry, Pa. State Coll., 1912-15, asso. prof. of dendrology and wood tech., 1915-21, prof. of dendrology and nature study, 1921-24, prof. of nature edn., head of dept. and dir. of nature camp, since 1924; chief wood inspector U.S. Naval Aircraft Factory, Phila., 1918-20. Fellow A.A.A.S.; mem. N.E.A. (life), Pa. State Edn. Assn. (life), Am. Assn. Univ. Profs., Am. Assn. Coll. Teachers, Am. Nature Study Soc. (past pres.), Nat. Council Supervisors Elementary Science, Nat. Assn. for Research in Science Teaching, Soc. Am. Foresters, Am. Ornithol. Union, Am. Nature Assn., Nat. Geog. Soc., Pa. Acad. Science, Nat. Soc. Coll. Teachers of Edn., Am. Science Teachers Assn., Acacia, Sigma Alpha Epsilon, Pi Gamma Mu, Xi Sigma Pi, Kappa Delta Pi, Phi Delta Kappa. Republican. Mason. Rotarian. Author: Survey of Nature, 1926; Trees of North America, Vol. I, The Conifers, 1933, Vol. II, The Broadleaves, 1934. Contbr. articles on nature study to mags. Home: 523 S. Atherton St., State College, Pa.

GREEN, Harold David, lawyer; b. New York, N.Y., Dec. 27, 1897; s. Alexander and Ray (Kienert) G.; student Pub. Sch. 6, Paterson, N.J., 1904-12, Paterson (N.J.) High Sch., 1912-16; LL.B., N.Y.U. Law Sch., 1919; m. Anne Steinberg, Nov. 8, 1921; children—Helen Rosalie, Marjorie Victoria. Admitted to N.J. bar, 1919, and since practiced at Paterson, N.J.; specializing in sch. law since 1929. Served as sergt., Co. B, N.G.N.J., Mexican Border, 1916; 1st sergt., 5th N.J. Inf., U.S. Army, during World War. Mem. bd. edn., Paterson, N.J., since 1926, pres. 1928-30, resigned 1930 to become counsel, asst. sec. and counsel since 1937; counsel Teaneck (N.J.) Bd. Edn. since 1934; sec. Barnet Memorial Temple since 1919. Mem. N.J. State Bar Assn., Passaic Co. Bar Assn., Y.M.-Y.W.H.A., Phi Epsilon Pi. Democrat. Jewish religion. K.P. Club: Preakness Hills Country (Paterson, N.J.). Home: 400 E. 40th St. Office: 121 Ellison St., Paterson, N.J.

GREEN, Harry, gen. insurance; b. Harrogate, Eng., Aug. 13, 1887; s. Henry George and Mary Jane (Atkinson) G.; student Western Coll., Harrogate, Eng., 1895-1902, Armstrong Coll. of Sci., Durham U., 1903-07; m. Mary Ann Pottinger, Aug. 25, 1915; children—Arline Dorothy (Mrs. Harold Gray), John Thomas. Came to U.S., 1907, naturalized, 1921. Began as engr., 1907; gen. fire ins. since 1917; v.p. and sec. Hildenberger & Green, Inc., gen. ins. and bonding, Allentown and Bethlehem, since 1924; dir. Lehigh Bldg. & Loan Assn. Republican. Episcopalian. Elk. Address: 128½ S. St. Cloud St., Allentown, Pa. Offices: 737 Hamilton St., Allentown, Pa.; 208 Union Bank Bldg., Bethlehem, Pa.

GREEN, Harry Joseph, lawyer; b. New York, N.Y., Feb. 12, 1906; s. Harry Henry and Rose (Achtsam) G.; student Baltimore City Coll., 1918-20, Fishburne Mil. Sch., Waynesboro, Va., 1920-22; LL.B., U. of Md., 1927; A.B., Johns Hopkins U., 1926, Ph.D., 1929; m. Guitelle Reisman, June 21, 1926; children—Mae Westmore, Harrie Ellin. Admitted to Md. bar, 1927, also to practice before Dist. of Columbia bar, 1932, and before Ct. of Appeals of Md., Supreme Ct. of U.S., Nat. Labor Relations Bd., Federal Trade Commn., Interstate Commerce Commn., U.S. Bd. of Tax Appeals and U.S. Treasury Dept.; partner law firm Weinberg, Sweeten & Green, Baltimore and Washington, D.C., since 1932; asst. dept of polit. science, Johns Hopkins U., 1927-28; asst. Dir. of Legislative Reference, State of Md., 1927-29; asst. atty. gen. of Md., 1931-35. Dir. Big Brother League, Baltimore Hebrew Congregation, Associated Jewish Charities; pres. Jewish Ednl. Alliance. V.p. and dir. Young Democrats, 1926-39. Mem. Am. Bar Assn., Md. Bar Assn., Baltimore Bar Assn., Am. Polit. Science Assn., Am. Internat. Law Assn., Phi Alpha. Clubs: Phoenix, Suburban, Chesapeake, Md. Sportsmen's (Baltimore). Home: Fordham Court. Office: 33d Floor, Baltimore Trust Bldg., Baltimore, Md.

GREEN, Irvin Taylor; prof. New Testament and church history, Bethany Coll. Address: Bethany College, Bethany, W.Va.

GREEN, John Frederick Carl, clergyman; b. Kratt, Schleswig, Germany, May 6, 1892; came to U.S., 1907; s. Friedrich and Dorothea (Koch) G.; grad. pub. schs., Soeby, Schleswig, 1907; spl. high sch. work, Billings, Mont., and Himes, Wyo., 1911-13; Ph.B., Shurtleff Coll., Alton, Ill., 1916; A.M., U. of Chicago Divinity Sch., 1918; B.D., Chicago Theol. Sem., 1919; m. Mamie Louise Snyder, Sept. 24, 1918. Ordained Congl. ministry, 1918; pastor of mission, Pana, Ill., 1918, Godfrey (Ill.) Congl. Ch., 1919-22, Batavia (Ill.) Congl. Ch., 1922-25, Madison (Ind.) Evang. Congl. Ch., 1925-26, McKeesport (Pa.) G.E.P. Congl. Ch. since 1926. Mem. McKeesport City Planning and Zoning Commn., of Bd. of Appeals of Zoning Bd. Pres. McKeesport Ministers' Assn., 2 yrs.; mem. Theological Circle (Pittsburgh). Democrat. Mason. Club: Optimist. Address: 322 Olive Av., McKeesport, Pa.

GREEN, Joseph Coy, govt. official; b. Cincinnati, O., Apr. 12, 1887; s. James Albert and Louise Washburn (Coy) G.; A.B., Princeton, 1908, A.M., 1909; grad. work U. of Grenoble, 1909, U. of Paris, 1909-10, 1913-14, Princeton, 1908-09, 1914-15; m. Harriet Stearns, June 15, 1912 (died 1912); m. 2d, Helen Kinsey, July 5, 1920 (died 1923); children—Suzanne, Helen; m. 3d, Gertrude Henshaw Norris, of Adamstown, Md., Feb. 22, 1927; 1 son, Joseph Norris. Fellow in history, Princeton, 1908-09, 1914-15; instr. in history, Bordentown Mil. Inst., 1910-11, Columbia U., 1911-13; mem. Commn. for Relief in Belgium, as rept. for Hainaut and Brussels and chief of inspection for Belgium and occupied area of France, 1915-17; mem. Am. Relief Adminstrn., as dir. for Rumania and later the Near East, 1918-19; asst. prof. of history and politics, Princeton, 1920-24, asso. prof. of history, 1924-30; mem. of staff of U.S. Dept. of State since 1930, as asst. in Div. of Western European Affairs, 1930-35, special rep. of U.S. at Internat. Inst. of Agr., Rome, 1931-32, special asst. to Am. Minister at Bern, 1931-32, chief Office of Arms and Munitions Control, 1935-39, chief div. of Controls since 1939, and exec. sec. Nat. Munitions

Control Bd. since 1935. Served as interpreter, lt. capt. maj., U.S.A., 1917-19; maj. in Mil. Intelligence Res. since 1936. Awarded A.E.F. Campaign medal with four clasps; chevalier Legion of Honor; chevalier Order of the Crown of Belgium; Comdr. Order of the Star of Rumania; medaille de la Reconnaissance Française; medaille Commemorative du Comite National (Belgium). Dir. Commn. for Relief in Belgium Ednl. Foundation. Mem. Council on Foreign Relations, Am. Hist. Soc., Acad. of Political Science, Am. Assn. of Univ. Profs., Am. Ethnol. Soc., Am. Anthropol. Assn., A.A.A.S. Editor of Am. Indian terms, Webster's Internat. Dictionary, 1929-35. Contbr. to reviews. Home: 1015 Avondale Av., Cincinnati, O.; and 10 Quincy St., Chevy Chase, Md. Office: Department of State, Washington, D.C.

GREEN, Otis Howard, univ. prof.; b. Monroe, Mich., Dec. 11, 1898; s. John Howard and Cora Letitia (Dike) G.; A.B., Colgate U., 1920; A.M., Pa. State Coll., 1923; Ph.D., U. of Pa., 1927; student Centro de Estudios Historicos, Madrid, Spain, summer 1922; m. Mabel Warburton Barnett, June 11, 1924; children—Eleanor Irving, Paul Barnett. Teacher of French and Spanish, The Peddie Sch., Hightstown, N.J., 1920-21; instr. in Romance langs., Pa. State Coll., 1921-23; instr. in Spanish, U. of Pa., 1923-28, asst. prof., 1928-36, asso. prof. of Romance langs., 1936-39, prof. since 1939, chmn. of dept. since 1938; visiting prof., U. of Colo., summers 1934, 36. Mem. Modern Lang. Assn. America, Am. Assn. Teachers of Spanish, Phi Beta Kappa, Kappa Delta Rho. Republican. Baptist. Author: The Life and Works of Lupercio Leonardo de Argensola, 1927. Asst. editor of Hispanic Review; contbr. to philol. jours. of America and Europe. Home: 4926 Sansom St., Philadelphia, Pa.

GREEN, Percy Warren, lawyer; b. Booth's Corner, Delaware Co., Pa., Aug. 18, 1889; s. Charles and Elizabeth Ellen (Talley) G.; B.S. in Economics, Wharton Sch. of Finance (U. of Pa.), 1911; A.M., U. of Pa., 1912; read law with William S. Hilles, of Wilmington, Del., 1913-16; m. Maria Ellen Reynolds, Dec. 17, 1931; children—Pennvia Ellen, Warren. Asst. in finance, Wharton Sch. of Finance (U. of Pa.), 1911; asst. prof. in finance and transportation, Washington State Coll., Pullman, Wash., 1912-13; dep. atty. gen. State of Del., 1917-19; chief deputy, 1919-21; atty. for Levy Court, Newcastle County, Del., 1921-22; asst. city solicitor, Wilmington, Del., 1921-23; chief dept. atty. gen. of Del., 1933; apptd. atty. gen. of Del., July 6, 1933, and elected Nov. 1934, for term of 4 yrs. from Jan. 1, 1935; chief atty. Legislature of Del., 1939. Mem. bd. of dirs. Interstate Commn. on Crime, Council of Defense; adminstr. for Del. of Interstate Parole and Probation Compact. Served as govt. appeal agt., World War. Republican. Methodist. Mason. Home: 1202 Lovering Av. Office: Equitable Bldg., Wilmington, Del.

GREEN, Robert Morris, vice-pres. Prudential Ins. Co.; b. Cincinnati, O., Feb. 12, 1892; s. James Albert and Louise (Coy) G.; A.B., Princeton U., 1913; m. Ellen Burchenal, Nov. 15, 1916; children—Robert Morris, Jr., James Albert 3d, John Burchenal, Ellen Burchenal, Charles Harrington, David Lonsdale, Leota Louise. In employ Procter & Gamble Co., Cincinnati, O., 1914-17; engaged in coal and iron bus., 1919-24; employed by Union Central Life Ins. Co., Cincinnati, O., 1924-32, treas same, 1928-32; asst. sec. Prudential Ins. Co., Newark, N.J., 1923-33, treas., 1934-38, vice-pres. since 1938. Served as 1st lt. F.A., U.S.A., 1916-19; with A.E.F. in France. Pres. West Essex Community Fund since 1935. Chmn. Bd. Editorial Direction of Princeton Alumni Weekly. Republican. Presbyn. Clubs: Princeton (New York City); Nassau (Princeton). Home: Beech Tree Lane, Essex Fells, N.J. Office: Prudential Ins. Co., Newark, N.J.

GREEN, Samuel; pres. Tastyeast, Inc. Address: 2144 E. State St., Trenton, N.J.

GREEN Wyman Reed, prof. biology; b. Moultrie Co., Ill., June 1, 1881; s. John Rogers and Mary Jane (Jones) G.; life diploma, State Teachers' Coll., Alva, Okla., 1907; AB., A.M., U. of Kan., 1911; Ph.D., U. of Chicago, 1919; m. Frances La Vergne Powers, June 16, 1920; (died August 1922); 1 son, Francis Powers; m. 2d, Sophie Anna Bachofen, June 2, 1929; children—Wyman Reed, Henry Albert. Assistant in biology, State Teachers' College, Alva, 1908-10; head department biology, Wichita (Kansas) High Sch, 1911-12; fellow University of Chicago, 1912-14; instr. zoölogy, Carleton Coll., Northfield, Minn., 1914-19, Northwestern U., 1919-20; head dept. biology, U. of Chattanooga, 1920-31; head dept. biology, Drew U., since 1931. Mem. Am. Assn. Univ. Profs., A.A.A.S., Am. Genetics Soc., Am. Assn. for Med. Progress, Wilson Ornithol. Club, Sigma Xi. Presbyn. Home: 7 Woodside Rd., Madison, N.J.

GREENAN, John Thomas, author, teacher; b. New York, N.Y., Nov. 25, 1890; s. John Thomas and Jennie (Cunningham) G.; student New Hampton (N.H.) Lit. Inst., 1910-11; A.B., Bates Coll., Lewiston, Me., 1915; A.M., Columbia U., 1919; m. Persis Kendall, Dec. 25, 1915; children—Sybil, Jeanne. Teacher of history, Revere (Mass.) High Sch., 1915-17, East Orange (N.J.) High Sch., 1917-37; head dept. social studies, C.J. Scott High Sch., East Orange, N.J., since 1937; instr. summer normal schs., N.J., Bates Coll., Summer Sch., Lewiston, Me., 1921-36. Mem. N.E.A., Nat. Council of Social Studies, Middle States and Md. Assn. of Teachers of Social Studies, Pi Gamma Mu. Independent Republican. Congregational. Mason (East Orange Lodge 208). Author: (with A. B. Meredith) Everyday Problems of Am. Democracy, 1924; Readings in Am. Citizenship, 1928; (with J. M. Gathany) Units in World History, 1934; Am. Civilization Today, 1934; From Then Until Now (with M. Louise Cottrell), 1936. Address: 312 N. Walnut St., East Orange, N.J.

GREENAWALT, Emerson Guy, supervising prin. of schools; b. July 30, 1890; s. George Albert and Mary Elizabeth (Fox) G.; ed. Franklin and Marshall Coll., Columbia U., Pa. State Coll.; m. Lola Harvey; 1 dau., Jane Elizabeth. Began as elementary grade teacher, Franklin Co., Pa.; teacher, Lancaster (Pa.) High Sch., 1919-20; asst. prin., Sunbury (Pa.) High Sch., 1920-22; supervising prin., Hummelstown, Pa., 1927-29; supervising prin., Susquehanna, Pa., since 1929. Served in U.S. Army, Camp Meade, during World War, 11 months; disch. as sergt. maj. Mem. Pa. State Edn. Assn., A.A.A.S., Am. Legion, Kappa Phi Kappa. Republican. Mem. Reformed Ch. Mason (K.T.). Club; Rod and Gun (Susquehanna). Home: 518 Church St., Susquehanna, Pa.

GREENBAUM, Frederick Rudolph, dir. of research, research chemist; b. Vienna, Austria, Feb. 14, 1896; s. Jacob and Josephine (Kisch) G.; came to U.S., 1921, and naturalized citizen, 1927; Chem. Engr., Polytechnicum of Vienna, 1918; D.Sc., U. of Vienna, 1921; m. Margaret Sperling, August 30, 1935. Research chemist for Calco Chemical Company, 1921-22; with Dermatological Research Labs., Phila, Pa., 1922-29; with G. D. Searle & Co., Chicago, Ill., 1929-33; research chemist and dir. of research, National Drug Co., Phila., Pa., since 1933. Mem. Am. Chem. Soc., Am. Pharm. Assn., German-Am. Technologists. Hebrew-Christian. Contbr. over 35 articles in med., pharm. and chem. mags. Also holds several U.S. patents on his inventions. Home: 450 W. Mt. Airy Av. Office: 4663 Stenton Av., Philadelphia, Pa.

GREENBAUM, Sigmund Samuel, dermatologist; b. Philadelphia, Mar. 17, 1890; s. Joseph and Sarah (Klein) G.; B.S., Central High Sch., Phila., 1909; M.D., Jefferson Med. Coll., Phila., 1913; m. Rae Reffowich, Nov. 27, 1922; children—Charles, Edwin, Carol, Janet. Practiced Phila. since 1913; prof. clin. dermatology and syphilology, U. of Pa.; grad. Sch. of Med., since 1935; attending dermatologist, Mount Sinai and Phila. Gen. hosps. since 1922; cons. dermatologist, Eagleville Sanitarium and formerly U.S. Vets. Administration; fellow in research, Inst. of Cutaneous Medicine. Served as capt. U.S. Med. Corps. Mem. A.M.A., Med. Soc. State of Pa., Phila. County Med. Soc., Am. Coll. of Physicians, Phila. Coll. of Physicians, Phi Delta Epsilon. Author: (with H. Prinz) Diseases of the Mouth, 1935. Contbr. to med. jours. Home: 1801 De Lancey Place, Philadelphia, Pa.

GREENBERG, Joseph; judge Dist. Court of N.J. Address: Hoboken, N.J.

GREENBERG, Reynold H., real estate; b. Baltimore, Md., Apr. 3, 1899; s. Bernard and Ray (Pimes) G.; ed. Baltimore City Coll., 1912-16, Johns Hopkins U.; 1916; m. Dora Wiel, June 21, 1921; children—Reynold H., Jr., Robert Ray, Lois Bernice. Began as ins. clk., 1916, then supt. audit dept., New Amsterdam Casualty Co. to 1918; in real estate business on own acct., 1919-28, mem. firm with bro., 1928-30, sec. and treas. Jos. J. & Reynold H. Greenberg, Inc., since 1930; pres. Wilkie Buick Co., Solidarity Bldg. & Loan Assn.; vice-pres. Phila. Marble & Tile Co.; pres. and treas. Rajore Co. Served as chief auditor, Emergency Fleet Corpn., Bristol, Pa., 1918-19; in U.S.N. Res. asso. chmn. Fed. Jewish Charities Drive for $4,000,000. Trustee Mt. Sinai Hosp.; founder and trustee Camp Council for Poor Girls; chmn. Nurses Training Sch. Com. for Mt. Sinai Hosp. Fellow Am. Inst. Property Management. Republican. Jewish religion. Clubs: Locust, Philmont Country. Home: 430 Ashbourne Rd., Elkins Park. Office: Architects Bldg., Philadelphia, Pa.

GREENBERG, Simon, rabbi; b. Horoshen, Russia, Jan. 8, 1901; s. Morris and Bessie (Chaidenko) G.; was brought to US., 1905 and naturalized citizen, 1924; ed. U. of Minn., 1920-21; A.B., Coll. of City of N.Y., 1922; Rabbi, Jewish Theol. Sem. New York, 1925; Ph.D. Dropsie Coll., Phila., 1932; grad. study Hebrew U. in Jerusalem, Am. Sch. for Oriental Research, Jerusalem, 1924-25; m. Betty Davis, Dec. 13, 1925; children— Moshe, Daniel Asher. Rabbi, Har Zion Temple, Phila., since 1925; lecturer in Jewish edn., Jewish Theol. Sem. since 1932, vis. lecturer in homilectics, 1938-39. Dir. Horace Berks Hosp. for Mental Diseases. Pres. Rabbinical Assembly of America, 1937-39, vice-pres., 1935-37, Dropsie Coll. Alumni Assn., 1938-39. Past pres. Avukah-Intercoll. Zionist Orgn., Phila. Branch of United Synagogue, Phila. Bd. Jewish Ministers. Mem. Chaplains Religious Council of U. of Pa., Bd. Dirs. Asso. Talmud Torahs of Phila., Bd. Dirs. Allied Jewish Appeal, Phila. Author: Living as a Jew To-day, 1939; Harishon—A Series of Texts for the Study of Hebrew. Contbr. sermons and articles to mags. Home: 2253 N. 53d St. Office: 2258 Georges Lane, Philadelphia, Pa.

GREENE, Arthur Maurice, Jr., mechanical engr., educator; b. Phila., Pa., Feb. 4, 1872; s. Arthur Maurice and Eleanor J. (Lowry) G.; grad. Phila. Manual Training Sch., 1889; B.S., U. of Pa., 1893, M.E., 1894, Sc.D., 1917; D.Eng., Rensselaer Polytech. Inst., 1922; studied in Germany, summers, 1896 and 1905; m. Mary Elizabeth Lewis, June 12, 1906. In charge of apprentice sch., Franklin Sugar Refinery, Phila., 1892-94; instr., Drexel Inst., 1894-95, U. of Pa., 1895-1902; prof. mech. engring., U. of Mo., 1902-07, and jr. dean Sch. of Engring., 1906-07; prof. mech. engring., Rensselaer Poly. Inst., 1907-22; dean Sch. of Engring., prof. mech. engring., Princeton U., since 1922. Consulting engr. for power plants and mfg.; expert in patent causes. Mem. World Power Conferences, 1930 and 1936. Former mem. Bcard of Edn., Princeton, N.J. Former mem. Nat. Research Council (engring. div.); chmn. power plant com. U.S. Fuel Administration for Rensselaer Co., N.Y.; "Four Minute Man"; mem. War Service League of Troy; mem. engring. council, war com. of tech. socs. Trustee Princeton Hosp.; formerly trustee Troy Public Library and v.p. Troy Y.M.C.A. Mem. Govs. Highway Safety Council of N.J. Fellow A.A.A.S., Am. Soc. M.E. (former mgr. and v.p.; chmn. research com.; mem. boiler code com.; chmn. com. on awards); mem. Franklin Inst., Soc. Promotion Engring. Edn. (pres. 1919-20), Soc. Engrs. Eastern N.Y. (ex-pres.), Am. Engring. Council, Newcomen Soc., Guild of Brackett Lecturers of Princeton Univ., Kappa Sigma, Sigma Xi, Phi Beta Kappa, Tau Beta Pi, Mu Phi Alpha; hon. mem. Princeton Engring. Assn. Awarded silver medal, Jugo-Slovakian Red Cross. Republican. Baptist. Mason. Clubs: University of Columbia, Mo. (life), Nassau (Princeton); Princeton (New York). Author: Elements of Steam Engineering (with H. W. Spangler and S. M. Marshall), 1902; Pumping Machinery, 1911; Elements of Heating and Ventilation, 1912; Heat Engineering, 1914; Elements of Refrigeration, 1916; Elements of Power Generation, 1933; Elements of Hydraulic Power Generation, 1934; Principles of Heating, Ventilating and Air Conditioning, 1936; Principles of Thermodynamics, Part I, 1938, Part II, 1939. Has traveled widely in America and Europe. Home: Farview, Fitz Randolph Rd., Princeton, N.J.

GREENE, Bartlett, advertising mgr.; b. Philadelphia, Pa., Jan. 28, 1880; s. Frank Bartlett and Jane Peterson (Deacon) G.; ed. Franklin Sch. and Friends Select Sch.; A.B., Brown U., 1901; m. Ruth Schenck, Feb. 14, 1917; children—Margaret Jane, Eleanor Louise. Began as salesman Remington Typewriter Co., 1902, located at Philadelphia, later Cleveland, mgr. offices at Binghamton, N.Y., and Toledo, O., 1905-10; became employed by Sterling Tire Corpn., Rutherford, N.J., 1911, later becoming secretary and salesmanager; joined western office Fidelity & Deposit Co. of Baltimore, 1925; agency supt. New York Indemnity Co., 1926-27, v.p., 1928-29; asst. sec. Nat. Assn. Ins. Agents since 1929; nat. advertising mgr. Am. Agency Bulletin. Mem. Alpha Delta Phi, Phi Beta Kappa. Republican. Club: Alpha Delta Phi (New York). Home: 28 West Drive, Marven Gardens, Margate, N.J. Office: 80 Maiden Lane, New York, N.Y.

GREENE, Edward McVitty, leather mfr., retired; b. Saltillo, Pa., May 19, 1871; s. Calvin and Amanda Jane (McVitty) G.; ed. Juniata Coll., 1889-90, West Chester State Normal, 1890-91, Bucknell U., 1891-94; m. Caroline W. Wittenmyer, Nov. 1, 1900; children—Edward McVitty, Jr., Waldo Wittenmyer. Mem. firm Calvin Greene & Son, 1895-1901; pres. Mount Union Tanning & Extract Co. since 1901, Union Poster Advertising Inc. since 1932, Porcion Land Co. since 1931, Encino Corpn. since 1938. Served as U.S. Federal Fuel Adminstr. for Huntingdon Co., Pa., 1917-19. Mem. Rep. State Com. of Pa., 4 yrs. Held several local polit. offices. Trustee Bucknell Univ. Mem. Huntingdon Hist. Soc., Phi Kappa Psi. Republican. Baptist. Mason (K.T.). Desc. of Scotch-Irish and English settlers who came to America 175 yrs. ago. Home: Huntingdon, Pa.

GREENE, Floyd L., pres. Gen. Refractories Co.; b. McConnellstown, Pa., Nov. 30, 1888; s. Wilson E. and Florence (Yocum) G.; student pub. sch.; Juniata Coll. (Huntingdon, Pa.) and business coll.; m. Ella M. Huyette, July 3, 1911; children—Anna Florence, Herbert E., Richard S., Jack H., Robert E. Began as sch. teacher near McConnellstown, Pa., later Centre Union, Pa.; traveled over central part of state for Pa. Forestry Dept.; started in mill, Standard Refractories Co., Claysburg, Pa., 1913, advancing through various positions to gen. supt. when co. absorbed by Gen. Refractories Co., Phila., Pa., 1922, and became dist. mgr. of Central Pa., Claysburg, Pa., later in exec. offices, Phila., as works mgr., v.p., 1924-36, exec. v.p., 1936-37, pres. since 1937, now also dir.; v.p. and dir. First Nat. Bank of Claysburg. Mem. Am. Refractories Inst. (dir. and mem. exec. com.). Mason (32°, Shriner); Elk. Clubs: Union League, Rolling Green Golf (Phila.); Duquesne (Pittsburgh); Bankers' (New York); South Shore Country (Chicago). Home: St. Davids, Pa. Office: 1600 Real Estate Trust Bldg., Philadelphia, Pa.

GREENE, Harry Washington, educator; b. New Bern, N.C., Feb. 28, 1897; s. Elvin and Sophia (Dudley) G.; student N.C. Coll. for Negroes, Durham, N.C., 1911-13; A.B., Lincoln U., Chester Co., Pa., 1917, A.M., 1918; grad. student Yale U., 1919-20; A.M. in Edn., Columbia U., 1927; m. Viola Loretta Johnson, Mar. 14, 1939. Engaged as dir. teacher training, Winston-Salem (N.C.) Teachers Coll., 1920-21; asst. prin. high sch., New Bern, N.C., 1921-22; dean Samuel Huston Coll., and dir. Summer School, Austin, Tex., 1922-28; dean Prairie View (Tex.) State Coll., dir. Summer School and dir. Bureau of Research, 1928-30; dir. teacher edn. W.Va. State Coll., Institute, W.Va., since 1930, prof. edn. since 1930. Gen. chmn. State Ednl. Expn., 1939. Trustee Samuel Huston Coll. Mem. N.E.A., Am. Assn. Sch. Administrs., Progressive Assn. of America, John Dewey Soc. of America, Supervisors of Student Teachers, Acad. Polit. & Social Sci., Am. Teachers Assn., W.Va. Teachers Assn., Nat. Adv. Com. on Edn. of Negroes, W.Va. State Policy Com. on Teacher Edn., Alpha Phi Alpha. Democrat. Methodist. Clubs: Research Council of Institute (chmn.); Business and Professional Men's (Charleston). Author: (monographs) Criteria of Teaching Excellence; Negro Leaders; An Adventure in Experimental Co-operative Teaching. Contbr. articles to School and Society Jour. of Negro Edn., Opportunity, etc. Home: W.Va. State Coll., Institute, W.Va.

GREENE, Herbert Eveleth; prof. emeritus English lit., Johns Hopkins U. Address: Johns Hopkins University, Baltimore, Md.

GREENE, John H., in gen. practice law since 1902; mem. W.Va. State Senate, 6th Dist. Address: Williamson, W.Va.

GREENE, (Richard) Laurence, writer; b. New York, N.Y., June 19, 1906; s. Richard Francis and Ellen (Keogh) G.; student pub. schs. and high sch., N.Y. City; m. Katherine Bosworth, Dec. 28, 1929. Began as newspaper reporter, 1924; employed on various Am. newspapers since 1924; now sub-editor Baltimore Sun. Author: America Goes to Press, 1936; The Filibuster, 1937; O'Mara (novel), 1938; The Era of Wonderful Nonsense, 1939. Office: Baltimore Sun, Baltimore, Md.

GREENE, Lloyd Belt, physician; b. Buckhead Plantations, Burke Co., Ga., July 24, 1893; s. John Alfred and Mary Jessie (Walton) G.; student Acad. of Richmond County, 1906-10, Porter Mil. Acad., Charleston, S.C., 1910-11; M.D., U. of Ga., 1917; post-grad. study, Paris, Vienna, 1924; married, June 9, 1923; children —George M., Mary W., Martha G. Lieut. Med. Corps, U.S. Navy, 1917-24; in practice of urology, Phila., since 1925; asst. prof. of urology, Grad. Sch., U. of Pa., since 1937; urologist Pa. Hosp.; Bryn Mawr Hosp., Burlington Co. Hosp. Lt. comdr. Med. Corps U.S.N.R. since June 1924. Mem. A.M.A., Am. Urol. Assn., Am. Bd. of Urology, Phila. Urol. Soc. (pres.), Alpha Kappa Kappa. Republican. Episcopalian. Clubs: Burlington County Country. Officers of U.S. Navy (Phila.). Home: 6807 Quincy St. Office: Medical Arts Bldg., Philadelphia, Pa.

GREENE, L(uther) Wilson, chem. engring.; b. Portsmouth, Va., Nov. 3, 1900; s. Luther Wilson and Ruth Virginia (Fulford) G.; B.S., N.C. State Coll., Raleigh, N.C., 1922; m. Elizabeth Eugenia Holland, Oct. 20, 1923; 1 dau., Barbara Louise. Employed as chemist N.C. State Highway Commn., 1922; research chemist paint, varnish and lacquer, E. I. duPont de Nemours and Co., Phila., 1922-29; chem. engr. research and munitions development divs., sr. chem. engr., chief plants dept., C.W.S., U.S.A. at Edgewood Arsenal, Md., since 1929. Served as res. officer, U.S. Army, 1922-37. Mem. Am. Chem. Soc., Am. Micros. Soc., Am. Oil Chemists' Soc., Gamma Sigma Epsilon, Kappa Iota Epsilon. Presbyterian. Contbr. many scientific papers and articles to chem. publs. Mem. staff, Chemical Abstracts. Home: Rogers St., Aberdeen, Md.

GREENE, Richard Thurston, lawyer; b. Port Henry, N.Y., June 29, 1867; s. James Gardner and Mary Helen (Rice) G.; B.S., Rutgers U., 1889; LL.B., Albany (N.Y.) Law Sch., 1891; m. Charlotte Louise Berry, June 21, 1896; children—Charlotte Louise, Helen (Mrs. James C. Heminway), Marion (Mrs. Ferdinand K. Thun), Karolyn (Mrs. John O. Cole), Thurston. Admitted to N.Y. bar and practicing atty. since 1891; dir. Lawyers Trust Co., Nat. Casket Co., Cutler Mail Chute Co., Nipissing Mines Co., Ltd., Nipissing Mining Co., Ltd. Pres. Montclair (N.J.) Bd. of Edn. Trustee Rutgers U., Montclair Y.M.C.A. Mem. Am. and N.Y. State bar assns., New York Co. Lawyers Assn., N.Y. Geneal. and Biog. Soc., New England Soc., U.S. Senior Golf Assn., Soc. of the Genesee, Delta Kappa Epsilon (ex-pres.). Republican. Conglist. (trustee First Ch.). Mason. Clubs: University, India House (New York); Montclair Golf; Hyannisport Golf (Cape Cod). Home: 239 S. Mountain Av., Montclair, N.J. Office: 61 Broadway, New York, N.Y.

GREENEWALT, Mary (Elizabeth) Hallock, pianist; b. in Beirut, Syria; d. of Samuel and Sara (Tabet) Hallock; educated under German Deaconess Sisters, Beyrouth; came to America, 1882; grad. Chelten Hills Sch., Phila., 1888; studied piano with Theodore Leschetizky, Vienna; grad. Phila. Musical Acad., 1893; m. Frank Lindsay Greenewalt, M.D., July 14, 1898; 1 son, Crawford Hallock. Piano soloist with Pittsburgh and Phila. symphony orchestras in tours; concertized in piano recital throughout country; lectured on rhythm at U. of Kan., Ia., Grinnell, Earlham, Holyoke and Vassar colls.; concertizing throughout America, 1909-10 and 1912-13. Hon. mem. Browning Soc.; mem. Illuminating Engrs.' Soc., Society of Arts and Letters; life member Woman Suffrage Soc. of county of Phila. Del. to 45th Annual Conv. the Nat. Am. Woman Suffrage Assn. Editor authorized textbook of the Leschetizky method by Marie Prentner. First to use a color lighting accompaniment shifting in sympathetic feeling with the phases of a musical composition during its performance. Inventor of basic patents dealing with the method for the use of light as a means of expression and with music; manufacturer of light and color players. Author: Light—Fine Art the Sixth, 1916. Magazine articles representing original research, "Pulse and Rhythm," 1903, and "Pulse and Verbal Rhythm," 1904; "Time Eternal," 1906. Hon. mem. Thursday Musical Club, Minneapolis, Minn.; chmn. 4th Congressional Dist. Nat. Woman's Party. Gold medallist, Phila. Conservatory; award gold medal Sesquicentennial Expn., Phila., 1926, for developing illumination as means of expression; adjudged inventor of light-color play as a means of human expression in combination with music, by Federal Dist. Court of Del. and Federal Circuit Court of 3d Dist. Coined words "nourathar" and "sarabet" to designate the art of light-color play and the instrument used. The Hist. Soc. of Pa. is repository of her light-color play documents. Address: Hotel du Pont, Wilmington, Del., and The Gladstone, Philadelphia, Pa.

GREENFIELD, Albert M(onroe), real estate broker and banker; b. in Ukraine, Aug. 4, 1887; s. Jacob and Esther E. V. (Serody) Greenfield; ed. at U. of Pa., 1905-06; m. Edna Florence Kraus, June 18, 1914 (divorced 1935); children—Gordon K., Elizabeth E. V., Carlotta, Patricia, Albert Monroe; m. 2d, Etelka J. Schamberg, Oct. 1, 1937. Real estate broker and banker since 1905; receiver and reorganizer of Producers and Consumers Bank, 1925-26; rehabilitation trustee for 17 building and loan assns., 1926-28; pres. Albert M. Greenfield & Co.; chmn. bd. Bankers Securities Corpn., Phila., Pa., Lit Bros. Dept. Store, Phila., Pa., City Stores Co., New York, Union Building Co. of Newark, N. J., Bankers Bond and Mortgage Guaranty Co. of America, New York, Bankers Bond & Mortgage Co. of Pa., Bankers Bond & Mortgage Co. of New York, Bonwit Teller Co., Phila., Mark Store, Miami; dir. Maison Blanche Co., New Orleans, La., Kaufman, Straus Co., Louisville, Ky., Loveman, Joseph & Loeb, Birmingham, Ala., B. Lowenstein & Bros., Memphis, Tenn., Phila. Record Co., Camden Courier-Post Co., New York Post Co., Mastbaum Loan System (hon.); trustee and chmn. of the reorganization managers of Phila. Rapid Transit Co.; dir. Bd. of City Trusts. Mem. City Council, 1918-19; dir. Sesquicentennial Expn. and chmn. finance com., 1926; apptd. chmn. Pa. Constitution Commemoration Com., 1938, awarded Pa. Distinguished Service medal in recognition of services as chmn. Mem. Philadelphia Chamber of Commerce (chmn. convention and tourists com.); chmn. com. on admission, discipline and discharge, Girard Coll.; mem. of com. of award

GREENFIELD, Kent Roberts, prof. history; b. Chestertown, Md., July 20, 1893; s. David Lee and Kate Mathews (Roberts) G.; Washington Coll., Chestertown, 1905-07; A.B., Western Md. Coll., 1911; Ph.D., Johns Hopkins, 1915; unmarried. Instr. in history and economics, U. of Del., 1915-16, asst. prof., 1916-19, asso. prof., 1919-20; prof. history, Rutgers, summers 1916, 17; asst. prof. history, Yale, 1920-30, Sterling fellow, leave of absence for research in Italy, 1929; prof. modern European history and chmn. of dept., Johns Hopkins, since 1930. Served as 2d lt. inf., U.S.A., 1918-19. Pres. Roland Park Country School. Mem. Am. Hist. Assn., Am. Hist. Assn. Univ. Profs., History Teachers Assn. Middle States and Md., Phi Beta Kappa, Presbyn. Clubs: Political Economy, P. L. Club, 16 W. Hamilton St. Club. Author: Sumptuary Law in Nürnberg—A Study in Paternal Government, 1918; Economics and Liberalism in the Risorgimento, 1934. Contbr. to Am. Hist. Review, Yale Review, Jour. of Modern History. Home: Tudor Arms, University Parkway, Baltimore, Md.

GREENLEAF, William Eben, coll. prof. and dean; b. Henniker, N.H., July 16, 1890 s. Eben Selden and Annie Eliza (Grover) G.; student Troy Conference Acad., Poultney, Vt., 1905-06, Hinesburg (Vt.) High Sch., 1907-09; A.B. (cum laude), Middlebury (Vt.) Coll., 1913; M.A., Yale, 1917, Ph.D., 1926; m. Elisabeth Bristol, Oct. 22, 1921; 1 son, Robert William. Prin., Pawlet (Vt.) High and Grade Sch., 1913-14; prof. biology Defiance (O.) Coll., 1915-16; visiting substitute instr. botany, Wesleyan U., Middletown, Conn., 1917; instr. zoology, Syracuse (N.Y.) U., 1921-23; instr. and asst. prof. zoology, Wesleyan U., Middletown, Conn., 1924-29; asst. prof. zoology, Marshall Coll., Huntington, W.Va., 1929-31, prof. since 1931, dean Coll. of Arts and Sciences since 1929. Served as pvt., student, head lab. asst., M.C., U.S. Army Med. Sch., Washington, D.C., 1918, 2d lt., S.C., 1918-19. Sub-dist. comdr. Near East Relief, Turkey and Caucasus Russia, 1919-20. Mem. Delta Sigma, Phi Beta Kappa, Gamma Alpha, Sigma Xi. Awarded jr. and sr. prizes in pedagogical essays, Middlebury Coll., 1912 and 1913. Republican. Presbyterian. Club: Huntington (W. Va.) Executives. Address: 1007 Euclid Pl., Huntington, W.Va.

GREENSLADE, Grover Rawle, dir. research; b. Moscow, Ida., May 21, 1886; s. James and Eliza (Rawle) G.; B.S. and M.S., Whitman Coll., Walla Walla, Wash.; M.A., U. of Wash., Seattle; Ph.D., U. of Wis., Madison; m. Esther Gunell, June 25, 1924. Designing engr. Gilbert Hunt Co., 1910-13; fellow, U. of Wis., 1914-15, mem. regent-faculty com., 1915-16, instr. physics, 1916-17, in charge instrn. in radio communication, Madison Cantonment, 1917-18, instr. engring. physics, 1918-20; physicist in charge heat-flow experimentation for Holland Tunnel, U.S. Bur. of Mines, 1921; chief physicist Flannery Interests, 1922; chief physicist Flannery Bolt Co., Bridgeville, Pa., 1922-33, dir. of research since 1937; chief chemist Am. Stentex Corpn., 1934, Pittsburgh Dry Stencil Co., 1935-36. Fellow Am. Physical Soc., A.A.A.S.; mem. Physical Soc. of Pittsburgh (v.p. 1932-34, pres. 1938-39), Am. Soc. Mech. Engrs., Army Ordnance Assn. Club: Pittsburgh Railway. Writer articles on spectra of metals, measuring smoke density, heat flow in mine tunnels, electrical testing of locomotive boilers, boiler sheet expansion, etc. Home: Greentree Rd., Crafton, Pittsburgh, Pa. Office: care Flannery Bolt Co., Bridgeville, Pa.

GREENSTONE, Julius Hillel, author; b. Russia, Apr. 27, 1873; s. Pesach David and Leah (Puskelinsky) G.; A.B., Coll. City of New York, 1900; rabbi Jewish Theol. Sem., 1900) A.B., U. of Pa., 1902, Ph.D., 1905, L.H.D. honoris causa, 1925; m. Carrie E. Amerach, 1902 (now deceased); m. 2d, Mrs. Ray Abeles, Sept. 5, 1916; children—Leah C. Farber, Gella G. Kraus, Deborah Greenstone. Teacher, Gratz Coll., Philadelphia, 1905-33, prin. since 1933. Mem. bd. dirs. United Synagogue of America. Editor: S. Morais' Italian Hebrew Litèrature, 1926. Author: The Religion of Israel, 1902; The Messiah Idea in Jewish History, 1906; Methods of Teaching the Jewish Religion in Junior and Senior Grades, 1915, revised edit. The Jewish Religion, 1920. Contributor to Rabbinic dept. Jewish Ency.; also to Jewish Quarterly Rev., Am. Jewish Year Book, etc.; dept. editor Jewish Exponent, Phila. Home: 1926 N. 13th St., Philadelphia, Pa.

GREENWAY, Walter Burton, clergyman, educator; b. Broylesville, Tenn., Aug. 18, 1876; A.B. from Washington (Tennessee) College, 1897 student Union Theol. Sem., N.Y. City, 1897-99; grad. study Columbia, 1899; grad. Princeton (N.J.) Theological Seminary, 1900; LL.D., Muskingum College, New Concord, O., 1931; also D.D., Washington College, Tenn.; m. Lillian Gilbert, June 28, 1905; children—Walter Samuel, William Lyndal, Dorothy Nancy. Ordained ministry Presbyn. Ch., 1900; pastor Elizabeth Av. Presbyn. Ch., 1900-05, Westminster Presbyn. Ch., Jersey City, N.J., 1905-11, Gaston Presbyn. Ch., Phila., Pa., 1911-19; gen. sec. dept. evangelism Presbyn. Gen. Assembly, 1919-22; pastor Bethany Temple Presbyn. Ch., Phila., 1922-28; pres. Beaver Coll. for Women since 1928. Chaplain, Camps Mills, Gordon and McClellan, World War. Vice pres. Stony Brook Sch. for Boys; trustee Washington Coll., Beman Manual Training Sch., Pa. State S.S. Assn., Phila., S.S. Assn., Pa. Anti-Saloon League, Phila. Sabbath Sch. Assn. Republican. Mason, Odd Fellow; mem. Royal Arcanum. Clubs: Union League, Princeton, City, Ministers. Author: Passion Week Sermons, 1926; Lenten Sermons, 1927; Sermons to Young People, 1927. Home: Jenkintown, Pa.

GREENWOOD, Harry Delbert, chem. and metall. engr.; b. Clinton, Mass., Nov. 10, 1875; s. Henry and Delilah (Manchester) G.; grad. Clinton High Sch., 1893; studied Worcester Poly. Inst., 1893-95; B.S., Cornell U., 1897; m. Emma J. Peterson, of Des Moines, Ia., Nov. 15, 1911; children—Helen G., Harry D. Chemist Everett Mills, Lawrence, Mass., 1897, Willimantic Linen Co., Willimantic, Conn., 1898, Nat. Steel Co., Youngstown, O., 1899, Juarez Mining Co., Juarez, Mex., 1900-01, Bingham Can Co., Midvale, Utah, 1902-03, U.S. Metals Refining Co., Carteret, N.J., 1903-36; owner H. D. Greenwood Co., chem. and metall. consultants, since 1936. Mem. Nat. Research Council. Mem. Am. Chem. Soc., Am. Electro Chem. Soc., Am. Soc. Testing Materials, Soc. Chem. Industry, British Inst. Metals. Republican. Unitarian. Mason (K.T., Shriner), Odd Fellow. Address: 883 Colonia Road, Elizabeth, N.J.

GREENZWEIG, Oscar Albert, banker; b. Kunkeltown, Pa., Jan. 6, 1878; s. George and Mary (Frantz) G.; ed. pub. schs.; m. Estella G. Knecht, Mar. 15, 1900; children—Albert, Ralph, Fred. Merchant, 1900-19; pres. Citizens Bank of Wind Gap since 1917. Served as chief burgess of Borough of Wind Gap, 2 terms; chief Wind Gap Fire Co. since 1920; mgr. Wind Gap Fire Co. Band since 1922; dist. forest fire warden since 1912. Trustee Easton Hosp. since 1934; mem. exec. com. Boy Scouts of America. Mem. Fraternal Patriotic Americans, Travelers Protecting Assn. Democrat. Lutheran. Club: Northampton County Motor (dir. and officer since 1922). Odd Fellow, Elk, Moose. Address: Wind Gap, Pa.

GREER, Charles Coover, judge; b. East Taylor Twp., Pa., Mar. 30, 1868; s. David Francis Asbury and Mary Jane (Coover) G.; grad. Johnstown (Pa.) High Sch., 1886, Dickinson Coll., Carlisle, Pa., 1892; m. Georgia Bratton, 1895 (died 1918); children—Mrs. J. C. Potter, Mrs. Hans Fiedler, Catharine, Robert B., Charles A.; m. 2d, Margaret Frances Kerr, Oct. 1919. City solicitor of Johnstown, Pa., 1899-1908; dist. atty. of Cambria Co., Johnstown, Pa., 1912-16; later fuel administrator of Cambria Co., Johnstown, Pa.; judge Court of Common Pleas of Cambria Co., Johnstown, Pa., since 1932. Mem. bd. of incorporators and dir., Mercy Hosp., Johnstown, Pa. Mem. Phi Beta Kappa, Phi Kappa Psi. Author: A Short Biography of Herbert Hoover. Home: Heidelberg Lane, Borough of Westmont. Office: 403 U.S. Bank Bldg., Johnstown, Pa.

GREER, Herbert Chester, steel mfr.; b. Sharon, Pa., Aug. 11, 1877; s. Charles and Mary (Park) G.; grad. Kiskiminetas Springs Sch., Saltsburg, Pa., 1895; B.S., Mass. Inst. Tech., 1899; m. Agnes J. Reeves, June 3, 1908; 1 dau., Jane. Began as steel mill employee with Sharon Steel Co., 1899; successively with Tenn. Coal, Iron & Steel Co., La Belle Iron Works, Preston County (W.Va.) Coke Co., and Reeves Mfg. Co. and Greer Steel Co. of Dover, O.; pres. Reeves Mfg. Co., Greer Steel Co., Preston Co. Coke Co., Preston Co. Light & Power Co., Greer Limestone Co., and W.Va. Newspaper Co.; owner of five newspapers in W.Va. Republican. Methodist. Mason. Clubs: Duquesne (Pittsburgh); Union (Dover); Everglades, Bath and Tennis (Palm Beach, Fla.). Home: Morgantown, W.Va.

GREER, Robert Bratton, lawyer; b. Johnstown, Pa., Sept. 19, 1896; s. Charles Coover and Georgia Boyd (Bratton) G.; A.B., Haverford Coll., 1920; LL.B., Harvard U. Law Sch., 1923; m. Virginia Brown, July 27, 1935; 1 son, Robert McPherson. Admitted to Pa. bar, 1923, and engaged in gen. practice of law at Phila., 1923-26, and in Media since 1927; mem. firm Greer and Johnson since 1934. Served as pvt. Base Hosp., U.S.A., 1917-19, with A.E.F. in France; 1st lieut. San. Corps, 1918. Mem. Pa. Bar Assn., Am. Legion. Republican. Club: Haverford. Home: Farnum Rd., Media, Pa. Office: 17 South Av., Media, Pa.

GREER, William Russell, v.p. Porcelain Enamel & Mfg. Co.; b. Baltimore, Md., June 28, 1892; s. William John and Mollie E. (Brown) G.; student Baltimore Poly. Inst., Johns Hopkins U.; m. Louise Browning Linhardt, Oct. 14, 1914; 1 dau., Dorothy Louise. Salesmgr. Porcelain Enamel & Mfg. Co., 1921-31, v.p. in charge of sales since 1931. Home: 6309 Mossway. Office: Eastern and Pemco Avs., Baltimore, Md.

GREGG, Albert Edmund, clergyman; b. County Derry, Ireland, June 25, 1893; s. William and Elizabeth (Evans) G.; came to U.S., 1913, naturalized, 1918; A.B., Muskingum Coll., New Concord, O., 1924; Th.B., Pittsburgh Theol. Sem., 1927; Th.M., Pittsburgh-Xenia Theol. Sem., 1933; (hon.) D.D., Cedarville Coll., Cedarville, O., 1930; m. Hazel M. Hartman, Sept. 23, 1919; 1 dau., Mary Ann. Ordained to ministry Presbyn. Ch., 1927; asst. minister First Reformed Presbyn. Ch., Pittsburgh, Pa., 1925-27, minister, 1927-38; minister Logan Memorial Presbyn. Ch., Audubon, N.J., since 1938. Served as pvt. inf., U.S.A., 1918-19 with A.E.F. in France and Italy. Mem. Am. Legion. Republican. Presbyn. Home: 18 W. Merchant St., Audubon, N.J.

GREGG, William C.; b. Pittsburgh, Pa., July 17, 1862; s. Cephas (educator) and Mary (Newton) G.; student U. of Neb., 1880-82; m. Mary A. Damarin, Sept. 18, 1889; children—Louis D., Otis T., W. Burr, Mrs. Rachel de Clairmont, Mrs. Mary Young. Inventor of ry. appliances; founded the Gregg Co., Ltd., of which is president. An authority on national parks, forests and reclamation; vice chmn. Southern Appalachian National Park Commission, 1924. In Y.M.C.A. service in France, 1918; visited (by request) Am. and British fronts and reported to hdqrs. on uses of light rys. Mem. Nat. Parks Assn., Council of Nat. Parks, Forests and Wild Life, Audubon Society, American Civic Assn., etc.; fellow Nat. Acad. Design.

Republican. Protestant. Clubs: Arts, Cosmos (Washington, D.C.); Nat. Arts (New York). Author: Three Months in France in 1918. Contbr. to mags. on travel and polit. economy. Collector of old masters and antiques. Home: 330 Prospect Av., Hackensack, N.J.

GREGORY, Ralph Amherst, banker; b. Hollisterville, Pa., Aug. 17, 1877; s. Marion A. and Lillian (Stevens) G.; m. Grace Peck, Sept. 24, 1907. Has been associated with Title Guaranty & Trust Co., and County Savings Bank, Scranton; now pres. and dir. Third Nat. Bank & Trust Co., Scranton. Served as major 109th Inf., 28th Div., World War; overseas, May 1918-June 1919. Awarded Distinguished Service Cross. Mem. Scranton Chamber of Commerce, Am. Legion, Army and Navy Legion of Honor. Mason (Shriner). Clubs: Scranton, Scranton Country. Home: 1611 Jefferson Av. Office: 120 Wyoming Av., Scranton, Pa.

GREGORY, Thomas B., oil and gas producer; b. Philadelphia, Pa., Oct. 15, 1860; s. William Sheed and Amanda Walton (Miller) G.; ed. Brooks Mil. Acad., Cleveland, O.; m. Adda S. Whitling, June 21, 1888; children—Ruth Whitling, Katherine Elizabeth (Mrs. Charles McGill Thomas). Began in oil business at Foxburg, Pa., 1885; mem. firm Crawford & Gregory, oil and gas producers; dir. Columbia Gas & Electric Corpn., Lone Star Gas Corpn., Wilmington, Del., Mountain Fuel Supply Co., Salt Lake City, Utah, Quaker State Oil Refining Corpn., Oil City, Pa., Union Heat & Light Co., Grove City, Pa. Asst. to dir. oil production, U.S. Fuel Administration, later dir. Bur. Natural Gas, same administration, World War. Mem. Am. Petroleum Inst., Am. Gas Assn. Episcopalian. Home: Emlenton, Pa. Office: Union Trust Bldg., Pittsburgh, Pa.

GREGORY, Waylande, sculptor, designer and ceramist; b. Baxter Springs, Kan., June 13, 1905; s. William Thomas and Louise (DeBlumer) G.; ed. Kan. State Teachers Coll., Kansas City Art Inst., Lorado Taft Studio Fellow U. of Chicago, Travel Study in Europe; m. Yolande Von Wagner, Apr. 7, 1930. Has followed profession as sculptor, designer and ceramist since 1922; exhbns. by invitation, Met. Mus., N.Y., Paris Expn., 1937, Modern Museum, Washington, D.C., San Diego Palace of Fine Arts, Whitney Mus. Am. Art, San Francisco Expn., Nat. Ceramic Exhbn., Syracuse, N.Y., Chicago Art Inst. and many others in America and Europe. Permanently represented by "Fountain of Atoms," World's Fair, N.Y.; Sem. Cloister sculptures in U. of Chicago; two groups, General Motors Corpn., N.Y. City; Colossal Fountain, Roosevelt Park, N.J. Holder many awards and prizes; mem. Nat. Ceramic Art Jury, 1938. Home: Mountain Top Studio, Bound Brook, N.J.

GREGORY, William Scott, architect; b. Clinton, N.J., Aug. 26, 1865; s. Milton A. and Mary C. (Bonnell) G.; student Newark (N.J.) private and pub. schs.; m. Loulu Van Syckel Robbins, Apr. 8, 1891 (died 1927); children—Mildred, Kenneth Robbins. Began as architectural draughtsman and student, Newark, N.J., 1882; office mgr. Cady, Bergh & See, architects, New York, 1890-1905; partner J. Cleveland Cady, architect, New York, 1905-18; individual practice as architect specializing in churches, parish houses and institutional bldgs., New York, since 1918. Trustee and pres. Presbyn. Home of the Synod of N.J. Mem. Am. Inst. of Architects, N.J. Soc. of Architects, Wednesday Club of Newark. Republican. Presbyterian. Home: 427 New England Terrace, Orange, N.J. Office: 171 Madison Av., New York, N.Y.

GREIFINGER, Marcus Harry, surgeon; b. Rahway, N.J., Mar. 25, 1900; s. Bernard and Rachel (Steinberg) G.; student Barringer High Sch., Newark, N.J., 1913-17, N.Y. U., 1918-20; M.D., U. of Md. Med. Sch., Baltimore, Md., 1924; unmarried. Interne Newark (N.J.) City Hosp., 1924-26; in pvt. practice medicine and surgery, Newark, N.J., since 1926; mem. surg. staff Newark City Hosp., St. James Hosp., Newark Memorial Hosp., Beth Israel Hosp., Newark. Served as private, U.S. Army, during World War, hon. disch., 1918. Fellow Am. Coll. Surgeons; sec. Essex County Med. Soc.; mem. Am. Legion. Jewish religion. Mason, Elk. Home: 22 Vassar Av. Office: 200 Ferry St., Newark, N.J.

GREINER, John E., consulting engr.; b. Wilmington, Del., Feb. 24, 1859; s. John and Annie (Steck) G.; B.S., Delaware Coll., 1880, later C.E., Sc.D.; Dr. Engring., Johns Hopkins University, 1937; m. Lily F. Burchell, December 16, 1886; children—Lillian Burchell, Gladys Houston. Practiced, Baltimore, since 1908; has served as cons. engr., B.&O. R.R., Erie R.R., Norfolk & Southern R.R., State of Pa., State of Md., etc.; designed and built nine bridges across the Ohio River and many others east of the Mississippi River; also railroad ocean terminals, dams and highways. Member American Railway Commission to Russia, 5 months, 1917. Chairman Port Development Commn., authorized to expend $50,000,000 in improving the port of Baltimore. Mem. Am. Inst. Consulting Engrs., Am. Soc. Testing Materials, Am. Ry. Engring. Assn. (chmn. com. which adopted specifications for iron and steel structures); hon. mem. Am. Soc. C.E. Clubs: University, Elkridge Fox Hunting. Home: Ruxton, Md. Office: 1201 St. Paul St., Baltimore, Md.

GREISHEIMER, Esther Maud, prof. physiology; b. Chillicothe, O., Oct. 31, 1891; d. William and Elizabeth (Andre) G.; B.S., in Edn., O. Univ., 1914; A.M., Clark U., 1916; Ph.D., U. of Chicago, 1919; M.D., U. of Minn., 1923. Began as instr. U. of Minn., 1918-21; asst. prof. of physiology, Wellesley Coll., 1922; asst. prof. of physiology, U. of Minn., then asso. prof., 1922-35; prof. physiology, Woman's Med. Coll. of Pa. since 1935. Mem. Am. Med. Assn., Am. Physiol. Soc., Zeta Tau Alpha, Phi Beta Kappa, Alpha Omega Alpha, Sigma Xi, Iota Sigma Pi, Alpha Epsilon Iota. Republican. Mem. M.E. Ch. Author: Physiology and Anatomy, 1932, 3d edit., 1936. Contbr. about 50 sci. articles to mags. and journs. Home: 212 W. Highland Av., Chestnut Hill, Pa. Office: Woman's Med. Coll., East Falls, Philadelphia, Pa.

GREISS, George Albert, clergyman; b. Alburtis, Pa., Oct. 22, 1874; s. George Gehris and Anna Boyer (Scheirey) G.; B.Ed., Kutztown State Teachers Coll., 1891, M.Ed., 1893; A.B., Muhlenberg Coll., 1896, A.M., 1903; B.D., Lutheran Theol. Sem., Gettysburg, 1899; (hon.) D.D., Gettysburg Coll., 1917; m. Daisy Irene Lonabaugh, June 6, 1900; 1 dau., Dorothy Lonabaugh (wife of Rev. Elmer Pierre Truchses). Ordained to ministry United Luth. Ch., 1898; pastor, New Bloomfield, Pa., 1899-1900; pastor St. Paul's Luth. Ch., Allentown, Pa., continuously since 1900; pres. Luth. Theol. Sem., Gettysburg, Pa., since 1938; pres. Fgn. Mission Bd. United Luth. Ch. in America since 1938; mem. Spl. Com. on Ch. Paper Policy, United Luth. Ch. in America; has been pres., v.p. and sec., Easton Pa. Conf., pres. and sec. E. Pa. Synod; treas. E. Pa. Synodical Missionary Bd. Republican. Mem. U. Luth. Ch. Mason (K.T., 32°). Home: 38 S. 8th St., Allentown, Pa.

GRESS, Ernest Milton, botanist; b. Fulton County, Pa., Aug. 1, 1876; s. George B. and Rebecca (De Shong) G.; M.E., Shippensburg (Pa.) Normal Sch., 1896; Ph.B., Bucknell U., Lewisburg, Pa., 1907; M.A., U. of Pittsburgh, 1912, Ph.D., 1920; m. Nora Booth Gress, May 16, 1901; children—LaRue Ernestine (Mrs. George Lehman), Margaret Rebecca (Mrs. Henry R. Tatnall), Dorothy Evelyn (Mrs. Russel Daugherty). Teacher pub. and high schs., Pa., 1893-1920; state botanist of Pa. since 1920. Mem. Bot. Soc. America, A.A.A.S., Pa. Acad. Science. Methodist. Mason. Author: Grasses of Pennsylvania, 1924; Common Wild Flowers of Pennsylvania, 1928; Poisonous Plants of Pennsylvania, 1934; also bulls. and mag. articles. Home: 2000 High St., Camp Hill, Pa. Address: Dept. of Agriculture, State Capitol, Harrisburg, Pa.

GRETH, Morris Samuel, college prof.; b. Berks Co., Pa., Apr. 22, 1895; s. David H. and Mary E. (Schultz) G.; ed. Keystone State Normal Sch., Kutztown, Pa., 1913-16; A.B., Muhlenberg Coll., 1922; B.D., Phila. Theol. Sem., 1926; A.M., U. of Pa., 1924, Ph.D., same, 1930; grad. study U. of Pa. since 1936; m. Marie Catherine Remmler, of West Collingswood, N.J., Aug. 7, 1928; 1 dau., Loretta Marie. Engaged in teaching, then prin. schs., 1916-22; ordained to Evang. Luth. Ch., 1925, and pastor, West Collingswood, N.J., 1925-31; instr. psychology and pedagogy, Luth. Sch. Christian Edn., Phila., Pa., 1927-30; prof. philosophy and sociology, Albright Coll., Reading, Pa., since 1930; exec. dir. edn., Reading Council Christian Edn. since 1935. Mem. bd. dirs. Berks Co. Guidance Inst. Mem. Am. Acad. Polit. and Social Sci., Rural Sociol. Soc. of America, Pa. State Edn. Assn., Am. Sociol. Soc., Am. Assn. Univ. Profs., Pi Gamma Mu, Theta Kappa Nu, Pi Tau Beta. Democrat. Lutheran. Club: Torch of Reading. Author: Leadership Training Through Local Church Agencies, 1930. Contbr. to rel. and professional jours. Home: R.F.D. No. 1, Temple, Pa.

GRICE, John Cleveland, lawyer; b. Sharpsburg, Md., July 6, 1888; s. Peter Newton and Sarah V. (Jefferson) G.; student Millersville State Normal Sch., 1908-10; LL.B., U. of Md. Law Sch., Baltimore, 1913; student Strayers Bus. Coll., Baltimore, summer 1912; m. Elta Marie Dorsey, Jan. 1, 1910; children—Martha Virginia (Mrs. John W. Roessner), Charles Cleveland. Admitted to Md. bar, 1913 and since in gen. practice of law at Hagerstown, Md.; admitted to practice before Supreme Ct. of the U.S., 1934; pres., treas. and sole propr. total stock Maryland Motor Co., Inc., wholesale and retail auto parts and supplies, distributors automobiles and accessories, Hagerstown, Md., since 1920; propr. Grice Ins. Agency since 1923; dir. and counsel Blue Ridge Transportation Co., Potomac Edison Co.; atty. for Central Chem. Corpn. of Md. and other corpns. Mem. bd. of govs. Dem. Orgn. Club of Washington Co. Mem. Am., Md., and Washington Co. bar assns. Democrat. Methodist. Odd Fellow, Elk, Fraternal Order of Police. Club: Fountain Head Country (Hagerstown, Md.); Concord (Baltimore). Home: 814 Oak Hill Av. Office: Grice Bldg., Hagerstown, Md.

GRIER, Albert Oliver Herman, editor; b. Milford, Del., Mar. 4, 1867; s. William George and Elma (Collins) G.; grad. Wilmington High Sch., 1885; m. Sarah Elizabeth Baylis, Dec. 24, 1895; children—George Martindale, Warren William, Albert Oliver Herman. Began as printer's apprentice on Wilmington (Del.) Every Evening, 1885, reporter, 1895-96, city editor, 1896-1927, editor, 1927-33; asso. editor Journal-Every Evening, 1933-34; editor Journal-Every Evening since 1934. Mem. Am. Soc. Newspaper Editors, Delmarva Press. Assn., Wilmington Soc. Fine Arts, Delaware Citizens Assn., Sons of Delaware. Democrat. Episcopalian. Odd Fellow. Clubs: Torch of Delaware, Church of Delaware (pres); Poor Richard Club (Philadelphia); Nat. Press (Washington). Contbr. articles to mags. Mem. advisory council Del. State Employment Service. Home: 114 W. 13th St. Office: News-Journal Bldg., Wilmington, Del.

GRIER, George Washington, Roentgenologist; b. Sewell, N.J., Nov. 7, 1882; s. Jesse Gyger and Clara (Chew) G.; student Bethel High Sch., 1898; M.D., Jefferson Med. Coll., Phila., 1904; m. Ida Hammer, Sept. 21, 1909; 1 son, Thomas Lee. Roentgenologist West Penn Hosp., 1906-16, St. Margaret's Hosp., 1910-20; Passavant Hosp. since 1916, St. John's Gen. Hosp. since 1920, Elizabeth Steel Magee Hosp., since 1921, Pittsburgh Diagnostic Clinic since 1925, Eye and Ear Hosp. since 1927, Falk Clinic since 1932, Butler Co. Memorial Hosp. since 1934, Children's Hosp. since 1936, Presbyterian Hosp.; acting roentgenologist Mercy Hosp., 1917-18; asst. roentgenologist Allegheny Gen. Hosp., Pittsburgh, 1913-17; asst. prof. roentgenology, U. of Pittsburgh, 1915-21, asso. prof., 1921-33, prof. since 1934. Mem. Am. Roentgen Ray Soc. (sec. 1917-20, pres. elect 1933-34, pres. 1934-35, chmn. bd. of censors since 1938), Am. Radium Soc. (sec. 1927-31, 2d v.p. 1931-32, 1st v.p. 1932-34, pres. elect 1934-35, pres. 1935-36, chmn. exec. com. since 1938), A.M.A. (sec. sect. on radiology 1929-32, chmn. 1932-33), Allegheny Co. Med. Soc. (mem. bd.

dirs. 1923-32, treas. 1932-33, pres. 1933-34), Pa. State Med. Soc. (mem. cancer commn. since 1929). Clubs: University (Pittsburgh); Shannopin Country. Writes numerous articles in med. journs. on radiology and radium, their uses in treatment of cancer, etc. Home: 142 Irwin Av., Ben Avon. Office: 8095 Jenkins Arcade Bldg., Pittsburgh, Pa.

GRIER, Thomas Campbell, head of The Grier Sch.; b. Birmingham, Pa., Dec. 8, 1903; s. Alvan Ruckman and Mary (Campbell) G.; ed. Blair Acad., 1917-18; grad. Haverford Sch., 1921; ed. Princeton, 1922-25; B.S., in M.E., Mass. Inst. Tech., 1927; m. Georgianna M. Parks, 1930 (divorced); children—Thomas Campbell, Jr., Bruce Ruckman. In employ E.I. du Pont de Nemours Co., 1927-31; asso. with father in The Grier Sch. for girls, founded by grandfather in 1857, Birmingham, Pa., 1931-32, pres., treas. and dir. The Grier Sch. since 1932. Served as pres. Birmingham Borough Council. Dir. Tyrone Chamber of Commerce. Mem. Nat. Assn. Prins. Schs. for Girls, Huntington Co. Hist. Soc. (dir.), Phi Beta Epsilon. Republican. Presbyn. (pres. bd. trustees Birmingham Presbyn. Ch.). Club: Pulpit Rock Hunt (M.F.H.) Home: Birmingham, Pa.

GRIEVE, Lucia Catherine Graeme, poet, lecturer; b. Apr. 30, 1862; d. Rev. David Graeme and Martha Lucy (Kinkead) G.; student Mrs. J. T. Benedict's French and English Sch., N.Y., 1871-78; A.B., A.M., Wellesley (Mass.) Coll., 1883; Ph.D., Columbia U., 1898; student Oxford U., Eng., 1896-97, Columbia U., 1924-25; unmarried. Sch. teacher, Young Coll., Thomasville, Ga., and elsewhere in the South, 1883-93; lecturer, chiefly on India, since 1898; for pub. sch. extension courses, New York, 1902-13. Mem. Am. Oriental Soc., Kipling Soc. (London), etc. Methodist. Club: Women's (Ocean Grove, N.J.). Parents being missionaries traveled widely; in India, 1902-04, following Kipling's trail and gathering lecture material. Author numerous poems. Address: 50 Heck Av., Ocean Grove, N.J.

GRIFFENBERG, Elbert Dickinson, confectionery mfr.; b. Wilmington, Del., May 15, 1904; s. Elwood Bryan and Rhoda (Dickinson) G.; grad. Tower Hill Sch., Wilmington, Del., 1922; A.B., Lehigh U., Bethlehem, Pa., 1926; m. Elizabeth Johnson, Oct. 27, 1928; children—Elbert Dickinson, Jr. Anne. Asso. with Reynolds Candy Co., mfrs. and retailers of candy, baked goods and ice cream, Wilmington, Del., since 1926, gen. mgr. since 1930, v.p. and treas. since 1934; v.p. and treas. Reynolds Realty Co. since 1934; dir. Wawasett Corpn. Mem. Mayor's Advisory Com., Wilmington, Del., since 1936; apptd. mem. Wilmington Zoning Commn., 1939. Mem. Nat. Assn. of Mfrs., Chamber of Commerce (dir.; chmn. retail sect., 1938), Phi Beta Kappa (hon.), Phi Gamma Delta, Alpha Kappa Psi (hon.), Sons of Am. Revolution. Republican. Episcopalian. Mason (Del. Consistory; Lu Lu Temple). Clubs: Univ., Lions, Whist, Advertising (Wilmington, Del.). Delaware Lehigh. Home: 718 Blackshire Rd. Office: 703 Market St., Wilmington, Del.

GRIFFIN, Bulkley Southworth, newspaper corr.; b. Springfield, Mass., Aug. 16, 1893; s. Solomon Bulkley and Ida (Southworth) G.; grad. Springfield Central High Sch.; A.B., Williams Coll., 1916; m. Isabel Kinnear, July 8, 1926; 1 dau., Charmian. Successively reporter, city editor and Washington corr. for Springfield Republican, 1916-22; head of Bulkley Griffin News Bureau, serving several New England newspapers with Washington news, since 1922. Served U.S. Navy and Army during World War; disch. as 2d lt., pilot, Army Air Service. Mem. Kappa Alpha. Home: 200 Raymond St., Chevy Chase, Md. Office: 1233 National Press Bldg., Washington, D.C.

GRIFFIN, Frederick Robertson, clergyman; b. Zanesville, O., May 3, 1876; s. Richard Andrew and Tabitha Folks (Taylor) G.; B.A., Bates College, Lewiston, Maine, 1898, D.D., 1923; S.T.B., Harvard University, 1901, D.D., 1936; m. Edith Josephine Bell, Oct. 9, 1901; children—Cynthia, Frederick Robertson. Ordained Unitarian minstry, 1901; pastor All Souls Ch., Braintree, Mass., 1901-09, Ch. of the Messiah, Montreal, Can., 1909-17, 1st Ch., Phila., since Oct. 1, 1917. Mem. Acad. Polit. Science of New York (life), Indian Rights Assn. (dir.), Pub. Edn. and Child Labor Assn. (dir.), Community Health and Civic Assn. (dir.), Joseph Priestley Conf. of Unitarian Chs. (pres. 1933-34), N.E. Soc. of Pa. (pres. 1934-36). Mem. bd. of preachers, Harvard, 1934-36; v.p. Seaman's Ch. Inst. Clubs: Union League, Contemporary (pres. 1929-31), Harvard. Home: 523 Oakley Road, Haverford, Pa. Office: 2125 Chestnut St., Philadelphia, Pa.

GRIFFIN, Isabel Kinnear, newspaper corr.; b. Rockbridge Co., Va., Dec. 31, 1899; d. John J. Lyle and Isabel (Lackey) Kinnear; ed. Lexington (Va.) High Sch. and Va. State Coll., Farmville, Va.; m. Bulkley Griffin, July 8, 1926; 1 dau., Charmian. Newspaper corr., Bulkley Griffin News Bureau, Washington, D.C., since 1924; served on Hartford (Conn.) Times, Springfield (Mass.) Union and other New England papers with the Griffin News Bureau. New Deal Democrat. Presbyterian. Club: Woman's National Press (Washington, D.C.). Home: 200 Raymond St., Chevy Chase, Md. Office: 1233 National Press Bldg., Washington, D.C.

GRIFFIN, Joseph Aloysius, chaplain, coll. prof.; b. Dickson City, Pa., Feb. 26, 1901; s. Charles D. and Julia E. (O'Connor) G.; student Dickson City (Pa.) pub. schs., 1907-19; B.A., Holy Cross Coll., Worcester, Mass., 1919-23; student St. Bernard's Sem., Rochester, N. Y., 1923-27; M.A., Catholic U. of America, Washington, D.C., 1930, Ph.D., 1932; student U. of Louvain, Belgium, 1930-31, Inst. Francaise, Cologne, Germany, summer 1931. Asst. pastor, East Stroudsburg, Pa., 1927, Blossburg, Pa., 1927-28, Williamsport, Pa., 1928; prof. history and chaplain, Marywood Coll., Scranton, Pa., 1932-38; head hist. dept., U. of Scranton, since 1938; chaplain St. Joseph's Hosp., Scranton, Pa., since 1938; examiner jr. clergy and candiates for Diocese of Scranton since 1932. Mem. Am. Catholic Hist. Assn. Democrat. Catholic. Author: The Contribution of Belgium to the Catholic Church in America, 1932; contbr. to Records of the Am. Catholic Hist. Soc., Emmanuel. Now preparing history of Diocese of Scranton. Home: 953 Main St., Dickson, Pa. Office: 2010 Adams Av., Scranton, Pa.

GRIFFIN, William Vincent, officer corpns.; b. Middletown, Conn., Jan. 1, 1886; s. John H. and Katherine (Stack) G.; Middletown High Sch.; LL.B., Yale, 1908, B.A., 1912; m. Isabel Shumard Carden, June 25, 1914; 1 son, William V. (deceased). Trustee Estate of James C. Brady, New York; pres. Brady Security & Realty Corporation; dir. Bank of Manhattan (New York), Compania Cubana, Central R.R. of N.J., Consolidated Railroads of Cuba, The Cuba Co., Cuba R.R. Co., Continental Oil Co., Manati Sugar Co., Motor Improvements, Inc., N.Y. Post-Grad. Hosp., Emigrant Industrial Savings Bank, Canadian Bell River, Ltd., Cuba Northern Railways, Dresser Manufacturing Co., Servel, Inc., Somerset Hills Development Corpn. Tiblemont Island Mining Co., Ltd., Am. Power & Light Co., Clarke, Sinsabaugh & Co., Inc., Dobie Mines, Ltd., Time, Inc. Trustee United Hosp. Fund of New York City, Yale Pub. Assn. Mem. Delta Kappa Epsilon, Phi Delta Phi, Scroll and Key. Catholic. Created Knight Comdr. Order of St. Gregory, 1926; Knight Official of the Crown of Italy, 1928; Papal Chamberlain—Cape and Sword 1929. Clubs: Broad Street, Recess, Grolier, Racquet and Tennis, Essex Fox Hounds, Union, Somerset Hills Country, Colony, River, Yale. Home: Peapack, N.J. Office: 140 Cedar St., New York, N.Y.

GRIFFING, Curtis Andrew, merchant; b. Linesville, Pa., Nov. 23, 1881; s. Albert Barnes and Edna (Wilmot.) G.; grad. Linesville High Sch., 1899; student Eastman Business Coll., Poughkeepsie, N.Y., 1899-1900; m. Ellen Miller, Nov. 11, 1903; 1 son, Curtis Edward. Partner A. B. Griffing's Sons since 1900, now mgr.; pres. Farmers & Merchants Bank, Linesville, since orgn. 1934. Mason. Home: West Erie St. Address: Linesville, Pa.

GRIFFITH, Beatrice Fox, (Mrs. Charles Frances G.), sculptor; b. Hoylake, Eng., Aug. 6, 1890; d. L. Webster and Beatrice (Bickerton) Fox, citizens of U.S.; grad. Bennett Sch., Milbrook, N.Y, 1908; ed. Pa. Acad. Fine Arts under Charles Grafly, 1921-23; m. Charles Frances Griffith, Feb. 27, 1919. Has followed profession as sculptor in Philadelphia since 1913; first exhibited marble, Acad. Fine Arts annual show, 1914; continued yearly exhibits in marble and bronze, Chicago, Buffalo, Phila., New York and other cities; represented by marble bust Sir J. C. R. Ewing, Lahore, India, marble bust Sir Wilfred Grenfell at St. Andrews Center of Labrador Hosp. Work; bronze bas-relief of Howard McClenahan, Franklin Inst., Phila.; also medalist and worker on illuminated mss. design, represented in hist. socs. and chs., most recent, two large tryptycts for side altars in Ch. of Nativity, R.C., Phila., 1939 Served at Army War Coll., Washington, D.C., modeled contour maps for M.I.Div. Office Chief of Staff, 1917-18. Dir. Womens Med. Coll. Mem. Pa. Mus. Art, Franklin Inst., Art Alliance. Awarded gold medal from King George V. occasion Silver Jubilee for spl. work in illuminated mss. design. Republican. Roman Catholic. Clubs: Acorn, Cosmopolitan (Philadelphia); Cosmopolitan (New York); Art Alliance. Home: Merion, Pa.

GRIFFITH, Edward, v.p. Glen Alden Coal Co.; b. Wilkes-Barre, Pa., Nov. 21, 1882; s. Samuel and Hannah M. (Jones) G.; student high sch., and Bloomsburg (Pa.) State Normal Sch.; m. Helen Leona Hughes, June 10, 1908; children—Helen Winifred, Edward Meredith. Began as clk. Lehigh and Wilkes-Barre Coal Co., 1902, successively chief clk. in exec. offices, asst. gen. supt. and asst. gen. mgr., gen. mgr., Feb. 1928-Dec. 1929; gen. supt. Glen Alden Coal Co., Scranton, Pa., 1930-34, v.p. and gen. mgr. since 1934; dir. Lehigh and Wilkes-Barre Coal Co. of Pa., Lehigh and Wilkes-Barre Coal Co. of N.J., First Nat. Bank of Wilkes-Barre. Clubs: Westmoreland, Franklin (Wilkes-Barre); Scranton (Scranton). Home: 44 Reynolds St., Kingston, Pa. Office: 310 Jefferson Av., Scranton, Pa.

GRIFFITH, Frederic Richardson, physician, educator; b. Phila., Pa., Sept. 17, 1873; s. David Reese and Sarah Jane (Richardson) G.; ed. U.S.N. sailing ship Saratoga as Pa. Sch. Ship under Admiral Sims, 1892; M.D., U. of Pa. Med. Sch., 1897; ed. U.S. Power Squadron Sch., 1917-18; grad. United States Navigation Sch., U. of Pa., 1919. Engaged in practice of medicine, dividing time annually with navigation seamanship under U.S. flag since 1897; founded and organized instn. of N.J. Schoolship as furthering development of merchant navy since 1920; with Gen. Frederick Gilkyson secured passage of State Schoolship Bill for N.J. Nautical & Maritime Acad. by N.J. Legislature, 1928; purchased by subscription Adm. Byrd S. Pole Ship, City of New York for N.J. Nautical Schoolship, 1937; supt.-comdr. N.J. Nautical & Maritime Acad., Port of Belmar, N.J.; holds chief officer (comdr. grade since 1924) certificate unlimited. Fellow N.Y. Acad. Medicine. Mem. N.Y. Hist. Soc., Nat. Geog. Soc. Mem. Religious Soc. Friends. Has invented various med., surg. and san. devices. Author: A Handbook of Surgery, 1904; Nurse's Textbook, 1904-06; The Third Mate (textbook on navigation-seamanship), 1921; The American Merchant Navy, 1926. Editor and pub. Sailors Almanac and Schoolship News Magazine. Contbr. articles on medicine and sci. navigation seamanship. Home: 500 9th Av., Belmar, N.J.

GRIFFITH, George Webster, lawyer; b. Ebensburg, Pa., Dec. 12, 1894; s. Webster and Alice (Zahm) G.; grad. Ebensburg High Sch., 1912; student Lawrenceville (N.J.) Sch., 1912-14; A.B., Princeton U., 1918; LL.B., U. of Pa., 1923; m. Gretchen Williams, June 24, 1925; children—George Webster, Webster II. Admitted to Pa. bar, 1923, and since practiced in Ebensburg; judge orphans court, Cambria Co., 1935; dir. First Nat. Bank, Ebensburg; sec. and dir. Motor Sales Co., Johnstown, Pa. Served in Am. Field Service with the French Army, 1917; 2d lt. 316th F.A., 81st Div., U.S. Army, with A.E.F., 1918-19. Mem. Am. Legion, Vets. of Foreign Wars, Phi Kappa Sigma, Phi Delta Phi. Republican. Presbyterian. Mason (Shriner).

Home: 503 W. Horner St. Office: Ebensburg Trust Bldg., Ebensburg, Pa.

GRIFFITH, Helen Sherman (Mrs. W. O. Griffith), author; b. at Des Moines, Ia.; d. Hoyt and Sara (Moulton) Sherman; niece of Gen. W. T. Sherman; educated The Misses Vinton Sch., Pomfret, Conn.; univ. extension course under Prof. Dallas L. Sharp; m. W. O. Griffith, Oct. 28, 1896; children—Helen Sherman, Florence Oglesby, Hoyt Sherman, John R. Republican. Episcopalian. Mem. Authors' League of America, Art Alliance of Phila., Phila. League Am. Penwomen (ex-pres.). Clubs: Boston Authors', Iowa Authors. Author: Her Wilful Way, 1902; Her Father's Legacy, 1904; Rosemary for Remembrance, 1911; The Lane, 1925; also Letty books (series), 10 vols.; Virginia books, 6 vols.; Louie Maude books (4 vols.); and short stories, plays, etc. Home: Chestnut Hill, Philadelphia, Pa.

GRIFFITH, Ivor, educator, chemist; b. Rhiwlas, Wales, Jan. 3, 1891; s. Rev. John William and Anne (Hughes) G.; came to U.S., 1907; P.D., Phila. Coll. Pharmacy and Science, 1912, Ph.M., 1920; Sc.D. hon. causa, Bucknell U., 1930; m. Carolyn Amanda Hobson, Mar. 28, 1914 (died Feb. 26, 1938); children—Doris Anne, Gwen Ivera. Has been director of Laboratories, Stetson Hosp., Philadelphia, since 1916; instr. mathematics, Phila. Coll. Pharmacy and Science, 1916-17, instr. pharmacy, 1917-22, prof. and dean pharm. div. since 1936; spl. lecturer Brooklyn Inst. Arts and Science; prof. organic chemistry, Wagner Inst. of Science, Phila., since 1925, also sec. faculty; director research, John B. Stetson Co., since 1924; dir. of research McNeil Laboratories, Phila. Editor American Journal of Pharmacy since 1921. President Gt. Fifth B. & L. Assn.; mem. bd. Stetson Hosp. Chem. investigations for Med. Supply Depot, Phila., during World War. Pres. St. David's Soc. (Phila.); fellow Am. Inst. Chemists, Royal Soc. of Arts, London; mem. Am. Pharm. Assn. (editor Formula Book, 1926), A.A.A.S., Am. Chem. Soc., Am. Soc. Bacteriologists, Pa. Acad. Science, Welsh Soc. of Phila., Kappa Psi. Republican. Presbyn. Mason. Author: Recent Remedies, 1927; "Lobscows," a science miscellany. Collab. editor United States Dispensatory, 1936; editor of Science Talks (14 vols.). Home: Rhiwlas, Elkins Park, Pa. Address: Stetson Hospital, Philadelphia, Pa.

GRIFFITH, James A(nthony), real estate and ins.; b. Pittsburgh, Pa., Sept. 20, 1872; s. Thomas and Margaret Catherine (Mitchell) G.; ed. pub. schs., Bellaire, O., Curry Coll. and Duff's Coll., Pittsburgh; m. Eliza Jane Faloon, Nov. 8, 1906; children—Jane Elizabeth, Mary Livingston. Began as realtor with E. T. Schaffner, Aug. 29, 1890; started in business of real estate and insurance for self, Jan. 1, 1900; in same community since 1890; dir. Iron and Glass Dollar Savings Bank (27 years); dir. and 1st vice-pres. Hill Top Bank; treas. Warrington Bldg. & Loan Assn. since 1919; one of organizers Hill Top Bank, Warrington Bldg. & Loan Assn., 31st Ward Bldg. & Loan. Treas. Baptist Orphanage and Home Soc. of Western Pa. (for over 25 yrs.). Republican. Baptist (trustee Knoxville Ch.). Mason. Club: South Hills Country (Pittsburgh). Home: 4720 Wallingford St. Office: 835 Warrington Av., Pittsburgh, Pa.

GRIFFITH, J(ohn) P. Crozer, M.D.; b. Phila., Jan. 5, 1856; s. Benjamin and Elizabeth (Crozer) G.; A.B., U. of Pa., 1st in class, 1877, M.D., 1881, Ph.D. (1st prize for thesis), 1881; m. Julia E. Jenks, 1882. Instr. clinical medicine, University of Pa., 1889-96; visiting physician St. Agnes Hosp., 1889, Howard Hosp., 1890; prof. clin. medicine, Phila., Polyclinic, 1891-1906; clin. prof. diseases of children, 1891-1913, prof. pediatrics, 1913—, U. of Pa.; visiting phys. Children's Hosp., 1891—; consulting phys. Women's Hosp., 1896—, St. Christopher's Hosp. for Children, 1901; consulting pediatrist Abington Memorial, Jewish, Misericordia and Babies Seashore hosps. Editor Proc. of Coll. of Phys. for several yrs. and of Internat. Clinics at its start. President board trustees Baptist Orphanage, Crozer Theological Seminary; chairman board managers Am. Bapt. Publ. Soc. Mem. Assn. Am. Physicians (treas. 1900-18), Am. Pediatric Soc., Phila. Pediatric Soc. (1st pres. and pres. at 30th anniversary), Am. Assn. Teachers of Diseases of Children, A.M.A., Coll. Physicians Phila., Am. Philos. Soc., Acad. Natural Sciences, Pa. Hist. Soc.; corr. mem. Société de Pediatrie de Paris. Author: The Care of the Baby, 1895; Diseases of Infants and Children, 2 vols., 1919; Diseases of Infants and Children, 1 vol., 1933, revised, 1936. Has written numerous contbns. to med. jours. Address: 1810 Spruce St., Philadelphia, Pa.

GRIFFITH, Stephen C., Jr., realtor and insurance Man; b. Morris Plains, N.J., Sept. 25, 1880; s. Stephen H. Griffith and Emily (Rielly) G.; student Morristown (N.J.) Pub. Sch., 1888-96; m. Gertrude Keeler, Apr. 15, 1903; children—Doris Gertrude (Mrs. J. Raymond Prideaux), Helen Winifred (Mrs. William H. Struble). Clk. in store, Morristown, N.J., 1895-97; in real estate and insurance business, Morristown, N.J., since 1889; pres. Stephen C. Griffith, Jr., Inc., real estate and insurance, Morristown, N.J., since 1899; treas. and dir. Morristown (N.J.) Packard Co. since 1920; dir. Morristown Trust Co., Morristown Bldg. & Loan Assn. Sec. and treas. Morris Co. Rep. Com. since 1911; freeholder, Morris Co., since 1925, dir. Morris Co. Bd. Freeholders since 1930. Dir. Morristown Y.M.C.A.; trustee Morris Co. Community Chest. Republican. Methodist. Mason (Shriner, Salaam Temple, Newark, N.J.; Lodge 188, Morristown), Elk (Morristown Lodge 815). Clubs: Rotary (Morristown, N.J.; pres. 1931-32); Spring Brook Country (Morristown, N.J.). Home: 19 Wetmore Av. Office: Park Sq. Bldg., Morristown, N.J.

GRIFFITHS, Hall McAllister, clergyman, editor; b. San Francisco, Calif., Jan. 16, 1900; s. Harry Howard and Elizabeth Regina (Geraldson) G.; A.B., U. of Calif., 1922; student Princeton Theol. Sem., 1923-25, Grad. Sch. of Princeton U., 1924-25; m. Catherine Hughena Macneil, Jan. 11, 1926; children—Catherine Elizabeth, John Gresham Machen. Asst. editor Sunday Sch. Times, 1922-23; ordained to Presbyn. ministry, 1925; pastor, Marion Bridge, N.S., 1925-26, Scotsburn, N.S., 1926-30; mng. editor Christianity Today, 1930-1935; pastor Hollond Memorial Presbyn. Ch., Phila., 1931-33; editor The Presbyterian Guardian, and gen. sec. the Presbyn. Constitutional Covenant Union, 1935-36; mgr. Independent Board for Presbyn. Foreign Missions, since 1937; lecturer in ch. history, Faith Theol. Sem. since 1937; editor Independent Board Bull. since 1937; pres. bd. trustees Reformation Fellowship, Inc.; mem. and sec. Independent Board for Presbyn. Foreign Missions, 1933-36. Contbr. tracts and articles to religious publs. Defense counsel in ecclesiastical cases, involving membership in the Independent Bd. for Persbyn. Foreign Missions, for Prof. J. Gresham Machen, President J. Oliver Buswell, Rev. Carl McIntire and Dr. Roy T. Brumbaugh. Elected commr. to Presbyn. Gen. Assembly, 1932, 34 and 35; unseated at 1935 assembly because of refusal to resign from The Independent Bd., as ordered by the Assembly of 1934; withdrew from denomination, 1936. Presiding Officer at organization of First Gen. Assembly of Presbyterian Ch. of America, 1936; ecclesiastical counsel Presbyn. Church of America, 1936; co-founder Bible Presbyterian Synod, 1937. Home: 616 W. Sedgwick St., Mt. Airy, Philadelphia, Pa. Office: 505 Otis Bldg., Philadelphia, Pa.

GRIGGS, Robert Fiske, botanist; b. Brooklyn, Conn., Aug. 22, 1881; s. Julian and Mary Eliza (Davison) G.; B.Sc., Ohio State U., 1903; M.S., U. of Minn., 1906; Ph.D., Harvard, 1911; m. Laura Amelia Tressel, June 27, 1907; children—Ruth, David Tressel, Julian Gladden, Rosamond. Asst. in tropical agr., U.S. Dept. Agr., 1901-02; prof. biology, Fargo (N.D.) Coll., 1903-05; spl. agt. Dept. Agr., in Tex., 1904; asst. prof. botany, Ohio State U., 1906-21; prof. botany, George Washington U., since 1921. Mem. Govt. expdns. to P.R., 1901, Guatemala, 1902, Alaska, 1913; dir. Nat. Geog. Soc. expdns. to Katmai Dist., Alaska., 1915-19, 30; discovered "Valley of 10,000 Smokes." Fellow Am. Assn. for Advancement of Science; mem. Botanical Soc. of America (chmn. of general sect. and mem. council, 1936), Ecol. Soc. of America, Washington Acad. Science (pres. 1933), Bot. Soc. Washington (recording sec., 1923; pres. 1928), Geol. Soc. Washington, Sigma Xi, Phi Beta Kappa, Sigma Gamma Epsilon; hon. life mem. Nat. Geog. Soc. Conglist. Club: Cosmos (Washington, D.C.). Author: The Valley of Ten Thousand Smokes (also trans. into German), 1927. Contbr. many scientific papers in tech. jours. Home: 39 E. Bradley Lane, Chevy Chase, Md. Address: George Washington University, Washington, D. C.

GRIM, George Austin, supt. county schs.; b. Rockland Twp., Pa., Feb. 16, 1876; s. William W. and Mary L. (Hottenstein) G.; ed. Kutztown State Normal Sch., 1888-94, Bucknell U., 1896-99, U. of Zurich, Switzerland, 1900-01, N.Y. Univ., 1905-06; m. Mabel A. Walter, June 11, 1905; children—Mary A. (Mrs. Jacob Knecht), Walter H., David H. Teacher in rural schools, 1894-96; prin. schools, Huntington Mills, 1899-1900; instr. Inst. Concordia, Zurich, Switzerland, 1900-01; teacher high sch., Nazareth, Pa., 1901-05; supt. co. schs., Nazareth, Pa., since 1905. Mem. Reformed Ch. Club: Rotary (Nazareth). Home: 50 S. Broad St., Nazareth, Pa.

GRIMES, William C(olumbus), lawyer: b. Tyler Co., W.Va., Dec. 5, 1876; s. Jacob C. and Cora Virginia (Haines) G.; student Franklin Coll., New Athens, O., 1896, O. Northern U., Ada, O., 1898-1902, W.Va. Univ., Morgantown, W.Va.; m. Zola Park Gump, Dec. 5, 1912. Engaged in teaching, pub. schs. of W.Va., 1896 to 1902; admitted to W.Va. bar, 1902, and engaged in gen. practice of law at Cameron, Marshall Co., 1903-12, at Keyser, Mineral Co., 1912-23, at Wheeling, Ohio Co., W.Va., since 1923; asso. with Eugene M. Prager as mem. firm Grimes and Prager, since 1937; served as mem. W.Va. Senate, 1908-12; asst. U.S. atty, 1921-23; candidate on Rep. ticket for governor, 1936. Served as chmn. local bd. Mineral Co. W.Va. during World War; chmn. com. fuel adminstrn. Mineral Co., 1918. Mem. Am. Bar Assn., Ohio Co. Bar Assn. Republican. Methodist. Elk. Club: Philosophers. Home: 200 Valley View Av., Wheeling, W.Va.; Route 3, West Alexander, Pa. Office: Riley Law Bldg., Wheeling, W.Va.

GRIMES, William Hearne, commercial banking; b. Washington, D.C., Oct. 4, 1871; s. Alexander Varden and Mary E. (Kirkland) G.; LL.B., Georgetown Univ. Law Sch., Washington, D.C., 1892, LL.M., 1893; A.B., Harvard, 1897; m. Isabelle Seguenot, Feb. 5, 1902; children—William Alexander, John Seguenot, Robert Sands (dec.). Mgr. credit and legal dept. shoe mfg. co., St. Louis, Mo., 1898-1909; asso. with Commercial Credit Co., commercial banking, Baltimore, since 1912, successively treas., v.p., pres., then vice chmn., 1912-39, dir. since 1913; dir. Textile Banking Co., Am. Credit Indemnity Co., Gleaner Harvester Corpn. Republican. Clubs: Maryland, Harvard of Maryland, Rolling Road Golf (Baltimore). Home: Catonsville, Md. Office: First Nat. Bank Bldg., Baltimore, Md.

GRIMM, Herbert L., editor The Times. Address: Gettysburg, Pa.

GRIMM, Karl Josef, prof. German; b. Steinbach-Wertheim A. M., Germany, June 10, 1871; s. Magnus and Biligildis (Schüssler) G.; student schs. in Germany, 1877-88, St. Jerome's Coll. (Berlin Kitchener, Canada), 1888-89, univs. of Rome, Italy, and Halle, Germany, 1890-91, Theol. Sem., Gettysburg, Pa., 1892-95; Ph.D., Johns Hopkins U., 1899; LL.D., Carthage Coll., 1938; m. Anna Catherine Broessel, June 18, 1902; children—Emma Hermine Louise, Gisela Adèle Elizabeth, Karl Joseph, Anna Dorothea. Came to U.S., 1891, naturalized citizen, 1900. Rayner Research fellow, Johns Hopkins U., 1899-1901; prof. modern lang., Ursinus College, Collegeville, Pa., 1901-06; prof. German lang. and lit., Gettysburg (Pa.) Coll., since 1906. Mem. Modern Lang. Assn. America, Phi Beta Kappa. Author: Euphemistic Liturgical Appendixes in the Old Testament, 1901; contributor to periodicals. Home: 238 Baltimore St., Gettysburg, Pa.

GRIMSHAW, Robert, engineer; b. Phila., Pa., Jan. 25, 1850; s. William and Marie Caroline (de la Croix) G.; prep. edn., Taylor's Acad., Wilmington, Del.; grad. Andalusia Coll., Pa., 1869; studied under Profs. Alexander and Guyot, Princeton, and in Paris, France; Ph.D.; m. Margaret Morton Dillon, Apr. 2, 1872 (died 1877); children—Charlotte (Mrs. Malcolm MacLear), Mary Morton (Mrs. Cornelius B. Hite), Edith Dillon (Mrs. Adolph Stelling); m. 2d, Marta Scharstein, of Kappeln, Schleswig-Holstein, Germany, May 15, 1914. Began practice, 1873; was mem. faculty New York U., Coll. City of N.Y. and Rutgers Univ.; served as consulting engr. for U.S. Govt., and various European govts. A founder Am. Soc. Mech. Engrs.; corr. sec. Polytechnic Soc.; ex-pres. James Watt Association Stationary Engineers; member National Institute of Social Sciences. Founder of "Blindaid," furnishing Braille printed matter. Republican. Episcopalian. Odd Fellow. Author: Why Manufacturers Lose Money, 1922; The Modern Foreman, 1923; Shop Kinks (6th Edit.); Machine Shop Chat, 1923; The Locomotive Catechism (30th edit.), 1923; also many other tech. works in English, German and French. Home: 321 Sylvan Av., Leonia, N.J.

GRIMSLEY, George Perry, geol. engr.; b. Granville, O., Feb. 21, 1868; s. Carson Porter and Mary (Evans) G.; A.B., Ohio State U., Columbus, O., 1890, A.M., 1891; Ph.D., Johns Hopkins U., 1894; grad. student U. of Chicago, 1896-97, Leland Stanford U., Palo Alto, Calif., 1900, Harvard, 1906; m. Clara M. Spencer, Dec. 25, 1901. Engaged as prof. geology and natural scis., Washburn Coll., Topeka, Kan., 1896-1905; prof. economic geology, W.Va. Univ., Morgantown, W.Va., 1905-08, also on geol. surveys, Ohio, Kan., Mich.; asst. state geologist W.Va. Geol. Survey, 1905-09; gen. mgr. Nat. Limestone Co., Martinsburg, W.Va., 1909-16; geol. engr. B.&O. R. R. Co., Baltimore, since 1916. Fellow A.A.A.S., Geol. Soc. America; mem. Kan. Acad. Sci. (hon.), N.Y. Acad. Sciences, Phi Kappa Psi, Sigma Xi. Republican. Presbyterian. Mason (32°). Club: Johns Hopkins (Baltimore). Author: Gypsum Deposits Kansas, 1899; Gypsum Deposits Michigan, 1904; Clays, Cement, Limestone, W.Va., 1905; Petroleum History U.S., 1909. Contbr. reports, bulls. sci. papers. Home: Hopkins Apts. Office: B.&O. R.R., Baltimore, Md.

GRING, Wilbur David, mfg. and r.r. exec.; b. Newport, Pa., Apr. 2, 1892; s. David and Emma (Caldwell) G.; ed. pvt. tech. sch.; unmarried. Employed as supt. motive power, Susquehanna River & Western R.R. and Newport & Sherman's Valley R.R., 1914-33; pres. and dir. Newport Home Water Co., 1920-26; engaged in mfg. of hosiery since 1933; vice-pres. and dir. Susquehanna River & Western R.R. since 1938. Republican. Home: Newport, Pa.

GRINNALDS, Jefferson Cleveland, city planning and zoning engr.; b. Accomac Co., Va., May 4, 1884; s. Jefferson Davis and Roberta Sarah (Twyford) G.; student Baltimore City Coll., 1899-1904, U. of Va., Charlottesville, Va., 1904-07, Johns Hopkins U., Baltimore, 1915-25, U. of Md., Baltimore, 1922-24; LL.B., U. of Md., Baltimore, 1915; m. Catherine Letitia Fleming, Nov. 4, 1914. Surveyor, draftsman, engr., Fairmont, W.Va., 1907-09; bridge, cofferdam and pier constrn., Fla. East Coast R.R., Pigeon Key, Fla., 1910; asst. engr. Topog. Survey Commn., Commrs. Opening Sts., City Planning Commn., Baltimore, 1910-20; supervisor Bartlett-Hayward Co., Baltimore, 1915-18; sec. and engr., Zoning Commns., Baltimore, 1921-29; cons. engr. on city planning and zoning, Baltimore, since 1920; sec.-eng. Bd. of Zoning Appeals, Baltimore, Md., since 1923; city planning expert on staff Advisory Com. on Zoning and City Planning, apptd. by Herbert Hoover while sec. of commerce, 1921-25; instr. city planning, Johns Hopkins U., Baltimore, 1924-26; lecturer zoning, Goucher Coll., Baltimore, 1924, U. of Md., Baltimore, 1925. Mem. Am. Soc. Planning Officials, Delta Sigma Pi. Democrat. Christian Scientist; first reader, Second Ch. of Christ, Scientist, Baltimore, 1936-39. Member Baltimore Rotary Club, 1924-27. Author: Zoning Laws for Raleigh, N.C., 1923; Zoning Laws for Frederick, Md., 1929; Zoning Laws for Salisbury, Md., 1931; numerous articles on city planning and zoning for tech. pubs.; co-author: Zoning Laws for Baltimore City, 1931. Home: 3200 Dorchester Rd. Office: City Hall, Baltimore, Md.

GRISCOM, John Milton, physician; b. Salem, N.J., Feb. 23, 1881; s. Walter D. and Mary M. (Bassett) G.; B.S., Swarthmore Coll., 1902; M.D., U. of Pa., Med. Sch., 1906; m. Mary W. Lippincott, Oct. 16, 1915; 1 dau., Mary L. After usual interneship, specialized in ophthalmology since 1908; exec. surgeon, Wills Hosp.; consulting ophthalmologist Jeanes Hosp., Phila., and Burlington County Hosp., Mount Holly, N.J.; prof. of ophthalmology, Grad. Sch. Med. Dept., U. of Pa.. Mem. com. Moorestown (N.J.) Friends Sch. Mem. Am. Med. Assn., Am. Ophthal. Soc., Am. Acad. Ophthalmology and Otolaryngology, Pa. State Med. Soc., Phila. County Med. Soc., Coll. of Physicians of Phila., Phi Kappa Psi. Republican. Mem. Religious Soc. of Friends. Club: Union League (Philadelphia). Home: Moorestown, N.J. Office: 255 S. 17th St., Philadelphia, Pa.

GRISCOM, Rodman Ellison, banker; b. Phila., Pa., Oct. 21, 1870; s. Clement Acton and Frances Canby (Biddle) G.; Ph.B., U. of Pa., 1889; m. Anne Starr, Feb. 17, 1897 (died June 14, 1919). Dir. Phila. Nat. Bank, Pennroad Corpn., Am. Scantic Steamship Co.; mgr. Western Savings Fund. Mem. Zeta Psi. Clubs: University, City, Midday, Nat. Golf Links (New York); Philadelphia (Phila.). Home: Haverford, Pa. Office: Land Title Bldg., Philadelphia, Pa.

GRISWOLD, Alexander Brown, investment banking; b. Baltimore, Md., Apr. 19, 1907; s. Benjamin Howell, Jr., and Bessie M. (Brown) G.; A.B., Princeton U., 1928; grad. student Trinity Coll., Cambridge, Eng., 1929; unmarried. Entered employ Alex. Brown & Sons, investment bankers, Baltimore, Md., 1930, mem. of firm since 1931; dir. Sharp & Dohme, Inc., Phila., The Canton Co., Baltimore, Md. & Pa. R.R. Co. Democrat. Clubs: Maryland, Merchants, Elkridge-Harford Hunt (Baltimore). Home: Solitude Farm, Monkton. Office: 135 E. Baltimore St., Baltimore, Md.

GRISWOLD, Benjamin Howell, Jr., lawyer, banker; b. Hagerstown, Md., Aug. 1, 1874; s. Benjamin Howell and Carrie G. (Robertson) G.; A.B., Johns Hopkins, 1894; LL.B., U. of Md., 1897; m. Bessie M., d. Alexander and Bessie (Montague) Brown, Dec. 7, 1904; children—Alexander Brown, Carolyn Howell (Mrs. J. McKenney W. Egerton), Benjamin Howell, Betty Tailer (Mrs. L. McLane Fisher). Admitted to Maryland bar, 1897; became senior mem. firm of Griswold, Thom & Jenkins, 1900; mem. Alex. Brown & Sons, bankers, since 1904, sr. mem. firm since 1924; judge advocate general of Maryland, 1916-20. President Board of Trade, Baltimore, 1915-21. President Alliance of Charitable and Social Agencies of Baltimore, 1916-21; member Maryland Council Defense; chmn. Md. Ednl. Survey Commn., 1915-16. Trustee Johns Hopkins; pres. bd. trustees Walters Art Gallery since 1933; chmn. code com. Investment Bankers under NRA, 1934-35; now chmn. Investment Bankers Conf., Inc. Clubs: Maryland, Johns Hopkins, Alpha Delta Phi; Links (New York). Home: Roland Park, Md. Address: Alex. Brown & Sons, Baltimore and Calvert Sts., Baltimore, Md.

GRISWOLD, Robertson, banker, lawyer; b. Baltimore, Md., Apr. 13, 1884; s. Benjamin Howell and Carrie Grieves (Robertson) G.; grad. Boys Latin Sch. (Dunham's), Baltimore, 1902; A.B., Johns Hopkins, 1905, grad. work, polit. science, 1905-06; LL.B., U. of Md., Baltimore, 1907; m. Abbie Sloan Roberts, Dec. 10, 1919; children—Robertson, Sloan, David Howell. Admitted to Md. bar, 1907; atty. United Rys. & Electric Co., Baltimore, 1907-09; mem. of law firm Griswold & Marshall, 1909-13, Ritchie, Janney & Griswold, 1913-16 asso. with Joseph C. France, atty.-in-law, 1916-17; asso. with banking house of Alex. Brown & Sons., 1919-20; v.p. Md. Trust Co., Baltimore, since 1920; dir. Houston Natural Gas Corpn. Served as mem. Battery A, Md. N.G., 1915-17; served during Mexican trouble, 1916; sergt. 110th F.A., U.S. Army, Pikesville, Md., Aug. 1917; commd. 1st lt., Air Service, Aug. 27, 1917; 2d R.O.T.C., Ft. Meyer, Va., 1917; adj., U.S. Sch. Mil. Aeronautics, Ithaca, N.Y., Sept. 1917-Nov. 1918; capt., Air Service, Apr. 1, 1918; Air Service Depot, Garden City, N.Y., Nov.-Dec., 1918; disch. Dec. 18. Mem. chmn. Municipal Aviation Commn., Baltimore. Trustee Endowment Fund, U. of Md., Am. Bankers Assn. (past pres. trust div.; mem. exec. com.; former chmn. com. on relations with the bar; former mem. exec. council; former chmn. com. on taxation); mem. Md. State Bar Assn. (treas.; mem. exec. council; former vice-pres.); mem. Johns Hopkins Alumni Assn. (past pres.); mem. Am. Bar Assn., Bar Assn. of Baltimore, Soc. of Colonial Wars State of Md. (lt. gov.), Md. Soc. Sons of the Revolution (bd. mgrs.), Alpha Delta Phi, Omicron Delta Kappa. Democrat. Episcopalian. Clubs: Maryland, Baltimore Country (treas., mem. bd. govs.), Merchants (v.p. and mem. bd. govs.); Alpha Delta Phi (New York). Home: 802 W. Belvedere Av. Office: Calvert and Redwood Sts., Baltimore, Md.

GRIZZELL, E(mit) Duncan, univ. prof.; b. Alexandria, Ky., Apr. 28, 1887; s. William Franklin and Margaret (Rees) G.; A.B., Yale U., 1915; A.M., U. of Pa., 1919, Ph.D., 1922; m. Ethyl Blackerby, Aug. 3, 1911. Asst. prof. secondary edn., U. of Pa., 1922-29, prof. since 1929; visiting prof. (summers), Trinity Coll., U. of Wis., U. of Mich., U. of Wash., O. State U., U. of Colo., U. of Va. Mem. survey staff for surveys of Philadelphia, Bethlehem and Wyomissing pub. schs. and George Sch. and Chestnut Hill Acad. Chmn. exec. com. Cooperative Study of Secondary Sch. Standards since 1933; chmn. Commn. on Secondary Schs., Middle States Assn. Colls. and Secondary Schs., since 1926; dir. com. on Implementation of Studies in Secondary Edn., Am. Council on Edn., 1939. Mem. A.A.A.S., Am. Hist. Assn., Am. Polit. Science Assn., Am. Acad. of Polit. and Social Science, Hist. Soc. of Pa., Am. Geographic Soc., Phi Delta Kappa. Baptist. Clubs: Yale (Philadelphia); Lenape (U. of Pa.). Author: Origin and Development of the High School in New England, 1922; Education, Principles and Practices, 1928; American Secondary Education, 1937; also many articles in professional mags. Home: 112 Crosshill Road (Carroll Park), West Park, Philadelphia, Pa. Office: University of Pa., Philadelphia, Pa.

GROBLEWSKI, Casimir C., physician and surgeon; b. West Nanticoke, Pa., Sept. 15, 1886; s. Albert G. and Helen (Switalski) G.; student Harry Hillman Acad., Wilkes-Barre, Pa., 1904-07; M.D., U. of Pa., 1911; m. Lucy S. Butkiewicz, Oct. 7, 1912; children—Lucia Kazimira (wife of Dr. Val B. Piskorski), Harry John. In gen. practice of medicine, Plymouth, Pa., since 1911; dir. and sec. First Nat. Bank of Plymouth; dir. and treas. Plymouth Lumber Co.; dir. and treas. Plymouth Realty Co. School dir. Plymouth Pub. Schs., 1923-35. Mem. A.M.A., Pa. Med. Soc., Luzerne Co. Med. Soc. Republican. Roman Catholic. Knight of Pythias. Home: 83 Academy St. Office: 241 E. Main St., Plymouth, Pa.

GROCE, William Marvin, pres. and gen. mgr. Bromo-Mint Co., Inc.; b. Danville, Pa., Feb. 8, 1903; s. William F. and Annie (McCormick) G.; B.S., Susquehanna U., 1923; Ph.B., Yale U., 1925; m. Helen Genevieve Emig, Jan. 4, 1928; children—Margie Lynn, William Marvin, 2d. Associated with Bromo-Mint Co. since 1925, beginning as special traveling representative, pres. and gen. mgr. since 1929. Mem. Inst. of Medicine Mfrs. (New York), Selinsgrove Chamber of Commerce, Susquehanna U. Alumni Assn., Yale Alumni Assn., Snyder County Sportsman's Assn. Republican. Methodist. Mason. Clubs: Bond and Key (Selinsgrove); Ammanot (New Haven). Mem. and violinist Milton (Pa.) Symphony Orchestra and Susquehanna Symphonic Society of Susquehanna Univ., Selinsgrove, Pa. Home: 503 N. Market St. Office: 107 N. High St., Selinsgrove, Pa.

GROEL, Frederick Henry, lawyer; b. Newark, N.J., Jan. 15, 1899; s. Charles and Augusta

(Schiener) G.; student South Side High Sch., Newark, N.J., 1914-17; A.B., Princeton U., 1921; LL.B., Harvard Law Sch., 1924; m. Audrey Berdine, June 15, 1929; children—Marjory Eve, Berdine. Admitted to N.J. bar as atty., 1924, and since practiced at Newark, N.J., admitted as counsellor-at-law, 1928; teacher sales, common law pleading, evidence and mortgages, N.J. Law Sch. (merged with U. of Newark, 1936), since 1927. Served as seaman, U.S. Navy, during World War. Mem. N.J. Ho. of Reps., 1926, 1927; asst. corpn. counsel, City of Newark, 1927-33. Trustee N.J. Hist. Soc. Mem. Delta Sigma Rho. Republican. Presbyterian. Clubs: Essex, Princeton (Newark, N.J.); Harvard of N.J. Home: 115 S. Munn Av., East Orange, N.J. Office: 11 Commerce St., Newark, N.J.

GROFF, June Gertrude, artist, painter; b. North Lawrence, O., June 26, 1903; d. John Milton and Belle (Lister) Groff; grad. Byron W. King's Sch., Pittsburgh, Pa., 1924; student N.Y. Univ., 1928-29, Pa. Acad. Fine Arts, Phila., 1931-36, Barnes Foundation, Merion, Pa., 1937-39. Began career as accompanist and contralto, Nat. Lyceum Bureau, 1924-25; held first one-man show in painting in oils and water colors, Pittsburgh, 1932, and since then has shown in Pa. Acad. Fine Arts, The Fellowship of Pa. Acad. Fine Arts, Friends Central Country Day Sch., Gimbels Contemporary Art Gallery, Art Alliance; one-man show at Am. Contemporary Art Gallery, 1938; exhibited at The Little Gallery, Washington, D.C., and Morton Galleries, New York City; represented in collections of Pa. Acad. Fine Arts, Fellowship of Pa. Acad. Fine Arts, Barnes Foundation, and in pvt. collections of Judge Francis Biddle, Walter S. Lister and others. Awarded Cresson European Traveling Scholarship from Pa. Acad. Fine Arts, 1935. Home and Studio: 736 Pine St., Philadelphia, Pa.

GROFF, Robert Armand, neurosurgeon; b. Phila., Pa., May 11, 1903; s. Henry Clemens and Estella (Rosenberger) G.; A.B., U. of Pa., 1925; M.D., U. of Pa. Med. Sch., 1928; m. Georgiana Ketchum Hallenbeck, of New York, N.Y., July 29, 1933. Interne U. of Pa. Hosp., 1928-30; instr. neurosurgery, U. of Pa. Med. Sch., 1930; asst. neurosurgery, Phila. Gen., Grad., Univ., hosps., 1930; vol. asst. neurosurgery, Peter Bent Brigham Hosp., Boston, Mass., 1931-32 and adjunct in surgery, Mt. Sinai Hosp., 1931; clin. clk., Nat. Hosp., Queen's Sq., London, Eng., 1933-34, asst. out patient dept., same, 1933-34; asst. in surgery, Presbyn. Hosp., 1934, Episcopal Hosp., 1936; asso. neurosurgery, U. of Pa. Med. Sch., 1936, asst. prof. same, Grade. Sch. of Medicine, 1937; cons. neurosurgeon, Women's Hosp., 1938; asst. surgeon in neurosurgery, Pa. Hosp., 1938. Served as 1st lt. R.O.T.C., 1928-38. Fellow Am. Coll. Surgs. Mem. Soc. for Research Nervous & Mental Diseases, Am. and Phila. neurol. socs., Am. Pa. State, and Phila. Co. med. socs., Alpha Sigma Phi, Phi Alpha Sigma. Republican. Lutheran. Club: Philadelphia Country (Bala). Home: Box 175 Righters Mill Rd., Penn Valley, Bala-Cynwyd, Pa. Office: Medical Tower, Philadelphia, Pa.

GROFF, Wilmer Krause, dist. supt. of schs.; b. Limerick, Montgomery Co., Pa., Jan. 19, 1880; s. Davis Fry and Mary Ann (Krause) G.; grad. West Chester Teachers Coll., 1899; B.S., U. of Pa., 1909; B.Pd., Keystone State Teachers Coll., 1911, M.Pd., 1916; A.M., Lafayette Coll., 1926; m. Mary Matilda Eisenberg, Aug. 22, 1900; children—Gordon E., Mary Kathryn (Mrs. Claude B. Wagoner), Davis F., Frank E. Supervising prin. of schools, Upper Dublin Twp., Montgomery Co., Pa., 1901-03, West Conshohocken, 1903-05, Jenkintown, 1905-12; prin. Cheltenham Twp. High Sch., Montgomery Co., 1917-18; dist. supt. of schools, Lansford, Pa., 1922-26; supervising prin., Easton Twp., Chester Co. since 1926, Tredyffrin Twp., 1931-34; dist. supt. of schools, Tredyffrin Co. since 1934. Mem. Reformed Ch. Home: Woodside Rd. at First Av. Office: First and Bridge Av., Berwyn, Pa.

GROH, John Lick, surgeon; b. Lickdale, Pa., Mar. 13, 1889; s. John Brightbill and Anna (Lick) G.; grad. Lebanon High Sch., 1908; M.D., U. of Pa., 1912; m. Anna B. Myers, June 15, 1913; children—Eleanor Elizabeth, John Richard, Lucille, Robert. Began gen. practice of medicine, 1913, surgery, 1918; chief surgeon and dir. Lebanon (Pa.) Sanatorium since 1920. Fellow A.M.A.; mem. Lebanon Co. Med. Soc. (mem. bd. censors since 1925), Pa. Hosp. Assn., Chamber of Commerce, Pa. Bd. of Assistance of Lebanon Co. Republican. Episcopalian. Clubs: Wyomissing (Reading); Lebanon Country (dir.), Hershey Country (dir.), Quentin Riding (dir.). Home: 419 Cumberland St. Office: Lebanon Sanatorium, Lebanon, Pa.

GRONDAHL, Lars Olai, dir. of research and engring.; b. Hendrum, Minn., Nov. 27, 1880; s. Peder Elias and Herborg (Huglen) Larson; student Concordia Coll., Moorhead, Minn., 1897-99; B.S., St. Olaf Coll., Northfield, 1904, M.S., 1905; Ph.D., Johns Hopkins, 1908; student U. of Chicago, summers 1903, 09, U. of Berlin, spring semester, 1914; m. Grace Elizabeth Fuller, Sept. 11, 1907; 1 son, Martin (dec.). Instr. physics, St. Olaf Coll., 1904-05; lecture asst. Johns Hopkins, 1906-08; prof. mathematics and physics, Spokane (Wash.) Coll., 1908-09; instr. physics, U. of Wash., 1909-12; instr. physics, Carnegie Inst. Tech., 1912-14, asst. prof., 1914-17, asso. prof., 1917-20; dir. research Union Switch & Signal Co. since 1920, dir. research and engineering since 1937. Commd. capt. U.S.A., later released for service with Naval Cons. Bd., World War. Mem. bd. dirs. Pittsburgh Acad., 1934-36; mem. Nat. 'Research Council, 1933-36; chmn. of exec. com. of Advisory Council on Applied Physics of Am. Inst. of Physics, 1936. Fellow A.A.A.S., Am. Phys. Soc. (mem. council 1933-36); mem. Am. Electro-chem. Soc., Am. Inst. Elec. Engrs., Franklin Inst., Phys. Soc. of Pittsburgh (organizer and past pres.), Pittsburgh Chamber of Commerce, Sigma Xi, Sigma Alpha Epsilon. Unitarian. Clubs: University, Longue Vue Country. Discoverer of copper-copperoxide rectifier and inventor various headlight, train control and signal devices. Home: 6937 Penn Av., Pittsburgh, Pa. Address: Union Switch & Signal Co., Swissvale, Pa.

GRONE, Robert Yocum, surgeon; b. Danville, Pa., Dec. 1, 1899; s. Alexander Henry and Florence (Shultz) G.; ed. Temple U. pre-med., 1919-22; M.D., Jefferson Med. Coll., 1926; m. Ethel Lloyd, Feb. 6, 1926; children—Alexander Robert, Joseph Lloyd. Interne Geisinger Mem. Hosp., Danville, Pa., 1926-27, chief resident in surgery, 1927-28, asst. surgeon, 1928-36; chief surgeon and supt. Shamokin State Hosp., 1936-38; in pvt. practice of surgery, Danville, Pa., since 1938. Served in U.S.N. during World War. Fellow Am. Coll. Surgs. Mem. Am., Pa. State, Columbia Co. med. assns., Phi Alpha Sigma. Mem. Am. Legion, Nat. Rifle Assn., Montour Co. Fish and Game Conservation Club, Pa. Rifle and Pistol Assn., Danville Gun Club. Republican. Presbyn. Mason (K.T., Shriner). Club: Acacia. Home: 101 W. Market St., Danville, Pa.

GROOVER, Clair, lawyer; b. E. Buffalo Twp., Union Co., Pa., Oct. 21, 1891; s. William H. and Kathryn (Brown) G.; student Bucknell U.; 1 yr. legal work, U. of Mich.; m. Margaret Schautz, Feb. 7, 1917; children—William Klein, Freddie Schautz. Admitted to practice before Pa. Supreme Ct., 1921; in practice of law at Lewisburg; now engaged in trial work in common pleas and federal cts., land title work and refinancing of individuals and business interests; spl. dep. atty. gen. Unemployment Compensation Bd. of Review. Mem. Speakers' Bur., Dem. State Com., addressing clubs on Pa. Unemployment Law. Served as capt. Troop D, 103d Cavalry, Lewisburg, 4 yrs.; 1st lt., 313th Inf., 79th Div., World War; engaged in battles of Meuse, Argonne, Verdun and Troyon Sector. Trustee Selinsgrove State Colony for Epilepsy. Ex-pres. Union Co. Bar Assn.; mem. Businessmen's Assn. (Lewisburg, Pa.), Am. Legion (comdr. 1922-33; past dep. dist. comdr.), Vols. Foreign Wars. Elder St. John's Reformed Ch.; teacher Men's Bible Class. Mason. Home: Third and St. George St. Office: 426 Market St., Lewisburg, Pa.

GROSE, C(larence) Herman, supt. of public schools; b. Nicholas Co., W.Va., Aug. 30, 1896; s. Walter R. and Maria (Rader) G.; B.S., W.Va. Wesleyan Coll., 1916; M.A., U. of Pittsburgh, 1927; m. Esther Mae Troeger, Aug. 29, 1931. High school teacher, Buckhannon, W.Va., 1914-15, Salem, W.Va., 1916-17, Huntington, W.Va., 1917-22; prin. Cammack Jr. High Sch., Huntington, W.Va., 1922-24, Ambridge, Pa., 1924-30; supt. of schs., Ambridge, 1930-31, Mt. Lebanon, Pa., 1931-35, Erie, Pa., since 1935. Served as corporal during World War. Dir. Erie Co. Health and Tuberculosis Assn., Erie Branch of Pa. Assn. for the Blind, Erie Social Hygiene Assn., Internat. Inst. Mem. N.E.A., Am. Assn. Sch. Adminstrs., Pa. Edn. Assn., Progressive Edn. Assn., Sons Am. Revolution, Am. Legion, Phi Delta Kappa. Presbyterian. Mem. Kiwanis Club. Contbr. to ednl. periodicals. Home: 3838 Sassafras St. Office: Public Library Bldg., Erie, Pa.

GROSE, Logan S(tephenson), clergyman; b. Nicholas Co., W.Va., Oct. 11, 1867; s. William and Rebecca (Stephenson) G.; student West Liberty Teachers Coll., West Liberty, W.Va., 1909-12; Ph.B., Bethany Coll., Bethany, W.Va., 1914; hon. D.D., W.Va. Wesleyan Coll., Buckhannon, W.Va., 1932; m. Ella G. Brown, Oct. 5, 1897 (dec.); 1 dau., Lois Margaret; m. 2d Mary Ruth Lowry, Apr. 9, 1934. Engaged in teaching in pub. schs., 1886-94; ordained to ministry M.E. Ch., 1894; dist. supt., 1929-35; mem. Gen. Conf. M.E. Ch., Atlantic City, 1932; pastor First Meth. Ch., New Martinsville, W.Va., since 1935. Trustee W.Va. Wesleyan Coll., Buckhannon, W.Va., since 1930. Republican. Methodist. Odd Fellow. Home: 25 College Av., Buckhannon, W.Va.

GROSH, Miriam, librarian; b. Brandon, N.Y.; d. Esta Edward and Mary (Gephart) G.; student Oberlin (O.) Coll., 1915-16 and 1916-17, Geneseo (N.Y.) State Normal Sch., 1917-18, Western Reserve Sch. of Library Science, 1925-26, Western Res. U., summers 1929 and 1930, B.S., 1930. Served in Bur. of Aircraft Production and Office of Air Service, Washington, D.C., 1918-20; asst. librarian Oberlin Coll. Library, 1921-31; now librarian Geneva Coll., Beaver Falls, Pa. Mem. Am. Library Assn., Pa. Library Assn., Am. Assn. Univ. Women, Spl. Library Assn., Mid-Western Dist. of P.S.E.A. Republican. Presbyterian. Club: College Hill Woman's (Beaver Falls). Home: 3226 6th Av., Beaver Falls, Pa.

GROSS, Edward Robert, univ. prof.; b. Nebraska City, Neb., Aug. 26, 1883; s. Charles Rudolph and Amelia (Wagner) G.; student Syracuse (Neb.) High Sch., 1899-1902; B.Ed., Neb. Teachers' Coll., Peru, Neb., 1913; B.Sc., U. of Neb., Lincoln, Neb., 1913; m. Mrs. Frankie Glasscock Schneider, Apr. 3, 1915; 1 foster son, Calvin Schneider. County sch. teacher, Burr, Neb., 1902-03; grain farmer, Burr, Neb., 1903-06; prin. high sch., Exeter, Neb., 1908-09; supt. of schools, Long Pine, Neb., 1909-11; instr. in carpentry, Sch. of Agr., U. of Neb., 1911-13; instr. in farm mechanics, Neb. School of Agr., Curtis, Neb., 1913-14; instr. to asso. prof. farm mechanics, Colo. State Coll., Fort Collins, Colo., 1914-18; extension agrl. engr., Miss. State Coll., Starkville, Miss., 1918-19, prof. and head dept., 1919-22; prof. and head dept. agrl. engring., Rutgers U. Coll. of Agr., New Brunswick, N.J., since 1922, in charge Agrl. Mus. since 1929. Fellow Am. Soc. Agrl. Engrs.; mem. New Brunswick Scientific Soc., Asso. Friends Rutgers Library, Nat. Farm Chemurgic Council. Presbyterian. Mason. Clubs: Kiwanis, Rutgers (New Brunswick, N.J.). Author bulletins and papers on septic tanks, poultry bldgs., ventilation, use of explosives, tractor farming, washing machines, stationary spraying plants, sprinkling irrigation. Del. 1st (Liege, Belgium, 1930) and 2nd (Madrid, Spain, 1935) Internat. Congress of Agrl. Engring. Home: 323 Lincoln Av., New Brunswick, N.J.

GROSS, John H., church official; b. Mount Pleasant, Pa., June 7, 1884; s. William H. and Samantha E. (Hickernell) G.; Mus.B., Findlay (O.) Coll., 1903, A.B., 1906, A.M., 1912; A.B., U. of Pittsburgh, 1912; student Western Theol. Sem., Pittsburgh, 1909-11; grad. Princeton Theol. Sem., 1912, Babson Inst., Wellesley, Mass., 1921; D.D., Coll. of Emporia (Kan.), 1924; m. Kathryn Nichols Davis, Feb. 26,

1908; children—Virginia Tallman, John William (dec.). Teacher of history, Ft. Scott, Kan., 1907-09; ordained Presbyn. ministry, 1912; pastor Covington, O., 1912-16, Marietta, 1916-20, Ft. Scott, Kan., 1922-25; treas. and investment officer Bd. of Pensions of Presbyn. Ch. in U.S.A., 1925-36, investment counsel since 1936. Chautauqua lecturer, summers, 1916-17. Overseas with Y.M.C.A., 1918-19. Dir. Lincoln Univ. (Pa.); trustee Princeton Theol. Sem. (N.J.), Presbyn. Hosp. (Phila.). Clubs: Tully Memorial Country, Penn Athletic, Manufacturers and Bankers. Home: Lansdowne, Pa. Office: Witherspoon Bldg., Philadelphia, Pa.

GROSS, John Messick, v.p. Bethlehem Steel Co.; b. York, Pa., Feb. 15, 1877; s. John Kunkel and Annie (Messick) G.; ed. private schs., York; m. Mary Robinson Boykin, 1911 (died 1921); m. 2d, Laura Merriam Curtis, July 1938. Employed by Pa. R.R. Co., 1896-1917; with Bethlehem Steel Co. since 1917, becoming v.p. and dir., 1927. Mem. Pa. Soc. (New York). Clubs: Maryland (Baltimore); Racquet (Philadelphia); India House (New York). Home: Four Oaks Farm. Office: Bethlehem Steel Co., Bethlehem, Pa.

GROSS, Juliet White (Mrs. John Lewis Gross), artist; b. Phila., Pa., June 19, 1887; d. George Philip and Clara (von Olhausen) White; grad. Phila. Sch. of Design for Women, 1908; student Pa. Acad. of Fine Arts, 1908-11, Atelier d'Edouard León, Paris, France, 1925-26; m. John Lewis Gross, Sept. 7, 1911 (died Oct. 8, 1932); children—John Lewis, Clarissa, Horace White. Head art dept., Ogontz Jr. Coll., Rydal, Pa. Awarded: grad. scholarship, Phila. Sch. Design; Cresson European scholarship, Pa. Acad. Fine Arts; Mary Smith prize, 1919; fellowship prize, Pa. Acad. Fine Arts, 1920; gold medal, Plastic Club, 1923; hon. mention Paris Salon, 1926. Home: 413 S. Carlisle St., Phila. Studio: 332 S. 13th St., Philadelphia, Pa.; (summer) Sellersville, Pa.

GROSS, Malcolm W.; mayor of Allentown for term ending 1939. Address: Allentown, Pa.

GROSSLEY, Richard Sylvester, coll. pres.; b. Gloster, Miss., July 11, 1883; s. Angus and Jane (Moore) G.; student Gloster (Miss.) Pub. Schs., Harper Inst., Gloster, Miss., Alcorn (Miss.) High Sch., 1903-07; B.S., Alcorn (Miss.) Agrl. & Mech. Coll., 1911; M.A., N.Y. Univ., 1936; grad. work, Univ. of Chicago, summer 1922, Cornell Univ., summer 1933, Columbia Univ., summers 1931 and 1932; hon. LL.D., S.C. State Coll., Orangeburg, S.C.; m. Helen Brooks Irving, August 3, 1920. Elementary grades teacher, Miss., 1911; dir. academic dept., Baton Rouge (La.) Coll., 1911-13, pres., 1914-16; supervisor rural schs., East Baton Rouge Parish, La., 1913-14; asst. supt. in charge of colored schs., Meridian, Miss., 1916-19; asst. state supervisor of pub. schs., Jackson, Miss., 1919-23; spl. agt., U.S. Dept. of Labor, part time 1919-21; state organizer Negro economics, Washington, D.C., part time, 1918-19; pres., State Coll. for Colored Students, Dover, Del., since 1923. Served in War Emergency Employment Service. Mem. Bd. of Dirs., Del. Children's Home Soc. Mem. N.E.A., Dept. of Sch. Administrators, Am. Teachers Assn., Kappa Delta Pi. Congregationalist. Mason (United Supreme Council, Scottish Rite; 33°; Corinthian Consistory No. 5, Wilmington, Del.). Address: State College, Dover, Del.

GROSSMAN, Max, hotel propr.; b. New York, N.Y., Sept. 8, 1889; s. Josef and Regina (Felberman) G.; C.E., Cornell U., 1912; m. Shirley Rosenberg, Oct. 3, 1922; children—Josef, Judith Regina, Louis Marshall. Began as civil engr. with Reading R.R. Co., 1912-13; propr. and operator Grossman's Hotel, Atlantic City, N.J., since 1913; dir. Bankers Trust Co., Chelsea Title Co. Served as mem. Water Policy Commn. State of N.J., 1929-38, Atlantic City Auditorium Commn., 1929-32, Atlantic City Poultry Commn., 1924-29. Vice-pres. Atlantic City Conv. Publicity Bur., 1930-35. Dir. Fed. Jewish Charities of Atlantic City; chmn. bd. dirs. Community Synagogue of Atlantic City, N.J. Mem. exec. com. N.J. State Hotel Assn.; sec. Avenue Hotel Assn. Republican. Jewish religion. Mason (32°, Shriner). Grotto. Hon. mem. Irem Temple, A.A.O.N.M.S., Wilkes-Barre, Pa. Clubs: Linwood Country, Shrine (Atlantic City). Home: 4702 Therese Pl. Office: Bankers Trust Co., Atlantic City, N.J.

GROSSMAN, Samuel Linn, surgeon; b. Slippery Rock, Pa., Feb. 27, 1891; s. John William and Miriam E. (Moore) G.; grad. Slippery Rock Teachers Coll., 1910; ed. Bucknell U., 1924-25; M.D., Jefferson Med. Coll., 1929; m. Mary Quinn, Oct. 19, 1935. Interne Mercy Hosp., Pittsburgh, 1929-30; engaged in practice of medicine specializing in urology and surgery at Harrisburg, Pa., since 1932; mem. dept. of urology, Harrisburg Hosp. Sec. Harrisburg Acad. of Medicine. Served as pvt. inf. U.S.A., 1917-18. Fellow Am. Coll. Surgs. Diplomate Am. Bd. Urology. Mem. Am. Urol. Assn., Phila. Urol. Soc., Pa. Med. Soc., Dauphin Co. Med. Soc., Am. Med. Assn., Harrisburg Acad. of Medicine. Republican. Presbyn. Mason. Club: Country (Harrisburg). Contbr. papers to med. journs. Home: 412 N. 2d St., Harrisburg, Pa.

GROSSNICKLE, Foster Earl, coll. prof.; b. Myersville, Md., Jan. 28, 1896; s. William Harland and Martha Ellen (Routzahn) G.; A.B., Blue Ridge Coll., New Windsor, Md., 1917; A.M., U. of Pa., 1919; student Columbia U. (part time), 1920-30, Ph.D., 1930; m. Blanche Orr Dumas, Dec. 22, 1922; 1 son, William Foster. High sch. teacher, Brunswick, Md., 1919-20, Nutley, N.J., 1920-25; teacher of Mathematics, Montclair (N.J.) Normal Sch., 1925-29; prof. of Mathematics, Jersey City (N.J.) Teachers Coll. since 1929; teacher summer sessions, Newark (N.J.) Teachers Coll., 1930-34, Syracuse (N.Y.) U., 1935, U. of Minnesota, 1939. Served in Psychol. Service, Camp Meade, 1918-19. Campaign mgr. for mayor of Nutley, N.J., in two elections, 1932, 1936; statistician for ednl. survey in N.J., 1928. Mem. N.J. State Normal Sch. Assn. (pres. 1929-30), N.J. Elementary Mathematics Assn. (pres. 1938-40), Am. Ednl. Research Assn., Phi Delta Kappa. Republican. Methodist. Club: Nutley (Nutley, N.J.). Author many articles in Jour. of Ednl. Research, Elementary Sch. Jour. Has done extensive research in teaching of division. Home: 53 Elm Pl., Nutley, N.J. Office: State Teachers College, Jersey City, N.J.

GROSVENOR, Gilbert Hovey, editor; b. Constantinople, Turkey, Oct. 28, 1875; s. Edwin Augustus and Lillian H. (Waters) G.; twin brother of Edwin Prescott G.; ed. prep. dept. Robert Coll., Constantinople, 1884-90; Worcester (Mass.) Acad., 1891-93; A.B., magna cum laude, Amherst Coll., 1897, A.M., 1901, Litt.D., 1926; LL.D., Georgetown U., 1921, William and Mary, 1930; Sc.D., South Dakota State Sch. of Mines, 1935; Litt.D., U. of Md., 1938; LL.D., Lafayette Coll., 1938; m. Elsie May, d. Alexander Graham Bell, Oct. 23, 1900; children—Melville Bell, Gertrude Hubbard (Mrs. Grosvenor Blair), Mabel, Lilian Waters (Mrs. Cabot Coville), Alexander Graham Bell (dec.), Elsie Alexandra Carolyn (Mrs. Walter K. Myers), Gloria. Taught in Englewood (New Jersey) Academy, 1897-98; assistant editor, 1899-1900, managing editor, 1900-02, editor-in-chief, 1903—, Nat. Geographic Magazine; also dir. Nat. Geog. Soc., 1899—, and pres. 1920— (during his directorship members increased from 900 to 1,150,000). Mem. Am. Antiquarian Soc., Assn. Am. Geographers, Washington Acad. of Sciences. Mem. bd. mgrs. Am. Assn. to Promote Teaching of Speech to the Deaf, Walter Reed Memorial Assn., Save the Redwoods League, Nat. Library for Blind; mem. advisory bd. Nat. Soc. D.A.R.; hon. corr. mem. geog. socs. of Australasia, Rio de Janeiro and Lima; trustee George Washington U., Clarke Sch., Northampton, Mass. Officer Legion of Honor (France); awarded Culver gold medal, Geographical Society Chicago, 1927. Dir. Am. Security and Trust Co., Equitable Coöp. Bldg. Assn., Chespeake & Potomac Telephone Co. Clubs: Chevy Chase, Cosmos (president 1922), Burning Tree, National Press, Cruising Club of America, Overseas Writers. Mem. Phi Beta Kappa, Sigma Xi and Psi Upsilon frats. Wrote: The Explorations of the 19th Century, in ann. report of sec. of the Smithsonian Instn., 1900; historical summary of polar exploration for Peary's "The North Pole," 1910. Author: Young Russia, 1914; The Land of the Best, 1916; Flags of the World (with Byron McCandless), 1917, (with W. J. Showalter), 1934; The Hawaiian Islands, 1924; Discovery and Exploration, 1924; A Maryland Pilgrimage, 1927; History of National Geographic Society, 1936; and numerous articles for magazines. Associate editor Proceedings 8th International Geographical Congress, 1905; Scientific Report of the Ziegler Polar Expedition of 1905-06. Editor: Scenes from Every Land, 1907, 2d series, 1909, 3d series, 1912, 4th series, 1917; Book of Birds (with Alexander Wetmore), 1937. Country home, "Wild Acres," at Bethesda, Md., is a bird paradise, holding Audubon Soc. and U.S. Biol. Survey record for greatest number land birds nesting in one acre adjacent house in U.S., 59 pairs in 1915. Lake 28 miles long, discovered in Alaska, 1919, named Grosvenor Lake in recognition of his encouragement of Alaskan explorations. Gilbert Grosvenor Range in Antarctic discovered and so named by Adm. Byrd, 1929. Crossed Pacific, San Francisco to Hong Kong, in Flying Clipper, May 1937. Home: "Wild Acres," Bethesda, Md.; (summer) Baddeck, N.S. Office: National Geographic Society, 16th and M Sts. N.W., Washington, D.C.

GROTON, Nathanael Babcock, clergyman; b. Westerly, R.I., Jan. 19, 1885; s. Wm. Mansfield and Hannah (Babcock) G.; A.B., Harvard U., 1907; S.T.B., Phila. Divinity Sch., 1920; m. Anna C. Heffern, Nov. 5, 1913; children—Nathanael Babcock, Jr., Anne. Ordained to ministry P.E. Ch., deacon, 1910, priest, 1912; curate Grace Ch., New York City, 1910-13; rector St. Thomas' Ch., Whitemarsh, Pa. since 1913. Served as civilian chaplain, Camp Hancock, Augusta, Ga., 1917-18. Mem. adv. com. Montgomery Co. Emergency Relief Bd., 1936-38; chmn. Montgomery County Bd. of Pub. Assistance since 1939. Mem. bd. mgrs., Childrens Aid Soc., Episcopal Hosp., Leamy Home, House of the Holy Child. Mem. Standing Com. Diocese of Pa. Mem. Founders and Patriots of America, Pi Eta Club (Harvard). Republican. Episcopalian. Club: Rotary (Ambler). Home: Whitemarsh, Pa.

GROVE, Harry A., educator; b. Welsh Run, Franklin Co., Pa., Sept. 9, 1888; s. Henry and Barbara (Resh) G.; grad. Mercersburg Acad., Mercersburg, Pa., 1906; Ph.B., Franklin & Marshall Coll., Lancaster, 1910; student Grad. Sch. in Edn., Pa. State Coll., summers, 1931-35, M.S. in Edn., 1935; m. Virginia Wilkinson (died Dec. 11, 1922); children—Virginia Barbara (dec.), Harry A.; m. 2d, Annie Fletcher, July 3, 1924. Teacher mathematics, Mercersburg Acad., 1910-15; supervising prin. Greencastle (Pa.) pub. schs., 1915-19; teller First Nat. Bank, Greencastle, 1919-20; merchant and newspaper editor, Greencastle, 1920-28; supervising prin. Greencastle pub. schs. since 1928. Del. to Pa. State Edn. Assn. at various times; del. to Nat. Edn. Assn., Detroit, 1937. Mem. Greencastle Draft Bd., World War. Pres. and sec. Greencastle Sch. Bd., 1920-28. Mem. N.E.A., Pa. State Edn. Assn. (mem. legislative com. of Dept. of Supervising Prins.), Franklin Co. Edn. Assn., Phi Kappa Sigma, Kappa Phi Kappa, Phi Delta Kappa. Republican. Presbyn (elder and Sunday sch. supt. Greencastle Ch.). Mason (Past Master). Home: 444 E. Baltimore St., Greencastle, Pa.

GROVE, John Bean, M.D.; b. Petersburg, W.Va., Mar. 20, 1887; s. John Bean and Annie Seymour (Welton) G.; student Petersburg pub. sch., 1895-1901, Potomac Acad., Romney, W.Va., 1902-04, Davis Elkins Coll., Elkins, W.Va., 1904-05; M.D., Coll. Phys. & Surgeons, Baltimore, 1909; m. Rosalie D. Sillings, Oct. 11, 1916. In gen. practice of medicine, Petersburg, W.Va., since 1909; pres. Central Tie & Lumber Co.; treas. and sec. Community Power Co.; dir. Grant Co. Bank. Mem. W.Va. State Road Commn. as advisor since 1933, present term expires, 1941; mem. Town Council of Petersburg, 1910-17; mem. sch. bd., 1930. Served as 1st lt., U.S. Med. Corps, 1918-19. Mem. A.M.A., Potomac Valley County Med. Assn. (past pres.), W.Va. State Med. Assn., W.Va. Tuberculosis and Health Assn. (dir.). Democrat. Presbyn. Mason. Club: Petersburg Kiwanis. Address: Petersburg, W.Va.

GROVE, Robert Eccles, advertising; b. Pittsburgh, Pa., Apr. 23, 1891; s. John Williamson and Eliza (Eccles) G.; grad. Central High Sch., Pittsburgh, 1910; B.S. in economics, U. of Pittsburgh, 1914; m. Louise Wolfe, Dec. 17, 1925. Began as salesman, 1914; asst. to pres. Tenn. Iron & Chem. Co., Pittsburgh, 1919-23; in advertising since 1923, now vice-pres., sec. and dir. Ketchum, MacLeod & Grove, Inc., advertising agents; sec. and dir. Ketchum, Inc. Served as 2d lt. Air Service, U.S. Army, 1917-18. Mem. Pittsburgh Chamber of Commerce. Mem. Am. Assn. Advertising Agencies, Pittsburgh Advertising Club (past pres.), Sigma Alpha Epsilon. Republican. Presbyterian. Clubs: Duquesne (Pittsburgh); Longue Vue (Verona, Pa.). Home: 116 Gladstone Rd. Office: Koppers Bldg., Pittsburgh, Pa.

GROVES, Frederick Hugh, manufacturer; b. England, Jan. 1, 1881; s. Samuel and Annie (Beckwith) G.; came to U.S., 1889, naturalized citizen; ed. pub. schs. and Duff's Coll., Pittsburgh; married; children—Hugh V., Frederick Nelson (M.D.), Dorothy Viola. Began as writer of advertising, 1909; pres. F. H. Groves Piano Co., Pittsburgh, 1912, Circle C. Oil Co., Pittsburgh, 1930, Grov-Lock Co., Pittsburgh, since 1937. Republican. Presbyterian. Mason (Shriner). Address: 2740 Glenmore Av., Pittsburgh, Pa.

GROVES, Hannah Cutler (Mrs. James Allison G.), artist; b. Camden, N.J., Dec. 30, 1868; d Edward Henry and Anne Elizabeth (Collings) Cutler; student Sch. of Design for Women, 1883-85, Temple U.; pupil Wm. M. Chase; m. James Allison Groves, June 15, 1898; children—Olga Cutler, Anne Braddock. Has followed profession as artist since 1884, specializing in portraits including miniatures; instr. various branches of art; awarded bronze medal for painting by Burlington Co. Agrl. Soc. (at age 16), 1884; awarded prize and diploma for best portrait, Southern Exposition, Montgomery, Ala., 1891; painted portrait-miniatures of King of Siam, Chulalonkorn, R.S., Prince Damrong of Siam, Pres. Woodrow Wilson, Hamilton King, minister to Siam, and many other noted men and women. Mem. Art Alliance of Phila., Cape May County Art League. Club: Haddon Fortnightly (Haddonfield). Home: 237 Hopkins Av., Haddonfield, N.J. Studio: 1714 Chestnut St., Philadelphia, Pa.

GROVES, John Stuart, chem. engr.; b. Smyrna, Del., July 16, 1881; s. James Henry and Emma Evelyn (Flowers) G.; student Wilmington (Del.) Friends' Sch., 1887-97, Wilmington (Del.) High Sch., 1897-1900; B.A., U. of Del., Newark, Del., 1904; unmarried. Research chemist, E. I. du Pont de Nemours & Co., Wilmington, Del., 1904-10, supt. of research, Georgetown, S.C., 1910-15, Hopewell Works, City Point, Va., 1915-19, in organic chemicals dept., production control, 1919-30, mgr. foreign tech. service, organic chemicals dept., since 1930. Mem. Am. Inst. Chem. Engrs., Am. Chem. Soc., S.A.R. (v.p., Del. sect.), Kappa Alpha. Democrat. Methodist. Clubs: Wilmington (Del.) Country, Wilmington (Del.); Concord (Pa.) Country; Sea View Golf (Absecon, N.J.); Rehoboth (Del.) Country; Arnold Fish and Game Preserve (Megannic, Can.); Del. Turf (Stanton, Del.). Home: 2307 Ridgeway Rd. Office: 5451 Nemours Bldg., Wilmington, Del.

GRUBB, William Robert, editor; b. Easton, Pa., Feb. 12, 1915; s. William Earl and Caroline (Norton) G.; grad. Bangor High Sch., 1932, Sch. of Journalism, Pa. State Coll., 1937; unmarried. Reporter Bangor Daily News, 1930-34, news editor, 1937, editor since 1937. Mem. at-large Delaware Valley Area Council, Boy Scout Com.; hon. mem. Apollo Male Chorus. Charter mem. Bangor Merchants Assn.; mem. Pa. State Alumni Assn., Delta Chi, Sigma Delta Chi. Presbyterian. Elk. Home: 218 S. Second St. Office: 17 S. Main St., Bangor, Pa.

GRUBBS, Barton, II, lawyer; b. Edgewood, Pa., Sept. 24, 1906; s. Thomas Scandrett and Caroline (Gasaway) G.; grad. Edgewood High Sch., 1923; A.B., Williams Coll., 1927; student Harvard Law Sch., 1927-28; LL.B., U. of Pittsburgh, 1930; m. Louise Hall Keeble, Mar. 2, 1936; children—Thomas Scandrett II, Donald Keeble. Admitted to Pa. bar, 1930, and since practiced in Pittsburgh; asso. Smith, Buchanan, Scott & Gordon, 1930-35; partner Rhea, Grubbs, Ewing & Hay, 1935-37, Rhea, Grubbs & Hay since 1937; justice of peace Borough of Edgewood, 1932-36. Mem. Allegheny County Bar Assn., Delta Upsilon, Phi Delta Phi, Phi Beta Kappa. Republican. Episcopalian. Clubs: Edgewood (Edgewood); Harvard-Yale-Princeton (Pittsburgh). Home: 235 W. Swissvale Av., Edgewood, Pa. Office: 928 Frick Bldg., Pittsburgh, Pa.

GRUBBS, Henry Alexander, univ. prof.; b. Bala, Pa., Mar. 7, 1904; s. Henry Alexander and Edith Clark (Holmes) G.; student Boys' Latin Sch., Baltimore, Md., 1917-19, Johns Hopkins U., 1919-20; student Princeton U., 1920-27, A.B., 1923, Ph.D., 1927; m. Mireille Masson, Feb. 17, 1931; 1 dau., Jacqueline Diane. Instr. French, Princeton U., 1927-30, asst. prof. French since 1931; asst. prof. French, Columbia U. Summer Session, 1936. Mem. Modern Lang. Assn. of America, Phi Beta Kappa. Democrat. Author (textbooks): Minimum French (with W. L. Wiley), 1935; First Readings in French Masterpieces (with Christian Gauss), 1939; also numerous articles and monographs. Home: 127 Jefferson Rd. Office: 43 McCosh Hall, Princeton, N.J.

GRUBER, Charles Michael, physician and teacher; b. Hope, Kan., Mar. 11, 1887; s. John Nicholas and Barbara (Ehrsam) G.; A.B., U. of Kan., 1911, A.M., 1912; Ph.D., Harvard, 1914; M.D., Washington U., 1921; student summers, U. of Wis., 1915, U. of Colo., 1917, 18, Rush Med. Coll., 1919, Puget Sound Marine Biol. Labs., 1910; m. Hermione Sterling, June 6, 1912; children—Cara Barbara, Charles Michael. Instr. in physiology, U. of Pa. Med. Sch., 1914-15; prof. of physiology and pharmacology, Albany Med. Coll., 1915-17; asso. prof. of same, U. of Colo., 1917-18, prof., 1918-20; asso. in physiology, Washington U. Med. Sch., 1920-21, asso. prof. of pharmacology, 1921-32; prof. of pharmacology, Jefferson Med. Coll., since 1932. Mem. Phila. Coll. Physicians, Phila. Co. Med. Soc., A.M.A., Am. Soc. for Pharmacology and Exptl. Therapeutics, Phila. Physiol Soc., A.A.A.S., Soc. for Exptl. Biology and Medicine, Calif. Soc. for Promotion Med. Research, Alpha Omega Alpha, Sigma Xi, Phi Sigma, Phi Beta Pi. Home: 128 Overhill Rd., Bala-Cynwyd, Pa. Office: Jefferson Medical College, Philadelphia, Pa.

GRUENBERG, Frederick Paul, civic worker; b. Minneapolis, Minn., Nov. 19, 1884; s. John and Charlotte (Mayberg) G.; ed. pub. schs., Minneapolis and New York City; student Coll. City of New York, 1898-99, DeWitt Clinton High Sch., 1899-1902; B.C.S., New York U., 1911; post-grad. study U. of Pa., 1916-18; m. Bertha Sanford, Dec. 29, 1909; children—Edith, John, 2d. Began as bookkeeper, 1902; engaged in financial and accounting work, Wall Street, 8 yrs.; dept. head Brown Bros. & Co., Philadelphia, 3 yrs.; with Philadelphia Bur. of Municipal Research, 10 yrs. (dir. 8 yrs.); treas. Bankers Bond & Mortgage Co. and Bankers Securities Corpn. (both of Philadelphia), 7 yrs.; apptd. pub. service commr. of Pa. by Gov. Pinchot, 1931, for term expiring 1940 (commn. abolished by Legislature, Mar. 31, 1937); directed nation-wide study of governmental research for Social Science Research Council, June 1937-38; exec. sec. City Charter Com. of Philadelphia since Dec. 1938; volunteer settlement resident, Southwark House and College Settlement, 1911-14; spl. lecturer, Hobart Coll., Geneva, N.Y., 1917-18; mem. faculty Pa. Sch. for Social and Health Work, 1917-24. Asst. in office of chmn. U.S. Shipping Bd., Washington, latter part of World War. Former trustee Nat. Farm Sch., Doylestown, Pa. Mem. Am. Polit. Science Assn. (mem. council 1921-24), Am. Acad. Polit. and Social Science, Nat. Municipal League, Governmental Research Assn. (chmn. 2 terms), Philadelphia Com. on Public Affairs, Philadelphia Chamber of Commerce (Taxation Com.), Lambda Sigma Phi, Phi Alpha Sigma. Ind. Republican. Mem. Ethical Soc. (former trustee). Clubs: Constitutional (Phila.); Rydal Country; Commonwealth Club of Pa. Home: 135 S. 17th St. Office: 726 Land Title Bldg., Philadelphia, Pa.

GRUGER, Frederic Rodrigo, artist, illustrator; b. Phila., Pa., 1871; s. John P. and Rebecca R. G.; ed. high sch., Lancaster, Pa., and Acad. Fine Arts, Phila.; m. Florence Felton Gray; children—Elizabeth Rodrigo, Frederic Rodrigo, Dorothy Gray. Home: Foxchase Rd., Chester Township, Morris Co. (P.O. Gladstone), N.J.

GRUMBINE, Harvey Carson, educator; b. Fredericksburg, Pa., May 1, 1869; s. Ezra (M.D.) and Annie (Beaver) G.; A.B., valedictorian, Albright College, Pa., 1888; Lafayette College, 1889; Ph.B., Wesleyan U., Conn., 1892; student Germanic and Romance philology, U. of Munich, 1897-1900, Ph.D., 1900; studied Bibliothèque Nationale, Paris, and British Mus., London; m. at Paris, C. Estelle Uhler, 1897. Asso. editor Lebanon (Pa.) Daily Report, 1892-94; on staff Philadelphia Record, 1894-95; prof. English and civics, Central State Normal Sch., Lock Haven, Pa., 1895-97; instr. English and German, Pa. State Coll., 1900-01; asst. prof. English, Washington U., St. Louis, 1901-02; prof. English lang. and lit., Coll. of Wooster, 1902-16; hon. fellow, 1916-18, lecturer, 1918-19, Clark U.; prof. English, 1919-25, W.Va. Univ. Author: Vol. XIV of Litterarhistorische Forschungen (Berlin), 1900; The Misfortunes of Arthur, 1900; Love, Faith and Endeavor, 1909; Stories from Browning, 1914; Humanity or Hate—Which? 1917; The Chase, 1928; The Web, 1929; also monograph Reflections of an Immature Introspectionist, 1917. Contbr. of verse and articles to Outlook, Putnam's, Scribner's, Unpartizan Review, etc. Alternate del. at large from Ohio to Nat. Progressive Conv. 1912. Mem. Am. Assn. of Univ. Profs., A.A.A.S., Chi Psi, Phi Kappa Phi, Pi Gamma Mu. Address "Meadow Bank," Lebanon, Pa.

GRUNDY, Joseph R., ex-senator; b. Camden, N.J., Jan. 13, 1863; s. Wm. H. and Mary Lamb (Ridgway) G.; ed. Swarthmore Coll. Became pres. Grundy & Co., Inc., mfr. woolens, 1920; pres. Farmers Nat. Bank of Bucks County; interested in numerous other business enterprises. A leader in Republican politics of Pa. for many yrs.; served as pres. Pa. Mfrs.' Assn.; mem. U.S. Senate, by apptmt. of Governor Fisher, 1929-30, to fill vacancy. Mem. Soc. of Friends. Home: Bristol, Pa.*

GRUVER, Elbert Asa, edn. of the deaf; b. Mt. Bethel, Pa., Feb. 18, 1869; s. Charles Baker and Christiana (Bachman) G.; A.B., Gettysburg Coll., 1892, A.M., same, 1896; (hon.) LL.D., Coe Coll., Cedar Rapids, Ia., 1928; m. Margaret Prindle Hinkley, Sept. 1, 1898; children—Eleanor (Mrs. Victor Hicks), Elbert Asa, Jr., Margaret H. 2d. Teacher and editor, Pa. Sch. for Deaf, 1892-98; supt. Lexington Sch. for Deaf, New York City, 1898-1908; supt. Rome (N.Y.) Sch. for Deaf, 1908-18; supt. Ia. Sch. for Deaf, Council Bluffs, Ia., 1918-25; supt. Pa. Sch. for Deaf, Mt. Airy, Phila., 1925-36; pres. Am. Assn. To Promote the Teaching of Speech to the Deaf, and The Volta Bur. for Diffusion of Knowledge Relating to the Deaf, both, Washington, D.C., since 1934. Served as mem. Physical and Mentally Handicapped Children White House Conf., 1926. Former mem. and ofcl. many socs. and assns. for social and polit. sci. and edn. Mem. Phi Beta Kappa. Republican. Presbyn. Mason. Rotarian. Home: 47 Woodale Rd., Philadelphia, Pa. Office: 1537 35th St.N.W., Washington, D.C.

GUBB, Larry E.; chmn. bd. and pres. Philco Radio & Television Corpn. Address: Tioga and C Sts., Philadelphia, Pa.

GUCKERT, William L., banker; b. Newark, O., Mar. 13, 1867; s. Frank and Magdalena (Schimpf) G.; student Curry Inst. of Pittsburgh, 1883-84; m. Laura M. Press, Oct. 11, 1892; 1 dau., Willa Press. Began as bookkeeper, 1884; sec. Workingmens Savings Bank & Trust Co., Pittsburgh, 1895-1904; vice-pres. First Nat. Bank of Allegheny, 1904-13, pres., 1913-14; vice-pres. Second Nat. Bank of Allegheny, 1914-30; pres. Second Nat. Bank of Pittsburgh, 1930-31; vice-pres. and mem. adv. bd. First Nat.

Bank at Pittsburgh, Federal St. Branch, since 1931. Mem. North Side Chamber of Commerce. Mem. Bankers & Bank Clerks Mutual Benefit Assn. Republican. Club: Duquesne (Pittsburgh). Home: 226 Waldorf St. Office: Federal St. and Park Way, Pittsburgh, Pa.

GUERIN, John J., real estate; b. Troy, N.Y., June 20, 1863; s. James and Margaret (Scanlon) G.; student pub. sch., N.Y. City, 1870-77; m. Jennie C. O'Connor, Feb. 29, 1892 (dec.); children—William, Mary, Thomas, Lillian, Leo. John, Joseph (dec.), Margaret (dec.), Francis (dec.); m. 2d Marie M. Grim, Apr. 27, 1920; children—Margaret, Ruth, Joseph. Engaged in real estate bus. in Phila., Pa.; now sec. Southern Savings & Loan Assn. Served in U.S. Marine Corps, 1883-88; awarded medal from U.S. Fgn. Service, Panama, 1885. Served as delinquent tax collector, 1900-14. Mem. Pa. Ho. of Reps., 1923-26. Mem. South Phila. Realty Bd. (pres.), South Phila. Business Mens Assn. (chmn. bd. govs.), United Business Mens Assn. (dir.). Democrat. Roman Catholic. K.C. Foresters of America. Moose. Red Men. Home: 2214 S. Broad St. Office: 1916 S. 6th St., Philadelphia, Pa.

GUERRISI, Girolamo, pres. Keystone Macaroni Mfg. Co.; b. Cittanova, Italy, Aug. 4, 1890; s. Girolamo and Catherine (Scullari) G.; m. Saveria Tallarita, Sept. 12, 1912; children—Catherine, Joseph, Mary, Raymond, Robert, Elenora Yolanda, Silvia, Henry-Jorens. Came to U.S., 1904, naturalized, 1920. Pres. and dir. Keystone Fruit Co. since 1910, Keystone Macaroni Mfg. Co. since 1914. Republican. Mason (Shriner). Home: 229 S. Fourth St. Office: 8 Water St., Lebanon, Pa.

GUERTIN, Arthur Henry, advertising exec.; b. Ottawa, Ont., Can., Dec. 29, 1883; s. William Henry and Rose G.; student high sch., art schs.; m. Lila Howland, Mar. 9, 1917; 1 son, Wilson Howland. Began as reporter, later newspaper artist; v.p. Federal Advertising Corpn., Paterson, N.J. Commr. for Paterson (N.J.) area, Boy Scouts of America. Mem. Paterson (N.J.) Chamber of Commerce (v.p.). Republican. Presbyterian. Mason. Clubs: Paterson Camera, Rotary (Paterson, N.J.). Home: Terrace Av., North Haledon, N.J. Office: 177 Gould Av., Paterson, N.J.

GUFFEY, Joseph F., U.S. senator; b. Westmoreland Co., Pa., Dec. 29, 1875; s. John and Barbaretta (Hough) G.; prep. edn., Princeton (N.J.) Prep. Sch.; student Princeton, 1890-92; unmarried. In U.S. postal service, Pittsburgh, Pa., 1894-99; sec. Philadelphia Co., public utilities, Pittsburgh, and affiliated corpns., 1899-1901; gen. mgr. Philadelphia Co., 1901-18; ex-pres. Guffey-Gillespie Oil Co., Atlantic Gulf Co., Columbia Syndicate. Mem. War Industries Bd., Petroleum Service Div., and dir. bur. of sales, alien property custodian's office, World War; mem. Dem. Nat. Com. from Pa. since 1920. U.S. senator from Pa. for term 1935-41. Home: Pittsburgh, Pa.; and 2929 Benton Pl., Washington, D.C.

GUIHER, James Morford, lawyer; b. Smithfield, Pa., Jan. 31, 1897; s. Dr. Horace B. and Maude F. (Brownfield) G.; A.B., W.Va. Univ., Morgantown, 1917; student George Washington U. Law Sch., Washington, D.C., 1919-20; LL.B., Harvard U. Law Sch., 1922; m. Ruth Souders, June 11, 1924; 1 son, James Morford, Jr. Admitted to W.Va. bar, 1922 and asso. with firm of Steptoe & Johnson, Clarksburg, W.Va., since 1922, mem. firm since 1924; served as mem. W.Va. Ho. of Dels., 1927; dir. Union Nat. Bank, Hornor-Gaylord Co., both of Clarksburg, W.Va. Served as 1st lt. Inf., U.S.A., 1917-20; severely wounded in action near Verdun, France, while serving with A.E.F. Awarded Order of Purple Heart (U.S.). Dir. Clarksburg Community Chest. Mem. Am., W.Va. State and Harrison Co. bar assns., Phi Beta Kappa, Sigma Nu, Scabbard and Blade. Republican. Methodist. Mason (32°, Shriner). Club: Clarksburg Country (v.p. and dir.). Home: 316 Buckhannon Av. Office: Union Nat. Bank Bldg., Clarksburg, W.Va.

GUILD, Lawrence Ridge, economist; b. Cleveland, O., Aug. 29, 1901; s. Albert Oswin and Jessie M. (Ridge) G.; B.A., Yale U., 1922, M.A., 1925, Ph.D., 1927; m. Elspeth Salmond Kydd, June 24, 1926; children—Lawrence Ridge, James Kydd. Prof. and head dept. of management engring., Carnegie Inst. Tech. since 1932. Mem. Pittsburgh Regional Labor Bd., 1934-35. Mem. Am. Econ. Assn., Nat. Assn. Marketing Teachers, Soc. Promotion Engring. Edn., Soc. for Advancement Management, Theta Xi, Phi Beta Kappa, Phi Kappa Phi (nat. sec.). Protestant. Contbr. to jours. Address: Carnegie Institute of Technology, Pittsburgh, Pa.

GUILFOIL, Paul Hayes, lawyer; b. Hartford, Conn., Aug. 2, 1886; s. Joseph Paul and Mary Agnes (Hayes) G.; student Hartford (Conn.) High Sch., 1899-1903; A.B., Trinity Coll., Hartford, Conn., 1908, A.M., 1909; LL.B., Columbia U. Law Sch., 1911; m. Sylvia Anastasia Nolan, Nov. 27, 1916; children—Paul Hayes, Jr., Philip Joseph. Gen. practice of law at New York since 1911; with legal dept., Travelers Ins. Co., Hartford, Conn., 1911-12, claim examiner and supervising adjuster, 1918-24; atty. Workmen's Compensation Publicity Bur., New York, 1913-14; mgr. claim dept. Employers Mutual Ins. Co., New York, 1914-15; claim examiner Globe Indemnity Co., New York, 1916-18; mgr. claim dept., asst. sec., v.p. and gen. counsel, Norwich Union Indemnity, New York, 1924-33; v.p. and gen. counsel Bankers Indemnity, Newark, N.J., since 1933; mem. of firm Van Orman & Guilfoil, attys., New York, since 1934. Mem. Internat. Assn. of Ins. Counsel, Casualty & Surety Club of N.Y. Catholic. Club: Maplewood (N.J.) Country. Home: 28 N. Crescent St., Maplewood, N.J. Office: 15 Washington St., Newark, N.J.

GUILLET, George Leroy, teacher of mech. engring.; b. Rochester, N.Y., Oct. 15, 1887; s. Charles and Jessie May (Roberts) G.; B.S., McGill Univ., Montreal, Can., 1908, M.S., 1909; m. Edna M. Sowry, July 22, 1925; 1 dau., Marilyn Elise. Asst. prof. of mech. engring., McGill U., 1909-14; factory engr. Bastian Bros., Rochester, N.Y., 1914-16; prof. of mech. engring., Queens U., Kingston, Ont., 1916-21; research engr. Johns Manville, Asbestos, Quebec, 1921-24; asso. prof. of mech. engring., Pa. State Coll., since 1924. Mem. Am. Soc. Mech. Engrs., Sigma Xi. Republican. Author: Kinematics of Machines, 1928. Contbr. many articles to tech. mags. Home: 233 Mitchell Av., State College, Pa.

GUION, Edward, physician; b. Yonkers, N.Y., July 20, 1878; s. William Morris and Sarah A. (Ormes) G.; M.D., Medico-Chirurg. Coll. (now U. of Pa.), Phila., 1899; m. Sarah Edie Fleming, 1901; children—Gertrude Edie, Edward, Jr., Eugene Fleming. Engaged in gen. practice of medicine at Atlantic City, N.J.; has been health officer Atlantic City, Ventnor City, N.J.; med. dir. and supt. Atlantic County Hosp. for Mental Diseases, N.J., since 1923; health officer, City of Northfield, N.J.; mem. staff Atlantic City Hosp., Pine Rest Sanitarium. Served as 1st lt. then capt. Med. Corps, U.S.A., 1917-19; now maj. Med. Res. Corps. Mem. A.M.A., N.J. State and Atlantic Co. med. socs., Am. Pub. Health Assn., N.J. Health and San. Assn. (sec., past pres.), Assn. Mil. Surgeons, N.J. Hosp. Assn. (pres.), Phila. Psychiatric Assn., Phila. Med. Club. Republican. Presbyterian (pres. bd. trustees First Ch.). Mason (32°). Elk. Clubs: Kiwanis of Pleasantville (past pres.); Tuna (Atlantic City); Atlantic County Game Preserve (Estelville). Home: Northfield, N.J.

GULDAHL, Ralph, professional golf; b. Dallas, Tex., Nov. 22, 1911; s. Olaf and Anna G.; grad. Woodrow Wilson High Sch., Dallas, Tex., 1929; m. Maydella LaVerne Fields, Apr. 11, 1931; 1 son, Ralph. Professional golfer, Franklin Hills Country Club, Detroit, Mich., 1931, St. Louis Country Club, 1932-33, Braidburn (N.J.) Country Club, 1938. Won Western Open championship at Davenport, Ia., 1936; Augusta Open at Augusta, Ga., 1936; Miami-Biltmore Open at Coral Gables, Fla., 1936; Western Open at Cleveland, O., 1937; U.S. Open, 1937; Canadian Open at Toronto, 1937; Western Open, St. Louis, Mo., 1938; U.S. Open, Denver, Colo., 1938. Mem. victorious Ryder Cup Team, 1927. Mem. advisory staff on sports New York World's Fair 1939; col. on Colo. Governor's Staff. Mem. Professional Golfers Assn.; hon. mem. Norwood Hills Country Club (St. Louis), Davenport (Ia.) Country Club. Home: Braidburn Country Club, Braidburn, N.J.

GULICK, Lee Nelson, prof. mech. engring.; b. Bacon Hill, N.Y., Sept. 11, 1893; s. Nelson Joseph and Harriet Helena (Lee) G.; B.S. in Mech. Engring., U. of Pa., 1916, M.E., 1927, M.A., 1930; m. Frances Reynolds Graham, June 12, 1920; children—Graham Lee, Robert Reynolds, Richard Wallace, Jane Lee. Supervisor machine shop tools and tool rooms Midvale Steel Co., 1916-20, jigs and fixtures, 1918-20, machine shop repairs, 1919-20; designer Paramount Rubber Co., 1920; consultant on design and shop operation problems for industrial concerns; instr. mech. engring., U. of Pa., 1920-22, asst. prof., 1922-27, prof. since 1927; in charge mech. practice div. since 1925. Mem. Am. Soc. Mech. Engrs., Alpha Chi Rho. Home: 33 Union Av., Bala-Cynwyd, Pa.

GULLICKSON, Otto Andrew, health and phys. edn.; b. Enderlin, N.D., July 18, 1893; s. Ever and Alida (Olson) G.; grad. Enderlin High Sch., 1913; student Teachers Coll., Valley City, N.D., 1913-14; B.P.E., Y.M.C.A. Coll., Springfield, Mass., 1918; B.S., Teachers Coll., Columbia, 1925, A.M., 1926; m. Helen Huber, May 22, 1926; step-daughter, Barbara Dejonge (Mrs. Gwyn William Edmonds), son, Donald Ever. Dir. of phys. edn., Boys Club, Springfield, Mass., 1915-18; athletic dir. Franklin and Marshall Acad., Lancaster, Pa., 1920-23; phys. dir., U. of Wyo., 1923-24; asst. Boy Scout commr., N.J., 1924-26; dir. of phys. edn., city schools, Charlotte, N.C., 1926-30; prof. of health and phys. edn., Marshall Coll., Huntington, W.Va., since 1930, trainer of athletic teams, 1930-37; dir. Life Summer Camp, Pottersville, N.J., 1926, Mt. Mitchell Camp for Boys, Burnsville, N.C., 1928. Served as lt. Machine Gun Co., U.S. Army, 1918-19; capt. Am. Red Cross, Fox Hills, S.I., N.Y., as head mechanotherapy dept. in rehabilitation of wounded soldiers. Organized Southern Interscholastic Golf Tournament, 1927-29, Buckeye Conf. Intramural Boxing Tournament, 1935. Mem. Am. Legion, Phi Delta Kappa, Sigma Alpha Epsilon. Republican. Episcopalian. Mason. Home: 1441 Edwards St., Huntington, W.Va.

GULLIKSEN, Finn H., electronic engr.; b. Oslo, Norway, Oct. 10, 1901; s. Gunvald and Borghild (Schulerud) G.; student Norwegian Inst. Tech., Norway; unmarried. Design engr. Elektrisk Bur., Oslo, Norway, 1924-25; electronic engr. Westinghouse Electric & Mfg. Co., East Pittsburgh, Pa., since 1925. Awarded nat. prize by Am. Inst. E.E. for best article on elec. engring. pub. during 1933. Club: Westinghouse (Pittsburgh). Author: Handbook for Basketweaving (pub. in Norway), 1931; Industrial Electronics, 1935; also numerous articles on electronic control devices pub. in tech. jours. Holder over 30 U.S. patents, principally in field of electronic industrial control and automatic regulation. Home: 5731 Center Av., Pittsburgh, Pa. Office: care Westinghouse Electric & Mfg. Co., East Pittsburgh, Pa.

GULLIVER, Robert Huntington, certified pub. accountant; b. New Haven, Conn., Feb. 26, 1891; s. Henry Strong and Harriet (Evans) G.; B.A., Yale, 1913; m. Alta Risdon, Aug. 25, 1917; 1 dau., Charlotte R. G. Began as accountant, Phila., Pa., 1913; junior accountant, Lybrand Ross Bros. & Montgomery, 4 years; owner Robert H. Gulliver & Co., accountants and auditors, Trenton, N.J., since 1920; sec. United Bldg. & Loan Assn. since 1922; gov. N.J. Bldg. & Loan League since 1925; dir. Federal Home Loan Bank of N.Y. since 1932. Served as ensign, U.S. Navy, 1917-19. Councilman, City of Trenton, N.J., 1935-39. Mem. Am. Inst. of Accountants, Am. Legion. Republican. Episcopalian. Home: 1404 W. State St. Office: Broad St. Bank Bldg., Trenton, N.J.

GUMAER, Alfred Herman, univ. prof.; b. Brooklyn, N.Y., June 5, 1873; s. Leander and Anne (Korff) G.; grad. Jersey City High Sch.; B.S. in Architecture, Columbia U.; student Godfroy Frenet Atelier, Paris; unmarried. Asst. prof., later prof. architectural history, Sch. of

Mines, Dept. Architecture, Columbia U., 1901-02, prof. history of art, 1902-06; prof. history of art, U. of Pa. since 1907. Mem. Archæol. Inst. America, Sigma Xi, Tau Sigma Delta, Lambda Chi Alpha. Clubs: Art Alliance, Lenape (Philadelphia); Columbia University (New York). Home: 331 S. 12th St., Philadelphia, Pa.

GUMMEY, Henry Riley, Jr., theologian; b. Phila., Jan. 12, 1870; s. Henry Riley and Mary (McFarland) G.; B.A., U. of Pa., 1890, M.A., 1893, B.D., 1895; grad. Gen. Theol. Sem., New York, 1893; D.D. in course, Philadelphia Divinity School, 1905; D.C.L., Univ. of the South, 1931; m. Margaret Upjohn, June 30, 1897; children—Henry Riley, Margaret McFarland. Deacon, 1893, priest, 1894, P.E. Ch.; curate St. Luke's Ch., Germantown, Phila., 1893-95; rector St. John's Ch., Germantown, 1897-1906, Grace Ch., Haddonfield, N.J., 1907-12; examining chaplain to bishop of N.J., 1908-14; prof. ecclesiastical history and polity, 1912-13, dogmatic theology and polity, 1913-14, U. of the South, Sewanee, Tenn.; rector St. James' Ch., Downingtown, Pa., 1914-29; prof. of liturgics, ch. polity and canon law, Phila. Div. Sch., since 1929. Examining chaplain to bishop of Pa., 1914-30. Mem. Hist. Soc. Pa. Author: The Consecration of the Eucharist, 1908; also articles and reviews in theol. periodicals. Home: 115 Bethlehem Pike, Chestnut Hill, Philadelphia, Pa.*

GUMMO, Blanchard Stanley, teacher, artist; b. Lock Haven, Pa., Feb. 3, 1906; s. Clarence Kent and Marilla Estella (Stouck) G.; student Central State Normal Sch., Lock Haven, 1918-21, Bucknell U., 1921-22; A.B. Yale 1926, B.F.A., Yale 1931; unmarried. Instr. in art, Bucknell University, 1931-34, asst. prof. of art, 1934-39, asso. prof. of art since 1939; field secretary Collectors of American Art, New York, since 1938, Exhibited paintings at Pa. Acad. Fine Arts, Art Inst. of Chicago, Corcoran Biennial, and other annual nat. exhibitions. Awards: medal for figure composition and portrait at 43d Annual Exhibit of Soc. of Washington Artists at Corcoran Gallery, for painting "After-thoughts of Heaven," 1935; 1st mention for oils at Springfield (Mass.) Art League for painting, "Still Life with Coffee Mill," 1938; 2d prize for oils, Harrisburg (Pa.) Art Assn., 1939. Mem. Delta Sigma, Theta Alpha Phi, Pi Alpha. Republican. Methodist. Clubs: Clinton County Country (Lock Haven, Pa.). Home: 131 S. Fairview St., Lock Haven, Pa. Address: 219 Market St., Lewisburg, Pa.

GUNBY, Walter Edwin, minister; b. in Sussex County, Del., Nov. 3, 1878; s. Jacob M. and L. J. (West) G.; grad. Buckingham High Sch., Berlin, Md., 1899; A.B., Washington Coll., Chestertown, Md., 1914, D.D. (hon.), 1923; grad. Dickinson Coll. Sch. of Religious Edn., Carlisle, Pa., 1927; m. Alberta B. Brittingham, Aug. 1, 1901; children—Olin Brittingham, Walter Edwin. Teacher Buckingham High Sch., Berlin, Md., 1900-03; joined Wilmington (Del.) Conf., M.E. Ch., 1903, ordained deacon, 1905, elder, 1907; pastorates: Queenstown, Md., 1903-05, Odessa, Del., 1905-07, Princess Anne, Md., 1907-12, Easton, Md., 1912-14, Dover, Del., 1914-18, Cambridge, Md., 1918-23, Newark, Del., 1929-35; dist. supt., Dover (Del.) Dist., Wilmington Conf. M.E. Ch., 1923-29, Wilmington (Del.) Dist. since 1935; pres. Conf. Bd. of Edn., M.E. Ch., 1923-33, mem. Gen. Bd. Edn., Chicago, Ill., 1928-32, mem. Gen. Conf., Kansas City, Mo., 1928, Gen. Conf., Columbus, O., 1936, mem. Bd. Temperance, Washington, D.C., since 1936; accredited lecturer, Standard Training Schs. of Religious Edn. since 1928. Chaplain of Senate, Assembly of Del., since 1932. Pres. Bd. Trustees, Wesley Collegiate Inst., since 1932. Methodist. Club: Cleric (Wilmington, Del.). Address: 2705 Harrison St., Wilmington, Del.

GUNN, Thomas McCheyne, mech. engring.; b. Joliet, Ill., Feb. 10, 1878; s. Thomas Morris and Mary Catherine (Waggoner) G.; A.B., U. of Wash., 1899, A.M., same, 1900; B.S. in Naval Architecture, Mass. Inst. Tech., 1905; m. Blanche Marguerite Gillieron, of Lausanne, Switzerland, Dec. 1,. 1919; 1 son, Lauren Thomas. Instr. mech. engring., U. of Me., and with U.S. Geol. Survey, 1905-07; marine designer, Fore River Shipbldg. Co., 1907-09; instr. thermodynamics and power plant design, also research work, Columbia U., 1909-12; in charge designing dept., Electric Boat Co., 1913-14, later tech. rep. same co. in Russia, followed by direction submarine boat constrn. for Russian Govt., 1914-17; chief specification branch ship constrn. div., U.S. Shipping Bd., 1917-19; cons. engr. and traveling in N. European states, 1919-21; tech. editor for Vacuum Oil Co., N.Y. City, specialist on lubrication refrigerating machinery, 1921-31; in charge equipment design and constrn., Research and Development Div., Gen. Labs., Socony-Vacuum Oil Co., Inc. since 1931; awarded patents submarine boat design and constrn., refrigerating machines and others. Mem. Am. Soc. Mech. Engrs. Republican. Presbyn. Mason. Kiwanian. Home: 223 Holroyd Pl., Woodbury. Office: Socony-Vacuum Oil Co., Paulsboro, N.J.

GUNNING, Harold D.; asst. surgeon Greenbrier Valley Hosp. Address: Ronceverte, W.Va.

GUNNISON, Sisson Boyd, leather mfg.; b. Erie, Pa., Aug. 19, 1888; s. Rolla and Annie (Sisson) G.; student Central High Sch., Erie, 1904; grad. Pratt Inst. Tech., Brooklyn, N.Y., 1908; m. Lenora Niemeyer, May 1913. Began as chemist with Trag. Schmitt & Sons, 1908; pres. Gunnison Bros., Inc., leather mfg., since 1930; pres. Girard Mfg. Co.; pres. Union Bank of Erie; dir. Armor Electric Mfg. Co. Mason (32°, Shriner). Clubs: Erie, Kahkwa Country, University (Erie). Home: 2700 Elmwood Av., Erie, Pa. Office: Girard, Pa.

GUNSTER, Joseph Frederick, lawyer; b. Lake Ariel, Pa., Aug. 27, 1894; s. Frederick W. and Margaret (Brehl) G.; ed. U. of Notre Dame (Ind.), 1911-12; A.B., Cath. U. of America, 1914; LL.B., Harvard U. Law Sch., 1917; m. Ruth Harris Work, Aug. 25, 1938. Admitted to Pa. bar, 1918; admitted to practice before Supreme Ct. of U.S., 1930; engaged in gen. practice of law at Scranton since 1918; mem. firm Gunster, Mackie and Murphy; served as asst. city solicitor of Scranton, 1920-21; counsel for important valuation and rate cases; dir. Third Nat. Bank & Trust Co., Scranton. Served at first O.T.C., Madison Barracks, N.Y.; 2d lieut. then 1st lieut. inf. U.S.A., 1917-19, with A.E.F. gen. hdqrs. in France. Past pres. Scranton Chamber of Commerce, Council of Social Agencies, Scranton and Dunmore. Trustee U. of Scranton, Community Welfare Assn. of Scranton and Dunmore. Chmn. Scranton Airport Commn. Pres. Lackawanna Hist. Soc. Republican. Roman Catholic. Clubs: Scranton, Scranton Country, Waverly, Abington Hills Hunt. Home: Scranton, Pa. Office: Scranton Life Bldg., Scranton, Pa.

GUNTHER, Charles Otto, prof. mathematics and ordnance engring.; b. New York, N.Y., May 21, 1879; s. Otto and Anna (Eybel) G.; M.E., Stevens Inst. Tech., 1900; m. Beatrice Disbrow, Feb. 19, 1901; children—Beatrix (wife of Dr. Frederick Britton Llewellyn), Jack Disbrow. Instr. mathematics, Stevens Inst. Tech., Hoboken, N.J., 1900-02, asst. prof., 1902-03, asst. prof. mathematics and mech. drawing, 1903-04, asst. prof. mathematics and mechanics, 1904-08, actg. prof. mathematics, 1908, prof. and head dept. mathematics since 1908, prof. mathematics and ordnance engring. since 1936, dean student activities, 1920-25, dean of sophomores, 1927-28. Served with Ordnance Dept. U.S.A., 1918-19, asso. with research and development in small arms and ammunition, Springfield Armory and Small Arms Ballistic Sta., Miami Beach, Fla.; now lt. col. Ordnance Dept. Reserve, U.S. A. Fellow A.A.A.S. Mem. Am. Soc. Civil Engrs., Am. Soc. Mech. Engrs., Army Ordnance Assn., Soc. Am. Mil. Engrs., Assn. Mathematics Teachers N.J. (past pres.), Societe Astronomique de France, Tau Beta Pi, Sigma Nu. Club: Officers of Army and Navy (New York). Author: Integration by Trigonometric and Imaginary Substitution, 1907; Identification of Firearms from the Ammunition Fired Therein, 1935. Home: Grand View-on-Hudson, N.Y. Address: Stevens Institute of Technology, Hoboken, N.J.

GUNTRUM, Emilie Ida, artist; b. Brooklyn, N.Y., June 26, 1899; d. Carl F. and Ida (Selg) G.; ed. N.Y. Sch. of Applied Design for Women, Art Students League, Nat. Academy of Design; studied under George B. Bridgman, Charles Hawthorne, George Luks, John Sloan and Hans Hofman. Has followed profession as artist at Elizabeth, N.J., since 1936; exhibited Montclair Museum, Newark Museum, Pa. Acad., Montross Gallery Contemporary Arts. Mem. Art Students League, New York, Alumnae N.Y. Sch. Applied Design for Women, Elizabeth Soc. of Arts Am. Artist Professional League, Studio Guild, Provincetown Art Assn. Democrat. Presbyterian. O.E.S. Home: 471 Madison Av. Studio: 1143 E. Jersey St., Elizabeth, N.J.

GUTHRIE, Charles Claude, physiologist; b. Gilmore, St. Charles Co., Mo., May 13, 1880; s. Robert McCluer and Frances (Hall) G.; grad. Woodlawn Inst., O'Fallon, Mo., 1897; M.D., U. of Missouri, 1901; Ph.D., University of Chicago, 1907; Sc.D., University of Pittsburgh, 1935. Instructor physiology, University of Missouri, 1901-02; demonstrator physiology, Western Reserve U., Cleveland, 1902-03; instr. physiology, U. of Chicago, 1903-06; prof. physiology and pharmacology, Washington U., 1906-09; prof. physiology and pharmacology, University of Pittsburgh since 1909. Protestant. Member Am. Physiol. Soc., Soc. Pharmacology and Exptl. Therapeutics, Soc. Exptl. Biology and Medicine, Sigma Xi, Alpha Omega Alpha. Author: Blood Vessel Surgery and Its Applications, 1912. Contbr. on physiol. problems. Major in Med. Reserve Corps, U.S.A. Address: Medical School, University of Pittsburgh, Pittsburgh, Pa.

GUTHRIE, Charles Ellsworth, denominational sec.; b. Terra Alta, W.Va., May 26, 1867; s. George E. and Nancy Catherine (Dawson) G.; ed. normal sch. and under pvt. tutors; Johns Hopkins, 1894-98; D.D., Dickinson, 1911; m. Beulah Cowan, Aug. 10, 1892 (died Feb. 21, 1934); children—Freedom Cowan (dec.), Mrs. Eleanor Wallace, Philip Dawson, Carl Strawbridge; m. 2d, Gladys Mae Snyder, Oct. 5, 1936. Ordained to the ministry of M.E. church, 1890; pastor, Hancock, Md., 1887, Rawlings, Md., 1888, Walkersville, Md., 1889, Pikesville, Md., 1890-92, Baltimore, 1893-1907, Washington, D.C., 1908-10, Wilkes-Barre, Pa., 1911-15, Buffalo, N.Y., 1916-17; gen. sec. Epworth League, 1917-24; pastor University Ch., Syracuse, 1924-26; supt. Buffalo Dist. of M.E. Ch., 1927-33; pastor Baker Memorial Ch., East Aurora, N.Y., 1934-36; became pastor, Coudersport, Pa., 1936. Pres. Interdenom. Young People's Union; mem. council of benevolent bds. M.E. Ch.; mem. Gen. Conf. M.E. Ch., 1920, 24, 32; apptd. by bishops as representative of M.E. Ch. to Sixth Ecumenical Meth. Conf., Atlanta, Oct. 1931; rep. of M.E. Ch. to Fed. Council of Chs. of Christ in America (com. on mercy and relief); mem. Council Internat. Friendship Through the Churches, 1927; trustee Genesee Wesleyan Sem., Blocher Homes (for aged), Williamsville, N.Y.; mem. bd. dirs. Methodist Home for Children (Williamsville, N.Y.). Mason (32°, K.T.). Republican. Home: 307 N. East St., Coudersport, Pa.*

GUTHRIE, Donald, surgeon; b. Wilkes-Barre, Pa., June 23, 1880; s. George W. and Sarah Hollenback (Wright) G.; Ph.B., Yale Univ., 1901; M.D., University of Pa., 1905; D.Sc., Lafayette College, 1937; m. Emily Franklin Baker, Dec. 2, 1916. Mem. surg. staff Mayo Clinic, Rochester, Minn., 1906-09; surgeon in chief Robert Packer Hosp. since 1910 and head of Guthrie Clinic, Sayre, Pa.; chief surgeon Lehigh Valley R.R.; also associate prof. of surgery, Graduate School of Medicine of University of Pa. Fellow Am. College of Surgeons (gov.), Southern Surg. Assn., Am. Surg. Assn., Surg. Research Soc.; mem. A.M.A., Pa. Med. Soc. (ex-pres.), N.Y.&N.E. R.R. Surgeons (ex-pres.), Internat. Surg. Assn., Royal Acad. of Medicine (Rome), Coll. of Phys. of Phila., Assn. Resident and Ex-Resident Phys. Mayo Clinic (ex-pres.), Assn. Railroad Chief Surgeons, Conf. Bd. Physicians in Industry, Am. Bd. of Surgery, Royal Hungarian Surg. Soc., Sons of Revolution, Sons of Colonial Wars, Delta Psi. Republican. Episcopalian.

GUTHRIE Clubs: Yale, Union (New York); Rittenhouse, St. Anthony, Racquet (Phila.). Contbr. articles, chiefly on surgical subjects. Home: Sayre, Pa.

GUTHRIE, Walter James, lawyer; b. Apollo, Pa., September 9, 1864; s. John Beatty and Mary Jane (Freetly) G.; grad. Blairsville (Pa.) Acad.; A.B., Allegheny Coll., 1884, A.M., 1889; m. Bella G. Giles, July 10, 1901; children—Douglas Giles (dec.), Laura Jean, Margaret Ruth (dec.), Walter J., Richard G. Admitted to Pa. bar, 1887, and began practice at Apollo; sec. and atty. for Pa., Gulf Oil Corpn., Pittsburgh, 1907-20; sec. and asso. gen. counsel for same and subsidiary corporations since 1920; vice-pres. Apollo Steel Company; dir. Apollo Trust Co.; sec. and asso. gen. counsel Mexican Gulf Oil Co., Venezuela Gulf Oil Co., Gulf Refining Co. (dir.), Western Gulf Oil Co., Gulf Exploration Co., Gulf Research & Development Corpn. Mem. Delta Tau Delta. Republican. Methodist. Mason (K.T., Shriner). Clubs: University, Duquesne, Pittsburgh Athletic Assn., Longue Vue Country, Alcoma Country. Home: 6568 5th Av., Pittsburgh, Pa.; also 1430 S. Bayshore Drive, Miami, Fla. Office: Gulf Bldg., Pittsburgh, Pa.

GUTMUELLER, William George, manufacturer; b. Brooklyn, N.Y., July 23, 1894; s. George and Anna (Brandmeier) G.; student Commercial High Sch., 1906-09; m. Helene A. Brede, June 7, 1919; children—Norma Jean, Phyllis Helene. Began as office boy Doehler Die Casting Co., Brooklyn, N.Y., 1909; successively in bookkeeping, payroll, production, estimating, and cost accounting depts. to present position of plant mgr.; v.p. Doehler Die Casting Co., Pottstown, Pa., since 1929. Served with 325th Inf., 82d Div., with A.E.F., during World War. Dir. Wyomissing Polytechnic Inst., Reading, Pa. Dir. Montgomery Co. Manufacturer's Assn., Norristown, Pa. Republican. Lutheran. Mason (32°, Lehigh Consistory). Club: Rotary (Pottstown, Pa.) Home: 443 Highland Rd. Office: Doehler Die Casting Co., Pottstown, Pa.

GUTTMACHER, Alan Frank, M.D.; b. Baltimore, Md., May 19, 1898; s. Adolf and Laura (Oppenheimer) G.; student The Park Sch., Baltimore, 1912-15; A.B., Johns Hopkins U., 1919; M.D., Johns Hopkins Med. Sch., 1923; m. Leonore Gidding, July 22, 1925; 1 dau., Ann. Instr. anatomy, Johns Hopkins U., 1924; instr. anatomy, U. of Rochester, 1925; interne, asst. and resident obstetrics Johns Hopkins Hosp., 1925-29; asst. resident and resident in gynecology Mt. Sinai Hosp., N.Y. City, 1927-28; asso. in obstetrics, Johns Hopkins U., 1933-39, asso. prof. since 1939; pvt. practice obstetrics and gynecology since 1929; on staff Johns Hopkins, Woman's, Union Memorial, Church Home, Sinai hosps. Mem. Am. Assn. Anatomists. Jewish religion. Author: Life in the Making, 1933; Into This Universe, 1937; also scientific and med.-hist. papers. Home: 2709 Lawina Road. Office: 1039 N. Calvert St., Baltimore, Md.

GUTTMACHER, Manfred S., psychiatrist; b. Baltimore, Md., May 19, 1898; s. Adolf and Laura (Oppenheimer) G.; A.B., Johns Hopkins U., 1919, M.D., 1923; m. Jocelyn Elizabeth McDonough, Nov. 29, 1928; children—Jonathan Adolf, Manfred Richard. Interne Johns Hopkins (Baltimore), Mt. Sinai (N.Y.), Boston Psychopathic hosps., and European Fellow, 1926-28; practice of psychiatry, Baltimore, since 1928; chief med. officer, Supreme Bench of Baltimore since 1930. Dir. Legal Aid Bur., Baltimore. Dir. Mental Hygiene Soc. of Md. (pres.); fellow Am. Psychiatric Assn. Club: Chesapeake (Baltimore, Md.). Home: 2704 Queen Anne Rd. Office: 511 Cathedral St., Baltimore, Md., and Court House, Baltimore, Md.

GYGER, Furman Holme, dairy farming; b. Kimberton, Pa., Dec. 9, 1888; s. John and Elizabeth Blower (Thomas) G.; ed. West Chester Normal Sch., 1905-09, grad., 1909; m. Francanna Colehower Hoffman, Aug. 26, 1914; children—Furman Hoffman, Edith Helen, Wayne Thomas (dec.). Began as teacher rural sch., 1909-13; engaged in dairy farming since 1913, took over father's farm as a tenant farmer, 1913, propr. of farm since 1926; rep. Eastern States Farmers' Exchange since 1926; agt. for Farmers & Traders Life Ins. Co. since 1917; agt. for Pomona Grange Fire Ins. Co. since 1921; dir. Interstate Milk Producers Cooperative; dir. and vice-prcs. Pomona Grange Fire Ins. Co. Served as mem. Pa. Ho. of Rep., 1927-28. Auditor, East Rikeland Twp., 1916-34. Dir. Chester Co. Agrl. Extension Assn. (past pres.). Trustee Pa. State Coll. since 1926. Mem. Upper Uwchlan Farmers Club (pres.), Gamma Sigma Delta. Awarded honor "Master Farmer" by Pennsylvania Farmer, mag., 1939. Mem. Nat., Pa. State, Pomona, Subordinate Grange. Mem. exec. com. Kimberton Grange; mem. exec. com. Pa. State Grange since 1933. Republican. Mem. Prot. Reformed Ch. (elder). Mason (K.T.). Club: Rotary of Phoenixville (dir.); Royal Shrine (Reading). Home: Kimberton, Pa.

H

HAAS, Alfred M., dentist; prof. of dental surgery and anesthesia, Temple U. Address: 2108 S. 17th St., Philadelphia, Pa.

HAAS, Francis Buchman, educator; b. Phila., Pa., June 6, 1884; s. Frederick and Emma (Roberts) H.; A.B., Central High Sch., Phila., 1904; Collegiate Certificate, Phila. Sch. of Pedagogy, 1906; B.S., Temple U., 1913, Pd.D., 1925; M.A., U. of Pa., 1922; LL.D., Juniata College, Huntingdon, Pa., 1934; m. Miriam Rider, June 26, 1916; children—Jean, Mary, Francis B. Teacher pub. schs., Y.M.C.A. evening sch., Girard Coll. Summer Sch., Phila.; later demonstration teacher, Sch. of Pedagogy, and teacher of mathematics, Phila. Evening High Sch.; apptd. mem. faculty, Sch. of Pedagogy, and supervisor research center, Phila., 1915; supervising prin. Breck Sch., Keyser-Meehan Sch., Benson Sch., 1916-20; asst. dir. teacher bur. of State Dept. Pub. Instrn., Pa., 1920; dir. administration bur. of same, 1922; commd. deputy supt. of pub. instn., 1925, supt., 1925-27; pres. State Teachers Coll., Bloomsburg, Pa., since 1927; member staff N.J. Edni. Survey, 1929; mem. Commn. for Study of Ednl. Problems, Pa.; chmn. Emily Jane Culver Scholarship Com. for Pa. Distinguished service medal, Pa. State Edn. Assn., 1928. Chmn. Columbia County Emergency Council on Adult Edn., Recreation and Youth, 1936. Mem. N.E.A., Pa. State Edn. Assn. (pres. 1932-33), Pa. Tuberculosis Soc. (dir.), Pa. Pub. Charities Assn. (dir.), Pa. Alumni Assn. Temple U., Alumni Assn. U. of Pa., Lambda Sigma, Phi Delta Kappa, Kappa Delta Pi, Phi Sigma Pi, Kappa Phi Kappa. Republican. Methodist (Official Board). Mason (33°). Clubs: Schoolmen's (Phila.); Rotary, Country, Craftsman, Consistory (Bloomsburg); Shrine (Wilkes-Barre). Home: R.D. 2, Bloomsburg, Pa.

HAAS, Harry J., banking; b. Luzerne Co., Pa., Jan. 20, 1879; s. John and Elizabeth H.; grad. Wyoming Sem. and Coll. of Business, Kingston, Pa.; grad. Evening Sch. of Accounts and Finance, U. of Pa., 1910; grad. Am. Inst. Banking, 1910; m. Rufie Watson Sanders, Oct. 28, 1914; 1 son, Joseph Sanders. Salesman and newspaper corr. until 1902; teller Berwick (Pa.) Nat. Bank, 1902-03; asst. treas. Berwick Savings & Trust Co., 1903-07; sec. and treas. Farmers & Mechanics Trust Co., West Chester, Pa., 1907; with Merchants Nat. Bank of Phila. (merged with First Nat. Bank 1910) since 1908, asst. cashier, 1908-1916, vice-pres. and dir. since 1924; dir. Philadelphia Bourse. Mem. Am. Bankers Assn. (pres. 1931-32), Pa. Bankers Assn. (pres. 1928), Assn. Reserve City Bankers, Phila. Chamber Commerce (chmn. banking and currency com.). Republican. Presbyn. Mason (Shriner). Clubs: Union League (dir.), Bank Officers' (pres.), Merion Cricket. Author: Golf Service for Caddies and Members. Home: Haverford, Pa. Office: First Nat. Bank, Philadelphia, Pa.

HAAS, John Franklin, clergyman; b. Corder, Mo., May 15, 1883; s. Jacob and Augusta (Sette) H.; A.B., Central Wesleyan Coll., Warrenton, Mo., 1908; S.T.B., Boston U., 1911; D.D., Neb. Wesleyan U., 1920; L.H.D., Coll. at Puget Sound, 1933; m. Addie Lorine Froeschle, Oct. 1908; children—Marjorie Eleanor (Mrs. John Hall Hopkins), Jane Frances. Ordained to ministry Meth. Ch.; pastor Dietz Memorial Ch., Omaha, Neb., 1911-12, Pearl Memorial Ch., Omaha, 1912-14, St. Lukes Ch., David City, Neb., 1914-18, Centenary Ch., Beatrice, Neb., 1918-23, First Ch., Eugene, Ore., 1923-29, First Ch., Tacoma, Wash., 1929-34, First Ch., Baltimore, since 1934. Home: 203 Southway, Baltimore, Md.

HAAS, Michael S.: pres. Metropolitan Savings Bank. Home: Latrobe Apts. Office: Charles and Saratoga Sts., Baltimore, Md.

HAAS, Robert Elliott, lawyer; b. Allentown, Pa., Dec. 12, 1890; s. Nathan A. and Emma H.; grad. Allentown High Sch., 1907; student Muhlenberg Coll., Allentown, Pa., 1907-08; Ph.B., Lafayette Coll., Easton, Pa., 1913; m. Una Wise, Oct. 7, 1914. Shoe mfr., 1913-15; admitted to Pa. bar, 1925, and since practiced in Allentown. Served in U.S. Army during World War. Mem. Pa. Legislature, sessions 1923, 25, 27. Nat. pres. Phi Delta Theta; pres. Lehigh County Bar Assn., 1938-39. Mem. Am., Pa. and Lehigh Co. bar assns., Am. Legion, Phi Delta Theta. Republican. Mem. Reformed Ch. Mason (32°), Elk. Home: 1208 Walnut St. Office: 502-504 Hamilton St., Allentown, Pa.

HABER, Isador, lawyer; b. Russia, Nov. 27, 1889; s. Hill and Bertha (Koenigsberg) H.; brought to U.S., 1893, naturalized, 1899; A.B. and A.M., Columbia U.; LL.B., Columbia U. Law Sch.; m. Olga C. Abeles, Nov. 14, 1918; 1 dau., Arlene Regina. Admitted to N.J. bar as atty., 1913; engaged in gen. practice of law at Union City, N.J.; served as judge First Jud. Dist. Ct. of Hudson Co. since 1937. Republican. Jewish religion. Mason. Home: 71 Columbia Terrace, Weehawken, N.J. Office: 708 Brookline Av., Union City, N.J.

HABER, Vernon Raymond, entomologist; b. Rossburg, Darke Co., O., Dec. 10, 1887; s. Jno. Francis and Margaret (Swinger) H.; student Greenville (Darke Co., O.) High Sch., 1906-08; B.Sc. in Agr., Ohio State U., 1914, M.A., 1916; post-grad. study Cornell U., 1917-18, U. of Minn., 1918-20; Ph.D. in zoology and entomology, Cornell U., 1924; m. Julia Moesel, Dec. 27, 1919. Asst. in entomology and zoology, Ohio State U., 1912-14, grad. asst., 1914-16; grad. asst. gen. biology, Cornell U., 1916-18; tutor biology, Edminster Sch., Ithaca, N.Y., 1917-18; research asst. entomology and animal biology, U. of Minn., 1918-20; deputy state nursery inspector, Minn. Dist. No. 8, 1918-20; asst. state entomologist, Raleigh, N.C., 1920-22; instr. extension entomology, Cornell U., 1923, instr. zool. lab., 1923; asst. prof., Dept. Zoology and Entomology, Pa. State Coll., 1924-26, asso. prof. since 1926. Fellow A.A.A.S.; mem. Am. Assn. Univ. Profs., Entomol. Soc. America, Am. Assn. Economic Entomologists, Sigma Xi, Pi Gamma Mu, Gamma Alpha, Delta Chi. Republican. Home: 355 W. Ridge Av., State College, Pa.

HABGOOD, Robert P(atton), newspaper editor and publisher; b. Bellefonte, Pa., May 21, 1871; s. William Henry and Sarah (Sircombe) H.; grad. Renovo (Pa.) High Sch., 1887; m. Daisy May Heffner, Nov. 3, 1897 (died March 11, 1910); children—Stuart Kinzer, Dorothy Gladys; m. 2d, Mary Ann Sheaffer, June 6, 1911; children—Robert Patton, Jr., Mary Ann. Began as car repairer's helper in railroad shops, 1887; then successively car accountant, gen. time keeper, railroad newspaper reporter and advertising man, editor and business mgr.; became owner Evening Star, 1903, and merged it with Record, 1908; owner Sunday Herald, 1922; all 3 published in same modern building since 1928; pres., treas., dir. and gen. mgr. Star Pub. Co., Record Pub. Co.; vice-pres. and dir. Era Pub. Co. Mem. Pa. State Legislature, 1907-15. Pres. Pa. State League Rep. Clubs, 1908-09; del. at large Rep. Nat. Conv., Chicago, 1908. Postmaster, Bradford, Pa., 1911-15 and 1924-36. Dir. Community Chest 13 yrs. (vice-pres. 7 yrs., pres. 6 yrs.); dir. Carnegie Pub. Library. Sec.-treas. Nat. P.M. Assn. (editor Nat. P.M. Gazette, 1929-34); mem. Am. Newspaper Pubs. Assn., Pa. Newspaper Assn. Ind. Republican. Presbyterian. Mason (32°, K.T., Shriner), Elk, Moose, K. of P. Clubs: Penn Hill Country,

Bradford (Bradford). Home: 73 W. Corydon St. Office: 10-16 St. James Pl., Bradford, Pa.

HACKEMANN, Louis Frederick, educator; b. Charleston, S.C., Feb. 5, 1905; s. Louis Frederick and Anna Catherine (Bosch) H.; A.B., Coll. of Charleston, 1926; A.M., Columbia, 1929; student Am. Acad. Rome, 1930, U. of Chicago, summer, 1932; unmarried. Instr. in Latin, Charleston (S.C.) High Sch., 1926-27; prof. of Latin and Greek, Lenoir-Rhyne Coll., Hickory, N.C., 1927-34, dean, 1930-34; headmaster of Allentown (Pa.) Prep. Sch. since 1934. Designated Student of Distinction, Am. Acad., Rome. Mem. Archæol. Inst. of America, Am. Assn. of Univ. Profs. Democrat. Lutheran. Clubs: Lehigh Valley Classical, Kiwanis. Address: Allentown Preparatory School, Allentown, Pa.

HACKENBERG, Joseph Lawrence, sch. supt.; b. Freeburg, Pa., Dec. 19, 1896; s. Waldo and Amanda (Steffen) H.; A.B., Susquehanna U., 1920; M.A., Pa. State Coll., 1929; Ph.D., 1935; m. Beulah D. Keim, Dec. 29, 1922; children—Shirley Mae, Nona Elizabeth, Charles Ray. Prin. Hooverville (Pa.) High Sch., 1920-22; supervising prin., Millheim, 1922-27; prin. Sandy Twp. High Sch., DuBois, Pa., 1927-30; supt. schs., Sandy Twp., DuBois, 1930-35, Windber, Pa., since 1935. Life mem. N.E.A.; mem. Am. Assn. Sch. Administrators, Pa. State Edn. Assn., Am. Legion (comdr. Post No. 444, Millheim, 1924-26); pres. Clearfield Co. Schoolmens Club, 1934-35. Republican. Presbyterian. Mason. Contributed to Jour. of Ednl. Sociology. Home: 1004 Cambria Av. Office: Somerset Av., Windber, Pa.

HACKER, Theodore Warren, civil engr.; b. New York, N.Y., Oct. 15, 1891; s. Theodore and Harriett Cabel (Blankenship) H.; student Baltimore Poly. Inst., 1908-12; C.E., Cornell U., 1917; m. Ethel Walker Mahon, Aug. 17, 1929; 1 dau., Martha Bolling. Civil engr. Norton, Bird & Whitman, 1917 and 1919-24, Whitman, Requardt & Smith, 1924-31; tech. adviser Siamese Govt., 1931-34; asso. Whitman, Requardt & Smith, cons. engrs., since 1934. Served as ensign, U.S. Naval Res. Force, 1918-19, World War. Mem. Am. Soc. Civil Engrs., Alpha Chi Rho. Democrat. Episcopalian. Clubs: Engineers, Cornell of Md., Severn River Assn. Home: "Tedshaven," Severna Park, Md. Office: Charles & Biddle Sts., Baltimore, Md.

HACKETT, E(dmond) Byrne, publisher; b. Kilkenny, Ireland, June 8, 1879; s. John Byrne (M.D.) and Bridget (Doheny) H.; ed. Kilkenny and Clongowes Wood colls., Ireland, St. Francis Coll., Crawley, Sussex, Eng.; hon. M.A., Yale, 1914; m. Margaret Carson, Dec. 11, 1903; children—Florence Mary D., Frances Byrne; m. 2d, Helen E. Plechner, Jan. 1923; 1 dau., Helen Byrne; m. 3d, Isabel La Monte, February 12, 1927. Came to America in 1899; with Doubleday, Page & Co., pubs., New York, 1901-07; head pub. dept., The Baker & Taylor Co., New York, 1907-09; 1st dir. Yale Univ. Press, New Haven, Conn., since 1909. Founder and pres. Brick Row Book Shop, New York. Clubs: Elizabethan (Yale); Yale, Grolier (New York); Quadrangle (Princeton). Home: Piedmont Farm, Bound Brook, N.J. Office: 55 Fifth Av., New York, N.Y.

HACKETT, James Lawrence, physician, surgeon; b. Driftwood, Pa., Sept. 5, 1895; s. John and Johanna (Fitzpatrick) H.; M.D., Georgetown U. Med. Sch., 1928; m. Freda Pauline Yetzer, Sept. 2, 1929; children—Pauline Ann, James Lawrence. Began gen. practice medicine and surgery, 1929; county med. dir., 1929; chief Tuberculosis Clinic, 1929; med. dir. Hygrade Sylvania Corpn., Emporium Plant, 1932. County chmn. Emergency Child Health Com. Fellow A.M.A.; mem. Elk County Med. Soc., Pa. State Med. Soc. Republican. Catholic. Elk. Club: Rotary International. Address: 8 W. Fourth St., Emporium, Pa.

HACKETT, Samuel Everett, steel exec.; b. Coralville, Ia., July 21, 1877; s. Thomas Ross and Amanda (Crozier) H.; ed. high sch. and business coll.; m. Bessie Bischoff, Sept. 20, 1906; children—Spencer Ross, David Everett (dec.). Clk. for Am. Tin Plate Co., Chicago, 1898, for Republic Iron & Steel Co., Chicago, 1899; mgr. order dept., and purchasing agt., Jos. T. Ryerson & Son, Chicago, 1899-1916; with Jones & Laughlin Steel Corpn. since 1916, as mgr. branch office and warehouse, Chicago, 1916-19, gen. mgr. of sales, Pittsburgh, 1919-23, v.p., 1923-34, pres., 1934-38, resigned as pres. Feb. 14, 1938. Mem. Am. Iron & Steel Inst. Republican. Presbyn. Clubs: Duquesne, Railway, Pittsburgh Athletic, Fox Chapel Golf (Pittsburgh). Home: 204 S. Lexington Av. Office: 1100 Union Trust Bldg., Pittsburgh, Pa.

HACKNEY, Henry Eastman, lawyer; b. Uniontown, Pa., Apr. 2, 1892; s. Jacob Sidwell and Mary (Eastman) H.; ed. Culver Mil. Acad., 1907-09; A.B., Princeton, 1913; LL.B., Harvard Law Sch., 1916; m. Elisabeth Moore Pendleton, Dec. 1, 1917; children—Henry Eastman, Jr., Reid, William Pendleton. Admitted to Pa. bar, 1916, and engaged in gen. practice of law at Uniontown, 1916-36; at Pittsburgh since 1936, mem. firm Reed, Smith, Shaw & McClay. Served as capt. later adjt. inf., U.S.A., 1917-19; honored by brigade citation for bravery in action. Mem. Am. and Pa. bar assns., Am. Law Inst. Republican. Presbyn. Clubs: Duquesne, University, Fox Chapel Golf. Home: Woodland Rd., Pittsburgh, Pa. Office: 747 Union Trust Bldg., Pittsburgh, Pa.

HACKNEY, H(iram) Hamilton, judge; b. Uniontown, Pa., Nov. 21, 1899; s. Edgar S. and Caroline (Hogg) H.; grad. St. Paul's Sch., Concord, N.H., 1918; A.B., Princeton U., 1922; grad. student Cambridge Univ., 1922-23; LL.B., Harvard, 1926; m. Alice Powell Smith, June 24, 1926; children—Alice Louise, Carol Elizabeth, Hiram Hamilton, Jr., George Edgar. Admitted to Md. bar, 1926, and began practice in Baltimore; counsel Legal Aid Bureau, Inc., Baltimore, 1929-39; judge Juvenile Court since 1939. Served in S.A.T.C., 1918. Trustee Community Fund of Baltimore; dir. Legal Aid Bureau of Baltimore. Democrat. Episcopalian. Club: Green Spring Valley Hunt (Garrison, Md.). Lives on a farm where he raises purebred Aberdeen-Angus cattle. Home: Finksburg, Md. Office: 311 St. Paul St., Baltimore, Md.

HACKNEY, Lilian; prof. mathematics, Marshall Coll. Address: Marshall College, Huntington, W.Va.

HADDEN, Samuel Bernard, neuropsychiatrist; b. Dunmore, Pa., May 19, 1900; s. Samuel and Ellen (MacDonnell) H.; grad. Dunmore High Sch.; M.D., U. of Pennsylvania Coll. and Med. Sch.; m. Alice O'Horo, October 18, 1924; children—Samuel, Michael, Alice. Successively asst. instr., instr. and asso. in neurology, U. of Pa., 1926-36; instr. neurology and pathology, Women's Med. Coll., 1927-28; asst. prof. and clin. prof., Temple U. Hosp., 1936-37; asst. neurologist Episcopal Hosp., 1926-32, neurologist, 1932-35; asst. neurologist Abington Memorial Hosp., 1926-36; now chief neurol. service Presbyn. and Fitzgerald Mercy Hosp.; visiting psychiatrist Philadelphia Gen. Hosp., 1926-38, visiting neurologist since 1938; consulting neurologist Bryn Mawr and Babies' hosps. Lt. comdr. U.S. Naval Reserve. Fellow Am. Coll. Physicians, Philadelphia Coll. Physicians. Mem. Am. Neurol. Soc., A.M.A., Mental Hygiene Com. of Pa., Philadelphia Neurol. Soc. (sec. 1932-36), Philadelphia Psychiatric Soc., Phi Alpha Sigma (v.p. nat. chapter). Republican. Catholic. Writer numerous articles on med. subjects. Home: 433 W. School Lane. Office: 37 S. 20th St., Philadelphia, Pa.

HADDOCK, John Courtney, coal operator; b. New York, N.Y., Nov. 24, 1893; s. John Courtney and Jennie Sharpe (De Wolfe) H.; Ph.B., Sheffield Scientific Sch. (Yale), 1915; m. Dorothy Tamzon Matlack, Oct. 5, 1916 (divorced Dec. 1936); 1 dau., Clare M.; m. 2d, Hope Bush Dillon, Nov. 3, 1937. Entered coal business, 1915; pres. Haddock Mining Co. since 1918; also pres. Candlemas Colleries Co., Silverbrook Anthracite Co.; v.p. First Nat. Bank, McAdoo, Pa.; v.p. and mgr. Alden Coal Co.; dir. Vulcan Iron Works, Wyoming (Pa.) National Bank. Served in U.S.N., World War. Dir. Wilkes-Barre Gen. Hosp. Fellow Royal Soc. of Arts; mem. Am. Inst. Mining & Metall. Engrs., Chi Phi. Clubs: Westmoreland (Wilkes-Barre); University, Yale, N.Y. Yacht (New York); Elizabethan (New Haven); Wyoming Valley Country. Home: 323 S. Franklin St. Office: Second Nat. Bank Bldg., Wilkes-Barre, Pa.

HADDON, Harry Harter, pres. Sunbury Daily Item; b. Northumberland, Pa., Sept. 16, 1898; s. John E. and Mary Elizabeth (Gaugler) H.; student Northumberland (Pa.) High Sch.; m. Emma E. Starook, Aug. 1, 1923; children—Harry, Roger S. Reporter, Sunbury (Pa.) Item, 1913-18, editor, 1918-27, part owner, 1927-37, pres. and mng. editor since consolidation of Sunbury Item with Sunbury Daily, 1937; dir. Sunbury Broadcasting Corpn. Elk, Moose, Odd Fellow, Jr. O.U.A.M. Clubs: Northumberland Co. Press, Sunbury (Pa.) Rotary. Home: 67 King St., Northumberland, Pa. Office: 2d and Market Sts., Sunbury, Pa.

HADLEY, Charles Frazer, physician, pres. Cambridge Investment Co.; b. Phila., Pa., July 7, 1878; s. Theodore Henry Hadley and Elizabeth Cake (Frazer) H.; student Rugby Mil. Acad., Wilmington, Del., 1888-89, Friends Sch., Wilmington, Del., 1889-90, Oswego (N.Y.) High Sch., 1892-95; M.D., Hahnemann Med. Coll., Phila., 1899; m. Eva Harriet Edwards, Apr. 26, 1905; children—Charles Frazer (M.D.), Frances Elizabeth (Mrs. Earl B. Keller, Jr.). Asst. surgeon at West Jersey Hospital, Camden, N.J., 1899-1912, chief gynecological dept. since 1912, chief of staff, 1924; pres. Cambridge Investment Co., Camden, N.J., since 1924. Mem. Camden Co. Med. Advisory Bd. during World War. Trustee West Jersey Presbytery (chmn. property com.). Fellow Am. Coll. Surgeons; mem. A.M.A., N.J. State, Camden Co. med. socs., Pi Upsilon Rho. Republican. Presbyterian. Mason (Royal Arch; K.T.; Shriner). Club: Germantown Medical (Phila., Pa.). Address: 210 W. Maple Av., Merchantsville, N.J.

HADLEY, Samuel H(iram), pres. Protected Home Circle; b. Hadley, Pa., Mar. 15, 1876; s. Ephraim and Mary Elizabeth (Lyons) H.; A.B., Grove City (Pa.) Coll., 1898; m. Agnes Reed, July 15, 1903. Began as school teacher, 1894; supt. schs., Sharon, Pa., 1902-13; cashier McDowell Nat. Bank, Sharon, 1913-24; pres. Protected Home Circle since 1924; dir. McDowell Nat. Bank, Sharon Bldg. & Loan Assn., Pa. Power Co., Sharon Hardware Mfg. Co., Masonic Assn. Republican. Presbyterian. Mason, Odd Fellow, Elk, Moose. Address: Sharon, Pa.

HADZSITS, George Depue, college prof.; b. Detroit, Mich., Jan. 30, 1875; s. George and Clemmy Louise (Depue) H.; A.B., U. of Mich., 1895, A.M., 1896, Ph.D., 1902; studied Am. Sch. Classical Studies at Rome, 1900-01; m. Gertrude Cronbach, Sept. 8, 1910; 1 dau., Marcia Louise. Acting asst. prof. Latin, U. of Cincinnati, 1903-05, U. of Wis., 1905-06; research fellow in classics, 1906-09, instr. Latin, 1909-11, asst. prof., 1911-23, prof. since 1923, U. of Pa.; prof. Latin, summers, U. of Colo., 1926, 27, 31, 32, University of Chicago, 1928, Leland Stanford University, 1933; visiting prof. American Academy in Rome, 1929-30. Mem. Am. Philol. Assn., Archœol. Inst. America, Phila. Oriental Soc., Phila. Classical Club (pres. 1916-17), Classical Assn. Atlantic States (pres. 1937-38), Phila. Soc. Promotion Liberal Studies (pres. 1919-20, 1921-23, 1925-27), Am. Assn. Univ. Profs., Phi Beta Kappa, Alpha Omega, Lambda Chi Alpha, Eta Sigma Phi (hon.), S.A.R. Republican. Episcopalian. Mason. Author: Prolegomena to a Study of the Ethical Ideal of Plutarch, 1906; also chapter on "Roman Religion," in Religions Past and Present, 1917; Handbook of the University of Pennsylvania Chapter of Phi Beta Kappa, 1919; Lucretius and His Influence, 1935. Editor-in-chief of the "Our Debt to Greece and Rome Library" of 40 to 50 volumes, 1922—; co-editor of "The Living Language," 2 vols. (with W. L. Carr), 1933-34. Contbr. numerous monographs and articles in classical jours. Home: 222 S. 43d St., Philadelphia, Pa.

HAFEY, William Joseph, bishop; b. Springfield, Mass., Mar. 19, 1888; s. James J. and Catherine (Mulcahy) H.; prep. edn., high sch., Chicopee, Mass.; B.A., Holy Cross Coll., Worcester, Mass., 1909; student Georgetown Law Sch., 1909-10; M.A., Mt. St. Mary's Sem., Emmitsburg, Md., 1914. Ordained priest R.C. Ch.,

1914; asst. pastor St. Joseph's Ch., Baltimore, Md., 1914-20; chancellor archdiocese of Baltimore, 1920-25; consecrated bishop Diocese of Raleigh, July 1, 1925; later coadjutor bishop and since Mar. 25, 1938, bishop of Scranton, Pa. Home: 315 Wyoming Av., Scranton, Pa.

HAFFNER, Thomas Nathaniel, engr.; b. Fullerton, Pa., Mar. 14, 1893; s. Nathan Adam and Mary Alice (Diefenderfer) H.; ed. high school and college extensions; m. Vorha May Baliman, June 14, 1927; children—Thomas Baliman, William Nathaniel. Began as machinist helper, 1908; draftsman, 1913-17; asst. engr., 1919-23; engr., later chief engr., Phoenix Portland Cement Co., Bath, Pa., 1923-29; supt. and chief engr. Keystone Portland Cement Co., Bath, Pa., since 1929. Served with infantry, U.S. Army, with A.E.F., 1917-19. Mem. Soc. Professional Engrs., Am. Legion. Presbyterian. Mason. Club: Engineers of Lehigh Valley. Home: 239 N. 7th St., Allentown, Pa. Office: Keystone Portland Cement Co., Bath, Pa.

HAGAN, James; dir. of athletics, U. of Pittsburgh. Address: University of Pittsburgh, Pittsburgh, Pa.

HAGAR, Ivan Drake, corpn. official; b. at Weybridge, Vt., Jan. 6, 1886; s. Henry B. and Katherine Drake (Valley) H.; A.B., Middlebury Coll., 1909; ed. Syracuse U., 1909-10; m. May Elida Williams, Aug. 19, 1911. Employed as chemist, Cementos Hidalgo S.A., Hidalgo, Nuevo Leon, Mex., and at Union Pacific R.R., Omaha, Neb., 1910-12; chief chemist, Mound City Paint & Color Co., St. Louis, Mo., 1912-18; sales engr., New Jersey Zinc Co., New York, 1918-20; production engr., Devoe and Raynolds Co., Inc., Brooklyn, N.Y., 1920-21; sales engr., Titanium Pigment Co., Inc., 1921-31, Eastern sales mgr., 1931-36, gen. sales mgr. and dir., 1936-37; v.p., dir. and gen. sales mgr., Titanium Pigment Corpn. since 1937; asst. mgr. Nat. Lead Co. Titanium Div. Mem. Am. Chem. Soc., Am. Soc. for Testing Materials, New York Sales Manager's Club, Kappa Delta Rho. Republican. Presbyn. Mason. Club: Downtown Athletic (New York). Home: 1 The Glen, Tenafly, N.J. Office: 111 Broadway, New York, N.Y.

HAGEDORN, Hermann, author; b. New York, July 18, 1882; s. Hermann and Anna (Schwedler) H.; A.B., Harvard, 1907; winter semester, U. of Berlin, 1907-08, Columbia, 1908-09; m. Dorothy Oakley, June 6, 1908; children—Mary Oakley, Dorothea Hermann, David Oakley. Instr. English, Harvard, 1909-11. Lyrics for Peterborough pageant, 1910; adapted The Witch, prod. New Theatre, New York, 1910; The House of Magic (masque, for William Winter testimonial meeting), prod. Century Theatre, New York, 1916; The Heart of Youth (for dedication of outdoor theatre at the Hill School, performed 1915). Delivered Phi Beta Kappa Poem, An Ode of Dedication, Harvard U., 1917; poem, The Three Pharaohs, for 150th anniversary Harvard Chapter of same soc., 1931; Crisis, for 25th anniversary Harvard Class of 1907; Harvard Tercentenary Ode "Harvard, What of the Light," 1936; principal address at dedication of memorial to Edwin Arlington Robinson, Gardiner, Me., 1936; poem "Noah" for 30th anniversary, Harvard class of 1907. Author: The Woman of Corinth, 1908; A Troop of the Guard, and Other Poems, 1909; Poems and Ballads, 1912; Faces in the Dawn (novel), 1914; Makers of Madness (play), 1914; The Great Maze—The Heart of Youth (poem and play), 1916; You Are the Hope of the World, 1917; Where Do You Stand? (appeal to Americans of German origin), 1918; Barbara Picks a Husband (novel), 1918; The Boys' Life of Theodore Roosevelt, 1918; That Human Being, Leonard Wood, 1920; Roosevelt in the Bad Lands (biography), 1921; Roosevelt, Prophet of Unity, 1924; Ladders Through the Blue (collection of poems), 1925; The Ten Dreams of Zach Peters, 1925; The Rough Riders (novel), 1927; The Book of Courage, 1929; Leonard Wood, a Biography, 1931; The Magnate, a biography of William Boyce Thompson, 1935; Brookings, a biography, 1936; Edwin Arlington Robinson (biography), 1938; This Darkness and This Light—Harvard Poems, 1907-1937 (privately printed). Editor: Fifes and Drums (a collection of poems of America at war), 1917; The Americanism of Theodore Roosevelt (selections from his writings and speeches), 1923; Memorial Edition of the Works of Theodore Roosevelt, 1923-25. With Porter Emerson Browne, Julian Street and Charles Hanson Towne founded the Vigilantes, Nov. 1916. Dir. movement for National Rededication, 1938. Trustee, sec. and exec. dir. Roosevelt Memorial Assn. Mem. Am. Inst. Arts and Letters; Edward MacDowell Assn. (dir. and v.p.). Quaker. Club: Century. Home: 21 Upper Mountain Av., Montclair, N.J. Address: Roosevelt House, 28 E. 20th St., New York, N.Y.

HAGEMAN, Aaron Martin, electro-chemistry; b. Bound Brook, N.J., Aug. 17, 1890; s. Andrew K. and Mary L. (Martin) H.; B.Sc., Rutgers U., 1912, M.Sc., same, 1913; Ph.D., U. of Wis., 1918; m. Elizabeth Walrath, Sept. 24, 1921; children—Robert Andrew, Mary Elizabeth, Jean Walrath. Employed as chemist, Westinghouse Lamp Co., Bloomfield, N.J., 1918-19, chief chemist, 1919-26, mgr. engring. dept., 1926-35, mgr. engring. dept. Westinghouse Lamp Div. of Westinghouse Electric & Mfg. Co. since 1935. Mem. Am. Inst. Elec. Engrs., Am. Electro Chem. Soc., Montclair Soc. Engrs., Phi Gamma Delta, Sigma Xi, Alpha Chi Sigma. Republican. Presbyn. Club: Deer Lake (nr. Boonton, N.J.). Home: 6 Fellswood Drive, Verona. Office: Westinghouse Electric & Mfg. Co., Bloomfield, N.J.

HAGER, William H., merchant; b. Lancaster, Pa., June 5, 1867; s. John Christopher and Margaret (Henderson) H.; student Franklin and Marshall Coll., 1885; m. Mary Wilson, Oct. 26, 1892; children—Edward T., William H., Nathaniel E., John Christopher, 3d, Redmond C. Began with Hager & Bro., Inc., dry goods, 1885, became partner, 1890, pres., 1897, chmn. bd., 1939. Pres. Lancaster Bd. Trade, 1899, 1900; was dir. Lancaster Chamber of Commerce; mem. Nat. Retail Code Authority, 1933-34. Trustee Am. Retail Fed. since 1936, treas. since 1936; trustee Franklin and Marshall Coll. since 1898; trustee Evang. Luth. Sem., Phila., since 1910; trustee Gen. Council Evang. Luth. Ch. of North America until merger with other bodies; trustee United Luth. Ch. in America, 1918-26. Mem. Pa. Dry Goods Assn. (organizer and pres. 1919-21), Pa. Retailers Assn. (organizer 1932 and since pres.), Nat. Retail Dry Goods Assn. (charter mem., dir.), Am. Acad. of Polit. and Social Science, Pa. German Soc., Diagnothian Lit. Soc., Cliosophic Soc., Lancaster Law and Order Soc., Phi Kappa Sigma. Club: Hamilton (Lancaster). Home: Columbia Av. Office: Hager & Bro., Inc., Lancaster, Pa.

HAGERT, Henry, mfg. lighting fixtures; b. Summit, N.J., May 3, 1895; s. Charles H. and Agnes (Haffelfinger) H.; ed. Episcopal Acad., 1906-13; B.S. in Econs., U. of Pa., 1917; m. Eleanor Fischer, June 16, 1923; children—Gabrielle, Thornton; m. 2d, Lee Murphy, of Swarthmore, Pa., Sept. 26, 1938. Employed as port steward Earnline Steamship Co., 1919-22; engaged in bus. on own acct. as designer and mfr. fine spl. lighting fixtures and art metal work since 1922. Served as sergt. (1st class) Med. Dept., U.S.A., 1917-19, with A.E.F. at Base Hosp. 20, France. Mem. Phila. Art Alliance, Arts and Crafts Guild of Phila., Soc. of Designers and Craftsmen, Phi Kappa Psi. Episcopalian. Home: 1923 Manning St., Philadelphia, Pa.; Dingman's Ferry, Pike Co., Pa. Office: 515 Madison Av., New York, N.Y.

HAGGERTY, Cecil Jerome, prof. of chemistry; b. Holyoke, Mass., Nov. 15, 1901; s. James Jerome and Eva Leanore (Harrow) H.; A.B. (cum laude), Williams Coll., Williamstown, Mass., 1923; Ph.D., Johns Hopkins U., 1926; m. Margaret Helen Molloy, June 28, 1930; 1 son, James Thomas. Prof. chemistry, Holy Cross Coll., Worcester, Mass., 1926-37, Manhattanville Coll. of the Sacred Heart, New York City, since 1937. Served as 2d lt., Res. Officers Chem. Warfare Service, U.S. Army, 1927-31, 1st lt., 1931-36, capt. since 1936. Fellow A.A.A.S., Am. Inst. of Chemists; mem. Am. Chem. Soc., Phi Beta Kappa, Sigma Xi, Gamma Sigma Epsilon. Horace Clark Scholar from Williams Coll. to Johns Hopkins U., 1923-25. Roman Catholic. Club: Worcester (Mass.) Chemists (v.p., 1934-35, pres., 1935-36). Contbr. to Jour. of Am. Chem. Soc., Am. Electrochem. Soc. Home: 930 Garrison Av., Teaneck, N.J. Office: Manhattanville College of the Sacred Heart, 133d St. and Convent Av., New York, N.Y.

HAGUE, Frank, mayor; b. Jersey City, N.J., Jan. 17, 1876; s. John D. and Margaret (Fagen) H.; ed. pub. schs. and pvt. tutors; m. Jennie W. Warner, Apr. 15, 1903; 1 son, Frank. Began in sheriff's office, Hudson Co., N.J., later mem. Street and Water Bd. of Jersey City; elected to first Bd. of Commrs., 1913, when the city govt. was changed to commn. form; mayor of Jersey City since 1917; present term expires 1941; mem. Dem. Nat. Com. since 1922 (vice chmn. since 1924). A founder of first Mother's Institute of N.J., and builder of first sch. for crippled children; trustee Pub. Library, Jersey City. Democrat. Elk, K.C. Club: Cartaret. Home: Boulevard and Duncan Av. Address: City Hall, Jersey City, N.J.

HAGUE, William Wilberforce, advertising counsel; b. Boston, Mass., Sept. 20, 1895; s. Rev. John R. and Harriet (Tanner) H.; student Fork Union Mil. Acad., Va., 1909-11, Mt. Hermon Sch., Mass., 1911-13; A.B., Washington and Jefferson Coll., 1916, A.M., 1920; A.M., U. of Lyons, France, 1920; m. Ellen Bell McDannald, Oct. 19, 1921; children—William Wilberforce III, John Allen. In advertising business (mail advertising service, direct mail advertising, etc.) for himself since 1920. Dir. Keystone Sch. of the Bible. Enlisted as private Pa. Nat. Guard, 1916; private and corpl., Mexican Border Campaign, 1916-17; sergt. and 2d lt. 110th Inf., 28th Div. and 30th Inf., 3d Div., with A.E.F. 13 months (twice wounded in action), 1917-19; 1st lt. Pa. Nat. Guard, 1919-25; capt. O.R.C. since 1925. Decorated Croix de Guerre (France), Order of Purple Heart (U.S.). Mem. Am. Legion, Vets. of Foreign Wars, Kappa Sigma, Delta Sigma Rho, Christian Laymen's Assn. Progressive Republican. Presbyterian. Clubs: Pittsburgh Advertising, Metropolitan (Pittsburgh). Home: Broad St., Library, Pa. Office: 823 Locust St., Pittsburgh, Pa.

HAGY, Henry B., banker; b. Reading, Pa., Aug. 2, 1864; s. William and Sarah A. (Bitler) P.; grad. high sch., Reading, 1883; m. Mary E. Eby, Oct. 11, 1899. Began with Kendall Bros., 1883; with H. T. & J. V. Kendall, bankers, 1884-86; with Pa. Trust Co., 1886, treas. and trust officer, 1904-12, 2d v.p., 1912-16, v.p., 1916-21, became pres., 1921, now retired; was mem. loan com., Nat. Credit Corpn. No. 2 of 3d Federal Reserve Dist. Chmn. first two Liberty Loan drives of Berks County, World War. Trustee and pres. bd. Y.M.C.A., Reading. Republican. Episcopalian (vestryman Christ Ch.). Clubs: Wyomissing, Berkshire Country. Home: Reading, Pa.

HAHN, Frank Eugene, architect, engr.; b. Philadelphia, Pa., Jan. 22, 1879; s. Henry and Clara (Heiman) H.; grad. Philadelphia Elementary pub. schs., 1892; prize scholarship, North East High Sch., 1896; B.S. in C.E., U. of Pa., 1900; m. Florence Steinbach, Dec. 14, 1910; 1 son, Frank Eugene. Engr. Philadelphia & Reading Ry. Co., 1900-03; with engring. dept. on subways Philadelphia Rapid Transit Co., 1903-04; mgr. and engr. Truscon Steel Co., Philadelphia, 1904-05; mem. firm Sauer & Hahn, architects and engrs., 1905-15; in private practice as pres. Frank E. Hahn, Inc., since 1915; dir. Loganian Bldg. & Loan Assn.; liquidating trustee (chmn.) Goward Bldg. & Loan Assn. Registered architect in Pa., N.Y., N.J. and Del.; registered professional engr. in Pa. Hon. dir. Y.M. and Y.W.H.A., Phila. Fellow Pa. Acad. Fine Arts; mem. Am. Inst. Architects, Pa. Soc. Professional Engrs. (pres. Phila. Chapter), Art Alliance. Republican. Jewish religion. Mason, Elk, Royal Arcanum. Clubs: Green Valley Country, T-Square, Stagecrafters Dramatic. Home: 1511 W. Oxford St. Office: 1700 Walnut St., Philadelphia, Pa.

HAHN, Frederick Charles, chemist; b. Springfield, Ill., Oct. 27, 1893; s. Louis Charles and Caroline Elizabeth (Ericson) H.; B.S. in Chem.

Engring., U. of Ill., 1916; M.S. in Chemistry, U. of Mich., 1917; Ph.D., Johns Hopkins U., 1923; m. Margaret Armstrong Kirby, May 17, 1919; 1 dau., Ann Caroline. Employed as research chemist, National Aniline & Chem. Co., 1919-21; research chemist and research group head, E. I. du Pont de Nemours & Co., Inc., 1923-37; asst. chem. dir., Plastics Dept., E. I. Du Pont de Nemours & Co., Inc., Arlington, N.J., since 1937. Served in C.W.S., U.S.A., 1917-18. Mem. Am. Chem. Soc., Phi Beta Kappa, Alpha Chi Sigma, Phi Lambda Upsilon, Gamma Alpha, Sigma Phi Epsilon. Republican. Episcopalian. Home: 337 Upper Mountain Av., Upper Montclair, N.J. Office: Arlington, N.J.

HAHN, Frederick E., violinist; b. N.Y. City, Mar. 23, 1869; s. Henry and Clara (Mayer) H.; ed. Eastburn Acad., Phila., Pa.; studied violin under father; grad. Leipzig Conservatory of Music, 1890 (1st prize for violin); unmarried. Toured U.S., 1890-91; 1st violinist Boston Symphony Orchestra, 1892; head of string quartet 25 yrs.; founder Hahn Conservatory of Music, Phila., 1902; pres. and dir. Zeckwer-Hahn Phila. Musical Acad. since 1917. Author: Practical Violin Study, 1930. Composer of violin works, songs and orchestra pieces, also editor violin pieces and études. Home: Bellerich Apt. Studio: 1617 Spruce St., Philadelphia, Pa.

HAHN, Lew, dept. stores; b. Jersey City, N.J., June 21, 1882; s. Lewis B. and Carrie Amelia (Van Tine) H.; ed. pub. schs.; m. Ethel Winifred Hesketh, May 28, 1910; children—Douglas Hesketh, Dane Francis. Newspaper work, N.Y. and Nev.; gold and silver mining, Nev., 1906-10; retail editor Fairchild Publications, New York, 1911-18; mng. dir. Nat. Retail Dry Goods Assn., 1918-28; pres. and gen. mgr. Hahn Dept. Stores (merger of 27 dept. stores throughout the country), 1929-31, chmn. bd., July 1931-Sept. 1933; pres. Hahn Dept. Stores Purchasing Corpn.; formerly mem. advisory bd. New York Trust Co., North Am. Inter-Insurers. Treas. and gen. mgr. Nat. Retail Dry Goods Assn.; mem. advisory com. Affiliated Underwriters; mem. bd. dirs. Prince Sch. of Edn. for Store Service, Boston; ex-pres. and mem. Council, Borough of Glen Rock, N.J. Chmn. Nat. Retail Code Authority until Jan. 1934; mem. industrial advisory bd. NRA, 1934-35; mem. business advisory and planning council U.S. Dept. of Commerce. Hon. mem. Eta Mu Pi (New York U.). Republican. Clubs: Union League (New York); Ridgewood Country, Bayhead Yacht. Writer, lecturer and teacher on getting goods from production to consumption. Author: (with Percival A. White) Merchants' Manual, 1926. Home: Ridgewood, N.J.*

HAHN, Theodore Ferdinand, clergyman; b. Lohardagga, India, July 23, 1877; s. Ferdinand and Dorothea (Voss) H.; student Gymnasium, Gütersloh, Germany, 1887-90, Breklum, Germany, 1890-93; student Bloomfield (N.J.) Coll., 1893-95, Bloomfield Theol. Sem., 1895-98, Hahnemann Med. Coll., New York, 1898-1901; M.D., Baltimore Med. Coll. (U. of Md.), 1902; m. Anna Margaret Scheer, Oct. 4, 1904; children—Herbert Ferdinand, Conrad, Theodore, Martin, Margaret. Came to U.S., 1893, naturalized, 1900. Began as evangelist while studying medicine, 1898; med. missionary, Gossner Mission, Purulia, India, 1902-04; missionary for A.B.C. F.M., El Fuerte, Mexico, 1904-07; missionary teacher, Guadalajara, Mexico, 1907-10; pastor Claiborne Av. Presbyn. Ch., New Orleans, La., 1910-14; pastor Av. B Dutch Reformed Ch., New York, 1914-16; pastor Hickory St. Presbyn. Ch., Scranton, Pa., since 1916. Dir. Bloomfield (N.J.) Theol. Sem.; curator Syrian Orphanage, Jerusalem, Palestine. Mem. Nat. Geog. Soc., World Calendar Assn. Republican. Home: 427 Hickory St., Scranton, Pa.

HAIG, Alfred Roland, lawyer; b. Philadelphia, Pa., Dec. 24, 1868; s. James Weir and Clara (Smith) H.; ed. Philadelphia pub. schs.; LL.B., U. of Pa., 1891; m. Cornelia E. Breitenbach, June 5, 1894; children—Roland B., Alfred Vernon, Robert L., Helen (Mrs. J. Russell Breitinger), Elsie (Mrs. Wallace L. Root). Admitted to Phila. bar, 1891, since in gen. practice of law; mem. law firms Harrity, Lowrey & Thompson, and Harrity, Thompson & Haig, 1898-1912; title officer Land Title & Trust Co., 1895-96; title and trust officer and dir. Roxborough Trust Co. (in liquidation), 1918-31; dir. Hardwick & Magee Co., J. E. Lonergan Co., H. Brinton Co. Mem. Am. Bar Assn., Pa. Bar Assn., Philadelphia Bar Assn. Republican. Presbyn. (trustee Leverington Presbyn. Ch.). Mason. Clubs: Union League, Lawyers' (Philadelphia). Author: The Law of Eminent Domain in Pennsylvania, 1891. Home: 443 Green Lane, Roxborough. Office: 2015 Land Title Bldg., Philadelphia, Pa.

HAIGHT, Clarence Michael, mining engr.; b. Poughkeepsie, N.Y., Sept. 11, 1884; s. Jacob Nelson and Anna Barbara (Spross) H.; Engr. Mines, Columbia U. Sch. Applied Sci., 1906; m. Helen Darlington Worrall, Sept. 26, 1911; children—Alice Barbara (Mrs. Charles Padley Shoemaker), Edith Darlington (Mrs. William C. Park, Jr.), Helen Elizabeth (dec.), Margaret Worrall. Began as mining engr. Adventure Cons. Copper Co., Greenland, Mich., 1906; mining engr., Mich. Copper Co., Rockland, Mich., 1907-11; mining engr. Oliver Iron Mining Co., Hibbing, Minn., 1911-12; asst. mine foreman, then mine foreman, New Jersey Zinc Co., Franklin, N.J., 1913-35, supt. Franklin Mine since 1936. Served on Victory and Liberty Loan coms., Franklin, N.J. during World War. Boy Scout Council mem. Mem. Bd. Edn., Franklin, N.J., since 1929, now vice-pres. Sec. Franklin Chapter Red Cross. Mem. Am. Inst. Mining & Metall. Engrs., Delta Upsilon. Republican. Presbyn. (treas. First Ch., supt. S.S. since 1916). Mason. Clubs: Walkill Country of Franklin (sec. and dir.); Lake Mohawk Country, Lake Mohawk Yacht (Sparta). Home: 8 Evans St. Office: New Jersey Zinc Co., Franklin, N.J.

HAIGHT, Thomas Griffith, judge; b. Freehold, N.J., Aug. 4, 1879; s. John Tyler and Mary Louise (Drummond) H.; ed. Princeton U. and New York Law Sch.; hon. LL.D., Princeton; m. Annie M. Crater, Oct. 18, 1905; children—Nancy, Catharine, David. Admitted to N.J. bar, 1900; practiced with Queen & Tennant, Jersey City, 1901-05, then with George G. Tennant until latter's appmt. as judge of court of Common Pleas, Hudson County, May 1913; city atty., Jersey City, 1911-13; co. counsel, Hudson County, 1913-14; judge of U.S. Dist. Ct., Dist. of N.J., 1914-19; U.S. circuit judge, 3d Jud. Circuit and judge U.S. Circuit Ct. of Appeals, 1919-20, resigned; mem. firm Wall, Haight, Carey & Hartpence, Jersey City, N.J. Democrat. Episcopalian. Mem. 2d Troop N.G.N.J., 2 yrs. Signal Corps, 5 yrs. Pres. Hudson Co. Bar Assn. Mason. Clubs: Lawyers, Princeton (New York); Nassau, Cannon (Princeton); Jersey City, Carteret (Jersey City); Knickerbocker Country; Englewood. Home: Englewood, N.J. Office: 15 Exchange Pl., Jersey City, N.J.

HAILE, LeRoy Yellott, real estate, ins.; b. Sweet Air, Baltimore Co., Md., July 9, 1895; s. Frederick D. and Marion C. (Guyton) H.; student Baltimore pub. schs., 1900-11, Poly. Inst., Baltimore, 1911-16; B.S., Johns Hopkins U. Sch. of Engring., 1922; m. Lillian Stabler, Feb. 9, 1924; children—Mary Anne, Rebecca Lillian, Charlotte Hazen, LeRoy Yellott, Edmund Frederick. Began as meat cutter Bel Air Market, Baltimore, 1916; rodman, later chief of field parties, Baltimore City Topographic Survey, 1916-17; in real estate and insurance business under own name since 1922; sec. First Federal of Towson (bldg. assn.); dir. in charge of real estate loans Towson (Md.) Nat. Bank; pres. Towson Co. (real estate holding co.). Served as sr. grade master engr., U.S. Army, Engring. Corps, 1917-19. Dir. Soc. Residential Appraisers. Democrat. Presbyterian. Mason, Odd Fellow. Club: Kiwanis (Towson, Md.; past pres.). Home: Towson, R.D. No. 6, Md.

HAINES, Amena Pendleton (Mrs. Oliver Sloan Haines; pen name, Amena Pendleton), writer; b. Chicago, Ill.; d. Bishop William Frederic and Mary Lawson (Young) Pendleton; ed. Acad. of New Ch., Bryn Athyn, Pa., 1897-1900, Training Sch. for Children's Librarians of Carnegie Library, Pittsburgh, 1901-03, Pomona Coll., Claremont, Calif., 1907-09; spl. French courses U. of Pa., and Cornell U.; m. Dr. Oliver Sloan Haines, of Phila., Pa., Nov. 15, 1930 (died 1936). Head Children's Dept. Rosenberg Library, Galveston, Tex., 1918-19; asst. librarian in charge Library of Acad. of the New Ch., Bryn Athyn, Pa., 1919-21; lecturer on literature for children, Coll. of Acad. of the New Ch., 1915-18 and 1919-21. Democrat. Mem. The New Ch. (Swedenborgian). Club: Women's City (Philadelphia). Author: Golden Heart and Other Stories, 1922. Co-editor (with Frances Jenkins Olcott): The Jolly Book for Boys and Girls, 1915. Editor and translator from French: Mystery of Castle Pierrefitte, by Eugenie Foa, 1927; The Strange Search, by Foa, 1929; Folktales of Brittany, by Elsie Masson, 1929; At the Inn of the Guardian Angel, by Ségur, 1931. Home: Bryn Athyn, Pa.

HAINES, Arthur Samuel, surgeon; b. Wilkinsburg, Pa., Sept. 26, 1891; s. James Low and Louise (Rush) H.; B.S., U. of Pittsburgh, 1914, M.D., 1916; m. Pearl Pierce, Apr. 23, 1932. In practice as physician and surgeon, Mt. Lebanon, Pittsburgh, since 1916; dir. Allegheny Co. Farm Loan Assn. Enlisted U.S. Army and immediately discharged for disability during World War. Fellow Am. Coll. Physicians; mem. Pa. Med. Soc., Allegheny County Med. Soc., Sons Am. Revolution, Sigma Alpha Epsilon, Nu Sigma Nu, Omicron Delta Kappa. Republican. Presbyterian. Mason. Clubs: Lions of Pittsburgh (dist. gov. Lions Internat. 1927); Pittsburgh Athletic Assn. Home: Route 1, Library, Pa. Office: 7 Alfred St., Mt. Lebanon, Pittsburgh, Pa.

HAINES, Benjamin W., investment banker; b. West Chester, Pa., Sept. 5, 1869; s. Franklin and Mary H. (James) H.; ed. pub. schs., West Chester, Pa.; m. Linda K. Hoopes, Nov. 4, 1897; children—William B., Linda. With David M. McFarland, conveyancing and investments, West Chester, Pa., 1886-99, partner McFarland & Haines since 1899; dir. Dime Savings Bank of Chester Co. since 1913, sec. of the bd. since 1928; dir. West Chester Bldg. & Loan Assn., Nat. Bank of Chester Co. and Trust Co. Dir. Chester Co. Hosp. Republican. Quaker. Club: West Chester (Pa.) Golf and Country (dir., past pres.). Home: 326 N. Church St. Office: 13 N. High St., West Chester, Pa.

HAINES, Harold Atlee, investment securities; b. Phila., Nov. 17, 1878; s. Lindley and Elizabeth (Atlee) H.; student Friends Select Sch., 1885-96; m. Florence Brearley Molten, Feb. 2, 1907; children—Alice Lalor, Harold Atlee. With Pa. R.R., 1899-1918, successively as clerk, 1899-1903, freight solicitor, Phila., 1903-04, Rochester, N.Y., 1904-06, Reading, Pa., 1906-10, Canadian freight agt., Toronto, 1910-12, div. freight agt., Baltimore, 1912-15, Phila., 1915-16, Pittsburgh, 1916-18; mem. firm Cadbury, Ellis & Haines, investment securities, 1920-38, retired. Served as private Battery A., Pa. Vols., Spanish-American War. Mem. United Spanish War Vets. Republican. Episcopalian. Club: Sunnybrook Golf (Flourtown, Pa.). Home: 105 Rex Av. Office: 1420 Walnut St., Philadelphia, Pa.

HAINES, Harry L., ex-congressman; b. Red Lion, Pa., Feb. 1, 1880; s. Benjamin Ambrose and Rebecca (Wallick) H.; ed. Pa. State Normal Sch., Lock Haven; m. Cora Ness, May 22, 1898; children—Henry Luther, Mary Rebecka (Mrs. Stuart S. Stabley), Charlotte Ruth, George Woodrow, Martha Jeanette. Mfr. cigars since 1906; chief exec. Red Lion Boro 3 terms, 1921-33; mem. 72d to 75th Congresses (1931-39), 22d Pa. Dist. Mason. Odd Fellow, Red Man. Democrat. Mem. United Brethren Ch. Clubs: Masonic, Lions. Home: Red Lion, Pa.*

HAINES, Thomas Harvey, psychologist, psychiatrist; b. Moorestown, N.J., Nov. 4, 1871; s. Zebedee and Anna Philips (Harvey) Haines; A.B., Haverford (Pa.) Coll., 1896; Ph.D., Harvard University, 1901; M.D., Ohio State University, 1912; special studies in neurology and psychiatry, Munich, Zurich and London, 1912-13; m. Helen Manley Hague, Aug. 15, 1912. Asst. prof. philosophy, prof. psychology, Ohio State Univ., 1901-15. First asst. phys., Boston Psychopathic Hosp., 1913-14, also prof.

psychology, Smith Coll. (part time); clin. dir. Ohio Bur. Juvenile Research, 1914-17; prof. medicine (nervous and mental diseases), Ohio State U., 1915-20. Field consultant and dir. mental health surveys for Nat. Com. for Mental Hygiene in Ky., Ala., Miss., La., Mo., Md., Ariz., N. Dak., 1917-22; dir. div. on mental deficiency, of Nat. Com. for Mental Hygiene, 1922-25. Psycho. examiner Camp Dix and Camp Stuart, 1917-18; mem. com. on psychol. exam. of recruits, Nat. Research Council, 1917; now psychiatrist at New York Hosp. Out-Patient Dept. Fellow A.A.A.S., A.M.A., Am. Psychiatric Assn.; mem. Med. Soc. of State of N.Y., Med. Soc. County of N.Y., N.Y. Soc. for Clin. Psychiatry, Am. Psychol. Assn., Phi Rho Sigma, Sigma Xi, Phi Beta Kappa. Mem. Religious Soc. of Friends. Author: Mental Measurement of the Blind, 1915; reports of mental hygiene studies in many states and bills offered to legislatures to improve administration in mental health fields; some fifty other titles in psychol. and med. jours. Home: 58 Tuxedo Road, Montclair, N.J. Office: 28 W. 54th St., New York, N.Y.

HAIRE, Frances Hamilton, dir. of recreation; b. Schell City, Mo., Jan. 9, 1895; d. Robert Donald and Maud (Maus) Haire; student Clinton (Mo.) High Sch., 1908-12, U. of Mo., Columbia, Mo., 1912-13, U. of Wis., Madison, Wis., 1918 (summer), Recreation Training Sch., Nat. Recreation Assn., 1921; grad. Sargent Sch. of Phys. Edn., Cambridge, Mass., 1915; unmarried. Teacher, phys. edn. dept., Lindenwood Coll., St. Charles, Mo., 1915-18; supt. of recreation, Beacon, N.Y., 1920-21; recreation organizer, Nat. Playground & Recreation Assn. of America (now Nat. Recreation Assn.), New York City, 1921-24; supt. of recreation, York, Pa., 1924; dir. of recreation for City of East Orange, N.J., since 1925. Gov. recreation dir., war dept. powder plant, Nitro, W.Va., during World War. Mem. Delta Gamma. Republican. Methodist. Author: The Folk Costume Book, 1926; The American Costume Book, 1934. Home: 40 Lenox Av. Office: City Hall, East Orange, N.J.

HAISTON, Frank; supt. of schools at Pottstown, Pa. Address: Pottstown, Pa.

HALBACH, Robert McCulley, physician; b. Lancaster, Pa., Jan. 20, 1894; s. William August and Emeline Thompson (McCulley) H.; B.S., Franklin and Marshall Coll., Lancaster, Pa., 1915, M.Sc., 1916; M.D., Johns Hopkins Med. Sch., 1920; m. Beatrice Mary Burrell, Oct. 30, 1924. Pathologist Amsterdam City Hosp., Amsterdam, N.Y., 1920-23, St. Luke's Hosp., New Bedford, Mass., 1923-25, Madison Gen. Hosp., Madison, Wis., 1925-26, South Side Hosp., Pittsburgh, 1926-27, N.Y. Orthopedic Dispensary and Hosp., 1930-33; chief resident Howard Hosp., Phila., 1927-28; med. officer, Admiral Farragut Naval Acad., Pine Beach, N.J., since 1934; pathologist, Royal Pines Hosp., Pinewald, N.J., since 1936. Lt. comdr. Med. Corps, U.S.N.R. since 1939. Mem. A.M.A., Am. Soc. Clin. Pathologists, Mass., N.J. State, and Ocean Co. med. socs., Alpha Kappa Kappa. Republican. Episcopalian. Home: 802 Main St., Toms River, N.J.

HALBERG, Elmer John, R.R. exec., lawyer; b. Warren, Pa., Dec. 13, 1896; s. John Frederick and Hilder (Nelson) H.; LL.B., Baldwin-Wallace U., Berea, O., 1922; LL.M., John Marshall Sch. of Law, Cleveland, O., 1924; m. Myrl Ray, Feb. 23, 1923. Admitted to practice before bar of Ohio, 1922, bar of Pa., 1930; atty. for N.Y., Chicago & St. Louis R.R. Co., Cleveland, O., 1922-30; v.p. and gen. counsel, Pittsburgh & Shawmut R.R. Co., Kittaning, Pa., since 1930; sec. and gen. counsel, Allegheny River Mining Co.; sec., gen. counsel and dir., Pittsburgh & Shawmut Coal Co., Allegheny River Supply Co. Mem. Boy Scouts of America (dir. Butler-Armstrong Area Council), Delta Theta Phi. Republican. Protestant. Elk. Clubs: Rotary (pres.), Kittanning Country (Kittanning, Pa.). Home: 304 Allegheny Av. Office: Shawmut Bldg., Kittanning, Pa.

HALBERT, LeRoy, clergyman; b. Belmont, N.Y., Sept. 5, 1882; s. Alexis LeRoy and Catharine Adorna (Bennett) H.; A.B., U. of Rochester, 1905; B.D., Rochester Theol. Sem., 1908; Th.D., Drew Theol. Sem., 1925; m. Rose A. Mecklei, July 9, 1907; children—Vincent Alexis, Rose Arlene. Ordained to ministry Northern Bapt. Ch., 1908; pastor, Meridian, N.Y., 1908; head worker Drummond Hall, Christian center, Minneapolis, Minn., 1910 to 1912; pastor, Belmont, N.Y., and various chs. in N.Y. and N.J., 1912-29; pastor, Punxsutawney, Pa., 1929-38, Sharon, Pa., since 1938. Trustee Camp Corbly Assn. Mem. Alpha Delta Phi. Past pres. New York City and Vicinity Bapt. Ministers Assn., Pa. Bapt. Ministers Union. Chmn. Pastoral Change Commn. in Pa. Bapt. Conv. Northern Baptist. Home: 305 W. State St., Sharon, Pa.

HALDEMAN, Paul Collins, mech. engr.; b. Westfield, Mass., July 25, 1879; s. John Henry and Virginia (Collins) H.; student Franklin and Marshall Acad., 1895-96; B.S., Pa. State Coll., 1901; m. Alice May Bromell, Apr. 23, 1907; children—Edw. B., P. Collins. Asst. master mechanic Lukens Steel Co., Coatesville, Pa., 1901-05; draftsman Semet Solvay Co., 1905-06; master mechanic Lukens Steel Co., 1906-25, chief engr. since 1925. Mem. Assn. Iron and Steel Engrs., Sigma Chi. Republican. Presbyterian. Home: 536 Chestnut St. Office: Lukens Steel Co., Coatesville, Pa.

HALDEMAN-JEFFERIES, Don, writer, poet, teacher; b. Gettysburg, Pa., June 21, 1889; d. James Wilson and Geogianne (Lupp) Haldeman; student pub. and pvt. schs., Adams County, Pa., Littlestown (Pa.) Acad., 1902-06, Millersville (Pa.) Teachers Coll., 1906-07, Temple U., Phila., evening school, 1927-33, Washington Sch. of Art, Washington, D.C., 1920-22; m. Edmund Landis Jefferies, Oct. 25, 1907 (died 1910); 1 dau., Ruth (Mrs. W. Lukens Hathaway). Teacher Easttown-Tredyffryn, Chester Co., Pa., 1910-13, Northampton, Bucks Co., Pa., 1923-27, Haverford, Pa., 1927-33; holds teachers state permanent certificate. Mem. Nat. League of Am. Pen Women, Soc. of Arts and Letters, Phila. Manuscript Club; formerly state pres. Am. Writers. Awarded various prizes from mags. and clubs for poetry, especially humorous verse. Republican. Episcopalian. Club: Women's Republican (Phila.). Author: Volume of Verse, 1929; Epileptic Fits (humorous verse), 1931; Nantucket, Manshope and Other New England Poems, 1931; Song of the Wissahickon and Other Poems, 1932; Humorous, Humane Side of Travel; now writing book on spl. edn. for Dept. Pub. Instrn. of Pa. Interested in mysticism, metaphysics and occult sciences; now organizing Internat. Bards (for poets). Home: 2208 Delancey St., Philadelphia, Pa., and "The Maples," Chalfont, Bucks Co., Pa. Office: Education Bldg., State Capitol, Harrisburg, Pa.

HALDENSTEIN, Alfred Augustus, chem. engring.; b. New York, N.Y., Jan. 31, 1895; s. Isidor and Rose (Miller) H.; B.S., Columbia, 1915, Chem.E., 1917; m. Dorothy M. Cohn, May 6, 1920; 1 dau., Barbara Jean. Employed as chem. engr., Barrett Co., 1917; chem. engr. National Adhesives Corpn. since 1919, sec. and dir. since 1932. Served as sergt. C.W.S., U.S.A., 1917-18. Mem. Am. Chem. Soc., Phi Beta Kappa, Sigma Xi, Phi Lambda Upsilon, Zeta Beta Tau. Republican. Jewish religion. Clubs: Engineers (Plainfield); Chemists (New York). Home: 11 Myrtle Av., Plainfield, N.J. Office: 820 Greenwich St., New York, N.Y.

HALDERMAN, J. Leonard, supervising prin. of schools; b. Pottstown, Pa., Jan. 9, 1900; s. John H. and Hannah (Funk) H.; grad. Pottstown High Sch., 1918; B.S., Pa. State Coll., 1922; M.S., U. of Pa., 1932; grad. student Temple U. (completing work for Ph.D.); m. Kathryn I. Neiman, Aug. 1, 1922; children—J. Leonard, Jane Bernice. Chemist Chipman Chem. Co., Houston, Tex., 1922-24; science teacher, N. Coventry Schs., Pottstown, Pa., 1924-25, Spring City, Pa., Schs., 1925-27; head science dept., Mahanry Twp. Schs., Mahanry City, Pa., 1927-31; supervising prin. N. Coventry Schools, 1931-36, Doylestown Borough Schs. since 1936. Served in U.S. Army, 1918-19. Dir. Boy Scouts of Bucks Co. Mem. N.E.A., Pa. State Edn. Assn., Pa. Schoolmen's Club, Delta Chi. Mem. Brethren Ch. (deacon). Club: Kiwanis of Doylestown (pres. 1938). Interested in scientific farming and helps operate the old homestead farm of the Haldeman estate at Pottstown, Pa. Address: Doylestown, Pa.

HALE, Charles Brockway, univ. prof.; b. Syracuse, N.Y., June 13, 1898; s. Francis Edwin and Jean (Brockway) H.; A.B., Cornell U., 1920, Ph.D., 1924; unmarried. Instr. English, Cornell U., 1920-25; asst. prof. English, U. of Md., College Park, Md., 1925-27, asso. prof., 1927-35, prof. English since 1935, chmn. of dept. since 1937. Served as pvt. inf., U.S.A., 1918. Mem. Modern Lang. Assn., Am. Assn. Univ. Profs. (mem. nat. council since 1938), Delta Sigma Phi, Phi Beta Kappa, Phi Kappa Phi, Alpha Psi Omega, Omicron Delta Kappa, Pi Delta Epsilon. Republican. Editor (with W. H. French), Middle English Metrical Romances, 1930; (with J. E. Tobin), Contrast and Comparison, 1931. Contbr. to ednl. jours. Home: 813 Madison Av., Hyattsville, Md.

HALE, George Clyde, dir. chem. research; b. Sullivan, Ind., Sept. 29, 1891; s. Charles and Rosetta (Bledsoe) H.; A.B., Indiana U., 1914, A.M., 1915, Ph.D., 1917; studied U. of Chicago, part of 1916; m. Mary Allen Raines, June 16, 1919; children—George Clyde, Allen Charles. Instr. chemistry, Indiana U., 1915-17; research work in explosives, U.S. War Dept., 1917-20; chief tech. dir. Ordnance Office, U.S. Army of Occupation, Coblentz, Germany, 1920-21; chief chemist Picatinny Arsenal, 1921-29, chief of chem. dept. since 1929. Sergt. U.S. Army, 1917-18. Mem. Am. Chem. Soc., Am. Inst. Chem. Engrs., Army Ordnance Assn., Alpha Chi Sigma, Sigma Xi. Democrat. Club: Chemists (New York). Writer of articles on explosives, fuse powders and pyrotechnics. Original inventor of gasless fuse or delay powders. Co-inventor flashless propellent powder now being used by U.S. Army. Home: 31 Elk Av. Address: Picatinny Arsenal, Dover, N.J.

HALF, Rudolph Seligman, merchant; b. Athens, O., Mar. 25, 1870; s. Isaac and Eva (Selig) H.; ed. pub. and private schs., Athens; m. Mildred Schweizer, Dec. 10, 1902; 2 sons, Ivan, Ernest; m. 2d, Clara Schweizer, Sept. 6, 1909; 1 son, Richard Samuel. Began as shipper in furniture factory, 1885; later furniture salesman, wholesale furniture and carpets; founded Half Bros. retail furniture store, 1899, pres. and dir. Felix Half & Bro., Inc., wholesale floor coverings; dir. Woodward-Wright Furniture Co. Mem. Pittsburgh Chamber of Commerce; vice-pres. Pittsburgh Wholesale Merchants Assn. Dir. Jewish Social Service Bur. of Pittsburgh. Republican. Jewish religion. Mem. K. of P. Clubs: Concordia, Carpet (Pittsburgh). Home: 5537 Darlington Rd. Office: 800 Penn Av., Pittsburgh, Pa.

HALL, Arthur A., univ. prof.; b. Taylor Co., W.Va., Dec. 16, 1880; s. William K. and Abalona (Knotts) H.; B.S. in M.E., W.Va. Univ., 1906; m. Edna Rightmire, Sept. 14, 1910; children—Evelyn Augusta (Mrs. Albert Wiley Friend), Ina Barnes (dec.), Arthur A., Jr. Student apprentice with General Electric Co., Schenectady, N.Y., 1906; engr. Elkins Power Co., 1907-09; engr. Union Utility Co., later W.Va. Traction & Electric Co., 1909-16; asso. with W.Va. Univ. since 1916, now prof. elec. engring.; served as city mgr., Morgantown, 1922-23; pres. and dir. Fidelity Bldg. & Loan Assn. Registered professional engr. in W.Va. Fellow A.A.A.S. Mem. Am. Inst. Elec. Engrs., W.Va. Acad. Sciences, W.Va. Univ. Scientific Soc. Republican. Methodist. Mason. Club: Lions. Home: 316 Forest Av., Morgantown, W.Va.

HALL, Clarence Arthur, chemist; b. at Philadelphia, Pa., March 4, 1874; s. Edwin and Anna M. (Ford) Hall; graduate of University of Pa., 1896; m. Mary Watson, December 3, 1907. Began as chemist for Lake Superior Carbide Works which later became Union Carbide Co., Sault Ste. Marie, Mich.; later with Pa. Salt Co.; now with Electric Storage Battery Co., Phila. Treas. bd. trustees, Presbytery of Phila., North. Mem. Franklin Inst. (mem. bd. mgrs.), The Bartol Research Foundation (chmn. bd. of mgrs.), Am. Chem. Soc., Am. Electrochem. Soc., Am. Ceramic Soc., Am. Inst. Chem. Engrs., Am. Inst. Mining and Metallurgical Engrs., Am. Physical Soc., Soc. of Chem. Industry, Faraday Soc.; fellow

Chem. Soc. of London. Home: 7951 Winston Rd., Chestnut Hill. Office: 19th St. and Allegheny Av., Philadelphia, Pa.

HALL, Clyde Willis, mining engring.; b. Trading Post, Kan., Nov. 23, 1889; s. Austin W. and Edith H. (Hill) H.; ed. Kan. State Agrl. Coll., 1910-11; B.S., U. of Mo. Sch. of Mines, 1914, Engr. of Mines, same, 1921; m. Fannie E. Mitchell, June 29, 1914; 1 dau., Marian Edith. Employed as mining engr. mines in Mex. and Colo., 1914-19; mine supt., Sonora, Mex., 1919-22; supt. silver mine, Chihuahua, Mex., 1922-25; vice-pres., gen. mgr. and dir., United Clay Mines Corpn., Trenton, N.J., since 1925; dir. Prospect Bldg. & Loan Assn., Trenton, N.J. Served as mem. Mayors Citizens Com., Trenton, N.J. Mem. Sigma Nu. Republican. Presbyterian (trustee). Home: 6 Kensington Av. Office: 101 Oakland St., Trenton, N.J.

HALL, Frank Hillman, lawyer; b. Washington, D.C., July 13, 1870; s. Hillman Allyn and Jennie (Carpenter) H.; A.B., Princeton, 1892; student George Washington U. Law Sch., 1892-93, N.Y. Law Sch., 1893-95; m. Alice Scudder, Apr. 22, 1897; children—Alice May (Mrs. Donald W. Sinclair), Frank Hillman; m. 2d, Frances B. Venino, of New York, Feb. 19, 1921. Admitted to N.J. bar, 1895, and began practice at Jersey City; mem. Dickinson, Thompson & McMaster, 1895-98, Thompson & Hall, 1898-1906, Steele, Otis & Hall, 1906-10; practiced alone, N.Y. City, since 1910; dir. and gen. counsel Corn Products Refining Co. Republican. Clubs: Whitehall (New York); Englewood, Knickerbocker Country (Englewood, N.J.); Havana (Cuba) Country. Home: 256 Lydecker St., Englewood, N.J. Office: 17 Battery Pl. New York, N.Y.

HALL, Fred Smith, social worker; b. Washington, D.C., June 2, 1870; s. Rev. George A. and Sarah S. (Smith) H.; A.B., Wesleyan U., 1893; Ph.D., Columbia, 1898; m. Jennie E. Orcutt, July 12, 1906. With U.S. Census Bur., 1899-1902; sec. New York Child Labor Com., 1903; asst. sec. City Club of New York, 1904-05; head worker Newark Neighborhood House, 1906-07; sec. Pa. Child Labor Assn., 1908-11; asso. dir. Charity Orgn. Dept., Russell Sage Foundation, 1911-28; editor Social Work Year Book, 1929-35; chmn. Com. for Social Action (N.J. area) of the Congl. and Christian Chs., 1937-38. Mem. Am. Assn. Social Workers, Nat. Conf. Social Work, Alpha Delta Phi. Conglist. Author: Sympathetic Strikes and Sympathetic Lockouts, 1898; American Marriage Laws (with Elizabeth Brooke), 1919; Medical Certification for Marriage, 1925; Child Marriages (with Mary E. Richmond), 1925; Marriage and the State (with Mary E. Richmond), 1929. Contbr. articles to professional pubns. Home: 173 Summit Av., Upper Montclair, N.J.

HALL, Frederick W(ilson), lawyer; b. Pittsburgh, Pa., Feb. 22, 1908; s. Peter B. and Rachel E. (Crispin) H.; Litt.B., Rutgers U., New Brunswick, N.J., 1928; LL.B., Harvard U. Law Sch., 1931; m. Jane Rowley Armstrong, July 18, 1936. Admitted to N.J. bar as atty., 1932, as counselor, 1936; in gen. practice of law at Newark since 1932; asso. with Arthur T. Vanderbilt, Newark, since 1931; served as mem. bd. edn., Bound Brook, N.J., since 1934. Mem. bd. trustees Bound Brook Presbyn. Ch. since 1938, pres. bd. since 1939. Mem. Am. Bar Assn., N.J. State Bar Assn., Essex Co. and Somerset Co. bar assns., Phi Beta Kappa. Democrat. Presbyn. Mason. Club: Down Town (Newark). Home: 17 E. High St., Bound Brook. Office: 744 Broad St., Newark, N.J.

HALL, John A(ugustus) F(ritchey), mayor of Harrisburg; b. Harrisburg, Pa., July 8, 1890; s. Samuel S. and Amanda (Feass) H.; grad. Central High Sch., Harrisburg, 1908, Dickinson Coll., 1912; m. Helen Irene Sebold, May 4, 1928; 1 son, John Augustus Fritchey. Teacher of English, Central High Sch., 1912-22; admitted to bar Dauphin Co., 1917, and began practice in Harrisburg; U.S. commr. Middle Dist. of Pa., 1919-22; city treas., Harrisburg, 1932-35; mayor of Harrisburg since 1936; dir. Harris Building & Loan Assn. Member Pa. House of Reps. 3 terms; former mem. State Vets. commn. Served in U.S. Navy during World War.

Mem. Am. Legion, Vets. of Foreign Wars, Phi Kappa Sigma. Methodist. Mason (32°, Shriner), Tall Cedars, Elk, Patriotic Order Sons of America: Club: Harrisburg Republican. Home: 2530 N. 2d St. Office: City Hall, Harrisburg, Pa.; Union Trust Bldg., Harrisburg, Pa.

HALL, John Howe, cons. metallurgist; b. South Portsmouth, R.I., June 20, 1881; s. David Prescott and Florence Marion (Howe) H.; A.B., Harvard U., 1903, A.M., same, 1904; m. Gertrude Earnshaw, Nov. 10, 1915; children—David Prescott, John Howe, Jr., Margaret Alward, Maud Elliott, Grisella Chrystie. Student, Bethlehem Steel Co., 1904, asst. supt. Crucible Steel Dept., 1905-06; metallurgist, Taylor Wharton Iron & Steel Co., 1906-13; cons. engr., 1913-15; metallurgist, Taylor Wharton Iron & Steel Co., 1915-30, tech. asst. to pres., 1930-37; consultant specializing in foundry work since 1937. Mem. Am. Inst. Mining Engrs (Henry M. Howe Memorial lecturer, 1929), Am. Soc. for Testing Materials, Electrochem. Soc., Am. Foundrymens Assn., Am. Soc. for Metals, Iron & Steel Inst. (Brit.). Awarded Whiting Gold Medal, A.F.A., 1924. Republican. Unitarian. Club: Harvard of New York. Author: The Steel Foundry, 2 edits., 1914, 1922, French translation, 1925. Co-author (with others):' A.B.C. of Iron & Steel, 1915. Contbr. many tech. papers. Home: 228 W. Willow Grove Av., Philadelphia, Pa.

HALL, Kent Bruce; mem. law firm Hall, Goodwin & Paul. Address: Board of Trade Bldg., Wheeling, W.Va.

HALL, Lyle G., pres. Stackpole Carbon Co.; b. St. Marys, Pa., Aug. 13, 1886; s. James K. P. and Kate (Hyde) H.; student St. Paul's Sch., Phillips Andover Acad. and Yale Univ.; m. Jane Grube, Jan. 1, 1928; children—Eugenia, Helen, Lyle. Pres. Stackpole Carbon Co., St. Mary's, Pa., Molded Materials, Inc., Ridgway, Pa.; v.p. St. Mary's Trust Co., St. Mary's Sewer Pipe Co., St. Mary's Clay Products Co., Russell Snow Plow Co. Asso. judge of Elk Co., Pa., since 1926. Dir. Children's Aid Soc. of Elk Co. since 1930; pres. Elk Co. Gen. Hosp. since 1938. Mem. Boy Scouts of America (pres. Bucktail Council, 1930-38; mem. exec. com., Region III, since 1937), Y.M.C.A. (pres., Ridgway, Pa., since 1932; mem. Pa. State Exec. Com. since 1937), Elk Co. Mfrs. Assn. (pres. since 1925), Am. Legion. Elk. Clubs: Elk Co. Country (Ridgway, Pa.); St. Mary's (Pa.) Country; Bath, Indian Creek (Miami Beach, Fla.); Everglades. (Palm Beach, Fla.). Home: 602 Hyde Av., Ridgway, Pa. Office: Stackpole Carbon Co., St. Mary's, Pa.

HALL, Mary Bowers (Mrs. Robert William H.); b. Saco, Me., Oct. 2, 1871; d. Roscoe and Sarah Abbie (Berry) Bowers; B.L., Smith Coll., 1895; A.M., Radcliffe Coll., 1898; spl. study, Mass. Inst. Tech., 1900-01; Ph.D., U. of Pa., 1909; m. Robert William Hall, aug. 4, 1908; children—Roberta Bowers (Mrs. William Bissell McLean), Marjorie Crossette (Mrs. James Osborn Fuller), Roscoe Bowers. Served as laboratory asst. in zoology and botany, Smith Coll. 1898-99; instr. zoology, Wellesley Coll., 1899-1908, actg. head dept. zoology, 1903-04. Fellow A.A.A.S.; mem. Am. Eugenics Soc., Birth Control Fed., Mass. Audubon Soc., Am. Assn. Univ. Women, N.E. Soc. of Pa., Phi Beta Kappa. Bennett Fellow at U. of Pa. Republican. Unitarian. Club: Lehigh University Woman's of Bethlehem. Home: 37 E. Church St., Bethlehem, Pa.

HALL, Ralph Emmons, chemist; b. Charlestown, O., Feb. 28, 1885; s. Franklin M. and Emma (Gilbert) H.; B.S., O. Wesleyan U., 1907, M.S., same, 1908; A.M., O. State U., 1911; Ph.D., U. of Chicago, 1916; (hon.) D.Sc., O. Wesleyan U., 1936; m. Dorothy Pierpont Murphy, Mar. 29, 1921; children—Marjorie Ellen, William Gilbert, Robert Murphy, Ralph Emmons, Jr. Engaged as asst. prof. chemistry, Ia. State Coll., 1916-17; phys. chemist, Geophys. Lab., Carnegie Instn., Washington, D.C., 1917-20, Firestone Tire & Rubber Co., Akron, O., 1920, Koppers Co., Pittsburgh, Pa., 1920-22, U.S. Bur. of Mines, Pittsburgh, Pa., 1922-26; dir. Hall Labs., Inc., conditioning of industrial water. Pittsburgh, Pa., since 1926. Served as capt. C.W.S., U.S.A., 1918. Mem. Am. Chem. Soc., Am. Soc. Mech. Engrs., Am. Soc. for Testing Materials, Phi Beta Kappa, Sigma Xi, Sigma Alpha Epsilon, Gamma Alpha. Patentee processes water conditioning. Contbr. tech. papers to socs. and sci. journs. Home: 99 Inglewood Drive. Office: 304 Ross St., Pittsburgh, Pa.

HALL, Robert Lee, physician, surgeon; b. Marion, Md., June 21, 1877; s. John Wesley and Mary Elizabeth (Coulbourn) H.; grad. Marion High Sch., 1894; M.D., U. of Md., Baltimore, 1901; m. Mary Fulton Hanna, Nov. 23, 1926; 1 son, Robert Lee. Began as clk. drug store, Crisfield, Md.; interne City Hosp., Baltimore, 1901-02; gen. practice of medicine and surgery, Pocomoke City, Md., since 1902; member courtesy staff Peninsula Gen. Hosp.; postmaster, Pocomoke City, 1928-36. Del. to Rep. Nat. Con., Chicago, 1912, when Theodore Roosevelt was nominated on ind. ticket; was an elector from Md. Mem. local Draft Bd. and physician, Worcester County, 1916-18. Mem. Rep. State Central Com., Worcester County, 1924-34. Fellow A.M.A.; mem. med. and Chirurg. Faculty of Md. (vice-pres. 1915, 1937; mem. Council since 1928), Worcester County Med. Soc. (charter mem.; served as sec.-treas. and pres. twice), Med. Alumni Assn. of U. of Md. (vice-pres. 1938-39). Republican. Presbyterian. Elk. Club: Lions (Pocomoke City, Md.). Home: 208 Walnut St. Office: 203 2d St., Pocomoke City, Md.

HALL, Robert William, biologist; b. Cincinnati, O., Aug. 17, 1872; s. Ephraim Gaylord and Alice Cogswell (Crossette) H.; Ph.B., Yale, 1895; A.B., Harvard, 1897, A.M., 1898, Ph.D., 1901; m. Mary Alice Bowers, Aug. 4, 1908; children—Mrs. Roberta Bowers McLean, Marjorie Crossette, Roscoe Bowers. Asst. in zoölogy, Harvard, 1896-99, Yale, 1899-1901; instr., Yale, 1901-02, Woods Hole, 1899-1901; head of dept. of biology, Lehigh Univ., 1902-37, prof. biology since 1937. Fellow A.A.A.S.; mem. Pa. Forestry Assn. (life), Sigma Xi (Yale Chapter). Home: 37 E. Church St., Bethlehem, Pa.

HALL, Sidney; v.p. U. S. Fidelity & Guaranty Co. Home: 1319 Park Av. Office: Calvert and Redwood Sts., Baltimore, Md.

HALL, Sobisca S.; otorhinolaryngological staff St. Mary's and Union Protestant hosps. Address: 134 S. 4th St., Clarksburg, W.Va.

HALL, Thomas John, 3d, tobacco planter; b. Tracys Landing, Md., Apr. 1, 1883; s. Thomas John, Jr., and Mary Esther (Loney) H.; student pvt. schs. in Md.; m. Isabella Frances Allen, Oct. 4, 1910; children—Thomas Allen Waters, Frances Barton Loney, Catherine Sandes, Mary Esther Cox. In wholesale notion bus., Baltimore, Md., 1898-1908; farming and propr. farms, Tracys Landing, Md., since 1908; served as justice of peace, 1916-23, 1928-34; rep. Anne Arundel County in Md. Farm Bur. Fed., 1922-23; mem. Anne Arundel Co. Welfare Bd., 1932-35 and since 1936, chmn., 1938-39. Dir. Anne Arundel Co. branch Md. Tuberculosis Assn., Annapolis and Anne Arundel Co. Pub. Library Assn. V-p. Anne Arundel Co. Council Parents Teacher Assn., 1930-32. Democrat. Episcopalian (lay reader St. James Parish since 1914, vestryman since 1921). Author: History Saint James Parish, 1932. Home: Lochlea, Tracys Landing, Md.

HALL, Van Byron, lawyer; b. Meigs Co., O., Mar. 30, 1870; s. Reynear Milton and Sarah Ann (Duvaull) H.; ed. Glenville (W.Va.) State Normal Sch.; m. Sarah Anne Boggs, Sept. 24, 1901; children—Byron William, Robert Milton, Boggs Charles, Harold Lee. Engaged in teaching pub. schs. of W.Va., 1887-98; admitted to W.Va. bar, 1896, and engaged in gen. practice of law at Sutton, 1896-1901, in practice with brother as Hall Bros., Sutton, W.Va., 1901-25; mem. firm Hines & Hall since 1929; prosecuting atty. of Braxton Co., 1921-24. Trustee Broaddus Coll., Phillippi, W.Va., 1920-28. Mem. W.Va. and Am. bar assns., Commercial Law League of America. Democrat. Baptist. Mason (K.T.). Club: Rotary of Sutton. Address: Sutton, W.Va.

HALL, Walter Phelps, prof. history; b. Newburgh, N.Y., May 5, 1884; s. William Kittridge and Anna (Bond) H.; A.B., Yale, 1906; Ph.D., Columbia, 1912; m. Margaret Nixon, 1923; children—Walter Phelps, Michael Garibaldi. Began as instr. in history, Amherst, 1909; with Princeton since 1913, as instr., asst. prof. and asso. prof. history, 1913-28, prof. since 1928, Dodge prof. since 1933. In Am. Field Service, France, 1917. Alumni trustee Hotchkiss Sch., 1930-32. Mem. Phi Beta Kappa, Sigma Alpha Epilson. Episcopalian. Club: Princeton (New York). Author: British Radicalism (1791-1797), 1912; Empire to Commonwealth, 1928; Mr. Gladstone, 1931; (with R. G. Albion) A History of England and The British Empire, 1937. Editor: (with E. A. Beller) Essays in Nineteenth Century Thought. Contbr. book reviews. Home: 12 Edgehill St., Princeton, N.J.

HALL, William M.; sch. physician W.Va. State Coll. Address: W.Va. State Coll., Institute, W.Va.

HALL, William Shafer, mathematician; b. Chester, Pa., June 27, 1861; s. Stephen Cloud and Mercie Emma (Baker) H.; C.E., Lafayette Coll., 1884 (Phi Beta Kappa Fraternity), M.E., 1885, M.S., 1887, LL.D. from the same college, 1934; Sc.D., Gettysburg College, 1922 (Tau Beta Pi); m. Rachel Estelle Kline, August 11, 1891; children—Rachel Elizabeth, Margaret (dec.), Mary Estelle, William Arthur (dec.), Eleanor Bassett. Tutor in Eng. and graphics, 1884-88, adj. prof. mining engring. and graphics, 1890-98, prof., 1898-1912, prof. tech. mathematics, 1912-14, prof. mathematics and head dept. since 1914, Lafayette Coll., also sec. of faculty. Fellow A.A.A.S.; mem. Math. Assn. of America, Am. Assn. Univ. Profs., Math. Assn. Middle States and Md., Pa. Soc. S.R. Republican. Presbyn. Elder. Mason (Past Eminent Comdr. K.T.). Author: Mensuration, 1893; Descriptive Geometry, 1904; Differential and Integral Calculus, 1897; Mine Surveying, 1911. Address: College Campus, Easton, Pa.

HALL, Wrayburn Benjamin, mem. Pa. State Ho. of Rep.; b. Ellisburg, Pa., Oct. 19, 1887; s. Horace H. and Sara Jane (Bishop) H.; student Ellisburg (Pa.) Grade Sch., 1895-99, Genesee (Pa.) High Sch., 1900-02, Canisteo (N.Y.) High Sch., 1903-04, Elmira (N.Y.) Free Acad., 1905-06; m. Edith May Webster, Mar. 31, 1931. Began as farmer, Ellisburg, Pa.; meter reader, repairman, lease foreman, Potter Gas Co., Potter County Gas fields, 1908-15; lumbering in Potter County, 1919-23; farming, Ellisburg, 1923-28; highway construction, Potter County, 1928-35; insurance underwriting since 1936. Mem. Pa. State Ho. of Rep. since 1936. Served with 78th Div., 312th Inf., Co. K, U.S. Army, A.E.F., 1918-19. Mem. Borough Council of Coudersport, Pa., 1934-38. Mem. Am. Legion. Republican. Methodist. Mason (past thrice potent master); lodge perfection trustee), Odd Fellow, Nat. Grange. Address: 501 Park Av., Coudersport, Pa.

HALLAM, Clement Benner, editor; b. Wilmington, Del., Aug. 30, 1876; s. Charles and Mary A. (Benner) H.; grad. Wilmington High Sch., 1893; unmarried. Began as a printer, 1894; reporter Wilmington Morning News, 1897-1907; city editor Wilmington Evening Journal, 1907-33; dir. and sec. Evening Journal Co., 1907-12; mng. editor Journal-Every Evening, 1933-36; exec. editor News-Journal papers, since Dec. 1, 1936. Mem. Del. State Athletic Commn., 1930-36, chmn., 1933-36; mem. bd. govs. Municipal Golf and Tennis Assn., 1922-37, pres., 1927-37. Republican. Mason. Home: 804 W. 5th St. Office: Orange and Girard Sts., Wilmington, Del.

HALLAM, William Alton, coll. prof.; b. Washington, Pa., Oct. 12, 1903; s. James Bradley and Virginia (Keaney) H.; B.S., Washington and Jefferson Coll., Washington, Pa., 1924; A.M., Johns Hopkins U., 1928, grad. student, 1931-32; m. Mary Lucretia McCuskey, Sept. 4, 1928; 1 dau., Hallie Lu. Engaged in teaching, high sch., Meyersdale, Pa., 1924; jr. instr. mathematics, Johns Hopkins U., 1925-28; prof. mathematics and head dept. mathematics, W.Va. Wesleyan Coll., Buckhannon, W.Va., since 1928, head of dept. physics since 1936. Served in Pa. N.G., 1921-25. Mem. Theta Kappa Nu. Democrat. Mem. M.E. Ch. Club: Lions of Buckhannon. Home: 13 E. Lincoln St., Buckhannon, W.Va.

HALLANAN, Walter Simms, oil official; b. Huntington, W.Va., Apr. 29, 1890; s. Thomas (M.D.) and Martha (Blake) H.; grad. Morris-Harvey Coll., Barboursville, W.Va.; m. Mary Imogene Burns, 1911; children—Walter Simms, Elizabeth Virginia. Mng. editor Huntington Herald-Dispatch, 1908-13; sec. to Gov. H. D. Hatfield, 1913-17; state tax commr., W.Va., 1917-23; pres. Plymouth Oil Co. since 1923; v.p. Big Lake Oil Co.; mem. bd. dirs. Republic Oil Refining Company, Kanawha Valley Bank, Reagan County Purchasing Co. In charge publicity bur., Republican State Com., W.Va., 1912; presdl. elector (chmn., W.Va.), 1920; mem. W.Va. State Senate, 1926; mem. Rep. Nat. Com. 2 terms, 1928-36, elected mem. exec. com., 1934. Became mem. exec. com. Nat. Tax Assn. 1921. Methodist. Elk. Clubs: Edgewood Country, Kanawha Country. Home: 1520 Kanawha St. Office: Kanawha Valley Bldg., Charleston, W.Va.

HALLETT, George Hervey, mathematician; b. Manchester, Me., Dec. 30, 1870; s. James Hervey and Sarah Louise (Hawkes) H.; student Lehigh U., 1889-90; A.B., U. of Pa. 1893, A.M., 1894, Ph.D., 1896; m. Gertrude Amy Hawkes, Feb. 21, 1894; children—George H., Henry M., Mrs. Rebecca Richie, Margaret E., Winslow N. Instructor in mathematics, 1894-1904, assistant prof., 1904-09, prof. 1909-33, Thomas A. Scott prof. of mathematics since 1933, University of Pa. Mem. Assn. Teachers of Mathematics of Middle States and Md., Pa. State Ednl. Assn. (ednl. council 1910-16), Am. Math. Soc., Pi Mu Epsilon, Sigma Xi, Phi Beta Kappa. Author: (with Robert F. Anderson) Elementary Algebra, 1917. Editor of math. texts of F. S. Crofts & Co., pubs. Home: West Chester, Pa.

HALLETT, Winslow Nichols, educator; b. Lansdowne, Pa., Dec. 5, 1907; s. George Hervey and Gertrude Amy (Hawkes) H.; student Westtown (Pa.) Friends Sch., 1920-22, Wilmington (Del.) Friends (High) Sch., 1922-24; A.B., U. of Pa., 1928, A.M., 1930, Ph.D., 1932; extension work in edn., Muhlenberg Coll., Allentown, Pa., 1938-39; m. Sarah Louise Hallett, Dec. 21, 1929. Asst. instr. of psychology, U. of Pa., 1928-31, instr., 1931-32; prof. of psychology and head of dept. of mathematics, Cedar Crest Coll., Allentown, Pa., 1932-35; adult edn. leader, Lehigh Co. (Pa.) Adult Education Program, Allentown, Pa., 1936-39. Mem. Am. Psychol. Assn. (asso.), Eastern Psychol. Assn., Am. Math. Soc., Math. Assn. of America, Am. Assn. for Adult Edn., Pa. State Assn. for Adult Edn., Pa. Conf. for the Edn. of Exceptional Children, Phi Beta Kappa, Sigma Xi (asso.), Pi Mu Epsilon. Mem. Soc. of Friends. Home: 902 N. 13th St., Allentown, Pa.

HALLEY, Albert Roberts, coll. prof.; b. Nashville, Tenn., Dec. 7, 1882; s. Robert Ambrose and Mary Jane (Houze) H.; student Nashville (Tenn.) pub. schs., 1890-1901, Johns Hopkins U., Baltimore, Md., 1919-20; M.D., Vanderbilt U., Nashville, Tenn., 1905, B.S., 1913, M.S., 1913; Ph.D., Harvard, 1923; m. Katherine Louise Campbell, Aug. 12, 1908; children —Alberta Louise, Albert Browning. M.D. in govt. service, Panama, 1906, 1907; physician, Fla. East Coast R.R., on Fla. Keys, summer 1911; teacher of German and Spanish, Meridian (Miss.) High Sch., 1911-12; head modern languages, Savannah (Ga.) High Sch., 1913-18; head Romance languages, Millsaps Coll., Jackson, Miss., 1918-19; head English Dept., U. of Tulsa (Okla.), 1922-23; asso. prof. English, U. of Fla., Gainesville, Fla., 1923-25; asst. prof. English, W.Va. U., Morgantown, W.Va., 1925-26; prof. of English, head of dept., Marshall Coll., Huntington, W.Va., since 1926. Served in Tenn. State Guard, 1899-1901. Mem. Phi Beta Kappa, Nat. Rifle Assn. Republican. Club: Tri-State Pistol (Huntington, W.Va.). Author numerous articles for learned pubs. and poetry. Address: 1721 Hildacrest, Huntington, W.Va.

HALLGREN, Mauritz Alfred, editor; b. Chicago, June 18, 1899; s. Alfred Aaron and Maria Katherine (Carlson) H.; ed. pub. schs., Chicago, and U. of Chicago; m. Elisabeth Steele, Oct. 12, 1921; children—Katherine, Elisabeth Lynn. Began as reporter Chicago Daily News, 1920; telegraph editor South Bend (Ind.) Tribune, 1920-22; asst. news editor Cincinnati Times-Star, 1922; editor for Associated Press, at Chicago, 1922-25; state dept. corr., Washington, D.C., for Internat. News Service and United Press, 1926-28; European corr., Berlin, for United Press, 1928-30; asso. editor The Nation, New York, 1930-34; became asso. editor Baltimore Sun, 1934. Served in U.S. Marine Corps, in France, June 1918-Sept. 1919. Author: Seeds of Revolt, 1933; The Gay Reformer, 1935; The Tragic Fallacy, 1937. Contbr. to mags. Home: Ellerslie Farm, Glenwood, Md.

HALLIDAY, Ernest Milton, clergyman; b. Vienna Twp., Genesee Co., Mich., July 26, 1878; s. James D. and Alcina (Colton) H.; A.B., U. of Mich., 1904; LL.B., 1906; A.M., Columbia, 1913; grad. Union Theol. Sem., 1917; D.D., Marietta Coll., 1924; m. Eleanor Armstrong, June 5, 1907; children—Dorothy, Lois, Ernest Milton. Instr. pub. speaking, U. of Ill., 1906-07, asso., 1907-12; ordained Congl. ministry, 1913; pastor Ocean Av. Ch., Brooklyn, 1913-22; gen. sec. Congl. Ch. Extension Bds., 1922-37; gen. sec. Bd. of Home Missions, Extension Div., since 1937; pres. Home Missions Council, 1935-36. Mem. Phi Beta Kappa, Delta Sigma Rho, Phi Alpha Delta. Home: Crestwood Drive, Mountain Lakes, N.J. Postoffice address: Denville, N.J. Office: 287 4th Av., New York, N.Y.

HALLIDAY, William Reeder, asso. prof. machine design; b. South Orange, N.J., Nov. 27, 1879; s. William Stirling and Mary Louise (Pierson) H.; M.E., Stevens Inst. Tech., 1902; grad. study, Purdue U. Sch. Engring. Teachers, summer 1929; m. Jane G. Caskey, Morristown, N.J., Feb. 13, 1907; 1 dau., Louise Reeder. Instr. Stevens Inst. Tech., 1902; labor foreman, Ill. Steel Co., S.Chicago, Ill., 1902-03; engring. asst., Continuous Rail Joint Co., Newark, N.J. and Rail Joint Co., New York, N.Y., 1903-05; instr. machine design, Stevens Inst. Tech., 1905-09, asst. prof. same, 1909-24, asso. prof. since 1924; consulting engr. since 1924. Served as mem. Bd. Edn., Morristown, N.J., 1909-15; mem. bd. dirs. Morristown Y.M.C.A. Mem. Am. Soc. Mech. Engrs., Soc. for Promotion Engring. Edn., Morris Co. Engrs. Club, Morristown Y.M.C.A. Republican. Presbyn. Home: 11 Altamont Ct., Morristown, N.J. Office: Stevens Inst. Technology, Hoboken, N.J.

HALLMAN, Ernest Clifton, minister; b. Chesapeake City, Md., Jan. 13, 1886; s. Samuel Allen and Annie Florence (Jenness) H.; student Chesapeake City (Md.) High Sch., 1900-04, Wilmington (Del.) Conf. Acad., 1904-05; A.B., Ph.B., Taylor U., Upland, Ind., 1909; m. May Taylor, Sept. 9, 1909; children—Raymond Wilson, Harold Taylor. Methodist minister, Millgrove, Ind., 1909-12, Dublin and Lewisville, Ind., 1912-14, Lynn and Spartansburg, Ind., 1915-18, Ocean View, Del., 1920-23, Tangier Island, Va., 1923-27, Berlin, Md., 1927-30, Brandywine Ch., Wilmington, Del., 1930-32, Denton, Md., 1932-34; dist. supt., Middletown Dist., Wilmington Conf. 1934-35, Dover Dist., 1935-39, Laurel (Del.) Dist. since 1939. Chmn. Delegation to Columbus Gen. Conf., 1936; mem. exec. com. Bd. of Foreign Missions. Mem. bd. trustees Wesley Collegiate Inst., Methodist Hist. Socs. (1st v.p. since 1935), Wilmington Conf. Hist. Soc. (pres. since 1923). Methodist. Mason (Royal Arch). Author: Brief History of the Wilmington Conference, 1939; Privateers, Pirates and the Peninsula, 1934; The Web of Life, 1923. Address: Laurel, Del.

HALLOWELL, A(lfred) Irving, anthropologist; b. Phila., Pa., Dec. 28, 1892; s. Edgar Lloyd and Dorothy (Edsall) H.; grad. Northeast High Sch., Phila., 1910; B.S., U. of Pa., 1914, A.M., 1920, Ph.D., 1924; m. Dorothy Kern, July 1, 1919; 1 son, William Kern. Social work, Phila., 1914-22; instr. in anthropology, Univ. of Pa., 1923-28, asst. prof., 1928-36, prof. since 1939. Mem. Am. Folk Lore Soc.

(vice-pres.), Phila. Anthropol. Soc. (vice-pres.). Am. Anthropol. Assn. (past sec.), Société des Americanistes de Paris. Contbr. to Am. Anthropologist, Am. Jour. Psychiatry, Jour. Am. Folk Lore, Am. Jour. Social Psychology, etc. Home: 319 Winona Av. Office: Bennett Hall, Univ. of Pennsylvania, Philadelphia, Pa.

HALLOWELL, Henry Richardson, investment banking; b. Phila., Pa., Aug. 12, 1898; s. John Wallace and Bertinia (Essen) H.; grad. William Penn Charter Sch., 1915; A.B., Yale, 1919; m. Dorothy Saylor, June 25, 1919; children—Henry Richardson, Dorothy Saylor, Bertinia, John Wallace III. With George H. McFadden & Bro., cotton merchants, Phila., 1919-21, agt. New Bedford, Mass., 1921-25; owner Henry R. Hallowell & Son, retail fruit merchants, Phila., 1925-30; salesman Lee, Higginson & Co., investment bankers, Phila., 1931-32, Bryan, Penington & Colket, investment bankers, 1933-37; mgr. investment dept. Eastman, Dillon & Co., Phila., since 1937; pres. Exchange Cold Storage Co.; dir. The Real Estate Trust Co. of Phila. Served in U.S. Navy, 1918. Dir. Broad St. Hosp., Phila.; dir. Chestnut St. Assn., Phila. Mem. Alpha Delta Phi. Republican. Presbyterian. Clubs: Union League, Phila. Country, Yale (Phila.). Home: "Berberrie," Merion Station. Office: 225 S. 15th St., Philadelphia, Pa.

HALLOWELL, Howard Thomas, pres. Standard Pressed Steel Co.; b. Hallowell, Pa., June 30, 1877; s. William J. and Anna (Thomas) H.; ed. Friends Sch. and Spring Garden Inst.; m. Blanche Nice, Oct. 28, 1905; children—Howard Thomas, Ruth Nice. Worked on farm until 1903; organized, 1903, and since pres. Standard Pressed Steel Co.; dir. Jenkintown Bank & Trust Co. Club: Old York Road Country. Has invented many items. Address: Jenkintown, Pa.

HALPERN, Leon Albert, dentist; b. Phila., Pa., June 29, 1890; s. Harry L. and Sara Leah (Girdany) H.; grad. Central High Sch., Phila.; D.D.S., Phila. Dental Coll. (dental school of Temple U.), 1914; graduate Dewey Sch. of Orthodontia, 1928; m. Dorothy Adelson, Aug. 27, 1916. In practice of dentistry, Phila., since 1914; instr. operative dentistry, Temple U., 1914-28, instr. in orthodontics, 1928-32, asso. prof. of operative dentistry since 1932. Served as 1st lt. Dental Officers Reserve, 1917-37. Mem. Gen. Alumni Assn. of Temple U. (pres. since 1937), Dental Alumni of Temple U. (past pres.), N.Phila. Assn. of Dental Surgeons (past pres.), Eastern Dental Soc. of Phila., Phila. County Dental Soc., Pa. Dental Soc., Am. Dental Assn., Psi Omega, Omicron Kappa Upsilon, Blue Key. Republican. Clubs: Manufacturers and Bankers (Phila.); Anglers (Margate, N.J.). Home: 5401 Lebanon Av., Philadelphia, Pa.

HALPRIN, Harry, physician; b. Russia, May 6, 1900; s. Samuel and Esther (Blecker) H.; came to U.S., 1910, naturalized, 1921; ed. Coll. City of N.Y., 1917-18, Columbia U., 1918-19; M.D., N.Y. Univ. & Bellevue Hosp. Med. Coll., 1923; m. Adelaide Oshrowitz, Mar. 29, 1925; children—Arthur Edward, Doris Pearl. Interne, Mountainside Hosp., Montclair, N.J., 1923-24, resident phys., 1924-25; in pvt. practice, Caldwell, N.J., since 1925, specializing in cardiology; asso. attdg. phys., chief of cardiac clinic, Mountainside Hosp.; cons. cardiologist, Essex Co. Isolation Hosp., Belleville, and Montclair Community Hosp., Montclair. Mem. Bd. Health, Caldwell, N.J.; sch. phys., Essex Fells, N.J. Pres. Jewish League of Caldwell, N.J. Fellow Am. Coll. Phys. Mem. Am. Med. Assn., Am. Heart Assn., Med. Soc. N.J., Essex Co. Med. Assn., Asso. Phys. of Montclair and Vicinity. Jewish religion. Mason. Elk. Club: Athletic (Caldwell); Caldwell-West Essex Kiwanis. Home: 8 Washburn Pl., Caldwell, N.J.

HALUSKA, John J., state senator; b. Cannonsburgh, Pa., May 9, 1902; s. John E. and Mary (Palko) H.; ed. high sch.; m. Anna P. Flesher, Jan. 26, 1924; children—Loretta, Gladys, J. Thomas. Pres. Patton Fire Co., 1925-30, Standard Motor Supply Co. since 1927, Motor Battery Mfg. Co. since 1930, Union Ins. Agency since 1936; v.p. First Nat. Bank of Patton since 1935. Mem. Patton Borough Council, 1932-34; burgess Patton Borough, 1934-38; mem. Pa. Ho. of Rep., 1935-37, Pa. State Senate since 1936. Trustee Spangler Hosp. since 1929. Democrat. Catholic. Moose, Eagle. Home: 413 Beech Av. Office: 413 Lang Av., Patton, Pa.

HAM, Ernest Leighton, hotel mgr.; b. Dresden, Me., June 11, 1893; s. Orrin LeForest and Effie Janet (Blinn) H.; ed. Bliss Business Coll. and U. of Pittsburgh; m. Jessie Lee Black, Sept. 23, 1920; 1 dau., Marjorie Louise. Dist. mgr. Mills Tea & Butter Corpn., Boston, 1914-17; sec.-treas. Guarantee Visible Sales Co., 1920-23; comptroller and asst. to pres. Guarantee Liquid Measure Co., Rochester, Pa., 1923-28; gen. mgr. Wayne Pump Co., 1928-31; engaged privately in income tax and accounting work, 1931-34; mgr. The Penn-Beaver Hotel, Rochester, Pa., since 1934; dir. Beaver Valley Community Hotel Co., Beaver Valley Hotel Equipment Co. Served as regt. sergt. major, Gen. Hdqrs., A.E.F., during World War. Dir. Rochester Gen. Hosp.; mem. bd. and sec. Salvation Army. Mem. Am. Hotel Assn., Pa. Hotels Assn., Hotel Greeters of America, Am. Legion. Republican. Episcopalian. Clubs: Rotary, American Turnerbund. Home: 218 Washington St. Office: Penn-Beaver Hotel, Rochester, Pa.

HAM, William Felton, public utilities; b. Lewistown, Me., Mar. 15, 1870; s. John Stockbridge Patten and Abigail Lincoln (Stetson) H.; student Bates Coll., Lewistown, 1891; m. Suzanne Mulford, Oct. 10, 1899. Entered pub. utility business, 1895; chmn. bd. Potomac Electric Power Co. Mem. Soc. Mayflower Descendants, S.R. Clubs: Metropolitan, Chevy Chase; Blue Ridge Rod and Gun (Va.); Alfalfa, Bay Head Yacht; Laurentian (Can.); Old Guard Society, Palm Beach, Fla. Home: 2621 Woodley Pl., Washington, D.C.; (summer) Bay Head, N.J.; and Turner, Me. Office: 10th and E Sts. N.W., Washington, D.C.

HAM, William Ross, physicist; b. Lewiston, Me., Feb. 10, 1879; s. John Lowell and Emily (Ford) H.; B.A., Bates Coll., Lewiston, Me., 1901; Ph.D., U. of Chicago, 1909; m. J. Elizabeth Dunmore, July 1908; children—Priscilla, John L. and Frank (twins), Nelson. Prof. physics, Pa. State Coll., since 1909, also head of dept. Capt. Ordnance Dept., U.S.A., June 1917-June 1919; maj. O.R.C., 1925. Mem. Am. Phys. Soc., Phi Beta Kappa, Sigma Xi, Phi Kappa Phi, Alpha Tau Omega. Wrote papers on polarization of Röntgen rays, depth of complete scattering of kathode rays, absorption in the ultra violet, relation between vapor tension and temperature, design of stereobinoculars (patents), reflection of electrons, energy of high velocity electrons, variation of photoelectric effect with temperature, equations of thermionic emission, diffusion of gases through metals. Club: Cosmos. Home: Boalsburg, Pa. Address: State College, Pa.*

HAMBLEN, Emily Stockbridge, writer; b. Hoboken Heights (now Jersey City), N.J., June 22, 1864; d. Eleazer and Nancy Emily (Woodhouse) H.; student Grammar Sch. No. 6, Jersey City, N.J., 1872-78, high sch., Jersey City, 1878-82; unmarried. Exec. of social service work, Norwich Conn., 1907-09; dir. ednl. work, Bur. of Social Service, Newark, N.J., 1909-10; exec. sec. Pub. Welfare Com. of Essex Co., N.J., 1911-13; dir. edn. and extension under State Bur. of Child Hygiene, N.J., 1918-20. Author: Friedrich Nietzsche and His New Gospel, 1911; On the Minor Prophecies of William Blake (London and New York), 1929; The Book of Job Interpreted; Illustrated with the Designs of William Blake, 1939. Home: care H. B. Timbrook, Stanhope, N.J. Office: 44 W. 56th St., New York, N.Y.

HAMBLIN, Adolph P.; football coach W.Va. State Coll. Address: W.Va. State College, Institute, W.Va.

HAMBLOCK, Leonard Charles, physician; b. Phila., Pa., Oct. 19, 1899; s. J. Charles and Kathrin (Schmid) H.; A.B., U. of Pa., 1921, M.D., 1925; m. Helen Koehler, Mar. 28, 1923. Interne Methodist Hosp., 1925-27; in practice as physician, Phila., since 1927; obstetrician and gynecologist in chief Meth. Episcopal Hosp., Phila., since 1937. Served in S.A.T.C. during World War. Fellow Am. Coll. Surgeons, A.M.A.; mem. Pa. State Med. Soc., Coll. of Physicians of Phila., Phila. Co. Med. Soc., Phila. Obstet. Soc., Am. Congress on Gynecology and Obstetrics, A.A.A.S., Med. Club of Phila., Phi Chi, Acacia. Mason (32°). Club: Union League (Phila.). Address: 2230 S. Broad St., Philadelphia, Pa.

HAMBURGER, Louis Philip, M.D.; b. Baltimore, Md., Sept. 18, 1873; s. Philip and Rachel (Bernei) H.; student Md. Coll. of Pharmacy, 1888-89; A.B., Johns Hopkins, 1893, M.D., 1897; grad. student U. of Berlin, 1898-99; m. Freda Rose Hamburger, Sept. 20, 1903; children—Louis Philip, Frederic. Began as physician, 1899; asso. in medicine, Johns Hopkins Med. Sch.; consultant Baltimore City Health Dept. since 1937; attending physician Johns Hopkins Hosp., Union Memorial Hosp., Sinai Hosp., Hosp. for Women of Md., Church Home and Infirmary, Bon Secours, Children's Hosp. Sch., West Baltimore Gen. Hosp. Mem. Med. Milk Commn.; mem. com. of revision of U.S. Pharmacopœia for Edition X, 1926. Mem. bd. dirs. Baltimore Chapter Am. Red Cross since 1939. Fellow Am. Coll. Physicians; mem. A.M.A., Southern Med. Soc., Baltimore City Med. Soc. (pres. 1931-32), Johns Hopkins Med. Soc. (pres. 1934-35), Md. Med. and Chirurg. Faculty, Am. Assn. Univ. Profs., A.A.A.S., Phi Beta Kappa. Democrat. Club: Johns Hopkins (Baltimore), University, Suburban. Contbr. to The Practitioners Library, 1937; also articles on internal medicine to jours. Home: 1207 Eutaw Place, Baltimore, Md.

HAMER, Alfred, organist; b. Bury, Eng., Jan. 6, 1898; s. Lewis and Annie (Robertshaw) H.; brought to U.S., 1905, naturalized, 1909; ed. pub. sch. and high sch., New Bedford, Mass.; mus. ed. N.E. Conservatory of Music, Boston, 1916-21, grad. with spl. honors, 1921; m. Victoria F. Hayward, May 27, 1925; 1 son, John Hayward. Began career as soloist in boy choir, 1911; organist and choirmaster, Ch. of the Messiah, Boston, Mass.; studied in Paris, France, with Ch. M. Widor, Andre Gedalge, 1921-23; organist and choir master, Ch. of the Advent, Boston; organist and choirmaster, Trinity Cathedral, Pittsburgh, Pa., since 1925; conductor of oratorios, choral socs. Served in U.S. Marines during World War. Mem. Sinfonia. Republican. Episcopalian. Mason. Home: 32 Elmwood St., Crafton, Pittsburgh, Pa.

HAMILL, James A., ex-congressman; b. Jersey City, N.J., Mar. 30, 1877; B.A., St. Peter's Coll., N.J., 1897; M.A., 1898, LL.D., 1912; LL.B., N.Y. Law Sch., 1899. Admitted to bar, 1900, and since in practice at Jersey City; admitted to bar of U.S. Supreme Court, 1918, N.Y. bar, 1922. Mem. N.J. Assembly, 4 terms, 1902-06; mem. 60th to 62d Congresses (1907-13), 10th N.J. Dist. and 63d to 66th Congresses (1913-21), 12th Dist.; then 1st asst. corpn. counsel of City of Jersey City, later corpn. counsel. Mem. New York Co. Lawyers Assn., Hudson Co. (N.J.) Bar Assn. Chevalier of French Legion of Honor. Democrat. Address: 239 Washington St., Jersey City, N.J.*

HAMILL, Samuel McClintock, pediatrician; b. Oak Hall, Pa., Nov. 3, 1864; s. Robert and Margaret E. (Lyon) H.; student Princeton, 1886; M.D., U. of Pa., 1888; m. Lila Clarke Kennedy, Apr. 17, 1895; children—Kennedy, Samuel McClintock, Hugh Maxwell. Practiced in Phila. since 1890; demonstrator physical diagnosis, 1892-94, instr. medicine, 1894-1901, U. of Pa.; prof. diseases of children, Phila. Polyclinic and Coll. for Graduates in Medicine, 1901-19; prof. same, Post-Graduate Department of Medicine, U. of Pa., 1919-20; consulting pediatrician, Presbyn. Hosp.; formerly visiting pediatrician to St. Christopher's Hosp. for Children and Phila. Polyclinic; chmn. sect. I, med. service, and chmn. follow-up com. of sect. I, White House Conference on Child Health and Protection. Mem. bd. mgrs. Babies' Hospital of Philadelphia. Mem. executive com. of Pa. mental hygiene com. of Public Charities Assn. Mem. Am. Med. Assn. (chmn. sect. on diseases of children, 1911), Am. Academy Pediatrics (pres. 1932), Am. Pediatric Soc. (pres. 1913-14), Med. Soc. State of Pa. (1st chmn. sect. on pediatrics), Phila. Pediatric Soc. (pres. 1901-02), Phila. Pathol. and Neurol. socs., Coll. of Physicians of Philadelphia. Chmn.

Pennsylvania Emergency Child Health Com.; mem. Gen. Med. Bd. and chmn. Nat. Child Welfare Com. of Council Nat. Defense; dir. child welfare for State of Pa., 1917-18; del. Cannes Med. Conf. of Red Cross Socs., 1919; pres. dirs. of Phila. Child Health Soc.; mem. Am. Assn. Study and Prevention Infant Mortality (pres. 1915-16), Am. Child Health Assn. (pres. 1931-35); former mem. trustees Lawrenceville Sch. Republican. Presbyn. Club: University. Home: 1822 Spruce St., Philadelphia, Pa.

HAMILL, William Howard, utilities exec.; b. Phila., Pa., July 26, 1904; s. William Danenberg and Gertrude Janet (Dasch) H.; student Germantown High Sch., Phila., 1918-22; diploma in constrn. engring., Drexel Inst. Evening Sch., Phila., 1927; m. Edith Long, Jan. 1, 1929; children—William Howard, Robert Charles. Began as stenographer, Phila., 1922; mgr. Williamstown Gas Co., Lykens, Pa., 1928-30; mgr. Crisfield (Md.) Light & Power Co., 1930, v.p. since 1936; mgr. Watertown (S.D.) Gas Co., 1931-34, Montana Dakota Power Co., Valley City, N.D., 1934-36. Congregationalist. Club: Rotary (Crisfield, Md.; pres. elect, 1939). Home: 203 N. Somerset Av. Office: 323 W. Main St., Crisfield, Md.

HAMILTON, Bryan, county supt. of schools; b. Elkwater, W.Va., Set. 15, 1896; s. Alexander Z. and Bernice (Bell) H.; B.S., Davis-Elkins Coll., 1923, A.B., 1925; A.M., W.Va. U., 1927, grad. study, 1938; m. Irene Lucille Moore, July 4, 1934. Teacher graded sch., Randolph Co., W.Va., 1918-23; high sch. teacher, Randolph Co., 1925-26; teacher of summer terms, Davis Elkins Coll., Elkins, 1928-33; elected county supt. of schs., Randolph County, W.Va., 1926, re-elected, 1930, apptd., 1935 and 1937; sec. Bd. of Edn., Randolph Co. Served in U.S. Army, 1918. Mem. N.E.A., W.Va. State Edn. Assn., County Supts. Orgn. of W.Va., Y.M.C.A., Am. Legion, 40 and 8, Chi Beta Phi, Alpha Sigma Phi. Democrat. Presbyterian (elder). Mason (32°, Shriner), Odd Fellow, K.P., Elk. Clubs: Rotary, Rod and Gun, Business Men's Assn. (Elkins); Masonic (Wheeling, W.Va.). Author of several articles published in hist. mags. and ednl. jours. Home: 136 Buffalo St., Elkins, W.Va.

HAMILTON, Charles Walter, oil executive; b. Ithaca, Mich., Apr. 8, 1890; s. Edward D. and Ella (Weidman) H.; grad. Ithaca Pub. Sch., 1908; student Alma (Mich.) Coll., 1908-09, Mil. Sch., Highland Falls, N.Y., 3 mos., 1909; A.B., U. of Okla., 1912; post-grad. study U. of Chicago, 6 mos., 1915; m. Irene Lucile Stroup, Oct. 26, 1916; children—Robert Dyer, Irene Elizabeth, Charles Walter (Jr.), Jean. With U.S. and Okla. Geol. Survey in Northeastern Okla., summer, 1910; U.S. Geol. Survey, N.D. and Mont., summer, 1911; asst. in Okla. Geol. Survey, offices, 1910-12; geologist Cia Mexicana de Petroleo, El Aguila, S.A., 1912-15; Roma Oil Co., Okla. and Kan., 1915-16; chief geologist Mexican Gulf Oil Co., Mexico, 1916-17; gen. agent Mexican Gulf Oil Co., Mexico, 1917-22; asst. to v.p., Gulf Oil Corpn., New York Production Div., N.Y. City, since 1923; pres. and dir. Danish American Prospecting Co. Mem. Am. Petroleum Inst., Am. Inst. Mining & Metall. Engrs., Am. Assn. Petroleum Geologists, Beta Theta Pi. Republican. Conglist. (pres. bd. trustees Union Ch., upper Montclair, N.J.). Clubs: Whitehall (N.Y. City); Deer Lake (nr. Boonton, N.J.); Upper Montclair (N.J.) Country. Home: 310 Highland Av., Upper Montclair, N.J. Office: 17 Battery Pl., New York, N.Y.

HAMILTON, Clyde Carney, entomologist; b. Salina, Kan., June 24, 1890; s. James Edward and Anna Elizabeth (Carney) H.; B.S., Kan. State Agrl. Coll., 1913; M.S., U. of Ill., 1916; grad. study, Cornell U., 1916-17, Ph.D., same, 1929; m. Vida M. Hawkins, Dec. 25, 1918; children—Rachel Jane, Carol Elizabeth. Asst. entomologist, Bur. of Entomology, U.S. Dept. Agr., 1917-18; extension entomologist, U. of Mo., 1918-19; asso. entomologist, U. of Md., 1920-25; asso. entomologist, N.J. Agr. Expt. Sta., asso. prof. entomology, Rutgers U., New Brunswick, N.J., since 1925. Mem. Entomol. Soc. of America, Nat. Shade Tree Conf. (pres. 1936-37), Am. Assn. Econ. Entomologists (chmn. Eastern Branch, 1938-39), Gamma Alpha, Sigma Xi. Republican. Presbyn. Mason. Kiwanian. Home: 616 S. 1st Av., Highland Park, N.J.

HAMILTON, Dewey Dallas, M.D., surgeon; b. Mannington, W.Va., Mar. 17, 1898; s. Dr. Millard F. and Bessie Lee (Bassnett) H.; student U. of W.Va., 1917-20, U. of Md., 1920-21; M.D., U. Electric Med. Coll., Cincinnati, O., 1925; m. Margaret Jeannette Morgan, Sept. 6, 1922; children—Thomas Millard, Jane Dallette. Interne City Hosp., Cincinnati, 1924-25; physician and surgeon, Cincinnati, O., 1925-27, Mannington, W.Va., since 1927; mem. staff Cook's Hosp., Fairmont, W.Va., since 1927; dir. Marion (W.Va.) County Hosp. Service. Served U.S. Army, World War. Pres. The George Washington Foundation, Berkeley Springs, W.Va. Mem. W.Va. State Med. Soc., Marion County Med. Soc., Phi Sigma Kappa, Mu Sigma Mu. Presbyterian. Mason. Home: 218 Market St. Office: 17 Market St., Mannington, W.Va.

HAMILTON, Francis Marion, prof. psychology, retired; b. Wells Co., Ind., Jan. 21, 1867; s. William Marshall and Mary Elizabeth (Beatty) H.; A.B., Ind. Univ., 1897, A.M., 1901; fellow U. of Chicago, 1903-05; Ph.D., Columbia U., 1907; m. Margaret Porch, June 16, 1904; 1 dau., Margaret Porch (dec.). Engaged in teaching, co. schs., Ind., 1887-95; asst. in psychology, Ind. Univ., 1897-98; asst. edn. dir., Central Y.M. C.A., Chicago, 1898-99; instr. psychology and edn., O. State U., 1899-1901; prof. psychology and edn., Wis. State Normal Sch., Platteville, 1901-03; asst. in psychology, Columbia U., 1906-07; prof. psychology and edn., N.Y. Training Sch. for Teachers, 1906-32, head of dept., 1911-32, retired, 1932. Mem. A.A.A.S., Am. Psychol. Assn., Sigma Xi. Independent Democrat. Conglist. Home: Leonia, N.J.

HAMILTON, Frank Watrous, pres. Ulster Iron Works; b. Groton, Conn., Dec. 14, 1886; s. Thomas and Eunice Ellen (Watrous) H.; student Norwich (Conn.) Free Acad., 1901-05; Ph.B., Sheffield Scientific Sch., Yale, 1908, E.M., Grad. Sch., 1910; post-grad. work Lehigh U., Bethlehem, Pa., 1908-09; m. Evelyn Hislop, Dec. 6, 1916; children—Frank Watrous, John Hislop. Shop apprentice, Jr. engr., sales engr. Lidgenwood Mfg. Co., New York, 1910-14; pres. Lyme Power Co., New London, Conn., 1914-17; mgr., v.p. Ulster Iron Works (founded 1827), Dover, N.J., 1919-26, pres. since 1926 and now principal owner; pres. Ulster Realty Co., Dover, N.J., since 1926; dir. Nat. Union Bank, Dover. Served successively as 1st lt., cap. and maj. comdg. 2d Bn., 304th Engrs. in France, U.S. Army, 1917-19. Pres. Dover (N.J.) Bd. of Edn. since 1930; pres. and trustee Morris Co. (N.J.) Y.M.C.A. since 1935; trustee Morris Co., W.Y.C.A. since 1939; mem. bd. mgrs. Shougurn Sanitorium. Mem. Delta Psi (Yale); former mem. Am. Iron & Steel Inst. Mason. Club: Yale (New York). Home: 35 Ann St. Office: Care Ulster Iron Works, Dover, N.J.

HAMILTON, George E., v.p. and ednl. dir. Keystone View Co.; b. Greenville, O., Mar. 18, 1882; s. Daniel and Barbara (Wilcox) H.; B.A., Earlham Coll., 1906; Rhodes scholar, Oxford U., 1904-07 (completed M.A. examinations); m. Daisy Cox; children—James C., George S., Robert C., Betty (dec.). Head dept. of Latin and in charge of athletics, Richmond (Ind.) High Sch., 1908-10; asst. mgr. D. C. Heath & Co., Chicago, 1910-19; salesman Keystone View Co., Chicago, 1919-24, ednl. dir., Meadville (Pa.) office, 1924-28; v.p. and ednl. dir. since 1928. Mem. Meadville Round Table. Episcopalian (sr. warden Christ Ch.). Mason. Club: Rotary. Author of widely used text materials in visual instruction. Home: 700 Chestnut St. Office: Keystone View Co., Meadville, Pa.

HAMILTON, Harry D(avid), lawyer; b. Washington Co., Pa., Jan. 21, 1874; s. Alexander T. and Sarah Samantha (Camp) H.; grad. Pittsburgh High Sch., 1895; A.B., and A.M., Washington and Jefferson Coll., 1899; LL.B., Western U. of Pa. (now U. of Pittsburgh), 1902; m. Mabel Hood, June 3, 1903; 1 dau., Elizabeth Hamilton (Mrs. J. Frank Cary). Admitted to Pa. bar, 1902, and since in gen. practice, Washington; senior mem. firm Hamilton & Pipes since 1917; dir., vice-pres. and gen. counsel Washington County Fire Ins. Co. Mem. City Council, Washington, 1912-32. Trustee Citizens Library, Washington. Mem. Washington Co., Pa. State and Am. bar assns., Phi Delta Phi. Republican. Presbyterian. Mason (32°, Shriner). Club: Bassett (Washington). Home: 262 Locust Av. Office: Washington Trust Bldg., Washington, Pa.

HAMILTON, Henry Alexander, school prin. and supt.; b. Elkwater, W.Va., July 17, 1904; s. Alexander Z. and Bernice (Bell) H.; A.B., Davis and Elkins Coll., 1929; A.M., W.Va. U., 1933; m. Bessie Zickefoose, Sept. 5, 1924; children—Milton Holmes, Le Moyne Lindbergh. Rural school teacher, Randolph County, W.Va., 1921-23; prin. Elkwater, Mill Creek and Third Ward, Elkins (W.Va.) elementary schools, 1923-33; prin. Adolph (W.Va.) High Sch., 1926-28, Elkins Jr. High Sch., 1933-36, and dir. elementary schs. in Randolph County, 1933-36; prin. Elkins High Sch., dir. high schs. in Randolph County since 1936. Mem. N.E.A., W.Va. Edn. Assn., Nat. and W.Va. Secondary Sch. Prins. Assns., Chi Beta Phi, Kappa Delta Pi. Democrat. Presbyterian. Mason, K. of P. Club: Rotary. Contbr. professional articles to jours. Home: 106 First St., Elkins, W.Va.

HAMILTON, Hughbert Clayton, prof. psychology; b. Cedar Rapids, Ia., Mar. 6, 1903; s. Leslie S. and Hattie Belle (Clayton) H.; A.B., Cornell Coll., Mount Vernon, Ia., 1925; A.M., Columbia U., 1926, Ph.D., same, 1929; m. Edna Louise Haas, May 16, 1927. Engaged as asst. in psychology, Barnard Coll., 1927-28; instr. in psychology, Temple U., Phila., Pa., 1928-32, asst. prof., 1932-38, asso. prof. psychology since 1938. Mem. Am. Psychol. Assn., Eastern Psychol. Assn., Sigma Xi. Roberts Fellow at Columbia Univ. Methodist. Club: Manufacturers and Bankers (Philadelphia). Office: Temple University, Philadelphia, Pa.

HAMILTON, James W(allace), lawyer; b. Pittsburgh, Pa., Nov. 30, 1884; s. John M. and Mary Ann (Wallace) H.; student Park Inst., 1899-1902; A.B., Kenyon Coll., 1906; m. Stella Mabel DeVeny, Oct. 12, 1920; 1 dau., Martha Ann. Admitted to Pa. bar, 1911, and began practice at Pittsburgh; with Carnegie Steel Co. since 1912, as atty., 1912-30, sec. and dir. since 1930 (company now known as Carnegie-Ill. Steel Corpn.); sec. and dir. Carnegie Land Co., Pittsburgh Limestone Corpn.; sec. Carnegie Natural Gas Co., Pa. & Lake Erie Dock Co., Pittsburgh and Conneaut Dock Co.; dir. U.S. Steel & Carnegie Pension Fund. Mem. Alpha Delta Phi. Republican. Presbyterian. Clubs: Duquesne, University (Pittsburgh); Shannopin Country (Ben Avon). Home: 6934 Church St., Ben Avon, Pa. Office: Carnegie Bldg., Pittsburgh, Pa.

HAMILTON, J(ohn) Taylor, bishop; b. Antigua, W.I., Apr. 30, 1859; s. Rev. Alan and Jane (Taylor) H.; prep. edn. Moravian boarding sch., Fulneck, Eng.; grad. Moravian Coll., Pa., 1875, Moravian Theol. Seminary, 1877; D.D., Lafayette College, 1901; L.H.D., from Moravian College, 1928; m. Cecelia Elizabeth Beck, June 7, 1886; children—Mrs. Constance Beck. Martin, Arthur Beck, Kenneth Gardiner. Teacher Nazareth Hall, 1877-81; pastor Second Moravian Ch., Phila., 1881-86; resident prof. Moravian Coll. and Theol. Sem., 1886-1903; mem. Moravian Mission Bd., Herrnhut, Germany, 1903; bishop of the Moravian Church since 1905; pres. gen. executive bd. of Moravian Ch., 1914-32; pres. Moravian Coll. and Theological Seminary, 1918-1928; pres. emeritus since 1928. Associate editor The Moravian, 1883-1893, sole editor, 1893-94 and 1897-99; mem. administrative bd. Moravian Ch. N., 1898-1903; sec. Soc. for Propagating the Gospel, 1886-98 and 1902, 03. Author: History of the Moravian Church in the United States (Am. Church History series), 1895; A History of the Moravian Church During the Eighteenth and Nineteenth Centuries, 1900; A History of Moravian Missions, 1901; Twenty Years of Pioneer Missions in Nyassaland, 1912; The Recognition of the Episcopate of the Moravian Ch. by Act of Parliament, in 1749, 1925; The Contacts of the Moravian Church with the Iroquois League, 1931. Home: 1444 Main St., Bethlehem, Pa.

HAMILTON, Milton Wheaton, coll. prof.; b. Fabius, N.Y., July 8, 1901; s. William Levi and Annie Belle (Wheaton) H.; student Fabius (N.Y.) secondary schs. and high sch., 1907-19, Central High Sch., Syracuse, N.Y., 1919-20; A.B. (cum laude), Syracuse (N.Y.) U., 1924, A.M., 1925; Ph.D., Columbia U., 1936; m. Margaret Lydia Gatchel, Aug. 30, 1927; children—Gwendolyn Lucille, Mary Elizabeth. Asst. in history, Syracuse U., 1924-25; prof. history, Albright Coll., Reading, Pa., since 1926. Mem. 5th Seminar in Mexico, Mexico City, 1930, summer session in internat. law, U. of Michigan, 1936. Mem. Am. Hist. Assn., N.Y. State Hist. Assn., Miss. Valley Hist. Assn., Fgn. Policy Assn., Pa. Hist. Assn., Hist. Soc. of Berks Co., Am. Assn. Univ. Profs. Alpha Chi Rho, Pi Gamma Mu. Republican. Author: The Spread of the Newspaper Press in N.Y. before 1830, 1933; The Country Printer, New York State, 1785-1830, 1936; Thurlow Weed's Nemesis in Norwich, 1938; contbr. articles for Dictionary of Am. History (forthcoming), book revs. in hist. jours. Home: 1722 N. 16th St. Office: Albright College, Reading Pa.

HAMILTON, Willard I., life ins.; b. Cleveland, O., Aug. 2, 1867; s. Edward L. and Sarah C. (Lum) H.; grad. Newark (N.J.) Acad., 1885; m. Lettie Thompson, Apr. 9, 1896 (died 1923); children—Ethel Hamilton, Raymond L., Stuart W.; m. 2d, Cornelia F. Foster, Mar. 16, 1927. With Prudential Life Ins. Co., 1885-1937, sec. 1912-37, v.p., 1918-37; now pres. Haskell Improvement Co., Inc. Pres. N.J. Chamber Commerce since 1924; chmn. bd. N.J. Water Policy Commn., 1925-1934; mem. N.J. Bd. of Agr., 1928-29. Republican. Presbyn. Clubs: Lake Valhalla Country (N.J.); Bald Peak Country (N.H.). Home: 71 Durand Rd., Maplewood, N.J.

HAMILTON, William Juél, mfr.; b. Albany, N.Y., Dec. 17, 1867; s. William August and Amanda Jane (Juél) H.; student Albany Boys Acad., 1875-84; M.E., Stevens Inst. Tech., Hoboken, N.J., 1889; m. Blodwyn May Joseph, Dec. 1, 1930. With Hendrik Mfg. Co., perforators and steel fabricators, since 1889, successively draftsman, purchasing agent, mech. engr., supt. constrn., and since 1910 sec. and dir.; sec. and dir. Hendrick Engring. Co.; v.p. & dir. Pioneer Dime Bank, Carbondale, Pa. Mem. Am. Soc. Mech. Engrs., Delta Tau Delta. Republican. Episcopalian. Clubs: Elkview Country (Carbondale); Scranton (Scranton); Engineers (New York). Home: 70 Lincoln Av. Office: 52 Dundaff St., Carbondale, Pa.

HAMILTON, William Thomas, lawyer; b. Hagerstown, Md., July 15, 1867; s. William Thomas and Clara (Jenness) H.; student St. James (Md.) Coll., 1881-83, St. Paul's Sch., 1883-85, Univ. of Munich, Germany, 1893-98; studied law in father's office, 1886 to 1888; m. Mary V. Jamison, Nov. 9, 1907; children—Mavin (Mrs. Eli Huston Brown III), Julia (Mrs. James Spencer Lee). Admitted to Md. bar, 1899, and since in gen. practice of law at Hagerstown, Md.; retired from active practice of law, 1924, to devote time to writing. Pres. Washington Co. Free Library; sec. Washington Co. Mus. Fine Arts. Democrat. Episcopalian. Author: Three Stages, Critical Essays, Clorinda Thorbald; contbr. articles to newspapers. Home: 175 S. Prospect St., Hagerstown, Md.

HAMLET, Harry Gabriel, rear adm., U.S. Coast Guard, retired; b. Eastport, Me., Aug. 27, 1874; s. Oscar Charles and Annie (Holland) H.; student Mass. Inst. Tech., 1892-93; grad. U.S. Coast Guard Acad., 1896; m. Francel Allen Hastings, Apr. 26, 1905; 1 dau., Jean Hastings. Ensign, Apr. 27, 1896; promoted through grades to rear-adm., comdt., June 14, 1932. Awarded Gold Life Saving Medal (U.S.); Silver Star (U.S.N.). Mem. Mil. Order World War, Am. Legion, National Sojourners Cararabao (foreign service order), Vets. Fgn. Wars, Sigma Alpha Epsilon, Pi Gamma Mu. Episcopalian. Mason (32°), Elk. Clubs: Army and Navy (Washington); Army and Navy (Chicago); Army and Navy (San Francisco); Columbia Country (Md.); Jibboom (New London, Conn.). Home: Port Townsend, Wash.; Chevy Chase, Md. Address: Coast Guard, Washington, D.C.

HAMLIN, Orlo J., banking; b. Smethport, Pa., June 23, 1873; s. Henry and Hannah (McCoy) H.; ed. St. Paul's Sch., Concord, N.H., 1885-88, Hobart Coll., 1890-94; m. Mirabel Folger, Jan. 4, 1899; children—Mirabel M. (Mrs. Robt. A. Digel), Hannah McCoy (Mrs. E. O'Neill Kane 3d), Susan Depew (Mrs. Lowell S. Oakes). Engaged in banking since 1892; pres. Hamlin Bank & Trust Co. since 1918; dir. Gaylord Container Corpn., Inc., Great Southern Lumber Co., First Nat. Bank of Eldred, Pa. Mem. Kappa Alpha. Republican. Episcopalian (sr. warden). Mason (K.T., 32°). Elk. Clubs: Masonic, Country (Smethport); Bradford (Bradford). Home: 911 Main St. Office: 333 Main St., Smethport, Pa.

HAMLIN, Percy Gatling, physician; b. Richmond, Va., Mar. 25, 1894; s. William Bernard and Ruth Evelyn (McIntosh) H.; M.D., Med. Coll. of Va., Richmond, 1916; student U. of Va. (academic), Charlottesville, Va., 1921, William and Mary Coll., Williamsburg, Va., 1922; m. Elizabeth Beverly Scott, Feb. 6, 1932; 1 dau., Elizabeth Stoddert. Interne Phila. Gen. Hosp., 1917-20; asst. physician, Westbrook Sanatorium, Richmond, Va., 1916-21; asst. physician, Eastern State Hosp., Williamsburg, Va., 1924-29; clin. dir. Friends Hosp. for Nervous and Mental Diseases, Phila., 1930-36; first asst. physician, Eastern Shore State Hosp., Cambridge, Md., since 1938. Served as lt. and capt., Med. Corps, U.S. Army, 1917-19, with A.E.F. attached to 12th inf. brig. and med. officer 2d Dragoon Gds., B.E.F. Awarded Mil. Cross (Brit.), 1918. Fellow Am. Med. Assn., Am. Psychiatric Assn. Diplomate Am. Bd. Psychiatry and Neurology. Democrat. Episcopalian. Mason. Contbr. to Va. Med. Monthly and U.S. Air Services. Home: State Hospital, Cambridge, Md.

HAMM, Homer Alexander, research chemist; b. St. Paul, Minn., Jan. 18, 1903; s. Conrad and Minnie Anna (Hensch) H.; student St. Paul (Minn.) Pub. Schs., 1910-17, George Weichbrecht Mechanics Arts High Sch., St. Paul, Minn., 1917-21; B.S., U. of Minn., Minneapolis, Minn., 1925; M.S., George Washington U., Washington, D.C., 1928; Ph.D., Johns Hopkins U., Baltimore, Md., 1936; m. Louella Martha Brinkman, Dec. 27, 1926; children—Homer Conrad, Carol Ann. Chemist, Am. Linseed Co., St. Paul, Minn., 1925-26, Nat. Bureau of Standards, Washington, D.C., 1926-33, Washington Naval Gun Factory, Washington, D.C., 1933-37; research chemist in charge of chem. lab., Talon, Inc., Meadville, Pa., since 1937; lab. asst., George Washington U., Washington, D.C., 1927-28; chemistry teacher, Meadville (Pa.) Night Schs., since 1937. Mem. Philos. Soc. of Washington, Sigma Xi (asso.), Alpha Chi Sigma, Phi Lambda Upsilon. Lutheran. Home: 946 B St. Office: Talon, Inc., Meadville, Pa.

HAMMAN, Louis, physician; b. at Baltimore, Dec. 21, 1877; s. John A. and Agatha (Haseneyer) H.; Calvert Hall Coll., Baltimore, 1893; A.B., Rock Hill Coll., Ellicott City, Md., 1895; studied Johns Hopkins, 1896; M.D., Johns Hopkins, 1901; m. Mary Brereton Sharretts, Oct. 10, 1906; children—Mary Sharretts, Ellen Power, Louis. Interne, 1901-02, resident phys., 1902-03, New York Hosp.; began practice at Baltimore, Mar. 1903; asst. in medicine, 1903-06, instr., 1906-08, asso., 1908-15, asso. prof. clin. medicine, 1915-32, asso. prof. medicine since 1932, Johns Hopkins U.; asst. visiting physician, Johns Hopkins Hosp., 1908-28, visiting physician since 1928. Mem. Assn. Am. Physicians, A.M.A., A.A.A.S., Phi Beta Kappa; corr. sec. Internat. Anti-Tuberculosis Assn. Catholic. Club: Elkridge. Contbr. on medical subjects. Home: 315 Overhill Rd. Office: 9 E. Chase St., Baltimore, Md.

HAMMER, Edwin Wesley, cons. engr.; b. Newark, N.J., Dec. 16, 1867; s. William Alexander and Anna Maria Nichols (Lawton) H.; descendant on maternal side of Michael Hillegas, of Phila., first treas. of United States, and the Pilgrim, John Howland, on paternal side of George Frederick Hammer of Pa.; ed. pub. schs. m. Emily Augusta Thompson, May 28, 1890; 1 son, Wesley Thompson. With Thomas A. Edison and Edison Cos., 1884-87; mgr. Edison Elec. Illuminating Co., Fall River, Mass., 1887-88; asst. engr. New York Edison Co., 1888-89; with Thomas A. Edison at Paris Expn., 1889-90, Northwestern Expn., 1890-91; engr. for legal dept. Edison Electric Light Co. and Gen. Electric Co., 1891-96; engr. Bd. of Patent Control, Gen. Electric Co., and Westinghouse Electric & Mfg. Co., 1896-1911; cons. practice since 1911; mem. firm Hammer & Schwarz; professional engr., State of N.Y. Served as commr. water supply East Orange, N.J.; consultant to U.S. Navy, 1917-18. Fellow Am. Inst. Elec. Engrs.; mem. Am. Soc. Mech. Engrs., N.Y. Elec. Soc., Franklin Inst., Am. Water Works Assn.; asso. Am. Electro-Therapeutic Association, Edison Pioneers. Mem. Society of Colonial Wars, S.R., N.E. Soc. of Oranges. Republican. Presbyn. Club: Bankers. Co-Author: The X-Ray, or Photography of the Invisible, 1896; Cataphoresis, 1898. An inventor and patentee and has had much to do with patents and inventions as technician and patent expert. Home: 286 Tillou Rd., South Orange, N.J. Office: 80 John St., New York, N.Y.

HAMMETT, Frederick Simonds, biologist; b. Chelsea, Mass., Nov. 18, 1885; s. Charles Freeman and Nellie Alice (Hunt) H.; A.B., Tufts, 1908; M.S., R.I. State Coll. of Agr. and Mechanic Arts, 1911; A.M., Harvard, 1914, Ph.D., 1915; m. 2d, Dorothy Wall Smith, Mar. 27, 1931; children—Frederick Simonds, Richard Lewis. Asst. in chemistry, Tufts, 1907-08; asst. chemist, R.I. Agrl. Expt. Sta., 1909-12; teaching fellow in biochemistry, Harvard Med. Sch., 1913-15, asst. comparative anatomy, 1914-15; prof. biochemistry and physiology, U. of Southern Calif., 1915-17; instr. histology, Harvard Med. Sch., 1917-18; fellow in biochemistry, Wistar Inst. Anatomy, Phila., 1919-22, asst. prof., 1922-27; dir. research, Research Inst. of Lankenau Hosp. since 1927; dir. and trustee Marine Field Sta. of same, N. Truro, Mass. Pres. Provincetown Art Assn.; fellow A.A.A.S.; mem. Am. Soc. Zoölogists, Am. Soc. Biochemists, Am. Physiol. Soc., Am. Genetics Assn., Phila. Co. Med. Soc. (hon.), Phi Beta Kappa, Sigma Xi. Club: Beachcombers (Provincetown). Mem. advisory council Yenching U., Peiping, China. Author "The Nature of Growth" and several scientific papers. Editor of Growth. Home: Provincetown, Mass. Address: Research Inst. of Lankenau Hospital, Philadelphia, Pa.

HAMMOND, Bernice Wharff, librarian; b. Bangor, Me., May 28, 1885; d. Joseph Henry and Mattie S. (Bartlett) Wharff; ed. Bangor Public Schools and short library courses; m. Roydon L. Hammond, Sept. 12, 1910; children—Ruth Mary, Joyce. Asst. librarian, Bangor (Me.) Pub. Library, 1904-10; librarian, Dover (Del.) Pub. Library, 1928-29; librarian State Library Commn. since 1929. Mem. D.A.R., Grange, Am. Library Assn., Del. Library Assn. (pres.), Fed. Clubs. Methodist. Home: 128 N. Governor's Av. Office: State Library Commn., Dover, Del.

HAMMOND, Frank Clinch, M.D.; b. Augusta, Ga., Mar. 7, 1875; s. Thomas and Mary Ann (Harries) H.; Boys' High Sch., Phila., 3 yrs.; M.D., Jefferson Med. Coll., Phila., 1895; hon. Sc.D., Temple U., 1929; unmarried. Interne St. Joseph's Hosp., Phila., 1895-96; instr. gynecology, Jefferson Med. Coll., 1896-1905; professor gynecology, Med. Dept. of Temple U. since 1923, hon. dean; gynecologist Temple Univ. Hosp., Phila. Hosp. for Contagious Diseases; obstetrician and gynecologist Phila. Gen. Hosp.; sr. attending obstetrician and gynecologist, Jewish Hosp.; cons. gynecologist, Newcombe Hosp. (Vineland, N.J.), Del. County Hosp., Riverside Hosp., Norristown, Pa. Editor Pa. Med. Jour. Med. aide to gov. of Pa., 1918. Fellow A.M.A.; mem. Pa. State Med. Soc., Phila. Co. Med. Soc. (ex-pres.), Obstet. Soc. of Phila. (ex-pres.), Phila. Clin. Assn. (ex-pres.); fellow Am. Coll. Surgeons. Republican. Episcopalian. Mason (32°). Clubs: Union League, Phila. Medical. Contbr. numerous articles to med. mags. and reviews. Home: 3311 N. Broad St., Philadelphia, Pa.

HAMMOND, Harry P., coll. dean; b. Asbury Park, N.J., Dec. 21, 1884; s. George A. and

Sarah J. (Snyder) H.; grad. Wilmington (Del.) High Sch., 1902; B.S. in civil engring., U. of Pa., 1909, C.E., 1915; hon. D.Eng., Case Sch. of Applied Science, 1931; m. Margaret L. Raymond, Sept. 8, 1913. Instr. in civil engring., U. of Pa., 1909-11, Lehigh U., 1911-12; asst. prof. of civil engring., Poly. Inst. of Brooklyn, 1913-18, prof., 1918-37; dean Sch. of Engring., Pa. State Coll., since 1938. Mem. Soc. for Promotion of Engring. Edn. (asso. dir. of investigation, 1924-29; dir. of summer schs., 1929-34, vice-pres., 1934-35, pres., 1936-37). Mem. Am. Soc. Civil Engrs., A.A.A.S., Am. Assn. Univ. Profs., The Newcomen Society of England. Congregationalist. Address: State College, Pa.

HAMMOND, Ogden Haggerty, diplomat; b. Louisville, Ky., Oct. 13, 1869; s. John Henry and Sophia Vernon (Wolf) H.; Ph.B., Yale, 1893; m. Mary P. Stevens, 1907 (died 1915); children—Mary Stevens, Millicent Vernon, Ogden Haggerty; m. 2d, Marguerite McClure Howland, Dec. 18, 1917; stepson, McClure Meredith Howland. Began in real estate business, 1907; now pres. Broadway Improvement Co.; vice-pres. First Nat. Bank of Jersey City; pres. Hoboken Development Co.; dir. Public Service Corpn. of New Jersey, Hoboken Land & Improvement Co. Dir. Morris & Essex Rd. of N.J.; dir. and v.p. Hoboken R.R. Warehouse & S.S. Connecting Co. Member N.J. House of Representatives 2 terms, 1914-17; del. Rep. Nat. Conv., 1916-24; A.E. and P. to Spain, Dec. 18, 1925-29; v.p. and treas. Nat. Civil Service Reform League. Presbyn. Clubs: Knickerbocker, Midday, Somerset Hills Country; Essex (Newark). Home: Bernardsville, N.J. Office: 1 Exchange Place, Jersey City, N.J.

HAMOR, William Allen, chemist, author; b. Du Bois, Pa., March 27, 1887; s. George Daniel and Margaret (Means) H.; student U. of Pittsburgh, 1904-07, M.A., 1913, honorary D.Sc., 1935; honorary Sc.D., Grove City (Pa.) Coll., 1932; unmarried. Research chemist, Coll. City of New York, 1907-14; asst. to dir. Mellon Inst. Industrial Research, Pittsburgh, Pa., 1914-16, asst. dir. since 1916; prof. chemistry, U. of Pittsbugh, 1915-18. Shale oil specialist, Can. Dept. of Mines, 1908; editorial staff, Science-History of the Universe, 1909-10, Jour. Industrial and Engring. Chemistry, 1912-14; contributing editor The Chemist, 1931-36. Mem. com. on airplane fuels, Nat. Research Council, 1917, vice chem. div. res. extension, 1921-24. Mem. exec. com. and chmn. tech. advisory com., Greater Pa. Council, 1932-34. Commd. maj. Chem. Warfare Service, U.S.A., Nov. 28, 1917; in France 10 mos. as asst. chief tech. div. C.W.S. of A.E. F.; hon. discharged, Dec. 6, 1918. Co-inventor of cellulosic food products and of processes of preserving foods and of distilling and plasticizing sulphur. Mem. Am. Soc. Testing Materials, Am. Chem. Soc., Electrochem. Soc., World Power Conf., Inst. of Metals, Am. Management Assn., Am. Pharm. Assn., Hist. Science Soc., Chamber Commerce of Pittsburgh, Sigma Xi, Sigma Gamma Epsilon, Pi Gamma Mu, Alpha Chi Sigma, Phi Lambda Upsilon; fellow A.A.A.S., Am. Inst. Chemists, Chem. Soc., London; corr. mem. Ufficio Consulenza Bibliografica, Torino. Companion Mil. Order Foreign Wars, Order of Washington; Chevalier Order of Lafayette. Clubs: University, Pittsburgh Faculty, Authors' (Pittsburgh); Chemists (New York). Author: History of Chemistry, 1909. Co-Author: The American Petroleum Industry, 1916; Examination of Petroleum, 1920; American Fuels, 1922; Science in Action, 1931; Glances at Industrial Research, 1936. Contbr. chapters Baskerville's Municipal Chemistry, 1911, Baker's The Preparation of Reports, 1924, and McKee's Shale Oil, 1925. Contbr. 14th ed. Ency. Britannica; also series of papers on the fuels, petroleums and oil-shales of America and repts. of investigations on chemistry of anesthetics. Contbr. of many articles to scientific and popular periodicals, especially on the value and management of industrial research. Devised symbolism in new building of Mellon Inst., 1935-36. Home: 322 Sixth St., Oakmont, Pa. Address: Mellon Institute, Pittsburgh, Pa.

HAMPSON, Harold Snover, lawyer; b. Warren, Pa., Dec. 18, 1897; s. Thomas Lee and Mary A. (Snover) H.; B.S. in Econs., U. of Pa., 1922; J.D., U. of Mich. Law Sch., 1929; m. Louise Goetchius, Aug. 28, 1924; children—Thomas Meredith, Harold Robert, Rodney Lee. Employed as salesman of bank advertising, 1922; in employ New Process Co., mail order mchts., Warren, Pa., 1923-27; admitted to Pa. bar, 1929 and since engaged in gen. practice of law at Warren; mem. Borough Council and chmn. Police Com. Served as one of the pvt. secs. to Gen. Pershing during the World War. Awarded citation for meritorious service in World War. Mem. Pa. State and Warren Co. bar assns., Warren Acad. Scis., Am. Legion. Republican. Presbyn. Mason. Rotarian. Home: 424 Conewango Av. Office: Warren Nat. Bank Bldg., Warren, Pa.

HAMRIC, Edwin Lee, dept. store mercht.; b. Sutton, W.Va., April 13, 1883; s. Newton Bland and Elzada (Matheny) H.; student pub. schs. and high sch., W.Va.; m. Mabel R. Hughes, June 10, 1908; children—Darrell Hughes, Dorothy E., Gertrude Eloise (Mrs. Dennis Petty), Anna Lee, Frederick L., Alice Carolyn. Employed as salesman in wholesale dry goods, 1901-23; engaged in bus. on own acct. as propr. dept. store, Parkersburg, W.Va., since 1923; vice-pres. and dir. Commercial Bank & Trust Co. since 1923. Served as pres. Wood Co. Bd. Edn. since 1935. Pres. Union Mission, Parkersburg, W.Va. Republican. Baptist. Mason (32°, Shriner). Club: Kiwanis of Parkersburg. Home: 1605 19th St. Office: 205 Third St., Parkersburg, W.Va.

HAMSHER, Mervin Roy, clergyman; b. Fayetteville, Pa., Oct. 3, 1882; s. Oliver Cromwell and Clara Anna (Hoffman) H.; ed. Franklin Co. (Pa.) pub. schs., 1887-99, Chambersburg (Pa.) Acad., 1899-1901; A.B., Gettysburg (Pa.) Coll., 1904, D.D., 1934; B.D., Gettysburg Theol. Sem., 1908; m. Eleanor W. Miller, June 23, 1909; children—Carl Miller, Paul Oliver; m. 2d, Mildred B. Burkholder, June 30, 1938. Teacher Richwood (O.) High Sch., 1904-05; ordained United Lutheran ministry, 1908; pastor Avonmore, Pa., 1908-10, Pittsburgh, 1910-13, Etna, 1913-14, York, 1914-21, Reisterstown, Md., 1921-23, Mechanicsburg, Pa., 1923-38; elected pres. Central Pa. Synod, 1938, for term expiring 1943; commr. from United Lutheran Ch. in Nat. Lutheran Council since 1932; pres. Synod of W. Pa., 1930-33. Dir. Gettysburg Theol. Sem., 1936-38. Mem. Phi Sigma Kappa. Home: 501 Edward St. Office: Central Pennsylvania Synod, 212 Locust St., Harrisburg, Pa.

HANAUER, Albert M., distiller and manufacturer; b. Pittsburgh, Pa., Feb. 27, 1865; s. Myer and Henrietta (Lehrberger) H.; grad. Pittsburgh Central High Sch., 1881; also studied under private tutors; m. Carrie Marx, June 1, 1905. Began as govt. bookkeeper Hamburger Distillery, 1882; became partner, 1889, sec. and treas., 1901, principal owner, 1904; pres. and sole owner since 1910; pres. Cotton Harvester Corpn. of America since 1928; dir. Lava Crucible Co., West Darlington Clay Co. Dir. Pittsburgh Chamber of Commerce, 1901-16. Local treas. Kief, Russia, Pogrom Relief, 1905; sec. local com. San Francisco Fire and Earthquake Relief; mem. exec. com. Dayton, O., Flood Relief; mem. exec. com. Greater Pittsburgh (resulting in making Allegheny City part of Pittsburgh); active in stopping removal of the historical Block House, relic of Ft. Pitt; Pa. commr. to St. Louis World's Fair; served on exec. com. of 2 Liberty Loan drives; personally guaranteed finances to Swiss Govt. for train which took 253 Americans to Rotterdam after outbreak of World War. Mem. U.S. Chamber of Commerce, Technical Verein; hon. mem. New England Geneal. Soc. Ind. Republican. Jewish religion. Mason (32°). Clubs: Bankers (New York); Concordia (Pittsburgh); Westmoreland Country (gov. 9 yrs.). Home: 5632 Aylesboro Av. Office: Oliver Bldg., Pittsburgh, Pa.

HANCE, Robert Theodore, prof. of biology; b. Cincinnati, O., Jan. 10, 1892; s. Robert Peter and Wilhelmina (Groger) H.; A.B., U. of Cincinnati, 1913, A.M., 1914; Ph.D., U. of Pa., 1917; m. Marion Turriff, July 2, 1920; children—Robert Turriff, Willa Theodora, Marion Turriff. Asst. in zoölogy, U. of Cincinnati, 1913-14; Harrison fellow in zoölogy, U. of Pa., 1914-16, asst. in zoölogy, 1916-18, Harrison research fellow, 1919-20, instr. in zoölogy, 1920-21; prof. and head of dept. of zoölogy, N.D. Agrl. Coll., 1921-23; Nat. Research Council fellow, 1923-25; asso. Rockefeller Inst. for Med. Research, 1925-27; prof. and head of dept. of zoölogy, U. of Pittsburgh, 1927-36; prof. of biology, U. of Pittsburgh since 1936; also guest grad. prof. of biology, Duquesne U., since 1938. Served as 1st lt. Sanitary Corps, U.S. Army, with A.E.F., 1918-19; chmn. dept. of zoölogy, A.E.F. Univ., Beaune, France, 1919. Fellow A.A.A.S.; mem. Am. Soc. Zoölogists, Am. Microscopical Soc. (former 1st vice-pres.), Pa. Acad. Science (pres. 1929), Sigma Xi. Author: The Machines We Are, 1929; Laboratory Experiments in General Zoölogy (with A. E. Emerson), 1928; Laboratory Experiments in General Zoölogy (with S. H. Williams), 1931; Visual Outlines of Zoölogy, 1938. Contbr. numerous articles to scientific and ednl. jours. Editor of Proceedings Pa. Acad. Sci. since 1939. Home: 1 Broadmoor Av., Pittsburgh, Pa.

HANCOCK, Walter Edgar, coll. prof.; b. Marietta, Tex., Sept. 17, 1884; s. Oliver Thomas and Emma Jane (Yeatman) H.; student Union Coll., Lincoln, Neb., 1905-06, Washington Missionary, Washington, D.C., 1907-09; A.B., George Washington Univ., Washington, D.C., 1912, A.M., 1913; Ph.D., Univ. of Tex., 1933; unmarried. Began as minister 7th Day Adventist Ch., then teacher in schs.; taught in Lone Park, Ont., 1906-07; prin. English sch. in Guatemala City, Guatemala, C.A., 1909-11; missionary and supt. North African Mission of Seventh Day Adventists in Spain and Algeria, 1913-21; connected with missionary and ednl. work in Chile and Argentina, S.A., 1922-28; part time instr., George Washington U., 1911-13, Univ. of Tex., 1930-34; prof. and head modern langs. dept., Salem Coll., Salem, W.Va., since 1935. Mem. Assn. of Profs. of Am. Colls. Democrat. Baptist 7th Day. Club: Kiwanis of Salem. Home: 54 Cherry St., Salem, W.Va.

HAND, Alfred, physician; b. Scranton, Pa., Feb. 7, 1868; s. Alfred and Phebe Ann (Jessup) H.; prep. edn., Sch. of Lackawanna, Scranton, Pa., 1875-84; A.B., Yale, 1888, Ph.B., 1889; M.D., U. of Pa., 1892; m. Louise Gregg, June 6, 1899; children—Phebe, Alfred, John Gregg, Benjamin Chapman. In practice of medicine, Phila., since 1892; visiting physician Children's Hosp., 1902-29, Methodist Hosp., 1904-15, Children's Hosp. of Mary J. Drexel Home since 1904; pediatrist Widener Memorial Sch. since 1906, Methodist Hosp., 1915-28; consulting physician Children's Hosp. since 1930, Methodist Hosp. since 1928; prof. pediatrics, Grad. Med. Sch., U. of Pa., since 1921. Mem. A.M.A., Pa. Med. Soc., Phila. Co. Med. Soc., Phila. Pathol. Soc., Phila. Pediatric Soc., Phila. Coll. of Physicians, Am. Pediatric Soc. Address: 1724 Pine St., Philadelphia, Pa.

HAND, George Trowbridge, civil engr.; b. Elizabeth, N.J., Dec. 1, 1872; s. James A. and Harriot M. (Trowbridge) H.; ed. pub schs. and business sch.; m. Margaret Healy, May 10, 1897 (died 1928); children—George Kenneth (died 1936), Margaret Jean, James Donald, Frederick Gordon. Rodman, Nat. Docks Ry. (now Lehigh Valley R.R.) at Jersey City, N.J., 1889; prin. asst. engr. Lehigh Valley's Jersey City terminals at Nat. Docks; asst. engr., terminal engr., div. engr., in charge Morris and Essex divs., D.,L. & W.R.R., 1891-1917; chief engr. Lehigh Valley R.R., 1917-37, cons. engr. since 1937; retired and pensioned, July 1, 1938. Mem. Am. Soc. C.E. Home: Denville, N.J. Office: Bethlehem, Pa.

HAND, Molly Williams, teacher, artist; b. Keene, N.H., Apr. 29, 1892; d. Rev. Aaron Wilmon and Matilda Butler (Williams) Hand; ed. Salem (N.J.) High Sch., 1907-10, Keyport (N.J.) High Sch., 1910-12, Pa. Acad. of Fine Arts, 1915-21, Art Students' League of N.Y., 1921-22; extension courses, New York Univ., Columbia U., Saturday winter courses; summer courses Rutgers Univ., 1915, 16, 26, Chautauqua, N.Y., summer 1925; unmarried. Elementary teacher, Monmouth Co., N.J., 1912-15, Union Co., N.J., since 1924; pvt. drawing and painting classes, Elizabeth, N.J., 1926-32, Roselle, N.J., since 1932; instr. in craft and landscape, Camp Kininga, Vt., 1930, 31, 32; exhibited: International Women's Art Show, London, 1931, Toronto, Can., 1937, other shows in N.Y., N.J., Pa. and other states. Represented permanently in Newark Museum by "Still Life, No. 1." Awards: first jury choice, Newark (N.J.) Art Week, 1932; first blue ribbon by Jr. League and Elizabeth (N.J) Woman's Club, 1928. Sec. Elementary teachers' unit, 1937 (chmn. 3d grade, 1936-37). Mem. State Com. for Circulation of Art, 1937-38, N.J. State Com. for Nat. Art Week, 1936. Mem. Am. Artists Professional League (mem. adv. bd., N.J. chapter), Nat. Assn. Women Painters and Sculptors (formerly mem. publicity com.), Elizabeth Soc. of Arts (past pres. and sec.), Westfield Art Assn., Art Students' League of N.Y. (life). Awarded scholarships, Pa. Acad. of Fine Arts, 1915-21; competitive scholarship to Art Students League; received award for distinguished service in Nat. Art Week, 1936, Am. Art Week, 1937; mem. Fellowship of Pa. Acad. of Fine Arts since 1917. Progressive Republican. Baptist. Club: Roselle (N.J.) Civic. Author of articles and lectures on art. Included in "Art and Artists in New Jersey" by Lolita Flockhart, 1938, with a reproduction of painting and brief biography. Home and Studio: 246 E. 6th Av., Roselle, N.J.

HAND, Thomas Millet, lawyer; b. Cape May, N.J., July 7, 1902; s. Albert Reeves and Sara Elizabeth (Millet) H.; LL.B., Dickinson Law Sch., Carlisle, Pa., 1922; m. Mary Mercer Worth, Mar. 1, 1930; 1 son, Thomas Millet, Jr. Admitted to N.J. bar as atty, 1924, as counselor, 1928; engaged in gen. practice of law at Cape May since 1924; served as clk. Cape May Co. Bd. of Freeholders, 1924-28; pros. atty. Cape May Co., 1929-34; mayor city of Cape May since 1937; city atty. for city of Cape May, 1931-37. Mem. Am. Bar Assn., N.J. State Bar Assn., Cape May Co. Bar Assn., Phi Kappa Psi. Republican. Mason. Clubs: Sea View Country (Absecon); Union League (Philadelphia). Home: 1020 Stockton Av. Office: 31 Perry St., Cape May, N.J.

HANDFORTH, Thomas, artist; b. Tacoma, Wash., Sept. 16, 1897; s. Thomas Jefferson and Ruby Edwardine (Shera) H.; student U. of Wash.; art edn., Nat. Acad. Design and Art Students' League, N.Y. City, Ecole des Beaux Arts and Académie Colarossi, Paris, Charles Hawthorne Sch., Provincetown, Mass.; unmarried. Etcher, lithographer, illustrator, portraitist. Represented in Metropolitan Mus. Art, N.Y. City; New York Public Library; Bibliothèque Nationale, Paris; Honolulu (H.T.) Acad. Arts; Pa. Mus., Phila.; Fogg Art Mus., Cambridge, Mass.; Omaha Art Mus.; Baltimore (Md.) Museum of Art; Library of Congress; Boston (Mass.) Museum of Fine Arts; also represented in Fine Prints of the Year, 1926-37; Fifty Prints of the Year, 1926-29. Awarded Emil Fuchs prize, Brooklyn Soc. Etchers, 1927; Charles M. Lea prize, Phila. Soc. Etchers, 1929; Guggenheim fellowship for study in Far East, 1931; purchase prizes, Northwest Soc. of Printmakers, 1934, Chicago Soc. for Etchers, 1937, Boston Soc. of Ind. Artists, 1937; Caldscott medal for "Mei Li," 1939. Illustrator of "Mei Li" by Thomas Handforth, 1938. Served as sergt. Med. Dept., U.S.A., 1918-19. Mem. Soc. Am. Etchers, Chicago Soc. Etchers, Zeta Psi. Illustrator of "Sidonie," by Pierre Coalfleet, 1921; Toutou in Bondage, by Elizabeth Coatsworth, 1929; Tranquilina's Paradise, by Susan Smith, 1930. Contbr. to Forum, Asia. Home: 604 Lindsey Rd., Wilmington, Del. Address: The Print Corner, Hingham Center, Mass.

HANEMAN, Frederick Theodore, retired editor; b. Wolgast, Germany, Sept. 20, 1862; s. Otto G. A. and Jenny K. E. (Fohmann) H.; Gymnasium at Greifswald and Marienburg; univs. of Bonn, Munich, Greifswald (M.D. 1888), and New York (D.D.S. 1891); came to America, 1888, naturalized, 1893; m. Laura Louise Siering, of New York, Nov. 18, 1899; 1 son, Vincent Siering. Practiced in New York and Phila.; mng. editor New York Med. Jour., 1905-13; contbr. Jewish Encyclopedia, 1899-1904, New Internat. Ency., 1914-16; asso. editor, College Standard Dictionary, 1916-20. Republican. Home: Brigantine, N.J.

HANEMAN, Vincent S(iering), lawyer; b. Brooklyn, N.Y., Apr. 25, 1902; s. Frederick T. and Laura L. (Siering) H.; LL.B., Syracuse U. Law Sch. (N.Y.), 1923; m. Helen L. Harris, June 17, 1923; children—Vincent S. Jr., Howard F. Admitted to N.J. bar as atty., 1924, as counselor, 1928; spl. master in chancery, 1938; supreme ct. commr., 1939; engaged in gen. practice of law as individual at Atlantic City, N.J., since 1925; mem. bd. edn. City of Brigantine, N.J., 1925-33, sec. of bd., 1925-28, mayor since 1933. Served as mem. N.J. Ho. of Assembly since 1938. Trustee Brigantine Community Ch., 1926-31. Mem. Am. and N.J. State bar assns., Atlantic Co. Bar Assn. (pres. since 1938), World Calendar Assn., Sigma Nu, Phi Delta Phi, Phi Kappa Phi, Justinian. Republican. Protestant. Elk. Red Man. Clubs: Golf and Country, Rod and Gun (Brigantine); Tuna (Atlantic City). Home: 313 27th St. S., Brigantine. Office: Guarantee Trust Bldg., Atlantic City, N.J.

HANEY, John Louis, educator; b. Phila., July 29, 1877; s. Hiram G. and Flora (Scherer) H.; A.B., Central High Sch., Phila., 1895, A.M., 1900; B.S., U. of Pa., 1898, Ph.D., 1901; Harrison scholar, 1898-99, fellow in English, 1899-1912, U. of Pa.; unmarried. Instr., 1900-04, asst. prof. English and history, 1904-05, prof. English philology, 1905-16, head English dept., 1916-20, pres. since 1920, Central High Sch., Phila. Vice-pres. Am. Theatre Realty Co.; vice-pres. and dir. John Church Co., Oliver Ditson Co., Theo. Presser Co. Secretary Presser House for Retired Music Teachers; trustee and sec. Presser Foundation; pres. Haney Family Association since 1928; associate trustee, University of Pa.; mem. advisory bd. Barnwell Foundation; editor, Barnwell Bulletin. Mem. Am. Philos. Soc., Mod. Lang. Assn. America, Am. Dialect Soc., Authors' League of America, Headmasters' Assn., Phi Beta Kappa, Alpha Chi Rho, Pi Gamma Mu. Clubs: Union League, Franklin Inn Club, Schoolmen's Club. Author: The German Influence on Coleridge, 1902; Bibliography of S. T. Coleridge, 1903; Early Reviews of English Poets, 1904; The Name of William Shakespeare, 1906; Good English, 1915; English Literature, 1920; The Story of Our Literature, 1923; rev. edit., 1937; The Haney Family, 1930; Shakespeare and Philadelphia, 1936; Morton W. Easton —A Memoir, 1938. Plays: Monsieur D'Or, 1910; Girard, 1919. Editor: Shakespeare's Mid-Summer Night's Dream, 1911; Bok's A Dutch Boy Fifty Years After, 1921; Bok's The Boy Who Followed Ben Franklin, 1924; Barnwell Addresses, 2 vols., 1931, 1937. Home: 6419 Woodbine Av., Overbrook, Philadelphia, Pa.

HANEY, Lewis Henry, economist; b. Eureka, Ill., Mar. 30, 1882; s. Conrad and Sada (Pavey) H.; Ill. Wesleyan U., Bloomington, 1899-1901; B.A., Dartmouth, 1903, M.A., 1904, Parker traveling fellowship, 1905; Ph.D., U. of Wis., 1906; m. Anna M. Stephenson, 1906; 1 dau., Hope. Instr. economics, U. of Ia., 1906-08; lecturer, New York U., 1908; asst. prof. economics, U. of Mich., 1908-10; asso. prof. economics, 1910-12, prof., 1912-16, U. of Tex.; in charge Federal Trade Commn. gasoline investigation, 1916; mem. economic advisory bd. of Federal Trade Commn., 1916-19; dir. bur. of research and publicity, Southern Wholesale Grocers' Assn., 1919-20; in charge cost of marketing div., U.S. Bur. of Markets, 1920-21; dir. New York Univ. Bur. of Business Research, 1920-32, and prof. economics since 1920. Special expert in (Federal) Census Bur., div. of methods and results, 1904; spl. examiner for Interstate Commerce Commn., 1909. Fellow of American Statistical Assn.; mem. American Economists Association, Chi Phi, Phi Beta Kappa. Clubs: Dartmouth (New York); Rock Spring, Rock Spring Riders (N.J.). Author: A Congressional History of Railways, Vol. I, 1908, Vol. II, 1910; History of Economic Thought, 1911, rev. edits., 1919, 1936; Business Organization and Combination, 1913, rev. edit., 1934; The Business of Railway Transportation, 1924; Business Forecasting, 1931; Brokers' Loans, 1932; Economics in a Nut Shell, 1933; How to Understand Money, 1935; Value and Distribution, 1939. Chief contbr. to Report on the Price of Gasoline in 1915, 1917; Price Fixing in the U.S. during the War, 1919. Contbr. on economic and statistical topics; syndicated daily financial column in New York Evening Journal since 1928. Home: 231 Wyoming Av., Maplewood, N.J. Address: New York University, 90 Trinity Pl., New York, N.Y.

HANKEY, William Laird, banker; b. Sardis, Pa.; s. George W. and Ellenor (Laird) H.; ed. Laird Inst. and U. of Pittsburgh (Ph.G.); m. Maude Chigston, 1905; children—William Russel, Donald Laird, Dorothy Blair, Sara Margaret, George Alton. Pharmacist and banking since 1902; vice-pres. First Nat. Bank, Wilmerding, since 1905; vice-pres. and dir. Arctic Refining Co.; dir. Grandview Cemetery Assn. Pres. and trustee Citizens Gen. Hosp., New Kensington, Pa. Democrat. Mem. United Presbyterian Ch. Home: New Kensington, Pa. Office: First Nat. Bank, Wilmerding, Pa.

HANKINS, James Henry, lumber exec.; b. Uniontown, Pa., Jan. 10, 1890; s. John Foster and Mary (Rankin) H.; student Kiskiminetas Springs Sch., Saltsburg, Pa., 1906-09, Washington and Jefferson Coll., Washington, Pa., 1909-11; m. Maybelle Pusch, Feb. 8, 1918. Automobile business, Tucson, Ariz., 1912-17; treas. and sec. Hankins-Paulson Co., mfrs. lumber, bldg. materials, Uniontown, Pa., since 1923; pres. Uniontown Thrift Corpn. since 1924. Served as Corpl. Motor Transport Corps 329, U.S. Army, Camp Lee, during World War. Dir. Uniontown Chamber of Commerce. Mem. Beta Theta Pi. Mason (K.T., 32°, Shriner), Elk, Eagle. Republican. Presbyterian. Clubs: Metropolitan (Pittsburgh); Uniontown Country, Rotary (Uniontown, Pa.). Home: 2 Charles St. Office: N. Beeson Blvd., Uniontown, Pa.

HANLEY, Edward James, corpn. sec.; b. Whitman, Mass.; Feb. 27, 1903; s. Francis Joseph and Mary Ellen (McGovern) H.; grad. Phillips Acad., Andover, Mass., 1920; B.S., Mass. Inst. Tech., 1924; M.B.A., Grad. Sch. Business Adminstrn., Harvard, 1927; m. Dorothy Ward, June 28, 1930. With Gen. Electric Co., 1927-36, as student engr., 1927-28, staff works accounts, 1931-34, asst. supt. wire and cable dept., 1934-36; sec. Allegheny Steel Co. since 1936; sec. Allegheny Ludlum Steel Corpn. Mem. Nat. Assn. Cost Accountants, Phi Kappa, Tau Beta Pi. Republican. Roman Catholic. Club: Pittsburgh Athletic Assn. Home: 1219 Carlisle St., Tarentum, Pa. Office: Allegheny Ludlum Steel Corporation, Brackenridge, Pa.

HANLIN, Fred A.; v.p. Weirton Steel Co.; officer or dir. several companies. Address: Weirton, W.Va.

HANLON, John, banking; b. Orange, N.J., Mar. 28, 1870; s. John and Mary Amelia H.; ed. Brooklyn Poly. Inst., Pennington Sem.; C.E., Princeton U., 1896; unmarried. Became mgr. Crown Point Mine, Prescott, Ariz., 1897; then mgr. Piedmont Cattle Co., later receiver Walnut Grove Storage Co.; pres. First Nat. Bank of Pennington, N.J. Office: First Nat. Bank, Pennington, N.J.

HANNA, Bernard F., banker; b. Harnedsville, Pa., Apr. 20, 1867; s. William and Catharine (Critchfield) H.; ed. local and state normal schs.; m. Mary B. Parks, Oct. 30, 1900. Teacher Pa. pub. schs., 1882-88; civil engr. L.&N. R.R., 1888-90; asst. roadmaster B.&O. R.R., 1890-99, roadmaster, 1899-1932; pres. and dir. Union Nat. Bank since 1934. Dir. Rockwood (Pa.) Borough Sch. Dist. Dir. Welfare Soc., Rockwood. Mem. County Bankers Assn. Republican. Mem. United Brethren Ch. (dir.). Club: Wild Life Sportsmen's. Home: 721 Broadway. Office: 656 Main St., Rockwood, Pa.

HANNA, Charles Augustus, banker; b. Cadiz, O., Dec. 28, 1863; s. Neri A. and Eliza Jane (Phillips) H.; ed. pub. schs., Cadiz; M.A., 1902, L.H.D., 1925; Marietta (O.) Coll.; m. Elizabeth Fleming Harrison, Oct. 19, 1905; children—Mrs. Elizabeth Harrison Howell, Mrs. Mary Eleanor Adams, Virginia Lee Phillips Hanna.

Banking at Lincoln, Neb., 1885-97; v.p. First Nat. Bank, 1891-97; also treas. Neb. Stock Yards Co.; nat. bank examiner for New York, 1899-1911; examiner for New York Clearing House, since 1911. Republican. Presbyn. Mem. N.Y., N.J., Pa., Ohio and Va. hist. socs., Soc. Colonial Wars, S.A.R. Clubs: Bankers', Metropolitan, Montclair Golf. Author: Historical Collections of Harrison County, O., 1900; Ohio Valley Genealogies, 1900; The Scotch-Irish, 1902; The Wilderness Trail, 1911. Home: 15 Rockledge Road, Montclair, N.J. Office: 77 Cedar St., New York, N.Y.

HANNA, Clinton Richards; b. Indianapolis, Ind., Dec. 17, 1899; s. Walter Parks and Elinor (Vestal) H.; B.S. in elec. engring., Purdue U., 1922, E.E., 1926; m. Dorothy Wilharm, June 8, 1926; children—Marilyn Louise, David Walter. With Westinghouse Electric & Mfg. Co. since 1922, research engr. on sound reproduction apparatus, amplifiers, etc., 1922-27, same on talking motion picture development, 1927-30, mgr. development div., research dept., 1930-36, mgr. electro-mech. div. research dept., since 1936. Mem. Am. Inst. Elec. Engrs., Inst. Radio Engrs., Soc. Motion Picture Engrs., Acoustical Soc. of America. Republican. Methodist. Writer numerous tech. papers presented before engring. assns. Home: 6940 Claridge Pl., Pittsburgh, Pa. Office: Westinghouse Electric & Mfg. Co., East Pittsburgh, Pa.

HANNA, Meredith, lawyer; b. Phila., Pa., Oct. 27, 1874; s. William Brantly and Mary (Hopper) H.; grad. William Penn Charter Sch., 1891; B.S., U. of Pa., 1895, LL.B., 1898; m. Marion Wiltbank Clark, Apr. 20, 1908; 1 son, William Clark. Admitted to Pa. bar, 1898, and began practice at Phila.; dep. prothonotary of Courts of Common Pleas since 1917. Served Light Battery A, Pa. Vol. Arty., Spanish-Am. War, 1898. Trustee Phila. Bapt. Assn., Bapt. Home of Phila. Mem. Phila. Bar Assn., Pa. Bar Assn., Law Acad., of Phila., Lawyers Club of Phila., Pa. Soc. Sons of the Revolution. Colonial Soc. of Pa., Descendants of War of 1812, St. Andrews Soc. of Phila., Netherlands Soc. of Pa., Order of Coif, Phi Kappa Psi. Republican. Baptist. Mason. Editor of Forms of Civil Practice. Home: 263 S. 21st St. Office: City Hall, Philadelphia, Pa.

HANNOCH, Herbert J., lawyer; b. Newark, N.J., Aug. 28, 1890; s. Abram and Tillie (Samuel) H.; LL.B., N.Y. Univ. Law Sch., 1910; m. Alice Siegel, Jan. 23, 1919; children— Louise A., Susanne H. Studied law in office Leo Stein and later became mem. firm; admitted to N.J. bar, as atty., 1911, as counselor, 1914; mem. firm Hannoch & Lasser since 1932. Served as counsel to Alien Property Custodian during World War. Vice-pres. Newark Beth Israel Hosp., Jewish Childrens Home, Newark, N.J. Dir. Conf. Jewish Charities. Del. Am. Jewish Com. Mem. Am. Bar Assn., N.J. Bar Assn., Essex Co. Bar Assn. (past pres.). Republican. Jewish religion. Clubs: Downtown (Newark); Mountain Ridge Country (West Caldwell). Home: 352 N. Ridgewood Rd., South Orange. Office: 17 Academy St., Newark, N.J.

HANNUM, Alberta Pierson, author; b. Condit, Ohio, Aug. 3, 1906; d. James Ellsworth and Caroline Adelle (Evans) Pierson; B.A., Ohio State U., 1927; student Columbia, 1928; m. Robert Fulton Hannum, Jan. 7, 1929; children— Joan, Sara Lee. Mem. Delta Gamma, Mortar Board. Republican. Methodist. Author: Thursday April, 1931; The Hills Step Lightly, 1934; The Third Book of the Highland Trilogy. Contbr. fiction to mags.; short story in "O'Brien's Collection of Best Short Stories of 1933"; lecturer. Regarded as an authority on southern highland life. Home: Moundsville, W.Va.

HANNY, William F., cartoonist; b. Burlington, Ia., Nov. 21, 1882; s. Gustave and Minnie (Hackman) H.; ed. grammar sch., and Art Students' League, New York; m. Alida Wikoff, Sept. 23, 1915. With St. Joseph (Mo.) News Press, 1912-22, except 1 yr. at Art Students' League; with Pioneer Press, St. Paul, 1922-24, Philadelphia Inquirer, 1924-34, Chicago Herald and Examiner, 1934, New York American, 1935-36, Chicago Herald and Examiner since 1937. Address: Swarthmore, Pa.

HANRAHAN, Edward Mitchell, surgeon; b. Binghamton, N.Y., Oct. 16, 1892; s. Edward M. and Julia (Stack) H.; A.B., Cornell U., 1915; M.D., Johns Hopkins U. Med. Sch., 1919; m. Evelyn Barton Randall, Feb. 3, 1923; children—Julia Stack, Edward Mitchell Jr. Interne and asst. resident, Johns Hopkins Hosp., 1919-21; asst. resident Union Memorial Hosp., Baltimore, 1921-22; grad. student in surgery, Vienna, Austria, 1922; instr. in surgery and anatomy, Johns Hopkins U. Med. Sch., 1923-36, asso. in surgery since 1936; asst. visiting surgeon, Johns Hopkins Hosp. since 1926; visiting surgeon, Baltimore City, Union Memorial hosps. Served in S.A.T.C., Med. Officers Res. Corps to 1930. Fellow Am. Coll. Surgeons. Mem. A.M.A., Southern Med. Assn., Am. Assn. for Thoracic Surgery, Am. Bd. Surgery (founders group), Halsted Club. Democrat. Episcopalian. Clubs: Gibson Island (Gibson Island); Alpha Delta Phi (New York). Contbr. to med. books and cyclopedias., also articles to journs. Home: Old Orchards, Ruxton. Office: 1201 N. Calvert St., Baltimore, Md.

HANSCOM, Clarence Dean, engineer; b. Chelsea, Mass., Dec. 29, 1894; s. Isaiah Clifford and Maud Hallet (Savage) H.; A.B., Harvard, 1917; student Mass. Inst. of Tech., 1917; m. Marceillite Thorn Ropes, June 7, 1924. Instr. of aeronautics, Naval Airplane Insps. Sch., Mass. Inst. Tech., 1917-18, Aeronautical Engring. Sch., Mass. Inst. Tech., 1918-19; aeronautical engr., Air Service, U.S. Army, 1918-20; asst. chief engr. Aerodynamical Lab., Mass. Inst. Tech., 1919-20; chief engr. Glenn L. Martin Co., airplane constrn., Cleveland, 1920-22; cons. aeronautical engr. since 1922; mem. tech. staff Western Electric Co., Bell Telephone Labs. since 1924; sec. and dir. Colonial Palm Products, Inc. Trustee Denville (N.J.) Pub. Library. Asso. fellow Inst. of Aeronautical Sciences; mem. Am. Acad. Air Law. Republican. Mason. Clubs: Lake Arrowhead, Tennis. Author of Aeronautical Sect. of Kent's Handbook, 10th edit., 1923; revised for publ. Aeronautical Engineering and Airplane Design by Alexander Klemin, 1918; asst. tech. editor Aviation and Aeronautical Engr., 1918-19; contbr. to tech. journs. Designed Martin Bomber MB-2, used in naval bombing experiments, 1921, and later; designed Glenn L. Martin wings No. 1-6, 2-F, 4-F. Home: Lake Arrowhead, Denville, N.J. Office: Bell Telephone Labs., 463 West St., New York, N.Y.

HANSELL, John Lewis, ins. agency; b. Ambler, Pa., Nov. 26, 1908; s. Isaac K.B. and Lydia J.C. (Edmunds) H.; ed. Cheltenham High Sch., Elkins Park, Pa., 1922-26; B.S. in econs., U. of Pa., 1930; m. Dorothy F. Woodward, Jan. 20, 1934. Engaged in gen. line of ins., Ambler, Pa., since 1930, asso. with father, I. K. B. Hansell; dir. Ambler Trust Co. An organizer Ambler Chamber of Commerce and first sec., 1932-38, now dir. Sec. Rotary Club since 1933. Mem. Phi Kappa Tau, Pi Lambda Sigma. Republican. Methodist (trustee Calvary M.E. Ch., Ambler, Pa.). Club: Rotary of Ambler. Home: 343 Mattison Av. Office: Knight Bldg., Ambler, Pa.

HANSELMAN, William Louis, research engr.; b. New York, N.Y., Feb. 4, 1897; s. William and Louise T. A. (Metz) H.; C. E., Rensselaer Poly. Inst., 1918; spl. courses, Columbia U. and Carnegie Inst. Tech.; m. Muriel A. Jackson, May 10, 1926. Asst. engr. of tests U.S. Ordnance Dept., 1918-19; metallographer and chief inspector Bethlehem Steel Co., Lackawanna plant, 1919-26; chief inspector and engr. of tests Talon, Inc., Meadville, 1926-38, research engr. since Jan. 1938. Mem. Am. Inst. Mining and Metall. Engrs., Am. Soc. Testing Materials, Am. Assn. Textile Chemists and Colorists, Meadville Chamber of Commerce. Republican. Protestant. Club: Meadville Country. Mason (K.T.). Home: 601 Chestnut St. Office: 626 Arch St., Meadville, Pa.

HANSON, Elisha, lawyer; b. Macon, Mo., Oct. 5, 1888; s. Elisha Adams and Jane Miriam (Dimmick) H.; ed. Owego (N.Y.) Free Acad., 1902-06, Bradley Inst., Peoria, Ill., 1906-07, Cornell U., 1910-11, George Washington U., 1921-24; m. Beatrice Marie Kurtz, Nov. 12, 1912; children—Kurtz McRoberts, Arthur Briggs, William Vernon. Reporter Peoria Journal, 1907-10; clk. of document room, Ho. of Rep., Washington, D.C., 1911-13; Washington corr. Lee Syndicate, 1912-14; asst. Washington corr. Chicago Tribune, 1913-17; sec. Senator Medill McCormick, 1917-22; admitted to D.C. bar, 1924, and practiced since at Washington; mem. firm Hanson, Lovett & Dale; gen. counsel of Am. Newspaper Pubs. Assn. Trustee and counsel National Geographic Society. Mem. Am. Bar Assn., Gamma Eta Gamma, Seal and Serpent. Republican. Mason. Clubs: Nat. Press, Chevy Chase, Nat. Capital Field Trial, Maryland Jockey, Eastern Fantail, Irish Setter of America, Blue Ridge Rod and Gun (Harpers Ferry, W.Va.). Home: Bethesda, Md. Office: 729 15th St. N.W., Washington, D.C.

HANSON, Ernest Roy, chemist; b. Moorehead, Minn., Oct. 30, 1900; s. Nels and Betsy (Erickson) H.; student Fargo (N.D.) pub. schs., 1906-14, high sch., 1914-17; B.S., Fargo (N.D.) Coll., 1921; M.S., Ph.D., Northwestern U., Evanston, Ill., 1925; m. Edith Ann George, Sept. 17, 1925; 1 dau., Roberta Mae. Chief chemist Halowax Corpn., Bloomfield, N.J., since July 1925. Mem. Am. Chem. Soc., Am. Inst. of Chem., Am. Inst. Chem. Engrs., Sigma Xi, Alpha Chi Sigma. Republican. Methodist. United Commercial Travelers, Modern Woodmen of America. Clubs: Chemists (New York); Greenbrook Country (Caldwell, N.J.). Home: 53 Church St. E. Office: 230 Grove St., Bloomfield, N.J.

HANSON, Henry W. A., clergyman, educator; b. Wilmington, N.C., Mar. 12, 1882; s. Louis and Augusta J. (Glameyer) H.; A.B., Roanoke Coll., 1901, A.M., 1904; B.D., Luth. Theol. Sem., Gettysburg, Pa., 1904, D.D., 1918; studied univs. Berlin, Leipzig and Halle; LL.D., Bucknell and Lafayette; m. Elizabeth Trimble Painter, 1904; children—Henry W. A., T. Painter, Robert De Lolle. Ordained Luth. ministry, 1904; pastor St. Luke's Ch., Pittsburgh, Pa., 1906-13, Messiah Ch., Harrisburg, 1913-23; pres. Gettysburg Coll. since Oct. 19, 1923. Pres. Bd. of Am. Missions of United Luth. Ch. since 1933. State chaplain Sunshine Soc. of Pa. Mem. staff preachers and lecturers War Work Commn. of Y.M.C.A., World War. Preacher at Harvard, U. of Pa., Pa. State Coll., U. of Minn., etc. Mem. Kappa Phi Kappa, Phi Beta Kappa, Scabard and Blade. Clubs: University, Rotary. Home: Gettysburg, Pa.

HANZSCHE, William Thomson, clergyman, editor; b. Baltimore, Md., July 28, 1891; s. William Thomson and Mary McLean (Hunt) H.; prep. edn., Baltimore Poly. Inst.; student Johns Hopkins, 1910-11; A.B., Washington and Lee U., 1913, D.D., 1928; student Union Theol. Sem., Richmond, Va., 1913-15; A.M., Princeton, 1916; B.D., Princeton Theol. Sem., 1916, M.S.Th., 1917; grad. study U. of Chicago, 1917-18; m. Miriam Elizabeth Woolf, Oct. 3, 1917; 1 dau., Elizabeth. Ordained Presbyn. ministry, 1917; served as chaplain Western Mil. Acad. and pastor Upper Alton Ch., Alton, Ill.; pastor Union Tabernacle, Phila, Pa., 1919-22, Prospect Street Ch., Trenton, New Jersey, since 1922; editor The Presbyterian Magazine, New York City, 1929-33; mem. operating com., Presbyterian Ch., 1927-32. Trustee Presbyterian General Assembly since 1936. Exchange preacher in Eng., summer 1934, in Germany and France, 1937. Mem. Delta Upsilon, Delta Sigma Rho, Phi Gamma Mu. Independent Republican. Kiwanian. Author: The Great Themes of Jesus, 1926; The Oracles of God, 1929; Our Presbyterian Church, 1933; The Presbyterians—A Stanch and Sturdy People, 1934; And They Went Forth, the story of 100 years, 1937. Contbr. articles to mags. Weekly speaker as "The Trailfinder," over Radio National Broadcasting Co. Blue Net Work, for Federal Council of Churches, 4 mos. each year. Home: Prospect and Spring Sts., Trenton, N.J. Address: 297 4th Av., New York, N.Y., and Prospect St. Church, Trenton, N.J.

HARBESON, John Frederick, architect; b. Phila., Pa., July 30, 1888; s. James Page and

Fredericka (Krauter) H.; B.S. in Architecture, U. of Pa., 1910, M.S. in Architecture, 1911; m. Georgiana Newcomb Brown, Oct. 5, 1916 (divorced 1929); children—John Frederick, Paul Cret. Began practice at Phila., 1911; instr. in perspective, Pa. Acad. Fine Arts, since 1916; asso. prof. architectural designs, Sch. Fine Arts, U. of Pa., since 1919; former chmn. dept. architecture; partner of Paul P. Cret, architect, Phila., since 1919. Prin. works: Pioneer Mother Monument (with Charles Grafly, sculptor), 1916; Mallory Memorial Fountain, Phila., 1917; Whitfield Memorial (with R. Tait McKenzie, sculptor). Awarded Arthur Spayde Brooke gold medal in design, U. of Pa., 1910; Walter Cope memorial prize, Phila. Chapter Am. Inst. Architects and T Square Club, 1913. Fellow Am. Inst. Architects; mem. Fairmont Park Art Assn., Sigma Xi. Presbyn. Clubs: University, Sketch, T Square (ex-pres.). Author: The Study of Architectural Design, 1926. Contbr. to Pencil Points, etc. Home: 6122 McCallum St., Germantown, Phila. Office: Architects' Bldg., Philadelphia, Pa.

HARBESON, William Page, univ. prof.; b. Phila., Pa., Nov. 27, 1882; s. James Page and Fredericka (Krauter) H.; student Central High Sch., Phila., 1900; LL.B., U. of Pa., 1910; unmarried. Admitted to Pa. Bar, 1910, and practiced 1910-15; instr. English dept., U. of Pa., 1910-20, asst. prof., 1920-27, prof. of English lit. since 1927. Republican. Episcopalian. Clubs: Lenape, Franklin Inn (Phila.). Asso. editor, U. of Pa. Law Review. Home: 6122 McCallum St. Office: College Hall, 35 Locust St., Philadelphia, Pa.

HARBISON, Francis Roy, lawyer; b. Fallbrook, San Diego Co., Calif., Aug. 27, 1882; s. James Henry and Lydia Ann (Heckert) H.; grad. Slippery Rock State Normal Sch., 1901; Ph.B., Grove City (Pa.) Coll., 1904; LL.B., U. of Pittsburgh, 1909; m. Laura Alice Adams, June 26, 1912; 1 dau., Eleanor Ruth. Admitted to Pa. bar, 1909, and since in practice, Pittsburgh; partner in firm Watson & Freeman, 1910-27; practice alone since 1927; sec., treas. and dir. Sutton Engring. Co.; dir. Pittsburgh Cut Stone Corpn. Sec. and dir. D. T. Watson Home for Crippled Children. Republican. Presbyterian. Mason. Home: Hunt Rd., Fox Chapel, Pa. Office: 1017 Park Bldg., Pittsburgh, Pa.

HARBISON, Ralph Warner, mfr.; b. Allegheny, Pa., Feb. 20, 1876; s. late Samuel Pollock and Emma Jane (Boyd) H.; A.B., Princeton, 1898; LL.D., Washington and Jefferson College, 1937; m. Helen Harris, 1905; children—Marjorie Stabler (adopted), E. Harris, Samuel P., Frederick H. Dir. Harbison-Walker Refractories Co., Pittsburgh (founded by father). Was member exec. com. War Work Council of Y.M.C.A. during the war; dir. and trustee Pittsburgh Y.M.C.A., Presbyn. Hosp. (Pittsburgh), Hosp. Council of Allegheny County; pres. bd. trustees Univ. Hosp., Pittsburgh; v.p. bd. trustees Pa. Coll. for Women; trustee Western Theol. Sem.; mem. gen. bd. Nat. Council Y.M.C.A.; mem. Internat. Bd. Y.M.C.A. Clubs: Lake Placid; Harvard-Yale-Princeton (Pittsburgh); Edgeworth, Allegheny Country (Sewickley). Home: Pine and Woodland Rd., Sewickley, Pa. Office: Farmers Bank Bldg., Pittsburgh, Pa.

HARBOLD, Peter Monroe, prof. education; b. Cumberland Co., Pa., Nov. 17, 1873; s. Peter and Leah H.; ed. Millersville (Pa.) State Normal Sch., 1896-99; Ph.B., Franklin and Marshall Coll., 1904; A.M., Harvard U., 1905; grad. study, Chicago, U. of Pa., U. of Wis.; (hon.) D.Sc., Franklin and Marshall Coll., 1916; m. Helen A. Keiser, July 24, 1907; children—Elizabeth K. (Mrs. Hans Westkott), Mary Leah. Employed as teacher in various schs., 1891-96; instr. history and edn., Millersville State Normal Sch., 1898-1902, supt. of training, 1905-11; supt. schs., Lancaster, Pa., 1911-12; prin. Millersville State Normal Sch., 1912-18; prof. edn., Franklin and Marshall Coll. since 1919. Served as Camp Ednl. Dir., Camp Meade, Md., 1918-19. Mem. N.E.A., Am. Assn. Univ. Profs., Pa. State Ednl. Assn., Phi Beta Kappa. Lutheran. Clubs: Fortnightly, Sphinx, Chisophic. Home: 343 College Av., Lancaster, Pa.

HARCUM, Edith Hatcher (Mrs. Octavius Marvin Harcum), educator; b. Richmond, Va., d. of William Eldridge and Virginia Oranie (Snead) Hatcher; B.L., Woman's College, Richmond, Va.; studied piano with Safonoff, New York, Philipp, Paris, Leschetizky, Vienna; m. Octavius Marvin Harcum, Feb. 17, 1913; children—Edith Virginia, William Marvin. Concert pianist; soloist with symphony orchestras; established music department Fork Union Mil. Acad.; former head of piano dept. Shipley Sch., Bryn Mawr, Pa.; founder and head of Harcum Junior Coll. and Harcum Summer School, Bryn Mawr, Pa. Clubs: Art Alliance, Plays and Players, Phila. Music. Home: Bryn Mawr, Pa.

HARDCASTLE, Alexander, retired lawyer; b. Caroline Co., Md., Jan. 27, 1862; s. Alexander and Catherine (Nandain) H.; student Princeton U., 1879, 1881-84; m. Clara Downes, Apr. 7, 1897. Engaged with father in raising peaches and fruit farming, 1884-90; studied law and admitted to Md. bar, 1894; in practice, Denton, Md., for few months; in practice at Baltimore, 1894-1938, when retired from active practice on account ill health; specialized in corpn. law, trusts, estates, and some gen. work; mem. firm Hardcastle & Wynn, 1901-05, in individual practice after 1905; instrumental in the formation and development of The Eastern Shore Soc. of Baltimore, 1913, now hon. mem. bd. govs. Served on Nat. Bds. during World War. Democrat. Presbyterian. Mason. Home: 1217 John St., Baltimore, Md.

HARDCASTLE, John Dudley, v.p. Spang Chalfant, Inc.; b. Carrolltown, Ill., Jan. 10, 1881; s. John C. and Marie E (Kyle) H.; student high sch.; m. Alice Mary Charles, Dec. 1, 1903; children—Dorothy, Ruth (Mrs. J. L. Barngrove), John Dudley, Jerome Charles. With Spang Chalfant, Inc., since 1904, mgr. sales, St. Louis, Mo., 1908-35, v.p., 1935-37, v.p. in charge sales, Pittsburgh, since Jan. 1937; dir. Fretz Moon Tube Co. Clubs: Duquesne, Oakmont Country (Pittsburgh). Home: 119 Hoodridge Drive, Mt. Lebanon, Pa. Office: Grant Bldg., Grant St., Pittsburgh, Pa.

HARDENBERGH, John Gerard, veterinarian; b. Berkshire, N.Y., Apr. 15, 1892; s. John Gerard and Mary DeFrancie (Wavle) H.; V.M.D., U. of Pa. Vet. Sch., 1916; m. Sara H. Keown, Oct. 1, 1919; children—James Gerard, Robert Bruce. Tech. asst., Gilliland Labs., Inc., Marietta, Pa., 1916-18; with N.J. Bur. Animal Industry, 1920-21; with Mayo Foundation for Med. Edn. and Research, Rochester, Minn., 1921-27; with Walker-Gordon Lab. Co., Inc., Plainsboro, N.J., since 1927; part-time instr. U. of Pa. Sch. Vet. Med. since 1938. Served as 2d lt. then 1st lt. Vet Corps, U.S.A., 1917-20. Mem. Am. Vet. Med. Assn. (exec. bd.), Am. Public Health Assn., Soc. Am. Bacteriologists, Internat. Assn. Milk Sanitarians (pres. 1937), Vet. Med. Assn. N.J. (sec. since 1931), N.J. Health Officers Assn., N.J. Health & San. Assn., Acacia, Sigma Xi, Phi Zeta, Alpha Psi (hon.). Republican. Conglist. Mason (32°, Shriner). Home: 166 Jefferson Rd., Princeton. Office: Walker-Gordon Lab. Co., Inc., Plainsboro, N.J.

HARDENBERGH, William Andrew, engr., editor; b. Galena, Ill., Aug. 6, 1888; s. Spencer and Elizabeth (Fetz) H.; B.E., Union Coll., Schenectady, N.Y., 1912; m. Alberta Sunderland, Aug. 25, 1915; children—Margaret, Kathryn. Employed as engr., Knoxville Power Co., Knoxville, Tenn., 1912-14; asst. editor, Municipal Journal, 1914-17; engr. U.S. Pub. Health Service, 1917-20; san. engr., Jefferson Co. Bd. Health, Birmingham, Ala., 1921-27; asso. editor, Public Works Mag., New York City, 1927-30, vice-pres. and dir. since 1930. Served as maj. San. Corps Res., U.S.A., 1923-34, lt. col. since 1934. Pres. Birmingham Chapter, Res. Officers Assn., 1926, Manhattan Chapter, N.Y., 1932, N.Y. State Dept., 1933-34. Mem. Am. Soc. Civil Engrs., Reserve Officers Assn., Delta Upsilon. Republican. Methodist. Author: Home Sewage Disposal, 1924; Sewerage and Sewage Treatment, 1936; Water Supply and Purification, 1938. Home: 70 Hamilton Rd., Ridgewood, N.J. Office: 310 E. 45th St., New York, N.Y.

HARDIN, Charles Roe, lawyer; b. Newark, N.J., Dec. 29, 1894; s. John Ralph and Jennie Josephine (Roe) H.; A.B., Princeton U., 1915; LL.B., Harvard U., 1919; m. Emma Downer, Mar. 6, 1920; children—Charles Roe, Jr., Dorothy Downer, William Downer, Robert Downer. Admitted to N.J. bar as atty., 1920, as counsellor, 1923; engaged in gen. practice of law at Newark, N.J., as mem. firm Pitney, Hardin and Skinner since 1923; dir. Nat. Newark & Essex Banking Co., American Ins. Co. Served as 1st lt. inf. U.S.A., 1917-19. Unsuccessful candidate N.J. State Senate, 1926. N.J. mem. Nat. Conf. of Commrs. on Uniform State Laws. Trustee Prospect Hill Sch., Newark Acad., Babies' Hosp., Bur. Municipal Research of Newark. Former trustee Newark Pub. Library. Mem. Newark Chamber of Commerce. Am., N.J. State bar assns., Essex Co. Bar Assn. (pres. 1935). Democrat. Episcopalian. Mason. Clubs: Essex, Down Town, Athletic (Newark); Somerset Hills Country (Bernardsville, N.J.); Princeton (New York). Home: 520 Parker St. Office: 744 Broad St., Newark, N.J.

HARDIN, John Ralph, lawyer and pres. Mutual Benefit Life Insurance Company; b. Sussex Co., N.J., Apr. 24, 1860; s. Charles and Abbie M. (Hunt) H.; A.B., Princeton, 1880, A.M., 1883; admitted to N.J. bar as atty., 1884, as counsellor, 1887; m. Jennie J. Roe, Feb. 1, 1894; children—Charles R., Elizabeth A. (Mrs. Wright D. Goss, Jr.), John R. Practiced, Newark, N.J., since 1884; mem. firm of Pitney, Hardin & Skinner; pres. Mutual Benefit Life Ins. Co. since Jan. 24; dir. National Newark & Essex Banking Co., Mutual Benefit Life Ins. Co., American Ins. Co., Howard Savings Instn., United N.J. Railroad & Canal Co., New Jersey Bell Telephone Company, Newark Eye & Ear Infirmary, Babies Hospital of Newark, Marcus L. Ward Home. Atty. Board of Health, Newark, 1887-90; alderman, Newark, 1890-91; mem. N.J. Ho. of Rep., 1891-92; mem. N.J. Constl. Conv. to suggest jud. changes, 1905; mgr. N.J. Epileptic Village, 1900-03; mem. Essex Co. Park Commn. since 1903; mem. Newark City Sinking Fund Commn. since 1904; mem. bd. mgrs. Institute for Advanced Study, Louis Bamberger and Mrs. Felix Field Foundation. Trustee (life) Princeton U. Democrat. Episcopalian. Mem. Am. Bar Assn., N.J. Bar Assn., Essex Co. (N.J.) Bar Assn. Mason. Clubs: Essex (Newark), Essex County Country (West Orange), Baltusrol Golf (Short Hills, N.J.), Somerset Hills Country (Far Hills, N.J.), Princeton, University (New York). Home: 40 Mt. Prospect Av. Office: 724 Broad St., and 300 Broadway, Newark, N.J.

HARDING, Constance, artist; b. Frederick, Md., Apr. 26, 1890; d. John Butterworth and Anna Mary (Trail) H.; student N.Y. Sch. of Fine and Applied Art, 1914, Art Students League, New York, 1914-15, Nat. Acad. of Design, 1927, Sch. of Industrial Art, Phila., 1920-21; studied under George Bridgeman, Frank Vincent DuMond, Winold Reiss, Dimitri Romanoffsky, Walter Goltz. Began as designer for John Wanamaker designing costumes for Bal Masque, 1916; designed for Albertina Rasch ballets; made impressionistic sketches for Pub. Ledger, Phila., 1916-17; designed textiles for Marshall Field, Cheney, Belding Bros., Mallinson, Mizel, Burton Bros., etc.; publicity work for School of Design, Phila., 1922; decorative painting, Strawbridge & Clothier, Phila., 1922; in charge of sales, Art Alliance, New York, 1920-21. Exhibited: textile designs, Hotel Vanderbilt, New York, 1918; life drawings, Art Students League, New York, 1929; landscapes and drawings, Hood Coll., Frederick, Md., 1938, College Park, Md., 1938, Chapter House of the Artists' Professional League, Baltimore, Md., 1939, Washington Co. Mus., Hagerstown, Md., Corcoran Mus., Washington, D.C., 1937. Mem. Artists' Professional League, Cooperative Concert Assn. Republican. Episcopalian. Author of article on "Venice and the Adriatic," pub. in The Bellman, 1919. Address: Frederick, Md.

HARDING, Ernest Arthur, educator; b. Paterson, N.J., Feb. 21, 1898; s. Samuel and Sarah (Steele) H.; B.S., Teachers Coll. of Columbia U., 1922, A.M., 1932; m. Helen S. Josten,

Aug. 12, 1922; children—Helen Patricia, Shirley Ann, Barbara Jean. Engaged in teaching, pub. sch., Plainfield, N.J., 1919-22; supervising prin., Peapack and Gladstone, N.J., 1922-28, Wallington, N.J., 1928-31; county supt. schs., Bergen Co., N.J., 1931-34; asst. state commr. of edn., Trenton, N.J., since 1934. Served as pvt. inf., U.S.A., 1918. Mem. Nat. Edn. Assn., Am. Assn. Sch. Adminstrs., Nat. Assn. State Dirs. Elementary Edn. (pres.), Am. Assn. Visiting Teachers, Nat. Elementary Prins. Assn., N.J. Council of Edn. (exec. com.), N.J. Mental Hygiene Assn. (exec. com.), Phi Delta Kappa. Methodist. Club: New Jersey Schoolmasters. Home: 197 Moore St., Princeton, N.J. Office: State Dept. Public Instrn., Trenton, N.J.

HARDING, George, artist; b. at Phila., Oct. 2, 1882; s. Joseph and Charlotte Elizabeth (Matthews) H.; brother Charlotte Harding Brown; ed. Pa. Acad. Fine Arts, and with Howard Pyle, 1902-03; also studied architecture; m. Anita Cotheal Nisbett, 1916; children—Anita N., George M. Sent to Newfoundland, northern ice fields and West Indies by Harper's, 1908, 10, 11; spl. artist, Harper's Mag., on journey around the world, working in Australia, New Guinea, Arabia, Dutch East Indies, Malay States, China, 1912-13. Mem. faculty Pa. Acad. of Fine Arts, dept. mural decoration. Mural decorations in First Nat. Bank, Corn Exchange Nat. Bank (Phila.), Germantown Trust Co.; war decoration State of Pa. Winner competition for mural decorations in U.S. Custom House, Phila., 1935, 2 panels in Post Office Bldg., Washington, D.C., 1936, murals in Phila. Post. Office, 1937, mural in Legislative Hall, U.S. Govt. Bldg., New York World's Fair, 1939; awarded E. T. Stotesbury prize Pa. Acad. of Fine Arts, 1938. Commd. capt. Engrs., U.S.A., Mar. 1918, and apptd. one of official artists of A.E.F.; made sketches and covered Château Thierry defense, Marne offensive, St. Mihiel offensive, Argonne-Meuse offensive, besides all American sectors from Amiens to Baccarat; accompanied Army of Occupation through Lorraine, Luxemburg and Germany; discharged, May 1919; commd. captain engrs., U.S.R., July 1919. Mem. Archtl. League New York, Soc. of Mural Painters, Soc. Am. Mil. Engrs.; fellow Royal Geog. Soc.; hon. mem. Tau Sigma Delta. Clubs: Art, Franklin Inn (Phila.) Home-Studio: Wynnewood, Pa.

HARDING, William Boyd, banker; b. Newark, N.J., Feb. 9, 1888; s. Thomas and Margaret (Boyd) H.; student Newark (N.J.) Pub. Schs., 1894-1906; m. Bess Inglin, Oct. 24, 1912; children—William Boyd, David Bruce, Mary Catharine, Richard (dec.). Began as runner, Merchants Nat. Bank, Newark, N.J., 1907; v.p. Merchants Newark (N.J.) Trust Co., 1907-27; organizer Hayes Circle Nat. Bank, Newark, N.J., 1926, pres., 1928-30; v.p. Federal Trust Co., Newark, N.J., since 1930; treas. J. L. Sommer Mfg. Co., Newark, N.J., since 1935; v.p. Goodyear Rubber Products Co., Newark, N.J., since 1928; organized Weequahic Trust Co., Newark, N.J., 1925; treas. and dir. Wallace Bldg. & Loan Assn., Opportunity Bldg. & Loan Assn.; dir. 14th Ward Bldg. & Loan Assn., Court House Bldg. & Loan Assn.; organized South Orange (N.J.) Trust. Co., 1926, dir. and mem. exec. com. since 1926. Trustee Masonic Bldg. & Loan Assn. Republican. Methodist. Mason. Club: Suburban Golf (Union, N.J.). Home: 235 Coudert Pl., S. Orange, N.J. Office: Federal Trust Co., Hayes Circle Branch, Newark, N.J.

HARDINGE, Harlowe, manufacturer; b. Denver, Colo., Mar. 17, 1894; s. Hal Williams and Bertha (Wilson) H.; student Collegiate Sch., New York, 1906-10, Tome School, Port Deposit, Md., 1910-12; M.E., Cornell U., 1916; m. Florence Donnelly, Mar. 22, 1929; 1 son, Harlowe De Forest, stepson, Byron Cantine. With Hardinge Conical Mill Co., New York, 1916-23 (except for World War period), beginning as office boy and becoming vice-pres. and gen. mgr., 1922; vice-pres. and gen mgr. Hardinge Co., Inc., also Steacy-Schmidt Mfg. Co. (subsidiary), mfrs. of mining, cement and allied heavy machinery, York, Pa., 1923-39, pres. since Apr. 3, 1939. Commd. 1st lt. Signal Corps, U.S. Army, Apr. 17, 1917, capt., July 25, 1918; with A.E.F., 1917-19, in charge training sect. of Radio Div., Air Service, Tank Corps and Artillery, Tours, France; received citation for "exceptionally meritorious and conspicuous services." Mem. Am. Inst. Mining and Metall. Engrs., Sigma Xi, Phi Kappa Sigma. Republican. Clubs: Rotary, Lafayette, Country (York). Home: Country Club and Grantley Roads. Office: Hardinge Co., Inc., York, Pa.

HARDINGE, Harold Jr., pres. Commonwealth Bank; b. Ellicott City, Md., Aug. 30, 1887; s. Harold and Mary L. (Hunt) H.; student pub. schs.; A.B., St. John's Coll., 1908, U. of Md., 1908; m. Elsie Evans Baxter, 1929; children—Dorothy Virginia, Mary Hunt, Harold III. Became runner Merchants Nat. Bank, Baltimore, Md. 1908; asst. cashier Patapoco Nat. Bank, Ellicott City, Md., 1919-21; investment banking at Baltimore, 1921-33; pres. and chmn. of bd. Commonwealth Bank, Baltimore, since 1933; dir. C. M. Pitt & Sons Co., Mt. Royal Hotel Co. Pres. and dir. St. Peters Sch. and Asylum; vestryman Grace and St. Peters Chs. Mem. Md. Hist. Soc., S.A.R. Episcopalian. Mason. Clubs: Baltimore (Md.) Country; Gibson Island (Md.). Home: 2450 Entaw Pl. Office: Commonwealth Bank, Baltimore, Md.

HARDMAN, Thomas Porter, dean law coll.; b. Horner, W.Va., May 13, 1886; s. Alonzo Clayton and Elizabeth Rebecca (Stalnaker) H.; ed. W.Va. Wesleyan Coll., 1905-07, W.Va. U., 1907-08, LL.B., 1914; Rhodes scholar, Oxford U., Eng., 1908-11, B.A. in Jurisprudence, M.A.; studied law, Harvard, 1911-13, Yale, 1914-15, J.D., 1915; m. Eleanor Brock, Sept. 2, 1922; 1 son, Thomas Brock. Connected with W.Va. U. since 1913, asst. prof. law until 1915, asso. prof., 1915-18, prof. law since 1918, also dean Coll. of Law since 1930; visiting prof. law, Yale, summer 1920. Served with W.Va. Revision and Codification Commn., part time 1923-25. Capt. Am. Red Cross in France, 1918. Mem. Am. Bar Assn., Am. Law Inst., W.Va. Bar Assn., Phi Delta Phi, Sigma Nu, Order of the Coif. Republican. Methodist. Contbr. to W.Va. Law Quarterly, also articles and book reviews to mags. Home: 601 Grand St., Morgantown, W.Va.

HARDT, Frank McCulley, v.p. Fidelity-Phila. Trust Co.; b. Frederick, Md., July 14, 1879; s. William McCulley and Mary Ida (Keller) H.; B.S., U. of Pa., 1901; m. Helen C. Liscom, Feb. 6, 1905; children—William McCulley II, Frances (wife of Thomas Francis Furlong, Jr., M.D.). Asst. cashier Nat. Bank of Northern Liberties, 1904-14; cashier and dep. gov. Federal Reserve Bank of Phila., 1914-18; v.p. Phila. Trust Co., 1918-26, merged into Fidelity-Phila. Trust Co. and v.p. since 1926; pres. Business Liquidation Corpn.; treas. Suburban Co.; dir. Phila. Life Ins. Co., Premier Shares, Inc., Warner Co., Pocono Hotels Corpn., etc. Mem. Community Fund of Phila. and Vicinity, Regional Planning Fed. Phila. Tri-State Dist. (mem. exec. com.), Bd. Christian Edn. (mem. advisory council); dir. Chancellor Hall, Inc.; v.p. Phila. Chamber of Commerce; v.p. Del. and Montgomery cos. council Boy Scouts; sec. U.S. Golf Assn. Mem. Am. Acad. Polit. and Social Science, Pa. Soc. S.R., Phi Delta Theta. Republican. Presbyterian (trustee and treas. Overbrook Ch.). Clubs: Union League (pres.), Midday (treas.), Bank Officers' (treas.), Merion Cricket (vice-pres.), Pine Valley Golf; Phila. Country. Home: "Springbank," Rolling Rd., Bryn Mawr. Office: 135 E. Broad St., Philadelphia, Pa.

HARDT, John William, banker; b. Frederick, Md., April 3, 1884; s. William McCulley and Mary Ida (Keller) H.; grad. Central High Sch., Phila., 1902; grad. U. of Pa., 1906; married, April 14, 1909. Asst. nat. bank examiner, 1906-07; with Franklin Nat. Bank, Phila., 1908-28, asst. cashier, 1910-16, cashier, 1916-21, vice-pres., 1921-28; Franklin Nat. merged with Phila. Nat., 1928; vice-pres. Phila. Nat. Bank since 1928; dir. Interstate R.R. Co., Phila. Treas. Phila. Chamber of Commerce; dir. Pa. Tuberculosis Soc. Mem. Phi Delta Theta. Republican. Presbyterian. Clubs: Union League, Midday (Phila.); Rolling Green Golf (Media, Pa.). Home: 1108 Remington Rd., Overbrook, Pa. Office: 1416 Chestnut St., Philadelphia, Pa.

HARDT, Walter Keller; b. Frederick, Md., Oct. 24, 1881; s. William McCulley and Mary Ida (Keller) H.; B.S., U. of Pa., 1905; m. Elizabeth Anne Williams, June 26, 1907; children—Elizabeth Mary, Richard Walter. Began as a certified pub. accountant, 1905; assistant cashier Fourth St. National Bank, 1909-12, v.p., 1912-26; v.p. Franklin Fourth St. Nat. Bank, 1926-28; became v.p. Phila. Nat. Bank, 1928; became pres. Integrity Trust Co., 1928; now dir. Commonwealth Title Ins. Co.; local dir. Am. Surety Co. Dir. Presbyn. Ministers Fund for Life Inc. Mem. Phi Delta Theta. Republican. Presbyn. Clubs: Midday, Down Town, University, Union League, Harris, Penn Athletic, Bank Officers of Phila. (Phila.); Merion Cricket (Haverford, Pa.). Home: Haverford, Pa.

HARDWICK, H. J. (Lt.); football coach U.S. Naval Acad. Address: U.S. Naval Academy, Annapolis, Md.

HARDY, Charles Oscar, economist; b. Island City, Mo., May 2, 1884; s. Charles Webster and Martha Louisa (Spilman) H.; A.B., Ottawa (Kan.) University, 1904, LL.D. from same university, 1935; Ph.D., Univ. of Chicago, 1916; m. Myra May Moore, 1909; children—Margaret Ruth, Frederick Leland. Teacher of mathematics, Hiawatha (Kan.) Acad., 1904-06; clk. govt. service, 1906-08; prof. history and economics, Ottawa U., 1910-18, dean of coll., 1916-18; lecturer, Sch. Commerce and Administration, U. of Chicago, 1918-19, asst. prof. finance, 1919-22; prof. finance, State U. of Ia., 1922-24; mem. research staff, Inst. Economics, Brookings Instn., Washington, D.C., since 1924. Mem. Am. Econ. Assn., Am. Statis. Assn., Phi Beta Kappa, Pi Kappa Delta and Alpha Kappa Psi fraternities. Baptist. Editor: Readings in Risk and Risk Bearing, 1924. Author: Risk and Risk Bearing, 1923 (with R. N. Owens); Interest Rates and Stock Speculation, 1925; Tax Exempt Securities and the Surtax, 1926 (with G. V. Cox); Forecasting Business Conditions, 1927; Credit Policies of the Federal Reserve System, 1932 (with H. G. Moulton and others); The American Transportation Problem, 1933; The Housing Program of the City of Vienna, 1934; Is There Enough Gold?, 1936; Odd Lot Grading on the New York Stock Exchange, 1939. Del. to Internat. Conf. sponsored by Carnegie Endowment for Internat. Peace, Chatham House, London, 1935. Home: R.R. 2, Silver Springs, Md. Office. 722 Jackson Pl., Washington, D.C.

HARDY, Fred Nichols, supervising prin. of schools; b. Lenox Twp., Susquehanna Co., Pa., May 16, 1889; s. William W. and Effie S. (Quick) H.; grad. Nicholson (Pa.) High Sch., 1906; grad State Normal Sch., Mansfield, Pa., 1911, Ped.B., 1914; B.S., Bucknell U., 1929; m. Florence E. Halliwell, Feb. 20, 1920; 1 dau., Ruth Annette. Teacher in rural school, Susquehanna Co., Pa., 1907-09; prin. of Auburn Twp. and Springville Twp. High Schs., 1911-16; partner in general store, Nichols, N.Y., 1916-22; selling general insurance, 1922-23; dir. community vocational school, Brooklyn, Pa., 1923-30; supervising prin. of schools, Port Allegany, Pa., since 1930. Enlisted as private in Signal Corps, U.S. Army, July 1917; trained at Camp Sherman, O., with 83d Div.; with A.E.F. in Chateau Thierry, San Mihiel and Argonne offensives; attended O.T.S. in France; disch. as 2d lt., May 1919. Mem. N.E.A., Pa. State Edn. Assn., Nat. Assn. Secondary Sch. Prins., Am. Assn. School Adminstrs., Am. Legion. Republican. Presbyterian. Mason (32°). Club: Rotary of Port Allegany (pres.). Address: Port Allegany, Pa.

HARE, Amory (Mrs. James Pemberton Hutchinson), author; b. Phila., Pa., Aug. 30, 1885; d. Hobart Amory and Rebecca Clifford (Pemberton) H.; ed. pvt. schs., Phila.; m. A. B. Cook, U.S.N., 1908; children—Mary Amory Cook, Hobart Amory Hare Cook; m. 2d, James Pemberton Hutchinson, M.D., Jan. 28, 1927. Mem. Poetry Soc. America, Alpha Pi, Acad. Am. Poets. Awarded Browning medal, 1924. Republican. Episcopalian. Clubs: Art Alliance, Altruscan, American Women's. Author: (verse) Tossed Coins, 1920; The Swept Hearth, 1922; The Olympians and other Poems, 1925; Sonnets,

1927; Tristram and Iscult, 1933; (novel) Deep Country, 1933; (plays) Hard Bargain, Passport, The Return of Hannibal, Private Enterprise. Contbr. to Atlantic Monthly, Scribner's, Harper's, Harper's Bazaar, Cosmopolitan, Mentor, Good Housekeeping. Initiator and dir. Am. Nat. Theatre and Acad. Movement (Federal Charter 1935). Home: Rocky Spring Farm, Media, Pa.

HARE, Jay Veeder, corpn. officer; b. Schodack, Rensselaer Co., N.Y., May 24, 1878; s. James Alfred and Elizabeth Niver (Veeder) H.; ed. High Sch., Johnstown, N.Y., Pierce Sch., Phila., Temple Coll. Law Sch., Phila.; m. Jean Weber, June 6, 1916; children—Jean Gilbert, Nancy Veeder. With Reading Co. since 1897; as clerk, 1897-1905; chief clerk, 1905-12; sec., 1912-38; sec. and treas. since July 1938; also sec. and treas. asso. companies; dir. Catawissa R.R. Co., Chestnut Hill R.R. Co., Mine Hill and Schuylkill Haven R.R. Co., Trestle Realty Corpn.; pres. Quaint Oak Bldg. & Loan Assn. Dir. Inter-County Hospitalization Plan, Inc., Abington, Pa. Fellow Royal Hort. Soc., London, Eng.; mem. Pa. Hort. Soc (mem. exec. council), Phila., Soc. for Promoting Agr., Hist. Soc. of Pa., N.Y. Hort. Soc., N.Y. Geneal. and Biog. Soc. Republican. Presbyterian. A.F. & A.M. (32°). Club: Union League of Phila. (dir.). Home: Trevose, Pa. Office: Reading Terminal, Philadelphia, Pa.

HARE, Mollie Woods (Mrs. John Ridgway Hare), educator; b. Duncannon, Pa., d. McClellan and Jeanne (Harkinson) Woods; ed. Phila. Normal Sch. Training Sch. (Vineland, N.J.), Temple Univ.; m. John Ridgway Hare, Aug. 19, 1919. Began as teacher pub. schs., Phila., 1901, later prin. Special Sch. of Phila. Pub. Schs.; founder, owner and prin. the Woods Schs., Langhorne, Pa., since 1915; founder Child Research Clinic of The Woods Schs., 1934, devoted to spreading broad knowledge and understanding of problems of exceptional children based on experience of The Woods Schs.; insts. held on the exceptional child, 1934, 35. Republican. Methodist. Home: Langhorne, Pa.

HARGER, George Downand, vice-pres. Prohibition Nat. Com.; b. Oneida, Co., N.Y., Oct. 1879; s. William P. and Sarah E. (Downend) H.; grad. Rome Free Acad.; married; children—Elizabeth, Helen; m. 2d, Grace Aleda Hershberger, Aug. 2, 1919; children—William L., J. Nevin. Formerly teacher in public schools, Oneida Co., N.Y., then salesman Rule & Co. of Royal Scroll; was prohibition county chmn., Oneida Co., N.Y., later Oswego Co., N.Y., has also served as sec. N.Y. State Prohibition Com., chmn. Prohibition Congl. Com. for Ontario, Seneca, Wayne and Yates counties, N.Y., now vice-pres. Prohibition Nat. Com.; chmn. Pa. Prohibition Com. since 1930; editor American Patriot (prohibition monthly). Author of The Two Titanic Tragedies of American History; The Pennsylvania Mess. Home: 61 Baldwick Rd., Crafton, Pittsburgh, Pa.

HARGEST, William M(ilton), judge; b. Winchester, Va., Aug. 5, 1868; s. Thomas Sewell and Virginia (Deffenderfer) H.; grad. Harrisburg Acad., 1886; grad. study, 1886-88; LL.D., Lebanon Valley Coll., 1922, Lafayette Coll., 1923; m. Kingsley LeGalliene, Oct. 17, 1895; children—Thomas Sewell II (dec.), William Milton. Began practice of law at Harrisburg, Pa., 1891; dep. atty. gen. State of Pa. 1909-20; pres. judge Common Pleas Court, 12th Pa. Dist., since 1920. Pres. Nat. Conf. of Commrs. on Uniform State Laws, 1930-33. Vice-pres. Harrisburg Y.M.C.A. Mem. Am. Bar Assn. Republican. Presbyn. Mason, Elk; mem. Royal Arcanum. Club: Harrisburg Country. Home: Riverside Drive, Harrisburg, Pa.

HARGIS, David Henry, minister; b. Crisfield, Md., Mar. 2, 1879; s. James Henry and Margaret A. (Sterling) H.; grad. Princess Anne (Md.) Coll., 1893; grad. Morgan Coll., Baltimore, Md., 1900, and also Theol. Dept., DD., 1919, Ph.B., Chicago (Ill.) Law Sch., Coll. Dept., 1905, D.D., Theol. Dept., 1912; postgrad. work, Howard U., Washington, D.C., 1912-13; m. Hattie R. Waters, May 2, 1906. Pub. sch. teacher, Princess Anne and Crisfield, Md., 1893-97; entered ministry, Del. Conf.,

M.E. Ch., 1900; pastorates: Atlantic City, 1901-03, Centreville, Md., 1905-09, Princess Anne, Md., 1909-11, Mt. Joy, Wilmington, Del., 1911-14, Salem, N.J., 1914-15, Cambridge, Md., 1915-17, Phila., Haven, 1923-29, Wilmington, Del., Ezion, since 1935; dist. supt. of Cambridge District, Bridgeville, Del., 1917-23, and Wilmington District, Wilmington, Del., 1929-35; treas. Del. Conf., M.E. Ch., 1912-18, mem. Bd. of Ministerial Traning since 1935, dean Del. and Washington Confs. Inst. since 1927; mem. M.E. Gen. Conf., 1920, 28, 32, 36; Phila. Area Rep. on World Service Commn., 1928-32; mem. Bd. of Home Missions and Ch. Extension since 1936; mem. Uniting Conf. of Methodism, Kansas City, Mo., 1939. Trustee Morgan Coll., Baltimore, Md. Mem. Nat. Ministers Conf. (ex-pres., Hampton, Va.), Phila. Conf. Preachers' Meeting (expres.). Mason (33°; Scottish Rite). Address: 200 E. 9th St., Wilmington, Del.

HARGROVES, Vernon Carney, clergyman; b. Nansemond Co., Va., Sept. 4, 1900; s. Robert Tatem and Emily Martha (Carney) H.; student U. of Richmond, 1918-20; A.B., Princeton U., 1922, A.M., 1927; Th.G., Southern Baptist Theol. Sem., 1925; m. Narcissa Bruce Daniel, Dec. 1, 1928; children—Narcissa Daniel, Emily Carney, Jeannette Snead. Ordained to ministry of Baptist Ch., 1925; minister Princeton (N.J.) Ch., 1925-27; Weatherford Memorial Ch., Richmond, Va., 1928-32, Second Bapt. Ch., of Germantown, Phila., since 1932. Served in S.A.T.C., 1918. Trustee Bapt. Inst., Phila., Nugent Home, Phila.; moderator Phila. Bapt. Assn. (trustee). Mem. Am. Bapt. Hist. Soc. (trustee), Phi Alpha, Phi Kappa Sigma. Democrat. Home: 48 E. Upsal St., Philadelphia, Pa.

HARING, (Harry) Albert, asso. prof. economics; b. Cleveland, O., June 11, 1901; s. Harry Albert and Inez Marie (Eccleston) H.; ed. Phillips Andover Acad., 1917-18; A.B., Yale, 1922, A.M., same, 1923, Ph.D., same, 1925; m. Ruth Marcia Goppelt, Jan. 31, 1935; children—David Philip, Robert Charles. Instr. econs., Yale U., 1925-26; asst. prof. econs., U. of N.C. Sch. of Commerce, 1926-29; asst. prof. econs., Lehigh U. Coll. Bus. Adminstrn., 1929-35; asso. prof. since 1935; consultant to large firms and engaged in market research since 1929. Served in R.O.T.C. at Andover, 1917-18, S.A.T.C. at Yale, 1918. Mem. Nat. Assn. Marketing Teachers (sec., treas. and dir. 1936), Am. Marketing Assn. (sec., dir., mem. exec. com., 1937-39), Am. Econ. Assn., Cum Laude of Andover, Phi Beta Kappa, Alpha Kappa Psi, Phi Kappa Sigma. Republican. Presbyn. Author: Retail Price Cutting and Its Control by Manufacturers, 1935; various monographs on selling and marketing. Contbr. articles to bus. mags and journs. Home: 1422 W. Market St., Bethlehem, Pa.

HARING, Fred Amasa, corpn. executive; b. Binghamton, N.Y., Jan. 29, 1878; s. John I. and Carrie (Herold) H.; grad. Binghamton High Sch., 1896; student Sheldon Sch. of Salesmanship, 1927; m. Jennie Mae Lown, Sept. 2, 1901. With Harris Pump & Supply Co. since 1914, vice-pres. and sales mgr. since 1922. Presbyterian. Mason (32°, Shriner). Mem. Pa. Soc. Clubs: Pittsburgh Athletic Assn.; Oakmont Country (Oakmont, Pa.); Pittsburgh Field (Aspinwall, Pa.); Bankers, Waldorf Astoria (New York). Home: 2283 Beechwood Boul. Office: Brady and Sidney Sts., S.S., Pittsburgh, Pa.

HARING, Malcolm Morrison, univ. prof.; b. Delanco, N.J., May 4, 1894; s. Rev. Dr. Harry Walter and Jennie Singer (Morrison) H.; A.B., Franklin and Marshall Coll., Lancaster, Pa., 1915; A.M., Princeton U., 1916; Ph.D., Columbia U., 1924; m. Miriam Crum Cassel, Sept. 3, 1923; children—Ruth Elizabeth, David Cassel, Mary Carolyn. Asst. in chemistry, Franklin & Marshall Coll., Lancaster, Pa., 1914-15; asst. in chemistry, Princeton U., 1916-17; prof. chemistry and head of dept., Lebanon Valley Coll., Annville, Pa., 1919-21; asst. in chemistry, Columbia U., 1921-23; prof. chemistry, U. of Md., College Park, Md., since 1923; cooperating expert Internat. Critical Tables, 1924-

28. Served as asst. inspr. powder and explosives, Ordnance Dept., U.S.A., 1917-19. Mem. Am. Chem. Soc., Electrochem. Soc., Alpha Chi Sigma, Phi Beta Kappa, Phi Lambda Upsilon, Sigma Xi. Republican. Presbyterian. Contbr. man sci. papers and articles. Home: 810 Baltimore Boul., Riverdale, Md.

HARKER, Samuel Augustus, clergyman; b. Camden, N.J., Nov. 26, 1872; s. John Church and Emma D. (Apgar) H.; A.B., Western Md. Coll., 1900; (hon.) A.M., Western Md. Coll., 1904, (hon.) D.D., same, 1932; m. Mary J. Lanning, May 3, 1903. Ordained to ministry Presbyn. Ch., 1904; pastor, Allenwood, N.J., 1903-08, Wildwood, N.J., 1908-11, Clayton, N.J., 1911-14, Tennant Memorial Ch., Phila., Pa., 1914-18; pastor, First Presbyn. Ch., Bloomsburg, Pa., since 1918; moderator Presbytery of West Jersey, 1910; commr. of Presbytery of Phila. to Gen. Assembly, Rochester, N.Y., 1915; moderator Presbytery of Northumberland, 1926, and commr. to Gen. Assembly, San Francisco, Calif., 1927; treas. Presbytery of Northumberland in Synod of Pa. Served as mem. Bd. Edn., Bloomsburg, Pa., 1938-41. Republican. Presbyn. Mason (K.T., 32°, Shriner). Jr.O.U.A.M. Clubs: Masonic, Rotary (Bloomsburg). Home: 236 W. 3d St., Bloomsburg, Pa.

HARKEY, William Franklin, clergyman; b. Matthews, N.C., Mar. 31, 1887; s. Marion L. and Isabella (Hargett) H.; A.B., Erskine Coll., Due West, S.C., 1910; B.D., Pittsburgh-Xenia Sem., Th.M., same, 1932; hon. D.D. Westminster Coll., New Wilmington, Pa., 1934; m. Ella Willery, Aug. 26, 1919. Ordained to ministry United Presbyn. Ch., 1913; pastor at Logans Ferry, Pa., Baltimore, Md., Washington, D.C., Houston, Pa.; pastor at Washington, Pa. since 1935. Served as chaplain, U.S.A. during World War. Served as dist. gov. Rotary Internat., 1935. Mem. Nat. Reform Assn. (dir.), Am. Legion. Republican. Presbyn. of U.S.A. Mason. Rotarian. Home: Washington, Pa.

HARKINS, John Franklin, clergyman; b. Blain, Pa., Feb. 21, 1891; s. Simon Edward and Mary Elizabeth (Stambaugh) H.; B.S., Susquehanna U., Selinsgrove, Pa., 1915, D.D., 1933; student Susquehanna Theol. Sem., 1915-18; A.M., Pa. State Coll., 1921; m. Mary Katherine Wagner, Sept. 18, 1918; children—John Wagner, William Edward. Ordained to ministry of United Luth. Ch. in America, May 20, 1918; pastor Grace Luth. Ch., State College, Pa., since 1918; also Luth. student pastor, Pa. State. Coll.; sec. Susquehanna Conf. of Central Pa. Synod, United Luth. Ch. in America. Dir. Susquehanna Univ., Selinsgrove, Pa. Mem. Phi Kappa Phi. Republican. Mason (32°). Club: Rotary of State College. Home: 114 S. Atherton St., State College, Pa.

HARKINS, Melvin Reece, prof. of physics, U. of Pa. Address: University of Pa., Philadelphia, Pa.

HARKNESS, Reuben Elmore Ernest, coll. prof.; b. Sarnia, Ont., Can., Oct. 27, 1884; s. Andrew and Isabella (McWhorter) H.; B.A., MacMaster U., Toronto, 1907; A.M., U. of Chicago, 1915, B.D., 1917, Ph.D., 1927; m. Ruth Elinore Thomas, Oct. 11, 1915; children—Elinore Ruth, Bruce Elmore. Came to U.S. 1911, naturalized, 1923. Ordained to Baptist ministry, 1910; pastor First Bapt. Ch., Belvidere, Ill., 1915-19, Union Congl. Ch. (Bapt. and Conglist), Waupun, Wis., 1919-24, Congl. Ch., Woodstock, Ill., 1924-27; prof. history of Christianity, Crozer Theol. Sem., Chester, Pa., since 1927; chaplain Wis. State Prison, 1923-24. Sec. Red Cross, Camp Grant, Rockford, Ill., 1918-19. Mem. Am. Bapt. Hist. Soc. (pres. since 1930), Am. Soc. Ch. History, Pi Gamma Mu. Independent Republican. Baptist. Editor: The Chronicle (quarterly mag.), The Crozer Quarterly. Contbr. articles to religious jours. Home: Crozer Campus, Chester, Pa.

HARLAN, Clarence Eugene, banking; b. Renovo, Pa., July 8, 1895; s. Howard and Georgianna Winifred (Pierce) H.; grad. Renovo High Sch., 1913; correspondence student Am. Institute of Banking, 1913-16, LaSalle Extension U., 1916-20; m. Pauline Elizabeth Shaffer, June

HARLAN 29, 1921; children—Robert E., William B., Mary Jane, Winifred LaRue, Margaret Ann. Began as clerk State Bank of Renovo, 1913, advancing to cashier, 1923-32; asst. to receiver for Pa. State Banking Dept., 1932-35; cashier Citizens Bank of Renovo, 1935-36, exec. vice-pres., sec. and dir. since Mar. 1936; treas. Renovo Utility Bldg. & Loan Assn., 1917-37; gen. agt. U.S. Fidelity & Guaranty Co., 1916-30; partner in firm Harlan & Wheeler, musical instruments, 1919-29. Dir. Pa. R.R. Y.M.C.A. Renovo. Republican. Episcopalian. Odd Fellow (past grand). Violinist since 1908; at various times leader of Smead's Orchestra, Strand Orchestra, Harlan Trio, Rialto Orchestra, Clinton Six, Harmony Four. Home: 137 6th St. Office: Citizens Bank, Renovo, Pa.

HARLAN, Henry David, lawyer; b. Churchville, Md., Oct. 23, 1858; s. David H. (med. dir. U.S.N.) and Margaret Rebecca (Herbert) H.; A.B., St. John's Coll., Md., 1878, A.M., 1884, LL.D., 1894; LL.B., Univ. of Md., 1881; LL.D., St. Lawrence Univ., 1935; m. Helen Altemus, Dec. 19, 1889; children—Helen (Mrs. R. Marsden Smith), Henry Altemus, Mary Leita (wife of Dr. John R. Paul), David. Admitted to bar, 1881; asso. prof. and later prof. elementary law and domestic relations, 1883-1900, prof. constl. law, 1900-13, prof. domestic relations, 1900-24, and treas. of the law faculty, 1883-1910, dean, 1910-32, dean emeritus since 1932, U. of Md.; chief judge Supreme Bench of Baltimore, Oct. 23, 1888-Jan. 1, 1914; counsel Fidelity Trust Co., Baltimore, since Jan. 1, 1914. Democrat. Mem. Standing Com. P.E. Ch., Diocese of Md., since 1912. Pres. trustees Johns Hopkins Hosp., since 1903; trustee Johns Hopkins U. since 1904. Home: 4909 Falls Road. Office: Fidelity Trust Co., Baltimore, Md.

HARLAN, Orla Kent, mech. engring.; b. Hollansburg, O., Jan. 25, 1872; s. Madison A. and Amanda (Peden) H.; B.Sc. in M.E., Purdue U., 1896, M.E., 1897, E.E., 1898; graduate study, Pa. State Coll., 1924-25; unmarried. Engaged in various engring. positions with r.r. cos., 1890-1908; staff position, dept. engring. and constrn., Panama Canal, 1909-13; chief draftsman and designer, Trenton (N.J.) Engine Works, 1915-16; electric locomotive div., Westinghouse Electric & Mfg. Co., 1918-19; asst. prof. mech. engring., Pa. State Coll., 1920-30; engaged in pvt. bus. and mech. engring. since 1931; produced and copyrighted a large scale Temperature-Entropy Diagram for Ammonia from minus 40 deg. F. to the critical temperature, showing the complete Dome and constant Quality lines at 10 per cent intervals. Served in power plant design sect., U.S. Steel Corpn. for war production, 1917-18; charter mem. 1st Batln. Mil. Engrs. Pa. N.G. Mem. Am. Soc. Mech. Engrs., Soc. Promotion Engring. Edn., Centre Co. Engrs. Soc. Awarded Pres. Theodore Roosevelt Service Medals, Panama Canal. Republican. Methodist. Author: Railway Car Design; also various tech. papers. Home: State College, Pa. Office: (temporary) Union City, Ind.

HARLEY, John Parker, surgeon; b. Dewart, Northland Co., Pa., Dec. 19, 1880; s. Dr J.H. and Ellen M. (Gosh) H.; grad. Lafayette Coll., 1902; M.D., Jefferson Med. Coll., 1905; m. Emily Riedel, May 1, 1909; children—Eleanor Louise (Mrs. Sedgwick Rusling Bennett), Emily Jane. Interne Williamsport Hosp., 1905-06; began gen. practice of medicine, 1906; surgeon Williamsport Hosp. since 1921. Served in U.S. Med. Corps, Base Hosp. No. 123, A.E.F., World War. Pres. Way Memorial Isolation Hosp. Commn., 1938; mem. bd. mgrs. Williamsport Hosp.; trustee James V. Brown Library. Mem. Pa. State Med. Soc. (trustee, councilor), Lycoming Co. Med. Soc. (pres. 1928), Williamsport Bd. of Trade, Am. Legion (comdr. Garrett Cochran Post No. 1, 1922). Lutheran. Club: Williamsport Kiwanis (pres. 1934). Home: 335 Rural Av. Office: 21 W. Fourth St., Williamsport, Pa.

HARLLEE, Chauncey Mitchell Depew, M.D.; b. Dallas, Tex., Apr. 7, 1893; s. Norman W. and Florence Bell (Coleman) H.; A.B., Howard U., 1914, M.D., 1918; m. Alma Augusta Mc-Guinn, June 29, 1921; 1 son, Chauncey M.D. Teacher anatomy to nurses, Mercy Hosp., 1921-34, teacher pediatrics Mercy Hosp. since 1934, chief pediatric staff since 1920, pres. staff since 1938. Fellow A.M.A.; mem. Philadelphia Co. Med. Soc., Philadelphia Pediatric Soc., Philadelphia Acad. Medicine, Omega Psi Phi (officer), Chi Delta Mu. Republican. Presbyn. (trustee Reeve Memorial Ch.) Clubs: Medical and Surgical Review (pres. 1934-35), Les Ceres. Contbr. to med. jours. Home: 5819 Arch St. Office: 5821 Arch St., Philadelphia, Pa.

HARLOW, Richard Cresson, football coach; b. Phila., Pa., Oct. 19, 1889; s. Louis Francis and Eugenia (Prichett) H.; prep. edn. Episcopal Acad., Phila., 1906-08; B.S., Pa. State Coll., 1912, M.S., 1913; m. Lila Naivette Gilpin, June 30, 1914; 1 dau., Katherine Jean. Football coach and instr. of zoology, Pa. State Coll., 1913-17, 1919-21; football coach and asso. prof. of ornithology, Colgate U., 1921-25; football coach and athletic dir., Western Md. Coll., 1925-34; football coach and curator of oology, Harvard, since 1934; also boxing instr. at Pa. State, Colgate and Western Md. Served with inf., U.S. Army, 1917-18; disch. as 2d lt. Mem. Am. Hort. Soc., Am. Ornithol. Union, Am. Rock Garden Soc., Nuttall Ornithol. Club, Phi Sigma Kappa, Phi Kappa Phi. Presbyn. Mason. Clubs: Rotary of Westminster, Md. (hon.); Gridiron (Boston). Contbr. to Auk and Oologist (ornithol. mags.), 1908-25; collaborated by measuring birds' eggs, 1936-39, for Bent's Life Histories of North American Birds. Home: Westminster, Md. Office: Harvard Athletic Assn., Cambridge, Mass.

HARMAN, J. Paul, clergyman; b. South Williamsport, Pa., Nov. 6, 1894; s. Hervey E. and Cora May (Jarrett) H.; A.B., Susquehanna U., 1916, B.D., 1921, M.A., 1923, D.D., 1939; post-grad. study, Alliance Francaise (Paris) and U. of Pittsburgh; m. Mary Elizabeth Holderman, Oct. 29, 1924; 1 son, John Paul. Ordained Lutheran ministry, 1921; pastor Holy Trinity Ch., Salem, O., 1921-23, Bethany Ch., Braddock, Pa., 1923-32, Zion's Evangelical Ch., Greensburg, Pa., since 1932. Served as 1st lt. 149th F.A. (Rainbow Div.), 1917-19; 1st lt., F.A., Officers Reserve Corps, 1927-29, capt., 1929-31; capt.-chaplain, 176th F.A., Pa. Nat. Guard, 1931-39. Trustee Thiel Coll. Pres. Westmoreland-Fayette Branch, Hist. Soc. of Western Pa., 1937-38; mem. Am. Legion. Republican. Mason. Clubs: Rotary. Home: 225 Westmoreland Av., Greensburg, Pa.

HARMAN, Susan Emolyn, coll. prof.; b. Speedwell, Tenn.; d. James Harvey and Frances Elizabeth (Travis) Harman; B.E., Peru (Neb.) State Teachers' Coll., 1916; A.B., U. of Neb. 1917, A.M., 1918; student U. of Chicago, summer 1926; Ph.D., Johns Hopkins, 1926; student Oxford Univ., England, summer 1928; unmarried. Asso. prof. of English, Peru (Neb.) State Teachers' Coll., 1918-20; asst. prof. of English, U. of Md., 1920-26, asso. prof. since 1926. Mem. Kappa Delta, Delta Kappa Gamma, Alpha Lambda Delta (faculty adviser). Republican. Methodist. Co-author (with Homer C. House): A Handbook of Correct English, 1926, A Descriptive English Grammar, 1931, College Rhetoric, 1935. Home: 5 Oak St., College Heights, Hyattsville, Md. Office: Univ. of Maryland, College Park, Md.

HARMAN, William Mahan, lawyer; b. Harman, W.Va., Sept. 13, 1900; s. John William and Myrtle Lillian (Miley) H.; student Ohio U., Athens, O., 1918-19, U. of Cincinnati, 1919-20; LL.B., U. of Southern Calif., Los Angeles, Calif., 1922; m. Louise Frances Poffenbarger, July 9, 1924. Admitted to W.Va. bar, 1922, and since practiced at Parsons, W.Va.; mem. firm J. W. and Wm. M. Harman, Parsons, W.Va., 1922-24; practiced since 1924; v.p. and dir. 1st Nat. Bank of Parsons, since 1934. Mem. Am. Bar Assn., Commercial Law League of America, Tucker Co. Bar Assn. Republican. Methodist. Address: Parsons, W.Va.

HARMESON, Glen W., football coach; b. Indianapolis, Ind., Mar. 9, 1908; s. Walter Lee and Grace Pearl (Apgar) H.; B.S., Purdue U., 1930; married; 1 son, Warren Glen. Engaged as asst. coach freshman football and asst. basketball coach, Purdue U., West Lafayette, Ind., 1930-31, coach varsity backfield and asst. basketball coach, 1932-33; head football and basketball coach, Lehigh U., Bethlehem, Pa., 1934-36, head football coach since 1936; reg. mem. two 1000 per cent teams football and basketball in Big Ten Competition, 1929-30; awarded four freshman numerals and nine maj. letters while attending Purdue U.; all Western Conf. selection in both football and basketball; all-Am. mention in football. Mem. Phi Delta Phi, Gimlet Club. Mem. Christian Ch. Club: Rotary of Bethlehem. Home: 1400 Broadway, Bethlehem, Pa.

HARMON, George Dewey, asso. prof. Am. history; b. Pittsboro, N.C., Aug. 23, 1896; s. Joseph Carson and Cynthia Jane (Petty) H.; A.B., Trinity Coll. (now Duke U.), 1921, A.M. same, 1922; Ph.D., U. of Pa., 1930; m. Gertrude McKay, Oct. 21, 1926; 1 dau., Patricia Laura. Engaged as teacher high sch., West Durham, N.C., 1921-22; asst. instr. Am. history, U. of Pa., 1922-25; instr. Am. history, Lehigh U., 1925-27, asst. prof., 1927-31, asso. prof. since 1931; teacher in summer schs., Wake Forest Coll., N.C., 1925, Duke U., 1926, 1930, 1934, 1937, Pa. State Coll., 1935. Served as 2d lt. inf., U.S.A., 1918, stationed at Pa. State Coll. Mem. Am. Hist. Assn., Pa. Hist. Assn., Lehigh Valley Torch Club, Pi Kappa Alpha, Phi Beta Kappa, Tau Kappa Alpha. Republican. Methodist. Contbr. articles to hist. mags. Contbr. about 16 articles to Dictionary of American History edited by James Truslow Adams (now in process of pub.). Home: 1831 Richmond Av., Bethlehem, Pa.

HARMON, Roy Lee, newspaperman, author; b. Boone County, W.Va., Oct. 7, 1900; s. Albert Sidney and Nettie May (Lucas) H.; grad. Scott Dist. High Sch., Danville, W.Va., 1916; student Morris Harvey Coll., 1919-21; m. Dorothy Marie Ball. Began as free lance writer in Barboursville, W.Va., 1919; editor Logan (W. Va.) Banner, 1923; reporter Herald-Dispatch, Huntington, W.Va., 1924-25; sports editor Huntington (W.Va.) Advertiser, 1926-27; editor Huntington Tribune, 1927-30; city editor New Smyrna (Fla.) Daily News, 1930; editor Wayne County (W.Va.) News, 1931-34; columnist Herald-Advertiser, 1930-36; sports editor Beckley (W.Va.) Post-Herald since 1937. Proposed laws for conservation of game and fish of W.Va., particularly anti-pollution statute. Poet laureate of W.Va. Democrat. Methodist. Author: Hill billy Ballads, 1938. Composer school songs, etc. Address: Beckley, W.Va.

HARMS, John Henry, clergyman; b. Savannah, Ga., Jan. 27, 1876; s. C. H. and Elizabeth (Bruker) H.; A.B., Newberry (S.C.) Coll., 1893, A.M., 1902; grad. Luth. Theol. Sem., Gettysburg, Pa., 1897; D.D., Erskine Coll., Due West, S.C., 1910; m. Sarah Bowers Wheeler, Apr. 20, 1898; children—Kathryn Wheeler (Mrs. W. C. Beasley), Elizabeth Wheeler (Mrs. John E. Slaughter, Jr.). Ordained Lutheran ministry, 1897; pastor Trinity Church, Chambersburg, Pennsylvania, 1897-1900, St. Paul's Ch., Newport, Pa., 1900-01, Bethlehem Ch., Harrisburg, 1902-08; pres. Newberry (S.C.) Coll., Oct. 1908-June 1918; pastor Ch. Holy Communion, Phila., 1918—. Mem. editorial staff Augsburg Teacher since 1909. Pres. Fed. of Chs., Phila.; pres. bd. dirs. Grace Coll., Luth. Bd. of Publ. Frequently del. to gen. ch. convs. Home: 2111 Sansom St., Philadelphia, Pa.

HARNE, Oliver Glenn, coll. prof.; b. near Garfield, Md., May 5, 1895; s. James Oliver and Anna Mary (Burrier) H.; ed. George Washington U., 1915-16, Army Med. Sch., Washington, D.C., 1917, U. of Md., 1919, Johns Hopkins, 1927-29; m. Amy Viola Brandenburg, June 23, 1928. Public school teacher, Frederick, Md., 1913-15; asso. prof. of pharmacology, George Washington U., 1919-20, U. of Md., 1920-28; asso. prof. of physiology, U. of Md., 1928-34, asso. prof. of histology, 1935-39. Served as C. O. Mobile Lab. No. 3, U.S. Army, 1917-19; with A.E.F. in Belgium and France. Mem. Am. Physiol. Soc., Md. Biol. Soc., Sigma Xi. Democrat. Mem. Evang. and

Reformed Ch. Clubs: Baltimore Press, Maryland Sportsman's. Home: 3210 Walbrook Av., Baltimore, Md.

HARNER, Nevin Cowger, religious educator; b. nr. Berlin, Pa., Feb. 5, 1901; s. James Philip and Myrtie Dare (Cowger) H.; A.B., Franklin and Marshall Coll., 1921; B.D., Theol. Sem. Ref. Ch. in the U.S., 1924; S.T.M., Union Theol. Sem., N.Y. City, 1925; Ph.D., Columbia, 1931; m. Flora Balch Morton, Aug. 2, 1926; children—Nevin Louis, Philip Balch. Part-time instr. in French, Franklin and Marshall Coll., 1922-23; ordained ministry Ref. Ch. in the U.S., 1924; dir. religious edn., Zion Ref. Ch., Lehighton, Pa., 1925-28; instr. in religious edn., Theol. Sem. of Ref. Ch. in the U.S., 1929-31, prof. christian edn. since 1931. Mem. Religious Edn. Assn., Cliosophic Soc., Law and Order Soc. (dir.), Phi Beta Kappa, Sigma Pi. Mem. edn. com., Pa. State S.S. Assn.; mem. permanent com. on christian edn., Eastern Synod Ref. Ch. in the U.S.; mem. exec. com. Lancaster Co. S.S. Assn.; dean of Leadership Training Sch., Lancaster; del. and speaker at Quadrennial Council of Alliance of Reformed Chs. throughout the World holding the Presbyn. System, Belfast, Ireland, 1933. Delegate to conferences on Life and Work at Oxford, and Faith and Order in Edinburgh, 1937. Author of Factors Related to Sunday School Growth and Decline in the Eastern Synod of the Reformed Church in the U.S., 1931; co-author with R. W. Roschy of How Can the Church Help the Home? Home: 631 College Av., Lancaster, Pa.

HARNEY, Julia Claudine, educator; b. Jersey City, N.J.; d. Thomas and Mary Agnes (Collins) Harney; student Jersey City Training Sch. for Teachers, Harvard, Columbia, Rutgers, Fordham and Cambridge Univ., England; B.S., New York U., 1918, A.M., 1920; Ph.D., 1931; LL.D., Coll. of St. Elizabeth, 1937; unmarried. Began as elementary teacher, Jersey City Pub. Schs., and since served successively as model teacher, instr. in music in training sch. for teachers, vice prin., prin., elementary and junior high school supervisor, and since 1936 asst. supt. of schools, all Jersey City Pub. Schs. Organist and choir dir., St. Michael's Ch., Jersey City. Mem. minimum wage bd. and exec. com. for cost of living survey, Dept. of Labor, State of N.J., 1937, 38, 39. Mem. N.E.A., Am. Assn. Sch. Adminstrs., Dept. of Supervisors and Dirs. of Instrn. of N.E.A., Nat. Soc. for Study of Edn., N.J. State Teachers Assn. (also Dept. of Elementary Prins. and Dept. of Music), Jersey City Teachers Assn., Jersey City Women Prins. Assn. (pres. 1923, 24), Alumni Assn. of New York U., Nat. Council Cath. Women, Cath. Summer Sch. of America (pres. Alumnae Auxiliary Assn. 1932, 33), Newark Archdiocesan Choir Guild (corr. sec. 1933-36), Mt. Carmel Guild of Archdiocese of Newark (sec. Jersey City unit since 1930), Pi Lambda Theta (pres. New York U. Chapter, 1934, 35). Kappa Delta Pi. Roman Catholic. Home: 302 Pavonia Av. Office: Administration Bldg., Jersey City, N.J.

HARNWELL, Gaylord P(robasco), prof. physics; b. Evanston, Ill., Sept. 29, 1903; s. Frederick W. and Anna L. (Wilcox) H.; A.B., Haverford Coll., 1924; M.Sc., Cambridge U. (Eng.), 1926; Ph.D., Princeton, 1927; m. Mary Louise Rowland, June 12, 1927; children—Mary Jane, Ann, Frederick William II (dec.), Robert Gaylord. Nat. research fellow Calif. Inst. Tech., 1927-28, Princeton, 1928-29; asst. prof. physics, Princeton U., 1929-36, asso. prof., 1936-38; prof. physics, chmn. physics dept., dir. Randal Morgan Lab. Physics, U. of Pa. since 1938. Fellow Am. Phys. Soc. Mem. Phi Beta Kappa, Sigma Xi. Republican. Episcopalian. Club: Nassau (Princeton). Home: 258 Kent Rd., Wynnewood, Pa.

HARPER, Francis, zoölogist; b. Southbridge, Mass., Nov. 17, 1886; s. William and Bertha (Tauber) H.; A.B., Cornell U., 1914, Ph.D., 1925; m. Mary Jean Sherwood, June 14, 1923; children—Mary Sherwood, Robert Francis, Lucy Lee, David Bartram. Employed by Am. Book Co., New York, 1906-12; scientific asst. U.S. Fisheries Lab., Beaufort, N.C., 1913; asst. in zoölogy, Cornell U. 1913-14; zoölogist Canadian Geol. Survey Expdn. to Great Slave Lake, 1914; asst. in natural science, Brooklyn Mus., 1915; spl. agent fisheries investigations N.Y. State Conservation Commn., 1916; asst. biologist U.S. Biol. Survey, 1916-17 and 1919-21; curator in zoölogy, Cornell U., 1921-22, instr. in zoölogy, 1922-25; instr. in zoölogy Biol. Station, U. of Mich., summers, 1923, 24; field zoölogist, N.Y. State Mus., summers, 1925, 26; sec., editor, and curator of mammals and fishes, Boston Soc. Natural History, 1925-29; field zoölogist expedition to Texas Academy of Natural Sciences, 1929; mem. scientific staff, Biological Abstracts, Philadelphia, 1929-35; research asso. Am. Com. for Internat. Wild Life Protection, Philadelphia, 1936-39; research asso. John Bartram Assn. since 1939. Mem. 312th Machine Gun Batt., 1917, 3d Officers' Training Sch., Camp Meade, 1918; served as 2d lt. Inf., 1918, 1st lt. Sanitary Corps, A.E.F., 1918-19. Mem. Am. Ornithologists' Union, Am. Soc. Ichthyologists and Herpetologists (v.p. 1934-35), Am. Soc. Mammalogists (corr. sec. 1931-32), Biol. Soc. Washington, Cooper Ornithol. Club, Wilson Ornithol. Club, Del. Valley Ornithol. Club, Acad. Natural Sciences Philadelphia, Phi Beta Kappa, Sigma Xi, Gamma Alpha. Mem. editorial bd. Ecology, 1934-36. Home: 224 S. Chester Road, Swarthmore, Pa. Address: Academy of Natural Sciences, Philadelphia, Pa.

HARPER, George McLean, university prof.; b. Shippensburg, Pa., Dec. 31, 1863; s. William Wylie and Nancy J. (McLean) H.; A.B., Princeton, 1884, A.M., Ph.D., 1891; m. Belle Dunton Westcott, May 9, 1895; children—Isabel Westcott, George McLean. Employed on New York Tribune, 1884; studied abroad, 1885-87; employed Scribner's Magazine, 1887-89; instr., 1889-91, asst. prof., 1891-94, prof. Romance langs., 1894-1900, English lit., 1900-26, Woodrow Wilson prof. of literature, Princeton, 1926-32, emeritus and spl. lecturer English lit., 1932. Dir. C.R.B. Ednl. Foundation, del. Am. Commn. for Relief in Belgium, 1915. Officer Order Crown of Belgium, 1919. Member Nat. Inst. Arts and Letters. Author: The Legend of the Holy Grail, 1893; Masters of French Literature, 1901; Life of Charles Augustin Sainte-Beuve, 1909; William Wordsworth, His Life, Works and Influence, 1916; John Morley and other Essays, 1920; Wordsworth's French Daughter, 1921; Dreams and Memories, 1922; Spirit of Delight, 1928; Literary Appreciations, 1937. Joint-translator Rein's Japan, Vol. II, 1888. Edited edits. of several French texts and addresses of President Wilson, 1918; Wordsworth, in the Modern Student's Library, 1923; introduction and notes to the Standard Oxford Edition of the Poetical Works of Wordsworth, 1933. Contbr. to the Coleridge Memorial Volume, 1934. Home: Princeton, N.J.

HARPER, Harry Clayton, state official; b. Hackensack, N.J., April 24, 1895; s. Henry and Lizzie (Van Saun) H.; student pub. sch. and high sch., Hackensack, N.J.; m. Bessie Brewster, Feb. 26, 1918; children—Mary Elizabeth, George Brewster. Professional baseball pitcher with Washington Senators, N.Y. Yankees, Boston Red Sox, 1913-23; formed Harper Bros. Inc., trucking and contractors, 1921-30; formed Foundation Constrn. Co., 1924-27, Consolidated Constrn. Corpn., 1929-30; served as sheriff Bergen Co., 1927-30; founded Harper Terminal, Inc., terminal, warehouses, mfg. industries, and industrial real estate, Hackensack, N.J., 1930, pres. and dir. since 1931; dir. Gilhaus Beverage Co., Inc., Hackensack, N.J., since 1933; served as civil service commr. State of N.J., 1934-39 and for term, 1939-44. Mem. Nat. Rep. League. Republican. Presbyn. Mason (32°, Shriner). Elk. Jr. O.U.A.M. Royal Arcanum. Clubs: Pioneer Masons, C.M.S. (Hackensack); Athletic (Newark); Country (Arcola); Country (Ridgewood); Friendship of New Jersey. Home: 370 Summit Av. Office: Administrative Bldg., Hackensack, N.J.

HARPER, Jacob M., lawyer; b. Roane Co., W.Va., Jan. 25, 1875; s. John L. and Jane (Hopkins) H.; student Glenville (W.Va.) State Normal Sch., 1893-96, W.Va. Univ. Law Sch., 1900-02; m. Bessie Kester, Sept. 12, 1901; children—Camille, Frances (Mrs. B. F. Whitney). Admitted to W.Va. bar and engaged in gen. practice of law at Spencer since 1901; mem. firm Harper & Baker since 1910; served as county supt. schs. Roane Co.; served as prosecuting atty. for Roane Co., W.Va. Democrat. Address: Spencer, W.Va.

HARPER, Samuel Williams, banker; b. Wheeling, W.Va., April 7, 1874; s. Henry Martin and Marion L. (Williams) H.; ed. Linsly Inst., Wheeling; m. Lillie E. Vance, Oct. 17, 1901; children—Louise E. (Mrs. D. T. Rownd), Nelson Vance, Virginia. Mgr. Harper & Bros., jobbers, Wheeling, 1891-1908; v.p. Consol. Telephone Co., 1908-15; pres. Southeastern Ohio R.R. Co., 1916-24; became pres. Wheeling Bank & Trust Co., 1919; now pres. Wheeling Dollar Savings & Trust Co. Chmn. personnel bur., Am. Red Cross, Washington, D.C., 1917-18. Trustee Linsly Inst., Children's Home. Republican. Presbyn. Mason. Clubs: Fort Henry, Wheeling Country; New York Athletic (New York). Home: Echo Point, W.Va. Office: Wheeling Dollar Savings & Trust Co., Wheeling, W.Va.

HARPST, Clifford Wayne, banking; b. Mercer Co., Pa., March 27, 1894; s. William Wayne and Mary Eva (Cochran) H.; ed. Sharon Coll. of Commerce, Sharon, Pa.; corr. courses, Alexander Hamilton Inst.; Am. Inst. of Banking; m. Mabel Elizabeth Lewis, Aug. 5, 1922; 1 dau., Marjorie Jane. Engaged in banking since 1914, vice-pres. McDowell Nat. Bank since 1934; vice-pres. and treas. McDowell Securities Co.; sec. Chestate Buildings, Inc.; dir. Citizens Mortgage & Security Co. Served in U.S.A. with A.E.F., 1918-19. Republican. Baptist. Mason. Home: 1049 Pearl St. Office: State St. at Chestnut Av., Sharon, Pa.

HARR, Luther, educator; b. Phila., Pa., April 10, 1896; s. Milton K. and Annie W. (Baum) H.; grad. William Penn Charter Sch., Phila., 1914; B.S., Wharton Sch. of Finance and Commerce, U. of Pa., 1918; A.M., U. of Pa., 1920, Ph.D., in economics, 1924; m. Kathryn Cressman, Aug. 21, 1919; children—Luther Cressman, Virginia Anne. Instr. in economics U. of Pa., 1919-21, instr. in finance, 1921-25, asst. prof., 1925-31, prof. of finance since 1931; econ. adviser and treas. Phila. Record, N.Y. Post, Courier Post Co. (Camden, N.J.) since 1934; sec. of banking Commonwealth, Pa., 1935-37; treas. City of Phila. since Jan. 1938; studied operation of English banking system in England, 1926-27; chmn. Pa. Bldg. and Loan Bd., 1937; chmn. Pa. Banking Bd., 1935-37; mem. Labor Disputes Arbitration Commn., Phila., since 1936; chmn. exec. com. Nat. Assn. of Supervisors of State Banks, 1936-37; chmn. Gov. Earle's Financial Survey Com., 1934; chmn. finance dept., Phila. Fed. of Churches. Served in R.O.T.C., 1917; statis. expert Ordnance Dept., U.S.A., 1917-18. Dir. Phila. Forum, Contemporary Club, Lutheran Brotherhood, Mary Drexel Home and Phila. Motherhouse of Deaconesses, Nat. Stomach Hosp., U. of Pa. Bi-Centennial Fund, Penn. Charter Alumni. Mem. Am. Acad. Polit. and Social Science, Acad. Polit. Science, Am. Econ. Assn., Am. Statis. Assn., Am. Assn. Univ. Profs., Am. Assn. Collegiate Schs. of Business, Luther Social Union, Delta Kappa Epsilon. Democrat. Lutheran. Mason, Moose. Clubs: Racquet, Whitemarsh Valley Country, Philadelphia Country, Penn Athletic (Phila.). Author: Branch Banking in England, 1929; Banking Theory and Practice (with W. Carlton Harris), 1928, revised, 1936. Contbr. articles to jours.; co-editor Webster's Internat. Dictionary. Home: 3101 W. Penn St., Germantown, Philadelphia, Pa. Office: City Hall, Philadelphia, Pa.

HARR, William R., lawyer; b. Washington, July 5, 1872; s. Peter and Adelaide L. H.; ed. pub. schools, D.C.; LL.M., Georgetown University, 1896; m. Martha B. Harvey, Aug. 1, 1900. Admitted to D.C. bar, 1897; sec. to Justice John M. Harlan, 1896-1901; atty., Dept. Justice, 1902-09; asst. atty. gen. of U.S., June 1909-Sept. 1913; mem. law firm Harr & Bates, 1913-27; commissioner Supreme Court, D.C., since 1930. Unitarian. Home: 36 Primrose St., Chevy Chase, Md. Office: Dept. of Justice Bldg., Washington, D.C.

HARRÉ, T. Everett, author; b. Marietta, Pa., Dec. 17, 1884; unmarried. On staff Phila. Press, 1905-07; spl. writer Phila. N. American, 1907-09; associate editor Hampton's, 1909-11, for which went North to meet Robert E. Peary on his return from his 8th Arctic expedition and with the collaboration of Elsa Barker secured the serial rights to story of trip to the North Pole; was first person after a 4 months' search, to get into touch, Oct. 1910, with Dr. Frederick A. Cook, the explorer, after his long disappearance, finding him in London, and securing the first exclusive statement for publication. Lit. and dramatic critic Phila. Evening Ledger, 1914. Spl. contbr. Am. Weekly of New York American, 1915-16; publicity dir. League for Nat. Unity and Nat. Civic Federation, 1917-20; mng. editor Nat. Civic Fed. Rev., 1919-21; spl. contbr. to Red Book Mag., also articles and stories in Cosmopolitan, Ladies' Home Jour., Liberty, The Dance, Good Housekeeping, etc. Author: The Eternal Maiden, 1913; Behold the Woman!, 1916 (both transl. into French); One Hour—and Forever, 1925; Beware After Dark, 1929; The Heavenly Sinner, 1935; You Can Not Miss That Inn, 1939; Grow Older, Keep Younger, 1940. Collaborated with Very Rev. Paul James Francis, Father General of Franciscan Soc. of the Atonement, Theresa Neumann—the Mystic Maid, 1939. Address: care Grace Morse, 15 W. 11th St., New York, N.Y.; (summer) Wrightsville, York County, Pa.

HARRINGTON, Emerson, Columbus, ex-gov.; b. Madison, Dorchester Co., Md., Mar. 26, 1864; s. John Edward and Mary Elizabeth (Thompson) H.; B.A., St. John's Coll., Annapolis, Md., 1884, M.A., 1886, LL.D., 1916; m. Mary Gertrude Johnson, June 20, 1893; children —Emerson C., Mary Virginia, William Johnson. Tutor prep. dept. and prof. Latin and mathematics, St. John's Coll. until 1886; prin. Cambridge Acad., 1886-89, and of its successor, the Cambridge High Sch., 1889-97; admitted to Md. bar, 1897; state's atty., Dorchester Co., 1899-1903; mem. State Ins. Commn., 1910-11; comptroller of treasury, Md., 1912-16; gov. of Md., 1916-20; mem. law firm Harrington & Harrington. Democrat. Mem. P.E. Ch. Club: Maryland. Home: Cambridge, Md.

HARRINGTON, Marshall C(athcart), asso. prof. physics; b. Rochford, O., Aug. 28, 1904; s. Marshall and Elizabeth Jane (Cathcart) H.; A.B., Princeton U., 1926, A.M., same, 1927, Ph.D., same, 1932; m. Betty Louise Bebout, Feb. 21, 1935. Instr. physics, Princeton U., 1927-29, research asst., 1930-31; asst. prof. physics and mathematics, Drew Univ., Madison, N.J., 1931-37, asso. prof. physics, same, since 1937. Mem. A.A.A.S., Am. Phys. Soc., History of Sci. Soc., Am. Assn. Physics Teachers, N.Y. Acad. Sci., Amateur Astronomers Assn., N.J. Science Teachers' Assn., Am. Assn. Univ. Profs., Astron. Soc. of the Pacific, Phi Beta Kappa. James W. Queen Fellow in Physics, Princeton U., 1926-27. Independent Democrat. Presbyn. Home: 30 Myrtle Av., Chatham, N.J. Office: Drew University, Madison, N.J.

HARRINGTON, William Watson, judge; b. Farmington, Kent Co., Del., June 30, 1874; s. Charles James and Mary Elizabeth (Watson) H.; A.B., Delaware Coll. (now U. of Del.), 1895; studied law in office of Edward Ridgely, of Dover, Del., 2 yrs. and at Harvard 1 yr.; m. Sarah Godwin, Oct. 26, 1909; children—Sarah Godwin, Mary Elizabeth Watson, Anna Banks. Admitted to Del. bar, 1898, and began practice at Dover; register of wills for Kent Co., succeeding father, deceased, by apptmt. of Gov. Tunnell, 1900-01; dep. atty. gen. for Kent Co., 1909-13; resident asso. judge for Kent Co., and mem. Supreme Court of Delaware, apptd. June 1921, and re-apptd., July 1933, apptd. chancellor Dec. 7, 1938. Editor Harrington's Delaware Law Reports. Trustee Delaware Coll. since 1900. Democrat. Episcopalian. Home: Dover, Del.

HARRINGTON, Willis F., v.p. and dir. E. I. du Pont de Nemours & Co. Office: Du Pont Bldg., Wilmington, Del.

HARRIS, Arthur Emerson, clergyman, educator; b. Montreal, Can., May 3, 1870; s. Edward and Sarah Maria (Gatland) H.; prep. edn. under tutors; grad. Crozer Theol. Sem., Chester, Pa., 1898; D.D., Bucknell University, Lewisburg, Pa., 1917; m. Anna Loomis Meredith, Oct. 29, 1902 (died Dec. 5, 1936). Telegrapher, 1888-92; in banking business, 1892-95; ordained Bapt. ministry, 1898; pastor successively at Newark, N.J., Meriden, Conn., and Phila., Pa., until 1926; asso. pastor with Russell H. Conwell, at Bapt. Temple, Phila., 7 yrs.; registrar and prof. psychology, sec. of faculty and dir. extension div., Eastern Bapt. Theol. Sem., Phila., 1925-38, prof. of Biblical introduction and sec. of Faculty since 1938. Republican. Club: Union League. Author: Perfected Character, 1894; Poems, 1895; Bible Books Outlined (O.T.), 1917; Bible Books Outlined (N.T.), 1918; The Psalms Outlined, 1925; The Household of Faith, 1938. Home: 181 E. Roosevelt Boul., Philadelphia, Pa.

HARRIS, Burtt, lawyer; b. Pittsburgh, Pa., Apr. 5, 1900; s. William and May Bevington (Burtt) H.; grad. Peabody High Sch., Pittsburgh, 1918, Pa. State Coll., 1920; B.S. in economics, U. of Pittsburgh, 1922; LL.B., U. of Pittsburgh Law Sch., 1927; m. Elizabeth Zoe Currier, Oct. 14, 1930; children—Dwight Currier, Burtt. Admitted to Allegheny Co. bar, 1928; in private practice of law since 1928; solicitor Pa. Bldg. & Loan Assn. of Pittsburgh. Sec. Jr. Bar Conf., Pa. Bar Assn., 1935-36; mem. exec. council Jr. Bar Conf., Am. Bar Assn., 1935-36. Served in U.S. Army, World War; hon. discharged, Dec. 19, 1918. Mem. Am. Bar Assn., Pa. Bar Assn., Allegheny Co. Bar Assn., Am. Legion, Phi Kappa Sigma, Alpha Kappa Psi, Phi Delta Phi. Republican. Christian Scientist. Home: 741 N. Negley Av. Office: 1207 Law and Finance Bldg., Pittsburgh, Pa.

HARRIS, Charles Willis, author, educator; b. Sugar Grove, Pa., Mar. 16, 1873; s. C. Perry and Annette Maria (Parks) H.; A.B., Lafayette Coll., 1895, A.M., 1897; grad. Princeton Theol. Sem., 1898; D.D., Jamestown (N.D.) Coll., 1912; m. Grace Doubleday, July 13, 1899; children—Mary Elizabeth (Mrs. Richard Brandt), Dorothy Frances (Mrs. Theodore Slager). Ordained ministry Presbyn. Ch., 1898; minister at Lisbon, N.D., 1899-1905, Bismarck, N.D., 1905-16, Bozeman, Mont., 1916-20; univ. pastor, Indiana U., 1920-27; prof. of religion and chaplain, Lafayette Coll. since 1927. Served with Y.M.C.A. in A.E.F., 1918-19. Mem. Am. Assn. Univ. Profs., Soc. of Bibl. Lit. and Exegesis. Club: Torch (Easton, Pa.). Author: The Hebrew Heritage, 1935. Home: 4 E. Campus, Easton, Pa.

HARRIS, Clinton Lee, prof. archtl. engring.; b. Fair Play, S.C., Jan. 28, 1886; s. Thomas Rayford and Margaret Elizabeth (Lee) H.; B.S. in C.E., The Citadel, Charleston, S.C., 1909; C.E., Pa. State Coll., 1916; m. Lula A. McGee, July 23, 1913; 1 son, Rhett Gibbes. Engaged as teacher and prin., high sch. and acads., 1909-13; with Pa. State Coll. continuously since 1913, instr. in drawing, 1913-17, asst. prof. archtl. engring., 1917-19, asso. prof., 1919-26, prof. since 1926, actg. head of dept., 1925-30, head dept. architecture, 1930-34; research asso., U.S. Bur. of Standards, 1932-33. Served as mem. Council Borough of State Coll., 1927-30, pres., 1930. Pres. bd. trustees, Wesley Foundation. Mem. Am. Soc. Civil Engrs., A.A.A.S., Soc. for Promotion Engring. Edn., Am. Assn. Univ. Profs., Sigma Xi, Sigma Tau, Scarab, Pi Gamma Alpha. Democrat. Methodist (vice pres. bd. trustees, St. Paul's M.E. Ch.). Club: Centre Hills Country. Author: The Influence of Neighboring Structures upon the Distribution of Wind Pressure on Tall Buildings, 1934. Home: 129 W. Prospect Av., State College, Pa.

HARRIS, Francis Waller, elec. engr.; b. Scottsville, Va., Oct. 22, 1886; s. Charles Bascom and Helen Godden (Crafton) H.; B.S. in E.E., Va. Poly. Inst., 1907; m. Sallie Elizabeth Fulton, Sept. 12, 1916; children—Sarah Frances, Marjorie Gertrude. Apprentice, Westinghouse Elec. & Mfg. Co., 1907-08; supt. Consol. Light & Power Co., Ronceverte, W.Va., 1908-09, gen. mgr., 1909-12; elec. engr. Valdosta Lighting Co., 1912; supt., later gen. mgr. Chester Valley Electric Co., 1912-26; v.p. Salem Lighting Co., 1915-16; treas. and gen. mgr. Merchants Ice Mfg. Co., Collingswood Ice Co., Atlantic Ice Mfg. Co., Parkersburg Ice Mfg. Co., 1917-26; pres. since 1926, Abington Electric Co., Mauch Chunk Electric Light & Power Co., Greencastle Electric Light & Power Co., Renover Edison Electric Light, Heat & Power Co., Renover Heating Co., Brockway Electric Light, Heat & Power Co., Page Power Co., Massanutten Power Corpn., Edmonson Electric Co., Damascus Electric Co.; pres. Mercersburg, Lehmasters & Marks Electric Light Co., Fulton Electric Light, Heat & Power Co.; pres. and dir. Mass. Water Co., vice-pres. and dir. Madison Power Co.; sec., treas., dir. and gen. mgr. Atlantic Ice Mfg. Co., Lawndale Merchants Ice Co.; v.p. and dir. Nat. Bank of Chester Valley; treas. Coatesville Industrial Co.; sec., treas. and dir. Newton-Langhorne Ice Co., Elizabethtown Ice Manufacturing Co.; gen. mgr. and dir. Republic Service Management Co.; dir. Republic Service Corpn. Mem. bd. mgrs. Coatesville Hosp.; mem. Bd. of Health, Coatesville; mem. Sch. Bd.; mem. Pa. Electric Associates, Coatesville Chamber of Commerce (dir.); pres. and dir. Coatesville Bldg. & Loan Assn.; dir. Eastern States Ice Assn.; asso. mem. Am. Inst. E.E. Republican. Presbyn. (trustee Coatesville Presbyterian Ch.). Clubs: Rotary (dir.), City, Coatesville Country, Chester County Automobile, Keystone Automobile; Union League (Phila.). Home: 1100 E. Lincoln Highway. Office: 15 N. 3d Av., Coatesville, Pa.

HARRIS, George Randolph, physician; b. Pittsburgh, Pa., July 2, 1891; s. George Randolph and Mary A. (Hoeh) H.; M.D., U. of Pittsburgh Med. Sch., 1914; grad. Med. Field Service Sch., Carlisle, Pa., 1921; Army Med. Sch., Washington, D.C., 1922; m. Sybil Maude Burton, Feb. 17, 1919; 1 son, George Randolph 3d. Engaged in pvt. practice of medicine, 1915-17, and in pvt. practice at Pittsburgh, Pa. since 1925; served as sec. and exec. sec. Allegheny Co. Med. Soc. since 1935; authorized med. examiner, Civil Aeronautics Authority; dir. Pittsburgh Dairy Council. Served as 1st lt. then capt. Med. Corps, U.S.A., 1917-22. Mem. Am. Med. Assn.; Aero-Med. Assn. of U.S.; Pa. State and Allegheny Co. med. socs. Democrat. Episcopalian. Mason. Home: Perrysville, Pa. Office: 500 Penn Av., Pittsburgh, Pa.

HARRIS, Harvey E(li), real estate; b. Bloomfield, N.J., Mar. 17, 1888; s. Eli and Lizzie (Cohen) H.; ed. pub. schs. and high sch., Bloomfield, N.J., grad. 1906; unmarried. In employ, Title Guarantee & Trust Co., N.Y. City, 1906-07; with Wimelbacher & Rice, gloves, 1907-08; with Holmes & Long, woolens, 1908-14; with M. Straus and Sons, leather, 1914-25; postmaster, Bloomfield, N.J., 1925-34; mem. firm Bloomfield Realty Co., since 1934, pres. Young Men's Bldg. & Loan Assn.; sec. "788" Holding Co., Inc. Served as pvt. F.A., U.S.A., 1917-19, with A.E.F. in France. Sec. and dir. Chamber of Commerce, Bloomfield, N.J. Mem. Am. Legion (past comdr. local post), Vets. Fgn. Wars. Republican. Jewish religion. B.P.O.E. (past dist. dep., grand exalted ruler). Mason. Home: 37 State St. Office: Bloomfield Bank & Trust Bldg., Bloomfield, N.J.

HARRIS, Henry Clayton, prof. and researcher in soils; b. Pike Rd., N.C., Dec. 12, 1898; s. Jesse Bryant and Jessie T. (Harrison) H.; grad. Whitsett (N.C.) Inst., 1917; A.B., U. of N.C., Chapel Hill, N.C., 1922; Ph.D., Cornell U., 1927; m. Martha Louise Robertson, Dec. 24, 1930; children—Henry Clayton, Anne Robertson. Teacher pub. schs., N.C., 1917; prin. Banner Elk (N.C.) High Sch., 1922; asst. in Agronomy Dept., Cornell U., 1924-26, instr. agronomy, 1926-27; prof. agronomy, Sam Houston State Teachers Coll., Huntsville, Tex., 1927-28; asst. prof. agronomy, U. of Del., Newark, Del., and asst. agronomist, Del. Agrl. Experiment Sta., since 1928. Served as pvt., S.A. T.C., U. of N.C., 1918, hon. disch., 1918. Fellow A.A.A.S.; mem. Am. Soc. Agronomy, Soil Science Soc. of America, Internat. Soc. of Soil Science, Assn. Official Agrl. Chemists, Am.

Soc. of Plant Physiology, Sigma Xi, Gamma Alpha. Independent Democrat. Clubs: Faculty (Newark, Del.); Cornell, U. of N.C. (Wilmington, Del). Author numerous articles on soil science and soil chemistry, fertilization, etc., in tech. pubs. Attended 3d Internat. Cong. of Soil Science, Oxford, Eng., 1935. Inspected many agrl. experiment stas. and colls. in Gt. Britain, Holland, Germany, Switzerland, France and throughout U.S. Address: 11 E. Park Pl., Newark, Del.

HARRIS, John Harold, physician; b. Newton, Kan., Jan. 5, 1896; s. William Henry and Martha A. (Houston) H.; A.B., Southwestern Coll., Winfield, Kan., 1920; M.D., Washington U. Med. Sch., St. Louis, Mo., 1923; M.M.Sc., U. of Pa. Grad. Sch. Medicine, 1934; m. LaRue Hamilton, June 9, 1924; children—John Harold, Jr., William Hamilton. Interne Univ. Hosp., Oklahoma City, 1923-24; in gen. practice of medicine at Great Falls, Mont., 1924-32, at Harrisburg, Pa. since 1934; specializing in radiology since 1934; radiologist, Carlisle Hosp., Carlisle, Pa. Served in Med. Corps, U.S.A., 1917-19. Mem. Am. Med. Assn., Am. and Phila. roentgen ray socs., Nu Sigma Nu. Republican. Presbyn. Mason (32°, Shriner). Clubs: Country (Harrisburg); Country (Carlisle). Home: 214 N. 17th St., Camp Hill, Pa. Office: 414 N. 2d St., Harrisburg, Pa.

HARRIS, John Henry, mgr. theaters and sports arenas; b. Pittsburgh, Pa., July 9, 1898; s. John Paul and Eleanor May (Davis) H.; grad. Crafton (Pa.) High Sch., 1917; LL.B., Georgetown, U., Washington, D.C., 1922; m. Lucille Miller, Jan. 22, 1932; 1 son, John Henry. Entered his father's business, 1922, and learned all phases of business; became mgr. Strand Theater, Youngstown, O., later also Harris Theater, McKeesport, Pa.; on father's death became mgr. all Harris interests, 1926; on uncle's death became gen. mgr., 1930; Harris Theaters sold to Warner Bros. Theaters, Inc., 1930; asst. to gen. mgr. Warner Theaters, New York, 1930; later mgr. Warner interests, Pittsburgh territory (80 theaters); resigned to manage Harris interests as gen. mgr. and exec.; pres. John P. Harris corpn., Harris Enterprises, Inc., Harris Amusement Co. (Detroit), Frank J. Harris Real Estate, Inc., Steel City Hockey, Inc., Pa. Sports & Enterprises; vice-pres. South Hills Theater Corpn., Penn Av. Theater, Inc., Perry Theater Corpn., Harris Amusement Co. of Pittsburgh, Harris Amusement Co. of East Liberty, Pa., North Side Theater, Inc.; sec. Youngstown Strand Co.; dir. Harris Theater Corpn., Washington Trust Co., Harris, Lawrence Co., Inc., Harris Amusement Co. of Pa. Served with R.O.T.C., June-Nov. 1918. Mem. Pittsburgh Chamber of Commerce. Chmn. City Neighborhood Div. of Community Fund of Pittsburgh since 1935. Trustee Western Penitentiary of Pa. One of 11 men who formed Variety Club (social organization of men in theatrical and amusement business), 1927, and first "chief barker" (pres.), 1927-29; a nat. orgn. of 21 clubs now form Variety Clubs of America (nat. pres. 1935-40). Mem. Am. Legion, Theater Mgrs. Assn., Delta Theta Pi. Republican. Catholic, (K.C.) Clubs: Variety, Rotary, Breakfast, University, Chartiers Heights Country, Pittsburgh Field, Metropolitan. Home: Royal York Apts. Office: 711 Clark Bldg., Pittsburgh, Pa.

HARRIS, John Tonner, telephone exec.; b. Bellefonte, Pa., Oct. 29, 1876; s. Henry Petrikin and Mary (Tonner) H.; student Pa. State Coll.; m. B. Mae Carter, Aug. 1, 1916; 1 son, John Tonner. With Central Pa. Telephone & Supply Co., 1898-1900, dist. mgr., Phillipsburg, Pa., 1900-01, dist. mgr. Altoona, Pa., 1901-07; traffic supervisor, Pa. Telephone Co., Harrisburg, Pa., 1907-08; div. traffic supervisor, Bell Telephone Co. of Pa., Harrisburg, Pa., 1908-20, Pittsburgh, 1920-23, gen. traffic mgr., Phila., 1923-26; v.p. and gen mgr. of central area, Harrisburg, Pa., 1926-38, operating v.p. and dir., Phila., since 1938; dir. Diamond State Telephone Co. Trustee Pa. State Coll. Dir. Pa. State Chamber of Commerce. Mason (Consistory; K.T.; Shriner). Club: Penn Athletic (Phila.). Home: The Mermont, Bryn Mawr, Pa. Office: 1835 Arch St., Phila, Pa.

HARRIS, Lynn H(arold), educator; b. at Milton, Pa., Nov. 26, 1885; s. James Lynn and Mary Annie (Polsgrove) H.; B.A., Dickinson Coll., 1906; M.A. in Philosophy, Boston U., 1909; M.A. in English, Yale, 1910, Ph.D., 1914; m. Rhoda Edna Reeser, Aug. 27, 1914; 1 dau., Elizabeth Reeser. Instr. English, Northwestern U., 1912-13; interim prof. English, Hamline U., 1913-14; instr. in English, U. of Ill., 1914-17; head English dept., U. of Chattanooga, 1917-20, Franklin Coll., 1920-23; pres. Beaver Coll. for Women, 1923-27; college acquired Beechwood, Inc., 1925, and moved from Beaver to Jenkintown, Pa.; pres. Howard Sem., West Bridgewater, Mass., 1927-37; dean and acting pres. Blue Ridge Coll., New Windsor, Md., 1937; pres. since April 1938. Ordained M.E. ministry. Mem. Modern Language Assn. America, Am. Assn. Univ. Profs., Tenn. Philol. Assn., Nat. Council Teachers of English, Am. Poetry Assn. (v.p. 1930-33), S.A.R., Phi Beta Kappa, Alpha Chi Rho, Pi Kappa Delta, Theta Alpha Pi. Mason. Editor: Ben Jonson's Catiline (critical edition), 1916. Contbr on religious and ednl. subjects. Home: New Windsor, Md.

HARRIS, Marian Dantzig, artist; b. Phila., Pa., Apr. 22, 1907; s. Louis and Frances (Dantzig) H.; student Wilmington (Del.) Pub. Schs., 1915-18; Wilmington (Del.) High Sch., 1918-22, Pa. Acad. of Fine Arts, Phila. (traveling scholarship), 1922-26; also Chester Springs (Pa.) Summer Sch., several summers; studied under Wayman Adams and Hugh Breckenridge; m. Mrs. Foster Gerard Lambert, 1928 (divorced, 1931). Exhibited: Pa. Acad. of Fine Arts, Nat. Acad. of Designs, Chicago Art Inst.; Art Club of Phila.; Albright Art Galleries (Buffalo, N.Y.), Memorial Art Gallery (Rochester, N.Y.), etc., one-man shows Ainslie Galleries, Babcock Galleries, Gimbels, Tricker Galleries, (all of New York), Bailey Galleries, Hartford, Conn.; awarded Georges A. Rhoads prize. Mem. Fellowship Pa. Acad. of Fine Arts, Plastic Club, Wilmington Soc. of Fine Arts, Am. Water Color Soc. Awarded Cresson Traveling Scholarship by Pa. Acad. Fine Artsfl 1925. Home: 920 Madison St., Wilmington, Del. Studio: 42 W. 58th St., New York, N.Y.

HARRIS, Mary Belle, federal instn. supt.; b. LaPlume, Pa.; d. John Howard and Mary (Mace) H.; A.B., Bucknell U., 1894, A.M., 1895; Ph.D., U. of Chicago, 1900; hon. LL.D., Bucknell Univ., 1927. Engaged in teaching Latin, 1900-12; studied in Europe, 1912-14; supt. women, workhouse, Blackwell's Island, N.Y., 1914-17; supt. Reformatory for Women, Clinton, N.J., 1918-19; supt. State Home for Girls, Trenton, N.J., 1919-25; supt. Federal Industrial Instn. for Women, Alderson, W.Va., since 1925. Trustee Bucknell Univ. Mem. Am. Assn. Univ. Women, Pi Beta Phi. Baptist. Club: Cosmopolitant (New York). Author: I Knew Them in Prison, 1936; Kalidasa; Poet of Nature, 1936. Contbr. to mags. Home: Alderson, W.Va.

HARRIS, Milton, textile research; b. Los Angeles, Calif., Mar. 21, 1906; s. Louis and Naomi (Hechman) H.; B.Sc., Ore. State Coll., Corvallis, Ore., 1926; Ph.D., Yale U., 1929; m. Carolyn Wolf, Mar. 30, 1934; children—Barney (adopted), John. Engaged as research chemist, Cheney Silk Mills, South Manchester, Conn., 1930-31; research chemist, Am. Assn. Textile Chemists, Washington, D.C., 1931-38; dir. research, Textile Foundation, Nat. Bur. of Standards, Washington, D.C., since 1938. Mem. A.A.A.S., Am. Chem. Soc., Am. Soc. Biol. Chemists, U.S. Inst. for Textile Research, Am. Assn. Textile Chemists and Colorists, Sigma Xi, Tau Beta Pi, Phi Lambda Upsilon, Gamma Alpha, Phi Kappa Phi, Phi Sigma Kappa. Home: 4815 Middlesex Lane, Bethesda, Md.

HARRIS, Philip H(oward), pres. and gen. mgr. Pa. Electric Co.; b. Portland, Me., Mar. 11, 1881; s. Newton W. and Lizzie (Huston) H.; B.S., in E.E., U. of Me., 1903; m. Ida Wright, June 8, 1911; 1 dau., Tillie C. Test course Gen. Electric Co., 1903-05; with Carolina Electric Power Corpn., 1905-06; in service dept. Westinghouse Electric & Mfg. Co., 1906-15, except 1 yr. when engr. Pocahontas Fuel Co.; with Pa. Electric Co. and its predecessor cos. since 1915, successively as supt. distribution, dist. supt., gen. supt., supt. power houses, and supt. power houses and engring. dept., gen. mgr. Pa. Electric Co., Johnstown Fuel Supply Co. and other subsidiaries in Western Pa. since 1928, now also pres. V.p. Cambria Co. Chapter, Am. Red Cross; dir. Cambria Library Assn., Conemaugh Valley Memorial Hosp. Dir. Johnstown Chamber of Commerce. Mason (Shriner). Club: Sunnehanna Country. Home: 414 Locust St. Office: 535 Vine St., Johnstown, Pa.

HARRIS, Stanley Edwards, physician; b. New York, N.Y., Sept. 24, 1894; s. Ira and Alice (Edwards) H.; A.B., Princeton U., 1917; M.D., U. of Pa., 1923; m. Margaret Dunham Roberts, June 1917; children—Stanley E., Margaret L.; Charles R., Lewis Thompson, Virginia A. Adjunct prof. of internal medicine, Med. Sch., Am. Univ. of Beirut, 1925-29, chmn. of dept. and asso. prof., 1929; asso. in medicine and cardiologist, Episcopal Hosp., Phila., since 1930; physician Student Health Service, U. of Pa., since 1931. Served as sergt. and bacteriologist, Pathol. Lab., Base Hosp. No. 9, U.S. Army, with A.E.F. at Chateauroux, France, 1917-19. Fellow Phila. Coll. Physicians; mem. Phila. Co. Med. Soc., Physiol. Soc. of Phila., Am. Heart Assn., A.M.A., Phi Beta Kappa, Alpha Omega Alpha, Alpha Kappa Kappa Mu. Contbr. articles on hypertension, coronary disease, etc., to med. jours. Home: 556 S. Lansdowne Av., Lansdowne, Pa. Office: 1520 Spruce St., Philadelphia, Pa.

HARRIS, Stephen, cons. engr.; b. Pottsville, Pa., Oct. 15, 1864; s. Stephen and Katharine (McArthur) H.; C.E., U. of Pa., 1886; m. Agnes Cointat, June 12, 1899; children—Eleonore (Mrs. Frank T. Gucker, Jr.), Katharine (Mrs. Henry Phillips, Jr.). Asst. engr. Nicaragua Canal Commn., 1897-1900, Philadelphia & Reading Ry. Co., 1903-04, Philadelphia Rapid Transit Co., 1905-08; asst. engr. on designs Dept. City Transit, Philadelphia, 1914-24, designing engr., 1924-32; engr. design Del. River Jt. Commn., 1933-36, cons. engr. since 1936. Registered professional engr. Pa. and N.J. Mem. Am. Soc. Civil Engrs. Republican. Presbyterian. Address: 119 W. Springfield Av., Chestnut Hill, Philadelphia, Pa.

HARRIS, Thomas Luther, sociologist; b. Modesto, Ill., Dec. 19, 1876; s. Sidney Thomas and Susan Elizabeth (McPherson) H.; A.B., U. of Ill., 1902; M.A., Ohio State U., 1905; Ph.D., U. of Wis., 1912; student Chicago Sch. Civics and Philanthropy; m. Georgine Ritland, Aug. 22, 1921; 1 dau., Susan Ritland. Asst. secretary Columbus (O.) Associated Charities, 1905-06; instr. sociology, U. of Pittsburgh, 1911; instr. social science, Dak. Wesleyan U., 1911-13; asst. prof. sociology, Carleton Coll., Northfield, Minn., 1913-15; prof. sociology, Miami U., 1915-21; asso. prof. sociology, 1921-23, prof. same, 1923, W.Va. U., also rural sociologist of Expt. Sta., W.Va. U. Coll. of Agr., 1926-29. Taught sociology, summer sessions, Univ. of Minn., 1915, Ohio State U., 1916, U. of Va., 1920. Mem. Am. Sociol. Soc., Am. Assn. Univ. Profs., Phi Beta Kappa. Methodist. Mason, Odd Fellow. Home: Morgantown, W.Va.

HARRIS, Virgil Bland, supt. of county schools; b. Little Birch, W.Va., May 22, 1905; s. George Robert and Nannie Catherine (Henderson) H.; ed. Glenville Normal Sch., 1922-24, Sutton High Sch., 1924-25, Marshall Coll., 1925; A.B., Glenville State Teachers Coll., 1929; student W.Va. U., 1937-38; also George Peabody Coll. (extension course), 1933-34; m. Macel Ellen Keener, Oct. 1, 1927; children—George Hampton, Virgil Bland, Nancy Jean, Virginia Anne, John Frederick. Teacher rural schools, Braxton Co., W.Va., 1925-29; teacher, Normantown (W.Va.) High Sch., 1929-31; prin. Gassaway (W.Va.) Grade Sch., 1931-34; asst. county supt., Braxton County Schools, 1934-36, supt. since 1936. Mem. N.E.A., State Supts. Assn., Central W.Va. Supts. Assn. Democrat. Baptist. Mason (past master). Clubs: Rotary (Sutton, W.Va.); Chamber of Commerce (Gassaway, W. Va.). One of a family of 8 children, born in rural sect., Braxton Co., W.Va., 7 of whom have college degrees. Home: Gassaway, W.Va. Office: Sutton, W.Va.

HARRIS, W. Carlton, prof. finance; b. Haddonfield, N.J., Aug. 4, 1890; s. Walter C. and Vernona E. (Malsbury) H.; LL.B., U. of Pa., 1913, Ph.D., 1930; m. Letitia M. Radcliffe, Feb. 8, 1923; 1 son, James R. Instr. finance, Wharton Sch. (U. of Pa.), 1920-23, asst. prof., 1923-31, prof. since 1931. Dir. rent relief Pa. State Emergency Relief Bd., 1934; spl. deputy sec. of banking, 1935-37; financial advisor, Camden, N.J., 1936-37, County of Camden, N.J., 1938; asst. treas. City of Philadelphia, 1938. Mem. Pa. State Bar Assn., Am. Acad. of Polit. and Social Science. Methodist. Clubs: Franklin Inn, Manufacturers and Bankers. Home: 3125 W Penn St., Philadelphia, Pa.

HARRIS, W. Hall, Jr., mem. law firm Harris & Thompson. Home: 31 E. Mt. Vernon Place. Office: Title Bldg., Baltimore, Md.

HARRISON, Benjamin Vincent, retired business exec.; b. Madison Co., N.J., Sept. 19, 1862; s. Daniel Vincent and Francis P. (Munn) H.; prep. edn. Montclair (N.J.) High Sch., 1868-79; A.B., Yale, 1883; m. Josephine French, Oct. 24, 1889; children—Dorothy (Mrs. Frederic P. Fiske), Helen Josephin (Mrs. Frank Lewis Soule), Benjamin Vincent, Francis French. Salesman N.J. Steel & Iron Co., Trenton, N.J., 1883-85, Palmer Smith & Co., Newark, N.J., 1885-88; began own leather business, New York, 1888, and proprietor, 1888-1907; pres. Benjamin V. Harrison Co., New York, 1901-27; treas. J. G. Curtis Leather Co., Ludlow, Pa., 1901-27; dir. Montclair Trust Co., 1914-37, chmn. bd., 1934-37. Pres. Montclair Bd. Edn., 1911-12. Dir. Family Welfare Soc.; v.p. Mountainside Hosp. Life Mem. Am. Mus. Natural History, Met. Mus. of Art. Awarded Citation for Distinguished Community Service, 1938. Republican. Presbyterian. Clubs: Graduates, Elihu (New Haven, Conn.); Yale (New York); Montclair (N.J.) Golf; Mastigouche (Quebec, Can.). Address: 54 S. Mountain Av., Montclair, N.J.

HARRISON, Bruce, lawyer; b. Duquesne, Pa., Aug. 21, 1891; s. Daniel and Mary Ellen (Sheppard) H.; ed. U. of Pittsburgh Sch. Econs., 1911-12; LL.B., U. of Pittsburgh Sch. of Law, 1915; m. Estella V. Beckman, Aug. 31, 1921; children—James Beckman, Bruce, Jr. Admitted to Pa. bar, 1915, and since engaged in gen. practice of law at Pittsburgh; asso. with firm Morris, Walker and Allen, 1915-17, with Morris, Walker and Boyle, 1917-29; mem. firm Morris, Walker Bothwell and Harrison, 1929-32; mem. firm Shrum, Harrison and Craig since 1933; sec., dir. and counsel Superior Paper Products Co. Served as pvt. inf. U.S.A., with A.E.F., 1918-19. Mem. Am., Pa. State, and Allegheny Co. bar assns., Commercial Law League of America. Republican. Presbyn. Mason (32°, Shriner). Home: 300 Orchard Drive, Mt. Lebanon. Office: 1508 Law & Finance Bldg., Pittsburgh, Pa.

HARRISON, Charles Custis, Jr., investments; b. Phila., Pa., April 27, 1876; s. Charles Custis and Ellen (Waln) H.; student St. Paul's Sch. (Concord, N.H.), and U. of Pa.; m. Marie Lemoines, Nov. 27, 1901; children—Mrs. John T. Nightingale, Mrs. James K. Davis, Mrs. John H. Hunter, 2d, Charles Custis, 3d. Mem. firm of Harrison & Co., Phila.; dir. U.S. Pipe & Foundry Co. Clubs: Radnor Hunt, Orange County Hunt. Home: The Plains, Va. Office: 123 S. Broad St., Philadelphia, Pa.

HARRISON, Charles J., Jr., b. Somerset, Pa., Dec. 2, 1884; s. Chas. J. and Margaret (Sanner) H.; ed. St. John's College; m. Gladys Speck, Oct. 6, 1912; children—Charles J. III, Frank S., Gladys S., Virginia W. Cashier and asst. treas. Somerset Co. Nat. Bank and Co. Trust Co., 1901-10; dir. Co. Trust Co. since 1912, pres. since 1934; real estate broker since 1910; engaged in ins. business with Edward A. Woods Agency (agents Equitable Life Ins. Soc. of U.S.), Pittsburgh, since 1910. Mem. Somerset Borough Council, later becoming pres.; justice of the peace, 20 yrs. Served as 1st lt., U.S. Army, Mexican border service, 1916. Dir. Somerset Community Hosp. 9 yrs. Odd Fellow. Home: 137 E. Church St. Office: Harrison Bldg., Somerset, Pa.

HARRISON, Earl G(rant), lawyer; b. Phila., Pa., April 27, 1899; s. Joseph L. and Anna (MacMullin) H.; grad. Frankford High Sch., Phila., 1917; A.B., U. of Pa., 1920, LL.B., 1923; m. Carol Rodgers Sensenig, April 2, 1923; children—Paul, Joseph Barton, Earl G., Jr. Admitted to Pa. bar, 1923, and since practiced in Phila.; asso. Saul, Ewing, Remick & Saul, 1923-32; partner Saul, Ewing, Remick & Saul since 1932; lecturer, U. of Pa. Law Sch., 1932-33, 1936-37. Vice-pres. Community Fund of Phila. and Vicinity since 1933; pres. Pub. Charities Assn. of Pa. since 1936; mem. bd. dirs. Phila. Forum since 1933; mem. bd. trustees Phila. Award since 1936. Trustee Pa. Sch. of Social Work and U. of Pa. Mem. Pa. Bar Assn. (mem. exec. com. 1934-37), Phila. Bar Assn. (bd. govs. 1934-37), U. of Pa. Law Sch. Alumni (vice-pres. since 1934), Alpha Chi Rho, Phi Beta Kappa, Delta Sigma Rho. Republican. Presbyterian. Club: University (Phila.). Home: Moylan, Rose Valley, Pa. Office: 2301 Packard Bldg., Philadelphia, Pa.

HARRISON, Edmund Pendleton Hunter, Jr., physician; b. Martinsburg, W.Va., Nov. 20, 1900; s. Edmund P. H. and Caroline Henderson (Webster) H.; A.B., Princeton U., 1922; M.D., Johns Hopkins U. Med. Sch., 1926; m. Miriam L. Washabaugh, Aug. 21, 1931. Interne Hosp. for Women of Md., Baltimore, 1926-27, Johns Hopkins Hosp., 1927-28; asst. resident, Johns Hopkins Hosp., 1928-30, resident obstetrician, 1930-31; instr. in obstetrics, Johns Hopkins U. Med. Sch. since 1931; asso. in obstetrics, U. of Md. Med. Sch. since 1933; mem. sr. staff, Hosp. for Women of Md. since 1932, Union Memorial Hosp. since 1934; obstetrician in chief, St. Joseph's Hosp., 1933-35. Served in S.A.T. C., 1918-19. Mem. Am. Med. Assn., Princeton Court, Pithotomy Club, Am. Soc. Colonial Wars. Democrat. Presbyterian. Home: 2903 N. Charles St., Baltimore, Md.

HARRISON, Francis Grillet, physician and surgeon; b. Phila., Pa., Apr. 23, 1891; s. Rollin Charles and Margretta (Cleland) H.; grad. Phila. Central High Sch.; M.D., U. of Pa., 1913; m. Amelia Gass, 1917; children—Francis, George B. Instr. in surgery, U. of Pa. Med. Sch., 1915-18; asso. prof. of urology, Grad. Sch., U. of Pa., since 1937. Served in U.S. Naval Reserve Force, 1917-18. Mem. Phila. Urol. Soc., Am. Urol. Assn., Phila. Coll. of Physicians, Delta Upsilon, Alpha Mu Pi Omega. Protestant. Clubs: Union League (Phila.); Merion Cricket. Home: Gladwyne, Pa. Office: 1900 Spruce St., Philadelphia, Pa.

HARRISON, H(enry) Norris, transportation official; b. Philadelphia, Pa., May 18, 1887; s. C. Leland and Catherine (Norris) H.; ed. St. Paul's Sch. and Mass. Inst. Tech.; m. Marjorie Mary Butler, Oct. 12, 1912; children—Robert Butler, C. Leland, Christopher Norris. Successively salesman, dist. supervisor traffic, division supt. and div. traffic employment mgr. Bell Telephone Co., 1910-25; treas. Fidelity Storage & Warehouse Co., 1925-27; v.p. Fidelity-20th Century Storage Warehouse Co., 1927-29, pres., 1929-37, chmn. bd. since 1937; v.p. Fidelity-20th Century Transportation Co., 1935-37, pres. since 1937; dir. of last three cos. named and DeLong Hook & Eye Co. Dir. Devitts Camp, Pa. Tuberculosis Assn.; dir. Better Business Bureau of Philadelphia. Pres. Delta Upsilon Assn. of Philadelphia. Democrat. Episcopalian. Clubs: Rittenhouse, Sunnybrook Golf, Chester River Yacht and Country. Home: R.F.D. 2, Centreville, Md. Office: 1811 Market St., Philadelphia, Pa.

HARRISON, Joseph F(rancis) X(avier), S.J., educator; b. at New York, N.Y., March 15, 1901; s. Michael and Agnes T. (Donovan) H.; ed. St. Andrew-on-Hudson, Poughkeepsie, N.Y., 1919-23, Weston Coll., Weston, Mass. (affiliated with Boston Coll., and Gregorian Univ., Rome, Italy), 1923-26, A.B., Boston Coll., 1925, A.M., same, 1926, Ph.D., Gregorian Univ., 1926; theological study, Woodstock Coll., Woodstock, Md., 1929-33. Entered S.J. (Jesuits) Aug. 14, 1919, at Poughkeepsie, N.Y.; ordained priest, June 21, 1932, Woodstock, Md.; Year of Ascetic Theology, St. Andrew-on-Hudson, 1934-35; engaged as teacher classics, Georgetown Prep. Sch., Garrett, Md., 1926-27, Xavier High Sch., N.Y. City, 1927-28, Georgetown Prep. Sch., 1928-29; prof. philosophy, St. Joseph's Coll., Phila., Pa., 1933-34, prof. psychology, 1935-39, asst. dean since 1939, also Faculty Moderator, dir. Coll. Placement Bur., dir. Coll. Publicity Dept., Coll. Newspaper, Coll. Year Book, Coll. Lecture Forum. Roman Catholic. Home: 18th and Thompson Sts., Philadelphia, Pa. Office: 54th St. and City Line, Philadelphia, Pa.

HARRISON, Thomas Randolph, mfg. industrial measuring instruments; b. New Kent Co., Va., Jan. 4, 1891; s. Chapman Leigh and Mary Ida (Nance) H.; ed. Va. Poly. Inst., 1907-11; B.S. in E.E., George Washington U., 1917; m. Susie Ruffin Coleman, June 27, 1916; children—Thomas Randolph, Jr., Sarah Powell, Richard Logan. Employed as elec. engr. with various cos., 1912-14; lab. asst. to asso. physicist, U.S. Bur. of Standards, 1915-20; physicist, Champion Porcelain Co., 1920-24; dir. research and tech. adviser, The Brown Instrument Co., mfr. industrial measuring instruments, Phila., Pa., since 1924. Mem. Am. Phys. Soc., Optical Soc. of America, Philos. Soc. of Washington, Franklin Inst. Honored by award of certificate of merit from The Franklin Inst. Home: 140 Hewett Rd., Wyncote. Office: The Brown Instrument Co., Philadelphia, Pa.

HARROP, George Argale, Jr., M.D.; b. Peru, Ill., Nov. 5, 1890; s. George Argale and Mary Belle (Cole) H.; U. of Wis., 1908-10; A.B., Harvard, 1912; M.D., Johns Hopkins University Medical School, 1916; research, University of Copenhagen, 1920-21; m. Esther Caldwell, Mar. 16, 1924; children—George Argale III, William Caldwell, David Cole. Interne and asst. resident phys. Johns Hopkins Hosp., 1916-21; resident phys. and instr. in medicine, Columbia U., 1921-23; asso. prof. medicine, Peking U. Med. Coll., China, 1923-24; asso. prof. medicine, Johns Hopkins, 1925-38 in charge chem. lab. and work in diseases of metabolism and endocrinology; dir. of research Squibb Inst. for Med. Research, New Brunswick, N.J., since 1938. Fellow Am. Scandinavian Foundation; mem. A.M.A., Assn. Am. Physicians, Am. Coll. Physicians, Am. Soc. for Clin. Investigation, Am. Soc. Biol. Chemists, Soc. for Exptl. Biology and Medicine, Société Biologique (Paris), Cosmopolitan Clinical Club, Am. Clin. and Climatol. Assn., Phi Beta Kappa, Alpha Omega Alpha, Phi Kappa Psi, Nu Sigma Nu. Club: Harvard (New York). Author: Management of Diabetes, 1925; Diet in Disease, 1930; also numerous articles on metabolism, diabetes, the use of diet in therapy, etc. Home: 33 Cleveland Lane, Princeton, N.J.

HARRY, Carolus Powel, clergyman; b. Norristown, Pa., Jan. 13, 1884; s. Charles Howard and Elizabeth (Longaker) H.; grad. William Penn Charter Sch., Phila., 1903; A.B., U. of Pa., 1907, A.M., 1912; student Phila. Sem., 1907-10; D.D., Carthage (Ill.) Coll., 1927; m. Lillian Dannaker, 1914; children—Ruth, John B. Teacher of history, George School, 1910-11; ordained to ministry Ministerium of Pennsylvania, 1911; pastor Ch. of the Holy Spirit, Reading, Pa., 1911-17; pastor for Luth. students, U. of Pa., 1917-22; sec. Bd. of Edn., United Luth. Ch., since 1922. Mem. Phi Beta Kappa. Clubs: St. Ambrose Soc. (St. Andrew Chapter, Phila.). Editor of Luther League Topics Quarterly since 1920; contbr. to Luth. periodicals. Author: Protest and Progress—A Reformation Manual, 1917; Everyday—A Manual of Devotions, 1935. Co-author: The Use of the Common Service. Home: 210 W. Fornance St., Norristown, Pa.

HARRY, David G.; b. Pylesville, Md., June 11, 1880; s. David and Maria J. (Warner) H.; student pub. schs. and high sch., Harford Co., Md., 1885-96; honors in agr., U. of Md., 1925; m. Sara L. Lanius, Dec. 5, 1908; children—Helen L. (Mrs. James J. DeRan, Jr.), David G., J. Charles. Engaged in farming since 1900; employed as dist. mgr. for ins. co., 1915-39; pres. Md. State Dairymen's Assn., 1918; vice-pres. Federal Land Bank, Baltimore, 1922-33; served as mem. Md. State Senate, 1922-27; pres. Southern States Cooperative, Richmond, Va., since 1938; dir. Farm Credit Administrn., Baltimore, Md., since 1922. Trustee Highland

High Sch., Streett, Md. Republican. Mem. Religious Soc. Friends. Mason. Grange. Home: R.D. 1, Pylesville, Md.

HARRY, Philip Warner, college prof.; b. Pylesville, Md., Aug. 9, 1877; s. David and Maria Jane (Warner) H.; ed. Georgetown (Ky.) Acad., 1893-94, Georgetown Coll., 1894-96; A.B., Johns Hopkins U., 1898, Ph.D., same, 1903; grad. study, Sorbonne, Paris, 1905-06; m. Elizabeth Eshleman, June 16, 1926. Instr. Romance langs., U. of Cincinnati, Northwestern U.; asst. prof. Romance langs., U. of Pittsburgh, 1909-14; associate professor of Romance langs., Colby College, 1914-22; professor of Romance langs., Franklin and Marshall Coll. since 1922. Served as Y.M.C.A. sec. with A.E.F. and dir. edn., Toulon, France, 1918-19. Mem. Modern Lang. Assn. of America, Assn. Coll. Profs., Lambda Chi Alpha. Mem. Religious Soc. of Friends. Clubs: University, Cliosophic. Editor textbooks of French and Spanish. Home: 828 Marietta Av., Lancaster, Pa.

HART, Cecil Albert, lawyer; b. Hackensack, N.J., June 6, 1905; s. Archibald C. and Lily L. (Fenwick) H.; LL.B., N.Y. Law Sch., 1927; m. Gertrude Hill, Sept. 4, 1929 (deceased); children—Victor Wellington, Irene Elsie; m. 2d Leta A. Decker, June 11, 1937. Engaged in gen. practice of law at Hackensack; pres. and dir. Fenwick-Reddaway Mfg. Co., Newark, N.J.; dir. Bogata Nat. Bank, Bogata, N.J. Mem. Phi Delta Phi. Democrat. Episcopalian. Mason. Elk. Club: Oritani Field (Hackensack). Home: 91 Cedar Av. Office: 210 Main St., Hackensack, N.J.

HART, Charles, pres. Delaware River Steel Co.; b. Doylestown, Pa., Jan. 5, 1869; s. Samuel and Ellen Yardley (Eastburn) H.; B.S., Swarthmore Coll., 1892; m. Florence McCurdy, Oct. 12, 1907; children—Natalie, Florence (Mrs. R. A. Montgomery), Eileen (Mrs. Morton McMichael), Lucia. Began as chemist, 1893; with Republic Iron & Steel Co., Youngstown, O., 1900-06, advancing to vice-pres. and gen. mgr.; pres. Inland Steel Co., Indiana Harbor, Ind., 1906-08; pres. Delaware River Steel Co., Chester, Pa., since 1909; partner Charles Hart & Associates, consultants on chem. and metall. problems; pres. and dir. Victoria Gypsum Mining & Mfg. Co.; dir. Chester-Cambridge Bank & Trust Co., Robert McCurdy Co. Mem. Am. Iron and Steel Inst., Am. Inst. Mining and Metall. Engrs., Army Ordnance, Eastern States Blast Furnace and Coke Assn., Phila. Soc. for Promoting Agr., Chicago Dist. Blast Furnace and Coke Assn., Franklin Inst., Bucks Co. Hist. Soc., Book and Key, Sigma Xi, Sigma Tau. Republican. Mem. Buckingham Friends Meeting. Club: India House (New York). Home: Creek Rd., Media, Pa. Address: Box 500, Chester, Pa.

HART, Edward J., congressman; b. Jersey City, N.J., Mar. 25, 1893; s. Dominic J. and Margaret (Connelly) H.; A.B., St. Peters Coll., 1913, M.A., 1914; Georgetown University Law Sch., 1924; m. Loretta A. O'Connell, Apr. 14, 1936. Admitted to bar of D.C., 1924 and to New Jersey bar, 1925; in practice at Jersey City since 1927; sec. Excise Commn., Washington, D.C., 1913-17; chief field deputy Internal Revenue Bur., 1918-21; asst. corpn. counsel of Jersey City, 1930-34; mem. 74th and 75th Congresses (1935-39), 14th N.J. Dist. Home: 96 Sherman Place. Office: 591 Summit Av., Jersey City, N.J.

HART, John Francis, cartoonist; b. Germantown, Phila., Pa., May 30, 1867; s. John and Thirza Mahala (Stagg) H.; ed. pub. schs., Germantown; m. Caroline E. Pettit, Apr. 6, 1895. Served apprenticeship as box wood engraver; later engaged in drawing posters; cartoonist on Phila. Press, 1908-13; puzzle cartoonist, Phila. North American, since 1915. Associated with C. W. Ervin in conducting a cartoon syndicate, supplying labor cartoons throughout U.S., 1916, 17; also syndicating through Bell syndicate. Socialist. Home: 169 Hansberry St., Germantown, Philadelphia, Pa.

HART, Robert S., v.p. Fidelity & Deposit Co.; b. Baltimore, Md., Sept. 9, 1871; s. Malcolm and Elizabeth Catherine (Shaw) H.; student pub. and private schs. and Baltimore City Coll.; m. Jane Beall Johnson, Dec. 14, 1893 (died June 28, 1936); children—Robert Malcolm, Archibald Murdoch; m. 2d, Eugenia Bratt Jones, July 17, 1937; one daughter, Eleanor Murdoch. Has been with Fidelity & Deposit Company since 1903, sec. since 1913, mgr. fidelity dept. since 1914, v.p. since 1920; sec., mgr. fidelity dept and v.p. Am. Bonding Co. since 1920. Home: 101 W. Monument St. Office: Fidelity Bldg., Baltimore, Md.

HART, Thomas, lawyer; b. Philadelphia, Pa., Nov. 24, 1894; s. Charles Byerly and Ida Virginia (Hill) H.; student Episcopal Acad., 1903-12; A.B., U. of Pa., 1916; LL.B., U. of Pa. Law Sch., 1929; m. Margaret Newbold Smith, May 15, 1918; children—Margaret Newbold, Thomas. Employed by J. B. Lippincott Co. publishers, 1916-17, Philadelphia Trust Co. (now Fidelity-Philadelphia Trust Co.), 1919-22; salesman Calbury, Ellis & Haines, investments, 1922-24; mem. administrative staff, U. of Pa., and dir. Houston Hall (first student union in America), 1924-29; admitted to Pa. bar, 1929; associated with law firm Hepburn & Norris, 1929-32; mem. of firm Hepburn & Norris since 1932; dir. Geyelin & Frank, Inc. (travel agency). Enlisted 1st Troop Philadelphia City Cavalry, Apr. 30, 1917; transferred to 103d Trench Mortar Battery, Jan. 1, 1918, commd. corporal; transferred to Intelligence Dept., 28th Div. and later to Air Service, U.S. Army; grad. as cadet major, U.S. Sch. of Military Aeronautics, Princeton, N.J., Oct. 5, 1918; hon. discharged, Dec. 17, 1918. Trustee and ex-sec. bd. The Episcopal Acad., Lankenau Hosp., Magee Memorial Convalescent Hosp.; mgr. Am. Oncologic Hosp., ex-pres., now dir. Phila. Charity Ball, Inc.; former pres., now mgr. Preston Retreat; dir. Athenaeum of Philadelphia. Am. Bar Assn., Pa. Bar Assn. (sec. Program Com.), Philadelphia Bar Assn., Juristic Soc., Soc. Colonial Wars (deputy gov. Commonwealth of Pa.), Am. Acad. Music (dir.), S.R., Soc. War of 1812, Gen. Soc. Colonial Wars (vice gov. gen.), Delta Psi; hon. mem. First Troop Phila. City Cavalry. Republican. Episcopalian. Clubs: Penn (sec. and dir.), Philadelphia, Merion Cricket, Union League, Mask and Wig; State in Schuylkill (sec.); Rabbit; St. Anthony (New York); Eagle Island Gunning (Salem, N.J.); Wharton Gun (Stretches Point, N.J.). Author: A Record of the Hart Family of Philadelphia, 1735-1920 (privately published). Home: Wynnewood, Pa. Office: 1500 Walnut St., Philadelphia, Pa.

HART, U. Shuman, banker; b. Huntingdon, Pa.; s. Barnett H. and Minnie (Shuman) H.; student at Bellefonte Academy, Bellefonte, Pa.; A.B., from Dickinson College; m. Dorothy E. Barth. With Banking Dept., Commonwealth of Pa., 1929-34; exec. vice pres. Citizens Nat. Bank of Hollidaysburg since 1934. Served as private Air Service, U.S. Army, Mar.-Nov. 1918. Mem. Phi Delta Theta. Republican. Methodist. Home: 314 Walnut St. Office: Citizens Nat. Bank, Hollidaysburg, Pa.

HART, Walter Lawrence, editor; b. Tunnelton, W.Va., Jan. 11, 1902; s. Thomas Dawson and Louella (Showalter) H.; ed. Tunnelton grade and high sch.; student W.Va. U., 1919-23; m. Mary P. Hart, Dec. 25, 1925; children—Mary Lou, Walter L., II. Began as newspapers reporter, 1922, later sports editor, columnist and editor; pres. Dominion-News Co. Mem. Reserve Officers Training Corps. Democrat. Elk, Moose. Club: Nat. Democratic (Washington, D.C.). Home: 219 Gingwood St. Office: Pleasant St., Morgantown, W.Va.

HARTE, Richard, pres. Ames Baldwin Wyo. Co.; s. Richard Hickman and Maria (Ames) H.; A.B., Harvard U., 1917; m. Mabel Webster, Aug. 16, 1917. Pres. and dir. Ames Baldwin Wyo Co. since 1931; officer or dir. many companies. Address: Parkersburg, W.Va.

HARTER, George Abram, emeritus prof. mathematics, U. of Del. Address: University of Delaware, Newark, Del.

HARTER, Nathan Warren, prof. mathematics; b. Seville, O., Feb. 15, 1887; s. William and Eliza Ellen (Peters) H.; A.B., Wittenberg Coll., 1908, A.M., same, 1909; grad. student U. of Pittsburgh, summers 1926-30; m. Besse Paula Roseberry, June 1, 1911; children—William Nathan, Elizabeth Margaret Roseberry, Nathan Francis Roseberry. Engaged as instr. physics and mathematics, Wittenberg Acad., 1909-11; prof. mathematics, Thiel Coll., Greenville, Pa. continuously since 1911, local treas. Thiel Coll., 1911-21, actg. dean, 1916-18; with Youngstown Y.M.C.A. Inst., Mathematics, 1923-27; dir. Thiel Coll. Summer Sessions, 1937-39; pres. Abrams-Orton Mfg. Co., 1915-18, N. W. Harter Mfg. Co., gas furnaces, 1918-25; treas. Greenville Consumers Co-operative Assn. Served as instr. S.A.T.C., Thiel Coll., 1918-19. Sec. Kiwanis Club, Greenville, 1922-26. Mem. Am. Math. Assn., Am. Assn. Univ. Profs., Phi Gamma Delta, Thiel Coll. Phi Mu Chi Sci. Club. Democrat. Lutheran. Clubs: Country, Chess, Tennis (Greenville). Home: 66 College Av., Greenville, Pa.

HARTGEN, Frederick Anthony, metallurgist; b. Reading, Pa., Oct. 14, 1899; s. Edward A. and Anna Catherine (Kemp) H.; student Carnegie Inst. Tech., Ohio State U., Columbus, U. of Minn., Minneapolis, and Carnegie Inst. Tech. Grad. Sch.; m. Harriet Frances Putnam, June 29, 1928; children—Nancy Jean, Roger Putnam, Frances Ann, Judith. Analyst Carpenter Steel Co., 1917-20; research asst. U.S. Bur. of Mines, Pittsburgh, 1920-21; mem. field staff U.S. Bur. of Mines, N.D., 1921; asst. to physicist on ventilation research Holland Tunnel, Pittsburgh, 1921-22; lab. asst., metall. dept., Ohio State U., 1922-23; lab. asst. research on blast furnaces, U.S. Bur. of Mines, Minneapolis, 1923-25, asst. metallurgist on study of physical chemistry of steel making, Pittsburgh, 1926-31; metallurgist A. O. Smith Corpn., 1931-32; research metallurgist Reading (Pa.) Iron Co., 1932-37; instr. ferrous metallurgy, Pa. State Coll. Extension, 1935; cons. metallurgist Empire Steel Casting Co., 1937-38; chief metallurgist in charge open hearth and electric steel making Nat.-Erie Corpn., Erie, Pa., since 1938. Mem. Am. Inst. Mining and Metall. Engrs. (mem. wrought iron com.). K.C. Writer numerous articles in tech. pubs. Holder U.S. patents 2072072 and 2072073, dealing with production of wrought iron or steel from iron ore by single step process. Home: 4625 Homeland Boul. Office: 1521 Raspberry St., Erie, Pa.

HARTLEY, Fred Allan, Jr., congressman; b. Harrison, N.J., Feb. 22, 1903; s. Fred Allan and Frances Alice H.; ed. high sch., Kearny, N.J., and Rutgers U.; m. Hazel Lorraine Roemer, Jan. 30, 1921; children—Henry Allan, Frances Lorraine, Fred Jack. Library commr., Kearny, 1923-25, police and fire commr., 1925-29; mem. 71st and 72d Congresses (1929-33), 8th N.J. Dist., and 73d to 76th Congresses (1933-39), 10th N.J. Dist. Republican. Protestant. Home: 52 Livingstone Av., Kearny, N.J.

HARTLEY, Ralph Vinton Lyon, research engr.; b. Spruce, Nev., Nov. 30, 1888; s. Robert and Matilda Elizabeth (Hutchison) H.; A.B., U. of Utah, 1909; B.A., Oxford U., Eng., 1912, B.Sc., same ,1913; m. Florence Vail, Mar. 21, 1916. Asso. with Western Electric Co. Engring. Dept. and its successor Bell Telephone Laboratories, Inc. since 1913, research on radio telephony, including part in Arlington demonstration of 1915, and on submarine detection problem during World War, supervision of research on telephone and telegraph transmission over wires, to 1933, individual research as permitted by health since 1933; served as instr. U. of Nev., 1909-10. Fellow A.A.A.S., Am. Phys. Soc., Acoustical Soc. of America, Inst. Radio Engrs. Mem. Am. Inst. Elec. Engrs. Rhodes Scholar from Utah, 1910-13. Home: 174 Summit Av., Summit, N.J. Office: 463 West St., New York, N.Y.

HARTMAN, Albert Leopold, prin. pub. schs.; b. Weippe, Ida., May 13, 1897; s. Charles William and Lena Hertel; B.S., State Teachers Coll., Emporia, Kan., 1921; ed. U. of Wis., summer 1923; A.M., Teachers Coll. of Columbia U., 1926; m. Mabel Virginia Cross, June 27, 1922; 1 dau., Virginia Lucille. Dir. Visual Edn. Service, State Teachers Coll., Emporia, Kan., 1921-22; supt. schs., Garfield, Kan.,

1922-25; dir. research, Bd. Edn., Montclair, N.J., 1926-28; prin. Edgemont and Watchung schs., Montclair, N.J. since 1928; instr. summer session, Rutgers U., 1931-38, and at U. of N.H., 1939. Served as 2d lt. inf. U.S.A., 1918. Mem. Nat. Edn. Assn., Am. Assn. Sch. Adminstrs., Nat. Soc. for Study Edn., Kappa Delta Pi, Phi Delta Kappa. Unitarian. Clubs: Cosmopolitan, Kiwanis (Montclair). Home: 104 Haddon Place, Upper Montclair, N.J. Office: Edgemont School, Montclair, N.J.

HARTMAN, Carl G., zoölogist; b. Reinbeck, Ia., June 3, 1879; s. Ossian W. and Sophia (Lemwigh) H.; State University of Ia., 1896-97; B.A., Univ. of Tex., 1902, M.A., 1904, Ph.D., 1915; m. Eva Rettenmeyer, June 23, 1919; children—Carl Frederick, Philip Emil, Paul Arthur and Bertha Grace. County superintendent of schools, Travis County, Texas, 1904-09; mem. faculty University of Tex., 1912-25, prof. zoölogy, 1923-25; now research asso. Lab. of Embryology, Carnegie Instn., Johns Hopkins Med. Sch. Mem. Nat. Acad. Science, Am. Soc. Zoölogists, A.A.A.S., Am. Assn. Anatomists, Am. Physiol. Soc., Am. Soc. Mammalogists, Soc. Exptl. Biology and Medicine, American Soc. of Naturalists, Sigma Xi, Phi Beta Kappa. Lutheran. Author: County Supervision of Schools, 1905; The First Book of Health (with L. B. Bibb, M.D.), 1912; The Human Body and Its Enemies (with same), 1912; Laboratory Manual in Human Physiology, 1915; Embryology, and Reproduction of the Opossum (series of articles), 1916-25; Menstruation and Reproduction in Monkeys (series of articles), 1925; Anatomy of the Rhesus Monkey, 1933; Time of Ovulation in Women, 1936. Home: 19 Merrymount Road, Baltimore, Md.

HARTMAN, Edwin Mitman, educator; b. nr. Applebachville, Bucks Co., Pa., Oct. 6, 1869; s. William Fulmer and Susan (Mitman) H.; State Normal Sch., Kutztown, Pa., 1890-91; A.B., Franklin and Marshall College, 1895, A.M., 1898 (Pd.D, same college, 1921); grad. Theological Seminary of Reformed Church in U.S., 1900; post-grad. study, U. of Pa.; m. Helen Russell Stahr (A.B., Wellesley, 1894), d. of John S. Stahr, June 5, 1905; children—Frances Andrews, William Fulmer, Charles Stahr. Teacher pub. schs., Bucks Co., Pa., 1886-90; prin. Franklin and Marshall Acad. since 1897; asst. to pres. Franklin & Marshall Coll., directing financial campaign, 1903-07; sec. dept. field work and dir. financial campaign of Forward Movement, Ref. Ch. in U.S., 1919-25; chmn. Civil Service Commission for Lancaster Dept. of Police, 1926-30; chmn. Lancaster City Shade Tree Commn. since 1929; pres. Head Masters' Club of Phila. Dist., 1928. Mem. Pa. German Soc., Phi Beta Kappa, Phi Sigma Kappa. Democrat. Home: Lancaster, Pa.

HARTMAN, Galen Campbell, lawyer; b. Independence, Pa., May 22, 1865; s. Robert Latour and Rebecca Jane (Perrine) H.; student Bethany Coll., 1880-82; LL.B., U. of Mich., 1885; m. Ada Blanche Taggart, Oct. 16, 1889. Admitted to Pittsburgh bar, 1885; in private practice of law since 1885. Mem. Am. Bar. Assn., Allegheny County Bar Assn., Acad. Science and Arts, S.A.R., Hist. Soc. of Western Pa., Pittsburgh Chamber of Commerce. Republican. Mem. Christian Ch. Clubs: U. of Mich. Alumni, Automobile Club of Pittsburgh (dir.), Athletic Assn. (Pittsburgh). Home: Bellefield Dwellings, 4400 Center Av. Office: Farmers Bank Bldg., Pittsburgh, Pa.

HARTMAN, Guy Nelson, county supt. of schools; b. Waynesboro, Pa., Aug. 30, 1890; s. John H. and Anna (Brindle) H.; A.B., Bridgewater (Va.) Coll., 1919; A.M., U. of Pa., 1921; B.D., Crozier Sem., 1921; grad. student U. of Pittsburgh and U. of Cincinnati (L.H.D. 1936); m. Edna Walker, June 10, 1917; children—John, Anna Caroline. Teacher of English, Meyersdale (Pa.) High Sch., 1921-24; prin. Garret (Pa.) High Sch., 1924-29; teacher of mathematics, Berlin (Pa.) High Sch., 1929-31; asst. supt., Somerset Co. Schs., 1931-34; supt. since 1934. Pres. County Sunday Sch. Assn.; pres. County Agrl. Assn. Rotarian. Mem. Pa. State Edn. Assn., N.E.A., Am. Sch. Adminstrs., Phi Delta Kappa. Home R.D. 2, Meyersdale, Pa. Office: Somerset, Pa.

HARTMAN, Ralph Ellis, clergyman; b. Harrisburg, Pa., Feb. 12, 1892; s. Rev. J. Stewart and Ella (Flickinger) H.; grad. Mercersburg (Pa.) Acad., 1909; A.B., Franklin and Marshall Coll., Lancaster, Pa., 1913; grad. Theol. Sem. of Ref. Ch. in U.S., Lancaster, Pa., 1916; m. Aurelia Hornberger, Sept. 21, 1916; children—Mary Jane, Ralph Ellis, Jr., Robert Frederick. Ordained to ministry Ref. Ch. in U.S., 1916; minister, Marysville, Pa., 1916-21; Quakertown, Pa., 1921-25, Latrobe, Pa., 1925-30; minister Grace Ch., Frederick, Md., since 1930; past pres. Spiritual Conf. of Ref. Ch.; pres. Synod of Potomac of Ref. Ch. in America; mem. and past pres. various city and co. ministerial assns. Mem. bd. trustees Potomac Synod; pres. bd. trustees Maryland Classis, Ref. Ch. Dir. Hood Coll., Frederick, Md. Mem. Phi Sigma Kappa. Republican. Mem. Ref. Ch. Clubs: Rotary of Quakertown, Pa. (charter mem.); Rotary of Latrobe, Pa. (past pres.); Lions of Frederick (past pres.). Home: 507 Elm St., Frederick, Md.

HARTMAN, Roland Clarence, magazine editor; b. Milwaukee, Wis., June 15, 1906; s. Arthur Charles and Augusta Dorothy (Baade) H.; student Milwaukee Co. (Wis.) Sch. of Agr., 1921-24; B.S.A., U. of Wis., 1929; m. Hazel Evelyn Fouts, June 29, 1931; 1 son—William Alan. Began as asso. editor Poultry Tribune, Mt. Morris, Ill., 1929-32; editor, Everybody's Poultry Mag., Hanover, Pa., since 1932; v.p., asst. sec.-treas., dir. Everybody's Poultry Mag. Pub. Co., Inc., Hanover, Pa., since 1936. Mem. Sigma Delta Chi, Alpha Zeta, Phi Kappa Phi. Lutheran. Author: Hatchery Management (with G. S. Vickers), 1932. Editor of National Poultry Digest, Hanover, Pa., since Jan. 1939. Address: 227 Meade Av., Hanover, Pa.

HARTMAN, Thomas H., banking; b. New Castle, Pa., Oct. 11, 1879; s. George William and Asemath (McConnell) H.; ed. pub. schs., New Castle, and Duff's Business Coll., Pittsburgh; unmarried. Began as clerk 1898; connected with Johnson interests as clerk, treas., auditor, etc.; pres. Lawrence Savings & Trust Co.; dir. Johnson Bronze Co., Bessemer Loam Land Co., Community Loan Co. Dir. Jameson Hosp., Y.M.C.A. Republican. Mem. United Presbyn. Ch. Clubs: Rotary, New Castle Field. Home: 235 Edgewood Av. Office: Lawrence Savings & Trust Co., New Castle, Pa.

HARTMAN, William Emory, clergyman; b. Freeland, Pa., Nov. 7, 1900; s. William Wade and Hester Anne (Tubbs) H.; grad. Harrisburg (Pa.) Central High Sch., 1917; A.B., Ohio Wesleyan U., Delaware, O., 1921; S,T.B., Boston U. Sch. of Theology, 1924; student Boston U. Grad. Sch., 1924-26, Ph.D., 1935; student Harvard Divinity Sch., Univ. of Berlin and Oxford, 1926-27; m. Naomi Dorcas Gum, May 28, 1924; children—Naomi Carolyn, Robert Hill. Minister Trinity Congregational Ch., Neponset, Mass., 1924-25; asst. prof. of philosophy, Allegheny Coll., Meadville, Pa., 1927-28; minister Calvary Meth. Ch., Berwick, Pa., 1928-30; Wesley Foundation pastor, State College, Pa., 1930-32; minister Allison Memorial Meth. Ch., Carlisle, Pa., since 1932; instr. of Bible, Dickinson Coll., since 1938. Mem. Sigma Alpha Epsilon, Pi. Delta Epsilon, Kappa Phi Kappa. Awarded Frank D. Howard fellowship, Boston U., 1926-27. Home: 234 W. High St., Carlisle, Pa.

HARTMANN, William V., oil exec.; b. Cincinnati, O., Sept. 12, 1871; s. Philip H. and Louise (Jaup) H.; ed. Franklin School, Cincinnati, O.; m. Elizabeth Hopkins, Oct. 24, 1894. Clerk, Alexander McDonald & Co., Cincinnati, O., 1888-92, merged with Standard Oil Co., 1892, asst. agt. of latter, Evansville, Ind., 1893-1903; salesman Gulf Refining Co., New York, 1903-05, asst. gen. sales mgr., Pittsburgh, 1905-12, gen. mgr., 1912-29, v.p. in charge of sales since 1929; dir. Gulf Oil Corpn., Gulf Refining Co., Gulf Exploration Co., Gulf Research & Development Co. Mem. Am. Petroleum Inst. (dir.). Dir. Homewood Cemetery, Pittsburgh. Republican. Episcopalian (vestryman, Ch. of the Ascension). Clubs: Duquesne, Pittsburgh Athletic Assn. (Pittsburgh); Longue Vue (Pittsburgh). Home: Schenley Apts. Office: Gulf Bldg., Pittsburgh, Pa.

HARTRIDGE, Emelyn Battersby, educator; b. Savannah, Ga., July 17, 1871; d. Alfred Lamar and Julia Smythe (Wayne) H.; A.B., Vassar, 1892; L.H.D., Smith Coll., Northampton, Mass., 1928. Founder The Hartridge Sch., Savannah, Ga., 1892; prin. The Hartridge Sch., Plainfield, N.J., since 1903, and pres. since incorporation, 1908, trustee and principal since 1933. One of organizers Plainfield Chapter of American Red Cross, 1914; organizer Plainfield Jr. Red Cross, 1917; treas. Plainfield Belgian Relief Soc., 1914-19; chmn. Plainfield Com. of Vassar Salary Endowment Fund, 1922-25; mem. standing com. Vassar Students' Aid, 1924-29; representative at large, Vassar Alumnæ Council (chmn. 1928-30); pres. Asso. Alumnæ of Vassar Coll., 1930-33; vice chmn. of exec. com. Co-operative Bur. for Women Teachers, 1928-31. Mem. Head Mistresses Assn. of the East (pres. 1924-28; chmn. pub. issues com. 1936-38), Internat. Student Hospitality Assn. (mem. advisory com.), Am. Assn. Univ. Women, Parents League of New York, Poetry Soc. of Ga., Progressive Edn. Assn. Episcopalian. Clubs: College, Monday Afternoon of Plainfield (pres. 1924-27); Cosmopolitan, Vassar (New York). Home: Oakwood, Plainfield, N.J.

HARTSHORNE, Richard, judge; b. Newark, N.J., Feb. 29, 1888; s. William Sydney and Margaret Bentley (Harrison) H.; grad. Newark (N.J.) Acad., 1905; Litt.B., Princeton U., 1909; LL.B., Columbia, 1912; m. Ellen Sahlin, of N.Y. City, Mar. 15, 1919; children—Richard, Nancy, John Fritz, Penelope. Admitted to N.Y. and N.J. bars, 1912, and began practice in Newark, N.J.; successively mem. firms Riker & Riker, Edward W. & Runyon Colie, Stewart & Hartshorne; special asst. U.S. atty. for N.J., 1925; pres. judge Court of Common Pleas, Newark, N.J., since 1931; prof. of constl. law and ins. law, N.J. Law Sch. Pres. Interstate Commn on Crime since 1935; chmn. N.J. Commn. of Interstate Co-operation; chmn. N.J. Commn. for State Labor Dept. Survey. Served as seaman, advancing to lit. (j.g.), U.S. Naval Reserve during World War; now lt. comdr. Mem. Am. Legion (chmn. nat. law and order com. since 1937; comdr. N.J. Dept., 1930), Sons Am. Revolution (nat. chancellor-gen. 1929-31; pres. N.J. Soc. 1928), Am. Bar Assn., N.J. Bar Assn., Essex Co. Bar Assn. Republican. Presbyn. Mason. Clubs: Essey (Newark); East Orange Tennis (East Orange, N.J.). Author of The Handbook on Interstate Crime Control (with John W. Woelfle), 1938; also co-author of booklet Our Children's Future, 1938. Contbr. to law jours., etc. Home: 132 Park St., East Orange, N.J. Address: Essex County Court House, Newark, N.J.

HARTSON, Joseph Tracy, mfg. aircraft; b. Spokane, Wash., Jan. 8, 1892; s. Millard Tracy and Margaret Slater (Roberson) H.; B.S. in C.E., U. of Wash., Seattle, Wash., 1914; m. Helen Patterson, Oct. 19, 1935. Employed as jr. engr. U.S. Geol. Survey, Tacoma, Wash., 1913-16; asst. to pres. (W. E. Boeing) and sec. Boeing Airplane Co., Seattle, Wash., 1917-20; mgr. The Sea Sled Co., Boston, Mass., and West Mystic, Conn., 1920-21; rep. at Detroit and Chicago, Standard Steel and Bearings, Inc., 1922-25; asst. sales mgr., then sales mgr., Wright Aeronautical Corpn., Paterson, N.J., 1925-29; asso. with Air Investors, Inc., N.Y. City; pres. Comet Engine Corporation, Madison, Wis., 1930-32; sales manager American Airways, Inc., Chicago, Ill., 1932-33; tech. expert, Federal Aviation Commn., Washington, D.C., 1934-35; with Manufacturers Aircraft Assn., N.Y. City, 1935; exec. vice-pres. and dir. The Glenn L. Martin Co., Baltimore, Md., since 1935; sec. and dir. Manufacturers Aircraft Assn.; dir. Air Investors, Inc., Commndr. lt. comdr. U.S.N. Res. Mem. Inst. Aeronautical Scis., Phi Delta Theta. Republican. Baptist. Club: Rodgers Forge Golf. Home: The Tuscany Apts., Baltimore, Md.

HARTT, George Montgomery, newspaper editor; b. N.Y. City, Dec. 10, 1877; s. George Le

Baron and Margaret Florence Montgomery (Hartt) H.; grad. Passaic High School, 1895; m. Marie Russell, Aug. 29, 1913 (died Oct. 6, 1928); m. 2d Dorothy Barber Goldsmith, June 10, 1930. Reporter, Passaic Daily Journal, 1895; with the Central Monthly, N.Y. City, 1896; then with the Passaic Daily News, 1896-1900, city editor, 1898-1900; with Paterson (N.J.) Morning Call, 1900; editor in chief Passaic Daily News, 1901-32, Passaic Herald-News (a consolidation) since 1932. Mem. Am. Soc. Newspaper Editors. Republican. Episcopalian. Clubs: Kenilworth (Passaic); Pica (Paterson) Upper Montclair Country (Montclair, N.J.). Home: 88 Boulevard. Office: 140 Prospect St., Passaic, N.J.

HARTUNG, Charles Amos, clergyman; b. Butler Co., Pa., Aug. 10, 1877; s. George Michael and Mary (Kline) H.; ed. West Sunbury Acad., 1896-97, Slippery Rock State Normal Sch., 1898-99; A.B., Allegheny Coll., 1907, A.M., 1910; ed. Drew Theol. Sem., 1908; hon. D.D., Allegheny Coll., 1930; m. Marjorie Roberts, Nov. 5, 1908; children—Charles C., Marjorie Thelma, Dorothy Elizabeth. Ordained to ministry M.E. Ch., deacons, 1908, elder, 1912; pastor, Cokeville, Pa., 1908-10, Windber, 1911-13, Homer City, 1914-16, Charleroi, 1917-18, Grove Av., Johnstown, 1919-22, Coraopolis, 1923-29, First Ch. Beaver Falls, 1930-36; pastor Sheraden Ch., Pittsburgh since 1936; mem. Bd. Ministerial Training Pittsburgh Conf. since 1917, chmn. since 1936; teacher and sec.-treas. Pittsburgh Area Summer Sch. for Ministerial Training, Mountain Lake Park, Md., 1929-36, teacher and dean since 1936; mem. and sec. pub. com. Pittsburgh Christian Advocate, 1916-20; mem. bd. dirs. Pittsburgh Conf. Hosp. and Home for Aged. Mem. Md. of Trade, Community Welfare Assn. Mem. M.E. Ch. Mason. Clubs: Kiwanis, Pittsburgh Methodist Preachers Book. Home: 2948 Chartiers Av., Pittsburgh (4), Pa.

HARTUNG, Walter H(enry), univ. prof.; b. Welcome, Minn., Jan. 4, 1895; s. Charles Henry and Mina (Bicknase) H.; A.B., Univ. of Minn., 1918; student Univ. d'Aix-Marseille, France, 1919; U. of Minn., 1922-23; Ph.D., U. of Wis., 1926; m. Corda Baumhoefner, June 15, 1926; children—Homer Arthur, Richard Walter, Victor Meyer. Engaged in teaching, high schs., Ore., Minn., S.D., 1920-22; asst. in chemistry, U of Wis., 1923-25; research chemist, Sharp & Dohme, Baltimore, Md., 1926-33, in charge chem. research, 1933-36; prof. pharm. chemistry, Sch. Pharmacy, U. of Md. since 1936. Served in U.S. Marine Corps, 1918-19 with A. E.F. in France. Fellow A.A.A.S., Am. Inst. Chemists. Mem. Am. Chem. Soc., Am. and Md. State pharm. assns., Franklin Inst., Phi Lambda Upsilon, Sigma Xi, Phi Delta Chi, Rho Chi. Lutheran. Contbr. to chem. and pharm. jours. Home: 5503 Stuart Av., Baltimore, Md.

HARTWELL, H(enry) Ameroy, physician; b. nr. Decorah, Ia., No. 2, 1874; s. Alex and Inger (Hartwell) H.; grad. Valder Bus. Coll., Decorah, Ia., 1892; student Highland Park Coll. Pharmacy, Des Moines, Ia., 1892-93; student Valparaiso (Ind.) U., 1904-05; M.D., Chicago Coll. Medicine & Surgery (now Loyola Univ.), Chicago, 1908; m. Fannie V. Osthoff, Oct. 30, 1904; children—Henry Ameroy Jr., Eleanor Inger. Served as apprentice in pharmacy, Minneapolis, Minn., 1893-96, pharmacist, 1896-98; pharmacist, Denver, Colo., 1899-1901, N.Y. City, 1902-04, Chicago, 1905-08; engaged in gen. practice of medicine at Weehawken, N.J., since 1908. Served with Vol. Med. Service Corps during World War; presented an ambulance to Am. Red Cross. Now patron mem. Am. Red Cross. Fellow A.M.A., N.Y. Acad. of Medicine. Mem. Am. Heart Assn., W. H. Luckett Clin. Soc., N.J. State Med. Soc., Hudson Co. Med. Soc., North Hudson Physicians Soc. Lutheran. Author: Perplexity, 1938; Dust of Our Time, 1936; The Living Aesculapius, 1937; What's Wrong With Me?, 1938; Uncle Sam Convalescing, 1940. Contbr. to Nat. Poetry Center, World's Fair. Wrote Christmas carol Faith Shall Never Die, adopted as Weehawken's Christmas carol, sung annually at municipal celebration. Home: 777 Boul. East, Weehawken, N.J.

HARTWELL, Oliver Whitcomb, civil engr.; b. Somerville, Mass., July 5, 1886; s. Haywood and Mary Reed (Whitcomb) H.; A.B. magna cum laude, Harvard U., 1908; m. Gladys E. Wood, Feb. 12, 1912; children—Mary Louise, James Haywood, Oliver Whitcomb, Jr., Carolyn Wood. Employed as asst. Mass. State Bd. Health, 1908-09; with U.S. Geol. Survey continuously since 1909, from jr. engr. to dist. engr., assignments in Salt Lake City, Albany, Boston, Harrisburg, and dist. engr. U.S. Geol. Survey, Trenton, N.J., since 1921. Served as 1st lt. Engrs. Corps, U.S.A., 1917. Mem. Am. Soc. Civil Engrs., Am. Geophys. Union. Methodist. Club: Engineers of Trenton, N.J. Home: 74 Oak Lane, Trenton, N.J. Office: 228 Federal Bldg., Trenton, N.J.

HARTZ, Robert E., prin. schs.; b. Palmyra, Pa., Sept. 17, 1894; s. Frank E. and Sarah (Balsbaugh) H.; A.B., Lebanon Valley Coll., 1916; grad. study, Lyons Univ., Lyons, France, 1919; m. Ruth M. Fasnacht, of Harrisburg, Pa., Sept. 3, 1920; children—Janet Marie, Helen Louise, Robert E., Jr. In employ Bethlehem Steel Co., Lebanon, Pa., 1916-17; teacher in high sch., 1920-27; supervising prin. of schs., Palmyra, Pa., since 1927. Served as corpl. A.S., U.S.A., 1917-19, with A.E.F. in France. Mem. A.A.A.S., Pa. State Edn. Assn. Republican. Mem. United Brethren in Christ. Club: Lions of Palmyra (pres.). Home: Oak and Grant Sts., Palmyra, Pa.

HARTZOG, Herbert Joseph, lawyer; b. Topton, Pa., Nov. 3, 1881; s. Israel Thompson and Martha Catherine (Welker) H.; A.B., Lehigh U., 1904; LL.B., U. of Pa., 1907; m. Ada Frederika Worsley, Nov. 19, 1912; children—Jane Worsley (Mrs. Richard E. Wengren), Margery Anne. Admitted to Pa. bar, 1907, Supreme Court of Pa., 1908, also to Federal Courts; practiced individually in Bethlehem since 1908. Trustee St. Luke's Hosp.; trustee Moravian Coll. for Women, Bethlehem. Mem. Northampton Co. Bar Assn. (pres. 1927-28), Pa. State Bar Assn., Am. Bar Assn., County Bd. of Benchers, Phi Beta Kappa, Phi Delta Theta. Episcopalian. Mason. Club: Saucon Valley Country. Home: 435 Seneca St. Office: Union Bank Bldg., Bethlehem, Pa.

HARVEY, Adelbert William, research chemist; b. Central Square, N.Y., March 8, 1894; s. Clarence D. and Charlotte ,Thiebeau) H.; ed. Colgate U., 1913-14; B.S. in chemistry, Syracuse U., 1917; M.S., U. of Pittsburgh, 1919, Ph.D., 1922; m. Marcella Schwer, June 22, 1921; 1 dau., Elizabeth Anne. Chemist with Federal Dye Corpn. and Aetna Chemical Co., 1917; instr. chemistry, U. of Pittsburgh, 1917-22; industrial fellow, Mellon Inst. since 1922. Mem. Am. Chem. Soc., Sigma Xi, Alpha Chi Sigma, Phi Lambda Upsilon. Republican. Methodist. Mason. Club: Faculty of University of Pittsburgh. Home: 455 Arden Rd., Mt. Lebanon, Pittsburgh, Pa.

HARVEY, Agnes Lewis, librarian; b. Mayfield, Ky.; d. John Isham and Margaret Lynn (Thompson) Harvey; ed. Stuart Hall, Staunton, Va., U. of W.Va., U. of Wis.; unmarried. Librarian Huntington (W.Va.) Public. Library since Oct. 1, 1908. Mem. Am. Library Assn., W.Va. Library Assn. Democrat. Episcopalian. Club: Woman's (Huntington). Home: 1327 Sixth Av. Office: Public Library, Huntington, W.Va.

HARVEY, Alexander, editor, author; b. Brussels, Belgium, Dec. 25, 1868; s. Alexander and Bridget Maria (Canavan) H.; came to America with parents at 2 yrs. of age; pub. sch. edn.; m. Eva Augusta Schubert, April 7, 1895. Reporter, Philadelphia Press, 1892, New York Evening Telegram, 1893; editor Irving Bacheller's Newspaper Syndicate, 1893-95, Twentieth Century, 1895-98: sec. to diplomatic agt. and counsel-gen. of U.S. in Egypt, 1898-99; asst. Sunday editor New York Herald, 1900; foreign editor Literary Digest, 1901-05; asso. editor Current Opinion. 1905-22; asso. editor Am. Monthly, 1922-29. Author: The Toe and other stories, 1913; William Dean Howells, 1917; Shelley's Elopement, 1919; Essays on Sophocles, 1922; Essays on Euripides, 1923; Oedipus, 1923; Essays on Jesus, 1924; Friends of Jesus, 1925;

Iphigenia, 1925; The Bacchantes, 1926; Love Life of Hellenic Heroines, 1927. Home: N. Hackensack, N.J.

HARVEY, Charles Woodroffe, clergyman; b. England, July 17, 1870; s. John and Margaret D. M. (Goyder) H.; came with parents to U.S., 1885. naturalized citizen; A.B., Harvard, 1899, A.M., same, 1901; ed. Swedenborgian Theol. Sch., Cambridge, Mass., 1896-1901, St. Catherines, Oxford, Eng., 1924-30; m. Leslie Clark Carter, Sept. 7, 1910; children—John Carter Helmsley, Dorothea Ward. Served as minister Swedenborgian Ch., Brookline, Mass., 1898-1911, instr. elocution and in ch. history, later prof., New Church Theol. Sch. (Swedenborgian), Cambridge, Mass., 1896-1911; pastor First Ch. of the New Jerusalem, Swedenborgian, Phila., since 1911; gen. pastor Pa. since 1918. Trustee Urbana (O.) Univ. and Jr. Col. since 1900. Republican. Swedenborgian. Club: Union League (Philadelphia). Home: 315 N. 35th St., Philadelphia, Pa. Office: 2129 Chestnut St., Philadelphia, Pa.

HARVEY, Edmund Newton, physiologist; b. Phila., Pa., Nov. 25, 1887; s. William and Althea Ann (Newton) H.; grad. Germantown (Pa.) Acad., 1905; B.Sc., U. of Pa., 1909; Ph.D., Columbia, 1911; m. Ethel Nicholson Browne, Mar. 1916; children—Edmund Newton, Richard Bennet. Instr. physiology, 1911-15, asst. prof., 1915-19, prof. 1919-33, H. F. Osborn prof. since 1933, Princeton U. Trustee Bermuda Biol. Station, Marine Biol. Laboratory, Woods Hole, Mass. Mem. A.A.A.S., Am. Soc. Naturalists, Am. Soc. Biol. Chemists, Am. Physiol. Soc., Soc. Exptl. Biology and Medicine, Am. Soc. Zoölogy, New York Zoöl. Soc., Bot. Soc. of America, Am. Philosophical Soc., National Academy of Sciences, Sigma Xi Fraternity. Awarded John Price Wetherill medal of Franklin Inst. of Pa., 1934. Author: The Nature of Animal Light, 1920; Laboratory Directions in General Physiology, 1933. Has made special studies in bioluminescence, cell permeability, nerve conduction, regulation in plants, ultrasonic radiation, cell surface tension, brain potentials, etc. Asso. editor Biol. Bull., Biol. Abstracts; mng. editor Jour. of Cellular and Comparative Physiology. Home: 48 Cleveland Lane, Princeton, N.J.

HARVEY, E(llis) Marshall, M.D.; b. London Grove, Chester Co., Pa., Feb. 5, 1869; s. Rolph Marsh and Anna (Marshall) H.; M.D., U. of Pa., 1893; m. Phebe Scarlett; children—Jane Scarlett, Anna Bartrain (Mrs. Alison G. Cernog), Ellis Marshall, Marjorie Scarlett (Mrs. James E. Pew), Rolfe Marsh, Phoebe Scarlett (Mrs. Scott West). Practice of medicine, Media, Pa., since Nov. 1893; physician County Home, Delaware Co., 30 yrs.; prison inspector and pres. of bd., 15 yrs.; trustee State Hosp., 15 yrs.; trustee E. V. King Hosp. Trust; dir. First Nat. Bank, Media. Served on Med. Bd. during World War. Mem. A.M.A., Pa., and County med. socs., Med. Club of Phila., Phi Kappa Psi. Republican. Mem. Soc. Friends. Mason (33°). Clubs: Manufacturers (Phila.); Media (Media). Home: 1 E. Jefferson St. Office: 101 E. Baltimore St., Media, Pa.

HARVEY, Frederic Addison, dir. research Harbison-Walker Refractories Co.; b. Kellogg, Ia., June 3, 1882; s. George Hobart and Mary (Lyman) H.; B.S., Grinnell Coll., 1904; M.S., U. of Calif., 1906, Ph.D., 1908; studied U. of Goettingen, 1909; m. Alice Wilson Kennedy, June 17, 1910; children—Margaret (Mrs. Adrian C. Hughes), Mary Wilson (Mrs. Newell Pottorf). Asso. prof. physics, Syracuse U., 1910-16; cons. engr. Semet Solvay Co., 1912-17, ceramic engr., 1917-20; ceramic engr. U. S. Refractories Co., 1920-26, Harbison-Walker Refractories Co., 1926-31; dir. research of latter since 1932. Fellow Am. Ceramic Soc.; mem. A.A.A.S., Am. Soc. Testing Materials, Am. Refractories Inst., Canadian Ceramic Soc., Ceramic Soc. (British), Deutsche Keramische Gesellschaft, Acacia, Phi Beta Kappa, Sigma Xi. Republican. Presbyterian. Mason (32°). Clubs: Alcoma Golf (Wilkinsburg); Mt. Union (Pa.) Rod and Gun. Home: 5724 Solway St. Office: 1800 Farmers Bank Bldg., Pittsburgh, Pa.

HARVEY, John Sykes Curtis, leather mfg.; b. Columbus, N.J., Aug. 15, 1872; s. Thomas Biddle and Mary (Sykes) H.; ed. Swarthmore Coll. Prep. Sch., 1887-88, Stewart Bus. Coll., 1888-89; m. Emily Bishop, Oct. 8, 1901; children—Anna (Mrs. J. Barclay Jones), J. S. Curtis, Jr., Thomas Biddle. In employ W. A. Lippincott & Co., Philadelphia, Pa., 1890-95; with John R. Evans & Co., Phila., since 1895, mem. firm since 1898; dir. Philadelphia Bourse. Republican. Mem. Religious Soc. Friends. Clubs: Union League (Philadelphia); Gulph Mills Golf (Gulph Mills, Pa.). Home: Radnor, Pa. Office: 2d and Erie Sts., Camden, N.J.

HARVEY, Lewis B., v.p., sec. and dir. Republic Service Corpn.; officer or dir. many companies. Home: Newtown Square, Delaware Co., Pa. Office: Industrial Trust Bldg., Wilmington, Del.

HARVEY, McLeod, clergyman; b. Newport, N.S., Can., July 3, 1862; s. William and Margaret (Miller) H.; came to U.S., 1898, naturalized, 1917; B.A., Dalhousie U., Halifax, N.S., 1889; diploma, Presbyn. Coll., Halifax, N.S., 1891; Ph.D., Clark U., Worcester, Mass., 1911; m. Amy Archibald, July 28, 1891; children—Jean Archibald (Mrs. Dean Albert Ricker), Ebenezer Erskine, Margaret Helena (Mrs. Ruy H. Finch), Amy McLeod (Mrs. Carl Elmer Farr), William McKenzie (dec.), Gertrude Elvira, Mary (dec.). Ordained to ministry Presbyn. Ch., 1891, and pastor chs. in Nova Scotia, 1891-98, chs. in Mass., 1898-1913; pastor, Washington, D.C., 1913-22, and prof. psychology, Howard U., 1913-23; prof. religious edn., Waynesburg College, Waynesburg, Pa., since 1923, also pastor, Clarksville, Nemacolin, and Jefferson since 1923; traveled to Near East twice and to Europe three times in religious work. Mem. Redstone Presbytery, Am. Sociol. Soc., Pi Gamma Mu, Phi Lambda Theta. Home: Waynesburg, Pa.

HARVEY, Walter Benjamin, M.D.; b. Mt. Summit, Ind., May 20, 1882; s. Samuel D. and Elizabeth (Beavers) H.; B.S., Earlham Coll., 1906; M.D., U. of Pa., 1909; m. Aurelia Bartlett, Feb. 1, 1911; children—Elizabeth, William, Janet, Benjamin. Interne Western Pa. Hosp., 1909-10; staff Presbyterian Hosp. since 1915. Served in World War at Camp Green and Base Hosp. 54, France, as orthopaedic surgeon. Citation Medaille D'Honneur Services de Sante, Paris, 1919. Mem. A.M.A., Pa. State Med. Soc., Allegheny Co. Med. Soc. Am. Legion, Vets. Foreign Wars. Mason (Shriner). Home: 3404 Delaware Av. Office: 940 Western Av., Pittsburgh, Pa.

HARVEY, (Marie) Zarina Hicks, (Mrs. Alfred Riva H.), organist, accompanist, teacher; b. Montclair, N.J., Sept. 30, 1899; d. William Henry and Harriette Babcock (Magovern) Hicks; ed. pub. schs. and high sch., Maplewood and South Orange, N.J., Dearborn Morgan Sch., Orange, N.J., studied piano about 15 years; ed. Guilmant Organ Sch., N.Y. City, 1919-22; grad. study, Flemington (N.J.) Children's Choir Sch., summer 1928; m. Alfred Riva Harvey, Aug. 31, 1935. Engaged as professional organist since 1921; teaching piano since 1923; asst. organist, First Presbyn. Ch., New York City, 1921; organist, Ch. of Our Saviour, Luth., N.Y. City, 1922; organist and mus. dir. Presbyn. Ch., Wyoming, N.J., 1923-28; asst. organist, First Presbyn. Ch., N.Y. City, 1929-34; organist-dir., First Luth. Ch., East Orange, N.J., 1936-38; organist dir., Bartholomew Luth. Ch., Elizabeth, N.J. since 1938. Mem. Am. Guild of Organists, Music Teachers Assn. of the Oranges, Alumni Assn. Guilmant Organ Sch. Presbyn. Home: 63 Salter Pl., Maplewood, N.J.

HARWOOD, Charles McHenry, editor; b. Shelbyville, Ky., Apr. 7, 1864; s. Charles McHenry and Lavinia (Winchester) H.; ed. pvt. schs., Shelbyville, and Chenault's Sch., Louisville; U. of Va., 1882-83; m. Martha L. Slavens, May 31, 1893 (died 1895). Began as reporter Kansas City Times, 1887; mng. editor Kansas City Evening News, 1889-91, Baltimore News, 1893-1900, Syracuse (N.Y.) Herald, 1901-07; asso. editor, 1907-08, editor, 1908-24, Baltimore News; asso. editor Baltimore Sun since 1924. Catholic. Home: Guilford, Md. Office: Baltimore Sun, Baltimore, Md.

HASEK, Carl William, prof. econs.; b. Franklin, Pa., July 6, 1889; s. George and Frances Hulda (Koessling) H.; A.B., Lehigh U., 1911; A.M., Harvard, 1914; Ph.D., Columbia U., 1925; m. Florence Theresa Hall, Sept. 2, 1914; children—Carl William, Jr., Robert Hall, George Frederick. Engaged in teaching, Bethlehem Prep. Sch., 1911-13; asso. with Pa. State Coll. since 1914, prof. econs. and head dept. econs. and sociology since 1930; dir. Pa. Business Survey, monthly report on business conditions; dir. Inst. of Urban Problems, Pa. State Coll. Mem. Am. Econ. Assn., Masaryk Sociol. Soc. Prague, Phi Beta Kappa, Delta Sigma Pi, Pi Gamma Mu, Phi Eta Sigma. Republican. Methodist. Home: 502 East Foster Av., State College, Pa.

HASKELL, Harry Garner, v.p. E. I. du Pont de Nemours & Co.; b. New York, N.Y., Sept. 30, 1870; s. Samuel and Mary Frances (Amory) H.; ed. private schs.; M.E., Columbia U., 1914; children—Elizabeth, Harry Garner. Vice-pres. and dir. E. I. du Pont de Nemours & Co. Home: Mount Salem Lane. Office: du Pont Bldg., Wilmington, Del.

HASLAM, George Stevenson, research chemist; b. Williamsport, Pa., Dec. 12, 1898; s. James Henry and Elizabeth (Long) H.; B.S., R.I. State Coll., 1924; m. Leona Esther Westfall, Aug. 7, 1928; 1 son, David Westfall. In employ New Jersey Zinc Co. (of Pa.) since 1924, lab. investigator, 1924-26, research chemist, 1926-27, chief Pigment Physics Sect., Research Div., Palmerton, Pa., 1927-31, chief Rubber Pigment Sect., Research Div. since 1931. Served in S.A.T.C. during World War. Mem. Am. Chem. Soc., Am. Soc. for Testing Materials, Theta Delta Chi. Republican. Lutheran. Club: Blue Ridge Country. Home: Residence Park, Palmerton, Pa.

HASLAM, Robert Thomas, chemical engineer; b. North Adams, Mass., Apr. 3, 1888; s. Robert Henry and Emma Dawson (Lynch) H.; grad. high school, Taunton, Mass.; B.S., in Chemical Engring., Massachusetts Institute of Technology, 1911. Asst. in qualitative and quantitative analysis, Mass. Inst. Tech., 1911-12; with Nat. Carbon Co., Cleveland, O., in Research Lab. and as asst. supt., 1912-20; prof. chem. engring., Mass. Inst. Tech., 1920-27, also dir. Research Lab. of Applied Chemistry and dir. Sch. of Chem. Engring. Practice, in charge of course in gas and fuel engrings., 1927-35; v.p. and gen. mgr. Standard Oil Development Co. (subsidiary of Standard Oil Co. of N.J.), 1935; v.p. Hydro Engring. and Chem. Co.; sales manager Standard Oil Co. of N.J. since 1935 and v.p. since 1937. Mem. Am. Inst. Chem. Engrs. (v.p. 1927; dir. 1928-31). Am. Petrolog. Inst., Soc. Automotive Engrs., Alpha Chi Sigma, Tau Beta Pi; fellow The Inst. of Fuel and Petroleum Technologists (British). Republican. Clubs: Chemists', Madison Square Garden, Baltusrol, Whitehall (New York). Author: Fuels and Combustion (with R. P. Russell), 1926; and one of co-authors of Britain's Fuel Problems. Contbr. Jour. Industrial Engineering and Chemistry, etc. Home: Short Hills, N.J.

HASLER, Frederick Edward, banker; b. Wethersfield, Essex, Eng., Feb. 28, 1882; s. Thomas and Jane Chatterson (Banyard) H.; ed. pvt. schs., Eng.; m. Marguerite Isabel Messent, Sept. 5, 1912; children—Audrey, Shirley, Marjory. Came to U.S., 1901, naturalized, 1918. Began as clk., London, 1899; chartering clk., J. H. Winchester & Co., New York, 1903-06; mgr. Am. Smelters S.S. Co., 1906-08; asst. to pres. Chesapeake & Ohio Coal & Coke Co., 1908-09; sr. partner Hasler Bros., 1909-23; v.p. Bank of America, 1923-26; pres. Internat. Trust Co., 1929-31; chmn. exec. com. Continental Bank & Trust Co. since 1931; dir. Haytian Corpn. of America, Homeland Ins. Co. of America, New York Shipbuilding Corpn. (Camden, N.J.), Crocker Wheeler Electric Mfg. Co., Munson S.S. Corpn., Ecuadorian Corpn., Ltd., Continental Safe Deposit Co. Major, U.S.A. Reserve. Trustee Wykeham Rise Sch., Washington, Conn., The Rumson (N.J.) Sch., Pan-Am. Soc., Inc., New York; mem. exec. com. Chamber of Commerce of State of N.Y.; dir. Am. Arbitration Assn. Republican. Episcopalian. Mason. Clubs: Pilgrims, Metropolitan, India House (New York); Country (Rumson, N.J.); Beach (Seabright, N.J.); Royal Yacht, Mid-Ocean (Bermuda). Home: Little Silver, N.J. Office: 30 Broad St., New York, N.Y.

HASLEY, Thomas Oliver, real estate broker; b. Pittsburgh, Pa., Jan. 20, 1887; s. William J. and Bertha E. (Welfer) H.; ed. pub. schs. and high sch., Pittsburgh, Pa., 1893-1902, Duff's Bus. Coll., 1903; m. Pearl Hinton, Dec. 2, 1913; 1 son, William J. Employed in various lines, 1904-07; foreman, estimator, then supt. bldg. and constrn. work, 1907-21; sec. and treas. W. J. Hasley Co., gen. contractors, 1921-33; dir. Highways, Bridges and Tunnels Allegheny Co., 1933-36; dir. Columbia Ice Co.; real estate broker, 1936-39; sec. and dir. North Hills Estates Land Co. Mem. and past pres. Squirrel Hill Bd. of Trade. Mem. Penn-Lincoln Highway Assn. Past pres. Squirrel Hill Rep. Club. Mem. and sec. com. Boy Scout Troop. Republican. Mem. Disciples (Christian Ch., mem. official bd. since 1918. Men's Bible Class since 1908). Mason (32°, Shriner), I.O.O.F. Home: 6773 Forward Av. Office: 750 Perry Highway, Pittsburgh, Pa.

HASSARD, Charles Thomas, school administrator; b. Phila., Pa., Sept. 15, 1896; s. Samuel D. and Mary (Thomas) H.; A.B., U. of Pa., 1918, A.M., 1927; grad. student Temple U., Phila., Pa., 1936-38, Rutgers U., New Brunswick, N.J., 1938; m. Marion F. Gardiner, Aug. 20, 1924; children—Charles Thomas, Jr. (dec.), Tom. Engaged in teaching, pub. schs., Hatboro, Pa., 1919-20; prin. high sch., Paulsboro, N.J., 1920-21; teacher sci., high sch., Haddon Heights, N.J., 1921-23; teacher chemistry and physics, high sch., Norristown, Pa., 1923-31; prin. high sch., Salem, N.J., 1931-34; supt. sch. system, Gloucester City, N.J., 1934-38; supervising prin. sch. system, Union, N.J., since 1938. Served as seaman to ensign, U.S.N. Res., 1918-22. Dir. Union Twp. Free Library, Union Co. Jr. Coll., Union Co. Music Sch. Former pres. Gloucester City Rotary. Mem. Am. Assn. Sch. Adminstrs., N.J. State Edn. Assn., Union Co. Supervisors Assn., Am. Legion. Republican. Episcopalian. Home: 995 Chestnut St. Union, N.J.

HASSE, Adelaide, bibliographer; b. Milwaukee, Wis.,; d. Dr. Herman E. and Adelaide (Trentlage) H.; ed. pub. schs. and pvt. tutors; unmarried. Asst. librarian, Los Angeles Pub. Library, 1889-95; librarian office supt. of documents, Washington,, 1895-97; librarian document dept., New York Pub. Library, 1897-1918; research work for War Labor Policies Bd., 1918-19; organized War Industries Bd. war records, 1919-21; office Asst. Sec. of War, statis. branch, 1921; bibliographer to Brookings Instn., Washington, 1923-32; chief of index div. U.S. Daily, 1929-39; research consultant, Works Progress Adminstrn., 1934-39. Lecturer at George Washington Univ., 1933-37. Editor: Bradford's Journal 1693 (the first book printed in New York); New York House Journal 1695; Index to Economic Material in U.S. State Documents, 14 vols.; also of Special Libraries (monthly mag.). Compiler of Bibliography of Explorations, 1899; Bibliography of Official Publications of Colonial New York, 1903; Index to U.S. Daily, vols. 1 and 6, 1926, 32. Home: Silver Spring, Md. Office: Auditorium, Washington, D.C.

HASSLER, Jacob Prugh, bursar; b. St. Clairsville, Bedford Co., Pa., Mar. 22, 1888; s. Edgar S. and Rilla J. (Prugh) H.; ed. state pub. and high schs., 1894-1907; A.B., Grove City Coll., 1911; grad. Cleveland Sch. Tech., 1917; m. Mary Elizabeth Dippman, Sept. 10, 1924; 1 son, Robert Edgar. Learned printing trade while in pub. sch.; clk. while studying accountancy; traveling auditor, U.S. Shipping Bd., 1919-22; engaged in printing business, 1922-24; bursar Grove City Coll. since 1924. City auditor Grove City Borough. Enlisted as sergt., Quartermaster Corps, Cleveland, July 1917; sent to France and advanced to 2d lt., Oct. 1918; hon. discharged, July 1919. Treas. and dir. Grove City Hosp. Mem. Assn. Univ. & Coll. Business Officers,

Eastern States. Republican. United Presbyn. Mason (32°). Home: 416 Bessemer Av. Address: Grove City College, Grove City, Pa.

HASSOLD, Carl Frederick Rudolph, broker; b. Philadelphia, Pa., Jan. 9, 1898; s. Frederick C. and Caroline (Schwammaele) H.; grad. Northeast High Sch., Philadelphia, 1916; student Univ. of Pa., 1916-17; m. Sara Montgomery, July 24, 1920; children—Frederick M., Robert M. Began with Bioren Co., brokers, as board boy, 1918, successively runner, clerk, bond trader and salesman, partner since 1925; pres. Kentucky-Ohio Gas Co., Fern Wood Vault Co., Fern Wood Cemetery Co.; vice-pres. Atlantic-Lafayette Hotel Co.; dir. Lackawanna-Wyoming Valley R.R. Served as seaman, U.S. Navy, 1917-18. Mem. New York and Philadelphia stock exchanges. Clubs: Union League, Racquet, Manheim Cricket (Philadelphia). Republican. Lutheran. Home: Pine Road, Chestnut Hill. Office: 1508 Walnut St., Philadelphia, Pa.

HASTINGS, Daniel O., ex-senator; b. Somerset Co., Md., Mar. 5, 1874; s. Daniel H. and Amelia Ellen (Parsons) H.; ed. under pvt. tutelage Prof. Charles F. Eastman, Wilmington, Del.; studied law, Columbian (now George Washington) U.; m. Garrie L. Saxton, Apr. 19, 1898 (died Feb. 7, 1930); m. 2d, Elsie Saxton, October 17, 1931. Admitted to Delaware bar, 1902; deputy attorney gen., Del., 1904-09; apptd. sec. of state, by Gov. Pennewill, Jan. 19, 1909, for term of 4 yrs.; resigned, June 16, 1909, and same day was apptd. asso. justice Sup. Court, resident in New Castle Co., for term of 12 yrs.; resigned Jan. 17, 1911, and made spl. counsel for legislature a few days later; city solicitor, Wilmington, 1911-17; apptd. judge Municipal Court, 1920, resigned 1929; apptd. U.S. senator by Gov. Robinson, Dec. 10, 1929, to fill unexpired term of Coleman du Pont, resigned; term expired Mar. 3, 1931; elected U.S. senator, term 1931-37; now practicing law; mem. firm Hastings, Stockly, Duffy & Layton, Wilmington. Republican. Methodist. Mason. Clubs: Wilmington, Wilmington Country, City, Young Men's Republican; Union League (Phila.); Metropolitan, Burning Tree (Washington, D.C.); Bankers (New York). Home: Kennett Pike. Office: Industrial Trust Bldg., Wilmington, Del.

HASTINGS, Glen Brown, cons. engr.; b. Wellsboro, Pa., Nov. 4, 1884; s. Hiram S. and Mary Rebecca (Brown) H.; ed. Mansfield Teachers Coll., 1902-03, Mercersburg Acad., 1903-04; B.S. in M.E., Pa. State Coll., 1908; corr. course, Alexander Hamilton Inst., 1915-16; m. Aimee Bliss Spicer, Sept. 9, 1908; 1 dau., Rebecca Brown. In employ The Tabor Mfg. Co., Phila., Pa., 1908-15, under supervision of Frederick W. Taylor, founder Taylor System Sci. Management; cons. engr., Chicago, Ill., 1915-19; cons. and valuation engr., Williamsport, Pa., since 1919. Mem. Phi Gamma Delta. Republican. Presbyn. Mason (32°). Home: 116 Loyalsock Av., Montoursville, Pa. Office: 143 W. 4th St., Williamsport, Pa.

HASTINGS, Penn Gaskill, newspaper publisher; b. Punxsutawney, Pa., April 13, 1875; s. William Penn and Emma L. (Evans) H.; ed. Milton (Pa.) High Sch.; m. Mabel C. Algert, Nov. 9, 1905; children—Margaret P., William Penn. Began as newspaper reporter, 1891; pres. Watsontown Boot & Shoe Co., 1908-34; pres. and gen. mgr. Standard Printing Co. since 1911; dir. First Milton Nat. Bank; dir. Milton Mfg. Co.; partner Hastings & Hastings. Democrat. Presbyterian. Mason. Clubs: Manufacturers, Rotary (Milton). Home: 4652 Locust St., Philadelphia, Pa. Office: Milton, Pa.

HASTINGS, Walter Scott, professor of modern langs.; b. Snow Hill, Md., Jan. 17, 1890; s. Laurence Hastings and Emma Sarah (Scott) H.; A.B., Princeton, 1910, M.A., 1911; Ph.D., Johns Hopkins, 1916; unmarried. Instr. French, Union Coll., Schenectady, N.Y., 1911-13; Johns Hopkins, 1915; master of French, Tome Sch. for Boys, Port Deposit, Md., 1919-20; Instr. French, Princeton, 1920-35, prof. modern langs. since 1935. Served as 1st lt. inf., World War; asst. mil. attaché, Am. Legation, Berne, Switzerland, 1919. Mem. Modern Lang. Assn., Assn. Am. Coll. Profs. Author: The Drama of Honoré de Balzac, 1917; Balzac and Souverain, 1927. Editor: Balzac's Cromwell, 1925; French Prose and Poetry (1850-1900), 1926; Balzac's Letters to His Family, 1934; The Student's Balzac, 1937. Contbr. articles. Home: 17 Springdale Road, Princeton, N.J.

HASTINGS, Willard Seth, pathologist; b. Spiceland, Ind., Sept. 30, 1884; s. Dr. Seth G. and Edith (Towell) H.; grad. Fairmount (Ind.) Acad., 1902; M.D., U. of Mich., 1909; m. Faith E. Olmstead, June 28, 1912; children—Edith L., Doris J., Frank W., Shirley E. Pathologist Burns Hosp., Cuero, Tex., 1914-15; research asso. and prof. pharmacology, Hahnemann Med. Coll., Chicago, 1915-20; pathologist Highland Hosp., Rochester, N.Y., 1920-25; dir. Cayuga Co. Lab., Auburn, N.Y., 1925-30; pathologist and dir. lab. Jeanes Hosp., Philadelphia, since 1930. Fellow Am. Med. Assn.; mem. Am. Assn. Pathologists and Bacteriologists, Am. Soc. Cancer Research, Am. Assn. for Study of Neoplastic Diseases, Phila. Pathol. Soc., mem. Society of Friends. Home: 45 E. Church Road, Elkins Park, Pa. Office: Jeanes Hosp., Fox Chase, Philadelphia, Pa.

HASWELL, John Robert, agr. engr.; b. Baltimore, Md., Aug. 6, 1886; s. James N. and Esther J. (England) H.; ed. Baltimore Poly. Inst.; C.E., Cornell U., 1909; m. Marion Paschall Frederick, Aug. 23, 1917. Drainage engr. U.S. Dept. Agr., 1910-20; prof. agrl. engring. extension, Pa. State Coll. since 1920. Registered professional engr., Pa. Served as capt. Engrs. Officers Res. Corps, U.S. Army, 1917-19. Fellow Am. Soc. Agrl. Engrs. (chmn. North Atlantic Sect. 1933); asso. mem. Am. Soc. C.E., Centre Co. Engrs. Soc., Soc. of 1st Div. A.E.F., "Tuscania" Survivors, Sigma Xi, Epsilon Sigma Phi (chief Alpha Omicron Chapter 1933). Presbyterian. Club: Centre Hills Country. Wrote many articles pertaining to agri. engring. Home: The Orlando, State College, Pa.

HATCH, David Arthur, asso. prof. mathematics; b. Weissport, Pa., Dec. 30, 1877; s. Arthur Augustus and Martha (Dodson) H.; ed. Lafayette Coll., 1894-96 and 1902-04, E.M., 1904; A.M., Columbia U., 1924; m. Marion Hertz, Sept. 7, 1910; 1 son, William Arthur. Began teaching in pub. schs., Easton, Pa., 1898-1902; engr. of mines, Hazleton, Pa., 1904-06; asst. supt. of mines, Kearney, Pa., 1906-08; engr. of mines, Hazleton, Pa., 1908-10; instr. Mathematics, Lafayette Coll., Easton, Pa., 1910-15, asst. Prof., 1915-24, asso. prof. since 1924. Mem. Math. Assn. of America, Am. Assn. Univ. Profs., Tau Beta Pi. Presbyterian. Home: 705 High St., Easton, Pa.

HATCH, Roy Winthrop, prof. edn.; b. Marshfield, Mass., Aug. 18, 1878; s. Luther Phillips and Elizabeth Wise (Clark) H.; A.B., Dartmouth Coll., 1902; A.M., Columbia, 1924; grad. study Harvard, 1904; m. Bertha May Roper, Aug. 23, 1906; children—Winslow Roper, David Lincoln, Grace Phillips. Teacher high sch., Hubbardston, Mass., 1902-03, Hingham, 1904-06, Lexington, 1906-09, Somerville, 1909-15, Dorchester High Sch., Boston, 1915-18; prof. edn. Horace Mann Sch., Teachers Coll. (Columbia), 1918-27, State Teachers Coll., Montclair, N.J., since 1927. Served as dir. 1st Boys' Working Res. Camp, Concord, Mass., World War. Mem. N.E.A., Assn. History Teachers Middle States and Md., Nat. Council Social Studies, N.J. State Social Studies Teachers Assn., Phi Gamma Delta, Phi Delta Kappa. Author: Training in Ciizenship, 1926; (with De F. Stull) Our World To-day, 1931; (with same) Journeys Through Our World Today, 1934; also chapts. in yr. books. Editor: Our New Wonder World, Vol. VII, 1932; (with others) Teaching of Current Events, 1929. Contbr. many articles to learned publs. Home: 584 Highland Av., Upper Montclair, N.J.

HATCHER, John Henry, judge; b. Bland, Va., June 29, 1875; s. Wilson Cary and Anne (Bulman) H.; student Emory and Henry Coll., 3 yrs., W.Va. U., 1 yr.; m. Leona Lyle Bowman, Apr. 12, 1900; children—Lois (Mrs. Frederick M. Simpson), Lyle (Mrs. Herman L. Bennett), John H. Admitted to W.Va. bar, 1899, and began practice at Beckley; mayor of Beckley, 1903; associated in practice with Judge W. H. McGinnis, title of McGinnis & Hatcher, 1907-20 inclusive; judge 10th Judicial Circuit of W.Va., 1921-24 inclusive; judge Supreme Court of Appeals, term 1925-28 inclusive; reëlected for term 1929-41. Republican. Methodist. Mason. Home: 714 Orange St. Office: Capitol Bldg., Charleston, W.Va.

HATFIELD, Charles James, M.D.; b. Phila., Pa., Jan. 23, 1867; s. Daniel Keyser and Margaret Alexander H.; A.B., Princeton, 1888, A.M., 1891, Sc.D., 1938; M.D., U. of Pa., 1900; studied U. of Göttingen, 1901, U. of Vienna, 1902; m. Louise Müller Spear, Sept. 14, 1901 (died Aug. 22, 1909). Practiced in Phila. since 1903; asso. dir. and chmn. bd. Henry Phipps Inst. for Study and Prevention of Tuberculosis. Ex-chmn. S.E. Pa. Chapter Am. Red Cross. Fellow Coll. Physicians of Phila.; mem. A.M.A., Nat. Tuberculosis Assn. (sec.), Sigma Xi. Trustee U. of Pa. Republican. Presbyn. Club: University. Home: 8614 Montgomery Av., Chestnut Hill, Phila. Office: Henry Phipps Institute, 7th and Lombard Sts., Philadelphia, Pa.

HATFIELD, Henry Drury, ex-senator; b. Logan Co., W.Va., Sept. 15, 1875; s. Elias and Elizabeth (Chafin) H.; A.B., Franklin Coll., New Athens, O., 1890; M.D., U. of Louisville, 1894, New York U., 1904; 5 post-grad. courses New York Polyclinic Med. Sch. and Hosp., also post-grad. New York Post-Grad. Sch. and Hosp. and Cornell U. Med. Coll.; LL.D., Bethany Coll., W.Va., 1915, also from Franklin Coll. and U. of W.Va.; m. Miss S. C. Bronson, Mar. 27, 1895; 1 dau., Hazel Hatfield (Mrs. John R. Sproul). Practiced at Eckman, W.Va.; commr. of health Mingo County, 1895-1900; surgeon Norfolk & Western Ry., 1895-1913, and cons. surgeon same, 1917-29; surgeon in chief W.Va. State Hosp. No. 1, Welch, W.Va., 1899-1913; visiting surgeon Kessler-Hatfield Hosp., Huntington, W.Va., and chief of surg. service Hatfield-Lawson Hosp., Logan, W.Va.; mem. County Court McDowell County, 1906-12; mem. State Senate, 1908-11 (pres. of Senate, 1911); gov. of W.Va., 1913-17; mem. U.S. Senate, term 1929-35. Served as maj. Med. Corps U.S. Army, May 1917-19; chief of surg. service Base Hosp. No. 36; now lt. col. Res. Was sec. Rep. Central Com. McDowell Co., W.Va., 8 yrs., chmn. Rep. Central Com. Cabell County 4 yrs. and mem. Rep. State Central Com., 1920-24; del. to Rep. Nat. Conv., 1916. Fellow Am. Coll. Surgeons, Southern Med. Assn.; mem. Am., W.Va., and Cabell County med. socs., Southern States Assn. Ry. Surgeons, Assn. Mil. Surgeons of U.S., Reserve Officers' Assn. of U.S., Am. Legion, etc.; hon. mem. McDowell County Med. Soc. Home: Huntington, W.Va.*

HATFIELD, Nina (Mrs. Thomas F. H.), librarian; b. Jersey City, N.J.; d. Carl F. and Martha (Jucker) Koester; grad. Hoboken Acad., 1888, Hoboken High Sch., 1889; ed. pvt. classes in art, Greenwich House Pottery; m. Thomas F. Hatfield, Apr. 27, 1897 (now dec.). Began as asst. librarian, Free Pub. Library, Hoboken, N.J., 1890-97; opened studio and taught painting and pottery; librarian, Free Pub. Library, Hoboken, N.J., since 1925. Dir. Girl Scouts, Keramic Soc. of Greater N.Y., N.Y. Soc. of Craftsmen. Mem. N.J. Library Assn., Special Library Assn., Zonta Club (dir.), McFeely Assn. Dir. State Art project, Jersey City Art Museum. Democrat. Conglist. Home: 606 River St., Hoboken, N.J.

HATHAWAY, Charles Montgomery, Jr., foreign service; b. Deposit, N.Y., Mar. 31, 1874; s. Charles Montgomery and Eliza (Grant) H.; B.A., Yale, 1899 (Phi Beta Kappa), M.A., 1901, Ph.D., 1902; m. Frances Elizabeth, d. of late Gen. Adoniram J. Warner, Sept. 1, 1904; 1 son, Elbridge W. Asst. prof. English Adelphi Coll., Brooklyn, N.Y., 1902-03; tutor in English, Columbia, 1903-05; instr. English and law, U.S. Naval Acad., 1905-11; Am. consul. Puerto Plata, Dominican Republic, 1911-13, Hull, Eng., 1914-17, Queenstown, Ireland, 1917-19, Bombay, India, 1921-22, Dublin, Ireland, 1922-24; consul gen., Dublin, Ireland, 1924-27, Munich, Germany, since 1927. On detail with Am. commr. in Hungary, at Budapest, 1920. Home: Olyphant, Pa. Address: Care Dept. of State, Washington, D.C.

HATHAWAY, Harle Wallace; b. Norwalk, O., Oct. 24, 1866; s. Israel Wister (D.D.) and Lucy Brownell (Fay) H.; A.B., Princeton, 1890 (class poet, commencement orator); A.M., 1894; grad. Princeton Theol. Sem., 1894; m. Eva Pauline Bellows, Apr. 2, 1895; children—Mildred Marie (Mrs. Leslie S. Betts), John Wallace. Ordained Presbyn. ministry, 1894; pastor Madison Av. Ch., Elizabeth, N.J., 1894-1903; mercantile business several yrs.; minister Eastminster Chapel, Germantown, Phila., 1907-10; pastor Covenant Ch., Germantown, 1911-25; became exec. secretary Presbytery of Philadelphia, North, 1925, honorably retired, October 1, 1938, still mem. several coms. Mem. Com. of 100, Phila.; mem. Reconstructed Fourth Assn.; organizer and pres. East Germantown Improvement Assn. Republican. Clubs: Union League, City. Writer of comments on Internat. Lessons in Union Quarterly since 1918. Mng. editor of Nassau Literary Mag. Home: Pelham Court, Germantown, Philadelphia, Pa.

HATHAWAY, Harrison Rountree, chartered life underwriter; b. Delhi, N.Y., Sept. 3, 1886; s. Charles and Cora Southworth (Rountree) H.; student Newark (N.J.) Acad., 1900-01, Hotchkiss Sch., Lakeville, Conn., 1901-06; Ph.B., Sheffield Scientific Sch. of Yale, 1910; C.L.U., Georgetown U., Washington, D.C., 1933; m. Marjorie Sybil Hooker, Sept. 29, 1915; children—Cynthia, Helen Hooker, Anne. Clk., bookkeeper, salesman Hathaway, Smith, Folds & Co., New York City, 1910-15; sec.-treas. Superior Thread & Yarn Co., New York City and Gloucester, N.J., 1915-27; salesman and agt. Sun Life Assurance Co. of Canada, Washington, D.C., since 1927; chartered life underwriter since 1933. Republican. Episcopalian. Club: Columbia Country. Address: 5016 Moorland Lane, Bethesda, Md.

HATHWAY, Marion (Mrs. Theodore R. Parker), educator and social worker; b. North Tonawanda, N.Y., July 31, 1895; d. William W. and Alice R. (Shelley) H.; A.B., Radcliffe Coll., 1916; A.M., U. of Chicago, 1927, Ph.D., 1933; m. Theodore R. Parker, June 6, 1936. Began teaching, 1916; with Y.W.C.A. Central Com., Denver, Colo., 1920-21; asst. dir. Bur. Attendance, Denver Pub. Schs., 1921-26; faculty, U. of Wash., 1927-31; faculty and asst. dir. Div. Social Work, U. of Pittsburgh, 1932-38; exec. sec. Am. Assn. Schs. of Social Work since 1938. Dir. Pittsburgh Community Fund. Mem. Am. Assn. Social Workers, Am. Assn. Univ. Profs. Democrat. Author: The Young Cripple and His Job, (social service monograph), 1928; Public Relief in Washington, 1853-1933 (with John Rademaker), 1934; The Migratory Worker and Family Life, 1937. Home: 4400 Center Av., Pittsburgh, Pa. Office: University of Pittsburgh, Pittsburgh, Pa.

HAUBER, Alois J.; b. St. Marys, Pa., Feb. 22, 1882; s. Sebastian and Philomena (Gregory) H.; ed. Williamsport Commercial Coll. and W. Va. Univ.; m. Clare Hanhauser, 1906; children—Joseph A. and Helen (Mrs. Clarence Dillson). In real estate business since 1905; pres. and gen. mgr. Builders & Mfrs. Supply Co.; vice-pres. and dir. Farmers & Merchants Bank, Industrial Finance Co., St. Marys Finance Co., St. Marys Mutual Ins. Co. Republican. Roman Catholic. K. of C., Eagle, Elk. Clubs: Catholic Men's Fraternal, Elk-Cameron Motor (St. Marys). Home: 128 State St., St. Marys, Pa.

HAUBERGER, George Henry, broker; b. Phila., Pa., May 12, 1873; s. Thomas Edward and Emeline (Rhoads) H.; ed. pub. schs. of Phila., and Eastburn Acad., Phila.; m. Ida May White, Oct. 25, 1898. Mem. Phila. Stock Exchange. Home: Warwick Hotel. Office: 1411 Walnut St., Philadelphia, Pa.

HAUCK, Anthony Moffatt, Jr., lawyer; b. Jersey City, N.J., July 24, 1901; s. Anthony and Eliza Jane (Moffatt) H.; student Wesleyan U., Middletown, Conn., 1923-25; LL.B., N.J. Law Sch., 1928; m. Virginia E. Brokaw, Sept. 14, 1929; children—Anthony Moffatt III, John Franz II, Robert Brokaw. Admitted to N.J. bar; asso. with firm Gebhardt & Gebhardt, Clinton, N.J., 1931; mem. firm Hauck, Felter & Lance since 1931; served as mem. N.J. Assembly, 1932; prosecutor of pleas, 1932-37; asst. atty. gen. of N.J. trying spl. criminal cases. Mem. troop com. Boy Scouts. Mem. Am., N.J. and Hunterdon Co. bar assns., Alpha Chi Rho, Delta Theta Pi, Seal and Scroll. Democrat. Presbyn. Mason. O.E.S. Grange. Club: North Hunterdon Rotary of Clinton (pres.). Home: Hampton, N.J. Office: Clinton, N.J.

HAUDENSHIELD, John Rochambeau, building and loan official; b. Scott Twp., Allegheny Co., Pa., Sept. 10, 1888; s. John E. and Mary Holmes (Burk) H.; grad. Carnegie High Sch., 1906, U. of Pittsburgh, 1911; m. Ella Mae Holliday, June 4, 1913; children—Mary Jane (deceased), John David. Bank clerk, 1910-13; cashier First Nat. Bank, West Middlesex, Pa., 1913-18; teller for trust company, 1918-26; salesman Frigidaire Co., 1926-31; sec. and dir. Beaver Falls Bldg. & Loan Assn. since 1932; sec. of liquidating com. Forbes Murray Bldg. & Loan Assn.; dir. First Federal Savings & Loan Assn., Carnegie; pres. Amherst Terrace Realty Co. Trustee Presbytery of Pittsburgh. Mem. Pa. House of Reps., 1939-40. Mem. Sons of the Am. Revolution (mem. state bd. control). Republican. Presbyterian. Home: 111 Ramsey Av., Carnegie, Pa. Office: Keystone Bank Bldg., Pittsburgh, Pa.

HAUGHT, Thomas William, educator; b. nr. Sistersville, W.Va., Nov. 25, 1871; s. Benjamin and Catherine (Shuman) H.; A.B., W.Va. U., 1896; student Harvard 1½ yrs.; M.A., W.Va. Wesleyan Coll., 1916, and D.Sc. from same college in 1929; spl. work, Johns Hopkins University; m. Helen Grace Wetmore, Mich., July 7, 1903; children—Thomas Wetmore, John William, Fred Benjamin, Florence Anna. Formerly teacher of science, W.Va. Wesleyan Coll., dean, 1909-29, acting pres. during four different periods, and prof. geology since 1929. Mem. Sigma Chi, Phi Beta Kappa. Republican. Methodist. Home: Buckhannon, W.Va.

HAUPT, William S., merchant; b. Shamokin, Pa., Aug. 15, 1878; s. Aaron H. and Sarah (Seiler) H.; ed. Shamokin pub. schs.; m. Ida V. Jones, June 25, 1902; children—Virginia M., Mary (Mrs. S. T. Siegfried). Merchant, Shamokin, since 1902; prop. Haupts' Dept. Store; dir. and chmn. real estate bd., Guarantee Trust & Safe Deposit Co., West Ward Bldg. & Loan Assn. Past pres. and dir. Shamokin Chamber of Commerce. Republican. Lutheran. Mason (Shriner), Woodmen of the World. Home: 1615 W. Arch St. Office: Spruce and Sixth Sts., Shamokin, Pa.

HAUSCHKA, Carola Spaeth, portrait painter; b. Phila., Pa., Apr. 29, 1883; d. Adolph and Harriett Reynolds (Krauth) Spaeth; ed. Lankenau Sch., Phila., 1892-1900, Walnut Lane Coll. Preparatory, 1900-02; grad. Phila. Mus. Acad., 1904 (gold medal, 1905); study with Leschetizky, Vienna, 2 yrs.; m. Hugo Hauschka(t), of Vienna, Oct. 8, 1907 (dec.); children—Theodor, Eleanor, Gertrude. Began career as musician; lived in Germany during World War; returned to U.S., 1921; studied art at Acad. Fine Arts, Phila., 1923-25, and since has studied and followed profession as portrait painter; exhibited, Copley Gallery, Boston; Plastic Club, Phila., Princeton Present Day Club, Am. Addison Gallery, Andover, N.Y. Contemporary Portraits, Tricker Gallery; many drawings of famous people; drawing of Einstein for Fortune Mag., Feb. 1936; conducts classes in art. Life mem. Fellowship of Acad. Fine Arts, Phila. Lutheran (attends regularly, Princeton Chapel, non-sectarian). Home: 34 Vandeventer Av., Princeton, N.J.

HAUSE, Nathan E., lawyer; b. Chester Co., Pa.; s. Daniel and Hannah (Quay) H.; student common and select schs.; studied in law office; m. Sarah Taft, Oct. 17, 1895; 1 dau., Mrs. Marjorie Quay Scheffer. Began as sch. teacher, serving 8 yrs.; salesman in gen. store, 4 yrs.; deputy prothonotary, Wayne Co., Pa., 4 yrs.; newspaper pub., 3 yrs.; cataloguer in library, 5 yrs.; chief clk. in auditor gen.'s dept., Pa., 10 yrs.; now engaged in gen. practice of law, Harrisburg, Pa.; dir. Harrisburg Bridge Co., Harrisburg Nat. Bank, Harrisburg Realty Co., West Harrisburg Market House Co., D. Bacon Co., McKay Co., J. Horace McFarland Co., Eagles Mere Land Co., United Ice & Coal Co. Mem. Pa. State Chamber of Commerce, Civic Club of Harrisburg, various legal orgns. Mason. Address: Telegraph Bldg., Harrisburg, Pa.

HAUSER, Conrad Augustine, church official; b. Frederick, Md., May 17, 1872; s. John Conrad and Mary (Rommel) H.; A.B., Johns Hopkins, 1894; grad. Theol. Sem. Ref. Ch. in U.S., Lancaster, Pa., 1897; studied U. of Berlin, 1900-01; A.M., U. of Pa., 1921, Ph.D., 1922; m. Sophia M. Hartig, Oct. 24, 1901; 1 son, Paul Martin Conrad. Ordained ministry Ref. Ch. in U.S., 1897; pastor successively Salem Ch., Frostburg, Md., St. Mark's Ch., Cumberland, and Emanuel Ch., Rochester, N.Y., until 1911; apptd. ednl. supt. for Publ. and S.S. Bd., Ref. Ch., Sept. 1911, editor, 1923, ednl. sec. and editor religious publs. same bd., 1925-38; dir. field promotion, Bd. of C.E. of Evang. and Reformed Ch. Mem. Com. on Edn. Pa. Council of C.E., and Phila. Council of C.E.; mem. Internat. Council of Religious Edn., Phi Delta Kappa. Author: A Course of Supplemental Lessons on the Sunday School, 1910; Outline Studies on the Old Testament, 1912; Outline Studies on the Church, 1915; Latent Religious Resources in Public School Education, 1924. Home: 43 Windsor Av., Highland Park (Upper Darby, P.O.), Pa. Office: 1505 Race St., Philadelphia, Pa.

HAUSMAN, Leon Augustus, coll. prof.; b. New Haven, Conn., Nov. 9, 1888; s. Augustus Clarence and Ella Amanda (Allen) H.; grad. Mt. Hermon (Mass.) Sch., 1910; B.A., Cornell U., 1914, M.A., 1916, Ph.D., 1919; m. Ethel May Hinckley, June 29, 1915. Instr. meteorology, Cornell U., 1914; instr. zoölogy, Miss. Agrl. & Mech. Coll., 1917-18; instr. biology and protozoölogy, Cornell U., 1918-22; asst. prof. zoölogy, Rutgers Coll., 1922-26, asso. prof., Rutgers Coll. and N.J. Coll. for Women, 1926-27; prof. zoölogy and head dept., N.J. Coll. for Women, since 1927; cons. ornithologist N.J. Agrl. Expt. Station. Mem. Am. Soc. Zoölogists, A.A.A.S., Am. Ornithologist Union, Phi Beta Kappa, Sigma Xi, S.A.R. Republican. Episcopalian. Clubs: Appalachian Mountain, Stanton Bird Club of Lewiston, Me., (hon. mem.), Wilson Ornithological. Writer many articles on mammalian hair, birds of N.J., protozoa and scientific articles; author of 10 booklets on birds of New Jersey. Contbg. editor Compton's Pictured Encyclopedia and Scientific American. Contbr. to Ency. Britannica. Home: 259 Harrison Av., New Brunswick, N.J.

HAUSMAN, William A., Jr., surgeon; b. Allentown, Pa., Nov. 18, 1878; s. William A. and Ida M. (Appel) H ; grad. high sch., Allentown, 1895; B.S., Muhlenberg Coll., Allentown, 1899, M.S., 1902, Sc.D., 1924; M.D., U. of Pa., 1902; m. Mary Repass, May 20, 1905; children—Mary Frances, Dorothy Hancock, Elizabeth Repass. Interne Allentown Hosp., 1902-03, pathologist, 1903-08; surgeon Sacred Heart Hosp., 1915-18, dean surg. dept. since 1918; dir. Second Nat. Bank. Cons. surgeon Draft Bd. No. 1, Allentown, World War. Trustee Muhlenberg Coll. Fellow Am. Coll. Surgeons; mem. Founders Group of Am. Bd. of Surgeons; mem. Am. and Pa. State med. assns., Lehigh County Med. Soc., Delta Theta, Phi Gamma Delta, Alpha Kappa Kappa (hon.). Democrat. Lutheran. Clubs: Livingston, Contemporary. Contbr. articles on surg. subjects. Home: College Drive, Park Ridge, Allentown. Office: 1116 Hamilton St., Allentown, Pa.

HAVEMEYER, Henry Osborne, ry. official; b. N.Y. City, Apr. 15, 1876; s. Theodore Augustus and Emily (de Loosey) H.; Yale, class of 1900; m. Charlotte Whiting, July 11, 1900. Pres. Brooklyn Eastern Dist. Terminal, 1906-21; treas. dir. Scranton-Lehigh Coal Co.; dir., v.p. and treas. Havemeyers & Elder, Inc.; dir. Kennecott Copper Corpn., Braden Copper Co., Chase Nat. Bank of N.Y., Cape Cruz Sugar Co.; trustee Nat. Surety Co. Mem. S.A.R., S.R. Republican. Catholic. Clubs: Knickerbocker, New York Yacht, Railroad, Recess, Yale, Tuxedo (N.Y.); Newport (R.I.), Casino, Newport Country, etc. Home: Mahwah, N.J. Office: 111 Broadway, New York, N.Y.

HAVENHILL, Robert Samuel, rubber technologist; b. Lawrence, Kan., Mar. 9, 1903; s. L. D. and Myra (Buck) H.; grad. Lawrence High Sch., 1921; B.S. in Chem. Engring., U. of Kan. Sch. of Engring., 1925; m. Monte Rey Breakey, June 10, 1925; children—Myra Winifred, John Robert. Analytical chemist B. F. Goodrich Co., 1925-26, rubber research chemist, 1926-28, raw materials development research, 1928-30; rubber technologist and development metallurgist St. Joseph Lead Co. since 1930. Mem. Am. Chem. Soc., Alpha Chi Sigma, Tau Beta Pi, Sigma Xi. Republican. Methodist. Holder of patents and writer on thermoplastic rubber adhesives, zno pigments, heat generation and hysterisis in rubber compounds, anistrophy of rubber compounds and electronics. Home: 1286 Corporation St., Beaver, Pa. Office: St. Joseph Lead Co., Monaca, Pa.

HAVENS, Charles W.; football coach Western Md. Coll. Address: Western Maryland Coll., Westminster, Md.

HAVENS, Paul Swain, coll. pres.; b. Lawrenceville, N.J., Sept. 19, 1903; s. Henry Clay and Anne Elizabeth (Swain) H.; student Lawrenceville (N.J.) Sch., 1916-21; A.B., Princeton, 1925; Rhodes Scholar, Oxford U. (Eng.), 1925-28, B.Litt., 1928, M.A., 1932; m. Lorraine Elizabeth Hamilton, Aug. 20, 1930; children—Anne Elizabeth, Mary Hamilon. Instr. in English, Princeton, 1928-30; dept. of English, summer session, George Washington U., 1930; asst. prof. of English, Scripps Coll., 1930-36; pres. of Wilson Coll., Chambersburg, Pa., since 1936. Mem. Modern Language Assn. of America, Kittochtinny Hist. Soc., Phi Beta Kappa. Presbyterian. Club: Princeton (Phila.). Address: Wilson College, Chambersburg, Pa.

HAVENS, Raymond Dexter, prof. English; b. Rochester, N.Y., July 25, 1880; s. Charles Wesley and Persis Elizabeth (Mack) H.; A.B., U. of Rochester, 1902; Ph.D., Harvard Univ., 1908; Litt.D., Univ. of Rochester, 1926; unmarried. Instructor mathematics, Pratt Inst. High Sch., 1902-04; mem. faculty U. of Rochester, 1908-25, prof. English, 1921-25; prof. English, Johns Hopkins, since 1925. Y.M.C.A. war work, 1917-19. Fellow Am. Acad. Arts and Sciences; mem. Psi Upsilon, Phi Beta Kappa. Democrat. Baptist. Author: The Influence of Milton on English Poetry, 1922. Joint editor Modern Language Notes. Home: 3700 N. Charles St., Baltimore, Md.

HAVILAND, James Thomas, insurance exec.; b. Aurora, Ill., June 20, 1889; s. William Crane and Florence (Hollister) H.; grad. West Aurora High Sch., 1907; studied Northwestern Univ., 1908-11, 1912-14, LL.B., 1914; B.S., Univ. of Chicago, 1912; m. Marjorie S. Benton, Mar. 25, 1916; children—Marjorie Benton, Nancy Jeanne. Admitted to Ill. bar, 1914; practiced at Chicago, 1914-17; atty. Lumbermens Mutual Casualty Co., Chicago, 1917-19, asst. sec. and mgr. Eastern Dept., same, Philadelphia, 1919-24, v.p. and eastern mgr. same and associated companies comprising Kemper group since 1924; v.p. and dir. Am. Motorists Ins. Co., Nat. Retailers Mutual Ins. Co., Federal Mutual Fire Ins. Co., James S. Kemper & Co.; pres. and dir. Philadelphia Automobile Club Insurors, Inc.; treas. and dir. Glen Cove Mutual Ins. Co., Eastern Adjustment Bureau; dir. Am. Underwriting Corpn. Chmn. management com. Philadelphia Safety Council. Mem. exec. com. Delaware County Rep. Com. Mem. Phi Kappa Psi. Mason. Clubs: Northwestern University (pres.), Union League, Kiwanis, Art, Penn Athletic (Philadelphia); Merion Cricket (Haverford); St. Davids (Pa.) Golf. Home: N. Wayne Av. and Eagle Road, Wayne, Pa. Office: 12 S. 12th St., Philadelphia, Pa.

HAVILAND, Walter Winchip, headmaster; b. Glens Falls, N.Y., Feb. 9, 1871; s. Harris G. and Adelia (Winchip) H.; ed. Glens Falls Acad., 1884-89; A.B., Haverford Coll., 1893; m. Olive Louise Robbins, June 17, 1902; children—Paul Robbins, Harris Goddard. Instr. mathematics and history, and dean of boys, Guilford Coll., N.C., 1893-96; instr. German and Bible, Friends Select Sch., Parkway, Phila, Pa., 1896-1911, headmaster same sch. since 1911. Mem. Nat. Edn. Assn., Progressive Edn. Assn., Headmasters Assn. Mem. Religious Soc. Friends. Home: The Knoll, Lansdowne, Pa.

HAWES, Edward McKean, lawyer; b. Braddock, Pa., Feb. 7, 1904; s. George Edward and Eva Cecelia (McKean) H.; student Harrisburg (Pa.) Tech. High Sch., 1918-22; A.B., Washington and Jefferson Coll., Washington, Pa., 1922-26; LL.B., U. of Pittsburgh Law Sch., 1929; m. Janet M. Laurie, July 15, 1930; 1 son, Edward Laurie. Admitted to Allegheny Co. (Pa.) bar, 1929, Supreme Ct. of Pa., 1929, Montgomery Co. (Pa.) bar, 1931; mem. firm Larzelere & Wright, attys. at law, Norristown, Pa., since 1936. Asst. dist. atty., Montgomery Co., Pa., 1931-32; dep. atty. gen. for Montgomery County, 1933-35. Mem. Pa. State Bar Assn., Montgomery Bar Assn. (dir.), Phi Gamma Delta, Delta Theta Phi. Republican. Presbyterian. Clubs: Kiwanis (pres. and dir.), Plymouth Country (Norristown, Pa.). Home: 1514 Plymouth Blvd. Office: 412 DeKalb St., Norristown, Pa.

HAWES, Raymond P., coll. prof.; b. East Providence, R.I., Apr. 11, 1891; s. Addison Sanger and Ella Dora (Jencks) H.; A.B. and A.M., Brown U., 1913; Ph.D., Cornell U., 1916; m. Marion Emsley, 1919; 1 son, Loring Emsley. Instr. Rice Inst., Houston, Tex., 1916-18, Princeton U., 1919-20; asst. prof. phil. and psychol., Goucher Coll., 1920-21, asst. prof. philosophy, 1921-23, asso. prof., 1923-30, prof. since 1930. Served in U.S. Army, Apr.-Dec. 1918. Mem. Am. Philos. Assn., Southern Soc. for Philosophy and Psychology, Phi Beta Kappa, Phi Delta Kappa. Home: 319 Taplow Road, Baltimore, Md.

HAWKEN, J. A.; editor Hagerstown Mail. Address: Herald-Mail Co., Hagerstown, Md.

HAWKES, Edward Matthias Zeh, physician; b. Schenectady, N.Y., Oct. 20, 1865; s. Edward Hoskins and Jane (Zeh) H.; A.B., Union Coll., Schenectady, N.Y., 1887, A.M., 1888; M.D., Coll. of Phys. & Surgs. of Columbia U., 1890; hon. D.Sc., Union Coll., 1930; m. Mary Everett Hawley, Aug. 31, 1905 (deceased); children—Stuart Zeh, Jane Hawley, Katherine Hawley (Mrs. Frederick Ballard Williams, Jr.). Engaged in gen. practice of medicine and surgery at Newark, N.J.; now gynecologist, Newark City Hosp. and chief dept. surgery, St. James' Hosp. (Newark), gynecologist, Presbyn. Hosp., Newark; consultant, Beth Israel Hosp., Newark, Essex Mountain Sanitarium, Essex Co. Hosp. for the Insane, Newark Eye and Ear Infirmary, St. Barnabas Hosp., Hosp. for Women and Children; med. dir. Presbyn. Hosp., Newark, N.J. Trustee Union Coll., Schenectady, N.Y. Fellow Am. Coll. of Surgeons; founder mem. Am. Bd. of Surgery; mem. Med. Soc. of N.J. (pres. elect), Soc. for Relief of Widows and Orphans of Med. Men of N.J. (bd. of trustees), Acad. of Medicine of Northern N.J. (past pres.), Essex Co. Med. Soc. (past pres.), Sigma Phi. Presbyn. Clubs: Essex (Newark); Essex County Country (West Orange). Home: 97 Heller Parkway. Office: 84 Washington St., Newark, N.J.

HAWKES, Stuart Zeh, physician and surgeon; b. Newark, N.J., Sept. 30, 1905; s. Edward Zeh and Mary Everett (Hawley) H.; A.B., Union Coll., 1926; M.D., Johns Hopkins U. Med. Sch., 1930; M.Sc.D. (surgery), N.Y. Univ. Med. Coll., 1937; m. Laura Jean Farrand, Apr. 16, 1932; children—Edward Zeh, Dudley Farrand, Richard Champenois. Interne, Newark City Hosp., 1930-32; asso. surgeon, Presbyn. and Babies hosps. since 1936; asst. surgeon, St. James', St. Barnabas', and Newark City hosps. since 1932; instr. in surgery, N.Y. Univ. Med. Sch. since 1938; cons. in surgery, Newark Eye & Ear Infirmary since 1934. Served as 1st lt. Med. Res. Corps U.S. Army since 1932. Fellow Am. Coll. Surgs. Mem. Am., N.J. State and Essex Co. med. assns., Am. Soc. Regional Anesthesia, Essex Co. Anat. & Pathol. Soc., Acad. of Medicine of Northern N.J., Clinicians' Soc., Newark, Practitioners' Club, Newark, Sigma Phi. Certified by Am. Bd. Surgery. Republican. Episcopalian (vestryman Trinity Cathedral, Newark). Club: Essex. Home: 382 Parker St. Office: 84 Washington St., Newark, N.J.

HAWKES, William F., editor; b. Bloomington, Ill., Oct. 20, 1897; s. William and Addie (Garland) H.; student Northwestern U., Evanston, Ill.; m. Flora E. Saxby, July 27, 1918; 1 son, William E. City editor Springfield (Ill.) News-Record, 1917-18; city editor St. Louis (Mo.) Star, 1920-29; managing editor Phila. (Pa.) Record since 1931. Clubs: Philadelphia Country, Penn Athletic (Phila.). Home: Rittenhouse Plaza. Office: Philadelphia Record, Philadelphia, Pa.

HAWKINS, Alfred Cary, soil technologist; b. Sewaren, Middlesex Co., N.J., June 15, 1887; s. Thomas W. and Ida A. (Wendell) H.; teachers certificate, N.J. State Normal Sch., Trenton, N.J., 1907; B.S. Columbia U., 1909; A.M., Princeton U., 1912; A.M., Ph.D., Brown U., Providence, R.I., 1916; m. Anne May Frost, Oct. 15, 1919; 1 dau., Barbara Anne. Asst. in mineralogy, Am. Mus. of Natural History, New York, 1909-10; asst., geology dept., Princeton, 1910-12; instr., geology dept., Brown U., 1912-16; oil geologist, 1916-18; U.S. Army, 1918-19; crystallographer E. I. du Pont de Nemours & Co., 1919-21; mgr. mineralogy dept., Ward's Natural Sci. Est., Rochester, N.Y., 1921-23; instr. in geology, U. of Rochester, N.Y., 1923-26; asst. prof. geology dept. Rutgers U., 1927-28, asso. prof., 1928-33; consulting geologist, 1933-35; soil technologist Soil Conservation Service, U.S. Dept. of Agr. since 1935. Served as sergt. 1st class, U.S. Signal Corps, 1918-19. Fellow A.A.A.S.,Mineral. Soc. of America, Meteorol. Soc. of Am., N.Y. Mineral. Soc., N.Y. Acad. of Sciences, Am. Legion (Post 25), 40 and 8 (Voiture 128), Plainfield (N.J.) Mineral. Soc. Rocks and Minerals Assn., Sigma Xi, Alpha Chi Rho (hon.). Author two books, 35 scientific papers. Address: 300 Livingston Av., New Brunswick, N.J.

HAWKINS, Arthur Hanson, M.D., surgeon; b. La Plata, Md., Dec. 27, 1868; s. Samuel and Jane (Robertson) H.; M.D., U. of Md. Coll. Phys. and Surgeons, 1895; m. Louise Brokenborough Price, 1901; children—Arthur Hanson, Helen Brokenborough; m. 2d, Lou Finzel, 1921. Began practice at Cumberland, 1901; chief surgeon, Memorial Hosp., Cumberland; consulting surgeon, Miner's Hosp., Frostburg, Md. Chmn. and surgeon, med. advisory bd., World War. Past pres. Allegany-Garrett County Med. Soc.; past pres. Med. and Chirurg. Faculty of Md. Fellow Am. Coll. Surgeons, A.M.A. Mason (32°, K.T., Shriner), Elk. Clubs: Cumberland Rotary (past pres.); University (Baltimore); Cumberland Country; AliGhan Shrine Country (Cumberland). Home: Hill Crest Drive, Allegany County, Md. Office: Medical Bldg., Cumberland, Md.

HAWKINS, Harry Calvin, official State Dept.; b. Reed City, Mich., Mar. 25, 1894; s. Harvey W. and Nettie (Thompson) H.; A.B., Olivet (Mich.) Coll., 1919; student U. of Mich., summer 1919; M.B.A., Harvard, 1921; m. Ruth Dayton Spencer, Dec. 9, 1917; children—Barbara Hope, Kathryn Mather. Spl. agt. U.S. Dept. of Commerce, 1921-22; asst. prof., U. of Va., 1922-23; drafting officer U.S. Dept. of State, 1924-25, 1927-30; fgn. service officer and vice-counsul of career, 1924-25; prof. of business adminstrn., U. of Ore., 1925-27, 1930-31; divisional asst. Dept. of State, 1931-35, asst. chief Div. of Trade Agreements, 1935-36, chief since 1936. Served as 1st lt. inf., U.S.A., 1917-19. Mem. Pan Xenia (fgn. trade fraternity). Co-Author: Merchant Shipping Industry (pub. under pen names H. C. Calvin and E. G. Stewart), 1925. Home: 12 W. Leland St., Chevy Chase, Md. Office: U.S. Dept. of State, Washington, D.C.

HAWKS, Edward, clergyman; b. South Wales, Feb. 1878; s. Edward (Longridge) and Maria Theresa (Hallam) H.; ed. private schools in England, Univ. of London, Univ. of Lennoxville (Quebec), Nashotah House Sem. (Wis.), St. Charles Sem. (Overbrook, Pa.); unmarried. Ordained an Episcopalian clergyman, 1905; tutor, Nashotah Sem., Wis., 1905-08; ordained Catholic priest, 1911; curate St. Edwards Ch., Phila., 1911-17; chaplain with Canadian Expeditionary Force in France, 1917-19; rector of St. Joan of Arc Ch., Phila., since 1919. Title Right Rev. Monsignor. Made Domestic Prelate of His Holiness the Pope, 1936; officier d' Academie. Mem.

British Officers Club, Phila. Author: William McGarvey and the Open Pulpit, 1935; The Difficulties of Myron Digby, 1935; A Pedigree of Protestantism, 1936; The Difficulties of Father Callaghan, 1939. Contbr. short stories and articles to mags.; columnist of Catholic Standard and Times, Phila., since 1920. Home: 2025 E. Atlantic St., Philadelphia, Pa.

HAWKS, Rachel Marshall (Mrs. Arthur Worthington Hawks), sculptor; b. Port Deposit, Md., Mar. 20, 1879; d. John Fulton and Annie Elizabeth (Deaver) Marshall; student Md. Inst. Sch. of Fine Arts, Baltimore, 1895-99, Rinehart Sch. of Sculpture, Baltimore, 1899-1901; m. Arthur Worthington Hawks, June 20, 1901; 1 son, Marshall. Has followed career as sculptor since 1901 specializing in garden sculpture; represented in garden late Ambassador Bingham, Louisville, Ky., Mrs. Geo. Beaham, Kansas City, Mo., G. L. Craig, Sewickley, Pa., Hockaday Sch. for Girls, Dallas, Tex.; fountain at Union Memorial Hosp., Maryland Casualty Co., both Baltimore; also portraits of people of prominence; busts and medallions. Democrat. Episcopalian. Club: Hardy Garden (Ruxton). Home: Ruxton, Md.

HAWLEY, William Chauncey, v.p. and supt. Pa. Water Co.; b. Cambridge, N.Y., Aug. 31, 1865; s. Charles T. and Fannie S. (Warner) H.; C.E., Rensselaer Poly. Inst., Troy, N.Y., 1886; m. Nellie N. Newton, Dec. 25, 1890; children—Margaret, William Chauncey. Resident engr. Cambridge (N.Y.) Water Works, June-Oct. 1886; asst. and principal asst. to Chester B. Davis, civil engr., engaged on surveys, making plans and constructing various water works and sewage systems, Chicago, Ill., 1887-93; asst. engr. on surveys and plans for additional water supply, Troy, N.Y., 1893-94; resident engr. Wilkins & Davison, Pittsburgh, on constrn. water works at Grafton, W.Va., 1894-95; asst. engr. to Robert Swan, Allegheny City, Pa., on design Montrose Pumping Sta. and 9½ miles of 60 inch riveted steel force main and in charge constrn. about 6 miles of latter, Feb.-Dec. 1895; engr. and supt. water dept., Atlantic City, N.J., 1896-1902; chief engr. and supt. Pa. Water Co., Wilkinsburg, Pa., 1902-36, v.p. and gen. supt. since 1936; dir. Standard Bldg. and Loan Assn., Wilkinsburg. Mem. Am. Soc. C.E., Engrs. Soc. Western Pa. (pres. 1 yr.), New England Water Works Assn., Pa. Water Works Assn. (pres. several yrs.; hon. life mem. since 1937), Am. Water Works Assn. Home: 131 Beech St., Edgewood, Pittsburgh, Pa. Office: 712 South Av., Wilkinsburg, Pa.

HAY, George, M.D., surgeon; b. Johnstown, Pa., Apr. 6, 1880; s. John Barnitz and Anna Margaret (Suppes) H.; student Johnstown (Pa.) Grade and High schs.; M.D., Jefferson Med. Coll., Phila., 1903; post-grad. work Johns Hopkins Hosp. and Med. Sch., Baltimore; m. Mary Louise Austin, Apr. 12, 1913; children—George Austin, Mariana Philips. In gen. practice medicine and surgery, Johnstown, Pa., since 1903; 2d asst. to acting chief of surg. staff Conemaugh Valley Memorial Hosp., 1903-23; health officer, city physician and physician-in-charge Johnstown (Pa.) Municipal Hosp. for Contagious Diseases, 1906-14; chief med. examiner Lorain Div. of Carnegie-Ill. Steel Corpn. since 1915; surgeon Nat. Radiator Corpn. (2 plants) and Century Specialty Co. since 1919; pres. Pennigan Oil Syndicate. Served as 1st lt., M.C., U.S. Army, Camp Greenleaf, Ga., and Evacuation Hosp. 57, Ga., 1918-19; capt., Med. Officers Res. Corps. until 1924. Chmn. finance com. for Pa. State Med. Conv., 1930; temp. pres. Physicians' and Dentists' Service Bur. of Johnstown, Pa., to form its orgn., 1938. Dir. Y.M.C.A.; ex-v.p. Community Chest; 1st v.p. Adm. Robt. E. Parry Council, Boy Scouts of America. Trustee Cambria Co. Med. Soc. since 1920, pres. 1932, now also dir.; business mgr. "Medical Comment" (official pub.), 1920-24, editor since 1934; compiled 80th Anniversary Edit. of Med. Comment, 1932, and authorized to edit 90th Anniversary Edition in 1942. Mem. Med. Soc. State of Pa., A.M.A., Am. Pub. Health Assn.; A.A.A.S., Phi Alpha Sigma. Mason (32°; Shriner; Commandery; K.T.; v.p. Masonic Temple Assn. of Johnstown). Address: Valley Pike and Hay Av., Johnstown, Pa.

HAY, George Asahel Frank, high sch. prin.; b. Junction City, Kan., May 14, 1897; s. Robert M. and Mary Susan (Hastings) H.; A.B., Colo. State Coll. of Edn., Greeley, 1923, A.M., 1927; m. Edmonia Richmond, June 9, 1928; children—Virginia Richmond, John Hastings. Engaged in teaching, rural schs., Kan., 1916-18; teacher pub. schs., Junction City, Kan., 1919, jr. high sch., 1919-21; prin. pub. sch., Webster Groves, Mo., 1922-25, jr. high sch., 1925-30, six-yr. high sch., 1930-31; prin. high sch., Ridgewood, N.J., since 1931. Served in U.S.A., 1918. Mem. Kappa Delta Pi, Phi Delta Kappa. Presbyn. Home: 249 Richards Rd., Ridgewood, N.J.

HAY, Homer William, supt. schs.; b. Rockwood, Pa., July 20, 1885; s. William and Hannah L. (Wolfersberger) H.; ed. California State Normal Sch., 1909-12; A.B., U. of Pittsburgh, 1924, A.M., same, 1927, Ed.D., same, 1934; m. Ella McVicker, July 2, 1913; children—Donald Arthur, Homer McVicker, Harold Stanley. Successively rural sch. teacher, grade sch. teacher, high sch. teacher, then prin. high sch.; now supt. schs., Somerset, Pa. Mem. Nat. Edn. Assn., Am. Assn. Sch. Adminstrs., Pa. State Edn. Assn., Phi Delta Kappa. Republican. Mem. Reformed Ch. Mason. Club: Rotary of Somerset. Home: 526 Taymare Av., Somerset, Pa.

HAY, Malcolm, lawyer; b. Pittsburgh, Pa., May 19, 1907; s. Southard and Eleanor (Humbird) H.; grad. Shady Side Acad., Pittsburgh, 1922, Phillips Acad., Andover, Mass., 1925; A.B., Yale U., 1930, LL.B., U. of Pittsburgh Law Sch., 1933; m. Martha Verner Leggate, Aug. 3, 1931; children—Eleanor Anne, Malcolm. Admitted to bar, 1933, and since in gen. practice of law; associated with Baker & Watts, 1933-35; partner Rhea, Grubbs & Hay since 1935. Sec. Zoning Bd. of Adjustment, Sewickley Borough; Democratic chmn. Sewickley Borough. First lt., 393d Inf., O.R.C., since 1931. Trustee Episcopal Diocese of Pittsburgh, Family Soc. of Allegheny County, Maternal Health Center. Mem. Phi Delta Phi. Mason. Clubs: Pittsburgh Golf, Harvard-Yale-Princeton (Pittsburgh); Edgeworth (Sewickley). Home: Backbone Road and Division St., Sewickley, Pa. Office: 928 Frick Bldg., Pittsburgh, Pa.

HAY, Southard, engr.; b. Pittsburgh, Pa., Oct. 24, 1878; s. Malcolm and Virginia Eleanor (Southard) H.; student Shady Side Acad., Pittsburgh, 1893-1897; grad. Phillips Acad., Andover, Mass., 1898 (pres. Class of 1898); Ph.B., Sheffield Scientific Sch. (Yale Univ.), 1901 (pres. Class of 1901); m. Eleanor Humbird, Apr. 21, 1906 (died Oct. 7, 1937); children—Malcolm, III, Eleanor Southard. Asst. to purchasing agent Harbison-Walker Co., 1901-03; partner Standard Contracting Co., 1903-05; v.p. Cuthbert Bros. Co., Inc. (established 1858, incorporated 1905), 1905-28, pres. since 1928; pres. Blagden Construction Corpn. of New York, 1928-29, now dir.; dir. Century Building Company, Inc.; Receiver Banking Dept. of Penna., 1931-32; dir. Reppert-Hay & Associates, Inc.; conservator U.S. Treasury Dept., 1932-33; dir. Dept. of Pub. Welfare, Pittsburgh, 1934-36; mem. Allegheny County Emergency Relief Bd., Pittsburgh, 1934-35. Dir. Children's Hosp.; trustee Homewood Cemetery; mem. bd. Travelers Aid Soc., Public Health Nursing Assn. (all of Pittsburgh); mem. Hospital Council of Allegheny County, Pa. Mem. and vice-pres. Yale Engring. Soc. of N.Y., Soc. Founders and Patriots of America, S.A.R., Soc. War of 1812, Soc. Kappa Omega Alpha, Phillips Academy, Soc. Book and Snake (Yale). Episcopalian. Democrat. Mason (Shriner). Clubs: Duquesne, Harvard-Yale-Princeton, Yale, Optimist Club of Pittsburgh, Junta (Pittsburgh); Graduate (New Haven, Conn.); Yale (New York); The Pennsylvania Society of N.Y. Published "Centennial Address on the Birthday of George Washington, Feb. 22, 1932, and a Brief Biography of Its Author, Samuel L. Southard"; also address delivered at 13th Annual Conf. of Hosp. Assn. of Pa., Pittsburgh, Apr. 11, 1934. Contbr. Yale Scientific Monthly. Home: 6212 Howe St. Office: Bessemer Bldg., Pittsburgh, Pa.

HAYDEN, Reynolds; sr. med. officer, U.S. Naval Acad.; capt. Med. Corps, U.S. Navy. Address: U.S. Naval Academy, Annapolis, Md.

HAYES, Albert Orion, univ. prof.; b. Granby, Que., Can., Mar. 16, 1882; s. Edwin Albert and Mary Emma (Mock) H.; B.S., McGill U., Montreal, Que., 1908, M.S., 1910; Ph.D., Princeton U., 1914; m. Camilla Louise Bordsen, Feb. 5, 1912; children—Marjorie, Marion (Mrs. Eric Browne). Jr. geologist, Canadian Geol. Survey, Ottawa, Ont., 1913-20, geologist, 1925-26; geologist, Whitehall Petroleum Co., Canada and Equador, S.A., 1920-22, Standard Oil Co. of N.J., Argentina and Bolivia, 1922-25; visiting prof., Lafayette Coll., Easton, Pa., 1926; visiting prof., Rutgers U., New Brunswick, N.J., 1926-28, prof. of geology since 1928. Mem. A.A.A.S., Geol. Soc. of America, Am. Inst. Mining and Metall. Engrs., Soc. of Econ. Geologists, Canadian Inst. of Mining and Metallurgy, Am. Assn. of Petroleum Geologists, Am. Polar Soc., Am. Geog. Soc. of N.Y., New Brunswick (N.J.) Scientific Soc., N.J. Archaeol. Soc., Sigma Xi. Reformed Ch. Club: Rutgers Univ. Outing (New Brunswick, N.J.). Dir. The Rutgers Geol. Museum, New Brunswick, N.J. Home: Highland Park, N.J. Office: Rutgers Univ., New Brunswick, N.J.

HAYES, Augustus W(ashington), college prof.; b. Pleasant Plains, Ill., July 2, 1884; s. Joseph Wright and Fannie Marie (Pierce) H.; B.S., U. of Ill., 1907; M.S., U. of Wis., 1915, Ph.D., 1920; m. Martha Fidelia Durham, June 14, 1917; children—John Durham, Howard Wright (deceased), Sarah Augusta. Instr. of sociology, Tulane U., 1920-21, asst. prof., 1921-23, asso. prof., 1923-25; asso. prof. of sociology, Iowa State Coll., 1925-26, U. of Mich., 1926; prof. and head of dept. of sociology, Marshall Coll., since 1926; acting dean, Coll. of Arts and Sciences, Marshall Coll., 1928-29. Partner, Hayes and Edwards since 1926 in operation of 536 acre farm, Sullivan County, Ind. Pres. Council Social Agencies, Huntington, W. Va., 1931-32; chmn. Tri-State Welfare Conf., Huntington, W.Va., 1932-36, 1939; mem. State Com. on Higher Edn. of W.Va., 1937-39; mem. com. edn. and training of W.Va. Conf. of Social Work since 1938; organizer and former mem. La. State Library Assn. (appointment made by the gov.). Mem. Ohio Valley Sociol. Soc., Am. Sociol. Soc., Acacia, Alpha Zeta, Alpha Kappa Delta, Pi Gamma Mu. Democrat. Presbyterian. Author: Community Organization, 1921; Rural Sociology, 1929; also 3 research studies in community organization, 1921, 22, 23. Home: 1024 Euclid Pl., Huntington, W.Va.

HAYES, E. V.; pres. Union Savings Bank. Address: 5th Av. and Grant St., Pittsburgh, Pa.

HAYES, J. Carroll, lawyer; b. West Chester, Pa., Mar. 28, 1869; s. William M. and Rachel H. (Russell) H.; A.B., Swarthmore Coll., 1889; A.B., Harvard, 1890; LL.B., U. of Pa. Law Sch., 1893; m. Louella Passmore, Sept. 25, 1894; children—William Waldo, George P., Ellen (Mrs. Paul Schulz, Germany), Margaret H. (Mrs. Harry E. Oppenlander). Admitted to Pa. bar, 1892, and since engaged in gen. practice of law at West Chester; asso. with son, William Waldo Hayes, since 1935; pres. Chester Co. Law Library Assn. Former mem. Pub. Sch. Bd. Pres. West Chester Relief Soc. Dir. and past pres. Chester Co. Hist. Soc. Mem. Delta Upsilon, Phi Beta Kappa (past pres. Swarthmore Chapter). Awarded prize for article on 1924 Meeting of Am. and Brit. Bars and comparison of the Two Legal Systems. Democrat. Mem. Religious Soc. Friends. Lecturer (illustrated) upon history and travel. Home: West Chester, Pa. Office: 121 N. High St., West Chester, Pa.

HAYES, John Russell, librarian; b. at West Chester, Pa., June 25, 1866; s. William Mordecai and Rachel Hutton (Russell) H.; A.B., Swarthmore, 1888; A.B., Harvard, 1889; LL.B., U. of Pa., 1892; univs. of Oxford and Strassburg, 1892-93; m. Emma Gawthrop, June 30, 1892; children—~~Esther Rachel~~, Katharine Russell, Eleanor Gawthrop. Instructor Enlish, 1893-95, assistant prof., 1895-1906, college librarian, 1906-27; librarian Friends Historical Library, 1927-

36, Swarthmore College, retired, 1936. Mem. Phi Beta Kappa, Delta Upsilon. Member Society of Friends (Quaker). Author: The Old-Fashioned Garden and Other Verses, 1895; The Brandywine, 1898; Swarthmore Idylls, 1899; Scholar's Ideal (Phi Beta Kappa ode), 1904; Old Quaker Meeting-Houses, 1909; Brandywine Days, 1910; In Memory of Whittier, 1910; Molly Pryce, 1913; Roger Morland, a Quaker Idyll, 1915; Collected Poems, 1916. Home: Embreeville, Pa.

HAYES, John William, labor leader; b. Phila., Dec. 26, 1854; s. Edward and Mary (Galbreath) H.; entirely self taught; m. Nellie A. Carlen, July 1882. With Pa. R.R. Co. as brakeman in early life; lost right arm, May 28, 1878, on N.Y. div. Pa. R.R. Learned telegraphy; worked at it until strike of 1883; mem. gen. exec. bd., 1884-88, sec.-treas., 1888-1902, gen. master workman, since Nov. 1902, Knights of Labor; was editor Journal of the Knights of Labor, and National Labor Digest. Pres. North Chesapeake Beach Land and Improvement Co. Home: North Beach, Md.

HAYES, Leslie David, univ. prof.; b. South Strafford, Vt., Mar. 27, 1876; s. Chauncey Ellis and Addie M. (Luce) H.; B.S., U. of N.H., Durham, N.H., 1897; M.E., Cornell U., 1908, grad. student, 1908-10; m. Emilie Christine Roths, June 15, 1907 (dec. 1921); children—Katherine Eloise (dec.), Chauncey Ellis, Betty Jane (dec.); m. 2d Vera Marriott, Apr. 2, 1923. Instr. manual training, Minneapolis, Minn., Bay City, Ishpeming, Mich., Appleton, Wis., Youngstown, O., 1898-1907; instr. machine design, Cornell U., 1907-10, asst. prof. machine design, 1910-18; mech. engr. U.S. Bur. Standards (on leave), 1917-18; prof. machine design and constrn., W.Va. Univ., Morgantown, W.Va., 1918-37, head dept. mech. engring. since 1937. Served as chmn. Progressive Party, Tompkins Co., N.Y., 1914-17. Registered professional engr. in W.Va. Mem. Am. Soc. Mech. Engrs., Soc. for Promotion Engring. Edn., Cornell Soc. Engrs., W.Va. Soc. Professional Engrs., W.Va. Univ. Sci. Soc., Kappa Sigma. Republican. Mem. Ch. of Christ Sci. Club: Rotary. Home: 804 College Av., Morgantown, W.Va.

HAYES, Lydia Young, work for the blind; b. Hutchinson, Minn., Sept. 11, 1871; d. Charles William Hardy and Mary Elizabeth (Grant) H.; ed. Foster Sch., Somerville, Mass., 1880-81, Perkins Instn. and Mass. Sch. for the Blind, Boston, Mass., 1881-89, Page Kindergarten Normal Class Cushman Sch., Boston, 1890-91, spl. courses N.Y. Univ., 1911-13. Engaged in various work for the blind and teaching, 1892-1900; called to N.J. to organize state work for blind and head N.J. Commn. for the Blind, 1910-37; ednl. and research consultant for N.J. Commn. for the Blind, consultant for Dept. for Deaf Blind at N.Y. Inst. for Edn. of Blind since 1937; lost sight in 1879 as result from an accident. Dir. John Milton Soc. N.Y. Mem. of Corpn. of Perkins Instn. and Mass. Sch. for Blind, Nat. Assn. Execs. of Commns. and State Assns. doing state wide work for blind (organizing pres. 8 yrs), Am. Assn. workers for the Blind. Del. to World Conf. on Work for the Blind, 1931; del. to World Conf. on Work for the Blind and chmn. Round Table on Deaf Blind, N.Y. City, 1931. Republican. Conglist. Clubs: Peapack Womens; Heptorean (Somerville, Mass.). Home: Far Hills, N.J. Office: 1060 Broad St., Newark, N.J., and also, 999 Pelham Parkway, New York, N.Y.

HAYES, Norman Trump, banking; b. Phila., Pa., Aug. 7, 1888; s. William Nathaniel and Mary (Trump) H.; ed. pub. sch. and high sch., U. of Pa. Wharton Sch. Finance; m. Elsie P. Phillips, Nov. 9, 1915; children—Norman T., Jr., Doris Phillips. Asso. with Philadelphia Nat. Bank continuously since entering its employ, 1904, advanced through various positions and now vice-pres. Served as dir. Pa. Economy League, Better Business Bur. of Phila., Chestnut St. Assn. Mem. Phila Humane Soc. Trustee Home for Incurables. For many yrs. active in banking edn. and adminstrn. and has held nat. offices in following orgns., Am. Bankers Assn., Am. Inst. of Banking, Assn. of Res. City Bankers. Mem. Pa. Soc. S.R. Republican. Presbyn. Mason. Clubs: Union League, Philadelphia Country, Skating, Rotary (Philadelphia); Skytop of Skytop, Pa. (dir.). Home: 115 Airdale Av., Rosemont, Pa. Office: 1416 Chestnut St., Philadelphia, Pa.

HAYES, Ralph; b. Crestline, O., Sept. 24, 1894; s. John and Margaret (Costello) H.; A.B., Western Reserve Univ., 1915; unmarried. Sec. City Club, Cleveland, O., 1915-16; pvt. sec. to sec. of war Dec. 1916-July 1918; asst. to sec. of war, Jan.-June 1920; asst. to pres. of Cleveland Trust Co., 1920-22; asst. to Will H. Hays, pres. Motion Picture Producers & Distributors of America, 1922-23; v.p. Chatham Phenix Nat. Bank & Trust Co., 1927-29; 2d v.p. Press Pub. Co. (New York World), 1929-30; v.p. Transamerica Corpn., 1930-31; exec. dir. New York Community Trust since 1923; v.p. The Coca Cola Co. since 1933; dir. Equitable Trust Co. (Wilmington, Del.). Pvt. 11th Division, Camp Meade, July-Sept. 1918; commd. lt. inf. at Ligny, France, Sept. 1918; liaison officer, between G.H.Q., A.E.F. and Am. Commn. to Negotiate Peace, Dec. 1918. Mem. Phi Beta Kappa (ex-pres. Alpha of Ohio), Delta Sigma Rho, Alpha Delta Phi (ex-treas.), Phi Delta Phi. Clubs: City (Cleveland—ex-treas., ex-sec., ex-dir.); Country (Wilmington); Broad Street (New York). Home: Crestline, O. Office: 101 W. 10th St., Wilmington, Del., and 120 Broadway, New York, N.Y.

HAYHOW, Edgar Charles, hospital supt.; b. N.Y. City, July 21, 1894; s. Henry Herbert and Lina Caroline (Buehlmaier) H.; B.S., Fordham; B.C.S., M.A., New York U., also grad. work same; unmarried. Successively asst. supt. Presbyterian, St. Luke's and Lenox Hill hosps., New York, 1916-24; supt. New Rochelle (N.Y.) Hosp., 1924-27; hosp. consultant, 1927-30; supt. Paterson (N.J.) Gen. Hosp. since 1930; lecturer on institutional management, New York U., 1924-28. Hosp. Service, B.E.F., later A.E.F., 1916-17; capt. Med. Administration Res. Corps, U.S.A.; adjt. Gen. Hosp. No. 157. Mem. Social Planning Council, Paterson Community Chest. Fellow Am. Coll. of Hosp. Adminstrs. (regent 1936-39); mem. Am. Acad. Polit. and Social Science, Paterson Tuberculosis and Health League (advisory council), Am., N.Y. State and Internat. hosp. assns., N.J. State Hosp. Assn. (pres.), Am. League for Human Rights, Lambda Sigma Phi, Phi Delta Kappa. Republican. Methodist. Clubs: Army and Navy (New York); Watchung Valley Country (Plainfield, N.J.). Contbr. to hosp. and social service mags. Mem. advisory council The Living Age. Home: 62 Eppirt St., East Orange. Address: Paterson General Hospital, Paterson, N.J.

HAYMAN, Joseph Lester, coll. dean; b. Whitesville, Del., June 3, 1896; s. Edwin Henry and Rosa Mary (White) H.; Ph.C., U. of Mich., Coll. of Pharmacy, Ann Arbor, Mich., 1919, B.S., 1919, M.S., 1925; m. Alice Lucille Bennett, Sept. 18, 1920; children—Alice Margaret, Joe Lester (dec.). Instr. in pharmacy, W.Va. Univ. Coll. Pharmacy, Morgantown, 1919-22, asst. prof. 1922-28, asso. prof. 1928-35, prof. since 1935; dir. Coll. of Pharmacy, 1936-38, dean of coll. since 1938. Mem. Nat. Drug Trade Conf. representing Am. Assn. of Colls. of Pharmacy, since 1933. Mem. Am. Pharm. Assn. (2d v.p. 1935-36), Nat. Conf. Pharm. Assn. Secs. (pres. 1932-33, exec. com. since 1931, sec.-treas. since 1937), W.Va. Pharm. Assn. (sec.-treas. since 1926), W.Va. U. Scientific Soc., Phi Lambda Upsilon, Phi Sigma, Rho Chi, Alpha Chi Sigma. Republican. Presbyn. Mason. Clubs: Rotary of Morgantown (pres. 1939-40); Faculty (W.Va. U.). Editor monthly bulls. W.Va. Pharm. Assn. since 1927. Mem. U.S. Pharmacopoeial Conv. 1930. Contbr. articles to drug trade jours. Home: 325 Ash St. Office: West Virginia Univ., Morgantown, W.Va.

HAYMOND, Frank Cruise; mem. law firm Haymond & Haymond. Address: Fairmont, W.Va.

HAYNE, Coe, author, clergyman; b. Tecumseh, Mich., Feb. 3, 1875; s. Marcus Eldon and Eleanor Currey (Tenbrook) H.; A.B., Kalamazoo College, 1899, Litt.D., 1932; A.B., U. of Chicago, 1900, grad. work, 1900-03; m. Ethel May Shandrew, July 1, 1909; children—Eldon William, Eleanor Shandrew, John Wrightwood, Mary Barbara. Contbr. to juvenile publs., 1904-07, 1909-16, ordained Bapt. ministry, 1907; pastor Eaton Rapids, Mich., 1907-09, Burlington Bapt. Ch., Salt Lake City, Utah, 1916-18; Y.M.C.A. service as interdivisional games mgr., Le Mans Area, France, 1918-19; asst. sec. lt. and publicity, Am. Bapt. Home Mission Soc., 1919-30, sec. since 1930; mem. bd. mgrs. Missionary Edn. Movement since 1923; vice-pres. Nat. Religious Publicity Council, 1937-38, pres. since 1939. Mem. Divinity Alumni Assn., U. of Chicago (pres. 1925-26). Republican. Author: Old Trails and New, 1920; By-Paths to Forgotten Folks, 1921; Race Grit, 1922; For a New America, 1923; Young People and the World's Work (monograph), 1927; The God of Yoto, 1928; Red Men on the Bighorn, 1929; Prisoners of Spirit Mountain, 1930; Vanguard of the Caravans, 1931; They Came Seeking, 1935; Baptist Trail Makers of Michigan, 1936; Cry Dance (novel), 1939. Collaborator: America Tomorrow, 1923; The Road to Brotherhood, 1924; The Moccasin Trail, 1923. Home: 6 Poplar St., Dumont, N.J. Office: 23 E. 26th St., New York, N.Y.

HAYNES, Roy Asa, ex-commr. prohibition of U.S.; b. Hillsboro, O., Aug. 31, 1881; s. Charles Elliott and Mary (West) H.; Western Reserve U., 1903-04; m. Katherine Logan Mason, Sept. 9, 1903. Editor of Dispatch, Hillsboro, O., since 1908. Active worker in prohibition campaigns for many yrs.; federal prohibition commr. by apptmt. of Presidents Harding and Coolidge, 1921-27; pres. Economy Fire Ins. Co., 1927-28; with Nat. Thrift Corpn., 1928-29; investment banking, 1929-30; mng. distributor for Eastern territory, Air-Way Electric Appliance Corpn., 1930-35, gen. sales mgr., same co., since 1936. Twice del. Gen. Conf. M.E. Ch., heading lay delegation from West Ohio Conf. Republican. Methodist. Mason (K.T.), Woodman. Author: Prohibition Inside Out, 1923. Home: Marchwood Apts., Germantown, Philadelphia, Pa. Office: care Airway Electric Appliance Corpn., Toledo, O.*

HAYS, Harry Clayton, banker; b. Huffsdale, Pa., Sept. 28, 1895; s. John Hunter and Flora (Truxell) H.; student Fredonia Inst.; m. Marie Chiew, Jan. 29, 1920; children—Alice Marie, Harry Richard. With Fredonia Nat. Bank, successively bookkeeper, asst. cashier, and cashier, pres. since 1933, now also dir. Mem. Am. Legion, Legion of Honor. Mason (32°), Odd Fellow. Home: First St. Office: Main St., Fredonia, Pa.

HAYS, Jo, supervising prin. of schools; b. York Co., Pa., Dec. 27, 1898; s. Morris Mills and Sarah (Krone) H.; grad. North York (Pa.) High Sch. 1916, Shippensburg (Pa.) State Teachers Coll., 1918; A.B., Pa. State Coll., 1923; Ed.M., Harvard (summers 1925-29); m. Helen Nelson McKain, Aug. 29, 1931; 1 son, Jo Nelson. Teacher and coach, Clarion (Pa.) High Sch., 1918-19; prin. of grade sch., Ridgeway Twp., Elk Co., Pa., 1919-20; prin. Orbisonia (Pa.) High Sch., 1920-21; teacher State College (Pa.) High Sch., 1923-24, prin. 1924-27; supervising prin. State College Pub. Schs. since 1927. Mem. N.E.A. (life mem.), Delta Sigma Rho, Kappa Phi Kappa, Phi Delta Kappa, Pi Gamma Mu, Phi Kappa Psi. Democrat. Methodist. Mason. Kiwanian. Home: 441 W. Fairmount Av. Office: New High School Bldg., State College, Pa.

HAYS, John Lashells, gen. counsel and sec. South Penn Oil Co.; b. Oil City, Pa., May 24, 1878; s. Frederic William and Elizabeth Ida (Lashells) H.; ed. Oil City pub. and high schs.; A.B., Washington & Jefferson Coll., 1901; m. Maude Bell Walker, Dec. 21, 1906; children—Frederic Walker, Katherine Elizabeth (dec.). Admitted to Pa. bar, 1903; mem. law firm F. W. & J. L. Hays, 1903-05; asso. counsel, sec. and dir. Barnsdall Oil Co., Bartlesville, Okla., 1906-18; asso. counsel South Penn Oil Co., Pittsburgh, 1918-34, gen. counsel since 1934; sec. and dir. since 1925; gen. counsel, sec. and dir. Clayco Gas Co.; dir. Pennzoil Co., Bradford Transit Co. Served as warrant officer Co. D, 16th Pa. Inf., U.S.V., Spanish-Am. War. Trustee and treas. First Presbyn. Ch., Bartlesville, 1907-18. Mem. Am. Bar Assn., Pa. Bar Assn., Allegheny Co. Bar Assn., Phi Kappa Sigma. Republican. Mason. Clubs: University, Stanton Heights Golf (Pittsburgh). Home: 3955 Bigelow Boul. Office: 1300 Chamber of Commerce Bldg., Pittsburgh, Pa.

HAYTHORN, Samuel Reese, director William H. Singer Memorial Laboratory; b. Danville, Ill., Sept. 10, 1880; s. William Quincey and Emma Louise (Reese) H.; M.D., U. of Mich., Ann Arbor, Mich., 1904; m. Mayme Hauser, June 25, 1908; 1 dau., Maraine (Mrs. Louis L. Bambas). Asst. pathologist and gynecologist, U. of Mich., Ann Arbor, Mich., 1904-06; pathologist, Mass. State Hosp., Boston, Mass., 1906-08; interne and asst., Boston City Hosp., 1908-09; asst. pathologist Harvard Med. Sch., 1909-10; instr. pathology, U. of Pittsburgh, 1910-11, asst. prof., 1911-13, fellow, 1912-13, prof. Med. Sch., 1921-33, dir. hygiene, 1921-26, asso. prof., preventive medicine, 1926-33; pathologist Allegheny Gen. Hosp., 1913-15; dir. William H. Singer Memorial Laboratory, Pittsburgh, 1915-21, since 1923. Mem. Med. Advisory Bd., State Dept. Health (Pa.), 1923-31. Mem. A.A.A.S., Assn. Pathology and Bacteriology (councilor since 1937), Soc. Exptl. Pathology (councilor, 1928-32, pres., 1932), Soc. Exptl. Biology, A.M.A., Am. Coll. Physicians, Pittsburgh Acad. Medicine (pres. 1927), Internat. Assn. Med. Mus. (councilor since 1936). Clubs: University, Stanton Heights Golf (Pittsburgh, Pa.). Home: 5431 Baywood St. Office: Allegheny General Hospital, Pittsburgh, Pa.

HAYWARD, Nathan, corpn. official; b. Boston, Mass., Aug. 27, 1872; s. James Warren and Sarah Bancroft (Howard) H.; student Roxbury Latin Sch., 1885-91; A.B., Harvard, 1895; S.B., Mass. Inst. of Tech., 1897; m. Anna Howell Lloyd, Apr. 30, 1907; children—Anna Howell, Nathan, Sarah Howard, Malcolm Lloyd, Esther Lloyd. Instr. in Mass. Inst. of Tech., 1897-98; with Bell Telephone Co. of Pa., as engr., later cons. engr., 1898-1922; pres. Am. Dredging Co. since 1917; Am. Shipyard Co. since 1919; dir. Bell Telephone Co. of Pa., Phila. & Reading Coal & Iron Corpn., Phila. & Reading Coal & Iron Co., Phila. Saving Fund Soc., Phila. Belt Line R.R. Co., Fidelity-Phila. Trust Co. Served asso. chief on War Industries Bd., World War. Pres. Franklin Inst., 1928-37; mem. bd. of overseers of Harvard U.; mem. advisory com. Pa. Hosp.; dir. Phila. Maritime Exchange, Phila. Bd. of Trade. Mem. Am. Philos. Soc., New England Soc. of Pa., Am. Inst. of Elect. Engrs., Newcomen Soc. (Eng.), Telephone Pioneers of America, Hist. Soc. of Pa., Acad. of Natural Sciences of Phila., Fairmount Park Art Assn., Nat. Assn. of River and Harbor Contractors, Dredge Owners Protective Orgn. Republican. Unitarian. Clubs: Harvard, Rittenhouse, Engineers (Phila.); Harvard, Fly (Boston); Harvard (New York); Jean Ribaut (Fla.); Manchester Yacht (Mass.). Home: Brook Rd., Wayne, Pa. Office: 12 S. 12th St., Philadelphia, Pa.

HAYWARD, William George, educator, sch. prin.; b. Passaic, N.J., Apr. 6, 1908; s. George Phelps and Vera (Heuser) H.; diploma, State Teachers Coll., Paterson, N.J., 1928; B.S., Rutgers U., New Brunswick, N.J., 1930; M.A., Teachers Coll., Columbia U., 1932, diploma for supt. of schs., 1935; m. Mabel Konig, Dec. 26, 1931; children—Doreen Phelps, Georgeanne Phelps. Asst. supt. of recreation, Paterson, N.J., 1927-28; teacher of elementary grades, Lodi, N.J., 1928-29; vice-prin. elementary sch., Roselle, N.J., 1929-33; supervising prin. Hohokus Twp. (N.J.) Schs., 1933-37; instr. extension div., Paterson (N.J.) State Teachers Coll. since 1935; instr. summer session, Montclair (N.J.) State Teachers Coll., 1937; prin. Elmwood Sch., East Orange, N.J., since 1937; instr. summer session, Newark (N.J.) State Teachers Coll., 1938, 39; instr. extension div., Montclair (N.J.) State Teachers Coll., 1939. Mem. N.E.A., N.J. State Edn. Assn., N.J. Schoolmasters Club, N.J. Elementary Prins. Assn. (exec. com.), Nat. Elementary Prins. Assn., N.J. Council of Edn., Advanced Sch. Teachers Coll. of Columbia U., Bergen Co. Schoolmen's Club (sec. 1936-37), Kappa Delta Pi, Phi Delta Kappa. Presbyterian. Club: Lions of the Oranges (East Orange). Contbr. to Elementary School Jour. and other ednl. jours. Home: 21 Whittier St. Office: Elmwood School, 339 S. Burnet St., East Orange, N.J.

HAZARD, Robert Culver, corpn. official; b. Salamanca, N.Y., Sept. 10, 1908; s. William Henry and Elizabeth Kennicott (Culver) H.; student Salamanca (N.Y.) High Sch., 1921-22, Phillips Andover Acad., Andover, Mass., 1923-25; A.B., Dartmouth Coll., Hanover, Mass., 1929; m. Catherine Louise Barnes, Oct. 11, 1930; children—Mary Elizabeth, Robert Culver. Clk. Union Trust Co. of Md., Baltimore, 1929-32; Fla. rep. Continental Mortgage Co. of Baltimore, 1932-33, asst. treas., 1933-34, v.p., 1934, dir. since 1935; v.p. John K. Culver, Inc., Baltimore, 1934-36, pres., 1937-38; chmn. Ackers Rugs, Inc., rug cleaning and sales, Baltimore, since 1938; pres. Culmor Co., Baltimore, since 1936; chmn. Glenbrook Pub. Co., Baltimore, since 1937; v.p. and dir. Brooklyn Curtis Bay Land Co. since 1937; dir. Md. Properties, Inc. Club: Dartmouth (Baltimore, Md.; pres. since 1939). Home: 2500 Gibbons Av. Office: 225 W. 25th St., Baltimore, Md.

HAZARD, Spencer Peabody, pres. R. D. Wood Co.; b. of Am. parents, London, Eng., Feb. 28, 1872; s. Samuel and Blanche Crissy (Peabody) H.; attended Germantown Acad., Philadelphia, Class 1889; m. Serena Bluxome Hawley, June 1, 1918; children—Georgiana, Samuel. Began as clerk Pa. R.R. Co., 1888; associated with R. D. Wood & Co., 1899-1934; pres. and dir. R. D. Wood Co. since 1934; pres. and dir. Florence Pipe Foundry & Machine Co.; sec., treas. and dir. Sand Spun Patents Corpn. Treas. and trustee Germantown Acad.; sec. Musical Fund Soc. Mem. Mil. Order Loyal Legion. Republican. Episcopalian (accounting warden St. Luke's Ch., Germantown). Clubs: Union League, Art, Philadelphia Country. Home: 3009 Queen Lane. Office: 400 Chestnut St., Philadelphia, Pa.

HAZELTON, William H., pres. Salem Nat. Bank & Trust Co.; b. Mullica Hill, N.J., Dec. 7, 1873; s. Collins A. and Julia (Harker) H.; student Gwynedd (Pa.) Friends Sch., 1885-87, Brunner's Acad., North Wales, Pa., 1887-90; m. Elsie F. Flinchbaugh, 1918. Student and clk. in law office of I. O. Acton, Salem, N.J., 1890-99; teller Salem (N.J.) Nat. Banking Co., 1899-1902; sec. Salem (N.J.) Glass Works, 1902-22; pres. Salem (N.J.) Nat. Bank & Trust Co. since 1922; dir. Franklin Bldg. & Loan Assn. Republican. Episcopalian. Mason. Club: Fenwick (Salem, N.J.). Address: 31 Chestnut St., Salem, N.J.

HAZEN, Carl Monroe, M.D.; b. Venango, Pa., Mar. 6, 1888; s. Francis Monroe and Elizabeth Ann (Minium) H.; student Allegheny Coll. Prep. Sch., Meadville, Pa., 1904-06; M.D., Cincinnati Eclectic Med. Coll., 1914; post-grad. study, New York Post-Grad. Med. Sch., 1919, Cook County (Ill.) Hosp., 1934; m. Mary Grace Denzler, June 2, 1917; children—Barbara Ann, Richard Denzler, Carl Monroe. Princ. Blooming Valley (Pa.) High Sch., 1908-10; in gen. practice of medicine, Titusville, Pa., since 1915; mem. and ex-pres. staff Titusville Hosp.; cons. mem. Grand View Sanitarium, Oil City, Pa.; dir. Titusville Trust Co., Titusville Community Loan Co. Mem. Pa. Med. Soc., Crawford Co. Med. Soc. (ex-pres.). Republican. Presbyterian. Mason (K.T., Shriner). Clubs: Titusville Country, Rotary. Home: 614 E. Main St. Office: Commercial Bank Bldg., Titusville, Pa.

HAZEN, Joseph Chalmers, clergyman; b. Beaver Co., Pa., Apr. 5, 1874; s. Shadrock Burney and Mary Jane (Booth) H.; A.B., Bucknell U., Lewisburg, Pa., 1899, A.M., 1902, D.D., 1919; grad. Div. Sch., U. of Chicago, 1902, D.B., 1903; D.D., Colgate, 1927; m. Ruth Burchard, Dec. 22, 1908; children—Joseph Chalmers, Burchard Miller, Mary Ruth. Ordained Bapt. ministry, 1903; pastor successively Kankakee, Ill., First Ch., Janesville, Wis., First Ch., Peoria, Ill., until 1923, North Orange Ch., Orange, N.J., from 1923 until retired. Mem. finance com., administrative com., Ministers and Missionaries Benefit Bd. and Bd. of Missionary Cooperation—all of Northern Bapt. Conv.; mem. bd. mgrs. N.J. Bapt. State Conv., pres. since 1937; pres. Ministers' Assn. of the Oranges; mem. exec. com. and radio commn. of Federal Council of Chs. of Christ in America. Pres. of bd. of trustees Internat. Bapt. Seminary, East Orange. Republican. Mason (32°, Shriner). Clubs: Kiwanis (ex-pres.); Essex County Country. Home: 55 Temple Way, Ivanhoe Park, Summit, N.J.

HAZEN, Joseph Norton, newspaper publisher; b. Lambertville, N.J., May 16, 1870; s. Phineas Kennedy and Emmaline (Arnett) H.; ed. Lambertville pub. schs.; m. Isabel Cooper, 1903 (died 1928); 1 son, John C. Began as reporter Lambertville Beacon, 1885; sole owner Beacon Pub. Co. since 1917. Known as dean of Hunterdon County publishers. Former asst. chief of fire dept. Democrat. Presbyn. Elk (former sec.), Odd Fellow. Home: 144 N. Union St. Office: 14 Bridge St., Lambertville, N.J.

HAZLEHURST, Thomas Huger, Jr., asso. prof. chemistry; b. Corinth, Miss., Mar. 11, 1906; s. Thomas Huger and Margaret (Smith) H.; A.B., Coll. of Charleston, S.C., 1923; Ph.D., Johns Hopkins U., 1927; m. Edith P. Blackburn, June 6, 1927; 1 son, Blackburn Huger. Engaged as instr. chemistry, Lehigh U., 1927-31, asst. prof. chemistry, 1931-39, asso. prof. since 1939. Mem. Am. Chem. Soc., Sigma Xi, Gamma Alpha. Democrat. Episcopalian. Co-author (with Harold V. Anderson), Qualitative Analysis, 1937. Contbr. articles to chem. jours. Home: 729 Sixth Av., Bethlehem, Pa.

HAZLETT, Adam James, pres. Eastern Rolling Mill Co.; b. Butter, Pa., 1889; s. James B. and Louisa (Troutman) H,; student Gettysburg Coll.; m. Rachael Witherow Skelly, Dec. 1912. Pres. and dir. Eastern Rolling Mill Co. since 1927. Home: 3911 Juniper Road, Guilford. Office: P.O. Box 1975, Baltimore, Md.

HAZLETT, Robert, banker; b. Wheeling, W. Va., Dec. 24, 1863; s. Robert W. (M.D.) and Mary Elizabeth (Hobbs) H.; prep. edn., Linsly Inst., Wheeling; C.E., Ohio State U., 1887; m. Anne Cummins, Mar. 18, 1909; children—Robert C., James C., Catharine H. Civ. engr., Washington, D.C., 1891-93, N.Y. City, 1893-95, Wheeling, 1895-1914; was county engr., Ohio Co., W. Va.; now chmn. bd. Wheeling Dollar Savings & Trust Co.; pres. Wheeling & Belmont Bridge Co.; pres. Greenwood Cemetery; dir. Ward Baking Co., Palace Furniture Co. Formerly mem. City Council, and also postmaster of Wheeling, 1911-14, W.Va. Ho. of Dels. and W.Va. State Senate; was vice-president for W.Va., Nat. Rivers and Harbors Congress. Treas. Linsly Inst. (trustee). Mem. Sigma Chi; asso. mem. Am. Soc. C.E. Republican. Presbyn. Elk. Club: Fort Henry. Home: Echo Point. Office: Wheeling Dollar Savings & Trust Co., Wheeling, W.Va.

HEAD, Leon Oswald, pres. Ry. Express Agency; b. Milner, Ga., Apr. 23, 1879; s. James Pinkney and Nancy Lamar (Reid) H.; student Central Coll., Walnut Springs, Tex., 1894-96; B.A., Ouachita Coll., 1898; m. Helen Bartlett Nold, Feb. 21, 1900; 1 dau., Helen Belle (Mrs. Erskine Girard). Express agt., Wells Fargo & Co., Lake Charles, La., 1901-03, route agt., Dallas, Tex., 1903-07, chief route agt., Houston, Tex., 1907-09, gen. agt., New Orleans, La., 1909-11, supt., Little Rock, Ark., 1911-13, efficiency supt., Houston, 1913-15, gen. supt., Los Angeles, Calif., 1915-16, asst. to v.p., San Francisco, 1916-18; asst. to v.p. Am. Ry. Express Co., 1918-27, v.p., 1927-29; v.p. Ry. Express Agency, Inc., 1929-32, pres. since 1932; pres. Ry. Express Motor Transport, Inc., Ry. Express Agency, Inc., of Calif., Ry. Express Agency, Inc., of Va.; dir. and mem. exec. com. Expressmen's Mut. Life Ins. Co.; dir. Western Union Telegraph Co., Wells Fargo & Co. of Cuba, Wells Fargo Latin-Am. Co., Wells Fargo Cuban-Mexican Corpn. Served as 1st lt. Ark. Vol. Inf., Spanish-American War. Dir. Transportation Assn. of America. Member Chamber Commerce State of New York. Democrat. Protestant. Clubs: Bohemian (San Francisco); Traffic (Chicago);

Railroad-Machinery, Traffic (New York), Sleepy Hollow Country. Home: Ambassador Hotel, New York, N.Y., and Island Farm, Center Bridge, Pa. Office: 230 Park Av., New York, N.Y.

HEAD, Walter Dutton, educator; b. Revere, Mass., Sept. 17, 1881; s. Abel and Mary Frances (Hancock) H.; A.B., Harvard, 1902; A.M., Columbia, 1913; m. Bernice E. Leighton, 1914; children—Lois Hancock, Richard Leighton. Teacher Volkmann Sch., Boston, Mass., 1902-04, St. Mark's Sch., Southborough, Mass., 1904-05, Phillips Exeter Acad., Exeter, N.H., 1905-11; prin. high sch., Haverhill, Mass., 1912-15, New Rochelle, N.Y., 1915-17; headmaster The Nichols Sch., Buffalo, N.Y., 1917-25, Montclair (N.J.) Acad. since 1925. Mem. Internat. Auxiliary Language Assn., Headmasters' Assn., Headmasters' Assn. of Country Day Schs., Phi Delta Kappa. Clubs: Rotary (pres. 1927-28; dist. gov. Rotary Internat. 1931-32; dir. and 3d v.p. 1934-35; chairman aims and objects com.), Montclair Golf; Harvard (Northern N.J. and New York). Author: Beginner's French Book, 1922. Editor: Contes Choisis de Daudet, 1917. V.p. bd. trustees Miss Beard's Sch. for Girls, Orange, N.J. Home: 20 Lloyd Rd., Montclair, N.J.

HEADINGS, Donald Moore, surgeon; b. McAlisterville, Pa., Aug. 13, 1899; s. Isaac G. and Mary L. (Moore) H.; ed. Franklin and Marshall Coll., 1916-18; A.B., Swarthmore Coll., 1920; M.D., Jefferson Med. Coll., 1924; m. Dorothy C. Schutt, Oct. 8, 1932; 1 son, Donald Moore, Jr. Interne, Montgomery Hosp., 1924, Episcopal Hosp., Phila., 1925-26; chief resident, Mary Drexel Hosp., Phila., 1927; asst. surgeon, Montgomery Hosp., Norristown, Pa., 1928-31, surgeon since 1931; chief surgeon, Riverview Hosp., Norristown, Pa., since 1935; surgeon Sacred Heart Hosp., Norristown, since 1937; cons. surgeon, Norristown State Hosp., 1931-38. Dir. Riverview Hosp. Fellow Am. Coll. Surgs. Mem. Schuylkill Valley Med. Club, Phila. Med. Club, Phi Sigma Kappa. Presbyn. Club: Plymouth Country. Home: Curren Terrace, Norristown, Pa. Office: 1327 DeKalb St., Norristown, Pa.

HEADLEE, Thomas J., entomologist; b. at Headlee, Ind., Feb. 13, 1877; s. Josephus and Ruann (Mattix) H.; grad. State Normal Sch., Terre Haute, Ind., 1900; A.B., Ind. U., 1903, A.M., 1904; Ph.D., Cornell U., 1906; m. Blanche Ives, Oct. 11, 1903; children—Mary Ruanna, Josephine (dec.), Miriam Esther, Ruth Margaret. Asst. entomologist, 1906-07, asso., July-Sept. 1907, State Agrl. Expt. Sta., N.H.; head dept. of entomology and zoölogy, State Agrl. Coll. and Expt. Sta., Kan., 1907-12; prof. entomology, Rutgers U., and entomologist N.J. Expt. Sta., and state entomologist, since Oct. 1912. Fellow A.A.A.S. (council, 1920-24); mem. Am. Assn. Econ. Entomologists (pres. 1929), Entomol. Soc. America (charter mem.), Sigma Xi, Phi Beta Kappa. Author of repts., bulls. and articles in tech. jours. Home: Dayton, N.J. Office: New Brunswick, N.J.

HEALD, Kenneth Conrad, geologist; b. Bennington, N.H., Mar. 14, 1888; s. Josiah Heald and Mary Katharine (Pike) H.; University of N.M., 1907-08; B.S. in Engring., Colorado Coll., 1912; studied Yale, 1912-14; D.Sc., University of Pittsburgh, 1928; m. Mary Marguerite Drach, Dec. 26, 1914; children—Mary Katherine, Kenneth Conrad. Field work, summers, U.S. Geol. Survey, until 1914, and full time, 1914-24, except 1918; chief of Sect. of Oil Geology, U.S. Geol. Survey, 1919-24 inclusive; asso. prof. petroleum geology, Yale, 1924-25; geologist with Gulf Oil Cos. (8 cos.) since June 1925. Engaged in exploration, S.A., 1912, 1919-20; lecturer on petroleum geology, U. of Chicago and Johns Hopkins, 1923, 24, U. of Pittsburgh since 1926. Capt. engrs., U.S.A., unattached, staff geologist, 1918. Mem. at large Nat. Research Council, 1925-26; mem. Am. Assn. Petroleum Geologists (rep. Nat. Research Council, 1921-25), Geol. Soc. America (rep. Nat. Research Council 1927), Soc. Economic Geologists, Am. Inst. Mining and Metall. Engrs., Geol. Soc. Washington, Army Ordnance Assn., Engrs. Soc. of Western Pa., Am. Statis. Assn., Am. Petroleum Inst.; fellow A.A.A.S., Royal Geog. Soc., Royal Soc. of Arts. Congregationalist. Clubs: Cosmos, Mid-River (Washington); Polygon, Pittsburgh Athletic Assn., Longue Vue Club, Harvard-Yale-Princeton (Pittsburgh); Chemists' (New York). Author: (bulls.) Geologic Structure of the Pawhuska Quadrangle, Okla., 1918; Structure and Oil and Gas Resources of Osage Reservation, Okla., 1922; Healdton Oil Field, Okla., 1915; Eldorado Oil Field, Ark., 1925; Geology of Ingomar Anticline, Mont., 1926. Contbr. papers dealing with geology, geophysics and oil field technology. Home: 100 Gladstone Road. Office: Gulf Oil Corpn., Gulf Bldg., Pittsburgh, Pa.

HEALD, William H., lawyer; b. Wilmington, Del., Aug. 27, 1864; s. Charles H. and Mary E. (Talley) H.; B.S., U. of Del., Newark, Del., 1883; LL.B., George Washington U., Washington, D.C., 1888; unmarried. In practice of law at Wilmington, Del.; dir. Equitable Trust Co., Del. R.R. Co. Mem. 61st and 62d Congresses (1909-13), Del. at large. Pres. bd. of trustees U. of Del. Mem. Sigma Nu, Phi Kappa Phi. Republican. Clubs: Wilmington, University, Wilmington Country (Wilmington, Del.). Home. Wilmington Apts. Office: 300 Equitable Bldg., Wilmington, Del.

HEALY, Fred Albert, publisher; b. Bristol, Ill., July 7, 1889; s. Arthur N. and Jennie E. (Palmer) H.; grad. West Aurora Pub. Sch., Aurora, Ill., 1903, West Aurora High Sch., 1908; B.S., U. of Ill., 1915; m. Alice Riley, Mar. 3, 1916; children—Doris Margaret, Frances. Salesman Osgood Lens Co., automobile accessories, 1915-17; with Curtis Publishing Co. since 1917, advertising solicitor, Chicago, 1917-21, mgr. Country Gentlemen, 1922-25, transferred to Detroit as manager, 1925, New York, Feb. 1928, advertising dir., Philadelphia, since Oct. 1928, v.p. and dir. since 1930; dir. Castanea Paper Co. Mem. Delta Tau Delta. Republican. Baptist. Clubs: Union League, Racquet, Poor Richard, Down Town (Philadelphia); Merion Cricket (Haverford); University (Chicago); Pine Valley Golf (Clementon, N.J.). Home: 116 Glenn Road, Ardmore, Pa. Office: Independence Sq., Philadelphia, Pa.

HEALY, James P.; chmn. bd. Carrollton Bank. Address: Baltimore St. and Carrollton Av., Baltimore, Md.

HEAPS, William James, educator; b. Baltimore County, Md., Feb. 17, 1868; s. James Anderson and Margaret (Wright) H.; A.B., Farmington (Ohio) Coll., 1892; A.M., Allegheny Coll., Pa., 1893; Ph.D., Taylor U., Upland, Ind., 1901; LL.B., Baltimore (Md.) Law Sch., 1903; spl. student in chemistry, Johns Hopkins Univ., 1904-08; m. Caroline Erdman, M.D., Sept. 1, 1909. Organizer and pres. Winfield Acad., Carroll Co., Md., 1894-1900; pres. Milton Acad., 1900-09; pres. Milton U. since Feb. 2, 1909. Rep. candidate for Congress, 2d Dist. of Md., 1915. Editor Sons of America since 1903; state sec. of Md. P.O.S. of A., 1905-31; past nat. pres. P.O.S. of A.; dir. United Patriotic Orphanage. As sec. of Francis Scott Key-birthplace-monument-com. raised funds for monument, dedicated June 12, 1915. During the war traveled extensively from Me. to Fla. lecturing and giving addresses in the interest of Liberty loans and War Saving stamps. Mem. A.A.A.S., Pi Gamma Mu, Sigma Beta Chi, Delta Chi; fellow Am. Geog. Soc. Mason (33°, K.T., Shriner). Clubs: Baltimore City, Optimist. Lecturer on patriotic and scientific subjects. Author: The Perfect Man; Autocracy vs. Democracy; The Book of Books; The Crisis; The "Milton Quizzer" for Pharmacy Students; Elementals in Religion; Claire Wellington; God in Genesis and Geology; The Slave and Other Poems. Editor of Sons of America for 30 yrs., Co-founder Patriotic Am. Civic Alliance (patriotic ednl. soc.). Home: Northway Apts. Office: 310 W. Hoffman St., Baltimore, Md.

HEARD, Drayton, lawyer; b. Pittsburgh, Pa., Dec. 12, 1887; s. George and Margaret Eaton (Neale) H.; grad. Shady Side Acad., Pittsburgh, 1906; A.B., Yale, 1910, LL.B., U. of Pittsburg, 1914; m. Elizabeth Ramsey Arrott, June 2, 1917; children—Drayton, George, Cyrus Ramsey. Admitted to Pa. bar, 1914, and since practiced in Pittsburgh; legal asst. in firm Sterrett & Acheson, 1914-19, partner 1919-29; partner with brother in Heard & Heard since 1929; dir. Pittsburgh Spring & Steel Co. Served as student officer in naval aviation in World War. Mem. Alpha Delta Phi, Phi Delta Phi. Clubs: Duquesne (Pittsburgh); Allegheny Country, Edgeworth and Sewickley Hunt (Sewickley). Home: 426 Woodland Rd., Sewickley, Pa. Office: 924 Grant Bldg., Pittsburgh, Pa.

HEARD, James Delavan, physician; b. Pittsburgh, Jan. 9, 1870; s. James B. and Emilie Lucretia (Delavan) H.; Western U. of Pa. 2 yrs.; M.D., U. of Pa., 1891, hon. Sc.D., 1938; post-grad. work same, 1891, univs. of Leipzig and Vienna, 1892-93; m. Edith van Rensselaer McIlvaine, Dec. 27, 1910. Interne, German Hosp., Phila., 1891-92; asso. prof. medicine, 1910-12, prof., 1912—, U. of Pittsburgh. During the war was lt. col., M.C.U.S.A. in charge med. service, Base Hosp. 27, A.E.F.; col. M.R.C., gen. Hosp. No. 27, 1924. Episcopalian. Mem. A.M.A., Assn. Am. Physicians, Pittsburgh Acad. Medicine, Med. Soc. State of Pa., Biol. Soc. U. of Pittsburgh. Mason (32°). Clubs: University, Pittsburgh Golf, Rolling Rock; Pot and Kettle (Bar Harbor, Me.). Home: 5720 Aylesboro Av., Pittsburgh, Pa.; (summer Bar Harbor, Me.). Office: 121 University Pl., Pittsburgh, Pa.

HEATH, Edwin Joseph, clergyman, educator; b. St. Jan, Danish West Indies, Dec. 27, 1880; s. George Octavius and Charlotte Elizabeth (Reinke) H.; prep. edn., Fulneck Sch., Leeds, Eng.; A.B., Moravian Coll., Bethlehem, Pa., 1904, A.M., 1916; B.D., Moravian Theol. Sem., 1907; D.D., Ursinus Coll., 1930; m. Mabel Mary Graham, Oct. 17, 1908; children—Barbara Mary, Edwin Clifford, Marian Graham. Came to United States, 1901, naturalized citizen, 1924. Ordained ministry Moravian Ch., 1904; supt. Moravian mission, Trinidad, B.W.I., 1907-11; pastor St. John's Ch., Antigua, B.W.I., 1911-14; also warden Antigua mission, and dir. Teachers' Training Coll., Antigua, 1911-14; exec. sec. Salem Acad. and Coll., Winston-Salem, N.C., 1914-26; pastor Immanuel Ch., Winston-Salem, 1915-20; head of history dept., Salem Coll., 1914-26; pres. Moravian Sem. and Coll. for Women, Bethlehem, since 1926. Mem. Am. Hist. Soc., Am. Acad. Polit. and Social Science, Nat. Assn. Biblical Instructors, Moravian Hist. Soc., Moravian Ch. Bd. of Christian Edn., Pa. Coll. Pres. Assn., Pi Gamma Mu. Democrat. Rotarian. Home: 87 W. Church St., Bethlehem, Pa.

HEATH, Louise Robinson; prof. philosophy and psychology, Hood Coll. Address: Hood College, Frederick, Md.

HEATH, William Pratt; v.p. Coca-Cola Co. Home: 206 Lambeth Road. Office: 1215 E. Fort Av., Baltimore, Md.

HEATHCOTE, Charles William, educator, author, clergyman; b. Glen Rock, Pa., Apr. 19, 1882; s. William T. and Eva (Frey) H.; A.B., Pa. Coll., 1905 (2d honor), A.M., 1908; grad. Gettysburg Theol. Sem., 1908; S.T.D., Temple U., 1910; A.M., U. of Pa., 1913; Ph.D., George Washington U., 1918; m. Emma Grace Bair, June 16, 1909; children—Eva B., Charles W. Tutor in Greek, Pa. Coll., 1905-07; prof. Greek and history, York Co. (Pa.) Acad., 1907-08; ordained Luth. ministry, 1908; pastor 2d Ch., Chambersburg, Pa., 1908-11, Bethel Ch., Phila., 1911-12; prof. ch. history and philosophy, Temple U., 1912-22; prof. social service, Beechwood Coll. for Young Women, 1915-22; head of dept. social science, West Chester State Normal Sch. (State Teachers Coll.), 1922—; entered Presbyn. Ministry, 1923. Active in Liberty Loan campaigns, World War. Pres. Franklin Co. (Pa.) S. S. Assn., 1908-11; dir. Phila. Sabbath Assn., 1913-18. Mem. Am. Soc. Ch. History, York Co. Hist. Soc., Kittochtinny Hist. Soc., Druid Fraternity and Pen and Sword Soc. (both Pa. Coll.), Am. Hist. Assn., Am. Acad. Polit. and Social Science, Chester Co. Hist. Soc. (mem. exec. bd.), Brandywine Battle Assn. (pres. since 1933), Am. Friends of Lafayette, Am. Civil Legion (life member), Phi Sigma Kappa, Kappa Phi Kappa, Pi Gamma Mu, Alpha Kappa Alpha; corr. member of Institut Historique et Héraldique de France. Fellow Royal Historical Society, England. President Colwyn-Philadelphia Board of Education, 1921-22. Mason (K.T.). Clubs:

City (Phila.); Rotary, X Club (West Chester); Authors' (London). Author: The Seventy-fifth Year, 1911; The Essentials of Religious Education, 1916; The Lutheran Church and the Civil War, 1919; Pilgrimage to Oberammergau, 1922; Battle of the Brandywine, 1923; Outlines of Modern Government, 1923, 3d edit., 1929; Essentials of Economics, 1923; Teaching of History, 1924; Son of the Morning, 1924; Story of Valley Forge, 1924; Essentials of United States History, 1925; Luke's Gospel, 1925; Story of the Declaration of Independence, 1926; Story of John's Gospel, 1926; History Project Problems, 1926; History of Chester County, 1927, 2d edit., 1929; Teaching the Social Studies, 1931; Signers of Declaration of Independence, 1932; Lincoln in Pennsylvania, 1935; Origins—Mayan Civilization, 1936. Editor in chief and co-author of Chester County History (unabridged), 1933. Contbr. on religious topics. Editor Chester Co. Hist. Bull., 1922-29 and 1930-36; asso. editor Social Science since 1928; advisor to Dr. Godcharles' 5 vol. History of Pennsylvania. Collector and owner rare mss. and first editions of early Am. history. Apptd. by Governor Pinchot to represent Pa. on Pennsylvania Day, at Valley Forge, to deliver address for years 1934 and 1935. Mem. advisory council The Living Age. Home: 215 S. Walnut St., West Chester, Pa.

HEATWOLE, Timothy Oliver; b. Dale Enterprise, Va., Feb. 18, 1865; s. David A. and Catharine (Driver) H.; Normall Coll., Harrisonburg, Va.; D.D.S., U. of Md., 1895; M.D., 1897; hon. D.Sc., St. John's Coll., Annapolis, Md., 1923; m. Mrs. Annie Blackwell Latham, June 17, 1914. Asso. prof. orthodontia, 1903-07, prof. dental materia medica and therapeutics, 1907-22, dean Sch. of Dentistry, 1911-37, asst. to pres., 1923-37, U. of Md. Retired Oct. 1, 1937. Mem. Md. Ho. of Rep., 1906; mem. City Council, Baltimore, 1907-19. Mem. Md. State Dental Assn., Va. and W.Va. state dental socs., Md. Pharm. Assn. Democrat. Presbyn. K.P. Club: Lions. Home: 1800 N. Charles St., Baltimore, Md.

HEBARD, Benjamin Morton, pub. utilities exec.; b. Boston, Mass., Apr. 9, 1874; s. Samuel C. and Annie A. (Spear) H.; ed. Chicago pub. schs.; m. Mary V. Campbell, Apr. 24, 1912; children—Laura H., Ethel Virginia. V.p. Internat. Utilities Corpn. since 1935, also several other utility companies. Home: 311 Woodside Av., Narberth, Pa. Office: Delaware Trust Bldg., Wilmington, Del.

HECHLER, F(red) G(eorge), coll. prof.; b. Dalton, Mo., Sept. 28, 1884; s. George and Elizabeth (Sasse) H.; B.S. in M.E., U. of Mo., 1908, M.E., 1910; m. Anna E. Griffith, Aug. 30, 1911; children—M. Catherine, Helen L., M. Jean. Instr. and asst. prof. mech. engring., Rensselaer Poly. Inst., 1908-16; with U.S. Engring. Dept., Albany, N.Y., 1914-15; mech. engr. U.S. Naval Engring. Expt. Station, Annapolis, Md., 1916-19; gen. mgr. Vibration Specialty Co., Philadelphia, 1919-22; prof. engring. research, Pa. State Coll., since 1922, dir. engring. expt. station since 1936. Licensed professional engr., Pa. Fellow A.A.A.S.; mem. Am. Soc. M.E., Nat. Research Council, Tau Beta Pi, Sigma Xi. Republican. Presbyterian. Club: University. Writer numerous bulls. and tech. papers on heat transmission and related subjects. Home: 343 E. Prospect Av., State College, Pa.

HECHMER, Carl Adam, Sr., civil engr.; b. Baltimore, Md., July 20, 1895; s. Adam and Anna E. (Beneze) H.; ed. Baltimore Poly. Inst., 1909-13; m. Eleanor M. Dove, Sept. 4, 1917; children—Carl Adam, Jr., Elizabeth Anne. Asst. engr. in electric power div., Consol. Gas & Electric Co., Baltimore, 1913-14; instrumentman Baltimore City Water Dept., 1914-15; draftsman Drafting Bureau, City of Baltimore, 1915-16; cost engr., then asst. pitometer engr. later Engr. Lime & Grade, Baltimore City Water Dept., 1916-18; resident engr. Bureau San. Engring., Md. State Dept. of Health, 1918; with Washington Suburban San. Dist. since 1918, as asst. engr. 1918-19, dept. engr. in charge maintenance and operation since 1919; also private practice as san. engr.; lecturer sch. for firemen, U. of Md., 1932-34, sch. for water and sewerage operators, Md.-Del. Assn., 1935-38; asst. instr. of municipal sanitation, U. of Md., 1937-39. Mem. Am. Water Works Assn. (mem. publ. com. 1930-38; chmn. plant management and operation div. 1933-34; trustee 4 States sect., 1935-36, and sec.-treas. since 1936) Am. Soc. Civil Engrs., Md.-Del. Water and Sewerage Assn. (pres. 1929-30). Author of numerous articles published in engring jours. Club: Patapsco Boating. Home: Riverdale, Md. Office: Hyattsville, Md.

HECHT, Edward, retired; b. Frankfurt-on-the-Main, Germany, Apr. 9, 1861; ed. schools of Frankfurt, Germany; m. Fannie B. Levi, Jan. 4, 1889; children—Eugene J., Norman L., Lester S., Carl E., Harold M. Merchant, men's wear, Lock Haven, Pa., 1888-1931; pres. West Branch Knitting Co., Milton, Pa., 1909-30; dir. Lock Haven Trust Co., Industrial Loan Co. Trustee Lock Haven Hosp. since 1912; trustee and treas. Annie Hallenbach Ross Free Library since 1908; trustee Playground Assn. Former dir. Lock Haven Chamber of Commerce. Elk. Rotarian. Home: 423 W. Main St., Lock Haven, Pa.

HECHT, Lee Isaac, judge; b. Havre de Grace, Md., Apr. 10, 1888; s. Isaac and Elizabeth (Weis) H.; grad. Havre de Grace High Sch., 1903; B.S., St. John's Coll., Annapolis, Md., 1907, M.A., 1909; LL.B., U. of Md., 1909; m. M. Dannenberg, Nov. 6, 1912 (died May 17, 1934); children—Isaac, Alan D.; m. 2d, Miriam R. Odenheimer, Sept. 3, 1937. Admitted to Md. bar, 1910; city solicitor, Havre de Grace, 1912; judge Appeal Tax Court, Baltimore, since 1923, pres. and chief judge since 1931; pres. Havre de Grace Banking & Trust Co. since 1916; dir. New Amsterdam Casualty Co., Baltimore. Mem. Md., Baltimore City, and Harford County bar assns. Democrat. Jewish religion. Mason (32°), Odd Fellow, Elk. Clubs: Phoenix, Suburban (Baltimore). Home: 3402 Bateman Av. Office: 1101-03 Union Trust Bldg., Baltimore, Md.

HECK, Robert Culbertson Hays, mechanical engr.; b. Heckton Mills, Pa., Oct. 30, 1870; s. John Lewis and Mary Frances (Hays) H.; M.E., Lehigh Univ., 1893; hon. Dr. Eng. from same univ., 1927; m. Anna Wilson, Sept. 10, 1902; children—Margaret Wilson, Robert C. H., Mary Hays. Instr. mech. engring., 1893-1903, asst. prof., 1903-07, prof. exptl. engring., 1907-08, Lehigh U.; prof. mech. engring., Rutgers Coll., 1908-35, research prof. of mech. engring. since 1935. Republican. Presbyterian. Fellow A.A.A.S.; mem. Am. Soc. Mech. Engrs., 1906, Soc. Promotion Engring. Education, Nat. Research Council, 1932-37, Tau Beta Pi, Phi Beta Kappa, Sigma Xi. Author: Notes to Supplement Holmes' Steam Engine, 1902; Manual for Course in Engineering Laboratory, Lehigh Univ., 1903; The Steam Engine and other Steam Motors, Vol. I, 1905, Vol. II, 1907; Notes on Elementary Kinematics, 1910; Notes on the Graphics of Machine Forces, 1910; The Steam Engine and Turbine, 1911; Steam Formulas, 1920; Mechanics of Machinery—Mechanism, Kinematics and Dynamics, 1925; Ideal Combustion-Engine Cycles, 1926. Home: 51 Adelaide Av., New Brunswick, N.J.

HECKEL, George Baugh, editor; b. Chester Co., Pa., Mar. 13, 1858; s. Edward Bowers (M.D.) and Harriet Rinehart (Baugh) H.; Ursinus Coll., Collegeville, Pa., 1874-75; med. dept. U. of Pa., 1877-79; m. Ellen Theresa McCloskey, June 27, 1893; children—James Edward, George Baugh, Frank Price. Western corr. Lockwood Press of New York, at Chicago, 1881-83; ed. ry. publs.; lit. editor of Rand-McNally & Co., Chicago, 1884-87; spl. rep. L. J. McCloskey & Co., varnish mfrs., 1888-89; owner, editor and pub. Drugs, Oils and Paints since 1890. Sec.-treas. Paint Mfrs.' Assn. of U.S., 1905, Nat. Varnish Mfrs.' Assn., 1909; sec. Am. Paint and Varnish Mfrs.' Association, 1926-1930; secretary emeritus Nat. Paint, Varnish and Lacquer Association, Inc., since 1930; adv. manager The New Jersey Zinc Company, 1907-19, now consultant; organizer, 1921, and secretary Fed. Paint and Varnish Production Clubs; sec. Agricultural Insecticide and Fungicide Mfrs. Assn., 1924. Mem. Am. Chem. Soc., Am. Soc. for Testing Materials. Republican. Catholic. Clubs: Union League, Merion Cricket. Joint Author: Jacob Valmont, Manager, 1885; A Paint Catechism, 1909, 4th edit., 1922; A Varnish Catechism, 1912-20; Materials of Paint Manufacture, 1925; The Paint Industry—Reminiscences and Comments, 1929; The New Paint, Varnish and Lacquer Catechism, 1936. Translator: Nouma Roumestan (from the French of Daudet), 1886; Journal of Marie Bashkirtseff, 1886; The Dream (from the French of Zola), 1888; Fromont, Jr., and Risler, Sr. (from the French of Daudet), 1895. Contbr. to mags., also Ency. Brit. Home: 200 S. 42d St. Office: Cunard Bldg., Philadelphia, Pa.

HECKERT, Winfield Walter, chemist; b. Kasson, Minn., Dec. 19, 1902; s. John Walter and Winifred Esther (Yahn) H.; student in William McGuffey Schs., Oxford, O., 1909-19; B.S. in Edn., Miami (O.) U., 1923; M.A., Ohio State U., 1926, Ph.D., 1928; m. Clarice Mary Upson, Sept. 9, 1933; 1 son, John Upson. High sch. teacher, Ansonia, O., 1923-25; grad. asst., Ohio State U., Columbus, O., 1926-27, Du Pont Fellow, 1928; research chemist Du Pont Exptl. Sta., Wilmington, Del., 1928-38; research supervisor Nylon Div., Rayon Dept., E. I. Du Pont de Nemours & Co., Wilmington, since 1938. Mem. Gamma Alpha, Phi Beta Kappa, Sigma Xi, Phi Lambda Upsilon, Am. Chem. Soc. Unitarian. Mason. Club: Du Pont Country (Wilmington, Del.). Has been asso. with development commercial processes for production of extended titanium pigments, organic delusterants for rayon, crush resistent, transparent velvet and nylon. Home: Ardentown, Del. Office: Du Pont Experimental Station, Wilmington, Del.

HECKSCHER, Maurice, lawyer; b. Phila., Pa., May 24, 1907; s. Stevens and Henrietta Armitt (Brown) H.; A.B. cumlaude, Harvard U., 1928; ed. Harvard U. Law Sch., 1928-30; m. Constance Antelo Butcher, June 24, 1929; children—Stevens 2d, Constance Devereux, Martin Anton. Admitted to Pa. bar, 1932 and since engaged in gen. practice of law at Phila.; mem. firm Duane, Morris & Heckscher since 1935; elected mem. 5 Yr. Plan Sect. Phila. Bar Assn., 1933; chmn. Com. of 21 for yr., 1937; elected to Bd. Govs. Phila. Bar Assn. for 3-yr. term, 1938. Mem. Bd. and vice-pres. Family Soc. of Phila.; mem. bd. mgrs. Zool. Soc. Phila.; mem. bd. dirs. Pa. Birth Control Federation. Mem. Am., Pa. State, Phila. bar assns., Juristic Soc. Republican. Episcopalian. Clubs: Philadelphia, Racquet, Harvard (Philadelphia); A.D. (Cambridge, Mass.). Home: Sheaff Rd., Ft. Washington, Pa. Office: 1617 Land Title Bldg., Philadelphia, Pa.

HEDENBURG, Oscar Fred, chemist; b. Webster, Mass., May 6, 1883; s. Fred and Anna C. (Swenson) H.; ed. Boston U., 1904-06; A.B., Wesleyan U., 1909, A.M., same, 1911; Ph.D., U. of Chicago, 1915; m. Lena R. Potter, Mar. 21, 1914 (died 1937); children—Lucy, Marian, John F.; m. 2d, Henrietta Kornhauser, Apr. 21, 1939. Research instr. in chemistry, U. of Chicago, 1913-16; Industrial Fellow, Mellon Inst. Industrial Research since 1916; pres. Chatterbox Products, Inc., mfrs. cosmetics, Pittsburgh, Pa., since 1939; chemist and dir. production, Rex Research Corpn., Toledo, O.; chemist and dir. Canada Rex Spray Co. Ltd., Brighton, Ont. Mem. Am. Chem. Soc., Am. Inst. Chemists, Sigma Xi, Phi Lambda Upsilon, Gamma Alpha, Beta Theta Pi. Republican. Clubs: Lions (Oakland); Pittsburgh Chemists. Home: 728 Summerlea St. Office: Mellon Institute, Pittsburgh, Pa.

HEDLEY, Evalena (Fryer), writer; b. West Chester, Pa.; d. John Plummer and Mary (Goheen) Fryer; acad. and mus. edn.; m. Thomas Wilson Hedley, librarian of Mercantile Library, Phila., June 16, 1904. Editor S.S. papers, for Presbyn. Bd. Publication, 1890-97; editorial staff Saturday Evening Post, 1899-1904; conducts woman's dept. in daily newspapers under name, "Grace Goodhouse." Mem. Sons and Daughters of Pilgrims, Huguenot Soc., D.A.R., Dames of Loyal Legion, W. P. Garden Society, Contemporary. Clubs: Philomusian, City History, Women's City. Compiler: Glimpses Through

Life's Windows. Contbr. to jours. and juvenile publs. Home: 1015 S. 47th St., Philadelphia, Pa.

HEDRICH, Arthur William; b. Chicago, Ill., July 7, 1888; s. Louis F. A. and Augusta (Neunuebel) H.; B.S., Northwestern U., 1914; C.P.H., Harvard-M.I.T. Pub. Health Sch., 1919; Sc.D., Sch. of Hygiene, Johns Hopkins, 1928; m. Helen Chandler Dyer, 1921; children—Arthur William, Lefa Cordelia, Louis Chandler, Nancy Louise. Asst. city chemist, and bacteriologist, Evanston, Ind., 1912-14; city chemist and dep. health officer, East Chicago, Ind., 1914-16; editorial asst. Am. Jour. Pub. Health, Boston, 1916-17; sec. Am. Pub. Health Assn., and editor Am. Jour. Pub. Health, 1917-23; director of surveys, Dept. of Health, Chicago, 1924-26; instr., later lecturer in vital satistics and epidemiology, Sch. of Hygiene, Johns Hopkins U., Baltimore, since 1927; consultant in vital statistics and epidemiology, U.S. Pub. Health Service since 1928; regional supervisor, chronic disease survey, 1934-35; chief Bur. of Vital Statistics, Md. State Dept. of Health, Baltimore. Mem. Alpha Chi Sigma, Phi Beta Kappa, Delta Omega. Home: 5925 Glenoak Av. Office: 2411 N. Charles St., Baltimore, Md.

HEDRICK, Charles Embury; prof. history, Marshall Coll. Address: Marshall College, Huntington, W.Va.

HEDRICK, G. C.; mgr., treas. and dir. Guyan Utilities Co.; officer or dir. many companies. Address: Beckley, W.Va.

HEELY, Allan Vanderhoef, educator; b. Brooklyn, N.Y., Feb. 2, 1897; s. Augustus Vanderhoef and Jessie (Ross) H.; grad. Phillips Acad., Andover, Mass., 1915; A.B., Yale, 1919; student Oxford U., England, 1929-30; A.M., Columbia, 1934; LL.D., Lafayette Coll., Easton, Pa., 1937; Litt.D., Princeton, 1938; m. Frances Torrey Thompson, June 25, 1927. With Wendell P. Colton Co., N.Y. City, advertising, 1919-21; asst. sec. Claflins, Inc., N.Y. City, wholesale drygoods, 1921-24; instr. English, Phillips Acad., 1924-34, asst. dean, 1933-34; headmaster The Lawrenceville (N.J.) Sch. since 1934. Mem. advisory com. Secondary Edn. Bd.; dir. Ednl. Records Bur. Served as 2d lt. field arty., U.S.A., 1918. Trustee Lawrenceville Sch.; mem. bd. mgrs. Marlboro (N.J.) State Hosp. Mem. Headmasters Club of Phila., Headmasters Assn., Alpha Delta Phi. Republican. Presbyterian. Clubs: Yale (Phila.); Elizabethan (New Haven); Yale, Century Assn., Coffee House (N.Y. City); Nassau, Prettybrook Tennis (Princeton). Address: Foundation House, Lawrenceville, N.J.

HEERMANCE, Radcliffe, college dean; b. at Rhinebeck, N.Y., Apr. 18, 1882; s. Martin and Nina (Radcliffe) H.; A.B., Williams, 1904, A.M., 1906; A.M., Harvard, 1908, Princeton, 1909; m. Elizabeth Platt Adams, Dec. 18, 1912 (died Oct. 27, 1919). Instr. Lawrenceville (N.J.) Sch., 1904-06, 1907-08; Scribner fellow in English, 1908, instr. English, 1909, asst. prof., 1912-21, supervisor of freshmen, 1921—, prof., 1922—, dir. of admission, dean of freshmen since 1925, Princeton U. Chmn. College Entrance Examination Bd., 1933-36. Commd. capt. inf. U.S.R., Nov. 27, 1917; maj. U.S.A., Aug. 20, 1918; comd. U.S. Training Detachment, Atlanta, Ga., 1918; prof. mil. sci. and tactics, Harvard, and comd. S.A.T.C., 1918; lt. col. O.R.C., 1923. Mem. Soc. War of 1812, Alpha Delta Phi, Holland Soc. of New York, Dutchess County Soc. of New York. Republican. Mem. Dutch Ref. Ch. Clubs: Nassau (Princeton); University, Princeton, Williams Club, Century, Ends of the Earth (New York); Army and Navy (Washington, D.C.). Home: 89 Mercer St., Princeton, N.J.

HEFFNER, Edward Hoch, prof. Latin; b. Dryville, Pa., Sept. 15, 1886; s. Henry and Amelia Diener (Hoch) H.; A.B., Franklin and Marshall Coll., Lancaster, Pa., 1911; A.M., Columbia, 1914; Ph.D., U. of Pa., 1916; Harrison fellow, 1915-16; m. Emma Wilhelmina Merkle, Sept. 17, 1925. Head of dept. Latin, Franklin and Marshall Acad., 1911-14; instr. in Latin, U. of Pa., 1914-26, prof. since 1926, asst. to dean of Grad. Sch., 1926-28. Mem. American Philol. Association, Archæol. Institute America (sec. for South Atlantic states), Am. Classical League, Classical Assn. Atlantic States, Phila. Classical Soc., Phila. Soc. for Promotion of Liberal Studies (ex-pres.), Phi Beta Kappa. Club: Phila. Classical. Asso. editor Am. Jour. Archæology, 1925-32. Contbr. to classical periodicals. Home: 220 S. Melville St., Philadelphia, Pa.

HEFFNER, Roy Jackson, asst. personnel dir.; b. Los Angeles, Calif., Sept. 21, 1890; s. John Henry and Jane (Jackson) H.; B.S. in E.E., U. of Calif., 1916; spl. study, Columbia U., fall 1918; grad. study, U. of Calif., 1919-20; m. Hazel K. Meddaugh, June 11, 1918; 1 son, Jackson Edward. Employed as engr., Western Electric Co., Chicago and N.Y. City, 1916-17; chmn. engring. extension, U. of Calif., 1919-20; ednl. dir. Hawaiian Dept., U.S.A., 1920-21; engr. Pacific Telephone & Telegraph Co., San Francisco, Calif., 1921-24, gen. supervisor employment and training, 1925-29; asst. ednl. dir., Bell Telephone Labs., Inc., N.Y. City, 1929-30, ednl. dir., 1930-36, asst. personnel dir. since 1936; trustee C. M. Ferguson Corpn., N.Y. City. Served as 1st lt., capt., then maj., A.S., U.S.A., 1917-19. Mem. Am. Management Assn., Soc. for Promotion Engring. Edn. Telephone Pioneers of America, Pi Kappa Phi, Tau Beta Pi, Eta Kappa Nu. Republican. Mason. Club: Morris County Engineers. Home: 32 Washington Av., Morristown, N.J. Office: 463 West St., New York, N.Y.

HEGNER, Robert William, zoölogist; b. Decorah, Ia., Feb. 15, 1880; s. Charles G. and Wilhelmina (Busch) H.; B.Sc., U. of Chicago, 1903, M.S., 1904; Ph.D., U. of Wis., 1908; m. Jane Zabriskie, Sept. 12, 1906; children—Janette La Tourette Zabriskie, Mary Elizabeth (dec.), Isabel McKinney (dec.). Instr. and asst. prof. zoölogy, U. of Mich., 1908-18; asso. prof. protozoology, Sch. of Hygiene and Pub. Health, Johns Hopkins, 1918-20; prof. and head of dept. med. zoölogy, same univ., since 1922; visiting prof. of parasitology, Sch. of Hygiene and Pub. Health, U. of the Philippines, 1929-30, London School of Tropical Medicine, 1926. Mem. scientific expedition to Mexico, 1903; del. to Royal Inst. Pub. Health, Brussels, Belgium, 1920; in chg. expdn. for study of tropical medicine, Porto Rico and Venezuela, 1921; del. to Internat. Congress on Health Problems in Tropical America, Jamaica, 1924; member Scientific Board of Gorgas Memorial Institute. Fellow A.A.A.S., Royal Inst. Pub. Health (London), Royal Soc. Tropical Medicine; mem. American Soc. Zoölogists, Am. Soc. Parasitologists, Am. Soc. Naturalists, Sigma Xi, Phi Beta Kappa; corr. mem. Belgian Soc. of Tropical Medicine. Unitarian. Author: Introduction to Zoölogy, 1910; College Zoölogy, 1912; Germ Cell Cycle in Animals, 1914; Practical Zoölogy, 1914; Diagnosis of Protozoa and Worms Parasitic in Man (with Dr. W. W. Cort), 1921; Outlines of Medical Zoölogy (with Dr. Cort and Dr. F. M. Root), 1923; Human Protozoölogy (with Dr. W. H. Taliaferro), 1924; Host-Parasite Relations between Man and His Intestinal Protozoa, 1927; Animal Parasitology (with Dr. F. M. Root and D. L. Augustine), 1929; Problems and Methods of Research in Protozoölogy (with Dr. Justin Andrews), 1930; Invertebrate Zoölogy, 1933; Parade of the Animal Kingdom, 1935; Big Fleas Have Little Fleas, 1938. Editor of Century Biol. series; contbg. editor Quarterly Rev. of Biology; mem. editorial board, Jour. of Morphology, Am. Jour. of Hygiene, Jour. of Parasitology. Contbr. to mags. Home: 218 Hawthorne Rd., Baltimore, Md.

HEHER, Harry, judge; b. Trenton, N.J., Mar. 20, 1889; s. John and Anne (Spelman) H.; student Cathedral Sch. and Trenton High Sch.; studied law pvtly.; m. Anne Egan, Aug. 5, 1925; children—Harry, John Robert, Garrett Martin. Admitted to N.J. bar, 1911, and practiced in Trenton until 1932; apptd. asso. justice N.J. Supreme Court ad interim, 1932, and for term of 7 yrs., 1933. Mem. N.J. State and Mercer Co. bar assns., N.J. Hist. Soc. Mem. Dem. nat. convs., 1924, 1928 and 1932, and chmn. state delegation. Catholic. Home: 42 Perdicaris Pl. Office: State House Annex, Trenton, N.J.

HEILBRON, Tillie Thompson, lawyer; b. Phila., Pa., Sept. 23, 1899; d. Abraham and Elizabeth (Neff) Thompson; student pub. sch. and high sch., Phila., 1906-16; Mus.B., LL.B., Syracuse (N.Y.) U., 1920; m. Seymour M. Heilbron, June 19, 1927; children—Amelia Thompson, Elizabeth Thompson. Admitted to Phila. bar, 1920, and since practiced at Phila.; mem. Phila. Legal Aid Soc. Staff since 1920. Asst. dist. atty. Phila. Co. (first woman apptd. in Pa.), 1925-32. Legislative chmn and chmn. of resolutions, State Fed. of Dem. Women. Mem. Lawyers Club, Am. Legion Auxiliary (pres., 1935-37), Girl Scouts of America, Alpha Epsilon Phi (legal chmn.). Democrat. Jewish religion. Home: Chancellor Hall, Phila., Pa., and Red Bridge Farms, Media, Pa. Office: North American Bldg., Philadelphia, Pa.

HEILBRUNN, Lewis Victor, biologist; b. Brooklyn, N.Y., Jan. 24, 1892; s. Victor and Matilda (Biedermann) H.; A.B., Cornell U., 1911; Ph.D., U. of Chicago, 1914; m. Marion Applebee Kerr, Jan. 13, 1923 (now deceased); 1 dau., Constance; m. 2d, Ellen Donovan, June 3, 1932. Asso. in zoology, Univ. of Chicago, 1914-16; instr., U. of Ill. Med. Sch., 1916-17; instr. of zoology, U. of Mich., 1919-21, asst. prof., 1921-29; Guggenheim Memorial Foundation fellow, 1927-28; asso. prof. of zoology, U. of Pa. since 1929. Trustee Marine Biol. Lab. since 1931. Served as 1st lt. Air Service, U.S. Army, 1917-19; received 3 citations; 1st lt., later capt. Air Corps Reserve, 1919-29. Fellow A.A.A.S.; mem. Am. Soc. Zoologists (v.p. 1932), Am. Physiol. Soc., Soc. Exptl. Biology and Medicine, Am. Soc. Naturalists. Author: The Colloid Chemistry of Protoplasm, 1928; Outline of General Physiology, 1937; etc. Former mng. editor Protoplasm monographs; mem. editorial bd. Physiol. Zoology. Address: Zoological Laboratory, Univ. of Pennsylvania, Philadelphia, Pa.

HEILMAN, Eugene Augustus, physician; b. Lebanon Co., Pa., Mar. 14, 1876; s. Wesley Marvin and Mary (Boyer) H.; student pub. schs., Lebanon Co., Pa., 1882-91; grad. State Normal Sch., West Chester, Pa., 1895; M.D., Temple U., Phila., Pa., 1911; m. Martha Jane Blair, May 25, 1899; children—Eugene Blair, William Blair, Wesley Marvin II, Horace Richard. Teacher pub. schs., Lebanon Co., Pa., 1891-94, Phila. since 1895; principal, Heston Sch., Phila. 1898-1927, Hanna Sch., 1927-36, Hamilton Sch. since 1936; in practice of medicine at Phila., specializing in ophthalmology since 1912. Mem. Phila. Co. Med. Soc., Med. Soc. State of Pa., A.M.A. Author: Practical Health Lessons, 1916; How to Live Longer, 1925. Home: 876 Wynnewood Rd., Philadelphia, Pa.

HEILMAN, Harry Anderson, lawyer; b. Kittanning, Pa., Sept. 25, 1875; s. William Milton and Emma L. (Anderson) H.; student Kittanning High Sch., 1889-91, Phillips Acad., 1891-95, Princeton Coll., 1895-96; LL.B., U. of Pa., 1899; m. Bessie Hulings, Apr. 10, 1901; children—Emma Elizabeth (Mrs. Ross Buchanan), Willis Hulings, William Milton (dec.), Mary Anderson, Harry Anderson. Admitted to Armstrong Co. bar, 1899; also to practice before courts of Allegheny County, Philadelphia, Armstrong County and Appellate Courts of Pa., also before U.S. Dist. and Circuit courts; actively in practice of law since 1899, giving particular attention to trial of cases, commercial and corpn. law and municipal law; pres. Safe Deposit & Title Guaranty Co.; v.p. Kittanning Thrift Corpn.; dir. Eljer Co. Trustee Armstrong Co. Gen. Hosp. Mem. Am. Bar Assn., Pa. Bar Assn., Armstrong Co. Bar Assn. Republican. Presbyterian. Mason (32°, K.T.), Elk. Clubs: Duquesne (Pittsburgh); Kittanning Country, Rotary (Kittanning, Pa.). Home: 409 N. McKean St., Kittanning, Pa.

HEILMAN, Russell Howard, research engr.; b. Ford City, Pa., Nov. 30, 1893; s. William Thompson and Anna Louise (Montgomery) H.; B.S., U. of Pittsburgh, 1921, E.E., 1923, M.E., 1927; m. Olive Irene Butler, Jan. 8, 1916; children—Helen Clare, Betty Louise. Asst. Mellon Inst., Pittsburgh, 1917-19, fellow, 1920-25, senior fellow specializing on heat-insulation since

1925. Mem. Am. Soc. M.E., Am. Soc. Heating and Ventilating Engrs., Am. Soc. Testing Materials, Am. Chem. Soc., Sigma Xi. Received Am. Soc. M.E. Junior Award, 1922, 1924. Republican. Methodist. Mason. Club: Fort Pitt Rifle (Pittsburgh). Author numerous articles on heat insulation, heat transmission, metal and asbestos ducts. Home: 2303 Beechwood Boul. Office: Mellon Inst., Pittsburgh, Pa.

HEILNER, Van Campen, editor, author, explorer; b. Phila., July 1, 1899; s. Samuel and Adelaide Lincoln (Breese) H.; studied Phillips Acad., Andover, Mass.; grad. Lake Placid-Florida Sch., 1918; M.S., Trinity Coll., Hartford, Conn., 1927; studied ichthyology under Dr. J. T. Nichols, Am. Mus. Natural History; m. Mary La Vie, of N.Y. City, June 28, 1919; children—Mary Van Campen, Samuel. Asso. editor Field and Stream; mem. firm Percy Heilner & Son; field rep. in ichthyology of Am. Mus. Natural History; ichthyologist Am. Mus. Natural History Expdn. to Peru and Ecuador, 1924-25; leader Heilner Far Western Alaskan Expdn. for Am. Museum Natural History, 1927; expedition for same into Cienaga de Zapata (or "Shoe Swamp"), south coast of Cuba, Mar. 1934 and Apr. 1935. Del., representing N.J., Atlantic Deeper Waterways Commn., 1922-35. First naturalist to make motion pictures successfully of the roseate spoonbill in its natural haunts; discovered several new species of West Indian fishes. Fellow Royal Geog. Soc., Royal Anthropol. Inst. (London), Am. Geog. Soc.; mem. Am. Mus. Natural History (hon. life), American Soc. of Mammalogists, Am. Soc. Ichthyologists and Herpetologists, Society of Colonial Wars, Sons of Revolution, Huguenot Soc., Bombay Natural History Soc.; asso. Am. Ornithologists' Union; hon. mem. British Sea Anglers Soc. Republican. Presbyn. Mason (32°). Clubs: Explorers (active mem.), P.E.N. Club, Camp Fire of America, New York Yacht (New York); Gooseville Gun (Hatteras, N.C.); Tuna (Santa Catalina, Calif.); Grand Island Lodge (Bath, Ill.); Bathing and Tennis (dir.). Author: The Call of the Surf (with Frank Stick), 1920; Adventures in Angling, 1922; Beneath the Southern Cross, 1930. Co-Author; American Big Game Fishing, 1935; Salt Water Fishing, 1937; A Book on Duck Shooting, 1939. Master of smallest motor boat ever to go from Atlantic City to Venezuela, 4000 miles. Decorated Order of Carlos Manuel de Cespedes (Cuba), 1937. Home: Spring Lake Beach, N.J., and Bimini, Bahama Islands. Address: 17 Battery Pl., New York, N.Y.

HEIM, Raymond Walter, univ. prof.; b. Williamsport, Pa., Oct. 13, 1886; s. David J. and Hulda (Schaeffer) H.; B.S., Pa. State Coll., 1913; student Cornell U., summer 1918; A.M., Teachers Coll. of Columbia U., 1921; m. Bess Fye, Aug. 5, 1913. Engaged in teaching, rural schs., Lycoming Co., Pa., 1905-09; supervisor vocational edn., Waterford Acad., Waterford, Pa., 1913-15; state supervisor vocational edn. dept. pub. instrn., Harrisburg, Pa., 1915-17; regional dir. vocational edn. for Federal Bur. for Vocational Edn., Washington, D.C., 1917-19; prof. vocational edn., U. of Del., Newark, Del., since 1919; state dir. of vocational edn., Dover, Del., since 1919; state adminstr. World War Orphans' Edn. since 1929; chmn. Del. State Employment Council, Newark, Del., since 1935. Mem. N.E.A., Am. Vocational Assn., Nat. Assn. State Dirs. (past pres.), Del. Vocational Assn. (past pres.), Phi Delta Kappa, Phi Kappa Phi, Alpha Zeta. Presbyn. Mason (32°, Shriner). Clubs: University, Faculty (Newark, Del.); Penn State, Rutgers Univ. (Wilmington). Contbr. articles Sch. Soc. publs.; A.V.A. Jour., Del. Sch. Jour., U. of Del. Press, etc. Home: 216 Orchard Rd., Newark, Del.

HEIMERDINGER, Leo H., chmn. bd. Pioneer Suspender Co.; b. Chicago, Ill., Sept. 16, 1877; s. Henry and Henrietta H.; ed. public schools of Chicago; m. Helen Holzheimer, July 31, 1906; children—Leo H., Bertha (Mrs. Michael Greenebaum), Alice (Mrs. Herbert Brandeis). Salesman Eagle Suspender Co., Philadelphia, 1894-1900; salesman Pioneer Suspender Co., Philadelphia, 1901-15, president, 1916-36, chmn. bd. since 1936; pres. Tower Nixon Frankfort Roosevelt Realty Co. Pres. Federation of Jewish Charities. Club: Locust (Philadelphia). Home: 1001 Valley Road. Office: 315 N. 12th St., Philadelphia, Pa.

HEIN, Carl, musical dir.; b. Rendsburg, Germany, Feb. 2, 1864; s. Fritz and Alwine (Schorr) H.; studied at Hamburg Conservatory Music; m. Marta Krüger, Jan. 1890 (died 1925); children—Illo, Yrsa, Castor, Pollux, Uarda. Came to U.S., 1890. Mem. Philharmonic Soc., Hamburg, Germany, 1885-90; mus. dir. German singing socs., etc., since 1890; dir. Franz Schubert Männerchor, 1890-1928, Mozart Verein, 1894-1927, Harmonie, 1891-1918, Concordia, 1894-1922, Einigheit, 1894-1923; now pres. New York Coll. Music. Mem. internat. jury of awards in music, San Francisco Expn., 1915, Sesquicentennial Expn., Philadelphia, 1926. Pres. United German Choral Dirs. America. Author: Thirty-one Daily Exercises for the Voice, 1915; Tone Production in 20 Lessons, 1918. Home: Woodcliff Lake, N.J. Office: 114-116 E. 85th St., New York, N.Y.

HEINE, H. Eugene, lawyer; b. Phila., Pa., Mar. 8, 1888; s. Joseph C. and Catherine Lucia (Klostermann) H.; A.B. and A.M. St. Joseph's Coll., Phila.; LL.B., Temple U.; m. Dorothy Mae Wicks, Aug. 9, 1922; children—Barbara Louise, H. Eugene, Richard Anthony, Rosalie Frances, Gregory Martin, Laurence Edward. Lecturer, St. Joseph's Coll., 1910-15; prof. law, Temple U., 1914-20; lecturer law and corpn. finance, U. of Pa., 1914-35; asso. counsel Bur. of War Risk Ins., 1917-18; gen. asst. city solicitor, Phila., 1920-32; spl. sr. counsel Div. of Closed Banks, Dept. of Justice, since 1932. Served as 1st lt., Chem. Warfare Service, U.S. Army, 1918-19. Mem. Phila. Charter Commn. since 1937; sec. City Parks Assn. since 1928; dir. and trustee Awbury Arboretum; dir. Phila. and Suburban Town Meetings, Inc. Mem. Phila. Chamber of Commerce, Steuben Soc., Am. Legion (past comdr.), Nat. Assn. Jews and Christians, German Soc. of Pa., Arion Singing Soc., Steuben Soc., Concord Group, Round Table. Mem. K.C. (4°; navigator Archbishop Ryan Gen. Assembly, 1920-22). Club: Penn Athletic (sec. since 1925). Home: 905 N. 64th St. Office: 2305 Philadelphia Saving Fund Bldg., Philadelphia, Pa.

HEINER, Gordon Graham, army officer; b. Washington, D.C., Nov. 2, 1869; s. Robert Graham and Helen Gordon (Slemaker) H.; B.A., U. of W.Va., 1889; grad. U.S. Mil. Acad., 1893; hon. grad. Arty. Sch., Fort Monroe, Va., 1910; m. Elizabeth Cloyd Kent, Nov. 12, 1895; children—Gordon G., Mary Grant, Robert Graham, Elizabeth Kent. Commd. 2d lt. 2d Arty., June 12, 1893; transferred to 4th Arty., Nov. 29, 1893; 1st lt., Mar. 2, 1899; capt. Arty. Corps, July 1, 1901; maj. Coast Arty. Corps, Jan. 24, 1910; lt. col., July 1, 1916; brig. gen. N.A., Aug. 5, 1917; col. C.A., Mar. 21, 1919; appt. comdr. Coast Defenses, Honolulu, T.H., Feb. 12, 1921; comd. Coast Defenses, Honolulu, 1921-23; exec. officer 2d Coast Arty. Dist., 1923-26; chief of staff, Field Arty. Group Organized Res., 3d Corps Area, hdqrs. Harrisburg, Pa., Apr. 6, 1926-Aug. 1928; comd. 30th C.A. Brig. and Fort Eustis, Va., Sept. 1928-May 1929; retired, Sept. 10, 1929. (For details as to career see Vol. XI, 1920-21.) Home: 313 Suffolk Road, Guilford, Baltimore, Md.

HEINLY, Charles Benjamin, high school prin.; b. Berks Co., Pa., June 20, 1874; s. David and Amanda (Levan) H.; B.E., Keystone State Normal Sch., Kutztown, Pa., 1895; A.B., Ursinus Coll., Collegeville, Pa., 1900, A.M., 1910, Ped.D., 1928; student Sch. of Theol., Phila., 1900-02, Columbia U., 1922-23; m. Grace Gristock, Aug. 23, 1903; 1 dau., Elizabeth Gristock (wife of Dr. John H. Frick, Jr.). Public school teacher, Berks Co., Pa., 1892-94; instr. in mathematics, Keystone State Normal Sch., 1901-02; instr. in science, York (Pa.) High Sch., 1903-19, prin., 1919-27; prin., William Penn Senior High Sch., York, since 1927; teacher of secondary edn., Elizabethtown Coll., summers 1928, 29. Asso. with Boy Scouts of America since 1917, chmn. court of honor; awarded Silver Beaver award 1935. Mem. bd. dirs. Ursinus Coll. Mem. N.E.A., Pa. State Edn. Assn. Home: 34 N. Keesey St. Office: College Av. and Beaver St., York, Pa.

HEINTZELMAN, C. H.; editor Coatesville Record. Address: Coatesville, Pa.

HEINZ, Howard, mfr.; b. Pittsburgh, Pa., Aug. 27, 1877; s. Henry John and Sarah Sloan (Young) H.; prep. edn., Shady Side Acad., Pittsburgh; B.A., Yale, 1900; LL.D., Juniata College, Huntingdon, Pa., 1926; m. Elizabeth Granger Rust, Oct. 3, 1906; children—Henry John, II, Rust. Began, 1900, in food product mfg. business estab. by father, 1869; became adv. mgr., 1905, sales mgr., 1907, pres. and chmn. bd. H. J. Heinz Co., 1919; dir. Pennsylvania R.R. Co., Mellon Nat. Bank of Pittsburgh. Trustee Carnegie Endowment for International Peace. Served during World War as mem. Nat. Council of Defense of Pa., also as follows: U.S. food administrator of Pa.; chmn. Food Supply Com. Nat. Council Defense, Pa.; zone chmn. U.S. Food Administration for Pa., Ohio, Va., W.Va., Md. and D.C.; mem. War Industries Bd. of Phila.; and mem. exec. com. Am. Relief Administration (European children's relief). Dir. gen. Am. Relief Administration for Southeastern Europe and Asia Minor, Jan.-June 1919. Pres. Sarah Heinz House, Pittsburgh; mem. bd. trustees U. of Pittsburgh, Carnegie Inst., West Pa. Hosp., W. Pa. Institution for the Blind (Pittsburgh), Shady Side Acad. (Pittsburgh); pres. Pittsburgh Regional Planning Assn.; v.p. Pittsburgh Symphony Soc.; dir. Carnegie Endowment for Internat. Peace, Boys' Club of America; mem. Nat. Industrial Conf. Bd., Inc., N.Y. City; trustee Commn. for Relief in Belgium, Ednl. Foundation, New York. Mem. Delta Kappa Epsilon. Republican. Presbyterian. Clubs: Duquesne, Pittsburgh Golf, Allegheny Country, Fox Chapel Golf, Harvard-Yale-Princeton, Rolling Rock (Pittsburgh); University, Yale, Recess (New York); Chicago (Chicago); Ristigouche Salmon (Quebec); American (London). Home: Morewood Heights, Wilkins and 5th Avs. Office: H. J. Heinz Co., Pittsburgh, Pa.

HEISERMAN, Clarence Benjamin, lawyer; b. Urbana, O., Sept. 18, 1862; s. Aaron and Maria Louisa (Stuart) H.; A.B., Ohio Wesleyan U., 1884; m. Lillian Brown, Oct. 29, 1890; 1 son, Robert Brown. Admitted to Ohio bar, 1887, and began practice at Urbana; pros. atty., Champaign Co., O., 1889-94; judge Court of Common Pleas, 2d Dist. of Ohio, 1894-1901, resigned; solicitor P.,C.,C.&St.L. Ry. Co., at Urbana; general solicitor Pa. Lines, at Pittsburgh, Pa., 1910-14, gen. counsel, 1914-21; gen. counsel Pa. system, at Phila., May 1, 1921-23, v.p. and gen. counsel, 1923-32, now spl. counsel. Mem. Am. and various state bar assns., Pa. Scotch-Irish Soc., Pa. Soc. of N.Y., Chi Phi. Republican. Presbyterian. Mason (32°). Clubs: Duquesne (Pittsburgh); Rittenhouse (Phila.). Home: Haverford, Pa. Office: Broad St. Station Bldg., Philadelphia, Pa.

HEISEY, Herman Biever, clergyman; b. Middletown, Pa., Dec. 10, 1890; s. John H. and Susan (Biever) H.; B.S.L., Juniata Coll., 1911, post-grad. work, 1912; m. Grace N. Nedrow, May 29, 1912; children—Helen Grace (Mrs. Christian S. Wenger), Kathren Mae (Mrs. Joseph A. Gibson), Kenneth Herman. Ordained to ministry Ch. of Brethren, 1910, became bishop 1915; student pastor, Saxton, Pa., 1911-12; missionary to India, 1912-14; pastor various chs. in Pa., also in Los Angeles and Long Beach, Calif.; pastor, Lewistown, Pa., since 1935; sec. Middle Dist. of Pa. Chs. of Brethren; a number of times rep. Annual Nat. Conv. on Standing Com.; has conducted many evangelistic campaigns; lectures on: "Pa, Ma, and the Youngster in the Family." Republican. Mem. Ch. of the Brethren. Home: 37 Shaw Av., Lewistown, Pa.

HEISEY, Victor Dewey, high sch. prin.; b. Lebanon, Pa., Aug. 22, 1898; s. Samuel A. and Lizzie (McCurdy) H.; A.B., Albright Coll., Reading, Pa., 1919; grad. work U. of Pa., summers 1921-26; A.M., Teachers Coll. Columbia U., 1931; m. May Eshelman, Aug. 25, 1927; 1 son, Victor Robert. Engaged in teaching high sch., Clearfield, Pa., 1919-23; supt. schs. Warwick Twp., 1923-26; prin. Pa. Av. High Sch.,

Cumberland, Md., 1926-36; prin. Fort Hill High Sch., Cumberland, Md., since 1936. Served as pvt. inf., U.S.A., 1918. Presbyn. Club: Rotary of Cumberland (past pres.). Home: 902 Hill Top Drive, Cumberland, Md.

HEISING, Raymond Alphonsus, radio research engr.; b. Albert Lea, Minn., Aug. 10, 1888; s. Charles and Anna A. (Fitzgerald) H.; E.E., U. of N.D., 1912; M.S., U. of Wis., 1914; m. Teresa A. Coneys, Nov. 25, 1920; children—William P., Charles R., Mary E. Research engr. Western Electric Co., Inc., 1914-25, Bell Telephone Labs., Inc., since 1925. Fellow Inst. Radio Engrs. (pres. 1939), Am. Inst. E.E., Am. Physical Soc., A.A.A.S. Awarded Morris Liebmann Prize by Inst. Radio Engrs., 1921. Republican. Mem. K.C. Contbr. many articles to scientific and engring. mags. Inventor numerous radio circuits and devices, some of basic importance (over 100 patents issued in U.S.); most widely known are on modulation and high efficiency amplification; invented and developed transmitter circuits used in radio telephone sets in U.S. Navy and Army during World War; participated in responsible capacity in engring. work establishing first transoceanic commercial radio telephone circuits, both long and short wave, and in ship-shore telephone circuits for transatlantic lines. Home: 232 Oak Ridge Av., Summit, N.J. Office: Bell Telephone Laboratories, Inc., 463 West St., New York, N.Y.

HEISLER, Roland Carlisle, lawyer; b. Milford, Del., Oct. 6, 1886; s. Charles C. and Minnie W. (Watson) H.; grad. Central High Sch., Philadelphia, 1906; studied U. of Pa. Coll., 1906-07; LL.B., U. of Pa. Law Sch., 1910; m. Hilda V. Hardesty, June 28, 1919; children—Edmond H., Charles C., Mary Ellen. Admitted to Pa. bar, 1910, since in gen. practice of law; mem. firm Drinker, Biddle & Reath since 1927. Served with A.E.F., as major 109th Inf., 28th Div., World War (wounded in action). Mem. Am. Bar Assn., Philadelphia Bar Assn., Am. Law Inst., Lawyers Club. Republican. Episcopalian. Mason. Clubs: Union League, Merion Cricket (Philadelphia). Home: 409 Penwyn Road, Wynnewood, Pa. Office: 1429 Walnut St., Philadelphia, Pa.

HEISS, Charles Augustus, pub. utility exec.; b. Catawissa, Pa., Mar. 22, 1878; s. Charles and Sophia (Marsh) H.; grad. Bloomsburg (Pa.) State Normal Sch., 1902; student Franklin and Marshall Coll., Lancaster, Pa., 1905-07; A.B., George Washington U., Washington, D.C., 1908; grad. student U. of Mich. Grad. Sch., 1908-10; (hon.) A.M., U. of Mich., 1928; (hon.) LL.D., Upsala Coll., East Orange, N.J., 1937; m. Anne E. Dreisbach, Jan. 2, 1909; children—Mary Ellen, M.D. (wife of Perry S. Boynton, Jr., M.D.), Anne Elizabeth, artist (wife of Carroll A. Boynton, atty.). Engaged in teaching in pub. and pvt. schs., 1896-1905; accountant and examiner, Interstate Commerce Commn., Washington, D.C., and Ann Arbor, Mich., 1907-13; accountant, Am. Telephone & Telegraph Co., New York, 1913-20, comptroller since 1920. Served as pres. bd. edn., East Orange, N.J., 1926-38. Vice chmn. N.J. State Bd. of Regents since 1929. Trustee, East Orange (N.J.) Gen. Hosp. and Overlook Hosp., Summit, N.J. Presbyterian. Club: Essex County Country (West Orange, N.J.). Home: Little Brook Farm, Pottersville, N.J. Office: 195 Broadway, New York, N.Y.

HEISS, Elwood David, prof. science; b. Martinsville, Pa., Dec. 30, 1899; s. George A. and Elizabeth (Oberdorff) H.; A.B., Lebanon Valley Coll., 1921; A.M., Columbia U., 1925, Ph.D., same, 1932; m. Hilda Grace Wood, Dec. 22, 1923; children—George Daniel, Elwood David, Jr., Betty Marie. Engaged as instr. science, high schs., 1921-25; prof. sci., Milwaukee State Teachers Coll., 1926-29; head of science dept., East Stroudsburg State Teachers Coll. since 1929. Mem. Nat. Edn. Assn., Nat. Assn. Biology Teachers, Nat. Assn. for Research in Sci. Teaching, Phi Delta Kappa. Republican. Presbyn. Mason. Rotarian. Author: Educational Biology, 1933; Modern Science Problems, 1936; Our World of Living Things, 1936; Science Problems of Modern Life, 1933; Modern Methods and Materials for Science Teaching, 1939. Home: 162 Analomink St., East Stroudsburg, Pa.

HEISSENBUTTEL, Ernest Gerhardt, prof. English; b. New York, N.Y., Jan. 11, 1903; s. George Frederick and Dora (Gartleman) H.; ed. Gettysburg Coll., 1922-25; A.B., Columbia U., 1926, A.M., same, 1930; grad. study, Columbia U., summers 1932-35; m. Jean Elizabeth McCormick, Aug. 18, 1932; 1 son, Robert Holmes. Engaged as instr. English, Gettysburg Coll., 1926-28, asst. prof., 1928-29; prof. English since 1930, head of Dept. English, Thiel Coll., Greenville, Pa., since 1930; formerly engaged in newspaper work at Middletown, N.Y., now adviser to publicity at Thiel Coll. Mem. Am. Assn. Univ. Profs., Tau Kappa Alpha. Democrat. Lutheran. Home: 9 Ridgeway Av., Greenville, Pa.

HELBERT, George Kingman, lawyer; b. Cheyenne, Wyo., Apr. 2, 1882; s. M. G. and Grace C. (Kingman) H.; grad. Haverford Sch., 1900; B.S. in mech. engring., Haverford Coll., 1904; LL.B., U. of Pa., 1911; m. Florence Hancock, Sept. 26, 1929. With Stohes & Smith Co., Phila., 1904, Maxwell Briscoe Motor Co., Tarrytown, N.Y., and Washington, D.C., 1905-06, Mercer Rubber Co., Trenton, N.J., and New York, 1907-08; admitted to Pa. bar, 1911, and has since specialized in patent, trade mark and copyright law, Phila.; dir. Hall Planetary Co., Parsons Ammonia Co. Grad. from 2d O.T.C., Fortress Monroe, Va., Dec. 1917; served as 1st lt. Coast Arty. Corps, U.S. Army in U.S. and in A.E.F., 1917-19. Mem. Am., Pa. and Phila. Bar Assns., Am. Patent Law Assn., Phila. Patent Law Assn., Psi Upsilon, Order of Coif. Republican. Episcopalian. Mason. Clubs: Union League of Phila., Phila. Country, Lawyers of Phila.; Sharswood Law; The Barracks (New York). Home: 305 W. Hortter St., Germantown, Pa. Office: 1900 Lincoln-Liberty Bldg., Philadelphia, Pa.

HELD, Jacob B., lawyer; b. Erie, Pa., Aug. 7, 1898; s. Andrew and Theresia (Hein) H.; A.B., U. of Pittsburgh, 1920; LL.B., U. of Pittsburgh Law Sch., 1923; m. Marie Carey, Nov. 26, 1925; children—John J., Mary Ann, Susan. Admitted to Pa. bar, 1923, and since engaged in gen. practice of law at Erie; served as city solicitor for Erie, 1924-32; county solicitor, Erie Co. since 1935; dir. and counsel Mutual Bldg. & Loan Assn. Served as lieut. U.S.A. Res. since 1920. Chmn. Rep. Co. Com., 1934-36. Mem. Pa. Bar Assn., Delta Theta Phi, Omicron Delta Kappa, Beta Gamma Sigma, Delta Sigma Rho. Republican. Roman Catholic. Home: 400 Arlington Rd. Office: Erie Trust Bldg., Erie, Pa.

HELD, Omar Conrad, personnel asst. to coll. dean; b. Santa Claus, Ind., Aug. 14, 1896; s. Jacob and Anna (Haas) H.; A.B., Ind. U., 1923, A.M., same, 1924, grad. study, same, 1924-26; Ph.D., U. of Pittsburgh, 1931; m. Eleanor Flatemersch, June 28, 1932; 1 son, George Conrad. Instr. in psychology, U. of Pittsburgh, 1926-28 and 1928-31, also personnel asst. to Dean of Coll. continuously since 1928, asst. prof., 1931-34, asso. prof. psychology since 1934. Served in U.S.N., 1918-19. Asso. mem. Am. Psychol. Assn. Mem. A.A.A.S., Assn. Applied Psychologists, Pa. Assn. Clin. Psychologists, Sigma Xi. Home: 7 Briar Cliff Rd., Ben Avon Heights, Pittsburgh, Pa.

HELFENSTEIN, Edward Trail, bishop of Md.; b. St. Louis, Mo., Apr. 7, 1865; s. Cyrus G. and Annie E. (Trail) H.; prep. edn., Frederick Acad. and Episcopal High Sch. of Va.; student Johns Hopkins, Va. Theol. Sem., D.D., 1916; m. Grace Fenton Nelson, Apr. 8, 1890; 1 dau., Grace Nelson (dec.). Deacon, 1889, priest, 1890, P.E. Ch.; rector Christ Ch., Rock Spring, Md., 1889-90, St. Mary's Parish, Frederick and Washington counties, 1890-1900, St. John's and St. Peter's Chs., Howard Co., 1900-20; archdeacon of Maryland, 1920-26; consecrated coadjutor bishop of Md., Dec. 28, 1926, bishop since Oct. 3, 1929. Deputy to Gen. Conv. P.E. Ch. 4 times. Home: Charles St. and University Parkway. Office: 105 W. Monument St., Baltimore, Md.

HELFFERICH, Donald Laurance, vice-pres. Ursinus Coll.; b. Bath, Pa., Apr. 24, 1898; s. Rev. William Ursinus (D.D.) and Nora Helena (Shuler) H.; grad. Mercersburg Acad., 1917; A.B., Ursinus Coll., 1921; LL.B., Yale Law Sch., 1924; m. Anna A. Knauer, of St. Peters, Pa., July 14, 1925; children—Ilse An, William Ursinus, II. Head legal dept. and asst. store mgr. Gimbel Bros., Inc., Phila., 1924-35; vice-pres. and mem. bd. dirs. Ursinus Coll., Collegeville, Pa., since 1935; sec. and dir. French Creek Granite Co.; vice-pres. and dir. Upper Darby Nat. Bank. Served as 2d lt. A.S., U.S.A., 1917-18. Dir. Family Welfare Soc. of Del. Co. Sec. and treas. Assn. of Trustees of Colls. of Pa. Mem. Pa. German Folklore Soc., Tau Kappa Alpha, Phi Delta Phi, Am. Legion (vice comdr. post). Republican. Mem. Evang. and Reformed Ch. Club: Yale (Philadelphia). Home: 114 Gladstone Rd., Lansdowne, Pa.

HELLER, Edgar William, manufacturer; b. Newark, N.J., Aug. 6, 1879; s. Frederick and Annie Josephine (Traud) H.; ed. Newark Acad., 1887-97, Yale (Sheffield Scientific Sch.), 1897-1900; m. Sara Edith Gaddis, Apr. 22, 1903; children—Edgar William, Elizabeth (Mrs. George D. Smith), Frederick, Sara (Mrs. Joseph F. Lord), Nancy Gaddis. Now pres. Lecourtenay Co., machinery, Newark, N.J.; mem. bd. dirs. Fidelity Union Trust Co., Franklin Savings Instn., Wilkinson-Gaddis Co., Inc. Served as food administrator and chmn. of Draft Bd. No. 2, Newark, during World War. Pres. Newark Eye and Ear Infirmary. Mem. Am. Soc. Mech. Engrs., Yale Engring. Assn. Clubs: Essex (Newark); Rumson Country (Rumson, N.J.); Batusrol Golf (Springfield, N.J.). Home: 368 Mt. Prospect Av. Office: 5 Maine St., Newark, N.J.

HELLER, Leighton James, lawyer; b. Phila., Pa., Jan. 16, 1901; s. James Leighton and Mary Frances (Skerrett) H.; A.B., Dickinson Coll., Carlisle, Pa., 1923, A.M., 1925; LL.B., Dickinson Coll. Law Sch., 1925; unmarried. Admitted to N.J. bar as atty., 1934, as counselor, 1938; engaged in gen. practice of law as individual at Camden, N.J., since 1934; served as police recorder, Clementon, N.J., 1925-33; pres. Clementon Sch. Bd., 1927-29; mayor, 1929-33; vice-pres. Nat. Bank of Clementon; dir. Clementon Bldg. & Loan Assn.; solicitor Signal Hill Bldg. & Loan Assn., Diligent Bldg. & Loan Assn. Albion, N.J. Mem. Camden County Bar Assn., Phi Kappa Psi. Republican. Presbyn. Mason (32°). Clubs: Lions, Clementon. Home: 50 Fulton Av., Clementon. Office: 12 N. 7th St., Camden, N.J.

HELLMUND, Rudolph Emil, electrical engr.; b. Gotha, Germany, Feb. 2, 1879; s. Louis and Katharina (Wenzel) H.; grad. realschule, Gotha, 1895; studied Tech. Coll., Ilmenau, and Univ. of Charlottenburg, 1896-99 and 1902-03; m. Hetty Borgmann, May 24, 1913. Came to U.S., 1903, naturalized citizen, 1920. Asst. to William Stanley, Great Barrington, Mass., 1904-05; designing engr. Western Electric Co., Chicago, 1905-07; with Westinghouse Electric & Mfg. Co. since 1907; apptd. chief engr., 1933, responsible for adequacy of company's engineering and design work, covering all branches of the orgn., also chmn. ednl. com., etc. Inventor elec. devices covered by more than 250 U.S. and foreign patents. Fellow Am. Inst. of E.E. Lutheran. Mason (K.T., Shriner). Awarded Benjamin Lamme medal, Am. Inst. E.E., 1929. Club: Pittsburgh Athletic. Writer of numerous papers and articles in Am. and European publs. Home: Swissvale, Pa.*

HELM, William P(ickett), journalist; b. near Warrenton, Virginia, May 4, 1883; s. William Pickett and Agnes Harwood (Marshall) H.; grad. high sch., Warrenton, 1896; m. Selma White Snyder, Oct. 29, 1921. Reporter Chattanooga (Tenn.) Times and other dailies, 1904-05; reporter, city editor, mng. editor Newark (N.J.) Morning Star, 1906-10; Associated Press corr., New York and Washington, D.C., 1911-17; asst. to v.p. Nat. Coal Assn., Washington, D.C., 1918-21; newspaper syndicate writer since 1921 and contbr. economic and financial articles to mags.; first economist to measure accurately the cost of Am. govt. (1923); founder, 1927, pres., 1927-28, Helm News Service; Washington corr. of daily newspapers since 1933. Dir. publicity, southern div., Rep. Nat. Com., 1928. Author:

The Truth About Taxes, 1924; History of the Anti-Saloon League (with Wayne B. Wheeler), 1926; The Federal Budget (with Gen. Herbert M. Lord), 1929; Washington Swindle Sheet, 1932. Contbr. to Collier's, World's Work, Liberty, Outlook, Nation's Business, American Mercury. Home: 606 Cecil Av., Riverdale, Md. Office: Colorado Bldg., Washington, D.C.

HELMBOLD, Theodore Raymond, physician; b. Saxonburg, Pa., Dec. 22, 1892; s. Louis August and Molinda (Christy) H.; grad. Cabot (Pa.) Inst., 1911; B.S., U. of Pittsburgh, 1918, M.D., 1920; m. Lillian Marie Straessley, Nov. 14, 1925. Interne Mercy Hosp., Pittsburgh, 1920-21, resident in pathology, 1921-22, asst. pathologist, 1922-24; pathologist to Passavant Hosp., Pittsburgh, 1924-31; pathologist South Side Hosp., Pittsburgh, since 1931; demonstrator in pathology, U. of Pittsburgh, since 1923. Certified by Am. Bd. of Pathology, 1936. Mem. Clin. Pathol. Soc. of Pittsburgh, Soc. of Biol. Research of U. of Pittsburgh, Allegheny Co. Med. Soc., Pa. State Med. Soc., A.M.A., Am. Assn. Pathologists and Bacteriologists, Am. Soc. Clin. Pathologists, Internat. Assn. Med. Museums, A.A.A.S., Sigma Alpha Epsilon, Nu Sigma Nu, Alpha Omega Alpha. Methodist. Mason. Clubs: University, Alcoma Country (Pittsburgh). Home: 5215 Celia Place. Office: South Side Hospital, Pittsburgh, Pa.

HELME J(ames) Burn, prof. architecture; b. Smiths Falls, Ont., May 29, 1897; s. James and Isabella Gray (Burn) H.; B.A.Sc., U. of Toronto, 1922, M.Arch., same, 1925; grad. study, Ecole des Hautes Etudes Urbaines à la Sorbonne, Paris, 1922-23, Ecole des Beaux Arts, Fontainebleau, summers 1927, 1928; A.M., Harvard U. 1930, grad. study, 1934-35; unmarried. Employed in various capacities with archtl. firms in Toronto, and city planning, 1919-25; asst. prof. architecture, Pa. State Coll., 1925-29, asso. prof., 1929-35, prof. architecture and head div. fine arts, Pa. State Coll. since 1935; resident consultant in Paris in connection Regional Plan of New York and Environs, summer 1927; guest lecturer on art, U. of Iowa, summer 1930. Served with Overseas Training Co., C.O.T.C., 1917-18. Mem. Am. Inst. Architects, Am. Assn. Univ. Profs., Am. Assn. Museums, Coll. Art Assn., Ontario Assn. Architects, Royal Archtl. Inst. Can., Town Planning Inst. Can., Scarab, Pi Gamma Alpha. Club: University of State College (dir.). Editor tech. bull. on low cost housing. Contbr. articles to professional journs. Home: University Club, State College, Pa.; also summer, Birklandbarrow, Smiths Falls, Ont.

HELRIEGEL, Florence J., lawyer; b. Ransom, Pa., Apr. 15, 1879; s. Oscar L. and Anna H.; student Scranton High Sch., Wood Business Coll., Dickinson Law Sch.; m. Magdalena Robinson, Oct. 24, 1906; children—Robinson R., Magdalen (wife of Dr. Mortimer Fruehan). Admitted to Pa. bar, 1902; mem. firm Donahoe & Helriegel; cashier South Side Bank & Trust Co., Scranton, 1902-12, dir., 1912-14, pres. since 1914; pres. Scranton Clearing House, 1932-34; pres. Westbrook Coal Co.; treas. Scranton Silk Machine Co. Pres. Anthracite Bankers Assn. Republican. Presbyterian. Home: 305 Arthur Av. Office: Mears Bldg., Scranton, Pa.

HELSON, Harry, prof. exptl. psychology; b. Chelsea, Mass., Nov. 9, 1898; s. William and Ida H.; A.B., Bowdoin Coll., 1921; A.M., Harvard U., 1922, Ph.D., same, 1924; m. Lida Anderson, Sept. 3, 1926; children—Henry Berge, Martha Alice. Engaged as instr. psychology, Cornell U., 1924-25, U. of Ill., 1925-26; asst. prof. psychology, U. of Kan., 1926-28; asso. prof. exptl. psychology, Bryn Mawr Coll., 1928-33, prof. since 1933. Served in Naval unit, S.A.T.C., 1918. Mem. Am. Psychol. Assn., Nat. Inst. Psychology, Optical Soc. America, Sigma Xi, Phi Beta Kappa, Sigma Nu. Fellow A.A.A.S. Delegate, Inter-Society Color Council. Contbr. articles to psychol. journs. Home: 418 Haverford Av., Narberth, Pa.

HELTON, Roy Addison, author; b. Washington, D.C., Apr. 3, 1886; s. Addison Smith and Marian Virginia (Hazard) H.; grad. Eastern High Sch., Washington, D.C., 1904; B.S., U. of Pa., 1908; m. Anne Watson, June 28, 1909; children—Frank Addison, Robert. Teacher of literature, Central Manual Training Sch., Phila., 1909, W. Phila. Boys High Sch., 1911-23, William Penn Charter Sch., 1923-30; lecturer on modern poetry, people of the southern mountains, etc.; research and planning supervisor, Pa. State Planning Bd., 1938. Mem. Sigma Phi Epsilon. Clubs: Contemporary, Franklin Inn. Author: Youth's Pilgrimage (verse), 1914; Outcasts in Beulah Land (verse), 1918; Jimmy Sharswood, 1924; The Early Adventures of Peacham Grew, 1925; Lonesome Water (Kentucky mountain verse), 1930; Nitchey Tilley (novel), 1934; Sold Out to the Future, 1935. Home: 1620 Pelham Rd., Beechwood, Upper Darby, Pa. Office: 928 N. 3d St., Harrisburg, Pa.

HELYAR, Frank George, univ. dir.; b. Boston, Mass., Feb. 6, 1883; s. James Putnam and Ada Marie (Gould) H.; student Brattleboro (Vt.) Pub. Schs., 1888-1900; B.S., U. of Vt., Burlington, Vt., 1905; m. Irma Maynard Hatcher, Apr. 25, 1908; children—Elizabeth Ada (dec.), James Edwin. Began as asst. to supt., Brattleboro (Vt.) Retreat Farm, 1905; insp. dept. feeds and feeding, Mass. Exptl. Sta., Amherst, Mass., 1905-06; dir. dept. of agr., Mt. Hermon Boys Sch., Mount Hermon, Mass., 1906-10; dir. N.Y. State Sch. of Agr., Morrisville, N.Y., 1910-17; dir. short courses in agr., Rutgers U., New Brunswick, N.J., since 1917, prof. animal husbandry since 1919, dir. resident instruction since 1929, appointed acting dean for all absences of dean, 1934; asso. in admnstrn., N.J. State Expt. Sta., 1917-19, acting dir., interims 1919-34. Mem. Gov's. Advisory Bd. on Agrl. Edn. in N.Y., 1911-17; chmn. Planning Bd., Raritan (N.J.) Twp. since 1930. Mem. N.Y. State Agrl. Soc. (life mem.; v.p., 1916-17), Alpha Kappa Pi (nat. first v.p., 1934-36; chmn. bd. of trustees since 1936), Theta Gamma, Alpha Zeta (nat. high censor, 1930-36; high chancellor since 1936), Phi Beta Kappa. Republican. Congregationalist. Mason (Royal Arch), Grange. Club: Lions (New Brunswick, N.J.). Home: 4 Rutgers St., Stelton, N.J. Office: College of Agriculture, Rutgers U., New Brunswick, N.J.

HEMINGWAY, Reginald S., lawyer; b. Beloit, Kan., July 8, 1884; s. George Henry and Sara Alberta (Swift) H.; ed. high sch., Bloomsburg, Pa., 1898-1902; A.B., Lafayette Coll., 1907; LL.B., U. of Pa. Law Sch., 1912; unmarried. Engaged as instr. mathematics, Pa. State Coll., 1907-09; admitted to Pa. bar, 1913, and since engaged in gen. practice of law at Bloomsburg; also mem. firm Hemingway & Wagner, Danville, Pa., since 1936; dir. Bloomsburg Bank-Columbia Trust Co.; sec. and dir. Bloomsburg Silk Mill; pres. and dir. Triangle Motor Co. Mem. Am., Pa. State, and Columbia Co. bar assns., Phi Delta Theta, Phi Delta Phi. Republican. Presbyn. Mason (K.T., 32°, Shriner). Elk. Clubs: Bloomsburg Country (pres. and dir.), Craftsman, Rotary (Bloomsburg); Wheel (Williamsport); Manufacturers (Milton); Valley Gun and Country (Elysburg); Painter Den (Benton); Pa. Soc. of New York (New York City). Home: 364 College Hill. Office: First Nat. Bank Bldg., Bloomsburg, Pa.

HEMPHILL, John, lawyer; b. West Chester, Pa., Sept. 6, 1891; s. E. Dallett and Rebecca (Mickle) H.; LL.B., Haverford Sch., 1908; student U. of Pa., 1912, and U. of Pa. Law Sch., 1915; m. Noma Spalding, Apr. 18, 1938; children (by former marriage)—Alexander, Dallett, Dolly. Admitted to Phila. bar, 1915; since in gen. practice of law; mem. law firm Lewis, Wolff, Gourley & Hemphill since 1938. Served as 1st lt., later capt., 47th Inf., 4th Div., U.S. Army, World War. Asst. sec. Dem. Nat. Conv., 1920; chmn. Speakers Bur. for Pa., 1928; candidate for gov. of Pa., 1930. Hon. consul of Latvia for Pa. since 1928. Mem. Am., Pa., Phila. bar assns., Maritime Law Assn. of U.S., Phi Kappa Sigma. Episcopalian. Club: Rittenhouse. Contbr. articles on legal and polit. subjects to Am. Mercury, Vanity Fair, The Outlook, etc. Home: 250 S. 17th St. Office: 208 S. Fourth St., Philadelphia, Pa.

HEMPHILL, Marguerite Flower; b. Enon Valley, Pa., Mar. 27, 1896; d. Albert Herman and Adelaide (Bean) Flower; direct desc. Gov. William Bradford; ed. Grand River Inst., Austinburg, O., 1910-14; B.O., Geneva Coll., Beaver Falls, Pa., 1916; also student Duquesne U.; m. George Robert Hemphill, June 5, 1918; 1 son, George R., II. Dist. del. Rep. Nat. Conv., 1928, del.-at-large, 1936; press. Pa. Council of Rep. Women, 1934-35; mem. Rep. State Exec. Com. since 1935; asst. sec. Pa. Rep. State Com., 1938; mem. Nat. Rep. Program Com. Dir. Beaver Co. Chapter, Am. Red Cross; mem. advisory com. on Women's Participation for Pa., New York World's Fair. Mem. D.A.R. Presbyn. Club: Outlook (Beaver Falls). Home: 607 Ninth St., Beaver Falls, Pa.

HENDERSON, Adelbert Andrew, mem. Allegheny County Bd. of Viewers; b. Franklin Co., O., June 21, 1873; s. Joseph and Martha Simpson (Robertson) H.; B.A., Ohio Wesleyan U., Delaware, O., 1895, M.A., 1898; C.E., Ohio State U., Columbus, 1898; m. Lena Weisman, May 29, 1900; children—Elizabeth Levitt, Thomas Johnson. Asst. in city engr's. office, Columbus, O., 1898-99; asst. engr. maintenance of way, Indianapolis (Ind.) Div., Pa. R.R. Co., 1899; junior civil engr. U.S. Engr's. Office, Cincinnati, 1899-1900; asst. and deputy county engr., Allegheny County, Pa., 1900-24; chief constrn. engr. Bur. of Bridges, Allegheny Co. Dept. of Pub. Works, 1924-32; mem. Allegheny Co. Bd. of Viewers since 1932; registered professional engr., Commonwealth of Pa. Mem. Am. Soc. C.E., Engr's. Soc. Western Pa., Am. Assn. of Engrs., Alpha Tau Omega, Phi Beta Kappa, Tau Beta Pi. Methodist (pres. bd. of trustees Ross Av. M.E. Ch., Wilkinsburg). Home: 603 Hill Av., Wilkinsburg, Pa. Office: City-County Bldg., Pittsburgh, Pa.

HENDERSON, Cam, athletic dir. and coach; b. Mannington, W.Va., Feb. 5, 1891; s. John H. and Catherine (Pethetel) H.; student Glenville (W.Va.) Normal Sch., 1910-11, Waynesburg (Pa.) Coll., 1912-14; A.B., Salem (W. Va.) Coll., 1917; m. Roxie Bell, Aug. 22, 1913; 1 dau., Camille Sue. Supt. of schs., Bristol, W.Va., 1917-20; athletic dir. and coach, Muskingum (Ohio) Coll., 1920-23, Davis Elkins (W.Va.) Coll., 1923-35, Marshall Coll., Huntington, W.Va., since 1935. Mem. Delta Sigma Phi. Given trophy by city of Huntington for the outstanding work done for the city. Buckeye Conference football championship, undefeated, Buckeye Conference basketball championship, undefeated, 1937-38. Presbyterian. Mason, Elk. Clubs: Rotary, Guyan Country (Huntington). Home: 1611 5th Av., Huntington, W.Va.

HENDERSON, Davis W(oodward), lawyer; b. Fayette Co., Pa., Dec. 25, 1875; s. Steward and Harriet (Woodward) H.; student pub. schs., Fayette Co., Pa., 1881-92; grad. State Normal Sch., California, Pa., 1892-94; A.B., Waynesburg (Pa.) Coll., 1897; m. Clelia Wyoming Knox, June 24, 1903; children—Davis Knox, Carolyn Harriett (Mrs. Clifford W. Brown). Admitted to Fayette Co., Pa., bar, 1900; pvt. practice, 1900-04, 1911-26, 1936-37; mem. firm Henderson, Parshall & Crow, attorneys, Uniontown, Pa., since Jan. 1938. Asst. dist. atty. Fayette Co., 1904-07, dist. atty., 1908-11; judge Court of Common Pleas, Fayette Co., 1926-36. Chmn. Rep. Co. Com., Fayette Co., 1902-03. Organizer Community Fund, Uniontown, Pa.; trustee Uniontown Hosp. Republican. Presbyterian. Mason, Elk. Clubs: Triangle, Uniontown Country (Uniontown, Pa.). Home: Derrick Av. Office: Cray Law Bldg., Uniontown, Pa.

HENDERSON, Earl Fletcher, surgeon; b. Mercer Co., Pa., Sept. 26, 1892; s. John F. and Emma (Buckley) H.; B.S., Grove City Coll., 1913; M.D., U. of Pa. 1918; M.S., U. of Minn., 1927; m. Jean Thompson, July 19, 1917; children—Mary Ellen, John F., Carol Jean, Robert E. Interne Western Pa. Hosp., Pittsburgh, 1918-19; in gen. practice of medicine, 1919-23; fellow Mayo Foundation, Rochester, Minn., 1924-26; asst. Mayo Clinic, 1927-28; in gen. practice surgery since 1929; mem. surg. staff Jameson Memorial Hosp., New Castle, Pa. Dir. New Castle Y.M.C.A. Fellow Am. Coll. Surgeons; mem. A.M.A., Pa. State Med. Soc. Republican. United Presbyterian. Clubs: New Castle Lions' (pres.), New Castle Civic Music Assn. (ex-pres.). Writer articles on surg. subjects, etc. Home: 306 Lincoln Av. Office: 364 First Nat. Bank Bldg., New Castle, Pa.

HENDERSON, George; in gen. practice of law since 1912; mayor of Cumberland, 1932-34; now atty. for many companies. Address: 64 Pershing St., Cumberland, Md.

HENDERSON, Harry Oram, univ. prof.; b. Elders Ridge, Pa., Nov. 5, 1889; s. Joseph Henry and Jennie Prudence (Telford) H.; B.S., Pa. State Coll., 1915, M.S., 1916; Ph.D., U. of Minn., 1928; m. Marian Clark Saltsman, May 29, 1918; 1 son, Robert Eugene. Employed as co. agrl. agt., Crawford County, Pa., 1916-18; dairy extension specialist, W.Va. Univ., Morgantown, 1919-20, asst. prof. dairy husbandry, 1920-24, asso. prof., 1924-28, prof. dairy husbandry and head dairy dept. since 1928; sec. and dir. Sanitary Milk & Ice Cream Co., Morgantown, W.Va. Treas. of Chestnut Ridge Recreation Center Assn. Mem. A.A.A.S., Am. Dairy Sci. Assn., Am. Assn. Milk Sanitarians, W.Va. Acad. Sci., Alpha Gamma Rho, Lambda Gamma Delta, Alpha Zeta, Phi Kappa Phi, Sigma Xi. Republican. Presbyn. Author: Dairy Cattle Feeding and Management, rev. edit., 1938. Home: 424 Grand St., Morgantown, W.Va.

HENDERSON, Joseph Hugh, official dept. pub. instrnr.; b. Vanderbilt, Pa., Aug. 23, 1897; s. Joseph B. and Cora S. (Bute) H.; A.B. Allegheny Coll., 1920; A.M., Columbia U. Teachers Coll., 1926; m. Mary Helen Hess, Aug. 18, 1923; children—Joseph Hugh, Jr., John Alfred. Prin. Derry Twp. high sch., 1924-27; supervising prin. pub. schs., Zelienople, Pa., 1927-29; statistician and edn. surveys adviser, Dept. Pub. Instrn., Harrisburg, Pa. since 1931. Mem. Nat. Edn. Assn., Pa. State Edn. Assn., Alpha Chi Rho, Phi Delta Kappa, Kappa Phi Kappa. Mem. M.E.Ch. Mason. Club: Harrisburg Kennel (treas.). Home: 406 E. Main St., Shiremanstown, Pa. Office: Harrisburg, Pa.

HENDERSON, Joseph W(elles), lawyer; b. Montgomery, Pa., Feb. 6, 1890; s. Samuel B. and Jean (Wells) H.; A.B., Bucknell U., Lewisburg, Pa., 1908, A.M., 1913; LL.B., Harvard, 1913; m. Anne K. Dreisbach, May 26, 1917; 1 son, J. Welles. Admitted to Pa. bar, 1913, and began practice at Philadelphia; mem. firm Rawle & Henderson since 1916. Spl. counsel on ins., Alien Property Custodian, 1918. Mem. Am. Bar Assn. (chmn. membership com. for Pa., 1924-25; mem. admiralty com. 1923-25, 1929; mem. pub. utilities sect. 1930-35; mem. gen. council 1935; mem. fidelity and surety com., insurance sect. 1935; state del. since 1936, bd. govs. 1937), Phila. Bar Assn. (mem. com. on judicial procedure 1933—, bd. govs. since 1937), Harvard Law Sch. Assn. (mem. council), Maritime Law Assn. (exec. com. since 1936), International Assn. Insurance Council (com. on fire and marine insurance; asso. editor Am. maritime cases 1931—), Phi Kappa Psi. Trustee Bucknell U.; chmn. Com. of Pa. State Bar Assn. to Consider Necessity for Constitutional Conv., 1933, Com. on Pa. Constitution since 1937. Decorated Officer and Chevalier of Order of Crown of Italy. Republican. Presbyn. Clubs: Union League, Philadelphia Cricket, Midday, Harvard, Sunnybrook. Home: 201 W. Gravers Lane, Chestnut Hill, Pa. Office: Packard Bldg., Philadelphia, Pa.

HENDERSON, Katharine C(reighton), (Mrs. Robert A. Henderson), mem. Dem. State Exec. Board; b. Altoona, Pa.; d. Henry T. and Mary A. (Harbaugh) Creighton; ed. Sisters of Charity, Convent, Mother House, Seaton Hill, Greensburg, Pa.; m. Robert Alvin Henderson, Apr. 23, 1902. Pres. Altoona Sunshine Soc. (women's civic and philanthropic organization; one of largest in Central Pa. Fed. Woman's Club) for 11 years; mem. State Speakers' Bur., organizer of Red Cross and Council of Nat. Defense, and county chmn. for Belgian Relief during World War; active in woman's suffrage movement (mem. speakers' bureau 1920); vice chmn. Dem. State Com. 1932-36, mem. Dem. State Exec. Com. Nat. Conv., Chicago, 1932, Phila., 1936, Catholic. Home: 849 25th St., Altoona, Pa.

HENDERSON, Leon, economist; b. Millville, N.J., May 26, 1895; s. Chester Bowen and Lida C. (Beebe) H.; A.B., Swarthmore (Pa.) Coll., 1920; post grad. work U. of Pa., 1920-22; m. Myrlie Hamm, July 25, 1925; children—Myrlie Beebe, Lyn, Leon. Instr. Wharton Sch. (U. of Pa.), 1919-22; asst. prof. economics Carnegie Inst. of Tech., 1922-23; dep. sec. Commonwealth of Pa., 1924-25; dir. consumer credit research, Russell Sage Foundation, N.Y. City, 1925-34; economic adviser and dir. research and planning div. NRA, 1934-35; mem. Nat. Industrial Recovery Bd., 1934-35; economic advisor U.S. Senate com. on mfrs., 1935; economist Dem. Nat. Campaign Com., 1936; cons. economist Works Progress Adminstrn., 1936-38; exec. sec. Temporary Nat. Econ. Com., 1938-39; Commr. Securities and Exchange Commn. since May 1939. Entered ordnance dept., U.S. Army, as pvt., 1917; promoted successively as ordnance sergt., 2d lt., 1st lt. and capt. of ordnance; hon. disch., 1919. Mem. Am. Econ. Assn., Am. Statis. Assn., Delta Upsilon. Democrat. Mason. Club: National Press. Contbr. to magazines. Home: Millville, N.J. Office: Securities and Exchange Commn. Bldg., Washington, D.C.

HENDERSON, Robert H(effner), lawyer; b. Huntingdon, Pa., July 13, 1898; s. Warren M. and M. Elizabeth (Heffner) H.; ed. Juniata Coll., 1915-16; A.B., Dickinson Coll., 1921, A.M., same, 1924; LL.B., Dickinson Coll. Law Sch., 1924; m. Blanche E. Metz, June 14, 1930; 1 dau., Mary Elizabeth. Admitted to Pa. bar, 1924, and since engaged in gen. practice of law at Huntingdon; mem. firm Henderson and Henderson; mem. Rep. State Com., 1934-35. Served in C.A., U.S.A. during World War. Mem. Huntingdon County and Pa. State bar Assns. Delta Chi. Republican. Mem. Reformed Ch. Mason. Club: Country (Huntingdon). Home: 409 4th St. Office: 306 Penn St., Huntingdon, Pa.

HENDERSON, Walter C.; b. Chelsea, Mass., July 6, 1876; s. William C. and Margaret (Robertson) H.; prep. edn. high sch., Somerville; LL.B., Boston U., 1903; A.B., George Washington U., 1926; m. Margaret L. Orpin, Oct. 21, 1908; 1 son, Fletcher O. Practiced in Boston, 1903-07; dist. law officer of Forest Service, 1908-10; admitted to bar U.S. Supreme Court, 1910; asst. to solicitor of Dept. of Agr., Washington, 1910-16; asst. chief. Biol. Survey, 1916-26, asso. chief since Jan. 1, 1927. Mem. Am. Ornithologists' Union, Am. Forestry Assn., Nat. Conservation Assn., Cooper Ornithol. Club, Am. Soc. Mammalogists, Biol. Soc. Washington, Nat. Assn. Audubon Socs., Epsilon Pi; fellow A.A. A.S. Republican. Episcopalian. Mason. Clubs: Cosmos, Kenwood Golf and Country. Home: 8 Magnolia Parkway, Chevy Chase, Md. Office: Biological Survey, Dept. Agriculture, Washington, D.C.

HENDRICKS, William Craig, surgeon; b. Bedford, Pa., Mar. 2, 1901; s. Irvin Washington and Elizabeth May (Craig) H.; grad. Mercersburg Acad., 1918; A.B., Haverford Coll., 1922; student U. of Chicago, 1924, Franklin and Marshall Coll., 1924-25; M.D., U. of Pa., 1929; m. Dorothy Helen Weaver, 1929; children—Barbara Joyce, William Craig. Interne Western Pa. Hosp., Pittsburgh, Pa., 1929-30, asst. visiting surgeon, 1930-32; visiting surgeon Brookville (Pa.) Hosp. since 1932. Mem. Jefferson County, Pa. State med. socs., Am. Med. Assn., Chi Phi. Republican. Home: 68 Walnut St. Office: 319 Main St., Brookville, Pa.

HENDRICKSON, David, artist; b. St. Paul, Minn.; Feb. 4, 1896; s. Frank and Carlotta (Johnson) H.; ed. St. Paul Inst. Fine Arts (part time), 1911-15, Best's Art Sch., San Francisco, 1919-20, Beaux Arts, Toulouse, France, spring 1919, various groups New York City since 1922; m. Margaret Ellen Renshaw, Apr. 15, 1923; 1 son, Ian David. Engaged as newspaper artist, St. Paul, Minn., 1913-17; advertising illustration, San Francisco, Calif., 1919-22; advertising, book and mag. illustration, New York City and New Hope, Pa., since 1922. Served with 25th Engrs. U.S.A., 1917-19, with A.E.F. in France; in Meuse-Argonne campaign. Mem. and recording sec. Soc. Am. Etchers, Inc., N.Y. City. Mem. Soc. Illustrators, Artists Guild, New York, Phillips Mill Community Assn., New Hope, Pa. Home: Sugan Rd., New Hope, Pa.

HENDRICKSON, Harold Alvin, gen. bldg. contractor; b. Englewood, N.J., Feb. 23, 1891; s. Winfield and Alice Gertrude (Ford) H.; student Manual Training High Sch., Brooklyn, N.Y., 1912-14; m. Katherine Schaefer, Aug. 12, 1917; children—Madeline, Harold Alvin, Mildred Janet. Apprentice carpenter, 1911-15, carpenter, 1915-17; supt. of constrn., draftsman and estimator, Davis Carpenter Co., N.Y. City, 1917-20; mem. firm H. A. Hendrickson & Co., gen. bldg. constrn., Red Bank, N.J., since 1920; dir. Red Bank Bldg. & Loan Assn. Mem. bd. edn. Red Bank, N.J., since 1926, pres. same since 1934; pres. Monmouth Co. Sch. Bds. Assn., 1937-38. Mem. exec. com. N.J. State Firemen's Assn. Dir. Red Bank Y.M.C.A.; mem. Monmouth Co. Vocational Sch. Survey Advisory Com. Mem. Gen. Contractor's Assn. of Red Bank (pres.), Holland Soc. of N.Y. Democrat. Club: Mason. Elk. Club: Monmouth Boat (Red Bank). Home: 82 Newman Springs Rd., Red Bank, N.J.

HENDRICKSON, John Harold, banker; b. Keyport, N.J., Nov. 9, 1889; s. John Schanck and Ella Stoutenborough (Longstreet) H.; student Keyport (N.J.) High Sch., 1896 to 1904, Trainers Pvt. Sch., Perth Amboy, N.J., 1905; m. Laura Ethel Cadoo, June 2, 1915; children—Betty Cadoo, Helen (dec.). Clk. Keyport (N.J.) Banking Co., 1907-09, asst. cashier, 1916-22, cashier 1922-29, v.p. dir. and trust officer since 1929; dir. 2d Keyport Loan Assn. Trustee Green Grove Cemetery, Keyport, N.J. Mem. Am. Inst. of Banking (pres. Monmouth chapter 1938-39). Republican. Reformed Church. Mason (Caesarea Lodge). Club: Holland Society (New York). Home: 99 Warren St. Office: care The Keyport Banking Co., Keyport, N.J.

HENDRIX, Nevins Byford; asso. in pathology and surg. pathology, U. of Md.; attending surgeon King's Daughter's Hosp.; visiting surgeon Charles Town (W.Va.) Gen. Hosp. and St. Joseph's Hosp., Baltimore; cons. surgeon B.&O. R.R. Address: 231 W. King St., Martinsburg, W.Va.

HENKE, Frederick Goodrich, college prof.; b. Alden, Hardin Co., Ia., Aug. 2, 1876; s. Edward William and Anna Margaret (Rudolph) H.; A.B., Morningside Coll., Sioux City, Ia., 1897; A.M., Northwestern U., 1908; Ph.D., U. of Chicago, 1910; m. Selma Aurora Hirsch, Sept. 4, 1901. Ordained M.E. ministry, 1900; pastor St. Paul's Ch., Kiukiang, China, 1901-04; dist. supt. Kiukiang, 1904-07; v.p. and prof. homiletics, William Nast Coll., Kiukiang, 1904-07; fellow in philosophy, Northwestern U., 1908-09; prof. philosophy and psychology, U. of Nanking, China, 1910-13; prof. philosophy and edn., Willamette (Ore.) U., 1913-14; acting. prof. same, 1914-16, Truman D. Collins prof. same since June 1916, Allegheny Coll., Meadville, Pa.; also dir. summer session. Pres. Assn. of Liberal Arts Colleges of Pa. for Advancement of Teaching, 1930-1938; chmn. Crawford County (Pa.) Council on Adult Edn., Recreation and Youth Program since 1935. Mem. N.E.A., Pa. State Edn. Assn. (pres. Dept. Higher Edn. 1938), Am. Philos. Assn., Royal Asiatic Soc., Phi Delta Kappa, Alpha Chi Rho, Phi Beta Kappa, Omicron Delta Kappa, Pi Gamma Mu, Kappa Phi Kappa (nat. treas.), Meadville Lit. Union. Mason. Republican. Author: The Psychology of Ritualism, 1910. Translator: The Philosophy of Wang Yang-Ming, 1916. Contbr. numerous articles to religious and philos. jours. Established first psychol. lab. in China, 1910; lecturer on ednl. subjects before teachers' institutes. Home: 643 William St., Meadville, Pa.

HENN, Arthur W(ilbur), zoologist and conservationist; b. Evansville, Ind., Mar. 8, 1890; s. August Wm. and Caroline (Weisheimer) H.; A.B., Ind. Univ., 1914, A.M., same, 1915; study Columbia U., 1915-17, (hon.) D.Sc., Westminster Coll., 1937; m. Martha Jean Findley, May 27, 1925. Began as sci. asst., Field Mus., Chicago, Ill., 1909; with Am. Mus. Natural History, N.Y. City, 1919-22; with Carnegie Mus., Pittsburgh since 1922; explorations in Andes of Colombia and Ecuador, S.A., 1912-14; initiated movement to improve Pittsburgh municipal zoo and now sec. Pittsburgh Zoological Soc., Inc.; active in conservation work, pres. Pymatuning Conservation Assn., Inc., Pa., mem. nat. exec. bd. Izaak Walton League of America. Served with Med. Dept., 326th Inf., U.S.A., 1918-19; with A.E.F. in France. Mem. Phi Beta Kappa, Sigma Xi, Phi Sigma. United Presbyn. Home: 1441 Squirrel Hill Av., Pittsburgh, Pa.

HENNEN, Ray Vernon, geologist; b. nr. St. Cloud, W.Va., June 18, 1875; s. William Harrison and Lydie Ann (White) H.; A.B., West Virginia U., 1900, B.S. in C.E., 1901; m. Cora May Hagan, June 26, 1907; children—Clara Ann (dec.), Kathleen Matilda, Ray V. (dec.). Engr. Carter Oil Co., Sistersville, W.Va., 1901-02; engr. and chief clk. W.Va. Geol. Survey, 1902-07, asst. geologist, 1907-18; chief geologist for Carter Oil Co. in expdn. to Peru, Patagonia, Argentine, S.A., 1913; in private practice as cons. geologist, 1918-19; asst. dir. Military Mapping of W.Va., 1918, until Armistice; chief geologist Transcontinental Oil Co., 1919-29, cons. geologist, 1929-30; dir. Big Lake Oil Co., Plymouth Oil Co., 1923-25; again in private practice as cons. geologist since 1930. Mem. Cadet Corps, W.Va. U., 2 yrs. Mem. Relief Bd. for Monongalia Co., W.Va., 6 mos., 1934. Fellow Geol. Soc. America; mem. Am. Assn. Petroleum Geologists, Am. Inst. Mech. Engrs., A.A.A.S., W.Va. Coal Mining Inst. Republican. Mason. Author of following reports: "Marshall, Wetzell & Tyler Counties," 1909, "Wirt, Roane and Calhoun Counties," 1911, "Doddridge & Harrison Counties," 1912, "Monongalia, Marion & Taylor Counties," 1913, "Wyoming and McDowell Counties," 1915, "Braxton and Clay Counties," 1917, "Fayette County," 1918, "Geologic Structure Contour Map of Wood, Pleasants and Ritchie Counties," 1910, the base and part of economic data for "State, Coal, Oil and Gas Map of W.Va.," "State R.R. Map of W.Va.," sr. author (with David D. Reger) of "Report on Preston County," 1914, "Logan and Mingo Counties," 1914; author of following papers in Am. Assn. Petroleum Geologists bulletins: "Memorial to Dr. I. C. White," "Big Lake Oil Pool, Reagan County, Tex."; senior author (with R. J. Metcalf) paper on "Yates Oil Pool, Pecos County, Texas," Am. Assn. Petroleum Geologists bulletin; pub. first complete detailed section of the Pottsville Series in W.Va., showing succession of all coal beds and other strata; 1918, compiled and pub. the first complete graphic section showing names and successions of all coal beds in W.Va.; 1923, recommended acquisition of oil and gas leaseholds that led to opening of great Yates oil pool of Pecos County, Tex. Home: 232 Grand St. Office: 816 Monongahela Bldg., Morgantown, W.Va.; (mailing address: Box 675).

HENNESSEY, John J(oseph), county commissioner; b. Heckshersville, Pa., Feb. 20, 1888; s. William F. and Mary (Hart) H.; student High School, Central High, Phila., 1900-03; m. Kathryn V. McBride, Apr. 29, 1915; children—Paul, Kathryn, Jack, Jeanne. Inspector U.S. Shipping Bd., 1917-22; business mgr. Catholic Union Review, nat. paper, 1922-25; sec. Benedict Service Club, 1925-28; pres. Henley & Co., mfg. agents, Phila., since 1928; examiner State Ins. Dept., 1932-35; county commr., Phila. Co. since 1935. Mem. Cath. Young Men's Assn. (pres. 1922-25), Cath. Laymen's Retreat, Knights of Columbus (4°), Archbishop Ryan Assn., Loyal Order of Moose. Democrat. Home: 1816 S. 56th St. Office: City Hall, Philadelphia, Pa.

HENNIGHAUSEN, Frederick H., mem. law firm Hennighausen & Stein. Address: 231 St. Paul Pl., Baltimore, Md.

HENNING, Stanley Raymond, prin. high sch.; b. Mehoopany, Pa., Sept. 13, 1890; s. John Casper and Juliette (Burgess) H.; diploma Phillips Exeter Acad., 1908-11; B.S., Pa. State Coll., 1915, grad. student, summers 1915-23; study U. of Pa. Extension Sch., 1930-36; m. Julia Decker, June 1, 1918; children—Stanley Phillip, Norma Elaine, Lois Marjory, Doris Julia, Sherman Christy (dec.), Carl Granville. Engaged in teaching, 1915-20; prin. high sch., Kingston Twp., 1920-24; teacher mathematics, G.A.R. Memorial High Sch., Wilkes-Barre, Pa., then supervisor mathematics, same, 1925-30, prin. since 1930. Served as twp. auditor, 10 yrs.; dir. bd. edn. Kingston Twp. Mem. Nat. Edn. Assn., Pa. State Edn. Assn., Secondary Sch. Prins. of Pa., Alpha Zeta, Phi Kappa Phi. Republican. Methodist (mem. official bd. Trucksville Ch.). Clubs: Craftsmens, United Sportsmen (Wilkes-Barre). Home: Trucksville, Pa. Office: Wilkes-Barre, Pa.

HENNING, William Lewis, coll. prof.; b. Defiance Co., O., Jan. 4, 1900; s. George Frederick and Lizzie S. (Brinck) H.; B.S., Ohio State U., Columbus, O., 1921; M.S., Pa. State Coll., 1923; student summer sch., U. of Wis., Madison, Wis., 1931,1932, 1933, 1934, 1935, 1936, Ph.D., 1937; unmarried. Asst. animal husbandry, Ohio State U., Columbus, O., 1921-22; instr. animal husbandry, Pa. State Coll., 1922-24, asst. prof. 1924-30, asso. prof.-1930-38, prof. since 1938; asso. with Henning Bros., mchts. hybrid seed corn, pure-bred livestock, Defiance Co., O. Served as apprentice, S.A.T.C., U.S. Navy, 1918-19. Mem. Am. Southdown Breeders' Assn. (sec.-treas. since 1924), A.A. A.S., Am. Soc. of Animal Production, Acacia, Alpha Zeta, Phi Kappa Phi, Sigma Xi, Phi Sigma, Gamma Sigma Delta. Lutheran. Mason (Consistory, Commandery, Shriner). Club: University (State College, Pa.). Home: 331 W. College Av. Office: 203 Agriculture Bldg., State College, Pa.

HENNINGER, Frank LaMont, clergyman; b. Williamsport, Pa., May 16, 1900; s. Frank Warren and Mary Clarinda (Parks) H.; A.B., Dickinson Coll., 1924, A.M., same, 1926; B.D., Drew Theol. Sem., Madison, N.J., 1926; Th.M., Drew U., 1928, Th.D., same, 1930; m. Harriet Seibert Stoner, Sept. 1, 1924; children—Carolyn Mary, William McDowell. Ordained to ministry M.E. Ch., 1926, and pastor various chs. in Pa., 1920-28; dir. student employment, Drew U., 1928, 30; pastor Danville, Pa., 1930-34; pastor Fifth St. Ch., Harrisburg, Pa., 1934-39; supt. Sunbury Dist., Central, Pa. Conf. M.E. Chs. since 1939; dir. Methodist Training Camp, Central Pa. Conf. M.E. Ch. Served in U.S.N., 1918. Served as sch. dir. Harrisburg Bd. Edn. since 1938; pres. Harrisburg Council of Christian Edn.; dean Harrisburg Sch. of Leadership in Christian Edn.; mem. exec. com. Dauphin Co. Council Christian Edn. Mem. Kappa Sigma, Tau Kappa Alpha. Republican. Mem. M.E. Ch. Mason (32°). Home: 148 Arch St., Sunbury, Pa.

HENNINGER, G(eorge) Ross, elec. engr., editor; b. Hamilton, O., May 22, 1898; s. George Henry Thomas and Harriet (Ross) H.; B.S. in E.E., U. of Southern Calif., 1922; m. Leah Katherine Craven, Nov. 16, 1923; children—Beverley Anne, Nancy Katharine. Employed in various capacities, Southern Calif. Edison Co., Los Angeles, while attdg. coll., 1917-22; in employ Westinghouse Electric & Mfg. Co., East Pittsburgh, Pa., 1922-23; asst. elec. protection engr., Southern Calif. Edison Co., 1923-24; engring. editor "Electrical West" mag., San Francisco, 1924-30; asso. editor publns. Am. Inst. Elec. Engrs., New York City, 1930-32, editor since Jan. 1, 1933. Active in work for Boy Scouts since 1916. Vice-pres. Teaneck, N.J., Taxpayers League, 1935-36. Trustee Haworth Municipal Library, Haworth, N.J., since 1936. Registered professional engr., State of New York. Mem. Am. Inst. Elec. Engrs. Republican. Methodist. Home: Hennessy St., Haworth, N.J. Office: 33 W. 39th St., New York, N.Y.

HENRETTA, James Edward, pres. Holgate Bros. Co.; b. Conneautville, Pa., Oct. 5, 1874; s. James and Birget (Bradley) H.; student Edinboro Normal; A.B., Allegheny Coll., Meadville, 1897; m. Antoinette Frances Wayave, Aug. 15, 1901; children—James Edward, William Terrence, Thomas Eugene, Frances May. Asst. prin. Waterford (Pa.) Acad., 1897-98; supervising prin. Kane Pub. Sch., 1898-1902; with Holgate Bros. since 1902, vice-pres., 1902-34, pres. since 1934; pres. Kane Mfg. Corpn., Kane Federal Savings & Loan Assn., vice-pres. Kane Bank & Trust Co. Trustee Clarion State Teachers Coll., 1933-37; dir. McKean Co. Tuberculosis and Health Soc.; dir. Y.M.C.A., Kane; pres. Alumni Assn. of Allegheny College. Mem. Phi Beta Kappa. Republican. Conglist. Mason. Club: Rotary. Home: 115 Dawson St. Office: Biddle and Welsh Sts., Kane, Pa.

HENRICI, Max, journalist; b. Economy (now Ambridge) Pa., June 8, 1884; s. Jacob and Viola (Irons) H.; grad. Pittsburgh Central High School, 1901; student U. of Pa., 1901-03; m. Ernestine Vaughan, May 28, 1910 (now deceased); 1 son, Anthony (deceased); m. 2d, Hilda Gundelfinger, Mar. 5, 1928. Sch. teacher, Barranquitas, P.R., 1903; reporter Pittsburgh Press, 1904-08, N.Y. Herald, 1908-10; city editor and news editor Spartanburg (S.C.) Herald, 1910-14; financial editor Pittsburgh Sun, 1915-17; editorial writer Pittsburgh Sun and Pittsburgh Post, 1919-27; editorial writer Pittsburgh Sun-Telegraph since 1928. Served as 2d lt. Air Service, U.S. Army, attached to Bureau Aircraft Production, during World War. Mem. Soc. of War of 1812, Sons of the Am. Revolution, Naturalists Club of Pittsburgh, Republican. Presbyterian. Author: Cy and Max Abroad (reprint of articles about travels in Europe and Africa, orginally published in Pittsburgh Sun; illustrated by Cyrus C. Hungerford, cartoonist); Forestry Needs (reprint of editorials in Pittsburgh Post); The Magical Growth of Pittsburgh Real Estate (pub. by Pittsburgh Real Estate Bd). Home: Route 3, Coraopolis, Pa. Office: Sun-Telegraph, Pittsburgh, Pa.

HENRY, Arnold Kahle, coll. dean; b. Marienville, Pa., Feb. 5, 1898; s. Samuel Mays and Emma (Kerr) H.; B.S. in Econ., U. of Pa., 1921, M.A., 1924, Ph.D., 1929; m. Lydia Leaming Cresse-Johnston, Aug. 1930. Instr. commerce and transportation, U. of Pa., 1921-30, asst. prof., 1930-37, asso. prof. transportation and pub. utilities, since 1937, asst. dir. student personnel, 1926-34, field sec., 1934-36, asst. dir. admissions, 1922-36, dir. admissions, 1936-39, dean of student affairs since 1939. Mem. S.A.T.C., 1918. Mem. Kappa Sigma. Republican. Clubs: Phila. Cricket, Lenape (Phila.). Home: 174 Hillcrest Av., Chestnut Hill, Philadelphia. Address: University of Pa., Philadelphia, Pa.

HENRY, George McClellan, lawyer, author; b. Newville, Pa., June 16, 1877; s. Alexander and Ellen (Miller) H.; LL.B., U. of Pa., 1904; m. Elise Koronski, Oct. 10, 1907 (died Jan. 10, 1929); 1 son, George McClellan. Admitted to Pa. bar, 1904, and since in practice at Phila. Served as private Co. I, 3d Regt., Pa. Vols., during Spanish-Am. War. Trustee, treas. and gen. counsel Joseph Priestly House, Inc. Mem. Phila. Bar Assn. Republican. Unitarian. Mason. Author: Pennsylvania Trial Evidence, 1914, 3d edit., 1939; Equity jurisdiction and Practice, 1933. Editor: Pennsylvania Digest of Decisions, 1936. Revised Sadler's Criminal Procedure in Pa., 1937. Contbr. to legal jours. Home: Leopard Rd., Berwyn, Pa. Office: Finance Bldg., Philadelphia, Pa.

HENRY, James Anderson, v.p. Weirton Steel Co.; b. Maysville, Ky., Feb. 4, 1885; s. Jefferson Thomas and Henrietta (Bruce) H.; ed. grammar and high schs.; m. Bertha Edwards, Feb. 24, 1909 (died June 28, 1927); m. 2d, Florence Peterson, May 11, 1929. With Weirton Steel Co. since 1927, beginning as asst. gen. mgr. of sales, now v.p. Home: Bryden Road, Steubenville, O. Office: Weirton Steel Co., Weirton, W.Va.

HENRY, John Thompson, civil engr.; b. Reedsville, Pa., Jan. 18, 1885; s. James Beatty and Jane Elizabeth (Thompson) H.; grad. Bellefonte (Pa.) Acad., 1904; B.S., Pa. State Coll., 1908; m. Ethel Rebecca Carothers, June 26, 1918; children—James Beatty, John Carothers, Robert McFarlane. Mining engr., 1908-16; safety engr., 1916-18; land surveying, gen. engring., cons. engr. since 1918; dir. Bellefonte Trust Co.; trustee and pres. bd. Centre County Hosp., Bellefonte; sec. and dir. Port Matilda (Pa.) Cemetery; pres. and dir. Port Matilda (Pa.) Fire Co.; dir. Presbyn. Home of

Huntingdon Presbytery, Hollidaysburg; trustee and pres. bd. Huntingdon Presbytery. Dir. Township Sch.; county surveyor and engr. and mem. Bd. of Viewers, Centre Co. Mem. Centre Co. Engrs. Soc., Phi Delta Theta. Republican. Presbyterian. Clubs: Engineers (Phila.). Address: Martha Furnace, Pa.

HENRY, Wilbur Frank, dir. athletics; b. Mansfield, O., Oct. 31, 1897; s. Ulysses Sherman and Bertha (Frank) H.; B.S., Washington & Jefferson Coll., 1919; m. Marie Floding, Sept. 16, 1927. Engaged as coach and player professional football, also propr. men's shop, Canton, O., 1920-29; coach professional football teams, Canton Bulldogs, 1920-23, New York Giants, 1926, Pottsville Maroons, 1924, 27; dir. athletics, Washington and Jefferson Coll., Washington, Pa. since 1929, asst. coach football, 1929-34, coach basketball, 1929-30. Served as pvt. inf., U.S.A., 1918. Mem. Alpha Tau Omega. Lutheran. Mason. Home: 308 E. Wheeling St., Washington, Pa.

HENSEL, George Washington, Jr., hardware mcht. and banker; b. Quarryville, Pa., May 3, 1866; s. George W. and Anna (Uhler) H.; ed. rural sch.; m. Josephine Martin, June 1, 1893. Served as postmaster, Quarryville, during President Cleveland's second adminstrn.; feature writer Philadelphia North American Weekly, 16 yrs.; mem. staff Philadelphia Inquirer, 12 yrs.; in hardware business (organized by father 1837) since 1882; pres. Quarryville Nat. Bank since 1908. U.S. Jury commr., Eastern Dist. of Pa., since 1935. Served continuously as mem. Dem. Co. Com. for 52 yrs., Nat. del., 1936; mem. bd. of Viewers of Lancaster County since 1924, Valley Forge Park Commn. since 1935, Bd. of Assistance of Lancaster Co.; pres. and dir. Martinsville Horse Detective Assn.; dir. Humane Soc. Mem. Pa. Soc. of New York, Lancaster Co. Hist. Soc., Pa. German Soc.; founder and pres. Chester and Lancaster Co. Old Fiddler's Assn. Democrat. Reformed Ch. Hibernating gov. and founder Slumbering Ground Hog Lodge, Quarryville. Contbr. to "Co-op Review." Address: Quarryville, Pa.

HENSLER, Carl Peter, clergyman; b. Pittsburgh, Pa., Nov. 7, 1898; s. Charles P. and Margaret (Klein) H.; student St. Vincent Prep. Sch., Latrobe, Pa., 1912-16; A.B., St. Vincent Coll., Latrobe, 1920; D.D., Univ. of Propaganda, Rome, Italy, 1924; student Catholic Univ. of America, Washington, D.C., 1932-33. Ordained priest Roman Catholic Ch., Mar. 15, 1924; asst. pastor St. Brendan R.C. Ch., Braddock, Pa., 1924-30; prof. of sociology and ethics, Cath. Univ. of Peking, Peiping, China, 1930-32; asst. pastor St. Lawrence Ch., Pittsburgh, since 1933. Co-founder St. Joseph House of Hospitality, Pittsburgh, 1938-39; co-chaplain Assn. Cath. Trade Unionists, 1938-39; one of three arbitrators selected to settle dispute between Pittsburgh Rys. and street car men's union, 1938; lecturer on labor problems. Contbr. of articles on economic questions to magazines. Democrat. Mem. K. of C. Home: 5325 Penn Av., Pittsburgh, Pa.

HEPBRON, James M(erritt), criminologist; b. Chestertown, Md., Feb. 17, 1891; s. Archer Maxwell and Lida Pleasanton (Merritt) H.; grad. Baltimore (Md.) City Coll., 1910; LL.B., U. of Md., 1913; studied penal and police methods and compilation of crime statistics, Europe, 1927-28; LL.D., Washington Coll., Chestertown, Md., 1930; hon. D.Sc., Temple University, Phila., 1934; m. Virginia Grace Carrick, December 17, 1913; 1 dau., Virginia (deceased). Pub. of law books, 1913-17; mem. Fosdick commn. on training camps, 1917-19; mem. U.S. Interdepartmental Bd., 1919-22; asst. dir. Baltimore Criminal Justice Commn., 1922-24, mng. dir. since 1924; instr. in criminology, Johns Hopkins, 1926-28, consultant, Pa. State Crime Commn., 1928; mng. dir. Community Fund of Baltimore since 1929. Mem. Governor's Advisory Com. on Unemployment Relief; mem. Governor's Com. on Inferior Courts, 1939; mem. com. on arrangements of Attorney General's Conf. on Crime; mem. Md. Commn. on Inter-State Compacts. Secretary U.S. Federation Justice, Goodwill Industries; consulting director Philadelphia Criminal Justice Assn.; chmn. finance com. Am. Prison Congress, 1931; consultant Washington Criminal Justice Assn.; pres. Nat. Assn. of Crime Commn. Execs., 1939; mem. of Md. Youth Commn., Mayor's Com. on Recreation (Baltimore); mem. bd. Baltimore Council of Social Agencies; chmn. Charities Endorsement Com., Baltimore Council of Social Agencies; dir. Community Placement Bur. of Baltimore. Trustee Morgan Coll. and Maryland Conference Social Work. Democrat. Methodist. Club: University. Contbr. to editorial page Baltimore Evening Sun, also articles and monographs including, "Probation and Penal Treatment in Baltimore," "Crime Commissions, Their Origin, Purpose and Accomplishments." In charge housing, feeding and med. care of Am. refugees in Spain until evacuation of Americans from Madrid. Home: 427 E. Lake Av. Office: 22 Light St., Baltimore, Md.

HEPPENHEIMER, Ernest J., judge; b. Jersey City, N.J., Feb. 24, 1869; s. Frederick and Christine (Hofer) H.; ed. Peekskill (N.Y.) Mil. Acad. and Phillips Acad., Andover, Mass.; m. Ruth Norris, Apr. 8, 1914. Mem. F. Heppenheimer's Sons, lithographers, New York, 1889-96; cattle ranching in Tex., 1889-97; organizer, 1897, and pres. since 1906, Colonial Life Ins. Co. of America. Pres. Bd. of Aldermen, Jersey City, 1910-13, also commr. of finance; Dem. presdl. elector, 1912; pres. N.J. Harbor Commn., 1912-13; apptd. judge Court of Errors and Appeals, by Gov. Woodrow Wilson, Mar. 1913; reappointed by Gov. Edge, 1919, for term which expired 1925. Dir. Northern Valley Nat. Bank, Tenafly, N.J.; dir. Trust Co. of N.J., Provident Instn. for Savings in Jersey City. Mem. Assn. Life Ins. Presidents. Episcopalian. Clubs: Cartaret, Knickerbocker Country. Home: Tenafly, N.J. Office: 921 Bergen Av., Jersey City, N.J.

HEPPENSTALL, Charles William, pres. Heppenstall Co.; b. Phila., Pa., June 12, 1872; s. Sam and Alice (Talbot) H.; student Indiana State Normal Sch., and Pa. State Coll.; m. Rachel Eleanor Bole, 1899; children—Charles William, Robert Bole, Rachel Eleanor; m. 2d, Helen Wells Quinn, Feb. 27, 1924. Began with Heppenstall Co. (then Tretheway Mfg. Co.), Pittsburgh, Pa., 1893, mgr., 1898-1920, pres., 1920-39, chmn. bd. since 1939. Home: W. Woodland Rd. Office: 4620 Hatfield St., Pittsburgh, Pa.

HEPPENSTALL, Robert Bole, steel mfr.; b. Pittsburgh, Pa., Jan. 12, 1904; s. Charles William and Rachel Eleanor (Bole) H.; grad. Peabody High School, 1921; A.B., Williams Coll., 1925; studied Carnegie Inst. Tech., 1925-26; m. Katherine Duncan Munroe, Aug. 19, 1926; children—Robert Bole, Edward Munroe, Charles Talbot, John Alexander. Began as apprentice Heppenstall Co., steel mfrs., 1925, advancing through various positions, becoming v.p. and dir., 1928; pres., 1939. Mem. Am. Inst. Mining and Metall. Engrs., Am. Iron and Steel Inst., Am. Soc. for Metals, Theta Delta Chi. Republican. United Presbyterian. Mason (Shriner). Clubs: Duquesne, Longue Vue, Pittsburgh Athletic Assn. (Pittsburgh). Home: 5714 Lynnehaven Road. Office: 4620 Hatfield St., Pittsburgh, Pa.

HERB, Charles Oliver, mech. engring., editor; b. Donaldson, Pa., Nov. 17, 1895; s. Samuel F. and Mary (Schlegel) H.; ed. Drexel Inst., Phila., evening courses mech. engring., 4 yrs.; m. Beulah Irene Herb, June 5, 1925; children—Marion Alice, Charles Oliver, Jr. Engaged as mech. draftsman, 1912-19; asso. with Industrial Press, New York, N.Y., since 1919, as associate editor Machinery mag. Mem. Am. Soc. Mech. Engrs. Republican. Mem. M.E. Ch. Mason. Author: Die Casting—Machines—Dies—Alloys, 1936; also numerous articles on engring. and mfg. in the metal-working industries. Home: 29 Oakley Av., Summit, N.J. Office: 148 Lafayette St., New York, N.Y.

HERBACH, Joseph, assn. official; b. Hungary, Aug. 18, 1873; s. Gimbel and Johanna (Goldberger) H.; student pub. sch., Phila., 1885-88; night course, Temple U., Phila., 1898, Union Coll., Phila., 1909; came to U.S., 1885, naturalized, 1896; m. Fannie Wiesler, Dec. 31, 1900; 1 dau., Harriett (Mrs. Leo Lichtenstein). Cigar mfr., Phila., 1896-1910; official sec. Eagleville Sanatorium, Phila., 1910-11; office exec. Sacks Bros., Phila., 1911-14; mgr. Girar Garment House, Phila., 1914-16; sec. and treas. Pannonia Beneficial Assn., Phila., since 1916; sec. dist. Grand Lodge, B'nai B'rith, comprising Pa., N.J., Del., W.Va., since 1918; founder, 1924, and editor Phila. Jewish Times, 1924-27; pres. Homewood Sch., Germantown and Wissahickon, Phila., 1926-31; now hon. pres.; chmn. Bur. of Jewish Children, 1918-26. Mem. Fed. of Jewish Charities, Phila. (dir., 1916-26, hon. dir. since 1931), Aleph Zadik Aleph (mem. supreme advisory council since 1927). Democrat. Jewish religion. B'nai B'rith. Home: Bennett Hall Apts. Office: 709 N. Franklin St., Philadelphia, Pa.

HERBEN, Stephen Joseph, prof. English philology; b. Montclair, N.J., Mar. 14, 1897; s. Rev. Stephen J. and Grace Ida (Foster) H.; B.Litt., Rutgers U., 1920 (as of 1918); M.A., Princeton U., 1921, Ph.D., 1924; m. Caroline Robbins, Sept. 21, 1932. Fellow Am. Scandinavian Foundation, U. of Copenhagen, 1922-23; spl. coach in Old English, Oxford U., 1923-24; contributing consultant C. & G. Merriam & Co., 1926-27; instr. English, Princeton U., 1924-28; asso. prof. English philology, Bryn Mawr Coll., 1928-37, prof. since 1937. Guest lecturer Sorbonne, Copenhagen, Bonn and various Am. univs. Mem. Delta Phi. Contbr. to mags. Home: 412 Berkley Road, Haverford, Pa.

HERBER, E(lmer) C(harles), educator; b. New Tripoli, Pa., Jan. 26, 1900; s. Alfred James and Amanda (Sieger) H.; A.B., Ursinus Coll., 1925; A.M., U. of Pa., 1929; m. Verna Weiss, June 15, 1929; 1 son, Charles Joseph. Science teacher, Springfield High Sch., Pleasant Valley, Pa., 1920-22, Palmerton (Pa.) High Sch., 1925-26; instr. in biology, Dickinson Coll., Carlisle, Pa., since 1929. Mem. A.A.A.S., Am. Soc. Parasitology, Pa. Acad. Science, Sigma Xi. Republican. Mem. Reformed Ch. Writer of several articles. Home: 416 W. South St., Carlisle, Pa.

HERBERT, James Cassidy, newspaper editor; b. Sharon, Pa., Apr. 6, 1875; s. George Dixon and Elba (Cassidy) H.; ed. pub. schs. and tutors; unmarried. Began as reporter York (Pa.) Gazette, 1893, mng. editor and editor, 1895-1904; news editor Harrisburg Patriot, 1905-12; city editor Harrisburg Telegraph, 1912-13; editor Lancaster News, 1914-15, The West Virginian, (Fairmont) 1915-21, The Exponent, Clarksburg, 1921-24, Morgantown Post, 1924-26; editor The West Virginian, and news editor Fairmont Times since 1926; dir. Marion Co. Securities Co. Mason. Rotarian. Office: Newspaper Bldg., Fairmont, W.Va.*

HERBERT, Robert Black, publisher; b. Greensburg, Pa., Dec. 29, 1886; s. Robert Watson and Margaret McGinley (Black) H.; student Greensburg pub. sch., 1893-1902, Kiskiminetas Sch., Saltsburg, Pa., 1902-06; Ph.B., Yale, 1910; m. Edith Angeline Huff, June 17, 1915. Bank clk., Greensburg, Pa., 1910-11; entered newspaper business with Daily Tribune, Greensburg, Pa., as clerk, 1911; worked in circulation dept. and advertising department; sec. and treas. Tribune Review Pub. Co., pubs. Greensburg (Pa.) Morning Review and Greensburg Evening Tribune since 1923. Served as 1st lt., Co. I, 110th Inf., 28th Div., U.S. Army, during World War; wounded in action, 1918; disch. from hosp., 1919. Dir. Greensburg Library Assn. Mem. Sigma Chi, Delta Phi Delta (prep. sch.). Awarded Purple Heart medal, 1918. Republican. Presbyterian. Elk. Clubs: Greensburg Country (Greensburg, Pa.); Harvard-Yale-Princeton, Polo, Pike Run Country (Pittsburgh, Pa.). Home: 337 Alexander St. Office: N. Main St., Greensburg, Pa.

HERBST, Josephine Frey, author; b. Sioux City, Ia., Mar. 5, 1897; d. William Benton and Mary Magdalena (Frey) Herbst; student Sioux City High Sch., Morningside Coll. (Sioux City), State U. of Ia.; A.B., U. of Calif., 1918; m. John Herrmann, October 21, 1925. Awarded Guggenheim fellowship, 1936. Author: Nothing Is Sacred, 1928; Money for Love, 1929; Pity Is Not Enough, 1933; The Executioner Waits,

1934. Contbr. fiction and articles to mags. Home: Erwinna, Pa.

HERD, John Victor, ins. exec.; b. Milwaukee, Wis., Apr. 12, 1902; s. John and Laura (Prescott) H.; m. Pauline May Hoffmann, Nov. 20, 1937. V.p. Fire Assn. Group of Ins. Cos., Phila., since 1934; dir. Lumbermen's Ins. Co., Phila. Nat. Ins. Co. Episcopalian. Home: Kenilworth Apts., Germantown. Office: 401 Walnut St., Philadelphia, Pa.

HERDIC, Carl Wesley, lawyer; b. Williamsport, Pa., Sept. 11, 1893; s. Charles and Nancy (Needler) H.; ed. Williamsport Commercial High Sch., 1907-09; m. Emily May Fisher, Nov. 15, 1919; children—Carl W., John Robert. Began as bookkeeper and stenographer, 1909; studied law in offices of Seth T. McCormick, Jr., and admitted to Pa. bar, 1921, and since engaged in gen. practice of law at Williamsport; asso. with Seth T. McCormick, Jr., 1921-36; mem. firm McCormick, Herdic and Furst since 1936; admitted to practice before Pa. Supreme and Superior cts. and Dist. Ct. of U.S.; dir. Williamsport Transportation Co., Williamsport Yellow Cab Co., Inc. Served as 2d lieut. inf. U.S.A. during World War. Past comdr. Post 1, Am. Legion. Dir. Williamsport Community Trade Assn., 1939 Pa. Legion Conv. Corpn. Mem. bd. trustees, Williamsport Y.W.C.A. Mem. Am., Pa. State and Lycoming Co. bar assns. Republican. Episcopalian. Mason (K.T., 32°, Shriner). Clubs: Country, Ross, Wheel (Williamsport). Home: Williamsport, Pa. Office: 429 Pine St., Williamsport, Pa.

HEREFORD, John Withers, lawyer; b. Hogsett, W.Va., July 22, 1897; s. Robert Esom and Grace Truman (Withers) H.; LL.B., W.Va. Univ. Law Sch., 1923; A.B., W.Va. Univ. 1925; m. Vivian L. Brown, Feb. 22, 1920; children—Virginia Grace, Wanda Frances, Vivian Johnie, Gloria Jean. Engaged in teaching in rural schs., 1913-16; admitted to W.Va. bar, 1923 and since engaged in gen. practice of law at Huntington; mem. firm Peyton, Winters & Hereford; asst. prosecuting atty. for Cabell Co., Huntington, W.Va., 1933-37; asst. U.S. atty. Southern Dist. of W.Va. since 1937. Served in U.S. Navy, 1917-18. Mem. W.Va. Bar Assn., Cabell Co. Bar Assn., Delta Sigma Rho, Delta Kappa Psi. Democrat. Baptist. Moose. Odd Fellow. Jr. O.U.A.M. Club: East Huntington Civic. Home: 2055 4th Av. Office: Federal Bldg., Huntington, W.Va.

HERGESHEIMER, Ella Sophonisba, artist, portrait painter; b. Allentown, Pa., Jan. 7, 1873; d. Charles Patterson and Elamanda (Ritter) H.; desc. Johannes DePeyster, who came to America, 1652, and helped draw up first charter of New Amsterdam; desc. Claes Martinzen Van Roosevelt, ancestor of the Roosevelt family; direct desc. Charles William Peale, early Am. portrait painter; desc. Anthony Hergesheimer, who came to N.Y., 1721, and later settled in Germantown, Pa., 1723; ed. Phila. Sch. of Design, 1891-93, Pa. Acad. Fine Arts, 1898-1902, Colorassi Art Sch., Paris, France, 1903-04; European study, 1902-05; private lessons in Italy, etc.; unmarried. Began as artist in Nashville, Tenn., 1907. Works: Portrait of Commodore Matthew Fontain Maury, one of the founders of Annapolis Naval Acad., hangs in Naval Acad.; Joseph W. Byrns, former speaker Ho. of Reps., in Speaker's Lobby, U.S. Capitol; Chancellor J. H. Kirkland, Vanderbilt U.; Exgov. M. R. Patterson, Tenn. State Capitol; also portraits of other prominent people of South. Awards: European scholarship while at Pa. Acad. Fine Arts; 1st prize for portrait Southern States Art League Exhbn.; medal for portrait Appalachian Expn., Knoxville, Tenn.; 1st prize and hon. mention many times for still life, block prints, etc. Mem. D.A.R., Fellowship Pa. Acad. Fine Arts, Tenn. Soc. Artists, Washington Water Color Soc., Comn. Museum Fine Arts, Hartford, Southern Print Makers, New Orleans Art Assn., Soc. Color Block Print-makers. Democrat. Lutheran. Clubs: Nat. Arts (New York); Phila. Prints (Phila.). Nashville Studio: 1807 21st Av., S., Nashville, Tenn. Home: 435 Windsor St., Reading Pa.

HERGESHEIMER, Joseph, author; b. Phila., Pa., Feb. 15, 1880; s. Joseph and Helen Janet (MacKellar) H.; ed. short period at a Quaker sch., Phila., and Pa. Acad. Fine Arts; m. Dorothy Hemphill, 1907. Author: The Lay Anthony, 1914; Mountain Blood, 1915; The Three Black Pennys, 1917; Gold and Iron, 1918; Java Head, 1919; The Happy End, 1919; Linda Condon, 1919; San Cristobal de la Habana, 1920; Cytherea, 1922; The Bright Shawl, 1922; The Presbyterian Child, 1923; Balisand, 1924; From an Old House, 1925; Hampico, 1926; Quiet Cities, 1928; Swords and Roses, 1929; The Party Dress, 1929; The Limestone Tree, 1931; Sheridan, 1931; Berlin, 1932; Tropical Winter, 1933; The Foolscap Rose, 1934. Also contbr. to mags. Home: The Dower House, West Chester, Pa.

HERING, George C., mem. law firm Hering, James & Hitchens. Address: Delaware Trust Bldg., Wilmington, Del.

HERMAN, Albert, physician; b. Phila., Pa., July 18, 1899; s. Hyman and Tillie (Silverstein) H.; A.B., Central High Sch., Phila., Pa., 1918; M.D., U. of Pa. Med. Sch., 1924; m. Sadye Jaspan, Dec. 27, 1925; children—Joyce, Carl. After usual interneships engaged in gen. practice of medicine at Phila.; former instr. medicine, U. of Pa.; former gastroenterologist, Jewish Convalescent Home; gastroenterologist, Skin and Cancer Hosp.; adjunct physician, Mt. Sinai Hosp. Served in U.S.N. R.F. Mem. Am. Med. Assn., Phila. Co. Med. Soc., Phi Lambda Kappa. Jewish religion. B'nai B'rith. B'rith Sholom. Home: 2135 S. 5th St., Philadelphia, Pa.

HERMAN, John Warren, treas. Lukens Steel Co.; b. Pomeroy, Pa., Jan. 22, 1899; s. William Louis and Naomi (Millard) H.; ed. high sch.; m. Margaret Antrim, Nov. 4, 1919; 1 dau., Margaret Myra. With Lukens Steel Co. since 1916, beginning as clerk, treas. since 1938. Home: 1301 E. Lincoln Highway. Office: Lukens Steel Co., Coatesville, Pa.

HERMAN, Leonora Owsley (Mrs. Leon Herman), artist and poet; b. at Chicago, Ill., July 2, 1890; d. Frederick and Lucie (Pace) Owsley; ed. Agnes Scott Coll., Decatur, Ga., Finch Sch., New York City, Colarossi's, Acad. Julien, Acad. Grande Chaumiere, all of Paris, France; m. Dr. Leon Herman, May 12, 1917. Engaged in mural painting; exhbns. at Phila. Acad. Fine Arts, Art Inst. Chicago, Corcoran Nat. Art Gallery, Washington, D.C., Nat. Arts Club, New York City. Mem. Poetry Soc. of America, Poetry Soc. of England, Nat. League Am. Pen Women, Phila. Art Alliance. Fellow Pa. Acad. Author: (verse) Rather Personal, 1934. Contbr. verse to Ladies' Home Journal, Literary Digest, The Novel (London), Poetry Review (London), etc. Home: 740 Beacon Lane, Merion, Philadelphia, Pa.

HERMAN, Samuel S., lawyer; b. Lancaster Co., Pa., Mar. 7, 1883; s. J. P. and Hannah (Snyder) H.; student Yeates Sch., Lancaster, Pa., 1895-1900; B.S., U. of Pa. (mem. and capt. varsity crew); m. Mildred S. Williams, June 26, 1912; children—Nancy Donaldson, Samuel S. (dec.). Admitted to Phila. bar, 1907, and since in practice at Phila.; mem. of firm Herman and Harris, Phila., since 1930. Asst. city solicitor of Phila., 1928-32. Mem. Am., Pa. bar assns., Historical Soc. of Pa., Sigma Nu, Delta Chi. Republican. Episcopalian. Clubs: University Barge, Le Coin d'Or, Lawyers' (Phila.); Varsity (U. of Pa.); West Chester (Pa.) Golf and Country, West Chester (Pa.) Hunt. Author: Real Estate and Conveyancing, 1911. Formerly part-time instructor in money and credit and banking, Wharton Sch. of the U. of Pa., and evening sch., U. of Pa. Home: West Chester, Pa. Office: 1518 Walnut St., Philadelphia, Pa.

HERMAN, Stewart Winfield, clergyman; b. York, Pa., Nov. 17, 1878; s. Simon Henry and Mary Lydia (Rupp) H.; prep. edn., York County (Pa.) Acad.; A.B., Gettysburg (Pa.) Coll., 1899, M.A., 1902, D.D., 1919; B.D., Gettysburg Sem., 1902; D.D., Carthage (Ill.) Coll., 1917; m. Mary O'Neal Benner, Oct. 21, 1908; children—Stewart Winfield, Mary Elizabeth, Martha Jane, Janice Bemmer (dec.). Ordained ministry Luth. Ch., 1902; pastor Wrightsville, Pa., 1902-03, Zion Luth. Ch., Harrisburg, Pa., since 1904. Pres. E. Pa. Synod, 1914-15; pres. Foreign Mission Bd. United Luth. Ch. since 1930; pres. publ. bd. United Luth. Ch. since 1934; mem. investment commn. United Luth. Ch. since 1931; sec. Pa. Council of Chs. since 1926; pres. Gettysburg Luth. Summer Assembly, 1912; mem. Synodical Mission Bd. and Examining Com., E. Pa. Synod. Dir. Irving Coll. (Mechanicsburg, Pa.), Grace Coll. (Washington, D.C.). Mem. Luth. Hist. Soc. (pres.), Ministerial Assn. Harrisburg and Dauphin County, Phi Sigma Kappa (grand chaplain), Phi Beta Kappa. Republican. Mason (Grand Chaplain Grand Lodge of Pa.); mem. Lions Internat. Clubs: University, Torch. Home: 121 State St., Harrisburg, Pa.

HERMAN, Theodore Frederick, theologian; b. Göttingen, Germany, Mar. 22, 1872; s. Henry and Caroline (Gardner) H.; Gymnasium, Göttingen; came to America, 1887; B.A., Calvin Coll., Cleveland, 1892; Theol. Sem. Ref. Ch., Lancaster, Pa., 1892-95; U. of Berlin, 1895-97; D.D., Franklin and Marshall Coll., 1910; m. Emma Lane Garrigan, July 19, 1899; children—Dorothea Elizabeth, Theodore Frederick, John Eldredge. Ordained Ref. Ch. ministry, 1897; asst. pastor Grace Ch., Cleveland, 1897-98; pastor, Salem Ch., Lafayette, Ind., 1898-1903, Allentown, Pa., 1903-09; prof. systematic theology, Theol. Sem. Ref. Ch., Lancaster, since Sept. 1909; prof. ethics Coll. for Women, Allentown, Pa., 1904-10. S.S. editor Reformed Church Messenger; editor Reformed Church Review. Mem. Am. Theol. Soc., Phi Kappa Sigma. Clubs: Contemporary (Allentown), Cliosophic (Lancaster). Address: 519 N. Pine St., Lancaster, Pa.

HERMAN, Burke Miller, prof. history; b. Middleburg, Pa., Sept. 1, 1888; s. Charles Wilson and Mary (Miller) H.; A.B., Pa. State Coll., 1912, A.M., same, 1916; grad. study, Columbia U., 1932-33; m. Bertie Virginia Coombs, Aug. 27, 1927. Engaged as teacher and athletic coach, high schs., 1912-15; asst. in history, Pa. State Coll., 1915-16, successively instr. history, asst. prof., asso. prof., 1916-35, prof. of history since 1936; athletic coach, Pa. State College, 1915-32. Served in 2d O.T.C. then 1st lt. inf., U.S.A., 1917-19 with A.E.F. Mem. Am. Hist. Assn., Pa. Hist. Assn., Beta Theta Pi. Republican. Presbyterian. Club: Centre Hills Country (State College). Home: Boalsburg, Pa.

HERMANN, John Herbert, surgeon; b. Arlington, N.J., Sept. 23, 1891; s. Edward F. and Effie B. (Crombie) H.; M.D., N.Y. Univ. Med. Sch., 1914; m. Laura B. Griffin, Sept. 9, 1915; children—John Herbert, Jr., Edward F. (dec.), Patricia Ann. In gen. prac. of medicine at Orange, N.J., since 1918, specializing in surgery since 1929; city physician, Orange, 1923-36; on Med. Advisory Bd. city of Orange since 1939; sr. attdg. surgeon, St. Mary's Hosp., Orange, N.J., since 1929, chief of staff, 1929-34, cons. surgeon, St. Vincent's Hosp., Montclair, N.J. Fellow Am. Coll. Surgeons; mem. Am. Med. Assn., Soc. Surgeons of N.J., Anat. and Pathol. Soc. Essex Co., Essex Co. Med. Soc., Bellevue Hosp. Alumni Soc., Nu Sigma Nu. Republican. Episcopalian. Home: 197 S. Centre St., Orange, N.J.

HERNDON, Edward Lilian, retired; b. Callaway Co., Mo., Sept. 11, 1863; s. Edward T. and Sarah Frances (Venable) H.; Engr. Mines and Metallurgy, Washington U., St. Louis, 1882; m. Bessie A. Tarr, Jan. 31, 1894; children—Edward Tarr, Hunter Venable. Engaged in various activities, St. Louis and Springfield, Mo., and Albany, N.Y., 1886-1903; treas. The Eastern Steel Co., Pottsville, Pa., 1903-26, receiver, 1926-32; retired, 1932. Mem. Legion of Honor of Am. Inst. Mining and Metall. Engrs. (more than 50 year membership). Republican. Episcopal. Clubs: Schuylkill Country (Pottsville); University, Winter Park (Fla.) Country. Home: (summer) 1240 Howard Av., Pottsville, Pa.; (winter) Alabama Hotel, Winter Park, Fla.

HERNDON, John Goodwin, Jr., coll. prof.; b. Washington, D.C., Nov. 26, 1888; s. John

Goodwin and Florence Early (Linton) H.; A.B., Washington and Lee, 1911, M.A., 1912; student U. of Wis., 1912-14, fellow in taxation, 1912-13; Ph.D., U. of Pa., 1931; student Harvard, 1929, U. of Geneva, Switzerland, 1930, U. of Mich., 1937; m. Grace Cordelia Middleton, Apr. 7, 1915; children—Dale Linton, Richard Middleton, Constance (dec.), Carol May. With Wis. Tax Commn., in charge corpn. income tax, 1912-14; expert, spl. agt., U.S. Bur. Labor Statistics, 1914-17; with personal income tax div., U.S. Bur. Internal Revenue, 1917-18; tax consultant Nat. City Co., 1918, Guaranty Trust Co., Phila. and London brs., 1919-20; tax consultant, 1921-28; asso. prof. economics, Ursinus Coll., 1927-28; asst. prof. economics and govt., Haverford Coll., 1929-33, asso. prof. govt. since 1933; spl. lecturer Am. Inst. of Banking, 1920-22, Haverford Coll., 1929, University of Pennsylvania, 1931-33, Swarthmore College, 1937. Secretary Am. delegation to gen. meeting governmental experts on double taxation, Geneva, 1928. Mem. Am. Acad. Polit. and Social Science, Foreign Policy Assn., Am. Polit. Science Assn., Hist. Soc. of Pa., S.R., Soc. 1812, Phi Sigma Kappa, Phi Beta Kappa, Delta Sigma Rho, Pi Gamma Mu. Democrat. Presbyn. Mason (32°). Author: Public Employment Offices in the U.S., 1918; Relief from International Income Taxation, 1932; Your New Income Tax, 1932; Our New Federal Taxes, 1934; also has written many articles for econ. jours., etc.; as chief investigator, Bureau of Budget, Washington, 1936-37, prepared "A Study of the Federal Ownership of Real Estate and of Its Bearing on State and Local Taxation." Editor in chief, Winston Business Encyclopedia since 1935. Home: 2 College Lane, Haverford, Pa.

HERPST, Martha Jane, artist; b. Titusville, Pa., Nov. 4, 1911; d. Henry Howard and Lou (Cupler) H.; ed. high sch., Titusville, Pa., 1926-27; grad. high sch., Tulsa, Okla., 1929; ed. Pa. Acad. Fine Arts, Phila., 1931, Grand Central Sch. of Art, New York City, 1931-33. Began painting in oils at age of 9 yrs.; sold first portrait at 12 yrs. of age; specializes in portraits; exhibited National Arts Club, New York, since 1933, Butler Art. Inst., Youngstown, O., 1938, Soc. of Independent Artists since 1936; represented in permanent collection of Nat. Arts Club. Mem. Nat. Arts Club, Soc. Independent Artists, New York City. Awarded medal from Grand Central Sch. of Art, 1932. Republican. Episcopalian. Home: 122 E. Main St., Titusville, Pa.

HERR, Benjamin Brubaker, prin. high sch.; b. Lancaster, Pa., Aug. 22, 1888; s. Elias L. and Katie (Brubaker) H.; A.B., Franklin and Marshall Coll., 1911; A.M., Columbia U., 1919; diploma in adminstrn., Teachers Coll. of Columbia U., 1919; m. Leah E. Bard, Dec. 24, 1913; children—Jane E., Nancy B. Engaged in teaching, pub. schs., Lancaster, Pa., 1905-07; instr. sci. and mathematics, high sch., Columbia, Pa., 1911-14; head sci. dept., high sch., Bethlehem, Pa., 1914-16; head sci. dept., high sch., Lancaster, Pa., 1916-30, asst. prin. senior high schs., 1930-32, prin. boys high sch., 1932-37, prin. sr. (co-ednl.) high sch., Lancaster, Pa., since 1937. Vice-pres. East-Central Interscholastic Foot Ball Conf. Mem. Franklin and Marshall Coll. Alumni Assn. (pres. Lancaster Chapter). Mem. Nat. Edn. Assn., Am. Assn. Sch. Adminstrs., Pa. State Edn. Assn. (pres. southern conv. dist.), Tau Kappa Alpha, Phi Delta Kappa. Republican. Mem. Reformed Ch. Mason (K.T., 32°, Shriner), Elk. Club: Lancaster Kiwanis (dir.). Home: 28 N. Lime St., Lancaster, Pa.

HERR, Benjamin Musser, sales engring.; b. Lancaster, Pa., July 15, 1883; s. Allan A. and Annie M. (Musser) H.; ed. Franklin and Marshall Acad., 1901-02; M.E., Cornell U., 1906; m. Mary Warren Brown, June 18, 1914; children—Benjamin Musser, Jr., Katherine Laelitia. Asso. with Westinghouse Machine Co., 1906-17, field engr., 1913, erection engr., 1915-17; supt. production Edwards Valve & Mfg. Co., East Chicago, Ind., 1917-19; engaged in sales engring. work selling power plant equipment and heat exchangers and propr. Herr-Harris Co., Pittsburgh, Pa. since 1919; dir. Buffalo Burial Park Assn. Mem. Am. Soc. Mech. Engrs. (chmn. Pittsburgh Sect.), Engrs. Soc. of Western Pa. Republican. Presbyterian. Mason. Clubs: University, Edgewood, Longue Vue (Pittsburgh); Gatineau Fish and Game (Canada). Home: 571 Briar Cliff Rd. Office: Fulton Bldg., Pittsburgh, Pa.

HERR, Dougal, adv. master in chancery of N.J.; b. Georgetown, D.C., Apr. 2, 1882; s. Charles and Helen (Dougal) H.; A.B., Princeton U., 1903; ed. N.Y. Law Sch., 1905-06; m. Josephine Fithian, d. Hon. Chas. Grant Garrison, N.J. Supreme Ct., Aug. 10, 1909; children—Geraldine Garrison (wife of A. Leslie Gibbins, M.D.), Garrison, William D., Linda. Admitted to N.J. bar, 1906 and engaged in gen. practice of law at Jersey City, 1906-11; mem. firm, Smith, Mabon & Herr, Hoboken, N.J., 1911-16, Hopkins & Herr, 1922-29; admitted as counselor at law in N.J., 1909; admitted to practice before the Supreme Ct. of the U.S., 1915; N.J. Supreme Ct. examiner, 1910, commr., 1911; spl. master in chancery, N.J., 1912, adv. master, 1920, standing advisory master since 1933; ceased active practice, 1933. Served as Mayor, Borough of Essex Fells, N.J., 1925-30. Pres. bd. trustees, Kingsley Sch. Mem. Am., N.J. State, Hudson Co. bar assns. Republican. Presbyn. Author: Marriage, Divorce and Separation, 2 vols., 1938. Contbr. articles on same subjects to legal journs. Home: Rensselaer Rd., Essex Fells, N.J. Office: Court House, Elizabeth, N.J.

HERR, Herbert T., Jr., pres. and chmn. bd. J. S. McCormick Co.; b. Denver, Colo., Feb. 18, 1898; s. Herbert T. and Irene (Viancourt) H.; student Culver (Ind.) Mil. Acad. and Philips Andover Acad., Andover, Mass.; B.S., Yale U.; m. Marion W. Tinker, Dec. 21, 1920; 1 dau., Marion Lysbeth. Spl. apprentice Westinghouse Electric & Mfg. Co., East Pittsburgh, Pa., 1921-22, steam service engr., 1923; salesman J. S. McCormick Co., Pittsburgh, 1924, v.p., 1925, v.p. and gen. mgr., 1926-32, pres. and chmn. bd. since 1932. Served in F.A., U.S. Army, World War. Mem. Berzelius Soc., Tau Beta Pi. Clubs: Longue Vue (dir.), University (dir.), Pittsburgh Athletic (dir.), Harvard-Yale-Princeton (Pittsburgh); Pine Valley Golf. Home: 217 S. Dallas Av. Office: 25th and A.V. R.R., Pittsburgh, Pa.

HERR, John Dow, clergyman; b. Poughkeepsie, N.Y., Feb. 8, 1901; s. John Philip and Margaret Cameron (Dow) H.; B. of Arch., U. of Pa., 1922; B.D., Drew Univ., 1926, Th.M., same, 1927, Th.D., same, 1929; m. Esther Williams Morton, Sept. 8, 1925; children—James Huganir, Robert Huganir. Ordained to ministry M.E. Ch., 1925; minister Asbury M.E. Ch., Phila., Pa. since 1935, prof. systematic theology, Temple U. Sch. Theology since 1929. Republican. Mem. M.E. Ch. Home: 312 S. 40th St., Philadelphia, Pa. Office: 3601 Locust St., Philadelphia, Pa.

HERR, John Kohr, mfr.; b. Strasburg, Pa., Jan. 13, 1882; s. Amos Kreider and Elizabeth (Kohr) H.; ed. public schools of Strasburg and Lancaster, Pa., Mercersburg Acad., 1902-04, Pa. State Coll., 1904-05; m. Maude Alice Frantz, Jan. 17, 1906; children—Elizabeth Georgia (Mrs. Benjamin Witmer), John Kohr, Richard Frantz, William Frantz. Machinist apprentice, Kreider Machine Co., 1897-1901; machinist and toolmaker, 1901-02; in 1907 organized Herr Mfg. Co., mfr. mattresses, bed springs, etc., continue as owner; mem. of Serta Associates, Inc.; pres. Eby Shoe Corpn.; trustee and treas. Conestoga Transportation Co.; dir. Northern Bank & Trust Co. (one of organizers). Mem. Lancaster Chamber of Commerce; treas. Mfrs. Assn. of Lancaster since 1921. Mem. Beta Theta Pi. Republican. Mason (32°, Shriner). Clubs: Hamilton, Lancaster Skeet and Gun, Lancaster Country; Tucquan of York Co. (fishing club organized 1879; mem. bd. govs.); Penn State of Lancaster. Home: 1020 Marietta Av. Office: 118 S. Christian St., Lancaster, Pa.

HERRICK, Cheesman Abiah, retired college president; b. Redwood, N.Y., July 21, 1866; s. Delos and Sophonia (Curtis) H.; student Ill. State Normal U., Normal, Ill., 1887-89; Ph.B., U. of Pa., 1894, Ph.D., 1899; LL.D., Lafayette, 1913, Muhlenberg, 1916, Univ. of Pa., 1930; m. Clara B. James, June 29, 1897. Taught ungraded country chs., Jefferson Co., N.Y., Winnebago Co., Ill., 1884-87; prin. town schs., at Hopedale and Minier, Tazewell Co., Ill., 1889-92; asst. sec. and lecturer of Am. Soc. for Extension of Univ. Teaching, 1894-95; instr. in history, 1895-98, dir. 1898-1909, dept. of commerce, Central High Sch., Phila.; prin. William Penn High Sch., Phila., 1909-10; pres. Girard Coll., Phila., 1910-36. Lecturer on commercial geography, Harvard Summer Sch., 1904; spl. agt. in commerce and advisor for commercial edn. of Federal Bd. for Vocational Edn., 1917-19. Mem. dept. jury awards St. Louis Expdn., 1904; del. 8th Internat. Geog. Congress. Life member Am. Historical Assn., Historical Society of Pennsylvania, Pennsylvania State Ednl. Assn. (president 1910); mem. N.E.A. (president business edn. sect. 1904), American Academy of Polit. and Social Science, Historical Society of Pennsylvania, Nat. Soc. Promotion Industrial Edn. (v.p. 1914-17, pres. 1917-18), Philadelphia Chamber of Commerce (chmn. edn. com. 1922-25; dir. and mem. exec. com., 1923-26), Phi Beta Kappa (U. of Pa.). Trustee U. of Pa., Presbyn. Author: Commercial Education, 1900; The Meaning and Practice of Commercial Education, 1904, Reclaiming a Commonwealth, 1911; History of Commerce and Industry, 1917; Outstanding Days, 1920. Editor: Macmillan Commercial Series of Text-books; English Readings for Commercial Classes, 1921; Call Him Not Dead, 1922; Stephen Girard, Founder, 1923; First Things, 1924; White Servitude in Pennsylvania, 1926; History of Girard College, 1927; More First Things, 1936; School Prayers, 1936. Address: The Delmar-Morris, Germantown, Philadelphia, Pa.

HERRMAN, Clinton S(imon), surgeon; b. Houtydale, Pa., May 1, 1896; s. Gerson and Clara (Feldman) H.; grad. Central High Sch., Phila., 1914; student U. of Pa., Arts and Science, 1914-15; M.D., U. of Pa. Med. Sch., 1919; m. Juliet Kind, Mar. 5, 1925; children—John Clinton, Terese Kind. Interne St. Joseph's Hosp., 1919-20; physician and surgeon, Phila., since 1920; now visiting surgeon St. Joseph's Hosp.; asso. surgeon Mt. Sinai Hosp.; demonstrator in anatomy, Temple U. Sch. of Medicine. Fellow Am. Coll. of Surgeons. Clubs: Medical (Phila.); Philmont Country. Address: 5106 N. Broad St., Philadelphia, Pa.

HERRMAN, William Gettier, physician; b. Norwood, O., June 13, 1890; s. Henry White and Katherine (Gettier) H.; A.B., Rutgers U., New Brunswick, N.J., 1912, A.M., 1916; M.D., N.Y. Med. Coll., 1916; m. Marjorie Barton Green, June 4, 1917; children—Jean Barton, Margaret Bushnell and William Gettier, Jr. (twins). Interne Cumberland St. Hosp., Brooklyn, N.Y., 1916-17, Metropolitan Hosp., N.Y. City, 1917; engaged in gen. practice of medicine at Asbury Park, N.J., 1919, specializing in radiology since 1921; attdg. radiologist, Monmouth Memorial Hosp., Long Branch, N.J., Fitkin Memorial Hosp., Asbury Park, N.J., State Hosp., Marlboro, N.J.; vice-pres. Reserve Bldg. & Loan Assn., Asbury Park, N.J., since 1927. Served with Med. Corps, U.S.A., 1917-19; with A.E.F. in France. Mem. bd. mgrs. Allenwood (county) Tuberculosis Sanitarium. Awarded Rutgers U. medal, 1938, for advancing medicine in N.J. Served on governor's com. on cancer, 1938-39. Fellow Am. Coll. Physicians, Am. Coll. of Radiology. Mem. A.M.A., Radiol. Soc. of North America, Am. Roentgen Ray Soc., Med. Soc. of N.J. (past pres.), Radiol. Soc. of N.J. (past pres.), Monmouth Co. Med. Soc. (past pres.). S.A.R., Delta Phi, Phi Alpha Gamma. Republican. Presbyn. (trustee First Ch.). Clubs: Rotary of Asbury Park (past pres.). Home: 211 Norwood Av. Deal. Office: 501 Grand Av., Asbury Park, N.J.

HERRON, David C(ampbell), mfr.; b. Monongahela, Pa., Oct. 28, 1879; s. Joseph A. and Mary (Campbell) H.; grad. Lawrenceville Sch., 1898; A.B., Princeton U., 1902; student U. of Pittsburgh, 1902-03; m. Julia Howe Abrams,

Oct. 25, 1906; 1 dau., Marjorie Anne. Clerk Alexander & Co., bankers, 1903-05, with Whitney & Co., 1905-06; with N.Y. Mail & Newspaper Transportation Co., 1906-09; sec. and treas. Herron, Webb Engring. Co., 1909-11; with Diamond Machine Co. since 1911, gen. mgr. since 1935, also sec. and treas. since 1911. Dir. Monongahela Cemetery Co. Republican. Presbyterian. Mason, Elk, Royal Arcanum. Home: 600 Meade St. Office: Diamond Machine Co., Monongahela, Pa.

HERRON, Samuel Davidson, mgr. Harriman Ripley & Co.; b. Pittsburgh, Pa., Oct. 16, 1897; s. Andrew W. and Jane N. (Jardine) H.; grad. Shadyside Acad., Pittsburgh, 1910-14; A.B., Princeton U., 1918; m. Louise L. Johnston, Jan. 5, 1921; children—Nancy Louise, S. Davidson, Jr. Salesman A. M. Byers Co., 1919-24; office mgr. with Hickman Williams & Co., Phila., 1924-27; salesman Graham Parsons & Co., 1927-33; manager of Pittsburgh office, Brown Brothers Harriman & Co., 1933-34, manager of Pittsburgh office, Brown Harriman & Co., Inc., 1934-39; mgr. Pittsburgh office, Harriman Ripley & Co. since Jan. 1, 1939. Republican. Presbyterian. Clubs: Allegheny Country, Oakmont Country, Pittsburgh. Home: 601 Academy Av., Sewickley, Pa. Office: 423 Union Trust Bldg., Pittsburgh, Pa.

HERSH, Edward Samuel, retired merchant; b. Petchau, Bohemia, Dec. 11, 1856; brought to U.S., 1866; s. Artolf and Catherine (Weil) H.; ed. Elizabeth Pub. Sch. No. 1; m. Lily Hackes, Oct. 9, 1889; children—Cecil, Austin (killed in Argonne Forest, 1918), Harry, Robert (all 4 sons served with A.E.F. during World War). Employed by Hirschbaum Bros. Dry Goods Store and later E. P. Williams Dry Goods Store, 1871-73; opened own dry goods store, 1873, operating under name of C. Hersh & Son; retired, 1918. One of organizers Elizabethport Banking Co. (only survivor of original bd. of dirs.). Former mem. Bd. of Zoning Commrs.; mem. Bd. of Adjustment. Dir. Family Welfare Soc. since 1919; dir. Y.M.H.A.; treas. B'nai Israel Cemetery Assn. Mem. Chamber of Commerce. Democrat. Mem. Temple B'nai Israel. Mason, Odd Fellow, K.P. Known as "Mayor of Frog Hollow" because of civic activity in vicinity of Elizabeth Av. and Third St. Home: 501 Linden Av., Elizabeth, N.J.

HERSHEY, Ezra Frantz, treas. Hershey Chocolate Corpn.; b. Lancaster Co., Pa., Sept. 1, 1879; s. Elias H. and Elizabeth (Frantz) H.; ed. pub. schs.; m. Mary Rohrer, Sept. 20, 1910; children—Frantz, Mary Elizabeth. Treas. and dir. Hershey Chocolate Corpn.; pres. and dir. Hershey Nat. Bank; treas. and dir. Hershey Estates, Hershey Corpn.; dir. Hershey Trust Co.; v.p. Harrisburg Council, Boy Scouts of America. Clubs: Hershey Civic, Hershey Country, Harrisburg Country. Home: Hershey, Pa.

HERSHEY, Milton Snavely, mfr.; b. Derry Twp., Dauphin Co., Pa., Sept. 13, 1857; s. Henry H. and Fannie (Snavely) H.; ed. pub. schs.; m. Catharine Sweeney, 1898 (died 1915). Began mfr. of chocolate at Lancaster, Pa., 1893; now chmn. bd. Hershey Chocolate Corpn., Hershey, Pa.; pres. Hershey Trust Co. Founder, 1905, chairman of board of managers Hershey Industrial Sch. for orphan boys; donated, 1918, fortune, estimated at $60,000,000, as a trust for the maintenance of the school. Republican. Home: Hershey, Pa.

HERSHNER, Newton Webster, M.D.; b. Gorsuch Mills, Md., July 26, 1878; s. Benjamin Franklin and Lucrecia Linthicum (Seitz) H.; M.D., U. of Md., 1906; m. Wilma A. Landis, June 18, 1912; children—Newton Webster, Robert Franklin. Sch. teacher, 1896-1901; physician at Mechanicsburg, since 1909; dir. First Bank & Trust Co. Mem. Kappa Psi. Republican. Methodist. Mason (32°). Club: Carlisle Country. Home: 213 W. Main St. Office: 211 W. Main St., Mechanicsburg, Pa.

HERTZLER, Jacob Oswald, lawyer; b. South Middleton Twp., Cumberland County, Pa., July 10, 1882; s. Samuel and Florence (Hollinger) H.; student pub. sch., S. Middleton Twp., 1888-1892; pub. sch., Carlisle, Pa., 1892-97; Dickinson Prep. Sch., Carlisle, Pa., 1897-99; Ph.B., Dickinson Coll., Carlisle, Pa., 1903, A.M., 1905; LL.B., W.Va. U., Morgantown, W.Va., 1905; m. Neuvia Gladfelter, Apr. 5, 1906. Admitted to W.Va. bar, 1905, practiced in W.Va., 1905-11; practiced in Erie, Pa., since 1911. Pres. Erie Co. Sabbath Sch. Assn., 1921-29; v.p. & dir. City Mission, Erie, since 1918; in charge faculty Camp Caledon for Girls, Erie, and trustee since 1921; supt. Luther Memorial Sunday Sch., Erie, 1915-24; teacher Luther Memorial Sunday Sch., Erie, 1911-15, and since 1924; mem. official bd. Luther Memorial Church, many past terms; dir. Erie Y.M.C.A. since 1914; dir. Erie Co. Sabbath Sch. Assn. since 1921. Mem. Phi Kappa Sigma, Delta Chi. Republican. Lutheran. Odd Fellow. Club: Kiwanis of Erie (past pres.). Home: 226 Shawnee Drive. Office: 1309 Erie Trust Bldg., Erie, Pa.

HERTZLER, William, banker; b. Port Royal, Pa., July 7, 1858; s. Noah and Susan (Garman) H.; A.B., Washington and Jefferson Coll., 1881; m. Mollie M. Kaufman, Jan. 7, 1898; 1 son, Penrose. Mem. Pa. Ho. of Reps., 1889-90, Pa. Senate, 1897-1901; clk. Com. of War Claims, Washington, D.C., 1902-09; pres. and dir. First Nat. Bank of Mifflintown since 1909; deputy sec. Commonwealth of Pa., 1911-15; file clk. U.S. Ho. of Reps., Washington, 1919-33. Mem. Pa. Soc. of N.Y. Republican. Presbyterian. Mason, Odd Fellow, Elk. Home: Port Royal, Pa.

HERVEY, John Gaines, univ. prof. and dean; b. Hillsboro, Tex., Feb. 26, 1900; s. William Edwin and Mollie (Revier) H.; B.A., U. of Okla., Norman, Okla., 1923, LL.B., 1925; Ph.D., U. of Pa., 1928; m. Hallie Holloway, Aug. 24, 1925; 1 dau., Janis Marilyn. Admitted to Okla. bar, 1925; asst. prof. internat. law., U. of Pa., 1928-30; asso. dean and prof. law, Temple U. Law Sch., Phila., 1930-38, dean since 1939. Pvt. U.S. Army, Sept.-Dec. 1918. Legislative adviser Pa. Senate Com., Revision of Pub. Service Co. Laws, 1932-33; utility consultant, Gov. of Pa., 1935-36. Mem. Am. Bar Assn., Pa. Bar Assn., Okla. State Bar, Pa. Hist. Soc., Acacia (nat. judge advocate, 1935-38), Phi Beta Kappa, Delta Sigma Rho. Democrat. Methodist. Mason. Author: Legal Effects of Recognition in International Law, 1928; Anti-Trust Laws of the U. S., 1930; co-author: Business and Government 4th edit., 1938; Readings in Internat. Law, 1929; contbr. articles to law reviews. Home: 9 N. Drexel Av., Upper Darby. Office: Temple U. Law Sch., Phila., Pa.

HERZBERG, Max J(ohn), educator, writer; b. N.Y. City, Mar. 29, 1886; s. Leopold and Mary H.; A.B., Columbia, 1906; m. Edna M. Newman, June 30, 1914; children—Richard A., Donald G. Head of English dept., Central High Sch., Newark, N.J., 1912-29; supervisor of English, pub. schs., Newark, 1929-33; instr. in English, Mercer Beasley Law Sch., 1925-27; instr. in extension courses, Rutgers U., 1927-29; and at Montclair (N.J.) State Teachers Coll. since 1936; prin. Weequahic High Sch., Newark, since 1933; lit. editor Newark Evening News, Pres. Stephen Crane Assn., 1924-30; was mem. com. that prepared syllabi in English for schs. of N.J., 1926, and now co-ordinator curriculum com. on high sch. English, Newark, N.J.; advisory editor The English Jour., 1933-34; mem. advisory com. Am. Sch. of the Air; 1st v.p. Nat. Council Teachers of English, 1935-36, chmn. of radio com. and co-chmn. com. on home reading; ex-pres. Newark Schoolmen's Club; dir. Carteret Book Club; vice-pres. N.J. High School Principals Assn.; mem. Listentome Club of the Oranges. Author: Speaking and Writing English (with collaborator), 1925; Myths and Their Meaning, 1928; New Style-Book of Business English, 1928; Outline of Contemporary American and British Literature, 1928; Secretarial Procedure (with collaborator), 1929; Romance (with collaborators), 1932; American Literature (with collaborators), 1933; Off to Arcady—Adventures in Poetry, 1933; English Literature (with others), 1934; Mark Twain Omnibus, 1935; Classical Myths, 1935; Albert Payson Terhune Omnibus, 1937; Americans in Action (with collaborator), 1937; Radio and the English Teacher, 1937. Editor Stories of Adventure, 1927; also sch. edits. of various works. Contbr. to Encyclopedia Britannica; editor of Word Study, a periodical for English teachers; contbg. editor The Scholastic; editor Photoplay Guides, Nat. Council Teachers of English, 1934-35; chmn. editorial com. Photoplay Studies, Dept. of Secondary Edn. of N.E.A. since 1935. Contbr. to mags.; broadcaster over various radio stations; author of inscriptions on 8 bronze tablets erected by Schoolmen's Club of Newark to mark historical occasions. Home: 135 Mercer Place, South Orange, N.J. Address: Board of Education, Newark, N.J.

HERZOG, Eugene, insurance; b. Pittsburgh, Pa., Aug. 18, 1880; s. Henry and Tillie (Klee) H.; student Allegheny (Pa.) High Sch.; m. Nell Stein, Apr. 22, 1907; 1 dau., Virginia. Clerk and stenographer, 1897-1907; iron pipe business, 1907-10; in ins. business since 1910; pres. Benswanger, Hast and Herzog (insurance), Kleelands, Inc. Trustee and dir., Montfiore Hosp., Gusky Orphange, Jewish Social Service Bur., Federation Jewish Philanthropies; mem. budget com. Community Fund. Mason. Republican. Jewish religion. Clubs: Concordia (trustee and dir.), Hundred (treas. and trustee), Westmoreland Country (Pittsburgh). Home: 5430 Beacon St. Office: 3010 Grant Bldg., Pittsburgh, Pa.

HESELBARTH, Thomas Kirk, real estate, insurance; b. Pittsburgh, Pa., July 9, 1897; s. William H. and Hattie R. (Fox) H.; B.S. in Economics, Wharton Sch. (U. of Pa.), 1921; m. Helen W. Snyder, Sept. 1, 1926. Began as salesman, W. H. Heselbarth & Sons, Inc., 1921; asst. sec., 1925-34, v.p., 1934-35, pres. since 1935; sec-treas. West End Federal Savings & Loan Assn. First lt., 393d Inf. Reserve. Dir. Woods Run Settlement House. Mem. Pittsburgh Real Estate Bd., U.S. Bldg. & Loan League, Am. Legion, Alpha Sigma Phi. Baptist. Mason. Home: 4307 Dakota St. Office: 506 S. Main St., Pittsburgh, Pa.

HESKETT, Charles Z., lawyer; b. Mill Creek, Pa., Oct. 12, 1892; s. Landon C. and Clara H.; student Piedmont (W.Va.) High Sch., 1907-11; LL.B., Dickinson Coll. Law Sch., 1917; m. Theresa Francis O'Leary, Oct. 8, 1925. Gen practice of law at Cumberland, Md., since 1917; city solicitor, Cumberland, Md., 1923-32, 1936-40; sec. Asso. Broadcasting Corpn. Served as lt., U.S. Army, 1918. Mem. Am., Allegheny Co. bar assns., Delta Chi. Republican. Lutheran. Mason (Shriner). Club: Cumberland (Md.) Country. Home: 607 Sedgewick St. Office: Clark-Keating Bldg., Cumberland, Md.

HESS, Arleigh Porter, investment banker; b. Philadelphia, Pa., Aug. 29, 1886; s. Albert W. and Susan W. (Wildeman) H.; ed. Philadelphia pub. schs., Central Manual Training Sch., Pierce Business Coll. and Banks Business Coll.; grad. Wharton Sch., U. of Pa., 1915; m. Annie B. McClelland, April 6, 1910; children—Arleigh Porter, William McClelland. Clerk Geo. S. Fox & Sons, 1901-17; with West Co., investment bankers, 1919-20; partner Schebener, Boenning & Co., 1920-26, Boenning & Co. since 1926, vice-pres. Walnut St. Assn.; sec. and dir. Hamburg Broom Works; treas. and dir. South Jersey Water Supply Co.; dir. Advance Bag & Paper Co., South Advance Bag & Paper Co., North La. & Gulf R.R. Co. Served as 1st lt. Ordnance Corps, 1918-19. Pres. bd. trustees Nat. Stomach Hosp. Mem. Phi Delta Epsilon. Republican. Methodist. Club: Kiwanis (Woodbury, N.J.). Home: Mulleca Hill, N.J. Office: 1606 Walnut St., Philadelphia, Pa.

HESS, Elam G(ross), owner Elam G. Hess; b. at Manheim, Pa., October 1, 1876; s. Levi H. and Salinda S. (Gross) Hess; educated Pa. Business Coll., Perkiomen Sch., Gettysburg Coll. and Sheldon Sch. of Scientific Salesmanship; m. Marcelia Edna Farmer, Oct. 5, 1910; children—Richard, Donald, Marcelia. Teacher Lancaster Co. pub schs., 1895-1900; with Underwood & Underwood (N.Y. City and London, England), 1907-11; became pres. Keystone Pecan Co., 1911, Pecano Manufacturing Company, 1929; owner Elam G. Hess since 1938. Inventor and patentee "Pecano Product," 1927, "Pecano Process," 1929. Republican. Lutheran. Mason. Club: Lancaster Health. Wrote: The Span of Life; The Meat That Grows on Trees; 800 Proved Pecan Recipes. Home: 101 S. Grant St. Office: 88 S. Grant St., Manheim, Pa.

HESS, Elmer, physician; b. Millville, N.J., May 31, 1889; s. Frederick and Mary (Theise) H.; ed. Peddie Sch., Hightstown, N.J., 1903-07; M.D., U. of Pa. Med. Sch., 1911; grad. study, Johns Hopkins U., 1919-21; m. Edna Africa, June 26, 1911; children—Celeste Remle (wife of Lt. P. W. Cann, U.S.N.), Camilla (dec.), Hope Noel, Elmer, Jr. (dec.). Physician in Indian Service of U.S., 1911-12; in pvt. practice of medicine and surgery at Erie, Pa., since 1912, specializing in urology since 1920; chief dept. urology, St. Vincent's Hosp. since 1920; senior urologist Hamot Hosp., Erie; cons. urologist, Corry (Pa.) Hosp., Erie Infants' Home, Warren State Hosp. Lieut., then capt. U.S.A. Med. Corps, 1917-19, with 15th F.A., 2d Div., A.E.F. Rep. nominee for mayor, Erie, 1919; pres. Erie Boys Club since 1919. Mem. governing com. Gorgas Memorial Inst. Fellow Am. Coll. Surgeons; mem. Am., Pa. State, and Erie Co. med. assns., Am. Urol. Assn., Western N.Y. and Ontario Urol. Assn., Pan-Am. Urol. Assn., Pan-Am. Med. Assn., Am. Legion, Forty and Eight; hon. mem. Detroit Urology Soc., Western Branch Soc. American Urology Assn. Diplomate American Board of Urology. Decorated Croix de Guerre, Verdun Medal, Chateau Thierry Medal (France); Three army citations (silver star), Victory Medal with 5 clasps (U. S.). Republican. Episcopalian. Clubs: Erie, Kahkwa. Contbr. to med. jours. Home: 4819 Highview Boul. Office: 501 Commerce Bldg., Erie, Pa.

HESS, George Hibbs, roentgenologist; b. New Salem, Pa., June 28, 1886; s. John Fuller and Harriet Ann (Hibbs) H.; student Washington & Jefferson Acad. and U. of Pa.; m. Marguerite Taylor, Nov. 8, 1916; children—Marguerite Taylor, George Taylor, Robert Hibbs. Roentgenologist Uniontown Hosp. since 1914. Fellow Am. Coll. Radiology, Am. Coll. Physicians, A.M.A.; mem. Am. Roentgen Ray Soc., Radiol. Soc. of North America, Pa. Radiol. Soc. (pres. 1922-23), Pa. State Med. Soc., Fayette Co. Med. Soc. (pres. 1928); diplomate Am. Bd. Radiology. Contbr. articles to Radiology. Home: 225 Derrick Av. Office: 104 Morgantown St., Uniontown, Pa.

HESS, H. Lloyd, pres. Lancaster Malleable Castings Co.; b. Lancaster Co., Pa., Oct. 28, 1895; s. Aaron B. and Fannie (Herr) H.; ed. Franklin and Marshall Acad.; m. Erla M. Garber, May 30, 1917; children—Dorothy P., H. Lloyd, Jr., Richard G., John Robert. Pres. and dir. Lancaster Malleable Castings Co. since 1933; dir. Penn Dairies, Inc. Vice-pres. Pa. State Industrial Conf.; mem. Lancaster County Com. since 1924. Trustee Moravian Ch., Lititz, Pa. Mason. Club: Lancaster Country Foremen's (pres. 1930). Home: 829 N. Duke St. Office: 100-152 Manheim Av., Lancaster, Pa.

HESS, Henry Lawrence, engineer; b. Plainfield, N.J., Dec. 14, 1887; s. Henry and Caroline Annie (Serle) H.; prep. sch., Friends Central Sch., Phila.; B.S. in Mech. Engring., Swarthmore, 1911, M.E., 1915; studied in Germany 3 yrs., in Holland one summer; m. Martha Adeline Sharples, 1916 (died 1926); children—Anne Serle, Carlisle, Martha Dorothea; m. 2d, Mary Ann Sanders, 1928. Began in the employ of Cadillac Co., Detroit, Mich., 1912; with Hess-Bright Manufacturing Co., 1912-13, Hess Steel Casting Co., of Bridgeton, N.J., 1913-15, Hess Steel Corpn., of Baltimore, Md., 1915-20; owner H. L. Hess Co., sales engrs., Phila., since 1920; pres. Hess Ives Co. Mem. Am. Soc. M.E., Delta Upsilon. Republican. Episcopalian. Clubs: Pleasantville Yacht, Atlantic City Tuna, Absecon Island Yacht. Active in track athletics. Home: Ansley Park, Pleasantville, N.J. Address: 1406 Dorset Lane, Overbrook Hills, Philadelphia, Pa.

HESS, Henry N., owner C. Hess & Sons; dir. various companies. Home: 1625 Wood St. Office: 1321-1322 Market St., Wheeling, W.Va.

HESS, Herbert William, univ. prof.; b. St. Louis, Mo., March 10, 1880; s. William Henry and Agnes Christina (Tuche) H.; A.B., Northwestern U., 1904; Ph.D., U. of Pa., 1914; unmarried. Teacher, Ft. Scott (Kan.) High Sch., 1904-05; St. Louis (Mo.) High Sch., 1905-09; promotive work and one of founders, City Coll. Law and Commerce, St. Louis, 1908-09; advertising and sales expert, 1914; instr. Wharton Sch., U. of Pa., 1909-14, head of merchandising dept., 1909-33, prof. since 1916. Mem. Am. Acad. of Polit. and Social Science, Am. Econ. Assn., Phila. Art Alliance, Am. Teachers of Advertising and Marketing, Beta Gamma Sigma, Sigma Kappa Phi. Clubs: Manufacturers and Bankers, Sales Manager's, Poor Richard (Phila.); Wranglers (Northwestern U.). Republican. Author: Productive Advertising, 1915; Creative Salesmanship, 1923; Advertising, Its Economics, Philosophy and Technique, 1930. Lecturer; advisory editor of The Plan, pub. by Middle Atlantic Lumberman's Assn., 1935-36. Home: Alden Park Manor, Germantown, Phila., Pa.

HESS, Leslie Elsworth, exec. v.p. J. G. Brill Co.; b. Beach Haven, Pa., Dec. 29, 1869; s. John I. and Almira (Everard) H.; student Wyoming Sem., Kingston, Pa.; m. Jennie Conover, June 18, 1896; children—Ruth, Dorothy, Helen, Eloise, Elizabeth. Began as telegraph operator and chief clerk to agent, D., L.& W. R.R., Kingston, Pa., 1891; works mgr. J. G. Brill Co., 1932-35, exec. v.p. and dir. since 1935. Home: 466 Windermere Rd., Drexel Hill, Pa. Office: 62d St. and Woodland Av., Philadelphia, Pa.

HESS, Sara M(ae), artist; b. Troy Grove, Ill., Feb. 25, 1880; d. Abram and Sara Jane (Foulk) H.; ed. Wheaton Coll., Ill., 1896-97, Art Inst., Chicago, 1899-1902, grad., 1902; study, Academie Julian, Paris, France, 1907-08. Engaged as art. instr., Benton Harbor (Mich.) Coll., 1902-06; supervisor drawing, pub. schs., Benton Harbor, Mich., 1908-10; art instr., pub. schs., Gary, Ind., 1910-18; artist and pvt. teacher, Hillsdale, N.J., since 1930; has exhibited, Salon, Paris, France, Nat. Acad. Design, N.Y. City, Am. Artists Exhbn., Chicago, N.J. Artists Exhbn., Montclair, N.J., and in many other cities; represented by paintings, Oshkosh Mus., Gary Memorial Gallery, John Vanderpool Memorial Mus., Chicago, Ridgewood Woman's Club, Westwood Woman's Club, both N.J.; Mem. Nat. Assn. Women Painters & Sculptors, N.Y. Soc. of Painters, Catharine Lorillard Wolfe Art Assn. N.Y., Orange Art Center, Orange, N.J., Ridgewood Art Assn. Republican. Conglist. Club: Sun Dial Garden (Hillsdale). Home: 10 Orchard St., Hillsdale, N.J.

HESSE, Frank McNeil, steel corpn. exec.; b. New Cumberland, W.Va., Oct. 19, 1894; s. Charles H. and Nell (McNeil) H.; ed. New Cumberland High Sch., and Bethany (W.Va.) Coll.; m. Tuckie Frances Gilcrest, 1914; children—Barbara Jean, Elinor Gail; m. 2d, Edith Josephine Richardson, 1936; 1 son, Frank McNeil. Began in accounting dept. Weirton Steel Co., 1912, became asst. auditor, 1921, auditor, 1923, asst. treas., 1925, treas., 1928; vice-pres., sec. and treas., Nat. Steel Corpn. since 1929; v.p., sec. and asst. treas. Great Lakes Steel Corpn.; dir., v.p., asst. sec. and asst. treas. Weirton Steel Co.; dir., v.p., sec. and asst. treas. The Hanna Furnace Corpn.; dir., v.p., asst. sec. and asst. treas. Hanna Iron Ore Co. of Del.; dir., v.p., sec. and treas. Weirton Coal Co. & Oak Hill Supply Co.; dir., v.p., treas. and asst. sec. Weirton Improvement Co.; v.p., sec. and treas. Midwest Steel Corpn.; v.p. Hanna Iron Ore Co. (Mich.); sec. and asst. treas. Michigan Steel Corpn.; dir. Bank of Weirton; dir. West Va. Mfrs. Assn. Mem. Am. Iron and Steel Inst., Controllers Inst., Kappa Alpha. Republican. Club: Duquesne (Pittsburgh). Home: 1414 N. Highland Av. Office: 2800 Grant Bldg., Pittsburgh, Pa.

HESSERT, Edmund Charles, surgeon; b. Oaklyn, N.J., Feb. 7, 1902; s. Emil Carl and Catherine (Martin) H.; B.S., Hahnemann Med. Coll., Phila., 1924, M.D., 1926; grad. study, U. of Pa., 1929-30; m. Frances Elizabeth Murphy, 1928; children—Edmund Charles, Frances Elizabeth. In pvt. practice at Camden, N.J., specializing in gynecology and obstetrics; mem. teaching faculty, Hahnemann Hosp.; mem. staff of West Jersey Hosp., Camden, N.J. Fellow Am. Coll. Surgeons; mem. Internat. Coll. Surgeons, Am. Med. Assn., West Jersey Soc. (past pres.), Germantown Homeo. Med. Soc. of Phila., Obstet. Soc. Phila. Roman Catholic. Club: Tavistock Country. Home: Colling Av., Collingswood, N.J. Office: 417 Cooper St., Camden, N.J.

HETRICK, Samuel L., M.D., banker; b. Asbury Park, N.J., July 5, 1879; s. Jacob A. W. and Linnie S. (Evans) H.; grad. Asbury Park (N.J.) High Sch., M.D., Hahnemann Med. Coll., Phila., 1900, 1896; bd. of regents diploma, N.Y.U., 1901; m. Louise F. Sherman, 1901. Licensed to practice medicine in N.Y. and N.J.; v.p. Commercial Trust Co. of N.J., Jersey City, N.J., since 1901. Mem. Alpha Sigma. Home: Deal, N.J. Office: 338 Grove St., Jersey City, N.J.

HETRICK, William Henry, clergyman; b. Shellsville, Pa., Oct. 13, 1877; s. David Henry and Amelia Anne H.; grad. Harrisburg (Pa.) High Sch., 1897; A.B., Gettysburg (Pa.) Coll., 1901; A.M., Gettysburg Luth. Theol. Sem., 1904, D.D., 1925; D.D., Western Md. Coll., 1920; m. Mary Margaret Deatrick, Apr. 27, 1905; children—Elizabeth Anne (Mrs. William Mercer Steele, Jr.), David William. Ordained to ministry of Evang. Luth. Ch., 1904; pastor Calvary Luth. Ch., Brooklyn, N.Y., 1904-07, Immanuel Luth. Ch., Phila., 1907-11, Grace Luth. Ch., Westminster, Md., 1911-20, Trinity Luth. Ch., Connellsville, Pa., since 1920. Pres. Greensburg Conf. of Pittsburgh Synod of Evang. Luth. Ch., 1933-35. Pres. of bd. Bethseda Orphans Home, Meadville, Pa., since 1929. Mem. Sigma Alpha Epsilon. Mason, K. of P. Club: Rotary of Connellsville (pres. 1931). Home: 110 E. Patterson Av., Connellsville, Pa.

HETZEL, Frederic V(alerius), consulting engr.; b. Phila., Pa., June 2, 1870; s. Herman V. and Emma Agatha (Fisher) H.; M.E., U. of Pa., 1890; m. Grace K. Brinton, Oct. 21, 1899; children—Sylvia B., Theodore B. With Link-Belt Co. since 1890, chief engr., 1906-20, consulting engr. since 1920. Mem. Chester Co. Hist. Soc., Franklin Inst., Hist. Soc. of Pa. Mem. Society of Friends. Club: Engineers (Philadelphia). Author: Belt Conveyors and Belt Elevators, 1922, 2d edit., 1925, 3d edit., 1939. Contbr. Kent's Mech. Engrs. Handbook (9th, 10th and 11th edits.) and to tech. jours. Granted several patents on elevating and conveying machinery. Home: 103 Dean St., West Chester, Pa.

HETZEL, Ralph Dorn, college pres.; b. Merrill, Wis., Dec. 31, 1882; s. Henry Clayton and Sadie (Dorn) H.; A.B., U. of Wis., 1906, LL.B., 1908; studied University of California, summer, 1909; LL.D., Dartmouth College, 1918, U. of Me., 1924, Bucknell University, 1927; Litt.D., Lafayette College, Easton, Pa., 1928; LL.D., Univ. of Pa., 1934, U. of N.H., 1937; m. Estelle Helene Heineman, Aug. 4, 1911; children—Ralph Dorn, Helene Estelle, Roger Harry, Harriett Elizabeth, Philip Edgar. Instr. English, 1908-09, asst. prof., 1909-11, prof. English and polit. science, 1911-13, dir. extension service, 1913-17, Ore. State Coll.; pres. New Hampshire Coll. Agr. and Mechanic Arts, 1917-23; pres. U. of New Hampshire, 1923-26; pres. Pa. State Coll. since Jan. 1927. Admitted to Wis. bar, 1908, Ore. bar, 1910. Mem. Nat. Advisory Council Lingnan University. Pres. Assn. of College Presidents of Pa., 1933. Mem. Com. for Consideration of Inter-Governmental Debts, 1933. Mem. Assn. Land-grant Colls. and Univs. (exec. com. 1924-32 and 1935-37), Nat. Assn. of State Universities (pres. 1934), Am. Council on Edn. (1st vice chmn.), Pa. Chamber of Commerce (dir.), Phi Beta Kappa, Delta Upsilon, Phi Delta Phi, Gamma Sigma Delta, Phi Kappa Phi, Kappa Phi Kappa, Pi Delta Epsilon, Phi Sigma Iota, Phi Eta Sigma. Republican. Conglist. Home: State College, Pa.

HEUER, Russell Pearce, chem. engr.; b. Philadelphia, Pa., June 13, 1896; s. Harry and Anna Lillie (Pearce) H.; grad. Central High Sch., Philadelphia, 1913; B.S. in Chem. Engring., U. of Pa., 1917, Chem. E., 1922, Ph.D., 1927; m. Elizabeth Lacy Crimian, of Phila., June 19, 1926; children—Russell Pearce, Charlotte Seabury. Began as chem. engr. Gen. Chem. Co., Marcus Hook, Pa., 1917; chem. engr. Philadelphia Brass Co., 1917-18, U.S. Bureau of Mines, 1918, Chase Metal Works,

1919-22; instr. in chem. engring., U. of Pa., 1922-28; chem. engr. General Refractories Co., since 1927, now also v.p. in charge of research and dir.; dir. Northwest Magnesite Co. Mem. Am. Inst. Mining & Metall. Engrs., Am. Ceramic Soc., Am. Inst. Chem. Engrs., Am. Chem. Soc., Electrochem. Soc., Am. Soc. for Testing Materials, Sigma Alpha Epsilon, Sigma Xi. Awarded Priestley Award, U. of Pa., 1917. Episcopalian. Clubs: Racquet, Philadelphia Country. Writer tech. papers relating to metallurgy and mfr. and use of refractory materials. Holder numerous patents relating to metallurgy of oxygen-free copper, operation of blast furnaces with acid slags, the desulfurization of pig iron and the manufacture of refractory materials from diverse raw materials including magnesite, chromite, silica, fire clay, diaspore, etc. Home: Ridgewood Road, Bryn Mawr, Pa. Office: 1600 Real Estate Trust Bldg., Philadelphia, Pa.

HEUSTIS, Charles Herbert, editor; b. South Acton, Mass., Dec. 12, 1855; s. Charles P. and Charlotte F. (Reed) H.; ed. high sch., Roxbury dist., Boston, Mass.; student Mass. Inst. Tech., 1872-76; m. Chestina F. Hamilton, Sept. 1894; 1 son, Waldo R. Began newspaper work with Phila. Times, 1877, night editor, 1878-86, mng. editor, 1886-89; mng. editor Phila. Inquirer, 1889-90, editor in chief, 1890-1934, asso. editor, 1934-36, retired, 1936. Health officer, Port of Phila., 1899-1919. Republican. Club: Union League. Home: Longport, N.J.

HEWETT-THAYER, Harvey Waterman, prof. modern langs.; b. Woolwich, Me., Sept. 21, 1873; s. Rev. Henry Otis and Sarah Eliza (Hewett) Thayer; A.B., Bowdoin Coll., Brunswick, Me., 1895; A.B., Harvard, 1896; post grad. work U. of Leipzig, Germany, 1898-99; Ph.D., Columbia, 1905; unmarried. Inst. modern langs., U. of Me., 1896-98; instr. German, Pratt Inst., Brooklyn, 1902-05; instr. Coll. City of N.Y., 1905; asst. prof. modern langs., Princeton, asso. prof., prof., since 1905, chmn. dept. of modern languages since 1936. Served as 1st lt. S.O.R.C., 1917-18; capt. U.S. Army, 1918-19. Mem. Modern Lang. Assn., Am. Assn. Univ. Profs., Modern Lang. Assn. of Middle States, Phi Beta Kappa, Theta Delta Chi. Democrat. Episcopalian. Club: Princeton (New York); Nassau (Princeton). Author: Lawrence Sterne in Germany, 1905; The Modern German Novel, 1924. Editor: Grete Minde (by T. Fontane), 1911; Anthology of German Literature in the Nineteenth Century, 1932. Contbr. reviews and articles on modern philology. Home: 3 Evelyn Pl., Princeton, N.J.

HEWITT, Arthur Challis, chief engr. Am. Lime & Stone Co.; b. Cincinnati, O., Feb. 6, 1888; s. Edward R. and Fanny M. (Sogle) H.; ed. Ohio Mechanics Inst. and Alexander Hamilton Inst.; M.E., U. of Cincinnati, 1912; m. Betty M. Allen, Oct. 23, 1913; 1 son, Allen Edward. Engr. Ill. Traction System, Springfield, Ill., 1912-13; engr. for W. G. Franz (cons. engr.), Cincinnati, 1913; chief engr. Security Cement & Lime Co., Hagerstown, Md., 1913-18; research engr. Aluminum Co. of America, Massena, N.Y., 1918-20; production mgr. and branch mgr. Porter Chem. Co., Hagerstown, 1920-25; chief engr. Am. Lime & Stone Co., Bellefonte, Pa., since 1925. Registered professional engr. in Pa. Borough engr., Bellefonte, since 1933. Dir. Centre Co. Library Assn.; former dir. Bellefonte Y.M.C.A. Ex-pres. Centre Co. Engrs. Soc. of Pa.; mem. Nat. Soc. Professional Engrs. Republican. Methodist. Mason. Clubs: University of State Coll., Nittany Country, Bellefonte Kiwanis (ex-pres.; dir.). Contbr. to tech. jours. Home: 237 E. Linn St. Office: American Lime & Stone Co., Bellefonte, Pa.

HEWITT, Charles Tredwell, clergyman; b. East Lynne, Mo., May 12, 1884; s. Thomas Jefferson and Mary Abagail (Farmer) H.; prep. edn. Prep. Dept., U. of Washington, Seattle, 1902; student McMinnville (Ore.) Coll., U. of Southern Calif. Coll., Occidental Coll., William Jewell Coll. D.D.; M.Litt., Webster U., Atlanta, Ga., 1932; m. Minnie Grace Darby, Oct. 9, 1911; 1 dau., Mary Kathryn (Mrs. Charles William Meadowcroft, III). Ordained to ministry of Baptist Ch., Cordova, Md., June 1909; pastor Division Street Bapt. Ch., Salisbury, Md., 1909-11, Harrisonburg, Va., 1911-14, Fourth Bapt. Ch., Baltimore, Hampden Bapt. Ch., Baltimore, 1913-22, St. Albans, W.Va., 1922-23, First Bapt. Ch., Martins Ferry, O., 1923-26; asso. pastor Bapt. Temple, Phila., 1926-31; pastor Calvary Bapt. Ch., Hackensack, N.J., 1931-34; pastor Fulton Av. Bapt. Ch., Baltimore, since 1934. Served as 1st lt., chaplain, 324th Inf., 81st Div., U.S. Army, 1918-19; with A.E.F. 9 months, past pres. Ministers Confs., Baltimore, Hackensack; mem. state bd. Md. Bapt. Union Assn. Mem. Am. Legion, chaplain Md. Guard Memorial Post; past chaplain Baltimore, Martins Ferry, O., Phila. posts; dept. chaplain, Md. 1921; chmn. child welfare (Dept. of Md.). Republican. Mason (Scottish Rite, Shriner). Former mem. Kiwanis Club, Martins Ferry, O., and Rotary Club, St. Albans, W.Va. Radio speaker, WCBM, and other stations. Home: 1835 W. Baltimore St., Baltimore, Md.

HEWITT, George, engr., architect; b. Paterson, N.J., Jan. 30, 1876; s. William and Mary (Rainey) H.; ed. Paterson pub. and high schs.; student Rogers & Magee Prep. Sch., 1891-92; M.E., Stevens Inst. Tech., 1896; m. Nellie Latham, Apr. 14, 1903; children—Frances Elizabeth, William Latham; m. 2d, Irma Marselus Post, Nov. 9, 1925; 1 son, Edward Speer. Mech. and structural engr. Passaic Rolling Mills, 1896-1906; mem. firm Lee & Hewitt, engrs. and architects, since 1906; county engr. and road supervisor Passaic County, 1934-38. Former mem. Passaic County Planning Bd. Served as engring. mgr. Boston Ordnance Office, World War, 1918. Treas. Passaic Valley Flood Control Commn.; trustee Paterson Orphan Asylum. Mem. Am. Soc. Civil Engrs., Am. Inst. Architects, Passaic County Engring. Soc.; State Assn. County Engrs. (ex-pres.). Democrat. Mem. Reformed Ch. Mason (Scottish Rite; Past Master Ivanhoe Lodge No. 88, F.&A.M.; Past Grand Marshall Grand Lodge F.&A.M. of N.J.). Organist and choir director in various churches; mem. Friday Afternoon Music Club. Home: 551 E. 29th St. Office: 152 Market St., Paterson, N.J.

HEYL, Lawrence, librarian; b. New York, N. Y., July 12, 1893; s. Lorentz and Annie (Olson) H.; student Coll. of City of N.Y., 1910-13; m. Bertha Sackmann, Aug. 12, 1916; 1 son, Lawrence, Jr. Employed as head of order dept. of U. of Minn. Library, Minneapolis, Minn., 1915-20; chief of acquisitions dept., Princeton Univ. Library, Princeton, N.J. since 1920, acting librarian since 1937. Mem. Am. Library Assn., Bibliog. Soc. of America, N.J. Library Assn. Democrat. Protestant. Home: 9 College Rd., Princeton, N.J.

HEYLIGER, William, author; b. at Hoboken, N.J., Mar. 22, 1884; s. Daniel and Ellen (Sullivan) H.; ed. pub. schs. and Sacred Heart Acad., Hoboken; m. Catherine C. McDermott, June 12, 1906; children—Ellen, Cecilia, Margaret, William, Jr., Elizabeth, Robert, Catherine, Donald. In mercantile business and newspaper work until 1912; contr. Youth's Companion. Roman Catholic. Author: Bartley, Freshman Pitcher, 1911; Bucking the Line, 1912; Captain of the Nine, 1912; Strike Three, 1913; Off Side, 1914; Against Odds, 1915; Don Strong of the Wolf Patrol, 1916; Captain Fair-and-Square, 1916; County Pennant, 1917; Don Strong, Patrol Leader, 1918; Fighting for Fairview, 1918; High Benton, 1919; Dan's Tomorrow, 1922; The Spirit of the Leader, 1923; Quinby and Son, 1925; Dorset's Twister, 1926; Fighting Captain, and Other Stories, 1926; Making of Peter Cray, 1927; Macklin Brothers, 1928; Jerry Hicks and His Gang, 1929; Jerry Hicks, Ghost Hunter, 1929; Yours Truly, Jerry Hicks, 1929; Builder of the Dam, 1929; Bean-ball Bill and Other Stories, 1930; Bill Darrow's Victory, 1930; Jerry Hicks, Explorer, 1930; Hot-Dog Partners, 1931; Quarterback Hothead, 1931; Johnny Bree, 1931; Boys Who Became President, 1932; Gallant Crosby, 1933; Ritchie of The News, 1933; Silver Run, 1934; Steve Merrill, Engineer, 1935; Dark Conquest, 1936; Mill in the Woods, 1936; Brave Years, 1937; Backfield Play, 1938; River Man, 1938. Home: 188 Teaneck Rd., Ridgefield Park, N.J.*

HEYWOOD, Harry B., publisher; b. Conshohocken, Pa., Dec. 6, 1867; s. William and Sarah A. (Lawson) H.; ed. pub. schs., Conshohocken; m. Laura Leedom, June 20, 1906 (died Sept. 18, 1920); children—Sarah Leedom, Lillian Leedom; m. 2d, Gertrude Gibson, May 19, 1923. Purchased Conshohocken Record, Dec. 1, 1890, editor and pub., 1890-94; organized Recorder Publishing Co., 1894, and since pres. and pub.; dir. First Nat. Bank; dir. Times-Chronicle Co., Jenkintown. Sch. dir., Conshohocken, 1 term; town councilman, Jenkintown, 3 terms. Pres. since founding in 1918 of Montgomery-Bucks Newspaper Assn.; vice-pres. Pa. Newspaper Assn., 1935. Republican. Home: 326 Summit Av., Jenkintown, Pa. Office: Hector and Forrest Sts., Conshohocken, Pa.

HIBBEN, Samuel Galloway, engr. elec. illumination; b. Hillsboro, O., June 6, 1888; s. Joseph M. and Henriette (Martin) H.; B.Sc., Case Sch. of Applied Science (Cleveland), 1910, hon. E. E., 1915; student U. of Paris, Sorbonne, France, 1918; m. Ruth Rittenhouse, Apr. 14, 1924; children—Eleanor Rittenhouse, Stuart Galloway, Barry Cummings, Craig Rittenhouse. Began as electrician, 1906; illuminating engr. Macbeth Evans Glass Co., Pittsburgh, Pa., 1910-15; cons. engr., Pittsburgh, 1915-16; with Westinghouse Lamp Co. since 1916, dir. of lighting since 1933. Served as 2d and 1st lt. U.S. Army, searchlight design Washington, D.C., and capt. sound ranging, A.E.F., World War. Mem. Am. Inst. Elec. Engrs., Soc. Am. Mil. Engrs., Illuminating. Engrs. Soc., Am. Soc. Agrl. Engrs., Illuminating Engrs. of London, Sigma Nu. Republican. Presbyn. Clubs: Engineers, Ohio Soc. of New York. Contbr. tech. articles. Home: 31 Clinton Av., Montclair, N.J. Office: 150 Broadway, New York, N.Y.

HIBBS, Ben, editor and writer; b. Fontana, Kan., July 23, 1901; s. Russell and Elizabeth (Smith) H.; A.B., U. of Kan., 1923; m. Edith Kathleen Doty, June 3, 1930; 1 son, Stephen Doty. News editor Fort Morgan (Colo.) Times, 1923, Pratt (Kan.) Tribune, 1924; prof. journalism, Hays (Kan.) State Coll., 1924-26; editor and mgr. Goodland (Kan.) News-Republic, 1926-27; managing editor Arkansas City (Kans.) Traveler, 1927-29; asso. editor Country Gentleman, Phila., Pa., since 1929. Mem. Phi. Beta Kappa, Sigma Delta Chi, Sigma Phi Epsilon. Republican. Methodist. Contbr. articles to Country Gentleman, Saturday Evening Post, Readers Digest and other nat. mags. Home: 713 Braeburn Lane, Penn Valley, Narberth, Pa. Office. Curtis Publishing Co., Philadelphia, Pa.

HIBSHMAN, Edward Kraatz, exec. sec. Penn State Alumni Assn.; b. Ephrata, Pa., Sept. 9, 1887; s. George and Mary (Kraatz) H.; B.S. in Agr., Pa. State Coll., 1909; m. Carrie Bowes, Mar. 24, 1913. Employed in state and federal cooperative tobacco investigations in Pa., 1909-12; asst. dir. Agrl. Extension, Pa. State Coll., 1912-20, asst. to pres. of coll. in pub. relations, 1920-30; exec. sec. Penn State Alumni Assn. since 1930; operate farms in Lancaster Co. which have been in family name since 1761. Mem. agrl. com. of Pa. Bankers Assn. since 1923. Pres. and former conv. dir. Am. Alumni Council. Former dir. Pennsylvania-New York Joint Stock Land Bank, Rochester, N.Y., and Joint Stock Land Bank, Cleveland, O. Served as sec. State Farm Products Show, 1917-25. Mem. Alpha Zeta, Phi Kappa Phi, Iota Lambda Sigma. Rotarian. Republican. Presbyn. Mason (K.T., 32°, Shriner). Home: 220 Frazier St. Office: 104 Old Main, State College, Pa.

HIBSHMAN, Eugene Emanuel, rabbi; b. Cleveland, O., Oct. 6, 1904; s. William and Elizabeth (Kohn) H.; B.A., U. of Cincinnati, 1925; B.H., Hebrew Union Coll., 1925; Rabbi, Hebrew Union Coll., 1928; studied Western Reserve U., summer, 1922, U. of Chicago, quarter, 1933. Rabbi Temple Beth Israel, Altoona, since 1928. Mem. Randolf McMullin Commn. (charitable) for Blair, Cambria and Huntingdon counties; dir. Blair Co. Chapter Am. Red Cross, Federation of Jewish Philanthropies of Altoona, B'nai B'rith. Mem. Central Conf. of Am. Rabbis, Hebrew Union College Alumni Assn., B'nai B'rith. Home: Penn-Alto Hotel. Address: 3004 Union Av., Altoona, Pa.

HICKERSON, Ainslee Earl, newspaper pub.; b. Hatfield, Mo., May 21, 1904; son of John L. and Virgie Iona (Snedaker) H.; grad. Mt. Ayr (Ia.) High Sch., 1923; A.B., State U. of Ia., 1928; m. Violette Jane Smith, June 16, 1934. Began as pub. Brownsville (Pa.) Telegraph, 1928; became mgr., sec. and treas. Phila. Suburban Newspapers, Inc., 1934, pres. since 1939; pub. Main Line Times, 69th St. News, Germantown Courier; treas. Brownsville Pub. Co. Mem. Acacia, Sigma Delta Chi. Republican. Presbyterian. Mason. Club: Rotary (Ardmore). Home: 104 Wynnedale Rd., Narberth, Pa. Office: 311 E. Lancaster Av., Ardmore, Pa.

HICKEY, David F., clergyman; b. Erie, Pa., Apr. 2, 1867; s. Matthew C. and Elizabeth (O'Callaghan) H.; ed. St. Bonaventure Coll., Alleghany, N.Y., Am. Coll., Louvain, Belgium; (hon.) LL.D., St. Bonaventure Coll., 1916. Ordained priest R.C. Ch., 1891; formerly pastor at Tidioute, Pa., Emlenton, Pa., and Johnsonburg, Pa.; rector St. Bernard Ch., Bradford, Pa. since 1915; apptd. Domestic Prelate with the title of Monsignor, by His Holiness, Pope Pius XI, 1928; made dean of Bradford District, 1927; appointed Vicar General of the Diocese of Erie by His Excellency Most Rev. John Mark Gannon, May 1939. Republican. Roman Catholic. Home: 98 E. Corydon St., Bradford, Pa.

HICKMAN, Joseph Newton Kurtz, univ. prof.; b. Lovettsville, Va., Aug. 17, 1876; s. George Luther Kurtz and Rosie Mae (Conard) H.; A.B., Gettysburg (Pa.) Coll., 1899, A.M., 1900; A.M., Columbia Univ., 1915; m. Bessie Fleming Keim, June 26, 1901; 1 dau., Elizabeth Mae (Mrs. Henry Pritting Zimmerman). Instr. Peekskill N.Y. Mil. Acad., 1900-03; head sci. dept. State Teachers Coll., Indiana, Pa., 1903-10; dean and head biology dept. Grove City Coll., Pa., 1910-12; supt. city schs., Lancaster, Pa., 1912-14; supervising prin. pub. schs., Flemington, N.J., 1918-20; master Lawrenceville (N.J.) Sch. for Boys, 1920-24; prof. edn., Rutgers U. (coll. for Women and Sch. of Edn.), New Brunswick, N.J., since 1924. Served as Army Y.M. C.A. sec. and ednl. dir., Camp Meade; asst. dir. Nat. Red Cross hdqrs., Washington, D.C.; mem. speakers com. for Relief in Belgium (Pa. com.). Mem. A.A.A.S., N.E.A., N.J. State Edn. Assn., Phi Beta Kappa, Phi Delta Kappa. Republican. Presbyn. Mason (K.T., Shriner). Clubs: Rutgers Alumni & Faculty (New Brunswick); Ingleside (Indiana, Pa.); Community (Sandy Point, Me.). Lecturer at edn. convs. Home: 109 Nichol Av., New Brunswick, N.J.

HICKOK, Paul Robinson, clergyman; b. Nebraska City, Neb., April 6, 1877; s. Rev. Francis M. (D.D.) and Mary Matilda (Robinson) H.; grad. prep. dept. Hastings (Neb.) Coll.; student Hanover (Ind.) Coll., D.D., 1920; B.A., Coll. of Wooster, O., 1897; grad. Auburn Theol. Sem., 1900; m. Mary, d. Rev. John Calvin Elliott, Sept. 6, 1900. Ordained Presbyn. ministry, 1900; asst. pastor "Old Stone" (First) Ch., Cleveland, O., 1900-02; pastor First Ch., Delaware, O., 1902-09; Metropolitan Ch., Washington, D.C., 1909-17; 2d Ch., Troy, N.Y., 1917-28, Forest Hill Church, Newark, N.J., since Nov. 1, 1928. Chaplain Fifth Infantry, Ohio N.G., 1900-09; dir. religious work Nat. War Work Council of Y.M.C.A. in group of camps of Washington Dist., 1918. Mem. Presbyn. Bd. of Ch. Erection since 1912; trustee Coll. of Wooster, 1915-22. Nat. Chaplain Alpha Tau Omega since 1916 (nat. pres. 1908-10). Mem. Pi Gamma Mu, Theta Phi. Republican. Mason (32°, K. T.). Dir. of "Told by Paul Hickok" sect. in Alpha Tau Omega "Palm" since 1928. Contbr. to mags. Home: 106 Heller Parkway, Newark, N.J.

HICKS, Ami Mali, artist, author; b. Brooklyn, N.Y., Jan. 3, 1876; d. George Cleveland and Josephine (Mali) Hicks; ed. Brooklyn (N. Y.) private schs., and art schs., Paris and Berlin, 1892; unmarried. Began as designer of metalwork, New York, 1896; designer Yale & Towne, Architectural Metal, Stamford, Conn., 1908-12; designer, Tiffany Studios, New York since 1921;, painter of costumes for theatrical productions The Miracle, Will Shakespeare, Road to Rome, Gilbour, and many others. Unitarian Quaker. Clubs: Town Hall (New York). Author: Craft of Handmade Rugs, 1914; Everyday Art, 1926; Color in Action, 1937. Home: Scotch Plains, N.J. Office: 141 E. 17th St., New York, N.Y.

HICKS-BRUUN, Mildred M. (Mrs. Johannes Hadeln Bruun), research chemist; b. Evington, Va., Jan. 30, 1900; d. Everdell Altamont and Minnie Hay (Patrick) Hicks; ed. by governess, 1905-12; grad. New London Acad., Forest, Va., 1917; B.A., Randolph-Macon Woman's Coll., Lynchburg, Va., 1921; studied Cornell U., summer, 1922, U. of Va., summer, 1923; M.S., U. of Iowa, 1925, Ph.D., 1930; student George Washington U., 1927-28, Columbia U., summer, 1929, U. of Ia., summer, 1928; m. Dr. Johannes Hadeln Bruun, May 1, 1930. Head dept. chemistry, Columbia (S.C.) Coll., 1921-23; head science dept., Biwabik (Minn.) High Sch., 1923-24; grad. asst., U. of Iowa, 1924-25; research chemists Am. Aniline Products Co., Lock Haven, Pa., 1925-26, Nat. Bureau of Standards, Washington, D.C., 1926-32, Sun Oil Co., Norwood, Pa., since 1932; cons. chemist Nat. Bureau of Standards since 1932. Mem. Am. Chem. Soc., Am. Petroleum Inst., Pa. Acad. Science, D.A.R., Nat. Woman's Party. Republican. Episcopalian. Writer various scientific articles on physical chemistry and petroleum research, in Jour. Physical Chemistry, Bur. of Standards Jour. of Research, Jour. Am. Chem. Soc., Industrial Engring. Chemistry. Home: 423 Riverview Road, Swarthmore, Pa. Office: Sun Oil Co. Laboratory, Norwood, Pa.

HIERS, Glen Sefton, chemist; b. Connersville, Ind., Aug. 17, 1896; s. Franklin Edward and Pearl Augusta (Sefton) H.; B.S., Miami U., 1919; A.M., Northwestern U., 1921; M.S., U. of Ill., 1924, Ph.D., same, 1926; m. Mildred Douthitt, June 15, 1920; children—Thomas Sefton, Richard Hyde. Employed as research chemist E. I. DuPont de Nemours Co., Wilmington, Del., 1926-28; research fellow Mellon Inst., Industrial Research, Pittsburgh, Pa., 1928-31; chief chemist Collins & Aikman Corpn., mfr. textiles, Phila., Pa., since 1931. Served in C.W.S., 1918. Mem. A.A.A.S., Am. Chem. Soc., Am. Assn. of Textile Chemists, Phi Beta Kappa, Sigma Xi, Phi Lambda Upsilon, Phi Kappa Tau. Republican. Episcopalian. Club: Cynwyd (Bala-Cynwyd). Home: 130 Cynwyd Rd., Bala-Cynwyd, Pa. Office: 51st & Parkside Av., Philadelphia, Pa.

HIGBEE, Donald Mestrezat, lawyer; b. Connellsville, Pa., Jan. 17, 1899; s. Edward Carter and Emma (Lint) H.; grad. Connellsville High Sch., 1917; A.B., Amherst Coll., 1921; LL.B., U. of Pittsburgh, 1925; m. Martha Elizabeth Port, Oct. 17, 1929; children—Martha Jane, Edward Carter, 2d. Admitted to Pa. bar, 1925, U.S. Supreme Ct., 1938, practiced in Connellsville and Uniontown, Pa., since 1925; mem. Higbee, Lewellyn & Higbee. Mem. Pa. and Am. Bar Assn. Home: 215 W. Cedar Av., Connellsville, Pa.

HIGBEE, William Smithers, M.D.; b. Philadelphia, Pa., Feb. 10, 1863; s. James Lane and Amanda (Carpenter) H.; ed. private schs.; m. Sara Leddenstrang, June 1, 1918. In gen. practice of medicine since 1884; physician Pa. Salt Mfg. Co. since 1898, Integrity Trust Co., Phila., 1932-37. Pres. Pa. State Bd. of Examiners for Registration of Nurses, 1909-19. Home: 5121 Pine St. Office: Delaware Av. and Shunk St., Philadelphia, Pa.

HIGBIE, Edgar Creighton, educator; b. Berlin, Wis., July 31, 1875; s. Columbus Jerome and Ann Electa (Wilson) H.; student U. of Minn. Sch. of Agr., Ripon College Acad., Carleton Coll. (Northfield, Minn.), U. of Chicago; A.B., U. of Minn., 1907, A.M., 1909; Ph.D., Columbia, 1921; m. Nellie May Leslie, June 15, 1904; children—Howard Ernest, Leslie Wilson. Dir. West Central Minn. Sch. of Agr., 1910-17; pres. Eastern S.D. State Teachers Coll., 1920-31, J. Ormond Wilson Teachers Coll., Washington, D.C., since 1931. Visiting instr., summer sessions, Boston U. and George Peabody Coll. for Teachers. Mem. N.E.A., Federal Schoolmen's Club, Phi Delta Kappa. Republican. Conglist. Mason. Home: 127 N. Chelsea Lane, Bethesda, Md.

HIGGINS, Charles Alfred, business exec.; b. Gillingham, Kent, Eng., July 2, 1888; s. George and Elizabeth Eleanor (Wheeler) H.; ed. private schs., England; m. Marion Dunham, of Wilmington, Del., June 4, 1920; 1 son, Charles Alfred. Came to U.S., 1915, naturalized, 1931. Chemist New Explosives Co., Ltd., Eng., 1910-15; chief chemist Union Powder Corpn., Parlin, N.J., 1915-16; asso. with Hercules Powder Co., Wilmington, Del., since 1916, as mgr. development dept., then v.p. and now pres. since 1939; dir. Equitable Trust Co., Continental Am. Life Ins. Co. Mem. Acad. of Polit. Sciences. Presbyn. Clubs: Wilmington, Wilmington Country, Concord Country, Vicmead Hunt, Burris Run Skeet, Hercules Country (all Wilmington). Home: 906 du Pont Rd., Westover Hills, Wilmington, Del. Office: Hercules Powder Co., Wilmington, Del.

HIGGINS, Henry Bertram, v.p. Pittsburgh Plate Glass Co.; b. Newburyport, Mass., Sept. 7, 1882; s. James Henry and Alice A. (Cheney) H.; A.B., Harvard U., 1904; m. Helen Agnew, Nov. 14, 1910; children—Elizabeth, James H., II. With Pittsburgh Plate Glass Co. since 1905, beginning as stenographer, Minneapolis Warehouse, 1905, asst. mgr., Minneapolis, 1910-12, local mgr., Kansas City, 1912, mgr. plate glass sales, Pittsburgh (gen. office), 1917-25, gen. sales mgr., 1925-28, v.p. and chmn. commercial dept. since 1928, now also dir.; dir. Montour Railroad. Mem. Borough Council, Edgeworth Borough, Pa. Trustee Magee Hosp., Pittsburgh. Republican. Presbyterian. Clubs: Duquesne, Edgeworth, Rolling Rock, Allegheny Country. Home: Woodland Road, Sewickley, Pa. Office: Grant Bldg., Pittsburgh, Pa.

HIGGINS, John Mark, physician; b. Sayre, Pa., Nov. 17, 1890; s. William P. and Mary (Cunneen) H.; grad. Sayre High Sch., 1908; M.D., Georgetown U., 1913; m. Eileen O'Donnell, Oct. 12, 1921; children—Eileen Loretta, Rita Ann. Interne Robert Packer Hosp., Sayre, Pa., 1913-14, resident house surgeon, 1914-15; practice of medicine, Sayre, since 1915; in charge div. of obstetrics, Robert Packer Hosp., 1918-28, organized div. of pediatrics, 1922, and since in charge. Served as 1st lt. Med. Corps, U.S. Army, 1918-19. Mem. Bd. of Edn., Sayre, since 1933, pres., 1935-37; chmn. Emergency Child Health Com. for Bradford Co., 1933-38. Fellow Am. Coll. Physicians, A.M.A., Am. Acad. Pediatrics; mem. Pa. State Med. Soc. (sec. pediatrix sect. 1936-38, chmn. 1938-39). Republican. Catholic. K. of C. Home: 600 S. Wilbur Av. Office: 114 W. Packer Av., Sayre, Pa.

HIGGINS, Nathan Bert, engr.; b. Morris Run, Pa., Feb. 15, 1885; s. Eleazer Ellsworth and Martha Ann (Lloyd) H.; B.S., Penn. State Coll., 1909; spl. courses elec. engring. Johns Hopkins U., 1920-22; m. Gertrude Meginney Hood, Dec. 24, 1909; children—Gertrude Atwell (dec.), Elizabeth Jean. Employed as draftsman and estimator with bridge cos., 1909-11; with Western Md. R.R. Co., 1912-13; chief draftsman, Pa. Water & Power Co., Baltimore, Md., 1914-17, engr. design and maintenance, 1918-19, asst. chief engr., 1920-29; asst. chief engr. Pa. Water & Power Co. and Safe Harbor Water Power Corpn., Baltimore, Md., 1929-33, chief engr. since 1933. Mem. Am. Inst. Elec. Engrs., Am. Soc. Mech. Engrs., Am. Soc. for Testing Materials, Am. Concrete Inst., Am. Welding Soc., Md. Acad. Scis., Engrs. Club Baltimore, Acacia. Registered as professional engr. in Pa. Clubs: Rodgers Forge Golf (Towson); Sherwood Forest (Sherwood Forest). Home: Lake Sta, Ruxton. Office: Lexington Bldg., Baltimore, Md.

HIGGINS, Robert Arlington, football coach; b. Corning, N.Y., Dec. 24, 1893; s. Michael Hennesey and Nancy (Purcell) H.; ed. Peddie Sch., Hightstown, N.J., 1911-14, Pa. State Coll., 1914-17, 1918; m. Virginia Gaylord, Dec. 6, 1922; children—Mary Ann, Virginia Gaylord, Nancy Purcell. Engaged as head football coach, West Va. Wesleyan Coll., 1920-24; head football coach, Pa. State Coll. since 1930. Served as capt. inf., U.S.A., 1917-18, with A.E.F. in France and Germany. Mem. Beta Theta Pi. Republican. Episcopalian. Home: 701 McKee St., State College, Pa.

HIGGINS, Ruth Loving, coll. dean, prof. history; b. Columbus, O., June 21, 1895; d. Charles and Jessie Hoover (Schatzman) H.; B.A., B.S. in Edn., Ohio State U., 1917, M.A. (scholarship), 1921, Ph.D. (2 fellowships), 1926; post grad. work U. of Wis., summer 1922, Cambridge U., Eng., summer 1929. Teacher history, civics, Ohio high schs., 1917-20, instr. history, polit. science, Elmira (N.Y.) Coll., 1924-25; asst. prof., Earlham Coll. Richmond, Ind., 1925-26; prof. and head of dept., Huntingdon Coll. (formerly Woman's Coll. of Ala.), Montgomery, 1926-34; mem. history faculty U. of Ala., summers 1930-31; dean and prof. history, Beaver Coll., Jenkintown, Pa., since 1934. Mem. Am. Hist. Assn., Miss. Valley Hist. Assn. (mem. exec. com.), Southern Polit. Science Assn. (sec. 1933), Nat. Assn. Deans of Women (editorial staff, 1935-38), N.E.A., Pa. Hist. Assn., Middle States Assn. of History and Social Science Teachers, Pa. Ednl. Assn., Am. Assn. Univ. Profs., O. State U. Assn., Am. Assn. U. Women (pres. of Montgomery br. 1929-31; v.p. Ala. div. 1933-34), Pa. Assn. Deans of Women (chmn. publs.), Delta Kappa Gamma. Presbyn. Club: Women's Univ. (Philadelphia). Author: Expansion in New York, with Especial Reference to Eighteenth Century, 1931. Contbr. hist. reviews. Home: Greenwood Terrace Apt., Jenkintown, Pa.

HIGGINS, Thomas Joseph, coll. pres.; b. Phila. Pa., Apr. 20, 1899; s. Thomas and Ellen (Slean) H.; grad. St. Joseph's Coll. High Sch., 1915; novitiate St. Andrew, Poughkeepsie, N.Y., 1915, A.B., A.M., Woodstock (Md.) Coll., 1922, theol. studies, 1925-29, Ph.D., 1931. Mem. Society of Jesus since 1915. Teacher, Boston Coll. High Sch., 1922-25; ordained to the priesthood, 1928; with St. Joseph's Coll., Phila., since 1929, as dean of men, 1929-32, dean of coll., 1932-33, pres. of coll. since 1933. Mem. Assn. of Coll. Pres. of Pa., Nat. Cath. Edn. Assn., Am. Acad. Polit. Science. Home: 18th and Thompson Sts. Office: 54th and City Line Av., Overbrook, Philadelphia, Pa.

HIGH, Samuel H., lawyer, banker; b. Norristown, Pa., July 17, 1875; s. Harry S. and Flora B. H.; LL.B., Franklin & Marshall Coll., 1899; m. Ada E. Pennypacker, Mar. 22, 1905; children—Samuel H., Gilbert P., Sarah B. Admitted to Pa. bar, 1899; since in gen. practice of law at Norristown; mem. law firm Hub, Dettra & Swartz since 1914; v.p. and trust officer Jenkintown Bank & Trust Co. since 1925. Solicitor for twps. of Cheltenham, Upper Moreland, Lower Moreland and Borough of Jenkintown. Home: Horsham, Pa. Office: 40 E. Airy St., Norristown, Pa.

HIGHBERGER, Elmer, Jr., physician; b. Greensburg, Pa., Nov. 15, 1904; s. Elmer and Lydia Ann (Schubert) H.; A.B., magna cum laude, Franklin and Marshall Coll., 1926; ed. Columbia U., summer 1925; M.D., Johns Hopkins U. Med. Sch., 1930; grad. study Harvard U. Med. Sch., 1930; unmarried. Interne Johns Hopkins and Baltimore City hosps., 1929, Baltimore City Hosps., 1930-31, asst. resident in medicine, 1931-32, resident in medicine, 1932-33; instr. medicine, Johns Hopkins Med. Sch., 1932-33; chief resident phys., Western Pa. Hosp., Pittsburgh, 1933-34, mem. med. staff, 1934-36; grad. study in tuberculosis and practice of internal medicine, asso. with Dr. Lawrason Brown, Saranac Lake, N.Y., 1935-37; med. dir. Grand View Instn., Oil City, Pa. since 1937; mem. staff internal medicine and instr. internal medicine Sch. of Nurses, Oil City Hosp., and cons. practice internal medicine since 1937. Served as 1st lt. Med. Res. U.S.A., Inactive, since 1932. Diplomate Am. Bd. Internal Medicine. Asso. Fellow Am. Coll., Phys. Fellow A.M.A., Am. Coll. Chest Phys. Mem. Pa. State, and Venango Co. med. socs., Phi Beta Kappa, Sigma Pi, Alpha Kappa Kappa. Republican. Mem. Reformed Ch. Mason. Clubs: Acacia, Kiwanis (Oil City). Home: Grand View Institution, Oil City, Pa.

HILDEBRANDT, Emanuel Henry Carl, mathematics; b. LaSalle, Ill., Sept. 21, 1902; s. Rev. Henry Carl Martin and Martha Caroline (Locher) H.; B.S., U. of Chicago, 1922; grad. study, U. of Chicago, 1928-29, summers 1923-29; A.M., U. of Mich., 1930, Ph.D., same, 1932; m. Elizabeth Arnold Tilden, Sept. 12, 1934; children—Ethel Caroline, Henry Francis. Engaged as teacher mathematics, high sch., Stevens Point, Wis., 1922-24, prin., 1924-28; instr. mathematics, U. of Mich., 1929-31; asst. prof. mathematics, De Pauw U., 1931-33; instr. mathematics, Brooklyn (N.Y.) Coll., 1933-34; instr. mathematics, N.J. State Teachers Coll., Upper Montclair, N.J., 1934-36, asst. prof. since 1936. Mem. Am. Math. Soc., Math Assn. of America, Inst. Math. Statistics, Nat. Council Teachers of Mathematics, Assn. of Math. Teachers of N.J., Sigma Xi. Mem. Evang. & Ref. Ch. Asso. editor, American Mathematical Monthly. Home: 43 Norman Road, Upper Montclair, N.J.

HILDENBERGER, Martin Joseph, gen. ins.; b. South Bethlehem, Pa., Jan. 25, 1884; s. Martin and Kate (Daley) H.; ed. pub. schs., South Bethlehem, Bethlehem Business Coll., Pub. Night Sch., Buffalo, N.Y.; m. Katherine V. Nolan, Apr. 29, 1908; children—Katherine Angela, Joseph Garret, Mary, Martin Joseph, Margaret Catherine, Anne Catherine, Gertrude Veronica, Lucy Elizabeth, Francis Thomas. Printer's apprentice, 1898-1901; printer, 1901-03; div. stenographer L.V.R.R., Buffalo, 1903-05; stenographer to vice-pres. Bethlehem Steel Co., 1905-07, to purchasing agent, 1907-09; buyer Bethlehem Steel Co., 1911-15; purchasing agt., Bethlehem Foundry & Machine Co., 1915-20; official court stenographer courts of Northampton Co., Easton, Pa., since 1921; entered insurance business, 1908; formed partnership with G. A. Hildenberger, 1912; organized Hildenberger-Goodwin, realty and insurance business, 1919; reorganized 1926, to Hildenberger & Green, Inc., gen. insurance, Bethlehem, Easton and Allentown, pres. since orgn.; dir. Bethlehem Nat. Bank, since orgn., 1934. Mem. South Bethlehem Bd. Sch. Dirs., 1905-10; former mem. Bethlehem Chamber of Commerce; former chmn. Dem. Ward Com. Mem. State of Pa. Agents Assn., Nat. Assn. of Ins. Agents. Mem. Holy Name Soc. (pres. local 20 yrs.); dist. pres. Lehigh-Northampton Regional Union, 1936-37. Democrat. Roman Catholic, K. of C. (sec. state Council 10 yrs.). Clubs: Jacksonian Democratic, American-Irish (Bethlehem). Home: 468 Montclair Av. Office: Union Bank & Trust Bldg., Bethlehem, Pa.

HILDNER, Richard Charles, asso. prof. mathematics; b. Pittsburgh, Pa., Sept. 23, 1907; s. Leonard F. W. and Rexa Mary (Langfett) H.; B.S., The Coll. of Wooster (O.), 1928; A.M., Ohio State U., 1930, Ph.D., same, 1933; unmarried. Engaged as substitute prof. mathematics, Mount Union Coll., Alliance, O., 1934-36, asst. prof., 1936-37, asso. prof. mathematics since 1937. Mem. Am. Math. Soc., Math. Assn. of America, Am. Assn. Univ. Profs., Sigma Xi, Phi Beta Kappa, Gamma Alpha. Democrat. Presbyn. Home: 1805 Morrell St., Pittsburgh, Pa. Office: Mount Union College, Alliance, O.

HILDT, Thomas, investment banker; b. Baltimore, Md.; s. George C. and Margaret (Thomas) H.; ed. Marston's Univ. Sch., Baltimore, Md.; m. Dorothy Ford, Nov. 24, 1909; children—Margaret, Thomas, John. Treas. Southern Electric Co., Baltimore, Md., 1907-09; asst. cashier Nat. Bank of Commerce, Baltimore, Md., 1909-10, cashier, 1910-12, v.p., 1914; v.p. Astor Trust Co., New York City, 1914-17; v.p. and mem. mng. com. Bankers Trust Co., New York City, 1917-21; pres. Merchants Nat. Bank, Baltimore, Md., 1921-24; partner Alex. Brown & Sons, Baltimore, since 1924; dir. and mem. exec. com. Sharp & Dohme, Inc., Phila., Pa.; dir. and mem. finance com. Canada Dry Ginger Ale, Inc., New York City. Served as chmn. of bankers com., Liberty Loan activities for 3d and 4th Liberty Loan and Victory Loan Drives in New York during World War. Fiscal agt. for State of Md., 1921-23. Clubs: The Links (New York City); Nat. Golf (Southampton, L.I. New York); Maryland (Baltimore, Md.). Home: 2 Wyndhurst Av. Office: 4 S. Calvert St., Baltimore, Md.

HILDUM, Clayton Edward, ry. official; b. Jamestown, N.Y., April 2, 1871; s. Edward Burke and Chloe Nichols (Wellington) H.; student Thiel Coll., 1893-95; A.B., Wittenberg Coll., 1897; m. Mary C. Schambs, July 5, 1899; children—Mary Elizabeth, Edward Barkdoll, Frederick Wellington. Clk. with Erie R.R. Co., 1898-1905; auditor in various depts., 1905-1913; mgr. accounting dept. U.S.R.R. Administrn., 1918-20; comptroller Lehigh Valley R.R., 1920-24, v.p., 1924-30, exec. v.p., 1930-38, now in special work for Lehigh Valley R.R. in coal region; pres. Coxe Bros. & Co., Inc., coal production. Served with U.S.N., Spanish-Am. War. Mem. Alpha Tau Omega. Republican. Clubs: Railroad, Traffic (New York). Home: 945 Woodland Av., Plainfield, N.J. Office: 143 Liberty St., New York, N.Y.

HILGENBERG, Carl George, mfg. exec.; b. Baltimore, Md., Oct. 1, 1873; s. Charles and Johanne (Lertz) H.; student Scheib Sch., Baltimore, Md.; grad. Deichmann Sch., Baltimore, Md.; m. Angelica Rogge, Jan. 11., 1898; children—Carl Rogge, Charles Edward, Angela Carr (Mrs. Joseph Marshall Gardiner). Asso. with Carr-Lowrey Glass Co., Baltimore, Md., since 1896, successively as office boy, sec., 1899-1901, pres., 1901-31, exec. chmn. since 1931; dir. Union Trust Co. of Md. Dir. Md. Workshop for the Blind. Clubs: Merchants, Baltimore Country (Baltimore, Md.); Gibson Island (Md.). Home: 12 Bishops Rd., Guilford, Baltimore. Office: 2201-2221 Kloman St., Baltimore, Md.

HILL, Arthur Middleton, transportation exec.; b. Charleston, W.Va., Mar. 23, 1892; s. Arthur Edward and Ellen Dickinson (Middleton) H.; ed. Central Missouri State Teachers College; m. Caroline Quarrier Staunton, June 29, 1918; children—Frederick Staunton, Caroline Quarrier. Pres. Atlantic Greyhound Corpn., Capitol Greyhound Lines, Charleston Transit Co., W.Va. Sand & Gravel Co.; Standard Brick & Supply Co.; v.p. and dir. The Greyhound Corpn.; dir. Truax-Traer Coal Co., Kanawha City Co., Kanawha Banking & Trust Co., Kanawha Land Co., Diamond Ice & Coal Co. Served as 2d lt., later capt. and asst. chief of staff, 77th Div., U.S.A., World War; grad. Army Gen. Staff Coll., Langres, France. Pres. Nat. Assn. Motor Bus Operators; mem. Joint Com. of Railroads and Highway Users; chmn. Motor Bus Code Authority NRA, 1933-35. Member American Automobile Assn. (dir.; mem. exec. com. 1928-35), Chamber Commerce of U.S. (dir. and mem. exec. com.), Am. Electric Ry. Assn. (mem. exec. com. 1932-34), Public Utilities Assn. W.Va. (pres. 1927-28), W.Va. Motor Transportation (pres. 1925-27), Southern W.Va. Automobile Club (pres. 1927-29). Republican. Episcopalian. Mason (32°, Shriner). Clubs: Rotary, Edgewood Country, Kanawha Country (Charleston); University, Metropolitan, Columbia Country, Burning Tree (Washington). Home: Staunton Rd., South Hills. Office: 1100 Kanawha Valley Bldg., Charleston, W.Va.

HILL, Bancroft, transportation exec.; b. Baltimore, Md., May 5, 1887; s. Charles Ebenezer and Kate Watts (Clayton) H.; student Johns Hopkins, 1906-07; B.S., Mass. Inst. Tech., 1911; m. Frances G. McCoy, May 5, 1915. Began as draftsman, 1915; consulting civil engr., harbor engr., pres. Harbor Bd. of Baltimore, engr. Port Development Commn., 1919-25; valuation engr. United Rys. & Electric Co., Baltimore, 1925-35; exec. v.p. Baltimore Transit Co., 1935-36, pres. since Apr. 1936. Author articles on costs, depreciation, valuation and earnings of pub. utilities. Home: 1812 Sulgrave Av., Mt. Washington Sta. Office: Court Square Bldg., Baltimore, Md.

HILL, Calvin Francis, banker; b. West Penn, Schuylkill Co., Pa., Jan. 8, 1877; s. Levi and Lydia Anna (Dengler) H.; student Lehighton (Pa.) pub. schs., 1884-90; m. Emma M. Geiger, Oct. 2, 1897; children—Wilmer Menno, Viola Lydia (Mrs. Allen T. Fink), Stanley Levi, Mabel Sally. Butcher, Newside, Pa., 1888-1912; railroader Lehigh Valley R.R. Co., 1890-92; farming and butcher, Newside, Pa., 1909-12; live stock dealer, Newside, Pa., 1922-23; founded

Neffs (Pa.) Nat. Bank, 1923, and pres. since 1923, chmn. bldg. com. for new bank bldg. opened 1938; one of organizers Union Bell Telephone Co., Best's, Pa., 1911, and pres. until merger, 1919, with Bell Telephone Co. of Pa.; one of organizers, 1930, of Lehigh Valley Milk Producers Assn., now Lehigh Valley Co-operative Farmers, of which dir. Spl. dep. game warden, 1923-27; sch. dir. Heidelberg Twp., Pa., 1915-21, 1921-27, pres., 1915-21, treas., 1921-28. Trustee Heidelberg Lutheran and Reformed Ch., 1914-18; one of organizers Young People's Soc. of Heidelberg Ch., 1910, and since treas. Mem. Bankers' Assn., Lehigh Co-operative Potato Growers' Assn. Awarded gold medal for potato production (466 bushels per acre), 1928. Republican. Evangelical Lutheran. Odd Fellow (Central Lodge, 636, Jordan, Pa.), United Order Am. Mechanics (Jr.; Allen Council 753). Address: Neffs, Pa.

HILL, Charles Chase, entomologist; b. Melrose, Mass., July 13, 1890; s. Charles Burrill and Harriet (Mendum) H.; student Harvard, 1911-12; B.S., Mass. State Coll., Amherst, Mass., 1914; m. Gertrude Sloane, Sept. 6, 1914; 1 dau., Karolyn Frances. Entomological research, U.S. Dept. of Agr., Nashville, Tenn., 1914-16, Knoxville, Tenn., 1916-17; mem. entomological staff, U.S. Research Lab., Carlisle, Pa., 1917-24; in charge of research lab., Bur. of Entomology and Plant Quarantine, Carlisle, Pa., since 1924. Mem. Am. Assn. of Econ. Entomologists, Pa. Acad. of Sciences, Entomol. Soc. of Washington (D.C.). Methodist. Author of numerous articles on cereal and forage insect pests, insect parasites and the morphology and embryology of certain hymenopterous parasites. Address: 231 Conway St., Carlisle, Pa.

HILL, Eben Clayton, M.D., Roentgenologist; b. Baltimore, Md., Oct. 9, 1882; s. Charles Ebenezer and Kate Watts (Clayton) H.; A.B., Johns Hopkins, 1903, M.D., 1907; matriculate research student, University of Freiburg, Germany, 1904, 05; graduate Army Medical School, 1909; m. Carolyn Sherwin Bailey, Oct. 14, 1936. Assistant in anatomy, Johns Hopkins University Medical Sch., 1907-08; practiced, Baltimore, 1907-08, Poughkeepsie, N.Y., 1913-20; pathologist and radiologist, 1911-13, Roentgenologist, 1912-20, Vassar Hosp. and Dispensary. Instr. 1920-21, asso. in Roentgenol. anatomy, 1921-22, lecturer Roentgenology Johns Hopkins, Roentgenologist U.S. Med. Advisory Bd., U.S.A., for N.Y., 1917-19. First lt. and capt., Med. Corps, U.S.A., 1908-13 (retired). Fellow A.A.A.S.; fellow and life mem. Am. Coll. Physicians, A.M.A.; mem. N.Y. and Dutchess Co. med. socs., Putnam Med. Society, Acad. of Medicine, Baltimore Med. Soc., Med. and Chirurg. Faculty of Md., Am. Roentgen Ray Soc., Soc. for Exptl. Biology and Medicine, Am. Congress Internal Medicine, Johns Hopkins Surg. Soc., Am. Assn. Mammalogists, Soc. of the Cincinnati (Va.), Soc. Descendants Order of the Garter. Republican. Episcopalian. Clubs: Army and Navy (Washington, D.C.); Maryland Club, Alpha Delta Phi, Psi Chi (hon.), Elkridge Fox Hunting. Contbr. research X-ray technic for studying collateral circulation, sacroiliac injuries and effects of rays on cellular life. Proved the necessity in 1909, of massive doses of diphtheria antitoxin in laryngeal and other serious cases of diphtheria; proved the importance, 1910, of carriers in the spread of diphtheria, and the relative unimportance of disinfection and fumigation; showed, 1912, that salvarsan, even in frequent dosages, is not specific in action, and is not the complete curative drug as supposed; invented radiopaque injection method, X-ray illuminator, an attachment for Sibley stove for army use in radiating heat and cooking, card system for recording hosp. med. histories, quickly removable surg. head bandage, mouth gag for use with stomach tube, opaque X-ray emulsion to study circulation, instrument to measure distortion in divergence of X-rays, design for illuminating X-rays based on three new principles. Completed in 1937 anatomical-surgical studies of sacro-iliac joint. Author of Cross Roads of the Mind, 1939. Address: Maryland Club, Baltimore, Md.

HILL, Edward Yates, clergyman; b. Rochester, Mo., Sept. 15, 1868; s. Rev. Isaac and Nancy Jane (Howard) H.; A.B., Baker U., Kan., 1891, D.D., 1905; grad. McCormick Theol. Sem., Chicago, 1894; A.M., Lake Forest (Ill.) U., 1895; m. Mary Moon, June 6, 1900; children—Helen, John Edward. Ordained Presbyn. ministry, 1894; minister Christ Chapel, Chicago, 1894-96; pastor 1st Ch., Warsaw, Ind., 1896-1900, 1st Ch., Logansport, Ind., 1900-04, 1st Ch., Phila. ("mother ch. of Presbyterianism in America"), since 1904. Am. exchange preacher to Great Britain in 1931. Trustee Gen. Assembly Presbyn. Ch. U.S.A., Presbytery of Phila., Tennent Coll. Dir. of Presbyn. Ministers' Fund for Life Ins.; mem. bd. of edn. Presbyn. Ch. U.S.A., 1907-18; dir. McCormick Theol. Sem., 1904-05; mem. Presbyn. Hist. Soc. (board mgrs.); vice-pres. Pa. Bible Soc.; Moderator of Synod of Pa., 1920-21. Clubs: Union League, Phi Alpha, Adelphoi, Buck Hill Golf. Author of papers and addresses on hist. and religious subjects. Home: 6339 Sherwood Road., Overbrook, Philadelphia, Pa.

HILL, E(rnest) Rowland, consulting engr.; b. Pompton, N.J., Jan. 29, 1872; s. Benj. Rowland, Jr., and Hetty M. (Van Duyne) H.; prep. edn., Pratt Inst., Brooklyn, N.Y.; M.E. and E.E., Cornell U., 1893; m. Grace G. Crider, June 1, 1904; 1 dau., Jean S. (Mrs. E. C. Johnson). Gen. shop training, Westinghouse Electric & Mfg. Co., 1893-95; spl. engr. same co., 1895-1901; engr. in chief British Westinghouse Electric & Mfg. Co., London, in charge of all elec., steam, mech. and gen. engring. work of the co., design and constrn. stations, lines, etc., in Gt. Britain, 1901-06; asst. to chief engr. of electric traction in electrification of New York Terminal and tunnels of Pa.R.R. and extension of electrification L.I.R.R., 1906-12; mem. firm Gibbs & Hill, consulting engineers for all electrification work on Pennsylvania R.R., Norfolk & Western Ry. and Virginian Ry.; changes and additions in Cos. Cob Power House and other electric power equipment of N.Y.,N.H.& H.R.R.; electrification of N.Y. Connecting R.R., I.C. R.R., Broad Street Subway, Phila.; engaged in consulting, designing and construction practice. Pres. member bd. Orange Memorial Hosp. Fellow Am. Inst. E.E.; mem. Am. Soc. C.E., Am. Inst. Cons. Engrs., Am. Soc. M.E., Inst. C.E. (London), S.A.R. Presbyn. Clubs: Railroad, Bankers, Rock Spring Country. Home: 111 S. Munn Av., East Orange, N.J. Office: Pennsylvania Station, 7th Av. and 32d St., New York, N.Y.

HILL, Grace Livingston, author; b. Wellsville, N.Y., April 16, 1865; d. Rev. Charles Montgomery and Marcia (Macdonald) Livingston; ed. Cincinnati Art Sch. and under pvt. tutors; m. Rev. Thomas G. F. Hill, Dec. 8, 1892 (died 1899); children—Margaret Livingston (Mrs. Wendell H. Walker), Ruth Glover (Mrs. Gordon Munce). Presbyn. Author: A Chautauqua Idyl, 1887; A Little Servant, 1890; The Parkerstown Delegate, 1892; Katharine's Yesterday, 1896; In the Way, 1897; Lone Point, 1898; A Daily Rate, 1899; An Unwilling Guest, 1901; The Angel of His Presence, 1902; According to the Pattern, 1903; The Story of a Whim, 1902; Because of Stephen, 1903; The Girl from Montana, 1907; Marcia Schuyler, 1908; Phoebe Dean, 1909; Dawn of the Morning, 1910; The Mystery of Mary, 1911; Aunt Crete's Emancipation, 1911; Lo, Michael, 1913; The Best Man, 1914; The Man of the Desert, 1914; Miranda, 1915; The Obsession of Victoria Gracen, 1915; The Finding of Jasper Holt, 1916; A Voice in the Wilderness, 1916; The Witness, 1917; The Red Signal, 1918; The Enchanted Barn, 1918; The War Romance of the Salvation Army, 1919; The Search, 1919; Cloudy Jewel, 1920; Exit Betty, 1920; The Tryst, 1921; The City of Fire, 1922; The Big Blue Soldier, 1923; Tomorrow About This Time, 1923; Re-creations, 1924; Not Under the Law, 1925; Ariel Custer, 1925; A New Name, 1926; Coming Through the Rye, 1926; Job's Niece, 1927; The White Flower, 1927; Crimson Roses, 1928; Blue Ruin, 1928; Duskin, 1929; The Prodigal Girl, 1929; Ladybird, 1930; The Gold Shoe, 1930; Silver Wings, 1931; The Chance of a Lifetime, 1931; Kerry, 1931; Happiness Hill, 1932; The Challengers, 1932; The Patch of Blue, 1932; The Ransom, 1933; Matched Pearls, 1933; The Beloved Stranger, 1933; Rainbow Cottage, 1934; Amorelle, 1934; The Christmas Bride, 1934; Beauty For Ashes, 1935; White Orchids, 1935; The Strange Proposal, 1935; April Gold, Mystery Flowers, The Substitute Guest, 1936; Sunrise, Daphne Deane, Brentwood, 1937; Marigold, 1938; Homing, Maris, 1938; also (under nom de plume of Marcia MacDonald) The Honor Girl, 1927; Found Treasure, 1928; Out of the Storm, 1929; The White Lady, 1930. Home: 215 Cornell Av., Swarthmore, Pa.

HILL, Harry Segner, co. supt. schs.; b. Mohnton, Pa., March 23, 1898; s. William Hartz and Sara Ann (Segner) H.; diploma Keystone State Normal Sch., Kutztown, Pa., 1916-18; A.B., Wheaton Coll., Ill., 1922; A.M., U. of Pa., 1927; Ed.D., Rutgers U., 1935; m. Margaret P. Kafes, Aug. 27, 1925; 1 dau., Barbara Ann. Engaged as teacher and supervising prin., Pa. and Del., 1918-20; instr. Latin and English, high sch., Trenton, N.J., 1922-26; prin. elementary schs., Trenton, N.J., 1926-37; psychologist, Trenton Bd. Edn., 1936-37; supervising prin. schs., Hightstown, N.J., 1937-39; co. supt. schs., Mercer Co., N.J., since 1939. Dir. Y.M.C.A. Mem. Nat. Edn. Assn., N.J. Edn. Assn., N.J. Schoolmasters Club, Phi Delta Kappa, Kappa Delta Pi. Republican. Presbyn. Mason. Club: Lions of Hightstown (dir.). Home: Hightstown, N.J. Office: Court House, Trenton, N.J.

HILL, Henry Clarke, penitentiary warden; b. Hamilton, Ill., Feb. 1, 1877; s. Thomas Alexander and Ellen White (Lynde) H.; grad. high sch., Galesburg, Ill.; student bus. coll., Galesburg; m. Blanche Colville, Nov. 14, 1900; children—Philip Colville, Blanche Joan (Mrs. Richard Seidel). Began as postal clk., Galesburg, 1899; post office insp., 1905-09; European rep. of New York Credit Men's Assn., 1909-12; asst. sales mgr. Thomas B. Jeffery Co., Kenosha, Wis., 1912-14; in charge automobile purchases for French War Dept., Paris, 1914-15; attending personal interests, 1916-29; warden Ill. State Penitentiary, 1929-32; apptd. warden Federal Penitentiary, Lewisburg, Pa., 1932. Pvt. 1st Arty. Bn., Ill. Vols., Spanish-Am. War; 1st lt. and q.m. Arty. Bn., Ill. N.G., 1900-04; maj. 10th Ill. Inf., Ill. N.G., 1917-20. Mem. S.A. R., Am. Prison Assn., Nat. Warden's Assn. (pres.), Police Chiefs Assn. of S. E. Pa. (hon.), Kappa Sigma (hon.). Spanish Am. Vets. Assn., Vets. of Foreign Wars. Baptist. Mason (32°, K.T., Shriner), K.P., Modern Woodman, Elk. Clubs: Rotary, Manufacturers, Otzinachson Country (Milton, Pa.); Galesburg (Ill.); Boca Raton (Florida). Address: U.S. Northeastern Penitentiary, Lewisburg, Pa.

HILL, James William, Jr., real estate; b. Baltimore, Md., Nov. 3, 1902; s. James William and Elizabeth (Campbell) H.; student Amherst Coll., Amherst, Mass., 1921-23; m. Anne Elizabeth Crockett, May 20, 1937; 1 son, James William III. Real estate business since 1923; mem. firm Piper & Hill, real estate brokerage, Baltimore, since 1933; dir. Title Guarantee & Trust Co., Baltimore. Mem. Nat. Real Estate Bd. Republican. Presbyn. Clubs: Maryland (Baltimore); Green Spring Valley Hunt (Garrison); Amherst (New York). Home: Ridgemead, Stevenson, Maryland. Office: 1010 N. Charles St., Baltimore, Md.

HILL, J(ohn) Ben(jamin), prof. botany; b. Lebanon, Ill., Dec. 12, 1879; s. Jesse B. and Emma (Bryan) H.; B.S. in Agr., U. of Mo., 1908; A.B., Cornell U., 1909; Ph.D., U. of Chicago, 1913; m. Helen C. Deuss, Sept. 3, 1916. Began as grad. asst. in botany, Cornell U., 1907-09; instr. botany, Pa. State Coll., 1909-13, asst. prof., 1915-19, prof. botany, Pa. State Coll. since 1920. Served as 2d lt. inf., U.S.A., 1918. Mem. A.A.A.S., Bot. Soc. America, Pa. Acad. Sci., Sigma Xi, Gamma Sigma Delta, Phi Kappa Phi, Phi Sigma Kappa. Republican. Home: State College, Pa.

HILL, J(ohn) B(oynton) P(hilip) Clayton, lawyer; b. Annapolis, Md., May 2, 1879; s. Charles Ebenezer and Kate Watts (Clayton) H.; A.B., Johns Hopkins Univ., 1900; LL.B., Harvard University, 1903; m. Suzanne Howell, d. late John Howell and Mary Grafton (Rogers)

Carroll, Oct. 28, 1913; children—Suzanne Carroll Clayton (Mrs. Phillips Huntington Clarke), Elise Bancroft Clayton, Catherine Coleman Clayton. Practiced at Boston, 1903-4, Baltimore and Washington, 1904-17; was member Hill, Randall & Leser (withdrew from firm, 1925, because of congl. duties); resumed practice, 1927, firm Howe, Hill & Bradley, now Hill, Ross & Hill, Baltimore, Washington and New York; U.S. atty. Dist. of Md., 1910-15; counsel for Baltimore and State of Md. in N.J-N.Y. Lighterage, Boston, Baltimore and Phila. Differential cases, 1930-33; spl. counsel State of Md. in Albany Port Differential. Pres. Artesian Water Co.; Rep. nominee Congress, 4th Md. Dist., 1908; Rep. candidate for nomination for mayor of Baltimore, 1915; del. Rep. Nat. Conv., 1916; pvt. Battery A, Mass. V.M., 1904; 2d lt., 1st lt., capt. 4th Inf., Md. N.G.; mil. observer 11th German Army Corps maneuvers, Sept. 1911; maj., judge adv. gen., Md. N.G., 1910-17; judge adv. 15th Div. Mexican border service, Aug. 26-Dec. 15, 1916; active duty, Aug. 3, 1917; mem. staff, 29th Div., Aug. 25, 1917-Dec. 10, 1918, then judge adv. and asst. G-3, Gen. Staff, 8th Army Corps, A.E.F., until its dissolution; liaison officer 17th French Army Corps during offensive north of Verdun, Oct. 1918; wounded, Bois d'Ormont, North of Verdun, Oct. 12, 1918; promoted lt. col., Oct. 22, 1918. Served in defense of center sector, Haute Alsace, July 25-Sept. 23, and Meuse-Argonne offensive, north of Verdun, Oct. 8-30, 1918; hon. discharged, May 9, 1919; col. R.C., comdg. 306th Cav. Member American Battle Monuments Commission; military observer 1st and 2d cavalry brigades, Interbrigade Manoeuvers, British Army, Salisbury Plains, Sept. 1933; apptd. mem. Md. Tercentenary Commn., 1934; apptd. brig. gen., the asst. adj. gen. State of Md., June 8, 1935. Decorated D.S.M. (U.S.); Legion of Honor (French); Croix de Guerre, with silver star, for "most distinguished services in the operations north of Verdun," Oct. 1918; La Solidaridad (Panama); Polonia Restituta (Poland); The Star of Abdon Calderon, 1st class (Ecuador). Mem. 67th Congress (1921-23), 3d Md. Dist.; reëlected to the 68th and 69th Congresses (1923-27), same dist.; not candidate for reëlection to House but candidate for Rep. senatorial nomination, 1926, 1934. Asst. in govt., Harvard, 1903; lecturer on Am. Government, Johns Hopkins, various periods to 1924, and at Harvard, 1924. Mem. Am. Bar Assn., Md. Bar Assn., Assn. Bar City of N.Y., Baltimore Bar Assn., Baltimore Assn. Commerce, Md. Hist. Soc., Am. Legion, Am. Officers of Great War, Vets. of Foreign Wars, Mass. Soc. of Cincinnati. Clubs: Maryland, Traffic, Maryland Polo, Green Spring Valley Hunt, Bachelor's Cotillon (Baltimore); Army and Navy, Cosmos (Washington); Harvard (New York); Annapolis Yacht (Annapolis). Author: Hill and Padgett's Annotated Public Service Commission Law of Md., 1913; The Federal Executive, 1916; National Protection—Policy, Armament and Preparedness, 1916. Contbr. to mags. Home: Maryland Hotel, Annapolis, Md.; Army and Navy Club, Washington, D.C. Office: Duke of Gloucester St. and Church Circle, Annapolis, Md.; Tower Bldg., Washington, D.C.; 17 State St., New York, N.Y.

HILL, J(oseph) Bennett, chem. engr.; b. Philadelphia, Pa., Oct. 3, 1891; s. Horace G. and M. Louisa (Bennett) H.; B.S. in Chemistry, U. of Pa., 1913, Ph.D., 1916, Chem. E., 1937; m. Margaret M. Howe, Oct. 24, 1929; children—J. Bennett, Priscilla. Research chemist and laboratory mgr. The Barrett Co., Frankford, Philadelphia, 1916-24; chief chemist Atlantic Refining Co., Phila., 1924-34; mgr. development div., Sun Oil Co., since 1934. Mem. Am. Chem. Soc., Am. Inst. Chem. Engrs., Am. Soc. Testing Materials, Soc. Automotive Engrs., Inst. Petroleum, Am. Petroleum Inst. Presbyterian (elder). Club: Springhaven (Wallingford, Pa.). Contbr. to scientific and trade jours. Home: 402 Wynmere Road, Wynnewood, Pa. Office: Sun Oil Co., Marcus Hook, Pa.

HILL, Lawrence Benjamin, prof. education; b. McKim, Tyler Co., W.Va., Nov. 16, 1876; s. Waitman T. and Emeline J. (Fletcher) H.; ed. Marshall Coll. State Normal Sch., Huntington, W.Va., 1897-1900; A.B., W.Va. U., 1906; A.M., U. of Neb., 1907; Ph.D., Columbia, 1921; m. Maud Rymer, Aug. 17, 1911; children—Lawrence Rymer, Grace Deyerle, Evelyn Marie. Teacher rural schs. and prin. grade sch. until 1899; prin. pub. schs., Guyandotte, W.Va., 1900-03; prin. Tyler County High Sch., 1908-12; pres. Concord State Normal Sch., 1913-18; asso. prof. edn., W.Va. U., 1918-20, prof. since 1920. Taught summers, Marshall Coll., 1924, 28, Fairmont State Teachers Coll., 1926, Rutgers U., 1930, U. of Calif., 1932, University of Maine, 1935. Member State Bd. of Edn., 1909-12; mem. W.Va. Public Sch. Survey Commn., 1923-24. Mem. N.E.A., W.Va. Edn. Assn., Supervisors of Student Teaching, Phi. Delta Kappa. Republican. Methodist. Author: Legislative Control of State Normal Schools, 1922. Home: Morgantown, W.Va.

HILL, Lewis Brown, physician; b. Lima, O., Feb. 18, 1894; s. Elmer and Jane (Agerter) H.; student Miami Univ., Oxford, O., 1909-12; M.D., Med. Coll. of Va., 1916; m. Ida Christian, Dec. 23, 1916; children—Mary Christian, Lewis Brown, Jr. Engaged in gen. practice of medicine at Baltimore, Md. Mem. Am. Psychoanalytic Soc. (pres.), Washington and Baltimore Psychoanalytic Soc. (past pres.), Phi Beta Pi. Mason (Shriner). Club: University. Home: 7101 Copeleigh Rd. Office: 700 Cathedral St., Baltimore, Md.

HILL, Minot James, elec. engr., real estate, ins.; b. Ogdensburg, N.Y., May 7, 1877; s. George H. and Sarah Jeannette (Bowden) H.; student Almond (Wis.) High Sch., Plainfield (Wis.) High Sch.; B.S. in elec. engring., U. of Wis., 1903; married, July 7, 1926; children—Jeannette, Minot James, Elizabeth. Became elec. engr. Westinghouse Elec. & Mfg. Co., 1903; then chief engr. and master mechanic Winnebago Traction Co., Oshkosh, Wis.; successively chief engr. Phila. & Western Ry. Co., Phila., pres. Eufaula (Ala.) Gas, Electric Light & Power Co.; gen. mgr. and dir. Trenton, Bristol & Phila. Ry. Co., Bristol, Pa.; now sec. and treas. latter: has also been gen. mgr. and dir. Salem & Pennsgrove Traction Co. (Salem, N.J.); vice-pres., dir. and mgr. N.J.&Pa. Ry. Co., vice-pres. Del. River Coach Co., Bristol, Pa.; now pres. North Eastern Salvage Co.; dir. and mem. exec. com. Bristol Trust Co.; vice-pres., dir. & gen. mgr. Pa., N.J. Ry. Co.; dir. Merchants & Mechanics Bldg. & Loan Co. Republican. Presbyterian. Mason (32°, Shriner), Elk (past exalted ruler). Club: Rotary (Bristol). Address: 405 Radcliffe St., Bristol, Pa.

HILL, Percival S., banker; b. Lausanne, Switzerland, Aug. 29, 1886; s. George R. and Rosalie Stuart (Carroll) H.; came to U.S., 1890, citizen by birth; student N.Y. Mil. Acad., Cornwall, N.Y., 1895-98, Haverford Sch., Haverford, Pa., 1898-1903; m. Isabelle Alter, Dec. 5, 1907; children—Rosalie Stuart (Mrs. Walter H. Cox, Jr.), Virginia Carroll (Mrs. Edgar A. Dunham, Jr.), Isabelle Alter (Mrs. Oscar E. Weissenborn), Percival S. Began in engr. corps, Pa. R.R. Co., 1905; engr. Latrobe-Connellsville Coal & Coke Co., Latrobe, Pa., 1907-08; cashier Farmers Nat. Bank, Neuville, Pa., 1909-13, Halifax (Pa.) Nat. Bank, 1914-19; v.p. and cashier Bank of Nutley (N.J.) since 1919. Republican. Episcopalian. Mason. Club: Yountakah Country (Nutley, N.J.). Home: 18 Stockton Pl. Office: Bank of Nutley, Nutley, N.J.

HILL, Roscoe R.; b. nr. Lilly, Ill., Feb. 22, 1880; s. Philip P. and Leona E. (Lindsey) H.; A.B., Eureka (Ill.) Coll., 1900, Litt.D., 1935; studied U. of Chicago and Ph.D., Columbia U., 1933; m. Edith Irene Rowell, August 6, 1902; children—Dorothy Irene (Mrs. Carl Oelhaf, Jr.), Lucile Elizabeth (Mrs. Victor E. Ferrall), Edith Frances. Teacher pub. schs., Minn. and Ill., 1901-02; ednl. work, Matanzas, Cuba, 1904-08; hist. research for Carnegie Instn., Washington, in Archives of the Indies, at Seville, Spain, 1911-13; lecturer in history, Columbia, 1913-14; instr. hist. extension teaching, same univ., 1914-15; asso. prof. and prof. history, U. of N.M., 1915-17, 1919-20; pres. Spanish Am. Normal Sch., N.M., 1917-19; regional economist for Latin America, Office Foreign Trade Adviser, Dept. of State, 1920; commr. Nicaraguan High Commn., 1920-28 and mem. Nicaraguan War Claims Commn., 1927-28; dir. for Spain of European Mission, Library of Congress, 1928-30; mem. Nicaraguan group, Inter-Am. High Commn.; official del. to 4th Pan-Am. Commercial Conf., 1931. Lecturer Conf. on Hispanic-Am. Affairs, George Washington U., summer 1933; asst. manuscript div. Library of Congress, 1933-35; editor Journals of the Continental Congress for 1787-89, 1933-37; del. to 2d Assembly of Pan-Am. Inst. of Geography and History, 1935; chief of Classification Div. The Nat. Archives, 1935—; special rep. to South America of Am. Com. of 3d World Power Conf., Feb.-April 1936; commr. to Latin America of Greater Tex. and Pan-Am. Expn., Feb.-April 1937; del. to II Congreso Internacional de Historia de América, 1937. Member American Historical Association, Academy Polit. Science, Am. Acad. Polit. and Social Science, N.M. Archæol. Soc., S.A.R., Phi Kappa Phi, etc.; corr. mem. Academia de la Historia (Madrid), Academia Hispano-Americana de Ciencias y Artes de Cadiz. Mem. Christian (Disciples) Ch. Author: Descriptive Catalog of the Documents relating to the History of the U.S. in the Papeles procedentes de Cuba, deposited in the Archivo General de Indias at Seville, 1916; Reports of High Commission, 1920-27; Fiscal Intervention in Nicaragua, 1933; also chapters on Central America in Wilgus, The Carribean Area, 1934; Los archivos españoles y los investigadores americanos in Colección de estudios . . . Altamira, 1936. Contbr. on Latin-Am. subjects in New Internat. Ency., 1914-16. Home: Leonia, N.J., and Albuquerque, N.M. Address: 4500 47th St., N.W., Washington, D.C.

HILL, Roy Linden, chem. engr.; b. Markham, Pa., Feb. 12, 1888; s. William W. and Mary (Yerkes) H.; student Ward Acad., Concordville, Pa., 1894-98, Swarthmore (Pa.) Prep. Sch., 1898-1904; A.B., Swarthmore (Pa.) Coll., 1908, M.A., 1909; m. Mabel Richardson, June 22, 1912 (died 1938); children—Roy Linden, Marjorie Hudson, Mary Elizabeth. Research chem. engr. E. I. du Pont de Nemours & Co., Wilmington, Del., 1909-16; asst. dir. exptl. lab. Atlas Powder Co., Wilmington, Del., 1917-19, dir., 1919-26, exec. chem. engr. and dir. chem. service sect. since 1926. Mem. Am. Chem. Soc., Am. Inst. of Chem. Engrs., Franklin Inst., Army Ordnance Assn., Sigma Xi. Quaker. Mason (Scottish Rite; Shriner). Home: 708 W. 23d St. Office: Atlas Powder Co., Wilmington, Del.

HILL, Samuel S., M.D., banker; b. Mercer Co., Pa., May 9, 1868; s. John Franklin and Margaret (Guthrie) H.; student Jefferson Acad.; M.D., Western Pa. Med. Coll. (now U. of Pittsburgh); m. Valeria E. Clymer, June 21, 1899; 1 son, Samuel Smith. Asst. physician Wernersville State Hospital, 1894-97, supt. and physician in chief, 1897-1928; pres. Wernersville Nat. Bank & Trust Co. Mem. A.M.A., Berks County Med. Soc., Am. Psychiatric Assn., Phila. Psychiatric Soc. Republican. Presbyterian. Mason. Club: University (Phila.). Address: Wernersville, Pa.

HILL, Theodore Case, engr.; b. Clymer, N.Y., Dec. 10, 1893; s. Clyde C. and Cora E. (Case) H.; attended Allegany Coll., 1915; B.S. in C.E., U. of Mich., 1917; post-grad. study, U. of Mich.; m. Ada Thompson, July 19, 1918; children—Katherine Thompson, Marie Estelle, Sara Ann. Resident engr., West Union, Ia., 1917; county engr., Bremer Co., Ia., 1917-18; partner Hill & Hill, cons. sanitary and municipal engrs., since 1920, specializing in design and construction of dams and storage reservoirs. County surveyor, Erie County, since 1932. Dir. North East Borough Bd. of Edn.; trustee Am. Legion Bldg. Endowment Fund. Served with Sanitary Corps, U.S. Army, 1918-19. Mem. Am. Soc. Professional Engrs., Am. Pub. Works Assn., Am. Soc. Municipal Engrs., Am. Legion, Pa. Vets. League (county com., Erie Co.), Sigma Alpha Epsilon. Republican. Presbyterian. Mason (Shriner; Past Master). Clubs: North East Sportsman, North East Service, U. of Mich. Union (life), Erie County Sportsman League. Wrote report on treatment of industrial waste for Am. City Mag. Home: 144 E. Main St., North East, Pa. Office: Marine Bank Bldg., Erie, Pa.

HILL, Walter Liddell, lawyer; b. Lewisburg, Pa., Aug. 7, 1875; s. David Jayne and Anna Amelia (Liddell) H.; ed. Lawrenceville Acad., Canandaigua Acad., U. of Rochester, Bucknell U., and U. of N.C. Law Sch.; (hon.) A.M., Bucknell U.; m. Rebecca Montgomery Stoughton, 1897; children—Rebecca Stoughton (Mrs. James Knickerbocker Peck), Walter Liddell, Jr., Anna Liddell (Mrs. Otto Carl Lorenz). Admitted to Pa. bar, 1900, and since in gen. practice of law at Scranton; mem. firm O'Malley, Hill, Harris & Harris; referee in bankruptcy, 1905-12; spl. dep. atty. gen. Pa., 1927-29; dir. Third Nat. Bank & Trust Co. of Scranton. Dir. Scranton Bd. Trade (v.p.), Scranton Chamber of Commerce, Scranton Y.M.C.A. Mem. Am. Pa. State, and Lackawanna Co. bar assns., Psi Upsilon. Republican. Baptist. Mason (32°). Home: 714 Taylor Av. Office: Scranton Electric Bldg., Scranton, Pa.

HILLEGASS, Charles E., banking; b. Milltown, near Pennsburg, Pa., Aug. 22, 1870; s. Jonathan P. and Hannah (Benner) H.; ed. Perkiomen Sem., Pennsburg, 1882-84, Central High Sch., Phila., 1889-90; m. Anna M. Bertolet, Oct. 14, 1896; children—Jonathan B., Charles E., Jr. Pres. Pennsburg Water Co.; vice-pres. Farmers Nat. Bank; dir. Perkiomen R.R. Democrat. Mem. Reformed Ch. Mason. Address: Pennsburg, Pa.

HILLEGASS, Foster Calvin, county commissioner; b. Pennsburg, Pa., Sept. 10, 1892; s. Dr. Charles Q. and Ella Hoch (Siegfried) H.; grad. Perkiomen Sch., Pennsburg, 1910; A.B., Franklin and Marshall Coll., 1914; m. Florence Gerhard Moll, Nov. 12, 1914. Editor Town and Country, weekly newspaper, Pennsburg, since 1914; partner in Aurora Theatre, Pennsburg, since 1918; county commr., Montgomery Co. since 1937; dir. Pennsburg Water Co. since 1921; dir. East Greenville Bldg. & Loan Assn. since 1929; dir. Farmers Nat. Bank, Pennsburg, since 1937. Served as mem. Pennsburg Borough Council, 1920-24. Vice-pres. and mem. bd. of trustees Perkiomen Sch. since 1925. Mem. Montgomery-Bucks Press League (dir.), Chi Phi. Republican. Mem. New Goshenhoppen Reformed Ch. Mason (32°). Club: Upper Perkiomen Rotary (past pres.). Home: 404 Main St., Pennsburg, Pa. Office: Court House, Norristown, Pa.

HILLEGASS, Jonathan Bertolet, lawyer; b. Phila., Pa., Sept. 13, 1898; s. Charles E. and Anna M. (Bertolet) H.; ed. Perkiomen Sem., Perkiomen Sch.; B.S., Franklin and Marshall Coll., 1920; ed. Harvard U. Law Sch., 1923-26; m. Ruth S. Hershey, Feb. 14, 1927; 1 son, Michael. Engaged as engr., Gen. Electric Co., Erie, Pa., 1920-23; admitted to Pa. bar, 1926 and since engaged in gen. practice of law at Norristown; mem. firm Hillegass & Moran since 1931; solicitor, Borough of Pennsburg, 1930-34, Borough of Red Hill, 1934-36; sec. and dir. Farmers Nat. Bank, Pennsburg Water Co., both Pennsburg; vice-pres. and dir. Perkiomen Transfer Inc., Pennsburg; sec., treas. and dir Perkiomen Ad. Co., Inc., Red Hill, Pa. Served in S.A.T.C., 1918. Chmn. activities com., Pa. Economy League since 1936. Pres. Pennsburg-East Greenville Rotary Club, 1934-35. Mem. Am. Inst. Elec. Engrs., Montgomery Co. Bankers Assn., Montgomery Co. Bar Assn., Sigma Pi (nat. pres., 1938-40). Republican. Mem. Reformed Ch. Mason (32°). Clubs: Plymouth Country (Norristown); Lehigh Country (Allentown). Home: 9th and Main Sts., Red Hill. Office: Norristown-Penn Trust Bldg., Norristown, Pa.

HILLER, Grace; physician Goucher Coll. since 1934. Address: Goucher College, Baltimore, Md.

HILLES, Robert L.; pres. Second Nat. Bank of Phila. at Frankford. Address: 4356 Frankford Av., Philadelphia, Pa.

HILLIARD, Thomas Jones, sales mgr.; b. Pittsburgh, Pa., Mar. 3, 1894; s. W. H. R. and Mary McM. (Jones) H.; grad. St. Pauls Sch., Concord, N.H., 1913; A.B., Princeton U., 1917; m. Marianna L. Talbott, Dec. 27, 1917; children—Mary Jones (Mrs. D. Eldridge Jackson, Jr.), Thomas Jones, Harry Talbott, Elsie Mead, William Raymond. Vice-pres. Car-

hill Petroleum Co., 1919-22; pres. Pittsburgh Oil Refining Co., 1922-26; pres. Waverly Oil Refining Co., 1926-30; vice pres. Standard Steel Spring Co., 1931-35; mgr. of sales Pittsburgh-Carnegie Ill. Steel Co., 1936-38, gen. mgr. of sales since 1938. Served as capt. Air Service, U.S. Army, during World War. Trustee Shady Side Hosp., Tuberculosis Hosp. Home: Route 2, Sharpsburg, Pa. Office: 434 5th Av., Pittsburgh, Pa.

HILLMAN, John Hartwell, Jr., corpn. exec.; b. Trigg Furnace, Trigg County, Ky., Apr. 27, 1880; s. John Hartwell and Sallie Murfree (Frazer) H.; m. Juliet Cummins Lea, June 27, 1907; children—John Hartwell, Juliet Lea, Margery Lea, Anne Elizabeth, Henry Lea, Mary Lea, Patricia Polk. Chmn. bd. Hillman Coal & Coke Co.; pres. Hecla Coal & Coke Co., J. H. Hillman & Sons Co., Pa. Industries, Inc.; also officer and director in many other cos. in coal, iron, steel and banking. Clubs: University, Duquesne, Fox Chapel, Pittsburgh Golf. Home: 5045 5th Av. Office: Grant Bldg., Pittsburgh, Pa.

HILLMAN, Julian Arthur, hotel mgr.; b. Washington, D.C., May 17, 1894; s. Joel and Sarah (Lulley) H.; student Washington (D.C.) Pub. Schs., 1900-07, Bordentown (N.J.) Mil. Inst., 1907-11; B.S. in Econ., Wharton Sch., U. of Pa., 1915; m. Madeleine Krauskopf, Sept. 19, 1919; children—Susanne K., Joel II, Julian Arthur, Sybil. v.p. and gen. mgr., Hotel Chelsea, Chelsea Hotel Corpn., Atlantic City, N.J., since 1934; dir. Pride of Atlantic Bldg. & Loan Assn. Served with U.S. Army, 1917-19; commd. 2d lt., Feb. 24, 1918, 1st lt. Aug., 1918. Trustee Nat. Farm Sch., Doylestown, Pa. Mem. Zeta Beta Tau, Mil. Order of World War. Republican. Jewish religion. Elk. Clubs: Linwood (N.J.) Country; Atlantic City Tuna, Morris Guards (Atlantic City, N.J.). Home: 131 S. Delancey Pl. Office: Hotel Chelsea, Atlantic City, N.J.

HILLS, Frederic Wheeler, cons. management engr.; b. Butler, N.J., Jan. 25, 1895; s. James Carter and Cathrine Julianna (Degnan) H.; ed. N.Y. Inst. Accountancy & Commerce, 1920-24, Coll. of City of N.Y., summers 1921-23, Pa. State Coll. Engring. Sch., 1926-27, Columbia U., evenings 1927-28, N.Y. Univ. Sch. Commerce, evenings 1927-28, N.Y. Univ. Coll. Engring., evenings 1932-33; m. Mildred Chambers Hood, of Rutherford, N.J., June 30, 1921; children—Carter Habbeshaw, Deborah Anne, Stuart Lee, Frederic Wheeler, Jr. Employed in various capacities as cost engr., accountant, market analyst, and management engr. with various industrials, public utilities, trade associations and professional firms from 1909-31; cons. industrial engr. with F. W. Hills & Assos., N.Y. City, 1931-35; senior expert accountant with Federal Communications Commn., 1935-36; on own acct., consultant in management, N.Y. City, since 1936. Served in U.S. Marine Corps and U.S. Navy, 1917-19. Mem. Am. Soc. Mech. Engrs., Nat. Assn. Cost Accountants, Soc. for Advancement of Management, Am. Legion, Alumni Assn. N.Y. Bus. Inst. Democrat. Protestant. Home: 165 Park Av., East Orange, N.J. Office: 551 Fifth Av., New York, N.Y.

HILLSTROM, David A., sec. and gen. mgr. Corry-Jamestown Mfg. Corpn.; b. Mullsjo, Sweden, Feb. 3, 1877; s. Carl A. and Helena (Sjoeberg) H.; student tech. and business schs., Sweden and U.S.; came to U.S., June 14, 1900, naturalized, 1905; m. Clara J. Swanlund, June 23, 1909; children—D. Armour, Clare A., Mary Helene. Sec. and gen. mgr. Crown Metal Constrn. Co., Jamestown, N.Y., 1909-12; mgr. Watson Mfg. Co., Jamestown, N.Y., 1912-20; organizer Corry-Jamestown Mfg. Corpn., Corry, Pa., 1920, and since sec., gen. mgr. and principal stockholder; dir. Nat. Bank of Corry, Pa., Corry Metal Corpn. State commr. 300th Commn.; mem. Corry Bd. of Edn., 1925-37 (pres. 1 yr.); pres. Corry Boy Scouts, 1923-26; pres. Chautauqua (N.Y.) Lutheran Assn.; mem. advisory bd. Bethesda Lutheran Orphanage, Meadville, Pa., Co. Tuberculosis Hosp., Erie, Pa. Dir. Gustaf Adolph Lutheran Orphanage, Jamestown, N.Y.,

Lutheran Old Folks Home, Jamestown, N.Y., Augustana Lutheran Foundation, Rock Island, Ill.; mem. bd. trustees St. Paul Lutheran Ch., Corry, Pa. Past pres. Corry Chamber of Commerce; mem. U.S. Chamber of Commerce, Swedish Chamber of Commerce in U.S.A., Y.M.C.A. (mem. state bd.). Knighted by H.M. the King, Gustaf V of Sweden, The Order of Vasa, 1926. Republican. Club: Rotary (Corry, Pa.). Home: 44 E. Congress St. Office: Main and Center Sts., Corry, Pa.

HIMEBAUGH, John Walter, lawyer; b. Centerville, Pa., May 19, 1899; s. Fred B. and May Florence (Ash) H.; student Meadville (Pa.) High Sch., 1914-18; B.S., Allegheny Coll., Meadville, Pa., 1923; LL.B., U. of Pittsburgh Law Sch., 1926; m. Pauline Boehm, Sept. 18, 1923. Admitted to Pa. bar, 1926, and since practiced at Erie; mem. firm Marsh & Eaton, 1927-35, Marsh, Spaeder, Himebaugh & Baur, 1935-38; pvt. practice since 1938; dir. Kress Gold & Silver Mining Co. Mem. S.A.T.C. during World War. Rep. candidate for Congress, 29th (Pa.) Dist., 1938. Organized and mem. Presque Isle Sportsman League; mem. Am. Legion, Vets. Fgn. Wars, Alpha Chi Rho, Phi Alpha Delta. Republican. Congregationalist. Mason (Shriner), Moose, Grange, Kiwanis. Clubs: East Erie Turners, Mannechor (Erie, Pa.). Operated orchestra for several years; soloist Erie Philharmonic Orchestra, saxophonist since 1918. Home: 4819 Sunnydale Boul. Office: 502 Ariel Bldg., Erie, Pa.

HIMES, Joseph Hendrix, ex-congressman; b. New Oxford, Pa., Aug. 15, 1885; s. George Thomas and Martha J. (MacKnight) H., Pa. Coll., Gettysburg, 1900-04, Pa. State Coll., 1904-07; m. Eilleen Canfield, May 6, 1915; children—Canfield MacKnight, Marilynn, Katrina. Began as cinder pitman in steel mills, and resigned, 1916, as gen. mgr. Carnahan Tin Plate & Sheet Co., Canton, O.; spent 1 yr. studying trade conditions in S. America. Mem. 67th Congress (1921-23), 16th Ohio Dist. Pres. Transportation Investment Co., Joseph H. Himes Co., Inc.; gen. partner brokerage firm of E. A. Pierce & Co., New York; dir. Acacia Mut. Life Ins. Co. of Washington, D.C., Pantepec Oil Co. of Venezuela, Electric Boat Co. (N.Y. City). Dir. Md. State Sch. for the Deaf, founder and pres. Group Hospitalization, Inc., Washington. Mem. Ohio societies of New York and Washington, Sigma Chi. Republican. Methodist. Mason (32°, Shriner). Clubs: Metropolitan, Burning Tree, Congressional Country (twice pres.; now gov.). Home: 2101 Connecticut Av., Washington, D.C.; and Prospect Hall, Frederick, Md. Office: Transportation Bldg., Washington, D.C.

HIMES, Leslie Roberts, lawyer; b. Armstrong Co., Pa., June 7, 1892; s. John Rutherford and Mary Alverta (Roberts) H.; ed. Grove City Coll., 1910-12; LL.B., U. of Mich. Law Sch., 1915; m. Helen Lytle, June 27, 1923; 1 dau., Margery Lytle. Admitted to Pa. bar, 1915, and since engaged in gen. practice of law at New Bethlehem; served as mem. Pa. Ho. of Rep., 1933-34. Served as ordnance sergt. C.A.C., U.S.A., with A.E.F. in France, during World War. Mem. Am. Legion, Sons of Union Vets. of the Civil War. Trustee Clarion State Teachers Coll., Clarion, Pa. Democrat. Presbyn. Mason (32°, Shriner). Home: New Bethlehem, Pa.

HIMSTEAD, Ralph E(bner) educator, editor; b. Blue Mound, Ill., Jan. 31, 1893; s. Christopher and Carolyn (Eelrich) H.; A.B., U. of Ill., 1916; LL.B., Northwestern U., 1921, A.M., 1924, J.D., 1924; S.J.D., Harvard, 1929; m. Dorothy Scott, of Evanston, Ill., Sept. 7, 1918; children—James, Scott. Prof. of polit. science, Cornell Coll., Mt. Vernon, Ia., 1919-24; Harris fellow in polit. science, Northwestern U., 1922-23; prof. of law, Syracuse U., 1924-36; gen. sec. Am. Assn. Univ. Profs., Washington, D.C., since 1936; research fellow Harvard Law Sch., 1928-29; teacher polit. science, Pa. State Coll., summers, 1925, 26; teacher law Northwestern U. Sch. of Law, summer 1927. Served as 1st lt. inf., U.S.A., instr. Central O.T.C., 1917-19. Mem. Am. Polit. Science Assn., Am. Soc. Internat. Law, Am. Assn. Univ. Profs., Phi Delta Phi, Phi Kappa Phi, Delta Sigma Rho, Acacia.

Methodist. Mason. Club: Cosmos (Washington, D.C.). Editor Bull. Am. Assn. Univ. Profs. Home: 210 Rosemary St., Chevy Chase, Md. Office: 744 Jackson Place, N.W., Washington, D.C.

HINCHMAN, William Rossiter, treas. West Penn Power Co.; b. Nutley, N.J., Jan. 26, 1897; s. John J. and Julia (Rossiter) H.; studied Brooklyn (N.Y.) Polytechnic Inst., 1908-14; M.E., Cornell U., 1918; m. Helen Gwendolyn Miller, of Brooklyn, N.Y., Jan. 16, 1931; children—William Rossiter. With Bell Telephone Co., spring and summer, 1919, Thompson & Starrett, 1919-21; with Am. Water Works & Electric Co., 1921-26, asst. treas., 1926-28; treas. West Penn Electric Co., 1928-35, v.p. since 1935; treas. and dir. West Penn Power Co., West Penn Rys. Co. Served as ensign for engring. duties, U.S. Naval Reserve, 1918-19. Mem. Phi Delta Theta. Presbyterian. Club: Longue Vue (Pittsburgh). Home: 5473 Kipling Road. Office: 14 Wood St., Pittsburgh, Pa.

HINCK, Claus F(rederick), Jr., prof. chemistry; b. New York, N.Y., Dec. 7, 1886; s. Claus Frederick and Johanna Elizabeth (Haase) H.; student Montclair (N.J.) Acad., 1893-1905, Columbia Coll., 1905-08; Ph.D., Heidelberg U., Germany, 1913; m. Luise Hofmeister, of Hilbersdorf, Silesia, Dec. 17, 1910; children—Elizabeth Charlotte (Mrs. David Greene Loomis), Claus Frederick, 3d. Asst. in chemistry University and Bellevue Hosp. Med. Coll., 1914-17; chief chemist E. I. du Pont de Nemours & Co., Lodi (N.J.) Works, 1917-19; chief chemist Lehn & Fink, Inc., Bloomfield, N.J., 1919-22; lived abroad, 1922-23; asst. prof. chemistry, Washington Square Coll., New York U., 1922-25; prof. chemistry and head dept., Coll. of Dentistry, New York U., since 1925. Fellow A.A.A.S., N.Y. Acad. Science; mem. Am. Chem. Soc., Phi Delta Theta, Sigma Xi, Phi Lambda Upsilon. Republican. Presbyn. Contbr. to scientific jours. Home: 150 Montclair Av., Montclair, N.J. Office: 209 E. 23d St., New York, N.Y.

HINDMAN, James Edward, lawyer; b. Altoona, Pa., July 6, 1875; s. John Adam and Anna Eliza (Brenaman) H.; attended Altoona High Sch., 1 yr., Franklin & Marshall Acad., Feb.-June 1896; spl. student Franklin & Marshall Coll., 1896-97; Ph.B., Lafayette Coll., 1900, M.S., 1903; student Dickinson Law Sch., 1901-02; LL.B., Pittsburgh Law Sch., 1903; m.Martha Ward, Oct. 16, 1915; children—James Edward, Martha Elizabeth, Helen Louise, John Ward. Messenger freight station, Pa. R.R., Altoona, Pa., 1892-93; admitted to Allegheny Co. bar, 1903; solicitor Wilkins Township, 3 yrs., Borough of Wilkinsburg, 5 yrs., Sch. Dist., Borough of Wilkinsburg since 1905; v.p., sec. and dir. State Theatres Corpn., Crystal Amusement Co.; sec. and dir. Times Theatres Corpn.; dir. North Am. Refractories Co. Mem. Pa. State Bd. for Examination of Public Accountants, 3 yrs., Allegheny Co. Bd. Law Examiners, 4 yrs., Com. on Grievances and Offenses of Common Pleas Court, Allegheny Co., since 1935; chmn. Legal Advisory Bd., Wilkinsburg, Pa. Four Minute Speaker, World War. Trustee Western Pa. Sch. for Deaf, Edgewood, Pa. Mem. Am., Pa. and Allegheny County bar assns., Am. Judicature Soc., Phi Kappa Psi, Delta Chi. Republican. Presbyn. Mason. Club: University (Pittsburgh). Breeder registered Guernsey Cattle, Quietude Farms, Huntingdon Furnace, Pa. Home: 1521 Penn Av., Wilkinsburg, Pa. Office: 335 Fifth Av., Pittsburgh, Pa.

HINDMAN, William Blake, clergyman; b. Joliet, Ill., June 4, 1888; s. Rev. William Murphy (D.D.) and Elizabeth Caroline (Blake) H.; A.B., in Lafayette Coll., 1910; student Princeton Theol. Sem., 1910-12, Princeton U. Grad. Sch., 1911-12; B.D., McCormick Theol. Sem., Chicago, 1913; (hon.) D.D., Lafayette Coll., 1925; m. Margaret Jane Ballard, Sept. 15, 1913; 1 dau., Jane Blake. Ordained to ministry Presbyn. Ch. U.S.A., 1913; minister Worthington, O., 1913-17, Bloomington, Ill., 1917-21, Aurora, Ill., 1921-28; minister First Presbyn. Ch., Uniontown, Pa., since 1928; del. to World Council Presbyn. Ch., Cardiff, Wales, 1925; served as chmn. Fort Necessity Memorial Assn., had charge reconstruction fort and establishment Fort Necessity Nat. Park and Mus.; authority on George Washington's early mil. career having discovered new source material. Served as chaplain U.S.A., 1918. Pres. Westmoreland-Fayette Cos. Hist. Soc. Mem. Princeton and Lafayette Coll. alumni assns., Friars Club, Theta Delta Chi. Republican. Mason (32°). Club: H.Y.P. (Pittsburgh). Author: Something New and Chinese, 1925; A Young Colonel from Virginia, 1931; History of National Highway, 1936. Home: 78 Morgantown St., Uniontown, Pa.

HINE, Willard Foster, consulting engr.; b. Fairchild, Wis., Aug. 15, 1886; s. Revillo Curtis and Kittie E. (Foster) H.; B.S. in E.E., U. of Wis., 1907; m. Edith Callanan, Feb. 18, 1914; children—Edith Gloria, Willard Foster. In employ Laclede Gas Co., St. Louis, Mo., 1907-11; chief gas engr. Pub. Service Commn., First Dist., State of N.Y., 1911-19; asso. with Milo R. Maltbie, pub. utility consultant, 1919-30; mem. firm, Hine Goldthwaite & Mylott, pub. utility consultants, New York, N.Y. since 1930; cons. gas engr., U.S. Bur. Standards, 1916-18; served as mem. Phila. Gas Commn., 1921; cons. valuation engr., Pub. Service Commn., State of N.Y. since 1935. Mem. Am. Gas Assn. Democrat. Roman Catholic. Home: 126 Stanmore Pl., Westfield, N.J. Office: 7 Dey St., New York, N.Y.

HINES, Cary C., lawyer; b. Alderson, W.Va., Mar. 10, 1874; s. Joseph P. and Lucy (Alderson) H.; student Concord Normal Sch., Athens, W.Va., 1892-93; A.B., W.Va. Univ., Morgantown, 1897; m. Elizabeth Morrison, Jan. 16, 1901; 1 dau., Virginia Ruth (Mrs. Caton Nelson Hill). Admitted to W.Va. bar, 1897, and since engaged in gen. practice of law at Sutton; mem. firm Linn, Bryne & Hines, 1897-1909, Hines & Morrison, 1909-19, Hines & Heavener, 1920-25, Hines & Davis since 1925; served as prosecuting atty. of Braxton Co., W.Va., 1909-12; propr. and operator Hines Coal Co., mines, Wainville, W.Va., 1918-30, now propr. but mines inactive; served as pres. Bd. Edn. of Braxton Co. Democrat. Mem. M.E. Ch. Mason (K.T., 32°, Shriner). Rotarian. Address: Sutton, W.Va.

HINES, Earle Garfield, pres. Gen. Theatres Equipment Corpn.; b. Arcadia, Ind., Nov. 19, 1880; s. William Harrison and Margaret Jane (Newby) H.; ed. Cincinnati schs. including 2 yrs. at U. of Cincinnati; m. Aida Alexandra Dowson, 1907; 1 son, Earle Dowson. Salesman with Harrison Williams, New York, 1911-14; with McGraw-Hill Co., 1915-17; pres. Livingston Radiator Co., 1917-21; with McGraw Hill Co., 1921-23; v.p. Am. Brown Boveri Electric Corpn., 1923-27; European travel, summer 1927; with Equitable Trust Co., New York, 1927-30, Chase Securities, 1930-34, Chase Nat. Bank, 1934-36; pres. and dir. Gen. Theatres Equipment Corpn. since 1936; pres. and dir. Internat. Projector Corpn.; dir. Abercrombie & Fitch Co., Cinema Bldg. Corpn., J. E. McAuley Mfg. Co., Nat. Theatres Corpn., Nat. Theatre Supply Co., Raybestos-Manhattan, Inc., Theatres Equipment Contracts Corpn., United Shipyards Inc., Strong Electric Corpn. Mem. Soc. Motion Picture Engrs. Clubs: Downtown Athletic, India House (New York); Verbank Hunting and Fishing (Verbank, N.Y.). Home: West Milford, N.J. Office: 92 Gold St., New York, N.Y.

HINES, Frank Brown, physician; b. Chestertown, Md., June 24, 1881; s. Dr. William Franklin and Mary (Emory) H.; student U. of Md., 1896-1900; M.D., Coll. Physicians and Surgeons, U. of Md., 1904; m. Miriam Louise Jessop, May 20, 1908; 1 son, Frank Brown. Gen. practice of medicine, Chestertown, Md., since 1904. Served as 1st lt., later capt., Med. Corps, U.S. Army, 1917-19; with A.E.F., 1 year; commd. major Med. Corps, Md. Nat. Guard, now lt. col. Mem. Kent County Med. Soc., Med. and Chirurg. Faculty of Md. (past pres.). Ind. Democrat. Episcopalian. Mason. Club: Chester River Country (Chestertown, Md.). Address: Chestertown, Md.

HINES, John Leonard, army officer; b. White Sulphur Springs, W.Va., May 21, 1868; s. Edward and Mary (Leonard) H.; grad. U.S. Mil. Acad., 1891; m. Rita S., d. Gen. William M. Wherry, U.S. Army, Dec. 19, 1898; children—Alice Grammer (wife of J. R. D. Cleland, U.S.A.), John Leonard. Commd. 2d lt. inf., June 12, 1891; promoted through grades to col. (temp.), Aug. 5, 1917; col. 16th Inf., Nov. 1, 1917; brig. gen. N.A., Apr. 12, 1918; maj. gen. U.S.A., Aug. 8, 1918 (temp.); brig. gen. regular army, Nov. 30, 1918; maj. gen., Mar. 5, 1921. Served at Ft. Omaha, Neb., 1891-96; acting q.m. 2d Inf., at Tampa, Fla., and Santiago de Cuba, 1898; Cienfuegos, Cuba, 1899, 1900; in Philippines, 1900-01, 1903-05, 1911-12, 1930-32; chief q.m. Camp of U.S. Troops, Jamestown Expn., 1907; asst. to chief q.m. Dept. of Mo., 1908-09; Nagasaki, Japan, 1910, 11; adj. Punitive Expedition into Mexico, 1916-17; asst. adj. gen. A.E.F., May-Oct. 1917; arrived in France, June 13, 1917; col. 16th Infantry, November 1, 1917; appointed comdr. 1st Brigade Inf., 1st Div., A.E.F., May 4, 1918; assigned to 4th Div., Aug. 25, 1918; apptd. comdr. 3d Army Corps, Oct. 11, 1918; comdr. 4th Div. Nov. 21, 1919; comdr. 5th Div., Sept. 25, 1920; comdr. 2d Div., July 11, 1921; comdr. 8th Corps Area, Oct. 6, 1921; dep. chief of staff, U.S.A., Dec. 5, 1922; chief of staff, Sept. 13, 1924; apptd. comdr. 9th Corps Area, Dec. 31, 1926; appointed comdr. Philippine Department, Oct. 2, 1930; retired from active service, May 31, 1932. Awarded D.S.M., 1919, "for services as regimental, brigade, division and corps comdr."; D.S.C., "for service in Soissons drive"; Silver Star Medal for service in Cuba, 1898"; Comdr. Legion of Honor and Croix de Guerre (French), 1918; Comdr. Order of Leopold (Belgian), 1918; Knight Comdr. of St. Michael and St. George (English), 1919; Order of the Crown (Italian), 1919; Medal of the Solidaridad (Panamanian), 1919; Grand Officer Kingdom of Cambodia (France), 1931. Mem. Soc. Santiago de Cuba. Home White Sulphur Springs, W.Va. Address: War Dept., Washington, D.C.

HINES, W. E., mem. law firm Hines & Hall. Address: Sutton, W.Va.

HINKLEY, John, lawyer; b. Baltimore, Mar. 1, 1864; s. Edward Otis and Anne M. (Keemlé) H.; A.B., Johns Hopkins, 1884; LL.B., U. of Md., 1886; unmarried. Sec. Am. Bar Assn., 1893-1909, mem. com. on professional ethics and grievances, 1923-1934; director of the Baltimore National Bank; now mem. firm Hinkley, Burger & Singley. Mem. Md. State Bd. Law Examiners, 1906-16. Capt. 5th Md. Inf. in Spanish War, May 14-Oct. 22, 1898; col. 5th Md. Inf., June 4, 1913-Feb. 28, 1917; Mexican border service, July 1, 1916-Feb. 24, 1917. One of Md. commrs. on Uniform State Laws since 1912, mem. com. on uniform commercial acts since 1921. Dir. Md. Sch. for the Blind, Friendly Inn Assn. Home: 808 Cathedral St. Office: 215 N. Charles St., Baltimore, Md.

HINRICHSEN, Arthur Feick, sales engring.; b. Newark, N.J., Feb. 7, 1889; s. August and Catherine H.; C.E., Princeton U., 1910; m. Eleanor Morgan, Mar. 14, 1914. Employed as field engr., Du Pont Powder Co., 1910-14; sales engr., Slocum, Arram & Slocum, 1914-19; engr. Am. Linseed Co., 1919-21; sales engr., Reed Engring. Co., 1921-28; engaged in bus. on own acct., sales engring. and mfrs. rep., as A. F. Hinrichsen, Inc. and pres. and treas. since 1928. Mem. Am. Soc. Heating & Ventilating Engrs., Am. Soc. Mech. Engrs., N.Y. Professional Engrs. Soc. Mem. Unity and New Thought. Clubs: Princeton (New York); Terrace (Princeton); Eastern Trades Golf Assn. of new York. Home: Mountain Lakes, N.J. Office: 50 Church St., New York, N.Y.

HINSDALE, Guy, M.D.; b. Brooklyn, Oct. 26, 1858; s. Theodore and Grace (Webster) H.; 7th in descent from Robert Hinsdale who came from Eng. and was a propr. of Dedham, Mass., 1637, and was slain by Indians in massacre at Deerfield, 1675; A.B., Amherst, 1878, A.M., 1881; M.D., U. of Pa., 1881; m. Mary P. Graham, Mar. 11, 1890; 1 dau., Jean Graham.

Assisted late Dr. S. Weir Mitchell and Dr. William Osler in hosp. and pvt. practice several yrs.; asso. prof. climatology. Medico-Chirurgical Coll., Phila., 1905-17; prof. climatology, Univ. of Pa., 1917-19; medical director White Sulphur Springs, Inc. An instr. in medicine and med. diagnosis, of student med. officers, U.S. Navy, Phila., 1917. Member American Academy Medicine (v.p. 1906-07), Coll. Physicians Phila., Phila. Med. Club, Am. Climatol. and Clin. Assn. (sec. 1894-1918, pres. 1919), Am. Neurol. Assn., A.M.A., Pa. Soc. Prevention Tuberculosis (pres. 1900-02), Am. Meteorological Soc., Internat. Soc. Med. Hydrology; fellow Royal Soc. Medicine, London; mem. Comite d'Honneur de Congrès Internat. du Tourisme, du Thermalisme et du Climatisme, Paris, 1937. Club: Medical Club of Philadelphia (honorary). Author: Syringomyelia (Alvarenga prize essay, Coll. Physicians, Phila.), 1895; Acromegaly (Boylston prize essay, Harvard), 1898; Vol. IV, System of Physiologic Therapeutics, 1902; Hydrotherapy, 1910; Atmospheric Air in Relation to Tuberculosis (Hodgkins prize essay of Smithsonian Instn.), 1914; sect. on Hydrotherapy, in The Oxford Medicine, 1919; also articles on "Mineral Springs in Modern Treatment," 1910, and "Heliotherapy" in Cyclopedia of Medicine, Phila., 1933; Climate and Disease, Bull. Am. Meteorol. Soc., 1936, 37, 38; and about 100 contbns. on med. topics. Home: The Greenbrier, White Sulphur Springs, W.Va.

HINSDALE, Katharine Lewis, librarian; b. Bridgeport, Conn.; d. Rev. Horace Graham and Charlotte Elouisa (Howe) H.; ed. pvt. schs. and Evelyn Coll. (not operated now), Princeton, N.J. Engaged as pvt. teacher to 1915; librarian Lakewood Pub. Library, Lakewood, N.J. since 1915. Served as mem. bd. mgrs. Paul Kimbell Hosp. of Lakewood and Ocean Co., 1913-26; mem. bd. dirs. Lakewood Community Service, Inc. since 1936. Republican. Presbyn. Club: Business and Professional Womens. Home: 211 Private Way. Office: Public Library, Lakewood, N.J.

HINTZ, Carl William Edmund, librarian; b. London, Eng., Oct. 14, 1907; s. Max Emil and Edith Helen (Newstead) H.; came to U.S., 1924, naturalized, 1937; A.B., DePauw Univ., Greencastle, Ind., 1932; A.B. in Library Science, U. of Mich., Ann Arbor, Mich., 1933; A.M. in Library Science, 1935; student U. of Chicago Grad. Library Sch., summer 1937; m. Frances Julia Bryant, June 5, 1939. Employed as jr. clk. British Passport Control Office, Berlin, Germany, 1922-24; clk. Studebaker Corpn., South Bend, Ind., 1924-27; asst. in charge circulation, DePauw U. Library, 1933-35, asst. librarian, 1935-37; librarian and asso. prof. library sci., U. of Md. since 1937. Mem. Am. Library Assn., Md. Library Assn., Middle Eastern Library Assn. (v.p. 1938-39), Md. Hist. Soc., Delta Upsilon, Delta Sigma Rho, Pi Sigma Alpha, Phi Eta Sigma. Methodist. Home: 6817 Georgia Av. N.W., Washington, D.C. Office: Univ. of Maryland, College Park, Md.

HIPSHER, Edward Ellsworth, musician, editor; b. Caledonia, O., March 28, 1871; s. Francis Marion and Elizabeth (Dickin) H.; grad. dept. of music, Valparaiso (Ind.) U., 1890, grad. study gold medalist, 1893; student Royal Acad. Music, London, 1894-95, 99; pupil of Carpi, Florence, Italy, 1914; hon. Mus. Doc. from Temple University in 1933; unmarried. Musical dir. Humeston (Ia.) Normal Coll., 1890-91, Mendota (Ill.) Coll., 1893-94, Holbrook Normal Coll., Fountain City, Tenn., 1898-1901, Marion (O.) Conservatory of Music, 1901-05, Southern Normal Inst., Douglas, Ga., 1905-07; dir. vocal dept. Centenary Coll., Cleveland, Tenn., 1909-10; musical dir. Marion Conservatory of Music and Claridon Tp. Schs., also condr. Marion Choral Soc., 1910-13; musical dir. Morris Harvey Coll., Barboursville, W.Va., 1913-20; associate editor The Étude since 1920. Dir. Phila. Operatic Soc., and Italo-American Philharmonic Orchestra. Mem. Phila. Music Teachers' Assn. (pres.), China Inst. of America, English-Speaking Union, Phila. Art Alliance, Philadelphia Society for Preservation of Landmarks (life), Ohio. Soc. of Philadelphia (exec. com.), Dickens Fellowship (exec. council), Arts and Sciences Soc. of Pa. (b.p. for music); founder-pres. The Mozart Society of Philadelphia Metropolitan Opera Guild, Italo-American Orchestra (mem. bd. dirs.), Italian Symphony Orchestra; associate Royal Academy Music, London. Author: Choir Book for Women's Voices, 1912; American Opera and its Composers, 1927; Choral Art Repertoire, 1933. Translator of libretto of Bizet's Pearl Fishers, 1928. Composer of songs, piano pieces and ch. music; contbr. to mags. Home: 1519 Pine St. Office: 1712 Chestnut St., Philadelphia, Pa.*

HIPWELL, Harry H., pres. Hipwell Mfg. Co.; b. New Brunswick, N.J., 1865; s. Thomas S. and Rebecca Ann H.; ed. high sch.; m. Lillian Grove; children—Harry H., Earl W. Pres. Hipwell Mfg. Co. since organization, 1899; dir. North Side Deposit Bank. Home: 3714 Perrysville Av. Office: 825-835 North Av., Pittsburgh, Pa.

HIRD, Emerson Freeman, physician; b. North Brookfield, Mass., Sept. 26, 1883; s. John Wood and Adeline Walter (Luce) H.; A.B., Western Reserve U., Cleveland, O., 1906; M.D., Boston Univ. Med. Sch., 1910; m. Helen Roberta Clark, July 26, 1917; 1 son, John Wood 2d. Interne Trull Hosp., Biddeford, Me., 1910-12; engaged in practice of medicine, Concord, N.H., 1912-13; interne West Jersey Homeopathic Hosp., Camden, N.J., 1913-14; engaged in practice of medicine at Bound Brook, N.J., since 1914; mem. auxiliary staff, junior pediatrician, Muhlenberg Hospital, Plainfield, 1929-30; visiting physician Somerset Hospital, Somerville, N.J., 1925-30. Served with Am. Red Cross, 1917-19. Awarded La Medaille Revolutionnaire (Czechoslovakia); Cruce a Regina Maria (Roumania). Mem. Am. Med. Assn., N.J. State Med. Assn., Alpha Sigma. Republican. Mason. Clubs: Rotary of Bound Brook. Home: 118 East Maple Av., Bound Brook, N.J.

HIRES, Charles E., Jr., pres. Charles E. Hires Co.; b. Philadelphia, Pa., April 27, 1891; s. Charles E. and Clara K. (Smith) H.; B.S., Haverford Coll., 1913; m. Ilsa M. Keppelmann, June 12, 1918; children—Charles E. III, Robert Gordon, Peter W. Began with Charles E. Hires Co., beverage mfrs., Philadelphia, 1913, pres. since 1925; pres. Hires Sugar Co. of Cuba, Charles E. Hires Co., Ltd. Clubs: Midday, Havana Country. Home: Wynnewood, Pa. Office: 206 S. 24th St., Philadelphia, Pa.

HIRES, Harrison S(treeter), manufacturing; b. Phila., Pa., May 31, 1887; s. Charles E. and Clara Kate (Smith) H.; prep. edn. Haverford Prep. Sch. and Phillips Brook Sch.; A.B. Haverford Coll., 1910; m. Christine Bronsdon Leland, Oct. 25, 1911; children—Claramary, William Leland. Vice-pres. and dir. Charles E. Hires Co., Hires Sugar Co. of Cuba, Charles E. Hires Co., Ltd., of Toronto, Hires Co. of Quebec, Ltd. Dir. and vice-pres. Phila. Art Alliance; trustee Phila. Coll. of Pharmacy and Science. Mem. Acad. Natural Sciences (life), Franklin Inst., Phila. Drug Exchange (twice pres.); Nat. Municipal League, Foreign Policy Assn.; Freethinkers of America, Inc., A.A.A.S., Pa. Acad. Science, Am. Genetic Assn., Am. Acad. Polit. and Social Science, Foreign Policy Assn. Clubs: Franklin Inn, Penn Athletic, Haverford, Penn, Contemporary (Phila.). Author: Reveries and Songs, 1926; Invitation and Other Poems, 1938. Contbr. articles and poems to periodicals. Home: Berwyn, Pa. Office: 206 S. 24th St., Philadelphia, Pa.

HIRSCH, Albert Carl, lawyer; b. Pittsburgh, Pa., July 17, 1890; s. Edward and Mary (Kern) H.; grad. Pittsburgh pub. schs., 1903, Commercial High Sch., 1906; LL.B., Pittsburgh Law Sch. (U. of Pittsburgh), 1915; m. Mary Elizabeth Fuhrer, July 18, 1911; children—Paul Kern, Vida Jane, Mary Emma. Stenographer Pa. R.R., 1906-10; official court stenographer Allegheny Co. (Pa.) Common Pleas Court, 1910-15, Orphans Ct., 1915-20; fellow and instr. Pittsburgh Law Sch., 1915-17; admitted to Pa. bar, 1915; in gen. practice of law, 1915-23; partner law firm Watson & Freeman, 1923-38, Hirsch, Shumaker, Demmler & Bash since May 1, 1938. Sec. Presbyn. Union, Pittsburgh. Mem. Am., Pa. and Allegheny Co. bar assns., Am. Judicature Soc., Pa. Soc. Republican. Presbyn. (elder). Mason (Scottish Rite, Shriner), Elk. Clubs: Pittsburgh Athletic, Masonic Veterans, Civic Club of Allegheny County, Agora (sec.), Highland Men's Bowling League (pres.). Home: 1035 N. Highland Av. Office: 418 Frick Bldg., Pittsburgh, Pa.

HIRSCH, Daniel, pres. First Nat. Bank & Trust Co. Address: Milford, Del.

HIRSCH, Isaac, wholesale wool and hides; b. Germany, Dec. 4, 1865; s. Samuel and Branetta (Lowenstein) H.; brought to U.S., 1866; ed. Allegheny Co. Acad., Cumberland, Md.; m. Ray Abrams, Feb. 26, 1895; 1 son, Sumner Alwyn. Began as clk. dept. store, Nashville, Tenn., 1880; mem. firm Hirsch Bros., wholesale wool and hides, Cumberland, Md., since 1886; dir. First Nat. Bank. Former pres. City Council; former chmn. Charter Commn., Municipal Light Commn.; former mem. Water Commn., State Tax Commn. Dir. Cumberland Free Library, Chamber of Commerce. Democrat. Jewish religion. Mason (32°). Club: Kiwanis of Cumberland (past pres.). Home: 726 Washington St. Office: 109 Cumberland St., Cumberland, Md.

HIRSCH, Isaac E., editor, pub.; b. Carver Co., Minn., May 11, 1859; s. Max and Helene (Einstein) H.; pioneer settlers of Minn.; ed. pub. schs. and grad. Old Central High Sch. of Pittsburgh, Pa., 1873; m. Margaret Bradley, 1885 (died May 2, 1935); 1 dau., Annette (wife of Dr. J. W. Frey, of Pittsburgh). Began as office boy foreign steamship and banking firm of Max Schamberg & Co., Pittsburgh, Pennsylvania, 1873, mgr., 1880, propr., 1887, and sold out to First Nat. Bank, Pittsburgh, 1900; part owner Pittsburgh Volksblatt, 1885, consolidating with Freiheits Freund, 1901; then v.p. Neeb-Hirsch Pub. Co. until dissolution, 1929. Mem. Acad. Science and Art (councilor, 1899-1921; pres. 1922), Art Soc. (dir. 1907-20). Mem. German-Am. Tech. Soc., Steuben Soc. America, Am. Turnerbund, Western Pa. Hist. Soc., Humane Soc. of Western Pa., Assn. of Masonic Vets. of Western Pa. Clubs: Civic, Press, German (pres. 1917-19). Author: Tante Lotte beim Freitag Nachmittag Kaffeeklatsch, 1887; poems set to music by various composers. Home: 214 Bellefield Av., Pittsburgh, Pa.

HIRSCH, Joseph, artist; b. Phila., Pa., Apr. 25, 1910; s. Charles S. and Fannie (Wittenberg) H.; A.B., Central High Sch., Phila., 1928; m. Ruth L. Schindler, Oct. 30, 1938. Water color sketches, 1931, pastel portrait studies, 1931-32, oil portraits, 1932-34, imaginary figure studies, 1935, murals, 1936-38; awarded 4 year scholarship (given by city of Phila.) to Pa. Mus. Sch. of Industrial Art, 1st prize in illustration, 1st prize in life drawing; Walter Lippincott Award, Pa. Acad. Fine Arts Annual Exhbn., 1934; 3d Hallgarten prize Nat. Acad. Design Annual Exhbn., N.Y., 1934; 1st honorable mention Prix de Rome Exhbn., Grand Central Gallery, 1935; Harriet Hale Wooley Fellowship to Paris, 1935-36; first one-man exhbn. Phila. Am. Contemporary Arts Gallery, 1937; exhibited in Phila., N.Y., Los Angeles, Chicago, Worcester, Washington, Cincinnati, San Francisco, Portland (Ore.), Paris; rep. in permanent collection N.Y. Mus. of Modern Art. Address: 900 Pine St., Philadelphia, Pa.

HIRSCHTHAL, Meyer, civil engring.; b. Krakau, Poland, Dec. 12, 1879; s. Jacob and Caroline (Poss) H.; brought to U.S., 1887, naturalized citizen; B.S., Coll. of City of N.Y., 1899; C.E., Columbia U., 1902; m. Regina Diamond, June 16, 1914; 1 son, Ellis Philip. Employed as draftsman in charge construction, Ransome & Smith, N.Y. City, 1902-03; estimator, cost engr., Roelbling Constrn. Co., N.Y. City, 1903-06; draftsman, cost engr., Henry Steers, Inc., 1906-07; designing draftsman, Del. & Lackawanna R.R. Co., 1907-15, asst. engr., 1915-20, concrete engr. since 1920; spl. lecturer on concrete structures at Columbia U., 1928-34; designer and patentee of slab forms for concrete without false work; developed use of girderless flat slab for r.r. loadings. Mem. Am. Soc. Civil Engrs., Am. Ry. Engring Assn., Am. Concrete Inst., Am. Soc. for Testing Materials, Jewish religion. Mason. Author: courses for Internat. Corr. Schs. Contbr. many articles on concrete design and constrn. to sci. jours. Home: 173 Riverside Drive, New York City, N.Y. Office: Hoboken, N.J.

HIRSCHWALD, Rudolph Mayer, lawyer; b. Litvia, Dec. 27, 1891; s. Abram and Johanna (Loewensohn) H.; came to U.S., 1892, naturalized, 1913; A.B., Central High Sch., Phila., 1908; student Sch. of Pedagogy, 1908-10; LL.B., U. of Pa., 1917; m. Rebecca Reinish, Sept. 7, 1919; children—Barry, Joanne. Admitted to Pa. bar, 1919, and began practice in Phila.; mem. firm Hirschwald, Goff & Rubin; asst. city solicitor City of Phila., 1936. Served in U.S. Navy, 1917-19. Mem. Am., Pa. State, and Phila. bar assns., Foreign Policy Assn., Lawyers Club, Am. Legion, Germantown Fellowship (former pres.). Jewish religion. Clubs: Philmont Country (Philmont, Pa.); Locust (Phila.). Home: 506 W. Springer St. Office: North American Bldg., Broad and Sansom Sts., Philadelphia, Pa.

HIRSH, Harry Bernheim, chmn. exec. com. Belmont Iron Works; b. Lancaster, Pa., Oct. 17, 1864; s. Leopold and Betty (Bernheim) H.; grad. Central High Sch., 1880; B.A., U. of Pa., 1883; m. Minnie Rosenberg, Apr. 30, 1891 (died Apr. 3, 1923); children—Elizabeth R. (Mrs. Horace T. Fleisher), Rose (Mrs. Morris Wolf), Margaret (wife of Conrad Valguarnera-Prince Niscemi); m. 2d, Edith Borden, Sept. 20, 1926. Asst. engr. Ore. Ry. & Navigation Co., 1883-84, Bur. of Surveys, Philadelphia, 1884-85; asst. engr. Belmont Iron Works, Phila., 1884-86, mgr. New York office, 1886-89, Philadelphia office, 1889-1919, president, 1919-36, chmn. exec. com. since 1936. Dir. Jewish Hosp. Assn., Indian Rights Assn. (both of Philadelphia), National Farm Sch. (Doylestown, Pa.). Clubs: Penn Athletic (Philadelphia); University of Pa. (New York, N.Y.). Home: 1901 Walnut St. Office: 2215 Washington Av., Philadelphia, Pa.

HIRSH, Sidney, pres. Globe Varnish Co.; b. Allegheny, Pa., Feb. 23, 1878; s. Herman and Hanna (Rosenberg) H.; ed. Fifth Ward Grade Sch., Allegheny High Sch., Park Inst. (all of Allegheny, Pa.); m. Gertrude Russack, Oct. 4, 1906; children—Louise B., Maxine S. With Globe Varnish Co. since 1895, successively as office asst., salesman and sec.-treas., pres. since 1932, dir. since 1916; dir. Russack Realty & Investment Co. Republican. Jewish religion. Club: Concordia (Pittsburgh). Home: 5718 Woodmont St. Office: Kelly & La Schall Sts., Pittsburgh, Pa.

HIRST, Lester Larsen, chemist; b. Paradise, Utah, Nov. 30, 1903; s. Charles Tarry and Caroline (Larsen) H.; B.S., Utah State Agrl. Coll., Logan, Utah, 1925; Ph.D., U. of Calif., 1929; m. Catherine George Wood, May 24, 1930; children—Margaret Ruth, Lester Larsen. Chemist U.S. Bureau of Mines, Pittsburgh, 1929-30; chemist with A. O. Smith Corpn., Milwaukee, Wis., 1930-32; chemist development dept., Standard Oil Co. of Calif., 1932-35; with Bureau of Mines, U.S. Dept. of Interior since 1935, building and operating small continuous coal hydrogenation plant. Mem. Am. Chem. Soc., Phi Beta Phi, Sigma Xi, Phi Lambda Upsilon. Home: 381 Greelee Rd., Brentwood, Pittsburgh, Pa. Office: 4800 Forbes St., Pittsburgh, Pa.

HIRT, William E., judge; b. Erie, Pa., May 13, 1881; s. Charles F. and Mary (Melhorn) H.; A.B., Princeton, 1904; (hon.) D.C.L., Thiel Coll., 1936; m. Emma LeJeal Spafford, Nov. 24, 1908; 1 son, John William. Admitted to Pa. bar, 1908, and engaged in gen. practice of law at Erie, 1908-20; apptd. Judge Ct. of Common Pleas 6th Jud. Dist. (Erie Co.) Pa., 1920, elected judge, 1921 for ten yr. term; reelected, 1931 for ten yr. term; president judge, 1936-39; apptd. judge Superior Court of Pa., Mar. 1939. Republican. Mason (K.T., 32°, Shriner). Clubs: Erie, Shriners', Kahkwa, University. Home: Erie, Pa.

HIRTZEL, Orris C., treas. and gen. mgr. Electric Materials Co.; b. Warren, Pa., May 29, 1869; s. Philip and Barbara Marian (Eichler) H.; ed. Duff's Business Coll., Pittsburgh; m. Beatrice E. Dewey, Sept. 17, 1902; 1 son, Philip D. Bookkeeper Penn Tanning Co. Div., U.S. Leather Co., 1892-96; treas. and gen. mgr. The Eureka Co., 1896-1913; detail and supply specialist Westinghouse Electric & Mfg. Co., East Pittsburgh, Pa., 1913-15; treas. and gen. mgr. The Electric Material Co., North East, Pa., since 1915; pres. Nat. Bank of North East since 1910; now also dir. of both cos. Democrat. Lutheran. Mason. Home: 20 Gibson St., North East, Pa.

HITCHCOCK, Clarence C., prin. city schs.; b. De Kalb, N.Y., Sept. 14, 1892; s. A. J. and Jane (Creighton) H.; B.S., St. Lawrence U., Canton, N.Y., 1914; A.M., Teachers Coll., Columbia U., 1928; Ph.D., N.Y. Univ., N.Y. City, 1938; m. Bernice L. Hastings, Nov. 25, 1915; 1 dau., Marjorie Elizabeth. Engaged as teacher and prin., Norfolk, N.Y., 1914-16, Cortland, N.Y., 1916-17; with state dept. edn., Albany, N.Y., 1917-20; supt. schs., St. Johnsbury, Vt., 1920-23, Bridgeton, N.J., 1923-27; supt. schs., Hasbrouck Heights, N.J. since 1927; part time instr. State Teachers Coll., Paterson, N.J., 1936-39. Mem. N.J. State Teachers Assn., N.J. Schoolmasters Club, N.J. Council of Edn., Phi Delta Kappa. Republican. Mem. Reformed Ch. Mason. Club: Lions. Home: 146 Hamilton Av., Hasbrouck Heights, N.J.

HITCHENS, William Frank, prof. architecture; b. Delmar, Del., Nov. 12, 1885; s. William Smith and Fannie Catherine (Parker) H.; B.S. in Architecture, U. of Pa., 1909. With Carnegie Inst. Tech. since 1913, prof. architecture and head of dept. of architecture since 1925. Registered architect of Pa. Served as 2d lt. F.A., U.S.A., 1918. Mem. Am. Inst. of Architects, Pa. State Art Commn., Sigma Xi. Home: 5726 Beacon St., Pittsburgh, Pa.

HITCHLER, Walter Harrison, dean of law; b. Plymouth, Pa., Feb. 20, 1883; s. Adolph Frederick and Alice Carey (Harman) H.; B.L., U. of Va., 1905; D.C.L., from Dickinson Coll., 1932; LL.D., from Saint Francis College, Loretta, Pa., 1932; unmarried. Editor Michie Pub. Co., Charlottesville, Va., 1905-06; teacher, Dickinson Sch. of Law, Carlisle, Pa., 1906-17; editor Statutory Law of Pa., 1919-22; teacher, Dickinson Sch. of Law, 1919-30, dean of sch. since 1930. Admitted to bars of Pa. and Va. Served as 2d lt. inf., U.S.A., 1918-19; 1st lt. O.R.C., 1919-23, capt. since 1923. Mem. Am. and Pa. bar assns. Raven Soc. (U. of Va.), Am. Law Inst. Episcopalian. Mason (K.T., Shriner). Clubs: Rotary, Carlisle Country; Penn Athletic (Philadelphia). Contbr. to Dickinson Law Review. Home: 301 S. College St., Carlisle, Pa.

HITE, Omar, newspaper man; b. Smithton, W.Va., Jan. 11, 1890; s. Rev. Raymond M. and Mary S. (Cochran) H.; grad. high school, 1907; student Campbell Coll., Holton, Kan., 3 yrs.; A.B., U. of Kan., 1913; m. June R. Barker, July 19, 1919; children—Howard Omar, Lois Elizabeth. Editorial staff, Ft. Worth (Tex.) Record, fall of 1913; telegraph editor Arkansas Gazette, Little Rock, Ark., 1914-15; editorial staff St. Louis Republic, 1915-17; with St. Louis Star, 1917; editorial staff and asst. day city editor, New York Herald, 1917-20; asso. editor Christian Herald, 1920-25, editor, 1925-28; mem. editorial staff New York Times since 1929. Served as 2d lt. inf., Camp Pike and Camp Funston, World War. Presbyn. Home: 54 Rodney St., Glen Rock, N.J. Address: New York Times, 229 W. 43d St., New York, N.Y.

HITTI, Philip K(huri), Orientalist; b. Shimlan, Mt. Lebanon, Syria, June 24, 1886; s. Iskandar and Sa'da (Nawfal) H.; B.A., with first honors, Am. U. of Beirut, Syria, 1908; Ph.D., Columbia, 1915; m. Mary George, May 22, 1918; 1 dau., Viola. Came to U.S., 1913, naturalized citizen, 1919. Teacher Am. High Sch., Lebanon, Syria, 1903-06; Am. U. of Beirut, 1908-13; lecturer, oriental dept. Columbia, 1915-20; prof. history, American University of Beirut, 1920-26; asst. prof. of Semitic lit., Princeton, 1926-29, asso. prof., 1929-36, prof. since 1936. Pres. Inter-collegiate Club of N.Y. City, 1915-20; founder, and pres. Syrian Edn. Soc., 1916; del. from Syria to World's Student Christian Federation, Constantinople, Turkey, 1910, and Lake Mohonk, N. Y., 1913; sec. War Work Council, City Coll. of New York, 1917-18; trustee École Nationale, Beirut, 1921-24; mem. administrative com. Near East Relief for Syria and Palestine, 1921-24; sec. Alumni Assn. American U. of Beirut, 1921-38; mem. Am. Schs. of Oriental Research since 1934; special editor, Webster's New Internat. Dictionary, 2d edit., 1934; dir. Summer Seminar in Arabic and Islamic Studies, joint auspices of Princeton U. and Am. Council of Learned Socs., 1935, 38. Mem. American Oriental Soc. (dir. 1927-29), Am. Hist. Assn., Linguistic Soc. America, Arab Acad. of Damascus; asso. mem. Islamic Research Assn., (Bombay), Archæol. Inst. of America. Club: Am. Oriental (New York). Author: The Origins of the Islamic State, 1916; Guide Book for Foreign Students in the U.S., 1921; The Semitic Languages Spoken in Syria and Palestine, 1922; The Syrians in America, 1924; Characteristics of Moslem Sects, 1924; Syria and the Syrians, 1926; An Arab-Syrian Gentleman and Warrior in the Period of the Crusades, 1929; The Origins of the Druze People and Religion, 1929; Kitab-al-I'tibar i-Usamah, 1930; History of the Arabs, 1937. Co-author Descriptive catalogue of the Garrett Collection of Arabic Manuscripts in Princeton University Library, 1938. Contributing editor Social Science Abstracts, 1928-32; contbr. of articles to Encyclopædia of the Social Sciences. Home: 106 Fitz Randolph Rd., Princeton, N.J.

HITTLE, James Monroe, lawyer; b. Hempfield Twp., Mercer Co., Pa., Feb. 17, 1877; s. Peter and Mary (Hause) H.; B.S., Fredonia Inst., 1897; LL.B., George Washington Law Sch., 1899; m. Estelle Moser, Nov. 9, 1909. Admitted to Pa. bar, 1900, and practiced in Mercer, 1900-05; in practice, Greenville, since 1905; dir. and counsel Farmers & Merchants Trust Co., Greenville, Pa.; borough solicitor and sec., Greenville, since Jan. 1, 1907; dir. Masonic Holding Assn. Trustee Greenville Hosp.; gov. Greenville Motor Club. Republican. Mem. Evangelical and Reformed Ch. Mason, K. of P. Clubs: Acacia, Greenville Country, Home: 62 Shenango St. Office: 222½ Main St., Greenville, Pa.

HITZ, Ralph, hotel management; b. Vienna, Austria, Mar. 1, 1891; s. Josef and Leopoldine (Gans) H.; ed. Vienna grade and high schs.; m. Myrtle Dahl, Sept. 25, 1915; 1 son, Ralph. Came to U.S., 1906, naturalized, 1915. Began in hotel business, 1906; mgr. Fenway Hall Hotel, Cleveland, O., 1926-27, Hotel Gibson, Cincinnati, 1927-29; mgn. dir. Hotel New Yorker, N.Y. City, 1929-31, pres. since 1931; pres. Nat. Hotel Management Co., Inc., since 1932; pres. Cincinnati Hotel Co., Van Cleve Hotel, Belmont Plaza Hotel; v.p. Book-Cadillac Properties, Inc.; dir. Dallas Hotel Co. Mem. Am. Hotel Assn. (chmn. accounting com.). Methodist. Mason (32°, Shriner), Elk, Eagle, Moose. Clubs: Riding and Polo (N.Y. City); Raritan Valley Country. Home: Pittstown, N.J. Office: Hotel New Yorker, New York City, N.Y.

HIXSON, Arthur Warren, chem. engring.; b. Mifflinburg, Pa., July 7, 1880; s. William E. and Anna E. (Shiffer) H.; A.B., U. of Kan., 1907, M.S., 1915; Ph.D., Columbia, 1918; m. Edetha M. Washburn, June 17, 1907; children—Arthur Norman, Rachel Marjorie. Assayer and metallurgist Detroit Copper Mining Co., Morenci, Ariz., 1906-08; chemist Ill. State Agrl. Expt. Sta., 1908-09; instr. and asst. prof. metallurgy and industrial chemistry, Ia. State U., 1909-17; chem. engr. Ia. State Geol. Survey, 1909-14; asso. prof. chem. engring., Columbia, 1919-27, prof. since 1927; asso., Tech. Advisory Corpn., 1921-26; cons. chem. engr. Fleischmann Co., 1922-27. Chem. eng. in charge production, High Explosives Div., Ordnance Bur., U.S.A., 1918-19; tech. adviser to Claims Board, U.S.A., 1919-21. Inventor of several processes for production of baker's yeast; specializes in process development and chem. plant design. Chmn. Am. Chem. Industries Tercentenary, 1935; chmn. Town Planning Commn., Leonia, N.J. Fellow A.A.A.S.; mem. Am. Chem. Soc. (chmn. N.Y. sect. 1934-35), Am. Electrochem. Soc., Am. Inst. Chem. Engrs., Soc. for Promotion Engring.

Edn., Soc. Chem. Industry of Gt. Britain, Sigma Xi, Tau Beta Pi, Phi Lambda Upsilon. Republican. Presbyn. Clubs: Chemists, Faculty, Columbia Univ. (New York); Englewood (N.J.) Golf. Home: 206 Hillcrest Av., Leonia, N.J.

HOADLEY, Frederick, pres. Newark Provident Loan Assn.; b. Princeton, N.J., Mar. 13, 1870; s. Philemon Lyman and Mary Aurelia (Olmstead) H.; grad. Newark High Sch.; m. Sarah Areson, of Montclair, N.J., June 22, 1898; children—Philemon, Frederick Areson. Archtl. student, draughtsman and architect, 1891-98; successively clerk, special agent, asst. sec. and sec. Am. Ins. Co., 1898-1936; retired 1936; dir. Newark Provident Loan Assn. since 1920, v.p. and treas., 1925-38, pres. since 1938; dir. Am. Ins. Co. Republican. Episcopalian. Home: 126 Bellevue Av., Upper Montclair, N.J. Office: 31 Clinton St., Newark, N.J.

HOAG, Clarence Gilbert, civic sec.; b. Lynn, Mass., Feb. 15, 1873; s. Gilbert Congdon and Louisa Phoebe (Oliver) H.; A.B., Haverford (Pa.) Coll., 1893, Harvard, 1894; post-grad. work, univs. of Berlin and Zürich, 1894-95; A.M., Harvard, 1898; m. Anna Scattergood; children—Mary Scattergood (Mrs. C. A. P. Lawrence), Gilbert Thomas, Garrett Scattergood, John Hacker. Instr. English, Bates Coll., 1898-1900, U. of Pa., 1901-08. General sec.-treas. Proportional Representation League, 1912-26, treas. and hon. sec. since 1926; treas. C. F. Taylor Trust. Mem. Soc. of Friends. Author: A Theory of Interest, 1914; (with G. H. Hallett, Jr.) Proportional Representation, 1926. One of the originators and first promoters (with Wm. Hoag) of the "Cincinnati Plan" of city government (applied in Cincinnati, Hamilton, etc.). Home: 619 Walnut Lane, Haverford, Pa.

HOBAN, Thomas Linus, judge; b. Scranton, Pa., Sept. 23, 1893; s. Thomas P. and Jane D. H.; A.B., Holy Cross Coll., 1913; LL.B., U. of Pa., 1917; unmarried. Admitted to Pa. bar, 1917, and practiced in Scranton, 1917-35; judge Court of Common Pleas, Lackawanna County, Pa., since 1935. Served as lt. of inf., U.S. Army, 1917-18; with A.E.F. and wounded in action; now lt. col. 109th Inf., Pa. Nat. Guard. Roman Catholic. Home: Hotel Casey. Office: Court House, Scranton, Pa.

HOBEIN, Charles Augustus, investment dealer; b. Brooklyn, N.Y., Sept. 30, 1881; s. Charles Augustus and Eliza Thompson (Buell) H.; B.Sc. in E.E., Elec. Engr., Ia. State Coll., Ames, Ia., 1903; m. Elsie Maida Galbraith, Apr. 10, 1907; children—Margaret Buell (Mrs. C. Worcester Bouck), Robert Galbraith, Kingsland. Elec. engr. St. Louis Transit Co., United Rys. Co., St. Louis, Mo., 1903-13; engr. for investment reports John Nickerson, New York, 1913-17; engring. reports and appraisals Republic Engrs., Youngstown, Ohio, and New York, and of Ford, Bacon & Davis, New York, 1917-19; vice-pres., sec.-treas. and mem. bd. of dirs. John Nickerson & Co., Inc., investment dealers, New York, since 1919; sec.-treas. and dir. Guardian Investors Corpn. since 1925. Guardian Safe Deposit Co., New York, since 1928; v.p., sec. and dir. Standard Utilities, Inc., New York, since 1932; treas. Utilities Coal Co., Huntington, W.Va., since 1930; dir. Ind. Ice & Fuel Co. Mem. Am. Inst. E.E., Montclair Soc. of Engrs., Beta Theta Pi. Republican. Episcopalian. Club: Downtown Athletic (New York). Home: 130 Edgemont Rd., Montclair, N.J. Office: 61 Broadway, New York, N.Y.

HÖBER, Rudolf Otto Anselm, prof. physiology; b. Stettin, Germany, Dec. 27, 1873; s. Anselm and Elise (Köhlau) H.; ed. Univs. of Freiburg, Erlangen, and Berlin, Germany, 1892-97, M.D., 1897; came to U.S., 1934; m. Margarete Marx, M.D., Aug. 10, 1901; children—Johannes Uto, Gabriele Lili (Mrs. Manfred Blaschy), Ursula Marie Elise, M.D. Engaged as prof. U. of Kiel, Germany, 1910-34; visiting prof. physiology, U. of Pa. Med. Sch. since 1934. Mem. Soc. of Exptl. Biology and Medicine, Am. Physiol. Soc., Sigma Xi. Spl. field of investigation, physicochemistry applied to physiology. Home: 6701 Cresheim Rd., Philadelphia, Pa.

HOBLITZELL, John D(empsey), Jr., real estate and ins.; b. Parkersburg, W.Va., Dec. 30, 1912; s. John D. and Juliette (Smith) H.; A.B., W.Va. Univ., Morgantown, 1934; m. Anna Rathbone Cochran, Oct. 7, 1932. Engaged in bus. of real estate and ins. brokerage at Parkersburg, W.Va., since 1934, vice-pres. and treas. Parkersburg Realty Co. since 1936; dir. White Star Laundry Co., Parkersburg, W.Va., since 1937. Mem. W.Va. Young Reps. (sec. 1934), Parkersburg Jr. Chamber of Commerce (pres. 1938-39), W.Va. Jr. Chamber of Commerce (pres. 1939). Mem. bd. govs. W.Va. Univ. Mem. W.Va. Golf Assn. (dir.), Am. Polit. Science Assn., Phi Kappa Psi. Republican. Episcopalian. Elk. Clubs: Elks, Country (Parkersburg). Home: Country Club Rd. Office: 512 Market St., Parkersburg, W.Va.

HOBLITZELLE, Harrison, pres. Gen. Steel Castings Corpn.; b. St. Louis, Mo., Oct. 17, 1896; s. George Knapp and Laura Trimble (Harrison) H.; student Smith Acad., St. Louis, 1908-13; A.B., Cornell U., 1917; m. Mary D. Jones, Jan. 14, 1920; children—George Knapp, Harrison. Clk., Commonwealth Steel Co., 1917, asst. purchasing agt., 1919, mgr. of purchases, 1922, vice-pres. and mgr. of purchases, 1926, vice-pres. and mgr. sales, 1929; vice-pres. and gen. mgr. Commonwealth Div. of Gen. Steel Castings Corpn., 1929-31, exec. vice-pres., 1931, pres. since Sept. 1931, also dir. and mem. exec. and finance coms.; dir. St. Louis Union Trust Co.; mem. bd. of mgrs. Western Saving Fund Soc.; mem. bd. of govs. Railway Business Assn.; mem. Pa. advisory bd. Am. Mutual Liability Ins. Co.; mem. state bd. Pa. Economy League; mem. 1937 Pa. Anthracite Coal Industry Commn. Trustee Thomas Skelton Harrison Foundation. Dir. Bryn Mawr (Pa.) Hosp. Mem. Am. Iron and Steel Inst., Newcomen Soc. (Eng.), Mo. Hist. Soc., Kappa Alpha. Ind. Democrat. Episcopalian. Clubs: Merion Cricket, Racquet, Gulph Mills Golf, Pine Valley Golf, Courts (Phila.); St. Louis Country, Round Table (St. Louis). Home: Conestoga Rd., Ithan, Pa. Office: General Steel Castings Corpn., Eddystone, Pa.

HOCKER, Carl DeWitt, telephone engring.; b. Rockville, Ind., Oct. 4, 1890; s. George E. and Harriet (Shortridge) H.; A.B., Wabash Coll., 1912; Ph.D. U. of Mich., 1915; m. Flora B. Ames, June 30, 1917; 1 dau., Eleanor E. Began as research chemist Western Electric Co., 1915; entire career with Bell Telephone Laboratories (formerly known as Engring Dept. of Western Electric Co.), now plant materials engr. Mem. Am. Chem. Soc., Am. Soc. Testing Materials, Phi Beta Kappa, Sigma Xi, Phi Lambda Upsilon, Gamma Alpha. Republican. Clubs: Columbian (East Orange); Crestmont Golf (West Orange). Home: 25 Grant Av., East Orange, N.J. Office: Bell Telephone Laboratories, 463 West St., New York, N.Y.

HOCKLEY, Chester F., pres. Davison Chem. Corpn.; dir. many companies. Home: Hyde, Md. Office: 20 Hopkins Pl., Baltimore, Md.

HODDESON, Samuel Isaac, chem. engring.; b. New York, N.Y., Apr. 5, 1892; s. Barnett and Rachel (Silverstein) H.; B.Sc., Rutgers U., 1914; m. Esther Wolfe, Mar. 4, 1917; children—Irene Rae, Burton Alan. Employed as chemist, N.J. Agrl. Expt. Sta., 1914-16; chemist, then chief chemist, Hercules Powder Co., 1916-24; supt. Minir-Edgar Co., 1924-28; supt. Am. Powder Co., 1928-31; tech. service and industrial surveys, Spl. Products Div. General Chem. Co. since 1931; pres. Property Owners Bldg. & Loan Assn., 1923-28, dir. since 1931. Served as tax assessor, City of New Brunswick, 1923-28. Mem. City Recreation Com., 1935. Active in local civic affairs as chmn., mem. exec. com. or officer of coms. of civic orgns. Trustee Jewish Community Center. Pres. Y.M.H.A., 1921-22, United Hebrew Sch., 1937-39. Mem. Tau Delta Phi. Democrat. Jewish religion. Mason. Elk. Home: 11 Llewellyn Pl., New Brunswick, N.J. Office: 40 Rector St., New York, N.Y.

HODGE, Charles, 4th, entomology and zoology; b. Louisville, Ky., Feb. 5, 1900; s. Charles and Peachey (Converse) H.; A.B., U. of Pa., 1922, Ph.D., same, 1932; m. Ruth Patrick, July 10, 1931. Engaged in teaching biology and chemistry, Pottstown High Sch., 1922-26; instr. zoology, U. of Pa., 1926-31, summer 1932; instr. zoology, Temple U., 1931-37, asst. prof. entomology and invertebrate zoology since 1937. Fellow A.A.A.S.; Am. Entomol. Soc., Am. Assn. Univ. Profs., Entomol. Soc. of America, Sigma Xi. Presbyn. Traveled in Brit. Guiana, collecting beetles, summer 1926. Home: 2119 Spruce St., Philadelphia, Pa.

HODGE, Mary Ashmun, asso. physician, Goucher Coll., 1925-27; prof. hygiene of Catherine Milligan McLane Foundation since 1927. Address: Goucher College, Baltimore, Md.

HODGE, Willard Wellington, prof. chem. engring.; b. Ripon, Wis., Aug. 22, 1884; s. Willard Addison and Elizabeth Ann (Pinch) H.; A.B., Ripon Coll., 1909; A.M., U. of Wis., 1912; A.M., Yale, 1913; student Columbia, summers 1921-23; unmarried. Instr. chemistry and physics, Green Bay (Wis.) High Sch., 1909-10; instr. in chemistry, Calumet (Mich.) High Sch., 1910-11; grad. asst. and research fellow Sheffield Scientific Sch., Yale, 1911-14; chem. engr. and factory supt., Gen. Labs. Co., Madison, Wis., 1914-15; prof. chemistry and physics, Albany (Ore.) Coll., 1915-17; instr. in chemistry, U. of N.D., 1917-18; asst. prof. chemistry, Ore. State Coll., 1918-20, asso. prof., summer 1920; prof. chem. engring. and head dept., W.Va. Univ., since 1921; asst. dir. W.Va. Univ. Engring. Expt. Sta., 1927-35, dir. since 1936; also consulting chem. engring. practice; industrial fellow for Am. Iron and Steel Inst., Mellon Inst. for Industrial Research (on leave from W.Va. Univ.), 1938-40. Mem. State Registration Bd. for Professional Engrs. of W.Va. since 1934. Chmn. com. on directory Nat. Council State Bds. Engring. Examiners; rep. Nat. Bureau Engring. Registration, N.E. Zone, 1938-39. Mem. Am. Inst. Chem. Engrs., Am. Chem. Soc., Soc. of Chem. Industry (London), Soc. for Promotion Engring. Edn., Am. Water Works Assn., Nat. Soc. Professional Engrs., W.Va. Acad. of Science, W.Va. Conf. on Water Purification, W.Va. Soc. Professional Engrs., Acacia, Sigma Xi, Tau Beta Pi, Phi Lambda Upsilon, Sigma Gamma Epsilon. Republican. Presbyn. Mason. Clubs: Kiwanis; Faculty (W.Va. Univ.); University (Pittsburgh). Contbr. to scientific and engring. jours.; author of bulletins on coal by-products, water purification, etc., pub. by W.Va. Engring. Expt. Sta. Home: 19 McLane Av., Morgantown, W.Va.

HODGES, Clarence Albert, prof. of physics; b. Covina, Calif., Dec. 13, 1889; s. James Rousseau and Olive (Judd) H.; grad. Los Angeles State Normal Sch., 1911; A.B., U. of Tex., 1921, A.M., 1924; student U. of Chicago, summers 1924, 25; Ph.D., Calif. Inst. of Tech., 1928; m. Cecilia Elizabeth Murphree, June 12, 1917; children—Evelyn Elizabeth, Margaret Helen, Amy Ruth. Teacher of rural school, Olive, Calif., 1911-12; prin. grammar schools, San Bernardino, Calif., 1912-14, Porterville, Calif., 1914-16, Holtville, Calif., 1916-18; tutor in physics, U. of Tex., 1921-23, instr., 1923-26; asst. prof. of physics, Temple U., 1928-35, asso. prof. since 1935. Served with 16th Div., Train Headquarters, and Mil. Police as sergt. major, U.S. Army, 1918-19. Mem. Am. Assn. Univ. Profs., Am. Assn. Physics Teachers, Rittenhouse Astron. Soc., Franklin Inst. (asso.), Phi Beta Kappa, Sigma Xi. Ind. Democrat. Presbyterian. Mason. Home: 6425 N. 13th St., Philadelphia, Pa.

HODGES, Fletcher, Jr., curator; b. Indianapolis, Ind., Aug. 6, 1906; s. Fletcher (M.D.) and Rebecca Traill (Andrews) H.; grad. Shortbridge High Sch., Indianapolis, 1924; A.B., Harvard U., 1928; m. Sarah Margaret Moore, of Indianapolis, Sept. 10, 1932; children—Fletcher, III, Arthur Carlisle. Began work in department store, 1928; associated with meat packing business, Chicago, 1929-31, Indianapolis, 1931; curator Foster Hall Collection, Indianapolis, 1931-36, Pittsburgh, since 1937. Sec. Stephen Foster Memorial Com., (U. of Pittsburgh). Republican. Episcopalian. Clubs: Literary (Indianapolis); Faculty (Pittsburgh). Author of bibliographical appendix in John Tasker Howard's biography, Stephen Foster, America's Troubadour, 1934; A Pittsburgh Composer and His Memorial, 1938; also various mag. articles on life and works of Stephen Collins Foster (Am. composer of middle 19th century). Home: 5812 Kentucky Av. Address: University of Pittsburgh, Pittsburgh, Pa.

HODGES, Harry, church official; b. Phila., Pa., Apr. 10, 1880; s. Robert and Josephine (Young) H.; student Phila. Sch. of Industrial Art, 1894-95, Central High Sch., Phila., 1895-99; unmarried. Dept. mgr. I. Snellenburg & Co., clothing mfrs., Philadelphia, 1900-16; exec. sec. Luther League of America, editor Luther League Review, 1916-28; exec. sec. Ministerial Bd of Pensions and Relief, United Lutheran Ch. in America, Phila., since 1929. Republican. Lutheran. Clubs: Manufacturers and Bankers (Phila.); Nat. Travel (N.Y.). Home: Manufacturers and Bankers Club. Office: Muhlenberg Bldg., Philadelphia, Pa.

HODGES, Leigh Mitchell, writer; b. Denver, Colo., July 9, 1876; s. Charles Hawley and Elizabeth P. (Mitchell) H.; grad. high sch., Carthage, Mo., 1894; student Sch. of Fine Arts, St. Louis, 1 yr.; m. Nadine Converse Skinner, Apr. 22, 1903; children—Mitchell Converse, Mary Leigh (Mrs. Harold G. Beeson). Became reporter then city editor, the Daily Ledger, Mexico, Mo., 1895-96; reporter, Kansas City Star, 1897-99; editorial staff, Ladies' Home Journal, New York and Phila., 1899-1901; started "The Optimist" column in Phila. Times, 1902, which was transferred to The North American, Phila., same year, and appeared continuously in that paper until 1925; now in Evening Bulletin, Phila.; mem. editorial staff The North American, 1906-15, contbg. editor, 1915-25. Inaugurated first publicity campaign for Red Cross Christmas seals, 1907. Mem. Acad. Natural Sciences, Philadelphia; hon. mem. Missouri Authors' Guild. Author: The Great Optimist and Other Essays, 1903; The Life Worth While, 1904; The Worth of Service, 1905; The Great Encouragement, 1913; Bird Guardians, 1915; The Bard at Home (Shakespeare Tercentenary masque), 1916; Processional (poem read at Cathedral of St. John the Divine, New York, by Bishop Manning), 1933. Compiler: Poems We Love, 1908. Home: Doyleston, Pa. Office: 311 S. Juniper St., Philadelphia, Pa.

HODGKISS, Harold Edward, entomologist; b. Cambridge, Mass., Apr. 8, 1879; s. Rev. Samuel and Margaret Elizabeth (Searles) H.; B.Sc., Mass. State Coll., 1902; B.Sc., Boston U., 1902; grad. study, Mass. State Coll., 1902-04; m. Emma Louise Knight, Nov. 29, 1905; children—Arthur Salisbury, William Searles. Engaged as asst. entomologist, N.Y. Agrl. Expt. Sta., Geneva, N.Y., 1904-07; field entomologist, U. of Ill., 1907-08; asst. entomologist, N.Y. Agrl. Expt. Sta., 1908-19; prof. of entomology extension and entomologist, Div. Agr. Extension, The Pa. State Coll. since 1919. Mem. A.A.A.S., Am. Assn. Economic Entomologists, Entomol. Soc. of America, Pa. Acad. of Science, Sigma Xi, Epsilon Sigma Phi. Republican. Episcopalian. Home: 147 W. Park Av., State College, Pa.

HOECHST, Coit Roscoe, educator; b. Adams Co., Pa., Nov. 16, 1886; s. Isaac H. and Sarah (Jacobs) H.; A.B., Bucknell U., 1907, A.M., 1908; Ph.D., U. of Pittsburgh, 1916; m. Jessie Mitten Hurst, 1909; children—Eleanor Hurst, Ruth Elizabeth; m. 2d, Margaret Iola Wagle, 1930. Engaged as instr. in high schs., 1908-14; instr. langs., Schenley High Sch., Pittsburgh, Pa., 1916-26; dir. extension edn., Pittsburgh Bd. Pub. Edn., since 1926, also teacher of methods, U. of Pittsburgh, summers since 1923. Mem. exec. bd. Am. Citizenship League, Pittsburgh Council on Adult Edn. (past pres.). Mem. Nat. Council on Immigration and Naturalization, Nat. Edn. Assn., Pa. State Edn. Assn., Pa. Modern Lang. Assn. (past pres.), Pa. Assn. Adult Edn., Phi Delta Kappa. Republican. Mem. Reformed Ch. Mason (32°, Shriner). Clubs: Unitey, Faculty of U. of Pittsburgh. Home: 3030 Iowa St., Pittsburgh, Pa. Office: Bellefield Av. and Forbes St., Pittsburgh, Pa.

HOEHLING, Adolph August, judge; b. Phila., Pa., Nov. 3, 1868; s. Rear Adm. Adolph August (U.S.N.) and Annie (Tilghman) H.; student Rensselaer Poly. Inst. and Lehigh U.; LL.B., Columbian (now George Washington) U., 1889, LL.M., 1890, LL.D., 1932; m. Louise G. Carrington, June 9, 1906; children—Louise Carrington, Adolph August. Admitted to D.C. bar, 1890, and practiced at Washington, D.C.; mem. firm of Hoehling, Peele & Ogilby, 1913-21; asso. justice Supreme Court of D.C., 1921-27; resigned to resume pvt. practice; v.p. Nat. Metropolitan Bank. Mem. Psi Upsilon, Phi Delta Phi. Republican. Episcopalian. Home: 5 Newlands St., Chevy Chase, Md.

HOEHN, Matthew Anthony, librarian; b. Newark, N.J., Feb. 4, 1898; s. Joseph and Elizabeth (Magin) H.; student St. Benedict's Prep. Sch., Newark, N.J., 1912-16, Columbia U. Summer Sch., 1924, Fordham U. Summer Sch., 1925; A.B., St. Anselm's Coll., Manchester, N.H., 1921; B.L.S., Columbia U., 1936. Instr. English, St. Benedict's Prep. Sch., Newark, N.J., 1925-26, instr. chemistry, 1927-33, librarian since 1927. In St. Vincent's Abbey, Novitiate, Latrobe, Pa., 1918-19; professed in Order of St. Benedict, 1919; in seminary of St. Anselm's Coll., Manchester, N.H., 1921-25; ordained to priesthood, June 6, 1925. Mem. Am. Library Assn., N.J. Library Assn., Catholic Library Assn., Columbia U. Library Assn. Catholic. Has large collection of bookplates of business firms' libraries. Address: 528 High St., Newark, N.J.

HOELZER, Virginia (Ida), artist; b. New York, N.Y., Mar. 8, 1917; d. Charles F. and Mary L. (Breithaupt) H.; ed. Art Inst., Chicago, 1931-32, Art Students League, N.Y. City, 1932-33, Yale U. Dept. Fine Arts, 1933-34, Columbia U. Teachers Coll., 1937-38, Nat. Acad., N.Y. City, 1936-38. Engaged as poster artist since 1934; conducted art sch. in Northfield, Mass., also taught pvtly.; poster artist in Bloomfield Pub. Library, Bloomfield, N.J. since 1934. Mem. Art Students League, N.Y. City. Episcopalian. Home: 463 Franklin St., Bloomfield, N.J.

HOEVELER, John Alexander, elec. and illuminating engr.; b. Madison, Wis., Feb. 26, 1889; s. John Peter and Anna (Weinman) H.; grad. Madison High Sch., 1906; B.S., U. of Wis., 1911, E.E., 1914; m. Lauretta Franceska Hollatz, Jan. 8, 1914; 1 son, John David. Illuminating engr. Vaughan & Meyer, consulting engr., Milwaukee, Wis., 1911-13, Nat. X-Ray Reflector Co., Chicago, 1913-17; engr. Industrial Commn. of Wis., Madison, 1917-26; chief engr. Pittsburgh Reflector Co., mfrs. silvered glass reflectors and lighting equipment, since 1926. Mem. Illuminating Engring. Soc. Home: 6 Nakoma Place, Mt. Lebanon, Pa. Office: 403 Oliver Bldg., Pittsburgh, Pa.

HOFF, Charles Worthington, banker; b. Baltimore Co., Md., Apr. 6, 1898; s. Charles Worthington and Violet Hand (Browne) H.; student Marstons' Univ. Sch., Baltimore, 1908-15; LL.B., U. of Md., 1925; m. Sarah Durant Yearley, Jan. 26, 1932; children—Charles Worthington III, Alexander Yearley. Clk. Union Trust Co. of Md., Baltimore, 1915-23, asst. sec. and asst. treas., 1923-24, treas. and asst. sec., 1924-27, v.p. since 1926; v.p. and dir. Lord Baltimore Hotel Co. since 1934; dir. Fidelity & Guaranty Fire Corpn., The Frank L. Wight Distilling Co., Unger & Mahon Inc., Md. Title Securities Corpn., Dietrich Bros. Served as 2d lt., F.A., O.T.S., Camp Zachary Taylor. Mem. Bachelor's Cotillion, S.R., Sons of Colonial Wars. Clubs: Rotary, Elkridge Kennels, Chesapeake (Baltimore). Home: 4202 Somerset Pl. Office: St. Paul and Baltimore Sts., Baltimore, Md.

HOFF, (George) Preston, tech. dir.; b. Shelby, O., May 1, 1899; s. Herman Cornelius and Nellie Jane (Wilson) H.; B.A., Ohio State U., Columbus, O., 1921, M.Sc., 1922, Ph.D., 1925; m. Eleanor Brown Hammond, Apr. 3, 1926; 1 son, Robert Preston. Research chemist, Commercial Chem. Co., Memphis, Tenn., 1925; research chemist rayon dept. E. I. du Pont de Nemours & Co., Wilmington, Del., 1925-27, research supervisor, 1927-28, asst. chem. dir. rayon, cellophane, acetate dept., 1928-35, research mgr. viscose rayon dept., 1935-38, tech. dir. Nylon Div. since 1938. Mem. Am. Chem. Soc., Sigma Xi, Phi Lambda Upsilon, Gamma Alpha, Alpha Chi Sigma. Republican. Presbyterian. Home: 1302 Woodlawn Av. Office: E. I. du Pont de Nemours & Co., Wilmington, Del.

HOFF, William Bruce; mem. law firm Hoff & Moore. Address: Parkersburg, W.Va.

HOFFBERGER, Harry; pres. Merchants Terminal Corpn., Baltimore Transfer Co. Home: 3305 Springdale Av. Office: Monument and Forrest Sts., Baltimore, Md.

HOFFHEIMER, G. M.; mem. law firm Hoffheimer & Stotler. Address: Clarksburg, W.Va.

HOFFMAN, Arthur G(ilman), industrialist; v.p. Great Atlantic & Pacific Tea Co.; v.p. Second Nat. Bank of Orange, N.J.; dir. Chase Nat. Bank of New York. Home: 93 Ridge St., Orange, N.J. Office: 420 Lexington Av., New York, N.Y.*

HOFFMAN, Dean Meck, newspaper man; b. Millersburg, Pa., Nov. 11, 1880; s. Issac White and Marian (Meck) H.; student Dickinson Prep Sch., 1897-98; A.B., Dickinson Coll., 1902; m. Ethel Wilcox Miller, Nov. 24, 1914; 1 son, Dean Mec. Reporter Harrisburg and Phila. Newspapers, 1902-10; city editor Harrisburg Patriot, 1911-12, mng. editor, 1912-17; mng. editor Patriot and Evening News, 1917-20, editor-in-chief since 1922. Trustee Dickinson Coll. Mem. Phi Beta Kappa, Phi Delta Theta (pres. since 1936). Democrat. Presbyterian. Mason. Clubs: Rotary, Pen and Pencil (Phila.). Editor: When Yesteryear Comes Back Again, 1932. Author: Electric Merger, 1927; Smashing the Home Front, 1919; Twenty Years Out, 1922. Home: 2139 Green St. Office: Patriot and Evening News, Harrisburg, Pa.

HOFFMAN, George Wright, univ. prof.; b. Rose Hill, Ia., Dec. 9, 1896; s. George Wright and Emma Edith (Crew) H.; A.B., Park Coll., Parkville, Mo., 1919; A.M., U. of Pa., 1922, Ph.D., same, 1925; m. Florence Fernstrum, June 15, 1922; children—Ann Armine, George Wright. Engaged as prof. econs., Highland Coll., 1919-20; instr. econs., U. of Pa., 1920-23, instr. in ins., 1923-25, asst. prof. ins., 1925-31, prof. ins. and marketing since 1931; asst. marketing specialist, U.S. Dept. Agr., apptmnts. varying length, 1923-26, cons. economist since 1926; cons., Federal Res. Bd., summer 1934; staff contbr. Twentieth Century Fund, 1933-35. Served as pvt., inf., U.S.A., 1918-19. Mem. Am. Econ. Assn., Am. Statis. Assn., Am. Farm Econs. Assn. Presbyn. Clubs: Cosmos (Washington, D.C.). Author: Hedging by Dealing in Grain Futures, 1925; Future Trading Upon Organized Commodity Markets, 1932; The Security Markets (co-author), 1935. Contbr. monographs and articles. Home: 7701 Parkview Rd., Upper Darby, Pa.

HOFFMAN, Harold Giles, ex-gov.; b. S. Amboy, N.J., Feb. 7, 1896; s. Frank and Ada Crawford (Thon) H.; grad. high school, S. Amboy, 1913; m. Lillie Moss, Sept. 10, 1919; children —Ada Moss, Lillie Moss, Hope. Enlisted as pvt., 3d N.J. Inf., 1917; promoted through grades to capt. Hdqrs. Co., 114th Inf.; participated in Meuse-Argonne campaign. Pres. Hoffman-Lehrer Real Estate Corpn. since 1925; pres. Mid-State Title Guaranty & Mortgage Co.; exec. dir. N.J. Unemployment Compensation Commn.; radio commentator on news, WOR; column writer "Of All Things" appearing daily in syndicate of N.J. newspapers. Mem. N.J. Ho. of Assembly, 1922-24; mayor of South Amboy, 1925-27; mem. 70th and 71st Congresses (1927-31), 3d N.J. Dist.; commr. of motor vehicles, N.J., 1930-35; gov. of N.J., 3 yrs., 1935-38. Maj. U.S. Res. since 1930. Vice-pres. Nat. Safety Council. Mem. Jr. Order U.A.M., Patriotic Sons America, Am. Legion, Vets. of World War. Republican. Methodist. Mason, Elk, Eagle; mem. Royal Arcanum. Author: Mile a Minute Men; Getting Away with Murder; The Crime, The Case, The Challenge. Home: 178 Broadway, South Amboy, N.J.

HOFFMAN, Harry Clyde, M.D.; b. Jenners, Pa., Feb. 2, 1877; s. Jacob and Sarah (Horner) H.; A.B., Gettysburg Coll., 1901; M.D., U. of Pa., 1905; m. Evelyn G. Day, Sept. 5, 1906; children—Edith C., Sara Elizabeth, Evelyn Day. Teacher public sch., 1892-96; interne West Penn

Hosp., 1905-06; engaged in gen. practice of medicine since 1906; mem. Connellsville State Hosp. since 1913; pres. Jackson Coal Co., 1917-23; dir. First Nat. Bank and Yaugh Trust Co., Connellsville, Pa., 1915-26; partner in bldg. South Side Private Hosp., 1910-13. Mem. Connellsville Bd. of Edn., 1927-32. Trustee Gettysburg Coll. since 1920; supt. Inner Mission Bd. of United Lutheran Ch. since 1926. Mem. Fayette Co. Med. Soc. (pres. 1911). Democrat. Lutheran. Mason. Club: Pleasant Valley Country. Home: 295 Wills Road. Office: 501-02 Second Nat. Bank Bldg., Connellsville, Pa.

HOFFMAN, Harry Frederick, physician; b. Minonk, Ill., Dec. 19, 1884; s. Frederick and Gustava (Schiebeck) H.; ed. U. of Buffalo, 1904-06; M.D., Hahnemann Med. Coll., 1910; m. Ruth Peabody, Taylorville, Ill., Mar. 4, 1913; 1 son, Charles Harry. Asst. phys. Norwich State Hosp., Norwich, Conn., 1910-12; asst. supt. and clin. dir., Allentown State Hosp., Allentown, Pa., since 1912; lecturer on mental diseases, Hahnemann Med. Coll., 1924-30, asso. prof. mental diseases, same, since 1930; lecturer psychiatry and mental hygiene, Lehigh U., 1927-39; lecturer psychiatry, Lafayette Coll., 1930-39. Diplomate Am. Bd. Psychiatry and Neurology. Fellow Am. Psychiatric Assn.; mem. Congress of Phys. Therapy, Pa. Phys. Therapy Soc., Am. Inst. Homœopathy, Lehigh Valley Homœ. Med. Soc., Homœ. Med. Soc. of Pa., A.A.A.S. Mem. Psi Omega, Pi Upsilon Rho, Sigma Xi. Mason. Home: Allentown State Hosp., Allentown, Pa.

HOFFMAN, James Franklin, clergyman; b. Marietta, O., June 11, 1876; s. Louis and Mary (Brown) H.; B.A., Mount Union Coll., Alliance, O., 1905, M.A., 1907, D.D., 1921; B.D., Drew Theol. Sem., 1908; m. Anna Snyder, Sept. 4, 1907; children—Mary Ellen, Helen Elizabeth. Ordained ministry M.E. Ch., 1908; pastor successively Smithfield, O., Bridgeport, Miles Park Ch., Cleveland Heights, now Ch. of the Savior, Central Ch., Springfield, until 1926, Walnut Hills-Avondale, Cincinnati, 1926-32, South Av. Ch., Wilkinsburg, Pa., since 1932. Del. to Gen. Conf. M.E. Ch., 1932; mem. Alpha Tau Omega, Literary Club of Springfield. Republican. Mason. Rotarian. Home: 735 South Av., Wilkinsburg, Pa.

HOFFMAN, James Irvin, chemist; b. Enterline, Pa., Oct. 26, 1893; s. Peter and Ida Elizabeth (Shoop) H.; A.B., Franklin and Marshall Coll., Lancaster, Pa., 1918; M.S., George Washington U., 1921; Ph.D., American U., Washington, 1930; m. Mabel Hemminger, Dec. 16, 1921; 1 son, John Drake. Chemist Atlas Powder Co., 1918, Nat. Bur. of Standards, 1919-39; adjunct prof. chemistry, American U., 1931-36; lecturer in analytical chemistry, U.S. Dept. Agr., Grad. Sch., since 1936; lecturer in chemistry of rarer elements, George Washington U., since 1938. Served as sergeant Inf., U.S. Army, and sergeant, 1st class, Chem. Warfare Service, 1918. Mem. Am. Chem. Soc., Washington Acad. Sciences, Phi Beta Kappa, Sigma Xi, Alpha Chi Sigma. Author: Chemical Analysis of Iron and Steel, 1931; Outlines of Methods of Chemical Analysis, 1938; also numerous journal articles on analytical chemistry. Home: 6402 Maple Av., Chevy Chase, Md. Office: Bureau of Standards, Washington, D.C.

HOFFMAN, John G., III; pres. J. G. Hoffman & Sons Co.; officer or dir. many companies. Address: Wheeling, W.Va.

HOFFMAN, Joseph Clare, clergyman; b. Montrose, Randolph Co., W.Va., Sept. 26, 1897; s. Wilson and Emma (Sylvania) H.; A.B., W.Va. Wesleyan U., 1921, D.D., 1932; S.T.B., Boston U. Sch. Theol., 1923; grad. student Union Theol. Sem.; m. Jessie Ernest, Nov. 6, 1925; children—Patricia Ann, Joseph Scott (dec.), David Ralph. Ordained to ministry M.E. Ch., 1923; pastor Belington, Va., 1923-25, Rainelle, 1926-29, Moundsville, 1930-34, Morgantown, 1935-37, Charleston since 1938. Trustee W.Va. Wesleyan Coll. Republican. Mason. Home: 109 Morris St., Charleston, W.Va.

HOFFMAN, Leon Hale, sec. and treas. Hoffman Bros. Drilling Co.; b. Trade City, Indiana Co., Pa., Aug. 8, 1877; s. Phillip H. and Sarah Jane (Clyde) H.; ed. Dilts Sch. (N. Mahoning Twp., Indiana Co.), and Covode Acad. (Cavode, Pa.); grad. Indiana (Pa.) State Normal Sch., 1900; m. Margaret Elizabeth Dilts, July 25, 1912; 1 dau., Sarah Jane. Teacher public schools, prin. of graded schools and teachers' training schools, 1897-1902; salesman and mgr. Pittsburgh office Dodd, Mead & Co., 1902-05; sec. and treas. Hoffman Bros. Drilling Co. (specialist in diamond core drilling and more especially testing bituminous coal properties) since 1909; mem. bd. dirs. Farmers & Miners Trust Co.; dir. Kurtz Coal, Lumber & Supply Co., Penn Wayne Gas Co. Republican. Presbyterian. Mason (Shriner). Club: Punxsutawney (Pa.) Country. Home: 998 E. Mahoning St. Office: County Nat. Bank Bldg., Punxsutawney, Pa.

HOFFMAN, Luther S., lumber; b. Monroe Co., Pa., May 24, 1856; s. Charles M. and Elizabeth (Smith) H.; ed. private sch., Stroudsburg, Pa., 1877-78, State Normal, Millersville, Pa., 1879; Orangeville (Pa.) Acad., 1879-80; m. C. Grace Keller, 1884; children—Ellen Elizabeth, Mary Emma (Mrs. M. Claude Rosinberry), Charles David (deceased), Oram Pester, Luther Keller (deceased). Teacher, 1876-85; foreman lumber yard, 1885-89; pres. East Stroudsburg Lumber Co., 1889-1938; pres. Monroe County Nat. Bank, 1921-31; vice-pres. Colonial Security Co. Mem. advisory bd. Gen. Hosp.; dir. Malta Temple Assn.; dir. East Stroudsburg Playground Assn. Awarded medal by Kiwanis Club, 1926, for distinguished service in the community. Mem. Knights of Malta. Republican. Lutheran (supt. of Sunday Sch., 35 yrs.; supt. emeritus, 15 yrs.). Club: Rotarian (Stroudsburg, Pa.). Home: 256 Washington St., Office: 226 Washington St., East Stroudsburg, Pa.

HOFFMAN, Milton J., theologian; b. Overisel, Mich., Jan. 31, 1886; s. Johannes and Jennie (Timmerman) H.; B.A., Hope Coll., Holland, Mich., 1909, M.A., 1912, D.D., 1918; winner Rhodes scholarship from Mich.; B.A., Oxford Univ. Eng., 1912; m. Anna Viola MacWhinnie, July 15, 1914; children—Lydia Viola, Mildred Patricia. Head of Latin dept., Hope Coll., 1913-17; pres. Central Coll., Pella, Ia., July 1, 1917-July 1, 1925; prof. ch. history, New Brunswick Theol. Sem., New Brunswick, N.J., since July 1, 1925. Ordained ministry Ref. Ch. in America, Dec. 1917. Mem. Holland-American Foundation, Assn. Am. Rhodes Scholars, an. Ch. History Soc., Phi Beta Kappa. Home: New Brunswick, N.J.

HOFFMAN, William Stamm, registrar Pa. State Coll.; b. Pottstown, Pa., Feb. 24, 1889; s. Jacob Smith and Harriet (Lingle) H.; B.S., Pa. State Coll., 1911, M.S., same, 1919; m. Margaret Hess, Jan. 2, 1917; children—Mary Dorman, Margaret Susan. Began as instr. engring., Pa. State Coll., 1911-13; instr. at Am. Univ. of Beirut, Syria, 1913-16; instr. engring., Pa. State Coll., 1916-19; asst. registrar Pa. State Coll., 1919-23, registrar since 1923. Mem. ex officio Pa. Com. on Secondary (accrediting) of the Middle States Assn.; mem. Am. Assn. Collegiate Registrars (pres. 1939-40); mem. Lambda Chi Alpha, Scarab, Pi Delta Epsilon. Republican. Lutheran. Contbr. papers on selective admissions to edn. journs. Editor, Bulletin Am. Assn. of Collegiate Registrars, 1929-32. Home: 356 E. Fairmount Av., State College, Pa.

HOFFMEIER, Frank Newcomer, physician; b. Middletown, Md., Sept. 15, 1876; s. Thomas Franklin and Sallie (Ankeney) H.; A.B., Franklin and Marshall Coll., Lancaster, Pa., 1900; M.D., Hahnemann Med. Coll., Phila., 1903; A.M., Franklin and Marshall Coll., 1903; m. Nellie McCardell, Dec. 29, 1908; 1 dau., Jean. Engaged in gen. practice of medicine at Hagerstown, Md., 1903-17; course in x-ray, Johns Hopkins U. Med. Sch., 1915; specializing in roentgenology since 1919; in charge roentgenological dept. Washington Co. Hosp., Hagerstown since 1915. Served as 1st lt., then capt., Med. Corps, U.S.A., 1917-19, roentgenologist evacuation hosp., Vladivostock, Siberia, 1918-19. Mem. Am. Med. Assn., Inst. of Homeopathy, N.A. Radiol. Soc., Southern Med. Assn., Washington Co. Med. Soc. Democrat. Evang. & Ref. Ch. Mason (K.T., 32°, Shriner). Home: 442 N. Potomac St., Hagerstown, Md.

HOFFROGGE, Fred W.; v.-p. New Amsterdam Castualty Co. Home: 516 Old Orchard Road. Office: 227 St. Paul Place, Baltimore, Md.

HOFMANN, Josef (Casimir), pianist; b. Cracow, Poland, Jan. 20, 1876; father pianist, capellmeister and composer; learned piano under father, in infancy, and at age of 7 attracted attention of Rubinstein; in 1887 came to U.S. where he was booked to give 80 concerts in one season, but after playing 42 concerts was compelled to abandon tour by interference of the Society for the Prevention of Cruelty to Children; returned to Europe and studied under Urban, Moszkowski and Rubenstein; married; children—Josefa (by 1st marriage), Anton, Edward, Peter (by 2d marriage). Has made many concert tours, America and Europe; director, dean and instr. piano, Curtis Inst. of Music, Phila., 1926-38; now devotes his time to concertizing. Composer of concertos and piano pieces; also a symphony and orchestra suite. Writer on mus. topics. Home: Mt. Pelerin, Switzerland; also Merion, Pa. Address: Curtis Inst. of Music, Rittenhouse Sq., Philadelphia, Pa.

HOFSTETTER, William Alfred, artist; b. Phila., Pa., July 15, 1884; s. John and Mary (Knoppel) H.; art edn. Drexel Inst., Phila., 1900-03, Pa. Acad. of Fine Arts, Phila., 1904-06; m. Frances Marie McKeone, Sept. 12, 1908; children—Elizabeth Frances (Mrs. James Rafferty), Mary Madeline. Artist and teacher of art in own studio since 1897. Exhibited at: Pa. Acad. of Fine Arts; Water Color Clubs of Baltimore, Rochester, Chicago; Palm Beach Art Center; Phila. Art Club and Art Alliance; Art Assn. of Newport, R.I.; Telfair Acad., Ga.; Pa. Museum of Art. Awards: 1st prize in oil at League of South Jersey Artists, 1938. Mem. Fellowship of Pa. Acad. Fine Arts, Phila. Art Alliance, Phila. Water Color Club, Germantown Art League (Phila.); League of South Jersey Artists (Atlantic City, N.J.). Home: 3801 Chestnut St. Studio: 2025 Walnut St., Philadelphia, Pa.

HOGAN, Charles Vincent, physician; b. Pottsville, Pa., Nov. 13, 1894; s. Sylvester J. and Alesia (Condon) H.; M.D., Hahnemann Med. Coll., 1919; m. Frances Swaving, Aug. 10, 1931. Interne Hahnemann Hosp., Phila., 1919-21, asst. chief resident, 1920-21; in practice medicine and surgery at Pottsville since 1921; pres. Bd. Health City of Pottsville since 1931; dep. coroner Schuylkill Co., 1928-35; asst. chief traumatic surgery, Pottsville Hosp. since 1932; industrial surgeon since 1921. Served in U.S.N. Res., 1917-21. Mem. Am. and Schuylkill Co. med. assns., Am. Legion. Roman Catholic. B.P.O.E. (state trustee Pa. State Elks Assn.). Club: Pottsville. Home: 317 W. Market St., Pottsville, Pa.

HOGAN, Franklin E., banker; b. Kane, Pa., Aug. 24, 1888; s. George W. and Nellie (Moyer) H.; ed. Kane pub. schs.; m. Jennie S. Nelson, Sept. 1, 1933. With First Nat. Bank, Kane, Pa., 1907-18; teller Kane Trust & Savings Co., 1918-26, treas. since 1926, v.p. and treas. since 1932, also dir.; treas. Westminster Heights, Inc., 1929-37. Sec. and treas. Kane Clearing House Assn. since 1934; treas. Roosevelt Highway Assn. of Pa. since 1929. Republican. Presbyterian. Mason, Elk, Eagle. Club: Acacia (Williamsport). Home: 24 Spruce Av. Office: 87-91 Fraley St., Kane, Pa.

HOGAN, John F., asso. urology, U. of Md.; urologist Franklin Sq. Hosp.; asso. urologist West Baltimore Gen. Hosp.; adjunct attending urologist South Baltimore Gen. Hosp.; cons. urologist Sydenham and Nursery and Childs' hosps. Address: 7 E. Preston St., Baltimore, Md.

HOGAN, Joseph Vincent, dredging and heavy constrn.; b. Watertown, N.Y., Oct. 17, 1885; s. James Maxwell and Mary Jane (O'Connor) H.; C.E., Cornell U., 1908; m. Margaret Louise Quigley, June 24, 1913; children—Evelyn Louise, Eileen, Rosemary Louise, Etheldreda Louise. Began as draftsman, then asst. engr. and res. engr., engring. dept. State of N.Y., 1908-15; field engr. and dist. mgr. various cos., 1915-21; chief engr. The Arundel Corpn., dredging, heavy constrn. and producers constrn. materials, Baltimore, Md., 1921-28, asst. to pres., 1928-34, pres. and dir. since 1934; pres. and dir. Arundel-Brooks Concrete Corpn.; vice-pres. and dir. Md. Slag Co.; dir. Richmond Sand & Gravel Co., Fidelity & Deposit Co. of Md., Baltimore Nat. Bank, Metropolitan Savings Bank, Pacific Constructors, Inc. Commd. lt. comdr. C. E. Corps, U.S.N. Res. Past v.p., now dir., Baltimore Assn. Commerce. Dir. and chmn. finance com. St. Mary's Industrial Sch.; chmn. bd. dirs. St. Vincent Infant Home; dir. Good Samaritan Hosp. Mem. Am. Soc. Civil Engrs. Democrat. Roman Catholic. Clubs: Engineers, Merchants, University, Chesapeake, Baltimore Country (Baltimore); Engineers, Cornell (New York). Home: 115 St. Albans Way. Office: Pier 2, Pratt St., Baltimore, Md.

HOGE, Ernest Kenworthy, pharmacist; b. Mt. Pleasant, O., Apr. 1, 1871; s. Kenworthy and Sarah A. (Jones) H.; Ph.G., U. of Pittsburgh Coll. Pharmacy, 1891; m. Katharine Clayland, Mar. 31, 1898. Actively engaged as pharmacist and propr. retail pharmacies since 1892, pres. and dir. Hoge Davis Drug Co., operating eight retail drug stores with gen. offices at Wheeling, W.Va., since 1913 (four stores in Wheeling, and one each in Elm Grove, Warwood, W.Va., and Bellaire, and Martins Ferry, O.); dir. Stanton Heater Co., Peoples Savings Bank. Mem. Am. Pharm. Assn., W.Va. Pharm. Assn. Republican. Presbyn. (elder). Mason. Rotarian. Club: Wheeling Country. Home: National Rd. Office: 1012 Main St., Wheeling, W.Va.

HOGG, Harold Kent, physician and surgeon; b. Cochronville, Pa., Sept. 3, 1900; s. Forrest W. and Emma (Fawkes) H.; student Cochronville High Sch., 1915-18, Porkesburg (Pa.) High Sch., 1918-19, Franklin and Marshall Coll., 1919-22; M.D., Temple U., 1926; m. Julia Resser, Sept. 13, 1927; children—Patricia Ann, Harold Kent. Gen. practice as physician, Quarryville, Pa., 1927-29; in medical practice, Lancaster, since 1929, gen. practice 1929-34, physician and surgeon since 1934; city dep. coroner since 1938. Comdg. officer Co. G, 103d Med. Regt., Nat. Guard Pa., since 1935. Mem. A.M.A., Pa. Med. Soc., Lancaster Med. Soc., Phi Sigma Kappa, Phi Chi, Am. Legion (Quarryville). Repub. Presbyterian. Elk. Clubs: Lancaster Country, Lions, University, Hamilton (Lancaster). Address: 802 N. Duke St., Lancaster, Pa.

HOGSETT, Everett Leon, lawyer; b. Ripley, W.Va., Mar. 31, 1879; s. James Samuel and Alice (Wolfe) H.; student Ohio Valley Coll., Ravenswood, W.Va., 1898-1900, W.Va. Univ., Morgantown, 1908-10; m. Cora Alice Greene, Feb. 10, 1901. Engaged in teaching in pub. schs., W.Va., 1897-1906, clk. and bookkeeper, 1906-07; studied law while teaching; admitted to W.Va. bar and engaged in gen. practice of law; then served as supt. schs.; now mem. firm Hogsett & Smith; dir. and counsel Huntington Realty Corpn. Served as mem. W.Va. Ho. of Rep., 1931; Rep. co. chmn., 1928-34; mem. Park Bd., Huntington, since 1934. Mem. Am. Bar Assn., W.Va. Bar Assn. Republican. Baptist. Clubs: Cabell Republican, Executives. Home: 124 11th Av. E. Office: 524 9th St., Huntington, W.Va.

HOISINGTON, Gregory; lt. col. U. S. Inf.; prof. mil. science and tactics, Johns Hopkins U. Address: Johns Hopkins University, Baltimore, Md.

HOLBROOK, Arthur A., mgr. water company; b. near Ithaca, N.Y., Mar. 5, 1870; s. Philip and Sarah J. (Fear) H.; ed. Wyoming Sem., Kingston, Pa.; m. Iva M. Scott, 1918. Began as publisher Kingston Times, 1888; later entered public utility field and active in that since 1898; gen. mgr. Monroe County Water Supply Co., Stroudsburg, Pa.; pres. Hamilton Water Co., Saylorsburg, Pa. Home: East Stroudsburg, Pa. Office: Stroudsburg, Pa.

HOLBROOK, Elmer Allen, educator; b. Fitchburg, Mass., June 23, 1881; s. John Perry and Martha (Allen) H.; B.S., Mass. Inst. Tech., 1904; E.M., U. of Ill., 1916; m. Sarah Kirby, Aug. 15, 1905 (died 1907); 1 dau., Katherine; m. 2d, Edith L. Brookfield, 1912; children—John Brookfield, Dorothy Mary, E. Allen, Ruth Estelle. Supt. Gould (Mont.) Mines Co., 1904, Ruby Gulch Mining Co., 1905; gen. supt. Daly Reduction Co., Hedley, B.C., 1906-09; consulting practice, 1909-10; prof. mining Nova Scotia Tech. Coll., Halifax, 1911-12; asst. prof. mining, 1913-14, prof. in mineral preparation, 1915-16, U. of Ill.; with U.S. Bur. Mines, 1917-22, asst. dir., 1920-22, also chief metal mining engr. and exec. officer of investigations br. of the Bur.; dean Sch. of Mines, Pa. State Coll., 1922-27, also acting dean Grad. Sch., 1925-27; dean, Schs. of Engring. and Mines, U. of Pittsburgh, since 1927; technical advisor N.R.A. in formation of the Bituminous Coal Code, 1933. Member American Inst. Mining and Metall. Engrs., Coal Mining Inst. America, Am. Standards Assn., Phi Gamma Delta, Sigma Xi, Theta Tau, Sigma Tau, Sigma Gamma Epsilon, Phi Kappa Phi. Methodist. Club: University. Author of many articles on mining and engring., etc. Home: 1543 Shady Av., Pittsburgh, Pa.

HOLCOMB, Richmond Cranston, naval officer, retired; med. historian; b. Brooklyn, N.Y., July 26, 1874; s. Charles Mortimer and Lucy Jane (Cranston) H.; M.D., Long Island Coll. of Med., 1896; m. Mary Browning, May 3, 1899; children—Richmond Cranston, Jr., Gladys Browning (Mrs. Joseph F. McDonnell, Jr.), Browning, Charles Mortimer. Interne St. Johns Hosp. and Brooklyn Hosp., 1896-98; actg. asst. surg., U.S.A., Spanish-Am. War, 1898; entered U.S.N., Dec. 1898, advanced regularly through grades from ensign to capt.; served in Philippines, 1899-1900, in Boxer trouble, China, 1900-1902; asst. surgeon gen. U.S.N. during World War; mem. Gen. Med. Bd., Council Nat. Defense, Com. Venereal Diseases, Gen. Munitions Bd., War Relief Bd. of Am. Red Cross; superintended constrn. and 1st comdg. officer Hosp. Ship "Relief"; comdg. officer Naval Hosp., League Island, Pa., on three occasions, and Naval Hosp., Norfolk, Va., 1926-30; retired from active service, 1932. Awarded Navy Cross with Citation, World War. Fellow Am. Coll. Surgs., Am. Med. Assn. Mem. Del. Co. Med. Soc. (bd. dirs.), S.R., Am. Legion, Alpha Kappa Kappa. Club: Army and Navy (Washington, D.C.). Author: A Century with Norfolk Naval Hospital (1830-1930), pub. 1930; Who Gave The World Syphillis?, 1937. Contbr. many papers on medico-naval and medical-historical investigations. Home: 306 S. Madison Av., Upper Darby, Pa.

HOLCOMBE, John Lee, army officer; b. Washington, D.C., Oct. 11, 1883; s. John Hite Lee and Ida (Taylor) H.; student U. of Va., Charlottesville, Va., 1902-05, Coast Artillery Sch., Ft. Monroe, Va., 1912-13, 1920-21, Command and Staff Sch., Leavenworth, Kan., 1922-23, Army War Coll., Washington, D.C., 1925-26; m. Katharine E. Burnham, Oct. 6, 1931; 1 son, John Lee. Began as 2d lt. C.A.C., U.S. Army, 1905-07, 1st lt., 1907-14, capt., 1914-18; major and lt. col. (temp.) inspector gen., U.S. Army, 1918-20, major, 1920-29, lt. col., 1929-35, col. since 1935. Served as insp. gen. Dept. of East and 17th Div. Regular Army during World War. Mem. Va. Historical Soc., Va. Soc. of Cincinnati, Aztec Club, Pitt Rifles, Am. Legion, Mil. Order World War, Scabbard and Blade, Sigma Tau. Democrat. Episcopalian. Clubs: Pittsburgh Athletic, Faculty, Longue Country (Pittsburgh). Home: Newstead, Gloucester, Va. Office: U. of Pittsburgh, Pittsburgh, Pa.

HOLDCRAFT, Paul Ellsworth, clergyman; b. Frederick, Md., Sept. 22, 1891; s. John Henry and Ella (Mehrling) H.; A.B., Eastern Coll., Manassas, Va., 1918; B.D. Westminster Theol. Sem., Westminster, Md., 1924, S.T.D., 1929; (hon.) D.D., Lebanon Valley Coll., Annville, Pa., 1938; m. Lola Grace McDonald, Dec. 28, 1910; children—Martha Romaine (Mrs. Calvin A. Keeney), Miriam Elaine, Rachel Evelyn. Ordained to ministry Ch. U.B. in Christ, 1913; pastor, Rayville, Md., 1910-12, Walkersville, Md., 1912-16, Keedysville, Md., 1916-20, 4th Church, York, Pa., 1920-21, Third Church, Baltimore, 1921-29; minister at Emmanuel Ch., Hagerstown, Md., since 1929. Served in Md. N.G., 1909-11. United Brethren. Author: History of Pa. Conference of U.B. Church, 1938. Writer numerous handbooks for ministers and ch. workers. Contbg. editor of U.B. S.S. literature since 1931. Editor, The Broadcaster, organ Pa. Conf. of U.B. Ch. Home: 812 Summit Av., Hagerstown, Md.

HOLDEN, Edwin Chapin, mining engr.; b. New York, Nov. 8, 1872; s. Albert James and Henrietta V. (Chambers) H.; B.S., Coll. City of New York, 1893; E.M., Sch. of Mines (Columbia), 1896; m. Grace E. Morgenroth, Sept. 19, 1908; children—Florence, Edwin C. Mining engr., supt. and mgr. various properties in British Columbia and U.S., 1897-1903; consulting mining engr., New York, 1903-08, with work in U.S., Can., Mex. and W.I.; prof. mining and metallurgy, U. of Wis., 1908-16; gen. mgr. Davison Sulphur & Phosphate Co., 1916-19; consulting engr., Davison Chem. Co. and Silica Gel Corporation, 1919-32; developing mines in British Columbia, 1930-34, and in Colo. since 1934. Member American Institute Mining and Metall. Engrs., Mining and Metall. Soc. America, Phi Gamma Delta, Sigma Xi. Unitarian. Co-Author: Mining Handbook. Home: 202 E. Chase St. Office: Garrett Bldg., Baltimore, Md.

HOLDEN, Hale Jr., vice-pres. Pullman Co.; b. Kansas City, Mo.; Apr. 30, 1900; s. Hale and Ellen Mitchell (Weston) H.; grad. Hotchkiss Sch., Lakeview, Conn.; A.B., Yale, 1922; m. Josephine Bell Cotton, Aug. 4, 1923 (died Mar. 12, 1937); children—Joan Holden, Hale III; m. 2d, Margaretta Harrison Fitler, May 3, 1938. Draftsman Pullman Co., 1922-23, sales agt., 1923-30, asst. to pres., 1930-31, vice-pres. since 1931; dir. Byron Weston Co. Served in U.S. Naval Reserve, active duty Sept.-Dec. 1918, inactive duty, 1919-22. Republican. Episcopalian. Clubs: Yale (New York); Gulph Mills Golf, Racquet (Phila.); Rolling Rock (Ligonier). Home: 31 Rose Lane, Haverford, Pa. Office: 1617 Pennsylvania Boul., Philadelphia, Pa.

HOLDEN, Robert F., investment banking; b. Brookline, Mass., Dec. 23, 1895; s. Fredrick Gurnray and Arabella (Proctor) H.; grad. Westminster Sch., Simsbury, Conn., 1913; A.B., Yale, 1918; m. Madeline Sands Heminway, Oct. 20, 1917; children—Cynthia, Robert Fletcher. Mgr. Phila. office Smith, Graham & Rockwell, 1928-31; partner Janney & Co., 1931-34; since 1934 partner Yarnell & Co., investment bankers and mems. N.Y. Stock Exchange; vice-pres. and dir. Salt Dome Oil Co.; pres. 400 Madison Av. Corpn.; dir. 2d and 3d Sts. Passenger Ry. Co., Central Airport, Inc. Mem. bd. mgrs. Childrens Hosp. of Phila. Mem. Scroll and Key, Psi Upsilon. Republican. Episcopalian. Clubs: Philadelphia, Racquet, Gulph Mills; Yale (New York and Phila.). Home: Haverford, Pa. Office: 1528 Walnut St., Philadelphia, Pa.

HOLLAND, J. Burnett, judge; b. Conshohocken, Pa., Jan. 5, 1887; s. James B. and Lidie (Sheard) H.; B.S., U. of Pa. Coll., 1908; LL.B., U. of Pa. Law Sch., 1912; m. Sarah A. Maule, Nov. 9, 1929 (dec.); m. 2d, Gertrude Green, Feb. 12, 1938; 1 son (adopted), David; step-children—Trudell and Stanley Green. Admitted to Pa. bar, 1912; second asst. dist. atty., Montgomery County, 1920-24, first asst. dist. atty., 1924-27; president judge Montgomery County Orphans Court, 38th Judicial Dist., since 1927; dir. Peoples Nat. Bank of Norristown. Dir. Clarke Conservatory of Music, Montgomery Hosp. of Norristown. Mem. Am. Legion, Vets. of Foreign Wars. Republican. Episcopalian. Club: Plays and Players (Philadelphia). Home: 1605 DeKalb St. Chambers: Court House, Norristown, Pa.

HOLLAND, Leicester Bodine, prof. fine arts; b. Louisville, Ky., May 23, 1882; s. James W. and Mary Boggs (Rupert) H.; grad. William Penn Charter Sch., Phila., 1898; B.S., U. of Pa., 1902, B.S. in Architecture, 1904, M.A. 1917, Ph.D., 1919; m. Louise Elizabeth Whetenhall Adams, Dec. 27, 1923; children—Barbara Adams, Marian Rupert, Lawrence Rozier. Architect and archtl. draftsman with Wilson

Eyre, Jr., Cram, Goodhue & Ferguson, and mem. firm of Howell & Holland, Phila., until 1912; teacher architectural design and history of architecture, U. of Pa., 1913-18; asso. prof. architecture, Am. Sch. of Classical Studies at Athens, 1919-22; prof. fine arts, Vassar, 1925-27, U. of Pa. since 1929; also chief div. of fine arts, Library of Congress since 1929. Fellow Am. Inst. Architects; mem. Archæological Institute of America, American Philos. Society. Clubs: Century Association, Philadelphia Sketch, Franklin Inn. Author: The Garden Blue Book, 1914; Traffic Ways about France in the Dark Ages, 1919; Ready Written Specifications (with Harry Parker), 1925. Contbr. Am. Jour. Archæology. Home: 4203 Pine St., Philadelphia, Pa. Address: Library of Congress, Washington, D.C.

HOLLAND, Moorhead B., banker, lawyer; b. Pittsburgh, Pa., Sept. 3, 1884; s. William J. and Caroline T. (Moorhead) H.; grad. Hill Sch., Pottstown, Pa., 1901; A.B., Princeton U., 1905; LL.B., U. of Pittsburgh, 1910; m. Frederica Morgan McKaig, of Pittsburgh, Jan. 21, 1931 (died Mar. 6, 1932); 1 dau., Muriel McKaig (adopted). Admitted to Allegheny Co. Pa., bar, 1910; asst. trust officer Safe Deposit & Trust Co. of Pittsburgh (now Peoples Pittsburgh Trust Co.), 1913-18, trust officer, 1918-23, v.p. in charge of trusts, 1923-37, chmn. trust com. since 1937; pres. and dir. Pittsburgh Incline Plane Co.; v.p. and dir. Union Storage Co. Trustee Carnegie Inst., Carnegie Inst. Tech.; mem. Carnegie Hero Fund Comm.; treas. and dir. Pittsburgh Orchestra Assn. Mem. Allegheny Co. Bar Assn. Republican. Presbyterian. Clubs: Duquesne, Pittsburgh Golf, Fox Chapel Golf (Pittsburgh); Allegheny Country (Sewickley, Pa.); Misquamicut Golf (Watch Hill, R.I.); Rolling Rock (Ligonier, Pa.). Home: 6821 Edgerton Av. Office: Fourth Av. and Wood St., Pittsburgh, Pa.

HOLLAND, Paul Leach, engineering; b. Keyser, N.C., Nov. 9, 1887; s. James Leonidas and Ina (Leach) H.; grad. Laurinburg (N.C.) High Sch., 1904; B.S., U.S. Naval Acad., Annapolis, Md., 1908; m. Anne Strobel Johnson, Dec. 25, 1917; children—Anne Randolph, Inez Leach, Eleanor Miot. Commd. ensign, U.S. Navy, 1910, retired as lt. comdr. (subject to call), 1915; instr. U.S. Naval Acad., 1917-19; public utility engring. and management, 1920-25; with Mees & Mees, consulting engrs., Charlotte, N.C., 1925-31; chief engr. Pub. Service Comm. of Md. since 1931. Asso. mem. Am. Soc. Civil Engrs. Democrat. Baptist. Clubs: Engineers of Baltimore (past pres.). Home: 3700 N. Charles. Office: 1701 Munsey Bldg., Baltimore, Md.

HOLLAND, Rupert Sargent, author; b. Louisville, Ky., October 15, 1878; s. James William and Mary B. (Rupert) H.; A.B., Harvard, 1900; LL.B., U. of Pa., 1903; m. Margaret Currier Lyon, Aug. 19, 1918; children—Richard Lyon, Eleanor Sargeant, David Thurston. Admitted to bar, 1903; chief atty. Legal Aid Soc., Phila., 1904-10; lecturer, Am. Soc. for Extension of University Teaching. Mem. bd. mgrs. Apprentices' Library of Philadelphia, Philadelphia City Inst., Wayne Library. Club: Franklin Inn. Author: The Count at Harvard, 1906; Builders of United Italy, 1908; The Man in the Tower, 1909; Historic Boyhoods, 1909; Historic Girlhoods, 1910; The Boy Scouts of Birch-Bark Island, 1911; Historic Inventions, 1911; Knights of the Golden Spur, 1912; Historic Poems and Ballads, 1912; Heart of Sally Temple, 1913; Historic Adventures, 1913; Historic Heroes of Chivalry, 1914; William Penn, 1915; The Boy Scouts of Snow-Shoe Lodge, 1915; Blackbeard's Island, 1916; Historic Events of Colonial Days, 1916; The Blue Heron's Feather, 1917; Lafayette, We Come, 1918; All 'Round Our House, 1919; Neptune's Son, 1919; The Man in the Moonlight, 1920; Refugee Rock, 1920; The Panelled Room, 1921; The House of Delusion, 1922; Peter Cotterell's Treasure, 1922; Lafayette for Young Americans, 1922; Crooked Lanes, 1923; The Mystery of the Opal, 1924; Minot's Folly, 1925; Pirates of the Delaware, 1925; Historic Ships, 1926; The Rider in the Green Mask, 1926; Historic Railroads, 1927; Red Beard of Virginia, 1927;

Historic Airships, 1928; The Splendid Buccaneer, 1928; Drake's Lad, 1929; Sons of Seven Cities, 1929; The Pirate of the Gulf, 1929; The Dauntless Company, 1930; Mad Anthony, 1931; Yankee Ships in Pirate Waters, 1931; A. Race for a Fortune, 1931; Captain Tripp, 1932; Rescue, 1932; How Murder Speaks, 1933; Big Bridge, 1934; The Sea Scouts of Birch-Bark Island, 1936; Plays of the American Colonies, 1937; The Boy Who Lived on London Bridge, 1938; also mag. articles and stories. Home: 216 Walnut Av., Wayne, Pa.

HOLLAND, Stanley Hall, physician and surgeon; b. Forest Hill, Md., Jan. 17, 1888; s. Evans Stanley and Martha Eliza (Lockard) H.; student Dickinson Coll., 1909-10; M.D., Coll. of Physicians and Surgeons, Baltimore, 1914; M.M.Sc. in surgery, U. of Pa. Grad. Sch. of Medicine, 1933; m. Katharene Rice, Aug. 1, 1917; children—Stanley Hall, Philip Brice, Kitty Lou. Interne McKeesport Hosp., 1914-15; physician and surgeon, McKeesport, Pa., since 1929. Served as 1st lt., regtl. surgeon, 156th Depot Brigade, U.S. Army, 1918-19. Mem. McKeesport Acad. of Medicine, Allegheny County Med. Soc., Am. Med. Assn., Phi Beta Pi. Address: 2700 Fifth Av., McKeesport, Pa.

HOLLANDER, Edward, lawyer; b. Austria, Mar. 8, 1874; s. Henry and Anna (Fuchs) H.; brought to U.S., 1881, naturalized, 18—; A.B., Coll. City of N.Y., 1895; LL.B., N.Y. Univ. Law Sch., 1903; grad. study, Columbia U. Grad. Sch., 1903-05; m. Beulah Riffenberg, Aug. 13, 1908; 1 dau. Ethel. Admitted to N.Y. bar, 1903; admitted to N.J. bar, 1906 and since engaged in gen. practice of law at Union City, N.J.; sr. mem. firm Hollander, Leichter and Klotz since 1935; admitted to practice before the Supreme Ct. of the U.S., 1919; served as pres. Sinking Fund Commn., Weehawken, N.J., 1924-25; mem. Bd. Edn., 1926-36, pres. bd. since 1930-36. Mem. Am. Bar Assn., N.J. State Bar Assn., Hudson Co. Bar Assn. Republican. Mason. B.P.O.E. Home: 28 Liberty Place, Weehawken, N.J. Office: 648 Bergenline Av., Union City, N.J.

HOLLANDER, Jacob H., economist; b. Baltimore, July 23, 1871; s. Meyer and Rosa (Meyer) Hollander; A.B., Johns Hopkins Univ., 1891, Ph.D., 1894; LL.D., Univ. of Glasgow, 1938; m. Theresa G. Hutzler, Jan. 22, 1906 (died May 3, 1916); children—Rosamond Hutzler (Mrs. Siegfried Weisberger), David Hutzler, Bertha Hutzler. Associate professor of finance until 1900, asso. prof. polit. economy, 1901-04, prof., 1904-25, Abram G. Hutzler prof. polit. economy since 1925, Johns Hopkins. Was sec. Bimetallic Commn. abroad in 1897; chmn. of municipal lighting commn., City of Baltimore, 1900; was apptd. by Sec. of War, 1900, spl. commr. to revise the laws relating to taxation in P.R., and while engaged in this service was apptd. by President McKinley as treas. of P.R.; organized treasury dept. and devised and introduced present revenue system ("Hollander law") of island, resigning Aug. 1901, after system was in successful operation; U.S. spl. agent on taxation in Ind. Ty., 1904; was sent by President Roosevelt as spl. commr. to Santo Domingo, 1905, to investigate its public debt; confidential agent of Dept. of State with respect to Dominican affairs, 1906-07; financial adviser of the Dominican Republic, 1908-10, and largely instrumental in readjusting its public debt. Umpire in Md. and Upper Potomac coal field, 1918-20; impartial chmn. and mem. bd. referees, Cleveland Garment Industry, 1921-32; associate editor Baltimore News, 1929-30; chmn. Tax Survey Commn. of Maryland, 1931-32. Mem. American Econ. Assn. (pres. 1921), American Statis. Assn., Am. Acad. Polit. and Social Science, Brit. Econ. Assn., Md. Hist. Soc., Am. Jewish Hist. Soc. Author: The Cincinnati Southern Railway—A Study in Municipal Activity, 1894; The Financial History of Baltimore, 1899; edited Letters of David Ricardo to J. R. McCulloch; Letters of David Ricardo to Hutches Trower (with James Bonar); Studies in State Taxation—with particular reference to the Southern States, 1900; Reprint of Economic Tracts, 1903—. Report on Taxation in Indian

Territory, 1904; Report on the Debt of San Domingo, 1906; David Ricardo, A Centenary Estimate, 1911; The Abolition of Poverty, 1914; War Borrowing, 1919; Economic Liberalism, 1925; Want and Plenty, 1932. Editor: Economic Essays in Honor of John Bates Clark, 1927; Ricardo's Notes on Malthus, 1928; Ricardo's Minor Papers on Currency, 1932. Home: 1802 Eutaw Pl., Baltimore, Md.

HOLLANDER, Lester, physician, dermatologist; b. Plavnicza, Hungary, Nov. 8, 1890; s. Edward and Sarah (Izsak) H.; brought to U.S., 1906, naturalized, 1911; M.D. first honors, U. of Pittsburgh, 1912; unmarried; 1 dau. (by adoption), Mildred Annette (Mrs. David Tynberg). Began as gen. practitioner, 1912; fellow in pathology Tuberculosis League Hosp., 1913-14; study to become specialist in skin diseases, New York, 1916, Europe, 1921-22; organized, 1923, Pittsburgh Skin and Cancer Foundation and since med. dir.; chief dermatology and syphilis Pittsburgh City Hosp., Montefiore Hosp., Crippled Children's Home, Leech Farm Tuberculosis Sanatorium. Mem. Volunteer Corps, World War. Mem. bd. Detention Home, Juvenile Court; chmn. Speakers Community Fund. Diplomate Am. Bd. Dermatology and Syphilis; fellow Am. Coll. Physicians; mem. A.M.A., Am. Radium Soc., Am. Acad. Dermatology. Home: 1323 Murdock Rd. Office: Jenkins Bldg., Pittsburgh, Pa.

HOLLANDER, Sidney, pharmaceutical mfr.; b. Baltimore, Md., Dec. 29, 1881; s. Edward and Fanny (Koshland) H.; Pharm. D., U. of Md., 1902; m. Clara D. Lauer, June 3, 1907; children—Edward D., Edith L. (wife of Dr. Frank Furstenberg), Sidney, Emily D. Began as mfg. druggist, 1902; pres. Md. Pharm. Co., since 1908; pres. Rem Co. since 1923. Trustee Bd. State Aid and Charities, Md.; pres. Nat. Council Jewish Feds. and Welfare Funds; v.p. Nat. Conf. of Social Work; mem. numerous civic and business bds. Jewish religion. Club: Chesapeake. Home: 2513 Talbot Road. Office: 2419 Greenmount Av., Baltimore, Md.

HOLLEY, Alfred Tilghman, pres. of Holley & Smith, Inc.; b. Hackensack, N.J., Feb. 15, 1872; s. Rev. Dr. William Welles (rector Christ Episcopal Ch. 40 yrs.) and Katherine Summer (Wyse) H.; desc. on paternal side of Holleys who landed at Saybrook, Conn., 1634, and the Welles, a Revolutionary family; on maternal side of Summers of Mass. and Morgans of Vt.; ed. Hackensack pub. schs. and Hasbrook Inst. (Jersey City); studied law, N.Y. Law Sch., 2 yrs.; married Miss Alice Beatrice Herbert, Apr. 22, 1914. Made extensive business trip to China and Japan; senior Holley & Smith, coal, hay and grain merchants, 1891-1909, pres. since incorporation, 1909; conducted retail coal business, 40 yrs.; dir. and mem. exec. com. Peoples Trust Co. of Bergen Co., Ridgefield Park Trust Co., Burns Bros.; pres. United Bldg. & Loan Assn. (Hackensack). Enlisted as private N.J. Nat. Guard, 1889; served in Spanish-Am. War; retired after 19 yrs. with rank of lt. col. Declined nomination to Congress, 1902; active in state politics, 25 yrs. Pres. Hackensack Retail Coal Dealers Assn. and successors Bergen Co. Fuel Merchants Assn., 30 yrs., Fuel Merchants Assn. of N.J. since 1934 (now serving 3d term); mem. S.A.R. Democrat. Episcopalian. Charter mem. Hackensack Lodge No. 658, B.P.O.E. (Grand Trustee Grand Lodge 6 yrs.); Mason. Clubs: Oritani Field (charter mem.), Hackensack Golf. Home: 320 Union St. Office: 200 State St., Hackensack, N.J.

HOLLEY, Ella Josephine, supervisor of schs.; b. New Haven, Conn.; d. Frank Corwin and Ella Josephine (Studwell) H.; diploma Stamford (Conn.) High Sch., 1901-05; State Normal Sch., New Haven, Conn., 1905-07; B.S., Columbia U. Teachers Coll., 1917, M.A., 1924; student summer sch. Clark U., Worcester, Mass., 1934; unmarried. Teacher elementary rural schs., Fairfield, Conn., 1907-10. 1910-11, 1911-12, 1914-15; teacher and prin. Green's Farm Sch., Westport, Conn., 1912-14; critic teacher, State Normal Coll., Bowling Green, O., 1917-19, State Normal Sch., Danbury, Conn.,

1919-20; teacher Old Trail Sch., Akron, O., 1925; state supervisor rural schs., New Castle Co., Del., since 1925. Life mem. N.E.A.; mem. Dept. Am. Assn. Sch. Adminstrs., Dept. Supervisors and Instrs., Dept. Rural Edn., Del. State Edn. Assn., New Castle Co. Edn. Assn., World Fed. Edn. Assns., D.A.R. (Caesar Rodney Chapter, Wilmington, Del.). Home: 402 Rodney Court Apts. Office: M-221 Delaware Trust Bldg., Wilmington, Del.

HOLLIDAY, Robert Cortes, author; b. Indianapolis, Ind., July 18, 1880; s. Wilbur F. and Minerva J. (Kendrick) H.; Art Students' League, New York, 1899-1902; U. of Kan., 1903-04; m. Estelle Alice Hickman, July 12, 1913 (divorced). Illustrator for mags., 1904-05; book-seller, Charles Scribner's Sons, 1906-11; librarian with New York Pub. Library, 1912; reference librarian, New York Sch. of Philanthropy, 1913; asst. lit. editor, New York Tribune, 1913-14; reporter and editor The Fishing Gazette, New York, 1915; with editorial dept. Doubleday, Page & Co., 1916; editorial dept. George H. Doran Co., 1917; asso. editor The Bookman, 1918, editor, 1919-20; contributing editor, 1921-23; lit. adviser Henry Holt & Co., 1921-23; staff writer for Leslie's Weekly, 1921; feature writer McNaught Syndicate, 1921; publicity work with John Price Jones, 1923; lit. critic for Life, 1923; account executive with Barton, Durstine & Osborn, 1923-24; journalism and advertising, 1925; instr. in writing for publication since 1926. Mem. Sigma Alpha Epsilon. Clubs: Players, Authors. Author: Booth Tarkington, 1918; The Walking-Stick Papers, 1918; Joyce Kilmer, A Memoir, 1918; Peeps at People, 1919; Broome Street Straws, 1919; Men and Books and Cities, 1920; Turns About Town, 1921; A Chat About Samuel Merwin, 1921; In the Neighborhood of Murray Hill, 1922; (with Alexander Van Rensselaer) The Business of Writing, 1923; Literary Lanes and Other Byways, 1925; Our Little Brother Writes a Play, 1928; Unmentionables—From Figleaves to Scanties, 1933. Contbr. to ednl. jours. and other publs.; lit. executor of Joyce Kilmer; occasional lecturer. Home: Stillwater, N.J. Address: 16 Gramercy Park, New York, N.Y.

HOLLINGER, D(aniel) Wilson, clergyman; b. Huntsdale, Pa., Dec. 3, 1877; s. Daniel H. and Laura V. (Fleming) H.; Ph.B., Dickinson Coll., 1898, A.M., same, 1900; grad. Princeton Theol. Sem., 1901; (hon.) D.D., Dickinson Coll., 1939; m. Elizabeth Gracey, June 15, 1899; children—Helen Elizabeth (dec.), Virginia (wife of Richard F. Stout, lt. comdr., U.S.N.). Ordained to ministry Presbyn. Ch. U.S.A., 1901; pastor, New Hope, Pa., 1901-06, Parkersburg, Pa., 1906-14, Bethany Presbyn. Ch., Trenton, N.J., since 1914; served as moderator, Presbytery of Chester, 1913, Presbytery of New Brunswick, 1920, Synod of Presbyn. Ch. U.S.A. of N.J., 1938. Trustee Presbyn. Home of Synod of N.J., Tennent Coll. of Christian Edn., Phila., Pa. Mem. Pi Gamma Mu. Republican. Presbyn. U.S.A. Mason (Chaplain Grand Lodge of N.J., 1931), I.O.O.F. Home: 426 Hamilton Av., Trenton, N.J.

HOLLINGER, John Adam, educator; b. Campbelltown, Pa., Aug. 16, 1877; s. John and Anne (Bomberger) H.; A.B., Franklin & Marshall Coll., 1903; M.A., Columbia U., 1913; Ph.D., U. of Pittsburgh, 1926; m. Adela Landis, Aug. 18, 1904; 1 dau., Catherine A. Teacher South Annville Twp. Elementary Sch., 1897-99, prin., 1903-04; teacher Dubois, Avalon High Sch., 1904-07; prin. Pittsburgh elementary schs., 1907-19; dir. Dept. of Science Education and Visual Instruction, Bd. of Pub. Edn., since 1919; lecturer in nature study, U. of Pittsburgh, summers, 1919-23, lecturer in edn., 1926-27; teacher U. of Denver, summer, 1930; lecturer in edn., U. of Pittsburgh, 1930-33, lecturer in psychology since 1937; teacher Pa. State Coll., 2 summer sessions. Dir. Gumbert Industrial Sch. for Girls, Assn. of School Film Libraries, Inc. Fellow A.A.A.S.; mem. N.E.A., Pa. State Edn. Assn., Bot. Soc. of Western Pa., Pittsburgh Zoöl. Soc., Phi Delta Kappa. Mem. Reformed Ch. Mason (Past Master). Clubs: Wildwood Country, Lions.

Contbr. to ednl. mags. Co-author of Elementary Science by Grades. Home: R.D.1, Allison Park, Pa. Office: 341 Bellefield Av., Pittsburgh, Pa.

HOLLINGSHEAD, W. Stewart, sales exec.; b. Riverton, N.J., Feb. 28, 1904; s. Richard M. and Emily H.; student Riverton (N.J.) Grammar Sch., 1909-16; diploma, Manlius (N.Y.) Mil. Sch., 1924; married, June 26, 1935; children—Wickliffe and Suzanne (twins). Began as salesman, 1925; now v.p. in charge sales, R.M. Hollingshead Corpn., Camden, N.J.; v.p. R.M. Hollingshead Co. of Canada, Ltd.; sec. Camden Blvd. Corpn. Mem. N.J. State Bd. of Conservation and Development. Republican. Episcopalian. Clubs: Riverton (N.J.) Country, Riverton (N.J.) Yacht. Home: Riverton, N.J. Office: 840 Cooper St., Camden, N.J.

HOLLINGSWORTH, Charles Baird, lawyer; b. Palo Alto, O., Mar. 3, 1867; s. Seymour L. and Susan (Smith) H.; student Washington and Jefferson Coll., 1 yr.; m. Lucie Freeman, Oct. 22, 1901. Admitted to Pa. bar, 1896, and since practiced in Greensburg; pres. and dir. Aladdin Theater Co., Irwin, Pa., Beaver Theater Co., Aliquippa, Pa.; vice-pres. and dir. Norwin Theater Co., Irwin, London Theater Co., London, O., Meigs Theater Co., Pomeroy, O.; dir. First Nat. Bank, Greensburg. Served with 10th Pa. Vols. during Spanish-Am. War. Trustee Torrance State Hosp. Mem. Westmoreland and Pa. bar assns. Democrat. Elk. Clubs: Greensburg Country; Oakmont Country (Oakmont, Pa.). Home: 524 N. Maple Av. Office: Coutter Bldg., Greensburg, Pa.

HOLLINGSWORTH, Herman Hale, surgeon; b. Lewisville, Ind., Jan. 17, 1894; s. Dr. Allen Scott, and Daisy (Reynolds) H.; grad. Goshen (Ind.) High Sch., 1911; A.B., Ind. U., 1917; grad. student, 1919-20; student Goshen Coll., 1913-14; M.D., U. of Pa., 1922; m. Ruth Helen Ikerd, Sept. 15, 1923; children—Helen Odette, Patricia Louise, Allen Hale. Interne Lankenau Hosp., Phila., 1922-25; surgeon, Armagh, Pa., 1925-26, Clifton, N.J., since 1926; asso. surgeon Passaic Gen. Hosp. since 1937. Served with Base Hosp. No. 32, U.S. Army, 1917-19; with A.E.F. 16 months; disch. as sergt. Mem. A.M.A., Am. Medico Legal Assn., Sigma Alpha Epsilon, Nu Sigma Nu. Republican. Episcopalian. Mason, Elk. Home: 86 1st St. Office: 785 Main Av. and 86 1st St., Clifton, N.J.

HOLLINSHEAD, Byron Sharpe, educator; b. Medford, N.J., Nov. 14, 1901; s. Charles I. and May (Darnell) H.; Ph.B., Brown U., 1928; A.M., Bucknell U., 1930; student Pa. State Coll., summer 1931, U. of Pa., summer 1932; m. Clara Stevens, Aug. 30, 1928; children—Byron Sharpe, Charles Thornton. Instr. in English, Bucknell U., 1928-34; dir. Sta. WDEL, Wilmington, Del.; 1930; mng. dir. Camp Hill for Boys, 1932-34; asst. dir. Bucknell U. Jr. Coll., Wilkes-Barre, Pa., 1933-34, head of English dept., dir. of athletics and dramatics, 1933-34; pres. Scranton Keystone Jr. Coll. since 1934. Pres. Jr. Coll. Council of Middle Atlantic States; dir. Scranton Country Day Sch. Mem. Am. Assn. Univ. Profs., Am. Acad. Polit. and Social Science, Sigma Tau Delta, Pi Delta Epsilon, Delta Upsilon. Republican. Mem. Soc. of Friends. Clubs: Rotary (dir.) Scranton (Scranton). Contbr. to periodicals. Home: La Plume, Pa.

HOLLINSHED, Ralph King, physician; b. Camden, N.J., Aug. 2, 1884; s. Thomas and Cornelia (Sanborn) H.; M.D., U. of Pa. Med. Sch., 1908; m. Martha Tuft Fox, Sept. 14, 1910; children—Sarah Cornelia (dec.), Janet Elizabeth. Interne Cooper Hosp., Camden, N.J., 1908-09; engaged in gen. practice of medicine and surgery at Westville, N.J., since 1909; mem. bd. of health, Westville, N.J., since 1914; mem. attdg. med. staff Cooper Hosp., Camden, N.J.; cardiologist, chief of the metabolism and heart sta. and cardiac clinic, Cooper Hosp.; pres. Westville Bldg. & Loan Assn., 1925-38. Served as mem. med. adv. bd. during World War. Certified by Am. Bd. of Internal Medicine. Fellow Am. Coll. Physicians. Mem. Am. Med. Assn., N.J. State Med. Soc., Gloucester

Co. Med. Soc. (sec. 1912-24, past pres.). Republican. Methodist. Mason (32°, Shriner). Home: 351 Broadway, Westville, N.J.

HOLLIS, Charles M., dentist; b. Greenwood, Del., Nov. 27, 1874; s. James M. and Elizabeth (Kinder) H.; student Greenwood (Del.) Pub. Schs., 1880-92; D.D.S., Medico-Chirurg. Coll., Phila., 1901; m. Mary A. Kinney, Dec. 14, 1904; children—Mary Elizabeth, Charles M. In practice at Seaford, Del., since 1901; State ins. commr., 1923-27; mem. Del. State Senate, 1929, 1931; dir. First Nat. Bank of Seaford (Del.) since 1926. Republican. Methodist. Mason, Odd Fellow. Address: Pine St., Seaford, Del.

HOLLISTER, Joseph Hillman, clergyman; b. Troy, N.Y., Mar. 22, 1882; s. William Henry and Julia Frances (Hillman) H.; grad. Troy Acad., 1900; A.B., Williams Coll., 1904, D.D. from same coll., in 1929; B.D., Union Theol. Sem., 1907; m. Katharine Lawder, June 28, 1917; children—Jane Crampton (dec.), Elizabeth Hillman, Mary Frances, William Hillman. Ordained ministry Presbyn. Ch., 1907; pastor Valatie, N.Y., 1907-11, Mt. Vernon, N.Y., 1911-26, Chevy Chase Presbyn. Ch., Washington, D.C., since 1926. Sec. Y.M.C.A., France, later acting chaplain Dunkirk Naval Air Sta., World War. Mem. Delta Kappa Epsilon. Home: 6302 Beechwood Drive, Chevy Chase, Md.*

HOLLOWAY, Edward Stratton, artist, author; b. Ashland, N.Y.; s. Rev. Charles Hoover and Rebecca (Stratton) H.; acad. edn. at private schs.; studied art at Pa. Acad. of Fine Arts, Philadelphia; m. Clara Augusta Githens. Splty. marines and landscapes; decorative designer—particularly of book covers and decorations; art director J. B. Lippincott Co., also mem. bd. dirs. Author: The Practical Book of Furnishing the Small House and Apartment; Practical Book of Learning Decoration and Furniture; Practical Book of American Furniture and Decoration—Colonial and Federal. Joint author: Practical Book of Interior Decoration. Contributor to art and literary periodicals. Home: 400 S. 15th St. Address: Care J. B. Lippincott Co., Philadelphia, Pa.

HOLLOWAY, Fred Garrigus, clergyman, educator; b. Newark, N.J., Mar. 28, 1898; s. Frank DeMott and Alice (Garrigus) H.; A.B., Western Md. Coll., Westminster, 1918, D.D., 1932; student Westminster Theol. Sem., 1918-19; B.D., Drew Theol. Sem., Madison, N.J., 1921; fellow Drew Univ., 1921-23; LL.D., Dickinson College, Carlisle, Pa., 1936; m. Winifred Maxwell Jackson, Apr. 12, 1923; children—Fred Garrigus, William Jackson. Ordained ministry Meth. Protestant Ch., 1921; pastor First Ch., Wilmington, Del., 1921-23, Wilton Heights Ch., Baltimore, 1923-24, Cherrydale, Va., 1926-29; prof. Bibl. langs., Westminster Theol. Sem., 1926-35, pres., 1932-35; pres. Western Md. Coll. since 1935. Mem. Md. Acad. Sciences. Rotarian. Author of articles on religion and edn. Home: Westminster, Md.

HOLLOWAY, Harry Vance, state supt. schs.; b. Selbyville, Del., July 13, 1875; s. Levin James and Mary Ellen (Morris) H.; A.B., Washington Coll., Chestertown, Maryland, 1895, A.M., 1898, LL.D., from the same college, 1932; Ph.D., University of Pa., 1914; m. Mabel Bailey Conner, June 29, 1905; children—Alice Bailey, Harry Vance, Mary Ellen. Teacher rural sch., 1895-96; prin. schs., Bethel, 1896-97, Felton, 1897-1902; supt. schs., New Castle, 1902-10, Bordentown, N.J., 1910-19, Kent Co., Del., 1919-21; state supt. pub. instrn., Del., since 1921. Organized state system of edn. in Del., 1921. Mem. N.E.A., Del. Ednl. Assn., Nat. Soc. for Study of Edn. Episcopalian. Mason. Rotarian. Address: Dover, Delaware.

HOLLOWAY, William Warfield, pres. Wheeling Steel Corpn.; b. Wheeling, W.Va., June 22, 1886; s. Jacob James and Mary Patterson (Du Bois) H.; student St. Paul's Sch., Concord, N.H., 1898-1904, Sheffield Scientific Sch. (Yale), 1904-07; m. Margaret Louise Glass, Apr. 26, 1911; children—William Warfield, James Alexander, Sallie Glass. Successively with La Belle Iron Works, Wheeling Corrugating Co.

and Whitaker Glessner Co., 1908-20; with Wheeling Steel Corpn. since 1920, pres. since 1930; pres. Bridgeport Nat. Bank; dir. Hazel-Atlas Glass Co., Fostoria Glass Co. Served as 1st lt., later capt., Ordnance Dept., U.S.A., World War. Dir. Am. Iron and Steel Inst. Mem. Book and Snake Soc. (Yale). Republican. Episcopalian. Clubs: Ft. Henry (Wheeling); Yale, Ohio Soc., Banker's (New York); Harvard-Yale-Princeton, Duquesne (Pittsburgh); Lotos (New York); Wheeling Country. Home: Pogue Run Rd., Wheeling. Address: Wheeling Steel Corpn., Wheeling, W.Va.

HOLLYDAY, Guy Tilghman Orme, mortgage loan correspondent; b. Baltimore, Md., Dec. 27, 1892; s. John Guy and Virginia May (Lannay) H.; grad. Boys Latin Sch., Baltimore, 1910; A.B., Johns Hopkins U., 1914; m. Louise Este Fisher, Jan. 28, 1926; children—Louise Este, Guy Tilghman, Virginia Lannay, Este Fisher. Real estate salesman M. & J. Brandt, 1914; asst. sec. Md. League for Nat. Defense, 1915-17; asst. to dir. Industrial Bur. of Bd. of Trade, Baltimore, 1919-21; sales mgr. Mortgage Guarantee Co., 1921-26, The Roland Park Co., 1926-32; v.p. Key Realty Corpn., 1932-35; mgr. Baltimore office, Randall H. Hagner & Co., Inc., since 1935; pres. and dir. Fiscal Mortgage Co. of Ala.; dir. Guilford Realty Co., Wyman Apts. Corpn., Title Guarantee & Trust Co. Mortgage Bankers Assn. of America. Served as 2d lt., 11th U.S. Cavalry, U.S. Army, later 1st lt. (temp.), 1917-19. Former pres. Real Estate Bd. of Baltimore, Apartment House Owners Assn. Dir. Commn. on Governmental Efficiency and Economy. Pres. Johns Hopkins Alumni Assn. (Baltimore); mem. Alpha Delta Phi. Democrat. Episcopalian. Clubs: L'Hirondelle (Ruxton, Md.); Johns Hopkins (Baltimore). Home: 119 Taplow Road. Office: 628 Munsey Bldg., Baltimore, Md.

HOLLYDAY, John David, banker; b. St. James, Md., Dec. 8, 1881; s. Samuel and Alice (Talbert) H.; student Hagerstown (Md.) High Sch., 1896-99; m. Laughty Duvall Middlekauff, June 7, 1913; children—Anna Jane (Mrs. Francis T. Hannigan), Sarah Louise, John Samuel. Clerk Cumberland Valley R.R., Hagerstown, Md., 1900-06; dep. register of wills for Wash. Co., 1906-19, register of wills, 1919-28; with Nicodemus Nat. Bank, Hagerstown, since 1919, v.p. and trust officer since 1928. Democrat. Lutheran. Odd Fellow (Potomac Lodge No. 31; Gilead Encampment No. 6), Jr. Order United Am. Mechanics (Antietam Council No. 38). Club: Monarch (Hagerstown, Md.). Home: Funkstown, Md. Office: Nicodemus Nat. Bank, Hagerstown, Md.

HOLMAN, Edward Lee, educator; b. Liverpool, Pa., Aug. 13, 1894; s. Adam Truman and Ida (Long) H.; prep. edn., New Bloomfield (Pa.) Acad., 1914-16; B.A., Gettysburg (Pa.) Coll., 1921, M.A., 1922; LL.B., Am. Extension U. (corr.), Los Angeles, Calif., 1929; m. Anna Helen Bower, Aug. 22, 1917; children—Ida Helen, Clark Lee, Elizabeth Anne, Carson Edward Richard. Reared on farm; began active career as country school teacher, 1912; served as assistant prin. Carson Long Inst. (mil. sch.), 1921-22, headmaster since 1922, prof. mil. science and tactics since 1926; trustee of the Institute; dir. Camp Carson since 1922. Served as pvt. and officer World War; now maj. U.S.R. Dir. gen. State Hemlocks Park Assn.; chmn. bd. Perry County (Pa.) Citizens Military Training Corps; chmn. Perry County Reëmployment Bd. (N.R.S.); chmn. Perry Co. Emergency Relief Board; pres. exec. com. Harrisburg Welfare Assn., Perry Co.; chmn. Perry Co. Dept. of Pub. Assistance Bd. Mem. "The Pennsylvanians" (1st pres. Perry County Chapter), Am. Legion Reserve Officers Assn., Perry Co. Hist. Assn. (pres.), Tau Kappa Alpha. Democrat. Lutheran. Club: Pike's Peak Summit Motor Club, Lions. Author: The Color of Life Is Red, or This Way Up, 1930. Home: New Bloomfield, Pa.

HOLMAN, William Kunkel, Bible publisher; b. Phila., Pa., Nov. 2, 1877; s. William Alfonso and Lena Gross (Kunkel) H.; ed. Protestant Episcopal Acad., Phila., 1888-95; m. Sarah Louise Sharp, of Phila., June 6, 1906; children—Sarah Louise (Mrs. Scott A. Lamb), Elizabeth Pennock (Mrs. Robert Baden Powell), Wilhelmina Kunkel (Mrs. Frederick Stephen Ball), Patience Burr. With A. J. Holman Co., Bible pubs., Phila., since 1897, beginning as stock boy; apprenticed as printer, 2 years, bookbinder, 1 year, leather gold worker, 1 year, gold stamper, 1 year; purchasing and managing, 1902-12, pres. and production mgr., 1912-30; pres. and sole owner since 1930. Mem. Home Civic Assn. (pres. 1918-22, now v.p.), Franklin Inst., Phila. Chamber Commerce, Phila. Bourse. Republican. Episcopalian. Club: Union League (Phila.). Home: Ithan, Delaware County, Pa. Office: 1224 Arch St., Philadelphia, Pa.

HOLMES, Dwight Oliver Wendell, coll. pres.; b. Lewisburg, W.Va., Nov. 15, 1877; s. John A. and Sarah (Bollin) H.; A.B., Howard U., 1901, hon. M.A., 1912; M.A., Columbia, 1915, Ph.D., 1934, LL.D., 1937; m. Lucy C. Messer, June 24, 1907; 1 son, Dwight Oliver Wendell. Teacher Summer High Sch., St. Louis, 1902; vice prin. and head of dept. of science, Douglass High Sch., Baltimore, Md., 1902-17; instr. in edn., Miner Normal Sch., Washington, D.C., 1917-19; registrar and prof. edn., Howard U., 1919-20, dean and prof. edn. Coll. of Edn., 1920-24, dean Grad. Sch., 1934-37; president Morgan College, Baltimore, since 1937. Pres. Baltimore Ednl. Assn., 1915-17, Gen. Alumni Assn. Howard U., 1912-15. Mem. Dept. Superintendence N.E.A., Am. Acad. Polit. and Social Science, Nat. Soc. Coll. Teachers of Edn., Pi Gamma Mu, Alpha Phi Alpha, Kappa Mu, Sigma Pi Phi. Rosenwald fellow, 1931-32. Methodist. Clubs: Schoolmasters Club of Baltimore (pres. 1915); Education (Washington). Author: The Evolution of the Negro College, 1934. Contbr. to Jour. of Negro Edn., Jour. of Negro History. Address: Morgan College, Baltimore, Md.

HOLMES, Ernest George Nosworthy, clergyman; b. England, Nov. 22, 1881; s. William N. and Emmalena H.; came to U.S., 1887, naturalized, 1902; Ph.B., Wesleyan U., Middletown, Conn., 1905; S.T.B., Boston U. Sch. of Theology, 1908; A.M., Lehigh U., 1935; m. Etta Eugenia Greenleaf, June 18, 1909; 1 son, William Eugene. Ordained to ministry M.E. Ch., 1908; mem. Wyoming Conf., 1908-13; minister in charge, White Haven, Pa., 1913-14; rector, Montrose, Pa. 1914-18, Carbondale, Pa., 1918-29; dean, Leonard Hall, Bethlehem, Pa., since 1929; ordained to ministry P.E. Ch., deacon, 1913, priest, 1914. Mem. Fullerton Philos. Club, Sigma Chi. Republican. Episcopalian. Mason. Home: 826 Delaware Av., Bethlehem, Pa.

HOLMES, Henry Donald, real estate and ins.; b. Newark, N.J., Feb. 20, 1887; s. Edward Cooke and Eliza Jane (Jenkinson) H.; ed. Worcester Acad., 1901-03; m. Susan Adams Wolfe, July 14, 1909; children—Susan Carolyn (Mrs. Donald Rockwell Sheldon), Edward Cooke III. In employ Western Electric Co., 1903-05, Austin-Gifford Co., 1905-06, Whitehead & Hoag Co., 1906-08; entered real estate and ins. agency with father, 1908, propr. Holmes Agency since 1920; dir. First Nat. Bank & Trust Co., Summit-Overlook Bldg. & Loan Assn. of Summit, N.J. Mem. Bd. Edn., Summit, 1920-34. Mem. Bd. Mgrs. Bonnie Burn Sanitorium (Tuberculosis Sanitorium of Union Co.) since 1935. Mem. Nat. Assn. Realtors, N.J. Bd. Realtors, Summit Real Estate Bd. (past pres.), Nat. Assn. Ins. Underwriters, Summit Assn. Local Underwriters (past pres.), N.J. Assn. Underwriters (pres.), S.A.R. (past pres. Passaic Valley Chapter). Republican. Presbyn. Mason. Clubs: Rotary of Summit (past pres.); Spring Brook Country (Morristown). Home: 74 Valley View Av., Summit, N.J. Office: 45 Maple St., Summit, N.J.

HOLMES, Henry Kenwood, banking; b. Pittsburgh, Pa., Nov. 2, 1894; s. William Henry and Florrie (Capper) H.; A.B., Harvard U., 1916; ed. Harvard U. Law Sch., 1915-16; m. Grace Nieman, Dec. 18, 1919; 1 son, Henry Kenwood, Jr. Asso. with First Nat. Bank at Pittsburgh, Pa., continuously since beginning as elk., 1921; asst. to the pres. since 1928; dir. First Nat. Bank at Pittsburgh, Federal St. Branch, Harris Stores Co., Nufer Cedar Co., Pittsburgh Gage & Supply Co., James B. Sipe & Co. Served as pvt. Ambulance Corps, later in A.S., U.S.A., 1917-19, dischd. as 2d lt. Republican. Episcopalian. Club: Harvard-Yale-Princeton (Pittsburgh). Home: 2151 Beechwood Boul., Pittsburgh, Pa. Office: 5th Av. and Wood St., Pittsburgh, Pa.

HOLMES, Howard Abbott, planning engr.; b. Youngstown, O., May 18, 1885; s. Bradner Pelton and Fanny (Abbott) H.; grad. Rayen High Sch., Youngstown, 1902; M.E., Cornell U., 1906; m. Lelah Corbin, Dec. 28, 1910; 1 son, Eugene Bradner; m. 2d, Edythe Marguerite Gillespie, June 23, 1934; children—George Abbott, Anne Marguerite. Cadet engr. J. G. White & Co. electrification of Newton & Northwestern R.R., Iowa, 1906-07; turbine erector Westinghouse Machine Co., East Pittsburgh, Pa., 1907; motor maintenance Mahoning & Shenango Ry. & Light Co., Youngstown, O., 1907-09; elec. and mech. expert aide Bureau of Yards and Docks, Washington, D.C., 1909-17; asst. elec. engr. Pa. Ohio Electric Co., Youngstown, O., 1917-20; elec. and mech. engr. Morris Knowles Inc., Pittsburgh, Pa., 1920-21; asst. elec. engr. later sec. engr. Duquesne Light Co., Pittsburgh, Pa., 1921-23; successively elec. engr., mgr. of power dept., chief engr. and now planning engr. in charge of investigations, design of transmission lines, substations and distribution lines, Monongahela West Penn Pub. Service Co. since 1923. Fellow Am. Inst. Elec. Engrs. Presbyterian. Mason (Royal Arch). Home: Cleveland Av. Ext. Office: 600 Bethlehem Bldg., Fairmont, W.Va.

HOLMES, Jesse Herman, college prof.; b. W. Liberty, Ia., Jan. 5, 1864; s. Jesse and Sara Morgan (Paxson) H.; B.S., U. of Neb., 1884, grad. student and librarian, 1884-85; grad. student, 1885-86 and 1888-90, Ph.D., 1890, Johns Hopkins; student Harvard Summer Sch., 1894, spl. student Oxford U., 1899-1900; m. Rebecca Sinclair Webb, June 16, 1892; children—Elizabeth Webb (dec.), J. Herman, Robt. S. Teacher Friends' Select Sch., Washington, 1886-88, 1890-93; collector bot. specimens for U.S. Herbarium, Dept. of Agr. in Potomac Valley, N.J., pine barrens and Rocky Mountains, 1888-90; teacher George Sch., Bucks Co., Pa., 1893-99; prof. history of religion and philosophy, Swarthmore Coll., 1900-34; emeritus prof. philosophy, 1934—. Socialist candidate for gov. of Pa., 1932, 34, 38; state chmn. for Pa. of Socialist party since 1935. Active worker, Society of Friends, especially in S.S. work. Lecturer and platform supt., Chautauqua Assn. of Pa., 1912-23. Pres. Nat. Federation Religious Liberals, 1915-27. Commr. for Am. Friends relief work in Europe, 1920. Mem. Phi Beta Kappa. Author of several courses of lessons on Old and New Testament, ch. history, etc., for Friends' Sunday schools. Home: 700 Manchester Av., Moylan, Pa.

HOLROYD, Roland, prof. biology; b. Manchester, Eng., May 9, 1896; s. Thomas and Annetta (Firth) H.; brought to U.S., 1904 and naturalized citizen, 1918; B.S. in biol., U. of Pa., 1918, A.M., 1920, Ph.D., 1923; hon. D.Sc., LaSalle Coll., 1928; unmarried. Asst. in botany, U. of Pa., 1916-18, instr., 1919-30; prof. biology and head of dept., LaSalle College, since 1920. Served in U.S.A., 1918-19. Mem. A.A.A.S., Am. Assn. Univ. Profs., Bot. Soc. of America, Bot. Soc. of Pa., Sigma Xi, Pi Gamma Mu. Episcopalian. Traveled extensively in Arctic of N.A., Europe, S.A., New Zealand and South Sea Islands. Contbr. papers in morphological botany. Home: 4614 Pilling St., Frankford, Philadelphia. Address: LaSalle Coll., Philadelphia, Pa.

HOLSINGER, Virgil Clair, prin. pub. schs.; b. nr. Williamsburg, Pa., Oct. 29, 1892; s. William Henry and Corena Jane (Gates) H.; Pd.B., Elizabethtown Coll., 1916; A.B., Juniata Coll., 1927; M.Ed., U. of Pittsburgh, 1937; m. Emma Besse Wright, Sept. 6, 1914;

children—Virgil Clair, Jr., Catharine May, Galen Wright, Jane Arlene, Anna Bessie. Engaged in teaching or attdg. sch. continuously since 1910 except four yrs., 1920-24 during which served as pastor of small ch. in addition to teaching pub. sch.; prin. high sch., Millvale, Pa., 1927-35, supervising prin. schs., Millvale, Pa., since 1935. Mem. Pa. State Edn. Assn., N.E.A. Republican. Mem. Church of the Brethren. Home: 907 Evergreen Av., Millvale, Pa.

HOLSOPPLE, James Quinter, psychologist; b. Parkerford, Pa., July 26, 1900; s. Frank Ferry and Grace (Quinter) H.; A.B., Juniata Coll., 1920; A.M., Johns Hopkins U., 1923, Ph.D., same, 1924; m. Nell Scott, Mar. 4, 1929; 1 son, James. Fellow in biol. scis. Nat Research Council, 1924-25; instr. Yale U., 1925-26; asst. prof. Psychology, Western Reserve U., 1926-29; psychologist, Cleveland City Hosp., 1928-29; extension lecturer, Columbia U., 1929-30; lecturer in abnormal psychology, Princeton U., since 1933; chief psychologist, Dept. Instns. and Agencies, State of N.J. since 1929. Pres. N.J. Assn. Psychologists, 1933-34; chmn. Bd. Affiliates, Am. Assn. Applied Phychologists; mem. Am. Psychol. Assn., N.J. Psychol. Assn., Phi Beta Kappa, Sigma Xi. Home: Titusville, N.J. Office: N.J. State Hospital, Trenton, N.J.

HOLSTINE, Russell McKendrew, banking; b. Talcott, W.Va., Sept. 27, 1886; s. Granger McKendrew and Isabell Susan (Wyant) H.; student Dunsmore Bus. Coll., Staunton, Va., 1901-03; m. Mary Pinkney, Oct. 1, 1907; 1 dau., Doris Isabel (Mrs. Henderson P. Kelly). Engaged in banking since 1914, asso. with Montgomery Nat. Bank, Montgomery, W.Va., since 1925, vice-pres. and cashier since 1929, sec. and treas. Montgomery Memorial Park Corpn. since 1934, New River Motor Co. since 1932. Democrat. Presbyn. Mason. Home: 215 Second Av. Office: Montgomery Nat. Bank, Montgomery, W.Va.

HOLT, Homer Adams, gov. of W.Va., lawyer; b. Lewisburg, W.Va., Mar. 1, 1898; s. Robert Byrne and Emma (McWhorter) H.; A.B., Washington and Lee U., 1918, LL.B., 1923; LL.D., W.Va. U., 1937; m. Isabel Hedges Wood, Mar. 22, 1924; children—Julia Kinsley, Isabel Drury. Instr. in mathematics, Washington and Lee U., 1920-23, prof. law, 1923-25; in practice of law, mem. firm Dillon, Mahan & Holt, Fayetteville, W.Va., 1925-33; atty. gen. of West Virginia, 1933-37; governor of West Virginia for term 1937-41. Served as private June-September 1918, and as 2d lieutenant C.A.C., U.S.A., Sept., 1918-May 1919. Mem. Am., W.Va. State and Fayette Co. bar assns., Am. Legion, Phi Beta Kappa, Phi Kappa Psi, Phi Delta Phi, Omicron Delta Kappa. Democrat. Presbyn. Mason, Elk, Moose. Home: Fayetteville, W.Va.; 1716 Kanawha St., Charleston, W.Va. Office: Governor's Office, Charleston, W.Va.

HOLT, Lee Cone, chemist; b. Harlan, Ia., Feb. 19, 1880; s. Lee Elwood and Eva Boise (Collier) H.; B.S., Pomona Coll., Claremont, Calif., 1901; Ph.D., U. of Mich., 1905; grad. study, U. of Berlin, 1907-08; m. Daisy Ellen Ben Oliel, June 18, 1907 (now deceased); children—Florence Lee (dec.), Helen Agnes, Lee Elbert. Instr. in chemistry, Pomona Coll., 1901-02, Carnegie research asst., 1903-05; instr. in organic chemistry, U. of Mich., 1905-08, asst. prof., 1908-13, asso. prof., 1913-16; with Dow Chem. Co., Midland, Mich., 1916-17, Semet Solvay Co., Syracuse, N.Y., 1917-18, Nat. Aniline & Chem. Co., Buffalo, N.Y., 1918-29, in charge research and development work, 1921-29, v.p., 1922-29; with Jackson Lab. of DuPont Co. since 1929. Mem. Am. Chem. Soc., Am. Inst. Chem. Engrs., Phi Beta Kappa, Sigma Xi. Republican. Contbr. articles to German and Am. chem. jours. Home: R.D. 3, Wilmington, Del. Office: Du Pont Co., Wilmington, Del.

HOLT, Rush Dew, U.S. senator; b. Weston, W.Va., June 19, 1905; s. Matthew Samuel and Chilelia (Dew) H.; A.B., Salem Coll., 1924; unmarried. Began as teacher Bedford City (Va.) High School, 1924; then instr. Salem (W.Va.) Coll.; athletic dir. St. Patrick's Sch., W.Va., 1925-28; became instr. Glenville (W.Va.) State Teachers Coll., 1927; mem. W.Va. House of Delegates, 1931-35; mem. U.S. Senate, from W.Va., term 1935-41. Democrat. Elk, Moose. Home: Weston, W.Va.

HOLTMAN, Dudley Frank, engineer; b. Chicago, Ill., Dec. 27, 1889; s. Frank and Hannah (Pierson) H.; B.S. in C.E. Armour Inst. Tech., Chicago, 1912; m. Bernice Graves, of Chicago, Jan. 27, 1921; children—Dorothy Jane, Frank Graves. Railroad location and constrn., 1912-1914; structural engr., 1914-16; sr. structural engr., Cent. Dist., Div. of Valuation, Interstate Commerce Commn., Chicago, 1916-18; asso. editor Am. Contractor, Chicago, 1918-19; asst. Advertising dir. Peoples Popular Monthly, Des Moines, Ia., 1920; construction engr., Nat. Lumber Mfrs. Assn., Washington, D.C., Jan. 1921-Dec. 1925; asst. dir. and construction engr., Nat. Com. on Wood Utilization, Washington, D.C., 1926-29, by apptmt. of Herbert Hoover, then sec. of commerce and chmn. of com.; H.M. Byllesby & Co. since 1930. Mem. Am. Soc. C.E. Author: Wood Construction, 1929. Home: 5616 Western Av., Chevy Chase, Md. Office: 744 Jackson Pl., Washington, D.C.

HOLTON, Charles Rudolph, v.p. Bethlehem Steel Co.; b. Iron Hill, Md., Apr. 1, 1887; s. William James and Catharine Fitten (Ash) H.; grad. Cecil County High Sch., Elkton, Md., 1900, Goldey Coll. (Business Sch.), Wilmington, Del., 1903; m. Grace Catharine Hershey, of Steelton, Pa., July 15, 1910 (died Oct. 11, 1927); children—Frances Hershey (Mrs. John Allen Aufhammer), Isabel Hershey (dec.), Elinor Friel; m. 2d, Irene Lewis Wilson, July 2, 1929. Office boy and stenographer Am. Bridge Co., Edge Moor, Del., 1901-03; stenographer Bush & Rayner, Wilmington, Del., 1903-04; stenographer and chief clerk Am. Bridge Co., Ambridge, Pa., 1904-06; sec. and asst. to v.p. Pa. Steel Co., Steelton, Pa., 1906-16; with Bethlehem Steel Co. since 1916, successively buyer, asst. purchasing agent, purchasing agent and v.p. in charge of purchases, now also dir.; dir. Bethlehem Steel Corpn. Asst. sec. of Council, Borough of Steelton, Pa., 1908-16. Mem. Am. Iron & Steel Inst., Engineer's Club of Lehigh Valley. Republican. Presbyterian. Clubs: Bethlehem, Saucon Valley Country (Bethlehem). Home: 1427 Prospect Av. Office: 703 E. Third St., Bethlehem, Pa.

HOLTZAPPLE, George Emanuel, M.D.; b. York Co., Pa., May 22, 1862; s. Israel E. and Christianna (Lecrone) H.; student York Collegiate Inst., York County Acad.; grad. course in philosophy, Lebanon Valley Coll.; Sc.D., Susquehanna U., 1925; m. Mahala Gladfelter, Jan. 9, 1886; 1 dau., Gertrude S.; m. 2d, Marie Schaeberle Van Natter, Jan. 7, 1932. In gen. practice of medicine; cons. physician and chmn. Neuropsychiatric Clinic, York Hosp. Dir. and past pres. York City Sch. Bd. Awarded certificate as internist by Am. Bd. Internal Medicine. Dir. York County Chapter, Am. Red Cross. Fellow Am. Coll. Physicians, A.M.A.; mem. A.A.A.S., Am. Pub. Health Assn., Pa. State Med. Soc. (ex-v.p.; mem. numerous coms.), York Co. Med. Soc. (ex-pres.). Club: Philadelphia Medical. Writer articles on med. subjects. Asso. editor Pa. Med. Jour., 10 yrs. Home: 10 E. Princess St. Office: 203 S. George St., York, Pa.

HOLTZMAN, Herbert P(eter), supt. of schs.; b. Jackson Twp., Lebanon Co., Pa., Jan. 4, 1887; s. Jonathan and Frany Smith (Witmer) H.; student Kutztown (Pa.) State Teachers Coll., 1904-06; Ph.B., Dickinson Coll., 1913; A.M., 1916; LL.B., Dickinson Law Sch., 1916; A.M, U of Pa. Sch. of Edn., 1923; B.S., U. of Pa. Sch. of Finance, 1936; m. Emily May Staudt, June 10, 1916; children—Franklin Herbert, Emily Verone. Teacher of ungraded schools, Berks Co., Pa., 1904, 1907-08; admitted to Pa. bar, 1916, and practiced at Reading, Pa.; supt. of schools, Fleetwood, Pa. (1917-24), West Reading, Pa., since 1924. Mem. N.E.A., Pa. State Edn. Assn., West Reading Bd. of Trade, West Reading Fire Co., Sinking Spring Fire Co., Nat. and Pa. State Grange, Pi Gamma Mu, Phi Delta Kappa, Theta Chi. Mem. Reformed Ch. Mason (K.T., 32°, Shriner), Red Men, Odd Fellows, Patriotic Order Sons of America. Home: 718 Reading Av., West Reading, Pa.

HOLZAPFEL, Henry, Jr.; v.p. Potomac-Edison Co. Home: 1017 Oak Hill Av. Office: 55 E. Washington St., Hagerstown, Md.

HOLZMAN, Mark Benjamin, physician; b. Phila., Pa., June 28, 1882; s. David and Diana (Sunclear) H.; student Horace Benney Sch., Phila., 1889-95; B.A., Central High Sch., Phila., 1899; M.D., Medico-Chirurg. Coll., Phila., 1904; m. Aimee Brown Arthur, Apr. 5, 1926; 1 son, Mark Benjamin. Mem. staff Homeopathic and Wilmington Gen. Hosps., courtesy staff of St. Francis Hosp. Served as 1st lt., M.C., U.S. Army, during World War. Mem. New Castle Co., Del. State, Am. med. socs., Del. Acad. of Medicine. Republican. Mason (Phila. Consistory; Lu Lu Temple). Address: S.E. corner 18th and Washington Sts., Hockessin, Del.

HOLZMANN, Albert William, univ. prof.; b. Newark, N.J., Nov. 29, 1894; s. Lawrence and Anna Barbara (Edling) H.; ed. Barringer High Sch., Newark, N.J., 1909-13; Princeton U., 1926-27, Heidelberg U., Germany, 1931; Litt. B., Rutgers U., New Brunswick, N.J., 1917; M.A., Columbia U., 1926, Ph.D., 1935; m. Marga Helena Edling, Sept. 5, 1924. Teacher of history and community civics, Paterson (N.J.) High Sch., 1921; sec. The Sodium Sulphate Co. of America, Newark, N.J., 1921-22; teacher of history and gen. science, Dover (N.J.) High Sch., 1923; instr. of German, Rutgers U., New Brunswick, N.J., 1923-27, asst. prof., 1927-31, asso. prof. of German language and literature since 1931, head of the German Dept. since 1934. Served as sergt., Corps of Interpreters, Intelligence Div., U.S. Army, 1917-18, 2d lt., 1918-20. Mem. Am. Assn. of Teachers of German (pres. N.J. chapter, 1938-40), Modern Language Assn. of America, Modern Language Teachers Assn. of N.J., Am. Assn. of Univ. Profs., Lambda Chi Alpha, Phi Beta Kappa (sec. Rutgers U. chapter 1928-31), Delta Phi Alpha. Elected mem. Schiller Acad., Munich, Germany, 1933; gen. adv. council, The Franklin Soc., 1935. Ind. Republican. Mem. Reformed Ch. Author: Family Relationships in the Dramas of August von Kotzebue, 1935; also "A Decade of Declamation," in Modern Language Journal, Nov. 1938. Translator numerous articles from German into English in the fields of ceramics and music. Dir. and co-dir. of plays: Goethe's Die Laune des Verliebten, Kotzebue's Schneider Fips, Lessing's Minna von Barnhelm, Gerhart Hauptmann's Die Versunkene Glocke, Schiller's Maria Stuart. Address: 22 Harrison Av., New Brunswick, N.J.

HOMAN, J(ames) Albert, lawyer; b. Atlantic City, N.J., Aug. 28, 1885; s. John Albert and Mary (Shone) H.; student pub. schs. and high sch., Atlantic City, N.J., grad. 1903; m. Stella Emmons, June 29, 1907; 1 dau., Mildred Elizabeth (Mrs. J. Walter Ireland, Jr.). Studied law in office Hon. John H. Backes, Trenton, N.J., 1907-12; admitted to N.J. bar as atty., 1912, as counselor, 1920; asso. with Hon. John H. Backes in practice, 1912-14; asso. with Hon. Malcolm G. Buchanan, 1914-19; mem. firm Homan & Buchanan, 1919-26; mem. firm Homan, Buchanan & Smith since 1926; supreme ct. commr. since 1935; spl. master in chancery since 1935; mem. N.J. Gen. Assembly, 1934; del. to Dem. Nat. Conv., 1931; Dem. presdl. elector, 1935; treas. and dir. United Railway Signal Corpn. since 1920. Trustee Trenton Sch. of Industrial Arts. Mem. Am. Bar Assn., N.J. Bar Assn. Democrat. Presbyn. Mason. Club: Carteret of Trenton (md. bd. trustees). Home: 1 Kensington Av. Office: Trenton Trust Bldg., Trenton, N.J.

HOMER, Harry Louis; asso. in surgery, Johns Hopkins U.; visiting surgeon Union Memorial Hosp., Church Home and Infirmary; surgeon-in-charge Out-Patient Dept., Johns Hopkins Hosp.; cons. surgeon Sheppard and Enoch Pratt Hosp., Towson, Md. Address: Riderwood, Md.

HOMRIGHAUSEN, Elmer George, clergyman, prof.; b. Wheatland, Ia., Apr. 11, 1900; s. Henry George and Sophia Julia (Mordhorst) H.; A.B., Mission House Coll., Plymouth, Wis., 1921; ed. Mission House Theol. Sem., 1921-23; Th.B., Princeton Theol. Sem., 1924; Th.M., U. of Dubuque, Ia., 1928, Th.D., same, 1930; A.M., Butler U., 1931; ed. U. of Chicago, 1926, 29; (hon.) D.D., Mission House Coll., 1931; m. Ruth Willa Strassburger, Sept. 17, 1923; children—Richard James, Ruth Karolyn, Elmer Paul, David Karl, Mary Elizabeth. Ordained to ministry Reformed Ch. U.S.A., 1924; minister, Freeport, Ill., 1924-29 and Carrollton Av. (Evang. & Ref. Ch.), Indianapolis, Ind., 1929-38; prof. of Christian edn., Princeton Theol. Sem. since 1938; spl. lecturer and asst. prof., Butler U., 1932-38; a vice-pres. N.J. Council Religious Edn.; transferred to Presbyn. Ch. U.S.A., 1938. Mem. Y.M.C.A. Bd., Princeton. Mem. Am. Ch. History Soc., Internat. Council Religious Edn., Phi Kappa Phi. Republican. Presbyn. U.S.A. Mason. Author. Christianity in America—A Crisis, 1937. Translator theol. works. Contbr. to religious publs. Lecturer. Home: 80 Mercer St., Princeton, N.J.

HOMSEY, Samuel Eldon, architect; b. Boston, Mass., Aug. 29, 1904; s. Elias S. and Margaret (Sabbag) H.; B.S. in Arch., M.S. in Arch., Mass. Inst. Tech., 1926; m. Victorine du Pont, Apr. 27, 1929; children—Coleman du Pont, Eldon du Pont. Began as architect, Boston, 1926; in practice at Wilmington, Del., since 1935; work mentioned in "Twice a Year" under map outstanding examples modern architecture by living Americans; work pub. in Architectural Forum, Architectural Record, Pencil Point; now mem. firm Victorine and Samuel Homsey, architects, Wilmington. Mem. A.I.A. Also watercolor artist with work represented in pvt. collections in Phila., Wilmington, Boston, Pasadena, Calif., Louisville, Ky., and Detroit. Awarded prizes by Wilmington Soc. of Fine Arts, 1936, 1938. Home: Old Baltimore Rd. Office: Delaware Trust Bldg., Wilmington, Del.

HOMSHER, Howard N., banker; b. Bart Twp., Pa., Mar. 12, 1864; s. John and Rachel E. (Coulter) H.; ed. high sch.; m. Anna G. Ludwig, Sept. 2, 1914; 1 dau., Olive (Mrs. McClure). Engaged in gen. merchandising business and farming, Bartville, Pa.; post master since 1909; pres. and dir. Christiana Nat. Bank since 1936. Presbyn. (treas. Middle Octorava Ch. 1909). Club: Lancaster Automobile (v.p.). Home: Bartville, Pa.

HONORÉ, Paul, mural painter; b. Crawford Co., Pa., May 30, 1885; prep. edn., Cass Tech. High Sch., Detroit, Mich.; art edn., Sch. of Fine Arts, Detroit, and Pa. Acad. Fine Arts, Phila.; pupil of Frank Brangwyn; m. Kate Ethel York, Feb. 1, 1911; children—Paul York, Ethel Mary. Specialist on murals, also wood block decorations for books. Represented by murals at Midland (Mich.) County Court House; Dearborn (Mich.) Pub. Library; 1st State Bank, Detroit; Highland Park (Mich.) High Sch.; Players Club, Detroit; Peoples Ch., Lansing, Mich.; Nat. Research Council, Washington, D.C.; Michigan Building at Century of Progress Expn., Chicago (now at Lansing, Mich.); Midland Country Club; Dearborn (Mich.) High School; Southeastern High School, Detroit, Michigan; etc. Awarded Marvin Preston prize, Mich. Artists Exhibit, Detroit Mus. of Art, 1917; Museum Founders prize, same, 1917; Walter Piper purchase prize, Scarab Club, Detroit, 1928. Mem. Mural Painters Soc. N.Y., Authors League, Soc. Arts and Crafts, Founders Soc. of Detroit Mus. of Art. Clubs: Scarab (Detroit); Nat. Arts (New York); Washington Arts. Made wood block decorations for Heroes from Hakluyt, Tales from Silverlands, Tales Worth Telling, Romantic Rascals, Frontier Ballads, Winged Horse, Winged Horse Anthology, etc. Founder Paul Honoré Fellowship, 1931. Home-Studio: Port Deposit, Md.

HOOBER, John Aaron, lawyer; b. Wrightsville, Pa., Jan. 27, 1867; s. Henry and Malinda (Holzapple) H.; student York (Pa.) Collegiate Inst., 1887-89; LL.B., Yale, 1891, M.L., 1892, D.C.L., 1893; m. Sarah A. Klinefelter, July 28, 1925; Admitted to Pa. bar, 1893, and practiced in York; pres. and treas. York Wall Paper Co.; pres. and dir. Susquehanna Casting Co.; treas. and dir. Joseph Black & Sons Co., dir. Enterprise Furniture Co., Diamond Silk Mill, Western Nat. Bank, Eastern Nat. Bank. Pres. Alumni Assn. of Law Dept., Yale. Democrat. Mem. United Lutheran Ch. in America; supt. Sunday sch.; mem. church council; mem. bd. dirs. Am. Missions of United Lutheran Ch. in America. Mason. Clubs: Graduates (New Haven, Conn.); Lafayette, Country (York). Home: 434 W. Market St. Office: 124 E. Market St., York, Pa.

HOOD, Alexander Bonbright, banker; b. Connellsville, Pa., June 15, 1872; s. Alfred Walters and Emily Long (Herbert) H.; ed. Connellsville pub. and high sch., 1878-88; m. Florence Haldeman, Oct. 15, 1905 (now deceased); 1 son, Alexander Haldeman; m. 2d, Florence B. Grim, May 18, 1932; Demurrage adjustor Pittsburgh Car Service, 1888-91; with Second Nat. Bank, Connellsville, since Feb. 1891, successively as bookkeeper, asst. cashier, cashier (1926) and since Nov. 1936 vice-pres.; dir. Second Nat. Bank, Connellsville, Pa.; sec. and dir. Peoples Bldg. & Loan Assn.; sec., treas. and dir. Connellsville Masonic Assn. and Hill Grove Endowment Assn. of Connellsville. Served in Nat. Guard of Pa. 15 yrs.; lt. Secret Service during World War. Republican. Presbyterian. Mason (32°). Home: Isabella Rd. Office: Second Nat. Bank, Connellsville, Pa.

HOOD, Ethel, painter, sculptor; b. Baltimore, Md., Apr. 9, 1908; d. John Mifflin and Ethel Gilpin (Painter) H.; student N.Y. Sch. of Illustration, N.Y. City, 1925-26, Academie Julian, Paris, Jan.-June 1927, Art Students League, N.Y. City, 1928-29. Painter and sculptor. Principal works: fountain figure owned by Max Schling, N.Y. City; portrait head of Francis Whitman, owned by Mrs. Ral Parr, Stevenson, Md.; portrait head of Miss Beatrice Lillie, 1939; portrait head Margaret Speaks (Am. soprano), 1939. Exhibited Baltimore Mus. of Art, 1933, 34, 35, 36 and 39, Pa. Acad., 1937, Corcoran Art Gallery (Washington Soc. of Artists exhbn.), 1939. Awarded bronze medal for sculpture, Washington Soc. Artists, 1939. Private exhbns.; Karl Freund Arts, Inc., New York, 1938; Decorators Club, New York, 1939. Mem. Nat. Assn. Women Painters and Sculptors, Nat. Sculpture Soc. Presbyterian. Clubs: Baltimore Country (Baltimore); Longshore Country (Westport, Conn.). Home: Wyman Park Apts., Baltimore, Md. Studio: 65 W. 56th St., New York, N.Y.

HOOD, Jean, asso. prof. nutrition extension; b. Saginaw, Mich., Oct. 14, 1903; d. Francis George and Katharine Lucas (Chambers) H.; ed. Simmons Coll., Boston, 1921-23; B.S., U. of Wis., 1927, M.S., 1939. Student interne, Peter Bent Brigham Hosp., Boston, 1927; chief dietitian, State of Wis. Gen. Hosp., Madison, 1928-29; lab. asst. agrl. bacteriology, U. of Wis., 1930; chief dietitian, Truesdale Hosp., Fall River, Mass., 1931-35; asso. prof. nutrition extension, Pa. State Coll., since 1935. Mem. Nat. and State Home Econs. assns., Nat. and State Dietetics assns., Am. Assn. Univ. Women, D.A.R., Phi Delta Gamma. Presbyn. Home: 133 W. Fairmount Av., State College, Pa.

HOOD, Richard, artist, etcher; b. Phila., Pa., July 13, 1910; s. Thomas Richard and Anne Lovering (Grubb) H.; student Montgomery Sch., Wynnewood, Pa., 1921-29, Sch. of Fine Art, U. of Pa., 1929-31; unmarried. Etcher since 1931. Exhibited in Internat. Exhbn. of Etching and Engraving, Chicago, 1936, 37, 38 and 39, Pa. Acad. Water Color Annual, 1937-38; New Horizons in Am. Art, Mus. Modern Art, N.Y. City; Prints for the People at Master Inst. United Arts, N.Y. City, 1937; American Art Today, N.Y. World's Fair, 1939. Prints in following pub. collections: Pa. State Coll.; Pa. State Dept. Banking, Harrisburg; Phila. Gen. Hosp.; Phila. Free Library; Pittsburgh Carnegie Library; 7 lithographs The Poe Book (limited edition, 125 copies), pub. 1934; 6 Dry Points—American Authors (limited edition, 50 copies), pub. 1934. Field supervisor of art Pa. Federal Art Project. Mem. Phi Kappa Sigma. Democrat. Episcopalian. Clubs: Phila. Sketch, Print (Phila.). Home: 314 N. 19th St., Philadelphia, Pa.

HOOK, John Inghram, lawyer; b. Pittsburgh, Pa., Aug. 28, 1889; s. George A. and Bertha Lotta (Kincaid) H.; ed. high schools, Waynesburg, Pa., and Waynesburg Coll.; studied law in office of F. W. Downey, Waynesburg, Pa.; m. Sara Graham Iams, June 19, 1915; children—John Inghram, Robert Aiken, James. Admitted to Pa. bar, 1914, and since practiced in Waynesburg; mem. firm Scott & Hook; dir. First Nat. Bank & Trust Co., Waynesburg. Trustee Waynesburg Coll. Democrat. Presbyterian. Address: Waynesburg, Pa.

HOOKER, Davenport, anatomist; b. Brooklyn, N.Y., May 13, 1887; s. Henry Daggett and Mary Theodora (Davenport) H.; grad. Polytechnic Prep. Sch., Brooklyn, 1903; grad. Hotchkiss Sch., 1904; B.A., Yale Coll., 1908; M.A., Yale U., 1909, Ph.D., 1912; Scott Hurtt fellow of Yale, Bonn and Naples, 1911-12; hon. D.Sc., University of Pittsburgh, 1939; m. Helen Millington Ferris, Apr. 14, 1917; 1 dau., Elizabeth Bradford. Asst. in biology, Yale U., 1908-09; instr. in anatomy, Yale Sch. of Medicine, 1909-14; asst. prof. histology, U. of Pittsburgh Sch. of Medicine, 1914-15; asst. prof. anatomy, Yale Sch. of Medicine, 1915-19; prof. anatomy and head of dept., U. of Pittsburgh Sch. of Medicine, since 1919. Capt. F.A. Reserves, 1919-23, Sanitary Reserves, 1923; major Sanitary Reserves since 1923. Trustee Community Sch. of Pittsburgh, 1928-30. Mem. Am. Assn. Anatomists (mem. exec. com. 1922-25), Am. Soc. Zoölogists, Am. Physiol. Soc., Soc. Exptl. Biology and Medicine, Phi Beta Kappa, Sigma Xi, Alpha Omega Alpha, Nu Sigma Nu; fellow A.A.A.S.; asso. fellow A.M.A. Conglist. Club: Graduate (New Haven). Mem. editorial bd. Journal Comparative Neurology since 1931, mng. editor since 1932; mem. advisory bd. Jour. Neurophysiology since 1938. Writer various scientific papers, etc. Home: 5410 Plainfield St., Pittsburgh, Pa.

HOOKER, Donald Russell, physiologist; b. New Haven, Conn., Sept. 7, 1876; s. Frank Henry and Grace (Russell) H.; B.A., Yale, 1899, M.S., 1901; M.D., Johns Hopkins, 1905; student U. of Berlin, 1906; m. Edith Houghton, June 14, 1905; children—Donald Houghton, Russell Houghton, Edith Houghton, Elizabeth Houghton, Beatrice Houghton. Asst. instr. and asso. in physiology, 1906-10, asso. prof. 1910-20, Johns Hopkins Med. Sch.; lecturer on physical hygiene, Johns Hopkins U. Mng. editor Am. Journal Physiology, since 1914; also mng. editor Physiological Revs. Mem. Am. Physiol. Soc. Home: 1016 St. George's Rd. Office: 19 W. Chase St., Baltimore, Md.

HOON, Merle R(ussel), surgeon; b. Mercer, Pa., Apr. 3, 1892; s. Hugh Beatty and Margaret E. (Brown) H.; B.A., Westminster Coll., 1910; student U. of Mich., 1914-16; M.D., U. of Pa., 1918; m. Marian Holliday, June 6, 1925; children—Margaret Holliday, Alexander Holliday, Nancy McGill. Fellow in surgery, Mayo Foundation, 1919-23; began practice of medicine, 1923; staff surgeon Presbyn. Hosp. since 1925. Pres. North Central Clin. Soc., 1938-39; sec. Pittsburgh Surg. Soc. since 1937. Republican. Presbyterian. Clubs: Duquesne, Oakmont Country. Author: Solid Sarcoma of the Ovary, 1922; Fibromata of the Ovary, 1923; Alkalosis Associated with High Gastro-Intestinal Tract Obstruction, 1926; Pancreatic Cyst, 1926. Home: 1239 Shady Av., Pittsburgh, Pa. Office: 5074 Jenkins Arcade Bldg., Pittsburgh, Pa.

HOOPER, Elizabeth, writer, artist, doll collector; b. Baltimore, Md., Oct. 6, 1901; d. Alcaeus and Florence (Gees) H.; student Johns Hopkins Univ., various courses, 1925-39. Studied art with pvt. instrs. and has followed profession of art since 1923; engaged in collecting dolls of various kinds from all over the world since 1929, collection now numbers over 600 pieces. Mem. Nat. League of Am. Pen Women, Am. Artists Professional League, Baltimore Water Color Club, Baltimore Mus. of Art, Doll Collectors of America, Inc., Nat. Doll and Toy Collectors Club, Inc., Sch. Art League of Baltimore. Republican. Methodist. Club: Womans (Roland Park). Author: Dolls the World Over, 3d edit., 1939; Royal Dolls, 1938. Contbr. to mags. Home: 3100 St. Paul St. Studio: 617 Hopkins Apts., Baltimore, Md.

HOOPER, Franklin Henry, editor; b. Worcester, Mass., Jan. 28, 1862; s. William R. and Frances (Nelson) H.; A.B., magna cum laude, Harvard, 1883; m. Grace M. Sessions, Oct. 19, 1887; children—Catharine B., Leverett F. With Century Co., pubs., New York, 1883-96 (one of editors of Century Dictionary); lit. adviser and mgr. for James Clarke & Co., pubs., 1896-99; with Ency. Britannica (except during war period) since 1899, Am. editor 10th edit., 1902, mngr. editor 11th edit., 1910, Am. editor 12th edit., 1922, 13th edit., 1926, 14th edit., 1928, and editor in chief, 1932-38, Ency. Britannica; also editor The World To-day, 1933-38; planned and edited These Eventful Years—The Twentieth Century in the Making (2 vols.), 1924; editor Britannica Junior—an Encyclopædia for Children (10 vols.), 1934. Mgr. New York office of British Ministry of Food, World War. Democrat. Episcopalian. Clubs: Harvard (New York and N.J.). Home: 30 Plymouth St., Montclair, N.J. Address: care Ency. Britannica, 342 Madison Av., New York, N.Y.

HOOPER, James Edward, mfg. textiles; b. Phila., Pa., Aug. 24, 1897; s. Robert P. and Marion Grant (Baylies) H.; C.E. Princeton U., 1918; m. Mildred W. Anderson, June 18, 1919; children—James Edward, Jr., Lawrence Lewis. In employ Wm. E. Hooper & Sons Co., cotton textile mfrs., Baltimore, Md., 1919-28, vice-pres. since 1928; dir. Hopkins Place Savings Bank, Baltimore, Fidelity & Guaranty Fire Corpn., Baltimore, Northern Central Ry. Co. Served as lt. (j.g.) U.S.N. during World War, comdg. officer Submarine Chaser No. 239, attached to Atlantic Fleet. Dir. Baltimore Assn. of Commerce; vice-pres. Community Fund of Baltimore, gen. chmn. Campaign 1937. Dir. Baltimore Chapter Am. Red Cross; dir. Community Placement Bureau. Dir. Home for Incurables. Republican. Episcopalian. Clubs: Maryland, Elkridge, Merchants (Baltimore); St. Andrew's Soc. (Philadelphia): Bachelor's Cotillion (Baltimore). Home: Ruxton Rd., Ruxton. Office: 3502 Parkdale Av., Baltimore, Md.

HOOPER, Robert P., cotton mfr.; b. Baltimore, Md., July 15, 1872; s. James E. and Sarah (Poole) H.; m. Marion Baylies, 1896; pres. Wm. E. Hooper & Sons' Co.; pres. Jefferson Med. Coll.; pres. Automobile Club, Phila.; dir. Lumbermen's Mutual Casualty Co. (Chicago), Nat. Retailers Ins. Co. (Chicago), Insurors (Pa.). Home: Chestnut Hill. Office: Juniper and Cherry, Philadelphia, Pa.

HOOPES, Darlington, lawyer; b. Vale, Harford Co., Md., Sept. 11, 1896; s. Price and Elizabeth (Tucker) H.; student George Sch., George School, Pa., 1909-13, U. of Wis., 1914-15; studied law privately; m. Hannah L. Foulke, Oct. 22, 1921 (died Jan. 9, 1923); m. 2d, Hazelette Miller, Oct. 16, 1925; children—Darlington, Rae, Delite. Admitted to Pa. bar, 1921, and practiced at Norristown, Montgomery Co., Pa., 1921-27; in practice at Reading, Pa., since 1927; asst. city solicitor of Reading, 1928-32, solicitor since 1936. Mem. Pa. House of Reps., 1930-36. Mem. Am., Pa. State, Montgomery County and Berks County bar assns., Nat. Lawyers Guild, Commercial Law League of America, Am. Fed. of Teachers. Socialist. Mem. Soc. of Friends. Home: 1521 Greenview Av. Office: 26 N. 6th St., Reading, Pa.

HOOVEN, Herbert Nelson, artist, author; b. Hazelton, Pa., Jan. 31, 1898; s. William S. and Maud (Madara) H.; student Pa. Mus. Sch. of Industrial Art, 1917-19, Pa. Acad. of Fine Arts, 1919-20, Beaux Arts Inst. of Design, New York, 1925; m. Ruth A. McBride, July 5, 1935; 1 dau., Heidi. Teacher of fine arts, U. of Mich., 1926-27, Valparaiso U., 1927-29, Ohio U., 1932-35, Syracuse U., 1936. Works: "Dunes" Peiping Mus., China; "Land of the Ojibway," San Joaquin Mus., Calif.; "On the Narragansett," Valparaiso U.; "Upper Shore, Lake Michigan," U. of Mich.; "Delaware Water Gap," Ohio U.; "Anthracite Coal Industry," Hazelton (Pa.) Library; "On the Lehigh Canal," Lehigh U.; "Wooded Shores of Cayuga," Cornell U.; "Foothills of the Alleghenies," U. of Mo. Honorable mention, Nat. Water Color Exhbn., Phila., 1931. Fellow Pa. Acad. of Fine Arts, Am. Artists Professional League, Soc. Ind. Artists. Author: Rig Veda, 1933; Pencilled Hands, 1934; The Laughing One, 1937. Home: Solebury, Bucks County, Pa.

HOOVER, Benjamin Andrew, physician, banker; b. Pleasant Hall, Pa., May 4, 1873; s. Abram W. and Elizabeth Ann (Rohrer) H.; student North Ind. Business Inst., 1894; M.D., Medico-Chirurg. Coll., Phila., 1901; post-grad. work, Johns Hopkins U., Baltimore, Md., 1907, 1917; m. Margaretta S. Shoemaker, July 7, 1903; children—Dr. Philip A., Robert Andrew, Margaretta Elizabeth. Teacher, Franklin Co. (Pa.) Pub. Schs., 1891-97; pvt. practice of medicine, Upper Strasburg, Pa., 1901-03; removed to Wrightsville, Pa., 1903; surgeon for Pa. Railroad, Wrightsville, Pa., 1904-39; examiner for Metropolitan, Prudential, Northwestern, Girard, Scranton, Provident, Equitable Life, Mass. Life, Travelers, Mutual Benefit of N.J. and Union Central ins. cos.; v.p. First Nat. Bank, Wrightsville, Pa., 1928-36, dir. since 1924, pres. since 1936; helped to organize Wrightsville (Pa.) Bldg. & Loan Assn., 1911, pres. since 1924. Examiner for Pensions for the Blind, Wrightsville, Pa., 1936; med. advisor and mem. Wrightsville (Pa.) Bd. of Health. Served as med. examiner, York Co. (Pa.) Draft Bd. during World War. Pres. Bd. of Trustees, Presbyn. Ch., Wrightsville, Pa., since 1918. Mem. A.M.A., Pa. State, York Co. med. socs., Pa. R.R. Surgeon's Assn., Am. Red Cross (pres., Wrightsville, Pa., chapter since 1917), Patriotic Order of Sons of America. Republican. Presbyterian. Odd Fellow. Club: Rotary Internat. (Wrightsville). Address: 121 N. 2d St., Wrightsville, Pa.

HOOVER, Clyde Wallace, supervising prin. of schools; b. West Fairview, Pa., Mar. 27, 1879; s. Abram and Margaret (Stough) H.; student Harrisburg Acad., 1895-97, Dickinson Prep. Sch., 1897-98; A.B., Dickinson Coll., 1902; m. Jessie Dersheimer, July 29, 1926. Prin., Chestnut Level Acad., Pa., 1902-04, Tunkhannock, Pa., Schools, 1904-19; supervising prin., East Pennsboro Twp. Schools, Enola, Pa., since 1919. Mem. N.E.A., Pa. State Edn. Assn., Cumberland Co. Principals Assn. Mem. Beta Theta Pi. Republican. Presbyterian (ruling elder). Mason (K.T., Shriner). Home: 24 Altoona Av. Office: High School, Enola, Pa.

HOOVER, Harvey Daniel, teacher of theology; b. New Oxford, Pa., June 17, 1880; s. Samuel E. and Jane J. (Gable) H.; student Gettysburg (Pa.) Coll., 1894-96; Susquehanna U., Selinsgrove, Pa., 1896-1902, A.B., 1899, A.M., 1900, B.D., 1902; Ph.D., Ill. Wesleyan U., Bloomington, Ill., 1907; S.T.D., Gettysburg, 1918, D.D., Wittenberg College, Springfield, O., 1922; Litt.D., Carthage (Ill.) College, 1935; m. Miriam Grace Stock, June 17, 1902; 1 dau., Dorcas Grace (Mrs. Paul H. Ensrud). Minister at Friedens, Pa., 1902-04, East Pittsburgh, 1904-07; prof. sociology and philosophy, Susquehanna U., 1907-09; prof. philosophy and edn., and pres. Carthage (Ill.) Coll., 1909-26; prof. practical theology (including sociology), Luth. Theol. Sem., Gettysburg, since 1926. Instr. Nawakwa Training Camp, Hanover Leadership Sch., York Training Sch. of Religious Edn.; lecturer on popular ednl., lit. and sociol. topics. Mem. N.E.A, Am. Sociol. Soc., Religious Edn. Assn., Luth. Hist. Acad., A.A.A.S., Nat. Hoover Assn., Am. Geog. Soc., S.A.R., Bookfellows, Am. Hymn Soc. (N.Y.), Hymn Society (London), Pi Gamma Mu. Sec. Common Service Book Com., and pres. Bd. of Deaconess Work, United Luth. Ch. America. Republican. Clubs: University (Chicago); Lions. Wrote: Master Mind; Lift Up Your Eyes; History of Carthage College. Editor: Light For Today, also of 5 vols. of Nat. Luth. Edn. Assn. Editor of Lutheran Church Quarterly. Home: Gettysburg, Pa.

HOOVER, J. M.; mem. law firm Hoover & Hoover. Address: Webster Springs, W.Va.

HOOVER, Samuel Earle; b. Phila., Pa., July 12, 1879; s. Frederick Lyman and Caroline (Seltzer) H.; student Peirce Sch. Business Adminstrn., 1896-97; m. Jennie Lachot, Oct. 1, 1902. Began as clk. F. L. Hoover & Sons Co., Phila., building constrn., 1897, pres. since 1933. Ruling elder Carmel Presbyn. Ch., Edge Hill Pa., since 1900; vice moderator Presbyn. Ch. in U.S.A., 1935; dir. Am. Sunday Sch. Union, Tennent Coll.; mem. exec. com., Federal Council of Chs. of Christ in America. Republican. Home: Greenwood Terrace, Jenkintown, Pa. Office: 1023 Cherry St., Philadelphia, Pa.

HOPE, Richard, educator; b. Pueblo, Colo., Aug. 12, 1895; s. William and Martha (Festner) H.; A.M., U. of Southern Calif., 1923, B.D., 1926; Ph.D., Columbia U., 1930; m. Lydia Koepsel, June 21, 1923. Pastor Bethel Lutheran Ch., University City, Mo., 1916-20, Grace Lutheran Ch., Los Angeles, Calif., 1920-25; prof. history and English, Concordia Collegiate Inst., 1926-28; lecturer philosophy, Columbia U., 1929-30; asso. prof. philosophy, U. of Pittsburgh, since 1930. Mem. Am. Philos. Assn. (Eastern and Western divs.), Am. Assn. Univ. Profs., Philos. Soc. of Pittsburgh. Republican. Club: University of Pittsburgh Faculty. Author: The Book of Diogenes Laertius, 1930. Writer of reviews and articles and newspaper editorial features. Home: 515 S. Aiken Av., Pittsburgh, Pa.

HOPE, William M.; mem. law firm Hope & Harmonson. Address: Dover, Del.

HOPKINS, Andrew Delmar, bioclimatist; b. Jackson Co., W.Va., Aug. 20, 1857; s. Andrew Evans and Miriam Florence (Evans) H.; early edn. at Jackson C.H., W.Va.; hon. Ph.D., W.Va. U., 1893; m. Adealia S. Butcher, Nov. 18, 1880; children—Roy Samuel, Edwin Butcher, Louise (dec.), Herbert Evans. Entomologist W.Va. Agrl. Expt. Sta., 1890-1902; v.-dir. same, 1897-1902; prof. econ. entomology, W.Va. U., 1896-1902; apptd. forest entomologist in charge forest insect investigations, Division of Entomology, U.S. Department of Agriculture, July 1, 1902; senior entomologist, 1904-23; spl. research in bioclimatics, 1923-31; collaborator in charge of bioclimatics, 1931. Fellow A.A.A.S. (emeritus life mem., 1938), Entomol. Soc. of America (v.p.); former mem. Assn. Econ. Entomologists (v.p. 1900, pres. 1901), Washington Acad. Sciences (former v.p.); mem. W.Va. Acad. Sciences (1st pres.), Entom. Soc. Washington (pres.), Am. Meteorol. Soc.; hon. mem. Soc. Econ. Biologists (Eng.), Biol. Soc. of Washington (pres. 1920). Author of numerous bulls., principally on forest tree insects and Scolytidæ and bioclimatics, including development of the bioclimatic law and science of bioclimatics, 1938. Club: Cosmos. Home: 1708 Washington Av., Parkersburg, W.Va.

HOPKINS, Annette B.; instr. English, Goucher Coll., 1911-14, asso. prof., 1914-18, prof. since 1918. Address: Goucher Coll., Baltimore, Md.

HOPKINS, Carleton Roper, high sch. prin.; b. Brooklyn, N.Y., Dec. 1, 1892; s. Horace Franklin and Esther Susan (Paton) H.; A.B., Coll. of City of N.Y., 1916; A.M., N.Y. Univ., 1921; B.S. in Edn., Teachers Coll. Temple U., Phila., Pa., 1923; student Brooklyn Law Sch., 1916-18, Johns Hopkins U., 1932; student various summer sessions, 1924-32; m. Gladys E. Hull, Oct. 25, 1919; children—Jeannette Ethel, Susan Esther. Teacher, N.Y. City high schools, 1916-21; prin. Cramer Grammar Sch., Camden, N.J., 1921-23; prin. Hatch Jr. High Sch., 1923-33; prin. Camden High Sch. since 1933; part time instr. Teachers Coll., Temple U., 1928-29, Drexel Inst., Phila., Pa., 1934-35. Served as sergt. Med. Corps, U.S.A., 1918-19; head edn. bur. war savings com.; chmn. com. on schs. Liberty Loan com. 2d federal res. dist.; awarded medal, U.S. Treasury Dept. Trustee and sec. Camden Pub. Libraries, 1924-29. Mem. Nat. Edn. Assn., N.J. State Teachers Assn., Camden Teachers Assn., Am. Legion. Phi Delta Kappa, Delta Kappa Epsilon. Ind. Republican. Presbyn. (elder). Mason. Clubs: University Glee of Philadelphia, Camden Lions (v.p. 1931). Home: 106 Harvard Av., Collingswood, N.J.

HOPKINS, James Bryant, asso. prof. Romance langs.; b. Bath, N.Y., July 2, 1875; s. Charles Elias and Catherine (Bryant) H.; A.B., Hamilton Coll., 1899; A.M., Cornell U., 1903; grad. study, Sorbonne, Paris, U. of Freiburg, Germany, 1903-04; student, Cornell U., summer 1915, Columbia U., summer 1916; student, Regia Università Italiana, Stranieri, 1934; m. Blanche Elizabeth Nolan, June 26, 1907; 1 dau., Elizabeth Catherine (wife of Lt. Albert T. Wilson, Jr.). Began as teacher pub. schs., N.Y. state, 1893-95; prof. Greek and French, Huron (S.D.) Coll., and Parsons Coll., Fairfield, Ia., 1899-1902; modern lang. master, Blees Mil. Acad., Macon, Mo., 1905-06; instr. mod. langs., Lafayette Coll., Easton, Pa., 1906-09, asst. prof. Romance langs., 1909-20, asso. prof. since 1920. Served as capt. Mo. N.G., 1905-06. Mem. Modern Lang. Assn., Assn. Teachers of Spanish, Assn. Teachers of French, Am. Assn. Univ. Profs., Phi Beta Kappa, Kappa Sigma. Republican. Presbyn. (elder). Mason. Rotarian. Author: Thoughts in Verse, 1936. Home: 614 Coleman St., Easton, Pa.

HOPKINS, James Stephenson, dentist; b. New Market, Md., Mar. 20, 1884; s. Dr. Howard Hanford and Margaret Mamtz (Downey) H.; grad. Deichmann Coll. Prep. Sch., Baltimore, 1902; student pvt. schs., New Market, Md., 1891-99; D.D.S., U. of Md., Baltimore, 1905; m. Elizabeth Finney Hopkins, Apr. 19, 1910; children—Amanda Wylie, Margaret Downey. In practice of dentistry, Bel Air, Md., since 1905; mem. Md. State Bd. Dental Examiners, 1917-39. Fellow Am. Coll. Dentists; mem. Am. Dental Assn., Md. State Dental Assn. (pres. 1925), Hartford-Cecil Dental Club (pres. 1934), Assn. of Dental Surgeons, Dental Ednl. Council of America (1929-30), Omicron Kappa Upsilon, Xi Psi Phi. Democrat. Episcopalian. Mason. Clubs: Rotary (Bel Air, Md.); Willoughby (Hartford Co., Md.). Address: Bel Air, Md.

HOPKINS, Robert Melvin, pres. Hopkins, Baumgartner & Co., Inc.; b. New Market, Md., Aug. 20, 1904; s. Howard Hanford and Alice Eleanor (Wood) H.; student Frederick (Md.) High Sch., 1919-21; A.B., Johns Hopkins U., Baltimore, Md., 1926; m. Frances Jillard Hurtt, June 20, 1938; 1 son, Robert Melvin. Asst. to statistician, Gillet & Co., bankers, Baltimore, 1926-29, v.p., 1935-38; helped to found Hopkins, Baumgartner & Co., Inc., securities dealers, Baltimore, 1938, and since pres. and dir.; pres. and dir. Peoples Water Service Co., Baltimore, since 1935; v.p. and dir. Master Printers Bldg. Operating Corpn.; dir. Greenway Apartment Co., Norfolk Portsmouth Bridge, Inc. Mem. Beta Theta Pi. Clubs: Gibson Island (Gibson Island, Md.); L'Hirondelle (Ruxton, Md.). Home: Ruxton, Md. Office: 407 Mercantile Trust Bldg., Baltimore, Md.

HOPKINS, Walter Cleary, bridge engr.; b. Newport News, Va., Sept. 5, 1892; s. Thomas Edenfield and Anna A. (Cleary) H.; grad. St. Vincents Acad., Newport News, Va., 1908; student Old Point Comfort Coll., Old Point Comfort, Va., 1908-09; bachelor Engring., N.C. State Coll., Raleigh, N.C., 1913; m. Hazel M. Herold, Sept. 17, 1917; 1 dau., Hazel Margaret. Began as draftsman with James A. Salter, architect, Raleigh, 1913, rodman J. G. White Engring. Corpn., Fla., 1913; draftsman Md. State Roads Commn., Baltimore, 1913-14, Western Md. Ry. Co., Baltimore, 1915-17; bridge draftsman B.&O. R.R. Co., Baltimore, 1917; engr. Newport News Ship Building and Dry Dock Co., Newport News, Va., 1919-20; bridge engr. Md. State Roads Commn. since 1920. Served successively as private, sergeant, master engr., 2d lt. and 1st lt., U.S. Army, Engring. Corps, 1917-19. Mem. Md. Assn. Engrs., Am. Roadbuilders Assn. (com. on elevated highways), Am. Assn. State Highway Officials, Atlantic Deeper Waterways Assn., Nat. River & Harbor Congress, Am. Shore and Beach Preservation Assn., Am. Welding Soc. (bridge com.), Engring. Foundation Welding Research Com., Mil. Order Foreign Wars, Delta Sigma Phi. Democrat. Catholic. Clubs: Engineers (Baltimore); Rolling Road Golf (Catonsville, Md.). Home: 22 Dutton Av., Catonsville, Md. Office: Federal Reserve Bank Bldg., Baltimore, Md.

HOPKINSON, Edward, Jr., banker; b. Philadelphia, Pa., Sept. 29, 1885; s. Edward and Abbie Woodruff (Dale) H.; A.B., U. of Pa., 1907, LL.B., 1910; m. May T. Sullivan, Oct. 9, 1911 (now dec.); children—Edward III, Ruth Ann, Francis, Joan, Martha, James; m. 2d, Edith Sullivan, Mar. 6, 1928; 1 son, John. In law practice at Phila. as mem. Dickson, Beitler & McCouch, 1910-26; partner Drexel & Co.,

bankers, Philadelphia, since 1926; partner J. P. Morgan & Co. since 1929; member board of managers Phila. Saving Fund Soc.; dir. Keystone Watch Case Corpn., Frankford & Southwark Phila. City Passenger Ry. Co., 2d & 3d St. Passenger Ry. Co., Pa. Fire Ins. Co., Riverside Metal Co., Phila. Electric Co., Ins. Co. of North America, Alliance Ins. Co., Indemnity Ins. Co. of N. America, Phila. Fire & Marine Ins. Co., Parkway Co., Baldwin Locomotive Works. Trustee U. of Pa. (chmn. bd. of law), Free Library of Phila., The Wistar Inst. Fund; mem. bd. of mgrs. Pa. Inst. for Instruction of Blind; chmn. eastern Pa. group Investment Bankers Assn. of America. Mem. Am. Philos. Soc., Zeta Psi. Episcopalian. Clubs: Philadelphia, Rittenhouse, Penn Athletic, Philadelphia Cricket, Sunnybrook Golf (Philadelphia); Incogniti (England). Home: 8700 Montgomery Av., Chestnut Hill, Pa. Office: 15th & Walnut Sts., Philadelphia, Pa.

HOPPER, Elmer Francis, paint mfg.; b. Newark, N.J., June 12, 1883; s. John Westervelt and Emma (Farrow) H.; ed. pub. sch. and high sch., Newark, Coleman's Bus. Coll.; m. Sarah Edith Hopkins, Dec. 10, 1909; children—Elmer F., Jr., Addison W. Asso. with Murphy Varnish Co., mfrs. paints, varnishes, lacquers, and enamels, Newark, N.J., since entering employ as office boy, 1901, sales clk., then salesman, 1905-19, sales mgr. since 1919, sales mgr. and dir. since 1924, vice-pres. Emveco Investment Co., Newark, N.J., since 1932. Past pres. Newark Kiwanis Club; pres. Civic Clubs Council, Newark, 1932-33. Past pres. Sales Mgrs. Council of Nat. Paint and Varnish Mfrs. Assn. Republican. Methodist. Mason (Shriner). Home: 29 Woodland Rd., Maplewood, N.J. Office: 224 McWhorter St., Newark, N.J.

HOPPER, Harry Boardman, investment banking; b. Phila., Pa., Nov. 19, 1884; s. Harry Samuel and Harriet M. (Bucknell) H.; B.S., Haverford Coll., 1906; grad. study Pa. State Coll., 1909; m. Dorothy Kerbaugh Goodwin, Apr. 24, 1912; children—Harry Samuel 2d, Elizabeth Anne, Deborah Lavinia Vanderslice. With Wm. G. Hopper & Co., investment bankers, 1908-18, member of firm since 1918, name changed to Hopper, Soliday & Co., 1928, mem. Phila. Stock Exchange, Investment Bankers Assn. of America. Trustee Am. Bapt. Publication Soc., and Bucknell U. Mem., Phi Delta Theta. Republican. Baptist. Clubs: Union League (Philadelphia); Merion Cricket (Haverford). Home: 315 Berkeley Rd., Merion, Pa. Office: 1420 Walnut St., Philadelphia, Pa.

HOPSON, Howard Colwell, lawyer, accountant, pub. utility consultant; b. Ft. Atkinson, Wis., May 8, 1882; s. Edgar Delos and Mary (Colwell) H.; student U. of Wis.; A.B., George Washington U., 1908, A.M., 1910. Admitted to D.C. bar, 1908; authorized to practice before U.S. Supreme Court, 1913; with Interstate Commerce Commn., 1907-08; head of Division Capitalization, Pub. Service Commn. State of N.Y. 1908-15; practiced as lawyer and pub. utility and tax consultant since 1915. Certified pub. accountant, states of N.Y. and Wis. Mem. Am. Inst. Accountants, Com. of 100 (Miami Beach, Fla.), Phi Delta Phi; asso. mem. Bar Assn. of D.C. Clubs: Lotos, Mid-Day, New York Athletic, Wall Street, Scarsdale Golf, Washington Irving Country, Westchester Country, Fort Orange (Albany); Surf (Miami Beach). Office: 61 Broadway, New York, N.Y.; also 26 Journal Sq., Jersey City, N.J.; and Munsey Bldg., Washington, D.C.

HOPWOOD, Josephine Lindsay Reed (Mrs. James Osborne Hopwood), public speaker; b. Phila., Pa.; d. Orville and Markanna (Leeds) Reed; B.S. in biology, U. of Pa., 1905; m. James Osborne Hopwood, June 20, 1907; (M.S., Yale, 1907; children—Dr. Josephine Lindsay, Margaret Scott (Mrs. Murry Culbertson Miller), William Jenks. Taught Americanization in Phila. Night Schools, 1901-05, science, Phila. High School for Girls, 1905-07, nature study, Bucks Hill Falls Nature School and in Friends Schools of Del. Co., 1918-30; speaker for Woman Suffrage Party, 1914-20; mem. Speaker's Bureaus, Rep. Party, 1920-39; associate dir. ednl. film service, Phila. Electric Co. since 1929. Speaker for Liberty Loan Com. during World War. Mem. bd. dirs.

Bedford St. Mission, 1914-26; mem. bd. Woman's Hosp., W. Phila., 1908-20; mem. Upper Darby Sch. Bd. (elective), 1920-32. Mem. Drexel Hill Woman's Club, Primes-Secane Woman's Club (founder), Writer's Club of Del. Co., Soroptimist Club Internat., Kappa Kappa Gamma, Pa. Council Republican Women, Upper Darby Council of Woman's Republican Club of Del. Co. (charter member), Del. Co. chmn. of legislation for State Fed. of Women's Clubs; dir. of the Citizenship School of Del. Co. Fed. Women's Clubs. Recipient of "Soroptimist Award" as outstanding woman of Del. Co., 1936; recipient of the Lions Club award for outstanding public service in Citizenship in Del. Co., 1936. Author of published stories and poems including Del. Co. Hymn; author of "Primer of Politics for Women Voters," 1928; "Primer of Information about These United States Today," 1934; co-author of "School of Politics Primer," 1930. Winner short story award, Del. Co. Fed. Clubs Contest, 1938. Home: Primos, Delaware Co., Pa. Office: 1000 Chestnut St., Philadelphia, Pa.

HORELICK, Samuel, pres. Pa. Transformer Co.; b. Minsk, Russia, Oct. 15, 1886; s. Morris and Bessie (Chirlin) H.; ed. high sch. in Russia; B.S. in E.E., Carnegie Inst. Tech., 1912; m. Esther Fannie Resnick, June 27, 1915; children—Martha Lillian, Arnold Leonard, Evelyn Rae. Came to U.S., 1904, naturalized, 1913. Chief engr. Pittsburgh Transformer Co., 1915-28; pres. and dir. Pa. Transformer Co. since 1929. Mem. Am. Inst. Elec. Engrs., Assn. of Iron and Steel Engrs., Nat. Elec. Mfrs. Assn. (Policy and Commercial Sects. of Transformer Div.), Pa. Electric Assn., Engrs. Soc. of Western Pa. Republican. Hebrew religion. Home: 1110 Cornell St., N.S. Office: 1701 Island Av., N.S., Pittsburgh, Pa.

HORN, Clarence A., biologist; b. McKeansburg, Pa., June 16, 1891; s. George B. and Hattie (Albright) H.; grad. Schuylkill Sem. (prep. sch.), 1912; B.S., Pa. State Coll., 1917; M.A., Columbia U., 1926; C.P.H., New York U., 1924; D.Sc., Albright Coll., 1928; m. Alma E. Barnet, Apr. 14, 1917; 1 dau., Janet H. Teacher in graded sch., Lilesville, N.C., Oct. 1912-May 1913; prof. biology, Tusculom Coll., Greeneville, Tenn., Sept. 1917-Feb. 1918; teacher science Ashland High Sch., Oct. 1919-June 1920; acting pathologist and instr. bacteriology Fountain Springs Hosp., Ashland, Pa., Nov. 1919-June 1920; prof. biology, W.Va. Wesleyan Coll., Buckhannon, W.Va., 1920-23; instr. bacteriology Buckhannon Hosp., 1921-22; instr. physiology, Columbia U., summers, 1921, 22, 23; prof. biology and dir. student health, Albright Coll., since 1924. Served as sergt. in charge of labs. Gen. Hosp. No. 14, Fort Oglethorpe, Ga., and technician Gen. Hosp. No. 36, Detroit, Feb. 1918-July 1919. Fellow and life mem. A.A.A.S., Am. Pub. Health Assn.; mem. Am. Assn. Tuberculosis Assn. for Study Internal Secretions, Long Island Biol. Assn., Am. Mus. Natural History, Pa. Acad. Sciences (v.p.), Pa. Pub. Health Assn., Hist. Soc. of Berks County, Reading Tuberculosis Assn., Reading Social Hygiene Com., Pi Gamma Mu, Kappa Upsilon Pi. Mem. Reformed Ch. Club: Torch (Reading). Chmn. Div. of Health of Social Agencies of Reading and Berks County. Home: 736 N. Third St., Reading, Pa.

HORN, Edgar George, editor; b. Chicago, Ill., Mar. 15, 1898; s. John Nicholas and Katharine Elizabeth (Bechtel) H.; ed. pub. schs. and high sch., Chicago; student Northwestern U., 1917-18; m. Mae E. Kelley, Aug. 10, 1920; children—Virginia Ann, Patricia Jane, Nancy Mae. Began as auditor with Audit Bur. Circulations, Chicago, 1918; gen. mgr. Sharon (Pa.) Daily Telegraph, 1920-24; v.p. and gen. mgr. Montee Pub. Co., pubs. mags. and books, Baltimore, Md., 1924-31, pres. since 1931; dir. Fleet McGinley, Inc. Mem. Racing Writers' Assn. (pres. since 1937). Democrat. Clubs: Baltimore Athletic (Baltimore); Gibson Island (Gibson Island, Md.). Author of several books on horse racing. Editor in chief, Turf and Sport Digest mag. Home: 5217 Springlake Way. Office: 511-13 Oakland Av., Baltimore, Md.

HORN, Robert Chisolm, coll. dean; b. Charleston, S.C., Sept. 12, 1881; s. Edward Traill and

Harriet (Chisolm) H.; grad. high sch., Charleston, 1896; student Coll. of Charleston, 1896-97; A.B., Muhlenberg Coll., 1900, Litt.D., 1922; grad. study Johns Hopkins, 1900-01; A.M., Harvard, 1904, grad. study, 1907-08, 1919; Ph.D., U. of Pa., 1926; m. Zelie Homer Soléliac, Aug. 24, 1911 (died June 29, 1936); children—Zelie Eleanor, Robert Chisolm, Harriet Chisolm, Edward Soléliac; m. 2d, Helen Ruth Richards, of Lebanon, Pa., Oct. 3, 1938. Began teaching in N.C. Mil. Acad., 1901; instr. in Greek Muhlenberg Coll., 1904, prof. Greek lang. and lit. since 1905, asst. to pres., 1921-29, acting pres., 1929-30 and 1936-37, dean since 1930; part-time professor Greek, U. of Pa., 1926-29. Mem. Archæol. Inst. America, Am. Philol. Assn., Classical Assn. of Atlantic States, Lehigh Valley Classical League, Alpha Tau Omega, Omicron Delta Kappa. Democrat. Lutheran. Clubs: Contemporary. Author: Followers of the Way, 1926; Use of the Subjunctive and Optative Moods in Non-Literary Papyri (monograph), 1926. Contbr. to Classical Journal, Art and Archæology, Lutheran Church Review, Classical Philology, The Lutheran, etc. Home: 2533 Washington St., Allentown, Pa.

HORNBOSTEL, Henry, architect; b. Brooklyn, Aug. 15, 1867; s. Edward and Johanna (Cassebeer) H.; Ph.B., Columbia, 1891, hon. M.A., 1912; Ecole des Beaux Arts, Paris, 4 yrs.; m. Martha Armitage, 1899; children—Lloyd, Caleb; m. 2d, Mabelle Sylvester Weston, 1932. Mem. firm of Palmer & Hornbostel; architects of New York City bridges, Hell Gate bridge, Carnegie Tech. Sch. (Pittsburgh), Albany Edn. Bldg., city halls, Pittsburgh, Wilmington, Del., Oakland, Calif., etc. Winner, 1925, design for $600,000 mausoleum, Marion, O., in memory of President Harding. Prof. of architecture, 1897-1900, lecturer, 1900-03, Columbia; now prof. architecture, Carnegie Tech. Schs. Dir. Allegheny County Parks and Airport; mem. Pa. State Parks Commn., Pa. State Planning Bd. Fellow A.I.A.; mem. Soc. Beaux Arts Architects (pres. 1915-16), League of Am. Architects, Am. Legion (comdr. Harwinton, Conn., Post). Served as maj., U.S.A.; gas officer 26th Div., Argonne, France. Club: University. Mem. Conn. State Grange. Home: Schenley Apts., Pittsburgh, Pa.; and The Elms, Harwinton, Conn. Office: 233 Oliver Av., Pittsburgh, Pa.

HORNE, Herman Harrell, university prof.; b. Clayton, N.C., Nov. 22, 1874; s. Hardee and Ida Caroline (Harrell) H.; A.B., A.M., U. of N.C., 1895; A.M., Harvard University, 1897, Ph.D., 1899; studied U. of Berlin, 1906-07; LL.D., Wake Forest (N.C.) Coll., 1924, Muhlenberg College, Allentown, Pa., 1927, University of North Carolina, 1934; m. Alice Elizabeth Herbert Worthington, Aug. 29, 1901; children—Julia Carolyn, Betsy Worthington, William Henry, Ida Battle. Instr. modern langs., U. of N.C., 1894-96; instr. philosophy, 1899-1900, asst. prof. philosophy and pedagogy, 1900-05, prof. philosophy, 1905-09, Dartmouth Coll.; prof. history of edn. and history of philosophy, New York U., since 1909. Lecturer in Harvard Summer Sch. of Theology, 1903, in Martha's Vineyard Summer Inst., 1902-04, U. of N.C. Summer Sch., 1903, Columbia U. Summer Session, 1905, Harvard Summer Sch., 1907, U. of Calif. Summer Session, 1909, N.Y.U., summers 1911-13, 1922—, Summer Sch. of the South, Knoxville, Tenn., 1914, Auburn Summer Schs., 1915-17, Southern Coll. of Y.M.C.A., summers, 1920, 21; Norton lecturer Southern Bapt. Theol. Sem., 1923; Carew lecturer, Hartford Theol. Foundation, 1935; James Sprunt lecturer, Union Theol. Sem., 1937; mem. Religious Edn. Assn., Am. Philos. Assn., Am. Acad. Polit. and Social Science, N.C. Historical Society, Soc. Coll. Teachers Edn., Phi Beta Kappa, Phi Delta Kappa; fellow A.A.A.S. Presbyn. Clubs: Authors (New York), Scholia. Author: The Philosophy of Education, 1904, 27; The Psychological Principles of Education, 1906; Idealism in Education, 1910; Free Will and Human Responsibility, 1912; Leadership of Bible Study Groups, 1912; Story-Telling, Questioning, and Studying, 1916; The Teacher as Artist, 1917; Jesus—Our Standard, 1918; Modern Problems as Jesus Saw Them, 1918; Jesus—The Master Teacher, 1920; Christ in Man-Making, 1925; Jesus as a Philosopher, 1927; This New Education, 1931; The Essentials of Leadership, 1931; John Dewey's Philosophy (pamphlet), 1931; The Democratic Philosophy of Education, 1932; Syllabus in The Philosophy of Education, 1934; Quintilian on Edn. (with Catherine Ruth Smith), 1936; The Philosophy of Christian Education, 1937; Introduction to Modern Education (with others), 1937; Tomorrow in the Making (with others), 1939. Editor: Simple Southern Songs, 1916; Songs of Sentiment (by Ida Caroline Horne), 1917; Romantic Rambles, 1925. Contbr. to Monroe's Cyclo. of Education and Nelson's Ency. of Sunday Schools. Home: Leonia, N.J.

HORNE, S. Hamill, physician; b. Indianapolis, Ind., June 25, 1876; s. Robert Gray and Martha Sarah (Hamill) H.; M.D., Jefferson Med. Coll., 1901; m. Mrs. Caroline S. Reed, Oct. 15, 1909; m. 2d, Louise E. Williams, Oct. 20, 1928; 1 son, S. Hamill. Engaged in practice of medicine at Phila. continuously since 1901. Served as capt. Med. Corps, U.S.A. attached to aviation service, during World War. Mem. Phila. Co. Med. Soc., Phi Alpha Sigma, S.R., Mil. Order Fgn. Wars. Republican. Episcopalian. Clubs: Racquet, Gulph Mills Golf. Home: Morris Av., Bryn Mawr, Pa. Office: N.E. Cor. 16th and Spruce Sts., Philadelphia, Pa.

HORNER, Charles Francis, pres. National Aeronautic Assn.; b. at Menomonee, Wisconsin, Aug. 1, 1878; s. William and Martha A. (Barron) H.; student Univ. of Neb., 1898-99; studied law; honorary Mus.D., Simmons Univ., 1932; m. Jessie Ridgway, Aug., 1904. Teacher and prin. pub. schs., 1894-97 and 1900; owner and mgr. cattle ranch, 1900-03; entered lyceum and Chautauqua work, Lincoln, Neb., 1906; founder and pres. Redpath-Horner Chautauquas, and Redpath-Horner Lyceum Bur.; pres. various country banks, Kan. and Colo., 1916-28; owner and editor Olathe (Kan.) Register, 1921-27; owner Central Lyceum Bur.; pres. Horner-Witte Concert Bur.; founder, 1914, Horner Inst. Fine Arts, now Kansas City Conservatory. Founded Horner Jr. Coll., 1929, transferred it to Kansas City U., 1933. Dir. Bur. of Pub. Relations of NRA, 1933; spl. asst. to adminstr. NRA, to Feb. 1, 1935; exec. asst. to pres. Nat. Aeronautic Assn., 1935, pres. since 1936. Member War Loan Com. and dir. Speakers' Bur. U.S. Treasury, World War; also mem. exec. com. Speakers' Bur. Nat. Red Cross and Mil. Entertainment Council of War Dept. Com. on Training Camp Activities; mem. advisory com. Speakers' Div. Com. on Pub. Information; chief of Speakers' Bur. Dem. Nat. Campaign for Woodrow Wilson, 1912, 16. Episcopalian. Mason. Clubs: Mission Hills Country (Kansas City); Nat. Press (Washington, D.C.). Author: The Speaker and the Audience; The Life of James Redpath. Editor of Nat. Aeronautics. Address: Kansas City, Mo.; and 108 Brookside Drive, Kenwood, Chevy Chase, Md. Address: National Aeronautic Association, Dupont Circle, Washington, D.C.

HORNER, Meyers Berkley, supt. pub. schs.; b. Meyersdale, Pa., Feb. 6, 1893; s. Milton C. and Magdalene H.; A.B., Juniata Coll., 1913; A.M., U. of Pittsburgh, 1926, Ph.D., same, 1938; (hon.) D.Sc. in Edn., Washington and Jefferson Coll., 1938; m. Lucille Ada Gump, Oct. 12, 1918; children—Hilda Louise, Mary Evelyn. Instr. in various colls. and high sch., 1913-20; prin. high sch., Coraopolis, Pa., 1920-26; prin. high sch., Washington, Pa., 1926-30, supt. schs. since 1930. Served as pvt. A.S., U.S.A., 1917-18, 1st lt. 1918-19. Dir. Community Chest, Washington Hosp., Boy Scouts. Mem. Nat. Edn. Assn., Phi Delta Kappa, Phi Sigma Pi. Republican. Mem. M.E. Ch. Mason. Club: Kiwanis. Home: 239 Allison Av. Office: 44 W. Wheeling St., Washington, Pa.

HORNER, Vaughan, manufacturer; b. Pittsburgh, Pa., May 27, 1892; s. William Stewart and Anne (Vaughan) H.; student Kiskiminetas Sch., Saltsburg, Pa., 1905-10, Haverford (Pa.) Sch., 1910-11; Litt.B., Princeton U., 1915; m. Marion Russell Sipe, June 1, 1920; children—William Stewart, II, Robert Vaughan. Sales apprentice, operating, traffic and sales depts. Am. Rolling Mill Co., Middletown, O., 1915-17; asst. to gen. mgr., later vice-pres. and gen. mgr. Pittsburgh Shovel Co., Pittsburgh, Pa., 1919-31; dir. of purchases, asst. to pres., treas. and dir. Ames, Baldwin, Wyoming Co., shovels, forks, rakes, hoes, since 1931. Served in Norton-Harjes Vol. Ambulance Service with French Army, 1917; Am. Ambulance Service with French Army, 1917-19. Decorated Croix de Guerre. Republican. Methodist. Mason. Clubs: Fox Chapel Golf (Pittsburgh); Parkersburg (W.Va.) Country. Home: 111 13th St. Office: Ames, Baldwin, Wyoming Co., Parkersburg, W.Va.

HORNER, Walter Woodward, teacher; b. Uniontown, Pa., Mar. 7, 1894; s. John Parker and Lida (Woodward) H.; grad. Fredericktown (Pa.) High Sch., 1914; grad. Normal Sch., California, Pa., 1917; B.S., Waynesburg (Pa.) Coll., 1924; A.M., Teachers Coll., Columbia, 1934; m. Mary Edna Rupert, June 26, 1919; children—Walter Rupert, John Robert, Mary Louise. Teacher of rural school near East Millsboro, Pa., 1914-16; teaching prin., New Kensington, Pa., 1917-18; teaching prin. of rural school near Monessen, Pa., 1919-20; teacher of mathematics, Redstone High Sch., Republic, Pa., 1924-25; teacher of mathematics Donora (Pa.) High Sch., 1925-30, prin., 1930-37; teacher of mathematics High Sch., Pittsburgh, since 1937. Served in U.S. Army, 9 months with A.E.F. in France, 1918-19. Mem. Pa. State Edn. Assn., Pittsburgh Teachers Assn., Delta Sigma Phi. Republican. Methodist. Mason. Club: Unity (Pittsburgh). Home: 509 Highland Place, Bellevue Branch, Pittsburgh, Pa.

HORNER, William Stewart, steel products mfg.; b. West Newton, Pa., Apr. 1, 1868; s. Gershon Blackburn and Lydia (Lawver) H.; ed. pub. schs. Pa.; m. Anne Mary Vaughan, Aug. 1890 (dec.); children—Vaughan, Lucille (Mrs. Clarence Bishop Steffey); m. 2d, Mary E. McCoy, Nov. 1920. Telegraph operator, B.&O. R.R., 1880; telegrapher and stenographer H. E. Collins & Co., later with O. M. Hartzell & Co., iron and steel brokers, Pittsburgh, 1889-99; became part owner Curtis Sheet Steel & Corrugating Co., Zanesville, O., 1902; became pres. Pittsburgh Shovel Works, 1902, merged with Ames, Baldwin, Wyoming Co. of which is now dir.; vice-pres. Am. Rolling Mill Co., also mem. exec. com. Trustee Allegheny Coll.; dir. Pittsburgh Y.M.C.A., Allegheny Gen. Hosp., Allegheny Co. Sabbath Sch. Assn. Republican. Methodist (trustee of Christ Ch.). Mason (K.T.). Clubs: Duquesne, Iron City Fishing (pres.), Oakmont Country. Home: 1028 N. Negley Av. Office: 1632 Oliver Bldg., Pittsburgh, Pa.

HORNEY, William R(aymond), lawyer; b. Queen Anne's Co., Md., May 11, 1898; s. Marion and Florence May (Melvin) H.; student St. John's Coll., Annapolis, Md., 1918-19; LL.B., U. of Md. Law Sch., 1923; unmarried. Admitted to Md. bar, 1923 and since engaged in gen. practice of law as individual at Centreville; served as state's atty. Queen Anne's Co., Md., 1927-35; U.S. Commr., 1936-37; dir. Queen Anne's Record-Observer Pub. Co. since 1936. Served as pvt. inf., U.S. Army, 1918. Mem. Phi Kappa Sigma. Democrat. Episcopalian. Club: Rotary of Centreville. Home: S. Commerce St. Office: Lawyers Row, Centreville, Md.

HORNSBY, Rogers; mgr. Baltimore Orioles baseball team. Address: Oriole Park, Greenmount Av. and 29th St., Baltimore, Md.

HORROW, Benjamin, lawyer; b. Woodbine, N.J., Dec. 21, 1906; s. David and Bessie H.; B.S. in Econ., Central High Sch., Phila., Pa., 1924; B.S. in Econ., U. of Pa., 1928, LL.B., 1931; unmarried. Admitted to Pa. and Phila. bars, 1932, and since practiced independently in Phila. Candidate Pa. Gen. Assembly, 1938. Founder Phila. Junior Bar Assn., 1934, pres., 1935; mem. Am. Bar Assn., Pa. State Bar Assn., Phila. Bar Assn., Brandeis Lawyers Soc., McKean Law Club (pres., 1931), B'nai B'rith, Tau Epsilon Rho, Sigma Alpha Rho (pres., 1929). Republican. Home: 4810 Conshohocken Av. Office: 2005 North American Bldg., Philadelphia, Pa.

HORSCH, William Grenville, research chemist; b. Newburyport, Mass., Apr. 28, 1890; s. William M. and Antoinette J. (Comley) H.; B.S., Mass. Inst. Tech., 1913; Ph.D., U. of Calif., 1917; m. Helen Gertrude Philbrick, Dec. 29, 1917; children—Helen P., Margaret. Engaged as electrochemist, U.S. Bur. Mines, 1918; research asso., Research Lab. of Applied Chemistry, Mass. Inst. Tech., 1919-22; acting mgr. Guggenheim Bros. Labs., New York, N.Y., 1922-24; chief chemist Vulcan Detinning Co., Pittsburgh, Pa., 1924-27; research chemist, Vacuum Oil Co., now Research & Development Div., Gen. Labs., Socony-Vacuum Oil Co., Inc., Paulsboro, N.J., since 1927. Served as 1st lt. C.W.S., U.S.A., 1918-19. Mem. A.A.A.S., Am. Chem. Soc., Am. Inst. Elec. Engrs., Electrochem. Soc., Sigma Xi, Alpha Chi Sigma. Indep. Republican. Unitarian. Club: Technology of Philadelphia. Awarded two patents. Contbr. articles in chem. and phys. fields. Home: 224 Briar Hill Lane, Woodbury. Office: General Laboratories, Paulsboro, N.J.

HORSEY, Harold Wolfe, banker; b. Laurel, Del., Nov. 4, 1893; s. Elmer Pancoast and Minnie (Wolfe) H.; student Dover (Del.) High Sch., 1909-13; B.S., U. of Del., Newark, Del., 1917; m. Phyllis Ridgely, Apr. 22, 1922; children—Philippa Lloyd, Henry Ridgely. Asst. examiner, Del. State Banking Dept., 1919-22; security salesman Laird & Co., Wilmington, Del., 1922-23; Del. State Bank Commr., 1923-36; exec. v.p. Union Nat. Bank, Wilmington, Del., since 1936. Trustee U. of Del., Newark, Del. Mem. Sigma Nu. Republican. Clubs: Wilmington Country, University (Wilmington, Del.). Home: Dover, Del. Office: Union Nat. Bank, Wilmington, Del.

HORTON, Clayton Reimer; b. Johnsonville, Pa., Sept. 9, 1905; s. William A. and Idella (Reimer) H.; grad. Bangor (Pa.) High Sch., 1922; student U. of Pa., 1923-24; B.S., Lafayette Coll., Easton, Pa., 1926, grad. student in chemistry, 1926-27; m. Helen I. Messinger, June 16, 1928; 1 dau., Sandra Irene. Began as partner with father in Horton Funeral Service (established by grandfather, 1870), Apr. 1927; vice-pres. and chmn. investment com. The Portland (Pa.) Nat. Bank; dir. Slate Belt Bldg. & Loan Assn. of Bangor, Pa. Served as mem. organization com. for Portland Nat. Bank in failure, 1931; mem. reorganization com. First Nat. Bank of Bangor, which closed 1933. Mem. Portland Borough Council since 1934. Mem. Portland Borough Rep. Com., 1934-38; mem. exec. com. Northampton Co. Rep. Com. since 1938. Mem. Northampton County Council State Chamber of Commerce. Mem. Eastern Pa. Funeral Dirs. Assn., Phi Kappa Tau. Lutheran. Mason (32°), Elk. Club: Kiwanis of Bangor (pres. 1934). Home: Delaware Av., Portland, Pa. Office: Bangor, R.D., Johnsonville, Pa.

HOSFORD, Charles Franklin, Jr., lawyer, coal exec.; b. Bloomington, Ill., Apr. 26, 1887; s. Charles Franklin and Mary Emma (Reiber) H.; A.B., Princeton, 1908; LL.B., Harvard, 1911; m. Jean Christie, June 20, 1916; children—Charles Franklin, Robert Christie, Jean Christie. Admitted to Pa. bar, 1911, and practiced at Butler, 1911-23; pres. Butler Consol. Coal Co., 1923-31; dir. Coal Control Assn. of Western Pa., 1933-34; became mem. Coal Code Authority, Western Pa., 1933, and mgr., 1934; served about 2 years in Washington, D.C., on Bituminous Coal Commn., resigning Nov. 3, 1938. Democrat. Lutheran. Home: Aspinwall, Pa.*

HOSKING, Herbert Tage, Jr., magazine editor; b. Phila., Pa., Dec. 24, 1905; s. Herbert Tage and Sarah Ann (Shute) H.; grad. Staunton (Va.) Mil. Acad., 1923, student Lehigh U., Bethlehem, Pa., 1923-24, Swarthmore (Pa.) Coll., 1924-28; m. Nancy Cornell Keffer, Sept. 4, 1929; 1 dau., Joan Arlington. Began as editorial apprentice, Chilton Co., Phila., pubs., 1928-32, mng. editor Journal of the Society of Automotive Engineers, New York, 1933-35, editor Automotive Industries, Phila., since 1935. Mem. Soc. of Automotive Engrs., Inc. (sec., Phila.; del. at dedication of Franklin Inst.), Am. Inst. of Graphic Arts (hon. v.p., 1936-38; mem. com. on traveling exhibitions), Phila. Graphic Arts Forum (founder, sec.), Art Alliance, Phila., Gutenberg Gesellschaft, Mainz, Germany. Protestant Episcopal. Contbr. arts. to professional jours. in Europe and America. Home: 115 Walsh Rd., Lansdowne, Pa. Office: 5601 Chestnut St., Philadelphia, Pa.

HOTCHKISS, Charles Harris Birchard, engr., editor; b. Wellsboro, Pa., Sept. 23, 1896; s. Arthur Harris and Ella (Hastings) H.; ed. O. Northern U., 1913-14; B.S., Pa. State Coll., 1918, M.E., same, 1924; m. Franchon Cummings, June 9, 1923. Instr. mech. engring., Pa. State Coll., 1920-23, asst. prof., 1923-25; asst. prof. heating and ventilating, Purdue U., 1925-30; editor Heating & Ventilating Magazine, N.Y. City since 1930. Served as pvt. trench mortar batln., U.S.A., 1918-19, with A.E.F. Mem. Ind. Coal Commn., 1928. Mem. Nat. Dist. Heating Assn., Am. Soc. Mech. Engrs., Am. Soc. Heating & Ventilating Engrs., Am. Soc. Refrigerating Engrs., Alpha Chi Rho, Phi Kappa Phi, Tau Beta Pi. Republican. Presbyn. Mason. Co-author (with Clifford Strock), Degree-Day Handbook, 1937; (with Clifford Strock) Air Conditioning Engineers Atlas, 1939. Home: 151 Sheridan Av., Hohokus, N.J. Office: 148 Lafayette St., New York, N.Y.

HOTELLING, Harold, mathematics and economics; b. Fulda, Minn., Sept. 29, 1895; s. Clair Alberta and Lucy Amelia (Rawson) H.; A.B., U. of Wash., 1919, M.S., 1921; student U. of Chicago, summer 1920; Ph. D., Princeton, 1924; m. Floy Tracy, Dec. 27, 1920 (died Oct. 2, 1932); children—Eric, Muriel; m. 2d, Susanna Porter Edmondson, June 14, 1934; 2 sons, George Alfred, William Edmondson. With weekly newspapers in State of Wash., 1915-16 and 1919; taught mathematics, Univ. of Washington, 1920-21, Princeton University, 1922-24; math. consultant Food Research Inst., Stanford, 1924-27; asso. prof. mathematics, Stanford, 1927-31; prof. economics, Columbia, since 1931. Fellow Econometric Soc., Inst. of Math. Statisticians, Royal Economic Soc.; mem. Am. Math. Soc., Am. Statis. Assn., Am. Assn. of Univ. Profs., Phi Beta Kappa, Sigma Xi; pres. Econometric Soc., 1936-37. Club: Columbia University Faculty. Asso. editor Annals of Mathematical Statistics, 1930, Econometrica, 1933. Contbr. to psychol., med. statis., math., econ., and other scientific publs. Home: 236 Morris Av., Mountain Lakes, N.J.

HOTSON, Leslie, author, teacher; b. Ontario, Can., Aug. 16, 1897; s. John H. and Lillie (Swayze) H.; A.B., Harvard, 1921, A.M., 1922, Ph.D., 1923; m. Mary May Peabody, Dec. 25, 1919. Dexter traveling scholar, summers 1922, 25; Sheldon traveling fellow, 1923-24; instr. in English, Harvard, 1924-25; asst. in English, Yale, 1925-26, Sterling senior research fellow, 1926-27; asso. prof. English, New York U., 1927-29; J. S. Guggenheim memorial fellow, 1929-31; prof. English, Haverford Coll., since 1931. Fellow Royal Soc. of Lit.; hon. mem. Elizabethan Club (Yale); mem. Phi Beta Kappa. Club: Athenæum (London). Author: The Death of Christopher Marlowe, 1925; The Commonwealth and Restoration Stage, 1928; Shelley's Lost Letters to Harriet, 1930; Shakespeare versus Shallow, 1931; I, William Shakespeare, 1937. Contbr. to Atlantic Monthly, London Times, etc. Home: 3 College Circle, Haverford, Pa.

HOUCK, Maurice E(lmer), supt. of schs.; b. Nescopeck R. D., Pa., May 22, 1886; s. Clinton (Rhodes) and Catherine (Remensnyder) H.; student Bloomsburg (Pa.) State Teachers Coll., 1907-10; A.B., U. of Mich., 1913; M.A., Pa. State Coll., 1929; m. Margaret Irene Meixell, June 17, 1914; children—Kenneth, William, Francis. With Public Schools of Berwick, Pa., since 1913, as teacher, 1913-16, prin., High Sch., 1916-20, supt. of schools since 1920. Mem. Y.M.C.A. (mem. bd. of dirs.), Patriotic Order of Sons of America. Republican. Methodist, (mem. bd. of dirs., Meth. Ch., Berwick, Pa.). Mason (32°). Club: Acacia (Berwick, Pa.). Home: 606 W. Front St. Office: High Sch., Berwick, Pa.

HOUCK, Samuel Clyde, banker, trust officer; b. Boyertown, Pa., Nov. 29, 1886; s. John G. and Phoebe (Hillegas) H.; ed. Boyertown pub. schs.; m. Mary E. Angstadt, June 8, 1916; children—Daniel A., John A., Ruth A. and Naomi A. (twins), Grace A., Mary A., Samuel A. and Esther A. (twins). Clerk Nat. Bank of Boyertown, 1907-21, teller, 1921-22, asst. cashier, 1922-23, cashier and sec. of bd. since 1923, sec. since 1930, trust officer since 1931. Mem. com. Y.M.C.A. Democrat. Treas. Reformed Ch. of the Good Shepherd. Home: 303 S. Reading Av. Office: corner Philadelphia and Reading Avs., Boyertown, Pa.

HOUGH, Lynn Harold, educator, clergyman; b. Cadiz, O., Sept. 10, 1877; s. Franklin M. and Eunice R. (Giles) H.; A.B., Scio College, Ohio, 1898; B.D., Drew Theol. Sem., 1905; postgrad. work, New York U.; D.D., Mt. Union-Scio Coll., 1912, D.D., Garrett Bibl. Inst., 1918; Th.D., Drew Theol. Sem., 1919; Litt.D., Allegheny Coll., 1922; LL.D., Albion Coll., 1923, Univ. of Detroit, 1928; L.H.D. University of Vt., 1932; D.D., Wesleyan University, Conn., 1924; LL.D., University of Pittsburgh, 1935; m. Blanche Horton, widow of the Rev. Stephen van R. Trowbridge, Oct. 13, 1936. Entered ministry of Methodist Episcopal Church, 1898; pastor Arcola, N.J., 1898-1904, 1st Church, Cranford, N.J., 1904-06, King's Park, N.Y., 1906-07, 3d Ch., L.I. City, N.Y., 1907-09, Summerfield Ch., Brooklyn, 1900-12, Mt. Vernon Pl. Ch., Baltimore, 1912-14; prof. hist. theology, Garrett Bibl. Inst., 1914-19; pres. Northwestern U., 1919-20; pastor Central M.E. Ch., Detroit, Mich., 1920-28, American Presbyn. Ch., Montreal, 1928-30; prof. of homiletics and christian criticism of life, Drew Theol. Sem., Drew Univ., since 1930, dean since 1934. Pres. Detroit Council Chs., 1926-28; v.p. Religious Edn. Assn., 1926-28; mem. Soc. Bibl. Lit. and Exegesis, Chicago Soc. Bibl. Research, Soc. Midland Authors; president Religious Education Council of Canada, 1929-30. Scottish Rite Mason (33°, Knight Templar). Clubs: Cliff Dwellers (Chicago); Sigma Chi, Century (N.Y. City); National Liberal, Authors' (London). Author: Athanasius, the Hero, 1906; The Lure of Books, 1911; The Theology of a Preacher, 1912; The Men of the Gospels, 1913; The Quest for Wonder, 1915; In the Valley of Decision, 1916; The Man of Power, 1916; The Little Old Lady, 1917; Living Book in a Living Age, 1918; The Significance of the Protestant Reformation, 1918; The Clean Sword, 1918; The Productive Beliefs (Cole lectures at Vanderbilt U.), 1919; Flying Over London, 1919; The Eyes of Faith, 1920; The Opinions of John Clearfield, 1921; Life and History, 1922; The Strategy of the Devotional Life, 1922; The Inevitable Book, 1922; A Little Book of Sermons, 1922; Twelve Merry Fishermen, 1923; Synthetic Christianity (Merrick lectures, Ohio Wesleyan U.), 1923; The Imperial Voice, 1924; The Lion in His Den, 1925; Evangelical Humanism (Fernley lecture, at Lincoln, Eng.), 1925; Adventures in the Minds of Men, 1927; Imperishable Dreams, 1929; The Artist and the Critic (Samuel Harris lectures, Bangor Theol. Sem.), 1930; Personality and Science (Ayer lectures, Colgate-Rochester Div. Sch.), 1930; The University of Experience, 1932; Vital Control (first vol. of Forest Essays), 1934; The Church and Civilization, 1934; The Great Evangel (Sam P. Jones Lectures on Evangelism), Emory University, Georgia, 1935; The Civilized Mind (2d vol. Forest Essays), 1937; Free Men (3d vol. Forest Essays), 1939. Mem. editorial bd. of Religion in Life, and of editorial com. of Intercollegian and Far Horizons. Lecturer on theol., lit. and philos. topics; sent to Great Britain to speak on the moral and spiritual aims of the war, by the Lindgren foundation of Northwestern U., 1918. Editor and contbr. to "Whither Christianity," 1929. Home: Drew Forest, Madison, N.J.

HOUGHTEN, Ferry Charles, dir. research lab.; b. Troy, Mich., Feb. 13, 1888; s. George and Pauline (Kaiser) H.; ed. Olivet (Mich.) Coll.; M.Sc., U. of Washington, 1915; m. Mattie Lincoln, July 12, 1916; children—Robert Lincoln, Richard Allen, Ruth Marian, James Wallace. Teaching fellow, U. of Wash., 1913-15; science teacher Ellensburg (Wash.) High Sch., 1915-16, Hoquiam High Sch., 1916-18; research engr. Am. Soc. Heating and Ventilating Engrs., 1920-24, nat. sec., 1924-26, dir. research lab., Pittsburgh, since 1926; lecturer U. of Pittsburgh. Pres. Tunnel Federal Savings & Loan Assn. V.p. Restland Mausoleum Assn.; dir. Restland Memorial Park, Inc. Mem. Com. on Heat Transmission, Nat. Research Council. Presbyterian.

HOUGHTON, Clinton Osborne; prof. biology, U. of Del. Address: University of Delaware, Newark, Del.

HOUGHTON, Frederick Percival, church official; s. William Lanyon and Annie Louise (Micklewright) H.; Lehigh U., 1911-12; grad. Gen. Theol. Sem., 1916; D.D., Pennsylvania Military College, 1937; m. Catherine Edwards, Nov. 22, 1924; children—Frederick Percival, John Robert. Deacon and priest P.E. Ch., 1916; curate St. Luke's Ch., Scranton, Pa., 1916-17; rector Ch. of the Epiphany, Glenburn, Pa., 1919-27, St. John's Ch., Lancaster, 1927-31; gen. sec. Nat. Council P.E. Ch., 1931-37; exec. sec. Diocese of Pa. since 1937. Served as chaplain 103d Engrs., 28th Div., U.S. Army; participated in Chateau Thierry defensive, Champagne-Marne defensive, Aisne-Marne offensive, Fismes sector, Oise-Aisne offensive, Meuse-Argonne offensive, Thiacourt sector; now lt. col.-chaplain Reserve Corps, U.S.A.; senior chaplain Pa. Nat. Guard. Mem. Delta Upsilon. Republican. Kiwanian. Home: 315 Bala Av., Bala-Cynwyd, Pa. Office: 202 S. 19th St., Philadelphia, Pa.*

HOUGHTON, William Morris, editor; b. of Am. parents, Lucerne, Switzerland, Oct. 4, 1882; s. William Addison and Charlotte Johnson (Morris) H.; grad. Phillips Acad., Andover, Mass., 1899; student Harvard, 1899-1900, Yale, 1900-01; A.B., Bowdoin, 1903; student in economics, Harvard, 1903-05, A.M., 1904; m. Hess Pringle, Sept. 1, 1909 (died July 2, 1930); children—Hess Pringle, Sarah Bryan (dec.), William Pringle. Reporter, feature writer and editorial writer, New York Tribune, 1906-17; publicity work, 1917-19, with Liberty Loan Com., New York Dist., Emergency Fleet Corpn., and U.S. Employment Service; adv. writer with William Green, Inc., 1919-21; editor Leslie's Weekly, 1921-22, asso. editor of Judge and sec. Leslie-Judge Co. 1922-27; editorial writer New York Herald Tribune, 1927-33; on editorial staff Literary Digest, 1933-35; editorial writer N.Y. Herald Tribune since 1935. Mem. Troop D, N.J. Cavalry, Mexican border, summer 1916. Mem. Psi Upsilon, Phi Beta Kappa. Episcopalian. Clubs: Players, Dutch Treat (New York). Home: 996 Leland Av., Plainfield, N.J. Office: 230 W. 41st St., New York, N.Y.

HOUSE, Edward John, pres. Appalacha Coal Co.; b. Pittsburgh, Pa., May 8, 1879; s. Edward and Ruth (Widney) H.; student Shady Side Acad., Pittsburgh, Pa., 1893-96, Andover (Mass.) Acad., 1896-97; B.S., Yale, 1900; m. Helen Horne, Dec. 6, 1910 (died Mar. 10, 1932); children—Edward John, William Pendleton, Helen. Pres. Appalacha Coal Co. since 1923, treas. and dir. Citizens Traction Co. and subsidiary cos.; sec. Union Fidelity Fire Ins. Co.; dir. Fidelity Trust Co. Author: A Hunter's Camp Fires, 1909. Home: 1415 Beechwood Boul. Office: Fidelity Trust Bldg., 341 4th Av., Pittsburgh, Pa.

HOUSER, Karl Musser, physician; b. Pennsylvania Furnace, Pa., Sept. 30, 1893; s. Luther Murray and Anna Catherine (Musser) H.; student Tyrone (Pa.) High Sch., 1908-09, Franklin and Marshall Acad., 1909-11; Ph.B., Franklin and Marshall Coll., 1915, hon. D.Sc., 1937; M.D., U. of Pa., 1921; m. Grace Ellen Shipley, Sept. 22, 1924; children—Karl Musser, Luther Murray, 2d. Teacher public schools, Clifton, Ariz., 1915-16; teacher, Mercersburg (Pa.) Acad., 1916-17; physician, Phila., since 1925; prof. of otolaryngology, University of Pennsylvania Med. Sch. Served in S.A.T.C., 1917-19. Fellow Am. Coll. Surgeons; mem. Am. Laryngol. Assn., Am. Otol. Soc., Am. Acad. Otolaryngology, Coll. of Physicians of Phila., A.M.A., Phi Alpha Sigma, Sigma Xi, Alpha Omega Alpha. Presbyterian. Club: Philadelphia Country. Home: 836 Bryn Mawr Av., Narbeth, Pa. Office: 2010 Spruce St., Philadelphia, Pa.

HOUSMAN, William F., lawyer; b. Steelton, Pa., Jan. 3, 1884; s. Charles and Kathryn (Houck) H.; student Highspire (Pa.) Pub. Schs., 1890-98; grad. Steelton (Pa.) Pub. Schs., 1904; Ph.B., Dickinson Coll., Pa., 1909, A.M., 1911, LL.B., Law Sch., 1911; m. Rose Loeb Fauble, Oct. 24, 1914; children—Jane Fauble, Kathryn Ann; m. 2d, Helen Sherman Potteiger, Mar. 15, 1923. Admitted to Dauphin Co. Pa. bar, 1912, and since in practice at Steelton; dir. and solicitor Steelton Bank & Trust Co. Mem. Steelton, Pa., Sch. Bd., 1918-23; dir. Steelton Welfare Assn., 1921-27. Mem. Phi Delta Theta, Delta Chi. Republican. Lutheran. Mason. Club: Carlisle Country (Carlisle, Pa.). Home: 415 Pine St. Office: Trust Co. Bldg., Steelton, Pa.

HOUSTON, G. Porter; v.p. and actuary U.S. Fidelity & Guaranty Co. Home: 1834 Linden Av. Office: U.S. Fidelity & Guaranty Bldg., Baltimore, Md.

HOUSTON, James Garfield, lawyer; b. Pittsburgh, Pa., Sept. 22, 1881; s. James Wilson and Sarah (McCutcheon) H.; A.B., U. of Pittsburgh, 1903, LL.B., 1906, M.L., 1918; m. Grace Preston, June 30, 1926. Admitted to Pa. bar, 1906; in gen. practice of law, 1906-36; mem. law firm Blaxter, O'Neill & Houston since 1936; asso. prof. law, U. of Pittsburgh (part time) since 1906. Served as capt., later major, O.R.C., 1917-19. Mem. Am. Bar Assn., Pa. Bar Assn., Allegheny County Bar Assn., Phi Delta Theta, Phi Delta Phi. Republican. Presbyn. Clubs: Duquesne, Fox Chapel Golf (Pittsburgh). Home: 116 Bayard Pl. Office: 1307 Oliver Bldg., Pittsburgh, Pa.

HOUSTON, Samuel Frederic; b. Germantown, Phila., Aug. 30, 1866; s. Henry Howard and Sallie S. (Bonnell) H.; Ph.B., U. of Pa., 1887; m. Edith A. Corlies, Nov. 9, 1887 (died 1895); m. 2d, Mrs. Charlotte Harding Shepherd Brown, Apr. 8, 1902. Pres. Real Estate Trust Co. of Phila.; v.p. Pa. Sugar Co.; dir. Corn Exchange Nat. Bank. Trustee U. of Pa. Mem. Am. Acad. Polit. and Social Science, Am. Econ. Assn., Geog. Soc. Phila. Episcopalian; mem. standing com. Diocese Pa. and formerly of Nat. Council P.E. Ch. President St. Andrews Society of Philadelphia. Chevalier Legion of Honor, 1927. Clubs: Rittenhouse, University, Church, St. Anthony, Union League, Corinthian Yacht, New York Yacht. Home: Chestnut Hill. Office: Real Estate Trust Bldg., Philadelphia, Pa.

HOUTZ, Harry Daniel, clergyman; b. near Myerstown, Lebanon Co., Pa., Feb. 17, 1885; s. Aquila G. and Emma Lizzie (Gibble) H.; desc. of Philip Houtz (who came to Phila., Aug. 29, 1734), through his son, Henry, who served as a soldier in the Revolutionary War; student Franklin and Marshall Acad., Lancaster, Pa., summer 1905; A.B., with honors, Albright Coll., Myerstown, Pa. (now located at Reading, Pa.), 1909, A.M., 1911; grad. student Cornell U., summer 1911; grad., with honors, Theol. Sem. of Reformed Ch. in U.S., Lancaster, Pa., 1912; B.D., Potomac U., Washington, D.C., 1920, Ph.D., 1921; m. Annie Priscilla Steiner, June 11, 1912; children—Lester Steiner, Myron Steiner (deceased), Ethel Mae (wife of Rev. Paul J. Slonaker), Florence Emily. Ordained by Lehigh classis of Reformed Ch., 1912; pastor Mahoning Charge, near Lehighton, 1912-25, East Berlin Charge, 1925-36, Selinsgrove, since 1938; supply pastor Salem Evang. and Reformed Ch., Shamokin, Jan.-May, 1938 and Messiah Evang. and Reformed Ch., Alvira, Pa., since May, 1938. Mem. bd. of trustees Gettysburg Classis, Evang. and Reformed Ch., 1934-36; mem. Corpn. of Am. Theol. Sem., Wilmington, Del. Mem. White Deer Valley Ministerial Assn., Allenwood, Pa.; mem. Snyder Co. Hist. Soc. Pres. Ministerial Assn., of Gettysburg Classis, 1931; pres. Lehigh Classis, 1921-22, Gettysburg Classis, 1930-31. Mem. Central Pa. Synod of the Evang. and Reformed Church since March, 1939. Democrat. Mason (32°). Author of pamphlet, The Reformation Memorial Record, 1917. Contbr. of "Houtz Families" in the 2-vol. edit. "Schuylkill County, Pa., Genealogy, Family History, Biography," 1916. Home: 514 N. 8th St., Selinsgrove, Pa.

HOUZE, Roger Joseph John, glass mfr.; b. Fostoria, O., Dec. 23, 1890; s. Leon J., Sr., and Irma (Andris) H.; student Point Marion (Pa.) High Sch. and Eastern Coll.; m. Mary Louise Steele, Nov. 9, 1921; 1 dau., LaVerne Elois. Sec.-treas. and sales mgr. L. J. Houze Convex Glass Co., Point Marion, Pa., since 1910, now also dir.; pres. Houze Window Glass Co., Point Marion, since 1914; v.p. and dir. Point Marion First Nat. Bank since 1936; dir. Point Marion Bridge Co. Past pres., now dir., Point Marion Sch. Assn. Dir. Evergreen Memorial Cemetery. Home: Prospect St. Office: P.O. Drawer E., Point Marion, Pa.

HOVDE, Brynjolf Jacob, univ. prof., adminstr. housing authority; b. Jersey City, N.J., May 17, 1896; s. Christian Joachim Mohn and Marie (Jacobson) H.; ed. Wittenberg Acad., Wis., 1910-12; A.B., Luther Coll., Decorah, Ia., 1916; A.M., State U. of Ia., 1919, Ph.D., same, 1924; m. Theresse Arneson, Nov. 24, 1921; children—Christian Arneson, Ellen Margrethe, Carl Frederick. Engaged as instr. Luther Coll., 1916-17, instr. and dean of men, 1919-23; asst. prof. history and polit. sci., Allegheny Coll., Meadville, Pa., 1924-27; asso. prof. modern European history, U. of Pittsburgh, 1927-38; dir. Dept. Pub. Welfare, City of Pittsburgh, 1936-38; adminstr. Housing Authority of City of Pittsburgh since 1938; spl. consultant in charge Management Division, U.S. Housing Authority, since July 12, 1939. Served as 2d lt. C.A.C., U.S.A., 1918. Mgr. Allegheny Co. Kennedy for Gov. Campaign Com., 1938. Mem. Am. Hist. Assn., Norwegian-Am. Hist. Assn., Am. Pub. Welfare Assn., Nat. Assn. Housing Officials. Awarded Guggenheim fellowship, 1930-31; Am.-Scandinavian Soc. fellowship, 1932. Democrat. Lutheran. Club: Faculty of University of Pittsburgh. Contbr. articles and monographs on modern European history, 2 vol. History of the Scandinavian Countries, 1720-1865. Home: 6311 Darlington Rd., Pittsburgh, Pa. Office: 1305 Law & Finance Bldg., Pittsburgh, Pa.

HOVEY, George Rice, educator; b. Newton Centre, Mass., Jan. 17, 1860; s. Alvah and Augusta M. (Rice) H.; A.B., Brown U., 1882, A.M., 1885; grad. Newton Theol. Instn., 1885; post-grad. work, same, 1885-86; D.D., Temple U., Phila., 1901, Brown, 1902; m. Clara K. Brewer, Sept. 15, 1890; children—Alvah Brewer (dec.), Ruth. Instr. Yale Summer Sch. of Hebrew, 1887; prof. Hebrew, 1887-97, N.T. Greek, 1890-97, Richmond (Va.) Theol. Sem.; pres. Wayland Sem. and Coll., Washington, D.C., 1897-99; prof. theology and philosophy, 1899-1919, pres., 1905-19, Va. Union U. (colored), Richmond, Va.; dir. Summer Normal Sch., Richmond, 1911-18; sec. for edn. Am. Bapt. Home Mission Soc., 1919-30; dir. Nat. Ministers' Inst., 1930-1935. Republican. Author: Hebrew Word Book, 1902; Alvah Hovey—His Life and Letters, 1927; The Bible—Its Origin and Interpretation, 1930; Christian Ethics for Daily Life, 1932; Bible Study—A Natural Method Illustrated, 1935. Home: Upper Montclair, N.J.

HOWARD, Benjamin Franklin, lawyer; b. New York, N.Y., Dec. 22, 1895; s. George Witten and Nannie (Pearl) H.; LL.B., Washington and Lee U. Law Coll., 1921; grad. student U. of Mich., Ann Arbor, 1921-22; m. Mary Hall Sinclair, Nov. 16, 1929. Admitted to W.Va. bar, 1922 and since engaged in gen. practice of law at Welch; served as city atty. Welch, W.Va., 1923-29, and asst. pros. atty. McDowell Co., 1923-29; judge 8th Judicial Circuit, W.Va., 1930-36; mem. firm Howard & Howard, Welch, W.Va., since 1937. Served as sergt. Signal Corps, U.S.A., 1918-19, with A.E.F. Past pres. and lt. gov. Kiwanis. Mem. Am., W.Va. State, and McDowell Co. bar assns., Sigma Delta Kappa, Am. Legion, Vets. Fgn. Wars, Forty & Eight. Republican. Episcopalian. Clubs: Masonic, McDowell County Country (Welch). Home: 977 Riverside Drive. Office: Wyoming St., Welch, W.Va.

HOWARD, Charles McHenry, lawyer; b. Baltimore, Md., May 8, 1870; s. McHenry and Julia Douglas (Coleman) H.; A.B., Johns Hopkins U., 1891; LL.B., U. of Md. Law Sch., Baltimore, 1893; m. Ellen N. Carter, June 16, 1898 (dec.). Admitted to Md. bar, 1893, and since engaged in gen. practice of law at Baltimore; mem. firm Venable, Baetjer & Howard since 1900. Trustee Peabody Inst., Johns Hopkins Hosp., Union Memorial Hosp., all of Baltimore. Mem. Am. Bar Assn., Am. Law Inst. (mem. council and exec. com.), Md. State Bar Assn., Baltimore City Bar Assn. Democrat. Episcopalian. Clubs: Maryland, University, Johns Hopkins (Baltimore). Home: 901 St. Paul St. Office: Mercantile Trust Bldg., Baltimore, Md.

HOWARD, Edgar Billings, archæologist; b. New Orleans, La., Feb. 28, 1887; s. Frank Turner and Emma Cora (Pike) H.; prep. edn. St. Paul's Sch., Concord, N.H., 1900-06; Ph.B., Yale (Sheffield Scientific Sch.), 1909; M.S., U. of Pa., 1930, Ph.D., 1935; m. Elizabeth Newhall, Oct. 1, 1910; children—Edgar Billings, Frank Turner, Charles Newhall Willing, Robert Pike. Bond salesman, 1910-11; export-import business with Wharton Sinkler & Robert Toland, 1922-28; scientific work as archæologist since 1928; research asso. Univ. Museum, Phila., since 1929, Carnegie Inst., Washington, D.C., since 1934. Served as capt. Hdqrs. Co., 313th Inf., U.S. Army, with A.E.F., during World War. Former pres. Sch. Bd., Radnor Twp., Pa.; sec.-treas. Howard Memorial Library, New Orleans; trustee Orthopedic Hosp., Phila. Mem. Soc. for Am. Archæology (pres.), Delta Psi. Republican. Episcopalian. Clubs: Yale (Phila.); Boston (New Orleans). Home: Bryn Mawr, Pa.

HOWARD, Edward G.; v.p. Electric Hose & Rubber Co. Home: 3714 Washington St., Wilmington, Del.

HOWARD, Frederick A., banker; b. Sussex Co., Del., Oct. 20, 1855; s. George W. and Leah Cannon (Poole) H.; student pub. schs., and Bryant and Stratton's Business Coll. of Phila.; m. Besse Dunn Pearce, May 1, 1882; children—John Pearce, Mary Anna, Besse Dunn, William Edward. Began as clk. Chester (Pa.) Post Office, 1873; in wholesale grocery business with brothers, 1880-1905; firm having previously acquired a 50-acre tract of land in First Ward of Chester, Pa., began development of property as suburban residential sect., giving name Park Pl. to tract where now resides; dir. First Nat. Bank of Chester since 1895, pres. since 1921. Active in civic affairs, servings many yrs. on Chester Hosp. Bd., Chester Free Library Bd., Bd. of Trade, etc.; helped acquire and develop pub. parks and pres. bd. for 15 yrs.; established and conducted with others Pub. Playgrounds, 1910-20, when taken over by the municipality. Food adminstr., Delaware County, during World War. Clubs: Penn (pres.), Chester (Chester, Pa.). Home: 108 W. 24th St., Park Pl. Office: Fifth and Market Sts., Chester, Pa.

HOWARD, G. W.; mem. law firm Howard & Howard. Address: Welch, W.Va.

HOWARD, John Duvall, investment bond broker; b. Baltimore, Md., Aug. 11, 1866; s. William and Octavia (Duvall) H.; ed. Baltimore Pub. Schs., 1873-79, Baltimore City Coll., 1879-82; m Mary Greenwood Smith, Nov. 3, 1897; children—Priscilla Dorsey, Mary Greenwood, Octavia Duvall (wife of Dr. Philip Barbour Price), Dr. John Eager. Began office boy, J. H. Fisher & Son, bankers, Baltimore, 1882, mem. of firm, 1891-1917; organized, 1917, and since sr. partner, John D. Howard & Co., investment bonds, Baltimore, Md.; dir. Mercantile Trust Co. Mem. Soc. of the Cincinnati of Md. Episcopalian. Clubs: Maryland, Merchants' (Baltimore, Md.). Home: 209 W. Monument St. Office: South & Redwood Sts., Baltimore, Md.

HOWARD, John Tasker, musician, composer, author; b. Brooklyn, N.Y., Nov. 30, 1890; s. John Tasker and Pamela Marvin (Hermance) H.; student at Williams College, 1909-13, honorary A.M., 1937; studied music with Paul Tidden, Howard Brockway and Mortimer Wilson; m. Ruth Hunter, June 7, 1916; children—Amy, Joan. Managing editor The Musician, New York City, 1918-22; ednl. dir. The Ampico Corpn., 1922-28; music editor McCall's Mag., 1928-30; editor music dept. Weedon's Modern Ency., 1931; editor music div. U.S. George Washington Bicentennial Commn. (medal of award 1933). Mem. Nat. Assn. for Am. Composers and Conductors. Authors' League of America, Am. Soc. Composers, Authors and Pubs., Am. Musicological Soc., Zeta Psi. Conglist. Clubs: Williams, Dutch Treat, The Bohemians (New York). Author: Our American Music, 1931; Stephen Foster, America's Troubadour, 1934; Ethelbert Nevin, 1935; (pamphlets) Studies of Contemporary American Composers, 1925-27, Series No. 2, 1929; A Program Outline of American Music, 1931; The Music of George Washington's Time, 1931; Music Associated with the Period of the Formation of the Constitution and with the Inauguration of George Washington, 1937. Editor and compiler: A Program of Early American Piano Music, 1931; A Program of Early and Mid-19th Century American Songs, 1931; A Program of Stephen Foster Songs, 1934. Composer of Fantasy on a Choral Theme, Foster Sinfonietta, March of the Grenadiers, for orchestra; also choral music, piano pieces and songs; composer and adapter of music for Percy MacKaye's folkmasque "Wakefield," 1931. Contbr. to Dictionary of Am. Biography, also mags., music jours. and encyclopedias. Radio broadcaster on NBC network since 1932. Lecturer. Home: 47 Lincoln St., Glen Ridge, N.J.

HOWARD, LeRoy D., physician and surgeon; b. Smithfield, Pa., Oct. 19, 1882; s. Absalom and Rebecca Jane (Core) H.; M.D., Jefferson Med. Coll., Phila., Pa., 1906; m. Edna Pearle Strorgis, June 23, 1909; children—Martha Rebecca (widow of John Morgan Mitchell, dec.), Mary Jean (dec.). Interne Jefferson Hosp., Phila., Pa., 1907-08; engaged in gen. practice of medicine and surgery at Fairmont, W.Va., since 1908; dir. Fairmont Gen. Hosp.; treas. Pine Bluff Coal Co. Past pres. Fairmont Kiwanis Club. Fellow Am. Coll. Surgeons; mem. A.M.A., W.Va. and Marion Co. med. socs., Alpha Omega Alpha. Republican. Methodist. Mason. Elk, K.P. Club: Kiwanis. Home: 612 Madison St. Office: Peoples Bldg., Fairmont, W.Va.

HOWARD, Philip Eugene, publisher; b. Lynn, Mass., Apr. 1, 1870; s. Eugene (M.D.) and Susan Ella (Nash) H.; B.A., University of Pennsylvania, 1891; LL.D., Houghton College, 1937; m. Annie Slosson, d. H. Clay Trumbull, Oct. 27, 1891; children—Philip Eugene, Henry Trumbull, Alice Gallaudet, Annie Trumbull. With the Sunday School Times, Philadelphia, 1891—; president and treasurer S.S. Times Company; western treasurer Alliance of Reformed Churches Throughout the World, 1910-1935. Guest of British Government in spl. study war work in British Isles and on Western Front, 1918. Mem. Phi Delta Theta, Phi Beta Kappa. Republican. Presbyn. Author: The Life Story of Henry Clay Trumbull, 1905; A Prayer Before the Lesson, 1911; Temptation—What It Is and How to Meet It, 1911; A History of World's Sunday School Conventions, 1912; Their Call to Service, 1915; The Many Sided David, 1917; Boy-Talks, 1920; When the Days Seem Dark, 1920; A Little Kit of Teachers' Tools, 1921; Father and Son, 1922; A New Invasion of Belgium, 1924; Living Through These Days, 1930. Editor: Sunday Schools the World Around, 1907. Wrote article on History of Sunday Schools in Internat. Ency. Home: 11 E. Central Av., Moorestown, N.J. Office: 323 N. 13th St., Philadelphia, Pa.

HOWARD, Philip Williams, investments; b. Cleveland, O., Dec. 3, 1903; s. Dr. William Travis and Mary Cushing (Williams) H.; A.B., Johns Hopkins U., 1925; grad. student Johns Hopkins U., 1926-27; m. Florence Freeman Blake, September 8, 1939. Was employed as statistician, Gillet & Co. and predecessors, Baltimore, 1927-37; mem. firm Mitchell, Murphy & Howard, brokers, Baltimore, 1937; with Smith, Barney & Co., brokers, Baltimore, 1938; investments New Amsterdam Casualty Co., Baltimore, Md., since 1939; sec., treas. and dir. Continental States Telephone Co., 1932-37. Mem. Beta Theta Pi. Clubs: Bachelors Cotillon, Maryland (Baltimore); Gibson Island (Gibson Island, Md.). Home: Northwood Apts. Office: 227 St. Paul St., Baltimore, Md.

HOWARD, Stanley Edwin, univ. prof.; b. Sherbrooke, P.Q., Sept. 29, 1888; s. George Henry and Hannah Bertha (Lambly) H., citizens of U.S.; A.B., Bates Coll., Lewiston, Me., 1910; A.M., Princeton U., 1913, Ph.D., 1916; m. Ethel Mae Chapman, June 24, 1913 (died 1923); children—Esther Caroline, Marshall Chapman; m. 2d, Helen Sibley, June 29, 1925; 1 son, Charles Sibley. Instr. Latin, Greek and pub. speech, Pennington Sch., Pennington, N.J., 1910-12; instr. econs. and sociology, Mount Holyoke Coll., South Hadley, Mass., 1913-14; instr. econs., Princeton U., 1916-17, Dartmouth Coll., Hanover, N.H., 1917-18; asst. prof. econs., Princeton U., Princeton, N.J., 1918-23, asso. prof. since 1923, chmn. dept. econs. and social instns. since 1934. Served with U.S. Shipping Bd., Washington, D.C., 1918. Mem. bd. overseers ("Alumni Trustee"), Bates Coll., Lewiston, Me. Mem. Am. Econ. Assn., Am. Accounting Assn., Am. Assn. Univ. profs., Phi Beta Kappa. Presbyn. Clubs: Springdale Golf (Princeton, N. J.); Mountain View Country (Greensboro, Vt.). Contbr. articles in field of econs. Home: 105 Fitz Randolph Rd., Princeton, N.J.; (Summer) Greensboro, Vt.

HOWARD, William Elmer, clergyman; born Athens, Mo., Dec. 26 1867; s. Rev. John Moses (D.D.) and Laura (Dameron) H.; ed. Cumberland U. (Tenn.), 1883-84; A.B., Waynesburg Coll., 1889, A.M., same, 1894; student Western Theol. Sem., 1889-92; (hon.) D.D., Waynesburg Coll., 1894; m. Luetta Matthews, Sept. 24, 1889; children—Helen Eugenia (Mrs. Kenneth Nathan Downs), Mary Etta (Mrs. Charles Franklin Troop), Sarah. Ordained to ministry Presbyn. Ch., 1892; minister at West Union, Pa., 1892-97, California, Pa., 1897-1900, Taylorville, Ill., 1900-05, Scio, O., 1905-08, Fayette City, Pa., 1908-11, Oakland, Pittsburgh, 1911-19, Hoboken, Pittsburgh, 1919-25, McCandless Av., Pittsburgh, 1925-34, McKees Rocks, Pittsburgh since 1934, also served as chaplain Pa. Senate, 1934-37. Awarded certificate for civilian service during World War. Pres. Class 1913 Chautauqua Lit. and Sci. Circle. Mem. S.A.R., Sigma Alpha Epsilon. Republican. Presbyn. Mason. Contbr. verse and articles to religious and secular publs. Home: 3426 Parkview Av., Pittsburgh, Pa.

HOWARD, William Travis, pathologist; b. Sans Souci, Statesburg, S.C., Mar. 13, 1867; s. John and Mary Catherine (Macleod) H. (both of Richmond, Va.); student U. of Va., 1885-87; M.D., U. of Md., 1889; grad. student Johns Hopkins, 1889-93; m. Mary Cushing Williams, of Baltimore, Aug. 15, 1896. Engaged in teaching and research in pathology since 1892; prof. pathology, Western Reserve U., Cleveland, 1894-1914; asst. commr. of health, Baltimore, 1915-19; lecturer vital statistics and biometry, Sch. Hygiene and Pub. Health, Johns Hopkins, 1919-25; asso. mem. Inst. of Biol. Research, same, 1926; voluntary associate in biology, 1930. Former bacteriologist Cleveland Bd. of Health. Pres. Am. Assn. Pathologists and Bacteriologists, 1902; mem. Assn. Am. Physicians, Med. and Chirurg. Faculty of Md. Club: Maryland. Author numerous papers on pathology, bacteriology and vital statistics, including Public Health Administration and The Natural History of Disease in Baltimore, Md., 1797-1920 (pub. by Carnegie Instn., Washington), 1924. Home: 835 University Parkway, Baltimore, Md.

HOWAT, John B., pres. Sharon Hardware Mfg. Co.; b. Braddock, Pa., Mar. 2, 1873; s. William and Margaret (Brown) H.; student Western U. of Pa. (now U. of Pittsburgh); m. Ida B. Boyle, Aug. 24, 1897. Pres. and treas. Sharon (Pa.) Hardware Mfg. Co. Address: 662 E. State St., Sharon, Pa.

HOWE, Edward Leavitt, banker; b. Princeton, N.J., Apr. 6, 1870; s. Edward and Hannah Tylee (Butler) H.; ed. Princeton U.; m. Isabel Charlotte Church, Dec. 8, 1916; m. 2d, Mrs. Dorothy Iona Campbell Hurd, Mar. 1, 1937. In banking business, Princeton, since 1888; chmn. bd. Princeton Bank and Trust Co.; pres. Princeton Water Co.; dir. Princeton Savings Bank. Mem. Am. Bankers Assn. (finance com.; exec. council; and rep. of N.J.); mem. spl. currency commn. of Am. Bankers Assn. to confer with Congress in preparation of Federal Reserve Act: mem. N.J. Bankers Assn., since its organization (pres. 1910-11; chmn. com. on agrl. development; hon. v.p.) Asso. gen. dir. Y.M.C.A. with Italian Army, Sept. 1918-Mar. 1919. Decorated Italian War Cross and Cavalier Crown of Italy. Mem. Am. Whig. Soc. (Princeton). Republican. Presbyn. Clubs: Nassau (Princeton), Bankers (New York). Author of Clearing of Country Checks (Trust Co.'s Mag.), 1914; Country Bankers and the Owen-Glass Bill (Acad. Polit. Sci., Vol. IV, No. 1). Home: Princeton, N.J.

HOWE, George, architect; b. Worcester, Mass., June 17, 1886; s. James Henry and Helen (Bradford) H.; grad. Groton (Mass.) Sch., 1904; A.B., Harvard, 1907; grad. in architecture, École des Beaux Arts, Paris, 1913; m. Marie Jesup Patterson, July 18, 1907; children—Helen, Ann. Began practice in Philadelphia, 1913; mem. firm Mellor, Meigs and Howe, 1916-28; architect for Phila. Saving Fund Soc. bank bldgs., Goodhart Hall of Bryn Mawr Coll., Coast Guard World War Memorial, Arlington Cemetery, 2 monuments in France for Am. Battle Monuments Commn., residences in Phila., etc.; practiced alone in Philadelphia, 1928-29; mem. firm Howe & Lescaze, 1929-38; architect for Ook Lane Nursery Sch., Phila.; Hessian Hills Sch., Croton-on-Hudson, N.Y.; Trans-Lux Theatre interiors; Phila. Saving Fund Society Office Bldg.; numerous residences, etc.; independent practice since 1933; architect for Phila. Evening Bulletin Bldg.; Childrens World, N.Y. World's Fair; residences, etc. Served as 1st lt., Corps of Interpreters, U.S.A., overseas May 1917-Aug. 1919. Mem. Am. Inst. Architects, Architectural League of New York, Société des Architectes Diplomés par le Gouvernement Français. Awarded gold medal, Phila. Chapter A.I.A., 1922 and 1939; Architectural League of New York, 1925. Episcopalian. Clubs: Philadelphia, T-Square, Coffee House. Author of numerous articles on modern architecture. Mem. archtl. advisory com. of Harvard and Princeton U. Pioneer in modern archtl. design. Home: 9189 Germantown Av., Chestnut Hill, Philadelphia, Pa. Office: 516 Bulletin Bldg., Philadelphia, Pa.

HOWE, John C., lawyer; b. Newark, N.J., Dec. 29, 1892; s. John and Annie G. (Fritz) H.; B.S., U. of Pa., 1914; ed. U. of Pa. Law Sch., 1914-15; LL.B., N.J. Law Sch., Newark, 1917; m. Rebecca Cousart, Nov. 27, 1917; 1 son, John III. Admitted to N.J. bar, 1920; mem. firm Howe & Freund; served as criminal ct. judge, Newark, 1925-33; mem. N.J. Assembly, 1923-24. Served as pvt. cav. N.J.N.G., 1917; ensign to lt. (j.g.) Pay Corps, U.S.N.R.F., 1917-19. Mem. Delta Theta Phi. Republican. Mason. Club: Athletic (Newark). Home: 83 Shephard Av. Office: 11 Commerce St., Newark, N.J.

HOWE, Samuel Burnett, author, educator; b. Groton, Tompkins Co., N.Y., July 15, 1879; s. Samuel Burnett and Sarah Malvina (Crain) H.; B.A., Union Coll., Schenectady, N.Y., 1903, M.A., 1913; m. Harriet Augusta Strowbridge, 1901; children—Miriam S., Robert B., Constance S., John S. Principal of high sch., Saugerties, N.Y., 1903-04; head of dept. of history, Plainfield (N.J.) High Sch., 1904-14; head of dept. of social science, South Side High Sch., Newark, 1914—; head of dept. of social sciences, N.J. State Summer Normal Sch., 1914-24; dept. of history, Extension and Summer Div. Hunter Coll., 1924-32; editor N.J. Jour. of Education, 1920-31. Mem. N.E.A., History Assn. of Middle States and Md. (dir.), Am. Hist. Association, N.J. Assn. Teachers of Social Studies (pres.), Gamma Sigma, Alpha Delta Phi. Was member of Commission of N.E.A. on revision of courses on social science in secondary schs. and chmn. of com. that prepared syllabi in the social studies for schs. of N.J., 1924. Democrat. Episcopalian. Mason. Author: Essentials in Early European History, 1912; Essentials in Modern European History (with Daniel C. Knowlton), 1917; Actual Democracy (with Margaret K. Berry), 1923. Home: 293 Seymour Av., Newark, N.J.; (summer) Camp Mirocojo, Cranberry Lake, Sussex Co., N.J.

HOWE, Thomas Dudley, prof. biology; b. Table Rock, Neb., Sept. 21, 1898; s. Edmund Dudley and Mary Frances (Viggers) H.; B.Sc., U. of Neb., 1921, A.M., same, 1922; Ph.D., U. of Wis., 1925; m. Clara Schnurer, Sept. 28, 1935. Engaged as instr. biology, James Millikin U., Decatur, Ill., 1925-27, Univ. of Ariz., 1928; prof. biology, Duquesne U., Pittsburgh, Pa., since 1929. Mem. A.A.A.S., Am. Assn. Univ. Profs., Bot. Soc., Phi Beta Kappa, Sigma Xi. Home: 3870 Beechwood Boul., Pittsburgh, Pa.

HOWELL, A(lfred) Brazier, comparative anatomist; b. Catonsville, Md., July 28, 1886; s. Darius Carpenter and Katherine Elinor (Hyatt) H.; studied Sheffield Scientific Sch. (Yale), 1908; m. Margaret Gray Sherk, Apr. 14, 1914; children—Elinor Gray, Margaret Travers, John Brazier, Jane. Spl. investigations in geog. variation and comparative anatomy of mammals; with U.S. Biol. Survey, 1918, scientific asst., 1923-27; collaborator U.S. Nat. Museum since 1926; lecturer in comparative anatomy, Johns Hopkins Med. Sch., 1928-1932, associate professor of anatomy since 1932. Mem. American Ornithologists' Union, Cooper Ornithol. Club (secretary 1913; trustee, 1920; vice-pres. 1921). Am. Soc. of Mammalogists (corr. sec., 1925-31, editor, 1936-38, vice-pres. since 1938); Am. Assn. Anatomists, Council for Conservation of Whales (exec. sec.); fellow A.A.A.S.; corr. mem. Internat. Office for Protection of Nature. Club: St. Elmo. Author 3 books and 160 contributions on mammals, birds, etc. Home: Ruxton, Md.

HOWELL, Benjamin Franklin, univ. prof.; b. Troy Hills, N.J., Sept. 30, 1890; s. Benjamin Franklin and Caroline Smith (Quinby) H.; B.S., Princeton U., 1913, A.M., same, 1915; Ph.D., Princeton, 1920; m. Claire Homan Mead, June 24, 1915; 1 son, Benjamin Franklin, Jr. Engaged as instr. geology, Princeton U., 1915-17, 1919-20; asst. prof. geology and paleontology, Princeton, 1920-26, asso. prof. since 1926; also prof. geology and paleontology, Wagner Free Inst. of Sci., Phila. since 1927; also lecturer on geology and paleontology, U. of Pa. since 1937; actg. curator of geology and paleontology, Acad. Natural Scis. of Phila. since 1938. Served as vice-pres. Academic Bd. of U.S.A. Sch. of Mil. Aeronautics at Princeton, N.J., 1917-19. Fellow Paleontol. Soc. (sec. since 1930), Geol. Soc. of America, A.A.A.S. Mem. Internat. Paleontol. Union (sec. since 1937), Paleontol. Research Inst., Acad. Natural Scis. of Phila., Paleontologische Gesellschaft. Asso. mem. Soc. Econ. Paleontologists and Mineralogists. Republican. Presbyn. Editor of Sect. of General Paleozoology of Biological Abstracts. Am. editor of Palaeontologisches Zentralblatt. Home: Fairlea, Princeton, N.J.

HOWELL, Clewell, physician; b. Wilmington, N.C., Mar. 12, 1898; s. Andrew Jay and Gertrude (Jenkins) H.; B.S., Davidson (N.C.) Coll., 1919; M.D., U. of Md. Med. Sch., Baltimore, 1924; m. Margaret E. Spragins, June 16, 1928; children—Clewell, Martha Tappan, Andrew Jay. Interne Union Memorial, Franklin Square, Johns Hopkins, Howard A. Kelly hosps., all of Baltimore, 1924-28; engaged in pvt. practice of pediatrics in Baltimore and Towson, Md., 1928-39, in practice at Towson since 1939; asso. in pediatrics, U. of Md. Med. Sch. since 1930; mem. staff U. of Md. Hosp., Union Memorial and West Baltimore Gen. Hosps. Mem. Am. Med. Assn., Am. Acad. Pediatrics, Baltimore Co. Med. Soc. (pres. 1938), Nu Sigma Nu. Democrat. Presbyterian. Club: Kiwanis of Towson, Md. Contbr. several articles to med. jours. Home: 702 Baltimore Av., Towson, Md.

HOWELL, Corwin, lawyer; b. Newark, N.J., Dec. 6, 1881; s. Francis K. and Emma (Corwin) H.; A.B., Princeton, 1903; LL.B., New York Law Sch., 1905; m. Elizabeth Lunn, June 14, 1910; 1 son, John Corwin. Instr. New York Law Sch., 1905-08; admitted to N.J. bar as atty., 1906, as counsellor, 1909; admitted to U.S. Supreme Ct., 1925, and engaged in gen. practice of law at Newark, N.J.; mem. firm Pitney, Hardin & Skinner since 1914; served as twp. committeeman, South Orange Twp. (now Maplewood Twp.), 1917-19; chmn. twp. com., 1919; mem. bd. sch. estimate, 1919. Trustee Protestant Foster Home Soc. of Newark, N.J., Children's Aid Soc. of Newark, N.J., Marcus L. Ward Home for Aged Mem. Mem. Am. Bar Assn., N.J. State Bar Assn., Essex Co. Bar Assn., Phi Beta Kappa. Republican. Episcopalian (former vestryman). Mason. Clubs: Country (Maplewood); Essex (Newark). Home: 10 Mountain View Terrace, Maplewood, N.J. Office: 744 Broad St., Newark, N.J.

HOWELL, Harry Ray, certified public accountant; b. Letart, Mason Co., W.Va., Nov. 21, 1892; s. Daniel Thomas and Mary Ann (Baier) H.; student Eastman Coll., Poughkeepsie, N.Y., 1914, Washington Sch. of Accountancy, Washington, D.C., 1919-20; m. Myra Myrtle Jones, Oct. 22, 1916; 1 dau., Blanche Esther. Teacher in public schs., Mason, Jackson and Kanawha Counties, W.Va., 1909-14; stenographer Willys-Overland Co., Toledo, O., 1914-15, B.&O. R.R., 1915; clerk-stenographer War Dept., Washington, D.C., 1916-20; staff accountant David A. Jayne & Co., Charleston, W. Va., 1920-24; practice of public accounting as Harry R. Howell Co., Charleston, W.Va., since 1925. C.P.A., W.Va., 1923. Treas. and dir. Union Mission Settlement; sec.-treas. Cavalier Apts., Inc., sec. Riverview Terrace, Inc.; mem. exec. com. Permanent Trust Fund Assn. Counselor Boy Scout div., Charleston Community Fund. Mem. Am. Inst. Accountants, W.Va. Soc. C.P.A.'s (sec.). Republican. Methodist (treas. Central Methodist Ch.). Club: Kanawha Country. Home: 1107 West Av. Office: 710 Kanawha Valley Bldg., Charleston, W.Va.

HOWELL, John Carnett, surgeon; b. Altoona, Pa., Apr. 11, 1901; s. William Henry and Regina Frances (Kempf) H.; grad. Atlantic City (N.J.) High Sch., 1918; pre-med. student U. of Pa., 1918-20, M.D., 1924; m. Henrietta Ida Keller, June 26, 1924; children—Henrietta Mary, Joan Augusta. Interne Presbyterian Hosp., Phila., 1924-26; clin. asst., Grad. Sch. of Medicine, U. of Pa., 1926-37, asst. surgeon, 1931-35, asst. prof. of Surgery since 1937; asso. in surgery radiological div., Phila. Gen. Hosp., 1927-34, visiting surgeon, same, since 1934; dispensary asst. in surgery Presbyterian Hosp., Phila., 1933, asst. in surgery since 1935; surgeon Babies Hosp., Phila., since 1934. Certified by American Board of Surgery, 1939. Fellow Am. Med. Assn., Am. Coll. of Surgeons, Coll. of Physicians of Phila., Phila. Acad. Surgery; mem. Phila. Co. Med. Soc., Pa. Med. Soc., Sigma Alpha Epsilon, Nu Sigma Nu. Home: 333 S. 18th St. Office: 326 S. 19th St., Philadelphia, Pa.

HOWELL, Robert Wilson, retired banker; b. Trenton, N.J., July 18, 1869; s. Charles Whitecar and Anne (Umpleby) H.; student Trenton (N.J.) pub. schs., 1875-86; m. Harriet Newton Bumstead, Feb. 13, 1892 (died 1934); children—Louise (Mrs. Donald B. Rice), Frances Kittinger (Mrs. Francis W. Johnson), Virginia Archibold (Mrs. Franklin R. C. Holbrook), Charles Robert. With Trenton (N.J.) Banking Co. since 1888, successively as corresponding clerk, personal ledger keeper, gen. ledger clk., note teller, receiving teller, paying teller, asst. to cashier, cashier, v.p., 1st v.p. (inactive as v.p.), vice-chmn. and dir.; retired, 1936. Mem. Trenton (N.J.) Park Bd., 1911. Treas. Trenton (N.J.) Red Cross, 1918-36. Mem. Trenton Chamber of Commerce (dir. 1913-16), Trenton Historical Soc. Republican. Anglo-Catholic (mem. chapter Trinity Cathedral). Address: 33 Atterbury Av., Trenton, N.J.

HOWELL, Roger, law dean; b. Baltimore, Md., Mar. 18, 1895; s. William Henry and Anne Janet (Tucker) H.; A.B., Johns Hopkins, 1914, Ph.D., 1917; LL.B., U. of Md., 1917; m. Katharine Louisa Clifford, Sept. 3, 1921; children—Louise Devens, Katharine Fairbanks, William Henry 2d (dec.), Anne Tucker, Roger. Admitted to Md. bar, 1916; began practice N.Y. City, 1919, with firm Cravath & Henderson, 1919; mem. firm Maloy, Brady, Howell & Yost, Baltimore, 1920-27; prof. law, U. of Md., since 1927, asst. dean of Law Sch., 1930-31, dean since 1931. Served as 2d lt., later 1st lt. and capt. inf., U.S.A., 1917-19. Mem. Am., Maryland State and Baltimore City bar assns., Phi Beta Kappa, Phi Gamma Delta. Democrat. Episcopalian. Clubs: Baltimore Country. Author: Privileges and Immunities of State Citizenship, 1918. Contbr. to legal publs. Home: 4705 Keswick Rd., Baltimore, Md.

HOWELL, William Henry, prof. physiology; b. Baltimore, Feb. 20, 1860; s. George Henry and Virginia Teresa H.; A.B., Johns Hopkins, 1881, Ph.D., 1884; hon. M.D., U. of Mich., 1890; LL.D., Trinity, 1901, U. of Mich., 1912, Washington U., 1915, U. of Edinburgh, 1923; Sc.D., Yale, 1911; m. Anne Janet Tucker, June 15, 1887; children—Janet Tucker (Mrs. Admont H. Clark), Roger, Charlotte Teresa (Mrs. Edward O. Hulburt). Asso. prof. physiology, Johns Hopkins, 1888-89; prof. physiology and histology, U. of Mich., 1889-92; asso. prof. physiology, Harvard, 1892-93; prof. physiology, 1893-1931, dean med. faculty, 1899-1911, asst. dir. Sch. Hygiene, 1917-26, dir., 1926-31, emeritus since 1931, Johns Hopkins U. Chmn. Nat. Research Council, 1932-33. Mem. Nat. Acad. Sciences, Am. Philos. Soc., etc.; hon. mem. English Physiol. Soc. Author: Text-book of Physiology, 1905. Editor of An American Text-book of Physiology, 1896. Home: 112 St. Dunstan's Rd., Baltimore, Md.

HOWELL, William Rabon, coll. prof. and registrar; b. Decatur County, Ga., Feb. 27, 1881; s. Elijah and Mary Virginia (Spear) H.; Ph.B., Milligan (Tenn.) Coll., 1904, A.B., 1905; A.M., Yale University, 1908, B.D., 1909, graduate student, Yale, 1909-11; student at Columbia, summers, 1926, 27; Ph.D., American U., Washington, D.C., 1929; m. Zorayda Mathis Brents, Sept. 3, 1918. Prof. of Latin and Greek, Atlantic Christian Coll., Wilson, N.C., 1904-05; vice-prin. Raeford Inst., Raeford, N.C., 1905-06; prof. of philosophy and edn., Washington Coll., Chestertown, Md., 1911-13; vice-prin. and prof. of edn., Beckley (W.Va.) Inst., 1913-16, prin., 1916-18; supt. dist. school, Attapulgus, Ga., 1918-19; prof. of polit. and social science, Washington Coll., since 1921, registrar since 1927; instr. in edn., Alfred U., summers 1929, 30. Served as chief clerk Draft Bd., Raleigh County, W.Va., 1917-18. Fellow Am. Geog. Soc.; mem. Am. Assn. Univ. Profs., Am. Assn. Collegiate Registrars, Md. Hist. Soc., Pi Gamma Mu, Theta Kappa Nu. Democrat. Mem. Christian Ch. Mason (32°, Shriner). Author: The Government of Kent County, Maryland, 1931. Home: 402 Washington Av., Chestertown, Md.

HOWER, Harry (Sloan), prof. physics; b. Parker, Pa., July 24, 1877; s. William H(enry) and Rebecca (Sloan) H.; B.S., Case Sch. Applied Science, 1899, M.S., 1907; grad. study, U. of Berlin, 1903-05; m. Sara Chester, June 23, 1909; children—Thomas Chester, Harry Sloan, Sara, William Henry II. Teacher physics, high sch., Conneaut, O., 1 yr., 1899-1900; instr. in physics, Case Sch. Applied Science, 1900-03, 1905-06; with Carnegie Inst. Tech. since 1906, prof. physics and head of dept. since 1915; cons. physicist. Designer of lenses for range lights for Panama Canal Commn., U.S. Light House Bd., U.S. Navy submarines, U.S. Army searchlight, Norwegian merchant marine, etc. Fellow Am. Physical Soc., A.A.A.S.; mem. Am. Optical Soc., Soc. Promotion Engring. Edn., Am. Ceramic Soc., Illuminating Engring. Soc., English Soc. Glass Technology, Pa. Acad. Science, Sigma Xi, Tau Beta Pi, Theta Xi. Republican. Episcopalian. Mason. Club: University. Home: 5709 Solway St., Pittsburgh, Pa.

HOWLAND, Alice Gulielma, educator; b. Wilmington, Del., Feb. 14, 1883; d. Charles S. and Mary (Shipley) H.; student Bryn Mawr Coll., 1901-02; grad. Carnegie Training Sch. of Children's Librarians, Pittsburgh, Pa., 1904; unmarried; adopted two girls. Asst. to prin., Miss Shipley's Sch., Bryn Mawr, 1905-06; state student sec. for N.Y. and N.J. for Nat. Bd. Y.W.C.A., 1906-08; prin. Utica (N.Y.) Female Acad., 1908-11; prin. and part owner, Shipley Sch., Bryn Mawr, since 1911. Trustee Lab. of Anthropology, Santa Fe, N.M.; dir. Bur. of Household Economics (Phila.); mem. Phila. Art Alliance, Nat. Assn. of Prins. of Schs. for Girls (pres. 1936-38). Quaker. Clubs: Cosmopolitan, Bryn Mawr (New York); Cosmopolitan, Acorn (Phila.). Address: Bryn Mawr, Pa.

HOWLAND, Anne Wallace, librarian; b. Athens, Ga.; d. Alexander McGhee and Frances Garland (Singleton) Wallace; ed. pvt. schs. and grad. Girls High Sch., Atlanta, Ga.; Sc.D. in library science, U. of Ga., 1929; m. Max Franklyn Howland, Feb. 18, 1908; 1 son, Wallace. Librarian Carnegie Library, Atlanta, Ga., 1899-1908; and dir. Library Sch., Carnegie Library, Atlanta, 1905-08; librarian Drexel Inst. Library and dean Drexel Inst. Sch. of Library Science, 1922-36, dean emeritus since Jan. 1, 1937. Mem. A.L.A. (v.p. 1902; council 1907, 24, 26), Ga. Library Assn. (pres. 1899), Ga. Library Commn. (sec. 1897), Pa. Library Assn. (pres. 1925), Pa. Library Club (v.p. 1929), Special Library Assn., Bibliog. Soc. America, Hist. Soc. of Pa. Democrat. Presbyn. Home: The Wellington. Address: Drexel Inst. Library, Philadelphia, Pa.

HOWLAND, Arthur Charles, univ. prof.; b. S. Danby, N.Y., Dec. 24, 1869; s. Charles and M. A. (Bassett) H.; A.B., Cornell, 1893; studied Göttingen and Leipzig, 1894-95, Cornell and U. of Pa., 1895-97; Ph.D., U. of Pa., 1897; m. Emily W. Berry, Sept. 3, 1902; children—Charles B., Arthur L., Emily H. Teacher English, Wyoming Sem., Kingston, Pa., 1893-94; instr. European history, U. of Ill., 1897-98; teaching fellow, U. of Pa., 1898-99; instr. history, Teachers Coll. (Columbia), 1899-1904; asst. prof. mediæval history, 1904-11, prof., 1911-34, Henry Charles Lea prof. European history since 1934, U. of Pa. Mem. Am. Hist. Assn., Assn. History Teachers Middle States and Md., Medieval Acad., Delta Phi, Phi Beta Kappa. Editor and translator: Ordeals, Compurgation, Excommunication and Interdict, 1898; The Early Germans, 1899. Editor: Mommsen's History of Rome (abridged), 1906. Joint Author: World History in the Making, 1927; World History Today, 1927. Clubs: University, Contemporary. Home: 9 Guernsey Rd., Swarthmore, Pa.

HOWLAND, Fred B(artlett), crude oil operator; b. Titusville, Pa., Jan. 23, 1873; s. Andrew B. and Emily Ann (Hill) H.; C.E., Princeton, 1894; m. Gertrude Lammers, June 2, 1897; 1 dau., Lois Bartlett (dec. wife of Charles P. Mason). Employed as understudy to gen. mgr., 1894-97; supt. Enterprise Transit Co. of Ind., 1897-1906; gen. mgr. Enterprise Transit Co. of Pa., 1905, The Kewanee Oil & Gas Co., 1908-37, Kewanee Oil Co. (successor and merger of two former cos.), producer crude petroleum in several states since 1937; dir. Second Nat. Bank. Served as sch. dir., Titusville. Dir. Midcontinent Oil & Gas Assn., Okla.-Kan. Div.; dir. Pinehurst (N.C.) Religious Assn. Republican. Presbyn. (mem. session First Ch.). Royal Arcanum. Clubs: Y.M.C.A., Country (Titusville); Country (Tulsa, Okla.); The Tin Whistles (Pinehurst, N.C.). Home: 501 N. Perry St. Office: Second Nat. Bank Bldg., Titusville, Pa.

HOWLAND, Harry Wagner, med. dir.; b. Academy Corners, Pa., 1884; s. Charles R. and Elizabeth D. (Smith) H.; M.D., U. of Md.; m. Helen P. Gaddis; children—Gaddis, A. Winfield. Surgeon Buffalo & Susquehanna R.R., 1930-34, B.&O. R.R. since 1934; mem. visiting staff since 1935 and now pres. and dir. Blossburg State Hosp.; med. dir. Tioga County since 1935; chief of staff Tuberculosis, Genito-Infectious Diseases, Prenatal and Child Health clinics. Mason (32°), Odd Fellow, Moose, Patrons of Husbandry. Address: 11 W. Main St., Galeton, Pa.

HOWLEY, Bartholomew M., physician; b. Greenock, Scotland, June 15, 1871; s. James and Helen (Maxwell) H.; student St. Leaurence Sch., Greenock, Scotland, 1878-85; M.D., New York U. Med. Coll., 1894; came to U.S., 1885, naturalized, 1885; m. Mary McColl, Sept. 14, 1910; children—Bartholomew M., Margaret M., Frances M. Began as physician, 1894; practiced in New York City, 1894-1915; with Manhattan Eye & Ear Hosp., 1900-07; practice restricted to eye, ear, nose and throat work since 1907; chief of eye, ear, nose and throat service, Middlesex and St. Peter's Hosp., New Brunswick, N.J., since 1920. Mem. Rutgers Med. Club, Acad. of Medicine Northern N.J., etc. Roman Catholic. Home: 15 N. 6th Av., Highland Park, N.J. Office: 419 George St., New Brunswick, N.J.

HOWORTH, John, surgeon; b. Scranton, Pa., Dec. 11, 1879; s. James and Catherine (Williams) H.; A.B., Bloomsburg State Teachers Coll., 1898; student, Cornell U., 1901; M.D., U. of Pa. Med. Sch., 1909; m. F. Loretta MacDaniels, Sept. 23, 1914; children—Catherine Miriam, Loretta Alice. Med. resident, Wilkes-Barre Gen. Hosp., 1909-11, mem. staff since 1911, now chief surgeon one of surg. divs.; surgeon Lehigh Valley R.R. Co. Served as mem. adv. bd. examiners during World War. Fellow Am. Coll. Surgs., N.E. Assn. Ry. Surgs. Mem. Am., Pa. State, and Luzerne Co. (past pres.) med. assns., Acacia, Phi Rho Sigma. Republican. Presbyn. (deacon First Ch.). Mason (K.T., Shriner). Clubs: Masonic, Y.M.C.A., Rotary, Irem Country, Wyoming Valley Motor. Home: 115 S. Franklin St., Wilkes-Barre, Pa.

HOWSON, Furman Sheppard, investment banker; b. Philadelphia, Pa., Feb. 9, 1879; s. Charles and Medora (Ware) H.; grad. Haverford Sch., 1896, Haverford Coll., 1900; unmarried. Associated with George B. Mifflin, civil engr., 1900; rep. with Rufus Waples of New York banking firm, J. & W. Seligman & Co., Philadelphia, 1901-12; partner Rufus Waples & Co., investment bankers, since organization, 1912; v.p. and dir. Grant Bldg. & Loan Assn. since 1933. Presbyterian. Club: Art (Philadelphia). Home: 401 Woodland Av., Wayne, Pa. Office: 1510 Chestnut St., Philadelphia, Pa.

HOY, Charles Winston, pub. utility exec., engr.; b. Troy, N.Y., June 22, 1877; s. Hugh and Catherine (Desonier) H.; B.S., Mass. Inst. Tech., 1904; studied U. of Pa., 1916-17; m. Angeline Riddle Gay, Sept. 28, 1905; 1 son, Harlan Winston. Foreman Hartford City Gas Co., Hartford, Conn., 1904-05; supt. Queensborough Gas & Electric Co., New York, 1905-06; gen. supt. and engr. Consumers Gas Co., Atlantic City, 1906-09, Atlantic City Gas Co., 1909-10; gen. mgr. New Jersey Gas Co., Glassboro, N.J., 1910-24; engr. Internat. Utilities Corpn., New York, 1924-29; gen. mgr. and engr. Internat. Pub. Utilities Corpn., 1929-31; v.p. and engr. Gen. Management Corpn., Philadelphia; since 1931; v.p., engr. and dir. Walnut Electric & Gas Corpn. since 1937; v.p. and dir. N. M. Pub. Utilities Corpn., North Attleboro Gas Corpn., South Carolina Utilities Corpn., Okla. Electric & Water Co., St. Johnsbury Gas Corpn., Vt. Lighting Corpn., Ware Gas Co.; trustee Wancat Associates; licensed professional engr., State of N.Y. Chmn. (Glassboro, N.J., sect.) Four Minute Men on Com. of Pub. Information, Red Cross and Liberty Loan Drive, World War. Mem. Am. Gas Assn.; ex-pres. N.J. Gas Assn. Republican. Episcopalian. Mason (A.A.O.N.M.S., A.A.S.R.). Clubs: Bankers of America, National Arts (New York); hon. mem. Rotary Internat. Home: 5 Focer St., Glassboro, N.J. Office: 1500 Walnut St., Philadelphia, Pa.

HOYLER, Cyril Nathaniel, prof. physics; b. Edmonton, Alberta, Can., Aug. 8, 1905; s. Rt. Rev. Clement (1st Moravian Bishop in Can.) and Mary Caroline (Gerdsen) H., citizens of U.S.; came to U.S., 1925; 1st class teacher's certificate, Edmonton Normal Sch., 1923; B.S., Moravian Coll., Bethlehem, Pa., 1928; grad. study, Columbia U., 1928-29; M.S., Physics, Lehigh U., 1935; m. Ethel Mary Schramko, June 20, 1934; 1 son, Carl Cyril. Began as teacher rural schs., Alberta, 1923-25; prin. Otoskwan (Alberta) Sch. Dist., 1924-25; instr. mathematics and German, jr. high sch., Irvington, N.J., 1928-29; instr. physics, Moravian Coll., Bethlehem, 1929-35, prof. physics since 1935; also asst. in physics and chemistry, Moravian Prep. Sch., 1930-32, also taught physics, Moravian Coll. for Women, Bethlehem, Pa., 1937-38; also engr. in design and constrn. elec. instruments and equipment for local mfrs. Mem. Am. Phys. Soc., Inst. Radio Engrs., Am. Assn. Physics Teachers. Republican. Moravian. Home: 418 Third Av., Bethlehem, Pa. Office: Moravian Coll., Bethlehem, Pa.

HOYT, Creig Simmons, prof. chemistry; b. Auburn, N.Y., Feb. 27, 1894; s. Frank E. and Florence (Simmons) H.; B.S., Grove City Coll., 1939; A.M., Cornell U., 1917; Ph. D., U. of Pittsburgh, 1933; m. Matilda Thompson, July

22, 1915; children—Creig Sieplein, Margaret Elizabeth. Engaged as chemist for Ayer and McKinney, 1912-13; instr. chemistry, Grove City Coll., 1913-17, asst. prof., 1917-20, prof. chemistry since 1920; also cons. chemist for a number of cos. Served as mem. bd. edn., Grove City, Pa., since 1934. Mem. Am. Chem. Soc., Sigma Xi, Phi Lambda Upsilon. Republican. Presbyn. Mason. Rotarian. Contbr. articles to tech. mags. Home: 631 S. Center St., Grove City, Pa.

HOYT, Ray; editor Prince George Post. Address: care Prince Georges Post, Inc., Hyattsville, Md.

HOYT, Sidney Merrill, v.p. Fidelity & Deposit Co. of Md.; b. Jamestown, N.Y., July 25, 1881; s. Sidney B. and Agnes A. (Merrill) .; B.S. in Civil Engring., U. of Mich., 1907; m. Evelyn E. Ouellette, June 1, 1910; 1 dau., Elizabeth O. (Mrs. John E. Conley, Jr.). Began as civil engr., 1907; now v.p. Fidelity & Deposit Co. of Md. (Baltimore), Am. Bonding Co. Served as capt. Constrn. Div., U.S. Army. Mem. Sigma Chi. Club: Baltimore Country. Home: 4121 Roland Av. Office: Fidelity & Deposit Co. of Md., Baltimore, Md.

HRON, Ralph Preston, coll. prof.; b. Kingman, Kan., May 31, 1886; s. Wencelas and Sarah Adaline (Frazier) H.; grad. Logan Co. High Sch., Guthrie, Okla., 1906; B.S., Epworth U. (now Okla. City U.), Oklahoma City, Okla., 1911; student Kansas U., Lawrence, Kan., summers 1912-13, Columbia U., 1929; Pharm. Chemist, M.A., U. of Okla., Norman, Okla., 1914, student summers 1930-31; m. Florence Louise Miller, Aug. 23, 1915. Teacher biology, Epworth U. Acad., Oklahoma City, Okla., 1909-11; teacher physics, Logan Co. High Sch., Guthrie, Okla., 1911-13; teacher biology, Salt Lake City (Utah) High Sch., 1914; head dept. physics and chemistry, Okla. Methodist U., Guthrie, Okla., 1915-19; prof. physics and head dept., Marshall Coll., Huntington, W. Va., since 1920, organized dept. of engring., 1921, and served as head until 1928; industrial experience with oil cos., Okla. and Kan., 1916-20, working on design of refinery, dehydration, gasoline absorption equipment, plant constrn., oil testing, and engring. research. Volunteered for Chem. Warfare Service, U.S. Army, 1917, but advised to remain at Okla. Methodist U. Mem. A.A.A.S., W.Va. Acad. of Science, Am. Assn. Physics Teachers, Phi Delta Kappa, Chi Beta Phi, Phi Delta Chi, Theta Kappa Nu. Democrat. Congregationalist. Mason (Scottish Rite, 32°). Clubs: Masonic, Congregational Mens (Huntington, W.Va.). Address: 1623 Crestmont Drive, Huntington, W.Va.

HUBACH, Louis Albert, pres. and treas. L. A. Hubach Co.; b. Wheeling, W.Va., Oct. 5, 1878; s. Frederick H. and Katherine (Beim-Esche) H.; ed. pub. schs. and business coll.; m. Bessie Lee Wheaton, Nov. 7, 1906; children—Bessie Algeo, Virginia May. Rug buyer Robert Keith Co., 1900-07; asst. and buyer of floor coverings Carson, Pirie, Scott & Co., Chicago, 1907-08; buyer floor coverings Joseph Horne Co., Pittsburgh, 1909-18, furniture and floor covering buyer, 1918-38, merchandise mgr. of home furnishings, 1930-34; pres. and treas. L. A. Hubach Co. since 1938. Club: Shannopin Country. Home: 508 Walnut Road. Office: 2017 Jenkins Arcade, Liberty Av., Pittsburgh, Pa.

HUBBARD, Charles Gillette, judge; b. Kane, Pa., Mar. 21, 1883; s. William and Mary Hungerford (Gillette) H.; A.B., U. of Mich. Law Sch., 1906; m. Mabel Sill, June 22, 1911; children—Genevieve Nourse, Helen Jane, Mary Gillette. Admitted to Pa. bar, 1906, and engaged in gen. practice of law at Kane until 1933; served as mem. Kane Bor. Sch. Bd., 1925-27; dist. atty. McKean Co., 1927-33; judge of Ct. Common Pleas, McKean Co., Pa., since 1934. Mem. Pa. Bar Assn. Republican. Methodist. Clubs: Rotary, Conopus (Smethport). Home: 9 Rose Hill Av., Smethport, Pa.

HUBBARD, Francis Alley, elec. engring.; b. Cambridge, Mass., Apr. 13, 1891; s. Sanford Benton and Emma Bates (Alley) H.; A.B., Harvard U., 1911; M.E.E., Harvard Grad. Sch. Applied Science, 1914; m. Genevieve Frances Mathews, June 21, 1916; children—Edwin Schuyler, Carolyn Emma. Instr. elec. engring., Cornell U., 1914-15; with engring. dept. Western Electric Co., 1915-23, Internat. Western Electric Co., 1923-25; asst. chief engr., Internat. Standard Electric Co., 1926-29, Internat. Telephone & Telegraph Co., 1927-29; v.p. and gen. mgr. Mexican Telephone & Telegraph Co., 1929; with dept. development & research, Am. Telephone & Telegraph Co., 1930-34; mem. tech. staff, Bell Telephone Labs., Inc., since 1934; established first S. Am. transcontinental telephone line, Montevideo-Buenos Aires-Santiago, 1928; transmission surveys, Sweden, 1920, Italy, 1922. Mem. Am. Inst. Elec. Engrs., N.Y. Elec. Soc., Harvard Engring. Soc. Republican. Baptist. Home: 52 Mountain Av., Maplewood, N.J. Office: 463 West St., New York, N.Y.

HUBBARD, John Charles, physicist; b. Boulder, Colo., Apr. 16, 1879; s. James Edwin and Rhoda Maude (Duke) H.; B.S., U. of Colo., 1901; Ph.D., Clark U., 1904; LL.D., Loyola Coll., Baltimore, 1938; m. Gertrude L. Pardieck, Feb. 9, 1929. Instr. in physics, at Simmons Coll., Boston, 1904-05; asst. prof. physics, New York U., 1905-06, Clark U., 1906-11; prof. physics, Clark Coll., 1911-16; professor and head of physics department, New York University, 1916-1927; prof. same, Johns Hopkins University since 1927; Dir. summer work in physics, New York U., 1906, U. of Colo., 1912-14; research engr., Western Electric Co., summer 1917. Commd. capt. Signal Corps, U.S.R., Div. Research and Insp., Sept. 29, 1917; active service in France, information sect. Office of Chief Signal Officer, A.E.F.; official historian, Signal Corps, A.E.F.; maj., Oct. 4, 1918; discharged, May 20, 1919. Officier d'Académie Instruction Publique, 1919. Fellow A.A.A.S., Am. Acad. Arts and Sciences, Am. Physical Soc.; mem. Optical Soc. America, Am. Acoustical Soc., American Association of Physics Teachers, American Assn. of Univ. Profs., Beta Theta Pi; rep. of Am. Inst. of Physics on Am. Engring. Standards Com.; member at large Div. of Physical Sciences of Nat. Research Council, 1931-33. Author various papers giving results of original physical research. Asso. editor Physical Rev., 1933-35. Address: 312 St. Dunstans Rd., Baltimore, Md.

HUBBARD, John W., corpn. official; b. Pittsburgh, Pa.; s. Charles White and Cleo (Winslow) H.; student Pa. Mil. Coll., Chester, U. of Pittsburgh; m. Cora M. Pack (died 1916); 1 dau., Cora W. (wife of John C. Williams, U.S.A.). Began as mfr., 1887; now chmn. bd. Hubbard & Co.; also chmn. bd. Ralston Steel Car Co.; pres. Sands Level & Tool Co., Campbell Transportation Co.; dir. New York Air Brake Co., Detroit Seamless Steel Tubes Co., Alton R.R. Co., Pittsburgh Oil & Gas Co., City Ice and Fuel Co. Episcopalian. Clubs: Duquesne, Pittsburgh Athletic, Pittsburgh Field (Pittsburgh); Lotos, New York Yacht (New York); Chicago Yacht; Longue Vue Country. Office: Granite Bldg., Pittsburgh, Pa.

HUBBARD, Wilbur Ross, lawyer; b. Chestertown, Md., Aug. 2, 1896; s. Wilbur Watson and Etta (Ross) H.; A.B., Yale U., 1920; LL.B., George Washington U. Law Sch., 1927; unmarried. Engaged as treas. Hubbard Fertilizer Co., Baltimore, Md.; 1920-24; admitted to bar D.C., 1927, and to Md. bar, 1928; in practice of law at Chestertown, Md., since 1929; served as mem. Md. Ho. of Dels., 1934-38; pres. Peerless Fertilizer Co., Chestertown, Md., since 1938; dir. Potomac Poultry Food Co., Summers Fertilizer Co. Served as 2nd lt. F.A., U.S.A. during World War. Del to Dem. Nat. Conv. Phila., 1936. Mem. Am. Bar Assn., Md. Bar Assn., Soc. Colonial Wars, S.R., M.F.H. Assn., New York. Democrat. Episcopalian (vestryman). Clubs: Green Spring Valley Hunt, Elkridge-Harford Hunt (Baltimore); Chester River Yacht and Country, Kent County Hounds (Chestertown). Address: Chestertown, Md.

HUBBS, Robert Colsher, clergyman; b. Phila., Pa., Sept. 29, 1899; s. William Colsher and Mary Lillian (Elliot) H.; grad. Germantown (Pa.) High Sch., 1919; student St. Stephen's Coll., 1919-21; A.B., Swarthmore Coll., 1924; student Gen. Theol. Sem., 1924-27; unmarried. Ordained to ministry of Episcopal Ch., June 1927; curate St. Bartholomew's Ch., New York, 1927-28; curate Christ Ch., Newark, N.J., 1928-30, priest-in-charge, 1930-31; vicar St. Ambrose's Ch., Phila., since Dec. 1931. Trustee St. Agnes House, Phila. Mem. Eulexian Soc. Home: 3427 N. Howard St. Office: Howard and Ontario Sts., Philadelphia, Pa.

HUBER, Charles Frederick; b. Pottsville, Pa., Dec. 22, 1871; s. August M. and Minna L. (Kopp) H.; ed. pub. schs.; m. Nelle Andrews Daugherty, Sept. 12, 1894 (died June 12, 1923); children—Paul Daugherty, Thomas Charles. Began with Lehigh & Wilkes-Barre Coal Co. as chmn. engring. dept., 1887, and successively div. engr., 1891-98, chief engr., 1898-1903, gen. supt., 1903-09, v.p. and gen. mgr., 1909-14, pres., 1914-29; chmn. bd. Glen Alden Coal Co., which acquired former co., since 1930 (except when acting as administrator for the anthracite industry, 1935-37); pres. The Lehigh & Wilkes-Barre Corpn. (Del.); chmn. Delaware, Lackawanna & Western Coal Co., Burns Brothers; v.p. First Nat. Bank of Wilkes-Barre. Pres. Anthracite Inst. Mem. Am. Inst. Mining and Metall. Engrs. Republican. Presbyn. Mason. Clubs: Westmoreland, Franklin, Wyoming Valley Country. Home: 24 South River St. Office: 16 South River St., Wilkes-Barre, Pa.

HUBER, Charles Henry, educator; b. Nebraska City, Neb., June 7, 1871; s. Prof. Eli (D.D.) and Mary Ellen (Deibert) H.; grad. Gettysburg (Pa.) Acad., 1888; B.A., Gettysburg Coll., 1892, M.A., 1895, Litt. D., 1914; grad. Gettysburg Theol. Sem., 1896; m. Louise Annan, Dec. 18, 1897; children—Elizabeth Annan (Mrs. William M. Welch II), Charles Henry. Master in Gettysburg Acad., 1892-96, headmaster since 1896; dir. women's div. Gettysburg Coll. since 1935; pres. Gettysburg Ice & Storage Co., Adams County Cold Storage Co.; vice-pres. Gettysburg Nat. Bank. Chmn Adams Co. Council of Defence, World War; mem. Gettysburg Town Council. Mem. Assn. Colls. and Prep. Schs. of Middle States, Phi Beta Kappa, Kappa Phi Kappa, Phi Gamma Delta. Republican. Lutheran. Clubs: Heteria Literary; Tumbling Run Game. Home: Gettysburg, Pa.

HUBER, Charles Joseph, dir. testing labs.; b. Attica, Ind., Aug. 24, 1886; s. Peter and Magdelena (Loibl) H.; B.S. in E.E., Purdue U., 1908, M.S., same, 1911; m. Ethel Lasier, Dec. 16, 1914; children—Mary Ellen, Carl Lasier. Began as lab. asst., Nat. Bur. Standards, Washington, 1908 to 1913; elec. engr., Larkin & Co., 1913-17; exec. engr., United Drug Co., 1920-23; Far-East mgr., United States Testing Co., Inc., at Shanghai, China, 1923-27; research dir., Cheney Bros., Manchester, Conn., 1927-31; dir. labs., United States Testing Co., Inc., Hoboken, N.J. since 1932. Captain Ordnance Dept., U.S. Army, 1917-19. Mem. A.A.A.S., Am. Inst. Elec. Engrs., Optical Soc. of America, Am. Inst. of Physics. Republican. Presbyn. Club: Shanghai Tiffin (New York). Home: 186 Godwin Av., Ridgewood. Office: 1415 Park Av., Hoboken, N.J.

HUBER, Frederick R., music; b. Baltimore, Md., Jan. 12, 1887; s. Robert and Mathilda Huber; ed. Baltimore City Coll., Peabody Conservatory of Music; unmarried. Teacher of piano, Peabody Conservatory; mgr. Peabody Summer Sch.; municipal dir. of music; local rep. Chicago and Met. Grand Opera cos.; mgr. Baltimore Choir Bur.; organist and dir., St. Marks R.C. Ch., St. Patricks R.C. Ch., Franklin St. Presbyterian Ch.; sec. and treas. Baltimore Opera Club; sec. and mng. dir. Lyric Theatre. Clubs: University, Baltimore Country (Baltimore); Bohemians (New York). Home: Homewood Apts. Office: Peabody Institute, 17 E. Vernon Pl., Baltimore, Md.

HUBER, John Franklin, teacher and research in anatomy; b. Ann Arbor, Mich., Nov. 8, 1904; s. Gotthelf Carl and Lucy Ann (Parker) H.; A.B., U. of Mich., 1925, M.D., 1929, A.M., 1927, Ph.D., 1933; m. Gladys Boutilier, Apr. 10, 1933; 1 dau., Candace. Asst. in anatomy, U. of Mich., 1926-28, instr. in anatomy, U. of Mich. Med. Sch., 1928-36; asso. prof. of anatomy, Temple U. Med. Sch. since 1936. Mem. Am. Assn. Anatomists, Physiol. Soc. of Phila., Galens (U. of Mich.), Alpha Sigma Phi, Phi Rho Sigma, Pi Delta Epsilon, Phi Sigma, Phi Beta Kappa, Phi Kappa Phi, Sigma Xi, Alpha Omega Alpha. Republican. Presbyterian. Home: Moreno Rd., Wynnewood, Pa. Office: Temple University Medical School, Philadelphia, Pa.

HUCKIN, LeRoy Booth, lawyer; b. Englewood, N.J., Dec. 24, 1898; s. Charles and Ada (Booth) H.; LL.B., N.Y. Law Sch., N.Y. City, 1919; m. Hazel Bentley, of Delmar, N.Y., Mar. 10, 1924; children—LeRoy Thomas, John Bentley. Admitted to N.J. bar as atty., 1920, as counsellor, 1923; engaged in gen. practice of law at Englewood since 1920; mem. firm Huckin & Huckin since 1922; served as police justice City of Englewood continuously since 1922; mem. Bergen Co. Safety Council. Mem. Am. Bar Assn., N.J. State Bar Assn., Bergen Co. Bar Assn. Independent Republican. Episcopalian. Club: Englewood. Home: 326 Murray Av. Office: 1 Engle St., Englewood, N.J.

HUDELSON, Earl, prof. education; b. Princeton, Ind., Oct. 16, 1888; s. William Crawford and Nancy Virginia (McClure) H.; grad. high sch., Princeton, Ind., 1907; B.A., Ind. U., 1911, M.A., 1912; Ph.D., Columbia, 1923; m. Helena Houf, Feb. 24, 1915; children—Virginia Louisa, William Henry. Instr. in English, Ind. U., 1911-12, Tome Sch., Port Deposit, Md., 1912-14; critic in English, Univ. High Sch., Bloomington, Ind., 1914-18; asst. in English, Teachers' Coll. (Columbia), 1918-19; prof. secondary edn., W.Va., U., 1920-23; prof. edn., U. of Minn., 1923-30; dean of Coll. of Edn., West Va. Univ., since 1930; teacher, summers, Ind. U., Teachers' Coll. (Columbia), univs. of Mich., Chicago and Minn., etc. Mem. N.E.A., Nat. Soc. for Study of Edn., Phi Beta Kappa, Phi Delta Kappa, Kappa Delta Pi. Author: Hudelson English Composition Scale (monograph), 1922; English Composition—Its Aim, Methods and Measurement (monograph), 1923; Hudelson Typical Composition Ability Scale (monograph), 1923; Class Size at the College Level, 1928. Editor and collaborator of Problems of College Education, 1928. Home: 305 Euclid Av., Morgantown, W.Va.

HUDGINS, Herbert Eugene, clergyman; b. Baltimore, Md., Nov. 20, 1900; s. John William and Metta L. (Jarvis) H.; prep. edn. Western Md. Prep. Sch., Westminster, Md., 1920-21; A.B., Western Md. Coll., 1925; S.T.B., Westminster (Md.) Theol. Sem., 1927, S.T.D., 1933; m. Frances Louise Browning, June 18, 1931; 1 dau., Jean Louise. Ordained to ministry Meth. Protestant Ch., 1927; pastor, Lewistown, Md., 1925-27, Doylesburg, Pa., 1927-31, Hampton, Va., 1931-33, Greenwood, Del., 1933-34, St. Paul's Ch., Baltimore, since 1934; instr. New Testament Greek, Westminster Theol. Sem., 1936-38. Home: 524 N. Linwood Av., Baltimore, Md.

HUDNUT, Herbert Beecher, clergyman; b. Port Jervis, N.Y., Feb. 4, 1894; s. William Herbert and Harriet Shew (Beecher) H.; grad. Rayen High Sch., Youngstown, O., 1911; A.B., Princeton U., 1916; S.T.B., Western Theol. Sem., Pittsburgh, 1926; m. Edith Suzanne Schaaf, June 3, 1924; children—Elizabeth Anne, Dorothy Ruth, Mary Joan, Herbert Beecher. Civil engring. work, Youngstown Sheet & Tube Co., 1911-12; sales Trumbull Steel Co., Warren, O., 1916; sales and advertising, Gen. Fireproofing Co., Youngstown, O., 1919-23; ordained to ministry of Presbyterian Ch., 1926; minister Cross Creek (Pa.) Presbyn. Ch., 1924-26; asso. minister City Temple, Dallas, Tex., 1926-28; minister Windermere Presbyn. Ch., East Cleveland, O., 1928-32; minister Presbyn. Ch., Bellevue, Pa., since 1932. Served as 2d lt. 115th Field Arty., U.S. Army, 1917-19. Mem. Bd. of Nat. Missions, Presbyn. Ch. in U.S.A., 1930-32; dir. Pittsburgh Community Fund, 1939-42. Trustee Children's Service Bureau of Pittsburgh; trustee Wood's Run Settlement. Mem. Dial Lodge (Princeton, U.). Home: 160 S. Euclid Av. Office: 45 N. Fremont Av., Bellevue, Pa.

HUDSON, Hoyt Hopewell, univ. prof.; b. Norfolk, Neb., July 6, 1893; s. Rev. Fletcher Edward and Mayme (Fitz) Randolph H.; A.B., Huron (S.D.) Coll., 1911; A.M., U. of Denver, 1913; student U. of Chicago, 1916-17; Ph.D., Cornell U., 1923; Litt.D., Huron Coll., 1938; m. Margaret Calvert Dille, Dec. 16, 1917; children—Randolph Hoyt, Michael Calvert. Teacher high schs., successively at Coeur d'Alene, Ida., Duluth, Minn., Cleveland, O., 1913-20; instr. pub. speaking Cornell U., 1920-23; asst. prof. English and pub. speaking, Swarthmore Coll., 1923-25; prof. English, U. of Pittsburgh, 1925-27; asso. prof. pub. speaking, Princeton, 1927-31, prof., 1931-33, prof. rhetoric and oratory since 1933, chmn. dept. of English since 1933. Research asso., Huntington Library, 1934. Lecturer summer schs. Cornell, 1924, 25, 29, U. of Colo., 1935, Harvard, 1937, U. of Calif. at Los Angeles, 1938. Trustee Princeton Country Day Sch. Mem. Phi Beta Kappa, Modern Lang. Assn. America, Nat. Assn. Teachers of Speech. Mem. Soc. of Friends. Clubs: Bookfellows (Chicago); Princeton (Phila.). Author: First Course in Public Speaking (with J. A. Winans), 1930. Translator: Kant's Religion within the Limits of Reason Alone (with T. M. Greene), 1934. Editor: Poetry of the English Renaissance (with J. W. Hebel), 1929; John Hoskins' Directions for Speech and Style, 1935. Mng. editor The Step Ladder, 1930, asso. editor since 1931; editor Quarterly Jour. of Speech, 1933-35. Home: 176 Western Way, Princeton, N.J.

HUDSON, Thomas Henry, judge; b. Kirby, Greene Co., Pa., Oct. 5, 1874; s. Samuel and Harriet Louisa (Mestrezat) H.; A.B., Waynesburg Coll., 1894; A.B., Princeton U., 1895; m. Lucille Scott Robinson, Oct. 16, 1906; children—Thomas H., Elizabeth Louise, Mary Hope. Read law with uncle, Hon. S. Leslie Mestrezat, justice Supreme Court of Pa.; admitted to Pa. bar, 1898, and began practice at Uniontown; asst. dist. atty., Fayette Co., Pa., 1902-05, dist. atty., 1905-08, county solicitor, 1912-15; president judge Court of Common Pleas of Fayette Co., 14th Jud. Dist., Jan. 1, 1926-Jan. 1, 1938; now in practice with son under firm name of Hudson & Hudson. Mem. Draft Bd., Fayette Co., World War, also head of Red Cross campaign for the county. Trustee Waynesburg Coll. Mem. Pa. State Bar Assn., S.A.R. (pres. Ft. Necessity chapter). Republican. Presbyterian. Clubs: Uniontown Country, Princeton of Western Pa. Home: 43 Lincoln St. Office: Blackstone Bldg., Uniontown, Pa.

HUEBNER, Grover Gerhardt; b. Manitowoc, Wis., Nov. 13, 1884; s. Frederick August and Wilhelmina (Dicke) H.; A.B., U. of Wis., 1905, A.M., 1906; Ph.D., U. of Pa., 1908; m. Hallie Madeline Beall, June 2, 1913; children—Robert Dinsmoor, Frederick Beall. Asst. prof., 1908, now prof. transportation and commerce, Wharton Sch. of Finance and Commerce (U. of Pa.); lecturer on transportation, Extension Dept., Columbia U., 1914, 15. Spl. statistician on tolls, Isthmian Canal Commn., 1911, 12. Economic advisor, U.S. Maritime Commn., 1937; trade expert, U.S. War Trade Bd., 1917; examiner, Federal Trade Commn., 1918; Mem. Am. Econ. Assn., Phi Beta Kappa. Author: Railroad Traffic and Rates, 1911; Agricultural Commerce, 1915; Principles of Ocean Transportation, 1918; Ocean Steamship Traffic Management, 1919; Railroad Freight Service, 1926; Principles of Transportation, 1928; Foreign Trade, 1930; Transportation by Water, 1935. Home: 26 S. Pennock Av., Highland Park, Upper Darby, Pa.

HUEBNER, Solomon Stephen, coll. prof.; b. Manitowoc, Wis., March 6, 1882; s. Frederick and Minnie W. (Dicke) H.; B.L., U. of Wis., 1902, M.L., 1903, Ph.D., U. of Pa., 1904, Sc.D., 1931; Harrison fellow, economics, U. of Pa., 1904; m. Ethel Elizabeth Mudie, June 24, 1908; children—Margaret Wilhelmina, John Mudie, Ethel Elizabeth, Esther Ann. Instr. ins. and commerce, 1904-06, asst. pro., 1906-08, prof. since 1908, U. of Pa. Expert to Com. on Merchant Marine and Fisheries of Ho. of Rep. and to U.S. Shipping Bd., for various periods, 1911-34. Spl. lecturer, Columbia, 1915-17, N.Y.U., 1917. Contbr. Am. Year Book, 1910-19 and since 1925. Member ins. advisory com., U.S. Chamber Commerce, 1924-30, sub-com. on marine ins. since 1930; mem. ins. advisory com. Phila. Chamber Commerce; mem. com. on causes of accidents of Nat. Conf. on Street and Highway Safety, also chmn. ins. com. of Nat. Conf., 1925; mem. Merchant Marine Conf. Com. on relation of the merchant marine to Am. foreign trade and nat. defense; chmn. pub. information com. of Phila. Fire Prevention Assn. Ednl. adviser Mass. Mut. Life Ins. Co., 1929-34; mem. com. ins. advisers Gen. Fed. Women's Clubs. Fellow Ins. Inst. America, Casualty Actuarial Soc.; mem. Am. Assn. of Univ. Teachers of Ins. (pres.), Am. Federation of Insurance (com. on edn), Am. Assn. Univ. Profs. (com. on ins.), Nat. Assn. Life Underwriters, American Philosophical Society, American Academy of Political and Social Science, Am. Inst. Banking, Am. Econ. Assn., Nat. Inst., Social Sciences, Union League Club of Philadelphia, Phi Beta Kappa, Beta Gamma Sigma, Pi Gamma Mu, Kappa Alpha Phi (hon. nat. pres.), Acacia. Pres. chmn. exec. com. and dir. Am. Coll. Life Underwriters, dean, 1927-34; mem. com. on life ins. of Am. Inst. for Endowments; adviser to com. on publicity of N.Y. Stock Exchange; mem. of com. considering reorganization of the U.S. Shipping Bur. and chmn. of the sub-com. on marine insurance, 1934; chmn. ins. sub-comn. of U. of Pa. Bequest Com.; mem. Casualty Actuarial Soc. Mason. Author: Steamship Agreements and Affiliations in the American Foreign and Domestic Trade, 1913; The Stock Exchange, 1918; Marine Insurance, 1920; Status of Marine Insurance in the United States, 1920; Legislative Obstructions to the Development of Marine Insurance in the United States, 1921; The Stock Market, 1921, 34; Property Insurance, 1922; Life Insurance, 1923, 35; The Human Value in Business Compared with the Property Value, 1924; The Economics of Life Insurance, 1927; Life Insurance as Investment, 1933. Home: 697 S. Highland Av., Merion, Pa.

HUFF, Wilbert James, chemist, chemical and gas engr.; b. Butler, Pa., Oct. 4, 1890; s. Leonidas Martin and Mary Ann (Weidhas) H.; A.B., Ohio Northern U., 1911, D.Sc., 1927; A.B., Yale, 1914, Ph.D. in Chemistry, 1917; m. Rachel Smith, May 11, 1918. With Barrett Co. Research Lab., N.Y. City, 1917-18; lt. Chem. Warfare Service, comdg. Princeton Research Detachment, U.S.A., 1918-19; research chemist U.S. Bur. Mines, 1919-20; in charge research div. Koppers Co. Labs., Pittsburgh, 1920-24; fellow Mellon Inst. Industrial Research, 1920-24; prof. gas engring., Johns Hopkins, 1924-37; prof. of chem. engring. and chmn. dept. chem. engring. and chmn. Div. of Physical Sciences, U. of Md., since 1937; consultant practice; chief chemist explosives div., U.S. Bureau of Mines, 1935-37, and consulting explosives chemist of that Bureau since 1937. Mem. Am. Chem. Soc. (chmn. gas and fuel div. and mem. of the council, 1935). Am. Inst. Chem. Engrs. (chmn. Md. sect. 1935), Am. Gas Assn. (chmn. chem. com. 1931), Southern Gas Assn., Am. Assn. Univ. Profs., Sigma Xi, Alpha Chi Sigma; hon. mem. Tau Beta Pi Fraternity; fellow A.A.A.S. Researches on rate of hydrolysis of hypophosphoric acid; researches on catalytic air oxidation of benzene to maleic acid; researches on cause of after-corrosion of firearms, origin of carbon disulfide in gas making, etc. Contbr. on chem. and engring. problems on explosives and on gas mfr., distribution and utilization. Home: 15 Hilltop Road, Sligo Park Hills, Silver Spring, Md.

HUFF, William Kistler, editor; b. Schnecksville, Pa., Oct. 11, 1888; s. Dr. Irvin F. and Isabel (Kistler) H.; A.B., cum laude, Harvard, 1910 (commencement speaker); m. Edna Elizabeth Jacoby, June 16, 1914; children—William Jacoby, Richard Jacoby. Asst. prin. high sch., Sellersville, 1910-11; instr. in English, U. of Me., 1911-12; master in history and English, Barnard Sch. for Boys, N.Y. City, 1912-14; sec. Am. Soc. for Extension of Univ. Teaching, Phila., 1914-21; exec. dir. Phila. Forum and editor Phila. Forum Mag. since 1921; sec. mgr., 1935, 1936, Robin Hood Dell Concerts, Inc. (summer concerts Phila. Orchestra); sec. and dir. General Credit, Inc., Washington, D.C. Mem. bd. of dirs. Legal Aid Soc.; mem. exec. com. Foreign

Policy Association; mem. bd. of dirs and sec.-treas. Phila. Opera Co. Mem. Am. Acad. Polit. and Social Science, Phila. Com. on Pub. Affairs. Clubs: Harvard, University, Franklin Inn, Town Hall (New York); Manufacturers and Bankers, Contemporary (sec.). Co-Author: This Is Russia, 1932. Home: Media and Weller Avs., Brookline. Office: Lincoln-Liberty Bldg., Philadelphia, Pa.

HUFFERD, Ralph William, research chemist; b. nr. Chanute, Kan., Aug. 5, 1892; s. Jacob Harvey and Belle (Woodward) H.; A.B., Washington U., St. Louis, 1915; A.M., U. of Ill., 1918, Ph.D., 1920; grad. study, U. of Graz, Austria, 1930-31; m. Margery Simpson, July 21, 1927. Asst. prof. chemistry, DePauw U., 1920-22, asso. prof., 1922-25, prof. chemistry, 1925-33; organic research chemist to search for new products from Pa. crude oil, Kendall Refining Co., Bradford, Pa., since 1936. Served as pvt. M.C., U.S.A. during World War, dischd. as corpl.; now maj. C.W.S. Res. Fellow Ind. Acad. Sci. Mem. Am. Chem. Soc., Sigma Xi, Phi Lambda Upsilon, Am. Legion, Res. Officers Assn. Republican. Mason. Home: 200 E. Main St., Bradford, Pa.

HUFNAGEL, Frederick Bernhard, steel mfr.; b. Mt. Vernon, N.Y., Oct. 31, 1878; s. Conrad Bernhard and Mary (Imhoff) H.; M.E., Cornell U., 1900; m. Ceora Wilson Thompson, June 18, 1910; children—Frederick Bernhard, Ceora Jennings. Began as draftsman Am. Steel & Wire Co., 1900; successively mill foreman, mgr., asst. supt., supt. and gen. supt. Jones & Laughlin Steel Co., 1901-20; pres. Pittsburgh Crucible Steel Co., 1921-25; pres. Crucible Steel Co. of America since 1926, chmn. bd. since 1937; chmn. bd. Toledo Ship Building Co.; pres. Crucible Fuel Co.; v.p. and dir. Gt. Lakes Steamship Co., Pittsburgh Crucible Steel Co. Trustee Grove City (Pa.) Coll. Mem. Kappa Sigma. Republican. Presbyn. Clubs: University (New York); Duquesne (Pittsburgh); Allegheny Country (Sewickley, Pa.); Round Hill (Greenwich); Blind Brook (Port Chester, N.Y.). Home: Dingletown Rd., Greenwich, Conn. Officer: 405 Lexington Av., New York, N.Y.; and Oliver Bldg., Pittsburgh, Pa.

HUFNAGEL, Henry Michael, banker; b. Fryburg, Pa., Dec. 28, 1880; s. Andrew and Lena (Rapp) H.; Master of Accounts, St. Vincent Coll., Beatty, Pa., 1899; m. Elizabeth Ruth Faller, July 31, 1907; children—Andrew, Frances Eleanor (Mrs. W. E. Quinlisk), Paul R. H., Leon C., James M., Betty F., Jeanne M., Henry M. Began as accountant, 1900; deputy treas. Clarion County, Pa., 1900-06, county clerk, 1906-09, prothonotary, 1909-16; asst. sec.-treas. Citizens Trust Co., 1916-20, trust officer, 1920-25, sec.-treas., 1925-28, pres. since 1928; dir. Sligo Nat. Bank, Sligo, Pa., First Nat. Bank, Fryburg, Pa. Democrat. Elk, K.C. Club: Pinecrest Country. Home: 2 Greenville Av. Office: Citizens Trust Co., Clarion, Pa.

HUGHES, Alvaroe Glenn, judge; b. Ravenswood, W.Va., Nov. 2, 1869; s. Lewis H. and Mary Ann (Lane) H.; student Wesleyan Coll., Buckhannon, W.Va., 1891-94; A.B., W.Va. Univ.; LL.B., W.Va. Univ. Law Sch., 1902; m. Nellie Jackson, Sept. 1, 1909; children—Helen Louise, Robert Glenn. Became teacher pub. schs., W.Va., 1890; admitted to W.Va. bar, 1902, and since engaged in gen. practice of law at Kingwood; county pros. atty., 1908-17; judge W.Va. Circuit Court, term 1921-44. Republican. Mem. M.E. Ch. Mason. Clubs: Rotary, Country (Kingwood); Masonic (Wheeling). Address: Kingwood, W.Va.

HUGHES, Don Emanuel, judge; b. Rock City, N.Y., Mar. 2, 1880; s. James Henry and Lucretia (Silviera) H.; grad. Olean (N.Y.) High Sch., 1900; B.A., Columbia U., 1904; unmarried. Prin. high sch., Pa., 1904-09; headmaster of schs., Bermuda, 1909-12; asso. judge of Sullivan Co., Pa., since 1935. Wrote lyrics for ballads "Waiting for Thee" and "Garden Behind the Moon." Address: S. Turnpike, Dushore, Pa.

HUGHES, Fred A., lawyer; b. Stone Mills, N.Y., Feb. 16, 1887; s. John D. and Carrie (Dickinson) H; student Scranton (Pa.) Central High Sch., 1902-06; A.B., U. of Pa., 1910, LL.B., Law Sch., 1912; m. Sarah Ethel Siddell, June 20, 1914; children—Fred A., Robert L., Howard S., John D. Admitted to Pa. bar, 1912, and since in practice at Scranton; trustee Dickson City (Pa.) Nat. Bank; dir. Lorenson Mfg. Co. Home: 533 Morgan St., Dickson City, Pa. Office: Lincoln Trust Co. Bldg., Scranton, Pa.

HUGHES, Frederic John, physician; b. Plainfield, N.J., July 21, 1876; s. John W. and Josephine (Owens) H.; student U. of Pa., 1894-95; M.D., Coll. of Phys. & Surgs. of Columbia U., 1899; m. Loretta F. Flanagan, Nov. 27, 1907; children—Dorothy T. (Mrs. Paul R. Brousse), Frederic J., Edward R. Interne St. Vincent's Hosp., 1899-1901, Sloane Maternity Hosp., 1901, N.Y. Foundling Hosp., 1901-02, Seaside Hosp., 1902, all in N.Y. City; engaged in gen. practice of medicine at Plainfield, N.J., since 1902; cons. pediatrician, Muhlenberg Hosp., Plainfield since 1928; consultant in internal medicine, Somerset Hosp., Somerville, N.J., since 1932. Mem. Rockefeller Tuberculosis Commn. to France, 1917-18; capt. Red Cross Tuberculosis Div., France, 1918. Trustee N.J. State Sanitorium for Tuberculous Disease; trustee Bonnie Burn Sanitorium, N.J. Fellow Acad. of Medicine, N.Y. Mem. Am. Med. Assn., N.J. State Med. Soc., etc. Roman Catholic. Clubs: Salmagundi, National Arts (New York). Home: 101 W. 7th St. Office: 706 Park Av., Plainfield, N.J.

HUGHES, Harold L(incoln), v.p. U.S. Steel Corpn.; b. Saugus, Mass., Nov. 2, 1879; s. James Riley and Laura Geraldine (Mansfield) H.; prep. edn. Lynn (Mass.) Classical High Sch., 1893-96; B.S., summa cum laude, Harvard, 1900; m. Jane Plunkett, of San Francisco, Feb. 9, 1903 (died June 27, 1930); 1 dau., Mary Caroline. With U.S. Steel Corpn. or its subsidiaries since 1901, beginning as draftsman Carnegie Steel Co., Pittsburgh, 1901-03; served in New York, 1903-05, Montreal, Can., 1905-07, Sydney, Australia, 1907-12, New York since 1913; v.p. U.S. Steel Corpn. since 1937. Treas. and dir. Am. Iron and Steel Inst. Republican. Clubs: Metropolitan, Harvard, India House (New York); Duquesne (Pittsburgh); Plainfield Country (Plainfield, N.J.). Home: 559 Belvidere Av., Plainfield, N.J.

HUGHES, Howard Larison, librarian; b. Trenton, N.J., Aug. 18, 1886; s. Joseph Edgar and Ann Matilda (Smith) H.; A.B., Princeton, 1911, A.M., 1925; m. Ethel Mary McKee, Apr. 26, 1917 (died Feb. 7, 1921); 1 son, David Lee; m. 2d, Mildred Rankin, Nov. 17, 1926, 1 dau., Avis Holloway. Asst. reference librarian, Princeton U., Aug.-Nov. 1911; librarian Free Pub. Library, Trenton, since Nov. 1911; camp librarian, A.L.A., Camp Dix, N.J., Nov. 1917-Mar. 1918. Mem. A.L.A., N.J. Library Assn. (pres. 1914-15 and 1933-34), Trenton Hist. Soc. (pres. 1932-33), N.J. Soc. S.R. Clubs: Rotary, Symposium. Wrote chapter on Schools and Libraries in a History of Trenton, 1679-1929. Home: 230 Hillcrest Av. Address: Free Public Library, Trenton, N.J.

HUGHES, I. Lamont, corporation official; b. at Mercer, Pa., Jan. 25, 1878; s. John and Mary Elizabeth (Ketler) H.; grad. high sch., North Braddock, Pa.; m. Elizabeth Little, 1902; 1 son, I. Lamont. Began in employ of Edgar Thomson Works of Carnegie Steel Co., Ltd., 1897; trans. to Donora (Pa.) Works of Am. Steel & Wire Co., 1901, then in 1905 to Youngstown dist. plants and also Greenville (Pa.) plants of Carnegie Steel Co.; apptd. asst. supt. all bar mills, Youngstown dist., 1906, later supt.; asst. gen. supt. Youngstown dist. plants, Jan. 1916; gen. supt. for Canadian Steel Corpn., at Ojibway, Ont., Can., June 1916; gen. supt. for U.S. Steel Ordnance Co. at Neville Island, Pa., June 1918; pres. Lorain Steel Co., Johnstown, Pa., May 1919; apptd. gen. supt. Carnegie Steel Co.'s operations in Youngstown dist., Jan. 1, 1920; elected v.p. Carnegie Steel Co., Jan. 1, 1925; elected v.p. in charge operations U.S. Steel Corpn., hdqrs. in N.Y. City, May 1, 1928; elected pres. Carnegie Steel Co., Sept. 1, 1930, exec. and dir., Oct. 1, 1935; v.p. Carnegie-Ill. Steel Corpn., 1935-36; pres. Carnegie Land Corpn., Conneaut Land Co., Sharon Coke Co., Bessemer Electric Power Co., Carnegie Libraries of Braddock, Homestead and Duquesne; dir. many cos. Mem. advisory board Pittsburgh Ordnance Dist.; trustee Grove City Coll. (Pa.), Carnegie Hero Fund Commn.; dir. U.S. Steel and Carnegie Pension Fund. Mem. Am. Iron and Steel Inst., Engrs. Soc. of Western Pa., Army Ordnance Assn., Chamber Commerce of Pittsburgh, Ohio State Chamber Commerce, Mich. Soc. S.A.R. Presbyn. Clubs: Duquesne, University, Longue Vue, Pittsburgh Athletic (dir.), Railway (Pittsburgh); Youngstown Club, Youngstown Country. Home: Woodland Rd., Pittsburgh, Pa.*

HUGHES, James H., U.S. senator; b. Kent Co., Del., Jan. 14, 1867; s. Eben and Rebecca Hurd; student Collegiate Inst., Dover, Del.; m. Caroline Taylor, Aug. 23, 1905; children—Caroline, Mary Adelaide (Mrs. W. Oakman Hay), James H. Admitted to Del. bar, 1890; mem. firm Hughes, Terry & Terry; sec. of state, State of Del., 1896-1901; U.S. senator from Del., term 1937-43; dir. Farmers Bank of Del. Mem. Am. Del. State and Kent Co. bar assns., S.A.R. Democrat. Mason. Home: Dover, Del.

HUGHES, James Whilden, lawyer; b. Washington, D.C., July 22, 1898; s. George Bond and Mary Jean (Robinson) H.; D.V.M., U.S. Coll. of Vet. Surgeons, Washington, D.C., 1918; LL.B., Washington Coll. of Law, Washington, D.C., 1928; m. Gertrude Ruth Tyrrell, Dec. 21, 1930. Engaged in practice vet. medicine in Ammendale, Prince Georges Co., Md., 1918-29; veternarian, Md. State Bd. Agr., Elkton, Md., 1929-30; admitted to Md. bar, 1929 and engaged in gen. practice of law at Elkton since 1930. Member Cecil County Com. of Boy Scouts of America. Served as sec. of Elkton Chamber of Commerce, 1934-35, pres., 1936-37. Dir. Cecil County Library, Children's Aid Soc. Mem. Bar Assn., Md. State Bar Assn., Am. Vet. Med. Assn. Cecil County Bar Assn. Republican. Seventh Day Adventist. Clubs: Rotary of Elkton (pres. 1938); North East River Yacht of Md. (dir.) Home: 108 Park Circle, Elkton, Maryland. Office: Peoples Bank Bldg., Elkton, Md.

HUGHES, John Henry, supt. schs.; b. Rathmel, Pa., Sept. 3, 1893; s. Edward and Jane (Bowser) H.; ed. Reynoldsville High Sch. and Clarion Teachers' Col.; B.Sc., U. of Pittsburgh, 1930, Ed.M., 1937; m. Alice Faye Cooper, Aug. 19, 1925; children— Richard Herbert, John Russell. Elementary Teacher, Jefferson Co., 1912-13, Allegheny Co., 1913-14; instr. Reynoldsville (Pa.) High Sch. 1914-17, prin., 1919-22; supervising prin. Reynoldsville pub. schs., 1922-31; supt. Jefferson Co. schs. since 1931. Served with A.E.F., during World War. Mem. N.E.A., Pa. State Edn. Assn., Am. Legion. Baptist. Club: Brookville Community (ex-pres.) Home: 446 Main St. Office: Court House, Brookville, Pa.

HUGHES, John Vernon, surgeon; b. Canada, June 7, 1897; s. Francis William and Eliza Honeyman (Lochead) H.; came to U.S., 1920, naturalized, 1923; ed. Univ. of Western Ont., London, 1913-17; M.B., Univ. of Toronto, 1918; m. Isabel McVittie, Aug. 28, 1922; 1 dau., Helen Margaret. Interne Bellevue Hosp., N.Y. City, 1920-21; engaged in practice of otolaryngology at Passaic, N.J. since 1922; sr. asst. aural surgeon, N.Y. Eye and Ear Infirmary since 1922; aural surgeon, Passaic Gen. Hosp. Served in Med. Corps, Canadian Army, 1918-20. Fellow Am. Coll. Surgs. Mem. Am. Bd. Otolaryngology. Presbyn. Club: City (Passaic). Home: 160 Ayerigg Av. Office: 150 Prospect St., Passaic, N.J.

HUGHES, Percy, university prof.; b. Peshawur, British India, Jan. 23, 1872; s. Thomas Patrick and Eliza (Lloyd) H.; Christ's Hosp., London, 1881-87; Diploma Teachers Coll. (Columbia), 1897; A.B., Alfred U., 1899; A.M., Ph.D., Columbia, 1904; m. Maude Williams, 1913; children (adopted)—Alfred Lloyd, Elizabeth Evelyn. Teacher in secondary schools, 1896-1901; instructor in philosophy, Alfred University, 1898-99; asst. in philosophy, Columbia, 1903-05; instr. in psychology and philosophy, U. of Minn., 1905-06; acting prof. philosophy and dir. extension courses, Tulane U., 1906-07; asst. prof. philosophy and edn., 1907-09, prof., 1909-21, prof. philosophy and psychology, Lehigh U., 1921-31, Clara H. Stewardson prof. philosophy since 1931. Fellow A.A.A.S.; mem. Am. Philos. Soc., Am. Assn. Univ. Profs., Am. Psychol. Assn., Sigma XI. Episcopalian. The Concept Action in History and in Nat. Sciences, 1905; Introduction to Psychology, 1926. Home: Belvidere, N.J.

HUGHES, Ray Osgood, educational author; b. Saxtons River, Vt., Nov. 13, 1879; s. Thomas Henry and Jennie Clara (Osgood) H.; grad. Vt. Acad., Saxtons River, 1896; A.B., Brown U., 1900; A.M., U. of Pittsburgh, 1924; m. Helene W. Hopkins, June 26, 1906. Instr., Williston Sem., Easthampton, Mass., 1900-01, Leland and Gray Sem., Townshend, Vt., 1901-02, Wellesley (Mass.) Boys' Sch., 1902-03, Keystone Acad., Factoryville, Pa., 1903-06, Westbrook Sem., Portland, Me., 1906-07, high sch., West Chester, Pa., 1907-11, 5th Av. High Sch., Pittsburgh, Pa., 1911-13; with Peabody High Sch., same city, 1913-29, vice-prin., 1926-29; dept. of curriculum study, Pittsburgh pub. schs., 1929-39, dir. of citizenship and social studies since 1939; instr. summer sessions Grad. Sch. of Edn., Harvard, 1926-30. Mem. A.A.A.S., Nat. Edn. Assn., American Hist. Assn., American Political Science Assn., Nat. Council for Social Studies (v.p. 1926-27, 1934, 1935; pres. 1936), Nat. Assn. Secondary Sch. Prins., Phi Delta Kappa. Baptist. Club: Unity. Author: Community Civics, 1917; Economic Civics, 1921; Elementary Community Civics, 1922; Problems of American Democracy, 1922; Textbook in Citizenship, 1923; New Community Civics, 1924; The Making of Our United States, 1927; American Citizenship Charts, 1929; Fundamentals of Economics, 1929; Workbook in Civics, 1930; Workbook in American History, 1931; Building Citizenship, 1933; The Making of Today's World, 1935; Workbook in World History, 1936; Building Citizenship Workbook, 1937; teachers' manuals to accompany various texts. Home: 5517 Beverly Pl. Office: Board of Education Bldg., Pittsburgh, Pa.

HUGHES, William Thomas, Jr., lawyer; b. Moundsville, W.Va., May 15, 1910; s. William T. and Retta (Donley) H.; prep. edn. Bellfonte Acad., Bellfonte, Pa.; A.B., W.Va. U., 1931, LL.B., 1933; m. Agnes May Jamison, Sept. 4, 1933; 1 dau., Donna Jane. Admitted to W.Va. bar, 1933 and since in practice, Morgantown; mayor of City of Morgantown, W. Va., since 1938; mem. City Council, Morgantown, 1937. Mem. Monongalia County Bar Assn., Mountain, Sphinx, Spiked Shoe, Kappa Sigma. Republican. Methodist. Club: Kiwanis. Home: Hopecrest. Office: Fidelity Bldg., Morgantown, W.Va.

HUGUS, Wright, lawyer; b. nr. Wheeling, W. Va., Nov. 8, 1890; s. Thomas J. and Annie V. (Wright) H.; A.B., Dartmouth College, 1913; LL.B., Harvard, 1916; m. Martha Majesky, Dec. 27, 1927; children—Mary Anne, Wright. Admitted to W.Va. bar, 1916, and began practice at Wheeling; mem. Schmidt, Hugus & Laas; gen. counsel Wheeling Steel Corpn.; mem. W. Va. Ho. of Delegates, 1921-23, state Senate (chmn. judiciary con. and floor leader), 1923-30; mem. and sec. W.Va. Constl. Commn., 1930; mem. bd. govs. W.Va. Univ. Served in World War 27 mos. 1st lt. inf., later capt., A.G.D. and maj., A.G.D., overseas 14 mos. Mem. Am. and Wheeling bar assns., W.Va. Bar Assn. (pres. 1935-36), Sigma Chi. Republican. Methodist. Mason. Clubs: Twilight, Ft. Henry, Wheeling Country (Wheeling); Dartmouth (New York). Home: Forest Hills, Wheeling. Office: Central Union Bldg., Wheeling, W.Va.

HULBERT, Gustavus Adolphus, cleryman, lecturer; b. Brookside, New Jersey, Mar. 29, 1876; s. John Foster and Sarah Elizabeth (Baird) Hulbert; A.B., Lafayette Coll., Easton, Pa., 1904; Columbia University, 1905, 06; grad. Union Theological Sem., 1907; D.D., Westminster Coll., Mo., 1919, Missouri Valley College, 1919; LL.D. from University of Dubuque, 1927; m. Laura Stowitts, Dec. 1, 1909; children—John Frederick, Robert Putnam. Ordained Congregational ministry, 1907; pastor Nutley, N.J., 1906-09, United Congl. Ch., Newport, R.I., 1909-13, St. Mary's Ch., Omaha, Neb., 1913-17, Kingshighway Presbyn. Ch., St. Louis, 1917-21, Brown Memorial Presbyn. Ch., Baltimore, Md., 1921—. Apptd. reconstruction superintendent young people's work in U.S. by the National Council of Congl. Ch., 1918. Trustee Westminster Coll., Lafayette Coll. Mem. Newport Hist. Soc., State Schs. Assn. of Pa. (mem. exec. and legislative committees). Mem. Judicial Commn. of Gen. Assembly Presbyn. Ch. in U.S.A., 1923; guest preacher, London, summer 1932, auspices Free Ch. Soc. Eng. and Wales; coll. speaker Union, Lafayette, Rutgers, Dubuque, Westminster colls., Union Sem., etc.; lecturer on "Ways to Truth," State Teachers Coll., Pa., 1934. Clubs: Eclectic, Maryland Country; Athletic (St. Louis). Author: Public Education, Our Greatest Public Utility, 1934. Contbr. to How We Got Our Bible (set of books), 1921. Home: (country) Henryville, Pa.*

HULBURT, Lorain Sherman, university prof.; b. Albany, Wis., Mar. 8, 1858; s. Chauncey D. and Sarah E. (Searles) H.; A.B., U. of Wis., 1883, A.M., 1888; Ph.D., Johns Hopkins U., 1894, LL.D. U. of South Dakota, 1927; studied in U. of Göttingen; m. Elizabeth Dorey, Aug. 3, 1886 (died July 20, 1910); children—Edward O., Lorrain C. Prof. mathematics and astronomy, U. of S.D., 1887-91; fellow in mathematics, Clark U., Worcester, Mass., 1891-92; instr. and asso. in mathematics, '1892-97, collegiate prof., 1897-1926, Johns Hopkins U., now emeritus. Fellow A.A.A.S., Am. Math. Soc.; mem. Math. Assn. of America, Phi Beta Kappa, Circolo Matematico di Palmero. Club: Johns Hopkins (Baltimore). Author: Differential and Integral Calculus, 1912. Home: 4515 Garrison Boul. Address: Johns Hopkins Univ., Baltimore, Md.

HULETT, George Augustus, chemist; b. Will Co., Ill., July 15, 1867; s. Frank Amos and Louise (Holmes) H.; Oberlin Coll., 1888-90; A.B., Princeton, 1892; Ph.D., U. of Leipzig, 1898; m. Dency Minerva, d. Dr. J. W. Barker, Aug. 15, 1904; 1 son, George Barker. Asst. in chemistry, Princeton, 1892-96; instr. phys. chemistry, 1899-1904, asst. prof., 1904-05, U. of Mich.; asst. prof. phys. chemistry, 1905-09, prof., 1909—, Princeton U. Mem. U.S. Assay Commn., 1906; chief chemist U.S. Bur. of Mines, 1912-13. Mem. Am. Chem. Soc., Am. Electrochem. Soc., Am. Phys. Soc., Am. Philos. Soc., Nat. Acad. Sciences; mem. Nat. Research Council (vice chmn. division of chemistry and chem. technology, 1927-28; chmn. of div. at Washington, D.C., 1928-29). Clubs: Cosmos (Washington, D.C.); Chemists' (New York). Mem. foreign service com. of Nat. Research Council, 1917; spent 4 months, mostly at battle fronts of French and English, to study orgn. and development of scientific activities in connection with warfare; mem. N.J. Commn., Workman's Compensation for Occupational Diseases, 1923-24. Asso. editor Jour. Physical Chemistry, 1923-27. Home: 44 Washington Rd., Princeton, N.J.

HULL, Bruce Harper, educator; b. Wheeling, W.Va., May 16, 1897; s. George W. and Sadie (Bruce) H.; grad. Lincoln High Sch., Wheeling, W.Va., 1915; B.S., magna cum laude, W.Va. State Coll., Institute, W.Va., 1925; B.D., Gammon Theol. Sem., Atlanta, Ga., 1931; A.M., U. of Mich., 1937; student U. of Chicago, Springfield (Mass.) Y.M.C.A. Coll., Ohio State U., summers; m. Martha Virginia Day, Aug. 20, 1919; foster children—Howard McDonald, Jacqueline Ray. Rural school teacher, Marion Co., 1919-21; civil service clerk, U.S. Naval Ordnance Plant, South Charleston, W.Va., 1921-22; prin. of schs., Logan, W.Va., 1922-28; pastor M.E. Ch., Lothian, Md., 1931-32; prin. high sch., Logan, W.Va., 1932 to 36; administrative asst. to state dir. National Youth Adminstrn., 1937; registrar W.Va. State Coll. since 1938. Served in Hdqrs. Co., U.S. Army, Washington, D.C., 1918. Secured support for erection of first state museum of Negro history and supervised constrn., Institute, W.Va., 1937. Mem. N.E.A., W.Va. State Teachers Assn., Am. Teachers Assn., Alpha Phi Alpha. Democrat. Methodist. Mason, Elk, Odd Fellow. Address: Institute, W.Va.

HULL, Lewis Madison, radio engr.; b. Great Bend, Kan., Feb. 27, 1898; s. Arthur St. Clair and Orlena June (Madison) H.; A.B., U. of Kan., 1917, A.M., 1918; Ph.D., Harvard, 1922; m. Helen H. Smith, Dec. 30, 1922; 1 dau., Carolyn June. Asst. and asso. physicist U.S. Bur. Standards, 1918-20, cons. physicist, 1920-22, also Whiting fellow, Harvard, 1920-22; dir. research Radio Frequency Labs., Boonton, N.J., 1922-28, now cons. engr.; pres. and dir. Aircraft Radio Corpn. since 1930. Mem. Radio Advisory Com. of Nat. Bur. of Standards, Engineering Com. of Nat. Advisory Council on Radio in Edn. Fellow Inst. Radio Engrs. (past pres.); asso. fellow Inst. Aeronautical Sciences; Am. Inst. Elec. Engrs., Am. Phys. Soc., Phi Beta Kappa, Sigma Xi. Republican. Conglist. Clubs: Lotos, Chemists (New York); University (Washington); Newark Athletic; Orange Lawn Tennis. Home: Boonton, N.J.

HULL, Robert Alonzo, banking; b. Scranton, Pa., Jan. 11, 1881; s. John Lorenzo and Florence Eugenia (Watres) H.; ed. Phillips Exeter Acad., Exeter, N.H., 1899-1901; A.B., Princeton, 1905; student Harvard U. Law Sch., 1906-07; m. Clara L. Woodruff, Dec. 3, 1912; children—Robert Alonzo, Jr., Lewis Woodruff, Barbara Hull, John Laurence. Asso. with Scranton Trust Co., now Scranton Lackawanna Trust Co. since 1908; admitted to Pa. bar, 1911; sec. Scranton Lackawanna Trust Co. since 1913; sec., treas. and dir. Scranton Mortgage Guaranty Co. since 1926. Served in 13th Pa., N.G., 1907-17; capt. inf., U.S.A., 1917-19, with A.E.F. Republican. Christian Scientist. Home: Clinton St., Waverly, Pa. Office: 506 Spruce St., Scranton, Pa.

HULL, William Isaac, college prof.; b. Baltimore, Nov. 19, 1868; s. Thomas Burling and Mary (Dixon) H.; A.B., Johns Hopkins, 1889, Ph.D., 1892; student Berlin, 1891, Leyden, 1907-08, Paris, 1914; m. Hannah Hallowell Clothier, Dec. 27, 1898; children—Mary Clothier, Elizabeth Powell. Associate professor history and economics, 1892-94, Joseph Wharton professor history and political economy, 1894-1904, professor history and internat. relations since 1904, Swarthmore Coll. Supt. summer charities, New York, 1896-97; examiner in history for Coll. Entrance Exam. Bd., 1900-05. Mem. Am. Hist. Assn., Hist. Soc. Pa., Am. Soc. Internat. Law, Phi Beta Kappa; fellow Royal Hist. Soc. Author: Maryland, Independence and the Confederation, 1891; Handbook of Sociology (with W. H. Tolman), 1893; History of Higher Education in Pennsylvania (with C. H. Haskins), 1902; The Two Hague Conferences and Their Contributions to International Law, 1908; The New Peace Movement, 1909; The Monroe Doctrine—National or International?, 1915; Preparedness the American vs. the Military Programme, 1916; The War-Method and the Peace-Method, 1929; India's Political Crisis, 1930; Willem Sewel of Amsterdam, 1934; William Penn and the Dutch Quaker Migration to Pennsylvania, 1935; Eight First Biographies of William Penn, 1936; William Penn—A Topical Biography, 1937; The Rise of Quakerism in Amsterdam, 1938. Trustee Church Peace Union. Home: Swarthmore, Pa.

HULLEY, Elkanah Bunce; b. Chester, Pa., Apr. 17, 1884; s. William Currie and Theresa (Bunce) H.; grad. Keystone Acad., Factoryville, Pa., 1903; B.S., Bucknell U., 1907; D.Eng., Stetson U., 1929; m. Mabel B. Moore, Dec. 22, 1908. Builder of houses (about 1,200), Pittsburgh, Pa., since 1912; pres. Liberty Housing Corpn. Mgr. Pittsburgh War Farms Commn., 1916-18; student O.T.C., Camp Taylor, Ky., 1918. Trustee John B. Stetson U. Mem. Phi Gamma Delta (editor in chief nat. jour., 1911-17). Republican. Baptist. Mason. Home: 2200 William Penn Highway, Wilkinsburg, Pa. Office: 838 Hazelwood Av., Pittsburgh, Pa.

HULLIHEN, Walter, university pres.; b. Staunton, Va., May 26, 1875; s. Walter Quarrier and Amelia Hay (Campbell) H.; B.A., M.A., U. of Va., 1896; post-grad. study, U. of Va., 1896-97, Johns Hopkins, 1897-1900, Ph.D., 1900; U. of Leipzig, Munich, Rome,

1907-08; D.C.L., U. of the South, 1922; LL.D., Temple U., 1925; m. Maude Louise Winchester, Sept. 14, 1907; children—Louise Winchester (Mrs. C. L. Walker), Frances Hay (Mrs. J. A. Woolley). Licentiate instructor in Latin, German and mathematics, U. of Va., 1895-96; fellow in Latin, Johns Hopkins, 1899-1900; teacher Latin and Greek, Univ. Sch., Baltimore, 1902-04; prof. Latin and Greek, U. of Chattanooga, 1904-09; prof. Greek, U. of the South, Sewanee, Tenn., 1909-12, dean Coll. Arts and Sciences, 1912-20; pres. U. of Del. since 1920; mem. bd. Columbia Oil, Shale & Refining Co. (Denver, Colo.). Mem. bd. dirs. Camp Alleghany, Ronceverte, W.Va., Camp Greenbrier, Inc., Alderson, W.Va. Maj. inf., asst. G-3, Staff 15th Div., U.S.A., 1918. Mem. Phi Beta Kappa, Delta Phi, Chevalier Legion of Honor (France). Democrat. Episcopalian. Home: Newark, Del.

HULLINGER, Edwin Ware, author, lecturer, motion picture producer; b. Chicago, Ill., Aug. 13, 1893; s. Henry Church and Lucy Ellen (Ware) H.; student Occidental Coll., Los Angeles, Calif., 1911-13; A.B., U. of Kan., 1917; grad. work, Columbia U. Sch. of Journalism, 1917; m. Helen Jean Sawyer, Nov. 20, 1933; children—Cynthia Ware, Mary Martha, Diane. Began on the staff of the Los Angeles Tribune, 1913, later with various Calif. papers and with Daily Capital, Topeka, Kan.; joined United Press, New York, 1917, and was made Mich. mgr. hdqrs. in Detroit; staff corr. in Eng., World War; trans. to Paris, 1919; corr. in Soviet Russia 1 yr. but deported for insistence on right of freedom of the press for foreign correspondents; corr. in Italy for New York Sunday Times, 1925-26; magazine writer and lecturer on internat. subjects. Mem. faculty, Dept. of Journalism, New York U., 1928, Univ. of Kan., 1936-37. Mem. Sigma Delta Chi, Phi Eta. Republican. Conglist. Mason. Author: The Reforging of Russia, 1925; The New Fascist State, 1928; Flesh Alley—A Story of Broadway (with Douglas Hertz), 1933. Produced motion picture The Private Life of Mussolini, 1938. Home: 121 Upper Mount Av., Atlantic Highlands, N.J. Address: Hullinger Productions, 121 Upper Mount Ave., Atlantic Highlands, N.J.

HULME, Norman, architect; b. Philadelphia, Pa., April 5, 1887; s. Arthur F. and Elizabeth E. (Smith) H.; ed. Drexel Inst. and U. of Pa.; m. Elisabeth R. Dubois, Aug. 17, 1922; children—Theodora E., Norman A., Elisabeth Anne, Robert D. Began practice as architect, 1920. Principal works: Philadelphia Coll. Pharmacy and Science, Reformed Episcopal Church of the Atonement (Germantown), Western Presbyn. Church (Washington, D.C.), etc. Dir. Keystone Automobile Club and affiliated insurance companies. Capt. Engrs. Reserve Corps, U.S. Army. Mem. Am. Inst. Architects, Philadelphia Art Alliance, Am. Legion, Mil. Order World War. Republican. Episcopalian. Clubs: Ben Franklin, Kiwanis. Home: Swarthmore, Pa. Office: 1524 Chestnut St., Philadelphia, Pa.

HULME, Thomas Wilkins, retired ry. official; b. Mount Holly, N.J., Aug. 11, 1868; s. Joseph S. and Abigail (Wills) H.; B.S. and C.E., Univ. of Pennsylvania 1889; m. Mary A. Oliphant, October 30, 1900; children—Alice Oliphant (Mrs. Frank T. Lloyd, Jr.), Mary Wills (Mrs. Courtlandt K. Schenck), Thomas Read, Katherine (Mrs. Harold L. Yoh). Began in real estate dept. Lehigh Valley R.R. Co., 1890, asst. real estate agt., 1893-1904; with Pa. R.R. Co., June-Nov. 1904; asst. real estate agt. N.Y. Connecting R.R. Co., 1904-05; with Pa. R.R. Co., 1905-38, as asst. real estate agt., 1905-13, real estate agt., 1913-18, gen. real estate agt., 1918-24, v.p. in charge real estate valuation and taxation, 1924-38, dir. 1932-38, retired Sept. 1, 1938; mgr. Western Savings Fund Society; dir. Corn Exchange Nat. Bank & Trust Co. Trustee U. of Pa., Bryn Mawr (Pa.) Hosp. Mem. Delta Phi. Republican. Episcopalian. Club: Merion Cricket (Haverford, Pa.). Home: Avonwood Rd. and Rose Lane, Haverford, Pa.

HULSART, John, banker; b. Squankum, N.J., Dec. 3, 1871; s. James Henry and Deborah Anne (Hyer) H.; student Peddie Sch. for Boys, Highstown, N.J., 1889-1902, Crozer Theological Sem., Chester, Pa., 1896-99; A.B., U. of Chicago, 1896; m. Mary D. Couse, Nov. 29, 1899 (died 1926); children—Emily Couse, James Burton; m. 2d, Cora Knapp Edell, May 3, 1930. Prof. theology, Bishop Coll., Marshall, Texas, 1899-1904; pastor Cherryville (N.J.) Baptist Ch., 1904-08; employed by Manasquan (N.J.) Nat. Bank since 1908, pres. and dir. since 1933. Mem. Manasquan (N.J.) Borough Council, 1914-17, Bd. of Edn., 1911-29. Mem. Manasquan Chamber of Commerce (v.p. since 1938). Baptist. Clubs: U. of Chicago Alumni of N.Y.; Kiwanis (Manasquan, N.J.). Home: 64 Curtis Av. Office: 107 Main St., Manasquan, N.J.

HULSE, Shirley Clark, civil engineer; b. Circleville, O., Jan. 6, 1879; s. Jonas Turney and Mary Louise (Clark) H.; C.E., Cornell U., 1902; m. Margaret Ann Reynolds, Nov. 22, 1906; children—Margaret Hartley (Mrs. Coolidge Ashcom Eichelberger), Shirley Clark, Jr. Employed as asst. engr. Ithaca Water Works Co., 1902-04; construction supt. on reinforced concrete work, New York City, 3 yrs.; supt., construction, engr. in charge, or field engr., mostly in connection with dams, hydraulic investigations, in N.Y., Pa., Tenn., Ore., Mexico, Nicaragua, and Colo.; vice-pres. Hartley Nat. Bank of Bedford, Pa., since 1907. Mem. Am. Soc. of Civil Engrs. Republican. Address: Bedford, Pa.

HULTON, John Gilmore, supt. pub. schs.; b. Oakmont, Pa., July 5, 1896; s. John and Ella (Kelso) H.; A.B., Franklin Coll., New Athens, O., 1918; M.Ed., U. of Pittsburgh, 1937; m. Lois Srodes, Aug. 24, 1921; children—John G., Jr., Richard K., Marjorie S. Engaged in teaching, high sch. Latrobe, Pa., 1919-22, prin. Latrobe High Sch., 1922-29; supt. pub. schs., Latrobe, Pa., since 1929. Served as ensign U.S.N.R.F. during World War. Dir. Latrobe Pub. Library, Latrobe Chamber of Commerce, Community Chest. Mem. A.A.A.S., Nat. Edn. Assn., Pa. State Edn. Assn., Phi Delta Kappa, Am. Vocational Assn., Am. Legion. Republican. Presbyn. Mason. Clubs: Kiwanis, Country (Latrobe). Home: 312 Chestnut St., Latrobe, Pa.

HUMES, E. Lowry, lawyer; b. Meadville, Pa., July 25, 1878; s. Homer J. and Delia E. (Lowry) H.; student Allegheny Coll., Meadville, Pa., 1896-99; m. Mary P. Eisele, April 16, 1904. Admitted to Pa. bar, 1900, and practiced in Meadville; mem. Pa. Ho. of Rep., 1913; U.S. Atty. Western Dist. of Pa., Sept. 10, 1913-Aug. 31, 1918, and Aug. 20, 1919-May 24, 1920; spl. asst. to U.S. atty.-gen., May 24, 1920-Mar. 1, 1921. Maj., judge-advocate U.S. A., Sept. 6, 1918. Mem. Registration Commn. of Pittsburgh, 1931. Democrat. Presbyn. Home: Roosevelt Hotel. Office: Plaza Bldg., Pittsburgh, Pa.

HUMES, Ralph Hamilton, sculptor; b. Phila., Pa., Dec. 25, 1901; s. John and Grace (Gann) H.; ed. Md. Inst. Art., 1923-25, Pa. Acad. Fine Arts, 1925-30; m. Janet Chapman, April 19, 1932. Has followed profession as artist and sculptor since 1923; represented in Brookgreen Gardens Mus., Pa. Acad. Fine Arts, Chester Springs, Pa., and in pvt. collections. Mem. Nat. Sculpture Soc., Fellowship Pa. Acad. Fine Arts, Conn. Acad. Arts, New Haven Paint & Clay Club, Soc. Washington Artists, Blue Dome Fellowship. Awarded First Cresson European Traveling Scholarship, 1929, Second Cresson European Traveling Scholarship, 1930; Ellen Speyer Memorial Prize, Nat. Acad. Design, 1932, also, 1937; Lindsey Morris Sterling Prize, New Haven Paint and Clay Club, 1932; hon. mention, Soc. Washington Artists Corcoran Gallery, 1932; New Haven Paint and Clay Club Prize, 1936; First Prize Washington Soc. Artists, 1937; Fellowship Prize of Pa. Acad. Fine Arts, 1937; Fla. Fed. Arts for best in show and best in exhbn. Episcopalian. Home: 3400 Del Monte Rd., Coconut Grove, Fla. Address: Shrewsbury, N.J.

HUMES, Samuel Hamilton, lawyer; b. Jersey Shore, Pa., Jan. 29, 1901; s. Samuel and Jessica Cole (Prindle) H.; student Jersey Shore (Pa.) pub. schs., 1907-14, Hill Sch., Pottstown, Pa., 1914-19; A.B., Williams Coll., Williamstown, Mass., 1923; LL.B., Harvard U. Law Sch., 1926; m. Elenor Kathryn Graham, July 19, 1929; children—Samuel, Graham, James Calhoun. Admitted to Allegheny County bar, and Pa. Supreme Ct., 1927; asso. with Dalzell, Fisher & Dalzell, Pittsburgh, Pa., 1926-29; with H. A. Baird formed firm Humes & Baird, Williamsport, Pa., 1929, and since mem. firm; dir. First Federal Bldg. & Loan Assn. Mem. Rep. State Com., 1934-36, 1936-38, since 1938; 1st asst. dist. atty., Lycoming Co., Pa., since 1936. Dir. Williamsport Y.M.C.A. Mem. Pa. Bar Assn., Lycoming Law Assn. Republican. Presbyterian. Odd Fellow (Amazon Lodge). Club: Ross (Williamsport, Pa.). Home: 515 Vallamont Dr. Office: 331 Pine St., Williamsport, Pa.

HUMKE, Herman Charles, clergyman; b. Ackley, Ia., Oct. 29, 1896; s. John F. and Hilka (Peters) H.; ed. Ellsworth Coll., Iowa Falls, Ia., 1915-16; A.B., Coe Coll., Cedar Rapids, Ia., 1919; B.D., McCormick Theol. Sem., Chicago, 1922; ed. Presbyn. Theol. Sem., Omaha, Neb., 1920-21; m. Ella Marie Stauffer, June 26, 1923. Ordained to ministry Presbyn. Ch. U.S.A., 1922; pastor, Rush City, Minn., 1922-23, Greenfield, Ia., 1923-27, Storm Lake, Ia., 1927-28; pastor, Presbyn. Ch., Punxsutawney, Pa., since 1928. Republican. Presbyn U.S.A. Club: Rotary of Punxsutawney (pres.). Home: 110 Church St., Punxsutawney, Pa.

HUMMEL, Arthur William, librarian; b. Warrenton, Mo., March 6, 1884; s. William Frederick and Caroline Wilhelmina (Wehking) H.; A.B., U. of Chicago, 1909, M.A., 1911; Ph.D., U. of Leyden, Netherlands, 1931; m. Ruth Emily Bookwalter, Oct. 8, 1914; children—Carol Emily, Arthur Milburn, Sharman Bookwalter. Teacher, Commercial U., Kobe, Japan, 1912-14; teacher of English, Ming-i Middle School, Fenchow, Shansi, China, 1915-24; lecturer in Chinese history, Yenching Sch. of Chinese Studies, Peiping, China, 1924-27, Columbia, 1930-32; dir. Far Eastern Seminar, Harvard University, 1932, University of California, Berkeley, 1934; lecturer in Chinese history, Columbia University Far Eastern Seminar, 1935, Berkeley, 1937; chief Div. of Orientalia, Library of Congress since 1927. Mem. Am. Council of Learned Socs. (chmn. Com. for Promotion of Chinese Studies), Am. Oriental Soc., Royal Asiatic Soc. Mem. Soc. of Friends. Author: The Autobiography of a Chinese Historian, 1931. Contbr. articles to jours. Home: 4615 Hunt Av., Chevy Chase, Md. Address: Library of Congress, Washington, D.C.

HUMMEL, Ernest Garfield, physician; b. Shiloh, N.J., Oct. 21, 1877; s. Lewis S. and Mary E. (Hall) H.; M.D., U. of Md. Med. Sch., Baltimore, Md., 1902; spl. course, Nursery and Childs Hosp., Baltimore, 1901-02; grad. study N.Y. Post Grad. Med. Sch., 1916-19; m. Rae Ella Hires, June 15, 1904; 1 dau., Mary Louise (Mrs. W. Lawrence Curry). Interne Md. Gen. Hosp., Baltimore, 1901-02; engaged in gen. practice of medicine at Shiloh, N.J., 1902-04, at Camden, 1904-16, pediatrics & gen. medicine; chief pediatric staff, Cooper Hosp., Camden, N.J., since 1916; engaged in Pediatric practice only since 1916; chief pediatric staff, Zerbrugge Hosp., Riverside, since 1934; consultant to Childrens Hosp., Lakeland, N.J., Camden Home for Friendless Children, Camden, N.J. Licentiate Am. Bd. Pediatrics. Fellow Am. Acad. Pediatrics. Mem. Am. Med. Assn., N.J. State Med. Soc. (chmn. pediatric sect. 1929-30), Camden Co. Med. Soc. (pres. 1932), Phila. Pediatric Soc. Presbyterian. Mason (32°). Home: 414 Cooper St., Camden, N.J.

HUMMER, Harry David, clergyman; b. Titusville, Pa., Nov. 5, 1895; s. Elias Wert and Mae (Hasbrouck) H.; A.B., Allegheny Coll., 1924; B.D., Drew Theol. Sem., 1927; Th.M., Drew U., 1928, Th.D., 1931; m. Grace Elizabeth Clay, Apr. 30, 1918; children—Lillian Mae, Martha Evelyn. Ordained to ministry Meth. Ch., joined Erie Conf., 1921, became deacon, 1923, elder, 1925; served as asst. prin. and prin. pub. schs. in Pa., 1915-21; minister, Lottsville, Pa., 1921-22, Lakewood, N.Y., 1922-24, Cliffwood, N.J., 1925-27, West Belmar, N.J., 1927-28, Farmingdale, N.J., 1928-34, Atlantic Highlands, N.J., 1934-36, Bordentown, N.J., since 1936; asst. in English dept., Brothers Coll. (Drew U.), since 1937; mem. faculty Summer Sch. of Theology, Ursinus Coll. Served in Tank Corps, U.S.A., 1918-19, with A.E.F. in France. Mem. Bd. Ministerial Training, N.J. Conf., Phi Beta Kappa, Kappa Phi Kappa. Methodist. Home: 112 Prince St., Bordentown, N.J.

HUMPHREY, Arthur F(ield) banker; b. Colorado Springs, Colo., Feb. 18, 1891; s. Arthur L. and Jennie (Field) H.; C.E., Princeton U., 1915; m. Marguerite Fendrick, Oct. 7, 1916; children—Virginia Shannon (Mrs. Thomas S. Jamison, Jr.), Arthur Field. Began with Fullston Fire Clay Co., 1916, asst. supt., 1917-18; dist. mgr. Massey Concrete Products Co., 1919-20; gen. manager Keystone Clay Products Co., 1920-29; vice-pres. First Nat. Bank, Greensburg, Pa., 1929-33; vice-pres. and dir. Pitt Nat. Bank, Pittsburgh, since 1933. Republican. Episcopalian. Club: Duquesne (Pittsburgh). Home: Greensburg, Pa. Office: Pitt National Bank, Pittsburgh, Pa.

HUMPHREY, Arthur Luther, mfr.; b. Buffalo, N.Y., June 12, 1860; s. Arthur K. and Hulda (Orcutt) H.; ed. high sch.; m. Jennie Field, Jan. 16, 1890; children—Arthur F., Frederick D. Farmer, later machinist's apprentice, advancing to superintendent of motive power. Served with U.P., S.P., A.T.&.S.F., Colo. Midland, Colo. Southern, and C.&.A. rys.; apptd. western mgr. Westinghouse Air Brake Co., 1903; gen. mgr. same co. at Pittsburgh, Pa., 1905, v.p., 1910, pres., 1919, executive director, 1932, chmn. board dirs., 1933-36, chmn. exec. com. since 1936; chmn. exec. com. Union Switch and Signal Co.; director Chamber Commerce of Pittsburgh (ex-pres.), First Nat. Bank (Pittsburgh), Canadian Westinghouse Co., Westinghouse Electric & Mfg. Co., Westinghouse Electric Internat. Co., Massey Concrete Products Corpn., Westinghouse Pacific Coast Brake Co. Mem. Colorado Ho. of Rep. 2 terms, 1893-95 (speaker of House, 1895). Industrial expert Ordnance Dept., U.S.A., World War. Mem. President's Conf. on Unemployment, Sept. 1921. Trustee U. of Pittsburgh, St. Margaret Memorial Hosp. Mem. Am. Soc. Mech. Engrs., Engineers' Soc. Western Pa. Republican. Episcopalian. Mason (K.T., Shriner). Clubs: Duquesne, Pittsburgh Athletic, Longue Vue, The Pittsburgh, Pike Run Country (Pittsburg); Engineers (New York); Congressional Country (Washington); Union League (Chicago). Home: 361 Maple Av., Edgewood, Pittsburgh. Address: Westinghouse Air Brake Co., Wilmerding, Pa.

HUMPHREY, George Selden, elec. engring.; b. Belleville, W.Va., Aug. 11, 1886; s. Edwin Jacob and Clara Ella (Stevenson) H.; Ph.B., Marietta Coll., O., 1907; B.S., Mass. Inst. Tech., 1910; m. Florence Opal Noon, June 5, 1912; children—Arthur Edwin, George Noon. Began as jr. engr., Telluride Power Co., Provo, Utah, then asst. engr., Knight Power Co.; distribution engr. Utah Power & Light Co., Salt Lake City, 1912-18; elec. engr. West Pa. Power Co., Pittsburgh, Pa., 1918-28; vice-pres. and chief engr. Potomac Edison Co., Hagerstown, Md., since 1928; vice-pres. Potomac Light & Power Co., Northern Va. Power Co., South Pa. Power Co. Mem. Am. Inst. Elec. Engrs., Phi Beta Kappa. Republican. Presbyterian. Club: Rotary of Hagerstown (past pres.). Home: 937 Oak Hill Av. Office: Potomac Edison Co., Hagerstown, Md.

HUMPHREY, Harold Phelps, banker; b. Osceola, Pa., June 29, 1881; s. Wilmot Grow and Sarah Elsa (Phelps) H.; student Cascadilla Sch., Ithaca, N.Y., 1898-1900; E.M. in Cer., O. State U., Columbus, O.; m. Catharine Gordon Sayre, Oct. 19, 1909; 1 son, Gordon Sayre. Began as ceramist, Cook Pottery Co., Trenton, N.J., 1904; ceramist, Northeastern Terra Cotta Co., Bradford, Pa., 1906-08; asst. supt. Cook & Co., Ford City, Pa., 1908-09; supt. Cook Pottery Co., Trenton, N.J., 1909-14, v.p. and gen. mgr., 1914-17; v.p. and gen. mgr. Washington Porcelain Co., Washington, N.J., 1917-29; v.p. First Nat. Bank, Washington, N.J., since 1929. Trustee First Presbyn. Ch., Washington, N.J. Mem. Am. Ceramic Soc., Phi Delta Theta. Republican. Presbyterian. Club: Kiwanis (Washington, N.J.). Address: First National Bank, Washington, N.J.

HUMPHREY, Harry Baker, plant pathologist; b. Granite Falls, Minn., Aug. 4, 1873; s. John Wadsworth and Adeline (Regester) H.; B.S., U. of Minn., 1899; Ph.D., Stanford, 1907; m. Olive Agatha Mealey, June 10, 1901; children—Llewellyn Mealey, Robert Regester, Helen Wadsworth (Mrs. John M. McLernon), Isabel Estella (Mrs. G. H. Godfrey), Harry Bartholomew, John William David. Secondary sch. teacher and prin., 1899-1903; instr. botany and grad. student, Stanford, 1904-07; bot. editor Cree Pub. Co., 1907-08; prof. botany, Wash. State Coll., 1908-13, vice dir. agrl. expt. sta., 1912-13; pathologist in charge cereal disease investigations, bur. plant industry, U.S. Dept. Agr., 1913-19, sr. pathologist, 1919-22, prin. pathologist since 1922; editor-in-chief Phytopathology since 1929; sec. Washington (D.C.) Coll. of Music; mem. faculty Grad. Sch. of U.S. Dept. of Agr. Fellow A.A.A.S.; mem. Canadian Geog. Soc., Am. Phytopathol. Soc. (councilor), Wash. Bot. Soc., Wash. Biol. Soc., Wash. Acad. Sciences, Minn. Hist. Soc., Sigma Xi. Club: Cosmos. Author of several botanical papers; joint author of handbook on Pisé de terre construction; contbr. bulls. and repts. on researches of cereal diseases. Home: Cabin John, Md. Address: U.S. Dept. Agriculture, Washington, D.C.

HUMPHREYS, Warren R., fire ins. exec.; b. Phila., Pa., Dec. 31, 1880; s. John C. and Lydia Mary (Farra) H.; ed. pub. schs., Phila.; m. Edna E. Edsall, Apr. 30, 1913; children—Elizabeth M. (Mrs. J. Lilburn Harwood), Edna Ruth. Began in banking, 1898, and since engaged in banking and fire ins.; vice-pres., treas. and dir. Mutual Fire Insurance of Germantown. Dir. Germantown Y.M.C.A. Republican. Baptist. Club: Union League (Phila.). Home: 270 Harvey St. Office: 5521 Germantown Av., Philadelphia, Pa.

HUN, John Gale, teacher; b. Albany, N.Y., Nov. 21, 1877; s. Edward Reynolds (M.D.) and Caroline (Gale) H.; A.B., Williams, 1899; Ph.D., Johns Hopkins, 1903; m. Leslie Crawford, June 26, 1906; children—Leslie C. (Mrs. Edward S. Morris), Elizabeth G. (Mrs. Robert G. McAllen), Carolyn G. (Mrs. Francis T. Miles). Teacher at Princeton University, 1903-14 (resigned); founder, 1914, and manager The Math School, Princeton, until 1917; headmaster Hun School, Princeton, since 1917. Pres. of Princeton Board of Education since 1930. Mem. Kappa Alpha. Clubs: Nassau (Princeton); Princeton, University, Williams (New York); Fort Orange (Albany). Author: (with C. R. MacInnes) Plane and Spherical Trigonometry, 1911. Address: Princeton, N.J.

HUNDLEY, John Mason, Jr., surgeon; b. Baltimore, Md., July 8, 1891; s. John Mason and Helen (Sweet) H.; A.B., St. John's Coll., Annapolis, Md., A.M., 1913; M.D., Johns Hopkins U., 1916; post grad. study in univs. of Kiel and Berlin, 1931; m. Emily Louise Holt, Dec. 1, 1923. House officer Union Protestant Infirmary, 1916-18; house officer Dept. of Gynecology, U. of Md., 1919-21, instr., 1921-29, asso., 1929-36, prof. and head of dept. since 1936; instr. in Dept. of Gynecology, Johns Hopkins Med. Sch., 1928-36. Served as 1st lt. Med. Corps, U.S.A. with A.E.F., 1918-19. Fellow Am. Coll. of Surgeons; mem. A.M.A., Southern Med. Assn. (councilor for Md.), Baltimore City Med. Soc., Md. State Med. Soc., Am. Urol. Soc., Am. Gynecol. Soc., Southern Surg. Soc.; N. Am. Obstet. and Gynecol. Club, Pithotomy Club, Phi Sigma Kappa. Democrat. Episcopalian. Clubs: Maryland (Baltimore); Gibson Island (Pasadena, Md.). Contbr. to med. jours. Home: 204 Ridgwood Rd. Office: 622 Med. Arts Bldg., Baltimore, Md.

HUNGERFORD, Churchill, Sr., filter mfg.; b. New Haven, Conn., Nov. 25, 1867; s. Henry and Mary E. (Churchill) H.; ed. pub. schs. and high sch., S. Norwalk, Conn.; m. Elizabeth Meck, Mar. 3, 1902; children—Churchill, David, Hayden, Grace Elizabeth (Mrs. David Luther Hillman), Edward, Barbara. Founded firm and mem. Hungerford & Terry, 1906-09, inc. 1909, and pres. 1909-37, chmn. bd. since 1937; organized Inversand Co., mfrs. zeolites, Clayton, N.J., and pres. since 1924; 1st vice-pres. Nat. Bank of Mantua, N.J. Mem. Mayflower Descendants, N.J. Soc., S.A.R. (past pres. So. Jersey Chapter). Republican. Presbyn. Mason. Clubs: Bankers and Manufacturers (Philadelphia); Ocean City Fishing (past pres.). Home: 201 Princeton Av., Wenonah, N.J. Office: Clayton, N.J.

HUNNER, Guy LeRoy, surgeon; b. Alma, Wis,. Dec. 6, 1868; s. John and Eudora (Cooke) H.; grad. high sch., Eau Claire, Wis., 1887; B.S., U. of Wis., 1893; M.D., Johns Hopkins, 1897; D.Sc., Dickinson Coll., Carlisle, Pa., 1913; m. Isabella Stevens, Sept. 10, 1902; children—Isabella Stevens (wife of Dr. John W. Parsons), Eudora Cooke (wife of John Meade, U.S.A.), John Stevens. Began practice surgery at Baltimore, Md., 1902; adjunct prof. of gynecology, Johns Hopkins U. Med. Sch. Mem. A. M.A., Southern Med. Assn., Southern Surg. Assn. (ex-pres.), Am. Gynecol. Assn., Am. Urol. Assn., Baltimore Co. Med. Soc., Baltimore City Med. Soc. (ex-pres.), Société Internationale d'Urologie, Phi Delta Theta. Democrat. Methodist. Contbr. chapters to med. textbooks, also to med. jours. Home: Pasadena, Md. Office: Medical Arts Bldg., Baltimore, Md.

HUNSAKER, Herbert Cason, coll. dean; b. White Salmon, Wash., Oct. 22, 1898; s. Daniel and Marietta (Beck) H.; A.B., U. of Wash., 1922; A.M., Teachers Coll. of Columbia U., 1928; ed. Harvard U. Law Sch., 1922-24, U. of Newark Sch. of Law; m. Lillian McLellan, Dec. 23, 1926 (divorced 1937); 1 son, Roderick C. Asst. in boys' club work and dir. dramatics, Denison House, Boston, 1923-26, also engaged in other work; asst. to pres. and registrar, N.J. Law Sch., Newark, N.J., 1926-29, asso. dir. Seth Boyden Sch. of Bus., same, 1929-32, dean Seth Boyden Sch., 1932-36, actg. dean, Dana Coll., 1935-36; dean College Arts and Sciences, University of Newark since 1936, on leave of absence, 1939-40. Served in S.A.T.C. 1918. Pres. Civic Clubs Council, 1937-38. Mem. Am. Bus. Club, Adv. Club, Newark. Mem. bd. dirs. N.J. Urban League; bd. mgrs. N.J. State Commn. for Blind; mem. corpn. Internat. Save the Children Fund. Mem. Eastern Assn. Coll. Deans and Advisers of Men, Am. Assn. Adult Edn., N.Y. Adult Edn. Council, N.J. Council Adult Edn. (pres. 1938-39), N.J. Guidance & Personnel Assn., Delta Upsilon, Delta Theta Phi, Delta Sigma Pi, Acacia. Presbyn. Club: Athletic (Newark). Home: Newark Athletic Club. Office: 40 Rector St., Newark, N.J.

HUNSICKER, Charles Owen, lawyer; b. Allentown, Pa., Aug. 18, 1878; s. James F. and Mary Elizabeth (Schrader) H.; prep. edn. Mercersburg Acad., 1894-96; A.B., Franklin and Marshall Coll., 1900; LL.B., U. of Pa., 1903; m. Lillian Leah Henninger, June 2, 1909; children—Mary Elizabeth (Mrs. Samuel C. Bond, Jr.), Robert Franklin. Admitted to Pa. bar, 1903, and since in practice at Allentown, Pa.; mayor City of Allentown, 1909-12. Trustee Allentown Hosp., Cedar Crest Coll. Republican. Mem. Evang. and Reformed Ch. of U.S. Home: 1451 Turner St. Office: 17 N. 7th St., Allentown, Pa.

HUNT, Bruce A.; editor Williamsport Sun. Address: 252 W. 4th St., Williamsport, Pa.

HUNT, Everett Lee, college prof.; b. Colfax, Ia., Oct. 14, 1890; s. Charles Reeve and Anna Belle (Johnson) H.; A.B., Huron (S.D.) Coll., 1913, D.Litt., 1938; M.A., U. of Chicago, 1921; m. Dorothy Rossman, June 24, 1919; 1 son, Alan Reeve. Instr. in debate and oratory, Huron Coll., 1913-18; asst. prof. public speaking, Cornell U., 1918-26; prof. rhetoric and oratory, Swarthmore Coll., 1926-32, acting dean of men, 1932-33; research at U. of Edinburgh, 1933-34; professor English, Swarthmore College since 1934, acting dean of men, 1938-39; visiting prof. pub. speaking, summers, U. of Ill., 1922, U. of Colo., 1928-31. Editor Quarterly Journal of Speech, 1927-30. Pres. Eastern Pub. Speaking Conf., 1922-24; mem. Nat. Assn. Teachers of Speech, Modern Lang. Assn. America, Am. Assn. Univ. Profs. Quaker. Club: Colorado Mountain (Boulder). Editor: (with A. M. Drummond), Persistent Questions in Public Discussion, 1924. Contributor to various publs. Home: 604 Elm Av., Swarthmore, Pa.

HUNT, Frank Raymond, asso. prof. economics; b. Port Washington, O., Mar. 8, 1898; s. Lewis H. and Dora B. (Howell) H.; A.B., Muskingum Coll., 1922; ed. U. of Ill., 1922-23; A.M., O. State U., 1925, grad. student, same, summers 1932-35-36; study Columbia U., summer 1929; m. Sara M. Speer, June 15, 1922 (dec.); children—Robert Speer, Doris Jane. Engaged as deptl. asst., U. of Ill., 1922-23; instr., O. State U., 1923-25; research asst., Bur. Pub. Rds., Washington, summer 1925; instr. economics, Lafayette Coll., Easton, Pa., 1925-27, asst. prof., 1927-29, asso. prof. econs. since 1929. Served as pvt. inf., U.S.A., 1918. Mem. Am. Econs. Assn., Nat. Tax Assn., Theta Chi. Presbyn. Club: Lafayette College Faculty. Home: 900 Porter St., Easton, Pa.

HUNT, Harriet Larned, educator; b. Fargo, N.D., 1893; d. William Edgar and Janet Barker (Rumney) H.; A.B., Smith Coll., 1913; grad. study U. of Wis., U. of Calif., Columbia; unmarried. Head of history dept., St. Timothy's Sch. for Girls, Catonsville, Md., 1917-18, 1919-20; head of history dept., Katharine Branson Sch., Ross, Calif., 1920-24; prin. Kent Place Sch., Summit, N.J., since 1924. Mem. Head Mistresses Assn. of the East, Nat. Assn. Prins. Schs. for Girls (v.p.). Episcopalian. Club: Women's University (New York). Address: Kent Place School, Summit, N.J.

HUNT, Henry Franklin, pathologist; b. Madisonville, Tenn., Sept. 22, 1899; s. Lewis A. and Mary Lee (Dawson) H.; ed. U. of Tenn., 1916-17; M.D., Vanderbilt U. Med. Sch., 1924; grad. study U. of Minn. Grad. Sch., Mayo Foundation, Rochester, Minn., 1926-29; m. Stella Cullum, June 17, 1924; 1 dau., Eloise Elizabeth. Chief resident phys. Knoxville Gen. Hosp., Knoxville, Tenn., 1925-26; actg. prof. pathology, U. of N.C., 1929; dir. labs., Geisinger Memorial Hosp. and Danville State Hosp., Danville, Pa. since 1929; consultant pathologist Northeastern Penitentiary, Lewisburg, Pa. since 1931. Served as lt. inf. U.S.A., 1917-18. Mem. Am., Pa. State, and Montour Co. med. assns., Am. Soc. Clin. Pathologists, Soc. Am. Bacteriologists, Am. Assn. for Study of Goiter, Assn. Ex-resident Phys. of Mayo Clinic, Pi Kappa Alpha, Alpha Kappa Kappa, Sigma Xi. Republican. Home: Red Lane, Danville, Pa.

HUNT, Levi Clarence, clergyman, educator; b. Seitzland, York Co., Pa., July 30, 1873; s. Levi Warner and Elizabeth (Nace) H.; A.B., Dickinson Coll., 1897, A.M., 1899 (D.D., 1916); B.D., Drew Theol. Sem., 1904; postgrad. work same, 1904-05, with lecture course, Columbia; m. Anna L. Frey, Sept. 6, 1905; 1 dau. (adopted), Dorothy Mackay Becker. Teacher pub. schs., 1890-92; prof. mathematics, Albright Coll., Myerstown, Pa., 1898-1901; ordained United Evang. ministry, 1899; pastor Columbia, Pa., 1897-98, M.E.Ch., Centerport, L.I., N.Y., 1901-04, Grace Ch., Reading, Pa., 1905-09, Germantown, 1909-13, Bangor, 1913-16; pres. Albright Coll., 1915-23; pastor Bethany United Evangelical Ch., Allentown, Pa., 1923-26, First Ch., Reading, Pa., 1926-31, Kemble Park, Phila., Pa., 1931-34, Grace Ch., Schuylkill Haven, Pa., since 1934. Mem. Pa. State Ednl. Assn., Sigma Alpha Epsilon, Phi Beta Kappa. Address: Schuylkill Haven, Pa.

HUNT, Percival, prof. English; b. Cedar Falls, Ia., Jan. 9, 1878; s. Henry Clay and Helen Marr (Garrison) H.; A.B., U. of Ia., 1900, A.M., 1904; Litt.D., U. of Pittsburgh, 1938; unmarried. Fellow in English, U. of Ia.; asso. prof., same, acting head of dept., 1916-19; prof. and head dept. of English, U. of Pittsburgh, since Sept. 1922. Mem. Modern Lang. Assn. America, English-Speaking Union, Phi Beta Kappa, Sigma Chi. Republican. Clubs: Faculty, Pittsburgh Athletic Assn. Author: (monographs) An Outline of Composition, 1930; Student Themes, 1938. Home: Schenley Apts., Pittsburgh, Pa.

HUNT, Rachel McMasters Miller (Mrs. Roy Arthur Hunt); b. Pittsburgh, Pa., June 30, 1882; d. Mortimer and Rachel H. (McMasters) Miller; ed. Miss Mittlebergers Sch., Cleveland, O.; m. Roy Arthur Hunt, June 11, 1913; children—Alfred Mortimer, Torrence Miller, Roy Arthur, Jr., Richard McMasters. Bookbinder, collector of books, first editions, pvt. press books; owns botanical library. Mem. Am. Civic Assn., Hort. Soc. of N.Y., Guild of Book Workers, N.Y. Republican. Episcopalian. Clubs: Twentieth Century, Pittsburgh Golf, Fox Chapel (Pittsburgh); Garden Club of America, Colony, Cosmopolitan (New York); Garden Club of Allegheny Co. Contbr. to mags. and journs. Home: 4875 Ellsworth Av., Pittsburgh, Pa.

HUNT, Roy Arthur, pres. Aluminum Co. of America; b. Nashua, N.H., Aug. 3, 1881; s. Alfred Ephraim and Maria Tyler (McQuesten) H.; grad. Shady Side Acad., Pittsburgh, Pa., 1899; A.B., Yale, 1903; m. Rachel McMasters Miller, June 11, 1913; children—Alfred Mortimer, Torrence, Roy Arthur, Richard McMasters. Machinists helper, New Kensington (Pa.) plant of Aluminum Co. of America, July, Aug., 1901, mill clk., 1903-05, cost clk., 1905-06, asst. supt., 1906-08, supt., 1908-14, gen. supt. fabricating plants at Pittsburgh, 1914-15, mem. bd. dirs. since 1915, vice pres. in charge fabricating plants, Pittsburgh, 1919-28, pres. since 1928; dir. Aluminum Goods Mfg. Co., Mellon Nat. Bank, Nat. Union Fire Ins. Co., Union Savings Bank of Pittsburgh, The Union Trust Co. Treas. and trustee Carnegie Inst. Tech., Carnegie Inst. of Pittsburgh, Carnegie Library of Pittsburgh; trustee Elizabeth Steel Magee Hosp., Mem. Engrs. Soc. Western Pa. Republican. Episcopalian. Clubs: Pittsburgh, Duquesne, Pittsburgh Golf, Allegheny Country (Pittsburgh); Yale, Cloud (New York). Home: 4875 Ellsworth Av., Pittsburgh, Pa. Office: Gulf Bldg., Pittsburgh, Pa.

HUNT, Theodore Brainerd, coll. prof.; b. Metuchen, N.J., Jan. 3, 1897; s. Alonzo C. (M.D.) and Elizabeth Evelyn (Ayers) H.; student Princeton U.; Docteur de l'Université de Paris; m. Lulu Jane Leathers, Sept. 8, 1921. Instr. English, U.S. Naval Acad., Annapolis, Md., 1919-22; asst. prof., U. of Hawaii, 1922-26; prof. English, Lafayette Coll., Easton, Pa., since 1928. Served in U.S. Navy, 1917-18. Mem. Am. Assn. of Univ. Profs., Modern Lang. Assn. of America, Shakespeare Assn. of America, Am. Legion. Clubs: Cloister Inn (Princeton, N.J.); Faculty (Easton, Pa.). Author: The Scenes as Shakespeare Saw Them (Parrot Presentation Volume), 1935; Le Roman Américain, 1830-1850 (Paris), 1937. Editor: The Lafayette Alumnus, 1930-35. Home: Middlesex Av., Metuchen, N.J. Address: Lafayette Coll., Easton, Pa.

HUNT, William Southworth, newspaper editor and pub.; b. Newark, N.J., Jan. 17, 1879; s. William Tallmadge and Lucy Bardine (Southworth) H.; grad. St. George's Hall, Summit, N.J. 1896; A.B., Yale, 1901, A.M., 1903; m. Lorentha Storms Lum, Sept. 9, 1903; 1 dau., Alice Southworth (Mrs. Charles Edward Burton, Jr.). Reporter N.Y. Herald, 1901-03, Newark Sunday Call, 1903-19; editor Newark Star-Eagle, 1919-24; mng. editor Newark Sunday Call, 1924-32; pres. Newark Call Printing and Pub. Co. since 1932. Mem. bd. mgrs. Howard Savings Inst.; mem. exec. com. Newark Pubs. Assn. N.J. Labor statistician, 1904; pres. South Orange Village, 1919-23; commr. N.J. state budget, 1924-25; pres. bd. trustees N.J. Training Sch. for Women, 1926-31. Mem. N.J. Hist. Soc. (trustee, pres. since 1936), Newark Mus. (trustee), Am. Numismatic Soc., Am. Philatelic Soc., Chi Delta Theta. Progressive Republican. Episcopalian. Mason. Clubs: Essex (Newark); Grolier (N.Y. City); Mory's (New Haven). Author: Frank Forester, 1927. Contbr. Newark Call (pseudonym Henry Hamlin) and various mags. Home: 368 Hillside Place, South Orange, N.J. Office: 91 Halsey St., Newark, N.J.

HUNT, Willis Roberts, asso. prof. biology; b. Essex, Conn., Feb. 13, 1893; s. Samuel Baldwin and Hattie Electa (Gladding) H.; Ph.B., Sheffield Sci. Sch. of Yale U., 1917, M.S., same, 1923, Ph.D., same, 1925; unmarried. Engaged in teaching secondary schs., 1919-23; plant and forest pathology work, Conn. Agr. Expt. Sta. and U.S. Dept. Agr., 1924-28; instr. biology, Lafayette Coll., Easton, Pa., 1928-29, asst. prof., 1929-36, asso. prof. biology since 1936. Served as 2d lt. Marine Corps, 1918. Fellow A.A.A.S. Mem. Soc. Am. Bacteriologists, Am. Assn. Univ. Profs., Sigma Xi, Gamma Alpha, Zeta Psi. Republican. Episcopalian. Mason (32°). Clubs: Faculty (Easton); Philadelphia Yale. Home: Essex, Conn. Office: Lafayette College, Easton, Pa.

HUNTER, Albert Clayton, bacteriologist; b. East Providence, R.I., Feb. 23, 1893; s. George Francis and Susan Frances (Salisbury) H.; B.S., R.I. State Coll., 1915; M.S., Brown Univ., Providence, R.I., 1917, Ph.D. 1918; m. Elizabeth H. Barker, Sept. 3, 1918. Bacteriologist U.S. Bur. Chemistry, 1918-27; in charge Bacteriol. Sect., U.S. Food and Drug Adminstrn., 1927-39; chief Bacteriol. Div., U.S. Food and Drug Adminstrn. since 1939. Mem. Soc. Am. Bacteriologists, Am. Pub. Health Assn., Washington Acad. of Scis., Sigma Xi, Assn. Official Agrl. Chemists. Author: Hygienic Fundamentals of Food Handling (with Charles Thom, 1924. Contbr. papers and bulletins on bacteriology of foods. Home: 716 Richmond Av., Silver Spring, Md.

HUNTER, Arthur, actuary; b. Edinburgh, Scotland, June 29, 1869; s. Robertson and Jane (Mitchell) H.; ed. George Watson's Coll., Edinburgh; LL.D., Edinburgh U.; m. E. May Borst, Oct. 16, 1894 (died Aug. 20, 1925); 1 dau., Virginia Calderwood (Mrs. Lewis E. Kimball); m. 2d, Ethel Merriam Parsons, Nov. 16, 1926. Came to U.S., 1892; actuary New York Life Ins. Co., 1904-18, chief actuary since 1918, 3d v.p., 1926-28, 2d v.p., 1928-31, v.p. since 1931. Chmn. Medico-Actuarial and Am.-Canadian Mortality Investigation, Medical Impairment and Occupational Studies, Blood Pressure Researches. Appointed chairman advisory board Division Military and Naval Insurance of Bureau of War Risk Insurance, Nov. 26, 1917. Chmn. ins. com. Am. Red Cross, 1917-18. Formerly pres. Montclair Art Mus.; trustee Montclair Community Chest; trustee Mountainside Hosp., Montclair. Decorated Chevalier Legion of Honor (France). Corr. member Inst. of Actuaries of Eng., of France, of Switzerland. Fellow Actuarial Soc. America (pres. 1916-18), Am. Inst. Actuaries, Faculty of Actuaries in Scotland, Casualty Actuarial Society, Royal Society Edinburgh; honorary member Association of Life Ins. Med. Dirs. Mem. St. Andrew's Soc. of N.Y. (pres.), Burns Soc. of N.Y. (past pres.), Pi Gamma Mu. Unitarian; sr. trustee of Unity Church. Clubs: Century, National Arts (New York); Montclair Golf. Has delivered numerous addresses to actuarial socs. and scientific bodies on subjects such as: Is Cancer Hereditary?; Heart Murmurs, Their Influence on Mortality; Mortality in Tropical Countries; Effect of Alcohol on Longevity; Blood Pressure, What Affects It?; etc. Author of Am. Annuitants' Mortality Table; asso. editor Alcohol and Man. Home: 124 Lloyd Rd., Montclair, N.J. Office: 51 Madison Av., New York, N.Y.

HUNTER, Charles W., constrn. engr.; b. Baltimore, Md., Feb. 13, 1882; s. James Welsh and Mary Loretta (Devereux) H.; student Baltimore City Coll.; M.E., Cornell U., 1905; m. Georgene Morrill, Feb. 18, 1918; children—Anne, Georgene Devereux. Constrn. engr., Astoria Light & Power Co., 1905-07, Retort Coke Oven Co., Cleveland, O., 1907-08, Peoples Gas Light & Coke Co., Chicago, Ill., 1908-10; gas engr., Stone & Webster, Boston, Mass., 1910-22; became v.p. Davis & Farnum Mfg. Co., Waltham, Mass., 1922; v.p. U.G.I. Contracting Co., Philadelphia, Pa., 1925-28; v.p. United Engrs. & Constructors, Inc., Phila., since 1928; dir. Dwight P. Robinson & Co., Day & Zimmermann Engring. & Constrn. Co., United Engrs. & Constructors of Argentine, Inc., Dwight P. Robinson Co. of Brazil, Inc., The U.G.I. Contracting Co. Organizer of Toluol div., Ordnance Dept., U.S.A., World War. Mem. Am. Soc. M.E., Am. Gas Assn., Franklin Inst., Delta Tau Delta. Republican. Catholic. Clubs: Midday, Philadelphia Country (Philadelphia). Home: Laurel Lane, Haverford, Pa. Office: 1401 Arch St., Philadelphia, Pa.

HUNTER, Frances Tipton, illustrator; b. Howard, Pa.; d. Mathew Mitchell and Laura Jane (Tipton) Hunter; student Pa. Mus. Sch. of Industrial Art, Phila., 1914-19, Pa. Acad. of Fine Arts, Phila., 1927-28; unmarried. Began as free lance illustrator, 1920; made illustrations for The Country Home, Woman's Home Companion, Good Housekeeping, Colliers; now painting magazine covers for Saturday Evening Post; also illustrations for numerous advertisements; published The Francis Tipton Hunter Picture Book, 1935. Mem. Artists Guild, Inc., Soc. of Illustrators (N.Y.), Alumni Assn. Acad. of Fine Arts (Phila.), Fellowship Acad. of Fine Arts, Phila. Republican. Methodist. Address: Garden Court Plaza, 47th and Pine St., Philadelphia, Pa.

HUNTER, Glenn, mem. law firm Hunter & Price. Address: Morgantown, W.Va.

HUNTER, J. Ross, surgeon Carbon Fuel Co. Address: 1117 Virginia St. E., Charleston, W.Va.

HUNTER, James Graham, cartoonist; b. La Grange, Ill., Feb. 2, 1901; s. William Clarence and Rebecca (Faul) H.; student Art Inst. Chicago, 1919-20 and 1924, Federal Schs., Minneapolis, 1921-22; m. Cornelia Isabel Seward, (great great grandniece of William Henry Seward), June 30, 1930. Free lance cartoonist since 1923; created "Jolly Jingles" for Chicago Sunday Tribune, 1924, and McClure Newspaper Syndicate, 1926-27; creator of "Isn't It The Truth!" page in Progressive Grocer since 1931; "Motor Laughs" and "Biceps Brothers" in Motor since 1932; "Sycamore Center" page in Southern Agriculturist since 1935; "Brainy Bill" strip in Boys' Life Mag. 1936; "Tubby" strip in Rural Progress 1936; "Rollicking Rhymes" cartoon series in Woman's Day since 1938; commercial advertising cartoons; political cartoons in New York daily newspapers; contbr. to Saturday Evening Post, Collier's, Country Gentleman, Am. Mag., Farm Journal, Nation's Business, Am. Boy, Successful Farming; also contbr. to Illustrated, Everybody's Weekly, Sunday Referee (London); Nat. Home Monthly, Maclean's, Le Bulletin Des Agriculteurs (Canada). Presbyn. Club: Cinema (Orange, N.J.). Home: 357 Lincoln Av., Orange, N.J.

HUNTER, James Norman, clergyman; b. Grove City, Pa., June 16, 1882; s. William John and Alice (Minich) H.; A.B., Grove City Coll., 1909; S.T.B., Western Theol. Sem., 1912; (hon.) D.D., Grove City Coll., 1933; m. Cora H. Eissler, May 30, 1913; children—Ruth Elizabeth, Helen Margaret, Mary Eleanor, Esther Jane, Myra Lucile. Engaged in teaching pub. schs., 1901-03, 1905-07; ordained to ministry Presbyn. Ch. U.S.A., 1912; pastor, Princeton, Pa., 1912-15, Bakerstown, 1916-19, Blairsville, 1919-30; pastor Avalon Presbyn. Ch., Pittsburgh, Pa. since 1930. Active in work of Boy Scouts since 1916; awarded Silver Beaver, 1933. Mem. Alpha Tau Epsilon. Republican. Presbyn. U.S.A. Mason (32°). Home: 326 S. Home Av., Avalon, Pittsburgh, Pa.

HUNTER, John Robert, Jr., architect; b. Hollidaysburg, Pa., July 11, 1898; s. John and Nancy Catharine Law (Gardner) H.; student Hollidaysburg (Pa.) High Sch., 1913-17, Pa. State Coll., 1918-22; m. Thelma Vera Davis, Dec. 16, 1922; children—John Davis (dec.), Joan Davis. In practice as John Hunter, Jr., architect, Hollidaysburg, Pa., 1922-27; partner Hunter & Caldwell, architects, Altoona, Pa., since 1927; pres. Phi Lambda Property Assn. since 1926. Served as pvt., S.A.T.C., 1918. Mem. A.I.A., Pa. Assn. Architects, Am. Legion, Lion's Paw Soc., Scarab, Parmi Nous, Druids, Sphinx, Alpha Chi Rho. Republican. Methodist. Mason. Clubs: The Art (Phila., Pa.); Kiwanis (Hollidaysburg, Pa.); Harrisburg (Harrisburg, Pa.). Home: 901 Spruce St., Hollidaysburg, Pa. Office: 3601 5th Av., Altoona, Pa.

HUNTER, Joseph, coll. pres.; b. Castlerock, Northern Ireland, April 27, 1873; s. John and Elizabeth (Thompson) H.; B.A., Magee Coll., Royal U. of Ireland, 1894; A.M., Princeton U., 1896; ed. Princeton Theol. Sem., 1894-97; D.D., Tusculum Coll., Greenville, Tenn., 1927; m. Bertha L. Williams, Oct. 25, 1899; children—John Desmond, Elizabeth Hezlett (Mrs. Alexander Hamilton Walsh, Jr.). Came to U.S., 1894, naturalized, 1915. Ordained Presbyn. ministry, 1897; pastor, Tamaqua, Pa., 1897-99, Berwick, Pa., 1899-1905; pastor Fifth Av. Presbyn. Ch., Newark, N.J., 1905-31; pres. and dir., Bloomfield Coll. & Sem., Bloomfield, N.J., since 1931. Served as chaplain, N.J. Res. World War. Mem. Greek Club of Essex Co., Kappa Chi. Republican. Presbyn. Mason. Club: Essex County Country (West Orange). Home: 46 Beach St., Bloomfield, N.J.

HUNTER, Lillian Acomb (Mrs. Livingston L. Hunter), trustee of estate; b. Cuba, N.Y., Jan. 6, 1864; d. James L. (M.D.) and Seraph (Oliver, M.D.) Acomb; B.Sc., Akron U., Akron, O., 1885; m. Livingston L. Hunter, Jan. 6, 1887 (dec.); children—James Livingston, Lella May (Mrs. William Floyd Clinger), Dorothy (Mrs. Marshall W. Ulf), Jahu Acomb. Executor and trustee L. L. Hunter Trust consisting of oil, lumber, banking and investment interests of dec. husband since 1902; treas. gen. Nat. Soc. D.A.R., 1920-23; nat. pres. Daughters of Am. Colonists, 1928-30; has held many offices in nat. orgns. Dec. with medal in recognition of work during World War (France); guest of French Govt., 1921. Mem. Daughters of Colonial Wars of Mass., Descs. of New Eng. Women, Ancient and Hon. Arty. Co. of Boston, Daughters of War of 1812, Kappa Kappa Gamma. Republican. Clubs: Womans (Tidionte); Shakespeake (Warren); Washington (Washington, D.C.); Bird and Tree, Chautauqua Woman's Club (Chautauqua, N.Y.). Home: 258 E. Main St., Tidionte, Pa.

HUNTER, Oscar Benwood, M.D., educator, pathologist; b. Cherrydale, Va., Jan. 31, 1888; s. Montgomery and Lillian Theresa (Edmonston) H.; M.D., George Washington U., 1912, A.B., 1916, A.M., 1917; m. Sidney Sophia Pearson, Dec. 26, 1914; children—Oscar Benwood, Frances Elizabeth, Mary Ellen, Margaret Pearson. Instr. in anatomy, George Washington U., 1912, prof. histology and embryology, 1913-16, prof. bacteriology and pathology, 1916-32, acting dean Dental Sch., 1918, asst. dean Med. Sch., 1918-32; pathologist George Washington U. Hosp. and Dispensary, 1916-32; sec. to The Doctors' Hosp.; cons. pathologist, Sibley Memorial Hosp. and Montgomery County Gen. Hosp.; prof. sanitary science, Central Training Sch. for Nurses; lecturer, Kober Foundation, Georgetown U., 1926; professorial lecturer Georgetown U. since 1935. Major Med. R.C. Fellow Am. Coll. Physicians; sec. Washington Med. Bldg. Corpn., Columbia Med. Bldg. Corpn. Mem. A.M.A., Am. Assn. Anatomists, Am. Soc. Bacteriologists, Am. Soc. Pathologists and Bacteriologists, Am. Therapeutic Soc., A.A.A.S., Southern Med. Assn., Tri-State Med. Soc., Galen-Hippocrates Soc., Med. Soc. D.C. (pres. 1928), Washington Med. Surg. Soc., George Washington U. Med. Soc. (pres. 1918-19), Am. Soc. of Clin. Pathologists, Am. Assn. for Study of Neoplastic Diseases, Am. Coll. of Physicians, Am. Assn. of Univ. Profs., Assn. of Military Surgeons of U.S., Reserve Officers Assn. of U.S., Washington Soc. of Pathologists (pres. 1937-38), Alpha Kappa Kappa; pres. Gen. Alumni Assn. of George Washington U., 1928-29 and 1929-30. Republican. Catholic. Clubs: University, Congressional, Torch, Kiwanis. Contbr. to Washington Med. Annals, Am. Jour. Clin. Pathology, Jour. A.M.A., Jour. Lab. and Clin. Medicine, etc. Home: 1 E. Bradley Lane, Chevy Chase, Md.*

HUNTER, Thomas Holland, v.p. Duer Spring & Mfg. Co.; b. Sewickley, Pa., Jan. 22, 1897; s. Charles Rowan and Mary (Dickson) H.; commissioned U.S. Naval Acad., Annapolis, Md., 1918; A.B., Pa. State Coll., State College, Pa., 1921; m. Elinor Campbell, April 25, 1929; children—Thomas Holland, Terry Campbell. Salesman Nat. Surety Co., N.Y. City, 1921-23; mgr. bond and ins. dept. John T. Reeves & Co. (private bankers), Beaver Falls, Pa., 1923-26; mgr. sales Fort Pitt Spring Co., McKees Rocks, Pa., 1926-30; v.p. Duer Spring & Mfg. Co. since 1930, now also dir.; dir. Acme Stamping & Mfg. Co., Pittsburgh. Mem. Delta Tau Delta. Republican. Presbyterian. Clubs: Edgeworth (Sewickley); Shannopin Country (Bon Avon Heights, Pittsburgh). Home: Davis Lane, Osborne, Sewickley, Pa. Office: Duer Spring & Mfg. Co., McKees Rocks, Pa.

HUNTINGTON, Park William, clergyman; b. Vicksburg, Pa., July 25, 1895; s. John Ephraim and Hester Amelia (Spotts) H.; A.B., Susquehanna U., Selinsgrove, Pa., 1917, A.M., 1928; B.D., Susquehanna Sem., 1921; S.T.M., Lutheran Sem., Mt. Airy, Pa., 1931; student U. of Pa. Grad. Sch., 1931-35; D.D., Am. Theol. Sem., Wilmington, Del., 1939; m. Marie Marguerite Romig, June 29, 1921; children—Park William, Marie Marguerite. United Lutheran cleryman, St. John's Lutheran Ch., Jersey Shore, Pa., 1921-26, St. Stephen's Lutheran Ch., Wilmington, Del., since 1926. Enlisted in Ambulance Corps, Sect. 574, U.S. Army, 1917, served as sergt. 1st class, Q.M.C., 1918, 2d lt., Q.M.C., 1918, hon. disch., 1919; 1st lt., Chaplain Corps, O.R.C, 1923-27, captain, 1927; captain and regimental chaplain, 198th Coast Arty., Del. N.G., 1927-36, maj. since 1936. Chmn. bd. trustees Wilmington Bible Coll. Mem. Am. Legion (post chaplain George W. Pepperman Post 36, Jersey Shore, Pa., 1921-25, post comdr., 1926; post chaplain J. Laurence Roberts Post 21, Wilmington, 1927-31, 1933-35, 1938-39, post comdr., 1932; dept. chaplain, Del., 1928, 1930, 1933, 1934, 1935; nat. chaplain, 1935.). Mem. 40 & 8, U.S. Army Ambulance Assn., Chaplains Assn. of Army of U.S., Phila. Dist. Assn. of Football Officials, Nat. Assn. Approved Basketball Officials, Pa. Intercollegiate Athletic Assn. Officials, Bond and Key, Phi Delta Kappa. Republican. Lutheran. Mason (Grand chaplain of Masonry of Del., 1927, 1929), Patriotic Order Sons of America, Odd Fellows. Clubs: Rotary (chaplain since 1929), Masonic of Del. (Wilmington, Del.; chaplain since 1928). Author: America Awake, 1938. Lecturer. Home: 806 W. 25th St. Office: 13th and Broom Sts., Wilmington, Del.

HUNTLEY, George William, Jr., pres. Pa. Powder Co., Carmoil Corpn.; b. Gibson Twp., Pa., March 16, 1867; s. George William and Luzerna (Shafter) H.; student Pa. State Coll. (prep. dept.), Dickinson Sem. (Carlisle, Pa.), Dickinson Sch. of Law (Carlisle); m. Margaret Metzger, Oct. 16, 1894; children—Floy, Geraldine, Margaret, Wilma. Began as foreman of logging camp; in practice of law, 1894-97. Pres. Pa. Powder Co., Emporium, Pa., since 1921; pres. Carmoil Corpn., Emporium, Pa., since 1937. Has been councilman, Town of Covington (Va.), Driftwood Borough (Pa.); elected to Pa. Gen. Assembly. Address: 134 W. 5th St., Emporium, Pa.

HUNTLEY, Louis Grow, geologist, petroleum engr.; b. Greenville, Mich., July 22, 1885; s. Charles L. and Antoinette A. (Grow) H.; B.S., Carnegie Inst. Tech., Pittsburgh, 1908; M.S., U. of Pittsburgh, 1922; m. Gladys I. Guy, Sept. 12, 1912; children—Gladys Margaret (Mrs. John B. Henry, Jr.), Louis Guy. Rodman Panama R.R., 1908; asst. engr. South Am. Development Co., Porto Bello Mines, Ecuador, 1909; asst. engr. Guayaquil & Quito R.R., prospecting and placer mining, 1910; oil geology, Ohio, 1911; asst. engr. Bur. of Mines, 1912; cons. oil geologist Johnson & Huntley, Pittsburgh, 1913-18; pres. Island Oil & Transport Corpn., N.Y. and Mexico, 1918-19; consultant and operating Johnson, Huntley & Somers, Pittsburgh, 1919-23; partner Huntley & Huntley, consulting geologists and petroleum engrs., since 1922. Mem. Am. Assn. Petroleum Geologists, Am. Inst. Mining and Metall. Engrs., A.A.A.S.; Fellow Am. Geog. Soc.; hon. mem. Sigma Gamma Epsilon. Clubs: Engineers, Explorers (New York). Co-author: Principles of Oil and Gas Production, 1916; Business of Oil Production, 1922. Contbr. to U.S. Bur. of Mines and to professional jours. Home: 1333 Squirrel Hill Av. Office: Grant Bldg., Pittsburgh, Pa.

HUNTON, Ella Grace, coll. dean and prof.; b. Roseville, O.; A.B., Thiel Coll., Greenville, Pa., 1900; M.A., Columbia U., 1918; summer student U. of Mich., 1901, 03, Roanoke Coll., Salem, Va., 1918, Instituto de Estudios Historicos, Madrid, Spain, 1923, U. of Chicago, 1930; unmarried. Teacher, Lima (O.) High

Sch., 1901-12; prof. of Latin, Elizabeth Coll., Salem, Va., 1912-22, dean, 1912-15; prof. of Latin and dean of women, Thiel Coll., Greenville, Pa., since 1922. Mem. Pa. Deans of Women, Nat. Deans of Women, Classical Assn. of Atlantic States, Am. Assn. of U. Profs. Democrat. Lutheran. Club: College (Sharon, Pa.). Address: Daily Hall, Thiel Coll., Greenville, Pa.

HUNTSMAN, Robert F. R., newspaper pub.; b. Newark, N.J., Mar. 19, 1868; s. John F. and Zerviah Fitz (Randolph) H.; ed. pub. schs.; m. Leontine Lissignolo, Aug. 4, 1891; children—Leontine A., Dorothy H. (Mrs. Daniel C. Adams, Jr.), Florence (Mrs. Edwin Dresser). Began as reporter Newark (N.J.) Evening News, 1886; pub. Brooklyn (N.Y.) Standard Union, 1917-27; pres. R.F.R. Huntsman Corpn. Republican. Presbyterian. Mason (K.T., Shriner). Clubs: Union League, Sphinx (pres.). Home: 835 Kensington Av., Plainfield, N.J.

HUOT, Constant John, glass mfr.; b. Fostoria, O., May 4, 1895; s. Joseph and Adele (Kopp) H.; grad. Carnegie Inst. Tech., 1917; m. Rose Babette Stussi, July 8, 1920; children—David Arthur, Marie Babette. Office work Union Switch & Signal Co., 1910-16; analytical chemist Duquesne Reduction Co., 1916-17; production mgr. and chemist Kopp Glass, Inc., mfr. of illuminating, signal and industrial glassware, Swissvale, Pa., 1919-37, vice-pres., dir. and gen. mgr. since 1937. Dir. Swissvale Pub. Schools. Mem. Illuminating Engrs. Soc., Am. Legion (past comdr. Swissvale post). Mason. Ancestors, both sides of family, associated with glass industry for several generations in Alsace-Lorraine, France, and U.S. Home: 2228 Hampton St. Address: Kopp Glass, Inc., Swissvale, Pa.

HURD, Peter, artist; b. Roswell, N.M., Feb. 22, 1904; s. Harold and Lucy Chew (Knight) H.; student N.M. Mil. Inst., 1917-20, U.S. Mil. Acad., 1921-23, Haverford Coll., 1923-24, Pa. Acad. of Fine Arts, and under N. C. Wyeth, 1924-26; m. Henriette Wyeth, June 22, 1929; children—Peter Wyeth, Ann Carol. Represented in permanent collections in Rochester, N.Y., Wilmington, Del., Chicago, Andover, Mass., Kansas City, and by mural frieze in fresco at N.M. Mil. Inst. Winner of competition for 3 mural panels in U.S. Terminal Annex Post Office, Dallas, Tex., 1938. Awarded first prize, 16th Internat. Watercolour Exhbn., Chicago Art Inst., 1937. Mem. Assn. of Grads. of U.S. Mil. Acad., Wilmington Soc. of Fine Arts. Club: Cap and Bells (Haverford Coll.). Illustrator of Books. Home: Chadds Ford, Pa., and San Patricio, N.M.

HUREVITZ, Meyer, realtor; b. Phila., Pa., July 27, 1898; s. Manuel and Anna (Haussmann) H.; ed. Central High Sch. and U. of Pa.; m. Frances A. Pressman, Jan. 21, 1923; children—June Rita, Manuel Donald. Engaged in real estate business since 1919, now operating under own name; v.p. Sphynx Bldg. & Loan Assn.; sec. Northern Liberties Finance Corpn., Girard Hall Bld. & Loan Assn.; dir. Realty Appraisal Co., Inc. Served as cadet, O.T.C., World War. Sr. mem. Soc. Residential Appraisers; mem. Phila. Real Estate Board, North Phila. Realty Bd., Alpha Epsilon Delta, Independent Young Men's Soc., Kurlander Verein. Republican. Home: 6873 N. 19th St. Office: S. W. Corner 6th and Girard Av., Philadelphia, Pa.

HURLEY, Emmet Daniel, wholesale druggist; b. Eric, Pa., Dec. 12, 1882; s. Daniel J. and Katherine (Hayden) H.; student Central High Sch., Erie, 3 yrs.; m. Irene Lee, Aug. 14, 1922; children—Emmet D., John Lee, Margaret Moston. Began as clerk in wholesale rug store, 1900, later traveling salesman for rugs and linoleums; began dealing in real estate at 21 yrs. of age; formed partnership Hurley & Hamberger, and opened up subdivision near Gen. Electric Co., Erie; built 65 houses, 14 stores; still own business; salesman for English shade cloth company, 1912-17, selling in all large cities, employment terminated when English plant was turned to making war munitions; partner W. P. Webster & Co., retail drug company, 1914; formed Erie Drug Co., wholesale and mfg. druggists, and since president; vice-president and dir. West Side Development Co., Citizens Mortgage Co.; dir. Security-Peoples Trust Co., Community Bldg. & Loans Assn. (all Erie). Gov. Erie Motor Club, 1918; became active in furthering good roads, helping form Trans-Pa. Highway Assn. and served as 1st sec. Incorporator St. Vincent Hosp. Mem. N.Y., Ohio and West Pa. Wholesalers Assn. Roman Catholic. Home: 467 Glenwood Boul. Office: 417 State St., Erie, Pa.

HURTZIG, William Garrett, pres. Wm. G. Hurtzig, Inc.; b. New York, N.Y., June 14, 1883; s. Charles Emile Frederick and Martha (Garrett) H.; student Morristown (N.J.) pub. schs., 1893-97, under pvt. tutor, 1899-1907; m. Ethel Miller, Sept. 6, 1917. Began as gen. ins. agt., Morristown, N.J., 1910; pres. Wm. G. Hurtzig, Inc., Ins. agency, Morristown, N.J., since 1924; treas. Hanover Bldg. & Loan Assn.; mem. bd. of mgrs. Morris Co. Savings Bank; dir. Excelsior Ins. Co. Mem. Bd. of Assessors, Town of Morristown (N.J.). Trustee Evergreen Cemetery, Morristown Green; pres. Morris Co. Children's Home; mem. bd. of govs., Morris Jr. Coll. Trustee, Washington Assn. of N.J. (sec.). Republican. Mason. Club: Forest Lake (Pike Co., Pa.). Home: 54 Morris Av. Office: 45 South St., Morristown, N.J.

HURWITZ, Abraham, journalist, editor; b. Brooklyn, N.Y., Jan. 3, 1888; s. Morris and Esther Rachel (Malakoff) H.; grad. high sch., Seattle, Wash.; student U. of Wash., 1906-09; admitted to Wash. bar, 1910, but did not practice; m. Charlotte Lippert, Apr. 20, 1918. Reporter successively with Seattle Post-Intelligencer, Seattle Times, Hoquiam Washingtonian, Seattle Star, 1908-14; city editor Seattle Star, 1914-16, editor, 1916-22; editor Jacksonville (Fla.) Journal, 1922-24, Reading (Pa.) Times since 1924. Also northwest corr. for Newspaper Enterprise Assn., 1916, and rep. and spl. writer for Kansas City (Mo.) Star, New York World, etc., various times. Helped draft first workmen's compensation act held constitutional in U.S. (Wash. state act); active in fight against convict leasing and flogging, Fla., 1922-23. Home: 1616 Alsace Road. Office: Reading Times, Reading, Pa.

HURWITZ, Max Zachary, retired merchant; b. Vilkomor, Lithuania, Sept. 14, 1886; s. Benjamin and Ethel (Margolies) H.; came to U.S., 1901; student under pvt. tutors; also extension courses in econs. and philosophy, Columbia U., 1918-21; m. Anna Lichtenstein, Jan. 1, 1924; 1 dau., Maxine Ethel. Founded store in Hoboken, 1902, which became largest dept. store in Hoboken; opened dept. store, Union City, 1921, two dept. stores, Jersey City, 1922; retired from retail business 1928, turning over first store (Hoboken) to employees and leasing remaining stores and property to chain stores operator; pres. Commercial Properties Corpn., M. Z. Hurtwitz Co. (investments), Hurwitz Realty Co., Washington Development Co., E. Maxine Co. Served as dir. Food Conservation Com. Hudson Co., also dir. several Liberty Loan and Red Cross drives during World War. Chmn. Hoboken Tercentenary Celebration, 1931. Dir. Council Boy Scouts (past pres.), Am. Red Cross, Hoboken Jewish Center. Dir. Christ Hosp. of Jersey City, Y.M.C.A., Y.W.C.A., Hoboken. Relief dir. for Hoboken, 1931-32. Mem. Acad. Polit. Science; dir. Hoboken Chamber of Commerce (ex-pres.), Hoboken Business Men's Assn. Independent Democrat. Jewish religion. Elk. Clubs: Kiwanis of Hoboken (past pres.); Tuna (Jersey City). Home: 135 Jewett Av., Jersey City. Office: 416 Washington St., Hoboken, N.J.

HUSEK, Joseph, editor; b. Ruzomberok, Czechoslovakia, Jan. 5, 1880; s. Joseph and Mary (Matousek) H.; came to U.S. 1903, naturalized, 1906; ed. Gymnasium, Ruzomberok; m. Anna Huska, of Ruzomberok, Aug. 30, 1903; children—Joseph (dec.), Martha (dec.), Stephanie Olga, Rosanne Vera. Employed as clk. Higher Appellate Ct., Ruzomberok, Czechoslovakia, 1899-1903; asst. editor, Slovak v Amerike, Slovak weekly, N.Y. City, 1904; editor and mgr. Jednota, official organ First Cath. Slovak Union, Middletown, Pa., 1904-38; pres. Slovak League of America, Assn. of Slovak Journalists of America; leader in movement resulting in signing of Pittsburgh Pact, May 30, 1918, by Pres. Thos. G. Masaryk, guaranteeing autonomy to Slovakia; mem. Diplomatic Reconstruction Commn. sent to Czechoslovakia by Slovak League of America, 1919. Mem. Czechoslovak Nat. Council in America, Friends of Slovak Freedom (founder, past pres.), Slovak Ednl. Inst. of America (founder, past pres.), Federation of Slovak Catholics (past pres.). Mem. Slovak League Delegation that visited Slovakia, 1938. Democrat. Roman Catholic. B.P.O.E. Home: Echo Knoll, Palmyra, Pa.

HUSEMEN, Lewis Edward, banker; b. Wheeling, W.Va., Mar. 25, 1873; s. Lewis and Veronica (Strobel) H.; ed. pub. schs. and Eastman Business Coll.; m. Clarice J. Jamieson, Oct. 12, 1916; 1 dau., Ann Louise (dec.). Accountant Wheeling Pottery Co., 1892-93, Western Union Telegraph Co., 1894-95; gen. clerk Lincoln Nat. Bank, Pittsburgh, 1896-1900; asst. sec. and treas. North Am. Savings & Trust Co., 1901-02; cashier Diamond Savings Bank, 1903-15; asst. cashier Diamond Nat. Bank, 1916-32; v.p. and cashier First Nat. Bank, Wilkinsburg, since 1933; treas. and dir. First Federal Savings & Loan Assn. Dir. East Borough Council, Boy Scouts of America. Sec. and treas. Tri-Valley Bankers' Assn.; dir. Wilkinsburg Chamber of Commerce. Republican. Presbyterian. Mason. Clubs: Bankers, Wilmas (Pittsburgh). Home: 810 Rebecca Av. Office: Penn Av. and Wood St., Wilkinsburg, Pa.

HUSSELTON, Thomas LaRue, sec. chamber of commerce; b. Williamsport, Pa., Aug. 26, 1895; s. Thomas Henry and Susan Martha (Bubb) H.; ed. U. of Pa., 1916-17, U.S. Naval Acad., 1918; m. Beth Barnett, Feb. 14, 1925; 1 dau., Joan. In employ Johns-Manville Corpn., 1912-17; with Victor Talking Machine Co., 1920-26; sec. Atlantic City Chamber of Commerce since 1927; pres. Tenncrest, Inc., operating The Shore Crest Hotel, Atlantic City, N.J. Served as yeoman, ensign, then lt. (j.g.), U.S.N., 1917-19. Pres. Columbia Regional Conf. Credit Bur. Execs., 1932. Mem. Nat. Assn. Commercial Orgn. Secs., N.J. Assn. Commercial Orgn. Secs. (pres. 1936). Republican. M.E. Ch. Club: Kiwanis of Atlantic City (past pres., lieut-gov., Delsea Div., N.J. Dist.). Home: 15 S. Quincy Av. Office: 2306 Pacific Av., Atlantic City, N.J.

HUSTON, Charles Lukens, mfr.; b. Coatesville, Pa., July 8, 1856; s. Dr. Charles and Isabelle Pennock (Lukens) H.; A.B., Haverford Coll., Pa., 1875; m. Annie Stewart, July 23, 1895. Clk. and bookkeeper, Huston & Penrose, and Huston, Penrose & Co. (now Lukens Steel Co.), 1875-80; assumed charge of puddle mill, 1881, plate mills, 1882, open hearth dept., 1891; became mem. firms, Huston, Penrose & Co., 1879, and Charles Huston & Sons, 1881; 2d v.p. Lukens Steel Co. until 1897, works mgr. until 1925, v.p. since 1897; dir. Belmont Iron Works, etc. Dir. of poor for Chester Co., Pa.; v.p. and dir. Montrose (Pa.) Bible Conf. Assn. Mem. Brit. Iron and Steel Inst.; asso. mem. Am. Soc. M.E.; mem. Am. Inst. Mining and Metall. Engrs., Franklin Inst. Presbyn. (elder). Home: 64 S. 1st Av., Coatesville, Pa.

HUSTON, Harland Watson, life ins.; b. Bethel, Del., Sept. 14, 1889; s. Irvin R. and Louise C. (Larrimore) H.; A.B., Washington Coll., Chestertown, Md., 1911; m. Margaret E. Sturgeon, June 25, 1921; 1 son, Harland W. Life ins. salesman Continental Am. Life Ins. Co., Seaford, Del., 1911-17; moved to Salisbury, Md., and entered agency work, mgr. of branch office, Salisbury, since 1926; dir. County Trust Co., Citizens Loan Co. Apptd. by Gov. Nice as mem. Casey Com., 1936, to study relief situation in State of Md. Chmn. Wicomico Co. Chapter, Am. Red Cross, 1936-37; dir. and chmn. Wicomico Welfare Bd.; dir. and past pres. Wicomico Children's Home; dir. Peninsula Gen. Hosp. Wicomico Free Library. Dir. Chamber of Commerce. Independent Democrat. Methodist. Mason (Shriner). Club: Rotary. Home: 301 E. William St. Office: Odd Fellows Bldg., E. Main St., Salisbury, Md.

HUSTON, McCready, writer; b. Brownsville, Pa., Mar. 11, 1891; s. Joseph Andrew and Elizabeth Entrikin (Fishburn) H.; ed. pub. schs.;

m. Daryl Greene, d. of W. W. Greene, of Uniontown, Pa., Sept. 22, 1913; children—Ruth Lindsey (Mrs. R. W. Peterson), Anne McCready, James McCready. With Uniontown (Pa.) Morning Herald, 1912-13, Pittsburgh Gazette Times, 1913-19; asso. editor South Bend (Ind.) Tribune, 1919-27; editor South Bend News-Times, 1929-32; mem. editorial staff Phila. Pub. Ledger, 1933-34; Scranton Republican, 1934; prof. journalism, U. of Pittsburgh, 1934-35; asso. editor Indianapolis (Ind.) Times, 1935-36; mem. editorial staff of United Features Syndicate, New York, 1936. Mem. Authors League America. Author: Hulings' Quest, 1925; The Big Show, 1927; Dear Senator, 1928; The King of Spain's Daughter, 1930; Solid Citizen, 1933; also articles and short stories in Scribner's Redbook, Harper's, Life, Saturday Evening Post, etc. Episcopalian. Home: Keswick Grove, N.J. Address: care Paul R. Reynolds & Son, 597 5th Av., New York, N.Y.

HUSTON, Stewart, sec. Lukens Steel Co.; b. Coatesville, Pa., May 9, 1898; s. Charles Lukens and Anne (Stewart) H.; ed. Haverford (Pa.) Sch. and Lehigh U., Bethlehem, Pa. Asst. metall. engr. Lukens Steel Co., mfrs. boiler plate, 1923-24, asst. open hearth supt., 1924-25, plant metallurgist, 1926-28, sec. since 1928; pres. and dir. Allegheny Ore & Iron Co.; mgr. and dir. Coach-and-Four Inn. Mem. Am. Soc. Metals, Am. Soc. Testing Materials, Am. Inst. Mining & Metall. Engrs., British Iron & Steel Inst., Delta Phi. Republican. Presbyterian. Collector early Americana. Home: 64 S. First Av. Office: 50 S. First Av., Coatesville, Pa.

HUTCHINS, Amos F.; instr. urology, Johns Hopkins U.; asso. visiting urologist Johns Hopkins Hosp.; urologist Calvert County Hosp.; visiting urologist Church Home and Infirmary and Bon Secours, Franklin Sq. and West Baltimore hosps. (all of Baltimore), also Emergency Hosp (Annapolis). Address: 1227 N. Calvert St., Baltimore, Md.

HUTCHINS, Elliott H.; prof. clin. surgery, U. of Md.; asst. visiting surgeon Johns Hopkins Hosp.; visiting surgeon Church Home and Infirmary, Mercy and South Baltimore Gen. hosps. Address: 1227 N. Calvert St., Baltimore, Md.

HUTCHINSON, Bennett Wertz, clergyman; b. Scottdale, Pa., Jan. 15, 1859; s. Wm. S. and Mary (Wertz) H.; A.B., O. Wesleyan U., 1883, A.M., same, 1886; S.T.B., Boston U. 1887; (hon.) S.T.D., Syracuse U., 1901; hon. LL.D. W.Va. Wesleyan Coll., 1927; m. Ruth A. Eastwood, July 14, 1886 (dec.); children—Mark Eastwood, Paul Eastwood. Engaged as teacher country schs., 1876; teacher Augusta (Ky.) Collegiate Inst. 1883-84; ordained to ministry M.E. Ch., 1887, and pastor in Brockton, Mass., and Providence, R.I., 1886-90; pres. W.Va. Wesleyan Coll., Buckhannon, W. Va., 1890-98; pres. Genesee Wesleyan Sem., 1898-1903; pastor Washington, Pittsburgh, Indiana and Connellsville, Pa., 1905-28; pastor, Oakmont, Pa., 1928-33, retired, 1933; mem. Pittsburgh Conf.; pres. Pittsburgh Conf. Ednl. Soc. since 1938. Trustee Beaver Coll., 1911-23, O. Wesleyan Univ., 1894-98. Republican. Methodist. Rotarian. Home: 3301 Iowa St., Pittsburgh, Pa.

HUTCHINSON, Charles Percy, lawyer; b. Trenton, N.J., Oct. 17, 1887; s. Barton Bellangee and Sarah Meirs (Hulme) H.; A.B., Princeton U., 1909; LL.B. (with hon.), N.Y. Law Sch., 1912; m. Laura Dorothea Reading, June 14, 1922; children—Sarah Ellen, Charles Percy. Admitted to N.J. bar, 1912, and since practiced at Trenton; mem. firm Hutchinson & Hutchinson, later Hutchinson & Bacon; now practicing alone. Served as 1st lt., capt., Inf., U.S. Army, during World War; 1st lt., capt., and maj. since 1929, N.J.N.G. County clk. (serving 3d term), Mercer County, N.J., since 1927. Mem. Mercer Co. Bar Assn., N.J. Sons of the Revolution, Union Rep. League (Trenton), Am. Legion (Trenton Post 93), Vets. Fgn. Wars (Trenton Post), Princeton Campus Club. Republican. Presbyterian. Mason (Trenton Lodge 5), Moose (Trenton Lodge 164). Club: Trenton (Trenton, N.J.). Home: 846 Parkside Av. Office: 702 Broad St., Trenton, N.J.

HUTCHINSON, John O.; mem. law firm Hutchinson, Crouse & Trail. Address: Beckley, W.Va.

HUTCHINSON, Paul Eastwood, lawyer; b. Buckhannon, W.Va., Nov. 29, 1891; s. Bennet W. and Ruth (Eastwood) H.; A.B., Ohio Wesleyan U., Delaware, O., 1913; LL.B., Western Reserve U., Cleveland, O., 1916; m. Lillian Ziegler, Apr. 22, 1925; children—William Ziegler, John Bennett. Asso. law firm Kelly & Cottrell, Cleveland, O., 1916-23; asso. Watson & Freeman, Pittsburgh, 1923-25; partner Sherriff, Lindsay, Weis & Hutchinson, Pittsburgh, since 1925 (specializing in corporate-federal tax and surety law); dir. and treas. Scholastic Corpn. Served as capt. inf., 88th Div., U.S. Army, 1917-19. Mem. Pittsburgh, Pa. and Am. bar assns., S.A.R. Am. Legion, Gyro, Delta Tau Delta, Phi Delta Phi. Republican. Methodist. Address: 72 Roycroft Av., Mt. Lebanon, Pittsburgh, Pa.

HUTCHINSON, Robert Parke, steel fabrication; b. Washington, D.C., May 24, 1882; s. Elias Smith and Mary Elizabeth (Seely) H.; M.E., Lehigh U., 1904; m. Elise Emily Myers, Nov. 6, 1906; children—Virginia Stuart (Mrs. Walter H. Gray), William Baxter Myers. Sales dept. Carnegie Steel Co., Pittsburgh, 1904-12; pres. and gen. mgr. Bethlehem Fabricators, Inc., since 1913. Home: Route 2, Bethlehem, Pa.

HUTCHISON, Albert Witt, chem. teacher; b. Carlisle, Pa., Mar. 19, 1905; s. William Albert and Mary Sophia (Loomis) H.; B.S., Dickinson Coll., Carlisle, Pa., 1925; M.S., Pa. State Coll., 1928, Ph.D., 1931; m. Claire Mabel Homan, Feb. 6, 1930; children—Mary Anne, William Witt, Nancy Claire. Instr. in chemistry, Pa. State Coll., 1931-33, asst. prof. since 1933. Mem. Am. Chem. Soc., Pa. Chem. Xi, Phi Lambda Upsilon, Sigma Pi Sigma, Phi Kappa Sigma. Democrat. Presbyterian. Contbr. articles on properties of solutions of electrolytes to Jour. Am. Chem. Soc. Home: 600 W. Fairmount Av., State College, Pa.

HUTCHISON, Charles Edward, clergyman; b. Boston, Mass., Sept. 29, 1872; s. Charles Edward and Mary Anne Elizabeth (Sargent) H.; A.B., Harvard U., 1893; B.D., Mass. Episcopal Theol. Sch., Cambridge, 1897; m. Louise Kendall, June 26, 1902. Ordained to ministry P.E. Ch., deacon, 1897, priest, 1898; curate Calvary Ch., N.Y. City, 1897-99; rector Grace Ch., Cincinnati, O., 1899-1902; vicar Ch. of the Ascension, Boston, Mass., 1902-06; rector Christ Ch., East Orange, N.J., since 1906. Trustee Bonnie Brae Farm. Clubs: Essex County Country (West Orange); Harvard of New Jersey; Harvard (N.Y. City). Home: 16 Prospect Terrace, East Orange, N.J.

HUTCHISON, Ralph Cooper, college pres.; b. Florissant, Colo., Feb. 27, 1898; s. Joseph Cooper and Estelle Katherine (Mosier) H.; Sterling (Kan.) Coll., 1914-16; A.B., Lafayette Coll., 1918, D.D., 1930; M.A., Harvard, 1919; Princeton Theol. Sem., 1919-22; Ph.D., U. of Pa., 1925; m. Harriet Sidney Thompson, Jan. 2, 1925; children—Mary Elizabeth, William Robert. Ordained ministry Presbyn. Ch., 1922; dir. religious edn. First Presbyn. Ch., Norristown, Pa., 1922-24; sec. young peoples work Presbyn. Bd. of Christian Edn., Phila., 1924-25; prof. philosophy and religion, Albarz Coll. of Teheran, Persia, 1925-26, dean 1926-31; pres. Washington and Jefferson College since 1931. With Aviation Service, U.S. Navy, Mar.-Nov. 1918. Trustee Albarz Coll. of Teheran, Western Theol. Sem. (Pittsburgh), Princeton Theol. Sem., Princeton, N.J. Mem. Sigma Alpha Epsilon, Pi Delta Epsilon. Presbyn. Clubs: Town Hall, University (New York); Duquesne, University (Pittsburgh); Rotary, Washington County Golf and Country. Contbr. to mags. Home: Washington, Pa.

HUTCHISON, Stuart Nye, clergyman; b. Pleasant Plains, N.Y., May 20, 1877; s. Sylvanus Nye and Sarah Matilda (Seeley) H.; A.B., Lafayette Coll., 1900, A.M., 1903; graduate Princeton Theol. Sem., 1903; D.D., Hampden-Sidney, 1916; m. Mary Hall Thompson, Dec. 2, 1907; children—Janet Louise, Stuart Nye, Richard Hall. Ordained Presbyn. ministry, 1903; asst. pastor South Park Ch., Newark, N.J., 1903-04; pastor 1st Ch., Steubenville, O., 1904-06, 1st Ref. Ch., Newark, N.J., 1906-10, First Presbyn. Ch., Norfolk, Va., 1910-21, East Liberty Ch., Pittsburgh, 1921—. Trustee Princeton Theol. Seminary, Western Theol. Seminary, Lafayette Coll., Wilson Coll., Grove City Coll. Mem. Presbyn. Bd. of Pensions. Mem. Delta Upsilon. Club: Duquesne. Author: The Soul of a Child, 1916; For the Children's Hour, 1918; Bible Boys and Girls, 1921; The Voice Within Us, 1932; Holy Ground, 1934. Home: 1301 Sheridan Av., Pittsburgh, Pa.

HUTCHISSON, Elmer, prof. physics; b. Cleveland, O., Dec. 29, 1902; s. Harry and Anna Bertha (Merrick) H.; B.S., Case Sch. Applied Science, 1923; M.S., Mass. Inst. Tech., 1924; Ph.D., U. of Minn., 1926; student U. of Berlin, Germany, 1929-30; m. Rose Valasek, Sept. 14, 1925. Instr., U. of Pittsburgh, 1926-27, asst. prof. physics, 1927-36, prof. and acting head dept. physics 1937-38, head since 1938; asst. dir. Am. Inst. of Physics, 1936-37; editor Jour. of Applied Physics since 1937. Awarded Charles A. Coffin fellowship, 1923-24. Fellow Am. Phys. Soc.; mem. Optical Soc. America, A.A.A.S., Am. Assn. Univ. Profs., Sigma Xi, Tau Beta Pi, Sigma Gamma Alpha. Clubs: University, Faculty (Pittsburgh). Author: Outline of Atomic Physics (with others) 1933; Laboratory Manual of Physics (with O. Blackwood), 1933. Contbr. articles to Phys. Rev. Home: 107 Fairfax Rd., Pittsburgh, Pa.

HUTSON, Frederick Leroy, univ. prof.; b. Pittsburgh, Pa., Apr. 12, 1875; s. John Speed and Hannah Sophronia (Snyder) H.; A.B., Denison Univ., Granville, Ohio, 1896, L.H.D., same university, 1935; Ph.D., U. of Chicago, 1907; m. Mrs. Sara Holmes Watts, Dec. 18, 1920; children—Holmes Leroy and (stepchildren) George Burghall Watts, William Wood Watts. Instr. classics, 1903-05, asst. prof. 1905-18 (leave of absence, 1906-07), prof. Greek and registrar, 1918-25 (leave of absence 1924-25), prof. classics since 1925, Princeton. Mem. Archæol. Inst. America, Am. Philol. Assn., Phi Beta Kappa, Sigma Chi. Republican. Club: Nassau (Princeton). Home: 42 Cleveland Lane, Princeton, N.J.

HUTTON, A. J. White, lawyer and prof. of law; b. Chambersburg, Pa., Mar. 20, 1877; s. Edward Noah and Alice Virginia (White) H.; student Chambersburg (Pa.) Acad., 1890-93; A.B., Gettysburg (Pa.) Coll., 1897, M.A., 1899; LL.B., Harvard Law Sch., 1902 (awarded scholarship for meritorious work); m. Matie Julia Smith, Dec. 20, 1905; children—Alice (Mrs. Robert M. Prather), Henry Smith, Edward Milton, Mary Julia. Began as elk. to com. on war claims, House of Reps., Washington, D.C., 1898; admitted to practice in Franklin Co. (Pa.), 1899, to practice in Supreme Ct. of Pa., 1914, to Superior Ct. of Pa., 1931; engaged in practice of law at Chambersburg, Pa., since 1902; prof. of law, Dickinson Sch. of Law, Carlisle, Pa., since 1902. Mem. Gen. Assembly of Pa. from Franklin Co., 1930-34 (rep. floor leader, chmn. of rules com., chmn. state govt. com., speaker pro-tem). Chmn. Franklin Co. Bd. of Law Examiners. Mem. Kittochtinny Historical Soc., Chamber of Commerce, Phi Beta Kappa, Alpha Tau Omega, Delta Chi. Republican. Lutheran. Clubs: Rufus Choate Law, Harvard (Phila.); Commercial (Chambersburg, Pa.). Contbr. numerous legal articles to Dickinson (Coll.) Law Review. Author: Hutton on Law of Wills in Pennsylvania, 1933. Home: 82 W. Queen St. Office: 209 Chambersburg Trust Bldg., Chambersburg, Pa.

HUTZLER, Albert David, merchant; b. Baltimore, Md., Nov. 22, 1888; s. David and Ella (Gutman) H.; A.B., Johns Hopkins U., 1909; m. Gretchen Hochschild, Apr. 5, 1911; children—Caroline (Mrs. Marcus M. Bernstein, Jr.), Albert David, Richard Hochschild. With Hutzler Bros. Co. since 1910, president since 1919; director Chesapeake & Potomac Telephone Co., Retail Research Assn. & Asso. Merchandising Corpn. Nat. Retail Dry Goods Assn. Pres. Asso. Jewish Charities, 1923-27 (hon. dir.); trustee Goucher

HYATT, Frank Kelso, coll. president; b. Chester, Pa., Nov. 19, 1885; s. Gen. Charles Eliot and Keziah West (Dyer) H.; father pres. Pa. Mil. Coll. many yrs.; grad. Gilbert's Acad., 1902, Swarthmore Prep. Sch., 1903; student Pa. Mil. Coll., 1903, LL.D., 1930; B.S. in Engring., Swarthmore Coll., 1907; m. Blanche L. Cramp, June 9, 1909; 1 son (died in infancy). With Pa. Mil. Coll. since 1907, asst. prof. mathematics, 1909-12, prof., 1912-29, treas. since 1916, v.p., 1917-30, succeeded father as pres., 1930, also trustee. Organizer, and capt. Troop Pa. N.G., 1910, lt. col. inf., 1917, col., 1930. Republican. Presbyn. Mason (K.T.). Clubs: Union League (Philadelphia); Chester, Spring Haven Golf, Pickering Hunt. Address: Pennsylvania Military College, Chester, Pa.

HYATT, Harriet Randolph, (Mrs. Alfred Goldsboro Mayor), sculptor, teacher; b. Salem, Mass., Apr. 25, 1868; d. Prof. Alpheus and Audella (Beebe) Hyatt; student The Misses Smith Sch., Cambridge, Cowels Art Sch., Boston, painting under Ross Turner, Triscott, Earnest Major and Dennis Bunker, sculpture under Henry Hudson Kitson; m. Dr. Alfred Goldsboro Mayor, Aug. 27, 1900; children—Alpheus Hyatt Mayor, Katharine Goldsboro Mayor Cook (divorced), Brantz Mayor, Barbara Snowden (Mrs. Theodore Davis Money). Professional artist since 1892; teacher since 1920. Exhibited in Boston, New York City, Chicago, Atlanta (awarded silver medal), San Francisco and in Salon, Paris; represented by sculpture in Mariner's Marine Park (Newport News), Brookgreen Gardens (S.C.), Guyot Hall, Princeton, the Howard C. Warren medal for the Soc. of Exptl. Psychologists, Cornell, Univ., Rear Adm. Goldsboro bust at Annapolis, etc. Taught night classes of Y.W.C.A., 6 yrs. Mem. Am. Artists Professional League, Soc. for Preservation N. E. Antiquities, N. E. Hist. & Geneal. Soc., Hist. Soc. Princeton, D.A.R. (regent Princeton chapter 10 yrs.), Daughters Colonial Wars, Daughters Am. Colonists, Women Descs. Ancient & Hon. Arty. Co. of Boston, Am. Women's Assn. Women's Nat. Rep. Club. Home: 280 Nassau St. Studio: Seven Gables, Princeton, N.J.

HYATT, Ralph W(esley), lawyer; b. Albany, N.Y., Apr. 23, 1871; s. John W. and Anna E. (Taft) H.; LL.B., Columbia U. Law Sch., 1893, LL.M., same, 1894; m. Maud R. Mueller, June 10, 1914; 1 son, John W. Admitted to N.J. bar, 1900; asso. with legal dept. The Prudential Ins. Co. of America continuously since entering its employ, 1895, now asso. gen. solicitor of same. Mem. Am. Bar Assn., N.J. State Bar Assn., Essex Co. Bar Assn. Club: Short Hills. Home: Windermere Terrace, Short Hills. Office: 763 Broad St., Newark, N.J.

HYDE, Louis Kepler, banker; b. Hydetown, Pa., July 30, 1865; s. Charles and Elizabeth (Kepler) H.; A.B., Yale, 1887; m. Verna May Emery, June 30, 1891. Pres. Plainfield Savings Bank, Muskogee (Okla.) Electric Traction Co., Shawnee-Tecumseh Traction Co., Riverside Coal & Timber Co., Union County Investment Co., Deka Development Co. Mem. Delta Kappa Epsilon. Club: Yale (New York). Home: Plainfield, N.J.

HYDE, Richard Elkins, educator; b. Martinsburg, W.Va., Apr. 22, 1895; s. Hiram Sydney and Sarah Anne (Hutchinson) H.; A.B., W.Va. Univ., Morgantown, 1921; grad. student Johns Hopkins U., Baltimore, Md., summers 1921-23; A.M., Columbia U., 1924; Ph.D., U. of Pittsburgh, 1929; m. Anna Baxter, Aug. 12, 1929; 1 dau., Barbara Ann. Instr. English, high sch., Pineville, W.Va., 1921-23, Mullens, W.Va., 1924-25; prof. edn., Fairmont (W.Va.) State Teachers Coll., 1925-30; dir. teacher training, Okla. Agrl. & Mech. Coll., Stillwater, Okla., 1930-33; dir. research, State Dept. Edn., Charleston, W.Va. since 1933. Served as pvt. inf. W.Va. N.G., 1917; sergt. Engrs. Corps, U.S.A., 1917-19; with A.E.F. Fellow A.A.A.S., Okla. Acad. Sci.; mem. Phi Beta Kappa, Kappa Delta Pi, Pi Gamma Mu. Democrat. Conglist. Club; Commons (W.Va. U.). Author: The Preparation and Partial Standardization of Unit Tests in American History, 1930; Exercises and Problems for High School Teachers, 1932; A Workbook for Apprentice Teachers in Secondary Schools, 1933. Contbr. bulls. and articles to ednl. journs. Home: 1584 Lee St., Charleston, W.Va.

HYDE, Roscoe Raymond, prof. immunology; b. Cory, Ind., Mar. 23, 1884; s. John Andrew and Mary Ann (Michaelree) H.; A.B., Ind. State Teachers Coll., Terre Haute, 1908; A.B. and A.M., Ind. U., 1909; Ph.D., Columbia, 1913; m. Elsie A. Coss, Sept. 18, 1910; children—Gertruda Martina, Margaret Irene, Edith Raymond. Asst. in embryology, Ind. U., 1908-09; asst. prof., later prof. and head of dept. zoology and physiology, Ind. Teachers Coll., 1909-19; fellow, Johns Hopkins, 1918-19, asso., 1919-22, asso. prof. immunology, 1922-28, asso. prof. filterable viruses and head of dept., 1928-32, prof. immunology and dir. of laboratories of filterable viruses and immunology since 1932. Visiting prof., U. of Chicago, 1930; mng. editor Am. Jour. Hygiene, 1927-32. Fellow A.A.A.S., Am. Soc. Zoölogists; Sigma Xi, Delta Omega (pres. Alpha chapter). Democrat. Contbr. to scientific publs. Home: 4101 Penhurst Av., Baltimore, Md.

HYDE, Walter Woodburn, university prof.; b. Ithaca, N.Y., May 14, 1870; s. Orange Percy and Eloise Flower (Davies) H.; A.B., Cornell, 1893; studied Am. Schs. Classical Studies, Athens and Rome, 1898-99, Göttingen and Halle, Germany, and Geneva, Switzerland, 1900-02; A.M., Ph.D., Halle, 1902; unmarried. Submaster, 1895-98, and headmaster, 1899-1900, Northampton (Mass.) High Sch.; instr. classics, Princeton, 1906; prof. Latin, U. of Tenn., 1908; instr. Greek, Cornell, 1909; instr. Greek, 1910-14, asst. prof., 1914-24, prof. Greek and lecturer in ancient history, 1924-30, prof. Greek and ancient history since 1930, U. of Pa. Mem. Am. Philol. Assn., Am. Oriental Soc., Am. Hist. Assn., Pa. Hist. Soc., Classical Assn. of Atlantic States, and of Classical (pres. 1923-24), Oriental (pres. 1922-23), and Anthropol. (pres. 1918-20) clubs of Phila., Sigma Phi Sigma, Phi Beta Kappa, Philomathean, Philobiblon Soc. Mason. Author: De Olympionicarum Statuis, 1903; Thessaly and the Vale of Tempe, 1912; Monasteries of Meteora and Greek Monasticism, 1913; Mountains of Greece, 1915; chapter on Greek Religion in Religious Past and Present, 1917; Olympic Victor Monuments and Greek Athletic Art (Carnegie Instn.), 1921; Greek Religion and Its Survivals, 1923; Roman Alpine Routes (Am. Philos. Soc.), 1935; contbr. chapters to Song of Songs, 1923, School Athletics in Modern Education, 1931, John C. Rolfe Memorial Volume, 1931, also to scientific jours., on Greek lit., religion, archæology, athletics, geography, history and legal antiquities. Editor: Am. and Medieval History in Natl. Ednl. Alliance Home Study Courses in History, 1937-38. Home: 4109 Locust St., Philadelphia, Pa.

HYMA, Nicholas, prof. chemistry, W.Va. Wesleyan Coll. Address: W.Va. Wesleyan Coll., Buckhannon, W.Va.

HYMES, Myron Barnard, lawyer; b. Barbour Co., W.Va., Mar. 24, 1897; s. Matthew E. and Olola (Thacker) H.; A.B., W.Va. Wesleyan Coll., Buckhannon, W.Va., 1920; LL.B., Harvard U. Law Sch., 1923; m. Cecile Marguerite West, Sept. 1, 1920; children— Cecile Marguerite, Myron Bernard, Jr., Charles Matthew, Carol Ann. Admitted to W.Va. bar, 1923, and engaged in gen. practice of law at Buckhannon since 1923, served as pros. atty. Upshur Co., W.Va., 1924-28; sec., treas. Upshur Loan Assn. since 1924. Served as pvt. inf., U.S.A., 1918. Chmn. troop com. and ct. of honor of Boy Scouts. Trustee W.Va. Wesleyan Coll., First M.E. Ch., both of Buckhannon. Republican. Methodist. Mason (K.T.), O.E.S. (worthy patron). Club: Lions of Buckhannon. Home: 67 Smithfield St. Office: Upshur Bldg., Buckhannon, W.Va.

HYNSON, William George, ins. co. exec. retired; b. Baltimore, Md., Mar. 8, 1872; s. William George and Anna Maria (Dushane) H.; student pub. schs. and Baltimore City Coll.; m. Lucy Erskine Bains, Oct. 4, 1902; children—William George, Jr., Richard. Asso. with United States Fidelity & Guaranty Co., Baltimore, Md., 1897-1939, successively asst. auditor, auditor, comptroller, treas. and dir., then vice-pres., 1923-29, retired as vice-pres. 1939, now dir. Served in Md. League of Nat. Defense, Am. Protective Legion, during World War. Mem. Huguenot Soc. of America, Md. Hist. Soc. Episcopalian. Club: Maryland (Baltimore). Home: The Knoll, Ruxton, Md.

HYSLOP, James Augustus, entomologist; b. Chicago, Ill., July 7, 1884; s. Charles George and Mary Agnes (Garvey) H.; B.S., Mass. Agrl. Coll., 1908; B.S., Boston U., 1908; M.S., Washington State Coll., 1911; m. Grace Geneva Anderson, Oct. 7, 1911; children—Charles Douglas, James Anderson, Rintha, Wynnifred. In charge first gipsy moth eradication work in Conn., 1906; cotton boll weevil parasite work, U.S. Dept. Agr., 1907; cereal and forage insect investigation, Dept. Agr., 1908-17; asst. at Pullman (Wash.) Field Sta., 1909-12; in charge Hagerstown (Md.) Field Sta., 1912-17; in charge all extension activities of Bur. of Entomology, World War; entomologist in charge Office of Insect Pest Survey and Pub. Relations, Bur. of Entomology, U.S. Dept. Agr., 1917-1934; entomologist in charge Division of Insect Pest Survey and Information, Bur. of Entomology and Plant Quarantine, U.S. Dept. Agr., 1934—. Fellow A.A.A.S., Am. Entomol. Soc.; mem. Am. Assn. Economic Entomologists, Washington Acad. Science, Washington Entomol. Soc. Has specialized in Elateridae. Home: Cameronia Farm, Silver Springs, Md.

I

IAMS, Samuel Harvey, physician; b. Waynesburg, Pa., May 30, 1879; s. John T. and Catherine (Harvey) I.; A.B., Princeton U., 1901; M.D., U. of Pa. Med. Sch., 1905; m. Elizabeth Rouse, Jan. 29, 1910; 1 son, Samuel Harvey, Jr. Interne Mercy Hosp., Pittsburgh, 1905-06; engaged in gen. practice of medicine at Princeton, N.J. since 1926; attdg. surgeon Princeton Hosp. since 1926; cons. surgeon Pt. Pleasant N.J. Hosp. since 1937. Served on draft bd. during World War. Mem. A.M.A., N.J. and Pa. State Med. Socs., Delta Kappa Epsilon. Republican. Presbyn. Clubs: Nassau (Princeton); Bay-Head Yacht (Bay Head, N.J.). Home: Library Pl. & Westcott Rd. Office: 34 Mercer St., Princeton, N.J.

ICKES, Harold L., Secretary of the Interior, lawyer; b. Frankstown Township Blair County, Pa., Mar. 15, 1874; s. Jesse Boone Williams and Martha Ann (McCune) I.; A.B., University of Chicago, 1897, J.D., cum laude, 1907; LL.D., Washington and Jefferson Coll. and Lake Forest Coll., 1933, Berea, Pa. Mil. and Tufts colls. and Northwestern U., 1934, U. of Ala., 1935; m. Anna Wilmarth Thompson, 1911 (died 1935); children—Mrs. ReQua Bryant, Wilmarth (dec.), Raymond, Robert; m. 2d, Jane Dahlman, of Milwaukee, May 24, 1938. Reporter, Chicago newspapers, 1897-1901; law practice, Chicago from 1907. Active in reform municipal politics since 1897; mgr. mayoralty campaign of John M. Harlan, 1905, and of Charles E. Merriam, 1911; chmn. Progressive County Com., Cook Co., Ill., 1912-14; chmn. Ill. Progressive State Com. 1914-16; mem. Progressive Nat. Com. and Nat. Exec. Com. 1915-16; mem. Nat. Campaign Exec. Com. in charge of Charles E. Hughes' campaign for President, 1916. Chmn. Ill. State Council Defense Neighborhood Com., 1917-Apr. 1918; Y.M.C.A. work in France with 35th Div. A.E.F., Apr. 1918-Jan. 1919; del. at large Progressive Nat. Conv., 1916, Rep. Nat. Convention, 1920, Democratic National Convention, 1936; president of People's Protective League, 1922; Ill. mgr. of Hiram W. Johnson Presidential campaign, 1924; mgr. campaign of Hugh S.

Magill, Independent Rep. candidate for U.S. Senator from Ill., 1926; chmn. Nat. Progressive League for Roosevelt and Garner, 1932. Sec. of Interior in cabinet of President Roosevelt since 1933, also administrator of Pub. Works Adminstrn. and oil administrator under NRA. Mem. Nat. Roosevelt Memorial Assn.; v.p. Roosevelt Memorial Assn. of Greater Chicago; pres. Chicago Forum Council, 1926-27. Mem. bd. Chicago Govt. Planning Assn.; Nat. Conservation Com.; chmn. People's Traction League, 1929-30. Mem. Am. Bar Assn., Ill. Soc. S.A.R., Phi Delta Theta, Phi Delta Phi, Pi Gamma Mu. Author: New Democracy, 1934; Back to Work, 1935. Clubs: University, Shawnee Country, Chicago Riding, Indian Hill (all Chicago); Nat. Press, Congressional Country (Washington, D.C.). Home: 900 S. Private Road, Winnetka, Ill.; and Headwaters Farm, Olney, Md. Office: Interior Bldg., Washington, D.C.

IGLEHART, Francis Nash, real estate broker; b. Baltimore, Md., Aug. 1, 1881; Charles Iredell and Anne (Calhoun) I.; ed. pub. sch., Baltimore, Marston Pvt. Sch., Baltimore, Johns Hopkins U. (Class 1903); m. Lucy James Cook, Nov. 16, 1907; children—Lucy James (Mrs. John Edgar Howard), Angelica Peale (Mrs. Warde B. Allan), Elizabeth Graham, Francis Nash. Began as real estate broker, Baltimore, 1905; pres. F. N. Iglehart & Co., Inc., Baltimore; pres. Motoramp Garages of Md.; dir. Dun-Bradstreet Corpn. Served as capt., Air Service, U.S. Army, with A.E.F. Mem. Soc. of Cincinnati of N.C., S.R., Md. Hist. Soc. Episcopalian. Clubs: Maryland, Elkridge, Merchants, Maryland Jockey, Baltimore Country, Bachelor Cotillion (Baltimore, Md.); Green Spring Valley Hunt (Garrison, Md.). Home: Stevenson, Baltimore Co., Md. Office: 11 E. Lexington St., Baltimore, Md.

IGLEHART, Joseph Alexander Wilson, broker; b. Baltimore, Md., Nov. 15, 1891; s. Paul and May (Wilson) I.; student Boy's Latin Sch., Baltimore, 1902-10; C.E., Cornell U., 1914; m. Jane Margaret Cary Ulman, Dec. 29, 1917; children—Jane Margaret Cary, Katharine Cary. Asso. with Brooke, Stokes & Co., Philadelphia, 1914-21, partner, 1920-21; partner J. A. W. Iglehart & Co., Baltimore, 1922-33; mgr. investment dept., Field, Glore & Co., New York, 1933-35; partner W. E. Hutton & Co., New York City, since 1935; dir. Columbia Broadcasting System, Nat. Gypsum Co. Served as pvt., Battery A, Md. F.A., 1915-16, 2d lt., F.A., 1916-17, capt., Battery F, 321st F.A., A.E.F., 1917-18, major, F.A., 1918. Mem. Delta Phi. Episcopalian. Clubs: Meadowbrook, Lunch (New York City); Valley Hunt, Baltimore Country (Baltimore, Md.); South River (Annapolis, Md.). Home: Lutherville, Md. Office: 14 Wall St., New York, N.Y.

IHRIG, Roscoe Myrl, educator; b. nr. Wooster, O., Sept. 21, 1881; s. Marion Brady and Sarah Loretta (Miller) I.; Ph.B., Coll. of Wooster, 1901; Ph.M., U. of Chicago, 1909, Ph.D., 1914; studied U. of Paris, 1907-08; m. Flavilla Grant, Aug. 16, 1910. Teacher secondary schs., 1901-07, 1909-12 and 1913-15; teaching fellow, U. of Chicago, 1912-13; instr., Coll. of Wooster, summers 1910-12, 14, 15 and 17; asst. prof., Carnegie Inst. Tech., 1915-16, asso. prof., 1916-18, prof. and head dept. modern langs., 1918-20, dir. evening courses since 1920, dir. summer sessions, 1918-33, dir. div. of gen. studies and dean of freshmen in engring. since 1926. Sec.-treas. Assn. of Urban Universities; mem. Pittsburgh Philos. Soc., Phi Beta Kappa, Phi Kappa Phi, Sigma Alpha Epsilon. Protestant. Club: Agora (Pittsburgh). Home: 1722 New Haven Av., Dormont, Pittsburgh, Pa.

IJAMS, George Edwin, asst. adminst. Veterans' Administration; b. Baltimore, Md., Sept. 29, 1888; s. George Edgar and Helen Elizabeth (Jordan) I.; ed. Baltimore grade schs. and Baltimore City Coll.; m. Mary Rawlings Addison, Feb. 7, 1912; children—George Edwin, Virginia, Barbara Ann. Served on Mexican Border in First Md. Cavalry, Nat. Guard, 1916; enlisted for World War service U.S.A. as private, subsequently entered R.O.T.C., Fort Myer, Va., 1917; served as capt. of inf., U.S. Army, at outbreak of World War; assigned to A.E.F., detachment of War Risk Ins. Bur.; drafted plan of soldier ins., used in the field; apptd. war risk ins. officer of 1st Div.; in that capacity wrote $200,000,000 ins. at the front, some of it under fire for which cited by Gen. Pershing for "exceptionally meritorious and conspicuous service"; joined staff of Brig. Gen. Charles G. Dawes, rendering service in Eng., Spain, Portugal, Switzerland, Italy and N. Africa, coöperating with mil. missions of allies; promoted to maj. and lt. col.; given spl. duties with demobilization and peace conf.; on return to U.S. apptd. asst. dir. Bur. War Risk Ins.; sent to Europe to negotiate reciprocal agreements with foreign countries for care disabled vets., 1921; dir. U.S. Vets. Bur. during its last yr.; has been asst. adminstr. Vet. Adminstrn. since orgn., in charge med. and domiciliary care, constrn. and supplies. Served 3 terms as comdr. in chief Mil. Order World War, its membership doubling during his adminstrn. Mem. Vets. Foreign Wars, Am. Legion, Heroes of '76, R.O.T.C. Assn. of U.S., Nat. Sojourners. Decorated Purple Heart (U.S.); Officer Order of Crown of Italy; Officer French Acad. (gold palms); Chevalier Legion of Honor (France). Home: 3201 Carlisle Av., Baltimore, Md. Office: Arlington Bldg., Washington, D.C.

IKELER, Kenneth Cole; prof. animal and dairy husbandry, U. of Md. Address: University of Maryland, College Park, Md.

ILL, Edward Joseph, M.D.; b. Newark, N.J., May 23, 1854; s. C. Fridolin and Julia (Rehman) I.; M.D., Coll. Phys. and Surg. (Columbia), 1875; Univs. of Strassburg, Vienna and Freiburg, 1875-76; m. Clothilde Dieffenbach, Jan. 10, 1878; children—Mrs. Clothilde Scheller, Edgar A., Mrs. Edna O'Malley, Mrs. Florence K. Hensler. In practice at Newark since 1876. Formerly surgeon Woman's Hosp. and med. dir. St. Michael's Hosp.; gynecologist, supervising obstetrician and trustee St. Barnabas Hosp.; consulting gynecologist, Beth Israel Hosp., Newark, All Soul's Hosp., Morristown, N.J., Mountain Side Hosp., Montclair, N.J., Rahway Memorial Hosp., Rahway, N.J.; dir. Prudential Insurance Co. of America. Member Bd. of Education, Newark, 1878-80; trustee Newark City Home, 1880-95. Republican. Mem. Southern Surg. and Gynecol. Assn.; v.p. for N.J. of Pan Am. Med. Congress, 1893; pres. Med. Soc. State of N.J., 1907; v.p., 1893, pres. 1899, exec. council, 1901-03, Am. Assn. Obstetricians and Gynecologists; pres. Acad. Medicine, Northern N.J.; chmn. for State of N.J. of Am. Soc. for Control of Cancer; pres. Soc. for Relief of Widows and Orphans of Med. Men of N.J.; fellow Am. Coll. Surgeons (chmn. judicial com. for N.J.); hon. fellow N.J. State Med. Soc. Home: 88 Treacy Av. Office: 1004 Broad St., Newark, N.J.

ILLINGWORTH, Ralph Walshaw, Jr., clergyman; b. State College, Pa., Sept. 1, 1899; s. Ralph Walshaw and Marion (Snyder) I.; prep. edn. Franklin and Marshall Acad., 1915-17; A.B., Princeton U., 1921; S.T.B., Western Theol. Sem., 1924; m. Edna Stewart, June 8, 1921; children—Ralph Stewart, Theodore Reynolds, Marion Elizabeth (deceased). Ordained to ministry of Presbyterian Ch., 1924; pastor Presbyn. Ch., Frederickstown, O., 1924-26, Philipsburg, Pa., 1926-36; supt. Presbytery of Huntingdon, Pa., since 1936. Dir. and sec. of bd. Huntingdon Presbytery Home for Aged. Mason (32°). Home: Pine Grove Mills, Pa.

ILLMAN, Adelaide Thomas, educator; b. Philadelphia, Pa., June 10, 1876; d. Charles and Adelaide (Litle) I.; student Philadelphia High Sch. for Girls, 1891-95, Philadelphia Normal Sch., 1895-98; B.S. in Edn., U. of Pa., 1929; A.M. in Edn., Columbia Univ. Teachers Coll., 1934; unmarried. Kindergarten teacher, Starr Center, Philadelphia, 1900-12; asst. Miss Hart's Training Sch. for Kindergartners, 1912-18; prin. Illman Training Sch. for Kindergarten and Primary Teachers, 1918-36, name changed, 1936, to Illman-Carter Unit for Kindergarten-Primary Teachers of School of Edn. of U. of Pa., thus becoming part of U. of Pa., and since dir. Mem. Pi Lambda Theta. Clubs: Women's University, Faculty Tea (Uni. of Pa., Philadelphia). Home: 30 W. Logan St., Philadelphia, Pa.

ILLMAN, George Morton, physician; b. Phila., Pa., May 13, 1878; s. Samuel H. and Annie R. (Lloyd) I.; ed. Temple U. Med. Prep. Sch., 1895-97; M.D., U. of Pa. Med. Sch., 1901; grad. study, U. of Vienna, U. of Berlin, 1901-02; m. Anna R. McCahan, Apr. 18, 1906. Specialized in internal medicine in pvt. practice in Phila., 1902-15; visiting and asso. physician, Temple U., Garretson, and Charity hosps., Phila., 1902-15; asso. prof. medicine, Temple U. Med. Sch., 1912-15; med. dir., Zurich Ins. Co., New York, N.Y., 1915-28, Home Ins. Co., New York, 1928-31; asso. prof. medicine, Temple U. Med. Sch. and mem. staff, Temple U. Hosp., Phila., Pa., since 1932; retired from active practice, 1931. Trustee Temple U. Mem. Am. Med. Assn., Pa. State and Phila. Co. med. socs. (past dir.), Phila. Clin. Assn. (past pres.), North Branch Phila. Med Soc. (past chmn.), Med. Club Phila. (past dir.). Republican. Presbyn. Mason (K.T.). Clubs: Union League, Penn Athletic (Philadelphia). Contbr. many articles to med. jours. Home: The Kenilworth, Alden Park, Germantown, Philadelphia, Pa.

IMBRIE, Andrew Clerk, retired business exec.; b. Jersey City, N.J., May 16, 1875; s. Charles Frederick and Charlotte Martha (Clerk) I.; student Halsey Collegiate Sch., New York, 1888-91; A.B., Princeton U., 1895; m. Dorothy Welsh, Jan. 12, 1918; children—Andrew Welsh, Frances Frazer. Began with Abbey & Imbrie, mfrs. fishing tackle, New York, 1895, treas., 1901-09, pres., 1909-16, when business was sold; rep. H.L. Crawford & Co., bankers, New York, and Amazon Pacific Ry. Co., in negotiations with Peruvian Govt., Lima, Peru, 1913; purchasing agt. U.S. Finishing Co., New York, operating five textile mills in Conn. and R.I., 1914-19, dir. and treas., 1916-32. Mem. of Com. of Fifty, Princeton U., 1905, formed to establish endowment; chmn. com. to organize Grad. Council of Princeton U., 1908, mem. Council since 1915, vice-chmn., 1922-23; trustee Princeton U., 1907-12; financial sec. of bd., 1909-12. Trustee Demilt Dispensary, New York, 1905-19, chmn. com. on med. staff, 1917-19, chmn. spl. com., 1919, to determine future orgn.; sec. Reconstrn. Hosp. (consolidation of Demilt Dispensary, the Clinic for Functional Reeducation and the Park Hosp.), 1924-26, v.p., 1928-29. Mem. exec. com. Friends of Princeton U. Library; chmn. visiting com. Princeton U. Dept. of Art and Archaeology; chmn. bd. of editorial direction Princeton Alumni Weekly, 1925-32; trustee Princeton Country Day Sch. since 1928, chmn., 1930-35. Republican. Presbyterian. Club: Princeton (New York). As undergrad. Princeton U., mem. Am. Whig Soc., awarded five prizes in lit., writing, pub. speaking. Editor Nassau Literary Mag., Class of 1895, sec. since 1894. Address: 20 Hibben Rd., Princeton, N.J.

INCH, Sydney Richard, pub. utility exec.; b. England, June 16, 1878; s. Reuben and Elizabeth (Down) I.; ed. Huish Sch. for Boys, Taunton, Eng., and Finsbury Tech. Coll., London, Eng.; m. Margaret B. Van den Broek, Apr. 25, 1904 (died Jan. 21, 1923); m. 2d, Alice Evans, Oct. 15, 1928. Began with Mont. Power Transmission Co., Butte, Mont., 1900; with Butte (Mont.) Electric & Power Co., 1901-03; mgr. Missoula (Mont.) Light & Water Co., 1903-12; gen. supt. Utah Power & Light Co., 1913-18, v.p. and gen. mgr., 1918-23; v.p. Electric Bond & Share Co., 1924-33, pres. since 1933; pres. Ebasco Services, Inc. Fellow Am. Inst. E.E. Republican. Mason. Clubs: Engineers, Bankers (New York); Rock Spring (W. Orange, N.J.). Home: Walnut Gate, N. Ridgewood Rd., S. Orange, N.J. Office: 2 Rector St., New York, N.Y.

INGBERG, Simon Hanson, research on fire resistance and prevention; b. Ringsager, Norway, June 24, 1877; s. Hans Olson and Christine (Ask) I.; came to U.S., 1881, naturalized, 1897; student Concordia Coll., Moorhead, Minn., 1895-97; C.E., U. of Minn., Minneapolis, Minn., 1909; M.S., U. of Ill., Urbana, Ill., 1910; m. Blanche Elizabeth McManus, June 18, 1912; children—Martin Howard (dec.), Kathryn Blanche, Philip Sigurd, Norval Owen, Lawrence Edward. Teacher Minn. pub. schs., 1897-1906;

instr. civil engring., Lehigh U., Bethlehem, Pa., 1910-11; structural designer James Stewart Co., Chicago, Ill., 1911-12, 1913-14, C.,M.&St.P. Ry. Chicago, 1912-13; asso. physicist Nat. Bur. of Standards, Washington, D.C., 1914-20, physicist, prin. engr. and chief fire resistance sect. since 1921. Sec. Federal Fire Council since 1930. Trustee Montgomery County (Md.) Pub. Sch. System. Mem. A.A.A.S., Wash. Philos. Soc., Am. Soc. for Testing Materials, Nat. Fire Protection Assn., Bldg. Officials Conf. of America, Sigma Xi. Am. Ethical Union. Royal Arcanum. Club: Edgemoor (Bethesda, Md.). Author many tech., scientific publs. on structural engring., fire resistance and prevention. Home: 7018 Hampden Lane, Bethesda, Md. Office: Nat. Bur. of Standards, Washington, D.C.

INGEBRITSEN, Otis Clarence, psychology; b. Hollandale, Wis., Apr. 9, 1893; s. Albert and Caroline (Rindy) I.; ed. State Normal Sch., Platteville, Wis., 1908-10, 1913-15; Ph.B., U. of Wis., 1924, Ph.M., same, 1926; Ph.D., U. of Chicago, 1931; grad. study, Cornell U., summer 1932; m. Mary Bishop, Aug. 13, 1929; children—Karl John, Donald Mace. Engaged in teaching rural schs., prin. sch., teacher high sch., 1910-23; instr. U of Wis., 1924-27, Syracuse U., 1927-29, Univ. of Chicago, 1929-31; prof. psychology, Queens-Chicora Coll., Charlotte, N.C., 1931-34; asso. prof. psychology, N.J. State Teachers Coll., Montclair, N.J. since 1934. Served as pvt. Field Hosp. service, U.S.A., 1917-19, with A.E.F. in France. Mem. Am. Psychol. Assn., N.J. Assn. Psychologists (pres.), Acacia. Conglist. Mason. Home: 115 Buckingham Rd., Montclair, N.J.

INGERSOLL, C(harles) Jared, ry. official; b. Philadelphia, Pa., Feb. 11, 1894; s. Charles Edward and Henrietta (Sturgis) I.; student St. Paul's Sch., Concord, N.H., 1908-13; C.E., Princeton, 1917; m. Marian Baird, Nov. 1, 1920; children—Anna Warren, Charles Jared, Sally Wister, Gainor Baird. With Midland Valley R.R., since 1920, chmn. bd. since 1932; chmn. bd. Kan., Okla. & Gulf R.R., Okla. City-Ada-Atoka Ry. Co.; pres. Muskogee Co., Sebastian County Coal & Mining Co.; mgr. Girard Trust Co., Western Savings Fund Assn.; dir. Pennsylvania R.R., Phila. & Western Ry. Co. Served as lt., j.g., U.S.N., World War. Democrat. Episcopalian. Club: Philadelphia. Home: Ft. Washington, Pa. Office: 135 Independence Sq., Philadelphia, Pa.

INGERSOLL, Frank Bostwick, lawyer; b. Pittsburgh, Pa., Nov. 22, 1893; s. Hartwell Bostwick and Susan Mary (Patterson) I.; LL.B., Cornell U., 1917; m. Melba Martin, Mar. 20, 1922. Admitted to Pa. bar, 1917, beginning in law office of Gordon & Smith, became partner, 1925, also partner of various successors, last being Smith, Buchanan & Ingersoll; dir. Armstrong Cork Co. Served as 1st lt. Ordnance Dept., 1st Army Hdqrs., later 3d Army Hdqrs., Demolition sect., A.E.F., World War. Mem. bd. govs. Pittsburgh Skin and Cancer Foundation, Legal Aid Soc., Kingsley Assn. Mem. Am. Law Inst., Am. Bar Assn., Pa. Bar Assn., Allegheny Co. Bar. Assn., Assn. Bar City of New York; Cornell U. Law Assn. (v.p.), Delta Chi. Republican. Mason. Clubs: Oakmont Country, (bd. of govs.), Fox Chapel Country, Duquesne, Lancaster Country. Home: R.D. 2, Sharpsburg, Pa. Office: 1025 Union Trust Bldg., Pittsburgh, Pa.

INGERSOLL, Robert Sturgis, lawyer; b. Philadelphia, Dec. 16, 1891; s. Charles Edward and Henrietta A. (Sturgis) I.; prep. edn., St. Paul's Sch., Concord, N.H.; Litt.B., Princeton U., 1914; LL.D., U. of Pa., 1921; m. Marion B. Fowle, Oct. 31, 1914; children—Robert Sturgis, George Fowle, Phebe Warren, Charles Edward, Harry. With editorial dept. of J.B. Lippincott & Co., Phila., 1914-17; mem. law firm Ballard, Spahr, Andrews & Ingersoll, since 1921; mgr. Phila. Savings Fund Soc.; dir. North Penn. R.R., Midland Valley Ry. Co., Muskogee Co. Served as 1st lt. inf., World War. Vice-pres. and mem. bd. mgrs. Phila. Zoöl. Soc.; trustee of Phila. Mus. of Art; trustee Fairmount Park Art Assn.; dir. Phila. Orchestra Assn.; Pa. chmn. Dem. Victory Fund Campaign, 1932. Episcopalian. Clubs: Philadelphia, Franklin Inn, Midday, Print Club of Phila. (ex-pres.); Ivy (Princeton, N.J.). Author: Open That Door, 1916. Home: Penllyn P.O., Pa. Office: Land Title Bldg., Philadelphia, Pa.

INGERSOLL, William Harrison, manufacturer; b. Delta, Eaton Co., Mich., Mar. 22, 1880; s. Arthur Nichols and Agnes Nancy (Wright) I.; student Pratt Inst., Brooklyn, N.Y., 1894-97; B.S., Poly. Inst., Brooklyn, N.Y., 1902; m. Frances Mary Evans, 1909; children—William Harrison, Frances Elizabeth, Lois Dorrit. Began as elec. engr., 1903; partner Robert H. Ingersoll & Bro., mfrs. Dollar Watch, New York; while dir. and gen. marketing mgr. Ingersoll Watches in charge sales and advertising business grew to world-wide concern; pres. Positype Corpn. of America, mfrs. photographic materials, New York; pres. Ingersoll Radipoint Co., mfrs. mech. pencils, New York; pres. Colloidal Minerals Co., New York; v.p. and gen. marketing mgr. DeForest Radio Co., New York; mem. Ingersoll, Norwell & Babson, marketing consultants, New York; dir. Hostiter Corpn.; advisor in marketing of numerous other articles; visiting lecturer at various times on marketing and advertising Harvard Sch. of Business Administrn., N.Y.U. Sch. of Commerce and Accounts, U. of Wis. Sch. of Commerce and Accounts, U. of Ill. Sch. of Commerce and Accounts. Nat. dir. of pub. speaking Com. on Pub. Information, Washington, D.C., during World War. Mem. Employer's Industrial Commn. sent by govt. to study European industrial conditions; organizer original Vigilance Com., out of which developed Nat. Better Business Burs.; organizer and dir. Am. Fair Trade Assn.; served as del. from U.S. and chmn. com. on distribution and unfair competition, Internat. Chamber of Commerce, Paris. Mem. Assn. of Nat. Advertisers (dir. and mem. exec. com.), Asso. Advertising Clubs of the World (dir. and mem. exec. com.), U.S. Chamber of Commerce (chmn. com. on distribution and unfair competition), Am. Soc. Sales Execs. (charter), Am. Marketing Soc. (charter, chmn. com. on mfrs. specialty marketing), Am. Mfrs. Export Assn. (treas.), Am. Marketing Assn., Alpha Delta Sigma. Clubs: Advertising (during term as pres. membership increased from 16 to 1,100), N.Y. Sales Managers (charter), National Arts (New York); Canoe Brook (Summit, N.J.). Home: 24 Mountain Av., Maplewood, N.J. Office: 370 Lexington Av., New York, N.Y.

INGHAM, Charles T(attersall), architect; b. Pittsburgh, Pa., Jan. 21, 1876; s. Tattersall and Ellen (Ward) I.; grad. high sch., Houtzdale, Pa., 1891; student U. of Pa., 1893-96; m. Cora Martha Rogers, Sept. 7, 1904; children—Charles Seth, Albert Joseph, Roger Ward, Cora May. Began practice as architect, Pittsburgh, 1897; mem. firm Ingham & Boyd since 1911. Prin. works of firm: Chatham Village Housing Development; Buhl Planetarium and Inst. of Popular Science; Historical Society of Western Pa. Bldg.; Henry Clay Frick Training Sch. for Teachers; Administration Bldg. of Bd. of Pub. Edn., gymnasium and dining hall for Shady Side Acad.; Waverly Presbyn. Ch. (all of Pittsburgh); also high-schs. at Edgewood, Wilkinsburg, Mt. Lebanon, all of Pa. Instr., Archtl. Sch., Carnegie Inst. Tech., 1917. Mem. Pa. State Bldg. Code Com., 1920, City of Pittsburgh Bldg. Code Com., 1920-24; ex-pres. Pa. State Bd. Examiners of Architects; mem. Commn. on Ch. Architecture, Diocese of Pittsburgh, P.E. Ch. Fellow and sec. Am. Inst. Architects (ex-dir.; ex-pres. Pittsburgh chapter); mem. Beta Theta Pi. Republican. Episcopalian. Mason (32°). Clubs: Duquesne, Pittsburgh Architectural (ex-pres.). Home: 917 Bellefonte St. Office: Empire Bldg., Pittsburgh, Pa.

INGHAM, John Albertson, clergyman; b. Meridian, N.Y., Jan. 13, 1868; s. Albert Constantine and Cynthia Amelia (Van Wie); A.B., Syracuse U., 1886, A.M., 1889, D.D., 1908; grad. Union Theol. Sem., 1892; m. Mary Bartlet Stebbins, N.Y., Sept. 28, 1892; children—Edward Stebbins, Caroline Lawrence (Mrs. James Marshall Plumer), Albert Van Wie. Teacher of mathematics, Centenary Collegiate Inst., Hackettstown, N.J., 1887-89 ordained ministry Presbyn. Ch., 1892; asst. pastor St. Nicholas Collegiate Ch., N.Y. City, 1892-93; pastor Irving-on-Hudson, N.Y., 1894-1910, 2d Ref. Ch., New Brunswick, N.J., 1910-20; sec. progress campaign com., Ref. Ch. in America, 1920-23; Sec. Progress Council, Ref. Ch. in America, 1923-37; stated clerk Gen. Synod. of Ref. Ch. in America since 1932, treas. since 1938. Mem. Presbyn. Bd. Ch. Erection, 1897-1910, Bd. Domestic Missions, Ref. Ch. in America, 1911-21. Mem. Am. Astron. Soc., Am. Assn. Variable Star Observers, Phi Beta Kappa, Psi Upsilon. Republican. Home: 332 Beechwood Pl., Leonia, N.J. Office: 25 E. 22d St., New York, N.Y.

INGLE, William, banker; b. Baltimore, Md., Aug. 27, 1858; s. William Pechin and Eliza (Crummer) I.; ed. pub. schs.; m. Harriet Page, of Baltimore, Dec. 12, 1883; children—Eliza, Margaret Page, Julia Pechin. Served as clk. Farmers & Merchants Nat. Bank, Baltimore, 1878-81; with Merchants Nat. Bank, Baltimore, 1881-1914, advancing to v.p.; chmn. bd. and federal reserve agt., Federal Reserve Bank, Richmond, Va., 1914-16; pres. Baltimore Trust Co., 1916-25, vice chmn. bd., 1925-27, retired, Feb. 1927. Episcopalian. Clubs: University, Merchants. Home: 1710 Park Av., Baltimore, Md.

INGLIS, William Wallace, manufacturer; b. Scranton, Pa., Jan. 19, 1871; s. John Scott and Janet Henderson (Lorimer) I.; student Scranton Pub. Schs., 1878-84; m. Gertrude Jayne Kennedy, Oct. 28, 1903 (died Jan. 5, 1937); children—Mary Elizabeth (Mrs. John Dodge Strong), John Scott 2d. Began as office boy Hillside Coal & Iron Co., Dunmore, Pa., 1884-88, chief clerk, 1888-1902; supt. Pa. Coal Co., Dunmore, Pa., 1902-09; gen. supt. Hillside Coal & Iron Co. and Pa. Coal Co., 1909-13, gen. mgr., 1913-16; gen. mgr. coal mining dept., D.L.& W. R.R. Co., 1916-17, v.p. and mgr. coal mining dept., 1917-21; pres. Keystone Mining Co., East Brady, Pa., since 1919; pres. Glen Alden Coal Co., Scranton, Pa., since 1921; pres. Shelocta Coal Co., East Brady, Pa., since 1921; chmn. Anthracite Bd. of Conciliation since 1927; dir. First Nat. Bank, Scranton, Pa., First Nat. Bank, Wilkes-Barre, Pa., Kingston (Pa.) Nat. Bank, D.L.& W. Coal Co., N.Y., Sprague & Henwood, Inc., Scranton, Pa., Nokomis Water Co., Factoryville, Pa., Honey Brook Water Co., Wilkes-Barre, Pa. Dir. Moses Taylor Hosp., Scranton, Pa. Mem. Y.M.C.A. Republican. Presbyterian. Mason (Royal Arch, Royal and Select Master, Knights Templar, Consistory, Shriner). Clubs: Scranton, Scranton Country (Scranton, Pa.); Westmoreland (Wilkes-Barre, Pa.). Home: 1025 Vine St. Office: 310 Jefferson Av., Scranton, Pa.

INGMANSON, John Harold, research chemist; b. Sycamore, Ill., April 9, 1898; s. Andrew Emil and Ellen (Johnson) I.; student U. of Ill., 1917-20; B.S., U. of Chicago, 1925; m. Myra Elizabeth Thompson, July 28, 1923; children—John Earl, Dale Eugene. Chemist, Sherwin Williams Co., 1919, Conley Foil Co., 1920-23; chem. engr. U.S. Foil Co., 1923-24, Tower Mfg. Co., 1925-27; works mgr. Crown Chem. Corpn., 1927-28; research chemists, Bell Telephone Labs., Inc., since 1928. Mem. Am. Chem. Soc., Am. Soc. for Testing Materials, Phi Lambda Upsilon. Republican. Mason. Contbr. papers on rubber and allied materials. Home: 183 Forbes St., Rahway, N.J. Office: 463 West St., New York, N.Y.

INGRAM, Martha Beardsley, business executive; b. Rock Rapids, Ia., Oct. 12, 1903; d. Frank Grenville and Mary Evanna (Riddell) Beardsley; A.B., Washington U., St. Louis, Mo., 1926, M.S., 1927, Ph.D., 1931; m. James Edward Ingram, Oct. 20, 1933. Teaching fellow in botany, Washington U., St. Louis, 1926-29, instr., 1929-31; prof. of biology, Sioux Falls (S.D.) Coll., 1931-33; sec.-treas. Davis Shoe Co., retail sale of shoes, Sharon, Pa., since 1936. Mem. Am. Bot. Soc., Phi Mu, Phi Sigma, Sigma Xi. Republican. Congregationalist. Clubs: Sharon College, "X" Club. Home: 359 E. State St. Office: 110 E. State St., Sharon, Pa.

INGRAM, William Albert, retired steel exec.; b. Bilston, England, Jan. 18, 1867; s. George and Jane (Cadman) I.; ed. Codsall Nat. Schs., Wolverhampton Tech. Inst., Metropolitan Sch. of Languages, London, Eng.; came to U.S., 1898, naturalized, 1911; m. Florence Timmis, Dec. 25, 1899; 1 dau., Florence Lillian. Confidential sec. to Rev. John Barton, Ch. Pastoral Aid Soc., London, Eng., later teacher of spl. subjects, London (Eng.) Bd. of Edn.; bookkeeper Rogers Locomotive Co., Paterson, N.J., 1901-06; in charge of comptroller's office, Am. Locomotive Co., New York, 1906-08; with Taylor-Wharton Iron & Steel Co., High Bridge, N.J., since 1909, sec. and treas., 1909-29, dir. since 1936; v.p. and dir. First Nat. Bank, High Bridge, N.J., since 1933; dir. High Bridge (N.J.) Bldg. & Loan Assn. Trustee Boy Scout Camp, Buck. Commr. High Bridge Borough (N.J.) Sinking Fund; pres. High Bridge Bd. of Edn., 1915-29. Republican. Episcopalian. Club: Railroad Machinery (New York). Address: High Bridge, N.J.

INNES, William Thornton, publisher, author; b. Phila., Pa., Feb. 2, 1874; s. William Thornton and Eleanor (Kirkbride) I.; grad. Friends' Central Sch., Phila., 1892; m. Mary Josephine Weber, Oct. 5, 1899; children—Evelyn Baldwin (Mrs. Austin Homer), Mary Thornton (Mrs. George McNeely Belsterling), Elizabeth Wevill (Mrs. Guyon Chadwick), Jean Woodside (Mrs. John Page Simpson). Began as copyholder in 1895; formed partnership with father in printing business, firm Innes & Son., 1897; upon retirement of father formed with brother Innes & Sons, 1910, which still continues; also operates Innes Pub. Co.; v.p. Graphic Arts Mutual Fire Ins. Co. Chmn. advisory com. printing div. Dobbins Vocational Sch. (Phila.). Past pres. Typothetæ of Phila. Mem. Acad. Nat. Sciences of Phila., Am. Mus. of Nat. History of N.Y. City. Club: Meridian of Phila. (past pres.). Author: Goldfish Varieties and Tropical Aquarium Fishes, 1917; The Modern Aquarium, 1929; Exotic Aquarium Fishes, 1935; The Complete Aquarium Book, 1936. Editor of the Aquarium (monthly mag.). Contbr. to Encyclopædia Britanica, and printing jours. Home: 1824 N. Park Av. Office: 129 N. 12th St., Philadelphia, Pa.

INSLEY, Herbert, scientist; b. Nanuet, N.Y., May 16, 1893; s. Earle and Annie (Hutton) I.; student Spring Valley (N.Y.) High Sch., 1906-10, Amherst (Mass.) Coll., 1910-11; B.S., Hamilton Coll., Clinton, N.Y., 1914; Ph.D., Johns Hopkins U., Baltimore, Md., 1919; m. Margarette Hiteshew, Oct. 8, 1921; children—Robert Hiteshew, Herbert Hutton. Scientific aide, Bur. of Standards, 1917-18; geologic aide and asst. geologist, U.S. Geological Survey, 1919-21; asst. and asso. petrographer, U.S. Bur. of Mines, 1921-22; petrographer and sr. petrographer, Nat. Bur. of Standards since 1922. Served as pvt. Chem. Warfare Service, U.S. Army, 1918-19. Fellow Mineralogical Soc. of America, Geological Soc. of America, Am. Ceramic Soc.; mem. Optical Soc. of America, A.A.A.S., Geol. Soc. of Washington, Washington Acad. of Science, Delta Tau Delta, Gamma Alpha. Democrat. Episcopalian. Author of numerous scientific papers. Home: 6710 Meadow Lane, Chevy Chase, Md. Office: Nat. Bureau of Standards, Washington, D.C.

INSLEY, T. S.; judge 1st Judicial Circuit of Md., term expires 1949. Address: Cambridge, Md.

IRELAND, Clarence Edward, prof. physics; b. Sullivan, Ill., Oct. 5, 1902; s. Joseph Hamilton and Louisa (Desjardin) I.; A.B., U. of Ill., 1926, M.S., 1928, Ph.D., 1932; m. Ruth Margarette Foster, Sept. 7, 1926; children—Cynthia, Ronald Joseph. Asst. in physics, U. of Ill., 1926-32; instr. in physics and mathematics, St. Peter's Coll., Jersey City, N.J., 1932-33, asst. prof. physics, 1933-35, prof. physics since 1935, chmn. dept. physics and mathematics since 1935. Mem. A.A.A.S., Am. Phys. Soc., Am. Assn. Physics Teachers, Theta Kappa Phi, Pi Mu Epsilon, Sigma Xi, Phi Eta. Roman Catholic. Mem. University Club of Hudson County (Jersey City). Home: Rochelle Park, N.J. Office: St. Peter's College, Jersey City, N.J.

IRELAND, Ritchie Alexander, physician and surgeon; b. White Oak, W.Va. Oct. 11, 1884; s. George Monroe and Mary Ellen (Law) I.; student W.Va. Wesleyan Coll., Buckhannon, W.Va., 1903-05; M.D., U. of Md. Coll. of Medicine, Baltimore, 1912; m. Ada Scott, Nov. 10, 1912; 1 son, James Dudley. Asst. prin. high sch., Pennsboro, W.Va., 1906-08; interne Kanawha Valley Hosp., Charleston, W.Va., 1913-15; doctor in charge Charleston (W.Va.) Health Dept., 1919-24, organized nursing service for dept., 1919; in charge Charleston Schs. Health Dept., 1928-32; pres. Mountain State Hosp., Charleston, since 1925; pres. W.Va. Hospital Association, 1928. Mem. medical appeal board, 6th W.Va. Dist., during World War; capt. M.R.C., U.S. Army, 1919-26. Mem. A.M.A., W.Va. Med. Soc. (chmn. pub. policy and legislative com. 1919-26), Kanawha Med. Soc. (sec. 1916-17, pres. 1918), Phi Beta Pi. Republican. Methodist. Mason. Home: 1207 Quarrier St. Office: Kanawha Bank & Trust Bldg., Charleston, W.Va.

IRLAND, George Allison, prof. elec. engring.; b. Lewisburg, Pa., Jan. 3, 1894; s. Thomas Edwin and Emma Priscilla (McCurdy) I.; B.S. in E.E., Bucknell U., 1915, E.E., same, 1922; M.E.E., Johns Hopkins U., 1925, Dr. Engring., same, 1932; m. Lillian A. Sindle, Sept. 16, 1924; children—Ruth Mitchell, Edwin Allison, Margaret Ann, Barbara Ellen. Draftsman, N.Y.C & H. R.R. Co., 1915-16; with Bethlehem Steel Co., 1918-20; instr. mech. drawing and elec. engring., Bucknell U., 1920-24, asst. prof. elec. engring., 1925-34, asso. prof., 1934-37, prof. since 1937. Served as pvt. to 2d lieut. Signal Corps, U.S.A., 1918. Fellow A.A.A.S.; mem. Am. Inst. Elec. Engrs., Soc. for Promotion Engring. Edn., Sigma Chi, Pi Mu Epsilon. Republican. Presbyn. Mason. Author and co-author, tech. papers of U.S. Bur. of Mines. Home: 5 Market St., Lewisburg, Pa.

IRVIN, Charles Henry, banker; b. Liberty, Pa., Oct. 29, 1866; s. William and Mary (Veil) I.; student Bethany (W.Va.) Coll., hon. LL.D., 1936; m. Fannie V. Williams, Sept. 27, 1893; children—William P., Helen (Mrs. James Wyckoff), Mary Louise (Mrs. Milo H. Olin), Frances (Mrs. Radford F. Pittam). Became asso. with father in mfr. sole leather and established firm of William Irvin & Son, 1888, assuming business at death of father, 1901, and continuing to operate tannery until 1916 (business sold to Armour and Co.); retired from active business, 1916; pres. Citizens' Nat. Bank of Big Run, Pa.; mgr. William Irvin Co. Mem. Pa. Ho. of Reps., 1923-27. Mem. sch. bd., Big Run, Pa., many years. Mem. Beta Theta Pi. Republican. Mem. Christian Ch. (supt. Bible Sch. 47 yrs.). Mason (32°). Home: Church St. Office: Citizens' Bank Bldg., Big Run, Pa.

IRVIN, Richard, architect, engr.; b. Pittsburgh, Pa., Sept. 12, 1884; s. Francis Orvill and Mary (Anderson) I.; grad. Pittsburgh Grade Sch., 1899, Pittsburgh High Sch., 1903, Sheffield Scientific Sch. (Yale U.), 1907; m. Cora Douglas, Feb. 1915 (died Dec. 16, 1918); 1 son, Richard. With Albert & Julius Kahn, Detroit (summers), 1903-07; draftsman, engr. and architect various firms in New York, Baltimore, Detroit, Kansas City and St. Louis, 1907-12; registered architect and professional engr., 1912; pres. and gen. mgr. Federal Enameling & Stamping Co., 1914; partner and originator Wirshing Peloubet Organ Co., 1916; was also v.p. and gen. mgr. Sligo Iron & Steel Co. Prin. works: 6 story bldg. for Geo. A. Kelly Drug Co.; 12-story office Bldg., Palace Hardware Co.; Fourth Avenue Garage, Pittsburgh; office bldg. West Penn Power Co.; altered and enlarged residence of Mrs. Wm. Thaw, Jr.; consulting architect for warehouses and garages of Consolidated Gas, Electric Light & Power Co., Baltimore, and one on L St., Washington, D.C.; also built and modernized several other large bldgs. in Erie and Pittsburgh, Pa. Co-inventor with Edward Shenk of modern type acoustical rectification, made improvements on concrete reinforcements, cribbing and steel beams. Dem. candidate for Congress, 1934. Dir. Pa. Assn. Architects. Mem. Assn. Architects of Western Pa., Soc. Professional Engrs., Am. Soc. Civil Engrs. Mason (Shriner), Ancient Accepted Scottish Rite, Elk. Club: Metropolitan (Pittsburgh). Home: 213 Charles St. (10). Office: 605 Starr Bldg., Third Av., Pittsburgh, Pa.

IRVIN, Robert Roy, chemist; b. Lawrence, Kan., June 11, 1887; s. John Alexander and Annie Greenwood (Smith) I; A.B., Kan. State U., 1916, M.S., 1917; m. Ester Elizabeth Brownlee, June 20, 1914; children—Howard Brownlee, John Martin. Research chemist, Mellon Inst. Industrial Research, Pittsburgh, 1917-32; research chemist National Grain Yeast Corpn., 1932-35, chief chemist since 1935. Fellow A.A.A.S.; mem. Am. Chem. Soc., Am. Assn. Cereal Chemists, Alpha Chi Sigma. Democrat. Home: 56 Haines Drive, Bloomfield, N.J. Office: Nat. Grain Yeast Corpn., Belleville, N.J.

IRVINE, William Burriss, banker; b. Smithfield, Jefferson Co., O., June 7, 1866; s. George Fleming and Rachael (Burriss) I.; ed. pub. schs. and Linsly Inst., Wheeling, W.Va.; m. Eva A. Drake, Feb. 25, 1886; 1 son, Russell Drake. Asst. cashier, Nat. Exchange Bank, Wheeling, 1898-1901; cashier Bank of Wheeling, 1901-07; v.p. and mgr. Nat. Bank of W.Va., 1907-26, pres. since 1926; also pres. Farmers Nat. Bank, Claysville, Pa. Mem. W.Va. Bankers Assn. (sec., 1907, 08, pres. 1909, 10), Wheeling Chamber of Commerce; ex-pres. Wheeling Assn. Credit Men; ex-treas. Wheeling Chapter Am. Red Cross. Republican. Methodist. Mason (K.T.). Clubs: Fort Henry, Twilight, Rotary. Home: Elmwood, Elm Grove, W.Va. Office: Wheeling, W.Va.*

IRVING, Laurence, biologist; b. Boston, May 3, 1895; s. Wm. Nathaniel and Esther (Messenger) I.; prep. edn., Roxbury Latin School; A.B., Bowdoin Coll., 1916, Charles Carroll Everett grad. scholar, 1916-17; A.M., Harvard U., 1917; Ph.D., Stanford U., 1924; m. Muriel Stevens, Aug. 16, 1917; m. 2d, Elizabeth Knox Hunter, June 12, 1925; children—Susan, William Nathaniel, Laurence. Instr., Menlo (Calif.) Sch., 1921-23; asst. in physiology, Stanford U., 1923-24, instr., 1924-25 asst. prof., 1926-27; Nat. Research Council fellow in biology, U. of Frankfurt, Germany, 1926-27; asso. prof. physiology, U. of Toronto, 1927-34, prof. exptl. biology, 1934-37; prof. biology, Swarthmore Coll., since 1937; lecturer physiology, U. of Pa., since 1937; instr. Marine Biol. Lab., Woods Hole, Mass., since 1931, in charge physiology course since 1934, trustee since 1935, sec. exec. com., 1936 and 1938-39. Served as lt., 165th Inf., with A.E.F. and Army of Occupation, 1917-19. Fellow A.A.A.S., Am. Physiol. Soc., Canadian Physiol. Soc., Am. Soc. Zoölogists; mem. Nat. Research Council (Div. Biology and Agr.); rep. on Div. of Chemistry and Chem. Technology; mem. Delta Kappa Epsilon, Phi Beta Kappa, Sigma Xi. Unitarian. Writer of articles on physiology of respiration in animals, etc. Editor: Jour. of Cellular and Comparative Physiology. Home: 311 Elm Av., Swarthmore, Pa.

IRWIN, Grattan G.; urologist Charleston Gen. Hosp. Address: 1017 Quarrier St., Charleston, W.Va.

IRWIN, Harold Seaton, prof. of law; b. Christiana, Pa., Aug. 11, 1901; s. Charles Fleming and Amy Marie (Skillman) I.; Ph.B., Dickinson Coll., 1923; LL.B., Dickinson Sch. of Law, 1925; A.M., Dickinson Coll., 1925; m. Dorothy E. Bayley, Aug. 21, 1926; children—Harold Seaton, Roger Bayley, Carol Ann. Admitted to Pa. bar, 1925, and prof. of law, Dickinson Sch. of Law since 1925; mem. faculty of Am. Inst. Banking, Harrisburg, Pa.; served as mem. Pa. State Bd. for Examination of Pub. Accountants, 1932-37. Mem. Phi Kappa Psi, Woolsack. Republican. Presbyn. Mason. Faculty Editor: Dickinson Law Review. Contbr. to legal journs. Home: 616 Highland Av., Carlisle, Pa.

IRWIN, James Robin, physician; b. Belleville, N.J., Aug. 18, 1891; s. Andrew and Jane Elizabeth (Dunbar) I.; B.P.E., Springfield (Mass.) Coll., 1914; M.D., U. of Pa. Med. Sch., 1918; m. Gladys A. Brown, Jan. 17, 1922. Interne St. Barnabas Hosp., Newark, N.J., 1918-20; engaged in gen. practice of medicine and surgery at Belleville, N.J., since 1920; attdg. surgeon, St. Barnabas Hosp., Newark, N.J.; mem. courtesy staff Mountainside Hosp., Montclair, Presbyterian and Crippled Children's hosps., Newark, N.J. Fellow Am. Coll. Surgeons. Mem. A.M.A., N.J. State and Essex Co. med. socs., Anat. Soc., Clinicians Soc., Asso. Physicians of Montclair and Vicinity, Phi Rho Sigma. Mem. Dutch Ref. Ch. Mason. Club: Upper Montclair Country. Home: 37 Clearman Pl. Office: 330 Washington Av., Belleville, N.J.

IRWIN, Orlando William, sales mgr.; b. Bellaire, O., Oct. 28, 1881; s. William David and Harriet (DeLong) I.; grad. Wooster Coll., 1904; B.S., Case Sch. of Applied Science, 1906, C.E., 1909; m. Nyda Lee Lewis, Aug. 16, 1904; children—Margaret Lee, William David. Held position of asst. chief draftsman, Lake Shore & Mich. Southern Ry., bridge Dept., Cleveland, 1906-11; draftsman Trucson Steel Co., Youngstown, O., 1911, chief draftsman, 1912-16, asst. sales mgr., 1917-25, v.p., 1925-35; sales mgr. concrete bar div. Carnegie Illinois Steel Co., Pittsburgh, since 1935. Mem. Concrete Reinforcing Steel Inst. (ex-pres.), Am. Soc. Civil Engrs., Am. Concrete Inst., Builders' Exchange. Republican. Presbyterian. Clubs: Rotary, Duquesne. Author: Distribution of Wheel Loads on Railroad Bridges, 1909; Competitive Cooperation, 1924; Selling Personality, 1922. Home: 5312 St. James Terrace. Office: Carnegie Illinois Steel Co., Pittsburgh, Pa.

IRWIN, Robert Benjamin, welfare work; b. in Rockford, Iowa, on June 2, 1883; s. Robert Payne and Hattie Edith (Chappell) I.; grad. Wash State Sch. for the Blind, 1901; B.A., U. of Wash., 1906; student Harvard, 1906-09, M.A., 1907; m. Mary Janet Blanchard, June 19, 1917; 1 son, Robert Benjamin (dec.). Supervisor classes for the blind, Cleveland (O.) pub. schs., 1909-23, also for classes for the blind, and sight-saving classes for partially blind children in various cities and towns of Ohio, 1915-23; dir. Bur. of Research and Edn. of the Am. Foundation for the Blind, N.Y. City, 1923-29, exec. dir., 1929—; mgr. Talking Book Studio, Am. Foundation for the Blind; president Clear Type Publishing Com., of Montclair, N.J. Mem. N.J. State Commn. for the Blind; pres. Am. Assn. of Workers for the Blind, 1923-27; chmn. subcom. on visually handicapped, White House Conf. on Child Health and Protection, 1930; chmn. orgn. com., New York World Conf. on Work for Blind, 1931; chmn. Am. Uniform Type Com. which arranged with British authorities for adoption of a uniform braille code for blind of English-speaking world, 1932. Mem. Am. Assn. of Social Workers. Unitarian. Editor of textbooks used in sight-saving classes in U.S.; author of monograph on blind relief legislation in the U.S., and other studies. Home: 36 Elston Rd., Upper Montclair, N.J. Office: 15 W. 16th St., New York, N.Y.

IRWIN, William Wallace, sch. supt.; b. Bovard, Pa., May 27, 1875; s. John T. and Louisa C. (Thompson) I.; ed. Slippery Rock State Teachers Coll. and Columbia U.; m. Blanche Christley, Aug. 11, 1915; children—Dorothy Belle Hughes. Teacher rural schs., 1896-99; prin. Mars pub. schs., 1899-1901, Dravosburg pub. schs., 1901-07; supt. Ford City, 1907-20, Meadville, 1920-26, Farrell since 1926; teacher Edinboro State Teachers Coll., summer, 1921, teacher Allegheny Coll., summers, 1922, 23. Mem. N.E.A., Pa. State Edn. Assn., Am. Assn. Sch. Adminstrs. Republican. Methodist. Mason. Club: Lions. Home: 1225 Washington St. Office: Haywood St. and Fruit Av., Farrell, Pa.

ISAACS, Asher, coll. prof.; b. Cincinnati, O., Mar. 13, 1902; s. Abraham and Rachel (Friedman) Isaacs; A.B. with honors, U. of Cincinnati, 1923, M.A., 1924; A.M., Harvard U., 1926, Ph.D., 1933; m. Flora Meyers, Aug. 28, 1927; 1 dau., Ruth Ann. Asst. in economics, U. of Cincinnati, 1922, grad. asst. in economics, 1923; instr. economics, U. of Pittsburgh, 1926-28, asst. prof., 1928-34, asso. prof., since 1934; mem. faculty Young Men's and Women's Hebrew Assn. Mem. Grad. Council, U. of Pittsburgh, chmn. Com. on Graduate Studies. Mem. Am. Economic Assn., Phi Beta Kappa. Republican. Mem. B'nai B'rith. Editor: Am. Jewish Outlook (weekly); contbg. editor: Orthodox Union (monthly). Writer numerous articles Dictionary Am. Biography. Home: 5534 Bartlett St., Pittsburgh, Pa.

ISANOGLE, Alvey Michael, prof. edn. and dean Sch. of Edn., Western Md. Coll. Address: Western Maryland College, Westminster, Md.

ISANOGLE, Anna Houck, registrar Western Md. Coll. Address: Western Maryland College, Westminster, Md.

ISHERWOOD, James Ernest, lawyer; b. Freedom, Pa., Dec. 10, 1897; s. Ernest and Anna (Young) I.; grad. Cannonsburg (Pa.) high Sch., 1914; A.B., Allegheny Coll., Meadville, Pa., 1919, A.M., 1920; certificate, U. of Poiters, Vienne, France, 1919; LL.B., U. of Pittsburgh, 1923; m. Dorothy May Curry, Aug. 8, 1923; children—James Earnest, Dorothy Jean, Robert Malvern. Admitted to Pa. bar, 1923; gen. practice of law, Waynesburg, 1923-27; partner firm Smith & Isherwood, Waynesburg, Pa., since 1927. Served as pvt., Inf., A.E.F., 1917-19; hon. disch. as 1st lt., 1919; now maj., Inf. Res., U.S. Army. Rep. state committeeman since 1936. Mem. Am. Legion (state comdr., Pa., 1935), Sigma Alpha Epsilon, Delta Theta Phi, Delta Sigma Rho. Cited for gallantry in action, U.S. Army, 1918. Republican. Methodist. Mason (K.T., Consistory, Shriner). Home: 230 Sherman Av. Office: 510 Peoples Bank Bldg., Waynesburg, Pa.

ISHERWOOD, James H., utilities exec.; b. Bradford, Pa., Oct. 20, 1898; s. Marion S. and Ellen M. (Anderson) I.; m. Elizabeth C. Cornell, Oct. 17, 1910; children—James Herman, Robert C., Mary Ellen, Elizabeth C. Operated lumber properties in W.Va., 1909-15; engaged in gasoline plant constrn. and operation, 1915-17; v.p. and mgr., Dempseytown Gas Co., 1917-25; v.p., dir. and gen. mgr., North Pa. Gas Co. and Asso. Cos., Port Allegany, Pa., since 1928, dir. Alum Rich Gas Co., Allegany Gas Co., Orrland Oil & Gas Co., Cameo Doll Co., First Nat. Bank. Pres. Borough Council of Port Allegany (Pa.). Mason. (Shriner). Clubs: Rotary (Oil City, Pa.); Valley Hunt (Bradford, Pa.); Cousesport (Pa.) Golf; Smithport (Pa.) Country. Home: 510 Main St. Office: Mill St., Allegany, Pa.

ISRAEL, Edward L., rabbi; b. Cincinnati, O., Aug. 30, 1896; s. Charles and Emma (Linz) I.; A.B., U. of Cincinnati, 1917; studied Harvard, summers, 1916, 17; B.H.L., Hebrew Union Coll., Cincinnati, 1914, Rabbi, 1919; LL.D., Washington (Md.) Coll., 1938; m. Amelia Dryer, Nov, 23, 1919; children—Charles Edward, Edward L. Acting chaplain Jewish Welfare Bd., Chaumont and Brest, France, 1919; rabbi B'rith Sholom Congregation, Springfield, Ill., 1919-20, Washington Av. Temple, Evansville, Ind., 1920-23, Har Sinai Congregation, Baltimore, since 1923. Mem. Bd. of govs., Hebrew Union Coll; 1st v.p. and chmn. of Social Justice Com. Synagogue Council of America since 1937; mem. Commn. on Social Justice of Central Conf. Am. Rabbis since 1926, chmn., 1927-33; pres. Baltimore Branch Am. Jewish Congress since 1934; mem. exec. com. World Jewish Congress; mem. Regional Nat. Labor Bd., 1934-35; summer lecturer, U. of N.C., 1927-29, U. of Va., 1931. Mem. Nat. exec. com. and chmn. administrative com. Seaboard Region, Zionist Orgn. America; mem. nat. exec. bd. Nat. Pub. Housing Conf. and Nat. Housing Com.; mem. and officer, Nat. Conf. Christions and Jews, League for Industrial Democracy, Am. Assn. for Social Security; mem. bd. trustees Christian Social Justice Fund, B'nai B'rith Hillel Foundation, Municipal Commn. on Employment Stabilization of Baltimore City (chmn.); chmn. Arbitration Com. Men's Clothing Industry, Baltimore, since 1935; mem. White House Conf. on Children in a Democracy, also mem. various local organizations. Mason (32°), Elk (hon. life mem.). Clubs: Woodholme Country (hon. life), Baltimore Interchurch (ex-pres.). Author: (with others) The Western Maryland Railway Strike, 1927; The Centralia Tragedy (in collaboration), 1930; also articles in mags. on religious, social and economic problems. Columnist of weekly syndicated column Nat. Conf. Christians and Jews News Service appearing in many secular and religious papers. Editor Bull. of Commn. on Social Justice of Central Conf. Am. Rabbis, 1927-33; contbg. editor The World Tomorrow, 1929-33; The Reconstructionist. Lecturer Jewish Chautauqua and various univs. and forums. Home: 3500 Shelbourne Rd. Office: 6300 Park Heights Av., Baltimore, Md.

ITTER, Harry Augustus, geologist; b. Hazleton, Pa., Mar. 26, 1899; s. Charles Justus and Anna Elizabeth (Smink) I.; Ph.B., Lafayette Coll., 1921, M.S., same, 1924; Ph.D., Columbia U., 1933; m. Marguerite Anna Zierdt, Sept. 5, 1923; 1 dau., Shirley Anne. Engaged as instr, geology, Lafayette Coll., 1921-26, asst prof., 1926-31, asso. prof. since 1931; prof summer schs., Rutgers U., 1929, Rochester U., 1930; asst. geologist with State of Pa. Geol. Survey, 1931-34; geologist for Nazareth Portland Cement Co. since 1935. Served as seaman 2d class, U.S. Naval Res., 1918-21. Mem. A.A.A.S., Am. Geog. Soc., Pa. Acad. Sci., N.Y. Acad. Sci., Am. Legion, Forty and Eight, Phi Beta Kappa, Sigma Xi, Kappa Phi Kappa. Republican. Mem. Reformed Ch. Clubs: Maroon, Faculty of Lafayette College (Easton). Prin. field of research, geomorphology; results of three yrs. research pub. in Bull. G3, 1938, Pa. Geol. Survey. Home: 641 Parsons St., Easton, Pa.

ITTNER, Martin Hill, chemist and chem. engr.; b. Berlin Heights, O., May 2, 1870; s. Conrad Smithman and Sarah Content (Hill) I.; B.Ph., Washington Univ., St. Louis, Mo., 1892, B.Sc., 1894, LL.D., 1938; A.M., Harvard U., 1895, Ph.D., 1896; hon. D.Sc., Colgate U., 1930; m. Emilie Younglof, Nov. 20, 1900 (dec.); children—Irving Hill, Lois Elizabeth (Mrs. Eldcn Bisbee Sullivan); m. 2d Hildegard Hirsché, July 21, 1934; 1 son, Robert Austen. Began as pvt. asst. to Dr. Walcott Gibbs, distinguished scientist; entered employ Colgate & Co., mfrs. soaps and toilet articles, Jersey City, N.J., Dec. 1896, and chief chemist, 1896-1928, when co. merged into Colegate-Palmolive-Peet Co. and chief chemist and chief chem, engr. latter since 1928. Mem. Am. Inst. Chem. Engrs. (pres. 1936-37), Am. Chem. Soc. (chmn. com. industrial alcohol since 1920), Soc. Chem. Industry, Am. Oil Chemists Soc., Am. Inst. Chemists. Past pres. The Chemists Bldg. Co. Republican. Mem. Christian Ch. Clubs: Harvard of N.J.; Chemists (trustee, past pres.), Harvard, Luncheon, Directors of Industrial Research (New York). Home: 50 Glenwood Av., Jersey City, N.J.

IVERSEN, Lorenz, pres. Mesta Machine Co.; b. Denmark, Apr. 15, 1876; s. Andreas and Elsie Marie (Christensen) I.; M.E., Univ. of Bingen am Rhine, Germany, 1902: m. Gertrude Maria Adlesperger, 1905; children—Mary Helen (Mrs. Frank A. Dixon), Pauline (Mrs. Casper Peter Mayer), Andreas Aluvicus, John Donald, Robert Francis; m. 2d, Fleda Levina Foust, Oct. 18, 1935. Came to U.S., 1897, naturalized, 1907. With Mesta Machine Co., Pittsburgh, since 1902, as draftsman, 1902-12, chief engr., 1912-27, v.p., dir. and gen. mgr., 1927-30, pres. since 1930; dir. Pa. Central Airlines. Pres. Pittsburgh Symphony Soc. (sponsoring Pittsburgh Symphony Orchestra). Mem. Engr. Soc. Western Pa., Am. Iron and Steel Inst. Clubs: Duquesne, University, Pittsburgh Athletic, Longue Vue, Oakmont (Pittsburgh); Woodmont Rod and Gun (Md.). Licensed private airplane pilot, 1938. Home: Woodland Rd. Office: Mesta Machine Co., Pittsburgh, Pa.

IVES, Herbert Eugene, physicist; b. Phila., Pa., July 31, 1882; s. Frederic Eugene and Mary Elizabeth (Olmstead) I.; B.S., U. of Pa., 1905; Ph.D., Johns Hopkins, 1908; hon. Sc.D., Dartmouth and Yale, 1928, Pa., 1929; m. Mabel Agnes Lorenz, Nov. 14, 1908; children—Ronald Lorenz, Barbara Olmstead (Madame Charles Beyer), Kenneth Holbrook. Asso. with Ives Kromskop Company, Philadelphia, 1898-1901; physicist, Bur. of Standards, Washington, 1908-09; physicist, Nat. Electric Lamp Assn., Cleveland, O., 1909-12, United Gas Improvement Co., Phila., 1912-18, Bell Telephone Laboratories, New York, 1919—. Commd. capt., Aviation Sect. Signal Corps, Jan. 1918, in charge exptl. work in airplane photography; discharged, May 1919, and commd. maj. R.C. Contbg. editor Lighting Journal, New York, 1913-15; asso. editor Jour. of Optical Soc. America. Fellow A.A.A.S. (v.p. Sect. B. 1938), Am. Inst. Elec. Engrs.; mem. Am. Philos. Soc., Am. Phys. Soc., Optical Soc. America (v.p. 1922-23, pres. 1924-25), Am. Astron. Soc., Franklin Inst., Am. Numismatic Soc., Nat. Acad. Sciences, Phys. Soc. of London, Phi Beta Kappa, Sigma Xi; pres. Physics Club of Phila., 1917-18; v.pres. Illuminating Engring. Soc. 1911-12; corr. mem. Brit. Illuminating Engring. Soc. Medals from Franklin Inst. for diffraction color photography, artificial daylight and studies of Welsbach mantle; John Scott medal and award, 1927, for electric telephotography and television; medal of the Optical Society for distinguished work in optics, 1937. Inventor apparatus for testing visual acuity, various photometric instruments, illuminating devices, means for producing artificial daylight, relief pictures, electrical photo-engraving, apparatus for transmission of pictures over telephone lines; in charge of experimental and development work culminating in first demonstration of television by wire and radio, 1927; developed scientific trichromatic palette for artists' use. De Forest lecturer, Yale, 1928; Lowell lecturer, Boston, 1932; Thomas Young orator Physical Society, London, 1933; Traill-Taylor memorial lecture, Royal Photographic Soc., 1933. Clubs: Cosmos (Washington); Salmagundi (New York). Author: Airplane photography, 1920. Contbr. to scientific journals, Encyclopædia Britannica, etc. Home: 32 Laurel Pl., Montclair, N.J.

IVINS, Haddon, newspaper editor, state librarian; b. Hightstown, N.J., Dec. 2, 1877; s. Robert Barclay and Cecelia J. (Haddon) I.; student pub. schs., Red Bank, N.J., State Sch., Trenton, N.J., 1898-1900; m. Ethel Tyson Wood, Dec. 2, 1905; children—Haddon Wood, Phyllis Cecelia (Mrs. Konrad Valentin). Employed as newspaper reporter, Red Bank, N.J., 1895-98, Perth Amboy, N.J., 1900-02, Jersey City, N.J., 1903-09; with adv. dept. N.Y. Times, 1909-10; with adv. dept. Saks & Co., N.Y. City, 1910-12; mgr. editor Hudson Dispatch, daily newspaper, Union City, N.J., 1912-26, editor since 1927; state librarian Commonwealth of N.J. since 1934. Mem. Chamber of Commerce and other civic orgns. Mem. Am. Newspaper Soc., Hudson Co. Press Club, S.R., Huguenot Soc., N.J. Hist. Soc. Democrat. Presbyn. Rotarian. Home: 298 Booth Av., Englewood. Office: 400 38th St., Union City, N.J.

IVY, Robert Henry, M.D.; b. Southport, Eng., May 21, 1881; s. Robert Sutcliffe and Annie Edith (Cryer) I.; D.D.S., U. of Pa., 1902, M.D., 1907; m. Norma C. Crossland, June 19, 1912; children—Cynthia Thompson, Robert Henry, Eleanor Anne, Peter Cryer. Practiced in Phila., 1907-15, Milwaukee, Wis., 1915-17. Capt., Med. R.C., 1917, and on duty office of Surgeon Gen., U.S.A., Washington, until Aug. 1918; maj., Feb. 1918, lt. col., Aug. 1919; A.E.F., France, Sept. 1918-Feb. 1919; on duty Surgeon Gen.'s Office and Walter Reed Gen. Hosp., Feb.-Oct. 1919; now col. M.R.C. Prof. maxillo-facial surgery, U. of Pa. since 1919, also trustee of Univ. Mem. Am. Pa. State and Phila. Co. med. socs., Am. Surgical Assn., Am. Coll. Surgeons, Coll. Physicians of Phila., Phila. Pathol. Soc., Phila. Acad. Surgery, Am. and Pa. State dental socs., Acad. Stomatology of Phila., Kaiserl. deutsch Akademie der Naturforscher, Loyal Legion. Republican. Clubs: University, Philadelphia Country (Philadelphia); Army and Navy (Washington); Springhaven. Author: Applied Anatomy and Oral Surgery, 1911; Applied Immunology (with B. A. Thomas), 1916; Essentials of Oral Surgery (with V. P. Blair), 1923; Fractures of the Jaws (with L. Curtis), 1931. Home: Lansdowne, Pa. Office: 1930 Chestnut St., Philadelphia, Pa.

J

JABLONSKI, Joseph S(tanley), professor of art; b. Poland, Feb. 9, 1898; s. Michael and Mary (Pastusiak) J.; came to U.S., 1910, naturalized, 1923; grad. East High Sch., Rochester, N.Y., 1919; A.B., Harvard, 1923, A.M., 1925; m. Jane Bartles, Apr. 13, 1929; children—Joan Elizabeth, Mary Jane. Asst. and tutor in fine arts, Harvard, 1924-26; free lance artist, Rochester, N.Y., and New York City, 1926-29; prof. of art, Marshall Coll., Huntington, W.Va., since 1929. One man shows of paintings, Memorial Art Gallery, Rochester, N.Y., 1929, 32; Marshall Coll. Art Gallery, 1930, 33; also exhibited paintings at Penn. Acad. of Fine Arts Exhibit in 1926, 27; the New York Watercolor Soc. show, 1928; Nat. Arts Club, N.Y. City, 1926, and various local exhibits in Rochester, N.Y., and Huntington, W.Va. Awarded first prize in Watercolor by the Memorial Art Gallery, Rochester, N.Y., in 1928. Awarded Pratt fellowship, Harvard, 1923-24. Mem. Am. Assn. Univ. Profs. Home: 1659 Washington Boul., Huntington, W.Va.

JACK, Horace Wesley, surgeon; b. Collingswood, N.J., Feb. 6, 1894; s. Thomas Weatherford and Elizabeth Lloyd (Atkinson) J.; M.D., Hahnemann Med. Coll., Phila., Pa. 1917; grad. study, Vienna, Austria, 1926 and 1930, Johns Hopkins Hosp., 1929, Temple U. Med. Sch., 1935, Cook County Hosp., Chicago, 1937; attended Mayo Clinic and other clinics; m. Pearle Crittenden Jones, Oct. 15, 1919; 1 dau., Carolyn Virginia. Engaged in gen. practice of medicine, specializing in surgery; in gynecol. dept. West Jersey Homeopathic Hosp., 1919, transferred to surg. dept., 1927, sr. surgeon since 1930, chief surgeon since 1933. Fellow Am. Coll. Surgeons. Home: 1 Tavistock Boul., Haddonfield, N.J. Office: 538 Cooper St., Camden, N.J.

JACK, James Ernest, lawyer; b. Worth Twp., Mercer Co., Pa., July 15, 1901; s. William L. and Maude (Gildersleeve) J.; grad. Slippery Rock (Pa.) State Normal Sch., 1921; B.S., Grove City (Pa.) Coll., 1926; LL.B., Duquesne U. Law Sch., 1931; m. Anne Irvine, Sept. 3, 1932; children—William I., Elizabeth A. Teacher Ellsworth (Pa.) Jr. High Sch., 1921-23; teacher Etna (Pa.) High Sch., 1926-31, prin., 1931-32; admitted to Crawford County bar, 1932; admitted to State Supreme Court and U.S. District Court, 1933; since 1932 in general practice of law. Pres. Titusville Sch. Bd.; trustee Benson Memorial Library. Mem. Crawford County Bar Assn., Pa. Bar Assn., Titusville Chamber of Commerce (dir.), Titusville Y.M.C.A. (dir.). Presbyterian. Republican. Mason, I.O. O.F., Rotarian. Home: 216 N. Kerr St. Office: 144 W. Spring St., Titusville, Pa.

JACK, William Griffith, physician, pres. Cecil Nat. Bank; b. Cecil Co., Md., Jan. 25, 1881; s. William Griffith and Sarah (Griffith) J.; student West Nottingham Acad., Colora, Md.; M. D., U. of Md., 1906; m. Margaret Caldwell, 1909; children—Jane Wright (Mrs. George Cashion), Sarah Griffith, Margaret Caldwell, William Griffith V. Practive of medicine at Port Deposit, Md., since 1906; pres. Cecil Nat. Bank, Port Deposit, Md., since 1933. Republican candidate for state comptroller of Md., 1938. Trustee Washington Coll., Chestertown, Md.; chmn. of bd. of mgrs. Eastern Shore State Hosp., Cambridge, Md. Mem. Cecil Co. Med. Soc., Med. and Chirurg. Faculty of Md., Alumni Assn. of West Nottingham Acad. (pres.), Phi Chi. Republican. Mason (Harmony Lodge No. 53, Port Deposit, Md.). Address: Port Deposit, Md.

JACKSON, Albert Atlee, banker; b. Stamford, Conn., May 28, 1867; s. Charles McClintock and Emily Boude (Haldeman) J.; ed. Episcopal Acad., Phila., and U. of Pa.; m. Lucy, d. John S. Runnells, Nov. 20, 1901. Began as clk. with Pa. R.R., 1884; became connected with Girard Trust Co. as clerk, 1889, pres., 1928-38, chmn. of bd. since 1938; dir. Western Savings Fund Soc., Buffalo & Susquehanna R.R. Corpn., Penn Mutual Life Ins. Co., Keystone Watch Case Corpn., Westmoreland Coal Co., Mem. Pa. Hist. Soc. Republican. Episcopalian. Clubs: Philadelphia, Rabbit, Sunnbrook Golf. Home: Chestnut Hill. Office: Broad and Chestnut Sts., Philadelphia, Pa.

JACKSON, Arthur Conrad, management engr.; b. Philadelphia, Dec. 11, 1879; s. Milton and Caroline (Swayne) J.; B.S. in Architecture, U. of Pa., 1901, student of engring., 1901-02; m. Edith Wilson, Apr. 27, 1907; children—Ruth, Caroline (Mrs. Leon A. Rushmore, Jr.), Edith W. (Mrs. Joseph H. Walter, Jr.), Elizabeth W. Began as apprentice with Miller Lock Co., Phila., 1902, and advanced to works mgr., sec. and treas. until 1926; works mgr. Phila. br. Yale & Towne Mfg. Co., 1926-28; cons. engr., specializing in management problems, Phila., 1928-34 and since 1936; administrator Tenn. Valley Asso. Coöperatives, 1934 and 1935. Sent to Germany by Food Administrator Hoover to organize child feeding, 1919. Chmn. of Friends (Quakers) Gen. Conf. 18 yrs.; mem. bd. dirs. George School, Newtown, Pa. Mem. Am. Soc. Mech. Engrs., Am. Management Assn., Verein Deutscher Ingenieure. Republican. Club: Union League. Home: 317 N. Chester Rd., Swarthmore, Pa. Office: Lincoln-Liberty Bldg., Philadelphia, Pa.

JACKSON, Charles Shattuck, banker; b. Parkersburg, W.Va., Aug. 22, 1887; s. Andrew Gardner and Mary (Shattuck) J.; student Va. Mil. Inst., Lexington, 1902-04; B.S., U.S. Mil. Acad., West Point, N.Y., 1908; m. Edith Carroll Reeder, May 26, 1917; children—Charles Reeder (deceased), John Jay, Carroll Shattuck. Commd. 2d lt., U.S. Army, 1908, and served 1908-11; resigned; oil producer, Parkersburg, W.Va., 1911-14, Tulsa, Okla., 1914-17, Baltimore, 1919-25; sec. and cashier Central Bank & Trust Co., Parkersburg, W.Va., 1925-29; sec. Federal Land Bank of Baltimore, 1929-31, v.p. and sec., 1931-32, pres. since 1932; sec. Federal Intermediate Credit Bank of Baltimore, 1929-31, v.p. and sec., 1931-32, pres., 1932-33; dir. Consol. Gas, Electric Light & Power Co. of Baltimore. Served as 2d lt., 11th U.S. Cav., 1908-11; capt. and adj. 2d Inf., W.Va. Nat. Guard, 1911-16; capt. Air Service, exec. officer, Wilbur Wright Field, Dayton, O., July 1917-Jan. 1918; capt. Air Service, Tours, France, and Aviation Acceptance Park, No. 1, Orly, France, Jan. 1918-Aug. 1918; maj. Air Service, Orly, France, Aug. 1918-Dec. 1918; resigned Feb. 17, 1919. Mem. Newcomen Soc. of England. Clubs: Maryland, The Elkridge, Gibson Island (Baltimore). Home: 222 E. 39th St. Office: 24th and St. Paul Sts., Baltimore, Md.

JACKSON, Chevalier, laryngologist; b. Pittsburgh, Pa., Nov. 4, 1865; s. William Stanford and Katharine Ann (Morange) J.; student Western U. of Pa., 1879-83; M.D., Jefferson Med. Coll., Phila., 1886; m. Alice Bennett White, July 19, 1899. Hon. prof. of broncho-esophagology, Temple U. Mem. A.M.A., Am. Laryngol. Assn., Am. Laryngol., Rhinol. and Otol. Soc., Pan Am. Med. Assn., Am. Coll. of Surgeons, Am. Bronchoscopic Soc., Am. Therapeutic Soc., Am. Assn. for Thoracic Surgery, Am. Acad. of Ophthalmology and Otolaryngology, Assn. des Medicins de Langue Française de l'Amerique du Nord, Phila. Co. Med. Soc., Penn. State Med. Soc., Coll. of Phys. of Phila., Phila. Laryngol. Soc., Phila., Pediatric Soc., Pittsburgh Acad. of Med.; hon. fellow Royal Soc. Medicine, Nat. Acad. of Medicine of Mexico, Swedish Med. Soc., Nat. Acad. of Medicine of Brazil, Scottish, French, Italian, Polish, Rumanian, Belgian and Spanish otolaryngol. socs. Decorated Officer Legion of Honor (France); Chevalier Order of Leopold (Belgium), Comdr. Order of Crown of Italy; Cross of Brazil. Clubs: Art and Rotary (Phila.). Author: Peroral Endoscopy and Laryngeal Surgery, 1914; Bronchoscopy, Esophagoscopy and Gastroscopy, 1934; Foreign Body in Air and Food Passages, 1934. Editor: (also contbr.) The Nose, Throat and Ear and Their Diseases, 1929; Bronchoscopy and Esophagoscopy. Contbr. to Systems of Surgery and Medicine. Developed the method of removal of foreign bodies from the lungs by the insertion of tubes through the mouth, also has contributed to development of laryngeal surgery. Home: Schwenkville, Pa. Address: 3701 N. Broad St., Philadelphia, Pa.

JACKSON, Earle Granville, ins. agency; b. Point Pleasant, W.Va., Aug. 23, 1885; s. Robert Conway and Elizabeth (West) J.; student Ohio Valley Coll., East Liverpool, O., 1902-05; m. Margaret Jane Snyder, July 28, 1914; children—Essie Jane (Mrs. Joseph Anderson Cole), Dorothy Louise, Earle Granville, Jr. Employed as life ins. salesman, Chester, W.Va., 1905-09; mgr. theatres in Colo., 1910-12; sales mgr. pub. co., 1914; engaged in bus. on own acct. as E. G. Jackson, Agency, gen. ins., Chester, W.Va., since 1915; dir. and chmn. bd. dirs. Masonic Temple Co. since 1928. Served as pres. sch. bd., Chester, W.Va., since 1936. Mem. Assn. of Ins. Agents of W.Va. (vice-pres. 1936). Republican. First Ch. of Christ Sci. Mason (32°, Shriner). Club: Country (East Liverpool, O.). Home: 119 Carolina Av., Chester, W.Va.

JACKSON, Elmer Martin, Jr., newspaper editor; b. Hagerstown, Md., Mar. 9, 1906; s. Elmer Martin and Blanche B. (Bower) J.; A.B., St. John's Coll., Annapolis, Md., 1927; m. Mary Waters Conard, Aug. 27, 1929; children—Elmer Martin 3d, Allen Conard, Pamela Conard. Sports writer, Hagerstown Daily Mail, 1921-23; corr. newspapers, 1923-27; sports editor, Evening Capital, Annapolis, Md., 1927-31; city editor, 1931-33; editor Evening Capital, Maryland Gazette, newspapers, Annapolis, Md., since 1933. Delegate Md. Legislature since 1939; mem. city council, Annapolis, Md., 1933-37. Lt. U.S.N. Res. since 1935. Pres. and dir. Library Assn. Pres. Annapolis Athletic Assn. Mem. Annapolis Zoning and Planning Commn., Md. State World's Fair Commn. Pres. Middle Atlantic States of Associated Press. Vice-pres. Port of Annapolis Propeller Clubs of U.S. (golf champion, 1938). Past pres. Civitan Club of Annapolis; past gov. Chesapeake Dist. Civitan Internat.; golf champion Civitan Internat. at Toronto, Can., 1935; awarded Civitan Citizenship Key, Birmingham, Ala. Awarded, King William Award, St. John's College, "for achievement," 1926. Democrat. Episcopalian. Elk. Clubs: Annapolis Yacht, University, Annapolitan, Naval Academy Golf, Annapolis Roads Beach and Golf, Baur Beach, Fish and Game Conservation Assn. (past officer); Fishing Fair Assn., Chamber of Commerce, Parent-Teachers Assn., Port of Marine Scribes. Author: Rat Tat, 1927; Annapolis, Three Centuries of Progress, 1937. Contributor to magazines. Home: 25 Franklin St. Office: 3 Church Circle, Annapolis, Md.

JACKSON, Eugene Joseph, retired merchant and banker; b. Ridgeway, Pa.; student St. Vincent Coll., Latrobe, Pa., 1889-90, Bucknell U., Lewisburg, Pa., 1890-91; m. Edith Handon, 1895 (died 1905); children—Mary Rita (Mrs. Harry Lang), Edith; m. 2d Emma Hanhauser, Nov. 1912 (died 1936); 1 son, John E. Began as order boy 1892, became mgr., 1897, later head of mines, Shawmut Commercial Co.; then mgr. Hall, Kaul & Hyde, St. Mary's Pa. (dept. store), and pres. Weedville State Bank. Pres. St. Mary's (Pa.) Borough Council. Has served as sheriff Elk Co., Pa., recorder of wills, head of Al Smith Assn. of St. Mary's Pa. Vice-pres. Andrew Kaul Hosp.; mem. Boys Club of America. Democrat. Roman Catholic. Elk. Clubs: Rotary, Country (St. Mary's, Pa.). Address: 150 N. Michael St., St. Mary's, Pa.

JACKSON, Frank Staples, supt. of schs.; b. Keeneyville, Pa., Nov. 1, 1872; s. Wallace E. and Mary Emmeline (Staples) J.; student Mansfield (Pa.) State Teachers Coll., 1894-96; Ph.B., Grove City (Pa.) Coll., 1911; post grad. work, Columbia U., 1914; m. Katharine Carr, Apr. 16, 1902; children—Jean Elizabeth, Mark Carr. Prin., Liberty (Pa.) Borough, 1897-98; asst. prin., Austin (Pa.) Borough, 1898-99; prin. Osceola (Pa.) Borough, 1899-1901, Big Run (Pa.) Borough, 1903-08; supt. of schs., Punxsutawney, Pa., 1908-38, emeritus supt. since 1938; lecturer in edn., Clarion (Pa.) State Teachers Coll., 1922-23; extension instr., Pa. State Coll., 1922-23; instr. in edn., Indiana (Pa.) State Teachers Coll., summers 1925, 1926, 1927. Trustee Punxsutawney (Pa.) Pub. Library. Mem. Am. Red Cross (former chmn.), Central Y.M.C.A. (dir. and trustee). Mem. state bd. Pennsylvania Interscholastic Athletic Assn. Republican. Presbyterian (elder; supt. of Sunday Sch.). Mason (Consistory). Clubs: Rotary, Punxsutawney Country, Punxsutawney Schoolmasters' (Punxsutawney, Pa.). Contbr. to numerous ednl. jours. Address: 207 Highland Av., Punxsutawney, Pa.

JACKSON, Frederick Brant, chmn. bd. Floridan Co.; b. Honeywell, Mo., Oct. 3, 1859; s. Gilson Adelbert and Helen Marr (Trask) J.; studied at Youngsville, Pa.; m. Donna A. Cummings; children—Helen, Allan C. Clk. in gen. mercantile stores and lumber yards, Castleton, N.D., 1873-75; mgr. steamboat and grain elevators north along Red River (transfer elevators at Fargo, N.D.), 1875-85; engaged in oil operations in Ohio and Superior Works, Warren, Pa., since 1885; chmn. bd. Floridan Co., mining and marketing fullers earth in Florida (principally used in decolorizing petroleum oils), Warren, Pa.; v.p. Warren Bank and Trust Co.; sec. Superior Oil Works. Home: 305 Fifth Av. Office: 220 Liberty St., Warren, Pa.

JACKSON, Frederick John Foakes, theologian; b. Ipswich, Eng., Aug. 10, 1855; s. Stephen and Catharine (Cobbold) J.; B.A., Trinity Coll. (Cambridge U.), 1879, M.A., 1882, B.D., 1903, D.D., 1905; D. Theol., Strasbourg, France; hon. D.Litt., U. of South, 1935; m. Anna Maria Everett, Oct. 1895 (died 1931); m. 2d, Clara Fawcett, widow of Arthur Jackson Tomlinson, 1932. Fellow, Jesus Coll., Cambridge, since 1886, dean and asst. tutor, 1895-1916; Briggs grad. prof. Christian instns., Union Theol. Sem., 1916-34. Lowell lecturer at Boston, 1916. Lecturer at Jewish Inst., New York, 1924, Gen. Theol. Sem., New York, 1925-26. Fellow Royal Hist. and Lit. socs.; Am. Acad. Arts and Sciences; hon. corr. mem. Institut Historique et Héraldique de France (medallist); hon. mem. Andiron Club (New York). Episcopalian. Past Grand Chaplain Grand Lodge of Eng., A.F. and A.M. Clubs: Century Association of New York City; United University (London, Eng.). Author: History of the Christian Church, 1891, 7th edit., 1921; Christian Difficulties, 1903; Biblical History of the Hebrews, 1903, 4th edit., 1921; St. Luke and a Modern Writer, 1916; English Society, 1750-1850 (Lowell Lectures), 1916; Introduction to Church History (590-1314), 1921; Anglican Church Principles, 1924; Studies in the Life of the Early Church, 1924; Life of St. Paul, 1926, 2d edit. Life and Letters series, 1933; Rise of Gentile Christianity, 1927; Peter, Prince of Apostles, 1927; Josephus and the Jews, 1930; The Church in England, 1931; Eusebius Pamphili, 1933; The Church in the Middle Ages, 1934; A History of Church Historians, 1939. Editor: Parting of the Roads, 1911; Faith and the War, 1916; Beginnings of Christianity (with K. Lake), Vol. I, 1919, Vol. II, 1922, Vol. III, 1926, Vols. IV and V, 1932. Home: Dana Pl., Englewood, N.J.

JACKSON, Frederick W., lawyer; b. New York, N.Y., July 3, 1883; s. George Thomas and Caroline G. (Weidemeyer) J.; student Collegiate Sch., New York, 1896-1900; A.B., Princeton U., 1904; LL.B., Columbia, 1907; m. Louise Bliven Shaw, June 4, 1913; 1 son, Frederick Willett. Asso. with Shearman & Sterling, attys., New York, since 1907, partner since 1919 (now specializing in corporation and financial law); dir. United Baltic Corpn. Served as corporal, Squadron A, Troop C., N.Y. Guard, 1918-19. Mem. Exec. Bd. of Mayor's Com. for Civic Progress, Summit, N.J. Dir. and trustee, Summit (N.J.) Y.M.C.A. Mem. Am., New York State, New York City bar assns., N.Y. Law Inst., Metropolitan Mus. of Art, Am. Museum of Natural History, N.Y. Zoöl. Soc., N.Y. Bot. Gardens, Phi Delta Phi, Tower Club (Princeton). Clubs: Princeton, Block Hall Luncheon (New York); Nassau (Princeton, N.J.); Canoe Brook Country (Summit, N.J.). Home: 100 Prospect Hill Av., Summit, N.J. Office: 55 Wall St., New York, N.Y.

JACKSON, Halliday Rogers, supt. city schs.; b. West Goshen, Pa., Oct. 17, 1881; s. Halliday and Emma (Kane) J.; B.E., State Normal Sch., West Chester, Pa., 1900; A.B., Swarthmore Coll., Pa., 1904; A.M., U. of Pa., 1933; m. Elizabeth Donald, Dec. 24, 1906 (dec.); children—Halliday Donald (dec.), John Schofield, Caroline Elizabeth, Eleanor Louise; m. 2d, Caroline W. Brown, Apr. 17, 1935. Engaged in teaching, Friends Central High Sch., Phila., Pa., 1904-05, high sch., Nesquehoning, Pa., 1906-07; supervisor schs., Mauch Chunk, Pa., 1907-15, Ventnor City, N.J., 1915-32; supt. city schs., Salem, N.J., since 1933. Dir. Salem Y.M.C.A. Pres. Library Commn. Mem. Nat. Edn. Assn., Am. Assn. Sch. Adminstrs., Soc. for Study of Edn., N.J. State Edn. Assn., Phi Beta Kappa, Delta Sigma Rho. Alumni dir. Swarthmore Coll. Mem. Religious Soc. Friends. Mason. Clubs: Rotary of Salem (past pres.). Home: 46 New Market St., Salem, N.J.

JACKSON, Harold Pineo, ins. exec.; b. Bar Harbor, Me., Feb. 18, 1889; s. Charles Augustus Goodrich and Ruby Mae (Pineo) J.; A.B., Dartmouth Coll., 1910; m. Grace Gillette Burnham, Dec. 1, 1917; children—Katherine Ruby, Charles Burnham, Ralph Pineo. Began as newspaper reporter, 1910; clk. with Am. Fidelity Co., 1911-1914; claim adjuster N.E. Casualty Co., 1914-16; examiner Zurich Ins. Co., 1916-17, Hartford Accident & Indemnity Co., 1919-21; supt. claim dept., later v.p., pres. and gen. mgr. Norwich Union Indemnity Co., 1921-30; pres. Bankers Indemnity Ins. Co. since 1930. Served as lt. 42d Div., A.E.F., U.S.A., 1918-19. Fellow Ins. Inst. of America. Mem. Am. Legion, Mayflower Soc., Huguenot Soc., Delta Tau Delta. Republican. Unitarian. Clubs: Dartmouth (New York); Essex (Newark); Essex Country. Home: 15 Mendl Terrace, Montclair, N.J. Office: 15 Washington St., Newark, N.J.

JACKSON, Hartley Harrad Thompson, zoölogist; b. Milton, Wis., May 19, 1881; s. Harrad and Mary (Thompson) J.; B.S., Milton Coll., 1904; M.A., U. of Wis., 1909; Ph.D., George Washington Univ., 1914; m. Anna M. Adams, of Rhinelander, Wis., Aug. 17, 1910. Head of science dept., Carthage (Mo.) Collegiate Inst., 1904-05; prin. pub. schs., Juda, Wis., 1905-06; prof. physics and chemistry, Lake Co. High Sch., Waukegan, Ill., 1906-08; asst. in zoölogy, U. of Wis., 1909-10; with Bur. Biol. Survey, U.S. Dept. Agr., since 1910, in charge mammal collection until 1925, biologist, in charge div. of biol. investigations, 1925-26; sr. biologist, in charge mammal collection, 1927-35; in charge of section of mammalogy, 1935-36; in charge section of wild life surveys since 1936. Condr. biol. explorations Mo., Wis., Ia., Minn., Ariz., Okla., Fla., Tenn., Va., Pa., N.H. Editor Jour. of Mammalogy, 1925-29; editor nature books pub. by C. C. Thomas. Fellow A.A.A.S. (council, 1922-26); member American Soc. Mammalogists (corr. sec., 1919-25; vice-pres., 1937, pres. since 1938), Biol. Soc. Washington (pres., 1931-33), Wis. Academy Science, Arts and Letters, Washington Academy Science (v.p., 1931-33), American Society Naturalists, Am. Ornithologists' Union (asso.), Cooper Ornithol. Club. Republican. Methodist. Club: Washington Biologists' Field Club. Contbr. many papers on mammals, birds, zoögeography, ecology and animal behavior. Home: 6313 Ridgewood Av., Chevy Chase, Md.

JACKSON, Howard W., mayor; b. Stemmers Run, Baltimore Co., Md., Aug. 4, 1877; s. Andrew C. J.; ed. pub. schs., Baltimore, Md.; m. Ella M. Galloway, Sept. 14, 1898; children—Carle A., Riall, Ella M. (Mrs. William H. Sheehan), Virginia. In ins. business; propr., Riall-Jackson Ins. Co. Mem. City Council, Baltimore, 1907; register of wills, Baltimore, 1909-23; mayor of Baltimore, 1923-27 and from 1931 for 2 terms 1931-39. Democrat. Methodist. Home: 5222 Springlake Way. Office: Chamber of Commerce Bldg., Baltimore, Md.

JACKSON, J. Roy, supt. schs.; b. New Buffalo, Pa., May 3, 1886; s. J. Benson and Caroline (Bair) J.; ed. New Buffalo pub. schs.; certificate and diploma Cumberland Valley Normal Sch., Shippensburg, Pa., 1908; Ph.B., Dickinson Coll., 1914; A.M., U. of Pittsburgh, 1927; m. Rhoda Myrtle McGeorge, May 13, 1916. Teacher rural sch., Moon Twp., Allegheny Co., Pa., 1908-09; prin. rural sch., Carnot, 1909-10; teacher mathematics and science, Coraopolis (Pa.) High Sch., 1914-16; supervising prin. Battles Memorial Sch., Girard, Pa., 1916-19; prin. New Brighton High Sch., 1919-22, Woodlawn High Sch. (now Harding High Sch.), Aliquippa, 1922-30, Beaver Falls High Sch., 1930-34; supt. schs., Beaver Falls since 1934; teacher methods in geography, nature study and arithmetic, Dept. of Edn. for Teacher Training, Geneva Coll., summers 1920-21, teacher orgn. and methods in gen. mathematics for junor high sch. and teacher of orgn., adminstrn. and supervision jr. high schs., summer 1922, teacher extension courses, 1922-23. Mem. N.E.A. (depts. of elementary, prins., secondary sch. prins., superintendence and dept. of high sch. teachers), Am. Vocational Assn., Nat. Soc. for Study of Edn., Pa. Edn. Assn., Mid-Western Conv. Dist., Dept. of Secondary Schs., Eastern Commercial Teachers Assn., Tri-State Commercial Ednl. Assn., Phi Delta Kappa, Iota Lambda Sigma. Republican. Presbyterian. Clubs: Rotary (pres., 1936-37), Beaver Valley Schoolmen's (pres., 1930-31). Home: 1215 8th Av. Office: 17th St. and 8th Av., Beaver Falls, Pa.

JACKSON, James Arthur, state law librarian; b. Montgomery, W.Va., Jan. 17, 1885; s. James Brutus and Emma (Hale) J.; ed. public schools, Charleston, W.Va., 1891-98, W.Va. State Coll., 1899-1901; m. Gertrude Diana Campbell, July 23, 1914; children—James Arthur, Jr. (deceased), Philip Ellsworth (deceased), Laura Mathews (Mrs. Joseph Cyrus Bradfield, III), Jane Lee, Barbara Ann. Messenger Supreme Court of Appeals and asst. librarian, Charleston, W.Va., 1901-20; Supreme Court (W.Va.) librarian, 1920-25, state law librarian since 1925. Republican. Baptist. Home: Institute, W.Va. Office: Supreme Court Bldg., Charleston, W.Va.

JACKSON, James Renwick, clergyman; b. Phila., Pa., Feb. 1, 1905; s. Samuel and Margaret (Carson) J.; desc. John Jackson of Scotland who sat in Westminster Assembly of Divines, London, 1643; student Temple U., 1927-32, Princeton Sem., 1933-35; m. Agnes McMullen, Aug. 2, 1924; children—Agnes Mae, James Renwick, Jr., Walter Thomas 2d. Ordained to ministry Presbyn. Ch.; 1932; minister Union Tabernacle Presbyn. Ch., Phila., Pa., since 1932; preached at Ocean City (N.J.) Tabernacle, 1935-36. Mem. Pension Com., Phila. Presbytery; commr. to Gen. Assembly, Columbus, 1937, and to Synod, 1938; counsellor Phila. Christian Endeavor Union, 1933. Mem. Northeast Ministerial Assn. of Phila., Y.M.C.A. Republican. Traveled in Canada, 1935, Mexico, 1936, Pacific Coast, 1937. Has 3 Presbyn. clergyman brothers. Home: 2168 E. York St., Philadelphia, Pa.

JACKSON, John J., lawyer; b. Cicero, N.Y.; s. Elias S. and Mary M. (Baum) J.; A.B., Olivet (Mich.) Coll., 1891, hon. M.A., 1893; m. Clara M. Sweet, Oct. 23, 1896; children—Gertrude (Mrs. William D. Bowers), Norma (Mrs. Harold G. Shirk), Andrew. In practice of law at Detroit, Mich., 1896-1909; became gen. atty. Westinghouse Electric & Mfg. Co., Pittsburgh, Pa., 1909; asst. treas. Westinghouse Lamp Co.; dir. Interborough Improvement Co., Turtle Creek & Allegheny River R.R. Co., Electric Bldg. & Loan Assn. Mem. Pa. State Chamber Commerce, Pittsburgh Chamber Commerce. Democrat. Presbyn. Clubs: University, Duquesne, Oakmont, Edgewood, Edgewood Country. Home: 343 Maple Av., Edgewood Park, Pittsburgh, Pa.*

JACKSON, Joseph (Francis Ambrose), writer, historian; b. Phila., Pa., May 20, 1867; s. Samuel and Barbara Marie (Dougherty) J.; ed. Spring Garden Inst., 1882-85, Pa. Acad. Fine Arts, 1887-88; m. Harriet Holmes Fletcher, Feb. 1, 1915. Began as newspaper reporter, 1887; art editor, Phila. Pub. Ledger, 1888-1902, news editor, 1904, feature writer, 1905-18; editor Building Magazine, 1922-25, Building Arts Magazine, 1925-26, The Pennsylvania Architect, 1939; asst. dir. Phila. Pageants, 1908, 1912; issued a series of lithographs of Phila., 1927-28. Hon. mem. Am. Inst. Archts. Life mem. Historical Soc. of Pa. Club: Philobiblon. Author: American Colonial Architecture, 1924; Development of American Architecture, 1926; America's Most Historic Highway, 1926; Poe's Philosophy of Animal Magnetism, 1928; Bibliography of Charles G. Leland, 1927; Encyclopedia of Philadelphia, 1931-33; See Philadelphia, 1937; Literary Landmarks of Philadelphia, 1939. Contbr. many articles to Dictionary of American Biography. Home: 113 S. 43d St. Office: 1110 Architects Bldg., Philadelphia, Pa.

JACKSON, Lloyd Earl, chem. engr.; b. Oswego, Kan., Dec. 6, 1892; s. Samuel S. and Edith M. (Burtiss) J.; B.S. in Chem. Engring., U. of Kan., Lawrence, Kan., 1916; student U. of Pittsburgh, 1921-28; m. Hazel Day, June 10, 1918; children—Hal Day, Lloyd Earl; m. 2d, Lydia Mouchron, Dec. 31, 1937. Control chemist, E. I. du Pont de Nemours & Co., Washburn, Wis., 1916-17; research chemist Empire Fuel & Gas Co., Bartlesville, Okla., 1917-20; petroleum chemist, U.S. Bur. of Mines, Pittsburgh, 1920; senior industrial fellow, Mellon Inst. Industrial Research, 1920-33; research on corrosion and dry cleaning, Crandall McKenzie and Henderson Co., Pittsburgh, since 1933; pres. and chem. engr. Spix Products Co., mfrs. chem. specialties for dry cleaning, dyeing, Pittsburgh, since 1933. Mem. Am. Chem. Soc., Am. Assn. Textile Chemists & Colorists, Nat. Assn. Dyers & Cleaners (hon.). Home: R.D. 1, Piteairn, Pa. Office: 7025 Chaucer St., Pittsburgh, Pa.

JACKSON, Naaman, lawyer; b. Boyd County, Ky., Nov. 13, 1873; s. Richard Clayton and Ann Elizabeth (Campbell) J.; ed. public schools of Ky.; married. School teacher, Ky. and W.Va., 1891-1902; admitted to W.Va. bar, 1903; in law practice, Logan, 1903-06; cashier, vice-pres. and pres. First Nat. Bank, Logan, W.Va., 1906-33; banking commr. W.Va., 1923-25; state senator, 1925-29; circuit judge, 1929-37; in practice of law, Logan, W.Va., since Jan. 1, 1937; pres. Clean Eagle Coal Co., Logan, W.Va. Trustee Logan College. Republican. Mason. Address: Logan, W.Va.

JACKSON, Ralph Garfield, mfr. floor coverings; b. Christiana, Pa., May 21, 1880; s. James J. and Josephine (Davis) J.; grad. George Sch., Newtown, Pa., 1901; A.B., Swarthmore (Pa.) Coll., 1905; m. Helen Moore, Jan. 10, 1911. Engr. Am. Pipe & Construction Co., 1905-14, Congoleum Co., 1915-20, Waltona Works, Inc., 1921-22; v.p. and dir. Sandura Co., Inc., since 1923; engaged mainly in development of new products and securing patents relative to same; pres. and dir. Kolor Thru Corpn.; v.p. and dir. Paulsboro Mfg. Co. Mem. Sigma Psi, Delta Upsilon, Book and Key. Republican. Quaker. Mason. Clubs: Union League (Philadelphia); Woodbury (N.J.) Country; ex-pres. Kiwanis (Paulsboro, N.J.). Home: 61 Bayard Av., Woodbury, N.J. Office: Finance Bldg., Philadelphia, Pa.

JACKSON, Samuel McCartney, II, lawyer; b. Apollo, Pa., Sept. 25, 1899; s. Frank Wilson and Caroline (Turney) J.; C.E., Pa. Mil. Coll., 1920; LL.B., U. of Pa. Law Sch., 1923; m. Martha R. MacCallum, June 26, 1929; children —Samuel M., III, Frank Wilson II, Malcolm MacCallum. Admitted to Pa. bar, 1925, since in gen. practice of law; dir. Apollo Trust Co.; vice-pres. and dir. First Federal Savings & Loan Assn. of Pittsburgh. Mem. Mil. Order Loyal Legion, Am. Legion, Sons Am. Revolution, Phi Gamma Delta. Republican. Presbyterian. Mason (32°). Clubs: Athletic Assn., Monarch (Pittsburgh). Home: 1129 Heberton Av. Office: 1220 Berger Bldg., Pittsburgh, Pa.

JACKSON, William H., pres. Pittsburgh-Des Moines Co.; b. Delaware, O., Mar. 19, 1868; s. John T. and Eliza A. (Faulkner) J.; B.C.E., Ia. State Coll., 1891; m. Minnie P. Long, Dec. 25, 1894; children—Ruth H., John E., William R. City engr., Fort Madison, Ia., 1892-93; mem. firm Jackson & Moss, engring. and constructing, Des Moines, Ia., 1894-99; v.p. Des Moines Bridge & Iron Works, 1900-21, now dir.; v.p. Pittsburgh- Des Moines Co., 1920-21, pres. since 1921; dir. Pittsburgh Nat. Bank, Horton Steel Works Clubs: Duquesne, Oakmont Country. Home: Schenley Apts. Office: Neville Island, Pittsburgh, Pa.

JACOB, Frederick Murray, dermatologist; b. Pittsburgh, Pa., Mar. 6, 1892; s. William Henry and Mary Ann (Murray) J.; M.D., U. of Pittsburgh Med. Sch., 1913; m. Regina Frauenheim, Apr. 14, 1921; children—Mary Regina, Walter Lindsay, Edward Frauenheim. Laboratory resident Mercy Hosp., Pittsburgh, 1914-15; Mellon fellow in pathology, U. of Pittsburgh, 1915-16, instr. in immunology, 1916-17; asst. in dermatology, Washington U., St. Louis, 1919-20; successively instr., asst. prof. now asso. prof. dept. dermatology, U. of Pittsburgh. Served as lt. Med. Corps, U.S.A., World War. Mem. Am., Pa. State and Allegheny Co. med. assns., Am. Dermatol. Assn., Alpha Omega Alpha. Catholic. Club: University. Home: 1159 Murrayhill Av. Office: Jenkins Arcade, Pittsburgh, Pa.

JACOB, William Paull, mfg. metal products; b. Wellsburg, W.Va., June 26, 1894; s. Wm. C. and Elizabeth (Paull) J.; A.B., Washington and Jefferson Coll., Washington, Pa., 1917; m. Helen Palmer, 1919; children—James P., Elizabeth P. Asso. with Eagle Manufacturing Co., mfrs. metal products, Wellsburg, W.Va., since 1919, now vice-pres. and dir.; dir. Municipal Mutual Ins. Co. of W.Va., Wellsburg, W.Va., Advance Federal Savings & Loan Assn. of Wellsburg. Commd. 2d lt. Aviation Sect., S.O.R.C. at close of World War. Mem. Beta Theta Pi. Republican. Presbyn. Mason. Clubs: Kiwanis (Wellsburg); Deep Creek Yacht (Deer Park, Md.). Home: Wellsburg, W.Va.

JACOBS, Disston Wright, clergyman; b. Kenton, Del., Oct. 11, 1886; s. Jonathan and Ellen A. (Greenwell) J.; B.D., Drew Theol. Sem. now Drew U., Madison, N.J., 1913; (hon.) D.D., Washington Coll., Chestertown, Md., 1932; m. Louise Gee, Mar. 15, 1913. Ordained to ministry Methodist Ch., 1915; pastor, Blades, Del., 1913-14, Rehoboth Beach, Del., 1915-17, Bridgeville, Del., 1918-20, Milford, Del., 1921-26, Newark, Del., 1927-28; supt. Wilmington Dist., 1929-34; minister, Snow Hill, Md., since 1935. Trustee Ocean Grove Camp Meeting Assn., Ocean Grove, N.J. Methodist. Mason (32°). Home: Federal St., Snow Hill, Md.

JACOBS, Harry S(ylvan), rabbi, author; b. New York, N.Y., Oct. 8, 1897; s. Moses Lionel and Libbie Gitl (Paltrowitz) J.; grad. Kearny (N.J.) High Sch., 1915; A.B., Coll. City of N.Y., 1919; A.M., Columbia U., 1925; Rabbi, Jewish Theol. Sem. of America, 1925; grad. study towards Ph.D., Columbia U., 1928-33. Rabbi, Queens Community Center, Elmhurst, L.I., 1921-24, Jewish Center, Middletown, N.Y., 1927-28, Young Israel Synagogue, Newark, N.J. 1929-34, Charleroi, Pa., 1935-36, Leominster, Mass. since 1938. Mem. bd. trustees Jewish Community Council, Fitchburg-Leominster. Mem. Y.M.H.A., Newark, N.J. Mem. N.Y. Bd. of Jewish Ministers, Rabbinical Assembly of America, Zionist Orgn. of America, B'nai B'rith. Author: Immigration Policy of America since 1917 (Columbia U. Grad. Essays, 1925), Critical Edition of Commentary of David Kimhi on Amos (doctor's thesis). Contbr. to book of sermons; reviewer books and plays for Anglo-Jewish press. Home: 178 Mapes Av., Newark, N.J.

JACOBS, Henry Barton, M.D.; b. Scituate, Mass., June 2, 1858; s. Barton Richmond and Frances Almira (Ford) J.; A.B., Harvard, 1883, M.D., 1887; asst. in botany Harvard, 1884-85; interne Mass. Gen. Hosp., 1887-88; m. Mary Frick Garrett, of Baltimore, Apr. 2, 1902. Practiced at Boston, 1888-90; asso. in medicine, Johns Hopkins, 1896-1904. Pres. Hosp. for Consumptives of Md.; mem. original bd. mgrs. Md. State Tuberculosis Sanatorium. Trustee, mem. executive com. Johns Hopkins Hosp., Peabody Inst. of Baltimore, Harriet Lane Home for Invalid Children, Ch. Home and Infirmary, Md. Inst., Children's Hosp. Sch.; pres. and dir. Redwood Library, Newport, R.I. Ex-mem. exec. com. Family Welfare Assn. of Baltimore. Fellow A.A.A.S.; original sec., dir. Nat. Tuberculosis Assn.; ex-pres. Md. Tuberculosis Assn.; mem. Laennec Soc. for Study of Tuberculosis (ex-pres.), Internat. Assn. Prevention Tuberculosis, A.M.A. Internat. Soc. History of Medicine, Nat. Civ. Service Reform League, Soc. for Preservation N.E. Antiquities, Archæol. Inst. America, Am. Fed. of Arts, English-Speaking Union (pres. Baltimore branch), American Bookplate Society, American Geog. Society, American Historical Association, Newport Hist. Soc., Md. Hist. Soc., Med. Library Assn.; ex-gov. Soc. Colonial Wars; member Soc. Mayflower Descendants. Vestryman, Grace and St. Peter's Chs., Baltimore, Md., and Trinity Church, Newport, R.I.; ex-pres. Churchmen's

Club; trustee and ex-treas. Md. Cathedral; mem. exec. council, Diocese of Maryland. Clubs: Grolier, Harvard, University (New York); Reading Room, Casino, Golf (Newport); Maryland, Elkridge, Merchants (Baltimore). Wrote article Some Distinguished American Students of Tuberculosis, 1902; also numerous other articles on subjects relating to tuberculosis, and on med. and hygienic topics. Associate editor Annals of Medical History. Home: (summer) Newport, R.I. Address: 11 W. Mt. Vernon Pl., Baltimore, Md.

JACOBS, Max, violinist, conductor, teacher; b. Rumania, Oct. 12, 1888; s. Abraham and Rachel (Yankovich) J.; brought to U.S., 1900; studied violin under Ovid Musin, harmony and composition, Columbia U. under MacWhood, later with Mortimer Wilson and Rubin Goldmark; m. Mona Jacobs, June 15, 1933. Played first violin with N.Y. Symphony, Russian Symphony and Peoples Symphony orchestras; concertmaster Am. Opera Co.; condr. Orchestral Soc. N.Y., 1913; headed Max Jacobs String Quartet, 1913-23; condr. Brooklyn Philharmonic Orchestra, 1914-17; organized N.Y. Chamber Symphony, 1924-28; condr. Trenton Symphony Orchestra, 1934-37; now condr. N.J. Chamber Symphony Orchestra, Young Men's Symphony Orchestra of N.Y. and Suffolk Co. Philharmonic Orchestra, Sayville, L.I. Served as bandmaster at Pelham Bay, N.Y. Naval Station, during World War. Condr. chamber symphony over leading radio stations. Democrat. Jewish religion. Author: Modern Scale Studies for Violin. Home: Hampton, N.J. Studio: 1013 Carnegie Hall, New York, N.Y.

JACOBS, Melvin Luther, dir. civil service; b. Coatesville, Pa., Jan. 26, 1911; s. Norris Thomas and Evalene (Lamping) J.; grad. Manor Twp. High Sch., Millersville, Pa., 1929; A.B., Franklin & Marshall Coll., Lancaster, Pa., 1933; LL.B., Temple U. Law Sch., 1936; m. Sylvia Thorson, Oct. 1936. Legal asst. Division of Unemployment Compensation, Harrisburg, Jan.-Apr. 1937; asst. dir. Civil service, Bd. of Review, Apr.-Dec. 1937, dir. civil service since Dec. 1937, asst. sec., Dec. 1937-Nov. 1938, sec. since Nov. 1938. Mem. Sharswood Court Hon. Legal fraternity. Baptist. Club: Carlisle Country (Carlisle, Pa.). Home: Paradise, Pa. Office: Board of Review, 3d and Foster Sts., Harrisburg, Pa.

JACOBS, Merkel Henry, physiologist; b. Harrisburg, Pa., Dec. 6, 1884; s. Michael William and Romaine (Merkel) J.; A.B., U. of Pa., 1905, Ph.D., 1908; grad. study U. of Berlin, 1908-09; m. Kate Eleanora Hodgson, Apr. 10, 1912; 1 son, Edward Hodgson. Instr. in zoölogy, U. of Pa., 1909-13, asst. prof., 1913-21, asst. prof. physiology, 1921-23, prof. since 1923; in charge instrn. in physiology, Marine Biol. Lab., Woods Hole, Mass., 1921-29, asso. dir., 1925-26, dir. 1926-38, trustee since 1938. Mem. editorial bd. Journal Cellular and Comparative Physiology, Physiological Reviews, Biol. Bull. and Jour. Exptl. Zoölogy. Was capt., Sanitary Corps, U.S.A., 1918-19. Fellow A.A.A.S.; mem. Am. Physiol. Soc., Am. Philos. Soc., Am. Soc. Zoölogists (v.p. 1928, pres. 1938), Am. Chem. Soc., Soc. Am. Naturalists, Physiol. Soc. Philadelphia (pres. 1920-22), Soc. Exptl. Biology and Medicine, Corpn. Marine Biol. Lab., Sigma Xi, Phi Beta Kappa, Sigma Chi. Contbr. sect. on permeability of the cell to General Cytology, 1924; also wrote Permeability of the Erythrocyte, 1931, and Diffusion Processes, 1935. Home: Route 2, Media, Pa.

JACOBS, Myrl Lamont, gen. mgr. quarries; b. Weldbank, Warren Co., Pa., May 16, 1885; s. Carl Bearse and Georgia (Truxel) J.; student Mercersburg (Pa.) Acad., and Marietta (O.) Coll.; E.M., Lehigh U., Bethlehem, Pa., 1910; m. Hermia Grace, Oct. 11, 1911; children—Barbara, Carl Bearse. Asst. engr. Astoria Light, Heat & Power Co., 1910-12, Mexican Light & Power Co., 1912-13, N.Y. Municipal Ry., 1913-16; cons. engr. F. H. Clement & Co., 1916; supt. quarries Bethlehem Steel Co., 1916-20, gen. mgr. quarries since 1934; gen. mgr. quarries Bethlehem Mines Corpn., 1920-34. Treas. Boys' Club of Bethlehem, Pa.; past pres. Bethlehem Council Boy Scouts of America. Mem. Am. Soc. Mining and Metall. Engrs., Am. Iron and Steel Inst., Engrs.' Club of Lehigh Valley. Vestryman and treas. Pro Cathedral Ch. of Nativity. Clubs: Bethlehem, University, Rotary, Saucon Valley Country (Bethlehem); Mining (New York). Home: 837 Tioga Av. Office: 701 E. Third St., Bethlehem, Pa.

JACOBS, Nathan Bernd, engr.; b. Pittsburgh, Pa., Dec. 18, 1891; s. Benjamin N. and Lottie (Pichel) J.; B.S. in san. engring., U. of Pittsburgh, 1914, San. Engr., 1917; m. Marie F. Oberndorf, of Pittsburgh, Pa., Sept. 17, 1918; 1 dau. Emily Nan. Asst. engr. Morris Knowles, Inc., 1914-17, division engr., 1917-21, asst. chief engr., 1921-32, pres. and chief engr. since 1932, now also treas. and dir.; mgr. Knowles-Main Appraisal Bureau, Pittsburgh and New York, since 1919; cons. engr. Maurice R. Scharff, New York; water consultant Dist. No. 2, Drainage Basin Study, Nat. Resources Com.; same, Interstate Commn. on Delaware River Basin. Studied development of utilities for houses in Europe for President's (Hoover) Conf. on Home Bldg. and Home Ownership, 1931. V.p. Irene Kaufmann Settlement, Emma Farm Assn.; mem. Maurice and Laura Falk Foundation, Pittsburgh Housing Assn., Ohio Valley Conservation and Flood Control Congress. Mem. Am. Inst. Consulting Engrs., Am. Soc. Civil Engrs., Am. Water Works Assn., Pa. Water Works Assn. (v.p.), Am. Soc. for Testing Materials, Am. Soc. Professional Engrs., Am. Pub. Health Assn., Internat. City Mgrs. Assn. Mem. Jewish religion. Clubs: Westmoreland Country (Verona, Pa.); Civic Club of Allegheny County (pres. 1936-38). Writer various published articles and speeches. Home: 6329 Bartlett St. Office: 507 Westinghouse Bldg., Pittsburgh, Pa.

JACOBS, Robert Lee, lawyer; b. Carlisle, Pa., Dec. 17, 1910; s. T. Ralph and Flora Alma (Lee) J.; A.B., Dickinson Coll., 1932; LL.B., Dickinson Sch. of Law, 1935; m. Ann Blaine Hays, June 9, 1937. Admitted to Cumberland Co. bar, 1935, Pa. Supreme Ct. bar, 1936; solicitor to Sheriff of Cumberland County, 1935-36; dir. Cumberland Valley Bldg. & Loan Assn., Carlisle, Pa.; mem. Pa. State Senate, 31st Dist., since 1936. Mem. Interstate Commn. on Delaware River Basin since 1937. Mem. Phi Kappa Psi. Democratic. Episcopalian (vestryman). Mason, Odd Fellow. Clubs: Kiwanis (dir.), Carlisle Country. Home: 29 Walnut St. Office: Sentinel Bldg., Carlisle, Pa.

JACOBS, Thomas Malone, lawyer; b. Millington, Md., May 21, 1904; s. Dr. William Henry and Mary Elizabeth (Malone) J.; A.B., St. John's Coll., Annapolis, Md., 1925; LL.B., Harvard Law Sch., 1930; unmarried. Clk. Central Fire Ins. Co., Baltimore, Md., 1925-26; Teacher Baltimore Poly. Inst., 1926-27; admitted to Md. bar, 1931; law clk. to Judge William C. Coleman, U.S. Dist. Ct., Baltimore, 1930-31; asso. Stewart, Pearre & Kieffner, lawyers, Baltimore, 1931-36; partner Pearre, Kieffner & Jacobs, lawyer, Baltimore, since 1936. Served as 2d lt., 5th Inf., Md. Nat. Guard, 1932-35. Mem. Am. Bar Assn. (state chmn. Jr. Bar Conf. 1938-39), Bar Assn. of Baltimore City, Jr. Bar Assn. of Baltimore City (v.p. 1935-36, pres. 1936-37), Kappa Alpha (Southern). Democrat. Episcopalian. Home: 2404 Monticello Rd. Office: 1061-9 Calvert Bldg., Baltimore, Md.

JACOBSON, Carl Alfred, prof. chemistry; b. Grantsburg, Wis., Jan. 25, 1876; s. of Carl John and Anna Britta (Asp) J.; B.S., Carleton Coll., Northfield, Minn., 1903, M.S., 1907; Ph.D., Johns Hopkins, 1908; spl. studies in 3 univs. of Europe, 1911, 12; m. Mary Edna Metzger, June 21, 1906; children—Ernest Howard (dec.), Alfred Marcel (dec.), Carl Metzger, John David, Joseph Edward, Samuel Odin, Robert Stanley. Fellow and research chemist at Rockefeller Inst. for Med. Research, New York, 1908-09; prof. agricultural chemistry, University of Nevada, and chief chemist Nevada Agrl. Expt. Station, 1909-18; fellow Johns Hopkins University, 1919-20; prof. chemistry, W.Va. U., 1920—. Fellow A.A.A.S.; mem. Am. Chem. Soc. (com. on nomenclature, spelling and pronunciation), Am. Assn. Univ. Profs., Phi Beta Kappa, Phi Kappa Phi, Phi Lambda Upsilon. Democrat. Methodist. Author: A Pronouncing Chemical Formula Speller and Contest Guide. Contbr. on elec. conductivity, phosphatides, chlorophylls, alfalfa constituents, enzymes, poisonous principles, oils, saponins, fluosilicic acid, fluosilicates, silica black and silica fluff, chemical spelling, chemical shorthand, etc. Inventor of various lab. apparatus, a calculating machine, and a new method for determining the solubility of solids at different temperatures; granted patent on a process for treating powdered coal. An organizer of Selco By-Products Co. of W.Va. (by-products of coal), Bluefield, (factory at Greer, W.Va.), 1938. Home: 447 Cedar St., Morgantown, W.Va.

JACOBSON, Lewis S., lawyer; b. Brooklyn, N.Y., Jan. 15, 1900; s. Eli and Eva (Cohen) J.; student Perth Amboy (N.J.) High Sch., 1912-16, Newark (N.J.) Normal Sch., 1916-18; LL.B., N.J. Law Sch., Newark, N.J., 1925; m. Rose M. Goldstein, Feb. 15, 1939; 1 son, Lynn Eduard. Pub. sch. teacher, Perth Amboy, N.J., 1918-26; in practice of law at Perth Amboy, N.J., since 1925; treas. Fidelity Petroleum Corpn. Mem. Perth Amboy, Middlesex Co., N.J. State and Am. bar assns. Home: 518 Tisdale Pl., Woodbridge, N.J. Office: 214 Smith St., Perth Amboy, N.J.

JACOBUS, David Dinkel, chemist; b. Jersey City, N.J., Feb. 16, 1900; s. David Schenck and Laura (Dinkel) J.; M.E., Stevens Inst. Tech., 1921; D.Sc., Mass. Inst. Tech., 1930; m. Margaret Penman, Feb. 24, 1926; children—David Penman, John Henry. Employed as draftsman and engr., Stone & Webster, Inc., 1922-26; instr., Mass. Inst. Tech., 1926-27, research asso., 1927-30; asst. prof. chemistry, Stevens Inst. Tech., Hoboken, N.J., 1930-39, asso. prof. since 1939; dir. chem. research, Keuffel & Esser Co. since 1936. Mem. A.A.A.S., Am. Chem. Soc., Am. Soc. Mech. Engrs. Home: Mt. Harmony Rd., Bernardsville, N.J. Office: care Keuffel & Esser Co., 300 Adams St., Hoboken, N.J.

JACOBUS, David Schenck, engineer; b. Ridgefield, N.J., Jan. 20, 1862; s. Nicholas and Sarah Catherine (Carpenter) J.; ed. in pvt. sch.; M.E., Stevens Inst. Tech., 1884 (Dr. Engring., 1906); spl. mechanical engineering; m. Laura Dinkel, Apr. 5, 1899; children—David D., Laura C. Instr., 1884-97, prof. experimental mechanics and engring. physics, 1897-1906, Stevens Inst. of Technology; advisory engr. The Babcock & Wilcox Co. since 1906, and now head of engring. dept. same. Chmn. Am. Soc. M.E., Boiler Code Com. Awarded Morehead medal by Internat. Acetylene Assn. for year 1935 for leadership in formulation codes and procedures. Trustee Stevens Inst. Tech. Has written many papers and is an authority in steam engring. Hon. mem. Am. Soc. Mech. Engrs. (pres. 1916-17); mem. Soc. Naval Architects and Marine Engrs., Am. Inst. Mining Engrs., Am. Math. Society, Society Promotion Engring. Edn., American Institute Electric Engineers, American Soc. Refrigerating Engrs. (pres. 1906-07), Am. Soc. Heating and Ventilating Engrs. (life), Am. Welding Soc. (pres. 1934-35), Franklin Inst., Holland Soc. New York; fellow A.A.A.S. Clubs: New York Railroad, Engineers. Home: 93 Harrison Av., Montclair, N.J. Office: 85 Liberty St., New York, N.Y.*

JACOBUS, George Richard, golf professional; b. Glen Ridge, N.J., June 2, 1899; s. George R. and Ethel (Lyons) J.; 1 son, George. Golf professional at Ridgewood (N.J.) Country Club since 1914; professional at Bobby Jones Golf Club, Sarasota, Fla., winter months since 1934. Served as private, U.S. Army, during World War. Mem. N.Y. World's Fair Sports Com. Mem. Professional Golfers' Assn. (pres. since 1932), U.S. Golf Assn. (mem. Greens Sect. Com.). Club: Ridgewood (N.J.) Country (hon. life mem.). Lecturer, radio speaker on golf. Address: Ridgewood Country Club, Ridgewood, N.J.

JACOBY, Wilmer Marshall, publicist; b. Phila., Pa., Apr. 4, 1884; s. John Freedley and Mary Frances (Denning) J.; ed. Central High Sch., Phila., 1896-99. Reporter Phila. Inquirer, 1902, Pittsburgh Gazette, 1903; city editor Pittsburgh Dispatch, 1904, 05; sports editor Pittsburgh Leader, 1906, polit. writer, 1907; polit. reporter Pittsburgh Chronicle Telegraph, 1908-11; exec. dir. Flood Commn. of Pittsburgh, 1912-33; sec. Retail Merchants Assn. of Pittsburgh, 1918-33; sec. Allegheny Co. Planning Commn., 1919-23; chmn. Zoning Bd. of Adjustment, Pittsburgh, 1923-33; mem. bd. advisors Inland Waterways Corpn. of U.S., operating Federal Barge Line, 1925-35; pub. Pittsburgh Sun-Telegraph and pres. Pitt Pub. Co., 1933-39; apptd. mem. Pa. Workmen's Compensation Bd. by Governor James, July 1, 1939. Mem. Pa. Forestry Assn., Pa. German Soc., Sons Am. Revolution, Pittsburgh Symphony Soc. Republican. Presbyterian. Clubs: Duquesne, Fox Chapel Golf (Pittsburgh); Harrisburg (Harrisburg); Union League (Phila.); Nat. Press Club (Washington, D.C.). Home: 1043 S. Negley Av. Office: Oliver Bldg., Pittsburgh, Pa.

JAEGER, Hans, educator; b. Warsaw, Poland, May 20, 1898; s. Adolf and Olga (Partowicz) J.; came to U.S., 1928; Ph.D., U. of Berlin, Germany, 1924; m. Eugenie Raff, July 16, 1929. Engaged as instr. German, Princeton U., 1928-30, asst. prof. since 1930. Mem. Modern Lang. Assn. America, Assn. Teachers of German, Goethe Gesellschaft. Lutheran. Author: Clemens Brentanos Frühlyrik, 1926. Editor (with G. Lüdtke): Kürschners Deutscher Gelehrten-Kalender, 1926; Die schönsten Geschichten und Novellen von W. H. Riehl, 1927; Moderne Einakter, 1938. Collaborator: Ferdinand Raimund als Schauspieler, 1925. Contbr. articles to publs. of Modern Lang. Assn. America and Germanic Review (Columbia U.). Home: 57 Jefferson Rd., Princeton, N.J.

JAEKEL, Frederic Blair, author; b. Hollidaysburg, Pa., May 6, 1882; s. Frederick and Cora A. (Blair) J.; Lafayette Coll., 1899-1901; B.S., Bucknell U., 1903; m. Edith Overholt McCain, Nov. 7, 1906; children—Virginia Overholt, Frederic Blair (dec.). On staff Phila. North American, 1906-07; spl. corr. Phila. Press at coronation of King George V and Queen Mary, June, 1911; spl. rep. Travel Magazine, in Holland, 1911, in Panama and Costa Rica, 1912; dramatic editor Evening Telegraph, Phila., 1917-18; editor, Bucks County Daily News, Doylestown, Pa., 1921-24; editor Camden (N.J.) Post-Telegram, 1924-25; now v.p. Osmond-Laurens, Inc. Presbyn. Fellow Royal Geog. Soc. Eng.; mem. Phi Gamma Delta, etc. Clubs: Phi Gamma Delta, Nat. Arts (New York); University (Phila.); Country (Doylestown); Nat. Press (Washington); Authors' (London). Author: The Lands of the Tamed Turk, 1910; Windmills and Wooden Shoes, 1912; Planning a Trip Abroad, 1912. Home: Glen Echo Farm, Doylestown, Pa. Office: 1700 Walnut St., Philadelphia, Pa.

JAFFE, Israel Max, executive; b. Baltimore, Md., July 24, 1891; s. Dr. Lewis Leonard and Hanah Ginsberg (Margolin) J.; prep. edn. public schools of Baltimore; student European theological school, 1900-06; m. Fannie L. Posner, Sept. 8, 1912 (died Oct. 4, 1933); children—Beaulah Judith (Mrs. Irv. C. Robins), Sidney Leroy, Arthur Hielman, Lewis Leonard, Norman David, Richard Allan; m. 2d, Anne Honick, Feb. 5, 1939. Began as farmer, 1907, later worker in oil field; owner Am. Button Works, New York, 1913-15; jr. partner Oram & Jaffe, dept. store, 1917-23; owner Jaffe Enterprises since 1923; pres. Style Center, Inc.; pres. Zimmerman Realty. Dir. Butler Chamber of Commerce, 1930; dir. Pa. State Coll. Parents Assn., 1933-36; treas. Rep. County Com., 1932; treas. Butler Boy Scouts since 1928. Awarded Silver Beaver, 1937. Republican. Jewish religion. Mem. B'nai B'rith, K.P. Club: Kiwanis of Butler. Home: 228 W. Penn St. Office: 100 N. Main St., Butler, Pa.

JAGELS, Claus Henry Carl, realty developer; b. New York, N.Y., Sept. 3, 1870; s. Claus H. and Anna (Kohnken) J.; student Hoboken (N.J.) Pub. Schs., 1876-84, Packard Business Coll., New York, 1884-85; m. Amelia M. Meschendorf, July 5, 1895 (died 1926); children—Carl Herbert, Dorothy Marie (Mrs. Thorman B. Givan); m. 2d, Amelia Marie Henke, July 30, 1927. Began as printer, Hoboken, 1885; formerly pres. Weehawken Trust Co., Union City, N.J., Second Bank & Trust Co., Hoboken, N.J., Jagels, a fuel corpn., Hoboken, N.J., Marie Antoinette Hotel, N.Y. City; treas. Crest Acre Corpn., Summit, N.J., since 1927. Pres. Summit (N.J.) Home for Children. Mem. Hoboken (N.J.) Chamber of Comemrce (pres.), Summit (N.J.) Bd. of Trade (pres.). Republican. Lutheran. Mason (32°), Royal Arcanum. Club: Masonic of Hoboken (N.J.). Address: 66 Hillcrest Av., Summit, N.J. Office: 77 River St., Hoboken, N.J.

JAMES, Albert Earl, lawyer; b. Sac City, Ia., Dec. 25, 1882; s. Joseph Henry and Mary Matilda (Smith) J.; prep. edn. Sac City Inst.; A.B., U. of Wis., 1905, A.M., 1908, LL.B., 1908; m. Ruth Ellen Varney, July 2, 1906; 1 dau., Betheva Ruth; m. 2d, Ida Elaine Dwinnell, Mar. 11, 1911; children—Eugenie Earl, Helen Muriel (Mrs. Carleton Wilson Wahl). Statistician Wis. Tax Commn., 1905-15; admitted to Wis. bar, 1908; dir. Taxpayers Assn. of N.M., 1915-18; head inventory sect., Bur. Internal Revenue, 1918-19; asso. with Greene & Hurd, attys., New York, 1920-24; mem. U.S. Bd. of Tax Appeals, Washington, D.C., 1924-26; personal practice of law, Washington, D.C., since 1926. Mem. A.B.A. Club: Wall Street (New York); Columbia Country (Chevy Chase, D.C.). Home: 6800 Meadow Lane, Chevy Chase, Md. Office: Union Trust Bldg., Washington, D.C.

JAMES, Albert William, lawyer; b. Cobden, Ill., June 12, 1902; s. Albert William and Alice (Broadway) J.; student Wilmington (Del.) High Sch., 1921-24; LL.B., Dickinson Law Sch., Carlisle, Pa., 1927; m. Madalin Wintrup, July 12, 1929; children—Albert William, Winthrop Broadway. Admitted to Del. bar, 1929, and since practiced at Wilmington, Del.; mem. firm Hering, Morris, James & Hitchens, attys.-at-law, Wilmington, Del., since 1929. Pres. Wilmington City Council since 1935; dep. atty. gen. for Del. State Tax Dept. since 1939 (four-yr. term). Mem. Del. State Bar Assn., New Castle Co. Bar Assn., Phila. Dickinson Coll. Alumni (pres. since 1938), Wilmington Community Concert Assn. (pres. since 1936), Phi Kappa Psi (Pa. Zeta Chapter of Dickinson Coll.). Republican. Methodist. Clubs: Torch (sec., treas. and dir.), Kiwanis, University, Whist, Masonic (Wilmington, Del.). Home: 4403 Tennyson Rd., Brandywine Hills. Office: 350 Delaware Trust Bldg., Wilmington, Del.

JAMES, Alfred Procter, prof. history; b. Fox Hill, Va., Feb. 7, 1886; s. Cyrus Rosser and Annie Elwood (Shields) J.; grad. Chesapeake Acad., 1903, Randolph-Macon Coll., 1906; student Oxford U., England, 1907-10, U. of Chicago, 1910-11, 13, 14, 15 and 21; m. Mable Elizabeth Williams, June 22, 1916; children—William Alfred. Instr. Latin, Randolph-Macon Coll., 1905-06; instr. Latin, Greek and history, Castle Heights Sch., Lebanon, Tenn., 1906-07; Rhodes scholar from Va., 1907-10; fellow in history, U. of Chicago, 1910-11; salesman Northwestern Mutual Life Ins. Co., Chicago, 1911-12; agt. Ginn & Co., 1912-16; instr. history, Ohio Wesleyan U., 1917; asst. prof. history, U. of Ark., 1917-18; asst. prof. history, U. of Pittsburgh, 1918-24, prof. since 1924. Mem. Am. Assn. Univ. Profs., Am. Hist. Assn., Miss. Valley Hist. Assn., Hist. Soc. of Western Pa., Pa. Hist. Assn., Phi Alpha Theta, Pi Lambda Mu, Phi Beta Kappa. Ind. Democrat. Methodist. Clubs: Faculty, Polygon (U. of Pittsburgh). Contbr. Miss. Valley Hist. Review, Western Pa. Hist. Mag., etc. Editor: Western Pa. Hist. Mag., 1922-27. Editor and compiler: The Writings of General John Forbes, 1938. Home: 101 Gladstone Road, Pittsburgh, Pa.

JAMES, Arthur Edwin, prof. inorganic chemistry; b. Elmsley Farm, West Chester, Pa., Jan. 21, 1897; s. John Edwin and Mary (Cope) J.; B.S., Pa. State Coll., 1921; A.M., U. of Pa., 1924; study, Columbia U., summer 1922; Ph.D., Cornell U., 1933; m. Alma I. Davis, Sept. 5, 1922; children—Barbara Ann, Arthur Dalton. Engaged as instr. chemistry, Lincoln U., Pa., 1921-22, asst. prof., 1922-24, prof. 1924-37, registrar, Lincoln U., 1923-31; prof. inorganic chemistry, Temple U. Sch. of Pharmacy, Phila., Pa., since 1937. Mem. bd. mgrs. Westtown Sch. Mem. Am. Chem. Soc., Am. Pharm. Assn., Phi Delta Kappa, Phi Lambda Upsilon, Sigma Phi Alpha, Chester Co. Hist. Soc. (dir.). Republican. Mem. Religious Soc. Friends. Club: "X" of West Chester, Pa. Home: 408 S. Walnut St., West Chester, Pa. Office: Temple University, Philadelphia, Pa.

JAMES, Arthur H.; judge Superior Court of Pa. for term 1933-43. Home: Plymouth, Pa.

JAMES, Ernest K., tax commr., lawyer; b. Maple Hill, N.C., June 29, 1895; s. Gibson J. and Annabelle (Murray) J.; A.B., Maryville (Tenn.) Coll., 1920; J.D., U. of Chicago, 1923; m. Mary Summers, July 6, 1929. Admitted to W.Va. bar, 1923, and since practiced at Charleston, W.Va.; mem. firm Campbell, McClintic and James, Charleston, since 1928. Served as lt., Air Service, U.S. Army, 1917-19. Mem. W.Va. State Legislature, 1934-36, State Dem. Exec. Com. since 1936; W.Va. state tax commr. since 1937. Democrat. Presbyterian. Mason. Home: Manor Place. Office: Charleston Nat. Bank Bldg., Charleston, W.Va.

JAMES, Frank Cyril, prof. of finance and economic history; b. London, Eng., Oct. 8, 1903; s. Frank and Mary Lucy (Brown) J.; student Grocers' Company's Sch., London, 1910-20; B. Commerce, London Sch. of Economics, 1923; A.M., U. of Pa., 1924, Ph.D., 1926; m. Irene L. V. Leeper, Aug. 26, 1926. Came to U.S., 1923. Clerk in Barclays' Bank, London, 1921-23; instr. in finance and transportation, U. of Pa., 1924-27, asst. prof. of finance, 1927-33, asso. prof., 1933-35, prof. since 1935, chmn. Grad. Faculty in Social Science, 1936-37, prof. of finance and economic history since 1938. Advisor in financial research Assn. of Reserve City Bankers, 1936; economist First Nat. Bank of Chicago, 1937-38; dir. Sch. of Commerce, Magill Univ., Montreal, 1939-40; mem. econ. advisory council Nat. Industrial Conf., Bd., N.Y.; mem. com. on financial research Nat. Bur. Econ. Research; dir. Am. Acad. of Polit. and Social Science. Fellow Royal Econ. Soc., London; mem. Inst. of Marine Engrs., London, Am. Econ. Assn., Economists Nat. Com. on Monetary Policy (exec. vice-pres.), Foreign Policy Assn. (chmn. exec. com.), Phi Beta Kappa. Clubs: Lenape (Phila.); Tavern, Quadrangle (Chicago); National Liberal (London). Author: Cyclical Fluctuations in the Shipping and Shipbuilding Industries, 1927; The Economics of Money, Credit and Banking, 1930; England Today, a Survey of Her Economic Situation, 1931; The Road to Revival, 1932; The Meaning of Money (with others), 1935; The Economic Doctrines of John Maynard Keynes (with others), 1938; The Growth of Chicago Banks (2 vols.), 1938; Economic Problems in a Changing World (with others), 1939. Home: 3425 Powelton Av., Philadelphia, Pa.

JAMES, Frederic, physician, doctor dental surgery, prof. dental histo-pathology; b. London, Eng., Dec. 26, 1895; s. James and Edith Amelia (Lee) J.; came to U.S. 1924; ed. London Hosp. Dental Sch., 1913-14; Licentiate in Medicine, Midwifery and Surgery (equivalent of M.D.) Soc. of Apothecaries, Guy's Hosp. Med. Sch., London, Eng., 1924; D.D.S., U. of Pa. Dental Sch., 1927; m. Lauretta Isabelle Reed, Sept. 24, 1927; 1 son, Frederic, Jr. Apptd. to faculty, U. of Pa. Dental Sch., dept. dental pathology, 1924-27; prof. dental histo-pathology, clin. pathology and periodontia, and dir. Henry Isaiah Dorr Research Lab., Temple U. Dental Sch. since 1927. Served as 2d lt. to actg. capt., R.A., 1914-18; twice wounded. Mem. A.A. A.S., Am. Dental Assn., Pa. State Dental Soc., North Phila. Assn. Dental Surgs., Research Soc. U. of Pa., Photographic Guild of Phila., Brit. Med. Assn., Royal Photographic Soc. of Gt. Britain, Sigma Xi, Delta Sigma Delta. Episcopalian. Author of textbooks: Principles Dental Histo-Pathology, Clinical Pathology and Therapeutics, 1934; Treatment and Control of Oral Infection, 1935. Contbr. many papers on oral pathol. conditions and treatments and research. Home: 1405 Sussex Rd., Wynnewood, Montgomery Co., Pa.

JAMES, Henry Duvall, cons. mech. and elec. engr.; b. Baltimore, Md.; s. Fleming and Mary Ella (Duvall) J.; grad. Episcopal Acad., Phila., Pa., 1891; B.S., U. of Pa., 1895, M.E., same, 1896; m. Elizabeth Louise Blakeslee, Jan. 14, 1908; children—Katharine Duvall, Curtis Blakeslee, Virginia Sartwell. In employ Otis Elevator

Co., 1897-1904; employed in various exec. positions in engring. dept. Westinghouse Electric & Mfg. Co., 1904-34; cons. engr. since 1934. Served as chmn. Zoning Bd., Edgewood, Pa. Trustee West Pa. Sch. for the Deaf. Fellow Am. Inst. Elec. Engrs.; mem. Engring. Soc. of W. Pa. (past pres.), Am. Canoe Assn. of U.S. (commodore 1910-11), Sylvan Canoe Club of Pittsburgh, Am. Philatelic Soc. of U.S. Republican. Episcopalian. Clubs: Westinghouse (Wilkinsburg); Church (Pittsburgh). Author: Controllers for Electric Motors, 1926. Contbr. several hundred articles to tech. papers. Granted over 150 patents. Home: 435 Locust St., Pittsburgh, Pa.

JAMES, Joseph Hidy, chemist; b. Jeffersonville, O., Nov. 3, 1868; s. John A. and Mary J. (Hidy) J.; B.S., Buchtel Coll., Akron, O., 1894; post-grad. work chemistry and physics, Columbia, 1897, chemistry, U. of Pa., 1898-99, Ph.D., 1899; m. Edith Mallison, Nov. 28, 1899; children—Mary Alice, Virginia, Josephine. Asst. chemistry and physics, Buchtel Coll., 1894-97; chief chemist Lake Superior Power Co., Sault Ste. Marie, 1899-1902; asst. prof. textile chemistry, Clemson (S.C.) Coll., 1902-05; asst. prof. tech. chemistry, 1905-06, asst. prof. chem. practice in charge dept. of chemistry, 1906-07, asso. prof., 1907-08, prof. chemistry from 1908 until retired, Carnegie Inst. Tech., Pittsburgh. Research and patents on acetylene storage and on oxidation products of petroleum. Mem. Am. Chem. Soc., Am. Inst. Chem. Engrs. Home: 5868 Douglas Av., Pittsburgh, Pa.

JAMES, Ralph Emerson, v.p. Charis Corpn.; b. Brooklyn, N.Y., Sept. 8, 1896; s. Henry Martin and Charlotte (Callum) J.; ed. Brooklyn grammar and high schs.; m. Sarah Louise Smith, Sept. 7, 1921; children—Ralph E., Palmer Judson, Eustace Anthony. Stenographer and circulation mgr. American Lithographic Co. and affiliates, Crowell Pub. Co., Mentor Assn., Knapp Co., Inc., 1913-22; with Charis Corpn. since 1922, v.p. and dir., 1926-39, pres. since 1939, sec. and dir. Charis, Ltd., New Toronto, Canada. With Norton-Harjes Ambulance Service, France-Am. Red Cross, Italy and Foreign Legion of France, Mar. 1917-Apr. 1919. Awarded Croix de Guerre. Trustee Community Chest; mem. council Boy Scouts of America. Republican. Presbyterian. Clubs: Lehigh Country, Livingston (Allentown). Home: 223 N. Marshall St. Office: 730 Linden St., Allentown, Pa.

JAMES, Reese Davis, associate prof. of English; b. Reading, Pa., Oct. 5, 1889; s. Edward William and Sara Jane (Graves) J.; A.B., U. of Pa., 1910, A.M., 1911, Ph.D., 1930; student Univ. of Clermont-Ferrand, France, 1919; m. Anna Gertrude Dunbar, Jan. 5, 1918; children—Edward William, David Dunbar. Began as teacher of English, Mercersburg Acad., 1911-12; newspaper and magazine writing, 1912-17; with the dept. of English, U. of Pa. since 1919, asso. prof. of English since 1937, dir. of courses in publishing since 1921. Served with 79th Div., U.S. Army, 1917-19; with A.E.F. in Argonne, St. Mihiel, North of Meuse, 1918. Mem. Am. Assn. Teachers of Speech, Phi Beta Kappa. Author: Old Drury of Philadelphia-A History of the Philadelphia Stage, 1800-35, pub. 1932. Home: Crooked Lane, Bridgeport, Pa. Office: Univ. of Pennsylvania, Philadelphia, Pa.

JAMESON, Robert Willis, corpn. official; b. Antrim, N.H., July 23, 1875; s. Nathan C. and Idabel B. (Butler) J.; ed. pub. schs. New York; m. Marie D'Arcy Buck, June 14, 1899; children—Caroline Mixer (Mrs. Joseph H. Currier), Isabel Butler (Mrs. William H. Chace). Began as clk., 1890; was with Wm. Carroll & Co., New York, 1901-1917; treas. and chmn. bd. Dominion Stores, Ltd., Canada, 1919-29; began with United Cigar Stores, 1929, pres. since 1933-36; now pres., dir. and mem. exec. com. United Stores Corpn., Tobacco Products of N.J. and Del.; dir. and mem. exec. com. Gold Dust Corpn. (now Hecker Products Corpn) Reiss Premier Co., Ward Baking Co. (exec. com. and dir.), McLellan Stores Co., McCrory Stores; dir. Best Foods, Inc.; chmn. bd. McCrory Stores Corpn., etc. Served with Am. Red Cross, overseas, 1918-19. Mem. Sons of Revolution. Democrat. Presbyn. Mason. Home: Antrim, N.H. Office: 15 Exchange Place, Jersey City, N.J.

JAMIESON, Crawford, lawyer; b. Trenton, N.J., June 13, 1902; s. M. William and Mary Ellen (Crawford) J.; ed. Princeton U., 1920-22, N.J. Law Sch., Newark, 1923-26; m. Mary Reddan, June 19, 1931; children—Martha Reddan, Mary Crawford, Thomas Crawford, Ellen Reddan. Admitted to N.J. bar as atty., 1927; engaged in gen. practice of law as individual at Trenton since 1928; also mem. firm Stockton & Jamieson, Princeton since 1936; served as mem. N.J. Ho. Assembly for Mercer Co., 1934-36, mem. N.J. Senate for terms, 1937-40. Mem. Am. Bar Assn., Mercer Co. Bar Assn. Democrat. Clubs: Trenton, Princeton of Trenton, Trenton Country. Home: Ivy Ct., Trenton. Office: 1 W. State St., Trenton; also, 90 Nassau St., Princeton, N.J.

JAMIESON, Lewis Crary, law and oil marketing; b. Warren, Pa., Aug. 3, 1889; s. Marcus W. and Emily (Crary) J.; ed. Williams Coll., 1908-10; LL.B., U. of Pa. Law Sch., 1913; m. Julia Bliss Chapin, Apr. 10, 1915 (dec.); children—Elizabeth Chapin (Mrs. Robert J. Lay), Emily Chapin; m. 2d, Mary A. Botchford, Warren, Pa., Mar. 16, 1922; children—Mary Botchford, Lewis Crary, Jr. Admitted to Pa. bar, 1913; mgr. Warren Refining Co., 1914-15; sec. Clarendon Refining Co., 1915-19; propr. Viking Oil Co., 1920-26, vice-pres. and gen. mgr. Viking Oil Corpn., 1926-32; pres. and dir. Warren Refining Co. since 1933; treas. and dir. Refiners Car Corpn.; pres. and dir. The Bey Mines, Ltd.; sec. and dir. Warren Airways, Inc. Served on Pa. Com. of Safety during World War. Mem. Phi Delta Theta, Phi Delta Phi. Republican. Episcopalian. Clubs: Conewango, Country. Home: Conewango Av. Office. 311 Market St., Warren, Pa.

JAMISON, David Lee, educator; b. Morgantown, W.Va., Oct. 15, 1867; s. John and Cinderella (Lynch) J.; B.A., U. of W.Va., 1888, LL.B., 1890; grad. study, Columbia U. Law Sch., 1890-91; U. of Chicago Div. Sch., 1894-95; grad. Rochester Theol. Sem., 1900; Th.D., Eastern Bapt. Theol. Sem., 1928; s. Janet Browse, Aug. 15, 1895; children—Donald (dec.), Mabel (dec.), Lee Browse, Gordon McLaren. In practice of law at Parkersburg, W. Va., 1891-94; ordained ministry Bapt. Ch., 1895; pastor Gas City, Ind., 1895-98, Fredonia, N.Y., 1900-05, Albion, N.Y., 1905-13, Albany, N.Y., 1915-25; prof. philosophy of religion, Eastern Bapt. Theol. Sem., Phila., since 1925. Y.M.C.A. sec. and acting chaplain of Machine-Gun Center, Camp Hancock, World War. Mem. Alpha Tau Omega. Republican. Mason (32°. Shriner; Grand Chaplain Masonic Order of N.Y. State, 2 yrs.). Clubs: Penn Athletic, St. Davids Golf (Philadelphia). Author: The Resurrection of Jesus, Considered from the Lawyer's Viewpoint, 1923; Philosophy Studies Religion, 1937. Traveled in Europe and the Orient. Home: St. Davids, Pa.

JAMISON, Jay N., life ins.; b. Emlenton, Pa., Feb. 15, 1883; s. Jeremiah T. and Mary Jane (Thomas) J.; ed. high sch.; m. Madelyn Helen Gantner, June 6, 1918; 1 son, Robert Gantner. With Reliance Life Ins. Co. since 1903, beginning as clerk; asst. sec., 1909-30, actuary, 1920-35, v.p., 1930-35, exec. v.p. and dir. since 1935. Mem. Pittsburgh Chamber of Commerce. Mason. Club: Pittsburgh Athletic. Home: Sunnyhill Farm, R.D. 2, McDonald, Pa. Office: Farmers Bank Bldg., Fifth Av. and Wood St., Pittsburgh, Pa.

JANES, Robert Brown, radio engring.; b. Burlington, Mass., Feb. 2, 1909; s. George Milton and Mary Alice (Helme) J.; ed. Washington and Jefferson Coll., 1924-25; B.S., Kenyon Coll., Gambier, O., 1928; grad. study, Harvard U., 1928-29; Ph.D., U. of Wis., 1935; unmarried. Engaged as instr. physics, Colgate U., 1929-31; asst. in physics, U. of Wis., 1931-35; engr. RCA Mfg. Co., Inc., Harrison, N.J., since 1935. Mem. Inst. Radio Engrs., Phi Beta Kappa, Sigma Xi, Gamma Alpha. Republican. Episcopalian. Mason. Contbr. articles on television to sci. publs. Home: 18 W. Van Ness Av., Rutherford. Office: RCA Mfg. Co., Inc., Harrison, N.J.

JANEWAY, Augustine S., exec. dir. Pa. Gen. State Authority; b. Huntingdon, Pa., Apr. 10, 1885; s. John L. and Linnard (Hildeburn) J.; midshipman U.S. Naval Acad., Annapolis, 1904-06 (resigned); m. Helen Gulick, Oct. 4, 1919; children—Helen, Julia, Augustine. Active in Pa. Nat. Guard since 1906, serving in infantry, cavalry and artillery; aid-de-camp to Maj. Gen. Charles M. Clements, 7th Div., Pa. Nat. Guard, during Mexican Border Campaign; commissioned capt. 28th Div., U.S. Army 1917; ordered to France, 1917, in advance of his division and attached to 57th Brit. Div. in Belgian trenches; assigned to 28th Regt., 1st Div., A.E.F., in Toul Sector and Cantigny later transferred as asst. chief of staff, 28th Div.; June 1918, assigned as asst. corps intelligence officer, 2d Army Corps; disch. Feb. 1919; aided in reorganizing Pa. Nat. Guard after war as asst. chief of staff, 28th Div.; apptd. dep. adj. gen., 1935; commd. col., 1935. Apptd. commander of all Commonwealth activities in flood of 1936; in charge of flood relief in Ohio and Mississippi River valleys, 1937; apptd. mil. comdr. when martial law was proclaimed in Cambria Co., 1937. Exec. dir. Pa. Gen. State Authority since Feb. 1937, in charge of $65,000,000 building program. Awarded Meritorious Service Medal by Gov. Earle, 1938, for "efficiency, leadership and fortitude" as chmn. Commonwealth Flood Relief Com. Mem. Am. Legion, Vets. of Foreign Wars, Mil. Order of World War, Soc. of Colonial Wars, Sons Am. Revolution. Clubs: Army and Navy, Army and Navy Country (Washington, D.C.); Harrisburg (Harrisburg, Pa.). Home: 1728 N. 2d St. Office: 2d and Locust Sts., Harrisburg, Pa.

JANNELLI, Vincent, artist and instr.; b. Andretta, Italy, Aug. 29, 1882; s. Joseph and Antonia (Del Franco) J.; came to U.S., 1898, naturalized, 1912; student Nat. Acad. of Design, N.Y. City, 1904-06, Royal Inst. Fine Arts, Naples, Italy, 1906-09, Rutgers U., New Brunswick, N.J., 1920-21, Columbia U., 1922-23; unmarried. Has followed profession as artist and instr. in art since 1909, at Newark, N.J., since 1922; art instr. Rutgers U., summer 1922; art instr. Newark Pub. Sch. of Fine and Industrial Art since 1922; exhibited at annual exhbns. Pa. Acad. Fine Arts, Phila., 1935, 36, 38, 39, Nat. Acad. of Design, N.Y. City, 1936, 15th Biennial Exhbn. of Contemporary Am. Oil Paintings, 1937, Corcoran Gallery of Art, N.J. State Annual Exhbns. at Montclair Art Mus., 1932-38, Newark Art Club Annual Exhbns. since 1931, N.J. Gallery, Spring Art Exhbns., Kresge Dept. Store, 1934-39. Awarded Kresge Popular Vote Prizes, 1934, 1938. Mem. Dante Alighieri Soc. Republican. Catholic. Home: 189 Hunterdon St., Newark, N.J.

JANNEY, Stuart Symington, lawyer; b. Harford Co., Md., Oct. 9, 1874; s. Johns Hopkins and Carolyn (Symington) J.; student Friends' Sch., Darlington, N.Y., 1884-88, Baltimore City Coll., 1889-91, Marstons Univ. Sch, 1891-92; A.B., Johns Hopkins U., 1895; LL.B., U. of Md., 1900; m. Frances M. Spencer, Nov. 29, 1905; children—Stuart Symington, J. Spencer, Elizabeth S., Richard M. Admitted to bar, 1901; mem. firm Ritchie, Janney, Ober and Williams, Baltimore; dir. Cottman Co., Am. Totaliator Co. Served as capt., maj., U.S. Vol., Inf., 1898-1900, maj., lt. col., U.S. Army, 1917-19. Dir. Md. Jockey Club. Awarded Div. Citation, World War. Democrat. Clubs: Maryland, Green Spring Valley Hunt (Baltimore, Md.). Home: Garrison P.O., Md. Office: Baltimore Trust Bldg., Baltimore, Md.

JANNEY, Walter Coggeshall, pres. Janney & Co.; b. Phila., Pa., June 25, 1876; s. Emmor K. and Mary Rhoads (Coggeshall) J.; grad. Wm. Penn Charter Sch.; A.B., Haverford Coll., 1898; student U. of Pa. Law Sch., 1898-1900; m. Pauline Flower Morris, Jan. 23, 1909; children—Walter C., Marian Morris, Anne F. (Mrs. Cumings), Margaret Morris, Priscilla Paul, Wistar Morris. Engaged in ranching in Wyo., 1900-04; mem. firm Janney & Burrough, sole leather mfrs., 1905-11; became employed by Montgomery, Clothier & Tyler, bankers, 1911, mem. same firm and successors, Montgomery & Co., 1913-21;

pres. Montgomery & Co., Inc. (now Janney & Co.) since 1921; dir. Boone County Coal Corpn., Second and Third Sts. Passenger Ry. Co. Mem. bd. Bryn Mawr Hosp., Haverford Coll., Philadelphia Museum of Art. Clubs: Philadelphia, Rittenhouse, Racquet, Radnor Hunt, Merion Cricket, Union League (Pa.); Boca Raton, Gulf Stream Golf (Fla.); Woods Hole Golf (Mass.). Home: Bryn Mawr Av., Bryn Mawr, Pa. Office: 1529 Walnut St., Philadelphia, Pa.

JANSSEN, Henry, textile mfr.; b. Barmen, Germany, Feb. 8, 1866; s. Wilhelm Albert and Anna Elisabeth Helena (Benner) J.; ed. tech. schs., Germany, and evening schs., Brooklyn, N.Y.; m. Wilhelmina Raeker, Sept. 25, 1890; children—Harry Frederick (dec.), Minnie Elsie (Mrs. John E. Livingood), Helen (Mrs. Richard C. Wetzel), Elsie (dec.). Came to U.S., 1888, naturalized, 1894. In mfg. bus., Reading, since 1892; pres. Textile Machine Works, Narrow Fabric Co., Delta Realty Co., Tulpehocken Farms, Inc., Henry Janssen Securities Co., Henry Janssen Foundation, North Wyomissing Heights Water Co.; v.p. Berkshire Knitting Mills, Delta Finance Co., Peoples Trust Co., Wyomissing Development Co.; dir. Berks County Trust Co., Wyomissing Building and Savings Assn., Wyomissing Disposal Co., Wyomissing Polytechnic Inst., Oberlaender Trust. Vice-pres. Carl Schurz Memorial Foundation; pres. bd. of mgrs. Reading Hosp.; affiliated with various philanthropic activities through Henry Janssen Foundation, Carl Schurz Memorial Foundation and Oberlaender Trust. Mem. borough council, Wyomissing, Pa., since 1906, Am. Academy of Polit. and Social Science, Am. Civic Assn., Army Ordinance Assn., Deutsche Verein (N.Y.), German Club, Tech. Soc. of Phila., German Soc. of Pa., Nat. Assn. of Audubon Socs., Nat. Municipal League. Clubs: Manufacturers, Automobile (Phila.); Wyomissing, Automobile, Country (Reading); Iris (Wyomissing); Berkshire Country. Home: Reading Boul., Wyomissing, Pa. Office: Reading, Pa.

JAQUETTE, Mrs. Henrietta Stratton, welfare worker; b. Stockton, Mo., Dec. 20, 1881; d. Daniel P. and Arabel (Barnes) Stratton; A.B., U. of Mich., 1904; A.M., U. of Pa., 1906; m. William A. Jaquette, June 14, 1907; children—William A., Arabel, Daniel Stratton, John Joseph. Prof. history, Western Coll. for Women, Oxford, O., 1906-07; lecturer on civics and current events. Pres. Delaware County Welfare Council since 1929; chmn. Delaware Co. Bd. of Pub. Assistance, 1938. V.p. Pa. Pub. Charities Assn. since 1935; pres. State Conf. on Social Work, 1936-37. Mem. Delta Gamma. Quaker. Club: Philadelphia Womens University. Wrote articles on social work adminstrn. in Pa. Editor: South After Gettysburg, Letters of Cornelia Hancock, 1937. Home: 605 Elm Av., Swarthmore, Pa.

JARMAN, G. W.; chmn. bd. Farmers & Merchants Bank. Address: Salisbury, Md.

JARRETT, Benjamin, congressman; b. Sharon, Pa., July 18, 1881; ed. pub. schs., Wheatland, Pa.; m. Agnes Boyle; children—Dorothy (Mrs. A. L. Brintz), Fred. Admitted to Pa. bar, 1907, and practiced in Farrell; mem. Pa. State Senate, 1911-13, Pa. State Workmen's Compensation Bd., 1919-23; mem. 75th and 76th Congresses (1937-41), 20th Pa. Dist. Home: 1209 Haywood St., Farrell, Pa.

JARRETT, Clarence L.; commr. of labor, State of W.Va., term expires 1941. Home: 809 Pennsylvania Av. Office: State Capitol, Charleston, W.Va.

JARRETT, Cora Hardy, novelist; b. Norfolk, Va., Feb. 21, 1877; d. Frederick and Charlotte Frances (Graves) Hardy; student Pollock-Stephens Inst., Birmingham, Ala., 1890-94; Miss Baldwin's Sch., Bryn Mawr., Pa., 1894-95; B.A., Bryn Mawr Coll., 1899; post grad. Sorbonne, Coll. de France, and Oxford U., Eng., 1899-1900; m. Edwin Seton Jarrett, C.E., June 26, 1906; children—Edwin Seton, William Armistead, Olivia Heather. Teacher English and Greek, Ward-Belmont Sem., Nashville, Tenn., 1902-03, of English, St. Timothy's Sch., Catonsville, Md., 1903-06. Clubs: Womans, Shepherdstown, W. Va., Cosmopolitan, New York; Present Day, Princeton, N.J. Author: The Cross Goes Westward, 1910; Peccadilloes, 1929; Night Over Fitch's Pond, 1933; Pattern in Black and Red (under pen name of Faraday Keene), 1934; The Ginkgo Tree, 1935; Strange Houses, 1936; I Asked No Other Thing, 1937; The Silver String, 1937. Contbr. fiction to mags. Home: Wild Goose Farm, Shepherdstown, W.Va.; and 144 Mercer St., Princeton, N.J.*

JARVIS, Anna (M.), founder of "Mother's Day"; d. Granville E. and Anna M. (Reeves) Jarvis; ed. private and public schools; unmarried. Long active in temperance movement and woman suffrage; founder of internationally observed Mother's Day as second Sunday in May; succeeded in having it officially recognized by Congress which in 1914 authorized annual display of U.S. flag on Capitol, consulates, etc.; now engaged in promotion of Mother's Day observance as pres. Mother's Day, Inc. Planned the official observance of Mother's Day for allied Army and Navy during the World War. Author of booklets, and plans for observance of Mother's Day. Address: Box 3473, Philadelphia, Pa.

JARVIS, Hugh; pres. Union Nat. Bank. Address: Clarksburg, W.Va.

JASPAN, Harry Jerome, lawyer; b. Phila., Pa., Aug. 28, 1897; s. Wolf and Anna (Zeeve) J.; A.B., Central High Sch., Phila., Pa., 1915; LL.B., Temple U. Law Sch., 1924; m. Florence Hirsch, Apr. 29, 1937. Admitted to Pa. bar, 1924, and since engaged in gen. practice of law at Phila.; served as asst. city solicitor, City of Phila., 1925-32; spl. dep. atty. gen. of Pa., 1934-36; mem. Pa. Senate for 4 yrs. from 1936. Home: 824 N. 7th St. Office: Market St. Nat. Bank Bldg., Philadelphia, Pa.

JAYNE, Horace Howard Furness, archæologist; b. Cape May, N.J., June 9, 1898; s. Horace and Caroline Augusta (Furness) J.; A.B., Harvard University, 1919; A.M., University of Pa., 1933; m. Henrietta M. E. Bache, 1928. With Pa. Museum since 1921, assistant, 1921-23, curator of Oriental art, 1923-26, chief of Eastern div. and curator of sculpture since 1926; dir. Museum of U. of Pa. Mem. 1st China expdn. of Fogg Museum of Harvard, 1923-24; mem. 2d expdn., field agt. in Asia for Harvard, 1924-25. Dir. Library Co. of Phila., Fairmount Park Art Assn.; pres. Edwin Forrest Home. Mem. Gesellschaft für Ostasiatische Kunst (Berlin), Am. Philos. Soc.; awarded Royal Crown of Italy. Clubs: Philadelphia (Phila.); Harvard (New York). Editor: Letters of Horace Howard Furness, 1920. Home: Wallingford, Pa. Office: University Museum, Philadelphia, Pa.

JEFFERIS, J. Walter, banker; b. Chester Co., Pa., Dec. 5, 1880; s. Thomas K. and Annie (Thomas) J.; student Martin Acad., Kennett Square, Pa., 1897-98; m. Elizabeth B. Pusey, Sept. 30, 1908. With Nat. Bank of Avondale (Pa.), 1898-1907; sec. and treas. Kennett Trust Co., Kennett Square, Pa., 1907-25, pres., 1925-30; with Nat. Bank & Trust Co., Kennett Square, since July 1930, as vice-pres. and trust officer, 1930-38, pres. since June 1938; dir. Bldg. and Loan Assn. of London Grove, Avondale, Pa.; dir. Progressive Bldg. & Loan Assn., Kennett Square. Dir. Kennett Consol. Sch., Kennett Square. Republican. Mem. Soc. of Friends. Mason (K.T., Shriner). Club: Kennett Square Golf and Country. Address: Kennett Square, Pa.

JEFFERS, Charles W.; pres. Wheeling Clearing House. Address: Wheeling, W.Va.

JEFFERS, Henry William; b. Harford, Pa., Jan. 4, 1871; s. Watson and Betsey Milburn (Oakley) J.; grad. Wyoming Sem., Kingston, Pa., 1894; B.S., Cornell U., 1899; hon. M.S., Rutgers U., N.J. Agrl. Coll., 1927; m. Anna C. Adams, July 14, 1898; children—Emily Adams, Watson (dec.), Henry W., Louise E. Mgr. Walker-Gordon Lab. Co., 1898-1918, pres. since 1918; dir. First Nat. Bank, Princeton, N.J. Mem. advisory bds., U.S. Dept. Agr. and U.S. Food Administration, World War; mem. N.J. State Bd. of Agr., 1916-27. Pres. Bd. Regents, N.J.; mem. bd. mgrs. N.J. Reformatory. Chmn. N.J. Rep. State Com., 1935-37. Conglist. Mason (32°, K.T., Shriner). Inventor of Jeffers bacteriology counter, Jeffers feed calculator, Rotolactor. Home: Plainsboro, N.J.

JEFFERS, Horace Carpenter, lawyer; b. Central Falls, R.I., Jan. 14, 1897; s. Horace and Alice Emma (Johnson) J.; student pub. schs., Central Falls, R.I., and Brattleboro, Vt., 1902-14; A.B., Brown U., Providence, R.I., 1918; student Law School, New York U., 1919-21; unmarried. Practicing atty. with firm King & Vogt, Morristown, N.J., since 1921; dir. Morristown Trust Co. Entered U.S. Army during coll., commd. 2d lt., F.A., 1918. Asst. U.S. atty., Dist. of N.J., 1929-31; dep. co. dir. Emergency Relief Administrn., 1931-35; chmn. Morristown Central Rep. Com., 1930-36. Trustee Morristown Sch. since 1936, Morristown Memorial Hosp. since 1935, Morristown Chapter Am. Red Cross since 1924, Morristown Neighborhood House since 1929. Mem. Am. Legion (N.J. Dept. vice-comdr., 1931-32), Morris Co. Bar Assn., Phi Beta Kappa, Sigma Phi Epsilon, Phi Delta Phi. Republican. Episcopalian. Mason (Morristown Lodge 188). Club: Brown University (New York). Home: 25 Colles Av. Office: 10 Washington St., Morristown, N.J.

JEFFERSON, Miles Matthew, coll. librarian; b. Parkersburg, W.Va., Nov. 9, 1905; s. John Rupert and Clara (Thomas) J.; grad. Sumner High Sch., Parkersburg, W.Va., 1923; A.B., magna cum laude, W.Va. State Coll., Institute, W.Va., 1927; A.M., Columbia, 1930, grad. student Sch. of Library Service, 1938-39; unmarried. Librarian W.Va. State Coll. since July 1, 1928. Mem. Am. Library Assn., Alpha Phi Alpha. Republican. Methodist. Home: Canty's Institute, W.Va. Office: Library, W.Va. State Coll., Institute, W.Va.

JEFFERY, Frank Moore, investment banker, retired; b. Corning, N.Y., Aug. 11, 1855; s. Edwin Avery and Mary Fletcher (Lee) J.; ed. schs., Corning, N.Y., New Haven, Conn., and Jersey City, N.J.; m. Frances Philene Campbell, Apr. 30, 1883 (died 1925); 1 son, F. Campbell Jeffery; m. 2d, Anna Caroline Hill, Sept. 8, 1926. Established printing business of Jeffery & Johnston, N.Y. City; later mem. firm Jeffery & Co., mfrs. springs and elec. goods; charter mem., dir., sec. and treas. Crocker-Wheeler Co., now Crocker-Wheeler Electric & Mfg. Co., Ampere, N.J., 1893-1900; engaged in investment banking as Frank Moore Jeffery, New York City, 1900-25; was dir. a number of banks and corpns.; inventor automatic spring machinery, revolving tempering oven, electric and other devices; retired from business, 1925, to engage in mus., lit. and art pursuits; painter various subjects in oil; exhibited at Palm Beach Art League; composer music-drama, anthems, sacred and secular songs pub. by well-known pub. houses. Mem. Palm Beach Art League, Order of Bookfellows. Graduate and mem. Chautauqua Hall in the Grove. Republican. Methodist. Contbr. music articles and verse to mags. and journs. Home: 82 Franklin Av., Ocean Grove, N.J.

JEFFERY, John Frederick, educator; b. Erie, Pa., Apr. 1, 1894; s. Fred and Helen Elizabeth (Stinchcomb) J.; grad. Harborcreek (Pa.) High Sch., 1912; B.S., Bucknell U., 1916, A.M., 1923; summer sch. and extension student U. of Pittsburgh; m. Alice Marie Hines, Aug. 16, 1917; children—Richard Clayton, Dorothy Margaret. Mech. engr. Bucyrus-Erie Shovel Co., 1916-17, Gen. Electric Co., 1917-18, Erie City Iron Works, 1918-20; teacher, Erie Pub. Schools, 1920-30, prin. Evening Sch., 1929-31, prin. Erie Tech. High Sch., 1931-38, dir. vocational edn. since 1937; visiting lecturer, U. of Pittsburgh since 1939. Served in U.S. Army, Aug.-Sept., 1917. Mem. Erie Teachers Assn., Pa. and Nat. Secondary Sch. Principals' Assns., Pa. State Edn. Assn., N.E.A., Pa. Vocational Assn., Am. Vocational Assn. Ind. Republican. Mem. United Presbyn. Ch. (trustee). Mason. Clubs: Lions, South Erie Turn Verein (Erie). Author: Mathematics for Metal Work, 1925; Machine Shop Projects (with Harry L. Cotter), 1927. Contbr. articles to Industrial Edn. Mag. Home: 919 W. 32d St. Office: Library Bldg., Erie, Pa.

JEFFERY, Oscar W., lawyer; b. Washington, N.J., June 7, 1872; s. Oscar and Emma (Wilde) J.; stud. Bordentown Mil. Inst., 1887-90; A.B., Princeton U., 1894; LL.B., New York Law Sch., 1896; m. Harriet Blythe, June 4, 1908 (died

1931); children—Suzanne Blythe, Frances, Margaret. Admitted to N.Y. State bar, 1896, becoming associated with law firm Wetmore & Jenner, became mem. firm, 1910; now mem. successor firm, Jeffery, Kimball & Eggleston, specializing mainly in patent, trade-mark, copyright and estate matters. Mem. and former pres. Englewood (N.J.) Bd. of Edn.; v.p. and mem. bd. N.J. State Bd. of Edn. since 1918. Mem. Am. Bar Assn., N.Y. State Bar Assn., Bar Assn of City of N.Y., Am. Patent Law Assn., New York Patent Law Assn. (past pres.). Republican. Presbyn. Clubs: Downtown Assn. (New York); Englewood, Englewood Field (Englewood); Colonial (Princeton); Knickerbocker Country (Tenafly, N.J.). Home: 185 Lincoln St., Englewood, N.J. Office: 20 Pine St., New York, N.Y.

JEFFERYS, Edward Miller, clergyman; b. Philadelphia, May 4, 1865; s. Charles Peter Beauchamp and Elizabeth (Miller) J.; A.B., U. of Pa., 1886, B.D., 1889, S.T.D., 1909; grad. Berkeley Div. Sch., 1889; m. Amy E. Faulconer, Apr. 24, 1895; children—Robert Faulconer, Charles Peter Beauchamp, Edward Miller (dec.). Deacon, 1889, priest, 1890, P.E. Ch.; curate, St. Peter's Ch., Phila., 1889; asst. rector St. John's Ch., Detroit, 1890-94; rector St. Paul's Ch., Doylestown, Pa., 1894-1902, Emmanuel Parish, Cumberland, Md., 1902-06; archdeacon Western Md., 1904-06; rector St. Peter's Church, Phila., 1906-37. Del. to Gen. Conv. P.E. Ch., 1919, 22, 25; pres. Standing Com. Diocese Pa. Chaplains U.S.A., May 1917-May 1919, in France, now major (chaplain) auxiliary, U.S.A. Clubs: Philadelphia, Army and Navy of Phila., British Officers Club of Phila., Corinthian Yacht (fleet chaplain); Penn Manor (Morrisville, Pa.). Author of numerous published sermons, addresses, etc. Home: Wheel Pump Lane, Chestnut Hill, Philadelphia, Pa.

JEFFERYS, William Hamilton, M.D., author, misisonary; b. Philadelphia, Pa., July 3 1871; s. Charles Peter Beauchamp and Elizabeth (Miller) J.; A.B., U. of Pa., 1894, A.M., 1897, M.D., 1898; m. Lucy Sturgis Hubbard, 1897 (deceased); children—Anne, Lucy Sturgis, Adelaide McCulloh, William Hamilton; m. 2d, Ann E. Prophet, 1931. Surgeon St. Luke's Hosp., Shanghai, 1901-13; prof. surgery, St. John's U., Shanghai, 1905-13; editor China Med. Jour., 1902-13; supt. Phila. City Mission, since 1915, and editor of The City Misisonary. Lecturer on Christian mysticism, Church Training School, Philadelphia, since 1915. President American Association of China, 1909-10; mem. China Med. Missionary Assn. (research, publn. and exec. cons.), Am. Soc. Tropical Medicine, Royal Asiatic Soc., Soc. Tropical Medicine, London, Delta Phi: fellow Coll. of Physicians of Phila.; hon. fellow China Med. Soc. (China). Episcopalian. Clubs: Shanghai, Shanghai Country (China); Authors' (London); Philadelphia, St. Elmo (Philadelphia). Author: The Great Mystery, 1900; Hospital Dialogue (in Shanghai dialect), 1906, (in Pekinese Mandarin), 1908; The Diseases of China, 1910; Life of Bishop Ingle, 1913; The Mystical Companionship of Jesus, 1919; The Shuffling Coolie, and Other Plays, 1913; How Can We Know the Way? 1921; The City Mission Idea, 1922; The Mystical Assurance of Immortality, 1924; Reasonable Faith; The Discovery of God; The Key to Divine Reality, 1934. Home: County Line Rd., Rosemont, Pa. Office: 225 S. 3d St., Philadelphia, Pa.

JEFFREY, Lon Cyrus, ins.; b. Fayette Co., Ind., Dec. 4, 1881; s. Cyrus and Olive (Moffitt) J.; student Fairview (Ind.) Grade and Jr. High Schs., 1887-95, Connersville (Ind.) Sr. High Sch., 1895-98, Business and Ins. Sch. U. of Pittsburgh, 1918-19; m. Alice Lynn Whitehead, June 25, 1905 (died 1931); 1 dau., Eileen Jane (Mrs. Carl Edward Lang); m. 2d, Anna Marie Domke, June 25, 1933. Began as salesman in men's furnishing store, Indianapolis, Ind., 1899-1906; dist. agent, Gen. Accident Ins. Co., Hamilton, O., 1906-07; asst. state spl. agt. for State of Ohio with Pa. Casualty Ins. Co., 1907-10, mgr. Pittsburgh office, 1910-12; mgr. Pittsburgh office Mass. Bonding and Ins. Co., 1912-13, mgr. accident and health depts., Mass. Bonding and Ins. Co. Home Office, 1914-15; formed Lon C. Jeffrey Co., Pittsburgh, gen. ins., 1915, and since pres.; mem. of firm Fahnestock & Jeffrey, Pittsburgh, realtors; sec.-treas. Pa. Registry Co., Nat. Placing and Underwriters Agency. Mem. Ins. Fed. of Pa., Pa. State Ins. Agts. Assn., Nat. Ins. Agts. Assn., Fire and Casualty Council, Pittsburgh Life Underwriters Assn., Pittsburgh Real Estate Bd., Pa. State, Nat. assns. of real estate bd., Pittsburgh Chamber of Commerce, Pittsburgh Accident and Health Assn. (dir.). Republican. Methodist. Mason (Crescent Lodge 576). Clubs: Keystone Athletic, Alcoma Country, Metropolitan, Pittsburgh Athletic, Insurance (Pittsburgh); Pa. Soc. (N.Y.). Home: Cathedral Mansions. Office: 324 4th Av., Pittsburgh, Pa.

JEFFRIES, Charles S., pres. Potomac Coal Co.; b. Frostburg, Md., Nov. 7, 1877; s. Samuel and Mary Susan (Hocking) Jeffries. Began in mining engr. corps, Consolidation Coal Co., Frostburg, Md., 1892, chief clk., 1903-12; managing partner, Annan & Jeffries since 1917; operating Frostburg (Md.) Big Vein Georges Creek Coal Co. since 1917; v.p. and dir. First Nat. Bank, Frostburg, Md., since 1914; pres. Potomac Coal Co., Inc., Frostburg, Md., since 1920; owner C. S. Jeffries Lumber Yard since 1914, Indian Hen Lumber Co., W.Va., since 1911; sales agt. A. P. Hoffa Coal Co., Barton, Md., since 1930. Pres. Miners Hosp., Frostburg, 1930-34; dir. Cumberland Fair Assn. Republican since 1932. Elk (Life). Club: Cumberland Country (Cumberland, Md.). Home: 68 W. Union, Frostburg, Md.

JENCKES, Earl S., receiver Fairy Silk Mills; b. Woonsocket, R.I., May 9, 1872; s. George W. and Martha (Hunt) J.; ed. Mass. Inst. Tech.; m. Grace Rankin, Dec. 9, 1897; children—Louise, George A. Salesman Draper Co., U.S. and Europe, 1895-1901; mng. dir. British Northrop Loom Co., Manchester, England, 1902-03; returned to U.S., 1904; supt. Paul Whitin Mfg. Co., 1904-08, Evansville Cotton Mills, 1909; successively supt., v.p. and pres. Joseph Bancroft & Sons Co. of Pa., 1910-31, retired; receiver Fairy Silk Mills since 1934; dir. Joseph Bancroft & Sons Co., Eddystone Mfg. Co. Mem. Wyomissing Borough Council. Pres. Wyomissing Pub. Library Assn. Clubs: Wyomissing, Berkshier Country. Home: 403 Wyomissing Boul., Wyomissing, Pa. Office: Shillington, Pa.

JENCKS, Millard Henry, publisher; b. Gravesville, N.Y., Nov. 5, 1881; s. George Rufus and Estelle (Payne) J.; B.S., St. Lawrence U., 1905; m. Ruth Kimball, 1909; 1 son, Kimball. Teacher and prin., pub. schs., 1905-09; admitted to N.Y. bar, 1908; asso. with Ginn and Co. since 1909, partner since 1923. Dir. War Camp Community Service, Camp Upton, 1917-18. Trustee St. Lawrence U., 1923-33, chmn. of bd. since 1934; mem. Council for Conf. on Canadian-Am. Affairs since 1935. Mem. Alpha Tau Omega, Phi Beta Kappa. Clubs: University, Salmagundi (N.Y. City), Golf (Montclair, N.J.). Home: 74 Overlook Rd., Upper Montclair, N.J. Office: 70 5th Av., New York, N.Y.

JENKINS, Arthur Hugh, editor; b. West Chester, Pa., Dec. 5, 1880; s. Howard Malcolm and Mary Anna (Atkinson) J.; grad. George Sch., Newtown, Pa., 1898; B.L., Swarthmore, 1901; m. Ann T. Roberts, June 2, 1915. Associated with uncle, Wilmer Atkinson, and brother, Charles F. Jenkins, in publication of The Farm Journal, 1903-35; circulation mgr. same, 1906-20, editor since 1921. Treasurer Farm Journal, Inc.; president Griscom Hall Association, Inc. Mem. American Country Life Assn., Assn. of Agrl. Editors, Agrl. History Assn., Am. Farm Economic Assn., Delta Upsilon. Republican. Quaker. Clubs: Nat. Press, Old York Road Country. Home: Jenkintown, Pa. Office: 230 S. 7th St., Philadelphia, Pa.

JENKINS, Charles Francis, publisher; b. Norristown, Pa., Dec. 17, 1865; s. Howard M. and Mary Anna (Atkinson) J.; ed. pub. schs.; LL.D., Haverford Coll., 1938; m. Maria G., d. Edward Cope, Feb. 12, 1890; children—Algernon Sidney, Mrs. Newlin T. Booth, C. Francis, Edward Cope. Pub. since 1883; dir. Farm Jour., Inc., Provident Trust Co., Commonwealth Title Co., Provident Title Ins. Co.; pres. Buck Hill Falls Co.; treas. Deemer Steel Casting Co., Buck Hill Water Co., Jeanes Hosp., Friends Intelligencer. Pres. bd. mgrs. Swarthmore Coll.; pres. Grandom Instn., Abolition Soc., v.p. English-Speaking Union (Phila. br.), Geneal. Soc. Pa.; v.p. council Hist. Soc. Pa.; hon. mem. Phi Beta Kappa. Mem. Society of Friends (Quaker). Author: Quaker Poems, a collection of verse relating to the Society of Friends, 1893; Guide Book to Historic Germantown, 1902; Washington in Germantown, 1905; Jefferson's Germantown Letters, 1906; Lafayette's Visit to Germantown, 1911; Tortola, 1923; Button Gwinnett—Signer of the Declaration, 1926. Established Hemlock Arboretum, "Far Country," 1932. Home: "Far Country," Kitchen's Lane, Germantown. Office: 232 S. 7th St., Philadelphia, Pa.

JENKINS, George Herbert, lawyer; b. Gwynedd, Montgomery Co., Pa., May 9, 1871; s. Algernon Sidney and Alice Ash (Davis) J.: grad. Friends Central Sch., Phila., 1888; LL.B., U. of Pa., 1893; m. Jessie Stockton Allen, Oct. 11, 1893 (deceased); 1 son, Dudley Allen; m. 2d, Mary Schofield Ash, June 9, 1903; children—Sarah Ash, Elisabeth Alice (Mrs. James Leland Dresser), Eleanor Foulke, Mary Schofield (Mrs. Harvey H. Valentine). Admitted to Pa. bar, 1893; dir. and counsel Perkiomen Valley Mutual Fire Ins. Co.; dir. and counsel Peoples Bldg. & Loan Assn. of North Wales. Vice-pres. and counsel Trustees of Phila. Yearly Meeting of Friends; treas. and counsel Incorporated Trustees Abington Quarterly Meeting of Friends; pres. and counsel Trustees Gwynedd Monthly Meeting of Friends. Trustee Schofield Normal and Industrial Sch., Aiken, S.C. Mem. Am., Pa. State, Phila. and Montgomery County bar assns., Welsh Soc. of Phila., Miller Law Club. Republican. Clubs: Lawyers (Phila.); Rotary of North Wales (past pres.). Home: Gwynedd, Montgomery Co., Pa. Office: Commercial Trust Bldg., Philadelphia, Pa.; 415 Swede St., Norristown, Pa.

JENKINS, John Clair, prin. city schs.; b. Crawford Co., Pa., Apr. 12, 1889; s. George Mark and Minerva (Watson) J.; A.B., Grove City Coll., 1914; M.Edn., U. of Pittsburgh, 1936; grad. study, Pa. State Coll., summers 1937-38; m. Rhea Myers, Dec. 31, 1919; children—Priscilla Mae, Richard Myers and John Robert (twins). Engaged as teacher rural schs. and graded and high schs., 1907-18; prin. high sch., Glassport, Pa., 1918-22; prin. schs., Girard, Pa., 1922-29; supervising prin. schs. Union City, Pa., since 1929. Served as pvt. inf., U.S.A., 1918. Dir. Union City Hosp., Union City Pub. Library. Mem. Nat. Edn. Assn., Pa. State Edn. Assn. Republican. Presbyn. Mason (32°). I.O.O.F. Grange. Home: 76 W. High St., Union City, Pa.

JENKINS, John E.; in gen. practice of law since 1922; local atty. for various large companies. Office: West Virginia Bldg., Huntington, W.Va.

JENKINS, John G(amewell), univ. prof.; b. South Amboy, N.J., May 30, 1901; s. Edward E. and Mary B. (Gamewell) J.; A.B., Cornell U., 1923; M.S., Ia. State Coll., Ames, Ia., 1927; grad. student U. of Ill., 1927-28; Ph.D., Cornell U., 1929; m. Valerie E. Frosch, Jan. 2, 1926; children—John Gamewell, Jr., Patricia Mavis. Instr. psychology, Ia. State Coll., Ames, Ia., 1924; asst. in psychology, U. of Ill., 1927-28; asst. in psychology, Cornell U., 1928-29; asst. prof. psychology, Ia. State Coll., 1929-30; asst. prof. psychology, Cornell U., 1930-38; prof. psychology and chmn. dept. psychology, U. of Md. since 1938. Fellow A.A.A.S. Mem. Am. Psychol. Assn., Am. Assn. Applied Psychology, Phi Kappa Phi, Sigma Xi. Author: Psychology in Business and Industry, 1935. Cooperating editor, Psychological Bulletin. Contbr. articles to psychol. jours. Home: Clagett Rd., College Park, Md.

JENKINS, T. Courtenay; partner Jenkins, Whedbee & Poe; mem. Baltimore Stock Exchange. Home: Lake Av., Roland Park. Office: 10 South St., Baltimore, Md.

JENKINS, Thomas Clifton, pres. Jenkins Arcade Co.; b. Pittsburgh, Pa., Nov. 22, 1869; s. Thomas Christopher and Eleanor Katherine

(Elliotte) J.; student U. of Western Pa. Prep. Sch. and Harvard U.; m. Clara Horton Shaw, Feb. 18, 1896; children—Elizabeth E., Mrs. Edwin M. Rhea. Pres. Jenkins Arcade Co., Pittsburgh, since 1911; dir. Fidelity Trust Co. of Pittsburgh. Trustee U. of Pittsburgh, 1908-16; dir. Pittsburgh Chamber of Commerce, 1910-12. Clubs: Harvard-Yale-Princeton, Pittsburgh, Duquesne, Pittsburgh Athletic, Longue Vue Country(Pittsburgh). Home: 801 Morewood Av. Office: Jenkins Arcade Bldg., Pittsburgh, Pa.

JENKINSON, Richard Dale, real estate and ins. broker; b. Bellevue, Pa., Sept. 22, 1882; s. William and Anna S. (Claney) J.; C.E., Cornell U., 1907; m. Helen Harvey, Nov. 6, 1913; children—Richard D., Harvey T. Engaged in real estate and insurance business since 1907, with brother, William, Jr., now operating under name of Jenkinson Realty Co.; dir. Bellevue Savings & Trust Co. Dir. Bellevue Sch. Dist., 1930-36. Mem. Phi Sigma Kappa. Republican. Episcopalian. Club: Cornell of Western Pa. Home: 15 N. Howard Av. Office: 507 Lincoln Av., Bellevue, Pa.

JENKS, John Story; b. Philadelphia, Pa., 1876; s. William H. and Hannah M. (Hacker) J.; student Haverford Coll., 1894-96; m. Isabella F. G. Morton, 1902; children—Thomas Story, Morton, Ann West. Clk. Girard Trust Co., 1897-99; partner firm Edward B. Smith & Co., bankers, 1900-08, Bertron, Griscom & Jenks, 1909-12; dir. Girard Trust Co., Fidelity-Phila. Trust Co., Ins. Co. of North America, Indemnity Ins. Co. of N. America, The Alliance Ins. Co. of Phila., Phila. Fire & Marine Ins. Co., Fidelity Bldg. Corpn., Muskogee Co., Midland Valley R.R. Co., Kan., Okla. & Gulf Ry. Co., Okla. City, Ada, Atoka Ry. Co., Pa. Salt Mfg. Co., trustee Penn Mutual Life Ins. Co. Mem. bd. mgrs. The Western Saving Fund Soc., The Morris Arboretum, Preston Retreat. Pres. Univ. Mus.; v.p. and trustee Phila. Mus. of Art (chmn. museum com.); trustee Thomas W. Evans Mus. and Inst. Soc., Fairmont Park Art Assn. Decorated Chevalier Légion d'Honneur (France), 1937. Mem. Am. Philos. Soc. Club: Philadelphia. Home: Seminole and Chestnut Avs., Chestnut Hill. Office: 123 S. Broad St., Philadelphia, Pa.

JENKS, Josephine, sculptress; b. Rye, N.Y., Dec. 30, 1903; d. Wm. P. and Bertha (Cooke) J.; student high sch. and one winter in France; art edn. under Ahron Ben Schmuel, winter 1932-33, Alfeo Faggi, Woodstock, N.Y., 1936, Milton Horn, winter 1939; m. James Carey Warren, June 9, 1923 (divorced 1936); children—Penelope, James C., Zoe. Worked with Boris Blai as asst. teacher, Oaklane Country Day Sch. of Temple U., Phila., 1931-32; has followed profession as artist, specializing in sculpture since 1931; exhibited Whitney Mus. 1st Biennial Exhbn. of Contemporary Sculpture, 1934, Century of Progress, Chicago, 1934, Montclair Mus., Newark Mus. and Exhbn. Contemporary Art, World's Fair, New York, 1939; represented in permanent collection Whitney Mus. Club: Analytical Psychology of New York. Home: Mt. Kemble Av., Morristown, N.J. Studio: 226 E. 15th St., New York, N.Y.

JENKS, Morton, investment banker; b. New York, N.Y., Jan. 26, 1907; s. John Story and Isabella Morton J.; ed. Chestnut Hill Acad., Phila., 1915-21; St. George's Sch., Newport, R.I., 1921-26; unmarried. Clerk Janney & Co., 1927-30; with Jenks, Gwynne & Co., 1931-35, mgr. Phila. office, 1932-35; partner Bioren & Co., mems. New York and Phila. Stock Exchanges and Chicago Bd. of Trade, investment banking and brokerage, since 1935; pres. and dir. Jenks Food Co.; dir. Keystone Wood Preserving Co. Member 1st City Troop, National Guard Pa., 1928-36. Treas. Com. of Seventy. Mem. bd. mgrs. Pa. Hosp., Maternity Hosp., Preston Retreat, Big Brothers Assn. Episcopalian. Clubs: Philadelphia, Racquet (Phila.); Union (New York). Home: Seminole and Chestnut Av. Office: 1508 Walnut St., Philadelphia, Pa.

JENNINGS, Burgess Hill, coll. prof., cons. engr.; b. Baltimore, Md., Sept. 12, 1903; s. Henry Hill and Mattie Whitfield (Burgess) J.; B. Engring., Johns Hopkins U., Baltimore, Md., 1925; M.S., Lehigh U., Bethlehem, Pa., 1928, M.A., 1935; m. Etta May Crout, Nov. 7, 1925; 1 son, Robert Burgess. Engr. Consol. Gas Electric Light & Power Co., Baltimore, 1924-25; Instr. and asst. prof. mech. engring, Lehigh U., Bethlehem, Pa., 1926-35, asso. prof. mech. engring. since 1935; cons. engr. Phila & Reading Coal & Iron Co., 1934-38; registered as professional engr. in Pa. Mem. Am. Soc. M.E., Am. Soc. Refrigerating Engrs., Soc. for promotion of Engring. Edn., Sigma Xi, Pi Tau Sigma, Pi Mu Epsilon (rep. on Nat. Research Council). Episcopalian. Club: Engrs. Club of Lehigh Valley (Bethlehem, Pa.). Author: Mechanical Engineering Laboratory Manual, 1930, 1937; Steam and Gas Engineering (co-author with Butterfield and Luce), 1933, 1938; Air Conditioning (co-author with Lewis), 1939; many articles in tech. jours. Research in refrigeration and internal combustion engines; inventor absorption refrigeration device. Home: 605 Norway Pl. Office: Lehigh University, Bethlehem, Pa.

JENNINGS, Dale C., lawyer; b. Pittsburgh, Pa., Sept. 28, 1879; s. William K. and Alice (Crawford) J.; grad. Shady Side Acad., Pittsburgh, 1896; A.B., Yale U., 1900; LL.B., U. of Pittsburgh Law Sch., 1903; unmarried. Admitted to bar, 1903; since in gen. practice of law; mem. firm Jennings & Jennings. Mem. Am., Pa. and Allegheny County bar assns. Republican. Presbyterian. Club: University (Pittsburgh). Home: 5226 Fifth Av. Office: 1101 Berger Bldg., Pittsburgh, Pa.

JENNINGS, Frank L.; instr. clin. surgery, Johns Hopkins U.; prof. clin. surgery, U. of Md.; asst. dispensary surgeon Johns Hopkins Hosp.; visiting surgeon Mercy and South Baltimore Gen. hosps.; surgeon Church Home and Infirmary. Address: 101 W. Read St., Baltimore, Md.

JENNINGS, Herbert Spencer, naturalist; b. Tonica, Ill., Apr. 8, 1868; s. Dr. George N. and Olive Taft (Jenks) J.; B.S., U. of Mich., 1893; A.M., Harvard, 1895, Ph.D., 1896; studied Jena (Germany), 1896-97; LL.D., Clark U., 1909; S.D., U. of Mich., 1918, University of Pa., 1933, Oberlin College, 1933; m. Mary Louise Burridge, of Tecumseh, Mich., 1898; 1 son, Burridge. Asst. prof. botany, Texas Agr. Coll., 1889-90; prof. botany, Mont. State Agrl. Coll., 1897-98; instr. zoölogy, Dartmouth Coll., 1898-99; asst. prof. zoölogy, U. of Mich., 1900-03; asst. prof. zoölogy, U. of Pa., 1903-05; prof. experimental zoölogy, 1906-10, Henry Walters prof. zoölogy and dir. zoöl. lab., 1910-38, emeritus prof. since 1938, Johns Hopkins Univ.; visiting prof., Keio University, Tokyo, 1931-32; George Eastman visiting professor and fellow of Balliol College, Oxford University, England, 1935-36; visiting prof. U. of Calif. at Los Angeles, 1939; Terry lecturer Yale University, 1933. Vanuxem lecturer, Princeton Univ., 1934. Specialist in research work on physiology of microorganisms, animal behavior, and genetics. Dir. U.S. Fish Commn. Biol. Survey of the Great Lakes, 1901; trustee Marine Biol. Lab., Woods Hole, Mass.; biometrician, U.S. Food Administration, 1917-18; mem. Nat. Research Council, 1922-25. Asso. editor Journal of Experimental Zoölogy, of Genetics, and of Biological Bulletin. Pres. American Zoöl. Society, 1908-09, American Society Naturalists, 1910-11; fellow Am. Acad. Arts and Sciences, A.A.A.S.; hon. fellow Royal Micros. Soc. Great Britain; mem. Nat. Acad. Sciences, Am. Philos. Soc., Phila. Acad. Natural Sciences; corr. member of the Russian Acad. of Science and of Société de Biologie de Paris. Author: Anatomy of the Cat (with Jacob Reighard), 1901; Behavior of Lower Organisms, 1906; Life and Death, Heredity and Evolution in Unicellular Organisms, 1919; Prometheus—or Biology and the Advancement of Man, 1925; The Biological Basis of Human Nature, 1930; Genetics of the Protozoa, 1929; The Universe and Life, 1933; Genetics, 1935; Genetic Variations in Relation to Evolution, 1935. Contbr. of numerous papers in zoöl. and physiol. jours. Home: 505 Hawthorn Road, Roland Park, Baltimore, Md.

JENNINGS, Ivan Frederick, certified public accountant; b. Spanishburg, W.Va., Feb. 13, 1894; s. Frederick and Laurinda (Hubbard) J.; ed. Piedmont Business Coll., Lynchburg, Va., 1915, Am. E.F. Univ., Beaune, France, 1919, Walton Sch. of Commerce, Chicago, 1928-31, Columbia U. (extension study), 1931-32; m. Kate Moye, Aug. 25, 1920. Public accountant Ivan F. Jennings, Welch, W.Va., 1931-34, C.P.A., State of W.Va., 1934; practice under own name since May 28, 1934; sec.-treas. Baxter & Co., Inc. Served with 11th Machine Gun Bn., U.S. Army, 1917-19. Mem. Am. Inst. Accountants, W.Va. Soc. C.P.A. (pres.), Am. Soc. C.P.A., W.Va. Soc. C.P.A., Am. Legion, Vets Foreign Wars. Republican. Baptist. Odd Fellow. Clubs: Skeet, Rifle (Welch); Iaeger Gun. Home: 280 McDowell St. Office: 203 First Nat. Bank Bldg., Welch, W.Va.

JENNINGS, O(tto) E(mery), biology; b. Olena, Huron Co., O., Oct. 3, 1878; s. Byron Emery and Jennie Ellen (Cowpe) J.; B.Sc. in agr., Ohio State U., 1903; Ph.D., U. of Pittsburgh, 1911, Sc.D., 1930; m. Grace Emma Kinzer, June 30, 1906. Florist, 1901-02, in Bot. Dept., 1902-04, Ohio State U.; custodian sect. of botany, 1904-08, asst. curator sect. of botany, 1908, curator of botany, 1915—, also dir. of edn., 1929—, Carnegie Museum of Pittsburgh. Lecturer in botany, Pittsburgh and Allegheny Kindergarten Coll., 1910-12; instr. botany, Lake Lab., Ohio State Univ., Sandusky, O., summer of 1905, and in ecology, 1910 and 1911; instr. in paleobotany, 1911-12, prof. paleobotany, 1912-13, prof. botany, 1913-35, head of dept., 1926-35, prof. biology and head of dept. since 1935; dir. Lake Lab. since 1931, U. of Pittsburgh. Fellow A.A.A.S. (gen. sec. 1918); mem. Bot. Soc. Western Pa. (pres.), Pa. Acad. Science (pres. 1924-25), Ohio Acad. Science, Pittsburgh Acad. Science and Art (pres.), Am. Fern Soc., Sullivant Moss Chapter, Sigma Xi, Townshend Chapter Alpha Zeta, Assn. Am. Geographers, Bot. Soc. America; hon. mem. Garden Club Allegheny Co.; ex-pres. Authors' Club of Pittsburgh. Unitarian. Editor "Bryologist," 1913-37. Author: Manual of Mosses of Western Pennsylvania; also various scientific articles in Annals Carnegie Mus. and various periodicals. Address: 241 Oakland Av., Pittsburgh, Pa.

JENSEN, Cyril Dewey, educator; b. Brownton, Minn., Aug. 17, 1898; s. Peder B. and Anna Marie (Thompson) J.; B.S., U. of Minn., 1921, C.E., 1931; M.S., Lehigh U., 1929; m. Bessie Evans, June 26, 1923; children—Grace Elizabeth, Thomas Evans. Engaged in highway location Minn. Highway Dept., 1921-23; instrumentman for hydroelectric surveys Northern States Power Co., 1923-25; instr., Lehigh U., 1925-29, asst. prof., 1929-33, asso. prof. civil engring. since 1933; welding engr. Lehigh Structural Steel Co., summer, 1930. Asso. mem. Am. Soc. Civil Engrs., Am. Welding Soc. Methodist. Wrote various articles pertaining to welding. Home: 1823 Maple St., Bethlehem, Pa.

JEPSEN, Glenn Lowell, geologist; b. Lead, S.D., Mar. 4, 1904; s. Victor Theodore and Katherine Elizabeth (Gallup) J.; student U. of Mich., 1922-23, S.D. State Sch. of Mines, Rapid City, S.D., 1923-25; B.S., Princeton U., 1927, Ph.D., 1930; m. Janet E. Mayo, June 14, 1933. Instr. English, S.D. State Sch. of Mines, 1924-25; instr. geology, Princeton U., 1930-34, asst. prof. geology since 1934, curator vertebrate paleontology since 1935; dir. Princeton U. Scott Fund expdns. Mem. A.A.A.S., Am. Soc. Mammalogists, Geol. Soc. America, Paleontol. Soc. America, Phi Beta Kappa, Sigma Xi. Club: Explorers (New York). Home: 176 Prospect St., Princeton, N.J.

JEPSON, Edwin C., ry. official; b. Wheeling, W.Va., Sept. 28, 1884; s. James and Elizabeth (Nuttall) J.; ed. Central Catholic High Sch., Wheeling, W.Va.; m. Mary Gundling, Apr. 21, 1910. Pres. Benwood & Wheeling Connecting Ry. since 1932. Home: Whitmar Farms. Office: 1134 Market St., Wheeling, W.Va.

JEPSON, Paul Newton, surgeon; b. Faribault, Minn., Oct. 12, 1893; s. Franklin Newton and Mae Belle J.; A.B., Carleton Coll., 1916; M.S. in orthopedic surgery, U. of Minn. Med. Sch., 1918; M.D., U. of Pa. Med. Sch., 1920; m. Dorothy Cannon, Dec. 30, 1922; children—Paul

Newton, Jr., Joel Bradshaw. First asst. in orthopedics, Mayo Clinic, Rochester, Minn., 1924, asso. in orthopedic surgery, 1925; orthopedic surgeon, St. Joseph's Hosp. (Phila.), St. Luke's and Childrens Hosp.; cons. orthopedic surgeon, Wilmington Gen. and Warren hosps. Fellow Am. Coll. Surgeons; mem. Am. Med. Assn., Phila. Orthopedic Club, Alumni Assn. of Mayo Foundation. Home: 1824 Spruce St., Philadelphia, Pa.

JESSUP, John Butler, banker; b. South Orange, N.J., Sept. 15, 1894; s. Henry Wynans and Mary Hay (Stotesbury) J.; student Black Hall (Conn.) Sch., 1906-07, Ridgefield (Conn.) Sch., 1908-11; A.B., Hamilton Coll., Clinton, N.Y., 1915; m. Marion Hall Zinderstein, June 11, 1921; children—Ann, John Butler. Clk. and stenographer E. I. du Pont de Nemours & Co., Hopewell, Va., 1916-17, div. head, treas. dept., Wilmington, Del., 1919-27; v.p. and dir. Equitable Trust Co., Wilmington, Del., since 1928; dir. Western Improvement Co., Diamond State Telephone Co. Served as pvt. to 1st lt., 107th Inf., A.E.F., 1917-19. Pres. Del. State Bd. Edn., 1937; mem. Wilmington Bd. Edn., Sinking Fund Commn.; dir. The Family Soc., Wilmington, since 1930, The Children's Bur. of Del. since 1933, Wilmington Gen. Hosp. since 1933, Group Hosp. Service, Inc., Visiting Nurses Assn., Bank Credit Bureau. Mem. Sigma Phi. Republican. Presbyterian. Clubs: Wilmington, Wilmington Country (Wilmington, Del.). Home: 2305 MacDonough Rd. Office: Equitable Trust Co., Wilmington, Del.

JETT, Ewell Kirk, radio engr.; b. Baltimore, Md., Mar. 20, 1893; s. John Covington and Elizabeth Woodrow (Bange) J.; ed. grade and high schs. and U.S. Naval schs.; m. L. Viola Ward, of Washington, D.C., Dec. 15, 1915; children—Geraldine Viola, Frances Elizabeth. Served in U.S. Navy, 1911-29, as radio electrician, 1912-17, warrant radio officer, 1917-19, ensign and lt., 1919-29, retired June 1929; asst. chief engr. Federal Radio Commn., 1929-37; chief engr. Federal Communications Commn. since 1938. Decorated Mexican campaign medal, Victory medal (U.S.). Fellow Inst. Radio Engrs. Methodist. Mason. Home: 6305 Hillcrest Place, Chevy Chase, Md. Office: Federal Communications Commn., Washington, D.C.

JETT, Page Covington, M.D.; b. Baltimore, Md., Sept. 8, 1905; s. Robert Starke and Lilian (Downing) J.; student Baltimore City Coll., 1920-23, Western Md. Prep. Sch., 1923-24; A.B., Johns Hopkins U., 1927; M.D., U. of Md. Med. Sch., 1931; m. Vashti Muinch, June 14, 1933; children—Linda Vashti, Robert Page. In gen. practice of medicine since 1933; physician to State Roads Commn.; mem. staff Calvert Co. Hosp. Mem. Calvert Co. Med. Soc. (ex-pres.), Southern Med. Soc., Southern Md. Med. Soc., Med. and Chirurg. Soc. of Md., Nu Sigma Nu. Democrat. Methodist. Club: Solomons Island (Md.) Yacht. Writer of scientific articles. Address: Prince Frederick, Md.

JEWETT, Arthur Crawford, educator; b. Bath, Me., Aug. 26, 1878; s. Edwin Hale and Lizzie L. (Chapman) J.; B.S., Mass. Inst. Tech., 1901; m. Blanche Lind von Beseler, May 7, 1903; children—Roger, Helen Hale. Instr. in mech. engring., U. of Me., 1903-05, prof. mech. engring., 1905-14; engring. mgr. Bird & Son, East Walpole, Mass., 1914-16; supt. various depts. Winchester Repeating Arms Co., 1916-24; mem. research staff Nat. Industrial Conf. Bd., N.Y. City, 1924-25; dir. Coll. of Industries, Carnegie Institute Tech., 1925-34. Exec. sec., Regional Labor Board, 1933-35; supervisor of labor management, Pa. dist. 15, Works Progress Adminstrn., 1935-36. Home: 5420 Plainfield St., Pittsburgh, Pa.

JEWETT, Fannie Frisbie (Mrs. Frank Baldwin Jewett); b. Rockford, Ill., Jan. 25, 1878; d. Willoughby L. L. and Clara Frances (Leach) Frisbie; A.B., Rockford Coll., Ill., 1899; grad. study, U. of Chicago, 1899-1903, Ph.D., 1904; m. Frank Baldwin Jewett, Dec. 28, 1905; children—Harrison Leach, Frank Baldwin, Jr. Trustee Rockford Coll., Rockford, Ill. Dir. Neighborhood Assn. of Milburn, N.J. Mem. Am. Assn. Univ. Women, Socratic Soc. of Rockford Coll., Sigma Xi. Republican. Conglist. Clubs: Engineering Woman's (New York); Short Hills Garden (Short Hills, N.J.). Home: Hobart Av., Short Hills, N.J.; (summer) "Cheesehahchamuk," Vineyard Haven, Mass.

JEWETT, Frank Baldwin, electrical engr.; b. Pasadena, Calif., Sept. 5, 1879; s. Stanley P. and Phebe (Mead) J.; A.B., Throop Poly. Inst. (now Calif. Inst. Tech.), 1898; Ph.D., U. of Chicago, 1902; D.Sc., New York U., Dartmouth, 1925, Columbia University and University of Wis., 1927, Rutgers U., 1928, U. of Chicago, 1929, Harvard, 1936; Dr. Engineering, Case School of Applied Science, 1928; LL.D. from Miami University, 1932; LL.D., Rockford Coll., 1929; m. Fannie C. Frisbie, Dec. 28, 1905; children—Harrison Leach, Frank Baldwin. Research asst. to Prof. A. A. Michelson, U. of Chicago, 1901-02; instr. physics and elec. engring., Mass. Inst. Tech., 1902-04; transmission engr. Am. Telephone & Telegraph Co., 1904-12; asst. chief engr., 1912-16, chief engr., 1916, vice-pres., 1922, Western Electric Co.; vice-pres. Am. Telephone & Telegraph Co., in charge dev. and res.; pres. Bell Telephone Laboratories, Inc., 1925. Maj. Signal Corps, U.S.R., 1917; lt. col. Signal Corps, U.S.A., Dec. 1, 1917; was advisory mem. Spl. Submarine Bd. of the Navy and mem. State Dept. Spl. Com. on Cables. Vice chmn. Engring. Foundation, 1919-25; chmn. Div. of Engring. and Industrial Research, Nat. Research Council, 1923-27; mem. President Roosevelt's Science Advisory Bd., 1933-35; now mem. Govt. Relations and Science Advisory Bd.; mem. Com. on Aids to Scientific Learning of Nat. Resources Com.; pres. and trustee N.Y. Mus. of Science and Industry; trustee Carnegie Instn. of Washington, Tabor Acad., Woods Hole Oceanographic Lab.; life mem. Mass. Inst. Tech. Corpn. Fellow Am. Inst. Elec. Engrs. (pres. 1922-23), Inst. Radio Engrs., A.A.A.S., Am. Physical Soc., Acoustical Soc. America, Am. Acad. Arts and Sciences; mem. Nat. Acad. of Sciences, Instn. of Elec. Engrs., New York Elec. Soc., Soc. for Promotion of Engring. Edn., Delta Upsilon, Sigma Xi, Tau Beta Pi. Awarded D.S.M. (U.S.); Fourth Order Rising Sun, 1923. Third Order Sacred Treasure, 1930 (Japan); Edison medal, 1928; Faraday medal, 1935, Washington Award, 1938; John Fritz Medal, 1939. Clubs: University Railroad-Machinery, Engineers, Century Assn. (New York); Short Hills (N.J.) Author of brochures, articles and pub. addresses on physical and elec. subjects. Home: Brantwood, Short Hills, N.J. Office: 195 Broadway, New York, N.Y.

JIULIANTE, Jessamine, lawyer; b. Erie, Pa., Apr. 26, 1899; s. Dominick and Nicoletta (Di-Tullio) J.; B.S., Wharton Sch. of Finance, U. of Pa., 1917; LL.B., Law Sch., U. of Pa., 1922; m. Rose Alfonso, Dec. 22, 1922; children—Jessamine S., Joyce Jacqueline, Joan Janet. Admitted to Pa. bar, 1922, and since practiced in Erie; asst. dist. atty., Erie County, 1928-32; asst. solicitor City of Erie, 1932-33; special dep. atty. gen. of State of Pa., since 1935. Served as sergt. Ordnance Corps, U.S. Army, 1917-19. Mem. Pa. State Bar Assn., Erie County Bar Assn., Am. Legion (comdr. Rogers Israel Post, Erie, 1927-29; comdr. 29th Dist.), Businessmen's Association (pres. 1928), Public Ownership League of Erie County (pres. 1937), Y.M.C.A., Sons of Italy (past del. to Supreme Council), Maennerchor, South Erie Turners Soc., Forty and Eight (past grand avocat). One of 25 students invited to Italy by Italian Govt., 1922. Democrat. Roman Catholic. Moose, Elk. Clubs: Presque Isle Sportsmen's League. Home: 1120 W. 10th St. Office: 25 E. 8th St., Erie, Pa.

JOCKERS, Ernst, prof. German lit.; b. Sand, Germany, Jan. 7, 1887; s. Jakob and Christina (Rieber) J.; M.A., U. of Strassburg, 1910, Ph.D., same, 1910; came to U.S., 1924, naturalized, 1932; m. Paula Annabert Büchler, May 18, 1925. Engaged as prof. modern langs. and dir. in various colls. in Europe, 1910-24; instr. German, Coll. of City of N.Y., 1925-26; asst. prof. German, U. of Pittsburgh, 1926-29; asst. prof. German literature, U. of Pa., 1929-34, prof. since 1934. Awarded Cross of Merit for service during World War. Dir. German Soc. of Pa., Phila. Mem. Modern Lang. Assn. of America, Am. Assn. Teachers of German, Goethe Soc. of Germany. Republican. Lutheran. Author: Three books pub. in Germany, 1911-17; Deutsch-Amerikanischer Musenalmanach, 1925; Die Deutschen Ihr Werden und Wesen, 1929; Wandlungen (verse), 1931. Contbr. articles, essays, criticisms, reviews, to European and Am. journs. and mags. Home: House Orplid, Doylestown, Pa.

JOHN, William Scott, lawyer; b. Morgantown, W.Va., Jan. 10, 1878; s. Lemuel N. and Julia A. (Boyers) J.; A.B., W.Va. U., 1900, LL.B., 1902; m. Estelle Cox, Dec. 17, 1902. Admitted to W.Va. bar, 1902; instr. in law, W.Va. U., 1902-03; asst. clk. Supreme Court of Appeals, W.Va., 1903-05; mem. W.Va. Ho. of Rep., 1917, 18, 19 (minority floor leader 1917-18, majority leader 1919); of spl. counsel for W. Va. in Ohio and Pa. gas cases, Supreme Court of U.S.; of counsel W.Va. 1929 Water Power Act (held unconstnl., 1931). Republican. Presbyn. Mason. Elk. Author original "work or fight" law in U.S. (enacted by W.Va. legislature, Feb. 1919); also author of first law adopted by any legislature in U.S. against Bolshevism and the red flag (enacted Mar. 1919). Engaged in reorganization of various banks of W.Va. by plan which he formulated. Author articles on banking which appeared in Review of Reviews. Home: Morgantown, W.Va.

JOHNS, Vernon, clergyman; b. Darlington Heights, Va.; s. William and Sallie Branch (Price) J.; grad. Va. Theol. Sem. and Coll., Lynchburg, 1915; Oberlin Coll. Grad. Sch. of Theology, 1918; m. Altona Trent, Dec. 23, 1927; children—Vernon, William, John. Ordained to ministry Bapt. Ch., 1918; pastor Court St. Ch., Lynchburg, Va., 1920-26; dir. Bapt. Ednl. Center, N.Y. City, 1926-29; pres. Va. Theol. Sem. and Coll., 1929-33; became pastor Holy Trinity Ch., Phila., 1933, First Ch., Charleston, W.Va., since 1937. Pres. Farm & City Products Co., Inc., since 1933. Kanawha Valley Consumers' Cooperative since 1937. Mem. Alpha Phi Alpha. Contbr. of "Human Possibilities" (sermon) to Best Sermons, 1926; writer pamphlets under the title "Pulpit Opinions." Address: 424 Shrewsbury St., Charleston, W.Va.

JOHNSEN, Sigurd Walter, physician; b. Chicago, Ill., July 29, 1895; s. Andrew and Dinah (Torgersen) J.; B.S., U. of Chicago, 1921; M.D., Cornell U. Med. Sch., 1925; m. Aletta H. Johnson, Dec. 23, 1922; children—Sigurd Edward, Miriam Aletta. Interne Passaic Gen. Hosp., 1925-26; engaged in gen. practice of medicine at Passaic, N.J., since 1926, specializing in internal medicine and gastro enterology since 1930; sr, attdg. phys. Passaic Gen. Hosp.; pres. Med. Dental Service Bur. of Passaic and Bergen Cos. Served as chief yeoman, U.S.N., 1917-19. Asso. fellow Am. Coll. Phys.; mem. Phi Beta Pi. Republican. Presbyn. Home: 82 Yantacaw Brook Rd., Montclair. Office: 49 Passaic Av., Passaic, N.J.

JOHNSON, Albert Rittenhouse, univ. prof.; b. Lambertville, N.J., Mar. 7, 1880; s. Clark B. and Sallie A. (Green) J.; student Reading's Pub. Sch., Delaware Twp., Hunterdon Co., N.J.; grad. Trenton State Normal Sch., 1900; B.Sc., Rutgers Coll., 1907, C.E., 1925; m. Ethel R. Hughes, Aug. 16, 1911; children—Edna Rittenhouse (Mrs. Philip L. Crecelius), Elizabeth Ann. Teacher and prin., North Branch, N.J., 1900-01, Succasunna, N.J., 1901-02, Stockton, N.J., 1902-03; in engring. dept. Hudson Cos. on construction Hudson and Manhattan R.R. tunnels, summer 1906 and June 1907-May 1908; river and harbor work for U.S. Govt., N.Y. City and Albany, N.Y., May-Oct. 1908; instr. mathematics and graphics, Rutgers U., 1908-11, asst. prof. same, 1911-17, asso. prof. civil engring., 1917-28, prof. structural design since 1928; has been employed by N.J. State Highway Dept., McClintic-Marshall Construction Co. and Hughes Foulkrod Co. of Philadelphia; pres. and dir. Highland Park Bldg. & Loan Assn. Mem. Phi Beta Kappa, Sigma Xi, Tau Beta Pi, Lambda Chi Alpha. Mason. Home: 68 N. Sixth Av., New Brunswick, N.J.

JOHNSON, Albert Williams, judge; b. Weikert, Pa., Nov. 28, 1872; s. Alanson and Sarah Alice (Catherman) J.; student Central Pa. Coll., New

Berlin; A.B., cum laude, Bucknell U., 1896; LL.D., Albright Coll. and Lebanon Valley Coll.; D.C.L., Bucknell U. and Juniata Coll.; m. Dora Miller, Nov. 1893 (died Oct. 9, 1909); children —Miller A., Alice Susannah (Mrs. Carl Schug), Donald M., Albert Williams, Paul E.; m. 2d, Mary C. Steck, Dec. 13, 1913; children—Mary Louise, William Steck, David Cadman, Frederick Welty, John Van Wert, Dianna Carl. Teacher, grammar and high sch., Lewisburg, Pa., 1896-1901; admitted to Pa. bar, 1898; instr. in law, Bucknell U., 1902-12. Mem. Pa. Ho. of Rep., 1901-02; president judge 17th Dist., Pa., 1912-22; solicitor Dept. of Edn., 1922-23; U.S. dist. judge, Middle Dist., Pa. since 1925, for life term. Trustee Bucknell U.; incorporator of Dickinson Law Sch., Carlisle, Pa. Mem. P.O.S. of A. (nat. pres., 1927-29), Kappa Sigma. Lutheran. Odd Fellow, Modern Woodman; mem. Royal Arcanum. Home: Lewisburg, Pa.

JOHNSON, Albert Williams, Jr., lawyer; b. Lewisburg, Pa., July 15, 1903; s. Albert Williams and Dora (Miller) J.; grad. Lewisburg High Sch., 1921; A.B., Bucknell U., 1925; student Harvard Law Sch., 1925-27; LL.B., Dickinson Law Sch., 1928; m. Virginia Lescure Lyon, Nov. 7, 1936; 1 son, Albert Williams 3d. Admitted to Pa. bar, 1928, and practiced in Wilkes-Barre, 1928-34, Williamsport since 1934; asst. dist. atty. Luzerne Co., Pa., 1932-34; pres. Tea Spring Lodge; dir. Hoff-Wilkinson Co., Federated Sportsman Assn. Mem. exec. com. Young Republicans of Lycoming Co.; Rep. candidate for dist. atty., Lycoming Co., 1939. Chmn. court of honor West Branch Council of Boy Scouts America. Mem. Am. Bar Assn., Pa. Bar Assn., Sigma Chi. Lutheran. Mason (32°, Shriner), Patriotic Order Sons of America. Club: Kiwanis, Wheel, Shrine, Young Men's Republican, Williamsport Country (Williamsport). Home: 641 Campbell St. Office: 120 W. 4th St., Williamsport, Pa.

JOHNSON, Alfred Hermann, musician and composer; b. Berlin, Pa., Mar. 27, 1900; s. John Nelson and Mary Rebecca (Heineymeyer) J.; A.B., Carnegie Inst. Tech., 1924, A.M., same, 1925; unmarried. Began career as teacher of music, organist and pianist, 1925; mem. faculty, Pittsburgh Mus. Inst. since 1925; organist and choir dir. Sewickley Presbyn. Ch. since 1929. Mem. Organist Guild (exec. com.), Sigma Alpha Epsilon, Phi Mu Alpha. Awarded three prizes for compositions by Pittsburgh Art Soc.; prize for composition by Phi Mu Alpha. Republican. Lutheran. Composer suites and songs pub. by leading music houses. Home: 422 Morewood Av. Office: 131 Bellefield Av., Pittsburgh, Pa.

JOHNSON, Allan Chester, prof. classics; b. Loch Broom, N.S., Can., Aug. 11, 1881; s. Leander and Hannah (Creelman) J.; A.B., Dalhousie U., Halifax, Can., 1904, LL.D., 1929; Ph.D., Johns Hopkins, 1909; fellow Am. Sch. of Classical Studies, Greece, 1909-11; m. Laura Williamson, Aug. 14, 1912. Came to U.S., 1912, naturalized citizen, 1932. Tutor in classics, Dalhousie U., 1904-06; lecturer in Greek, U. of Alberta, 1911-12; asst. prof. classics, Princeton, 1912-22, asso. prof., 1922-23, prof. since 1924. Trustee Am. Acad. in Rome. Mem. Am. Philol. Assn., Phi Beta Kappa. Co-Author: (with Frank Frost Abbott) Municipal Administration in the Roman Empire, 1926. Editor: (with H. B. Van Hoesen) Greek Papyri in the Princeton Collection, 1930; Princeton University Studies in Papyrology; (with H. S. Gehman and E. H. Kase) John H. Scheide Biblical Papyri. Author: Roman Egypt, 1936. Contbr. articles on Greek history to Am. Jour. Philology, Am. Jour. Archæology, etc. Home: 3 College Rd., Princeton, N.J.

JOHNSON, Amandus, educator, author, explorer; b. Sweden, Oct. 27, 1877; to U.S. in infancy; A.B., Gustavus Adolphus Coll., St. Peter, Minn., 1904; A.M., U. of Colo., 1905; scholarship, Yale, 1905 (resigned); Harrison fellow U. of Pa., 1906-08, Ph.D., 1908, fellow, 1908-10; traveled and engaged in research in Europe; hon. D.Litt., U. of Gothenburg, 1921; m. Helen M. Chadwick, May 27, 1912. Asst. in modern langs., U. of Colo., 1904-05; instr. Scandinavian langs., U. of Pa., 1910-15, asst. prof., 1915-22; dir. Educational West African Expdn., 1922-24; pres. New Sweden Memorial Commn. since 1924, also pres. Swedish-Am. Sesquicentennial Expn., Phila.; dir. American-Swedish Historical Mus., Philadelphia. Lecturer U. of Upsala, spring of 1909; official rep. Swedish Acad. Sciences and of Swedish Govt. at 19th Congress of Americanists, Washington, D.C., 1915; pres. Soc. of Arts and Letters, 1917-19; chmn. hist. sect. of Am. Div. of Göthenburg Exhbn., 1922; sec. Swedish Colonial Soc.; mem. of Kungl. sällsk. för utg. av hands rör Skand. hist. (Stockholm); pres. Am. Sons and Daughters of Sweden. Stipend from University of Upsala, 1926. Knight Order of Vasa (Sweden), 1926; also Knight Order of the North Star (Sweden). Republican. Lutheran. Author: The Swedish Settlements on the Delaware (2 vols.), 1911; The Swedes in America (Vol. I), 1914; Contributions of Swedes to American Progress, 1921; I Marimbans Land, 1929; Instruction for Johan Prints, 1930; Mbundu-English-Portuguese Dictionary with Grammar of Mbundu Language, 1931; Journal and Biography of Nicholas Collin, 1936; also numerous hist. and philol. articles. Editor and transl.; Lindeström's Geographia Americæ, 1925; Samuel Gustaf Hermelin's Report on Mines in the United States in 1783, 1933. Home: 400 Master St. Office: American Swedish Hist. Museum, Philadelphia, Pa.

JOHNSON, Arthur Newhall, civil engr.; b. Lynn, Mass., Nov. 11, 1870; s. David Newhall and Amanda Malvina (Richardson) J.; S.B. in civ. engring., Lawrence Scientific Sch. (Harvard), 1894; hon. Dr. Engring., University of Maryland, 1924; m. May Louise Ash, of Lynn, Sept. 12, 1900. Instr. descriptive geometry, Harvard, 1895-96; asst. engr. Calumet and Hecla Mine, Calumet, Mich., 1896-97; asst. engr. Mass. Highway Commn., 1897-98; state highway engr. of Md., 1898-1905; chief engr. U.S. Office of Pub. Roads, Washington, 1905; state highway engr. of Ill., 1906-14; with Bur. Municipal Research of New York, 1914-16; consulting highway engr., Portland Cement Assn., Chicago, 1916-20; dean College Engineering, University of Maryland, 1920-36, dean emeritus since 1936. Chairman Highway Research Bd., Nat. Research Council, 1923-26; del. to Pan Am. Road Congress, Buenos Aires, 1925. Mem. Am. Soc. C.E., Am. Soc. Testing Materials. Club: Cosmos (Washington). Author of various reports on road work and articles on same subject in tech. mags. Received Bartlett award for outstanding contribution to highway progress, 1933. Home: 2824 St. Paul St., Baltimore, Md.

JOHNSON, Benjamin Alvin, judge; b. Salisbury, Md., Dec. 23, 1887; s. Rufus and Tabitha Wise (Davis) J.; A.B., Washington Coll., 1911; student Baltimore Law Sch., 1911-12; m. Ethel Frances Halloway, of Newark, Md., Oct. 20, 1915; children—Alvin Halloway (dec.), William Benjamin, Rufus Clay, Martha Jane (dec.), Frances Perdue, Mary Jane. Admitted to Md. bar, 1913; city solicitor Town of Salisbury, practicing atty. and mem. firm Long & Johnson, 1915-34; chief justice 1st Judicial Circuit Court of Md. since 1934. Mem. bd. of gov. and visitor, Washington Coll. Mem. Kappa Alpha. Democrat. Elk. Club: Green Hill Country. Home: 237 S. Division St., Salisbury, Md. Address: Court House, Salisbury, Md.

JOHNSON, Benjamin M., v.p. and gen. mgr. Whitaker Paper Co.; b. Jackson, O., July 29, 1884; s. William M. and Jennie (Alexander) J.; grad. Columbus (O.) Grade Sch., 1898, East High Sch., 1902; A.B., Ohio State U., 1907; m. Gladys W. Hill, May 8, 1912; children—Samuel W., Benjamin M., Charles Theodore, Robert E., Miriam. In paper business since 1902, beginning as office boy, became salesman, 1908, district mgr., 1909, and sales mgr., 1922, v.p., gen. mgr., dir. and mem. exec. com. Whitaker Paper Co., since 1925. Mem. Phi Kappa Psi. Republican. Methodist. Clubs: Metropolitan, Shannopin Country. Home: 21 Briar Cliff Road, Ben Avon Heights. Office: 1005 Beaver Av., Pittsburgh, Pa.

JOHNSON, Benjamin Slemmons, clergyman; b. nr. Cadiz, O., Jan. 7, 1884; s. Benjamin Harrison and Martha Jane (Welch) J.; A.B., Bethany Coll., 1907; A.M., Yale U., 1912; B.D. Yale Divinity Sch., 1912; m. Elizabeth Glass, June 20, 1912 (dec.); children—Margaret Elizabeth (Mrs. James L. Herbald), Dorothy Mae, Ben S., Jr.; m. 2d Virginia S. Hall, Oct. 12, 1922; children—J. Willard, Mary Elizabeth, Virginia Jeannette. Ordained to ministry Christian Ch., 1907; pastor, Greensburg, Pa., 1907-10, 1914-21, New Haven, Conn., 1910-12, Norwalk, O., 1912-14, Steubenville, O., 1921-26; pastor First Christian Ch., Bluefield, W.Va., since 1926; erected new ch. bldg., Greensburg, Pa., during second pastorate; rep. Christian Chs. of W.Va. on Recommendation Com. at Internat. Convs., 1929-30; pres. W.Va. State Conv., 1928. Trustee Bethany Coll. Mem. Kappa Alpha. Mem. Disciples of Christ. Club: Lions of Bluefield. Baccalaureate and commencement speaker on many occasions. Home: 333 Hancock St. Office: 601 Bland St., Bluefield, W.Va.

JOHNSON, Buford Jeannette, psychologist; b. Thomson, Ga., Aug. 23, 1880; d. Preston Brooks and Ella (Morris) J.; A.B., LaGrange (Ga.) Coll., 1895; A.M., Johns Hopkins, 1915, Ph.D., 1916. Asso. psychologist, Lab. of Social Hygiene, Bedford Hills, N.Y., 1916-17; with Bureau Ednl. Expts., N.Y. City, 1917-20; psychologist and chmn. research com., 1920-22; asso. prof. psychology, Johns Hopkins, 1920-24, prof., 1924-38. Trustee Roland Park Country Sch. Fellow A.A.A.S.; mem. Am. Psychol. Assn., Southern Soc. Philosophy and Psychology, Nat. Inst. Psychology, Soc. for Research in Child Development, Phi Beta Kappa, Sigma Xi. Clubs: Cosmopolitan (New York); College, Hamilton (Baltimore). Author: Mental Growth of Children, 1925; Habits of the Child, 1929; Child Psychology, 1932, Mental Measurements Monograph Series. Home: Greenway Apts., Baltimore, Md.

JOHNSON, Charles B.; mem. law firm Johnson & Johnson. Address: Clarksburg, W.Va.

JOHNSON, Charles Meredith, corpn. official; b. Philadelphia, Pa., Aug. 7, 1897; s. Josiah Meredith and Rosa Isabel (Heron) J.; grad. West Philadelphia High Sch., Philadelphia, 1915; m. Harriett E. Cochran, Aug. 9, 1927; 1 son, Charles Meredith, Jr. Associated with J. H. Weaver & Co., producers bituminous coal, since 1917, dir. and sec. since 1923, treas. since 1929; sec. and treas. W.Va. Northern R.R. Co., Dawson Coal Co., Heisley Coal Co., Monroe Coal Mining Co., Cambria Twp. Light, Heat & Power Co., Revloc Supply Co., Hines Coal Co., Irona Coal Co.; sec., treas. and dir. Conner Water Co., Senwick Water Co., Heisley Store Co., Mildred Supply Co., Rosemont Coal Co., Red Lands Coal Co., Summit Realty Co.; sec. and asst. treas. Cambria & Indiana R.R. Co., Cambria Improve-Co.; sec. United Eastern Coal Sales Corpn. Served in U.S. Navy, 1918. Mem. Pa. Soc., Am. Legion, Forty & Eight. Republican. Catholic. Club: Penn Athletic. Home: 540 Shadeland Av., Drexel Hill, Pa. Office: Broad St. Station Bldg., 1617 Pennsylvania Boul., Philadelphia, Pa.

JOHNSON, Charles Morris, chemist and metallurgist; b. Alliance, O., Aug. 15, 1869; s. George Washington and Evalina (Hutchins) J.; prep. edn. Western U. of Pa. Prep. Sch., 1882-85; Ph.B., Western U. of Pa. (now U. of Pittsburgh), 1889; Ph.M.; m. Mary Alma Yost, Aug. 15, 1898; children—Alma Evalina, George Warren, Amy Pauline (Mrs. Theodore Klotzbaugh), Carroll Morris, Celia Wetherald. Asst. chemist Park Plant, 1889-1900; chief chemist Park Plant, Crucible Steel Co. of America since 1900; dir. of research dept. Park Plant, 1918-26, metallurgist Tungsten Plant of Crucible Steel Co. of America, 1910-25. Fellow A.A.A.S., Am. Inst. Chemists, Am. Geog. Soc.; mem. Am. Soc. for Metals, Am. Soc. Testing Materials, Am. Chem. Soc., Sigma Xi. Presbyterian. Author: Rapid Methods for the Chemical Analysis of Special Steels, Steel-Making Alloys and Graphite, 1909. 4th edit., 19—. Contbr. many articles on alloys of steel, etc., to scientific jours.; contbr. to Colliers New Encyclopedia. Holder of several patents on steel processes. Home: 731 Orchard St., Avalon, Pittsburgh, Pa.

JOHNSON, Charles William Leverett, securities brokerage; b. Gambier, O., Aug. 12, 1870; s. William Woolsey and Susannah Leverett (Batcheller) J.; A.B., Johns Hopkins U., 1891, Ph.D., 1896; m. Ella Blakistone Conway, July 12, 1922; 1 son, Charles Leverett Batcheller (dec.). Instr. Greek, Yale U., 1897-1900; instr. Latin, Princeton U., 1901-03; bought a seat on the Baltimore Stock Exchange, 1905 and since engaged in securities brokerage individually in Baltimore; pres. Baltimore Stock Exchange, 1934-39; interested in collection of antiques having inherited a considerable collection of silver, faience and wood carvings from mother. Mem. Soc. of Colonial Wars (sec. Md. Soc.), Alpha Delta Phi, Phi Beta Kappa. Episcopalian. Clubs: University (treas.), Johns Hopkins (Baltimore). Home: 909 St. Paul St. Office: 210 E. Redwood St., Baltimore, Md.

JOHNSON, Clarence Rudolph, artist; b. Maxtown, O., Sept. 11, 1894; s. Cary W. and Lina (Moss) J.; ed. Columbus Art Sch., 1912-15, Pa. Acad. Fine Arts, 1915-18, Art school in Paris, France, 1919-21; m. Margaret Dickinson Crozer, Sept. 9, 1931. Artist, painter, since 1920. Exhibited at: Nat. Acad. of Design, N.Y., Chicago Art Inst., Carnegie Inst. (Pittsburgh), Corcoran Gallery of Art (Washington, D.C.), Pa. Acad. of Fine Arts, etc. Awards: Cresson traveling scholarship, 1917; 2d Toppan prize, 1918; 1st Hallgarten prize, 1925; Mr. and Mrs. Augustus Peabody prize at Art Inst. of Chicago, 1926; bronze medal Nat. Acad. of Design, Sesqui-centennial Expn., 1926; hon. mention, Art Club of Phila., 1926. Home: Lahaska, Pa.

JOHNSON, David Dale, prof. of English; b. Parkersburg, W.Va., Oct. 22, 1875; s. David Dye and Julia (Dale) J.; A.B., Marietta (O.) Coll., 1896, grad. student 1896-97, hon. A.M., 1908, Litt.D., 1927; A.M., W.Va. Univ., 1904; student Harvard, 1908; m. Jane M. Plumer, Aug. 10, 1909; children—Frances Dale (deceased), Katherine Plumer (Mrs. Travis C. Johnson), David Dale, Carol Dana. Instr. Parkersburg (W.Va.) High Sch., 1896-97, 1898-1902, Marietta (O.) Acad., 1897-98; instr. of English, W.Va. U., 1902-10, asst. prof., 1910-12, asso. prof., 1912-20, prof. of English, since 1920, head dept. of English since 1929. Mem. W.Va. Edn. Assn., Phi Beta Kappa; former mem. Modern Lang. Assn., Am. Assn. Univ. Profs. Baptist. Club: Morgantown Kiwanis (past pres.). Home: 20 Campus Drive, Morgantown, W.Va.

JOHNSON, Edward Sooy, surgeon; b. Snow Hill, Md., Jan. 8, 1886; s. William David and Sallie Margaret (Kelly) J.; grad. Snow Hill Acad., 1905; M.D., U. of Md., 1912; m. Lillian Diehl, July 12, 1919; 1 dau., Barbara Grace. Clinical asst. Univ. Hosp., 1911-12; resident in surgery St. Joseph's Hosp., Baltimore, 1912-13, sr. resident of hosp. and resident in surgery, 1913-15; specializing in surgery since 1915; asso. prof. of surgery, U. of Md. Sch. of Medicine and Coll. of Physicians and Surgeons, since 1929; mem. staff Univ. Hosp., St. Joseph's Hosp., Church Home and Infirmary, West Baltimore Gen. Hosp.; chief surgeon Franklin Square Hosp. Served as capt. Med. Corps, U.S. Army, 1917-19; with Base Hosp. Unit No. 42, A.E.F.; dir. Mobile operating team, No. 101, France; now lt. comdr. U.S. Naval Res. in charge surg. div., Baltimore Unit. Fellow Am. Coll. Surgeons; mem. Am. Bd. Surgery (a founder); F.A.M.A., Baltimore Med. Soc., Med.-Chirurg. Faculty of Md., Baltimore County Med. Soc. Democrat. Episcopalian. Mason. Club: University (Baltimore). Home: 203 Chancery Rd., Guilford, Baltimore, Md. Office: 1123 St. Paul St., Baltimore, Md.

JOHNSON, Eldridge Reeves, founder Victor Talking Machine Co.; b. Wilmington, Del., Feb. 6, 1867; s. Asa S. and Caroline (Reeves) J.; ed. Spring Garden Inst., Phila.; A.E.D., U. of Pa., 1928; m. Elsie Reeves Fenimore, Oct. 5, 1897; 1 son, Eldridge Reeves Fenimore. Founder, 1894, of business, inc., 1901, as Victor Talking Machine Co. of which was pres. until 1927. Trustee U. of Pa. Mem. Am. Philos. Soc. Republican. Episcopalian. Clubs: Union League, Rittenhouse, New York Yacht. Owner of yacht "MS Caroline." Home: Moorestown, N.J. Address: 608 West Jersey Trust Bldg., Camden, N.J.

JOHNSON, Elizabeth Forrest, educator; b. Frederick, Md., Sept. 21, 1881; d. Chapman Love and Mary Margaret (Shriver) J.; A.B., Vassar, 1902, and grad. work same. Headmistress of The Baldwin Sch., Bryn Mawr, Pa., since 1915. Mem. Head Mistresses' Assn., Phi Beta Kappa. Democrat. Episcopalian. Clubs: Cosmopolitan, College, Contemporary (Phila.). Address: The Baldwin School, Bryn Mawr, Pa.

JOHNSON, Elmer Ellsworth Schultz, educator; b. New Berlinville, Berks Co., Pa., June 26, 1872; s. Allen T. D. and Susanna K. (Schultz) J.; grad. Perkiomen Sch., Pennsburg, Pa., 1895; A.B., Princeton, 1899; B.D., Hartford Theol. Sem., 1902, Ph.D., 1911; D.D., Franklin and Marshall Coll., 1924; m. Agnes Gerhard, Sept. 7, 1899; 1 son, Rolland Gerhard. Pastor First Schwenkfelder Ch., Phila., 1902-04; at Wolfenbüttel, Germany, as mem. Corpus Schwenkfeldianorum editorial staff, 1904-19; pastor Hereford Mennonite Ch., Bally, Pa., since 1921; prof. mediæval and modern ch. history, Hartford Theol. Sem., since 1923. Mem. editorial staff The Schwenkfeldian (organ of Schwenkenfelder Ch. of America) since 1903; editor in chief Corpus Schwenkfeldianorum (letters and treatises of Casper von Schwenkfeld, 1490-1561), 14 vols. to 1935. Trustee of Perkiomen School, United Society of Christian Endeavor; custodian of Schwenkfelder Hist. Library, Pennsburg, Pa. Mem. Hist. Soc. of Conn., Pa. German Soc., Berks and Montgomery cos. hist. socs., Hist. and Natural Science Soc. of Perkiomen Region. Owner with son of Hereford Hills Orchard. Address: Hereford, Pa., Pennsburg, Pa., and Hartford Theol. Sem., Hartford, Conn.

JOHNSON, Emma, ednl. dir.; b. York, Pa.; d. Michael and Virginia Haller (Upp) J.; student Pa. State Coll., 1914-16; B.S., Teachers Coll. of Columbia U., 1917, M.A., 1928; unmarried. Teacher pub. schs., York, Pa., to 1914; teacher home econs., State Teachers Coll., Pittsburg, Kan., summer 1917, also lecturing and presenting food conservation demonstrations; mem. N.Y. State Food Conservation Unit in charge Bronx Sect., 1917-19; in dept. rural edn., Cornell U. Coll. of Agr., 1919-23, administrating and supervising home econs. work in rural town under Jr. Project Program; business experience in home econs., Los Angeles, Calif., 1923-25; asst. prof. home econs. dept., U. of Ark., Fayetteville, Ark., 1925-27; dir. dept. of early childhood edn., Temple U., Phila., 1928-35, responsible for preparation nursery sch., kindergarten, primary teachers, dir. enlarged dept. early childhood and elementary edn. since 1935, preparing teachers for elementary grades also. Mem. Am. Asso. Univ. Women (Phila. branch), Am. Assn. Univ. Profs., Nat. Assn. Nursery Edn. (mem. governing bd., 1936-39), Nat. Assn. Childhood Edn., Progressive Edn. Assn., Pa. Assn. Adult Edn. (pres. dept. for family life edn. since 1936), Pa. State Edn. Assn., N.E.A., State Assn. of Childhood Edn. (1st v.p. since 1939). Author: (with Helen Goodspeed) Care and Training of Children, 1929; Care and Guidance of Children, 1938. Address: 312 W. Hortter St., Philadelphia, Pa.

JOHNSON, Emory Richard, university prof.; b. Waupun, Wis., Mar. 22, 1864; s. Eli and Angeline (Nichols) J.; B.L., U. of Wis., 1888, M.L., 1891; Ph.D., U. of Pa., 1893 (Sc.D., U. of Pa., 1913); m. Orra L. March, Sept. 5, 1894 (died, 1923); m. 2d, Hedwig Anna Schroeder, December 24, 1930. Instr. economics, Haverford Coll., 1893-96; prof. transportation and commerce, U. of Pa., since 1896; dean Wharton Sch. Finance and Commerce, 1919-33. Expert on transportation, U.S. Industrial Commn., 1899; mem. U.S. Isthmian Canal Commn., 1899-1904; expert on valuation of ry. property for U.S. Census Bur., 1904-05; expert on traffic, Nat. Waterways Commn., 1909; apptd., 1911, to report on Panama Canal traffic, tolls and measurement of vessels; mem. Pub. Service Commn. Pa., 1913-15; dir. Phila. Maritime Exch., 1907-28. Editor Annals of Am. Acad. Polit. and Social Science, 1901-14; arbitrator of dispute between S.P. Co. and Order of Railroad Telegraphers, 1907; mem. bd. that prepared an Economic History of the U.S., 1904-1930. Asst. dir. Bur. of Transportation, War Trade Bd., 1917—; rate expert, U.S. Shipping Bd., 1918-19; transportation expert Chamber Commerce U.S.A., 1919-21, 1923 and 1925. Chairman Research Council upon Operation and Effect of the Eighteenth Amendment, 1931. Chmn. Spl. Com. on Panama Tolls and Vessel Measurement Rules, 1936-37. Pres. National Institute Social Sciences, 1918-22; pres. Assn. of Collegiate Schs. of Business, 1920-21; mem. Am. Econ. Assn., Geog. Soc. Phila. (pres. 4 terms), Am. Philos. Soc., Society of Puritan Descendants, S.A.R., Colonial Soc. of Pa. Decorated by Emperor of Japan with medal of Order of the Rising Sun (3d rank), by Chinese Government, medal of Order of Chia-Ho (2d rank), 1926. Clubs: Print, Merion Cricket Club. Author: Inland Waterways, Their Relation to Transportation, 1893; American Railway Transportation, 1903; Ocean and Inland Water Transportation, 1906; Elements of Transportation, 1909; Railroad Traffic and Rates, 1911; Panama Canal Traffic and Tolls, 1912; Measurement of Vessels for the Panama Canal, 1913; History of Domestic and Foreign Commerce of the United States, 2 vols., 1915; The Panama Canal and Commerce, 1916; Principles of Railroad Transportation, 1916; Principles of Ocean Transportation, 1918; The Ocean Freight Service (with Prof. G. G. Huebner), 1925; Interpretative Essays on China and England, 1927; Principles of Transportation (with collaborators), 1928; Transportation by Water (with Profs. G. G. Huebner and A. K. Henry), 1935; Government Regulation of Transportation, 1938; also author of papers on railways and economics, Report to Isthmian Canal Commission on Industrial and Commercial Value of Isthmian Canal, 1901, to U.S. Shipping Bd. on Ocean Rates and Terminal Charges, 1919, to U.S. Bd. of Review on Traffic and Revenues of Proposed Trans-Florida Canal, 1934, and articles in econ. mags. and reports in bulls. of U.S. Dept. Labor and Bur. of the Census. Home: Hamilton Court. Address: University of Pa., Philadelphia, Pa.

JOHNSON, Frederick Green, newspaper pub.; b. Wilkes-Barre, Pa., Oct. 22, 1890; s. Frederick Charles (M.D.) and Georgia (Post) J.; prep. edn., Harry Hillman Acad. (now Wilkes-Barre Acad.); A.B., Cornell U., 1913; studied Columbia U. Sch. of Journalism, 1913-14; m. Kathleen MacBeth Cable, Apr. 9, 1914 (died 1916); 1 dau., Kathleen Cable; m. 2d, Thelma Rhea Neiger, June 25, 1921; children—Eleanor Lindsey, Marjory Holt, Marilyn, Frederick G., Gail; m. 3d, Lillian Yow Weller. With U.S. Marine Corps, Res., in U.S. and overseas, Dec. 1917-Apr. 1919. Mem. Pa. Soc. Sons of the Revolution, Wyoming Hist. and Geol. Soc., Wyoming Commemorative Assn. Republican. Episcopalian. Mason (32°, Shriner). Club: Westmoreland. Office: The Record, Wilkes-Barre, Pa.

JOHNSON, George, univ. prof.; b. Edinburgh, Scotland, July 4, 1872; s. James B. and Annie Wares (Todd) J.; came to America, 1882; A.B., U. of Pa., 1893, Ph.D., 1911; grad. Princeton Theol. Sem., 1896; m. Florence DeBaun, Sept. 8, 1897; children—Archibald DeB., Catherine P., Mary T. Ordained Presbyn. ministry, 1896; missionary at Chilpancingo, in State of Guerrero, Mex., under the Bd. of Foreign Missions of the Presbyn. Ch. in U.S.A., 1896-1902; prof. of theology and philosophy, Lincoln U., Pa., since 1902, dean of the Coll., 1908-37, dean of the Univ., since 1937; lecturer in Apologetics, Princeton Theol. Sem., 1923-28; Stone lecturer, Princeton Theol. Sem., 1931-32. Mem. Am. Philos. Assn., Aristotelian Soc. (London), A.A. A.S. Republican. Address: Lincoln University, Chester Co., Pa.

JOHNSON, George Brinton, lawyer; b. Chester Co., Pa., Feb. 8, 1858; s. Benjamin D. and Elizabeth (Coale) J.; ed. Chester Co. pub. schs. and Westtown Friend's Boarding Sch.; m. May Cooke, May 29, 1889; 1 dau., Marjorie J. (Mrs. Stafford Good). Admitted to Chester Co. and Phila. Co. bar, 1880; since in gen. practice of law in state and federal courts; active in political reform and establishing a nonpartisan judiciary. Admitted to practice before U.S. Supreme Ct. and Federal and State courts of Philadelphia, Chester and Delaware counties, Pa. Mem. Am. Bar Assn. Republican. Mem. Soc. of Friends. Home: 447 N. Church St. Office: 22 E. Market St., West Chester, Pa.

JOHNSON, George William, congressman; b. nr. Charles Town, Jefferson Co., W.Va.; s. George Dallas and Ann Elizabeth (Henry) J.; A.B. and LL.B., W.Va. Univ., 1894; m. Mary A. McKendree; children—Mildred Elizabeth, George McKendree. Practiced law at Martinsburg, W.Va., later at Parkersburg; orchardist; established Washington Jersey Farms, Wood Co., W.Va.; served as city atty. Martinsburg, asst. prosecuting atty. Parkersburg and referee in bankruptcy, U.S. Dist. Court of W.Va.; gen. counsel W.Va., Pub. Service Commn.; mem. 68th and 73d to 76th Congresses (1923-25 and 1933-41), 4th W.Va. Dist. Formerly mem. bd. regents State Normal Sch., W.Va. Democrat. Episcopalian. Mason (32°), K.P., Kiwanian, Elk. Home: Parkersburg, W.Va.*

JOHNSON, Gerald White, newspaper man; b. Riverton, N.C., Aug. 6, 1890; s. Archibald and Flora Caroline (McNeill) J.; A.B., Wake Forest Coll., 1911; Litt.D., 1928; studied U. of Toulouse, France; LL.D., Coll. of Charleston, S.C., 1935; LL.D., U. of N.C., 1937; m. Kathryn Dulsinea Hayward, Apr. 22, 1922; 2 daughters. Established Thomasville (N.C.) Davidsonian, 1910; with Lexington (N.C.) Dispatch, 1911-13; with Greensboro (N.C.) Daily News, 1913-24; prof. journalism, U. of N.C., 1924-26; editorial writer Baltimore Evening Sun, 1926-39, The Sun since 1939. Served with 321st Inf., 81st Div., U.S.A., 1917-19; with A.E.F. in France 1 yr. Democrat. Author: The Story of Man's Work (with W. R. Hayward), 1925; The Undefeated, 1926; What Is News? 1926; Andrew Jackson—An Epic in Homespun, 1927; Randolph of Roanoke—A Political Fantastic, 1929; By Reason of Strength, 1930; Number Thirty Six, 1933; The Secession of the Southern States, 1933; The Sunpapers of Baltimore (with Frank R. Kent, H.L. Mencken and Hamilton Owens), 1937; A little Night-Music, 1937; The Wasted Land, 1937; America's Silver Age, 1939. Club: West Hamilton St. Home: 1310 Bolton St. Address: care Evening Sun, Baltimore, Md.

JOHNSON, Guy Roche, engr.; b. Longdale, Va., Apr. 11, 1894; s. Guy R. and Edith Ashley (Whelen) J.; Engr. of Mines, Lehigh U., 1916; m. Dorothy Marion Jones, June 2, 1923; 1 son, Guy Roche III. Engr. Florence (Wis.) Iron Co., 1916, W.R. Shanklin Engring. Co., Joplin, Mo., 1917, Cerro de Pasco Copper Co., Peru, 1917-20; asst. to train master Reading Co., Harrisburg, Pa., 1920-28; engr. Pa. Pub. Utility Commn., Harrisburg, since 1928. Episcopalian. Clubs: Engineers, Harrisburg Country (Harrisburg). Home: 2347 N. Second St. Office: North Office Bldg., Harrisburg, Pa.

JOHNSON, Helgi, prof. geology and paleontology; b. Akureyri, Iceland, Feb. 3, 1904; s. Gisli and Gudrun (Finnsdotter) P.; came to U.S., 1929; B.Sc., U. of Manitoba, 1926; Ph.D., U. of Toronto, 1929; m. Helen Mary Hunter, Sept. 12, 1933. Engaged as student demonstrator in chemistry, U. of Manitoba, 1924-26; research asst. and class asst. geology, U. of Toronto, 1926-29; asst. Geol. Survey of Can., 1925-31; instr. geology, Rutgers U., New Brunswick, N.J., 1929-33, prof. geology since 1933; geologist (temp.), Geol. Survey of Newfoundland since 1936; research in paleozoic paleontology and stratigraphic geology. Mem. A.A.A.S., Paleontol. Soc., N.J. Archæol. Soc., Sigma Xi. Unitarian. Clubs: University Outing, Rutgers (New Brunswick). Home: Route 3, Highwood, New Brunswick, N.J.

JOHNSON, Henry R.; mem. staff Cook Hosp. Address: 320 Jefferson St., Fairmont, W.Va.

JOHNSON, Herbert, cartoonist; b. Sutton, Neb., Oct. 30, 1878; s. Joseph William and Mary Hollingsworth Bagley J.; Western Normal Coll., at Lincoln, Neb.; State U. of Neb., 1899-1901; spl. courses, Columbia; m. Helen L. Turner, Jan. 8, 1908; children—Herberta Hollingsworth, Katharine Turner. Asst. cartoonist, Denver Republican, 1896; head of art and engraving depts., Kansas City Journal, 1897-99; free lance cartoonist in New York, 1903-05; mgr. Sunday art dept., Phila. North American, 1906-09, cartoonist, North American, 1908-12; art editor, cartoonist, Saturday Evening Post, 1912-15, cartoonist Saturday Evening Post. Mem. Soc. Illustrators, Phi Delta Theta (Neb. Alpha Chapter). Mem. Soc. of Friends. Clubs: Phila. Sketch, Phila. Art, Franklin Inn, Union League, Old York Road Country; Players (New York). Home: Morningside Farm, Huntingdon Valley, Pa.

JOHNSON, Holger J(oseph), life insurance; b. Middletown, Conn., Aug. 4, 1896; s. Joseph and Hannah (Erickson) J.; prep. edn. Mt. Hermon Prep. Sch. and New Britain (Conn.) High Sch.; A.B., U. of Pittsburgh, 1922; m. Muriel Cole, Apr. 25, 1925; children—Nancy Carol, Joan Sinclair. Agent Conn. Mutual Life Ins. Co., Pittsburgh, 1922-26; asst. supt. of agencies, Home Office of Conn. Mutual, Hartford, Conn., 1926-28; gen. agent, Penn Mutual Ins. Co. of Phila., in Pittsburgh since May 1, 1928. Served in U.S. Navy Reserve during World War. Vice-pres. Metropolitan Com. of Y.M.C.A.; mem. Internat. Com. of Y.M.C.A.; vice chmn. Pittsburgh Community Fund, 1937; trustee U. of Pittsburgh; mem. bd. dirs. Ins. Fed. of Pa. Pres. Nat. Assn. of Life Underwriters, 1938-39. Mem. Penn Mutual Gen. Agents Assn. (former treas., vice-pres., pres.), Pittsburgh Life Underwriters Assn. (former pres.), Pa. State Assn. Life Underwriters (former pres.), Nat. Assn. of Life Underwriters (former conv. chmn., program chmn., chmn. gen. agts. and mgrs. sect.; nat. membership chmn., 1935; nat. edn. chmn., 1935-37; nat. vice-pres., 1937-38). Republican. Baptist. Clubs: Duquesne, Longue Vue, University, Pittsburgh Field (Pittsburgh). Contbr. to periodicals on life insurance business; speaker before life insurance underwriters' assns. Home: 540 Glen Arden Drive. Office: 1309 Clark Bldg., Pittsburgh, Pa.

JOHNSON, Howard Cooper, lawyer; b. Camden, N.J., Jan. 18, 1876; s. George K. and Sallie Kaighn (Cooper) J.; student Eastburn Acad., Phila., 1885-92; B.L., Swarthmore (Pa.) Coll., 1896; LL.B., U. of Pa., 1899; m. Edith Lamb, Apr. 16, 1903; children—Robert E. L., Howard Cooper, George K. III. Admitted to Pa. bar, 1899; in gen. practice, Phila., 1899-1927; asso. counsel Penn Mutual Life Ins. Co., 1902-27; pres. Starr Savings Bank, 1924-29; v.p. and gen. counsel Strawbridge & Clothier since 1927; pres. College Realty Co.; v.p. WFIL Broadcasting Co.; pres. bd. trustees Jeanes Hosp., 1928-30; mgr. and v.p. Swarthmore Coll.; chmn. Phila.-Com. of Pa. Economy League; pres. bd. trustees Central Soup Soc.; pres. Trustees of Phila. Yearly Meeting of Friends; advisory trustee Woman's Hosp., Phila.; mem. Philadelphia Financial Advisory Commn.; pres. Philadelphia Merchants Association. Mem. Am. Pa. State and Phila. bar assns., Law Acad. of Phila., Am. Geneal. Soc., Colonial Soc. of Pa., N.J. Soc. of Pa., Pa. Mus. Art, Franklin Inst., Delta Upsilon, Book and Key. Republican. Mem. Soc. Friends. Clubs: Union League, University, Lawyers, Kiwanis, Swarthmore, Rose Tree Hunt, Corinthian Yacht (Phila.); Players (Swarthmore); Northeast Harbor (Me.) Fleet; Southwest Harbor (Me.) Country; Keystone Auto. Home: ''Coleshill,'' Moylan, Pa. Office: 801 Market St., Philadelphia, Pa.

JOHNSON, John Bertrand, physicist; b. Gothenburg, Sweden, Oct. 2, 1887; s. Carl Bernard and Augusta (Thorson) J.; came to U.S., 1904, naturalized, 1913; B.S., U. of N.D., 1913, M.Sc., 1914; Ph.D., Yale U., 1917; m. Clara Louisa Conger, June 24, 1919; children—Bertrand Conger, Alan William. Employed as physicist, Engring. Dept., Western Electric Co., 1917-25; physicist, Bell Telephone Labs., New York City since 1925. Mem. A.A.A.S., Am. Physical Soc., Franklin Inst. of Pa., Phi Beta Kappa, Sigma Xi, Gamma Alpha. Republican. Research in ionization, electronics, cathode rays, fluctuation phenomena, television. Home: 57 Elm St., Maplewood, N.J. Office: 463 West St., New York, N.Y.

JOHNSON, John C(hristopher), prof. biology; b. Sterling, Colo., Feb. 25, 1891; s. John and Anna Helena (Berg) J.; A.B., Colo. State Coll. of Edn., 1911; ed. U. of Chicago, summers 1913, 1916; M.S., U. of Calif., 1915, Ph.D., same, 1919; grad. study, Columbia U., Harvard U., 1926; m. Vera Adams, July 23, 1915 (dec.); children—John Christopher, Jr., Clea Marie; (adopted children)—Clarence Everett Johnson, Lawrence Leverett Johnson (twins); m. 2d, Mildred Fischer, June 2, 1934. Instr. biology, agr. and edn., Colo. State Normal, Gunnison, Colo., 1911-14; asst. in zoölogy, U. of Calif., 1914-15; asso. prof. biology, Colo. State Coll. of Edn., Greeley, Colo., 1915-18; prof. biology and dean of coll., Western State Coll., Gunnison, Colo., 1919-28, v.p., same, 1927-28; dir. div. of sci. and prof. biology, Pa. State Teachers Coll., West Chester, Pa. since 1928; dir. Rocky Mountain Biol. Lab., Crested Butte, Colo. since 1928. Served as pvt. San. Corps, U.S.A., 1918-19. Mem. Town Council, Gunnison, Colo., 1922-24. Trustee The Rocky Mountain Biol. Lab. Mem. Nat. Edn. Assn., Pa. Acad. Sci. (past pres., dir.), Phi Delta Kappa, Sigma Xi, Kappa Delta Pi, Beta Beta Beta. Republican. Presbyn. Mason. Rotarian. Home: 26 Price St., West Chester, Pa.

JOHNSON, Josiah Barton, physician; b. Allegheny, Pa., Apr. 10, 1877; s. Josiah Barton and Kate (Doane) J.; M.D., U. of Pittsburgh Med. Sch., 1899; m. Mary E. Sibel, Dec. 10, 1907 (dec.); 1 son, Josiah Barton; m. 2d, Margaret Wiseman, Apr. 10, 1928; children—William Ward, Joel David. Engaged in pvt. practice of medicine in Pittsburgh, 1899-1902, in Ligonier, Pa., since 1902. Served as capt. Med. Corps, U.S.A., 1918-19; capt. M.C., Pa. N.G. since 1927. Mem. A.M.A., Pa. State Med. Soc., Westmoreland Co. Med. Soc., Nu Sigma Nu. Republican. Lutheran. Mason. Club: Country (Ligonier, Pa.). Home: 230 W. Main St. Office: 232 W. Main St., Ligonier, Pa.

JOHNSON, Kate Burr (Mrs. Clarence A. Johnson), social worker; b. Morganton, N.C., Feb. 14, 1881; d. Frederick Hill and Lillian (Walton) Burr; Queen's Coll., Charlotte, N.C.; studied summers N.Y. Sch. Social Work, U. of N.C.; m. Clarence A. Johnson, Apr. 14, 1903 (died Sept. 9, 1922); children—Clarence A., Frederick Burr. Dir. Bur. Child Welfare of N.C. State Bd. Charities and Pub. Welfare, 1919-21; commr. pub. welfare, N.C., 1921-30; supt. N.J. State Home for Girls, Trenton, since 1930. Vice-pres. N.C. Conf. for Social Service, 1915-16; pres. N.C. Federation Women's Clubs, 1917-19; mem. State Com. for sale of Liberty Bonds, 1917-18. Chmn. com. on state and local orgns. for handicapped, White House Conf. on Child Health and Protection. Mem. Am. Assn. Social Workers, Nat. Conf. of Juvenile Agencies, N.J. Conf. of Social Work, Am. Prison Assn., League of Women Voters. Democrat. Episcopalian. Address: State Home for Girls, Trenton, N.J.

JOHNSON, Laurence Bicknell, educator; b. Phila., Pa., Sept. 24, 1901; s. Julius Bicknell and Elizabeth (Long) J.; student Avon (N.Y.) High Sch., 1913-16, Pa. State Coll., 1922-24; B.A., Central High Sch., Phila., 1918; B.A., U. of Pa., 1922; M.A., Teachers Coll. of Columbia U., 1933; unmarried. Teacher, Pa. State Coll., 1922-24; prof. of English, U. of the Philippines, Manila, P.I., 1924-27; copy editor Manila (P.I.) Tribune, 1926; asst. city editor Manila Daily Bulletin, 1926-27; fgn. corr. N.Y. Evening Post and Chicago Tribune, 1926-27; county editor New Brunswick (N.J.) Home News, 1927; dir. of information, Rutgers Prep. Sch., New Brunswick, N.J., 1927-28; editor Newark Sch. Bulletin, Newark (N.J.) Bd. of Edn., 1928-33; now field sec., N.J. Edn. Assn.; mng. editor N.J. Ednl. Review since 1934. Mem. N.J. Edn. Assn., N.E.A., Sch. Pub. Relations Assn. (ex-pres.), Ednl. Press Assn. (ex-pres.), Pi Kappa Alpha. Independent Republican. Baptist. Club: Advertising (New York City). Author: Interpreting the Schools. Co-author: College Composition; Test Your Bids; How's Your Culbertson. Home: 150 N. Munn

Av., East Orange, N.J. Office: 605 Broad St., Newark, N.J.

JOHNSON, Lester Fremen, headmaster; b. Lewes, Del., July 17, 1897; s. John Burton and Lucy Walter (Dutton) J.; A.B., Dickinson Coll., Carlisle, Pa., 1919; M.S., U. of Pa., 1938; m. Ella Virginia Frazer, Aug. 25, 1920; children—Ella Elizabeth, Lester Fremen. Instr. mathematics, Wesley Collegiate Inst., Dover, Del., 1920-25; instr. mathematics, York Collegiate Inst., York, Pa., 1925-34, instr. and headmaster since 1934. Served in U.S.N., 1918. Mem. York Chamber of Commerce. Mem. Theta Chi, Phi Delta Kappa. Methodist. Club. Rotary (York, Pa.). Home: 832 McKenzie St., York, Pa.

JOHNSON, Lewis Edgar, banker; b. Monroe Co., W.Va., Sept. 29, 1860; s. William B. and Agnes R. (Hinchman) J.; ed. pub. and pvt. schs.; grad. Eastman Business Coll., Poughkeepsie, N.Y., 1880: m. Jane Ella Johnson, May 2, 1889; children—Mary Pauline, Agnes (Mrs. Joseph B. Vernon), Ellen Langley. Hardware and furniture business, with George K. Gwinn, at Alderson, since 1883; cashier Greenbrier Valley Bank, Alderson, 1896-1900, pres. 1900-09; pres. First Nat. Bank (consolidation of Greenbrier Valley Bank and First Nat. Bank) since 1909; dir. Federal Reserve Bank of Richmond; sec. and treas. Greenbrier Milling Co.; partner firm Johnson & George (farming), etc. Served as county chmn. Draft Bd., World War. Democrat. Presbyn. Home: Alderson, W.Va.

JOHNSON, Lewis Howes, telephone engring.; b. Thomaston, Me., May 11, 1886; s. Merritt Austin and Nora Clementine (Howes) J.; S.B., Mass. Inst. Tech., 1909; m. Blanche Wilda Robinson, June 10, 1909; children—Ralph Edward, Mary Helen (Mrs. George Marius Stein Albertsen), Elizabeth Ann. Mem. tech. staff, engring. dept. Western Electric Co., 1909-25; mem. tech. staff, Bell Telephone Labs. since 1925. In charge of engring. telephone and telegraph equipment for A.E.F. during World War. Sr. mem. and navigator, U.S. Power Squadrons; lt. comdr. N.Y. Power Squadron. Mem. Am. Inst. Elec. Engrs., Science Forum, N.Y. Elec. Soc., Telephone Pioneers of America, S.A.R. Republican. Methodist. Clubs: Town Hall, Technology, Harlem Yacht (New York); Huntington Yacht (Huntington, N.Y.); Rockland Community Yacht (Rockland, Me.). Home: 61 Garfield Av., Madison, N.J. Office: 463 West St., New York, N.Y.

JOHNSON, Louis Arthur, asst. sec. of War; b. Roanoke, Va., Jan. 10, 1891; s. Marcellus A. and Katherine Leftwich (Arthur) J.; LL.B., U. of Va., 1912; m. Ruth F. Maxwell, Feb. 7, 1920; children—Lillian Maxwell, Ruth Katherine. Began practice at Clarksburg, W.Va., 1912; mem. firm Steptoe & Johnson, Clarksburg and Charleston; dir. Union Nat. Bank, Community Savings & Loan Co. (both Clarksburg). Became civilian aide to Sec. of War, State of W.Va., 1933; mem. Federal Advisory Council of U.S. Employment Service under Dept. of Labor; apptd. by President asst. sec. of War, June 28, 1937. Served as capt., inf., overseas 1 yr., World War; lt. col. Inf. Res. Decorated Comdr. Legion of Honor (France). Mem. W.Va. Ho. of Rep., 1917 (chmn. Judiciary com.; majority floor leader). Nat. comdr. Am. Legion, 1932-33. Del. to Dem. Nat. Conv., 1924. Mem. Am., W.Va. State and Harrison Co. bar assns., Assn. Bar City New York, Nat. Soc. S.A.R., Reserve Officers Assn. of U.S., F.I.D.A.C. (v.p. for U.S. 1933-34), Delta Chi, Delta Sigma Rho, Raven. Democrat. Episcopalian. Mason, Elk. Clubs: Bohemian (San Francisco); Metropolitan, Army and Navy, Burning Tree, Chevy Chase (Washington, D.C.); Rotary (ex-pres.), Clarksburg Country; University, Midday, Drug and Chemical (New York). Home: 239 E. Main St. Office: Union Nat. Bank Bldg., Clarksburg, W.Va.; and War Dept., Washington, D.C.

JOHNSON, Norman Gardner, chemist; b. Oakland, Calif., July 4, 1902; s. George and Gerda Maria (Bark) J.; B.Sc., U. of Wash., 1925; m. Elizabeth B. Benford, July 5, 1930; children—Barbara Elizabeth, Carolyn Gardner. Chemist, Eastern Lab., E. I. Du Pont de Nemours & Co., Inc., Gibbstown, N.J., 1926-38, head of explosives div. since 1938; awarded a number of patents pertaining to high explosives; dir. Wenonah Bldg. & Loan Assn. Mem. Am. Chem. Soc., Tech. Assn. Paper & Pulp Industry, Sigma Xi, Phi Lambda Upsilon, Pi Kappa Phi. Republican. Contbr. tech. articles to scientific jours. Home: 9 N. Jackson St., Wenonah, N.J. Office: Eastern Labs., Gibbstown, N.J.

JOHNSON, Philander Chase, editor; b. Wheeling, W.Va., Feb. 6, 1866; s. Sylvanus E. and Martha A. (Mann) J.; ed. in Cincinnati; m. Washington, Oct. 21, 1890, Louise Covert (dec.); m. 2d, Mrs. Mary A. Hagman, d. of late Brig.-Gen Daniel W. Adams, C.S.A., Apr. 8, 1908. Conducted humorous and lit. depts. in Merchant Traveler, Chicago, and Washington (D.C.) Critic, also Capital, column "Postscripts" in Post; now editorial contbr. to Washington Star. Since July 15, 1891, has written for that paper daily contbns. of miscellaneous verse and dialogue, under caption, "Shooting Stars," also reviews of theater. Mason (32°, Shriner). Club: Gridiron. Author: Sayings of Uncle Eben, 1897; Now-a-Day Poems, 1900, Senator Sorghum's Primer of Politics, 1906. Song verse of the war ballad, "Somewhere in France is the Lily," 1917. Home: Rockville Pike, Rockville, Md.*

JOHNSON, Ralph Grant, pres. R. G. Johnson Co.; b. Washington, D.C., Mar. 19, 1882; s. Jerome F. and Eliza (Woodruff) J.; C.E., Lehigh U., 1904; m. Adella Barnes, Nov. 5, 1910; children—Marian J., Priscilla, Woodruff B., R. Grant, Jr. With Dravo Contracting Co., Pittsburgh, 1904-17, v.p., 1916-17; pres. R. G. Johnson Co. since 1917; dir. and mem. exec. com. Citizens Nat. Bank of Washington; dir. George Washington Hotel Co. Dir. Washington Hosp. Republican. Presbyterian. Clubs: Duquesne, University (Pittsburgh); Gibson Island (Md.). Home: Redstone Lane. Office: Washington Trust Bldg., Washington, Pa.

JOHNSON, Robert Lee, professional baseball player; b. Pryor, Okla., Nov. 26, 1906. Began as baseball player, 1929, with Wichita, Pueblo and Portland (Ore.) teams; outfielder with Phila. Am. League team since 1933. Mem. Am. League All-Star Team, 1938, 1939. Address: care Phila. American League Baseball Club., Philadelphia, Pa.

JOHNSON, Robert Wilkinson, Jr., surgeon; b. Baltimore, Md., June 3, 1891; s. Robert W. and Julia Watts Hall (Brock) J.; A.B., Princeton U., 1912; M.D., Johns Hopkins U. Med. Sch., 1917; m. Rose Gordon Haxall, June 5, 1917; children—Robert Wilkinson III, John Triplett Haxall, Rose Gordon. Asst. in orthopedic surgery, Johns Hopkins U. Med. Sch., 1919-26, instr., 1926-29, asso. since 1929; prof. orthopedic surgery, U. of Md. Med. Sch., 1929-31; engaged in practice orthopedic surgery, Baltimore, Md., since 1919, mem. firm Drs. Bennett, Johnson & Eaton since 1919. Served in Med. Res. U.S.A., 1917-19, attached to B.E.F. Trustee Calvert Sch., Children's Hosp. Sch., Playground Athletic League, St. Paul's P.E. Ch. Mem. Am. Med. Assn., Am. Orthopedic Assn., Am. Acad. Orthopedic Surgeons, Phi Beta Kappa. Episcopalian. Clubs: University, Elkridge (Baltimore); Colonial (Princeton). Home: 16 Midvale Rd. Office: 4 E. Madison St., Baltimore, Md.

JOHNSON, Robert William, M.D., surgeon; b. Springfield, S.C., Nov. 4, 1888; s. Hansford Robert and Ada (Udora) J.; student Windsor (S.C.) High Sch., 1900-04; M.D., U. of Md., 1915; m. Helen Marr Forsyth, 1917; children—Vivian Helen, Robert William, Roma Geraldine, Veatrice Clarice. Employed by village store, Windsor, S.C., 1904, Jones Furniture Co., Augusta, Ga., 1905-11; asst. supt. Euduwood Sanatorium, 1915-16; interne St. Agnes Hosp. and Md. Gen. Hosp., Baltimore, then supt. South Baltimore Hosp.; now in gen. practice medicine and surgery; instr. surgery and allied subjects, U. of Md.; pres. Southern Land Co., Security Development Corpn., Ake-O-Dyne Co.; DuPont Cemetery Co. Served as 1st lt., Med. Corps, Md. Nat. Guard on Mexican Border; British ship surgeon, 3 mos.; capt. Med. Corps, serving in gen. hosps. in France and U.S., 2 yrs., World War. Mem. A.M.A., Md. State Med. Soc., Baltimore City Med. Soc., Md. Acad. Medicine and Surgery, Brooklyn Bd. of Trade (mem. bd. govs.), Chi Zeta Chi. Democrat. Baptist. K.P., Odd Fellow, Redman. Home: 3614 Sixth St. Office: 3564 Hanover St. and 117 W. Saratoga St., Baltimore, Md.

JOHNSON, Robert Wood, pres. Johnson & Johnson; b. New Brunswick, N.J., April 4, 1893; s. Robert Wood and Evangeline (Armstrong) J.; ed. at Lawrenceville Sch. and by pvt. tutors; m. Elizabeth D. Ross, Oct. 18, 1916 (divorced); 1 son, Robert Wood; m. 2d, Margaret Shea, Sept. 19, 1930; 1 dau., Sheila. Entered the family firm of Johnson & Johnson, mfrs. of surgical dressings, 1910, v.p., 1918-30, v.p. and gen. mgr. 1930-32, pres. since 1932; dir. of subsidiaries. Mem. City Council of Highland Park, N.J., 1918-19, mayor, 1920-22. Pres. Middlesex Gen. Hosp., New Brunswick, 1921-27. Patron of Am. Mus. of Natural History. Episcopalian. Clubs: Racquet and Tennis, New York Yacht, Cruising, River (New York); Stony Brook Hunt, Pretty Brook Tennis (Princeton); Mt. Royal (Montreal); Porcupine (Bahamas). Home: Princeton, N.J. Office: Johnson & Johnson, New Brunswick, N.J.

JOHNSON, Russell Conwell, dir. athletics and baseball coach; b. Parkerford, Pa., Oct. 9, 1894; s. Harry Wm. and Alice Rambo (Shantz) J.; B.S., Ursinus Coll., 1916; m. Mary H. Seiz, June 11, 1919; 1 son, Donald Seiz. Began as pitcher in professional baseball, 1916; pitcher, Phila. Athletics, 1916, 17, 19, 27, 28, Baltimore, 1928, Allentown, 1929; with Oil City, Shamokin, and Allentown, 1920-26; baseball coach, Bucknell U., 1922, Lehigh U., 1925-27; exptl. and research work, Bethlehem Steel Coke Plant, Bethlehem, Pa., 1923-25; dir. athletics and baseball coach, Ursinus Coll., since 1930. Served as chief storekeeper, U.S.N.R.F., 1918. Pres. Collegeville Sch. Bd.; mem. Collegeville-Trappe Joint Sch. Bd. Mem. Middle Atlantic States Coll. Athletic Conf. (pres. 1936-37), Middle Atlantic Intercollegiate Football Assn. (sec.-treas.), Eastern Collegiate Athletic Conf. (sec.-treas.), Eastern Pa. Collegiate Basketball and Baseball Leagues (past pres.). Republican. Baptist (teacher Men's Bible Class). Mason. Home: 44 6th Av., Collegeville, Pa.

JOHNSON, Theodore, pres. Johnson Metal Products Co.; b. McKeesport, Pa., Jan. 18, 1888; s. Otto G. and Anna J.; student high sch., and commercial coll.; m. Kathryne Buchner, June 15, 1911; children—Donald, David, Jean. Engaged in tool making, 1905-10; musician and teacher, 1910-15; mech. and steam engring., 1915-24; pres. and chmn. of dirs. Johnson Metal Products Co., Erie, Pa., since 1924. Home: 356 E. 29th St. Office: 1316 Holland St., Erie, Pa.

JOHNSON, Thomas Hope, physicist; b. Coldwater, Mich., Sept. 12, 1899; s. Henry Elmore and Anna (Darling) J.; A.B., Amherst (Mass.) Coll., 1920; grad. study, U. of Chicago, 1922-23; Ph.D., Yale Grad. Sch., 1926; m. Mrs. Anna Benedict, Jan. 24, 1930. Grad. student and instr. mathematics, U. of Me., Orono, Me., 1920-21; instr. mathematics and physics, Moses Brown Sch., Providence, R.I., 1921-23; research fellow Yale U., 1927; Bartol Fellow, Bartol Research Foundation, Swarthmore, Pa., 1927-30, asst. dir. since 1930; research asso. of Carnegie Instn. of Washington since 1933; instr. Grad. Sch., U. of Pa., 1935-38; instr. physics, Swarthmore (Pa.) Coll. since 1936; mem. Editorial Bd., Phys. Review since 1938. Served as lt. comdr., E-V(s), U.S.N.R., since 1937. Fellow Am. Phys. Soc., A.A.A.S., Am. Geophys. Union; mem. Sigma Xi, Delta Upsilon. Honored as ninth Joseph Henry Lecturer of Washington Philos. Soc. Presbyterian. Contbr. many sci. articles. Organized expdns. for Cosmic Ray Measurements to Mexico, 1933, Panama & Peru, 1933, Mexico, 1934, Northern Manitoba, 1937, Panama, 1939. Home: "Meriwether," Westtown, Pa. Office: Bartol Research Foundation, Swarthmore, Pa.

JOHNSON, Virgil Lamont, architect, engr.; b. Mannsville, Jefferson Co., N.Y., June 10, 1868; s. Levi and Harriet C. (Baker) J.; prep. edn., Adams (N.Y.) Collegiate Inst.; spl. course in architecture, U. of Pa., 1898; m. Elizabeth W. Johnson, June 10, 1901; children—Katharine, Elenore, Harriette, Ruth, Virgil. Began in Buffalo, 1894; settled in Phila., 1901; chief structural engr. for over 160 public sch. bldgs. for Phila. Bd. of Edn. Mem. Am. Inst. Architects. Home: 29 W. Upsal St., Germantown, Philadelphia, Pa.

JOHNSON, William Hallock, educator; b. New York, Dec. 3, 1865; s. John Edgar and Fanny Elizabeth (Hallock) J.; A.B. Princeton, 1888, A.M., 1897; Union Theol. Sem., 1891, grad. student, 1901-02; Princeton Theological Seminary, 1894-96, grad. student, 1896-97, B.D., 1897; also D.D., Princeton University, 1935; Ph.D., Columbia U., 1902; D.D., Centre Coll. of Ky., 1914; U. of Jena, summer semester, 1904; m. Virginia Sherrard, June 22, 1905; children—Hallock Sherrard, Roswell Park. Ordained Presbyn. ministry, 1897; prof. logic and psychology, Centre Coll., Danville, Ky., 1897-1901; instr. N.T. lit. and exegesis, Danville Theol. Sem., 1897-1901; became prof. Greek and N.T. lit., Lincoln U., Pa., 1903, acting pres., 1925, pres. 1926-36, now emeritus. L.P. Stone lecturer, Princeton Theological Sem., 1913-14, 1930-31. Trustee Princeton Theological Sem., 1929. Mem. Phi Beta Kappa. Author: The Free-Will Problem in Modern Thought, 1903; The Christian Faith Under Modern Searchlights, 1916; Can the Christian Now Believe in Evolution?, 1926. Humanism and Christian Theism, 1931. Contbr. to religious jours. Address: 9 Hamilton Av., Princeton, N.J.

JOHNSTON, Alfred Meahan, banker; b. Pittsburgh, Pa., Oct. 11, 1876; s. George B. and Sarah Jane (French) J.; grad. Pittsburgh High Sch., 1894, Iron City Coll., Pittsburgh, 1895; m. Kathryn McKean, Sept. 3, 1902; children—George Stuart, Alfred McKean, Wallace Coulson, Dorothy Lucile, Jean Carol. Clerk Keystone Chem. Co., Pittsburgh, 1895-96; stenographer Nat. Bank of Commerce, Pittsburgh, 1896-1901; with The Old Freeport Bank since Apr. 15, 1901, cashier, 1901-30, pres. since Jan. 19, 1930; vice-pres. Kerr Coal Co., Freeport. Republican. Mem. United Presbyterian Ch. Mason (32°, Shriner), Odd Fellow. Mem. Kiwanis Club of Freeport (treas. since 1937). Home: 319 4th St. Office: 5th St., Freeport, Pa.

JOHNSTON, Archibald, steel mfr.; b. Phoenixville, Pa., May 30, 1865; s. Joseph and Martha E. (Stroman) J.; M.E. Lehigh U., 1889; m. Estelle S. Borhek, Feb. 11, 1891. Entered employ Bethlehem Steel Co., physical testing dept., 1889; later in charge erection and operation gun forging plant, same co. (the first to be established in America); took charge of erection, and later supt. of armor plate dept. (also first to be built in America); asst. gen. supt., later gen. supt., and from 1908 v.p. Bethlehem Steel Co., retired, 1927. First mayor City of Bethlehem, Pa., 1917-21; chmn. City Planning Commn. Trustee Moravian Coll. and Theol. Sem., Bethlehem. Republican. Moravian, Mem. Am. Soc. M.E., Am. Inst. Mining and Metal Engrs., Am. Iron and Steel Inst., Iron and Steel Inst. (Great Britain), Pan-Am. Soc. the U.S., Theta Delta Chi. Home: R.D. 1, Camel's Hump, Bethlehem, Pa.*

JOHNSTON, Cecil C., banker; b. Hazel Dell, Pa., Aug. 3, 1879; s. Jordan and Nancy Jane (Boots) J.; ed. rural schs. Lawrence Co., Pa.; married 1st, Aug. 12, 1901; 1 son, Henry C.; m. 2d, Belle Nickols, Oct. 20, 1917; children—William D., Charles C., Sylvia Joan. Sch. teacher, 1898-1901; bank clerk, 1901-06, cashier, 1906-18, pres., 1918-20; vice-pres. Crawford County Trust Co. (merger of Commonwealth Bank and Crawford County Trust Co.) since 1920; pres. and dir. Townville (Pa.) State Bank; dir. and asst. treas. Meadville Telephone Co.; dir. Meadville Malleable Iron Co., Reznor Mfg. Co., Mercer, Pa., Cochranton Telephone Co. Mem. sch. bd., Meadville, 12 yrs. (pres. of bd. 6 yrs.). Trustee Meadville Y.M.C.A., Y.W.C.A. Republican. Baptist. Mason (32°, K.T.). Mem. Meadville Round Table. Home: 593 Chestnut St. Office: Crawford County Trust Co., Meadville, Pa.

JOHNSTON, Emma Louisa, writer; b. Paterson, N.J.; d. James and Alice (Ridings) J.;
A.B., Adelphi Coll., 1899; (hon.) A.M., Adelphi Coll., 1915. Began as teacher in pub. schs., Brooklyn, N.Y., 1882; teacher, Brooklyn Training Sch. for Teachers, 1885-1902; prin. Maxwell Training Sch. for Teachers, Brooklyn, N.Y., 1904-28, retired 1928. State pres. for N.J., Nat. League of Am. Pen Women (also pres. Paterson Branch). Republican. Episcopalian. Clubs: Paterson Women's College, Paterson Branch, National League of American Pen Women. Co-author (with William H. Maxwell), School Composition, 1902; (with William H. Maxwell and Madalene D. Barnum), Speaking and Writing, 1915; (with Madalene D. Barnum), Book of Plays for Little Actors, 1907. Author: (verse) Questing Spirit, 1936, awarded first prize in biennial award from Nat. League Am. Pen Women, 1938. Home: 81 Carroll St., Paterson, N.J.; Summit Av., Campgaw, N.J.

JOHNSTON, Harry Lang, newspaper editor; b. Hollidaysburg, Pa., Apr. 1, 1873; s. William Noble and Laura (Lang) J.; ed. pub. schs.; m. Annie Cherry Bunker, May 4, 1899; children—Helen Louise (Mrs. J. Lewis Hammitt, Jr.), Anna Margaret (Mrs. Frederick B. Sheldon). Began career in employ Democratic Standard, Hollidaysburg, Pa., 1889; asso. with Altoona Mirror since 1900, editor since 1908. Democrat. Baptist. Odd Fellow. Clubs: Blairmont Country, Rotary. Home: 3508 Oneida Av. Office: 1000 Green Av., Altoona, Pa.

JOHNSTON, Henry Rust, banker; b. Chicago, Ill., Feb. 13, 1888; s. James Wright and Bessie (Rust) J.; grad. University High Sch., Chicago, 1905; A.B., Williams Coll., 1909; LL.B., cum laude, New York Law Sch., 1912; m. Helen Earle, May 20, 1914; children—Douglas Earle, David Prince, Alexander Rust. Admitted to N.Y. bar, 1912, and began practice at N.Y. City; mem. firm Greene & Hurd until 1917; asst. to pres. Mercantile Trust Co., 1919-21; with Chatham Phenix Nat. Bank & Trust Co. (now Mfrs. Trust Co.), 1921-33, was v.p. and dir.; vice-pres. and dir. Case, Pomeroy & Co., 1933-38, pres. since 1938. Served in U.S.N. Flying Corps, World War. Chmn. Nat. Interfraternity Conf., 1925-26, instituting system of ann. surveys of scholarship of male students in 120 colls. and univs. of U.S. Mem. Borough Council of Essex Fells, N.J., 2 terms 1929-35, pres. 1935; mem. N.J. State Prison Bd., Trenton, since 1934. Trustee Williams Coll., 1926-31; pres. Soc. of Alumni of Williams Coll., 1933-36. Mem. Delta Kappa Epsilon. Republican. Episcopalian. Clubs: University, Williams, Down Town Assn. (New York); Montclair (N.J.) Golf, Pine Valley Golf. Donor of Amherst-Williams Trophy of Trophies, 1919. Home: Forest Rd., Essex Fells, N.J. Office: 1 Cedar St., New York, N.Y.

JOHNSTON, Howard Malcolm, railroad exec.; b. Clarion Twp., Clarion Co., Pa., May 15, 1891; s. Thomas Grant and Alfaretta (Potter) J.; student grade sch.; m. Augusta (Snyder) Hetrick, Feb. 20, 1919; 1 adopted step-son, Eugene Ralph. Warehouseman, Lake Erie, Franklin & Clarion R.R., Clarion, Pa., 1908-09, sta. agt., 1909-15, chief clerk, 1915-18, acting auditor, 1918-19, auditor, 1919-20, auditor and treas., 1920-36, dir. since 1922, v.p., treas. and gen. mgr. since 1936. Mem. Am. Short Line R.R. Assn., Assn. of Am. Railroads (freight claim div.). Mason (Royal Arch; K.T.; Scottish Rite; Consistory), Odd Fellow. Club: Washington (Franklin, Pa.) Home: 58 S. Fifth Av. Office: Ninth Av., Clarion, Pa.

JOHNSTON, John, chemist; b. Perth, Scotland, Oct. 13, 1881; s. James and Christina (Leslie) J.; B.Sc., Univ. Coll. (U. of St. Andrews), Dundee, Scotland, 1903; work in chemistry, Univ. Coll., 1903-05, U. of Breslau, Germany, Prof. Abegg, 1905-07; research asso. in physical chemistry, Mass. Inst. Tech., 1907-08; D.Sc., U. of St. Andrews, 1908; hon. M.A., Yale, 1919; hon. D.Sc., New York U., 1928, Lehigh, 1929; m. Dorothy Hopkins, July 17, 1909; children—Helen Leslie, John Murray, William Valentine. On staff of Geophysical Lab., Carnegie Instn. of Washington, 1908-16; in charge research dept. for Am. Zinc, Lead and Smelting Co., St. Louis, 1916-17, U.S. Bur. of Mines, 1917-18; sec. Nat. Research Council, Washington, 1918-19; prof. chemistry and chmn.
chemistry dept. Yale, 1919-27; dir. of research, U.S. Steel Corpn., 1927—. Mem. Nat. Research Council. Mem. Am. Chem. Soc., A.A.A.S., Franklin Institute, American Electrochemical Society (pres. 1933-34), American Society for Metals, American Institute Mining and Metall. Engineers, American Iron and Steel Inst., British Iron and Steel Inst., Faraday Soc., Inst. Metals, Verein deutscher Eisenhüttenleute. Clubs: Century, Chemists' (New York); University (Pittsburgh); Short Hills. Home: Short Hills, N.J. Address: U.S. Steel Corpn. of Del., 436 7th Av., Pittsburgh, Pa.

JOHNSTON, John Harold, univ. exec.; b. Brooklyn, N.Y., Aug. 2, 1898; s. John and Katherine C. (Schade) J.; B.S., Rutgers U., 1920; m. Lucile E. Knight, June 16, 1928; children—Robert Chapman, David Knight. Exec. sec., Leopold Schepp Foundation, N.Y. City, 1926-36; asst. to pres. of Rutgers Univ. since 1936. Mem. N.J. State Com. Y.M.C.A.; mem. Personnel Services Com., Nat. Council Y.M.C.A.; ex-pres. Ridgewood (N.J.) Y.M.C.A. Mem. Pi Kappa Alpha (past nat. sec.). Republican. Mem. Reformed Ch. in America. Home: 40 Harrison Av., Highland Park, N.J.

JOHNSTON, Lemuel Roy, educator; b. Haw River, N.C., Jan. 23, 1892; s. John William and Virginia (Hall) J.; A.B., U. of N.C., Chapel Hill, N.C., 1914; M.A., Teachers Coll., Columbia, 1925; Ph.D., New York U., 1936; m. Annie Laurie Wicker, June 28, 1921; 1 dau., Rebecca Holt. Teacher mathematics and science, Oak Ridge (N.C.) Inst., 1914-17 and 1919-20; teacher mathematics, High Point (N.C.) High Sch., 1921-22, prin. 1922-33; instr. in edn., summer schs., U. of N.C. Womans Coll. 1926, Duke U., Durham, N.C., 1928, 29, 30 and 31, New York U., 1932, 33, 34, 35 and 36, U. of N.C. 1937 and 38; prin. Hawthorne (N.J.) High Sch., 1933-37; prin. Clifford J. Scott High Sch., E. Orange, N.J., since 1937. Served as 1st lt., 113th F.A., Hdqrs. Co., Adj. 19th F.A. Brig., 1917-19. Mem. N.J. Council of Edn., Nat. Assn. of Secondary Prins., N.J. Schoolmasters Club, N.J. High Sch. Prins. Assn., Kappa Delta Pi, Phi Delta Kappa. Presbyterian. Mason. Address: 21 Sherman Av., E. Orange, N.J.

JOHNSTON, Percy Hampton; banker; b. Lebanon, Ky., Jan. 1, 1881; s. William Johnston and Bluford (Oliver) J.; ed. pub. schs.; m. Belle Rogers; children—Percy H., Dorothy Belle. Began as clk. Marion Nat. Bank, Lebanon, 1897; apptd. nat. bank examiner, 1907, and became chmn. of examiners in states south of Ohio River and east of Miss. River, later one of nat. bank examiners at large; apptd. cashier Citizens Nat. Bank, Louisville, Ky., 1913; v.p., 1916; sr. v.p. Chem. Nat. Bank (now Chemical Bank & Trust Co.), New York, 1917-20, pres., 1920-35, chmn. bd. dirs. since Jan. 1935; also dir. many corpns. Presbyterian. Clubs: Bankers, Santee, The Links, Recess (New York); Ristigouche Salmon, Baltusrol. Home: 32 Pleasant Av., Montclair, N.J. Office: 165 Broadway, New York, N.Y.

JOHNSTON, Richard Holland, librarian; b. Windsor, Ont., Can., May 6, 1868; s. Rev. Hugh (D.D.) and Eliza (Holland) J.; B.A., U. of Toronto, 1889; post-grad. work in theology, Victoria Coll., 1889-92; m. Elizabeth Deborah, d. William Thode, of Baltimore, Md., 1900; children—Hugh Libertus, Richard Holland, Mary Alice. Librarian Victoria Coll., 1892-96; reference desk, Library of Congress, 1897-1910; librarian Bur. of Ry. Economics Library of the Association of American Railways (special collection of 175,000 items pertaining to rys.) since 1910. Fellow Am. Library Inst.; mem. A.A.A.S., A.L.A., Special Libraries Assn. (ex-pres.), Bibliog. Soc. America. Clubs: University (Washington, D.C.) Wrote: Bibliography of Thomas Jefferson, 1905; Special Libraries, 1915, revised edit., 1931. Compiler of Railway Economics, 1912. Home: Silver Spring, Md. Office: Transportation Bldg., Washington, D.C.

JOHNSTON, S(amuel) Paul, editor; b. Pittsburgh, Pa., Aug. 3, 1899; s. James Irvin and Bertha Wilson (Gill) J.; student Carnegie Inst. Tech., 1917-19; B.S., in mech. engring., Mass. Inst. Tech., 1921; m. Carol Bates Rhodes, Dec.

28, 1923; children—Mary Carol, James Irvin II. Began as apprentice Aluminum Co. of America, 1921, in operating dept. New Kensington Works, 1921-22, Pittsburgh office, 1922-23, Massena (N.Y.) plant, 1923-28 (asst. supt., 1925-28), staff chief engr., Pittsburgh, 1928-29; writing, 1930-31; asst. editor Aviation, 1931-34, asso. editor, 1934-35, acting editor, 1935-36, editor since Apr. 1936. Served in R.O.T.C. and in Air Service, U.S.A., May-Dec. 1918; now lieut. comdr. U.S.N.R. Mem. Com. on Award for Collier Trophy for 1937. Mem. advisory com. N.Y. World's Fair, 1939, aviation com. Merchants Assn. N.Y.; hon. mem. maintenance com. Air Transport Assn.; Asso. fellow Inst. Aeronautical Sciences. Author: Aviation Handbook (with E. P. Warner), 1931; also author aeronautics sect. Kent's Mechanical Engineer's Handbook (with E. P. Warner), 1936. Contbr. to Aviation and other jours. Home: 847 Shadowlawn Drive, Westfield, N.J. Offices: 330 W. 42d St., New York, N.Y.

JOHNSTONE, Arthur Edward, composer; b. London, Eng., May 13, 1860; s. Frank E. and Minnie (DeFries) J.; was brought to America, 1868; ed. Coll. City of New York; studied piano with Dr. William Mason, and organ and theory with Samuel Prowse Warren and higher composition with Dr. Leopold Damrosch; m. Clara Archer Butler, June 28, 1885. Has made a specialty of composition including piano methods and music for pub. sch. text books; won medal, 1902, for best original setting of "America," offered by Soc. of the Cincinnati. Composer, with Harvey Worthington Loomis, of all the music (6 books) comprising the "Foresman System of Pianoforte Instruction," an innovation, utilizing the modern player piano as a means of teaching how to play the piano by hand; also with same, Lyric Music Series, 4 vols. Was exec. editor Art Publication Soc., dir. Progressive Series Teachers Coll. and prof. of harmony and lecturer on music appreciation, Washington U. summer sessions; now teaching harmony, composition, and piano. Address: 21 N. Franklin St., Wilkes-Barre, Pa.

JOHNSTONE, Burton Kenneth, architect, prof. architecture; b. Chicago, Ill., Jan. 20, 1907; s. Burton Clermont and Margaret (Wulff) J.; B.S. in Architecture, U. of Ill., 1928; ed. Lake Forest Foundation for Architecture and Landscape Architecture, summer 1928; B.F.A., Yale U., 1929; grad. study, Am. Acad. in Rome, Italy, 1929-32, F.A.A.R., 1932; m. Helene Estelle Hetzel, Aug. 27, 1938. Engaged as asst. in design, U. of Ill., 1928, Yale U., 1929; asst. prof. archtl. design, Pa. State Coll., 1933-35, asso. prof. and head dept. architecture, 1936-38, prof. and head dept. architecture since 1938. Mem. Soc. for Promotion Engring. Edn., Pa. Assn. Architects, Scarab (nat. pres.), Pi Kappa Alpha, Tau Beta Pi, Sigma Tau. Awarded Prix de Rome in Architecture, 1929. Republican. Lutheran. Home: Glennland Apt., State College, Pa.

JOHNSTONE, Edward Lehmann, educator; b. Vineland, N.J., April 1, 1902; s. Edward Ransom and Olive (Lehmann) J.; student pub. and high schs., Vineland, N.J., also Rutgers U., 1921-22; m. Angie Lirio, Feb. 17, 1934; 1 dau., Susan. Editor Winter Park (Fla.) Herald, 1922-24; dir. Patient Welfare, Woodbine Colony, Woodbine, N.J., 1924-25, asst. supt., 1929-30, supt. since 1930; engaged in publicity and advertising, Orlando, Fla., 1925-26; supervisor of occupational therapy, State Hosp., Greystone Park, N.J., 1927-29. Chmn. Cape May Co. Welfare Bd. since 1933; dir. Emergency Relief Adminstrn., Cape May Co., 1933-34; chmn. Nat. Re-employment Service, Cape May Co., 1933-34; trustee N.J. Welfare Council. Mem. Nat. Conf. Juvenile Agencies (sec. and editor The Proceedings since 1930), Am. Assn. on Mental Deficiency, Am. Prison Assn., Nat. Jail Assn., Nat. Conf. Social Work, Supts. Conf.; consultant Ednl. Policies Commn. U.S. Baptist. Mason (32°, Shriner). Clubs: Yacht, Tuna (Ocean City, N.J.); Juniper Hunting (Astor, Fla. and Louisville, Ky.). Contbr. papers on care and training of mental defectives. Address: Woodbine Colony, Woodbine, N.J.

JOHNSTONE, Edward Ransom, humanitarian; b. Galt, Ont., Can., Dec. 27, 1870; s. William and Jane (Ransom) J.; pub. schs., Cincinnati; hon. M.Sc. Princeton, 1923; m. Olive Lehmann, June 16, 1898; children—Carol, Edward Lehmann, Earl Ransom, Douglas Davidson. Officer, Cincinnati House of Refuge (reformatory), 1889; teacher pub. schs., Hamilton Co. and Cincinnati, 1889-93; teacher and prin. Ind. Sch. for Feeble Minded Youth, 1893-98; asst. supt., 1898-1900, supt. 1900-22, exec. dir. since 1922, Training Sch. for the Feeble Minded, Vineland, N.J. With army Edn. Corps of A.E.F., during World War. Consultant N.J. State Dept. of Instns. and Agencies; mem. Am. Commn. to Serbia, 1919-20; chmn. com. on mental deficiency, White House Conf., 1930-31. Decorated Order of St. Sava of Serbia, 1920. Mem. Am. Assn. on Mental Deficiency (pres. 1902 and 1927), Nat. Conf. Social Work, N.J. State Conf. Social Welfare (pres. 1903), N.E.A, N.J. State Council of Edn., Am. Prison Assn., State Prison and Parole Board (pres. since 1927), N.J. Crime Commn. (chmn. com. on edn., 1935), A.A.A.S., Eugenics Research Assn. Baptist. Editor The Training School Bulletin (monthly publ.). Dir. Tradesmen's Bank, Millville Utilities; pres. Electric Light Co. Vice-pres. Advisory Bd. of North Jersey Branch Expt. Station. Home: Vineland, N.J.

JOHNSTONE, Henry Webb, v.p. Merck & Co., Inc.; b. Mexico City, Mex., Oct. 13, 1892; s. Andrew and Minnie S. (Webb) J.; grad. Wm. Penn Charter School, Philadelphia, 1912; A.B., Yale U., 1916; grad. study, Columbia U., summer 1916; m. Beatrice G. Grieb, June 9, 1917; children—Henry Webb, Jr., Barbara Grieb. Instr., Middlesex Sch., Concord, Mass., 1916-17; employed in various capacities with Colgate & Co., Jersey City, N.J., 1919-29; investment counselor, Brookmire Econ. Service, N.Y. City, 1929-30; asso. with Merck & Co., Inc., mfg. chemists, Rahway, N.J., since 1930, successively dir. of planning and plant mgr., v.p. in charge of operations since 1936; dir. Am. Products Co., Riedsville, N.C. Served as 1st lt. U.S.A., 1917-19, with A.E.F. in France. Awarded Croix de Guerre (France). Mem. Zeta Psi. Republican. Presbyn. Clubs: Racquets (Short Hills); Chester River Yacht and Country. Home: Delwick Lane, Short Hills, N.J. Office: care Merck & Co., Inc., Lincoln Av., Rahway, N.J.

JONES, Addison, concert pianist, teacher, composer; b. Washington, Pa., June 6, 1906; s. John McIlvaine and Charlotte Lucinda (Streator) J.; musical edn., Fontainebleau Sch. of Music, France, summer 1925; studied with Isidor Philipp, Camille Decreus, Nadia Boulanger, Paris, France, 1925-26; with Emil von Sauer, Vienna, Austria, 1926-30; unmarried. Debut, Vienna and Berlin, 1930, New York, 1933, Chicago, 1934; concert appearances throughout U.S.; soloist with Pittsburgh Summer Symphony Orchestra, Youngstown and Wheeling Symphony Orchestras, Chicago Civic Orchestra. Dir. Washington (Pa.) Sem. Sch. of Music. Compositions: Virtuostique Fantasie, Intermezzo, Caprice, Puck, Valsotique. Home: 437 E. Chestnut St., Washington, Pa.

JONES, Adrian Hamilton, lawyer, banker; b. Ebervale, Pa., Dec. 26, 1885; s. Joseph H. and Martha E. (Brior) J.; student Lehigh U., Bethlehem, Pa.; LL.B., Dickinson Law Sch., Carlisle, Pa.; m. Naomi O. Winters, Dec. 9, 1914; children—Elwood Hamilton, Bruce Adrian. Began practice of law, Hazleton, Pa., 1909; sch. dir. West Hazleton Sch. Dist., 1909-17; solicitor West Hazleton Borough since 1909, West Hazleton Sch. Dist. since 1910, Black Creek Twp. (Pa.) Sch. Dist. since 1912, Conyngham Borough, Pa., since 1913, Exeter Twp. (Pa.) Sch. Dist., 1930-31, Sugarloaf Twp. (Pa.) Sch. Dist., 1931-33, West Hazleton Bldg. & Loan Assn. since 1936; pres. and dir. Miners Bank & Trust Co. of West Hazleton since 1936; dir. Hazleton Thrift & Loan Corpn., West Hazleton Bldg. & Loan Assn., Hazleton Floral Co. V.p. branch of County Assessors, Luzerne Co., Pa., since 1931. Mem. Pa. Sch. Dirs. Assn. (past sec.), Hazleton Chamber of Commerce. Club: Rotary (Hazleton). Home: 237 N. Broad St., West Hazleton, Pa. Office: 222-223-224 Markle Bldg., Hazleton, Pa.

JONES, Archbold Marion, pediatrician; b. Smithburg, W.Va., Oct. 20, 1901; s. Edwin Camden and Georgia (Smith) J.; B.S., U. of W.Va., 1923; M.D., Med. Coll. of Va., 1925; m. Lois Boone, Aug. 9, 1929; 1 son, Archbold Marion. Began gen. practice of medicine, 1925; pediatrician since 1928; mem. staff Camden Clark and St. Joseph Hosps. Fellow Am. Acad. Pediatrics; mem. Delta Tau Delta, Phi Beta Pi. Methodist. Mason. Club: Parkersburg Country. Home: 939 Julian St. Office: Strong Bldg., Parkersburg, W.Va.

JONES, Arthur Julius, prof. edn.; b. Grinnell, Ia., Mar. 21, 1871; s. Publius Vergilius and Lavinia (Burton) J.; A.B., Grinnell (Ia.) Coll., 1893; student U. of Chicago, summer 1894; Ph.D., Teachers Coll. (Columbia), 1907; m. Ethel Louise Rounds, June 26, 1899; children—Burton Wadsworth, Donald Prentiss. Asst. in biology, Grinnell Coll., 1893-95; teacher of biology, Central High Sch., Minneapolis, 1895-98; supt. schs., Redwood Falls, Minn., 1898-1904; teacher Charlton Sch., New York, 1905-06; head Dept. of Edn., R.I. State Normal Sch., Providence, 1907-11; head Dept. of Edn., U. of Me., 1911-15; asst. prof. secondary edn., 1915, prof. since 1919, U. of Pa.; prof. edn., summer sch., U. of Chicago, 1919, U. of Wash., 1929, U. of Wis., 1931, U. of Hawaii, 1932, Cornell U., 1933. Mem. N.E.A., Nat. Soc. Coll. Teachers of Edn., Nat. Soc. for Study of Edn., Nat. Vocational Guidance Assn., Phi Beta Kappa, Phi Kappa Phi, Phi Delta Kappa, Kappa Phi Kappa. Presbyn. Wrote: Continuation Schools in the United States (bull. U.S. Bur. Edn.), 1907; Education and the Individual, 1926; Principles of Guidance, 1930; The Education of Youth for Leadership, 1938; also various articles in ednl. mags. Home: Swarthmore, Pa.

JONES, Barclay Lincoln, headmaster; b. South China, Me., May 19, 1893; s. Isaac Lincoln and Lora (Sibley) J.; diploma Oak Grove (Me.) Sem., 1910, Moses Brown Sch., Providence, R.I., 1911; Ph.B., Brown U., 1916; Ph.D., U. of Chicago, 1924; m. Esther Louise Coffin, Sept. 4, 1917; children—Louise Henrietta, Frances Smiley, Hoylande Coffin, Irma Wilcox. Instr. sports and gymnasium while attdg. sch., 1910-12; instr. mathematics and gymnasium, Hill Sch., 1916-17; instr. chemistry, Westtown Friends Sch., 1917-22; headmaster Friends' Central Sch., Overbrook, Phila., Pa. since 1924. Served as pres. Brookline Civic Assn. since 1938. Mem. Bd. Corporators of Haverford Coll., Exec. Com. Haverford Friends Sch. Mem. Headmasters Assn. (nat.), Headmasters Assn. (Phila.), Country Day Sch. Assn. of U.S., Friends Council on Edn., N.E.A. Dept. of Superintendence, Progressive Edn. Assn., Theta Delta Chi, Phi Beta Kappa, Sigma Xi. Republican. Mem. Religious Soc. Friends. Rotarian. Home: 400 Strathmore Road, Brookline, Upper Darby, Pa. Office: Friends Central School, Overbrook, Philadelphia, Pa.

JONES, Benjamin Charles, lawyer; b. Tyrone, Pa., June 9, 1896; s. Claude and Stella (Armor) J.; student Pa. State Coll., 1912-14; Litt. B., Princeton U., 1916; LL.B., U. of Pa., 1921; student Univ. of Paris, France, 1919; m. Kathleen Adaline Stover, Aug. 28, 1929; children—Benjamin Charles, David Mattern, Kathleen Elizabeth. Admitted to Pa. bar, 1921; practiced in Phila., 1921-25, in Tyrone, Pa., since May 1925; pub. Tyrone Daily Herald, daily newspaper, since 1924, and Williamsburg Journal, weekly, since 1938; dir. First Blair County Nat. Bank. Served as 1st lt. 311th Machine Gun Bn., 79th Div., U.S. Army, with A.E.F., during World War; now col., comdg. 103d Cav., Pa. Nat. Guard. Decorated Silver Star medal (World War). Chmn. Blair Co. Rep. Com. and mem. State Rep. Com., 1932-34; Rep. nominee for Congress, 1936. Mem. Blair Co. Bar Assn. Presbyterian. (pres. bd. trustees First Ch., Tyrone). Elk, Moose, Odd Fellow. Clubs: Union League (Phila.); Frankstown Hunt (Altoona, Pa.). Home 303 W. 11th St. Office: First Nat. Bank Bldg., Tyrone, Pa.

JONES, Benjamin Franklin III, steel mfr.; b. Pittsburgh, Pa., Mar. 15, 1895; s. Benjamin Franklin, Jr., and Sue Duff (Dalzell) J.; prep.

edn., St. Paul's Sch., Concord, N.H.; student Princeton, 1915-17; m. Katharine W. Holdship, June 27, 1927. Asst. treas. and asst. sec. Jones & Laughlin Steel Co., 1919-23; sec. Jones & Laughlin Steel Corpn., 1923-27, vice-pres. and sec. since 1927; dir. Union Trust Co., Mellon Nat. Bank, Nat. Union Fire Ins. Co. Dir. Allegheny Gen. Hosp. Second lt. F.A. Res. Corps, Aug. 1917-Dec. 1918. Republican. Presbyn. Clubs: Pittsburgh, Duquesne, Princeton, Pittsburgh Golf (Pittsburgh); Racquet and Tennis (New York); Allegheny Country (Sewickley). Home: 203 Creek Drive, Sewickley, Pa. Office: Jones & Laughlin Steel Corpn., Pittsburgh, Pa.

JONES, Benjamin R., Jr., lawyer; mem. Bedford, Waller, Jones & Darling. Office: Wilkes-Barre, Pa.*

JONES, Burwell Walter, clergyman; b. Teloga, Ga., Aug. 14, 1889; s. Floyd Washington and Martha (Hemphill) J.; A.B., Trinity U., Tex., 1912; ed. Princeton Theol. Sem., 1912-15; A.M., Princeton U., 1916; m. Ruby Saxon, June 2, 1915; children—Mary Gladys, Helen Louise. Ordained to ministry Presbyn. Ch., 1915; pastor, Presbyn. Ch., Delta, Pa. since 1915. Served as sch. dir., 1932-36, vice-pres. York Co. Sch. Dirs., 1936. Democrat. Presbyn. Mason (past master). Club: Lions (Delta). Home: Delta, Pa.

JONES, Charles B., owner Thompson & Jones; officer or dir. many companies. Home: 3400 Parkside Drive. Office: Bourse Bldg., Baltimore, Md.

JONES, Charles Sherman, aviation; b. Castleton, Vt., Jan. 11, 1894; s. John and Helen (Sherman) J.; grad. high sch., Rutland, Vt.; student Middlebury (Vt.) Coll., Harvard Sch. of Physical Edn.; m. Marguerite Williams, Oct. 31, 1917; children—Charles Sherman, Deborah Harrison. Served with Air Corps, U.S.A., 1917-18; with Curtiss-Wright Corpn., airplane mfrs., 1919-1933; now pres. Casey Jones Sch. of Aeronautics, J. V. W. Corpn. (Newark). Mem. Phi Beta Kappa, Chi Psi. Clubs: Advertising (New York). Winner of 2d place, New York-Toronto race, 1919; winner of Am. Derby, Kansas City, Mo., 1921; winner 2 1st places and 2d place, Nat. Air Races, Omaha, Neb., 1921; 2d place, On to Detroit race, 1922; winner of On to St. Louis race, 1923, On to Dayton race, 1924, Central Union speed race, 1924; won 2 events, Nat. Air Races, Mitchel Field, 1925, 1st and 2d places, Philadelphia, 1926, winner of race for cabin ships, Chicago, 1930. Home: Washington Crossing, Pa. Office: 534 Broad St., Newark, N.J.

JONES, Clement Ross, engineer; b. Knottsville, W.Va., Apr. 19, 1871; s. Uriah and Pernissa Jane (Ford) J.; B.S., C.E., W.Va. U., 1894, M.E., 1897; Worcester Poly Inst., summer 1896; Stevens Inst. Tech., summer 1897; M.M.E., Cornell, 1900; m. Elizabeth Charles Gambrill, July 22, 1915; 1 son, Ross Gambrill. Mem. engring. firm Jones & Jenkins, 1894-98; asst. in mech. engring., 1895-97, instr., 1897-99, asst. prof., 1899-1901, prof. and head dept., 1901-11, dean Coll. Engring. and prof. steam and exptl. engring., W.Va. Univ., 1911-1932, dean emeritus and prof. power engring., 1932—. Sec. engring. sect. Land Grant Coll. Assn., 1921-24, mem. com. on engring. expt. sta., 1924-27; chmn. engineering sect. of same assn., 1928-29. Editor Experiment Station Record, 1921-24. Chmn. fuel com., 1917-18. Grad. as No. 1, and 1st lt. adj. W.Va. Corps of Cadets, 1894; 1st lt. W.Va. N.G.; 1894; capt. 1896. Fellow A.A.A.S.; mem. Am. Soc. M.E., Am. Soc. for Testing Materials, Soc. Promotion of Engring. Edn., The Newcomer Soc., W.Va. Acad. Science, Sigma Xi, Phi Beta Kappa, Tau Beta Pi, S.R. (pres. W.Va. state soc.). Republican. Methodist. Mason (K.T., Shriner). Rotarian. Author of numerous articles and addresses on engring. and related topics. Home: 317 Willey St., Morgantown, W.Va.

JONES, Clement Russell, med. educator; b. Waynesburgh, O., Nov. 30, 1871; s. Charles H. and Laura C. (Christy) J.; M.D., Columbus (O.) Med. Coll., 1892; m. Margaret Elson, Nov. 23, 1898; children—R. Elson, Clement Russell, C. Christy. Prof. of pathology, Dental Sch., U. of Pittsburgh, 1896-1920, prof. of materia medica and therapeutics and principles of medicine since 1938. Formerly treas. Am. Coll. of Physicians, Phila. Mem. A.M.A., Pa. State and Allegheny Co. med. socs. Home: 5806 Beacon St., Pittsburgh, Pa.

JONES, David Robert, clergyman; b. Aber, North Wales, Great Britain, Dec. 6, 1879; s. Robert Merion and Margaret (Edwards) J.; came to U.S., 1888, naturalized 1896; A.B., Princeton, 1907; student Auburn Theol. Sem., 1907-10; hon. A.M., Princeton, 1918; m. Anna Moses, June 10, 1907; children—Robert Moses, Martha Bowen, Edward Huss. Employed in coal mines, 1891-93; clk. in hardware store, 1895-1902; ordained to ministry Presbyn. Ch., 1910; pastor, Tonawanda, N.Y., 1910-17, Syracuse, N.Y., 1917-21, Dunkirk, N.Y., 1921-33; pastor First Presbyn. Ch., Greenville, Pa. since 1933. Presbyn. Home: 321 Main St., Greenville, Pa.

JONES, E. Ray; sec. of State of Md. Address: State House, Annapolis, Md.

JONES, Edgar Alexander, lawyer; b. Corpus Christi, Tex., July 12, 1892; s. Edward Augustus and Elizabeth (Spann) J.; student Staunton Mil. Acad. 1908-09, St. John's Coll., Annapolis, Md., 1909-13, U. of Md. Law Sch., 1920-21; m. Sally Waterman Gray, July 27, 1916; children—Maud Garland, Alexander Gray. Engaged in farming, 1913; admitted to Md. bar, 1921, and since engaged in gen. practice of law at Princess Anne; pres. Mutual Fire Ins. Co. of Somerset & Worcester Counties. Democrat. Episcopalian. Home: 166 Beckford Av. Office: Mutual Ins. Bldg., Princess Anne, Md.

JONES, Edmund Lloyd, physician; b. Slatington, Pa., Feb. 24, 1894; s. John H. and Mary (Easterday) J.; student Keystone State Normal Sch., Kutztown, Pa., 1911-12, Muhlenberg Coll., Allentown, Pa., 1913-14; M.D., Jefferson Med. Coll., Phila., Pa., 1919; grad. student U. of Pa. Grad. Sch. of Medicine, Phila., 1922-23; m. Thelma Turner, Aug. 23, 1923; children—Mary Josephine, Gwendolyn, Jacqueline, Robert Lloyd, Geraldine. Served as resident, Jefferson Hosp., Phila., Pa., 1919-21; chief resident, Grant Hosp., Columbus, O., 1921-22; engaged in practice of medicine at Wheeling, W.Va. since 1924, specializing in diseases of eye, ear, nose and throat since 1924; mem. Wheeling Clinic. Served in S.A.T.C., 1918. Fellow Am. Coll. Surgeons. Mem. A.M.A., Am. Acad. Ophthalmology and Otolaryngology, W.Va. State and Ohio Co. med socs., Alpha Kappa Kappa, Alpha Omega Alpha. Mem. Reformed Ch. Mason. Home: Martins Ferry, O. Office: Wheeling Clinic, Wheeling, W.Va.

JONES, Edward H(enry), clergyman; b. Wales, Ia., Oct. 22, 1903; s. Dr. Robert H. and Margaret Ann (Davis) J.; ed. high sch. and U. of Calif., Los Angeles, 1917-21; A.B., Occidental Coll., 1924; Th.B., Princeton Theol. Sem., 1927; A.M., Princeton U., 1927; m. Dorothy May Griffiths, of Los Angeles, Calif., Aug. 28, 1931; children—Doreen Marie, Robert Griffith. Ordained to ministry Presbyn. Ch., 1927 and pastor Gettysburg Presbyn. Ch., Gettysburg, Pa., 1927-31; pastor State Coll. Presbyn Ch., State Coll., Pa. since 1931; served as commr. to Gen. Assembly Presbyn. Ch., U.S.A., 1931 and 1936; moderator Presbytery of Huntingdon, 1938-39; pres. State Coll. Ministerium, 1935. Chmn. bd. trustees, Westminster Foundation at State Coll. Mem. Tau Kappa Alpha, Phi Beta Kappa. Republican. Club: Kiwanis of State College (pres. 1935). Author: Travel Impressions of Europe and Palestine, 1928; A History of the Gettysburg Presbyterian Church, 1931; Intellectual Citizenship, 1924; devotional magazine "To-Day," October, 1935. Home: 301 E. Beaver Av., State College, Pa.

JONES, Edward Sherman, corpn. exec.; s. Edward (pioneer anthracite operator of Pa.) and Mary Elizabeth (Jones) J.; student high sch., Blakely, Pa., Wyoming Sem. and Wyoming Commercial Coll., Kingston, Pa.; unmarried. Gen. mgr. Jones & Simpson Co., and Raymond Coal Co., 1892-1900, Crescent Electric Co., 1894-1905, Forest Mining Co., 1896-1901; pres. First Nat. Bank and Citizens' Bank, Olyphant, Pa., 1902-16, Kanawaha & W.Va. R.R., 1903-16; sec-treas. North End Coal Co. 1910-22; now pres. and dir. Blue Creek Coal and Land Co., Forest Store Co.; v.p. Meadow River Coal and Land Co.; dir. First Nat. Bank of Scranton, New River Co. (mem. exec. com.), Scranton-Lackawanna Trust Co., Klotz Throwing Silk Co. Founded, 1908 and since pres. Mid Valley Hosp.; pres. Mid Valley Community Chest, Mid Valley Hosp. Assn.; dir. Am. Red. Cross, Boy Scouts of America; actively identified with Salvation Army movement. Dir. Scranton Chamber of Commerce, Lackawanna Hist. Soc.; mem. Am. Inst. Mining and Metall. Engrs. Presbyn. (pres. bd. trustees Olyphant Ch.). Clubs: Scranton, Kiwanis, Scranton Country (Scranton). Author: Glacial Pot Holes of Lackawanna County. Delivered Memorial Day Address before Am. Legion; frequent speaker on travelogues, having visited total of 65 countries; made 23,000 mile trip to Australia and New Zealand. Prime mover toward constrn. county road, Scranton to Carbondale, Lackawanna Co., Pa. Home: "Tyn-y-vron," 200 Blakely St., Blakely, Pa. Office: Brooks Bldg., Scranton, Pa.

JONES, Emmett L.; mem. consultant staff Memorial Hosp. Address: 7 S. George St., Cumberland, Md.

JONES, Ernest Ray, lawyer; b. Deer Park, Md., Dec. 14, 1886; s. Wilbur C. and Olive (Forman) J.; student W.Va. Wesleyan Coll., Buckhannon, W.Va., 1903-07; A.B., O Wesleyan U., Delaware, O., 1910; LL.B., U. of Md. Law Sch., Baltimore, 1913; m. Nancy Forman, May 26, 1915 (dec.); 1 son, Lewis Ray; m. 2d, Maud Bowman, Oct. 6, 1920; children—Wilbur C., Audrey C., Thomas Stuart. Admitted to Md. bar, 1913 and since engaged in gen. practice of law at Oakland; served as state's atty. Garrett Co., 1916-19; sec. of state of Md., 1936-38; dir. First Nat. Bank of Oakland, First State Bank of Grantsville, Md. Trustee W.Va. Wesleyan Coll., Buckhannon, W.Va. Mem. Am. and Garrett Co. bar assns., Commercial Law League of America, Phi Beta Kappa, Delta Sigma Rho. Republican. Methodist. Mason. Odd Fellow. K.P. Clubs: Rotary (Oakland); Alexander Hamilton (Baltimore). Home: Second St. Office: First Nat. Bank Bldg., Oakland, Md.

JONES, Frank Cazenove, manufacturer; b. New York, N.Y., Aug. 14, 1887; s. Frank Cazenove and Harriet Cazenove (Lamar) J.; g.g.s. Capt. Jacob Jones, comdr. U.S. sloop of war Wasp, War of 1812; student King Sch., Stamford, Conn., 1902-04, Noble and Greenough Sch., Dedham, Mass., 1904-07, Harvard, 1907-09; m. Gladys Kemp, N.Y., July, 1909 (divorced); m. 2d, Helen Griffith, June 30, 1917; children—Frank Cazenove, Helen Griffith. Began as clk. for B. T. Babbit, Inc., New York, Oct. 1909; with Edgar A. Wilhelmi, Inc., New York, as treas., 1911-14; with Jones & Cammack, of New York, as partner, 1915-17; with The Okonite Co., Passaic, N.J., as treas. since 1919, pres. and gen. manager since 1932; also pres. The Okonite-Callender Cable Co.; dir. N. Y. Lubricating Oil Co. Served as 1st lt. 2d Plattsburg O.T.C.; trench warfare sect. Engring. Div., Ordnance Dept., World War. Mem. Aztec Soc. of 1847. Mem. Business Advisory Council, Dept. of Commerce, 1936-38. Republican. Clubs: Union, Engineers, Harvard, Downtown Athletic (New York); Rockaway Hunting (Cedarhurst, L. I.); Montclair Golf, Montclair Athletic. Home: 237 Upper Mountain Av., Montclair, N.J. Office: The Okonite Co., Passaic, N.J.

JONES, Franklin Taylor, univ. prof.; b. Ridley Park, Pa., Jan. 2, 1904; s. Franklin Ellis and Ella Marie (Taylor) J.; A.B., Rutgers Univ., New Brunswick, N.J., 1926; B.D., Drew Univ., Madison, N.J., 1929; A.M., Columbia U., 1932; m. Florence Holroyd, June 18, 1928; children—Taylor Ellis, Christopher Curtiss. Instr. history, Brothers Coll. of Drew Univ., Madison, N.J., 1928-30, asst. prof. history, 1930-34, assoc. prof., 1934-39, prof. history since 1939; registrar of Drew Univ. since 1929. Pres. N.J. Consumers Cooperative, Inc. Mem. Am. Hist. Soc., Am. Assn. Collegiate Registrars,

Phi Beta Kappa. Methodist. Home: Madison, N.J.

JONES, George Ellis, coll. prof.; b. Tipton, Eng., June 7, 1879; s. John and Annie (Greaves) J.; student Parsons Coll., Fairfield, Ia., 1900-03; A.B., Kan. State Teachers Coll., Emporia, Kan., 1909; M.A., Ph.D., Clark Univ. Worcester, Mass., 1915; came to U.S., 1885, naturalized citizen; m. Henriette Matilda Schlegel, Aug. 26, 1920; children—George Ellis, Charles Bruce. Teacher rural schs., Ia., 1898-99; supt., Moran (Kan.) schs., 1905-08; principal, Marion (Kan.) High Sch., 1909-12; fellow, Clark U., Worcester, Mass., 1912-15; prof. psychology, U. of Pittsburgh, since 1915; sec.-treas. Van Buren Point Assn., Inc. Fellow A.A.A.S., N.E.A., Pa. State Edn. Assn., Nat. Soc. for Study of Edn., Nat. Soc. Coll. Teachers of Edn. Club: U. of Pittsburgh Faculty (Pittsburgh, Pa.). Author: Training in Education, 1916; Tuberculosis Among School Children, 1913; co-author (with W. H. Burnham) Hygiene and War, 1917. Home: 73 Harwood St. Office: 2109 Cathedral of Learning, U. of Pittsburgh, Pittsburgh, Pa.

JONES, Harrison, v.p. The Coca-Cola Co.; b. Marion, Va., May 23, 1887; s. Sam D. and Elizabeth (Harrison) J.; A.B., U. of Ga., 1907; LL.B., U. of Mich., 1910; m. Kathryn Gordon, Oct. 8, 1913. With Coca-Cola Co. for many years, beginning as asst. sales mgr., now v.p. Home: 730 W. Pace's Ferry Road, Atlanta, Ga. Office: DuPont Bldg., Wilmington, Del.

JONES, Harrison Tilden, building and loan exec.; b. Farmington, W.Va., Dec. 4, 1876; s. Robert Tisdel and Virginia (Davis) J.; ed. public schools of W.Va., 1882-97, Mountain State Business Coll., Parkersburg, W.Va., 1900-01; m. Katherine Leslie Hamilton, Oct. 29, 1902; 1 son, Robert Harold. School teacher, Marion County, W.Va., 1897-1902; mgr. Jones and Davis Grocery Store, Fairmont, W.Va., 1903-06; asso. with hardware business, Fairmont, W.Va., 1906-15; pres. E. C. Rowand, clothing business, Fairmont, W.Va., 1915-24; organized Standard Bldg. & Loan Assn., Fairmont, 1924, and since dir., sec. and gen. mgr.; dir., sec.-treas. and gen. mgr. Evergreen Realty Co., Fairmont, since 1929. Mem. W.Va. State Legislature, 1923-24. Mem. W.Va. Bldg. & Loan League (1st vice-pres., 1938; mem. advisory com. U.S. League on state legislation 1939). Mem. Woodmen of the World (del. nat. conv. St. Louis, Mo., 1925, Los Angeles, 1927; head clerk Woodmen of the World, (dist. composed of W.Va., Md., Del. and D.C., 1913-25). Democrat. Methodist. Mason. Clubs: Rotary, Town Hall (Fairmont). Home: 605 Coleman Av. Office: 104 Main St., Fairmont, W.Va.

JONES, Harold Walter, physician; b. Newark, N.J., Feb. 1, 1891; s. Walter Clearwater and Abbie Lucretia (Reynolds) J.; ed. Peddie Sch., 1912-13; M.D., Jefferson Med. Coll., 1917; m. Elizabeth Hughes Farquhar, May 23, 1925; children—Harold Farquhar, Patricia Ann. Interne Jefferson Hosp., 1917-18, chief resident phys., 1919-21; demonstrator in medicine, asso., asst. prof. and asso. prof. medicine, Jefferson Med. Coll. since 1928; asst. phys., Phila. Gen. Hosp., 1921-28; phys., Memorial Hosp. since 1928; asst. phys., Jefferson Hosp. since 1927, hematologist and dir. div hematology since 1938. Served as 1st lt., Med. Corps, U.S.A., 1918-19, instr. sch. mil. medicine, Ft. Oglethorpe, Ga., and med. cons., dir. sect. nephritis, Gen. Hosp., Lakewood, N.J.; now capt. Med. Corps Res. Mem. bd. corporators, Peddie Sch., Hightstown, N.J. Fellow Am. Coll. Phys.; mem. Assn. Am. Phys., Am., Pa. State and Phila. Co. med. assns., Coll. Phys. Phila., Interurban Clin. Club, Alpha Omega Alpha, Alpha Kappa Kappa. Republican. Presbyn. Clubs: University (Philadelphia); Rolling Green Golf (Springfield, Pa.). Home: 323 Aubray Rd., Wynnewood, Pa. Office: 1930 Chestnut St., Philadelphia, Pa.

JONES, Harry Albert, lawyer; b. Monongahela, Pa., June 9, 1873; s. Isaac Warren and Mary Agnes (McIlvaine) J.; A.B., Washington and Jefferson Coll. 1895, A.M., 1898; LL.B. Pittsburgh Law Sch., 1897; m. Ruth Crawford, June 7, 1906; children—Katharine Crawford (Mrs. Gordon L. Uhl), Henry Addison. Admitted to Pa. bar, 1897; practiced in Pittsburgh, 1897-1909, Washington, Pa., since May 1909; asso. legal dept. Monongahela River Consol. Coal & Coke Co., 1899-1909; solicitor Washington County Poor Dist., 1916-26; sec. State Assn. Dirs. of Poor, 1927-33; mem. Poor Law Commn., 1922-25; author of Gen. Poor Relief Act of 1925; dir. Washington Ice Co. Sec. and dir. Washington Hosp.; dir. Y.M.C.A.; mem. advisory bd. Y.W.C.A. Republican. Methodist. Mason (K.T., Shriner). Home: 65 Morgan Av. Office: Washington Trust Bldg., Washington, Pa.

JONES, Harry Christian, state employment commr.; b. Baltimore, Md., Aug. 23, 1869; s. William H. and Amelia R. (Beckmyer) J.; grad. Baltimore City Coll.; m. Elizabeth Gill, 1891 (died 1935); children—Helen Gill (Mrs. W. Stewart Anderson), Marian Elizabeth (Mrs. W. F. Lehnert, Jr.), Henry Lawrence, Ruth Katherine (Mrs. E. Starr Coale). Entered grain business as office employee, 1885; mem. firm H. C. Jones & Co., grain exporters, Baltimore, Md., 1908-32, retired, 1932; chmn. Civil Service Commn., Baltimore, 1922-31; chmn. War Memorial Commn. of Md. since 1921; mem. Port Development Commn. of Baltimore, 1926-32; serving as state employment commr. of Md. since 1935 and for term, 1937-43, administrative head of civil service of Md.; nationally known as an authority in administrn. of merit system in pub. employment. Served as pvt. to col. Md. N.G., 1887-1917; col. inf. U.S.A. since 1917; comd. 113th and 318th Inf., A.E.F. in France; chief of staff 80th Res. Div. U.S.A., 1927-32. Mem. Civil Service Reform League, Nat. Civil Service Assembly of U.S. and Can. Awarded citations for service with A.E.F. Republican. Methodist. Mason (K.T., 32°, Shriner, Jesters). Home: 117 W. 29th St., Baltimore, Md.

JONES, Henry Albert, olericulturist; b. Ottawa, Ill., May 6, 1889; s. John Wallace and Rosa (Wergin) J.; student Sch. of Agr., Lincoln, Neb., 1909-12; B.S.A., U. of Neb., Lincoln, Neb., 1916; Ph.D., U. of Chicago, 1918; m. Louise Frances White, June 15, 1916; children—Mary Elizabeth, Myron White, Joy Irene, Henry Albert. With Bur. of Markets, U.S. Dept. Agr., Washington, D.C., 1918; asso. prof. of vegetable crops, U. of W.Va., Morgantown, W.Va., 1919-20; prof. of vegetable crops, U. of Md., College Park, 1920-22; prof. of truck crops, U. of Calif., Berkeley, Calif., 1922-36; prin. olericulturist Bur. of Plant Industry, U.S. Dept. of Agr., Horticultural Sta., Beltsville, Md., since 1936. Mem. A.A.A.S., Botan. Soc. of America, Am. Soc. Plant Physiology, Am. Soc. Hort. Science, Alpha Zeta, Sigma Xi, Farm House. Home: 310 Jackson Av., University Park, Hyattsville, Md. Office: Horticultural Sta., Beltsville, Md.

JONES, Henry Warren, public accountant; b. Pittsburgh, Pa., Oct. 10, 1879; s. J. Warren and Annie Louise (Drane) J.; ed. Pittsburgh pub. and high schs.; m. Flora Baldinger Daum, Feb. 18, 1907. Began as bookkeeper for A. E. Jones Co., painting contractor, 1900; collection mgr., later credit man, H.J. Heinz Co., Pittsburgh, 1907-12; office mgr. Lutz & Schramm Co., Cincinnati, 1912-14; asst. claim agent Westinghouse Electric & Machine Co., Pittsburgh, 1914-18; asst. collection mgr. Goodyear Tire & Rubber Co., 1918-22; owner H. W. Jones Co., accountants, since 1922; sec. and dir. A. E. Jones Co. Republican. United Presbyterian. Writer on religious and sociological topics. Home: 1612 Seaton St. Office: 422 Bessemer Bldg., Pittsburgh, Pa.

JONES, H(erman) Ennis, broker; b. Phila., Pa., Aug. 7, 1895; s. Herman Wildermere and Mary Amanda (Brown) J.; ed. Palmyra (N.J.) High Sch., Drexel Inst., Phila., Temple U.; m. Marie Frances Cross, Sept. 12, 1918; children—H. Ennis, Marvin Cross. Began as office boy Phila. Trust Co., 1912, holding various positions, 1912-17; with Am. Internat. Shipbuilding Corpn., 1917-21, successively as clerk, asst. to hull engr. and on staff of pres.; with Franklin Trust Co., 1921-31, successively as teller, mgr. branch office, asst. to pres. in charge of personnel and advertising, asst. sec. and treas., vice-pres. in charge business development; special representative Hulse Cook & Co., tax specialists, 1932-33; associate Ward, Wells & Dreshman Co., 1934, 35; exec. dir. Taxpayers Forum of Pa., 1935; asst. to pres. of Albert M. Greenfield & Co. since Sept. 1935. Treas. and dir. Benjamin Franklin Memorial, Inc., since 1928; asst. to chmn. and mem. exec. com. Pa. Constitution Commemoration Com. since 1937; dir. Mercy Hosp., Phila. Mem. Bd. of Edn., Beverly Township, N.J. Formerly dir. Phila. Chamber of Commerce, Financial Advertisers Assn. of America. Episcopalian (vestryman Christ Ch., Riverton, N.J.). Mason (32°). Clubs: Kiwanis, Poor Richard, Goats (Phila.). Home: 2628 Cove Rd., Merchantville, N.J. Office: Bankers Security Bldg., Philadelphia, Pa.

JONES, Horace Conrad, mfr., banker; b. Conshohocken, Pa., June 16, 1857; s. Ellwood and Rachel (Conrad) J.; ed. U. of Pa. 1 yr., class of 1877; m. Linda Loch, Feb. 5, 1889; 1 son, Spencer L. Pres. The H. C. Jones Co.; chmn. bd. First Nat. Bank of Conshohocken; dir. Norristown-Penn Trust Co., Lee Rubber & Tire Co., Buck Hill Falls Co. Trustee Carson Coll. for Orphan Girls. Mem. Hist. Soc. of Pa., Hist. Soc. of Montgomery Co. Mem. Soc. of Friends. Clubs: Union League, Gulph Mills Golf. Home: Conshohocken, Pa.

JONES, J. S. William, prof. mathematics; b. Chance, Md., Nov. 19, 1866; s. Benjamin J. M. and Arianna (Scott) J.; A.B., Washington Coll., Chestertown, Md., 1889, A.M., 1892; ScD., 1918; Litt.D., Franklin and Marshall Coll., Lancaster, Pa., 1928; post grad. work at U. of Chicago, U. of Pa., Columbia, Cambridge (Eng.), U. of Southern Calif.; m. May L. Matthews, Sept. 7, 1896 (died Mar. 10, 1923); children—Alan Morrison (dec.), Miriam Elizabeth, Margaret Olivia (dec.), Mary Virginia; m. 2d, Ethel S. Fox, of Chestertown, Md., July 17, 1935. Teacher pub. schs. Somerset Co., Md., 1884-86; prin. Harrington (Del.) High Sch., 1889-92; prof. mathematics Washington Coll. since 1892, act. pres., 1918-19, dean since 1923, sec.-treas. alumni assn. since 1916. Mem. A.A.A.S., Am. Alumni Council, Eastern Assn. Coll. Deans and Advisers of Men, Eastern Shore Soc., Kappa Alpha (Southern). Club: Chester River Yacht and Country. Home: Chestertown, Md.

JONES, James Sumner, soldier, mcht.; b. Wheeling, W.Va., April 23, 1881; s. Henry and Anna (Stone) J.; grad. Linsly Inst., Wheeling, 1896; student Washington and Jefferson Coll., Washington, Pa., 1897-99; grad. U.S. Mil. Acad., 1903; m. Marguerite Westinghouse Sands, Oct. 4, 1905; children—Wilbur Stone, Pearson Sands. Commd. 2d lt. Cav., U.S.A., 1903; 1st. lt., 1911; resigned Oct. 1913; maj. lt. col. and col. Adj. Gen.'s Dept., U.S.A., staff of Gen. Pershing, June 1917-July 1919; brig. gen. Adj. Gen.'s R.C. since July 1923. With Stone & Thomas, Inc., dept. store, Wheeling, since 1913, except 1917-19, now pres.; pres. Security Trust Co.; dir. M. Marsh & Son, Inc., Ohio Valley Drug Co., Clarksburg Drug Co., Stone & Thomas, Inc., Hazel Atlas Glass Co., U.S. Stamping Co., Sterling Products Co., Wheeling Tile Co., Wheeling & Belmont Bridge Co. Member Wheeling (W. Va.) Park Com. Awarded D.S.M. (U.S.); Legion of Honor (French); Order of The Crown (Italian). Republican. Episcopalian. Mason (33°). Clubs: Ft. Henry (Wheeling); Army and Navy (Washington, D.C.). Home: Orchard Av., Woodsdale. Address: Stone & Thomas, Wheeling, W.Va.

JONES, John Lloyd, county treas.; b. Rhos, North Wales, Eng., Feb. 14, 1881; s. Lloyd and Harriet J.; student Ruabon Coll. for Boys, Eng.; m. Sarah Ann James, Nov. 5, 1902; children—Edward, Kenneth, Ifan. Began as office boy with Jenkins & Jones, contractors, Johnstown, North Wales, later serving in various capacities until 1900, chief office administr. and sec.-treas., 1900-11; came to Johnstown Oct. 1912; with Cambria Steel Company (now Bethlehem Steel Company) at Johnstown, Pa., until

1930, beginning in time dept. and advancing to accounting dept. Mem. of Dirs. of Poor, Cambria Co., Pa., 1931-35; county treas., 1936-39. Dir. Handelian Chorus and United Male Chorus; music dir. First Brethren Ch., Johnstown, Pa., 15 yrs.; vice-regional dir. State Fed. of Men's Bible Classes. Club: Rotary. Wrote many ch. hymns and anthems. Home: 1413 Mulberry St., Westmont Boro, Johnstown, Pa. Office: Court House, Ebensburg, Pa.

JONES, John Paul, soil conservation; b. Davidsonville, Md., May 9, 1897; s. Stephen Collison and Nettie Johnson (Harper) J.; student Anne Arundel Acad., Millersville, Md., 1911-14; B.S., U. of Md., 1918, M.S., 1921; Ph.D., Cornell U., 1926; m. Mildred Woodward, Sept. 18, 1926; children—Kenneth Woodward, Sylvia Perry, Donald Harper. Asst. plant physiologist, Md. Agr. Expt. Station, 1919-21; instr. botany, Cornell U., 1921-23; asst. research prof. Agronomy, Mass. State Coll., 1923-26, research prof., 1926-30; agronomist Koppers Research Corpn., 1930-32; consulting agronomist U.S. Steel Corpn., 1932-35; chief agronomist Soil Conservation Service, U.S. Dept. Agr., 1935, asso. regional conservator, 1935-37, regional conservator since 1937. Served as 2d lt., U.S. Inf., 1918. Fellow A.A.A.S.; mem. Am. Soc. Agronomy, Am. Soc. Plant Physiologist, Phi Kappa Phi, Sigma Xi, Acacia. Home: 919 Lindale Av., Drexel Hill, Pa. Office: Center Bldg., Upper Darby, Pa.

JONES, Kenneth Barzillai, physician; b. Church Creek, Md., Nov. 10, 1885; s. Edwin Barzillai and Margaret Ellen (Richardson) J.; M.D., U. of Md. Med. Sch., Baltimore, Md., 1911; grad. student Johns Hopkins U. Med. Sch., 1911-12; m. Margaret C. Nicholson, June 8, 1908; children—Jacob Lawton, Marguerite L. (Mrs. Robert C. Camp). Interne Baltimore City Hosp., 1912-13; asst. physician Trenton State Hosp., 1913; phys. in chief Baltimore City Hosp. Insane Dept., 1913-14; asst. supt. Rosewood State Training Sch., 1914-17; first asst. phys. Letchworth Village, 1920-21; supt. Univ. Hosp., Baltimore, Md., 1921-23; supt. Relay Sanitarium, 1923-24; supt. Dist. Training Sch., Laurel, Md., 1924-34; supt. Rosewood State Training Sch., 1934-37; supt. Eastern Shore State Hosp., Cambridge, Md., since 1937. Served as lt. to maj. Med. Corps, U.S.A., 1917-20; attached to B.E.F., 1917-19. Fellow Am. Psychiatric Assn.; mem. Am. Med. Assn., Am. Assn. on Mental Deficiency, Med. and Chirurg. Faculty of Md., Eastern Shore Soc. Republican. Episcopalian. Mason. Clubs: Rotary (Cambridge); Monday Evening (Washington, D.C.). Home: Eastern Shore State Hospital, Cambridge, Md.

JONES, Lawrence E., builder, engr., collector; b. Stotts City, Mo., Feb. 26, 1888; s. Columbus D. and Katherine (Payne) J.; A.B., William Jewell Coll., Liberty, Mo., 1911; m. Edna Withers, Sept. 26, 1914. Pioneer in development of coöperative apartments in America, among them Alden Park, Phila.; pres. Alden Park Corpn., Chelten Av. Bldg. Corpn., Kenilworth Bldg. Corpn., Cambridge Bldg. Corpn. Trustee Park Coll., Parkville, Mo.; Mayfair Corpn., Phila. Clubs: Racquet, Philobiblon, Rose Tree Fox Hunting, Philadelphia Country (Phila.); Grolier (New York). Designed machinery which produced practically all cartridge clips for U.S. Army, World War. Address: Apt. 301 Kenilworth, Alden Park, Philadelphia, Pa.

JONES, Lawrence J.; attending surgeon Dr. Jones' Private Hosp. and Delaware Hosp. Address: 1012 Delaware Av., Wilmington, Del.

JONES, Livingston Erringer, banker; b. Germantown, Pa., March 30, 1878; s. Thomas Firth and Cornelia (Erringer) J.; prep. edn., Penn Charter Sch., Phila.; A.B., Princeton, 1899; m. Edith Bolling, May 23, 1908; children—Livingston Eric, Cornelia Livingston (Mrs. Dew), Peyton (Mrs. Burnett). With Reeves, Parvin & Co., wholesale grocers, Phila., 1899-1913; pres. Savings Fund Soc. of Germantown, 1913-22, mgr. since 1922; pres. First Nat. Bank, Phila., since 1922; dir. Fire Assn. of Phila., Reliance Ins. Co., Am. Pulley Co., Hamilton and Dayton Corpn., Saving Fund Soc. of Germantown; trustee Penn Mutual Life Ins. Co. Trustee and v.p. Welfare Federation; trustee, Germantown Hosp.; vice-pres. Asso. Hosp. Service of Phila. Republican. Episcopalian. Clubs: University, Sunnybrook Golf, Bras Coupé, Rittenhouse. Home: Crefeld St., Chestnut Hill, Phila. Office: 1500 Walnut St., Philadelphia, Pa.

JONES, Lloyd Meredith, phys. edn.; b. Attica, Kan., July 16, 1900; s. Lewis Albert and Mary Ann (Williams) J.; grad. Attica (Kan.) High Sch., 1917; A.B., U. of Wichita, 1922; A.M., Columbia U., 1927, Ph.D., 1935; m. Theresa Averill Dower, Dec. 20, 1929; children—David Lloyd, Barbara Theresa. Teacher phys. edn. public schs., Wichita, Kan., 1921-26; instr. phys. edn., Western State Teachers Coll., Kalamazoo, Mich., 1927-28; asso. prof. phys. edn., W.Va. Univ. since 1928. Pres. Recreation Council Monongalia County since 1937. Mem. A.A.A.S., Am. Assn. Univ. Profs., N.E.A., W.Va. Scientific Soc., W.Va. Acad. of Science, W.Va. Edn. Assn., Coll. Phys. Edn. Assn., Am. Assn. for Health, Phys. Edn. and Recreation, Nat. Soc. for Study of Edn., Phi Delta Kappa, Kappa Delta Pi. Republican. Methodist. Mason (32°, Shriner), Acacia, Am. Legion. Author: A Factorial Analysis of Ability in Fundamental Motor Skills, 1935; A Survey of Recreational Opportunities and Problems in Monongalia County, W.Va., 1938. Contbr. numerous articles to professional jours. Home: 301 Frst St., Morgantown, W.Va.

JONES, Loren Farquhar, radio engring.; b. Kirkwood, Mo., July 4, 1905; s. Edward Fairfax Berkley and Cecil Bodly (Hough) J.; B.S. in E.E., Washington U., 1926; ed Stanford U. Grad. Sch. Bus. Adminstrn., 1928-29; unmarried. Employed as radio engr., Gen. Electric Co., Schenectady, N.Y., 1926-28, at Oakland, Calif., 1928-29, supervision of installation broadcasting stas., WTIC, WENR, WFAA, 1929-30; engring. duties in Rome, Italy, for RCA Mfg. Co., 1930, and engring. conf., Moscow and Leningrad, U.S. S.R., 1931; with RCA Mfg. Co., Camden, N.J., 1931-37, in Moscow, U.S.S.R., 1937-38, coordinator television projects, 1938-39; engring. rep. RCA Mfg. Co. in Washington, D.C., since 1939. Mem. Inst. Radio Engrs., Sigma Xi, Sigma Alpha Epsilon. Private pilot's license since 1929. Episcopalian. Club: Falcon Aero Club, Inc., of Camden, N.J. (pres.). Home: Alden Park Manor, Germantown, Phila., Pa. Office: RCA Mfg. Co., Camden, N.J.

JONES, Mark Manderville, cons. economist; b. Cedar Falls, Ia., May 25, 1890; s. Fred Soule and Ada (Thompson) J.; student East Waterloo (Ia.) High Sch., 1903-05; m. May Irene Rinehart, Feb. 19, 1916; children—Helen May, Andrew Rinehart. Successively chief clk., gen. freight and passenger agt., and traffic mgr. Waterloo, Cedar Falls and Northern Ry.; traffic mgr. William Galloway Co., Waterloo, Ia.; successively industrial sec. Chamber of Commerce, Oakland, California; director of personnel Thomas A. Edison Industries, Orange, N.J.; director economic staff Curtis, Fosdick and Belknap, New York; now consulting economist; pres. Alcon Belting Co.; vice-chmn. com. on econonic policy, Nat. Assn. of Mfrs.; pres. Am. Leather Belting Assn.; chmn. Power Transmission Council. Served as dir. div. of trade tests, Com. on Classification of Personnel in the Army. Mem. Am. Management Assn. (dir.), Transportation Assn. of America (v.p.). Republican. Presbyn. Clubs: Union League (New York); Lake Placid; Portage Country (Akron, O.). Contbr. to periodicals; specialist on organization, philanthropy, labor and enterprise system. Home: R 2, Princeton, N.J. Office: 270 Park Av., New York, N.Y.; 74 S. Canal St., Akron, O.

JONES, Marshall John H., pres. Jones Collieries, Inc.; b. Monongahela, Pa., Aug. 1899; s. John H and Sara (Walker) J.; ed. Princeton U. and U. of Edinburgh (Scotland); m. Virginia Amanda A. Bingler, June, 1925; children —Ann Marshall, Marshall John H. Engaged in coal industry in all its various phases since beginning of active career, 1914; pres. Jones Collieries, Inc., since 1936; dir. Six States Coal Corpn., Pa. Security Sales. Mem. Am. Inst. Mining Engrs. Protestant. Clubs: Colonial, Congressional Country (Washington, D.C.); Chesapeake Bay Yacht; Princeton (New York and Phila.); H.Y.P. (Pittsburgh). Home: Paper Mill Road, Chestnut Hill, Pa. Office: 80 Wall St., New York, N.Y.

JONES, Montfort, univ. prof.; b. Cambria, Wis., July 4, 1890; s. William Gabriel and Eunice (Evans) J.; student Beloit (Wis.) Coll., 1908-10; A.B., U. of Wis., 1912, A.M., 1914; m. Eleanor Lloyd, Aug. 2, 1916. On faculty, U. of Pittsburgh, since 1915, prof. of finance since 1924. Mem. Am. Econ. Assn., Beta Gamma Sigma, Alpha Kappa Psi. Republican. Mason. Home: 6423 Kentucky Av., Pittsburgh, Pa.

JONES, Owen, clergyman; b. Aug. 17, 1901; s. William Lewis and Elizabeth (Williams) J.; ed. Blue Ridge Coll., New Windsor, Md., 1922-23; A.B., Muhlenberg Coll., 1927; B.D., Southern Sem., Richmond, Va., 1931; m. Mamie M. Kelchner, June 9, 1928; children—Owen Kelchner, Harry Williams. Ordained to ministry Congl. Ch.; now pastor, Scranton, Pa.; formerly pres. and moderator Ministerium of Northeastern Assn. of Congl. and Christian Chs. of Pa. Mem. Delta Theta. Republican. Conglist. Club: Amici Trigintia (Scranton). Home: 210 W. Market St., Scranton, Pa.

JONES, Paul Reese, supervising prin. of schools; b. Kingston, Pa., Feb. 6, 1905; s. Isaac and Alice (Reese) J.; B.S. in edn., State Teachers Coll., Mansfield, Pa., 1928; A.M., Teachers Coll., Columbia, 1933; student U. of Va., summer 1928, Rutgers U., 1939; m. Mabel Claire Cochran, May 3, 1931; 1 dau., Susanne Gwendolyn. Prin. Auburn Twp., Pa., 1926-28; supervising prin., Sonestown, Pa., 1928-30, Pemberton, N.J., 1933-36, Palmyra, N.J., since 1936. Mem. N.J. Council of Edn., N.J. Schoolmasters Club, South Jersey Schoolmen's Club, Phi Delta Kappa. Methodist. Mason. Rotarian. Address: Palmyra, N.J.

JONES, Reginald Lamont, elec. engr.; b. New York, N.Y., Feb. 28, 1886; s. Albert Sinclair and Clara E. (Bishop) J.; B.S., Mass. Inst. Tech., 1909, M.S., 1910, Sc.D., 1911; m. Marion E. Babcock, Oct. 2, 1917; children—Elizabeth, Reginald Lamont, Peter Babcock. Began as mem. research staff Western Electric Co., 1911, Bell Telephone Laboratories, Inc., 1925, dir. of apparatus development since 1928; dir. Summit (N.J.) Trust Co. Served as capt. U.S. Signal Corps, 1917-18. Summit Bd. of Edn. Mem. Am. Physical Soc., Am. Inst. E.E., Acoustical Soc. America, A.A.A.S. Republican. Congregationalist. Club: Salmagundi (New York). Home: 190 Oakridge Av., Summit, N.J. Office: 463 West St., New York, N.Y.

JONES, Robert, pres. First Federal Savings and Loan Assn. of Pittsburgh. Home: 7429 Church Av., Ben Avon, Pa. Office: 600 Grant St., Pittsburgh, Pa.

JONES, Rufus Matthew, college prof.; b. S. China, Me., Jan. 25, 1863; s. Edwin and Mary G. (Hoxie) J.; A.B., Haverford Coll., 1885, A.M., 1886, LL.D., 1922; studied in U. of Heidelberg, 1887, U. of Pa., 1893-95; A.M., Harvard, 1901, D.D., 1920; in Oxford U., 1908, Marburg, 1911; Litt.D., Penn Coll., 1898; LL.D., Swarthmore, 1922; D.Th., Marburg, 1925; LL.D., Earlham, 1929; S.T.D., Columbia, 1933; D.D., Yale, 1935; LL.D., Williams, 1936; S.T.D., Colby, 1937; m. Sarah H. Coutant, July 3, 1888; 1 son, Lowell Coutant (dec.); m. 2d, Elizabeth Bartram Cadbury, Mar. 11, 1902; 1 dau., Mary Hoxie. Prin. Oak Grove Sem., Vassalboro, Me., 1889-93, instr., 1893-1901, asso. prof., 1901-04, prof. philosophy, 1904-34, Haverford Coll., now emeritus; editor Friends' Review, 1893, The American Friend, 1894-1912, Present Day Papers, 1914-15. Coll. preacher, Harvard, Cornell and Stanford universities. Trustee Bryn Mawr Coll., 1896— (pres. bd. 1916-36); trustee Brown University, Yenching Univ. Minister Society of Friends; chmn. Am. Friends Service Com. European Relief, 1917-28, 1934—; mem. Appraisal Commn. Foreign Missions in Orient, 1931-32. Mem. Commn. on Phila. Award. Mem. Kant-Gesellschaft, Am. Philos. Soc., Phi Beta Kappa. Author: Life of Eli and Sibyl Jones, 1889; Practical Christianity, 1899; A Dynamic Faith, 1900; A Boy's Religion from

Memory, 1902; Autobiography of George Fox, 1903; Social Law in the Spiritual World, 1904; The Double Search, 1905; The Abundant Life, 1908; Quakerism, A Religion of Life, 1908; Studies in Mystical Religion, 1909; The Children of the Light, 1909; Clement of Alexandria, 1910; The Quakers in the American Colonies, 1911; Stories of Hebrew Heroes, 1911; Spiritual Reformers in the Sixteenth and Seventeenth Centuries, 1914; The Inner Life, 1916; St. Paul the Hero, 1917; The World Within, 1918; The Story of George Fox, 1919; The Remnant, 1920; Nature and Authority of Conscience, 1920; A Service of Love in War Time, 1920; Later Periods of Quakerism, 1921; The Boy Jesus and His Companions, 1922; Spiritual Energies in Daily Life, 1922; Religious Foundations, 1923; Fundamental Ends of Life, 1924; The Life and Message of George Fox, 1924; The Church's Debt to Heretics, 1925; Finding the Trail of Life, 1926; The Faith and Practice of the Quakers, 1927; New Studies in Mystical Religion, 1927; The New Quest, 1928; The Trail of Life in College, 1929; Some Exponents of Mystical Religion, 1930; George Fox: Seeker and Friend, 1930; Pathways to the Reality of God, 1931; A Preface to Christian Faith in a New Age, 1932; Mysticism and Democracy in the English Commonwealth, 1932; Haverford College—A History and an Interpretation, 1933; Re-Thinking Religious Liberalism, 1935; The Testimony of the Soul, 1936; Some Problems of Life, 1937; The Eternal Gospel, 1938. Home: Haverford, Pa.; (summer) South China, Me.

JONES, Russell Neal, gen. supt. Castanea Paper Co.; b. Shippensville, Pa., Dec. 13, 1895; s. William N. and Martha A. (Baker) J.; B.S., Carnegie Inst., Tech., in E.E., 1920; m. Mary L. Yarger, May 2, 1918; children—Mary Jane, Martha L. Asst. chief engr. Castanea Paper Co., 1920-22, chief engr. 1922-26, supt. 1926-34, gen. supt. since 1934; dir. Johnsonburg Nat. Bank. Chmn. Am. Red Cross, Johnsonburg. Republican. Methodist (trustee 1st Ch.). Mason. Club: Acacia. Contbr. to Radio Journal. Home: 701 Penn St. Office: 100 W. Center St., Johnsonburg, Pa.

JONES, Thomas Roy, industrialist; b. Kingman, Kan., Apr. 26, 1890; s. Joseph Francis and Emma Laura (Miller) J.; B.S., U. of Kan., 1913; post grad. work, Harvard Sch. of Business Administration, 1916-17; m. Anna Margaret Seymour, Dec. 25, 1923; children—Chalmer Eaton, Margaret Seymour. Began as civil and mech. engr., 1907; was works mgr. of the motor works dept. of Moline Plow Co. (Rock Island, Ill.); asst. gen. mgr. Cincinnati Milling Machine Co., v.p., gen. mgr. Harris-Seybold-Potter Co. (Cleveland); pres. and gen. mgr. Am. Type Founders, Inc., mfrs. of printing presses and type, since 1932; pres., gen. mgr. Am. Type Founders Sales Corpn.; pres. Nat. Printing Equipment Assn.; chmn. exec. com., Am. Management Assn.; v.p. Comité International de l'Organisation Scientifique. Dir. N.J. State Chamber of Commerce. Served as 1st lt. ordnance, 1918, capt. gen. staff, 1919, World War. Club: Union (Cleveland). Home: 130 Hobart Av., Summit, N.J. Office: 200 Elmora Av., Elizabeth, N.J.

JONES, Vincent, dir. dept. mus. edn.; b. Los Angeles, Calif., Oct. 29, 1894; s. Lemuel R. and Alice Maude J.; ed. U. of Southern Calif., 1919-20, Inst. Mus. Art, and Columbia U., 1921-22; B.S. in Music, N.Y. Univ., 1927, A.M., same, 1928; Ph.D. in Music, Harvard U., 1934; unmarried. Engaged as teacher music, harmony and theory, various schs., 1917-23; teacher, Combs Conservatory, Phila., Pa., 1923-24; successively, asst. prof., asso. prof. and prof. music edn., N.Y. Univ., 1925-36; prof. music edn. and dir. dept., Temple U. Teachers Coll., Phila., Pa. since 1936. Mem. Nat. Sinfonia. Conglist. Author: Revised Alchin Applied Harmony, 1930, 1931, 1935; Essentials in Teaching Harmony, 1931. Author (with Bernice White): Harmonic Dictation, 1932. Composer vocal, piano, and violin music. Home: 2039 N. Broad St., Philadelphia, Pa.

JONES, Walter Adelbert, civic leader; b. Kent, Portage Co., O.; s. Walter Rozelle and Lydia (Davidson) J.; desc. John Morton of Delaware Co., Pa., signer Declaration of Independence; student Ohio Wesleyan U., Delaware, O.; m. Emma Butler. V.p. and dir. Carbo-Oxygen Co., Hiawatha Oil & Gas Co., Plymouth Oil Co.; dir. Republic Oil Co., Republic Oil & Refining Co. Presidential mem. on Bituminous Coal Code Authority under NRA, 1933; pres. Good Neighbor League, Inc., 1937; chmn., 10 yrs., Pa. Turnpike Commn. which is building all-weather super-highway from Harrisburg to Pittsburgh at cost of approximately $60,-000,000. Pres. bd. trustees Ohio Wesleyan U. for many yrs.; trustee Am. Univ., Washington, D.C. Mem. S.A.R. Clubs: Duquesne, Pittsburgh Athletic, Oakmont Country (Pittsburgh); Columbus, Faculty of Ohio State U. (Columbus); National Press, Burning Tree Country, Congressional Country (Washington, D.C.); Bankers' of America (New York). Home: 325 6th Av. Office: 223 4th Av., Pittsburgh, Pa.

JONES, Webster Newton, educator; b. Rich Hill, Mo., July 29, 1887; s. Jenkins S. and Annie Davis (Lewis) J.; A.B., U. of Mo., 1908, A.M., 1909; Ph.D., Harvard U., 1920; m. Nettie Donald Haire, Aug. 31, 1918; children—Webster Newton, William Cary. Instr. chemistry, Purdue U., 1909-10; Austin teaching fellow, Harvard U., 1910-12; instr. chemistry, U. of Me., 1912-13, U. of Mo., 1913-14, Radcliffe Coll., 1914-15; asst. prof. chemistry, U. of Mont., 1915-18; research chemist B. F. Goodrich Co., 1919-24; mgr. Gen. Chem. Labs., 1925-27, tech. supt., 1927, gen. supt. processing div., 1928-32; dir. Coll. of Engring., Carnegie Inst. Tech. since 1932. Served as 1st lt., U.S. Army, 1918; chem. expert War Trade Bd., 1919; major U.S. Army Res. Corps. Mem. A.A.A.S., Am. Chem. Soc., Am. Inst. Chem. Engrs., Soc. for Promotion Engring. Edn., Engrs. Soc. of Western Pa., Engrs. Council for Professional Development, Pittsburgh Personnel Assn. Republican. Presbyterian. Writer articles on engring. subjects. Home: 562 Briar Cliff Road, Pittsburgh, Pa.

JORDAN, Emory V.; asso. urologist Mountain State Hosp. Address: 714 Lee St., Charleston, W.Va.

JORDAN, Frank Craig, astronomer; b. Cordova, Ill., Sept. 24, 1865; s. John Henry and Louisiana (Craig) J.; B.Ph., Marietta Coll., 1889, M.A., 1892; Ph.D., University of Chicago, 1914; Sc.D. Marietta (Ohio) College, 1929; m. Cora A. Ross, June 22, 1893; 1 son, Frank Warren (dec.); m. 2d, Mrs. Harriet C. Roy, Nov. 25, 1909; 1 son, William. Inst. astronomy and mathematics, Marietta Coll. 1889-1900, high sch., Portland, Ore., 1900-02, at Colorado Springs, Colo., 1902-05; fellow Yerkes Obs., Williams Bay, Wis., 1905-08; with Allegheny Obs. since 1908; asst. prof. astronomy U. of Pittsburgh, 1910-19, prof. since 1919; asst. dir. Allegheny Obs., 1920-30, dir. since 1930. Mem. A.A.A.S., Am. Astron. Soc., Internat. Astron. Union, Pittsburgh Physical Soc., Phi Beta Kappa, Sigma Xi. Democrat. Presbyterian. Has specialized in photometry; determined light curves of many short period variable stars. Home: 49 Riverview Av., Pittsburgh, Pa.

JORDAN, George, pres. Drovers & Mechanics Nat. Bank; b. Conewago Twp., York Co., Pa., May 1, 1884; s. Henry E. and Anna Mary (Hollerbush) J.; student York County Acad., and Pa. Business Coll. (Lancaster); m. Jennie G. Bentzel, June 26, 1910; children—Helen M., Sara L., Mary Isabel. Teacher pub. schs., Conewago Twp., York Co., Pa., 1902-05; became individual bookkeeper Drovers & Mechanics Nat. Bank, York, Pa., 1905, various positions in bank to 1915, asst. cashier, 1915, cashier, 1915-20, v.p. and cashier, 1920-36, dir. since 1928, pres. since 1936. Mem. York Co. Bankers' Assn. (ex-pres.), Sons of Vets. (York). Home: 138 Springdale Rd. Office: 30 S. George St., York, Pa.

JORDAN, James Shannon, physician, oculist; b. Pittston, Pa., Oct. 7, 1903; s. William and Mary (Shannon) J.; B.S., U. of Scranton, 1927; M.D., Jefferson Med. Coll., 1930; grad. study, U. of Pa., 1932-33; m. Mae O'Rourke, June 8, 1936; children—Arthur, James. Resident physician Wills Hosp., 1933-34; in practice of medicine and oculist at Scranton since 1934. Dir. Pa. Assn. for the Blind. Mem. Am. Med. Assn., Pa. State Med. Soc., Am. Acad. of Ophthalmology and Otolaryngology. Wills Hosp. Soc., Alpha Omega Alpha. Roman Catholic. K.C. Club: Scranton Country. Home: 1210 Richmond St. Office: Medical Arts Bldg., Scranton, Pa.

JORY, Herbert Godfrey, architect; b. Baltimore, Md., Nov. 20, 1877; s. John Godfrey and Margaret (Wagner) J.; student Baltimore City Coll., 1892-96; grad. Sch. Architecture of U. of Pa., 1900; m. Bessie Hollstein, July 5, 1904; 1 son, John Godfrey 2d. Archtl. draftsman with office of George Archer, Baltimore, 1900-02; with office of Supervising Architect, U.S. Treasury Dept., 1902-11; in bus. on own acct. as architect, Baltimore, Md. since 1911; mem. Archtl. Commn. City of Baltimore, 1913-19. Served as 1st lt. then capt. constrn. div., Q.M.C., U.S.A., 1917-19; capt. through grades to col. Q.M.C. Res., 1920-37. Dir. and sec. South Baltimore Gen. Hosp., 1914-37. Mem. Am. Inst. Architects, Mil. Order of World War, Mil. Order of Fgn. Wars. Democrat. Lutheran. Home: 405 E. Lake Av. Office: Munsey Bldg., Baltimore, Md.

JOSEPH, Charles Homer, journalist; b. Little Falls, N.Y.; s. Harris and Rose (Jackson) J.; student Warwick (N.Y.) Grade Sch., 1880-92, Packard's Business Coll., New York City, 1893-94; m. Caroline Schoenfield, Oct. 15, 1907 (died 1933); children — Alexander Henry, Charles Homer. Began as newspaper man with Warwick Dispatch, 1891; editor Jewish Criterion, Pittsburgh, 1894-1933; edited monthly magazine, Kitkats, 1901-03; publicity dir. Frank and Seder Dept. Store, Pittsburgh, 1907-33; asst. pub. Pittsburgh Sun-Telegraph since 1933. Dir. George Junior Republic, Grove City, Pa. Jewish religion. B'nai B'rith. Club: Concordia (Pittsburgh). Home: Hampton Hall. Address: care Sun-Telegraph, Pittsburgh, Pa.

JOSEPH, Emrys Sibbering, cons. ins. accountant; b. Ruabon, South Wales, Jan. 21, 1880; brought to U.S., 1884; s. Rev. Watkin B. and Mary (Sibbering) J.; ed. pub. schs.; m. Mary Davis, Dec. 6, 1905; children—Margaret (Mrs. Samuel F. Hinkle), Mary Elizabeth. Office boy, stenographer and bookkeeper, various companies, 1894-1906; mgr. insurance agency, Scranton, 1906-10; spl. agt. N. H. Fire Ins. Co., 1910-20; owner ins. agency, Harrisburg, 1920-35; deputy ins. commr., Pa., 1935-39; pres. Unit System Co., insurance accounting, since 1939. Democrat. Presbyterian. Mason (Shriner), Elk. Club: Harrisburg. Wrote: Accounting and Office Methods; Insurance Agency Accounting and Management. Originator and designer of accounting system for ins. agencies known as "Joseph System." Home: 1918 N. 2d St., Harrisburg, Pa.

JOSLIN, Charles Loring, pediatrist; b. Sudlersville, Md., Nov. 10, 1887; s. Charles Lober and Anor (Gooden) J.; student Wilmington Acad., Dover, Del., 1904-07; M.D., U. of Md., 1912; post-grad. work Johns Hopkins Med. Sch., 1913-15, New York Postgrad. Med. Sch., 1915; m. Hester L. Riddle, Mar. 2, 1918; children—Mary Margaret Leavenworth, Charles Loring, Blackburn Smith, Light Leavenworth. Began practice of pediatrics, 1916; instr. pediatrics, U. of Md., 1920-22, asso. in pediatrics, 1922-24, asst. prof., 1924-27, asso. prof., 1927-30, prof. clin. pediatrics, 1930-34, prof. pediatrics since 1934. Served as lt., then capt. Med. Corps, 315th F.A., 80th Div., A.E.F., World War. Licentiate Am. Board of Pediatrics. Fellow Am. Acad. Pediatrics; mem. A.M.A., Southern Med. Assn., Med. and Chirurg. Faculty of Md., Baltimore City Med. Soc., Baltimore Co. Med. Soc., Nu Sigma Nu. Home: 4400 Roland Av. Office: 706 Medical Arts Bldg., Baltimore, Md.

JOSLIN, Theodore Goldsmith, publicist; b. Leominster, Mass., February 28, 1890; s. Frederick Alonzo and Hannah Gammage (Hapgood) J.; grad. high sch., Leominster, 1908; m. Rowena Hawes, June 15, 1912; children—Richard Hawes, Robert Edward. With Associated Press, 1908-13; state political correspondent, Boston Evening Transcript, 1913-16; Washington corr.

Boston Evening Transcript, 1916-31; sec. to President Hoover, 1931-33; Washington rep. Babson Statis. Orgn., Inc., 1933-36; pres. News-Journal Co., Wilmington, Del., 1936-39; dir. dept. of public relations, E. I. du Pont de Nemours Co. since 1939. Conglist. Clubs: Nat. Press, Gridiron, Wilmington, Wilmington Country. Author: Hoover Off the Record, 1934. Home: "Hillhome," Greenville, Del.

JOST, Arthur Cranswick; physician; b. Guysborough, N.S., Oct. 17, 1874; s. Burten and Sarah Annie Muncy (Norris) J.; A.B., Acadia U., Wolfville, N.S., 1893; student Dalhousie U., Halifax, N.S., 1893-94; M.D., McGill U., Montreal, Que., 1895, M.D.C.M., 1897; m. Carrie Victoria Louise Martin, July 23, 1906; children —Victor Arthur, Burton Norris; m. 2d, Clara Delene Reed, July 29, 1934; came to U.S., 1928, naturalized, 1934. Gen. practice, Guysborough, N.S., 1897-1916; Co. health officer, Guysborough Co., 1900-16; divisional health officer, insp. of health and provincial health officer, N.S. Provincial Bd. of Health, Halifax, Nova Scotia, 1919-28; dep. registrar gen. and insp. of penal institutions, Halifax, N.S., 1925-28; Del. state health officer, Dover, Del., since 1929. Served as lt. col., C.E.F., 1916-19. Exec. sec. Del. State Bd. of Health since 1928; Del. state registrar since 1929. Mem. Co., State, Nat. health socs. Baptist. Home: 55 S. Bradford St. Office: State Board of Health, Dover, Del.

JOY, James Richard, editor, librarian; b. Groton, Mass., Oct. 16, 1863; s. Richard Pickering and Mary (Hartwell) J.; B.A., Yale, 1885, M.A., 1888; Litt.D., Syracuse U., 1905; LL.D., Dickinson Coll., 1916; m. Emma Prentice McGee, Jan. 20, 1891 (died April 6, 1934); children—Helen, Alice, Gertrude. Asst. editor "Our Youth," 1885-99; S.S. editorial department Methodist Book Concern, New York, 1890-1904; asst. editor, 1904-15, editor, 1915-36, The Christian Advocate, New York, also chmn. editorial bd., retired, 1936; mem. editorial bd. Religion in Life. Pres. Nat. Assn. Meth. Hist. Socs.; librarian N.Y. Meth. Hist. Soc. Trustee Am. Bible Soc., Drew U., Methodist Hosp. (Brooklyn); mem. Methodist Bd. of Fgn. Missions. Del. M.E. Gen. Conf., 1908-36; sec. Class of 1885, Yale Coll. Clubs: Graduate (New Haven); Yale (New York). Author: The Greek Drama, 1887; Outline History of England, 1888; Grecian History 1890, 1900; Rome and the Making of Modern Europe, 1892; Twenty Centuries of English History, 1898; Thomas Joy and His Descendants, 1900; Ten Englishmen of the XIVth Century, 1902; John Wesley's Awakening, 1937. Home: 960 Cedar Brook Rd., Plainfield, N.J., and 29 Perry St., New York, N.Y. Office: 150 5th Av., New York, N.Y.

JOYCE, Claude Alexander, lawyer; b. Stuart, Va., Feb. 19, 1898; s. Richard Lee and Emma Lou (Spencer) J.; A.B., William and Mary Coll., Williamsburg, Va., 1920; LL.B., Washington and Lee U. Law Coll., 1923; m. Myra Elizabeth Bardin, July 19, 1934; 1 son, James Bardin. Admitted to W.Va. bar, 1923 and since engaged in gen. practice of law at Logan; atty. City of Logan 1930-31; municipal judge, Logan, W.Va., 1931-32; pros. atty. of Logan Co., 1933; mem. firm Bland & Joyce since 1930; sec. and treas. Altizer Coal Land Co., and Union Coal Land Co., Logan, W.Va.; dir. Elk Creek Coal Land Co. Served as 2d lt. inf., U.S.A., 1918. Democrat. Baptist. Mason. Address: Logan, W.Va.

JOYCE, Harry B., cons. engr.; b. Baltimore, Md., Feb. 25, 1889; s. Harry S. and Catherine (Burkert) J.; student Baltimore Poly. Inst.; M.E., Cornell U., 1912; m. Mabel E. Snell, Dec. 18, 1926; 1 dau., Phyllis. Test foreman New York Edison Co., 1913-15, asst. operator, 1915-16; power engr. United Electric Light & Power Co., New York, 1916-18 and 1919-20; mem. firm Johnson & Benhem (cons. engrs.), N.Y. City and Kansas City, Mo., 1920-21; chief engr. Centrifugal Fan Co., 1921-22; mgr. synchronous dept. Ideal Electric & Mfg. Co., Mansfield, O., 1922-25; sales mgr. Burke Electric Co., 1925-29; in private practice as consulting engr. since 1929. Mem. City of Erie Bldg. Commn. and Appeals Bd., City of Erie Civil Service Examining Commn., Pa. State Examining Bd. for Professional Engrs. Served as major, Construction Div., Q.M. Corps, World War. Club: Lions. Home: 501 Liberty St. Office: 616 Commerce Bldg., Erie, Pa.

JOYCE, Hazelton Austin, lawyer; b. Cambridge, Md., Jan. 25, 1878; s. Hazelton Austin and Emma Frances (Tull) J.; A.B., Western Md. Coll., Westminster, 1899, A.M., 1902; LL.B., U. of Md. Law Sch., Baltimore, 1902; m. Nona Harrington, April 6, 1909 (dec.); m. 2d, Agnes Julia Conroy, Jan. 2, 1913; children —1 son, 3 daus., died in infancy. Admitted to Md. bar, 1902, and since engaged in gen. practice of law at Cambridge, Md., and Baltimore; asso. with firm William, Homer, France & Smith, 1902-03; city atty. for Cambridge, Md., 1903-10; chief examiner of Md. Ins. Dept., 1910-22; supt. surety claims dept. U.S. Fidelity & Guaranty Co., Baltimore, Md., 1922-25; dep. ins. commr. of Md. since 1927; served as mem. Md. Ho. of Dels., 1910-12. Served as pvt. Md. N.G., 1900-03. Democrat. Episcopalian. Mason (K.T., 32°, Shriner). Home: Lennox Av., Severna Park. Office: Lexington Bldg., Baltimore, Md.

JOYCE, John St. George, dir. pub. relations; b. Ireland, Feb. 19, 1884; s. John St. George and Mary Teresa (Foy) J.; brought to U.S., 1886; ed. Central High Sch., Phila., Pa., 1898-1900, Pa. Mus. Sch. Industrial Art, 1900-01, Acad. of Fine Arts, 1901-02; Hon. Alumnus, Temple U., 1935, in recognition of services to Univ.; m. Katharine T. Murray, Feb. 8, 1906. Ed. in art but father was journalist 50 yrs. and every mem. family in journalism so entered newspaper work; reporter Phila. papers, 1905-09; asst. city editor Public Ledger, 1909-23; asst. city editor North American, 1923-24; on editorial staff Evening Bulletin, 1924-25; dir. pub. relations, Temple U. since 1925, conducted nation-wide publicity campaign of Russell H. Conwell Foundation in behalf Temple U., 1925-26; during journalistic career acted as pub. relations counsel for many nat., state and civic orgns. Served as Dir. Publicity for U.S. Shipping Bd. Recruiting Service during World War. Personally commended by Pres. Franklin D. Roosevelt for efficient handling of publicity in connection with visit of Pres. to Temple U. to receive hon. degree, 1936. Home: 129 S. Carol Boul., Highland Park, Pa.

JUDGE, Wade Williams, merchant; b. Mansfield, Pa., June 2, 1893; s. Tom W. and Myra Lee (Williams) J.; student Mansfield State Normal Sch., 1908-11; B. Economics, Wharton Sch., U. of Pa., 1915; m. M. Yolande Clark, Jan. 25, 1918; children—Tom William, Clark Voorhees. Began with T. W. Judge Co., department store, 1916, mgr. 1916-17, partner with H. G. Peterson in ownership since 1920; pres. First Nat. Bank, Mansfield, Pa. Served as corpl. Motor Supply Train, 79th Div., U.S. Army, at Camp Meade and with A.E.F., 1917-19. Treas. and dir. Mansfield Borough Sch. Dist. Mem. Delta Upsilon. Episcopalian. Mason. Club: Corey Creek Golf (Mansfield). Home: 47 College Av. Office: 6 S. Main St., Mansfield, Pa.

JUDGE, William John, pres. Nat. Fuel Gas Co.; b. Corry, Pa., April 5, 1873; s. William and Joanna (Allen) J.; ed. pub. schs.; m. Anna M. Scholl, Oct. 6, 1909; 1 son, Philip Scholl. Pres. Nat. Fuel Gas Co. since 1919; dir. many other pub. utility cos. Home: 36 Glenwood Rd., Montclair, N.J. Office: 30 Rockefeller Plaza, New York, N.Y.

JUDKINS, Malcolm Faulkner, engr.; b. Seattle Wash., May 23, 1906; s. Elmer Eugene and Ruby Elizabeth (Copp) J.; B.S. in Chem. Engring., U. of Wash., 1928; M.S. in Chem. Engring., Carnegie Inst. Tech., 1929; m. Hazel Carolyn Moorman, Aug. 31, 1929; 1 son, Alan Faulkner. Analytical chemist Northwest Testing Labs., Seattle, 1924-28; research fellow U.S. Bur. of Mines, Metall. Adv. Bd., 1929; chief engr. Firthite Div., Firth-Sterling Steel Co., since 1929. Mem. Am. Soc. for Metals, Am. Inst. Mining and Metall. Engrs., Am. Soc. Mech. Engrs. (chmn. spl. research com. on cutting of metals), Am. Soc. Tool Engrs. (treas. Pittsburgh chapter). Republican. Presbyterian. Club: Camera of Clairton, Pa. Contbr. to Machinery, Am. Machinist. Delivered numerous addresses before tech. socs. Home: 1821 Evans Av. Office: Firth-Sterling Steel Co., McKeesport, Pa.

JUDSON, James Edward; prof. biology, W.Va. Wesleyan Coll. Address: W.Va. Wesleyan College, Buckhannon, W.Va.

JULIAN, Alvin Frederick, athletic coach; b. Reading, Pa., Apr. 5, 1901; s. Frank and Marie (Faust) J.; B.S., Bucknell U., Lewisburgh, Pa., 1923; m. Gertrude Steffenberg, Nov. 28, 1925 (divorced); 1 son, Alvin Frederick; m. 2d, Lena Viola Tobias, Sept. 5, 1931; 1 son, Franklin Tobias. Played professional baseball with Reading (Pa.) Internat. Club and professional football with Pottsville (Pa.) Maroons, 1923-25; athletic coach Albright Coll., Reading, Pa., 1925-31; coach professional football clubs, 1931-33; coach, high sch. Ashland, Pa., 1933-36; head coach, Muhlenberg Coll., Allentown, Pa., since 1936; chosen in Pop Warner's All American Selection, 1922. Mem. Am. Football Coaches Assn., Franklin Home Assn., Phi Kappa Psi. Republican. Roman Catholic. Elk. Club: Lehigh Country (Allentown, Pa.). Home: 430 N. 22d St., Allentown, Pa.

JUMP, Henry Draper, physician; b. Dover, Del.; s. Robert Broadaway and Elizabeth (Draper) J.; prep. edn. Wilmington Conf. Acad.; student Johns Hopkins; M.D., U. of Pa., 1893; m. Mary Irwin, Apr. 18, 1895. Began as physician, Phila., Sept. 1893; outpatient physician to Med. Sch., U. of Pa., 1894-1905, instr. in medicine, attending physician Phila. Gen. Hosp.; prof. applied therapeutics, Woman's Med. Coll., 1923-38. Dir. Phila. Child Health Soc. Served as maj. Med. Reserve, 1917, lt. col., 1918. Mem. A.M.A., Med. Soc., State of Pa. (ex-pres.), Phila. Co. Med. Soc. (ex-pres.). Episcopalian. Mason. Home: 2019 Walnut St., Philadelphia, Pa.

JUSTICE, Daniel Webster, clergyman; b. Brooklandville, Md., Aug. 7, 1893; s. John Stephen and Adella Maude (Kieffer) J.; prep. edn., Conway Hall, Carlisle, Pa., 1914-17; student Wesleyan U., Middletown, Conn., 1917-18; A.B., Johns Hopkins, Baltimore, 1922; S.T.B., Boston U. Sch. of Theology, 1925; A.M., Boston U. Grad. Sch., 1927; m. Norma Lavada Gaver, Nov. 24, 1923; children—Phyllis Ann, Norma Sue, Nancy Lee. Bookkeeper and private sec., 1910-14; ordained to ministry of Meth. Ch., 1925; pastor Orangeville, Md., 1919-22, West Harford, Md., Circuit, 1927-29, Glyndon, Md., 1930-33; pastor Govans Meth. Ch., Baltimore, since 1934; mem. of faculty Baltimore Conf. Young Peoples Summer Inst., 1931-39; instr. and dean of leadership training schools, Internat. Council Religious Edn., 1928-34. Chmn. bd. of management, Hood Coll. Summer Sch. of Christian Edn.; trustee Anti-Saloon League of Md.; dir. Council of Churches and Christian Edn. of Md. and Del.; chmn. exec. com. Baltimore Meth. Preachers Meeting, 1936-37; pres., 1937-38; mem. legislative com., 1939; trustee Commn. on Conf. Claimants' Endowment Fund of Baltimore Annual Conf. of Meth. Ch. since 1939; mem. bd. of edn. Baltimore Annual Conf. of Meth. Ch., also mem. ministerial qualifications com. and social service commn. Mem. Theta Phi, Commons Club of Wesleyan U. (now Sigma Chi), Kappa Delta Pi. Democrat. Mason. Home: 5208 York Rd., Baltimore, Md.

K

KABAKJIAN, Dicran Hadjy, univ. prof.; b. Armenia, Nov. 7, 1875; s. Hadjy and Elizabeth (Arzoumanian) K.; B.A., Anatolia Coll. Marsovan, 1896; M.S., U. of Pa., 1908, Ph.D., 1910; came to U.S., 1905, naturalized, 1911; m. Dicranouhi Kuludjian, 1911; children—Armen, Raymond, Alice, Lillian, Louise. Principal, Normal Sch., Sivas, Turkey, 1897-1905; instr. physics, U. of Pa., 1910-18, asst. prof., 1918-25, prof. since 1925. Mem. Amer. Phys. Soc., Am. Assn. Univ. Profs., Sigma Xi. Christian (Protestant). Contbr. of scientific articles to Phys. Review. Home: 105 E. Stratford Av., Lansdowne. Office: University of Pa., Philadelphia, Pa.

KAEMMERLING, Effie Barnhurst (Aldis Dunbar, pen name), writer; b. Phila., Pa. Aug. 3, 1870; d. Henry Rohrman and Emily (Gregory) Barnhurst; ed. pub. schs., Phila. and Erie, Pa., Erie Acad., mus. edn. in violin and composition; m. Rear-Admiral Gustav Kaemmerling, U.S.N., Sept. 3, 1888 (div.); children—Gustav Henry, Gordon (1st lt. inf. U.S.A., killed in action, France, 1918). Active in War Relief Work with Devastated France Com., 1917-18; awarded medal (France). Mem. Author's league of America (under pen name). Republican. Engaged in writing under pen name Aldis Dunbar since 1891. Author: The Sons of Cormac (London), 1904, re-issued in U.S., 1920; The Light Bearers (Greek history tales), 1924; Once There Was a Prince, 1928. Contbr. short stories mostly juvenile, much pub. verse, articles. Home: 403 W. 6th St., Erie, Pa.

KAERCHER, George H., lawyer; b. Phila., Pa., May 20, 1888; s. George R. and Annette (Hughes) K.; student Hotchkiss Sch., Yale, U. of Pa.; m. Elizabeth D. Beahm, Feb. 21, 1924. Admitted to bar, 1912, and since in practice at Pottsville, Pa.; solicitor banks, coal and utility cos., Pottsville; dir. Pardee Land Co., The Miners Nat. Bank of Pottsville. Sec. Pottsville City Planning Commn. Clubs: Pottsville, Schuylkill Country (Pottsville, Pa.). Home: 1702 Mahantouge St. Office: 508 Thompson Bldg., Pottsville, Pa.

KAGAN, Louis R(obert), lawyer; b. Jersey City, N.J., June 26, 1905; s. Robert and Rachel (Schachnow) K.; LL.B., N.Y. Univ., 1926, LL.M., same, 1930; m. Constance S. Lockman, Aug. 5, 1931; 1 son, Leonard. Admitted to N.J. bar as atty., 1927, as counsellor and master in chancery, 1930; admitted to practice before the Supreme Ct. of the U.S., 1936; admitted to practice before various Federal Commns., 1936, U.S. Bd. Tax Appeals, 1937; engaged in practice of law at Jersey City, N.J. since 1927. Mem. Hudson Co. Dem. Speakers Bur. Mem. Ednl. Com. Y.M.C.A., Jersey City. Mem. Y.M.H.A. Mem. Commercial Law League of America, Hudson Co. Bar Assn., Sigma Tau. Democrat. Jewish religion. Mason (32°). Elk. Clubs: Allied Democratic, Men's Council of Jersey City. Office: 921 Bergen Av., Jersey City, N.J.

KAGAN, Pescha (Mrs. David Glick), pianist; b. Pittsburgh, Pa., Oct. 28, 1912; d. Alexander B. and Sara (Ginsburgh) K.; ed. College of Music, Cincinnati, O., Curtis Inst. of Music, Phila., Pa.; m. David Glick. Began mus. career as concert pianist, 1926; has appeared with leading symphony orchestras in all the large cities; soloist in broadcasting debut with Pittsburgh Symphony Orchestra, 1936. Awarded gold medal by College of Music, Cincinnati, O., 1926. Home: 114 Hall Av., Washington, Pa.

KAHLER, Arthur D., athletic coach; b. Arkansas City, Kan., Dec. 27, 1898; s. Peter D. and Sarah E. (Blevins) K.; A.B., Southwestern Coll., 1923; m. Helen June Radley, Mar. 17, 1923; children—Arthur D., Conrad Andrew. Coach of football, basketball and track, Lyons (Kan.) High Sch., 1923-25, Coffeyville (Kan.) High Sch., 1925-28; athletic dir. and coach, Sterling (Kan.) Coll., 1928-31; head basketball coach and asst. coach in football and track and instr. in phys. edn., Brown U., Providence, R.I., 1931-35, head basketball coach and instr. in phys. edn., 1935-38; head football coach, Dickinson Coll., Carlisle, Pa., 1935-38, head football and track coach (asso. prof. in phys. edn.) since 1938. Record, 1923-38: football—won 92 games, tied 11, lost 22. Mem. Nat. Football Coaches Assn., Nat. Basketball Coaches Assn. Mason. Home: 361 W. High St., Carlisle, Pa.

KAHLER, Hugh MacNair, writer; b. Phila., Pa., Feb. 25, 1883; s. Frederick A. and Margaret (MacNair) K.; A.B., Princeton, 1904; m. Louise, d. of Spencer Kingsley, Oct. 15, 1907; 1 dau., Kingsley. Contbr. to Saturday Evening Post, Collier's, Country Gentleman, Ladies' Home Jour., etc. Clubs: Cap and Gown, Nassau (Princeton); Players, Princeton (New York). Author: The Six Best Cellars (with Holworthy Hall), 1919; Babel, 1921; The East Wind, 1922; The Collector's Whatnot (with Booth Tarkington and Kenneth L. Roberts), 1923; Father Means Well, 1930; Hills Were Higher Then, 1931; The Big Pink, 1932. Home: Princeton, N.J.

KAHN, David Harman, bd. commerce exec. sec.; b. Parkersburg, W.Va., July 25, 1888; s. Samuel and Menna (Davis) K.; B.S., W.Va. Univ., 1911; m. Fannie Bryan, Feb. 26, 1917; children—David Harman, Jr., Charles Samuel. Engaged in bus. on own acct. as mcht., Parkersburg, W.Va., 1911-33; exec. sec. Parkersburg Bd. of Commerce since 1933; dir. Bentley Oberwig Desk Co. Past pres. Community Chest now dir. Democrat. Jewish religion. Mason (32°). B'nai B'rith. Club: Rotary of Parkersburg (past pres.). Home: 1401 21st St., Parkersburg, W.Va.

KAIN, George Hay, lawyer; b. York, Pa.; Apr. 13, 1877; s. William Henry and Clara Maria (Hay) K.; prep. edn., York County Acad.; grad. York Collegiate Inst., 1893; B.S., Gettysburg (Pa.) Coll., 1897, M.S., 1900; LL.B., Harvard, 1902; m. Cara Bahn Watt, Jan. 1, 1901; children—George Hay, Richard Morgan, William Henry. Instructor in mathematics, prep. dept. Gettysburg Coll., 1897-98; admitted to Pa. bar, 1902, and practiced since at York; mem. firm Cochran, Williams & Kain, 1912-30; v.p., dir. and counsel York Trust Co., The York Water Co., York Suburban Water Co.; dir. and counsel The Farmers Fire Ins. Co., Yorktown Land Co. Trustee York County Acad. (pres.), York Collegiate Institute. Mem. Am., Pa. State and York County bar assns., Phi Beta Kappa, Phi Delta Theta. Republican. Lutheran. Mason. (K.T.; Dist. Dep. Grand Master Grand Lodge of Pa. since 1911). Club: Lafayette. Home: 45 Springettsbury Pl. Office: 57 E. Market St., York, Pa.

KALBFUS, Edward Clifford, naval officer; b. Mauch Chunk, Pa., Nov. 24, 1877; s. Daniel and Mary Electra (Jones) K.; grad. U.S. Naval Acad., 1899; m. Syria Florence Brown, May 13, 1905. Commd. ensign, U.S. Navy, 1901; promoted through grades to rear admiral, 1931. Participated in Spanish-Am. War, 1898, Philippine Insurrection, 1900-01, Cuba Pacification, 1905, Mexican occupation, 1914; captain U.S.S. Pocahontas, World War, later captain U.S.S. Iowa, Trenton, California; mem. staff Naval War Coll., 1927-29; chief of staff, Battleship Divs., Battle Fleet, 1930; dir. War Plans, Navy Dept., 1931; commander Destroyers, Battle Force, U.S. Fleet, 1931-34; pres. Naval War Coll., 1934-36; vice admiral, commander Battleships, Battle Force, U.S. Fleet, 1937; admiral, commander Battle Force, U.S. Fleet, 1938. Member Military Order of Carabao. Episcopalian. Clubs: Army and Navy (Washington, D.C.); hon. mem. Cruising Club of America. Home: State College, Pa. Address: Navy Dept., Washington, D.C.

KALICHEVSKY, Vladimir Anatole, chem. engineering; b. Tiflis, Russia, Apr. 9, 1895; s. Anatole Joseph and Maria (Grodekov) K.; student Corps of Pages of H.I.M. Emperor of Russia, 1910-14, War Coll. (Russia), 1917; B.S. in Chem. Engring., Calif. Inst. Tech., 1924; m. Valentina Fedorenko, Aug. 31, 1924; 1 dau., Kira. Came to U.S., 1921, naturalized, 1928. Lecturer tactics and surveying, Paulovskoe Mil. Coll., Russia, 1917; asst. Russian mil. attaché in Denmark, 1917-19; officer with Royal Rumanian Mission in Vladivostok, Siberia, and Tokyo, Japan, 1920; mgr. topographical dept., Chukotsk Peninsula Mining Corpn., Tokyo, Japan, 1920-21; research chemist, Union Oil Co. of Calif., 1924-29; research chemist Standard Oil Development Co., 1929-31; sect. supervisor Socony-Vacuum Oil Co., Inc., Paulsboro, N.J., 1931-37, gen. supervisor research and development dept. since 1937. Inventor processes in petroleum refining. Served from sub-lt. to capt. Imperial Russian Guards, 1914-17; in Siberia, Civil War, 1919-20. Awarded Medaille de Sauvetage (France); sword with inscription "For Bravery''; a number battle rewards (Russia). Name carved on Marble Plate of Corps of Pages as having best scholastic record. Mem. Am. Chem. Soc. Republican. Greek Catholic. Contbr. monographs and articles on petroleum refining. Home: 24 N. Woodland Av., Woodbury, N.J.

KALISKI, Jesse, textile mfr.; b. New York, N.Y., Nov. 17, 1885; s. John Ephriam and Hannah (Manheimer) K.; student N.Y. Pub. High Sch., 1897-99, Cooper Union Sch. of Engring., 1899-1902; m. Beryl Kahn, Nov. 25, 1914; children—Juliette Alliene, Edward Jay. Sec. and treas. Heather Handkerchief Works, Jersey City, N.J., since 1916; v.p. and sec. Kaliski Realties, N.Y. City, since 1932. Mason (Shriner). Elk. Clubs: Westchester Yacht (Mamaroneck, N.Y.); Inwood Beach (Inwood, L.I.). Home: 1 W. 67th St., New York, N.Y. Office: 106 Cambridge Av., Jersey City, N.J.

KALLENBACH, Walter Dustin, evangelist, lecturer; b. Everett, Mass., July 20, 1905; s. John Henry and Eva Frances (Dustin) K.; desc. Hannah Dustin; B.S., U. of Va., 1931; student Southern Bapt. Theol. Sem., 1931-32; B.D., Eastern Bapt. Theol. Sem., 1933, Th.M., 1934; Th.D., Pikes Peak Sem., 1936; Ph.D., Webster U., Atlanta, Ga., 1938; m. Shelburne Wyly, May 19, 1932; 1 dau., Shelburne Brashear. Began as musician, lost his sight as a result of hunting accident, 1927, and returned to college; began evangelistic work while student in Phila.; has held services in many of the large cities of U.S., also in univs. and penal instns., winning many converts. Mem. Phi Beta Kappa. Baptist. Knight of Malta, Knight of Mystic Chain, Browning Soc. of Haverhill, Mass. Ind. Republican. Club: Quill (Louisville). Author: The Higher Significance of the Gospel, 1938. Author of booklets, Salvation and What Follows, 1937; Message and Authorship of Hebrews, 1938; Law and Commandments, 1938; That Men May Know, 1938. Contbr. articles to religious jours. Home: 750 Concord Av., Drexel Hill, Pa.

KALLOK, John, clergyman; b. Suche, Slovakia, Sept. 14, 1907; s. John and Elizabeth (Bakajsa) K.; ed. St. Procopius Coll., Lisle, Ill., 1927-29, St. Procopius Sem., Lisle, Ill., 1929-30, Greek Catholic Theol. Sem., Uzhorod, Czechoslovakia, 1930-34; grad. study, Duquesne U., 1937. Ordained priest Greek Cath. Ch., 1934; pastor, St. Peter's and St. Paul's Ch., Granville, N.Y., 1934-36; pastor, St. George's Ch., West Aliquippa, Pa., since 1936. Mem. Sigma Alpha (Slovak students' frat.), Greek Cath. Union, Jednota. Democrat. Greek Catholic. Rotarian. Author (pamphlet), The Eastern Catholic Church, 1936. Has written two plays, "Half and Half" and "Fraternity Knights." Founder and editor, Chrysostom, only monthly in English devoted to Eastern Catholics. Contbr. articles to religious pubs. Home: 324 River Av., West Aliquippa, Pa.

KALODNER, Harry Ellis, U.S. dist. judge; b. Phila., Pa., Mar. 28, 1896; s. David and Ida (Miller) K.; prep. edn. public schools of Phila.; LL.B., U. of Pa., 1917; m. Tillie Poliner, Dec. 20, 1925; children—Philip P., Howard I. Began as reporter, 1912; admitted to Pa. bar, 1919; practice in Phila. 1919-35; mem. editorial staff Phila. North American, 1919-25; mem. editorial staff Phila. Record, 1928-34; sec. of revenue Commonwealth of Pa., Aug.-Dec. 1935; judge of Court of Common Pleas, Phila. Co., 1936-37; judge U.S. Dist. Court, Eastern Dist. of Pa., since July 1938. Served in O.R. T.C., May-June 1917; Judge Adv. Gen. Dept., with A.E.F., Sept. 1918-Apr. 1919. Mem. exec. bd. Zionist Orgn. of Phila.; mem. bd. dirs. Jewish Welfare Soc., Homewood Sch., Y.M. and Y.W.H.A., Hebrew Sheltering and Immigrant Aid Soc., Northern Liberties Hosp. Awarded hon. mention Pulitzer prize for journalism, 1931, 32. Mem. Am., Pa. and Phila. bar assns., Am. Legion. Democrat. Elk, Moose, B'nai B'rith. Club: Lawyers. Home: 5829 Woodbine Av. Address: 311 Customs House, Philadelphia, Pa.

KALTMAN, David Lyman, wholesale druggist; b. New York, N.Y., Apr. 5, 1897; s. Israel and Sarah Rose (Itzkowitz) K.; Ph.G., Columbia U. Sch. Pharmacy, 1917; m. Pauline Lein, Apr. 12, 1917; children—Phyllis, Mildred. Asso. with M. Lein Chem. Works, 1918; organized and mem. firm D. Kaltman & Co., 1919-20;

acquired M. Lein Chem. Works, combined both cos. and inc. as D. Kaltman & Co., Inc., and pres. since 1920; organized Ogden Realty Co. and pres. since 1927, Hutton Realty Co. and pres. since 1937. Mem. exec. com. of Drug & Chem. Sect. of N.Y. Bd. of Trade. Past pres. Jersey City Lions Club. Past pres. Druggists' Sundries Assn. Chmn. Wholesalers Div. Joint Distribution Com. Mem. bd. govs. Temple Emanuel, Englewood. Jewish religion. Home: 400 Manor Rd., Englewood. Office: 126 Webster Av., Jersey City, N.J.

KAMENS, Benjamin M(aurice), furniture mcht.; b. Pittsburgh, Pa., Feb. 28, 1889; s. Henry and Ray (Frankenstein) K.; student pub. schs. and high sch., Pittsburgh, Pa., 1903-06; m. Idaline Kline, Oct. 27, 1914; children—Ruth Lee, Helen Sue. Employed as accountant with one firm in Baltimore, 1907-13; engaged in retail furniture bus. on own acct. as mem. firm Kline Furniture Co., Cumberland, Md., since 1913; vice-pres. Community Loan & Finance Co., Cumberland, Md., since 1926. Pres. Cumberland Chamber of Commerce. Vice-pres. Md. League of Retail Mchts. Democrat. Jewish religion. Club: Cumberland Country. Home: 317 Cumberland St. Office: 405 Virginia Av., Cumberland, Md.

KAMMAN, William Frederick, prof. modern langs.; b. Holland, Ind., Jan. 30, 1885; s. Henry William and Sophia Engel (Meyer) K.; A.B., Ind. U., 1913, A.M., same, 1914; student U. of Leipzig, Germany, 1914; Ph.D., U. of Pa., 1917; B.S., U. of Pittsburgh, 1921; m. Ida Elizabeth Geiss, Dec. 23, 1917; children—Elizabeth Wilhelmina, Grace Eleanor, Carol Ruth. Began as teacher country schs., 1903, then, teacher in high schs.; teaching fellow at Ind. U.; asst. in German, U. of Pa., 1914-17; instr. to asst. prof. of modern langs., asso. prof., then prof. and head of dept. of modern langs., Carnegie Inst. of Tech. since 1917. Mem. Modern Lang. Assn. of America, Modern Lang. Assn. of Pa., Modern Lang. Assn. of Pittsburgh, Verein für Niederdeutsche Sprachforshung. Republican. Lutheran. Author: Socialism in German American Literature, 1917. Contbr. articles on mod. langs. to mags. Home: 5711 Solway St., Pittsburgh, Pa.

KANE, E. Kent, oil and gas exec.; b. Kushequa, Pa., Apr. 19, 1902; s. Elisha K. and Zella Ellen (Hays) K.; B.S., Princeton U; LL.B., U. of Pittsburgh; m. Alma Ray Bryan, Mar. 17, 1929; children—Zella Ellen, Cornelia Ray, Marjorie Bryan. Pres. Kane Gas Light & Heating Co., Citizens Gas Co., McDade Gas Co., Warren Co. Gas Co., Mt. Jewett Gas Co., Kane Plumbing Co., Inc., Amity Oil & Gas Co., Hazelhurst Gas Co., Mountain Gas Co., Northwestern Permagas Corpn., Kane Industrial Gas Corpn., Pa. Cos. Gas Corpn.; v.p. Kane Realty Co., Kane Real Estate, Inc., Kanesholm Oil Co. (Kane, Pa.). Mem. Pa. Ho. of Rep., representing McKean Co., since 1934. Home: Kushequa, Pa. Office: 22 Greeves St., Kane, Pa.

KANE, Evan O'Neill, exec.; b. Kushequa, Pa., Aug. 11, 1899; s. Elisha Kent and Zella Ellen (Hays) K.; grad. Kane (Pa.) High Sch., 1917; student Oberlin (O.) Coll., 1917-18; B.S., Princeton U., 1921; m. Hannah McCoy Hamlin, June 19, 1926; children—Hannah Elizabeth, Orlo Hamlin, Evan O'Neill, Eugenia Mary. Supt. Kushequa Brick Co., Kushequa Keramic Co. and Garage, Kane, Pa., since 1928; trustee Elizabeth D. Kane Estate, 1929; organized Kane Estate, Inc., and Kane Realty Corpn., 1930, and since pres.; treas. Northwestern Pa. Gas Co. and subsidiaries since 1933; dir. Simpson-Cooper Oil Co., oil producing, 1928-37, partner same since 1937; vice-pres. Kane Industrial Gas Co. since 1932; partner Lannigan Run Property, oil producing. Mem. Borough Council 1930-33. Served as private inf., U.S. Army, Aug.-Dec. 1918. Mem. bd. mgrs. Kane Summit Hosp., Kane. Regional dir. Boy Scouts; dir. Kane Y.M.C.A. Mem. Cloister Inn Club (Princeton U.). Republican. Mem. Union Ch., Kushequa. Club: Rotary of Kane (past pres.). Home: 117 Dawson St. Office: 87 Fraley St., Kane, Pa.

KANE, Francis Fisher, lawyer; b. Philadelphia, June 17, 1866; s. Robert Patterson and Elizabeth (Fisher) K.; A.B., Princeton, 1886, A.M., 1889; LL.B., U. of Pa., 1889; unmarried. Admitted to Pa. bar, 1889; formerly mem. Beck, Robinson & Kane, Phila., now practicing alone. Democratic nominee for Pa. Ho. of Rep., 1890; 1st asst. U.S. atty. Eastern Dist. of Pa., 1896-1900; nominee for mayor of Phila., 1903; U.S. atty. Eastern Dist. of Pa., by appmt. of Pres. Wilson, from Sept. 10, 1913-20, resigned. Served in Vienna as Am. rep. Friends' Relief Mission, 1923. Pres. Pa. Prison Soc. Mem. Hist. Soc. Pa., Phila. Geog. Soc., Shakespeare Soc. of Phila., Phi Kappa Sigma. Episcopalian. Clubs: University, Univ. Barge. Recipient of the Philadelphia award of Bok Foundation, 1936. Home: 200 E. Johnson St., Germantown. Office: Guarantee Trust Bldg., Philadelphia, Pa.

KANN, Gustave Herman, steel abrasive mfr.; b. Pittsburgh, Pa., Dec. 22, 1886; s. Myer Milton and Bertha (Friedlander) K.; student Carnegie Inst. Tech., 1905-08; m. Evelyn B. Solomon, Aug. 18, 1914. Began as mgr., 1908; with Carnegie Steel Co., 1908-10; with Pittsburgh Crushed Steel Co. since 1910, pres. since 1915; pres. Globe Steel Abrasive Co., Am. Steel Abrasives Co., Steel Shot & Grit Co., Ambassador Apts., Inc.; v.p. Triumph Fusee & Fireworks Co., Brackenridge (Pa.) Brewing Co., Hopkan Rivet Co. and Acme Protection Equipment Co. of Pittsburgh; dir. Globe Varnish Co. Vice-pres. Alumni Fed. of Carnegie Inst. of Tech., Young Men and Women's Hebrew Assn. (Pittsburgh); dir. Walter P. Steffen Memorial Fund (Pittsburgh). Served in U.S.N., 1917-18. Republican. Jewish religion. Mason. Clubs: Concordia, Hundred (Pittsburgh); Westmoreland Country. Home: Schenley Hotel. Office: 61st St. and Allegheny Valley Railroad, Pittsburgh, Pa.

KANN, James Jay, mfg. hosiery; b. New York, N.Y., May 7, 1897; s. Arthur James and Amelia M. (Jay) K.; ed. U. of Vt., 1913-15; B.J., Columbia U., 1918; unmarried. In employ Anglo-South American Bank, 1920-25; pres. State Textile Corpn., 1925-32; pres. Cromwell Hosiery Mills, 1932-37; pres. and dir. Wilmington Hosiery Mills, Inc., hosiery mfrs., Wilmington, Del., since 1927; pres. Amera Securities Corpn.; dir. Phila. & Reading Coal & Iron Co.; dir. and chmn. finance com. Cosden Petroleum Corpn., Fort Worth, Tex.; chmn. N.Y., N.H. & Hartford R.R. Bondholders Com. Served as Am. sec., Agence Economique et Politique de France, 1919-20. Served as capt. Royal Air Force, 1917-19. Treas. Am. Mission to Poland, 1919. Awarded Croix de Guerre (France); Order of White Eagle (Poland); D.S.C. (U.S.) Republican. Episcopalian. Clubs: Bankers, Chemists (New York); Brandywine Hunt (Lenape, Pa.); Royal Air Force (London); Phyllis Court (Henly, Eng.). Home: Fox Hollow, Chadds Ford, Pa. Office: 4014 Du Pont Bldg., Wilmington, Del.; 320 5th Av., New York, N.Y.

KANNER, Leo, physician; b. Klekotow, Austria, June 13, 1894; s. Abraham and Clara (Reissfeld) K.; came to U.S., 1924, naturalized, 1930; M.D., U. of Berlin, 1919; m. June Lewin, Feb. 14, 1921; children—Anita, Albert Victor. Asst. Univ. Hosp., Berlin, 1920-23; sr. asst. phys. Yankton State Hosp., S.D., 1924-28; commonwealth fund fellow in psychiatry, Johns Hopkins Hosp., 1928-30; dir. Children's, Psychiatric Clinic, Johns Hopkins Hosp. since 1930; asso. prof. psychiatry, Johns Hopkins U. Med. Sch. since 1933; mem. adv. bds. of Child Study Assn., Baltimore Branch, Baltimore Assn. for Nursery Sch. Edn.; psychiatric consultant Baltimore City Juvenile Ct.; psychiatrist Frederick Co. Md. Mental Hygiene Clinic. Served in Austrian Army, 1914-18. Dir. Child Study Home of Md., 24-Hour Day Sch., Wild Rose Shore, Annapolis, Md. Fellow Am. Psychiatric Assn. Mem. Am. Soc. Med. History, Am. History of Medicine Soc., Nervous and Mental Research Assn., Baltimore City Med. Soc., Bd. of Md. Refugee Adjustment Com. Democrat. Jewish religion. Mason (32°). Author: Folklore of the Teeth, 1928; Folklore and Cultural History of Epilepsy, 1930; Medical Folklore, 1931; Judging Emotions from Facial Expression, 1931; Christian Franz Paullini, 1934; Child Psychiatry, 1935, 2d edit., 1937; Historical Notes on Rumination in Man, 1936. Contbr. about 85 articles to med. journs. Home: 4510 Wentworth Rd. Office: Johns Hopkins Hospital, Baltimore, Md.

KANTNER, Franklin E., lawyer; b. Reading, Pa., June 30, 1902; s. Harry F. and Maude (Frishmuth) K.; LL.B., Dickinson Law Sch., 1923; m. A. Dorothy Morgan, Feb. 14, 1935. Admitted to bar, 1923; since in gen. practice of law under own name; v.p. and dir. Penn Title Ins. Co.; pres. Chancellor Hosiery Mills, Inc.; dir. Ferdinand Goetz Sons Co. Mem. Delta Chi. Republican. Clubs: Wyomissing, University, Reading Country (Reading). Home: 1553 Mineral Spring Road. Office: 200 Am. Casualty Co. Bldg., Reading, Pa.

KAPLAN, Eliah, physician; b. Poland, Oct. 12, 1884; s. Joshua Hersall and Sarah Rebecca (Arkin) K.; came to U.S. 1903, and naturalized citizen, 1912; M.D., Jefferson Med. Coll., 1913; M.Sc.M., U. of Pa. Grad. Med. Sch., 1921; m. Ina Rabinovitz, Mar. 14, 1917; children—Joshua H., Sherman O. Engaged in gen. practice of medicine at New Castle, Pa., since 1913; mem. med. staff Jameson Memorial Hosp., New Castle Hosp. Fellow Am. Coll. Physicians; mem. Pa. State and Lawrence Co. med. socs. Republican. Jewish religion. B'nai B'rith. Elk. Home: 223 N. Mercer St., New Castle, Pa.

KAPLAN, Frank R(aphael) S(elig), lawyer; b. Russia, May 26, 1886; s. Abraham and Bessie (Ezralet) K.; brought to U.S., 1889, naturalized 1892; A.B. Washington and Jefferson Coll., 1907, A.M., 1912; LL.B., U. of Pittsburgh, 1910; m. Madeline May Roth, Nov. 28, 1918; children—Irving Meyer Joseph, Lois Edna, Margery Elaine. Admitted to Pa. bar, 1910, and practised in McKeesport, and in Pittsburgh since 1910; sec., treas. and dir. Copperweld Steel Co. Formerly mem. and pres. bd. of edn., McKeesport, Pa.; trustee McKeesport (Pa.) Hosp. Mem. Am., Pa. and Allegheny County bar assns.; hon. mem. Phi Epsilon Pi. Jewish religion. Mason, B'nai B'rith (former pres. dist. grand lodge). Clubs: Concordia, Westmoreland Country, Hundred (Pittsburgh). Home: 5251 Fair Oaks St. Office: Frick Bldg., Pittsburgh, Pa.

KAPP, Cecil Abram, elec. engring.; b. Oxford, O., Dec. 18, 1895; s. Charles and Iona J. (Ramsey) K.; ed. O. Northern U., 1913-14; E.E., U. of Cincinnati, 1919; m. Mabel Ferguson, Apr. 29, 1922. Employed as elec. engr., Roane Iron Co., Rockwood, Tenn., and W.Va. Engring. Co., Williamson, W.Va., 1919-20; co-ordinator, Co-operative Dept., Ga. Sch. Tech., Atlanta, 1920-22; asso. with Drexel Inst. Tech., Phila., Pa., since 1922, dir. co-operative edn. since 1922. Served in S.A.T.C., 1918. Mem. Am. Inst. Elec. Engrs., Soc. for Promotion Engring. Edn. Mason. Clubs: Overbrook Country, Manufacturers and Bankers (Philadelphia). Home: 1105 N. 63d St., Philadelphia, Pa.

KAPPEL, John Frank, jewelry; b. Pittsburgh, Pa., July 26, 1889; s. John and Marie K.; studied Iron City Business Coll., 1903-04; m. Edna I. Duysters, Aug. 27, 1913; children—Edna Mae, Marilyn, Richard W., Patricia Ann. Sec., treas. and dir. W. J. Kappel Co., Pittsburgh; sec., treas. and dir. Aug. Loch Co., Kappel Wholesale Jewelry Co. (both of Pittsburgh); sec. and dir. Busch Jewelry Co. (New York and Chicago); sec. and dir. Howard Jewelry Co. (Buffalo); pres. East Park Bldg. & Loan Assn. Republican. Lutheran. Mason (K.T.). Clubs: Lions, Syria Temple, Shannopin Country (Pittsburgh). Home: 8 Bonvue St. Office: 109 Sixth St., Pittsburgh, Pa.

KAPPEL, William J., pres. William J. Kappel Co.; b. Allegheny, Pittsburgh, Pa., Mar. 18, 1885; s. John and Marie (Franke) K.; ed. business coll., Pittsburgh; m. Olive Pearl Dean; children—William D., Herbert J., Virginia M., Wallace J., Ruth Christman. Pres. William J. Kappel Co., Pittsburgh, Pa., since 1922, August Loch Co., Pittsburgh, since 1929, Busch Jewelry Co., New York, since 1927, Busch Jewelry Co., Chicago, since 1937, Howard

Jewelry Co., Buffalo, N.Y., since 1925; Kappel Wholesale Jewelry Co. of N.J., Newark, N.J., since 1932; dir. Workingmans Savings Bank & Trust Co., East Park Bldg. & Loan Assn. Republican. Lutheran. Mason (Syria Temple Shrine). Clubs: Monarch, Shannopin Country (Pittsburgh). Home: Kent Rd., Ben Avon Heights. Office: 109 Sixth St., Pittsburgh, Pa.

KAPPES, Charles William, lawyer; b. Town of Union, now Union City, N.J., May 5, 1880; s. Charles Adolph and Sophia (Koeberlein) K.; LL.B., N.Y. Univ. Law Sch., 1903; m. Erna A. Braunstein, Nov. 1, 1911; children—Charles William, Jr., S. Winifred. Admitted to N.J. bar as atty., 1906, as counselor, 1912; engaged in gen. practice of law at Union City, N.J., since 1906; mem. firm Kappes, Hille & Curran since 1920, vice-pres. Weehawken Bldg. & Loan Assn. since 1931. Trustee North Hudson Hosp., Weehawken, N.J. Mem. Am. Bar Assn., N.J. State Bar Assn., Hudson Co. Bar Assn., (pres. 1932-33). Episcopalian. Mason (32°, Shriner). Elk. Clubs: North Hudson Lawyers. Home: Saddle River. Office: 708 Bergenline Av., Union City, N.J.

KAPPES, William Carl, surgeon; b. Clifton Forge, Va., July 16, 1899; s. George Lewis and Elizabeth James (Johnson) K.; student U. of Richmond, 1918-20; M.D., Med. Coll. of Va., Richmond, 1924; m. Frances Louise Kenney, June 20, 1928; children—William Carl, Jr., Charles Kenney. Became interne and resident C. & O. Hosp., Huntington, W.Va., 1924; attdg. surgeon C. & O. Hosp. and St. Marys Hosp.; mem. staff W. W. Kinson Surg. Clinic. Served in S.A.T.C., 1918. Fellow Am. Coll. Surgeons; mem. Kappa Sigma. Democrat. Episcopalian. Home: 316 N. Boul. Office: 1119 6th Av., Huntington, W.Va.

KARCHER, Joseph T., lawyer; b. Sayreville, N.J., Sept. 10, 1903; s. Joseph T. and Katherine Virginia (Quaid) K.; LL.B., N.J. Law Sch. (now U. of Newark), 1927; m. Ellen Stokes Joseph, Nov. 25, 1927; children—Joyce Marie, Evelyn. Admitted to N.J. bar as atty., 1928, as counsellor, 1931; police judge, Borough of Sayreville, N.J., 1929-32; mem. N.J. Ho. Assembly, 1930-32; deputy surrogate, Middlesex Co., 1932-38; corpn. counsel for Borough of Sayreville and Twp. of E. Brunswick, 1938-39; became spl. master in chancery, 1938. Mem. Middlesex Co. Bar Assn. Democrat. Mem. K.C. Club: Lions. Home: 507 Main St. Office: 61 Main St., Sayreville, N.J.

KARICKHOFF, Oda Earle, coll. prof.; b. Rural Dale, W.Va., March 14, 1880; s. Henry Nicholas and Permelia (Strader) K.; student W.Va. Conf. Sem., 1898-1901; A.B., W.Va. Wesleyan Coll., Buckhannon, 1905; A.M., Harvard, 1907; grad. student Harvard and Boston U.; m. Myrtle Mauzy, Sept. 8, 1926; children—Elizabeth Marie, Michael. Supt. of boys' work, Riverside Settlement, Cambridge, Mass., 1906; resident Elizabeth Peabody Social Settlement, Boston, 1907-12; Boston sec. North Am. Civic League for Immigrants, 1909-15; prof. of sociology and economics, Salem Coll., W.Va., 1915-19; prof. sociology and economics, W.Va. Wesleyan Coll. since 1919. Republican. Methodist. Mason (K.T.). Club: Lions (Buckhannon). Home: 38 Arnold Av., Buckhannon, W.Va.

KARR, Robert McNary, theologian; b. Bloomington, Ind., Sept. 1878; s. John and Mary Elizabeth (Alexander) K.; A.B., Monmouth (Ill.) Coll., 1907, A.M., 1909, D.D., 1922; grad. Pittsburgh Theol. Sem., 1909; m. Annis Bertha Marshall, Aug. 6, 1909; children—Margaret Elizabeth, Robert Livingstone, Katherine Louise, Frances Mary. Ordained ministry U.P. Ch., 1909; pastor successively Tacoma, Wash., Kansas City, Mo., and Oakmont, Pa., until 1922; prof. systematic theology and homiletics, Xenia Theol. Sem., St. Louis, Mo., 1922-30, also v.p., 1923-30; prof. systematic and bibl. theology, Pittsburgh-Xenia Theol. Sem., Pittsburgh, Pa., since 1930, also registrar since 1930. Editor and author (with others) Children of the Covenant, 1921. Home: 236 Hilands Av., Ben Avon Boro, Pittsburgh, Pa.

KASE, Paul George, glass mcht. and artist; b. Reading, Pa., Nov. 4, 1895; s. James M. and Martha (Weis) K.; grad. Reading High Sch., 1913; ed. Pa. Acad. Fine Arts, 1913-16; m. Jane Louise Keffer, Nov. 22, 1921; children—Paul G., Jr., Jane L., David E. Began career as designer in stained glass, 1918, studio at Reading, Pa.; designed stained glass for portion of Riverside Ch. and Cloisters Mus., both New York City, St. Florian Ch., Detroit, Mich., Christ Ch., Winnetka, Ill., Skinner Hall of Music, Vassar Coll., St. Carthage Ch., Phila.; asso. with J. M. Kase, Inc., gen. glass mchts., Reading, Pa., since 1916, treas., 1932-36, pres. since 1936. Served as pvt. inf., U.S.A. during World War. Mem. Fellowship Pa. Acad. Fine Arts, Am. Legion. Roman Catholic. Club: Reading Country. Home: 427 Friedensburg Rd. Office: 30 N. 8th St., Reading, Pa.

KASEL, Frank Valentine, pres. Janson Steel & Iron Co.; b. Columbus, Pa., Aug. 17, 1879; s. Frank Peter and Catherine Elizabeth (Janson) K.; student Holy Trinity Parochial Sch., Columbia, Pa., 1885-95, Dickinson Business Coll., 1895-99; m. Elizabeth Veronica Barth, June 11, 1901; children—Frank X., William B. Began as bookkeeper Janson Iron Co., 1900; now pres. Janson Iron & Steel Co., Columbia, Pa.; dir. First Columbia Nat. Bank, Home Bldg. & Loan Assn., Grand pres. and dir. Pa. Catholic Beneficial League; dir. Columbia Hosp. Democrat. Catholic. K.C., Order of Alhambra, Elk, Eagle. Home: 904 Locust St. Address: P. O. Box 89, Columbia, Pa.

KATENKAMP, William E.; chmn. Nat. Central Bank. Address: Baltimore and Holliday Sts., Baltimore, Md.

KATZ, Daniel, psychologist; b. Trenton, N.J., July 19, 1903; s. Rudolph and Regina (Fletcher) K.; A.B., U. of Buffalo, 1925; A.M., Syracuse U., 1926, Ph.D., 1928; m. Christine Ross Braley, Sept. 1, 1930; children—Joanna Braley, Jean Braley. Instr., Princeton U., 1928-31, asst. prof. psychology since 1931. Mem. Am. Psychol. Assn., Soc. for Psychol. Study of Social Issues, Am. Assn. Univ. Profs., Sigma Xi, Phi Beta Kappa. Co-author (with F. H. Allport): Students' Attitudes, 1931; (with R. L. Schanck), Social Psychology, 1938. Contbr. chapter, "Personality," to Psychology, a Factual Text-book. Home: 7 College Rd., Princeton, N.J.

KATZ, David, business exec.; b. Albany, N. Y., March 12, 1888; s. Jacob and Belle (Anton) K.; student high sch. and business coll.; m. Emma H. Hayden, Sept. 30, 1922. Examiner of accounts, Pub. Service Commn., State of N.Y., 1916-22; accountant, investigation and reports, Day & Zimmerman, Phila., Pa., 1922-25, asst. treas. and asst. sec., 1926-38, treas. since 1938; treas. Cold Springs Bleachery since 1938; v.p. Great Lakes Utilities Corpn. and subsidiaries since 1937; dir. Cold Springs Bleachery, L. F. Grammes & Sons. Mason (32°, Shriner). Clubs: Penn Athletic, National League Masonic (Phila.). Home: 1520 Spruce St. Office: 620 Packard Bldg., Philadelphia, Pa.

KATZ, Sidney Hershberg, chem. engring.; b. Gilmore, Pa., Feb. 1, 1884; s. Ellis and Jennie (Kleinmaier) K.; B.S. in Chem. Engring., Ohio State U., 1909; student Columbia U., 1913; M.S., U. of Pittsburgh, 1923, Chem. E., 1924, Ph.D., 1926; unmarried. Research chemist National Carbon Co., Cleveland, O., 1909; chem. engr., John D. Owens & Son, Owens, O., 1909-10; instr. in chemistry, N.H. Univ., Durham, N.H., 1910-14; in charge various research work U.S. Bur. of Mines, Pittsburgh, Pa., 1914-29; prin. chemist, Edgewood Arsenal, C.W.S., U.S.A. since 1929; engaged at Safety in Mines Research Bd. of Grt. Britain, Sheffield, Eng., as exchange research worker from U.S. Bur. of Mines, 1928-29. Served as 1st lt. C.W.S., U.S.A., 1918-19; now major, C.W. Reserve. Mem. A.A.A.S., Am. Chem. Soc., Sigma Xi, Tau Beta Pi, Alpha Chi Sigma. Mem. K. of P. Club: Officers (Edgewood Arsenal). Home: Edgewood Arsenal, Edgewood, Md.

KATZENBACH, G. A.; pres. Broad Street National Bank. Address: Trenton, N.J.

KATZENELBOGEN, Solomon, physician; b. Ouman, Russia, Dec. 3, 1890; s. Moise and Eva K.; came to U.S., 1928, naturalized 1933; M.D., U. of Geneva Med. Sch., 1918; m. Nina Gandjoumoff, 1916; 1 dau., Eva. Post. grad. work U. of Zürich, 1918-20; research asst., resident, U. of Geneva Med. Sch., 1920-25, head of lab. internal medicine, 1925-28, privat docent internal medicine, 1925-28; asso. in psychiatry, Johns Hopkins U. Med. Sch., 1928-36, asso. prof. psychiatry, 1936-38; dir. labs. and research, St. Elizabeth's Hosp., Washington, D.C., since 1938, clin. prof. George Washington Med. School, 1939. Fellow Am. Coll. Physicians, Am. Psychiatric Assn.; mem. Am. Neurol. Assn., Soc. Exptl. Biology and Medicine. Author: The Cerebrospinal Fluid and Its Relation to Blood, 1935. Contbr. to med. and psychiatric jours. Home: 5921 Wilson Lane, Bethesda, Md.

KAUFFMAN, Daniel, bishop; b. Richfield, Pa., June 20, 1865; s. David Demuth and Elisabeth (Weiney) K.; student pub. schs., Morgan Co., Mo., and Mo. State Univ. (1884-85); m. Ota Josephine Bowlin, Aug. 17, 1887 (died March 5, 1890); 1 son, James Arthur (deceased), and a daughter (died in infancy); m. 2d, Mary Catherine Shank, Feb. 6, 1902; children—Homer Matthew, Eunice (deceased), Paul Raymond (deceased), Alice Ruth (Mrs. Fred Gingerich), Fannie Esther, John Mark (deceased). Pub. sch. teacher, 1883-96; sch. commr. Morgan Co., Mo., 1889-1901; minister Mennonite Ch. since 1893; ordained bishop, 1897; editor Gospel Witness, 1905-08, Gospel Herald since 1908; pres. Goshen Coll., 1922-23. Author of about 20 books on Christian doctrine, church history, and Christian living. Address: 800 Walnut Av., Scottdale, Pa.

KAUFMAN, Anton, editor and publisher; b. Csenger, Hungary, Oct. 6, 1882; s. Ludwig and Julia (Berger) K.; came to U.S., 1905, naturalized, 1910; student Univ. of Berlin, Germany, 1900-05, Ph.D. in History, 1904; m. Fannie Newman, March 14, 1909 (died 1939); children—Theodore N., Herbert, Julian M., Leonard B. Employed as reporter, Berliner Morgenzeitung, 1900-03, 1904-05; employed by several English and German newspapers, 1905-14; established Detroit Jewish Chronicle and editor and publisher, 1914-18; established Newark Jewish Chronicle, Anglo-Jewish newspaper, and editor and pub. since 1921; pres. Jewish Chronicle Pub. Co., Anka Publications, Inc., Traffic Bldg. & Loan Assn.; vice-pres. Progressive Merchants Bldg. & Loan Assn., Legal Publications, Inc.; dir. Normal Bldg. & Loan Assn. Served in 12th Hungarian Regt., 1903-04, disch. as lt. Served on Liberty Loan and Red Cross drives in Detroit during World War. Active in community affairs. Dir. N.J. Anti-Tuberculosis League. Mem. N.J. Press Assn., Newark Chamber of Commerce. Jewish religion; mem. B'nai B'rith. Club: Progress. Editor in chief, Newark Jewish Community Blue Book, 1927. Author: Jews in Napoleonic Era, 1910. Home: 302 Seymour Av. Office: 190 Badger Av., Newark, N.J.

KAUFMAN, Charles Milton, banker; b. Llewellyn, Pa., July 2, 1862; s. Elias and Lydia Ann (Haertter) K.; ed. pub. schs., Tower City, Pa.; unmarried. Began as slate picker Brookside Colliery, 1878; mgr. country store, 1885-92; gen. mgr. Williams Valley R.R. Co., 1892-1908, dir. since 1892; pres. Tower City Nat. Bank since 1902; established Greenwood Cemetery, 1896. Republican. Lutheran. Mason (past master). Club: Philharmonic (Tower City). Address: Tower City, Pa.

KAUFMAN, David E., lawyer; b. Bradford Co., Pa., May 15, 1883; s. Marks and Rachel K.; LL.B., Dickinson Sch. of Law, Carlisle, Pa., 1904; Doctor of Laws, Social Sciences and Polit. Economy, U. of San Simon, Cochabamba, Bolivia, 1928; unmarried. Admitted to Pa. bar, 1904, and began practice with Judge A. C. Fanning, Towanda; E.E. and M.P. to Bolivia, 1928-30; E.E. and M.P. to Siam, July 1930-1933; now associated in law practice with Brown & Williams; apptd. and acting as trustee Philadelphia Rapid Transit Co. Decorated Grand Cross, Order of Condor of the Andes, Bolivia, (1st Am. to receive this honor). Clubs: Manufacturers and Bankers Club, Locust, Philmont (Phila.); Press Club of Bolivia (organizer; hon. pres.). Home: Bellevue-Stratford Hotel. Office: 1421 Chestnut St., Philadelphia, Pa.

KAUFMAN, George S., newspaperman, playwright; b. Pittsburgh, Pa., Nov. 16, 1889; s. Joseph S. and Nettie (Schamberg) Myers K.; ed. pub. schs.; m. Beatrice Bakrow, 1917. Conducted daily humorous column, Washington Times, 1912-13, New York Evening Mail, 1914-15; subsequently on dramatic staffs, New York Tribune and New York Times. Author: The Butter and Egg Man, 1925. Co-Author: (plays) Someone in the House, 1918; Jacques Duval, 1920; Dulcy, 1921; To the Ladies, 1922; Merton of the Movies, 1922; Helen of Troy, New York (musical), 1923; The Deep Tangled Wildwood, 1923; Beggar on Horseback, 1924; Be Yourself (musical), 1924; Mimick, 1924; The Cocoanuts (musical), 1925; The Good Fellow, 1926; Strike Up the Band (musical), 1927; The Royal Family, 1927; Animal Crackers (musical), 1928; June Moon, 1929; The Channel Road, 1929; Once in a Lifetime, 1930; The Band Wagon (musical), 1931; Eldorado, 1931; Of Thee I Sing (musical), 1931; Dinner at Eight, 1932; Let 'Em Eat Cake (musical), 1933; The Dark Tower, 1933; Merrily We Roll Along, 1934; Bring on the Girls, 1934; First Lady, 1935; Stage Door, 1936; You Can't Take It With You, 1936; I'd Rather Be Right (musical), 1937; The Fabulous Invalid, 1938; The American Way, 1939. Home: Holicong, Pa.

KAUFMAN, Harry Keva, concert pianist; b. New York City, Sept. 6, 1893; s. Keva and Fanny (Shapiro) K.; student City Coll. of New York; student of Sigismund Stojowski at the Inst. of Musical Art, New York; student of Dr. Josef Hofmann at the Curtis Inst. of Music; m. Lilian Lewez, Nov. 17, 1921; children—Howard Keva, Curtis Casimir. Alto in synagogues, New York, 1902-04; accompanist and soloist since 1909; has been accompanist for Toscha Seidel, Erica Morini, Alma Gluck, Efrem Zimbalist; appeared as soloist in Phila. and New York with Phila. Orchestra under Stokowski, Smallens and Iturbi; in Venice Festival with La Scala Orchestra under Reiner; soloist with Philharmonic Orchestra under Hadley; soloist for first Gershwin Memorial Concert, New York Stadium, playing Concerto in F under Smallens and Rhapsody in Blue under Grofe; soloist with Manhattan Orchestra under Nikolai Sokoloff; assisting artist with Musical Art and Gordon String Quartets; official accompanist, Curtis Inst. of Music, Phila., since 1923, head dept. of accompanying since 1925; now vocal coach and teacher ensemble. Mem. Bohemian and Beethoven assns. of New York. Home: Hotel Meurice. Office: Curtis Institute of Music, Philadelphia, Pa.

KAUFMAN, Morgan S., lawyer; b. Kelme, Lithuania; s. Marks and Rachel K.; LL.B., Dickinson Sch. of Law, Carlisle, Pa.; unmarried. In practice of law at Scranton, Pa.; U.S. referee in bankruptcy, Middle Dist. of Pa., 1913-36; pres. Pa. Range Boiler Co. of Phila. Del. Rep. Nat. Conv., 1932. Trustee Fairview State Hosp., 1926-34. Republican. Mason, Elk. Clubs: Locust (Phila.); Lawyers' (New York City). Address: Mears Bldg., Scranton, Pa.

KAUFMAN, Reuben, rabbi; b. in Russia, June 1, 1890; s. Louis and Gertrude Minnie (Novosholsky) K.; brought to U.S., 1893, naturalized, 1900; A.B., Clark Coll., Worcester, Mass., 1911; A.M., Columbia U. 1912; Rabbi (valedictorian), Jewish Theol. Sem. of America, N.Y., 1915, D.H.L. 1917; m. Lilian Prigoff, Mar. 27, 1921; children—Sarah Miriam, Edward Joseph. Rabbi Mt. Sinai Congregation, N.Y. City, 1915-16, South Norwalk, Conn., 1916-18, Utica, N.Y., 1919-25, East Midwood Jewish Center, Brooklyn, N.Y., 1925-28; rabbi Temple Emanuel, Paterson, N.J., since 1928. Served as dir. religious activities in Am. Embarkation Center, Le Mans, France, 1919. Pres. Rabbinical Assn. of N.J., 1933-36; hon. chaplain Reuben Kaufman Post, Jewish War Vets., since 1935. Mem. Clark Scholarship Soc. Patentee Hebrew lotto game, automatic pencil, index tabs. Mason (32°, Shriner). Author Hebrew text-books. Composer: "Reverie" for violin and piano. Home: 349 E. 36th St., Paterson, N.J.

KAUFMAN, Samuel, lawyer; b. Newark, N.J., Dec. 31, 1893; s. Isaac and Dena (Kadan) K.; B.A., Columbia Coll., 1914; LL.B., Columbia Law Sch., 1916; M.A., Columbia Sch. of Polit. Science, 1916; m. Sylvia R. Meltzer, Oct. 4, 1923; children—John Meltzer, Andrew Lee. Admitted to N.J. bar, 1916; since in gen. practice law; mem. law firm Bilder, Bilder & Kaufman since 1919; dir. and counsel Warranty Bldg. & Loan Assn. Mem. Am. Bar Assn., N.J. State Bar Assn., Essex County Bar Assn., Phi Sigma Delta. Club: Mt. Ridge Country. Home: 446 Parker St. Office: 60 Park Pl., Newark, N.J.

KAUFMANN, Albert George, ins. official; b. Pittsburgh, Pa., July 8, 1886; s. Leonhard and Karolina (Deckler) K.; student pub. schs. and business coll.; m. Lillian Cryder, Aug. 17, 1909 (died 1920). Began as clerk Birmingham Fire Ins. Co., dir. since 1931, pres. since 1934. Home: Brentwood, Pa. Office: 1812 E. Carson St., Pittsburgh, Pa.

KAUFMANN, Arthur C., v.p. Gimbel Brothers, Inc.; b. Pittsburgh, Pa., May 7, 1901; s. Morris D and Sophie (Coblens) K.; student Pittsburgh pub. schs.; m. Dorothy Blatt, Jan. 19, 1936; 1 dau., Susan Louise. Began as stock boy Kaufmann & Baer Co. (dept. store); mng. dir. and v.p. McCreery & Co., 1928-35; now v.p. and exec. head Gimbel Brothers, Inc., and Gimbel Brothers Bank & Trust Co., Phila. Home: Ardmore, Pa. Office: 9th and Chestnut Sts., Philadelphia, Pa.

KAUFMANN, Edgar J., pres. Kaufmann Dept. Stores. Address: Fifth Av. and Smithfield St., Pittsburgh, Pa.

KAUFMANN, Helen Loeb, author; b. New York, N.Y., Feb. 2, 1887; d. Herman Albert and Selina (Loeb) Loeb; A.B., Barnard Coll., 1908; m. Mortimer J. Kaufmann, Aug. 12, 1907; children—George Mortimer, Richard Edward, Ruth (Mrs. Russell Abbot Ames). Mem. Beethoven Assn., Phi Beta Kappa. Clubs: Women Pays, Town Hall (New York). Author: Minute Sketches of Great Composers (with E. E. Hansl), 1932; Artists in Music of Today (with E. E. Hansl), 1933; From Jehovah to Jazz: the Story of American Music, 1937. Contbr. to mags. Home: Mackenzie Farms, Hampton, N.J. Office: 59 W. 12th St., New York, N.Y.

KAVANAUGH, E. P.; sec. Baltimore Sun. Office: Sun Bldg., Baltimore, Md.

KAY, James, physician; b. England, Mar. 9, 1891; s. Richard and Agnes (Doig) K.; brought to U.S., 1897, naturalized citizen, 1912; M.D., Jefferson Med. Coll., 1914; m. Mary W. Kennedy, Aug. 31, 1918; 1 son, Richard. Interne Memorial, Abington, and Episcopal hosps., 1914-17; visiting phys. Episcopal Hosp. since 1920; clin. prof. medicine, Temple U. Med. Sch. since 1929; cons. phys. Kensington Hosp. for Women since 1930. Fellow Coll. of Physicians of Phila.; Mem. A.M.A., Pa. State Med. Assn., Phila. County Med. Soc. Republican. Presbyn. Club: Torresdale-Frankford Country. Home: 600 W. Olney Av., Philadelphia, Pa.

KAY, J(ames) LeRoy, paleontologist; b. Mona, Utah, Mar. 25, 1892; s. John J. and Mary (Bascom) K.; ed. dist. sch. and Uinta Stake Acad., Vernal, Utah; m. Lola York, Dec. 21, 1915; children—Edytha, Oma, Orpha, Kathryn. Field asst. to Earl Douglass, 1915-22; acting curator vertebrate paleontology, Carnegie Museum, since 1922. Home: 836 Farragut St., Pittsburgh, Pa.

KAY, Robert Gillespie, wholesale lumber; b. Phila., Pa., Mar. 3, 1863; s. Alexander and Catherine (Graham) K.; student Beck Sch., Phila.; m. Mary Cope Scott, June 1896; children—Dorothy (Mrs. Benjamin H. Shoemaker, III), David Alexander. Began as clerk Stevenson & Sons lumber office, 1880; partner Kay Lumber Co., wholesale lumber, Phila. Became comptroller for Chester County, Pa., 1918. Former pres. Lumbermen's Exchange of Phila., Phila. Wholesale Lumber Dealers' Assn.; former trustee Nat. Wholesale Lumber Dealers' Assn. Republican. Clubs: Union League, St. Andrews' Soc. (Phila.); West Chester Country. Home: 522 N. Church St. Office: 133 S. 12th St., Philadelphia, Pa.

KAY, Robert H. C., mem. law firm Kay, Casto & Amos. Address: Charleston, W.Va.

KAYS, Henry T., vice-chancellor of N.J., banker; b. Newton, N.J., Sept. 29, 1878; s. Thomas M. and Marielle Ryerson (Anderson) K.; student Newton (N.J.) Pub. Sch., 1885-96, English and Classical Sch., Newton, N.J., 1896-99; A.B., Princeton U., 1903; m. Katherine Van Blarcom, Aug. 1918. Began as lawyer, 1910; mem. bd. freeholders, Sussex Co., N.J., 1910-11, co. counsel, 1911-12, 1917-35; mem. N.J. Assembly, 1913, 1914, 1915; N.J. State Senator, 1918-24; judge N.J. Ct. of Errors and Appeals, 1924-35; vice-chancellor of N.J. since 1935; pres. Sussex and Merchants Nat. Bank, Newton, N.J., since 1928. Served as food adminstr. for Sussex Co., N.J., during World War. Dir. Newton (N.J.) Library Assn. Mem. U.S. Bar Assn., N.J. Bar Assn. Democrat. Clubs: Princeton, Lawyers, University (New York); Essex (Newark, N.J.). Home: 97 Main St. Office: 95 Spring St., Newton, N.J.

KEAGY, Gula Bauder, artist and mezzo-soprano; b. Newcastle, Pa.; d. Charles Harrison and Tace Jane (Loraine) Bauder; student Artists League of Pittsburgh, Conservatory of Westminster Coll., also pvt. study under well-known music tutors; married Clinton D. Keagy. Has been engaged as artist, designing and art work for many business concerns, covers for magazines and free lance work in New York City; mezzo-soprano soloist with New Castle Civic Orchestra, 1934, also Pa. Welsh Choir, 1934, Womens' Pittsburgh Symphony, 1935; bi-weekly radio broadcasts from Pittsburgh; concerts in Western Pa. and E. Ohio; with Manhattan Light Opera Co., N.Y. City. Mem. Star, White Shrine. Presbyn. Club: Music (New Castle). Home: 4 W. Clenmoore Boul., New Castle, Pa.

KEAN, Hamilton Fish, ex-senator; b. Ursino, Union Twp., Union Co., N.J., Feb. 27, 1862; s. John and Lucy (Halsted) K.; grad. St. Paul's Sch., Concord, N.H.; m. Katharine Taylor Winthrop, January 12, 1888; children—John, Robert Winthrop. Dealer in securities and farmer; served as officer and dir. various cos. Sec. and treas. Republican Com. of Union County, N.J., 1884-1906; mem. Rep. State Com., 1905-19, Rep. Nat. Com., 1919-28; del. at large Rep. Nat. Conv., Chicago, 1916; mem. U.S. Senate, term 1929-35. Episcopalian. Clubs: Metropolitan, Knickerbocker, Union, Down Town (New York); Metropolitan (Washington, D.C.). Home: "Ursino," Union Co., N.J.

KEAN, John Scott, aeronautical engr.; b. Phila., Pa., Jan. 10, 1898; s. Thomas Joseph and Elizabeth Minnie (Robb) K.; student U. of Pa., 1916-18; unmarried. Design engr. U.S. Naval Aircraft Factory, Phila., 1918-22, project engineer, 1922-33, senior aeronautical engr., aeronautical materials labs., since 1933. Mem. Inst. of Aeronautical Sciences, Aircrafters. Mason (Radiant Star Lodge). Author articles on seaplanes in Aviation mag. Home: 1630 N. Sydenham St. Office: U.S. Naval Aircraft Factory, Philadelphia, Pa.

KEANE, Raymond Richard, realtor, builder; b. Camden, N.J., Mar. 4, 1895; s. Thomas J. and Ellen E. (Moran) K.; ed. Woodbury (N.J.) High Sch., 1908-09, Camden (N.J.) High Sch., 1909-11, Temple U., 1912-13, U. of Pa., 1913-14, Pierce Business Coll., 1915-16, Lincoln Prep. Sch., 1916-17, Neff Coll., Phila., 2 yrs.; m. Anna Krimm, June 14, 1916; 1 dau., Elaine Marie. In various capacities Hurley Dept. Store, Phila., 1915-17; mfr. of brass beds, Phila., 1919-24; real estate business, Atlantic City, N.J., 1924-29, Phila. since 1929; pres. Keane Management Co.; v.p. Nat. Realty Appraisal Co.; pres. Apartment Owners and Mgrs. Assn., Phila.; pres. Apartment Operators Co., of Pa.; pres. Apartmentor Mag. Pub. Co. Served as chief petty officer, advancing to ensign, U.S. Navy, 1917-19; with U.S. Naval Radio Unit in France 6 months. Mem. West Phila. Realty Bd. (past vice-pres.), Phila. Real Estate Bd. (chmn. golf com.; vice chmn. property management com.); pres. Neff Coll. Alumni; mem. Am. Legion. Roman Catholic. Clubs: Jefferson Golf (Jefferson, Pa.); Near Deer Hunting (Mt. Pocono, Pa.); Aronomink Golf. Former business mgr. Realty News; pub. Apartmentor, mag. for apartment business. Contbr. to newspapers.

Home: 1901 S. Darby Rd. Office: 111 S. 34th St., Philadelphia, Pa.

KEARNEY, Francis X., instr. surgery, U. of Md.; asso. in surgery Mercy Hosp. Address: 814 N. Calvert St., Baltimore, Md.

KEARNEY, George Fairchild, president newspaper; b. Philadelphia, Pa., June 4, 1895; s. George and Emilie S. F. (Corey) K.; A.B., Central High Sch., Phila., 1913; B.S., U. of Pa., 1917; unmarried. Began as newspaper reporter for Phila. Telegraph, 1911; special feature writer in Europe for Public Ledger, 1913; reporter Phila. Press, (foreign corr. 1920), Phila. Evening Bulletin, 1921-29; with Public Ledger, Phila., since 1929, suc. as promotion mgr. later asst. to editor of Evening Public Ledger, 1929-35, gen. mgr. Ledger Syndicate, 1935-39, pres. Evening Public Ledger since 1939. Served with Base Hosp. 20, U.S. Army, with A.E.F., also with Chief Surgeon Office, Service of Supply. Republican. Clubs: Writeabout, Franklin Inn, Art Alliance, Down Town (Phila.); National Press (Washington, D.C.). Home: 2041 Delancey St. Office: Public Ledger Bldg., Philadelphia, Pa.

KEARNS, William Joseph, lawyer; b. Newark, N.J., Aug. 12, 1864; s. William Joseph and Elizabeth (Cogan) K.; ed. St. Patrick's Cathedral Sch. and St. Benedict's Coll., Newark, N.J.; LL.B., Univ. of City of New York, 1886; m. Katherine L. D. Tighe, Feb. 17, 1890 (died Jan. 6, 1920); children Rev. John Chrysostom, Anthony Paul, Mary Rose (Mrs. Arthur F. X. Connolly), Agnes Annunciata (Mrs. Victor D. Smythe), Anna Gabriella Bernadette (Mrs. John M. DeCoster), Basil Leo, Cyril Soter. Law stenographer, 1883-87; admitted to N.J. bar as atty, 1887, counsellor, 1892; admitted to U.S. Supreme Court bar, 1915, practiced in Newark since 1887; master in chancery since 1888; Supreme Court Commr. since 1905; mem. N.J. Legislature, 1893; city atty., City of Newark, N.J., since 1916; counsel to sheriff of Essex Co., N.J.; diocesan counsel R.C. diocese of Newark, 1902-29; former counsel for Ruthenian Greek Catholic Diocese in U.S. Roman Catholic. K. of C. (past dist. dep.; past grand knight Newark Council). One of original contbrs. to Catholic Encyclopedia. Home: Clairvaux Manor, Bernards Twp., Basking Ridge P.O., N.J. Office: 17 Market St., Newark, N.J.

KEATH, Charles Koehler, pres. and mgr. Keath Planing Mill Co.; b. Penn Twp., Lancaster Co., Pa., Mar. 14, 1886; s. Michael and Sara Ann (Koehler) K.; student The Little Red School by the Roadside (Pleasant View), Penn Twp., Pa., 1892-1903, Pa. Business Coll., Lancaster, Pa., 1904-05; m. Lillian Mae Harnish, June 29, 1909. Began as stenographer, Apr. 1903; organized, 1912, Keath Planing Mill Co., mfrs. custom woodwork, Lititz, Pa., and since pres. and mgr.; dir. Lititz Springs Nat. Bank, Lititz Community Hotel Co. Dir. Lititz Bd. of Education. Mason (Lamberton Lodge 476, Rajah Temple A.A.O.N.M.S.). Republican. Lutheran. Club: Rotary (Lititz, Pa.; charter mem.). Home: 301 Front St., Lititz, Pa.

KEATING, Thomas J.; judge 2d Judicial Circuit of Md., term expires 1953. Address: Centerville, Md.

KEATOR, Alfred Decker, librarian; b. Accord, N.Y., June 9, 1886; s. Thomas Oliver and Sarah Jane (Decker) K.; studied State Normal Sch., New Paltz, N.Y., 1902-06; B.A., Amherst, 1910; B.L.S., State Library Sch., Albany, N.Y., 1913; m. Margaret Sievewright Dick, Feb. 5, 1915. Branch librarian Brooklyn Pub. Library, 1912; head of technology dept., Minneapolis Pub. Library, 1913-16; asso. librarian Carleton Coll., 1916-18; librarian U. of N.Dak., 1918-28; asso. prof. library science, 1921-28; librarian Reading (Pa.) Pub. Library since 1928. Asst. librarian Camp Humphreys, Va., 1918. Mem. A.L.A. (councillor 1917, 1919-21), Bibl. Soc. America, Minn. Library Assn. (pres. 1917), N.D. Library Assn. (pres. 1919-21), Pennsylvania Library Assn. (pres. 1933-34), Institute of Am. Genealogy, Berks County Hist. Soc., N.Y. Geneal. Biog. Soc., S.A.R., Holland Soc. of New York. Republican. Conglist. Mason. Club: Rotary Internat. Wrote: "Congregationalism in Grand Forks," also "American Magazines of Today." Contbr. to professional periodicals. Home: Reading, Pa.

KEBOCH, Frank Daniel, supt. city schs.; b. Berrysburg, Pa., Nov. 20, 1878; s. Isaac and Caroline (Miller) K.; M.Pd., Millersville State Normal Sch., 1907; A.B., Lebanon Valley Coll., 1915; A.M., U. of Pittsburgh, 1925; hon. A.M., Susquehanna U., 1912; m. Polly Louise Deibler, July 14, 1900; children—Mildred Miriam (Mrs. George D. Headley), Franklin Deibler (dec.). Engaged in teaching since 1895, teacher in pub. schs. then prin. schs.; supt. schs., Aspinwall, Pa., since 1917. Mem. Phi Delta Kappa. Republican. Presbyn. Mason (32°). Home: 121 Emerson Av., Aspinwall, Pittsburgh, Pa.

KEE, John, congressman; b. Glenville, W.Va., Aug. 22, 1874; s. Jasper Newton and Louisa (Campbell) K.; student Glenville State Normal Sch., 1887-90, W.Va. U., 1898-99; m. Maude Elizabeth Frazier, Sept. 7, 1926; 1 son, James. In practice of law, Glenville, 1897-1900; with South Penn Oil Co., 1900-02; counsel for Virginian Ry. Co., 1902-10; practiced at Bluefield, W.Va., 1910-16, and since 1918; spl. legal work, Mexico, 1916-18. Mem. W.Va. State Senate, 1923-27; mem. 73d to 76th Congresses (1933-41), 5th W.Va. Dist. (mem. Com. on Foreign Affairs). Mem. Phi Sigma Kappa. Democrat. Episcopalian. Odd Fellow, K.P., Elk. Home: Woodland Drive. Office: 1531 New House Office Bldg., Bluefield, W.Va.

KEEBLE, Glendinning, fine arts director; b. Pittsburgh, Pa., Feb. 24, 1887; s. Martin Edward and Anne (Glendinning) K.; student N.Y. Sch. of Art, 1903-08; pvt. studies, 1908-11; unmarried. Art and music editor Pittsburgh Gazette Times, 1912-23; assist. prof. dept. of music, Carnegie Inst. Tech., 1914-24, dir. College of Fine Arts since 1924. Mem. Am. Assn. of Univ. Profs, Art Society of Pittsburgh, Phi Kappa Phi, Phi Mu Alpha, Tau Sigma Delta. Republican. Episcopalian. Home: 120 Ruskin Av. Office: Carnegie Institute of Technology, Pittsburgh, Pa.

KEECH, Edward P., Jr.; mem. law firm Keech, Carman, Tucker & Anderson. Home: 203 Ridgewood Road. Office: Maryland Trust Bldg., Baltimore, Md.

KEECH, Finley, clergyman; b. Netcong, N.J., Sept. 23, 1894; s. George Thompson and Amy B. (Willever) K.; A.B., Bucknell U., 1922; B.D., Rochester Theol. Sem., 1925; m. Mary Elizabeth Peifer, Aug. 8, 1924; children—Finley Morris and William Thompson (twins), Herbert Randolph. Ordained to ministry Bapt. Ch., Penfield, N.Y., 1925; minister, Newark, N.J., 1925-27, Rahway, N.J., 1927-35; minister, First Bapt. Ch., Harrisburg, Pa., since 1935; mem. bd. mgrs. and mem. exec. com., Pa. Bapt. Conv. Pres. Harrisburg Ministerial Assn., 1938-39. Baptist. Mason. Clubs: Kiwanis, Keystonians (Harrisburg). Contbr. articles to religious publs. Home: 2119 N. Second St., Harrisburg, Pa.

KEEDY, Edwin Roulette, prof. law; b. Boonsboro, Md., Jan. 19, 1880; s. Reuben Miller and Anne Elizabeth (Roulette) K.; A.B., Franklin and Marshall Coll., 1899; LL.B., Harvard Univ., 1906; LL.D., Franklin and Marshall College, 1927; unmarried. Asso. prof. law, Ind. U., 1906-09; prof. law, Northwestern U., 1909-15, U. of Pa. since 1915. Spl. Commr. Am. Inst. Crim. Law and Criminology to investigate administration of criminal law in England, 1909, Scotland, 1911. Investigated administration of criminal law in France, 1931-32. Pres. Am. br. Internat. Law Assn., 1929; co-reporter (with W. E. Mikell) for criminal procedure, Am. Law Inst.; mem. Am. Bar Assn., Internat. Prison Congress, Internat. Union of Penal Law, Am. Inst. Criminal Law and Criminology (pres. 1924), Am. Law Inst., Phi Beta Kappa, Phi Kappa Psi, Phi Delta Phi. Democrat. Mem. Reformed Ch. in U.S. Commd. maj. judge advocate, March 15, 1918, lt. col., Oct. 29, 1918, col., July 10, 1919; mem. Bd. of Rev. Judge Advocate Gen's. Dept., Aug. 8, 1918-Aug. 9, 1919. Clubs: University, Franklin Inn, Phila. Country, Art Alliance, Harvard (New York); Authors' (London). Author: Cases on Agency; Cases on Administration of Criminal Law; also many legal articles. Home: University Club. Office: 3400 Chestnut St., Philadelphia, Pa.

KEEFE, David Andrew, consulting engr.; b. Athens, Pa., Jan. 28, 1869; s. Marcus and Mary (Pyne) K.; ed. pub. schs. of Athens and Athens Acad.; m. Clara Angela Wingerter, Sept. 24, 1913; children—Mary Clare, David A. Practiced, Athens, since 1896; pres. Merchants & Mechanics Nat. Bank, Sayre, Pa.; dir. Athens Nat. Bank, Chemong Telephone Co., W.,S.& A. R.R.; consulting engr. for Bradford, Luzerne and Carbon counties, Pa.; designer of reinforced concrete pier at Atlantic City, etc. Del. Rep. State Conv. 1912. Catholic. Mem. Am. Soc. C.E., Engineers' Soc. Pa., etc. Clubs: Rotary and Shepard Country. Home: Athens, Pa.*

KEEFER, Arthur Charles, lawyer; b. Sheldrake, N.Y., Aug. 22, 1898; s. Walter E. and Amy (Galbreath) K.; student Surrattsville High Sch., 1912-15, Md. State Coll., 1916-17; LL.B., George Washington U., 1922; grad. study, Catholic U. of Md., 1937-39; unmarried. Admitted to bars of Md. and Dist. of Columbia, 1921; engaged in practice of law, Md. and D.C., since 1921; mem. law firm Ray and Keefer; corpn. counsel Mt. Rainier, Prince Georges Co., Md., 1922-27 and 1929-31; dir. Prince Georges Bank & Trust Co., Hyattsville, Md.; prof. real property, Washington Coll. of Law since 1935; mem. Bd. Pub. Welfare, Prince Georges County, 1935-38. Mem. Ho. of Delegates (Md.) from Prince Georges Co., 1922-24; del. Rep. State Conv., 1923 and 1927. Mem. Ct. of Appeals Md. and D.C. and Supreme Ct. of U.S. Mem. D.C. Bar Assn., Prince George's Bar Assn., Sigma Delta Kappa. Republican. Methodist. Mason. Clubs: University (Washington, D.C.); Beaver Dam Country, Kiwanis (past pres.; lt. gov. Capital Dist. Kiwanis Clubs). Contbg. editor to Trust Companies mag. Home: 3740 31st St., Mt. Rainier, Md. Office: 900 F St. N.W., Washington, D.C.

KEEFER, Brua Cameron, Jr., pres. Brua C. Keefer Mfg. Co.; b. Williamsport, Pa., May 27, 1892; s. Brua Cameron and Charlotte (Saylor) K.; student Bellefonte Acad., 1908-10; A.B., Cornell U., 1914; m. Rebecca Foresman, Nov. 3, 1920; 1 son, Brua Cameron, III. Began as asst. mgr. Brua C. Keefer Mfg. Co., mfrs. musical instruments, 1914, now pres.; prop. Keefer Stations (tires and gasoline); pres. Brua C. Keefer Sch. of Music; dir. Williamsport Nat. Bank. Served as ensign U.S.N.R.F. during World War. Mem. Chi Phi. Republican. Presbyterian. Clubs: Williamsport Country, Big Bear Creek Fishing (vice-pres.), Ross (Williamsport). Home: 912 W. 4th St., Williamsport, Pa.

KEEFER, Clarence Edward, san. engring.; b. Baltimore, Md., July 10, 1891; s. David B. and Ella (Bosman) K.; B.E., Johns Hopkins U., 1919; m. Margaret J. Tyson, Oct. 22, 1938. Employed as engr. with Md. State Rds. Commn., the Roland Park Co., Baltimore, Baltimore Sewage Commn., B.& O. R.R. Co., 1909-15; in employ Bur. of Sewers of Baltimore since 1919, in charge of design, constrn. and operation of all pumping stas. and sewage treatment plants in Baltimore City. Mem. Am. Soc. Civil Engrs., Am. Pub. Health Assn., Am. Pub. Works Assn., Md.-Del. Water and Sewage Assn., Inst. of Sewage Purification (Eng.), Die Deutsche Gesellschaft fur Bauwasen (Germany). Democrat. Methodist. Club: University (Baltimore). Home: 1918 Mount Royal Terrace. Office: Municipal Office Bldg., Baltimore, Md.

KEELER, Harold R., physician; b. Harleysville, Pa., Feb. 27, 1894; s. Vincent Z. and Alice G. (Raudenbush) K.; Ph.B., Lafayette Coll., Easton, Pa., 1917; M.D., U. of Pa., 1921; m. Evelyn Grant, June 24, 1925; children—Grant, Harold R. Asst. visiting physician Methodist Episcopal Hosp., Phila., 1926-33, chief in medicine since 1933; certified by Am. Bd. Internal Medicine. Fellow Coll. of Physicians of Phila.; Fellow Am. Coll. Physicians; mem. A.M.A. Republican. Methodist. Author articles on endocarditis, leukemia, etc., in med. jours. Home: 735 Ormond Av., Drexel Hill. Office: 1824 Spruce St., Philadelphia, Pa.

KEEN, Edward Oscar, minister; b. Reading, Pa., Dec. 26, 1871; s. Reuben and Rebecca

(Davis) K.; grad. Reading High Sch., 1889; A.B., Gettysburg Coll., 1892, hon. A.M., 1895; student Theol. Sem. of Reformed Ch. in U.S., Lancaster, Pa., 1893-1896; D.D., Franklin and Marshall Coll., 1927; m. Augusta Koller, Nov. 25, 1897; children—Margaret Evelyn, Edward Koller. Ordained to ministry Reformed Ch., Aug. 2, 1896; pastor St. Paul's and Harbaugh congregations, Waynesboro, Pa.; 1896-1913; pastor Memorial Reformed Ch., York, Pa., since Jan. 1, 1914. Mem. bd. trustees York County Acad., York, Pa. Mem. York Co. Ministerial Assn., York County Hist. Soc., Phi Delta Theta, Phi Beta Kappa. Mason (K.T., 32°), Odd Fellow. Club: Cleric (sec.). Home: 625 S. Duke St., York, Pa.

KEEN, John Harold, newspaperman; b. Reading, Pa., Aug. 10, 1897; s. Owen Horace and Mary Ellen (Haws) K.; student Reading (Pa.) High Sch., 1912 to 1916; m. Myra Theresa Sassano, Jan. 11, 1930. Newspaper reporter, sports editor, later legislative corr., 1916-19; Harrisburg (Pa.) bur. mgr., later Ohio State bus. mgr., Internat. News Service, 1919-20; night city editor Washington (D.C.) Herald, 1920-25; city editor Phila. Daily News, 1925-30, columnist, drama critic and mng. editor since 1930. Senate award and merit trophy from Northeast High Sch., Phila., 1934. Republican. Lutheran. Clubs: Variety (Phila.); Nat. Press (Washington, D.C.). Home: 4414 Walnut St. Office: Philadelphia Daily News, Philadelphia, Pa.

KEENAN, J. Hilary, judge; b. Greensburg, Pa., Jan. 23, 1885; s. Edward W. and Anna (Eason) K.; student St. Mary's Sem., Greensburg, Pa., 1894-98; A.M., St. Vincent's Coll., Latrobe, Pa., 1902; LL.B., Dickinson Sch. of Law, Carlisle, Pa., 1907; m. Anne Bates, April 27, 1921. Admitted to Pa. bar, 1908, and began practice in Greensburg; chief clerk Selective Service Headquarters for State of Pa., Harrisburg, 1918-19; with claim depts. of several surety companies, New York and Newark, 1920-25; private practice of law, Greensburg, Pa., 1925-33; U.S. marshal, Western Dist. of Pa., 1933-35; mgr. State Workman's Ins. Fund, Harrisburg, 1935-36; apptd. judge Court of Common Pleas, 10th Judicial Dist. of Pa., Westmoreland Co., to fill unexpired term, Feb. 1936, elected for 10-year term, Nov. 1937. Chmn. Westmoreland County Dem. Com., 1930-36. Mem. Acad. Polit. Science, Westmoreland County Hist. Soc., Delta Chi. Roman Catholic. Club: Central Democratic (Harrisburg). Home: 419 W. Main St. Office: Court House, Greensburg, Pa.

KEENAN, James F., pres. Haugh & Keenan Storage & Transfer Co.; b. Pittsburgh, Pa., March 4, 1861; s. Owen and Catharine (Gaytons) K.; ed. pub. schs. of Pittsburgh, Pa.; m. Phebe Eyrich, April 17, 1888; children—Virginia K. (Mrs. Nicoladse), Ruth K. (Mrs. Rockwell). Pres. Haugh & Keenan Storage & Transfer Co., Pittsburgh, since 1889; chmn. of bd., Commonwealth Trust Co., Pittsburgh; dir. Schenley Farms Co. Pres. bd. of trustees Pittsburgh Hosp. Mem. Pa. Furniture Warehousemen's Assn. (pres. Pittsburgh chapter since 1900), East Liberty (Pa.) Chamber of Commerce (mem. bd. govs.), Pittsburgh Real Estate Bd. Catholic. Clubs: Pittsburgh Athletic Assn. (dir.), Duquesne (Pittsburgh). Home: Schenley Apts. Office: Centre and Euclid Avs., Pittsburgh, Pa.

KEENAN, Joseph Berry, lawyer; b. Pawtucket, R.I., Jan. 11, 1888; s. Bernard A. and Sarah (Berry) K.; A.B., Brown, 1910, M.A., 1910, LL.B., Harvard Law Sch., 1913; m. Charlotte Quigley, July 7, 1920; children—William Quigley, Joseph Berry, Betty Jean, John David. Admitted to Ohio bar, 1913, and since in practice at Cleveland; mem. firm Day, Day & Wilkin, 1919; apptd. spl. asst. to atty. gen. of Ohio to investigate crime, 1919; formed firm Keenan & Butler, 1930; apptd. spl. asst. to atty. gen. of U.S., to investigate crime, July 1933, asst. atty. gen. of U.S., in charge of criminal division of Dept. of Justice, Oct. 1933, asst. to the Attorney General since Jan 1936. Served with cav. Mexican border, 1916; with 137th field arty., A.E.F., 1917; commd. 1st lt. judge adv. gen.'s dept. Cited by Gen. Pershing "for meritorious service"; cited by French govt. "for distinguished service." Mem. Am. Ohio State, Cuyahoga Co. and Cleveland bar assns. Democrat. Catholic. Home: 10 Hesketh St., Chevy Chase, Md. Office: 520 Woodward Bldg., Washington, D.C.

KEENAN, Peter, artist, writer; m. Belfast, Ireland, Aug. 20, 1896; s. Peter and Ann (Irwin) K.; ed. Christian Brothers Sch., Belfast, Ireland, 1904-09, Ulster Provincial Sch., Lisburne, Ireland, 1909-11, Univ. of London, 1918; art edn. Slade Sch. of Art, London, 1919-21; m. Marie Sloop, Jan. 2, 1922; children—Seamus, Terrence, Art, Brian, Shiela. Ran away from home at age 15 and became cabin boy on ship, later clerk at Los Palmos, Canary Islands; went to Australia, 1912, and worked on Sydney Bulletin; joined Royal Irish Rifles, British Army, as private, 1914, advancing through grades to capt., commd. on field; twice wounded and decorated with Mil. Cross for bravery; retired, 1920; worked on London newspapers and mags. after war; came to U.S., 1921; worked on Evening Bulletin, Phila., 1921-38; United Business Pubs., 1923-32; Internat. Syndicate, 1926-30; Christy Walsh Syndicate, 1925-26; editor and pub. New Hope Mag. of Art, since 1934; pres. Tri-Dimensional Co., N.Y.; pres. Bucks Co. Sch. of Art. Has exhibited painting in Royal Hibernian Acad., New English Belfort Art Gallery, Midtown Gallery (New York), New Hope, Boyce Gallery (Phila.), etc. Published and illustrated: Zero to Eighty, by Dr. E. F. Northrup, 1938; Irish Folk Tales, 1938. Catholic. Address: Edison, Bucks Co., Pa.

KEENER, Martin M., pres. of Keener Mfg. Co.; b. Strasburg, Pa., Oct. 1, 1892; s. John Bally and Elizabeth (Martin) K.; student Teachers Coll., Millersville, Pa., 1911, Emerson Inst. of Efficiency, New York, 1915; m. Iva M. Gontner, Dec. 1, 1921; children—Jean Elizabeth, Patricia Ann. Teacher, Lancaster County schools, 1910-11; chief clerk First Nat. Bank of Strasburg, Pa., 1912-17; gen. mgr. Keener Mfg. Co., tag makers, Lancaster, Pa., since 1918, sec., 1918-23, treas. since 1918, pres. since 1923, dir. since 1918. Mem. Mfrs. Assn. of Lancaster, Young Republicans. Mem. Reformed Ch. Club: Rotary (Lancaster, Pa.). Author address before State Legislature on Speaker's birthday. Home: Lampeter, Lancaster Co., Pa. Office: 407-11 Lancaster Av., Lancaster, Pa.

KEEVIL, Charles Samuel, prof. chem. engring.; b. Woodside, L.I., Oct. 3, 1899; s. Charles James and Paulina M. (Harrer) K.; B.S., Mass. Inst. Tech., 1923, M.S., same, 1927, D.Sc., same, 1930; m. Charlotte W. Thropp, May 28, 1924 (dec.); 1 son, Charles Samuel, Jr.; m. 2d, Etta Pence, Sept. 12, 1938. Employed as chem. engr., Magnetic Pigment Co., Trenton, N.J., 1923-26; instr. chem. engring., Mass. Inst. Tech., 1927-30; prof. and head dept. chem. engring., Ore. State Coll., 1930-36; prof. and head dept. chem. engring., Bucknell U. since 1936. Mem. Am. Inst. Chem. Engrs., Sigma Xi, Theta Delta Chi, Phi Lambda Upsilon. Republican. Baptist. Home: 135 Brown St., Lewisburg, Pa.

KEFFER, Frances Alice, artist; b. Des Moines, Ia., Jan. 6, 1881; d. William Byron and Ellen (Skinner) K.; grad. Pratt Inst., Brooklyn, N.Y., 1903; student Alexander Robinson Traveling Art Sch., abroad, 1908-09. Engaged in teaching art, 1903-18, professional artist since 1918, specializing in flowers and landscapes; exhibited Nat. Acad. Design, Allied Artists of America, Chicago Art Inst. and many other cities; permanently represented in pub. schs., Des Moines, Ia., and Bloomington, Ill. Mem. Nat. Assn. Women Painters and Sculptors, Orange Art Center, Ridgewood Art Center. Republican. Mem. Christian Ch. Club: Sun Dial Garden (Hillsdale, N.J.) Home: 10 Orchard St., Hillsdale, N.J.

KEGEL, Will Christian, pres. and mgr. Ellwood City Ledger; b. Muscatine, Ia., Aug. 31, 1853; b. Muscatine, Ia., Aug. 31, 1853; s. George Frederick and Dora (Reuling) K.; ed. high school and business coll.; m. Marie Griswold, June 4, 1890 (died Mar. 31, 1933); children—Marguerite Griswold, William Francis. Began as bookkeeper Muscatine (Ia.) Daily Journal, 1875, later compositor; with F. W. Mahin purchased Clinton (Ia.) Daily Herald, 1882; bus. mgr. Des Moines (Ia.) Daily Capital, 1885; mgr. Hutchinson (Kan.) Daily News, 1891; advertising mgr. and asst. bus. mgr. Dubuque (Ia.) Telegraph, 1893; Iowa rep. Barnhart Bros., type founders, 1893; purchased Defiance (O.) Daily Express, 1903; Painesville (O.) Daily Telegraph, 1917; purchased Montclair (N.J.) Herald, 1922; purchased Ellwood City (Pa.) Ledger, 1924, now pres. and mgr. Dir. Ellwood Red Cross; Sponsor All-American Derby. Home: 49 Pittsburgh Circle. Office: 835 Lawrence Av., Ellwood City, Pa.

KEHOE, Arthur Henry, pub. utility exec.; b. Bennington, Vt., Feb. 18, 1889; s. Charles S. and Etta M. (Wilkins) K.; B.S. in E.E., U. of Vt., 1911; m. Eliza Hart, July 17, 1915; children—Edward Charles, Hester, Arthur Henry, Jr., Charles W. Began as engring. asst. United Electric Light & Power Co., 1911, distribution engr., 1914-19, supt. transmission and distribution, 1919-21, elec. engr., 1921-32; vice-pres. United & N.Y. Edison Co., 1932-35, dir., 1935; vice-pres. and dir. N.Y. Edison Co., Inc., 1935; engr. constrn., Consolidated Edison Co. of N.Y., Inc., 1936-38, vice-pres. since 1936; dir. N.Y. & Queens Electric Light & Power Co. since 1935; registered professional engr. State of N.Y. Fellow Am. Inst. E.E., Edison Electric Inst. (v.p.), Nat. Fire Protection Assn. (dir.), N.Y. Elec. Soc. (jr. past pres.), Phi Delta Theta, Phi Beta Kappa. Clubs: Yountakah County (Nutley, N.J.); Engineers, New York Fraternity (New York). Home: 67 W. Pierrepont Av., Rutherford, N.J. Office: 4 Irving Pl., New York, N.Y.

KEIM, George de Benneville, retired banker; b. Philadelphia, Pa., Oct. 27, 1884; s. George de Benneville and Elizabeth Archer (Thomas) K.; ed. Farnum Sch., Beverly, N.J., and Peirce Sch. of Bus. Administration, Phila.; m. Crystine Fleeta Bowers, 1919. In leather business, Phila., later in banking business until retired, 1930; dir. several banks and corpns., Port of New York Authority since 1930. Mem. Liberty Loan Com., Phila., World War. Del. N.J. to Rep. Nat. Conv., 1928, 32, 36; mem. N.J. State Finance Com., Hoover campaign, 1928; sec. Republican Nat. Com., 1930-36; chmn. N.J. State Rep. Finance Com., 1930; mem. N.J. Rep. State Com. for Burlington Co., N.J. Appointed chmn. Commission on Historic Sites in State of N.J., 1929; chmn. N.J. U.S. Constitution Commn.; chmn. N.J. World's Fair Commn. 1938. Trustee St. Mary's Hall, Burlington, N.J., Temple U., Phila.; mem. bd. mgrs. Burlington County Hosp. Trustee Yorktown (Va.) Sesquicentennial Assn.; chmn. N.J. Washington Bicentennial Com. Mem. Gen. Soc. Colonial Wars (gov. gen. 1930-36; ex-gov. N.J. Soc.), Soc. Colonial Wars in Commonwealth of Pa., Soc. of the Cincinnati, Order of Merit, Baronial Order of Runnemede, Pa. Soc. S.A.R., Soc. S.R. State of N.J., Colonial Soc. Pa., Huguenot Soc. America, Huguenot Soc. N.J., Huguenot Soc. S.C., Universalist Hist. Soc. (sec.), Transatlantic Soc., Nat. Security League, Soc. War of 1812, Navy League, Pan Am. Soc. U.S., N.J. Historical Society, Welcome Society. Episcopalian. Clubs: Metropolitan, Bankers, Recess, Downtown Athletic, Rockwood Hall, Circumnavigators, Union League, Racquet (New York); Corinthian Yacht, Rose Tree Fox Hunting, Philadelphia Country (Philadelphia); Seaview Golf (Absecon, N.J.); Riverton (N.J.) Country; Everglades, Bath and Tennis (Palm Beach, Fla.); Metropolitan (Washington); Maryland (Baltimore); Westmoreland (Richmond, Va.); Pendennis (Louisville, Ky.); Detroit Athletic. Home: Edgewater Park, Burlington Co., N.J.

KEIPER, Charles Andrew, newspaperman; b. Northampton Co., Pa., July 26, 1881; s. Elijah Henry and Ellen Rebecca (Keller) K.; ed. pub. schs. Nazareth and Easton and high sch., Easton, Pa., 1888-95; m. Stella Rebecca Laros, Oct. 20, 1909; children—Mary Elizabeth (Mrs. Harold E. Hosier), Charles Andrew, Jr. Engaged as printer, writer, instr. in pub. schs., reporter, editor and lecturer; church sch. supt. and lay ch. official since 1910; writer of verse, also on nature and industrial subjects; critic in English literature and essayist. Served as pub. speaker in

World War. Campaign speaker for Dem. Party. Dir. Stroudsburg Y.M.C.A. Democrat. Evang. Lutheran. I.O.O.F. Patriotic Order Sons of America. Home: 321 N. 5th St., Stroudsburg, Pa. Office: The Sun Printery, East Stroudsburg, Pa.

KEIRNS, May Elizabeth, prof. Latin and Greek; b. Ottumwa, Ia., Oct. 9, 1883; d. William and Adaline (Jenkins) K.; A.B., Parsons Coll., Fairfield, Ia., 1906; A.M., Stanford U., Calif., 1915; Ph.D., U. of Chicago, 1930. Engaged in teaching high schs., Ia., 1906-14, high sch. Fort Smith, Ark., 1915-21; prof. of Latin, Tex. Presbyn. Coll. for Women, 1921-23, Tarkio Coll., Mo., 1923-27; prof. of classics, Juniata Coll., Huntingdon, Pa., since 1929. Mem. Am. Philol. Assn., Classical League, Classical Assn. of Middle West & South, Am. Assn. Univ. Women. Republican. Presbyn. Home: 301 18th St., Huntingdon, Pa.

KEISER, Clarence Elwood, clergyman, archaeologist; b. Lyons, Pa., Oct. 12, 1884; s. William Henry and Fianna (Carl) K.; B.E., Kutztown State Teachers Coll., 1900, B.S., same, 1902; A.B., Muhlenberg Coll., 1905; student Mt. Airy Luth. Theol. Sem., 1905-08; A.M., U. of Pa., 1910; Ph.D., Yale, 1911; grad. student U. of Leipzig, Germany, summer 1911; m. Eva Mae Heilman, June 24, 1914; children—William Edwin, Russell Elwood. Ordained to ministry Luth. Ch., 1908; pastor, Millersville, Pa., 1908-09; asst. curator Yale Babylonian Collection, New Haven, Conn., 1912-14; instr. English Bible, Smith Coll., Northampton, Mass., 1914-15; work on pvt. Babylonian Collection of James B. Niles, Brooklyn, N.Y., 1915-21; continued research in Babylonian antiquities since 1921; supplied pulpits since 1909. Mem. United Luth. Synod of New York. Mem. Am. Oriental Soc. Awarded a Certificate of Merit in Genealogy by Inst. Am. Genealogy, 1939. Democrat. Lutheran. Author: Cuneiform Bullae of the Third Millenium B.C., 1914; Letters and Contracts from Erech., 1917; Selected Temple Documents of the Ur Dynasty, 1919; Patesis of the Ur Dynasty, 1919; A System of Accentuation for Sumero-Akkadian Signs, 1919; Historical, Religious and Economic Texts and Antiquities (with Dr. Nies), 1920. Contbr. "Historical Relationships of the Old Testament" to Luthern Commentary on the Old Testament. Home: Lyon Station, Pa.

KEISTER, Clinton Lee, banker; b. The Dalles, Ore., July 15, 1897; s. Edwin and Cora Gertrude (Starrett) K.; student U. of Pa., 1914-17, U. of London, Eng., 1919; m. Marie E. Ryan, June 29, 1918; children—Mary Lee, Jean, Ann, Frances. With Commonwealth Trust Co., Harrisburg, 1919-22; with Dauphin Deposit Trust Co., Harrisburg, Pa., since 1922, asst. trust officer and asst. sec., 1925-27, trust officer and sec., 1927-29, v.p. and trust officer since 1929; dir. Harrisburg Steel Corp. Served with U.S. Army, 1917-19; with A.E.F. Mem. Harrisburg Chamber of Commerce (treas. and dir. since 1937). Republican. Roman Catholic. Club: Harrisburg (Pa.) Country (sec.-treas. since 1920). Home: 3315 N. 2d St. Office: 213 Market St., Harrisburg, Pa.

KEISTER, H. S., mem. surg. staff Cook Hosp. Address 322½ Main St., Fairmont, W.Va.

KEISTER, John Ridinger, lawyer; b. Irwin, Pa., June 5, 1887; s. Joseph M. and Bella (Ridinger) K.; A.B., Allegheny Coll., Meadville, Pa., 1909; LL.B., Harvard Law Sch., 1912; m. Marie Delin, Nov. 21, 1918; 1 son, Stephen Ridinger. Admitted to Westmoreland Co. bar, 1912; dist. atty. Westmoreland Co. (Pa.), 1926-29; Socialist candidate Congress, 28th Pa. Dist., 1934. Mem. Phi Beta Kappa, Phi Kappa Psi. Democrat. Methodist. Advocate production for use not profit, collective ownership basic industries and utilities. Home: R.D. 5. Office: Woolworth Bldg., Greensburg, Pa.

KEITH, John DeKalb, pres. Emmitsburg R.R. Co.; b. Waynesboro, Pa., June 11, 1879; s. William Henry and Helen Anna (Hines) K.; student Stevens Hall Pa. Coll., and U. of Mich.; m. Mary Stair Swope, Oct. 26, 1912; children—Nancy McCurdy, Keith-Johnson, John Burgoyne, Helen Swope. Receiver East Berlin R.R. Co., 1903-05; pres. Emmitsburg R.R. Co. since 1912; pres. Reaser Furniture Co. since 1932; also dir. various companies. Home: 218 Carlisle St. Office: First Nat. Bank Bldg., Gettysburg, Pa.

KELCEY, Guy; b. at Dunchurch, Ontario, Can., June 1, 1889; s. George Henry and Mary (Tully) K.; brought to U.S., 1899; B.S., Carnegie Inst. Tech., 1914; m. Grace Elizabeth Saxe, Oct. 2, 1918; children—Theodosia Saxe, Virginia Saxe. In employ city engr's. office, Lackawanna, N.Y., 1907-08; with Peoples Savings & Trust Co. and E. W. Clark & Co., Pittsburgh, Pa., 1914-17; with Rush Machinery Co., Pittsburgh, Pa., 1919-20; mgr. traffic engring. div. Am. Gas Accumulator Co., Elizabeth, N.J., 1920-31, sales mgr. its subsidiary, Signal Service Corpn., mfrs. traffic devices, since 1931. Served as bombing and engr. pilot, A.S., U.S.A., 1917-19. Tech. dir. Eno Foundation for Traffic Control. Mem. Am. Soc. Civil Engrs., Inst. Traffic Engrs. (former dir.), Quiet Birdmen, Delta Upsilon. Episcopalian. Club: Lotos (New York). Has participated in evolution and development of betterment traffic conditions on sts. and rds. Contbr. many articles and papers. Lecturer before wide variety of groups on traffic problems and improvement. Mem. various assns. and socs. concerned with traffic safety and highways. Home: 739 Highland Av., Westfield, N.J.

KELLAM, Frederic Jefferson, surgeon; b. Princess Anne, Va., July 21, 1891; s. A. E. and Clara O. (Eaton) K.; ed. Randolph Macon Acad., 1907-09, Randolph Macon Coll., 1909-11; M.D., Med. Coll. of Va., Richmond, 1915; m. Dorothy Ann Minter, Dec. 15, 1915; children—Frederic J., Jr., Margaret Ann. Interne Sarah Leigh Hosp., 1915-16; engaged in gen. practice at Indiana, Pa. since 1921, specializing in surgery since 1927; mem. staff Indiana Hosp. Fellow Am. Coll. Surgs. Mem. Am., Pa. State, and Va. State med. assns. Republican. Presbyn. Mason. Clubs: Hunt, Country (Indiana); Rolling Rock Hunt (Ligonier); Pennsylvania Society. Home: R.F.D. No. 7 Indiana, Pa. Office: Indiana Theatre Bldg., Indiana, Pa.

KELLENBERGER, Keith E., advertising exec.; b. Yates Center, Kan., Dec. 5, 1883; s. Marcus Elwood and Lula (Warwick) K.; student Ottawa (Kan.) U., 1902-04; B.S. in E.E., Purdue U., Lafayette, Ind., 1907; m. Opal Ferne Sharp, July 10, 1907; children—Prenton, Miriam, Evelyn. Signal apprentice Pa. R.R., Logansport, Ind., and Canton, O., 1907-10; signal inspector Chicago Passenger Terminal, C.&N.W.Ry., 1910, div. signal foreman, 1910-11, constrn. signal inspector, 1911-13, signal supervisor, 1913-14; senior ry. signal engr. Bur. of Valuation, Interstate Commerce Commn., Chicago, Ill., 1914-17; editor Ry. Signal Engr. and signal editor Ry. Age, Chicago, 1917-24; eastern mgr. Nat. Safety Appliance Co., Chicago, 1924-26; v.p. and dir. Nat. Train Control Co., Chicago, 1924-26; advertising mgr. Union Switch and Signal Co., Swissvale, Pa., since 1926; v.p., treas. and dir. Hann Lithoprint Co., Williamsport, Pa., since 1932. Mem. Nat. Industrial Advertising Assn. (nat. dir.), Advertising Affiliation of America (dir.), Direct Mail Advertising Assn. (dir.), Pittsburgh Advertising Club (dir.), Pittsburgh Chamber of Commerce, Inst. of Ry. Signal Engrs., Assn. of Am. R.Rs. (signal sect.), Western Soc. of Engrs., Automobile Club of Pittsburgh (dir.). Presbyterian. Club: Chicago Engineers. Author: Maintenance of Way Cyclopedia (signal section), 1921; co-author: The Invention of the Track Circuit, 1921; articles in EMF Elec. Year Book, 1924-25. Home: 245 Maple Av., Edgewood (Pittsburgh), Pa. Office: 1789-1807 Braddock Av., Swissvale, Pa.

KELLER, Edward Luther, coll. prof.; b. Harrisburg, Pa., Mar. 8, 1904; s. Harry Levi and Ida (Windsor) K.; grad. Harrisburg Tech. High Sch., 1921; B.S., Pa. State Coll., 1925; m. Dessa Belle Buoymaster, Nov. 6, 1926; 1 son, Edward Windsor. Began as salesman John J. Nesbitt Co., 1925; instr. engring. extension, Pa. State Coll., 1926-30, asst. prof., 1930-34, asso. prof., 1934, acting head of dept., 1934, dir. of dept., 1935, prof. engring. extension, since 1937. Mem. Pa. Vocational Assn., Am. Vocational Assn., Pa. State Assn. for Adult Edn., Pittsburgh Personal Assn., Alpha Tau Omega (mem. nat. vocational advisory bd.), Gamma Omega Alumni Assn. of Alpha Tau Omega (pres.). Republican. Presbyn. Club: Centre Hills Country (State College). Home: 610 N. Burrowes St., State College, Pa.

KELLER, Frederick Eugene, physician; b. Brook Co., W.Va., Nov. 2, 1892; s. John Milton and Nora (Fuller) K.; Ph.C., Phila. Coll. Pharmacy, 1913; M.D., Jefferson Med. Coll., 1917; m. Ruth Lock, Jan. 29, 1917; 1 son, John Milton. After internship engaged in gen. practice of medicine and surgery at Phila. since 1920; asso. med. dir. Anderson Hosp. Served in Med. Corps, U.S.A., 1917-19; former capt. Med. Res. Corps. Fellow Am. Coll. surgeons; mem. Am., Pa. State, and Phila Co. med. assns., Medico-Legal Soc., Obstet. Soc. of Phila., Poetry Soc. of London, Theta Kappa Psi. Republican. Methodist. Mason (K.T., 32°, Shriner). Home: 3025 Frankford Av., Philadelphia, Pa.

KELLER, Harry Hexamer, mech. engr.; b. Phila., Pa., Apr. 11, 1898; s. Harry Frederick and Henrietta (Hexamer) K.; A.B., Central High Sch., Phila., 1916; B.S. in M.E., U. of Pa., 1920, student Law Sch., 1929-31, (hon.) M.E., 1930; m. Susannah G. Beury, July, 1923; children—Emma Louise, Harry Hexamer. Employed as constrn. engr., 1920-22; sales engr. Vilter Mfg. Co., 1922-26; treas. Sales & Engring. Co., 1922-23, pres., 1923-30; builder and prof. engr., 1924-31; asso. as engr. with Bitting Inc., New York since 1931; pres. Efficiency Homes Corpn., real estate development and bldg. since 1938; licensed professional engr. in Pa., also licensed real estate broker. Served in Inf., O.T.C., during World War. Mem. Am. Soc. Mech. Engrs., Sphinx Senior Soc., Varsity Club, Hare Law Club, Hexagon Sr. Soc., Am. Legion, Sigma Alpha Epsilon. Evang. Lutheran. Club: Seven O'Klockers. Contbr. articles on prefabricated bldg. and bldg. methods to mags. Designed and patented many parts for prefabricated structures and developed unit panel system; holder chem. and mech. patents. Home: 423 Newbold Rd., Jenkintown, Pa.; 5 S. Cambridge Av., Ventnor, N.J. Office: 45 Maplewood Av., Philadelphia, Pa.

KELLER, Henry, Jr., univ. prof.; b. Bellefonte, Pa., June 11, 1895; s. Harry and Anne Mary (Orvis) K.; B.S., Pa. State Coll., State College, Pa., 1920; M.S., U. of Wis., Madison, Wis., 1922, Ph.D., 1931; student Columbia U., 1924-25; also student Harvard U.; m. Eleanor Schofield Parker, Feb. 5, 1921; children—Henry Parker, Kenneth Parker. Engaged as asst. in agrl. econs., U. of Wis. 1920-22; asst. prof. agrl. econs., Rutgers U., New Brunswick, N.J., 1922-27, asso. prof., 1927-28, prof. agrl. econs. since 1928. Served as 1st lt. inf., U.S.A., 1917-19; with A.E.F. in France; wounded in action, Fismette, 1918; awarded medal of Purple Heart (U.S.). Mem. Am. Econ. Assn., Am. Statis. Assn., Am. Farm Econs. Assn., Econometric Soc., Phi Kappa Sigma. Democrat. Presbyn. Elk. Clubs: Plainfield Country, Rutgers (New Brunswick); Forsgate Country (Jamesburg, N.J.). Home: 419 Lincoln Av., Highland Park, New Brunswick, N.J.

KELLER, Hiram Harpel, pres. judge; b. Bedminster, Pa., Aug. 9, 1878; s. Lewis and Emma Jane (Harpel) K.; prep. edn. Sellersville High Sch., and West Chester Normal Sch.; A.B., Gettysburg (Pa.) Coll., 1901, A.M., 1904; LL.B., U. of Pa., 1904; unmarried. Admitted to Phila. Co. bar, 1904, Bucks Co. bar, 1905; county solicitor Bucks Co., 1915-18; dist. atty. Bucks Co., 1918-26; workmen's compensation referee, 1st Dist., Pa., 1927-29; additional law judge, Bucks Co., 1929-30; pres. judge Common Pleas Court, 7th Judicial Dist., Doylestown, Bucks Co., since 1930. Pres. bd. of trustees Melinda Cox Free Library, Doylestown; trustee Mercer Fonthill Museum, Gettysburg Coll. Mem. Am. Bar Assn., Pa. Bar Assn., Bucks Co. Bar

KELLER, John Calvin, coll. teacher; b. Sidney, N.Y., May 7, 1898; s. Joseph Winfield and Emma M. (Shiber) K.; grad. Johnson City (N.Y.) High Sch., 1917; B.S., Colgate U., 1921; Ph.D., Cornell U., 1926; m. Florence Kohl, Dec. 20, 1929. Asst. in chemistry, Cornell U., 1921-26; instr. in chemistry, Lehigh U., 1926-27; asst. prof. in chemistry, Muhlenberg Coll., since 1927. Mem. Am. Assn. Univ. Profs., Alpha Chi Sigma, Sigma Xi. Republican. Presbyterian. Home: 39 N. 15th St., Allentown, Pa.

KELLER, John Orvis, ednl. adminstr.; b. Bellefonte, Pa., Apr. 1, 1893; s. Harry and Anna Mary (Orvis) K.; student Bellefonte (Pa.) Acad., 1899-1906; grad. Bellefonte (Pa.) High Sch., 1909; B.S. in Industrial Engring., Pa. State Coll., 1914; M.S. in Engring., Pa. State Coll., 1919; m. Mary Lyons Gans, June 18, 1919; children—John Gans, Henry, Mary Jane, Anna Orvis. Rancher, guide, Wyo., 1912; surveyor San Pedro, Los Angeles & Salt Lake R.R., 1913; draftsman Utah Power & Light Co., Salt Lake City, Utah, 1913; safety engr. Ocean Accident & Guarantee Corpn., serving variously in New York City, Chicago, Ill., Omaha, Neb., Pittsburgh, Pa., 1914-16; instr. industrial engring., Pa. State Coll., 1916-19, asst. prof. and acting head dept., 1919, asso. prof., 1921-22, prof. and head dept., 1922-25, prof. and head dept. engring. extension, 1925-34, asst. to pres. in charge extension since 1934; asso. prof. mech. engring., Ia. State Coll., Ames, Ia., 1919-21; while teaching industrial engring. spent summers in various capacities with various industrial firms. Served as 2d lt., Ordnance Dept., U.S. Army, Camp Hancock, Ga., during World War; maj. Ordnance Res., since 1927. Mem. Soc. for the Promotion of Engring. Edn., Am. Assn. Univ. Profs., Am. Legion, Res. Officers Assn., Pa. Assn. for Adult Edn., Nat. Com. on Edn. by Radio, Nat. Univ. Extension Assn. (chmn. radio com. since 1930), Phi Kappa Sigma, Psi Chi, Tau Beta Pi. Republican. Presbyterian. Club: Centre Hills Country (State College, Pa.). Author: (pamphlet) General Business Economics, 1928; numerous articles on industrial engring., etc., in tech. mags. Home: 218 E. Prospect Av. Office: President's Office, State College, Pa.

KELLER, Joseph Steddam, manufacturer; b. Phila., Pa., July 4, 1859; s. Francis and Katherine (Laudenslager) K.; ed. private schs. in Phila.; m. Elizabeth Hunter, Feb. 3, 1885; children—Joseph Walter, Albert Samuel (deceased), Elizabeth (Mrs. James Gay Gordon, Jr.). Began as retail feed dealer, 1880; with Pratt Food Co., mfrs. table cereals, animal and poultry feeds, brewers corn goods, disinfectants, etc., since 1885, pres. since 1907; pres. and dir. Pratt Food Co. of Can. Ltd., Service Grain Co. treas. and dir. Harleigh Cemetery Co., Meadow Land & Improvement Co. Pres. Springfield Twp. Sch. Bd., 1916-22. Republican. Mem. Friends Meeting Ch. Mason (32°). Club: Union League (Phila.). Home: 249 N. Latchs Lane, Merion, Pa. Office: 130 Walnut St., Philadelphia, Pa.

KELLER, Joseph Walter, manufacturer; b. Phila., Pa., Feb. 27, 1886; s. Joseph Steddam and Elizabeth (Hunter) K.; grad. Friends Central Sch., 1904; A.B., Swarthmore Coll., 1907; grad. work U. of Pa., 1908; m. Anne Catherine Miller, Mar. 30, 1928; 1 dau., Elizabeth Anne. With Pratt Food Co., mfrs. of table cereals, animal and poultry feeds, brewers corn goods, disinfectants, etc., since 1907 v.p., sec. and dir., 1932-39, pres. since 1939; pres. and dir. Pratt Food Co. of Can. Ltd., Service Grain Co. Mem. Chicago Board of Trade. Served as 1st lt. Cav., Pa. N.G., 1908-09; 1st lt. advancing to lt. col. F.A., U.S. Army, 1917-19; col. F.A. Reserve Corps since 1925. Decorated 3 campaign medals, 2 decorations (Purple Heart and A..O..A..). Mem. Am. Legion (comdr. Merion Post, 1939-40), Sons of Revolution, Mil. Order World War, Field Artillery and Army Ordnance Assns., etc. Republican. Mem. Friends Meeting Ch. Club: Penn Athletic. Home: 225 Upland Rd., Merion, Pa. Office: 130 Walnut St., Philadelphia, Pa.

KELLER, Oliver James, newspaper editor; b. Lancaster, Pa., Feb. 9, 1898; s. William Heustis and Anna (Dickey) K.; grad. Yeates Sch., Lancaster, 1914; A.B., Williams Coll., 1918; m. Rosalind Lodge Thomas, Nov. 5, 1920; children—Daniel S., Oliver J. Reporter and copy reader Lancaster Examiner, 1919, asso. editor, 1919-20; editor Lancaster Examiner-New Era, 1920-27; gen. mgr. Pittsburgh (Pa.) Post-Gazette, 1927, editor and vice-pres. since 1928. Served as 2d lt., aerial observer, Air Service Reserve, U.S.A., Jan. 1918-Mar. 1919. Mem. Phi Gamma Delta. Republican. Mem. Reformed Ch. Clubs: Duquesne, Pittsburgh Golf, Fox Chapel. Home: 631 Pitcairn Pl. Office: Grant St. and 2d Av., Pittsburgh, Pa.

KELLER, William Huestis, judge; b. Montgomery County, Md., Aug. 11, 1869; s. Daniel S. and Martha E. (Huestis) K.; A.B., Franklin and Marshall Coll., 1891, LL.D., 1920, LL.B., George Washington U., 1893; m. Anna Dickey, Oct. 18, 1893; children—Daniel S. (killed in action in France), Elizabeth D. (Mrs. Robert E. Miller), Oliver J., Martha E. (Mrs. Edmund Rowland), Mary D. Admitted to Pa. bar, 1893, and began practice at Lancaster; mem. firm Steinmetz & Keller, 1894-99, Coyle & Keller, 1899-1919. First dep. atty. gen. of Pa., 1915-19; judge Superior Court of Pa. since 1919, reëlected in 1929, president judge since Jan. 7, 1935. Del. to Rep. Nat. Conv., 1908, 12. Trustee Franklin and Marshall Coll., Home for Friendless Children, Lancaster Gen. Hosp. Mem. Am. and Pa. State bar assns., Pa. Soc. S.R., Phi Beta Kappa, Phi Kappa Sigma. Republican. Mem. Evangelical and Reformed Ch. Mason. Clubs: Union League, Art (Phila.); Hamilton; Lancaster Country. Home: 1061 Wheatland Av. Office: 124 E. King St., Lancaster, Pa.

KELLETT, Donald S., football coach; b. Brooklyn, N.Y., July 15, 1909; s. David S. and Grace E. (Thompson) K.; ed. Peekskill Mil. Acad., 1927-28; B.S. in Econs., U. of Pa. 1934; m. Dorothea L. Tevis, Mar. 20, 1937; 1 dau., Dona L. Coach of football, Ursinus Coll., Collegeville, Pa., since 1938. Mem. Kappa Sigma. Congregationalist. Club: Penn Athletic. Home: Park Av., Collegeville, Pa.

KELLETT, William Wallace, pres. Kellett Autogiro Corpn.; b. Boston, Mass., Dec. 20, 1891; s. W.W. and Francis Revere (Flagler) K.; student Princeton U., 1913; m. Virginia Fink, March 10, 1928. Am. rep. H. & M. Farman, Paris, France, 1919-27; pres. B.B.T. Corpn. of America, Phila., 1925-30; treas. Scialytic Corpn. of America, Phila., since 1926; pres. Kellett Autogiro Corpn., Phila., Pa., since 1929; v.p. and dir. Central Airport Inc., Camden, N.J., since 1930; chmn. exec. com. Ludington Airlines, Phila., 1929; pres. Seversky Aircraft Corpn., Farmingdale, L.I., N.Y. Mem. bd. of trustees Temple U. 1938. Member State of Pa. Govs. Aviation Council, Aeronautical Chamber of Commerce of America (v.p. 1938), Aero Club of Pa. (pres. 1927). Democrat. Episcopalian. Clubs: Whitemarsh Valley Hunt, Phila. Aviation Country (Phila.). Home: The Barclay, Rittenhouse Sq. Office: Island Rd. and Laycpck Av., Philadelphia, Pa.

KELLEY, Arthur Pierson, botanist; b. Malvern, Pa., Aug. 15, 1897; s. Albanis Ashmun and Sarah Rebecca (Groff) K.; B.S. in Biology, U. of Pa., 1920, A.M., same, 1921, Ph.D., same, 1923; grad. study, Johns Hopkins U., 1929-30; unmarried. Began as instr. in botany, Rutgers U., 1922; asst. prof. botany, Rutgers U., 1926-28; asso. ecologist, U.S. Forest Service, 1928-29; dir. Landenberg Lab. since 1936. Corr. mem. Victoria Inst. (Phila. Soc. of Great Britain). Patron Evolution Protest Movement of London. Baptist. Editor of The Landenberg Review. Home: Landenberg, Pa.

KELLEY, Augustine Bernard, exec. coal and coke industry; b. New Baltimore, Pa., July 9, 1883; s. Abraham Francis and Mary Elizabeth (Kegg) K.; St. Benedict's Parochial Sch., Greensburg, Pa., 1890-1900, Greensburg (Pa.) Grade Sch., 1900-01, Greensburg High Sch., 1901-04, U.S. Military Acad., 1904-05; m. Ella Marie Bates, June 24, 1913; children—Augustine Regis, Robert Vincent, Richard Bates, Joy Hilory, Paul Aloysius, Marcella Marie, Therese Eleanor, Katherine Anne, James Reeves. Coke inspector and clerk, H.C. Frick Coke Co., Scottdale, Pa., 1907-09 at Standard Mine, Mt. Pleasant, Pa., asst. supt., Coal Brook Mine, Connellsville, Pa., 1909-10, Whitney Mines, Latrobe, Pa., 1910, supt. Dearth Mines, Uniontown, Pa., 1910-13; supt. mines, Hillman Coal & Coke Co., 1913-20; with Humphreys Coal and Coke Co., Greensburg, Pa., 1920-38, becoming treas., gen. mgr. and dir.; with Ideal Supply Co., Greensburg, Pa., 1923-38, becoming treas., gen. mgr. and dir.; assisted in organizing Atlas Fuel Co., New York and Pittsburgh, pres. and dir. 1920-23; organized, 1937, Old Basin By-Product Coal Co., with mine at Mutual, Westmoreland Co., Pa., and since pres., gen. mgr. and dir.; organized, 1924, The French Dye Works, Greensburg, Pa., wholesale cleaners and dyers, and since pres.; receiver, Lacosto Coal Co., and Fairfield Coal Co., 1924-26. Mem. Bd. of Education, Greensburg, Pa., 1935-36. Trustee Seton Hill Coll., Greensburg, Pa., 1938-39. Assisted in organizing Soc. of St. Vincent de Paul, Greensburg, Pa., 1934, and since pres. Mem. Am. Inst. Mining and Metall. Engrs., Am. Mining Congress, Coal Operators Assn. of Western Pa. (mem. scale com.), Assn. of Graduates of U.S. Mil. Acad. (life mem.), Army Athletic Assn. Democrat. Clubs: Metropolitan (Pittsburgh); Greensburg Country (chmn. tennis com., mem. membership com.). Lecturer on Regulation of Coal Industry, Labor Problems in the Industry, Collective Bargaining and Unionization before Nat. Cath. Conf. on Industrial Problems, Cincinnati, 1935, Phila., 1936, Indianapolis, 1937; lecturer before Am. Mining Congress, 1928 and 1937. Contbr. to trade, technical and Cath. jours. Home: 231 Westmoreland Av. Office: Greensburg, Pa.

KELLEY, James Francis, clergyman, coll. pres.; b. Kearney, N.J., July 27, 1902; s. James F. and Frances (Shaw) K.; A.B., Seton Hall Coll. (South Orange, N.J.), 1920, A.M., 1921; Licencie en Philosophie, U. of Louvain, Belgium, 1934, Ph.D., 1935. Ordained priesthood R.C. Ch., 1928. Prof. of edn. and French, Seton Hall Coll., 1928-32, head of dept. of philosophy, 1935-36, pres. since 1936; lecturer Immaculate Conception Sem. since 1935; prof. of philosophy, Coll. of St. Elizabeth since 1936. Mem. Am. Catholic Phlios. Assn. Address: Seton Hall College, South Orange, N.J.

KELLEY, Louise, prof. of chemistry; b. Franklin, N.H., Oct. 10, 1894; d. Elmer Daniel and Etta Emma (Ingalls) K.; student Franklin (N.H.) High Sch., 1907-12; B.A., Mount Holyoke Coll., South Hadley, Mass., 1916, M.A., 1918; Ph.D., Cornell U., 1920; unmarried. Asst. in chemistry, Mount Holyoke Coll., South Hadley, Mass., 1916-17; instr. chemistry, Wheaton Coll., Norton, Mass., 1917-18; grad. fellow, Cornell U., 1918-20; asst. prof. chemistry, Goucher Coll., Baltimore, Md., 1920-23, asso. prof., 1923-30, prof. chemistry since 1930. Mem. Am. Chem. Soc., A.A.A.S., Am. Inst. of Chemists, Am. Assn. of Univ. Women, Am. Assn. of Univ. Profs., Phi Beta Kappa, Sigma Xi. Republican. Methodist. Clubs: College, Johns Hopkins, Soroptimist (Baltimore). Asst. editor: Chem. Reviews since 1929, The Jour. of Phys. Chemistry since 1937. Home: Franklin, N.H. Address: Goucher Coll., Baltimore, Md.

KELLEY, Richard Carlyle, mfr. upholstery fabrics; b. Coldwater, Mich., Sept. 30, 1882; s. Edmund Levi and Catherine (Bishop) K.; A.B., U. of Ia., 1903; post grad. work, U. of Chicago (summer sch.), 1905-08; M.A., Teachers Coll., Columbia U., 1918; m. Anna Zimmermann, Aug. 10, 1915; children—Joan Catherine, Richard Carlyle, Susan Dorothea, Marian, Anita, Donald Edmund, Janet Nancy (dec.). Teacher and educational dir., Graceland Coll., 1903-04; prin. Lamoni (Ia.) High Sch., 1904-05, Columbian Sch., Independence, Mo., 1905-07, Ottumwa

(Ia.) Pub. Schs., 1907-08; dir. manual arts, Sioux City, Ia., 1908-11; dir. trade sch., Philippine Islands, 1911-13; dir. manual arts, U. of Ia., 1914-17; supervisor Federal Bd. for Vocational Edn., Washington, D.C., 1918-19; sec., treas. and dir. John Zimmermann & Sons, mfrs. upholstery fabrics, Phila., since 1919. Dir. pub. schs., Cheltenham Twp., Montgomery Co., Pa., since 1929. Mem. Phi Delta Kappa. Republican. Clubs: University, Cedarbrook, Country (Phila.). Home: Elkins Park. Office: Erie and Castor Avs., Philadelphia, Pa.

KELLOGG, Herbert Morris, pres. Dushare First Nat. Bank; b. New Albany, Pa., June 7, 1869; s. Morris and Minnie (Hawthorne) K.; student pub. schs., New Albany, Pa., 1875-87; m. Florence Scureman, July 14, 1891; 1 son, Herbert Morris. Treas. Colley Twp. (Pa.), 1895-96; mgr. and part owner Kellogg & Christian, retail proprietary medicines, Lopez, Pa., since 1898; owner and mgr. jewelry store, Lopez, Pa., since 1892; postmaster Lopez, Pa., 1905-15; dir. Dushare (Pa.) First Nat. Bank since 1905, pres. since 1937. Republican. Methodist. Mason (Lodge 163, life mem.). Address: Lopez, Pa.

KELLY, Evander Francis, sec. Am. Pharmaceutical Assn.; b. Carthage, N.C., July 2, 1879; s. John Evander and Penelope (Kelly) K.; grad. Union Home (N.C.) High Sch., 1896; student State Coll., Raleigh, N.C., 1896-97; Pharm.D., Sch. of Pharmacy, U. of Md., 1902; hon. Sc.D., Temple Univ., 1933; m. Marian Low, October 11, 1906; children—Evander Francis, Kenneth Low, Kathleen Dammers (Mrs. James Bruce Kilgore), Lauchlin McIver. Began as pharmacist, 1899; pharmacist Sharpe & Dohme, Baltimore, 1902-11; instr. in Pharmacy, U. of Md., 1903-06, asso. prof., 1906-17, prof., 1917-26, dean, 1918-26, advisory dean since 1926; prof. of chemistry, Dental Sch., U. of Md., 1914-21; lecturer in pharmacy, Johns Hopkins Med. Sch. since 1933; sec. Md. Pharm. Assn. since 1907; sec. Am. Pharm. Assn. since 1926. Mem. Md. State Bd. of Health since 1920; mem. bd. trustees U.S. Pharmacopœia since 1930; trustee Endowment Fund of U. of Md.; chmn. Am. Council on Pharm. Edn. Awarded Remington medal, 1923. Fellow A.A.A.S.; mem. Md. Pharm. Assn., Am. Pharm. Assn. (life), Md. Acad. Science (life), Rho Chi (hon.), Kappa Psi, Phi Delta Chi, Alpha Zeta Omega, Rho Pi Phi. Democrat. Presbyterian. Club: Torch (Washington, D.C.). Home: Texas, Md. Office: 2215 Constitution Av., Washington, D.C.

KELLY, Frances Hamerton, librarian, ednl. dir.; b. Woodville, Pa., Nov. 18, 1883; d. Robert Hamerton and Margaret (Winstein) K.; A.B., Wellesley (Mass.) Coll., 1910; certificate, N.Y. State Library Sch., Albany, 1911; unmarried. First asst. Carnegie Library of Pittsburgh, 1914-15; readers asst., Stations Div., Pittsburgh, 1915-16; branch librarian, Pittsburgh 1916-20; head dept. of work with schs., 1920-27; instr. Carnegie Library Sch., Carnegie Inst. Tech., 1920-27, asso. dir. since 1927. Mem. Am. Library Assn., Pa. Library Assn. (pres. 1936), Special Libraries Assn. (employment and salaries com.), Am. Assn. Univ. Women, Dickens Fellowship. Clubs: Monday Luncheon, College, Women's City (dir. 1937-39), Wellesley (Pittsburgh). Author: 'Professional Training of the Elementary School Librarian (Elementary School Libraries 12th Yearbook), 1933; contbr. to library jours. Home: 383 Lehigh Av. Office: 4400 Forbes St., Pittsburgh, Pa.

KELLY, Frances Marie ("Francine Markel"), journalist; b. Philadelphia; d. Edward Augustine and Rebecca Marie (McGoldrick) K.; educated at Hallahan Catholic Girls' High School; post graduate work at Price School of Journalism; Academy of the Sacred Heart and Berlitz Sch. of Languages—all Philadelphia. On writing staff Ledger Syndicate, Phila., 1931-35, Watkins Syndicate, Inc., Phila., since June 1935, producing a daily column "Good Taste" and another daily culture feature, "The Polisher," both of which she created and which are now being pub. by leading newspapers of the U.S., Can., Australia and the Philippines. Editor, Watkins Syndicate since 1937. Author of "The Knowmeter," "The Helpful Quiz," "Check Your Knowledge"; also many magazine articles. Home: 35 N. Robinson St. Office: 2214 Chestnut St., Philadelphia, Pa.

KELLY, Herbert Thomas, physician, internal medicine, metabolic diseases; b. Lee County, N.C., April 27, 1899; s. John Thomas and Fanny (Farrell) K.; student U. of N.C.; M.D., Jefferson Med. Coll., 1925; special course in diabetes, Frederick W. Allen, 1926; grad. course in advanced cardiology, Harvard Grad. Med. Sch., 1932; m. Margaret G. Campbell, June 26, 1935; 1 dau., Lois Yolande. Interne Grad. Hosp., Phila., 1925-26; asst. in urology, Grad. Sch. of U. of Pa., 1926-29, asso. in cardiology, 1929-32, asso. in medicine since 1932; asst. physician dept. of diseases of metabolism, Phila. Gen. Hosp., 1927-28, asso. in cardiac clinic, 1928-32; asso. visiting physician diabetic clinic, Presbyn. Hosp., Phila., since 1933, chief of med. clinic, 1933-35; chief of diabetic clinic Grad. Hosp. of U. of Pa., 1933-35; consultant internists Pa. R.R. since 1927, Pa.-Reading Seashore Lines since 1934. Fellow Am. Coll. Physicians, A.M.A., Phila. Coll. Physicians; mem. Phila. Co. Med. Soc., Pa. Med. Soc., Am. Med. Editors and Authors Assn., Phila. Metabolic Assn. Mason. Clubs: Junto, Art Alliance (Phila.). Home: 6709 Lincoln Drive. Office: 1900 Spruce St., Philadelphia, Pa.

KELLY, Howard Atwood, surgeon; b. Camden, N.J., Feb. 20, 1858; s. Henry Kuhl and Louisa Warner (Hard) K.; B.A., U. of Pa., 1877, M.D., 1882; LL.D., Aberdeen, 1906, Washington and Lee U., 1906, U. of Pa., 1907, Washington Coll., 1933, Johns Hopkins Univ., 1939; m. Laetitia Bredow, June 27, 1889; children—Olga Elizabeth Bredow, Henry Kuhl, Esther Warner (Mrs. Henry G. Seibels), Friederich Heyn, Howard Atwood, William Boulton, Margaret Kuhl (Mrs. Douglas Warner), Edmund Bredow, Laetitia Bredow (Mrs. Winthrop K. Coolidge). Founder of the Kensington Hospital, Philadelphia; associate prof. obstetrics, U. of Pa., 1888-89; prof. gynecology and obstretics, 1889-99, gynecology, 1899-1919, emeritus prof. since 1919, Johns Hopkins U.; gynecol. surgeon, 1899-1919, consulting gynecologist since 1919, Johns Hopkins Hosp.; surgeon and radiologist Howard A. Kelly Hosp. since 1892; Hunterian lecturer Mansion of Lord Mayor of London, 1928; hon. curator Div. of Reptiles and Amphibians, U. of Mich. Hon. fellow Royal Coll. Surgeons (Edinburgh), Edinburgh Obstet. Soc., Glasgow Obstet. and Gynecol. Soc., Royal Acad. Medicine in Ireland, Obstetrico Gynecol. Soc. of Kiev (Russia), Obstet. Soc. of London; mem. Am. Gynecol. Soc. (pres. 1912), Chicago Gynecol. Soc., Am. Urol. Assn., Roentgenol. Soc., Seaboard Med. Assn., Va. and N.C. med. socs.; fellow Southern Surg. and Gynecol. Soc., Am. Radium Soc.; Am. Coll. of Surgeons, A.A.A.S., Am. Geog. Soc., British Gynecol. Society, Maryland Academy of Sciences (life member); fellow Natural History Society of Maryland; mem. Nat. Assn. Audubon Socs., Phila. Acad. Natural Sciences, N.Y., Zoölogical Soc., N.Y., Bot. Gardens, Am. Mus. of Natural History, Am. Soc. Ichthyologists and Herpetologists, Assn. Française d'Urologie (Paris), Société Internationale d'Histoire de la Médecine, Philos. Soc. of Gt. Britain, British Mycol. Soc., Deutsche Gesellschaft für Pilzkunde; hon. mem. Societa Italiana di Ostetricia e Ginecologia (Rome), Gesellschaft für Geburtshülfe und Gynekologie zu Berlin, Société d'Obstetrique et de Gynécologie (Paris), Société Française de Gynécologie, Gesellschaft für Geburtshülfe zu Leipzig, Royal Med. Soc. of Edinburgh, Obstetrico-Gynecol. Soc. of Moscow, Peruvian Surg. Soc.; corr. mem. Société de Chirurgie de Paris, K.K. Gesellschaft der Aerzte in Wien, Roumanian Acad. Science; asso. foreign mem. Société d'Obstetrique, de Gynecologie et de Pediatrie de Paris. Comdr. Order of Leopold (Belgium), 1920; Order of Cross of Mercy (Serbia), 1922; Cross of Charity of the Kingdom of the Serbs, Croats and Slovenes, 1926. Author: Operative Gynecology (2 vols.), 1898, 1906; The Vermiform Appendix and its Diseases (with Elizabeth Hurdon), 1905; Walter Reed and Yellow Fever, 1906, 07, 23; Gynecology and Abdominal Surgery (edited with C. P. Noble), Vol. I, 1907, Vol. II, 1908; The Stereo Clynic, 84 sections, 1908—; Medical Gynecology, 1908, 1912; Appendicitis and Other Diseases of the Vermiform Appendix, 1909; Myomata of the Uterus (with T. S. Cullen), 1909; Cyclopedia of American Medical Biography (2 vols.), 1912; Some Am. Med. Botanists, 1913; Diseases of the Kidneys, Ureters, and Bladder (with C. F. Burnam—2 vols.), 1914, 1922; American Medical Biographies (with W. L. Burrage), 1920; A Scientific Man and the Bible, 1925; Gynecology, 1928; Dictionary of American Medical Biography (with W. L. Burrage), 1928; Electrosurgery (with Grant E. Ward), 1932; also some 500 scientific articles. Home: 1406 Eutaw Pl. Sanatorium: 1412-20 Eutaw Pl., Baltimore, Md.

KELLY, J. Howard, retired banker; b. Pleasant Unity, Pa., May 11, 1870; s. Dr. James H. and Nancy (Gamble) K.; student Greensburg (Pa.) Sem., 1891-93, Washington and Jefferson Coll., 1893-94; m. Gertrude Pearsall, May 20, 1902; children—Eleanore (Mrs. Raymond G. Sellars), George Robert. Began as teacher, 1888; was prin. Jeannette (Pa.) High Sch.; bookkeeper Old Meadow Rolling Mill Co., Scottdale, 1897, Nat. Tin Plate Co., Monessen, Pa., 1898-1900; pres. First Nat. Bank & Trust Co., Monessen, 1906-31; vice-pres. and treas. Monessen Foundry and Machine Co. since 1902; dir. Monessen Thrift and Loan Co. Address: 126 6th St., Monessen, Pa.

KELLY, John Alexander, prof. of German; b. Chilhowie, Va., Sept. 2, 1889; s. Francis Alexander and Elizabeth Strother (Patton) K.; A.B., Emory and Henry Coll., 1911; A.M., Columbia U., 1916; grad. study, U. of Va., 1916-17; Ph.D., Columbia U., 1920; grad. study, U. of Berlin, 1926-27. Instr. langs., Emory & Henry Coll., 1911-12; actg. adjunct prof., Hendrix Coll., Ark., 1912-13; instr., McCallie Sch., Chattanooga, Tenn., 1913-15; instr. U. of Va., 1916-17 and summers 1917, 1920; instr. Haverford Coll., 1920-21, asst. prof. German, 1921-27, asso. prof. 1927-37, prof. since 1937; was grad. in piano and harmony, Va. Intermont Coll., 1907. Served in U.S.N.R.F. active duty, 1918. Mem. Modern Lang. Assn. of America, Goethe Soc. of America, Va., Pa. and East Tenn. hist. socs., S.A.R., Soc. of War of 1812, Phi Beta Kappa, Sigma Alpha Epsilon. Democrat. Episcopalian. Author: England and the Englishman in German Literature of the Eighteenth Century, 1921; German Visitors to English Theaters in the Eighteenth Century, 1936. Editor: Thomas Mann's Tonio Kroeger, 1931. Contbr. many articles and reviews. Home: Haverford Coll., Haverford, Pa.

KELLY, Lewis Hoke, coal operator; b. Latrobe, Pa., May 4, 1890; s. Joseph McQuaide and Emily (Hoke) K.; student Mercersburg (Pa.) Acad., 1906-09; Ph.B., Lafayette Coll., 1913; m. Jess Morgan, Aug. 1, 1935. Began as engineer, 1913; salesman Nat. Fuel Co., 1916-17; salesmgr. Internat. Fuel & Iron Corpn., 1920, v.p., 1921-24; v.p. in charge sales Pittsburgh Terminal Coal Corpn., 1925-27, also dir.; v.p. and dir. Continental Coal Co., 1928-35; pres., treas. and dir., Pittsburgh & Fairmont Coal Co. since 1935. Served as 1st lt. Ordnance Dept., U.S.A., 1917-18; capt. Q.M.C., A.E.F., 1918-19. Dir. Am. Coal Distributors' Assn. Mem. Phi Kappa Psi. Republican Presbyterian. Clubs: Duquesne, Pittsburgh Traffic, Pittsburgh Athletic Assn. (Pittsburgh); N. Y. Railroad (New York); Oakmont Country (Oakmont, Pa.). Home: 601 St. James St. Office: 906 First National Bank Bldg., Pittsburgh, Pa.

KELLY, Lon Hamman, lawyer; b. Sutton, W.Va., Jan. 28, 1871; s. John McH. and Alzira Virginia (Hamman) K.; LL.B., Washington and Lee U., 1893; m. Bertha Gorrell, of Sutton, Mar. 3, 1897 (died 1904); children—Robert G., Mrs. Janet Savage; m. 2d, Nellie Kiddy, June 19, 1907; 1 dau., Virginian Elizabeth. Admitted to W.Va. bar, 1893; mem. Brown, Jackson & Knight. Mayor of Sutton, 1896; pros. atty. Braxton Co., W.Va., 1897-1900; asst. U.S. atty. Southern Dist. of W.Va., 1916-17, and U.S. atty., Oct. 1917-22; nominated by Dem. Party for Judge Supreme Ct. of Appeals of W.Va., 1924. Pres. W.Va., State Bar

Assn., 1933-34; gov. Rotary Internat., 24th Dist., 1935-36. Presbyn. Mason, K.P. Home: Charleston, W.Va.

KELLY, Mervin J(oe), dir. research; b Princeton, Mo., Feb. 14, 1894; s. Joe F. and Mary Etta (Evans) K.; B.S., U. of Mo., 1914; M.S., U. of Ky., 1915; Ph.D., U. of Chicago, 1919; D. Eng., U. of Mo., 1936; m. Katharine Milsted, Nov. 13, 1919; children—Mary Katharine, Robert Milsted. Research physicist, Western Electric Co., 1918-25; research physicist Bell Telephone Labs., N.Y. City, 1925-30, dir. vacuum tube development, 1930-36, dir. research since 1936. Fellow Am. Physical Soc., Am. Inst. E.E., Am. Inst. Radio Engrs., Am. Acoustical Soc.; mem. A.A.A.S., Franklin Institute, Sigma Nu, Tau Beta Pi, Sigma Xi. Clubs: Short Hills (Short Hills); Canoe Brook Country (Summit); Salmagundi (New York). Home: Windermere Terrace, Short Hills, N.J. Office: care Bell Telephone Laboratories, 463 West St., New York, N.Y.

KELLY, Michael B.; otorhinolaryngologist and ophtalmologist Wheeling Hosp. Address: 56 14th St., Wheeling, W.Va.

KELLY, Thomas Charles, physician; b. Phila., Pa., Feb. 22, 1882; s. Dr. Joseph V. and Emma (Ferguson) K.; A.B., LaSalle Coll., 1900, A.M., same, 1907; M.D., U. of Pa. Med. Sch., 1904; m. Bernadine Eagan, Nov. 29, 1911; 1 dau., Kitty. Interne Univ. Hosp., Phila., 1904-06; engaged in practice of medicine at Phila., Pa., since 1907; asst. prof. pediatrics, U. of Pa. Med. Sch.; asso. in pediatrics, U. of Pa. Grad. Sch. of Medicine since 1934; physician, St. Christophers Hosp.; pediatrist, Misericordia Hosp.; cons. pediatrist, St. Mary's, and Fitzgerald-Mercy hosps. Fellow Am. Coll. of Physicians, Coll. of Physicians of Phila.; mem. Am. Clinical and Climatol. Assn., Am. Acad. of Pediatrics. Republican. Roman Catholic. Club: Philadelphia Country. Home: 105 School Lane, Philadelphia, Pa.

KELLY, Thomas Raymond, asso. prof. philosophy; b. Chillicothe, O., June 4, 1893; s. Carlton W. and Madora (Kersey) K.; B.S., Wilmington (O.) Coll., 1913; S.B., Haverford Coll., 1914; B.D., Hartford (Conn.) Theol. Sem., 1919, Ph.D., same, 1924; grad. study Harvard U., 1930-32; m. Lael Macy, May 29, 1919; children—Lois Lael, Richard Macy. Instr. Pickering Coll., Newmarket, Ont., 1914-16; prof. Wilmington (O.) Coll., 1919-21; prof. philosophy, Earlham Coll., Richmond, Ind., 1925-30, also, 1932-35; lecturer, Wellesley Coll., 1931-32; prof. philosophy, U. of Hawaii, Honolulu, 1935-36; asst. prof. philosophy, Haverford Coll., Haverford, Pa., 1936-38, asso. prof. since 1938. Mem. Am. Philos. Assn., Phi Beta Kappa. Mem. Religious Soc. Friends. Author: Explanation and Reality in the Philosophy of Emile Meyerson, 1937. Home: Haverford College, Haverford, Pa.

KELSEY, Albert, architect; b. St. Louis, Mo., Apr. 26, 1870; s. Albert Warren and Janette Garr (Washburn) K.; Univ. of Pa., 1896; studied in Paris, 1897-98 (traveling scholarship in architecture, U. of Pa.); m. Henrietta L. Allis, Jan. 18, 1898; children—Albert Washburn, Charlotte Elizabeth, Charles Cashman. Practiced at Phila. since 1894; architect for the "Model City," St. Louis, 1903; designed plans for Pan. Am. bldgs., at Washington, D.C., in association with Prof. Cret; Carson Coll., bldgs. nr. Phila.; Sacred Heart Acad., Madison, Wis.; etc.; chmn. com. of experts for construction of Phila. Parkway; mem. various town planning commns.; an organizer Regional Planning Fed. of Phila. Tri-State District; architectural advisor Pan-Am. Union and dir. Columbus Memorial Lighthouse Competition, Santo Domingo. Decorated Commander of Isabella la Catolica by Alfonso XIII. Mem. bd. of dirs. Fairmount Park Art Assn.; member bd. of govs., English-Speaking Union. Pres. Architectural League America, 1908-09; fellow of American Institute of Architects; member of Architectural League of New York, Pa. State Assn. Architects (pres. 1916-17), Numismatic Soc. Democrat. Clubs: Franklin Inn, Philobiblon, T-Square, Art (Phila.); Metropolitan (Washington). Office: Architect's Bldg., Philadelphia, Pa.

KELSEY, Carl, college prof.; b. Grinnell, Ia., Sept. 2, 1870; s. Carl James and Mary Maria (Sutherland); K.; A.B., Ia. (now Grinnell) Coll., 1890; Andover Theol. Sem., 1892-95; univs. of Göttingen and Berlin, 1896, 97; Ph.D., U. of Pa., 1903; m. Gertrude H. Haldeman, Sept. 2, 1896. Teacher high school, Marshalltown, Ia., 1891, 92; in social work, Helena, Mont., 1895; Buffalo and Boston, 1897; Chicago, 1898-1901; Harrison fellow in sociology, 1901-03, instr., 1903-04, asst. prof., 1904-06, prof. sociology, 1906—, U. of Pa. Asst. dir. New York Sch. of Philanthropy, 1905-13. Dist. supt. of War Risk Ins., June 1918-May 1919. Republican. Mem. Am. Academy Polit. and Social Science (sec. 1906-12, v.p. 1912-25), Am. Econ. Assn., Am. Sociol. Soc. Clubs: Century (New York); Cosmos (Washington). Author: The Negro Farmer, 1903; The Physical Basis of Society, 1916, 28. Home: Mendenhall, Pa.

KELSEY, Frederick Trowbridge, lawyer; b. Orange, N.J., Dec. 26, 1886; s. Frederick Wallace and Ella A. (Butts) K.; grad. Cartaret Acad., Orange, N.J., 1903; A.B., Yale, 1907; LL.B., N.Y. Law Sch., 1909; m. Anna Welles Whitney, May 13, 1913 (died 1925); children—Whitney Trowbridge, Elinor Kelsey; m. 2d, Joan Skolnik, May 28, 1926; 1 son, Frederick Trowbridge. Admitted to N.Y. bar, 1909, and since practiced in N.Y. City; mem. firm McLean, Hayward & Kelsey, 1910-13, Lewis & Kelsey, 1913-25, Lewis, Garvin & Kelsey, 1925-33, Lewis & Kelsey since 1933. Sec. and dir. Park-Lexington Co., Inc., Smith Victory Corpn.; dir. Colonial Trust Co., Lake Placid Co., Rock Spring Co. Mem. Am. and N.Y. State bar assns., Bar Assn. City of N.Y., County Lawyers Assn., Phi Beta Kappa. Ind. Republican. Episcopalian. Clubs: Bankers, Union League (N.Y. City); Rock Spring (West Orange); Lake Placid (Essex Co., N.Y.). Home: 361 Ridgewood Rd., South Orange, N.J. Office: 120 Broadway, New York, N.Y.

KELSO, James Anderson, theologian; b. Rawal Pindi, India, June 6, 1873; s. Alexander P. and Louisa M. (Bolton) K.; A.B., Washington and Jefferson Coll., 1892, D.D., 1902; B.D., Western Theol. Sem., Pittsburgh, 1896; student U. of Berlin, 1896-97, U. of Leipzig, 1899-1900, Ph.D., summa cum laude, 1900; LL.D., Coll. of Wooster, Ohio, 1919; m. Wilhemina Wise, June 29, 1898. Ordained Presbyn. ministry, 1898; instr. Hebrew, 1897-1900, prof. Hebrew and O.T. lit. since Sept. 1900, acting pres., 1908-09, pres. since May 1909, Western Theol. Sem. Lecturer Am. Sch. Oriental Research, Jerusalem, 1922-23. Dir. Ministers Mutual Life Ins. Co. Mem. Bd. of Christian Edn., Presbyn. Ch., 1929-32; mem. board of dirs. Presbyn. Ministers' Fund; trustee Presbyn. Hosp. Moderator Pittsburgh Presbytery, 1931, Synod of Pa., 1935; exchange preacher to Great Britain, 1938. Mem. Soc. Bibl. Lit. and Exegesis, Archæol. Inst. America, Am. Oriental Soc.; foundation mem. Phi Beta Kappa. Club: Penn Athletic. Author: Die Klagelieder, Der massoretische Text und die Versionen, 1901; Hebrew-English Vocabulary to the Book of Genesis, 1917; A History of the Hebrews in Outline, 1921; The Hebrew Prophet and His Message, 1922. Contbr. to Hastings' Dictionary of Ethics and Religion, Hastings' Dictionary of the Bible, Standard Bible Dictionary. Contbr. to religious and secular press. Home: 725 Ridge Av. N.S., Pittsburgh, Pa.

KELSO, James Leon, prof. Old Testament; b. Duluth, Minn., Oct. 21, 1892; s. Evan Edward and Bertha (Walle) K.; A.B., Monmouth (Ill.) Coll., 1916, D.D., 1926; Th.M., Xenia Theol. Sem., St. Louis, Mo., 1918, Th.D., 1927; A.M., Ind. U., 1921; m. Adolphina Pearson, Jan. 28, 1920. Ordained ministry U.P. Ch., 1918; pastor Bloomington, Ind., 1918-23; prof. Old Testament, Xenia Theol. Sem., 1923-30, Pittsburgh-Xenia Theol. Seminary since 1930; member staff of archæological excavations, Tell Beit Mirsim, Palestine, 1926, 30, 32; pres. staff of Bethel Archæol. expdn., 1934. Mem. Am. Oriental Soc., Archeol. Inst. America. Republican. Archæol. editor S.S. Times since 1934; contbg. editor to Bibliotheca Sacra since 1934. Address: Pittsburgh-Xenia Theol. Seminary, Pittsburgh, Pa.

KEMLER, Joseph I.; asso. in ophthalmology, U. of Md.; mem. attending staff Sinai Hosp.; mem. staff Baltimore Eye, Ear and Throat Charity Hosp., Mercy Hosp. Dispensary; otolaryngologist Mt. Pleasant Sanatorium. Address: 1908 Eutaw Place, Baltimore, Md.

KEMMERER, Edwin Walter, economist; b. Scranton, Pa., June 29, 1875; s. Lorenzo Dow and Martha H. (Courtright) K.; A.B., Wesleyan U., 1899, LL.D., 1926; fellow in economics and finance, Cornell, 1899-1901, Ph.D., 1903; LL.D., Occidental Coll., 1928; Dr., honoris causa, Central U., Ecuador, also from all univs. of Bolivia, 1927; D.C.S., Oglethorpe Univ., 1933; D.Sc., Rutgers Univ., 1933; LL.D., Columbia University, 1935; m. Rachel Dickel, Dec. 24, 1901; children—Donald Lorenzo, Ruth. Instructor economics and history, Purdue U., 1901-03; financial adviser to U.S. Philippine Commn., spl. reference to establishment gold standard in P.I., 1903; chief div. of currency, P.I., 1904-06; asst. prof. polit. economy, 1906-09, prof. economics and finance, 1909-12, Cornell U.; prof. economics and of finance, Princeton U., 1912-28, Walker professor international finance since 1928, also director International Finance Section; financial adviser to Govt. of Mexico, 1917, and to Government of Guatemala, 1919; U.S. Trade Commr. in S.A., 1922; chmn. Commn. of Am. Financial Advisers in Columbia, 1923. Mem. Gold Standard Inquiry Commn. for Union of S. Africa, 1924-25; expert on currency and banking to Dawes Com., 1925; chmn. Am. Commn. of Financial Advisers for Chile, 1925; chmn. Am. Commn. of Financial Advisers to Poland, 1926, to Ecuador, 1926-27, to Bolivia, 1927; pres. Am. Commn. Financial Advisers to the Republic of Colombia, 1930, to Peru, 1931; president of American Commn., Financial Experts to China, 1929; joint chmn. Hines Kemmerer Commn. to make economic survey of Turkey, 1934; pres. Economists' National Committee on Monetary Policy, 1937-39. Mng. editor Economic Bulletin, 1907-10. Contbr. econom. mags. Fellow Am. Statistical Assn., Am. Acad. of Arts and Sciences; mem. Acad. of Polit. Science, Am. Economic Assn. (pres. 1926), Am. Philos. Soc., Council on Foreign Relations. Awarded gold medal by Government of Colombia, for services to Colombia, 1923; Commander's Star, Order of Polonia Restituta, 1926; Order of Merit, First Class, Ecuador, 1927; Order of the Crown (Belgium), 1937. Trustee Wesleyan Univ. since 1936, Scranton Keystone Junior Coll. since 1935. Mem. Delta Kappa Epsilon, Phi Beta Kappa. Mason (Shriner). Author: Report on the Advisability of Establishing a Government Agricultural Bank in the Philippines, 1906; Report on the Agricultural Bank of Egypt, 1906; Money and Credit Instruments in Their Relation to Gen. Prices, 1907, revised, 1909; Seasonal Variations in the Relative Demand for Money and Capital in the United States (in report of Nat. Monetary Commn.), 1910; Modern Currency Reforms, 1916; The United States Postal Savings System, 1917; Monetary System of Mexico, 1917; The A B C of the Federal Reserve System, 1918, 11th rev. edit., 1938; Six Lectures on the Federal Reserve System, 1920; High Prices and Deflation, 1920; Kemmerer on Money, 1934; Money—The Principles of Money and Their Exemplification in Outstanding Chapters of Monetary History, 1935. Co-Author: Facing the Facts, 1932. Home: Princeton, N.J.

KEMMERER, John L., lawyer, corpn. official; A.B., Amherst, 1893, M.A., 1896; LL.B., Harvard, 1896; m. Frances Mott Ream, 1906. Dir. Kemmerer Coal Co., Whitney & Kemmerer, Am. Reinsurance Co., Newmont Mining Corpn.; trustee Am. Surety Co. of New York. Clubs: Recess, New York Yacht, Baltusrol Golf. Home: Short Hills, N.J. Office: 15 Exchange Place, Jersey City, N.J.

KEMNER, E. Fred, realtor; b. Phila., Pa., May 15, 1901; s. John and Caroline (Uhland) K.; student Central High Sch., Phila., and Temple U.; m. Florence S. Frey. Industrial engr. The Austen Co., Phila., 1918-22; in real estate business for himself, 1922-29; vice-pres.

Heyer, Kemner, Inc., Phila., since 1929. Certified property mgr. by Am. Inst. Real Estate Management. Mem. North Phila. Realty Bd. (pres. 1932), Pa. Real Estate Bd. (vice-pres. 1934, chmn. com. on rates, etc., 1938-39), Phila. Real Estate Bd. (vice-pres. 1934-35, dir. 1939; chmn. conv. com. 1938-39), Nat. Assn. Real Estate Bds. (mem. com. on rates, 1939), Bucks County Real Estate Bd., Montgomery County Real Estate Bd., N.E. Phila. Chamber of Commerce, Soc. of Residential Appraisers (charter mem.). Republican. Lutheran. Mason. Artisan. Clubs: Torresdale Country; Jeffersonville Country. Home: 807 Kerper St. Office: 7319 Rising Sun Av., Philadelphia, Pa.

KEMP, Alvin F., sch. supt.; b. District Twp., Berks Co., Pa., June 18, 1876; s. John F. and Fietta (Fronheiser) K.; B.S. State Teachers Coll., Kutztown, Pa., 1900, Muhlenberg Coll., Allentown, Pa., 1913; A.M., U. of Pa., 1921; m. 2d, Ella C. Pilgert, Jan. 15, 1921; children (by previous marriage)—Harvey W., John W., Viola F., Edna F. Teacher ungraded rural elementary schs., 1894-1905; supervising prin. high sch., 1905-15; asst. co. supt. schs., 1915-26; co. supt. schs., Berks Co., Pa., since 1926; pres. Mertztown Bldg. and Loan Assn.; dir. Mountain Telephone Co. Mem. Red Cross, Mental Health Clinic, Children's Aid Soc. Mason, Odd Fellow, Grange, Patriotic Order Sons Ameriea. Club: Schoolmen's (Reading, Pa.). Author: The School Director at Work; The New School; The School Budget; Marking and Rating for Home Reports; Pupil Mortality; Research Problems in Rural Education; Common Sense in Education; The Efficient School. Home: Mertztown, Pa. Office: Reading, Pa.

KEMP, Anna Mary, librarian; b. Westside, Ia., Dec. 26, 1881; d. James Orpheus and Harriett Agnes (Snyder) K.; Mus.B., Bethany (W. Va.) Coll., 1905, A.B., 1906, Mus.M., 1907; student Chautauqua Library Sch., summers 1916, 1922, Columbia U. Library Sch., summer 1927. Engaged as instr. English, high sch., Amherst, O., 1909-11, Mansfield, O., 1911-13; with pub. library, Mansfield, O., 1913-18; with Westinghouse Electric and Mfg. Co. office, Mansfield, O., 1918-22; librarian Bethany Coll., Bethany, W. Va., since 1922. Mem. Am. Library Assn., W.Va. Library Assn., Alpha Xi Delta. Republican. Mem. Christian Ch. Home: Bethany, W.Va.

KEMP, Archie Reed, research chemist; b. Groton, S.D., Apr. 24, 1894; s. Frederick and Alice (Cassandra) K.; B.S., Calif. Inst. Tech., 1917, M.S., 1918; m. Ruby R. Stokesbary, Nov. 10, 1916; children—Vera Lucile, Marilyn Lenore, Warren Reed, Ernest Eugene. Chemist Western Electric Co., 1918-25; research chemist Bell Telephone Labs., Inc., N.Y. City since 1925, in charge organic chem. research; holder of a large number of patents. Fellow Instn. Rubber Industry, London; mem. Am. Chem. Soc. (chmn. rubber div., 1938; official rep. to London Rubber Technology Conf. (May 1938), Sigma Alpha Pi. Republican. Methodist. Mason. Clubs: Chemists, Java Tiffin (New York). Contbr. to Rubber Chemistry and Technology; also about 32 articles to scientific jours. Home: 170 Lexington Av., Westwood, N.J. Office: 463 West St., New York, N.Y.

KEMP, Hal, orchestra leader; b. Marion, Ala., Mar. 27, 1904; s. Thomas Dupree and Leila (Rush) K.; A.B., Alexander-Graham Coll., Charlotte, N.C., 1922; A.B., U. of N.C., Chapel Hill, N.C., 1926; m. Betsy Collins Slaughter, Jan. 14, 1932; children—Sally Rush, Hal, Jr. Propr. and dir. Hal Kemp Orchestra since orgn. 1925. Mem. Sinfonia, Delta Sigma Phi, Phi Mu Alpha, Legion of Honor-DeMolay. Methodist. Club: Lambs (New York), (also golf, country, etc., local). Home: Dover, N.J. Office: 551 Fifth Av., New York, N.Y.

KEMP, Robert D.; pres. Artisans' Savings Bank. Home: 2409 Delaware Av. Office: 505 Market St., Wilmington, Del.

KEMP, William Beck, univ. prof.; b. Baltimore County, Md., Mar. 3, 1890; s. John McKendree and Sara (Beck) K.; graduated Franklin High Sch., Reistertown, Md., 1908; Hopkins, and George Washington U.; Ph.D., Am. U., 1928; m. Louise Cobey Jan. 12, 1915; children—Margaret, William Beck. Teacher high sch., Frederick County, Md., 1912-13; instr. of science, U. of W.Va., 1913-14, asst. prof., 1914-16; extension agronomist, U. of Md., 1916-18; prin. Sparks High Sch., Baltimore County, Md., 1918-21; asso. prof. of agronomy, U. of Md., 1921-28, prof. and head of dept. of genetics and statistics since 1928. Fellow A.A. A.S.; mem. Theta Chi, Phi Kappa Phi, Sigma Xi, Alpha Zeta. Episcopalian. Contbr. articles on genetics, statistics, plant breeding to jours. Home: College Park, Md.

KEMPEL, Arthur B(ushnell), rubber mfr.; b. Akron, O., Oct. 28, 1888; s. Charles W. and Nellie M. (Bushnell) K.; grad. Akron High Sch., 1906; m. Fern M. Martin, June 22, 1912; children—Ethel Fern (Mrs. Kenneth L. Broderick), Arthur Bushnell, Mary Jane. With Thomas Edison Co. in development of storage battery, 1906-10; development dept. Diamond Rubber Co., 1910-12, Goodrich Rubber Co., 1912-17; vice-pres. and gen. mgr. Rex-Hide, rubber mfrs., since 1917. Sch. dir. East Brady, Pa., Pub. Schs. since 1930. Mem. Am. Chem. Soc. Club: Ridgeview Country (East Brady). Address: East Brady, Pa.

KEMPER, A. Judson, physician; b. Freemansburg, W.Va., Aug. 18, 1873; s. Reuben A. and Rosamond (Hitt) K.; m. Pearl Swisher, Nov. 1, 1905; children—Pearl Maurine (Mrs. Lloyd H. Young), Rachel Annabel, William Judson. Engaged in farming and teaching in pub. schs. of W.Va.; now in gen. practice of medicine and surgery at Clarksburg, W.Va.; serving as county health officer since 1931; vice-pres. Harrison Co. Bank; pres. Lost Creek Lumber & Concrete Co. Served as med. mem. co. draft bd. during World War. Baptist. Mason (32°). Club: Kiwanis (Clarksburg). Home: Lost Creek, W.Va. Office: Clarksburg, W.Va.

KENDALL, John Wiley, business exec.; b. Myersdale, Pa., Nov. 23, 1897; s. Samuel A. and Minnie E. (Wiley) K.; student Friends Select Sch., Washington, D.C., 1909-11, Western High Sch., Washington, D.C., 1911-14; Haverford (Pa.) Coll., 1914-18; A.B., Princeton U., 1920; unmarried. Began as salesman Kendall Lumber Co., Pittsburgh, 1921, sales mgr., sec. and dir., 1921-36, pres. since 1936; gen. mgr. and dir. Preston R.R. Co., Pittsburgh, since 1921; dir. Stanley Coal Co., Crellin, Md., since 1926; dir. Garrett (Pa.) Water Co. since 1927, vice-pres. since 1933. Served as ensign U.S. N.R.F., 1918-22, as instr. piloting flying boats. Mem. Charter Club (Princeton). Republican. Presbyterian. Clubs: University (Pittsburgh); Princeton (New York). Composer of 2 published songs: When God Gave Me You, 1934; I Dream of Bermuda, 1936. Managed Nixon Theatre Players, Inc., in summer stock, 1928. Home: Myersdale, Pa. Address: Box 14, Pittsburgh, Pa.

KENDIG, H. Evert; dean faculty of pharmacy, U. of Pa. Address: 1812 Spring Garden St., Philadelphia, Pa.

KENDRICK, W. Freeland, ex-mayor; b. Phila., June 24, 1874; s. William D. and Margaret K.; married Mabel Bernard. Mayor of Phila., term Jan. 1924-Jan. 1928. Republican. Mason. Past Imperial Potentate A.A.O.N.M.S. Originator of idea of Shriners' hosps. for crippled children, now operating in various cities. Home: 5425 Woodbine Av. Office: Widener Bldg., Philadelphia, Pa.

KENNA, Joseph Norris, judge; b. Charleston, W.Va., Jan. 10, 1888; s. Senator John Edward and Annie (Benninghaus) K.; law student U. of Va., 1908-10; m. Louise Mounteastle, June 22, 1916; children—Nancy, Lee Mounteastle. Admitted to W.Va. bar, 1910; in office Chilton, McCorkle & Chilton, 1910-12; mem. firm Loeb & Kenna, 1912-19; asst. U.S. atty., Southern Dist. W.Va., 1919-22; mem. firm Avis & Kenna, 1922-24; mem. W.Va. Ho. of Delegates, 1931-32; judge Supreme Court of Appeals, W.Va., since Jan. 1, 1933. Mem. Phi Kappa Psi, Phi Delta Phi. Democrat. Presbyn. Mason (32°, Shriner), K.P. Club: Edgewood Country. Home: 625 Swarthmore Av., Charleston, W.Va.

KENNEDY, Ambrose J(erome), congressman; b. Baltimore, Md., Jan. 6, 1893; s. Ambrose J. and Annie (McDonald) K.; ed. Calvert Hall Coll. and Poly. Inst., Baltimore; m. Mary E. Dailey, Aug. 9, 1910; children—Mary B., Margaret A., Ambrose J., John D., Mildred, Jerome. Began as clk., Howard T. Williams & Co., ins., Baltimore, 1909; with Benson M. Greene & Co., 1915-24; in ins. business for self, 1924-32; v.p. Poor, Bowen, Bartlett & Kennedy, Inc., since 1932. Mem. Md. Ho. of Rep., 1918; mem. City Council, Baltimore, 1922-26; mem. Md. State Senate, 1926; state parole commr., Md., 1929-32; mem. 73d to 76th Congresses (1933-1941), 4th Md. Dist. Dir. Baltimore Catholic League. Catholic. Elk. Club: Merchants: Home: 914 E. Biddle St. Office: 26 S. Calvert St., Baltimore, Md.

KENNEDY, Andrew M(illiken), vice-pres. Pittsburgh Coke & Iron Co.; b. Youngstown, O.; s. James Patterson and Jennie (Milliken) K.; grad. Lehigh Univ., 1912; m. Nan Roper, June 7, 1916; children—Andrew M., D'Arcy P., Mary A., James P. Supt. steel plant, Trumbull Steel Co., 1916-23; gen. mgr. Sharpsville Furnace Co., 1923-28; works mgr. Davison Coke & Iron Co., Neville Island, 1928-37; vice-pres. Pittsburgh Coke & Iron Co. (formerly Davison Coke & Iron Co.) since July 1937; vice-pres. and gen. mgr. Hunter Steel Co., Neville Island, since Nov. 1938. Mem. Am. Iron and Steel Inst., Eastern States Blast Furnace and Coke Oven Assn., Am. Welding Soc., Am. Foundrymen's Assn., Am. Inst. Mining and Metall. Engrs. Clubs: Duquesne, Edgeworth, Propeller Club of U.S. (Pittsburgh). Address: 27 Thorn St., Sewickley, Pa.

KENNEDY, Charles William, coll. prof.; b. Port Richmond, S.I., N.Y., Jan. 13, 1882; s. T. Livingstone and Marie Alice (Bush) K.; grad. Phillips Acad., Exeter, N.H., 1899; Princeton, 1899-1900; A.B., Columbia, 1902; New York Law Sch., 1903-04; M.A., Princeton, 1905; Charles Scribner fellowship, 1905-06, Ph.D., 1906; studied University of Munich, 1907-08. Instr. English, 1906-07, Porter Ogden Jacobus fellowship, 1907-08, instr. English, 1908-10, asst. prof., 1910-19, associate professor, 1919-21, professor English since 1921, Princeton University. Commissioned 1st lt. Ordnance R.C., May 28, 1917; capt., Ordnance Dept., N.A., Jan. 22, 1918; on active duty, July 12, 1917-Jan. 10, 1919; service with A.E.F., Sept.-Dec. 1918. Member Modern Language Association of America, Association Teachers of English in N.J., Huguenot Society America, Phi Beta Kappa, Sigma Chi. Episcopalian. Clubs: Tiger Inn, Nassau (Princeton); Princeton (New York). Author: The Legend of Juliana, 1906; The Poems of Cynewulf, 1910; The Caedmon Poems, 1916; The Walls of Hamelin, 1922; College Athletics, 1925; Sport and Sportsmanship, 1931; Old English Elegies, 1936. Address: The Nassau Club, Princeton, N.J.

KENNEDY, John A., newspaper pub.; b. St. Paul, Minn., Dec. 21, 1898; s. Charles C. and Mary M. (Sullivan) K.; grad. Trinity Coll., Sioux City, Ia., 1918; B.S., Coe Coll., Cedar Rapids, Ia., 1922; B.C.L., Georgetown U., 1923; m. Viera Hines, Nov. 19, 1924 (divorced 1932); 1 son, John Hines; m. 2d, Ellen Bruce Lee, Nov. 21, 1932; children—Patricia Henry, Davis Lee. On staff Sioux City Tribune, 1918, Cedar Rapids Rep. and Cedar Rapids Gazette, 1919-22, Washington (D.C.) Herald, 1922-35; conducted several investigations of wide-spread abuses in various federal governmental agencies resulting in conviction of offenders of conspiracy; purchased control of Exponent, Clarksburg, W.Va., Dec. 5, 1935. Pres. and gen. mgr. W.Va. Network, Ohio Valley Broadcasting Corpn., Charleston Broadcasting Co. Pres. Exponent Corpn.; mem. bd. Nat. Assn. of Broadcasters. Served as pvt. U.S. Army, World War. Mem. bars of Ia. and D.C. Awarded Pugsley prize of $1,000 for most noteworthy work by a Washington corr., 1929. Clubs: Metropolitan, National Press, Chevy Chase (Washington, D.C.); Racquet and Tennis (New York). Home: 422 W. Pike St., Clarksburg, W.Va.; and "Graceland," Elkins, W.Va.

KENNEDY, John B., school supt.; b. Landisburg, Pa., Oct. 27, 1891; s. Charles B. and Anna C. (Emlet) K.; student Millersville (Pa.)

Normal, 1910-13, Dickinson Coll., Carlisle, Pa., 1920-22, Bucknell U., Lewisburg, Pa., 1927-30; m. Ruth Carl, Aug. 17, 1915; children—John L.; Charles C. High school teacher and athletic coach, 1913-23; teacher and high sch. principal, Columbia, Pa., 1923-30; supt. of schools, Columbia, Pa., since 1930. Lutheran. Mason. Club: Rotary (Columbia, Pa.; pres. 1937-38). Home: 825 Walnut St. Office: High School Bldg., Columbia, Pa.

KENNEDY, Matthew G.; v.p. and gen. mgr. Delaware Electric Power Co.; officer or dir. various other companies. Home: 717 Blackshire Road. Office: 600 Market St., Wilmington, Del.

KENNEDY, O'Neil; editor The News Standard. Address: Uniontown, Pa.

KENNEDY, Paul Stuart, varnish mfg.; b. Rockland, Me., Sept. 26, 1888; s. William Francis and Clementine Starr (McAllister) K.; B.S., Worcester Poly. Inst., Mass., 1910; m. Eva Mildred McAfee, Nov. 17, 1926. Began career as newspaper reporter and spl. writer, 1902; asso. with Murphy Varnish Co., Newark, N.J., continuously since entering employ as chemist, 1910, successively chief chemist, tech. dir., gen. supt., sales mgr., then vice-pres. and dir. since 1926; vice-pres. Essex Varnish Co. since 1926. Served as 2d lt. Camouflage Corps, 20th Engrs., U.S.A., 1917-19, with A.E.F. Chmn. Lacquer Inst. Nat. Chmn. Industrial Sales Div., Nat. Paint, Varnish & Lacquer Assn. Mem. Am. Soc. Mech. Engrs. Roman Catholic. Clubs: Essex (Newark); Crestmont Golf (West Orange). Home: 493 Ridgewood Av., Glen Ridge, N.J. Office: 224 McWhorter St., Newark, N.J.

KENNEDY, R. Lewis, lawyer. Office: 780 Broadway, Bayonne, N.J.

KENNEDY, Reid, pres. Monongahela Trust Co.; b. Washington Co., Pa., Jan. 14, 1865; s. Dr. David S. and Nancy W. (Kelly) K.; A.B., Westminster Coll., New Wilmington, Pa., 1889; m. Martha E. West, Dec. 21, 1901. Pres. Monongahela Trust Co., Homestead, Pa.; pres. Hays (Pa.) Nat. Bank and First Nat. Bank, Homestead, Pa.; sec. and dir. Henderson Coal Co. Clubs: Duquesne Longue Vue Country (Pittsburgh); Orlando Country (Fla.). Home: 6553 Beacon St., Pittsburgh, Pa. Office: 143 E. 8th Av., Homestead, Pa.

KENNEDY, Thomas, labor union official; b. Lansford, Pa., Nov. 2, 1887; s. Peter and Mary (Boyle) K.; ed. pub. schs., Lansford, Pa., 1893-99, and private study; m. Helen Melley, July 23, 1912; children—Helen M., Thomas. Began as mine worker at age of 12; became active in labor union, holding offices, and later becoming active in United Mine Workers of America, pres. Dist. 7, Hazleton, Pa., 1910-25, internat. sec.-treas. since 1925; lt.-gov. of Commonwealth of Pa., 1935-39. Mem. Nat. Catholic Welfare Council, Am. Assn. for Old Age Security, Am. Assn. for Labor Legislation, Am. Acad. of Polit. and Social Science. Democrat. Catholic. K.C., Eagle. Home: 134 S. Poplar St., Hazleton, Pa. Office: United Mine Workers Bldg., Washington, D.C.

KENNEL, Louis, artist, scenic painter; b. North Bergen, N.J., May 7, 1886; s. Jean Baptiste and Barbara (Hess) K.; studied under pvt. tutors, perspective under Ernest Qros, George Bridgeman of Art Students League, Wm. H. Lippincott at Acad. of Design, and George Melrose; m. Irene Lenora Arnold, Apr. 24, 1907; 1 dau., Muriel Irene Margaritha. Employed as asst. scenic artist in Ernest Qros Studio, 1903; mgr. and head of Unitt and Wuks studio, 1909-17; pres. Kennel & Entwiste, Inc., since 1917; propr. Louis Kennel Scenic Studios since 1919; executed scenic display in Electric Utility Bldg., N.Y. World's Fair; executed over 500 productions among them, Street Scene, The Storm, Outward Bound, Decoration for White Horse Inn at Center Theatre. Professional athlete in basketball and baseball. Mem. United Scenic Artists Assn. Protestant. Mason. Home: 200 E. Madison Av., Dumont, N.J.; (summer) Hainesville, Sussex Co., N.J. Office: 741 Monroe St., North Bergen, N.J.

KENNELL, Henry B., pres. Citizens Nat. Bank & Trust Co.; b. Slatington, Pa., June 2, 1868; s. John W. and Sarah Jane (Brown) K.; student high sch.; m. Emma C. Obert, Sept. 25, 1890; children—Marie O., Dorothea C. Asst. cashier First Nat. Bank, Lehighton, Pa., 1888; with Joseph Obert Co., Inc., Lehighton, Pa., since 1888, sec. and treas. since 1907; became cashier Citizens Nat. Bank & Trust Co., Lehighton, Pa., 1902, now pres.; dir. Joseph Obert Co., Inc. Mem. Zions Evangel. and Reformed Ch. Mason (33°, Shriner). Club: Rotary (Lehighton, Pa.; ex-pres.). Home: corner 3d and Alum Sts. Office: Citizens National Bank & Trust Co., Lehighton, Pa.

KENNEY, John Andrew, physician; b. Albemarle Co., Va., June 11, 1874; s. John and Caroline (Howard) K.; student Hampton Inst., Hampton, Va., 1893-95, 1896-97; student Shaw Univ., Raleigh, N.C., 1895-96, 1897-1901, M.D., 1901; (hon.) D.Sc., Lincoln U., Oxford, Pa., 1934; (hon.) LL.D., Shaw Univ., 1938; m. Alice Talbot, Dec. 28, 1902 (dec.); m. 2d, Frieda Frances Armstrong, Oct. 29, 1913; children—John Andrew, Jr., Oscar Armstrong, Howard Washington, Harriet Elizabeth. Interne Freedmens Hosp., Washington, D.C., 1901-02; res. physician, dir. hosp. and Nurses Training Sch., Tuskegee, Ala., 1902-24, for 22 yrs.; founded John A. Andrew Clinics, 1912; physician, Newark, N.J., since 1924; personal physician to late Booker T. Washington; surgeon and chief John A. Andrew Memorial Hosp., a founder John A. Andrew Clin. Soc., 1918; founded Kenney Memorial Hosp., Newark, N.J., 1927, continued as pvt. hosp. and donated same to community as Christmas present, 1934, deeded to Booker T. Washington Community Hosp. Assn. representing the colored people of N.J., now med. dir., chief surgeon and mem. bd. trustees. Mem. John A. Andrew Clin. Soc. of Tuskeegee, N.J. State Med. Soc., Acad. of Medicine Northern N.J., North Jersey Med. Soc., A.M.A., Nat. Med. Assn. (sec. 1904-12, pres. 1912), N.J. State Med. Soc., Essex Co. Med. Soc., Zeta Boulé. Republican. Baptist. Mason. Club: Tuskegee Alumni (Tuskegee, Ala.). Founded Journal of N.M.A., 1908, asso. editor and bus. mgr., 1908-16, editor since 1916. Pub. The Negro in Medicine, 1912. Home: 34 Irving St., Montclair. Office: 134 W. Kinney St., Newark, N.J.

KENT, A(rthur) Atwater, mfr., inventor; b. Burlington, Vt., Dec. 3, 1873; s. Prentiss J. (M.D.) and Mary Elizabeth (Atwater) K.; ed. Worcester Poly. Inst.; hon. E.E., University of Vermont, 1924; Doctor of Engineering, Worcester Polytechnic Institute, 1926; D.Sc., Tufts College, 1927; m. Mabel Lucas, 1906; children—Arthur Atwater, Elizabeth Brinton (Mrs. William Laurens Van Alen), Virginia Tucker (Mrs. Cummins Catherwood), Jonathan Prentiss (adopted). Established, 1902, the Atwater Kent Manufacturing Works, Philadelphia, for manufacture of telephones and small volt meters; added mfr. of the unisparker (for which John Scott Medal was awarded in 1914), panoramic sights, clinometers, fuse setters and angle of sights for the army during World War; business incorporated, 1919, as the Atwater Kent Mfg. Co., of which is pres.; started mfg. radio receiving sets, 1922. Mem. com. on general problems of radio broadcasting, 3d and 4th Nat. Radio Confs., 1924, 25; sponsored multi-station broadcasting of world's greatest musical artists, beginning Oct. 1925. Mem. bd. mgrs. Franklin Inst.; mem. bd. dirs. Zoöl. Soc. of Phila., Bryn Mawr Hosp.; mem. Sons of Am. Revolution. Clubs: Bar Harbor (Me.); Rittenhouse, Union League, Racquet, Radnor Hunt, Merion Cricket, Corinthian Yacht, New York Yacht. Sponsored Nat. Radio Audition to discover young singers. Home: Ardmore, Pa.; (summer) Bar Harbor, Me. Office: 4700 Wissahickon Av., Philadelphia, Pa.

KENT, Clarence Hammond, coll. prof.; b. Ft. Wayne, Ind., Oct. 16, 1892; s. John Hammond and Florence (Hood) K.; B.S., Purdue U., Lafayette, Ind., 1915, M.S., 1925; Ph.D., U. of Mich., Ann Arbor, Mich., 1931; m. Rachel Avis Fitch, Dec. 20, 1919. Test dept. Erie R.R., 1910-13; application engr. Westinghouse Electric and Mfg. Co., Pittsburgh, Pa., 1915-17, 1919-20; instr. U. of Nevada, Reno, Nev., 1920-22, asst. prof., 1922-26, asso. prof., 1926-28; prof. and head dept. mech. engring., U. of Ark., Fayetteville, Ark., 1928-31; prof. mech. engring., Pa. State Coll., since 1931. Served as 1st lt., Engrs., U.S. Army, during World War. Mem. Am. Soc. M.E. (chmn. Central Pa. Sect. since 1936), Soc. for Promotion of Engring. Edn., A.A.A.S., Am. Assn. Univ. Profs., Scabbard and Blade, Acacia, Sigma Xi, Phi Kappa Phi, Eta Kappa Nu, Phi Tau Sigma, Pi Mu Epsilon. Protestant. Mason (Shriner). Author articles on thermal stresses, alloys, etc., in engring. jours. Home: 127 Buckhout St. Office: Pa. State Coll., State College, Pa.

KENT, Donald W., pres. Electric Heating Equipment Co.; b. Clifton Heights, Pa., July 25, 1893; s. Samuel L. and Anna (Ahrens) K.; B.S., U. of Pa., 1915; m. Kathleen Denniston, May 6, 1916; children—Jean, Kathleen, Donald W. Mgr. Burdett Oxygen Co., Phila., 1914-17; pres. Gas Equipment Engring. Corpn., Phila., Pa., since 1921-31; pres. Electric Heating Equipment Co., Phila., since 1931. Served as lt. j.g., Air Force Balloon Sect., U.S. Naval Res., during World War. Clubs: IV Street (Phila.); Gibson Island Yacht (Gibson Island, Md.). Home: White Marsh, Pa. Office: 26 S. 32d St., Philadelphia, Pa.

KENT, Everett, lawyer; b. East Bangor, Pa., Nov. 15, 1888; s. Charles V. and Mary K.; grad. high sch., 1906; LL.B., U. of Pa., 1911; m. Daisy Allen Speer, Nov. 22, 1911; children—Sarah Elizabeth (Mrs. Kenneth C. Proctor), Mary Louise (Mrs. John MacMaster), James Everett. Admitted to Pa. bar, 1911, practicing at Bangor; solicitor Northampton Co. Prison Inspectors, 1912-16; county solicitor Northampton County, 1920-24; mem. 68th and 70th Congresses (1923-25 and 1927-29), 30th Pa. Dist.; atty. for county controller, Northampton Co., since 1933. Del. to Dem. Nat. Conv., 1936; special dep. atty. gen. of Pa., 1936-37. Democrat. Home: 16 S. 3rd St. Office: 11 Broadway, Bangor, Pa.

KENT, Everett Leonard, manufacturer; b. Delaware Co., Pa., June 25, 1889; s. Henry T. and Louise (Leonard) K.; ed. William Penn Charter Sch., Cornell U. (class of 1911); m. Helen Irwin, 1915; children—William Irwin, Everett L., Jr. (deceased), Warren Thompson. Pres. Kent Mfg. Co., Clifton Heights; pres. Clifton Heights Nat. Bank; pres. Kent-Hampton Sales Co., New York; dir. Pa. Mfrs. Ins. Co. Home: Merion, Pa. Office: Clifton Heights, Pa.

KENT, Frank Richardson, journalism; b. Baltimore, Maryland, May 1, 1877; s. Thomas Marine and Mary (Richardson) K.; ed. public and private schools; hon. M.A., University of Maryland, 1911; awarded P.B.K. William and Mary College, 1934; Litt.D., Oglethorpe U., 1937; m. Minnie Whitman, Jan. 5, 1907 (died April 28, 1910); 1 son, Frank R.; m. 2d, Elizabeth Thomas, 1916. Reporter Baltimore American 1 yr.; began with Baltimore Sun, 1898, polit. reporter 10 yrs., Washington corr. 2 yrs.; sec. and treas. Md. Agrl. Coll., 1910-11; mng. editor Baltimore Sun, 1911-21, vice-pres. since 1921; writer of column on politics syndicated in more than 100 papers. Member advisory board Pulitzer School of Journalism, Columbia Univ.; mem. board of trustees St. John's Coll., Annapolis. Democrat. Episcopalian. Clubs: Maryland, Elkridge (Baltimore); Cosmos, National Press (Washington); American (London). Author: The Story of Maryland Politics, 1911; The Great Game of Politics, 1923; History of the Democratic Party, 1925; Political Behavior, 1928; Without Gloves, 1934. Home: Lombardy Apartments. Office: The Sun, Baltimore, Md.

KENT, John Irvin, lawyer; b. Meadville, Pa., Apr. 4, 1904; s. Orville Clare and Marion (Adrian) K.; A.B., Allegheny Coll., 1925; LL.B., U. of Pa., 1928; m. Dorothy Tamplin Hughes, Aug. 19, 1929; 1 son, John Hughes. Admitted to Pa. bar, 1928, and began practice in Meadville; partner with brother, Robert F., under name Kent & Kent since Feb. 1938. Mem. Crawford Co. Bar Assn. (sec.), Theta Nu Epsilon, Sigma Alpha Epsilon, Phi Delta Phi. Republican. Episcopalian (vestryman Christ Episcopal Ch.). Mason (past master, past high priest), Eagle. Clubs: Taylor Hose Co. (pres.),

Iroquois Boating and Fishing (Meadville). Home: 366 Park Av. Office: 353 Center St., Meadville, Pa.

KENT, Orville Clare, judge; b. North Shenango Twp., Crawford Co., Pa., June 15, 1876; s. John O. and Mary (Free) K.; grad. Linesville High Sch.; B.S., Allegheny Coll., 1896; studied law in office of Joshua Douglas, Esq., Meadville, Pa.; m. Marion Letitia Irvin, Apr. 14, 1903; children—John Irvin, Marion Adrain (Mrs. R. Graham Fithian), Fay Elizabeth (Mrs. John C. Chisholm, Jr.), Robert Free. Admitted to Pa. bar, 1900, and began practice in Meadville; dist. atty. Crawford Co., Pa., 1906-12; county solicitor, Crawford Co., 1912-16; elected judge 30th Judicial Dist. of Pa., 1927, for term 1928-38, re-elected for term, 1938-48. Mem. Crawford Co. Bar Assn., Sigma Alpha Epsilon. Republican. Methodist. Mason (32°), Elk, Eagle. Home: 709 Alden St. Address: Judges Chambers, Meadville, Pa.

KENT, Roland Grubb, philologist; b. Wilmington, Del., Feb. 24, 1877; s. Lindley Coates and Anna (Grubb) K.; B.A., Swarthmore Coll., 1895 (Phi Beta Kappa, president of the chapter, 1912-15, v.p., 1915-18, 1924-27), B.L., 1896, M.A., 1898; studied U. of Berlin, 1899-1900, Munich, 1900-01, Am. Sch. Classical Studies, Athens, 1900-02, U. of Pa., 1902-04, Ph.D., 1903; m. Gertrude Freeman Hall, July 12, 1904. Instr. Lower Merion High Sch., Ardmore, Pa., 1896-99; Harrison fellow in classics, 1902-03, Harrison research fellow in. classics, 1903-04, U. of Pa.; instr. Greek and Latin, 1904-09, asst. prof. comparative philology, 1909-16, prof. since 1916, U. of Pa. Lecturer in Sanskrit, Bryn Mawr Coll., 1910-11, 1912-14; prof. comparative philology, Ohio State Univ., summer 1921; delivered lectures at Sorbonne, Paris, June 1925; member of the administrative committee and professor of comparative philology, Linguistic Institute, New Haven, Conn., summers, 1928, 1929, Ann Arbor, summers, 1937, 1938. Decorated Chevalier Legion of Honor (France), 1934. Fellow Am. Acad. Arts and Sciences, 1934; mem. Am. Oriental Soc. (dir. 1917-20, 1924-27; v.p. 1923-24; pres. 1934-35), Am. Philol. Assn., Classical Assn. Atlantic States, Am. Assn. Univ. Profs. (charter mem.), Société de Linguistique de Paris, Oriental Club Phila. (sec.-treas. 1909-19; pres. 1919-20 and 1934-35); Classical Club Phila. (v.p. 1908-09; pres. 1909-10); Association Guillaume Budé (Paris; président du Comité Américain), Société des Études Latines (Paris), Linguistic Society America (founder, sec.-treas. since 1924), Philadelphia Classical Soc., Loyal Legion, Indogermanische Gesellschaft. Decorated Officier de l'Instruction Publique (French), 1926. Episcopalian. Author: Language and Philology (vol. 22 of Hadzsits and Robinson's Our Debt to Greece and Rome), 1923; The Textual Criticism of Inscriptions (monograph), 1926; The Sounds of Latin, 1932. Editor of W. R. Newbold's The Cipher of Roger Bacon, 1928. Editor and translator of Varro de Lingua Latina, 2 vols., 1938. Contbr. to Am., English, French and German philol. periodicals. Home: 204 St. Mark's Sq. Office: Bennett Hall, Univ. of Pa., Philadelphia, Pa.

KENT, Russell Hathaway, exec. engr.; b. Upper Darby, Pa., Aug. 31, 1891; s. Henry Thomas and Louise (Leonard) K.; student Penn Charter Sch., Phila., Pa., 1903-08; M.E., Cornell U., 1912; m. Dorothy Curtis, Nov. 19, 1914; children—Russell Hathaway, Laurence Shackford, Barbara Bartlett. Student engr. Westinghouse Electric & Mfg. Co., Pittsburgh, Pa., 1913-14; junior engr. Bur. of Chemistry, U.S. Dept. of Agr., Washington, D.C., 1914-16; exec. and engr. Kent Mfg. Co., wool textiles mfg., Clifton Heights, Pa., since 1916, dir. since 1921. Mem. Am. Soc. M.E., Am. Chem. Soc. Republican. Club: Union League (Phila.). Home: 431 Riverview Rd., Swarthmore, Pa. Office: Clifton Heights, Pa.

KENWORTHEY, Charles Edward, lawyer; b. Milford, Pike Co., Pa., Mar. 7, 1901; s. William Bartle and Corinne Howard (Reed) K.; A.B., U. of Pa., 1922, student Med. Sch., 1921-22, LL.B., 1925; m. Elizabeth Parker Prichard, Oct. 5, 1927; children—Anne, Reed Prichard (dec.), Pamela, Elizabeth. Admitted to Pa. bar, 1925; with Murray, Aldrich & Roberts, New York City, 1925-26, Evans, Bayard & Frick, Phila., since 1926, mem. of firm since 1935. Sub-chmn. Civil Service Com., The Com. of Seventy, Phila. Trustee Hahnemann Med. Coll. and Hosp., Phila. Mem. Juristic Soc. (pres.), Phila. Bar Assn. (mem. bd. govs.), Phila. Voluntary Defender Assn. (dir.), U. of Pa. Law Alumni Assn. (bd. mgrs.), Phi Kappa Sigma (nat. treas.), Phi Delta Phi. Republican. Episcopalian. Clubs: Racquet (Phila.); Merion Cricket (Haverford, Pa.). Home: Mill Creek and Righter's Mill Rd., Ardmore, Pa. Office: 1335 Land Title Bldg., Philadelphia, Pa.

KENWORTHY, J. Miller, physician; b. Elkton, Md., Jan. 19, 1883; s. Joseph Wardman and Minnie (Miller) K.; grad. Media (Pa.) High Sch., 1902; M.D., Hahnemann Med. Coll., Phila., 1906; m. Estelle Weyl, 1909; 1 son, Joseph Miller. In practice of medicine, Phila., since 1909; asso. prof. of urology, Hahnemann Med. Coll. and Hosp., Phila., consultant in urology, Crozer Hosp., Chester, Pa. Served as capt. Med. Corps, U.S. Army, 1917-19. Mem. County, State and Nat. Med. (homeopathic) Socs., Phi Alpha Gamma. Republican. Mason (32°, K.T., Shriner). Home: 4523 Pine St. Office: 1930 Chestnut St., Philadelphia, Pa.

KENYON, Elmer, theatrical press rep., lecturer; b. Pittsburgh, Pa., June 11, 1886; s. Thomas and Rosalia (Gloeckler) K.; ed. U. of Pittsburgh, 1909-10; A.B. cum laude, Harvard U., 1913. Engaged as prof. literature, Bourbonnais, Ill., 1913-16; teacher, Schenley High Sch., Pittsburgh, 1916-29; press rep., lecturer, The Theatre Guild, New York, N.Y., 1929-31; head drama dept., Carnegie Inst. Tech., 1931-36; press rep., lecturer, The Theatre Guild since 1936. Served as pvt. engrs., Camp Humphreys, during World War; overseas with Signal Corps as German interpreter for six months after Armistice. Pres. Pittsburgh Drama League, 1923-29; a nat. dir. Drama League of America, 1927-30. Home: 4116 Bigelow Boul., Pittsburgh, Pa. Office: Theatre Guild, 245 W. 52d St., New York, N.Y.

KEPHART, Alvin Evans, lawyer; b. Ebensburg, Pa., Dec. 21, 1905; s. John William and Florence May (Evans) K.; ed. Lawrenceville (N.J.) Sch., 1919-23; A.B., Princeton, 1927; LL.B., Harvard U. Law Sch., 1930; m. Ruth Bond Hill, June 28, 1929; children—Susan Hill, Katharine Evans. Admitted to Pa. bar, 1930 and since engaged in gen. practice of law at Phila.; asso. with Montgomery and McCracken, attys. since 1931; asst. city solicitor, law dept. City of Phila., 1930-37; counsel Inter-State Milk Producers Coöperative. Mem. Pa. State, Phila. Co., Cambria Co. bar assns., Juristic Soc., Harvard Law Sch. Assn., Lawyers Club of Phila., Law Acad. Republican. Conglist. Mason. Clubs: Union League, Clover (Philadelphia). Home: 1826 Delancey Place, Philadelphia; summer, Kephill Farm, Yerkes, Pa. Office: 1421 Chestnut St., Philadelphia, Pa.

KEPHART, John William, jurist; b. Wilmore, Cambria Co., Pa., Nov. 12, 1872; s. Samuel A. and Henrietta B. (Wolfe) K.; early edn. Soldiers Sch., Allegheny Coll.; LL.B., Dickinson Coll., Pa.; LL.D., Allegheny (Pa.) Coll., Dickinson Coll., Lafayette Coll., U. of Pa., Villanova Coll., St. Francis Coll., U. of Pittsburgh, Juniata Coll.; m. Florence M. Evans, December 1, 1904; children—Alvin Evans, Henrietta F., John William. Admitted to Pa. bar, 1894, and practiced at Ebensburg; engaged in many business enterprises; county solicitor Cambria Co., 1906-14; judge Superior Court of Pennsylvania, 1914-18 inclusive; justice Supreme Court of Pa. since Jan. 1919, term of 21 yrs.; chief justice since January 6, 1936. Actively identified with ednl. affairs of Dickinson Coll. Law Sch. and Allegheny Coll. Mem. Am. Law Inst., Am. Bar Assn., Pa. Bar Assn., Alumni Assn., Dickinson Coll. (pres.). Republican. Lutheran. Clubs: Art, Clover, Union League, Hist. Soc. (Phila.); Lincoln. Home: Ebensburg, Cambria Co., Pa.

KEPPEL, Alvin Robert, religious sec.; b. Buffalo, N.Y., Apr. 10, 1896; s. John and Salome (Henn) K.; A.B., Ohio Wesleyan U., 1917; grad. student Ohio State U., 1923; m. Bernice Eulalia Crimm, June 18, 1919; children —Junia Evelyn, Robert Alvin. High Sch. instr., 1917-20; prin. Marietta (O.) Jr. High Sch., 1920-24; prin. Marietta jr. and sr. high schs., 1924-30; dir. of teacher training Marietta Coll., 1927-29; exec. sec. Evang. Bd. of Religious Edn., 1930-36; nat. exec. sec. Bd. of Christian Edn., Evang. and Reformed Ch., since 1936. Sec. Council of Church Boards of Edn.; mem. Nat. Protestant Com. Boy Scouts of America. Mem. officers auxiliary U.S.N.R.F., 1918. Mem. Ohio High Sch. Prins. Assn., Internat. Council of Religious Edn. (exec. com.), Ednl. Commn. Pa. State Council of Religious Edn., Kappa Delta Pi, Sigma Phi Epsilon. Mem. Evang. and Reformed Ch. Clubs: Rotary, Jr. Reading (Marietta). Author: The Christ of the Church School, 1930. Author and pub. Keppel's Six Year High School Cumulative Record System. Home: 627 Shadeland Av., Drexel Hill, Pa. Office: 1505 Race St., Philadelphia, Pa.

KERIGAN, Florence, author and editorial asst.; b. Haverford, Pa., Dec. 4, 1896; d. John Joseph and Elizabeth (Harvey) K.; ed. pub. sch. Bryn Mawr, Pa., 1903-11, Lower Merion High Sch., Ardmore, Pa., 1911-15. In employ Curtis Pub. Co., Phila., Pa., 1916-17; statis. clk., Firestone Tire and Rubber Co., Phila., 1917-21, Stephen F. Whitman Co., 1921-25; editorial asst. Am. S.S. Union, Phila., Pa., since 1925. Presbyn. Clubs: Professional Writers, Fiction Guild (Philadelphia). Author: (plays), The Lady of the Lilacs, 1925; The Eyes That See, 1925; The Daughter of the Duke of Ballyhoo, 1926; (books), June's Quest, 1931; The Secret of the Maya Well, 1936. Contbr. juvenile stories, articles, and verse to mags. and jours. Home: Haverford. Office: 1816 Chestnut St., Philadelphia, Pa.

KERLIN, Robert Thomas, educator, author; b. Newcastle, Mo., Mar. 22, 1866; s. Thomas L. and Nancy (Jeffries) K.; A.M., Central Coll., Fayette, Mo., 1890; studied Johns Hopkins, 1889-90, U. of Chicago and Harvard; Ph.D., Yale, 1906; m. Adeline K. Koster, July 10, 1907; children—Katharine Elizabeth, Elsa Adeline, Constance Lee. Prof. English, Mo. Valley Coll., 1890-94; in active ministry M.E. Ch., S., 1895-98; chaplain 3d Mo. Vols. in Spanish-Am. War; prof. English, Mo. Valley Coll., 1901-02, Southwestern U., 1902-03, State Normal, Warrensburg, Mo., 1903-06; instr. English, Yale, 1906-07; prof. lit., State Normal Sch., Farmville, Va., 1908-10, Va. Mil. Inst., Lexington, 1910-21, State Normal Sch., West Chester, Pa., 1922-27. Asso. editor of Arena, 1905-10. Lecturer on English lit., U. of Vt. Summer Sch., 1911-17. Instr. A.E.F. Univ., Beaune, France, 1919; lecturer in lit., Phila. Labor Coll., 1925-27; at Lincoln U., 1927; prof. English, Potomac State Coll., Keyser, W.Va., 1927-33. Lecturer in English lit. and European history, Western Maryland Coll. since 1933. Author: Mainly for Myself (poems), 1897; The Camp Life of the Third Regiment, 1898; The Church of the Fathers, 1901; Theocritus in English Literature, 1909; The Voice of the Negro, 1920; Negro Poets and Their Poems, 1923. Editor of Milton's Minor Poems in Johnson's English Classics. Home: 615 Memorial Av., Cumberland, Md.

KERN, Frank Dunn, botanist; b. Reinbeck, Ia., June 29, 1883; s. William Sloane and Emma (Dunn) K.; B.S., U. of Ia., 1904; M.S., Purdue, 1907; Ph.D., Columbia, 1911; D.Sc., U. of P.R., 1926; m. Jessie Rhoda Adair, Aug. 21, 1907; children—Sue Emma (Mrs. H. C. Musser), Frances Louise. Spl. agt. Bur. Plant Industry, U.S. Dept. Agr., 1904-05; asst., later asso. botanist Purdue U. Agrl. Expt. Sta., 1905-13; instr. cryptogamic botany, Purdue U., 1910-11; research scholar, N.Y. Bot. Garden, Jan. each yr. for 4 yrs.; univ. fellow in botany, Columbia, 1910-11; prof. and head Dept. of Botany, Pa. State Coll., since 1913, also dean Grad. Sch.; dean Colls. of Agr. and Engring., U. of Porto Rico (while on leave absence from Pa. State College, 1925-26 and 1933-34). Awarded medal for pub. instruction, Venezuela, 1934. Fellow Am. Assn. Advancement of Science, Ind. Acad. Science; mem. Bot. Soc. America, Am. Phytopathol. Soc., Pa. Acad. Science, Torrey Botanical Club, Deutsche Botanische Gesellschaft, Alpha Zeta, Phi Kappa Phi, Sigma Xi, Gamma Sigma Delta, Phi Eta Sigma. Has specialized in researches in plant rusts, and other fungous diseases in plants. Home: 140 W. Fairmount Av., State College, Pa.

KERN, Howard Lewis, lawyer; b. Charles City, Ia., Feb. 4, 1886; s. Samuel Lewis and Lydia (Healey) K.; A.B., Cornell Coll., Mt. Vernon, Ia., 1907; LL.B., Harvard, 1911; m. Edna Luella Francis, Aug. 8, 1913; children—Myrna, Virginia Jean. With Cravath & Henderson, N.Y. City, 1911-13; atty. gen. of Porto Rico, term 1914-21; actg. gov. by designation of the President during absences of gov., 1917, 18, 19; resigned, Sept. 1, 1919; mem. law firm Armstrong, Keith & Kern, New York City, 1920-28; asst. gen. atty. Internat. Telephone & Telegraph Corpn., 1928-35, and since 1938; gen. counsel Postal Telegraph-Cable Co., Mackay Radio & Telegraph Co., Commercial Cable Co., 1930-38. Alternate, Porto Rican Delegation Dem. Nat. Conv., 1920, 24. Presbyn. Mem. Am. Bar Assn., Assn. Bar City of New York, Pan Am. Soc., Phi Beta Kappa. Clubs: Harvard, Harvard Law, Down Town Assn. (New York); Jefferson Islands Club (Md.); Metropolitan (Washington, D.C.); Baltusrol Golf. Home: 530 Ridge St., Newark, N.J. Office: 67 Broad St., New York, N.Y.

KERN, John Dwight, prof. English; b. Germantown, O., Sept. 14, 1900; s. Harry and Charlotte Elizabeth (Spring) K.; A.B., Heidelberg Coll., 1922; A.M., Harvard, 1924; Ph.D., U. of Pa., 1933; m. Florence Cochrane, Dec. 22, 1927 (dec.); children—John Dwight, Jr., Elizabeth Hunter; m. 2d, Marion Dougherty, Oct. 3, 1936. Instr. English, Rensselaer Poly. Inst., 1924-26; instr. English, Temple U. 1926-27, prof. English since 1927. Mem. Modern Lang. Assn. of America, Am. Assn. Univ. Profs. Democrat. Author: Constance Fenimore Woolson, 1934. Home: 1512 Spruce St. Office: Temple University, Philadelphia, Pa.

KERN, Richard Arminius, M.D.; b. Columbia, Pa., Feb. 20, 1891; s. Rev. George and Wilhelmine (Maurer) K.; A.B., U. of Pa., 1910, M.D., 1914; m. Donna A. Couch, Aug. 19, 1927; children—Richard Bradford, Donna Natalie. Interne and sr. med. resident Univ. Hosp., 1914-17; instr. in medicine, U. of Pa., 1919-23, asso. 1923-28, asst. prof., 1928-34, prof. clin. medicine since 1934, Louis A. Godey fellow in medicine, 1927-31; prof. clin. Medicine, grad. Sch. of Med, U. of Pa., since 1934; visiting physician Hosp. of the U. of Pa.; also chief of med. outpatient dept. and allergy sect. Mem. Bd. of Health, Lower Merion Township, since 1934. Served as lt. M.C., U.S.N., during World War; now lt. comdr. M.C., U.S.N.R., and sr. officer N.R. Unit of Specialists at Hosp. of U. of Pa. Fellow Am. Coll. Physicians; mem. A.M.A. Assn. Am. Physicians, Soc. for Clin. Investigation, Am. Clin. and Climatol. Assn., Assn. for the Study of Allergy (ex-pres.), Soc. for the Study of Asthma and Allied Conditions (ex-pres.), Assn. Mil. Surgeons, Phila. Pathol. Soc., Phila. Physiol. Soc., Phila. Allergy Soc. (ex-pres.), Coll. of Physicians of Phila., Sigma Xi, Alpha Omega Alpha, Phi Chi. Republican. Mem. Evangelical and Reformed Ch. Clubs: University (Phila.); Philadelphia Country (Balacynwyd, Pa.). Contbr. many papers to med. jours. Asst. editor Am. Jour. of Med. Sciences since 1925. Home: 1239 Remington Rd., Wynnewood, Pa. Office: University Hospital, 36th and Spruce Sts., Philadelphia, Pa.

KERN, William Franklin, football coach; b. Kingston, Pa., Sept. 3, 1906; s. Martin Anthony and Katherine (Lukas) K.; prep. edn. Wyoming Sem., Kingston, 1922-23; A.B., U. of Pittsburgh, 1928; m. H. Velletta McCullough, of Pittsburgh, June 30, 1934; children—John Carey, Barbara Ann. Asst. football coach, U. of Wyo., 1928; with Standard Sanitary Mfg. Co., 1928-30; asst. coach, U. of Pittsburgh, 1930-36; football coach, Carnegie Inst. Tech., Pittsburgh, since 1937. Mem. Phi Kappa, Omicron Delta Kappa. Roman Catholic. Club: Metropolitan (Pittsburgh). Home: 239 Suncrest St., Pittsburgh, Pa.

KERNEY, James, Jr.; editor Trenton Times. Address: Trenton, N.J.

KERR, Charles Matthew, Jr., sec. Farmers Fire Insurance Co.; b. Wrightsville, Pa., Feb. 27, 1898; s. Charles M. and Blanche S. (McConkey) K.; student Princeton U.; m. Catharine H. Rosenmiller, Mar. 31, 1927; 1 dau., Catharine. Served in various capacities Farmers Fire Ins. Co., York, Pa., 1920-38, sec. since 1938; partner M. B. Evans Ins. Agency and E. K. McConkey & Co. since 1920. Home: Wyndam Rd., Wyndam Hills. Office: 53 E. Market St., York, Pa.

KERR, Duncan J(ohn), ry. pres.; b. Glasgow, Scotland, Dec. 3, 1883; s. Alexander and Barbara Balfour (Sleigh) K.; B.S., C.E., U. of Glasgow, 1904; m. Elizabeth Muir Hendrie, May 6, 1911; children—William S., Alexander D., John D., Douglas H., Elsie M. Came to U.S., 1904, naturalized, 1919. Rodman Pa. R.R., 1904-08; constrn. work Chicago, Milwaukee & Puget Sound R.R., 1908-10, Ore. Trunk Line & Spokane, Portland & Seattle Ry., 1910-13; engr. Great Northern Ry., St. Paul, Minn., 1913, asst. to v.p. of operations, 1936; also pres. Cottonwood Coal Co. and Somers Lumber Co. (subsidiaries of Great Northern Ry.) for 10 years; asst. to pres. Lehigh Valley R.R., 1936, pres. since 1937. Served as chief engr. and asst. to exec. v.p. U.S. R.R. Adminstrn. during World War. Mem. Am. Soc. Civil Engrs. (received Arthur M. Wellington award 1933), Am. Ry. Engrs. Assn. Clubs: Railroad and Machinery, Traffic, Railway (New York). Home: Sayre, Pa. Office: 143 Liberty St., New York, N.Y.; Bethlehem, Pa.

KERR, Hugh T., clergyman; b. in Elora, Ont., Canada, Feb. 11, 1871; s. William and Annie (Thomson) Kerr; B.A., University of Toronto, 1894, M.A., 1895, LL.D., 1937; student, Knox Coll., Toronto, 1894-95; graduate of Western Theological Sem., 1897; D.D., College of Emporia, Kan., 1908; D.D., U. of Pittsburgh, 1918; LL.D., Washington and Jefferson Coll., 1920; m. Olive M. Boggs, June 12, 1902; children—Anna Boggs (Mrs. John Watson Harmeier), Hugh Thomson, Donald Craig. Ordained Presbyn. ministry, 1897; pastor Oakland Ch., Pittsburgh, 1897-1901. First Ch., Hutchinson, Kan., 1901-07, Fullerton Av. Ch., Chicago, 1908-13, Shadyside Presbyn. Ch., Pittsburgh, since 1913. Lecturer systematic theology and religious pedagogy, McCormick Theol. Sem., Chicago, Ill., 1910-11. Clubs: Duquesne, Longue Vue, The Cleric. Author: Children's Story Sermons, 1911; Children's Missionary Story-Sermons, 1915; The Highway of Life, 1917; How to Teach the Life of Christ, 1917; From Port to Listening Post, 1918; How to Teach the New Testament, 1918; My First Communion, 1920; Children's Gospel Story Sermons, 1921; Children's Nature Story Sermons, 1923; The Gospel in Modern Poetry, 1926; Old Things New, 1931; Children's Worship Story-Sermons, 1931; The Christian Mission in America, 1933; After He Had Risen, 1934; A God-Centered Faith, 1935; Faith and Life, 1937; Children's Everyland Story-Sermons, 1937. Pres. Presbyn. Bd. Christian Edn.; mem. bd. Western Theol. Sem. Moderator Gen. Assembly Presbyn. Ch., U.S.A., 1930-31. Home: 827 Amberson Av., Pittsburgh, Pa.

KERR, Samuel Logan, engineer; b. Phila., Pa., July 15, 1899; s. Matthew Henry and Margaret MacLean (Logan) K.; B.S. in M.E., U. of Pa., 1921, M.E., same, 1924; student Ecole Speciale des Travaux Publics, Paris, France, 1919; unmarried. Employed as research asst., I. P. Morris Corpn., 1921-24, asst. hydraulic engr., 1924-27, asst. chief engr., 1927-29; research engr., I. P. Morris & De La Vergne Inc., 1929-35; mgr. automatic control work, 1928-35; sr. mech. engr., U.S. Engr. Office, Eastport, Me., 1935-36; chem. engring. div., United Engineers & Constructors, Inc., design and constrn. chem. plants, Phila., Pa., since 1937. Served as pvt. and sergt. Med. Corps, U.S.A., 1918-19, with A.E.F.; capt. Specialist Res. Ordnance Dept. U.S.A., 1930-38; maj., Chief Arty. Div. Phila. Ordnance Dist., U.S.A., since 1938. Mem. Am. Soc. Mech. Engrs., Am. Soc. Civil Engrs., Engring. Inst. Canada, Army Ordnance Assn., Am. Water Works Assn., Am. Welding Soc., Am. Chem. Soc., Res. Officers Assn., Am. Legion, Theta Xi, Tau Beta Pi. Inventor of hydraulic, chem. and speed control apparatus. Received Jr. Award, Am. Soc. Mech. Engrs., 1921. Republican. Presbyn. Clubs: Engineers, Philadelphia Cricket (Philadelphia); Army and Navy (Washington); U. of Pa. (New York). Contbr. many papers on engring. topics. Home: 30 E. Mt. Pleasant Av. Office: 1401 Arch St., Philadelphia, Pa.

KERR, Wilbur Franklin, univ. registrar; b. Columbus, N.J., Nov. 2, 1879; s. Harry Holloway and Mary Elizabeth (Ridgway) K.; student Princeton Model Sch., Princeton, N.J., 1889-91; m. Lydia Rebecca Young, Apr. 10, 1901; children—Lydia Rebecca (Mrs. Jacob Irving Macfarland), Wilbur Franklin, Jr. Employed as clk. Princeton U., 1891-1911; asst. registrar, Princeton Univ., Princeton, N.J., 1912-26, registrar since 1926; dir. Nassau Bldg. & Loan Assn. since 1930. Served in N.J.N.G., 1900-08. Vice-pres. bd. edn. Borough of Princeton since 1935. Mem. Am. Assn. Collegiate Registrars, Patriotic Order Sons of America. Republican. Presbyn. Mason. Home: 103 Jefferson Rd. Office: 211 Nassau Hall, Princeton, N.J.

KERSTETTER, Daniel C., banker; b. Trevorton, Pa., Feb. 14, 1889; s. Isaac H. and Matilda (Frahn) K.; grad. of Trevorton (Pa.) High Sch., 1905; grad. Am. Inst. of Banking; m. Roma Ida Kressly, Sept. 23, 1914; children—Robert Daniel Kressly, Margaret Roma Kressly. Teller First Nat. Bank, Trevorton, Pa., 1906-11; cashier New Tripoli (Pa.) Nat. Bank, 1911-30; treas. Hamburg (Pa.) Savings & Trust Co. since 1930, also vice-pres. since 1938. Treas. Welfare Fed. of Berks Co., Hamburg Dist., since 1932; treas. St. Johns Evang. Luth. Ch., Hamburg; past pres. Reading Chapter, Am. Inst. Banking. Republican. Lutheran. Mason (32°, Shriner). Clubs: Rotary, Cinosam (Hamburg). Home: 649 State St. Office: 52 S. 4th St., Hamburg, Pa.

KESSEL, Oliver Dennis, lawyer; b. Ripley, W.Va., Jan. 12, 1901; s. Edward Dennis and Ella (Corbin) K.; A.B., W.Va. Univ., Morgantown, W.Va., 1924; LL.B., W.Va. Univ. Law Sch., 1928; m. Katharyn Hartman, Sept. 8, 1930; children—Katharyn Elaine, Sandra Ellen. Admitted to W.Va. bar, 1928 and since engaged in gen. practice of law at Ripley; served as pros. atty. of Jackson Co., W.Va., 1929-33; dir. and atty. First Nat. Bank of Ripley, W.Va., since 1933. Mem. Am. Bar Assn., W.Va. Bar Assn., Kappa Sigma. Republican. Mem. M.E. Ch. Mason. Clubs: Ripley Rotary. Home: 733 Church St. Office: Court St., Ripley, W.Va.

KESSEL, Russel; staff surgeon Mountain State Hosp.; visiting surgeon St. Francis Hosp.; surgeon Kessel Emergency Hosp., Ripley, W.Va. Address: 1021 Quarrier St., Charleston, W.Va.

KESSLER, Henry Howard, M.D., surgeon; b. Newark, N.J., Apr. 10, 1896; s. Simon and Bertha (Portugues) K.; A.B., Cornell U., 1916; M.D., Cornell U. Med. Coll., 1919; A.M., Columbia U. Grad. Sch., 1932, Ph.D., 1934; m. Jessie Winnick, Dec. 25, 1918; children—Sanford, Jerome, Joan. Interne Newark City (N.J.) Hosp., 1919-20; in practice of medicine and surgery at Newark, N.J., since 1921, specializing in orthopedic surgery since 1923; attending orthopedic surgeon Newark City Hosp., Newark Beth Israel Hosp., Hosp. and Home for Crippled Children, Hasbrouck Heights Hosp. Lt. Comdr. U.S.N.R. Med. Corps. V(S). Awarded gold medal, Am. Acad. Orthopedic Surgs., 1936. Fellow Am. Coll. Surgs.; diplomate Am. Bd. Orthopedic Surgery. Med. dir. N.J. Rehabilitation Commn., Democrat. Jewish religion. Author: Accidental Injuries, 1931; Occupational Disease Legislation, 1932; The Crippled and Disabled, 1935. Hunterian lecturer, London, Eng., 1935. Home and Office: 53 Lincoln Park, Newark, N.J.

KETCHUM, Carlton Griswold, public relations and adv.; b. Yankton, S.D., Feb. 17, 1892; s. Lester and Luna L. (Beard) K.; student Oberlin (O.) Coll., 1910-11; B.S. in Econ., U. of Pittsburgh, 1916; m. Mildred Caroline Storey, Oct. 8, 1914; 1 son, David Storey. Successively newsboy, messenger, stenographer, clerk, private sec., 1900-12; asst. to dir. of univ. extension, U. of Pittsburgh, 1912-14, asst. registrar, 1914-16; publicity man, asso. campaign dir., campaign dir. since 1916; with brother organized, 1919, Ketchum, Inc., campaign direction and public relations, and since v.p. and dir.; organized, 1922, Ketchum, Mac Leod & Grove, adv. agency, and since v.p. and dir.; finance counsellor Republican Nat. Com. since 1937. Served as private, sergeant and 2d lieut., U.S. Army, Dec. 1917 to Jan. 1919. Former chmn. U. of Pittsburgh Alumni Council, Am. Legion (past comdr. Pa. Post No. 5), Omicron Delta Kappa. Republican. United Presbyterian. Mason. Clubs: Duquesne, University, Rotary (Pittsburgh). Home: 530 Glen Arden Drive. Office: Koppers Bldg., Pittsburgh, Pa.

KETCHUM, Dickerson Albert, natural gas operator; b. Oakland Valley, N.Y., Sept. 11, 1877; s. Dickerson Ambrose and Susan Jane (Williams) K.; student Wallkill Acad., Middletown, N.Y., 1892-96; C.E., Cornell U., 1900; m. Mabel E. Van Buskirk, Feb. 12, 1901 (died 1938); children—Robert Dickerson (M.D.), Marion Cornelia (Mrs. John T. Collins). In employ N.Y. State Barge Canal, Syracuse, and Central R.R. of N.J. in N.Y., 1900; civil engr. National Transit Co., Oil City, Pa., 1901-05; with L.V. R.R., Buffalo, N.Y., 1905-07; with Nat. Transit Co., Oil City, Pa., 1907-12; asso. with United Fuel Gas Co. and Columbia Gas & Electric Cos., Charleston, W.Va., continuously since 1912, successively engr., asst. gen. supt., gen. supt. then vice-pres. since 1932; vice-pres. Warfield Natural Gas Co., Cincinnati Gas Transportation Co., Atlantic Seaboard Corpn., Central Ky. Natural Gas Co., all Charleston Group Cos. of Columbia Gas & Electric Corpn. Republican. Episcopalian. Mason. Club: Lions of Charleston. Home: 2915 S. Kanawha Av. S.E. Office: United Fuel Gas Co., Charleston, W.Va.

KETCHUM, George, public relations and adv.; b. Blair, Neb., Aug. 19, 1893; s. R. Lester and Luna Louise (Beard) K.; grad. Prep. Dept., Maryville (Tenn.) Coll., 1908; student U. of Pittsburgh, 1913-16; m. Thelma June Patton, Dec. 7, 1920; children—Richard Malcolm, Janet. Stenographer, bookkeeper, clerk various employers, 1905-12; sec. to chancellor, U. of Pittsburgh, 1912-16; with Frederic Courtenay Barber and Assos., New York City, dirs. of financial campaigns for philanthropic instns., 1916-17; pres. and dir. Ketchum, Inc., public relations and institutional finance, since 1919; pres. and dir. Ketchum, MacLeod & Grove, Inc., Pittsburgh, adv. agency, since 1919. Served as cadet and 2d lieut., Air Service, U.S. Army, with A.E.F., 1917-19. Mem. Omicron Delta Kappa (U. of Pittsburgh chapter). Republican. Presbyterian. Mason (Bellefield Lodge 680, Pittsburgh). Clubs: Duquesne, Longue Vue, Amen Corner (Pittsburgh). Home: 401 S. Linden Av. Office: Koppers Bldg., Pittsburgh, Pa.

KETELS, Luther Henry, clergyman; b. Marion, Ia., Jan. 16, 1887; s. Oluf V. and Julia (Grill) K.; student Barringer, Newark (N.J.) High Sch., 1902-06; B.D., Drew Sem., Madison, N.J., 1912; A.B., Columbia U., 1912, M.A., 1916; student Johns Hopkins U., Baltimore, Md., 1912-13, U. of Pa., 1917-18; Th.D., Drew U., 1925; m. Vera L. Treible, Sept. 19, 1916; children—Vera Madelyn, Donald Luther, Patricia Ann. Minister, student churches, Dover, N.J., 1908-09, Brooklyn, N.Y., 1909-12, Baltimore, Md., 1912-13; minister, Swarthmore (Pa.) Ch., 1913-16, Ridley Park (Pa.) Ch., 1916-18, Bethlehem Ch., Wesley, Pa., 1918-24, Cynwyd (Pa.) Ch., 1924-25, Union Ch., Phila., 1925-28, St. Stephens Ch., Phila., 1928-30, Central Ch., Frankford, Pa., 1930-36, Holy Cross Ch., Reading, Pa., since 1936. Served as 1st lt. chaplain, U.S. Army, during World War. Methodist. Address: 329 N. 5th St., Reading, Pa.

KETLER, Frank Courtney, supt. twp. schs.; b. Grove City, Pa., Mar. 26, 1892; s. Isaac Conrad and Esther Matilda (Gilson) K.; A.B., Grove City Coll., 1911; ed. U. of Pa., 1919-20; A.M., Columbia U. Teachers Coll., 1929, Ph.D., 1931; m. Ethel Crews, Sept. 17, 1919; children—Franklin Courtney, Robert Edward. Engaged in teaching, high sch., Transfer, Pa., 1911-12, Grove City, Pa., 1912-13; supervising prin. schs., Midland, Pa., 1913-17, 1921-28; instr. English, Grove City Coll., Grove City, Pa., 1920-21; supt. schs., Berlin, N.H., 1930-32, Cheltenham Twp., Pa., since 1932. Served as lt. then capt. cav., U.S.A., 1917-19. Mem. Nat. Edn. Assn. Dept. Sch. Adminstrs., Pa. State Edn. Assn., Phi Delta Kappa. Republican. Presbyn. Mason. Home: 8013 Hillcrest Av., Elkins Park, Pa.

KETLER, Weir Carlyle, educator; b. Grove City, Pa., Mar. 14, 1889; s. Isaac Conrad and Matilda (Gilson) K.; A.B., Grove City Coll., 1908, A.M., 1911; A.B., Yale, 1910 (highest honor group); LL.D., Buena Vista College, Ia., 1921, also University of Pittsburgh, Pa., in 1928; Litt.D., Allegheny Coll., Pa., 1922; m. Ellen Bell, Aug. 26, 1914; children—Eleanor, Elizabeth, George Conrad, William Richard, David Weir. Instr., 1908-09, asst. prof. mathematics, 1910-11, prof. history and economics, 1911-13, asst. to pres. 1914-15, acting pres. 1916, pres. since June 13, 1916, Grove City Coll. Mem. bd. govs. Bur. of Ednl. Records and Research; pres. Presbyn. Coll. Union, 1930-31, Western Pa. Coll. Assn., 1931-32, Pa. Coll. Presidents Assn. 1932-33; also pres. higher edn. sect., Pa. State Edn. Assn., 1927-28; mem. Com. on Higher Instns. of Middle States Assn. Colleges and Secondary Schs., 1932-36; mem. Bd. Christian Edn., Presbyn. Ch., State Council of Edn., 1928-36; chmn. Com. on Social Edn. and Action, Presbyn. Ch., U.S.A. Trustee Grove City Hosp.; mem. bd. dirs. Princeton Theol. Sem. Elder Presbyn. Ch. Club: Grove City Country. Rotarian. Home: Grove City, Pa.

KETTERER, Lillian H. (Mrs. Gustav Ketterer), official Gen. Fed. Womens Clubs; b. Phila., Pa.; d. William H. and Anna Kate (Evans) Harner; ed. St. Mary's Convent, Bessie V. Hicks Sch., Neff Coll.; (hon.) Master of Interpretation, Bessie V. Hicks Sch.; m. Gustav Ketterer, Oct. 26, 1904; 1 dau., Antoinette Harner. Founder mem. Temple U. Womens Club, 1910, recording sec. and pres.; served as pres. Phila. Fed. Women's Clubs and Allied Orgns.; jr. pres. State Fed. Pa. Women; state comdr. Women's Field Army of Am. Soc. for Control of Cancer; chmn. dept. legislation, Gen. Fed. Women's Clubs, 1938-41; pres. Pa. Housing and Town Planning Assn.; parliamentarian Recording Libraries Assn. of North America; chmn. Consumers Adv. Council, Phila. Chamber of Commerce. Organized Perkiomen Valley Women's Club, Montgomery County, Pa., 1934; mem. exec. com. Nat. Com. on the Cause and Cure of War since 1939. Awarded distinguished service medal by bd. of dirs. of Am. Soc. for the Control of Cancer for contribution to cancer control, 1939; cited by Gov. George H. Earle for a meritorious service medal as one of Pennsylvania's distinguished benefactors in working for public betterment and civic improvement in the City of Phila. and throughout the state, 1939. Appointed by Frances Perkins, sec. U.S. Dept. of Labor, on com. to advise on ways to further labor legislative programs. Mem. Women's Joint Congl. Com., Washington, D.C.; mem. advisory com. Economic Program of the Federal Works Progress Adminstrn. Patroness Astron Senior Honor Soc., Temple U. Mem. Pa. Economy League (exec. com.), State Minimum Wage Bd. for Women and Minors Employed in Hotel Occupations, Adv. Bd. Salvation Army, Speakers Com. Am. Red Cross Roll Call, Pa. and Germantown hist. socs., Geneal. Soc. of Pa., Fairmount Park Com., City Parks Assn. Phila., Assn. of Women in Pub. Health. Honored by One Thousand Dollar Gimbel Award as outstanding woman in Phila., 1933. Republican. Baptist. Clubs: Art Alliance, Temple U. Women's (Philadelphia); Womens (Germantown). Home: 458 W. Bringhurst St., Germantown, Philadelphia, Pa.

KEYLOR, Josiah B., M.D.; b. Lancaster Co., Pa., Oct. 24, 1857; s. Milton and Rebecca (Beyer) K.; grad. Millersville (Pa.) Normal Sch., 1879; M.D., Coll. of Physicians and Surgeons, Baltimore, Md., 1885; registered pharmacist, 1891; m. Lillian Rakestraw, 1895; 1 dau., Mrs. Kathryn Bair. Began gen. practice of medicine, 1885; asso. mem. staff Coatesville (Pa.) Hosp.; one of founders, and since pres. Atglen National Bank, Altglen, Pa.; one of founders, Quarrysville Nat. Bank. Dem. candidate for Pa. Ho. of Reps., 1925. Awarded hon. certificate from Pa. Med. Soc. for 50 yrs. successful practice medicine, 1935. Mem. Pa. Med. Soc., Chester Co. Med. Soc. I.O.R.M. (past chief), Odd Fellow (past grand), Mason (past master; Royal Arch; Oxford Commandery, K.T.). Clubs: Coatesville (Pa.) Y.M.C.A., Coatesville Country. Address: Cochranville, Pa.

KEYSER, W. R.; editor Welch News. Office: care Welch Publishing Co., Welch, W.Va.

KEYWORTH, William Albert, chmn. of bd. First Nat. Bank, York, Pa.; b. York, Pa., June 22, 1868; s. Charles Augustus and Mary J. (Castor) K.; ed. pub. schs. of York and York Collegiate Inst.; m. Bella Weiser Carl, Nov. 5, 1896; 1 son, Charles Carl (deceased). With First Nat. Bank, York, since 1885, successively as asst. to cashier, note clerk and cashier, 1896-1900, pres., 1910-34, chmn. of bd. since 1934; treas. Martin Carriage Works (now Martin-Parry Corpn.), 1900-05; mem. bd. dirs. Martin-Parry Corpn. Charter member of Royal Fire Company. Treas. Y.M.C.A. for many years; treas. York County Red Cross during World War. Mem. Pa. Soc. of N.Y. Republican. Lutheran. Mason (K.T.). Clubs: Lafayette, Country, Keystone Automobile, Temple (York). Home: 326 E. Market St. Office: First Nat. Bank, York, Pa.

KIBLER, Alton Lewin, chemist; b. Trappe, Md., Dec. 6, 1880; s. James Latimer and Angelica Rebecca (Arnold) K.; A.B., Randolph Macon Coll., Ashland, Va., 1904; M.S., George Washington U., 1909, Ph.D., 1912; grad. student Univ. of Berlin, 1909-10, Technische Hochschule, Karlsruhe, Germany, 1910; m. Mabel Anne Dailey, Sept. 1, 1915 (died Aug. 22, 1928); children—Alton Lewin (deceased), Dorothy Virginia, Mary Josephine; m. 2d, Mildred Moore McCullough, Dec. 10, 1929. Research chemist, DuPont de Nemours & Co., Wilmington, Del., 1912-15; chief chemist Picatinny Arsenal, Dover, N.J., 1915-20; supt. of operations for recovery of platinum, Old Hickory Powder Plant, Tenn., 1920-21; with Edgewood (Md.) Arsenal since 1921, as asst. chief organic dept., 1921, chief phys. dept., 1922-28, chief of information div. since 1928. Served as maj. Ordnance Dept., U.S. Army, 1918-19. Mem. Am. Chem. Soc., Kappa Alpha (Southern). Democrat. Methodist. Translator of Brunswig's Explosives, 1912. Contbr. articles on explosives, recovery of platinum from contact mass, chem. warfare, etc., to jours. Home: 1707 Lakeside Av., Baltimore, Md. Office: Edgewood Arsenal, Md.

KIBLER, John Thomas, grain and coal dealer, athletic dir.; b. Queen Anne Co., Md., July 17, 1886; s. Charles Wilmer and Julia (Tucker) K.; Chestertown (Md.) High Sch., 1904; B.P.T., Temple U., Phila., 1908; student Yale U. Summer Sch., 1908-10; m. Bessie Perry, Apr. 21, 1920; children—John Thomas, Mary Jane. Dir. of athletics and coach of baseball and basketball, Lehigh U., Bethlehem, Pa., 1908-09; asst. dir. of athletics, head coach of baseball and basketball, Ohio State U., Columbus, O., 1909-12; dir. of athletics and head coach of all sports, Washington Coll., Chestertown, Md., since 1913; mem. of firm C. W. Kibler & Sons, grain and coal dealers, Chestertown, Md., since 1913. Served as capt., 23d Inf., 2d Div., U.S. Army, during World War. Pres. Kent and Upper Queen Anne Gen. Hosp. Bd. Mem. Md. Intercollegiate Basketball League (pres.), Md. Intercollegiate Baseball League (pres.), Nat. Basketball Coaches Assn., Nat. Baseball Coaches Assn., Eastern Shore Baseball League (pres., 1937), Kappa Alpha, Omicron Delta Kappa. Awarded D.S.C., 1918; Silver Star, 1918; Croix de Guerre, 1918. Democrat. Episcopalian. Mason (K.T.; Shriner). Club: Chester River Yacht and Country (pres., 1934-37). Played professional baseball for ten yeads and managed teams in Ohio State League and Texas League. Address: Chestertown, Md.

KIDDE, Walter, mech. engr.; b. in N.J., Mar. 7, 1877; s. F. E. and Mary O. (Lang) K.; grad. Hoboken Acad., 1892; M.E., Stevens Inst. Tech., 1897; E.D., 1935; m. Louise Carter, Oct. 22, 1902; children—Walter Lawrence, John Frederick, Mary (Mrs. W. E. Morgan). Engring. practice at N.Y. City, 1900—; now pres. Walter Kidde & Co., Walter Kidde Constructors; trustee N.Y., Susquehanna & Western R.R. since 1937; mem. board of dirs. Vreeland Corpn.; dir. Hudson Trust Co., Union City, N.J.; dir. Firemen's Ins. Co. of Newark. Was chmn. joint water com. which originated a comprehensive plan for water supply for Northern N.J. Mem. N.J. advisory bd. U.S. Pub. Works Administration, 1933. Mem. N.J. State Highway Commn., 1922-26. Trustee Stevens Inst. Tech. (chmn. bd., 1928-35); treas. N.J. Conf. Social Work, 1913-38; v.p. N.J. Welfare Council; mem. N.J. State Sanatorium for Tuberculosis, 1914-18. Mem. Am. Soc. M.E., N.Y. State Chamber of Commerce (mem. arbitration com.), N.J. State Chamber of Commerce (pres. 1935-37, now v.p. and chmn. cost of govt. com., was chmn. State Com. to Make Zoning Effective, 1929). Episcopalian; jr. warden St. Luke's Ch., Montclair; v.p. Brotherhood of St. Andrew in U.S.A., 1900-38; mem. Nat. Council of P.E. Ch. in U.S.A. (mem. trust fund com.). Clubs: Whitehall (New York); Essex (Newark, N.J.); Nat. Golf Links, Montclair Golf, Quantuck Beach; Yeoman Hall (Charleston, S.C.). Home: 56 Gates Av., Montclair, N.J. Office: 140 Cedar St., New York, N.Y.

KIEB, Ormonde Anton, real estate and ins.; b. Springfield, Mass., Aug. 17, 1901; s. August Anton and Harriet (Livingston) K.; student Franklin and Marshall Coll., Lancaster, Pa., 1920-21, 1923-25; m. Gladys Chandler, Nov. 14, 1928; 1 dau., Elizabeth Livingston. Salesman E. J. Maier Corpn., real estate, Newark, N.J., 1925-26, Berry Bros. Inc., Newark, N.J., 1926-29; in bus. on own acct. as broker, Newark, N.J., 1929-30; vice-pres. B. J. Quinn Jr., Inc., 1931-32; mem. firm Thoms-Kieb Co., 1932-33; organized and inc. The Kieb Company, real estate and ins. brokerage, Newark, N.J. and pres. since 1933. Dir. Newark Y.M.C.A. Boys Camp Com. Professional mem. Inst. of Real Estate Management. Mem. Nat. and N.J. State assns. of real estate bds. and Newark Board. Mem. Phi Sigma Kappa. Treas. Alumni Club of Northern N.J. of Franklin and Marshall Coll. Republican. Episcopalian. Club: Rotary of Maplewood (past pres.). Treas. Inter-Service Clubs Com., South Orange and Maplewood. Home: 18 Colonial Terrace, Maplewood. Office: 917 Broad St., Newark, N.J.

KIEFER, Paul James, prof. mech. engring.; b. Camden, Ind., Nov. 26, 1886; s. Rev. Cornelius Joseph and Ellinore Loretta (Cainan) K.; A.B., Wittenberg Coll., Springfield, O., 1908; B.S., Case Sch. Applied Science, Cleveland, O., 1911, M.E., 1930; grad. student U. of Pa., 1916-18; m. Lucile Brubaker, of Springfield, O., June 12, 1913; children—Marjorie Brubaker (deceased), Paul James. Machinist, draftsman, surveyor, 1906-11; power plant designing and constrn., U.S. and Can., for Internat. Harvester Co., 1911-13; instr. mech. engring., U. of Pa., 1913-18; asst. prof. mech. engring., U. of Ill., 1919-20; asso. prof. mech. engring., U.S. Navy Postgrad. Sch., 1920-25, prof. and chmn. dept. since 1925. Served as ensign, lt. (j.g.), U.S. Navy, 1918-19. Chmn. Annapolis City Planning Commn., 1935-37. Mem. Am. Soc. Mech. Engrs., Am. Soc., Naval Engrs., Am. Meteorol. Soc., Am. Assn. Univ. Profs., Phi Kappa Psi. Presbyn. Mason. Clubs: Rotary (Annapolis); Officers (U.S. Naval Acad.); Army and Navy (Washington, D.C.). Author: Principles of Engineering Thermodynamics (with M. C. Stuart), 1929. Contbr. articles to tech. jours. Home: Ferry Farm. Office: Postgraduate School, Naval Academy, Annapolis, Md.

KIEFFER, Richard Fulton; surgeon Church Home and Infirmary, Union Memorial and South Baltimore Gen. hosps.; visiting surgeon Waynesboro (Pa.) Hosp.; consulting surgeon Western Maryland Ry. Address: 18 W. Franklin St., Baltimore, Md.

KIEHL, Eugene Phillips, mech. and elec. engring.; b. Phila., Pa., Sept. 26, 1892; s. Eugene Edward and Matilda Collins (Phillips) K.; B.S. in E.E., U. of Pa., 1912; m. Ida Jean Hopkin, Feb. 7, 1918; children—Doris Jane, Eugene Robert, Elizabeth Ann, Ruth Matilda. Engaged in elec. engring. since 1915, mech. and elec. engring. since 1921; served as instr., Phila. Trades Sch., 1917; spl. lecturer, U. of Pa. Towne Sci. Sch., 1927-28; professional engr. in Pa. Served at Mil. Training Camp, Plattsburg, N.Y., 1916. Mem. Am. Soc. Mech. Engrs. (past chmn. Phila. Sect.). Club: Engineers. Contbr. papers engring. topics for socs. and mags. Home: 551 Kathmere Rd., Brookline, Delaware Co., Pa. Office: 900 Sansom St., Philadelphia, Pa.

KIENLE, Roy Herman, research chemist; b. Easthampton, Mass., Apr. 27, 1896; s. Edmund Frederick and Emily Mary (Hupfer) K.; B.S., Worcester Poly. Inst., 1916; M.Sc., Union Coll., Schenectady, N.Y., 1927; grad. study, Mass. Inst. Tech., 1928; Ph.D., Rutgers U., 1938; m. Ruth Lynn Hine, June 17, 1920; children—Lawrence Frederick, Robert Nelson. Chemist Works Lab., General Electric Co., Pittsfield, Mass., 1916, Research Lab., Schenectady, N.Y., 1916-17, U.S. Bur. Mines, Washington, D.C., 1917-18; research chemist Research Lab., General Electric Co., Schenectady, N.Y., 1919-33; dir. phys. chemistry lab. Research Dept., Calco Chemical Co., Bound Brook, N.J., since 1933. Served as 1st lt. C.W.S., U.S.A., 1918-19, chief Incendiary Div., Am. Univ. Exptl. Sta., Washington, D.C. Fellow Am. Inst. of Chemists; mem. Am. Chem. Soc., Faraday Soc. of London, Sigma Xi. Conglist. Mason. Clubs: Raritan Valley Country (Somerville); Chemists (New York). Home: 560 Church St., Bound Brook, N.J.

KIFT, Jane Leslie, writer and editor; b. West Chester, Pa.; d. Joseph, Jr. and Helen (Graham) K.; D.D.S., U. of Pa. Coll. of Dental Surgery. A grad. in dental surgery but never in practice; engaged in writing since leaving coll.; contbr. articles to woman's page, Public Ledger, Phila.; daily garden feature syndicated since 1924; garden editor, Pictorial Review, 1932-33; contbr. series articles to Ladies' Home Journal, 1931; editor garden page, Sunday issue, Phila. Inquirer since 1934. Republican. Episcopalian. Clubs: Business and Professional Womens, Art Alliance of Phila., Women Writers of Phila. (pres.). Author: Woman's Flower Garden, 1927; Hope Chest (with Loraine Bowman), 1926; Success With House Plants (with Karin Brober Nedenberg), 1932. Contbr. hort. articles to leading mags. Home: 35th and Powelton Av., Philadelphia, Pa. Office: Public Ledger Syndicate, Philadelphia, Pa.

KILBORN, William T., mfg. metal products; b. Portland, Me., Sept. 23, 1897; s. James E. and Caroline (Goss) K.; ed. Phillips Andover Acad.; m. Marguerite Duttenhofer, Nov. 22, 1925. Asso. with Flannery Bolt Co., Bridgeville, Pa., since 1933, pres. and dir. since 1934; dir. Colonial Trust Co., Pittsburgh, Pa., Freehold Bank of Pittsburgh, Pa.; dir. Keystone Driller Co., Beaver Falls, Pa. Republican. Presbyterian. Club: Duquesne (Pittsburgh). Home: 6500 Beacon St., Pittsburgh, Pa. Office: Bridgeville, Pa.

KILDUFFE, Robert A(nthony), physician; b. Phila., Pa., May 8, 1884; s. Robert Ormsby and Caroline (Bazin) K.; A.B., St. Joseph's Coll., Phila., Pa., 1908; M.D., U. of Pa. Med. Sch., 1913; (hon.) A.M., St. Joseph's Coll., 1911; m. Adelaide Long, June 12, 1918. Interne Chester Hosp., Chester, Pa., 1913-14, chief resident and resident pathologist, 1914-15; engaged in pvt. practice, and pathologist Chester Hosp., 1915-17; pathologist Pittsburgh Hosp., Pittsburgh, Pa., and dir. labs. and city bacteriologist to McKeesport Hosp. and City of McKeesport, Pa., 1920-24; dir. labs. Atlantic City Hosp., Atlantic City, N.J., since 1924, also city bacteriologist of Atlantic City; pathologist, Atlantic County Hosp. for Tuberculous Diseases, Atlantic Co. Hosp. for Mental Diseases, Betty Bacharach Home for Crippled Children, Municipal Hosp., Jewish Seaside Home, all of Atlantic City, N.J.; chief of Tumor Clinic, Atlantic City Hosp.; pres. med. staff Atlantic City Hosp., 1939, Atlantic Co. Hosp. for Tuberculous Diseases, 1939. Served as 1st lt. to maj. Med. Corps, U.S.A., 1917-19, regtl. surgeon, then comdg. officer field hosp., A.E.F., chief bacteriol. div. and epidemiologist on staff chief surgeon. Fellow Am. Med. Assn.; mem. Am. Soc. Bacteriologist, Assn. of Mil. Surgeons, Am. Soc. Clin. Pathologists (past pres.), N.J. State and Atlantic Co. med. socs., N.J. Soc. Clin. Pathologists (vice-pres., chmn. exec. com.), Omega Upsilon Phi, Sigma Xi. Author: The Clinical Interpretation of the Wassermann Reaction, 1926; The Clinical Interpretation of Blood Chemistry, 1927; The Clinical Interpretation of Blood Examinations, 1931; A Manual of Clinical Laboratory Procedure, 1926; Bacteriology and Applied Immunology for Nurses, 1931; Bacteriology, Pathology and Applied Immunology for Nurses, 3d edit., 1939; Clinical Urinalysis, 1939. Editor in chief, Am. Jour. of Clinical Pathology since 1936; asso. editor and abstract editor, Jour. of Laboratory and Clinical Medicine; asso. editor Internat. Med. Digest, Diagnostica e Technica di Laboratorio (Naples). Asso. editor, Cyclopedia of Medicine and contbr. many articles to first and second edits. Contbr. 350 articles to med. jours. of U.S. and Europe. Home: 108 S. Nassau Av., Margate. Office: Atlantic City Hosp., Atlantic City, N.J.

KILE, Orville Merton, agricultural economist, publicist; b. New Vienna, O., Feb. 17, 1886; s. Morris and Morrie (Zinn) K.; B.Sc. in Agr., Ohio State U., 1912; grad. study same; m. Ruth Flora Clinton, Aug. 18, 1925. Agrl. extension lecturer, Ohio State U., 1912-13; with W.Va. U. as editor publs. and lecturer, 1913-16; mgr. ednl. bur. Nat. Assn. Fertilizer Mfrs., 1916-19; asst. Washington rep. Am. Farm Bur. Federation, 1920-21; mem. bd. dirs. Nat. Press Building Corporation. Active in orgn. of farm bloc in Congress. Mem. Nat. Grange, Am. Farm Economic Assn. Methodist. Club: Nat. Press. Author: The Farm Bureau Movement, 1921; The New Agriculture, 1932. Contbr. agrl. and polit. articles to mags. and newspapers. Home: Glen Echo Heights, Md. Office: Nat. Press Bldg., Washington, D.C.

KILEY, Moses E., R.C. bishop, Diocese of Trenton. Was head of St. Vincent de Paul Soc. and Men's Mission, Chicago, 1918; later supt. Asso. Cath. Charities of Chicago Archdiocese and head of Holy Cross Mission; chmn. dirs. group Nat. Charities Assn., 1924-26; spl. adviser Am. College, Rome, Italy, 1926-34; consultore to Vatican's Russian Commn., 1929; bishop of Trenton since Mar. 1934. Address: Trenton, N.J.

KILKER, Adrian Jerome, clergyman, educator; b. Girardville, Pa., Aug. 21, 1901; s. Michael Ambrose and Catherine Loretta (Conville) K.; A.B., St. Charles Sem., Overbrook, Pa., 1924, A.M., same, 1934; J.C.B., Cath. Univ. of America, Washington, D.C., 1925, J.C.L., same, 1925, J.C.D., same, 1926. Ordained priest R.C. Ch. in Phila, Pa., May 29, 1924; curate, Wayne, Pa., 1926-28, St. Patrick's Ch., Phila., Pa., 1928-32, Narberth, Pa., 1932-33; prof. English and fundamental moral theology, St. Charles Sem., Overbrook, Pa., 1933-38; adminstr. St. Monica's Parish, Berwyn, Pa., since 1938; prof. metaphysics and social sci., Immaculata Coll., 1926-34; held positions on Archdiocesan Curia, Defender of the Bond, 1931-33, Prosynodal Judge, 1933-34, Vice-Officialis, 1934-36, Officialis, 1936-38. Roman Catholic. Author: Extreme Unction, 1927. Contbr. articles to eccles. jours. Home: St. Monica's Rectory, Berwyn, Pa.

KILLIAN, John Allen, biochemist; b. Philadelphia, Pa., Jan. 4, 1891; s. Mark and Sarah Anne (Bradley) K.; A.B., Central High Sch., Phila., 1909, St. Joseph's Coll., Phila., 1913; A.M., Fordham U., N.Y. City, 1915, Ph.D., 1921; grad. study Columbia, 1915-16; m. Marie Frances Fitzpatrick, Sept. 1, 1917; children—Francis Mark, Joan Allen, Elizabeth Marie. Instr. chemistry, Fordham U., 1913-16; instr. in biochemistry, N.Y. Post Grad. Med. Sch. and Hosp., 1916-26, prof. 1926-33; established Killian Research Labs. for analytical and research work in biochemistry, bacteriology and pathology, 1933, pres. and dir. since 1933. Served as capt. Sanitary Corps, U.S.A. Mem. Am. Chem. Soc., Am. Soc. Biol. Chemists, Soc. for Exptl. Biology and Medicine, Am. Gastro-Enterological Assn., Am. Urol. Assn., Am. Pub. Health Assn. Republican. Club: Chemists.

Contbr. to tech. jours. Home: 334 Robin Rd., Englewood, N.J. Office: 49 W. 45th St., New York, N.Y.

KILLIAN, John Calvin, church official; b. Reading, Pa., July 6, 1870; s. John D. and Katharine (Helena) K.; ed. Lebanon Valley Coll.; grad. Crozer Theol. Sem., 1894; D.D. Western Baptist Theol. Sem., Portland, Ore., 1934; m. Addie E. Smith, Sept. 3, 1899 (died July 31, 1931); m. 2d, Luella E. Adams, May 27, 1934. Ordained ministry Baptist Church, 1894; pastor Hammonton, N.J., 1894-1898; associate pastor First Ch., Trenton, 1898-1900; pastor successively Alderson, W.Va., New Britain, Pa., Grace Ch., Trenton, until 1910; with Am. Bapt. Publ. Soc., 1910-20; pastor First Ch., Parkersburg, W.Va., 1920-24; field rep. Northern Bapt. Conv., 1924-27; field rep. Am. Bapt. Publ. Soc. since 1927; sec. Colporter-Missionary Work of Am. Bapt. Publ. Soc. and Am. Bapt. Home Mission Soc., 1932. Mason. Home: 868 Stuyvesant Av., Trenton, N.J. Office: 1701 Chestnut St., Philadelphia, Pa.

KILLORAN, Clair John, lawyer; b. Weiser, Ida., Apr. 12, 1905; s. Charles J. and Ada (Percifield) K.; grad. Emmett (Ida.) High Sch., 1922; A.B., U. of Ida., 1928; LL.B., Georgetown U., 1932; m. Anne Regina Biggs, Nov. 30, 1935. Admitted to Dist. of Columbia bar, 1933, Del. bar, 1934; mem. firm Borton, Melson & Killoran, Wilmington, Del., 1934, Melson & Killoran since 1935; dep. atty. gen. of Del., 1937-39; chief dep. atty. gen. for term, 1939-43. Mem. Am. Bar Assn. (chmn. Jr. Bar Conf. for Del. 1939), Kappa Sigma. Republican. Clubs: Wilmington Country, University, Elks (Wilmington). Home: 1500 N. Broom St. Office: Citizens Bank Bldg., Wilmington, Del.

KILMER, Aline (Murray) (Mrs. Joyce Kilmer), author; b. Norfolk, Va., Aug. 1, 1888; d. Kenton C. and Ada (Foster) Murray; ed. Rutgers Prep. School, New Brunswick, N.J., and Vail-Deane School, Elizabeth, N.J.; m. Joyce Kilmer, author, June 9, 1908 (died July 30, 1918); children—Kenton, Deborah (Sister Michael, C.S.B.), Christopher. Author: (poems) Candles That Burn, 1919; Vigils, 1921; Hunting a Hair Shirt and Other Essays, 1923; The Poor King's Daughter, 1925; Emmy, Nicky and Greg, 1927; A Buttonwood Summer, 1929; Selected Poems, 1929. Lecturer on poetry and kindred subjects, 1919-26. Regular contributor to Liberty, 1926-27; occasional contbr. to various mags. Home: Stillwater, N.J.

KILPATRICK, Ellen Perkins, artist; b. Baltimore, Md.; d. William D. and Rebecca H. (Perkins) Kilpatrick; ed. Bryn Mawr Sch., 1888-95, Bryn Mawr Coll., 1895-97; unmarried. Artist, specializing in oil painting. Treas. Ogunquit Art. Assn., 1933-38, mem. bd. of dirs., 1932-38; mem. bd. of dirs. Handicraft Club of Baltmore, and Colonial Dames of America; mem. Southern States Art League, Am. Assn. Professional Artists. Served as Red Cross canteen worker, directrice at Nantes and Bordeaux, France, 1917-18. Presbyterian. Clubs: Mount Vernon, Friends of Art (Baltimore). Home: 1027 St. Paul St., Baltimore, Md.

KILPATRICK, Mary Grace, artist; b. Baltimore, Md.; d. William David and Rebecca H. (Perkins) K.; student Bryn Mawr Sch., Baltimore, Madam Bertrand's Sch., Neuilly-sur-Seine, France; A.B., Bryn Mawr Coll., 1900. Artist since 1927. Vice-chmn. Women's Overseas Service Bur. of Md. Red Cross; vice-chmn. Food Production Com. of Md. Council of Defense (Woman's Div.); sec. Women's Land Army of Md. Chmn. Md. branch Am. Assn. Univ. Women, 1922-25; prof. mem. Ogunquit Art Assn., Municipal Art Soc., Mus. of Art of Baltimore, Colonial Dames America, Southern States Art League. Presbyterian. Clubs: Baltimore Water Color (treas. 1936-39), College (pres. 1922-25), Mt. Vernon (Baltimore). Editor Civic League News, 1922-33. Home: 1027 St. Paul St., Baltimore, Md.

KIM, Gay B(ong), physician; b. Korea, June 5, 1896; s. Hyung Kuen and (Chungjoo) Kim; came to U.S., 1917; student U. of Hawaii, Hawaii, T.H., 1916-17; B.S., Boston Univ., Boston, Mass., 1920, Ch.B., 1921; M.D., Boston Univ. Med. Sch., 1922; grad. study, Johns Hopkins U. Med. Sch. and Hosp., 1923-24; m. Ellen Chung, May 26, 1929; children—Marion Mikiung, Robert Misoo. Interne St. Mary's Hosp., Phila., Pa., 1922-23; pathologist, St. Joseph's Hosp., Paterson, N.J., since 1924. Diplomate of Am. Bd. of Pathology. Mem. Am. Med. Assn., Am. Soc. Clin. Pathologists, Am. Assn. for Study of Neoplastic Diseases, N.J. Soc. of Clin. Pathologists, N.J. State Med. Soc., Passaic Co. Med. Soc. Methodist. Home: 452 Totowa Rd. Office: St. Joseph Hosp., Paterson, N.J.

KIMBALL, Charles Nathaniel, lawyer; b. Parkville, Mo., Sept. 20, 1871; s. Chester Frayer and Sarah Margaret (Boydston) K.; grad. Phillips Acad., Andover, Mass., 1899; student Harvard Law Sch., 1899; m. Mary Jane McGlinchey, July 3, 1904; children—Chester Frayer, Mary Boydston, Walter Sugden. Admitted to Pa. bar, 1894; member of the firm of Kimball & Sugden; active in organizing and operating gas and oil companies in W.Va., Okla., Ill., Kan., Ohio, Wyo. and Ky. since 1907; pres. Old Hundred Gold Mining Co. (Silverton, Colo.), Gen. Petroleum Engrs., Inc.; dir. Star News Pub. Co., Sistersville Tank & Boiler Works, Wells Hotel Corpn., First Tyler Bank & Trust Co., Agnew Torpedo Co., Sistersville Cemetery Assn. Mayor Sistersville, W.Va., 1 term; mem. W.Va. Rep. State Com. since 1916, state chmn., 1934-36; del. at large from W.Va. to Rep. Nat. Conv., Cleveland, 1936; del. from W.Va. to Progressive Nat. Conv., Chicago, 1916. Mem. Am. Bar Assn., Pa. Soc. of Order of Founders and Patriots of America, N.E. Historic Geneal. Soc. (life mem.), Mass. Soc. Mayflower Descs. (life mem.), Gov. and Company of Mass. Bay in New England (life mem.), Theta Nu Epsilon. Republican. Episcopalian. Mason, K.T., Shriner (life mem.), Elk (life mem.). Clubs: Country (Sistersville); Chautauqua (N.Y.) Golf; Harvard of Western Pa. (Pittsburgh). Home: 809 Main St., Sistersville, W.Va.; (summer) Chautauqua, N.Y. Office: Thistle Bldg.

KIMBALL, Fiske, museum dir., architect; b. Newton, Mass., Dec. 8, 1888; s. Edwin Fiske and Ellen Leora (Ripley) K.; A.B. from Harvard, 1909, M.Arch., 1912; Ph.D., University of Michigan, 1915; m. Marie, d. Julius Gœbel, June 7, 1913. Assistant at Harvard, 1900-10; instructor, University of Illinois, later assistant professor architecture and fine arts, University of Michigan, 1912-19; prof. art and architecture, U. of Va., 1919-23; Morse prof. lit. of arts of design, in charge Dept. of Fine Arts, New York University, 1923-25; director Philadelphia Museum of Art since 1925. Has served on editorial bds. of Art and Archæology, Architectural Record, Art Bulletin, Gazette des Beaux-Arts and New England Quarterly; in charge Am. sect. of Allgemeines Künstler Lexikon, 1920-26; chmn. Va. Art Commn., 1920-23; mem. State Bd. for Examination of Engrs. and Architects, 1920-23, Thomas Jefferson Memorial Commn., since 1935; Holder Sachs Research Fellowship, 1916-17; lecturer, Met. Mus., 1919-25, U. of Chicago, 1921, Nat. Acad. Design, 1923-25. Architect of McIntire Amphitheatre, Gymnasium, University Apts., U. of Va.; and many other bldgs.; university architect N.Y. Univ. since 1924. Engaged in restoration of important Am. houses, among them home of Thomas Jefferson, "Monticello," Va., of Robert E. Lee, Stratford, Va., mansions of Fairmount Park, Phila., and on advisory bd. for restoration of Williamsburg, Va., advisory bd. for Rockefeller Center, New York, advisory board Nat. Park Service since 1935; mem. Thomas Jefferson Memorial Commn. Mem. A.I.A. (past pres. Va. Chapter), Am. Assn. of Museums (ex-pres., Assn. of Art Museum Directors, Phi Beta Kappa and Delta Upsilon fraternities. Clubs: Century (New York); Rittenhouse, Art Alliance, T-Square (Phila.); Farmington Country (Va.). Author: Thomas Jefferson, Architect, 1916; A History of Architecture (with G. H. Edgell), 1918; Domestic Architecture of the American Colonies, 1922; American Architecture, 1928; Samuel McIntire. Editor of Foundations of Classic Architecture, 1919. Frequent contbr. lit. and art mags. in America and Europe, also to Ency. Britannica, Webster's Dictionary, Dictionary of Am. Biography, etc. Home: Lemon Hill, Fairmount Park. Office: Philadelphia Museum of Art, Fairmount, Phila., Pa.

KIMBERLY, George Maney, life ins. broker; b. Asheville, N.C., Aug. 1, 1870; s. John and Elizabeth (Maney) K.; student pub. schs., Nashville, Tenn.; m. Alice Roberts, June 3, 1903; children—George M. (dec.), Florence (Mrs. Kimberly Stone), Robert C., Alice R., Lucy Huxley. Employed as clk. N.C.&St.L. Ry., Nashville, Tenn., 1887-96; clk. Withington & Russell Co., Nashville, Tenn., 1896-97; agt. Mutual Benefit Life Ins. Co., Detroit, Mich., 1897-98; gen. agt. Phenix Mutual Life Ins. Co., Baltimore, Md., 1898-1926; life ins. broker at Baltimore, Md., since 1926; dir. New Amsterdam Casualty Co., New York, Am. Indemnity Co., Baltimore, Black & Decker Mfg. Co., Towson, Md.; vice-pres. and dir. Bartgis Bros. Co., Ilchester, Md.; vice-pres. and dir. The Baltimore Co., Baltimore, Md.; dir. Md. Title Securities Co. Served as pres. Catonsville Improvement Assn., 1923-25, 1937-39; vice-pres. Babies Milk Fund Assn. Democrat. Episcopalian. Club: University (Baltimore). Home: "Belle Grove," Catonsville. Office: New Amsterdam Bldg., Baltimore, Md.

KIMBROUGH, Robert Alexander, Jr., obstetrician and gynecologist; b. Jackson, Tenn., Aug. 6, 1899; s. Robert Alexander and Martha (Conn) K.; A.B., Mississippi Coll., Clinton, Miss., 1918; M.D., U. of Pa., 1922; m. Agnes McComb, July 12, 1928; children—Robert Alexander III, William McComb. Interne, U. of Pa. Hosp., 1922-24, resident in gynecology, 1924-25; now chief in obstetrics and gynecology Pa. Hosp., Phila., asst. gynecologist Univ. Hosp., cons. obstetrician Chester Co. Hosp., asso. prof. obstetrics, Grad. Sch. U. of Pa. Mem. Coll. of Physicians of Phila., Am. Gynecol. Soc. Contbr. med. articles to jours. Home: 255 Kent Rd., Wynnewood, Pa. Office: 807 Spruce St., Philadelphia, Pa.

KINCAID, Wallace Patton, banking; b. Summersville, W.Va., Feb. 2, 1886; s. Robert Alexander and Mary (Patton) K.; grad. Greenbrier Mil. Sch., Lewisburg, W.Va., 1908; unmarried. Began as bookkeeper Nicholas County Bank, Summersville, W.Va., 1901, asst. cashier, 1902-06; asst. cashier First Nat. Bank, Richwood, W.Va., 1908-09; resigned to organize Farmers & Merchants Bank of Summersville, W.Va., and cashier since opening, 1910, exec. vice pres. and cashier since 1933. Democrat. Presbyn. Mason (K. T., Shriner). O.E.S. Office: Farmers & Merchants Bank, Summersville, W.Va.

KINCAID, William Morris, musician and teacher; b. Minneapolis, Minn., Apr. 26, 1895; s. William Morris and Ellen (Douglas) K.; ed. pub. schs., Honolulu, T.H., 1901-07, high sch., Charlotte, N.C., 1907-11, Inst. of Mus. Art, 1911-16; m. Helen Gooding, June 12, 1920. Mem. N.Y. Symphony Orchestra, 1914-18; mem. N.Y. Chamber Music Soc., 1919-21; mem. Phila. Orchestra since 1921, solo flutist; mem. faculty and teacher flute, Curtis Inst. of Music since 1923. Home: 247 S. Juniper St., Philadelphia, Pa.

KIND, Paul A., mfr. gelatins; b. Aussig, Bohemia, Apr. 22, 1895; brought to U.S., 1900; s. Maurice and Hermine (Fischl) K.; student Camden (N.J.) City Schs., Ridley Coll. (St. Catherine, Ont.) and Philadelphia Coll. Pharmacy and Sciences; m. Edith M. Clement, Apr. 21, 1919; children—Edith H., Eleanora M., Paul A. Began as chemist Kind & Knox Gelatine Co. (mfg. affiliate of Knox Gelatine Co., Johnstown, N.Y.), gelatine mfrs., 1913, treas. and gen. mgr. since 1919; dir. Haddonfield Nat. Bank, Northern Bldg. & Loan Soc. Entered U.S. Army, Sept. 1917, serving 20 mos.; now major U.S. Army Specialists Res. Trustee Philadelphia Coll. Pharmacy and Science. Mem. Am. Chem. Soc., Alpha Sigma. Clubs: Union League (Philadelphia); Chemist (New York); Army and Navy (Washington, D.C.); Tavistock Country (Tavistock, N.J.). Home: Kings Highway, Audubon, N.J. Office: care Knox Gelatine Co., N. 5th St. above Erie St., Camden, N.J.

KINDER, James S., prof. edn.; b. Millersville, Mo., Oct. 19, 1895; s. Robert F. and Emma (Reynolds) K.; B.S., Southeast Mo. State

Coll., 1921; student Univ. Coll. of Wales, Gt. Britain, 1919, U. of Mo., summer 1922; A.M., Columbia U., 1923, Ph.D., 1934; m. Mary Clare Lett, Sept. 11, 1919. Engaged in teaching high schs., prin. and supt. schs., Mo., 1916-17, Utah, 1919-20; vis. prof. Southwestern La. Inst., Lafayette, La., 1923, 26, Geneva Coll., summer 1933, U. of Pittsburgh, summers 1925, 37, 38; prof. edn. and head dept. edn., Pa. Coll. for Women, Pittsburgh, Pa., since 1923; dir. PCW Film Service since 1938. Served in U.S. Army, 1918-19, with A.E.F. in France. Mem. Nat. Edn. Assn., Pa. State Edn. Assn., Am. Assn. Univ. Profs., Phi Delta Kappa. Democrat. Mason. Author: The Internal Administration of the Liberal Arts College, 1934. Contbr. articles to edn. jours. Home: 5839 Beacon St., Pittsburgh, Pa.

KING, Caroline B(lanche), editor and author; b. Chicago, Ill.; d. Robert William and Caroline (Warren) Campion; educated Lake View High School, Chicago, and under private instruction; m. J. M. McIlvaine King (dec.); 1 dau. living, Mrs. Mary Grace Ramey. Was Sunday editor of Phila. Press, 1909-13; editorial staff Evening Telegraph, 1913-17; apptd. U.S.A. dietitian by Surgeon Gen. Gorgas, 1917 (first dietitian apptd.); lectured and conducted soldiers' cooking classes; went to France with Base Hosp. 116, Mar. 1918; asso. editor The Country Gentleman since 1924. Mem. Phila. Art Alliance, Nat. Home Econ. Assn. Republican. Episcopalian. Author: Caroline King's Cook Book, 1917; Rosemary Makes a Garden. Home: "Arborcote," Beechwood, Philadelphia, Pa.

KING, Charles Daly, author; b. New York, N.Y., Feb. 17, 1895; s. Robert Courtney and Ella Bourdette (Daly) K.; grad. Newark Acad., 1912; A.B., Yale, 1916; A.M., Columbia, 1928; m. Mildred Georgina Sisson, of Maplewood, N.J., Oct. 23, 1923; 1 dau., Valerie Daly. Gen. partner Robert C. King & Co., factors, New York, 1921-26; treas. Hampton, Weeks & Marston, Inc., advertising, New York, 1931-33; now writer. Served as 2d lt., 128 F.A., 35th Div., U.S. Army, 1917-19, with A.E.F.; 1st lt. F.A. Reserve, 1921-25; capt. 391st F.A., Reserve, 1925-26. Asso. mem. Am. Psychol. Soc.; mem. N.Y. Acad. Sciences, A.A.A.S., Empire State Soc., S.A.R., Soc. Colonial Wars in State of N.J., Phi Beta Kappa. Clubs: Yale (New York); Essex County Country (West Orange, N.J.); Orange Lawn Tennis (South Orange); Authors (London); Bermuda Tennis, Somerset Lawn Tennis and Croquet (Bermuda). Author: Beyond Behaviorism, 1923; Integrative Psychology (with E. H. Marston), 1931; Psychology of Consciousness, 1932; Obelisks at Sea, 1932; Obelisks en Route, 1933; Obelisks Fly High, 1934; The Curious Mr. Tarrant, 1935; Careless Corpse, 1937; Arrogant Alibi, 1938. Contbr. to publs. of London and U.S. Home: 119 Woodland Av., Summit, N.J.; Cedar Hill, Somerset, Bermuda.

KING, Charles Glen, chemist; b. Entiat, Wash., Oct. 22, 1896; s. Charles Clement and Mary (Bookwalter) K.; B.S., Wash. State Coll., 1918; M.S., U. of Pittsburgh, 1920, Ph.D., 1923; grad. study Columbia, 1926-27, Cambridge (Eng.) U., 1929-30; m. Hilda Bainton, Sept. 11, 1919; children—Dorothy, Robert Bainton, Kendall Willard. By-products specialist, State of Wash., 1918-19; instr. chemistry, U. of Pittsburgh, 1920-26, asst. prof., 1927-30, prof. since 1930; research asst. Columbia, 1926-27; isolated vitamin C, 1932; synthesis of vitamin C, 1933; DeLamar lecturer, Johns Hopkins, 1936. Served as pvt. 12th Inf., Machine Gun Co., 1918, World War. Mem. Am. Chem. Soc. (sec. 1935, chmn. biol. div. 1936, chmn. Pittsburgh section 1938), Am. Soc. Biol. Chemists (sec. since 1938), Am. Inst. Nutrition, Am. Inst. Chemists, A.A.A.S., Am. Dairy Science Assn., Am. Public Health Assn., Sigma Xi, Phi Beta Kappa. Baptist. Mason. Clubs: Chemists, University. Home: 1015 Celeron Av., Pittsburgh, Pa.

KING, Helen Dean, zoölogist; b. Owego, Tioga Co., N.Y., Sept. 27, 1869; d. George Alonzo and Leonora Louise (Dean) K.; A.B., Vassar, 1892; fellow in biology, Bryn Mawr, 1896-97, A.M., Ph.D., 1899; univ. fellow for research in zoölogy, P. of Pa.; unmarried. Student asst. in biology, Vassar, 1894-95; teacher science, Baldwin Sch., Bryn Mawr, Pa., 1899-1907; asst. in anatomy, 1909-10, asso., 1910-13, asst. prof. embryology, 1913-27, Wistar Inst., Phila., mem. same, 1927—. Fellow A.A.A.S.; mem. American Society Zoölogists (vice-president, 1937), American Society Naturalists, Wistar Institute (mem. advisory bd.), Soc. Exptl. Biology and Medicine, American Association Anatomists, Marine Biol. Lab. Assn. (Woods Hole, Mass.), Am. Genetic Assn., Eugenics Research Assn., Phi Beta Kappa, Sigma Xi. Republican. Episcopalian. Contbr. on regeneration, sex determination, inbreeding, domestication, etc. Home: 17 Elliott Av., Bryn Mawr, Pa.

KING, Henry Stouffer, banker; b. Baltimore, Dec. 24, 1849; s. Henry S., Sr., and Susan (Johnson) K.; ed. St. Timothy's Hall, Catonsville, Md.; m. Ella Wynn, Nov. 8, 1877; children—Henry W., R. Glenn, Ralph Ashley (dec.), Roy Livingston (dec.), Edward Stouffer. Original incorporator, 1894, and first and only pres. Security Storage & Trust Co., Baltimore; original incorporator, Hopkins Place Savings Bank. Incorporator and prin. organizer Md. Asylum and Training Sch. for Feeble Minded; pres. Rosewood State Training Sch. Presbyn. Home: (country) Riderwood, Baltimore County, Md.; (city) 2921 N. Calvert St., Baltimore, Md.

KING, Howell Atwater, educator; b. Manchester-by-the-Sea, Mass., Sept. 8, 1896; s. Edward Gilbert and Theodora (Atwater) K.; B.C.S., U. of Md., 1925; D.C.S., Chicago Law Sch., 1931; m. Gladys C. Passano, Jan. 15, 1920; children—Charlotte Howell, Mary-Louise Atwater, Gladys Theodora, Arabelle Knight. Appt. asst. dean U. of Md., 1924; exec. sec. and prof. accounting, U. of Baltimore, 1925, exec. dean, 1925-33, pres., Nov. 1933-Jan. 1936, also sec. bd. trustees; City Service Commissioner, Baltimore; special rep. U.S. Treasury Department since 1936. Served in World War 3 yrs.; 29th divisional citation for bravery. Mem. Nat. Assn. Cost Accountants, Nat. Association American Law Schools (pres.), Pi Gamma Mu (lt. gov. Md. chapter), Pi Delta Tau, Delta Sigma Pi. Mem. advisory com. Baltimore City Democrats. Episcopalian. Clubs: University, Sovereign, Tall Story (dir., treas.). Home: 4303 Keswick Rd. Office: 847 N. Howard St., Baltimore, Md.

KING, James Wesley, lawyer; b. Burrell, Armstrong Co., Pa., Sept. 29, 1859; s. George and Mary (Fiscus) K.; m. Ida Lillian Cooper, May 25, 1887 (dec.); children—James Perry, Fennimore Cooper. Admitted to Armstrong County bar, 1886; in gen. practice of law, 1886-1914; president judge Armstrong County, 1914-24; again practiced law since 1924; dir. Armstrong County Trust Co. Ex-pres. Armstrong County Bar Assn.; mem. Armstrong County Hist. Soc. (pres.), Pa. Hist. Soc. Mem. exec. bd. and lay pres. of church council St. John's Evang. Lutheran Ch. Contbr. to mag. of Western Pa. Hist. Soc. Home: N. McKean St. Office: Empire Bldg. Market St., Kittanning, Pa.

KING, Jessie L.; instr. physiology, Goucher Coll., 1911-15, asso. prof., 1915-19, prof. since 1919. Address: Goucher College, Baltimore, Md.

KING, John Theodore, physician; b. Baltimore, Md., Sept. 18, 1889; s. John Theodore and Mary B. (Gees) K.; A.B., Princeton U., 1910; M.D., Johns Hopkins U. Med. Sch., 1914; m. Charlotte M. Baker, Sept. 14, 1916; children—John T., III, Joseph D. B., Virginia M., James Sydney. Interne Johns Hopkins Hosp., Baltimore, 1914-16; engaged in consultation practice of medicine, Baltimore, since 1919; asso. prof. of medicine, Johns Hopkins U., 1939; visiting physician, Union Memorial Hosp. since 1925, Bon Secours Hosp. since 1924, Hosp. for Women of Md. since 1923, Johns Hopkins Hosp. since 1938; cons. physician, Sydenham Hosp. since 1925; physician in chief, City Hosps. since 1939. Trustee Buckingham Sch., Buckeystown, Md., Sheppard & Enoch Pratt Hosp., Towson, Md. Fellow Am. Coll. Physicians; mem. Am., Southern, Baltimore City med. socs., Assn. Am. Physicians, Congress of Am. Phys. and Surgs. (sec.), Am. Soc. for Clin. Investigation, Am. Clin. and Climatol. Assn., Med. and Chirurg. Faculty of Md., Interurban Clin. Club, Phi Kappa Psi, Sigma Xi, Alpha Omega Alpha. Democrat. Clubs: Maryland (Baltimore); Gibson Island (Gibson Island). Home: 219 W. Lanvale St. Office: 1210 Eutaw Pl., Baltimore, Md.

KING, Joseph Thomas, pres. First Nat. Bank of Lawrenceville; b. Canton, Pa., Jan. 21, 1876; s. Patrick and Bridget (Dwyer) K.; student pub. schs.; m. Martha Louise Rooney, Sept. 15, 1903; children—Hugh Carney, Allan Edward, Joseph Thomas, Mary Ella, Martha Louise. Telegraph operator and sta. agt., Lawrenceville, Pa., 1895-1906; in mercantile business, Lawrenceville, 1906-36; pres. First Nat. Bank of Lawrenceville since 1930. Chmn. Dem. County Com. Elk. Home: Main St. Office: First National Bank of Lawrenceville, Lawrenceville, Pa.

KING, Karl Clarence; b. Plevna, Kan., Jan. 26, 1897; s. Clarence William and Della (Parker) K.; student Kan. State Teachers Coll., 1915-16, Columbia U., 1918-19, U. of Pa., 1920-21; m. Lora Gould, Sept. 1, 1921; children—Lora Eileen, Karla Wanda. Reporter Daily Drovers Telegram, Kansas City, Mo., 1917-18; reporter during college work in New York and Phila.; vice-pres. and gen. mgr. Starkey Farms Co., Morrisville, Pa., 1922-29; since 1929 vice-pres. and gen. mgr. King Farms Co., one of largest vegetable farms, annual payroll being over $300,000; vice-pres. and gen. mgr. King Supply Co., farm supplies, trucks and machinery; dir. Vulcanized Rubber Co., Morrisville Bank. Served as chief quarter master, naval aviation, during World War. Mem. Sigma Nu, Pi Kappa Delta. Republican. Methodist. Clubs: Penn Manor (pres.), Rotary (Morrisville); Carteret (Trenton, N.J.); Trenton Country. Address: Morrisville, Pa.

KING, LeRoy Albert, university professor; b. at York, Pa., August 10, 1886; s. Albert and Arabella (Stoner) K.; grad. Millersville (Pa.) State Normal Sch., 1905; B.S., Teachers Coll. (Columbia), 1910; A.M., Columbia, 1916; Ph.D., U. of Pa., 1920; m. Estella Adelle Hoffman, August 24, 1915; children—John Albert, Joseph Hoffman, Jane Louise. Prof. edn. and supt. Training Sch., Central State Normal Sch., Lock Haven, Pa., 1910-14; supt. schs. in Pa., 1914-17; instr., U. of Pa., 1917-26, prof. ednl. administration since 1926; prof. edn. summer sessions State Coll. of Pa., Univ. of Calif., U. of Southern Calif., University of Pittsburgh, Elizabethtown College; lecturer U. of N. Dak.; dir. Bur. of Ednl. Measurements, and sec. Schoolmen's Week Ednl. Conv., U. of Pa., since 1917, also editor proc. same. Mem. Pa. State Council of Edn., 1928-36, chmn. finance commn. Pres. Pa. Pub. Edn. and Child Labor Assn. Mem. Ednl. Research Assn., N.E.A., Pa. State Ednl. Assn., Nat. Soc. for Study of Edn., Nat. Soc. Coll. Teachers of Edn., Phi Delta Kappa, Kappa Phi Kappa, Acacia. Republican. Presbyn. Mason. Clubs: Undine Barge, Lenape, Schoolmen's (Philadelphia). Writer of Status of the Rural Teacher in Pennsylvania (Bull., U.S. Bureau Edn.), 1921; (joint) Survey of Fiscal Policies of State of Pa. in Field of Edn., 1922; Rept. on Appropriations and Subsidies (Ednl. Survey of Pa.), 1925. Participated in series of ednl. surveys, Bethlehem, 1937, Philadelphia, 1937. Contbr. to ednl. periodicals. Home: 1 Shirley Rd., Narberth, Pa.

KING, Morland, prof. elec. engring; b. Brooklyn, N.Y., Nov. 22, 1881; s. Samuel Warner and Mary Ellen (Jeffrey) K.; B.S. in E.E. (commencement honors and Blatchford oratorical prize), Union Coll., Schenectady, N.Y., 1905, M.E.E., 1906, hon. Sc.D., 1930; m. Angelica Van Vranken Olmstead, Sept. 2, 1913; children—Margaret Leslie, Sherwood, Angelica Van Vranken. Instr. in elec. engring., Union Coll., 1906-14, asst. prof., 1914-20; asso. prof., Lafayette Coll., Easton, Pa., 1920-21, prof. and head of dept. elec. engring. since 1921; with testing dept. Gen. Electric Co., Schenectady, summer 1905, transformer engring. office, summer 1907, standardizing lab., summer 1916, radio engring. dept., summers 1917, 18, 19; with motor power dept. Interborough Rapid Transit Co., summer 1915; supervisor student training, Internat. Motor Co., summer 1928, 29. Fellow Am. Inst. E.E.; mem. Soc. Promotion Engring. Edn., Am. Assn. Univ. Profs., Alpha Delta Phi, Sigma Xi,

Tau Beta Pi. Republican. Unitarian. Clubs: Engineers Club of Lehigh Valley; Country Club of Northampton County. Home: 6 E. Campus, Easton, Pa.

KING, Robert Waldo, physicist; b. Sioux Falls, S.D., May 13, 1890; s. William Leonard and Harriet (Lucas) K.; A.B., Cornell, 1912, Ph.D., 1915; m. Dorothy Muriel Babcock, Dec. 28, 1922; children—Robert Waldo, Jerome Babcock. Instr. physics, Cornell U., 1913-17; physicist Western Electric Co., 1917-20; engr. Am. Telephone & Telegraph Co., 1920-27; asst. dir. publ. Bell Telephone Labs., 1927-29; asst. tech. rep. in Europe, Am. Telephone & Telegraph Co., 1929-35; assistant to president Bell Telephone Labs. since 1935. Fellow American Physical Society, A.A.A.S.; mem. Am. Inst. E.E., New York Electrical Soc. (1st v.p. 1938-39), Sigma Xi. Clubs: Racquets (Short Hills, N.J.); Salmagundi (New York). Unitarian. Republican. Editor Bell System Tech. Jour., 1922-28, 1935 —. Author: Profitable Science in Industry. Contbr. papers on tech. subjects. Home: Hemlock Rd., Short Hills, N.J. Office: 195 Broadway, New York, N.Y.

KING, Victor Louis; b. Nashville, Tenn., Mar. 14, 1886; s. Louis Andrew and Christine (Hartman) K.; student Kansas City (Mo.) Central High School, 1899-1903, Dartmouth College, Hanover, N.H., 1903-06; Ph.D., U. of Zurich, Switzerland, 1911; grad. study Federal Polytechnikum, Zurich, Switzerland, 1911-12; m. Eugènie Catherine Ruegger, Sept. 7, 1907; children—Victor Ruegger, Jamie Hartman, Gene Giovanni, Thomas Andrew. Smelter supt. Vermont Copper Co., South Stafford, Vt., 1906-09; works mgr. Hoffman LaRoche Chem. Co., Grenzach, Germany, 1912-15, built several factories for Thomas A. Edison, Inc., West Orange, N.J., 1915; tech. dir. Charles Pfizer & Co., Brooklyn, N.Y., 1916; tech. dir. Calco Chemical Company, Inc., Bound Brook, N.J., since 1918. Built phenol and picric acid plants and served as chief of dyestuffs section War Industries Bd., during World War. Dir. Carlstadt Mutual Bldg. & Loan Assn.; mem. of Council of Am. Inst. Chem. Engrs.; Amateur Fencers Assn. of America; Phi Gamma Delta. Awarded Silver Beaver by Boy Scouts America, 1936. Congregationalist. Mason (K.T.). Clubs: Chemists, New York City; Raritan Valley Country Club, Sommerville, N.J.; Lavallette Yacht Club, Lavallette, N.J. Home: Middlebrook Road. Office: Calco Chemical Co., Inc., Bound Brook, N.J.

KING, Warren Thomas, public relations counsellor; b. Little Rock, Ark., Sept. 26, 1890; s. John Thomas and Mary Alleluiah (Rogers) K.; grad. Little Rock High Sch., 1907, and business college, 1908; LL.B., U. of Ark., 1910; LL.B., Columbia, 1912; m. Lucia Featherstone, Aug. 23, 1927; children—Lucia Featherstone, Mary Rogers, Phoebe Douglas. Admitted to Ark. bar, 1912, and practiced in Little Rock, 1912-14; sec. Pub. Service Bureau, Camden, Ark., 1915-17, Chamber of Commerce, Greenwood, S.C., 1919-21; farmer Pulaski County, Ark., 1921-23; asst. mgr. Little Rock C. of C., 1923-25; real estate, Little Rock, Ark., 1925-26; dir. of civic development, Baltimore, 1927-38; organization service, public relations, promotional campaigns, business research, since 1939. Served in inf., U.S. Army, 1917-19; disch. as capt. Democrat. Presbyterian. Home: 10 Linden Terrace, Towson, Md. Office: Mercantile Trust Bldg., Baltimore, Md.

KING, Willard Vinton, banker; b. Brooklyn, Nov. 3, 1868; s. William Vinton and Belle F. (Boyd) K.; A.B., Columbia, 1889; m. Mary Spingler van Beuren, Apr. 26, 1904. Began as messenger Produce Exchange Bank, New York, 1890, later with Continental Trust Co., of which became sec., 1898, v.p., 1901 (company merged with New York Security and Trust Co., 1904, later known as New York Trust Co.); pres., 1908-23, Columbia Trust Co., which absorbed Knickerbocker Trust Co.; now retired; dir. 2d Av. Ry., Aztec Land & Cattle Co., Manati Sugar Co., New York Life Insurance Co., United Artists Theatre Corpn., First Nat. Bank of Morristown, N.J. Trustee Columbia University, Archæol. Inst. America, New York Assn. for the Blind, Museum of American Indian. Served as pvt. to sergt. maj., 22d Regt. N.Y.N.G., 1891-96. Mem. Phi Beta Kappa, Delta Upsilon. Protestant. Clubs: University, Columbia Univ. Author: Benefits and Evils of the Stock Exchange, 1913. Home: Convent, N.J. Office: 115 Broadway, New York, N.Y.

KING, Wyncie, illustrator, caricaturist; b. Covington, Ga., Sept. 21, 1884; s. George Whitfield and Susie Davis (Brown) K.; ed. pub. schs.; m. Hortense Flexner, Apr. 30, 1919. Cartoonist with Nashville Banner and Nashville Daily News, 1905; with Louisville Courier Jour., Chicago Record Herald and New York Evening World, 1905-10; cartoons, caricatures and feature drawing with Louisville Herald, 1911-21; made caricatures for editorial page, Public Ledger, Phila., 1921-22; worked for Public Ledger, Life, Judge and New York Times; illustrator Saturday Evening Post, 1925. Water color caricatures exhibited at Louisville Art Assn., Art Inst. Chicago, Pa. Acad. Fine Arts, etc. Mem. Artists Guild. Clubs: Franklin Inn, Philobiblon, Print Club of Phila. Home: Millbank Rd., Bryn Mawr, Pa.

KINGDON, Arthur Frederick, lawyer; b. London, Eng., Dec. 2, 1889; s. Abraham and Elizabeth Ann (Crawley) K.; came to U.S., 1907, naturalized 1916; student pvt. and pub. schs. (Eng. and Can.), summers, W.Va. Univ. extension Columbia University and LaSalle Extension University; m. Alva Retz (dec.); children—Arthur and Frederick (twins), Kathryn (Mrs. Richard Framoton), Helen, Ann. Admitted to W.Va. bar and engaged in gen. practice of law at Bluefield; later admitted to Va. bar; referee in bankruptcy, 1917-23. Mem. Am. Law Inst., Am. Bar Assn., Va. State Bar Assn., W.Va. State Bar Assn. (pres. 1930), Mercer Co. Bar Assn. (pres. 1924-25). Republican. Presbyn. Club: Lions of Bluefield. Home: 1100 College Av. Office: Law & Commerce Bldg., Bluefield, W.Va.

KINGDON, Frank, college pres., clergyman; b. London, Eng., Feb. 27, 1894; s. John and Matilda (Caunt) K.; A.B., Boston U., 1920; post grad. work Harvard, 1920-21, Mich. State Coll., 1926; m. Gertrude Littlefield, Feb. 27, 1915; children—John Gilmore, Frank Oliver, David Charlton, Gertrude Matilda, Barrie Knight. Came to America, 1912, naturalized, 1918. Ordained Meth. ministry, 1912; member East Maine Conf., 1912-16, New England Southern Conf., 1916-20, New England Conf., 1920-23, Michigan Conf., 1923-28, Newark Conf., since 1928; president Dana College, Newark, N.J., 1934-35; pres. U. of Newark, 1936. Campaign chmn. Newark Community Chest, 1935, 36 and 37; pres. Welfare Federation, Newark, N.J.; chmn. Save The Children Fund of America; mem. bd. of trustees N.J. Conf. of Social Work, Drew U. (Madison, N.J.), Essex (N.J.) County Jr. Coll., Centenary Collegiate Inst. (Hackettstown, N.J.), Newark Mus. Mem. Phi Beta Kappa, Kappa Chi. Clubs: Rotary, Athletic, Contemporary, Deer Lake, Essex, Down Town. Author: Humane Religion, 1930; When Half-Gods Go, 1933. Contbr. articles, verse. Home: 9 Clearview Terrace, W. Orange, N.J. Office: 37 Fulton St., Newark, N.J.

KINGMAN, Russell Barclay, pres. Metal Textile Corpn.; b. East Orange, N.J., Dec. 17, 1884; s. Thomas Sewall and Anna Helena (Jenks) K.; grad. Newark Acad., 1903; m. Ethel Kimberley Spencer, Dec. 17, 1908; children—Elsa (Mrs. F. Stark Newberry), Barclay Alden. Began learning tanning trade, 1903; employed by C. L. & R. E. Smith, 1903-05, Comstock Hoff Co., 1905-06; partner Walton Advertising Agency, Boston, 1906-08; advertising mgr. Rogers & Wise Publications, 1908-11; New England representative Condé Nast Publications, 1911-13, Doubleday, Page & Co., 1913, Curtis Pub. Co., 1913-18; pres. Purity Cross, Inc., 1918-24; founder 1924, and since pres. and dir. Metal Textile Corpn.; pres. and dir. Metal Textile Corpn. of Canada, Ltd.; dir. Boston Food Products Co., Sinfra Corpn. Created and produced emergency trench ration, widely used in "No Man's Land" during World War. Decorated Chevalier Legion of Honor (French), 1939. Trustee Bureau of Associated Charities;

hon. pres. New Jersey Symphony Orchestra; hon. mem. Local 16, A.F. of M., A.F. of L. Mem. French Inst. in U.S., Soc. Mayflower Descendants, Beethoven Assn. (New York); v.p. New England Soc. of the Oranges; treas. U.S. Lawn Tennis Assn. (mem. advisory and finance, Davis Cup, Internat. Play, Tennis Supplies, membership and sectional advisory coms.); pres. Alliance Francaise des Oranges; hon. mem. Nat. Canners Assn. Republican. Episcopalian. Clubs: Rock Spring Country (bd. govs.), Berkeley Tennis (v.p.), both of Orange; Beethoven Assn., Bankers, Bohemians (New York). Collector and player of ancient musical instruments; amateur cellist, concertized coast to coast in America and in Europe. Inventor about 50 products and processes. Home: 382 Oakwood Av., Orange, N.J. Office: 4 Central Av., West Orange, N.J.

KINGSBURY, Dana William, physician and surgeon; b. Luzerne Co., Pa., July 12, 1852; s. Daniel H. and Lucy E. (Chapin) K.; M.D., Coll. of Phys. and Surgs., Baltimore, Md., 1882; m. Emma S. Sharpless, Dec. 31, 1882; children—Oscar J. (M.D.), Eben P., Russell J., Arthur, Erma (Mrs. Thomas Muir), Marjorie (wife of Dr. L.C. Rummage), Marian (Mrs. Luke C. Christian). Engaged in gen. practice of medicine and surgery at Nanticoke, Pa., continuously since 1882; surgeon Pa. R.R. since 1882; vice-pres. Nanticoke Nat. Bank. Served as pres. Bd. No. 9 Luzerne Co. during World War. Mem. A.M.A., Pa. Med. Soc., Luzerne Co. Med. Soc. Republican. Methodist. Home: 137 State St., Nanticoke, Pa.

KINGSBURY, Edwin Foster, physicist; b. Hamilton, N.Y., Dec. 24, 1886; s. Edwin Lemuel and Sarah (Foster) K.; student Colgate Acad., Hamilton, N.Y., 1902-06; B.S., Colgate U., 1910; m. Caroline Ellen Woodcock, June 29, 1912; children—Winfred Foster, Helen Edwina. Engr. and physicist United Gas Improvement Co., Phila., 1910-18; engr. Eastman Kodak Co., Rochester, N.Y., 1919-20; physicist Western Electric Co., New York, 1920-25; physicist Bell Telephone Labs., New York, since 1925. Served as 1st lt., later capt., Air Service, Bureau of Aircraft Production, U.S. Army, 1918-19. Awarded Edward Longstreth Medal of Merit by Franklin Inst., 1919. Fellow A.A.A.S., Am. Phys. Soc.; mem. Optical Soc. American. Methodist. Home: 121 Woodward Av., Rutherford, N.J. Office: 463 West St., New York, N.Y.

KINGSBURY, Franklin Laflin, research chemist; b. Indianapolis, Ind., Aug. 13, 1900; s. Frank Enoch and Pearl Viola (Laflin) K.; B.S. in Chem. Engring. (with special honors), U. of Ill., 1924; m. Leatha Holliday, June 3, 1933; 1 son, John Franklin. Began as control chemist, 1924; chief chemist and chem. engr., Titanium Pigment Co., St. Louis, Mo., 1925-38; research chemist, Titanium Div., Nat. Lead Co., South Amboy, N.J., since 1938. Mem. A.A.A.S., Am. Chem. Soc., Tribe of Illini. Home: 666 River Rd., Fair Haven, N.J.

KINGSBURY, Susan Myra, social economist; b. San Pablo, Calif., Oct. 18, 1870; d. Willard B. and Helen (De Lamater) K.; A.B., College of Pacific, 1890, LL.D., 1937; A.M., Leland Stanford Jr. Univ., 1899; Ph.D., Columbia, 1905; LL.D., Mills College, 1937. Teacher history, Lowell High Sch., San Francisco, 1892-1900; instr. history, Vassar Coll., 1904-05; dir. investigation for Mass. Commn. on Industrial and Tech. Edn., on relation of children to industries, 1906; prof. economics, Simmons Coll., Boston, 1906-15; Carola Woerishofer prof. social economy and dir. Carola Woerishofer graduate dept. of social economy and social research, Bryn Mawr College, 1915-1936, now emeritus. Mem. Am. Sociol. Assn., Kappa Alpha Theta, Phi Beta Kappa. Author: (with M. Fairchild) Factory, Family and Woman in the Soviet Union, 1935. Editor: (series) Economic Relations of Women; Records of the Virginià Company of London (Library of Congress). Home: Bryn Mawr, Pa.

KINKEAD, Eugene F., ex-congressman; b. in Ireland, Mar. 27, 1876; s. Thomas C. and Nora (Barrett) K.; came to America with parents, 1880; A.M., Seton Hall Coll., N.J., 1895;

LL.D., St. Peter's Coll., Jersey City, N.J.; m. Anna O'Neill, Sept. 29, 1909. V.p. Jersey Rys. Advertising Co., Orange Publishing Co.; chmn. exec. com. Hibernia Trust Company (now Colonial Trust Company) of New York. Alderman, Jersey City, and pres. board of aldermen, 1898; mem. 61st and 62d Congresses (1909-13), 9th N.J. Dist., and 63d Congress (1913-15), 8th Dist.; sheriff Hudson Co., N.J., 1914-17. Settled Standard Oil Strike in Bayonne, N.J., 1915, when 9,300 men were out; as a result of the settlement an 8-hour day was established by the Standard Oil Co. for the first time in its history and in addition the men received 10% increase in wages. Democrat. In mil. service for period of the war; commd. maj. Mil. Intelligence Div. U.S.A. Home: South Orange, N.J. Office: 57 William St., New York, N.Y.

KINNARD, Leonard Hummel, telephone official; b. Harrisburg, Pa., Sept. 5, 1869; s. Leonard Hervey and Mary Elizabeth (Hummel) K.; ed. high sch. and business coll.; m. Sarah Elizabeth Peters, Apr. 4, 1893; 1 son, Leonard Richard. Mgr. Pa. Telephone Co. (Bell), respectively, at Carlisle, Lancaster and Harrisburg, 1891-96; div. supt., Harrisburg, 1896-1902, gen. supt., 1902, gen. mgr., 1902-07; at Phila. with Bell Telephone Co. of Pa. and associated cos. since 1907, advancing to pres. Sept. 1919, chairman board, 1933-34; retired; dir. Bell Telephone Co., Pa. Co. for Ins. of Lives and Granting Annuities, Fidelity-Phila. Trust Co., Pa. Salt Mfg. Co., Barber Asphalt Co., Inc., Pa. Fire Ins. Co. During World War mem. Phila. Com. on Nat. Defense, Advisory Com. on Purchase of Army Supplies, and Utilities sect. of War Chest Com.; mem. advisory bd. Phila. Ordnance Dist. Mem. bd. mgrs. Franklin Inst. Mem. Phila. Telephone Pioneers America (pres. 1924). Democrat. Lutheran. Clubs: Rittenhouse, Pocono, Pocono Lake Preserve (Pa.). Home: Wister Rd., Wynnewood, Montgomery Co., Pa. Office: 1500 Walnut St., Philadelphia, Pa.

KINNEY, Antoinette Brown; b. N.Y. State; d. Joseph Addison and Mary J. (Daniels) Brown; B.L., U. of Mich., 1887; m. Clesson S. Kinney, Dec. 1, 1889 (dec.); 1 son, Selwyn Perez. Organizer Utah State Federation Women's Clubs; hon. v.p. Gen. Fed. Women's Clubs; chmn. legislative com. of State and City Federation; organizer and mgr. Federation Coll. Loan Fund; past. pres. League of Women Voters of Utah; and actively identified with other women's orgns. and officer or dir. various corpns. Mem. Utah State Senate, 1919 and 1921; regent U. of Utah; dir. State Humane Soc.; past pres. Assn. Collegiate Alumnæ; regent D.A.R. Republican. Unitarian. Home: 6729 Penn Av., Pittsburgh, Pa.

KINSLEY, Carl, electrical engr. and physicist; b. Lansing, Michigan, Nov. 25, 1870; s. William Wirt and Mary (Jewell) K.; A.B., Oberlin, 1893, A.M., 1896; M.E., Cornell U., 1894; scholar, Johns Hopkins, 1898-99; student Cavendish Lab., Cambridge, Eng., 1905; m. Harriet Buchly, June 1, 1901 (died Oct. 19, 1910); m. 2d, Prudence Ellis, June 7, 1913; children—Colony, Stephanie, Penelope, and Roger (dec.). Instructor in physics and electrical engineering, Washington Univ., 1894-99; elec. expert for War Dept., 1899-1901; fellow in physics, 1901, instr., 1902, asst. prof., 1903, asso. prof., 1909-19, U. of Chicago. Served in U.S. Army, as maj. Signal Corps, Dec. 1917-Aug. 1919; detailed to Gen. Staff and made chief of Sect. 10 of Mil. Intelligence Division, for radio, telegraph and telephone operations; cons. engr., elec. research and development, 1919—. Republican. Congregationalist. Fellow A.A.A.S., Am. Physical Soc., Am. Inst. Elec. Engrs.; mem. Am. Soc. Testing Materials, Sigma Xi. Clubs: Cosmos (Washington); Engineers (New York); Plainfield Tennis. Has invented methods and apparatus of printing telegraph systems, storage batteries, radio circuits and method for non-destructive testing of steel. Contbr. engring. jours. and scientific mags. on radio, telegraphy, alternating currents, testing of steel, etc. Home: 508 Belvidere Av., Plainfield, N.J. Office: 32 West 40th St., New York, N.Y.*

KINSLEY, John Franklin, educator; b. Glencoe, O., Mar. 23, 1888; s. William Marion and Anne Virginia (Bare) K.; B.S., Mount Union Coll., 1909; grad. study U. of Pittsburgh, 1919-23; m. Odessa Mae Cook, Aug. 25, 1909; children—William Allen, Kathryn Virginia (Mrs. Malcolm Mahoney). Dir. bus. edn., California State Normal Sch., 1909-12; successively office mgr., teacher high sch., bus. sec. Y.M.C.A., teacher high schs., eastern dist. sales mgr., gen. sales mgr., then pres. The Pittsburgh Academy since 1932. Trustee The Pittsburgh Acad. Mem. Nat. Edn. Assn., Nat. Commercial Assn., Eastern Commercial Assn., Pittsburgh Tri-State Assn. Democrat. Methodist. Mason. Clubs: Metropolitan, Kiwanis, Junto. Home: 321 Beverly Rd., Mt. Lebanon, Pittsburgh. Office: 531 Wood St., Pittsburgh, Pa.

KINSLOE, Charles Lambert, electrical engineer; b. Lock Haven, Pa., Oct. 15, 1881; s. Frank and Ida (Lambert) K.; grad. Central State Normal Sch., Lock Haven, 1899; B.S., Pa. State Coll., 1903, M.S. in E.E., 1907; m. Margaret White Buckhout (Vassar, 1908), July 14, 1909; children—Helen Lambert, Margaret White, Elizabeth. Student engr. Westinghouse Electric & Mfg. Co., Pittsburgh, Pa., 1903; engr. Phila. Electric Co., 1904-05, United Gas Improvement Co., Phila., 1905-06; instr. elec. engring., U. of Pittsburgh, 1906-07; with Pa. State Coll. since 1907, actg. head dept. elec. engring., 1907-09, head of dept. since 1909; also consulting practice. Mem. Am. Inst. E.E., Soc. for Promotion Engring. Edn., Sigma Chi, Eta Kappa Nu, Sigma Tau, Sigma Xi, Phi Kappa Phi, Triangle. Republican. Mason. Home: State College, Pa.*

KINSOLVING, Arthur Barksdale, clergyman; b. Middleburg, Loudoun Co., Va., Feb. 20, 1861; s. Rev. Ovid (D.D.) and Lucy Lee (Rogers) K.; prep. edn., Episcopal High Sch. of Va.; U. of Va., 1882-83; grad. Theol. Sem. Va., 1886; D.D., Washington and Lee U., 1905; m. Sally Bruce, Feb. 5, 1896; children—Mrs. Magill James, Arthur Lee, Mrs. Beverly Ober, Anne Seddon (Mrs. John N. Brown), Herbert Leigh, Sally Archer, Lucinda Lee. Deacon, 1886, priest, 1887, P.E. Ch.; rector St. John's Ch., Warsaw, Va., 1886-89, Christ Ch., Brooklyn, N.Y., 1889-1906, St. Paul's Ch., Baltimore, Md., since 1906; spl. preacher U. of Va., Washington and Lee U., etc. Mem. Central Diocesan Council; chmn. Nat. Com. on Christian Edn.; dep. to Gen. Conv. (P.E. Ch.), 10 times. Trustee Episcopal High Sch. of Va., Hannah More Acad.; pres. St. Paul's Boys' Sch., Baltimore. Mem. Delta Kappa Epsilon. Democrat. Clubs: University, Eclectic; New York Club (Episcopalian). Author: Story of a Southern School, 1922; Texas George—Life of Bishop George H. Kinsolving. Home: 24 W. Saratoga St., Baltimore, Md.

KINSOLVING, Sally Bruce, author; b. Richmond, Va., Feb. 14, 1876; d. Thomas Seddon and Mary (Anderson) Bruce; ed. pvt. schs. and at home of grandfather, Charles Bruce, of Staunton Hill, Va.; m. Rev. Arthur B. Kinsolving, D.D., Feb. 5, 1896; children—Bruce (Mrs. Magill James), Arthur Lee (rector Trinity Ch., Boston), Eleanor (Mrs. Beverly Ober), Anne Seddon (Mrs. John N. Brown), Herbert Leigh, Sally Archer, Lucinda Lee (Mrs. Egbert G. Leigh III). Contributor verse to newspapers and magazines since 1907. Vice-president Woman's Auxiliary in Md. of P.E. Ch., 1913-21, and del. to two triennial convs.; co-organizer and v.p. Ch. Service League of P.E. Ch. in Md., 1920-22; v.p. Md. br. Girls Friendly Soc. of America, 1913-21; transferred from Colonial Dames of New York to Colonial Dames of Md., 1914; initiator Poetry Soc. of Md., 1923, pres., 1929-38; mem. C.L.G., associated with Order of the Holy Cross; associate Community of All Saints, 1934; mem. Poetry Soc. of America, Catholic Poetry Soc. of America; mem. exec. com. of E.A. Poe Assn. in Md.; elected mem. Phi Beta Kappa Soc. (Alpha Chapter), Coll. of William and Mary, Va., 1934; elected hon. mem. Tudor and Stuart Club, Johns Hopkins; hon. mem. Woman's Literary Club and hon. pres. Lizette Woodworth Reese Memorial Assn., Baltimore. Author: Depths and Shallows, 1921; David and Bathsheba, and Other Poems, 1922; Grey Heather, 1930; also P.B.K. address, Rhythm and Art, Drew U., May 1935, and P.B.K. poem, Founders' Day, William and Mary Coll., Dec. 5, 1935. Home: 24 W. Saratoga St., Baltimore, Md.

KINZER, J. Roland, congressman; b. Lancaster Co., Pa., Mar. 28, 1874; A.B., Franklin and Marshall Coll., 1896; m. Bertha Snyder. Admitted to Pa. bar, 1900, and began practice at Lancaster; del. Rep. Nat. Conv., Kansas City, Mo., 1928; elected to 71st Congress Jan. 1930, to fill vacancy and was reëlected 72d to 76th Congresses (1931-41), 10th Pa. Dist. Home: Lancaster, Pa.

KIP, Frederic Ellsworth, mfr.; b. Passaic, N.J., Jan. 1, 1862; s. Nicholas J. and Susan P. (Worcester) K.; ed. pub. schs.; m. Charlotte Bishop Williams, Oct. 15, 1884. Began as office boy in commn. house of Libby, Bartlett & Kimball, New York, 1878; entered lubricating dept. Standard Oil Co., 1880; stock clk. dry goods commn. house, 1881; salesman and mgr. pile fabric dept. of Frederick Vietor & Achilles, New York, 1883-92; purchased with others, the Am. pile fabric plant of Sir Titus Salts Co., Bridgeport, Conn., 1892; pres. Kip-Armstrong Co.; with others bought the Griswold Worsted Co. of Darby, Pa., 1902, and now pres. same; pres. Salts Textile Mfg. Co., Bridgeport, Conn., and Lyons, France. Mem. Holland Soc. Republican. Home: Montclair, N.J.*

KIPLINGER, Willard Monroe, journalist; b. Bellefontaine, O., Jan. 8, 1891; s. Clarence E. and Cora (Miller) K.; A.B., Ohio State U., 1912. Began as reporter Ohio State Jour., 1912-14; reporter and editor Asso. Press, Columbus, 1914-16, financial writer, editor, at Washington, covering war financing, 1916-19; business and financial writer, editor and pub. Kiplinger Washington Letters, since 1920. Mem. Sigma Delta Chi, Sigma Pi. Unitarian. Clubs: University, Nat. Press, Arts, Cosmos. Contbr. econ. articles to leading mags.; editorial advisor various mags.; advisor various econ., ednl. and journalistic orgns. Author of Inflation Ahead (with Frederick Shelton), 1935. Home: R.F.D. 3, Bethesda, Md. Office: Nat. Press Bldg., Washington, D.C.

KIPP, Walter Adriance, lawyer; b. New York, N.Y., Feb. 25, 1877; s. Stanley Calum and Sadie Brinckerhoff (Adriance) K.; ed. pvt. schs. and Rutherford (N.J.) pub. schs.; m. Janet Streat, Oct. 30, 1906; children—Walter Adriance, Virginia (Mrs. Bradford M. Harrington), Derick Brinckerhoff. Began as lawyer, Rutherford, N.J., 1899, as mem. firm Copeland, Luce & Kipp; later Kipp, Ashen & Kipp; judge Dist. Court of 2d Judicial Dist., Bergen Co., N.J., 1929-34; mem. Bergen Co. Bd. Freeholders, 1923-29. Mason (Boiling Spring Lodge). Republican. Presbyterian. Clubs: Rotary (Rutherford, N.J.); Yountakah Country (Nutley, N.J.). Home: 52 Addison Av. Office: 10 Ames Av., Rutherford, N.J.

KIRACOFE, Edgar S., prof. edn.; b. Mt. Solon, Va., Dec. 18, 1894; s. John S. and Sarah (Cool) K.; A.B., Bridgewater Coll., 1921; A.M., U. of Va., 1925, Ph.D., same, 1932; m. Helen E. Miller, June 18, 1925; children—Betty, Nancy Virginia. Began as teacher, Nokeville Sem., 1916-18; dir. athletics and coach of sports, Bridgewater Coll., 1921-29; prof. edn., Elizabethtown Coll., Pa., 1932-37; head dept. edn., Juniata Coll., Huntingdon, Pa., since 1937; instr. in U. of Va. summer sch. since 1932. Mem. Nat. Edn. Assn., Pa. State Edn. Assn., Phi Delta Kappa. Mem. Ch. of Brethren. Author: Athletics and Physical Education in the Colleges of Virginia, 1932. Home: 1800 Moore St., Huntingdon, Pa.

KIRBY, Allan Price, corpn. exec.; b. Wilkes-barre, Pa., July 31, 1892; s. Fred Morgan and Jessie (Owen) K.; student Wyoming Sem., 1906-08, Lawrenceville (N.J.) Sch., 1908-10; Lafayette, Easton, Pa. Coll., 1910,12; m. Marian G. Sutherland, Feb. 14, 1918; children—Grace Jessie, Fred Morgan II, Ann Sutherland, Allan P. Office mgr. Bathurst (New Brunswick) Lumber Co., 1914-15; treas. Jenkins-Kirby Packing Co., 1915-22; pres. Kirby-Davis Co., 1922-34; vice-pres. 2d Nat. Bank, Wilkes-Barre, 1924-34; pres. Imperial Motor Corpn. since 1934; dir. Alleghany Corpn., F. W. Woolworth Co., Pere Marquette Ry. Co., N.Y.C.&St.L. R.R. Co., Terminal & Shaker Heights Realty Co.,

White Sulphur Springs, Inc., Pathé Film Corpn. Mem. U.S. Naval Res. Treas. Wilkes-Barre Inst., Angeline Elizabeth Kirby Memorial Health Center; trustee Lafayette Coll., Wyoming Hist. Assn. Mem. Zeta Psi. Republican. Episcopalian. Mason (32°). Clubs: Metropolitan, The Recess (N.Y. City); Everglades, Gulf Stream Golf, Boca Raton, Bath and Tennis (Palm Beach, Fla.); Westmoreland, Wyoming Valley Country (Wilkes-Barre); Clove Valley Rod and Gun (Lagrangeville, N.Y.); Union League (Phila.). Home: Convent, N.J. Office: 26 Journal Square, Jersey City, N.J.

KIRBY, C. Valentine, art educator; b. Canajoharie, N.Y., 1875; s. Frank and Frances (Devendorf) K.; grad. high sch., Canajoharie, 1893; student Union Coll.; student Art Students' League and Chase Sch. of Art, New York, 4 yrs., also Europe; hon. A.M., Union College, 1922; Pd.D. (hon.), Franklin and Marshall College, 1937; Dr. Fine Arts, Lebanon College, 1937; m. Florence J. Beach, Mar. 20, 1902; 1 son, Donald Beach. Teacher of fine and industrial arts, pub. schs. of Denver, 1900-10; dir. art instrn., Buffalo, N.Y., 1911-12, Pittsburgh, 1912-20; state dir. of art, Pa., since 1920. Lecturer various univs., Carnegie Inst. Tech.; Am. rep. and speaker Internat. Art Congress, Dresden, 1912; assisted in survey of art in Am. industry, 1920. Mem. Am. Fed. Arts, N.E.A., Pa. State Edn. Assn., Eastern Arts Assn., Western Arts Assn., Art Alliance, Phila., Psi Upsilon, S.R.; mem. Federated Council Art Edn.; mem. bd. of govs. Nat. Assn. for Art Edn.; mem. yearbook com., Nat. Assn. for the Study of Edn.; mem. Am. Com. 6th Internat. Art Congress, Prague, 1928. Democrat. Unitarian. Mason (32°, Shriner). Clubs: Sketch (Phila.); University, Torch Club (Harrisburg). Author: The Business of Teaching and Supervising the Arts, 1927. Co-Author: Graded Art Textbooks; Art Education in Principle and Practice. Designer of book plates; contbr. on art subjects. Home: 601 N. Front St. Office: State Dept. of Public Instruction, Harrisburg, Pa.

KIRBY, David, educator; b. Grantsville, W.Va., Feb. 27, 1896; s. William Atha and Clara Monda (Kimble) K.; grad. Morris Harvey Coll. Acad., Barboursville, W.Va., 1917; A.B., Morris Harvey Coll., 1921; student U. of Pa., summer 1924; A.M., W.Va.U., 1928; grad. student State U. of Iowa, summer 1928, U. of Cincinnati, 1929; m. Vennie Mae Copley, Sept. 20, 1922; children—Davene, Rosaclaire. Teacher in public school, Calhoun County, W.Va., 1913-14; instr., Morris Harvey Coll. Acad., 1919-21; instr. in history, Morris Harvey Coll., 1923-27, prof. of edn. 1927-31; prof. of edn., Davis and Elkins Coll., Elkins, W.Va., 1931-33; sec. W.Va. State Bd. of Edn. since 1933. Mem. N.E.A., W.Va. Edn. Assn., Am. Assn. Sch. Adminstrs., Nat. Soc. Coll. Teachers of Edn., Kappa Delta Pi. Democrat. Methodist. Mason. Home: 315 Central St., Swanns Hill. Office: 105 State Capitol, Charleston, W.Va.

KIRBY, Dunne Wilson, physician; b. Phila., Pa., Oct. 15, 1901; s. Edmund William and Annette (Candy) K.; grad. Peddie Sch., Hightstown, N.J., 1919; B.S., Hahnemann Coll. of Science, Phila., 1921; M.D., Hahnemann Med. Coll., 1928; m. Zelma Maude Kunsman, Nov. 11, 1927; children—Sarah Louise, Peter Andrew, Timothy Stephen. Resident physician, St. Luke's and Children's Hosp., Phila., 1928-29; asso. with Dr. G. H. Wells in his private practice, 1929-32; in practice since 1929, specializing in internal medicine and diagnosis; asst. physician and electro-cardiographer Hahnemann Hosp.; lecturer on medicine, Hahnemann Med. Coll.; lecturer on infectious diseases, Hahnemann Hosp. Sch. of Nursing. Mem. Phila. Alumni Assn. of Peddie Sch. (mem. exec. com.; past pres.); pres. Gen. Alumni of Peddie School, 1939-40. Fellow Am. Coll. Physicians; mem. County, State and Nat. Med. Socs., Pi Upsilon Rho (nat. sec.-treas. since 1931). Republican. Episcopalian. Clubs: Germantown Cricket (Phila.); Medinah Athletic of Chicago (non-resident). Home: 4341 Manayunk Av. Office: Hardt Bldg., Philadelphia, Pa.

KIRBY, Francis J.; asso. in surgery, U. of Md.; surgeon St. Joseph's, Bon Secours and Mercy hosps. (Baltimore), Annapolis Emergency Hosp. (Annapolis) and St. Mary's Hosp. (Leonardtown); cons. surgeon Mt. Hope Retreat. Address: 110 E. North Av., Baltimore, Md.

KIRBY, Fred Morgan, capitalist; b. Brownville, Jefferson Co., N.Y., Oct. 30, 1861; s. William and Angeline E. (Slater) Kirby; educated in public schools; m. Jessie Amelia Owen, May 27, 1886 (died April 10, 1933); children—Allan Price, Summer Moore. Was in the employ of Moore & Smith, dry goods, Watertown, 1876-84; removed to Wilkes-Barre, Pa., and associated with C.S. Woolworth in 5 and 10-cent store; purchased interest of partner, 1887, and became owner of 96 stores, located in nearly every state east of Miss. River; merged interests with F. W. Woolworth Co. and retired Jan. 1, 1912; v.p. F. W. Woolworth Co., New York; dir. Miners Nat. Bank of Wilkes-Barre; pres. Wilkes-Barre Ry. Co. Member board dirs. Wilkes-Barre Hosp., Wyoming Sem., Wilkes-Barre Y.M.C.A., trustee Lafayette Coll., Easton, Pa., to which has given $100,000 to found Kirby Chair of Civil Rights; also gave $100,000 to Wyoming Sem. to insure the teaching of civil rights there; erected Kirby Hall of Civil Rights, Lafayette College, at a cost of approximately $500,000, 1930; also erected Angeline Elizabeth Kirby Memorial Health Center, Wilkes-Barre, Pa. (cost $2,000,000; designed to last 300 years), 1931. Republican presdl. elector for Warren G. Harding, 1920. Episcopalian. Mason (33°). Clubs: Westmoreland, Franklin, Press, Wyoming Valley Country, Scranton (Scranton, Pa.); Fox Hill Country (Pittston, Pa.); Metropolitan, Bankers, Union League, Hardware (New York). Home: 202 S. River St. Office: Miners Nat. Bank Bldg., Wilkes-Barre, Pa.

KIRBY, R(obert) S(tearns), extension plant pathologist; b. Battle Creek, Mich., Mar. 18, 1892; s. Emery Davis and Amanda (Stearns) K.; student Colo. A. and M. Coll., 1913-14; B.S., N.M. A.&M.A. Coll., 1916; M.S., Ia. State Coll., 1917; Ph.D., Cornell U., 1923; m. Ora Walker, Dec. 23, 1917; 1 son, Robert Emery. Employed as asst. pathologist, U.S. Dept. Agr., 1918-20; instr. in extension plant pathology, Cornell U., 1920-24; asst. prof. plant pathology, asso. prof. then prof., extension div., Pa. State Coll., since 1924. Fellow A.A.A.S.; mem. Am. Phytopathol. Soc. (sec.), Acacia, Sigma Xi. Republican. Methodist. Mason (K.T., Shriner). Home: 251 S. Barnard St. Office: Botany Bldg., State College, Pa.

KIRCHER, Edward A(ugust Theodore), investment banking; b. Chicago, Ill., Mar. 21, 1890; s. Julius (D.D.) and Emma (Bandow) K.; A.B., U. of Ill., 1911, A.M., 1912, Ph.D., 1914; m. Naomi Kemm Wish, Oct. 7, 1924; children—Charlotte Elise, Naomi Jane, Ann Louise. Instr. mathematics, Mass. Inst. Tech., 1914-15; Benjamin Peirce instr. mathematics, Harvard U., 1915-17; with Nat. City Co., 1919-34; with Harriman Ripley & Co., Inc. (formerly Brown Harriman & Co., Inc.), since 1934. Mem. First Plattsburg Training Camp and First Fortress Monroe Training Camp, May-Aug. 1917; capt. Coast Arty. Reserve, Boston Harbor, until Dec. 1917, 55 Arty., C.A.C., A.E.F., until Nov. 1918. Awarded Silver Beaver, Boy Scouts of America, 1935; hon. grad. Army Heavy Arty. Sch., Mailly, France, 1918. Commr. Watchung Council Boy Scouts of America, Plainfield, 1922-27. Mem. Phi Beta Kappa, Sigma Xi. Co-Author: Yields of Bonds and Stocks. Collaborator: Regimental History of 55th Artillery, C.A.C., A.E.F. Contbr. to Jours. Republican. Lutheran. Home: 701 Belvidere Av., Plainfield, N.J. Office: Harriman Ripley & Co., Inc., 63 Wall St., New York, N.Y.

KIRCHER, Ellis Corson, realtor; b. Camden, N.J., Apr. 15, 1897; s. Thomas Scott Jr. and Eva Justice (Corson) K.; student pub. and high schs., Camden, N.J. Became ins. clk. Smith-Austermuhl Co., 1916, dir. and jr. officer, 1932; in real estate business at Camden, N.J., since 1932, pres. E. C. Kircher, Inc., realtors, Camden; treas. Walt Whitman Bldg. & Loan Assn., Camden. Candidate for Camden City Commn., 1935 (withdrew), for Bd. of Chosen Freeholders, 1937 (defeated). Pres. Camden Co. Real Estate Bd.; has been interested in various civic activities for 20 yrs., including several Chamber of Commerce promotions. Republican. Methodist. Club: Engineers of Camden (chmn. bd. of govs.). Home: 1113 Sylvan Av., Oaklyn, N.J. Office: 431 Market St., Camden, N.J.

KIRK, Harris Elliott, clergyman; b. Pulaski, Tenn., Oct. 12, 1872; s. John Harvey and Katherine (McCord) K.; grad. Southwestern U., Memphis, Tenn., 1897, D.D., 1905, LL.D., 1925; LL.D., Davidson Coll., Davidson, N.C., 1937; m. Helen O. McCormick, June 24, 1897; children—Harris Elliott, Mary Louise (wife of Dr. Julius Lane Wilson), Helen Lucretia (Mrs. Harry J. Verner, Jr.). Ordained Presbyn. ministry, 1897; pastor Cottage Ch., Nashville, Tenn., 1897-99, 1st Ch., Florence, Ala., 1899-1901, Franklin St. Ch., Baltimore, Md., since 1901; ann. lecturer on historical Christianity, Princeton U., 1923-29, Goucher Coll., 1925-28; prof. Bibl. lit., Goucher, since 1928, lecturer Gen. Conf. Christian Workers, Northfield, 1917-26, mission confs. in China, summer of 1924; summer preacher Westminster Chapel, London, 1922-40; Sprunt lecturer Union Theol. Sem., Va., 1916; Carew lecturer Hartford Theol. Sem., 1916; spl. lecturer on homiletics and psychology, Hartford Sem., 1919-24; alumni lecturer New Brunswick Theol. Sem., 1920; faculty lecturer, McCormick Theol. Sem., 1922; university preacher Princeton, Yale, U. of Va., etc.; Shepard lecturer Bangor Theol. Sem., 1928; Reinicker lecturer P.E. Seminary in Va., 1929; Cole lecturer, Vanderbilt, 1930; Otts lecturer, Davidson Coll., 1930; McNair lecturer, U. of N.C., 1931; Rockwell Lectures, Rice Inst., Houston, Tex., 1939. Moderator Va. Synod., 1911; elected moderator Gen. Assembly Presbyn. Ch. in U.S., 1928; director Persbyn. Ministers' Fund for Life Ins., Phila.; trustee Peabody Inst., Mary Baldwin Coll. Mem. Sigma Alpha Epsilon. Clubs: University, P. and L., Arts and Letters; Nat. Liberal (London). Author: The Religion of Power, 1916; The Consuming Fire, 1919; One Generation to Another, 1924; The Spirit of Protestantism, 1930; The Glory of Common Things, 1930; Stars, Atoms and God, 1932; A Man of Property, 1935; A Design for Living, 1939; also numerous articles in mags. Home: 502 Cathedral St., Baltimore, Md.

KIRK, James T.; has served as judge and mayor of Elizabeth. Address: Elizabeth, N.J.

KIRK, Mabel Eleanor, asso. prof. edn.; b. Hamilton Co., Neb., Aug. 6, 1888; d. Joseph and Virginia (Eller) K.; ed. State Teachers Coll., Kearney, Neb., 1906-09; A.B., U. of Neb., 1921; A.M., Teachers Coll. of Columbia U., 1924; grad. study, Northwestern U., 1939. Engaged as teacher rural schs., high schs., co. supt. schs., Neb., Mon. and Minn., and asst. state leader Boys' & Girls' 4-H Clubs, Nebr., 1909-24; supervising teacher, Frederick Co. Schs., Frederick, Md., 1924-25; teacher summer sessions, U. of Neb., 1922, 24; asst. prof. edn. Pa. State Coll., 1925-29, asso. prof. since 1929. Mem. Nat. Edn. Assn., Am. Assn. Univ. Women, Am. Assn. Univ. Profs., Phi Beta Kappa, Pi Lambda Theta. Baptist. Home: 205 E. Beaver Av., State College, Pa.

KIRK, William, chem. and engring. management; b. Greenfield, Ia., Oct. 23, 1890; s. David Samuel and Eliza (Gregg) K.; A.B., Tarkio Coll., Mo., 1912; A.M., U. of Neb., 1914; Ph.D., Cornell U., 1916; m. Merry Irene Irwin, June 20, 1916; children—William, Jr., Margaret Jane, Elizabeth Ann, Robert Irwin. Research chemist, Eastern Labs., E. I. Du Pont de Nemours & Co., Inc., Gibbstown, N.J., with six months in Eng., 1916-18, div. leader on research on intermediates, Jackson Lab., 1918-21; supt. in charge mfg. intermediates, Du Pont Dye Works, 1921-27, supt. in charge intermediates and azo colors, 1927-29; asst. mgr. Du Pont Dye Works, Pennsgrove, N.J., since 1930. Mem. Sch. Bd., Pennsgrove, N.J. Active in Boy Scout work. Awarded Silver Beaver, Boy Scouts of America. Fellow Am. Inst. Chemists, Am. Inst. Chem. Engrs.; mem. Am. Chem. Soc., Gamma Alpha, Alpha Chi Sigma, Sigma Xi. Republican. Presbyn. Mason.

Home: Maple Av. & State St. Office: Du Pont Dye Works, Pennsgrove, N.J.

KIRKBRIDE, Mabelle Mills (Mrs. Harry Carson K.), pub. speaker; b. Lancaster, Mo., Feb. 12, 1889; d. John C. and Minnie A. (Mott) Mills; B.Pd., Kirksville Mo. Teachers Coll., 1907; grad. Washington (D.C.) Sem., 1908; m. Dr. Harry Carson Kirkbride, Dec. 15, 1910; children—Jane Mills (wife of Dr. L. Stowell Gary, Buffalo, N.Y.), Katherine Mills, Harry Carson, Jr. Began as teacher English, high sch., Kirksville, Mo., 1908; engaged in polit. work at Norristown, Pa., since 1921; served as mem. Pa. Ho. of Rep., 1929-34; sec. Banking Com. Pa. Legislature, 1934-36; custodian vital records Register of Wills' Office of Montgomery Co. since 1936. Served as vice chmn. Montgomery Co. Rep. Com., 1921-36; state dir. and corr. sec. Pa. Council Rep. Women; mem. Rep. State Com., Mothers Assistance Bd., 1923-36; organizer, past pres. and hon. pres. Montgomery Council Rep. Women, and Norristown Council Rep. Women. Mem. D.A.R., U.S. Daughters of 1812, Y.W.C.A. (dir. 15 yrs.), Sigma Sigma Sigma, Business and Professional Womens Club of Norristown. Republican. Presbyn. Clubs: Plymouth Country (Norristown); West Norristown Womens. Home: 814 De Kalb St., Norristown, Pa.

KIRKPATRICK, Alton, mech. engring.; b. Phila., Pa., Nov. 24, 1889; s. William Henry Green and Margaret Weaver (Keyser) K.; B.S. in M.E., U. of Pa., 1911; (hon.) M.E., U. of Pa., 1925; m. Margaret Lamson Aldrich, Feb. 16, 1918. Employed as cable tester, American Telephone & Telegraph Co., 1911-12; with C. H. Wheeler Mfg. Co., Phila., Pa., successively, test engr., asst. to works mgr., erecting engr., supt. marine auxiliary shop, 1912-19; with Albert C. Wood, cons. engr., Phila., Pa., 1919-35, mem. firm Wood & Kirkpatrick, cons. engrs., since 1935; registered professional engr. in Pa. Mem. Am. Soc. Mech. Engrs., Nat. Assn. Power Engrs. Republican. Presbyn. Home: 192 N. Lansdowne Av., Lansdowne, Pa. Office: Stock Exchange Bldg., Philadelphia, Pa.

KIRKPATRICK, Forrest Hunter, coll. dean; b. Galion, O., Sept. 4, 1906; s. Arch Melvin and Mildred (Hunter) K.; A.B., Bethany Coll., Bethany, W.Va., 1927; student Univ. of Dijon, France, 1926; A.M., Columbia U., 1932; grad. student U. of Pittsburgh, 1933, U. of London, Eng., 1937; unmarried. Served on faculty Bethany Coll., Bethany, W.Va., since 1927 with several leaves of absence, dean of freshmen, 1927-31, dean of personnel since 1931; mem. bd. edn. of Disciples of Christ; mem. exec. council of Am. Coll. Personnel Assn.; organized and developed first program of student personnel adminstrn. in W.Va. at coll. level. Mem. Beta Theta Pi, Kappa Delta Pi, Phi Delta Kappa. Republican. Disciples of Christ. Mason (32°). Clubs: Fort Henry (Wheeling); University (Pittsburgh). Home: Bethany, W.Va.

KIRKPATRICK, Harlow Barton, property management; b. Anna, Ill., July 26, 1879; s. Cornwall E. and Frank M. (Hubbard) K.; grad. Union Acad., Anna, Ill., 1896; B.S. in civil engring., U. of Ill., 1901; m. Elizabeth G. Hillman, Feb. 26, 1908; children—Eleanor Millward (Mrs. Charles B. Saints), Harlow Barton, John Gaylord, Elizabeth Hillman (Mrs. S. Lewis Hotchkiss), Francis Hubbard, William Alexander. Rodman C.&N.W. Ry., 1901; instr., U. of Ill., 1901-02; instrumentman C.&N.W. Ry., 1902-04; instr., Syracuse U., 1904-05; engr. Bur. Pub. Works, Philippine Islands, 1905-07; engr. Arnold Co., Chicago, 1907-08; irrigation engr. Bur. Pub. Works, Philippine Islands, 1908-10; harbor engr. Sanitary Dist., Chicago, 1910-11; with Koppers Co. since 1912; pres. Koppers Bldg., Inc. Dir. Pittsburgh Chamber of Commerce (pres. 1935, 37). Mem. Better Traffic Com. of Pittsburgh; dir. Better Business Bureau, Building Owners and Managers Assn., Pittsburgh. Mem. Phi Delta Theta. Republican. Episcopalian. Mason. Club: Duquesne (Pittsburgh) Home: 4405 Schenley Farms Terrace. Office: Koppers Bldg., Pittsburgh, Pa.

KIRKPATRICK, Martin Glen, editor, writer; b. South English, Ia., Dec. 18, 1889; s. Martin Van Buren and Frances Virginia (Beery) K.; student Central U., Pella, Ia., 1912; B.S., Ia. State Coll., 1917; m. Eloise A. Dalrymple, Aug. 14, 1919; children—Virginia Lois, Barbara Jean. Teacher pub. schs., Ia., 1908-12; chautauqua supt., Jones Chautauqua System and Lincoln Chautauqua, 1912-14; farm editor Des Moines (Ia.) Daily Register, 1916-17; asso. editor The Farm Journal since 1917. Mem. Pa. Minn., N.J. and Ia. hort. socs., Am. Rose Soc., Northwest Farm Mgrs. Assn., Gamma Sigma Delta, Sigma Delta Chi. Republican. Baptist. Club: Nat. Press. Contbr. articles on farm management. Home: 203 Morgan Av., Collingswood, N.J. Office: The Farm Journal, Philadelphia, Pa.

KIRKPATRICK, Sidney Dale, chemical engr., editor; b. Urbana, Ill., Apr. 2, 1894; s. Frederick Dilling and Virginia Mae (Hedges) K.; B.Sc., U. of Ill., 1916, grad. study, 1916-17; m. Bonnie Jean Hardesty, Aug. 6, 1919; children—Mary Jane, Dale. Chemist and editor, Ill. State Water Survey, 1916-17; chem. advisor U.S. Tariff Commn., 1917-18, spl. expert with same, 1919-21; with McGraw-Hill Pub. Co., N.Y. City, since 1921, as asst. editor Chemical & Metallurgical Engineering (mag.), 1921-25, asso. editor, 1925-28, editor, 1928, and since 1928 cons. editor chem. engring. series of text and reference books; director McGraw-Hill Book Co. Served as 2d lt. and 1st lt. S.C., A.E.F., 1918-19; chem. advisor Am. Commn. to Negotiate Peace, 1919. Mem. Am. Inst. Chem. Engrs. (dir. 1932-35 and since 1937), Am. Electrochem. Soc. (dir. 1933-35; v.p. 1931, 1935), Am. Chem. Soc. (councillor 1939), Sigma Xi, Phi Lambda Upsilon, Alpha Chi sigma, Sigma Delta Chi, Theta Delta Chi. Awarded silver anniversary medal Am. Inst. Chem. Engrs., 1932. Republican. Methodist. Clubs: Chemists (trustee), Western Universities. Editor: Twenty Five Years of Engineering Progress, 1933; also cons. editor Chemical Engring. series (18 titles). Contbr. to Chemical & Metallurgical Engring. Home: 52 Woodcrest Av., Millburn, N.J. Office: 330 W. 42d St., New York, N.Y.

KIRKPATRICK, William Huntington, U.S. dist. judge; b. Easton, Pa., Oct. 2, 1885; s. of Hon. William S. (former atty. gen. of Pa.) and Elizabeth H. (Jones) K.; A.B., Lafayette Coll., 1905; law dept. U. of Pa., 1905-06; m. Mary Stewart Wells, May 17, 1913; children—William S. Miles. Admitted to Pa. bar, 1908; mem. 67th Congress (1921-23), 26th Pa. Dist.; U.S. dist. judge for Eastern Dist. of Pa., Mar. 3, 1927—. Maj. and lt. col. Judge Adv. Gen.'s Dept., and mem. Bd. of Review of Courts Martial, World War. Republican. Presbyn. Home: Easton, Pa.

KIRKWOOD, Maclean, telephone engring.; b. Toronto, Ont., Apr. 19, 1891; s. Alexander and Emily Frederica (Stow) K.; came to U.S., 1912, naturalized, 1923; B.A.Sc., U. of Toronto, 1912; m. Bernice Silverman, Sept. 11, 1919; children—Esme Alison, Nancy Carol, Maclean, Jr. Employed as elec. engr., Crocker-Wheeler Co., Ampere, N.J., 1912-13; with engring. dept., Am. Telephone & Telegraph Co., 1913-19, with dept. operation and engring. since 1919; treas. Indian Hill Water Assn.; pres. Crystal Brook Sound Beach Corpn. Neighborhood commr. Boy Scouts of America. Pres. bd. trustees, Whitehall M.E. Ch. of Towaco, N.J. Mem. Am. Inst. Elec. Engrs., Canadian Soc. of N.Y. Methodist. Clubs: United States Power Squadrons (Brooklyn); Nonowantuck Yacht (Mount Sinai, L.I., N.Y.). Home: Indian Hill, Towaco, N.J. Office: 195 Broadway, New York, N.Y.

KIRNER, Walter Raymond, organic chemist; b. Chicago, Ill., July 23, 1895; s. Benedict A. and Anna K.; B.S., U. of Ill., 1918, M.S. same, 1920; Ph.D., Harvard U., 1924; grad. study, U. of Graz, Austria, U. of Munich, Germany, Univ. Coll., London, Eng., 1929-30; m. Juvanta Harper, Sept. 10, 1925; 1 son, Stephen Harper. Instr. organic chemistry, Middlebury Coll., 1923; instr. organic chemistry, Rice Inst., 1924-26, asst. prof. in charge organic chemistry div., 1926-31; organic chemist, Coal Research Lab., Carnegie Inst. Tech., since 1931, lecturer in organic chemistry, same, since 1937. Served as lt. C.W.S., 1917-18; asst. in charge Chemistry Lab., Lakehurst Proving Grounds. Mem. Am. Chem. Soc., Alpha Chi Sigma, Gamma Alpha, Phi Lambda Upsilon, Sigma Xi. Austin Fellow and Du Pont Fellow in Chemistry, Harvard U. Club: Pittsburgh Chemists (chmn. 1936). Contbr. many articles to sci. jours. Home: 215 Richland Lane, Pittsburgh, Pa.

KIRVEN, Frank Douglas, ins. exec.; b. Columbus, Ga., Mar. 31, 1882; s. Richard Munroe and Nettie (Moore) K.; student pub. schs., Columbus, Ga., 1889-98; m. Miriam M. Whitaker, Oct. 18, 1911; children—Thirza Alma (Mrs. John A. Zerbe), Miriam. Banking business in Ga. and Ala., 1902-09, N.Y. State, 1909-12, Ala., 1912-17; comptroller Manhattan Life Ins. Co., New York, 1917-28, v.p. since 1928. Home: 269 Bay Av., Glen Ridge, N.J. Office: 120 W. 57th St., New York, N.Y.

KISER, Robert William, retail and wholesale fuel merchant; b. Pittsburgh, Pa., Apr. 24, 1878; s. David Oliver and Margaret (Black) K.; student Pittsburgh Central High Sch., 1893-98; B.S., U. of Pittsburgh, 1901; m. Elizabeth Campbell Sands, Oct. 21, 1902; children—Jean Miller (dec.), Robert William. Began as bookkeeper, June 1900; acquired half interest in Alex. Black Coal Co., 1901, with father as partner; took over entire business when father retired, 1912, and since proprietor. Mem. Retail Coal Mchts. Assn. of Greater Pittsburgh, Y.M.C.A. United Presbyterian. Club: Rotary (Pittsburgh). Home: 4377 Schenley Farms Terrace. Office: 3126 Liberty Av., Pittsburgh, Pa.

KISKADDON, J. Fulton, clergyman; b. Kittanning, Pa.; s. Frank and Melvina J. (Sarver) K.; A.B., A.M., Washington and Jefferson Coll.; student Western Theol. Sem., 1912-15, U. of Chicago Divinity Sch., 1916, U. of Edinburgh, Scotland, 1924-25; m. Edith J. McClellan, Oct. 15, 1918. Ordained to ministry Presbyn. Ch.; pastor, Oxford, Ind., 1915-18, Covington, Ind., 1918-20, Tecumseh, Mich., 1920-24; pastor, Presbyn. Ch., North East, Pa., since 1925. Pres. trustees of Erie Presbytery. Mem. Internat. Council of Christian Edn., Am. Rheumatism Assn. (lay mem.). Presbyn. Mason. Author: Scientific Support for Christian Doctrines, 1933. Home: 63 Gibson St., North East, Pa.

KISNER, Ralph, lawyer; b. Millville, Pa., Apr. 6, 1878; s. Hendy and Mary (Shoemaker) K.; ed. Greenwood Sem., Millville, Pa., Bloomsburg (Pa.) Normal Sch., Pierce's Business Coll., Phila.; m. Marie Fetterman, June 19, 1912. Taught rural sch., 1896-98; entered law office Hon. James Scarlet, Danville, Pa., 1898, and asso. with him until his death, 1920, then practiced alone until 1936, retiring on account of health; solicitor Danville Borough, and Montour Co., 1912-36; dist. atty. Montour Co., 1903-06; dir. Danville Nat. Bank since 1918. Chmn. Four-Minute Men, pres. Montour Co. advisory bd., and active in Red Cross and Liberty Loan drives during World War. Republican. Mason, K.P., Elk (hon. life mem.). Club: Williamsport (Pa.) Wheel. Address: 106 W. Market St., Danville, Pa.

KISSAM, Philip, asso. prof. civil engring.; b. West Orange, N.J., July 5, 1896; s. Coleman Embury and Anne Higbee (Green) K.; ed. Princeton U., 1915-17, 1919-20, C.E. 1920; m. Dorothy Marie Wurtenberg, Oct. 21, 1922; 1 dau., Dorothea Anne. Employed in student course, Winchester Repeating Arms Co., 1920-21; instr. civil engring., Princeton U., 1921-26, asst. prof., 1926-35, asso. prof. since 1935; practicing civil engring. and land surveying; organized and directed N.J. Geodetic Control Survey, 1933-37; chiefly known for advancing utilization of the state systems of plane coordinates. Served as 2d lt. pursuit pilot A.S., U.S.A., 1917-19. Mem. Am. Soc. Civil Engrs., Am. Geophys. Union, Am. Soc. Photogrammetry, Soc. for Promotion Engring. Edn., Nat. Soc. Professional Engrs., Soc. Am. Mil. Engrs., Am. Rd. Builders Assn., N.J. Soc. Professional Engrs., Princeton Engring. Assn., Sigma Xi. Republican. Episcopalian. Home: 15 Newlin Rd., Princeton, N.J.

KITSON, Arthur, Jr., lawyer; b. Media, Pa., July 10, 1888; s. Arthur and Fannie E. (Aschenbach) K.; student Chestnut Hill Acad., Phila.,

Pa., 1898-1905; B.S. in Econ., U. of Pa., 1909; LL.B., Temple U., 1914; m. Maria van Arcken, Oct. 4, 1930. Bank clerk, Chelten Trust Co., Phila., 1909-13; admitted to Phila. bar, 1913, and in practice at Phila., 1913-21; v.p. and trust officer Franklin Trust Co., Phila., 1921-31; in practice of law at Phila. since 1931; v.p. and dir. Phila. Bronze & Brass Corpn. Ensign U.S. N.R.F., 1917-18. Nonpartisan in politics. Club: Seaview Golf (Absecon, N.J.). Home: 15 S. Pembroke Av., Margate City, N.J. Office: 938 Land Title Bldg., Philadelphia, Pa.

KITTLE, Frank G., lawyer, editor; b. Philippi, W.Va., Aug. 27, 1887; s. George Monroe and Charity Ellen (Poling) K.; A.B., Ohio State U., 1913, LL.B., 1915; unmarried. Admitted to W.Va. bar, 1916, and since practiced in Philippi; editor of The Philippi Republican, Philippi, since 1918; sec.-treas. Mountain State Water Co.; vice-pres. Maryland Coal Co. of W. Va., Maryland Coal Co. of Allegheny County, Md.; pres. Philippi Pub. Co.; asst. treas. Consumers Gas Utility Co. 2d lt., F.A., U.S. Army, May-Dec., 1918. Mem. Barbour Co. Bar Assn. (pres. 1935-39), Phi Kappa Psi, Phi Delta Phi, Theta Nu Epsilon. Republican. Methodist. Club: Stag (Philippi). Home: 2 Glade Av. Office: 109 Court St., Philippi, W.Va.

KITTO, Charles White, clergyman; b. Pen Argyl, Pa.; s. Charles and Emily (Winsboro) K.; ed. East Stroudsburg State Teachers Coll., 1905-07; A.B., Dickinson Coll., 1912; student Drew Theol. Sem., 1912-13; A.M., U. of Pa., 1920; (hon.) D.D., Dickinson Coll.; m. Dina Jackson, July 11, 1913; children—Richard Charles J., Dorothy Lillian. Engaged in teaching, 1907-09; ordained to ministry M.E. Ch. and entered Phila. Conf., 1912; pastor Pottsville, Pa., 1925-30, St. James Ch., Phila., 1930-36; dist. supt. Phila. Conf. since 1936. Trustee Dickinson Coll., Methodist Hosp. of Phila., Preachers Aid Soc. Trustee bd. Phila. Conf. Mem. Uniting Conf. Meth. Church, 1939. Mem. Beta Theta Pi. Republican. Methodist. Mason (grand chaplain of Pa.). Club: Union League (Philadelphia). Home: 916 N. 64th St., Philadelphia, Pa. Office: Wesley Bldg., Philadelphia, Pa.

KITTREDGE, Arthur Edmund, mech. engring.; b. South Portland, Me., Nov. 7, 1900; s. George Edmund and Lelia (Spencer) K.; B.S., U. of Me., 1923; m. Phyllis M. Bangert, June 1, 1925. Employed as engr., Westinghouse Electric & Mfg. Co., 1923-26; engr., American Brown Boveri, 1926-27; engr., Cochrane Corpn., Phila., Pa., since 1927, chief engr. since 1937. Mem. Tau Beta Pi. Home: 225 Crystal Lake Av., Audubon, N.J. Office: Cochrane Corpn., Philadelphia, Pa.

KIZIS, Andrew C., banking; b. Pittston, Pa., Sept. 12, 1898; s. Charles and Anna (Walukas) K.; ed. pub. sch. and high sch., Pittston, Pa., 1905-17; m. Eva Comorosky, Sept. 23, 1925; children—Regina, Andrew C., Jr., Anthony J., Albert. Employed as clk. First Nat. Bank, Pittston, 1917-23; asst. cashier, Liberty Nat. Bank, Pittston, 1923-30, cashier, 1930-32, vice-pres., cashier and dir. since 1932. Served in U.S.N., 1917-18. Pres. Sch. Dist., Swoyerville, Pa., 1930-37. Pres. Pittston Clearing House Assn. Treas. Greater Pittston Chamber of Commerce. Roman Catholic. Elk. Clubs: Elks, Fox Hill Country. Home: 10 Delaware Av., West Pittston, Pa. Office: 2 N. Main St., Pittston, Pa.

KLAER, Harvey, clergyman; b. Milford, Pa., Dec. 31, 1874; s. John and Maria (Bull) K.; A.B., Lafayette Coll., 1896, A.M., same, 1899; student Princeton Theol. Sem., 1896-99; A.M., Princeton U., 1898; hon. D.D., Lafayette Coll., 1926; m. Mary Elizabeth Lee, Apr. 12, 1900; children—Alfred Lee, Harvey, Jr. Ordained to ministry Presbyn. Ch., 1899; pastor, Easton, Pa., 1898-1913, Harrisburg, 1914-24; asso. dir. evangelism Presbyn. Bd. Nat. Missions, 1924-32; sec. Federation of Chs., Harrisburg, and vicinity, 1920-24; pastor First Presbyn. Ch., Olney, Phila., Pa., since 1933. Republican. Presbyn. Club: Presbyterian Ministers Social Union. Author: A Church Evangelistic Program, 1925; Sunday School Evangelism, 1926; Bible Studies in Personal Work, 1927; What the Minutes Say to the Minister, 1929; Preparing the Heart, 1929; Seeking and Finding Men, 1930; Being a Presbyterian, 1930; Home Visitation Evangelism, 1931. Home: 237 W. Tabor Rd., Philadelphia, Pa.

KLAIN, Zora, educator; b. Norway, Me., Oct. 14, 1884; s. Maurice and Rebecca (Harkins) K.; A.B., Clark U., 1912; student Johns Hopkins U., summers, 1912-15; M.A., Pa. State Coll., 1918; Ph.D., U. of Pa., 1924; m. Mary Christine Dudley, Apr. 28, 1919; children—Priscilla Alden, Evangeline MacDowell, Dudley O'Sullivan. Teacher McDonogh Sch., 1912-15, Pa. State Coll., 1915-22; teacher, summers, Duke U., 1923-25, U. of Rochester, 1924-25; prof. and head dept. edn., New Jersey Coll. for Women, Rutgers U. since 1925; visiting prof. edn., U. of Pa., summers, 1926, 27, 28, 38. Mem. bd. of trustees Neighborhood House, New Brunswick. Mem. Am. Assn. Univ. Profs., N.E.A., Coll. Teachers of Edn., Phi Delta Kappa, etc. Author: Quaker Contributions to Education in North Carolina, 1925; Educational Activities of New England Quakers, 1928. Contbr. to various jours. Home: 10 Rutgers St., Stelton, N.J.

KLARMANN, Emil G., chemist; b. Austria, Dec. 31, 1900; s. Oscar and Regina (Trompeter) K.; came to U.S., 1924, naturalized, 1930; Chem. Engr., Tech. Inst., Bruenn, 1922; D.Sc., U. of Halle, 1924; m. Alvine Ganeau, Oct. 10, 1935. Research chemist for Lehn and Fink Products Corpn., Bloomfield, N.J., 1924-26, chief chemist since 1926; awarded patents for chem. discoveries. Mem. A.A.A.S., Am. Chem. Soc., Am. Inst. Chem. Engrs. Contbr. articles to scientific publs. Home: 153 Franklin St., Bloomfield, N.J.

KLAUSNER, Bertram, rabbi; b. Newark, N.J., Nov. 18, 1908; s. Jacob and Rebecca (Rosenberg) K.; grad. South Side High Sch., Newark, N.J., 1926; A.B., New York U., 1930; rabbi, Hebrew Union Coll., Cincinnati, O., 1936 unmarried. Rabbi Congregation Beth El, Glens Falls, N.Y., 1936-37; rabbi Temple Beth El, Fairmont, W.Va., since 1937. Dir. Jewish Student Foundation, W.Va. Univ., Morgantown, since 1937. Mem. Central Conf. Am. Rabbis, B'nai B'rith. Reformed Jewish religion. Home: Elks Club, Fairmont, W.Va.

KLAUSNER, David Maurice, lawyer; b. New York, N.Y., Aug. 20, 1896; s. Mayer and Sarah (Berman) K.; A.B., Columbia U., 1916; LL.B., Columbia U. Law Sch., 1918; m. Mildred S. Miller, June 2, 1925; children—Robert Benjamin, William James. Admitted to N.J. bar, 1919, counsellor at law, 1922, engaged in gen. practice at Jersey City since 1919; mem. firm, Kinkead & Klausner, 1923-33, in practice alone since 1933; Supreme Ct. Commr. of N.J., 1930; spl. Master in Chancery, 1936. Served as seaman, U.S.N., 1918. Pres. Hebrew Home for Orphans & Aged of Hudson Co.; vice-pres. Internat. Inst. of Jersey City; past pres. B'nai B'rith Council of State of N.J.; past vice-pres. Council of Social Agencies of Jersey City; dir. Jersey City Y.M.H.A. and Jewish Community Center. Mem. Am. Bar Assn., N.J. State Bar Assn., and Hudson Co. Bar Assn. (trustee), Conf. of Co. Bar Assns. of N.J. (exec. com.), Am. Legion, Brotherhood of Temple Beth-El. Democrat. Jewish religion. Mason, B'nai B'rith, K.P., B.P.O.E. Club: Lions of Jersey City. Home: 117 Kensington Av., Jersey City, N.J. Office: 26 Journal Sq., Jersey City, N.J.

KLEEB, Henry Adam, lithographer; b. Dudelsheim, Germany, Sept. 19, 1876; s. Henry Christ and Katharina (Schwarz) K.; came to U.S., 1881, became citizen through father's naturalization, 1890; student 8th Ward Allegheny City (now 26th Ward Pittsburgh) Pub. Sch., 1882-88; m. Anna Amelia Schmittdiel, Feb. 19, 1903; children—Grace Catherine (Mrs. William P. Flynn), Alice Estella (Mrs. Elmer Broerman), Helen (dec.), Robert Henry, Howard William, Ruth Mary. Began as cash boy, Kaufmann's Dept. Store, Pittsburgh, 1888; salesman Jos. Horne Co., Pittsburgh, 1892-97; bookkeeper, Pa. Savings Fund, Pittsburgh, 1900-04, 1st Nat. Bank of Allegheny, Pittsburgh, 1904-14; auditor and asst. treas. Macbeth-Evans Glass Co., Pittsburgh, 1914-19; v.p. and dir. Bloomfield Trust Co. and Garfield Bank, Pittsburgh, 1915-31; pres. Bankers Lithographing Co., Pittsburgh, mfrs. bank and commercial stationery, 1919-35; v.p. and dir. since 1935. Mem. Nat. Assn. Cost Accountants. Republican. Lutheran. Mason (past master Allegheny Lodge 223, F.&A.M.; Islam Grotto No. 35 M.O.V.P. E.R.). Clubs: Malsi, Permas (Pittsburgh). Home: 2914 Norwood Av. Office: Forbes Field, Pittsburgh, Pa.

KLEFFMAN, Albert Henry, clergyman; b. Scotland, Pa., May 29, 1896; s. John Edward and Ella Amanda (Lucking) K.; student Chambersburg (Pa.) High Sch., 1911-13; A.B., Lebanon Valley Coll., Annville, Pa., 1916, D.D., 1936; A.M., Princeton U., 1919; student Princeton Theol. Seminary, 1916-19; student Johns Hopkins University, 1920-23; unmarried. Minister Fulton Av. Presbyn. Ch., Baltimore, Md., 1919-27; stated supply Lakeland Presbyn. Ch., Baltimore, Md., 1924-27; minister West Presbyn. Ch., Wilmington, Del., since 1927; moderator Presbytery of New Castle, Del., 1929; moderator of Synod of Baltimore, Md., 1939. Mem. Princeton Theol. Sem. Alumni Assn. of Phila. (pres. 1936), Presbyn. Ministers Social Union of Phila. (pres. 1937). Presbyterian. Mason (Eureka Lodge 23, Wilmington, Del.; Grand Chaplain of Del., 1936-38). Clubs: Cleric (Wilmington, Del.); Canterbury Cleric (Phila., Pa.), Alumni Friars (Princeton, N.J.; pres. 1939). Home: 1013 Park Pl. Office: 8th and Washington Sts., Wilmington, Del.

KLEIN, Arthur Warner, prof. mech. engring.; b. New Haven, Conn., Nov. 17, 1880; s. Joseph Frederic and Ada Louise (Warner) K.; M.E., Lehigh U., 1899; m. Josephine Russell Brock, July 10, 1907; 1 dau., Dorothy Brock (Mrs. David Perry Nichols). Began as cadet engr. Essex & Hudson Gas Co., Newark, N.J., 1900; cadet engr. and asst. to supt., Atlanta Gas Light Co., 1901-03; prof. mech. engring., civil engring. and physics, Grove City Coll., 1903-04; with Lehigh U. since 1904, instr. mech. engring., 1904-08, asst. prof., 1908-10, asso. prof., 1910-15, prof. mech. engring. since 1915. Mem. A.A.A.S., Am. Soc. Mech. Engrs., Soc. for Promotion Engring. Edn., Tau Beta Pi, Bach Choir, Engrs. Club of Lehigh Valley. Democrat. Episcopalian. Home: 43 Wall St. Office: Packard Laboratory, Lehigh University, Bethlehem, Pa.

KLEIN, Charles, judge; b. Atlantic City, N.J., Sept. 16, 1900; s. Samuel and Esther (Grün) K.; LL.B., Temple U. Sch. of Law, 1921; student Villanova Coll. Extension Sch., 1921-22; m. Rosalie S. Benson, June 30, 1933. Admitted to Pa. bar, 1921, and since engaged in gen. practice of law at Phila.; spl. counsel, Dept. of Banking of Pa., 1927-31; spl. dep. atty. gen. of Pa., 1931-34; counsel joint legislative com. of Pa. investigating milk industry; govs. counsel Pub. Service Commn. investigation; judge Orphan's Ct., Phila., since 1934. Dir. Jewish Hosp., Jewish Welfare Soc., Big Brothers Assn. Mem. exec. com. Gen. Alumni Assn. of Temple U. Jewish religion. Club: Caveat of Philadelphia (vice-pres.). Home: 206 S. 13th St. Office: 542 City Hall, Philadelphia, Pa.

KLEIN, Charles Herbert (Chuck), professional baseball player. Outfielder with Phila. Nat. League Baseball Team, 1928-34, 1936-39, Chicago Nat. League, 1934-35, Pittsburgh Nat. League since 1939; won Nat. League batting championship, 1933. Mem. Nat. League All-Star Team, 1933. Address: care Pittsburgh National League Baseball Club, Pittsburgh, Pa.

KLEIN, Frederic Shriver, coll. prof.; b. York, Pa., Oct. 22, 1904; s. Harry Martin John and Mary Winifred (Shriver) K.; ed. Franklin and Marshall Acad., 1914-19; A.B., Franklin and Marshall Coll., Lancaster, Pa., 1923; A.M., Columbia U., 1927; m. Florence Haenle, June 7, 1932; children—Joan Haenle, Frederic Ferree. Instr. high sch., Milford, Pa., 1923-25; instr. history, Washington Square Coll., New York U., 1926-28; instr. history, Franklin and Marshall Coll., Lancaster, Pa., 1929-37, asso. prof. since 1939; organizer and condr. European tours since 1929; travel agt. Trans-Atlantic Passenger Conf. since 1937; condr. Franklin & Marshall Coll. Symphony Orchestra since 1930. Mem.

Am. and Pa. hist. assns., Lancaster Co. Hist. Soc., Phi Kappa Psi, Pi Gamma Mu. Reformed Ch. Club: University (Lancaster, Pa.). Author: An Introduction to Historical Method, 1931; The Spiritual and Educational Background of Franklin and Marshall College, 1939; Research Methods in History, 1939; co-editor (with H. M. J. Klein) Franklin and Marshall College Studies, 1938; contbr. hist. articles to mags. and papers. Home: 1050 Maple Av., Lancaster, Pa.

KLEIN, Harry Martin John, coll. prof.; b. Hazelton, Pa., Dec. 9, 1873; s. George and Rebecca (Schaeffer) K.; student Muhlenberg Coll., 1889-91; A.B., Franklin and Marshall Coll., 1893, Ph.D., 1907; Litt.D., Franklin and Marshall College, 1935; studied U. of Berlin, 1899; student Theol. Sem. Ref. Ch., Lancaster, Pa., 1893-96; m. Mary Winifred Shriver, Sept. 14, 1899; children—Richard Henry, Frederic Shriver, Philip Shriver. Ordained ministry Ref. Ch. in U.S., 1896; pastor Grace Ch., York, Pa., 1896-1905, Zion Ch., Allentown, Pa., 1905-10; Audenried prof. history and archæology, Franklin and Marshall Coll., since 1910. Prof. history, U. of Pittsburgh Summer Sch., 1912. Pres. Eastern Synod of Ref. Ch., 1914-15. Mem. Am. Acad. Polit. and Social Science, Pa. Association of Planning Commissioners (pres.), Lancaster Chamber of Commerce (pres. 1931-32), Phi Gamma Delta, Phi Beta Kappa, Tau Kappa Alpha. Pres. Hist. Soc. of Reformed Ch. in U.S. Contributor articles on history, religion and philosophy to various periodicals. Editor The History of Lancaster County, Pa., 1923. Author: A Century of Education at Mercersburg, 1936. Home: 450 President Av., Lancaster, Pa.

KLEIN, Jacob M., lawyer; b. New York, N.Y., Feb. 1, 1889; s. Max and Leah (Beerman) K.; grad. Perth Amboy (N.J.) High Sch., 1907; student New York Law Sch., 1908-11; m. Agnes Sayler, Dec. 1917; children—Jacob M., Jane. Admitted to bar, 1911; now in practice at Perth Amboy, N.J.; counsel to Port Raritan Dist. Commn. since 1932. Enlisted in U.S. Army, Dec. 1917; stationed at Ft. Thomas, Ky., Camp Taylor, Louisville, Ky., Camp Johnson, Jacksonville, Fla., Camp Sherman, Chillicothe, O.; disch. with officers commn. Apr. 1919. Pres. Perth Amboy Chamber of Commerce 8 years; mem. exec. com. Troop 6, Boy Scouts of America, Perth Amboy. Mem. Perth Amboy Bar Assn., Middlesex County Bar Assn. (v.p. 1939), N.J. Bar Assn., Am. Legion, Y.M.C.A., Y.M.H.A. Democrat. Elk. Clubs: Raritan Yacht, Metuchen Golf and Country, Lions (pres. 1928-29). Home: 178 Rector St. Office: National Bank Bldg., Perth Amboy, N.J.

KLEIN, John Warren, college pres. emeritus; b. Reading, Pa., Mar. 28, 1872; s. John and Sally (Custer) K.; B.A., Willamette Univ., Salem, Ore., 1897, M.A., 1898; D.D., Ursinus Coll., 1910; LL.D., Lebanon Valley College, Pa., 1934; m. Anna Lanz, Nov. 24, 1898; children—Ruth Anna (Mrs. Herman DeMund), John Norman, Esther Adella (Mrs. Richard T. Williamson). Ordained ministry Evangelical Church, 1893, occupying various pulpits; head department of history Schuylkill Coll., Reading, Pa., 1918-23, v.p. and treas., 1923-28; v.p. and treas. Albright Coll., Reading, 1928-32, pres., 1932-38. Ex-dir. Berks County Trust Co. Trustee Homeopathic Hosp.; dir. Teachers' Protective Union; former mem. Reading City Planning Commn. Mem. N.E.A. Mason (Shriner). Clubs: University, Wyomissing, Kiwanis. Contbr. to religious and ednl. publs. World traveler and lecturer. Home: 1209 Orchard Rd., Reading, Pa.

KLEIN, Louis Amos, veterinarian; b. Phila., Pa., May 10, 1871; s. Albert and Mary Elizabeth (Shoemaker) K.; Sch. of Vet. Medicine, V.M.D., U. of Pa., 1897; m. Sue Boyd Harris, Apr. 9, 1901. Gen. practice, 1897-98; vet. insp., U.S. Bur. Animal Industry, 1898-99, 1902-04; prof. vet. medicine, Ia. State Coll., Ames, 1899-1902; prof. vet. science, Clemson (S.C.) Agrl. Coll., 1904-07; dep. state veterinarian of Pa., 1907-09; prof. vet. hygiene and pharmacology, Sch. of Vet. Medicine, U. of Pa., since 1909, dean faculty, 1909-30. Mem. advisory bd. Office of Surgeon Gen. of U.S.A.;

service with A.E.F. in France. Mem. Am. and Pa. vet. med. assns., Alpha Psi, Omega Tau Sigma, Sigma Xi. Republican. Presbyn. Mason. Author: Principles and Practice of Milk Hygiene, 1917. Translator: Fröhner's General Therapeutics, 1914. Home: Moylan, Pa. Address: School of Veterinary Medicine, University of Pa., Philadelphia, Pa.

KLEIN, William Henry, cement mfg.; b. Milwaukee, Wis., Apr. 2, 1884; s. Louis and Christina (Befort) K.; ed. pub. sch. and high sch., Kansas City, Mo., 1890-1901; B.S., U. of Mich., 1906; m. Jessie Creswell Booker, June 15, 1909 (dec.); children—William Frederick, Philip Merlin, Louis Edward, David Alwyn; m. 2d, Jean Altrude Smith Jan. 7, 1930; 1 son, Richard Ashley. With Kansas Portland Cement Co., chemist to supt., 1906-11; gen. supt. Dixie Portland Cement Co., Richard City, Tenn., 1911-26; gen. mgr. southern div., Pennsylvania-Dixie Cement Corpn., Chattanooga, Tenn., 1926-33, gen. operating mgr., Nazareth, Pa., 1933-37, vice-pres., dir., and gen. operating mgr., same, at Nazareth, Pa., since 1937. Mem. A.A.A.S., Am. Concrete Inst., Am. Soc. for Testing Materials. Republican. Mem. Christian Ch. Mason (K.T., Shriner). Clubs: Pomfret (Easton); Northampton County Country; Mountain City (Chattanooga, Tenn.). Home: 221 N. 14th St., Easton, Pa. Office: Nazareth, Pa.

KLEITZ, George, wholesale jeweler; b. Germany, June 6, 1874; s. George and Dorothie (Meyer) K.; came to U.S., 1881, naturalized, 1895; student pub. sch., Wilmington, Del., 1881-88; m. Louisa B. Bacher, Apr. 19, 1900; children—George Theodore, Louisa M. (Mrs. Henry Ingram Law), Katherine P., Howard W. Employed with Walter H. Thompson, jeweler, Wilmington, Del., 1889-90; started in jewelry business with brother Bernard Kleitz, 1891; pres. B. Kleitz & Bros. Co., wholesale jewelers, Wilmington, Del., since 1935. Lutheran. Home: 2206 Delaware Av. Office: 601 Market St., Wilmington, Del.

KLIEFORTH, Alfred Will, fgn. service officer; b. Mayville, Wis., Oct. 10, 1889; B.A. U. of Wis., 1913; m. Barbara Leslie, Feb. 20, 1918; children—Alexander A., Leslie A. Attaché Am. Legation, Stockholm, Sweden, 1916; asst. mil. attaché Am. Embassy to Russia, 1916-19; apptd. economic expert on Russia and Poland, Dept. of State, 1929, consul, Mar. 1, 1923; consul at Berlin, Germany, 1924-27, Riga, Latvia, 1927-29; sec. Am. Embassy, Berlin, 1929-33; sec. of Legation, Vienna, 1933-35; consul general, Cologne, Germany, since 1935. Commd. 1st lt. inf., 1918. Catholic. Club: Metropolitan (Washington, D.C.). Home: Boalsburg, Pa. Address: Department of State, Washington, D.C.

KLIMM, Lester Earl, coll. prof.; b. Brooklyn, N.Y., June 6, 1902; s. George Stephen and Minnie Alfreda (Rhood) K.; student Hartford (Conn.) Pub. High Sch., 1916-1920, Middlebury (Vt.) Coll., 1920-22; B.S., Columbia U., 1924; Ph.D., U. of Pa., 1930; m. Mary Elizabeth Lee, Dec. 21, 1927; 1 dau, Elizabeth Lee. Instr. geography, Wharton Sch., U. of Pa., 1924-30, asst. prof., 1930-35, asso. prof. since 1935; dir. student personnel, Wharton Sch. of Finance and Commerce, U. of Pa. since 1937. Fellow Social Science Research Council (Ireland), 1933-34. Mem. Assn. Am. Geographers, Alpha Sigma Phi, Beta Gamma Sigma. Mason. Author: (with O. P. Starkey and N. F. Hall) Introductory Economic Geography, 1937. Editor of Bulletin of Phila. Geog. Soc., 1931-33; contributor to geographical publications. Home: 4643 Locust St. Office: U. of Pennsylvania, Philadelphia, Pa.

KLINE, Burton, newspaper man, author; b. Williamsport, Pa.; s. Isaac Newton and Jane (Clapp) K.; prepared for coll. at Dickinson Sem., Williamsport, Pa.; Harvard, 1902-04; m. Madeleine Mesinger, May 12, 1909; 1 dau., Jane. With Boston Transcript, 1904-18, magazine editor, same, 1912-18; Sunday editor of New York Tribune, 1918-19; publicity mgr. Greater N.Y. Hoover Com., 1920; spl. asst. to sec. of labor, 1921-22, 1924-31; magazine editor Phila. Public Ledger, 1922; mem. U.S. George Washington Bicentennial Commn., 1931-

32; N.J. director Federal Writers' Projects, 1935-36. Clubs: Harvard (New York City); Newspaper (Boston); Engineers' (Phila.). Author: An Onslaught on Fame—A Satire, 1901; The Embarrassment of Mr. Perkins, 1912; Struck by Lightning, 1916; The End of the Flight, 1917; Canardia, 1920; The Gallant Rogue, 1921; A Merchant's Horizon (with A. Lincoln Filene), 1923; The Puppet-Show on the Potomac (by Rufus Dart II), 1933; Humanity in Court (with Hon. Norman S. Dike, Justice N.Y. Supreme Court), 1934; also numerous short stories and critical articles. Republican. Home: Westfield, N.J.

KLINE, Earl Kilburn, univ. prof.; b. Harper, Kan., Mar. 14, 1884; s. Elijah William and Charlotte (Birkett) K.; A.B., U. of Okla., Norman, Okla., 1907; B.A., Oxford U., England, 1910, M.A., 1913; student Goettingen and Leipzig, Germany, 1910-13, U. of Ill., Urbana, Ill., 1915-16, Centro de Estudios Historicos, Madrid, Spain, summer 1926; m. Anna Maria Frauenheim, Aug. 17, 1914. Instr. modern langs., Kansas U., Lawrence, Kansas., 1913-14, Whitman Coll., Walla Walla, Wash., 1914-15, U. of Ill., Urbana, Ill., 1915-16; prof. modern langs., U. of Wyo., Laramie, Wyo., 1916-20, U. of Chattanooga (Tenn.), 1920-32; prof. modern langs., Brothers Coll., Drew U., Madison, N.J., since 1932. Mem. Modern Lang. Assn., Spanish Teachers Assn., Assn. of Univ. Profs. Methodist. Has spent 7 yrs. in study and travel in England, Germany, France, Spain. Address: 13 Woodcliff Drive, Madison, N.J.

KLINE, Emanuel, real estate and ins.; b. Philadelphia, Pa., Mar. 29, 1883; s. Moritz and Lena (Friedman) K.; student Upper Pittsgrove Twp. Sch., Norma, N.J., 1888-93, Pub. Sch., Phila., 1893-95, German St. Sch., 1895-98, Temple U., 1898-1900, Internat. Corr. Sch., 1900-05; m. Hettie Jalkowe, Aug. 16, 1908; children—Sylvia (Mrs. Harry Rantz), Jerome, Jesse A., Ruth, Daniel, Leonard, Maurice. Worked on father's farm, summers, 11 yrs.; employed by brother in grocery store, 3 yrs.; entered real estate business since 1907; federal negotiator Phila. Housing Authority; pres. Equity Tent Credit Union; sec. Central City Businessmen's Assn., Woodbury Heights Land Development Co. Was at one time actively interested in politics; drafted first Federal Deposit Insurance Act. Del. to United Business Men's Assn., several yrs., also mem.; mem. South Phila. Realty Bd., North Phila. Realty Bd., Phila. Real Estate Bd. Winner various prizes for essays in local newspaper. Mem. Temple Emanu-El. Mason, K.P. Clubs: Dover Fishing, Izaak Walton League, Zionists of America. Home: 1980 W. Sparks St. Office: 255 S. 5th St., Philadelphia, Pa.

KLINE, I. Clinton, ex-congressman; b. Mt. Pleasant, nr. Sunbury, Pa., Aug. 18, 1858; s. Herman Garner and Mary (Bassett) K.; A.B., Lafayette Coll., 1893, A.M., 1897; unmarried. Admitted to Pa. bar, 1894, and since practiced at Sunbury; also practiced for some time in Washington, D.C.; admitted to Superior and Supreme courts of Pa. and Supreme Court of U.S.; made stumping tour of Pa. for Rep. Party, 1898, and of N.H. and N.J., 1924; mem. 67th Congress (1921-23), 17th Pa. Dist. Traveled through 8 countries of Europe, 1925, and around the world, 1927. Mason. Address: 235 Market Sq., Sunbury, Pa.

KLINE, J. Simpson, lawyer; b. Upper Augusta Twp., Northumberland Co., Pa., Jan. 1, 1861; s. Herman G. and Mary (Bassett) K.; student Lafayette Coll., Easton, Pa.; unmarried. School teacher, Bloomsburg, Pa., until 1889; admitted to Pa. bar, 1891, and since practiced in Sunbury; pres. and solicitor Northumberland Co. Ry. Co. since 1918; dir. and solicitor First Nat. Bank of Sunbury since 1916, chmn. of finance com. for 5 years; dir. Lewisburg Nat. Bank; dir. Lewisburg Bridge Co.; dir. and treas. S. & S. Transit Co.; vice-pres. and dir. Sunbury Water Co.; local solicitor for Pa. R.R. Co. Trustee and pres. Mary M. Packer Hosp. for over 15 years. Republican. Presbyterian. Mason (K.T., Shriner). Home: 122 N. Front St., Sunbury, Pa.

KLINE, John Robert, prof. mathematics; b. Quakertown, Pa., Dec. 7, 1891; s. Henry K. and Emma (Osman) K.; A.B., Muhlenberg Coll., Allentown, Pa., 1912, Sc.D., same college, 1934; A.M., University of Pennsylvania, 1914, Ph.D., 1916; Guggenheim fellow, Univ. of Göttingen, 1925-26; m. Anna B. Shafer, June 1, 1915; 1 son, John Shafer. Instr. in mathematics, U. of Pa., 1917-18, Yale, 1918-19; asso. in mathematics, U. of Ill., 1919-20; asst. prof. mathematics, U. of Pa., 1920-28, prof. since 1928; visiting professor, Bryn Mawr Coll., 1935-36. Mem. bd. examiners in mathematics, Coll. Entrance Exam. Bd. Mem. Am. Math. Society, (asso. editor of bulletin, council, and asso. sec.), A.A.A.S. (v.p. and chmn. Sect. A. 1938), Math. Assn. of America, Deutsche Mathematiker Vereinigung, Polish Math. Soc., Alpha Tau Omega. Presbyn. Mason. Contbr. to Trans. Am. Math. Soc., Fundamenta Mathematicæ, etc. Asso. editor Trans. Am. Math. Soc., also of Am. Jour. Mathematics. Home: 529 Riverview Av., Swarthmore, Pa.

KLINE, Sidney DeLong, banker and lawyer; b. West Reading, Pa., June 15, 1902; s. Simon Sydenham and Elda M. Esther (DeLong) K.; A.B., Dickinson Coll., 1924; LL.B. and M.A., Dickinson Sch. of Law, 1926; m. Leona Clarice Barkalow, Aug. 4, 1928; children—Joan Clarice, Sidney DeLong, Jr., Robert Cornelius. Admitted to Berks and Phila. Co. bars, 1926, and to practice before Superior and Supreme Cts. of Pa., 1926; asst. to trust officer, Mutual Trust Co., Phila., July 5, 1926-28; asst. trust officer, Union Bank and Trust Co., Phila., 1928-29; trust officer Colonial-Northeastern Trust Co., 1929-32; v.p. and trust officer Berks County Trust Co. (formed by merger of Colonial-Northeastern Trust Co. and Berks County Trust Co.), Reading, Pa., since July 1, 1932; pres. Orange Lake Development Corpn., Reading Med. Arts Bldg. Corpn.; dir. Am. Casualty Co., Carsonia Park Co., Reading Hotel Corpn., Cassel's Stores, Inc. Trustee Welfare Fed. of Reading and Berks Co., Hist. Soc. of Berks Co. Mem. Phi Kappa Psi (mem. bd. trustees Pa. Zeta Chapter). Democrat. Reformed Church. Clubs: Wyomissing, Berkshire Country (Reading, Pa.). Home: 62 Grand View Boul., Wyomissing Hills, West Lawn, Pa. Office: 35 N. 6th St., Reading, Pa.

KLINE, Whorten Albert, educator; b. York Co., Pa., Apr. 24, 1864; s. Daniel and Margaret A. (Ruby) K.; A.B., Ursinus Coll., Collegeville, Pa., 1893, A.M. and B.D., 1896 (Litt.D., 1913); U. of Pa., 1897-1901; unmarried. Teacher pub. schs., Pa., 1883-86; instr. Latin, Ursinus Acad., 1893-96; instr. Latin, Ursinus Coll., 1896-1903, prof. Latin lang. and lit. since 1903, dean since 1909. Ordained minister Ref. Ch. in U.S., 1896. Mem. Classical Assn. Middle States and Md., Phila. Bot. Club. Republican. Address: Ursinus College, Collegeville, Pa.

KLINEDINST, David Philip, lawyer; b. York, Pa., July 31, 1870; s. John and Margaret Anna (Wagner) K.; ed. York (Pa.) pub. schs., 1876-88, York Collegiate Inst., 1892-94, Pricketts Coll. of Commerce, Phila., Pa., 1894-95; LL.B., Yale Law Sch., 1897; m. Mary Moulson, of Rochester, N.Y.; children—Mary Ellen, David Moulson, Elizabeth Wakefield, Ruth, Thomas John. Admitted to Pa. and Conn. bars, 1897, and since practiced in York, Pa.; pres. and treas. York Motor Co. since 1920; city solicitor, York, Pa., 1899-1903 (two terms); mem. Pa. State Senate, 1907-10. Trustee Children's Home, York; mem. bd. mgrs. York Benevolent Soc. Mem. Young Men's Dem. Assn. Democrat. Lutheran. Home: 145 W. Springettsbury Av. Office: 33 & 34 Central National Bank Bldg., York, Pa.

KLINGEL, Joseph William, realtor; b. Phila., Pa., Oct. 1, 1886; s. Joseph Henry and Matilda (Breininger) K.; ed. Banks Business Coll., Phila., 1902-03, Central High Sch., Phila., 1904-05, Temple U., 1916-18; m. Anna Marie Mader, Sept. 14, 1910; children—Joseph Victor, Anna Paulina. With Phila. & Reading Ry. Co., 1899-1918, beginning as messenger boy and advanced to soliciting freight agent; in real estate business since 1918; organized Klingel, Wilson, Schmid, realtors, Phila., 1930. Mem. N. Phila. Realty Bd. (dir.), Phila. Real Estate Bd., S. Phila. Realty Bd., W. Phila. Realty Bd. Republican. Roman Catholic. Home: 822 W. Lehigh Av. Office: 9th and Lehigh Av., Philadelphia, Pa.

KLINGELHOFER, Edward Kohne, manufacturer; b. Pittsburgh, Pa., Nov. 2, 1894; s. George Edward and Ada Louise (Kohne) K.; student Shady Side Acad., Pittsburgh, 1908-13, Cornell U., 1917; m. Margaret Stoner, Dec. 28, 1920; 1 son, Edward Kohne. Began in minor position with Pittsburgh Bridge and Iron Works, structural steel fabricators, 1917, successively asst. to pres., v.p. and gen. mgr., pres. since 1930. Dir. Am. Inst. of Steel Construction. Mem. Sigma Chi. Republican. Presbyterian. Clubs: Duquesne, Harvard-Yale-Princeton (Pittsburgh); Allegheny Country; Edgeworth (Sewickley, Pa.). Home: 33 Thorn St., Sewickley, Pa. Office: 1910 Union National Bank Bldg., Pittsburgh, Pa.

KLINGER, Allen Connable; prof. history Marshall Coll. Address: Marshall College, Huntington, W.Va.

KLINGINSMITH, John Glenn, investment management; b. Greenwood Twp., Crawford Co., Pa., Jan. 11, 1890; s. Charles Chester and Esther (Brush) K.; grad. Edinboro (Pa.) State Normal Sch., 1911; A.B., Allegheny Coll., Meadville, Pa., 1916; m. Ruth Pearl McMaster, Oct. 20, 1917. Security salesman Harris Forbes & Co., New York, Sept. 26, 1916-Oct. 15, 1918, mgr. Pittsburgh office until Jan. 1, 1926; asst. mgr. bond dept. Peoples Pittsburgh Trust Co., Jan. 1, 1926-June 1, 1932; treas. and dir. Pa. Industries, Inc. and sec.-treas. and dir. Pa. Bankshares and Securities Corpn., Pittsburgh, management of investment co. portfolios and supervision of bank portfolios in which co. stock holder since 1932; v.p. 1st Nat. Bank, Etna, Pa.; dir. Ky. Natural Gas Co., Owensboro, Ky., Peoples Nat. Bank, Tarentum, Pa., Arsenal Bank, Pittsburgh. Trustee Allegheny Coll., Zoar Home, Allison Park, Pa. Member Pittsburgh Chamber of Commerce, Delta Tau Delta Fraternity. Republican. Methodist (trustee Christ M.E. Ch., Pittsburgh). Clubs: Duquesne, University, Bankers, Bond (Pittsburgh). Home: 5501 Beacon St. Office: 1914 Grant Bldg., Pittsburgh, Pa.

KLONOWER, Henry, dir., teacher edn. and certification; b. Phila., Pa., Sept. 14, 1888; s. Oscar and Sophia (Heintz) K.; grad. Central Manual Training High Sch.; B.S., Central High School, Phila.; grad. Phila. Sch. of Pedagogy, Phila., 1910; B.S., U. of Pa., 1915, A.M., 1920; student Temple U., 1921, Columbia, summer 1920; hon Pd.D., Ursinus Coll., Collegeville, Pa., 1936; m. Elizabeth Luburg Peddrick, 1915 (died 1916). Teacher elementary schs., Phila., 1910-16, Sch. of Pedagogy, Phila., 1916-18, high sch., Radnor, Pa., 1918-20; dir. in charge secondary certification and placement, Dept. Pub. Instrn., Pa., 1920-25, dir. Teachers Bur., 1925-34, chief Teacher Div., 1934-36; dir. Teacher Edn. and Certification, Pa. Dept. Pub. Instrn., since 1936. Sec. Bd. of Pres. of State Teachers Colls. since 1925; sec. Nat. Assn. of State Dirs. of Teacher Training and Certification, 1932-33, pres. since 1933; pres. interstate Conf. on Common Problems in Teacher Edn., Columbia U., 1937-38; chmn. com. on teacher edn. and visual instrn., Am. Council on Edn. Mem. R.O.T.C., Ft. Niagara, N.Y., 1917; farm insp. Sch. Mobilization Com., 1918. Mem. Am. Acad. Polit. and Social Science, Am. Assn. Pub. Sch. Adminstrs. (life), N.E.A., Pa. State Edn. Assn.; Phi Sigma Pi, Kappa Phi Kappa, Phi Delta Kappa. Mason. Clubs: Schoolmen's, U. of Pa. Alumni Assn. (Phila.). Compiler: Syllabi for State Teachers Colls. courses in Preparation of Elementary and Secondary Sch. Teachers, 1932. Contbr. to Public Education and other publs. on teacher edn. Home: 1430 W. Grange St., Philadelphia. Pa. Office: Dept. of Public Instruction, Harrisburg, Pa.

KLONOWSKI, Henry Theophilus Thomas, clergyman; b. Scranton, Pa., Mar. 8, 1898; s. Ladislaus and Apollonia (Kurzydlowska) Klonowski; A.B., St. Thomas Coll., Scranton, Pa., 1916; ed. St. Francis Sem., St. Francis, Wis., 1916-17, SS. Cyril and Methodius Sem., Orchard Lake, Mich., 1917-19, Collegio Capranica and Gregorian Univ., Rome, Italy, 1919-20, S.T.B., 1920; S.T.L., Angelico Univ., Rome, 1923, S.T.D., same, 1924. Ordained priest R.C. Ch. in Rome, Aug. 8, 1920; mng. editor "Angelicum," Rome, 1923-24; adminstr. Parish of St. Mary (Polish), Wilkes-Barre, Pa., 1921; asst. pastor, Dickson City, Pa., 1925; chaplain, Maloney Home, Scranton, Pa., 1928-38, also prof. religion, Marywood Coll., 1928-38, also prof. Latin and head of dept., U. of Scranton, 1928-38; sec. Diocesan Tribunal, 1928-37; sec. Diocesan Bd. Examiners of Jr. Clergy and Seminarians since 1928; Dep. Visitor for Religious (Nuns) since 1937; vice official of the Diocesan Tribunal since 1937; pastor parish of the Sacred Hearts of Jesus and Mary, Scranton, Pa., since 1938. Mem. bd. of examiners, Dept. of Public Assistance, 1938. Trustee Univ. of Scranton. Mem. Am. Cath. Philos. Assn., Am. Classical League. Roman Catholic. Asso. editor "Catholic Light" since 1934. Home: 1213 Prospect Av., Scranton, Pa.

KLOPP, Henry Irwin, psychiatrist; born at Stouchsburg, Pa., Jan. 1, 1870; s. Jerome and Katherine (Groh) K.; student Palatinate (now Albright Coll.), Myerstown, Pa., 1885; M.D., Hahnemann Med. Coll., 1894; D.Sc., Muhlenberg Coll., Allentown, Pa., 1927; m. Elizabeth Ladora Stump, Dec. 28, 1898; 1 dau., Mrs. Robert E. Bender. With Westboro (Mass.) State Hosp., 1892-1912; supt. and phys. in chief Allentown State Homeo. Hosp. since 1912; asso. prof. psychiatry Hahnemann Med. Coll., 1912-30, clin. prof. mental diseases since 1930; dir. mental clinics Allentown and Sacred Heart Hosps. (Allentown), St. Luke's Hosp. (Bethlehem), Easton (Pa.) Hosp., etc.; spl. neuropsychiatric examiner U.S.P.H. Service, 1919-21. Fellow Am. Coll. Physicians; mem. Am. Psychiatric Assn., Phila. Psychiatric Assn., N.E. Psychiatric Assn., Am. Inst. Homeopathy, Pa. State Homeo. Med. Soc. (v.p.), Am. Congress on Internal Medicine, and many others; apptd. mem. Pa. governing com. Gorgas Memorial, 1929. Mem. German Reformed Ch. Clubs: Contemporary, Lehigh Valley Torch. Contbr. numerous articles to med. jours. Home: Allentown, Pa.*

KLOSKY, Simon, research chemist; b. Mobile, Ala., Feb. 4, 1895; s. Peter J. Rabby and Vincenza Klosky; A.B., Mt. St. Mary's Coll., Emmitsburg, Md., 1914, A.M., same, 1916; Ph.D., Johns Hopkins U., 1921; m. Kathryn Gloninger, June 21, 1919; children—Marilyn, Rosilyn, Simon III, Peter, Henry Spalding, Philip Michael, Kathryn. Employed as research chemist, Edgewood Arsenal, Md., 1921 to 1922; instr., chemistry dept., Catholic Univ., Washington, D.C., 1923-28; chem. patent expert U.S. War Dept., Washington, D.C., 1928; chemist, research dept., Am. Agricultural Chem. Co., New York, N.Y., since 1928, dir. Research Lab., Newark, N.J., since 1936. Served as 1st lt. A.S., U.S.A., 1917-18, with A.E.F. Mem. Am. Chem. Soc., Kappa Alpha. Democrat. Roman Catholic. Home: 137 Livingston Av., New Brunswick. Office: 120 Lister Av., Newark, N.J.

KLOSTERMAN, Julius August, physician and univ. prof.; b. Jersey City, N.J., Dec. 10, 1898; s. August Julius and Theresa (Neuhauser) K.; B.S., N.Y. Univ., 1929, M.S., same, 1930, Ph.D., same, 1932; M.D., Cornell U. Med. Sch., 1936; m. Sarah Grace Hickcox, July 31, 1927. Employed as lab. asst., Rockefeller Inst., 1917-25; instr. in bacteriology, N.Y. U., 1925-26, asst. prof., 1926-27, asst. prof. bacteriology and immunology, 1927-29, lecturer in bacteriology, 1929-32, asst. prof., 1932-34, asso. prof. since 1934; cons. bacteriologist Holy Name Hosp. (Teaneck, N.J.), and Parkway Hosp., Beekman Street Hosp., New York, 1939. Served in S.A.T.C., 1917; 1st lt. Med. Res. Mem. A.A.A.S., Am. Med. Assn., Assn. Mil. Surgs., Am. Assn. Bacteriologists, Harvey Soc., Sigma Xi, Nu Sigma Nu. Republican. Roman Catholic. Club: Army and Navy. Home: 40 Maplewood Av., Bogota, N.J. Office: 477 1st Av., New York, N.Y.

KLOTZ, John R(hoderic) MacPherson, chemist; b. Newark, N.J., Jan. 2, 1887; s. Samuel

Willet and Laura (Stickle) K.; B.S., U. of Pa., 1909; m. Margaret Carpenter, Dec. 6, 1916; children—Margaret Eugenia, John R. MacPherson III. Employed as chemist, Barrett Mfg. Co., 1909-15; mgr. Newport Co., 1915-22; cons. chemist at Montclair, N.J., since 1922. Served as sec. Chemists Club, 1916-21, trustee same, 7 yrs. Mem. Am. Chem. Soc., Am. Inst. Chem. Engrs. Episcopalian. Clubs: University, Chemists (New York); Rittenhouse (Philadelphia). Home: 165 Midland Av., Montclair, N.J.

KLUGE, Albert Carl, woven label mfg.; b. New York, N.Y., June 25, 1892; 's. Adolph Carl and Grace Mary (Mackey) K; Textile Engr., Phila. Textile Coll., 1913; grad. study Wharton Sch. of U. of Pa., 1913-15; unmarried. Began as silk and cotton weaver and supt. Artistic Weaving Co., mfr. cotton and silk woven labels, Pompton Lakes, N.J., 1915-18, advanced to vice-pres. then pres., treas. and dir. Artistic Weaving Co., world's largest woven label mfr., 141 W. 36th St., New York, N.Y., since 1918; pres. and treas. Chatham Mills, Inc., Pittsboro, N.C., vice-pres. First Nat. Bank, Pompton Lakes, N.J., since 1935; dir. Citizens Trust Co., Paterson, N.J., since 1924. Mem. Phi Delta Theta. Mason (32°, Shriner). Elk. Clubs: Athletic (New York); Hamilton (Paterson); North Jersey Country (Paterson, N.J.). Home: 205 Ringwood Av., Pompton Lakes, N.J. Office: 141 W. 36th St., New York, N.Y.

KLUMPP, James Sybert, surgeon; b. Owosso, Mich., Jan. 21, 1893; s. Frederick J. and Alice (Hanna) K.; B.S. in Medicine, U. of Mich. Med. Sch., 1918, M.D., 1920; m. Reba T. Griffith, June 7, 1919; 1 dau., Mary Alice. Interne Guthrie Hosp., Huntington, W.Va., 1920-21, house physician, 1921-22; sr. attdg. surgeon St. Marys Hosp., Huntington since 1929; attdg. surgeon Memorial Hosp., Huntington since 1930; chief of staff St. Marys Hosp., 1934-35. Commd. comdr., U.S.N.R. Med. Corps. Fellow Am. Coll. Surgeons. Mem. Am. Med. Assn., W.Va., State Med. Soc., Cabell Co. Med. Soc., Med. Review Soc. Republican. Presbyn. Mason. Clubs: Cabell, Guyan Country (Huntington); Army and Navy (Washington, D.C.). Home: 1328 Neel St. Office: Chesapeake & Ohio Bldg., Huntington, W.Va.

KNANDEL, Herman Clyde, prof. poultry husbandry and head dept.; b. Ilion, N.Y., May 18, 1892; s. Herman Charles and Ida (Kling) K.; B.S., Cornell U., 1914; m. Georgia Haller, July 7, 1915; 1 dau., Jean Frances. Engaged as instr. poultry husbandry, Bristol Co. Agrl. Sch., 1914-16; extension specialist in poultry husbandry, Pa. State Coll., 1916-20, head of dept. poultry husbandry since 1920. Mem. Poultry Sci. Assn. (past pres.), Alpha Zeta, Alpha Gamma Rho, Gamma Sigma Delta. Republican. Presbyn. Mason (trustee Ch., State College, Pa.). Mason. Clubs: Rotary, Centre Hills Country. Contbg. poultry editor, Pennsylvania Farmer, Poultry Tribune. Poultry editor, Comfort Mag. Author of technical articles and bulletins pub. by Pa. State Coll. Home: 329 Ridge Av., State College, Pa.

KNAPP, Harry Butler, surgeon; b. Darwin, Minn., Aug. 9, 1876; s. Ovid Butler and Jennie (McNeal) K.; M.D., U. of Ill. Med. Sch., 1904; m. Dr. Nettie Evans, Sept. 12, 1904; children—Helena M. (Mrs. C. Dudley Clawson), Betty M. (Mrs. Jewel A. Abbey), Harry B., Jr. Employed as surgeon, South Porto Rico Sugar Co., Ensanada, P.R., 1907-10; in pvt. practice at Ionia, Mich., 7 yrs.; asso. surgeon, Battle Creek Sanitarium, 1919-25; surgeon, Nichols and Leila Hosps., Battle Creek, Mich. 1925-34; surgeon, Wellsboro Hosp., Wellsboro, Pa., since 1934; pres. Wellsboro Hosp. Corpn., Wellsboro, Pa. Served as capt. Med. Corps, U.S.A., 1918-19. Fellow Am. Coll. Surgs. Mem. A.M.A., Pa. State Med. Soc. Republican. Conglist. Mason (32°). Clubs: Kiwanis of Battle Creek (pres. 1929); Rotary of Wellsboro (pres. 1938-39). Home: 21 West Av., Wellsboro, Pa.

KNAPP, Rolla Sherwin, pres. Moffitt Creek Lumber Co.; b. Menomonie, Wis., 1872; s. John H. and Valeria (Adams) K.; A.B., Har-

482

vard, 1894; m. Emily Baer Connard, 1915. Began as newspaper reporter, Milwaukee Journal, 1895; engaged in lumbering and mining, California, 1901-06; pres. Moffitt Creek Lumber Co., Yreka, Calif., since 1904. Club: Pomfret. Home: 609 Weygadt Drive. Office: Drake Bldg., Easton, Pa.

KNAUER, Wilhelm Frederick, lawyer; b. Holmesburg, Phila., Pa., Oct. 11, 1894; s. Adolf Joseph and Mary (Rexer) K.; grad. Northeast High Sch., 1912; B.S. in economics, U. of Pa., Wharton Sch., 1916, LL.B., 1920; student U. of Lyon, 1919; unmarried. Admitted to Pa. bar, 1920, and since practiced in Phila.; special dep. atty. gen., 1926-34; counsel Pa. Alcohol Permit Bd., 1928-33, counsel Pa. Liquor Control Bd., 1933-35; dir. dept. supplies and purchases, City of Phila., 1936; dir. and trust officer Northeast Nat. Bank of Phila. Elected as rep. Constitution Revision Commn., 1920. Engaged in relief work, Germany, 1915. Served as mem. Troop A, 1st Pa. Cav., on Mexican Border, 1916; in 1st O.T.C., Ft. Niagara, 1917; 2d lt. Intelligence Service, 114th Inf.; 29th Div., U.S. Army, with A.E.F. in St. Mihiel and Argonne offensives, 1917-19. Mem. Pa. Bar Assn., Phila. Bar Assn., Wilson Law Club, Lawyers Club, Pa. Hist. Soc., Am. Legion, Vets. of Foreign Wars, Delta Sigma Phi. Republican. Mem. German Lutheran Ch. Mason, Odd Fellow. Clubs: Germantown Cricket, Pen and Pencil (Phila.); Collectors (New York). Home: Holmesburg, Phila. Office: 2126 Land Title Bldg., Philadelphia, Pa.

KNEVELS, Gertrude, author; b. Fishkill-on-Hudson (now Beacon), N.Y., Apr. 2, 1881; d. Daniel Crommelin Ver Planck and Mary Louisa Van (Wagenen) K.; ed. in pvt. schs. and at Geneva, Switzerland and Florence, Italy. Democrat. Club: Pen and Brush (New York). Author: The Wonderful Bed (children's book), 1911; Dragon's Glory (play), 1925; Octagon House (mystery-novel), 1926; By Candle-light, 1927; The Diamond Rose Mystery, 1928; Molly Moonshine (book for girls), 1930; Out of the Dark (mystery story), 1932; Lovers' Luck, 1934; Of Love Beware, 1936; also short stories and plays for amateurs. Home: 50 Wheeler St., West Orange, N.J.*

KNIFFEN, Frederick, chemist; b. at Alcove, N.Y., Dec. 2, 1872; s. Franklin and Elizabeth (Winn) K.; B.S., Wesleyan U., Middletown, Conn., 1895, M.S., 1896; m. Lillian May Bassett, July 2, 1898; children—Florence Elizabeth, Charles Franklin. Asst chemist U.S. Naval Torpedo Sta., Newport, R.I., 1897-99, chem. 1905-06; asst. chemist U.S. Smokeless Powder Factory, Indian Head, Md., 1899-05; asst. supt. E. I. du Pont de Nemours & Co. powder plant, Parlin, N.J., 1906-10; asst. operating dir. smokeless powder dept., Wilmington, Del., 1910-22; v.p. Fairfield Rubber Co., Wilmington, 1914-18, du Pont Fabrikoid Co., 1912-18; pres. Claymont Trust Co., Claymont, Del., since 1924. Methodist. Clubs: Rotary, Wilmington Whist. Home: Holly Oak, Del. Office: 7031 du Pont Bldg., Wilmington, Del.

KNIFFIN, Herbert Reynolds, coll. prof.; b. Hornell, N.Y.; s. Herbert Potter and Stella (Reynolds) K., student Cooper Union Sch., N.Y. City, Nat. Acad. Design, N.Y. City, Art Student's League, N.Y. City; grad. diploma Fine Arts and Education, Teachers Coll., Columbia U., 1909; private study, Munich, Germany, 1911; student Academie De LaCluse and Academie Mont Parnasse, Paris, France, 1919-25; m. Henrietta Pyre, 1915; 1 dau., Stella Elizabeth (Mrs. H. W. Jefferson, II). Asst. supervisor art schools, Newark, N.J., 1909-12; prof. fine and industrial arts, U. of Pittsburgh, 1912-17; dir. Art Schs. of Ethical Culture Soc. for Women, Rutgers U., since 1929; lecturer U. of Calif., Berkeley, 1923, U. of Tenn., Knoxville, 1914, U. of Calif., Los Angeles, 1924-25. Exhibited at Nat. Acad. Design, Am. Water Color Soc., N.Y. Color Soc., Architectural League (all of N.Y. City), Salon D'Automn, Paris, Carnegie Inst., Pittsburgh. Chmn. N.J. State Art Com. Author: Masks, 1931. Contbr. to art and edn. periodicals. Home: 29 Baldwin St., New Brunswick, N.J.

KNIGHT, Augustus Smith, M.D., retired; b. Manchester, Mass., Nov. 21, 1864; s. John and Deborah (Carleton) K.; grad. Phillips Acad., Andover, Mass., 1884, Harvard, 1887; M.D., Harvard, 1891; m. Anita Merle-Smith, July 28, 1930; 1 son, Augustus Smith. Practiced in N.Y. City as med. dir. Metropolitan Life Ins. Co., 1899-1934. Pres. bd. of mgrs. N.J. State Hosp. for Mental Diseases, Greystone Park, N. J.; pres. bd. of trustees of Somerset Hosp., Somerville, N. J.; trustee and chairman of house com. of Neighborhood House and Hosp., Inc., Keene Valley, New York. Fellow American College Surgeons; mem. Am. Psychiatric Assn., Assn. for Research in Nervous and Mental Diseases, Nat. Com. for Mental Hygiene (chmn. bd. dirs.), Harvard Med. Soc. of New York, Med. Soc. of N.J., Somerset County Med. Soc. (N.J.). Republican. Episcopalian. Clubs: Harvard (New York); Harvard (Boston); Essex Fox Hounds (Peapack, N.J.); Keene Valley (N.Y.) Country (pres.) Home: Far Hills, N.J.

KNIGHT, Edward Wallace, lawyer; b. Newport, N.H., Apr. 30, 1866; s. Edward Boardman and Hannah Elizabeth (White) K.; A.B., Dartmouth, 1887, A.M., 1925; m. Mary Catherine Dana, Jan. 25, 1893 (died Sept. 14, 1935); children—Edward Dana, Elizabeth Swift, Mary Ethel. Admitted to W.Va. bar, 1889; mem. firm Brown, Jackson & Knight, 1892—; gen. counsel Virginia Ry. Co. and its predecessors, 1902-28, consulting counsel, 1929—; v.p. Central Trust Co. of Charleston; dir. Kanawha Valley Bank, Greenbriar Valley Bank (Lewisburg, W.Va.), Virginian Electric, Inc., Slab Fork Coal Co., New River Coal Co., etc. Member City Council, Charleston, 1891-94; vice-chairman West Virginia Constitutional Commission, 1929-30. Trustee Dartmouth College, 1925-35; member Phi Beta Kappa, Theta Delta Chi. Democrat. Presbyn. Mason. Clubs: Edgewood Country (Charleston); Dartmouth College (New York). Home: 1208 Kanawha St. Office: Kanawha Valley Bldg., Charleston, W.Va.

KNIGHT, Harry S. lawyer; b. Watsontown, Pa., Mar. 6, 1868; s. Frederick H. and Anna (Schoch) K.; ed. Wyoming Sem.; m. Mary B. Martin, June 16, 1897; 1 son, Frederick H. Admitted to Pa. bar and since engaged in gen. practice of law; mem. of law firm of Knight and Kivko; dir. U.S. Fidelity & Guaranty Co. of Baltimore, First Nat. Bank of Sunbury, Sunbury Converting Works, Huntingdon Specialty Co., Seaboard Silk Mills, Ross Realty Co. Pres. bd. trustees Sunbury Pub. Library; vice chmn. Sunbury Chapter Am. Red. Cross. For many yrs. active in Am. Bar Assn., past mem. exec. com. and bd. govs.; sec. since 1936 and ex-officio mem. Bd. Govs. and Ho. Dels.; past pres. Pa. Bar Assn.; mem. Bar Assn. City of New York. Episcopalian (sr. warden St. Matthews P.E. Ch., Sunbury). Clubs: Rotary (past pres.), Susquehanna Valley Country (Sunbury); Union League (Philadelphia); Manufacturers (Milton); Country (Williamsport). Home: 103 Chestnut St. Office: Bittner Trust Bldg., Sunbury, Pa.

KNIGHT, Seymour H., supervising engr.; b. Eau Claire, Wis., Oct. 21, 1875; s. Carleton H. and Alice (Grant) K.; student pub. schs.; m. Eugenia Philbrook, Nov. 10, 1900; 1 dau., Lois. In C.&N.W. R.R. shops Kaukauna, Wis., 1892-94; asst. to city engr., Eau Claire, Wis., 1895-98; principal asst. engr. on railroad work in Ohio, Great Northern Constrn. Co., 1899-1902; chief engr. Indiana Union Traction Co., railroad constrn. in Ind. and Ill., 1902-04; chief engr. Carolina Constrn. Co., S.C., 1904-05; ry. and hydraulic engr. on work in 10 states with W. H. Schott, cons. engr., Chicago, 1905-07; cons. engr. and western rep. on ry., bridge and hydraulic work in Pacific Northwest, Wallace Coates Engring. Co., Chicago, 1907-08; contracting engr. with Northwest Bridge Works, Portland, Ore., 1909; chief engr. on bridge, bldg., irrigation and power plant work. Engring. Constrn. Co., Spokane, Wash., 1909-17; senior civil and advisory engr. on design, constrn., valuation and reports on wide range industrial and pub. utility plants in U.S. and Can., Day and Zimmerman, Inc., Phila., 1918-23; supervising engr. Chicago River Bridge Survey, 1924-25; supervising engr. Sesqui-Centennial Expn., Phila., 1926, Strawbridge & Clothier, Phila., since 1927. Mem. Am. Soc. C.E., Am. Soc. M.E., Soc. Am. Mil. Engrs. (mil. engr. mem.), United Spanish War Vets. Club: Llanderich Country. Home: 615 Manda Rd., Penfield, Delaware Co., Pa. Office: 8th and Market Sts., Philadelphia, Pa.

KNISELEY, John Blair, clergyman; b. Brookville, Pa., Dec. 27, 1888; s. Daniel P. and Catherine Ann (Shaffer) K.; A.B., Susquehanna U., 1913; A.M., Susquehanna U. Theol. Sem., 1916, B.D., 1916; hon. D.D., Susquehanna U., 1931; m. Mary Mae Graybill, June 15, 1916; children—Karl Eugene, Paul Wilbur, Jean Arlene, Ruth Louise. Ordained to ministry United Luth. Ch. in America, 1916; pastor, Port Royal, Pa., 1916-20, DuBois, Pa., 1920-25, Northumberland, Pa., 1925-34; pastor Mt. Zion Ch., Pittsburgh, Pa., since 1934. Dir. Susquehanna U., Selinsgrove, Pa. Dir. Luth. Summer Assembly at Susquehanna U. for 5 yrs.; sec. Susquehanna U. Alumni Assn., 11 yrs., pres., 4 yrs. Mem. Pi Gamma Mu, Phi Mu Delta. Republican. Lutheran. Mason (K.T., 32°, Shriner). Club: Kiwanis. Home: 47 Waldorf St., N.S. Pittsburgh, Pa. Office: 3936 Perrysville Av., N.S., Pittsburgh, Pa.

KNISKERN, Philip Wheeler, real estate, loans, appraising; b. Hastings, Mich., Mar. 25, 1889; s. Albert Decatur (brig. gen. U.S.A.) and Estelle (Wheeler) K.; B.C.E., U. of Mich., 1911; m. Karine Nessen, Sept. 4, 1917; children—Edith Estelle, Philip Nessen. With Thompson-Starrett Co., engrs., New York, 1912-15, Kniskern Co., Chicago, 1915-17 and 1919-20; appraiser and negotiator, real estate loan dept. Chicago Trust Co., 1921-22; examiner and appraiser, city loan div. Metropolitan Life Ins. Co., New York, 1923; mgr. real estate loan dept. Reliance State Bank, Chicago, 1924; v.p. Nat. Surety Co., New York, 1925-27; pres. Nat. Reserve Corpn., 1927-29; v.p. and gen. mgr. Continental Mortgage Guarantee Co., 1929-32; pvt. appraisal practice since 1932; appraisal adviser to Federal Home Loan Bank Bd., Washington, D.C., 1933-35; now pres. and dir. First Mortgage Corpn.; director Quaker City Federal Savings and Loan Assn., First Federal Savings and Loan Assn. of New York. Village trustee Bronxville, N.Y., 1932-34. Served as capt. Engr. O.R.C., World War, on constrn. chem. plants and in charge purchase, storage and distribution of forage for Army in U.S. Gov. and first pres. Am. Inst. Real Estate Appraisers; dir. and mem. exec. com. Nat. Assn. Real Estate Bds.; mem. exec. com. Appraisal Com. Phila. Real Estate Bd.; mem. Beta Theta Pi. Republican. Methodist. Mason. Clubs: Union League, Penn Athletic (Phila.); Commonwealth (Chicago). Speaker and writer on real estate appraisal and financial subjects. Wrote "Real Estate Appraisal and Valuation." Home: Swarthmore, Pa. Office: 1604 Walnut St., Philadelphia, Pa.

KNISS, C. Asher, pres. Keystone Telegraph Press; b. Herndon, Pa., May 22, 1889; s. Samuel B. and Mary (Albert) K.; student Carnegie Inst. Tech.; m. Anna E. Benner, June 26, 1911. Mgr. Myers Printing Co., 1908-14; pres. Keystone Telegraph Press, Mifflinburg, Pa., since 1918. Union County health dir. since 1934. Mason (Mifflinburg Lodge 270). Club: Kiwanis (Mifflinburg, Pa.). Home: 226 Green St. Office: 360 Walnut St., Mifflinburg, Pa.

KNOTTS, Earle Paul, physician; b. Ridgely, Md., Mar. 26, 1895; s. Louis J. and Agnes (Lynch) K.; prep. edn. Washington Coll. Prep. Sch., 1911-12; B.S., Washington Coll., 1916; M.D., U. of Md. Med. Sch., 1920; post grad. work, Harvard, 1925, 32, Rush Medical Sch., 1927, McGill Univ., 1929, Johns Hopkins Hosp., 1936; m. Marjorie Todd, May 3, 1922; children—Elizabeth Agnes, Willard Todd. Health officer, Newberry, S.C., 1920-23; gen. practice of medicine, Denton, Md., since 1923; mem. med. staff Easton Hosp., Easton, Md. Examiner in medicine Md. State Bd. of Med. Examiners; chmn. Military Com. and Armory Bd., Denton. Fellow A.M.A.; mem. Southern Med. Soc., Md. Med. Soc., Caroline County Med. Soc. (pres.

1936), Am. Legion, Denton Business Men's Assn. (vice-pres. 1939), Nu Sigma Nu. Democrat. Roman Catholic. K. of C. Club: Denton Rotary (pres. 1939). Address: Denton, Md.

KNOTTS, James Owen, judge; b. Ridgely, Md., May 28, 1892; s. Louis J. and Agnes L. (Lynch) K.; student Washington & Lee U., Lexington, Va., 1911-12; LL.B., U. of Md., 1914; m. Margaret S. Knotts, Dec. 30, 1910; children—Margaret Jane, Mary Ann, James Owen. Admitted to bar, 1914; practiced at Denton, Caroline Co., Md., 1914-33; apptd. asso. judge, 2d Judicial Circuit of Md., 1933, elected for 15-year term, 1934. Del. Dem. Nat. Conv. 1932. Mem. bd. visitors and govs. Washington Coll., Chestertown, Md.; dir. Emergency Hosp., Easton, Md. Mem. Md. Bar Assn. (v.p. 1937-38), Caroline County Bar Assn. (pres. 1933), Alpha Tau Omega. Mem. K.C. Club: Denton Rotary (pres. 1926). Address: Denton, Md.

KNOWLES, Archibald Campbell, clergyman; b. Phila., July 11, 1865; s. George Lambert and Matilda Josephine K.; ed. U. of Pa., class of '85; attended lectures at Cambridge and London, England; D.D., Nashotah, 1937; m. Mary Clements Stocker, Apr. 20, 1893; children—Margaretta Lewis (Mrs. Stevenson H. Walsh, Jr.), Mary Clements Stocker (Mrs. Alan Maxwell Palmer, died 1933). Was ordained deacon, 1898, priest, 1899, P. E. Church; rector St. Alban's Ch., Olney, Phila. Author: The Belief and Worship of the Anglican Church, 1895; Joscelyn Vernon, 1898; Turning Points, 1898; The Triumph of the Cross, 1900; Come Unto Me, 1901; The Holy Christ Child, 1905; The Life of Offering, 1906; The Practice of Religion (now in its 47th edition), 1906; Adventures in the Alps, 1913; Reminiscences of a Parish Priest, 1935; Franklin Delano Roosevelt —The Great Liberal, 1937. Was engaged in banking and other business enterprises for ten years before entering ministry. Has traveled extensively in Europe, specially interested in ecclesiastical art and architecture; rebuilt St. Alban's Church as a memorial to his father, in the style of French Decorated Gothic of the 13th Century. Home: 555 Pelham Rd., Germantown, Philadelphia, Pa.

KNOWLES, Frank Raymond, commercial engr.; b. Dunbar, Pa., June 25, 1903; s. George W. and Grace M. (Stewart) K.; student high sch., Cleveland, 1917-20, corr. and night sch., Cleveland, 1920-21; m. Genevieve Borski, June 17, 1936. In elec. accuracy lab. General Electric Co., Cleveland, O., 1920-22, in charge lab., 1922-25, asst. illuminating engr., Chicago, 1925-28; illuminating engr., Pa. Electric Co., Johnstown, Pa., 1928-35, organizing illuminating engrng. sect., 1928, dir. commercial engrng. dept. since 1935. Mem. Illuminating Engrng. Soc. (local rep.), Am. Soc. Heating and Ventilating Engrs. (asso.). Author articles for trade pubis. and speeches before service clubs. Home: Box B-340, R.D. 4. Office: 535 Vine St., Johnstown, Pa.

KNOWLES, Richard, educator; b. Boston, Jan. 1, 1889; s. Charles Sumner and Nina (Adams) K.; student St. Mark's Sch., Southboro, Mass. 1901-05. A.B., Harvard, 1908; LL.B., 1911, Ph.D., 1930; A.M., U. of Pa., 1936; m. May Ashley, Sept. 23, 1916; children—Mary, Hope, Nina, Charles Sumner, Sylvia. Admitted to Mass. bar, 1911, and practiced in New Bedford; mem. New Bedford Common Council, 1912-13, pres. 1913; mem. Mass. Ho. of Rep., 1914-15, Senate, 1916-17; master St. Mark's Sch., 1918-31; headmaster Great Neck (N.Y.) Prep. Sch., 1931-35; headmaster William Penn Charter Sch. (country day sch. for boys), Philadelphia, since Apr. 1935. Republican. Unitarian. Clubs: Germantown Cricket, Phila. Cricket, New Bedford Yacht. Home: 8605 Seminole St., Chestnut Hill, Philadelphia. Address: William Penn Charter School, Germantown, Philadelphia, Pa.

KNOWLES, William Gray, judge Municipal Court of Philadelphia since 1913. Home: 2102 De Lancy St., Philadelphia, Pa.

KNOWLTON, Daniel Chauncey, author, educator; b. Cazenovia, N.Y., July 16, 1876; s.

Charles M. and Martha Jane (Badley) K.; grad. Cazenovia Sem., 1893; A.B., Cornell, 1898, Ph.D., 1906; student Bonn U., Germany, 1903-04; m. Lou Osburn, Aug. 11, 1898; children—Daniel Chauncey, Donald Blackstone. Asst. in English, Cornell, 1898-99; head dept. of history, high sch., Ithaca, 1900-03; President White traveling fellow, Cornell, 1903-04; head dept. of history, high sch., Montclair, N.J., 1904-07; asst. in history, high sch., N.Y. City, 1907-08; asst., head of dept. and supervisor history and social studies, high schs. of Newark N.J., 1908-20; in charge history and civics, Lincoln Sch., Teachers Coll., 1920-26; asst. prof. visual instrn., Yale, 1926-28; research asso. (asso. prof. rank) in visual instrn., same, 1928-29; lecturer Harvard and Boston univs., 1929; head of history dept. Fieldston Sch., New York, 1929; asso. prof. edn., New York Univ., 1930-1932, prof. of education since 1932. Assistant editor Illustrated Current News Ednl. Service, 1927-30; now asso. editor Education; on staffs summer schs., Harvard, etc. Mem. Am. Hist. Assn., Am. Assn. Univ. Profs., N.E. History Teachers Assn., Assn. History Teachers of Middle States and Md., Nat. Acad. Visual Instrn. (exec. com.), S.A.R., Phi Beta Kappa, Phi Delta Kappa, Pi Gamma Mu, Kappa Delta Pi, Presbyn. Club: Graduate. Author: The Government of New Jersey, 1909; (with S. B. Howe) Essentials in Modern European History, 1917; Making History Graphic, 1925; History and the Other Social Studies in Jr. High School, 1926; Motion Pictures in History Teaching, 1929; The Knowlton Workbook in American History, 1930; Our America—Past and Present, 1938. Editor: Illustrated Topics in Ancient, Medieval and Modern History, 1920; Wall Maps of European History, 1920; asso. editor Larned History for Ready Reference, also (series) Westward March of Man (4 vols.) 1933-34, Home Study Courses in Ancient, European and American History, etc. Mem. ednl. staff Literary Digest, 1919-26. Home: 97 N. Mountain Av., Montclair, N.J.

KNOX, Charles Webster, scientist; b. Brooklyn, N.Y., Nov. 24, 1896; s. John and Matilda Louise (Drescher) K.; B.S., Cornell U., 1921; M.S., Ia. State Coll., Ames, Ia., 1923, Ph.D., 1926; m. Mary Elizabeth Fatula, Feb. 7, 1920; children—Charles Webster, Jr., Margaret Louise, Philip Henry, James Alfred, Agnes Joan, Rita Ann, Joan Marie, Mary Lou, John Vincent. Instr. poultry husbandry, Ia. State Coll., Ames, Ia., 1921-23, asst. prof., 1923-26, asso. prof., 1926-31; geneticist, U.S. Dept. Agr., Bur. Animal Industry, Div. Animal Husbandry, 1931-35, sr. geneticist since 1935, at The Agricultural Research Center, Beltsville, Md. Served as 1st lt. R.O.T.C., 1920; now 2d lt. U.S.A. Res. Mem. Sigma Xi. Home: Laurel View Farm, Scaggsville Rd., Laurel, Md.

KNOX, Harry Edward, surgeon; b. New Castle, Pa., Apr. 2, 1892; s. John H. and Lida (DeNormande) K.; M.D., Jefferson Med. Coll., 1915; m. Margaret Reid, July 30, 1917; 1 son, Harry Edward, Jr. Interne, St. Christopher Hosp., 1915, Lankanau Hosp., 1916-18; surgeon to Newport News Shipbuilding & Dry Dock Co., 1919-22; engaged in practice at Phila., Pa. since 1922; chief surgeon, St. Christopher's Hosp. for Children, Phila. Hosp. for Contagious Diseases; surgeon, Germantown Hosp., Ogontz Sch., Rydal, Pa.; asso. surgeon, Episcoal Hos.; asso. in surgery, U. of Pa. Med. Sch. since 1925; treas. Phila. Acad. of Surgery. Served in U.S.N. Res., 1918-19. Fellow Am. Coll. Surgeons, Phila. Acad. Surgery, Phila. Coll. Physicians. Mem. Am. and Phila. Co. med. assns., Am. Surg. Bd., Phi Rho Sigma. Republican. Presbyn. Mason. Clubs: Medical (Philadelphia); Old York Rd. Country (Jenkintown). Home and office: 719 66th Av., Philadelphia, Pa.

KNOX, Paul Waddell, lawyer; b. Waynesburg, Pa.; s. I. H. and Theodosia K.; A.B., Yale, 1914, LL.B., 1916; m. Florence Welch, Oct. 18, 1919; children—Patricia Alden, John Paul, Richard Havely. Admitted to Pa. bar, 1917, and since 1919 practiced at Phila.; formerly dist. counsel U.S. Shipping Bd.; mem. firm Rambo, Rambo and Knox. Served in U.S.

Navy, 1917-19; hon. disch. as lt., j.g., Pres. bd. Stevens Sch., Philadelphia. Mem. Pa. Bar Assn., Maritime Bar Assn. Republican. Methodist. Mason. Home: Lincoln Drive, Germantown. Office: Girard Trust Co. Bldg., Philadelphia, Pa.

KNOX, Robert Welch, lawyer; b. Buffalo Twp., Washington Co., Pa., Jan. 31, 1869; s. William and Wilhelmina (Meloy) K.; A.B., Washington and Jefferson Coll., Washington, Pa., 1893; LL.B., U. of Buffalo, N.Y., 1895; m. Sarah Agnes Chaney, June 30, 1904; children —Ruth Elizabeth, Sarah Charlotte. Admitted to Pa. bar, 1896, and since practiced at Washington, Pa.; judge of Common Pleas Court, Washington Co., since Jan. 2, 1939. Chmn. Dem. Co. Com., Washington Co., Pa., 1903-05; delegate Dem. Nat. Conv., Denver, Colo., 1908, St. Louis, Mo., 1916. Trustee Pa. Training Sch., Morganza, Pa., since 1935; dir. and trustee Washington (Pa.) Y.M.C.A. Democrat. Protestant. Club: Basset (Washington, Pa.). Home: 249 N. Wade Av. Office: Court House, Washington, Pa.

KNOX, Samuel Lippincott Griswold, cons. engr.; b. New York, N.Y., Nov. 28, 1870; s. Andrew and Annabel Grace (Douglas) K.; student Coll. City of New York, 1885-87; M.E., Stevens Inst. Tech., Hoboken, N.J., 1891; m. Edith Somerville Rulison, Sept. 16, 1897 (died Nov. 24, 1936); children—Nelson Rulison, Alexander Douglas. Chmn. com. of mech. design and engr. in charge drafting dept. General Electric Co., 1900-02; v.p. general manager and chief engineer Bucyrus Co., S. Milwaukee, Wis., mfrs. excavating machinery, 1902-10, designing and mfg. much of machinery used in constrn. of Panama Canal, also placer gold dredges of the period.; cons. engr., later v.p. and gen. mgr. Natomas Consol., of Calif., gold dredging and land reclamation, also pres. Pacific Engring. & Constrn. Co. and Pacific Dredging Co., building jetties on Pacific Coast, river correction and levee bldg., Sacramento and San Joaquin rivers, 1911-17; chmn. mech. engring. div. Nat. Research Council, Washington, D.C., also chief cons. engr. U.S. Navy Anti-Submarine Base, New London, Conn., 1917-20, devised improvement of secondary and turret guns of battleships, also apparatus for enemy airplane location; scientific attaché Am. Embassy, Rome, Italy, 1918-19; cons. engr.; pres. Lombard Tractor Co., 1927-28; now pres. Knox Engring. Co., Englewood, N.J., developing high efficiency automatic steam power plants for unit ry. cars; dir. and mem. exec. com. Lamson Co. (pneumatic tube and other service conveyors), Am. Pneumatic Service Co.; dir. Boston Pneumatic Transit Co., New York Mail & Newspaper Transit Co., Peter Clark, Inc. Mem. Am. Soc. Mech. Engrs., Pilgrims of U.S., Kappa Alpha. Episcoplian. Clubs: University, Town Hall (New York). Address: 95 S. Woodland St., Englewood, N.J.

KNOX, Stuart Kelsey, cons. engr.; b. Three Rivers, Mich., May 8, 1879; s. David and Maria Louise (Kelsey) K.; B.S. in C.E., U. of Mich., 1903; m. E. Isabel Lane, June 8, 1914 (dec.); 1 son, Stuart Kelsey, Jr. Employed as inspr. U.S.A. Engrs., 1903; instrument man, Irrigation and Drainage Surveys, Tex., 1904; successively time-keeper, material man and supt. of constrn. on large building contracts in Baltimore, Washington and New York for Thompson-Starret Co., N.Y. City, 1904-07; supt. of constrn., The Foundation Co., N.Y. City, 1907; successively prin. asst. engr., asso. and co-partner, cons. engring. business headed and conducted under firm name of Nicholas S. Hill, Jr., N.Y. City, 1908-34; in bus. on own acct. as cons. hydraulic and sanitary engr., New York City, since 1934. Served as engr. in charge of design. Camp Merritt, N.J. and design and constrn. housing developments for U.S. Housing Bur. during World War. Mem. Am. Soc. Civil Engrs., Am. Water Works Assn., N.E. Water Works Assn., N.Y. State Sewage Works Assn. Former mem. Am. Soc. Mech. Engrs. and Am. Pub. Health Assn. Author of articles in Trans. of the Am. Soc. Civil Engrs., Proceedings of the Am. Water Works Assn., and Technical Press. Home: 25 Warfield St., Mont-

clair, N.J. Office: 11 Broadway, New York, N.Y.

KNOX, William Francis, lawyer; b. Connellsville, Pa., Jan. 29, 1885; s. Alfred C. and Annie E. (Wilson) K.; A.B., Yale, 1907; LL.B., U. of Pittsburgh, 1910; m. Ruth Thoburn, June 29, 1916; children—William Francis (deceased), James Thoburn. Admitted to Pa. bar, 1910; asst. trust officer Safe Deposit & Trust Co. (now Peoples-Pittsburgh Trust Co.), 1910-13; practised law alone, 1913-16; mem. law firm Moorhead & Knox since 1916. Pres. Y.M.C.A. of Pittsburgh since 1938. Home: 8 Robin Rd. Office: Oliver Bldg., Pittsburgh, Pa.

KNUTSEN, Martin Halvor, prof. bacteriology; b. Kimball, S.D., Nov. 21, 1887; s. Andrew Martin and Lettie (Thomas) K.; B.S., U. of Wis., 1914, M.S., 1916; grad. study, State Coll. of Wash., 1916-18; m. Bernice Rosseau, June 21, 1919; children—Martin Halvor, Jr., Lettie Bernice. Engaged as bacteriologist, Wash. State Coll., 1916-18; asso. with Pa. State Coll. since 1919, prof. bacteriology since 1928. Served as 2d lt. San. Corps, U.S.A., 1918-19; now 1st lt. San. Res. Corps. Mem. bd. health, State College, Pa., since 1925. Mem. Soc. Am. Bacteriologists, Am. Pub. Health Assn., Am. Assn. Univ. Profs., Am. Legion (past comdr. local post). Democrat. Mason (K.T.). Home: 217 W. Park Av., State College, Pa.

KOCH, Alfred, clergyman, educator; b. Arzheim-Palatinate, Oct. 19, 1879; s. Joseph and Margaret (Geier) K.; S.T.D., Univ. of Rome, 1911. Joined Benedictine Order (O.S.B.), 1916; ordained priest R.C. Ch., 1905; prof. Greek, Latin and French, Sem. of Sutri, Prov. of Rome, 1906-12; came to U.S., 1912; prof. Latin and German, Sacred Heart Mission House, Girard, Pa., 1912-16; prof. of exegesis, introduction and hermeneutics, St. Vincent Sem., Latrobe, 1917-30; archabbot of St. Vincent, 1930. Pres. Benedictine Soc. of Westmoreland County, Pa., since 1930. Address: St. Vincent Archabbey, Latrobe, Pa.

KOCH, Carl Elwood, real estate and ins.; b. Pittsburgh, Pa., July 6, 1898; s. John A. and Elizabeth (Knerler) K.; grad. Fifth Av. High Sch., Pittsburgh, 1917; spl. study, U. of Pittsburgh, evenings, 1926-30; unmarried. Employed by various concerns in Pittsburgh and Toronto, Can., as office mgr. and salesman, 1917-26; engaged as real estate and ins. broker at Pittsburgh since 1926; prop. Carl E. Koch Co. since 1926; asst. sec. and dir. Security Savings Fund & Loan Assn. since 1926; in employ Fed. Housing Administrn. as rental housing appraiser for Western Pa. and W.Va. Served in S.A.T.C. during World War. Mem. Am. Inst. Real Estate Appraisers, Nat. Assn. Real Estate Bds., Soc. Residential Appraisers, Pittsburgh Real Estate Bd. Mem. Evang. Ch. Mason (K.T., Shriner). Home: 908 Steuben St. Office: 20 Wabash Av., Pittsburgh, Pa.

KOCH, Carleton S., steel mfr.; b. Buffalo, N.Y., Dec. 31, 1875; s. H. H. and Harriet (Coe) K.; student Buffalo High Sch., 1890-94; B.S., Mass. Inst. Tech., 1898; m. Jane Nicholson, Jan. 11, 1911; 1 son, Richard. Served as instr. Mass. Inst. Tech., 1898; pres., mgr. and dir. Fort Pitt Steel Casting Co., McKeesport, Pa., since 1906. Republican. Presbyterian. Home: 437 Maple Av., Edgewood, Pa. Office: McKeesport, Pa.

KOCH, Caspar Petrus, organist, composer, author, teacher; b. Karnap, Germany; Nov. 25, 1872; s. Theodor and Elizabeth (Jockenhoever) K.; came to U.S., 1881, naturalized, 1897; ed. St. Francis Sem., St. Francis, Wis., 1889-92, Kirchenmusikschule, Regensburg, Germany, 1903, pvt. teachers in Berlin, 1901-03; hon. Mus. D., Duquesne U., 1922; m. Myra Singenberger, June 30, 1904; children—Arthur John, Dorothy Ann (wife of Dr. John Howard), Theodore Albert, Paul William. Engaged as organist Ch. of Most Holy Trinity, Pittsburgh, Pa., 1892-1901, 1903-25; organist St. Cecilia Ch., Regensburg, Germany, 1903; city organist of Pittsburgh since 1904; instr. piano and organ, Carnegie Inst. Tech. since 1914; pvt. organist to Emil Winter, Pittsburgh, since 1925. Mem.

Am. Musicol. Soc., Sinfonia Fraternity of America, Musicians Club. Mem. St. Paul's Cathedral. Author: Book of Scales for Organ; Bach's Symphonies as Organ Trios; The Organist's Gradus ad Parnassum (ms.). Composer numerous organ transcriptions pub. by leading mus. publishers. Contbr. articles on mus. subjects. Has given about 1,500 organ recitals in Europe and America. Home: 334 N. Craig St., Pittsburgh, Pa.

KOCH, Frank, lawyer; b. North Arlington, N.J., June 7, 1873; s. Louis and Amelia (Weaver) K.; student North Arlington (N.J.) Grammar Sch., 1878-84, 13th St. Seh., New York, 1884-86, Scranton (Pa.) High Sch., 1886-89; m. Edith Stremlau, Oct. 7, 1903; children—Calvin Stremlau, Edith Amelia (Mrs. Palmer York Epler). Began as lawyer North Arlington, N.J., 1898; partner firm Koch and Koch, Arlington, N.J., since 1930; sec. Fairlawn Manor Land Co., Arlington, N.J., since 1924; dir. First Nat. Bank & Trust Co. of Kearny, N.J. Served as corp. and acting commissary sergt., Co. L, 2nd N.J. Inf., during Spanish-Am. War. Borough clk., North Arlington, N.J., 1896; clk. bd. of edn., bd. of health, North Arlington, 1898-1901; tax collector of Borough of North Arlington, 1898-1901; mem. Borough Council, 1901-02, borough atty., 1903, North Arlington; police recorder, Kearny, N.J., 1906, 1907. Mason (Truine Lodge, Arlington, N.J.; Scottish Rite, Jersey City; Shriner, Salaam Temple, Newark, N.J.), Elk. Republican. Home: 110 S. Midland Av. Office: 102 Midland Av., Arlington, N.J.

KOCH, Julius Arnold, chemist; b. Bremen, Germany, Aug. 15, 1864; s. Arnold and Amanda (Wenke) K.; came to America with parents in infancy; ed. pub. and high schs., Pittsburgh; grad. Pittsburgh Coll. of Pharmacy, 1884; Pharm.D., 1895; studied U. of Munich, 1896, U. of Heidelberg, 1897; Ph.D., Scio (O.) Coll., 1905; D.Sc., Washington and Jefferson Coll., 1907; Ph.M., Phila. Coll. of Pharmacy and Science, 1922; m. Albertine M. Strunz, Oct. 17, 1889 (died Feb. 28, 1900); children—Adele M. (dec.), Florence S., Elsa A.; m. 2d, Alice M. Cope, July 15, 1927. Entered drug business as apprentice, 1880, became proprietor, 1885, sold out business, 1891; dean since 1891, prof. pharmacy, 1891-99, chemistry since 1899, Pittsburgh Coll. of Pharmacy; prof. chemistry, med. dept. U. of Pittsburgh, 1900-13. Chmn. exec. com. Am. Conf. Pharm. Faculties, 1908-20; ex-pres. Pa. Pharm. Soc.; pres. Am. Pharm. Assn., 1922-23; pres. Pittsburgh Br. Am. Pharm. Assn.; mem. Deutsche Chemische Gesellschaft, Soc. Chem. Industry (London), Am. Chem. Soc., A.A.A.S. Author: Chemical Laboratory Tables, 1898; Laboratory Manual for Pharmaceutical Students, 1904. Reporter on the Progress of Pharmacy and editor Year Book of Am. Pharm. Assn., 1915-16; mem. Revision Com. U.S. Pharmacopœia, 1910-20. Home: 5463 Wilkins Av., Pittsburgh; (winter) Ocala, Fla. Office: 1431 Boul. of the Allies, Pittsburgh, Pa.

KOCHER, Edward Henry, mfr. and inventor; b. Newark, N.J., May 4, 1878; s. Henry and Elizabeth (Albert) K.; ed. Newark Schools; supplemented by night and correspondence courses in electrical and mech. engring.; m. Lillian Addis, Apr. 8, 1903; children—Addis Edward, Roger Henry (dec.). Began as office clerk with Edison General Electric Co., Harrison, N.J., 1894; apprentice machinist with Hewes & Phillips Iron Works, Newark, N.J., 1896-1900; mechanical draftsman, 1901; inspector Jersey City Water Supply Co., Boonton, N.J., 1902-05; chief draftsman, General Storage Battery Co., 1906; personal asst. to Thomas A. Edison, Edison Labs., West Orange, N.J., 1910; supt. Bijur Motor Lighting Corpn., New York City, 1911-14, works mgr. same, Hoboken, N.J., 1914-18, mfg. engr. Bijur Motor Appliance Corpn., Hoboken, N.J., 1918-23, factory mgr. and treas. Bijur Lubricating Corpn., N.Y. City, 1923-32; pres., gen. mgr. and dir. Bijur Lubricating Corpn., mfr. lubricating systems for machinery, Long Island City, N.Y., since 1932; pres., gen. mgr. and dir. Auto Research Corpn., patents and engring. development, Dover, Del., since 1932. Mem. Soc. Am. Mil. Engrs., Army Ordnance Assn., Am. Soc. Mech. Engrs., Soc. Automotive Engrs., Edison Pioneers. Republican. Mason. Clubs: Morris County Engineers, Deer Lake of Morris County. Home: Reserve St., Boonton, N.J. Office: 4301 22d St., Long Island City, N.Y.

KOCHIN, Elihu Wolf, rabbi; b. Rumsisock, Russia; s. Rabbi Eliezer and Teige Rachel (Becker) K.; ed. in Russia; came to U.S., 1905 and naturalized citizen, 1911; m. Bessie Reznik; children—Dr. Louis M., Dr. Morris L., Milton, Esther, Mary (Mrs. Frank Kopelson), Judith (Mrs. Abe Cohen), Eva (Mrs. Meyer Broz). Rabbi at Dombrovitz, Ukraine, Russia, 1900-05; rabbi at Pittsburgh, Pa., since 1905. Mem. Agudath of Orthodox Rabbis of America. Orthodox Jewish religion. Home: 1602 Center Av., Pittsburgh, Pa.

KOEHLER, Walter Allos, prof. chemical engineering; b. Mishicot, Wis., Mar. 25, 1893; s. Louis Carl and Ottilie (Dallmann) K.; grad. Manitowoc (Wis.) High Sch., 1911; B.S. in Chem. Engring., U. of Wis., 1919, Ch. E., 1920, Ph.D., 1923; M.S., U. of Ill., 1922; m. Laura Harker, Aug. 11, 1923; children—Elizabeth Louise, Walter Harker. Engr. research lab., Carborundum Co., Niagara Falls, N.Y., 1920-21; instr. chem. engring., W.Va. U., 1924, asst. prof., 1924-29, prof. chem. and ceramic engring. since 1929; specialization in ceramics and electro-chemistry. Mem. Am. Inst. Chem. Engr., Am. Ceramic Soc., Electrochem. Soc., Am. Chem. Soc., W.Va. Acad. of Science, Tau Beta Pi, Sigma Xi, Phi Lambda Upsilon, Sigma Gamma Epsilon. Registered professional engr. W.Va. Presbyn. Author: Applications of Electrochemistry, 1935. Contbr. tech. articles. Home: 412 Linden St. Address: Mechanical Hall, Morgantown, W.Va.

KOERBER, George Albert, prof. elec. engring., U. of Del. Address: University of Delaware, Newark, Del.

KOESTER, Edwin Ferdinand, surveys and traffic engr.; b. Baltimore, Md., Sept. 14, 1892; s. Herman Frederick and Kina (Haas) K.; student Baltimore (Md.) Poly. Inst., 1906-10; C.E., Cornell U., 1913; m. Malinda Lawton, Apr. 21, 1915; children—Suzanne, Margery. Field asst. B.&O. R.R., Pittsburgh, Pa., summer 1912; draftsman Am. Bridge Co., Edgemoor, Del., 1913-14; in garage business, Wilmington, 1914-16; asst. engr. Street and Sewer Dept., Wilmington, Del., 1916-19, engr. in charge of surveys, 1919-33, surveys and traffic engr. since 1933. Dir. Del. Safety Council; chmn. Mayor's Traffic Adv. Com., Wilmington, Del.; mem. Bd. of Park Commrs., Wilmington, Del. Mem. Inst. of Traffic Engrs., Am. Pub. Works Assn., Del. Automobide Assn. (mem. bd. of dirs.). Mason (Del Consistory; 32°). Club: Cornell of Del. (Wilmington). Home: 414 W. 22d St. Office: P.O. Box 2, Wilmington, Del.

KOHLER, Charles Henry, mech. and elec. engring.; b. Jones Point, N.Y., July 18, 1881; s. Charles H. and Mary A. (Osterhout) K.; E.E., Pa. State Coll., 1907; M.E., Drexel Inst., 1908; m. Louise Clearwater, Jan. 15, 1909; children—Charles Henry, Jr., Wellington Clearwater, Myrabel Louise. Employed as draftsman, inspr., and designer, by various cos., 1908-31; employed in piping design and layout, Phila. Dept. of Water, Phila., Pa., 1931-34; sr. mech. engr., Eastern State Penitentiary, Phila., Pa., 1934-38; in bus. on own acct. as cons. engr. since 1938; registered professional engr. in Pa. Served in 6th U.S. Provisional Training Regt. Inf. O.T.S. Lt. inf. Pa. N.G. Mem. Fed. Architects and Engrs., Nat. Soc. Professional Engrs., Pa. Soc. Professional Engrs., Lambda Epsilon Delta. Republican. Episcopalian. Home: 611 N. 32d St., Philadelphia, Pa.

KOHLER, Edwin L(awrence), lawyer; b. Allentown, Pa., Jan. 4, 1901; s. J. Herbert and Nellie M. (Seip) K.; student Allentown Prep. Sch., 1913-17; B.A., Muhlenberg Coll., 1920; B.L., U. of Pa., 1923; m. Katharine E. Stuart, Dec. 24, 1924; children—Jean Frances, Mary Louise (deceased). Admitted to Pa. bar, 1923, and began practice in Allentown; asst. Am. Law Inst., 1923; on legal staff Pa. Power & Light Co., Allentown, 1924; gen. practice since 1924; partner in law firm Helfrich & Kohler, 1928-38; dir. and solicitor Lehigh Title Guarantee Co., Security Bldg. Assn.; solicitor Jordan Bldg. & Loan Assn. Mem. Lehigh Co. Bar Assn., Alpha Tau Omega. Republican. Presbyterian. Elk. Clubs: Brookside Country, Lions (Allentown). Home: 24 N. 18th St. Office: 508 Hamilton St., Allentown, Pa.

KOHLER, Milton, jeweler; b. Hanover, Pa., Aug. 10, 1852; s. Jesse and Sarah (Kindig) K.; student pub. sch., Hanover, Pa., 1858-65, pvt. sch., Hanover, 1865-70; m. Mary Bittinger, May 23, 1877; children—Mary Ethel, Milton Leroy (dec.), Elsie Naomi (Mrs. Richard J. Kingston), Harry Bittinger, Helen Ruhamah (Mrs. Joseph Faries Denniston), Jesse Earl. Learned watchmaker trade, 1870-75; established watchmaker and jeweler business 1875; founded Milton Kohler & Sons, jewelers and optometrists, Hagerstown, Md., 1920, and since in business; dir. and only living charter mem. Nicodemus Nat. Bank (formerly Peoples Nat. Bank of Hagerstown, Md., organized 1894); dir. Blue Ridge Fire Ins. Co. (formerly Mutual Fire Ins. Co.). Republican. Presbyterian. Home: 417 N. Potomac St. Office: 27 W. Washington St., Hagerstown, Md.

KÖHLER, Wolfgang, coll. prof.; b. Reval, Esthonia, Jan. 21, 1887; s. Franz and Minni (Girgensohn) K.; student Gymnasium, Wolfenbüttel, 1896-1905, Tübingen, Bonn and Berlin Univs., Germany, 1905-09; came to U.S., 1935; m. Lili Harleman, July 9, 1927; 1 dau., Karin. Privatdozent, Frankfurt On Main, Germany, 1912-21; dir. anthropoid station, Tenerife, Canary Islands, 1913-20; prof. psychology, Göttingen U., Germany, 1921-22; prof. psychology and philosophy, Berlin U., Germany, 1922-35; prof. psychology, Swarthmore (Pa.) Coll., since 1935. Mem. Am. Psychol. Assn. Soc. of Exptl. Psychologists. Author: Die Physischen Gestalten in Ruhe und in Stationären Zustand, 1920; Mentality of Apes, 1925; Gestalt Pyschology, 1929; Place of Value in a World of Facts, 1938. Home: 401 Walnut Lane. Office: Swarthmore College, Swarthmore, Pa.

KOHLSTEDT, Edward Delor, clergyman, educator, administrator; b. Minneapolis, Minn., Sept. 11, 1874; s. Conrad William and Wilhelmine (Kuhlmeyer) K.; grad. East Side High Sch., Minneapolis (salutatorian); grad. Garrett Biblical Inst., Evanston, Ill., B.D., 1899, S.T.D., 1922; grad. Lawrence Coll., Appleton, Wis. A.M., 1911, D.D., 1917; LL.D., Dakota Wesleyan U. Mitchell, S.D., 1926; m. Hannah Carrie Sandmeier, Sept. 21, 1899. Entered ministry M.E. Ch. and united with Wis. Conf., 1898; ordained deacon, 1899, elder, 1901, Meth. Episcopal Ch.; pastor Wis. chs., 1898-1914; supt. Milwaukee dist., 1914-18; St. Paul Area sec. and gen. dir. field activities for Com. on Conservation and Advance, 1918-22; pres. Dak. Wesleyan U., 1922-27; exec. sec. Bd. Home Missions and Ch. Extension, M.E. Ch., since May 7, 1927. Chmn. Wis. Conf. delegation to Gen. Conf. M.E. Ch., Des Moines, Ia., 1920; del. to Ecumenical Conf., London, Eng., 1921, Atlanta, Ga., 1931; transferred to Dakota Conf., 1922, chmn. Dak. delegation to Gen. Conf. M.E. Ch., Springfield, Mass., 1924, Kansas City, 1928, Atlantic City, 1932, Columbus, 1936; mem. Joint Com. on Unification M.E. Ch. and M.E. Ch., S., 1920-28; mem. uniting conf. Am. Methodism, Kansas City, 1939; mem. univ. senate, M.E. Ch., 1924-27; mem. Bd. Home Missions and Ch. Extension M.E. Ch. since 1924; mem. exec. com. Federal Council Chs. of Christ in America; pres. Home Missions Council, 1937-38; pres. Board for Christian Work in Santo Domingo, 1936-37. Mem. Phi Kappa Phi, Pi Kappa Delta, Sigma Tau Delta. Mason (32°). Contbr. on Christian service themes. Home: 251 High St. Office: 1701 Arch St., Philadelphia, Pa.

KOHMAN, Girard Theodore, chemist; b. Dillon, Kan., Nov. 28, 1897; s. Henry and Elizabeth (Rhumold) K.; B.S., U. of Kan., 1920; Ph.D., Yale U., 1923; m. Ella A. Shank, Aug. 30, 1923; children—Warren Girard, Wayne Elbert. Employed as research chemist, Western Electric Co., 1923-34; research chemist, Bell Telephone Labs., New York, N.Y., since 1934. Served in U.S.N., 1918-22. Mem. Am. Chem. Soc., Alpha Chi Sigma, Tau Beta Pi, Sigma Xi, Gamma Alpha, Sigma Tau. Republican. Baptist. Contbr. sci. articles to tech. journs. Home: 133 Ashland Rd., Summit, N.J. Office: 463 West St., New York, N.Y.

KOHN, Bernard, physician; b. Phila., Pa., Mar. 12, 1876; s. Simon I. and Julia (Tim) K.; M.S., U. of Pa., 1896, M.D., 1899; m. Elsa A. Leberman, Nov. 2, 1903; children—Bernard A., Lewis L., Elise (Mrs. Paul Friedman). Med. insp. Phila. Bur. of Health, 1903-12; supervisor pub. sch. med. inspection, Phila. 1912-18, dir., 1918-20; med. dir. Max and Sarah Bamberger Seashore Home, Longport, N.J. 1912-36, Community Health Center of Phila., 1920-36; visiting physician Jewish Hosp., Phila., 1907-37, cardiologist since 1921; cardiologist Nat. Stomach Hosp., Phila., since 1937. Hon. dir. Nat. Farm Sch., Doylestown, Pa., Community Health Center of Phila., Max and Sarah Bamberger Seashore Home. Life mem. Phila. Co. Med. Soc. Republican. Jewish religion. Club: Physicians Motor (Phila.). Address: 1520 Spruce St., Philadelphia, Pa.

KOLB, Louis John, mfr.; b. New York, June 25, 1865; s. John Gotlieb and Sarah Elizabeth (Kaiser) K.; grad. Rugby Academy, Phila.; A.B., U. of Pa., 1887; LL.D., Juniata Coll.; m. Caroline Kaiser, Mar. 20, 1895. V.p. Real Estate Trust Co.; dir. Keystone Telephone Co., Internat. Equities, Phila. Mfrs. Mut. Fire Ins. Co. Lt. col. and a.d.c. on staff Gov. Brumbaugh of Pa. Pres. Hahnemann Hosp.; mem. bd. dirs. Graduate Hosp., U. of Pa., St. Luke's Hosp., Children's Homeopathic Hosp. Mem. Union League of Phila. (dir.). Republican. Presbyn. Mason. Clubs: Union League, Poor Richard (pres.), Art, Philadelphia Country, Germantown Cricket, Five O'Clock, Ledger, University, Penn Athletic, Auto Club of Phila.; Whitemarsh Valley Country, and Seaview Country (Atlantic City, N.J.); Locust Club, Wissahickon Farms, N.C., Egypt Mills; Boca Raton (Fla.). Home: School Lane, Germantown. Office: 1629 Locust St., Philadelphia, Pa.

KOLBE, Parke Rexford, coll. pres.; b. Akron, O., Apr. 23, 1881; s. Carl F. and Jennie (Yergin) K.; A.B., Buchtel Coll., 1901, A.M. 1902; studied U. of Göttingen, 1901-02, U. of Heidelberg, 1907 and 1910-12, Ph.D., 1912; LL.D., Temple U., 1933, U. of Akron, 1934; m. Lydia Voris, June 17, 1905. Prof. Modern langs., Buchtel Coll., 1905-13, pres. Feb. 4-Dec. 1913; pres. Municipal U. of Akron, 1913-25; pres. Polytechnic Inst. of Brooklyn, 1925-32; pres. Drexel Inst. since 1932. Mem. Federal Sch., Survey Commn. to Hawaiian Islands, 1919; head of U.S. Bur. of Edn. Survey Commn. to U. of Ariz., 1922. Past pres. Assn. of Urban Univs.; first vice chairman American Council on Edn.; mem. Kurpfalz (Heidelberg), Phi Delta Theta. Republican. Universalist. Rotarian. Clubs: University (Akron, O.); University (Washington); Century (New York); Rittenhouse, Manufacturers, Bankers (Phila.). Author: The Colleges in Wartime and After, 1919; Urban Influences on Higher Education in England and the United States, 1928. Editor: Heinie's Harzreise, 1909; Die Variation bei Otfrid, 1912. Contbr. to ednl. and philol. publs. Address: Drexel Institute of Technology, Philadelphia, Pa.

KOLLER, Edmund Leonard, dir. art schs.; b. Hanover, Pa., Dec. 8, 1877; s. Rev. Jesse Cramer (D.D.) and Alice Geneva (Heathcote) K.; A.B., Pa. Coll., Gettysburg, Pa., 1898; M.A., Drexel Inst., Phila., Pa., 1901; m. Leonora Edwards, Sept. 24, 1905; 1 dau., Alice (Mrs. Joseph Leopold). Began as illustrator and designer, Phila., Pa., 1901; designer stained glass and interior decorations, Pittsburgh and Phila., 1901-04; writer textbooks and prin. art schs., Internat. Corr. Schs., Scranton, Pa., 1904-08, writer textbooks and dir. art schs, 1908-38; lecturer and writer on art subjects; designer of Civil War Soldiers' Monument, Hanover, Pa.; designer many memorial stained glass windows in Phila. and Pittsburgh chs. Served by work for Camouflage Div., U.S.A. and poster work during World War. Mem. Am. Federation of Arts, Eastern Arts Assn., Alpha Tau Omega. Republican. Methodist. Home: 540 Jefferson Av., Scranton, Pa.

KOLLER, James Roosevelt, lawyer; b. Myerston, Pa., Oct. 27, 1906; s. James and Mary Ellen K.; B.A., Albright Coll., Reading, Pa.; LL.B., U. of Pa.; unmarried. In gen. practice of law at Lebanon, Pa., since 1931; dir. Tulpehocken Mutual Fire Ins. Co., Myerston, Pa. Mem. Patriotic Order Sons of America, Pi Gamma Mu; hon. mem. Myerston (Pa.) Civic Club. Elk. Clubs: Lions of Lebanon (1st v.p.) Home: 43 E. Main Av., Myerston, Pa. Office: 824 Cumberland St., Lebanon, Pa.

KOLLMORGEN, Frederick Ludwig George, optical engr.; b. Stettin, Germany, Sept. 16, 1871; s. Ludwig and Anna (Langefeld) K.; came to U.S., 1905, naturalized, 1913; student Univ. of Berlin, Germany, 1890-93; m. Agnes E. Hunt, April 28, 1896 (dec.); children—Dorothea, Hildegard Iris (Mrs. Robert E. Garst), Ernest Otto; m. 2d, Edith M. L. Mounteney, Oct. 20, 1920. Chief optical adviser, Carl Reichert, Vienna, Austria, 1898-1900, Ross, Ltd., London, Eng., 1900-02, Keuffel & Esser Co., Hoboken, N.J., 1905-15; chief optical adviser and pres. Kollmorgen Optical Corpn., design and mfr. optical equipment for army and navy, especially periscopes for submarines, Brooklyn, N.Y., since 1915. Fellow A.A.A.S. Mem. Optical Soc. of America. Republican. Protestant. Home: 248 Morris Av., Mountain Lakes, N.J. Office: 767 Wythe Av., Brooklyn, N.Y.

KOLMER, John Albert, physician; b. Lonaconing, Allegany Co., Md., Apr. 24, 1886; s. Leonard and Selma Louisa (Reichelt) K.; grad. Charlotte Hall Mil. Acad., 1904; A.B., U. of Md., 1905; M.D., U. of Pa., 1908, Dr.P.H., 1914; M.Sc., Villanova, 1915, D.Sc., 1921, LL.D., 1927; D.Sc., La Salle Coll., 1935; L.H.D., St. Joseph's Coll., 1935; m. B. Cecilia Herron, Sept. 18, 1912. Prof. of medicine, Temple Univ. Sch. of Medicine; dir. Research Institute Cutaneous Medicine; cons. pathologist St. Vincent's and Misericordia hosps. Fellow A.M.A., Coll. Physicians of Phila.; Am. Coll. of Physicians; mem. Am. Assn. Immunologists (pres.), Am. Soc. Clin. Pathologists (pres.), Alpha Kappa, Sigma Xi, etc. Catholic. Author: Infection, Immunity and Biologic Therapy, 1915; Manual of Laboratory Diagnostic Methods, 1925; Chemotherapy and Treatment of Syphilis, 1926; Serum Diagnosis by Complement Fixation, 1928; Acute Infectious Diseases (with Jay Frank Schamberg), 1928; Approved Laboratory Technic (with Fred Boerner), 1931. Contbr. to Frazier's Spinal Surgery and Keen's Surgery. Home: Bala-Cynwyd, Pa. Office: 2101 Pine St., Philadelphia, Pa.

KONKLE, Burton Alva, writer; b. Albion, Ind., Apr. 25, 1861; s. Simon Kenton and Cornelia Gale (Andrews) K.; Lake Forest (Ill.) Coll., 1882-86; McCormick Theol. Sem., Chicago, 1889-92; U. of Chicago, Apr.-Dec. 1896; M.A., Huron Coll., 1906; m. Susie Montague Ferry, June 28, 1900; 1 dau., Winifred Ferry (Mrs. Charles E. Fischer). Teacher, pub. schs., later prin. pub. schs., Avilla and Wawaka, Ind., 1876-82; in historical work, various parts of U.S., vacations 1882-86; ordained ministry Presbyn. Ch., 1894; pastor Libertyville, Ill., 1893, Georgetown, Colo., 1894; engaged in hist. writing in vacations, 1888-97, full time, Phila., since 1897. Life mem. Hist. Society of Pa. Established hist. sect. of Pa. Bar Assn.; a founder of Pa. Hist. Club. Republican. Author: Life and Times of Thomas Smith of The Continental Congress, 1904; Life and Speeches of Thomas Williams (2 vols.), 1906; Life of Chief Justice Ellis Lewis, 1908; George Bryan and the Constitution of Pennsylvania, 1922; John Motley Morehead and the Development of North Carolina, 1922; History of the Presbyterian Ministers' Fund (oldest life insurance company in the world); Joseph Hopkinson, author of "Hail Columbia," 1931; The Life and Letters of Chief Justice Benjamin Chew, 1932; Life and Writings of James Wilson, Constitutionalist (6 vols.); David Lloyd and the First Half Century of Pennsylvania; Thomas Willing and the First American Financial System, 1937; Land o'Lakes, a Hoosier Tale of North, South, West and East; The Life of Nicholas Biddle. Contbr. to periodicals. Mem. Pa. Constitution Celebration Com. Home: 307 S. Chester Rd., Swarthmore, Pa. Office: 1300 Locust St., Philadelphia, Pa.

KONRAD, Henry Rudolph, supervising prin. schs.; b. Amsterdam, N.Y., Dec. 10, 1893; s. Rev. Otto Carl and Anna (Gerlach) K.; A.B., Wesleyan U., Middletown, Conn., 1914; A.M., Columbia U. Teachers Coll., 1932; m. Mary Bingley Hostetter, Dec. 24, 1917; 1 dau., Henrietta Bingley. Engaged in teaching at Tuckahoe, N.J., Hanover and Pottsville, Pa., 1914-25; prin. high sch., Dover, Pa., 1925-30; supervising prin. schs., Port Carbon, Pa., since 1930. Served as pvt. inf., U.S.A., 1917-18; capt. inf. U.S.A. Res. Mem. Commons Club, Schoolmens Club of Pottsville. Republican. Lutheran. I.O.O.F. Home: Washington St., Port Carbon, Pa.

KONVITZ, Joseph, rabbi; b. Kaisedorys, Lithuania, Apr. 15, 1878; s. Elijah Chaim and Feige (Gobst) K.; ordained rabbi at sems. of Slabodka, Lithuania, 1898, Slutsk, Poland, 1899; came to U.S., 1915, naturalized, 1926; m. Welia Ridvas-Wilowsky, Aug. 15, 1899; children—Ben Zion, Solomon Albert, Rose (Mrs. Benjamin Nessanbaum), Dr. Milton Ridvas, Philip. Rabbi, Shadavow and Kavarsk, Lithuania, 1901-06; dean Palestine Theol. Sem., Safed, Palestine, 1906-15; rabbi United Synagogues, Elizabeth, N.J., 1915-19, United Orthodox Congregations, Trenton, N.J., 1919-24, Anshe Russia Synagoge, Newark, N.J., 1924-35, Beth Joseph Synagogue, Newark, N.J., since 1935. Chaplain N.J. State Penitentiary, 1919-24; v.p. Central Relief Com.; trustee Home for Aged, Jerusalem; hon. pres. Girls' Orphan Home, Jerusalem; mem. Advisory Bd. Yeshiva Coll., Rabbi Isaac Elchanan Sem.; mem. Exec. Bd. Torah Vodath Sem.; chmn. bd. of dirs. Mercaz Achivuch, Palestine. Mem. Union of Orthodox Rabbis of U.S. and Can. (pres. 1933-39, hon. pres. 1939), Am. Palestine Soc. (pres. since 1930), Am. Alumni of Slabodka Sem. (v.p.), Kollel America Palestine Soc. (v.p.), Ezras Torah Fund (v.p.), Am. Publ. Com. of Talmud (v.p.), United Palestine Appeal (nat. commn.), Independent Order Brith Abraham (mem. reserve fund bd.), Etz Chaim (exec. com.), Relief of Holy Institutions, Jerusalem (exec. com.). Author responsa, articles in Ozar Israel Hebrew Encyclopedia. Judge Ontario, Can., Supreme Court rabbinical tribunal, 1926. Address: 781 S. 10th St., Newark, N.J.

KONVITZ, Milton Ridvas, lawyer and univ. prof.; b. Palestine, Mar. 12, 1908; s. Joseph and Welia (Ridvas-Wilowsky) K.; brought to U.S., 1915, naturalized, 1926; B.Sc., N.Y. Univ., 1928, A.M., same, 1930, J.D., same, 1930; Ph.D., Cornell U., 1933; unmarried. Law clk. with Kalisch & Kalisch; admitted to N.J. bar, 1931; sage fellow in philosophy, Cornell U., 1932-33; asso. with Senator John Milton, Jersey City, 1933-35; pvt. practice Newark since 1936; faculty, N.Y. Univ. Sch. of Law since 1938; counsel Newark Housing Authority since 1938. Mem. Am. and Essex Co. bar assns., Nat. Lawyers Guild, N.Y. Co. Lawyers Assn., Am. Philos. Assn., Am. Polit. Sci. Assn., Brit. Inst. Philosophy, Menorah Assn., Conf. on Jewish Relations, Am. Acad. for Jewish Research, N.J. Civil Liberties Union (dir.), N.J. Urban League (dir.), N.J. Guild Assos. (dir.), Newark Community Forum and Inst. (dir.), Soc. for Libraries of N.Y. Univ., Am. Jewish Hist. Soc., Am. Assn. of Univ. Profs., Nat. Assn. of Housing Officials, Am. Bar Assn. (com. on comparative housing laws), Newark Welfare Council; chmn. com. on administrative law, N.Y. City Chapter, Nat. Lawyers Guild. Awarded first prize, Law Quarterly Rev., 1929. Jewish religion. Club: Cornell (Essex). Editor, N.Y.U. Law Quarterly Review, 1928-30. Contbr. to philos. and law jours.; consultant N.J. Guide, 1939. Home: 781 S. 10th St. Office: 744 Broad St., Newark, N.J.

KONZELMANN, Frank Williamson, M.D.; prof. clinical pathology, Temple U. Address: 3638 N. 21st St., Philadelphia, Pa.

KOON, Thomas Walter, in gen. practice of medicine for many years; now mayor of Cumberland. Address: 221 Baltimore Av., Cumberland, Md.

KOONS, Tilghman Benjamin, retired railway officer; b. Treichlers, Pa., May 29, 1852; s. Daniel and Sarah (Shipe) K.; ed. pub. schs., tutored by Prof. Atwaters and student special business course Eastman's Sch., Poughkeepsie, N.Y.; m. Cornelia E. Benjamin, of Lincoln Park, N.J., May 30, 1876 (died Nov. 8, 1931); children—Mrs. Norman H. Probasco, Chauncey B., Lucius T. Began as telegraph operator D., L. & W.R.R., Dec. 1872; in service of gen. freight agent, L.V.R.R., Mauch Chunk, Pa., 1873-78; in service of Central R.R. Co. of N.J., 1880-1926, as soliciting freight agent, Elmira, N.Y., 1880, gen. agent, div. freight and passenger agent, Mauch Chunk, 1887-98, gen. freight agent, N.Y. City, 1898-1902, freight traffic manager, 1902, v.p. and freight traffic mgr. Jan. 1, 1913-26, vice-pres. in charge of freight traffic, 1924-26; pensioned Nov. 1, 1926. Mem. Academy Political Science, Pennsylvania Society of New York. Republican. Presbyterian. Clubs: Railroad-Machinery (New York). Home: 440 W. 7th St., Plainfield, N.J.

KOONTZ, Amos R., surgeon; b. Marksville, Va., Feb. 12, 1890; s. Hubert Lee and Annie (Brown) K.; A.B., Coll. of William and Mary, Williamsburg, Va., 1910, B.S., 1910, A.M., 1911; student U. of Chicago, summers 1910-11; M.D., Johns Hopkins U. Med. Sch., 1918; m. Besse E. Stocking, July 3, 1920; 1 son, James W. II. Instr. biology, William and Mary Coll., Williamsburg, Va., 1910-14; interne and resident surgeon Johns Hopkins Base Hospital Unit, Union Protestant Infirmary and Hebrew Hosp., 1917-21; engaged in pvt. practice of surgery at Baltimore since 1921; asso. in surgery, Johns Hopkins U. Med. Sch. since 1933; surgeon Diagnostic Clinic, Johns Hopkins Hosp. since 1929, asst. vis. surgeon since 1934; mem. staff Union Memorial, Sinai hosps., Church Home and Infirmary, Hosp. for Women of Md. Served as pvt. to 1st lt. Med. Corps., U.S.A., 1917-19. Mem. Alumni Bd. of Coll. of William and Mary, Williamsburg, Va. Fellow Am. Coll. Surgeons, Am. Med. Assn. Mem. A.A.A.S., Assn. of Mil. Surgeons of U.S., Southern Med. Assn., Med. & Chirurg. Faculty of Md., Baltimore City Med. Soc., Clin. Club of Baltimore, Theta Delta Chi, Phi Beta Kappa, Sigma Xi, Pithotomy Club. Clubs: University, Maryland (Baltimore); Maryland Polo (Stevenson); Gibson Island (Gibson Island). Contbr. to med. publs. Home: 1623 Bolton St. Office: 1014 St. Paul St., Baltimore, Md.

KOONTZ, Arthur Burke, lawyer; b. Nicholas Co., W.Va., Jan. 29, 1885; s. John and Alice (Groves) K.; student Marshall Coll., Huntington, W.Va., 1903-07; LL.B., Yale Law Sch., 1910; m. Mazie Watson Sipe, Dec. 15, 1915; children—Mary Watson, Arthur Burke, Jr., Alice Ann. Admitted to W.Va. bar, 1910 and since engaged in gen. practice of law in Charleston; organized Union Trust Co., Charleston, W.Va., 1913, and was elected v.p. and gen. counsel; v.p., dir. and counsel Charleston Nat. Bank (with which Union Trust Co. was consolidated) since 1929; dir. Federal Home Loan Bank of Pittsburgh since 1936. Nominee for gov. of W.Va., 1920; active in local civic affairs, mem. Chamber of Commerce, City Planning Commn., Community Chest and others. Mem. bd. govs. W.Va. Univ. since its creation, 1927, now pres. bd. Mem. Am., W.Va. State, Charleston City bar assns., Order of Coif, Phi Alpha Delta, Phi Beta Kappa. Democrat. Episcopalian. Mason (K.T., 32°, Shriner). Clubs: Edgewood Country (Charleston); Maryland (Baltimore); Yale (New York). Home: South Hills, Charleston. Office: Union Bldg., Charleston, W.Va.

KOONTZ, Norman Clair, supt. of public schools; b. Indiana Co., Pa., Dec. 12, 1882; s. Samuel Henry and Eliza (Fleming) K.; A.B., Grove City (Pa.) Coll., 1909; A.B., Yale, 1911; A.M., Columbia, 1926; m. Mary Belle

KOONTZ Martin, Sept. 7, 1911; children—Norman Clair, Beatrice Louise, Rosemary June, John Paul. Teacher of rural schools, Indiana Co., Pa., 1902-04; prin. elementary school, DuBois, Pa., 1904-06; prin. Indiana (Pa.) High Sch., 1909-10; Tyrone (Pa.) High Sch., 1911-12; supt. of schools, Cooperstown, N.D., 1912-15, Jamestown, N.D., 1915-22, Titusville, Pa., 1922-28; supt. of public schools, Indiana, Pa., 1928-38; instructor Grove City (Pa.) Coll., summers 1915, 18, Indiana (Pa.) Teachers Coll., 1929, 31. Mem. N.E.A., Nat. Soc. for Study of Edn. Republican. Presbyterian. Clubs: Cosmopolitan, Shakespeare (Indiana, Pa.); Yale (Pittsburgh). Contbr. to professional jours. Home: 468 S. 7th St. Office: 95 N. 4th St., Indiana, Pa.

KOONTZ, Paul Rodes, clergyman; b. Rayville, Md., Oct. 30, 1890; s. Josiah Perry and Amanda Jane (Rodes) K.; A.B., Lebanon Valley Coll., Annville, Pa., 1911; B.D., Bonebrake Theol. Sem., Dayton, O., 1914; grad. study Johns Hopkins U., 1927; (hon.) D.D., Lebanon Valley Coll., 1926; m. Elizabeth Agnes Lau, Nov. 21, 1917; children—Martha Jane, Miriam Elizabeth. Ordained to ministry U. B. Ch., 1914; pastor, Carlisle, Pa., 1914, Myersville, Md., 1914-15, Lemoyne, Pa., 1915-19, Mechanicsburg, Pa., 1919-25; pastor Otterbein Memorial Ch., Baltimore, Md. since 1925; reading sec. Gen. Conf. U. B. Ch. since 1929; pres. Bd. Christian Edn. Pa. Conf. since 1937. Republican. U. B. Ch. Mason. Home: 1000 W. 38th St., Baltimore, Md.

KOOP, William H., insurance exec.; ed. pub. schools and Cooper Union, N.Y. City. Began with German (now Great) Am. Ins. Co., N.Y. City, 1894; pres. and dir. Great Am. Ins. Co. since 1928; chmn. bd. N.C. Home Insurance Co.; pres. Great Am. Indemnity Co., Am. Alliance Ins. Co., Am. Nat. Fire Ins. Co., County Fire Ins. Co., Mass. Fire & Marine Ins. Co., Rochester Am. Ins. Co., Detroit Fire & Marine Ins. Co., One Liberty St. Realty & Securities Corpn., Great Am. Investing Co.; mem. exec. com. Nat. Bd. Fire Underwriters; dir. Fire Companies' Adjustment Bur.; pres. and trustee Am. Foreign Ins. Assn.; trustee Insurance Executive Association; director Nat. Bd. of Fire Underwriters Bldg. Corpn., Sanborn Map Co. Served as chmn. Explosion Conf.; also served as pres. Eastern Automobile Conf., New York Fire Ins. Exchange, New York Bd. Fire Underwriters and Nat. Bd. of Fire Underwriters. Home: Essex Fells, N.J. Office: 1 Liberty St., New York, N.Y.

KOOPMAN, John Ruloef, artist and instr.; b. Falmouth, Mich., June 5, 1881; s. John and Jennie (Bunning) K.; student O. Northern U., Ada, O., 1899-1902, Chase Sch., N.Y. City, 1903-06, N.Y. Sch. of Fine and Applied Art, N.Y. City, 1908-09; m. Caroline F. Lanterman, Nov. 28, 1913. Instr. drawing and painting, Brooklyn Inst. of Arts & Scis., Brooklyn, N.Y. since 1926; instr. life and antique, Grand Central Sch. of Art, N.Y. City, 1928-33; instr. water color painting class, N.Y. Sch of Fine and Applied Art, 1930-31; spl. critic and instr. out of door painting class, Montclair Art Mus., 1938-39; mem. adv. bd. N.Y. Sch. of Fine & Applied Art; awarded first water color prize annual exhbn. Mich. artists, Detroit, 1924; water color purchase prize, Mich. State Fair, 1924; Joseph Isidor prize award, N.Y. Water Color Club, 1929. Mem. N.Y. Water Color Soc., N.Y. Water Color Club, N.J. Water Color and Sculpture Soc., Chatham N.J. Art Club. Club: Salmagundi (New York). Home: Rainbow Lakes, Denville, N.J.

KOPF, Harry Daniel, pres. Hammond Iron Works; b. Warren, Pa., Mar. 16, 1881; s. Martin and Mary K.; grad. Warren High Sch., 1899; m. Mary Yates, Oct. 6, 1908; children—Elizabeth Yates (Mrs. Louis H. Hall, Jr.), Robert Yates, Harry Daniel. With Hammond Iron Works since 1900, now pres.; vice-pres. and dir. Warren Axe & Tool Co.; dir. De Luxe Metal Furniture Co. Republican. Mason. Clubs: Conewango, Conewango Valley Country. Home: 509 Market St. Office: Hammond Iron Works, Warren, Pa.

KOPP, Charles Leonard, supt. of schs.; b. Linboro, Md., May 5, 1887; s. William Leonard and Margaret Elizabeth (Stough) K.; student elementary schs., Linboro, Md., 1893-1901, high sch., Glenville, Pa., 1901-05; A.B., Gettysburg (Pa.) Coll., 1909, D.Sci. in Edn. (hon.), 1937; student Johns Hopkins U., 1914-19; M.A., Columbia U., 1925; m. Anna Ursula Sterner, Aug. 20, 1920 (died 1932); m. 2d (Leona) Grace Shatzer, Aug. 24, 1938. Teacher in mil. schs., St. John's, Ossining, N.Y., 1909-10; prin. high sch., New Freedom, Pa., 1910-15; supervising prin., Westfield, Pa., 1915-18; prin. high sch., Clearfield, Pa., 1919-23, Allegany High Sch., Cumberland, Md., 1923-28; supt. of schs., Cumberland, Md., since 1928. Served as sergt. major, U.S. Army, 1918-19. Dir. advisory bd. Salvation Army, Y.M.C.A. League for Crippled Children, Asso. Charities, Cumberland, since 1928, v.p. and dir. Community Chest, Cumberland, since 1937, Chamber of Commerce since 1930; dir. Boy Scouts of America. Mem. Md. State Teachers Assn. (pres. 1937-38), N.E.A. (advisory com. on salaries), Phi Sigma Kappa, Phi Beta Kappa. Democrat. Mason. Clubs: Rotary (pres. 1936-37), Cumberland, Cumberland Country (Cumberland, Md.). Address: 108 Washington St., Cumberland, Md.

KOPP, John Wilbur, supervising prin. of schools; b. Tower City, Pa., Aug. 5, 1907; s. Chappeth L. and Ellen (Heberling) K.; grad. Tower City High Sch., 1925; B.S., Albright Coll., Reading, Pa., 1929; student Pa. State Coll., summers 1929-31; A.M., New York U., 1935; m. Violet Burdell Yoder, July 6, 1930; 1 son, John Bernard. Teacher and coach, Wisconisco (Pa.) High Sch., 1929-34; prin., teacher of history and coach, Lykens (Pa.) High Sch., 1934-36; supervising prin. Joint Sch. Dist., Williamstown, Pa., since 1936. Mem. Ch. Council of Luth. Ch.; supt. Sunday Sch., Luth. Ch., Lykens, Pa., 1934-36. Pres. Upper Dauphin Scholastic League, 1929-36. Mem. N.E.A., Pa. State Edn. Assn., Secondary Prins. Assn. of Pa., Dauphin Co. Prins. Assn., Kappa Delta Pi. Republican. Lutheran. Mason, K. of P. Club: Rotary of Williamstown. Address: Market St., Williamstown, Pa.

KOPPELMAN, Walter, brokerage; b. Baltimore, Md., Mar. 25, 1875; s. John George and Elizabeth Estelle (Fritz) K.; student pub. schs., Baltimore, Md., Baltimore City Coll., 1889-91; m. Grace Lawrence Dunderdale, Nov. 29, 1911; children—Grace Forbes, Sarah Parker (Mrs. William Bradford Banks), Walter Jr., John Van Cortlandt. Successively, clk., bank teller, bond salesman; now in bus. on own acct. as stock broker and mem. Baltimore Stock Exchange; dir. Guilford Assn. Mem. Md. Bankers Assn. Democrat. Episcopalian. Clubs: Merchants (Baltimore); Gibson Island (Gibson Island); Lake Placid (Lake Placid, N.Y.). Home: 102 Millbrook Rd. Office: 219 E. Redwood St., Baltimore, Md.

KORB, Carl R., banker; b. Pittsburgh, Pa.; s. Louis and Mary A. (Roemhild) Korb; m. Margaret G. Hanrahan; children—Margaret Ann, Donald C. Has been associated with The Union Trust Co. of Pittsburgh since 1915, now v.p.; pres. Tuco Corpn., Pittsburgh; dir. Babcock Coal & Coke Co., Babcock Lumber Co., Babcock-Carrier Florida Co. Dir. Suburban Gen. Hosp., Bellevue, Pa. Mem. bd. trustees Ben Avon (Pa.) Presbyn. Ch. Mem. Pittsburgh Chamber of Commerce. Presbyterian. Clubs: Duquesne (Pittsburgh); Shannopin Country (exdir.). Home: 7074 Woodland Av. Office: 5th Av. and Grant St., Pittsburgh, Pa.

KORB, Robert T., pres. Korb-Pettit Wire Fabrics & Iron Works, Inc.; b. Phila., Pa., Aug. 14, 1888; s. Edward and Kathryn (Toussant) Korb; student Peirce Business Coll., Phila., 1914-15, Drexel Inst. of Tech., Phila., 1915-16; m. Margery Elizabeth Simmons, July 15, 1911; 1 dau., Margery Roberta. Pres. Audubon (N.J.) Wire Cloth Co., 1917-32; pres. Korb-Pettit Wire Fabrics & Iron Works, Inc., Phila., since 1933. Episcopalian. Home: 252 Chrystal Lake Av., Audubon, N.J. Office: 1505-15 N. Mascher St., Philadelphia, Pa.

KORNER, Jules Gilmer, Jr., lawyer; b. Kernersville, Forsyth Co., N.C., July 24, 1888; s. Jules Gilmer and Polly Alice (Masten) K.; student Guilford (N.C.) Coll., 1902-04; A.B., Trinity Coll. (now Duke U.), 1908, A.M., 1909; law student, same, 1909, 10; Harvard, 1910, 11; business course Oak Ridge Inst., 1912; m. Susan Leonard Brown, Oct. 3, 1917; 1 son, Jules Gilmer. Admitted to N.C. bar, 1911, and began practice at Winston-Salem; mem. firm Alexander, Parrish & Korner, 1914, Alexander & Korner, 1915; associate with L. M. Swink, 1916-17; mem. firm, Swink, Korner & Hutchins, 1919-21; spl. atty., Bur. Internal Revenue, 1921-23; asst. solicitor same, in charge Penal Div., 1923-24; apptd. mem U.S. Bd. Tax Appeals, by President Coolidge, July 16, 1924, chmn. bd. Apr. 1, 1925-Apr. 15, 1927; resigned as chmn. and mem. bd. and resumed practice specializing in state and federal income and estate tax matters; law partner David H. Blair, former commr. of internal revenue, 1921-30, Richard S. Doyle and George D. Brabson. Enlisted in U.S. Navy, May 1917; grad. Officers' Material Sch., summer 1918; commd. ensign, later lt.; personnel officer Naval Overseas Transportation Service; trans. to R.O.C., Sept. 25, 1919. Mem. Duke Univ. Alumni Assn. (pres.), North Carolina Soc. of D.C. (pres.), Southern Soc. of Washington, Kappa Sigma. Republican. Clubs: Duke Univ. Alumni Club of D.C. and Md. (v.p.), University, Inquirendo, Chevy Chase, Congressional Country (Washington, D.C.); Twin City, Forsyth Country (Winston-Salem). Home: 5636 Western Av., Chevy Chase, Md. Address: Transportation Bldg., Washington, D.C.

KORNS, Charles B(yron), Sr., physician; b. Somerset Co., Pa., July 11, 1882; s. Edmund and Agnes (Sipe) K.; student Franklin and Marshall Acad., 1904-05; M.D., cum laude, Baltimore Med. Coll., 1909; m. Bessie Elda Miller, Sept. 14, 1910; children—Charles Byron (M.D.), Miller J. (M.D.). Public school teacher, 1901-04; gen. practice as physician, Sipesville, since 1909. Dir. First Nat. Bank, Somerset, Pa.; pres. Sipesville Water Co. Chmn. Somerset Co. and Rep. Com.; del. to Nat. Conv., Chicago. School director. Memberships A.M.A. Pa. Med. Soc., Somerset Co. Med. Soc. Mem. Reformed Church. Mason. Address: Sipesville, Pa.

KOSER, John McCrea, real estate, ins.; b. Newville, Pa., Sept. 22, 1892; s. Howard M. and Martha (McCrea) K.; student Newville High Sch., 1908-11; m. Charlotte E. Freyer, Mar. 31, 1923; children—George McCrea, John McCrea. Began as farmer, 1912; telephone exchange mgr. Newville, Pa., 1913-14; mgr. sanitary co., Pittsburgh, 1914; recording clerk Edgar Thompson Steel Works, 1915; inspector munitions, 1916; telephone installation and switchboard expert, 1917; with telephone Co., Phila., 1920, chief operator Phila. Electric Bur., 18 mos.; became real estate salesman, 1923; pres. and owner Koser Bros. Realtors since 1931. Served with A.E.F., 23 mos. Active in local Y.M.C.A. Boys Movement. Awarded several war medals. Dir. Ardmore Chamber of Commerce; mem. Am. Legion (comdr. Post 136), Vets. Foreign Wars, Business Men's Assn. Phila. Real Estate Bd. Republican. United Presbyn. Home: 24 Wellington Road. Office: 6 Anderson Av., Ardmore, Pa.

KOSSLER, Herman Stanislaus, banker; b. Pittsburgh, Pa., Nov. 13, 1882; s. William and Mary Agetha (Beck) K.; student Duquesne U. High Sch., Pittsburgh, 1895-98; Ph.G., U. of Pittsburgh, 1903, Phar.D., 1906; m. Estella Emma Epp, May 29, 1907; children—Robert William, Anna Mary (Mrs. Erick F. Moeller). Began as drug clerk, Apr. 1900; owner retail drug store, Pittsburgh, Pa., 1904-38; instr. mathematics, U. of Pittsburgh, 1903-30; v.p. and dir. West End Bank, Pittsburgh, 1934-39, pres. since 1939; dir. Kosta Bldg. Dir. Pittsburgh Coll. of Pharmacy. Republican. Roman Catholic. Home: 71 Dinsmore Av., Crafton, Pa. Office: S. Main and Wabash Sts., Pittsburgh, Pa.

KOTHNY, Gottdank L(ebrecht), mech. engr.; b. Troppau, Austria, Apr. 25, 1881; s. Erasmus and Johanna (Hoschek) K.; came to U.S., 1904, naturalized, 1921; M.E., Tech. Coll., Reichenberg, 1899; spl. courses, Tech. Coll., Prague, 1900-01; m. Rosa Kallies, June 1,

1918. Employed as design engr. in New York, 1904-07, and in France, Eng., and Japan, 1907-14; cons. engr. Westinghouse Machine Co., Pittsburgh, Pa., 1914-16; exec. engr. and dir. C. H. Wheeler Mfg. Co., Phila., 1916-29; v.p. and gen. mgr. Sperry-Sun Well Surveying Co., underground well surveying and oil production services, Phila. since 1929; inventor Radojet air pump; has patented many air ejectors, condensers, and well surveying instruments and tools. Received Edw. Longstreth Medal of Merit from Franklin Inst. awarded 1920 for invention Radojet air pump. Fellow Am. Soc. Mech. Engrs. Mem. Am. Inst. Mining & Metall. Engrs., Soc. Naval Architects & Marine Engrs., Am. Petroleum Inst., Franklin Inst. of Pa. Civil mem. Am. Soc. Naval Engrs. Republican. Roman Catholic. Clubs: Racquet (Phila); Merion Cricket (Haverford); Pickering Hunt (Phoenixville); Philadelphia Skating (Ardmore). Home: West Valley Rd., Strafford, Pa. Office: 1608 Walnut St., Philadelphia, Pa.

KOTZEN, Earl Louis, hosiery mfg.; b. Lithuania; s. Solomon J. and Bessie (Siegal) K., citizens of United States; came to U.S., 1894; ed. public school, Reading, Pa.; unmarried. Vice-pres. Howard C. Mohn Hosiery Co., Inc., Adamstown, Pa.; treas. Hanna Mfg. Co., Reading, Pa. Served as asso. chmn. Pinchot for Governor Com. for Berks Co., 1931. Mem. Bd. Mgrs. Reading Hosp. Republican. Jewish religion. Elk. Club: Kiwanis (Reading). Home: 515 N. 8th St., Reading, Pa.

KOUES, Helen; see Bodine, Helen Koues.

KOUWENHOVEN, Frank Wolfert, univ. prof.; b. Brooklyn, N.Y., Jan. 13, 1893; s. Tunis Garret Bergen and Phebe Florence (Bennett) K.; M.E., Poly. Inst. of Brooklyn, N.Y., 1916; m. Alice H. Witherell, Sept. 6, 1921; children—Phyllis, Gertrude Bergen, Alice Witherell. Employed as steam tester, Brooklyn Edison Co., Brooklyn, N.Y., 1916-17, Transit Development Co., Brooklyn, N.Y., 1917; engr. of tests, N. Y. Steam Co., N.Y. City, 1917-19; battery process engr., Winchester Repeating Arms Co., New Haven, Conn., 1919-20; with mech. engineering dept., John Hopkins U. since 1920, instr. mech. engring., 1920-30, asso. in mech. engineering, Johns Hopkins U. since 1930, Served in Air Service, U.S.A., 1918. Mem. Bd. of Control, Baltimore Safety Council, since 1937. Mem. Am. Soc. Mech. Engrs., St. Nicholas Soc. of Nassau Island, Brooklyn, Sigma Psi. Democrat. Presbyn. Club: Engineers (Baltimore). Home: 4310 Rugby Rd., Baltimore, Md.

KOUWENHOVEN, William Bennett, elec. engineer; b. Brooklyn, N.Y., Jan. 13, 1886; s. Tunis Gerrit Bergen and Phoebe Florence (Bennett) K.; E.E., Brooklyn Poly. Inst., 1906, M.E., 1907; Diplom Ingenieur, Kalsruhe Technische Hochschule, Baden, Germany, 1912, Doktor Ingenieur, 1913; m. Abigail Baxter Remsen, June 22, 1910; 1 son, William Gerrit. Asst. in physics, Brooklyn Poly. Inst., 1906-07, instr. in physics and elec. engring., 1907-10; instr. in elec. engring., Washington U., 1913-14; same, Johns Hopkins, 1914-17, asso. in elec. engring., 1917-19; engring. supt. Winchester Repeating Arms Co. (leave of absence from Johns Hopkins), 1919-20; asso. prof. elec. engring., Johns Hopkins, 1919-30, prof. and asst. dean Sch. of Engring., 1930-38, prof. and dean sch. of Engring. since Sept. 1938; cons. engr. U.S. Bur. Mines, U.S. Bur. Standards. Instr., rank of capt., R.O.T.C., World War. Fellow A.A. A.S.; mem. Am. Inst. E.E. (v.p. 1931-33; dir. 1935-39; chmn. Baltimore sect. 1922-31), Am. Soc. for Testing Materials, Tau Beta Pi, Sigma Xi, Pi Kappa Phi. Democrat. Presbyn. Clubs: Johns Hopkins Baltimore Engineers, Gibson Island. Contbr. many articles and papers on electrical measurements, electric shock and magnetic analysis to Trans. Am. Inst. E.E., Electrical World, Proc. Am. Soc. for Testing Materials, etc. Home: 334 St. Dustan's Rd., Baltimore, Md.

KOVACS, Koloman, pres. Royal Mfg. Co.; b. Hungary, May 8, 1868; student European Law Sch.; m. Gizella Kovacs, 1888; children—Sam S., Daniel, Martin, Jennie (Mrs. Joseph Weishaus). Came to U.S., 1907. Employed in retail drug store, Duquesne, Pa., 1907-13; organized, 1913, and since pres. Royal Mfg. Co. of Duquesne (mfg. and marketing drugs and chemicals) branch factories at Brooklyn, N.Y., Chicago, Ill., and Kansas City, Mo. Home: 119 S. 4th St. Office: 19-23 N. First St., Duquesne, Pa.

KOYL, George Simpson, architect, educator; b. Evanston, Wyo., Feb. 8, 1885; s. Rev. Charles Henry and Caroline (Emigh) K.; grad. North Denver High Sch., Denver, Colo., 1902; B.S. in Architecture, U. of Pa., 1909, M.S., in Architecture, 1911; fellow Am. Acad. in Rome, 1911-15; m. Adelaide Wight Howard, Oct. 10, 1924. Began as architectural draftsman, in office of F. E. Edbrooke, Denver, 1902; with Cass Gilbert, architect, N.Y. City, 1915-17 and 1918-19, McKim, Mead and White, 1920-24; chief designer and consultant County and City Bldg., of Denver, 1925-27; practiced alone, 1928-29; mem. Rich. Mathesius & Koyl, 1929-32; critic in design, Columbia U., 1928, Princeton, 1928-29; instr. and asst. prof. New York U., 1929-32; dean Sch. of Fine Arts, U. of Pa., since 1932. Mem. bd. mgrs. House of Detention for Witnesses and Untried Prisoners for the County of Philadelphia; mem. architects advisory com. Phila. Housing Authority. Prin. works: Ridgewood (N.J.) Woman's Club Bldg.; Hospital, Littleton, N.H.; memorial to James Cardinal Gibbons, Washington, D.C. Served as lt. Air Service, A.E.F., 1917-18. Trustee Am. Acad. in Rome; fellow Am. Inst. Architects; mem. Archæol. Soc. America, Architectural League of N.Y., Art Alliance of Phila., 1st Reserve Aero Squadron Assn., Soc. American Etchers (asso.), Sigma Xi, Tau Sigma Delta, Sigma Phi Sigma. Republican. Clubs: Lenape, University; University of Pa. of New York; asso. mem. Orpheus Club. Home: 4400 Spruce St. Address: School of Fine Arts, Univ. of Pa., Philadelphia, Pa.

KRABILL, Verlin Christian, educator; b. Defiance Co., O., Oct. 18, 1898; s. John William and Florence Mary (Bosserman) K.; student one room sch., Defiance County, Ohio, 1904-09, elementary and high sch., Denton, Md., 1909-16; A.B., Blue Ridge Coll., New Windsor, Md., 1920; M.A., U. of Md., 1929; m. Anna Louise Arnold, June 22, 1921 (died 1931); children—Verlin Arnold, Emma Louise; m. 2d, Mary Lynn Hostetler, Feb. 10, 1933; 1 dau., Betty Katherine. Teacher Greensboro (Md.) High Sch., 1920-22, Brunswick (Md.) High Sch., 1922-23, Frederick (Md.) High Sch., 1923-27; prin. Tri-County High Sch., Queen Anne, Md., 1927-28, Pocomoke High Sch., Pocomoke City, Md., since 1928. Republican. Presbyterian. Club: Rotary (Pocomoke City, Md.). Home: Walnut St. Office: Market St., Pocomoke City, Md.

KRAEMER, Joseph, lawyer; b. Kamenetz, Russia, Apr. 18, 1889; s. Jacob and Kiriam (Schurberg) K.; brought to U.S., 1893; LL.B., N.Y. Univ. Law Sch., 1909; m. Tania Kupperman, Dec. 23, 1913; children—Louis Brandeis, Daniel, Miriam Faith. Admitted to N.J. bar as atty., 1910, counsellor, 1913; admitted to practice before the Supreme Ct. of the U.S., 1925; N.J. Supreme Ct. Commr., 1929; engaged in gen. practice of law at Newark since 1910, mem. firm Kraemer, Siegler & Siegler since 1921. Treas. Essex Co. Dem. Com. Trustee, Oheb Shalom Synagogue. Mem. exec. com. Order Sons of Zion. Dep. mem. exec. council, World Zionist Orgn.; mem. exec. com., Zionist Orgn. of America. Mem. Am., N.J. State and Essex Co. bar assns., Com. of One Hundred for Defense of Human Rights. Democrat. Jewish religion. Mason. Home: 74 Baldwin Av. Office: 790 Broad St., Newark, N.J.

KRAEMER, Manfred, physician; b. Newark, N.J., July 27, 1904; s. Leopold and Eleanore (Bachman) K.; A.B., Univ. of Pa., 1926; M.D., U. of Pa. Med. Sch., 1929; grad. study, U. of Vienna, Austria, 1932, Sch. Trop. Medicine and Hygiene, London, Eng., 1932; m. Evelyn Waldron, Newark, N.J., Mar. 9, 1932; 1 son, Waldron. Engaged in practice of medicine at Newark, N.J., since 1931; chief Gastro-intestinal Clinic, Newark Presbyn. Hosp.; gastroenterologist, St. James Hosp.; mem. staff, Newark City Hosp.; courtesy staff, Beth Israel, St. Barnabas, St. Michael's hosps.; instr. clin. medicine, N.Y. Med. Coll., 1936-37. Served as 1st lt. Med. Res. Corps, U.S.A., since 1935. Fellow Am. Coll. Phys., Am. Med. Assn., Royal Soc. Trop. Medicine and Hygiene. Mem. Internat. Gastroenterol. Assn., N.J. Gastroenterol. Assn. (v.p. 1938-39), N.J. Med. Soc., Essex Co. Med. Soc., Acad. of Medicine of Northern N.J. Ind. Republican. Hebrew religion. Clubs: Rotary (Newark); Officers of Army and Navy (New York). Contbr. to med. jours. Home: 35 Nairn Pl. Office: 31 Lincoln Park, Newark, N.J.

KRAFT, John F., pres. Washington Tin Plate Co., Washington, Pa.*

KRAMER, Clarence R., lawyer; b. Clearfield, Pa., Apr. 28, 1893; s. Aaron G. and Jane Elizabeth (Reed) K.; ed. high sch., Clearfield, Pa., 1908-12, U. of Mich. Law Sch., summers 1915-17; m. Ruth C. Cooper, Oct. 4, 1922; children—Dorothy Ann, Marjorie Jane, Carl A. (foster son). Also studied law in office of father; admitted to Pa. bar, 1918 and since engaged in gen. practice of law at Clearfield; mem. firm Kramer and Kramer, 1918-34, and on death of father, in practice alone since 1934; admitted to practice before Supreme Ct. of Pa., U.S. District Ct. and the Supreme Ct. of the U.S.; pres. of bd. Clearfield Pub. Co., pub. Clearfield Times, weekly newspaper. Served as Chmn. Dem. Co. Com. since 1936; Dem. nominee for Congress, 23d Cong. Dist., 1926. Democrat. Methodist. Mason, I.O.O.F., Red Man. Home: 117 Nichols St. Office: 219 Market St., Clearfield, Pa.

KRAMER, Roland Laird, educator; b. Phila., Pa., Feb. 26, 1898; s. John Howard and Agnes (Laird) K.; grad. West Phila. High Sch., 1915; B.S., U. of Pa., 1918, A.M., 1921, Ph.D., 1923; m. Mildred Rose Cramer, June 9, 1920; 1 dau., Jeanne Mildred. Instr. in commerce and transportation, Wharton Sch., U. of Pa., 1919-23, asst. prof., 1923-31, prof. since 1931; special agent U.S. Bureau of Foreign and Domestic Commerce, Washington, D.C., 1923, 31; sec. Latin Am. Round Table and Conf., Inst. of Politics, Williamstown, Mass., 1928, 29, 30; sec. Far Eastern Round Table and Conf., same, 1932; special editor of marine transportation terms, revision of Webster's New Internat. Dictionary, 1929; sr. econ. analyst, for special adviser to the President on foreign trade, 1935; business specialist Foreign Trade Zones Bd., Washington, D.C., 1936; special expert U.S. Maritime Commn., 1938-39; mem. Am. Council, Inst. of Pacific Relations. Served in S.A. T.C., Oct.-Dec. 1918. Mem. Foreign Traders Assn. of Phila., Inc. (sec. since 1934), Propeller Club (pres. U. of Pa. port). Democrat. United Presbyterian. Author: History of Export and Import Rates (thesis), 1924. Co-author: Railroad Freight Rate Structures, Eastern Territory, 1925, Western Territory, 1926; Foreign Trade, Principles and Practices (with G. G. Huebner), 1930. Contbr. articles to periodicals also govt. bulletins. Home: 825 Ormond Av., Drexel Hill, Pa. Office: Univ. of Pennsylvania, Philadelphia, Pa.

KRANER, Hobart McKinley, ceramic engr.; b. Columbus, O., Nov. 3, 1896; s. John W. and Sophia (Lauer) K.; B. of Ceramic Engring., Ohio State U., Columbus, O., 1921, M.Sc., 1922, Ceramic Engr., 1938; m. Frances Angela Wilson, Sept. 5, 1928; 1 son, Hobart Wilson. Research asst., U.S. Bur. of Mines, Columbus, O., 1922-23; research engr., A. C. Spark Plug Co., Flint, Mich., 1923-24; supt., Ill. Electric Porcelain Co., Macomb, Ill., 1924-25; research engr. Westinghouse Co., E. Pittsburgh, Pa., 1925-30, supt. porcelain plant, Derry, Pa., 1930-32; research engr. Corhart Refractories Co., Louisville, Kl., 1932-35; research engr., refractories research, Bethlehem Steel Co., Bethlehem, Pa., since 1935. Fellow Am. Ceramic Soc.; mem. Alpha Chi Sigma, Sigma Xi. Author numerous articles on porcelain, refractories, glass, etc., mfr. in ceramic and engring. jours. Holder numerous ceramic, etc., patents. Home: 215 Wall St. Office: 701 E. 3d St., Bethlehem, Pa.

KRANTZ, John Christian, Jr., univ. prof.; b. Baltimore, Md., Oct. 8, 1899; s. John Christian and Johanna Fredericka (Steinmann) K.; Pharm. B., U. of Md. Sch. Pharmacy, 1923, M.S., 1924, Ph.D., 1928; m. Helen King, June 15, 1921; 1 dau., Margaret Claire. Asso. prof. chemistry, U. of Md. Sch. Pharmacy and Dentistry, Baltimore, 1921-26, prof. chemistry, 1926-27; dir. pharm. research, Sharp & Dohme, Baltimore, Md., 1927-30; chief bur. of chemistry, Md. State Dept. Health, 1930-35; prof. pharmacology, U. of Md. Sch. of Medicine since 1933. Served in S.A.T.C., 1918. Mem. Am. Chem. Soc., Pharmacol. Soc., Soc. for Exptl. Biology and Medicine, Sigma Xi. Awarded Simon medal, Ebert Prize in Chemistry, 1929. Presbyn. Clubs: University, Grachur, Iroquois Canoe, Homeland Ice Skating (Baltimore). Home: 3401 Crossland Av., Baltimore, Md.

KRATZ, Albert Roger, dean theol. sem.; b. Silverdale, Pa., Jan. 20, 1894; s. Albert Phillips and Malinda Shutt (Bean) K.; ed. Kutztown State Teachers Coll., 1909-11; A.B., Northwestern U., 1919; B.D., Garrett Bib. Inst., Evanston, Ill., 1921; grad. study, Cornell U., summers 1922-25, U. of Pa., 1926-28; m. Esther Rosenberger, Sept. 1, 1919; 1 dau., Irma Joan. Employed as teacher pub schs., 1911-16 ordained to ministry Evang. Ch., 1921; prof. Evang. Sch. Theology, Reading, Pa., 1920-26, dean since 1926; chmn. dept. social service, Pa. Council of Chs. Dir. Social Welfare League, Hoipe Rescue Mission, Reading, Pa. Mem. Am. Acad. Polit. and Social Sci., Reading Ministerial Assn. (past pres.), Pi Gamma Mu. Republican. Evangelical. Author: Is There a Social Gospel?, 1926; The Wisdom of Preaching, 1930; From Economics to Christianity, 1934; Christ or Caesar, 1938; Called to Be Teachers, 1939. Home: 730 Wyomissing Boul., Berkshire Heights, Pa. Office: Evang. Sch. of Theology, Reading, Pa.

KRATZ, John Aubel; b. Baltimore, Md., Feb. 20, 1884; s. John and Jennie Elizabeth (Aubel) K.; A.B., Johns Hopkins, 1906; m. Mary Luella Hunter, Nov. 25, 1913; children—Jean Aubel, Elinor Hunter, John Hunter, Martha Bacon. Instr. and head Dept. of Commerce, Baltimore City College, until 1920; chief Rehabilitation Div., U.S. Office of Education since 1921. Mem. Nat. Rehabilitation Assn., Am. Vocational Assn. Protestant. Author: Standard Shorthand, 1916; Vocational Rehabilitation in the United States, 1927. Home: 4302 Springdale Av., Baltimore, Maryland. Address: Dept. of the Interior, Washington, D.C.

KRAUSE, Allen Kramer, M.D., medical research; b. Lebanon, Pa., Feb. 13, 1881; s. George Derr and Jeanie Julia (Kramer) K.; A.B., Brown U., 1901; grad. sudent in biology, same univ., 1901-03, A.M., 1902; M.D., Johns Hopkins, 1907; Litt.D. (honorary), Norwich University, 1935; m. Clara Fletcher, Oct. 10, 1906; children—Gregory, Francis, Fletcher. Asst. and instr. pathology, Johns Hopkins, 1907-09; asst. dir. Saranac (N.Y.) Lab., 1909-16; asso. prof. medicine and dir. Kenneth Dows Tuberculosis Research Labs., Johns Hopkins, 1916-29; in charge Tuberculosis Dispensary, Johns Hopkins Hosp., and asso. phys. Johns Hopkins Hosp., 1916-29; pres. The Desert Sanatorium, Tucson, Ariz., 1929-37; clin. prof. medicine, Stanford U., 1929-37; clin. prof. medicine, U. of Southern Calif., 1932-37. Lecturer in medicine, Johns Hopkins. Managing editor Am. Rev. of Tuberculosis, 1916, editor since 1922; editor Am. sect. of "Tubercle" (London) since 1924; collaborator, Zeitschrift für Tuberkulose (Berlin), Arch. Med.-Chirurg. de l'Appareil Respiratoire (Paris); lecturer Trudeau School of Tuberculosis, 1916-29; counsellor Med. Council U.S. Vets. Bur., 1924—. Awarded Trudeau Medal, 1931. Mem. Assn. Am. Physicians, Am. Society Clin. Investigation (hon.), Am. Climatol. and Clin. Asn., Am. Assn. Pathologists and Bacteriologists, Am. Assn. Anatomists, Am. Soc. Bacteriologists, Am. Soc. Exptl. Pathologists, Am. Pub. Health Assn., Nat. Tuberculosis Assn., Internat. Union Against Tuberculosis, Am. Soc. Med. Editors, Assn. Study Internal Secretions, Harvey Soc. (hon.), Los Angeles Clin. and Path. Soc. (hon.), Bronx County (N.Y.) Med. Soc. (hon.), Pima Co. Med. Soc. (hon.), St. Louis (Mo.) Med. Soc. (hon.), Theta Delta Chi, Phi Beta Kappa, Sigma Xi, Alpha Omega Alpha; fellow Am. Coll. Phys., A.A.A.S., American Geographical Soc. Democrat. Protestant. Clubs: Century Assn. (New York City); Cactus (Denver); Pacific Interurban Clinical, Interurban Clinical (hon.). Author: Rest and Other Things, 1922; Environment and Resistance in Tuberculosis, 1923; The Evolution of Tubercle, 1927; also numerous articles on tuberculosis. Contbr. to Nelson's Loose Leaf System of Medicine, Osler's Modern Medicine, Cecil's Text-Book of Medicine, Piersol's Cyclopedia of Medicine, and Ency. Britannica. Address: Cambridge Arms, Baltimore, Md.

KRAUSE, George Derr, hardware mcht.; b. Lebanon, Pa., Dec. 8, 1858; s. George and Catharine (Shindel) K.; desc. John Peter Shindel, who came to America, 1751, and served in Continental Army; A.B., Muhlenberg Coll., 1879, A.M., 1892; grad. study U. of Pa.; m. Jeanie J. Kramer, of Allentown, Pa., May 2, 1880 (died 1902); children—Allen K., Charles William (dec.), Geo. Franklin (dec.), Elamina (Mrs. Donald W. Rich), James Roger (dec.), Maxwell; m. 2d, Mrs. Harriet A. Neifert, of Reading, Pa., Oct. 21, 1920. Asso. with George Krause Hardware Co. continuously since 1879, pres. since (bus. inc., 1902) death of father, 1906, bus. in continuous operation at Lebanon, Pa., since founded by grandfather, John D. Krause, 1833; first vice-pres. Lebanon County Trust Co.; pres. Pennsylvania Chautauqua since 1899, dir. since 1896; pres. Mt. Lebanon Cemetery Assn. since 1922; has served as treas. Pa. Wholesale Hardware & Supply Assn. since 1904, former pres. Ephrata & Lebanon St. Ry. Co. Served as mem. then pres. Select Council, Lebanon, Pa., 1906-10; del. to Dem. State Conv.; served three times as Dem. Presdl. Elector of Pa. Mem. Pa. Soc. of New York, Chi Phi. Democrat. Lutheran. Elk. Clubs: Rotary, Steitz (Lebanon); Hardware (Phila. and New York); honored on 80th birthday by Hardware Club with dinner, 400 guests. Home: 14 S. Third St. Office: 35 S. 8th St., Lebanon, Pa.

KRAUSE, Maxwell, hardware merchant; b. Lebanon, Pa., Dec. 23, 1890; s. George Derr and Jeanie (Kramer) K.; Ph.B., Brown U., Providence, R.I., 1910; m. Helen Guthrie, Oct. 23, 1911; children—James Guthrie, Allen Herschel, George Derr, 2d. Entered Geo. Krause Hardware Co. (founded by great-grandfather 1833), 1910; served in various capacities, vice-pres. and gen. mgr. (4th generation to manage the business) since 1929, dir. Lebanon County Trust Co. Vice-pres. and asst. treas. Pa. Wholesale Hardware and Supply Assn. Mem. Theta Delta Chi. Democrat. Lutheran. Clubs: Quentin (Pa.) Riding, Pen and Pencil (Phila.). Home: 106 E. Chestnut St. Office: 35 S. 8th St., Lebanon, Pa.

KRAUSS, Franklin Brunell, asso. prof. Latin; b. Quakertown, Pa., March 5, 1901; s. Morris Edelman and Flora Virginia (Erney) K.; A.B., U. of Pa., 1922, A.M., same, 1924, Ph.D., same, 1930; student at Am. Sch. Classical Studies, Rome, Italy, summer 1926; m. Martha Katherine Zeeb, June 15, 1935; 1 dau., Gloria Madeline. Engaged as instr. Latin, U. of Pa., 1922-31, asso. prof. Pa. State Coll., since 1931. Mem. Am. Philol. Assn., Linguistic Soc. of America (foundation mem.), Classical Assn. of Atlantic States, Assn. Am. Univ. Profs., Pa. State Edn. Assn., Philomathean Literary Soc., Phi Sigma Iota, Phi Eta Sigma, Eta Sigma Phi, Phi Beta Kappa, Delta Chi. Democrat. Lutheran. Club: State College Literary. Author: The Omens, Portents, and Prodigies Recorded by Livy, Tacitus, and Suetonius, 1930. Contbr. articles on classical subjects to ednl. jours. Home: 28 Orlando Apts., State College, Pa.

KRAUSZ, Charles Edward, chiropodist; b. Phila., Pa., July 25, 1902; s. Charles Henry and Louise (Krauskopf) K.; D.S.C., Temple U. Sch. Chiropody, 1923; grad. study, Ill. Coll. Chiropody, Chicago, 1933; m. Alice Worrall, Nov. 25, 1937. Engaged in profession as chiropodist, Phila., Pa., since 1923; prof. didactic chiropody, Temple U., since 1931; guest lecturer at British Chiropody Council Conv., London, 1938. Mem. Nat. Assn. Chiropodists (past v.p., pres. since 1938), Chiropody Soc. Pa. (sec. 1930-34, pres. 1934), Blue Key, Pi Epsilon Delta. Received Temple Univ. Alumni Award for meritorious service, 1935. Republican. Mennonite. Mason (K.T., Shriner). I.O.O.F. Club: Northeast Shrine (Rockledge). Contbr. sci. papers to jours. of chiropody. Co-editor (with others), Chiropody Quiz Compends., 3d edit. Editor of Chiropody Index. Home: 7342 Tabor Av. Office: 926 W. Lehigh Av., Philadelphia, Pa.

KRAYBILL, David Barto, educator; b. at Maytown, Pa., Dec. 28, 1886; s. Franklin Engle and Adeline (Barto) K.; A.B., Franklin and Marshall Coll., Lancaster, Pa., 1911; A.M., Columbia, 1916; Ph.D., Pa. State Coll., 1927; m. Ellen Kathryn Millar, July 25, 1917; children—Margaret Adeline, William Henry. Teacher rural schs., Lancaster Co., Pa., 1905-08; prin. high sch., Lampeter, Pa., 1911-18; state supervisor Bur. of Vocational Edn., Dept. Pub. Instrn., Harrisburg, Pa., 1919; dir. rural community vocational sch., Lampeter, 1919-24; asst. in dept. rural edn., Pa. State Coll., 1924-25; supt. pub. schs., Redstone Tp., Republic, Pa., 1925-29; supt. schs., Wheeling, W.Va., 1929-33; dean of instrn., New River State Coll., Montgomery, W.Va., 1933—. Attended O.T.C., Camp Lee, Va., 1918. Mem. N.E.A. and Dept. Superintendence of same, Nat. Vocational Guidance Assn. America, Am. Vocational Assn., Nat. Platoon Sch. Assn., Pa. State Edn. Assn., W.Va. State Edn. Assn., Wild Life League of W.Va., Am. Legion, Lambda Chi Alpha, Kappa Delta Pi. Pa. del. to N.E.A. Conv., Minneapolis, Minn., 1927. Republican. Lutheran. Mason. Clubs: Rotary (chmn. vocational guidance com.), Masonic Forum. Home: Montgomery, W.Va.

KREBS, Charles Edward, mining engr., geologist; b. New Martinsville, W.Va., May 19, 1870; s. John W. and Elizabeth J. (Hubacher) K.; student Magnolia High Sch., New Martinsville, W.Va., 1884-85; B.S., in civil engring., W.Va. U., 1894; m. Donnie Carr, Feb. 22, 1899 (died 1903); m. 2d, Josephine Paden Stephens, Nov. 22, 1905 (died 1920); 1 son, Charles Gregory. Teacher of rural schs., Wetzel Co., W.Va., 1894-95; transitman Taylor, Romine & Scott, McKeesport, Pa., on ry. survey Charleston, Clendenim & Sutton R.R., W.Va., 1895-96; resident engr., same ry., constrn., W.Va., 1895-96, W.Va. Southern Ry., 1896-98; mem. firm Clark & Krebs, civil and mining engrs., Kanawha Falls, later Charleston, 1898-1931; pres. Charles E. Krebs, Inc., Charleston, since 1931; mem. W.Va. State Examing. Bd. for examination of mine inspectors and foremen, 1908-12; asst. geologist, W.Va. Geol. Survey, 1909-15; cons. geologist Pure Oil Co. and others since 1917. Dir. Charleston Chamber of Commerce, 1915-26; past pres. Charleston Chapter Am. Assn. Engrs.; former sec. Charleston Div. Am. Soc. Mining and Metall. Engrs. Republican. Presbyterian. Mason (32°, Shriner). Rotarian. Author of geol. reports and surveys. Authority on coal mining and oil and gas development. Address: 502 Charleston Nat. Bank, Charleston, W.Va.

KREBS, Frank Philip, lawyer; b. Tamaqua, Pa., Oct. 1, 1864; s. Philip A. and Elizabeth (Portz) K.; student Tamaqua (Pa.) High Sch., 1870-81; B.Sc., Lafayette Coll., Easton, Pa., 1885; LL.B., U. of Pa., 1887; m. Mary Henrietta Hobart, Apr. 26, 1914. Admitted to Pa. bar, 1887, and practiced at Tamaqua since 1890. Mem. town council, Tamaqua, Pa., 1887-1901; pres. Tamaqua Sch. Bd., 1902-06; pres. Commrs. of Water-Works, Tamaqua, Pa., since 1913. Dir. Peoples Trust Co. Republican. Mem. Reformed Ch. Elk. Home: 112 E. Broad St. Office: 12 W. Broad St., Tamaqua, Pa.

KREBS, W. W., editor The Tribune. Address: Johnstown, Pa.

KREHBIEL, Otto Frederick, physician; b. New York, N.Y., Mar. 17, 1879; s. Augustus and Louise (Kanenbley) K.; A.B., Coll. of City of N.Y., 1898; M.D., Coll. of Phys. & Surgs. of Columbia U., 1902; grad. student univs. of Leipzig, Strassburg, Berlin, Vienna, 1905-07; m. Jessie E. Fellows, June 29, 1909.

Interne Lenox Hill Hosp., N.Y. City, 1902-05; engaged in pvt. practice internal medicine at New York, 1907-14; engaged in hosp. lab. work, 1918-20; asso. in cancer research at Inst. of Cancer Research of Columbia U., 1920-37; retired from active work in cancer research, 1937. Mem. Med. Soc. of County of New York (1907-1938), Am. Assn. for Cancer Research. Home: Shrewsbury Township, N.J. Address: Box 133, Red Bank, N.J.

KREIDER, Charles Daniel, educator, editor; b. Lancaster, Pa., Dec. 29, 1867; s. William Eugene and Mary Josephine (Demuth) K.; A.B., Moravian Coll. and Theol. Sem., Bethlehem, Pa., 1892; m. Emily Augusta Hammer, June 29, 1898 (now dec.); children—Alice Hammer (dec.), Josephine Hammer, Albert Hammer (dec.). Instr. Nazareth Hall, 1890-96 instr. Moravian College, and Moravian Seminary and Coll. for Women, Bethlehem, 1896-97; asst. prin., 1897-98, prin., 1898-1912, Linden Hall Sem., also treas. same; pastor Schoeneck Moravian Congregation, Nazareth, 1912-14; editor, The Moravian, official organ, 1913-38; vice prin. Nazareth Hall, 1914-18; exec. sec. Denominational U.S. Service (war) Commn., 1918-20; pastor V. Moravian Congregation, Phila., 1918-20; recording sec. Provincial Elders' Conf. (governing board of the Moravian Church in America, Northern Province) since 1922; secretary Society for Propagating the Gospel (oldest incorporated missionary soc. in U.S.), since 1922, also editor annual vol. of "Proceedings" of same; sec. Synod and editor journal, Eastern Dist., Northern Province, Moravian Ch. in America, 1924; also sec. Synod and editor journal, Northern Province (U.S. and Can.), 1925, 30; editor The Moravian Missionary (monthly) since 1926, business mgr. since 1938; sec. bd. Moravian Coll. and Theol. Sem. Deacon, 1898, presbyter, 1908, Moravian Church. Republican. Sec-treas. Moravian Ednl. Assn., 1911-18; president local Dickens Fellowship, 1914-18. Author papers and contbns. on ednl. and hist. subjects. Pub. U.S. Service edit., 187th ann. vol. Moravian Daily Texts. Home: Nazareth, Pa.

KREIDER, Henry K., minister; b. Campbelltown, Pa., Jan. 10, 1873; s. Rev. John F. and Mary B. K.; ed. pub. schs. Lebanon Co. and 6 terms Annville Summer Normal; m. Alice Johnston, Oct. 11, 1894 (died Aug. 10, 1896); m. 2d, Kate R. Hoffman, June 15, 1899; children—Ethan A., John H., Herbert H., Mary C., Grace E. (Mrs. Joseph A. Stoner), Anna R. (Mrs. John H. Engle). Rural sch. teacher, 1891-1901; agriculture, 1901-29; pres. Campbelltown Bank; pres. Campbelltown Water Co.; sec. Campbelltown Telephone Co. Mem. Brethren in Christ Ch., minister, Campbelltown, 1900-12, bishop Dauphin and Lebanon Counties since 1912; sec. of exec. bd. Brethhen in Christ of U.S., Can. and Fgn. Countries since 1924, del. to 36 annual Gen. Confs. and assisted in moderating at 12; chmn. Messiah Rescue and Benevolent Home, Harrisburg, Pa. Address: Campbelltown, Pa.

KREIDER, William Erb, shoe mfr.; b. Palmyra, Pa., Sept. 21, 1887; s. David Addison and Minnie Edna (Erb) K.; ed. Palmyra Pub. Schs. and Lebanon Business Coll.; m. Lydia Bertha Kreider, May 1, 1906; children—David Heilman, Mildred Irene, William Lester (deceased), Chester Wilhelm (deceased). Began as shoe salesman, 1907; dir. W. L. Kreider's Sons Mfg. Co., Inc., Palmyra, since 1920, pres. since 1930; dir. and pres. Kreider-Creveling Shoe Co., Boston; dir. Palmyra Bank & Trust Co. Dir. Palmyra Chamber of Commerce; dir. Nat. Boot and Shoe Mfrs. Assn., New York; pres. and dir. Palmyra Athletic Assn. Mem. First United Brethren in Christ Ch., mid-week class leader, teacher S.S. class since 1904, teacher adult Bible class since 1920, treas. bd. of trustees; trustee of Official Bd. United Brethren in Christ. Republican. Home: 420 E. Main St. Office: Harrison and Arch St., Palmyra, Pa.

KREIDER, William H., lawyer; b. Annville, Pa., Aug. 19, 1874; s. Henry and Mary A. (Hoverter) K.; A.B. and A.M., Lebanon Valley Coll., Annville, Pa.; LL.B., Yale, 1896, M.L., 1897. Admitted to Pa. bar and since practiced at Phila. Mem. City Council, Phila.,

1905-07; mem. and sec. Civil Service Commn., 1907-11, 1916-20, pres., 1924-36. Mason (K.T., 32°, Shriner). Club: Lawyers (Phila.). Home: 5003 Walnut St. Office: 711 Harrison Bldg., Philadelphia, Pa.

KREIDLER, William Alfred, bacteriologist; b. Tatamy, Pa.; s. Charles Meyer and Ella (Whitesell) K.; grad. Bethlehem (Pa.) High Sch., 1913; B.S., Lehigh U., 1920, M.S., 1924; Ph.D., U. of Pa., 1926; m. Pearl Grube, July 10, 1917; children—Lucille Ellen, Ruth Adele, William Alfred (deceased), Robert Dale. Teacher of science, Easton (Pa.) High Sch., 1920-21; instr., Lehigh U., 1921-24; instr., later asst. prof., of bacteriology, U. of Pa., 1924-32; bacteriologist Phila. Gen. Hosp., 1924-31; asst. prof. of bacteriology, Jefferson Med. Coll., 1932-37, asso. prof. since 1937. Served as private U.S. Army, 1918-19. Mem. Soc. Am. Bacteriologists, Physiol. Soc., Sigma Xi. Republican. Methodist. Contbr. professional articles to med. jours. Home: 212 Barrington Rd., Upper Darby, Pa. Office: Jefferson Medical College, Philadelphia, Pa.

KREMER, David Nathaniel, physician; b. Phila., Pa., Mar. 28, 1890; s. Michael and Rebecca (White) K.; student Central High Sch., Phila., 1904-07; M.D., U. of Pa., 1911; m. Minna Gaber, Mar. 25, 1917; children—Howard, Edwin, Adele. House physician Pa. State Hosp. for Insane, Harrisburg, Pa., 1913-14; physician Pa. R.R., Pittsburgh and Phila., 1914-17, mem. commn. for Pa. R.R. at Mexican Border, 1916; asst. med. insp. Phila. Bd. of Health, 1912-22; instr. medicine, U. of Pa. Med. Sch., since 1922; visiting physician St. Agnes Hosp., Phila., since 1934; asst. visiting physician, Phila. Gen. Hosp., since 1933; specialist in internal medicine since 1930. Fellow Am. Coll. Physicians; mem. A.M.A., Pa. State Med. Assn., Phila. Co. Med. Soc. Jewish religion. Mason. Author numerous articles in med. mags. Address: 1918 Pine St., Philadelphia, Pa.

KREMP, Laura Amelia Miller (Mrs. Joseph P. Kremp), artist; b. Chester, Pa., May 12, 1856; d. Lewis and Mary Ann (Dixon) Miller; ed. Convent of the Holy Child Jesus, Sharon Hill, Pa.; m. Joseph P. Kremp, May 4, 1888; children—Lewis Miller, Marie Ada. Awarded prizes in archtl. drawing at sch.; engaged in crafts, needle work of all kinds; judge of needle work at Atlanta Cotton States Exposition; organized and was pres. many yrs. Ladies Auxiliary of St. Joseph's Hosp., Reading, Pa.; began painting and taught self when 70 yrs. old; first painting accepted for exhbn. in annual Water Color Show of Pa. Acad. Fine Arts and showed here regularly for ten yrs.; invited to exhibit Pa. Mus.; exhbns., New York City, Washington, D.C., Phila., Hollywood, Calif., and many other cities. Republican. Roman Catholic. Home: 1601 Mineral Springs Rd., Reading, Pa.

KREMP, Marie Ada Miller, teacher and dir. of dancing, artist; b. Reading, Pa.; d. Joseph P. and Laura (Miller) Kremp; student Sharon Hill (Pa.) Acad., Cleveland (O.) Museum School, Pennsylvania Academy of Fine Arts, and private teachers; unmarried. Solo dancer, 1934-35; teacher of dancing since 1935; dir. of actors in the dance since 1938; teacher of art and portrait painter since 1937; dir. of Echo Dell Players, creative dancing, Reading, Pa. Works: Portraits of Nancy Crage, Jasper Deeter, J. B. Nolan, Kozloff (dancer). Mem. Sharon Hill Alumnae, Fellowship of Pa. Acad. of Fine Arts (Phila.). Catholic. Home: 1601 Mineral Spring Rd. Studio: 1605 Mineral Spring Rd., Reading, Pa.

KRESGE, Elijah Everitt, clergyman, educator; b. McMichaels, Pa., Nov. 4, 1875; s. Linford and Elizabeth Anna (Everitt) K.; A.B., Franklin and Marshall Coll., Lancaster, Pa., 1898; B.D., Eastern Theol. Sem. of Ref. Ch. in U.S., Lancaster, 1901; Ph.D., U. of Pa., 1913; m. Edna Schultz Gerhard, June 10, 1902; children—Marian Gerhard, Karl Everitt. Ordained ministry Ref. Ch. in U.S., 1901; pastor Dubbs Memorial Ch., Allentown, Pa., 1902-22; prof. psychology, Cedar Crest Coll. for Women, Allentown, Pa., 1904-09, acting pres., 1908; prof.

philosophy, Franklin and Marshall Coll., since Sept. 1922. Chmn. Pa. State Dist. of World Alliance for Promotion Internat. Friendship and Good-will, 1920-23; chmn. Com. on Education, 1920-24, pres. since 1930, Social Service Commn. of Reformed Church in U.S.; mem. Bd. of Education of Reformed Ch., Bd. Visitors Eastern Theol. Sem. Mem. exec. com. Pa. League for Economic Security. Mem. Am. Acad. Polit. and Social Science, A.A.A.S., American Association Univ. Profs., Phi Beta Kappa, Sigma Pi, Phi Upsilon Kappa, Pi Gamma Mu. Mason. Author: Immanuel Kant's Doctrine of Teleology, 1914; The Church and the Ever-Coming Kingdom of God, 1922. Contbr. Proceedings of World Alliance of Presbyn. and Reformed Churches, 1928, 37. Home: 432 State St., Lancaster, Pa.

KRESSLEY, George Smith, clergyman; b. Maxatawney, Pa., Feb. 8, 1877; s. Percival N. and Martha R. (Smith) K.; ed. Keystone State Normal Sch., 1890-93; A.B., Muhlenberg Coll., 1898, A.M., same, 1901; student Luth. Theol. Sem., 1898-1901, Goettingen Univ., Germany, summer 1910; (hon.) Litt.D., Muhlenberg Coll., 1913; m. Anna R. Fretz, Aug. 5, 1902; 1 dau., Helen Elizabeth (widow of Paul Richard Hess, M.D.). Ordained to ministry Luth. Ch., 1901; prof. fgn. langs., Keystone State Normal Sch., 1901-17; supervisor fgn. langs., pub. schs., Allentown, Pa., 1917-29; sec. of benevolence, Luth. Ministerium of Pa. since 1929. Trustee of Muhlenberg Coll. since 1934. Republican. Lutheran. Home: 906 N. Fifth St., Reading, Pa. Office: 1228 Spruce St., Philadelphia, Pa.

KRETSCHMANN, Theodore William, prof. Bible and religion; b. Phila., Pa., May 13, 1868; s. Christian Ernst and Wilhelmina Christiane (Kuemmerle) K.; A.B., U. of Pa., 1888, A.M., same, 1891, B.D., same, 1891, Ph.D., same, 1892; m. Margaret Graham Finley, of Philadelphia, Pa., Oct. 4, 1894; children—Theodore Ernest (dec.), Dorothy Anna (dec.), Philip Miller, Herbert Finley, Stephen William (dec.). Ordained to ministry Luth. Ch., 1891; instr. Hebrew, Mt. Airy Luth. Theol. Sem., Phila., Pa., 1892-98; pastor, Chestnut Hill, Phila., Buffalo, N.Y., W. Phila., Pa., 1891-1919; prof. Hebrew and O.T. and theology, Pacific Luth. Theol. Sem., Seattle, Wash., 1919-24; prof. Hebrew, O.T. and practical theology, Susquehanna U. Sch. Theology, 1924-33; prof. Bible and religion, Susquehanna U., Selinsgrove, Pa. since 1933. Mem. Am. Oriental Soc., Nat. Assn. Bib. Instrs., Central Pa. Synod of Luth. Ch., Phi Beta Kappa, Pi Gamma Mu. Lutheran. Author: History of Christ Lutheran Church of Chestnut Hill, Philadelphia, 1896; The Church's Treasures, 1923. Contbr. articles to religious journs., and to books of worship, especially The Old Testament Commentary on "Messiah—The Hope of Israel." Home: R.D. 1, Selinsgrove, Pa.

KREUTZINGER, Edmund Philip, printing exec.; b. Mt. Vernon, Ind.; s. James Knight and Anna Margaret K.; student Ind. U., Bloomington, Ind., 1907-11; m. Edith Hill, Dec. 4, 1919. High sch. prin., Boonville, Lafayette, Laporte, Ind., 1911-17; mgr. export dept. Am. Colortype Co., printers, lithographers, pubs., Clifton, N.J., since 1919, dir. since 1930; dir. Osborne Co., Ltd., London, Eng., Osborne Co., Ltd., Johannesburg, South Africa, Osborne Co., Ltd., Sydney, New South Wales. Entered training camp for U.S. Army, Indianapolis, Ind., Apr. 1917, served as instr., F.A. Sch., Camp Taylor, Ky., 1917-18; disch. as 1st lt., 1918. Home: 147 Christopher St., Montclair, N.J. Office: 9 Brighton Rd., Clifton, N.J.

KRIBS, David Alson, botanist; b. Thief River Falls, Minn., Jan. 2, 1896; s. Alson E. and Prudence (McCord) K.; grad. Grand Rapids (Minn.) High Sch., 1915; B.S., U. of Minn., 1924, M.S., 1927; Ph.D., Yale, 1929; student Harvard, 1929-31, Cornell U., summer 1931; m. Katherine Carson, Nov. 24, 1918; children—David Alson, Patricia Katherine. Football coach, Brookings (S.D.) High Sch., 1921-22; instr. of forestry, U. of Minn., 1924-27; Sterling research fellow, Yale, 1927-29; Nat. Research fellow, Harvard, 1929-31; instr. of botany, Pa. State Coll. 1931-37, asst. prof. since 1937. Served as master mechanic 1st class U.S. Navy, 1917-19. Mem. Soc. Am. Botanists, Soc. Am. Foresters, Torrey Bot. Club, Sigma Xi, Sigma Delta Psi, Gamma Sigma Delta, Xi Sigma Pi. Episcopalian. Home: 1347 Scotland Av., Chambersburg, Pa. Address: Pa. State College, State College, Pa.

KRICK, Charles Shalter, ry. official; b. Reading, Pa., Mar. 16, 1866; B.S., Lafayette Coll., 1887, hon. D. Eng. Began as rodman asst. engr.'s office, Schuylkill div., Pa., R.R., July 11, 1887, and has continued with same rd. successively as rodman at Altoona until 1890, asst. supervisor Tyrone div., 1890-92, Phila. div., 1892-95, acting supervisor Schuylkill div., 1895-96, supervisor same div., 1896-97, middle div., 1897-1900, Pittsburgh div., 1900-03, asst. engr. Eastern and Susquehanna divs., Jan.-Aug. 1903, Phila. terminal div., 1903-06, prin. asst. engr. Phila., Baltimore & Washington R.R., 1906-10, supt. New York Terminal div., 1910-12, Manhattan div., 1912-14, supt. Phila. terminal div., 1914-15, acting gen. supt. N.J. div., 1915-16, gen. supt. same div., 1916-18, asst. gen. mgr. lines East, 1918-20, gen. mgr. Eastern region, 1920-23, vice-pres. Eastern Region, 1923-36, retired, 1936, Pa. System. Home: St. Davids, Delaware Co., Pa.

KRIEBEL, William F., banker; b. Montgomery Co., Pa., Mar. 16, 1890; s. Jacob A. and Emma K.; ed. Peirce Sch., Phila., Pa., and Temple U.; m. Mabel Burtt, 1916; children—William Burtt, Howard B., John A. Asso. with The Pennsylvania Company for Insurance on Lives and Granting Annuities, Phila., Pa. since starting as clk., 1911; vice-pres. and cashier since 1926. Mem. Phila. Yearly Meeting Soc. of Friends. Am. Inst. of Banking. Club: Aronimick Country (Phila.). Home: Possum Hollow Rd., Rose Valley, Moylan, Pa. Office: 15th and Chestnut Sts., Philadelphia, Pa.

KRIEGER, Abraham; pres. Gunther's Brewing Co. Home: Arlington Park Apts. Office: 1211 S. Conklin St., Baltimore, Md.

KRISS, Max, biochemist; b. Ostropol, Russia, May 2, 1889; s. Joseph and Fannie (Shatz) K.; came to U.S., 1910, and naturalized citizen, 1916; B.S., Pa. State Coll., 1918, M.S., 1920; grad. study, Yale, 1929-30, fellow, 1934-35; Ph.D., Yale, 1936; m. Sima Charny, Apr. 12, 1918; 1 son, Joseph Pincus. Asst. in animal nutrition, Pa. State Coll., 1918-20, asso., 1920-29, asso. prof. of animal nutrition, 1929-37, prof. since 1937. Mem. A.A.A.S., Am. Chem. Soc., Am. Inst. of Nutrition, Am. Soc. Biology and Medicine, Am. Soc. Animal Production, Sigma Xi. Jewish religion. Contbr. many articles dealing mainly with respiratory metabolism of animals under different conditions of nutrition. Home: 825 W. Beaver Av., State College, Pa.

KRISTELLER, Lionel Paul, lawyer; b. Newark, N.J., Oct. 30, 1891; s. Julius and Minnie (Newman) K.; student Newark Acad., 1902-08; m. Helen B. Salmon, June 1, 1919; 1 dau., Lois. Began as office boy in law offices, 1909; admitted to New York bar, 1914, N.J. bar, 1915, as counsellor, Nov. 1918, U.S. Supreme Ct., Mar. 1923; apptd. Supreme Ct. Commr. of N.J., Dec. 5, 1924, spl. master chancery of N.J., Feb. 2, 1937; mem. law firm Kristeller & Zucker since 1939; dir. Merchants & Mfrs. Ins. Co. of N.Y.; sec. N.J. Good Humor, Inc. Enlisted in U.S. Army, July 1918; hon. discharged, Dec. 1918. Mem. Am. Bar Assn. (chmn. Ins. Law Sect.), N.J. State Bar Assn. (vice-chmn. Ins. Sect.; chmn. Ethics and Grievances Com.), Assn. Bar City of N.Y., Essex County Bar Assn. (ex.-sec.), Internat. Assn. Ins. Counsel. Democrat. Jewish Religion. Mason, Elk. Clubs: Down Town (Newark); Lawyers (N.Y.). Essex County; Blue Goose Internat. Home: 385 Highland Av. Office: 744 Broad St., Newark, N.J.

KRIVOBOK, Vsevolod Nicholas, univ. prof., research dir.; b. Russia, Nov. 1, 1894; s. Nicholas Simon and Anna (de Yaremenko) K.; student St. Petersburg Poly. Inst., Russia, 1913-14; B.S., magna cum laude, Harvard Engring. Sch., 1921, Met. E., 1922, Sc.D., 1924; came to U.S., 1915, naturalized, 1924. Mem. Russian Arty. Commn. and Russian Mission of Ways and Communication, in U.S., 1917-19; prof. metall., Carnegie Inst. Tech., 1924-34, mem. metall. research bur., 1924-29, part-time prof. metall. since 1934; cons. metallurgist numerous steel cos., 1924-29; cons. metallurgist Rustless Iron and Steel Corpn., Baltimore, Md., 1929-34; asso. dir. research Allegheny Ludlum Steel Co., Pittsburgh, since 1934. Mem. Am. Soc. for Metals, Am. Inst. Mining and Metall. Engrs., Am. Soc. for Testing Materials (com. mem. and chmn. since 1924). British Inst. of Metals. Greek Orthodox Ch. Clubs: University, Long View (Pittsburgh, Pa.); Rolling Rock, Rolling Rock Hunt, Ligonier, Pa. Author numerous articles in professional and trade mags. Home: 6607 Woodwell St. Office: Carnegie Institute of Technology, Pittsburgh, Pa.

KROGH, Detlef M(arius) Ferdinand, physician; b. Hamburg, Schleswig-Holstein, Germany, Mar. 10, 1867; s. Hans and Juliane (Mathiesen) K.; came to U.S., 1882, naturalized, 1888; grad. Am. Gymnastic Union, 1888, Indianapolis (Ind.) Normal Coll., 1906, B.S., 1908. M.D., Jefferson Med. Coll., Phila., Pa., 1896; m. Caroline Nunge, Dec. 24, 1890 (died 1934); children—Karl Nunge, Violet Barbara, Alexander Waters Ransley, Pearl June, Harold Ferdinand, Grace May. Instr. Turner's Gymnasium, Johnstown, Pa., 1888-89; instr. gymnastics Wheeling (W.Va.) Female Sem., and Turner's Gymnasium, 1889-93; teacher gymnastics, Southwark, Phila., 1893-1904; asst. in out-patient dept., Jefferson Med. Coll., Phila., 1896-1901; spl. teacher gymnastics, Phila. Pub. Schs., Sch. of Pedagogy, 1908-12; asso. editor Mind and Body mag., 1908-28; phys. dir. pub. and junior high schs., lecturer in hygiene, Newark, N.J., 1913-18; asst. in gymnastics, Evander Childs High Sch., New York, 1919; in pvt. med. practice at Phila., 1896-1912 and since 1919. Dist. supervisor Med. Assistance Bd., Phila., since 1918. Mem. W. Phila. Med. Assn., Alumni Assn. of Coll. of Gymnastics, Jefferson Med. Coll. Alumni Assn., Phila. Co. Med. Soc., Pa. Med. Soc., A.M.A. Author various articles on phys. edn. and hygiene in Mind and Body mag. Address: 5923 Chester Av., Philadelphia, Pa.

KROHN, Israel, lawyer; b. New York, N.Y., Sept. 4, 1895; s. Morris and Jennie (Fabrikant) K.; student Easton (Pa.) pub. schs., 1900-06, high sch. 1906-10; LL.B., N.Y.U. Law Sch., 1912; Ph.B., Lafayette Coll., Easton, Pa., 1917; unmarried. Admitted to Pa. bar, 1920, and since practiced at Easton, Pa.; partner Gen. Crayon Co., Easton, Pa.; treas. Jersey Materials Co., Phillipsburg, N.J. Served as sergt., 111th Ordnance Dept. Co., U.S. Army, during World War, Sec. Easton (Pa.) War Memorial & Community Hall Assn., 1920; mem. bd. govs. Y.M.H.A. and Y.W.H.A. since 1911. Mem. Pa. and Middle Atlantic Fed. of Y.M. and Y.W.H.As. and Kindred Assns. (pres. 1931-32), Easton Zionist Soc. (pres., 1917), Jewish Community Center (pres., 1914-33), Pa. Com. for George Washington Forest in Palestine (vice-chmn.), Am.-Jewish Joint Distribution Com. (mem. nat. council), United Palestine Appeal for Eastern and Central Pa. (mem. provisional exec. council), Nat. Coordinating Com. for aid to Refugees, Am. Bar Assn., Pa. Bar Assn., Northampton Co. Bar Assn., Commercial Law League of America, Am. Legion (1933 commdr. Post 9; mem. Americanism Com., Dept. of Pa.), 40 & 8 (avocat, voiture 697), Jewish War Vets. of U.S. (commdr. Post 85), Civic League of Easton (pres. 1925-30), Easton City Guard (hon. mem.). Democrat. Jewish religion. Mason, Elk, K.P., Independent Order B'nai B'rith. Clubs: Pomfret, Lions (Easton, Pa.); Berkeley Country (Kutztown, Pa.) Home: 112 Parker Av. Office: Easton Trust Bldg., Easton, Pa.

KROUSE, Luther Adolph, clergyman; b. Reading, Pa., Apr. 28, 1897; s. Harry K. and Mary (Rippien) K.; A.B., Muhlenberg Coll., 1919; student Luth. Theol. Sem., Phila., Pa., 1919-22; grad. study U. of Pittsburgh, 1930-31; m. Grace M. Yocom, June 18, 1924; children—Luther Samuel, David Harry. Ordained to ministry Luth. Ch., 1922; pastor, Ridgway, Pa., 1922-28, Wilkinsburg, Pa., 1928-32; pastor Emmanuel Luth. Ch., Pottstown, Pa. since 1932. Served in Hosp. Corps, U.S.N., 1918-19. Mem. Phi Kappa Tau. Republican. Lutheran. Mason. Club: Kiwanis of Pottstown. Home: 239 Chestnut St., Pottstown, Pa.

KRUEGER, Wabun Clarence, extension agrl. engr.; b. Sawyer, Wis., Feb. 19, 1897; s. Frank A. and Ida (Krueger) K.; B.S. in Agr., U. of Wis., 1921; student U. of Tenn., Knoxville, Tenn., 1921-24; m. Gertrude Mount Caldwell, Mar. 10, 1923; children—Robert Wabun, Donald Edward, Richard Caldwell, Russell Lee. Employed in teaching rural schs., N.D., 1915-16; instr. agrl. engring. and farm mechanics, U. of Tenn., 1921-25; instr. marble setters sch., U. of Tenn., 1924-25; project dir., Commn. on Application of Electricity to Agr., State of Wis., 1925-28; extension specialist in rural electrification, N.J. Joint Commn. on Rural Electrification, 1928-30; extension specialist agrl. engring., N.J. Coll. Agr. and Expt. Sta., New Brunswick, N.J. since 1929. Served in inf., motor transport instrn., U.S.A., 1918. Mem. Am. Soc. Agrl. Engrs., New Brunswick Sci. Soc., New Brunswick Current Problems Club, Alpha Zeta, Farmhouse Fraternity, Nat. Geographic Soc. Presbyn. Club: Rutgers of New Brunswick. Home: Dayton, N.J.

KRUMBHAAR, E(dward) B(ell), M.D., pathologist; b. Philadelphia, Pa., Aug. 1, 1882; s. Charles Hermann and Mary Ellis (Bell) K.; prep. edn., DeLancey Sch., Phila., 1894-95, Groton (Mass.) Sch., 1895-1900; A.B., Harvard, 1904; M.D., U. of Pa., 1908, Ph.D., 1916; m. Helen Dixon, Mar. 14, 1911; children—Peter, David. Resident pathologist, Pa. Hosp., 1908-09; instr. in medicine, U. of Pa., 1912-15, asso., 1915-16, asst. prof. research medicine, 1916-20, asso. prof. Grad. Sch. Medicine, 1920-27, prof. pathology since 1927; dir. labs., Phila. Gen. Hosp., 1920-27, cons. pathologist, 1927—; same, Bryn Mawr Hosp., 1921—; editor Am. Jour. Med. Sciences, "Clio Medica." Served as lt., later capt. and maj., Med. Corps, U.S.A., France, 1917-19; now lt. col. M.R.C. Mem. A.M.A., A.A.A.S., Assn. Am. Physicians, Am. Soc. Exptl. Pathology, Am. Assn. Pathology and Bacteriology, Am. Assn. Med. History, Sigma Xi, Alpha Omega Alpha, Delta Kappa Epsilon. Democrat. Episcopalian. Clubs: Racquet, Lenape, Whitemarsh Hunt. Author: Spleen and Anemia, 1917; History of Pathology, 1937; also more than 100 med. articles, and chapters in med. books. Address: Box 4378, Chestnut Hill, Philadelphia, Pa.

KRUMPELMANN, John Theodore; dean of men and prof. German, Marshall Coll. Address: Marshall College, Huntington, W.Va.

KRUPP, Harry Z., wholesale druggist; b. Lansdale, Pa., Jan. 17, 1882; s. Henry D. and Mary Ann (Zimmerman) K.; student Lansdale, (Pa.) High Sch. and Peirce Business Coll., Phila., Pa.; m. Amelia Wynn, May 28, 1913; 1 dau., Mary Elizabeth. Began with Phila. Wholesale Drug Co., 1902, now treas. and gen. mgr.; dir. Northern Trust Co., Phila. Drug Exchange. Mem. Federal Wholesale Druggists Assn. (ex-pres.). Mason (32°). Clubs: Union League (Phila.). Home: 630 Columbia Av., Lansdale, Pa. Office: 10th and Spring Garden Sts., Philadelphia, Pa.

KRUSE, Theophile Karl Theodore, univ. prof.; b. Sappington, Mo., March 3, 1888; s. Rev. Samuel and Amalia (Mueller) K.; A.B., U. of Mo., Columbia, Mo., 1912, A.M., 1913, Ph.D., 1918; student U. of Chicago, summer 1915; m. Bertha Claire Powell, Sept. 9, 1925. Asst. in physiology and pharmacology, U. of Mo., Columbia, Mo., 1912-14, instr., 1914-16; instr. physiology and pharmacology, U. of Pittsburgh Sch. of Medicine, 1916-19, asst. prof., 1919-20, asso. prof., 1920-21, prof. since 1931. Served in research div., C.W.S., U.S. Army, 1918. Mem. Am. Legion. Republican. Mem. Evang. Ch. Author numerous pharm., etc., articles in scientific jours. Home: 528 Overlook Drive, Mt. Lebanon, Pa. Office: U. of Pittsburgh, Pittsburgh, Pa.

KRUSE, William Charles, Jr., engring.; b. Buffalo, N.Y., Oct. 30, 1900; s. William Charles and Elizabeth A. (Murphy) K.; ed. U. of Pittsburgh, 1917-19, U. of Kan., 1919-21; m. Jessie E. Pollard, Feb. 9, 1927; children—Donald Frederick, Carl Murray. Engr. with Kruse, Graham & Howe, Buffalo, N.Y., 1921-27; engr., Carrier Engring. Co., Newark, N.J., 1927, Nat. Air Filler Co., New York, N.Y., 1927-30; engaged in engring. bus. on own acct. as Kruse Engring. Co., ventilation and dust collection, Newark, N.J., since 1931; licensed engr. in N.Y. State. Mem. Am. Soc. Heating & Ventilating Engrs. Republican. Conglist. Clubs: Downtown (Newark); Braidburn Country (Madison). Home: 32 University Ct., South Orange, N.J. Office: 24 Commerce St., Newark, N.J.

KRUSEN, Wilmer, college pres.; b. Richboro, Pa., May 18, 1869; s. John and Elizabeth (Sager) K.; student Medico-Chirurg. Coll., Phila., Pa., 1889-90, U. of Pa., 1890-91; M.D., Jefferson Med. Coll., Phila., 1893; LL.D., U. of Pittsburgh, 1916; hon. D.Sc., Temple U., 1927, Franklin and Marshall Coll., 1933; m. Elizabeth Gilbert, June 19, 1895; children—Edward Montgomery, Francis Hammond, Carolyn Armitage (Mrs. Karl W. H. Scholz). Began as pharmacy clk., 1886; became prof. gynecology, Temple U., 1902, now med. v.p.; dir. health and charities, Phila., 1916-20; dir. health, same, 1924-28; pres. Phila. Coll. of Pharmacy and Science since 1927. Mem. Prison Bd., Phila. Turstee Temple U. Mem. A.M.A., Pa. State and Phila. Co. med. assns. Republican. Unitarian. Mason (33°). Clubs: Rotary (pres. 1932-33), Union League, Phila. Yacht. Contbr. professional journals. Home: Media, Pa. Address: Philadelphia College of Pharmacy and Science, Philadelphia, Pa.

KRUT, John A., business exec.; b. Pittsburgh, Pa., Feb. 17, 1889; s. John Anthony and Philomena (Soulier) K.; student Pittsburgh Acad., Duquesne U. (Pittsburgh); m. Catherine Eccleston, Jan. 28, 1914; children—Catherine A., Dorothy E. Accountant Arbuthnot-Stephenson Co., Pittsburgh, 1909-26; became accountant G. C. Murphy Co., McKeesport, Pa., 1927, now v.p., sec.-treas. and dir.; dir. Union Nat. Bank, McKeesport, Pa. Mem. Controllers' Inst. of America (dir.), Pittsburgh Control (dir.). Home: 1420 Carnegie Av. Office: 531 5th Av., McKeesport, Pa.

KUDNER, Arthur Henry, advertising; b. Lapeer, Mich., Dec. 7, 1890; s. Henry Clay and Leonora R. (Cutting) K.; ed. Lapeer High Sch.; m. Madelin Thayer, Aug. 1, 1933; children—Arthur, Karyl. Began as reporter on father's newspaper, Lapeer; concert singer, 1912; reporter Detroit Free Press, 1912-13, 1915, N.Y. World, 1914; adv. writer Cheltenham Adv. Agency, 1915; adv. writer Erwin, Wasey & Co., Chicago and New York, 1916-18, chief copywriter, 1919-29, pres., 1929-35; pres. Arthur Kudner, Inc., since Oct. 1, 1935; pub. relations and advertising advisor to leading Am. corpns.; mem. Business Advisory Council to the Dept. of Commerce. Writer of Red Cross and Liberty Loan advertisements, 1917. Served in R.O.T.C. and U.S.A., 1918. Received Harvard award for best written advertisement, 1929. Mem. Am. Assn. of Adv. Agencies (chmn. of bd., 1934). Clubs: Yacht (N.Y. City); Chicago (Chicago); Bohemian (San Francisco); Surf (Miama Beach). Contbr. to Atlantic Monthly. Home: Grasonville, Md. Office: 630 5th Av., New York, N.Y.

KUEHNER, Quincy Adams, prof. edn.; b. Little Gap, Pa., June 22, 1879; s. Augustus and Christiana (Eckhart) K.; grad. Fairview Acad., Brodheadsville, Pa., 1898; A.B., Muhlenberg Coll., Allentown, Pa., 1902, A.M., 1905; univ. scholar and Harrison fellow, Univ. of Pennsylvania, 1902-04, Ph.D., 1912; LL.D., Lenoir-Rhyme College, 1937; m. Katherine E. Follweiler, Aug. 18, 1915. Teacher, high schs., Pa., 1905-20; prof. edn. and dean of summer sch., Lenoir-Rhyme Coll., Hickory, N.C., 1920-22; prof. philosophy of edn., Temple University, since 1922. High sch. insp. Burke and Catawba counties, N.C., 1920-22. Mem. A.A.A.S., Am. Acad. Polit. and Social Science, American Assn. of Univ. Profs., Religious Edn. Assn., Nat. Education Assn., Pennsylvania State Educational Assn., Hist. Soc. of Pa., Pa. German Soc., Phi Delta Kappa, Pi Gamma Mu; charter asso. Federal Council Chs. of Christ in America. Democrat. Lutheran. Clubs: Social Science, Acacia, Religious Book Club, Cedar Brook Country. Wrote: The Evolution of the Modern Concept of School Discipline, 1913; A Philosophy of Education, 1935. Lecturer on ednl. and religious subjects. Home: 15 W. Wharton Av., Glenside, Pa.

KUHLMANN, G(arrett) Edward, clergyman; b. Woodville, O., Sept. 26, 1882; s. John Henry and Mary (Cline) K.; A.B., Capital Univ., Columbus, O., 1903; ed. Luth. Div. Sch., 1903-06; study and travel abroad, 1906-07; m. Hattie Koebe, May 9, 1916; children—Ellen Jane, John Edward, Marjorie June. Ordained to ministry Luth. Ch., 1907; pastor, Oshkosh, Wis., 1907-26; pastor, Good Hope Luth. Ch., Oil City, Pa., since 1926; recognized for achievement in painting: has exhibited in many galleries; specializes in landscapes and eccles. work; paintings in many Luth. chs., especially in St. Louis. Republican. Lutheran. Club: Rotary of Oil City (past pres. 2 terms). Author: Journeys on Highway Ten, 1930; Thy Way, 1930; God's Children at Prayer, 1931; He Will Teach Us, 1933; Bearers of Heavenly Gifts, 1934; Watch Yourself Go By, 1935. Home: 107 W. First St., Oil City, Pa.

KUHN, C. John, insurance exec.; b. New York, N.Y., Dec. 31, 1897; s. Lewis and Theresa (Tuckhammer) K.; student West High Sch., Rochester, N.Y., 1911-12, 1917-18; B.S., U. of Rochester, 1922; m. Virginia Mansfield, Sept. 10, 1927; children—Thomas Mansfield, C. John. Asst. treas., U. of Rochester, N.Y., 1923-27; mgr. statistical dept. J. G. White & Co., New York, 1927-31; mgr. investment advisory dept. Hayden Stone & Co., New York, 1931-32; asst. treas., Firemen's Ins. Co., Newark, N.J., 1932-35, 3d v.p. 1935-39; 2d v.p. since 1939; 2d v.p. Loyalty Group Ins. Cos., Newark, N.J., since 1939; treas. and dir. Essex House, Newark, N.J., since 1934, also pres. 1934-38; mem. board of dirs. Laicremmoc Realty Company, Broad & Market Corporation. Served as pvt. in U.S. Army, 1918. Dir. West Essex (N.J.) Social Service, Inc., Broad St. Assn., Newark, N.J. Mem. Am. Statis. Soc., Acad. of Polit. Science, Phi Beta Kappa, Alpha Delta Phi. Republican. Baptist. Clubs: Newark (N.J.) Athletic, Montclair Athletic, Montclair Dramatic (pres. since 1939, also dir.), Skeet (Loantaka, N.J.). Home: 7 Bradford Way, Upper Montclair, N.J. Office: 10 Park Pl., Newark, N.J.

KUHN, Ernest Guy, county supt. of schools; b. Mannington, W.Va., May 6, 1897; s. William Ellis and Viola Ellen (Ice) K., A.B., Fairmont (W.Va.) Teachers Coll., 1928; A.M., W.Va. Univ., 1938; m. Margaret Jeannette McQuaid, Oct. 30, 1920; children—Byron Guy, Martha Jean. Teacher Wadestown (W.Va.) High Sch., 1917-18, Blacksville (W.Va.) High Sch., 1922-24; prin. Farmingon (W.Va.) High Sch., 1924-30, Grafton (W.Va.) High Sch., 1930-31; supt. of schs., Grafton, 1931-33; asst. county supt. of schs., Taylor County, W.Va., 1933-35, county supt. since 1935. Served in U.S. Navy, 1918; now 1st lt. Q.M. Reserve. Mem. N.E.A., W.Va. State Edn. Assn.; Nat. Assn. Secondary School Prins.; Am. Legion (post comdr., Grafton, 1934), W.Va. Athletic Assn. (pres. 1930), Kappa Delta Pi. Past pres. Lions Club, Farmington. Republican. Methodist. Club: Rotary of Grafton (pres. 1935). Home: 431 W. Main St. Office: Bank and Trust Bldg., Grafton, W.Va.

KUIPER, Rienk Bouke, prof. practical theology; b. The Netherlands, Jan. 31, 1886; s. Klaas and Maaike (de Bruyn) K.; brought to U.S., 1891, naturalized, 1896; A.B., U. of Chicago, 1907; A.M., Ind. U., 1908; student Calvin Sem., 1908-11; B.D., Princeton Theol. Sem., 1912; m. Marie Janssen, of Grand Rapids, Mich., June 18, 1911; children—Marietta Rolena (Mrs. Edward Heerema), Klaudius (D.D.S.), Kathryn Junia (dec.). Ordained to ministry Christian Reformed Ch., 1912; pastor Christian Reformed and Reformed in America chs. in Mich., 1912-29; prof. systematic theology, Westminster Theol. Sem., Phila., Pa., 1929-30; pres. Calvin Coll., Grand Rapids, Mich., 1930-33; prof. practical theology, Westminster Theol. Sem., Phila., Pa. since 1933, and pres. of the faculty since 1937. Pres. bd. trustees, League of Evang. Students. Served as moderator Fourth Gen. Assembly of Orthodox Presbyn. Ch., 1938. Mem. Phi Beta Kappa. Author: Christian Liberty, 1913; While The Bridegroom Tarries, 1919; As to Being Reformed, 1926; Not of the World, 1929; Co-author, Is Jesus God?, 1912. Contbr. many articles to rel. journs. Home: 6636 Boyer St., Philadelphia, Pa.

KUIZENGA, John E., clergyman, educator; b. Muskegon, Mich., Dec. 20, 1876; s. Eildert and Johanna K. (Soldaat) K.; A.B., with highest honors, Hope Coll., Holland, Mich., 1899, D.D., 1916; grad. Western Theol. Sem. of Ref. Ch. in America, Holland, 1904; Morris fellow in philosophy, U. of Mich., 1914-15, A.M., 1915; studied U. of Chicago Div. Sch.; m. Anna J. Mulder, Aug. 7, 1901; 1 dau., Marion Ruth. Teacher of English, Northwestern Classical Acad., Orange City, Ia., 1900-03; ordained ministry Ref. Ch. in America, 1904; pastor Ref. Ch., Graafschap, Mich., 1904-06; prof. Bible and philosophy, Hope Coll., 1906-15; prof. practical theology, Western Theol. Seminary of Reformed Church in America, 1915-28, prof. systematic theology, 1928-30, also pres., 1924-30; Stuart prof. apologetics and Christian ethics, Princeton Theological Seminary, since 1930. Delivered lectures on apologetics and religious edn. at various theol. seminaries; mem. of faculty of Winona Summer Sch. of Theology for several years; also mem. summer confs., etc. Pres. Gen. Synod Reformed Ch. in America, 1924-25. Mem. Victoria Inst. Republican. Author of series of Bible lessons for children and young people and articles in theol. jours. Editor The Leader, a Reformed Church weekly, for about ten years. Home: 31 Alexander St., Princeton, N.J.

KULL, Irving Stoddard, univ. prof.; b. Genoa City, Wis., Apr. 12, 1884; s. Philip Henry and Grace Helen (Stoddard) K.; student pub. schs., Genoa City and Lake Geneva, Wis., 1890-1902; A.B., Beloit (Wis.) Coll., 1909; M.A., Ind. U., Bloomington, Ind., 1911; grad. student U. of Chicago, 1915-17; m. Nellie May Myers, Aug. 6, 1912; children—Blaisdell Myers, Robert Irving, Martha Edith. Teacher country schs., Wis., 1902-05, Beloit (Wis.) Coll. Prep. Sch., 1909-10; fellow in history, Ind. U., Bloomington, Ind., 1910-11; instr. history Denison U., Granville, O., 1911-13, asst. prof., 1913-15; asst. in history, U. of Chicago, 1915-17; asso. prof. history, Rutgers U., New Brunswick, N.J., 1918-26, prof. of history and head dept. history and political science since 1926, Vorhees prof. history since 1932; also extra-mural lecturer in American foreign affairs. Trustee League of Nations Assn. of N.J. Mem. Am. History Assn., Miss. Valley Hist. Assn., N.J. Hist. Assn., Phi Beta Kappa, Tau Kappa Epsilon. Dutch Reformed Ch. Editor: New Jersey, A History, 4 vols., 1930; contbr. articles to jours. Specialist in Am. history. Home: 203 Lincoln Av., Highland Park, N.J. Office: Rutgers U., New Brunswick, N.J.

KULP, Clarence Arthur, prof. of insurance; b. Chalfont, Pa., Aug. 23, 1895; s. Jacob Slifer and Katie Wolf (Stauffer) K.; B.S. in economics, Wharton Sch., U. of Pa., 1917; A.M., Grad. Sch., U. of Pa., 1921, Ph.D., 1924; m. Naomi Benner Alderfer, of Souderton, Pa., Feb. 16, 1918; children—Robert Alderfer, Donald Alderfer. With U. of Pa. since 1919, as instr. in economics, 1919-20, instr. in insurance, 1920-24, asst. prof., 1924-28, prof. of ins. since 1928; lecturer in ins., Columbia, since 1937; consultant Social Security Bd., since 1937; mem. senior research staff, Social Security Commn. of Social Science Research Council, 1935-38; lecturer in economics and finance, Am. Inst. of Banking, Phila., 1920-35; research asso., dept. industrial research, U. of

Pa., 1930-32; chmn. Pa. Com. on Workmen's Compensation, 1933-34; mem. for Pa. on Commn. on Unemployment Ins., 1931-32; tech. advisor Pa. Commn. on Unemployment Reserves, 1933; statis. editor Dept. of State, Pa., 1924-26; dir. N.H. Conf. on Unemployment Compensation, 1939. Served with U.S. Army, 1917-19; with A.E.F. 9 months. Mem. bd. Family Soc. of Phila.; mem. social security com. of Social Science Research Council. Fellow Casualty Actuarial Soc. (chmn. edn. com., asst. editor of Proceedings), Am. Assn. for Labor Legislation (mem. exec. com.), Beta Gamma Sigma, Delta Sigma Phi. Mem. United Presbyn. Ch. Club: Lenape (Phila.). Author: Discounting of Dividends by Stock Market, 1924; Casualty Insurance, 1928; Social Insurance Coordination, 1938. Editor: Social Insurance, Vol. 170, Annals of Am. Acad. Polit. and Social Science, 1933. Contbr. to professional jours. Home: 413 Netherwood Rd., Upper Darby, Pa. Office: Logan Hall, Univ. of Pennsylvania, Philadelphia, Pa.

KUMMEL, Henry Barnard, geologist; b. Milwaukee, Wis., May 25, 1867; s. Julius M. F. and Annie (Barnard) K.; A.B., Beloit Coll., valedictorian, 1889, A.M., 1892; A.M., Harvard, 1892; Ph.D., U. of Chicago, 1895; m. Charlotte F. Coe, June 20, 1899 (dec.); children—Charlotte Proctor, Lucy Barnhard; m. 2d, Mrs. Anna G. Williams, Sept. 1, 1934. Instructor Beloit College Academy, 1889-91; assistant in geology, Harvard U., 1891-92; fellow geology, U. of Chicago, 1892-95; asst. geologist, N.J. State Geol. Survey, 1892-98; asst. prof. physiography, Lewis Inst., Chicago, 1896-99; asst. state geologist, 1899-1902, state geologist, New Jersey, 1902-37; director Conservation and Development of New Jersey, 1922-37; retired, 1937; executive officer, Forest Commission of New Jersey, 1905-15. Asso. editor Journal of Geography, 1897-1901. Fellow Geol. Soc. America, A.A.A.S.; pres. Assn. Am. State Geologists, 1908-13; v.p. Geol. Soc. America, 1931. Contbr. numerous papers to geol. jours. and reports. Home: 100 Abernethy Drive, Trenton, N.J.

KUMMER, Frederic Arnold, author-playwright; b. Catonsville, Md., Aug. 5, 1873; s. Arnold and Mary Morris (Pancoast) K.; C.E., Rensselaer Poly. Inst., Troy, N.Y., 1894; m. Clare Rodman Beecher, 1895; children—Marjorie Beecher (Mrs. Roland Young), Fredericka (deceased); m. 2d, Marion J. McLean, June 14, 1907; children—Marion McLean (Mrs. Ernest E. Wachsmuth), Frederic Arnold, Joseph Talbot Tennant. Asst. editor Railroad Gazette, 1894-96; chief engr. Am. Wood Preserving Co., 1896-98; gen. mgr. Eastern Paving Brick Co., Catskill, N.Y., 1898-1900; gen. mgr. and chief engr. U.S. Wood Preserving Co., 1900-07; lit. work since 1907. Corporate mem. Am. Soc. C.E.; mem. Soc. Am. Dramatists and Composers, Authors' League America, Chi Phi. Author: The Green God, 1911; The Brute, 1912; A Song of Sixpence, 1913; A Lost Paradise, 1914; The Second Coming (collaboration), 1916; The Painted Woman, 1917; The Web, 1919; The Battle of the Nations, 1919; Peggy-Elsie (collaboration), 1919; Pipes of Yesterday (collaboration), 1921; Plaster Saints, 1921; The Earth's Story (child's book of knowledge), vol. 1, 1922, vol. 2, 1923, vol. 3, 1924; Phryne, 1924; The Road to Fortune, 1925; Love's Greatest Mistake, 1927; Ladies in Hades, 1928; Maypoles and Morals, 1929; Gentlemen in Hades, 1930; Forbidden Wine, 1931; The Golden Piper, 1932; Red Clay, 1933; Manhattan Masquerade, 1934; Design for Murder, 1936; Death at Eight Bells, 1937; The Scarecrow Murders, The Twisted Face, The Great Road, 1938; Leif Erikson The Lucky, 1939; also of following plays: Mr. Buttles, 1910; The Other Woman, 1910; The Brute, 1912; The Diamond Necklace, 1912; The Painted Woman, 1913; The Magic Melody (musical comedy, with music by Sigmond Romberg), 1919; My Golden Girl (musical play, music by Victor Herbert), 1919; The Bonehead, 1920; The Voice, 1923; Song of Omar (play, with music by Harry Tierney), 1935; The Captive (grand opera with score by Gustav Strube), 1938. Wrote under pseudonym Arnold Fredericks: One Million Francs, 1912; The Ivory Snuff Box, 1912; The Blue Lights, 1915; The Little Fortune, 1915; The Film of Fear, 1917; The Mark of the Rat, 1929; The Spanish Lady, 1933. Contbr. short stories, serials, etc., to mags., and author of many motion pictures, including The Slave Market, The Yellow Pawn, Motherhood, The Ivory Snuff Box, The Belgian, etc. Home: 224 W. Lafayette Av., Baltimore, Md.

KUMP, Herman Guy, ex-gov.; b. Capon Springs, W.Va., Oct. 31, 1877; s. Benjamin Franklin and Margaret (Rudolph) K.; student Shenandoah Normal Coll.; LL.B., U. of Va., 1905; LL.D., W.Va. University; m. Edna Scott, Oct. 9, 1907; children—Cyrus Scott, Frances Irvine, Margaret Rudolph, Elizabeth Logan, Mary Gamble, Benjamin Franklin. Admitted to W.Va. bar, 1905, and began practice at Elkins; pros. atty. Randolph Co., 1908-16; judge Circuit Court, W.Va., 1928-32; gov. of W.Va., term 1933-37; pres. Citizens Nat. Bank of Elkins. Served as capt. ordnance, U.S.A., 1918. Mayor of Elkins, 1921-23. Mem. W.Va. Bar Assn., Rotary Internat., Phi Delta Theta, Am. Legion. Democrat, Elk. Presbyn. Home: Elkins, W.Va.

KUN, Joseph Lorenz, judge; b. Ungvar, Hungary, Nov. 27, 1882; s. Lorenz and Betty (Adler) K.; brought to U.S., 1886, and naturalized citizen; B.S., Central High Sch., Phila., Pa., 1901; LL.B., U. of Pa. Law Sch., 1904; m. Effie B. Weil, Mar. 17, 1907; children—Ruth Hannah (Mrs. Emil Cohn, Jr.), Claire Weil (Mrs. I. Jerome Stern), Joseph Weil. Admitted to Pa. bar, 1904, and since engaged in gen. practice of law at Phila.; dep. atty. gen. of Pa., 1916-20; spl. asst. U.S. Atty., 1922-26; mem. firm Sundheim, Folz and Kun, 1922-27; judge Common Pleas Ct. since 1927. Mem. bd. overseers, Gratz Coll. Dir. Fed. Jewish Charities. Hon. dir. Y.M.H.A. and Y.W.H.A. Mem. Am. Acad. Polit. and Social Sci., Pa. and Phila. bar assns., Phi Beta Delta. Republican. Jewish religion. B'nai B'rith. Clubs: Penn Athletic, Locust, Ashbourne Country. Home: Chateau Crillon. Office: 242 City Hall, Philadelphia, Pa.

KUNKEL, Beverly Waugh, biologist; b. Harrisburg, Pa., Oct. 27, 1881; s. Charles A. and Eliza B. (Waugh) K.; grad. Lawrenceville (N.J.) Sch., 1898; Ph.B., Yale, 1901, Ph.D., 1905; studied U. of Freiburg, 1911-12; m. Caroline T. Jennings, June 24, 1908; children—Mary T., Sarah W. Asst. in biology, 1901-05, instr., 1905-12, Yale; prof. zoölogy, Beloit (Wis.) Coll., 1912-15; prof. biology, Lafayette Coll., since 1915. Studied in London, 1925. Fellow A.A.A.S.; mem. Am. Soc. Zoölogists, Am. Assn. Anatomists, Am. Assn. Univ. Profs., Sigma Xi, Delta Phi. Conglist. Contbr. numerous papers chiefly on vertebrate embryology and the relations of the colleges to intellectual leadership. Home: Easton, Pa.

KUNKEL, George, lawyer; b. Harrisburg, Pa., Mar. 10, 1893; s. George and Mary (Minster) K.; A.B., Franklin and Marshall Coll., Lancaster, Pa., 1915; LL.B. and A.M., Dickinson Sch. of Law, Carlisle, Pa., 1920. Admitted to Pa. bar, 1920, and since practiced at Harrisburg; state senator 15th Dist., Dauphin Co., Pa., 1936-40. Served as lt., 79th Div., A.E.F., during World War. Mem. Am. Legion, Vets. Fgn. Wars, Disabled Am. Vets., Phi Kappa Sigma. Democrat. Reformed Church. Mason (Harrisburg Consistory, Shriner), Moose. Home: 601 N. Front St. Office: Keystone Bldg., Harrisburg, Pa.

KUNKEL, John Crain, congressman; b. Harrisburg, Pa., July 21, 1898; s. John C. and Louisa Espy (Sergeant) K.; student Harrisburg (Pa.) Acad.; B.S., Yale, 1919; LL.B., Harvard, 1926; unmarried. Admitted to Pa. bar, 1926; mem. 76th Congress (1939-41), 19th Dist. of Pa.; dir. Harrisburg Trust Co.; chmn. bd. Citizens Trust Co. Served in S.A.T.C. during World War. Mem. Am. Legion. Elk, Moose. Republican. Home: 17 S. Front St. Office: 20 S. River St., Harrisburg, Pa.

KUNKEL, Louis Otto, botanist; b. Mexico, Mo., May 7, 1884; s. Henry and Katie Price (Spencer) K.; B.S. in Edn., U. of Mo., 1909, A.B., 1910, A.M., 1911; student Henry Shaw Sch. Botany, St. Louis, Mo., 1911-12; Ph.D., Columbia, 1914; grad. study U. of Freiburg, Germany, 1915-16; m. Johanna Caroline Wortmann, Sept. 4, 1915; children—Henry George, Otto Wortmann, Walter Relph, Paul Spercer. Asst. in botany, U. of Mo., 1908-11; Columbia, 1912-13, research asst., 1913-14; pathologist U.S. Dept. Agr., 1914-20; asso. pathologist, expt. sta. Hawaiian Sugar Planters Assn., 1920-23; pathologist Boyce Thompson Inst. for Plant Research, Yonkers, N.Y., 1923-32; mem. Rockefeller Inst. Med. Research since 1931. Fellow A.A.A.S.; mem. Nat. Acad. Science, Bot. Soc. America, Am. Phytopathological Soc., Phi Beta Kappa, Sigma Xi, Alpha Zeta, Phi Delta Kappa. Joint Author: Filter Viruses, 1928. Home: Princeton, N.J. Office: Rockefeller Institute for Medical Research, Princeton, N.J.

KUNKELMAN, Merle Rea, clergyman; b. Phila., Pa., June 5, 1875; s. Rev. John Alleman and Mary Rebecca (Rea) K.; A.B., Thiel Coll., Greenville, Pa., 1894, M.A., 1897; student Phila. Theol. Sem. at Mt. Airy (Luth.), Phila., 1894-97, U. of Pa. (tutor and grad. work with scholarship), 1898-1901; m. Isabel Campbell Atwood, Dec. 25, 1902; children—William Rea, Mary Isabel (Mrs. Frank H. Miller). Pastor, St. Andrew's-by-the-Sea, Atlantic City, N.J., 1900-05, Good Shepherd, Overbrook, Phila., 1906-07, Edinboro Parish, Cambridge Springs, Pa., 1915-20, Grace Ch., Franklin, Pa., 1920-25, Mt. Calvary, McKees Rocks, Pa., 1925-31, Christ Ch., Charleroi, Pa., 1931-35; supply and student pastor, U. of Pittsburgh, since 1936, Carnegie Inst. Tech., since 1936, Pa. Coll. for Women, Pittsburgh, since 1936; pastor St. Matthew's Lutheran Church, Leetsdale, Pa., since 1939. Sch. dir., Cambridge Springs, Pa., 1919-20. Dir. Thiel Coll., Greenville, Pa., 1930-36, Phila. Theol. Sem., 1931-36. Republican. Lutheran. Clubs: Calendar (Pittsburgh); Kiwanis (Charleroi, Pa.). Address: 128 Broad St., Leetsdale, Pa.

KURNIKER, Max Waldemar, physician; b. Cottbus, Germany, July 7, 1872; s. Adolph and Marian (Born) K.; student Friedrichs Gymnasium, Berlin, 1886-89, Berlin Univ., 1889-92; student Eclectic Med. Coll., New York City, 1892; M.D., Coll. of Physicians and Surgeons, Columbus, O., 1895; M.A., Academy, Toulouse, France, 1889; 1 dau., Helen Katherine Vermillion. Came to U.S., 1892, naturalized, 1900. Began as newspaper man on Pittsburgh Volksblatt, 1895; in med. practice, Pittsburgh, since 1906. Author: The Cosmic Cycle, 1934. Contbr. to mags. and newspapers. Home: Center and Bellefield Av. Office: 314 Empire Bldg., Pittsburgh, Pa.

KURRELMEYER, William, university prof.; b. Osnabrück, Germany, Jan. 17, 1874; s. Eberhard and Bernhardine (Veditz) K.; A.B., Johns Hopkins, 1896, Ph.D., 1899; m. Carrie May Herrmann, June 18, 1902; children—Bernhard, Carrie May. Prof. modern langs., Franklin and Marshall Coll., 1899-1900; instr. asso., asso. prof. and prof., Johns Hopkins, since 1900. Mem. Modern Lang. Assn. America; pres. Goethe Soc. of Md. and D.C., Soc. for History of Germans in Md. Editor: H. von Kleist's Michael Kohlhaas, 1902; Die erste deutsche Bibel, 10 vols., Tübingen, 1904-15; Wielands Gesammelte Schriften (vols. 6, 9, 11-15, and 21), Berlin, 1928-39; Hesperia, Schriften zur germanischen Philologie. Author: Die Doppeldrucke in ihrer Bedeutung für die Textgeschichte von Wielands Werken, 1913; Index to Publications of the Mod. Lang. Assn., 1919. Contbr. to philol. jours. Co-Editor: Modern Language Notes. Home: 1529 Linden Av., Baltimore, Md.

KURTH, Wilfred, ins. official; b. New Britain, Conn., Sept. 24, 1875; ed. pub. schs., New Britain; m. Ethel A. McLean, July 31, 1901. Began with Hartford (Conn.) br. of Scottish Union and Nat. Ins. Co., 1891-1902; mgr. Canadian business of Home Ins. Co. of N.Y., 1902-16, sec. of co., 1916-20 v.p. and sec., 1920-29, elected dir., 1925, pres., 1929-37; pres. Franklin Fire Ins. Co. of Phila., City of New York Ins. Co., Gibraltar Fire Insurance Co., New Brunswick (N.J.) Fire Ins. Co., Carolina Ins. Co., Homestead Fire Ins. Co., Ga. Home Ins. Co., Nat. Liberty Ins. Co. of America, Baltimore Am. Ins. Co. of N.Y., Paul Revere Fire

KURTZ, Charles C.; pres. Charles C. Kurtz & Sons Co. Home: 1207 Van Buren St. Office: Kurtz Bldg., Wilmington, Del.

Insurance Co. of N.Y., The Home Indemnity Company of N.Y., Home Fire Securities Corpn., Interzone Corporation (chairman of the board); ex-pres. Nat. Bd. Fire Underwriters; U.S. mgr. Halifax Fire Ins. Co.; dir. Underwriters Laboratories, Ltd. (Chicago). Mem. Am. Foreign Ins. Assn. (pres.), Ins. Soc., New England Soc., New York Chamber Commerce. Clubs: Union League, Drug and Chemical, Blue Goose, Ridgewood Country, Arcola Country, Down Town Assn., Recess, Bankers, Turf and Field, Terrace. Home: Ridgewood, N.J. Office: 59 Maiden Lane, New York, N.Y.

KURTZ, Charles C.; pres. Charles C. Kurtz & Sons Co. Home: 1207 Van Buren St. Office: Kurtz Bldg., Wilmington, Del.

KURTZ, Charles T., pres. and gen. mgr. Kurtz Bros.; b. Tamaqua, Pa., Nov. 16, 1874; s. John C. J. and Eliza A. (Meyers) K.; ed. Shamokin (Pa.) High Sch.; m. Pauline L. Stutz, Apr. 18, 1900; children—Charles T., Jr.; Robert M., John L. Asso. with Kurtz Bros., mfg. stationers, printers, school supplies, as pres. and gen. mgr. since 1894; vice-pres. and treas. Moshannon Smithing Coal Co.; dir. Clearfield Trust Co. Dir. Chamber of Commerce; dir. Am. Red Cross (former chmn.); vice-pres. and dir. Clearfield Y.M.C.A. Clubs: Clearfield, Curwensville Golf. Home: 3 W. Front St. Office: 4th and Reed Sts., Clearfield, Pa.

KURTZ, Jacob Banks, ex-congressman; b. Delaware Twp., Juniata Co., Pa., Oct. 31, 1867; s. Abraham H. and Mollie (Bergey) K.; student Dickinson Coll., Carlisle, Pa., A.M., 1893; LL.B., law sch. same coll., 1893; m. Jennie Stockton, of Washington Co., Pa., Sept. 4, 1895; children—Dorothy Stockton, Jay Banks. Began practice at Altoona, Pa., 1893; dist. atty. Blair Co., Pa., 2 terms, 1905-12; chmn. Com. Pub. Safety and Council of Defense, World War; mem. 68th to 72d Congresses (1923-33), 21st Pa. Dist., reëlected to 73d Congress (1933-35), 23d Pa. Dist. Republican. Presbyn. Home: Altoona, Pa.

KURTZ, John Frederick, Penna. State official; b. Connellsville, Pa.; s. Henry and Emma A. (Enos) K.; m. Edna Kay Kimmell, Nov. 11, 1925. Began as sec. Chamber of Commerce, Connellsville, Pa., 1910; coal and coke operator, Connellsville Coal & Coke Co., Connellsville, Pa., to 1929; bank director; treas. Connellsville Bldg. & Loan Assn.; state dir. of Federal programs, Dept. of Public Assistance, Harrisburg, Pa. Home: 214 Pine St. Office: 147 N. Cameron St., Harrisburg, Pa.

KURTZ, John Robert, supt. of public schools; b. Myerstown, Pa., Nov. 16, 1884; s. Edwin Harry and Fannie (Krall) K.; m. Hester N. Neufarth, Nov. 4, 1922. Athletic coach and science teacher, Goddard Sem., Barre, Vt., 1911-13; coach and teacher, Leland U., New Orleans, 1915; prin. and coach Vienna (Ill.) High Sch., 1916-17; coach and science teacher Vandergrift (Pa.) High Sch., 1918, prin., 1919-32; supt. of schools, Vandergrift, since 1932. Pres. Chamber of Commerce, 1934-36; chmn. local Red Cross chapter, 1938; vice-pres. Westmoreland Co. Boy Scouts, chmn. Court of Honor. Mason. Club: Kiwanis (pres. 1937). Home: 113 E. Adams St. Office: Franklin Av., Vandergrift, Pa.

KUSSY, Nathan, author, lawyer; b. Newark, N.J., July 13, 1872; s. Gustav and Bella (Bloch) K.; grad. Newark High Sch., 1890; LL.B., New York Law Sch., 1894; m. Tennie Levi, April 25, 1900 (died Dec. 26, 1935); children—Hazel M. (Mrs. Raymond H. Cohn), Bella N. (Mrs. Milton Bernstein). Practiced in Newark since 1895; mem. Bd. of Edn., 1898-1902; asst. city atty. 1917-21. Mem. Authors League America, Dramatists' Guild. Democrat. Jewish religion. Author: Grinmar, 1907; The Abyss, 1916; The Victor (pub. in England), 1922; also playlets—The President Speaks; The Diamond Necklace; The Schemers; Crooks (pub. by War Dept., U.S.A., for performance at cantonments, World War). Home: 77 S. Munn Av., East Orange, N.J. Office: 790 Broad St., Newark, N.J.

KUYKENDALL, Clark Porter, foreign service officer; b. Towanda, Pennsylvania, May 10, 1896; s. Benjamin and Louise (Porter) Kuykendall; graduate of high school, Towanda, 1913; A.B., Columbia University, 1920; m. Kathrine Nicolaysen, June 28, 1930. Vice consul at Amsterdam, Netherlands, 1920-23; vice consul and consul, Batavia, Java, 1923-27; consul at Oslo, Norway, 1928-30, Bergen, 1930, Naples, Italy, 1930-33, Cherbourg, France, 1933-35; 1st sec. Am. Legation and consul at Kaunas, Lithuania, 1935-38; consul Free City of Danzig since 1938. In Ambulance Service, U.S. Army, France, 1917-19. Awarded Croix de Guerre (France). Member Alpha Sigma Phi, Sigma Delta Chi. Episcopalian. Club: Columbia Univ. (New York). Home: Towanda, Pa. Address: Am. Consulate, Danzig, Free City of Danzig.

KUZNETS, Simon Smith, economist; b. Kharkov, Russia, Apr. 30, 1901; s. Abraham and Pauline (Friedman) K.; B.S., Columbia, 1923, M.A., 1924, Ph.D., 1926; m. Edith H. Handler, June 5, 1929; children—Paul, Judith. Fellow Social Science Research Council, 1925-27; mem. staff, Nat. Bur. Econ. Research, since 1927; asst. prof. econ. statistics, U. of Pa., 1930-34, asso. prof., 1934-35, prof. since 1935. Mem. Am. Econ. Assn., American Statis. Assn. (v.p. 1935; fellow since 1938). Econometric Soc., Social Sci. Research Council (bd. dirs. since 1938). Jewish religion. Author: Cyclical Fluctuations, 1926; Secular Movements in Production and Prices, 1930; Seasonal Variations in Industry and Trade, 1933; National Income and Capital Formation, 1937; Commodity Flow and Capital Formation, 1938. Contbr. to econ. jours. Home: 2 Bent Road, Bowling Green, Media, Pa. Office: 1819 Broadway, New York, N.Y.; also Wharton School of Finance and Commerce, University of Pennsylvania, Philadelphia, Pa.

KYLE, Frank Posey, supervising prin. city schs.; b. Airville, Pa., Feb. 23, 1900; s. Bertram Bryan and Rebecca (Barley) K.; B.S., Albright Coll., 1923; A.M., Teachers Coll. of Columbia U., 1928; grad. study at Teachers College, summer 1929, N.Y. Univ., Saturdays, winters 1930-32; m. Florence Flinchbaugh, Oct. 1919; children—Richard Eugene, Jay Frank. Instr. sci., high sch., Mauch Chunk, Pa., 1923-26; teacher mathematics and prin., Mauch Chunk, Pa., 1926-30; prin. Lansford Jr.-Sr. high sch., 1930-32; teacher mathematics, high sch., Bogota, N.J., 1932-33; life ins. salesman, Red Lion, Pa., 1933-34; supervising prin. pub. schs., Burnham, Pa. since 1934. Served in Pa. N.G., 1936-39. Mem. bd. dirs. Burnham Y.M.C.A. Mem. Mifflin Co. Tuberculosis Commn. Mem. Pa. Acad. Sci., Zeta Omega Epsilon, Tau Kappa Alpha. Republican. Mem. Evang. Ch. Mason. Home: Red Lion, Pa. Office: Burnham, Pa.

KYLE, William Joseph, lawyer; b. Milroy, Pa., Aug. 26, 1867; s. Charles and Ann (Campbell) K.; B.S., State Teachers Coll., Lock Haven, Pa., 1887; LL.B., State U. of Ia., 1895; m. Gertrude Bell Shaffer, Jan. 3, 1900; children—Richard Shaffer, Charles Derrick, William Joseph, Emory Relmond (all lawyers). Admitted to Pa. bar, 1895, and since practiced in Waynesburg; sr. mem. firm. Kyle & Reinhart. Trustee Waynesburg (Pa.) Coll. Mem. Greene Co., Pa. State and Am. Bar Assns., Phi Delta Phi. Republican. Presbyterian. Elk. Club: Greene County Country. Home: 115 N. Richhill St. Office: 502 Peoples Bank Bldg., Waynesburg, Pa.

KYNETT, Alpha Gilruth, clergyman; b. Davenport, Ia., Aug. 3, 1858; s. Rev. Alpha Jefferson and Althea Pauline (Gilruth) K.; A.B., Wesleyan U., 1878, A.M., 1881; taught in Rugby Acad. and studied law, 1878-82; B.D., Drew Theol. Sem., 1884; A.M., Ohio Wesleyan U., 1893; D.D., Cornell Coll., Ia., 1897; S.T.D., Wesleyan U., 1918; m. Elizabeth H. Hardy, 1884 (now deceased); children—Elizabeth Hardy, Alpha Hardy (dec.), Eleanor Gilruth, Dorothy Dale, Alpha Gilruth (dec.), Katharine Hardy (dec.), Gerald Penfield, Olivia Sterner (dec.), Willard Carpenter; m. 2d, Catharine A. Hardy, 1910 (now deceased). Ordained Methodist Episcopal ministry, 1886; pastor in Philadelphia Conference at Darby, 1884-87, Oxford, 1887-89, Pine Grove, 1889-90, Pottstown, 1890-92, St. Stephen's Ch., Phila., 1892-97, Central Ch., Frankford, Phila., 1897-99, Fortythird St. Ch., Phila., 1899-1901; presiding elder, S. Dist. Phila. Annual Conf., 1901-07; recording and field sec., 1907-16, centenary rep. and asst. treas., 1916-19, asst. in church extension since 1919, Board of Home Missions and Church Extension of M.E. Ch.; retired, 1929. Mem. Bd. Ch. Extension M.E. Ch., 1896-1916, Bd. Missions, 1904-12, Nat. Bd. Temperance, Prohibition and Pub. Morals, 1916-24; del. Gen. Conf., M.E. Ch., 1904, reserve del., 1908, 12, del., 1916, 20; del. Ecumenical Conf., 1912; pres. Phila. Conf. Branch of Retired Ministers Nat. Assn. Mem. Phi Beta Kappa, Pi Gamma Mu, Psi Upsilon. Mason (32°). Home: 4820 Beaumont Av., Philadelphia, Pa.

KYNETT, Harold Havelock, advertising agt.; b. Phila., Pa., Sept. 13, 1889; s. Harry Havelock and Emeline Goodsell (Westcott) K.; grad. Central High Sch., Phila., 1907; B.S., U. of Pa., 1912; m. Edna Isabel Gallager, Jan. 21, 1915; 1 dau., Mary Elizabeth. Reporter Phila. Press. North American, 1908-13; copy writer N. W. Ayer & Son, advertising agency, 1913-14, Richard A. Foley, 1914-18; exec. Dippy & Aitkin, advertising, 1918-20; senior partner Aitkin-Kynett Co., advertising agency, since 1920; lecturer in marketing, Wharton Sch., U. of Pa., since 1915; dir. Audit Bur. of Circulations; dir. Investment Corpn. of Phila. Dir. Chas. Morris Sch. of Advertising and Journalism. Mem. Am. Assn. Advertising Agts., Phi Gamma Delta. Republican. Methodist. Clubs: Lotos, Phi Gamma Delta, Advertising (New York); University, Poor Richard, Midday, Corinthian Yacht, Aronimink Golf (Phila.). Author of books on print collecting: Amiable Vice, Illusion, Nostalgia, Harbor Lights. Contbr. to advertising jours. Home: Edgehill Rd., Wayne, Pa. Office: 1400 S. Penn Square, Philadelphia, Pa.

L

LABATUT, Jean, architect, prof. of architecture; b. Martres-Tolosane, France, May 10, 1899; s. Dominique and Gabrielle (Clarac) L.; ed. Ecole St. Stanislas, College du Caousou, Lycee National, Ecole des Beaux Arts et des Sciences Industrielles (all Toulouse, France) and Ecole Nationale Superieure des Beaux Arts de Paris, France; m. Mercedes Terradell, June 10, 1929. Began as practicing architect in France, 1924; consultant city planner for Havana, Cuba, 1926-28; asso.-architect and asso. landscape architect for the town, church, residence and gardens of Castillega de Gusman near Seville, Spain, 1926-31; prof. of architecture, Am. Summer Sch. of Fine Arts, Palais de Fontainebleau, France, since 1927; prof. of architecture (chief critic of archtl. design), Princeton U., since 1928; consultant to Bd. of Design of New York World's Fair, architectural designer of the fountains for the water, light and sound displays and designer of the spectacles, 1937-39. Served in Engring. Corps, French Army, 1918-19. Awarded Laureat de l'Institut de France, 1923; Premier 2d Grand Prix de Rome, 1926; 1st in internat. competition for civic center, plaza and monument to Cuban patriot, Jose Marti, Havana, Cuba, 1938-39; medal Societe des Artistes Francais, 1925; registered architect State of N.J. Mem. Am. Inst. of Architects, French Soc. of City Planners, Societe des Artistes Francais, Beaux Arts Inst. of Design. Archtl. League of New York. Club: Nassau (Princeton); Princeton (New York). Home: Maybury Hill, Snowden Lane. Office: McCormick Hall, Princeton Univ., Princeton, N.J.

LABRECQUE, Theodore Joseph, lawyer; b. Portland, Ore., Mar. 8, 1903; s. Herman F. and Clara (Thibault) L.; ed. Manhattan Coll., 1920-21; LL.B., Fordham U. Law Sch., 1924; m. Marjorie Uprichard, Jan. 31, 1931; children—Theodore J., Jr., Katherine, Thomas. Admitted to N.J. bar as atty., 1925, as counsellor, 1928; admitted to practice before Interstate Commerce Commn., 1936; engaged in gen. practice of law at Red Bank, N.J., since 1925; mem. firm

Quinn, Parsons & Doremus, 1929-37, Parsons, Labrecque & Borden since 1937. Mem. Am. and Monmouth Co. bar assns., Cath. Lawyers Guild, Commercial Law League of America. Mem. Nat. Sweepstakes Regatta Assn. (dir.). Democrat. Roman Catholic. B.P.O.E. Clubs: Y.M.C.A. (dir.), Lions (pres.), Monmouth Camera (v.p.), Fair Haven Yacht (gov.), Monmouth Boat. Home: Conover Lane, Red Bank, N.J.

LA BRUM, J(ohn) Harry, lawyer; b. Phila., Pa., Aug. 9, 1897; s. Thomas J. and May Theresa (Conlen) LaB.; LL.B., Georgetown U., 1925; grad. student Cambridge U., England; m. Catharine Agatha Foley, June 29, 1921; 1 dau., Agatha Mary. Admitted to Pa. bar, 1925, and since practiced in Phila.; mem. firm Conlen, LaBrum & Beechwood; special atty. gen. for Commonwealth of Pa., 1936-37. Mem. Am. Bar Assn.; vice-pres. 3d Judicial Dist., 1932-33; mem. admiralty and maritime law com.; 1933-35, vice-chmn. marine and inland marine ins. com., 1934-35, chmn., 1935-37; mem. standing com. on Am. citizenship, 1935-37; mem. council of sect. on insurance law, 1937-39; chmn. com. to cooperate with U.S. Const. Sesquicentennial Commn., 1937-39; mem. council public utility law sect., 1938-39; mem. Pa. com. on admissions, 1938-39. Mem. Pa. Bar Assn.; mem. com. on civil laws, 1934-38; chmn. com. on Am. citizenship, 1935-39. Mem. Phila. Bar Assn. (mem. bd. govs.), Assn. Practitioners before Interstate Commerce Commn., Internat. Assn. Ins. Counsel, Foreign Traders Assn., Am. Legion, Port of Philadelphia Maritime Society, Phi Alpha Delta (supreme justice). Clubs: Art, Union League, Racquet, Philadelphia Country, Whitemarsh Valley Country, Lawyers, Caveat, Marine, Traffic (Phila.); India House (New York); Executives League of America. Home: 1830 N. 69th St., Overbrook, Phila. Office: 1507 Packard Bldg., Phila., Pa.

LACKEY, Sylvester Jacob, physician; b. Chicora, Pa., Aug. 12, 1883; s. William Ernest and Mary Anna (Frederick) L.; student Chicora (Pa.) grade schs., 1889-1900, Allegheny Coll., Meadville, Pa., 1901-03, Western Pa. Med. Coll., Western U. of Pa. (now U. of Pittsburgh), Pittsburgh, 1904-08; m. Ethel Lydia Kamerer, Sept. 30, 1904; children—Evelyn Romayne (Mrs. Leroy Drake), Lucille Geraldine (Mrs. Harry H. Arnold), Vivian Susanna (Mrs. Amor M. Deemer), Sylvester Kamerer (dec.). Physician, Limestone, Pa., 1908-17, Clarion, Pa., since 1917; on staff Brookville (Pa.) Hosp., Brookville, Pa., Oil City (Pa.) Hosp. Mem. Pa. State Med. Soc., Clarion Co. Med. Soc., Phi Rho Sigma. Republican. Presbyterian. Mason (K.T., Shriner, Syria Temple). Home: 131 Seventh Av. Office: 543 Main St., Clarion, Pa.

LACY, George Rufus, physician; b. Marble Falls, Tex., Sept. 3, 1886; s. George W. and Adelia J. (Tate) L.; ed. U. of Tex., 1907-09; M.D., Vanderbilt U. Med. Sch., 1913; m. Caroline M. Dodson, July 25, 1917; children—George Rufus, Jr., Ann Elizabeth. Instr. Vanderbilt U. Med. Sch., 1913-15; bacteriologist, Singer Lab., Pittsburgh, Pa., 1915-18, 1919-23; with Rockefeller Foundation at Manila, P.I., 1923-25; prof. bacteriology and immunology, U. of Pittsburgh since 1925. Served in Med. Corps, U.S.A., 1918-19. Fellow Am. Coll. Physicians; mem. A.M.A., Am. Soc. Pathology and Pathologists and Bacteriologists, Soc. Am. Bacteriologists, Soc. Exptl. Pathology. United Presbyn. Home: 1364 Navahoe Drive, Mt. Lebanon. Office: Sch. of Medicine, U. of Pittsburgh, Pittsburgh, Pa.

LADD, George Tallman, mechanical engr.; b. Edinburgh, O., May 17, 1871; s. George Trumbull and Cornelia Ann (Tallman) L.; student Sheffield Scientific Sch. (Yale), 1891; M.E., Cornell, 1895; m. Florence Ewing Barrett, Sept. 2, 1910. With P.&L.E. Ry. Co., Pittsburgh, 1891-93; designer Brooks Locomotive Works, Dunkirk, N.Y., 1895-98; mech. engr. in charge engine and boiler sales, Bass Foundry & Machine Co., Ft. Wayne, Ind., 1898-1909; consulting engr., Pittsburgh, 1909-10; pres. and treas. The George T. Ladd Co., engrs., Pittsburgh, 1910-25; pres. Ladd Water Tube Boiler Co., 1925-28; pres. and gen. mgr. United Engineering & Foundry Co., Pittsburgh, since 1928; pres. Ladd Securities Co., Ladd Equipment Co.; chmn. Pittsburgh Testing Laboratory, Woodings-Verona Tool Works; v.p. Davis Brake Beam Co., Johnstown, Pa.; dir. Columbian Enameling & Stamping Co. (Terre Haute, Ind.), United Engring. & Foundry Co., Combustion Engring. Co., Inc. (New York), Heyl & Patterson, Inc., First Nat. Bank (Pittsburgh), Pa.-Central Airlines Co., Flannery Bolt Co., Pittsburgh Steel Co., Pittsburgh Br. of Federal Reserve Bank of Cleveland. Trustee Follansbee Bros. Co. Dir. Pittsburgh Chamber of Commerce. Pres. Employers Assn. Pittsburgh. Trustee Carnegie Inst. and Carnegie Inst. of Techn., Pittsburgh, Bucknell univ.; dir. Allegheny Gen. Hosp., Pittsburgh. Lt. comdr. U.S.N.R.F., in charge construction 14-inch naval railway mounts and 7-inch caterpillar mounts, which were in service in France, August 1918, with naval railway batteries, World War; was mem. advisory bd. Pittsburgh Dist., U.S. Fuel Administration. Designed and built largest water tube boilers in world, operating at Fordson Plant, Ford Motor Co., Detroit. Mem. Am. Soc. M.E., Engring. Soc. of Western Pa. (pres.), Am. Iron and Steel Inst., U.S. Naval Inst., Amerian Geog. Soc., Pa. Soc. Mason (32°, K.T., Shriner). Republican. Clubs: Duquesne, Pittsburgh Athletic, Montour Heights Golf, Country of Pittsburgh, Harvard-Yale-Princeton; Edgeworth (Sewickley, Pa.); Chicago Athletic (Chicago); Cornell, Yale, Lotos, Engineers' (New York). Home: Coraopolis Heights, Pa. Office: First Nat. Bank Bldg., Pittsburgh, Pa.

LADENBURG, Rudolf Walter, prof. physics; b. Kiel, Germany, June 6, 1882; s. Albert and Margarete (Pringsheim) L.; Ph.D., U. of Munich, 1906; post. grad. work, Cambridge, Eng., 1906-07; m. Else Uhthoff, Aug. 15, 1911; children—Margarete (Mrs. Hubert Ladenburg), Kurt, Eva Marie. Came to America, 1931. Univ. instr. and professor at Breslau, 1908-25; was scientific honorary member Academy Goettingen Faculty, Frankfurt Am.-Main, and Kaiser Wilhelm Gesellschaft, Berlin; prof. U. of Berlin, 1925-31; Brackett research prof. physics, Princeton U. since 1931. Awarded German Iron Cross. Contbr. scientific books and articles. Home: 55 Princeton Av. Address: Palmer Physical Laboratory, Princeton, N.J.

LADNER, Albert H., Jr., lawyer; b. Phila., Pa., Oct. 21, 1882; s. Albert H. and Emma S. (Konzelman) L.; ed. public schools and Central High Sch., Phila., and Temple U.; m. Lillian Guenthoer, Apr. 14, 1909; children—Albert H., III, Robert A. Began as clerk in coal office, 1902; admitted to Phila. bar, 1906, and established firm Ladner & Ladner, since in practice as mem. firm; gen. counsel, L.O.O.M.; atty. Phila. Lodge No. 54 since 1913. Capt. 2d Inf., Pa. N.G.; served with Vet. Corps, 2d Regt., U.S. Army, during World War. Mem. Co. Bd. Law Examiners, Phila. Co.; registration commr., Phila. Co., 1915-18, 1927-30; mem. Phila. Zoning Commn.; U.S. Collector Internal Revenue, 1st Pa. Dist., 1931. Mem. Am., Pa. and Phila. bar assns., Law Acad., Sons of Vets. of Civil War, Phila. Zool. Soc., Pa. Acad. Fine Arts, Mooseheart Alumni Assn., Strollers, Germon Soc. of Pa., Phila. Turngemeinde, Fraternal Home Ins. Soc., Ins. Fed. of Pa., Royal Order of Jesters. Mem. Legion of Honor. Republican. Lutheran. Mason (past master Columbia Lodge No. 91; past potentate Lu Lu Temple; mem. Chapter and Commandery of Scottish Rite Bodies, Cross of Constantine, Phila. Council, Masonic Vets.), Moose (chmn. Nat. Membership Com.; gov. Mooseheart; mem. exec. com. Supreme Lodge; chmn. Charity Bd.; mem. Foundation and past supreme dictator; past dictator Phila. Lodge No. 54 since 1913, vice dictator since 1925, dictator, 1936-40), Elks, Eagles, Maccabees, Royal Arcanum. Clubs: Lawyers, Phila. Rifle, Lambskin (Phila.); Koran Grotto (Phila.); Irem Country (Wilkes-Barre, Pa.); Lu Lu Temple Country (Phila.). Home: 4700 Pine St. Office: 1501 Walnut St., Philadelphia, Pa.

LADNER, Grover Cleveland, lawyer, jurist; b. Phila., Pa., Jan. 8, 1885; s. Albert Henry and Emma (Konzelmann) L.; ed. U. of Pa. Wharton Sch., 1902-03; LL.B., U. of Pa. Law Sch., 1906; m. Mary C. Davis, Aug. 20, 1907; 1 dau., Katherine Helen (Mrs. M. P. Sargent). Admitted to Pa. bar, 1906 and since engaged in gen. practice of law at Phila.; mem. Commn. to Revise Banking Laws of Pa., 1917-23; spl. counsel, Phila., Pa., 1927-29; dep. atty. gen. of Pa., 1935-37; mem. Dern-Lonergan Commn. to report on Fed. control of stream pollution, 1934-36; mem. commn. for Pa. to negotiate Interstate Anti-Pollution Compact between 7 states of Ohio River Basin, 1937-38; judge of Orphans Ct., Phila., since 1937. Served as Dem. presdl. elector for Pa., 1936. Nat. Dir. Izaak Walton League; pres. Pa. Fed. Sportsmen's Clubs. Active in conservation work. Cited by Gov. of Pa. for Meritorious Service Medal for "distinguished service in the cause of conservation, 1938. Mem. Philadelphia Bar Assn., Pennsylvania Bar Assn., American Bar Assn., Phi Sigma Kappa. Democrat. Lutheran. Elk. Moose. Patriotic Order Sons of America. Clubs: Penn Athletic, White Marsh Valley Country. Author: Ladner on Conveyancing in Pa., 1913. Contbr. articles on conservation and stream pollution. Home: 415 S. 47th St., Philadelphia, Pa. Office: 429 City Hall, Philadelphia, Pa.

LAESSLE, Albert, sculptor; b. Phila., Pa., March 28, 1877; s. Henry Christian and Caroline Louise (Metzger) L.; grad. Spring Garden Inst., Phila., 1896, Drexel Institute, Philadelphia, 1897; graduate in art, Pa. Academy of Fine Arts, 1901; studied with Michel Béquine, Paris, 1904-07; m. Mary Prudden Middleton, June 7, 1905; children—Albert Middleton, Paul. Awarded Stewardson prize, 1902, Cresson traveling scholarship, 1904-07 (both Pa. Acad. Fine Arts); bronze medal, Buenos Aires, 1910; gold medal, San Francisco Expn., 1915; Fellowship prize, Pa. Acad Fine Arts, 1915; first prize for sculpture in "Americanization through Art" exhbn., Phila., 1916; George D. Widener memorial gold medal, Pa. Acad. Fine Arts, 1918; fellowship gold medal, same acad., 1923; gold medal, Sesquicentennial Exposition, Phila., 1926; hon. mention, Art Institute of Chicago, 1920; James E. McClees prize, Pennsylvania Academy Fine Arts, 1928; 2d prize for best decorative group for garden, park or other outdoor placement, 1928. Represented in permanent collections Pa. Acad. Fine Arts, Phila. Art Club, Met. Mus. (New York), Carnegie Inst. (Pittsburgh), Peabody Inst. (Baltimore), Calif. Palace of Legion of Honor, Reading (Pa.) Mus. of Art, Johnson Square, Camden, N.J.; the bronze "Billy," purchased by the Fairmount Park Art Commn., Phila., 1917; "The Bronze Penguins," purchased by Fairmount Park Art Commn., 1918; Pennypacker Memorial, Logan Circle Parkway, Phila., 10th issue medal for Soc. of Medalists. Instr. in construction, Pa. Academy of Fine Arts, also instr. in sculpture, Summer Sch., same. Mem. National Sculpture Soc., Am. Soc. Painters, Sculptors and Gravers, Société des Amis de la Médaille d'Arts (Brussels), Fellowship of Pa. Acad. Fine Arts, Nat. Inst. of Arts and Letters. National Academician, 1932. Home: 511 Runnymede Av., Jenkintown, Pa.

LaFAVRE, Harry Buyer, surgeon, U.S. Navy; b. Sandusky, O., Sept. 9, 1893; s. Francis Gustavus and Ada Mae (Buyer) L.; student Ohio Wesleyan U., 1911-13; M.D., Ohio State U., 1917; grad. student Harvard Med. Sch., 1917, Rockefeller Inst., 1918, Naval Med. Sch., Washington, D.C., 1931-32; m. Carol Edith Miller, July 31, 1925. Commd. lt. (jr. grade) Med. Corps, U.S. Navy Reserve, May 11, 1917, regular service, Sept. 1917; advanced to lt. comdr., June 1925; served in transport service, as port med. officer, Nantes, France, and in naval hosp., Brest, during World War, 1917-19; stationed at Cleveland, O., 1919-23, Naval Hosp., Santo Domingo, and Naval Station, Guantanamo, Cuba, 1923-25, Milwaugee, Wis., 1925-29, U.S.S. Patoka, 1929-31, naval powder factory, Indian Head, Md., 1932-36, Phila. since 1936. Decorated World War and Dominican Occupation medals. Mem. A.M.A., Md. Med. Soc., Assn. Mil. Surgeons, Phi Rho Sigma, Delta Tau Delta. Methodist. Mason, H.B.L., Eastern Star. Home. State Rd., Springfield, Pa. Office: Customs House Bldg., Philadelphia, Pa.

LAFEAN, Edward Charles; b. York, Pa., April 21, 1867; s. Charles and Charlotte (Kottcamp) L.; student pub. schs., York, Pa., 1872-81;

Ph.G., hon. mention, Phila. Sch. of Pharmacy, 1886; m. Katherine Herman, Nov. 28, 1888 (died May 1933); children—Earle Bernard, Paul Herman (dec.), Raymond Guy. Began as drug store errand boy, 1881; in drug store of L. E. Sayre, Phila., 1884-86, working by day and attending sch. of pharmacy at night; in drug business as mem. firm A. H. Lafean and Bro., York, Pa., 1886-1914; sold interest in drug business, 1914, and was apptd. gen. organizer Nat. Council Jr. Order of United Am. Mechanics, editor official publ. The American, 1916-17, ins. dept., Pittsburgh, 1917-18, pres. and gen. mgr. ins. dept., 1918-29; now retired; v.p. The American Publ. Co. Mem. Jr. O.U.A.M. (past state councilor of State Council of Pa., Nat. Fraternal Congress (mem. bd. govs. 2 yrs.), Royal Arcanum, Mutual Artisans. Republican. Lutheran. Mason (past master Zeredatha Lodge, York, Pa.; past high priest Horrell Chapter R.A.M.; past comdr. York Commandery K.T.). Clubs: Arts & Sciences, Syria Auto (Pittsburgh); Amateur Cinema League, Nat. Travel, Universal News Photographers (New York). Since retirement has traveled around world several times, visiting more than 100 countries and taking nearly 100,000 ft. of moving pictures which are being shown gratuitously to churches, Y.M.C.A, Y.W.C.A., Boy Scouts, colleges and schools. Home: 4411 Schenley Terrace, Pittsburgh, Pa.

LAFFERTY, Theodore Thomas, asso. prof. philosophy and edn.; b. Foyil, Okla., June 3, 1901; s. Roy Henderson and Nannie (Hodges) L.; A.B., Okla City U., 1924; A.M., U. of Chicago, 1926, Ph.D., 1928; m. Isabel Ella Morrison, Oct. 29, 1924. Began as instr. mathematics, Agrl. and Mech. Coll., Jonesboro, Ark., 1924-25; instr. philosophy, U. of Chicago, 1928-30; instr. philosophy and psychology, Lehigh U., Bethlehem, Pa., 1930-34, asst. prof. education, 1934-37, asso. prof. philosophy, and edn. since 1937; propr. farm of 165 acres, Foyil, Okla., and farm of 114 acres, Bethlehem, Pa. Served as pvt. to sergt.-maj. j.g., U.S.A., 1916-20, mainly in Philippine Islands; 1st lt. F.A., (A.A.) N.A., 1924-25. Mem. Am. Philos. Assn., Am. Ednl. Research Assn. Democrat. Methodist. Contbr. articles to jours. philosophy and edn. Home: Route 1, Nazareth, Pa.

LAFFOON, Carthrae Merrette, elec. engr.; b. Coldwater, Kan., Aug. 14, 1888; s. Mark and Kate Brown (Carthrae) L.; E.E., U. of Mo., Columbia, Mo., 1914, A.M., 1915; m. Kittie Kuhns Painter, Nov. 22, 1916; children—Carthrae Merrette, Christopher Painter, Louis Marchand. Design engr. Westinghouse Electric & Mfg. Co., East Pittsburgh, Pa., power engring. dept., 1916-26, sect. engr. large turbine generator sect., generator dept., 1926-31, sect. engr. turbine generators, hydraulic generators, synchronous condensers and frequency converters, generator dept., 1931-35, mgr. alternating current generator engring., generator div., since 1936; extension lecturer, U. of Pittsburgh Grad. Sch. since 1930. Zone finance chmn. Westmoreland Co. (Pa.) Boy Scouts. Mem. Am. Inst. E.E. (chmn. elec. machinery com. since 1938), North Huntingdon Twp. (Pa.) Sch. Bd. Presbyterian. Club: Century (Irwin, Pa.). Author numerous articles and papers presented before tech. socs. Home: Penglyn Pl., Irwin, Pa. Office: Braddock Av., East Pittsburgh, Pa.

LAHEY, Richard; visiting prof. fine arts, Corcoran Sch. of Art, Washington D. C. Address: Goucher Coll, Baltimore, Md.

LAIDLEY, Lowell Terry, banker and merchant; b. Carmichaels, Pa., Dec. 11, 1875; s. Alvin D. and Anna (McClintock) L.; student Duff's Business Coll., Pittsburgh, 1892-93; m. Katherine Heinbeck, Feb. 10, 1903; children—Mary Katherine, Alvin D, Antoinette H. Mgr. commercial dept. Hidalgo Mining Co., Parral, Chihuahua, Mexico, 1900-02; propr. Laidley's Dept. Store, Carmichaels, Pa., since 1904; pres. First Nat. Bank, Carmichaels, since 1923; treas. and dir. Home Bldg. & Loan Assn., Carmichaels, since 1924; dir. South Penn Telephone Co. of Pa., South Penn Telephone Co. of W.Va. Democrat. Presbyterian. Club: Rotary (Carmichaels, Pa.; pres. 1933-34). Address: Carmichaels, Pa.

LAING, John, coal mining; b. nr. Glasgow, Scotland, Aug. 24, 1865; s. Alexander and Elizabeth (MacAlpin) L.; brought to U.S., 1867; ed. pub. schs., Mercer County, Pa.; m. Margaret Slagle, Oct. 6, 1903; children—Louisa, Gertrude, Margaret. Worked in mines of Fayette Co., W.Va., until 1890; assisted in organizing Sun Coal Coa., Royal Coal Co. and the Lanark, Rush Run, Cunard McAlpine and Morrison coal cos., all in W.Va.; later organized and developed the Main Island Creek, MacBeth, McKay and Wyatt coal cos.; pres the Wyatt Coal Sales Co., the sales agency for all the mines in which he is interested; pres. Beckley Fire Creek Coal Co.; dir. Kanawha Valley Bank. Chief Dept. of Mines of W.Va., 1908-13. Pres. Y.M.C.A. of Charleston; pres. Union Mission. Republican. Presbyn. Mason (32°), Elk. Home: 1325 Quarrier St. Office: Kanawha Valley Bldg., Charleston, W.Va.

LAIRD, George S., pres. Laird Schober Co., Inc.; b. Phila., Pa., Oct. 13, 1877; s. Samuel S. and Mary E. (Schober) L.; student Germantown (Pa.) Acad.; m. Kathryn Knowles, June 1, 1904; children—Catherine, George S. Began with Laird, Schober & Co., shoe mfrs., becoming partner, now pres. operating corpn., Laird, Schober Co., Inc. Club: Huntingdon Valley Country. Home: 212 Highland Av., Abington, Pa. Office: 22d and Market Sts., Philadelphia, Pa.

LAIRD, John Baker, clergyman; b. Lancaster Co., Pa., Feb. 14, 1866; s. Clarkson and Anna (O'Neill) L.; A.B., Lafayette Coll., 1892, A.M., 1895 (D.D., 1903); grad. Princeton Theol. Sem., 1895; unmarried. Ordained Presbyterian ministry, 1895; pastor Frankford Ch., Phila., since 1895. Has served as moderator of Presbytery and of Synod of Pa. Trustee Lafayette Coll.; pres. Red Cross auxiliary of 18,000 members; organizer and trustee Frankford Hosp.; pres. trustees Wilson Coll. for Women; dir. and trustee Princeton Theological Seminary; trustee and former pres. bd. Lincoln University; mem. Bd. of Nat. Missions of Presbyn. Ch. and trustee Bd. of Publication same ch.; many times mem. Gen. Assembly; mem. Council Ref. Chs. and Presbyn. Alliance. Pres. Pennsylvania Scotch-Irish Society, 1912-13; dir. Frankford Hist. Soc. Republican. Clubs: Adelphia, Union League, Country. Contbr. numerous religious and ednl. articles. Dir. of "The Presbyterian." Home: 4315 Frankford Av., Philadelphia, Pa.

LAIRD, John Wesley, clergyman; b. in Scotland, Oct. 5, 1882; s. Thomas and Jane (Patterson) L.; brought to U.S., 1888; grad. Wyoming Sem., Kingston, Pa., 1905; Ph.B., Syracuse U., 1909, D.D., 1916; student Yale Divinity School (class of 1916); LL.D., Albion Coll., 1921; m. Margaret Lila Keller, June 13, 1908. Supplied Congl. Ch., W. Pittston, Pa., 1904-05, M.E. Ch., Vernon Center, N.Y., 1905-06; ordained, 1908; pastor Vernon, N.Y., 1907-10, Grace Ch., Bronx, 1910-12, Winsted, Conn., 1912-14, First Ch., New Haven, 1914-18, Mt. Vernon Place Ch., Baltimore, Md., 1918-21; pres. Albion Coll., Mich., 1921-24; minister Brighton Presbyn. Ch., Rochester, N.Y., 1925-37, Doylestown (Pa.) Presbyn. Ch., 1937; prof. philosophy and social ethics, Sch. of Theology, Temple U., Phila., since 1937. Dir. religious work, Y.M.C.A. at Camp Meade, Md., 1917. Mem. Phi Gamma Delta. Mason, Odd Fellow. Author: The Role of the Educated Man, 1921. Home: 501 W. Hortter St., Germantown, Philadelphia, Pa.

LAIRD, Richard Drum, judge; b. Greensburg, Pa., June 30, 1872; s. Francis V. B. and Hetty (Welty) L.; ed. Greensburg High Sch. and Grove City Coll.; m. Clara E. Dalbey, Nov. 15, 1904; children—Rachel Dalbey, John Keenan, Emily Drum (Mrs. Nevin A. Cort, Jr.); m. Martha Erickson, June 6, 1936. Admitted to Pa. bar, 1898, and practiced in Greensburg; dist. atty., 1933-37; apptd. judge Common Pleas Court, 10th Judicial Dist., Pa., June 1937, elected for full term of 10 yrs. Nov. 1937. Served as officer 10th Pa. Vol. Inf. in Spanish-Am. War and Philippine Insurrection, 1898-99. Dir. Greensburg Pub. Sch., Westmoreland Hosp. Democrat. Presbyterian. Mason (K.T., 32°, Shriner). Home: 545 N. Main St. Office: Court House, Greensburg, Pa.

LAIRD, Robert Malcolm, judge; b. Petersburg, Pa., Oct. 18, 1895; s. Edwin Walter and Eleanor (Giles) L.; student Huntingdon (Pa.) High Sch., 1910-14; A.B., Gettysburg (Pa.) Coll., 1920; LL.B., Dickinson Sch. of Law, Carlisle, Pa., 1927; M.A., Dickinson Coll., 1927; m. Helen Mar O'Neill, June 30, 1926; children—Eleanor Giles, Robert Malcolm. Admitted to York Co. bar, 1928, and since practiced at Hanover, Pa.; mem. firm Laird & Buchen, attys.; apptd. judge Court of Common Pleas, York County, Pa., July 21, 1939. Capt., A.E.F., 1917-18. Mem. Kappa Delta Rho. Republican. Lutheran. Home: Stock St., Hanover, Pa. Address: Court House, York, Pa.

LAIRD, Walter J., v.p. and trust officer Wilmington Trust Co. Home: 2502 Willard St., Wilmington, Del.

LAIRD, Warren Powers, architect; b. Winona, Minn., Aug. 8, 1861; s. Matthew James and Lydia (Powers) L.; ed. pub. and state normal schs., Winona, Minn., and at Cornell U.; instr. at latter, 1886-87, and at U. of Pa., 1890-91; 6 yrs. practice and study with architects, in Minn., Boston, and New York, and 1 yr. travel and study in Europe (1882-90); Sc.D., U. of Pa., 1911, LL.D., 1932; m. Clara Elizabeth, d. Dr. Charles and Mary (Hall) Tuller, Nov. 15, 1893; children—Mary Hall (Mrs. John Dashiell Myers), Helen Powers (dec.). Prof. architecture, 1891-1932, and dean Sch. of Fine Arts, from founding, 1920-32, emeritus prof. architecture since 1932, U. of Pa. Lecturer Princeton U., 1932-33. Consulting architect of state, municipal and other pub. and pvt. bodies in many states and Can. Award of Merit, Gen. Alumni Soc. University of Pa., Founders Day, 1936. Mem. nat. advisory council Lingnan University, Canton, China, trustee, 1909-26. Mem. Pa. State Art Commn., 1928-36. Mem. Great Council of Cathedral of Washington, D.C., Tri-State Regional Planning Federation of Phila. (dir.); mem. Phila. Zoning Commn., 1929. Fellow Am. Inst. Architects; pres. Assn. Collegiate Schs. of Architecture, 1912-21; mem. Am. Civic Assn., Phi Beta Kappa, Sigma Xi (pres. Pa. Chapter, 1916-17), Tau Sigma Delta; hon. mem. Soc. Architects of Uruguay, Central Soc. Architects of Argentina; del. 3d Pan-Am. Congress of Architects, Buenos Aires, 1927, as rep. U.S. Govt., Univ. of Pa. and A.I.A.; chmn. architectural jury, art competition, 10th Olympics, Los Angeles, 1932; mem. permanent com. Internat. Congress of Architects, 1925-35; U. of Pa. del. to Internat. Congress of Univs., Havana, 1930. Mem. bd. of overseers P.E. Div. Sch. Phila., 1925-35; mem. Ch. Bldg. Commn. of Diocese of Pa., Com. on Ch. Architecture of Gen. Council Lutheran Ch. of N.A.; mem. vestry Memorial Ch. of St. Paul, Overbrook, Phila., 1898-1933 (rector's warden 1914-1925). Hon. mem. Archtl. Alumni Soc. of U. of Pa., Art Alliance of Phila.; former mem. Archæol. Inst. of America, Coll. Art Assn., Art Teachers Assn. of Phila., Pa. Scotch-Irish Soc., Merion Civic Assn.; mem. Order of Founders and Patriots of America. Clubs: Art, Contemporary, T-Square, Lenape. Home: Warwick Hotel, Philadelphia, Pa.

LAIRD, William R., surgeon Laird Memorial Hosp. Address: Montgomery, W.Va.

LAKE, Kirsopp, theologian, historian; b. Southampton, Eng., Apr. 7, 1872; s. George Anthony (M.D.) and Isabel Oke (Clark) L.; B.A., Lincoln Coll., Oxford, 1895, M.A., 1897; Arnold essay prizeman, 1902; D.D., St. Andrews Univ., 1911; Th.D., Leiden Univ., 1921; Litt.D., Univ. of Michigan, 1926; Ph.D., Heidelberg Univ., 1936; m. Helen Courthope Forman, Nov. 10, 1903; m. 2d, Silva Tipple New, December 16, 1932. Curate of Lumley, Durham, 1895, of St. Mary the Virgin, Oxford, 1897-1904; prof. ordinarius, U. of Leyden, Holland, 1904-13; prof. early Christian lit., Harvard, Sept. 1914-19; Winn professor ecclesiastical history, 1919-1932, professor of history, same university, 1932-38. Paid visits to Mt. Athos and other libraries to investigate Greek MSS., summers since 1903; dir. archaeol. expedition to Serabit, 1930, 35, to Samaria, 1932-34, to Lake Van, 1938-39. Fellow Am. Acad. Arts and Sciences. Awarded medal, British Acad., 1936. Corr. mem. Preussische Akademie der Wissenschaft. Clubs: St. Botolph (Boston); Century (New York). Author: Text of the New Testament, 1898; Codex I of the Gospels, 1900; Texts from Mt. Athos, 1901; The Athos Leaves of Codex H—Paul, 1904; The Historical Evidence for the Resurrection of Jesus Christ, 1905; The Athos Leaves of the Shepherd of Hermas, 1908; Professor von Soden's Treatment of the Text of the Gospels, 1909; The Earlier Epistles of St. Paul, 1910; The Codex Sinaiticus, 1911; The Stewardship of Faith, 1914; The Beginnings of Christianity, Vol. I, 1920, Vol. II, 1922, Vol. III, 1926, Vols. IV and V, 1933; Landmarks in the History of Early Christianity, 1921; The Codex Sinaiticus, Vol. II, 1921; Immortality and the Modern Mind, 1922; Religion Yesterday and Tomorrow, 1925. Translator: The Apostolic Fathers, 1912; Eusebius, 1927; The Serabit Inscriptions (Harvard Theol. Studies), 1927; The Caesarean Text of Mark, 1928; Six Collations of N.T. MSS., 1933; Dated Greek minuscule MSS., Fasc. I & II, 1934, Fasc. III & IV, 1935, Fasc. V & VI, 1936, Fasc. VII & VIII, 1937; Studies and Documents, Vols. I & II, 1934, Vols. III, IV & V, 1935, VI, VII, VIII & IX, 1936-37; Paul, His Heritage and Legacy, 1934; An Introduction to the New Testament, 1937. Home: 522 Oakley Road, Haverford, Pa.

LAKIN, Harry Allen, physician; b. Frederick, Md., Jan. 16, 1876; s. Francis T. and Mary F. (Gary) L.; A.B., Western Md. Coll., 1896; ed. N.Y. Univ. and Bellevue Hosp. Med. Coll., 1899-1902; M.D., Univ. of Md., 1903; (hon.) A.M., Western Md. Coll., 1903; m. Alice M. Taughinbaugh, March 5, 1905; 1 dau., Frances Isabelle. Engaged in gen. practice of medicine at Harrisburg, Pa., since 1903; asst. med. examiner, Pa. R.R. Co., 1910 to 1919; chief of dept. anesthesia, Harrisburg Polyclinic Hosp. since 1924. Fellow Internat. Coll. Anesthetists, Am. Soc. Anesthetists, A.M.A. Mem. Internat. Anesthesia Research Soc., Asso. Anesthetists of U.S. and Can., Eastern Soc. Anesthetists (pres.), Pa. State and Dauphin Co. med. socs. Mem. Reformed Ch. Home: 10 S. 20th St., Harrisburg, Pa.

LALLY, J. P., business exec.; b. Pittsburgh, Pa., March 29, 1892; s. P. J. and Jennie (McMahon) L.; student pub. schs.; m. Helen Mangan, Nov. 23, 1920; children—Jean Ann, Joan Glynn, Jack Robert. Vice-pres. and dir. Copper Range Co., Pittsburgh; managing dir. C. G. Hussey & Co., copper rolling mills, Pittsburgh. Clubs: Pittsburgh Athletic Assn. (Pittsburgh); St. Clair Country. Home: 93 Hoodridge Drive, Mt. Lebanon, Pa. Office: 2850 Second Av., Pittsburgh, Pa.

LAMB, Carl Sherman, glass mfr.; b. Gurnee, Lake Co., Ill., Feb. 2, 1874; s. Charles H. and Mary A. (Sherman) L.; student Waukegan (Ill.) Pub. and High Schs., 1880-92, Northwestern U., Evanston, Ill., 1895-96; B.L., Chicago Coll. of Law (dept. of Lake Forest U.), 1899; m. Elizabeth M. Overman, March 14, 1901; children—Richard Overman, Eunice Helen (Mrs. Harold M. Tenney). Began as office boy with George F. Kimball, Chicago, glass jobber, 1892, remaining until bus. purchased, 1896, by Pittsburgh Plate Glass Co., with whom continued in Chicago, 1896-1907, in gen. office, Pittsburgh, 1907-10, asst. gen. counsel, 1910-38, asst. sec. 1921-25, sec. since Jan. 20, 1925; chmn. bd. and dir. Brown Graves Co.; pres. and dir. Pittsburgh Coal Exchange; sec. and dir. Chandler Boyd Co. Mem. council, Boro of Edgewood, Pa., 1915-25 (pres. 2 yrs.). Republican. Episcopalian. Mason. Clubs: Metropolitan, Edgewood, Edgewood Country. Home: 1025 S. Trenton Av., Wilkinsburg, Pa. Office: 2200 Grant Bldg., Pittsburgh, Pa.

LAMB, Charles Rollinson, architect; b. New York; s. Joseph and Eliza (Rollinson) L.; m. Ella Condie. Ex-pres. Arts Realty Co.; pres. J. & R. Lamb Corpn. Splty. ecclesiastical architecture, memorial and hist. art; architect Dewey arch, erected in Madison Sq., New York, by Nat. Sculpture Soc. to commemorate home-coming of Admiral Dewey; also of the Court of Honor, Hudson-Fulton Celebration, 1909, and chmn. of the committee on stands and on decoration; ex-v.p. Architectural League, Nat. Sculpture Soc.; v.p. Am. Fine Arts Soc.; ex-pres. Art Students' League, Municipal Art Soc.; ex-sec. Soc. Mural Painters; trustee Nat. Arts Club; mem. S.R., S.A.R. (ex-trustee), Nat. Soc. Arts and Crafts; dir. Boy Scouts America, etc. Clubs: National Arts (bd. of govs.), Church. Home: Cresskill, N.J.*

LAMB, Ella Condie, artist; b. N.Y. City; d. James and Ellen (Harrison) Condie; studied in New York under William M. Chase, Walter Shirlaw, and C. Y. Turner; in England under Hubert Herkomer, R.A.; in Paris under R. Collin; m. Charles Rollinson Lamb; children—Richard C. (dec.), Karl B., Katharine S., Donald W., J. Condie. Specialty portrait and decorative painting; among important examples of mural work are paintings in Flower Memorial Library, Watertown, N.Y.; "Governor Baldwin Memorial," St. John's Ch., Detroit; "Sage Memorial," Cornell U.; reredos in St. Mary's Ch., Wayne, Pa.; "Russell Memorial," Wells Coll.; "Hobart Memorial," Briarly Sch., New York, etc. Dodge prize, Nat. Acad. Design, 1889; hon. mention, Chicago Expn., 1893, Buffalo Expn., 1901; gold medal, Atlanta Expn., 1895. Life mem. Art Students' League of N.Y.; artist life mem. Nat. Arts Club; mem. Art Center, Nat. Soc. of Mural Painters. Studio: Lambs Lane, Cresskill, N.J. *

LAMB, Hugh Louis, bishop; b. Coatesville, Pa., Oct. 6, 1890; s. Matthew J. and Anna (Coyle) L.; grad. high sch., Coatesville, 1907; grad. Overbrook Theol. Sem., Phila., 1912; S.T.D., Am. Coll., Rome, Italy, 1915; studied Catholic U., Washington, D.C., 1916-17. Ordained priest R.C. Ch., 1915; asst. rector Annunciation Ch., Phila., 1915-17, Ch. of the Holy Child, Phila., 1917-18; prof. Overbrook Theol. Sem., 1918-21; sec. to Cardinal Dougherty, 1921-23; asst. supt. Diocesan Schs., Phila., 1923-26; chancellor Archdiocese of Phila., 1926-36; made domestic prelate by Pope Pius XI, 1927; protonotary apostolic, 1929; now auxiliary bishop of Phila. and vicar general, Phila. Address: 4625 Springfield Av., Philadelphia, Pa.

LAMB, Karl Barré, pres. J. & R. Lamb; b. New York, N.Y., Nov. 8, 1890; s. Charles R. and Ella (Condie) L.; grad. Friends Sem., N.Y. City, 1908; Chem.E., Columbia U., 1912; m. Clara Mateos, June 5, 1923; children—Charles Anthony, Barea. Engaged in gen. engring. work, 1912-15; asst. merchandise mgr. and tech. dir. John Wanamaker, 1915-17; mem. Industrial Investigation Bd. of Am. Peace Commn. (exec. officer Belgian Mission), 1919; chem. engr. and dir. research and development Am. Cotton Oil Co., 1919-23; v.p. and dir. Stamscott Co., Hopewell, Va., 1922-23; treas. and dir. J. & R. Lamb, 1924-29, pres. and dir. since 1929; treas. and dir. The Zanorsky Co. Mem. council, Tenafly, N.J., 1933-39, pres., 1937-39; police commr., 1938. Served as capt., 7th Army Corps, A.E.F., 1918. Mem. Am. Inst. Chem. Engrs., Delta Psi. Republican. Episcopalian. Clubs: Columbia University (N.Y. City); Aldecress Country (Englewood, N.J.). Address: Tenafly, N.J.

LAMB, Richard Weller, v.p. Family Loan Soc.; b. Brightseat, Md., Nov. 11, 1897; s. Roscoe Graham and Annie (Weller) L.; ed. Ga. Sch. of Technology; m. Lois Douglas, April 26, 1919; children—Richard Eugene, Madlin Mariya. With Family Loan Soc., Inc., since 1928, now v.p. and dir. Home: Kennett Square, Pa. Office: Odd Fellows Bldg., Wilmington, Del.

LAMB, William Hollinshead, lawyer; b. Phila., Pa., April 17, 1885; s. John Gordon and Abbie Browning (Hollinshead) L.; student Germantown Acad., 1896-1902, Wharton Sch., U. of Pa., 1902-06; m. Edith Cochran, May 15, 1918; children—Pauline Cochran, Jane Browning. Began as clerk studying law in father's office, 1907; admitted to Pa. bar, 1911, and practiced in Phila., 1911-17; asst counsel Bell Telephone Co. of Pa. and Diamond State Telephone Co., 1917-19; atty., both cos., 1919-34, gen. counsel, both cos., since Nov. 1, 1934; dir. The Bell Telephone Co. of Pa. Mem. Am. Bar Assn., Pa. Bar Assn., Philadelphia Bar Assn., Beta Theta Pi (Phi chapter). Republican. Episcopalian. Clubs: Phila. Country (Phila.); Spring Lake Golf and Country (Spring Lake, N.J.); Bay Head Yacht (Bay Head, N.J.). Home: 348 Penn Rd., Wynnewood, Pa. Office: 1835 Arch St., Philadelphia, Pa.

LAMBDIN, Henry Lyle, clergyman; b. Rutledge, Tenn., Nov. 18, 1892; s. Samuel Jackson and Dorthula (Young) L.; A.B., Carson-Newman Coll., Jefferson City, Tenn., 1911, A.M., 1912; A.M., N.Y. Univ., 1915; B.D., Drew Theol. Sem., Madison, N.J., 1914; Ph.D., Drew Univ., 1935; m. Cornelia Vivian Morrow, Oct. 9, 1917; children—Doris Evelyn, Patricia Vivian, Miriam Louise. Ordained to ministry Meth. Ch., 1915; asso. pastor, Centenary Ch., Newark, N.J., 1914-19; pastor, Arlington, N.J., 1919-20, Port Jervis, N.Y., 1921-22; pastor Summit Meth. Ch., Summit, N.J., since 1923. Trustee Drew Univ., Madison, N.J., since 1936. Methodist. Home: 58 De Forest Av., Summit, N.J.

LAMBERT, Gerard Barnes, corpn. official; b. St. Louis, Mo., May 15, 1886; s. Jordan Wheat and Lily (Winn) L.; grad. Smith Acad., St. Louis, 1904; Litt.B., Princeton, 1908; student Columbia Architectural School, 1908-10; m. Rachel Lowe, June 25, 1908; children—Rachel, Gerard B., Lily; m. 2d, Grace Lansing Mull, April 18, 1936. Pres. Gerard B. Lambert Co., lumber and cotton, 1912-28; gen. mgr. Lambert Pharmacal Co., 1921-23, pres., 1923-28; pres. Lambert & Feasley, 1926-28; pres. The Lambert Co., 1926-28, now dir.; pres. Gillette Safety Razor Co., 1931-34, dir., chmn. exec. com., 1934-36. Served as 1st lt. Air Service, U.S.A., Eng. and France, World War; capt. Air Service R. C., 1918-20. Chmn. visiting com., Dept. Art and Archaeology, Princeton. Mem. Archaeol. Inst. America (pres. N.J. Soc.), Southern Soc. (N.Y. City). Adviser to Federal Housing Administrator, Washington, D.C., June 1938-Feb. 1939. Republican. Episcopalian. Clubs: Knickerbocker, Coffee House, Princeton, Creek, Deepdale, Racquet and Tennis, Ivy, New York Yacht (rear commodore), Seawanhaka-Corinthian Yacht, Nat. Golf, Shinnecock Golf; Seminole, Gulf Stream, Bath and Tennis (Palm Beach, Fla.); Myopia, Tennis and Racquet, Algonquin, Dedham Country and Polo, Eastern Yacht, Brookline Country (Boston); Manchester (Mass.) Yacht; Porcupine (Nassau, B.W.I.); etc.; permanent hon. mem. Royal Thames Yacht and Lymington Yacht (London, Eng.). Home: Princeton, N.J. Office: 250 Park Ave., New York, N.Y.

LAMBERT, Oscar Doane, prof. polit. science and dean of coll., W.Va., Wesleyan Coll. Address: W.Va. Wesleyan College, Buckhannon, W.Va.

LAMBERT, William Vincent, animal geneticist; b. Stella, Neb., Sept. 13, 1897; s. George W. and Addie L. (Keister) L.; B.S. in Agr., U. of Neb., 1921; M.S., Kan State Coll., Manhattan, 1923; Ph.D., U. of Calif., Berkeley, 1931; m. Esther W. Posson, Sept. 15, 1923; children—Marilyn Marya, Carol Anne. Instr. genetics, Ia. State Coll., Ames, 1923-27, asst. prof. genetics, 1927-29, asst. prof. genetics, 1930-36; sr. animal husbandman in charge genetics investigations, Bur. Animal Industry, U.S. Dept. Agr., Beltsville, Md. since 1936. Fellow A.A.A.S. Mem. Am. Soc. Zoologists, Am. Soc. Naturalists, Genetics Soc. of America, Am. Genetics Assn., Soc. Animal Production, Sigma Xi, Phi Kappa Phi. Club: Cosmos (Washington). Home: 712 Spring St., Silver Spring, Md.

LAMBERTON, Chess, banker; b. Franklin, Pa., Nov. 1, 1877; s. Robert G. and Louella (Chess) L.; ed. Grove City (Pa.) Coll., 1897-98; grad. Eastman Business Coll., Poughkeepsie, N.Y., 1899; m. Lauretta L. Lamberton, Aug. 11, 1925. In banking business at Franklin since 1898; pres. and trust officer Lamberton Nat. Bank, Franklin; pres. First Nat. Bank (Cochranton, Pa.); dir. Joy Mfg. Co., Sylvania Producing Co., Industrial Silica Corpn. (Youngstown). Mem. N.G. Pa., 1899-1913, retiring as adj. gen. Chmn. Venango Liberty Loan Orgn.,

World War, also of War Savings Stamps Assn. Republican. Presbyn. Mason (K.T., 32°), Elk, Moose, Eagle. Clubs: Franklin; Wanango (Reno, Pa.). Home: Franklin, Pa.

LAMBERTON, Robert, banker; b. Franklin, Pa,. May 4, 1886; s. Robert G. and Jessie King (Judson) L.; student Culver (Ind.) Mil. Acad. and Eastman's Business Coll.; m. Myra Moorhead Plumer, Sept. 29, 1909; children—Robert Gilfillan, Jessie Margaret, Charles Plumer, Harry Willson. Vice-pres., cashier and dir. The Lamberton Nat. Bank, Franklin, Pa., since 1919; president and dir. Waterford Water Supply Co. since 1928; v.p. and dir. Northern Development Co., Inc., since 1928. Mem. Pa. Game Commn. since 1935. Mason, Elk, Eagle, Moose. Office: 13th and Liberty Sts., Franklin, Pa.

LAMBIE, Joseph Sioussa, industrial engr.; b. Pittsburgh, Pa., Mar. 23, 1887; s. James Baird and Mary Montgomery (Brown) L.; C.E., U. of Pittsburgh, 1907; m. Glennah Gertrude Dulin, June 20, 1912; children—Mary Lillian, Richard Alan, Ruth Irene, Lois Janet. Draftsman Standard Bldg. Constrn. Co., Pittsburgh, 1907; asst. engr. Bur. of Filtration, Pittsburgh, 1908-09; instr. civil engring., U. of Pittsburgh, 1909-14, asst. prof., 1914-19, asso. prof., 1919-29, lecturer in civil engring. since 1929; operating mgr. Concrete Products Co. of America, Pittsburgh, since 1929. Served as lt., Engring. Corps, U.S. Army, 1917-18, asst. supervising constructing quartermaster, Norfolk, Va. and Charleston, S.C., Port Terminals. Mem. Am. Soc. C.E. Soc. for Promotion of Engring. Edn., Am. Soc. for Testing Materials, Am. Concrete Inst., Engineering Soc. of Western Pa., Acad. of Science and Art, Nat. Geog. Soc. Republican. Presbyterian. Home: 1303 Singer Pl., Wilkinsburg, Pa. Office: Diamond Bank Bldg., Pittsburgh, Pa.

LAMBORN, Louis Emmor, educator; b. Still Pond Kent. Co., Md., Aug. 16, 1890; s. Louis and Mary Rebecca (Taylor) L.; grad. Baltimore City Coll., 1909; A.B., Dickinson Coll., Carlisle, Pa., 1916; m. Florence Jean Wagner, Feb. 15, 1913; children—Robert Louis, Elizabeth Jean. Rancher and miner, Salmon, Ida., 1912-15; teacher, 1916, later vice prin. Friends Sch., Baltimore; headmaster McDonogh Sch., Md., since 1926; also mgr. summer camps for boys and girls. Enlisted in U.S. Army, June 1917; capt. inf., Nov. 1917; maj. cav., Res., Feb. 1919. Mem. Kappa Sigma. Mem. Soc. of Friends. Mem. Harvard Club of Md. Home: McDonogh, Md.

La MER, Victor Kuhn, educator, chemist; b. Leavenworth, Kan., June 15, 1895; s. Joseph Secondule and Anna Pauline (Kuhn) LaM.; A.B., U. of Kan., 1915; Ph.D., Columbia, 1921; student U. of Chicago, 1916, Cambridge U., England, 1922-23, Copenhagen, Denmark, 1923; m. Ethel Agatha McGeevy, July 31, 1918; children—Luella Belle, Anna Pauline, Eugenia Angelique. Chemist and high sch. teacher chemistry, 1915-16; research chemist, Carnegie Inst. of Washington, 1916-17; asst. in chemistry, Columbia, 1919-20, instr., 1920-24, asst. prof., 1924-28, asso., 1928-35, prof. since 1935; visiting prof. Stanford U., 1931, Northwestern U., 1928; Priestley lecturer, Pa. State Coll., 1932. Mem. Jury of Award, Nichols medal, since 1934 (chmn. 1934-1937). First lt. Sanitary Corps, U.S.A., 1917-19. Fellow N.Y. Acad of Science; mem. Am. Chem. Soc., Faraday Soc. (Eng.), Sigma Xi, Phi Lambda Upsilon, Phi Chi, Epsilon Chi. Republican. Conglist. Clubs: Faculty (Columbia). Translator and editor of Fundamentals of Physical Chemistry by Arnold Eucken (with Eric Jette) 1925. Asso. editor of Jour. Chem. Physics, 1933-36. Contbr. to scientific jours. Home: 353 Moore Av., Leonia, N.J.

LAMME, Maurice Allison, engr.-chemist; b. Bozeman, Mon., Sept. 5, 1881; s. Edwin Bates and Susie Louise (Welch) L.; B.S., Mon. Agrl. Coll., 1903; A.M., Columbia U., 1904, Ph.D., same, 1909; m. Mabel P. Foster, Aug. 7, 1906; children—Mary Louise, Margaret Harriet (Mrs. Kenneth S. McIver. Engaged as tutor, Columbia U., 1904-07, instr., 1907-12; dir. Instituto de Geologia y Perforaciones, Montevideo, Uruguay, 1912-19; asst. dir. Caulk Labs., Milford, Del., 1919-20; geologist, Standard Oil Co., Venezuela, 1922; engr. Western Electric Co., Kearny, N.J., since 1923. Mem. Am. Chem. Soc., A.A.A.S., Sigma Xi. Democrat. Episcopalian. Home: 32 Mountain Av., Maplewood, N.J.

LAMMERS, Martin William, life ins.; b. Grass Lake, Mich., Oct. 30, 1896; s. Henry and Mary C. (Noon) L.; B.S., U. of Notre Dame, 1919; ed. Northwestern U., 1919-20; m. Ruth Marie Poe, Oct. 9, 1925; children—Martin William, Jr., Charlene Adelaide. Began in real estate office of Henry Lammers, Jackson, Mich., 1920-22; asso. with American Central Life Ins. Co., 1922-33, successively, salesman, supervisor, home office field supt., then branch mgr. at Philadelphia since 1933. Pres. and dir. Phila. Chapter, Chartered Life Underwriters; treas. Phila. Life Underwriters Assn. Mem. Phi Rho Sigma. Republican. Clubs: Old York Road Country (Jenkintown); Notre Dame Alumni (Philadelphia). Home: 516 Cheltena Av., Jenkintown, Pa. Office: Lincoln-Liberty Bldg., Philadelphia, Pa.

LAMONT, William Hayes Fogg, univ. prof.; b. New York, N.Y., Mar. 26, 1891; s. Charles and Hester (Wallace) L.; A.B., Washington and Lee U., Lexington, Va., 1915; M.A., Columbia U., 1917; Ph.D., U. of Pa., 1933; m. Hetty Slack Moore, Dec. 3, 1932; 1 son, James Wallace. Teacher of English, N.Y. Mil. Acad., Cornwall, N.Y., 1915-16; served as seaman, Submarine Chaser No. 118, U.S.N., 1917-18; teacher of English, Princeton Prep Sch., 1918-21; prof. of English literature, Rutgers U., New Brunswick, N.J., since 1922; spl. lecturer, summer sessions, Columbia U., 1938-39. Mem. Nat. Council of Teachers of English (com. on college reading), Modern Language Soc. of America, Beta Theta Pi. Democrat. Universalist. Critic on books by Am. Women, Chicago World's Fair, 1934; judge for Annual Literary Competition of Women's Federation of N.J., 1926-36; judge of 1st novels for Contemporary Arts Assn., New York, 1933. Lecturer on current literature to literary groups throughout Middle Atlantic and New England States; radio lecturer. Compiler of numerous reading lists including Sixty Great Novels of All Time. Prepared contemporary Am. sect. of Good Reading for Nat. Council of Teachers of English. Home: 104 N. 2d Av. Office: Rutgers Univ., New Brunswick, N.J.

La MOTTE, William Oscar; chief eye, ear, nose and throat dept. Delaware Hosp.; cons. otolaryngologist Delaware State Hosp., Wilmington; cons. ophthalmologist and otolaryngologist Kent Gen. Hosp., Dover; otolaryngologist St. Francis Hosp., Wilmington. Address: 601 Delaware Av., Wilmington, Del.

LAMPE, William Edmund, official Evang. and Reformed Ch.; b. Frederick, Md., May 23, 1875; s. Christian Lewis Charles and Mary Eva (Babel) L.; grad. Frederick (Md.) Acad., 1892; A.B., Princeton, 1896, A.M., 1898, Ph.D., magna cum laude, 1908; grad. Theol. Sem. Ref. Ch., Lancaster, Pa., 1899; LL.D., Catawba College, Salisbury, N.C., 1937; m. Anna Lenora Thomas, Dec. 28, 1899; children—Mary Elizabeth, William Thomas, Grace Evelyn, Harold Christian, John Edmund, Carl Anspach, Anna Kathryn. Ordained ministry Reformed Ch. in U.S., 1900; missionary, Sendai, Japan, 1900-07; also teacher of English, Greek and N.T. theology, North Japan Coll., 1900-05, and chmn. Foreign Community of Sendai, 1903-07; organizer, 1908, sec., 1908-16, Layman's Missionary Movement of Reformed Ch.; recording sec. World's S.S. Assn., 1916-24; same, Foreign Missionary Conf., N.A., 1917-22, 28, 29; sec. United Missionary and Stewardship Com., Reformed Ch., 1914-26; secretary Exec. Com. of Gen. Synod Reformed Ch. in U.S., 1926-34; now sec. Gen. Synod of Evang. and Reformed Ch. and of its Com. on Constitution and Charter. Pres. United Stewardship Council Chs. of Christ, 1933, Civic League of Philadelphia. Mem. of Am. Acad. Political and Social Science, Anti-Saloon League of Pa. (chmn. exec. com.), Anti-Saloon League of America (dir.), American Whig Soc. (Princeton), Phi Beta Kappa, Lambda Chi Alpha (honorary). Republican. Clubs: Overbrook Assn. (ex-pres.), Penn Athletic. Author: The Japanese Social Organization, 1910. Home: 5004 Pine St. Office: 1505 Race St., Philadelphia, Pa.

LAMSA, George Mamishisho, author; b. Mar Bishoo, Kurdistan, Aug. 5, 1892; s. Jando Peshah and Sarah (Yokhanan) L.; A.B., Archbishop of Canterbury's Coll., Urmiah, Persia, 1907; student English Sch., Van, Turkey, 1907-08, Va. Theol. Sem., Alexandria, Va., 1918-21; unmarried. Came to U.S., 1916, naturalized, 1923. Field sec. Archbishop Canterbury's Assyrian Mission in America, 1925-31. Translator of scriptures from Aramaic. Fellow Royal Society of Arts, London, England. Author: The Secret of the Near East, 1924; The Oldest Christian People, 1926; Key to the Original Gospels, 1931; My Neighbor Jesus, 1932; The Four Gospels (from Aramaic), 1933; Gospel Light, 1936; Modern Wisdom, The Shepherd of All Psalms (translation from Aramaic), 1939. Contbr. articles to mags. Discoverer of the origin of the English alphabet. Founder Christian Jewish Mohammedan Soc. to bring an understanding between Christians, Jews and Mohammedans, 1923. Address: 1222 Arch St., Philadelphia, Pa.

LANAHAN, Henry, lawyer; b. Baltimore, Md., April 19, 1873; s. Daniel and Susan (Dilworth) L.; grad. Baltimore City Coll., 1893; A.B., Johns Hopkins, 1896; LL.B., Nat. U. Sch. Law, 1909; M.P.L. George Washington U., 1910; m. Genevieve Turner, Oct. 7, 1903; m. 2d, Mrs. Lillian Wendell Van Arsdale, of East Orange, N.J., Dec. 2, 1916; stepson, William Kenneth Van Arsdale. Prof. physics, Md. Agrl. Coll. (now U. of Md.), 1898-1906; asst. examiner, U.S. Patent Office, 1906-10; admitted to D.C. bar, 1910, N.J. bar, 1913; counsel and asst. gen. counsel Thomas A. Edison, Inc., and subsidiaries, West Orange, N.J., 1910-21, gen. counsel and dir. since 1922, vice-pres. since 1934. Mem. Am. Bar Assn., New York Patent Law Assn., Essex Co. Bar Assn., Phi Beta Kappa. Home: 27 Gap View Road, Short Hills, N.J. Office: Edison Office Bldg., West Orange, N.J.

LANAHAN, William W.; partner W. W. Lanahan & Co.; officer or dir. several companies. Home: Towson, Md. Office: Calvert Bldg., Baltimore, Md.

LANCASTER, Edward Lee, prof. econs.; b. Phila., Pa., Aug. 12, 1898; s. Richard and Mary Emma (Le Fetre) L.; B.S. in Econs., U. of Pa. Wharton Sch. Accts. and Finance, 1921; M.S., Franklin and Marshall Coll., 1924; m. Caroline Elizabeth Kullmann, Dec. 27, 1921; children—Edward Lee, Jr., and Richard Alexander (twins). Instr. bus. adminstrn., N.C. State Coll., 1921-22; instr. bus. adminstrn., Franklin and Marshall Coll., 1922-24, asst. prof. 1924-30, asso. prof., 1930-38, prof. econs. and bus. adminstrn. since 1938. Served as pvt. Marine Corps, U.S. 1918-19. Trustee Nat. Endowment, Delta Sigma Phi. Mem. Delta Sigma Phi, Pi Gamma Mu. Republican. Mem. Reformed Ch. Home: 422 State St., Lancaster, Pa.

LANCASTER, Henry Carrington, univ. prof.; b. Richmond, Va., Nov. 10, 1882; s. Robert Alexander and Williamine Cabell (Carrington) L.; B.A. and M.A., U. of Va., 1903; Ph.D., Johns Hopkins, 1907; hon. M.A., Amherst, 1912; m. Helen Converse, d. John Bates Clark, June 11, 1913; children—John Huntington, Helen Carrington, Maria Dabney, Henry Carrington, Robert Alexander. Instr. Romance langs., 1907-08, asso. prof., 1908-10, prof., 1910-19, Amherst; prof. French literature and chmn. department of Romance langs., Johns Hopkins, since 1919; visiting prof., New York U. since 1930. Taught summer session, U. of Chicago, 1916, 24; asso. editor Modern Lang. Notes, 1919-28, editor in chief since 1928; editor Johns Hopkins Series in Romance Lit. and Langs.; corr. Rev. d'histoire litt. de la France since 1921. Dir. Foyer at Lizy-sur-Ourcq and Am. ednl. dir. of Foyers du Soldat, France, Dec. 1917-Dec. 1918. Dir. Am. Univ. Union (Paris); Hyde exchange lecturer in French univs., 1924-25. Decorated Chevalier Legion of Honor (France), 1932. Democrat. Presbyn. Mem. Modern Language Assn. of America (exec. council, 1920-23, 30;

vice-pres. 1931, 38; pres. 1939), Société des anciens textes français, Société des textes, français modernes. Am. Philos. Soc., American Association of University Professors, Delta Tau Delta, Phi Beta Kappa. Author: The French Tragi-Comedy, 1907; Pierre Du Ryer, Dramatist, 1912; Le Mémoire de Mahelot et d'autres décorateurs de l'Hôtel de Bourgogne et de la Comédie Française, 1920; La Calprnède, Dramatist, 1920; Jean Mairet, Chryseide et Arimand, 1925; A History of French Dramatic Literature in the Seventeenth Century (Part I, 2 vols.), 1929, (Part II, 2 vols.), 1932, (Part III, 2 vols.), 1936; Du Ryer, Alcionée, 1930; saül, 1931; Five French Farces, 1937; Editor: Racine, 1934. Clubs: University, Johns Hopkins. Home: 604 Edgevale Rd., Baltimore, Md.

LAND, John Nevin, supervising prin. of schools; b. Center Hall, Pa., March 26, 1886; s. Thomas S. and Sarah Marie (Yearick) L.; A.B., Franklin and Marshall Coll., 1907; student Cornell U., summer 1909, U. of Chicago, summer 1913; A.M., U. of Pa, 1935; m. Laura Esther Altenderfer; children—Sarah Agnes, Phoebe Jane. Prin. public schools, Alexandria, Pa., 1907-08, Wyomissing, Pa., 1908-10; supervising prin. Hamburg, Pa., Pub. Schs. since 1910. Life mem. N.E.A., Am. Assn. Sch. Adminstrs., Pa. Hist. Soc., Pa. Genealogical Soc., Phi Delta Kappa, Chi Phi. Mason. Address: 141 S. 3d St., Hamburg, Pa.

LANDAU, Hyman Jacob, rabbi; b. in Russia, Dec. 5, 1895; s. Gershon Lieb and Gussie L.; came to U.S., 1910, naturalized, 1934; A.B., N.Y. Univ., 1918, A.M., same, 1920; LL.B., N.J. Law Sch., Newark, 1927; J.S.D., N.Y. Univ. Law Sch., 1928; Ph.D., Drew Univ., 1936; Rabbi, Jewish Theol. Sem., N.Y. City, 1920; study, Beth Midrosh Lorabonim, Hatoras Horaah, Brooklyn, N.Y., 1933; m. Clara Brown, May 4, 1924; 1 dau., Marilyn. Formerly rabbi, Hoboken Jewish Center, Hoboken, N.J., and Union City Jewish Community Center; rabbi Congregation Agudas Achim, Orange, N.J., since 1930. Dir. Jewish Edn. Assn. of Newark, N.J. Mem. Rabbinical Assembly of Jewish Theol. Sem. of America. Mem. Orange Chevera Shaas Talmudical Group. Democrat. Jewish religion. B'nai B'rith. I.O.B.A. Home: 100 N. Essex Av., Orange, N.J.

LANDER, William Peter Sirius, clergyman; b. Brooklyn, N.Y., Aug. 13, 1891; s. William and Charlotte (Wolter) L.; ed. Columbia U., 1911-14; S.T.B., Gen. Theol. Sem., N.Y. City, 1915; m. Lotta Ray Edwards, June 30, 1915; children—Mary Barbara, Virginia Ray, William Wolter, Richard Ernest. Ordained to ministry P.E. Ch. deacon, 1915, priest, 1916; successively rector, Forest Hills, N.Y., Glendale, N.Y., Forest Hills, N.Y.; rector, Holy Trinity, West Palm Beach, Fla., 1926-32; rector, Church of the Good Shepherd, Rosemont, Pa., since 1933; gen. sec. and treas. American Church Union, Inc. Served in chaplain's res. corps, U.S.A. Republican. Episcopalian. Clubs: Penn Athletic (Philadelphia); Tuscawilla (Palm Beach). Home: Rosemont, Pa.

LANDERS, Howe Stone, ins. exec.; b. Martinsville, Ind., Oct. 17, 1885; s. John Bothwell and Idawile (Gardner) L.; A.B., De Pauw U., 1905; student U. of Ill., 1905; LL.B., Ind. Law Sch., 1908; m. Shirley McNutt, March 26, 1919; children—Georgianna, Shirley Mary. Admitted to Ind. bar, 1908; asso. in practice with William A. Ketcham, 1908-15; mem. Ind. State Industrial Commn., 1915-19; spl. counsel U.S. Fidelity & Guaranty Co., 1919-25; atty. mgr. Met. Casualty Ins. Co., New York, 1925-31, v.p. and gen. counsel, 1931-32, pres. since 1932; v.p. and gen. counsel Commercial Casualty Ins. Co., Newark, N.J., 1931-32, pres. since 1932; also pres. Empire Properties Corpn., Interstate Debenture Corpn., Unified Debenture Corpn., Met. Service Corpn., Park Lane Hotel Co.; dir. First Reinsurance Co. of Hartford. Mem. Phi Kappa Psi. Democrat. Episcopalian. Mason. Clubs: Montclair Golf, Meridian Hills Country. Home: 332 Ridgewood Av., Glen Ridge, N.J. Office: 10 Park Place, Newark, N.J.

LANDES, William Grant; b. Lancaster, Pa., May 31, 1865; s. John Shoemaker and Catharine (Wanner) L.; grad. high sch., Lancaster, 1881; hon. C.E.D. Susquehanna U., 1922; m. Bertha N. Lukens, June 18, 1890. Watchmaker and jeweler, Sheldon, Ill., until 1893; insp. Elgin Watch Co., 1894-97; traveling salesman, 1897-1903; gen. sec. Pa. State S.S. Assn., 1004 22; gen. sec. World's S.S. Assn., 1922-27. Attended 6 world's convs., Rome, Washington, D.C., Zurich, Tokyo, Glasgow and Los Angeles; mem. exec. com. Internat. S.S. Assn. 5 yrs.; as statis. sec. World's S.S. Assn. reported membership of 30,296,531 in 1920; was general secretary N.Y. State Council of Churches and Religious Edn., 1927-34. Address: 63 W. Plumstead Av., Lansdowne, Pa.

LANDES, William Stuart, chemical mfg.; b. Sheldon, Ill., Nov. 15, 1892; s. William Grant and Bertha Nell (Lukens) L.; B.S. in chem. engring., U. of Pa., 1914; m. Ruth Wunderlich, of Lansdowne, Pa., Oct. 1919 (divorced 1938); 1 dau., Alice Hope; m. 2d, Mrs. Callene Thomas Cassedy, of New York, Aug. 1938 (now deceased). Research chem. engr. Westinghouse Lamp Co., Bloomfield, N.J., 1914-16; sales engr. Atwater Kent Mfg. Co., Phila., 1919-21; with Celluloid Corpn., Newark, N.J., since 1921, successively as mfg. supt., works mgr., asst. to v.p., v.p. in charge of mfg. and research, 1921-31, pres. since 1931; v.p. and dir. Vitalite Co. Enlisted as private, 1st Inf., N.J. Nat. Guard, Feb. 1916, and served on Mexican border; with 113th Inf., 29th Div., U.S. Army, 1917-19; with A.E.F. 11 months; wounded in Meuse Argonne offensive; disch. as capt., June 1919. Decorated D.S.C. (U.S.), Croix de Guerre and Chevalier Legion of Honor (France), D.S.M. (State of N.J.). Pres. bd. trustees Ironbound Community and Industrial Service, Newark, N.J.; v.p. and dir. Newark Chamber of Commerce; dir. and past pres. N.J. Employers Assn. Trustee Newark Municipal Research Bureau; mem. tech. advisory com. Newark Coll. of Engring.; dir. and past pres. N.J. Housing League. Mem. Am. Chem. Soc., Am. Inst. Chem. Engrs., Soc. Automotive Engrs., Am. Legion. Republican. Clubs: Newark Athletic, Down Town, Essex (Newark, N.J.); Univ. of Pennsylvania (New York); Canoe Brook Country (Summit, N.J.). Home: 120 N. Oraton Parkway, East Orange, N.J. Office: 290 Ferry St., Newark, N.J.

LANDIS, Mark Homer, mech. engr., mfg.; b. Lancaster, Pa., Dec. 16, 1885; s. Frank Frick and Elizabeth (Hershey) L.; prep. edn., high sch., Waynesboro, Pa. and Mercersburg (Pa.) Acad.; M.E., Cornell U., 1908, M.M.E., 1909; m. Ethel Marie Hartman, June 16, 1910 (died Jan. 17, 1937). Machinist apprentice, summers 1899-1902, full time, 1902-04; sec. and treas. Fred. Frick Clock Co., 1909-13; gen. mgr. and mech. engr. Landis Engring. & Mfg. Co., 1913-20, pres. and gen. mgr. since 1920; pres. and gen. mgr. Geiser Mfg. Co., 1928-39; pres. and treas. Frank F. Landis Patents, Inc.; pres. Erd Co., Inc.; treas. Madeira Development Co.; dir. Landis Machine Co. (exec. com.). Trustee Waynesboro Hosp. Mem. Am. Soc. Mechanical Engineers, Society Automotive Engineers. Republican. Mason (Shriner), Elk. Clubs: Sinfonia, Waynesboro Country; Fountain Head Country (Hagerstown). Home: 228 Philadelphia Av., Waynesboro, Pa.

LANDIS, William Paine, lawyer; b. Camden, N.J., Sept. 2, 1873; s. Joseph Christian and Elizabeth Meadows (Gardner) L.; student North East Sch., Camden, N.J., 1881-85, Cooper Sch., Camden, 1885-88; Private Tutors in Law, Phila., Pa., 1888-97; m. Mary Tinsman Worman, Jan. 20, 1904; children—Emily Haney (Mrs. Charles N. Moffett), Mary Alice (Mrs. Alexander S. Fleming), Josephine Elizabeth (Mrs. Paul P. Ulrich), Julia Gardner, Elizabeth Fraser. Admitted to Phila. bar, 1897, Montgomery Co. bar, 1913, to practice before Supreme Ct. Pa., 1900; asst. trust officer Merion Title and Trust Co., Ardmore, Pa., Apr.-July 1901, trust officer and title officer, 1901-20, resigned to resume practice of law at Ardmore; pres. 69th St. Terminal Title and Trust Co., 69th St. Centre, 1924-26; v.p. and trust officer Ardmore Nat. Bank and Trust Co., 1926-30; senior partner Landis and Kain, ins. and real estate, since 1920. Mem. Legal Adv. Bd. under Selective Service Law during World War. Pres. Bd. of Health, Lower Merion Twp., Montgomery Co., Pa. Mem. Am., Pa., and Montgomery Co. bar assns. Republican. Episcopalian (asst. accounting warden and vestryman St. Mary's Ch., Ardmore). Mason. Club: Rotary (Ardmore; past pres.). Home: 124 Ardmore Av. Office: Lancaster and Cricket Avs., Ardmore, Pa.

LANDIS, William Weidman, coll. prof.; b. Coatesville, Pa., Feb. 15, 1869; s. Isaac Daniel and Anna Mary (Davis) L.; Ph.B., Dickinson Coll., 1891, A.M., 1894; student Johns Hopkins, 1891-94, and student-asst. in mathematics, 1892-95, Sc.D., 1907. Prof. mathematics, Thiel Coll., Pa., 1894-95; prof. mathematics and astronomy, Dickinson College since 1895. Republican. Methodist. Mem. Am. Math. Society, Circolo Matematico di Palermo, Phi Delta Theta, Phi Beta Kappa. Mem. 5th Internat. Math. Congress, Cambridge, Eng., 1912. Contbr. Am. Math. Monthly, Popular Astronomy, Rendiconti del Circolo Matematico di Palermo. Y.M.C.A. war service, June 1918-Sept. 1919, with 3d Italian Army; was in the trenches on the lower Piave several months and in battle, Oct. 24-Nov. 4, 1918; regional dir. of all work with 3d Army about 6 months. Awarded hon. rank of maj., Cross of War, Cross of Third Army (Italian); Chevalier Crown of Italy. Home: Carlisle, Pa.

LANE, Frederick William, chemist; b. Springfield, Mass., Feb. 17, 1889; s. Frederick Lester and Nellie Idella (Wade) L.; B.S., Mass. Inst. Tech., 1914; grad. student U. of Me., Orono, Me., 1915-16; Ph.D., Yale U., 1920; m. Gertrude E. Burt, Sept. 22, 1928; 1 son, Frederick Marvin. Asst. instr. organic chemistry, Mass. Inst. Tech., Boston, Mass., 1913-15; instr. chemistry, U. of Me., Orono, Me., 1915-16; asst. instr. chemistry, Yale U., 1916-17, instr., 1917-20; petroleum chemist, U.S. Bur. of Mines, Pittsburgh, 1920-22, Washington, D.C., 1922-24, Bartlesville, Okla., 1924-29; sr. chemist, C.W.S., U.S.A., Edgewood Arsenal, Edgewood, Md., since 1929. Mem. A.A.A.S., Am. Chem. Soc., Sigma Xi, Alpha Chi Sigma, Gamma Alpha. Republican. Club: Officers (Edgewood Arsenal). Home: Edgewood Arsenal, Edgewood, Md.

LANE, Nathaniel Franklin, physician; b. Hartford, Vt., Mar. 21, 1863; s. Alonzo Franklin and Mary Weston (Lyman) L.; grad. Vineland (N.J.) High Sch.; M.D., Hahnemann Med. Coll., 1891; m. Naomi R. Walker, 1887; children—Franklin Fayette, Charles Walker, Albert Lyman; m. 2d, Beatrice A. Driscol, 1916. Began as telegraph operator, 1885; asso. with Hahnemann Med. Coll. Hosp. since graduation 1891, successively in dispensary, asst. in hosp., clin. prof. of gynecology, retired on account of age; chief gynecological dept., Broad St. Hosp. Address: 2045 Chestnut St., Philadelphia, Pa.

LANE, Otho Evans, fire insurance exec.; b. Franklin, O., Oct. 6, 1880; s. John Van Tyl and Cornelia (Frances) L.; B.S., Miami U., Oxford, O., 1901, LL.D., 1931; m. Nell Cameron, Sept. 30, 1908. Clerk Western Electric Co., Chicago, 1899-1901; inspr. Ins. Survey Bur., Chicago, 1902; spl. agt. Traders Ins. Co. in Wis. and Mich., 1903-05; spl. agt. and adjuster Providence Washington Ins. Co. in Wis., Mich., Minn., 1905-07; state agt. and adjuster Scottish Union and Nat. Ins. Co. at Denver, 1907-12; asst. mgr. U.S. Branch, Yorkshire Ins. Co. of York, Eng., 1912-16; v.p. Niagara Fire Ins. Co., N.Y., 1916, pres., 1917-29; pres. Fire Assn. of Phila. and Reliance Ins. Co. of Phila. since 1930; pres. Lumbermen's Ins. Co. and Phila. Nat. Ins. Co. since 1934; dir. Fire Assn.; First Nat. Bank & Trust Co., Phila.; mem. bd. mgrs. Western Savings Fund Soc. Phila.; trustee Ins. execs. Assn. Mem. Eastern Underwriters Assn., Phi Beta Kappa. Clubs: Rittenhouse, Down Town (Phila.); Radnor Hunt, Drug and Chemical (New York). Home: Woodcock Farm, Westtown, Chester Co., Pa. Office: 401 Walnut St., Philadelphia, Pa.

LANE, Robert Ripley, newspaperman; b. Fitzwilliam, N.H., Sept. 27, 1880; s. Horace H. and Evelyn N. (Alexander) L.; student Amherst Coll., 1898-1900, 1903-04; m. Catherine Cecilia Gibson, Oct. 11, 1910; 1 son, Robert Philips.

Teacher high schs., Pa. and Mass., 1901-03; reporter and copy-reader World, Herald, Sun and News (Baltimore) successively, 1904-10; editorial writer, legislative corr., news editor and asst. mng. editor Baltimore Star, 1910-12; began with Newark News, 1912, editorial writer, 1920-25, Washington corr., 1925-34, became editorial writer, 1934. Mem. Chi Phi. Clubs: Gridiron, National Press (Washington, D.C.). Frequent lecturer on pub. affairs. Home: 6 Iris Road, Summit, N.J. Office: 215 Market St., Newark, N.J.

LANE, William Preston, Jr., lawyer; b. Hagerstown, Md., May 12, 1892; s. William Preston and Virginia Lee (Cartwright) L.; B.L., U. of Va., 1915; m. Dorothy Byron, Jan. 17, 1922; children—Dorothy Byron, Jean Cartwright. Admitted to Md. bar, 1916, and since in practice, Hagerstown, Md.; atty. gen. of Md., 1930-34; became pres. Herald-Mail Co., 1923; now chmn. exec. com. Hagerstown Trust Co.; dir. Fairchild Aircraft Corpn. Served as capt., later maj. and asst. div. adj., 29th Div., U.S.A., World War; received War Dept. citation. Del. to Dem. Nat. Conv., Houston, 1928, Chicago, 1932; presidential elector for Md., 1936. Democrat. Episcopalian. Elk. Home: 943 Terrace, Hagerstown, Md.

LANFEAR, Vincent Wesley, sch. administration; b. Elgin, Tex., Jan. 2, 1894; s. John Wesley and Mary (Moore) L.; B.A., U. of Tex., 1917, M.A., 1919; Ph.D., Columbia, 1922; m. Leslie Margaret Hofer, Sept. 10, 1919; 1 dau., Mary Vivian. Instr. in mil. aeronautics, U. of Tex., 1917-18, instr. in economics, 1918-20, asst. prof., 1920-21; instr. in economics, Columbia, 1922; asst. prof. polit. economy, Yale, 1923-24; prof. finance, U. of Pittsburgh, 1925-26, dir. evening div. of U. of Pittsburgh, 1927-33, dean of men since 1933. Member National Association of Deans of Men, American Econ. Assn., Assn. Urban Univs., Am. Assn. Adult Edn., Pittsburgh Chamber Commerce, Omicron Delta Kappa, Delta Mu Delta, Beta Gamma Sigma. Republican. Methodist. Mason. Clubs: University, Faculty. Author: Business Fluctuations and the American Labor Movement, 1915-22, 1924; Metal Industry of New York City and Environs, 1924. Home: 5289 Forbes St., Pittsburgh, Pa.

LANG, George F.; pres. Carr-Lowrey Glass Co.; b. Baltimore, Md., Dec. 20, 1883; s. Frederick C. and Mina (Magaw) L.; student Baltimore City Coll.; m. Marion N. Gift, Oct. 11, 1920. V.p. Carr Lowrey Glass Co., 1926-31, pres. since 1931. Home: 102 St. Albans Way. Office: Kloman and Wenburn Sts., Baltimore, Md.

LANG, Harold Locke, prof. of biology and public health; b. Franklin, N.H., Mar. 5, 1887; s. John A. and Caroline A. (Glines) L.; S.B., Mass. Inst. Tech., 1910; m. Lillian Adelaide Stanley, May 15, 1912; children—John Stanley, Harold Bickford. Asst. instr., Mass. Inst. of Tech., 1910-12; scientific asst., U.S. Dept. Agr., 1912-17, consulting specialist, 1917-20; prof. of biology and public health, Carnegie Inst. of Tech. since 1917. Fellow Am. Pub. Health Assn.; mem. Soc. of Am. Bacteriologists, A.A.A.S., Am. Assn. Univ. Profs., Sigma Xi, Phi Kappa Phi, Theta Chi. Episcopalian. Home: 403 Pasadena Drive, Fox Chapel, Pa. Office: Carnegie Institute of Technology, Pittsburgh, Pa.

LANG, Leon Solomon, rabbi; b. Palestine, May 9, 1898; s. David and Annie (David) L.; brought to U.S., 1898, naturalized citizen; B.S., Columbia U., 1927; A.M., Columbia U. Teachers Coll., 1929; Rabbi, Jewish Theol. Sem. of America, 1927; m. Rebecca Greenspan, Dec. 25, 1921; children—Ezra Johanan, Hedvah Ann. Began career as ednl. dir., Nat. Young Judea, 1920-22; exec. dir. Soc. for Advancement of Judaism, 1922-25; rabbi, Nyack, N.Y., 1926-27; rabbi, Cong. Oheb Shalom, Newark, N.J., since 1927; pres. Nat. Young Judea, 1928-29; treas. Rabbinical Assembly Amer., 1937-39, v.p., 1939-40. Mem. Newark Labor Relations Bd. since 1937, arbitrator in several labor disputes. Mem. Essex Co. Conf. of Jews and Christians. Dir. Conf. of Jewish Charities, Jewish Edn. Assn. Essex Co. Jewish religion. B'nai B'rith. Club: Kiwanis of Newark. Home: 109 Johnson Av., Newark, N.J. Office: 672 High St., Newark, N.J.

LANGE, Edward Henry, research engr.; b. Baltimore, Md., Jan. 4, 1892; s. John and Augusta (Hetz) L.; M.E., Cornell U., 1912; A.M., Harvard U., 1916; grad. student Johns Hopkins U., 1916; m. Beatrice Agnes Greene, May 13, 1936. Asst., phys. development, Carnegie Lab., Brookline, Mass., 1913-15; asst. physicist, U.S. Bur. of Standards, 1917; asst. examiner U.S. Patent Office, 1918; instr. U.S. Naval Acad., 1920-22; asst. prof. elec. engring., Post Grad. Sch. of U.S. Naval Acad., 1922-25; research engr., Ware Radio Corpn., New York, 1926; asso. dept. elec. engring., Johns Hopkins U., 1928-31; engaged in patent research and development on own acct., Baltimore, Md., since 1931. Served as ensign U.S.N.R.F., 1919, exptl. work on submarine detection devices, New London, Conn. Mem. Inst. Radio Engrs., Am. Phys. Soc., Sigma Xi, Sigma Tau. Republican. Lutheran. Contbr. sci. papers to jours. and proceedings of socs. Awarded many patents in automotive and radio development and in other fields. Home: 3801 Hillsdale Rd. Office: 4301 Maine Av., Baltimore, Md.

LANGE, Ernest Otto Albert, coll. prof.; b. Fond du Lac, Wis., Sept. 27, 1891; s. Christopher Frederick and Millie (Sells) L.; B.S. in E.E., U. of Wis., Madison, Wis., 1915; m. Jessie Mabel Thompson, Dec. 24, 1916; children—Donald, Ernest, Robert. Cadet engr. Westinghouse Electric & Mfg. Co., East Pittsburgh, Pa., 1915-16; instr. elec. engring. and athletics, U. of Wisconsin, Madison, Wis., 1916-19; with Stone, Huddle, Freeman, cons. engrs., Madison, Wis., summer 1917; asst. prof. elec. engring., Drexel Inst. Tech., Phila., Pa., 1919-25, asso. prof. since 1925, varsity basketball coach, 1924-27, 1935-38; with Phila. Elec. Co. summer 1927. Vestryman Trinity Ch., Swarthmore, Pa. Mem. Am. Inst. E.E. (mem. student activities com.), Soc. for Promotion of Engring. Edn., Theta Xi. Episcopalian. Author: Electric Laboratory Manual, 1927. Home: Baltimore Pike, Swarthmore, Pa. Office: Drexel Institute of Technology, Philadelphia, Pa.

LANGE, Linda Bartels, prof. bacteriology; b. New York, N.Y., Jan. 15, 1882; d. John Daniel and Alvina (Bartels) L.; A.B., Bryn Mawr Coll., 1903; M.D., Johns Hopkins U. Med. Sch., 1911. Interne, N.Y. Infirmary Women and Children, 1911-12; fellow Rockefeller Inst., 1912-14; pathologist H. A. Kelly Hosp., Baltimore, 1914-15; instr. pathology, U. of Wis. Med. Sch., 1915-16; instr. in medicine, Johns Hopkins Med. Sch., 1916-19, fellow Sch. Hygiene and asso. prof. bacteriology, 1919-37; prof. bacteriology and immunology, Woman's Med. Coll., Phila., since 1937. Pres. bd. trustees Haines Falls Free Library, Haines Falls, N.Y. Mem. A.A.A.S., Soc. Am. Bacteriologists. Home: 6357 Wayne Av. Office: 3300 Henry Av., Philadelphia, Pa.

LANGFELD, Herbert Sidney, psychologist; b. Phila., Pa., July 24, 1879; s. Charles and Flora R. L.; A.B., Central High Sch., Phila., 1897; Haverford Coll., 1897-98; Ph.D., Berlin, 1909; m. Florence Hoffman Purdy, Oct. 6, 1904; m. 2d, Mary Brita Bergland, of Baltimore, June 11, 1932. Sec. naval attaché, Am. Embassy, Berlin, 1902-03; research fellow, 1909-10, instr., 1910-15, asst. prof., 1915-22, asso. prof., 1922-24, acting dir., Psychol. Lab., 1917-19, dir., 1919-22, Harvard; prof. and dir., Psychol. Lab. since 1924; Stuart prof. of psychology since 1937, Princeton. Fellow A.A.A.S. (v.p. 1931); mem. Am. Psychol. Assn. (sec. 1917-19, pres. 1930, honorary president New York branch 1935-36). Research secretary Y.M.C.A., in France, 1918. Republican. Episcopalian. Clubs: Harvard (Boston); Harvard, Princeton (New York). Author: On the Psycho-physiology of a Prolonged Fast, 1914; An Elementary Laboratory Course in Psychology (joint author), 1916; The Aesthetic Attitude, 1920; Problems of Personalities (joint author and editor); Psychology, A Factual Textbook (joint author and editor), 1935; A Manual of Psychological Experiments (joint author and editor), 1937; Introduction to Psychology (joint author and editor), 1939. Editor of Psychol. Review (formerly editor of Psychol. Monographs). Home: Elm Road, Princeton, N.J.

LANGFORD, George Shealy, entomologist; b. Blythewood, S.C., Mar. 9, 1901; s. Clark and Kizzie (Timms) L.; B.S., Clemson Agrl. Coll., Clemson, S.C., 1921; M.S., U. of Md., College Park, Md., 1924; grad. student Colo. Agrl. Coll., Fort Collins, Colo.; Ph.D., O. State U., Columbus, O., 1929; m. Mary Riley, Sept. 9, 1926; children—Marilyn, George Shealy, Jr. Teacher of science, high sch., Lillington, N.C., 1921-22; grad. asst., U. of Md., 1922-24; deputy state entomologist, Fort Collins, 1924-27; asst. in zoölogy, O. State U., 1927-28; research, Crop Protection Inst., O. Expt. Sta., Wooster, O., 1928-29; specialist in insect control, U. of Md., since 1929, and asso. prof. entomology since 1937. Mem. Am. Assn. Econ. Entomologists, Entomol. Soc. of America, Washington Entomol. Soc., Sigma Xi, Epsilon Sigma Phi. Club: Rotary of College Park. Contbr. papers and articles on entomol. subjects to scientific bulls. Home: College Park, Md.

LANGMUIR, Dean, investment counsel; b. Elmsford, N.Y., June 18, 1886; s. Charles and Sadie (Comings) L.; grad. De Witt Clinton High Sch., N.Y. City, 1904; A.B., Williams Coll., Williamstown, Mass., 1910; m. Ethel M. Ivimey, Dec. 17, 1911; children—Robert Vose, Evelyn. Accountant for Western Electric Co., 1910-11; dept. comptroller City of Schenectady, N.Y., 1912; expert accountant N.Y. Pub. Service Commn., 1912-16; partner Thompson & Black, financial and industrial investigations, N.Y. City, 1916-21; with Irving Trust Co., and other banks, liquidating and operating various corpns., 1921-22; with Equitable Trust Co. of New York, 1922-26; in charge research dept. Scudder, Stevens & Clark, investment counsel, 1926-28; with Lazard Freres, 1929-30; v.p. in charge of research, Distributors Group, Inc., 1930-33; pres., Dean Langmuir, Inc., investment counsel, since 1933. Served as maj. U.S. Army Signal Corps, also Bur. of Aircraft Production, 1917-18. Trustee New Sch. for Social Research. Fellow Royal Econ. Soc. Mem. Acad. Polit. Science, Am. Econ. Assn., Am. Acad. Polit. and Social Science, Am. Statis. Assn., St. Andrews Soc., Phi Beta Kappa, Phi Gamma Delta. Presbyn. Clubs: University, India House, Lawyers, Ausable (New York). Contbr. to financial publs. Home: 105 Dana Pl., Englewood, N.J. Office: 90 Broad St., New York, N.Y.*

LANING, Harris, naval officer; b. Petersburg, Ill., Oct. 18, 1873; s. Caleb Barrett and Mary Esther (Harris) L.; prep. edn., Peekskill Mil. Acad.; grad. U.S. Naval Acad., 1895; m. Mabel Clare Nixon, July 24, 1900; 1 dau., Hester Marie. Commnd. ensign, U.S.N., May 19, 1891; advanced through grades to rear adm. Served on U.S.S. Philadelphia. Oregon and Mohican, 1895-98; served on U.S.S. Monadnock and comdr. U.S.S. Panay, Philippine Insurrection; with dept. English and law, U.S. Naval Acad., 1900-02; on U.S.S. Dolphin, 1902-05; in dept. ordnance and gunnery, U.S. Naval Acad., 1905-07; navigation officer U.S.S. Nebraska in cruise around world with Battle Fleet, 1907-10; in charge athletics and head of dept. of navigation, U.S. Naval Acad., 1910-13; comdr. U.S.S. Cassin and Reserve Destroyer Flotilla, 1913-16; with chief of Naval Operations, later in charge officer personnel div., Bureau of Navigation, asst. chief of bureau and acting chief, World War; chief of staff, Destroyer Force, U.S. Fleet, 1919-21; student, later head of dept. of tactics, Naval War Coll., 1921-24; comdr. U.S.S. Pennsylvania, 1924-26, U.S. Naval Training Sta., San Diego, Calif., 1926-27; apptd. chief of staff, U.S. Battle Fleet, 1927; comdr. Battleship Div. Two, U.S. Fleet, 1928-30; pres. U.S. Naval War Coll., 1930-33; comdr. cruisers, U.S. Fleet, with rank of vice admiral, 1933-35, comdr. Battle Force, with rank of admiral, 1935-36; comdt. Third Naval Dist. and comdt. United States Navy Yard, New York, 1936-37; retired, 1937; gov. U.S. Naval Home, Phila., since 1937. Decorated with Navy D.S.C.; campaign medals, Spanish-Am. War, Philippine Campaign, China Relief Expdn., Mexican Campaign, Dominican Campaign, World War (all U.S.); Order of Avis (Portugal); gold medal, as capt. of the United States Rifle Team winning first place in the Olympic Games, Stockholm, 1912. Episcopalian. Mason. Clubs:

Army and Navy, Army and Navy Country (Washington); New York Yacht. Home: Petersburg, Ill. Address: U.S. Naval Home, Philadelphia, Pa.

LANKARD, Frank Glenn, Biblical literature; b. Garnett, Kan., Sept. 1, 1892; s. William Irving and Rosetta May (McNatt) L.; U. of Kan., 1912-13; A.B., Baker U., Baldwin, Kan., 1916; S.T.B., Boston U., 1919; M.A., Northwestern U., 1921; B.D., Garrett Bibl. Inst., 1923; Ph.D., Northwestern U., 1926; m. Myrtle Etna Denlinger, Aug. 7, 1917. Asso. prof. Bibl. lit. and religious edn., U. of Chattanooga, 1922-23, prof., 1923-24; instr. Northwestern U., 1924-25, asst. prof. Bibl. lit., 1925-29; prof. Bibl. lit., Drew U. since 1929, dean Brothers Coll. (Drew) since 1931. Ordained ministry M.E. Ch., 1921. Mem. Soc. Bibl. Lit. and Exegesis, Religious Edn. Assn., Am. Assn. Univ. Profs., Nat. Assn. Bibl. Instrs. (pres. 1937), N.E.A., Eastern Assn. of Deans and Advisers of Men (pres. 1938-39), Pi Kappa Delta, Phi Beta Kappa, Phi Delta Kappa. Republican. Club: Rotary (Madison). Author: A History of the American Sunday School Curriculum, 1927; Difficulties in Religious Thinking, 1933; The Bible and the Life and Ideals of the English Speaking People, 1935; The Wanted Generation, 1937. Home: 11 Academy Rd., Madison, N.J.

LANKFORD, Henry Marshall, physician; b. Princess Anne, Md., Feb. 26, 1881; s. Henry Fillmore and Ida (Marshall) L.; A.B., Western Md. Coll., Westminster, Md., 1901; M.D., Johns Hopkins U. Med. Sch., 1905; m. Catherine Fitzsimmons, Dec. 23, 1908 (dec.); children—Catherine Marshall (Mrs. David J. Carver, Jr.), Henry Fillmore, 2d; m. 2d, Marguerite Harms, of Bogalusa, La., Feb. 2, 1939. Engaged in practice of medicine at Princess Anne, Md., since 1905; surgeon for Pa. R.R. Co. since 1923, examiner for nearly all the large ins. cos.; dep. med. examiner for Somerset Co. Served as capt. Med. Corps, U.S.A. during World War. Mem. Am. Med. Assn., Med. and Chirurg. Faculty of Md., Somerset Co. Med. Soc. Presbyn. Mason. Club: Rotary of Princess Anne. Home: "Beckford." Office: 69 Prince William St., Princess Anne, Md.

LANNING, Robert Lee, clergyman, editor; b. Cambridge, O., Aug. 5, 1872; s. George and Keziah (Speers) L.; A.B., Ohio Northern U., 1893, A.M., 1895; student Pittsburgh-Xenia Theol. Sem., 1895-98; D.D., Whitworth Coll., Tacoma, Wash., 1909; LL.D., Monmouth (Ill.) Coll., 1938; m. Nellie Fulton, 1900; m. 2d, Belle Edie, 1918; children—Robert Lee, George Edie. Ordained ministry U.P. Ch., 1898; pastor U.P. Ch., Everett, Wash., 1900-12, New Castle, Pa., 1913-18; asso. editor Bd. of Publ. U.P. Ch., 1918-26, editor since 1926, editor and gen. mgr. since 1935. Mem. Internat. S.S. Lesson Com. (now incorporated in Internat. Council of Religious Edn.), since 1918 (chmn. home daily Bible readings com., 1922—; chmn. com. for meeting British lesson com., 1937—). Trustee (sec.-treas. bd.) Gen. Assembly of the U.P. Ch. Republican. Home: 1234 Biltmore Av., Dormont, Pa. Office: 209 9th St., Pittsburgh, Pa.

LAPLACE, Louis Borsch, physician; b. Phila., Pa., Dec. 13, 1903; s. Ernest and Catherine (Borsch) L.; A.B., Georgetown U., 1924; M.D., U. of Pa. Med. Sch., 1928; m. Delphine Hollingsworth, May 4, 1935; children—Liane Delphine, Ernest. Interne Pa. Hosp., Phila., 1928-30; asst. dept. clin. research, Univ. Coll. Hosp., London, Eng., 1930-31; asst. Med. Univ. Clinic, Leipzig, Germany, 1932-33; fellow in medicine, Nat. Research Council, 1932; instr. physiology, U. of Pa. Med. Sch., 1933, instr. in medicine since 1934; asso. in cardiology, U. of Pa. Grad. Sch. Medicine since 1935; phys., Misericordia Hosp.; asst. phys. Phila. Gen. Hosp.; cons. cardiologist, Shriners Hosp. for Crippled Children, Phila. Orthopedic Hosp., Eastern State Penitentiary; phys. to French Consulate in Phila. Served as lt. Med. Corps, U.S.N.R.F. Fellow Am. Coll. Phys., Phila. Coll. Phys., A.M.A. Mem. Phila. Co. Med. Soc., Physiol. Soc. Phila., Alliance Francaise (v.p.), Phi Kappa Sigma, Nu Sigma Nu, Sigma Xi. Club: University. Home: 2222 Rittenhouse Sq. Office: 1900 Rittenhouse Sq., Philadelphia, Pa.

LARAMY, Robert Edward, sch. supt.; b. Catasauqua, Pa., Jan. 18, 1875; s. Charles and Elizabeth Ann (MacDaniel) L.; student Ulrich's Prep. Sch., Bethlehem, Pa., 1890-92; B.A., Lehigh U., Bethlehem, Pa., 1896, M.A., 1899; m. Mary Emily Brodhead, Nov. 23, 1901; children—William John, Rachel Elizabeth, Robert Edward, Mary Brodhead, Margaret Ellen. Instr., Moravian Schs., Bethlehem, Pa., 1896-1903; principal, Bethlehem High Sch., 1903-05; supt. schs., Phoenixville, Pa., 1905-13, Easton, Pa., 1913-22, Altoona, Pa., 1922-38; retired 1938; acting prof., Dept. of Edn., Lafayette Coll., Easton, Pa., since 1939. Mem. Bethlehem (Pa.) City Council, 1902-05; mem. Commn. on Study of Sch. System of Pa., 1922-23, Commn. on Study of Financial Support of Schs. for Blind and Deaf, 1927-30. Mem. bd. trustees Phoenixville (Pa.) Hosp., 1910-13; trustee Pa. Sch. Employees Retirement Assn., 1918-25. Mem. Alumni Assn. of Lehigh U. (pres. 1909-10), Pa. State Edn. Assn. (chmn. and treas. permanent fund since 1935), Advisory Alumni Council of Lehigh U. Coll. of Liberal Arts (chmn. since 1938), Easton (Pa.) Community Chest (mem. organizing com., 1921), Ninety-Six Club (pres. 1932-33) of Dept. of Sch. Adminstrs. of N.E.A., A.A.A.S., Phi Beta Kappa, Sigma Chi. Republican. Methodist. Club: Rotary (Bethlehem, Pa.). Author: Pennsylvania Civics, 1920; Manual—Guidance and Character, 1937; articles on lacrosse; asso. editor Youth's Digest since 1938. Address: 643 N. New St., Bethlehem, Pa.

LARDNER, Henry Ackley, engineer; b. Oconomowoc, Wis., Oct. 1, 1871; s. Richard and Catharine (Breck) L.; B.S. in E.E., U. of Wis., 1893, E.E., 1895; m. Ethel Anne Elmore, Sept. 17, 1902; children—Dorothy Ann, Richard Penn. V.p. J. G. White Engring. Corpn., N.Y. City. Mayor of Montclair, N.J., 1924-28. Past pres. N.J. State League of Municipalities; v.p. Bd. of Edn., Montclair; past pres. Montclair Community Chest; v.p. United Engring. Trustees, Inc. Fellow Am. Inst. E.E., Am. Soc. M.E.; mem. Montclair Soc. Engrs. (pres. 1930-31) S.A.R., Sigma Chi; ex-pres. New York Elec. Soc. Episcopalian. Clubs: Engineers, Lawyers (New York). Home: Montclair, N.J. Office: 80 Broad Street, New York, N.Y.

LARDNER, John J(oseph), educator; b. Baltimore, Md., Oct. 9, 1893; s. John and Catherine (Cryan) L.; M.A., St. Mary's U., Baltimore, 1917; S.T.L., Catholic U., Washington, D.C., 1921; S.T.D., Angelico U., Rome, 1927. Prof. philosophy, St. Mary's Sem., Baltimore, 1927-29, prof. theology and vice-pres., 1929-30, vice-pres. since 1934; rector St. Patrick's Sem., 1930-34. Address: St. Mary's Seminary, Baltimore, Md.

LARER, Richard White, surgeon; b. Phila., Pa., Oct. 4, 1877; s. William F. and Frances Ella (White) L.; M.D., Hahnemann Med. Coll., 1898; m. Sara Webb, June 26, 1906. In gen. practice medicine at Phila. since 1898, specializing in surgery since 1915; lecturer med. ethics and med. econs., Hahnemann Med. Coll., 1925-39; lecturer psychology, training schs. for nurses, St. Luke's Children's and Women's Homeopathic hosps., 1925-39; sr. surgeon, St. Luke's Children's Hosp.; chie. surgeon Women's Homeopathic Hosp. Fellow Am. Coll. Surgeons. Republican. Presbyterian. Home: 1407 E. Columbia Av., Philadelphia, Pa.

LARGENT, Robert Joseph, coll. prof.; b. PawPaw, W.Va., Dec. 16, 1877; s. Joseph and Martha Cornelia (Powell) L.; student prep. sch., Morgantown, 1896-99; A.B., W.Va. U., 1903; student Harvard U., 1908-09; A.M., U. of Chicago, 1923; m. Virginia Rider, July 3, 1906; 1 son John Joseph. Teacher, Marshall Coll., 1904-08; employed in U.S. Marshal's Office, Dept. of Justice, Washington, D.C., 1909-12; instr. Latin and history, Marshall Coll., 1912-22; dean Coll. of Arts and Sciences, 1924-28, prof. history since 1928. Mem. Am. Hist. Assn., Miss. Valley Hist. Assn., N.E.A., W.Va. Edn. Assn., W.Va. Acad. Science. Presbyn. (elder 1st Ch., Huntington, W.Va.). Contbr. to Indiana Teacher, W.Va. Review and Marshall Review. Home: 621 Elm St., Huntington, W.Va.

LARKIN, Charles Rozier, physicist and asso. prof. physics; b. Washington, D.C., Dec. 10, 1899; s. James Reid and Blanche D. (Faris) L.; A.B., U. of Va., 1923, A.M., 1925, Ph.D., 1929; unmarried. Engaged as instr. physics, U. of Va., 1922-23, instr. mathematics, 1923-28, research asso., 1928-29; asst. prof. physics, Lehigh U., Bethlehem, Pa., 1929-37, asso. prof. since 1937. Mem. Am. Phys. Soc., Optical Soc. of America, Seismol. Soc., Phi Beta Kappa, Sigma Xi. Independent Democrat. Clubs: Colonnade (University, Va.); Farmington (Charlottesville, Va.). Home: Manassas, Va. Office: Lehigh University, Bethlehem, Pa.

LARKIN, Fred Viall, univ. prof.; b. Verona, Wis., Apr. 2, 1883; s. Edwin Newcomb and Eudora (Viall) L.; B.S., U. of Wis., 1906, M.E., 1915; m. Nell Grant Wright, June 30, 1910; children—Franklin Jonathan, Richard Newcomb. Engr. and supt. Telluride (Colo.) Power Co., 1906-09; supt. Empire Engring. Corpn., Spencerport, N.Y., 1909-11; engr. Terry & Tench Co., Inc., N.Y. City, 1911-12; instr. mech. engring., Lehigh U., Bethlehem, Pa., 1912-13, asst. prof., 1913-15; asst. gen. supt. Harrisburg (Pa.) Pipe & Pipe Bending Co., 1915-19; prof. mech. engring., Lehigh U., since 1919, joint organizer industrial engring. curriculum, 1926, dir. since 1927, organizer comprehensive exam. for engring. sophomores, 1927, dir. rehabilitation of power plant, 1928; consultant on industrial management since 1919. Made trip around the world, sabbatical year, 1931-2. Mem. Am. Soc. M.E., Soc. for Promotion of Engring. Edn., Am. Management Asso. Republican. Methodist. Clubs: Rotary, Engineers' (Bethlehem, Pa.); Saucon Valley Country (Bethlehem, Pa.). Author numerous tech. articles. Home: 135 Wall St. Office: Lehigh University, Bethlehem, Pa.

LARNER, Chester Waters, hydraulic engr.; b. Elizabeth, N.J., Mar. 3, 1881; s. William Hill and Frances (Worthington) L.; student Baltimore (Md.) Poly. Inst., 1893-97. Designer Cramps Shipyard, Phila., Pa., 1902-06; hydraulic engr. Wellman-Seaver-Morgan Co., Cleveland, O., 1907-17; pres. Larner-Johnson Valve & Engring. Co., Phila., 1918-22; pres. Larner Engring. Co., cons. engrs., Phila., since 1922; pres. Larner Machine Co. since 1927. Asso. mem. U.S. Naval Cons. Bd., 1916-18. Mem. Am. Soc. M.E., Am. Soc. C.E., Am. Inst. E.E., Engring. Inst. of Canada, British Inst. M. E., British Inst. C. E. Republican. Club: Union League (Phila.). Pioneer in design hydraulic machinery for water power plants; designed and built primary equipment for many larger plants in U.S. and Canada and designed machinery for plants in almost every civilized country. Home: "The Kenilworth," Germantown, Pa. Office: Lincoln-Liberty Bldg., Philadelphia, Pa.

LAROQUE, Herbert E.; ophthalmologist St. Joseph's Hosp. Address: 1800 N. Charles St., Baltimore, Md.

LARRABEE, Albert S., lawyer; b. Lakewood, N.J., Dec. 29, 1899; s. Albert S. and Rose (McKee) L.; student Brown U., 1919-22; A.B., Yale U., 1924; LL.B., Harvard U. Law Sch., 1927; unmarried. Admitted to N.J. bar as atty., 1928, as counselor, 1931; engaged in gen. practice of law as individual at Lakewood, N.J., since 1928; dir. Lakewood Trust Co. since 1935. Served as sec. Ocean Co. Rep. Exec. Com. since 1928. Mem. Ocean Co. Bar Assn. (pres., 1937-39), N.J. Soc. Colonial Wars. Republican. Episcopalian (vestryman All Saints Ch.). Clubs: Rotary (Lakewood); Island Heights Yacht. Home: 15 Lexington Av. Office: 251 Second St., Lakewood, N.J.

LARRABEE, Don Marshall, pres. judge court of common pleas; b. Emporium, Pa., Mar. 11, 1877; s. Marcellus Marshall and Georgiana (Mayo) L.; A.B., Allegheny Coll., 1899; LL.B., U. of Pa. Law Sch., 1902; m. Olive E. Moore, Oct. 7, 1903; children—Don Lincoln, David Marcell, John Amsden. Admitted to Pa. bar, 1902, and engaged in gen. practice of law at Williamsport, 1905-31; elected judge ct.

common pleas, Lycoming Co., 1931, for ten yr. term. Served as exec. sec. Lycoming Co. Chapter, Pa. Council Nat. Defense, 1917-18. Chmn. Rep. Co. Com., 1910-11. Trustee Dickinson Jr. Coll., Williamsport, Pa. First pres. Consol. Sportsmen of Lycoming Co. (3,000 mem. organized for fish and game conservation). Mem. Am. Hist. Assn., Pa. Bar Assn., Sigma Alpha Epsilon (presided at installation of chapter at U. of Pa., 1901). Republican. Mem. M.E. Ch. Mason (K.T.). I.O.O.F. Clubs: Howard of Knights Templar, Black Forest Hunting and Fishing. Writer monograph, The Journals of George Washington and His Guide, Christopher Gist, on the Historic Mission to the French Forts in 1753. Delivered the address at unveiling William McKinley bronze memorial at Centennial, Allegheny Coll., 1915. Home: 601 Glenwood Av., Williamsport, Pa.

LA RUE, Daniel Wolford, prof. psychology; b. Newton Twp., Lackawanna Co., Pa., Oct. 9, 1878; s. Daniel Wolford and Abigail Ann (Warren) L.; grad. State Normal Sch., East Stroudsburg, Pa., 1898 (valedictorian); A.B., Dickinson Coll., 1904 (valedictorian), A.M., 1905; A.M., Harvard, 1907, Ph.D., 1911; studied Columbia, 1908, Cold Spring Harbor, N.Y., 1913; m. Mabel Scudder Guinnip, Dec. 24, 1907; 1 son, Daniel Wolford. Teacher and prin. elementary sch., Chinchilla, Pa., 1898-1900; same, Grammar Sch., Boonton, N.J., 1900-01; supervising prin. schs., Milford, Del., 1904-06; supt. schs., Augusta, Me., 1907-10; prof. psychology and prin., head of dept., State Teachers Coll., East Stroudsburg, 1911—; lecturer Harvard Grad. Sch. of Edn.; mem. ednl. survey, Honesdale, Pa., 1921. Served as capt. Sanitary Corps, U.S.A., Jan.-Dec. 1918; chief psychol. examiner, Camp Meade, Md. Mem. N.E.A., Am. Eugenics Soc., Inc., Pa. State Ednl. Assn., Phi Beta Kappa, Nat. Com. for Mental Hygiene; research worker, A.A.A.S., on value of a phonetic alphabet, 1919. Fellow American Association Advancement Science. Unitarian. Author: Outline of a Study of the Self (with Dr. Robert M. Yerkes), 1914; Making the Most of the Children, 1916; The Science and the Art of Teaching, 1917; Psychology for Teachers, 1920; The Child's Mind and the Common Branches, 1924; Mental Hygiene, 1927. Contbr. Jour. of N.E.A., Educational Forum, etc. Home: East Stroudsburg, Pa.

LA RUE, Edwin Davis, banking; b. East Bound Brook, N.J., Dec. 11, 1901; s. William Burrell and Adella (Worthington) La R.; grad. high sch., Plainfield, N.J.; student accounting, Pace & Pace; tax courses, N.Y. Univ.; m. Gladys Haight, June 3, 1922; children—Edwin Davis, Jr., Richard W. Began as clk. Union Trust Co., New York, N.Y., 1917, later merged into Central Union Trust Co. and finally Central Hanover Bank & Trust Co., asst. sec. in trust dept. of combined instn., specializing in estate adminstrn. to 1934; v.p. and trust officer Montclair Trust Co. Republican. Baptist. Club: Kiwanis (Montclair). Home: 21 Sutton Pl., Verona, N.J. Office: 475 Bloomfield Av., Montclair, N.J.

La RUE, Mabel Guinnip, author; b. nr. Honesdale, Pa.; d. William Baker and Florence R. (Scudder) Guinnip; ed. Del. Valley Acad., Damascus, Pa., Pa. State Teachers Coll., East Stroudsburg, Syracuse U.; m. Daniel Wolford La Rue, Dec. 24, 1907; 1 son, Daniel Wolford 3d. Taught pub. schs., N.Y. and Pa., Pa. State Teachers Coll., East Stroudsburg; writer of juvenile fiction since 1920. Elected honorary member Eugene Field Society. Republican. Unitarian. Author: The F-U-N Book, 1923; Under the Story Tree, 1924; In Animal Land, 1924; The Billy Bang Book, 1927; Little Indians, 1930; The Good Time Book, 1931; Zip, The Toy Mule, 1932; Hoot-Owl, 1935; The Tooseys, 1938. Contbr. to Story Parade and other magazines for children. Home: East Stroudsburg, Pa.

LA SALLE, Dorothy Marguerite, educator; b. Lake Geneva, Wis., June 2, 1895; d. Charles Onézine and Mary (Lawson) La S.; B.S., Columbia U., Teachers Coll., 1917, A.M., same, 1931. Engaged in teaching, Detroit, Mich., and Greenwich, Conn., 1917-20; teacher, State Normal Sch., Bloomsburg, Pa., 1921-22; asst. supervisor, second asst., first asst., pub. schs., Detroit, Mich., 1922-26; staff mem., Child Study Assn., New York City, 1926-29; exec. sec. Com. on Sch. Child, White House Conf. on Child Health and Protection, 1929-31; dir. health and phys. edn., pub. schs., East Orange, N.J., since 1931; asst. prof. U. of Wash. summer sch., 1923, U. of Wis. summer sch., 1939. Mem. exec. council N.J. Phys. Edn. Assn.; past mem. exec. com. Dance Sect. and Women's Athletic Sect., Am. Assn. for Health, Phys. Edn. and Recreation. Mem. Nat. Edn. Assn., Progressive Edn. Assn., Am. Assn. of Health, Phys. Edn. and Recreation, N.J. Teachers Assn., N.J. Phys. Ed. Assn. Episcopalian. Author: Play Activities, 1926; Rhythms and Dances, 1926; Physical Education for the Class Room Teacher, 1937. Co-author (with A. S. Barr and others), Standards for Elementary School Practice, 1925. Editor, The School Health Program, 1932. Contbr. articles to mags and journs. Home: 111 Halsted St., East Orange, N.J.

LASSER, Aaron, lawyer; b. Newark, N.J., Aug. 8, 1895; s. Louis and Sarah (Eisner) L.; student Cornell U., 1914-16; LL.B., N.J. Law Sch., 1918; m. Hazel Yuells, Mar. 15, 1924; children—Lawrence L., John Owen. Admitted to N.J. bar; supreme ct. commr., 1931; spl. master in chancery, 1937; mem. firm Hannoch & Lasser; prof. of law, Univ. of Newark; admitted to practice before the Supreme Ct. of the U.S., 1939. Served in U.S.N. during World War. An organizer, then pres., dir. and trustee Y.M.H.A. and Y.W.H.A. of Newark; a founder Mercer Beasley Sch. of Law, Newark. Mem. finance com. Amateur Athletic Assn.; trustee and sec. Univ. of Newark. Mem. Am., N.J. State, and Essex Co. bar assns., Acad. Polit. Science, Am. Legion, Lambda Alpha Phi. Jewish religion. Mason (32°). B'nai B'rith. Elk. Clubs: Down Town (Newark); Mountain Ridge Country (West Caldwell); Carteret Book; Cornell of Northern N.J. Co-editor: Practice, Pleading and Procedure in New Jersey, 1936. Home: 31 Washington Park, Maplewood, N.J. Office: 17 Academy St., Newark, N.J.

LASSER, Jacob Kay, public accountant; b. Newark, N.J., Oct. 7, 1896; son of Morris and Rebecca L.; student New York U., 1915-17; B.S., Pa. State Coll., 1920, Industrial Engr.; m. Terese Reuben, Jan. 1, 1924; children—Donald Judd, Barbara Ann. C.P.A., State of N.Y., 1923; in practice as mem. firm J. K. Lasser & Co., New York, since 1923. Served in U.S. Navy, 1917-18. Mem. Am. Inst. Accountants, N.Y. Soc. C.P.A., N.J. Soc. C.P.A., Nat. Assn. Cost Accountants. Clubs: Engineers (New York); Mountainridge (West Caldwell, N.J.). Author: Federal Securities Act Procedure (with J. A. Gerardi), 1934; Your Income Tax, 1939. Home: 307 West End Rd.; South Orange, N.J. Office: 1440 Broadway, New York, N.Y.

.LATHAM, Harold Strong, author; b. Marlboro, Conn., Feb. 14, 1887; s. Charles Arthur and Minnie Alice (Strong) L.; A.B., Columbia, 1909; unmarried. With the Macmillan Co., pubs., since 1909, now vice-pres., dir. and in charge gen. pub. dept. Republican. Universalist. Clubs: Players, Columbia University, Nat. Arts, Phi Sigma Kappa (New York); Unteora (Catskill Mountains). Author: Under Orders—The Story of Tim and the Club, 1918; Marty Lends a Hand, 1919; Jimmy Quigg, Office Boy, 1920; At the Sign of the Feather, 1924, 30; The Perry Boys; The Making of Larry; The Thirteenth Domino. Home: 17 Pleasant Pl., Arlington, N.J.

LATHEM, Abraham Lance, clergyman; b. Hanover Twp. 30 miles west of Pittsburgh, Pa., May 26, 1866; s. Robert and Eliza (Lance) L.; B.A., Washington and Jefferson Coll., 1890; student Western Theol. Sem., Allegheny, Pa., 1891; grad. Princeton Theol. Sem., 1893; Ph. D., Wooster U. (now Wooster Coll.), 1901; D.D., Washington and Jefferson Coll., 1915; m. Elizabeth McKeag, May 16, 1893; children—Lance B., Helen G. (Mrs. John C. Taber), Elizabeth A., Evangeline (Mrs. Ewing Hill Buysse). Ordained Presbyn. ministry, 1893; pastor Martinsburg and Duncansville chs., Blair Co., Pa., 1893-95, N. 10th Street Ch., Phila., 1895- 1904, 3d Ch., Chester, Pa., since Feb. 1904. Started "Summer Bible School" movement in Chester, Pa., 1911, which has extended through U.S. and into foreign countries; pres. and dir. Summer Bible School Assn. Prohibitionist. Author: The Way of Life, 1911; The Gospel by John (a study), 1927; Character Building, 1928; The Acts (a study), 1934; Sunrise, 1937; also various booklets pertaining to the Bible. Home: 434 E. Broad St., Chester, Pa.

LATIMER, Thomas E(dwin), physician and surgeon; b. Charles Co., Md., May 12, 1874; s. James Brawner and Mary Louisa (Sedwick) L.; B.Sc., St. John's Coll., Annapolis, Md., 1894; M.D., U. of Md. Med. Sch., 1907; (hon.) A.M., St. John's Coll., 1898; m. Eleanor Grace Gourley, June 17, 1901. Engaged in gen. practice of medicine and surgery at Hyattsville, Md., since 1908. Served as chmn. Rep. State Central Com. for Prince George Co., Md., 1902-08. Chmn. local Red Cross Chapter, 1920-24. Mem. Am. Med. Assn., Med. and Chirurg. Faculty of Md., Prince George Co. Med. Assn. Republican. Episcopalian. Mason. Home: 40 Franklin St., Hyattsville, Md.

LATTA, Harrison Wainwright, retired engr.; b. Phila., Pa., Sept. 11, 1871; s. James William and Susan Eyre (Withers) L.; student Central High Sch., Phila., Pa., 1884-88; B.S., U. of Pa., 1891, C.E., 1891; m. Ella Fritz Roberts, Nov. 17, 1903. Engr. corps Pa. R.R., Pa. and N.J., 1891-94; asst. engr. Peoples Traction Co., Phila., 1894-96; div. engr. Union Traction Co., Phila., 1896-98; mem. firm Latta and Terry, engrs. and contractors, Phila., 1898-1915, Latta and Roberts, 1915-33; retired 1933. Mem. Am. Soc. C.E. (pres. Phila. sect. 1923-24), Loyal Legion, Phi Delta Theta. Republican. Episcopalian. Clubs: Union League (Phila.). Address: 4418 Spruce St., Philadelphia, Pa.

LAUBENSTEIN, Franklin Jonas, lawyer; b. Minersville, Pa., Sept. 3, 1878; s. Albert L. and Mary Ida (Roads) L.; student Lehigh U., 1895-96; LL.B., Dickinson Law Sch., 1899 and 1902; m. Sarah Edna Kuhn, Jan. 1, 1915. Admitted to W.Va. bar, 1900, and began practice at Clarksburg, 1900; admitted to Pa. Supreme Court, 1905, and since practiced at Ashland, Pa.; pres. Laubenstein Mfg. Co.; solicitor Ashland Savings & Loan Assn., Citizens Saving & Loan Assn. Mem. Am. Bar Assn., Pa. Bar Assn., Schuylkill Co. Bar Assn. Republican. Lutheran. Elk. Clubs: Ashland Gun and Country, Fountain Springs Country. Home: 308 S. 2d St. Office: Post Office Bldg., Ashland, Pa.

LAUCHHEIMER, Sylvan Hayes, lawyer; b. Baltimore, Md., Jan. 22, 1870; s. Meyer Henry and Babette (Eichberg) L.; A.B., Johns Hopkins U., 1890; LL.B., U. of Md. Law Sch., Baltimore, Md., 1892; m. Florence Ambach, Apr. 27, 1905. Admitted to Md. bar, 1892 and since engaged in gen. practice of law at Baltimore; mem. firm Lauchheimer & Lauchheimer since 1925; served as asst. city solicitor and dep. city solicitor of Baltimore, 1905-11; dir. following corpns. in Baltimore, Md., Commercial Credit Co., Green Realty Corpn., The Hecht Co., S. Kann Sons Co., Muskin Shoe Co., Oliver Realty Co., J. Schoeneman, Inc., Schloss Bros. & Co., Inc., Shufac Realty Corpn., Stanley Mfg. Co., United States Fidelity & Guaranty Co. Mem. Am., Baltimore City bar assns., Md. State Bar Assn. (pres. 1921-22), Am. Law Inst., Phi Beta Kappa. Democrat. Jewish religion. Mason. Clubs: Chesapeake, Johns Hopkins, Phoenix, Suburban, University (Baltimore). Home: Riviera, 3-A, Lake Drive and Linden Av. Office: 111 N. Charles St., Baltimore, Md.

LAUDENSLAGER, Ray V., supt. of schools; b. Selinsgrove, Pa., Feb. 25, 1901; s. William Lincoln and Jane M. (Comfort) L.; grad. Selinsgrove High Sch., 1919; A.B., Susquehanna U., 1923, A.M., 1929; grad. student New York U., 1930-33; m. Grace C. Cawley, Nov. 11, 1922; children—Meredith Jane, Phyllis Marie. Teacher, Clearfield (Pa.) High Sch., 1923-24; prin., Chestnuthill Twp. Schools, 1924-28; supervising prin., Weatherly, Pa., Pub. Schs., since 1928. Mem. N.E.A., Pa. State Edn. Assn., Phi Mu Delta. Republican. Lutheran. Mason, Odd

Fellow. Club: Rotary (Weatherly, Pa.). Home: Eurana Av. Office: Spring St., Weatherly, Pa.

LAUER, Conrad Newton, pub. utility exec.; b. Three Tuns, Montgomery Co., Pa., Nov. 25, 1869; s. Herman and Margaret Lukens (Clayton) L.; ed. pub. and pvt. schs., Montgomery Co.; hon. M.E., Stevens Inst. Tech., 1930; m. Katherine Pierrepont Ifill, Nov. 2, 1893; children—Ida Felicia (Mrs. George Potter Darrow, Jr.), Harry Ifill. Time clk. to plant supt. Link Belt Co., 1893-1902; industrial engr., Dodge & Day (later Day & Zimmerman, Inc.), 1902-17, sec. and gen. mgr., 1917-19, treas., 1919-26, v.p., 1926-29; pres. and dir. Phila. Gas Works Co. since 1929; v.p. and dir. The United Gas Improvement Co., Cold Spring Bleachery, Bates, Inc., Baldwin Locomotive Securities Corpn., Baldwin-Southwark Corpn., Cramp Brass & Iron Foundries Co., Federal Steel Casting Co., I. P. Morris & De La Vergne, Inc.; dir. and chmn. exec. com. Sharp & Dohme, Inc., Baldwin Locomotive Works; dir. Welsbach Co. Mem. Am. Acad. Polit. and Social Science, Princeton Engring. Assn. (hon.), Art Club of Phila. Chmn. industrial com., Phila., 2d and 3d Liberty Loan drives. Mem. Phila. Gas Commn. (sec.); v.p., mem. bd. and exec. com. Regional Planning Fed. of Phila. Tri-State Dist.; mem. bd. mgrs. Beneficial Saving Fund Soc. Trustee Stevens Inst. Tech., Welfare Fed. Mem. Am. Soc. M.E. (ex-pres.), Am. Gas Assn. (mem. exec. com., pres., dir., mem. exec. bd.), Soc. for Advancement of Management, Franklin Inst., Newcomen Soc. of London, Pa. State Chamber Commerce, Phila. Chamber Commerce (v.p., mem. exec. com.), Pa. Acad. Fine Arts. Republican. Episcopalian. Mason. Clubs: Manufacturers, Engineers, Racquet, Poor Richard, University, Midday, Penn, Wanderers, Union League, Orpheus (Phila.); Engineers, India House (New York); Manufacturers Country (Oreland, Pa.). Author: Engineering in American Industry. Home: "Westlawn" Penllyn, Montgomery Co., Pa. Office: 1401 Arch St., Philadelphia, Pa.

LAUFFER, George Nevin, clergyman; b. Apollo, Pa., Nov. 24, 1878; s. Jacob D. and Elizabeth (Ament) L.; prep. edn. Apollo Public Schools and private tutoring; A.B., Gettysburg Coll., 1899, A.M., 1902, D.D., 1921; B.D., Luth. Theol. Sem., Gettysburg, Pa., 1902; m. Naomi Myers, Oct. 8, 1902. Ordained to ministry of Lutheran Ch., 1902; pastor Trinity Ch., McKeesport, Pa., 1902-03, First Luth. Ch., New Oxford, Pa., 1903-10, Zion Luth. Ch., Newville, Pa., 1910-15, St. John's Ch., Steelton, Pa., 1915-19, Christ-Second Luth. Ch., Altoona, Pa., 1919-31; pastor St. John's Luth. Ch., Kittanning, Pa., since 1931. Trustee Tressler Orphans' Home, Loysville, Pa., 1916-19; sec. West Pa. Synod, 1914-15; pres. Allegheny Synod, 1929-31; dir. Theol. Sem., Gettysburg, Pa., 1930-31; mem. Bd. of Deaconess Work of United Luth. Ch., 1926-38; del. to United Luth. Ch. Convs., 1924, 30, 36; pres. East Conf., Pittsburgh Synod, 1934-38. Mem. Sigma Alpha Epsilon. Republican. Lutheran. Mason. Home: 220 N. Jefferson St., Kittanning, Pa.

LAUFFER, Vada Dilling Kuns, musician; b. McPherson, Kan.; d. John Leslie and Maria Ann (Dilling) Kuns; student McPherson (Kan.) Coll., 1909-10, Washburn Coll., Topeka, Kan., 1910-12; B.M., Bethany Conservatory of Music, Lindsborg, Kan., 1918; studied with Arthur Freidheim, Alexander Siloti, Isidor Philipp, Katherine Ruth Heyman; m. Ernst Lauffer, Sept. 7, 1935. Began as pianist and teacher, Cleveland, O., 1918; head of music dept., Central Coll. and Acad., McPherson, Kan., 1914-16; instr., Laurel Sch., Cleveland, O., 1918-20; pvt. teacher, Phila., since 1920; made musical debut, Phila., 1922. Mem. women's com. of Phila. Chamber String Simfonietta. Republican. Episcopalian. Clubs: Play and Players, Phila. Music, Art Alliance (Phila.). Address: 1632 Pelham Rd., Beechwood, Upper Darby, Pa.

LAUGHLIN, George (McCully), Jr., steel mfr.; b. Pittsburgh, Pa., Feb. 25, 1873; s. George M. and Isabel B. (McKennan) L.; prep. edn., Shadyside Acad., and St. Paul's Sch., Concord, N.H.; student freshman yr. Sheffield Scientific Sch. (Yale), class of 1895; m. Henrietta Z., d. John Z. Speer, Jan. 10, 1895; children—George M., Katharine S. (Mrs. Erl C. B. Gould), Isabel, John S. Connected with Jones & Laughlin Steel Corpn. since 1893, made v.p. and mem. exec. com., 1923, now dir. Mem. Delta Psi. Republican. Episcopalian. Clubs: Pittsburgh, Duquesne, Pittsburgh Golf, Allegheny Country, Fox Chapel Golf; Racquet and Tennis (New York). Home: Woodland Rd. Address: Jones & Laughlin Steel Corpn., Pittsburgh, Pa.

LAUGHLIN, Irwin (Boyle), diplomat; b. Pittsburgh, Pennsylvania, April 26, 1871; s. Maj. George McCully and Isabel Bowman (McKennan) L.; B.A., Yale University, 1893; m. Thérese, d. Adrian Iselin, Sept. 18, 1912; children—Gertrude (wife of Lt. Hubert Winthrop Chanler, U.S. Navy), Alexander (deceased). Entered office of Jones & Laughlin, Ltd., steel manufacturers, Pittsburgh, 1894; treas. Jones & Laughlin Steel Co., 1900-03. Pvt. sec. to Am. minister to Japan, 1903-05; 2d sec. Am. Legation at Tokyo, 1905-06; sec. Legation at Bangkok and consul gen. for Siam, 1906-07; 2d sec. Legation at Peking, Mar.-Sept. 1907; 2d sec. Embassy at St. Petersburg, 1907-08; sec. legation to Greece and Montenegro, 1908-09; 2d sec. Embassy at Paris, Aug.-Dec. 1909; sec. spl. Embassy to Sultan of Turkey, Oct.-Nov. 1910; sec. Embassy at Berlin, Dec. 21, 1909-Sept. 1912 (chargé d'affaires June-Oct. 1911); sec. Embassy at London, 1912-17 (chargé d'affaires, Dec. 15, 1912-May 24, 1913, July-Oct. 1916, May-July and Oct.-Dec. 1918), and was counselor of the Embassy, 1916-1919, when took extended leave of absence; on duty at Conf. for Limitation of Armament, as sec. to Henry Cabot Lodge, 1921. E.E. and M.P. to Greece, 1924-26; ambassador to Spain, 1929-33. Representative for U.S. on Internat. Commn. for the Advancement of Peace between U.S. and Denmark; mem. bd. regents Smithsonian Instn., 1923-35. Republican. Mem. Hist. Soc. Pa., Psi Upsilon, Scroll and Key (Yale), Mil. Order Loyal Legion. Clubs: Pittsburgh, Pittsburgh Golf (Pittsburgh); University, Knickerbocker (New York City); Metropolitan (Washington); Touring Club de France; St. James's, Burlington Fine Arts (London). Home: Pittsburgh, Pa. Address: Meridian House, Crescent Place, Washington, D.C.

LAUGHLIN, Ledlie Irwin, educator; b. Pittsburgh, Pa., Apr. 25, 1890; s. James Ben and Clara Belle (Young) L.; grad. St. Paul's Sch., Concord, N.H., 1908; Litt.B., Princeton, 1912; m. Roberta Moody Howe, Sept. 25, 1925; children—Leighton Howe, James Ben II, Ledlie Irwin, Jr., Robert Moody. Asso. with Jones & Laughlin Steel Co., Pittsburgh, Pa., in various positions, 1912-17, then in sales dept. including sales mgr. of Buffalo Office, 1919-28; asst. to dean of freshman, Princeton Univ. since 1928; dir. Jones & Laughlin Steel Corpn. Served as 1st lt. inf. U.S.A. then capt., regtl. personnel adjt., 1917-19, with A.E.F. Trustee Princeton Country Day Sch. Mem. Pewter Collectors Club of Boston. Republican. Clubs: Nassau, Pretty Brook Tennis (Princeton); Hyannis Port and Hyannis Port Yacht (Hyannis Port, Mass.); Princeton (New York). Now preparing a book on American pewter. Home: Drakes Corner, Princeton, N.J. Office: Nassau Hall, Princeton, N.J.

LAUGHLIN, Samuel O., Jr.; pres. Wheeling Tile Co.; officer or dir. many companies. Address: Wheeling, W.Va.

LAUGHLIN, Sara Elizabeth, social worker; b. Wheeling, W.Va.; d. James and Sara Ann (Bloomer) Laughlin; ed. St. Joseph's Acad., New York Sch. of Social Work, and U. of Pa.; unmarried. Formerly dir. Big Sister Council, Rochester, N.Y.; now counselor parish schools, White-William Foundation, Phila., since 1921. Chmn. social service com. of Internat. Fed. of Cath. Alumnæ since 1930; mem. bd. dirs. Phila. Social Service Exchange; mem. vocational guidance com. Women's Univ. Club. Mem. Am. Assn. Social Workers, Vocational Guidance Assn., Delta Kappa Gamma. Democrat. Roman Catholic. Home: 5106 Spruce St., West Philadelphia, Pa. Office: White-William Foundation, 21st and Parkway, Philadelphia, Pa.

LAURIE, Frank Alan, univ. prof.; b. Corry, Pa., Dec. 2, 1887; s. Frank and Mary (Workman) L.; B.S., U. of Pa., 1909, also A.M. and Ph.D.; study, U. of Lausanne, Switzerland, 1910; m. Dessa C. Ebbert, Feb. 6, 1917; children—Jean Dunlap, Frances Ebbert. Engaged as instr. English, Roberts Coll., Constantinople, Turkey, 1909-11; instr. in French and asst. to dean of coll., U. of Pa., 1911-14; became instr. English, U. of Pa., 1915, now prof. Mem. Sigma Phi Sigma. Episcopalian. Home: 121 County Line Rd., Bryn Mawr, Pa.

LAURITZEN, John Irvin, plant physiologist; b. Moroni, Utah, July 28, 1884; s. Peter and Caroline (Jensen) L.; B.S., Utah State Coll. Agr., Logan, Utah, 1914; Ph.D., Cornell U., 1918; m. Edna Stephenson, Feb. 17, 1925; 1 son, John Irvin, Jr. Asst. botanist, Utah State Coll., Logan, Utah, 1912-13, instr., 1913-14; asst. plant physiologist, Cornell U., 1915-16, instr., 1917; asst. pathologist, Bur. Plant Industry, U.S. Dept. Agr., 1918-19, pathologist, 1920-30, sr. physiologist since 1930; career has been devoted to research work in plant pathology and plant physiology, and of late, research in physiology of sugar cane. Mem. A.A.A.S., Am. Phytopathol. Soc., Am. Soc. Plant Physiologists, Washington Acad. Scis., Sigma Xi. Club: Cosmos (Washington). Home: 4005 Leland St., Chevy Chase, Md.

LAVERTY, Elizabeth Stevens, artist; b. Scranton, Pa.; d. Guy Ernest and Maud Manderson (McLean) Stevens; art. edn. St. Botolph Art Sch., Boston, Pa. Museum Sch. of Industrial Arts; m. Maris Alexander Laverty, March 27, 1926. Artist in water colors since 1921. Exhibited at: Pa. Acad. Fine Arts, 1933, 34, 35, 36, 38; Corcoran Art Gallery, Washington Water Color Club, Washington, D.C., 1934; Am. Water Color Soc., New York, 1934; Phila. Art Alliance, 1933, 34, 35, 36, 37, 38. Awards: Beaux Arts medal, Museum School of Industrial Arts, 1921. Mem. Phila. Water Color Club, Phila. Art Alliance, Alumni Assn. of Museum School of Industrial Arts, Skating Club, Humane Soc. (Phila.), Soc. of Sponsors of the U.S. Navy. Home: Derwen Rd., Merion, Pa.

LAW, Clyde Otis, gen. agt. life ins. co.; b. Lawford, W.Va., Oct. 14, 1883; s. Martin L. and Mida (McKinley) L.; B.S., W.Va. Wesleyan Coll., Buckhannon, 1909; M.B.A., Harvard U. Sch. Bus. Adminstrn., 1913; m. Maude Lininger, June 24, 1914; children—Helen (Mrs. Thorold S. Funk), John M., Margery. Employed as dist. agt. for Northwestern Mutual Life Ins. Co. of Milwaukee, Wis., at Clarksburg, W.Va., 1913-19, gen. agt. for state of W.Va. and five counties in O., at Wheeling, W.Va. since 1920; served as mem. Commn. on Unification of Meth. Chs. consummated at Kansas City, Mo., 1939. Pres. bd. trustees W.Va. Wesleyan Coll., Buckhannon, W.Va. since 1933. Mem. Kappa Alpha. Republican. Methodist. Clubs: Fort Henry, Rotary (Wheeling). Home: 120 Edgwood St. Office: Hawley Bldg., Wheeling, W.Va.

LAW, Harrison, insurance analyst, pub. ins. data; b. Brooklyn, N.Y., Feb. 20, 1876; s. Samuel H. and Jennie (Benson) L.; student public sch., Brooklyn, N.Y., 1881-89, gen. studies including accounting, stenography, Y.M.C.A., Brooklyn, 1889-93; m. Grace Isabel Davis, Mar. 1900; children—Jean I., Dr. Harrison E., George W. Began as file clk. German Am. Ins. Co. (now known as Great American), New York, 1894; as mgr. local exchange dept. (now reinsurance dept.), instrumental in having first reinsurance co. admitted to U.S. (The Kolnische), 1898; statistician and compiler fire insurance data, The Spectator, New York, 1900-02; originated Laws, Taxes & Fees, pub. by Spectator Co.; asst. loss clk. London & Lancashire Ins. Co., New York, 1902-04; proofchecker, Loss com., N.Y. Bd. Underwriters, 1904-05; mgr. loss dept. and adjuster National Union Ins. Co., Pittsburgh, Pa., 1905-06, Eagle Fire Co. (to handle San Francisco losses), New York, 1906-07; assisted in orgn. N.J. Fire Ins. Co., 1910; organized Eagle Fire Ins. Co., Newark, N.J., as reinsurance co., 1913; consultant in orgn. of loss depts. and automobile depts. in various ins. cos., 1907-18; mgr. ins. dept. and statistician Nat. Acceptance Co., Boston, Mass., 1918-19; independent adjuster of losses for cos. since 1920; mgr. Automobile Adjusting Co., Newark, N.J., since 1920;

started publishing statistical tables as hobby after leaving Spectator Co., 1900, now issue annually Law's Statistical Tables (fire and marine cos.), Laws Comparative Tables (liability cos.), The Ins. Broker-Agent (laws of all states applying to brokers), Return Premium Tables, Fire Insurance Co. Directory. Mason (life mem., Brooklyn, N.Y.). Clubs: Blue Goose Internat., Masonic (Nutley, N.J.). Address: 44 Whitford Av., Nutley, N.J.

LAW, Margaret Lathrop, writer; b. Spartanburg, S.C.; d. William Adger and Lucy Lathrop (Goode) L.; A.B., Wellesley Coll., 1912; A.M., U. of Pa., 1918. Began career as writer feature articles for Phila. Public Ledger; engaged in publicity work for Pa. Museum and Sch. Industrial Art, Phila. Served with Y.M.C.A. with A.E.F. at end of World War. Mem. Shakespeare Soc. at Wellesley, Colonial Dames of America, Phila. Art Alliance, Women's Overseas League. Republican. Presbyn. Clubs: Cosmopolitan (Phila.); Wellesley (Phila.). Author: Horizon Smoke, 1932; From Gold to Green, 1933; Where Wings Are Healed, 1936; White Camellias and Black Laughter, 1939. All four are books of verse from which author gives poetry recitals before clubs and literary gatherings. Contbr. articles and short stories to many leading mags. and also verse to gen. mags. and poetry jours. Home: 440 W. Chestnut Av., Chestnut Hill, Pa.

LAW, Marie Hamilton, dean and prof. library science; b. Pittsburgh, Pa., Dec. 3, 1884; d. Benjamin Snodgrass and Mary (Thompson) L.; A.B., Washington Coll., 1905; A.M., U. of Pa., 1926, Ph.D., same, 1932; B.S. in Library Science, Carnegie Inst. Tech., 1931. Gen. asst., Carnegie Library of Pittsburgh, 1907-17; registrar and instr., Carnegie Library Sch., 1912-18, asst. to prin., 1918-20; librarian, Employers Assn., Pittsburgh, 1920-22; instr., Sch. of Library Sci., Drexel Inst. Tech., Phila., 1920-22, vice dir. and asso. prof., 1925-36, dean and prof. since 1937, librarian since 1937. Mem. Am. Library Assn., Assn. Am. Library Schs., Pa. Library Assn., Spl. Libraries Council Modern Lang. Assn., Hist. Soc. of Pa., Phi Kappa Phi. Republican. Presbyterian. Clubs: Women's University, Drexel Women's, Pennsylvania Library (Phila.). Home: 243 W. Tulpehacken St. Office: Drexel Inst. of Tech., Philadelphia, Pa.

LAWALL, Charles Elmer, Univ. pres.; b. Catasauqua, Pa., Nov. 21, 1891; s. Charles Elmer and Maria (Thomas) L.; E.M., Lehigh U., 1914, M.S., 1921; LL.D., Waynesburg Coll., 1939; m. Marjorie Berger, Apr. 29, 1920; 1 son, Charles Elmer. Testing engr. Pittsburgh Testing Lab., 1914; chemist N.J. Zinc Co., Palmerton, Pa., 1915-16; mining engr. Peal Peacock & Kerr, St. Benedict, Pa., 1916-17; metallurgy dept. Gen. Motors Co., Detroit, 1917; mining engr. Bethlehem Steel Co., Bethlehem, Pa., 1917-18; research engr., Bethlehem, Pa., 1919-21; instr. geology, Lehigh U., 1921; became asst. prof. W.Va. U., Sch. of Mines, 1921, later prof. and dir.; acting pres. W.Va. U., 1938-39, pres. since 1939. Served in U.S. Army, France, 1918-19. Chmn. papers and programs com. Coal Div., Am. Inst. Mining Engrs.; sec. and treas. W.Va. Coal Mining Inst. since 1930; mem. Coal Mining Inst. of America. Presbyn. Home: 1549 University Av., Morgantown, W.Va.

LA WALL, Elmer H., mining engr.; b. Bethlehem, Pa., Dec. 7, 1861; s. Alan J. and Marie Antoinette (Toengeux) LaW.; student Lehigh U., Bethlehem, 1878-82; m. Carolyn Johns, June 14, 1888; children—Elise (Mrs. Henry Ellsworth Bemis), Marie (Mrs. Charles Stone Murley), Claire (Mrs. Benjamin Crampton). Asst. engr. Lehigh Valley R.R. Co., 1882-86; mining engr. successively with Estate of Charlemgne Tower, Morea Coal Co., New Boston Coal Co.; chief engr. Diamond Water Co.; city engr., Hazelton, Pa.; now dir. Internat. Correspondence Schs. Home: Wilkes-Barre, Pa. Office: International Correspondence Schools, Scranton, Pa.

LaWALL, Harold Jacob, utilities official; b. Bloomsburg, Pa., May 5, 1880; s. John Jacob and Emma Jane (Boas) LaW.; student Bloomsburg (Pa.) State Normal Sch., 1890-96, Peirce Business Coll., Phila., Pa., 1898-99, Pace and Pace Inst. of Accounting, New York City, 1905-06; m. Helen Gordon Schuyler, Apr. 6, 1912; 1 dau., Miriam (Mrs. Frederick C. Geiger). Bookkeeper Creasy and Wells Lumber Co., Bloomsburg, Pa., 1896-98; asst. bookkeeper and paymaster Manning Maxwell & Moore, Phila., 1899-1900; clk. engring. and operating dept. United Gas Improvement Co., Phila., 1900-04, asst. chief clk., 1904-19, chief clk., 1919-22, statistician, 1922-27, budget mgr., 1927-34, asst. to operating v.p. since 1934; v.p. Chester County Light and Power Co., Kennett Square, Pa., since 1936. Mem. Phila. Chamber of Commerce (mem. tax com.), Am. Gas Assn. (mem. gen. accounting com.), Edison Electric Inst., Pa. Gas Assn. Republican. Protestant. Mason (Corinthian Lodge 368). Home: 38 Tenmore Rd., Haverford, Pa. Office: 1401 Arch St., Philadelphia, Pa.

LAWRANCE, Charles Lanier, aircraft engr.; b. Lenox, Mass., Sept. 30, 1882; s. Francis Cooper and Sarah Egleston (Lanier) L.; A.B., Yale, 1905, hon. A.M., 1927; student École des Beaux Arts, Paris, 3 yrs.; hon. D.Sc., Tufts, 1928; hon. A.M., Harvard, 1929; m. Emily M. G. Dix, 1910; children—Emily, Margaret, Francis Cooper. Engaged in engineering since 1915, with special interest in development of aircraft engines; founder, 1917, and president until 1923, Lawrance Aero Engine Corpn., N.Y. City; corpn. merged with Wright Aeronautical Corpn., 1924, and was pres. same until corpn. was merged, 1929, with Curtiss-Wright Corpn., of which was v.p. in charge of engring. and research, resigned, 1930; organized Lawrance Engineering & Research Corpn. of which is pres.; pres. C. L. Lawrance Corpn. (realty). Ensign N.Y. Naval Militia, 1916-17; assigned by Navy Dept. to aeronautical research, World War. Fellow Royal Aeronautical Soc., Eng.; mem. Soc. Automotive Engrs., Aeronautical Chamber Commerce of America (pres. 1931-32). Decorated Chevalier Legion of Honor (France). Republican. Episcopalian. Clubs: Yale, Brook. Home: 151 E. 63d St., New York, and East Islip, L.I., N.Y. Office: Linden, N.J.

LAWRENCE, David Leo.; b. Pittsburgh, Pa., June 18, 1889; s. Charles B. and Catherine (Conwell) L.; student pub. schs.; m. Alice Golden, June 8, 1921; children—Mary, Anna May, Brennen, David. Mem. Pittsburgh Registration Commn., 1914-24; collector internal revenue, U.S. Dept. Internal Revenue, Pittsburgh, 1933-34; became sec. of Commonwealth of Pa., 1935. Dir. Roselia Foundling Asylum. Clubs: Pittsburgh Athletic Assn. (Pittsburgh); Castle Shannon Country. Home: 355 S. Aiken Av. Office: Benedum-Trees Bldg., Pittsburgh, Pa.

LAWRENCE, Granville A(llen), ophthalmologist; b. Phila., Pa. Nov. 30, 1883; s. Thomas Allen and Mary Estelle (Watson) L.; grad. Central Manual Training High Sch., Phila., 1902; M.D., Temple U., Phila., 1909; m. Mathilde Exton, Dec. 8, 1909; children—Mabel Exton (Mrs. Myron E. Whitney), Granville Allen. In gen. practice of medicine, 1909-13; specializing in diseases of the eye since 1913. Served on Med. Advisory Bd. during World War. Mem. bd. dirs. Northeastern Hosp., Phila. Mem. A.M.A., Pa. Med. Soc., Phila. Co. Med. Soc., Am. Acad. Ophthalmology, Phila. Clin. Soc., Phi Chi. Republican. Reformed Episcopal Ch. (vestryman). Mason (K.T., Shriner). Club: Torresdale Country (Phila.). Home: 6805 N. 10th St. Office: Medical Arts Bldg., Philadelphia, Pa.

LAWRENCE, James Cuthbert, chem. engr.; b. Toms River, N.J., July 20, 1888; s. James and Martha Scott (Purdie) L.; A.B., B.S. in Chem. Engring., U. of Mo., 1910; grad. study, Royal Tech. Coll., Glasgow, Scotland, 1916-17; m. Mary S. Logan, Feb. 23, 1911; children—James Cuthbert, Jr., Harry Logan, Mary-Martha (Mrs. James P. Sill, Jr.), Ian MacLaren, Virginia, Jean Bertram. Mgr. and chem. engr., Forest Products Chem. Co., Memphis, Tenn., 1911-14; dir. Blair, Campbell & McLean Ltd., Glasgow, Scotland, 1914-18; pres. Am. Chem. Machinery Co., Phila., Pa., 1918-23; chem. engr. in charge Organic Chem. Dept. Engring., E. I. du Pont de Nemours & Co., Wilmington, Del., since 1923. Served as (hon.) capt. British Army, 1915-18. Mem. Am. Inst. Chem. Engrs., Kappa Sigma, Alpha Chi Sigma. Republican. Presbyn. Club: Springhaven Country (Wallingford). Home: Maple Brae, Moylan, Pa. Office: Du Pont Bldg., Wilmington, Del.

LAWRENCE, Joseph Stagg, economist; b. Budapest, Austria-Hungary, Oct. 19, 1896; s. Joseph Schmalz and Elizabeth (Stumpf) L.; brought to U.S., 1903; grad. Masten Park High Sch., Buffalo, N.Y., 1915; student U. of Grenoble, France, Mar.-June 1919; grad. Princeton U., 1923; m. Ann Werner, Feb. 2, 1919; children—Mary Josephine, Joseph Stagg. Teacher Princeton U., 1924-26, 1927-29, New York U., 1926-27; vice-pres. Equity Corpn. (mem. exec. com.); vice-pres. Am. General Corpn. Enlisted as pvt. inf., U.S. Army, at outbreak of World War; served in three major engagements in France; hon. discharged as 1st lt. Fellow Inst. of Economics, 1929-30; mem. Am. Economic Assn., Phi Beta Kappa. Club: Princeton. Author: Stabilization of Prices, 1928; Wall Street and Washington, 1929; Banking Concentration in the United States, 1930; Understanding Money, 1932. Mem. pub. relations com. N.Y. Stock Exchange; economist and v.p. for Analytical Research Bur. Editor Econostat, Bradstreets; asso. editor World's Work, Review of Reviews. Home: Newton, N.J. Office: 50 Pine St., New York, N.Y.

LAWRENCE, Josephine, author; b. Newark, N.J.; d. Elijah Wiley (M.D.) and Mary Elizabeth (Barker) L.; ed. pub. schs. and spl. courses New York U. Editor children's page, Newark (N.J.) Sunday Call, since 1915; household editor (woman's page), same, since 1918; wrote "Man in the Moon" stories, broadcast bi-weekly, 1921; also wrote first story for children for radio broadcast, 1921. Member of Authors' League of America. Democrat. Presbyterian. Author: Brother and Sister Series (4 books), 1921-22; Rosemary, 1922; Man in the Moon Story Book, 1922; Rainbow Hill, 1924; Elizabeth Ann Series (4 books), 1923-25; The Berry Patch, 1925; Linda Lane Books (2 books), 1925; Next Door Neighbors, 1926; Rosemary and the Princess, 1927; The Two Little Fellows (3 books), 1927; Glenna, 1929; Christine, 1930; Wind's in the West, 1931; (novels) Head of the Family, 1932; Years Are So Long, 1934; If I Have Four Apples, 1935; The Sound of Running Feet, 1937; Bow Down to Wood and Stone, 1938; A Good Home with Nice People, 1939. Home: Newark, N.J.

LAWRIE, Ritchie, Jr., registered professional engr.; b. Edinburgh, Scotland (parents Am. citizens), Oct. 7, 1890; s. Ritchie and Lida (McDowell) L.; B.S., Carnegie Inst., 1911; m. Helen Lowther, Mar. 7, 1914; 1 dau., Frances Lawrie. Successively asst. supt., supt. and asst. to gen. supt. Thompson-Starrett Co., building constrn., Pittsburgh and Chicago, 1911-17; dir. Housing Bur., 1918-20; partner Lawrie & Green, Harrisburg, Pa., architects, since 1920; dir. Central Trust Co., Harrisburg, Harrisburg Gas Co. Mem. Harrisburg Chamber of Commerce. Served as 1st lt. Ordnance, United States Army, during World War. Mem. Pa. Soc. Professional Engrs., Am. Inst. Architects, Am. Legion. Presbyterian. Mason (32°). Elk. Clubs: Harrisburg Country, Rotary (dist. gov. 34th dist. Rotary Internat., 1933-34). Home: 110 Shamokin St. Office: 111 S. Front St., Harrisburg, Pa.

LAWS, Bertha Margaret, headmistress Agnes Irwin Sch.; b. Phila., Pa., July 28, 1879; d. Jesse A. T. and Virginia (Cantrell) L.; A.B., Bryn Mawr (Pa.) Coll., 1901; grad. study, U. of Pa., Columbia U., Am. Acad. at Rome, Italy, summer 1927. Recording sec., Bryn Mawr (Pa.) Coll., 1901-03; instr. and sec., Agnes Irwin Sch., Wynnewood, Pa., 1901-15, sec. and treas., 1915-28, headmistress since 1928. Served with Am. Red Cross, in Paris and Rome, 1917-19. Mem. Headmistresses Assn. of the East, Nat. Assn. of Principals of Girls' Schools. Episcopalian. Club: Women's University (Phila.). Home: The Drake, Philadelphia, Pa. Office: Wynnewood, Pa.

LAWS, George Malcolm, physician; b. Paulsboro, N.J., Sept. 15, 1881; s. Dr. George C. and Elizabeth M. (Roe) L.; B.S., U. of Pa., 1902, M.D., 1905; m. Elizabeth

Williams, Aug. 25, 1914; children—George Malcolm, Elizabeth. Interne Univ. Hosp., Phila., 1905-06; began as asst. instr. in surgery and advanced through grades to asso. in surgery, U. of Pa. Med. Sch., 1908-23, now asst. prof. gynecology, Grad. Sch. of Medicine; gynecologist, Presbyn. Hosp., Phila., since 1933. Served in Med. Corps, U.S. Army, 1917-19, with A.E.F. in France; now maj. Med. Corps Res. Fellow Phila. Coll Phys., Phila. Acad. Surgery; mem. Obstet. Soc. Phila., Pathol. Soc., Phi Alpha Sigma, Alpha Omega Alpha. Republican. Episcopalian. Mason. Club: Philadelphia Country. Home: 1907 Spruce St., Philadelphia, Pa.

LAWSON, Aubrey Francis, physician and surgeon; b. Berlin, W.Va., Mar. 5, 1887; s. Albert Francis and Elisabeth (Swisher) L.; M.D., Univ. of Md. Med. Sch., 1911; m. Lotta L. Vandervort, Feb. 3, 1917; children—Nancy Elisabeth, John Francis. Began as co. surgeon, Wildell Lumber Co., Wildell, W.Va., 1913-14, Davis Colliery Co., Bower and Coalton, W.Va., 1914-16; asst. to Dr. A. C. Harrison, Mercy Hosp., Baltimore, Md., 1916-17; med. examiner B.&O. R.R., Connellsville, Pa., 1917-18; asso. with Dr. T. F. Law and founded Gen. Hosp. of Weston, W.Va., 1920, individual owner since 1928; has built up the clinic to 44-bed hosp. with training sch. for nurses in connection; dir. Citizens Bank, Weston, W.Va., since 1939. Served as capt. Med. Corps, U.S.A., 1918-19, with A.E.F. in France. Fellow Am. Coll. Surgeons. Mem. Lewis Co. Med. Soc. (pres.), Phi Chi. Republican. Presbyn. Mason. Club: Lions of Weston. Home: 204 High Av. Office: General Hosp., Weston, W.Va.

LAWSON, Evald Benjamin, coll. pres.; b. Brockton, Mass., July 24, 1904; s. Benjamin and Edla Sofia (Johanson) L.; A.B., Upsala Coll., East Orange, N.J., 1925; B.D., Augustana Theol. Sem., Rock Island, Ill., 1928; student Columbia, 1928-29, Bibl. Sem., New York, 1929-35; Th.D., 1937; student Union Theol. Sem., 1935-37; unmarried. Ordained to ministry Lutheran Ch., 1928; pastor Trinity Luth. Ch., White Plains, N.Y., 1928-38; pres. Upsala Coll., since 1938. Mem. Am. Soc. Ch. History, Kyrkohistoriska Föreningen (Uppsala U., Sweden). Contbr. to Augustana Quarterly. Address: Upsala College, East Orange, N.J.

LAWSON, George Benedict, educator; b. Brooklyn, N.Y., Aug. 11, 1867; s. Albert Gallatin and Eliza (Knight) L.; grad. Poly. Inst. of Brooklyn, 1884; A.B., Colgate, 1888, A.M., 1891, D.D., 1912; grad. study Hamilton Theol. Sem., 1888-89, Union Theol. Sem., 1889-91; m. Kate P., d. Prof. J. J. Lewis, Feb. 3, 1892 (died 1916); children—Margaret Louise, Elizabeth Knight; m. 2d, Margaret E. Holstein, June 8, 1927; 1 son, George Benedict. Ordained Bapt. ministry, 1892; successively pastor Delhi, N.Y., Bennington, Vt., Pleasant Street Church, Worcester, Mass., Brattleboro, Vt., until 1908; principal Vt. Acad., Saxtons River, 1908-16; prof. edn. and philosophy, Pa. Coll. for Women, Pittsburgh, 1916-22; prof. philosophy, Bucknell U. since 1922. Chaplain Vt. N.G., 1900-10; 1st lt. Tank Corps, U.S.A., 1918. Mem. A.A.A.S., Am. Assn. Univ. Profs., Delta Kappa Epsilon. Home: Lewisburg, Pa.

LAWSON, James Henry, supt. of schs.; b. Elk Valley, Tenn., Jan. 12, 1890; s. Madison and Mary (Boling) L.; B.S., U. of Chicago, 19—; Ed.D., U. of Pittsburgh, 19—; m. Mary Louise Harrison, June 9, 1921; children—Lucile DeGrief, James Henry, Margaret Louise, William Elrod, Jay DeGrief, Charles Madison. Head of mathematics dept., McKeesport (Pa.) High Sch., 1920-24, asst. prin., 1924-35; supt. of schs., McKeesport, Pa., since 1935. Vice-pres. McKeesport Council, Boy Scouts of America; mem. advisory bd. Salvation Army; dir. Y.M.C.A., McKeesport Community Fund. Mem. Pa. Edn. Assn. (ex-pres. McKeesport Branch, v.p. Western Conv. Dist.), Am. Assn. Sch. Adminstrs., N.E.A., Am. Legion. Elk Club: Rotary (McKeesport, Pa.). Author various articles on ednl. subjects. Home: 1320 Centennial Av. Office: Shaw Av. Bldg., McKeesport, Pa.

LAWSON, Octo Gerald, univ. librarian; b. London, Can., Oct. 1, 1895; s. Peter Hutty and Mary Alice (Waugh) L.; came to U.S., 1924, naturalized, 1939; A.B. Toronto (Can.) U., 1921; student Victoria U., Theol. Sch., Toronto, Can., 1922; M.R.E., Boston (Mass.) U., 1923, grad. study, 1925; B.S., Columbia U., Sch. of Library Service, 1929; m. Marian Helliwell, June 14, 1923; 1 son, John Wellesley. Minister, Meth. Ch. of Can., West Lorne, Can., 1923-24; dir. of religious edn., First Presbyn Ch., Bradford, Pa., 1925-27; reading room asso., N.Y.U. Washington Sq. Coll., 1929-30; librarian, Drew U., Madison, N.J., since 1930. Mem. Boy Scouts of America (field commr. of reading, Morris-Sussex Council), Am. Library Assn., A.A.A.S., Am. Soc. of Ch. History, Spl. Libraries Assn., N.J. Library Assn. Presbyterian. Home: 120 Central Av. Office: Rose Memorial Library, Drew Univ., Madison, N.J.

LAWSON, Walter Eastby, research chemist; b. Dunlap, N.D., Dec. 12, 1892; s. Torrey O. and Emma (Eastby) L.; B.S., U. of Wash., 1917, M.S., same, 1922; Ph.D., Johns Hopkins U., 1925; m. Emma Stuart Dunbar, Oct. 8, 1918; children—Dunbar, Walter Eastby, Jr. Chief research chemist, Cuba Cane Sugar Corpn., Havana, 1920-21; biochemist, Edgewood Arsenal, 1921-25; research chemist, Expt. Sta., E. I. du Pont de Nemours & Co., 1925-33, dir. Eastern Lab., E. I. du Pont de Nemours & Co., Gibbstown, N.J., since 1933. Served as 2d lt. to capt., U.S. Marine Corps, 1917-20. Fellow A.A.A.S., Franklin Inst. Mem. Am. Chem. Soc., Am. Inst. Chem. Engrs., Sigma Xi, Phi Beta Kappa, Phi Lambda Upsilon. Republican. Episcopalian. Mason (32°). Clubs: Country (Woodbury); Du Pont Country (Wilmington, Del.). Consultant, Chem. Warfare Service. Home: 114 Delaware St., Woodbury, N.J. Office: Eastern Laboratory, Gibbstown, N.J.

LAYCOCK, Charles Wilbur, banker; b. Harveyville, Luzerne Co., Pa., Oct. 3, 1860; s. Adam Clark and Clarissa Ann (Millard) L.; ed. Wyoming Sem., Kingston, Pa.; m. L. Jennie Clapp, June 5, 1890; children—Charles Harold, Robert Clark, Millard Day. Bookkeeper 2d Nat. Bank, Wilkes-Barre, Pa., 1882-90; cashier Anthracite Savings Bank, 1890-1910; with New York and Phila. banking house, 1910-13; cashier Miners Bank of Wilkes-Barre, 1913-15, v.p., 1915-24, pres. since 1924; dir., sec. and treas. Wilkes-Barre Ry. Corpn.; director Stevens Coal Company. Trustee of Wyoming Sem.; dir. Pa. State Chamber Commerce, Wilkes-Barre-Wyoming Valley Chamber Commerce; treas. Wyoming Hist. and Geol. Soc. Republican. Methodist. Mason (33°, K.T., Shriner). Clubs: Craftsmen's, Westmoreland, Irem Temple Country. Home: 243 N. Maple Av., Kingston, Pa. Office: Miners Nat. Bank of Wilkes-Barre, Wilkes-Barre, Pa.

LAYNG, Frank Rahn Shunk, Jr., civil engr.; b. Salem, O., Sept. 9, 1878; s. Frank R. S. and Estelle (Tower) L.; grad. high sch., Pittsburgh, 1896; student U. of Pittsburgh, 1896-97; m. Belle Kennedy Chase, Jan. 19, 1905; children—Frank Chase, Evelyn Louise, Edwin Tower. Rodman Pa. R.R., 1897-1900; with Bessemer & Lake Erie R.R. since 1900, as draftsman, 1900-02, asst. engr., 1902-03, engr. of bridges, 1903-06, engr. of track 1906-28, asst. chief engr., 1928-31, chief engr. since 1931; dir. Greenville Nat. Bank. Pres. Greenville Hosp., 1918-28; pres. Greenville Sch., 1918-28. Trustee Greenville Hosp. Mem. Am. Ry. Engring. Assn. (dir.), Am. Soc. Civil Engineers, Engrs. Soc. Western Pa., Hist. Soc. Western Pa., Am. Soc. for Testing Materials, Am. Iron and Steel Inst., Ry. Signal Assn., Am. Wood Preservers Assn. Republican. Methodist. Mason. Clubs: Greenville Country; Railroad (New York); Railway (Pittsburgh). Home: 387 S. Main St. Office: 160 Main St., Greenville, Pa.

LAYTON, Caleb S., lawyer; b. Georgetown, Del., Apr. 1, 1886; s. Caleb R. and Anne E. (Sipple) L.; grad. Mercersburg (Pa.) Acad., 1903; B.S., U. of Pa., 1907; student U. of Pa. Law Sch., 1908-10; m. Helene H. Mustard, Dec. 31, 1913; children—Virginia L., Ann S., Rodney M. Practiced at Wilmington, Del., since 1910; city solicitor, Wilmington, 1923-31; mem. firm, Richards, Layton & Finger; dir. Equitable Trust Co.; represented Weirton Steel Co. in case against NRA, challenging right of Congress to enact statutes affecting commerce not of an interstate or foreign nature. Trustee St. Andrew's Sch., Middletown, Del. Episcopalian. Clubs: Wilmington, Wilmington Country. Home: 908 du Pont Rd. Office: du Pont Bldg., Wilmington, Del.

LAYTON, Daniel J., judge; b. Georgetown, Del., Aug. 1, 1879; s. Caleb Rodney (physician) and Anna (Sipple) L.; student Drew Acad., 1895-96; A.B., U. of Pa., 1900; student U. of Pa., Law Sch., 1900-02; m. Laura Huber, 1906; children—Caleb Rodney, Daniel J. Admitted to Del. bar, 1903; dep. atty. gen. of Del., 1919-22, atty. gen., 1922-23; chief justice of the Supreme Court of Del. since 1933. Republican. Episcopalian. Home: Georgetown, Del. Address: Sussex Co. Court House, Del.

LAZARON, Morris Samuel, rabbi; b. Savannah, Ga., Apr. 16, 1888; s. Samuel Louis and Alice (De Castro) L.; B.A., U. of Cincinnati, 1909, M.A., 1911; studied Hebrew Union Coll., Cincinnati, 1905, 1914; m. Pauline Horkheimer, May 1, 1916 (died Apr. 25, 1933); children—Morris Samuel, Harold Victor, Clementine. Rabbi Congregation Leshem Shomayim, Wheeling, W.Va., 1914, Baltimore Hebrew Congregation since 1915. Chaplain during World War, now maj. chaplain, O.R.C. Mem. nat. exec. com. Am. Mcht. Marine Library Assn.; mem. Central Conf. Am. Rabbis; mem. bd. dirs. Am.-Jewish Joint Distribution Com.; mem. nat. council of Am. Provident Soc.; mem. exec. com. Nat. Conf. of Jews and Christians. Democrat. Mason (33°). Clubs: Suburban Country, Woodholme Country, Civitan. Author: Religious Services for Jewish Youth; Side Arms; Consolations of Our Faith; Seed of Abraham; Ten Jews of the Ages, 1930; Common Ground, 1938; also wrote various booklets and pamphlets. Contbr. to Jewish and gen. mags. Home: "Tel-Elim," Naylor Lane, Pikesville, Md.

LEACH, Henry Goddard, author, editor; b. Phila., Pa., July 3, 1880; s. Dr. Alonzo Lemuel and Jennie (Goddard) L.; A.B., Princeton, 1903; A.M., Harvard, 1906, Ph.D., 1908; m. Agnes Lisle, d. T. Wistar Brown, Feb. 20, 1915; adopted children—Annis Leach, Jeffery E. Fuller. Master, Groton Sch., 1903-05; traveling fellow, Harvard, in Denmark, 1908-10; instr. in English, Harvard, 1910-12; sec. Am.-Scandinavian Foundation, New York, 1912-21, pres., 1926—; curator Scandinavian history and lit., Harvard, 1921-31; editor The Forum, 1923—. Secured economic support, 1919, for exchange of 40 students annually between U.S.A., and Scandinavian countries; v.p. Am. unit P.E.N.; trustee Carnegie Ch. Peace Union; pres. Poetry Soc. America, 1934-37. Comdr. of Vasa Order and Comdr. of North Star (Sweden); Comdr. of the Dannebrog (Denmark); Comdr. of St. Olav (Norway); Knight of Falcon (Iceland). Mem. Soc. Mayflower Descendants, Soc. Colonial Wars, S.R. Clubs: Ausable, Century, Church (pres. 1923-26), Harvard, Piping Rock (New York); Faculty (Cambridge); Gulph Mills (Phila.); Saville (London). Author: Scandinavia of the Scandinavians, 1915; Angevin Britain and Scandinavia, 1921. Lecturer and contbr. to periodicals. Home: 170 E. 64th St., New York, N.Y., and Villanova, Pa. Office: 570 Lexington Av., New York, N.Y.

LEACH, Howard Seavoy, librarian; b. Penobscot, Me., May 14, 1887; s. George Elmer and Hattie Gertrude (Grindle) L.; A.B., Wesleyan U., Conn., 1913; A.M., Princeton, 1915; library training at Princeton U. under Dr. E. C. Richardson, 1913-15; unmarried. Sergt. U.S. Army, 1918; asst. librarian Camp Meade, and Librarian Camp Lee; librarian U.S.S. George Washington, May-July, 1919; reference librarian Princeton U. Library, 1919-24; librarian Lehigh U. since 1924. Mem. A.L.A., Pa. Library Assn., Archæol. Inst. America (pres. Bethlehem Chapter 1938), Am. Bibliog. Soc. Republican. Methodist. Clubs: Bethlehem, Sigma Chi. Author: List of Collections of English Drama in American Libraries, 1916; An Essay Towards a Bibliography of the Published Writings and Addresses of Woodrow Wilson (Mar. 1917-Mar. 1921), 1923; Bibliography of Howard Crosby Butler, 1924; Bibliography of Woodrow Wilson (1875-1924); Wilson—Public Papers, 6 vols.; (with R. M. Smith) The Shakespeare Folios and the Forgeries of Shakespeare's Handwriting in the Lucy Packer Linderman Memorial Library, Bethlehem, 1927. Contbr. to mags. on library subjects. Home: Bethlehem, Pa.

LEACH, Paul R., newspaperman; b. Lafayette, Ind., Sept. 10, 1890; s. Harvey Allen and Emma (Field) L.; ed. high sch., Lafayette; m. Clara Bronson, Apr. 15, 1912; children—Paul R., Elizabeth Jane. Mem. editorial staff Chicago Daily News since 1910, war corr., 1917-18, political and economic writer since 1920, Washington corr. since 1933. Mem. Am. Press Soc., Sigma Delta Chi. Mason (32°). Author: That Man Dawes, 1930. Contbr. short stories and articles to mags. Clubs: Columbia Country, National Press, Gridiron (Washington). Home: 107 E. Oxford St., Chevy Chase, Md. Office: 901 Colorado Bldg., Washington, D.C.

LEACH, Walter, forestry; b. Blossburg, Pa., Jan. 25, 1892; s. Harvey Brightman and Irene (Wheeler) L.; g.g.s. Dr. Harvey Leach, pioneer doctor in Tioga Co.; desc. Rev. Peter Bulkely, founder of Concord, Mass.; grad. Mansfield (Pa.) State Teachers Coll., 1910; B. Forestry, Pa. State Forest Sch., Mont Alto, 1914; m. Annamary Dean, July 25, 1924; children—Walter, Elizabeth Ann, Charles Daniel. With Dept. of Forests and Waters, Commonwealth of Pa., since 1914, as topographer, forester, dist. forester, research forester—stationed in Centre, Perry, Union, Tioga, Huntingdon, Cameron, Franklin, Dauphin and Lycoming counties; for years at Blackwells, Snow Shoe, Mount Union, Driftwood, Mont Alto and Harrisburg. Served in Intelligence Sect., Headquarters Co., 314th Inf., U.S. Army, during World War. Mem. Soc. Am. Foresters, Am. Legion. Mem. Evangelical Ch. Mason (32°, Shriner). Home: Mansfield, Pa. Office: Jersey Shore, Pa.

LEAF, Leonard; chmn. bd. and pres. Nat. Bank of Pottstown. Address: Pottstown, Pa.

LEAKE, Lowell LaVerne, editor; b. Prescott, Ia., Jan. 2, 1898; s. Ervin Francis and Mamie Leona (Adkins) L.; ed. Drake U. (Des Moines), 1916-17, Drury Coll. (Springfield, Mo.), 1918 and 1919-20; m. Frances Bruce Ross, May 11, 1921; children—James Ross, Charles Ervin, Lowell. Newspaper reporter, 1920; mng. editor Akron (O.) Press, later Akron Times-Press, until 1926; Sunday editor Rocky Mountain News, 1926-28, Pittsburgh Press, 1928-29; mng. editor Buffalo Times, 1929-30; with United Press, New York, 1930-33; editor Youngstown (O.) Telegram, 1933-36; asst. mng. editor The Washington (D.C.) Post since 1936. Mem. White House Corrs. Assn., Am. Soc. Newspaper Editors. Club: National Press. Home: 102 W. Woodbine, Chevy Chase, Md. Address: The Washington Post, Washington, D.C.

LEAMAN, William Gilmore, Jr., physician, coll. prof.; b. Phila., Pa., Sept. 3, 1898; s. William Gilmore and Eleanor (Pelly) L.; student U. of Pa. Coll. Dept., 1916-18, M.D., Med. Sch., 1922; post grad. work in cardiology, Harvard, 1929; m. Anne Hankins, Jan. 7, 1924; 1 dau., Nancy Anne. Interne Univ. Hosp., Phila., 1922-24; asso. in medicine, Woman's Med. Coll. of Pa., Phila., 1931-38, asst. prof. of medicine in charge dept. cardiology since 1938; in practice medicine since 1924; cardiologist Woman's Coll. Hosp., Phila., 1931; asst. visiting physician Phila. Gen. Hosp. since 1932; cardiologist St. Luke's and Children's Hosp., Phila., since 1933, Roxborough Memorial Hosp., Phila., since 1934; cardiologist Northeastern Hosp., Phila., since 1937. Fellow Am. Coll. Physicians, Phila. Coll. Physicians; mem. A.M.A., Am. Heart Assn., Phila. Co. Med. Soc., Med. Soc. of State of Pa., Am. Soc. for Study of Med. History. Episcopalian. Author numerous articles in med. jours. Address: 3700 Baring St., Philadelphia, Pa.

LEANDER, Hugo Austin, industrial executive; b. Cambridge, Mass., Dec. 2, 1894; s. Carl and Clara W. (Carlson) L.; B.S., Harvard, 1916; student New York U., Grad. Sch. of Business Adminstrn., 1921-23; m. Marguerite Reynolds McFarland, Nov. 29, 1917; children—Jeanne Marguerite, Hugh Austin. Special accountant Union Pacific System, 1916-18; traveling auditor, Gen. Electric Co., Schenectady, N.Y., 1918-21; supervisor of methods Del. & Hudson Co., New York, 1921-24; mgr., Arthur Andersen & Co., New York, 1924-26; financial and industrial-consultant Bonner, Brooks & Co., New York, 1926-29; pres. Am. Rayon Products Co., New York, 1927-28; vice-pres. Am. Founders Co., New York, 1930-35; vice-pres. Am. Gen. Corpn., 1935-36; mgr. industrial dept., Van Alstyne, Noel & Co., New York, 1936-38; vice-pres. and dir. Reynolds Metals Co. since 1938, Richmond Radiator Co. since 1938; dir. Fulton Sylphon Co., Bridgeport Thermostat Co., Robertshaw Thermostat Co. Served as sergt. maj., 547th Engrs., U.S. Army, during World War. Clubs: Harvard (New York, N.J. and Va.); Country of Va.; Deep Run Hunt. Home: West Rd., Short Hills, N.J. Office: 810 E. Franklin St., Richmond, Va.

LEARY, Lewis Gaston, clergyman; b. Elizabeth, N. J., Aug. 3, 1877; s. George S. and Joanna (Gaston) L.; B.Sc., Rutgers, 1897; M.A., New York U., 1900, Ph.D., 1905; Union Theol. Sem., 1897-99; grad. McCormick Theol. Sem., Chicago, 1900; post-grad. work same, 1903-04; D.D., U. of Vt., 1927; m. Beatrice E. Knight, Dec. 15, 1904; children—Lewis Gaston, George Knight, Mary Emily, William Gillett. Ordained Presbyn. ministry, 1900; instr. in Am. Univ., Beirut, Syria, 1900-03; pastor Blauvelt, N.Y., 1904-07, Huguenot Memorial Ch., Pelham Manor, N.Y., 1907-27, West Milford, N.J., since 1935. Professor of Biblical literature, Vassar College, 1921-22; conducted People's Radio Vespers, 1927. Lecturer and contbr. numerous articles connected with O.T., Palestine, out-of-the-way parts of Europe, and young people's problems. Mem. Phi Beta Kappa. Clubs: Clergy, Theta, Phi Beta Kappa (New York). Author: The Christmas City, 1911; The Real Palestine of To-day, 1911; Andorra, the Hidden Republic, 1912; Syria, the Land of Lebanon, 1913; The Bible When You Want It, 1932; Problems of Protestantism, 1933. Editor: From the Pyramids to Paul, 1935. Address: West Milford, N.J.

LEATHERMAN, Clarence Gordon, clergyman; b. Lewistown, Md., Dec. 26, 1875; s. Levi Calvin and Elizabeth (Derr) L.; student U. of Md., 1895-97; A.B., Roanoke Coll., Salem, Va., 1900, A.M., same, 1904; B.D., Gettysburg Sem., 1903; (hon.) D.D., Gettysburg Coll., 1928; m. Elfie Irene Cramer, Nov. 19, 1903; children—Paul Kramer, Levi Henry (dec.), Clarence Daniel. Ordained to ministry Luth. Ch., 1903; pastor Trinity Ch., Lemoyne, Pa., 1903-06, Bethany Ch., New Castle, Pa., 1906-11, St. Pauls Ch., Vandergrift, Pa., 1911-16, Immanuel Ch., Manchester, Md., 1916-23; pastor Zion Luth. Ch., Hummelstown, Pa., since 1923; treas. Synod of East Pa., 1928, 29, pres., 1930, 31; del. to convs. U. Luth. Ch., 1928-34. Dir. Gettysburg Sem. Republican. Lutheran. Home: 20 N. Rosina St., Hummelstown, Pa.

LEATTOR, William Leslie, banking; b. McVeytown, Pa., June 24, 1897; s. William J. and Hannah (Roche) L.; ed. pub. sch. and high sch., Doylestown, Pa., 1906-17; m. Leonora Hibshman, Aug. 21, 1927. Employed as bank clk., 1921-23; asst. cashier, Lambertville Nat. Bank, Lambertville, N.J., 1923-25; cashier First Nat. Bank, Riegelsville, Pa., 1925-34, pres. and dir. since 1934; dir. Riegelsville Bldg. & Loan Assn. Served as pres. Riegelsville Borough Council. Served as private U.S.A. during World War. Mem. Am. Legion. Republican. Mem. Reformed Ch. Mason (K.T., 32°). Home: Riegelsville, Pa.

LEAVITT, Frederic Headley, neuropsychiatrist; b. Trenton, N.J., May 27, 1888; s. Charles B. (M.D.) and Anna M. (Headley) L.; ed. U. of Pa., pre-med., 1906-08; M.D., U. of Pa. Med. Sch., 1911; m. Jeanette Haag, June 19, 1929; 1 dau., Jeanette Anna. Interne Phila. Gen. Hosp., 1911-13; asst. phys., Phila. Gen. Hosp. dept. neurology, 1913-21; asst. phys., Phila. Orthopedic Hosp. since 1913; neuropsychiatrist, Chestnut Hill Hosp. since 1915, Reading Hosp. since 1925, Am. Stomach Hosp. since 1930, Lankenau Hosp. since 1935; cons. neuropsychiatrist, Phila. Children's Hosp. since 1915; chief dept. psychiatry, Phila. Gen. Hosp. since 1930; neuropsychiatrist, U.S. Vets. Bur., 1921-30; asst. prof. neurology, U. of Pa. Grad. Sch. Medicine since 1925, asso. in psychiatry Med. Sch., U. of Pa. since 1933. Served as 1st lt. then capt. Med. Corps, U.S.A., 1917-19; with A.E.F. in France. Republican. Presbyn. Clubs: Medical, Aesculapian (Philadelphia). Home: 2923 Rising Sun Rd., Ardmore, Pa. Office: 1527 Pine St., Philadelphia, Pa.

LEBER, Charles Tudor, missionary sec.; b. Baltimore, Md., Nov. 11, 1898; s. George Greenbury and Laura (Tudor) L.; A.B., Johns Hopkins U., 1920; S.T.B., Princeton Theol. Sem., 1923; D.D., Washington and Jefferson Coll., 1936; m. Elizabeth Louise Heath, May 12, 1923; children—Charles Tudor, Elizabeth Adelaide, Donald Heath. Ordained ministry Presbyterian Ch., 1923; pastor Westminister Ch., Trenton, N.J., 1923-24, Forest Park Ch., Baltimore, 1924-28, Green Ridge Ch., Scranton, Pa., 1928-36; sec. Bd. of Foreign Missions of Presbyn. Ch. in U.S.A. since 1936; official visitation Presbyn. Missions in Syria, Iraq, Iran, India, Siam, Philippines, China, Chosen, Japan, 1936-37; mem. Gen. Council of Presbyn. Ch. in U.S.A.; chmn. exec. com. Foreign Missions Conf. of North America. Served in U.S. Navy, 1917-18. Trustee Alborz Coll. of Teheran, Iran. Mem. Delta Upsilon, Omicron Delta Kappa. Mason. Contbr. to religious jours. Home: 92 Edgemont Rd., Upper Montclair, N.J. Office: 156 Fifth Av., New York, N.Y.

LEBHERZ, William Bennett, mfg. exec.; b. Frederick, Md., Dec. 4, 1885; s. William Henry and Margaret (Bennett) L.; student St. John's Literary Inst., Frederick, Md., 1895-1903; m. Harriett Behney, Apr. 29, 1914; children—Adele Marie (Mrs. Jacques Davidson), Harriett Margaret, William Bennett, Thomas Behney, Katherine Elizabeth. Clerk Helfenstein Insurance Agency, Frederick, Md., 1903-05; office mgr. Ox Fibre Brush Co., Frederick, Md., 1905-09; gen. mgr. Royal Brush & Broom Co., Toledo, O., 1909-17; treas. Gallaudet Aircraft Corpn., East Greenwich, R.I., 1917-22; v.p. and treas. The Everedy Co., Frederick, Md., since 1922. Catholic. K.C. Club: Catoctin Country (Frederick, Md.). Home: 203 E. 2d St. Office: 8 East St., Frederick, Md.

LE BRUN, Pierre Napoleon, banking; b. Montclair, N.J., July 5, 1896; s. Michel Moracin and Maria Olivia (Steele) LeB.; A.B. honoris causa, Amherst Coll., Amherst, Mass., 1919; B.S., Columbia U., 1922; m. Margaret Eleanor Boyle, June 26, 1923; children—Pierre Lajus, Elenor Carey, Olivia, Richard Michel. Began as clk., Farmers Loan & Trust Co., N.Y. City, 1920; clk., Metropolitan Bank, N.Y. City, 1921, Chase Nat. Bank, N.Y. City, 1921; instr., Tome Sch., Port Deposit, Md., 1922-25; asst. cashier Cecil Nat. Bank, Port Deposit, Md., 1925-33, vice-pres. and dir. since 1933; dir. Mutual Fire Ins. Co. of Cecil Co. since 1938, Water Witch Fire Co. since 1939. Served as q.m. 2d class, U.S.N.R.F., 1917-21, active service 1917-19, overseas with minesweeping detachment. Awarded Victory medal. Mem. Cecil Co. Welfare Bd. since 1933, chmn. since 1934. Mem. bd. mgrs. Children's Aid Soc. of Cecil Co. Local committeeman and asst. scoutmaster Boy Scouts of America. Mem. Am Red Cross, Lincoln Farm Assn., Alpha Delta Phi, Soc. Colonial Wars, Descs. Colonial Govs., Colonial Order of Crown, Am. Legion. Republican. Roman Catholic. K.C. Clubs: Conowingo Fishing, Cecil Co. Rod and Gun. Address: Cecil Nat. Bank, Port Deposit, Md.

LEBSON, Abram Allen, lawyer; b. May 11, 1902; s. Michael and Bessie (Krupenin) L.; LL.B., N.Y. Law Sch., 1923; m. Dorothy Helen Jacobs, of Hackensack, N.J., Sept. 2, 1925; children—Marion Doris, Joan Aline. Admitted to N.J. bar as atty., 1924, as counsellor, 1928; admitted to practice before Supreme Ct. of U.S., 1933; served as magistrate, Palisades Interstate Park, N.J., 1925-31; judge First Jud.

Dist. Criminal Ct., Bergen Co., 1931-36; municipal atty. for Fairview, Cresskill and Tenafly, many yrs.; supreme ct. commr., spl. master in chancery; candidate for N.J. Assembly on Dem. ticket, 1925-26; dir. Englewood Mutual Loan & Bldg. Assn., Englewood Sewerage Co. Dir. and counsel Englewood Hosp. Assn.; mem. bd. mgrs. Englewood Community Chest. Mem. Am. and N.J. State bar assns., Bergen County Bar Assn. (past pres.), Sigma Omega Psi. Mem. Englewood High Sch. Alumni Assn. (past pres.), Northern Valley Civic Music Assn. (v.p.). Democrat. Jewish religion. Mason. Elk. Clubs: Englewood Rotary (past pres.), Tuscan Craftsman (past pres.). Home: 231 Sunset Av. Office: 39 Park Pl., Englewood, N.J.

LeCLERE, John Burk, box mfr.; b. Cincinnati, O., Feb. 2, 1892; s. Louis and Caroline (Burk) LeC.; student Woodward High Sch., Cincinnati, O., 1906-10; A.B., U. of Cincinnati, 1914, grad. student, 1915-16; student Harvard Grad. Sch. of Bus. Adminstrn., 1919-20; m. Helen Trow, Jan. 4, 1921; children—Thomas Craig, Suzanne. Dir. of personnel, H. J. Heinz Co., 1920-26; production mgr., F. J. Kress Box Co., Pittsburgh, Pa., 1926-28, sec. 1929-32, sec. and treas., 1933, v.p., gen. mgr. and dir. since 1934; chmn. bd. and pres. Clarksburg Paper Co. since 1933. 1st lt., 3d Div., U.S. Army, 1917-19. Mem. exec. com. Nat. Container Assn., mem. Pi Kappa Alpha. Presbyterian. Clubs: Harvard of Western Pa. (Pittsburgh); Wildwood Country (Allison Park, Pa.). Home: Oak Hill Farms, Allison Park, Pa. Office: 1 28th St., Pittsburgh, Pa.

LEDERER, Erwin Reginald, chem. engr.; b. Vienna, Austria, May 21, 1882; s. Josef Ignatius and Berta (Pekarek) L.; Chem. E., U. of Heidelberg, 1904; Ph.D., U. of Vienna, 1905; M.E., Technol. Inst., Vienna, 1905; spl. grad. work New York U., 1921; children—Elizabeth, Louise. Came to U.S., 1912, naturalized, 1919. Chemist and asst. supt. for Vacuum Oil Co. in Rumania and Austria-Hungary, 1906-12; chemist Standard Oil Co. of N.J., 1912-13; chief chemist Atlantic Refining Co., 1914-16; gen. supt. Galena Signal Oil Co., 1917-19; mgr. Atlantic Gulf Oil Corpn., 1920-22; v.p. La. Oil Refining Co., 1922-25; v.p. Tex. Pacific Coal & Oil Co., 1925-35, dir. since 1935; pres. Bradford (Pa.) Oil Refining Co. since 1936. Mem. Am. Chem. Soc., Am. Inst. of Chem. Engrs., Inst. of Petroleum Technologists (Eng.), Am. Soc. Automotive Engrs., Am. Soc. for Testing Material, Am. Petroleum Inst., Natural Gasoline Assn. of America (ex-pres.). Episcopalian. Clubs: Bradford, Bradford Country, Valley Hunt. Contbr. of papers to tech. jours. and assns.; co-author books on petroleum technology. Home: 23 Sanford St. Office: Bradford Oil Refining Co., Bradford, Pa.

LEDERER, Lewis George, grain mcht.; b. Baltimore, Md., Jan. 5, 1892; s. Henry Andrew and Frances (Richardson) L.; student Baltimore City Schs., 1898-1909, Baltimore City Coll., 1907-11, Johns Hopkins U., 1911-15; m. Ruth Virginia Lindau, Oct. 18, 1920; 1 son, George Richardson. Began as grain buyer in sch. vacations, 1911; asso. with Lederer Bros., grain mchts., Baltimore, since 1915, partner since 1920; chmn. bd. dirs. Colonial Trust Co. since 1939. Served as lt., Air Service, A.E.F., 1917-19. Mem. Am. Rifle Assn., Phi Gamma Delta. Club: Johns Hopkins (Homewood, Md.). Marine pilot and navigator, Weems System of Navigation, 1939. Home: 514 Woodlawn Rd., Roland Park. Office: 304 Chamber of Commerce Bldg., Baltimore, Md.

LEDERER, Lucy Christine Kemmerer, artist; b. Milton, Pa.; d. William and Kathryn E. (Krumrine) Kemmerer; student Simmons Coll., Pratt Inst.; B.S., Pa. State Coll.; m. Col. Eugene H. Lederer, June 29, 1918; 1 son, Eugene William. Served as teacher in Pa. high schools from 1915-18. Has exhibited work at Corcoran Art Gallery, Washington, D.C., 1935; Chicago Art Inst., 1937; Conn. Acad. Fine Arts, Hartford, 1936; Cincinnati Museum of Art, 1936; Pa. Acad. Fine Arts, 1938; Nat. Assn. Women Painters, 1938; Pa. State Coll., 1938; Bucknell U., 1937; Reading (Pa.) Museum, 1938. Represented in permanent collections: Pa. State Coll., Jo Hays, Central Pa. Hist. Museum. Mem. Art Alliance of Phila., Am. Legion Auxiliary, D.A.R. Presbyterian. Home: State College, Pa.

LEE, Blair, ex-senator; b. Silver Spring, Md., Aug. 9, 1857; s. Samuel Phillips (adm.) and Elizabeth (Blair) L.; A.B., Princeton, 1880, A.M., 1883; LL.B., Columbian (now George Washington) U., 1882, LL.M., 1883; m. Anne Clymer Brooke, Oct. 1, 1891 (died Dec. 24, 1903); children—Edward Brooke, Phillips Blair, Arthur Fitzgerald (dec.). Admitted to bar of D.C. and Md.; Dem. nominee for Congress, 6th Md. Dist., 1896 (defeated); elected mem. Md. state senate, 1905; reëlected, 1909; candidate for Dem. nomination for gov. of Md., 1911, and defeated by vote in convention of 64 to 65; elected to U.S. Senate Nov. 4, 1913, for period expiring Mar. 3, 1917. Pres. Soc. Lees of Va., 1922-34; mem. Soc. of the Cincinnati (Va.). Home: Silver Spring, Md.*

LEE, Charles Marston, prof. Greek and Latin, coll. dean; b. Corvallis, Ore., Feb. 7, 1888; s. Rev. George Hewit and Nettie Anna (Cooke) L.; A.B., Miami U. Oxford, O., 1910; A.M., U. of Cincinnati, 1917; grad. study, Am. Acad. in Rome, 1924; Ph.D., U. of Pittsburgh, 1937; m. Alice H. Stewart, June 11, 1913; children—Jonathan Stewart, Sara Rebecca, Walter Marston, Margaret Isabella, Ellen Norville, Stewart Munro. Engaged in teaching, high sch., Mt. Washington, O., 1910-11, elementary sch., Cincinnati, O., 1911-16, prin., 1917-18; prof. Greek and Latin, Geneva Coll., Beaver Falls, Pa., since 1918, sec. faculty since 1918, dean Geneva Coll. since 1923. Served as pvt. Home Guards, Cincinnati and mem. Am. Protective Assn. during World War. Mem. Am. Classical League, Classical Assn. Atlantic States, Classical Assn. Pittsburgh and Vicinity, Eastern Assn. Coll. Deans, Pa. State Edn. Assn., Classical Soc. of Am. Acad. in Rome. Reformed Presbyn. Contbr. articles on Varro, Latin writer. Home: 2823 Fourth Av., Beaver Falls, Pa.

LEE, Elsworth M., civil engr., architect; b. Paterson, N.J., June 20, 1876; s. Wm. Gregory and Hester Graham (Ackerson) L.; ed. Paterson pub. schs. and New York U.; m. Mary E. Christie, June 8, 1898; children—Carlton Elsworth, Gregory Christie. Began as draughtsman, 1895, becoming engr., 1900; engaged in steel mill designing and estimating, 1900-02, contracting and architectural work, 1902-06; mem. firm Lee & Hewitt, engrs. and architects, since 1906. Served as production engr. Ordnance Dept. Loading Sect., 1918-19 Mem. Am. Soc. Civil Engrs., Am. Inst. Architects. Democrat. Mem. Reformed Ch. in America. Mason (Past Master); Elk (hon. life mem.). Home: 262 E. 30th St. Office: 152 Market St., Paterson, N.J.

LEE, Frederic Paddock, lawyer; b. Lincoln, Neb., Jan. 6, 1893; s. George Sterling and Maud Maria (Paddock) L.; Ph.D., Hamilton Coll., Clinton, N.Y., 1915; M.A., Columbia, 1916, LL.B., 1918; m. Marian A. Armstrong, June 22, 1918; children—Eleanor, Sterling, Barbara, Richard Curry. Admitted to bar, 1918; asst. draftsman Legislative Drafting Service, U.S. Ho. of Rep., 1919-23; legislative draftsman, U.S. Senate, 1923-24, legislative counsel of same, 1924-30; mem. law firm of MacCracken & Lee, Washington, D.C., 1930-34; mem. bd. and gen. counsel Federal Alcohol Control Adminstrn., 1934-35; mem. law firm Alvord & Alvord, Washington, D.C., since 1935; prof. law Georgetown U., 1929-35. Pres. Montgomery County (Md.) Civic Federation, 1931-33; dir. Social Service League, Montgomery County, 1931-37; mem. Md. Nat. Capital Park and Planning Commn., 1934-35. Served as pvt., 2d lt. inf., 1918; 2d lt. inf., O.R.C., 1918-23; capt. judge advocate, O.R.C., 1924-29. Mem. Am. and D.C. bar assns., Assn. Bar City of N.Y., Am. Soc. Internat. Law, Delta Upsilon. Democrat. Clubs: University (Washington); Columbia Univ. (New York). Contbr. on legal subjects. Home: 6915 Glenbrook Rd., Bethesda, Md. Address: Munsey Bldg., Washington, D.C.

LEE, Harry Winfield, lawyer; b. Shenandoah, Pa., Apr. 24, 1894; s. W. Thomas and Mary Jane (Preston) L.; grad. Mercersburg Acad., 1912; student Pierce Business Sch., Phila., 1913; LL.B., Dickinson Sch. of Law, 1918; m. Mildred H. Price, Oct. 28, 1920. Admitted to Pa. bar, 1920, and since practiced in Reading; mem. firm Stevens & Lee. Trustee Homeopathic Hosp., Reading. Served in infantry, U.S. Army, 1918. Mem. Berks Co. Bar Assn., Delta Chi. Republican. Methodist. Mason, Elk. Clubs: University, Wyomissing, Reading Country (Reading, Pa.). Home: Route 2, Muhlenberg Park, Reading, Pa. Office: 18 S. 5th St., Reading, Pa.

LEE, Henry, publisher; b. Hamlet, Ill., May 25, 1884; s. Graham and Anna Sarah (Fisher) L.; ed. Aledo (Ill.) High Sch., Met. Business Coll., Chicago; m. Pearl Anderson, Dec. 20, 1910; children—Doris Carol (Mrs. George Weaver Porter), Henry. With Railway Age (publ.) later with. Railroad Gazette (consolidation) through grades from mem. news staff to treas., 1905-11; following formation of Simmons Boardman Pub. Co., dir., later v.p. and treas., 1911-29, pres. since 1931; v.p. Simmons Boardman Pub. Corpn., 1929-32, pres. since 1932; v.p. Am. Builder Pub. Corpn., 1929-33, pres. since 1933. Served as chmn. business press dir. U.S. Liberty and Victory Loans, World War; mem. Surplus Property Com. U.S. War Dept. Mem. National Pubs. Assn. (dir.), Asso. Business Papers, Inc. Republican. Methodist. Clubs: Downtown Athletic, Engineers, New York Railroad, Railroad Machinery (New York); Seaview Golf, Lake Hopatcong Country. Home: 246 Rugby Rd., Brooklyn, N.Y., and Hopatcong, N.J. Office: 30 Church St., New York, N.Y.

LEE, Henry Haworth, pres. Pennroad Corpn.; b. Pawtucket, R.I., Nov. 3, 1880; s. Frank L. and Clara M. (Haworth) L.; grad. Media (Pa.) High Sch., 1897; m. Edith Carpenter Green, Oct. 9, 1912; children—Henry Haworth, William L. With Pa. R.R., 1898-1929, asst. treas., 1918-24, treas. same and affiliated cos., 1924-29; pres. Pennroad Corpn. since 1929; dir. Pa. Co. for Insurances on Lives and Granting Annuities, Pittsburgh & W.Va. Ry. Co., Canton Co., Northern Trust Co. (Phila.); mem. bd. mgrs. Beneficial Savings Fund Soc. Republican. Episcopalian. Clubs: Union League, Rittenhouse (Phila.); Rolling Green Golf (Media, Pa.); Wilmington Country. Home: Moylan, Pa. Office: Delaware Trust Bldg., Wilmington, Del.

LEE, Howard Burton, lawyer; b. Wirt Co., W.Va., Oct. 27, 1882; s. Stephen S. and Virginia (Quick) L.; student Marshall Coll., Huntington, W.Va., 1902-05; LL.B., Washington and Lee U., 1909; m. Ida Hamilton, Mar. 5, 1907. Admitted to W.Va. bar, 1909, and began practice at Bluefield; referee in bankruptcy, Southern Dist. of W.Va., 1912-16; pros. atty. Mercer Co., W.Va., 1912-24; atty. gen. of W.Va., 2 terms, 1925-33. Republican. Presbyn. Mason. Author: The Criminal Trial in the Virginias; The Story of the Constitution. Home: 1412 Jackson St. Office: Union Bldg., Charleston, W.Va.

LEE, Howard Hall Macy; v.p. Safe Deposit & Trust Co. Home: 1930 Mount Royal Terrace. Office: 13 South St., Baltimore, Md.

LEE, James Augustine, chem. engring., mng. editor; b. New Iberia, La., Aug. 7, 1894; s. Charles Hill and Dora Glassel (Weeks) L.; A.B., Washington & Lee U., Lexington, Va., 1917, B.S., same, 1917; grad. study, Mass. Inst. Tech., 1917-18; A.M., Columbia U., 1925; m. Margaret Bateman Lee, June 6, 1931; children—James Augustine, Jr., David Weeks. Was chemical engr., Federal Dyestuff & Chem. Co., Kingsport, Tenn., 1917, Citizens Gas Co., Indianapolis, Ind., 1919-20, Western Electric Co., New York, N.Y., 1920-25, Bell Telephone Labs., N.Y. City, 1925-28; with McGraw-Hill Pub. Co., New York, N.Y., since 1928; mng. editor mag., Chemical & Metallurgical Engineering since 1932. Served in C.W.S., U.S.A., 1918. Mem. Am. Chem. Soc., Electrochem. Soc. (mem. bd. of dirs.), Tech. Assn. Pulp & Paper Industry, Am. Soc. for Testing Materials, Am. Inst. Chem. Engrs., Royal Soc. of Arts (British). Democrat. Episcopalian. Mason (K.T.). Club: Country (Glen Ridge). Home: 286 Rutledge Av., East Orange, N.J. Office: 330 W. 42d St., New York, N.Y.

LEE, John, research chemist; b. Barnard Castle, Eng., Sept. 3, 1901; s. Harry and Eleanor

(Skelton) L.; came to U.S., 1927, naturalized, 1939; Ph.C., Glasgow Royal Tech. Coll., 1921; B.S., Brooklyn Poly. Inst., 1931; Ph.D., U. of Zürich, 1934; m. Mary Louise Vaughan, Sept. 24, 1932; 1 dau., Elinor Jane. Employed as pharm. chemist, Eng., 1921-27; research chemist, E. R. Squibb & Sons, Brooklyn, N.Y., 1928-32; chief research chemist, Hoffman-La Roche, Inc., Nutley, N.J., since 1934. Mem. Am. Chem. Soc., German Chem. Soc. Episcopalian. Home: 38 Overlook Terrace. Office: Hoffman-La Roche, Inc., Nutley, N.J.

LEE, John Curry, banker; b. Pottsville, Pa., Mar. 6, 1894; s. John Curry and Phebe (Atkins) L.; student Mackensie Sch., Dobbs Ferry, N.Y., 1910-12; B.S., Lafayette Coll., Easton, Pa., 1917; m. Virginia Giesen, Oct. 4, 1934; 1 son, John Curry 4th. With Harris Forbes & Co., New York, 1922-24; with City Nat. Bank, Pottsville, Pa., since 1924, pres. and dir. since 1934; vice-pres. Pottsville Clearing House Assn., 1939. Pursuit pilot, 2d lt., 213 Aero Squadron, 3d Pursuit Group, A.E.F., during World War. Mem. K.R.T. (Lafayette Coll.), Am. Legion, Theta Delta Chi. Episcopalian. Clubs: Pottsville (pres.); Schuylkill Country (Orwigsburg, Pa.). Home: Pottsville, Pa. Office: City National Bank, Pottsville, Pa.

LEE, John Harvey, clergyman; b. Bovina Center, N.Y., June 16, 1875; s. Rev. James B. (D.D.) and Jane I. (Campbell) L.; ed. Monmouth Coll., Monmouth, Ill., 1891-93; A.B., Hamilton Coll., Clinton, N.Y., 1895; grad. study, Harvard U. Grad. Sch., 1895-96; ed. Xenia Theol. Sem., Xenia, O., 1896-99, New Coll., Edinburgh, Scotland, 1899-1900; (hon.) D.D., Macalester Coll., Minn., 1926; m. Elizabeth Junia Park, Oct. 2, 1902; children—John Park, Catharine. Ordained to ministry United Presbyn. Ch., 1901; pastor, Columbus, O., 1901-02; pastor Second Presbyn. Ch., Germantown, Phila., Pa., continuously since 1902. Served in Nat. War Work of Y.M.C.A., 1917-18; chaplain Pa. N.G., 1920-27. Trustee of Gen. Assembly of Presbyn. Ch. U.S.A. Mem. Theta Delta Chi. Democrat. Presbyn. Club: Union League (Philadelphia). Home: 6135 Greene St., Germantown, Philadelphia, Pa.

LEE, John Munson, manufacturer; b. Philipsburg, Pa., Sept. 21, 1901; s. Thomas James and Carrie Bowman (Munson) L.; student Philipsburg Pub. Schs., 1907-16, Kiskiminetas Springs Sch., Saltsburg, Pa., 1916-17, Army & Navy Prep. Sch., Washington, D.C., 1918-21; A.B., Pa. State Coll., State Coll., Pa., 1925; m. Eugenia Row Mitchell, Feb. 4, 1928 (died Jan. 15, 1939). Began as asst. to father in coal operation, 1925; sec. Citizens Bldg. & Loan Assn., 1925-28; gen. mgr. Chester Mine, 1926-34; sec.-treas. Lee Metal Products Co., Inc., mfrs. metal equipment for food and chemical processing industries, 1928-32, pres. and treas. since 1932. Mem. Canning Machinery and Supplies Assn., Sigma Alpha Epsilon. Republican. Presbyterian. Mason (R.A.M.; K.T., Comdr. 1935-36). Clubs: Philipsburg Country, Rotary (Philipsburg). Home: Curtis Park. Office: Lee Metal Products Co., Philipsburg, Pa.

LEE, Linwood Lawrence, geologist, soils specialist; b. Trenton, N.J., Jan. 11, 1894; s. William James and Laura (Beatty) L.; B.S., Rutgers U., 1916; ed. Princeton U., 1924-25, U. of London, Eng., 1929-31; hon. D.Sc., U. of London, 1931; m. Lucy M. Litterst, Sept. 22, 1923; 1 son, Linwood Lawrence, Jr. Asst. to state geologist of N.J. in charge soil survey, 1916-25; asst. prof. soils, Rutgers U. Coll. Agr., 1925-29, research specialist land utilization, N.J. Agrl. Expt. Sta.; fellow, Rockefeller Foundation Internat. Edn. Bd., Europe, 1929-31; research fellow, Nat. Research Council, Europe, 1931; mem. staff Rothamsted Exptl. Sta., Harpenden, Eng., 1929-31; asst. prof. soils, Rutgers U., 1931-34, research specialist land utilization, N.J. Agrl. Expt. Sta.; with Agrl. Adjustment Administrn., 1934; with U.S. Dept. Interior, 1935; state coördinator soil conservation service, U.S. Dept. Agr. since 1935. Served as lt. inf., U.S.A., during World War. Mem. Internat. Soc. Soil Sci., Soil Sci. Soc. America, Am. Soc. Agronomy, Am. Geophys. Union, N.J. Parks & Recreation Assn., N.J. Hort. Soc., N.J. Pub. Health Assn., New Brunswick Sci. Soc., Sigma Xi, Kappa Sigma, Rutgers Club. Episcopalian. Grange. Clubs: Union (New Brunswick); Country (Trenton). Home: Hillcrest, River Rd., New Brunswick, N.J.

LEE, Manning de Villeneuve, illustrator; b. Summerville, S.C., Mar. 15, 1894; s. Brig. Gen. Joseph and Gertrude Marie (Sweeny) L.; prep. edn., Porter Mil. Acad., Charleston, S.C.; art study Pa. Acad. Fine Arts, 1914-15, 1919-22; grad. F.A. Sch., Saumur, France, Heavy Arty. Tractor Sch., Vincennes, Army Antiaircraft Sch., Arnouville, 1918; m. Eunice Celeste Sandoval, Apr. 8, 1922; 1 son, Richard Sandoval. Prin. works: portrait of Freas Styer, U.S. Mint, Phila.; 5 marine paintings, U.S. Naval Acad., Annapolis, Md. Illustrator of books and also for mags.; books illustrated include Blue Fairy Book and Red Fairy Book (by Lang), Historic Ships, Historic Airships and Historic Railroads (by Rupert Sargent Holland), Kidnaped (Robert Louis Stevenson), When You Grow Up to Vote (by Eleanor Roosevelt), etc. Awarded medal, Charleston Expn., 1901; Cresson traveling scholarship, Pa. Acad. Fine Arts, 1921; 2d Toppan prize, same, 1922. Served with 1st Va. F.A., Mexican border, 1916; 2d lt. F.A., U.S.A., 1917-19. Mem. Southern States Art League. Companion Mil. Order Foreign Wars of U.S. Democrat. Episcopalian. Home: Boxwood Farm, Ambler, Pa. Studio: 234 Walnut St., Philadelphia, Pa.

LEE, Philip Francis, ins. co. exec.; b. Baltimore, Md., Mar. 24, 1884; s. Columbus O'Donnell and Hannah Anne (Tyson) L.; LL.B., U. of Md. Law Sch., Baltimore, 1906; m. Margaret L. Wilson, Nov. 1, 1904; children—Philip F., Jr., Augustus W., J. Tyson, Georgine I. Admitted to Md. bar, 1906; asso. with U.S. Fidelity & Guaranty Co., casualty and surety bonds, Baltimore, Md., since 1915, vice-pres. and agency dir. since 1932. Democrat. Roman Catholic. Clubs: Maryland, Merchants, Elkridge, Bachelors' Cotillon (Baltimore). Home: R.F.D. 2, Frederick. Office: Redwood and Calvert Sts., Baltimore, Md.

LEE, Walter Estell, surgeon; b. Phila., Pa., July 22, 1879; s. William Estell and Nellie Florence (Dickerson) L.; M.D., U. of Pa., 1902; m. Margaret Gordon, June 14, 1911; 1 dau., Jean Gordon. Res. pathologist Pa. Hosp., 1902-03, resident anesthetist and chief resident phys., 1904-08; interne Germantown Hosp., 1903-04; at present surgeon to Pennsylvania, Graduate, Germantown, Children's, Bryn Mawr and Burlington Co. hosps. Res. officer Med. Corps, U.S.A., 1911-14; Med. Corps, French Army, 1915-16; Med. Corps, U.S.A., 1917-19; officer Med. Res. Corps, U.S.A. since 1919 (maj. 1919, now lt. col.). Fellow Am. Coll. Surgeons; mem. Internat. Surg. Soc., Am. Surg. Assn., Am. Assn. Thoracic Surgeons, A.M.A., Pa. State Med. Soc., Am. Soc. Clin. Surgery, Phila. Acad. Surgeons, Coll. of Phys. of Phila., Phila. Pediatric Soc., Kappa Sigma, Alpha Mu Pi Omega. Republican. Presbyterian. Mason. Club: University of Phila. Author: Textbook of Surgery (with F. T. Stewart), 1931; Manual of Surgery (with F. T. Stewart), 1928. Coeditor of Progressive Medicine, 1919-33; chmn. editorial bd. Annals of Surgery since 1935. Contbr. to surg. jours. Address: 1833 Pine St., Philadelphia, Pa.

LEE, William Porter, clergyman, retired; b. Crestline, O., Dec. 19, 1865; s. Samuel Porter and Rebecca Porter (Hall) P.; A.B., Macalester Coll., St. Paul, Minn., 1889; A.M., Princeton U., 1891; B.D., Princeton Theol. Sem., 1892; Ph.D., Coll. of Wooster (O.), 1903; hon. D.D., Macalester Coll., St. Paul, Minn., 1910; m. Pamela R. Clark, Mar. 1, 1893; 1 dau., Virginia Clark (Mrs. Andrew R. Wight, Jr.). Ordained to ministry Presbyn. Ch., 1892; began as pastor of a mission in Germantown which eventually became the Westside Presbyn. Ch. with membership of over 1250 and property of over $450,000, pastor continuously, 1892-1938, retired 1938. Republican. Home: 309 Sylvania Av., Glenside, Pa.

LEECH, Carl Graydon, sch. supt.; b. Jamestown, Pa., Dec. 22, 1887; s. Richard Van Dyke and Lucy Anna (Wolfe) L.; A.B., Franklin and Marshall Coll., Lancaster, Pa., 1907; A.M., U. of Pa., 1910, Ph.D., 1932; m. Alma King Johnson, June 11, 1913; children—Janet King (Mrs. Frank F. Silloway), John Graydon, Howard Johnson. Principal, Oley (Pa.) High Sch., 1907-09, Riegelsville (Pa.) Acad., 1910-16; supervising principal of schs., Quakertown, Pa., 1918-22; principal, Glen-Nor High Sch., Glenolden, Pa., 1922-25; co. supt. of schs., Delaware Co., Pa., since 1925. Mem. N.E.A., Lambda Chi Alpha, Phi Delta Kappa. Republican. Presbyterian. Mason. Club: Rotary (Media, Pa.). Author: The Constitutional and Legal Basis of Education in New Jersey, 1932. Home: 317 Trites Av., Norwood. Office: Court House, Media, Pa.

LEECH, Edward Towner, editor; b. Denver, Colo., June 17, 1892; s. Edward Palmer and Henrietta May (Reasoner) L.; grad. West Denver High Sch., 1910; student, U. of Colo., 1910-12; m. Pauline Bohanna, July 27, 1914; children—Edward Palmer, Robert Henry; m. 2d, Rose Loretta Roche, Apr. 15, 1931; children—Kathleen Patricia, Johanna May. Began on Denver Republican, 1909; editor Denver Express, 1916-17, Memphis (Tenn.) Press, 1917-21; founder and editor, Birmingham (Ala.) Post (for Scripps-Howard Newspapers), 1921-26; editor Rocky Mountain News, 1926-31, Pittsburgh Press since 1931. Mem. Delta Tau Delta. Mason. Clubs: Duquesne, Pittsburgh Athletic Assn. Home: 78 Hoodridge Drive, Mt. Lebanon, Pa. Office: The Pittsburgh Press, Boul. of the Allies, Pittsburgh, Pa.

LEECH, George L., bishop; b. Ashley, Pa., May 21, 1890; s. William Dillon and Helen Mary (FitzSimons) L.; ed. St. Charles Sem., Overbrook, Pa., 1913-20; J.C.D., Cath. U. of America, 1922. Ordained priest R.C. Ch.; sec. Apostolic Delegation, Washington, 1923-29; rector St. Patrick's Church, Pottsville, Pa., 1929-35; apptd. titular bishop of Mela and auxiliary bishop of Harrisburg, Pa., July 6, 1935; bishop of Harrisburg since Dec. 19, 1935. Trustee Am. Eccles. Review. Address: 111 State St., Harrisburg, Pa.

LEEDS, Morris Evans, mfr.; b. Phila., Pa., Mar. 6, 1869; s. Barclay R. and Mary (Maule) L.; ed. Westtown Boarding Sch., 1883-86; B.S., Haverford Coll., 1888; studied U. of Berlin, 2 semesters, 1892-93; Dr. of Engring., Brooklyn Polytechnic Inst., 1936; m. Hadassah J. Moore, June 10, 1926; children—Esther Hallett, Mary Maule. Pres. Leeds & Northrup Co. since 1903. Inventor of elec. and temperature measuring instruments. Went to France, June 1917, as spl. commr., with first party of Am. Red Cross, representing Am. Friends Service Com. to assist in relief work in France. Dir. Phila. Chamber of Commerce. Pres. of corpn. and board of managers of Haverford Coll.; pres. Bd. of Pub. Edn. of Phila.; trustee Germantown Friends' Sch., Christiansburg Industrial Inst. Fellow Am. Inst. E.E., A.A.A.S.; mem. Am. Physical Soc., Acad. Natural Sciences, Am. Soc. Steel Treating, Franklin Inst., Assn. Scientific Apparatus Makers of U.S. (pres. 1920-26), Metal Mfrs.' Assn. of Phila. (pres. 1924-30), Phi Beta Kappa. Awarded Edward Longstreth Medal of Merit, Franklin Inst., 1920, for invention of Leeds & Northrup recorder. Quaker. Clubs: Engineers, University (Phila.); Huntington Valley Country (Pa.); Engineers (New York); Cosmos (Washington). Mem. Industrial Advisory Bd. of NRA, 1933-35, mem. business advisory council U.S. Dept. of Commerce. Home: 1025 Westview St., Mt. Airy. Office: 4901 Stenton Av., Philadelphia, Pa.

LEES, George Cooper, pres. U.S. Axle Co., Inc.; b. in Eng., Mar. 1881; s. William Kelsall and Alice (Radcliffe) L.; B.S., Mass. Inst. Tech.; m. Bertha Butler, 1911; children—John Butler, Elizabeth. Pres. U.S. Axle Co., Inc., Pottstown, Pa., since 1920, also dir.; dir. Curtiss & Smith Mfg. Co. Episcopalian (vestryman Christ Episcopal Ch., Pottstown, Pa.). Elk. Club: Brookside Country (Pottstown, Pa.; dir.). Home: 203 Rosedale Av. Office: Water St., Pottstown, Pa.

LEETCH, Robert Graham, clergyman; b. Washington, D.C., Jan. 23, 1877; s. John and Victoria Imogen (Winship) L.; grad. Washington (D.C.) High Sch., 1896; A.B., Lafayette Coll., Easton, Pa., 1900, D.D., 1925; A.M., Princeton U., 1902; m. Louise Day Pierce, Feb. 25, 1903; children—Robert Graham, Louise Pierce (Mrs. Talbot T. Speer), George Norman Pierce, Helen Haldane (Mrs. Joseph S. Hall), David Winship. Ordained to ministry of Presbyn. Ch., 1904; pastor First Presbyn. Ch., Far Rockaway, N.Y., 1904-12; pastor First Ch. of Evans, community ch., Derby, N.Y., 1912-22; pastor Second Presbyn. Ch., Baltimore, since 1923. Mem. bd. of govs. Presbyn. Hosp., Baltimore. Mem. Phi Kappa Psi. Home: 4201 Charlcote Rd., Baltimore, Md.

LEFEVER, Clarence Homer, physician; b. Meadville, Pa., Dec. 22, 1874; s. David Harper and Alice A. (Gaut) L.; B.E., Edinboro Normal Coll., 1891, M.E., same, 1893; A.B., Allegheny Coll., 1898; M.D., U. of Pa. Med. Sch., 1902; hon. A.M., Allegheny Coll., 1902; m. Cecilia McKenna, Jan. 4, 1905. After interneship engaged in gen. practice of medicine at Erie, Pa., since 1903; staff phys., St. Vincent Hosp., Erie, Pa., 1907-35, chief of med. staff and cons. phys. since 1935; mem. asso. staff, Hamot Hosp. Mem. Erie Co. Med. Soc. (sec. 1908-09, pres. 1936), Phi Beta Kappa. Democrat. Catholic. Knight of St. John, Eagle. Home: 448 W. 28th St. Office: 805 W. 26th St., Erie, Pa.

LEFEVRE, Edwin, author; b. Colon, Colombia, Jan. 23, 1871; s. Henry L. (American) and Emilia (de la Ossa) L.; ed. pub. schs., San Francisco, 1880-84, Mich. Mil. Acad., Orchard Lake, Mich., 1884-87; studied mining engring., Lehigh U., 1887-90; m. Martha Moore, Jan. 22, 1902; children—Edwin, Reid. In journalism since 1890. Author: Wall Street Stories, 1901; The Golden Flood, 1905; Sampson, Rock of Wall Street, 1907; "H. R.," 1915; The Plunderers, 1916; To the Last Penny, 1917; Simonetta, 1919; Reminiscences of a Stock Operator, 1923; The Making of a Stock Broker, 1925. Mem. Am. Inst. Arts and Letter. Home: Atlantic City, N.J.

LeFEVRE, Laura Zenobia (Zenobia Bird), writer; b. Strasburg, Pa.; d. George Newton and Laura (Long) LeF.; ed. pub. schs. and under pvt. tutors; grad. business coll., West Chester, Pa., 1909. Stenographer in law office, West Chester, 1909; sec., editorial dept., Ladies Home Jour., 1910-13; stenographer, law offices, 1913-15; mem. editorial staff The Sunday Sch. Times since 1915. Presbyn. Author (under pen name): Under Whose Wings, 1928; Eyes in the Dark, 1930; The Return of the Tide, 1932; Sally Jo, 1934; Stoke of Brier Hill, 1936. Home: 5851 Willows Av. Office: 325 N. 13th St., Philadelphia, Pa.

LEFFERTS, Walter, educator; b. Phila., Pa., Dec. 12, 1875; s. John and Helen Campbell (Rich) L.; A.B., Temple U., 1905; Ph.D., U. of Pa., 1917; m. Marie Weber, July 15, 1920. Served as prin. Locust St., Morton Key, Marshall and Hanna schs., Phila., Pa., 1905-26; prin. Fitz Simons Jr. High Sch., 1926-38. Served on Research Bur. of War Trade Bd., 1918. Pres. Phila. Teachers Assn., 1925-28. Republican. Clubs: Schoolmen's, Art Alliance. Author: Noted Pennsylvanians, 1913; American Leaders, 1918; Our Own United States, 1925; Neighbors North and South, 1926; Our Neighbors in South America, 1927; Settlement and Growth of Pennsylvania, 1925; Our City and Our State, 1935. Home: 4411 Pine St., Philadelphia, Pa.

LEFFLER, George Leland, asso. prof. econs.; b. Maryville, Mo., Jan. 11, 1899; s. Charles David and Adelaide Viola (Reeves) L.; A.B., U. of Kan., 1927; A.M., U. of Wis., 1930, Ph.D., 1931; m. Vada Morris, Sept. 8, 1932. In employ Irving-Pitt Mfg. Co., Kansas City, Mo., 1927; on research staff, U. of Wis., 1928-32; instr. econs., 1930-32; statistician, various depts. State of Wis., 1931-32; asst. prof. finance, U. of Toledo, 1932-34; dep. co. auditor, Toledo, O., 1935 and 1937; asso. prof. finance, U. of Toledo, 1934-37; asso. prof. econs., Pa. State Coll. and asst. dir. Pa. Business Survey since 1937. Served as pvt. inf., U.S.A., 1918. Mem. Am. Econ. Assn., Phi Beta Kappa, Alpha Kappa Psi, Pi Gamma Mu. Republican. Presbyn. Writer monographs and tax studies. Home: 405 Arbor Way, State College, Pa.

LEFFLER, Ross L.; b. Butte, Mont., Aug. 7, 1886; s. John R. and Ouida E. (Cole) L.; student U. of Mich., 1903-05; m. Erma M. Wernke, Aug. 2, 1910. Asst. supt. of rolling mill, Duquesne Works, Carnegie Steel Co., 1027 31, supt., 1931-35, dir. of personnel, 1935; mgr. of industrial relations, Pittsburgh Dist. Carnegie-Ill. Steel Corpn., 1935-38; dir. industrial relations, Carnegie-Ill. Steel Corpn. since 1938. Mem. Pa. Game Commn., 1927-31, 1934-38, pres., 1928-31, vice-pres., 1937-38, chmn. organization analysis com., 1937-38; pres. Internat. Assn. Game, Fish and Conservation Commn., 1933; chmn. 17th Am. Game Conf., New York City, 1929; vice-pres. and mem. exec. bd. Duquesne Sportsmen's Club. Chmn. Region 3 camping com., Boy Scouts of America, 1938; mem. personnel advisory com. Boy Scouts, 1938; chmn. Allegheny County Council, West, Boy Scouts; asso. chmn. Community Fund, Allegheny Co., 1938; mem. com. on Moral Court work, Y.M.C.A., 1938. Mem. Am. Iron and Steel Inst. Pres. Lewis & Clark Club since 1934; mem. Good Fellowship Club. Author of pamphlet, Game Conservation in Pennsylvania. Home: 1403 Michigan Av., McKeesport, Pa. Office: 434 Fifth Av., Pittsburgh, Pa.

LEFSCHETZ, Solomon, mathematician; b. Moscow, Russia, Sept. 3, 1884; M.E., École Centrale, Paris, France, 1905; Ph.D., Clark U., 1911; m. Alice Berg Hayes, July 3, 1913. With Westinghouse Electric & Mfg. Co., Pittsburgh, Pa., 1907-10; fellow Clark U., 1910-11; instr. mathematics, U. of Neb., 1911-13; instr. mathematics, 1913-16, asst. prof., 1916-19, asso. prof., 1919-23, prof., 1923-25, U. of Kan.; visiting prof., Princeton University, 1924-25, asso. prof., 1925-28, prof., 1928-32. H.B. Fine Research prof., 1933—. Mem. Am. Math. Soc. (pres. 1935-36), Math. Assn. America, A.A.A.S., National Academy Sciences, Am. Philosophical Soc., Société Math. de France, Circolo Matematico di Palermo, Nat. Res. Council Committees on Rational Transformations and on Analysis Situs, Soc. Royale d. Sc. de Bohême, Jednota Mat. Fis. of Prague. Awarded Bordin prize by French Acad., for work in algebraic geometry, 1919; Bôcher prize, by Am. Math. Soc., 1924. Author of L'Analysis Situs et la Géometrie Algébrique, 1924; Topology, 1930. Asso. editor Bulletin des Sciences Mathématiques; editor Annals of Mathematics. Home: 129 Broadmead, Princeton, N.J.

LEGG, Clarence Angle, statistician; b. Legg's Mills, N.Y.; s. Peter John and Louise W. (Schaefer) L.; ed. pub. schs., Kingston, N.Y., pvt. sch., Ithaca, N.Y., Eastman Bus. Coll., Poughkeepsie, N.Y.; m. Florence E. Cornell, of Chicago, Ill., Aug. 10, 1918. Began as statistician for Armstrong Commn., New York, N.Y., 1905, then with P. B. Armstrong, publisher, to 1917; independent life ins. actuary, Chicago, Ill., 1917-22; propr. C. A. Legg & Co., statisticians, 80 Wall St., N.Y. City since 1922; propr. National Auditing Co., same address since 1930; exec. sec.-treas. Nat. Assn. of Retail Beverage Dealers of N.J., Inc., Newark, N.J., since 1933. Served as cons. efficiency engr. McCook Field, Dayton, O., during World War. Republican. Methodist. Elk. Clubs: Athletic (Newark); Players Boat (Fair Haven). Home: Biltmore Hotel, Newark, N.J.; (summer) Fair Haven, N.J. Office: 80 Wall St., New York, N.Y.; also Raymond-Commerce Bldg., Newark, N.J.

LEGG, Thomas Henry, physician and surgeon; b. Queen Anne Co., Md., Dec. 11, 1880; s. James Richard and Susan Anna Carter (Tanner) L.; A.B., Western Md. Coll., Westminster, 1902; student George Washington U., Washington, D.C., 1903-05; M.D., U. of Md. Med. Sch., Baltimore, 1907; m. Evelyn Clara Repp, May 10, 1910; children—Doris Evelyn (Mrs. Lewis Edward Crumpacker), Susan Shirley (dec.). Employed as prin. sch., Bladensburg, Md., 1902-04; interne Univ. of Md. Hosp., Baltimore, 1907-08; engaged in gen. practice of medicine and surgery at Union Bridge, Md., since 1908. Served in vol. Med. Service Corps during World War. Mem. Carroll Co. Bd. of Edn. (pres. 1935-39); asso. mem. Eastern Shore Soc., Baltimore, Md. Democrat. Meth. Protestant (trustee M.P. Ch., Union Bridge). Club: Kiwanis of Taneytown, Md. Address: Main and Thomas Sts., Union Bridge, Md.

LEGRAIN, Leon; Clark research prof. of Assyriology and curator Babylonian sect. Univ. Museum, Univ. of Pa. Address: University of Pa., Philadelphia, Pa.

LeGRYS, Herbert James, chem. engring.; b. Troy, N.Y., Apr. 26, 1901; s. Walter John and Harriet (Van Decar) LeG.; Chem.E., Rensselaer Poly. Inst., 1924; unmarried. Employed as research chemist, Fisk Rubber Co., Chicopee Falls, Mass., 1924-25; chemist, Stackpole Carbon Co., St. Marys, Pa., 1925-29, chief chemist since 1929. Mem. Am. Chem. Soc., Am. Soc. for Testing Materials, A.A.A.S., Electrochem. Soc., Nat. Soc. Professional Engrs., Pa. Soc. Professional Engrs., Faraday Soc., Eng., Deutsche Bunsen Gesellschaft, Germany. Republican. Presbyn. B.P.O.E., Moose. Club: Country (St. Marys). Home: 305 E. Erie Av., St. Marys, Pa.

LEH, Howard Harrison, cement mfr.; b. Siegfried, Pa., Feb. 7, 1889; s. T. Frank and Sarah E. (Bachman) L.; student Lerches Sch. and Lafayette Coll.; m. Jennie M. Roth, June 6, 1909; children—Ruth Roth, Ethel Margaretta. Chemist Penn-Allen Cement Co., Nazareth, Pa., 1909-10; chemist and engr. Cowell Portland Cement Co., Cowell, Calif., 1910-13; v.p. and engr. Leh Engring. Co., San Francisco, Calif., 1913-15; chemist Lehigh Portland Cement Co., Mason City, Ia., 1915-17; mgr. and engr. Gilmore Portland Cement Co., Gilmore City, Ia., 1917-18; Utah Portland Cement Co., Salt Lake City, Utah, 1918-19; supt. and engr. Phoenix Portland Cement Co., Nazareth, Pa., 1919-29; gen. mgr. Keystone Portland Cement Co., Bath, Pa., since 1929; dir. and cons. engr. Limestone Products Corpn. of America, Newton, N.J. Mem. Nazareth (Pa.) Y.M.C.A., Nazareth Sch. Bd. Mason (De Molay Consistory, 32°, Shriner). Clubs: Engrs. of the Lehigh Valley, Livingston, Shrine (Allentown, Pa.); Mink Pond (Bushkill, Pa.). Home: 326 S. Broad St., Nazareth, Pa. Office: Bath, Pa.

LEH, John, merchant and banker; b. Allentown, Pa., May 22, 1867; s. Henry and Sally Angelina (Trexler) L'ch; grad. Allentown High Sch., 1884; m. Irene Estella Keck, Jan. 17, 1893; children—John Henry, George Edward, Robert (dec.). Began as salesman H. Leh & Co., dept. store, Allentown, Pa., June 1884, mem. firm since 1887; pres. Merchants Nat. Bank from 1936-39. Trustee Y.M.C.A. (Allentown). Republican. Mem. Evangelical Congregational Ch. (trustee). Home: 1549 Hamilton St. Office: 626-632 Hamilton St., Allentown, Pa.

LEH, John Henry, dept. store exec.; b. Allentown, Pa., May 24, 1899; s. John and Irene E. (Keck) L.; student Lawrenceville (N.J.) Prep. Sch., 1912-17; A.B., Princeton U., 1921; m. Dorothea Seler Backenstoe, Sept. 8, 1921. With H. Leh & Co., department store, Allentown, Pa., since 1921, sales mgr. and partner since 1923; partner Leh & Koch, real estate, Allentown, since 1923, Leh Bros., real estate, Allentown, since 1929; pres. Allentown Airport Corpn. since 1934; dir. Second Nat. Bank of Allentown; trustee Earle Theater Bond Holders, Allentown. Mem. Allentown Chamber of Commerce (chmn. airport com. since 1929, dir. retail div.). Lutheran. Club: Lehigh Country, Kiwanis (mem. bd. dirs.), Princeton of Eastern Pa. (Allentown, Pa.). Licensed commercial pilot. Home: 1318 Linden St. Office: 626 Hamilton St., Allentown, Pa.

LEHMAN, George Mustin, consulting engr.; b. Lebanon, Pa., May 13, 1863; s. Benjamin Bringhurst and Susanna (Mustin) L.; brother of Ambrose Edwin L.; ed. Episcopal Acad., Lebanon, Pa.; m. Corinne May Stockton, Nov. 12, 1891 (died Feb. 6, 1933); 1 son, George Stockton (deceased). Aid, assistant and topographer Geol. Survey of Pa., 1882-89; chief assistant engr. surveys for extension Gettysburg & Harrisburg R.R., Gettysburg, Pa., to Washington, D.C., Brooklyn, Bath & West End R.R., N.Y., topographic and geologic survey, Navassa Island,

W.I., relief map of same, later, elec. ry. surveys, 1889-90; engr. location and constrn. Great Falls Water Power & Imp. Co.'s. canal, dams and location town (now Roanoke Rapids, N.C.), 1890-93; chief asst. engr. charge surveys for ship canal from Delaware River to Raritan Bay, 1894; principal assistant engineer in charge of surveys and estimates for the Lake Erie and Ohio River Canal, from Pittsburgh to Lake Erie, 1895-96; U.S. assistant engineer on improvement Allegheny, Pa., West Fork, W.Va., Youghiogheny, Pa., rivers, etc., assisted in inspection and report for permanent U.S. Army camp sites, Conewago Valley and Somerset, Pa., 1896-1903; constructed large relief map, Pittsburgh and vicinity, for Pittsburgh Chamber of Commerce, 1903-04 (gold medal at St. Louis Expn., 1904); engr. of parks, Pittsburgh, 1905; incorporator and chief engineer Lake Erie and Ohio River Canal Co., 1905—; sec.-member Pittsburgh Flood Commn. and engr. in charge investigations, surveys, and plans for flood prevention and protection (suggested commission and reservoir control), 1908—; chief engineer Lake Erie and Ohio River Canal Board to 1917; investigations and report on modes and costs of transportation by canal and river, 1917, 21. Reported to Com. on Inland Waterways of U.S. Railroad Administration on various canals as a war measure; production engr., and claims adjustment, U.S. Ordnance Dept., 1918-19; engr. Dept. of Internal Affairs of Pa., 1920; chief div. of Waterways, same, 1921-23 (resigned and division abolished); cons. practice since 1923, on waterway engring., including transportation methods; egineer River Front Improvement and River-Rail Terminal Plans of Department of Public Works; chief engineer of L.E.&O.R. Canal Bd. Mem. Am. Soc. C.E., Swedish Colonial Soc., Phila., Pa. Forestry Assn. (council), Engineers Soc. Western Pa., Flood Commn. of Pittsburgh, Pittsburgh Chamber of Commerce, Rivers and Harbors Congress (Washington), Propeller Club, The Pa. Soc. (N.Y. City). Home: Royal York Apts., Bigelow Boul. Office: County Office Bldg, Pittsburgh, Pa.

LEHMAN, James Alphonsus, surgeon; b. Phila., Pa., Mar. 12, 1904; s. Joseph Davis and Frances (Kelly) L.; grad. La Salle Prep. Sch., Phila., 1921; student U. of Pa., 1921-24; M.D., Jefferson Med. Coll., 1928; m. Adelaide Asadorian, Dec. 12, 1933; children—James Alphonsus, Richard Michael. Interne, U. of Pa. Grad. Hosp., 1928-29; post grad. study in surgery, Cleveland Clinic, 1929-33; in practice as surgeon, Phila., since 1933; attending surgeon Memorial Hosp.; asso. surgeon Chestnut Hill, Fitzgerald Mercy and Woman's Coll. hospitals; asst. surgeon St. Joseph's Hosp.; asso. in surgery, Woman's Med. Coll. Fellow Am. Coll. Surgeons, A.M.A.; mem. Am. Assn. for Study of Goiter; Phila. Co. Med. Soc., Pa. Med. Soc. Republican. Roman Catholic. Club: Phila. Cricket. Home: 3323 Queen Lane. Office: 1815 Spruce St., Philadelphia, Pa.

LEHMAN, William Parry, lawyer; b. Fairmont, W.Va., June 19, 1903; s. Albert L. and Jessica (Parry) L.; B.S., W.Va. Univ., Morgantown, 1924; LL.B., W.Va. Univ. Law Sch., 1927; m. Katherine Bartlett Valliant, Sept. 24, 1932; 1 dau., Katherine Valliant. Admitted to W.Va. bar, 1927, and engaged in gen. practice of law at Charleston, 1927-28; opened office in Fairmont, 1928, and since engaged in gen. practice of law; commr. in chancery of circuit ct. Marion Co., 1929-36; Rep. nominee for prosecuting atty. Marion Co., 1936. Served as sec. Marion Co. Rep. Exec. Com., 1932-36; vice-pres. W.Va. Young Rep. League, 1938-40. Mem. Am., W.Va. State and Marion Co. bar assns., W.Va. Soc. Sons of the Revolution, Delta Tau Delta, Phi Delta Phi. Republican. Baptist. Mason (K.T.). Club: Kiwanis. Home: 813 Fourth St. Office: Home Savings Bldg., Fairmont, W.Va.

LEHN, Homer Martin Boger, supt. of schs.; b. Lebanon Co., Pa. Oct. 18, 1878; s. Martin and Catherine Elizabeth (Boger) L.; A.B., Lebanon Valley Coll., Annville, Pa., 1908; A.M., Grove City (Pa.) Coll., 1921; grad. study Harvard and U. of Pittsburgh and U. of Chicago, 1908-31; m. Katie Elizabeth Henry, May 20, 1905; children—Homer Vincent, Roberta Ruth. Teacher, rural schs., East Hanover Twp. and North Annville Twp. (Pa.), 1895-1901; principal, North Annville Twp. Schs., 1902-08; high sch. teacher, Greenville, Pa., 1909-13; supervising principal, Grove City, Pa., 1913-35, supt. of schs. since 1935. Mem. N.E.A., Pa. State Edn. Assn., Patriotic Order Sons of America, Knights of Pythias. Republican. Lutheran. Clubs: Commercial, Rotary (Grove City, Pa.). Home: 147 State St. Office: Grove City, Pa.

LEHR, Anna Marguerite Marie, coll. prof.; b. Baltimore, Md., Oct. 22, 1898; d. George and Margaret (Kreuder) Lehr; student Western High Sch., Baltimore, Md., 1912-15, U. of Rome, Italy, 1923-24, Johns Hopkins U. (fellow by courtesy), Baltimore, Md., 1931-32; A.B., Goucher Coll., Baltimore, Md., 1919; Ph.D., Bryn Mawr (Pa.) Coll., 1925; unmarried. Instr. in mathematics, Bryn Mawr (Pa.) Coll., 1924-29, asst. prof., 1929-37, asso. prof. since 1937; mem. examining com. Coll. Entrance Examination Bd. since 1935. Mem. Am. Math. Soc., Math. Assn. of America, Am. Assn. U. Profs., Am. Assn. U. Women, Phi Beta Kappa. M. Carey Thomas fellow, Bryn Mawr, 1920; European fellow, Am. Assn. U. Women, 1923. Club: Women's University (Phila.). Home: Bryn Mawr. Office: Bryn Mawr Coll., Bryn Mawr, Pa.

LEIBENSPERGER, George F(ranklin), physician; b. Berks Co., Pa., Aug. 12, 1892; s. Frank D. and Emma L. (Kunkel) L.; diploma, Keystone State Teachers Coll., Kutztown, Pa., 1913; student Muhlenberg Coll., 1918-21; M.D., U. of Md. Med. Sch., 1925; m. Jennie K. Merkel, June 26, 1919; children—Maclowe Franklin, Randolph Jacob, Charles Merkel. Engaged in teaching sch., 1913-16; interne Bay View Hosp., Baltimore, 1925-27, also St. Joseph's Hosp., Reading, Pa., 1927-28; engaged in gen. practice of medicine and surgery at Kutztown, Pa., since 1928; mem. Berks Co. Med. Soc., Pa. State Med. Soc., A.M.A., Phi Chi. Republican. Lutheran. Mason. Home: 24 E. Main St., Kutztown, Pa.

LEICH, Chester, artist; b. Evansville, Ind., Jan. 31, 1889; s. Charles and Wilhelmine (Lemcke) L.; ed. in U.S. and abroad; studied in Italian and German art schs., 1911-15; grad. work, U. of Munich, 1911; m. Jean Graham Townley, July 8, 1927; 1 dau., Mary Townley. Works: "Landing at Ulvik" and "Village Street, Bedford," reproduced in Fine Prints of the Year, 1930 and 1932. Represented by etchings in permanent collections at Nat. Collection of Fine Arts, Washington, D.C.; Library of Congress; Museum of N.M. at Santa Fe (etchings); Soc. of Am. Etchers; Roerich Mus., New York; Nat. Acad. of Design Library; Contemporary Arts Bldg., New York World's Fair (drypoint, Norwegian Village). Temple of Fine Arts and History, Evansville, Ind. Award of Merit, Exhbn. of Artists of N.J., 1932; medal of merit for black and white, Exhbn. of Artists of N.J., Montclair Art Museum, 1938, for drypoint "Rio Grande Country," prize for black and white, Fine Arts Assn., Tucson, Ariz., 1938, for drypoint "Village Street, Bedford." Mem. Soc. of Am. Etchers, Chicago Soc. of Etchers, Phila. Soc. of Etchers, Am. Artists Professional League, Ind. Soc. of Printmakers. Home: Leonia, N.J.

LEICHTER, Walter, lawyer; b. West Hoboken, N.J., Apr. 14, 1903; s. Herman and Mary (Hollander) L.; ed. Columbia U., 1920-21; LL.B., N.Y. Univ., 1924; unmarried. Admitted to N.J. bar as atty. 1924, and since engaged in gen. practice of law at Union City; mem. firm Hollander, Leichter & Klotz; vice-pres. Weehawken Home Owners Assn. Dir. Jewish Community Center of North Hudson, N.J. (pres. 1934-35). Active in civic movements and charitable orgns. Mem. N.J. State Bar Assn., Hudson Co. Bar Assn., North Hudson Lawyers Club. Independent Republican. Jewish religion. Mason. Club: Spring Meadow Golf and Country (Allenwood, N.J.). Home: 28 Liberty Pl., Weehawken. Office: 648 Bergenline Av., Union City, N.J.

LEIGHTON, Alan, phys. chemist; b. Concord, N.H., Mar. 26, 1890; s. Fred and Irene (Harnden) L.; B.S., U. of N.H., Durham, N.H., 1912; student Cornell U., 1912-14; m. Rachel Courser, Nov. 16, 1915; children—John, Constance. Engaged as asst. in phys. chemistry, Cornell U., 1913-14; jr. chemist radio activity, U.S. Bur. Mines, Denver, Colo., 1914-16; research chemist, Goodyear Rubber Co., Akron, O., 1916-17; asst. chemist, U.S. Bur. Mines, Pittsburgh, Pa., 1917-20; chemist and sr. chemist, U.S. Bur. of Dairy Industry, Washington, D.C., since 1920. Served as fire marshal, Town of Cottage City, Md., 1922-33, health officer, 1924-26, commr., 1923-24 and since 1938. Mem. Am. Chem. Soc., Am. Dairy Sci. Assn., Alpha Chi Sigma, Sigma Xi. Conglist. Home: 25 Hamilton St., Cottage City, Md.

LEIGHTON, Henry, coll. prof.; b. Canandaigua, N.Y., Feb. 20, 1884; s. Peter and Jeanie (Hall) L.; A.B., Cornell U., 1908; m. Jessie Cipperly, Aug. 25, 1909; children—Helen Elizabeth (Mrs. Ralph Cannon), Harry. Instr. geology, Cornell U., 1906-08; geologist N.Y. State Geologic Survey, 1908-10; instr. geology, U. of Pittsburgh, 1910-13, asst. prof., 1913-17, prof. since 1917; head dept. geology since 1930. Fellow A.A.A.S., Geol. Soc. of America, Soc. of Econ. Geologists; mem. Sigma Xi. Republican. Lutheran. Home: 1250 Rebecca Av., Wilkinsburg, Pa. Office: U. of Pittsburgh, Pittsburgh, Pa.

LEINBACH, Paul Seibert, clergyman, editor; b. Womelsdorf, Pa., Sept. 21, 1874; s. of Rev. Thomas Calvin and Maria R. (Seibert) L.; A.B., and A.M. (first honor), Franklin and Marshall, 1895; grad. Reformed Ch. Theol. Sem. Lancaster, Pa., 1898; D.D., Heidelberg, 1912; Litt. D., Franklin and Marshall, 1921; m. H. Belle Martin, May 26, 1898 (died Mar. 28, 1908); children—Thomas Martin (dec.), Joseph Nevin, Paul Harold; m. 2d, Helen S. DeLong, Aug. 2, 1910; 1 son, John DeLong. Ordained ministry Ref. Ch. in U.S., 1898; pastor Grace Ch., Altoona, Pa., 1898-1900, Trinity Ch., Pittsburgh, 1900-05, 1st Ch., Easton, 1905-13, Hamilton Grange Ref. Ch., New York, 1913-17; editor in chief Reformed Church Messenger since 1917; exec. sec. Publ. and S.S. Board Ref. Ch., 1925-29; exec. sec. Bd. Christian Education, 1929-30, pres., 1930-38. Pres. Editorial Council Religious Press of America, term 1924-34; editor in chief The Messenger, combined English organ Evang. and Ref. Chs., since Jan. 1, 1936. Sec. Gen. Bd. Home Missions Ref. Ch. in U.S., 1905-13; pres. Eastern Synod, 1911-12; 1st v.p. Gen. Synod, 1911-12; editor denominational S.S. lit., 1907-15. Mem. Federal Council of Churches, 1905-38 (exec. and administrative committees). Mem. Am. Relief Commn. to Near East, 1919; mem. exec. com. and bd. trustees of Internat. Council of Religious Edn.; mem. bd. dirs. Periodical Publisher's Inst. Mem. Am. Soc. Ch. History, Am. Acad. Polit. and Social Science, Pa. Acad. of Fine Arts, Phi Beta Kappa, Alpha Sigma, Phi Alpha. Republican. Mason. Rotarian. Home: 1520 Spruce St. Office: Schaff Bldg., Philadelphia, Pa.

LEIPER, Henry Smith, church official; b. Belmar, N.J., Sept. 17, 1891; s. Joseph McCarrell and Fanny Heywood (Smith) L.; grad. Blair Acad., Blairstown, N.J., 1909; B.A., Amherst, 1913, D.D. from same univ., 1930; grad. Union Sem., N.Y. City, 1917; M.A., Columbia, 1917; studied Chinese at N. China Union Lang. Sch., Peking, 1919; m. Eleanor Lansing Cory, May 15, 1915 (died Jan. 30, 1935); children—Juliet McCarrell, Henry Martyn Welling; m. 2d, Elizabeth Glover Olyphant, July 1935. Ordained ministry Presbyterian Church, 1915, transferred to Congregational Church, 1920; traveling sec. Student Vol. Movement, 1913-14; acting pastor Rutgers Presbyn. Ch., N.Y. City, 1914-16; served with Army Y.M.C.A., Siberia, 1918; missionary, A.B.C.F.M., Tientsin, China, 1918-22; mem. governing bd. China Internat. Famine Commn., 1919-20; Chinese Internat. Friendship del. to Japan, 1921; asst. sec., A.B.C.F.M., N.Y. City, 1922-23; editor Congl. Nat. Council's Commn. on Missions, 1923-29; asso. corr. sec. Am. Missionary Assn., N.Y. City, 1924-1927; editor The Potter's Wheel; asso. editor The Congregationalist, 1927-30; speaker for Am.

chs. at 400th anniversary of Augsburg Confession, Augsburg, 1930; pres. Union Sem. Alumni Council, 1931; contributing editor Federal Council Bulletin, 1930—; in charge Am. Ch., Paris, 1932; exec. sec. Am. Sect. Universal Christian Council for Life and Work, also same, Dept. of Relations with Chs. Abroad, Federal Council of Chs. of Christ in America, since 1930; mem. exec. coms. European Central Bur. for Inter-Ch. Aid (Geneva), World Conf. Faith and Order (Lausanne), Universal Christian Council (Stockholm), Nat. Conf. of Jews and Christians (New York), Council on Exchange of Preachers between Great Britain and America; mem. Am. Soc. World Council of Churchs (provisional com.); Council of Five on Christian World Movements, Commn. on Internat. Justice and Good Will, Am. Com. on Religious Rights and Minorities; trustee Am. Coll. (Madura, India); sec. Am. and Foreign Christian Union; sec. Am. Com. for Christian German Refugees; exec. dir. China Famine Relief. Recipient of Pi Lambda Phi tolerance medal, 1937. Mem. Am. Acad. of Polit. and Social Science, Beta Theta Pi, Delta Sigma Rho. Conglist. Clubs: Amherst, Clergy, Quill (New York); Shanghai Tiffin (pres.). Author: Blind Spots—Experiments in Cure of Race-Prejudice, 1929; The Ghost of Caesar Walks—The Conflict of Nationalism and World Christianity, 1935; Christ's Way and the World's—in Church, State, and Society, 1936; World Chaos or World Christianity, 1937. Co-Author: Younger Churchmen Look at the Church, The Church Through Half a Century. Lecturer on Orient, race relations, European relations. Writer numerous magazine articles and book reviews. Home: 1 Paulin Boul., Leonia, N.J. Office: 297 4th Av., New York, N.Y., and 41 Avenue de Champel, Geneva, Switzerland.

LEISENRING, Edward Barnes, coal operator; b. Nice, France, Jan. 12, 1895; s. Edward Barnes and Annie (Wickham) L.; came with parents to U.S., 1895; ed. Hotchkiss Sch., Lakeville, Conn.; B.S., Yale, 1917; m. Margaret Patterson Pierce, May 26, 1917; children—Ann Wickham, Mary Pierce, Carolyn Bertsch, Edward Barnes. Associated with engring. corps, Hazle Brook Coal Co., and became mine supt., v.p., 1923-26, pres., 1926-28; chmn. bd. Stonega Coke & Coal Co.; pres. Westmoreland Coal Co., Wentz Corpn., Va. Coal & Iron Co.; v.p. Gen. Coal Co.; bd. mgrs. Lehigh Coal & Navigation Co.; dir. Whitehall Cement Mfg. Co., Lehigh & N.E. R.R. Co. Seaman, 2d class, U.S.N.R.F., later ensign and lt. j.g., 1917-19. Mem. Delta Psi. Republican. Clubs: Philadelphia, Rittenhouse, Racquet (Philadelphia); St. Anthony (New York); Gulph Mills Golf; Merion Cricket; Radnor Hunt. Home: Glenn Rd., Ardmore, Pa. Office: Fidelity-Philadelphia Trust Bldg., Philadelphia, Pa.

LEISER Andrew Albright, Jr., lawyer; b. Lewisburg, Pa., Feb. 6, 1879; s. Andrew Albright and Susan Matilda (Brickenstein) L.; ed. Bucknell Acad., 1891-94; A.B., Bucknell U., 1898; A.B., Yale, 1899; unmarried. Admitted to Pa. bar, 1901, Pa. Supreme Court bar, 1903, bar of Mass., 1916; counsel for Pa. Telephone Co., 1906-08, during merger with Bell Telephone Co.; counsel Fisk Rubber Co., Chicopee Falls, Mass., 1915-30, sec., 1921-30; engaged in private practice of law, Lewisburg, Pa., since 1930; dir. Mifflinburg (Pa.) Body Co. Mem. Phi Kappa Psi. Republican. Elk. Clubs: Union League (Philadelphia); Yale (New York). Home: 522 St. George St., Lewisburg, Pa. Office: 124 Market St., Lewisburg, Pa.

LEISTER, John Swivel, civil engring. and asso. prof.; b. Lincoln, Neb., May 30, 1895; s. John B. and Margaret (Swivel) L.; C.E., Lafayette Coll., 1915; m. Margaret Gale Stinchcomb, Sept. 24, 1927; children—Margaret Ann, John Stinchcomb, Gale Campbell. In employ of engineering department of Pennsylvania Railroad and Central R.R. of N.J., 1915-18; maintenance engr., D. G. Dery Corpn., 1919-22; structural engr. with various cos., 1922-25; asst. prof. struct. engring., Purdue U., 1925-26; dir. pub. bldgs. for Am. Occupation of Haiti, 1926-32; asst. civil engr. Bur. Yds. & Docks, U.S.N., 1933-34; asst. prof. civil engring., U. of Ala., 1934-37; asso. prof. civil engring., Pa. State Coll. since 1937. Lt. comdr. C.E.C. V(s) U.S.N.R. Mem. Am. Ry. Engrs. Assn., Am. Soc. Civil Engrs., Soc. for Promotion Engring. Edn. Licensed professional engr. in Ala. Democrat. Lutheran. Mason. Home: 440 W. Beaver Av., State College, Pa.

LEITCH, Alexander, sec. Princeton Univ.; b. Paterson, N.J., Dec. 7, 1900; s. Charles and Louise (Flood) L.; A.B., Princeton U., 1924; m. Mary Lancaster, July 30, 1938. Engaged as dir. Bur. of Appointments and Student Employment, Princeton Univ., 1924-25, dir. Pub. Information, 1925-28, asst. to the Pres., 1928-35, sec. of the Univ. since 1935. Mem. Grad. Council of Princeton Univ. (sec. 1927-29). Presbyn. Clubs: Nassau, Terrace, Springdale Golf (Princeton); Princeton of New York (New York City). Home: Pretty Brook Rd. Office: Nassau Hall, Princeton, N.J.

LEITCH, Andrew, coll. prof.; b. Glencoe, Ontario, Canada, Dec. 16, 1885; s. Alexander and Katharine (McFarlane) L.; B.A., Butler U., Indianapolis, 1911, M.A., 1912; B.D., Yale U., 1914, Ph.D., 1919; student Columbia U., summers, 1921-23, U. of Pa., summer, 1929, U. of Chicago, summer, 1928, Harvard U., summer, 1936; m. Pearl R. Shipley, Dec. 28, 1911 (died 1927); children—Roy Yale, Katharine; m. 2d, Mary M. Horton, June 17, 1930. Came to U.S., 1908, naturalized, 1925. Teacher pub. schs., Ontario, 1904-07; prof. psychology and head of dept., Bethany Coll. since 1920; prof. ednl. psychology, Butler U., summers, 1924-30. Hooker Dwight fellow, Yale U., 1914-15, Currier fellow, 1915-19. Mem. A.A.A.S., N.E.A., Am. Psychol. Assn., Am. Assn. Univ. Profs., Soc. Psychol. Study of Social Issues, W.Va. Acad. Science, Phi Kappa Phi. Ind. Republican. Mem. Disciples of Christ (trustee, Bethany Memorial Ch.). Mason. Address: Bethany, W.Va.

LEITH, Hugh, clergyman; b. Hazleton, Pa., July 11, 1875; s. James and Mary (McCullough) L.; A.B., Washington and Jefferson Coll., 1897; student Western Theol. Sem., 1899-1902; hon. D.D., Center Coll., Danville, Ky., 1914; m. Pauline Watson Brown, Oct. 8, 1903; 1 child, Yoder Poignand. Ordained to ministry Presbyn. Ch., 1902; pastor, Zelienople, Pa., 1902-09, Lancaster, O., 1909-13, Covington, Ky., 1913-21, Wilkinsburg, Pa., 1921-29; pastor Presbyn. Ch., Mt. Lebanon, Pa., since 1929. Served as chaplain Ky. N.G., 1914-15; chaplain, U.S.A., 1918. Trustee Pikeville Coll., Pikeville, Ky. Republican. Mason (32°). Home: 751 Shady Drive East, Mt. Lebanon, Pa.

LEITH-ROSS Harry, artist; b. Mauritius (British colony), Jan. 27, 1886; s. Frederick Arbuthnot and Sina (van Houten) L.; ed. U. of Birmingham, Eng., 1901-02, Académie Delécluse and Académie Julian, Paris, 1909-10, Art Students' League, New York, 1910-13; m. Emily Slaymaker, July 20, 1925; 1 dau., Emily Elizabeth. Came to U.S., 1903, naturalized citizen, 1918. Served as 2d lt. inf., U.S.A., World War. Winner of Porter prize, Salmagundi Club, N.Y. City, 1915; Charles Noel Flagg prize, Conn. Acad. Fine Arts, 1921; 2d prize, Duxbury, Mass., 1921; landscape prize, New Haven Paint and Clay Club, 1924; Ranger Fund purchase award, N.A.D., 1927; Burton Mansfield prize, New Haven Paint and Clay Club, 1928; Grant prize, New Rochelle, N.Y., 1930; Providence (R.I.) Art Club prize, 1932; Art Center prize, Ogunquit, Me., 1932; Downes prize, New Haven, 1934; Geo. A. Zabriskie purchase prize, Am. Water Color Soc., 1937; lay members' prize Salmagundi Club, 1938. Nat. Academician. Mem. Am. Water Color Soc. Clubs: Salmagundi, N.Y. Water Color, Philadelphia Water Color. Home: New Hope, Pa.

LEITZEL, Frank Octave, v.p. Lewis Foundry & Machine Co.; b. Washington, D.C., Mar. 24, 1887; s. Stuart Milton and Cora (Gigoness) L.; B.S. in Mech. Engring., Pa. State Coll.; m. Martha Irvin, Dec. 17, 1918; children—William I., F. Stuart, Martha J. Became spl. apprentice Am. Locomotive Co., 1907; asst. gen. mgr. H. K. Porter Co., 1909-19; mgr. sales and engring.-welding Blaw-Knox Co., 1919-35; v.p. and dir. Lewis Foundry & Machine Co. since 1935. Home: 6421 Monitor St. Office: Lewis Foundry & Machine Co., Pittsburgh, Pa.

LEMAN, G(rant) W(illiam), supervising prin. of schools; b. Pittsburgh, Pa., July 10, 1896; s. George and Melinda (Funk) L.; A.B., Ohio State U., 1919, A.M., 1925; Ph.D., New York U., 1932; m. Gladys Neidhold, June 16, 1926; 1 dau., Marian Laverne. Public school teacher in Wis. and Minn., 1919-24; prin. Gallia (O.) Acad. High Sch., 1924-25; supervising prin. Jr. and Sr. High Sch., Wakefield, Mich., 1925-27; asst. prof. of edn. and supervisor of student training, U. of Ark., 1927-30; asst. dir. of student teaching, N.J. State Teachers Coll., Montclair, 1931-32; asst. in edn., New York U., 1932-33, instr. in edn., 1933-34; lecturer in edn., 1938-39; prin. Training Sch. for Teachers, Bucknell U., summers 1934, 1935; instr. in visual edn., N.J. State Teachers Coll., Paterson, 1936-40; supervising prin. of schs., Bogota, N.J., since 1934. Mem. N.E.A., N.J. State Teachers Assn., N.J. Council of Edn., N.J. Visual Edn. Assn. (mem. exec. com.), Bergen County Supervising Prins. Assn. (exec. com.), Kappa Delta Pi, Phi Delta Kappa, Gamma Phi. Presbyterian. Contbr. to ednl. jours. Home: 138 Park Place. Office: Main St. and River Rd., Bogota, N.J.

LEMMI, Charles W.; asst. prof. Italian and French, Goucher Coll., 1921-27, asso. prof., 1927-37, prof. since 1937. Address: Goucher College, Baltimore, Md.

LEMMON, Lyman Newill, clergyman; b. Mt. Pleasant, Pa., Jan. 3, 1891; s. Milton David and Nettie Jeanette (Wright) L.; A.B., Franklin Coll. (later Muskingum Coll.), 1917; S.T.B., Western Theol. Sem., 1922; D.D., Davis & Elkins Coll., 1939; m. Elizabeth Martha Walter, June 28, 1922; 1 dau., Lillian Elizabeth. Licensed to preach Redstone Presbytery, 1919; ordained to ministry by Kittanning Presbytery, 1922; pastor Worthington and West Glade Run Presbyn. Ch., 1922-24, Upper Path Valley Ch., Carlisle Presbytery, 1924-29; pastor Warwood Presbyn. Ch., Wheeling, W.Va., since 1929; prin. Washington Twp. High Sch., Westmoreland Co., Pa., 1919-20, and 1920-21; instr. young people's confs. Mem. Presbyterian Ministers Assn. (pres.). Contbr. articles and poems to relig. jours. Home: 125 N. 21st St., Wheeling, W.Va.

LeMON, Melvin William, musician; b. Paradise, Utah, Apr. 23, 1906; s. George W. and Elizabeth (Thomas) LeM.; grad. South Cache High Sch., Hyrum, Utah, 1921; B.S., Utah State Agrl. Coll., 1925; Mus.B., U. of Rochester, Eastman Sch., 1929, Mus.M., 1930; m. Beth Thurber, 1929 (died Jan. 5, 1935); 1 son, Melvin William; m. 2d, Jane Orwig, June 20, 1936. Organist Christian Science Ch., Rochester, N.Y., 1927-32; instr. in music, Bucknell U., 1932-33, asst. prof. of theory and organ since 1933, condr. of Glee Club since 1932, condr. of Band since 1934; organist St. Paul's Ch., Williamsport, Pa., 1932-35, Baptist Ch., Lewisburg, Pa., since 1935. Pres. Lewisburg chapter of Pa. Assn. of Organists. Mem. Phi Mu Alpha, Phi Kappa Phi, Phi Kappa Alpha. Republican. Baptist. Co-author: The Miner Sings and other publications of Pa. folk music. Collector and transcriber of Pa. folk music. Home: 1411 Market St., Lewisburg, Pa.

LENFESTEY, Nathan Coggeshall, banker; b. Marion, Ind., Mar. 1, 1890; s. William Lomax and Sarah (Coggeshall) L.; student De Pauw U., 2½ yrs.; B.S., Dartmouth, 1913; M.C.S., Amos Tuck Sch. of Administration and Finance (Dartmouth), 1914; m. Jeannette Hazen Ricketts, Feb. 14, 1919; children—William Richard, John Francis, Virginia, Janet. Began in banking business at Marion, 1907; cashier Nat. City Bank, New York, since 1919; pres. Parmley Apts., Inc.; v.p., sec. and treas. Internat. Banking Corpn.; dir., treas. and sec. Nat. City Safe Deposit Co.; dir., v.p., sec.-treas. Nat. City Realty Corpn.; dir., sec. and treas. Forty Four Wall St. Corpn.; dir. First Nat. Bank & Trust Co. and 1st Securities Corpn. (Summit. N.J.), State Title & Mortgage Guaranty Co. (Summit). Mem. Phi Beta Kappa, Phi Kappa Psi. Methodist. Clubs: Bankers, Dartmouth, Phi Kappa

Psi. Home: 30 Essex Rd., Summit, N.J. Address: 55 Wall St., New York, N.Y.

LENGLER, Frederick Kullman, manufacturer; b. Scranton, Pa., Aug. 1, 1887; s. Charles A. and Katharine (Kullman) L.; ed. Scranton Pub. Schs., 1891-99, Internat. Correspondence Sch., 1900-03, Scranton Business Coll (night school), 1904-08, Scranton Tech. Night Sch., 1909-12; m. Errilla Schooley, Oct. 15, 1913; children—Robert Edward, Marion Katharine (deceased). With Internat. Textbook Co., 1899-1903; with Simpson & Watkins (name changed later to Simpson & Brady), anthracite coal dealers, 1903-24, also sec. West End Coal Co., Shickshinny Store Co., Am. Universal Mill Co., Nat. Graphite Lubrication Co. and sec. treas. River Coal Co., Tower Coal Co.; sec. Estate of Chas. R. Connell since 1924; dir. Lackawanna Mills, mfrs. knitted goods and paper boxes, 1929-30, receiver, 1930-31, sec. and treas. since 1931; executor and trustee Estate of Bernard L. Connell since 1931; dir. Am. Record Corpn., 1929-30; mgr. and pres. Internat. Investors, 1935. Pres. Scranton Civil Service Commn.; mem. Scranton Recreation Commn.; Rep. committeeman county dist. Formerly active in Audubon Parent-Teachers Assn., and Boy Scout work. Republican. Methodist (mem. official bd. and religious edn. com. of Elm Park Ch.). Mason. Clubs: Y.M.C.A.; Travel (Harrisburg). Home: 1618 Olive St. Office: Connell Bldg., Scranton, Pa.

LENHARD, Raymond, Earl, physician and surgeon; b. Baltimore, Md., Jan. 14, 1898; s. Frederick William and Louise (Pruitt) L.; A.B., Johns Hopkins U., 1918; M.D., Johns Hopkins U. Med. Sch., 1922; m. Mary Coe Neiberger, Apr. 15, 1930; 1 son, Raymond Earl, Jr. Interne Johns Hopkins Hosp., Baltimore, 1922-23, 1924-25, Toronto Gen. Hosp., 1923-24; engaged in practice of medicine at Baltimore since 1927, specializing in orthopedic surgery since 1922; visiting orthopedist to the Johns Hopkins Hosp., Children's Hosp. Sch., Union Memorial Hosp., St. Joseph's Hosp.; instr. in orthopedics, Johns Hopkins Med. Sch. Mem. Am. Med. Assn., Baltimore City Med. Soc., Phi Beta Kappa, Alpha Kappa Kappa. Democrat. Lutheran. Clubs: Hopkins Alumni, Forum. Home: 217 Saint Dunstan's Rd. Office: 1107 Saint Paul St., Baltimore, Md.

LENHERT, George Roy, Jr., radio engring.; b. Maytown, Pa., May 27, 1903; s. George R. and Violet (Houseall) L.; B.S. in E.E., Drexel Inst., 1931; grad. study, Capitol Radio Engring. Inst., Washington, D.C., 1932-35; m. Margaret V. Smith, Sept. 10, 1927; 1 dau., Esther Elizabeth. Employed as mgr. radio sales and service, Phila., 1925-28; consulting radio engring., 1931-36; propr. and mgr. Metropolitan Radio & Electric Co., Phila., 1928-34; radio engr. for various radio stations; chief engr. Associated Broadcasting Corpn., Cumberland, Md., since Jan. 1937. Asso. mem. Inst. Radio Engrs, Republican. Methodist. Home: 4013 Spring Garden St., Philadelphia, Pa.

LENNIG, Frederick 6th, engr. and elec. construction; b. Phila., Pa., s. George G. and Margaret (Birmingham) L.; ed. sci. class, Central High Sch., Phila., Pa., 1890-95, elec. engring., Spring Garden Inst., 1897-99; m. Charlotte Hauseman Duling, 1910. Established Lennig Bros. Co., engrs. and constructors mostly elec. and steam driven elec. power plants, Phila., Pa., and propr. and pres. Lennig Bros. Co., Inc., since 1907; designed for U.S. Govt. first fire alarm system installed in Naval Powder Mag., Fort Mifflin; designed, built and operated one of first broadcasting stations in U.S., 1922, later purchased by WHAT, Phila., and now in operation. Served with 1st regt. Pa. N.G., assigned as personal body guard to Pres. Wm. McKinley on visit to Phila. Merit Badge councilor, Boy Scouts. Former mem. Engineers Club. Mem. Soc. Am. Mil. Engrs., S.R. Republican. Episcopalian (vestryman Christ Ch. and St. Michaels, Germantown). Mason. Home: 22 E. Mt. Pleasant Av., Chestnut Hill. Office: Spring Garden & Ninth Sts., Philadelphia, Pa.

LENT, Frederick, clergyman, coll. pres.; b. Freeport, N.S., June 10, 1872; s. Shippy and Euphemia (Moore) L.; brought to U.S., 1875; B.A., Brown, 1900, M.A., 1901; B.D., Newton Theol. Instn., 1900; Ph.D., Yale, 1906; D.D., Brown, 1922; LL.D., Colgate, 1922; m. Estelle Bolles, 1896. Ordained Bapt. ministry, 1895; pastor Calvary Ch., Salem, Mass., 1896-98, Oaklawn, R.I., 1898-1901, 1st Ch., New Haven, Conn., 1903-18; instr. Bibl. lit., Brown U., 1900-01, Yale, 1903-07, 1909-10; pres. Elmira Coll., 1918-35; pres. Internat. Bapt. Sem., E. Orange, N.J., since 1935. Trustee Bapt. Ministers' Home Soc., 1912-18; trustee American Baptist Home Mission Society, 1912-35. Member American Oriental Society, Phi Beta Kappa, Chi Phi. Republican. Club: Rotary. Wrote: The Life of Simon Stylites, 1914; Three Minute Talks, 1933. Home: East Orange, N.J.

LENTZ, Edwin Warner, clergyman; b. Lebanon Co., Pa., Aug. 15, 1863; s. Jonathan and Maria (Warner) L.; A.B., Ursinus Coll., 1895; A.M., U. of Pa., 1902; B.D., Ursinus Sch. of Theology, 1894 (hon.) D.D., Ursinus Coll., 1918; m. Flora Snell Rahn, Aug. 23, 1893; children—Frederick Rahn, Edwin Warner, Jr. (dec.). Began as teacher in pub. schs., 1879; head master St. John's Mil. Acad., Haddonfield, 1896-98; dean Ursinus Acad., 1898-99; ordained to ministry Ref. Ch. U.S., 1899; pastor, Rayenford, Pa., 1899-1904, Steelton, Pa., 1904-08; pastor St. Johns Ref. Ch., Bangor, Pa., 1908-37, resigned 1937 to follow study and writing. Served as pres. Eastern Pa. Classic Ref. Ch., 1911-18, pres. Eastern Synod, 1925-26. Republican. Mem. Ref. Ch. in U.S. Mason (K.T., 32°). Club: Kiwanis of Bangor (charter mem.). Home: 232 South 39th St., Philadelphia, Pa.

LENTZ, Maxwell Jacob, dentist; b. Newark, N.J., Sept. 19, 1898; s. Joseph Jerome and Sarah (Hausman) L.; student Clifton (N.J.) High Sch., 1911-15; D.D.S., N.Y.U. Coll. of Dentistry, 1918; unmarried. Began as dentist, 1919; chief dental dept. Passaic (N.J.) Gen. Hosp. since 1924; attending dental surgeon Midtown Hosp., New York, since 1919, Hasbrouck Heights (N.J.) Hosp. since 1934; pres. Dumore Corpn., Passaic, N.J., since 1937; v.p. Pride of N.J. Bldg. & Loan Assn., Passaic, N.J., since 1924; dir. Clifton (N.J.) Nat. Bank. Served in U.S. Army, 1918. Mem. Clifton Bd. of Edn., 1927-35. Mem. Passaic City Dental Soc., N.J. State Dental Soc., Am. Dental Assn., N.Y. Inst. of Clin. Oral Pathology, Alpha Omega, Omicron Kappa Upsilon. Mason. Club: Preakness Hills (N.J.) Country. Home: 315 Lexington Av., Clifton, N.J. Office: 655 Main Av., Passaic, N.J.

LENTZ, Valentine ("Dutch"), athletic dir.; b. Baltimore, Md., Aug. 3, 1897; s. William and Julianna (Stahl) L.; B.S., St. John's Coll., Annapolis, Md., 1918; student U. of Md., 1917-18, Northwestern U., Chicago, 1933; m. Pauline M. Raabe, Nov. 23, 1918; children—Mary Julianna, Pauline Francis, Valentine II, William Hubert, Richard Clemens, Harry Claude. Engaged as asst. prof. and dir. athletics, St. John's Coll., Annapolis, Md., 1919-20; instr. pub. schs., Baltimore, and coach at Calvert Hall Coll., Baltimore, Md., 1920-28; coach, Marston Sch., 1929; asst. athletic dir. and basketball coach, St. John's Coll., Annapolis, Md., 1930-36, athletic dir. since 1936; played professional baseball, 1919-28, football, 1919-27, basketball, 1919-30. Served as lt. inf., U.S.A., 1917-19, mem. Res. since 1919. Mem. Assn. Basketball Coaches (exec. com.), Nat. Bd. Basketball Ofcls. (past pres.), Am. Football Coaches Assn. Lutheran. Club: Baltimore Athletic (Baltimore). Home: Pines on Severn, Arnold, Md.

LENTZ, William Jacoby; prof. veterinary anatomy and mgr. Veterinary Hosp., Univ. of Pa. Address: University of Pa., Philadelphia, Pa.

LENZ, Charles Otto, consulting engr.; b. Providence, R.I., May 14, 1868; s. Otto C. and Mary L. (Jordan) L.; ed. Mory and Goff Private Sch., Providence, 1884-88, Mass. Inst. Tech., 1888-92; m. Elizabeth C. Carver, Oct. 25, 1899; children—Winthrop C., Virginia C. (Mrs. Douglas G. Levick, Jr.), Janet C. (Mrs. Proctor B. Baker). Engring. dept. Gen. Electric Co., New York, 1892; asso. with Frederick Sargent as asst. engr. in charge power equipment, World's Columbian Expn., Chicago, 1892-93; 1st asst. engr. Sargent & Lundy, cons. engrs., Chicago, 1895-1900; asst. engr. in charge of design and constrn. J. G. White & Co., New York, 1900-05; engr. Sanderson & Porter, New York, 1905-08; cons. engr. 1908-31 (most important work: design and constrn. of 108,000 h.p. hydro-electric development of Tallulah Falls for Ga. Power Co.); mech. engr. Gibbs & Hill, part time, 1933-36, Parsons, Klapp, Brinckerhoff & Douglas, part time, 1933-36, Gibbs & Hill, full time, since 1936. Republican. Episcopalian. Home: 612 Clifton Av., Newark, N.J. Office: Gibbs & Hill, Pennsylvania Railroad Bldg., New York, N.Y.

LEONARD, Adna Wright, bishop; b. Cincinnati, O., Nov. 2, 1874; s. Adna Bradway and Caroline Amelia (Kaiser) L.; A.B., New York U., 1899; B.D., Drew Theol. Sem., 1901; Am. Sch. Archæology, Rome, 1901-03; D.D., Ohio Northern, 1909; LL.D., Coll. of Puget Sound and U. of Southern Calif.; also S.T.D. from Syracuse University, June 1926; m. Mary Luella Day, Oct. 9, 1901; children—Adna Wright, Phyllis Day. Ordained M.E. ministry, 1899; pastor Green Village, N.J., 1898, First Church, San Juan, P.R., 1900, American M.E. Ch., Rome, 1901-03 (also teacher in Meth. Theol. Sch.), Grace Ch., Piqua, O., 1903-05 Central Ch., Springfield, 1905-08, Walnut Hills Ch., Cincinnati, 1908-09, 1st Ch., Seattle, Wash., 1910-16; elected bishop M.E. Ch., May 1916. Del. Gen. Conf. M.E. Ch., 1916. Pres. Bd. of Edn. of Meth. Ch. Mem. Psi Upsilon (Delta Chapter). Mason (33°, K.C.C.H., Shriner). Author: The Shepherd King; The Roman Catholic Church at the Fountain Head; Evangelism in the Remaking of the World; Hearthstone League Book of Remembrance; Ancient Fires on Modern Altars; Decisive Days in Social and Religious Progress. Home: 336 S. Graham St. Office: 3012 Koppers Bldg., Pittsburgh, Pa.

LEONARD, Joseph Stephens, army officer; b. Marshall, Mo., Feb. 3, 1888; s. Abel and Mittie (Stephens) L.; B.S., U.S. Mil. Acad., 1910; grad. Inf. Sch., 1925, Command & Gen. Staff Sch., 1926; m. Gwladys E. Owen, Sept. 7, 1929. Entered U.S.A. as 2d lt. inf., 1910, and promoted regularly through grades to colonel, 1939; prof. mil. science and tactics, Lehigh U., Bethlehem, Pa., since 1937; mem. of Gen. Staff, 18th Div., Fort Sam Houston, Tex., during World War. Presbyn. Mason. Clubs: Bethlehem (Bethlehem); Army and Navy (Washington, D.C.). Home: 414 Cherokee St., Bethlehem, Pa.

LEONARD, Lester Carpenter, lawyer; b. Long Branch, N.J., Nov. 29, 1897; s. George Willis and Julia Knapp (Carpenter) L.; student Cornell U.; LL.B., Cornell U. Law Sch., 1922; m. Edna M. Birchall, Nov. 1, 1924; children—Lester C., Jr., Carol Lynn. Admitted to N.J. bar, 1922; served apprenticeship under former Atty. Gen. Edmund Wilson; mem. firm Applegate, Stevens, Foster, Leonard & Reussille, Red Bank, N.J., 1927-30; assoc. mem. firm Williams & Leonard, Newark, N.J., 1931-35; in practice alone, Red Bank, N.J., since 1930; spl. counsel to Commr. Banking and Ins. of N.J., 1935; apptd. Supreme Ct. Commr., 1936; spl. asst. atty. gen. of N.J., 1936; spl. counsel to Gov., N.J., 1937; apptd. Spl. Master in Chancery, 1938. Served in U.S.N. during World War. Republican. Methodist. Home: Rambler Hedge, Little Silver, N.J. Office: 65 Broad St., Red Bank, N.J.

LEONARD, Walter Churchill, pres. Standard Floor Co.; b. Coudersport, Pa., Dec. 25, 1893; s. Fred C. and Estella (Cook) L.; student Coudersport (Pa.) High Sch., 1908-11, Harrisburg (Pa.) Acad., 1911-12; A.B., Yale, 1916; m. Aurelia Mansfield, Dec. 22, 1917; 1 son, Walter Churchill. Salesman Pa. Rubber Co., Pittsburgh, Pa., 1916, Jeannette, Pa., 1919-24; with Standard Floor Co., Pittsburgh, Pa., since 1924, pres. since 1939. Served as 1st lt., 310th F.A., 79th Div. during World War. Mem. Beta Theta Pi. Presbyterian. Club: Harvard Yale Princeton (Pittsburgh). Home: 614 Bellefonte St. Office: Gulf Bldg., Pittsburgh, Pa.

LEONARDS, Thomas C(athcart), lawyer; b. Phila., Pa., July 15, 1890; s. Leonard and

Maria (Cathcart) L.; A.B., Central High Sch., Phila., 1907; LL.B., U. of Pa., 1913; m. Gwendolyn E. Taylor, Oct. 12, 1920; children —Marie Elizabeth, Thomas Cathcart, Jr., Emilie Taylor. Admitted to Pa. bar, 1913, and since engaged in gen. practice of law at Phila.; mem. firm Mesirov and Leonards since 1926. Pvt. ordnance, U.S. Army, 1917-19, with A.E.F. in France. Mem. Phila. and Pa. bar assns., Kappa Sigma, Am. Legion. Intercollegiate gymnastic champion, 1913; former holder of a number of minor lawn tennis titles. Republican. Episcopalian. Clubs: Penn Athletic, Racquet, Pennsylvania Varsity, Lawyers, Right Angle (Philadelphia); Merion Cricket (Haverford). Home: Rock Creek Rd., Bryn Mawr, Pa. Office: 918 Packard Bldg., Philadelphia, Pa.

LEONHART, James Chancellor, educator; b. Parkersburg, W.Va., Mar. 18, 1897; s. William Henry and Dorah Catherine (Chancellor) L.; student Marshall Coll., Huntington, W.Va., 1910-16, W.Va. Univ., 1922-23; B.Litt., Sch. of Journalism of Columbia U., 1925; A.B., Johns Hopkins U., 1926; m. Gail Anderson, Dec. 29, 1923; 1 dau., Willa Claire. Employed as reporter, The News, Bronx and Manhattan, N.Y. City, 1923-25; reporter, Baltimore Sun, 1925-26; instr. English and adviser The Press, Forest Park High Sch., Baltimore, 1926-27; instr. English, Baltimore City Coll., Baltimore, Md., 1927-29, adviser of publs., 1929-31, dir. journalism since 1931. Contbr. and gen. editor, One Hundred Years of the Baltimore City College, 1939. Established The Collegian, student weekly newspaper, 1929. Adviser, The Green Bag (founded 1896), sch. annual, since 1930. Dir. edn. div. J. Ramsay Barry & Co., Inc., ins. brokers, Baltimore, since 1936. Served as 1st sergt. U.S. Marines, 1917-21, overseas service, as 1st sergeant; U.S. Marine Detachment, U.S.S. Pittsburgh, flagship of Am. forces in European waters, 1918-21; awarded Good Conduct Medal, 1st enlistment; World War Ribbon with one bronze star. Mem. Nat. Assn. Journalism Dirs., Pub. Sch. Teachers Assn. of Baltimore, Md. State Teachers Assn., Phi Delta Theta, Sigma Delta Chi. Democrat. Episcopalian. Mason (Scottish Rite). Club: Optimist (Baltimore). Contbr. to The Bulletin of Education (Baltimore). Home: 1901 E. 31st St., Baltimore, Md.

LEONIAN, Leon Hatchig, univ. prof.; b. Van, Armenia, Feb. 27, 1888; s. Hatchig and Anna L.; came to U.S., 1910, naturalized, 1925; B.S. in Agr., U. of Ky., Lexington, Ky., 1916; M.S., U. of Mich., Ann Arbor, 1917, Ph.D., 1922; m. Nell Almyra Lanham, Aug. 21, 1924; children—Phillip Marshall, Armen Lanham, John Fulton. Asst. horticulturist, S.C. Expt. Sta., 1917; asst. prof. biology, N.M. Agrl. Coll., 1918; asst. plant pathologist, W.Va. Univ. and W.Va. Agrl. Expt. Sta., Morgantown, W.Va., 1922-26, asso. prof., 1927-36; prof. mycology, W.Va. Univ., and mycologist W.Va. Expt. Sta. since 1937; also engaged in spare time plant breeding work under firm name, Lyondel Gardens, seeds of delphinium, poppy and hemerocallis are bred and sold. Fellow A.A.A.S.; mem. Am. Phytopathol. Soc., Bot. Soc. America, Mycol. Soc., Am. Soc. Plant Physiologists, Sigma Xi. Democrat. Author: How to Grow Delphiniums, 1935. Editor: Yearbook of American Delphinium Society. Contbr. articles and monographs to sci. publs. and papers pertaining to gardening. Home: 836 Price St., Morgantown, W.Va.

LEOPOLD, Eugene Joseph, physician; b. Baltimore, Md., Dec. 1, 1879; s. Joseph and Rosa (Weiller) L.; A.B., Johns Hopkins U., 1901; M.D., Johns Hopkins Med. Sch., 1905; grad. study, Berlin, Munich, Germany, 1905-07, Munich, Tübingen, Germany, 1912; m. Sadie H. Frank, Sept. 4, 1918. Engaged in gen. practice of medicine at Baltimore, Md., since 1907; asst. vis. phys. Johns Hopkins Hosp., in charge Diabetic Clinic, Johns Hopkins Hosp. Dispensary, instr. in medicine, Johns Hopkins U. Med. Sch.; vis. phys. and chmn. med. bd., Sinai Hosp., Baltimore. Served as capt. Med. Corps, U.S.A., 1918-19. Fellow Am. Coll. Physicians; mem. A.A.A.S., Am. Med. Assn., Med. & Chirurg. Faculty of Md., Baltimore City Med. Soc. Jewish religion. Home: 200 W. Lafayette Ave., Baltimore, Md.

LEOPOLD, Samuel, M.D.; b. Phila., Pa., Sept. 25, 1879; s. Samuel and Hannah L.; student Northeast Manual Training Sch.; student U. of Pa., coll. dept., M.D., Med. Sch., 1902; m. Clara Greenberg, April 29, 1918; children— Janet, Marjorie, Richard. Began as physician, 1902; instr. in neurology, 1907-11; asso. in neurology and neuropathology, U. of Pa., since 1912; now chief of neuropsychiatric dept., Municipal Ct. of Phila. Home: 12 Asbury Av., Melrose Park, Pa. Office: 1923 Spruce St., Philadelphia, Pa.

LEROUX, Jules, president Leroux & Co., Inc., consul of Belgium; b. Brussels, Belgium, Oct. 28, 1887; s. Jules and Emilie (Ponslet) L.; grad. chemistry, economics; m. Berthe Jacqmain, June 27, 1918; children—Jacques, André. Pres. Comptoir Commercial de Dinant, Belgium; gen. managing dir. Crédit Général du Congo, Belgium and Africa; v.p. Belgian American Rayon Corpn., Hartford, Conn., John J. Deery Co., New York and Montreal; pres. Leroux & Co., Inc., Phila., Pa. Consul of Belgium for Eastern Pa. Member Military Order of Foreign Wars of U.S., Mil. Order of World War. Served as officer, Belgian Army; del. of Belgian Commn. for purchase of war supplies in U.S.; official rep. of Belgian Govt. in Allied Provisions Export Commn., New York, during World War. Decorated Knight Order of Leopold, Knight of the Crown of Belgium, Comdr. of the Industrial Merit of Portugal. Club: Union League (Phila.). Home: 6452 Woodbine Av. Office: 1220 Spring Garden St., Philadelphia, Pa.

LERRIGO, Peter Hugh James; b. Birmingham, Eng., Oct. 6, 1875; s. George and Mary (Watkins) L.; came to U.S., 1886; M.D., New York Homœ. Med. Coll. and Hosp., 1898; M.D., Medico-Chirurg. Coll., Phila., 1902; post-grad. work, Post-Grad. Sch. of Medicine, New York, 1910; D.D., Franklin (Ind.) College, 1923; D.D., Bates College, Lewiston, Me., 1932; m. Edith Mary Dowkontt, Aug. 20, 1902; children —George Dowkontt (dec.), Hugh D. (dec.), Edith Mary, Florence Lillian. Served in the Philippines as medical missionary of the American Baptist Foreign Mission Society, 1902-13; joint secretary for N.E. of Foreign and Home Mission Soc. and Publn. Soc., 1914-15; exec. sec. Five Yr. Program of Northern Bapt. Com., 1916-18; candidate sec. Foreign Mission Soc., 1919-21; now home sec., med. dir. and sec. for Africa, Foreign Mission Soc. Republican. Opened mission at Capiz, P.I., 1903; built Emmanuel Hosp., Capiz, P.I., 1909; sent to Belgian Congo, 1920, 28, 35, to report on work of Foreign Mission Soc.; chmn. Com. of Reference and Counsel, Foreign Missions Conf. of N.A., 1928, 29, pres. of conf., 1932; mem. Internat. Missionary Council, 1935; missionary inspection tour, Japan, China, Philippines, Burma, India, Assam, 1930-31. Author: Stature of a Perfect Man, 1920; Rock-Breakers, 1922; God's Dynamite, 1924; Anita, a Tale of the Philippines, 1924; The World Thrust of Northern Baptists, 1928; Northern Baptists Rethink Missions, 1933; Omwa? Are You Awake?, 1936. Home: 174 Summit Av., Summit, N.J. Office: 152 Madison Av., New York, N.Y.

LESER, Oscar, lawyer; b. at St. Louis, Mo., Oct. 16, 1870; s. Frederick and Emilie (Vogel) L.; A.B., Central High Sch., Phila., 1887; LL.B., from University of Pa., 1891; m. Annette Agnus, 1896; children—Felix Agnus, Frederica (wife of Richard D. Sears, Jr.), C. C. Fulton. Began practice at Baltimore, 1898. Member Appeal Tax Court, Baltimore, 1901-14 (pres. 1908-14); mem. State Tax Commn., 1914-37; chmn., 1935-37; judge Supreme Bench of Baltimore City, 1937-38. Rep. nominee for U.S. Senate, 1938. Mem. Nat. Municipal League, Nat. Econ. League, Nat. Tax Assn. (pres. 1936-37), Baltimore Mus. of Art, Municipal Art Society, Civil Service Assn. Md., Am., Maryland and Pa. bar assns., Bar Assn. Baltimore, Sharswood Law Club (Phila.). Republican. Clubs: University, Maryland; University (Phila.); University of Pennsylvania (New York, N.Y.). Writer and speaker on topics pertaining to taxation, public finance and government. Home: 3915 N. Charles St. Office: American Bldg., Baltimore, Maryland.

LESH, John Andrew, univ. prof.; b. Snydersville, Pa., Sept. 24, 1879; s. Stogdell Stockes and Mary Elizabeth (Fabel) L.; Ph.B., Taylor U., Ind., 1906; B.D., Drew Theol. Sem., 1908; A.M., U. of Pa., 1909; Ph.D., New York U., 1915; summer sessions Harvard and Columbia; m. Ora Frances Nabring, Sept. 19, 1906; 1 son, Richard Olover (dec.). Head dept. of edn., Ind. State Normal Sch., 1909-11; head dept. history and economics, State Teachers' Coll., Marysville, Mo., 1911-14; head dept. of edn., N.C. State Coll. for Women, Greensboro, N.C., 1915-18; head dept. polit. and social science, 1918-22, head dept. of Am. history and economics, 1922—, Temple U. Mem. Am. Hist. Assn., Am. Polit. Science Assn., Am. Acad. Polit. and Social Science, Am. Assn. Univ. Profs. Phi Delta Kappa, Kappa Sigma Phi. Democrat. Methodist. Mason. Club: City. Lecturer on polit. and sociol. topics. Home: 2127 N. Uber St., Philadelphia, Pa. Died Aug. 6, 1939.

LESHER, Amos Yerkes, lumber merchant; b. Huntingdon Valley, Pa., June 19, 1877; s. James Bell and Catherine (Yerkes) L.; student Huntingdon Valley (Pa.) High Sch. to 1892, Pierce Business Sch., 1892-93; m. Flora J. Quail, 1902 (deceased); children—Charles Q., James E., m. 2d, Emilie Fricke, 1917. Began as bookkeeper and stenographer, 1893; in lumber business, Phila., Pa., since 1895; with Charles F. Felin & Co., 1896-1903, co-partner, 1903-15, v.p., 1915-28; pres. The Lumber and Millwork Co., Phila., Pa., successors to Chas. F. Felin & Co., Inc., since 1928. Dir. North Phila. Trust Co., Phila. Reserve Supply Co., Lumbermans Mutual Casualty Co. (Chicago). Republican. Presbyterian. Mason (32°). Clubs: Union League (Phila.); Manufacturers Golf and Country (Oreland, Pa.); Columbus Fish and Game (Quebec, Can.). Home: Ambler, Pa. Office: 3812 Old York Road, Philadelphia, Pa.

LESHER, Carl Eugene, engineer, economist; b. La Junta, Colo., Nov. 20, 1885; s. David and Rosa Clair (Barnes) L.; grad. Colo. Sch. of Mines, 1908; m. Lois Quick, Mar. 1911; children—Carl E., Barbara. With U.S. Geol. Survey, Washington, D.C., 1910-17; dir. statistics U.S. Fuel Administration, 1917-18; again with U.S. Geol. Survey, 1919; dir. Bur. of Economics, Nat. Coal Assn., 1920; editor Coal Age, New York, 1920-23; chief engr. U.S. Coal Commn., 1923; with Pittsburgh Coal Co. since 1924, asst. to pres. until 1927, exec. v.p. since Jan. 1927. Mem. Am. Inst. Mining and Metall. Engrs., Am. Econ Assn., Engineering Soc. Western Pa. Methodist. Clubs: Shannopin Country, Duquesne. Author of Govt. repts. on coal covering years 1915-19, also Geol. Survey repts. on coke and by-products for same period; History of Coal Distribution (3 vols.); Prices of Coal and Coke (1913-19), 1920. Contbr. to "What Coal Commission Found" (Williams and Wilkins), 1925; "Marketing of Minerals," 1925, many articles in mags. Home: Wilson Drive, Ben Avon Heights. Office: Pittsburgh Coal Co., Oliver Bldg., Pittsburgh, Pa.

LESLEY, Frank W., utilities exec.; b. Scotia, N.Y., Jan. 17, 1896; s. John J. and Ann (Porter) L.; student U. of Pa., 1918-22; m. J. Almeda Trout, July 12, 1930; 1 dau., Lois Ann. Began as accountant T. S. Johnson Sons Co., Phila., 1922; mem. consol. corpn. unit, Income Tax Div., U.S. Treasury Dept., 1922-28; comptroller Pa. Gas & Electric Co., York, Pa., 1928-36, treas. and dir. since 1936; treas. and dir. Interborough Gas Co.; sec. Conewago Gas Co., Peoples Light Co. of Pittston, Petersburg & Hopewell Gas Co. Enlisted U.S. Army, 1917, commd. 2d lt., 1918, hon. disch., 1919; now capt. Inf. Res. Republican. Lutheran. Mason. Clubs: Lafayette, Country of York (York, Pa.). Home: 1633 2d Av. Office: 127 W. Market St., York, Pa.

LESSENBERRY, David Daniel, educator; b. Barren Co., Ky., Sept. 7, 1896; s. James David and Martha Belle (Sanders) L.; B.C.S., Bowling Green Coll. of Commerce, Bowling Green, Ky., 1925; B.S., Duquesne U., Pittsburgh, 1929; A.M., New York U., 1933; grad. student New York U.; m. Elona Jean Spence, Aug. 28, 1926 (died June 27, 1933). Began as office worker; teacher of commercial subjects,

Allegheny (Pa.) High School, 1919-27; vice prin. Business High School, Pittsburgh, 1927-29, prin. 1929-30; dir. courses in Commercial edn., U. of Pittsburgh, since 1930. Mem. Nat. Commercial Teachers Fed. (former pres.), Tri-State Commercial Teachers Assn. (mem. bd.), N.E.A., Business Edn. Dept., N.E.A., Southern Business Educators Assn., Progressive Edn. Assn., Pa. State Edn. Assn., Phi Delta Kappa, Delta Delta Lambda, Phi Delta Kappa, Delta Pi Epsilon. Democrat. Baptist. Home: Fox Chapel Rd. Office: University of Pittsburgh, Pittsburgh, Pa.

LETCHWORTH, George Everett, Jr.; b. Johnstown, Pa., July 15, 1896; s. George Edward and Mary (Easton) L.; grad. Uniontown (Pa.) High Sch., 1916; A.B., Pa. State Coll., 1922; LL.B., U. of Pa., 1925; m. Beatrice L. Singer, July 6, 1925; 1 son, George Everett. Admitted to Pa. bar, 1925, and since practiced in Phila.; mem. teaching staff, Wharton Sch., U. of Pa., 1925-30, Charles Morris Price Sch. since 1935. Served in U.S. Army, with A.E.F., 1917-19. Dir. Osteopathic Hosp., Phila., Charles Morris Price Sch. Mem. Sigma Nu, Phi Delta Phi, Scabbard and Blade. Republican. Methodist. Mason. Club: Poor Richard of Philadelphia. Home: 7607 Torresdale Av. Office: 1500 Walnut St., Philadelphia, Pa.

LEUBA, James Henry, psychologist; b. Neuchâtel, Switzerland, Apr. 9, 1868; s. Henri and Cecile (Sandoz) L.; B.Sc., Neuchâtel, 1886; came to U.S., 1887; Ph.D., Clark U., 1895; studied Leipzig, Halle, Heidelberg, Paris, 1897-98; m. Berthe A. Schopfer, Jan. 6, 1896; children—Clarence James, Gladys Aline. Prof. psychology, Bryn Mawr Coll., 1889-1933, emeritus since 1933. Fellow A.A.A.S.; Author: The Psychological Origin and the Nature of Religion, 1909; A Psychological Study of Religion, 1912; The Beliefs in God and Immortality, 1916; The Psychology of Religious Mysticism, 1925; God or Man—a Study of the Value of God to Man?, 1933. Address: Bryn Mawr, Pa.

LEUBUSCHER, Frederic Cyrus, lawyer; b. New York, N.Y., Sept. 1, 1858; s. Louis Mortimer and Catherine (Horner) L.; A.B., Coll. City of N.Y., 1878; LL.B., Columbia U., 1880; m. Aurelia Lange, Nov. 30, 1903 (dec.); children—Frederic Henry, Mary Catherine. Admitted to N.Y. bar, 1880; mem. law firm Leubuscher Kayser & Oliver until 1935; candidate for judge of gen. sessions, N.Y. City, 1887. Pres. Hervey George Sch. of Social Science. Mem. Am. Bar Assn., N.Y. County Lawyers Assn., Independent in politics. Lutheran. Mason. Club: Fells Brook (Essex Fells, N.J.). Author: The George-Hewitt Campaign of 1886. Home: Essex Fells, N.J. Office: 225 Broadway, New York, N.Y.

LEUKEL, George Allen, clergyman; b. Shrewsbury, N.J., Oct. 23, 1886; s. Jost Wilhelm and Katharine (Wied) L.; student Eatontown (N.J.) Pub. Sch., 1892-1900, Red Bank (N.J.) High Sch., 1900-03; B.A., Rutgers U., New Brunswick, N.J., 1907, M.A., 1911; diploma, Princeton (N.J.) Theol. Sem., 1910; grad. work, U. of Berlin (Germany), 1910-11; m. Marian S. MacFadden, Sept. 8, 1910; children—Marian Katharine (dec.), George Allen, Mary Elizabeth, Ruth Anna. Ordained by Lehigh (Pa.) Presbytery, Presbyn. Ch. in U.S.A., 1911; pastor, Ashland, Pa., 1911-15, Little Britain Presbyn. Ch., Nottingham, Pa., 1915-21, Kennett Square (Pa.) Presbyn. Ch. since 1921. In Y.M.C.A. War Service during World War. Mem. Phi Beta Kappa. Presbyterian. Address: 213 S. Broad St., Kennett Square, Pa.

LEUTHAUSER, Theodore Charles, editor; b. Newark, N.J., May 21, 1905; s. Theodore and Laura (Waechter) L.; student Newark Acad. and U. of Pa.; m. Matilda Lengel, Feb. 14, 1929. Editor New Jersey Frei Zeitung, 81 yr. old German newspaper, Newark, N.J., since 1934. Lutheran. Mason. Home: 137 Mulberry St., Newark, N.J. Office: 190 Badger Av., Newark, N.J.

LE VAN, Gerald Wilberforce, physician; b. Baltimore, Md., Sept. 24, 1895; s. Charles Wilberforce and Harvene Estelle (Bowers) LeV.; student Baltimore City Coll., 1910-11, Juniata Coll., Huntingdon, Pa., 1911-13; B.S., Franklin and Marshall Coll., Lancaster, Pa., 1917; M.D., Jefferson Med. Coll., Phila., Pa., 1921; m. Esther Gay Bourne, Sept. 15, 1922; children—Esther Bourne, Margaret Eleanor. Interne O. Valley Gen. Hosp., Wheeling, W.Va., 1921-22; engaged in gen. practice of medicine, Uniontown, Md., 1922-23; in gen. practice at Boonsboro, Md., since 1923; mem. staff Washington County Hosp. Served as mem. R.O.T.C. Past mem. bd. trustees Boonsboro High Sch.; past pres. Boonsboro Parent Teachers Assn. Mem. Cumberland Valley Med. Soc. (pres. 1930), Med. & Chirurg. Faculty of Md., Edward P. Davis Obstet. Soc., Washington County Med. Soc., Phi Sigma Kappa, Theta Kappa Psi. Democrat. Evang. Ref. Ch. Club: Lions of Boonsboro (pres. 1938-39). Home: S. Main St., Boonsboro, Md.

LEVENGOOD, Brooklyn Boyer, physician; b. Glendale, Pa., June 21, 1868; s. William W. and Matilda (Boyer) L.; ed. U. of Md., 1887-88; M.D., Jefferson Med. Coll., 1889; m. Eva Keyser, Oct. 3, 1889 (dec.); children—Eva Williams (dec.), Robert P. (dec.); m. 2d, Estelle M. Smith, Mar. 28, 1906; children—Rodman Whitley, Elizabeth (Mrs. Cecil A. Phelps), William James. After usual internship engaged in gen. practice of medicine at Bellwood, Pa., since 1889; surgeon Pa. R.R. Co.; examiner for ins. cos.; dir. First Nat. Bank of Bellwood. Served as 1st lt. Med. Corp, U.S.A. Res., 1918. Mem. Am. Med. Assn., Pa. State and Blair Co. med. socs. Democrat. Mason. Home: 517 Main St., Bellwood, Pa.

LEVENSON, Joseph, dentist; b. Phila., Pa., Sept. 19, 1898; s. Israel and Minnie (Molitz) L.; student Woodbine (N.J.) High Sch., 1909-13; D.D.S., Univ. of Pa. Dental Coll., 1916; unmarried. Engaged in practice of dentistry, Elizabeth, N.J., 1916-18; upon disch. from army in Dec. 1918 began practice dentistry at Woodbine, N.J., and continued since 1918; vice-pres. Woodbine Nat. Bank since 1929. Served as 1st lt. Dental Corps, U.S.A., 1918; now capt. Dental Res. Corps, U.S.A. Elected mayor of Woodbine, 1938. Mem. Am. Dental Assn., Southern Dental Soc., N.J. State Dental Soc., Am. Legion. Democrat. Jewish religion. Address: Adams Av., Woodbine, N.J.

LEVER, John Howard, clergyman; b. Pawtucket, R.I., Jan. 21, 1886; s. John and Jessie Benton (Dean) L.; grad. Classical High Sch., Providence, R.I., 1904; A.B., Brown U., 1908; D.D., Cambridge Episcopal Theol. Sch., 1911, S.T.M., 1915; student Harvard, 1908-10; m. Cora Ella Medbury, June 8, 1911; children—John Medbury, Katherine. Supt. of St. Louis City Mission, 1913-20; supt. of social service, Diocese of Mich., Protestant Episcopal Ch., 1920-22; ordained Episcopal Ch., 1912; rector Ch. of the Advocate, Phila., 1922-26, Holy Trinity Ch., Lincoln, Neb., 1926-30, All Saints Ch., Worcester, Mass., 1930-33, St. John's Free Ch., Phila., since 1933; preacher on Shaw Foundation, St. Louis, 1921. Home: 1011 Fillmore St., Philadelphia, Pa.

LEVERING, Edwin W., Jr., v.p. U.S. Fidelity & Guaranty Co. Home: Ruxton, Md. Office: Calvert & Redwood Sts., Baltimore, Md.

LEVERING, Howard Allen, highway engr.; b. Levering, O., Jan. 8, 1887; s. Frank Orlando and Byrdess Ellen (Leiter) L.; E.M., O. State Univ., Columbus, O., 1910; m. Eugenia May McDougal, June 24, 1914. Was mining engr., Island Creek Coal Co., Holden, W.Va., 1910-11, Pocahontas Consol. Coal Co., Berwind, W.Va., 1911-14; mining engineer gas and oil, Frank O. Levering, Mt. Vernon, O., 1914; assistant testing engineer, State Highway Dept. of O., Columbus, O., 1914-18; county rd. engr. of Wayne Co., W.Va., 1918-22; asst. engr. and sr. engr., second dist., State Rd. Commn. of W.Va., Huntington, W.Va., 1922-38, resident engr. of constrn. in charge constrn. in 5 counties since 1938. Served in univ. cadets, O. State Univ. Dir. and past pres. Ceredo-Kenova Chamber of Commerce. Mem. Am. Soc. Civil Engrs., Am. Assn. Engrs. (nat. past pres.), W.Va. Soc. Professional Engrs., W.Va. Rd. Builders Assn. (past v.p., sec., dir.), Central O. Valley Development Assn. (v.p., dir.), Huntington Engrs. Club, O. State Univ. Alumni Assn., Alpha Sigma Phi, Gamma Phi, Sphinx. Democrat. Conglist. (deacon, trustee First Ch.). Mason. Club: Automobile of Huntington (dir.). Home: 799 C St., Ceredo. Office: 2224 Fifth Av., Huntington, W.Va.

LEVERING, J(ohn) P(ercy) Wade, manufacturer; b. Baltimore, Md., Dec. 3, 1912; s. Ernest Douglas and Grace Bennett (Wade) L.; student Gilman Country Sch., Baltimore, 1923-30, Lawrenceville (N.J.) Sch., 1930-32; m. Marie (Elizabeth) du Pont, Oct. 23, 1935; 1 dau., Elise du Pont. Board boy Westheimer & Co., Baltimore, Sept. 1932-Apr. 1933; seaman Bull Steamship Lines, Apr.-June 1933; laborer Nat. Sash Weight Corpn., Baltimore, June-Sept. 1933, asst. treas., 1937-38, pres. and treas., July-Dec., 1938, chmn. of bd. and treas. since Dec. 1938; laborer Levering Bros., Inc., Baltimore, Sept. 1933-Jan. 1934, office boy, 1934-35, sec., 1935-37, v.p., 1937-38, pres., treas. and dir. since June 1938; dir. Homewood Apt. Co., Calvert Ct. Co., Cecil Constrn. Co. Baptist. Clubs: Elkridge, Bachelors Cotillion (Baltimore, Md.). Home: Malvern Av., Ruxton, Md. Office: 200 Key Highway, Baltimore, Md.

LEVERING, William Wallace, corpn. official; b. Phila., Pa., July 2, 1878; s. William A. and Josephine (Carpenter) L.; student Friends Central Sch., Phila., Class 1896; m. Mabel Shute, 1903; children—William Wallace, Estelle (Mrs. Henry McD., Chestnut), Katharyn S., Barbara F. Began as errand boy Belknap, Johnson & Powell, 1895; now pres. and dir. Lansdale (Pa.) Water Co., Hatboro (Pa.) Water Co., Lancaster (Pa.) Suburban Water Co., Wayne (Pa.) Sewerage Co., Toms River (N.J.) Water Co.; v.p. and dir. Chestertown (Ind.) Electric Light & Power Co. Republican. Baptist. Clubs: Union League (Phila.); Old York Road Country (Jenkintown, Pa.); Island Heights Yacht (Island Heights, N.J.). Home: Jenkintown, Pa. Office: Girard Trust Bldg., Philadelphia, Pa.

LEVIN, Harry O.; mem. law firm Levin, Weinberg & Goldstein. Address: Union Trust Bldg., Baltimore, Md.

LEVIN, Jack, pub. utility expert, economist, lawyer; b. Portland, Ore., June 23, 1898; s. Rev. Max and Anna Toba (Cohan) L.; student Shattuck Sch., Portland, Ore., 1903-12, Lincoln High Sch., Portland, 1912-16; B.A., Reed Coll., Portland, Ore., 1920; LL.B., Northwestern, Portland, Ore., 1923; post-grad. student U. of Ore., U. of Wash., Columbia U., 1925-29, grad. sch. American U., 1929-32, Ph.D., 1932; m. Lillian Shapiro, June 26, 1932; children, Anina Toba, Maureen Judith. Admitted to Oregon bar, Federal bar, 1923; director public utility research Peoples Legislative Service, Washington, D.C., 1929-32; valuation expert, St. Paul, Minn., 1932; valuation expert counsel Pub. Utility Commn., Washington, D.C., 1932; chief legal research, NRA, Washington, 1932-33, consultant constl. and anti-trust law, 1933-34; spl. counsel to adminstr. Rural Electrification Adminstrn., Washington, 1935-36, rate expert, 1937-38, chief, in charge of personnel edn., Div. of Engring. and Operations, since 1938. Served in R.O.T.C., U.S. Army, Presidio, San Francisco, 1918; hon. disch., 1918. Mem. Federal Bar Assn., Nat. Lawyers Guild, B'nai B'rith. Clubs: Open Court, Patrick Henry's (Washington, D.C.). Co-author: The Valuation and Regulation of Public Utilities, 1933; Industrial Planning Under the Codes, 1935; author: Power Ethics, 1931; numerous economic and legal articles; legal chapter on President's Great Plains Drought Com. Report. Has made studies and surveys of Am. prisons and European economic conditions. Home: 301 Baltimore Av., Takoma Park, Md. Office: Rural Electrification Administration, Washington, D.C.

LEVIN, Leonard S., lawyer; b. Pittsburgh, Pa., July 20, 1874; s. Samuel and Mary (Leavitt) L.; grad. Duquesne Coll.; studied law in office of Joseph Stadtfeld, and U. of Pittsburgh Law Sch.; m. Stella May Fink, March 1, 1906; children— Mary, Robert Fink, Lenore. Practiced, Pittsburgh, 1902—; asst. city atty. under Mayors Hays and Guthrie, 1903-09, asst. solicitor Allegheny Co. since Jan. 1936. mem. legislative Com. Credit Assn. Western Pa. Interested in boys' work; pres. George Junior Republic of Western Pa.; v.p. Nat. Assn. Junior Republics; mem. bd. govs. B'nai B'rith Orphanage and Home for Friendless Children, Erie, Pa.; trustee Irene Kaufmann Settlement, Jewish Home for the Aged. Author: Pa. Bulk Sales Act and other legislation. Club: Westmoreland Country. Home: 1715 Denniston Av. Office: Grant Bldg., Pittsburgh, Pa.

LEVIN, Louis, physician; b. New York, N.Y., Aug. 7, 1897; s. Samuel and Mary (Lidsky) L.; M.D., Jefferson Med. Coll., 1919; grad. study, U. of Pa. Grad. Sch. of Medicine, 1925-26; m. Marion Anderson, July 1, 1920; children—Jonas Anderson, Robert Barney. Interne Western Pa. Hosp., Pittsburgh, 1919-20; engaged in gen. practice of medicine at Trenton, N.J., 1920-27, limited to diseases of heart since 1927; cardiologist to St. Francis Hosp. since 1926, N.J. State Prison since 1928, N.J. State Hosp., 1929-32; asst. phys. Heart Clinic Pa. Hosp., Phila., Pa., 1926-36. Served in S.A.T.C., 1918. Fellow Am. Med. Assn. Mem. Am. Heart Assn., Phi Delta Epsilon. Author: Living Along with Heart Disease, 1935. Contbr. sect. on Medicine and Doctors in Vol. II of A History of Trenton, 1929; many articles on heart disease in med. jours. since 1927. Home: 651 W. State St., Trenton, N.J.

LEVIN, Max, psychiatrist; b. Latvia, May 10, 1901; s. Raymond and Lena (Friedman) L.; came to U.S., 1904, naturalized, 1922; A.B., Johns Hopkins U., Baltimore, Md., 1920, M.D., Med. Sch., 1924; m. Shulamith Dennenberg, Oct. 13, 1928; 1 son, David Carl. Mem. resident staff, Henry Phipps Psychiatric Clinic, Johns Hopkins Hosp., Baltimore, Md., 1924-27; dir. psychiatric clinic, Fed. of Jewish Charities, Phila., Pa., 1927-31; clin. dir. Harrisburg (Pa.) State Hosp., 1931-37; chief psychiatrist Pittsburgh City Hosp., Mayview, Pa., since 1937. Mem. A.M.A., Am. Psychiatric Assn., Phi Beta Kappa. Jewish religion. Author many articles on neurology and psychiatry in med. jours. Address: Mayview, Pa.

LEVINE, Joseph, rabbi; b. McKeesport, Pa., Dec. 18, 1907; s. Rabbi Wolf and Sarah (Cooper) L.; A.B., Univ. of Pittsburgh, 1930; ed. Jewish Inst. of Religion, 1930-31, Jerusalem, Palestine, 1931-33; m. Betty Kaufman, May 14, 1933; 1 dau., Naomi Claire. Rabbi since 1934; rabbi, Glasgow Progressive Synagogue, Glasgow, Scotland, 1934-35; rabbi, Temple Sholom, Plainfield, N.J., since 1936. Mem. adv. bd. of Community Chest, Plainfield, N.J. Mem. bd. dirs. Jewish Community Centre; exec. com. N.J. Zionist Region. Chmn. InterFaith Com., Plainfield Ministers Assn. Mem. Pub. Relations Com., Council of Jewish Organs. of Plainfield. Mem. Ministers' Assn., Sigma Alpha Mu. Awarded Judge Irving Lehman Trophy, 1929. Democrat. Jewish religion. Mason. B'nai B'rith. Author: (with introduction by Mrs. Stephen S. Wise) Echoes of the Jewish Soul, 1931. Home: 612 Madison Av., Plainfield, N.J.

LEVINE, Philip, physician, bacteriologist, serologist; b. Kletzk, Russia, Aug. 10, 1900; s. Morris and Fay (Zirulick) L.; came to U.S., 1908, naturalized, 1917; B.S., Coll. of City of N.Y., 1919; M.D., Cornell U. Med. Sch., 1923, A.M., same, 1925; m. Hilda Lillian Perlmutter, May 1, 1938. Interne Beth Moses Hosp., Brooklyn, N.Y., Oct., 1923-25; on research staff, Rockefeller Inst., 1925-32; mem. faculty, U. of Wis. Med. Sch., 1932-35; bacteriologist and transfusion service, Beth Israel Hospital, Newark, N.J., since 1935; also in practice at 1089 Madison Av., N.Y. City; co-discoverer with Dr. Landsteiner, Nobel Prize Winner, 1930, of the M and N blood factors, 1928; consulted as expert for blood tests in paternity disputes in Courts of N.Y. by Corpn. Counsel's Office, N.Y. City; expert for blood tests in paternity disputes in N.J. and throughout U.S.; author Wis. law granting courts authority to order blood tests in paternity disputes in Wis.; sponsor similar bill in N.J. Served in S.A.T.C., 1919. Mem. Bd. Med. Control of Blood Transfusion Betterment Assn., N.Y. City. Mem. Harvey Soc., Am. Assn. Immunologists, N.Y. Acad. Medicine, Am. Genetic Assn., N.J. State Med. Soc., Sigma Xi. Jewish religion. Contbr. med. papers. Home: 1133 Bergen St., Newark, N.J. Office: Beth Israel Hosp., Newark, N.J.

LEVINE, William, corpn. official; b. Dec. 29, 1881; s. Moses and Jennie (Goldberg) L.; A.B., Coll of City of N.Y., 1901; LL.B., New York U., 1907; m. Mary Plotz, March 12, 1911. Chmn. bd., pres. and dir. Roebling Coal Co. since 1919. Address: 1440 Broadway, New York, N.Y.; and 134 Freylinghuysen Av., Newark, N.J.

LeVINESS, Charles Thabor, lawyer; b. Baltimore, Md., June 13, 1902; s. Charles Thabor and Alice J. (Dorman) LeV.; A.B., Princeton U., 1923; LL.B., U. of Md. Law Sch., 1926; m. Hildegarde Denmead, April 17, 1933; 1 son, Garner Denmead. Employed as newspaper reporter on Baltimore Sun, 1923-26; admitted to Md. bar, 1926 and engaged in gen. practice of law at Baltimore since 1927; mem. firm Hargest, LeViness, Duckett and McGlannan since 1934; mem. adv. bd. Maryland Law Review; served as asst. atty. gen. of Md., 1935-39; chmn. liquor license commrs. of Baltimore since 1939. Served as 1st lt. U.S.A. Res., 1923-29; 1st lt. F.A., Md. N.G., 1929-31. Mem. Am., Md. State, Baltimore City bar assns., Internat. Assn. of Ins. Counsel, Phi Kappa Sigma. Democrat. Episcopalian. Clubs: Baltimore Country (Baltimore); Princeton (New York). Home: 106 Oakdale Rd. Office: Munsey Bldg., Baltimore, Md.

LEVINSOHN, Sandor A., physician; b. New York, N.Y., Mar. 9, 1897; s. Louis and Anna (Glick) L.; ed. Cornell U., 1913-14; M.D., N.Y. Univ. & Bellevue Hosp. Med. Coll., 1918; m. Bertha Jackson, June 27, 1920; children—Anita Helene, Miriam Barbara. Interne Barnert Memorial Hosp., Paterson, N.J., 1918-20; engaged in gen. practice of medicine at Brooklyn, N.Y., 1920-25; post grad. study in Europe, 1925-26; specializing in pediatrics since 1926; vice-pres. med. bd. and attdg. pediatrician, Barnert Memorial Hosp., Paterson, N.J. Commd. 1st lt. Med. Corps, U.S.A., 1918, placed on inactive list. Resigned 1920. Fellow Am. Acad. Pediatrics, Am. Med. Assn. Diplomate Nat. Bd. Pediatrics. Mem. Sigma Alpha Mu. Jewish religion. B'nai B'rith. Clubs: Mens of Temple Emanuel, Paterson (past pres.); Pistol of Ridgewood (vice-pres.); Preakness Hills Country of Wayne Twp. (2d v.p.). Translator of Lust-Levinsohns Treatment of Children's Diseases, 1930. Home: 656 E. 29th St., Paterson, N.J.

LEVINTHAL, Abraham Allen, lawyer; b. Phila., Pa., May 26, 1895; s. Bernhard L. and Minna (Kleinberg) L.; ed. Central High Sch., Phila., Temple U. Law Sch., 1914-18; m. Passie R. Ellis, Dec. 25, 1918; children—Marvin I., Deljean. Admitted to Pa. bar, 1918 and since engaged in gen. practice of law at Phila.; mem. firm Levinthal and Levinthal since 1938; asst. city solicitor since 1936. Dir. Central Talmud Torah, Yeshiva Mishkan Israel. Past pres. Chevra Bikur Cholim; mem. exec. bd. Jewish Progressive Order of the West, Independent Order Brith Sholom; mem. Independent Order Brith Abraham, Jewish Youth Council in Phila. (dir.), Brith Achim Beneficial Assn. (pres.); formerly treas. of Philadelphia Council B'nai B'rith; del. to Am. Jewish Congress; first sec. and one of the organizers of Har Zion Temple. Home: 2401 N. 54th St. Office: 1600 Bankers Securities Bldg., Philadelphia, Pa.

LEVINTHAL, Bernard Louis, rabbi; b. Vilna, Russia, May 12, 1865; s. Rabbi Abraham and Sarah L.; ed. in Russian schs.; grad. High Rabbinical Insts. of Kovno and Wilna, Russia, 1888; m. Minna, d. Rabbi Elazer Kleinberg, Mar. 1886. Came to U.S., 1891; minister of the United Orthodox Hebrew Congregations of Phila. since 1891. Founder Hebrew Free Schs., Free Burial Soc., Kosher Meat Assn., and other Hebrew assns. of Phila.; founder and now pres. Orthodox Rabbinical Assn. of America, Hebrew Talmudic Inst., Phila.; founder and prin. Hebrew High Sch., Phila.; mem. Am. Jewish Com.; hon. v.p. Federation of Am. Zionist; mem. bd. of delegates of civil and religious rights of Jews; organized Council of Jewish Clubs of Phila.; mem. delegation of Am. Jewish Congress to Peace Conf., Paris. Mem. faculty, Rabbinical Coll. of America, New York. Address: 716 Pine St., Philadelphia, Pa.

LEVINTHAL, Louis Edward, judge; b. Phila., Pa., Apr. 5, 1892; s. Bernard Louis and Minna (Kleinberg) L.; student Central High Sch., Phila., 1906-10; A.B., U. of Pa., Coll. Dept. 1914, LL.B., Law Sch., 1916, LL.M., 1918; m. Lenore Chodoff, Dec. 5, 1916; children—Sylvia Betty (Mrs. Herbert I. Bernstein), Cyrus. Admitted to Phila. bar, 1916; mem. Phila. Co. Bd. of Law Examiners, 1917-37; lecturer on bankruptcy and corporate reorganization, U. of Pa. Law Sch., 1933-36; spl. counsel to Pub. Service Commn. of Pa. in connection with reorganization of Phila. Rapid Transit, 1935-37; judge Common Pleas Ct. No. 6, Phila., since 1937. Mem. Gov.'s Commn. on Constl. Revision, 1935. Dir. Fed. of Jewish Charities; trustee Public Charities Assn. of Pa. 1939; dir. Jewish Welfare Soc. of Phila. (hon.); trustee Gratz Coll.; chmn. publication comm., Jewish Publ. Soc. of America, 1939. Mem. Asso. Talmud Torahs of Phila. (pres. 1929-34), Zionist Orgn. of Phila. (pres. 1926-29); chmn. administrative com. Zionist Organization America, 1939. Mem. Order of Coif, Phi Beta Kappa. Democrat. Jewish religion. Clubs: Locust (Phila.), U. of Pa. of N.Y. Author: Mayer Sulzberger, P.J., 1927; History of Bankruptcy Law, 1918. Home: 1901 Walnut St., Phila. Office: City Hall, Philadelphia, Pa.

LEVITSKY, Louis Moses, rabbi; b. Russia, May 12, 1898; s. Samuel and Freida (Wolowick) L.; was brought to Can., 1904, came to U.S., 1916, and naturalized citizen, 1924; ed. pub. schs. and high sch., Montreal, Can., 1905-16; A.B., Coll. of City of N.Y., 1920; student Harvard, summer 1921; Rabbi, Jewish Theol. Sem. of America, 1923, D.H.L., same, 1933; m. Dr. Anna L. Levy, Nov. 27, 1929; 1 dau., Barbara. Rabbi of Temple Israel, Wilkes-Barre, Pa. since 1922. Served as chmn. edn. com. Chamber of Commerce; pres. Rotary Club, 1936-37; first chmn. Council of Social Agencies, 1924; vice chmn. Community Welfare Campaign, 1936; mem. co. com. Nat. Youth Adminstrn.; mem. com. on church and social work, Pa. Conf. Social Workers. Has served as mem. several mediation bds. in various labor disputes. Mem. exec. com. United Synagogues of America, Rabbinical Assembly of America; mem. Soc. for Biblical Literature. Democrat. Jewish religion. Mason. Author: Social Life in Pumbadita (in preparation for pub., 1939); A Jew Looks at America, 1939. Contbr. articles on Jewish edn. to mags. Home: 217 S. Franklin St., Wilkes-Barre, Pa.

LEVY, Benjamin E.; chmn. bd. Coty, Inc.; also officer and dir. various subsidiaries. Office: care Coty, Inc., Wilmington, Del.

LEVY, Herbert, lawyer; b. Baltimore, Md., July 22, 1896; s. Jacob I. and Lillie (Panitz) L.; student pub. schs., Baltimore, 1904-10, Baltimore City Coll., 1910-13; LL.B., U. of Md., Baltimore, 1913-16; m. Bess Lipsitz, Nov. 28, 1934; children—Jane Frances, Sally Harriet. Admitted to Md. bar, 1917, and since practiced at Baltimore; mem. firm Tydings, Sauerwein, Levy and Archer, Baltimore, since 1930. Served as yeoman, 2d class, U.S.N.R. F., 1918-19. Asst. atty.-gen. of Md., 1923-30. Dir. Baltimore Hebrew Coll., Chizuk Amuno Congregation, Mt. Pleasant Sanatorium. Mem. Am. Bar Assn., Md. Bar Assn., Baltimore City Bar Assn. Democrat. Jewish religion. Now preparing for Am. Law Inst.; Maryland Annotations to the Restatement of the Law of Contracts. Home: 2501 Queen Anne Rd. Office: Union Trust Bldg., Baltimore, Md.

LEVY, Leon, corpn. official; b. Phila., Pa., June 6, 1895; s. David and Fannie (Feigenbaum) L.; student S. Phila. High Sch., 1909-12; D.D.S., U. of Pa., 1915; Sc.D. (hon.), Pa. Mil. Coll., 1919; m. Blanche Paley, Sept. 22, 1927; 1 son, Robert P. Began as dentist 1915-26; with W.C.A.U. Broadcasting Co., Phila., 1926-27; sec. Columbia Broadcasting System, 1928-33; dir. Yellow Cab Co. (Phila.),

Columbia Broadcasting System, Transradio Press, Inc. Served in U.S. Navy, 1917-19. Mem. Elec. Assn., Acad. Polit. Science, Benj. Franklin Inst. Clubs: Locust, Philmont, Penn Athletic, Variety, Poor Richard (Phila.). Home: School House Lane. Office: 1622 Chestnut St., Philadelphia, Pa.

LEVY, Maurice Ambrose, clergyman; b. Townsend, Mass., Sept. 13, 1874; s. Adolph Maximilian and Ellen (Stickney) Léve; A.B., Williams College, 1897, D.D. from same college, 1928; grad. Newton Theol. Instn., 1900; m. L. Mable Deland, June 14, 1899; 1 son, Rev. Maurice Eugene. Ordained Baptist ministry, 1898; pastor First Church, Hingham, Mass., 1898-1901, First Ch., Medford, 1901-07, First Ch., Newton, Newton Center, 1907-14, Greene Av. Ch., Brooklyn, N.Y., 1914-19, First Ch., Pittsfield, Mass., 1919-1932. First Church, Williamsport, Pa., 1932—. Mem. bd. mgrs. Am. Bapt. Foreign Mission Soc., 1909-21; rec. sec. Northern Bapt. Conv. and editor Annual, 1912-28; corr. sec. Northern Bapt. Conv., 1928—; mem. bd. mgrs. Conf. of Bapt. Ministers in Mass., 1924-27; recording sec. and dir. Mass. Bapt. Conv., 1929-32, pres., 1927, 28; trustee Newton Theol. Instn., 1909-30, and 1931-33; mem. exec. com. Pa. Council Chs. since 1935; chaplain Ancient and Hon. Arty. Co., Boston, 1913-14; pres. Conf. of Bapt. Pastors State of N.Y., 1917-18; mem. Advisory Council American Bible Soc. since 1937; vice-pres. Ministers Council of Northern Baptist conv. since 1938. Pres. Pittsfield Chamber of Commerce, 1928-30. Mem. Phi Beta Kappa, Sons of Vets. Mason. Odd Fellow. Clubs: Kiwanis, Advertising. Frequent speaker before civic and religious bodies. Home: 1051 W. 4th St., Williamsport, Pa.

LEVY, Raphael, prof. of Romance langs.; b. Baltimore, Md., Nov. 4, 1900; s. Max and Dora (Pollack) L.; A.B., Johns Hopkins U., 1920, A.M., 1922; grad. study, U. of Paris, France, 1922-23; Ph.D., Johns Hopkins U., 1924; m. Helen Silverman, June 30, 1929; 1 son, Manford Harold. Engaged as instr. French, Baltimore City Coll., 1922; instr. French, U. of Wis., 1924-29; prof. Romance langs., U. of Baltimore since 1931. Dir. Baltimore Hebrew Coll. Mem. Modern Lang. Assn. America, Anglo-Norman Text Soc., Société des anciens textes français. Awarded J. S. Guggenheim fellowship in Europe, 1929; Johnston scholarship at Johns Hopkins U., 1930; Am. Council Learned Socs. grants, 1932, 1936; Am. Philos. Soc. grant for research, summer of 1939; hon. mention Institut de France, 1933. Mem. Zionist Orgn. America, Conf. on Jewish Relations. Democrat. Jewish religion. Author: The Astrological Works of Abraham ibn Ezra, 1927; Recherches lexicographiques sur d'anciens textes français d'origine juive, 1932; Li Coronemenz Looïs: Glossaire, 1932; Répertoire des lexiques du vieux français, 1937; An Introduction to Current Affairs, 1938; The Beginning of Wisdom, 1939. Contbr. over 50 articles and revs. to learned jours. in France, Eng., Holland, Portugal, and U.S. Home: 2246 Eutaw Pl., Baltimore, Md.

LEWALD, James, physician; b. Cincinnati, O., July 29, 1888; s. Oscar and Jennie (Soloman) L. M.D., Washington Univ. Med. Sch., St. Louis, Mo., 1911; student U. of Pa. Grad. Sch. of Medicine, 1917; m. Alice Wahlert, Nov. 15, 1913; 1 son, James Henry. Interne City Hosp., St. Louis, Mo., 1911-12; asst. physician, City Sanitarium, St. Louis, Mo., 1912-14, asst. supt., 1914-22; specialist in neuro-psychiatry, U.S. Vets. Bur., St. Louis, 1922-24; supt. and psychiatrist, St. Louis Training Sch., 1924-34; supt. Dist. Training Sch., Laurel, Md., since 1934; asst. in clin. psychiatry, Washington U., St. Louis, 1916-34; prof. clin. psychiatry, Georgetown Univ., Washington, D.C. since 1936. Served as 1st lt. Med. Corps, U.S.A., neuro-psychiatric sect., 1917-19. Fellow A.M.A., Am. Psychiatric Assn. Mem. Am. Assn. on Mental Deficiency, Dist. Med. Soc., Phi Rho Sigma. Mason (32°). Club: Torch (Washington). Home: District Training School, Laurel, Md.

LEWELLYN, Charles Lewis, lawyer; b. Germantown, Pa., Aug. 18, 1885; s. Lewis Cass and Sarah Ellen (Hague) L.; student S. Western State Normal Sch. (California, Pa.), 1901-04; LL.B., West Va. U., Morgantown, W.Va., 1908; m. Irene Catherine Buttermore, Nov. 18, 1920; children—Gregg Higbee, Charles Lewis, Nancy Louise. Admitted to Pa. bar, 1911, and since practiced at Uniontown, Pa.; mem. firm Higbee, Lewellyn & Higbee, Uniontown, since 1911; sec. Carter Ice Cream Co., Uniontown. Mem. Phi Kappa Psi. Democrat. Presbyterian. Mason, Elk. Club: Triangle (Uniontown, Pa.). Home: 68 Union St. Office: Union Trust Bldg., Uniontown, Pa.

LEWIN, William, teacher, editor; b. New York, N.Y., Aug. 12, 1889; s. Marcus and Yetta (Mindlin) L.; A.B., N.Y. Univ., 1911; A.M., Columbia U., 1916; Ph.D., N.Y. Univ., 1933; research work in edn., others univs., 1928-30; m. Mildred Fuerstman, June 27, 1920 (divorced 1929); m. 2d, Ruth E. Meyer, Aug. 5, 1930; children—Lawrence, Ann. Engaged in teaching, pub. schs., Newark, N.J. since 1911; chmn. English dept., Weequahic High Sch. since 1938; conducted expts. with ednl. films, 1919-29; organized Am. photoplay-appreciation movement as chmn. photoplay com., under auspices Nat. Council Teachers of English, 1931-34; pres. and mng. editor, Educational and Recreational Guides, Inc.; mng. editor, Photoplay Studies since 1935; instr. in edn., N.Y. Univ., 1932. Chmn. Motion Picture Com., Dept. Secondary Edn. of N.E.A. Mem. Phi Beta Kappa. Pres. Schoolmen's Club of Newark, 1924-25. Democrat. Jewish religion. Author: Speaking and Writing English (with Max J. Herzberg); Photoplay Appreciation; Story of American Journalism; Pageant of New Jersey History; Newark, 1666-1926; What Shall We Name the Baby?; and numerous ednl. articles, study plans, etc. Home: 172 Renner Av., Newark, N.J.

LEWIS, Allen, artist; b. Mobile, Ala., Apr. 7, 1873; s. Seth Francis and Ida (Clark) L.; ed. pub. schs., Buffalo, N.Y.; studied Buffalo Art Students' League, under George Bridgman; École des Beaux Arts, Paris, under Gérôme; m. Bessie Jayne, May 2, 1917. Exhibited at various salons and at Paris Expn., 1900, under name of Arthur Allen Lewis; returned to U.S., 1902; teacher wood engraving and color printing, etching and illustration, Art Students' League, New York, 1924-32; teacher of wood engraving and etching, New School for Social Research, N.Y. City, 1932-34. Was awarded the Logan prize, Chicago Soc. of Etchers, 1916; Noyes prize, Brooklyn Soc. of Etchers, 1917; bronze medal, St. Louis Expn., 1904; gold medal, San Francisco Expn., 1915; silver medal for woodcut, Sesquicentennial Expn., Phila., 1926; Nathan I. Bijur prize, soc. of Am. Etchers, 1928; John G. Agar prize, Nat. Arts Club, 1928. Works on perm. exhbn. at Harvard Univ. Library, Met. Mus., New York; New York Pub. Library; Brooklyn Mus. Arts and Sciences; Art Inst. Chicago; Cleveland Mus.; Detroit Mus.; British Mus.; Bibliothèque Nationale, Paris; etc. Nat. Academician; mem. Brooklyn Soc. of Etchers (1st pres.), Am. Inst. Graphic Arts (v.p. 1928-29), Print Makers of Calif. Republican. Presbyn. Illustrated: Undine; Journeys to Bagdad; Diverse Proverbs; Paul Bunyan; Short Stories (by Walt Whitman); Petronius; Calico Bush; Hepatica Hawks; Once at Woodhall; Society Faces the Future. Home: Basking Ridge, N.J.

LEWIS, Arthur Montague, pres. Globe Automatic Sprinkler Co.; b. Richmond, Va., Sept. 14, 1881; s. Louis and Jane Elizabeth (Owen) L.; student Richmond (Va.) pub. schs., 1887-96. Temple U., Phila., Pa., 1899-1900; m. Natalie Stover Willits, Nov. 17, 1904; 1 dau., Mary Frederica (Mrs. Wheeler H. Page). V.p. and gen. mgr. Internat. Sprinkler Co., Phila., 1900-10; treas. Automatic Sprinkler Co. of America, New York, 1910-13; pres. Asso. Automatic Sprinkler Co., Phila., 1913-15; v.p. and gen. mgr. Globe Automatic Sprinkler Co., Phila., 1915-31, pres. since 1931; dir. Consolidated Equipment Co., Merchant and Evans Co. Republican. Episcopalian. Club: Leash (New York). Home: Stamford, Conn. Office: 2035 Washington Av., Philadelphia, Pa.

LEWIS, Arthur Willis, lawyer; b. Lansford, Pa., Sept. 22, 1904; s. Rev. Willis Arthur and Jennie M. (Sinclair) L.; LL.B., South Jersey Law School, Camden, 1930; m. Alberta H. Lewis, Feb. 22, 1936; 1 son, Robert Sinclair. Admitted to N.J. bar as atty., 1931, and since in general practice, Camden; mem. of law firm Bleakly, Stockwell, Lewis & Zink; prof. practice at law, South Jersey Law Sch. since 1933; dir. Fidelity Mutual Bldg. & Loan Assn., Camden, N.J., Camden Optional Bldg. & Loan Assn., Guarantee Bldg. & Loan Assn., Twin Cities Bldg. & Loan Assn., Stockton Bldg. & Loan Assn., Am. Bldg. & Loan Assn., Mickle Bldg. & Loan Assn., Cramer Hill Bldg. & Loan Assn. Vice-pres. Camden Co. Bldg. & Loan League. Trustee West Jersey Homeopathic Hosp., Camden, N.J. Mem. Camden County, Burlington County and N.J. State bar assns. Republican. Presbyn. Home: 714 Thomas Av., Riverton. Office: West Jersey Trust Bldg., Camden, N.J.

LEWIS, Burdette Gibson, statistician, economist; b. Jamestown, Pa., Jan. 1, 1882; s. Ransome Stella and Rosaline (Braden) L.; A.B., U. of Neb., 1904; post-grad. work, U. of Wis., 1904-05, Cornell U., 1905-07; hon. Sc.D., Rutgers, 1924; m. Pearl Merriam Archibald, Aug. 9, 1910; children—Burdette Gibson, Archibald Ross, Jane Alleyne, Patricia Merriam. Spl. agt. Wis. State Tax Commn., 1904, Interstate Commerce Commn., Washington, 1907; statistician Pub. Service Commn., 1st Dist., N.Y., 1907-10; asst. to pres. Bd. of Aldermen, City of New York, 1910-13; dep. commr. of correction, 1914-15, commr. of correction, City of New York, Dec. 28, 1915-Dec. 31, 1917; exec. asst. to v.p. and gen. mgr. Air Nitrates Corpn., N.Y., Jan. 14-June 11, 1918; state commr. institutions and agencies of N.J., June 12, 1918. Mem. N.J. Commn. for Rehabilitation of Civilian Handicapped Persons, and Commn. to Revise and Codify the Poor Laws. Formerly trustee Nat. Training Sch. for Community Workers; formerly v.p. Am. Inst. Criminal Law and Criminology; formerly pres. Am. Assn. Pub. Officials; mem. Am. Econ. League, Acad. Polit. Science, Nat. Conf. Social Work, Am. Prison Assn., Phi Kappa Psi; pres. Nat. Conf. Juvenile Agencies, 1924-25; v.p. J. C. Penney-Gwinn Corpn.; pres. Farm and Town Realty Corpn.; pres. Foremost Dairy Products Corpn., 1928-31; chmn. bd. Equitable Assessment Assn., N.Y.; rep. of Am. Pub. Welfare Assn., Chicago, 1932-37; dir. of Investigation of Pub. Relief Agencies in Dist. of Columbia for 74th Congress Coms. on Appropriation, Senate and Ho. of Reps., 1938. Regent U. of Miami, 1926—. Gold medal, Nat. Com. on Prisons and Prison Labor, 1925. Presbyterian. Clubs: Seminole (Jacksonville); Nassau (Princeton). Author: The Offender in His Relation to Law and Society, 1917; Correctional and Penal Treatment (Part IV of the Cleveland Foundation Survey of Criminal Justice in Cleveland), 1921; A Plan for Reuniting the States, 1933. Contbr. on financial topics. Home: 57 Cleveland Lane, Princeton, N.J. Office: Woolworth Bldg., New York, N.Y.

LEWIS, Charles Borie, cons. engr. and appraiser; b. Phila., Pa., Oct. 12, 1873; s. John T. Lewis, Jr. and Elizabeth McKean (Borie) L.; student Episcopal Acad., Phila., 1887-90, Princeton U., 1891-95; m. Grace Gough, Nov. 6, 1900. Engr. Madeira Hill & Co., Phila., 1895-98, Pa. Iron Works, Phila., 1898-99; in gen. practice as cons. engr., Denver, Colo., 1900-03; cons. engr. Los Angeles (Calif.) Gas & Electric Co., 1903-05; cons. engr. successively with Mitchell Mining Co., Los Angeles, Calif., and Berkeley Exploration and Development Co., Mexico, 1905-10; organized Lewis Motor Truck Co., mfg. motor trucks, San Francisco, Calif., 1910, and continued in business until 1915; cons. engr. in charge motor and automobile exhibits, Panama Pacific Internat. Exhbn., San Francisco, 1915; western appraiser, Mortgage Loan dept., Equitable Life Assurance Soc., Chicago, 1921-25, cons. engr. and appraiser, Phila., since 1931; sec. and asst. treas. Bankers Bond and Mortgage Co., Phila., 1925-30. Served as private, cavalry U.S. Army, Spanish-Am. War, 1898; capt., Ordnance Dept.,

U.S. Army, Engring. Bur., 1917-20; camp Ordnance officer, Camp Lewis, Wash., 1917-18; adj., Augusta (Ga.) Arsenal, 1918; ordnance officer, Southeastern Dept., Charleston, S.C., 1918-20. Republican. Episcopalian. Home: 259 S. 20th St. Office: Suite 1109-1500 Chestnut St., Philadelphia, Pa.

LEWIS, Charles Fletcher, dir. The Buhl Foundation; b. Gibsonton, Pa., Jan. 8, 1890; s. William Henry and Maria (Fletcher) L.; A.B., Allegheny Coll., Meadville, Pa., 1900; grad. study, U. of Pittsburgh, 1911-12, LL.D., from the same university, 1934; m. Jessamine De-Haven, June 12, 1915. Instr. in Latin and history, Alden Acad., Meadville, 1909-11; newspaper work, 1912-28; became connected with Pittsburgh Sun, 1916, chief editorial writer, 1919-27; editor Pitstburgh Record, 1928; dir. The Buhl Foundation since 1928; trustee and dir. Boggs & Buhl, Inc.; pres. Chatham Realty Co. (Chatham Village, large-scale housing demonstration); mem. com. on large scale operations, President's Conference on Home Bldg. and Home Ownership, 1931; mem. Housing Advisory Council of Federal Housing Adminstrn., 1934-35; mem. Planning Commn., City of Pittsburgh since 1934; mem. bd. of dirs. Pittsburgh Fed. of Social Agencies. Trustee Buhl Planetarium, Pa. Coll. for Women, also of Zoar Home. Mem. Delta Tau Delta, Sigma Delta Chi, Omicron Delta Kappa. Mason. Clubs: Duquesne, University. Writer of pamphlets: "The Truth About the Schools," 1922; "Sourcebook on the Constitution," 1927. Editor: Pittsburgh Sun Handbook of Politics, 1922-27; also "The Pennsylvania Papers," 1921 (discussion of state constl. problems by leading Pennsylvanians). Office: Farmers Bank Bldg., Pittsburgh, Pa.

LEWIS, Charles Lee, author, educator; b. Doyle, White Co., Tenn., Mar. 7, 1886; s. Mason Avery and Sarah Louisa (Richards) L.; A.B., U. of Tenn., 1906; A.M., Columbia, 1911; m. Flora Louise Quarles, July 30, 1914; children—Mary Louise, Richard Quarles. Teacher of English, Robert Coll., Constantinople, Turkey, 1911-16; teacher of English, United States Naval Academy, 1916-25, associate professor, 1925-35, prof. since 1935. Historian of Md. Soc., S.A.R.; mem. Sons of Confederate Veterans, Maryland Historical Society, Miss. Valley Historical Assn., Thomas Jefferson Bi-Centenary Assn. (hon. vice-pres.), Annapolis Public Library Association, Near East College Assn., Institut Littéraire et Artistique de France. Mem. Phi Kappa Phi. Democrat. Disciple of Christ. Clubs: Annapolis University, Naval Acad. Officers' Club. Author: Famous American Naval Officers, 1924; Life of Matthew Fontaine Maury—Pathfinder of the Seas, 1927; Famous Old-World Sea Fighters, 1929; Admiral Franklin Buchanan—Fearless Man of Action, 1930; The Romantic Decatur, 1937. Editor: Four Centuries of Literature—English and American (with Allan Westcott and Carl Jefferson Weber), 1925. Contbr. to Dictionary Am. Biography and Dictionary of Am. History. Home: 41 Southgate Av., Annapolis, Md.

LEWIS, David John, congressman; b. nr. Osceola, Pa., May 1, 1869; s. Richard Lloyd and Catharine (Watkins) L.; never attended sch.; learned to read in Sunday sch.; m. Florida M. Bohn, Dec. 19, 1893. Employed in coal mine from age of 9 to 23; studied law and Latin; admitted to bar, 1892, and since in practice at Cumberland. Mem. Md. Senate, 1902-04; Dem. nominee for 61st Congress, 1908; elected 62d to 64th and 72d to 75th Congresses (1911-17, 1931-39), 6th Md. Dist.; mem. U.S. Tariff Commn., Apr. 1917-Mar. 1925. Mem. Nat. Acad. of Sciences (physics sect.). Home: Cumberland, Md.

LEWIS, Dean (De Witt), surgeon; b. Kewanee, Ill., Aug. 11, 1874; s. L. W. and V. Winifred L.; A.B., Lake Forest (Ill.) U., 1895; M.D., Rush Med. Coll., 1899; D.Sc., U. of Ireland; m. 2d, Norene Kinney, Dec. 26, 1927; children—Julianne, Dean, Mary Elizabeth. Asst. in anatomy, 1900-01, asso. 1901-03, instr. in surgery, 1903-19, asso. prof. 1919-20, prof. 1920-24, Rush Med. Coll.; prof. surgery, U. of Ill., Jan.-July 1925; prof. surgery, Johns Hopkins U., and surgeon in chief to Johns Hopkins Hosp., 1925-39. Mem. Am. Surg. Assn., Am. Assn. Anatomists, Am. Physiol. Soc., Am. Soc. Clin. Surgery, Interurban Surg. Soc., Southern Surg. Assn., Western Surg. Assn., Baltimore Med. Soc., A.M.A. (ex-pres.); hon. mem. Wis. State Med. Soc., Royal Coll. Surgeons of Ireland, Royal Australian Coll. of Surgeons; Eclat Club. Editor Archives of Surgery, and Internat. Surgical Digest. Served as lt. col. World War. Awarded D.S.M. Home: 210 Goodwood Gardens, Roland Park, Baltimore, Md.

LEWIS, Edwin, prof. theology; b. Newbury, Eng., Apr. 18, 1881; s. Joseph and Sarah (Newman) L.; student Mt. Allison U., Can., Middlebury Coll., Vt., United Free Ch. Coll., Glasgow, Scotland; A.B., N.Y. State Coll. for Teachers, 1915; B.D., Drew Theol. Sem., 1908, Th.D., 1918; D.D. from Dickinson College, Carlisle, Pa., 1926; m. Louise Newhook Frost, Jan. 5, 1904. Came to America, 1904, naturalized citizen of U.S., 1916. Ordained M.E. ministry, 1904; pastor Velva, N.D., 1904-05, North Chatham, N.Y., 1910-12, Rensselaer, N.Y., 1913-16; instr. in English, N.Y. State Coll. for Teachers, 1915-16; instr. Greek and theology, 1916-18, adj. prof. systematic theology, 1918-20, prof., June 8, 1920—, Drew Theol. Sem. Republican. Author: Jesus Christ and the Human Quest, 1924; A Manual of Christian Beliefs, 1927; God and Ourselves, 1931; Great Christian Teachings, 1933; A Christian Manifesto, 1934; The Faith We Declare, 1939. Joint editor The Abingdon Bible Commentary. Contbr. on theol. and lit. topics. Home: Madison, N.J.

LEWIS, Edwin James, mech. engring.; b. Auburn, N.Y., July 3, 1875; s. Edwin and Sarah (Bartlett) L.; M.E., Cornell U., 1899; m. Charlotte Agnes Johnson, Mar. 4, 1903; children—James Edwin, Sarah Helene (Mrs. Richard Earl Contryman). Employed in engring. depts. r.r.s at Chicago, Ill., 1899-1902; inspr. motive power, Pa. R.R., Columbus, O., 1902-03, gen. foreman, Lancaster, O., 1903-04, asst. to master mechanic, Pa. R.R., Columbus, O., 1904-10; engr. and supt. Climax Mfg. Co., locomotive builders, Corry, Pa., 1910-29; supt., treas. and dir. McInnes Steel Co., Corry, Pa., since 1931. Served as dir. bd. edn. sch. dist., Corry, Pa. Republican. Presbyn. Mason (K.T.). Home: 60 E. Bond St., Corry, Pa.

LEWIS, Edwin Owen, judge; b. Richmond, Va., July 12, 1879; s. Louis and Jane Elizabeth (Owen) L.; student Richmond (Va.) Coll., 1895-96; LL.B., U. of Pa., 1902; m. Eleanor Lord, Apr. 26, 1905 (died 1935); children—Carolyn Montague (Mrs. W. Wyclif Walton), Eleanor Lord (Mrs. Adkins Lowell). Admitted to Pa. bar, 1902; in practice at Phila., 1902-24; mem. Phila. Common Council, 1907-09, asst. city solicitor, 1912-15; 1st asst., 1915-16, mem. bd. of recreation, 1914-16; judge Common Pleas Ct. No. 2, Phila. Co., since 1923 (elected without opposition, 1923, 1933). Pres. Phila. Sch. of Design for Women, Moore Inst. of Art, since 1917. Dir. Athenaeum Library (Phila.) since 1929, Pa. Acad. of Fine Arts since 1934. Mem. Pa. Soc. Sons of the Revolution (v.p. and gen. delegate, 1935), Soc. of Colonial Wars (chancellor gen., 1936). Hist. Soc. of Pa. (v.p., 1938). Ind. Republican. Episcopalian. Clubs: Phila. Skating, Merion Cricket (Phila.). Author: The Street Railway Situation in Philadelphia, 1907; Recreation of the Colonial Background, 1931. Home: 6350 City Line, Overbrook. Office: 344 City Hall, Philadelphia, Pa.

LEWIS, Elizabeth Foreman, author; b. Baltimore, Md., May 24, 1892; d. Joseph Francis and Virginia D. (Bayly) L.; ed. Tome Sch., 1906 to 1909, Md. Inst. of Fine Arts, Baltimore, 1909 to 1910; student Bryant and Stratton Secretarial Sch., Baltimore, 1916 to 1917; studied Bibl. Sem. of N.Y., 1917; m. John Abraham Lewis, Jan. 28, 1921 (died 1934); 1 son, John Fulton. Asst. treas. Woman's Foreign Missionary Society, Shanghai, 1917-18; teacher dist. schs., Chungking, W. China, 1918-19, Hwei Wen Boarding Sch. for Girls, Nanking, and Boys' Acad., Nanking, 1919-21. Methodist. Author: Young Fu of the Upper Yangtze, 1932 (awarded John Newbery Medal, A.L.A. 1933; pub. also in Eng. and transl. into several European langs. and transcribed into Braille in U.S. and Eng.); Ho-Ming, Girl of New China, 1934 (also pub. in Eng. and Scandinavia); China Quest, 1937 (transcribed into Braille); Portrait from a Chinese Scroll, 1938; also short stories in juvenile mags. and anthologies. Home: Briar Cliff-on-Severn, Arnold, Md.

LEWIS, Florence P.; instr. mathematics, Goucher Coll., 1908-11, asso. prof. 1911-20, prof. since 1920. Address: Goucher College, Baltimore, Md.

LEWIS, Francis A(lbert), lawyer; b. Phila., Pa., Feb. 14, 1889; s. Francis A. and Blanche (McClelland) L.; student Episcopal Acad., Phila., 1897-1903, Haverford (Pa.) Sch., 1903-06; B.S. U. of Pa., 1910; student Harvard Law Sch., 1910-12, U. of Pa. Law Sch., 1912-13; m. Louise B. Brock, April 24, 1915; children—Francis Albert, Tyler, Lawrence. Admitted to Pa. bar, 1913; asso. with Duane, Morris & Hechscher, Phila., 1913-17, partner, 1917-34; mem. firm Schnader & Lewis, Phila.; counsel for Liquidating Div. of Dept. of Banking of the Commonwealth of Pa., 1933-35. Dir. Land Title Bank & Trust Co., Phila., Catawissa R.R. Co., Phila. Served as seaman, 2d class, U.S.N., July-Nov. 1917, ensign, Nov. 1917-Oct. 1918, lt. J.G., Oct.-Dec. 1918. Treas. Corpn. for Relief of Widows and Children; mgr. Episcopal Hosp. Mem. Soc. Colonial Wars, Delta Psi. Republican. Episcopalian (vestryman Old St. Peters Ch. and St. James the Less). Clubs: Philadelphia, Union League (Phila.); Gulph Mills Golf (Gulph Mills, Pa.). Home: Fishers Rd., Bryn Mawr, Pa. Office: 1719 Packard Bldg., Phila., Pa.

LEWIS, George, F.S.C.; prof. mathematics; b. Washington, D.C., April 12, 1888; s. William H. and Eleanore V. (Craig) Mathews; A.B., LaSalle Coll., Phila., 1917; A.M., U. of Pa., 1922; (hon.) D.Sc., Duquesne Univ., 1925. Engaged in teaching mathematics and physics, Rock Hill High Sch., 1909-13; instr. mathematics and physics, LaSalle Coll., High Sch., 1913-17; asst. prof. mathematics and physics, LaSalle Coll., 1917-22; entered religious order Christian Brothers, 1904; prof. mathematics and physics, St. Thomas Coll. (now Univ. of Scranton) and vice-pres. coll., 1922-25, pres. coll., 1925-31; prof. mathematics, LaSalle Coll. since 1934, also dean since 1938. Fellow, A.A.A.S. Roman Catholic. Home: LaSalle College, Philadelphia, Pa.

LEWIS, George Francis, lawyer; b. New York, N.Y., Nov. 21, 1885; s. Francis Cornelius and Sarah Elizabeth (Kelley) L.; student Mt. Hermon (Mass.) Boys Sch., 1902-04; LL.B., Cornell U., 1907; m. Elizabeth Lofgren, March 2, 1912; children—Robert Gibson, George Francis. Admitted to N.Y. bar, 1907; mem. of firm Tibbetts, Lewis, Lazo & Welch; v.p. and counsel Technicolor, Inc., Technicolor Motion Picture Corpn.; sec. Gen. Electric X-Ray Corpn.; counsel Heyden Chem. Corpn., Am. Aniline Products Corpn. Mem. Am. and N.Y. state bar assns. Delta Chi. Mason. Clubs: Downtown Athletic, Cornell, Essex Fells Country. Home: Essex Fells, N.J. Office: 15 Broad St., New York, N.Y.

LEWIS, George William, aeronautical engr.; b. Ithaca, N.Y., March 10, 1882; s. William H. and Edith (Sweetland) L.; M.E., 1908, Cornell U., M.M.E., 1910; Sc.D., Norwich University, Northfield, Vermont; m. Myrtle D. Harvey, Sept. 9, 1908; children—Alfred William, Harvey Sweetland, Myrtle Norlaine, George William, Leigh Kneeland, Armin Kessler. Instr. in engring., Cornell U., 1908-10; prof. engring., Swarthmore Coll., 1910-17; engr. in charge Clarke Thompson Research, 1917-19; salesmgr. Phila. Surface Combustion Co., 1919; exec. officer Nat. Advisory Com. for Aeronautics, 1919-24; dir. aeronautical research Nat. Advisory Committee for Aeronautics, Washington, D.C., since 1924. Served as mem. Com. on Power Plants for Aircraft of National Advisory Committee for Aeronautics, 1918-22, vice-chmn. since 1922; chmn. contest board National Aeronautical Assn.; mem. committee on judges Daniel Guggenheim Safe Aircraft Competition, 1927-29; mem. bd. judges Wright Medal Award, 1928-29, chmn. bd., 1930; mem. bd. of award Manly Memorial Medal since 1929; mem. Guggenheim

Medal Bd. of Award, 1930-35. Mem. Inst. of Aeronautical Sciences (v.p.), Soc. Automotive Engrs. (v.p. 1931); mem. War Dept. Spl. Committee on Army Air Corps (Baker Bd.), 1934. Awarded Daniel Guggenheim medal, 1936. Presbyn. Clubs: Cosmos, Kenwood. Home: 6502 Ridgewood Av., Chevy Chase, Md. Address: Navy Bldg., Washington, D.C.

LEWIS, H. B.; pres. Charleston Clearing House. Office: Charleston Clearing House, Charleston, W.Va.

LEWIS, H. Edgar, corpn. official; b. Pontardulais, Wales, July 24, 1882; s. William E. and Emily Ann (Williams) L.; Martins Ferry (O.) High Sch.; m. Lottie May Ruch (died 1918); children—Emily (Mrs. Robert W. Gillespie, Jr.), James Edgar; m. 2d, Helen Sanders, Sept. 7, 1920; 1 son, Edgar Sanders. Came to U.S. 1896; entered employ Bethlehem Steel Co., 1906, and advanced through grades to exec. v.p., 1916-30; chmn. exec. com. Jeffrey Mfg. Co., 1930-36; chmn. of bd. Jones & Laughlin Steel Corpn., 1936-38, chmn. and pres. since 1938; dir. Jeffrey Mfg. Co., British Jeffrey-Diamond, Ltd., Kelsey-Hayes Wheel Co., Kelsey-Hayes Wheel Co., Ltd., Ohio Malleable Iron Co., Galion Iron Works & Mfg. Co. Mem. Pittsburgh Chamber of Commerce. Republican. Episcopalian. Pres. Pittsburgh Convention and Tourists Bureau, 1938. Clubs: Metropolitan, Cloud (New York); Duquesne, Fox Chapel Golf, Pittsburgh Golf (Pittsburgh); Detroit Athletic; Oakland Hills (Detroit); Rolling Rock Country, Oakmont Country. Home: 5420 Darlington Rd., Pittsburgh, Pa. Office: Jones & Laughlin Steel Corpn., 3d Av. and Ross St., Pittsburgh, Pa.

LEWIS, Harry Irving, vice-pres. American Type Founders, Inc.; b. Salem, Mass., July 26, 1892; s. Alvin L. and Florence S. (Potter) Lewis; B.S., Mass. Inst. Tech.; m. Guiguitte Gluck de la Villeguérif, 1923; children—Aimee Florence Guiguitte, Robert Leonard. Mech. engr. Dolphin Jute Mills, 1915; supt. Lamond & Robertson Co., 1916-17; chief engr. Bishop & Babcock Co., 1919-21; pres. Lewis & Woolard, Inc., sec.-treas., dir. Siebel Inst. of Tech., Chicago, partner O. G. Halvorsen Co., asso. editor Ice & Refrigeration, 1921-24; sales mgr. Am. Engring. Co., 1924-28; sales mgr. Gen. Refrigeration Co., 1928-29; v.p. and gen. mgr. J. L. Morrison Co., gen. mgr., Seybold Machine Co., 1930-34; v.p. Am. Type Founders Co., Elizabeth, N.J., since 1934. Served as 1st lt. U.S. Army, 1917-18; now lt. col. Ordnance Res. Mem. Army Ordnance Assn., Am. Soc. Mech. Engrs., Automobile Mfrs. Assn., Soc. Am. Mil. Engrs., Reserve Officers Assn., Am. Soc. Refrigerating Engrs. Holds patents for automatic spacer and multiple spindle drill. Home: 1021 Lawrence Av., Westfield, N.J. Office: Am. Type Founders, Inc., Elizabeth, N.J.

LEWIS, Harry Joseph, merchant; b. Manasquau, N.J., April 20, 1889; s. Julius Lewis and Florence (Lippman) L.; ed. Manasquau (N.J.) High Sch. and Rider Coll., Trenton, N.J.; m. Cecile Klopstock, 1913; children—Doris Roseland, Jane Lenore, Richard Ellas. Owner Lewis' Dept. Store, Belmar, N.J.; v.p. Belmar (N.J.) Nat. Bank; pres. Monmouth Co. (N.J.) Sch. Bds.; v.p. Belmar (N.J.) Bd. of Edn. Mason. Club: Kiwanis (past pres.). Home: 701 10th Av. Office: 1001 F St., Belmar, N.J.

LEWIS, Harry Rauch, pres. Hyvis Oils, Inc. and Conewango Refining Co.; b. Parkersburg, W.Va., June 13, 1897; s. Leopold H. and Bertha (Rauch) L.; student Howe Military Acad., Howe, Indiana, 1910-15, U. of Mich., 1915-17, 1919-20; m. Margaret Hubbard, July 10, 1926; children—Harry, John, Margaret. Salesman Fred G. Clark, Inc., Cleveland, O., 1918-24; pres. Conewango Refining Co., Warren, Pa., since 1924, Hyvis Oils, Inc., Warren, Pa., since 1933. Served in U.S. Army, 1917-19. Mem. Pa. Grade Crude Oil Assn. (dir.), Nat. Petroleum Assn. (dir.). Democrat. Episcopalian. Mason, Elk. Clubs: Conewango, Conewango Valley Country (Warren, Pa.). Home: 408 Conewango Av. Office: Market St., Warren, Pa.

LEWIS, H(enry) H(arrison) Walker, lawyer; b. Hoboken, N.J., Feb. 10, 1904; s. Edwin Augustus Stevens and Alice Stuart (Walker) L.; student Morristown (N.J.) Sch., 1915-21; A.B., Princeton U., 1925; LL.B., Harvard Law Sch., 1928; m. Eleanor Randall Nelson, Oct. 7, 1938. Admitted to Md. bar, 1928, and since practiced at Baltimore, Md.; asso. with Piper, Carey & Hall, Baltimore, 1928-31; in law dept. U. S. Fidelity Co., Baltimore, 1931-33; atty. Pub. Works Administrn., Washington, D.C., 1933-34; gen. counsel Allied Mortgage Cos., Inc., and Associated Mortgage Cos., Inc., real estate and mortgage liquidation, Baltimore, since 1934, v.p. since 1935. Democrat. Episcopalian. Home: 1207 Bolton St. Office: 301 Keyser Bldg., Baltimore, Md.

LEWIS, Herbert Frederick, gen. mgr. Oakland Beach Co.; b. Brookville, Pa., Apr. 23, 1909; s. Herbert Grant and Mayme (McGiffin) L.; student Brookville (Pa.) High Sch., 1914-26, Allegheny Coll., Meadville, Pa., 1926-29, Am. Inst. of Banking, Pittsburgh, 1932, U. of Pittsburgh, 1933; unmarried. Began as ins. clerk Pa. Surety Co., Pittsburgh, 1929-31; clerk Peoples-Pittsburgh Trust Co., Pittsburgh, 1931-33; mgr. Oakland Beach Hotel, Conneaut Lake, Pa., since 1933; pres. and gen. mgr. Oakland Beach Co. since 1933; owner Silver Shores Restaurant, Conneaut Lake, Pa., since 1938. Mem. Pa. Hotel Assn., Pa. Restaurant Assn., Sigma Alpha Epsilon. Republican. Presbyterian. Address: Oakland Beach Hotel, Conneaut Lake, Pa.

LEWIS, James Edward, chairman Harbison-Walker Refractories Co., Pittsburgh; dir. Farmers Deposit Nat. Bank, Reliance Life Ins. Co. Office: Farmers Bank Bldg., Pittsburgh, Pa.

LEWIS, Leicester Crosby, clergyman; b. N.Y. City, Mar. 30, 1887; s. George Washington and Maria Elizabeth (Sharkey) L.; A.B., Columbia, 1910, A.M., 1911; B.D., Gen. Theol. Sem. of P.E. Ch., New York, 1912; student univs. of Berlin, Tübingen and Freiburg, 1912-14; Ph.D., Univ. of Pa., 1925; S.T.D. from Columbia University, 1936; m. Beatrix Elizabeth Baldwin, June 1, 1915; children—Leicester Crosby, Richard Warrington Baldwin, Virginia Adelaide. Deacon P.E. Ch., 1911, priest, 1912; curate Christ Ch., Ridgewood, N.J., 1911-12; prof. ecclesiastical history, Western Theol. Sem. and chaplain St. Mary's Sisters, Chicago, 1913-20; head dept. ch. history, Episcopal Acad., Phila., 1922-29, chaplain, 1931-32, hon. chaplain since 1932; asst. Holy Trinity Ch., Lansdale, Pa., 1922-29; dir. sch. of religious edn., St. James Ch., Phila., 1931-32; rector Ch. St. Martin-in-the-Fields, Chestnut Hill, Phila., since 1932; lecturer, Philadelphia Divinity Sch. since 1937; examining chaplain to bishop of Pa.; chaplain Soc. of Companions of the Holy Cross and St. Ursula's Guild for Teachers; exec. chmn. Am. Church Union; pres. Phila. Clericus; pres. Thirty Club; overseer Phila. Divinity Sch.; v.p. House of the Holy Child (Ambler, Pa.); trustee House of Rest for the Aged (Phila.). Mem. American Society Church History, Church Hist. Soc., Am. Philosophical Assn., Gesellschaft für Kirchengeschichte, Société d'Histoire Ecclésiastique de la France, Classical Club, Alpha Chi Rho. Founder (with S. A. Mercer) Anglican Theological Review, 1918 and since coeditor. Contbr. monographs and articles on philosophical and religious subjects. Home: 7737 St. Martin's Lane, Philadelphia, Pennsylvania.

LEWIS, Lloyd Griffith, surgeon; b. Remsen, N.Y., Nov. 10, 1902; s. John G. and Nettie (Griffith) L.; A.B., Hamilton Coll., Clinton, N.Y., 1924; M.D., Johns Hopkins U. Med. Sch., 1928; m. Lois Gray Falconer, Aug. 16, 1930; 1 son, John Richard. Interne, Johns Hopkins Hosp., 1928-29; asst. res. surg., Emergency Hosp., Washington, D.C., 1929-30; asst. res. urologist, Johns Hopkins Hosp., 1930-32, res. urologist, 1932-33, asst. vis. urologist since 1933; instr. urology, Johns Hopkins Med. Sch., 1930-37, asso. in urology since 1937; urologist to diagnostic clinic, Johns Hopkins Hosp. since 1934; dispensary urologist Johns Hopkins Hosp., 1930-38, urologist in charge dispensary since 1938. Mem. Alpha Kappa Kappa. Democrat. Episcopalian. Club: University. Contbr. urol. articles to med. journs. Home: Riderwood, Md. Office: 101 W. Read St., Baltimore, Md.

LEWIS, Ludwig Clifford, ins. co. official; b. Phila., Pa., Feb. 18, 1891; s. Edwin Clifford and Amelia Read (Collis) L.; grad. Episcopal Acad., 1909; student U. of Pa., 1909; m. Lucy Sturgis Jefferys, Apr. 14, 1923; children—Ludwig Clifford, Jr., Edwin Mower 3d, Lucy Sturgis Jeffreys, Anne Jefferys. Asso. with Ins. Co. of North America continuously since entering employ as clk., 1909, asst. sec., 1924, marine sec., 1929, vice-pres. since 1937; vice-pres. Alliance Ins. Co. of Phila., Phila. Fire and Marine Ins. Co. Served in A.S., U.S.N. Res., 1918. Trustee Southern Home for Destitute Children, Episcopal Acad. Mem. Delta Phi. Episcopalian. Clubs: Racquet, St. Elmo; Merion Cricket (Haverford). Home: Villa Nova, Pa. Office: 1600 Arch St., Philadelphia, Pa.

LEWIS, Mahlon Everett, lawyer; b. Minneapolis, Minn., Apr. 4, 1901; s. Harlow Satterlee and Grace (Everett) L.; ed. high sch. Ben Avon Heights, Pa., 1916-20; A.B., Lafayette Coll., 1924; LL.B., U. of Pittsburgh Law Sch., 1927; m. Janet Fraser, Dec. 22, 1928; children—Harlow Satterlee II, Fraser, Sally Hathaway. Admitted to Pa. bar, 1927 and since engaged in gen. practice of law at Pittsburgh; asso. with firm Alter, Wright and Barron, 1927-36; mem. firm Stewart and Lewis since 1936; prof. of law, U. of Pittsburgh Law Sch. since 1927; dir. Allegheny Trust Co., Bold Baking Corpn. Served as burgess Ben Avon Heights Borough, 1929-37. Mem. Am., Pa. and Allegheny Co. bar assns., Order of Coif, Chi Phi, Phi Alpha Delta. Republican. United Presbyn. Clubs: Duquesne (Pittsburgh); Shannopin Country (Ben Avon Heights). Home: 21 Devon Lane, Ben Avon Heights, Pa. Office: 1017 Park Bldg., Pittsburgh, Pa.

LEWIS, Margaret Sarah, artist and teacher; b. York, Pa., Feb. 8, 1907; d. Melchinger Oliver and Sarah Jane (Ammon) L.; grad. high sch., York, Pa., 1924; ed. Md. Inst. Art, Baltimore, Md., 1925-29; B.S., Teachers Coll. of Columbia U., 1935. Asst. supervisor of art York Sch. Dist. since 1929; dir. arts and crafts, camp, Barton, Vt., summer 1936, camp, Lake Champlain, Vt., summer 1937; one-man exhbn. water color paintings at Md. Inst. Art, 1938, at Martin Memorial Library, York, Pa., 1938; paintings exhibited in galleries, N.Y. City, Baltimore, Hagerstown, Md., Wichita, Kan.; traveling exhbns. East and middle West; local dir. Nat. Art Week for York Co. since 1936; designer scenery for York Little Theatre. Mem. Eastern Arts Assn., Md. Inst. Art Alumni Assn., York Art Club (sec.). Awarded European traveling scholarship from Md. Inst. Art. Republican. Lutheran. Home: 255 Roosevelt Av., York, Pa.

LEWIS, Marion L., publisher, banker; b. Valparaiso, Ind.; s. Sylvester A. and Maria (Hansford) L.; ed. Valparaiso U.; m. Mabel E. Mosher, Dec. 23, 1905; children—Bruce Mosher, Koradine (Mrs. Sanford L. Smith). Began teaching in public schools in Ind., Kans. and Iowa; then selling encyclopedia and general book publications in N.J., N.Y. and through the Southern States; in publishing business since 1907; pres. Lewis Hist. Pub. Co., New York, N.Y.; pres. First Nat. Bank, Nutley. Pres. Nutley Library Bd.; mem. Nutley Bd. of Edn.; trustee Centenary Jr. Coll., Hackettstown, N.J. Mem. Sons Am. Revolution. Republican. Methodist. Clubs: Yountakah Country (Nutley). Home: 501 Prospect St. Office: First National Bank, Nutley, N.J.

LEWIS, Mary Fanning Wickham (Mrs. Shippen L.), writer; b. Phila., Pa., June 8, 1898; d. Samuel and Maria Porter (Landis) Porcher; diploma, Wissahickon Heights Sch., 1915, Dana Hall, Wellesley, Mass., 1916; m. Shippen Lewis, November 19, 1930; step-children—Dora Lewis (Mrs. Hunter Moss), Mary Emlen Lewis (Mrs. J. William Townsend 3d), Louise W. Lewis. Trustee Pennhurst State Sch. (for feeble-minded boys and girls). Awarded Browning Soc. prize for verse, 1925. Democrat. Episcopalian. Author (under name of Porcher): The Tilted Cup (verse), 1926; (girls adventure books) Cherique, 1928; Gloom Creek, 1929. Contbr. stories and articles to mags. Home: Hartwell and Navajo Sts., Chestnut Hill., Philadelphia, Pa.

LEWIS, Mary Ruth Hadley, physician; b. Sabina, O., 1879; d. Ellis and Emma (Hadley) Lewis; B.S., Wilmington Coll., 1911; M.D., Woman's Med. Coll. of Pa., 1911; unmarried. Interne Woman's Hosp., Phila., 1911-12, asst. in pediatrics, 1912-13, asst. and asso. in obstetrics, 1913-28, med. dir. since 1928; lecturer in hygiene and physician to women, Swarthmore Coll., 1912-23; asst. med. inspr. Phila. Pub. Schs., 1913-18; asst. and asso. in obstetrics, West Phila. Hosp. for Women, 1913-23, chief in obstetrics, 1923-28, med. dir. 1918-28; dir. Asso. Hosp. Service of Phila.; del. Internat. Congress Med. Women, Edinborough, 1938. Fellow Am. Coll. Hosp. Adminstrs. (charter fellow), A.M.A.; mem. Pa. Med. Soc., Phila. Co. Med. Soc., Phila. Hosp. Assn., Pa. Hosp. Assn., Am. Hosp. Assn., Am. Med. Women's Assn., Internat. Med. Women's Assn., Women's Internat. League for Peace and Freedom, Internes Assn. of Woman's Hosp. of Phila., Rose Valley Folk, Rose Valley Swimming Pool Assn. Mem. Soc. of Friends. Clubs: Medical Women, Physicians Motor, National Travel, Anna E. Broomall (Phila.). Home: "Fairywood," Route 3, Media, Pa. Office: Preston and Parrish Sts., Philadelphia, Pa.

LEWIS, Orville Garrett, surgeon; b. Washington Co., Pa., Oct. 7, 1877; s. Homer Estine and Mary Elizabeth (Jordan) L.; student Waynesburg (Pa.) Coll., 1896-98; M.D., U. of Pittsburgh Med. Coll., 1904; m. Queen Elizabeth Fulton, June 1, 1921; children—William Franklin, Orville Garrett. Sch. teacher, Washington Co., Pa., 1898-99; mem. surgical staff Washington (Pa.) Hosp., since 1908. Served as capt., M.C., U.S. Army, 1918-19. Fellow A.M.A.; mem. Founders Group of Am. Bd. of Surgery, Washington Co. Med. Soc., Pa. State Med. Soc. Republican. Presbyterian. Mason (32°, Shriner). Home: 315 E. Wheeling St. Office: 6 S. Main St., Washington, Pa.

LEWIS, Robert T., printing and pub.; b. Wales, Dec. 20, 1872; s. Robert and Elizabeth (Hughes) L.; brought by parents to U.S., 1873 and naturalized through papers of parent; ed. country schs. to 1887; m. Cordelia Jamison, Aug. 3, 1899; children—Loran L., Thomas S., Donald B., Betty. Engaged in business of printing and publishing since starting as printer, 1888; propr. R. T. Lewis Printing Co. since 1911; dir. Sheraden Bank. Served as del. Rep. Nat. Conv., Cleveland, from 33d congl. dist. of Pa. Trustee Adrian Coll., Adrian, Mich. Republican. Methodist. I.O.O.F. Club: Monarch of Pittsburgh (sec.). Home: 631 Sherwood Av. Office: 316 Market St., Pittsburgh, Pa.

LEWIS, Thomas Morgan, lawyer; b. Plymouth, Pa., Nov. 21, 1891; s. Morgan V. and Gwennie (Morgan) L.; ed. Wyoming Sem., Kingston, Pa., 1909-13; LL.B., U. of Pa. Law Sch., 1916; m. Adelaide Bodenstine, July 14, 1919. Admitted to Pa. bar, 1916, and since engaged in gen. practice of law at Wilkes-Barre; served as asst. dist. atty., 1923-26, dist. atty. Luzerne Co., 1926-36; solicitor Plymouth Borough since 1923; local atty. D.L.& W. R.R. Co.; dir. and counsel First Nat. Bank, Plymouth, Pa. Mem. Pa. Bar Assn., Wilkes-Barre Law Library Assn. Republican. Mem. First Christian Prot. Ch. Mason (32°, Shriner). Clubs: Kiwanis (Plymouth); Franklin, Westmoreland (Wilkes-Barre); Irem Temple Country (Dallas). Home: 135 W. Main St., Plymouth, Pa. Office: Miners Bank Bldg., Wilkes-Barre, Pa.

LEWIS, Vivian M., vice chancellor; b. Paterson, N.J.; s. Isaac Arriston and Hannah (Davies) L.; LL.D., Lafayette College, Pennsylvania; m. September 27, 1916, Charlotte A. Jörgensen; children—Henry C., John C. Admitted N.J. bar, 1892; practiced in Paterson; judge advocate, 2d Regt. N.J.N.G., 1896-99, retired with rank of capt.; mem. Gen. Assembly, 1898-99, 1900; leader Rep. majority, 1900; city counsel, Paterson, 1904; counsel State Bd. Health, 1900-04; clerk in chancery, 1904-09; commr. of banking and ins., 1909-12; Rep. candidate for gov. of N.J., 1910, against Woodrow Wilson; vice chancellor N.J., Apr. 3, 1912—; trustee for policy holders of Prudential Ins. Co. of America. Mem. N.J. Hist. Soc. Clubs: Hamilton, Arcola, Somerville, North Jersey, Union League, Pacific, Sankaty Head Golf. Home: Paterson, N.J.

LEWIS, Warren Harmon, univ. prof.; b. Suffield, Conn., June 17, 1870; s. John and Adelaide E. (Harmon) L.; student Chicago Manual Training Sch., 1886-89; B.S., U. of Mich., 1894; M.D., Johns Hopkins, 1900; m. Margaret Reed, May 23, 1910; children—Margaret Nast, Warren Reed, Jessica Helen. Asst. in zoölogy, U. of Mich., 1894-96; asst. in anatomy, 1900, instr., 1901-03, asso., 1903-04, asso. prof., 1904-13, prof. physiol. anatomy, 1913—, Johns Hopkins U. Research asso., dept embryology, Carnegie Instn. of Washington, 1919—. Trustee Mt. Desert Island Biological Laboratory (pres. 1933-37). Mem. Nat. Academy of Sciences, American Association Anatomists (president 1934-36), American Physiol. Society, Am. Society of Naturalists, Internat. Soc. for Exptl. Cytology (pres.); fellow A.A. A.S.; hon. mem. La Société de Médecine de Gand. Club: Johns Hopkins. Has published papers on Development of the Arm, Muscular System and Skull in Man, Development of the Eye in Chick, Experimental Studies on development of the eye, ear, nervous system, brain, muscular system, cyclopia, etc.; cultivation of living tissues outside the body in artificial media; mitochondria and experimental cytology; studies on the cultivation of human lymph nodes and cell degeneration; cinematographs of living developing rabbit eggs, of normal and of malignant cells; studies on malignant sarcoma cells and young mammalian eggs. Editor 20th, 21st, 22d and 23d edits. of Gray's Anatomy. Co-author of General Cytology. Co-editor of Archiv für exper. Zellforschung. Home: 202 Hawthorn Rd., Roland Park, Baltimore, Md.

LEWIS, Willard Potter, librarian; b. Watertown, N.Y., Aug. 10, 1889; s. Benjamin Morgan and Jennie Noa (Potter) L.; grad. DeWitt Clinton High Sch., N.Y. City, 1907; B.A., Wesleyan U., Conn., 1911, M.A., 1912; B.L.S., New York State Library Sch., Albany, N.Y., 1913; m. Harriet Edna Stillman, Apr. 9, 1914; children— Robert Stillman, Barbara Evelyn, Walter Morgan, Donald Richey. Asst. N.Y. State Library, 1912-13; librarian, Albany (N. Y.) Y.M.C.A., 1913-14, Baylor U., 1914-19; organizer and librarian, Camp McArthur Library, Waco, Tex., Oct.-Dec. 1917; librarian U. of New Hampshire, 1919-29, Wesleyan U., Middletown, Conn., 1929-31, Pa. State Coll. since 1931; resident dir. N.H. Summer Library Sch., 1920-26; lecturer Conn. Pub. Library Summer Sch., 1926-30; dir. Pa. State Coll. Summer Library Sch. since 1932. Mem. A.L.A. (chmn. agrl. libraries sect. 1927-28; sec., treas. coll. and reference sect. 1935-38; sec., Assn. of College and Reference Libraries, 1938—), N.H. Library Assn., (pres. 1922-24), Pa. Library Assn. (v.p. 1932-33; chmn. coll. libraries sect. 1935-36), Am. Assn. Univ. Profs., Sigma Chi, Pi Gamma Mu. Democrat. Methodist. Home: 510 E. Prospect Av., State College, Pa.

LEWIS, William Ditto, librarian; b. Chicago, Ill., July 14, 1896; s. Theodore Porter and Edith Emily (Kemp) L.; prep. edn. pub. schs., Delta, O.; A.B., Oberlin (O.) Coll., 1919; student Library Sch. of N.Y. Pub. Library, 1920-22; m. Ruth Marilla Curtis, Sept. 5, 1925. Teacher Birmingham (O.) High Sch., 1919-20; asst. in stacks N.Y. Pub. Library, 1920-22, reference asst., econs. div., 1922-26, reference asst., information desk, 1926-30; librarian U. of Del., Newark, Del., since 1930. Mem. Am. Library Assn., Del. Library Assn., Am. Assn. Univ. Profs. Home: 25 Amstel Av. Office: Memorial Library, University of Delaware, Newark, Del.

LEWIS, William Dodge, educator, author; s. John E. and Anna J. (Van Ornum) L.; B.A., Syracuse U., 1892, M.A., 1895, Pd.D., 1917; Litt.D., Susquehanna U., 1921; m. Louise Graff, Sept. 19, 1893; children—Jessie Louise, Frederick Howard. Grammar sch. prin., head dept. of English, and high sch. prin., pub. schs., Syracuse, until 1909; prin. William Penn High Sch., Phila., 1910-19; dep. supt. pub. instrn., Pa., 1919-23; editor The John C. Winston Co., Phila., 1923—. Mem. Phi Kappa Psi, Phi Beta Kappa. Methodist. Author: Democracy's High School, 1914. Joint Author: Practical English for High Schools, 1st course, 1916, 2d course, 1927; Knowing and Using Words, 1917; Silent Reading Series, 1920; The New Silent Readers, 1931; The Reading Hour Series, 1931. Joint Editor: The Winston Simplified Dictionary, 1919, advanced edition, 1926; English for Use, 1926; Dictionary for Schools, 1935; also several English classic texts and mag. articles. Home: 38 E. Greenwood Av., Lansdowne, Pa.

LEWIS, William Draper, lawyer; b. Philadelphia, Apr. 27, 1867; s. Henry and Fannie Hannah (Wilson) L.; B.S., Haverford, 1888; LL.B., and Ph.D., U. of Pa., 1891; m. Caroline Mary Cope, June 22, 1892. Instr. legal hist. instns., Wharton Sch., U. of Pa., 1891; lecturer on economics, Haverford Coll., 1890-96; prof. of law and dean law dept., U. of Pa., 1896-1914, prof. of law until Sept. 1924; dir. of Am. Law Inst. since June 1, 1923. Author: Federal Power Over Commerce and Its Effect on State Action, 1891; Our Sheep and the Tariff, 1891; Restraint of Infringement of Incorporeal Rights, 1904; Life of Theodore Roosevelt; Interpreting the Constitution, 1938; also numerous articles on legal, economic and historical topics for periodicals. Editor: Lewis' Edition Greenleaf's Evidence, 3 volumes, 1896; Wharton's Criminal Law, 10th edit., 2 vols., 1895; Lewis' edit. Blackstone's Commentaries, 4 vols., 1897; Digest of Decisions of United States Supreme Court and Circuit Court of Appeals, 1 vol., 1897; Pepper & Lewis' Digest of Statutes of Pennsylvania (co-editor), 3 vols., 1896, and 4 vols., 1911; Digest of Decisions and Encyclopædia of Pennsylvania Laws, 23 vols.; Great American Lawyers, 8 vols., 1907-08; Pepper & Lewis' Cases on Law of Association, Part I-IX (co-editor), 1909-10. Chmn. resolutions (platform) com. 1st and 2d Prog. Nat. Convs., Chicago, 1912 and 1916; Prog. candidate for gov. of Pa., 1914. Home: Aubury, Germantown, Phila. Office: 3400 Chestnut St., Philadelphia, Pa.

LEWIS, William Mather; b. Howell, Mich., Mar. 24, 1878; s. James and Mary (Farrand) L.; student Knox Coll., Galesburg, Ill., 1896-98; A.B., Lake Forest (Ill.) Coll., 1900, LL.D., 1924; A.M., Ill. Coll., 1902; studied abroad, 1913-14; LL.D. from Norwich U., 1925, Temple U., 1927, Lehigh U., 1928, Dickinson Coll., 1933, St. John's, Maryland, 1934, Univ. of Rochester, 1935, U. of Pa., 1935, Columbia, 1936; Litt.D., Knox Coll., 1930; L.H.D., Hobart, 1935, New York U., 1936; m. Ruth Durand, Dec. 20, 1906; 1 dau., Sarah Durand (Mrs. W. E. Betts). Instr., Ill. Coll., 1900-03, Lake Forest Coll., 1903-06; headmaster Lake Forest Acad., 1906-13; exec. sec. Nat. Com. Patriotic Socs., 1917-19; dir. savings div. United States Treasury Department, 1919-21; chief of edn. service, Chamber of Commerce, U.S.A., 1921-23; president George Washington University, 1923-27; president Lafayette College since 1927. Mayor Lake Forest, Ill., 1915-17; mem. Bd. of Review, 1915; pres. Bd. of Edn., 1911-13. Lecturer McCormick Theol. Sem., 1909-12; spl. lecturer Colo. Teachers Coll., 1923-26. Mem. Assn. of Am. Colleges (v.p. 1929-30; treas. 1930-31; pres. 1934-35), S.A.R., Loyal Legion, N.Y. Hist. Soc., St. Andrews Soc., Kappa Phi Kappa, Phi Delta Theta, Phi Beta Kappa. Pres. Assn. Urban Univs., 1924-25; pres. Middle States Assn. Colls. and Secondary Schs., 1932-33; trustee Princeton Theol. Sem., Barrington Sch. (Great Barrington, Mass.); mem. Greater Pa. Council; mem. bd. regents Mercersburg Acad.; mem. advisory bd. Northwestern Mil. and Naval Acad.; moderator Presbyn. Synod of Pa., 1933-34; dir. Presbyn. Ministers Fund Ins., Phila.; Elder Presbyn. Ch. Pres. Huguenot Soc. of Pa. Mem. Nat. Com. for Columbus Memorial Light House. Clubs: Cosmos (Washington, D.C.); Penn Athletic (Phila.); Pomfret, Northampton Country (Easton); Greenwoods Country (Winsted, Conn.). Editor: The Voices of Our Leaders, 1917; Liberty Loan Speakers' Hand Books, 1918. Author: From a College Platform, 1932; also of articles in The Analyst, Independent, etc., and addresses on ednl. and economic subjects. Chevalier Legion of Honor (France). Home: Easton, Pa.

LEWITH, Edward L., real estate and insurance broker; b. Wilkes-Barre, Pa., Nov. 1, 1879; s. Lewis and Josephine (Freeman) L.; student high sch. and Wyoming Sem.; unmarried. Pres. Wilkes-Barre Hotel Co., Caswith Corpn., v.p. Wyoming Valley Bldg. and Loan Assn.; sec. Guarantee Title & Mortgage Co., Am. Auto Accessory Stores; treas. Hebrew Loan Assn.; dir. Miners' Nat. Bank; v.p. Greater Wilkes-Barre Real Estate Bd.; chmn. Wilkes-Barre Planning Commn.; v.p. Property Owners Assn., Wilkes-Barre Chamber of Commerce. Masons (Consistory; Shriner), B'nai B'rith (treas. temple). Writer articles on real estate taxes. Home: 240 S. River St. Office: 426-428 Miners Bank Bldg., Wilkes-Barre, Pa.

LEWTON, Frederick Lewis, technologist; b. Cleveland, O., Mar. 17, 1874; s. George Washington and Annie Louise (Taylor) L.; student Rollins Coll., Winter Park, Fla., 1888-90, Drexel Inst., Phila., Pa., 1891-95; A.B., George Washington Univ., Washington, D.C., 1922; (hon.) D.Sc., Rollins Coll., 1930; m. Emilie Marie Hempel, June 29, 1898 (dec.); children—Lilian Louise (Mrs. John B. Hopkins), Myrtle Ivy (Mrs. Irving Rothrock), Rhoda (Mrs. John Jennings), Norma (Mrs. Peter C. Michaelson); m. 2d Blanche B. Clark, July 24, 1930. Asst. chemist, Baldwin Locomotive Works, Phila., Pa., 1895; instr. chemistry, Drexel Inst., Phila., Pa., 1895-1904; econ. botanist, Commercial Mus., Phila., Pa., 1896-1904; asst. botanist, U.S. Dept. Agr., Washington, D.C., 1904-12; curator div. textiles, U.S. Nat. Mus., Washington, D.C., 1912-38, curator div. crafts and industries since 1938; dir. Northwestern Federal Savings & Loan Assn., Smithsonian Instn. Employees Federal Credit Union, both, Washington, D.C. Mayor town of Takoma Park, Md., 1932-36. Trustee Takoma Park, Md., Library. Mem. Washington Acad. Scis., Phila. Acad. Nat. Scis. Presbyterian. Home: 217 Albany Av., Takoma Park, Md.

LEWY, Frederic Heinrich, M.D., univ. prof.; b. Berlin, Germany, Jan. 28, 1885; s. Dr. Heinrich and Anna (Milchner) L.; M.D., U. of Berlin, Germany, 1910; came to U.S., 1934, naturalized, 1939; m. Flora Maier, July 9, 1924. Research fellow, Internat. Inst. Brain Anatomy, Zuerich, Switzerland, 1905-06, neurophysiology, U. of Berlin, Germany, 1907-08; head dept. of neurophysiology, Physiological Inst. of U. of Breslau, 1908-10; research fellow, Neuropathological Inst., U. of Munich, Germany, 1910-12; head of lab., Neurological Clinic, U. of Breslau, Germany, 1912-14; head dept. of neurology, 2d Med. Clinic, U. of Berlin, 1919-31; clin. prof. neurology, Sch. of Medicine, 1923-34; dir. Neurological Inst., 1931-33; prof. neurophysiology and consultant in neurology, U. of Pa. Sch. of Medicine, since 1934. Mem. Assn. for Research Nervous and Mental Diseases, Am. Physiol. Soc., Am. Assn. Neuropathologists, Am. Hosp. Assn. Author books, monographs, papers on organic neurology, its physiology and pathology, the relation of nervous diseases to nutrition and industrial poisons. Home: Hamilton Ct., 39th and Chestnut Sts. Office: 3400 Spruce St., Philadelphia, Pa.

LICHLITER, Levi G.; b. Salisbury, Pa., June 6, 1901; s. Christian S. and Minnie (Enos) L.; student at Mercersburg (Pa.) Academy, Albright College, Reading, Pa., and George Washington University, Washington D.C.; m. Louise A. Heffley, Jan. 1, 1926; children—Effie Lou, Sandra Lee. Dir. athletics and instr. history, Boswell High Sch., 1921-25; engaged in banking business, 1925-33; mgr. Pittsburgh Office, Home Owners' Loan Corpn., 1933-34; established and managed own office, Johnstown, Pa., 1934-35; chmn. Pa. Securities' Commn., 1935-37; Pa. Labor Relations Bd., Harrisburg, Pa., since 1937. Sec.-treas. Somerset Co. Bankers' Assn. Home: 2712 Lexington St. Office: South Office Bldg., Harrisburg, Pa.

LICHTENBERGER, James Buchanan, lawyer; b. Dauphin Co., Pa., Oct. 19, 1876; s. Paris and Emma (Donecher) L.; A.B., Princeton U., 1904; LL.B., U. of Pa. Law Sch., 1909; Gowen Fellow, U. of Pa. Law Sch., 1909-11; m. Mary S. Stackhouse, May 19, 1923. Began as teacher pub. schs., York Co., Pa., 1895-97, Steelton, Pa., 1897-1900; prof. Mercersburg Acad., 1904-06; admitted to Pa. bar, 1911, and since engaged in gen. practice of law at Phila.; lecturer, U. of Pa. Law Sch., 1911, U. of Pa. Towne Sci. Sch., 1911-19; asso. editor Law Review, U. of Pa., 1909, grad. editor, 1911; counsel and mem. adv. bd. Pa. Co. for Insurances on Lives and Granting Annuities; pres. and dir. Phila. Union Bus Terminal, Inc.; vice-pres. and dir. Laguna Co.; sec. and dir. Colonial Holding Co., Excess Reins. Co. of America. Mem. Am., Pa., and Phila. bar assns., Phila. Law Acad. Republican. Lutheran. Mason (K.T., 32°). Clubs: Lawyers, Penn Athletic, Princeton, Art, Racquet (Philadelphia); Merion Cricket (Haverford); Nassau, Cap and Gown (Princeton). Home: Golf House Rd. and College Av., Haverford. Office: 1917 Packard Bldg., Philadelphia, Pa.

LICHTENBERGER, James Pendleton, sociologist; b. Decatur, Ill., June 10, 1870; s. Conrad H. and Elizabeth (Nesbit) L.; A.B., Eureka (Ill.) Coll., 1893; A.M., Hiram (O.) Coll., 1902; fellow New York Sch. of Philanthropy, 1908-09; Ph.D., Columbia, 1909; m. Martha A. Cantrell, June 20, 1892; children—Muriel E. (Mrs. J. B. Leopold), Yolande V. (Mrs. J. V. Pequignot). Minister Disciples of Christ; pastor Canton, Ill., 1896-99, Buffalo, N.Y., 1899-1902, N.Y. City, 1902-08; prof. sociology, U. of Pa., since 1900. Mem. Am. Acad. Polit. and Social Science (sec. since 1912), Am. Sociol. Soc., Beta Gamma Sigma. Republican. Author: Development of Social Theory, 1923; Divorce—A Social Interpretation, 1931. Home: 71st St. at Greenhill Road., Philadelphia, Pa.

LICHTENTHAL, Daniel, lawyer; b. Odessa, Russia, April 5, 1905; s. Chaskel and Sarah L.; LL.B., Temple U. Law Sch., 1927; m. Anne L., Jan. 2, 1932. Admitted to N.J. bar as atty., 1927, as counsellor, 1931; engaged in gen. practice of law at Riverside, N.J., since 1927; dir. First Nat. Bank of Riverside, N.J.; solicitor for Riverside and Delran Twps. Chmn. Burlington Co. Dem. Com. Mem. N.J. State Bar Assn., Burlington Co. Bar Assn. (pres.). Democrat. Jewish religion. Mason. Elk. Moose. Home: 131 Bridgeboro St., Riverside, N.J.

LICHTENTHALER, Henry Phillips, ins. agency exec.; b. Montoursville, Pa., Jan. 29, 1890; s. Thomas Carlin and Charlotte Emma (Bastian) L.; ed. pub. sch. and high sch., Montoursville, Pa., U. of Pittsburgh Night Sch; m. Elizabeth Madeline Klinger, June 2, 1920; children—Lois Madeline, Janet Louise, Elizabeth Ann. Employed successively with Nat. Union Fire Ins. Co., Pittsburgh Underwriters, K. William Schuchman; asso. with Freehold Real Estate Co., Pittsburgh, Pa., since 1912, dir. and v.p. in charge ins. since 1935; dir. Freehold Bldg. & Loan Assn., Falcon Chem. Co. Served as 1st lt. inf. U.S.A., 1917-19. Mem. Pa. Assn. Ins. Agts. (dir.), Pittsburgh Assn. Ins. Agts. (dir.), Ins. Club of Pittsburgh (dir.). Republican. Episcopalian. Mason (K.T., Shriner). Home: 256 LeMoyne Av., Mt. Lebanon, Pittsburgh, Pa. Office: 311 Fourth Av., Pittsburgh, Pa. Office: 311 Fourth Av., Pittsburgh, Pa.

LICK, Maxwell John, surgeon; b. Albion, Pa., Oct. 24, 1884; s. Chauncey V. and Mary A. Lick; A.B., Allegheny Coll., 1908; M.D., U. of Pa., 1912; studied abroad, 1925; m. Mary E. McLaughlin, July 1915; children—Maxwell Robert (dec.), Mary. Practicing physician in Erie, Pa., since 1912; surgeon on staff St. Vincent's and Hamot Hosps. since 1917, surgeon in chief Hamot Hosp. since 1938; surgeon to N.Y.C. R.R. and N.Y.C.& St.L. R.R. since 1917; lecturer. Pres. Med. Soc. of State of Pa.; ex-pres. Erie Co. Med. Soc.; fellow Am. Coll. of Surgeons; mem. A.M.A., Phi Beta Kappa, Alpha Omega Alpha, Phi Delta Theta, Phi Alpha Sigma. Republican. Methodist. Mason. Clubs: Erie, Kahkwa, Shrine. Contbr. to med. jours. Home: 149 W. 8th St., Erie, Pa.

LIDDELL, Donald Macy, engineer; b. Lawrenceburg, Ind., Feb. 28, 1879; s. Oliver Brown and Josephine (Major) L.; prep. edn., high sch., Denver, Colo., A.B. (chem. and physical course), Johns Hopkins, 1900; m. Edith Stabler, Dec. 2, 1905; children—Donald M., Jr., Edith Jordan (Twiss). With Detroit Copper Mining Co., Morenci, Ariz., 1900-01, Baltimore Copper Smelting & Rolling Co., 1901-05, U.S. Metals Refining Co., Chrome, N.J., and Grasselli, Ind., 1905-10; asso. editor and mng. editor Engineering and Mining Jour., New York, 1910-16; consulting engr. with Merrill, Lynch & Co., 1916-17; partner firm Weld & Liddell, consulting engrs., 1919-36; president Calvert Court Co., Cecil Constrn. Co., Homewood Apartment Co., Moa Bay Co. (Cuba). Union County Coprn.; dir. Nat. State Bank, Elizabeth, N.J.; asst. sec. Superior Steel Corpn., Carnegie, Pa., Capt. A.S., O.R.C., active service, Feb. 2, 1918-May 20, 1919; with Reserve, July 6, 1919-Sept. 22, 1924; commd. maj. Res., Sept. 22, 1924, lt. col., Nov. 20, 1930; chief engr. War Credits Board, Dec. 2, 1917-April 25, 1918. Member Mining and Metall. Soc. America, Am. Institute Mining Engrs., Elizabeth Music Assn., Loyal Legion, Military Order Foreign Wars, Beta Theta Pi, Phi Beta Kappa. Republican. Club: Mining (treas.). Author. Metallurgists and Chemists Handbook, 1916; Handbook of Chemical Engineering, 1922; Handbook of Non-Ferrous Metallurgy, 1926; also about 100 articles in tech. jours. Co-Author: The Principles of Metallurgy, 1932; Mineral Resources of the United States and Its Capacity to Produce, 1934; Chessmen, 1937. Originated selenium recovery methods in use in most Am. copper refineries; several waterproofing methods for stucco work; first successful commercial water-mix method for magnesium-oxichloride stucco. Home: Elizabeth, N.J. Office: 33 Rector St., New York, N.Y.

LIEBERMAN, Abraham, lawyer, judge; b. Union City, N.J., Aug. 28, 1899; s. Benjamin and Rebecca (Berelson) L.; LL.B., N.Y. Univ. Law Sch., 1923; unmarried. Admitted to N.J. bar as atty., 1923 and since in gen. practice of law at Union City and Weehawken; serving as Judge Police Ct., Weehawken, since 1932. Served in U.S.A., 1918. Hon. mem. Internat. Chiefs of Police Assn., N.J. Assn. Chiefs of Police, Police Benevolent Assn. of N.J., Superior Police Officers of N.J. Mem. Jewish Community Center of North Hudson (past v.p.), Hebrew Orphans Home, Jewish Home for Convalescents. Mem. Am. Bar Assn., Federal Bar Assn., N.J. State and Hudson Co. bar assns., North Hudson Lawyears Club, Am. Legion. Jewish War Veterans. Democrat. Clubs: Preakness Hills Country (Paterson); Grand Street Boys (New York). Home: 85 Liberty Pl., Weehawken. Office: 657 Bergenline Av., Union City, N.J.

LIEBLICH, Joseph Tomas, lawyer; b. Paterson, N.J., July 18, 1884; s. S. Harry and Sophia (Perlman) L.; E.E., Cooper Union Inst., 1902; LL.B., Lincoln and Jefferson U., 1913; m. Ida Edith Rosen, Sept. 1, 1907; children—Selma Vera (Mrs. Raymond Kramer), Ruth Shirley (Mrs. Herbert N. Davis), Dan Parke. Elec. engr., Otis Elevator Co., 1903-05; fire companies adjuster, 1905-10; admitted to N.J. bar as atty., 1914, counsellor at law, 1920; engaged in gen. practice of law and fire adjusting, Paterson, N.J., since 1914; admitted to practice before the Supreme Ct. of the U.S., 1932; apptd. spl. master in chancery, N.J., 1937; president Hansen & Sinclair, Selray Investment Co.; dir. Fortune Bldg. & Loan Assn.; counsel Property Owners Assn. Mem. Central Republican Club. Trustee Barnert Memorial Temple. Mem. Am., N.J. State and Co. bar assns. Republican. Reformed Jewish Cong. Mason. I.O.O.F. K.P. Clubs: Lambs, Square, Preakness Hills Country. Home: 548 15th Av., Paterson, N.J. Office: 20 Smith St., Paterson, N.J.

LIFTER, Morris, dairyman; b. Tilzit, Germany, Aug. 24, 1874; s. Michael and Flora (Joel) L.; came to U.S., 1878, naturalized, 1885; ed. public schools of Phila., m; Effie B. Campbell, Nov. 16, 1915. Began as ice cream mfr., Lifter Ice Cream Co., Phila., 1893-1919; asst. treas. head purchasing dept. and mem. bd. dirs. Abbott's Dairies, Inc., Phila., since 1919. Charter mem. Pa. and N.J. Ice Cream Assn. (past pres., mem. bd. dirs., chmn. finance com.); dir. Nat. Ice Cream Mfrs. Assn.; pres. J. J. Lifter Bldg. & Loan Assn. (charter mem., mem. bd. dirs.). Republican. Jewish religion. Mason (32°), Elk (chmn., mem. bd. trustees). Clubs. Manufacturers and Bankers, Poor Richard (Phila.). Home: 4418 Spruce St. Office: 31st and Chestnut Sts., Philadelphia, Pa.

LIGGETT, Sidney Sharp, retired corpn. exec.; b. Pittsburgh, Pa., May 13, 1876; s. Sidney B. and Emma Catherine (Stevenson) L.; student Rensselaer Poly. Inst., Troy, N.Y.; m. Gertrude Irwin, Oct. 6, 1909; children—Elizabeth Irwin (Mrs. Harlow W. Culbertson), Laura Sharp (Mrs. David B. Oliver, II). Manager of bond department of Union Trust Company of Pittsburgh, later v.p.; chmn. bd. Nat. Credit Corpn., 1930-32; mem. exec. com. Reliance Life Ins. Co. since 1920; retired from active business, 1934; dir. Farmers Deposit Nat. Bank, Farmers Deposit Trust Co., Reliance Life Ins. Co. Mem. Borough Council, Edgeworth Borough, Pa., 6 yrs. Dir. Allegheny Gen. Hosp., many years, retiring, 1937. Clubs: Pittsburgh; Rolling Rock (Ligonier, Pa.); Allegheny Country; Sewickley (Pa.) Hunt. Home: 7 Oliver Rd., Sewickley, Pa.

LIGHT, Harry Henry, iron manufacturer; b. Lebanon, Pa., Sept. 22, 1862; s. Samuel L. and Maria E. (Henry) L.; student Lebanon (Pa.) High Sch., 1878, Eastman Business Coll., Poughkeepsie, N.Y., 1878-80; married, 1887; children—Vara L. (Mrs. William H. Keller), B. Joyce (Mrs. Thomas Sidney Quinn), F. Marie (Mrs. Roy M. Bowman), Pauline Emma (Mrs. Wm. Henry Worrilow), Eloise Henry (Mrs. James H. Stewart). Began as clerk in gen. store, 1879; pres. Lebanon (Pa.) Valley Iron & Steel Co., 1011 17; pres. Schuylkill Haven (Pa.) Rolling Mill, 1914-19; pres. Lebanon Drop Forge Co., Avon, Pa., since 1920. Dir. Lebanon (Pa.) Steel Foundry, Consol. Market House Co., Lebanon, Pa. Zion Lutheran Ch. (trustee). Mason. Home: 330 N. 9th St., Lebanon, Pa. Office: Avon, Pa.

LIGHT, V(ernal) Earl, prof. of biology; b. North Annville, Pa., Jan. 9, 1892; s. John Felix and Emma Rebecca (Reese) L.; student Annville High Sch., 1906-08, Lebanon Valley Acad., 1908-09; A.B., Lebanon Valley Coll., 1916, M.S., 1926; Ph.D., Johns Hopkins, 1929; m. Cora Grace Heilman, Dec. 22, 1917; children—Mary Grace, V(ernal) Earl, John Henry, Ruth Eleanor, Anna Louise, James Frederick. Teacher Fairview Country Sch. (ungraded), North Annville Twp., Pa., 1910-13; teacher, Annville (Pa.) High Sch., 1916-18, Uniontown (Pa.) High Sch., 1918-20, Wyomissing (Pa.) High Sch., 1920-21, Annville High Sch., 1921-26; asso. prof. of biology, Lebanon Valley Coll., Annville, since 1929. Mem. A.A.A.S., Am. Soc. Zoologists (asso.), Pa. Acad. Science (sec.-treas.), Pa. State Edn. Assn., Sigma Xi, Gamma Alpha. Republican. Mem. United Brethren Ch. Mason. Home: Route 1, Annville, Pa.

LIGHTCAP, John Steel, Jr., lawyer; b. Latrobe, Pa., Dec. 16, 1900; s. John Steel and Mary (Zahniser) L.; B.S., Washington and Jefferson Coll., Washington, Pa., 1922; LL.B., U. of Pittsburgh, 1928; m. Martha Doty, June 15, 1935; 1 son, John Steel, III. Admitted to Pa. bar, 1928; asst. dist. atty., Westmoreland Co., Pa., 1928-29; gen. practice, Latrobe, Pa., since 1929; treas. and dir. Fullman Mfg. Co., dir. Latrobe Bldg. & Loan Assn., Community Loan Co. (Latrobe), Latrobe Finance Co., Connellsville Mine & Supply Co. Vice-pres. and dir. Latrobe Chamber of Commerce. Mem. Westmoreland County and Pa. State bar assns., Washington and Jefferson Alumni Assn. of Westmoreland County (pres.), Lambda Chi Alpha, Delta Theta Chi. Republican. Presbyterian. Mason. Clubs: Latrobe Country, Rotary, Lamas (Latrobe). Home: 721 Spring St. Office: Latrobe Trust Co. Bldg., Latrobe, Pa.

LILLY, Austin Jenkins, lawyer; b. Conewago, Pa., Dec. 24, 1883; s. Henry Joseph and Mary Helen (Jenkins) L.; student pub. schs., 1891-96; Calvert Hall Coll., Baltimore, 1897-1901, Loyola Coll., Baltimore, 1907-11; LL.B., U. of Md., 1907; m. Helen Scott Browne; children—Austin Jenkins, Sarah Lee (Mrs. Cumberland Dugan), Thomas Horace Bowyer Browne. Admitted to bar of Md., 1907, and since in practice at Baltimore; admitted to bar of Okla., 1910, N.C., 1914; asst. editor Baltimore Catholic Mirror, 1907, editor, 1908-09; in claim div. Md. Casualty Co., Baltimore, 1910-14, legal dept., 1914-23, gen. counsel, 1923-33, v.p., 1933-35, asst. gen. counsel since 1935. Mem. Gov's. Commn. on Workmen's Compensation Legislation, 1931, Gov's. Commn. on Blue Sky Legislation, 1931-32; mem. Standing Com. on Financial Responsibility of Motor Vehicle Owners. Mem.-designate Law Com., Assn. of Casualty and Surety Execs., and Legal Com., Nat. Bur. of Casualty and Surety Underwriters (New York); fellow Ins. Inst. of America; mem. Baltimore, Md. State and Am. bar assns., Phi Kappa Sigma, Ins. Soc. of Baltimore, Soc. of Colonial Wars of Md., St. George's Soc. of Md. Democrat. Catholic. Clubs: University, Phi Kappa Sigma (Baltimore). Home: 2742 St. Paul St. Office: 701 W. 40th St., Baltimore, Md.

LILLY, Edwin Belwood, insurance exec.; b. New York, N.Y., Nov. 17, 1875; s. George W. and Alvina R. (Krug) L.; ed. public schools, New York, and corr. courses, Cornell, Columbia; m. Claribel Smith, Feb. 5, 1896; children—George Belwood, Edwin Milton. Began as bank clerk, 1892; with Manhattan Bank, New York, 1892-1919, later with Ridgewood Trust Co., advancing to vice-pres.; pres. Consol. Engraving Co., New York, 1927-31; owner of Lillygraphic Service, New York, 1931-39; pres. Lilly Agency, Inc., gen. ins., since 1931. Mem. Ridgewood Bd. of Edn., 1912-38, vice-pres., 15 years, pres., 8 years. Served as private N.Y. Vol. Cav. during Spanish Am. War; capt. N.J. Militia Reserve during World War. Republican. Presbyterian. Mason, Elk, Jr. Order, Royal Arcanum. Home: 393 Stevens Av. Office: 45 N. Broad St., Ridgewood, N.J.

LILLY, Scott Barrett, coll. prof.; b. Poweshiek Co., Ia., May 27, 1885; s. Lyman A. and Lelia (Barrett) L.; B.S., Mich. State Coll., East Lansing, Mich., 1907; C.E., Cornell U., 1909; m. Jean McCoy, Sept. 14, 1908; children—Mary Alice, Scott Barrett. Instr. civil engring., Cornell U., 1907-10; asst. prof. civil engring., Swarthmore (Pa.) Coll., 1910-17; asst. plant engr. Merchant Ship Bldg. Corpn., Bristol, Pa., 1917-1918; cons. civil engr., Phila., 1918; with J. N. Kinney, contracting engr., New York, 1918-21; with Ohio Locomotive Crane Co., N. Y. office, 1922-23; sales engr., Philip T. King, cranes, New York, 1924; resident engr. in charge constrn., Florida Rock Products Co., Tampa, Fla., 1925-26; sales engr. Philip T. King, 1926-28; prof. civil engring., Swarthmore (Pa.) Coll., since 1929, chmn. div. of engring. since 1936. Mem. Am. Soc. C.E., Am. Concrete Inst., Soc. for Promotion of Engring. Edn., Am. Assn. Univ. Profs., Tau Beta Pi, Sigma Tau, Sigma Xi. Republican. Episcopalian. Co-author (with John A. Miller): Analytic Mechanics, 1914, revised, 1935; article in engring. jour. Home: 600 Elm Av. Office: Swarthmore College, Swarthmore, Pa.

LINCOLN, Charles Monroe, newspaper exec.; b. Bath, Me., Mar. 15, 1866; s. George Mitchell and Frances Lucretia (Berry) L.; m. Annie Palmer Fisher, 1892. In newspaper work, New Haven, Conn., and Philadelphia, Pa., until 1895; mem. staff New York Herald, various editorial positions, including editor Paris edition, 1895-1907; mng. editor New York World, 1910-20; mng. editor New York Herald, 1920-24; mem. editorial staff New York Times since 1924. Pres. James Gordon Bennett Memorial Corpn. Hon. life pres. New York Herald Alumni Assn.; mem. S.A.R. Club: Pine Valley. Explored route for canal across Nicaragua. Home: Montclair, N.J. Office: N.Y. Times, New York, N.Y.*

LINCOLN, Edmond Earl, economist; b. Neb., Feb. 5, 1888; s. Charles Sanford and Christiana (Bayless) L.; B.A., O. Wesleyan U., 1909; selected from Ohio as Rhodes scholar to Oxford U., 1908; B.A., Honor Sch. of Modern History (Oxford), 1910; M.A., Oxford, 1914; Ph.D. in banking, finance and pub. utilities, Harvard, 1917; m. Edith Walker, August 14, 1915; children—Elinore, Robert Edmond. Engaged part time in industrial work (principally contracting and building), 1902-08; teacher in Ohio public schools, 1903-04; professor and head of English department, Mt. Union Coll., 1911-12; prof. and head dept. of history and economics, 1912-14, sec. of faculty, 1913-14, St. John's Coll.; on faculties of Harvard University Economics Department and Graduate School of Business Administration, 1914-22, specializing in finance, public utilities and applied economics; also lecturer in industrial and financial courses of university extension and Radcliffe College. Traveled widely in foreign countries; winner of first prize in Hart Schaffner & Marx economic essay contest, 1917. In charge of numerous investigations in pub. utility problems and financial administration since 1915; expert spl. agt. U.S. Census Bur., in charge of report on central electric light and power stations in U.S., 1918-20; mem. com. on business finance, 1920-21, com. on pub. utilities, 1921-22, Boston Chamber Commerce; mem. Merchants Assn. New York (com. on city transit, 1924—; chmn. 1926-27); mem. com. on costs of distribution, Chamber of Commerce of U.S., 1925-26, and of finance department committee, 1929-31; mem. Chamber of Commerce of the State of N.Y., Wilmington Chamber of Commerce. Chief statistician and economist, Western Electric Co., Inc., New York, 1922-27; with Internat. Telephone & Telegraph Corpn., 1927-31; with E. I. du Pont de Nemours & Co. since 1931. Trustee Mount Union Coll. Mem. Am. Econ. Assn., Am. Statis. Assn., Royal Econ. Soc. (London), Harvard Econ. Soc., Am. Management Association (director), Acad. Polit. Science, Am. Acad. of Polit. and Social Science, Am. Assn. for Labor Legislation, Economic Club of N.Y., Pan-Am. Soc. Bd. of Trade for German-Am. Commerce, Foreign Policy Assn., Nat. Assn. Mfrs. (mem. various coms.), Am. Chem. Soc., A.A.A.S., Am. Mus. Natural History, Oxford Society (life mem.), Phi Beta Kappa. Club: Harvard, Bankers Club of America, Lotos, Nat. Republican (New York); Wilmington Club, Wilmington Country. Mason. Author: The Result of Municipal Electric Lighting in Massachusetts, 1918; Central Electric Light and Power Stations (1917), 1920; References in the Economic History of Europe and of the United States, 1920; Problems in Business Finance, 1921; Applied Business Finance, 1923, 11th edit., 1931; Steps in Industry, 1926; Testing Before Investing, 1926; Applied Economic History, 1932; also mag. articles, etc. Home: 907 Westover Road, Wilmington, Del. Office: du Pont Bldg., Wilmington, Del.

LINCOLN, John Joseph, coal operator; b. Oak Hill, Pa., Oct. 11, 1865; s. Abel Thomas and Elizabeth Dinah (Haines) L.; student State Teachers Coll., West Chester, Pa., 1883-85; C.E., Lehigh U., Bethlehem, Pa., 1889; m. Rachel Lloyd Hutchinson, Oct. 11, 1899; children—Lloyd Stanley (dec.), John Joseph, Jr., Elizabeth Hutchinson (Mrs. Leland M. Burr, Jr.), Pemberton Hutchinson. Designer steel structural work, 1889, topographic work with U.S. Geol. Survey, 1890-92; mem. firm Harris and Lincoln, civil engrs., Elkhorn, W.Va., 1892-93; vice-pres. and gen. mgr. Crozer Coal & Coke Co., Elkhorn, since 1912, Upland Coal & Coke Co., Elkhorn, since 1899, Crozer Land Assn., Elkhorn, since 1895; treas. American Coal Co. of Allegheny Co., McComas, W.Va. since 1930. Mem. Am. Inst. Mining & Metall. Engrs., Phi Delta Theta. Republican. Clubs: University (Washington); Shenandoah (Roanoke, Va.); Bluefield Country (Bluefield, W.Va.). Home: Elkhorn, W.Va.

LINCOLN, Joseph Crosby, author; b. Brewster, Mass., Feb. 13, 1870; s. Joseph and Emily (Crosby) L.; ed. Brewster and Chelsea, Mass.; m. Florence E. Sargent, May 12, 1897; 1 son, Joseph Freeman. Asso. editor League of America Wheelmen Bulletin, 1896-99; moved from Boston to New York, 1899. Author: Cape Cod Ballads, 1902; Cap'n Eri, 1904; Partners of the Tide, 1905; Mr. Pratt, 1906; The Old Home House, 1907; Cy Whittaker's Place, 1908; Our Village, 1909; Keziah Coffin, 1909; The

Depot Master, 1910; Cap'n Warren's Wards, 1911; The Woman Haters, 1911; The Postmaster, 1912; Rise of Roscoe Paine, 1912; Mr. Pratt's Patients, 1913; Cap'n Dan's Daughter, 1914; Kent Knowles, "Quahaug," 1914; Thankful's Inheritance, 1915; Mary 'Gusta, 1916; Extricating Obadiah, 1917; Shavings, 1918; The Portygee, 1919; Galusha the Magnificent, 1921; Fair Harbor, 1922; Doctor Nye, 1923; Rugged Water, 1924; Queer Judson, 1925; The Big Mogul, 1926; The Aristocratic Miss Brewster, 1927; Silas Bradford's Boy, 1928; (with Freeman Lincoln) Blair's Attic, 1929; Blowing Clear, 1930; All Alongshore, 1931; Head Tide, 1932; Back Numbers, 1933; Storm Signals, 1935; Cape Cod Yesterdays, 1935; Great Aunt Lavinia, 1936; Storm Girl, 1937; A. Hall & Co., 1938; Christmas Days, 1938. Clubs: Players (New York); Franklin Inn, Arts (Phila.). Contrbr. short stories, verse, etc., to various mags. Home: Villa Nova, Pa.; (summer) Chatham, Mass.

LINCOLN, Rollo Basil, engineer; b. Knox, Pa., Mar. 13, 1885; s. Alfred Lyman and Rebekah (Walls) L.; student Westinghouse Tech. Night Sch., East Pittsburgh, Pa., 1905-07, Carnegie Inst. Tech., 1907-09; m. Emma Jane Glenn, May 19, 1909; children—Martha, Hazel, Edwin, Roy, Janet. Chief engr. Hoskins Mfg. Co., Detroit, Mich., 1912-20; engr. of tests Hayes Wheel Co., Jackson, Mich., 1920-21; plant mgr. Hiram Walker & Sons Metal Products, Ltd., Walkerville, Ontario, 1921-23; supt. Electric Alloys Co., Morristown, N.J., 1923-24; mech. designer Jones & Laughlin Steel Co., Pittsburgh, Pa., 1924-25; engr. Westinghouse Electric & Mfg. Co., East Pittsburgh, 1925-34; dir. Nat. Weld Testing Bur., Pittsburgh, since 1934; engr. in charge physical tests Pittsburgh Testing Lab. since 1936. Registered professional engr., Pa. Mem. Am. Soc. Mech. Engrs., Am. Welding Soc., Am. Soc. for Metals, Am. Soc. for Testing Materials, Science of Metals Club. Republican. Presbyterian. Mason. Club: Railway (Pittsburgh). Author numerous papers on welding. Home: 631 Princeton Boul., Wilkinsburg, Pa. Office: 1330 Locust St., Pittsburgh, Pa.

LINDBACK, Christian R., dairyman; b. near Copenhagen, Denmark, July 6, 1877; s. Albert C. and Marie (Rützoü) L.; came to U.S., 1881, became citizen through father's naturalization; grad. West Bend (Wis.) High Sch., 1895; m. Mary Falls, Apr. 28, 1910. Began as buttermaker with father in a creamery in Wis.; Later became sales rep. DeLaval Separator Co., of New York, then joined Creamery Package Mfg. Co., Chicago having charge of Phila. territory; v.p. Abbotts Dairies, Inc., Phila., 1912-14, pres. since 1914; farmer. Pres. Phila. Milk Exchange. Trustee Bucknell U. Mem. Internat. Ice Cream Mfrs. Assn. (dir.; pres. 1929-31). Clubs: Union League, Philadelphia Country (Phila.); Seaview Golf (Absecon, N.J.); Bath, Indian Creek, Surf, Committee of One Hundred (Miami Beach, Fla.). Home: 107 S. Princeton Av., Ventnor, N.J. Office: 3043 Chestnut St., Philadelphia, Pa.

LINDBORG, Carl, artist; b. Phila., Pa., Nov. 27, 1902; s. Carl John and Mina (Jonason) L.; ed. Phila. Mus. Art, Pa. Acad. Fine Arts, Julian Acad., Paris, France, 1928-29. Acad. L'Hote, Paris, 1929-30; married. Has followed profession as artist since 1931; paintings exhibited in Phila., Washington, New York City, Chicago, and Paris; represented Pa. Acad. Fine Arts, Phila., Museum Art, Allentown, Private Collections. Mem. bd. mgrs. Fellowship Pa. Acad. of Fine Arts. Awarded gold medal Fellowship Exhbn. at Art Club, Phila., 1937. Mem. Am. Fed. of Arts. Republican. Home: 500 Pembroke Av., Lansdowne, Pa. Studio: 807 Green St., Philadelphia, Pa.

LINDEMAN, Eduard Christian, teacher, author: b. St. Clair, Mich., May 9, 1885; s. Frederick and Frederika Johanna (von Piper) L.; B.S., Mich. Agrl. Coll., 1911; hon. H.M., Springfield Coll., 1937; m. Hazel Charlotte Taft, August 29, 1912; children—Doris Eleanor, Ruth Christine (Mrs. Donald O'Neil), Elizabeth Taft, Barbara. Worked as laborer until 21; editor The Gleaner, Detroit, Mich., 1911-12; social work, Lansing, 1912-14; teacher and extension worker, Mich. Agrl. Coll., 1915-17; teacher Y.M.C.A. Coll., Chicago, 1918-19, N.C. Coll. for Women, 1919-21, New York Sch. of Social Work since 1924. Lecturer New Sch. for Social Research, New York, 1925-27, Pendle Hill, 1933-34, Temple U., 1934-35, U. of Calif., 1936, 38. Mem. exec. com. Am. Assn. for Adult Edn., Pub. Edn. Assn., Progressive Edn. Assn.; consultant Nat. Council of Parent Edn., 1929-33; mem. Council World Assn. for Adult Edn., Inst. of Pacific Relations. Dir. of research for workers, Ednl. Bur. America, 1926-27; dir. Dept. of Community Organization for Leisure, Works Progress Adminstn., Washington, D.C., since 1935, planning consultant for professional and service div., 1939, pres. N.J. State Conf. of Social Work, 1934; chmn. N.J. Library Planning Com. and N.J. Social Planning Com. since 1934; adviser Nat. Housing Assn. since 1933; chmn. ednl. com. New York council on Housing; mem. exec. com. New York Council on Adult Edn. since 1933. Chmn. Survey Com. Nat. Council for the Conservation of Human Resources, 1937; chmn. Hunterdon County Library Commn., 1927-39; advisor Inst. for Propaganda Analysis, 1937, pres., 1938-39; mem. bd. Council Against Intolerance. Advisory editor Rural America. Mem. advisory com. White House Conf. on Children in Democracy, 1939; chmn. sub-com. on leisure of President's Interdepartmental Com. for Reorganizing Federal Govt., 1938, 39; mem. advisory com. Am. Youth Congress; mem. exec. com. Pioneer Youth of America; chmn. com. on academic freedom of Civil Liberties Union; chmn. advisory com. Wm. C. Whitney Foundation. Trustee Nat. Child Labor Com., Internat. Community Center, Nat. Gallery for Indian Art. Mem. Nat. Conf. of Social Work, Internat. Conf. of Social Work. Mem. Am. Sociol. Soc., A.A.A.S., Am. Country Life Assn., Acad. Polit. Science, Teachers' Union of New York, Social Service Employees Union, Am. Assn. Social Workers, Friends of Am. Democracy (mem. advisory com.), Council on Family Relations. Conglist. Clubs: City, Franklin Inn. Author: College Characters (essays and verse), 1912; The Community, 1921; Social Discovery, 1924; The Meaning of Adult Education, 1926; Urban Sociology, 1928; Dynamic Social Research, 1933; Social Education, 1933; Wealth and Culture, 1935. Contbg. editor The New Republic. Home: High Bridge, N.J.

LINDENMUTH, Anson William, clergyman, lecturer; b. Hamburg, Pa., May 30, 1874; s. Joseph and Sara (Kauffman) L.; B.E., Keystone (Pa.) State Normal (now Teachers Coll.), 1893, M.E., 1896; A.B., magna cum laude, Muhlenberg Coll., Allentown, Pa., 1902, A.M., 1905; grad. Luth. Sem., Mt. Airy, Phila., 1905; Ph.D., Potomac U., Washington, D.C., 1913; m. Elizabeth S. Moll, July 18, 1896 (died Oct. 25, 1929); children—Marion Moll (Mrs. Edgar E. A. Rabenold), Luther Moll, Anson William; m. 2d, Emma Agnes Werley Wisser, Aug. 11, 1931. Public school teacher, near Hamburg, Pa., and Akron, Pa., 1893-98; instr. in Latin and Greek, Keystone Normal Sch., 1903; instr. in history, Allentown (Pa.) Prep. Sch., 1918-19; ordained to ministry of Luth. Ch., 1905; pastor Amityville, Pa., 1905-10, Pottstown, Pa., 1910-14; pastor Allentown, Pa., since 1914. Served on various coms. in Allentown Confs. and Luth. Ministerium of Pa., now chmn. Com. on Evangelism and Luth. Students in Luth. instns.; mem. Bd. of Inner Missions, Ministerium of Pa.; former pres. Luth. Pastoral Assn. and Ministers' League of Allentown. Mem. Odd Fellows. Contbr. to church paper and mem. News Letter staff of United Luth. Ch. Extensive traveler in Europe, Mediterranean countries, including Palestine, and U.S. and Can. Home: 1436 Turner St., Allentown, Pa.

LINDLEY, Ernest Kidder, journalist, author; b. Richmond, Ind., July 14, 1899; s. Ernest Hiram and Elisabeth (Kidder) L.; student Ind. U., Bloomington, 1916-17; A.B., U. of Ida., 1920; B.A., Oxford U., Eng. (Rhodes scholar), 1923; m. Betty Grimes, Oct. 5, 1929; children—Jonathan, Christopher, Mark. Began as reporter, Wichita Beacon, 1924; reporter N.Y. World, 1924-31, political writer and Albany correspondent, 1928-31; political writer New York Herald Tribune, 1931-37, with Washington Bureau, 1933-37; chief Washington bureau Newsweek since 1937; author syndicated column on political affairs since 1937. Second lieut. U.S. Army, World War. Mem. Phi Kappa Psi, Phi Beta Kappa. Clubs: National Press (Washington); American Alpine Club; Alpine Club of Eng. Author: Franklin D. Roosevelt—A Career in Progressive Democracy, 1931; The Roosevelt Revolution—First Phase, 1933; Half Way with Roosevelt, 1936; (with Betty G. Lindley) A New Deal for Youth, 1938. Contbr. to mags. Home: Erwinna, Pa. Office: National Press Bldg., Washington, D.C.

LINDQUIST, Raymond Irving, clergyman; b. Sumner, Neb., Apr. 14, 1907; s. Elmer Henry and Esther (Nyberg) L.; A.B., Wheaton Coll., Ill., 1929; ed. Columbia U. Law Sch., 1929-30; Th.B., Princeton Theol. Sem., 1933; A.M., Princeton U., 1933; hon. D.D., Cumberland U., 1939; m. Ella Sofield, Sept. 16, 1930. Ordained to ministry Presbyn. Ch., U.S.A., 1934; dir. Christian Edn., Third Presbyn. Ch., Newark, N.J., 1932-34; serving as minister (11th in succession), historic Old First Ch. Presbyn., founded 1719, Orange, N.J., since 1934. Dir. Stony Brook Sch. for Boys, Stony Brook, L.I.; dir. Am. Tract Soc. Awarded Princeton Sem. Fellowship in Comparative Religions, Hugh Davies Homilectics Prize, Grace Erdman Prize in English Bible. Mem. Pi Kappa Delta. Contbr. to nat. religious periodicals. Presbyn. U.S.A. Home: 11 High St., Orange, N.J.

LINDSAY, Alexander Pitcairn, lawyer; b. Pittsburgh, Pa., Nov. 9, 1883; s. Samuel Stewart and Helen Rush (Pitcairn); student Pittsburgh (Pa.) Pub. Schs., 1896-98, Pittsburgh (Pa.) Cent. High Sch., 1898-1900; A.B., Acad. of New Church, Bryn Athyn, Pa., 1904; A.M., LL.B., Northwestern U. (Law Sch.), Chicago, 1908; m. Rena May Heilman, Apr. 12, 1911; children—Alexander Heilman, Helen Elizabeth, Anne Pitcairn. Admitted to Pa. bar 1909 and since practiced at Pittsburgh; mem. firm Sherriff, Lindsay, Weis & Hutchinson, Pittsburgh, since 1926; v.p. and dir. Hi-Voltage Equipment Co., Cleveland, O., v.p. and dir. Murlin Mfg. Co., Phila., Pa., Safety First Supply Co., Pittsburgh, Pa. Dir. Coll. Acad. of New Church. Mem. Am., Pa., and Allegheny Co. bar assns., Order of Coif. Republican (chmn. Asso. Republican Workers of Allegheny Co.). Swedenborgian Ch. (dir., mem. exec. com. Gen. Ch. of New Jerusalem). Home: 579 Briar Cliff Road. Office: 1406 Law and Finance Bldg., Pittsburgh, Pa.

LINDSAY, George Easby, real estate brokerage; b. Baltimore, Md., May 31, 1901; s. George Carey and Flora (Woodall) L.; student pvt. and pub. schs., Baltimore, Md.; grad. U. of Md. Sch. of Commerce, Baltimore, 1925; m. Dorothy Frances Corning, Sept. 11, 1929; 1 son, James Corning. Asso. with firm of Geo. W. Lindsay & Sons, real estate, established 1857, Baltimore, Md., since 1926, mem. firm since 1926; dir. Western Nat. Bank of Baltimore since 1936, Druid Hill Federal Savings & Loan Assn. of Baltimore since 1934. Mem. Real Estate Bd.; Delta Sigma Pi. Democrat. Episcopalian. Home: 411 Gitting Av. Office: 116 N. Paca St., Baltimore, Md.

LINDSAY, George LeRoy, dir. music pub. schs. Phila.; b. Ashbourne, Pa., Jan. 23, 1888; s. George Alexander and Mary (Perkins) L.; A.B., Temple U., 1916; Mus.B., Temple U. College of Music, 1917; under private teachers and Columbia Coll. of Music, 1904-09; hon. Mus.D., Temple U., 1936; m. Louise Downs, June 26, 1926; 1 dau., Mary Louise. Engaged as organist and teacher of piano, Phila., since 1906; organist in various Phila. chs.; pvt. teacher piano; instr., Columbia Coll. of Music, Phila., 1908-12; supervisor of music, pub. schs., Phila., 1918-25, dir. of music since 1925; spl. instr., Temple Univ., 1920-26, Columbia U., 1929, 30, Am. Inst. of Normal Methods, 1920-25, U. of Pa., 1931-33. Dir. Music Educators Nat. Confs.; vice-pres. Eastern Music Educators Confs. (pres., 1936-37). Mem. N.E.A., Pa. State Edn. Assn., Phila. Teachers Assn., Phi Delta Kappa, Phi Mu Alpha, Sinfonia. Republican. Presbyn. Mason (K.T.). Club: Philadelphia Schoolmens. Editor and writer; Educational Vocal Technique, 2 vols., 1936. Editor, Educational Orchestra Folios 1 and 2, 1934, 36. Joint compiler (with Gartlan, Smith), Assembly Songs for Intermediate. Compiler, Most Popular Operatic Songs, 1930. Composer anthems, vocal solos, organ numbers, etc. Home: 431 W. Upsal St., Philadelphia, Pa.

LINDSEY, Edward Sherman, judge; b. Warren, Pa., Dec. 17, 1872; s. Wilton Monroe and Emma (Sherman) L.; ed. Phillips Exeter Acad., Dartmouth Coll., 1890-91; LL.B., New York Law Sch., 1893; m. Mildred M. Crosby, May 28, 1895 (died May 31, 1937). Practiced at Warren, 1895-1920. Mem. Pa. Ho. of Rep., 1915; pres. judge 37th Jud. Dist. of Pa., 1920-22. Treasurer and asso. editor Jour. of Am. Inst. Criminal Law and Criminology. Mem. Am. Bar Assn., Pa. Bar Assn., Am. Soc. Internat. Law, Internat. Congress Americanists, Selden Soc., Am. Anthropol. Assn., Am. Polit. Science Assn., Am. Sociol. Soc., Am. Hist. Assn., Am. Folk-Lore Soc., Am. Soc. Naturalists, N.Y. Acad. Sciences; fellow A.A.A.S., Am. Geog. Soc. Author of Indeterminate Sentence and Parole System, 1925; The International Court, 1931; and numerous articles in legal periodicals. Home: Warren, Pa.

LINEN, James Alexander, Jr.; b. Scranton, Pa., Oct. 11, 1884; s. James Alexander and Anna (Blair) L.; grad. Lawrenceville Sch., 1902; A.B., Williams Coll., 1907; m. Genevieve Tuthill, Oct. 22, 1908; children—James Alexander, Harriet Tuthill, Mary, Sally Strong. Receiver for Scranton (Pa.) Steam Pump Co., 1910-13; v.p. and treas. Scranton Pump Co., 1913-16; treas United Service Co., 1920-23; pres. Lincoln Trust Co., 1923-28; chmn. of bd. Internat. Corr. Sch. and affiliated instns., 1928-37; now pres. Internat. Educational Pub. Co.; dir. Haddon Press & Haddon Craftsmen; conservator Union Nat. Bank, Scranton, Pa., 1933. Mem. Scranton City Council, 1913-16, pres., 1915-16; chmn. Scranton Chapter Am. Red Cross, 1938.; pres Scranton Community Chest, 1932-33, incorporator and mem. original bd. of dirs. Charities Assn. of Pa. Served as 2d lt., 13th Pa. Inf., Mexican Border, 1916-17; capt. and personnel adjutant, Machine Gun Training Center, U.S.A., 1917-19. Trustee Scranton Keystone Jr. Coll. Mem. Sigma Phi. Republican. Presbyterian. Clubs: Williams (New York); Scranton (Scranton). Home: Waverly, Pa. Office: International Correspondence Schools, Scranton, Pa.

LINGELBACH, Anna Lane; b. Shelbyville, Ill., Oct. 10, 1873; d. Oscar F. and Mary E. Lane; A.B., Ind. U. 1895; studied U. of Chicago, Sorbonne, Paris; Ph.D., U. of Pa., 1916; m. William E. Lingelbach, 1902; children—William E., Anna, Robert Lane. Lecturer in history, Bryn Mawr Coll., 1918-19; prof. history Temple U. since 1922. Mem. Phila. Bd. Pub. Edn. since 1920, vice-pres. since 1938; mem. Presbyn. Bd. of Christian Education; pres. Phila. Fed. of Women's Clubs and Allied Orgns., 1933-35; chmn. Dept. of Internat. Relations, State Federation of Pa. Women, 1934-38; pres. West Phila. Women's Com. for Phila. Orchestra since 1935; trustee Tennent Coll. of Christian Edn.; del. Anglo-Am. Hist. Conf., London, 1931 and 1936; dir. Crime Prevention Assn. Mem. Pa. Soc. Colonial Dames (chmn. Sulgrave Manor Endowment Fund Com., 1923-24), Am. Hist. Assn., Am. Assn. Univ. Women, Pa. Hist. Soc., Phila. Com. of 70, Genealogical Soc. of Pa., Kappa Kappa Gamma, Phi Beta Kappa; mem. exec. bd. Republican Women of Pa. Clubs: New Century (pres. 1925-29), Acorn, Women's University, Art Alliance. Contbr. articles to Am. Hist. Rev., Dictionary Am. Biography and other publs. Home: 4304 Osage Av., Philadelphia, Pa.

LINGELBACH, William E., univ. prof.; b. Shakespeare, Ont., Can., March 17, 1871; s. John and Mary (Young) L.; A.B., U. of Toronto, 1894, fellow, 1894-95; U of Leipzig, 1895-96, U. of Chicago, 1897-98; Ph.D., U. of Pa., 1901; m. Anna Lane, 1902; children—William E., Anna, Robert Lane. Instr. history, Mich. Mil. Acad., 1898-99; instr. 1900-03, asst. prof., 1903-08, prof. modern European history, since 1908, U. of Pa., dean Coll. of Arts and Sciences since 1939. Mem. Am. Hist. Assn. (chairman exec. com. 1935-37); Am. Philos. Soc. (mem. council 1924-27; sec. since 1935), National Inst. Social Sciences, Geog. Soc. Phila. (pres. 1914-16, 1918-20), Hist Teachers' Assn. of Middle States and Maryland (pres. 1926-27), American Academy of Political and Social Science, Academy of Political Science, Chi Psi Fraternity; mem. exec. com. Council Am. Learned Socs. (sec.-treas. 1929-34; chmn. since 1938). Dir. war issues course, S.A.T.C, 3d Fed. Dist., 1917-18; mem. Nat. Bd. Hist. Research, 1917-18; mem. council Am. Hist. Assn., 1914-18, chmn. com. on history in the schs., 1923. Presbyterian. Clubs: Lenape, University, Phila. Cricket. Author of The Internal Organization of the Merchant Adventures of England, The Laws and Ordinances of the Merchant Adventures, The Doctrine and Practice of Intervention, England and Neutral Trade in the Napoleonic Wars and Now, Paradoxes of Post War Europe, Democracy and the Control of Foreign Affairs and other studies. Home: 4304 Osage Av., Philadelphia, Pa.

LININGER, Frederick Fouse, coll. prof.; b. Martinsburg, Pa., July 29, 1892; s. Levi and Mary (Fouse) L.; studied Huston Twp. Sch., Blair County, 1898-1910; Lock Haven (Pa.) State Teachers Coll., 1910-12; B.S., Pa. State Coll., 1917; M.S., Cornell U., 1926, Ph.D., 1928; m. Mildred Tobias, April 9, 1917; children—Fred Tobias, Jean Lois. Engaged in agrl. extension service as county agent, Mercer Co., Pa., 1917-18; farmer, 1918-20; supervisor of agr., Morrison Cove Vocational Sch., 1920-23, dir., 1923-25; asst. prof. agrl. economics, Pa. State Coll., 1926-28, asso. prof., 1928-29, prof. since 1929, head of dept. since 1938; while on leave of absence, engaged in research at Brookings Instn., 1933-34. Mem. N.E.A., Am. Acad. Polit. and Social Science, Pa. State Edn. Assn., Am. Farm Econ. Assn., Internat. Conf. of Agril. Economists, Alpha Zeta, Delta Sigma Rho, Gamma Sigma Delta, Phi Delta Kappa, Phi Kappa Phi, Sigma Xi. Democrat. Presbyn. Mason (Scottish Rite). Author: Dairy Products Under the Agricultural Adjustment Act; Consumer Cooperation Here and Abroad; various bulls. on marketing and farm management in Pa. Home: 159 W. Park Av., State College, Pa.

LINN, William Bomberger, judge; b. Ephrata, Pa., Dec. 20, 1871; s. Valentine and Mary (Bomberger) L.; LL.B., U. of Pa. Law Sch., 1897; Hon. LL.D., Franklin and Marshall Coll., 1934; D.C.L., Hahnemann, 1939; m. Josephine Stewart Wood, June 4, 1902; children—Anne Wood, Mary Bettina, Thomas Wood. Admitted to Pennsylvania bar, 1897, and practiced at Philadelphia, 1897-1919; judge Pennsylvania Superior Ct., 1919-32; justice Pa. Supreme Ct., 1932. Episcopalian. Clubs: Rittenhouse, Art (Phila.). Author numerous articles on legal subjects. Home: 6374 Overbrook. Office: City Hall, Philadelphia, Pa.

LINSON, Corwin Knapp, artist; b. Brooklyn, N.Y., Feb. 25, 1864; s. William Van Keuren and Maria Louisa (Knapp) L.; studied at Acad. Julian and École des Beaux Arts, Paris (1st prize in composition, also hon. mention in composition and drawing); pupil of Gérome, and Lefebvre and Jean Paul Laurens; m. Annie G. Prickitt, d. Hon. William A. Prickitt, U.S. consul, at Reims, France, July 20, 1898; children—Elizabeth Louise, Rosalind Van Keuren. Returned to U.S., 1901; illustrator for many yrs.; McClure's Mag., Scribner's, Century, Ladies' Home Jour., Delineator, etc.; desinger of 5 memorial windows in Baptist Temple, Brooklyn, memorial window in Presbyterian Church, Rumson, N.J.; painted mural in baptistry of Central Baptist Church, Atlantic Highlands, N.J. Exhibited at National Academy Design, New York; New York Water Color Club; New York Water Color Soc.; Art Inst., Chicago; Corcoran Gallery, Washington, D.C.; Pa. Acad. Fine Arts; Buffalo Expn., 1900; St. Louis Exposition, 1904, etc. Portraits, Mark Hopkins, former pres. Williams College; Hon. Edmund Wilson, former atty. gen. State of N.J.; Dr. Hunter McGuire; Col. Charles Jefferson Wright, founder of New York Military Academy; John Willard Raught in Scranton Museum; etc. Mem. of Allied Artists of America, American Federation of Arts, New York Water Color Club, Salmagundi Club, Baptist. Illustrator: I.N.R.I. (by Rosegger); The Lost Word (Henry Van Dyke); Life of the Master (Ian Maclaren); Modern Athens (George Horton). Contbr. descriptive articles to mags. Home-Studio: 27 Hooper Av., Atlantic Highlands, N.J.

LINSZ, Henri Phillips; surg. consultant and mem. surg. staff Ohio Valley Gen. and Wheeling hosps. Address: 2224 Chapline St., Wheeling, W.Va.

LINTON, Edwin, coll. prof.; b. E. Bethlehem, Pa., March 14, 1855; s. Joseph and Naomi (Harry) L.; A.B., Washington and Jefferson Coll., 1879; Ph.D., Yale, 1890; m. Margaret McKnight, d. Rev. James I. Brownson, July 9, 1885; children—Eleanor Acheson (Mrs. Eliot Round Clark), Edwin S. (dec.). Instr. math., 1879-81; grad. student Yale, 1881-82; prof. geology and biology, Washington and Jefferson Coll., 1882-1920, prof. emeritus, 1920; hon. fellow in zoölogy, U. of Mo., 1920-22, parasitology, med. supt. U. of Ga., 1922-26; hon. fellow zoölogy at Univ. of Pa. since 1926. Scientific work for U.S. Fish Commn., at Woods Hole, Mass., summers of 1882-87, 87, 89, 1898-1900, 1903-36, in Yellowstone Nat. Park, summer of 1890; Beaufort, N.C., summers of 1901-02; Bermuda, 1903; Tortugas, 1906-08. Awarded silver medal, Paris Expn., 1900. Joseph Leidy memorial medal, Acad. Nat. Sci., Phila., 1937. Fellow A.A.A.S. (v.p. sect. F, 1925); mem. Am. Soc. Naturalists, Am. Soc. Voölogists, Ga. Acad. Science, Washington Acad. Sciences, Am. Soc. Parasitologists, Sigma Xi. Wrote various zoöl. papers in reports and bulls. of U.S. Fish Commn. and U.S. Nat. Mus., etc. Address: Zoölogical Laboratory, University of Pa., Philadelphia, Pa.

LINTON, Frank B. A., artist; b. Philadelphia, Pa., Feb. 26, 1871; s. Edwin Ruthven and Sarah (Piper) L.; ed. École des Beaux Arts and Académie Julian, Paris, France, 1890-98; studied with Thomas Eakins, Phila., 1900-09. Painted portraits of Pres. Mathis Baldwin of Baldwin Locomotive Works, Dean Ruther Weaver of Hahnemann Med. Coll. (both phila.), Dr. Jennings of Johns Hopkins, and other notables. Awarded gold medal, Paris Salon, 1927; Officer d' Academie (France), 1927. Mem. N.Y. Soc. Pennsylvanians, Internationale Union des Beaux Arts et des Lettres (Paris). Democrat. Methodist. Club: Art. Home: 2037 De Lancey Pl., Philadelphia, Pa.

LINTON, Morris Albert, life ins. exec.; b. Germantown, Phila., Pa., Apr. 4, 1887; s. Morris and Ruth A. (Leeds) L.; B.S., Haverford (Pa.) Coll., 1908 (Phi Beta Kappa), A.M., 1910; grad. study, Federal Polytechnic, Zurich, Switzerland, 1908-09, University of Michigan, 1910; LL.D. from Miami University, 1934; m. Margaret Stokes Roberts, Dec. 8, 1914; children—Morris Albert, Elizabeth. Began with Provident Life and Trust Co. (now Provident Mut. Life Ins. Co. of Phila.), 1909, v.p. 1916-31, pres. since 1931; dir. Provident Trust Co., Friends Fiduciary Corpn. Mem. bd. Haverford Coll.; pres. Moorestown Welfare Assn.; chmn. Moorestown Friends Sch.; mem. advisory council Social Security Bd. Past pres. Actuarial Society America; fellow Am. Inst. Actuaries, Inst. of Actuaries (London). Quaker. Clubs: University, Haverford (Phila.); Lake Placid (N.Y.); Pine Valley (N.J.) Golf; Am. and Swiss Alpine clubs. Author of many articles on social security and life insurance. Home: 315 E. Oak Av., Moorestown, N.J. Office: 46th and Market Sts., Philadelphia, Pa.

LIPPINCOTT, Horace Mather, author; b. Phila., Pa., Apr. 20, 1877; s. Robert Cook and Cynthia Shoemaker (Mather) L.; grad. Germantown Acad., 1892; Ph.B., U. of Pa., 1897; m. Sarah S. Jenkins, June 20, 1914; 1 son, Horace Mather. Trustee Germantown Acad.; alumni soc. U. of Pa., 1912-30. Mem. Pa. Hist. Soc., Friends Hist. Soc. (dir.). Republican. Quaker. Club: University. Author: Mather Family of Cheltenham, Pennsylvania,

1910; The Colonial Homes of Philadelphia and Its Neighborhood, 1912; A Portraiture of the People Called Quakers, 1915; George Washington and the University of Pennsylvania, 1916; Early Philadelphia, Its People, Life and Progress, 1917; The University of Pennsylvania; Franklin's College, 1919; An Account of the People Called Quakers in Germantown, Philadelphia, 1923; George Fox (a pageant), 1924; Philadelphia, 1926; A History of Germantown Academy (for 175th anniversary), 1935; also pageants for Germantown Friends' Meeting, George School and Abington Friends' Meeting. Editor The General Magazine and Historical Chronicle (the graduate quarterly mag. of U. of Pa.) and the Pennsylvania Gazette (monthly). Home: East Lane, Chestnut Hill, Pa. Address: University of Pennsylvania, Philadelphia, Pa.

LIPPINCOTT, Joseph Wharton, author, pub.; b. Phila., Pa., Feb. 28, 1887; s. Joshua Bertram and Joanna (Wharton) L.; B.S. in Economics, U. of Pa., 1908; m. Elizabeth Schuyler Mills, Oct. 29, 1913; children—Joseph Wharton, M. Roosevelt Schuyler, Elizabeth Schuyler. With J. B. Lippincott Co. since 1908, v.p., 1915-26, pres. since 1926. With U.S.N.R.F., World War. Trustee Moore Inst., Mercantile Library, Abington Hosp.; asso. trustee of U. of Pa.; master of Oak Hill Beagles. Mem. Pa. Soc. Mayflower Descendants (gov. 1926-27), S.R., Franklin Inst., Phila. Zoölogical Soc., Acad. Natural Sciences, Zeta Psi, National Assn. of Book Publishers (president 1929), American Booksellers' Association. Republican. Clubs: Explorers, Philadelphia, Publishers Lunch, Franklin Inn, Huntingdon Valley Country, Wilderness, Masters of Foxhounds Assn. Author: Bun, A Wild Rabbit, 1918; Red Ben, the Fox of Oak Ridge, 1919; Gray Squirrel, 1921; Striped Coat, the Skunk, 1922; Persimmon Jim, the Possum, 1924; Long Horn, Leader of the Deer, 1928; The Wolf King, 1933; (with G. J. Roberts) Naturecraft Creatures, 1933; The Red Roan Pony, 1934; Chisel Tooth, the Beaver, 1936; Animal Neighbors of the Countryside, 1938. Home: Bethayres, Pa. Office: 227 East Washington Sq., Philadelphia, Pa.

LIPPINCOTT, J(oshua) Bertram, publisher; b. Huntingdon Valley, Pa., Aug. 24, 1857; s. Joshua Ballinger and Josephine (Craige) L.; grad. Episcopal Acad., Phila., 1873; U. of Pa., 1 yr., class of '78, hon. B.A., 1907, LL.D., 1935; m. Joanna Wharton, Apr. 21, 1885; children—Joseph Wharton, Marianna (Mrs. Wm. Paul O'Neill), Sarah (Mrs. Nicholas Biddle), Bertram. Entered publishing business, 1875; v.p., 1886-1911, pres., 1911-26, chmn. bd. since 1926, J. B. Lippincott Company; dir. Farmers & Mechanics Nat. Bank. Dir. of Mercantile Library, Am. Acad. of Music. Mem. Geog. Soc. Phila., Hist. Soc. Pa., Am. Philos. Soc., Art Alliance of Phila. Republican. Clubs: Union League, Art, University, Rittenhouse, Franklin Inn. Home: 1712 Spruce St. Office: 229 S. 6th St., Philadelphia, Pa.

LIPPINCOTT, Martha Shepard, writer; b. Moorestown, N.J.; d. Jesse and Elizabeth (Holmes) L.; ed. Swarthmore Coll. Began writing poetry when a school girl in 1886; since 1895, has made it life work; contbr. poems, stories, articles and book reviews to many mags., newspapers and religious papers in U.S., Can., Eng., Ireland and Scotland. Mem. Soc. of Friends; widely called "The Quaker Poetess." Author: Visions of Life, 1901; also a large number of poems and songs, among the latter of which are: Guide Thou My Bark (sacred solo), Thou Wilt Guide My Journey Through (same), That All Thy Mercies May Be Seen (quartette), Teach Me Thy Will, For Thy Own Dear Self, To My Valentine, My Love for All Eternity, Sleep Little Birdies, Faith and Trust (sacred solo), etc. and many gospel songs. Home: 6204 Jefferson St., West Philadelphia, Pa.

LIPPITT, Walter Otis, supt. of public schools; b. Davenport, Ia., 1880; s. Otis Russell and Adella (Conaro) L.; B.S., Carleton Coll., Northfield, Minn., 1903; A.M., U. of Minn., 1911; grad. student Teachers Coll., Columbia; m. Lois Garvey, June 11, 1908; children—Ronald Otis,

Vernon Garvey, Gordon Leslie. Supt. of schools, Minn., 1904-29; supt. of schools, Westwood, N.J., since 1929. Vice-pres. Minn. Edn. Assn., 1922-24. Mem. N.E.A., Nat. Assn. Sch. Administrators, Nat. Soc. for Study of Edn. Republican. Methodist. Mason. Club: Westwood Rotary. Home: 259 Kinderkarnack Rd. Office: High School Bldg., Westwood; N.J.

LISLE, Clifton, author; b. Phila., Pa., Nov. 27, 1891; s. Robert Patton and F. Hollingsworth (Lyman) L.; ed. DeLancey Sch., Phila., Pa., 1901-09; A.B., U. of Pa., 1913. Has followed writing as a profession since 1914; English master, William Penn Charter Sch., Phila., Pa. since 1929. Served as 1st lieut., later capt., Inf. U.S.A., 1917-19, with A.E.F.; col. 316th Inf. U.S.A. Res., 1936. Decorated Medaille de Verdun, Medaille de St. Mihiel (France); Silver Star and Cluster (U.S.); Pa. Fed. Service Medal. Mem. Soc. of Colonial Wars, S.R., Mil. Order of the Loyal Legion, Mil. Order Fgn. Wars, St. Andrews Soc., Geneal. Soc. Republican. Episcopalian. Clubs: Philadelphia (Philadelphia); Radnor Hunt (Malvern, Pa.); Treweryn Beagles (Berwyn). Author: Diamond Rock, 1920; Saddle Bags, 1923; Sandy Flash, 1922; Hobnails and Heather, 1928; History of 316th Infantry, 1938. Contbr. to leading Am. and fgn. mags. Writer hunting and war verse. Home: Wayne, Pa.

LISSE, Martin William, prof. chemistry; b. Bridgeton, N.J., June 2, 1891; s. Rev. Heinrich Friederich Felix and Martha (Hornig) M.; B.S., Pa. State Coll., 1914; M.S., U. of Washington, Seattle, 1916; Ph.D., Pa. State Coll., 1929; grad. study U. of Wisconsin, 1922; m. Mary Parks, Dec. 30, 1919; children—Mary Louise, Miriam Martha. Teaching fellow, U. of Wash., Seattle, 1914-16; instr. of chemistry, Northwestern U., Evanston, Ill., 1916-17; asst. prof. chem. agr., Pa. State Coll., 1917-26, asso. prof. biophys. chemistry, 1926-29, prof. since 1929. Mem. Am. Chem. Soc., Phi Kappa Phi, Gamma Sigma Delta, Phi Lambda Upsilon, Sigma Xi, Alpha Pi Mu, Alpha Epsilon Delta. Republican. Lutheran. Author: Biocolloids, 1938. Contbr. to sci. mags. Home: 712 McKee St., State College, Pa.

LITSINGER, Elizabeth Clunet, librarian; b. Elizabeth, N.J., July 12, 1905; d. William Hawkins and Eliza (Clunet) L.; A.B., Goucher Coll., Baltimore, Md., 1927; B.S., Columbia U. Sch. of Library Service, 1930. Assistant, Goucher Coll. Library, Baltimore, 1927-29; documents asst., Enoch Pratt Free Library, Baltimore, Md., 1930-33, head Md. Dept. since 1934. Mem. Am. Library Assn., Md. Library Assn., Md. Hist. Soc. Democrat. Methodist. Home: 1503 Mt. Royal Av. Office: Enoch Pratt Free Library, Cathedral, Franklin & Mulberry Sts., Baltimore, Md.

LITTAUER, Kalman, librarian; b. Union Hill, N.J., July 9, 1901; s. Solomon and Minnie (Rosen) L.; student Union Hill (N.J.) High Sch., 1917-21, New York U. Sch. of Commerce, 1921-24; New Jersey Law Sch., Newark, N.J., 1924-25, library science, State Teachers Coll., N.J. since 1935; m. Helen Kelly, Oct. 3, 1930; children—Barbara, Nancy. Office and sales mgr. K. J. Littauer, Realtors, Union City, N.J., 1921-29; sec. to mayor, Union City, N.J., 1929-32; sec. to dir. pub. affairs, Union City, 1932-35; librarian, Union City, since 1935. Active enlistment in 102d Cav., Essex Troop, N.J.N.G., since 1939. Mem. Am. Library Assn., N.J. Library Assn., Spl. Libraries Assn. Democrat. Jewish religion. Mason (Ezra Lodge 215), Elk (Lodge 1357). Club: North Hudson Exchange, Union City, N.J. Home: 213 Palisade Av. Office: Main Library, 43d St., Union City, N.J.

LITTEL, Charles Lester, pres. junior coll.; b. Bertrand, Neb., Aug. 13, 1885; s. Charles and Amanda (Atkinson) L.; A.B., Neb. Univ., 1912; A.M., Stanford U., 1926; Ed.D., N.Y. Univ., 1935; m. Bernice Warner, May 26, 1907; 1 dau., Estella Marie. Engaged in teaching rural schs., then prin. sch. and acad., supt. schs., in Neb., 1902-22; teacher and supt. schs. in Wash., 1922-30; instr. N.Y. Univ., 1930-31; prin. high sch., Teaneck, N.J., 1931-33; pres.

Junior Coll. of Bergen Co. since 1933, also pres. bd. trustees. Served as Dist. Red Cross Chmn. during World War. Mem. bd. dirs. Teaneck Bd. Commerce. Mem. Nat. Edn. Assn. (life), Am. Assn. Sch. Adminstrs., N.J. State Jr. Coll. Assn. (v.p.), Phi Delta Kappa. Republican. Presbyn. Mason (32°, Shriner). K.P. B.P. O.E. I.O.O.F. Clubs: Rotary, Bergen County Schoolmasters (Hackensack); Teaneck Men's Club (pres.). Contbr. to edn. journs. Home: 793 Cedar Lane, Teaneck, N.J.

LITTER, David Hiram, pres. chem. sales orgn.; b. Odessa, Russia, Nov. 12, 1887; s. Loeb and Sara (Jenkins) L.; brought to U.S., 1891, naturalized, 1912; LL.B., N.Y. Law Sch., 1912; m. Mary Scheck, June 30, 1912; 1 dau., Florence Beatrice (Mrs. Milton H. Ohringer). In employ Robert Grant, iron and steel, N.Y. City, 1900-03; chief clk. Central R.R. of N.J., Newark and Elizabethport, 1903-10; traveling freight rep. Central States Dispatch, 1910-14; dir. purchases, Calco Chem. Co., Bound Brook, N.J., 1914-21; pres. and dir. D. H. Litter Co., Inc., mfrs. sales agts for raw materials to paint, varnish, linoleum, and allied industries, New York, N.Y. since 1924; dir. Peterson Chem. Co., Lodi, N.J., Travis Colloid Research Co., New York, N.Y. Mem. Nat. Paint, Varnish & Lacquer Assn. Jewish religion. Mason (32°, Shriner). Club: Chemists (New York). Home: 136 S. Centre St., South Orange, N.J. Office: 500 Fifth Av., New York, N.Y.

LITTLE, Arthur W., printer; b. New York City, Dec. 15, 1873; s. Joseph James and Josephine (Robinson) L.; ed. pvt. schs. and business coll., New York; m. Marguerite Lanier Winslow, Apr. 19, 1897 (died Mar. 21, 1926); children—Winslow, Arthur W.; m. 2d, Charlotte Houston Fairchild, Apr. 27, 1927 (died Sept. 2, 1927); m. 3d, Mary Alice Van Nest Barney June 30, 1928 (died Apr. 18, 1939). Joined father's co., J. J. Little & Co., printers, 1891; now chairman board dirs. J. J. Little & Ives Co. Served pvt. and corpl. Company 1, 7th Regt. N.G.N.Y., 1891-98; capt. Co. D, 171st Regt. N.G.N.Y., 1898; 1st lt. Co. I, 71st Regt., 1899; capt. and a.d.c. to Gen. George Moore Smith, 1900-10; maj. insp.-gen. 1st Brigade, 1910-12. Served in World War with 15th N.Y. Inf., colored, later 369th U.S. Inf.; capt. Co. F, regtl. adj., and maj. 1st Battalion, Apr. 13, 1917-Feb. 28, 1919; in all actions with Gouraud's 4th Army (French), bet. Apr. 7, 1918, and armistice, Nov. 11, 1918; wounded in action, Sept. 12, 1918. Chevalier Legion of Honor and 4 Croix de Guerre (2 palms, one gold star, one silver star); U.S. Silver Star citation for gallantry; Comdr. Order of Black Star (French); Order of Purple Heart (U.S.). Colonel 15th Inf. (colored), N.Y. N.G., Jan. 5, 1921; bvt. brig. gen., Dec. 31, 1922; resigned Apr. 8, 1925. Episcopalian. Mason (life), Elk. Mem. Business Advisory and Planning Council of U.S. Dept. of Commerce, 1933-34; mem. Industrial Advisory Board of NRA, 1934. Mem. S.R., Sons of Vets., Am. Legion, Vets. of Foreign Wars, Nat. Farmers Union (life, hon.). Home: White Sulphur Springs, W.Va.; and 863 Lexington Av., New York, N.Y. Office: 435 E. 24th St., New York, N.Y.

LITTLE, E(dward) H(erman), pres. Colgate-Palmolive-Peet Co.; b. Mecklenburg Co., N.C., Apr. 10, 1881; s. George W. and Ella Elizabeth (Howie) L.; ed. pub. schs., Mecklenburg Co., N.C., and Greys Acad., Huntersville, N.C.; m. Suzanne Heyward Trezevant, Nov. 24, 1910. Began as salesman Colgate & Co., in N.C. and S.C., 1906, dist. mgr. Memphis, Tenn., 1906-10; resigned on account of health and went to Denver, Colo., for recuperation; became salesman Palmolive Co., 1915, dist. mgr. at Los Angeles 1919-23, New York, 1923, Eastern div. mgr., 1924, asst. gen. sales mgr., 1926, mgr. foreign business, 1926-33, dir. since 1927, v.p., 1933-38; pres. Colgate-Palmolive-Peet Co. since 1938. Presbyterian. Office: 105 Hudson St., Jersey City, N.J.

LITTLE, Ernest, coll. prof.; b. Johnstown, N.Y., June 9, 1888; s. John and Martha Jane (Snook) L.; B.S., U. of Rochester, 1911, M.S., 1913; A.M., Columbia, 1919, Ph.D., 1924;

DSc., Phila Coll. of Pharmacy and Science, 1939; grad. student, U. of Graz, Austria, 1931; m. Margaret Lucy Weaver, July 1, 1913; children—John Ernest, Robert Weaver. Instr., U. of Rochester, 1911-14; instr. in leather chemistry, Pratt Inst., Brooklyn, 1914-18; asst. prof of chemistry, Rutgers U., 1918-20, asso. prof., 1920-24, prof. of analytical chemistry, 1924-28; prof. of physics and chemistry, N.J. Coll. of Pharmacy (now Rutgers Univ. Coll. of Pharmacy), 1918-26, dean and prof. of chemistry since 1926. Mem. Com. of Revision of Pharmacopœia of U.S., 1930-40 (mem. exec. com.). Past pres. Bd. of Edn. of Highland Park, N.J., Treas "The Indicator," pub. of N.Y. and North N.J. Sects. Am. Chem. Soc. Rutger's Medalist. Mem. Am. Chem. Soc., N.J. Chem. Soc., Am. Leather Chemists Assn., N.J. Pharm. Assn. (ex-pres.), Am. Pharm. Assn., Am. Assn. of Colls. of Pharmacy (ex-pres., chmn., exec. com. since 1936), Kappa Psi, Phi Lambda Upsilon, Sigma Xi, Phi Beta Kappa. Mem. Reformed Ch. Club: Newark Rotary (past pres.). Home: 237 Benner St., Highland Park, N.J. Address: 1 Lincoln Av., Newark, N.J.

LITTLE, Lawrence Calvin, coll. prof.; b. Couley, La., May 24, 1897; s. Henry Calvin and Minnie (Brett) L.; student Tulane U., New Orleans, La., 1921-23; A.B., Davidson (N.C.) Coll., 1925; A.M., Duke U., Durham, N.C., 1929; student Yale U., 1930-31, Columbia U., summer 1938; D.D., Adrian (Mich.) Coll., 1931; m. Katherine McKenzie, Dec. 30, 1922; children—Katherine Alice, Marjorie Evelyn, Betty, Lawrence (dec.). Engaged in teaching, pub. schs., La., 1917-19; ordained to ministry Meth. Protestant Ch., 1920; pastor, Hicks Circuit, 1918-19; asst. to county supt. pub. edn., Winn Parish, La., 1919-20; all-South field sec., United Soc. C.E., 1920-21; pastor, Concord, N.C., 1923-24; asso. pastor, Greensboro, N.C., 1925-26; exec. sec. Bd. Young People's Work and Christian Edn., 1926-32; instr. religious edn., Duke Univ., 1929-30; instr. in edn., Yale U., 1930-31; prof. religious edn., Western Md. Coll., Westminster, Md., since 1931; mem. ednl. commn., Internat. Council Religious Edn. Mem. Kappa Delta Pi. Democrat. Methodist. Mason. Club: Kiwanis of Westminster. Home: 52 College Av., Westminster, Md.

LITTLE, Marou Brown (Mrs. William F. Little), mem. State Bd. of Education; b. Boston, Mass.; d. Thomas Webb and Marou (Yenetchi) Brown; grad. Latin Sch., (for girls), Boston, 1895; A.B., Vassar Coll., 1899; student Columbia U. and Rutgers U.; m. William Francis Little, July 21, 1910 (died Apr. 19, 1939); children—William Francis, Richard Walter. Began as teacher, Battin High Sch., Elizabeth, N.J., later became head of Greek and Latin Dept., Rye (N.Y.) Sem. Active in edln. work for many years; mem. commn. to promote Nat. Child Welfare Program, Children's Year, 1918; del. to Pres. Hoover's White House Conf., 1930; mem. exec. bd. N.J. Congress of Parents and Teachers 14 years, now hon. vice pres.; mem. bd. dirs. N.J. Tuberculosis League since 1928; mem. advisory bd. N.J. Dental Soc.; mem. Council State Emergency Relief Adminstrn., 1932; sec. Woman's Auxiliary Rahway Memorial Hosp.; mem. N.J. State Bd. of Edn. since 1933; mem. planning com. of Citizens State Com. on Edn.; mem. exec. com. N.J. Council on Adult Edn.; mem. N.J. Recreation Commn., N.J. Health Survey Commn. Mem. Am. Assn. Univ. Women, D.A.R., Vassar Alumnae Assn., Nat. Amateur Athletic Fed. (exec. com.), N.E.A., N.J. State Teachers Assn., Organization for Pub. Health Nursing, Am. Assn. for Adult Edn., Nat. Congress of Parents and Teachers. Awarded medal for "distinguished service to edn." by N.J. State Teachers Assn., 1936 Republican. Episcopalian. Home: 216 Elm Av., Rahway, N.J.

LITTLE, Peter Joseph, lawyer; b. Loretto, Pa., April 23, 1869; s. William Albert Bernard and Susan (Storm) L.; student St. Francis Coll., Loretto, Pa., 1888-90; m. Bertha May O'Connor, Oct. 12, 1898; children—Joseph Francis, Margaret Brown, Frances Shields, Mary (sister Angelica), Clare Ceo, James, Genevieve Solomon, Marjorie McLaughlin. Admitted to Cambria Co. bar, 1893, and since in practice at Ebensburg, Pa.; mem. firm Kittell & Little, 1893-1903, Little & McCann, 1903-06; in practice alone since 1906. Mem. Procedural Rules Com. apptd. by Pa. Supreme Ct. to promulgate uniform rules for cts. of Pa. Pres. Cambria Co. Hist. Soc., 1935-38 (recently erected monument to Robert E. Peary at Cresson, Pa.). Republican. Roman Catholic. Home: 317 N. Center St. Office: High and Center Sts., Ebensburg, Pa.

LITTLEDALE, Clara Savage (Mrs. Harold Aylmer Littledale), editor; b. Belfast, Me., Jan. 31, 1891; d. John Arthur and Emma (Morrison) Savage; A.B., Smith Coll., 1913; m. Harold Aylmer Littledale, Dec. 20, 1920; children—Rosemary, Harold Aylmer. Reporter N.Y. Evening Post, 1913-14; press chmn. Nat. Am. Woman Suffrage Assn., 1914-15; asso. editor Good Housekeeping, 1916-18, fgn. corr. 1918-19; free lance writer, 1919-26; editor Parents' Mag. since 1926. Mem. Am. Assn. of Univ. Women, Child Study Assn. of America, Am. Assn. for Adult Edn., Nat. Com. for Mental Hygiene, Nat. Council of Parent Edn. Contbr. fiction and articles to mags. Home: Hardwell Rd., Short Hills, N.J. Address: Parents Mag., 9 E. 40th St., New York, N.Y.

LITTLEPAGE, Thomas Price, lawyer; b. Spencer Co., Ind., Jan. 6, 1873; s. Thomas Price and Caroline C. (Barnett); L.; student Ind. State Normal, Terre Haute; LL.B. and LL.M., George Washington U.; m. Ella Tasch, April 14, 1900; children—Ellen (Mrs. Willard L. Hart), John Marshall, Louise (Mrs. W. B. Fletcher, Jr.), Thomas Price, James Hemenway. Admitted to D.C. bar, 1910, and practiced since at Washington; v.p. Bank of Bowie (Md.); dir. Liberty Nat. Bank. Former pres. Washington Chamber Commerce. Republican. Mason. Clubs: Cosmos, Alfalfa, Tenuvus. Received gold medal and citation from Cosmopolitan Club "as citizen who performed most outstanding unselfish service to City of Washington during 1934." Home: Bowie, Md. Office: Bowen Bldg., Washington, D.C.

LITZ, Moroni Orson, in practice of law at Welch, W.Va., for many years; now in practice at Charleston; justice Supreme Court of W.Va., 1923-37. Office: Kanawha Banking & Trust Bldg., Charleston, W.Va. *

LIVA, Paolo Francesco, physician; b. Italy, April 29, 1890; s. Giusto and Margherita (Visentin) L.; came to U.S., 1905, naturalized, 1923; Ph.G., Brooklyn Coll. of Pharmacy, 1912, Pharm.D., 1913; M.D., Long Island Coll. Hosp., 1923; m. Lucia Andreozzi, April 26, 1916; children—Vinicio Giusto, Yolanda Margherita, Matilda Brigida, Edward Louis. Began as pharmacist apprentice, Brooklyn, 1907; pharmacist until 1922; interne Hackensack (N.J.) Hosp., 1923-24; physician, Lyndhurst, N.J., since 1924; attending physician in medicine and dermatology Hackensack (N.J.) Hosp.; attending physician in dermatology. Newark City Clinic; physician to Lyndhurst Police Dept. Fellow Am. Coll. Physicians; mem. A.M.A., N.J. State Med. Soc., Long Island Coll. Hosp. Alumni Assn. Republican. Roman Catholic. Address: 280 Stuyvesant Av., Lyndhurst, N.J.

LIVELY, Chauncy C(linton), coll. dean, head dept. psychology and edn.; b. Greene Co., Pa., Dec. 14, 1883; s. John S. and Martha Elvira (Riggs) L.; B.Sc., Waynesburg Coll., 1909; A.M., Oskaloosa Coll., Ia., 1917; Ph.D., Central U., Indianapolis, 1923; m. Luella Grace King, July 20, 1910; children—Virginia Agnes, Lenora Martha (Mrs. Fred M. Hill), Robert Lee, Chauncy King, John Roger, Grace Elizabeth, Richard George, Pataricia Jane. Engaged as teacher, various schs: and Waynesburg Coll., 1902-09; prin. and head dept. sci., high sch., Brookville, Pa., 1909-14, same high sch., Latrobe, Pa., 1914-18; prin. high sch., Charleroi, Pa., 1918-28; head dept. psychology and edn., Waynesburg Coll., since 1928, dean of coll. since 1929, dir. Summer Session since 1930. Fellow A.A.A.S., Royal Soc. of Arts, London. Mem. Am. Genetic Assn., Pa. State Edn. Assn., Pa. Acad. Sci., Brit. Inst. Philosophy, Phi Lambda Theta. Republican. Presbyn. Woodman. Home: 511 Ross St., Waynesburg, Pa.

LIVELY, Frank, judge; b. Monroe Co., W. Va., Nov. 18, 1864; s. Col. Wilson and Elizabeth (Gwinn) L.; grad. Concord Normal Sch., Athens, W.Va., 1882; LL.B., W.Va. U., 1885; m. Annie E. Prince, Jan. 1, 1890; children—Wm. T., Jas. P., Frank W. (dec.), Frederick, Mrs. Jenny Fontaine, Harry W. (dec.). Began practice at Hinton, 1886; pros. attorney, Summers Co., W.Va., 1900-04; asst. atty. gen., W.Va., 1905-06; pardon atty., 1906-09; 1st asst. atty. gen. W.Va., 1909-20; judge Supreme Court of Appeals, W.Va., term 1920-33. Republican. Unitarian. Mason (33°, Shriner). Home: Charleston, W.Va.

LIVELY, William Thompson, lawyer; b. Hinton, W.Va., May 8, 1891; s. Frank and Annie (Prince) L.; LL.B., W.Va. Univ. Law Sch., Morgantown, 1913; m. Mary Donnally, Nov. 27, 1919; children—Willam Thompson, Jr., Mary Willis. Admitted to W.Va. bar, 1913 and engaged in gen. practice of law at Charleston since 19—; mem. firm Lively and Lively since 1913; served as divorce commr., Kanawha Co., 1917-32; sec. and atty. Community Savings & Loan Co., Lewis Oil Co.; dir. and atty. W. L. Smith & Co., wholesale dry goods, Charleston, W.Va.; trustee and atty. Charleston Federal Savings & Loan Assn. Served as seaman, U.S.N. during World War. Served as councilman, City of Charleston, 1919-23. Trustee Charleston High Sch. Stadium Corpn., Charleston Y.M.C.A. Mem. W.Va. State, Kanawha County bar assns., Delta Tau Delta, Mountain and Sphinx. Republican. Presbyn. Mason (32°). Clubs: Rotary, Kanawha Country, Edgewood Country (Charleston). Home: 2010 Quarrier St. Office: Security Bldg., Charleston, W.Va.

LIVENGOOD, Horace Rutherford, physician; b. Salisbury, Pa., Dec. 4, 1876; s. Dr. Theodore F. and Alice (Stutzman) L.; grad. Pingry Sch., Elizabeth, N.J., 1894; student Columbia U. Sch. of Mines, 1894-95; M.D., Coll. Physicians and Surgeons of Columbia U., 1899; m. Lilah Hewson, Nov. 5, 1905; 1 son, Hugh. Interne Elizabeth Gen. Hosp., 1900-01; engaged in gen. practice of medicine at Elizabeth, N.J., since 1901; coroner of Union Co., 1904-07; mem. bd. health, Elizabeth, N.J., 1910-14; jail physician, 1915-25; attdg. phys. Elizabeth Gen. Hosp. (vice-pres. of med. bd.) and mem. Clin. Soc. (pres. 1915). Served as surgeon N.J. N.G., 1906. Served as lt. then capt. Med. Corps, U.S.A during World War. Mem. Elizabeth Chamber of Commerce. Fellow Am. Coll. Phys. Mem. A.M.A., N.J. State and Union Co. med. socs., Acad. Medicine of Northern N.J. Certified by the Nat. Bd. as specialist in internal medicine. Republican. Presbyterian. Elk. Contbr. pamphlets on med. subjects. Home: 587 Westminster Av., Elizabeth, N.J.

LIVERSIDGE, Horace Preston, pub. utility exec.; b. Norristown, Pa., Sept. 29, 1878; s. Thomas and Elizabeth (Jarrett) L.; grad. Drexel Inst., Philadelphia, 1897, grad. study in elec. engring., 1897-98; m. Sara B. Moore, Oct. 14, 1902; children—Preston Moore, Robert Passmore, Thomas Kinnard. With Edison Electric Light Co. (Phila. Electric Co. since 1902) since 1898, successively insp., sub-sta. operator, asst. supt. main generating sta., supt. electric plant constrn., asst. elec. engr., supt. main generating plant, operating engr., asst. chief engr., until 1924, v.p. and asst. chief engr., 1924-26, v.p. and gen. mgr., 1926-38, dir. since 1936, pres. since 1938; pres. and dir. Phila. Electric Power Co., The Susquehanna Electric Co., The Susquehanna Power Co., Phila. Hydro-Electro Co., Deepwater Light & Power Co., Electric Realty Corpn., Philadelphia Steam Co., Susquehanna Utilities Co.; v.p. and dir. South Pennsgrove Realty Co. and Deepwater Operating Co.; dir. Wayne Steam Heat Co., The Proprs. of Susquehanna Canal, Conowingo Land Co. of Cecil County, Howard Improvement Co., Sowego Water & Power Co. Elec. Testing Labs., Inc., Central-Penn Nat. Bank of Phila., Ins. Co. of North America, Indemnity Ins. Co., Phila. Fire & Marine Ins. Co., Alliance Ins. Co. Trustee Drexel Inst. and Jefferson Med. Coll. and its Hosp.; mgr. Franklin Inst. of Phila.; dir. Kensington Hosp.; mem. operating com. Edison Electric Inst.; mem. advisory bd. The Salvation Army. Mem. Assn.

Edison Illuminating Cos. (ex-pres.), Electric Association of Philadelphia (ex-pres.), Am. Soc. M.E., Am. Inst. E.E., Illuminating Engring. Soc. Granted James H. McGraw Award for Co-operation, 1932. Republican. Presbyn. Clubs: Union League, Engineers, Midday, Art, Philadelphia Country (Philadelphia); Aronimink (Newton Square, Pa.); Seaview Golf (Absecon, N.J.); Neighborhood (Bala-Cynwyd). Home: 202 Clwyd Rd., Bala-Cynwyd, Pa. Office: 1000 Chestnut St., Philadelphia, Pa.

LIVESAY, Edward Alexander, univ. prof.; b. Frankford, W.Va., Oct. 22, 1889; s. John Granvil and Elizabeth (Robinson) L.; B.S., Va. Poly. Inst., Blacksburg, Va., 1912, M.S., 1916; A.M., U. of Mo., Columbia, Mo., 1917; M.S., Harvard U., 1925, D.Sc., 1928; m. Helen Hungate, Dec. 27, 1919; children—Betty Jane, Virginia Lee, Alice Marie, Nelle Maxine. Instr. agrl. physics, Va. Poly. Inst., 1914-16; asst. county agt. leader, U. of Mo., 1917-19; prof. animal husbandry, W.Va. Univ., Morgantown, W.Va., animal husbandman, W.Va. Agrl. Expt. Sta., Morgantown, W.Va., since 1919; judge of livestock at many state and dist. fairs. Mem. W.Va. Scientific Soc., Am. Soc. of Animal Production, Alpha Gamma Rho, Gamma Alpha, Alpha Zeta. Presbyn. Mason. Club: Kiwanis (Morgantown). Contbr. articles on animal nutrition and breeding. Home: 18 W. Front St., Morgantown, W.Va.

LIVINGOOD, Frederick George, prof. of education; b. Punxsutawney, Pa., Sept. 19, 1893; s. Samuel Kline and Rebecca Margaret (Shaeffer) L.; grad. Slippery Rock (Pa.) State Normal Sch., 1913; B.S., Albright Coll., Reading, Pa., 1922; Ed.M., Harvard, 1924, Ed.D., 1925; m. Marguerite Irene Kline, July 10, 1925; children—Frederick George, John Kline. Teacher Farrell (Pa.) schs., 1913-16, bldg. prin., 1916-18; head of dept. of edn., Washington Coll., Chestertown, Md., since 1925; instr., summer schs., Albright Coll., 1925, Seton Hill Coll., Greensburg, Pa., 1930, 31. Ednl. sec. Y.M. C.A., Camp Eustis, Va., 1918-19. Mem. Am. Assn. Univ. Profs., Nat. Soc. Coll. Teachers of Edn., N.E.A., Nat. Soc. for Study of Edn., Am. Psychol. Assn., Md. State Teachers Assn. (pres. upper Eastern Shore Region (1939-40), Pa. German Soc., Phi Delta Kappa, Tau Kappa Alpha, Lambda Chi Alpha, Pi Gamma Mu, Omicron Delta Kappa. Methodist. Mason (Shriner). Contbr. to ednl. pubs. Home: Chestertown, Md.

LIVINGSTON, A(lfred) E(rwin), prof. of pharmacology; b. Frost, O., Dec. 6, 1883; s. William Henry and Lydia E. (Place) L.; B.S., Ohio U., 1910, M.S., 1911; Ph.D., Cornell U., 1914; m. Mabel Howell, Sept. 12, 1912; children—Wendell Howell, Philip Reid, Janet, Beatrice. Instr. of biology, Ohio U., Athens, O., 1909-11; instr. of physiology, Cornell U., 1911-14; pharmacologist, Bureau of Chemistry, U.S. Dept. of Agr., Washington, D.C., 1914-16; asso. in physiology, U. of Ill., Coll. of Medicine, Chicago, 1916-18; pharmacologist, U.S. Pub. Health Service (rank of past asst. surgeon), Washington, D.C., 1918-21; asst. prof. of pharmacology, U. of Pa., Sch. of Medicine, 1921-29; prof. and head of dept. of pharmacology, Temple U., Sch. of Medicine, since 1929. Mem. Am. Physiol. Soc., Am. Soc. for Pharmacology and Exptl. Therapeutics, Physiol. Soc. Phila., Phi Beta Kappa, Sigma Xi. Republican. Methodist. Contbr. numerous articles to professional jours. Home: 120 W. Wayne Av., Wayne, Pa. Office: Temple University School of Medicine, Philadelphia, Pa.

LIVINGSTON, Benjamin Thomson, clergyman and prof. evangelism; b. Scotland, Aug. 21, 1869; s. David and Margaret (Thomson) L.; came to U.S., 1882, naturalized, 1891; A.B., Brown U., 1897; grad. Newton Theol. Instn., 1900; (hon.) D.D., Eastern Bapt. Theol. Sem., 1935; m. Deborah King Knox, Aug. 27, 1897 (now dec.); children—Helen Reid (dec.), David Knox; m. 2d, Anne B. Atwood, Oct. 27, 1928. Ordained to ministry Bapt. Ch., 1898; student pastor, Osterville, Mass., 1897-99; pastor at Providence, R.I., 1899-1913, Bangor, Me., 1913-17; sec. Rhode Island Bapt. Conv., 1917-21; exec. sec. Evangelistic Assn. of N.E.,

Boston, Mass., 1921-26; sec. evangelism, Am. Bapt. Home Mission Soc. for Northern Bapt. Conv., N.Y. City, 1926-30; prof. evangelism, Eastern Bapt. Theol. Sem., Phila., Pa., since 1930. Trustee Newton Theol. Instn., Newton Center, Mass. Mem. Delta Tau Delta. Republican. Baptist. Mason (32°). Home: Osterville, Mass. Office: 1814 S. Rittenhouse Sq., Philadelphia, Pa.

LIVINGSTON, Burton Edward, plant physiologist; b. Grand Rapids, Mich., Feb. 9, 1875; s. Benjamin and Keziah (Lincoln) L.; B.S., U. of Mich., 1898; Ph.D., U. of Chicago, 1902; m. Grace Johnson, 1905 (divorced, 1918); m. 2d, Marguerite A. Brennan Macphilips, 1922. Asst. in plant physiology, U. of Mich., 1895-98; fellow and asst. in plant physiology, U. of Chicago, 1899-1905; soil expert U.S. Bur. Soils in charge of fertility investigations, 1905-06; staff mem. dept. bot. research, Carnegie Instn., Washington, 1906-09; prof. plant physiology, Oct. 1909-32, prof. plant physiology and forest ecology, 1932—, dir. lab. of plant physiology, 1913—, Johns Hopkins. Mem. Nat. Research Council. Fellow Am. Acad. Arts and Sciences; mem. Am. Philos. Soc., Bot. Soc. America, American Soc. Naturalists (pres. 1933), Ecol. Soc. America, American Society Plant Physiologists (pres. 1934). Permanent mem. A.A.A.S., 1920-31, general secretary, 1931-34. Author: Rôle of Diffusion and Osmotic Pressure in Plants, 1903; Distribution of Vegetation in U.S., as Related to Climatic Conditions (with F. Shreve), 1921. Editor: Physiological Researches; English edit. Palladin's Plant Physiology, 1918; Botanical Abstracts, 1918-20. Inventor: porous cup atmometer (for measuring evaporation as climatic factor); radio-atmometer (for measuring sunshine); auto-irrigator (for automatic control of soil moisture in potted plants); instruments for measuring water-supplying and water-absorbing power of soils. Writer of many tech. papers. Home: Riderwood, Md. Address: Johns Hopkins Univ., Baltimore, Md.

LIVINGSTON, Herman, chem. engring.; b. Pittsburgh, Pa., Aug. 26, 1876; s. Max and Laura (Weidemeyer) L.; B.S., U. of Pa., 1897; m. Elizabeth S. Talmage, June 18, 1906; 1 son, John T. Employed as engr., United Gas Improvement Co., 1898-1915; chem. engr., Aetna Explosives Co., 1915-18; chem. engr. Calco Chem. Co., Bound Brook, N.J., 1918-23; engaged in profession of cons. engring., N.Y. and N.J., since 1924. Licensed professional engineer, N.Y. and N.J. Mem. Franklin Inst. of Pa. Republican. Clubs: Chemists, Raritan Valley Country. Home: 1341 Marlborough Av., Plainfield, N.J. Office: 701 Spring St., Elizabeth, N.J.

LIVINGSTON, Philip Atlee, publisher; b. Brooklyn, N.Y., Apr. 29, 1901; s. William and Mary Margaret (O'Brien) L.; grad. Narberth (Pa.) High Sch., 1919; A.B., U. of Pa., 1923; m. Carol Lukens Cummings, Oct. 10, 1925; m. 2d, Mary Ellen Cooper, June 15, 1931. Editor Our Town, local newspaper, Narberth, Pa., 1921-38; editor and pub. Bala-Cynwyd News, 1923-37, Ardmore (Pa.) Main Liner, 1925-37; editor Cassinia, ornithological annual, pub. by Delaware Valley Ornithol. Club, Phila., 1928-30; vice-pres. Suburban Publications, Inc., Wayne, Pa., 1931-34; pres. Livingston Pub. Co., pubs. and printers specializing in scholastic field, since 1934. Mem. Pa. Forestry Assn. (dir.), Am. Ornithogists' Union (asso.), Photographic Guild of Phila., Delaware Valley Ornithological Club. Awarded Achievement medal by Poor Richard Club of Phila., 1933. Republican. Episcopalian. Home: 620 Manor Rd., Penn Valley, Narberth, Pa. Address: 209 Haverford Av., Narberth, Pa.

LIVINGSTONE, Roy M(onte), lawyer; b. Tamaqua, Schuylkill Co., Pa., Jan. 11, 1886; s. Sigmund and Lena (Stern) L.; grad. William Penn Charter Sch., Phila., 1901; student U. of Pa., Wharton Sch., 1901-03; LL.B., U. of Pa., 1906; m. Mabel Bennett, Apr. 30, 1913. Admitted to Pa. bar, 1906, and since practiced in Phila.; vice-pres. Broad & Walnut Corpn.; vice-pres. City Bond & Mortgage Corpn.; dir. Inventions Holding Corpn. Republican. Club: Phil-

mont Country (Philmont, Pa.). Home: 1901 Walnut St. Office: 1324 Walnut St., Philadelphia, Pa.

LIZZA, Bedy, manufacturer; b. in Italy, May 4, 1888; s. Justino and Lucia L.; ed. schools of Italy; m. Margaret Catabile, Oct. 30, 1919; children—Justin Wilbur, Frederick Louis, Bedy Richard, Harry. Came to U.S. in 1903, naturalized, 1909. Sec. and treas. Continental Fireworks, 1912-34; pres. and mgr. Keystone Fireworks & Specialty Co., mfrs. commercial and exhibition fireworks, since 1934. Mem. Sons of Italy, Masons, Elks. Address: N. 2d St., Dunbar, Pa.

LLEWELLYN, Frederick Britton, research engr.; b. New Orleans, La., Sept. 16, 1897; s. Frederick Thomas and Virginia (Britton) L.; ed. Staunton (Va.) Mil. Acad., 1916-17; M.E., Stevens Inst. Tech., 1922; Ph.D., Columbia U., 1928; m. Beatrix Gunther, Feb. 25, 1924; 1 dau., Barbara Elizabeth. Employed as research engr., F. K. Vreeland Lab., 1922-23; with Western Electric Co., 1923-25; research engr., Bell Telephone Labs., New York, N.Y. since 1925. Served in U.S.N., 1918-19, U.S.N.R., 1919-22. Dir. Inst. Radio Engrs., 1939-41. Fellow A.A.A.S., Phys. Soc., Inst. Radio Engrs. Mem. Montclair Soc. Engrs., Sigma Xi. Awarded Morris Liebmann Prize, Inst. Radio Engrs., 1935. Republican. Baptist. Author: Electron Inertia Effects, 1939. Contbr. sci. papers to tech. mags. and journs. Home: 72 Afterglow Av., Montclair, N.J. Office: 463 West St., New York, N.Y.

LLEWELLYN, Lee, engr.; b. Morgantown, W.Va., Sept. 20, 1885; s. William Alexander and Elizabeth Ellen (Martin) L.; engineering graduate W.Va. Univ.; m. Caroline Virginia Hess, Oct. 11, 1905; children—Alice Virginia, Robert Lee. Designing Heyl & Patterson, 1905-12; exec. v.p. Pittsburgh Coal Washer Co., 1912-35, v.p. and dir. since 1935; engr. sales dept., Koppers-Rheovaleur Co., Pittsburgh, Pa., since 1935. Burgess Borough of Dormont, Pa. Mason. Clubs: Duquesne, Almas (Pittsburgh). Inventor coal washing equipment and pig iron casting equipment. Home: 2801 Broadway Av. Office: 950 Koppers Bldg., Pittsburgh, Pa.

LLOYD, Frank T., judge; b. Middletown, Del., Oct. 29, 1859; s. Horatio G. and Caroline E. (Newell) L.; grad. Middletown Acad., 1875; studied law pvtly.; m. Mary Pelouze, Feb. 22, 1887; children—Mrs. Ethel Lea Davis, Frank T., Mrs. Mary P. Davis. Admitted to Pa. bar, 1882, N.J. bar, 1897, counsellor, 1900; mem. N.J. legislature, 1896-97; prosecutor of pleas, Camden Co., N.J., 1899-1906; judge Circuit Court of N.J., 1906-24; asso. justice Supreme Court of N.J., 2 terms, 1924-38; now mem. Starr, Summerill & Lloyd, Camden, N.J. Pres. Camden County Library Assn. Member American and N.J. State bar assns., local bar assns., Am. and English socs. for psychical research, Am. Acad. Polit. and Social Science. Republican. Presbyn. Home: Merchantville, N.J. Office: 330 Market St., Camden, N.J.

LLOYD, Frank Tilghman, Jr., lawyer; b. Camden, N.J., June 25, 1895; s. Frank Tilghman and Mary (Pelouze) L.; ed. Princeton U., 1913-15; LL.B., Temple U., 1920; unmarried. Admitted to N.J. bar, as atty., 1919, counsellor at law, 1923; engaged in gen. practice of law at Camden, N.J. since 1920; mem. firm Starr, Summerill & Lloyd since 1926. Served as 1st lt. A.S., U.S.A., 1917. Republican. Presbyn. Clubs: Tavistock Country (Tavistock, N.J.); Seaside Park Yacht (Seaside Park, N.J.). Home: 6507 E. Maple Av., Merchantville, N.J. Office: 330 Market St., Camden, N.J.

LLOYD, Howard Huntley, instr. chemistry, Goucher Coll., 1916-17, asso. prof., 1917-19, prof. since 1919. Address: Goucher College, Baltimore, Md.

LLOYD, Morton Githens, engr.; b. Beverly, N.J., Sept. 10, 1874; s. Clement E. and Irene Emma (Githens) L.; B.S., U. of Pa., 1896, Ph.D., 1900, E.E., 1908; Harvard, 1897-98; Friedrich Wilhelms Universität, Berlin, 1898-99; m. Ethel Tucker Maurer, June 20, 1907; children—Miriam, Richard Louis. Instr. physics

U. of Pa., 1899-1902; lab. asst., asst. physicist and asso. physicist, Bur. of Standards, Washington, 1902-10; tech. editor, Electrical Review and Western Electrician, Chicago, 1910-16; electrical engineer and chief safety codes sect., Nat. Bur. of Standards, 1917—. Fellow Am. Inst. E.E.; mem. Washington Acad. Sciences, Am. Assn. Engrs., U.S. Nat. Com. of the Internat. Commn. on Illumination, Internat. Asso. of Elec. Inspectors (pres.), Franklin Inst., Federal Interdepartmental Safety Council, Federal Accident Statisticians, Sigma Xi, Am. Assn. for Labor Legislation, Philos. Soc. Washington, National Fire Protection Assn., Nat. Safety Council, Am. Soc. Safety Engrs. (past pres.), Safety Code Correlating Com.; hon. member Internat. Municipal Signal Assn.; pres. Washington Safety Soc.; del. to Montgomery County Civic Fed.; sec. Community Assn. of Sect. 3 Chevy Chase. Member Internat. Elec. Congress, St. Louis, 1904, Turin, 1911, Internat. Engring. Congress, San Francisco, 1915; Internat. Congress on Illumination, Saranac, N.Y., 1928. Awarded Edward Longstreth medal, Franklin Inst., 1910. Contbr. to scientific and tech. publs. Home: Chevy Chase, Md. Office: National Bureau of Standards, Washington, D.C.

LLOYD, Stacy Barcroft, banker; b. Camden, N.J., Aug. 1, 1876; s. Malcolm and Anna (Howell) L.; student Lawrenceville Sch., 1892-94; A.B., Princeton, 1898; LL.B., U. of Pa., 1901; m. Eleanor B. Morris, Oct. 25, 1902; children—Ellen Douglas (Mrs. Lloyd Dunham), Stacy Barcroft, Morris. Admitted to Pa. bar, 1901, and asso. with firm Reed & Pettit, 1901-06; asst. gen. solicitor, later asst. gen. counsel, Pa. R.R., 1906-21; v.p. Phila Saving Fund Soc., 1921-34, pres. since 1934; dir. Phila. Nat. Bank, Provident Mut. Life Ins. Co., Merchants Fund, Baltimore & Eastern R.R. Co. Asso. counsel for Pa. of the U.S. Food Administration, 1917-18. Commd. maj. judge-advocate, July 1918, and served in France and Italy until June 1919; honorably disch. Aug. 1919. Republican. Episcopalian. Clubs: Philadelphia, Princeton. Gulph Mills Golf (Phila.); Princeton (New York); Ivy (Princeton). Home: Ardmore, Pa. Office: 1212 Market St., Philadelphia, Pa.

LOANE, William Paul Coppinger, clergyman; b. Phila., Pa., Mar. 1, 1902; s. William Coppinger and Helen Fallan (Brown) L.; A.B., Hobart Coll., 1927; B.D., Berkeley Divinity Sch., 1930. Ordained to ministry P.E. Ch., deacon, 1930, priest, 1931; asst. minister, Old Saint Peter's Ch., Phila., Pa., 1930-35; rector Ch. of the Incarnation, Drexel Hill, Pa. since 1935; mem. Commn. on Music and Ch. Schs., Diocese of Pa.; nat. rep. Knights of St. John on Nat. Council of Youth Orgns. P. E. Ch.; chmn. Administrn. Diocesan Summer Conf. Trustee Camp Taitt. Mem. Kappa Sigma. Traveled extensively in U.S.A. and abroad. Home: 338 Riverview Av., Drexel Hill, Pa.

LOBB, Hugh Rowland, clergyman; b. Ocean Mines, No. 1, Clearfield Co., Pa., Dec. 16, 1879; s. Thomas Trown and Annie Rebecca (Rowland) L.; grad. Brisbin (Pa.) High Sch., 1900; student Clearfield (Pa.) Business Sch.; grad. Findlay (O.) Coll.; correspondence course student of Temple U.; m. Ida May Blowers, Nov. 8, 1905; children—Bernita Blowers (Mrs. Nathan Hale Segner), Hugh Rowland. Began in bituminous mines of Pa. at age of 13; as a young man had charge of coal office and company store; earned way through college as coal miner during summers; ordained to ministry of Churches of God, 1905; pastor Columbia, Pa., 1905-07, Newville, Pa., 1907-12, Alverton, Pa., 1912-18, Shippensburg, Pa., 1918-27, First Ch., Harrisburg, Pa., 1927-33, Roaring Spring, Pa., 1933-38; pastor, Mechanicsburg, Pa., since 1938. Pres. East Pa. Eldership, 1922; pres. Gen. Eldership, 1933-37; pres. of Corpn. of Gen. Eldership, 1933-37; hon. vice-pres. Lord's Day Alliance of U.S.; denominational rep. of Am. Bible Soc.; mem. exec. com. Pa. Council of Churches. Mem. Gen. Eldership Bd. of Missions; chmn. East Pa. Eldership Bd. of Edn. and mem. Bd. of Supervision and Appointment. Trustee Findlay Coll. (chmn. East Pa. Eldership expansion program com.). Ind. Republican. Home: 29 W. Marble St., Mechanicsburg, Pa.

LOBECK, Armin Kohl, prof. geology; b. N. Y. City, Aug. 16, 1886; s. Adolph Christian and Elmire Celeste (Voullaire) L.; A.B., Columbia, 1911, A.M., 1913, Ph.D., 1917; m. Bertha Merrill, Dec. 25, 1917; children—Elmire, Merrill. Instructor Phila. Coll. Pharmacy, 1911-14; asst. prof. U. of Wis., 1919-24, asso. prof., 1924-29; prof. geology, Columbia, since 1929. Mem. geog. sect., Am. Commn. to Negotiate Peace, Paris, World War. Fellow A.A.A.S., N.Y. Acad. Science; mem. Geol. Soc. of America, Assn. of Am. Geographers, Sigma Xi. Republican. Presbyn. Club: Men's Faculty (Columbia U.). Author: Block Diagrams, 1924; Guide to Geology of Allegany State Park, 1927; Airways of America, 1933; Geomorphology, 1939. Contbr. maps, block diagrams, guides and articles to geol. and geog. publs. Home: 251 Sunset Av., Englewood, N.J.

LOBINGIER, Ella Hanlon, (Mrs. Chauncey Lobingier), asst. dir. edn. extension; b. Pittsburgh, Pa., Oct. 16, 1870; d. James and Anna Burns (Hanlon) Hanlon; A.B., summa cum laude, U. of Pittsburgh, 1915, grad. study, 1915-17; grad. study, Pa. State Coll., 1923; m. Chauncey Lobingier, June 27, 1916; step-children—George Danby, John Huston. Engaged as teacher grade sch., asst. prin., prin. schs., Pittsburgh, Pa., 1887-1919; instr. U. of Pittsburgh, 1919-21; asso. prof. and asst. dir. Edn. Extension of Pa. State Coll. since 1921. Trustee Lawrenceville Neighborhood House (pres. bd.). Mem. Nat. Edn. Assn. (life), Am. Assn. Sch. Adminstrs. Dept. Supervisors and Dirs. Instrn., Assn. Childhood Edn., Pa. State Edn. Assn., Pi Lambda Theta. Republican. Attends Community Ch. Clubs: Civic, Women's (Bradford Woods). Home: Bradford Woods, Pa. Office: 424 Duquesne Way, Pittsburgh, Pa.

LOBLEIN, Eldon Leon, pres. Vannote Lumber Co.; b. New Brunswick, N.J., Jan. 13, 1888; s. Eldon Leon and Emma (Hendricks) L.; grad. New Brunswick (N.J.) High Sch., 1905; student Rutgers U., New Brunswick, N.J., 1905-07; V. M.D., U. of Pa., 1910; m. Helen Mae Oram, Sept. 1, 1910; children—Eldon Oram, Margaret Catherine (Mrs. John E. Orchard), Janet, Mary Anne. Gen. practice as vet. throughout N.J., 1910-26; teacher and lecturer vet. science and instr. short courses in agr., Rutgers U., New Brunswick, N.J., 1910-20; examiner, State Bd. of Vet. Examiners, N.J., 1915-20; consultant to N.J. State Bd. of Health, 1915-26, Dept. of Animal Industry State of N.J., 1915-26; veterinarian Squibb Biological Labs., New Brunswick, N.J., 1918-22, Union County Med. Milk Commn., Wood Brook Farms, 1920-26; retired from vet. practice, 1926; pres. Vannote Lumber Corpn., Point Pleasant, N.J., since 1926; pres. River and Ocean Front Land Co.; v.p. Ocean Co. Nat. Bank; sec. and treas. Bay Sites Development Corpn.; dir. Swift Business Machines Corpn.; pres. Point Pleasant Bldg. & Loan Assn. Mem. N.J. State Ho. of Rep., 1913, 1914; mem. Middlesex Co. (N.J.) Bd. of Freeholders, 1918-19, 1920. Mem. N.J. Vet. Med. Assn. (sec. 1913-20), Delta Kappa Epsilon. Episcopalian. Club: Bay Head (N.J.) Yacht (Commodore). Home: 177 Livingston Av., New Brunswick, N.J.; 341 Ocean Front, Bay Head, N.J. Office: Vannote Lumber Co., Point Pleasant, N.J.

LOCHER, Roy W.; asso. prof. clin. and operative surgery, U. of Md.; visiting surgeon Mercy, St. Joseph's South Baltimore Gen. and West Baltimore Gen. hosps. and Church Home and Infirmary. Address: 31 E. North Av., Baltimore, Md.

LOCKE, Albert Wentworth, banking; b. Sylvan Mills, W.Va., Jan. 29, 1874; s. William B. and Rebecca (Wrick) L.; student West Liberty Teachers Coll., West Liberty, W.Va., 1896-99; m. Ada Virginia Ingram, June 20, 1910; 1 dau., Anna Virginia. Engaged in teaching pub. schs., 1894-98; supt. pub. schs., Pleasants County, 1899-1907; in office sheriff of Pleasants Co., 1917-29; mcht. Eureka, and Parkersburg, W.Va., 1908-17; oil producer, St. Marys, W.Va., 1928-39; pres. Pleasants County Bank, St. Marys, W.Va., since 1932; treas. McBride Gas Co., Nina Gas Co., Williamson Oil Co., Jamison Gas Co., all St. Marys, W.Va. Served as pres. county bd. edn., Pleasants Co., since 1933. Democrat. Methodist. Mason (32°, Shriner), Odd Fellow. Club: Masonic (Wheeling). Home: 612 Fourth St. Office: 323 Second St., St. Marys, W.Va.

LOCKE, Alfred Cookman, clergyman; b. nr. New Castle, Pa., Feb. 20, 1875; s. James Hamilton and Eleanor (Piper) L.; diploma Slippery Rock State Teachers Coll., 1897; Ph.B., Grove City Coll., 1901; student Garrett Bib. Inst., Evanston, Ill., 1915-16; (hon.) D.D., Allegheny Coll., 1930; m. Nellie May Hess, July 24, 1901; children—Ethel Rowena (Mrs. Harry William Hagmann), Alfreda Mae (Mrs. Forest Burton Irwin). Engaged in teaching pub. schs. and student pastor, 1897-1901; admitted to Erie Conf., M.E. Ch., 1901, ordained deacon, 1903, elder, 1905; pastor various chs. Pa. and N.Y., 1901-28; supt. Erie and Jamestown Dists., 1928-34; pastor M.E. Ch., Franklin, Pa., since 1934; mem. Gen. Conf., 1932. Dir. Corpn. of Erie Conf. and Cribbs Home. Mem. Pi Gamma Mu. Republican. M.E. Ch. Mason (K.T., 32°). Club: Kiwanis of Franklin (former pres. Du Bois, Pa., club). Home: 1116 Liberty St., Franklin, Pa.

LOCKE, Charles Addam, lawyer; b. Phila., Pa.; s. John Jacob and Emma (Weise) L.; grad U. of Pittsburgh; unmarried. Admitted to Pa. bar, 1897, and since practiced in Pittsburgh. Mem. Metropolitan bd. of dirs. Y.M.C.A of Pittsburgh; trustee Church Club of Pittsburgh; mem. bd. of govs. Law Alumni Assn., U. of Pittsburgh. Major Judge Advocate Department, U.S. Army, during World War; also as chmn. all Y.M.C.A. camps in Pittsburgh Dist. and as mem. Draft Bd. Mem. Allegheny County and Am. bar assns., Acad. Science and Art, Western Pa. Hist. Soc., Sons of Vets. of U.S.A, Phi Gamma Delta. Episcopalian. Clubs: Duquesne, University, Church (Pittsburgh). Home: Iroquois Apts. Office: Berger Bldg., Pittsburgh, Pa.

LOCKE, John Harold, steel exec.; b. Cambridge, Mass., Oct. 19, 1888; grad. Mechanic Arts High Sch., Boston, Mass., 1904; B.S., Mass. Inst. Tech., 1908; grad. student Harvard U., 1909-10; m. Virginia Maddox, Oct 9, 1915; children—Virginia, John Harold, Jr. Research asst. Westinghouse Lamp Co., 1910-12; with Commonwealth Steel Co., 1912-29, as draftsman and later asst. to gen. mgr.; company bought by Gen. Steel Castings Corpn., 1929, and since then with Gen. Steel Castings Corpn., successively as asst. gen. mgr., gen. mgr. of Commonwealth Div., mgr. of operations of corpn., and since 1932, vice-pres. Mem. Theta Chi. Republican. Congregationalist. Clubs: Merion Cricket (Haverford, Pa.); Seigniory (Quebec, Can.). Home: Villanova, Pa. Office: Eddystone, Pa.

LOCKHART, Henry, Jr., banker; b. Millerstown, Pa., Sept. 30, 1877; s. Henry and Ellen (Burns) L.; ed. Bates Acad., Millerstown, Pa., and privately; m. Aletha Swift, of San Antonio, Tex., 1903; children—Henry, IV, Meredith A., David G. With Am. Smelting & Refining Co., El Paso, Tex., 1898-99, at Monterrey, Agascalientes, Torreon, City of Mexico, Sonora (Mexico), 1900-08; banking exec., New York, 1908-17; Goodrich-Lockhart Co., New York, 1923-32; partner Blair & Co., Inc., and successor corpn. Bancamerica-Blair, Inc., bankers, New York, 1932-38; engaged in personal operations since 1938; chmn. bd. dirs. New York Shipbuilding Corpn.; dir. Shell Union Oil Corpn., Shell Pipe Line Corpn., Shell Oil Corpn., Commercial Solvents Corpn., Aviation and Transportation Corpn., Walworth Co., Inc., North Am. Refractories Co., Interstate Co. In charge of Mission on Aeronautics (to Allies) and mem. Inter-Allied Aviation Com. during World War. Dir. and mem. bd. mgrs. New York Bot. Gardens; trustee Broad Street Hosp. Fellow Am. Geog. Soc. Republican. Episcopalian. Clubs: Racquet and Tennis, Metropolitan, Recess, Talbot Country, Grolier, Madison Square Garden (New York); Piping Rock (Locust Valley); Pacific Union (San Francisco); California (Los Angeles). Home: Longwoods, Md. Office: New York Shipbuilding Corpn., Camden, N.J.

LOCKLEY, Lawrence Campbell, market analyst; b. Salem, Ore., Nov. 21, 1899; s. Fred and Hope (Gans) L.; student Ore. Agrl. Coll., Corvallis, 1917-18; B.A., U. of Calif., 1920, M.A., 1921; M.A., Harvard, 1929, Ph.D., 1931; m. Phyllis Harrington, May 11, 1920; children—Robert Campbell (died July 2, 1937), Neil Harrington; m. 2d, Naomi M. Hewes, of Phila., Nov. 19, 1938. Reporter Oregon Journal, Portland, 1917 and 1920; associate in English, University of Calif., 1921-27; also cons. work, 1921-27; mem. research staff Harvard Grad. Sch. Business Administration, 1929-30; asst. prof. business administration and head of dept. orgn. and management, Temple U., 1930-32, became prof. of marketing and head of dept. of marketing 1932. Tech. expert U.S. Census of Business, 1935; now with div. of commercial research Curtis Pub. Co., Phila. Mem. S.A.T.C., Corvallis, Ore., 1918. Mem. Am. Econ. Assn., Nat. Assn. of Marketing Teachers, Beta Gamma Sigma, Sigma Phi Epsilon, Pi Gamma Mu, Alpha Delta Sigma. Republican. Presbyn. Author: Faulty Paragraphs for Composition Classes (with Phyllis H. Lockey), 1923; Making Letters Build Business, 1925; A Road Map to Literature (with P. H. Houston), 1926; Principles of Effective Letter Writing, 1927, revised edit., 1933; Vertical Coöperative Advertising, 1931. Co-Author: Advertising Agency Compensation, 1934. Editor: Lessons in California History, by Harr Wagner and Mark Keppel, 1924. Contbr. to Printers' Ink, Advertising & Selling, etc. Address: Curtis Publishing Co., Philadelphia, Pa.

LOCKWOOD, Charlotte Mathewson, organist; b. Granby, Conn., Feb. 24, 1903; d. Ernest H. and Lottie (Davis) M.; Mus.Bac., Salem Acad. and Coll., Winston-Salem, N.C., 1922; Sac.Mus.M., Union Theol. Sem., 1931; pvt. organ pupil Clarence Dickinson, N.Y. City, 1922-28, Charles Marie Widor, Paris, 1930, Günther Ramin, Leipzig, 1932; m. Edward B. Lockwood, 1924 (divorced 1930); m. 2d, John Stuart Garden, Oct. 20, 1935. Organist First M.E. Ch., Reidsville, N.C., 1914-18, First Presbyn. Ch., Danville, Va., 1918-19, Renolda Presbyn. Ch., Winston-Salem, N.C., 1919-20, First Presbyn. Ch., Greensboro, N.C., 1920-22, Congl. Ch., Scarsdale, N.Y., 1923-26, Sinai Synagogue, N.Y. City, 1923-25, West End Synagogue, N.Y. City, 1925-36; now organist, choir dir. Crescent Av. Presbyn Ch., Plainfield, N.J., teacher of singing, Hartridge Sch., Plainfield; teacher at Union Theol. Sem.; made transcontinental tour of organ recitals, spring 1935. Fellow Am. Guild of Organists (passed examinations 1925). Author: 7 sacred anthems for chorus, pub. separately, 1930-35; 12 vesper hymns for classic melodies, pub. in 1 vol., 1932; 4 organ duets (with Dr. C. Dickinson) pub. separately, 1931. Home: Murray Hill, N.J.*

LOCKWOOD, Dean Putnam, educator, librarian; b. of Am. parents, Rio Janeiro, Brazil, May 13, 1883; s. Robert Minturn and Ellen (Dean) L.; prep. edn., Smith Acad., St. Louis, Mo.; A.B., Harvard, 1903, A.M., 1904, Ph.D., 1907; m. Esther Greenleaf Abercrombie, May 27, 1911; 1 son, Robert Minturn. Instr. Harvard, 1909-10; asst. prof. Columbia, 1911-15, acting librarian, 1916-17; asso. prof. Latin, Haverford (Pa.) Coll., 1918-23, prof. and librarian, 1923-27, and since 1928; prof. in charge Sch. of Classical Studies, Am. Acad., Rome, 1927-28. Mem. Am. Philol. Assn., Medieval Acad. America, Am. Assn. Univ. Profs., Phi Beta Kappa. Author: A Survey of Classical Roman Literature, 1934. Home: 6 College Circle, Haverford, Pa.

LODGE, George, lawyer; b. Claymont, Del., Oct. 15, 1862; s. William C. and Emma A. (Lore) L.; student Reynolds Sch., Wilmington, Del., 1872-73, Rugby Acad., Wilmington, 1873-80; M.A., U. of Pa., 1883; unmarried. Admitted to Del. bar, 1887; pres. and counsel Del. Bldg. & Loan Assn., Claymont, since 1923; mgr., dir. and counsel Claymont (Del.) Enterprises, Inc., since 1918; sec., dir. and counsel Claymont (Del.) Trust Co. since 1923; dir. Del. Trust Co. Mem. Del. Ho. of Reps., 1887. Served as adj. gen., Del., 3 yrs. Democrat. Episcopalian. Mason. Club: Wilmington (Wilmington, Del.). Home: Claymont, Del. Office: 1112 King St., Wilmington, Del.

LOEB, Arthur, contractor, broker; b. Lafayette, Ind., June 29, 1872; s. Simon and Rosa E. (Wolf) L.; student Rugby Acad., Phila., 1886-89, U. of Pa., 1889-91; m. Emma Gerstley, Nov. 11, 1901; children—Elinor Gerstley, William Simon, George Arthur. Worked as shoemaker for father's firm, Saller Lewin & Co., 1889-93; mem. firm Rosenau & Loeb, mfrs. of hosiery, 1893-1906; vice-pres. Keystone State Constrn. Co., gen. contractors, since 1906; special partner Theo. Prince & Co., brokers, New York, 1927-32; vice pres. Alliance Investment Co.; dir. Southern Transport. Co., Hotel Barbizon, New York. Dir. Glen Mills Schs.; dir. Fed. of Jewish Charities; dir. M. & S. Bamberger Home United Campaign. Republican. Jewish religion. Mason. Clubs: Philmont Country, Locust (Phila.). Home: 1701 Locust St. Office: 213 S. Broad St., Philadelphia, Pa.

LOEB, Howard A., banker; b. Philadelphia, Pa., July 25, 1873; s. August B. and Mathilde (Adler) L.; ed. Friends Central Sch., Phila.; B.S., U. of Pa., 1893, M.E., 1894. Practiced engring., 1894-1907, as officer and dir. Francis Bros. & Jellett, Inc.; became v.p. Tradesmens Nat. Bank, Phila., 1907, elected pres., 1915, and on merger with Guarantee Trust & Safe Deposit Co. and Chelten Trust Co., 1928, elected chairman Tradesmens Nat. Bank and Trust Co.; also chairman Chelten Corpn. and Chelten Title Co.; dir. Tradesmens National Bank and Trust Company, Chelten Corpn., Chelten Title Co., Integrity Trust Co. (Phila.), South Chester Tube Co., South Chester Terminal and Warehousing Company, Horn & Hardart Co., Securities Corpn. Gen., Sharp & Dohme, Liberty Mutual Ins. Co. (Pa. advisory bd.), Patterson Oil Terminals, Inc., Terminal Transport Co. Mem. exec. com. Federal Advisory Council; mem. Phila. Clearing House Assn.; chmn. advisory com. Phila. Agency of the Reconstruction Finance Corpn. Mem. Am. Acad. Polit. and Social Science, Acad. Natural Sciences, Pennsylvania Museum and Sch. of Industrial Art, Foreign Policy Association. Clubs: Manufacturers and Bankers, Down Town, Midday, Bank Officers', Locust, Ashbourne Country, Rydal Course (Phila.); U. of Pa. Club, Bankers (New York). Home: Elkins Park, Pa. Office: 320 Chestnut St., Philadelphia, Pa.

LOEB, Oscar, stock broker; b. Phila., Pa., Sept. 26, 1879; s. Simon and Rosa E. (Wolf) L.; student Central High Sch., 1893-96, Drexel Inst., 1896-97, U. of Pa., 1897-1900; m. Rebecca W. Thomas, Nov. 11, 1907; children—Bettina R. (Mrs. Alfred D. Katz), Thomas O. Began as clerk in brokerage office, 1900; became mem. Phila. Stock Exchange, 1901, New York Commodity Exchange, 1935. Writes column "Observation Car" in Jewish Exponent; former editor Town Crier magazine. Dir. Hebrew Edn. Soc., Eagleville Sanatorium, Jewish Chautauqua Soc., Rodeph Shalom Congregation. Mem. Am.-Jewish Hist. Soc., Pa. Soc. of N.Y. Republican. Clubs: Rydal Course (Rydal, Pa.); Univ. of Pennsylvania Club of New York. Home: 6704 N. 12th St. Office: Stock Exchange Bldg., Philadelphia, Pa.

LOECHEL, Lloyd Orlando, dentist; b. Garett Co., Md., Nov. 23, 1891; s. Samuel and Ellen (Keim) L.; grad. Franklin and Marshall Acad., 1911; D.D.S., U. of Pa. Dental Sch., 1914; m. Sara Glatfelter, Mar. 12, 1920; children—Sylvia Ellen, Lloyd Orlando. In active practice of dentistry, Columbia, Pa., since 1914 (except War period); dir. Columbia Trust Co., Home Bldg. & Loan Assn. Served as 1t. later capt., Dental Corps, U.S. Army, during World War. Mem. Am. Dental Assn., Harris Dental Soc. Republican. Lutheran. Mason (K.T., Shriner). Address: Columbia, Pa.

LOESCHE, William H., banking; b. Phila., Pa., Dec. 22, 1888; s. Charles and Sophia L.; ed. pub. sch. and Northeast High Sch., Phila.; m. Minnie E. Jeffer, June 16, 1909; 1 son, William H., Jr. Asso. with Girard Trust Co. since 1918, trust officer since 1928; dir. Keystone Portland Cement Co., Bird Coal Co., Frank C. Snedaker & Co., Lumbermen's Ins. Co., Phila. Nat. Ins. Co. Served as mem. Bd. Pub. Edn. of Phila. since 1932. Republican. Mem. Reformed Episcopal Ch. Mason. Clubs: University, Old York Road Country. Home: 6400 N. 8th St. Office: Broad and Chestnut Sts., Philadelphia, Pa.

LOETSCHER, Frederick William, clergyman; b. Dubuque, Ia., May 15, 1875; s. Christian and Mary L.; A.B., Princeton, 1896, A.M., 1901, Ph.D., 1906; B.D., Princeton Theol. Sem., 1900; U. of Berlin, 1901-02, U. of Strassburg, 1902-03; D.D., Lafayette, 1914; LL.D., Dubuque, 1918; m. Mary Aletta McClelland, Apr. 18, 1901; children—Lefferts Augustine, Helen Mildred, Frederick William. Ordained Presbyn. ministry, 1903; instr. ch. history, 1903-07, mem. bd. dirs., 1908-10, prof. homiletics, 1910-13, prof. ch. history, 1913—, Princeton Theol. Sem.; pastor Oxford Ch., Phila., 1907-10. Lecturer on church history at Biblical Sem. (New York), 1922-23, and at New Brunswick (N.J) Theological Sem., 1924-25. Member of Presbyterian Hist. Soc. (councilor 1907—; editor Journal 1912—); director Presbyterian Ministers' Fund of Philadelphia. Member American Society Church History (councilor, secretary, and editor of papers 1918-33, pres. 1934), Am. Hist. Assn., Phi Beta Kappa. Republican. Author: Schwenckfeld's Participation in the Eucharistic Controversy of the Sixteenth Century, 1906; also articles in Princeton Theol. Review and other mags. Address: 98 Mercer St., Princeton, N.J.

LOEWER, Charles Hastings, banking; b. Nanticoke, Pa., Jan. 21, 1895; s. George and Ernestine (Doberstein) L.; grad. Nanticoke High Sch., 1912; B.B.A., U. of Wash., Seattle, 1924; m. Ernestine Rebecca Smith, Oct. 19, 1934; children—Margaret Belle, Helen Jane. With First Nat. Bank, Nanticoke, 1912-18; nat. bank examiner, 1925-27; with First Nat. Bank, Hazelton, Pa., since 1928, exec. vice-pres. and trust officer since 1934. Served in the U.S. Navy, 1918-19. Republican. Presbyterian. Mason (32°). Home: 633 N. Church St. Office: West Broad St., Hazleton, Pa.

LOGAN, Frank Albert, banker; b. Audubon, Pa., Jan. 25, 1892; s. Morris Mark and Blanche S. (McManus) L.; grad. Norristown (Pa.) High Sch., 1910; m. Margaret A. Bollinger, Oct. 27, 1920; 1 dau., Peggy Ann. In banking since 1910; vice-pres., cashier and dir. Bridgeport Nat. Bank; sec. and dir. Upper Merion Bldg. & Loan Assn.; dir. Schuylkill Valley Protective Bldg. & Loan Assn. Served in Marine Corps during World War. Republican. Methodist. Mason. Home: 209 W. Fomance St., Norristown, Pa. Office: Bridgeport Nat. Bank, Bridgeport, Pa.

LOGAN, Harry Allison, business exec.; b. Summit City, McKean Co., Pa., Nov. 20, 1881; s. Ryland M. and Eugenia (Allison) L.; student Warren County (Pa.) pub. schs., 1887-97, Erie (Pa.) Business Coll., 1897-99; m. Helen Temple, Jan. 8, 1922; children—Harry Allison, Helen Marian. Clk. and bookkeeper in veneer factory, Warren, Pa., 1899-1902; helped organize United Refining Co., Warren, Pa., 1902; beginning as accountant and advancing to v.p.; treas., gen. mgr. and dir. since 1907; helped organize Elk Refining Co., Charleston, W.Va., 1914, and since pres.; pres. Emblem Oil Co., Warren, since 1928, Red Star Lubrication Service, Inc., Jamestown, N.Y., since 1929; v.p. Tiona Petroleum Co., Phila., since 1923, J. L. Yerdon & Co., Bradford, Pa., since 1928; v.p. and dir. Warren Bank & Trust Co. since 1934. Served as mem. various coms. of Nat. Petroleum War Service Com., organized in connection with Oil Div. of U.S. Fuel Administrn., during World War. Mem. refinery sub-com. of planning and co-ordination com. for petroleum industry and regional refinery com., Regional Dist. 1, Planning and Co-Ordination Com., during administrn. fair competition code under N.R.A. Mem. Nat. Petroleum Assn. (v.p. 1926 and dir. since 1912), Pa. Grade Crude Oil Assn. (dir. and mem. exec. com. since 1931), Am. Petroleum Inst. (dir. since 1935). Republican. Episcopalian. Clubs: Conewango, Conewango Valley Country (Warren, Pa.); Bradford (Bradford,

Pa.); Pa. Society of N.Y., Cloud (New York City). Address: Warren, Pa.

LOGAN, James Jackson, lawyer; b. York Co., Pa.; s. John N. and Ella M. (Coover) L.; Ph.B., Lafayette Coll., 1900, M.S., same, 1903; grad. student Dickinson Coll. Law Sch.; m. Louise Keyworth; children—John Tyler, Mary Castor. Admitted to Pa. bar, 1901, and since engaged in gen. practice of law at York; rep. of Pa. Atty. Gen. in York Co. Served with 4th Pa. Vol. Inf. in Spanish-Am. War, in Puerto Rico campaign. Mem. Sch. Bd. of York. Dir. Pa. Sch. Dirs. Assn. Home: Merion Road, York, Pa. Office: Continental Sq., York, Pa.

LOGAN, Thomas, pres. Parkersburg Nat. Bank. Address: Parkersburg, W.Va.

LOGUE, James Gibson, pediatrician; b. July 23, 1889; s. Charles T. and Ada (Dreisbach) L.; M.D., U. of Pa. Sch. of Medicine, 1914; student New York Post Grad. Hosp., 1922-23; m. Helen Margaret Stouck, July 11, 1914; children—James Gibson, Helen Elizabeth. Chief pediatric staff, mem. bd. mgrs., Williamsport (Pa.) Hosp. since 1936. Fellow Am. Acad. Pediatrics; licentiate Am. Bd. Pediatrics; mem. Lycoming Co. Med. Soc. (pres. 1938-39), Pa. Med. Soc. (chmn. and sec. sect. of pediatrics, 1930-32). Mem. Reformed Church. Home: 362 Market St. South. Office: 25 W. Third St., Williamsport, Pa.

LOHR, William Shannon, prof. civil engring.; b. Centre Hall, Pa., Oct. 29, 1887; s. James Hale and Annie Jane (Welsh) L.; ed. Central Manual Training Sch., Phila., 1902-05; B.S. in C.E., U. of Pa., 1909, C.E., same, 1924; m. Frances Hubbard, Dec. 27, 1911; children— Dorothy Hubbard (Mrs. Robert H. Woolston), Audrey Frances. Instr. civil engring., U. of Pa., 1909-12, 1915-16, Lafayette Coll., 1912-15; employed with engring. cos., 1916-20; asso. prof. civil engring., Lafayette Coll., 1920-30, prof. since 1930; engr. bridge div., Me. State Highway Commn., Augusta, Me., summers 1926, 1928-29, 1931; also cons. engr.; registered professional engr. in Pa. Mem. Am. Soc. Civil Engrs., Am. Soc. for Testing Materials, Soc. for Promotion Engring. Edn., Am. Soc. for Metals, Am. Assn. Univ. Prof., Nat. Soc. Prof. Engring., Pa. Soc. Prof. Engring., Sigma Xi, Tau Beta Pi. Republican. Presbyn. Club: Faculty of Lafayette Coll. (past pres.). Contbr. to engring. mags. Home: 624 Parsons St., Easton, Pa.

LOIZEAUX, Charles E., lumber mcht., banking; b. Vinton, Ia., Jan. 22, 1889; s. Joshua D. and Catherine L. (Geddes) L.; ed. pub. sch. and high sch., Plainfield, N.J.; m. Berta, dau. Col. S. Rolfe Millar, of Front Royal, Va., Nov. 16, 1921; children—Charles E., Jr., Elaine Millar. Asso. with J. D. Loizeaux Lumber Co., Plainfield, N.J., continuously since entering emply as clk., 1908, now pres.; pres. Loizeaux Builders Supply Co., Elizabeth, N.J.; pres. Mid City Trust Co., Plainfield, N.J. Served as pvt. inf. to capt. machine gun batl., U.S.A., 1917-19, with A.E.F. in France; awarded citation from Gen. Pershing for meritorious services; awarded service medal by State of N.J. Served in Plainfield Common Council, 1916-17; mayor of Plainfield two terms. Served as mem. N.J. Senate, 1932-38, and for term, 1938-41; actg. gov. N.J. during absence of Gov. A. Harry Moore. Mem. Vets. Fgn. Wars, Am. Legion, Chamber of Commerce. Republican. Baptist. Mason, B.P.O.E., Jr. O.U.A.M. Club: Country (Plainfield). Home: 955 Belvidere Av. Office: 861 South Av., Plainfield, N.J.

LOMAN, Harry James, univ. prof.; b. North Wales, Pa., Mar. 19, 1896; s. Augustus Homer and Estella (Christman) L.; B.S. in Econ., U. of Pa., 1918, M.A., 1921, Ph.D., 1923; m. Blanche Bernd, July 1, 1918; children—Janet Marie, James Gilbert. Expert in ins. U.S. Bur. of War Risk Ins., Washington, D.C., 1919; instr. in ins., U. of Pa., 1919-21, asst. prof., 1921-26, prof. since 1926, vice dean, Wharton Sch., 1933-39, asso. dean since 1939, dir., grad. course in business administrn., since 1938; holds various ins. consultant positions. Served in U.S. Navy, 1918-19. Mem. Am. Assn. Univ. Teachers of Ins. (pres. 1936-38), Am. Econ. Assn., Am. Assn. Univ. Profs., Lambda Chi Alpha, Beta Gamma Sigma. Mem. Reformed Ch. Mason. Author: Insurance of Foreign Credits, 1923; Taxation in Its Relation to Life Insurance, 1927; co-author (with Robert Riegel): Insurance Principals and Practices, 1921; various articles on ins. Home: 1209 Drexel Av., Drexel Hill. Office: 36th St. and Woodland Av., Philadelphia, Pa.

LOMAX, Paul Sanford, prof. education; b. Laclede, Mo., May 3, 1890; s. James Wesley and Alsina Arabella (Artlip) L.; B.S., U. of Mo., 1916; student U. of Dijon (France), 1919, Harvard, summers 1922, 23; Ph.D., New York U., 1927; m. Emily Bertha Tschann, Dec. 25, 1919 (died June 16, 1928); 1 dau., Lucille Bertha; m. 2d, Beatrice Marie Loyer, of New Washington, Ohio, August 15, 1929; children— Jeanne Marie, Donald Loyer. Was teacher in the public schools of Mo., 1908-13, Univ. of Mo. High Sch., 1914-16; prof. commerce N.M. Normal U., 1916-18; specialist commercial edn. Fed. Bd. Vocational Edn., 1919-20, N.Y. State Dept. Edn., 1920-21; dir. business edn. pub. schs., Trenton, N.J., 1921-24; prof. edn., New York U. since 1924. Served as ord. sergt., Ordnance Dept., U.S.A., World War. Mem. N.E.A. (ex-pres. business edn. dept.), Nat. Assn. Commercial Teacher Training Instns. (expres.), Nat. Commercial Teachers' Fed., Nat. Soc. College Teachers of Edn., Eastern Commercial Teachers Assn. (ex-pres.), National Council of Business Education (ex-pres.), for Curriculum Study, Am. Assn. of Sch. Administrators, Guidance and Personnel Assn. of N.J., Am. Acad. of Polit. and Social Science, N.Y. Acad. of Public Education, American Legion, Delta Pi Epsilon, Phi Delta Kappa. Republican. Presbyterian. Mason. Author: Commercial Teaching Problems, 1928; Problems of Teaching Elementary Business Training (with B. R. Haynes), 1929; Problems of Teaching bookkeeping (with P. L. Agnew), 1930; Problems of Teaching Shorthand (with J. V. Walsh), 1930; Problems of Teaching Economics (with H. A. Tonne), 1932; Problems of Teaching Arithmetic (with J. J. W. Neuner), 1932; Teaching Principles and Procedures for Gregg Shorthand (with E. C. Skene and J. V. Walsh), 1932; Problems of Teaching Typewriting (with H. Reynolds and M. H. Ely) 1935. Editor yearbooks of Eastern Commercial Teachers Assn., 1928, 29, 30, Journal of Business Education, 1929-38; mem. editorial council, Journal of Educational Sociology. Home: 21 Beach Pl., Maplewood, N.J.

LONDON, William, physician; b. Newark, N.J., Dec. 27, 1896; s. Solomon Bernard and Bertha (Featherman) L.; ed. N.Y. Univ., 1913-14; M.D., N.Y. Univ. & Bellevue Hosp. Med. Coll., 1918; m. Lillian Mann, July 17, 1924; children—Barbara, Nancy, Thomas. Interne Gouverneur Hosp., N.Y. City, 1918; res. phys. pediatric service, N.Y. Nursery & Childs Hosp., 1919, attdg. pediatrician, out-patient dept., same, 1920-27; engaged in practice of medicine limited to diseases of infants and children in Perth Amboy, N.J. since 1920; sr. attdg. pediatrician, Perth Amboy Gen. Hosp. since 1924. Served as 1st lt. Med. Res. Corps, U.S.A., 1918-20. Med. dir. Middlesex Co. Camp for Undernourished Children. Fellow Am. Acad. Pediatrics, A.M.A. Licentiate Am. Bd. Pediatrics. Mem. N.J. Med. Soc., Middlesex Co. Med. Soc., Zeta Beta Tau. Jewish religion. Home: 173 Kearney Av. Office: 255 State St., Perth Amboy, N.J.

LONG, Breckinridge, lawyer; b. St. Louis, Mo., May 16, 1881; s. William Strudwick and Margaret M. (Breckinridge) L.; A.B., Princeton, 1904, A.M., 1909; student St. Louis Law Sch. (Washington U.), 1905-06; hon. LL.M., Washington U., 1920; m. Christine Alexander Graham, June 1, 1912; 1 dau., Christine Blair. Admitted to Mo. bar, 1906; began practice in St. Louis, 1907; 3d asst. sec. of state, by appmt. of President Wilson, Jan. 22, 1917- June 7, 1920; Dem. nominee for U.S. Senate from Mo., 1920; del. Dem. Nat. Conv. 1928 (mem. com. on platform resolutions); then practicing internat. law. A.E.&P. to Italy, 1933-36; ambassador on special mission to Brazil, Argentina and Uruguay, 1938; Am. commr. U.S. and Italy. Treaty for Advancement of Peace since 1939. Trustee Princeton U., 1937-41. Mem. Commn. on Revision of Judicial Procedure, Mo., 1914. Presbyterian. Clubs: Metropolitan, Chevy Chase (Washington, D.C.); Author: Genesis of the Constitution of the United States, 1925. Home: Montpelier Manor, Laurel, Md. Office: 726 Jackson Place N.W., Washington, D.C.

LONG, C. W.; mem. law firm Long & Robins. Address: Salisbury, Md.

LONG, Charles Ramsay, editor and publisher; b. Pittsfield, Ill., Nov. 4, 1872; s. Jesse Green and Caroline Farwell (Ramsay) L.; grad. high sch. Pittsfield, Ill., 1890; m. Gertrude H. Jones, Sept. 8, 1925. Began as office asst. and solicitor of advertising, 1892; bus. mgr., later mem. firm., and pres. and treas. Chester Times, newspaper also commercial job printing, since 1926; dir. Chester-Cambridge Bank and Trust Co. Active in Liberty Loan drives during World War. Vice-pres. and dir. Delaware Co. Chamber of Commerce; chmn. Del. Co. Com. of Pa. Economy League. Dir. J. Lewis Crozer Library. Mem. Pa. Newspaper Pub. Assn. (past pres.), Colonial Soc. of Pa., Delaware Co. Hist. Soc. Republican. Conglist. Mason. Rotarian. Clubs: Chester, Springhaven, Keystone Automobile (Chester); Union League (Philadelphia); National Press Club (Washington, D.C.) Address: 18 E. 8th St., Chester, Pa.

LONG, Clarence Edward, consulting engr.; b. Bendersville, Pa., Mar. 24, 1888; s. Daniel Abraham and Mary Elizabeth (Shenk) L.; B.S. in civil engring., Bucknell U., Lewisburg, Pa., 1908; special work Purdue U., LaFayette, Ind., 1908-09; draftsman Jones & Laughlin Steel Co., Pittsburgh, 1909-11; office engr. Carnegie Steel Co., Munhall, Pa., 1911-13; part time instr., Carnegie Inst. Tech., Pittsburgh, 1910-14; private practice of engring. since 1913, consultant in design and construction of industrial and municipal works; expert testimony in litigation; regional surveys for development of industry and transportation. Mem. Am. Soc. Civil Engrs. Republican. Presbyterian. Mason (32°, Shriner). Home: 249 Maple Av., Edgewood, Pittsburgh, Pa. Address: Box 1922, Pittsburgh, Pa.

LONG, Daniel Edward, pres. Chambersburg Ice & Cold Storage Co.; b. Fayetteville, Pa., Mar. 15, 1872; s. Daniel M. and Annie E. (Wingert) L.; student Cumberland Valley State Normal Sch., Shippensburg, Pa., 1889-91, Dickinson Sch. of Law, Carlisle, Pa., 1897-99; m. Mary Ellen Crawford, 1904. Vice-prin. Bel Air (Md.) Acad., 1894-97; pres. Chambersburg Ice & Cold Storage Co. since 1935, Pub. Opinion Co., newspaper publishers, Chambersburg, Pa. since 1912; dir. Chambersburg Trust Co. Dist. atty., Franklin Co., Pa., 1904-11; Rep. nat. elector, 1912; mem. cabinet of Gov. Brumbaugh of Pa., 1916-18, of Gov. Sproul, 1919; mem. Pa. State Senate, 1920-24; del. to Rep. Nat. Conv., 1932. Trustee Eastern Penitentiary of Pa., 1926-31. Mem. Am., Pa. and Franklin Co. bar assns., Pa. Cold Storage Warehousemen, Chambersburg and U.S. chambers of commerce, Am. Red Cross, Tuberculosis Soc., Delta Chi. Republican. United Lutheran (mem. Laymen's Movement for Stewardship). Mason, K.P. Club: Rotary (Chambersburg, Pa.). Home: Fayetteville, Pa. Office: Chambersburg Trust Bldg., Chambersburg, Pa.

LONG, Edgar Fauver, univ. prof.; b. Bridgewater, Va., Oct. 26, 1886; s. Caleb and Fannie Catherine (Mullendore) L.; A.B., Blue Ridge Coll., New Windsor, Md., 1911; student U. of Pa., 1911-12; A.M., U. of Kan., Lawrence, 1914; Ph.D., Johns Hopkins U., 1932; m. Edith M. Cressman, June 11, 1913. Employed as prin. elementary sch., 1907-08; prof. English, McPherson Coll., McPherson, Kan., 1912-16; head dept. English, high sch., Wilmington, Del., 1916-17; prin. high sch., Boonsboro, Md., 1918-25; instr. edn., U. of Md., College Park, Md., 1925-26, asst. prof. edn., 1926-33, asso. prof., 1933-35, prof. edn. since 1935. Mem. Am. Assn. Univ. Profs. (local pres. 1933-34), N.E.A., Assn. Coll. Teachers of Edn., Alpha Gamma Rho, Phi Kappa Phi, Phi Beta Kappa. Republican. Mason. Home: College Heights, Hyattsville, Md.

LONG, Esmond Ray, pathologist; b. Chicago, Ill., June 16, 1890; s. John Harper and Catherine Belle (Stoneman) L.; A.B., U. of Chicago, 1911, Ph.D., 1919; M.D., Rush Medical College (Univ. of Chicago), 1926; post-graduate studies German University of Prague; m. Marian Boak Adams, June 17, 1922; children—Judith Baird, Esmond Ray. Asst. in pathology, U. of Chicago, 1911-13; asst. desert laboratory of Carnegie Instn. of Washington, at Tuscon, Ariz., 1914-15; Trudeau fellow, Saranac Lab., Saranac Lake, N.Y., 1918, 20; instr. pathology, 1919-21, asst. prof., 1921-23, asso. prof., 1923-28, prof., 1928-32, U. of Chicago; prof. pathology, U. of Pa., since 1932; also dir. lab., Henry Phipps Inst., for Study, Treatment and Prevention of Tuberculosis, 1932-35, and dir. of the Inst. since 1935; spl. consultant on tuberculosis, U.S. Office of Indian Affairs, since 1935; mem. Nat. advisory health council, U.S. Pub. Health Service. Mem. Nat. Research Council (chmn. Div. of Med Sciences 1936-39), Nat. Tuberculosis Assn. (dir.; pres. 1936-37), A.A.A.S. (v.p. and chmn. Section on Med. Sciences 1936-37; mem. exec. com. since 1938, A.M.A., Assn. Am. Physicians, Am. Assn. Pathologists and Bacteriologists (pres. 1936-37), Am. Public Health Assn., Am. Assn. for History of Medicine, Soc. Biol. Chemists, Am. Soc. Exptl. Pathology, Soc. Exptl. Biology and Medicine, College of Physicians, Philadelphia, Pathol. Soc. of Philadelphia (pres. 1936-38) Author: The Chemistry of Tuberculosis, 1923, 2d edit., 1932; Tuberculosis—Its Cause and Prevention, 1925; A History of Pathology, 1928. Compiler: Selected Readings in Pathology, 1929. Contbr. to med. jours., especially on tuberculosis. Address: Henry Phipps Institute, Philadelphia, Pa.

LONG, John Cuthbert, author; b. Babylon, L.I., N.Y., Aug. 22, 1892; s. Rev. Dr. John Dietrich and Elizabeth Trott (Audoun) L.; A.B., Amherst Coll., 1914; unmarried. On editorial staff Springfield (Mass.) Union, 1915-17, Automotive Industries, 1917-18, also spl. corr. for various papers including Christian Science Monitor and Boston Evening Transcript; mgr. ednl. dept. Nat. Automobile Chamber of Commerce, 1920-30; mgr. of publs. Bethlehem Steel Co. since 1930; editorial staff The New Yorker, 1927-30; contbg. editor N.Y. American, 1928-30. Served as dir. War Camp Community Service, 1918-20. Mem. Nat. Conf. on Street and Highway Safety, 1925, 1926 and 1927. Mem. Am. Hist. Assn., Pa. Hist. Assn., Theta Delta Chi, Delta Sigma Rho. Presbyn. Clubs: Saucon Valley Country (Bethlehem, Pa.); National Arts, Amherst, (New York). Author: Public Relations, 1924; Bryan, The Great Commoner, 1928; Lord Jeffery Amherst—A Soldier of the King, 1933; Mr. Pitt, the Earl of Chatham, 1940. Contbr. articles and reviews to leading mags. Home: Kenridge Farms. Office: Bethlehem Steel Co., Bethlehem, Pa.

LONG, John Robinson, retired paper mfr.; b. Cambridge, Ill., May 6, 1864; s. William Munro and Amanda (Andre) L.; ed. Livermore (Pa.) Pub. Schs., Livermore (Pa.) Acad. and pvt. schs. and tutors, Pittsburgh, Pa.; m. Mary A. Myers, 1884 (died 1903); children—Vern Edward, Walter John, Myrtle, May (Mrs. James E. Knox); m. 2d, Janet Deemar Long, 1909. Began in stock dept., Tarentum (Pa.) Paper Mills, 1884, foreman, 1886, supt., 1888-1911, gen. mgr., 1911-27; retired, 1927; dir. and v.p. Peoples Nat. Bank of Tarentum (Pa.). Prospect Cemetery Assn., Tarentum, Pa. Former pres. Tarentum Council, Tarentum Sch. Bd. Dir. Allegheny Valley Hosp. Republican. Methodist. Mason. Invented and patented insulating paper for high voltage cables. Home: Kittanning, Pa. Office: Peoples Nat. Bank, Tarentum, Pa.

LONG, John William, educator; b. Sussex Co., Del., Nov. 3, 1882; s. Richard Wilson and Jane (Adkins) L.; prep. edn., Wilmington Conf. Acad. (now Wesley Collegiate Inst.), Dover, Del.; A.B., Dickinson Coll., Carlisle, Pa., 1907, D.D., 1922; student Drew Theol. Sem., Madison, N.J.; m. Mildred Lee Lewis, Oct. 1, 1907; children—Gladys Elizabeth (Mrs. Earl Zimmerman McKay), Olive Mildred, Dorothy Frances, John William, George Richard, Jean Frazier, Henry Lewis. Ordained ministry M.E. Ch., 1907; pastor successively at Littlestown, Dillsburg, Clearfield and State College (all in Pa.), until 1921; pres. Williamsport Dickinson Sem., since 1921. Pres. Edn. Assn. of M.E. Ch.; statis. sec. Central Pa. Conf. M.E. Ch. 4 yrs.; delegate Methodist Ecumenical Conference, 1931. Organizer, dir. until 1921, Wesley Foundation of Pa. State Coll. Mem. Edn. Assn. Middle States and Md., Sigma Alpha Epsilon. Republican. Mason (32°), Rotarian. Address: Williamsport Dickinson Seminary, Williamsport, Pa.

LONG, Joseph Harvey, newspaper pub.; b. nr. Jonestown, Pa., May 21, 1863; s. Edward Christian and Sarah (Roebuck) L.; student pub. schs. and high sch., Pittsburgh, Pa.; hon. LL.D., Marshall Coll., 1936; m. Cora Hildreth Thompson, June 12, 1884; children—Luther Thompson, Virginia (dec.), Paul Walker, Edward Harvey. In employ Wheeling Sunday Leader, 1881-82, Erie Dispatch, 1882-84, Oswego (N.Y.) Palladium, 1884-86, Wheeling (W.Va.) Register, 1886-90; joined in orgn. Wheeling Evening News, 1890, sold interest, 1893, purchased Huntington (W.Va.) Herald, 1893, sold Herald, 1895 and purchased the Advertiser, Huntington, W.Va.; acquired Huntington Herald Dispatch with three sons and Mr. Gidean, and chmn. bd. Huntington Publishing Co. since 1927; dir. First Huntington Nat. Bank, Huntington Ohio Bridge Co., Ohio Valley Bus Co. Served as postmaster Huntington, W.Va., 1916-21. Col. on staff of gov.; mem. Governor's Tax Com., 1925. One of four state dels. to Dem. Nat. Conv., Chicago, Ill., 1932. Pres. Huntington Chamber of Commerce. Democrat, Conglist. Mason (K.T.). Clubs: Guyan Country, Gypsy (Huntington). Home: Park Hills. Office: Cor. 5th Av. and 10th St., Huntington, W.Va.

LONG, Mason, prof. English; b. Bellegrove, Pa., Sept. 30, 1892; s. David Ensminger and Clara Zellers (Miller) L.; A.B., Lebanon Valley Coll., 1916; A.M., Pa. State Coll., 1923; grad. study, Yale U., 1927-29, Cornell U., 1932; m. Esther Katherine Moyer, June 10, 1919. Asso. sec. of Y.M.C.A., Danville, Va., 1916-17; instr. English, Mercersburg (Pa.) Acad., 1917-19; vice-prin. Troy Conf. Acad., Poultney, Vt., 1919-20; instr. English, Pa. State Coll., 1920-23, asst. prof 1923-28, asso. prof. English lit., 1928-36, prof. since 1936. Mem. Phi Kappa Phi. Republican. Presbyn. Author: Handbook of English Grammar, 1925; A College Grammar, 1928; Poetry and Its Forms, 1935; The New College Grammar, 1935; The Bible and English Literature, 1935. Contbr. to mags. Home: 255 W. Park Av. Office: Liberal Arts Bldg., State College, Pa.

LONG, Newell Blaine, banker; b. Burnside, Pa., Oct. 4, 1891; s. Charles C. and Sarah Catherine L.; student Indiana State Normal, 1907-09; m. Helen Levengood, Feb. 22, 1919; children—Joan, Betty Lorraine. Began as bank clerk, 1912; pres. and dir. First Nat. Bank, Bellefonte, Pa. Republican. Presbyterian. Mason. Club: Nittany Country (Bellefonte). Home: W. Lion St. Office: First Nat. Bank, Bellefonte, Pa.

LONG, Perrin Hamilton, physician; b. Bryan, O., April 7, 1899; s. James Wilkinson and Wilhelmina Lillian (Kautsky) L.; B.S., U. of Mich., 1920; M.D., U. of Mich. Med. Sch., 1924; m. Elizabeth D. Griswold, Sept. 6, 1922; children—Perrin Hamilton, Jr., Priscilla Griswold. Resident physician, Thorndike Memorial Lab., Boston City Hosp., Boston, Mass., 1924-25, interne fourth med. service, 1925-27; vol. asst., Hygienic Inst., Frieburg, Germany, 1927; asst. and asso., Rockefeller Inst. for Med. Research, 1927-29; asso. in medicine, Johns Hopkins U. Med. Sch., 1929-37, asso. prof. since 1937; lecturer in epidemiology, Johns Hopkins U. Sch. Hygiene and Pub. Health since 1936; asst. and asso. physician, John Hopkins Hosp. since 1929. Served as driver, Am. Field Service, 1917; pvt. A.S., U.S.A., 1917-19, with A.E.F. Awarded Croix de Guerre (France), 1918. Gov. Nat. Farm Chemurgic Council since 1937. Mem. Am. Soc. for Clin. Investigation, Harvey Soc., Soc. of Am. Bacteriologists, Zeta Psi, Alpha Omega Alpha, Sigma Xi. Presbyterian. Clubs: 14 W. Hamilton St., Johns Hopkins University (Baltimore). Contbr. many med. articles to jours. Home: 307 Thornhill Rd. Office: Johns Hopkins Hospital, Baltimore, Md.

LONG, Theodore Kepner, lawyer; b. Millerstown, Pa., Apr. 26, 1856; s. Abraham and Catharine (Kepner) L.; ed. Millerstown (Pa.) High Sch., and State Normal Sch., Millersville; New Bloomfield (Pa.) Classical Acad.; spl. studies at Yale; LL.B., Yale Law Sch., 1878; m. Kate Carson, Nov. 25, 1885. Editor Mandan (N.D.) Daily Pioneer, 1882; compiled Long's Legislative Hand Book for Dakota, 1883; began practice of law, 1884; state's atty. for dist. west of the Mo. River, Dak. Ter., 1885; atty. N.P. R.R., Bismarck, Dak. Ter., 1887; settled in Chicago, 1894. Legal adviser in formation of Ill. Life Ins. Co., 1899, and gen. counsel same, 1899-1907; assisted in organizing Western Trust & Savings Bank, 1903, and gen. counsel same, 1903-07; retired from active practice, 1908. Founded, 1914, and since pres. Carson Long Inst. (prep. and vocational instrn.), New Bloomfield, Pa. Alderman 6th Ward, Chicago, 1909-15. Mem. Chicago Bar Assn. Republican. Episcopalian. Mason, K.T., Shriner. Clubs: Union League, South Shore Country (Chicago). Home: "The Maples," New Bloomfield, Pa.; (winter) 130 4th Av. N., St. Petersburg, Fla.

LONG, Urah Willis, lumberman; b. Selbyville, Del., Sept. 2, 1887; s. Isaiah Willis and Joanna May (Williams) L.; student Selbyville (Del.) High Sch., 1893-1903, Wilmington Conf. Acad., 1903-04; B.S., U. of Md., 1908; m. Ethel May Melson, June 29, 1911; 1 dau., Virginia Mae. Began as mcht., Selbyville, Del., 1908; in wholesale and retail lumber business since 1914; with I. W. Long & Son, Selbyville, Del., since 1919, mgr. and partner since 1919. Methodist. Mason (Past Master, Del. Consistory. Address: Selbyville, Del.

LONG, William Franklin, educator; b. Boyertown, Pa., Apr. 18, 1871; s. Franklin Diener and Anna Maria (Wanner) L.; B.E., Keystone State Normal Sch., 1891; A.B., Franklin & Marshall Coll., 1897; studied (summers) U. of Chicago, U. of Pittsburgh, Cornell U., Harvard U. and U. of Pa.; m. Cora Anna Swope, June 14, 1900; children—Catherine Maria (Mrs. Edward E. Helm), Carl Franklin, Elizabeth Anne. Teacher ungraded schs., Longswamp, Pa., 1887-90, graded schs., Weatherly, Pa., 1891-93, Keystone State Normal Sch., 1894-97; prin. Johnstown High Sch., 1897-1908; teacher Pittsburgh High Schs. (Central and Schenley), 1908-18; with depts. of mathematics and astronomy, Franklin & Marshall Coll., since 1918, head of dept. since 1925. Mem. Am. Math. Assn. Democrat. Mem. Reformed Ch. Mason. Home: 612 Race Av., Lancaster, Pa.

LONGACRE, David Fenstermacher, clergyman; b. Weissport, Pa., May 7, 1897; s. Rev. Jacob Hoppes and Irene Deborah (Fenstermacher) L.; A.B., Muhlenberg Coll., 1918; B.D., Luth. Theol. Sem., 1923, S.T.M., same, 1927; m. Clara B. Andrews, June 17, 1922; children—Jacob Andrews, David Wilson. Ordained to ministry Luth. Ch., 1922; pastor Christ Luth. Ch., Stouchsburg, Pa., Altalaha-Rebersberg, Elias-Newmanstown, 1922-26; pastor St. John's Luth. Ch., Boyertown, Pa., since 1926; pres. Reading Conf. of Evang. Luth. Ministerium of Pa. and adjacent states, 1932-37. Served in Med. Corps, U.S.A. during World War. Chaplain Am. Legion post, Boyertown, Pa. Trustee Topton Orphans Home, 1922-39. Mem. Luth. Pastoral Assn. of Reading (past pres.). Republican. Lutheran. Club: Rotary of Boyertown (past pres.). Home: 115 N. Reading Av., Boyertown, Pa.

LONGAKER, John H., lawyer; b. Pottstown, Pa., Jan. 29, 1902; s. Anson D. and Cora E. (Nagle) L.; grad. Keystone Acad., Factoryville, Pa., 1919; A.B., Lafayette Coll., Easton, Pa., 1923; LL.B., Temple U. Law Sch., Phila., Pa., 1929; m. Harriett M. Wentz, Oct. 24, 1923; children—Adeline M, John H., Barbara Ann. Admitted to Montgomery Co., Pa., bar, 1930, to practice before Pa. Supreme Ct., 1930, Dist.

Ct. of U.S. for Eastern Dist. of Pa., 1931; mem. Pa. Ho. of Reps., 1934-38; dir. Pottstown (Pa.) Savings & Loan Assn.; solicitor, Borough of Pottstown (Pa.) since 1936. Dir. Pottstown (Pa.) Y.M.C.A.; mem. Pottstown Historical Soc. (dir.), Sigma Chi. Republican. Baptist (supt. Sunday Sch.). Mason, Odd Fellow. Clubs: Lions (Pottstown, Pa.); Lafayette Coll. of Montgomery Co. (Norristown, Pa.). Author speeches pub. in Legislative Jour. of Gen. Assembly, 1935-38, and on industrial taxation, teachers tenure, motor police. Winner George Wharton Pepper Prize and pres. Class of '23, Lafayette Coll. Home: 500 N. Franklin St. Office: 310 Security Trust Bldg., Pottstown, Pa.

LONGCOPE, Warfield Theobald, M.D.; b. Baltimore, Mar. 29, 1877; s. George von S. and Ruth (Theobald) L.; A.B., Johns Hopkins, 1897; M.D., Johns Hopkins Med. Sch., 1901; m. Janet Percy Dana, Dec. 2, 1915; children—Barbara, Duncan, Mary Lee, Christopher. Resident pathologist of Pennsylvania Hospital, Philadelphia, 1901-04; director Ayer Clinical Laboratory, same, 1904-11; asst. prof. applied medicine, U. of Pa., 1909-11; asso. prof. practice of medicine, 1911-14, Bard prof., 1914-21, Columbia; asso. visiting phys., 1911-14, dir. med. service Presbyn. Hosp., New York, 1914-21; prof. medicine Johns Hopkins Med. Sch. and phys. in chief Johns Hopkins Hosp., 1922—. Commd. maj., Med. O.R.C., 1917; on active duty med. div., Office of Surgeon Gen. U.S.A., Washington, Aug. 1917-July 1918; col., Medical Corps, U.S.A., A.E.F., July 1918-Jan. 1919. Member Association of Am. Physicians, A.M.A., Soc. Exptl. Biology and Medicine, Am. Soc. for Advancement Clin. Investigation, Am. Soc. Exptl. Pathology, A.A.A.S., N.Y. Acad. Medicine, N.Y. Clin. Soc., Am. Soc. Pharmacology and Exptl. Therapeutics, Am. Assn. Pathologists and Bacteriologists, Am. Assn. Immunologists, Harvey Soc., Medico Chirurg. Faculty of Md., Baltimore City Med. Soc.; fellow Am. Coll. Phys., Am. Acad. Arts and Sciences. Extensive investigations in clin. medicine and in pathology. Home: 3 St. Martin's Rd., Guilford, Baltimore, Md.

LONGENDYKE, William Frederick, pharmacist; b. Bridgeville, Del., Jan. 4, 1884; s. Benjamin Franklin and Margaret (Kleber) L.; Ph.G., Medico Chirurg. Coll., Phila., Pa., 1909; m. Anna McMurray, Oct. 8, 1917; children—William Harlan (dec.), Betty M. Served as apprentice in drug store, Phila., Pa., 1905-07; drug store, U. Gilbert Ruff, Phila., 1905-07; sr. pharmacist, Richard H. Lackey, Phila., 1910-12; pharmacist and mgr. Dr. W. F. Haines & Co. drug store, Seaford, Del., 1912-25, mem. firm since 1925, sr. mem. firm and mgr. since 1925. Served as pres. Seaford bd. edn., 1936-38. Pres. Seaford Chamber of Commerce since 1939; pres. Seaford Merchants Assn., 1936-38. Dep. collector of port Seaford, Del., 1927-29. Pres. Hobbs & Longendyke Minstrels, charitable orgn., since 1915. Trustee Del. State Hosp. Mem. Del. State Pharm. Soc. Republican. Presbyterian. Mason. Clubs: Kiwanis, The Izaak Walton (Seaford). Home: Arch St. Office: High St., Seaford, Del.

LONGSDORF, Harold Hamilton, physician; b. Belvue, Neb., July 28, 1858; s. William Henry and Lydia Rebecca (Haverstick) L.; student Centreville Acad., Dickinson, Pa., 1865-73, Newville (Pa.) Acad., 1873-75; A.B. and A.M., Dickinson Coll., 1879; M.D., Coll. of Physicians & Surgeons, Baltimore, Md., 1882; m. Anna Eleanor Ernst, Feb. 18, 1885; children—Harold Ernst (M.D.), Helen (Mrs. John Theodore Mohler). Teacher in public schools, 1879-80; gen. practice of medicine over a territory with a 20-mile radius from Dickinson since 1882; mem. med. staff Carlisle Hosp.; school examiner, 4 yrs.; coroner's physician and acting coroner, 12 yrs.; Cumberland Co. jail physician since 1936; dir. Farmers Trust Co., Carlisle, since 1908; pres. Centreville Cemetery Assn. since 1897. Served as school dir. 12 yrs.; pioneer in advocating consolidated schools, writing a bulletin for State Dept. Pub. Instruction on that subject, 1902; former pres. Cumberland Co. Sch. Dirs. Assn. Served on Final Exemption Draft Bd., Harrisburg, during World War. Mem. Cumberland Co. Med. Soc. (pres. 1906 and 1937), Pa. State Med. Soc., Am. Med. Soc., Am. Acad. Medicine, Alumni Assn. Coll. Physicians and Surgeons (pres. 1896), Sons of Vets., Chi Chi. Democrat. Mem. United Presbyn. Ch., Newville (elder). Clubs: Old Town Mountain (Carlisle); Elks. Home: Dickinson, Pa.

LONGSTRETH, Walter Cook, lawyer; b. Phila., Pa., Feb. 13, 1881; s. Samuel Noble and Mary Hance (Cook) L.; A.B., Amherst Coll., 1901; LL.B., U. of Pa. Law Sch., 1904; m. Emily Corson Poley, June 15, 1926. Admitted to Pa. bar, 1904, and since engaged in gen. practice of law, individually, at Phila.; mem. of Phila. Com. on Public Affairs (treas., 1936-38). Mem. of delegation of eight sent by Am. Com. for Relief in Ireland to investigate conditions in Ireland, 1921. Mem. Nat. Lawyers Guild, Phila. Bar Assn., Sharswood Law Club, Phi Kappa Psi. Mem. Bd. of Sch. Visitors of 22nd Ward, Phila., 1916-20; pres. of Bd. in 1920; chmn. of Phila. Peace Council, 1927-28. Socialist. Mem. Religious Soc. Friends. Author of pamphlet: Regarding Military Training at Universities, 1925. Home: 33 E. Upsal St. Office: 1218 Chestnut St., Philadelphia, Pa.

LONN, Ella, coll. prof.; b. La Porte, Ind., Nov. 21, 1879; d. John and Nellie (Pambla) L.; A.B., U. of Chicago, 1900; A.M., U. of Pa., 1910, Ph.D., 1911; grad. student, U. of Berlin, Germany, 2 seminars, 1913, Sorbonne, Paris, France, 1913-14. Employed as teacher in secondary schs., 1902-08; instr., asst. prof., history and German, Grinnell (Ia.) Coll., 1914-18; asst. prof. of history, Goucher Coll., Baltimore, 1918-19, asso. prof., 1919-23, prof. of history since 1923. Mem. Am. Hist. Assn., Am. Assn. Univ. Profs. (chmn. membership com.), Middle States Assn. of History and Social Sci. Teachers (pres., 1936-37), Phi Beta Kappa. Republican. Clubs: Women's Civic League College Club, League of Women Voters. Author: Reconstruction in Louisiana, 1918; Government of Maryland, 1922; Desertion During the Civil War (pub. by Am. Hist. Assn.), 1928; Salt as a Factor in the Confederacy, 1933; Foreigners in the Confederacy, 1939. Contbr. articles to hist. publs. Lecturer. Home: 2435 N. Charles St., Baltimore, Md.

LOOK, Arnold Evert, college pres.; b. Bath, N.Y., Oct. 6, 1896; s. Newman Simmons and Lydia Ella (Shults) L.; B.Th., Southern Theol. Sem., 1917; A.B., McMaster U., 1919; B.D., Crozer Theol. Sem., 1920; A.M., U. of Pa., 1920; Th.M., Crozer Theol. Sem., 1922; Ph.D., Yale, 1927; fellow Dropsie Coll., 1921-22; m. Lillian Mildred Lupton, May 7, 1920; children—Arnold Evert, Jr., Donald Lupton, Lillian Emma. Ordained to ministry Baptist Ch., 1917; various student pastorates, 1917-23; pastor, Upland Baptist Church, 1923-25; pastor Shelton Conglist. Ch., 1925-27, grad. student, and instr. Yale Theol. Sem., 1925-27; prof. Internat. Y.M.C.A. Coll., 1927-31; pres. Ellis Coll., Newtown Square, Pa., since 1931; mem. exec. com. Pa. State Y.M.C.A. Mem. Soc. Bib. Lit. and Exegesis, Nat. Assn. Bib. Insts., World, Nat., and Pa. State edn. asns., Progressive Edn. Assn., Middle States Assn. Nat. and Pa. councils for social work, Phila. Headmasters Assn. Republican. Conglist. Club: Rotary (Media, Pa.). Home: Newtown Square, Pa.

LOOMIS, Nathaniel Edward, oil refining exec.; b. Grand Rapids, Wis., Mar. 16, 1888; s. Alba Levi Parsons and Frances Sarah (Peck) L.; grad. Windsor (Wis.) High Sch., 1904; B.S., Beloit (Wis.) Coll., 1908; M.S. in Chem., Syracuse (N.Y.) U., 1909; Ph.D. in Chem., Johns Hopkins U., Baltimore, Md., 1911; m. Lucile Didlake, June 8, 1916; 1 son, Arthur Hale. Instr. chemistry, Bowdoin Coll., Brunswick, Me., 1911-12, asst. prof., 1913; instr. phys. chemistry, Purdue U., Lafayette, Ind., 1914, asst. prof., 1915-18; chief chemist Standard Oil Co. of Ind., Wood River, Ill., 1918; chief chemist Standard Oil Co. of N.J., Elizabeth, N.J., 1918, dir. exptl. div., 1919 to 1927, mgr. tech. service div., 1927-33, mgr. tech. service div. and asst. to v.p., 1933-36; v.p. in charge tech. service depts., Standard Oil Development Co., New York, since 1936, dir. since 1936; dir. and v.p. Filtrol Corpn. Home: 748 Boulevard, Westfield, N.J. Office: 26 Broadway, New York, N.Y.

LOOMIS, Ruth, coll. dean.; b. North Manchester, Conn., Aug. 11, 1864; d. Rev. Henry and Frances Elizabeth (Craft) L.; A.B., Vassar, 1885; studied La Sorbonne and École Normale Supérieure, Sèvres, Paris, France, 1892; Litt.D., Colo. Coll., 1917. Instr. English, Vassar, 1886-95; dean of women, Colorado Coll., Colorado Springs, 1896-1917. Mem. League of Nations Assn., Nat. Soc. of Colonial Dames in the State of N.Y., Phi Beta Kappa. Home: 211 Private Way, Lakewood, N.J.

LOOPER, Edward Anderson, M.D., otolaryngologist; b. Silver City, Ga., Dec. 16, 1888; s. John Anderson and Jennie (Stewart) L.; M.D., U. of Md., 1912; Emory U., 1908-10; Ophthal. D., U. of Colo., 1913; m. Lola Patenall, Jan. 15, 1920; children—Edward A., Lola Elise, Sybil Ann. Began practice as specialist in eye, ear, nose and throat, Baltimore, Md., 1913; prof. diseases of nose and throat, U. of Md., since 1921; laryngologist, University Hosp. since 1921, chief of ear, nose and throat service, Baltimore City Hosps., since 1933; mem. bd. of govs. and surgeon, Baltimore Eye, Ear and Throat Hosp., since 1930; mem. exec. com. and mem. staff Woman's Hosp. since 1931; oto-laryngologist Md. State Sanatorium for Tuberculosis since 1922; oto-laryngologist, Eudowood Sanatorium for Tuberculosis since 1920; laryngologist, Md. Gen., St. Agnes, Franklin Square, West Baltimore Gen., and Nurses and Child's Hosps.; mem. staff, Union Memorial and Mercy Hosps.; cons. laryngologist Kernan Hosp. for Crippled Children; bronchoscopist and esophagoscopist, University Hosp. and U.S. Marine Hosp.; cons. oto-laryngologist, Provident Hosp.; oto-laryngologist Baltimore City Hosps. for Tuberculosis, Edward McCready Memorial Hosp., Crisfield, Md.; and Havre de Grace Hosp., Md. Served as 1st lt. Med. Reserve Corps, U.S. Army, 1918; instr. and capt., Ft. Oglethorpe; in France 2 yrs.; maj., Med. Reserve Corps. Fellow Am. College Surgeons (mem. advisory council com. for otolaryngology), A.M.A.; mem. Am. Bronschoscopic Soc. (vice-pres.), Am. Rhinol., Laryngol. and Otol. Soc., Am. Acad. Ophthalmology and Oto-Laryngology, Am. Laryngol. Assn., Internat. Coll. of Surgeons (past state regent) Med. and Chirurg. Faculty of Md., Baltimore City Med. Soc., Southern Med. Soc. (past councillor). Democrat. Baptist. Clubs: Baltimore Country, Gibson Island Country. Author: The Diagnosis and Treatment of Laryngeal Tuberculosis, 1937. Home: 504 Overhill Rd., Roland Park, Baltimore. Office: 104 W. Madison St., Baltimore, Md.

LOOSE, Jacob C., pres. Mauch Chunk Nat. Bank; b. Meyerstown, Pa., July 6, 1866; s. Jacob A. and Emma E. (Spangler) L.; student pvt. schs. and Dickinson Law Sch. (Carlisle, Pa.); m. Alice M. Bear, Nov. 17, 1892; 1 son, Alan S. Admitted to bar and since practiced at Mauch Chunk, Pa.; pres. Mauch Chunk Nat. Bank; dir. Progressive Bldg. & Loan Assn. Home: 306 Centre St., East Mauch Chunk, Pa. Office: 3 Broadway, Mauch Chunk, Pa.

LOOSE, Katharine Riegel, writer; b. Centreport, Pa., June 18, 1877; d. Charles G. (M.D.) and Sarah E. (Riegel) L.; ed. Reading (Pa.) Sem., 1884-93; A.B., Bryn Mawr Coll., 1898; studied also at Convent de l'Assompcion, Paris, and Crainische Schule, Berlin. Republican. Presbyn. Author: Hearts Contending, 1910; House of Yost, 1923. Contbr. short stories to Scribners, Century, and Harpers Mag. Home: 221 S. 5th St., Reading, Pa.

LOPATTO, John S(imon), lawyer; b. Lithuania, Sept. 16, 1882; s. Simon and Ursula (Starkus) L.; came to U.S., 1892, and naturalized citizen, 1903; ed. Wyoming Sem., Kingston, Pa., 1900-04; LL.B., U. of Pa. Law Sch., 1907; m. Mary Skritulsky, June 24, 1913; children—Mary Margaret, Edward Wilson, John, Richard Henry. Admitted to Pa. bar, 1907 and since engaged in gen. practice of law at Wilkes-Barre; served as Borough Solicitor, 1902-12; asst. dist. atty. of Luzerne Co., 1916-20; mem.

Lithuanian-Swedish Conciliation Com., 1927-39. Mem. Lithuanian Delegation at Peace Conf., Versailles, 1919. Dec. with Order of Gedeminas (Lithuania). Democrat. Roman Catholic. Home: 136 Park Av. Office: 703 Miners Bank Bldg., Wilkes-Barre, Pa.

LOPEZ, Aaron M., supt. hospital; b. Charleston, S.C., Aug. 12, 1884; s. Aaron M. and Cordelia (Cohen) L.; ed. Cooper Union Night Sch., New York, N.Y., 1903-05, Poly. Inst. Tech., Brooklyn, evenings, 1905-06, Cornell U., 1910-11; m. Elizabeth Lyons, Jan. 27, 1912; children—Aaron M., Jr., John L., Elizabeth L. In employ N.Y. Telephone Co. and Nat. Bridge Works, 1903-13; asst. gen. sec. Bur. of Charities, Brooklyn, N.Y., 1913-21; gen. sec. Family Service Soc., Erie, Pa., and supt. Erie Gen. Dispensary, 1921-29; steward, Warren State Hosp., Warren, Pa., 1929-37; supt. Warren Gen. Hosp. since 1937. Served as chmn. Vacant Lot Garden Com. of Brooklyn, and exec. sec. Disaster Relief Com. Am. Red Cross, Met. Area of N.Y., during World War. Dir. and v.p. Warren Co. Boy Scouts. Past pres. Pa. State Conf. Social Workers. Mem. Am. Assn. Social Workers, Hosp. Assn. of Pa., Warren Acad. of Sci., Am. Coll. of Hosp. Administrators. Republican. Presbyterian. Home: 16 Fourth Av. Office: 2 Crescent Park West, Warren Pa.

LORD, Charles S., newspaper man; b. Center Co., Pa., Mar. 11, 1882; s. John and Mary Jane (Losh) L.; ed. pub. schs., Reynoldsville, Pa.; unmarried. Began as apprentice in office The Star, weekly newspaper, Reynoldsville, Pa., 1897, became foreman, then, propr. and editor since 1912; vice-pres. and dir. First Nat. Bank. Served as mem. Pa. Ho. Rep., 1933-34. Republican. Mem. M.E. Ch. Elk. Home: 402 Main St. Office: 537 Main St., Reynoldsville, Pa.

LORD, Edward Thomas Sumner, publisher; b. Limington, Me., Nov. 18, 1871; s. William Godding and Mary Shepard (Clark) L.; A.B., Dartmouth, 1891, A.M., 1894; Litt.D., Bates College, Lewiston, Me., 1939; m. Agnes Halladay, Apr. 18, 1905; children—William Shepard, George Alexander, Edward Sumner, Elizabeth Halladay. Instr. English and mathematics, Worcester (Mass.) Acad., 1891-92; N.E. agt. D. C. Heath & Co., pubs., 1892-93; mgr. ednl. dept. Charles Scribner's Sons, 1893-1901; pres. Lothrop Pub. Co., Boston, 1901-02; vice-pres., dir. and mgr. ednl. dept., Charles Scribner's Sons, 1902—; chmn. Glen Ridge Trust Co. Mem. Am. Hist. Assn., N.E.A., Phi Beta Kappa, Delta Kappa Epsilon. Democrat. Conglist. Clubs: Dartmouth College of New York, D.K.E., Glen Ridge Country, Glen Ridge. Home: 78 Lincoln St., Glen Ridge, N.J. Office: 597 Fifth Av., New York, N.Y.

LORD, Edwin Byron, chamber of commerce exec.; b. Stillwater, Me., Dec. 21, 1867; s. Edwin F. and Maria F. (Henderson) L.; A.B., U. of Me., 1888; m. Mabel S. Gilmore, Jan. 28, 1888; children—Hazel M. (dec.), Beulah M. (dec. wife of Benjamin Hubbard), Erma R. (Mrs. Clarence Gunderman), Thelma A., Virginia A. (Mrs. J. A. Taylor), Veryl G., Rosa M. (Mrs. W. P. Farrell). Began as station agt. Me. Central R.R., Stillwater, Me., 1880-88; adv. mgr. Phila. Herald, 1888-90; mng. editor Yankee Blade (founded 1842), Boston, 1890-94; sales mgr. The Wilbur Co., Milwaukee, Wis., 1894-1900; sales mgr. Rex Co., Omaha, Neb., 1900-10; with J. Walter Thompson Co., 1910-15; mng. sec. Chamber of Commerce, Massillon, O., 1915-22; exec. vice-pres. and mgr. Jersey City Chamber of Commerce, Jersey City, N.J., since 1922. Republican. Episcopalian. Clubs: Rotary, Carteret (Jersey City). Home: 64 Livingston Av., Arlington, N.J. Office: 1 Newark Av., Jersey City, N.J.

LORD, Ernest A., pres. South Jersey Title & Finance Co.; b. Wilmington, Del., Feb. 18, 1876; s. Alexander and Catherine (Parker) L.; student Washington Coll., Chestertown, Md., 1891-93, Goldey's Business Coll., Wilmington, Del., 1894-96; m. Louise Bohlin, Mar. 31, 1897. Clk. Independence Nat. Bank, 1897-1901; with Girard Nat. Bank, 1901-03; Marine Trust Co., Atlantic City, N.J., 1903-33; with South Jersey Title & Finance Co., Atlantic City, N.J., since 1903, now pres. real estate officer Guarantee Trust Co., Atlantic City, since 1933; v.p. and dir. Neptune Mortgage & Finance Co., Atlantic City; pres. and dir. Trident Bldg. & Loan Assn., Atlantic City; dir. and trustee Atlantic Coast Bldg. & Loan Assn. Republican. Methodist. Home: Northfield, N.J. Office: Guarantee Trust Co., Atlantic City, N.J.

LORD, William A(dgate), lawyer and brig. gen.; b. Jersey City, N.J., Oct. 7, 1870; s. Charles D. and Lucy A. (Fay) L.; grad. Orange High Sch., 1889, Blackstone Inst., 1897; m. Sarah H. Roberts, Apr. 16, 1903; children—William A., Jr., Mary R. (Mrs. Everett H. Holmes), Genevieve F. (Mrs. Austin G. Beveridge), Sarah (Mrs. J. Milton Lent). Began as newspaper reporter, 1889-96; clk. Orange Dist. Ct., 1895-99; admitted to N.J. bar as atty., 1899, counsellor, 1901; in gen. practice of law at Orange since 1899, Newark since 1918; mem. N.J. legislature, 1901-03; Orange City counsel, 1904-13; mayor of Orange, 1919-21. Served as 2d lt. 2d N.J. Vol. Inf. in Spanish-Am. War, maj. N.J.N.G. on Mexican border, 1916 and in World War; col. O.R.C. and brig. gen. N.J.N.G. in which served for more than 25 yrs. Mem. Essex Co., N.J. and Am. Bar. Assn. New Eng. Soc. of Orange, Y.M.C.A., Mil. Order of Fgn. Wars, Mil. and Naval Order of Spanish-Am. War, U. Spanish War Vets, Fgn. War Vets., Am. Legion. S.A.R. (past pres. Maplewood Chapter), N.J. Soc. of War of 1812 (pres.). Republican. Presbyn. (trustee First Ch.). Mason (K.T., Shriner). Home: 32 New England Rd., Maplewood, N.J. Office: 744 Broad St., Newark, N.J.; also, 308 Main St., Orange, N.J.

LOREE, Leonor Fresnel, railway pres.; b. Fulton City, Ill., Apr. 23, 1858; B.S., Rutgers, 1877, M.S., C.E., LL.D.; Dr. Engring., Rensselaer Polytech. Inst., 1933. Entered ry. service, 1877, as asst. in engr. corps Pa. R.R.; transitman, engr. corps U.S.A., 1879-81; leveler, transitman and topographer, preliminary survey, Mexican Nat. Ry., from Rio Grande River to Saltillo, Mex., 1881-83; with Pa. R.R. Co. as asst. engr. Chicago div. 1883-84, engr. maintenance of way, I.&V. div., 1884-86, engr. m. of w., Chicago div., 1886-88, engr. m. of w., Cleveland and Pittsburgh div., 1888-89, supt. Cleveland & Pittsburgh div., 1889-96, gen. mgr., 1896-1901, 4th v.p. Pa. Lines W. of Pittsburgh, Jan. 1-June 1, 1901; pres. Baltimore & Ohio R.R. Co., June 1, 1901-Jan. 1, 1904; pres. Rock Island Co. of N.J. and chmn. exec. C., R.I. &P. Ry. Co. and S.L.&S.F. Ry. Co., Jan. 1-Oct. 4, 1904; chmn. exec. com., 1906-36, chmn. bd. dirs., 1909-36, Kansas City Southern Ry. Co.; pres., chmn. exec. com. and mem. bd. mgrs. Del. & Hudson Co., 1907-38; also director various corporations. Trustee Rutgers University. Brackett member of Princeton Engineering Association; trustee and 1st v.p. N.Y. Genealogical and Biographical Soc.; v.p. Chamber of Commerce of State of N.Y., 1922-28, pres., 1928-30, mem. exec. com. since 1931; mem. Royal Commn. on Rys. and Transportation (Can.). Judge of transportation. Chicago Expn., 1893; pres. Am. Ry. Assn., 1899-1901; chmn. U.S. delegation Internat. Ry. Congress, Paris, 1900; one of 7 Am. members of Permanent Commn. of Internat. Ry. Congress, Brussels, Belgium. Apptd. mem. Nat. War Labor Bd., Washington, D.C., Apr. 1918. Home: "Bowood," West Orange, N.J.

LORIMER, Graeme, author, editor; b. Wyncote, Pa., Feb. 9, 1903; s. George Horace and Alma Viola (Ennis) L.; grad. William Penn Charter Sch., Phila., 1919; B.A., U. of Pa., 1923, studied U. of Pa. Law Sch., 1924; m. Sarah Moss, Oct. 2, 1926; children—Sarah Lee, Belle Burford, George Horace II, Anna Hunter Moss. Began as asst. editor Country Gentleman, 1926; asso. editor Ladies' Home Journal, 1930-31; asso. editor Saturday Evening Post since 1932. Mem. Psi Upsilon. Baptist. Clubs: Rittenhouse, Franklin Inn, Phila. Cricket, Players. Author: (with wife) Men Are Like Street Cars, 1932; Stag Line, 1934; Heart Specialist, 1935; Acquittal, 1938. Home: Conshohocken, Pa.

LORIMER, Sarah Moss, author; b. Bala, Pa., Mar. 25, 1906; d. Frank Hazlett and R. Anna (Hunter) Moss; prep. edn., Shipley Sch. (Bryn Mawr, Pa.) and Agnes Irwin Sch., Phila.; student Smith Coll., Northampton, Mass., 1923-24; m. Graeme Lorimer, Oct. 2, 1926; children—Sarah Lee, Belle Burford, George Horace II, Anna Hunter Moss. Episcopalian. Clubs: Acorn, Cosmopolitan. Author: (with husband) Men Are Like Street Cars, 1932; Stag Line, 1934; Heart Specialist, 1935; Acquittal, 1938; also short stories (with husband) in Ladies' Home Jour. Home: Conshohocken, Pa.

LOSCHE, George Frederick, lawyer; b. New York, N.Y., June 11, 1894; s. George Frederick and Karoline (Dopke) L.; LL.B., Fordham U. Law Sch., 1915; grad. study, N.Y. Univ., 1915-16, U. of Aix-Marseilles, France, 1918-19; m. Hattie H. Holmes, June 27, 1920; children—Bruce Holmes, Barbara Evans, Kent Alan, Craig Kendall. Admitted to N.Y. bar, 1916; admitted to N.J. bar, 1922 and since engaged in gen. practice of law at Hackensack; mem. firm Losche and Mounier; counsellor at law since 1927; spl. master in chancery; supreme ct. commr.; served as judge Bergen Co. 5th Judicial Dist. Ct., 1929-30; prosecutor Bergen Co., 1930-34; trustee Bank of Bogota. Served as pvt. then corpl. inf., U.S.A., 1918-19. Mem. N.J. State Bar Assn., Bergen Co. Bar Assn. Republican. Mem. M.E. Ch. Home: 194 Norma Rd., Teaneck, N.J. Office: 210 Main St., Hackensack, N.J.

LOSER, Paul, supt. of schools of Trenton. Home: 110 Kensington Av. Office: Board of Education, Trenton, N.J.

LOTKA, Alfred James, mathematician; b. of Am. parents at Lemberg, Austria, Mar. 2, 1880; s. Jacques and Marie (Doebely) L.; B.Sc., Birmingham (Eng.) U., 1901, D.Sc., 1912; M.A., Cornell U., 1909; grad. study, U. of Leipzig, Germany, 1901-02, Johns Hopkins, 1922-24; m. Romola Beattie, Jan. 5, 1935. Asst. chemist Gen. Chem. Co., 1902-08; asst. in physics, Cornell U., 1908-09; examiner U.S. Patent Office, 1909; asst. physicist U.S. Bur. of Standards, 1909-11; editor Scientific Am. Supplement, 1911-14; chemist Gen. Chem. Co., 1914-19; supervisor math. research, Statis. Bur. Metropolitan Life Ins. Co., 1924-33, gen. supervisor, 1933-34; asst. statistician Metropolitan Life Ins. Co. since 1934. Fellow Am. Statis. Assn., A.A.A.S., Royal Econ. Soc., Population Assn. America (pres. 1938-39), Econometric Soc.; mem. Internat. Union for Scientific Investigation of Population Problems, Am. Math. Soc., Am. Pub. Health Assn., Am. Econ. Assn., Swiss Actuarial Soc., Washington Acad. Science, Sigma Xi. Club: Cornell (New York). Author: Elements of Physical Biology, 1925; The Money Value of a Man (with L. I. Dublin), 1930; Length of Life (with L. I. Dublin), 1936; Théorie Analytique des Associations Biologiques, 1934—; Twenty Five Years of Health Progress (with L. I. Dublin), 1937; also numerous publications in scientific and tech. jours. on math. analysis of population, math. theory of evolution, actuarial mathematics applied to problems of population and of industrial replacement. Home: Beattie Park, Red Bank, N.J. Office: 1 Madison Av., New York, N.Y.

LOTT, Howard Ridge, investments; b. Phila., Pa., July 9, 1902; s. Charles Fulmer and Katherine (Ridge) L.; grad. Frankford High Sch., Phila., Pa., 1919; B.S., U. of Pa., 1923; m. Rose Marie Schenkel, Apr. 25, 1925; children—Geraldine Marie, Joan Barbara. Teacher, Camden High Sch., 1923-25, Germantown Evening Sch., 1923-28; with Phila. Rapid Transit Co., 1925-26; with Mitten Bank Securities Corpn. (now Transit Investment Corpn.) since 1925, vice-pres. and dir. since 1934; vice-pres. and dir. Penn Steel Castings Co.; pres. and dir. Diamond Silver Co. Mem. Colonial Soc. of Pa. Republican. Episcopalian. Clubs: University, Penn Athletic (Phila.). Home: Towpath, New Hope, Pa. Office: Mitten Bldg., Philadelphia, Pa.

LOTT, Leigh Melvin, supt. of schools; b. Carbondale, Pa., Jan. 6, 1899; s. John and Ella (Manning) L.; grad. Auburn (Pa.) High Sch., 1916, Mansfield (Pa.) State Normal Sch., 1920; A.B., Wesleyan U., Middletown, Conn., 1926; A.M., U. of Pa., 1931; m. Helen M. Jones,

Aug. 21, 1926; children—Robert Morton, Marion Millicent. Teacher Starkey Sem., Lakemont, N.Y., 1920-22; supervising prin., Frenchtown, N.J., 1926-31; supt. of schools, Salem, N.J., 1931-33; supt. of schools, Bridgeton, N.J., since 1933. Served in U.S. Army, 1918. Chmn. Red Cross Roll Call, Bridgeton, since 1936. Trustee Bridgeton Y.M.C.A. since 1938, Johnson-Reeves Playground since 1934. Mem. Am. Assn. Sch. Adminstrs., South Jersey Schoolmen's Club (past pres.), N.J. Edn. Assn., Phi Sigma Kappa. Episcopalian. Mason. Club: Bridgeton Rotary (pres. 1939-40). Home: Franklin Drive. Office: High School Bldg., Bridgeton, N.J.

LOTTE, Charles Walter, pres. Lotte Chem. Co.; b. Phila., Pa., May 19, 1894; s. Edward F. and Mary Viola (Collom) L.; A.B., Bucknell U., Lewisburg, Pa., 1914, A.M., 1921; m. Helene M. O'Byrne, Dec. 1, 1938. With Nat. Silk Dyeing Co., East Paterson, N.J., 1914-30, advancing to plant mgr.; pres. Lotte Chemical Co., Inc., chemical mfrs. and jobbers, Paterson, N.J., since 1932. Served as capt. of Q.M. Corps, U.S. Army, May 1917-Dec. 1918. Pres. N.J. Christian Endeavor Union, 1920-25; pres. State Y.M.C.A., 1925-26; commr. pub. works, Paterson, 1929-38; pres. Paterson Chamber of Commerce, 1935-36; dir. Paterson Y.M.C.A.; trustee Broadway Bapt. Ch. Mem. Am. Assn. Textile Chemists and Colorists. Republican. Mason (Shriner), Elk. Clubs: Hamilton (Paterson); Arcola Country (Arcola, N.J.). Home: 581 Broadway. Office: 4th Av. and Boulevard, Paterson, N.J.

LOUCHERY, Charles William, lawyer; b. Salem, W.Va., Mar. 9, 1888; s. Daniel Carson and Mary Catherine (Lynch) L.; A.B., W.Va. Univ., Morgantown, 1911; LL.B., U. of Wis. Law Sch., 1913; m. Mildred Lamberd, May 24, 1917; 1 son, Daniel Lamberd. Admitted to W.Va. bar, 1913 and since engaged in gen. practice of law at Clarksburg; also interested in real estate and in production of oil and gas since 1921; dir. Merchants Nat. Bank of W.Va., Clarksburg, since 1921, White-Bailey, Inc., Clarksburg, W.Va.; sec., treas., and dir. Richwood Oil Co., Clarksburg; sec. and dir. Harrison-Ritchie Oil & Gas Co., Clarksburg; mem. firm C. Burke Morris, Trustee. Served as chmn. Harrison Co. Exec. Com. Rep. Party, 1926. Mem. W.Va. Bar Assn., Harrison Co. Bar Assn. (pres. 1936), Sigma Chi. Republican. Mem. M.E. Ch. Club: Clarksburg Country (pres. 1939). Home: 558 E. Main St. Office: Goff Bldg., Clarksburg, W.Va.

LOUCHHEIM, William S., engr. and contractor; b. Elkins Park, Pa., Dec. 23, 1904; s. Jerome Henry and Etta O. (Lovenstein) L.; grad. Abington (Pa.) High Sch., 1921; C.E., Cornell U., 1925; m. Jean Benoliel, Dec. 28, 1925; children—Patsy B., William S. Asst. supt. Keystone State Constrn. Co., 1925-26; vice-pres. Keystone State Corpn., 1927-33; field engr. Middlesex Pipe Line Co., 1936; partner Louchheim, Brown & MacDonough, gen. contractors, since 1934; pres. C. & W. Corpn.; treas. Spacarb Phila. Co.; dir. Warner Co. Vice chmn. 1937 United Campaign; dir. Big Brother Assn. Asso. mem. Am. Soc. Civ. Engrs.; mem. Am. Concrete Inst. Republican. Clubs: Locust, Engineers, Philmont (Phila.); Engineers (New York). Home: Scotford Rd., Mt. Airy, Pa. Office: 1321 Arch St., Philadelphia, Pa.

LOUCKS, William Negele, prof. economics; b. Somerset, O., Dec. 13, 1899; s. Daniel Webster and Minnie Alice (Negele) L.; A.B., Heidelberg U., Tiffin, O., 1922; A.M., O. State U., 1923; Ph.D., U. of Pa., 1928; m. Olive Lucille Wagner, Sept. 10, 1924; 1 dau., Janet Ann. Engaged as instr, econs., U. of Pa., 1923-29, asst. prof., 1929-35, asso. prof. econs., 1935-39; served as dir. staff of spl. advisers, Consumers Advisory Bd., NRA, 1933; on staff Pa. State Emergency Relief Bd., 1934; on staff Pa. Works Progress Adminstrn., 1935. Served in S.A.T.C., 1918. Mem. Am. Econ. Assn., Pi Kappa Delta, Pi Gamma Mu, Delta Sigma Phi. Mem. Evang. and Reformed Ch. U.S.A. Author: The Philadelphia Plan of Home Financing, 1929; The Stabilization of Employment in Philadelphia through the Long Range Planning of Municipal Improvement Projects, 1931. Co-author: Comparative Economic Systems; Capitalism, Socialism, Communism, Fascism, Cooperation. Contbr. various articles in econs. field. Home: 501 Anthwyn Rd., Merion, Pa.

LOUD, Frederick Ellsworth, pres. Murray Oil Products Co.; b. East Weymouth, Mass., Mar. 25, 1890; s. Henry K. Loud and Josephine Florence (Pratt) L.; student pub. schs., Mass., 1895-1909; m. Rosenna McFaul, Nov. 4, 1914; children—Ruth Virginia, Charlotte Ann. Chemist Marden-Orth & Hastings, Boston, Mass., 1911-14, asst. supt. Chicago plant, 1914-17, gen. mgr., Blue Point, L.I., N.Y., 1917-20; organized, 1920, and since pres. Murray Oil Products Co. of Pa., Phila.; organized, 1924, and since pres. Murray Oil Products Co. Inc. of N.Y., New York; founded, 1927, and since pres. Industrial Oil Products Corpn. of Calif., Los Angeles. Mem. Nat. Paint, Varnish and Lacquer Assn., Ail Trades Assn. of Phila. Republican. Mason (Consistory; Shriner). Club: Seaview Golf (Absecon, N.J.). Home: 1015 Park Av., Collingswood, N.J. Office: Margaret and Pearce Sts., Philadelphia, Pa.

LOUDEN, Adelaide Bolton, illustrator; b. Phila., Pa.; d. Charles W. and Lydia E. (King) Bolton; A.B., Mt. Holyoke Coll., S. Hadley, Mass.; art student Pa. Acad. of Fine Arts; m. Norman P. Louden, 1922. Illustrator for J. B. Lippincott Co., John C. Winston Co., Altemus Co., all Phila., since 1923; advertising illustrator for various advertising agencies; instr. in illustration, costume design and interior decoration, Wildcliff Jr. Coll., Swarthmore, Pa., since 1938; exhibited at Pa. Acad. of Fine Arts, 1921, 36, Phila. Art Alliance, 1921. Republican. Author and illustrator: Historic Costumes, 1936. Home: Quakertown, Pa. Office: 712 N. 20th St., Philadelphia, Pa.

LOUDEN, Samuel L., clergyman; b. West Sunbury, Pa., July 13, 1876; s. John Montgomery and Hannah (Campbell) L.; A.B., Grove City Coll., 1902, A.M., same, 1906; student Pittsburgh-Xenia Sem., 1903-06; (hon.) D.D., Grove City Coll., 1927; m. Emma Gertrude Ray, July 5, 1906; children—John Ray, Rolland English and Roberta Elizabeth (twins). Ordained to ministry United Presbyn. Ch., 1906; pastor Sandy Lake, Pa., 1906-11; pastor, Mars, Pa., since 1911; mem. Home Missions Com. Bd. Am. Missions. Served as moderator Lake and Allegheny presbyteries. Pres. Butler Co. S.S. Assn. several yrs. Presbyn. Club: Kiwanis of Mars. Home: Mars, Pa.

LOUDON, Edward Whitmer, physician and surgeon; b. Altoona, Pa., Mar. 4, 1874; s. William and Rebecca (Bridenbaugh) L.; B.S., Gettysburg Coll., 1896; M.D., U. of Pa., 1901; m. Cora Lee Kerlin, Oct. 8, 1902; Engaged in gen. practice, Altoona, Pa., since 1902; resident physician Altoona Hosp., 1901-02; med. insp. Logan Twp. Schs., Blair (Pa.) Co., since 1918; chief examiner Prudential Ins. Co. of Newark (N.J.) for Altoona (Pa.) dist. since 1918; examiner Knights Life Ins. Co., Pittsburgh, Pa., since 1928; chief examiner Tuberculosis Clinic of Altoona Hosp., 1933-37. Mem. Blair Co. Med. Soc., Pa. State Med. Soc., Am. Med. Soc., Sigma Chi. Republican. Presbyterian (Elder Ward Av. Presbyn. Ch., Altoona). Address: 3721 6th Av., Altoona, Pa.

LOUGHNER, Josiah Robert, clergyman; b. Jeannette, Pa., Oct. 31, 1877; s. Joseph and Rebecca (McCreery) L.; A.B., Washington and Jefferson Coll., 1904, A.M., 1905; B.D., Western Theol. Sem., 1909; student Univ. of Marburg, Germany, 1909-10; m. Maudress Montgomery, Mar. 12, 1906. Ordained to ministry of Presbyterian Ch., May 1908, by Shenango Presbytery; pastor Moravia Presbyn Ch., Lawrence Co., Pa., 1908-12, Portersville Presbyn. Ch., Butler Co., Pa., 1912-16, Bethel Presbyn. Ch., Washington Co., Pa., 1916-25; prin. Beulah Park Bible Sch., also Bible conf. work and evangelistic work, 1925-33; pastor Scrubgrass Stone Presbyn. Ch., Emlenton, R.D. No. 2, Venango Co., Pa., since 1933. Traveled in Egypt and Palestine, summer 1929. Address: Route 2, Emlenton, Pa.

LOUGHRIDGE, Jonathan Edwards, physician; b. Peoria, Ill., Jan. 13, 1887; s. Samuel Orr (M.D.) and Effie Margaret (Edwards) L.; A.B., Williams Coll., 1908; M.D., U. of Pa. Med. Sch., 1914; m. Dorothy Cookman Halsted, June 25, 1921; children—John Halsted, James Barry. Resident phys., Germantown (Phila.) Hosp., 1914-15 and mem. staff continuously since 1915, consultant in medicine since 1929. Mem. Am. Med. Assn., Phila. Co. Med. Soc., Phi Alpha Sigma. Republican. Presbyn. Club: Physicians Motor (Philadelphia). Home: 6225 Greene St., Philadelphia, Pa.

LOUTHAN, James Straine, physician and banker; b. South Beaver Twp., Beaver Co., Pa., Apr. 28, 1854; s. James and Nancy (Straine) L.; student Darlington Acad. and Westminster Coll. (New Wilmington, Pa.); M.D., Cleveland (O.) Med. Coll.; m. Ida May Johnson, June 20, 1883; children—Mrs. Roy Briarly, Mrs. Charles Babbitt. In practice of medicine at Beaver Falls, Pa.; sr. mem. firm Drs. Louthan, Patterson & Smith; surgeon N.Y. Central Lines R.R.; mem. staff Beaver Valley Gen. and Providence hosps.; pres. Farmers Nat. Bank of Beaver Falls; dir. Ingram-Richardson Mfg. Co., Standard Steel Specialty Co. Mem. Beaver Co. and Pa. State Med. socs., Beaver Falls Bd. of Trade. Republican. Mason (K.T., Shriner). Clubs: Rotary, Beaver Valley Country (Beaver Falls, Pa.). Home: 1414 8th Av. Office: 1417 7th Av., Beaver Falls, Pa.

LOUTREL, Cyrus Henry, pres. The Nat. Lock Washer Co.; b. East Orange, N.J., Nov. 26, 1885; s. Cyrus Francis and Harriet Amanda (Powles) L.; grad. Carteret Acad., Orange, N.J., 1903; Ph.B., Sheffield Scientific Sch., Yale, 1907; student spl. courses Mass. Inst. Tech.; m. Ethel McCluney, Dec. 15, 1908; children—Harriet (Mrs. Charles Gordon Zug, Jr.), Cyrus Henry, John McCluney. With Am. Pulley Co., Phila., Pa., 1907-11; factory supt. Nat. Lock Washer Co., mfrs. spring washers, ry. and bus windows and window equipment, drop forgings, rheostats, resistors, elec. apparatus, Newark, N.J., 1911-17, pres. since 1917; pres. and dir. The Nat. Lock Washer Co. of Wis. since 1926; mem. bd. mgrs. Half Dime Savings Bank, Orange, N.J.; dir. Hardwick, Hindle, Inc., Newark, N.J. Mem. N.J. Ho. of Reps., 1925, 1926. Treas. of Trustees Record Ambulance, Orange, N.J.; trustee Schs. for Industrial Edn. of Newark, N.J. (Newark Coll. of Engring., Newark Tech. Sch.). Fellow in perpetuity The Met. Mus. of Art, New York; mem. Am. Soc. M.E., Soc. of Automotive Engrs., Yale Engring. Assn., N.J. State Chamber of Commerce (dir.), Delta Psi (St. Anthony). Episcopalian. Clubs: Essex (Newark, N.J.); Orange Lawn Tennis (South Orange, N.J.); Rock Spring Country (West Orange, N.J.); Mason's Island Yacht (Mason's Island, Mystic, Conn.). Home: 270 Irving Av., South Orange, N.J. Office: 40 Hermon St., Newark, N.J.

LOVE, Charles Hervey, chemist; b. Easton, Pa., June 17, 1905; s. Hervey and Edith May (Brands) L.; grad. Easton High Sch., 1923; B.S. in chemistry, Lafayette College, Easton, Pa., 1927, Chem. E., 1935; m. Gwendolyn Frances Reeder, Feb. 28, 1936; 1 son, Charles Hervey. Control and research chemist E. I. du Pont de Nemours & Co., 1927-29; chief research chemist C. K. Williams & Co., 1929-37, dir. tech. service since 1937. Mem. Officers Reserve Corps. Fellow A.A.A.S.; mem. Am. Chem. Soc. (chmn. Lehigh Valley Sect. 1939-40), Phi Beta Kappa, Tau Beta Pi, Alpha Chi Rho, Alpha Chi Sigma. Republican. Presbyterian. Clubs: Country of Northampton County; Pomfret; Maroon. Home: Green Pond Farms. Office: 640 N. 13th St., Easton, Pa.

LOVE, Charles Marion, Jr., lawyer; b. Huntington, W.Va., Jan. 10, 1902; s. Charles Marion and Minnie Elizabeth (Moore) L.; student Univ. of Va., Charlottesville, Va., 1920-21; A.B., W.Va. Univ., Morgantown, 1924; LL.B., W.Va. Univ. Law Sch., 1926; m. Naomi Nale, Feb. 3, 1927; children—Naomi, Lucy Temple, Charles Marion III. Admitted to W.Va. bar, 1926, and since engaged in gen. practice of law at Charleston; served as co. atty., Kanawha Co., 1932; asst. U.S. atty. for Southern Dist. W.Va. since 1934. Mem. W.Va. Bar Assn., Charleston City Bar Assn., Order of Coif, Kappa Alpha, Phi Delta Phi. Democrat. Presbyn. Club: Edgewood

Country. Home: 4 Manor Pl. Office: Security Bldg., Charleston, W.Va.

LOVE, Mrs. Estelle Lippincott, pres. J. B. Sheppards and Sons, Inc.; b. Phila., Pa., Nov. 18, 1893; d. Alfred Harmer and Estelle (Taylor) Lippincott; student Ogontz Sch., Rydal, Pa., 1911-13; m. Donald Martin Love, Aug. 13, 1918; children—Donald Martin, Mortimer Crane, Patricia Lippincott, John Beresford, 5th, Estelle Lippincott. Entered business, 1931, pres. J. B. Sheppards and Sons, Inc., Phila., since 1934. Republican. Episcopalian. Home: 626 Love Lane, Wynnewood, Pa. Office: 212-14 S. 17th St., Philadelphia, Pa.

LOVE, George; mem. law firm Love & Love. Address: Fayetteville, W.Va.

LOVE, John William, clergyman; b. Weston, Mo., Nov. 17, 1887; s. William Marvin and Mary Julia (Graves) L.; ed. Camden Point Mil. Inst., Camden Point, Mo., 1901-04; A.B., Christian U., Canton, Mo., 1909, A.M., 1911; m. Besse Blye Lucas, June 7, 1912; children—Merrill Arthur, Betty Grace. Ordained to ministry Disciples of Christ Ch., 1911; pastor Burlington Junction, Mo., 1912-15, St. Joseph, Mo., 1915-21; pastor First Christian Ch., Washington, Pa., since 1921; mem. bd. mgrs. United Christian Missionary Soc., Indianapolis, Ind.; mem. Pa. Commn. Christian Edn.; mem. Pa. Com. Pension Fund of Disciples of Christ. Chmn. Coke Region Administrative Com. Republican. Club: Kiwanis of Washington, Pa. (past pres.). Home: 340 Allison Av., Washington, Pa.

LOVE, William Samuel, Jr., physician; b. Baltimore, Md., May 7, 1898; s. Dr. William S. and Esther Ann (Ebaugh) L.; A.B., Johns Hopkins U., 1918; M.D., U. of Md. Med. Sch., Baltimore, 1923; m. Emma Margareta Magdalena Barton (Ankarcrona), Apr. 10, 1930; children—Alexander Kirkland (Barton), William Samuel, IV, Thomas Ankarcrona, James Holm, Margaret Ankarcrona. Asst. resident in medicine, Univ. Hosp., Baltimore, Md., 1923-24, resident physician, 1924-25; with Brit. Med. Research Council, Dept. Clin. Research, London, Eng., 1925-26; asst. attdg. physician, Univ. Hosp., 1926-29, attdg. physician and cardiologist since 1929; instr. medicine, U. of Md. Med. Sch., 1926-30, asso., 1930-34, asst. prof., 1934-36, asso. prof. medicine since 1936; chief heart clinic, Univ. Hosp. since 1926; cons. physician, Sheppard and Enoch Pratt Hosp. since 1929, Springfield State Hosp. since 1938; cardiologist, Bon Secours Hosp., 1937-39, attdg. physician and cardiologist since 1939. Served as 1st lt. and capt., Md. N.G., M.C. and Inf., 1927-36. Fellow Am. Coll. Physicians, A.M.A. Mem. Am. Heart Assn., Southern Med. Soc., Med. and Chirurg. Faculty of Md., Baltimore City Med. Soc., Kappa Alpha, Alpha Kappa Kappa, Theta Nu Epsilon. Democrat. Episcopalian. Clubs: Johns Hopkins, Fifth Regiment Officers Assn. (Baltimore). Home; 209 Ridgemeade Rd. Office: 2211 Eutaw Pl., Baltimore, Md.

LOVEJOY, Arthur Oncken, univ. prof.; b. Berlin, Germany, Oct. 10, 1873; s. Wallace Williams and Sara Agnes (Oncken) L.; A.B., U. of Calif., 1895; A.M., Harvard, 1897; studied U. of Paris, 1898-99; LL.D., U. of Calif., 1924; unmarried. Asst. and asso. prof. philosophy, Leland Stanford Jr. U., 1899-1901; prof. philosophy, Washington U., St. Louis, 1901-08; prof. philosophy, U. of Mo., 1908-10; prof. philosophy, Johns Hopkins, 1910-38, emeritus prof. since 1938; lecturer in philosophy, Columbia, 1907-08, Harvard, 1932-33, 1937-38. Fellow A.A.A.S.; mem. Am. Philos. Assn. (pres., 1916-17), Am. Assn. of Univ. Profs. (pres., 1919), Am. Philos. Soc. Author: The Revolt Against Dualism, 1930; Primitivism and Related Ideas in Antiquity (with G. Boas), 1935; The Great Chain of Being, 1936. Contbr. to Jour. Philosophy, Jour. Ethics, Hibbert Jour., Mind; editor of Jour. History of Ideas; collaborator Essays in Critical Realism, 1920. Home: 827 Park Av., Baltimore, Md.

LOVELAND, Charles Noyes, mayor; b. Wilkes-Barre, Pa., Nov. 26, 1872; s. George and Julia Lord (Noyes) L.; student Wilkes-Barre (Pa.) Acad., 1885-90; A.B., Yale, 1894; m. Mabel Huidekoper Bond, June 7, 1900; children—Rose C. (Mrs. John E. Toulmin), Charles Noyes, George. Dir. of sts. and pub. improvements, Wilkes-Barre, Pa., 1913-15, dir. parks and pub. property, 1918-19; mayor, City of Wilkes-Barre, since 1933; dir. First Nat. Bank of Wilkes-Barre. Trustee James Sutton Home, Mill Memorial Library; dir. Wilkes-Barre Gen. Hosp., Y.M.C.A., Community Welfare Fed. Republican. Presbyterian. Home: 104 W. River St. Office: 1111 Miners Bank Bldg., Wilkes-Barre, Pa.

LOVELAND, Henry M., pres. H. M. Loveland & Son; b. Cohansey, N.J., Apr. 9, 1872; s. Anthony S. and Emma (Johnson) L.; student Horse Branch (N.J.) Pub. Sch., 1878-96, S. Jersey Inst., Bridgeton, 1896-1900; grad. Rutgers Coll.; m. Attie D. Burt, Jan. 17, 1899; 1 son, Heber A. Founded H. M. Loveland & Son, ins., Bridgeton, N.J., 1932; 1st vice-pres. and dir. Farmers & Merchants Bank, Bridgeton, since 1905; head S. Jersey claim dept., Selected Risks Ins. Co.; dir. Selected Risks Indemnity Co., Selected Risks Fire Co., Farmers and Traders Life Ins. Co., Syracuse, N.Y., Farmers Reliance Ins. Co., Trenton, N.J. Mason, Grange. Club: Kiwanis (Bridgeton, N.J.). Home: 72 W. Commerce St. Office: 107 E. Commerce St., Bridgeton, N.J.

LOVELL, Earl B., civil engr.; b. Marathon, N.Y., May 2, 1869; s. Ransom Marlow and Dorcas (Meacham) L.; grad. Marathon Acad., 1886, Cascadilla Sch., Ithaca, 1887; C.E., Cornell, 1891; m. Ida L. Peck, Oct. 4, 1899; children—Robert Marlow, Helen Louise (dec.), Esther Hope, Gordon Peck, Ruth Caroline. Asst. engr. M.C. R.R., 1891-93; instr. civ. engring., Lafayette Coll., 1893-96, Cornell U., 1896-98; adj. prof. civ. engring., 1898-1901, asso. prof., 1901-7, prof., 1907—, chmn. dept. civ. engring., 1916-34, Columbia U. Advisory engr. and mgr. survey dept. Lawyers Title & Trust Co. (now Lawyers Title & Guaranty Co.), New York, 1907-33; pres. Earl B. Lovell, Inc., engring. and surveying since 1933; chmn. Assn. of Dept. Heads, 1923-24; consulting engr. for Portland Cement Lumber Co., 1923-24. Owner "Lovell Farms," Marathon, N.Y. Pres. Assn. of City Surveyors, Greater New York, 1919-22; asso. mem. Am. Soc. C.E.; mem. Tau Beta Phi, Sigma Xi. Republican. Episcopalian. Has specialized in railroad engring. and masonry constrn. Home: 67 Myrtle Av., Montclair, N.J. Office: 141 Broadway, New York, N.Y.

LOVELL, Ralph L., mechanical engr.; b. Millbury, Mass., Aug. 2, 1865; s. William L. and Jane E. (Harris) L.; M.E., Worcester Poly. Inst., 1888; m. Miss M. L. Brackett, June 24, 1896; 1 son, Frederick H. With Gen. Elec. Co., Lynn, 1888-94; with Newport News Shipbuilding Co., 1894-1904; asst. chief engineer, 1904-10, chief engineer, 1910-14, Fore River Shipbuilding Co., Quincy, Mass.; consulting engr. and patent expert, 1914-16; marine engr. with Theodore E. Ferris, naval architect and engr., New York, 1916-17; chief engr. U.S. Shipping Bd. Emergency Fleet Corpn., Washington and Phila., 1917-19; pres. Adams, Lovell & Burlingham, consulting marine engrs., New York, 1919-22; engr. with Bethlehem Shipbuilding Corpn., Elizabeth, N.J., 1924-29; with United Dry Docks, Inc., Staten Island, N.Y., since 1929, now chief engr.; chief engr. Bethlehem Steel Co., shipbuilding div., Staten Island Works, since 1938. Home: Cranford, N.J.

LOVETT, Henry, physician and banker; b. Langhorne, Pa., Dec. 5, 1865; s. Samuel and Anne (Banes) L.; M.D., Jefferson Med. Coll., Phila., Pa., 1888; m. Lily J. Hill, 1892; 1 son, Charles H. In practice of medicine at Langhorne, Pa., since 1888; pres. Peoples Nat. Bank and Trust Co. of Langhorne since 1912; pres. Langhorne Spring Water Co. since 1910; dir. Bucks Co. Contributionship of Morrisville, Pa., Bristol Trust Co. Republican. Methodist. Club: Union League (Phila.). Address: 360 S. Bellevue Av., Langhorne, Pa.

LOVINS, William Thomas, lawyer; b. Wayne Co., W.Va., Aug. 27, 1887; s. James Harvey and Nancy Josephine (Sink) L.; LL.B., Washington & Lee U. Law Sch., Lexington, Va., 1914; m. Grace Huff, Dec. 31, 1925; 1 son, Walter McCallister. Admitted to W.Va. bar, 1914, and engaged in gen. practice of law at Huntington since 1915 except for absence in army; pres. and dir. First Nat. Bank of Kenova, W.Va. Served as 2d lt. to capt. of inf. U.S. Army, 1917-18; now lt. col. Reserve Corps, U.S. Army. Member Am. Bar Assn., Cabell Co. Bar Assn., Delta Theta Phi. Democrat. Mason (K.T., 32°, Shriner), Brotherhood R.R. Trainmen, B.P.O.E. Home: 520 Fifth Av. Office: First Huntington Nat. Bank Bldg., Huntington, W.Va.

LOVITT, John Valentine, lawyer; b. Nova Scotia, Aug. 25, 1898; s. John Harold and Florence (Hardwicke) L.; B.A., U. of Pa., 1920; B.C.L., Oxford Univ., England, 1924, M.A., 1926; unmarried. Admitted to Pa. bar, 1926; partner in firm Ballard, Sparks, Andrews & Ingersoll; instr. in finance, U. of Pa. since 1928. Served in U.S. Naval Aviation during World War. Trustee Second Presbyn. Ch. of Germantown. Rhodes Scholar from Pa. to Oxford, 1921; now sec. Pa. Com. for Selection of Rhodes Scholarships. Pres. Soc. of the Alumni of U. of Pa., 1934-38. Mem. Phila. and Pa. bar assns., Kappa Sigma, Sphinx; barrister-at-law Inner Temple, Eng. Clubs: University, Philadelphia Cricket (Phila.). Home: 243 W. Tulpehocken St. Office: Land Title Bldg., Philadelphia, Pa.

LOWE, Boutelle Ellsworth, author, educator; b. Marion, N.Y., Mar. 24, 1890; s. Ralph and Clara (Ellsworth) L.; A.B., Denison U., Granville, O., 1911; A.M., U. of Rochester, 1912; Ph.D., Columbia, 1918; m. Louise Alberta Caroline Klein, June 28, 1926. Prin. high sch., Machias, N.Y., 1912-14; dept. social science, East High Sch. and Washington Jr. High Sch., Rochester, 1914-16, Evander Childs High Sch., N.Y. City, 1916-17; vol. war service, 1917-18; teacher Courtney Sch. (pvt.), N.Y. City, 1919-20, Hackensack High Sch. since 1920, head dept. of social sciences, 1929-37, prin. since 1937; prin. Hackensack Summer Sch., 1933-36; pres. of Language Inst., Inc., N.Y. City, 1918-34; prof. economics, Jr. Coll. of Bergen Co., Hackensack, N.J., since 1933. Trustee Secondary Sch. Teachers' Assn. of State of N.J., 1934-37; mem. Royal Soc. for Encouragement of Arts (Eng.), N.E.A., Am. Acad. Polit. and Social Science, Am. Assn. Labor Legislation, History Assn. of Middle States and Md., Phi Beta Kappa; organized local fraternity, now Gamma Iota Zeta Chap. of Lambda Chi Alpha. Author: International Education for Peace, 1929; The International Protection of Labor (new enlarged edit.), 1935. Contbr. articles on labor since 1912. Home: 125 Lawrence Av., Hasbrouck Heights, N.J.

LOWE, Elias Avery, palæographer; b. Oct. 15, 1879; s. Charles and Sarah (Ragoler) L.; student Coll. of City of New York, 1894-97; A.B., Cornell U., 1902; graduate study at Halle; Ph.D., University of Munich, 1907; D.Litt. (honorary), Oxford, 1936; fellow Am. Sch. at Rome, 1908-10; m. Helen Tracy Porter, Feb. 8, 1911; children—Prudence Holcombe, Frances Beatrice, Patricia Tracy. Lecturer in palæography, Oxford U., Eng., since 1913, reader since 1927; Sandars reader, Cambridge U., 1914; asso. in palæography, Carnegie Instn., Washington, D.C., 1911—; prof. palæography, Inst. for Advanced Study, Princeton; mem. Corpus Christi Coll. Fellow Mediæval Acad. America; corresponding fellow of British Academy; member Oxford Philol. Soc., Bezan Club, Phi Beta Kappa; corr. mem. Hispanic Soc. America and Acad. of Madrid. Clubs: Authors, American. British-American, North Oxford Golf. Author: Die Ältesten Kalendarien aus Monte Cassino, 1908; Studia Palæographica, 1910; The Beneventan Script, 1914; The Bobbio Missal, 1920; An Unknown Sixth Century Fragment of Pliny's Letters (with E. K. Rand), 1922; Codices Lugdunenses Antiquissimi, 1924; English Handwriting (with Robert Bridges and Roger Fry), 1926; "Handwriting" in Legacy of the Middle Ages, 1926; Regula S. Benedicti, 1929; Scriptura Beneventana, 1929; Codices Latini Antiquiores, Vol. I, 1934, Vol. II, 1935, Vol. III, 1938. Contbr. to Hermes, Classical Quarterly, Classical Rev., Jour. Theol. Studies, English Hist. Revue, Speculum, etc. Address: Institute for Advanced Study, Princeton, N.J.; also Corpus Christi College, Oxford, England.

LOWENGARD, Leon, printing and pub.; b. Harrisburg, Pa., Apr. 6, 1886; s. Joseph and

LOWENTHAL, Sophia (Spitz) L.; ed. pub. sch. and high sch., Harrisburg, Pa., 1891-1904; unmarried. Engaged in bus. since 1904; in newspaper pub. since 1912, pub. Harrisburg Sunday Courier, propr. Courier Press (gen. printing). Served in U.S.A. during World War. Republican. Jewish religion. Mason, Elk, Kiwanian. Home: 416 Briggs St. Office: 210 N. 3d St., Harrisburg, Pa.

LOWENTHAL, Alexander; b. Cincinnati, O., Jan. 12, 1898; s. Philip and Jenny (Gloss) L.; A.B., Yale, 1920, LL.B., 1921; m. Anne Fineman, Dec. 18, 1935. Dealer in investment securities as partner Rosenbloom & Lowenthal, 1923-29; pres. Development Corpn. of Pittsburgh since 1931; sec. and dir. Falk & Co. Dir. Y.M.&Y.W. Hebrew Assn., Jewish Home for Aged, United Jewish Fund, Workers Sch. of Western Pa. Home: 144 N. Dithridge St. Office: 4628 Bayard St., Pittsburgh, Pa.

LOWNDES, Tasker Gantt, banking; b. Cumberland, Md., July 30, 1883; s. Lloyd and Elizabeth (Tasker) L.; A.B., Yale Univ., 1907; student U. of Md. Law Sch., 1907-09; unmarried. Admitted to Md. bar, 1909 and engaged in gen. practice of law at Cumberland, 1909; dir. and vice-pres. Second Nat. Bank, Cumberland, Md., 1921; pres. and dir. since 1921. Served as pres. State Bd. Edn. of Md. Dir. and treas. Cumberland Free Pub. Library, Memorial Hosp. (Cumberland). Republican. Episcopalian. Mason (32°, Shriner). Clubs: Country (Cumberland); Maryland (Baltimore). Home: 27 Washington St. Office: Baltimore St., Cumberland, Md.

LOWNDES, W. Bladen; pres. Fidelity Trust Co.; officer or dir. many companies. Home: Roland Av. and Evansdale Road, Roland Park. Office: Charles and Lexington Sts., Baltimore, Md.

LOWNDES, William Bladen, Jr., banker; b. Mt. Savage, Md., Oct. 7, 1903; s. W. Bladen and Hannah Parker (Randall) L.; student Gilman Sch. and Hill Sch.; m. Clarke Dulany, Oct. 3, 1925; 2 daughters. Pres. Lowndes Savings Bank & Trust Co. since 1933. Home: 112 Witherspoon Road, Baltimore, Md. Office: Lowndes Savings Bank & Trust Co., Clarksburg, W.Va.

LOWNES, John Barton, physician and surgeon; b. Worcester, Pa., June 2, 1886; s. Charles Thomas and Mary Cassel (Heist) L.; ed. Brown Prep. Sch.; M.D., Jefferson Med. Coll., 1906; m. Kathryn D. Weis, Sept. 11, 1907. Interne State Hosp., Ashland, Pa., 1906, Samaritan Hosp., Phila., 1907; in gen. practice medicine and surgery, specializing in urology since 1907; asso. with genito-urinary dept., Jefferson Med. Coll. and Hosp. continuously since 1907; urologist, Germantown Hosp. since 1917, Jewish Hosp. since 1925; cons. urologist, Northeastern Gen. Hosp. since 1920; also cons. urologist, Montgomery, Riverview, Norristown, and Sacred Heart hosps. all of Norristown. Certified urologist by Am. Bd. Urology. Mem. Am., Pa. State and Phila. Co. med. assns., Am. Urol. Assn., Phila. Urol. Assn., Sigma Phi Epsilon, Phi Beta Pi. Republican. Episcopalian. Mason. Club: Union League. Home: 321 E. Durham St., Mt. Airy, Pa. Office: Medical Arts Bldg., Philadelphia, Pa.

LOWRIE, Robert Newell, physician; b. Jerseytown, Pa., Nov. 10, 1888; s. James Wm. and Priscilla (Bryson) L.; ed. Easton Acad., 1904-07; M.D., Medico-Chirurg. Coll., 1911; m. Laura Rae Essick, Oct. 14, 1913; children—James Allison, Robert Newell, Jr. (dec.), Betty Jane, Walter Olin. Interne St. Francis Hosp., Pittsburgh, 1911-12; engaged in gen. practice of medicine at Braddock, Pa., since 1912, specializing in pediatrics; mem. staff Braddock Gen. Hosp.; dir. Braddock Community Discount Co., Physicians Pharmacy, Inc. Mem. Am. and Allegheny Co. med. assns., Phi Rho Sigma. Republican. Presbyn. Club: Rotary of Braddock. Home: 210 Hawkins Av., North Braddock, Pa. Office: 436 Liberty St., Braddock, Pa.

LOWRIE, Walter, clergyman; b. Phila., Apr. 26, 1868; s. Samuel Thompson and Elizabeth A. (Dickinson) L.; A.B., Princeton, 1890, A.M., 1893, D.D., 1930; Princeton Theol. Sem.,

1890-93, U. of Griefswald, 1893-94, U. of Berlin, 1894; fellow Am. Sch. Classical Studies, Rome, 1895-96, and 1889-1900; m. Barbara Armour, 1918. Deacon, 1895, priest, 1897, Protestant Episcopal Church; rector Trinity, Southwark, Phila., 1903-04, Trinity Ch., Newport, 1905-07. St. Paul's Am. Ch., Rome, 1907-1930. Honorary canon of Trinity Cathedral, Trenton. Author: The Doctrine of St. John, 1899; Monuments of the Early Church, 1901; The Church and Its Organization, 1904; Gaudium Crucis, 1905; Abba, Father, 1908; Problems of Church Unity, 1924; Fifty Years of St. Paul's Church, and The Birth of the Divine Child, 1926; Jesus According to St. Mark, 1929; Religion or Faith, 1930; Our Concern with the Theology of Crisis; Kierkegaard, 1937. Address: Cedar Grove, Princeton, N.J.

LOWRIGHT, Wallace John, physician; b. Center Valley, Pa., Mar. 4, 1881; s. James Harvey (M.D.) and Anna Catherine (Harlacher) L.; M.D., Medico-Chirurgical, Coll. of Phila., 1898; m. Mabel E. Kline, Apr. 11, 1903 (dec.); 1 son, Wallace John, Jr. (M.D.); m. 2d, Elsie Gross, Nov. 8, 1932. Interne Hazelton Hosp., 1899; med. dir. Lehigh Co. Hosp., 1902-14; mem. staff, Quakertown Hosp. and Allentown Hosp.; chmn. bd. dirs. Coopersburg Nat. Bank. Served in U.S.A. Med. Res. since 1898. His father practiced medicine at Center Valley, 1881-1928, his son now in practice at Center Valley since 1930. Mem. Lehigh Co. and Pa. State med. socs., Patriotic Order Sons of America. Mem. Reformed Ch. Mason (K.T., 32°, Shriner). I.O.O.F. Club: Lions of Coopersburg. Home: Center Valley, Pa.

LOWRY, Edward George, Jr., lawyer; b. New York, N.Y., Mar. 5, 1903; s. Edward George and Elizabeth (Lahey) L.; A.B., Harvard U., 1925; B.A., Baliol Coll., Oxford U., Oxford, Eng., 1928; LL.B., Columbia U. Law Sch. 1929; m. Ruth Driver, Aug. 24, 1928; children—Ruth Elizabeth, Edward George III. Admitted to Mass. bar, 1929 and asso. with Hale & Dorr, Boston, 1929-32; atty. Reconstruction Finance Corpn., Washington, D.C., 1932-33; spl. asst. to the sec. of the Treasury; gen. counsel, and bd. mem. Federal Alcohol Control Adminstrn., 1933-34; vice-pres. and gen. counsel Maryland Casualty Co., Baltimore, Md., since 1934, dir. since 1939. Club: Merchants (Baltimore). Home: Towson, Md. Office: 701 W. 40th St., Baltimore, Md.

LOWRY, Ellsworth, educator; b. Martinsville, Ill., July 20, 1886; s. Lewis Taylor and Eliz. M. (Sweet) L.; A.B., Tex. U., 1909, grad. study, 1909-10; A.M., Columbia U., 1913; grad. study, U. of Minn., 1916-17; Ph.D., U. of Pittsburgh, 1931; m. Ethel Stryker, Sept. 3, 1914; children—Elizabeth Jean, David Tod, Donald Stryker. Began as teacher, 1911; head dept. edn., Upper Ia. Univ., 1913-16; prin. training sch., State Normal Sch., Winona, Minn., 1917-20; dist. supt. in charge City Normal Sch., Indianapolis, 1920-23; dir. extension, State Normal Sch., Indiana, Pa., 1923-28; asst. dir. extension, Pa. State Coll. since 1928, also asso. prof. edn. Republican. Mem. United Presbyn. Ch. Home: 520 Locust St., Butler, Pa.

LOWRY, H(omer) H(iram), research dir.; b. Peking, China (of American parents) Oct. 6, 1898; s. George Davis and Cora (Calhoun) L.; A.B., Ohio Wesleyan U., Delaware, O., 1918; du Pont fellow, Princeton U., 1918-20, A.M., 1919-20, A.M., 1919, Ph.D., 1920; m. Helen Mary Smith, June 30, 1920; children—Helen Louise, Barbara. Chem. research Western Electric Co., New York, N.Y., 1920-25; physical chemist Bell Telephone Labs., New York, 1925-30; dir. coal research lab., Carnegie Inst. Tech., since 1930. Chmn. com. of chem. utilization of coal, Div. of Chemistry and Chem. Tech., Nat. Research Council. Fellow A.A.A.S., Inst. of Fuel (London); mem. Am. Chem. Soc., Am. Gas Assn., Am. Inst. Mining and Metall. Engrs., Am. Inst., Engrs. Soc. of Western Pa., Eastern States Blast Furnace and Coke Oven Operators Assn. Foreign Policy Assn., Nat. Econ. League, Am. Acad. of Polit. and Social Science. Lt. comdr. U.S. Naval Reserve. Author numerous papers on gas absorption, coal, carbon, theory of dielectrics, insulating materials. Address: Carnegie Institute of Technology, Pittsburgh, Pa.

LOWRY, Oscar Raymond, clergyman; b. Cedar Falls, Ia., Sept. 8, 1909; s. Oscar and Mamie King (Swindell) L.; A.B., Wheaton Coll., Ill., 1930; grad. Moody Bible Inst., Chicago, 1932; Th.B., Princeton Theol. Sem., 1936; m. Millie Whisler, June 17, 1938. Ordained to ministry Presbyterian Ch., Trenton, N.J., 1936; pastor, Union Beach, N.J., 1932-34; pastor, Second Presbyn. Ch., Trenton, N.J., 1936-37; pastor, Ridgeview Community Presbyn. Ch., West Orange, N.J. since 1937. Mem. adv. bd. Goodwill Home & Rescue Mission, Newark, N.J. Mem. Aristonian Literary Soc., Wheaton Coll., Ill. Republican. Presbyn. Study: 174 S. Valley Rd., West Orange, N.J.

LOWRY, W(elles) Norwood, univ. prof.; b. Carbondale, Pa., Jan. 25, 1900; s. Dr. Welles James and Flora May (Hammond) L.; grad. Carbondale High Sch., 1917; B.S. in elec. engring., Bucknell U., 1922, M.S., 1923; Ph.D., Cornell U., 1929; m. Thelma May Drake, Sept. 1, 1925; children—Joanne Drake, Welles Norwood. Employed by Consol. Telephone Co., Carbondale, Pa., 1917-18; asst. in physics, Bucknell U., 1920-22, teaching fellow in physics, 1922-23, instr. in physics, 1923-29, asst. prof., 1929-34, asso. prof. since 1934, social adviser, 1932-37. Served in S.A.T.C., 1918. Fellow A.A.A.S.; mem. Am. Phys. Soc., Sigma Xi, Pi Mu Epsilon, Kappa Delta Rho. Republican. Presbyterian. Mason (past master). Home: 206 S. 13th St., Lewisburg, Pa.

LOWY, Alexander, coll. prof.; b. New York, N.Y., Mar. 31, 1889; s. David and Fannie (Weiss) L.; B.S., Columbia, 1911, A.M., 1912, Ph.D., 1915; m. Dora Landberg, Dec. 23, 1915; children—Evelyn F., Muriel A., Alexander D. Asst. in electrochemistry, Columbia U., and teaching in N.Y. City until 1918; prof. of organic chemistry, U. of Pittsburgh, since 1918; holder of numerous U.S. patents on chem. research discoveries. Vice-pres. Am. Electrochemical Soc., 1930-33, chmn. of its publication com. since 1931. Mem. Am. Chem. Soc. (chmn. Pittsburgh sect.), Am. Assn. of Univ. Profs., Sigma Xi, Phi Lambda Upsilon, Sigma Alpha Mu. Jewish religion. Club: Faculty. Author: Introduction to Organic Chemistry, 1922; Study Questions in Organic Chemistry, 1923; Laboratory Methods in Organic Chemistry, 1926; Industrial Organic Chemicals and Dye Intermediates, 1935. Home: 5425 Normlee Place, Pittsburgh, Pa.

LOWY, Harry P.; pres. Lippman & Lowy; v.p. Sussex Fire Ins. Co.; dir. Ajax Fire Ins. Co., Eagle Fire Ins. Co., Essex Fire Ins. Co. Address: 60 Park Place, Newark, N.J.

LOXTERMAN, Howard B., engring. exec.; b. Pittsburgh, Pa., Jan. 9, 1883; s. William and Eva (Catley) L.; student Pittsburgh Commercial High Sch.; m. Elizabeth F. Whalen, Apr. 25, 1906; 1 son, Henry Russell. Constrn. engr., City of Pittsburgh, 1901-06; with Blaw Knox Co., Pittsburgh, since 1906, now v.p., dir., sec., and gen. sales mgr.; dir. Blaw Knox Internat. Corpn., A. W. French & Co., Blaw Knox Constrn. Co., Hoboken Land Co. Home: 407 Glen Arden Drive. Office: Blaw Knox Co., Pittsburgh, Pa.

LOY, A. Clinton, county supt. schs.; b. Ruckman, W.Va., Jan. 29, 1906; s. James M. and Mary R. (Snyder) L.; A.B., Marshall Coll., Huntington, W.Va., 1930; A.M., W.Va. Univ., Morgantown, W.Va., 1937; m. Henrietta Antoinette Wise, Oct. 3, 1931. Engaged as prin. elementary schs. Hampshire Co., W.Va., 1925-29; teacher high sch., Kanawha Co., 1930-33; prin. high sch., Romney, W.Va., 1933-35; supt. schs. Hampshire Co., W.Va., since 1935. Mem. Nat. Edn. Assn., Am. Assn. Sch. Administrs., W.Va. State Edn. Assn., W.Va. Assn. Sch. Supts. Democrat. Club: Lions of Romney. Home: Romney, W.Va.

LOY, Melvin Parsons, coll. prof.; b. Ruckman, W.Va., Oct. 21, 1890; s. William Henry and Clerza Ann (Poland) L.; A.B., Marshall Coll., 1926; A.M., Ohio State Univ., 1931; student W.Va. Univ., summers 1924-26; m. Charlotte E. Turley, June 30, 1917; 1 dau., Ann

Louise. Engaged in teaching pub. schs., 1909-17; prin. high sch., 1917-19; prin. jr. high sch., 1920-22; prin. jr. high sch., South Charleston, 1922-23, supt. schs., 1923-25; asso. prof. biology and head dept. biology, Marshall Coll., Huntington, W.Va., since 1926. Mem. W.Va. State Edn. Assn., W.Va. Acad. Science, Chi Beta Phi. Republican. Baptist. Mason. Modern Woodmen. Clubs: Lions, Executive (Huntington). Home: 1924 Underwood Av., Huntington, W.Va.

LUBLINER, Abram J., lawyer; b. Pocahontas, Va., Oct. 25, 1900; s. Sander and Hannah (Bergman) L.; student Emory and Henry Coll., Emory, Va., 1918-20; LL.B., Washington and Lee Univ. Law Sch., Lexington, Va., 1922; unmarried. Admitted to W.Va. bar, 1922, and since engaged in gen. practice of law at Bluefield; ast. pros. atty., 1925-29; served as mem. W.Va. Ho. of Dels., 1931-35. Mem. Mercer County, W.Va., State and Am. bar assns., Zeta Beta Tau. Democrat. Mason (32°, Shriner), Elk, Moose. Home: 625 North St. Office: 209-12 L. & C. Bldg., Bluefield, W.Va.

LUCAS, Edwin Adams, lawyer; b. Elgin, Ill., Mar. 24, 1892; s. Dr. George N. and Lucy E. (Blackburn) L.; A.B., Swarthmore Coll., 1914; LL.B., U. of Pa. Law Sch., 1917; m. Bretta Crapster, Jan. 26, 1918; children—Caroline Louise, Margaret Brettun. Admitted to Pa. bar, 1919, and since engaged in gen. practice of law at Phila.; asso. with Biddle, Paul & Jayne, Phila., 1919-20; atty. Pa. R.R., 1920-22; asso. with Dickson, Beitler & McCouch and successor, Drinker, Biddle & Reath, 1922-30, mem. firm since 1930. Served in O.T.C., 1917; 2d lieut. to capt. F.A., U.S.A., 1917-19, with A.E.F., 1918-19. Mem. Am. Law Inst., Order of the Coif, Phi Delta Phi, Kappa Sigma. Republican. Mem. Religious Soc. of Friends. Club: Union League. Home: Villa Nova, Pa. Office: 1429 Walnut St., Philadelphia, Pa.

LUCAS, Emil A., corpn. official; b. Pittsburgh, Pa., Sept. 14, 1894; s. Julius F. and Amelia (Hollatz) L.; student Carnegie Inst. Tech.; m. Elsie Catherine Grunert, Oct. 2, 1918. Began as asst. chemist Crucible Steel Co., 1915; became works mgr. Molybdenum Corpn. of America, 1920, v.p. in charge operations since 1930, also dir. Address: Washington and York, Pa.

LUCAS, Francis Ferdinand, scientist, engr.; b. Glens Falls, N.Y., Aug. 7, 1884; s. Frank and Mary (Bateman) L.; ed. special courses; hon. D.Sc., Lehigh U., 1931; m. Rose Jennet Howe, Sept. 19, 1905; 1 daughter, Mrs. Marie Jennet Wilson. With Bell telephone companies since 1902; member tech. staff Bell Telephone Labs., Inc., since 1925, in charge of microscopical analysis laboratories; cons. metall. expert Watertown Arsenal, U.S. War Dept., 1928-36. Awarded Henry Marion Howe medal by Am. Soc. for Steel Treating, 1924; medal by Royal Photographic Soc. of Great Britain, 1926 and 1929; John Price Wetherill medal, Franklin Inst., 1935. Del. Internat. Congress for Testing Materials, Amsterdam, Holland, 1927, Zurich, Switzerland, 1931, World Engr. Congress, Tokyo, Japan, 1929; scientific advisory trustee Internat. Cancer Research Foundation. Mem. Am. Society for Metals, Franklin Inst., Am. Society for Testing Materials (mem. research com. on fatigue of metals; metallography com. E-4), Engring. Research Foundation (mem. com. on welding D-4), Am. Inst. Mining and Metall. Engrs., New Internat. Soc. for Testing Materials, Am. Chem. Soc., N.Y. State Hist. Soc., Assembly Point Assn. (pres.). Republican. Presbyn. Mason. Club: New York Engineers (chmn. com. on admissions; mem. bd. govs.). Contbr. numerous articles and repts. of researches to tech. and scientific publs. Developed high power metallography, ultra violet microscopy and optical sectioning of living cells, applied ultra violet microscope to study of living cells, new method for bringing out latent fingerprints and ultra violet camera and viewing chamber for study of such prints; metallography and examination on structure of materials; investigation of fatigue of metals. Home: 245 Rutledge Av., East Orange, N.J. Office: 463 West St., New York, N.Y.

LUCAS, Harry Percy, investment and utilities exec.; b. Baltimore, Md., Mar. 8, 1876; s. Harry P. and Annabelle (Merryman) L.; student pvt. schs. and U. of Md. Law Sch.; m. Anna Wilson Edgar, 1908; 1 son, Edgar Merryman. Became clk. B.&O. R.R., 1895; now partner J. C. M. Lucas Co., Baltimore; sec. treas. and dir Gen. Utilities Operating Co., investment trust, Baltimore; sec. and treas. Ky. Electric Power Co., Narbonville, Ky. Clubs: Maryland, Baltimore Country, Green Spring Valley Hunt (Baltimore, Md.). Home: Brooklandville, Md. Office: Standard Oil Bldg., Baltimore, Md.

LUCAS, James Clarence Merryman, pub. utility exec.; b. Baltimore, Md., Mar. 24, 1873; s. Harry P. and Annabelle (Merryman) L.; student Baltimore City Coll., 1890-92; m. Emma Findlay Brogden, Jan. 14, 1920. Began in elec. contracting business, Baltimore, 1894; organizer, 1914, since pres. Gen. Utilities & Operating Co.; dir. Mercantile Trust Co., Eutaw Savings Bank. Episcopalian. Home: 100 University Parkway. Office: Standard Oil Bldg., Baltimore, Md.

LUCAS, William Albert, chem. and industrial engring.; b. Elizabeth, N.J., Aug. 5, 1885; s. William Siebert Albert and Lydia Gertrude (Parkinson) L.; Chem.G., Cooper Union Inst., 1905, B.S., and Chem.E., same, 1908; m. Isabel Smith, Oct. 18, 1915 (died 1919). Employed as lab. asst., technologist Grasselli Chem. Co., Grasselli, N.J., 1901-06; chief engr., supt. and dir., Butterworth-Judson Co., Newark, N.J., 1906-13; adv. engr. Chile Exploration Co., Braden Copper Co., Chile, S.A., 1913-15; supt. operations, Butterworth-Judson Corpn. at Newark, N.J., Curtis Bay, Md. and Medford, Mass., 1915-19; cons. engr., L. L. Summers & Co., N.Y. and Chicago, 1919-21; asst. to pres., Granton Chem. Co., N.Y. City, 1921-27; cons. engr., Marsden-Sewell Corpn., N.Y. City, 1927-33; cons. engr. Peyton-Hunt Co., N.Y. City since 1933. Supervised mfg. munitions for U.S., England, France, and Russia, 1915-19. Mem. Am. Inst. Chemists, Am. Chem. Soc., Am. Assn. Cons. Chemists & Chem. Engrs., N.J. State Soc. Professional Engrs. and Land Surveyors. Republican. Methodist. Mason (32°, Shriner). Club: Masonic (Elizabeth). Home: 572 Monroe Av., Elizabeth, N.J. Office: 350 Madison Av., New York, N.Y.

LUCASSE, Walter W(illiam), prof. of chemistry; b. Kalamazoo, Mich., Mar. 9, 1895; s. John Matthew and Nellie (Hoek) L.; A.B., Kalamazoo (Mich.) Coll., 1917; M.A., Clark U., Worcester, Mass., 1920, Ph.D., 1921; m. Phyllis Blanchard, May 1, 1925. Jr. gas chemist U.S. Bureau of Mines, 1918; instr. in chemistry, Worcester Poly. Inst., 1921-22; instr. in chem., U. of Pa., 1922-27, asst. prof., 1927-36, asso. prof. since 1936. Fellow A.A.A.S.; Am. Chem. Soc., Am. Assn. Univ. Profs., Sigma Xi, Alpha Chi Sigma. Home: 247 S. 38th St. Office: Harrison Lab., Univ. of Pennsylvania, Philadelphia, Pa.

LUCE, Bente Smith, banker; b. Perryopolis, Pa., Nov. 29, 1885; s. Samuel and Elizabeth (Gallery) L.; student business coll., 1904-05; spl. work, Hiram (O.) Coll., 1906-07, Ohio Northern U., Ada, O., 1907-08; m. Edna Catherine Browneller, Dec. 17, 1908; children—Muriel Catherine, Wayne Smith, Byron Browneller, Richard Galley. Bookkeeper First Nat. Bank of Perryopolis, Pa., 1908-20, asst. cashier, 1920-26; cashier and dir. Union Nat. Bank, Carnegie, Pa., 1926-30; cashier and dir. Old Nat. Bank of New Brighton, Pa., 1930-34; cashier, v.p. and dir. First Nat. Bank, Beaver Falls, Pa., since 1934. Republican. Mem. Christian Ch. Mason (Shriner). Home: Patterson Heights. Office: 1201 Seventh Av., Beaver Falls, Pa.

LUCIONI, Luigi, artist; b. Malnate, Italy, Nov. 4, 1900; s. Angelo and Maria (Beati) L.; student Cooper Union Art Sch., 1916-20, Nat. Acad. of Design, 1920-25; unmarried. Came to U.S., 1911, naturalized, 1922. Represented in Met. Mus. of Art, Whitney Mus. of Am. Art, Denver Art Mus., Nelson Gallery of Art, Pa. Acad. of Fine Arts, Neb. State Capitol, Canajoharie Mus., Phillips Memorial Gallery (Andover, Mass.); Library of Congress, Washington, D.C. (2 etchings); Victoria and Albert Museum, London (1 etching). Awarded Tiffany medal, 1928; Allied Artists medal of honor, 1929; Nat. Arts Club prize for flower painting, 1939. Asso. Nat. Acad. Catholic. Club: Coffee House. Home: 403 New York Av., Union City, N.J. Studio: 64 Washington Sq., New York, N.Y.

LUCKETT, Thomas James, lawyer; b. Washington, D.C., June 24, 1897; s. John Francis and Sarah Jane (Robey) L.; LL.B., Columbus U. Law Sch., Washington, D.C., 1925; m. Helen G. Henderson, Oct. 8, 1921; children—Thomas James, Gloria M. Admitted to Dist. of Columbia bar, 1925, Md. bar, 1930; in practice Capitol Heights, Md., since 1925; mayor, Capitol Heights, 1926-36. Served on Mexican border with 3d D.C. Inf. and 110th Field Arty., U.S. Army, 1916-19; with A.E.F. 12 months; capt. U.S. M.C. Reserve, 1929-35. Mem. Dist. of Columbia Bar Assn., Prince Georges County Bar Assn. Address: Capitol Heights, Md.

LUDLOW, Theodore Russell, bishop; b. Valley Creek, Tex., July 14, 1883; s. Samuel Russell and Mary Hoagland (Vermilye) L.; A.B., Austin Coll., Sherman, Tex., 1903, D.D., 1923; LL.B., Columbia, 1907, A.M., 1907; student Harvard Grad. Sch., 1908-09; B.D., Episcopal Theol. Sch., 1911; m. Helen Roosevelt Lincoln, June 7, 1911; children—Theodore Lincoln, James Minor, Ogden Roosevelt. Ordained to ministry Episcopal Ch., 1911; prof. of polit. science, Boone, U., Wuchang, China, 1911-16; polit. adviser to Provisional Govt., Wuchang, China, 1911-12; rector St. Paul's Ch., Newton Highlands, Mass., 1920-23; lecturer on canon law, Episcopal Theol. Sch., 1922; dean Grace Cathedral, Topeka, Kan., 1923-27; sec. for adult edn., Nat. Council P.E. Ch., 1927-31; rector Ch. of the Holy Communion, South Orange, N.J., 1931-36; suffragan bishop diocese of Newark, N.J., since 1936. Served as welfare worker with Chinese Labor Batt., with A.E.F., during World War; formerly chaplain 94th Div., O.R.C. Trustee Hosp. of St. Barnabas, Bonnie Brae Farm for Boys, Arthur Fund, Inc., Gertrude Butts Memorial Home Assn. Mem. Liberal Evangelical Assn. Author: I Am a Vestryman, 1937. Contbr. articles to The Churchman and other church magazines. Home: 380 Hillside Place, South Orange, N.J. Office: 99 Main St., Orange, N.J.

LUDLOW, William Orr, architect; b. New York, N.Y., May 24, 1870; s. Rev. James Meeker and Emma (Orr) L.; M.E., Stevens Inst. Tech., 1892; m. Abbie Hartwell, June 10, 1902; children—David Hartwell, William Hartwell. Engaged as archtl. draftsman with Carrere & Hastings, architects, New York City, 1892-95; sr. mem. firm Ludlow & Valentine, architects, 1895-1909; sr. mem. firm Ludlow & Peabody, 1909-35; sr. mem. firm Ludlow & Ludlow, Summit, N.J., since 1935; work includes 40 coll. bldgs., 30 chs. and large number banks, hosps. and wide variety of bldgs. (more than 400 in all); architect for office bldg. of New York Times, the Johns-Manville Bldg., and 48-story Chase Tower, also bldgs. in India and Greece. Gov. New York Building Congress. Fellow Am. Inst. Archts. (national chmn. Com. on Public Information). Mem. N.J. Soc. of Archts., Washington Soc. N.J., Madison Hist. Assn., Delta Tau Delta, Tau Beta Pi. Presbyn. (elder). Home: Madison, N.J. Office: Commercial Bldg., Summit, N.J.

LUDLUM, Seymour DeWitt, physician, psychiatrist, neurologist; b. Goshen, N.Y., Aug. 1, 1876; s. John Frank and Loisa May (Minturn) L.; B.S., Rutgers U., New Brunswick, N.J., 1897; M.D., Johns Hopkins U., Baltimore, Md., 1902; m. Mabel Stewart, Oct. 9, 1920; 1 son, Seymour DeWitt. Chief of staff, neuro-psychopathic dept., Phila. Gen. Hosp., since 1910; med. dir. and owner, Gladwyne Colony, pvt. sanitarium for mental and nervous diseases, Gladwyne, Pa., since 1912, dir. Gladwyne Research Lab. for Mental Research since 1912; prof. of psychiatry, U. of Pa. Grad. Sch. of Medicine, since 1914. Mem. Am. Psychiatric Assn., Am. Neurological Assn., A.M.A., Am. Chem. Soc., Phila. Co. Med. Soc., Johns Hopkins Surgical Soc., Assn. Research Nervous and Mental Diseases, Eugenic Research Assn., Am.

Therapeutic Assn. Republican. Presbyterian. Clubs: Univ., Philobiblon, Med. of Phila., Aesculapian, Med. Lit. (Phila.). Author of about 50 articles on research in mental and nervous diseases. Home: 1827 Pine St., Philadelphia, Pa. Office: Gladwyne Colony, Gladwyne, Pa.

LUEHRING, Frederick William, prof. physical edn.; b. nr. Hanover, Kan., Dec. 11, 1882; s. William and Emelia (Werner) L.; Ph.B., N. Central Coll., Naperville, Ill., 1905; Ph.M., U. of Chicago; Ph.D., Columbia, 1939; m. Emma Amanda Hatz, June 26, 1907 (died 1929); children—Mary Emmeline, Frederick William (dec.); m. 2d, Ellen Andrea Davidson, of Minneapolis, Minn., Dec. 5, 1930; 1 son, Davidson. Prof. and dir. phys. edn. and athletics, Ripon (Wis.) Coll., 1906-10; asst. prof. and asso. dir. hygiene and phys. edn., Princeton, 1911-20; prof. and dir. phys. edn. and athletics, U. of Neb., 1920-22, U. of Minn., 1922-30; prof., asst. to dean and dir. div. of instrn., dept. health and phys. edn., University of Pennsylvania since 1931; made survey of physical education in the Philadelphia public schools, 1937. Member Nat. Collegiate Swimming Rules Com. since foundation, 1913, chmn. since 1914; mem. Am. Olympic Com., X and XI Olympiads; chmn. Olympic men's swimming com., 1934-36; mem. White House Conf. on Child Health and Protection, 1930-31. Mem. Am. Phys. Edn. Assn., Soc. Dirs. Phys. Edn. in Colls. (pres. 1921), N.E.A., Am. Assn. Univ. Profs., Amateur Athletic Union (mem. Nat. bd. govs.), Nat. Collegiate Life Savings Soc. (mem. bd. govs.), Phi Delta Kappa Kappa Delta Pi, Phi Epsilon Kappa, Phi Kappa Sigma, Dolphins. Conglist. Mason (32°). Club: Lenape (Phila.). Author of Standards for the Swimming Pool, and various pamphlets on swimming, life-saving; contbr. to phys. edn. jours. Home: Swarthmore, Pa.

LUFTMAN, Harry Irvin, sec. N.J. State Housing Authority; b. Roumania, May 14, 1898; s. Samuel and Sara (Leaderman) L.; brought to U.S., 1905, naturalized, 1914; ed. Baltimore (Md.) High Sch. and Nat. U., Washington, D.C.; m. Lillian A. Vaeth, 1919 (divorced 1934); 1 son, Harry Irvin. Served as 2d lt. Ordnance Dept., U.S. Army, 1917-19; disch. as C.O., Elizabeth Port Proving Grounds; zone finance officer entire Eastern Div., to wind up Govt. contracts in East after war, 1919. Pres. and gen. mgr. United Drive-It-Yourself Corpn., Roanoke, Va., 1924-32; judge Small Cause Court of Union County, Hillside, N.J., 1929-33; sec.-treas. Harry I. Luftman, Inc., real estate, mortgages and ins., Hillside, N.J., since 1937; dep. dir. and sec. N.J. State Housing Authority, Newark, since 1934. Campaign mgr. for Mayor Thomas Williams, Elizabeth, N.J., 1932; sec. Union County Rep., chairman, 1933-35; Rep. chmn. Hillside, N.J., 1938; del. Rep. Conv. for Repeal of 18th Amendment. Sec. N.J. Council Housing Authorities. Mem. Am. Legion, Rep. Vets. of N.J., Rep. Club of Union County. Odd Fellow, Elk. Home: 160 Grumman Av., Hillside, N.J. Office: 1060 Broad St., Newark, N.J.

LUHN, John Andrew, lawyer, exec. ins. cos.; b. Barnesville, Md., Sept. 10, 1878; s. Charles Andrew and Sarah Catherine (McLain) L.; LL.B., U. of Md. Law Sch., 1903; m. Hannah Catherine Layfield, Aug. 19, 1905; 1 dau., Catherine Layfield. Engaged in teaching pub. schs. Montgomery Co., Md., 1898-1901; admitted to Md. bar, 1903, and in pvt. practice, Baltimore, 1903-04; with legal dept. Am. Bonding Co., Baltimore, Md., 1904-13, when merged with Fidelity & Deposit Co. of Md., and continued with this corpn. since 1913; now vice-pres. and counsel in charge of claims and litigation, Fidelity & Deposit Co. of Md.; dir. and vice-pres. in charge of claims and litigation, American Bonding Co. of Baltimore. Mem. Baltimore Bar Assn., Md. Bar Assn., Am. Bar Assn. Democrat. Presbyn. Clubs: Baltimore Country, Casualty and Surety (Baltimore). Home: 2408 Elsinore Av. Office: Fidelity Bldg., Baltimore, Md.

LUHR, Augustine, physician; b. St. Marys, Pa., Sept. 15, 1886; s. Joseph J. and Frances (Krug) L.; ed. Villa Nova Coll., 1900-04; M.D., Jefferson Med. Coll., 1908; grad. study, N.Y. Post Grad. Med. Sch., 1922, Vienna, Austria, 1927, Harvard U. Med. Sch., 1937; m. Gertrude M. Wall, Oct. 15, 1913; children—Jordan T., Hubert W., Pierre and Eymard C. (twins). Res. phys., St. Josephs Hosp., Phila., 1908-10; in pvt. practice of medicine and surgery at Phila., 1910, then in practice at St. Marys, Pa., since 1910; propr. pvt. hosp. at St. Marys, Pa. Served as mem. Vol. Med. Res. Corps during World War. Former mem. U.S. Pension Examination Bd., Elk Co. Served as coroner Elk Co. Roman Catholic. K.C. Home: 326 Centre St. Office: Medical Arts Bldg., St. Marys, Pa.

LUKENBACH, Frank K., pres. First Blair Co. Nat. Bank; b. Indianapolis, Ind., Mar. 28, 1869; s. Abram and Amanda (Kreamer) L.; student Bellefonte (Pa.) pub. schs., 1879-82; m. Mildred Bouse West; 1 dau., Catherine (Mrs. E. Loyd Tyson). Began as boy in banking house, W. F. Reynolds and Co., Bellefonte, Pa., 1882, and served as clerk to 1892; cashier First Nat. Bank of Philipsburg, Pa., 1892-1902; v.p. Blair Co. Nat. Bank, Tyrone, Pa., 1902-32; pres. First Blair Co. Nat. Bank (merged with First Nat. Bank), Tyrone, Pa., since 1932; dir. Am. Lime and Stone Co., Phila. Trustee Altoona (Pa.) Hosp.; dir. Tyrone (Pa.) Chamber of Commerce. Republican. Protestant. Home: 1055 Lincoln Av. Address: First Blair Co. Nat. Bank, Tyrone, Pa.

LUKENS, Edward Clark, lawyer; b. Elizabeth, N.J., Sept. 29, 1893; s. Lewis N. and Edith (Clark) L.; grad. Episcopal Acad., Phila., 1911; A.B., Princeton U., 1915; LL.B., U. of Pa., 1920; m. Frances B. Day, May 12, 1923; children—Alan Wood, Anne Blakiston, Frances Day. Admitted to Pa. bar, 1920, and since in gen. practice in Phila.; mem. firm Adams, Childs, McKaig & Lukens; lecturer in business law Towne Scientific Sch., U. of Pa.; pres. Northwood Cemetery Co. Served as 1st lt., 320th Inf., 80th Div., U.S. Army, with A.E.F., 1917-19. Mem. Phila. Co. Bd. of Law Examiners. Mem. Am. Law Inst., Phi Kappa Sigma. Republican. Presbyterian. Clubs: Princeton, Philadelphia Cricket (Phila.); Mountain View Country (Greensboro, Vt.). Home: Allens Lane, Mt. Airy, Phila. Office: Integrity Bldg., Philadelphia, Pa.

LUKENS, Francis D(ring) W(etherill), physician; b. Phila., Pa., Oct. 5, 1899; s. William Weaver and Isabella Macomb (Wetherill) L.; prep. edn. Hoosac Sch., Hoosick, N.Y., 1912-17; A.B., Yale, 1921; M.D., U. of Pa., 1925; grad. student Johns Hopkins U. Hosp., 1928-30; m. Emma Martyn George, Oct. 10, 1933; children—Marian Martyn, Isabella Wetherill. Interne Pennsylvania Hospital, Philadelphia, 1925-27, resident physician, 1927-28; instructor in medicine, Univ. of Pennsylvania, 1930-36, asst. prof. of medicine and dir. George S. Cox Med. Research Inst. since 1936. Mem. Am. Physiol. Soc,. Soc. Exptl. Biology and Medicine, Soc. Clin. Investigation, Phi Kappa Sigma. Episcopalian. Home: 34 W. Levering Mill Rd., Bala-Cynwyd, Pa. Office: Maloney Clinic, 362 Spruce St., Philadelphia, Pa.

LUKENS, Hiram Stanhope, prof. chemistry; b. Phila., Pa., Sept. 30, 1885; s. Joseph C. and M. Louisa (Stanhope) L.; B.S., U. of Pa., 1907, Ph.D., same, 1913; m. Marguerite D. Perrine, of Phila., Pa., Nov. 6, 1912; 1 son, William P. Asso. with U. of Pa. continuously since 1907, instr. chemistry, 1907-13, asst. prof., 1913-21, prof. since 1921, dir. dept. of chemistry and chem. engring. since 1932, Blanchard prof. since 1937, actg. dean, Towne Sci. Sch., 1937-38; tech. dir. Royal Electrotype Co. 1918-32; vice-pres. and tech. dir., Solidon Products, Inc., 1923-32. Served as civilian mem. Gas Defense Div., C.W.S., 1918. Mem. Div. of Chemistry and Chem. Technology, Nat. Research Council, 1934-37. Mem. A.A.A.S., Am. Chem. Soc., Electrochem. Soc., Am. Inst. Chem. Engrs., Am. Electroplaters Soc. (hon.), Soc. for Promotion Engring. Edn., Phila. Inst. Cons. Chemists and Chem. Engrs., Franklin Inst., Sigma Xi, Alpha Chi Sigma, Tau Beta Pi. Republican. Presbyn. Mason. Clubs: Rittenhouse, Engineers, Lenape (Philadelphia); Univ. of Pa., Chemists (New York); Absecon Island Yacht (Absecon, N.J.). Contbr. many sci. articles to learned publs. Holds a number of patents on his inventions. Home: 5843 Woodbine Av., Overbrook, Philadelphia, Pa.

LUKENS, Robert McDowell, physician; b. Phila., Pa., Oct. 5, 1887; s. Harry Walker and Emma Catherina (Freund) L.; M.D., Jefferson Med. Coll., 1912; m. Irene Phy, June 28, 1916; 1 son, Robert. Interne Jefferson Hosp., Phila., Pa., 1912-14; post grad. training in otolaryngology, pvt. assn. Dr. D. Bradin Kyle, 1914-16; engaged in practice of medicine at Phila., Pa., specializing in diseases of ear, nose and throat since 1919; asst. prof. bronchoscopy, Jefferson Med. Coll. Served in med. corps, R.A. Gt. Britain and U.S.A. during World War. Awarded Cambria Bar (Gt. Britain). Mem. Am. Med. Assn., Bronchoscopic Soc. (treas.), Am. Laryngol., Rhinol. and Otol. Soc., Am. Laryngologic Assn., Phila. Co. Med. Soc. Republican. Mem. Christian Ch. Mason. Clubs: Boulevard Mens (pres.), Masons, Wildwood Crest Fishing, Greater Wildwood Yacht (rear commodore). Home: 1308 Hunting Park Av., Philadelphia, Pa. Office: 1923 Spruce St., Philadelphia, Pa.

LUM, George Vernon, banker; b. Chatham, N.J., July 5, 1881; s. George Edward and Addie B. (Genung) L.; student Chatham (N.J.) High Sch., 1886-96, Morristown (N.J.) High Sch., 1896-97, St. George's Hall, Prep. School, Summit, N.J., 1898-99; m. Florence Taylor, June 10, 1908; children—George E. T., Hazel Pollard, Janet Spencer. Began as runner Summit Trust Co., Summit, N.J., 1899, and has filled every position to v.p. (v.p. since 1927); charter mem. and treas. Chatham (N.J.) Bldg. & Loan Assn. since 1908. Collector and treas. Borough of Chatham, 1911-23. Republican. Presbyterian (mem. Ogden Memorial Presbyn. Ch., Chatham). Mason (Overlook Lodge 163, past master; Royal Arch; Council; Commandery), Elk. Clubs: Kiwanis (Summit, N.J., charter mem.); Spring Brook Country Club (Morristown, N.J.). Home: Chatham, N.J. Office: The Summit Trust Co., Summit, N.J.

LUM, Hermann Arthur, educator; b. Madison, N.J., Oct. 2, 1891; s. Arthur Remington and Elizabeth (Whittaker) L.; B.S., Pa. State Coll., 1913; grad. work, Berkeley Divinity Sch., 1918-20; m. Flora Katharine Bowden, Sept. 14, 1921; 1 son, Arthur Remington. Sec. of College Y.M.C.A., Pa. State Coll., 1913-14; sec. Wesleyan U. of Conn. Christian Assn., 1914-20; track coach, Wesleyan U., 1918-20; Am. rep. of Amer. U. at Cairo, Egypt, and sec. of its Bd. of Trustees since 1920. Mem. Haddonfield, N.J., Bd. of Edn. since 1934, pres. since 1937; mem. Bd. of Dirs. Camden County Y.M.C.A., pres. for 2 years; mem. local com. Haddonfield (N.J.) Y.M.C.A. Mem. Haddonfield Hist. Soc., Haddonfield Contemporary Club (bd. mgrs.), Appalachian Mountain Club, Phi Kappa Psi. Republican. Episcopalian. Club: University (Phila.). Makes frequent trips to Egypt; speaker and writer on present day Egypt. Home: 217 Hawthorne Av., Haddonfield, N.J. Office: Land Title Bldg., Philadelphia, Pa.

LUM, Ralph Emerson, lawyer; b. Chatham, N.J., Apr. 21, 1877; s. Frederick Harvey and Alice Elizabeth (Harris) L.; prep. edn., St. Paul's Sch., Garden City, L.I., 1893-96; A.B., Columbia, 1900; post-grad. study, New York U., 1900-01; m. Sylvia Swinnerton, Aug. 21, 1902; children—Philip Livingston Swinnerton, Ralph Emerson, Mary dePeyster (Mrs. Johan Docker Hansen). Began practice, 1900, as mem. firm of Guild & Lum, later Lum, Tamblyn & Sommer, Lum, Tamblyn & Colyer, now Lum, Tamblyn & Fairlie, representing the Firemen's Ins. Co., Eastwood-Nealley Corpn., Sears, Roebuck & Co., Holme & Co., L. Bamberger & Co., Health Products Corpn.; dir. Fidelity-Union Trust Co., Eastwood-Nealley Corporation, Newark Tidewater Terminal Co.; counsel for Trustee of Susquehanna & Western R.R. since 1937. State chairman (New Jersey) World Court; chairman Morris County (N.J.) Rep. Com.; dir. Community Chests and Councils; ex-pres. Newark Welfare Federation. Trustee Pawling (N.Y.) Sch. Mem. Am. Bar Assn., N.J. Bar Assn. (ex-pres.), Newark Music Foundation (v.p.), Phi Kappa Psi, Phi Delta Phi. Mason (33°); Past Grand Master Masons of N.J. Clubs: Essex (Newark); Canoe Brook

Country (Summit, N.J.); Columbia Univ. (N.Y. City); Hollywood Adirondack (N.Y.). Home: 16 Chandler Rd., Chatham, N.J. Office: 605 Broad St., Newark, N.J.

LUMMIS, Katharine, coll. prof.; b. Natick, Mass.; d. Henry and Jennie (Brewster) Lummis; student Lawrence Coll., Appleton, Wis.; A.B., Stanford U., 1907, A.M., 1911, Ph.D., same, 1917; grad. study Am. Acad., Rome, Italy, 1910-11, Johns Hopkins U., 1914-16. Instr. Latin, Coll. of the Pacific, San Jose, Calif., 1912-14; grad. asst. in Latin, Stanford U., 1916-17; dean and prof. classics, Sweet Briar Coll., Sweet Briar, Va., 1917-23; dean, Wells Coll., Aurora, N.Y., 1923-28, prof. classics, 1928-38. Mem. Phi Beta Kappa. Awarded University Fellowship Johns Hopkins Univ., 1915. Episcopalian. Home: 942 S. 49th St., Philadelphia, Pa. Office: Wells College, Aurora, N.Y.

LUNAS, Lawrence John, elec. engring.; b. Balfour, N.D., Sept. 2, 1905; s. John and Matilda Lunas; B.S. in E.E., University of North Dakota, 1926; M.S., University of Pittsburgh, 1939; m. Pauline Howell MacGahan, June 19, 1931; children—Anne Elizabeth, John Paul. Was graduate student of course including engineering and design schools, Westinghouse Electric & Mfg. Co., East Pittsburgh, Pa., 1926-28; in employ Westinghouse Electric & Mfg. Co., Newark, N.J., since 1928, in responsible charge engring. work and designer various types portable and switchboard type indicating and recording instruments; holds U.S. and fgn. patents on various designs; registered professional engr. N.J. Mem. Am. Inst. Elec. Engrs., Phi Alpha Epsilon, Sigma Xi, Sigma Tau, Montclair Soc. Engrs., Nat. Geographic Soc. Republican. Episcopalian. Contbr. many articles to elec. and engring. jours. and papers to proceedings of A.I.E.E. Home: 14 Westland Rd., Cedar Grove (P.O., Verona). Office: 95 Orange St., Newark, N.J.

LUND, C. Harrison, lawyer; b. Erie, Pa., Sept. 7, 1888; s. Nels P. and Catherin (Sabe) L.; student Pa. State Coll. and U. of Chicago; LL.B., Temple U., 1916; m. Gladys Freeman, Apr. 18, 1922; children—John F., Sarah M., David H. Admitted to Pa. bar, 1916, and began practice in Phila., asso. with Buckman & Buckman, 1916-17; gen. practice of law in Erie, Pa., since 1919, specializing in promotion and organization of corpns.; asst. dist. atty., 1924; pres. Development Corpn. of Erie; pres. Sullivan Motor Sales Co.; owner Lunds Grape Juice Co. Served in U.S. Army, 1917-19; now capt. Judge Advocate Corps, Reserve Republican. Episcopalian. Club: Press (Erie). Address: 332 E. 6th St., Erie, Pa.

LUND, Frederick Hansen, psychologist; b. Kairanga, New Zealand, Apr. 4, 1894; s. Hans Hansen and Johanne (Höll) L.; prep. edn., Dana Coll., Blair, Neb., 1914-18; A.B., U. of Neb., 1921, A.M., 1923; Ph.D., Columbia, 1925; m. Adelia P. Butcher, June 1, 1924. Came to U.S., 1913, naturalized citizen, 1918. Instr. in psychology, U. of Neb., 1922-23, Columbia U., 1925-27; prof. of psychology, Bucknell U., Lewisburg, Pa., 1927-30, Temple U., Phila., since 1930. Sec. of com. on emotions and the educative process of Am. Council on Edn.; mem. Am. Psychol. Assn., Am. Assn. Univ. Profs., Theta Upsilon Omega, Phi Beta Kappa. Democrat. Lutheran. Author: Psychology—The Science of Mental Activity, 1927, Emotions of Men, 1930; Psychology—An Empirical Study of Behavior, 1933; Emotions—an Experimental and Physiological Study, 1938; also many tech. articles. Home: 1110 Prospect Av., Melrose Park, Philadelphia, Pa.

LUNT, William Edward, college prof.; b. Lisbon, Me., Jan. 13, 1882; s. Edward Henry and Katherine Garcelon (Flagg) L.; A.B., Bowdoin, 1904; A.M., Harvard Univ., 1905, Ph.D., 1908, traveling fellow of Harvard in Europe, 1907-08 and 11; hon. L.H.D., Bowdoin College, 1929; m. Elizabeth Elliott Atkinson, Dec. 5, 1910; children—William Edward, Jr., Robert Henry. Asst. in govt., Harvard, 1905-07; instr. history, U. of Wis., 1908-10; Thomas Brackett Reed prof. history and polit. science, Bowdoin, 1911-12; prof. English history, Cornell U., 1912-17; Walter D. and Edith M. L. Scull prof. English constl. history, Haverford Coll., since 1917. Chief of Italian div. of Am. Commn. to Negotiate Peace, Paris, 1918-19. Fellow Mediæval Academy of America (council 1932-35; v.p.), Royal Historical Soc.; mem. Am. Hist. Assn., Am. Soc. Ch. History, Zeta Psi, Phi Beta Kappa. Author: The Valuation of Norwich, 1926; History of England, 1928, rev. edit., 1938; Papal Revenues in the Middle Ages, 1934; Financial Relations of the Papacy with England to 1327, 1939; also articles on the history of mediæval papacy, etc. Home: Haverford, Pa.

LUONGO, Romeo Andoino, physician; b. Pittsburgh, Pa., Nov. 4, 1893; s. Michele and Maria Teresa (Addobati) L.; M.D., U. of Pittsburgh, 1922; grad. study, U. of Pa. Grad. Sch. of Medicine, 1926-27, M.Med.Sc., 1932, D.Sc., 1935; m. Maria A. Perfetti, June 29, 1927; children—Romeo, Maria Teresa, Laura Mae. In practice of medicine at Phila., specializing in otolaryngology. Asso. in otolaryngology, U. of Pa. Grad. Sch. of Medicine. Mem. Am. Bd. of Otolaryngology since 1930. Fellow Am. Coll. Surgeons, Am. Acad. Ophthalmology and Otolaryngology, Am. Med. Assn., Pa. State Med. Assn., Phila. Co. Med. Assn., Phila., Laryngol. Assn., Am. Laryngol, Otol. and Rhinol. Assn. Contbr. articles to med. jours. Home: 2054 Locust St., Philadelphia, Pa.

LUSCOMBE, Albert Paul, banker; b. Somerville, Mass., July 5, 1901; grad. Bentley Sch., Boston, Mass., 1923; m. Rebecca Homan Hale, Jan. 1, 1924; children—Betty Ella, Paul Albert. Clk. in accounting Federal Res. Bank of Boston, Mass., 1917-24, mgr. Havana (Cuba) Agency, 1924-27; nat. bank examiner, New York, 1927-34; exec. v.p. Rutherford (N.J.) Nat. Bank, 1934-37; exec. v.p. and dir. Peoples Nat. Bank & Trust Co., Belleville, N.J., since 1938. Mason. Home: 191 Whitford Av., Nutley, N.J. Address: Belleville, N.J.

LUTZ, Albert Clay, supervising prin. schs.; b. Middletown, Md., July 27, 1882; s. John Lewis and Mary (McBride) L.; A.B., Roanoke Coll., Salem, Va., 1907; A.M., Columbia U. Teachers Coll., 1924; ed. Johns Hopkins U. Summer Sch. Edn., 1916-18; m. Emily Pauline Rudy, Aug. 27, 1908; children—Catherine Emily, George Albert, Sereta Pauline, Carlton Edward. Engaged in teaching pub. schs. and prin. schs. in Md. and Del., 1907-20; supervising prin. and dist. supt. schs., Duryea, Pa., 1920-22; supervising prin. schs., Moosic, Pa., since 1926; successful in promoting track field activities; in 13 yrs. Moosic schs. have acquired 43 cups and trophies for athletic achievements; has sch. band of 50 to 60 pieces; local preacher Meth. Ch. Republican. Methodist. Mason. Club: Fellowship Circle. Home: 727 Minooka Av., Moosic, Pa.

LUTZ, Athey Ragan, orthopedic surgeon; b. Orkney Springs, Va., Aug. 24, 1900; s. Albert and Clara Virginia (Biller) L.; student John Marshall High Sch., Richmond, Va., 1916-20, U. of Richmond, 1920-23; M.D., Med. Coll. of Va., 1927; unmarried. In practice of orthopedic surgery since 1932; mem. staff St. Joseph Hosp., Camden-Clark Hosp., both of Parkersburg, W.Va.; mem. orthopedic staff Crippled Children's Div., W.Va. Dept. Public Assistance. Diplomate Am. Bd. Orthopedic Surgery; mem. Am. Acad. Orthopedic Surgeons, A.M.A., Southern Med. Assn., W.Va. State Med. Assn., Parkersburg Acad. Medicine. Democrat. Episcopalian. Clubs: Rotary International, Parkersburg Country (Parkersburg). Address: 1044 Market St., Parkersburg, W.Va.

LUTZ, Edwin George, artist, writer; b. Phila., Pa., Aug. 26, 1868; s. John Martin and Ernestine (Bachmann) L.; student Pa. Mus. Sch. of Industrial Art, 1886-89, Pa. Acad. of Fine Arts, 1889-92; studied at Academie Julien, Paris, and Academie Colorossi, Paris, 1904-07; unmarried. Advertising and commercial artist, designer and contbr. to mags. since 1900; artist on New York World, 1895-1900; created animated cartoons during early development of the art; since 1913, author of numerous textbooks for adults and children on practical drawing. Home: 119 Howard St., Dumont, N.J.

LUTZ, Frank Eugene, biologist; b. Bloomsburg, Pa., Sept. 15, 1879; s. Martin Peter and Anna Amelia (Brockway) L.; A.B., Haverford (Pa.) Coll., 1900; A.M., U. of Chicago, 1902, Ph.D., 1907; studied Univ. Coll., London, Eng., 1902; m. Martha Ellen Brobson, Dec. 30, 1904; children—Anna, Eleanor, Frank Brobson, Laura. Entomologist, Biol. Lab. of Brooklyn Inst., 1902; asst. in zoöl. dept., U. of Chicago, 1903; resident investigator, Sta. for Experimental Evolution (Carnegie Instn.), Cold Spring Harbor, 1904-09; asst. curator invertebrate zoölogy, 1909-16, asso. curator, 1916-1921; curator of entomology since 1921, also editor of tech. papers, Am. Mus. Natural History, and 1925-28 in charge of Station for the Study of Insects, Tuxedo, N.Y.; lecturer Columbia U., 1937. Fellow A.A.A.S., N.Y. Acad. Sciences, Entomol. Soc. America (pres., 1927); mem. Am. Soc. Zoölogists, Sigma Xi, Phi Beta Kappa, etc. Baptist. Mason. Author: Field Book of Insects, 1917. Contbr. numerous papers on variation, heredity, assortive mating, entomology, etc. Home: Ramsey, N.J.

LUTZ, George Washington, merchant; b. Wheeling, W.Va., July 17, 1855; s. Sebastian and Anna (Truschler) L.; mainly self-ed.; m. Lugene E. Hombrook, July 25, 1878 (now dec.). In mercantile business, Wheeling, 1872—; dir. Gee Elec. Co., Security Trust Co.; organizer and pres. Market Auditorium Co. 3 yrs. Club: Carroll. Democrat. Catholic. Elk. Home: Elm Grove, W.Va.

LUTZ, Harley Leist, economist; b. nr. Chillicothe, O., July 30, 1882; s. Ira and Minnie (Leist) L.; A.B., Oberlin Coll., 1907; LL.D. from same college 1932; A.M., Harvard University, 1908, Ph.D., 1914; m. Rachel A. Young, Dec. 31, 1909; children—Robert Gordon, Martha Jane, Barbara. With Oberlin Coll., 1909-23, prof. economics, 1909-23; head of dept., 1914-23; prof. economics, Stanford, 1923-28; professor of public finance, Princeton, 1928. Economic adviser Joint Taxation Com. 83d Ohio General Assembly, 1919; spl. adviser Washington Tax Investigating Com., 1922; mem. Commn. of Financial Advisers to Chile, 1925, to Poland, 1926; adviser Tax Investigation Commission of Utah, 1929; dir. New Jersey Tax Survey Commission, 1930-31. Decorated Comdr. Order of Polonia Restituta. Mem. Nat. Tax Assn. (pres. 1927-28), Am. Econ. Assn., Academia de Sciencia Economica (Chile), Phi Beta Kappa. Conglist. Author: The State Tax Commission, 1918, A Handbook of Classification of Property for Taxation, 1919; Report of Joint Special Committee on Taxation, 1919; Public Finance, 1924, 29, 36; The Georgia System of Revenue, 1930; The System of Taxation in Maine, 1934; The Fiscal and Economic Aspects of the Taxation of Public Securities, 1939. Co-Author: An Introduction to Economics, 1923 (New Introduction to Economics 1933). Home: 56 Battle Rd., Princeton, N.J.

LUTZ, Roland Bruce, clergyman; b. Phila., Pa., June 29, 1897; s. William Dellet and Margaret Ann Jane (Hillyer) L.; Litt.B., Princeton U., 1918, A.M., same, 1921; Th.B., Princeton Theol. Sem., 1921; (hon.) D.D., Beaver Coll., 1936; m. Sara Caroline Swartz, Aug. 9, 1921; children—Lois Virginia, Roland Bruce, Jr., Gordon Dellet. Ordained to ministry Presbyn. Ch., 1921; pastor Temple Ch., Phila., Pa., 1921-25, Faith Ch., Baltimore, Md., 1925-28; pastor Presbyn. Ch., Abington, Pa., since 1928; moderator Presbytery of Phila. North, 1931; mem. Council of Synod of Pa.; chmn. Adv. Com. on Christian Approach to the Jews, Presbyn. Bd. Nat. Missions. Served as 2d lt. F.A., U.S.A., 1918. Trustee Tennent Coll. Christian Edn., Phila. Mem. Forward Movement Com. of Princeton Theol. Sem., Presbyn. Ministers Social Union, Phila., Phi Beta Kappa. Republican. Presbyn. Clubs: Huntingdon Valley Country (Abington); Canterbury Cleric (Philadelphia); Friars (Princeton). Home: 4 S. York Rd., Abington, Pa.

LUTZ, William Filler, clergyman; b. Bedford, Pa., July 25, 1872; s. John and Catherine (Filler) L.; desc. John L., capt. Washington's Bodyguard at Valley Forge; A.B., Pa. Coll., 1894, A.M., 1897; ed. U. of Pa., 1896-97, Phila. Divinity Sch., 1897-1900; grad. study, U. of Pa., 1916-36; m. Ethel Freas Hogeland, Sept.

8, 1924; stepson, Russell Hogeland. Ordained to ministry P.E. Ch., 1900; successively asst. St. Mark's, Phila., rector Christ Ch., Eddington, Pa., asst. Am. chaplain, Nice, France, and actg. British chaplain, Nice and the Riviera, rector St. Michael and All Angels, Woolwich, London; rector Trinity Memorial Ch., Ambler, Pa., since 1924; asst. in psychology, U. of Pa., 1920-32; dir. Camp Ocean Wave, Trinity House Sch. since 1920. Mem. A.A.A.S., Am. Psychol. Assn., Am. Child Health Assn., English Speaking Union, Pa. Hist. Soc., Geneal. Soc., Pa. Camp Dirs. Assn., S.R., Huguenot Soc., Soc. Colonial Wars, Colonial Soc. of Pa. (since 1937 chaplain), Pa. Soc. Sons of Revolution (chaplain 1939), St. Andrew's Soc. of Phila., and Desc. Knights of the Garter. Clubs: Penn Athletic, Art Alliance (Philadelphia). Home: Ambler, Pa.

LYFORD, Oliver Smith, exec. and cons. engr.; b. Cleveland, O., Mar. 21, 1870; s. Oliver Smith and Lavinia A. (Norris) L.; Ph.B., Yale, 1890; post-grad. work, Cornell U.; m. Frances Lyman Meigs, Jan. 1896; children—Mrs. Margaret Sheldon, Olive Meigs. Chief engr. Westinghouse Electric & Mfg. Co., 1897-99; v.p. and gen. mgr. Siemens & Halske Electric Co., 1899-1901; cons. engr. and mng. engr. Westinghouse, Church, Kerr & Co., 1902-12; pvt. practice, 1913-16; maj. and lt. col., Ordnance Dept., U.S.A., 1917-18; v.p. Finance & Trading Corpn., 1919-22; pvt. practice, 1923; v.p., gen. mgr. Lawrence Investing Co., and Lawrence Park Heat, Light & Power Co., 1924-26; v.p. Brooklands, Inc., since 1927; v.p. Santa Clara Lumber Co. Republican. Presbyn. Fellow Am. Inst. E.E.; mem. Berzelius Soc. (Yale), Kappa Alpha (Cornell). Club: Yale (New York). Home: 125 Dana Place, Englewood, N.J. Office: 230 Park Av., New York, N.Y.

LYFORD, Richard Taylor, clergyman; b. Concord, N.H., Jan. 6, 1896; s. James Otis and Susan Ayer (Hill) L.; A.B., Harvard, 1917; S.T.B., Episcopal Theol. Sch., Cambridge, Mass., 1925; m. Dorothy W. Emery, June 21, 1926; 1 son, Richard T., Jr. Ordained to ministry P.E. Ch.; curate, St. Paul's Ch., Concord, N.H., 1925-26; vicar, St. Andrew's Ch., Longmeadow, Mass., 1926-31; rector, St. Asaph's Ch., Bala, Pa., since 1931. Served as pvt. F.A., U.S.A., 1917-19, with A.E.F. Dir. Phila. City Inst. Episcopalian. Home: St. Asaph's Rectory, Bala-Cynwyd, Pa.

LYMAN, Robert Ray, pres. Citizens Safe Deposit and Trust Co. of Coudersport and Gray Chem. Co.; b. Roulette, Pa., Oct. 9, 1894; s. Milo and Kittie Calista (Thompson) L.; B.S., Pa. State Coll., 1917; m. Lorena Mae Williams, July 15, 1920; children—Robert Ray, Betty Jane, Lois Ann. Pres. Citizens Safe Deposit and Trust Co. of Coudersport, Pa., since 1934, Gray Chem. Co., Roulette, Pa., since 1935; dir. Potter County Garage, Mfrs. Charcoal Co., Wood Distillers Co. Pres. Coudersport Borough Council, 1932-35. Republican. Presbyterian. Mason (Coudersport Consistory). Address: Coudersport, Pa.

LYNCH, Charles F., lawyer; b. Franklin Boro, N.J., Jan. 9, 1884; s. Patrick H. and Margaret (Crawley) L.; ed. pub. schs.; studied law as clk. in offices of Michael Dunn, Paterson, N.J., and Pierce & Greer, N.Y. City; married. Admitted to N.J. bar, 1906; associated in practice with Hon. William Hughes, Paterson, N.J.; candidate on Dem. ticket for N.J. Gen. Assembly several times; apptd. 2d asst. U.S. dist. atty., Dist. of N.J., June 1, 1913, 1st asst., Sept. 1, 1914; apptd. U.S. dist. atty., June 1916; U.S. Dist. judge, Dist. of N.J., by appmt. of President Wilson, 1919-25 (resigned); city counsel, Paterson, for term expiring Jan. 1, 1940. Mem. N.J. State, Passaic Co. and Essex Co. bar assns. Knight of Columbus, Elk. Clubs: Hamilton, North Jersey, Deal Golf, Spring Lake Tennis, Democratic, Newark Athletic, Sky Top. Home: 350 E. 38th St., Paterson, N.J. Office: 2316 Raymond Commerce Bldg., Newark, N.J. City Hall, Paterson, N.J.

LYNCH, Clay F., coke mfr.; b. Dunbar, Pa., Nov. 12, 1880; s. Thomas and Sarah (McKenna) L.; student Georgetown Coll., Washington, D.C., 1898-1902; m. Eleanor Head, Nov. 19, 1923.

Vice-pres. and gen. supt. H. C. Frick Coke Co., Scottdale, Pa., 1915-39, retired; vice-pres. and dir. First Nat. Bank of Scottdale; dir. First Nat. Bank of Latrobe, Pa.; dir. Richardson Co. and Carthage Mills Inc., Cincinnati. Democrat. Roman Catholic. Home: Bally-Duff, Greensburg, Pa. Office: 110 Broadway, Scottdale, Pa.

LYNCH, Clyde Alvin, coll. pres.; b. Harrisburg, Pa., Aug. 24, 1891; s. John Henry and Carmina Blanche (Keys) L.; prep. edn. Lebanon Valley (Pa.) Acad.; A.B., Lebanon Valley Coll., 1918, A.M., 1925, D.D., 1926; B.D., Bonebrake Theol. Seminary, 1921; A.M., University of Pa., 1929, also Ph.D., 1931; LL.D., Albright College, 1937; m. Edith L. Basehore, June 30, 1914; children—Rose Eleanor, John Howard. Ordained ministry United Brethren in Christ, 1916; pastor successively Centerville Circuit Chamber Hill and Ebenezer, Linglestown and Rockville (all of Pa.) until 1918; pastor Antioch and Pyrmont, O., 1918-21, Ephrata, Pa., 1921-25, 2d Ch., Phila., 1925-30; asst. instr. in psychology, U. of Pa., 1929-30; prof. homiletics and practical theology, Bonebrake Theol. Sem., Dayton, O., 1930-32; pres. Lebanon Valley Coll., Annville, Pa., since 1932. Pres. Southern Conv. Dist., Pa. State Edn. Assn. 1931-38, mem. exec. com., 1938-39; mem. Pa. State Y.M.C.A. (exec. com.). Mem. Federal Council of Chs. of Christ in America (exec. com.); mem. Bd. of Christian Edn. of United Brethren Ch. Mem. A.A.A.S., Am. Psychol. Assn., Pa. Acad. of Science, Dept. Sch. Adminstrs. N.E.A. Republican. Mason (32°, Shriner). Clubs: Lions of Lebanon (hon.), Rotary (Lebanon); University, Torch (Harrisburg, Pa.). Contbr. to ch. publs. Lecturer on religious, civic and ednl. subjects. Home: Annville, Pa.

LYNCH, Lawrence Robinson, lawyer; b. Clarksburg, W.Va., May 29, 1890; s. Charles Wesley and Mary Virginia (Robinson) L.; grad. Clarksburg (W.Va.) High Sch., 1908; A.B., Ohio Wesleyan U., Delaware, O., 1913; A.M., Columbia U., 1914; LL.B., Harvard Law Sch., 1917; m. Gretchen Marie Spindler, Aug. 30, 1916; children—Barbara Virginia, Martha Gretchen, Charles Wesley. Licensed to practice law, W.Va., 1917; law clk. Supreme Ct. of Appeals of W.Va., 1918-21; in pvt. practice, Clarksburg, W.Va., since 1921; assisted in revision and codification of statutes of W.Va., now the revised code of W. Va., 1923-30; dir. Empire Nat. Bank, Clarksburg. Pres. Clarksburg Chamber of Commerce, 1930, 31, 36, 37, dir. since 1929; mem. Clarksburg Pub. Library Bd. since 1928; chmn. Clarksburg Charter Bd. for Revision of City Charter, 1939. Vice-pres. bd. of trustees W.Va. Wesleyan Coll., Buckhannon, W.Va., since 1939, mem. since 1929. Mem. Am. Bar Assn., W.Va. Bar Assn., Harrison County Bar Assn. (pres. 1932), Harvard Law Sch. Assn., Order of the Coif, Phi Delta Theta. Republican. Methodist. Mason (32°). Club: Clarksburg (W.Va.) Country. Author: The West Virginia Coal Strike, 1912-13, in Polit. Science Quarterly, Dec., 1914. Home: 411 Lee Av. Office: 216 Court St., Clarksburg, W.Va.

LYNCH, Ralph, physician; b. Greensburg, Pa., Jan. 23, 1896; s. Thomas and Sarah (McKenna) L.; B.S., Dartmouth Coll., 1917; M.D., U. of Pa. Med. Sch., 1923; m. Katherine Gans, Jan. 21, 1925; children—Hugh McKenna, Ralph, Jr., Hilary Gans, David M. Interne Mercy Hosp., Pittsburgh, 1923-26, Montreal Gen. Hosp., 1926-27, Peter Bent Brigham Hosp., Boston, 1927-28; in pvt. practice of medicine at Pittsburgh, Pa., since 1928; phys. to Mercy Hosp., Presbyn. Hosp.; cons. phys., City of Pittsburgh Hosp.; asst. prof. medicine, U. of Pittsburgh Med. Sch. since 1938. Served Med. Dept., U.S.A., 1917-19. Fellow Am. Coll. Phys. Mem. Alpha Delta Phi. Roman Catholic. Clubs: Pittsburgh Golf, Fox Chapel Golf (Pittsburgh); Rolling Rock (Ligonier). Home: Hunt Rd. R.F.D. No. 2, Sharpsburg, Pa. Office: Mercy Hospital, Pittsburgh, Pa.

LYNETT, Edward James, editor, pub.; b. Dunmore, Pa., July 15, 1856; s. William and Catherine (Dowd) L.; ed. pub. schs. and Pa. State Normal Sch., Millersville, Pa.; m. Nellie A. Ruddy, Sept. 30, 1896 (died Nov. 4, 1924); children—William R., asst. pub. Scranton Times,

Elizabeth R., Edward J. Began as solicitor Scranton Daily Avalanche; reporter Sunday Morning Free Press, Scranton, 1877; became pub. and proprietor The Scranton Times, 1895 (circulation was 3,000, now is 55,000); dir. U.S. Lumber Co., Miss. Central Rd. Co., Internat. Corr. Schs., Internat. Ednl. Pub. Co., International Textbook Company. Delegate to Democratic Nat. Conv. 6 times between 1900-32. Mem. Pa. State Mine Cave Commn., 1911; mem. State Council of Defense, 1917. Trustee University of Scranton, Mercy Hospital, St. Patrick's Orphanage, St. Michael's Boys Industrial School, Maryknoll Preparatory College. Member Scranton Chamber of Commerce, Am. Newspaper Pubs. Assn., N.Am. Newspaper Alliance, Nat. Editorial Assn., Pa. Newspaper Pubs. Assn., Associated Adv. Clubs of the World, Associated Press. Catholic. Club: Scranton. Home: 841 Clay Av. Office: Times Bldg., Penn Av. and Spruce St., Scranton, Pa.

LYNETT, William R., asst. pub. Scranton Times; b. Scranton, Pa., Sept. 10, 1899; s. Edward James and Ellen (Ruddy) L.; A.B., St. Thomas Coll., Scranton, 1917; A.M., Catholic U., Washington, D.C., 1918; unmarried. Began as newspaper reporter Scranton (Pa.) Times, 1918; asst. pub. Scranton Times since 1924; dir. North Am. Newspaper Alliance, First Nat. Bank of Scranton, Scranton Lackawanna Trust Co.; trustee Community Welfare Assn.; mem. Pa. Anthracite Coal Commn., 1937. Served in U.S.N.R.C., Phila., Aug.-Dec., 1918. Mem. Pa. Com. Pub. Assistance and Relief, 1936-37. Trustee U. of Scranton; dir. Mercy Hosp. Democrat. Roman Catholic. Clubs: National Press (Washington, D.C.); Scranton, Scranton Country. Home: 841 Clay Av. Office: The Scranton Times, Scranton, Pa.

LYNN, Frank S.; prof. clin. surgery, U. of Md.; visiting surgeon University Hosp. of U. of Md., Franklin Sq., St. Agnes and Bon Secours hosps. Address: 101 W. Read St., Baltimore, Md.

LYON, Adrian, judge; b. Pluckemin, Somerset Co., N.J., July 25, 1869; s. William L. and Ursula (Sebring) L.; LL.B., New York Law Sch., 1894; m. Cornelia Post, May 8, 1895; 1 son, Howard S.; admitted to N.J. bar, 1892; supt. schs., Perth Amboy, 1894-95; city atty., 1895-98; pres. Perth Amboy Savings Instn. since 1899; mem. N.J. Legislature, 1900-01; judge Perth Amboy Dist. Court, 1901-09; referee in bankruptcy, 1913-30; judge Middlesex County Court of Common Pleas, 1909-11, and since 1930. Mem. Am., N.J. State and Middlesex County bar assns., N.J. State Bankers Assn. (pres., 1914), S.A.R. (pres., 1922, 23). Treas. Perth Amboy Gen. Hosp. since 1905; pres. Perth Amboy Y.M.C.A. since 1912; chmn. Gen. Bd. Nat. Council Y.M.C.A., 1925-35; mem. Gen. Council Presbyn. Ch., U.S.A., 1931-37; trustee Princeton Theol. Sem. Republican. Clubs: Union League (New York); Rotary, Masonic. Address: 84 Gordon St. Office: 210 Smith St., Perth Amboy, N.J.

LYON, B.B. Vincent, physician; b. Erie, Pa., Mar. 29, 1880; s. George Armstrong and Rose (Vincent) L.; A.B., Williams Coll., 1903; M.D., Johns Hopkins U. Med. Sch., 1907; Sc.D., Williams Coll., 1931; grad. study in Europe, 1914, 1923, 1927, 1937; m. Clara Armstrong, Jan. 11, 1910; children—Rose Vincent (Mrs. Lawrence Price Sharples), B.B. Vincent, Jr., Armstrong. Interne German (Lankenau) Hosp., 1907-09; clin. asst. out-patient med. dispensary, U. of Pa., German, Presbyn. and Jefferson Hosps., Phila., 1910-13; asst. phys. Jefferson Hosp. since 1929, founder and chief of clinic, out-patient stomach dept. since 1912; demonstrator in medicine, Jefferson Med. Coll., 1910-20, asso. in medicine, 1920-28, asst. prof., 1929-37, asso. prof. in medicine since 1937. Served as lt. (s.g.) Med. Corps. U.S.N. R.F., 1917-19, Naval Base Hosp., Brest, France, also with Marine Corps and U.S.A. in France. Mem. Am. Com. and del. to 1st Internat. Cong. of Gastro-Enterology, Brussels, Belgium, 1935; hon. mem. Soc. Gastro-Enterology, Brussels. Mem. Pithotomy Club of Johns Hopkins, Sigma Phi. Republican. Presbyn. Clubs: Medical (Philadelphia); Williams (New York). Author of monograph, Non-Surgical Drainage of the Gall Tract, 1923. Contbr. to med. books and cycs. and many articles to med. mags. Home: Rosemont, Pa. Office: 2031 Locust St., Philadelphia, Pa.

LYON, George Marshall, pediatrician; b. Union City, Pa., Feb. 8, 1895; s. Marshall Allen and Harriet Bell (Law) L.; teacher training, Marshall Coll., Huntington, W.Va., 1909-13; B.S., Denison U., 1916; M.D., Johns Hopkins U., 1920; m. Virginia Berkeley Sutherland, June 24, 1922 (died June 20, 1926); children—Virginia Berkeley, Natalie Sutherland, Harriet Elizabeth; m. 2d, Theeta Carrington Searcy, July 29, 1927; 1 son, George Marshall. Resident house officer Johns Hopkins Hosp., 1919-21; pediatrician Holzer, Memorial and St. Mary's hosps. since 1925; chief of staff Memorial Hosp., 1931-33; dir. sch. health program, Cabell County pub. schs., 1933-39; lecturer post-grad. confs., Va., 1934, 35, W.Va., 1936, 37, Miss., 1938. Chmn. W.Va. White House Conf. on Child Health and Protection, 1933; official rep. U.S. Govt. to 7th Pan-Am. Congress on the Child, Mexico City, 1937; mem. advisory com. on maternal and child health, Children's Bur., United States Dept. Labor, 1938, 39. Engaged in gas research, U.S. Bur. of Mines and Chem. Warfare Service, U.S.A., 1918; hon. discharged, Med. Emergency Relief Corps, 1917, S.A.T.C., 1918; lt. comdr. Medical Corps, U.S. Naval Res., since 1935. Awarded Victory Medal, World War. Dir. hospitalization and emergency med. relief, Am. Red Cross, Huntington Flood, 1937. Fellow American Academy Pediatrics (chairman committee on post-graduate education since 1935), Society for Research in Child Development; mem. Am. Pediatric Soc., Phi Gamma Delta, Nu Sigma Nu. Republican. Presbyn. Mason. Clubs: Guyan Country, Gypsy (Huntington). Writer many articles on epidemic meningitis, acute poliomyelitis, school health and child health problems, infant mortality studies and many other clin. subjects. Home: 111 Kingshighway. Office: 955 Fourth Av., Huntington, W.Va.

LYON, Howard Suydam, banker; b. Perth Amboy, N.J., Jan. 27, 1896; s. Adrian and Cornelia (Post) L.; grad. Perth Amboy High Sch., 1913; student Tome Inst., 1913-14; Litt.B., Princeton U., 1918; m. Mildred Derry, Aug. 13, 1921; 1 son, Roger Adrian. Clerk Nat. Bank of Commerce, New York, 1919-23; nat. bank examiner, 1923-25; exec. v.p. Phillipsburg Nat. Bank & Trust Co., 1925-33, Somerville Trust Co. since 1933. Served as chief machinist mate and ensign, U.S. Naval Res., 1917-18; lt. (j.g.) Naval Militia, N.J., 1920. Trustee Somerset Hosp.; mem. bd. mgrs. Epileptic Village, Skillman, N.J. Republican. Mem. Reformed Ch. Clubs: Bankers (New York); Raritan Valley Country (Somerville). Home: 246 Altamont Pl. Office: 50 West Main St., Somerville, N.J.

LYON, James Alexander, M.D.; b. Broome Co., N.Y., Feb. 28, 1882; s. Henry and Katherine (Murray) L.; high sch., Goshen, N.Y., and pvt. tutoring; student, Ohio U. and Syracuse U.; M.D., Md., Med. Coll., Baltimore, 1906; grad. study, Harvard Med. Sch., Nat. Heart Hosp. (London), and Univ. of Vienna; m. Irene Elizabeth Moore; 1 dau., Elizabeth. Interne Bay View Hosp., Baltimore, 1906-07; asst. physician Loomis Sanatorium, Liberty, N.Y., 1907-09; asst. supt. and physician Mass. State Sanatorium for Tuberculosis, Rutland, Mass., 1909-16; prof. clinical cardiology, Georgetown U. Med. Sch.; attending cardiologist The Doctors' Hosp., Inc., Children's and Emergency Hospitals; chief cardiac clinics, Children's and Emergency Hospitals; mem. med. staff Georgetown U. Hosp.; mem. Med. Council of United States Veterans Bureau; mem. med. bd. of advisers The Sidwell Friends Sch.; mem. bd. of dirs. Washington Loan and Trust Co., The Inter-Am. Horse Show Assn., Inc., Health Security Adminstrn., Inc., The Doctors' Hosp., Inc., Washington, D.C. Served as lieut., capt. and maj. Med. Corps, U.S. Army, 1916-25; Mexican border service, 1916-17; joined A.E.F., Oct. 1917 (51st Brig., 26th Div.); organized and commanded Camp Hosp. No. 4, Neufchateau, France, Oct. 1917; attached to Evacuation Hosp. No. 19 (French), Soisson Sector, Jan.-Mar. 1918; graduate, U.S.A. Sanitary Sch., Longue, France; battalion surgeon, 104th U.S. Inf., 26th Div., May 1918-Apr. 1919; asst. chief med. service, U.S. Base Hosp., Camp Devens, Mass.; chief med. service, Base Hosp., Camp Shelby, Miss., and Gen. Hosp. No. 8, Otisville, N.Y., 1919; asst. attng. surg., U.S. Army Dispensary, Washington, D.C., 1919-23; detached service, Med. Dept., U.S.A., London and Vienna, 1923-24; post surg., Fort Wayne, Detroit, Mich., 1924-25; resigned, July 1925, to enter private practice in Washington, D.C. As batt. surg., 104th U.S. Inf., participated in battles of Champagne-Marne, Aisne-Marne, Meuse-Argonne, St. Mihiel, Ile de France, Lorraine, defense of Toul; citations, in Gen. Orders (Nos. 28 and 74), 26th Div., A.E.F. (Aisne-Marne, Meuse-Argonne); decorations, Victory Medal (with 5 campaign clasps), Silver Star, and Purple Heart (U.S.A.); citations, French Army Corps, Army of the East (Verdun), decorations, Croix de Guerre with Gold Star, Grande Guerre, Verdun and Chateau Thierry Campaign Medals (France). Fellow A.M.A., Am. Coll. Physicians (life mem.), Am. Board of Internal Med., New York Academy of Med., A.A.A.S.; mem. Internat. Med. Soc. (treas.), Pan Am. Med. Assn. (trustee; pres. Washington chapter), Am. Heart Assn., Washington Heart Assn. (ex-pres.), Assn. for Study of Internal Secretions, Am. Therapeutic Soc. (ex-vice pres.), Am. Assn. of the Hist. of Med., Southern Med. Soc., Med. Soc. of D.C., Washington Med. and Surg. Soc., The Hippocrates-Galen Soc. of Washington, D.C., Assn. Mil. Surgeons of U.S., Mil. Order of Foreign Wars (surg. gen. of Nat. Commandery; past comdr Washington Commandery), Mil. Order of World War (life mem.; junior vice comdr., Washington Commandery), Mil. Order of Purple Heart, Mil. Order of Carabao, Am. Inst. Banking, N.Y., English Speaking Union, Museum of Natural History of N.Y., Columbia Historical Soc., Phi Chi, Phi Delta Theta. Clubs: Army and Navy (ex-mem. bd. of govs.), Metropolitan (Washington, D.C.); Chevy Chase, Burning Tree, Woodmont Rod and Gun (med. bd. of govs., Md.). Contbr. to med. journals on diseases of heart and circulation. Home: "Glenview Farm," Baltimore Boul., Rockville, Md. Office: 1801 I St. N.W., Washington, D.C.

LYON, John Denniston, retired banker; b. Pittsburgh, Pa., Jan. 24, 1861; s. Alexander Parker and Eliza Thaw (Denniston) L.; grad. Lawrenceville, N.J., Sch., 1878; m. Maude Fleming Byers, Feb. 18, 1896; 1 dau., Martha Byers (Mrs. H. Nelson Slater). Began with William R. Thompson & Co., Pittsburgh, 1890; with N. Holmes & Sons, 1900-05; elected v.p. Union Nat. Bank, 1905, and dir. Safe Deposit & Trust Co. (now Peoples Pittsburgh Trust Co.), of which became pres., 1913; dir. A. M. Byers Co., Pittsburgh Coal Co. Federal dir. Nat. War Savings Com., World War. Republican. Presbyn. Clubs: Pittsburgh, Duquesne, Allegheny Country; Knickerbocker, Racquet and Tennis, The Brook, Links, Piping Rock, Nat. Golf Links (New York). Home: Sewickley, Pa. Office: 1602 Clark Bldg., Pittsburgh, Pa.

LYON, Julian Milton, physician; b. Absecon, N.J., Dec. 19, 1894; s. Melvern Seymour and Hannah L. (Crosby) L.; B.Sc., Rutgers Coll., 1919; M.D., Harvard U. Med. Sch., 1923; unmarried. Interne Presbyterian Hosp., Phila., 1924-26; resident physician N.Y. Nursery and Child's Hosp., 1926-27; engaged in practice of pediatrics, Ardmore, Pa., since 1927; asst. prof., Dept. of Pediatrics, Grad. Sch. of Medicine, U. of Pa. Mem. Am. Med. Assn., Phila. Co. Med. Soc., Am. Acad. Pediatrics, Phila. Pediatric Soc., Delta Upsilon. Methodist. Home: 40 Llanfair Rd., Ardmore, Pa.

LYON, Leland; chmn. bd., pres. and dir. Atlas Powder Co. Home: 901 N. Broom St. Office: Delaware Trust Bldg., Wilmington, Del.

LYON, Leverett Samuel, economist; b. Sollitt, Ill., Dec. 14, 1885; s. Edward Payson and Charlotte (Rose) L.; Beloit Coll., 1906-07; Ph.B., U. of Chicago, 1910; LL.B., Chicago-Kent Coll. of Law, 1915; A.M., U. of Chicago, 1919, Ph. D., 1921; m. Lucille Norton, June 26, 1915; children—Richard Norton, David Mansfield. Head dept. civic science, Joliet Twp. High Sch., 1910-14, 1915-16; admitted to Ill. bar, 1916; asst. in economics, 1916-17, instr., 1917-19, asst. prof., 1919-23, asso. prof., 1923, U. of Chicago; dean Sch. Commerce and Finance, prof. economics and head of dept., 1923-25, Washington U.; prof. economics, Robert Brookings Grad. Sch. of Economics and Government, 1925-29; mem. research staff and dir. ednl. activities and public relations of the Brookings Institution, 1929-32, exec. v.p. since 1932; dep. asst. adminstr. for trade practice policy, NRA summer 1934. U.S. del. to the International Congress on Business Education, Amsterdam, 1929, London, 1932. Editorial asst. U.S. Food Adminstrn., World War. Mem. Am. Economic Assn., Am. Statistical Assn., American Marketing Assn. (pres. 1933), Phi Kappa Psi (nat. pres. 1936-38), Sigma Delta Rho, Phi Delta Phi, Beta Gamma Sigma, Alpha Kappa Psi. Clubs: Cosmos, Chevy Chase (Washington); Quadrangle (Chicago). Author: Elements of Debating, 1913; Eight Lessons (in Bulletin of National and Community Life), 1917; A Survey of Commercial Education in the Public High Schools of the United States, 1919; A Functional Approach to Social Economic Data, 1920; Education for Business, 1922, 3d edit., 1931; Making a Living, 1926; Salesmen in Marketing Strategy, 1926; Hand-to-Mouth Buying, 1929; Some Trends in the Marketing of Canned Foods, 1930; Advertising Allowances, 1932; The Economics of Free Deals, 1933; A Preliminary Analysis for a Program of Economic Education, 1937. Joint Author: Our Economic Organization, 1921; Business Cases and Problems, 1925; Vocational Readings, 1927; ABC of the NRA, 1934; The National Recovery Administration, 1935; The Economics of Open Price Systems, 1936; Government in Relation to Economic Life, 1939. Joint Editor: Textbooks in The Social Studies (11 vols.). Contbr. to professional and other jours. Home: Persimmon Tree Road, Cabin John, Md. Office: 722 Jackson Pl., Washington, D.C.

LYONS, Louis Willard, treas. Westinghouse Electric & Mfg. Co.; b. Pittsburgh, Pa.; s. Andrew and Katherine (McCauley) L.; student commercial schs.; m. Claralee Duva, Nov. 22, 1904; 1 dau., Katherine Elizabeth. Asso. with Westinghouse Electric & Mfg. Co., Pittsburgh, Pa., since 1903, treas. since 1935; dir. Credit Assn. of Western Pa., Electric Ry. Equipment Securities Corpn., First Nat. Bank & Trust Co. of East Pittsburgh, Turtle Creek & Allegheny River R.R. Co., Westinghouse Inter-Works Ry. Co. Mem. Pittsburgh Chamber of Commerce. Mason (32°). Clubs: Bankers, Oakmont County, Edgewood Country (Pittsburgh); Bankers of America (New York). Home: 6712 Beacon St. Office: 306 Fourth Av., Pittsburgh, Pa.

LYTLE, William Torrance, clergyman; b. Pittsburgh, Pa., Dec. 23, 1889; s. William Wilson and Mary (Torrance) L.; grad. with 2d honor, Wilkinsburg (Pa.) High Sch., 1908; A.B., Monmouth (Ill.) Coll., 1912; grad. with 2d honor, Pittsburgh-Xenia Theol. Sem., 1915; D.D., Westminster Coll., New Wilmington, Pa., 1929; m. Hazel Alice Pierce, Aug. 25, 1915; children—Mary Elizabeth, William Pierce. Ordained to ministry United Presbyterian Ch., 1915; minister U.P. Ch., Mt. Pleasant, Pa., 1915-16; minister Ben Avon U.P. Ch., Ben Avon, Pittsburgh, since Nov. 1, 1916. Moderator Allegheny Presbytery, 1925; mem. bd. dirs. Pittsburgh-Xenia Theol. Sem., 1925-27; mem. exec. com. Pittsburgh Union Ministers Assn., 1934; pres. Alumni Assn. of Pittsburgh-Xenia Theol. Sem., 1932-33; mem. United Presbyn. Bd. of Publication and Bible Sch. Work since 1939. Home: 502 Walnut Rd., Ben Avon, Pittsburgh, Pa.

M

MABON, Thomas McCance, physician; b. Pittsburgh, Pa., Aug. 11, 1890; s. John Steele and Jane Hurst (McCance) M.; B.S., Princeton, 1913; M.D., Harvard U. Med. Sch., 1917; m. Marjorie Arnold, Dec. 28, 1921; children—John Steele (dec.), Thomas McCance, Jr. Interne Mass. Gen. Hosp., Boston, 1917-18, Allegheny Gen. Hosp., Pittsburgh, Pa., 1918-19; physician at Presbyterian Hosp., Magee Hosp., and Falk Clinic, Pittsburgh.; asso. prof. of preventive medicine and hygiene, later asst. prof. of medicine, Sch. of Medicine, U. of Pittsburgh since 1921; engaged in practice of medicine at Pittsburgh since 1920. Served as 1st lt. Med. Corps, U.S.A., 1918-19. Fellow A.M.A., Am. Coll. Phys., Am. Pub. Health Assn. Certified by Am. Bd. Internal Medicine. Mem. Pa. State and Allegheny Co. med. socs., Pittsburgh Acad. Medicine (sec.). Republican. Club: Harvard of Boston. Home: 5446 Kipling Rd., Pittsburgh, Pa.

MacARTHUR, Angus, vice-pres. Koppers Co.; b. Duluth, Minn., Nov. 29, 1888; s. Angus and Mary (McAlpine) MacA.; B.S. in M.E., U. of Wis., 1911; m. Zela Smith. Employed in various capacities to 1918; works supt., Minneapolis Gas Light Co., 1918-20; sales engr., Koppers Constrn. Co., Pittsburgh, Pa., 1920-21; asst. supt. Chicago By-Product Coke Co., Chicago, Ill., 1921-23; dist. engr. Koppers Construction Co., Chicago, Ill., 1923-27; v.p. and mgr. Connecticut Coke Co., New Haven, Conn., 1927-30; v.p. and dist. mgr., Koppers Gas & Coke Co., New York and Pittsburgh, 1930-36; v.p. and dir. Koppers Co., Pittsburgh, since 1936; pres. and dir. Connecticut Coke Co., Phila. Coke Co.; v.p. and trustee Eastern Gas & Fuel Assns.; dir. Brooklyn Borough Gas Co., Montreal Coke & Mfg. Co. Mem. Am. Iron and Steel Inst., Am. Gas Assn., Soc. of Gas Lighting, Eastern States Blast Furnace and Coke Oven Assn. Republican. Methodist. Clubs: Duquesne, Oakmont Country. Home: Park Mansions. Office: Koppers Bldg., Pittsburgh, Pa.

MACARTNEY, Clarence Edward Noble, clergyman; b. Northwood, O., Sept. 18, 1879; s. J. L. (D.D.) and Catherine (Robertson) M.; B.A. from Univ. of Wisconsin, 1901; M.A., Princeton, 1904; grad. Princeton Theol. Sem., 1905; D.D., Geneva College, 1914, Litt.D., same college, 1933; LL.D., Washington and Jefferson Coll., 1939; unmarried. Ordained Presbyterian ministry, 1905; pastor 1st Church, Paterson, N.J., 1905-14, Arch St. Ch., Phila., 1914-1927; First Church, Pittsburgh, since 1927. Dir. Westminster and Princeton theol. seminaries; moderator Presbyn. Ch. in U.S.A., 1924-25. Stone Foundation lecturer, Princeton Theol. Sem., 1928; Ott lecture, Davidson Coll., 1934; Davis lectures, Hiram Coll., 1937, Smythe lectures, Columbia Theol. Sem., 1939. Author: The First Presbyterian Church, Paterson, N.J. (hist. sketch), 1913; The Minister's Son, 1917; Twelve Great Questions About Christ, 1923; Lincoln and His Generals, 1925; Putting on Immortality, 1926; Highways and Byways of the Civil War, 1926; Of Them He Chose Twelve, 1927; Christianity and Common Sense, 1927; Wrestlers with God, 1930; Things Most Surely Believed, 1931; Lincoln and his Cabinet, 1931; The Way of a Man with a Maid, 1931; Sermons from Life, 1932; Parables of the Old Testament, 1916. Compiler Great Sermons of the World, 1927; Paul the Man, 1928; Sons of Thunder, 1929; Parallel Lives of the Old and New Testaments, 1930; Heroes of the Old Testament, 1935; Bible Epitaphs, 1936; Not Far from Pittsburgh, 1936; Right Here in Pittsburgh, 1937; Peter and His Lord, 1937; Bible Epitaphs, 1938; More Sermons from Life, 1939; The Bonapartes in America, 1939. Contbr. lit. and hist. articles to mags. Address: First Presbyn. Church, Pittsburgh, Pa.

MacBRIDE-DEXTER, Edith, physician; b. Grove City, Pa., May 3, 1887; d. Robert and Ellen (Bigler) MacBride; B.S., Grove City (Pa.) Coll., 1906; M.D., Woman's Med. Coll. of Pa., Phila., 1910; post-grad. work in ophthalmology, New York Eye and Ear Infirmary, 1917, Clinics in London, England, 1925, 1927, Vienna, Austria, 1927; m. Allen T. Dexter, Nov. 16, 1929. Resident physician, St. Vincent's Hosp., Erie, Pa., 1910-11, chief resident physician, Jan.-July 1917; gen. practice, Grove City, Pa., and physician to girl students at Grove City (Pa.) Coll., 1912-17; in practice of ophthalmology, Erie, Pa., 1917-19, now in Sharon, and mem. staff, Buhl Hosp., Sharon, 1919-35; teacher of nurses, Buhl Hosp., 1920-35; ophthalmologist to Sharon (Pa.) Works, Westinghouse Co., 1923-35; sec. of health, Commonwealth of Pa., 1935-39. Chmn. Adv. Health Bd., Sanitary Water Bd.; mem. Ohio-Pa. Pymatuning Commn., 1935-39; member Water and Power Resources Board, State Bd. of Med. Edn. and Licensure, State Anat. Bd., State Dental Council and Examining Bd., State Bd. of Undertakers, Pennsylvania Constitution Commemoration Committee and Pennsylvania Adv. Committee on Women's Participation for New York World's Fair. Awarded Meritorious Service Medal and cited by Gov. for distinguished pub. health work during floods in 1936. Mem. Mercer Co., Pa. State med. socs. (past v.p. Pa. soc.), A.M.A., State and Provincial Health Authorities of N. America, Pa. Pub. Health Assn. (chmn. exec. com., 1935-39), Am. Pub. Health Assn. Democrat. Presbyn. Home: 894 Linden St. Office: Boyle Bldg., Sharon, Pa.

MAC CALLUM, John Archibald, clergyman; b. Gananoque, Ont., Can., Feb. 2, 1874; s. Peter and Mary (Kane) M.; B.A., Queen's U., Kingston, Ont., 1899; student Columbia, 1900-03; B.D., magna cum laude, Union Theol. Sem., 1903; D.D., Lafayette, 1915; m. Josephine Dickson Russell, May 30, 1904. Ordained Presbyn. ministry, 1903; pastor Washingtonville, N.Y., 1903-07, 1st Ch., Chestnut Hill, Phila., 1907-10, Walnut St. Ch., Phila., since 1910. Is the 23d mem. of immediate family connection to be ordained to Presbyn. ministry. Only official rep. of Am. chs. at 13th Internat. Congress On the Lord's Day, Edinburgh, 1908. Pres. Phila. Housing Assn.; mem. Com. for Slum Clearance in Phila.; mem. Presbyn. Bd. of City Missions, Phila.; trustee Temple Univ.; mem. bd. dirs. Presbyn. Ministers Fund (chmn. finance com.); sec. and mgr. Ministers Mutual Life Ins. Co., Boston, Mass.; chmn. Phila. Com. on Race Relations; first pres. Com. of 100 (clergy), 1933-35; chmn. bd. 1935—; pres. Union Theol. Alumni Assn., 1923-24; chmn. Phila. Advisory Com. on Housing; lecturer Inst. of Pub. Affairs, Charlottesville, Va., 1936, 37; chmn. N. Am. Com. to Aid Spanish Democracy (Phila.). Clubs: Union League, Phi Alpha, Contemporary (pres. 1933-35); University (Boston). Author: Now I Know, 1924; The Great Partnership, 1926. Editor of Presbyterian Tribune, New York. Contbr. to mags., revs. and weekly papers. Home: 3925 Walnut St. Office: 3936 Sansom St., Philadelphia, Pa.

MAC CALLUM, William George, pathologist; b. Dunnville, Ont., Apr. 18, 1874; s. Dr. George Alexander and Florence O. (Eakins) M.; B.A., U. of Toronto, 1894; M.D., Johns Hopkins, 1897; unmarried. Asso. prof. pathology, 1900-08, prof. pathol. physiology, 1908-09, Johns Hopkins U.; prof. pathology, Columbia U., 1909-17; prof. pathology and bacteriology, Johns Hopkins U., since 1917. Contbr. to med. jours. on pathol. subjects. Fellow A.A.A.S.; mem. Assn. Am. Physicians, Nat. Acad. Sciences; hon. fellow Royal Soc. Medicine, London, England; hon. mem. Soc. Medicorum Sverana, Stockholm, 1918. Author: Text-book of Pathology, 1916. Contbr. to Johns Hopkins Hosp. Bull., Jour. A.M.A., Jour. Experimental Medicine, etc. Home: 701 St. Paul St. Address: Johns Hopkins Hospital, Baltimore, Md.

MacCARTER, William J., Jr., lawyer; b. Phila., Pa., Sept. 17, 1890; s. William J. and Margaret (Caterson) MacC.; grad. West Chester (Pa.) State Normal Sch., 1910; LL.B., U. of Pa. Law Sch., 1915; m. Mary Comerford, Aug. 13, 1923; 1 dau., Gloria. Admitted to Pa. bar, 1915, and since in practice at Chester, Pa.; asst. dist. atty., Delaware Co., Pa., 1919-20, 1st asst. dist. atty., 1920-28, dist. atty., 1928-36; dir. Glen-Nor Bldg. Assn. Mem. Am. Legion. Republican. Presbyterian. Mason (32°), Elk. Clubs: Aronomink Golf (Newtown Square, Pa.); Skytop (Skytop, Pa.). Home: 14 Swarthmore Av., Ridley Park, Pa. Office: 502 Crozer Bldg., Chester, Pa.

MAC CLINTOCK, Paul, prof. geology; b. Aurora, N.Y., Feb. 2, 1891; s. William D. and Lucia Porter (Lander) MacC.; B.S., U. of Chicago, 1912, Ph.D., 1920; m. Elizabeth S. Copeland, Sept. 1925; children—Lucia Lander, Copeland. Engaged as instr. U. of Chicago, 1920-25. asst. prof., 1925-28, asso. prof., 1928; Knox Taylor prof. Princeton U. since 1929. Served as corpl. to 2d lt. Engrs., U.S.A., 1917-18. Mem. Geol. Soc. America, A.A.A.S., Sigma Xi, Alpha Delta Phi. Home: 170 Prospect Av., Princeton, N.J.

MacCLOSKEY, James Edward, Jr., lawyer; b. Pittsburgh, Pa., Dec. 16, 1876; s. James Edward and Catherine Hayes (Houston) MacC.; A.B., Harvard, 1900, LL.B., 1902; m. Helen Irwin, Nov. 1, 1905; children—Katharine, Helen (Mrs. Howard F. Rough). Admitted to Pa. bar, 1902, and since practiced in Pittsburgh; chmn. bd. of dirs. Harbison-Walker Refractories Co.; mem. bd. of dirs. Union Trust Co. of Pittsburgh, Bellefield Co., Hotel Schenley. Vice-pres. and trustee Hosp. Service Assn. of Pittsburgh; pres. and trustee Shadyside Hosp.; sec. and treas. Pittsburgh Park and Playground Soc.; vice-pres. Pa. Coll. for Women. Republican. Unitarian. Clubs: Duquesne, Longue Vue (mem. bd. govs.), University, Harvard-Yale-Princeton (Pittsburgh). Home: 1301 Inverness Av. Office: Farmers Bank Bldg., Pittsburgh, Pa.

MacCOLL, Alexander, clergyman; b. Glasgow, Scotland, Dec. 27, 1866; s. Hugh and Janet (Roberton) M.; ed. Glasgow High Sch. and Univ., and Union Theol. Sem. (non grad.); D.D., Rutgers, 1914; m. Grant Stuart Hally Craig, June 15, 1892; children—Ailsa Craig, Alexander Meredith. Came to U.S., 1886, naturalized citizen, 1898. Editor New Bedford (Mass.) Evening Journal 5 yrs.; ordained ministry, 1897; asst., N. Ref. Ch., Newark, N.J., 1896-97; minister Congl. Ch., Briarcliff Manor, N.Y., 1897-1907, S. St. Presbyn. Ch., Morristown, N.J., 1907-11, 2d Ch., Phila., since 1911. Trustee Gen. Assembly Presbyn. Ch. in U.S.A.; univ. preacher many yrs., Princeton, Harvard, etc. Clubs: Union League, University, Phi Alpha, Merion Cricket. Author: A Working Theology, 1909; The Sheer Folly of Preaching, 1923. Address: 21st and Walnut Sts., Philadelphia, Pa.

MacCOLLUM, Isaac James, physician; b. Fenwick Island, Del., Aug. 18, 1889; s. Orlando L. and Mary E. (James) MacC.; student pub. sch., Roxana, Del., 1895-1907, West Chester (Pa.) State Normal Sch. (now State Teachers Coll.), 1907-10; M.D., Jefferson Med. Coll., Phila., Pa., 1914; m. Marion M. Maclay, Oct. 25, 1915. Resident physician Del. Hosp., Wilmington, Del., 1914-15; in gen. practice medicine, Wyoming, Del., since 1916; surgical staff Kent Gen. Hosp., Dover, Del., since 1927; examiner for over 20 life insurance companies (awarded medal by Met. Life Co. for 20 yrs. service); dir. Baltimore Trust Co., Selbyville, Bridgeville and Camden, Del., since 1935, vice-pres. since 1937. Pres. Wyoming (Del.) Bd. of Health since 1916. Trustee Del. State Hosp., Farnhurst, Del. Mem. Kent Co. Med. Soc., Del. State Med. Soc. (pres. 1930), A.M.A., Jefferson Med. Coll. Alumni Assn. Democrat. Methodist. Mason (Shriner, Lu Lu Temple), K.P., Odd Fellow. Speaker on 20th anniversary of graduation from Jefferson Med. Coll. at Alumni Assn. and to graduating class. Address: Wyoming, Del.

MacCOY, William Logan, attorney and banker; b. Phila., Pa., Mar. 4, 1885; s. Alexander Watt and Emma Martha (Logan) M.; grad. Haverford (Pa.) Sch., 1902; A.B., Princeton U., 1906, LL.B., U. of Pa., 1910; m. Marguerite Pascal Wood, Oct. 16, 1912; children—Janet Morris (Mrs. Robert F. Edgar), Marguerite Wood (wife of Arthur M. Rogers, M.D.). Teacher Haverford Sch., 1906-07; admitted to Pa. bar, 1910; law clerk with Duane, Morris & Heckscher, Phila., 1910-11; since 1911 successively mem. law firms of MacCoy, Evans & Hutchinson, then MacCoy, Evans, Hutchinson & Lewis, and now MacCoy, Brittain, Evans & Lewis; pres. and dir. Provident Trust Co. of Phila. since Feb. 1, 1938; dir. Commonwealth Title Co., Provident Title Co., Goodall Rubber Co. Served in Naval Aviation during World War; commd. ensign U.S.N.F.R. Dir. Haverford Sch.; trustee Bryn Mawr Presbyn. Ch.; mgr. Bryn Mawr Hosp.; dir. Big Brother Assn.; dir. Phila. Orchestra Assn.; chmn. Phila. Co. Emergency Relief Bd., 1933-34. Mem. Phila., Pa. and Am. bar assns., Legal Club, Junior

Legal Club, Am. Inst. of Banking, Reserve City Bankers Assn., Pa. Scotch-Irish Soc., Hist. Soc. of Pa., Zeta Psi, Cap and Gown Club of Princeton. Republican. Presbyterian. Clubs: Rittenhouse, Midday, Corinthian, Merion Cricket, Contemporary, Princeton (Phila.). Home: City Av., Overbrook, Phila. Office: Provident Trust Bldg., Philadelphia, Pa.

MAC CREADIE, William Thomas, asso. prof. mathematics; b. Pawtucket, R.I., July 8, 1888; s. Thomas and Sarah (Knipe) Mac C.; student Phillips Acad., Andover, 1905-07; B.S. in M.E., Mass. Inst. Tech., 1911; A.M., Harvard U., 1924; Ph.D. in Mathematics, Cornell U., 1928; m. Vera Johnson, Aug. 1, 1916. Asso. with Stone & Webster and Lockwood, Greene & Co., 1911-13; prof. mathematics, Norwich U., Northfield, Vt., 1913-16; instr. engring., R.I. State Coll., Kingston, R.I., 1916-17; prof. mathematics, Norwich U., 1917-23; instr. mathematics, Cornell U., 1924-27; asso. prof. mathematics, Bucknell U., Lewisburg, Pa., since 1928. Republican. Episcopalian. Mason. Contbr. to Proceedings of the Nat. Acad. of Sci. Home: 42 13th St., Lewisburg, Pa.

MacDADE, Albert Dutton, judge; b. Lower Chichester Twp., Pa., Sept. 23, 1871; s. Joseph Walker and Amy Manwarren (Hedden) MacD.; student Chester (Pa.) High Sch., 1885-88, Chester (Pa.) Acad., 1889-90; LL.B., U. of Pa. Law Sch., 1894; m. Mabel Troth, Oct. 5, 1899; children—Millicent Troth (Mrs. Lyle G. Durham), Dutton Troth; m. 2d, Jessie G. Kimes, February 17, 1924, at Palm Beach, Fla.; m. 3d, Clara P. Wood, Feb. 21, 1939, at Ormond, Fla. Admitted to Delaware Co. bar, 1894, and practiced at Chester, Pa., 1894-1928; dist. atty., Del. Co., Pa., 1906-12; Pa. state senator, 1921-28; judge, Ct. of Common Pleas, Del. Co., Pa., since 1928; presidential elector, 9th Senatorial Dist., Pa., 1934. Served as Minute Man during World War. Mem. Del. Co., Pa. Bar Assn., Am. Bar Assn. (del. to London Conf., 1924). Decorated Cavalieri Order of the Crown of Italy. Republican. Protestant Episcopalian. Mason. Clubs: Union League (Phila.); Penn (Chester, Pa.). Home: 2304 Edgmont Av., Chester, Pa. Office: Court House, Media, Pa.

MAC DONALD, Harry, stock broker; b. Germantown, Pa., May 30, 1888; s. Robert and Annie (Clarke) Mac D.; ed. pub. schs.; m. Mabel Neville Lea, May 25, 1915; children—Doris Louise (Mrs. Albert J. Deisinger, Jr.), Barbara Lea. Began as board boy in brokers office, 1902; now resident partner in charge Germantown office Mac Donald & Co., stock brokers, mems. N.Y. Stock Exchange, Phila. Stock Exchange, N.Y. Curb Asso. Mem. Business Men's Assn. of Germantown (dir.). Trustee Calvery Presbyn. Ch., Wyncote, Pa. Republican. Clubs: Union League (Phila.); Huntingdon Valley Country (mem. house com.); Lions. Home: Wyncote, Pa. Office: 18 W. Chelten Av. Bldg., Germantown, Pa.

MacDONALD, Harry Baldwin, banker; b. Trenton, N.J., Dec. 8, 1870; s. Thomas Eastborn and Jane (Field) MacD.; student Rutgers Prep. Sch., New Brunswick, N.J., Miss Pardee's Pvt. School, Elizabeth, N.J., and special business course C. T. Miller's School, Newark, N.J.; m. Jeannette W. Simpson, Apr. 24, 1901; 1 dau., Helen Howat (Mrs. Charles A. Eaton, Jr.). Began as clerk Plainfield (N.J.) Savings Bank, 1888, now sec., treas. and dir.; sec. and treas. Somerset Union and Middlesex Lighting Co.; treas. and dir. Monarch Investment Co., Plainfield, N.J. Chmn. North Plainfield (N.J.) Twp. Com.; first mayor, Borough of Watchung, N.J. Mem. Soc. of Mayflower Descendants in State of N.J. (mem. bd. assts. and treas.). Republican. Presbyn. Club: The Fosgate Country (Jamesburg, N.J.). Home: Valley Rd. Office: 102 E. Front St., Plainfield, N.J.

MacDONALD, Robert, Jr., stock broker; b. Dublin, Ireland, Jan. 14, 1883; s. Robert and Annie (Clarke) MacD.; brought to U.S., 1885, naturalized, 1904; ed. pub. schs.; m. Alice C. Byram, June 8, 1910; children—Robert Byram, Catharine Clarke. Partner MacDonald & Co., stock brokers, mems. N.Y. Stock Exchange, Phila. Stock Exchange; vice-pres. and dir. Ross Tacony Crucible Co.; dir. F. W. Tunnell & Co. Gov. Phila. Stock Exchange. Republican. Episcopalian. Clubs: Union League, Phila. Cricket, Fourth Street (Phila.); Huntingdon Valley Country (Abington, Pa.). Home: 352 Roumfort Rd. Office: 234 Real Estate Trust Bldg., Philadelphia, Pa.

MacDOWELL, John Lazier, physician; b. Kingston, Ont., Aug. 29, 1879; s. Robert John and Elda Lucinda (Lazier) MacD.; came to U.S., 1904, naturalized, 1915; B.A., Queens U., Kingston, Ont., 1900, M.D., C.M., 1903; unmarried. Interne Manhattan Eye, Ear and Throat Hosp., New York, 1904-06; engaged in practice of ophthalmology and otology at Perth Amboy, N.J., since 1906; asst. surgeon, Manhattan Eye and Ear Hosp., N.Y. City, 1906-23; chief of staff ophthalmology and otology, Perth Amboy Gen. Hosp., since 1909. Mem. Am. Med. Assn., N.Y. Medico Surg. Soc., Phi Sigma Kappa. Republican. Presbyterian. Home: 113 Market St., Perth Amboy, N.J.

MacELREE, Mary Eyre, musician; b. West Chester, Pa., Nov. 5, 1884; d. Wilmer Worthington and Ella (Eyre) MacE.; ed. West Chester State Normal Sch., mus. conservatories in Phila., Baltimore, and Vienna, Austria, organ and composition under Ralph Kinder and Newell Robinson. Concert pianist, organist, and teacher of music, Nat. Cathedral Sch. for Girls, Mt. St. Alban, Washington, D.C., 1919-35; teacher piano, pipe organ, theory and appreciation of music, Mary Lyon Sch. and Wildcliff Jr. Coll., Swarthmore, Pa., 1935-38; pvt. teacher and substitute organist First Presbyn. Ch., West Chester, Pa., since 1938; has appeared in pub. piano recitals. Colleague of Am. Guild of Organists. Republican. Presbyn. Former mem. Arts Club, Washington, D.C., Art Alliance, Phila. Home: 609 S. High St., West Chester, Pa.

MAC ELWEE, Roy Samuel, consulting engineer; b. Parkville, Michigan, Apr. 12, 1883; s. Rev. Samuel J. and Anna Belle (Mozingo) M.; prep. edn., Hudson River Mil. Acad.; B.S., Columbia, 1907; studied several European univs.; A.M., Ph.D., U. of Berlin, 1915; m. Ellen Mohlau, 1912; m. 2d, Sarah Smyrl, of Philadelphia, Pa., 1923; children—Anne Frances, Roy Samuel, Sarah Margaret. Clerk, salesman, branch mgr. Internat. Harvester and Otis Elevator cos. in European cities, 1899-1914; chief clk. U.S. Consulate Gen., Berlin, 1915; lecturer on economics and foreign trade, port and terminal engineering, Columbia, 1916-19; professor Sch. of Foreign Service, Georgetown Univ., 1919, dean, 1921-22; prof. Coll. of Charleston, 1923, S.C. Mil. Coll. (Citadel), 1927. Asst. mil. instr. Columbia U. Training Corps, 1917; commd. 1st lt. R.R. Transportation Corps of U.S. Army, Feb. 12, 1918; served as aide to General Goethals; lieutenant colonel S.S. O.R.C.; agt. Federal Bd. Vocational Edn., 1918; 2d and 1st asst. dir. and dir. U.S. Bur. Foreign and Domestic Commerce, Jan. 1, 1919-Mar. 31, 1921; chmn. U.S. Economic Liaison Com.; chmn. U.S. Interdepartment Com. for Commercial Aviation, 1919-21; mem. Com. for Commercial Use of Army Bases; commr. of Port of Charleston, S.C., 1923-30; vice-president (for South Carolina) Great Lakes-St. Lawrence Tidewater Assn., Nat. Rivers and Harbors Congress; dir. Atlantic Deeper Waterways Assn., Am. Bur. of Shipping; del. of U.S.A. to 14th Internat. Navigation Congress, Cairo, Egypt, 1926; lecturer European univs., engring. socs., and chambers of commerce, Paris and Berlin, 1926. Member Am. Statis. Assn., Soc. Terminal Engrs. (v.p.), American Society of Civil Engineers, Soc. Am. Mil. Engrs., Am. Soc. Mech. Engrs., Soc. Naval Architects and Marine Engrs., New York Society Professional Engrs., Nat. Society Professional Engrs., Licensed Professional Engrs. of New York, Pan-Am. Soc., Military Order World War, American Legion, 40 and 8, Theta Delta Chi, Delta Phi Epsilon (co-founder and 1st nat. president), Sec. Am. Assn. Port Authorities, Navy League (chmn. for S.C.), Verein Deutsche Ingenieure, Hafenbau Technische Gesellschaft, Assn. Internat. Permanente des Congrés de Navigation; fellow Am. Geog. Soc. Episcopalian. Decorations: Officer Polonia Restituta (Poland); Comdr. Crown of Rumania; Chevalier Crown of Italy; Officer Order of Leopold II (Belgium); medals—Victory, D.C. Mil. Engineers. Clubs: University (Washington); Columbia Univ., Theta Delta Chi, Whitehall (New York). Author: Bread Bullets, 1917; Vocational Education for Foreign Trade and Shipping, 1918; Ports and Terminal Facilities, 1919, 25; Training for Foreign Trade, 1920; Training for the Steamship Business, 1920; Port Development, 1925; Port Glossary, 1927; The Ports of Rumania, 1927; The Great Ship Canals, 1929; Wesen und Entwicklung der Hamburger Hafenbau-politik. Translator: Delbrüch's Government and the Will of the People. Co-Author: Paper Work in Export Trade, 1920; Economic Aspects of the Great Lakes-St. Lawrence Ship Channel, 1921, Wharf Management, 1921. Contbr. numerous articles to mags. Drew waterfront and port development plan for Toledo, O., Cleveland, O., Canaveral, Fla., and Turiamo, Venezuela, also fixed bridge report, Chicago, port plans for Green Bay and Marinette, Wis., Sandusky, O., Rochester, N.Y.; designed and supervised constrn. Charcotte Terminal, Port of Rochester, N.Y., etc. Home: 619 Turner Av., Drexel Hill, Pa. Office: 101 W. 58th St., New York, N.Y.

MACFADDEN, Bernarr, physical culturist; b. nr. Mill Springs, Mo., Aug. 16, 1868; s. Wm. R. and Elizabeth (Miller) M.; ed. pub. schs.; m. Mary Williamson, 1912; children—Helen Byrnece, Beulah, Braunda, Beverly, Berwyn, Brewster. Founder, 1898, and pub. Physical Culture Magazine, True Story (mag.), 1919, True Romances, 1923, Dream World, Love and Romance, 1924, True Detective Mysteries Mag., 1925, Master Detective Mag., 1929; also publisher Liberty Weekly, Photoplay, Movie Mirror, True Detective, etc.; president and chmn. bd. Macfadden Publications, Inc. Founder of "Physcultopathy" (healing through physical culture), Macfadden Institute of Physical Culture, American Institute for Physical Education, and of Bernarr Macfadden Foundation Inc. (latter sponsors Castle Heights Mil. Acad., Physical Culture Hotel, Dansville, N.Y., Macfadden-Deauville Health Hotel, Miami Beach, Fla., Bernarr Macfadden Foundation School, Briarcliff, N.Y. Mem. Italy-America Soc., Nat. Aeronautic Assn., Com. of One Hundred (Miami Beach, Fla.). Unitarian. Clubs: N.Y. Athletic, Congressional Country. Author of Ency. of Physical Culture, and numerous health books. Home: Newark, N.J. Office: Chanin Bldg., New York, N.Y.

MACFARLAND, Charles Stedman, clergyman; b. Boston, Dec. 12, 1866; s. Daniel and Sarah Abigail (Crafts) M.; grad. Chapman Sch., 1881, and E. Boston High Sch., 1884; B.D., Yale, 1897, Ph.D., 1899; D.D., Ursinus and U. of Paris; S.T.D., Geneva; LL.D., Elon; m. Mary Perley Merrill, Mar. 9, 1904; children—Charles S., James M., Lucia M. Hogan; m. 2d, Genevieve Dayton, Jan. 22, 1938. Gen. mgr. T. O. Gardner & Co., Mfrs., Boston and New York, 1885-92; gen. sec. Y.M.C.A., Melrose, 1892-93; asst. pastor Maverick Congl. Ch., E. Boston, 1893-94; student Yale U., 1894-99, instr. 1900; ordained Congl. ministry, 1897; teaching, 1899-1900; minister Maplewood Ch., Malden, Mass., 1900-06; pastor S. Norwalk, Conn., 1906-11; social service sec., 1911-12, general sec., 1912-31, now gen. sec. emeritus, Federal Council of the Churches of Christ in America. Lecturer on philos., scientific and theol. subjects; book review editor The Messenger and The Federal Council Bulletin; editor Corpus Confessionum; lecturer at univs. of Berlin, Prague, Athens, Strasbourg, also at Rollins College, Winter Park, Florida. National field scout commissioner Boy Scouts of America. Chaplain (lt. col.) O.R.C., U.S.A. V.p. Universal Christian Conference on Life and Work; Am. mem. Central Bur. European Chs., Geneva; chmn. Huguenot-Walloon-New Netherlands Commn., 1924; trustee Ch. Peace Union; pres. of the Mountain Lakes Historical Society. Me. Phi Beta Kappa. Decorated Officier Legion of Honor (France); Order of Leopold (Belgium); Order of Phoenix (Greece); Chevalier Order of the Holy Sepulchre (Jerusalem). Clubs: Yale, Clergy (New York City); University (Winter Park, Florida); Graduates (New Haven, Conn.). Author: The Spirit Christlike; The Infinite Affection; Jesus and the Prophets; Spiritual Culture and Social Service; Christian Service and the Modern World; The Great Physician; The Progress of Church Federation; Christian Unity in Practice and Prophecy, 1933; The New Church and the New Germany, 1934; Chaos in Mexico, 1935; Contemporary Christian Thought, 1936; Across the Years, 1936; Trends of Christian Thinking, 1937; Steps Toward the World Council, 1938; The Christian Faith in a Day of Crisis, 1939. Editor, part author: The Christian Ministry and the Social Order; The Churches of the Federated Council; Christian Unity at Work; The Churches of Christ in Council; The Church and International Relations, 2 vols.; The Church and International Relations—Japan; Christian Cooperation and World Redemption; The Churches of Christ in Time of War; The Churches of America in France; The Old Puritanism and the New Age; International Christian Movements. Contbr. to mags. Home: Mountain Lakes, N.J. Office: 297 Fourth Av., New York, N.Y.

MacFARLAND, George Arthur, univ. prof.; b. Phila., Pa., Nov. 3, 1887; s. George Henry and Elizabeth (Dickson) MacF.; grad. Central High Sch., Phila., 1906; B.S. in Econ., U. of Pa., 1910, M.A., 1926; m. Laura Ethel Ayer, Nov. 9, 1911; children—George Arthur, Ann. Instr., Boy's Evening High Sch., Phila., 1906-10; instr., Wharton Sch. of Finance and Commerce, U. of Pa., 1909-19, asst. prof., 1919-26, asso. prof., 1926-34, prof. of accounting since 1934, sec. Evening and Extension Schs. of Accounts and Finance, 1913-17, chmn. dept. of accounting since 1937; chmn. exec. com. Wharton Sch. Faculty, U. of Pa., since 1930. Vice-pres. Am. Accounting Assn., 1939-40. Dir. Jenkintown Improvement Assn. Mem. Beta Gamma Sigma, Alpha Chi Rho. Republican. Presbyterian (trustee, Grace Presbyn. Ch., Jenkintown, Pa.). Club: Lenape, Phila. Co-author: A First Year in Bookkeeping and Accounting, 1913; Accounting Fundamentals, 1936. Spl. editor for words and phrases in bookkeeping and accounting, Merriam-Webster's Internat. Dictionary, 1934. Home: 216 Greenwood Av., Jenkintown, Pa. Office: Logan Hall, Univ. of Pennsylvania, Philadelphia, Pa.

MACFARLANE, Charles Edward, chemist; b. Frankfurt, Germany, June 17, 1900; s. Samuel Sterrett and Ida (Willett) M.; parents American citizens; came to U.S., 1916; B.S. in Chem., Johns Hopkins U., Baltimore, Md., 1920; m. Margaret Lindsay Reber, Feb. 23, 1929; children—Samuel Graham, John Willett. Chemist, Westinghouse Air Brake Co., Wilmerding, Pa., 1920-27, asst. chief chemist, 1927-38, chief chemist since 1938. Mem. Am. Chem. Soc., Am. Soc. for Metals, Am. Soc. for Testing Materials, Kappa Alpha. Republican. Presbyterian. Home: 315 Beech St., Edgewood, Pa. Office: Westinghouse Air Brake Co., Wilmerding, Pa.

MacGILLIVRAY, Charles Daniel, vice-pres. Baldwin Locomotive Works; b. Cambridge, Mass., Apr. 21, 1896; s. Alexander Allan and Florence MacG.; grad. Cambridge High Sch., 1914; student Boston Coll., 1914-16; special courses at Princeton and U. of Pa.; m. Eleanor Rodriguez, May 22, 1927; children—Eleanor Joanne, Charles Daniel, Joyce Anne, Robert Bruce. Office and warehouse mgr. Wm. C. Robinson & Sons Co., New York and Phila., 1919-20; salesman Wahl Co., Chicago, Jan.-Dec. 1921; sec. to pres. Gen. Sugar Co., Havana, Cuba, 1922-27; office mgr. Fisher & Co., New York, 1927-29; with Baldwin Locomotive Works since 1929, successively as asst. sec., sec., and since 1938 vice-pres.; sec. Midvale Co., Phila., Baldwin-Southwark Corpn., Eddystone, Standard Steel Works, Burnham, Pelton Water Wheel Co., San Francisco, Whitcomb Locomotive Co., Rochelle; dir. Flannery Bolt Co., Pittsburgh. Served in 8th Inf., Mass. Nat. Guard, 1913-16; U.S. Navy, ensign Supply Corps, 1916-19; U.S. Naval Reserve Force, 1919-25. Republican. Catholic. Club: Aronimink Golf (Newton Square, Pa.). Home: 453 Turner Av., Drexel Hill, Pa. Office: 123 S. Broad St., Philadelphia, Pa.

MacGILVARY, Norwood, painter, teacher; b. of Am. parents at Bangkok, Siam, Nov. 14, 1874; s. Rev. Daniel (D.D.) and Sophia (Bradley) M.; A.B., Davidson (N.C.) Coll., 1896; U. of Calif., 1896-97, Mark Hopkins Inst., San Francisco, 1897-98; pupil of Jean Paul Laurens, Académie Julian, Paris, 1904-06, also of Myron Barlow, Etaples, France; studied in galleries of Holland and Italy; m. Adeline Kaji, 1918; children—Winifred Sophia, Daniel Bradley. Figure and landscape painter; formerly illustrator for mags.; asso. prof. painting, Carnegie Inst. Tech., Pittsburgh, since 1921. Exhibited Salon, Paris; Nat. Acad. Design, New York; Pa. Acad. Fine Arts, Phila.; Corcoran Gallery, Washington, D.C.; Carnegie Inst., Pittsburgh; Art Inst., Chicago; Kansas City Mus., etc. Represented in permanent collections Nat. Gallery, Washington, D.C., by "Twilight after Rain." Silver medal, for "Nocturne," San Francisco Expn., 1915; 1st prize, Associated Artists, Pittsburgh. Mem. Am. Water Color Soc., Associated Artists of Pittsburgh, Sigma Alpha Epsilon, Tau Sigma Delta. Clubs: Salmagundi (New York); Architectural (Pittsburgh). Home: 8 Roselawn Terrace, Pittsburgh, Pa. Address: Carnegie Inst. Technology, Pittsburgh, Pa.

MacGINNIS, Henry Ryan, artist and instr. art; b. Martinsville, Ind., Sept. 25, 1875; s. John Calvin and Katherine Elizabeth (Ryan) MacGinnis; student Art Sch. under William Forsyth, J. O. Adams and T. C. Steale, Indianapolis, Ind., 1896-97; studied Royal Acad., Munich, Germany, 1900-04, under Collin and Courtrois, Paris, France, 1904-05. Artist since 1898; exhibited Omaha Expn., 1898; exhibited with Soc. Western Artists since 1899, Pa. Acad. Fine Arts since 1900, most of important exhbns. in U.S. since 1905; mural decoration, Trenton, N.J., decoration in tile, Woodhaven, L.I.; many portraits of notables; head of fine arts dept., Sch. Industrial Arts, Trenton, N.J., since 1907. Mem. Allied Artists of America, Am. Artists Professional League, Hoosier Salon of Ind. Received Hon. Mention Award, Royal Acad., Munich, Germany. Republican. Club: Salmagundi (New York City). Home: 42 W. State St. Rear, Trenton, N.J. Mail address: School of Industrial Arts, Trenton, N.J.

MACGOWAN, Birkhead; asso. rhinolaryngologist Mercy Hosp.; attending otorhinolaryngologist Sydenham Hosp.; surgeon Presbyterian Eye, Ear and Throat Charity Hosp.; mem. staff Church Home and Infirmary. Address: 101 W. Read St., Baltimore, Md.

MacGREGOR, Lawrence John, pres. Summit Trust Co.; b. Itasca, Ill., Dec. 9, 1892; s. John Hope and May E. (Sherer) MacG.; student Evanston (Ill.) High Sch., 1906-10; Ph.B., U. of Chicago, 1916; student Edinburgh U., Scotland, 1919; m. Mary Elizabeth Childs, Oct. 6, 1923; children—Lois Alward, Samuel Childs, John Duncan. With Halsey Stuart & Co., New York, 1919-25, Bank of America, New York, 1925-29, N.Y. Trust Co., 1929-33; pres. and dir. Summit (N.J.) Trust Co. since 1933, Summit Title & Mortgage Guaranty Co. since 1933; dir. Jersey Central Power & Light Co. Served in U.S. Army, with A.E.F., 1918-19. Pres. Council of Social Agencies, Summit, N.J., since 1938; trustee and treas. Kent Pl. Sch. since 1924; trustee Summit Y.W.C.A. since 1935. Mem. Phi Beta Kappa, Beta Theta Pi. Presbyterian (trustee New Providence Presbyn. Ch.). Clubs: Wall Street (New York); Baltusrol Golf (Springfield, N.J.). Home: Ard Coille, Chatham, N.J. Office: Summit, N.J.

MACHEN, Arthur Webster, lawyer; b. Baltimore, Md., Mar. 18, 1877; s. Arthur Webster and Mary Minnie Gresham M.; Univ. Sch. for Boys, Baltimore, 1888-93; A.B., Johns Hopkins, 1896; LL.B., Harvard, 1899; m. Helen Chase Woods, Dec. 1, 1917; children—Mary Gresham, Arthur Webster, Elizabeth Hall. Admitted to Md. bar, 1899, and since practiced in Baltimore (with father to 1915); mem. firm Armstrong, Machen & Allen since 1925. Special asst. to atty. gen. of United States, 1914, 15. Chmn. Tax Revision Commn. of Md., 1929. Mem. Am., Md. and Baltimore bar assns., Phi Kappa Psi, Phi Beta Kappa. Democrat. Presbyn. Clubs: Maryland, Merchants (Baltimore). Author: Modern Law of Corporations, 1908; Federal Corporation Tax Law of 1909, 1910. Home: Ruxton, Md. Office: 1209 Calvert Bldg., Baltimore, Md.

MACHT, Ephraim, real estate, builder; b. Kovno, Russia, Nov 15, 1866; s. Moses and Esther M.; came to U.S., 1887, naturalized, 1888; student Talmudical and Rabbinical Schs. in Russia; m. Annie Morowitz, 1887; children—Rebecca (wife of Dr. Joseph I. Kemler), Morris, Sarah (Mrs. Benjamin Samler). Engaged in business on own account as real estate operator and builder in Baltimore since 1891; organized New Calvert Bldg. & Loan Assn., 1906, now pres.; organized Sterling Realty Co., 1909; organized Welsh Constrn. Co., 1912, now pres.; pres. The Macht Co., Eastern State Bldg. & Loan Assn., Internat. Realty & Development Co.; has built approximately 10,000 dwellings in Baltimore and vicinity, also office bldgs., apartment houses, etc. A founder Jewish Home for Consumptives, 1908. Pres. Hebrew Coll. and Teachers Training Sch.; vice-pres. Bd. Hebrew Edn. Dir. Asso. Jewish Charities, Hebrew Home for Aged and Infirm, Talmud Torah Soc. Jewish religion. Clubs: Chesapeake, Mercantile, Woodholme Country. Home: 701 Lake Drive. Office: Macht Bldg., Baltimore, Md.

MacINTOSH, Aden B., clergyman; b. Morrisburg, Ont., May 10, 1871; s. Barney U. and Maria (Garlough) MacI.; brought to U.S., 1883, naturalized, 1885; A.B. and A.M., Thiel Coll., Greenville, Pa.; student Luth. Theol. Sem., Mt. Airy, Phila., 1893-96; D.D., Muhlenberg Coll., 1919; m. Lillie E. Wagoner, Apr. 24, 1897; children—Walter Bruce, Dorothy Wagoner (Mrs. E. Bagby Pollard). Ordained to ministry Luth. Ch., 1896; pastor, Spring City, Pa., 1896-1902, Bethlehem, 1902-12, Norristown, 1912-21, Lancaster, Pa., since 1921. Served as chaplain, U.S.A., 1918-19, with A.E.F. Dir. Mt. Airy Theol. Sem. Republican. Lutheran. Club: Lancaster Country. Home: 516 Race Av., Lancaster, Pa.

MacINTOSH, Mark, athletic dir.; b. Providence, R.I., Apr. 12, 1903; s. John and Annie (Brown) MacI.; B.S., Rhode Island State Coll., Kingston, R.I., 1926; M.S., Northwestern U., 1935; post-grad. work, U. of Pa. and Columbia; m. Doris Buchanan, Jan. 3, 1925. Coach of football, basketball and track, Warwick (R.I.) High Sch., 1926-27; dir. of athletics and phys. edn., Lake Forest (Ill.) Coll., 1927-33, Arizona State Coll., Flagstaff, 1933-36, Swarthmore (Pa.) Coll. since 1936. Mem. Am. Football Coaches Assn., Am. Assn. for Health and Phys. Edn. Colleges, Phys. Edn. Assn., Lambda Chi Alpha. Republican. Episcopalian. Club: Rotary (Swarthmore, Pa.). Author of several books and articles on athletic coaching and phys. edn. for professional jours. Home: Swarthmore Apartments. Office: Swarthmore Coll., Swarthmore, Pa.

MACK, Connie (Cornelius McGillicudy), baseball mgr.; b. East Brookfield, Mass., Dec. 23, 1862. Began as catcher on East Brookfield baseball team, 1883; catcher on professional team, Meriden, Conn., 1884; catcher, Hartford, Conn., team (New England League), 1885, Washington, D.C., team (Nat. League), 1886-89; Buffalo, N.Y., team (Brotherhood League), 1890; mgr. Pittsburgh team (Nat. League), 1891-96; catcher mgr. Milwaukee team (Western League), 1897-1900; mgr. Phila. Athletics (Am. League) since 1901. Won Am. League pennants, 1902, 05, 10, 11, 13, 14, 29,30, 31; won World Series, 1910, 11, 13, 29, 30. Awarded Bok prize for distinguished service to Phila., 1929. Address: Philadelphia American League Baseball Club, Philadelphia, Pa.

MACK, John Sephus, pres. G. C. Murphy Co.; b. Indiana Co., Pa., Mar. 9, 1880; s. John McCrory and Sarah Ellen (Murphy) M.; ed. pub. schs., Indiana Co., Pa., and bus. coll., Johnstown, Pa.; m. Margaret L. Gordon, Jan. 31, 1907; children—John Gordon, James S. Began as stockroom clk. McCrory Stores Corpn., Johnstown, Pa., 1899, advancing to gen. mgr., 1908; with G. C. Murphy Co., McKeesport, Pa., since 1911, pres. and chmn. bd. since 1912; pres. and dir. Mack Realty Co. Trustee McKeesport Hosp., Indiana (Pa.) Hosp., Westminster Coll., New Wilmington, Pa. Republican. Presbyterian. Elk. Clubs: Duquesne (Pittsburgh); Youghiogheny Country (McKeesport); Metropolitan, Indiana Country (Indiana, Pa.); Republican,

Union, Bankers, Aldine (New York). Home: 1317 S. Union Av. Office: 531 Fifth Av., McKeesport, Pa.

MACK, Warren Bryan, prof. vegetable gardening; b. Flicksville, Pa., Jan. 18, 1896; s. Oscar and Anna Maria (Lockard) M.; Ph.B., Lafayette Coll., 1915; B.Sc. in Hort., Pa. State Coll., 1921; M.Sc., Mass. State Coll., 1924; Ph.D., Johns Hopkins U., 1929; m. Pauline Gracia Beery, Dec. 27, 1923. Instr. sci. high sch., 1915-18; tester, N.Y. Edison Co., 1919; instr. pomology, Mass. State Coll., 1921-23; instr. horticulture, Pa. State Coll., 1923-24, asst. prof. vegetable gardening, 1924-26, asso. prof., 1926-30, prof., 1930, head of dept. horticulture, Pa. State Coll. since 1937. Served as 2d lt. F.A., U.S.A., 1918. Fellow A.A.A.S. Mem. Am. Soc. Hort. Sci., Am. Soc. Plant Physiologists, Bot. Soc. of America, Phi Beta Kappa, Phi Kappa Phi, Sigma Xi, Gamma Sigma Delta, Alpha Zeta. Democrat. Episcopalian. Known as artist in wood engraving. Home: 245 E. Hamilton Av., State College, Pa.

MACKALL, Paul, vice-pres. Bethlehem Steel Co.; b. Alexandria Co., Va., May 15, 1886; s. James McVeen and Evanina F. (Evans) M.; M.E., Lehigh U., 1907; unmarried. With Bethlehem Steel Co. since July 1, 1907 (except during World War), looper, Bethlehem, 1907-08, St. Louis office, 1908-10, Chicago office, 1910-16, made Western sales rep., 1915, asst. to gen. sales agt., Bethlehem, 1916-28, vice-pres. in charge sales since Aug. 1, 1928, dir. since 1932. Requested by War Industries Bd. to organize iron and steel div.; sent to Europe with 10 men to represent steel on Inter-Allied Munitions Council, later pres. steel com., 1917-18. Republican. Episcopalian. Clubs: Cloud, Links, Racquet and Tennis, India House, Nation Golf Links of America (New York); University (Chicago); Racquet (Phila.); Saucon Valley Country (Bethlehem); Travellers (Paris). Home: Route 4, Bethlehem, Pa. Office: Bethlehem Steel Co., Bethlehem, Pa.

MACKALL, Robert McGill, artist; b. Baltimore, Md., Apr. 15, 1889; s. Charles and Eliza Bowie (Mackenzie) M.; student Baltimore City Coll., 1903-07, Md. Inst. Sch. of Art, 1907-09, Art Students League, New York, 1909-11, Royal Acad., Munich, Germany, 1911-12, Julian Acad. and Colarossi Acad., Paris, France, 1912-14; m. Ethel Ruth Palmer, Dec. 17, 1938. Portrait and mural painter; artist in stained glass; instr. Md. Inst. Sch. of Art since 1933, Notre Dame Coll. of Md. since 1937. Works: (decorations) Soldiers memorial altar, St. Luke's P. E. Ch., main auditorium, Md. War Memorial Bldg., chancel, First English Luth. Ch., banking hall, Baltimore Trust Bldg., over mantel decoration and facade decorations Municipal (Peale) Museum (all Baltimore); chancel window, Christ P. E. Ch., Luray, Va.; lobby decorations and portrait Woodrow Wilson Hotel, New Brunswick, N.J., and Logań Theatre, Phila.; reconstructed State House, St. Mary's City, Md.; ballroom, Emerson Hotel, and lobby, Centre Theatre and Friends Sch., Baltimore; stained glass window, All Saints Ch., Frederick, Md. Portraits in Stafford Court House, Va., Constitution Hall, Washington, D.C.; Johns Hopkins, Municipal, Union Memorial and Church Home hosps., Court House, Baltimore; also private residences. Served as capt., C.A.C., U.S. Army, 1918-19; with A.E.F. Mem. Municipal Art Commn. of Baltimore. Mem. Nat. Soc. Mural Painters, Archtl. League of New York, Mural Artists Guild of N.Y. Home: 2423 Pickwick Rd., Baltimore, Md.

MACKAY, John Alexander, clergyman, educator; b. Inverness, Scotland, May 17, 1889; s. Duncan and Isabella (Macdonald) M.; M.A. with 1st class honors in philosophy, U. of Aberdeen, Scotland, 1912; B.D., Princeton Theol. Sem., 1915; U. of Madrid, 1915-16; D. Litt., U. of Lima, Peru, 1918, U. of Bonn, Germany, 1930; D.D., Princeton, LL.D., Ohio Wesleyan U., 1937; LL.D., Albright Coll., 1938; D.D., Aberdeen U., 1939; m. Jane Logan Wells, Aug. 16, 1916; children—Isobel Elizabeth, Duncan Alexander Duff, Elena Florence, Ruth. Ednl. missionary, Presbyn. Ch., Lima, 1916-25; prof. philosophy, Nat. U. of Peru, 1925; lecturer and writer under S.Am. Fed. of Y.M.C.A.s, 1926-32; residing successively in Montevideo and Mexico City; Merrick lecturer Ohio Wesleyan U., 1932; sec. Presbyn. Bd. Foreign Missions, 1932-37; pres. Princeton Theol. Sem. and prof. of ecumenics since 1937. Trustee Mackenzie Coll., Sao Paulo, Brazil; chmn. Student Volunteer Movement; chmn. University Christian Missions. Club: Nassau (Princeton). Author: Mas Yo os digo, 1927; El Sentido de la Vida, 1931; The Other Spanish Christ, 1932; That Other America, 1935. Home: 86 Mercer St., Princeton, N.J.

MACKAY, Robert West, banker; b. Warren, Pa., Aug. 19, 1889; s. Robert and Joanna Lind (Summerton) M.; student Warren (Pa.) High Sch., 1905-09, Grad. Sch. of Banking, Am. Bankers Assn., Rutgers Univ., New Brunswick, N.J., summer 1935, 36, 37; m. Louise Johnson Rogers, Jan. 27, 1921; children—Robert West (dec.), Joanna Louise. Messenger boy Warren (Pa.) Nat. Bank, 1905-06, bookkeeper, 1907-12, head bookkeeper, 1913-15, teller, 1916-17, asst. trust officer, 1920-22, cashier since 1923, dir. since 1934; dir. Denver Producing and Refining Co., Oklahoma City. Served as capt. Inf., U.S.A., 1917-19, asst. camp personnel adj. Camp Lee, Va., 1918-19. Dir. and treas. Sch. Dist. of Warren Borough, Pa., since 1929. Dir. and sec.-treas. Watson Memorial Home, Warren, Pa.; dir. Y.M.C.A., Warren Chamber of Commerce; chmn. publicity Boy Scout Council. Republican. Presbyterian (treas. First Presbyn. Ch., Warren, Pa.). Mason (North Star Lodge 241; Occidental Chapter 235; Warren Commandery 63, K.T.). Elk (Warren Lodge 223). Home: 311 Poplar St. Office: Warren Nat. Bank, Warren, Pa.

MACKAY, William Andrew, artist; b. Phila., Pa., July 10, 1876; s. Frank F. and Elizabeth J. Sneathen (Bond) M.; student Coll. City of N.Y., Academie Julian, Paris, and Am. Acad. in Rome, 1906-07; pupil of Benjamin Constant and Jean Paul Laurens. Worked as apprentice under Frank Millet, Columbian Expn., Chicago, 1893; painter of murals and decorations; decorated ceiling of U.S. Senate Reading Room; represented by his work in Federal Bldg., Cleveland, Civic Opera House, Chicago, Minn. Capitol Bldg., Baltimore Customs House; Murals in N.Y. State Roosevelt Memorial Bldg., New York. Chief Camouflage artist 2d Dist., U.S.A., World War. Mem. Archtl. League, Am. Art Assn. in Paris. Episcopalian. Mason. Club: Players (New York). Home: Coytesville, N.J. Studio: 209 W. 40th St., New York, N.Y.*

MacKELLAR, James Malcolm, physician, business exec.; b. New York, N.Y., June 10, 1882; s. Archibald and Jane (Malcolm) MacK.; student Nyack (N.Y.) High Sch., 1897-1901; M.D., Cornell U. Med. Sch., 1905; unmarried. Interne City Hosp. Blackwell's Island, New York, 1905-07; in practice at Tenafly, N.J., since 1907; roentgenologist Nyack (N.Y.) Hosp., 1912-22; mem. surg. staff Englewood (N.J.) Hosp. since 1922; pres. Tenafly (N.J.) Lumber & Supply Co. since 1936. Served as 1st lt., M.C., U.S. Army, 1918-19. Fellow Am. Coll. Surgeons, A.M.A. Republican. Presbyterian. Mason. Home: 38 E. Clinton Av. Office: 26 E. Clinton Av., Tenafly, N.J.

MACKENZIE, Alastair St. Clair, educator; b. Inverness, Scotland, Feb. 17, 1875; s. Alastair Forbes and Christina Douglas (Macdonald) M.; M.A., Glasgow U., 1892; U. of Edinburgh, 1892-93; Oxford U., 1893-94; LL.B., U. of Ky., 1912; LL.D., Ky. Wesleyan U., 1911; Litt.D., Cumberland, 1913; unmarried. Prof. English and logic, Sept., 1899, prof. English and comparative lit., 1910-16, dean of Grad. Sch., 1912-16, State University of Ky.; pres. Lenox College, Hopkinton, Ia., 1916-17; research work in New York, 1918-28; editorial work since 1928. Institute lecturer since 1905; Ropes Foundation lecturer, University of Cincinnati, 1911-12; lecturer on comparative literature, U. of Tenn., 1912. Sec. Am. Iona Soc., 1926-28; fellow Royal Soc. of Lit.; mem. Royal Asiatic Soc. (London), Am. Philol. Assn., Modern Lang. Assn., N.E.A., Alpha Delta Sigma (pres. 1923); hon. mem. Inst. de Sociol. (Bruxelles). Mason (K.T.). Clubs: University, Masonic, Caledonian and Filson. Author: History of Lexington Lodge (F. and A.M.), 1904; The Evolution of Literature, 1911 (translated into Spanish, 1913); History of English Literature, 1914. Collaborator on Library of Southern Literature (15 vols.), 1910. Contbr. to lit. and other periodicals. Home: 70 2d St., Weehawken, New Jersey.*

MACKENZIE, Donald, prof. theology; b. Ross Shire, Scotland, May 30, 1882; s. Donald and Janet (Mackenzie) M.; student Nicolson Inst., at Stornoway, 1900; M.A., University of Aberdeen (Scotland), 1905; grad. United Free Ch. College, Aberdeen, 1910; student Univ. of Halle (Germany), 1909, U. of Berlin, 1909; D.D., Washington and Jefferson Coll., 1931, University of Aberdeen, 1934; m. Alice A. Murray, Sept. 7, 1910; children—Alice M. (wife of Rev. William T. Swain, Jr.), Elizabeth M., Janet C., Donald C. Came to U.S., 1928. Asst. prof. logic and metaphysics, Aberdeen U., 1906-09; ordained to ministry United Free Ch., 1910; pastor, Scotland, 1910-28; Elliott lecturer Western Theol. Sem., Pittsburgh, 1926, prof. theology, 1928-33; Sprunt lecturer Union Theol. Sem., Richmond, Va., 1933; prof. of Biblical theology, Princeton Theol. Sem. since 1933. Author: Christianity—The Paradox of God, 1933..Contbr. to religious and philos. publs. Home: 31 Library Rd., Princeton, N.J.

MACKENZIE, George Washington, physician; b. Phila., Pa., Sept. 12, 1871; s. George Washington and Caroline M. (Lee) M.; M.D., Hahnemann Med. Coll., Phila., 1893; post grad. study, U. of Vienna, Austria; m. Alice V. Derr, Mar. 15, 1905; 1 son, George W. III (dec.). Engaged in gen. practice of medicine at Phila. since 1893, specializing in otolaryngology since 1908; chief of staff, W. Phila. Homeo. Hosp., 1908-16, St. Luke's Childrens Hosp., Ear, Nose and Throat Dept. since 1928; cons. otolaryngoligist, McKinley Hosp., Trenton, N.J. since 1918, Blair Memorial Hosp., Huntingdon, Pa., W. Jersey Homeo. Hos., Camden, N.J. since 1913, Crozer Hosp., Chester, Pa. since 1918; asso. prof. otology, U. of Pa. Grad Sch., 1918-22; instr. pvt. courses in diseases of eye, ear, nose and throat since 1918; dir. Intensive European courses in medicine since 1922; dir. Mackenzie Post Grad. Med. Sch., Phila., 1939. Awarded gold medal, U. of Vienna, 1931. Fellow Am. Coll. Surgs., Am. Acad. Ophthalmology and Otolaryngology. Mem. A.M.A., Pa. and Phila. Co. med. socs., Am. Laryngol., Rhinol. and Otol. Soc., Phila. Laryngol. Soc., Med. Club, Phila. Co. Homeo. Med. Soc., Homeo. Med. Soc. of State of Pa., Am. Inst. Homeopathy, Internat. Homeo. League. Episcopalian. Home: 269 S. 19th St., Philadelphia, Pa.

MACKERT, Charles LeRoy, prof. physical edn.; b. Sunbury, Pa., Feb. 4, 1894; s. Philip and Mary Kathryn (Rothermal) M.; student Lebanon Valley Coll., Annville, Pa., 1915-17; B.S., U. of Md., College Park, Md., 1921, A.M., 1924; student Teachers Coll. of Columbia U., 1927-30, George Washington U., Washington, D.C., 1937-1939; m. Hazel Tenney, Sept. 5, 1931; 1 son, Charles LeRoy, Jr. Employed as coach freshman athletics, U. of Md., 1921-27; instr. in edn., Lebanon Valley Coll., Annville, Pa., 1930-31; prof. phys. edn., U. of Md., College Park, Md. since 1931; employed as professional football player, 1921-27; part-time instr., Lincoln Sch., N.Y. City, 1927-30. Served as 2d lt. inf., U.S.A., 1917-19. Mem. Am. Football coaches Assn., Coll. Phys. Edn. Assn., Nat. Health, Phys. Edn. and Recreation Assn., Am. Assn. Univ. Profs., Kappa Alpha. Democrat. Mem. Reformed Ch. Mason. Clubs: "M" at U. of Md. (College Park); Kiwanis of Prince George Co., Md. Home: 8 Beechwood St., Hyattsville, Md.

MACKEY, Richard Joseph, lawyer; b. Jersey City, N.J., Sept. 19, 1892; s. James Thomas and Margaret (Allen) M.; ed. Fordham Coll., 1908-09; A.B., Columbia U., 1912, A.M., same, 1914; LL.B., Columbia U. Law Sch., 1914; m. Anne O'Brien, July 1, 1920; children—James Thomas, Anne Mercedes (Nancy). Admitted to N.Y. bar, 1915 and engaged in practice of law in New York City since 1915; mem. firm Mackey & Herrlich, 1450 Broadway, New

York, N.Y., since 1929; admitted to N.J. bar as atty., 1919, counsellor at law, 1922 and engaged in gen. practice alone in Jersey City since 1919. Served as ensign, U.S.N., 1917-19, deck officer U.S.S. Manchuria, transport. Mem. Cath. Lawyers Guilds of N.Y. and N.J., Assn. of Bar of City of N.Y., Hudson Co. (N.J.) Bar Assn., Columbia U. Law Alumni Assn., Sigma Nu, Delta Theta Phi. Roman Catholic. Clubs: New York Athletic, Catholic (New York). Home: 93 Mt. Prospect Av., Verona, N.J. Office: 195 Arlington Av., Jersey City, N.J.; also, 1450 Broadway, New York, N.Y.

MACKIE, Alexander, clergyman and pres. life ins. co.; b. Frankford, Phila., Pa., Sept. 26, 1885; s. Alexander John Howie and Alice Bolton (Cooper) M.; A.B., Princeton U., 1907, A.M., same, 1909; study, Princeton Theol. Sem., 1907-10; (hon.) D.D., Parsons Coll., Fairfield, Ia., 1923; m. Ethel Dean Walton, Nov. 14, 1911. Ordained to ministry Presbyn. Ch., 1910; minister, Sherwood Ch., Phila., Pa., 1910-11, Tully Memorial Ch., Sharon Hill, Pa., 1911-36; pres. Presbyn. Ministers Fund for Life Ins., Phila., Pa., since 1936. Trustee Coll. of the Ozarks, Clarksville, Ark. Mem. Princeton Terrace Club. Treas. Canterbury Cleric, Presbyn. Ministers Social Union, Twentieth Century Cleric, all of Phila. and The Symposium, Princeton, N.J. Republican. Presbyn. I.O.O.F. Clubs: Penn Athletic, Manufacturers and Bankers (Philadelphia). Author: The Gift of Tongues, 1921. Home: Hamilton Ct., 39th & Chestnut St., Philadelphia, Pa. Office: 1805 Walnut St., Philadelphia, Pa.

MacKINNEY, Paul R., pres. United Dyewood Corpn.; b. Providence, R.I., Aug. 27, 1885; s. Herbert G. and Mary (Bartlett) MacK.; ed. Brooklyn High Sch., 1899-1902; m. Abigail McKelvey Detes, June 25, 1908; 1 son, Francis P. With United Dyewood Corpn., New York, beginning as vice-pres., pres. since 1938; pres. Am. Dyewood Co., N.Y. Color & Chemicals Co. Republican. Clubs: Union League, Princeton, Madison Square Garden (New York); Essex County Country, Essex Fells Country; Oakmont Shooting. Home: Essex Fells, N.J. Office: 22 E. 40th St., New York, N.Y.

MacKINNON, George V., hat mfr.; b. Dundee, Scotland, Jan. 4, 1882; s. Samuel and Agnes (Valentine) MacK.; brought by parents to U.S., 1888; Central High Sch., Phila., Pa., 1896-97; grad. Peirce Sch. of Business Administration, 1900; m. Imogene Derbyshire, Mar. 16, 1910; 1 dau., Alice I. (dec.). Began as errand boy, J. P. Twaddell & Co., retail shoes, Phila., 1897; clk., Thos. Cocker & Co., brush mfrs., 1897-99, Welsbach Commercial Co., 1899-1900; with John B. Stetson Co., hat mfrs., since 1900, elk., bookkeeper, chief accountant to 1917, treas. until 1924, v.p. in charge finance, 1924-28, president since 1928; pres. John B. Stetson Co., Ltd. (Canada); pres. John B. Stetson Bldg. & Loan Assn.; treas. Goodwill Industries of Phila.; dir. Fidelity-Phila. Trust Co., Phila. Mfrs. Mutual Fire Ins. Co., Fidelity Mutual Life Ins. Co. Director Philadelphia Chamber of Commerce; pres. and dir. Stetson Hospital of Phila.; dir. S.E. Pa. chapter Am. Red Cross. Trustee Methodist Episcopal Orphanage. Ex-pres. St. Andrew's Soc. Republican. Methodist. Clubs: Manufacturers', Midday, Union League, Kiwanis (Philadelphia); Old York Road Country (Jenkintown, Pa.). Home: Washington Lane, Jenkintown, Pa. Office: 5th St. and Montgomery Av., Philadelphia, Pa.

MACKLIN, John Farrell, corpn. official; b. Worcester, Mass., Oct. 17, 1883; s. Robert and Margaret (Wray) M.; student St. Paul's Sch., 1904-06, U. of Pa., 1906-10; m. Phoebe Mildred Weaver, June 12, 1915 (died 1936); children—Ida Weaver (Mrs. Lilley), John Heisley Weaver. Athletic dir. Pawling (N.Y.) Sch., 1910-11; dir. of athletics and physical edn. Mich. State Coll., 1911-16; asso. with J. H. Weaver & Co., coal producers since 1917, pres. since 1934; also pres. asso. and affiliated cos.; pres. W.Va. Northern R.R. Co.; v.p. Cambria & Ind. R.R. Co.; dir. Cambria Township Light, Heat & Power Co., Phila. Nat. Bank. Trustee Bucknell U.; advisory trustee Villanova Coll. Stadium of Mich. State Coll. named "Macklin Field" in recognition of his services as football coach. Dir. Nat. Coal Assn.; mem. Phi Gamma Delta. Republican. Episcopalian. Mason, Elk. Clubs: Union League, Racquet, Art, Penn Athletic, Phila. Country, Bala Golf, Whitemarsh Golf (Phila.); Bachelors, Sunnehanna Golf (Johnstown); Pine Valley Golf (Pine Valley, N.J.); Seaview Golf (Absecon, N.J.); Westchester Country (Rye, N.Y.); Downtown Athletic (New York); Ebensburg Country. Home: Green Hill Farms, Overbrook, Phila. Office: 1617 Pennsylvania Boul., Philadelphia, Pa.

MacLAREN, Malcolm, electrical engr.; b. Annapolis, Md., June 21, 1869; s. Donald and Elizabeth Stockton (Green) M.; A.B., Princeton, 1890, E.E., 1892, A.M., 1893; m. Angelina Post Hodge, June 1900; children—Malcolm, Angelina Hodge, Wistar Hodge, Elizabeth Green. Engr. with Westinghouse Electric & Mfg. Co., Pittsburgh, 1893-98 and 1905-08, London, Eng., 1898-1900; chief elec. engr., British Westinghouse Electric & Mfg. Co., Manchester, Eng., 1900-05; prof. elec. engring., Princeton, 1908-37; retired. Commd. capt., Engr. R.C., Dec. 1917; maj. N.A., Apr. 1918; lt. col., Engr. R.C., July 1919; col., 1924; on duty at Washington during service. Mem. Am. Inst. Elec. Engrs. Republican. Presbyn. Home: Princeton, N.J.

MACLAY, Robert Barr, farm equipment; b. Belleville, Pa., Nov. 16, 1893; s. William Barr and Elizabeth Mary (Campbell) M.; student Franklin and Marshall Acad., Lancaster, Pa., 1908-09; Ph.B., Franklin and Marshall Coll., 1913; m. Grace Virginia Royer, March 22, 1917; children—Robert Barr, Marlin Hugh (deceased), Harry Elwood, William Nevin, Donald Merle. High sch. instr., 1913-17; farm mgr., 1917-21; since 1921 senior partner Maclay and Campbell, retail farm equipment; treas., sec. and dir. Kishacoquillas Valley R.R. Co.; vice-pres. and dir. Kishacoquillas Valley Mutual Fire Ins. Co. Charter mem. Belleville Chamber of Commerce (sec. 2 yrs., pres. 2 yrs.). Pres. Mifflin Co. Sabbath Sch. Assn., 1935-38. Mem. Sons Am. Revolution, Lambda Chi Alpha. Republican. Presbyterian (elder since 1927). Address: Belleville, Pa.

MacLEAN, Angus Lloyd, instr. ophthalmology, Johns Hopkins U., asst. visiting ophthalmologist Johns Hopkins Hosp. Address: 1201 N. Calvert St., Baltimore, Md.

MacLENNAN, Alexander Gordon, clergyman; b. Sidney, N.S., Can., March 8, 1889; s. Duncan and Annie M.; student Dalhousie U., Halifax, 1911-13; B.A., Antioch Coll., Yellow Springs, O., 1915; student Lane Theol. Sem., 1916; B.D., Xenia (O.) Theol. Sem., 1917; D.D., Buena Vista (Ia.) Coll., 1926; m. Leanna Taylor, Dec. 5, 1917. Came to U.S., 1913, naturalized citizen, 1923. Ordained Presbyn. ministry, 1915; pastor Yellow Springs, 1915-17; regional Y.M.C.A. dir. in France, 1917-18; pastor Boston, Mass., 1918-21, Bethany Ch., Phila., 1921-28, Shadyside United Presbyn. Ch., Pittsburgh, since 1928. Mem. bd. dirs. Stony Brook Assembly (L.I.), China Inland Mission, S. African Gen. Mission, Dudley Bible Inst., Wanamaker Inst. (Phila.), Stony Brook Sch. for Boys. Republican. Mason. Editor: Prayers of John Wanamaker, 1923; Prayers in Bethany Chapel, 1925; John Wanamaker Leads in Prayer, 1925. Home: 4752 Bayard St., Pittsburgh, Pa.

MacLEOD, Donald Campbell, clergyman; b. Inverness Co., N.S., Can., Nov. 13, 1868; s. Angus Finlay and Mary (Campbell) M.; A.B., Franklin Coll., New Athens, O., 1895; A.M., 1898, D.D., 1912; grad. Western Theol. Sem., Pittsburgh, 1898; m. Georgia Porter, Nov. 21, 1899. Ordained Presbyn. ministry, 1898; pastor Meadville, Pa., 1898-99, 1st Ch., Washington, D.C., 1899-1913 (successor to late Rev. T. DeWitt Talmage), 1st. Ch., Springfield, Ill., 1913-18, Central Presbyn. Ch. (U.S.), St. Louis, 1918-23, Dundee Presbyn. Ch., Omaha, 1923-29; sec. Presbytery of St. Louis, 1929; pastor Lower Brandywine Presbyn. Ch., Wilmington, Del., since 1933. Democrat. Address: 1407 Delaware Av., Wilmington, Del.

MAC MILLAN, Charles Wright, physician; b. Savannah, Ga., Nov. 6, 1895; s. Charles William and Harriett Eloise (Bessellieu) MacM.; ed. U. of Tenn., 1914-15; M.D., Vanderbilt U. Med. Sch., 1919; m. Elizabeth Taylor Chester, June 18, 1921; children—Susan Willard, Elsie Parson, Charles Wright, Jr. Resident phys. Davidson Co. Tuberculosis Hosp., Nashville, Tenn., 1918-19; interne Hillman Hosp., Birmingham, Ala., 1919-20; pathologist Passaic Gen. Hosp., Passaic, N.J., 1920-24, St. Mary's Hosp., 1921-25; clin. asst. and instr. pediatrics, N.Y. Post-Grad. Med. Sch. and Hosp., 1924-27, clin. asst. and instr. laryngology, 1927-29; clin. asst. in otology, Manhattan Eye, Ear & Throat Hosp., N.Y. City, asst. surgeon, 1930-31; asso. in otolaryngology, N.Y. Post Grad. Med. Sch. & Hosp., 1931-34; consultant in otolaryngology, Passaic Co. Tuberculosis Sanatorium since 1929; asst. attdg. otolaryngologist, Mountainside Hosp., Montclair since 1936, St. Mary's Hosp., Passaic, 1927-36. Served in S.A.T.C., 1918-19. Fellow Am. Coll. Surgns. Licentiate Am. Bd. Otolaryngology. Mem. A.M.A., N.J. and Passaic Co. med. socs. (pres. Passaic Co. Med. Soc. 1935-36), Asso. Phys. Montclair & Vicinity, Acad. Medicine Northern N.J., Sterilization League of N.J. (pres.), Alpha Kappa Kappa, Beta Theta Pi. Republican. Conglist. (deacon). Rotarian. Home: 4 Duryea Rd., Montclair, N.J.

MAC MILLAN, Edward Allen, civil engr.; b. Perrineville, N.J., Feb. 14, 1893; s. William Tennant and Mary Elizabeth (Allen) MacM.; C.E., Princeton U., 1915; m. Helen Grover Applegate, of Hightstown, N.J., June 20, 1923. Engaged as instr. civil engring., Princeton U., 1915-17; supt. of bldgs. and grounds Princeton U. since 1921. Served as capt., Corps of Engrs., U.S.A., 1917-19 with A.E.F. in France; now lt. col. Corps of Engrs., Reserve. Mem. Am. Soc. Civil Engrs., Soc. Am. Mil. Engrs., Phi Beta Kappa, Sigma Psi. Home: Princeton, N.J. Office: Princeton University, Princeton, N.J.

MacMILLAN, Hugh Ross, clergyman; b. Maple Lake, Can., Mar. 4, 1872; s. Angus and Christie (Ross) MacM.; came to U.S., 1893, naturalized, 1904; B.S., Colgate Coll., 1902; student Colgate Sem., 1901-03; hon. D.D., Franklin Coll., Franklin, Ind., 1926; m. Eugenia Viola Smith, Aug. 29, 1907; 1 dau., Alice Christie (dec.). Ordained to ministry Bapt. Ch., 1903; various pastorates, 1903-11; promotion sec. Bapt. Missions, 1914-17; various pastorates, 1917-28; pastor First Bapt. Ch., Bradford, Pa., since 1928; mem. Pa. Bapt. Conv. Bd. since 1929. Mem. Phi Kappa Psi. Republican. Baptist. Mason. Club: Rotary of Bradford. Home: 61 Congress St., Bradford, Pa.

MacMURRAY, John Van Antwerp, diplomatic service; b. Schenectady, N.Y., Oct. 6, 1881; s. Junius W. and Henrietta (Van Antwerp) M.; B.A., Princeton, 1902, M.A., 1907, LL.D., 1930; LL.B., Columbia, 1906; D.C.L., Wesleyan Univ., 1925; LL.D., Union College, 1930; m. Lois R. Goodnow, Feb. 19, 1916; children—Joan Goodnow, Frank Goodnow, Lois Van Antwerp. Admitted to N.Y. bar, 1906; apptd. sec. legation and consul gen. at Bangkok, Siam, May 10, 1907; 2d sec. Embassy, St. Petersburg, Russia, 1908-11; asst. chief div. of information, Dept. of State, Apr.-July 1911; asst. chief and chief Div. of Near Eastern Affairs, 1911-13; sec. Legation, Peking, 1913-17; apptd. counselor of Embassy, Tokyo, Nov. 10, 1917; assigned on spl. detail in charge Legation at Peking, June 18, 1918; reassigned to Embassy, Tokyo, Oct. 15, 1918; apptd. chief of Div. of Far Eastern Affairs, Dept. of State, Aug. 20, 1919. Expert asst. on Pacific and Far Eastern affairs to Am. commrs., Internat. Conf. on Limitation of Armament, Washington, 1921; observer for Govt. at Chinese-Japanese negotiations for settlement of Shantung question, 1921-22; apptd. asst. sec. of state, Nov. 18, 1924; minister to China, 1925-29, chmn. Am. delegation to Spl. Conf. on Chinese Customs Tariff, 1925-26; Am. mem. Internat. Conciliation Commn. under 1929 Treaty with Estonia; minister to Estonia, Latvia and Lithuania, 1933-

36; ambassador to Turkey since Jan. 1936; asst. chairman International Wheat Advisory Com., 1933-38; chairman Joint Preparatory Com. on Philippine Affairs, 1937-38. Dir. Walter Hines Page Sch. of Internat. Relations, Johns Hopkins, 1930-35. Hon. chancellor Union Coll., 1929-30. Editor: Treaties and Agreements with and concerning China, 1894-1919, 2 vols., 1921. Home: Brooklandville, Md. Address: Dept. of State, Washington, D.C.

MACNEILL, Norman Merle, M.D.; b. Grand Narrows, Nova Scotia; s. Edward A. and Elizabeth (MacDougall) M.; came to U.S., 1906, naturalized, 1925; ed. pub. schs., Nova Scotia, and St. Francis Xavier U., Antigonishe, N.S.; M.D., Jefferson Med. Coll., Phila., 1916; unmarried. Interne St. Joseph's Hosp., Phila., 1916-17; asst. physician Pa. Hosp. (dept. of mental and nervous diseases), Phila., 1919-22; asst. demonstrator in pediatrics, Jefferson Med. Coll., Phila., 1921-39, asst. prof. of pediatrics, 1934-39; asst. pediatrist, Jefferson Hosp., Phila., 1934-39; pediatrist St. Joseph's Hosp., Phila., 1923-39; St. Simon's Mission Settlement, Phila., since 1925. Capt., Canadian Army Med. Corps, 1917-19. Fellow A.M.A., Am. Acad. Pediatrics, College of Physicians of Philadelphia; mem. Philadelphia Co. Med. Soc., Phila. Pediatric Soc., Phi Rho Sigma (nat. v.p.). Roman Catholic. Club: British Officers (Phila.; charter mem.). Author numerous articles on diseases of children. Home: Suffolk Manor. Office: 5116 N. 5th St., Philadelphia, Pa.

MACPHERSON, Elwood Hall, physician; b. Morristown, N.J., Dec. 20, 1897; s. Frank and Emma F. (Hall) M.; student Morristown (N.J.) High Sch., 1914-18, New York Univ., premedical, 1919-20, George Washington U., 1918; M.D., Long Island Coll. Hosp., 1924; m. Rose F. Sulmonetti, June 24, 1926; children—Douglas Kay, Malcolm Lauder. Interne, Elizabeth (N.J.) Gen. Hosp., 1924-25; in practice at Millburn, N.J., since 1925; attending physician and electrocardiologist, Overlook Hosp., Summit, N.J.; physician in charge, Millburn (N.J.) Neighborhood House Clinic, since 1925; mem. med. adv. com. Morris Jr. Coll., Morristown, N.J.; med. advisor Millburn (N.J.) Day Nursery Sch., 1937-39; med. advisor Adult Edn. Com. of Millburn since 1939. Health officer of Millburn (N.J.) Twp. since 1926; mem. Millburn (N.J.) Bd. of Health; mem. Millburn (N.J.) Council of Social Agencies. Mem. A.M.A., N.J. Med. Soc., Essex Co. Med. Soc., Summit Med. Soc. (sec.), Am. Heart Assn., Essex Co. Heart Com., Acad. of Medicine of Northern N.J. Address: 34 Rawley Pl., Millburn, N.J.

MacQUEEN, Lawrence Inglis, business counsel; b. Milledgeville, Ga., Jan. 26, 1889; s. Donald and Martha (Windsor) MacQ.; A.B., Centre Coll., Ky., 1909; A.M., U. of Cincinnati, 1912; m. Madge Blount, 1912; children—Donald Blount (deceased), Marjorie, Lawrence Prince. Teacher, Frederickburg Coll., Va., 1909-11; pres., Synodical Coll., Mo., 1912-14; mem. faculty, Southwestern Presbyn. U., Tenn., 1914-20, U. of Pittsburgh, 1921-36; exec. mgr. Credit Assn. of Western Pa., 1923-30; exec. sec. Builders Supply Club and Nat. Fed. of Builders Supply Assns., 1930-36; since 1936 owner MacQueen Service, management counsel, specializing in construction materials; dir. Universal Sanitary Mfg. Co., Indiana Brass Co., Barnes, Inc. Mem. Sigma Alpha Epsilon, Delta Sigma Pi, Beta Gamma Sigma. Presbyn. Address: 2067 Beechwood Boul., Pittsburgh, Pa.

MacRAE, Allan Alexander, prof. theology; b. Calumet, Mich., Feb. 11, 1902; s. Dr. John and Eunice Caroline (Jennison) MacR.; A.B., Occidental Coll., Los Angeles, Calif., 1922, A.M., 1923; Th.B., Princeton Theol. Sem., 1927; M.A., Princeton U., 1927; Ph.D., U. of Pa., 1936; student U. of Berlin, Germany, 1927-29, 1931, Am. Sch. of Oriental Research, Jerusalem, Palestine, 1929; unmarried. Instr. Semitic philology and Old Testament criticism, Westminster Theol. Sem., Phila., 1929-30, asst. prof. Old Testament, 1930-37; pres. and prof. Old Testament, Faith Theol. Sem., Wilmington, Del., since 1937. Mem. Independent Bd. for Presbyn. Fgn. Missions since 1937. Mem. Am. Oriental Soc., Phi Beta Kappa, Tau Kappa Alpha. Republican. Bible Presbyterian. Mem. Sierra Club of Calif. Home: 1205 Delaware Av. Office: 1617 W. 14th St., Wilmington, Del.

MADDEN, Francis James, M.D.; b. Cleveland, O., May 31, 1870; s. Cornelius S. and Ellen (McGarity) M.; student Wilkinsburg (Pa.) pub. schs., 1879-88; M.D., Western U. of Pa., Pittsburgh, 1895; m. Justina Whalen, Apr. 15, 1896; m. 2d, Mary E. Kennelley, May 5, 1920; 1 son, Paul F. Began gen. practice of medicine, 1895. Councilman, City of Duquesne, Pa., since Jan. 1938. Mem. A.M.A., Pa. State Med. Soc. Democrat. Catholic. Woodman. Home: 4 N. Third St. Office: Corner N. 3d and W. Grant Av., Duquesne, Pa.

MADDEN, John Thomas, prof. accounting; b. Worcester, Mass., Oct. 26, 1882; s. Michael James and Mary Teresa (Lawton) M.; B.C.S., summa cum laude, New York U. Sch. of Commerce, Accounts and Finance, 1911; hon. M.A., Holy Cross Coll., hon. ScD., U. of Newark; m. Anna Marie Callahan, September 3, 1912 (died Aug. 3, 1933); children—Annette Jeanne, Ruth, Jane Louise, Marjorie Helen. Certified pub. accountant, N.Y., 1911, State of New Jersey, 1926. With New York U. Sch. of Commerce since 1911, head Dept. Accounting Instrn., 1917-22, asst. dean Sch. of Commerce, Accounts and Finance, 1922-25, actg. dean 1925, dean since 1925; pres. Alexander Hamilton Inst., 1929-35; pres. Internat. Accountants Soc. since 1929. Decorated Commander Order of Crown (Roumania); Commander Order of Leopold II (Belgium). Dir. Institute International Finance; mem. N.J. State Soc. Certified Public Accountants since 1927. Mem. Am. Economic Assn., American Assn. Univ. Instrs. in Accounting (pres. 1921), Am. Inst. Accountants, N.Y. State Soc. Certified Pub. Accountants (dir. 1923), Nat. Assn. Cost Accountants (dir. 1939), Acad. Polit. Science, Pan-Am. Soc., Merchants Assn., N.Y. City, Am. Assn. Labor Legislation, Am. Management Assn., Am. Arbitration Assn., Foreign Policy Assn., Delta Mu Delta, Theta Nu Epsilon (nat. pres. 1925-28), Alpha Kappa Psi (nat. pres. 1920-21), Beta Gamma Sigma. Catholic. Club: Accountants. Author: Principles of Accounting, 1918; Accounting Practice and Auditing, 1919; Elementary Accounting Problems (with A. H. Rosenkampff), 1920; Foreign Securities (with Marcus Nadler), 1929; International Money Markets (with Marcus Nadler), 1934; America's Experience as a Creditor Nation (with Marcus Nadler and Dr. Harry Sauvain), 1936; Auditing (with A. H. Rosenkampff and P. E. Bacas), 1939. Pres. Am. Assn. of Collegiate Schs. of Business, 1928-29; mem. Council on Accountancy of N.Y. State Dept. of Edn. Home: 710 Berkeley Av., Orange, N.J. Office: Washington Sq., New York, N.Y.

MADDEN, Joseph Warren, lawyer, administrator; b. Damascus, Stephenson Co., Ill., Jan. 17, 1890; s. William James and Elizabeth Dickey (Murdaugh) M.; grad. high sch., Freeport, Ill., 1906; grad. Northern Ill. State Normal Sch., DeKalb, Ill., 1908; A.B., U. of Ill., 1911; J.D., U. of Chicago, 1914; m. Margaret Bell Liddell, July 16, 1913; children—Mary Esther, Joseph Warren, Robert Liddell, Margaret Elizabeth, Murdaugh Stuart. Prof. law, U. of Okla., 1914-16; practiced law, Rockford, Ill., 1916-17; prof. law, Ohio State U., Columbus, O., 1917-21, also pvt. practice; dean Coll. of Law and prof. law, W.Va. U., 1921-27; prof. of law, U. of Pittsburgh, 1927-38; chmn. Nat. Labor Relations Bd., Washington, D.C., since 1935; acting prof. law, Stanford, 1930-31; visiting prof. of law, U. of Chicago, 3 summers to 1928, Cornell U., summer 1930, Stanford U., summer 1933. Spl. asst. in office of atty. gen. of U.S., summer 1920; assisted W.Va. Revision and Codification Commn. in revising property statutes, 1925; adviser on property and torts to Am. Law Inst. since 1934; chmn. Hill Dist. Community Council, and mem. bd. Federation of Social Agencies, Pittsburgh; mem. Gov's. Commn. on Special Policing in Industry; mem. bd. dirs. Pittsburgh Housing Assn. Mem. Am. Bar Assn., Am. Law Inst., Pa. State Bar Association, Delta Upsilon, Phi Alpha Delta, Order of the Coif. Democrat. Presbyn. Author: Cases on Persons and Domestic Relations, including Marriage and Divorce, 1928; Treatise on the law of Domestic Relations and Persons, 1931. Editor: (with H. A. Bigelow) Cases on Rights in Land, 1934; Introduction to Real Property (with same), 2d edit., 1934. Contbr. on legal topics. Home: 4323 Andover Terrace, Pittsburgh, Pa. Office: Shoreham Bldg., Washington, D.C.

MADDOX, William Percy, associate prof. polit. sci.; b. Princess Anne, Md., Nov. 21, 1901; s. Robert Franklin and Ella Virginia (Hoblitzell) M.; A.B., St. John's Coll., Md., 1921; B.A. (Oxon.), Oxford, Eng., 1925; Ph.D., Harvard, 1933; m. Andree Marie Pellion, Sept. 8, 1928. Employed as reporter on Baltimore Evening Sun, 1921-22; instr. polit. sci., U. of Ore., 1925-27, asst. prof., 1927-28; actg. asso. prof. polit. sci., U. of Va., 1928-29; instr. in govt., Harvard U., 1930-36; asst. prof. politics, Princeton U., 1936-38; asso. prof. polit. sci., U. of Pa., since 1938. Mem. Council on Fgn. Relations, Am. Council, Inst. of Pacific Relations, Am. Polit. Sci. Assn., Am. Acad. Polit. and Social Sci., Phi Sigma Kappa. Honored by award Rhodes Scholarship from Md. Democrat. Clubs: Lenape, Harvard (New York). Author: Foreign Relations in British Labor Politics, 1934. Contbr. articles to mags. Address: Dept. of Political Science, Univ. of Pennsylvania, Philadelphia, Pa.

MADEIRA, Percy Child, coal mining; b. Phila., Pa., Nov. 14, 1862; s. Louis Cephas and Adeline Laura (Powell) M.; ed. Episcopal Acad., Phila.; m. Marie V. Marié, Jan. 18, 1888 (died 1893); m. 2d, Elise Donaldson Creswell, July 28, 1915. Began in office of A. Taylor Co., 1879; organized Percy C. Madeira Co., 1886, Madeira, Hill & Co., 1893; now pres., Colonial Colliery Co., Hale Coal Co., Janesville Coal Co., Madeira-Hill Coal Mining Co., Natalie Store Co., Saltsburg Colliery Co., Rockhill Coal & Iron Co., etc. Mem. Anthracite Coal Operators' Assn. (pres. 1916-25). Mem. 1st Troop Phila. City Cav., 1893-1901. Republican. Episcopalian. Author: Hunting in British East Africa, 1909. Home: Ogontz, Pa. Office: Morris Bldg., 1421 Chestnut St., Philadelphia, Pa.*

MADEIRA, Percy Childs, Jr., banking; b. Phila., Pa., Feb. 8, 1889; s. Percy Childs and Marie Virgine (Marié) M.; grad. DeLancey Sch., Phila., 1906; A.B., Harvard, 1910; LL.B., U. of Pa., 1913, M.A., 1933; m. Margaret T. Carey, May 2, 1914; children—Percy Childs, 3d, Francis King Carey, Eleanor Irwin Carey. Admitted to Pa. bar, 1913, and began practice in Phila.; asso. with firm of Morgan, Lewis & Bockins, 1913-21; partner in firm of Ballard, Spahr, Andrews & Madeira (now Ingersoll), 1921-27; vice-pres. Madeira, Hill & Co., coal operators, 1927-34; vice-pres. in charge of trust dept., Land Title Bank & Trust Co. since 1934; dir. Erben-Harding Co., Jesup & Moore Paper Co., Adelphia Hotel Corpn. Served as 1st lt. 313th Inf., 79th Div., U.S. Army, and capt. 313th Cav. later 56th F.A., during World War. Vice-pres. and trustee Univ. Museum; trustee Pa. Soc. Deaf and Dumb; dir. Family Soc. of Phila. Fellow Royal Geog. Soc., Am. Geog. Soc., Delta Psi. Republican. Clubs: Phila., Gulph Mills Golf (Phila.); Explorers (New York). Author of report on "An Aerial Expedition to Central America," pub. in Jour. Univ. Mus., 1931, and various small articles on miscellaneous subjects. Home: W. Sch. Lane and Vaux St. Office: 100 S. Broad St., Philadelphia, Pa.

MAEDER, LeRoy M. A., physician; b. Minneapolis, Minn., May 30, 1898; s. Carl J. and Lucinda A. (Weishaar) M.; ed. St. John's U., Collegeville, Minn., 1916-17; A.B., U. of Minn., 1920, A.M., 1921; M.B., U. of Minn. Med. Sch., 1921, M.D., 1922; LL.B., U. of Pa. Law Sch., 1927; grad. study in Vienna, Austria, 1930-32; unmarried. Resident and asst. chief resident phys., Phila. Gen. Hosp., 1922-23; phys. Internat. Health Bd., Rockefeller Foundation, 1924; psychiatrist, Phila. Hosp. for

Mental Diseases, 1924-25, Pa. Hosp. for Nervous and Mental Diseases, 1925-27; med. dir. Pa. Mental Hygiene Com. of Pub. Charities Assn. of Pa., 1925-35; supt. Fairmount Farm (pvt. mental hosp.), 1927-29; in pvt. practice of neurology, psychiatry, and psychoanalysis since 1927; mem. bd. dirs. Fairmount Farm, Inc. Served in U.S. Army, 1918. Fellow A.M.A., Am. Psychiatric Assn., Coll. of Physicians, Phila., Pa. Psychiatric Soc. (sec.-treas.); mem. Pa. State, and Phila. Co. med. socs., Am. Psychoanalytic Assn., Am. Orthopsychiatric Assn., N.Y. Psychoanalytic Soc., Phila. Psychiatric Soc., Philadelphia Psychoanalytic Society (secretary-treasurer), Phila. Neurol. Soc., Sigma Xi, Alpha Omega Alpha. Home and office: Chancellor Hall, 206 S. 13th St., Philadelphia, Pa.

MAGAW, Elden Samuel, univ. prof.; b. Downs, Kan., Jan. 24, 1906; s. James Willis and Ella Mabel (Uglow) M.; grad. Concordia (Kan.) High Sch., 1924; student Kansas State Coll., Manhattan, 1924-27; A.B., U. of Okla., 1928, LL.B., 1931; grad. student, Georgetown U. Sch. of Law, Washington, D.C., 1937-39, S.J.D., 1939; m. Mildred Holloway, June 29, 1933. Admitted to Okla. State bar, 1931; in gen. practice of law, Oklahoma City, Okla., 1931-33; prof. law, Temple U. Sch. of Law, since 1933; prof. insurance, contracts and agency, 1933-39. Mem. Okla. State Bar Assn., Phi Alpha Delta, Acacia. Democrat. Methodist. Mason. Club: Tredyffrin Country (Paoli, Pa.). Author: Legal Aspects of Administrative Hearings and Findings, 1939. Contbr. to legal periodicals. Home: 7261 Pine St., Upper Darby, Pa. Office: 672 Public Ledger Bldg., Philadelphia, Pa.

MAGEE, F. Earle, M.D.; b. Sandy Lake, Pa., Nov. 13, 1882; s. William Campbell and Malinda (McClure) M.; grad. McElwaine Collegiate Inst., 1904; M.D., U. of Pittsburgh Sch. of Medicine, 1908; student Chicago Eye, Ear, Nose and Throat Coll., 1914; post-grad. work Phila. Polyclinic (now U. of Pa. Grad. Sch. of Medicine), 1915; m. Mabel Wallace (pres. Pa. Fed. Womans Clubs), June 12, 1912; children—Helen Margaret (dec.), Frank Earle. In practice medicine at Oil City, Pa., specializing in treatment of eye, ear, nose and throat. Dir. Pa. Assn. for the Blind. Fellow A.M.A.; mem. North Western Pa. Eye, Ear, Nose and Throat Soc. (pres. 1932-35), Venango Co. Med. Soc. (pres. 1939), Western Pa. Eye, Ear, Nose and Throat Soc., Pa. Med. Soc., Am. Acad. Ophthalmology and Otolaryngology. Mason (32°, Erie Consistory). Writer articles on Sphenopalatine Ganglion Neurosis, The Management of Maxillary Sinus Infections, etc., in Pennsylvania Med. Jour. Home: 116 Wyllis St. Office: 222 Seneca St., Oil City, Pa.

MAGEE, James M., ex-congressman; b. Evergreen, Pittsburgh, Apr. 5, 1877; s. Frederick M. and Hannah Mary (Gillespie) M.; A.B., Yale, 1899; LL.B., U. of Pa., 1902; m. 2d, Mary L. Gittings, children (by former marriage)—Mary J., Edward J. Admitted to Pa. bar, 1903, and began practice at Pittsburgh; mem. 68th and 69th Congresses (1923-27), 35th Pa. District; ex-chmn. Pennsylvania Securities Commn. Commd. 1st lt. U.S.A.S., 1917, later capt.; now lt. col. U.S. Res. Chmn. bd. trustees Elizabeth Steel Magee Hosp., Pittsburgh Maternity Dispensary. Mem. Am., Pa. and Allegheny Co. bar assns., Pa. Hist. Soc. Republican. Episcopalian. Mason, Odd Fellow, Moose. Clubs: Duquesne, Law (Pittsburgh); Rolling Rock (Ligonier, Pa.). Home: 5628 Forbes St. Office: Magee Bldg., Pittsburgh, Pa.

MAGEE, John Fackenthal, mfg. exec.; b. Easton, Pa., Nov. 16, 1892; s. Charles Morford and Anna Margueretta (Fackenthal) M.; student Lafayette Coll., Easton, Pa., 1909-13; m. Elizabeth Atwood Nightingale, Mar. 22, 1917; childen—Elizabeth Nightingale, John Fackenthal. Plant and staff engr. Alpha Portland Cement Co., Easton, Pa., 1913-16, supt. Martens Creek (Pa.) Plant, 1916-19, production engr., 1920-21, chief engr., 1922-25, mgr. operations, 1926-32, v.p. in charge operations and dir. since 1932; pres. Taylor Stiles & Co.,

Riegelville, N.J., since 1937. Trustee Lafayette Coll. since 1933. Republican. Presbyterian. Clubs: Pomfret, Northampton County Country (Easton, Pa.). Home: 613 Paxinosa Av. Office: First National Bank Bldg., Easton, Pa.

MAGEE, Russell Stuart, physician; b. Philadelphia, Pa., Nov. 24, 1898; s. Harry Stuart and Margaret (Wagner) M.; A.B., Central High Sch., Phila., 1917; B.S., Hahnemann Coll. of Science, 1919, M.D., Hahnemann Med. Coll., Phila., 1923; m. Helen Kathryn Pusey, July 27, 1923; children—Russell Stuart, Harrison Pusey. In practice as physician, Audobon, N.J., since 1924; prof. med. terminology, Hahnemann Med. Coll., Phila., since 1930, lecturer history of medicine, since 1938, asso. in therapeutics since 1934; on surg. staff St. Luke's Hosp., Phila., since 1927. Served in S.A.T.C., 1918-19. Mem. bd. of edn., Audobon, N.J., since 1939. Fellow A.M.A.; mem. Pan-Am. Med. Assn., Germantown Med. Soc., Alpha Sigma. Republican. Episcopalian. Club: Tavistock (N.J.) Country. Address: 201 White Horse Pike, Audubon, N.J.

MAGENAU, John Martin, vice-pres. Erie Brewing Co.; b. Erie, Pa., Aug. 15, 1881; s. David and Bertha (Riedinger) M.; ed. grammar and high schs., Erie; m. Florence M. Koehler, Oct. 25, 1904; children—Ruth M., Jackson D., John Martin. Clerk in grocery store, 1900-02; clerk in post office, 1902-06; with Erie Brewing Co. since 1906, vice-pres. and sec. since 1919; dir. Bank of Erie, Mutual Bldg. & Loan Assn.; treas. Parade St. Market Co. Pres. Stadium Comm., Erie; mem. City Planning Commn.; incorporator Erie Cemetery. Republican. Lutheran. Mason, Eagle, Elk, Moose. Club: Erie. Home: 2323 Sassafras St. Office: 22d and State Sts., Erie, Pa.

MAGER, Gus (Charles A.), artist, cartoonist; b. Newark, N.J., Oct. 21, 1878; s. Charles August and Lina (Vollmer) M.; ed. pub. schs. and high sch., Newark, N.J.; art ed. Newark Sketch Club, Graphic Art League, Newark, N. J.; m. Matilda Stunzi, Jan. 30, 1907; 1 son, Robert Augustus. Began in office of jewelry factory, then designer jewelry; cartoonist on N. Y. newspapers and for sydicates; creator, "Knocko the Monk," "Hawkshaw the Detective," "Un-Natural History" in Popular Science mag., "Game Gimmicks" in Outdoor Life mag.; exhibited paintings in three one-man shows in New York City and two in Newark; represented in many pvt. collections also Whitney Mus. of N.Y. City, Newark Mus., Field Foundation and others; apptd. painting authority on com. of selection for N.J. of Contemporary Art at N. Y. World's Fair, 1939. Dir. Salons of America, art soc. Mem. Painters, Sculptors and Gravers, Modern Artists N.J. Home: 204 Prospect St., South Orange, N.J.

MAGIDSON, Frank, pres. Pittsburgh Tag Co.; b. Russia, Aug. 18, 1886; s. Louis and Toby (Schein) M.; ed. pub. schools of Chicago; came to U.S., 1894; m. Mattie Ada Davis, Jan. 17, 1909; children—Phyllis (Mrs. Samuel Allen Jubelirer), Roslyn, Helen, Herbert, Jean. Organized Rapid Spring Co., Pittsburgh, 1923, pres. until 1932; organized Pittsburgh Hanger Co., 1926, and operated until 1927; pres. Pittsburgh Tag Co. since 1928; pres. Pittsburgh Wire Co. since 1936. Republican. Jewish religion. Mason. Home: 5529 Beacon St. Office: 318 Penn Av., Pittsburgh, Pa.

MAGIE, David, prof. classics; b. N.Y. City, Jan. 20, 1877; s. David and Margaret (McCosh) M.; A.B., Princeton, 1897, A.M., 1899; Ph.D., U. of Halle, 1904. Instr. Latin, 1899-1905, preceptor classics, 1905-11, prof. since 1911, Princeton. Mem. Am. Philol. Assn., Archæol. Inst. America. Presbyn. Home: 101 Library Pl., Princeton, N.J.

MAGILL, Frank Stockton, teacher; b. Lewistown, Ill., July 15, 1875; s. John Fulton and Ellen S. (McCabe) M.; B.A., Parsons Coll., Fairfield, Ia., 1896; M.A., magna cum laude, Washington and Jefferson Coll., Pa., 1906, LL.D., from the same college, 1935; m. Anne Nelson, Oct. 27, 1910; children—M. Margaret, Frances H., T. Nelson, John F., Anne N. Teacher of English, Purdue U., Lafayette, Ind., 1904-1906; acting dean, Wilson College, Chambersburg, Pa., 1906-07; head master, Penn Hall Sch. for Girls, Chambersburg, Pa., since July 1, 1910; also sec.-treas. Penn Hall Co. Mem. Univ. Assn. America, Pi Gamma Mu. Mem. Pa. legislature, 1918-21. Republican. Presbyn. Address: Chambersburg, Pa.

MAGILL, James P., investment banker; b. Phila., Pa.; s. Andrew and M. Eleanor (Ash) M.; prep. edn. Westtown Boarding Sch.; B.S., Haverford Co.; m. Ruth Marshall, Partner Eastman, Dillon & Co. since 1924; gov. Phila. Stock Exchange; dir. Phila. Dairy Products Co. Served with Base Hosp. No. 10, U.S. Army, with A.E.F., 1917-19. Overseer William Penn Charter Sch. Republican. Mem. Soc. of Friends. Clubs: Racquet, Sunnybrook Golf (Phila.). Home: Scotforth Rd. Office: 225 S. 15th St., Philadelphia, Pa.

MAGILL, Walter Henderson, univ. prof.; b. Phila., Pa., Dec. 11, 1878; s. Andrew and Mary Eleanor (Ash) M.; B.S. in edn., U. of Pa., 1920, A.M., same, 1922, Ph.D., same, 1930; m. Josephine Adair Andrews, June 28, 1911; children—Eleanor Elizabeth, Charles Andrews, Jean Ash, Arthur Andrews, James Phineas II, Donald Adair, Lincoln Clark. Began as asst. prof. industrial edn., U. of Pa., 1920; employed in tech. and administrative depts., Bell Telephone Co. of Pa., 1899-1909; instr. electricity, Phila. Trades Sch., 1909-12; teacher mathematics, physics, and shop, Westown Sch., 1912-19; prof. industrial edn., U. of Pa., since 1930. Dir. Howard Instn., Germantown Friends Sch. Mem. N.E.A., Nat. Soc. for Study of Edn., Nat. Soc. Coll. Teachers of Edn., Am. Assn. Univ. Profs., Am. Vocational Assn., A.A.A.S., Pa. State Edn. Assn., Pa. Vocational Assn. Mem. Religious Soc. Friends. Home: 117 Carpenter Lane, Philadelphia, Pa.

MAGILL, William Seagrove, surgeon, pathologist; b. Lynne, Conn., July 7, 1866; s. William Alexander and Mathilda Wakefield (Smith) M.; A.B., Amherst Coll., 1887, A.M., 1892; B.L. B.S., U. of Paris, 1889, M.D., 1894; studied Institut Pasteur, Paris, 1892-97, U. of Zurich, 1894; m. Camille Grandclement, Princess of Graves, Russia, 1915 (died at Amherst, Mass., 1928); 1 son, William Camille. Prof. pathology and dean, Coll. of Medicine, U. of W.Va., 1900-01; research bacteriologist Carnegie Lab., New York, 1901-03; spl. investigator, Paris, Berlin, Vienna, Munich, 1903-08; surgeon New York Nose, Throat and Lung Hosp., 1908-09; dir. labs., N.Y. State Dept. Health, 1909-14; owner and operator Wolfram (tungsten) Mines, Portugal, 1917-22. First lt. U.S.A. Med. Reserve Corps, 1909-15; chief interpreter Internat. Tuberculosis Congress, Washington, D.C., 1909, and Internat. Congress of Hygiene, Washington, 1912. Lt. gen. M.C., Russian Imperial 3d Army, 1914-15. Inventor of processes and products mostly concerning milk in dry form for which over 400 patents have been issued. Fellow Am. Acad. Medicine; mem. Internat. Univ. Com. (founder, Paris, 1896), etc. Extensive contbr. on med. subjects. Home: Morgantown, W.Va.

MAGNESS, John Robert, pomologist; b. Amity, Ore., Nov. 9, 1893; s. Robert Newton and Ollie (Barendrich) M.; B.S., Ore. Agrl. Coll., Corvallis, Ore., 1914, M.S., 1916; Ph.D., U. of Chicago, 1923; m. Iva Grace Moore, June 5, 1921; children—Robert Moore, John Newton, Donald Eaton. Research asst. in horticulture, Ore. Agrl. Coll., Corvallis, 1914-17; science asst. in U.S. Dept. Agr., 1917-20, asst. physiologist, 1920-21, physiologist, 1922-27; prof. horticulture and head of dept., State Coll. of Washington, Pullman, Wash., 1927-29; prin. pomologist, U.S. Dept. Agr., U.S. Hort. Sta., Beltsville, Md., since 1929. Fellow A.A.A.S.; mem. Am. Soc. for Hort. Sci. (past pres.), Am. Soc. for Hort. Sci., Am. Soc. Plant Physiologists, Alpha Gamma Rho, Sigma Xi, Phi Beta Kappa. Democrat. Presbyn. Home: 5 Valley View Av., Takoma Park, Md. Office: U.S. Hort. Sta., Beltsville, Md.

MAGOON, Charles Alden, research in horticulture; b. St. Albans, Me., Oct. 14, 1883; s. Lindley Hoag and Elizabeth Shepherd (Bates)

M.; A.B., Bates Coll., Lewistown, Me., 1910; student Mass. Inst. Tech., 1910-11, U. of Minn., Minneapolis, 1915-16; Ph.D., Am. Univ., Washington, D.C., 1924; m. Ella Briggs Russell, Sept. 3, 1913. Employed as bacteriologist and chemist, Boston Biochem. Lab., Boston, Mass., 1911-13; asso. prof. bacteriology, asst. bacteriologist, bacteriologist, State Coll. of Washington and Wash. Agrl. Expt. Sta., Pullman, Wash., 1913-18; research in fruit and vegetable utilization in U.S. Dept. Agr., Washington, D.C., 1918-36; sr. bacteriologist, and investigations in grape production and utilization since 1936. Mem. local civic improvement orgns. Mem. A.A.A.S., Soc. Am. Bacteriologists, Am. Phytopathol. Soc., Am. Soc. for Hort. Sci., Bot. Soc. of Washington, Phi Beta Kappa, Hyattsville Hort. Soc. Independent Democrat. Club: Cosmos (Washington). Home. 216 W. Madison Av., Riverdale. Office: U.S. Hort. Station, Beltsville, Md.

MAGRADY, Frederick W., lawyer; b. Pottsville, Pa., November 24, 1863; s. William and Isabel (McConaghy) M.; B.E., Bloomsburg State Normal Sch., 1890, M.E., 1892; LL.B., Dickinson Sch. of Law, 1909; m. Mary Kiefer. Began practice at Mt. Carmel, Pa., 1909; mem. 69th to 72d Congresses (1925-33), 17th Pa. Dist.; v.p. Shamokin and Mt. Carmel Transit Co.; dir., solicitor First Nat. Bank (Mt. Carmel), Mt. Carmel Water Co.; pub. speaker in drives, World War; dir. Four Minute Men. Mem. Am., Pa. and Northumberland Co. bar assns. Mason (K.T.); mem. I.O.O.F (Grand Master of Pa., 1924-25), P.O. Sons of America (state pres. 1921-22). Republican. Home: 501 W. Av. Office: 13 W. 3d St., Mt. Carmel, Pa.

MAGRAW, James Finney, physician; b. Thomas Run, Md., April 22, 1886; s. James Martin and Katherine Whitely (Stump) M.; M.D., U. of Md. Med. Sch., Baltimore, 1909; m. Helen Edna Daugherty, April 29, 1925; 1 son, James Finney, Jr. Interne University Hosp., Baltimore, 1909-10; engaged in gen. practice of medicine at Perrysville, Md., since 1911; pres. Nat. Bank of Perryville, Md., since Jan. 1939; vice-pres. Home Bldg. & Loan Assn. of Cecil Co. since 1936; dir. Community Fire Co. of Perryville. Mem. Cecil County Med. Soc., Medico-Chirurg. Faculty of Md., Cecil County Med. Soc. (pres.), Cecil County Rod & Gun (dir.). Democrat. Presbyn. Mason. Address: Aikin Av., Perryville, Md.

MAGRUDER, Warren Keach, life ins.; b. Baltimore, Md., Feb. 8, 1887; s. Edward B. and May Annie (Keach) M.; student Baltimore City Coll. to 1904; m. Mary Dorsey Mitchell, Jan. 11, 1913; 1 son, Warren Alexander Edward. Employed as clk. McCubbin, Goodrich & Co., 1905-06; clk. and salesman, Nat. Surety Co., 1906-07; salesman, Philip F. Gehrman & Co., 1907-09; salesman, John Hancock Mutual Life Ins. Co., Baltimore, 1909-12; mgr. Guardian Life Ins., Co., 1912-15; supervisor and asst gen. agt. Conn. Mutual Life Ins. Co., Baltimore, 1915-29, gen. agt. since 1929. Served as mem. field arty., Md.N.G., 1916-17; 2d lt. U.S.A., 1918-19; 1st lt. artr. U.S.A. Res., 1919-24. Mem. bd. mgrs. Henry Watson's Children's Aid Soc. Mem. Baltimore Life Underwriters Assn. (past pres.), Gen. Agts. and Mgrs. Assn. (past pres.), Soc. Colonial Wars, S.A.R., Southern Md. Soc., Am. Clan Gregor Soc., Wednesday Club, Execs. Assn. Mem. for 5 yrs. exec. com. Am. Nat. Lawn Tennis Assn. Awarded tennis championship State of Md., singles once, doubles twice. Independent Democrat. Methodist. Clubs: Baltimore Country (member board of governors), Maryland, Merchants (Baltimore). Home: 4305 Wendover Rd. Office: Baltimore Trust Bldg., Baltimore, Md.

MAGUIRE, Frank P., chief health and phys. edn.; b. Plains, Pa., March 5, 1890; s. William Vincent and Ellen L. (Mullally) M.; prep. edn. Plains Twp. (Pa.) High Sch., 1896-1908, Holy Cross Prep. Sch., 1909-10; A.B., Holy Cross Coll., 1914, hon. A.M., 1919; student Teachers Coll., Columbia, summer 1920; Ph.D., New York U., 1933; m. Helen Frances Monahan, Nov. 30, 1922; children—Frank Arthur, Donald Bruce, Burton Todd, Malcolm Roy. Dean of men, State Teachers Coll., East Stroudsburg, Pa., 1914-36; state dir. of health and phys. edn., Pa. Dept. of Pub. Instrn. since 1936. Served as sergt. I Co., 3d Batt., Chem. Warfare Service, U.S. Army, 1918. Mem. Community Chest Bd. and Park Commn., East Stroudsburg, Pa. Mem. N.E.A., Pa. State Edn. Assn., Am. Phys. Edn. Assn., Pa. State Phys. Edn. Assn., Eastern Intercollegiate Football Officials Assn., Nat. Assn. of Approved Basketball Officials, Am. Legion, Beta Pi, Kappa Delta Pi. Elk. Club: Hungry (Reading). Home: 229 E. Brown St., East Stroudsburg, Pa. Office: Dept. of Public Instruction, Harrisburg, Pa.

MAGUIRE, John Francis, dentist; b. Wilmington, Del., July 20, 1905; s. Charles Francis and Reba May (Hudson) M.; student U. of Del., 1923-25, U. of Pa., 1925-26; D.D.S., U. of Md., 1930; M.S.D., Northwestern U., 1931; m. Jean Elizabeth Kennedy, Feb. 19, 1938; 1 son, Charles. In gen. practice of dentistry since 1932; mem. Del. State Bd. of Health since 1937. Mem. R.O.T.C., 1923-25. Mem. Druids, Gamma Delta Pi, Phi Kappa Tau, Psi Omega. Catholic. Clubs: Monarch Service, University (Wilmington). Home: 1004 Madison St. Office: 500 Delaware Av., Wilmington, Del.

MAHAFFEY, Pearl, coll. prof.; b. Taylorsville, O., Oct. 1, 1879; d. John Wesley and Malissa (Robinson) M.; A.B., Miami Univ., Oxford, O., 1908; A.M., Columbia U. 1922. Engaged in teaching in rural schs., O., 1900-03; teacher, pub. schs., Middletown, O., 1903-04, Hillsboro, O., 1904-08; instr. French and German, Bethany (W.Va.) Coll., 1908-18, prof. modern langs. since 1922; sec. Y.W.C.A., Spartanburg, S.C., 1918-21. Mem. Modern Lang. Assn., Am. Assn. Univ. Women, Am. Assn. Univ. Profs. Republican. Mem. Disciples of Christ. Home: Pendleton St., Bethany, W.Va.

MAHAN, C. E., Jr.; mem. law firm Mahan, Bacon & White. Address: Fayetteville, W.Va.

MAHON, John Dougherty, ins. exec.; b. Ellicott City, Md., Apr. 15, 1885; s. John J. and Bridget A. M.; student Rock Hill Coll. and Strayer's Business Coll.; m. Gertrude E. Ells, Jan. 29, 1913; children—Gertrude Elizabeth, Dorothy Annette, Joseph Ells. Began as stenographer, 1903; spl. agt. Fidelity & Deposit Co., 1905-11, asst. sec., 1911-14; v.p. New Amsterdam Casualty Co., Baltimore, since 1914; pres. Commercial & Farmers Bank; v.p. and dir. Am. Indemnity Co. Democrat. Catholic. Club: Rolling Road Golf (Catonsville, Md.). Home: Ellicott City, Md. Office: 227 St. Paul St., Baltimore, Md.

MAHONEY, Bertha Winter (Mrs. Thomas Sullivan M.); b. Erie, Pa., Apr. 7, 1892; d. George Joseph and Catherine (Moyer) Winter; grad. Erie Normal Sch., 1911; spl. summer courses, Columbia U.; m. Thomas Sullivan Mahoney, June 25, 1925. Engaged as teacher in elementary schs., Erie, Pa., 1911-19; prin. elementary schs., 1919-25; elected to Bd. Edn. of Erie, 1932, served as pres. bd., 1937-38, re-elected by popular vote for term 1938-44, first woman to be so re-elected. Trustee Edinboro State Teachers Coll. (vice-pres. 1936-40). Mem. bd. dirs. Erie Social Hygiene Assn.; mem. Girl Scout Council of Erie. Pres. Erie Council of Cath. Women, Rosary Soc. of St. Peter's Cathedral. Mem. Ladies Auxiliary Knights of St. John, Cath. Daughters of America (regent Erie), Bishop Gannon Guild, Ladies Cath. Benevolent Assn. Apptd. by Bishop Gannon as Diocesan Rep. in charge of all girls' activities, also field sec. his dept. of Confraternity of Christian Doctrine; vol. worker and has no salaried position in all this work. Democrat. Roman Catholic. Home: 409 Lincoln Av., Erie, Pa.

MAHONEY, Charles Harold, prof. olericulture. U. of Md. Address: University of Maryland, College Park, Md.

MAHOOD, Alexander Maitland, pub. service commr.; b. Princeton, W.Va., Sept. 3, 1900; s. William Maitland and Kate Alexander (Straley) M.; student Fishburne Mil. Sch., Waynesboro, Va., 1914-17; LL.B., U. of Va., Charlottesville, Va., 1922; m. Gladys Shumate, July 20, 1928; children—Alexander Maitland, William Henderson. Admitted to W.Va. bar, 1922; city atty., Princeton, W.Va., 1924-28; asst. prosecuting atty., Mercer County, W.Va., 1928-29; mem. Pub. Service Commn. of W.Va., Charleston, since 1930 (reappointed 1935). Served as 1st sergt., O.T.C., 1918. Chmn. Rep. Exec. Com. for Mercer County, 1926-30. Mem. Nat. Assn. of R.R. and Utilities Commrs. (pres. Apr. 1937-Nov. 1938; mem. exec. com.), W.Va. Bar Assn., Am. Legion, Phi Kappa Sigma, Phi Delta Phi. Republican. Baptist. Elk, Moose, K.P. Club: Charleston (W.Va.) Tennis. Home: 501 Nancy St. Office: Capitol Bldg., Charleston, W.Va.

MAIHL, Viola Ruth, librarian; b. Paterson, N.J., Mar. 11, 1903; d. John Ulrich and Mary (White) M.; grad. high sch., Paterson, N.J., 1920; ed. Simmons Coll., Columbia U. Employed as library asst. Paterson Free Pub. Library, 1920-27; asst. hosp. librarian, U.S. Vets. Bur., Hines, Ill., 1927; librarian, Free Pub. Library, Linden, N.J., since 1928. Mem. Am. Library Assn., N.J. Library Assn. (v.p. 1937-38), Spl. Libraries Assn. Mem. Christian Ch. Club: Linden College. Home: 521 Westminster Av., Elizabeth. Office: Free Pub. Library, Linden, N.J.

MAINZER, Francis Stanislaus, surgeon; b Erie, Pa., Nov. 26, 1898; s. Frank and Margaret Hubler M.; grad. St. Bonaventure High Sch., 1919; grad. St. Bonaventure Pre-Medical, 1921; B.S., St. Bonaventure, 1923; M.D., Jefferson Med. Coll., 1926; m. Dorothy Kirkwood, July 19, 1929; children—Francis Kirkwood, Thomas Richard, John Edward, Peter James. Interne St. Vincents Hosp., Erie, Pa., July 1926-27; asso. surgeon Waterworth Clinic, full time, 1927-35; asso. surgeon J. C. Blair Memorial Hosp. Mem. Pa. State Med. Soc.; Huntingdon County Med. Soc.; fellow Am. Coll. of Surgeons since 1933; fellow Am. Med. Assn.; Am. Med. Editors and Authors Assn., Soc. for the Study of Glands of Internal Secretion; charter mem. Am. Neisserian Soc.; Theta Nu Epsilon, Omega Epsilon Phi, Theta Kappa Psi, Kappa Delta Phi. Major, Officers Reserve Corps, U.S. Army. Republican. Catholic. K. of C., Elks. Author of 30 articles published in various jours. Co-author: Encyclopedia Sexualis. Address: Huntingdon, Pa.

MAIRS, Thomas Isaiah, educator; b. Browning, Mo., Apr. 16, 1871; s. Joseph Watson and Mary Elizabeth (Curtis) M.; B.Agr., U. of Mo., 1896, B.S., and M.S., 1900; grad. student, Mich. State Agrl. Coll., Lansing, Mich., and University of Ill., 1896-97; m. Charlotte Marie Riley, July 30, 1902 (died July 24, 1929); children—Thomas Isaiah, John Curtis, Edward Shrader. Supt. field experiments, U. of Ill., 1896-97; asst. in agr. and supt. coll. farm, U. of Mo., 1897-1901; prof. agrl. edn., and supt. corr. courses in agr., Pa. State Coll., since 1901. Fellow A.A.A.S.; mem. Am. Genetic Assn., Am. Assn. for Advancement of Agrl. Teaching, Alpha Zeta, Gamma Sigma Delta. Republican. Presbyn. Mason. Specialized in pub. sch. agr. and instruction by correspondence. Author: Some Pennsylvania Pioneers in Agricultural Science, 1928; also wrote chapters on edn. and orgn. in Rural Pennsylvania, 1905. Home: State College, Pa.

MAJOR, James Arthur, lawyer; b. New York, N.Y., June 2, 1900; s. John Frederick and Louise (Pfrender) M.; LL.B., N.Y. Law Sch., 1928; m. Ann Mae Donahue, Apr. 4, 1929; 1 son, James Arthur II. Admitted to N.J. bar as atty., 1929, as counsellor at law, 1932; mem. firm Major, Back & Carlsen, Hackensack, N.J., since 1934. Mem. Lawyers Club of Bergen Co. Democrat. Reformed Ch. Mason (William L. Daniels Lodge; Royal Arch, Henry S. Haines Chapter). Home: 66 Romaine Av., Maywood, N.J. Office: 130 Main St., Hackensack, N.J.

MAJOR, Randolph Thomas, chemist; b. Columbus, O., Dec. 23, 1901; s. David R. and Mary (Campbell) M.; A.B., U. of Neb., Lincoln, Neb., 1922, M.S., 1924; Ph.D., Princeton U., 1927; m. Grace E. Lowe, July 8, 1928; children—Mary Elizabeth, Randolph Thomas, Jr., Anne Campbell, Jane Wyman. Engaged in teaching, high sch., Albion, Neb., 1922-23; research asso., Princeton U., 1927-30; dir. pure research Merck & Co., Inc., 1930-37, dir. research and development, Merck & Co., Inc., Rahway, N.J., since 1937. Mem. A.A.A.S., Am. Chem. Soc. (chmn.-elect N. Jersey Sect. 1939), Chemists Club of N.Y., Phi Beta Kappa, Sigma Xi. Republican. Conglist. Club: Colonia Country (Colonia). Home: 1210 Denmark Rd., Plainfield. Office: Merck & Co., Inc., Rahway, N.J.

MAKOVER, Abraham Bernard, lawyer; b. Baltimore, Md., Feb. 9, 1896; s. Bernard and Rose (Sworzyn) M.; student Cornell U., 1913-14; LL.B., U. of Md. Law Sch., Baltimore, Md., 1917; m. Celeste Greenberg, Apr. 22, 1918 (dec. 1920); 1 dau., Jeanne Amelie; m. 2d, Idella Porter, Dec. 19, 1935. Admitted to Md. bar, 1917, and engaged since 1919, in gen. practice of law at Baltimore; mem. firm Makover and Kartman, in practice at Baltimore (since 1930) and Washington, D.C. (since 1938). Served as pvt. to sergt. then 2d lt., U.S.A. Res., 1918. Mem. Am. Bar Assn., Md. State Bar Assn., Bar Assn. Baltimore City. Democrat. Jewish religion. Author: (biography) M. M. Noah, 1917. Home: 2440 N. Charles St. Office: Baltimore Trust Bldg., Baltimore, Md.

MALCHEREK, Karl August, asso. prof. music; b. Bebra, Germany, Apr. 25, 1872; s. Johann and Marie (Vaternahm) M.; came to U.S., 1899, naturalized, 1911; ed. Realgymnasium, Conservatory of Music, Darmstadt, Dr. Hoch's Conservatory, Frankfurt a/M, Germany; (hon.) Mus.D., Beaver Coll., 1925; m. Nettie M. Showalter, May 28, 1907. Instr. violin, Darmstadt Conservatory of Music; concertmaster, Palmengarten Orchestra, Frankfurt; first violinist, Museum's Orchestra, Frankfurt; first violinist, Theodore Thomas Orchestra, Chicago, Ill., 1899-1902; first violinist, Pittsburgh Symphony Orchestra, 1902-10; head of violin dept., Beaver Coll., 1910-25; asso. prof. violin, Carnegie Inst. Tech. since 1912. Home: Cathedral Mansions, Pittsburgh, Pa., and Juniata St., Hollidaysburg, Pa.

MALCOLM, Gilbert, exec. sec. and treas. Dickinson Coll.; b. New York, N.Y., Oct. 13, 1892; s. Thomas Duff and Annie Elder (Bissett) M.; Ph.B., Dickinson Coll., 1915, A.M., same, 1917; LL.B., Dickinson Coll. Law Sch., 1917; m. Helen F. Bucher, Nov. 6, 1919 (died 1921). Employed as reporter, Harrisburg Patriot, 1917-18, state editor, 1919-20; with Tax Audit Co., Phila., Pa., 1920-22; endowment sec., Dickinson Coll., 1922-34, treas. since 1925, exec. sec. since 1934; editor The Dickinson Alumnus since 1923. Served as pvt. inf. U.S.A., 1918-19, with A.E.F., asso. editor The Lorraine Cross newspaper 79th Div.; 1st lt. Pa.N.G., 1920-22. Mem. Am. Alumni Council, Raven's Claw, Beta Theta Pi, Omicron Delta Kappa. Republican. Lutheran. Mason (K.T.). Club: Kiwanis of Carlisle (past pres.). Home: Boiling Springs, Pa.

MALCOLM, Ola Powell, home economist; b. Plainview, Tex., Dec. 19, 1889; d. Robert F. and Laura (Tisdel) Powell; ed. Friends' Central Sch., Phila.; domestic science course, State Coll., Columbus, Miss.; grad. Drexel Inst., Phila., 1913; m. Dr. Robert Cummings Malcolm, Oct. 6, 1935. Assisted father in directing vacant lot gardening in Phila. and Cleveland; dir. domestic science dept., Sch. of Organic Edn., Fairhope, Ala., 1910-11; teacher domestic science and sch. gardens, summer schs., Cleveland, 1911-12; asst. state agt. in charge extension work for women and girls, La. State U., 1913, 14; with U.S. Dept. of Agr. since 1914, in charge home demonstration work in fifteen Southern states, with title of senior home economist. Presbyterian. Author: Successful Canning and Preserving, 1917; also home economics bulls., U.S. Dept. Agr. Sent to France, summer 1921, to direct unit of workers on food preservation, under auspices French minister agr. and Am. Com. for Devastated France; also sent by U.S. Dept. Agr., to Spain and Italy, to study methods used in preserving and utilizing Spanish pimientos and other fruits and vegetable products and to secure other information to use in home demonstration work; sent again to France, 1922, for purpose of organizing and establishing home demonstration work in France. Assisted many yrs. planning study and travel for agts. of foreign govts. Sent to U.S. to study home demonstration work. Mem. Epsilon Sigma Phi. Home: 7 Oak Pl., Alta Vista, Bethesda, Md.*

MALCOLM, Talbot Marion, lawyer; b. Huntington, Ind., Feb. 12, 1898; s. Leslie Joseph and Florence Anne (Rathell) M.; prep. edn. Hornell (N.Y.) High Sch., 1910-13, Salamanca (N.Y.) High Sch., 1913-14; A.B., Cornell U., 1918; LL.B., Columbia, 1920; m. Margaret Elizabeth Richart, Jan. 23, 1923; children—Talbot Marion, Bruce Leslie, Allen Rufus, Margaret Louise. Law clerk with Murray, Prentice & Howland (now Milbank, Tweed & Hope), 1920; admitted to N.Y. bar, 1921; sent to Japan, China, Philippines, Singapore and Java on legal business for firm, 1921-22; became asso. with Phillips & Avery, New York, 1923, mem. of firm since 1929; specializing in trial work of firm and since 1937 tax and corpn. work; sec. Cairns Corpn.; dir. Home Bldg. and Loan Assn. Served with U.S. Marine Reserves Flying Corps, 1918. Mem. Westfield, N.J., Bd. of Edn. since 1932, pres. since 1937. Charter mem. and 1st treas. Community Players, Westfield. Mem. Sigma Phi Epsilon, Phi Delta Phi, Sphinx Head (Cornell). Republican. Presbyterian. Mason (past master). Clubs: New York Downtown Athletic; Echo Lake Country, Cornell (past pres.), and College Men's (past pres.), of Westfield, N.J. Home: 737 Boulevard, Westfield, N.J. Office: 1 Wall St., New York, N.Y.

MALE, Arthur J., manufacturer; b. Buffalo, N.Y., Aug. 14, 1889; s. Phillip and Emma (Vellacott) M.; ed. grammar and high schs., Buffalo, 1894-1906; m. Eleanor Lewis Durham, July 21, 1919; 1 son, Edward Durham. Began in aircraft construction, 1916; sec., treas. and dir. Bonney Forge & Tool Works since 1920; pres. and dir. Auto Craft Tool Co.; sec. and dir. Nassau Products Co. Served in Naval Aviation as constructor and pilot, 1917-19. Clubs: Lehigh Country, Livington (Allentown, Pa.). Home: 934 N. 26th St. Address: Allentown, Pa.

MALICK, Robert E., publisher; b. Shamokin, Pa., June 4, 1896; s. Charles C. and Kathryn M.; B.S., Pa. State Coll., 1920; m. Gertrude L. Lytle, March 13, 1924; children—Richard, Jean, Miriam. Entered offices of Shamokin (Pa.) Daily News, 1922, later becoming reporter, city editor seven yrs., sec., 1926-33; engineered, 1933, merger of Daily News with Daily Dispatch; sec. News-Dispatch, 1933-34, pres. since 1934, treas. since 1938; dir. News Pub. & Printing Co. (pubs. of News-Dispatch), Market St. Nat. Bank of Shamokin. Served overseas with U.S. Army during World War. V.p. Susquehanna Council Boy Scouts of America. Mem. Pa. Newspaper Publishers Assn., Am. Legion, Vets. of Foreign Wars, Sigma Pi. Mason, Elk. Clubs: Rotary (past pres.), Kiwanis of Shamokin (charter mem.). Home: 504 N. Market St. Office: 701-703 N. Rock St., Shamokin, Pa.

MALLALIEU, Wilbur V(incent), clergyman; b. Baltimore, Md., May 10, 1876; s. John Barclay and Mary (Catherine) (Amos) M.; student Baltimore City Coll., 1892-95; A.B., Dickinson Coll., Carlisle, Pa., 1899; B.D., Drew Theol. Sem., 1902; grad. study same and New York U., Free Ch. Coll., Glasgow, Scotland; S.T.D., Wesleyan U., Middletown Conn., 1916; D.D., Dickinson Coll. Carlisle, Pa., 1935; m. Gertrude Seville, Feb. 23, 1910; 1 foster dau., Wanda (wife of Fred W. Beib, M.D.). Ordained ministry M.E. Ch., 1903; pastor Roland Park, Md., 1903-11, Union Ch., Washington, D.C., 1911-14, Summit, N.J., 1914-18; capt. Am. Red Cross, in charge home service, U.S. Gen. Hosps. No. 3 and No. 27, and Fort Wadsworth, N.Y., 1918-20; pastor Englewood, N.J., 1920-22, First M.E. Ch., Akron, O., 1922-28, First M.E. Ch., Charleston, W.Va., 1928-33, Grace Ch., Harrisburg, Pa., since 1933; preacher in various colleges since 1905. Chmn. Com. of 100, Washington, D.C., 1913; trustee Y.W.C.A., Akron and Charleston. Mem. Phi Beta Kappa, Phi Delta Theta. Home: 216 State St., Harrisburg, Pa.

MALLERY, Otto Tod; b. Willets Point, N.Y., April 27, 1881; s. Major John Conrad (grad. U.S. Mil. Acad., 1867) and Anna Louise (Winslow) M.; A.B., Princeton, 1902; post-grad. work, U. of Pa. and Columbia; m. Rosamond Robinson Junkin, Nov. 2, 1910 (died 1915); children—Otto Tod, Rosemary; m. 2d, Louise Marshall, 1918; children—Bayard, David. Field sec. Playground and Recreation Assn. of Phila., 1908, treas., 1910, pres. since 1926; pres. Pub. Education Assn. of Philadelphia, 1911-14; sec. Bd. of Recreation, Phila., 1912-15, pres. 1915-16; mem. Pa. State Industrial Bd., 1915-23; dir. Playground and Recreation Assn. America, 1912—; nat. exec. com. and dir. War Camp Community Service, 1918; mem. staff of War Labor Policies Bd., 1918; staff of Arthur Woods, asst. to sec. of war, as chief of Federal Aid and Works Sect., War Dept., 1919; exec. sec. Pa. Emergency Pub. Works Commn., 1917-23. Trustee Am. Acad. Polit and Social Science, Carson Coll. for Orphan Girls. Treasurer National Assn. for Labor Legislation, 1927-31; mem. President's Conf. on Unemployment (mem. econ. advisory com. and exec. sec. pub. works com.), 1921; mem. governing board Gen. Com. on Limitation of Armaments, 1921; Am. observer at Canadian Govt. Unemployment Conf., Ottawa, 1922; spl. investigator of industrial relations for U.S. Coal Commn., 1923; mem. Nat. Com. on Seasonal Operations in the Construction Industries, 1923; sr. business specialist U.S. Dept. Commerce, 1930; mem. state advisory com. of Nat. Youth Administrn. since 1936; mem. Pa. State Planning Bd. since 1936; mem. Phila. City Charter Commn., 1937; econ. advisor to U.S. delegation to Internat. Labor Office and reporter of Public Works Com., Geneva, 1937. Clubs: Franklin Inn (Phila.); Cosmos (Washington, D.C.). Part author of Business Cycles and Unemployment, 1923. Address: 1427 Spruce St., Philadelphia, Pa.

MALLETT, Daniel Trowbridge, publisher; b. New Haven, Conn., April 16, 1862; s. Dr. Samuel and Elizabeth Ann (Turney) M.; ed. Hopkins Grammar Sch., New Haven, Conn.; m. Elsie Lyle Suydam, 1908; children—Samuel Rowland, Elizabeth, Margery (Mrs. B. F. Parsons), Daniel Turney. Hardware mcht., New Haven, Conn., 1883-90; hardware editor, Metal New York, 1892-94; founded, 1984, Hardware Dealer's Magazine; established Rating Register of Hardware Mchts., 1910; now retired; dir. Austin, Nichols Co. Republican. Methodist. Author: When, 1890; Ideas for Hardware Merchants, 1892; Life of Admiral Dewey, 1898; Hardware Merchants of the World, 1910; Mallett's International Index of Artists, 1935. Has one of the largest pvt. collections in U.S. of reproductions of paintings, sculpture, etchings. Address: 363 Prospect Av., Hackensack, N.J.

MALLETT, John Purington, engineer; b. Topsham, Me., Jan. 20, 1869; s. Isaac Emery and Mary (Purington) M.; student town schs., Topsham, Me., 1873-85, town high schs., Brunswick, Me., 1886-88; E.E., Tufts Coll., Medford, Mass., 1894; m. Charlotte Ballou, Sept. 13, 1899 (died 1937); children—Priscilla, Russell Ballou, John Purington, Walter Woodman. Designing engr. Westinghouse Electric & Mfg. Co., Pittsburgh, Pa., 1894-1900; chief engr. Northern Electric & Mfg. Co., Madison, Wis., 1900, Diehl Mfg. Co., Elizabeth, N.J., 1908-14; cons. engr. Soc. for Electric Development, New York, 1914-17; cons. engr., New York City, since 1919; chief engr. and 1st v.p. Gas-it Corpn., mfg. spl. gas for cutting metals, welding, brazing, heat treating, New York, since 1938; chief engr. and 1st v.p. Malletane Gas. Corpn., South Kearny, N.J., since 1938. Served as maj., Chem. Warfare Service, Gas Defense Div., U.S. Army, during World War. Fellow Am. Inst. E.E.; mem. Delta Upsilon. Republican. Unitarian. Odd Fellow. Home: 515 Chilton St., Elizabeth, N.J. Office: Malletane Gas Corpn., South Kearny, N.J.

MALLON, Henry Neil, pres. S. R. Dresser Mfg. Co.; b. Cincinnati, O., Jan. 11, 1895; s. Guy Ward and Hannah (Neil) M.; student Taft Sch., Watertown, Conn., 1909-13; A.B., Yale, 1917; unmarried. With Continental Can Co., Chicago, Ill., 1919-20; with U.S. Can Co., Cincinnati, as factory mgr., later gen. mgr.

and dir., 1920-29; pres. and general manager Dresser Mfg. Co., Bradford, Pa., since 1929, pres. Dresser Mfg. Co., Ltd., Toronto, Can., since 1932; chmn. of the bd. Bryant Heater Co., Cleveland, O., Clark Bros. Co., Olean, N. Y.; dir. Pharis Tire & Rubber Co., Petrolite Corpn. Mem. Am. Petroleum Inst., Am. Gas Assn. Episcopalian. Clubs: Bradford, Valley Hunt, Pennhills (Bradford, Pa.); Union, Kirtland Country (Cleveland, O.); Yale, University, Lunch (New York). Home: 132 Clarence St. Office: Dresser Mfg. Co., Bradford, Pa.

MALLON, Joseph, real estate; b. Manayunk, Phila., Pa., Oct. 23, 1879; s. James Joseph and Sarah Ann (Mellon) M.; student private, pub. and parochial schs., 1885-92, Roman Catholic High Sch., 1892-97; m. Hurley, Oct. 25, 1905; children—Joseph Hurley (dec.), Mary Ellen (Mrs. Joseph A. Hayden), William Kirby, Sara M. (Mrs. Ralph Holden Belcher), James Edward, Jerome Hurley. Clk. in title dept. Continental Title & Trust Co., Phila., 1898-1902; conveyancer, real estate and insurance broker, 1902-03; asst. title officer Continental Title & Trust Co., 1904-07, real estate officer, 1907-12; real estate officer Continental Equitable Title & Trust Co., 1912-35; expert real estate appraiser, realtor and fire ins. broker since 1935; sec. Summit Bldg. & Loan Assn. since 1907, Northern Realty Co. since 1909. Asso. mem. Draft Bd., Germantown and Chestnut Hill, 1917-18. Mem. Phila. Real Estate Bd., Nat. Assn. Real Estate Bds., Soc. Residential Appraiser, Pa. Hist. Soc., Friendly Sons of St. Patrick. Republican. Catholic. Clubs: Germantown Republican, Yachtsmen's (sec.). Home: 143 E. Gorgas Lane, Mt. Airy. Office: Commercial Trust Bldg., Philadelphia, Pa.

MALLORY, Clifford Day, shipping; b. Brooklyn, N.Y., May 26, 1881; s. Henry Rogers and Cora (Pynchon) M.; student Lawrenceville (N. J.) Sch., 1896-1900; m. Rebecca Sealy, Jan. 3, 1911; children—Margaret Pynchon, Clifford Day, Barbara Sealy. Began as clk., C. H. Mallory & Co., 1900; sec. Mallory S.S. Co., 1907-13; v.p. same and Clyde S.S. Co., 1913-17; asst. dir. operation U.S. Shipping Bd., 1917-19; pres. C. D. Mallory & Co., shipping, since 1919; pres. Malston Co., Mallory Transport Lines, Lehigh & Lackawanna Corpn., Ardmore Steamship Co., Inc., C. D. Mallory Corpn., Seminole S.S. Corpn.; vice-pres. and dir. Swiftarrow S.S. Co., Swiftlight S.S. Co., Swiftscout S.S. Co., Swiftsure S.S. Co.; dir. The Putnam Trust Co., Hasler & Company, Inc., Vamar Steamship Co., Inc., Seatrain Lines, Inc., Am. Protection & Indemnity Assn., Inc., Waterways Oeperating Co., Inc., P. R. Mallory Co. Dir. Navy League of U.S.; trustee Webb Inst. Naval Architecture. Mem. Soc. Naval Architects and Marine Engrs. Republican. Presbyn. Clubs: India House, Whitehall, New York Yacht, Indian Harbor Yacht, Seawanhaka-Corinthian Yacht, Cruising Club America, Royal Nassau Sailing; Round Hill, Field (Greenwich). Home: Old Church Rd., Greenwich, Conn. Office: 11 Broadway, New York, N.Y.; and Exchange Place, Jersey City, N.J.

MALLORY, Virgil S(ampson), mathematics; b. Union City, N.J., Aug. 14, 1888; s. Eugene Lester and Adele May (Reeder) M.; A.B., Columbia, 1914, A.M., 1919, Ph.D., 1939; m. Lauris Baum, Sept. 22, 1914; children—Ruth Adele, Virgil Standish. Instr. in mathematics, Wright Oral Sch., N.Y. City, 1908-11; asst. prin. high sch., Dumont, N.J., 1914-18; head of math. dept., high sch., East Orange, N.J., 1918-28; also instr., extension courses, Columbia, 1918-27, spl. lecturer, 1918-29; asso. prof. mathematics, State Teachers Coll., Montclair, N.J., 1928-34; prof. and head math. dept. since 1934. Mem. Council of Edn. Survey Com., N. J. high schs., 1924; reader Coll. Entrance Examination Bd., 1925-28. Made survey of Rahway (N.J.) pub. schs., 1931. Fellow A.A. A.S.; mem. N.E.A., Math. Soc. America, Am. Math. Assn., Nat. Council Teachers of Mathematics (dir. since 1936), N.J. Mathematics Teachers (pres. 1932-33, mem. council since 1928), Brit. Math. Soc., N.Y. Soc. for Exptl. Study of Edn., Mass. Soc. Mayflower Descendants, Alden Kindred, S.A.R., Kappa Delta Pi, Presbyn. Author: Modern Plane Geometry (with John C. Stone), 1929; Modern Solid Geometry (with same), 1930; First Year Algebra Manual for Teachers (with same), 1930; Objective Tests in Algebra (with same), 1930; A Second Course in Algebra (with same), 1931, revised edit., 1937; Higher Arithmetic (with same and F. E. Groosnickle), 1931; Ninth Year Mathematics, Part 1, Algebra, 1931, Part 2, Geometry, 1932; Diagnostic Tests, Demonstrative Geometry, 1933; Junior High School Mathematics (with John C. Stone and C. N. Mills), 1934; Mathematics for Everyday Use (with John C. Stone), 1935; First Year Algebra (with same), 1936; New Plane Geometry (with same), 1937; Achievement Tests in Plane Geometry (with same), 1937; New Solid Geometry (with same), 1937; New Higher Arithmetic (with same), 1938; Achievement Tests in First Year Algebra, 1939; Relative Difficulty of Certain Topics in Mathematics, 1939. Lecturer. Contbr. to professional publs. Home: 351 Springdale Av., East Orange, N.J.

MALMAR, Ruth May, librarian, artist; b. Brooklyn, N.Y., May 28, 1891; d. Esaias and Isabella (Cadiz) M.; grad. Richmond Hill High Sch., 1911; ed. Cornell U. summer 1922, Syracuse U., summers 1932, 38, Columbia U. Extension study over period, 1911-20, N.J. State Teachers Coll., Montclair, N.J., 1936, 1938. Employed in various pub. libraries and sch. libraries, Greater N.Y. and Glen Ridge, N.J., 1913-32, librarian of Commercial Museum, Haaren High School, since 1933; artist in oil and water colors since 1932; studied art, Syracuse U. Art Summer Sch., 1932, L'Ecole des Beaux Arts, Fontainebleau, France, 1933, also pvt. study under Paul Gill, Ruth Randall, Stanislav Rembiski and others; exhibited in France, Brooklyn Museum, N.J. State Annuals, Rockefeller Centre, Architectural League and many other important exhbns. Served as member Protestant Big Sisters in juvenile ct. follow up work, 15 yrs. Mem. Prison Aid Soc., Caldwell Penitentiary. Mem. Am. Artists Professional League, Art Centre of Oranges, High Sch. Teachers Assn., N.Y. City. Republican. Conglist. Home: 18 Pierson Pl., Montclair, N.J. Office: Haaren High Sch., New York, N.Y.

MALONE, Clarence Franklin ("Jack"), mng. editor; b. Rochester, Pa., Aug. 22, 1904; s. Jesse Frank and Mary C. (Field) M.; grad. high sch., Rochester, Pa., 1923; student Geneva Coll., Beaver Falls, Pa., 1927-28; m. Theodora H. Hetche, Aug. 16, 1930. In employ Jones and Laughlin Steel Corpn., Aliquippa, Pa., American Bridge Co., Ambridge, Pa., Fry Pump Co., Rochester, Pa.; began as reporter for Daily Times, 1928, managing editor since 1931. Has served as pub. dir. and on coms. for many civic and charitable orgns. and campaigns in Beaver Co.; also served on church bds. and coms. and teacher of boys' S.S. class. Past sec. Kiwanis Club now merged with Rotary Club. Republican. Evang. Ch. Mason. Clubs: Rotary (past dir.), Exchange (past sec.). Home: 439 Wagamond Av., Rochester. Office: Times Bldg., Beaver, Pa.

MALONE, Kemp, philologist; b. Minter, Miss., Mar. 14, 1889; s. John W. and Lillian (Kemp) M.; A.B., Emory Univ., 1907, Litt.D., 1936; Ph.D., Univ. of Chicago, 1919; grad. study, University of Copenhagen, 1915-16, U. of Iceland, 1919-20, Princeton University, 1920-21; m. Inez René, d. of J. Henry Chatain, Apr. 28, 1927. Teacher Tech. High Sch., Atlanta, 1909-11; Carnegie Foundation exchange teacher to Prussia, 1911-13; instr. in German, Cornell U., 1916-17; asst. prof. English, U. of Minn., 1921-24; lecturer in English, Johns Hopkins, 1924-25, asso. prof. English, 1925-26, prof. since 1926. Visiting prof. summers, U. of Wash., 1925, Yale (Linguistic Inst.), 1928-29, U. of Chicago, 1932-33. Founder (with Louise Pound) of American Speech, mng. editor, 1925-32; editor Hesperia Ergänzungreihe; mem. bd. editors Modern Lang. Notes, Am. Jour. Philology; mem. adv. bd. Speculum, 1930-33, English Jour., 1932, Am. Speech, 1933. Served as 1st lt. Adj. Gen.'s Dept., U.S.A., 1917-18, capt., 1918-Feb. 1919. Fellow Am. Geog. Soc., A.A. A.S.; asso. Am.-Scandinavian Foundation; mem. Mediæval Acad. America (councillor 1934-37), Soc. for Study of Mediæval Lang. and Lit., Am. Philol. Assn., American Association University Professors, Soc. for Advancement of Scandinavian Study (v.p. 1923-24), Nat. Council Teachers of English, Linguistic Soc. America (v.p. 1938), Modern Language Association of America, Shakespeare Association of America, American Iona Society, Irish Texts Society (mem. consultative com.), English-Speaking Union of U.S., Sögufjelag Islands, Islenzkt Bokmentafjelag (hon. 1937), Vereinigung der Islandfreunde, Viking Soc., Internat. Council for English, History of Science Soc., Phil Beta Kappa, Sigma Nu. Democrat. Episcopalian. Clubs: Maryland, University, Johns Hopkins, Tudor and Stuart (pres. 1938-39). Author: The Literary History of Hamlet, 1923; The Phonology of Modern Icelandic, 1923. Editor: Studies in English Philology, 1929; Deor, 1933; Widsith, 1936; The Dodo and the Camel, 1938. Contbr. verse and articles to many philol. and lit. jours. Home: 2710 Maryland Av., Baltimore, Md.

MALONE, Watson, lumber merchant; b. Phila., Pa., Feb. 18, 1881; s. Bernard Taylor and Creacie Crane (Strickler) M.; student Germantown Acad., 1890-98; West Jersey Mil. Acad., Bridgeton, N.J., 1898-99; U. of Pa., 1902-03; m. Anne Newell Dunn, Apr. 17, 1909; 1 son, Watson, III. Began as laborer in 1899 with Watson Malone & Sons, wholesale and retail lumber (established 1854) foreman, 1905-10, salesman, 1910-21, partner 1921-35, owner since 1935; dir. Kensington Nat. Bank, Pa. Lumbermen's Mutual Fire Ins. Co. Trustee Germantown Acad. since 1939. Mem. Beta Theta Pi. Republican. Episcopalian. Clubs: Racquet (Phila.); Germantown Cricket. Home: 11 Railroad Av., Haverford, Pa. Office: 1001 N. Delaware Av., Philadelphia, Pa.

MALONEY, Clifton, pres. Phila. Life Ins. Co.; b. Phila., Pa., June 7, 1872; s. Andrew J. and Susan (Noble) M.; grad. Rugby Acad., Phila., 1888; A.B., U. of Pa., 1892, LL.B., 1895; m. Florence Paul, Oct. 29, 1904; 1 son, Paul. Admitted to Pa. bar, 1895, and practiced in Phila.; pres. Phila. Life Ins. Co. since Sept. 21, 1921. Mem. Phi Delta Theta. Republican. Mem. Soc. of Friends. Home: 3310 Baring St. Office: 111 N. Broad St., Philadelphia, Pa.

MALOY, William M., in gen. practice of law since 1899; mem. law firm Maloy & Brady. Office: Fidelity Bldg., Baltimore, Md.

MAN, E. Lester, lawyer, ins. agt.; b. Wilkes-Barre, Pa., Sept. 17, 1893; s. Eugene L. and Sarah (Fisher) M.; LL.B., Georgetown U. Law Sch., 1915; m. Celia Cohen, May 10, 1917; children—Frances, Eugene. Admitted to D.C. bar, 1916; admitted to Pa. bar, 1919 and since engaged in gen. practice of law at Scranton; entered ins. bus. 1920, pres., treas. and dir. Man & Levy, Inc. gen ins. agency. Chmn. budget com. Scranton Community Chest; dir. and chmn. finance com. Visiting Nurse Assn., Scranton. Dir. and chmn. adult edn., Temple Israel; dir. and chmn. athletics, Y.M.H.A.; past pres. Scranton Zionist Dist.; past pres. Lackawanna Valley Underwriters Exchange. Mem. Lackawanna Bar Assn., Pa. Assn. Ins. Agts (dir.). Jewish religion. Mem. B'nai B'rith. Clubs: Lions (Scranton); Fox Hill Country (Pittston). Home: 1611 Madison Av., Scranton, Pa. Office: Scranton Nat. Bank Bldg., Scranton, Pa.

MANCHESTER, Charles, clergyman; b. Burritt, Ill., Dec. 28, 1858; s. Charles T. and Climena (Crowell) M.; A.B., Park Coll., Mo., 1883, A.M., 1887, and D.D., 1898 from same; B.D., Oberlin Theological Seminary, 1886; m. Lovana Thomas, Dec. 24, 1884 (died July 24, 1926); children—Bertha Ione (Mrs. H. E. Garner), Ray George and Roy Charles (twins), Pansy Elizabeth, Hazel Climena (deceased), Paul Thomas, Lois Sarah (Mrs. C.B. Harding); m. 2d, Ruth Gealy, November 23, 1929. Ordained minister in "Church of God" (a Baptist denomination), Sept. 6, 1878; pastor Mt. Carroll, Illinois, 1886-88, Decatur, Ill., 1888-89, Milmine and Lodge, Ill., 1889-90; preacher of Barkeyville, Pa., ch., 1890-96; prin. Barkeyville (Pa.) Acad., 1890-96; prof. Greek and philosophy, 1896-1901, philosophy and theology, 1901-04, acting pres., 1896-1900, pres. 1900-04, Findlay (O.) Coll.; also pastor Findlay Coll. Ch., 1896-1903; pastor Wooster, O., 1904-05. Ch. of God, Phila., 1905-08, Columbia, Pa., 1908-09; pres. Ft. Scott, Kan., Collegiate Inst., July 1909-13; pastor Ch. of God, Ft. Scott, 1911-13, Ft. Wayne, Ind., 1913-16, Idaville, Ind., 1916-17, Collamer, Ind., 1917-18, Milmine and Lodge, Ill., 1918-19; prof. English Bible and history, dean Summer Sch., Winona Coll., 1917-18; instr., mathematics, Purdue U., 1918-19; prof. mathematics, Defiance Coll., 1919-20; prof. Greek and pub. speaking, 1920-21, prof. Greek N.T. and mathematics, 1921-22, prof. pub. speaking and N.T. Greek, 1922-31, same college; pastor at Butler, Pa., until retirement, Oct. 1, 1938. Sec. of Bd. of Missions of General Eldership of "Church of God," 1893-1901. Founder "The Missionary Signal," and its editor, 1893-96. Pres. Ft. Wayne Ministerial Assn., 1914-16. Home: (summer) 1233 Buffalo St., Franklin, Pa.; (winter) Jacksonville Beach, Fla.

MANCILL, Frank H., lawyer; b. Port Kennedy, Pa., Aug. 26, 1891; s. Francis Shunk and May (Hoy) M.; ed. Wharton Sch., U. of Pa.; LL.B., U. of Pa., 1914; m. M. Louise Gibney, Sept. 22, 1915; 1 dau., Mary Elizabeth. Admitted to Pa. bar, 1914, bar of U.S. Supreme Court, 1932; mem. firm Mancill & Shallow, Phila.; instr., Wharton Sch., U .of Pa., 1915-20; asst. prof., Drexel Inst. of Tech., 1917-20. Pres. Bd. of Commrs. of Lower Merion Twp., 1932-35; dir. Merion Civic Assn. Mem. Phila., Pa. State, Am. and Federal bar assns., Franklin Inst., Baronial Order of Runnemede, Soc. of Descendants of Knights of Most Noble Order of the Garter, Sigma Phi Epsilon. Republican. Roman Catholic. Clubs: Lawyers, Union League, Philadelphia Country (all Phila.). Home: "Lauraston," 394 N. Latches Lane, Merion Station, Pa. Office: Packard Bldg., Philadelphia, Pa.

MANCUSI-UNGARO, Lodovico, physician; b. Sarno, Italy, Dec. 14, 1881; s. Edmund and Eugenia (Nob-Petrillo) M-U.; came to U.S., 1901, naturalized, 1911; M.D., N.Y. Univ. Med. Sch., 1906; m. Frances Groves Chambers, June 12, 1929; children—Giovanna, Pier Lodovico, Mario. Interne St. James Hosp., Newark, N.J., 1906-07; asst. surgeon, St. James Hosp., Newark, 1907-14, asso. surgeon, 1914-21, visiting pediatrician, 1921-26, cardiologist and dir. cardiac clinic since 1926; cons. cardiologist, N.J. State Dept. Instns. and Agencies since 1929; cons. cardiologist North Newark Hosp.; attdg. cardiologist Essex Co. Isolation Hosp. since 1932; physician City Hosp. since 1936; physician cardiac clinic, Beth Israel Hosp., N.Y. City since 1932. Served as physician local draft bd. No. 1, Newark, 1917. Fellow Am. Coll. Physicians, Acad. Medicine of Northern N.J., Am. Med. Assn.; mem. Am. Heart Assn., N.J. State and Essex Co. med. socs. Democrat. Home: 156 Mt. Prospect Av., Newark, N.J.

MANCUSI-UNGARO, Themistocles, lawyer; b. Sarno, Italy, Sept. 11, 1883; s. Edmund and Eugenia (Petrillo) M-U.; came to U.S., 1900, naturalized, 1905; ed. Almo Seminario di Sarno; m. Marguerite Grimaldi, June 30, 1910; children—Edmund T., Harold R. Began as law clk., 1901, studied law and admitted to N.J. bar as atty., 1907; engaged in gen. practice of law at Newark, N.J. since 1907; senior mem. firm Mancusi-Ungaro and Mancusi-Ungaro since 1937; served as judge 2d Criminal Ct. of City of Newark, 1915-18. Mem. Am. Bar Assn., Essex Co. Bar Assn. Awarded Chevalier of the Crown of Italy. Republican. Presbyn. Mason (32°, Shriner, Jester). Elk. I.O.O.F. Sons of Italy (past supreme treas., past grand master and hon. grand master for life of N.J.). Standard bearer T. Mancusi-Ungaro Assn. Mem. Y.M.C.A., Newark. Clubs: Athletic, Kiwanis, Advertising (Newark). Home: 25 Oakland Terrace. Office: 24 Branford Pl., Newark, N.J.

MANGES, Edmund Longinus, clergyman; b. Somerset Co., Pa., Dec. 1, 1885; s. Rev. Edmund and Margaret (Whisker) M.; A.B., Gettysburg Coll., 1908, A.M., same, 1911; grad. Gettysburg Theol. Sem., 1911; B.D., Union Theol. Sem., New York City, 1912; (hon.) D.D., Gettysburg Coll., 1933; m. Grace Blocher, Apr. 17, 1913; children—Frances May, Kathryn Grace, Nellie Margaret. Ordained to ministry Luth. Ch., 1912; Luth. Student pastor, U. of Ill., Urbana, Ill., 1912-13; pastor Lemoyne, Pa., 1913-17, St. James Luth. Ch., Huntingdon, Pa. since 1920; sec. Allegheny Synod U. Luth. Ch. America, 1922-23, vice-pres. since 1937, pres. Juniata Conf., 1923-24 and 1934-35. Served as chaplain and 1st lt. F.A., U.S.A., 1917-19, also supply train and inf.; capt. O.R.C. Ch. Res., 1925, maj. since 1937. Trustee Gettysburg Theol. Sem., 1929-37. Mem. Sigma Alpha Epsilon. Republican. Lutheran. Mason. Home: 525 Mifflin St., Huntingdon, Pa.

MANN, Alexander, bishop; b. Geneva, N.Y., Dec. 2, 1860; s. Duncan Cameron and Caroline Brother (Schuyler) M.; B.A., Hobart Coll., N.Y., 1881, S.T.D., 1900; S.T.B., Gen. Theol. Sem., 1886, S.T.D., 1923; LL.D., Kenyon and Allegheny colls., 1923; m. Nellie Gerrish Knapp, 1896. Deacon, 1885, priest, 1886, P.E. Ch.; asst. minister, St. James Ch., Buffalo, N.Y., 1885-86; asst. minister, 1887-1900, rector, 1900-05, Grace Ch., Orange, N.J.; rector Trinity Ch., Boston, 1905-23. Elected bishop of Washington, 1908, but declined, for reason that his work in Boston was still unfinished; elected suffragan bishop of Diocese of Newark, 1915, but declined; elected bishop of Western N.Y., 1917, but declined; consecrated bishop of Pittsburgh, Jan. 25, 1923. Pres. House of Clerical and Lay Deputies of Gen. Conv. of P.E. Ch., 1913, 16, 19, 22. Mem. Phi Beta Kappa. Republican. Clubs: Duquesne, Longue Vue Country. Home: 5565 Aylesboro Av. Office: 325 Oliver Av., Pittsburgh, Pa.

MANN, Fletcher W(ills), lawyer; b. Monroe Co., W.Va., Dec. 24, 1899; s. Joseph Davidson and Ella (Skaggs) M.; student Concord State Coll., Athens, W.Va., 1919-22; A.B., W.Va. Univ., 1928; LL.B., W.Va. Univ. Law Coll., Morgantown, W.Va., 1930; m. Hope Smith, 1920; children—Mavis Andre, Jean Elizabeth, Jack Alfred. Engaged in teaching pub. schs. in W.Va., 1916-20; prin. high sch., Greenville and Peterstown, W.Va., 1923-27; admitted to W.Va. bar, 1930 and engaged in gen. practice of law at Beckley since 1930; mem. firm McGinnis & Mann since 1934; mem. Am. Bar Assn., W.Va. Bar Assn., Raleigh County Bar Assn., Order of Coif, Phi Beta Kappa, Phi Delta Phi, Delta Sigma Rho. Republican. Baptist. Mason. Club: Lions of Beckley. Home: Harper Road. Office: 19 S. Heber St., Beckley, W.Va.

MANN, Manley Burr, supt. city schs.; b. West Fulton, N.Y., Apr. 1, 1883; s. Almerien and Maria (Chapman) M.; LL.B., Cornell U., 1904; student extension, N.Y. Univ.; m. Anna Lee Pitcher, Oct. 18, 1904; 1 dau., Gwendolin (Mrs. Paul L. Bates). Engaged as county supt. schs., Schoharie Co., N.Y., 1909 to 1913; prin. schs., Neshanic, N.J., 1913-15; supervisor schs., Bloomfield, N.J., 1915-16; supervising prin. schs., South Bound Brook, N.J., 1916-18, Dunellen, N.J., 1918-23, Woodstown, N.J., 1923-26; supt. schs., Boonton, N.J., since 1926. Vice-pres. Boonton Chamber of Commerce since 1936. Mem. N.J. Edn. Assn., N.J. Schoolmasters Club (pres. 1937-38), Morris Co. Prins. Assn. (pres. 1928-29). Republican. Presbyn. Mason. Clubs: Kiwanis (pres. 1936); Cornell (New York). Home: 329 Forbush St., Boonton, N.J.

MANN, Thomas Andrew, realtor; b. Ireland, Apr. 3, 1888; s. Andrew J. and Annie (Anderson) M.; brought to U.S., 1903; student Bellaghy, Co. Derry, Ireland, 1894-1903, Temple Coll., 1916-18; m. Elizabeth Hudson, July 29, 1914; children—William T., Andrew H., Margaret E., Norman H., Warren A. Employed by William J. Crockett, 1903-07, Robert P. Cameron, his successor, 1907-14; in business for self as realtor since 1919; conveyance McPherson Square Bldg. & Loan Assn., North Kensington Bldg. & Loan Assn., United Links Bldg. & Loan Assn., Mutual Friends Bldg. & Loan Assn., Harrowgate Bldg. & Loan Assn. Sec. and treas. Orange Home, Inc., Hatboro, Pa. Sec. Greater Kensington Business Men's Assn., 1917-36; mem. Phila. and North Phila. real estate bds. Mem. Orangemen. Republican. Methodist. Mason, Odd Fellow. Home: 4666 Castor Av. Office: 3141 G St., Philadelphia, Pa.

MANNING, Frank Leroy, asso. prof. mathematics; b. Otisville, N.Y., Mar. 4, 1898; s. Albert and Hattie Elmira (Green) M.; B.S., Cornell U., 1919; M.S., Rutgers U., 1924; student, Butler, U. of Pa., U. of Michigan, Cornell U., summers 1926-32; Ph.D., Cornell, 1935; m. Mabelle Wright, Dec. 30, 1925; children—Barbara Ann, John Randolph. Engaged as lab. asst. and part time instr., Rutgers U., 1923-24; high sch. teacher and prin., 1924-28; instr. Clarkson Coll. Tech., 1928-30; asst. prof. mathematics, Ursinus Coll., Collegeville, Pa., 1930-35, asso. prof. since 1935. Served in U.S.N., 1917-18. Mem. Math. Assn. of America. Republican. Mem. Evang. & Reformed Ch. Mason. Home: 68 Sixth Av., Collegeville, Pa.

MANNING, Helen Herron Taft, coll. dean; b. Cincinnati, O., Aug. 1, 1891; d. William Howard (27th President of U.S.) and Helen (Herron) Taft; prep. edn., Nat. Cathedral Sch., Washington, D.C., and Baldwin Sch., Bryn Mawr, Pa.; A.B., Bryn Mawr Coll., 1915; M.A., Yale Univ., 1916, Ph.D., 1924; LL.D., George Washington University, 1937; m. Frederick Johnson Manning, of Braintree, Mass., July 15, 1920; children—Helen Taft, Caroline. Dean of Bryn Mawr Coll., 1917-19 and since 1925, acting pres. 1919-20, 1929-30. Clubs: Cosmopolitan (New York); Women's University (Philadelphia). Home: 215 Roberts Rd., Bryn Mawr, Pa.*

MANSFIELD, Donald Bruce, prof. of law; b. Hamilton, O., Jan. 31, 1910; s. Paul Chandler and Katharine Simon (Marr) M.; A.B., Kenyon Coll., Cambier, O., 1930; LL.B., Duke U., Durham, N.C., 1933; J.S.D., Yale, 1935; unmarried. Admitted to Ohio bar, 1933; prof. of law, Temple U., Phila., 1934-38; atty. Securities and Exchange Commn., Washington, D.C., since 1938 (on leave of absence from Temple U.). Mem. Phi Kappa Sigma, Phi Delta Phi, Phi Beta Kappa, Order of Coif, Juristic Soc. Clubs: University (Phila.); Brookside Country (Canton, O.). Home: 4323 Pine St. Office: 672 Public Ledger Bldg., Philadelphia, Pa.

MANSFIELD, Capt. J(ohn) Clark, official U.S. Ry. Mail Service; b. Phila., Pa., Dec. 11, 1875; s. John Clark and Catherine (Hoctor) M.; m. Ella Mae Carey, of Forty Fort, Luzerne Co., Pa., Feb. 25, 1902; children—Charlotte Sponsler (Mrs. Charles Andrew Stover), Katherine Hoctor (Mrs. Edward Hoopes III; awarded Carnegie Hero Medal, 1932), Clark. Official U.S. Ry. Mail Service, Pittsburgh, Pa., since 1912. Served as pvt., 2d Pa. Inf., U.S. Vols., Spanish Am. War; 2d and 1st lieut. 2d Inf., Pa. Nat. Guard, 1908-12; comdr. 209th Air Squadron, U.S. Army, World War; capt. Air Corps Res., U.S. Army, since 1929. Mem. bd. trustees Pa. State Soldiers and Sailors Home, Erie, Pa., since 1929, pres. bd. since 1934. Mem. United Spanish Vets. (state comdr. 1928-29), Am. Legion (comdr. Sewickley Post 4, Pa., 1919-21), Pittsburgh Chapter of S.A.R. (pres. 1934-35), Pa. Soc. of Order of Founders and Patriots of America (gov. 1937-38), Colonial Soc. of Pa., Soc. of Colonial Wars (22 ancestors), Sons of Union Vets. of Civil War, Western Pa. Hist. Soc., Mil. Order of Crusades (6 ancestors); hon. life mem. Ladies of Grand Army of the Republic, United Daughters of the Confederacy. Republican. Episcopalian. Clubs: Army and Navy (Washington, D.C.); Pittsburgh Athletic. Home: 1213 Milton Av., Regent Sq., Pittsburgh, Pa. Office: Federal Bldg., Pittsburgh, Pa.

MANSFIELD, Myron Gorton, consulting engr.; b. Bergen, N.Y., Feb. 26, 1889; s. George W. and Ada (Clothier) M.; C.E., Syracuse (N.Y.) U., 1913; C.E., Coll. of Applied Sciences, Syracuse, N.Y., 1913; m. Ida Hoffman, July 28, 1917. Inspector, Pittsburgh Rys., 1913-14; resident engr., City of York, Pa., 1914-16; resident engr. engaged in explorations, Chester, Nova Scotia, 1916; design engr., construction engr. and operator, Morris Knowles, Inc., consulting engrs., Pittsburgh, 1916-22, div. engr. and sec. since 1922, v.p. since 1932. Mem. Pittsburgh Chamber of Commerce. Republican. Protestant. Clubs: Rotary, University, Allegheny Co. Civic (Pittsburgh). Home: 6841 Reynolds St. Office: 507 Westinghouse Bldg., Ninth St., Pittsburgh, Pa.

MANSFIELD, William Douglass, pres. and editor The Daily News, McKeesport, Pa.; b. Elizabeth Twp., Pa., Mar. 6, 1878; s. James MacDonald and Helen Mar (Douglass) M.; student Douglas Business Coll., McKeesport, 1895-96; m. Margaret Alice Butler, Feb. 15, 1908 (died 1934); 1 son, William Douglass. Real estate and insurance broker, 1900-27; mem. Pa. State Senate, 1923-35 (chmn. Com. on Edn., 1925-33); county commr., Allegheny Co., Pa., 1932-36; pres. Daily News Pub. Co., McKeesport, Pa., since 1925, editor Daily News since 1927; chmn. of the bd. First Nat. Bank of McKeesport (Pa.) since 1937; chmn. McKeesport (Pa.) Housing Authority since 1937. Trustee McKeesport Hosp., McKeesport Y.M.C.A. Republican. Methodist. Mason. Clubs: Youghiogheny Country (McKeesport); Amen Corner, Bankers' (Pittsburgh); Kiwanis (McKeesport). Home: 540 Sixth Av. Office: Daily News Bldg., McKeesport, Pa.

MANSON, Frederic E., editor; b. Searsmont, Me., July 6, 1860; s. Rev. Edwin and Viola (Pattee) M.; A.B., Bates Coll., 1883, A.M., 1886; m. Alma B. Millay, May 20, 1892 (died Jan. 9, 1909); children—Frances V., Alice E.; m. 2d, Catherine P. Rentz, June 21, 1911; children—Helen Rentz, Catherine J., Ann P. Editor Augusta (Me.) Journal, 1888-91, Lowell (Mass.) Evening Mail, 1891-92; New England news editor Boston Journal, 1892-93; mng. editor "Grit" (weekly), Williamsport, Pa., 1895-1928, now editor in chief. Republican. Episcopalian. Mason (33°). Author of "Pennsylvania Masonry" and several Masonic brochures. Contbr. to Goulds' History of Freemasonry Throughout the World. Home: Williamsport, Pa.

MANSUY, John L., M.D.; b. Gamble Twp., Lycoming Co., Pa., Oct. 29, 1869; s. Augustus and Emma A. (Lush) M.; student Teachers Normal Sch., Muncy, Pa.; M.D., U. of Md., 1897; m. Laura F. Bertin, June 30, 1904; children—Walter L. (deceased), John L. (deceased), Milton B. Began as teacher Lycoming Co., 1886, taught 7 yrs. and then took up study of medicine; after graduation as M.D., U. of Md., practiced in Cross Fork, Pa., 1897; gen. practice in Ralston, Pa., since 1898; physician Pa. R.R., Ralston; Lycoming Co. med. dir. for Pa. Dept. of Health, 1935-39; med. inspr. of schs; successful in diagnosis and treatment of anthrax; pres. First Nat. Bank; pres. Ralston Walter & Water Power Co. Pres. Lycoming Co. Bd. of Sch. Dirs. since 1903; mem. Lycoming Co. Dem. Com. since 1903. Mem. Lycoming Co. Med. Soc. (past pres.). Democrat. Catholic. Address: Ralston, Pa.

MANTINBAND, Charles, rabbi; b. New York, N.Y., April 2, 1895; s. Samuel and Delia (Gottlieb) M.; B.S., Coll. of City of New York, 1916; M.A., Columbia, 1924; student Jewish Inst. of Religion and Hebrew Union Coll.; m. Anna Kest, April 4, 1918; children—Judith Carol, William Lion. Exec. sec. Y.M.H.A., Mount Vernon, N.Y., and Memphis, Tenn., 1916-17; field worker Jewish Welfare Bd., 1917-19; student dir. Intercollegiate Menorah Assn., 1919-21; rabbi Vassar Temple, Poughkeepsie, N.Y., 1923-26, Temple Beth Ha-Sholom, Williamsport, Pa., since 1926; chaplain State Industrial Home, Muncy, Pa., 1926-39, U.S. N.E. Penitentiary, Lewisburg, 1931-34. Mem. Bur. of Friendly Counsel of Lycoming Co.; mem. State Inter-racial Com. Republican. Mason. Lecturer; writer. Home: 1057 W. 4th St., Williamsport, Pa.

MANZETTI, Leo P(eter), clergyman, music; b. Evian-Les-Bains, Savoy, France, April 27, 1867; s. Anthony and Matilda (Viglino) M.; student, Coll. in France, Sem., Aosta, Italy; music in France, Italy and Germany; grad. Kirchenmusikschule, Ratisbone, Bavaria, 1903; came to U.S., 1903. Ordained to ministry R.C. Ch., priest, 1892; asst. pastor, St. Marcel and Villeneuve, 1892-94; organist Aosta Cathedral and editor in chief diocesan weekly, 1894-97; organist and choirmaster St. Rita's Ch., N.Y. City, 1903-05; organist and choirmaster, Cathedral, prof. ch. music, St. Mary's Sem. of the West, and Cincinnati Coll. Music, Cincinnati, O., 1905-07; organist and choirmaster, St. Leo's Ch. and dir. music, K.C. Choral Club, St. Louis, Mo., 1907-11; dir. music, St. Mary's Univ. and Sem., Baltimore, Md., 1911-27; mem. faculty Peabody Conservatory Music, Baltimore, Md., chaplain at St. Mary's Orphanage, Roland Park, Md., since 1911; made Pvt. Chamberlain to the Pope with title of Monsignor, 1918; awarded title of Maestro of Ch. Music by Pontifical High Sch. of Ch. Music, Rome, 1922; assisted in organizing Soc. of St. Gregory of America, 1913. Mem. Acad. of St. Anselm, Aosta, Italy, 1936. Roman Catholic. Composer of more than 30 mus. works, including an accompaniment to the Gregorian Kyriale, now in its sixth edit.; completed an organ accompaniment of Gregorian Chant for all the Vespers, which may revolutionize the art of harmonizing Gregorian melodies; has been entrusted with revision of St. Basil's Hymnal. Contbr. to leading mus. publs. of U.S., France, and Italy. Author several brochures. Nephew of Innocent Manzetti (1826-77), called the Prince of Inventors and Mechanics of Aosta, Italy (invented telephone to work with electricity, 1864; papers and schemes of invention later sold to an American inventor). Address: 625 W. Cold Spring Lane, Roland Park, Md.

MARBAKER, Edward Ellsworth, chemical engineer; b. Trenton, N.J., June 28, 1888; s. William Ellsworth and Rosemary (Douglass) M.; B.S., U. of Pa., 1910, Ph.D., 1914, Ch.E., 1930; m. Mabel Price, Oct. 22, 1914; children—Ethel Price, William Ellsworth. Asst. chemist Westinghouse Lamp Co., Bloomfield, N.J., 1910-15, chief chemist, 1915-17; chief chemist, Alexander Bros., Phila., 1917-19, chief engr., 1919-20; chief chemist Cleveland (O.) Wire Div., Nat. Lamp Works, Gen. Electric Co., 1920; industrial fellow, Mellon Inst. of Industrial Research, Pittsburgh, 1920-28, and since 1935; v.p. Industrial Research and Engring. Co., Pittsburgh, 1929-34. Mem. Am. Chem. Soc. (vice-chmn. Phila. sect., 1920; chmn. Pittsburgh sect., 1929-30, leather div., 1920-21), Franklin Inst., Am. Ceramic Soc. (mem. edn. com., data com., since 1936, publ. com. since 1938), Am. Inst. Chem. Engrs. (chmn. Pittsburgh sect., 1935-37; mem. local sect. com., 1934-37, membership com. since 1937), Sigma Xi, Phi Lambda Upsilon. Republican. Episcopalian. Contbr. to Jour. of the Am. Chem. Soc., Transactions of the Am. Foundrymen's Assn. and other technical jours. Home: 5562 Hobart St. Office: 4400 5th Av., Pittsburgh, Pa.

MARBLE, Dean Richmond, asso. prof.; b. West Bloomfield, N.Y., Sept. 27, 1902; s. Harry Raymond and Effie M. (Cottrell) M.; B.S., Cornell U., 1926, M.S., same, 1928, Ph.D., same, 1930; m. Anna Hamlin, April 10, 1928; children—Jean Marie, Patricia Ann. Engaged in farming, 1919, employee on Poultry Instrn. Plant of Cornell U., 1922-23; part-time instr. poultry husbandry, Cornell U., 1926-30; asst. prof. poultry husbandry, Pa. State Coll., State College, Pa., 1930 to 1933, asso. prof. since 1933 and engaged in research in poultry sci. Mem. World's Poultry Sci. Assn., Poultry Science, Acacia, Sigma Xi, Phi Kappa Phi, Gamma Sigma Delta. Awarded Roberts Scholarship, Cornell U., 1925. Republican. Methodist. Mason. Author: Judging Poultry for Production (with J. E. Rice, and G. O. Hall), 1930. Asso. editor, Poultry Science. Contbr. bulls. and research papers. Home: 301 Hartswick Av., State College, Pa.

MARBLE, John Putnam, geochemist; b. Worcester, Mass., May 30, 1897; s. Joseph Russel and Emily Greene (Chase) M.; A.B., Williams Coll., Williamstown, Mass., 1918; student Clark Coll., Worcester, Mass., 1919; A.M., Harvard U., 1928, Ph.D., 1932; grad. student George Washington U., 1932-33; m. Adelaide Holme Maghee, May 21, 1921; children—Katharine Chase, Richard Almy, Rosamond Holme, John Putnam, Jr. Employed as. clk and salesman, J. Russel Marble & Co., Worcester, Mass., 1919-26; research geochemist since 1931, vice-chmn. com. on measurement of geologic time, Div. of Geology and Geography, Nat. Research Council since 1937; ofcl. del. from U.S. Govt., Nat. Acad. Scis., Smithsonian Instn., to 17th Internat. Geol. Cong., U.S.S.R., 1937. Served as pvt. C.W.S., U.S.A., 1918-19. Fellow A.A.A.S., Am. Minerol. Soc., Soc. for Research on Meteorites. Mem. Am. Chem. Soc., Electrochem. Soc., Phi Beta Kappa, Alpha Chi Sigma, Gamma Alpha. Independent Republican. Mem. Religious Soc. Friends. Clubs: Chevy Chase (Chevy Chase); Cosmos (Washington); Williams (New York); University (Boston); Harvard Faculty (Cambridge); Worcester (Worcester, Mass.); Nantucket Yacht (Nantucket, Mass.). Home: 37 E. Bradley Lane, Chevy Chase, Md. Office: 321 U.S. National Museum, Washington, D.C.

MARBURG, Louis Christian, elec. and mech. engr.; b. of Am. parents, Wiesbaden, Germany, March 8, 1876; s. Francis and Henrietta (Stauff) M.; classical edn. in Latin and Greek, Gymnasium, Wiesbaden, 1885-94; student Tech. Coll., Berlin, 1895-96, Hanover, 1896-97, Darmstadt, 1897-98; m. Gertrude Wells, Sept. 13, 1913; children—Louis Hellmuth, Hildegarde (Mrs. Howard Hennington), Donald, Rolland, Dorothea. Before entering college and during vacations, employed by Sulzer Bros., engine builders, Winterthur, Switzerland, and Siemens & Halske, Berlin; elec. engr. Sprague Electric Co., Watsessing, N.J., 1898-99, Gen. Electric Co., Schenectady, N.Y., 1899-1904, Bullock Electric Co., Cincinnati, and Allis Chalmers Co., Milwaukee, 1904-09; sec., treas. and dir. Marburg Bros., Inc., since 1909. Chmn. Joint Conf. Com. which created Am. Engring. Council, 1919. Fellow Am. Inst. Elec. Engrs.; mem. Am. Soc. Mech. Engrs., Soc. Automotive Engrs.; Pres. Montclair Soc. Engrs., 1926-27, Council on Foreign Relations. Unitarian. Clubs: Engineers, Railroad-Machinery, New York Economic (New York). Home: 10 Prospect Av., Montclair, N.J. Office: 90 West St., New York, N.Y.

MARBURG, Theodore, publicist; b. Baltimore, Md., July 10, 1862; s. William A. and Christine (Munder) M.; ed. Princeton Prep. Sch., 1876-79, Johns Hopkins, 1880-81, Oxford, Eng., 1892-93; École Libre de la Science Politique, Paris, 1893-95; U. of Heidelberg (summer semesters), 1901, 03; hon. A.M., Johns Hopkins, 1902; LL.D., Dickinson Coll., 1912, Univ. of Cincinnati, 1917; LL.D., Rollins Coll., Winter Park, Fla., 1928; m. Fannie Grainger, Nov. 6, 1889. Children—Madame A. W. L. Tjarda Van Starkenborgh Stochouwer (wife of Gov. Gen. of the Netherlands East Indies), Francis Grainger, Charles Louis. United States minister to Belgium, 1912-14. Trustee Johns Hopkins University. Pres. American Soc. Judicial Settlement Internat. Disputes, 1915-16; chmn. com. foreign organization League to Enforce Peace (one of organizers); organized Munipical Art Society, Baltimore, 1900, serving as sec., pres., now chmn. exec. com.; mem. American Econ. Assn. (v.p. 1899-1901), Am. Polit. Science Assn., Am. Soc. Internat. Law, Phi Beta Kappa; chmn. exec. com. Am. Peace Congress, 1911; hon. pres. Md. Peace Soc., v.p. Internat. Federation of League of Nations Socs., 1925, and head of Am. delegation to Assembly of League of Nations Socs., Warsaw 1925, London 1926, Berlin 1927. Clubs: Metropolitan (Washington); Century, Pilgrims, Authors (New York); Pilgrims, Authors' (London); Maryland, University (Baltimore). Author: World's Money Problem, 1896; The War with Spain, 1898; Expansion, 1900; The Peace Movement Practical, 1910; Silent Thoughts on Judicial Settlement, 1911; Philosophy of the Third American Peace Congress, 1911; League of Nations, 1917; In the Hills (collection of poems), 1924; Development of League of Nations Idea, 1932; Bobbylinkapoo (poem), 1937; 'The Story of a Soul' (drama), 1938. Translator: Emile Levasseur's Elements of Political Economy. Contbr. to revs. Home: 14 W. Mt. Vernon Pl., Baltimore, Md.

MARBURY, Ogle, lawyer; b. Howard Co., Md., Aug. 23, 1882; s. Ogle and Eleanora Brevitt (Mackenzie) M.; A.B., Johns Hopkins U., 1902; LL.B., U. of Md. Law Sch., 1904; m.

Eliza G. Cronmiller, Aug. 17, 1915; 1 dau., Anne Tasker Ogle. Admitted to Md. bar, 1904 and since in gen. practice individually at Baltimore and Laurel, Md.; mem. Md. Ho. of Dels., 1910-12; asst. atty. gen. of Md., 1916-20, actg. atty. gen., 1918; chmn. State Bd. Prison Control of Md., 1920-23; del. at large Dem. Nat. Conv., 1920; atty. bd. edn. Prince George Co., Md., 1916-37; city solicitor of Laurel, Md., since 1929; atty. county commrs. Prince George Co. since 1937. Democrat. Episcopalian. Home: 320 Washington Av., Laurel, Md. Office: Union Trust Bldg., Baltimore, Md., and Laurel, Md.

MARBURY, William Luke, Jr., lawyer; b. Baltimore, Md., Sept. 12, 1901; s. William Luke and Silvine von Dorsner (Slingluff) M.; student Boys Latin Sch., Baltimore, 1909-16, Episcopal High Sch., Alexandria, Va., 1916-18; A.B., U. of Va., Charlottesville, 1921; LL.B., Harvard, 1924; m. Natalie Jewett Wheeler, Dec. 3, 1935; children—Luke, Anne. Admitted to Md. bar, 1925, and since practiced at Baltimore; mem. firm Marbury, Gosnell & Williams, Baltimore, 1925-30, and since 1931; asst. atty. gen., Md., 1930-31. Trustee Peabody Inst., Baltimore, Baltimore Mus. of Art. Mem. Am. Bar Assn., Phi Beta Kappa. Democrat. Episcopalian. Clubs: 14 West Hamilton St., Merchants, Baltimore Country (Baltimore, Md.). Home: 43 Warrenton Rd. Office: Maryland Trust Bldg., Baltimore, Md.

MARCEAU, Henri, curator; b. Richmond, Va., June 21, 1896; s. Louis and Jeanne (Cottè) M.; B.Arch., Columbia, 1920; fellow in architecture, Am. Acad. Rome, 1925 (Rome prize in architecture); m. Rebecca Alvord, Aug. 17, 1927; 1 dau., Elizabeth Bartlett. Instr. archtl. design, U. of Pa., 1926, asst. prof., 1927; curator John G. Johnson Collection since 1927; curator fine arts, Pa. Mus. of Art, 1929-33, asst. dir. since 1933; mem. advisory com. Walters Art Gallery, Baltimore, Md. Commd. 2d lt. F.A., U.S.A., World War. Mem. Fairmount Park Art Assn. (sec. since 1930), Phila. Art Alliance (sec. 1932-33, v.p. 1933), Arts and Crafts Guild (pres.), Delta Upsilon. Republican. Clubs: University, Art Club, Art Alliance. Author: William Rush—First American Sculptor, 1937. Home: 3423 Warden Drive. Address: Philadelphia Museum of Art, Philadelphia, Pa.

MARCH, Matthias L(evengood), lumber merchant; b. Douglas Twp., Berks Co., Pa., July 10, 1862; s. Isaac Fagley and Sarah R. (Levengood) M.; ed. Red Sch. House, No. 9, and Amityville Acad., 1868-78; m. Sarah Jane Ludwig, Feb. 23, 1883 (died Sept. 5, 1888); children—William Allen, Ethel Naomi (Mrs. Walter K. Jamison); m. 2d, Lilla May Kerger, Oct. 25, 1894; children—Matthias Russell, Anna Levengood (Mrs. William Ernst Campbell) John Ellsworth, Robert Irwin, George Kreiger, Elizabeth May (Mrs. Biron Ganser). Began as sch. teacher, 1878; entered business Jan. 1886; with I. F. March's Sons, lumber merchants, Bridgeport, Pa. since 18—; partner Jones Lumber Co., Conshohocken, Pa.; dir. Montgomery Nat. Bank, Norristown Water Co.; pres. and dir. Fame Bldg. and Loan Assn.; treas. and dir. Paxtang Cemetery Assn. Served as burgess and sch. dir., Bridgeport. Trustee Luth. Theol. Sem., Mt. Airy, Pa. Republican. Lutheran. Mason (K.T.). Clubs: Union League (Phila.); Plymouth Country; Rotary of Norristown. Home: 1421 DeKalb St., Norristown, Pa. Office: Bridgeport, Pa.

MARCH, William Allen, lumber and mill work; b. Monacacy, Pa., Jan. 1, 1884; s. Matthias Levengood and Sarah Jane (Ludwig) M.; grad. Pottstown (Pa.) High Sch., 1904; C.E., Princeton U., 1908. Began as yardsman, I. F. March's Sons, lumber, building supplies, boxes, 1908, now mgr.; dir. Norristown-Penn Trust Co.; pres. and dir. Valley Forge Hotel Co.; dir. Pa. Real Estate Exchange; dir. Fame Bldg. & Loan Co.; sec. and dir. Paxtang Cemetery Co. Dir. Norristown Chamber of Commerce (past pres.); chmn. advisory bd. Salvation Army, Norristown; prison inspr. for Montgomery Co., Pa. Served as capt. Battery C, 2d Pa. F.A., on Mexican Border. June 1916-Mar. 1917; capt. 108th F.A., U.S. Army, July-Sept. 1917, maj. 3d Batt., Sept. 1917-May 1918; maj. 1st Batt., 108th F.A., May 1918-May 1919 (with A.E.F., 28th Div., in Champagne sector, Oise-Aine, Lorraine sector, Meuse-Argonne, Ypres-Lys); col. 108th F.A., Pa. Nat. Guards, since 1919. Decorated Croix de Guerre (Belgium). Pres. Pa. Nat. Guard Assn. Mem. Hist. Soc. of Phila., Geneal. Soc. of Phila. Republican. Lutheran. Mason. Clubs: Plymouth Country (Norristown); Union League, Princeton (Phila.); Quadrangle (Princeton). Home: 1421 DeKalb St., Norristown, Pa. Office: Bridgeport, Pa.

MARCKS, Frederick Augustus, supt. of schools; b. Upper Milford Twp., Lehigh Co., Pa., Feb. 11, 1887; s. Edwin and Hannah (Henninger) M.; student Emmaus (Pa.) High Sch., 1901-04, Allentown (Pa.) Prep. Sch., 1904-05; A.B., Muhlenberg Coll., 1909; grad. work at Lehigh U. and U. of Pa.; m. Olivia Eleanor Swambach, Aug. 18, 1908; children—Thalia Olive (Mrs. C. Harold Shafer), Carl Arthur, Elisabeth Louise, Donald Alton. Teacher Nazareth (Pa.) High Sch., 1909-10, prin. 1910-15; supervising prin. Nazareth Pub. Schools, 1915-37, supt. since 1937. Mem. Pa. State Edn. Assn. Lutheran. Mason. Home: 366 Belvidere St., Nazareth, Pa.

MARCUM, John Roy, lawyer; b. Wayne, W.Va., Aug. 12, 1883; s. John St. Clair and Emma (Wellman) M.; grad. Marshall Coll., Huntington, W.Va., 1901; LL.B., W.Va. Univ. Law Sch., Morgantown, W.Va., 1905; unmarried. Admitted to W.Va. bar, 1905 and since engaged in gen. practice of law at Huntington; mem. firm with father as Marcum & Marcum, 1905-32; mem. firm Marcum & Gibson since 1932. Past pres. Rotary Club. Past vice-pres. Y.M.C.A. Past commr. Huntington Boy Scouts of America. Dir. Huntington Union Mission Settlement (Children's Home), Camp Anthony Wayne. Mem. Am., W.Va. State bar assns., Cabell County Bar Assn. (past pres.), Kappa Alpha. Democrat. Episcopalian (vestryman St. Peter's Ch.). Club: Executives. Home: 432 Sixth Av. Office: First Huntington Nat. Bank Bldg., Huntington, W.Va.

MARGARETTEN, Morris, lawyer; b. New York, N.Y., Jan. 3, 1899; s. John and Mary (Rosenberg) M.; student Perth Amboy (N.J.) High Sch., 1912-16, Newark (N.J.) Normal Sch., 1916-18; night study N.J. Law Sch., Newark, N.J., 1920-23, LL.B., 1923; m. Pauline Avchen, Dec. 27, 1922; children—Judith Mae, Beatrice Claire. Pub. sch. teacher, Roselle, N.J., Jan.-June, 1919, Perth Amboy, N.J., 1919-23; admitted to N.J. bar, 1923, and since in pvt. practice at Perth Amboy, N.J. Served as sergt., S.A.T.C., Columbia U., 1918, hon. disch. 1918. Spl. asst. atty. gen. of N.J. in connection with condemnation of properties for highway purposes, 1932-33. One of organizers Boy Scouts, Perth Amboy, N.J., 1919, pres. Raritan Council, Boy Scouts, 1933-35, chmn. advisory com. since 1938; pres. Perth Amboy Jewish Community Center, 1931-33, mem. bd. dirs. since 1923; mem. nat. exec. com. Jewish Welfare Bd. since 1937; pres. N.J. Fed. Y.M.-Y.W.H.A.'s since 1937; pres. Council of Social Agencies, Perth Amboy, 1936; mem. bd. dirs. Congregation Shaarey Tefiloh since 1928, Perth Amboy Hebrew Sch. since 1928. Mem. Am. Legion (Perth Amboy Post), Jewish War Vets. of U.S. (judge advocate, Dept. of N.J., 1933), Middlesex Co. Bar Assn., Perth Amboy Bar Assn., Lambda Alpha Phi. Awarded Silver Beaver by Boy Scouts of America for meritorious service to boyhood, 1935. Republican. Jewish religion. Home: 99 Lewis St. Office: 280 Hobart St., Perth Amboy, N.J.

MARGIE, Peter Michael, pres. Wilkes-Barre Baseball Club; b. Pittston City, Pa., Apr. 25, 1896; s. Frank and Frances M.; student pub. schs.; m. Claire Margaret Holleran, June 30, 1932. Began as breaker boy in anthracite coal mines, 1907; became theatre usher and motion picture operator, 1913, later theatre mgr. and real estate dir. Comerford-Publix since 1933; salesman Standard Brewing Co., 1932, gen. mgr. for Luzerne Co. and dir. since 1932; pres. and owner Wilkes-Barre (Pa.) Baseball Club (Eastern League) since 1936. Prothonotary for Luzerne County. Home: 116 Exeter Av., West Pittston, Pa. Office: Court House, Wilkes-Barre, Pa.; 888 Wyoming Av., Kingston, Pa., and American Theater Bldg., Pittston, Pa.

MARGIOTTI, Charles Joseph, lawyer; s. Joseph and Fortunata (Reca) M.; grad. Ind. State Teachers Coll., 1912; LL.B., U. of Pa. Law Sch., 1915; Litt.D., St. Francis Coll., Loretto, Pa., 1934; m. Denise Wery, Feb. 5, 1918; children—Juliette Charlotte, Charles Joseph. Began at 11 as water boy, later laborer in brick yards; worked way through teachers coll. and law sch.; began practice at Punxsutawney, 1915; has appeared before courts in 38 counties in Pa. and in eight different states; atty. gen. of Pa., 1935-38. Dir. Punxsutawney Nat. Bank. Mem. Allegheny County Bar and Jefferson County Bar. Trustee St. Francis Coll., Loretto, Pa.; v.p. Adrian Hosp. Assn., Punxsutawney. Mem. Am. and Pa. State bar assns., Phi Sigma Pi Eta, Phi Alpha Zeta. Elk. Mem. Knights of Columbus, Eagles, Moose, Foresters of America. Club: Penn Athletic. Home: William Penn Hotel, Pittsburgh, Pa. Address: 720 Grant Bldg., Pittsburgh, Pa.

MARGOLIS, Jacob, lawyer; b. Pittsburgh, Pa., May 31, 1886; s. Julius and Anna (Willinsky) M.; student Washington and Jefferson Coll., Washington, Pa., U. of Pittsburgh Law Sch.; m. Florence Kaminsky, Jan. 31, 1911; children—Judith, Frederick Julian, Louise. Admitted to bar and now in practice at Pittsburgh; editor Detroit (Mich.) Jewish Chronicle, 1922-27, asso. editor since 1927. Lecturer on economics, sociology and pacifism. Home: 6435 Bartlett St. Office: 902 Grant Bldg., Pittsburgh, Pa.

MARIL, Herman, artist; b. Baltimore, Md., Oct. 13, 1908; s. Isaac Harry Becker and Celia M.; student Baltimore Poly. Inst., 1922-26, Md. Inst. of Fine Arts, Baltimore, Md., 1926-28; unmarried. Has had one-man exhbns. in Baltimore, Washington, Phila., New York, and other cities; exhibited in museums and colls. throughout the U.S.; represented in collections at Exhbn. of Contemporary Am. Painting, San Francisco Fair and New York Worlds Fair, Phillips Memorial Gallery, Baltimore Mus. of Art, Crane Collection, Howard Univ. Gallery and in many pvt. collections, also in White House and Labor Dept. Bldg.; now engaged on mural for new post office at Alta Vista, Va.; instr. painting, Cummington Sch., Mass. during summer months. Color stencil print, "The Farm," selected for distribution by Am. Artists Group, Inc. Mem. artists' com., Baltimore Mus. of Art. Mem. Am. Artists Congress, Baltimore Artists Union. Awarded $100 Prize for best work in All-Md. exhbns. of painting and sculpture, Baltimore Mus. Art, 1935. Home: 3810 Park Heights Av., Baltimore, Md.

MARINARO, Carmen Vincent, lawyer; b. Soldier, Pa., Sept. 17, 1902; s. Nicholas M. and Philomena (Capriola) M.; student St. Fidelis Sem., Herman, Pa., 1915-22; LL.B., Georgetown U., 1926; m. Rose M. Colucci, Sept. 28, 1932; 1 dau., Patricia Ann. Admitted to Pa. bar, 1929, and since practiced in Butler. Dir Butler Community Chest; pres. and dir. Butler Conf. Catholic Charities. Mem. Butler County Bar Assn. Democrat. Catholic. Elk, Moose, K. of C. (dist. dep. 18th Dist.). Home: 223 Christy Av. Office: Butler County Nat. Bank Bldg., Butler, Pa.

MARIS, Albert Branson, judge; b. Phila., Pa., Dec. 19, 1893; s. Robert Wood and Elma (Branson) M.; LL.B., Temple U., 1918; grad. Drexel Inst. of Tech., July 3, 1917; children—William Robinson, Robert Wood. Admitted to Pa. bar, 1918, practiced in Phila., 1919-36, mem. firm White, Maris and Clapp; apptd. U.S. dist. judge, Eastern dist. of Pa., June 22, 1936; apptd. U.S. circuit judge, 3d Circuit, June 24, 1938. Dem. county chmn. Delaware Co., 1924-30; mem. Dem. State Com., 1930-34; mem. council Borough of Yeadon, Pa., 1935-36. Served as 2d lt. coast arty., U.S.A., 1918. Dir. Elwyn (Pa.) Training Sch. Mem.

Am., Pa. State, Phila. and Federal bar assns., Assn. of the Bar of the City of N.Y., Am. Judicature Soc. Mem. Soc. of Friends. Clubs: University, Constitutional, Ben Franklin, Caveat (Phila.); Rolling Green Golf (Media, Pa.). Editor of The Legal Intelligencer, Phila., 1933-36. Home: 554 S. Lansdowne Av., Yeadon, (Lansdowne P.O.), Pa. Office: Custom House, Philadelphia, Pa.

MARK, Joseph Sidney, surgeon; b. Arad, Hungary, Nov. 16, 1892; s. Maurice and Sidonia (Buchs) M.; came to U.S., 1906, naturalized, 1916; grad. DeWitt Clinton High Sch., New York, 1910; M.D., Univ. and Bellevue Hosp. Med. Coll., New York, 1914; m. Vivienne Delany, Sept. 6, 1922. House surgeon, Elizabeth (N.J.) Gen. Hosp., 1914-15; gen. practice of surgery, Woodbridge, N.J., since 1915; med. dir. U.S. Metals Refining Co., Carteret, N. J.; visiting surgeon Rahway Memorial Hosp. (past pres. med. staff); adjunct visiting surgeon Perth Amboy Gen. Hosp. Served in Med. Corps, U.S. Army, during World War. Dir. Middlesex County Anti-Tuberculosis League. Mem. A. M.A., N.J. State Med. Soc., Middlesex County Med. Soc. (past pres.), Acad. of Medicine of Northern N.J., Elizabeth Clinical Soc., Assn. of Industrial Physicians (N.J. and U.S.). Mason (32°). Clubs: Rotary (Woodbridge); Colonia Country (Colonia, N.J.). Special work on industrial poisoning. Contbr. articles on lead poisoning to jours. Address: 102 Green St., Woodbridge, N.J.

MARKELL, William Ody, orthopedic surgeon; b. Monongahela, Pa., Mar. 25, 1886; s. William Thomas and Mary (Hodgson) M.; M.D., U. of Pittsburgh Med. Sch., 1914; unmarried. Interne Mercy Hosp., 1914-15; engaged in practice of medicine specializing in orthopedic surgery since 1916. Served as capt. Med. Corps U.S.A., 1918-19, with A.E.F. in 1919. Mem. Acad. Orthopedic Surgery, Acad. of Medicine of Pittsburgh, Nu Sigma Nu. Republican. Mason. Clubs: University, Edgewood Country. Home: 413 Whitney Av. Office: 7133 Jenkins Arcade, Pittsburgh, Pa.

MARKEY, D(avid) John; b. Frederick, Md., Oct. 7, 1882; s. J. Hanshew and Ida (Williard) M.; student Western Md. Coll., 1900-01; grad. Md. Agrl. Coll., 1904; m. Mary Edna Mullenix, June 13, 1907 (died 1935); children—D. John, Mary Elizabeth. Asso. Eugene J. Canten Co., Inc.; v.p. New England Products Exchange, Inc.; dir. Automatic Gun, Inc. Mem. Am. Battle Monument Commn. since 1924. Organized West Md. Chamber of Commerce, 1923, pres., 1923-25; pres. Frederick Bd. of Trade, 1912-13; pres. of first commercial orgn. to join U.S. Chamber of Commerce; pres. Frederick Chamber of Commerce, 1921-24; pres. Frederick Y.M.C.A.; aide to Gen. Pershing, 2d A.E.F., 1927. Enlisted in Md. Nat. Guard, 1898; private 1st Md. Inf., Spanish-Am. War, Major Mexican Border Campaign, 1916; maj. 112th Machine Gun Batt. and lt. col. 114th Inf., 29th Div., U.S.A., with A.E.F. 1917-19; now brig. gen. Md. Nat. Guard. Decorated D. S.M. (U.S.); Officer Legion d'Honneur (France); Officer Order of the Crown (Belgium). Mem. Am. Legion (past dept. comdr. and mem. nat. exec. com.). Republican. Mem. Reformed Ch. of U.S. Mason. Clubs: Army and Navy (Washington, D.C.); Catoctin County (Frederick). Address: Frederick, Md.

MARKLE, David Lloyd, prof. elec. engring.; b. Hublersburg, Pa., Oct. 7, 1883; s. William Henry and Caroline Elizabeth (Yocum) M.; B.S. in E.E., Pa. State Coll., 1909, E.E., same, 1914; m. Lila Annette Dietrich, Nov. 24, 1910; children—Inez Annette (Mrs. Horace W. Miller), Hugh Dietrich, Sarah Louise, David Lloyd, Robert Louis, Catherine Elizabeth. Began as student engr., Westinghouse Electric & Mfg. Co., 1909-10; asst. in elec. engring., Pa. State Coll., 1910-11, instr., 1911-15, asst. prof., 1915-21, asso. prof., 1921-38, prof. elec. engring. since 1938; also part time professional practice of elec. and illuminating engring. Registered professional engr. in Pa. Mem. Am. Inst. Elec. Engrs., Phi Kappa Tau, Phi Kappa Phi, Sigma Tau, Eta Kappa Nu. Republican. Mem. Reformed Ch. Conducted investigation of tungsten filament incandescent lamp characteristics. Home: 334 S. Burrowes St., State College, Pa.

MARKLE, Donald, coal operator; b. Hazleton, Pa., Aug. 29, 1892; s. Alvan and Mary (Dryfoos) M.; student Hill Sch., Pottstown, Pa., 1906-11; Ph.B., Sheffield Scientific Sch. (Yale), 1914; student Lehigh U., 1914-16; m. Mary Orme, Feb. 10, 1917; children—Mary Orme, Donald, Gordon Orme, Eckley Coxe, Joan, Dorothy, Isabel Parham. Began as inside coal mine foreman and worked successively in various depts. mining industry; pres. Markle Corpn. since 1928, Jeddo-Highland Coal Co. since 1926; pres. and chmn. bd. Hazlebrook Coal Co.; chmn. bd. Fuel Service Co.; director Virginia Coal and Iron Company, General Coal Co., Highland Coal Co., Markle Bank & Trust Co. Served as 2d lt., later capt. and maj. A.E.F., World War; awarded Verdun Medal; citation by Gen. Pershing for "exceptional meritorious and conspicuous service" as comdg. officer 4th Am. Train. Mem. Am. Inst. Mining Engrs., Delta Psi. Republican. Presbyn. Mason. Clubs: St. Anthony, Yale, University, Whitehall (New York); Midday, Racquet (Phila.). Home: Jeddo, Pa.

MARKLE, John, 2d, tel. traffic supervisor; b. Hazleton, Pa., May 22, 1902; s. Alvan and Mary (Dryfoos) M.; grad. The Hill School, 1920; B.S., Yale Scientific Sch., 1924; m. Pauline Penolope Powers, Feb. 2, 1929; children—John, Brinton Bayard, William Lowell. With Lehigh Telephone Co., 1924-28, as engring. asst.; 1924-26, methods supervisor, 1926-27, traffic engr., 1927-28, dist. traffic supt., 1928-30; dist. traffic supt. Bell Telephone Co. of Pa., 1930-39, gen. traffic supervisor for co. since 1939; director Hazleton Auto Bus Co., Markle Corpn., Jeddo Highland Coal Company, Hazlebrook Coal Co., Fuel Service Co.; vice-pres. and dir. North Branch Bus Co. Mem. Chi Phi. Republican. Mason. Clubs: Yale (New York); Union League (Phila.); Westmoreland of Wilkes-Barre (vice-pres.). Home: 104 N. 25th St., Camp Hill, Pa. Office: 210 Pine St., Harrisburg, Pa.

MARKS, Harold Kemmerer, prof. music; b. Emmaus, Pa., May 12, 1886; s. Clement A. and Kate M. (Kemmerer) M.; A.B., Muhlenberg Coll., 1907; (hon.) Mus.D., Muhlenberg Coll., 1930; studied music with noted teachers in New York City, Brooklyn and Phila.; m. Edna I. Clauss, Oct. 19, 1910. Has followed profession as organist and teacher of music since 1907; organist St. John's Luth. Ch., 1913-32; dir. music, high sch., Allentown, Pa., 1908-16; head vocal dept., Cedar Crest Coll., 1909-11; organist and prof. music, Muhlenberg Coll. since 1913. Mem. Alpha Tau Omega. Democrat. Lutheran. Mason. Composer sacred songs, anthems and organ numbers. Home: 428 N. 29th St., Allentown, Pa.

MARKS, Lewis Hart, M.D.; b. New Orleans, July 14, 1883; s. Ferdinand and Fanny (Bensadon) M.; M.D., Tulane U., 1906; post-grad. Johns Hopkins and Harvard univs.; m. Miriam Sears (playwright), July 19, 1931. Supt. Emergency (yellow fever) Hospital, New Orleans, epidemic of 1905; voluntary asst. Royal Inst. for Exptl. Therapeutics, Frankfort-on-the-Main, 1907, asst., 1908, member Inst., 1910, being first foreigner and youngest man ever apptd. to this position in Germany; resigned 1912 to become dir. Inst. for Med. Research, Frankfort (an instn. founded for Dr. Marks, by a com. of Am. philanthropists); instn. closed on account of war; returned to U.S., 1917; founder and mgr. pharmaceutical div., Nat. Aniline & Chem. Co., 1920-25; exec. sec. Industrial Alcohol Institute, 1926-33; president American Hyalsol Corpn. and Am. Hydronapthane Corpn. since 1932, Continental Distilling Corpn. since 1933; consultant in chem., distillery and pharm. industries. Officer Order of Mil. Merit, 1st Class (Spain); holder of Red Cross Medallion, 1st Class (Germany), Red Cross Officer Cross (Austria). Fellow A.A. A.S.; hon. mem. German Soc. for History of Medicine; mem. Am. Inst. of Chemists, Am. Chem. Soc., Soc. of Am. Bacteriologists, Soc. Chem. Industry (Great Britain), Phi Rho Sigma. Clubs: Chemists of New York (pres. 1933-35); University (Washington, D.C.). Author scientific publications, appearing chiefly in German med. periodicals, also many papers appearing in Am. publications. Home: Paoli, Pa. Office: 1800 W. Lehigh Av., Philadelphia, Pa.

MARKS, Mary Helen, educator; b. Burgettstown, Pa., Jan. 3, 1886; d. Samuel Ferree and Sara Eliza (Fredericks) M.; A.B., Smith Coll., 1909; hon. A.M., Pa. Coll. for Women, 1927; L.H.D., Pa. Coll. for Women, 1938; unmarried. Began as teacher Latin and mathematics, Tidioute (Pa.) High Sch., 1910; field sec. Pa. Coll. for Women, 1916-19, registrar, 1919-22, dean, 1922-32, dean, actg. pres., 1932-35, dean, 1935—. On adv. board, Washington Sem. Member N.E.A., Am. Assn. Univ. Women, Nat. Assn. Deans, Administrative Women in Edn., Pa. State Edn. Assn., Pa. Dean's Assn., Western Pa. Dean's Assn. (v.p. 1932-35), Pittsburgh Council on Adult Edn. Presbyterian. Clubs: Pittsburgh Coll. (v.p. 1931-33), Colloquium (pres. 1922-23), Monday Luncheon (pres. 1928-29). Address: Pennsylvania College for Women, Pittsburgh, Pa.

MARLATT, Clyde Douglas, chem. mfg. exec.; b. Newark, N.J., Oct. 2, 1892; s. Dennis Sharp and Loretta (Bell) M.; B.S., Princeton U., 1913; m. Mary Jeannette Benjamin Nichols, June 9, 1920; children—Clyde Douglas, Jeannette Nichols. Instr. chemistry, Swarthmore (Pa.) Coll., 1913-15, Montclair (N.J.) High Sch., 1915-16; chemist Martin Dennis Co., Newark, N.J., 1916-18, supt., 1918-23, asst. to pres. since 1923. Mem. bd. edn., Essex Fells, N.J., since 1933, pres. since 1934. Mem. Am. Chem. Soc., Princeton Engring. Assn., The Mfg. Chemists Assn. of America (mem. exec. com. since 1933), Employers Assn. of North Jersey (dir.), The Cloister Inn (Princeton U.). Republican. Presbyterian. Clubs: Princeton (New York); Essex Fells (N.J.) Country. Home: Old Chester Rd., Essex Fells, N.J. Office: 859 Summer Av., Newark, N.J.

MARLIER, Raymond Murray, architect; b. Pittsburgh, Pa., Sept. 27, 1894; s. George F. and Mary A. (Murray) M.; ed. Duquesne U. Prep., 1909-12, Carnegie Inst. Tech., 1912-17; m. Esma Grace McClellan, June 11, 1919; children—Raymond M., Jr., Mary Grace, Joan, Rita. Has followed profession as architect at Pittsburgh since 1919; served as chmn. Bldg. Com., Duquesne U. since 1936; chief architectural supervisor, Federal Housing Adminstrn., W. Pa., 1934-37. Served as pilot A.S., U.S.A., 1917-19. Airport advisor to State of Pa., 1933-34. Mem. Aviation Adv. Bd. Allegheny Co. since 1936. Mem. Am. Inst. Architects (past pres. Pittsburgh Chapter), Pa. Assn. Architects (pres. 1938-39), Duquesne U. Alumni Assn. (past pres.), Alpha Tau Omega. Roman Catholic. K.C. Club: Aero of Pittsburgh (past pres.). Home: 222 W. Prospect Av., Ingram, Pa. Office: Empire Bldg., Pittsburgh, Pa.

MARLIN, Harry Halpine, clergyman, writer; b. Shelocta, Indiana Co., Pa., Aug. 19, 1869; s. Thomas Jefferson and Elizabeth (Hutchison) M.; A.B., Tarkio (Mo.) Coll., 1894; grad. Pittsburgh Theol. Sem., 1897; D.D., Monmouth, 1919; m. Norma Henrietta Fenderich, May 20, 1915. Ordained ministry U.P. Ch., 1897; pastor 11th Ch., Pittsburgh, 1897-1900, 4th Ch. East End, Pittsburgh, 1900-24, 4th Ch., East End, Cleveland, O., 1925-28. Member editorial staff United Presbyterian since 1917, contributing 2 pages weekly under "Current Events and Comment," also numerous articles and sketches. Sec. Social Service Com. of U.P. Ch. many yrs.; mem. Commn. on the Ch. and Social Service of Federal Council Chs. of Christ in America, 1913-25. Mem. S.A.R. Newspaper columnist. Asso. editor Bibliotheca Sacra, 1930-34. Address: New Castle. Pa.*

MARQUARD, William B., coll. prof.; b. Dayton, O., May 12, 1881; s. John M. and Mary M.; student Ohio State U.; m. Helen C. Decker, 1912; 1 dau., Catherine. Chemist, South Sharon (Pa.) By-Product Coke Co., 1903-04; phys. dir. Buhl Club, Sharon, Pa., 1905-06, supt. 1906-07; instr. of applied mechanics, Lafayette Coll., Easton, Pa., 1907-11, asst. prof., 1911-

MARQUARDT, Carl Eugene, coll. prof.; b. Higginsville, Mo., Sept. 16, 1884; s. Rev. Carl L. and Lou:se (Guenther) M.; grad. high sch., St. Joseph, Mich., 1905; B.A., University of Michigan, 1909; M.A., Pennsylvania State Coll., 1912; Ph. D., University of Pennsylvania, 1915; Ed.M., Harvard, 1924; m. Delia Florence Schenbeck, Aug. 17, 1910; children—Helen Louise, Gretchen Irmgard, Carl Eugene (dec.), Delia Florence, Carroll Quentin. Instr. in German, 1909-13, asst. prof. and asso. prof., 1913-19, asso. prof. French, 1919-23, prof. Romance philology since 1923, Pa. State Coll., also coll. examiner since 1920. Asst. in German, U. of Pa. (on leave of absence), 1913-15; Austin scholar, Grad. Sch. of Edn., Harvard (leave of absence), 1923-24. Fellow A.A.A.S.; mem. Am. Assn. of Univ. Profs., Phi Kappa Phi, Tau Kappa Epsilon, Phi Beta Kappa, Phi Delta Kappa, Phi Sigma Iota (nat. treas.), Phi Eta Sigma, Kappa Delta Pi, Kappa Gamma Psi. Republican. Baptist. Club: Center Hills Country. Home: State College, Pa.

MARQUIS, Dean Wilson, physician; b. Cedar Falls, Ia., Dec. 15, 1900; s. Rollin Ruthwin and Irene.(Shumaker) M.; grad. Lawrenceville Twp. (Ill.) High Sch., 1918; B.S., Wooster (O.) Coll., 1922; M.D., Cornell U., 1926; m. Helen Van der Veer Boyd, April 6, 1929; children—Joan Riddle, Jennifer Lee, Dean Anthony. Interne Meth. Episcopal Hosp., Brooklyn, N.Y., 1926-27; private practice, East Orange, N.J., since 1928; practice limited to internal medicine; formerly asso. in medicine N.Y. Post Grad. Med. Sch., Columbia; now asso. attending physician Allergy Clinic, N.Y. Post Grad. Hosp.; asst. attending physician Orange Memorial Hosp., N.J.; attending physician Essex County Hosp. for Contagious Diseases, N.J.; consultant in medicine N.J. Orthopædic Hosp., N.J. Served as lt. Med. Corps Reserve, 1926-36. Fellow Am. Coll. Physicians, A.M.A.; mem. N.Y. Med.-Surgical Soc., Clin. Soc. of the Oranges and Vicinity, Nu Sigma Nu. Republican. Presbyterian. Club: Rock Spring (West Orange, N.J.). Home: Park Place, Short Hills, N.J. Office: 144 Harrison St., East Orange, N.J.

MARQUIS, Sarah, steamship and travel agt.; b. Greensburg, Pa., July 8, 1897; d. John A. and Martha M. (Neilson) M.; grad. Ossining (N.Y.) Sch. for Girls, 1914; B.A., Coe Coll., Cedar Rapids, Ia., 1918; student Columbia U., 1919; unmarried. Asst. in edn. dept., Bd. of Home Missions, Presbyn. Ch., New York, 1919-23; asso. with W. A. Pratt Tours, Cedar Rapids, Ia., 1923-34; bought business on Mr. Pratt's death, 1935, and moved it to Jamesburg, N.J., continuing it as steamship and travel agency, opened New York office, 1937. Mem. English Speaking Union, Kappa Delta. Democrat. Presbyterian. Club: National Arts (New York). Home: Jamesburg, N.J. Office: 156 5th Av., New York, N.Y.

MARRINER, Guy Vincent Rice, dir. of music; b. Auckland, New Zealand, Apr. 9, 1898; s. Herbert Arthur and Winifred Alice (Rice) M.; ed. Kings Coll., Auckland, 1908-12, Wanganui Collegiate Sch., New Zealand, 1912-17; studied piano with Theresa Nelson, N.Y. City, 1924-30; unmarried. Began as concert pianist, 1921; made debut in London, Eng. 1930; lived in Vienna, Austria, 1930-33, and concertized Eng., Holland, Germany, Poland and Italy; began lecture-recitals, Philadelphia, 1934; apptd. mus. adviser to dir. Franklin Inst., Philadelphia, 1935, asso. dir. in charge of music since Dec. 1935; teacher pianoforte and harmony; lecturer in music, U. of Pa., since 1937. Served as 2d lt. inf., pilot in flying sch., New Zealand 1918. Episcopalian. Clubs: Franklin Inn, Art Alliance; British Empire (London). Home: St. George's Rd., Mt. Airy, Pa. Office: Franklin Institute, Philadelphia, Pa.

MARRIOTT, Ross W., mathematics and astronomy; b. Paxton, Ill., Dec. 30, 1882; s. Joshua H. and Elizabeth (Kelley) M.; B.S., Valparaiso (Ind.) U., 1904; A.B., Ind. U., 1906; A.M., Swarthmore, 1907; Ph.D., U. of Pa., 1911; m. Marian Redfield Stearne, Sept. 8, 1915; 1 dau., Alice Elizabeth. Instr. in mathematics, Swarthmore, 1907-10, asst. prof., 1910-22, asso. prof., 1922-27, prof. since 1927. Mem. Swarthmore Coll. Eclipse Expdns., Mexico, 1923, New England, 1925, Sumatra, 1926, 29, New England, 1932; mem. U.S. Naval Obs. Eclipse Expdn., 1930. Research ballistician on spl. aircraft ammunition, E. I. duPont de Nemours & Co., 1918. Fellow A.A.A.S., Royal Astron. Soc.; mem. Am. Astron. Soc., Am. Math. Soc., Math. Assn. America, Sigma Xi. Republican. Quaker. Contbr. research papers on astron. subjects. Home: 213 Lafayette Av., Swarthmore, Pa.

MARSALIS, Thomas, stocks brokerage; b. Dallas, Tex., Feb. 5, 1884; s. Thos. L. and Elizabeth J. (Crowdus) M.; A.B., Harvard U., 1904; m. Lillian Davenport, June 6, 1914; 1 dau., Barbara (Mrs. Chas. E. Lucke, Jr.). Engaged in stocks brokerage, N.Y. City, since 1904, mem. firm Thomas Marsalis & Co. since 1916; dir. Queenstown Bank of Md. Served as 1st lt. M.T.C., U.S.A., 1918. Democrat. Episcopalian. Clubs: Chesapeake Bay Yacht, Talbot Country (Easton); Woodmont Rod and Gun (Hancock, Md.). Home: Queenstown, Md. Office: 19 Rector St., New York, N.Y.

MARSELLA, Loreto, teacher, conductor, composer; b. Italy, Nov. 21, 1874; s. Pasquale and Marianna (Palombo) M.; student pub. and high schs., Italy, 1880-92, music sch., Italy, 1879-95; studied music, harmony, counterpoint and composition with A. Bellandese, Marchetti A. Vessella and D'Onofrio; classic and philosophy with D'Cafolla, 1888-92; m. Assunta Piacitelli, Nov. 28, 1898; children—Alessandro Lucis, Ettore Pasquale, Dante S. Francesco, Italo Vitterio Tullio, Italia Marianna Vittoria (Mrs. Gabriele Sisca). Came to U.S., 1895, naturalized, 1906. Music teacher and orchestra and band conductor, Providence, R.I., 1895-1907; owner Marsella Conservatory of Music, since 1908, Phila. and Norristown, Pa.; composer many marches and symphonies, classic and semi-classic songs, romances and serenades; also grand opera "The Alloween Dance" (lyric from Dr. Francesco Cubicciotti); now actively engaged in ednl. and recreational Federal projects. Awarded 4 gold medals for merit, 1 silver medal for composition from Roma Turin World Fair, 1911. Mem. Am. Federation of Musicians; trustee Lodge Antorio Neuci Order Sons of Italy (hon. pres. Holy Savior Lodge). Catholic. Home: 201 Jacoby St., Norristown, Pa.

MARSH, Anne Steele (Mrs. James R. M.), painter and graphic artist; b. Nutley, N.J., Sept. 7, 1901; d. Frederic Dorr and Mary (Thyng) Steele; ed. Y.W.C.A. Art Sch., 1917-19, Cooper Union Art Sch., 1919-20; studied with Wm. Palmer; m. James R. Marsh, Jan. 17, 1925; children—Reginald, Janet, Peter. Designer interior decorations and tapestries, 1920-21; teacher occupational therapy, 1921-26; began exhibiting paintings and graphic art, 1933; one man exhibitions of water colors, Baltimore, 1935, Florida, 1936, N.Y. City, 1935, 1937, N.J., 1938; instr. art, Buxton Country Day Sch., 1938-39; awarded hon. mention, Print Club of Phila., 1935, Asbury Park Soc. Fine Arts, 1938, N.J. Gallery, Newark, 1936, 1937, 1939. Print selected for World's Fair Exhbn. of Contemporary Art, 1939. Mem. Am. Artists Cong., Modern Artists of N.J., N.J. Water Color and Sculpture Soc., N.J. Artists Union; mem. N.J. sponsoring com. of Federal Art Projects. Home: Essex Fells, N.J.

MARSH, James Ingraham, lawyer; b. Pittsburgh, Pa., Feb. 21, 1890; s. Joseph W. and Anna Rose (Ingraham) M.; student Shady Side Acad., 1900-05, Lawrenceville Sch., 1905-07; A.B., Princeton U., 1911; LL.B., U. of Pittsburgh, 1914; m. Mary Glyde Wells, Jan. 4, 1919; children—Louise Dewey, Mary Glyde, James Ingraham, Jr. Admitted to bar, 1914; 1st asst. U.S. atty., 1926-36. Rep. candidate for Congress, 1938; mem. State Affairs Com., Civic Club, Allegheny County. Mem. Am. Bar Assn., Pa. State Bar Assn., Allegheny County Bar Assn., S.A.R., Am. Legion, Phi Delta Phi. Presbyterian. Mason (32°). Clubs: Duquesne, Fox Chapel Golf. Home: 4701 Wallingford St. Office: Columbia Bldg., Pittsburgh, Pa.

MARSH, Joseph Franklin, coll. pres.; b. Toll Gate, W.Va., Jan. 29, 1877; s. Jefferson and Angelina (Cunningham) M.; B.Pd., W.Va., Wesleyan Coll., Buckhannon, 1901, Pd.D., 1927; A.B., W.Va. Univ., 1907, .A.M., 1912; m. Florence Catharine Keller, May 29, 1922; 1 son, Joseph Franklin. Began teaching, 1894; supt. schs., Harrisville, W.Va., 1902-05; prin. Fairmont High Sch., 1908-09; asst. state supt. schs., W.Va., 1909-15; sec. State Bd. of Regents, 1915-19; sec. State Bd. of Edn., and dir. vocational edn., 1919-29; pres. Concord State Teachers Coll. since 1929. Served as exec. sec. State Food Administration, W.Va., World War, also four-minute man. Mem. Am. Commn. to Study Cooperation in Europe, 1913. Mem. N.E.A. and Dept. of Superintendence same, Am. Vocational Assn. (life), W.Va. State Education Assn. (bldg. com.), W.Va. Athletic Assn. (eligibility com.), Phi Beta Kappa. Republican. Methodist. Mason. Clubs: Rotary (Princeton, W.Va.); Mountain (Morgantown). Author: The Teacher Outside of the School, 1928; also various brochures and bulls. Editor W.Va. School Journal, 1921-25. Home: Athens, W.Va.

MARSH, Ray Stanley, horticulturist, univ. prof.; b. Morgan Co., Ind., Dec. 17, 1894; s. Curtis B. and Hattie M. (Cox) M.; student Purdue U., Lafayette, Ind., 1914-17, U. of Chicago, 1924-25; B.S., M.A., U. of Mo., Columbia, Mo., 1923; m. Ruth Moon, Oct. 20, 1917; 1 son, David Fielding. Began as newsboy, Kokomo, Ind., 1911; instr., U. of Mo., Columbia, Mo., 1920-23; acting prof. Bethany (W.Va.) Coll., 1923-24; asst. in plant physiology, U. of Chicago, 1924-25; asst. prof. horticulture, U. of Ill., Urbana, Ill., 1925-36; prof. horticulture, W.Va. Univ., Morgantown, W.Va., since 1936. Mem. Acacia, Gamma Alpha, Sigma Xi. Club Kiwanis (Morgantown, W.Va.). Address: 724 College Av., Morgantown, W.Va.

MARSH, Ritchie T(hompson), lawyer; b. Waterford, Pa., Nov. 15, 1870; s. Wilson and Elmina (Sedgwick) M.; ed. public schools, Erie, Pa., and Edinboro State Teachers Coll.; m. Clara Margaret Roberts, Sept. 27, 1911; 1 dau., Winifred. School teacher, 1893-99; admitted to Pa. bar, 1899, and practiced in State and Federal Courts of Pa.; U.S. referee in bankruptcy since 1926; mem. law firm Marsh, Spaeder, Bauer & Marsh, Erie. Trustee Erie Public Library, Edinboro State Teachers Coll., St. Vincent's Hosp. Republican. Presbyterian. Mason (32°, K.T., Shriner). Home: 636 W. 10th St. Office: Ariel Bldg., Erie, Pa.

MARSH, Robert Price, prof. biology and hygiene; b. Chester, N.J., Mar. 30, 1889; s. George Price and Sarah Miller (Babbitt) M.; student Middlebury Coll. (Vt.), 1910-12; B.S., New York U., 1921; M.S., Rutgers U., 1923, Ph.D., 1924; m. Kate Conover Garland, Aug. 9, 1919. Began as teacher pub. schs., N.J., 1912; research asst. and lab. instr., Rutgers U., 1921-24; actg. prof. biology, Gettysburg Coll., 1924-25, prof. biology and hygiene and head of dept. since 1925. Served with Engrs. Corps, U.S.A., 1918-19, with A.E.F., in 3 maj. engagements; taught in army schs. in France. Fellow A.A.A.S.; mem. Am. Soc. Plant Physiologists, Bot. Soc. of America, Soc. Exptl. Biology and Medicine, Am. Assn. Univ. Profs., Beta Beta Beta (nat. vice-pres.), Sigma Xi, Delta Kappa Epsilon. Republican. Lutheran. Mason (K.T., 32°, Shriner). Home: 100 Broadway, Gettysburg, Pa.

MARSH, Theodore McCurdy, lawyer; b. East Orange, N.J., Aug. 27, 1883; s. Stanford and Gertrude Mercer (McCurdy) M.; A.B., Yale U., 1904; LL.B., Columbia U. Sch. Law, 1907; A.M., Columbia U. Grad. Sch., 1907; m. Lillian Hillyer, Apr. 10, 1913; children—Lillian Hillyer, Gertrude McCurdy, Matilda Lucille, Dorothea Couthouy. Admitted to N.J. bar as atty., 1907, counsellor, 1910; since admission, engaged in gen. practice of law at Newark; mem. firm, Raymond, Mountain, Van Blarcom and Marsh, 1912-18, Raymond, Marsh & Ellis, 1918-20; mem. firm, Riker & Riker, 1920-35, and Child, Riker, Marsh & Shipman since 1935; served as city counsel, East Orange, 1919-22; borough atty., Borough of Mantoloking; prof. law, Mercer Beasley School of Law, 1926-36, U. of Newark Law Sch. since 1936. Served as capt., N.J. State Militia, 1917-19; capt. then maj., N.J.N.G., 1919-21; lt. col. 113th inf., 1921; lt. col. J.A.G. Dept., 1922-24; lt. col. 44th inf. div., 1924-28. Trustee Mercer Beasley Sch. Law, 1926-36, U. of Newark since 1936; trustee N.J. Orthopaedic Hosp. and Dispensary (pres., 1930-38), Hosp. Council Essex Co. Mem. Am., N.J. and Essex Co. bar assns., Phi Beta Kappa, Beta Theta Pi, Phi Delta Theta. Independent Republican. Episcopalian (vestryman and warden Grace Ch.). Clubs: Rotary of Newark (dir.), Rock Spring (trustee, sec. since 1927). Coeditor (with Aaron Lasser), case-book, Marsh and Lasser Pleading, Practice and Procedure in New Jersey, 1937. Home: 20 East Highland Av., East Orange. Office: 744 Broad St., Newark, N.J.

MARSHALL, Berry Carroll, (Mrs. E. Kennerly M., Jr.), physician; b. Columbus, O., May 30, 1889; d. Thomas B. and Katherine (Berry) Carroll; B.S., Ohio State U., 1911; grad. student U. of Wis., 1911-13; M.D., Johns Hopkins U. Med. Sch., 1917; m. E. Kennerly Marshall, Jr., Sept. 17, 1917; children—Katherine Berry, Julia Brown, Richard Kennerly. Dispensary physician, Phipps Clinic, Johns Hopkins Hosp. since 1928; instr. psychiatry, Johns Hopkins Med. Sch. since 1929; psychiatrist, Baltimore Juvenile Ct. since 1929. Fellow Am. Psychiatric Assn. Mem. Orthopsychiatric Assn., Baltimore City Med. Soc., Kappa Kappa Gamma. Clubs: College, Altrusa, 14 E. Hamilton St. (Baltimore). Home: 419 Hawthorne Rd. Office: Juvenile Court, Baltimore, Md.

MARSHALL, Charles D(onnell), bridge builder; C.E., Lehigh U., 1888; m. Dora Noble; children—Elizabeth P., John N., Dorothy C., Charles Donnell, Mary M., Jane I. Chmn. bd. Koppers Co.; pres. Union Shipbuilding Co.; v.p. Hughes-Foulkrod Co.; dir. Bethlehem Steel Corpn., Granite City Steel Co., Nat. Enameling and Stamping Co., U.S. Glass Co. Trustee Lehigh U. Home: 6300 Fifth Av. Office: Koppers Bldg., Pittsburgh, Pa.

MARSHALL, Charles Henry, field engr.; b. Wilmerding, Pa., Jan. 15, 1893; s. Charles Homer and Nancy Ann (Rupp) M.; E.E., U. of Pittsburgh, 1916; m. Iona Abraham, Feb. 4, 1914; 1 son, Homer Abraham. Testing engr. in charge phys. and exptl. labs. Westinghouse Electric & Mfg. Co., East Pittsburgh, Pa., 1916-28; mem. tech. staff apparatus development dept., Bell Telephone Labs., Inc., New York, 1928-32; cons. engr. on materials, material testing, Short Hills, N.J., 1932-34; field engr. Baldwin-Southwark Corpn., Phila., Pa., since 1934; con. engr. Mem. Am. Soc. for Testing Materials. Republican. Protestant. Odd Fellow (Past Grand). Holder several patents on materials testing equipment. Home: 42 Whitney Rd., Short Hills, N.J. Office: Baldwin-Southwark Corpn., Philadelphia, Pa.

MARSHALL, Edward Wayne, vice-pres. and actuary; b. Lumberton, N.J., Feb. 24, 1889; s. William B. and Anna B. Marshall; grad. Haddonfield High Sch., student U. of Pa.; m. Viola B. Craig; children—Virginia C., Edward Wayne, William B., David L. Actuarial dept. Penn Mutual Life, 1909-11, Provident Life & Trust, 1911-17; asst. actuary Fidelity Mutual Life, 1917-20; with Provident Mutual Life Ins. Co. since 1920, successively asst. actuary, 1920-24, asso. actuary, 1925-28, actuary, 1928-30, vice-pres. and actuary since 1931; dir. Friends Fiduciary Corpn. Fellow Actuarial Soc. of Am. (vice-pres.; mem. council; mem. joint com. on mortality and actuarial studies; fellow Am. Inst. Actuaries; mem. Am. Statis. Assn. Mem. Soc. of Friends. Clubs: Tavistock Country (Haddonfield, N.J.); Ozone Golf. Home: 574 Warwick Rd., Haddonfield, N.J. Office: 4601 Market St., Philadelphia, Pa.

MARSHALL, E(li) Kennerly, Jr., pharmacologist and physiologist; b. at Charleston, S.C., May 2, 1889; s. Eli Kennerly and Julia Irene (Brown) Marshall; B.S., College of Charleston, 1903, Ph.D., in Chemistry, Johns Hopkins U., 1911, M.D., 1917; studied Halle, Germany, summer 1912; m. Alice Berry Carroll, Sept. 17, 1917; children—Katherine Berry, Julia Brown, Richard Kennerly. Ast. and asso. in physiol. chemistry, Johns Hopkins, 1911-14; asso. and asso, prof. pharmacology, same univ., 1914-19; prof. pharmacology, Washington U., 1919-21; prof. physiology, Johns Hopkins, 1921-32, prof. of pharmacology since 1932. Editor Jour. of Pharmacology and Experimental Therapeutics, 1932-37; associate editor of the Journal of Pharmacology and Experimental Therapeutics since 1937. Captain Med. Corps U.S.A., 1918. Fellow A.A.A.S.; mem. Am. Physiol. Soc., Am. Soc. Biol. Chemists, Am. Soc. Pharmocology and Exptl. Therapeutics, Assn. of Am. Physicians, Gamma Alpha, Phi Beta Pi. Home: 419 Hawthorn Rd., Roland Park, Baltimore, Md.

MARSHALL, James Edwin, lawyer; b. Butler Co., Pa., Aug. 13, 1877; s. James M. and Ruth Ann (Riddle) M.; B.E., Slippery Rock State Teachers Coll., 1894; A.B. and A.M., Grove City (Pa.) Coll., 1898, LL.D., 1938; LL.B., U. of Pa., 1903; m. Alberta Cronenwett, 1904 (now deceased); children—John Howard, Ruth Helen (deceased); m. 2d, Josaphine Hammond, 1934. Admitted to Pa. bar, 1903, and since practiced in Butler, Pa.; admitted to all State and Federal Courts including Supreme Ct. of U.S. Dir. Butler Y.M.C.A., Boy Scouts; dir. Pa. Soc. for Crippled Children. Served as Y.M.C.A. war sec. in France during World War. Republican. Presbyterian. Mason. Club: Rotary of Butler. Home: 244 W. Pearl St. Office: Butler County Nat. Bank Bldg., Butler, Pa.

MARSHALL, John; mem. law firm Marshall & Forrer. Address: Parkersburg, W.Va.

MARSHALL, John, chemist; b. Huntington, W.Va., May 12, 1891; s. Norman Fitz-Hugh and Mary Virginia (Ball) M.; student U. of N.M. Prep., Albuquerque, 1907-08, U. of N. M., 1908-9; Chem.E., U. of Va., Charlottesville, Va., 1913; m. Dorothea Bechtel, June 3, 1916; children—John, Delia Page, Thomas Ball, Mary Ball. Chemist E. I. du Pont de Nemours & Co., Eastern Lab., Gibbstown, N.J., 1913-20, asst. dir. Eastern Lab., 1921-26, dir. Phila. (Pa.) Lab., 1927-33, asst. chem. dir. finishes div., Wilmington, Del., 1933-36, chem. dir. finishes div. since 1936. Mem. Am. Chem. Soc., Franklin Inst., Pi Kappa Alpha, Tau Beta Pi. Episcopalian. Club: Rolling Green Golf (Media, Pa.). Home: Lincoln Av., Swarthmore, Pa. Office: du Pont Bldg., Wilmington, Del.

MARSHALL, John G., lawyer; b. Big Beaver Twp., Beaver Co., Pa., Oct. 2, 1880; s. Marvin and Sarah (Garvin) M.; student Grove City, (Pa.) Coll. and U. of Pa. Law Sch.; m. Lulu Schoeller, Aug. 4, 1921; children—Mary Louise, John Schoeller. Mem. firm Moorhead & Marshall, Beaver; dir. Ft. McIntosh Nat. Bank, Beaver, The Freedom (Pa.) Nat. Bank. Deputy sheriff, Beaver Co., 1903-06; mem. Pa. Ho. of Reps., 1919-25. Presbyterian. Home: 329 Iroquois Pl. Office: Beaver Trust Bldg., Beaver, Pa.

MARSHALL, Leon Carroll, college prof.; b. Zanesville, O., March 15, 1879; s. John Wesley and Rachel (Tanner) M.; A.B., Ohio Wesleyan U., 1900 (LL.D., 1918); A.B., Harvard, 1901, A.M., 1902; m. Mary Brown Keen, Sept. 1, 1903; children—Mary Rachel, Leon Carroll, Margaret, Barbara. Prof. economics, Ohio Wesleyan U., 1903-07; asst. prof. polit. economy, 1907-08, asso. prof., 1908-11, prof., 1911-28, dean Coll. of Commerce and Adminstrn., 1909-24, dean Sch. of Social Service Administrn., 1918-24, dean Senior Colls., 1911-18, chmn. dept. polit. economy, 1918-28, dir. work in economics and business, 1924-28, U. of Chicago; visiting prof. Sch. of Law, Columbia U., 1926-27; prof. of law, The Inst. of Law, Johns Hopkins U., 1928-33, also visiting prof. edn. since 1935; prof. polit. economy, American U., since 1936; vice-chmn. of Nat. Labor Board, 1934; dep. asst. adminstr. for policy, NRA, 1934; mem. and exec. sec. Nat. Industrial Recovery Bd., 1934-35; dir. NRA Div. of Review, 1935-36. Asso. editor Journal of Political Economy. Apptd. chief of sect. on industrial service, Council of Nat. Defense, Dec. 1917; sec. Advisory Council of Dept. of Labor, Jan. 1918; dir. industrial relations, Emergency Fleet Corpn., May 1918; economic advisor, War Labor Policies Bd., June 1918. Mem. Am. Acad. of Arts and Sciences, Am. Economic Assn., Am. Sociol. Soc., Am. Statis. Assn., Am. Polit. Science Assn., Phi Beta Kappa. Clubs: Quadrangle, University (Chicago). Author or joint author: Outlines of Economics, 1910; Bibliography of Economics, 1910; Materials for the Study of Elementary Economics, 1913; Quartermaster and Ordnance Supply, 1917; Readings in Industrial Soc., 1918; Our Economic Organization, 1920; Business Administration, 1921; Social Studies in Secondary Schools, 1922; The Story of Human Progress, 1923; Readings in the Story of Human Progress, 1925; Modern Business, 1926; Collegiate Education for Business, 1928; Outlines of the Economic Order, 1929; The Emergence of the Modern Order, 1929; Production in the Modern Order, 1929; The Coördination of Specialists Through the Market, 1929; Judicial Statistics, 1930; Maryland Trial Court Criminal Statistics for 1930, 31; Comparative Judicial Criminal Statistics—Ohio and Maryland, 1931; Comparative Judicial Criminal Statistics—Six States, 1932; Ohio Criminal Statisics, 1932; Judicial Criminal Statistics, 1932; The Divorce Court, Vol. I, Maryland, 1932; Judicial Criminal Statistics in Maryland for 1931, 1932; Expenditure of Public Money for the Administration of Justice in Ohio, 1933; The Divorce Court, Vol. II, Ohio, 1933; The Improvement of Divorce Statistics in Ohio, 1933; Unlocking the Treasuries of the Trial Courts, 1933; National Crisis Series, 1934; Hours and Wages Provisions in NRA Codes, 1935; The National Recovery Administration—an Analysis and Appraisal, 1935; Curriculum Making in the Social Studies, 1936; also numerous articles on ednl. and econ. subjects in jours. Joint Editor: Lessons in Community and National Life, 1918; Textbooks in the Social Studies (13 vols.). Editor of Materials for the Study of Business (40 vols.); publications issued by NRA Division of Review (150 vols.). Home: 7007 Rolling Road, Chevy Chase, Md.

MARSHALL, Loyal S(ylvester), supervising prin. of schools; b. Hazel Dell, (now Ellwood City), Pa., Aug. 6, 1893; s. Thomas C. and Florence (Newton) M.; grad. Ellwood City High Sch., 1911; A.B., Geneva Coll., Beaver Falls, Pa., 1915; grad. student U. of Pittsburgh, Pa. State Coll.; m. Marie Smith, Oct. 8, 1915; children—Goldie Lucille, Betty Jane, Loyal Smith, Mildred Marie. Worked as carpenter during summer vacations while college student; worked in steel mill, 1915-17; taught Slippery Rock Twp. High Sch., Princeton, Pa., 1917-18; teacher of mathematics and coached athletics Slippery Rock Teachers Coll., 1918-19; supervisor of schools, Patton Twp., Allegheny Co., Pa., 1919-21; West Deer Twp., Allegheny Co., 1921-22; supervising prin. of schools, Springdale, Pa., since 1922. Scoutmaster for 9 years. Mem. N.E.A., Am. Assn. Sch. Administrs., Pa. State Edn. Assn., Allegheny Co. Prin. Round Table (vice-pres. 1929-30, pres. 1930-31). Mem. United Presbyn. Ch. (elder). Club: Kiwanis of Springdale (sec.). Home: 347 Butler St. Office: 331 School St., Springdale, Pa.

MARSHALL, Mortimer Villiers, prof. of education; b. Yarmouth, Nova Scotia, May 26, 1898; s. Frederic Lakeland and Minnie (Knollin) M.; student Yarmouth (Nova Scotia) Acad., 1911-16; B.A., B.S., Acadia U., Wolfville, Nova Scotia, 1921; Ed.M., Ed.D., Harvard, 1929; m. Vera Gould Goreham, June 29, 1927; children—Mary Bernice, Lydia Jane. Came to U.S., 1929. Country school teacher, Carleton, N.S., 1921-22; instr. mathematics and hygiene, Nova Scotia Normal Sch., 1922-27; instr. in science, Horton Acad. of Acadia U., 1927-28; asst. prof. of edn., Franklin and Marshall Coll., 1929-30, prof. since 1931; supt. of schs., Yarmouth, N.S., 1930-31. Served in Canadian Army, 1916-19. Mem. A.A.A.S., Am. Assn. Univ. Profs., Phi Delta Kappa. Baptist. Mason. Club: Torch (Lancaster). Home: 227 Atkins Av., Lancaster, Pa.

MARSHALL, R. E.; mem. law firm Marshall & Carey. Office: First Nat. Bank Bldg., Baltimore, Md.

MARSHALL, Roy Kenneth, astronomer; b. Glen Carbon, Ill., Aug. 21, 1907; s. Richards and Minerva Sarah (Westbrook) M.; A.B., Ohio Wesleyan U., Delaware, O., 1929; A.M., U. of Mich., 1930, Ph.D., 1932; m. Frances Marian Madison, Oct. 23, 1934; 1 son, Roy Kenneth. Began as lecturer in astronomy, Adler Planetarium, Chicago, 1932; research asst., Yerkes Observatory and Harvard Observatory, 1934-35; instr., later asst. prof., of mathematics and astronomy, Wilson Coll., Chambersburg, Pa., 1935 to 1939; occasional lecturer, Adler Planetarium, Chicago, Hayden Planetarium, New York, Fels Planetarium, Phila.; asst. dir. Buhl Planetarium and Inst. of Popular Science, Pittsburgh, since 1939. Fellow Royal Astron. Soc. (London), A.A.A.S.; mem. Am. Astron. Soc., Brit. Astron. Assn., Royal Astron. Soc. of Can., La Societe Astronomique de France, Sigma Pi Sigma, Sigma Xi. Address: Buhl Planetarium, Pittsburgh, Pa.

MARSHALL, Samuel Mathewson Donnell, physician; b. Milford, Del., Oct. 2, 1884; s. Dr. George William and Mary Louise (Donnell) M.; student Milford (Del.) pub. schs., 1890-1900; B.A., U. of Del., Newark, Del., 1905; M.D., U. of Pa., 1909; m. Ruth Thorp Heisler, Feb. 27, 1918; children—Barbara Thorp, Samuel Mathewson Donnell. Interne M.E. Hosp. Phila., 1909-10; resident house surgeon Wills Eye Hosp., Phila., 1912-13; chief eye, ear, nose and throat diseases, Milford (Del.) Memorial Hosp.; pres. Milford Bd. of Health; dir. First Nat. Bank & Trust Co. of Milford. Served as capt., M.C., Base Hosp. 123, A.E.F., during World War. Republican. Mason (Shriner). Club: Phila. Medical. Address: Milford, Del.

MARSHALL, Thomas Randolph, lumber; b. Seaville, N.J., May 29, 1883; s. Ellis Hughes and Lydia Ann (Gandy) M.; student Temple Coll., Phila., 1899-1902; Ph.B., Brown U., Providence, R.I., 1907; A.M., Yale, 1908; student U. of Pa. Law Sch., 1908-09; m. Flora K. Allen, Jan. 3, 1911. With Ellwood Allen Lumber Co., Phila., since 1910, successively as mgr., junior partner, head of firm; dir, Pa. Lumberman's Mutual Fire Ins. Co. Treas. Northeastern Hosp. of Phila. Past pres. Lumbermen's Exchange of Phila. Mem. Retail Lumbermen's Assn. of Phila. (dir., past pres.); Middle Atlantic Lumbermen's Assn. (dir.); past pres. Phila. Lumbermen's Golf Club. Mem. Pa. Soc. of N.Y., Phi Beta Kappa, Phi Delta Theta, Miller Law Club. Republican. Methodist. Clubs: Union League, Brown Alumni of Phila. (vicepres.), Phi Delta Theta Alumni (Phila.); Old York Road Country (Jenkintown, Pa.). Home: 1005 Stratford Av., Melrose Park, Pa. Office: Trenton Av. and Ann St., Philadelphia, Pa.

MARTENEY, Charles Walton, clergyman; b. Handy Camp, W.Va., Oct. 24, 1905; s. Odus Cooper and Martha Ann (Crites) M.; A.B., W.Va. Wesleyan Coll., 1926; B.D., Crozer Theol. Sem., 1929, M.Th., 1930; m. Lorene Rathje, Mar. 16, 1930; children—Pierre J., Eugene Robert. Ordained Bapt. ministry, 1927, minister, Reading, Pa., 1927-29, Bapt. Ch., Ridley Park, Pa., since 1929; founder and dir. Crum Lynne Mission, Crum Lynne, Pa., since 1934; dir. finance com. Pa. Bapt. Conv., 1934-36; mgr. Pa. Bapt. Conv., 1934-38. Founder Boys Model Airplane Club, Ridley Park, Pa., 1938. Trustee Pub. Library, Ridley Park, Pa. Mem. Ministerium, Chester, Pa. Republican. Baptist. Home: 103 Delaware Av., Ridley Park, Pa.

MARTENS, James Hart Curry, univ. prof.; b. Brooklyn, N.Y., Jan. 1, 1901; s. James William and Genevieve (Curry) M.; C.E., Cornell U., 1921, M.S., 1923, Ph.D., 1926; m. Vivian Stone, June 17, 1931; children—James Mason, William Stephen. Asst. in geology, Cornell U. 1921-24, instr. geology, 1924-27; asst. geologist, Fla. Geol. Survey, 1927-29; asst. prof. geology, W.Va. Univ., Morgantown, W.Va. 1929-35, asso. prof. since 1935; cooperating mineralogist, W.Va. Geol. Survey since 1931; engagements as geologist, summers, 1923-30, including pvt. expdn. to Northern Quebec, 1924, geologist Rawson-MacMillan expdn. of Field Mus. to Labrador, Greenland and Baffin Land, 1926. Mem. Am. Geog. Soc., Geol. Soc. of America, Mineral. Soc. of America, Appalachian Geol. Soc., W.Va. Acad. Sci., Sigma Xi, Sigma Xi, Sigma Gamma Epsilon, Phi Kappa Phi. Home: 308 Spring Rd., Morgantown, W.Va.

MARTI, Fritz, univ. prof.; b. Winterthur, Switzerland, Jan. 1, 1894; s. Johann Gottfried and Lina (Netscher) M.; came to U.S., 1923, naturalized, 1930; P.D. of M.E., Swiss Federal Inst. Tech., Zürich, 1918; grad. student U. of Zürich, Switzerland, 1918-20; Ph.D., Univ. of Berne, Switzerland, 1922; grad. student, Teachers Coll. of Columbia U., summer 1932; m. Gertrude E. Austin, June 5, 1937; 1 dau., Judith Anne. Engaged as teaching fellow and instr. philosophy, U. of Ore., Eugene, Ore., 1923-25; lecturer in philosophy, Haverford (Pa.) Coll., 1926-27; instr. and asst. prof. philosophy, Goucher Coll., Baltimore, Md., 1925-32; asso. prof. philosophy, Hollins (Va.) Coll., 1932-35; prof. philosophy, U. of Md. since 1935 and head of dept. of philosophy since 1936; condr. courses in history of art, and philosophy, Grad. Sch., U.S. Dept. Agr. since 1939. Served as pvt. to 1st lt. Swiss Army, 1914-22, tech. instr. training courses of motor car service. Mem. Am. Philos. Assn., Southern Soc. for Philosophy and Psychology, Brit. Inst. of Philosophy. Democrat. Author: A Philosophical Glossary, 1933; Schelling's Lectures on the Method of Academic Study, 1939. Home: 11 Hesketh St., Chevy Chase, Md. Address: University of Maryland, College Park, Md.

MARTIEN, James Carey, pres. William Martien & Co., Inc.; b. Baltimore, Md., Dec. 10, 1875; s. William and Virginia (Conradt) M.; ed. pub. schs., Baltimore, 1885-95; m. May Mealy, Apr. 23, 1903; children—Helen May (Mrs. Lawrence B. Fenneman), Ethel Reba (Mrs. George H. Blackwell), William, Louise Carey. Began as clk., steamship agency, Baltimore, 1895; entered William Martien & Co., real estate, Baltimore, 1899, pres. since 1919; dir. Roland Park Co. Chmn. bd. of zoning appeals, Baltimore, 1923-26; pres. Baltimore Assn. of Commerce, 1926-28; pres. Real Estate Bd. of Baltimore, 1907. Pres. Md. Baptist Union Assn., 1925-27, Baltimore Baptist Ch. Extension Soc. since 1929; treas. Baptist Home of Md.; dir. Y.M. C.A., Baltimore. Democrat. Baptist. Clubs: Chesapeake, Merchants, Baltimore Country (Baltimore, Md.). Home: 1813 Thornbury Rd. Office: 3200 Baltimore Trust Bldg., Baltimore, Md.

MARTIN, Adam Hershey, supervising prin. schs.; b. New Holland, Pa., Sept. 12, 1890; s. Eli W. and Hester (Hershey) M.; A.B., Franklin and Marshall Coll., 1917; A.M., Columbia U., 1922; grad. student U. of Pa., 1931-39; m. Lottie Mae Cooper, June 27, 1923; 1 son, David Cooper. Began as teacher rural schs., 1909; prin. pub. schs., Duncansville, Pa., 1917-18, Nazareth, 1919-22; supervising prin. pub. schs. West York, Pa., 1922-28; sales mgr. Fishels Bakery, West York, Pa., 1928-30; supervising prin. pub. schs., West York, Pa., since 1930. Mem. Nat. Edn. Assn., York Co. Sch. Mens Club (past pres.), Phi Delta Kappa, Phi Kappa Tau. Mem. Prot. Reformed Ch. Mason (K.T., Shriner). Clubs: Exchange of West York (past pres.); Lions (past pres.), Tall Cedars, Shrine (York). Home: 50 N. Clinton St., York, Pa.

MARTIN, Adam Oscar, architect; b. Dublin, Pa., Sept. 28, 1873; s. Jonas and Mary Catherine (Crouthamel) M.; student Drexel Inst., Phila., Pa., 1892-94; m. Minerva Fretz, Jan. 18, 1896; children—Margaret F., Fred F. In practice architecture since 1896; senior mem. firm A. Oscar Martin & Son, registered architects, Doylestown, Pa., since 1921; dir. and mem. exec. com. Doylestown Trust Co. since 1934. Co. engr., Bucks Co., Pa., 1900-16. Mem. A.I.A. Republican. Mem. Reformed Ch. Mason (32°, Shriner), Odd Fellow, Moose. Clubs: Kiwanis, Doylestown Country (Doylestown, Pa.). Home: 153 Shewell Av. Office: 14-15 Hart Bldg., Doylestown, Pa.

MARTIN, Alfred, mfr., banker; b. South Staffordshire, Eng., Nov. 2, 1877; s. Richard and Lucy (Robinson) M.; brought to U.S., 1884, naturalized, 1898; ed. Pittsburgh pub. and high schs., 1885-1902; m. Johanna Cuthbert, Mar. 10, 1903; 1 son, Alfred Cuthbert. In business since 1903, now pres. and treas. West Penn Mfg. & Supply Corpn., metal stampings, Brackenridge, Pa.; pres. Allegheny Valley Trust Co., Verona, Pa., since 1925. Has served on council and bd. of health (pres.), Oakmont, Pa. Republican. Episcopalian. Club: Pittsburgh Athletic. Home: 611 Pennsylvania Av. Office: 808 3d Av., Brackenridge, Pa.; also Verona, Pa.

MARTIN, Arthur C., pres. Kittaning Brick & Fire Clay Co.; b. Pittsburgh, Pa., May 25, 1883; s. Sherwood C. and Ella (Coe) M.; student Shadyside Acad., Pittsburgh, 1898-1900, Bordentown (N.J.) Mil. Inst., 1900-03, Dartmouth Coll., 1903-04, U. of Pa., 1904-06; m. Flora Belle Morrow, 1918; children—Sherwood C., Roberta M. Salesman Kittanning Brick & Fire Clay Co., Pittsburgh, 1906-22, v.p., 1922-32, pres. since 1932; dir. Yingling-Martin Brick Co., W. B. Martin Stone Co. Republican. Protestant. Mason. Clubs: Duquesne (Pittsburgh), Rolling Rock, Westmoreland Hunt, Westmoreland Polo, Greensburg Country (Greensburg, Pa.). Home: (winter) 697 Morewood Av., Pittsburgh, Pa.; (summer) "Woodcrest Farm," R.F.D. 4, Greensburg, Pa. Office: Empire Bldg., Pittsburgh, Pa.

MARTIN, Asa Earl, prof. Am. history; b. Johnson Co., Mo., Nov. 15, 1885; s. Isaac R. and Mary Donah (Smith) M.; B.A., William Jewell Coll., Liberty, Mo., 1908, M.A., 1912; studied U. of Chicago 3 summers; Ph.D., Cornell U., 1915; m. Anna Elizabeth Fox, June 6, 1912; children—Milton Fox, Marion (Mrs. R. B. Blum). Teacher history and civics, Westport High Sch., Kansas City, Mo., 1908-13; instr. Am. history, 1915, asst. prof., 1916-18, prof. and head dept. history and polit. science, 1918-30, prof. Am. history since 1930, Pa. State Coll. Member Am. Historical Assn., Pennsylvania Historical Association, American Assn. of Univ. Profs., Hist. Soc. Western Pa., Kappa Alpha (Southern), Delta Sigma Pi, Phi Kappa Phi. Republican. Methodist. Club: Centre Hills Country. Author: Our Negro Population—A Sociological Study of the Negroes of Kansas City, Missouri, 1913; The Anti-Slavery Movement in Kentucky Prior to 1850, 1918; Pennsylvania History Told by Contemporaries (with H. H. Shenk), 1925; History of the United States, 1783-1865, Vol. I, 1928, Since 1865, Vol. II, 1931, rev. edit., 1938. History of the United States, 1492-1865, 1934; also numerous his. articles. Home: State College, Pa.

MARTIN, Carl Neidhard, banker; b. Phila., Pa., Dec. 4, 1874; s. Robert Thomas and Bertha (Neidhard) M.; A.B., Central High Sch., Phila., 1894; Ph.B., U. of Pa., 1896; m. Aline Skillman Taylor, Dec. 5, 1900; children—Carl Neidhard, Evelyn (wife of Edward Jack Wilbraham, M.C., British Army), Hollinshead Taylor, Roberta, Oliver. Clk. with Peter Wright & Sons, shipping, Phila., 1896, Pa. R.R. Co., 1897, Ervin & Co., brokers, 1899; in partnership with father, R. T. Martin & Co., brokers, 1900-12; organizer firm of Martin & Co., investment bankers, 1913, pres. since 1927 of Martin & Co., Inc.; sec. and treas. Trenton, Bristol & Phila. Street Ry. Co., 1909-15, pres. 1915-35; sec. and treas. Salem & Pennsgrove Traction Co., 1916-21, pres., 1921-33; pres. Pa.-N.J. Ry. Co., 1924-35; v.p. Pa. Joint Stock Land Bank, 1928-35; dir. Better Bus. Bur., 1926-33; mem. governing com. Phila. Stock Exchange, 1920-32; mem. exec. com. Eastern Group, Investment Bankers Assn., 1931. Served as pvt. Light Battery, Pa. Vols., Spanish-Am. War; chmn. citizens com., 3d Federal Res. Dist., Liberty Loan campaign, and mem. Selective Draft Bd., World War. Dir. Phila. Charity Ball Assn. (pres. 1927-32). Mem. Zeta Psi. Republican. Episcopalian. Clubs: Bond, Mask and Wig. Home: Pine Creek Farm, Anselma, Pa. Office: Packard Bldg., Philadelphia, Pa.

MARTIN, Charles Ellison, utilities exec.; b. Carolina, R.I., Feb. 19, 1899; s. Charles Edward and Nellie (Bailey) M.; C.E., Cornell U.,

1921; m. Louise Carr, Sept. 6, 1927; children—Charles Edward II, Shirley Louise. Cadet engr. Pub. Service Gas and Electric Co. of N.J., Newark, N.J., 1921-25; supt. Gardner (Mass.) Gas Fuel and Light Co., 1925-28; mgr. Iron Mountain (Mich.) Gas Co., 1928-30; supt. gas dept. Eastern Shore Pub. Service Co., Cambridge, Md., 1930-32; gen. mgr. Central Pa. Gas Co., Bellefonte, Pa., since 1932, dir. since 1935; pres. Slatington (Pa.) Gas Corpn. since 1937. Mem. Centre Co. (Pa.) Engrs. (pres. since 1939), Am. Gas Assn., Bellefonte (Pa.) Chamber of Commerce. Republican. Protestant. Mason (Shriner). Clubs: Kiwanis (Bellefonte, Pa.; v.p.); University (State Coll., Pa.). Home: 119 W. Linn St. Office: West High St., Bellefonte, Pa.

MARTIN, Christian Frederick, mfr. musical instruments; b. Nazareth, Pa., Sept. 9, 1894; s. Frank Henry and Jennie Otilia (Keller) M.; grad. Nazareth High Sch., 1911; student Perkiomen Sch., 1912; A.B., Princeton U., 1916; m. Daisy Belle Allen, June 23, 1920; children—Frank Herbert, Pamela Susan. With C. F. Martin & Co., Inc., mfrs. guitars, mandolins and ukuleles (business established by great-grandfather, 1833), since 1911; began as apprentice guitar maker; vice-pres. and factory mgr. since 1921. Served as Y.M.C.A. war work sec., 1917-19. Mem. Nazareth Sch. Bd., 1925-37, pres., 1931-37; mem. Easton Area Council, Boy Scouts of America. Trustee Moravian Coll. and Theol. Sem., Bethlehem, Pa.; supt. Nazareth Moravian Sunday Sch. since 1927. Mem. Northampton Co. com. of Pa. Economy League since 1937. Mem. Nat. Assn. of Musical Merchandise Mfrs. (pres. since 1936). Mem. Delta Sigma Rho. Clubs: Nazareth Lions (pres. 1928); Maskinoza Rod and Gun (Bushkill, Pa.). Home: 315 E. Center St. Office: C. F. Martin & Co., Inc., Nazareth, Pa.

MARTIN, Clarence Eugene, lawyer; b. Martinsburg, W.Va., Mar. 13, 1880; s. Morgan W. and Ella Genevieve (Mulligan) M.; LL.B., U. of W.Va., 1899, LL.D., 1933; LL.M., Catholic U. of America, 1901; LL.D., Dickinson, 1933; m. Agnes G. McKenna, Sept. 28, 1904; children—Morgan V., Clarence E. (both lawyers). Admitted to W.Va. bar, 1901, and began practice at Martinsburg; city attorney Martinsburg, 1904-06; member firm Martin & Seibert. W.Va. mem. Conference on Uniform State Laws since 1925; member of West Virginia Judicial Council since 1933; pres. W.Va. Constitutional Conv. to ratify 21st Amendment, 1933. Trustee Catholic U. of America. Mem. Am. Bar Assn. (pres. 1932-33), Am. Soc. Internat. Law (exec. com. 1934-37), Am. Judicature Soc., W.Va. Bar Assn. (pres. 1924), Am. Law Inst., Am. Hist. Assn., Am. Cath. Hist. Assn. (pres. 1927), Am. Acad. Polit. and Social Science. Apptd. Knight Comdr. of St. Gregory by Pope Pius, 1929. Democrat. Clubs: Rotary, Opequon Golf; University (Washington, D.C.). Home: 418 S. Queen St. Office: Peoples Trust Bldg., Martinsburg, W.Va.

MARTIN, Edgar Stanley, editor, educator; b. Gorham, N.Y., Mar. 8, 1873; s. William and Elizabeth (McIntyre) M.; grad. Keuka Coll., N.Y., 1894; N.Y. State Normal Coll., Albany, N.Y., 1898; spl. courses sociology and education univs. of Chicago, Pittsburgh and Ohio State; B.A., Central U., 1901; m. Gertrude Bishop, Dec. 24, 1898; children—Clinton Stanley, Margaret Elizabeth, Ruth Alice. Prin. high sch., Tully, N.Y., 1898-1901; prin. John G. McMynn Sch., Racine, Wis., 1901-10; dir. Washington Park Recreation Center, Pittsburgh, Pa., 1910; sec. Dept. of Recreation, Columbus, O., 1910-11, also commr. Franklin Co. (O.) Council Boy Scouts America; supt. play grounds of D.C., also commr. and scout exec., 1911-15; mem. Nat. Council Boy Scouts of America, 1910-15, sec. editorial board since 1915, nat. dir. of publications and editor of Scouting since 1931. Pres. Am. Swimming Assn., 1923-25; instructor in scoutmastership of Columbia Univ., 1925-28. Member Pi Gamma Mu, Phi Delta, Republican. Methodist. Mason. Clubs: Nat. Arts, Swiss Alpine; National Press (Washington, D.C.). Home: 158 Harrison St., E. Orange, N.J. Office: 2 Park Av., New York, N.Y.

MARTIN, Edward, lawyer, banker; b. Washington Twp., Greene Co., Pa., Sept. 18, 1879; s. Joseph T. and Hannah M. (Bristor) M.; A.B., Waynesburg (Pa.) Coll., 1901; LL.D., Washington and Jefferson Coll.; m. Charity Scott, Dec. 1, 1908; children—Edward, Mary C. Admitted to Pa. bar, 1905, and began practice at Waynesburg; president Dunn Mar Oil & Gas Company, Consumers Fuel Company (Wheeling, W.Va.), Chartiers Discount Company, Inc. (Washington, Pa.); director Citizens National Bank, Washington County (Pa.) Fire Ins. Co.; auditor gén. of Pa., term 1925-29, state treas., term 1929-33. Chmn. Rep. State Com. Served as pvt. Spanish-Am. War and as lt. col., World War; brig. gen. and comdr. 55th Inf. Brig., Pa. N.G. Trustee Waynesburg Coll. Republican. Presbyn. (elder). Mason (33°), Elk. Home: Washington, Pa.

MARTIN, Mrs. Florence Arminta DeLong (Minta Martin); b. Clark Co., Ia., Jan. 11, 1864; d. Andrew Jackson and Alta Myra (Bozarth) DeLong; grad. Afton (Ia.) High Sch., 1881; m. Clarence Y. Martin, Nov. 9, 1882 (died June 1, 1935); 1 son, Glenn Luther. School teacher, Afton, Ia., 1881-82. Actively interested in aviation; adviser and helper to her son, Glenn Martin, pres. Glenn L. Martin Co., airlane mfrs., Baltimore; one of first women to fly; flew with son on China Clipper on his 25th anniversary flight from Newport Beach, Calif., to Avalon, Catalina Island; travels extensively. Republican. Presbyterian. Home: Ambassador Apts., Baltimore, Md.

MARTIN, Francis C., banker; b. New Baltimore, Pa., 1878; s. Solomon B. and Elizabeth B. (Findlay) M.; student Calif. State Teachers' Coll.; m. Agnes Stover, 1903; children—Donald S., Mrs. Agnes Skillen, David. Read law and did court work three yrs.; with United States Nat. Bank, Johnstown, Pa., 1901-12; cashier Dollar Deposit Bank of Johnstown (later Nat. Bank of Johnstown), 1912-23, consolidated with U.S. Nat. Bank of Johnstown, 1923, v.p. and cashier since 1934, director since 1938. Chmn. Citizens' Com. during 1937 Steel Strike, Johnstown. Mem. Johnstown Chamber of Commerce (pres. 1937, 38). Presbyn. (teacher adult Bible class, 16 yrs.). Mason. (Blue Lodge, Council, Commandery, Knights of Constantine, Shriner). Clubs: Shrine, Kiwanis (Johnstown, Pa.) Home: 97 Fourth Ave., Westmont. Office: 216 Franklin St., Johnstown, Pa.

MARTIN, George Clark, med. dir.; b. Conemaugh, Pa., Aug. 10, 1899; s. Dr. George and Mary (Clark) M.; B.S., Washington and Jefferson Coll., Washington, Pa.; M.D., Temple U. Med. Sch., 1928; m. Mary Edna Rector, July 31, 1923; children—Patricia, Mary Olive. Mem. staff Indiana (Pa.) Memorial Hosp. since 1931; co. med. dir., Indiana Co., Pa., since 1935. Indiana Co. Dem. campaign mgr., 1938. Pres. Ind. Co. Med. Soc., 1939. Mem. Am. Med. Assn. of Vienna (Austria), Druids, Phi Kappa Psi, Phi Sigma Mu, Phi Beta Kappa. Democrat. Presbyterian. Mason. Club: Masonic (Indiana, Pa). Address: Franklin St., Clymer, Pa.

MARTIN, George E., physician; b. Volant, Pa., May 20, 1896; s. Joseph Scott and Ella (Weller) M.; B.S., Westminster Coll., New Wilmington, Pa., 1922; M.D., U. of Pittsburgh, 1925; m. Mildred Jones, 1923; children—Evelyn, Joseph. Interne St. Francis Hosp., Pittsburgh, 1925-26; resident physician Tuberculosis League Hosp., Pittsburgh, 1926-35; supt. Pittsburgh Tuberculosis Hosp. since 1935. Served with 12th F.A., U.S. Army, 1917-19; with A.E.F., disch. as sergt. maj. Fellow A.M.A.; mem. Acad. Chest Physicians. Presbyterian. Address: Pittsburgh Tuberculosis Hospital, Pittsburgh, Pa.

MARTIN, Glenn L., airplane manufacturer; b. Macksburg, Iowa, Jan. 17, 1886; s. Clarence Y. and Minta (DeLong) M.; educated Kansas Wesleyan University, hon. D.Sc., 1933; Dr. Engring., University of Md., 1939; unmarried. Began in 1907 to build gliders; designed and built pusher type airplane, 1908, and taught self to fly; established one of the first airplane factories in the U.S., 1909; constructed airplanes of various types, including monoplanes and water aircraft; gave exhibition flights in U.S. and Canada, 1909-16; qualified for F.A.I. Aviators' Certificate, Aug. 9, 1911; holds Aviation Certificate No. 56, and Expert Aviator's Certificate No. 2, Aero Club of America; incorporated Glenn L. Martin Co., Santa Ana, Calif., 1911; moved factory to Los Angeles, 1912; received two medals for over-ocean flight, Newport to Catalina, Calif., 1912 (to which bars were added May 10, 1937, commemorating 25th Anniversary of flight by re-enactment of flight in Martin-built China Clipper); built airplanes for exhibition flying and sport use until 1913, when first order was received from War Department for Model TT, later adopted by Army for training purposes; produced several new models for U.S. Army, and built 24 airplanes for the govts. of Holland and Netherlands East Indies; factory was employing about 150 men constructing aircraft; merged interests with Wright Co., resulting in the Wright-Martin Aircraft Corpn. of New York, 1917; withdrew from Wright-Martin Co., and organized The Glenn L. Martin Co., Cleveland, 1918, designed and built first American designed airplane for Liberty engines and produced Martin bombers for U.S.Army and Navy and mail planes for Post Office (over 440 for Navy). Pres. East End Mgrs. Assn. of Cleveland, 1924-26; dir. Cleveland Chamber of Commerce, 1924-26. Plant relocated at Middle River, Baltimore, 1929; expansions in 1937 and 1939; plant now producing Martin bombers for U.S. and foreign govts. and Martin ocean transport flying boats for over-ocean transport. Pres. and chmn. of bd. The Glenn L. Martin Co. Fellow Royal Aeronautic Soc. London; mem. Nat. Aeronautic Assn.; corr. mem. Lilienthal Soc. for Aeronautical Research; asso. mem. Soaring Soc. of America, Md. Flying Club; mem. Nat. Aeronautic Assn. (Ohio gov., pres. Cleveland Chapter, 1924-26; Md. gov.), Inst. of Aeronautical Sciences (pres., 1936; hon. Fellow since 1937). Trustee Baltimore Assn. Commerce; mem. S.A.E. Wright Bros. Com. Clubs: Los Angeles Athletic, Vermejo (Los Angeles); Chesapeake, Maryland Sportsmen's Luncheon Club; Baltimore Country (Baltimore); Early Birds, Maryland Yacht Club, Annapolis Yacht Club. Presented with Collier Trophy by President Roosevelt for greatest achievement in aeronautics in America in 1932. Delivered Wright Memorial Lecture before Royal Aeronautic Soc., London, 1931. Received Civic Award from Advertising Club of Baltimore for outstanding business achievement during 1937. Delivered Van Rensselaer Lecture before Drexel Inst., Phila., 1938. Home: Ambassador Apts., Canterbury Rd. and 39th St. Office: The Glenn L. Martin Co., Baltimore, Md.

MARTIN, Hershel Ray, professional baseball; b. Birmingham, Ala., Sept. 19, 1909; s. Albert and Jessie May (Davis) M.; diploma high sch., Ponca City, Okla., 1930; student Okla. A. and M. Coll., 1931-32; m. Adelaide Mary Nash, Nov. 19, 1933. Playing professional baseball since 1932; third baseman, Monroe, La., 1932, Springfield, Ill., 1933, Elmira, N.Y., 1934, Bloomington, Ill., 1935, Houston, Tex., 1936; third baseman, Phila. Club., Nat. League, 1937-38; chosen to play on all-star team, Three-I League, 1935, Tex. League, 1936, and Nat. League, at Cincinnati, O., 1938; mgr. Vienna Community Sale; propr. Ridge View Hereford Farm, Vienna, Mo. Baptist. Home: Vienna, Mo. Address: Philadelphia Nat. League Baseball Club, Philadelphia, Pa.

MARTIN, J. Willis, mem. staff emergency Hosp. Address: 185 Prince George St., Annapolis, Md.

MARTIN, James Prangley, manufacturer; b. Lancaster, Pa., Nov. 10, 1880; s. Henry and Alice (Holden) M.; ed. Lancaster Pub. Schs., 1886-92, Millersville State Normal Sch., 1893-94, Drexel Inst., 1900-01; m. Margaret Kreider, Oct. 1, 1902; children—James Kreider, Alice Mary. Began as machinist apprentice, 1896; machinist trade, 3½ yrs., pattern makers trade, 1 yr., draftsman, 2 yrs., salesman, 10 yrs.; organized mfr. brick making machinery, 1919, and since managed same for Lancaster (Pa.) Iron Works, Inc., now vice pres.; dir. Lancaster Brick Co. Invented Martin automatic brick machine; built many brick plants on Hudson River and in New England; developed mixer for concrete, glass, ceramic industries. Served in 11th Pa. Inf. during Spanish-Am. War. Republican. Mem. Reformed Ch. Mem. Artisans Order of Mutual Protection. Club: Hamilton (Lancaster). Home: 356 College Av. Office: Lancaster Iron Works, Inc., Lancaster, Pa.

MARTIN, James Sankey, clergyman; b. Guernsey Co., O., May 22, 1861; s. John and Mary Hannah (McWilliams) M.; A.B., Geneva Coll., Pa., 1887 (first honors), M.A., 1893; D.D., Temple U., 1911; m. Edith Amelia Copeland (A.B., Geneva Coll., 1886), May 21, 1891 (she died December 31, 1925); children—Sloane C., Donald K., Mrs. Mary E. Hathaway Boren; m. 2d, Mrs. Anna George, March 12, 1928. Principal of the Parnassus (Pa.) Academy, 1887-88; professor Latin, rhetoric and mathematics, Geneva Coll., 1889-92; mem. Board of Corporators Geneva Coll.; ordained ministry Ref. Presbyn. Ch., 1893; pastor Newcastle, Pa., 1893-1909; gen. supt. Nat. Reform Assn., Feb. 1, 1909-24; exec. sec. Geneva Coll., Beaver Falls, Pa., since 1924; corr. sec. Geneva Coll. Alumni Assn. since June, 1925. Editor for yrs. The Christian Statesman; editor Ref. Presbyn. Standard, 1896-1912; editor Geneva Alumnus. Chmn. bd. Nat. Reform Assn. Organizer and gen. dir. 2d and 3d World's Christian Citizenship Conf., Portland, Ore., 1913, and Pittsburgh, Pa., 1919. Leader, nation-wide anti-Mormon crusade, 1912-24. Author of many booklets on Christian citizenship; platform speaker. Home: Beaver Falls, Pa.

MARTIN, Jay Roy, mfg. concrete products; b. Collamer, Pa., Sept. 13, 1892; s. Rankin F. and Effie May (Gibson) M.; ed. Stevens Trade Sch., Lancaster, Pa., 1910-13; m. Erva Louise Mount, June 4, 1919; 1 dau., Betty Jane. Engaged in mfg. concrete products as Martin Bros., Inc., Yardville, N.J. since 1913, pres. since 1913; one of founders of Yardville Nat. Bank, dir. since 1925, pres. since 1937; treas. N.J. Farm Show since 1936. Served as dir. Mercer Co. Red. Cross Chapter since 1936. Dir. Mercer Co. Automobile Trade Assn. Treas. Stevens Trade Sch. Alumni Assn. Republican. Presbyn. Mason (K.T., Shriner). Elk. Odd Fellow. Jr.O.U.A.M. Clubs: Sunnybrae Country (Yardville); Mercer County Sportsmans; Engineers (Trenton). Home: 3947 S. Broad St. Office: 4391 S. Broad St., Yardville, N.J.

MARTIN, John Charles, newspaper publisher; b. Hagerstown, Md., Aug. 31, 1882; s. David C. and Anne Catherine (Little) M.; ed. high sch., Hagerstown; m. Alice Wedgwood Pillsbury, Apr. 12, 1909; children—Isabel Wedgwood, Harrison Pillsbury, Edith Curtis, John Stanwood, David Cutter. In machinery business 10 yrs., with Wagner Electric Co., St. Louis, Mo., Westinghouse Electric Co., Pittsburgh, Pa., Allis-Chalmers Co. and Chain Belt Co., Milwaukee; made treas. Public Ledger Co., Phila., 1913, now retired from active business. Republican. Clubs: Union League, Racquet, Huntingdon Valley Country (Phila.); Boca Raton Club (Fla.). Office: Lincoln Liberty Bldg., Philadelphia, Pa.

MARTIN, Joseph Bernard, pres. and owner J. B. Martin Motors, Inc.; b. Newark, N.Y., 1893; s. John and Velista K. (Van Gillewee) M.; m. Marie Verstrate, Oct. 19, 1916; children—Jane Elizabeth, Eleanor Ann. Began as water boy at age of 10, 1903; helped farmers harvest cucumbers for 50 cents a day at age 12; repair work in garage, 1909-11; chauffeur, 1911-12; factory worker, 1912-14; organized, 1916, bicycle and tire shop, Newark, N.Y., moving into larger quarters, 1918, and starting to sell cars in which business continued at Newark, N.Y., handling principal makes, 1918-26; handled Chrysler distribution, Harrisburg, Pa., 1926-39; pres. and owner J. B. Martin Motors, Inc., one of largest garages and service stations in central Pa. since 1929; dir. Capital Bank and Trust Co. Vice-pres. and dir. Internat. Investors Fund System, Inc., Baltimore, Md. Mem. bd. dirs. Harrisburg Chamber of Commerce; mem. Allison Hill Civic Assn. Elk (life). Club: Kiwanis (Harrisburg, Pa.). Home: 102 Park Terrace, Paxtang, Pa. Office: South 15th St., Harrisburg, Pa.

MARTIN, Joseph Henry, newspaper pub.; b. Wilmington, Del., Jan. 10, 1875; s. Peter Francis and Margaret (Bridgman) M.; ed. Wilmington pub. schs.; m. Florence Upton, Dec. 11, 1900; children—Florence (Mrs. John B. France), Joseph Henry. Began as reporter Evening Journal, Wilmington, 1891; with Norfolk (Va.) Virginian, 1893, Norfolk Pilot, 1894-95; city editor, mgr., mng. editor The Sunday Star, Wilmington, 1895-1912, gen. mgr., 1912-18, owner, editor and gen. mgr. since 1918; pres. The Star Pub. Co., pubs. The Star and gen. printers, Wilmington, since 1914; dir. Interstate Amiesite Co., Wilmington since 1924; pres. Colprovia Paving Co., Wilmington, since 1936. Dir. Wilmington Boys' Club. Mem. Del.-Mar.-Va. Press Assn. Home: 907 Broom St. Office: 309 Shipley St., Wilmington, Del.

MARTIN, Kingsley Leverich, engineer; b. Brooklyn, N.Y., June 16, 1869; s. Charles Cyril and Mary Asenath (Read) M.; grad. Poly. Inst. Brooklyn, 1888; M.E., Stevens Inst. Tech., 1892; m. Elizabeth Saxe Johnson, Feb. 2, 1895. Asst. engr. Brooklyn Bridge, 1892-96; engr. in charge Williamsburgh Bridge, 1905; chief engr. Dept. of Bridges, N.Y. City, 1908-09; commr. of bridges, N.Y. City, 1910-11; v.p. The Foundation Co., 1911-13, Am. Writing Paper Co., 1913-15; pres. The Engineer Co. since 1916. Served in 2d Batt. Naval Militia, N.Y., Spanish-Am. War; comdr. of batt., 1911-13. Mem. Am. Soc. M.E. Home: 54 Gates Av., Montclair, N.J. Office: 17 Battery Pl., New York, N.Y.

MARTIN, LeRoy Albert, clergyman; b. Morristown, Tenn., Jan. 15, 1901; s. Burton McMahan and Julia Zona (Haggard) M.; A.B., U. of Chattanooga, Tenn., 1924; S.T.B., Boston U. Sch. of Theology, 1928; M.A., Drew U., Madison, N.J., 1931; m. Ruth Duckwall, Aug. 10, 1927; 1 dau., Julia Carolyn. Instr. of English, Baylor Sch., Chattanooga, Tenn., 1924-25; ordained deacon, 1927, elder, 1928; minister First Methodist Ch., Bristol, Tenn., 1928-30; Grace Methodist Ch., Paterson, N.J., 1932-36, Trinity Methodist Ch., Hackettstown, N.J., 1936-37, First Methodist Ch., Madison, N.J., since 1937. Mem. Newark (N.J.) Annual Conf. of Methodist Ch. Mem. Delta Chi. Methodist. Clubs: Wranglers, Monday (New York); Madison (N.J.) Golf. Address: 22 Madison Av., Madison, N.J.

MARTIN, Luther III, retired business exec.; b. Germantown, Phila., Pa., Sept. 9, 1873; s. Luther and Sarah (Winslow) M.; student Germantown (Pa.) Acad. Prep. Sch., 1885-92; U. of Pa., 1892-96; m. Catherine Abeel Muller, 1895; children—Elizabeth Muller, Catherine A. (dec.), Luther IV (dec.), Winslow (dec.); m. 2d, Lillian Lewis, Dec. 13, 1925. Supt. factory L. Martin & Co., Phila., 1896-1902, firm took over Ebony Color Works, Cincinnati, 1902, and incorporated as The L. Martin Co., for which supt. production, sales mgr., and treas., 1902-05; v.p. and mgr. production Wilckes, Martin, Wilckes Co., New York, 1905-31, when merged with Swan Corpn. for which chmn. bd., 1931-32, until merged with Montsano Chem. Co.; v.p., dir., mgr. sales for U.S. and Europe, United Oil and Natural Gas Products Corpn., Monroe, La., Houston, Tex., and New York, 1919-24; retired 1932. Served in Secret Service during World War and mem. several fund raising coms. for prosecution of the war. Trustee Germantown (Pa.) Acad., U. of Pa. Mem. Gen. Alumni Soc. of U. of Pa. (pres. 1936-38), The Associated Pa. Clubs (pres. 1936), Pilgrims of the U.S., Am. Acad. Polit. and Social Science, S.A.R., Germantown Hist. Soc. Chosen most outstanding and distinguished U. of Pa. man for 1938 by U. of Pa. Club of N.Y. and name inscribed on club's honor cup. Republican. Episcopalian. Clubs: U. of Pa. (New York); Morristown (Morristown, N.J.); Morris Co. Golf (Morristown, N.J.); Guernsey Cattle (Peterboro, N. H.); Cricket (Germantown, Pa.). Pres. Philomathean Soc., Germantown Acad., 1891-92; pres. Class of 1892; v.p. Class, U. of Pa., 1896. Home: Kenelm Farms, Washington Valley, Morristown, N.J.

MARTIN, Mildred Palmer (Mrs. Linton P. Martin), dept. editor on newspaper; b. Phila., Pa., Sept. 24, 1902; d. Edward Carlton and Mathilda Edith (Yarrow) Palmer; grad. Friends Central Sch., 1920; m. C. Harold Cain, Nov. 22, 1920 (died 1923); m. 2d, Linton Martin, June 10, 1927. Began as reviewer motion pictures on Phila. Inquirer, 1926, motion picture editor since 1933. Republican. Episcopalian. Contbr. Radio Digest, Evening Bulletin (Phila.). Home: 269 S. 17th St. Office: Phila. Inquirer, Philadelphia, Pa.

MARTIN, Newton E(lmer), structural steel; b. New Holland, Pa., Sept. 11, 1881; s. Isaac Groff and Kate (Mohler) M.; student pub. schs., New Holland, Pa., 1887-98; m. Cora Sweigert, 1905; 1 daughter, Ethel Virginia. Served a four-year machinist apprenticeship beginning at the age 18; organized N. E. Martin, structural steel plant, Leola, Pa., 1907, and since proprietor; treas. and dir. Enterprise Telephone Co., New Holland, Pa., 1916-33; began development Leola (Pa.) Water Works, 1937, and since proprietor; dir. Leola Nat. Bank. Protestant. Address: Leola, Pa.

MARTIN, Paul, clergyman, educator; b. Ashland, Ky., April 21, 1862; s. Edwin W. and Narcissa (McCurdy) M.; A.B., Princeton, 1882, A.M., 1914; grad. Princeton Theol. Sem., 1886; U. of Halle and U. of Berlin, 1887-88; m. Lucy Gilman Abbott, May 11, 1891 (died March 19, 1921); 1 son, Willard; m. 2d, Catherine M. Reeve, Dec. 16, 1927. Ordained Presbyterian ministry, 1888; pastor Knox Ch., Omaha, 1888-89, Palisades, N.Y., 1890-99; promoter of foreign missions, 1900-02; in lit. work, 1904-05; registrar and sec. of faculty of Princeton Theol. Sem., 1906-32, now emeritus. Independent Republican. Club: Springdale Golf. Collaborator on Index Encyclopædia to Periodical Articles on Religion, 1890-99, 1906; occasional articles for religious press. Address: Princeton, N.J.

MARTIN, Renwick Harper, educator, lecturer; b. Sugartree, O., Sept. 14, 1872; s. John and Mary Hannah (McWilliams) M.; A.B., Geneva Coll., Beaver Falls, Pa., 1895; grad. Ref. Presbyn. Theol. Sem., Pittsburgh, 1899; studied Columbia; D.D., Westminster, 1917; m. Alice Anna Garrett, May 14, 1912; children—Renwick Garrett, Robert Donald (dec.), Mary Alice. Ordained ministry Ref. Presbyn. Ch., 1899; pastor College Hill Ch., Beaver Falls, 1899-1916; sec. trustees Geneva Coll., 1907-16; pres. Geneva Coll., 1916-20 (resigned); lecturer for Nat. Reform Assn., 1920-24 (resigned); dir. Sabbath Observance of Presbyn. Ch., 1924-28 (resigned); pres. Nat. Reform Assn. since 1928; moderator of Synod, Ref. Presbyn. Ch. of N.A., 1932-33; pres. Nat. Temperance and Prohibition Council, 1938. Author: The Day (a manual on the Christian Sabbath), 1933; Six Studies on the Day, 1935. Editor of The Christian Statesman. Home: Beaver Falls, Pa. Office: 209 9th St., Pittsburgh, Pa.

MARTIN, Robert Wayne, artist; b. California, Pa., July 16, 1905; s. Leonard Philip and Ada Pauline (Beasell) M.; ed. Washington and Jefferson Coll., 1924-25; B.Sc. in Art, Edinboro, 1928; ed. Carnegie Inst. Tech., U. of Pittsburgh, Phila. Mus. Sch. Industrial Art, Temple U.; m. Florence C. Curtis, June 27, 1934. Instr. fine arts, Donora (Pa.) High Sch., 1928-32; dir. fine arts, Radnor Secondary Schs., Wayne, Pa., since 1932; exhibited in many large cities in all the states and in leading galleries and mus. of art; rep. in permanent collections of Phila. Art Alliance, Pa. State Coll., and in many pvt. collections; eccles. work, altar pieces, etc., in St. Francis Ch., Rutherfordton, N.C., St. John's, Donora, Pa., St. Thomas', Canonsburg, Pa., Annunciation, Phila. and others. Mem. Nat. Edn. Assn., Pa. State Edn. Assn., Progressive Edn. Assn., Pa. Art Teachers Assn. (vice-pres.), Descendants of the Am. Revolution, Scarab, Beta Xi. Democrat. Episcopalian. Club: Sword (Philadelphia). Home: R.F.D. No. 3, "Ellerslie House" Quakertown, Pa.

MARTIN, Sydney Errington, architect; b. Phila., Pa., Sept. 6, 1883; s. Robert Thomas and Bertha (Neidhard) M.; B.S., U. of Pa., 1908; study in Europe, 1910; m. Margaret

Crozer Fox, Oct. 16, 1915; children—Margaret Crozer, Sydney Errington, Crozer Fox, Harriet. Mem. firm Thomas & Martin, architects, Phila., since 1919. Served as capt., Engrs. Corps, U.S. Army, during World War. Pres. Meadowbrook (Pa.) Sch. Bd., 1930-32. Trustee Lankenau Hosp. since 1924, U. of Pa. since 1937; dir. Southeastern Chapter of Red Cross, 1933-36, Acad. of Fine Arts since 1936, University Museum since 1937. Fellow A.I.A.; trustee Fairmount Park Art Assn. (v.p. since 1936); mem. U. of Pa. Gen. Alumni Soc. (pres. 1934-36); chmn. bd. Sch. of Fine Arts, U. of Pa., since 1937. Republican. Episcopalian. Clubs: Sunnybrook Golf, Rittenhouse. Home: Ridge Pike, Upper Roxborough, Pa. Office: Architects Bldg., Philadelphia, Pa.

MARTIN, Thomas Wesley, pres. Citizens Nat. Bank of Martinsburg; b. Baltimore, Md., Jan. 22, 1873; s. James L. and Sarah J. M.; student pub. schs., Baltimore; married, 1906; children—Thomas Wesley, Helen A. (Mrs. Francis C. Chambers). Became hotel steward, 1889, later dining car steward; now pres. Martinsburg (W.Va.) Hotel Corpn., Citizens Nat. Bank of Martinsburg, Berkeley Woolen Co. (Martinsburg), Martinsburg Clearing House Assn., Martinsburg Bldg. & Loan Assn.; dir. Potomac Light & Power Co. Republican. Mason (Shriner), Elk. Address: Shenandoah Hotel, Martinsburg, W.Va.

MARTIN, William Eli, physician; b. Reisterstown, Md., July 26, 1881; s. William and Rebecca (Fitch) M.; M.D., U. of Md. Med. Coll., 1909; m. Hannah M. Bailey, Feb. 6, 1885; 1 son, William Bailey. Engaged in gen. practice of medicine at Randallstown, Md., continuously since 1909; served as health officer 2d dist., Baltimore Co., since 1934; vice-pres. Randallstown Bank. Mem. Am. Med. Assn., Southern Med. Assn., Med. & Chirurg. Faculty of Md., Baltimore Co. Med. Soc., Phi Chi. Republican. Mason (S.R.). Home: Randallstown, Md.

MARTIN, William Hope, dean and dir.; b. Carlisle, Pa., June 3, 1890; s. William and Sarah Catharine (Morrison) M.; B.A., U. of Me., 1915; M.S., Rutgers U., 1917, Ph.D., 1918; m. Eugenia Mary Rodick, Sept. 11, 1918. Asst. plant pathologist, N.J. Agrl. Expt. Station, 1915-18, asso. plant pathologist, 1919-23, plant pathologist since 1923, dir. of research since 1935, dean and director since June 10, 1939; dir. New Brunswick Trust Co. Served as 2d lt., Air Service, World War. Mem. New Brunswick Bd. of Edn. Fellow A.A.A.S.; mem. Am. Phytopathol. Soc., Potato Assn. America, Sigma Chi, Sigma Xi, Alpha Zeta. Lutheran. Clubs: Rutgers, Union (New Brunswick). Writer numerous articles on plant diseases in scientific jours. Home: 2 Delevan St., New Brunswick, N.J. Address: N.J. Agrl. Experiment Station, New Brunswick, N.J.

MARTINET, Marjorie Dorsey, artist; b. Baltimore, Md., Nov. 3, 1886; d. Oscar Conway and Anna Cora (Walker) M.; ed. private schools and tutors; extensive study of art in museums and galleries of Europe and U.S. ; grad. Md. Inst., 1904; studied Rhinehart Sch. of Sculpture, 1904-05, Pa. Acad. Fine Arts, 1905-10; studied under Wm. M. Chase and Cecelia Beaux; awarded Cresson European Scholarship by Pa. Acad. Fine Arts, 1909, Thouron prize for composition, same, 1909. Instr. drawing, Drexel Inst., Phila., 1908, advanced life class drawing and painting, 1910-11; dir. Martinet Sch. of Art, Baltimore, since 1912. Exhibited Peabody Inst., Pa. Acad Fine Arts, Plastic Club, Art Club of Phila., Sequi-Centennial (one man show) Baltimore Mus. of Art, 1930. Exhibited 49 paintings at Newman Galleries, Phila., 1936; group included portraits, landscapes, character portraits, still life and compositions, including "Spring," "An Autumn Song," "Orange and Gold," "A Spaniard," "The Half Breed," "Chief White Wing," "In Old Seville," "Jim Tree," "A Cowboy," "Wholesale Fish Market, Baltimore," "Japanese Persimmons," "Old Slave Quarters, Gwynn's Falls, Md.", oil painting, was one of 20 selected in 1937 to represent U.S. by jury of National Association of Women Painters and Sculptors for International Exhibition of Women's Art at Toronto, Canada (25 countries exhibiting). Works: The Court Robe, Singing Leaves, Gwynn Falls Winter, Justina Albereda and her Parrot, Enrique, Chestnut Lane in December, Indian Summer Rest, Chief Star Eagle, Kathleen, My Grandmother, Baltimore Harbor. Chmn. art com. of Lizette Woodworth Reese Memorial Assn., Baltimore, for Reese Symbolic Memorial Tablet by Beatrice Fenton, of Phila.; also for Pratt Library, Baltimore, since 1939. Mem. Fellowship Pa. Acad. Fine Arts, Phila. Art Alliance (professional artist mem.), Baltimore Museum of Art Federation of Arts (Washington), Nat. Assn. of Women Painters and Sculptors of New York, Woman's Lit. Club of Baltimore. Home: 4102 Ridgewood Av. Studio: 10 E. Franklin St., Baltimore, Md.

MARTINO, Antonio Pietro, artist; b. Phila., Pa., Apr. 13, 1902; s. Carmen and Clementina (Baranello) M.; ed. Spring Garden Inst., Phila., Pa., Phila. Mus. Sch. Industrial Art; m. Mary J. Hofstetter, June 22, 1927; children—Anthony, Marie Clementina. Has followed profession as artist and painter since 1917; represented in John Wanamaker Collection, Carlisle (Pa.) Museum, Reading (Pa.) Mus., Pa. Acad. Fine Arts, Phila. Water Color Club, and in many pvt. collections; mem. firm Martino Studios, advertising art service, Phila., Pa.; awarded hon. mention, Phila. Sketch Club, 1925, Art Club, 1925; medal Phila. Sketch Club, 1926; J. Francis Murphy Memorial Prize, Nat. Acad. of Design, 1926; bronze medal, Phila. Sesqui-Centennial Expn., 1926; First Hallgarten Prize, Nat. Acad. Design, 1927; Wanamaker Regional Art Purchase Prize, 1934; First Hallgarten Prize, Nat. Acad. Design, 1937; Jennie Sesnan Medal, Pa. Acad. Fine Arts, 1938; purchase recommendation, Va. Mus. Fine Arts, 1938; First Hon. Mention, Annual Exhbn. Da Vinci Alliance, 1938. Asso. mem. Nat. Acad. of Design. Mem. Phila. Water Color Club (dir.), Da Vinci Alliance. Home: 127 N. Gross St., Philadelphia, Pa. Studio: 27 S. 18th St., Philadelphia, Pa.

MARTLAND, Harrison Stanford, physician; b. Newark, N.J., Sept. 10, 1883; s. William Henry and Ida Carlyle (Bucklish) M.; A.B., Western Md. Coll., Westminster, Md., 1901; M.D., Coll. Phys. & Surgs. of Columbia U., 1905; m. Myra Cee Ferdon, Nov. 15, 1910; children—Gloria Ferdon (wife of Edgar Athalston Lawrence, M.D.), Harrison Stanford, Jr. Interne N.Y. City Hosp., 1905-07; pathologist, Russell Sage Inst. of Pathology, N.Y. City, 1907-09; pathologist Newark City Hosp. since 1909; chief med. examiner, Essex Co., N.J., since 1925; prof. forensic medicine, N.Y. Univ. Coll. of Medicine since 1935. Served as 1st lt. to lt. col. Med. Corps, U.S.A., 1917-19; col. Med. Res. since 1925. Trustee Dazian Fund for Med. Research, New York, N.Y. Fellow A.M.A., N.Y. Acad. of Medicine, N.J. Med. Soc. Mem. N.Y. Pathol. Soc. (past pres.). Contbr. more than 50 papers; first description radium poisoning; first description of punch drunk; contbr. chapters to books and med. cycs. Home: 180 Clinton Av. Office: City Hospital, Newark, N.J.

MARTS, Arnaud Cartwright, financial counsellor, univ. pres.; b. Reeds Corners, N.Y., Oct. 9, 1888; s. Rev. William G. and Irene A. (Cartwright) M.; prep. edn., East Aurora (N.Y.) High Sch., 1902-05; A.B., Oberlin Coll., 1910; LL.D., Hillsdale Coll., 1936; m. Ethel A. Daggett, Oct. 16, 1920. Formerly identified with boys' work, Pittsburgh, Pa.; became connected with Standard Life Ins. Co., Pittsburgh, 1914, elected v.p. and dir., 1917; served as asso. nat. dir. $18,000,000 campaign for War Camp Community Service, World War, also as mem. Nat. Com. of 35 in charge United War Work Campaign for $175,000,000; after close of the war continued work of raising funds for philanthropic purposes; an organizer and pres. Marts & Lundy, Inc., financial counsellors for philanthropic institutions, New York; firm has raised over $200,000,000 for colleges, chs., hosps. and other agencies; pres. of Bucknell U. since 1935; trustee Crozer Sem.; dir. Am. Mission to Lepers. Mem. S.A.R., Sons of Union Vets. of Civil War, Phi Beta Kappa. Conglist. Clubs: Town Hall, Advertising, University (New York). Contbr. to mags. Home: Plainfield, N.J. Office: Lewisburg, Pa.; and 521 5th Av., New York, N.Y.

MARVEL, N. Clyde, attending surgeon South Baltimore Gen. Hosp.; asso. surgeon Mercy Hosp.; visiting surgeon Church Home and Infirmary, St. Joseph's and Md. Gen. hosps. Address: 1301 St. Paul St., Baltimore, Md.

MARVIN, Dwight Edwards, clergyman, author; b. Greenwich, Washington Co., N.Y., Feb. 22, 1851; s. Rev. Uriah and Margaret J. (Stevens) M.; grad. Alexander Inst., White Plains, N.Y., 1869; grad. Auburn Theol. Sem., 1880; studied Union Theol. Sem., 1881; Ph.D., Franklin Coll., New Athens, O., 1900; m. Ida N. Whitman, Sept. 17, 1874; children—Charles Ingalls, Caroline Whitman, Dwight Marvin, Rowland Whitman (dec.). Ordained Congl. ministry, 1882; pastor 1st Ch., East Albany, N.Y., 1881-84, Plymouth Ch., Utica, 1884-88, 1st Ch., Germantown, Phila., 1888-1900, Flatbush Presbyn. Ch., Brooklyn, 1902-10. Mem. Folk-Lore Soc. (Eng.), Sons Am. Revolution, Order Founders and Patriots of America. Republican. Author: The Christman, 1908; Professor Slagg of London, 1908; The Church and Her Prophets, 1909; The Harksborough Committee, 1915; Fireside Prayers, 1921; Sunset Thoughts, 1921; The Antiquity of Proverbs, 1922; The Passing of the Caravans, 1924; The Wonderful City, 1924; The Castle of the Soul, 1924; The Chariot of God, 1925; The Wings of Time, 1929; Knowing God, 1931; Devotional Lyrics and Other Poems, 1933; In the Splendor of His Presence, 1934; Vanished Barriers, 1935; Abba Father, 1936; When and Where, 1937; Home and the Children, 1937; The Chariot-Stars, 1936; When Christ Was Born, 1937; Abide With Me, 1938; also The Looming Cross; Cloud Islands; Highlands of the Sky; Historic Child Rhymes. Compiler: Curiosities in Proverbs, 1916. Owner of a notable library pertaining to folk-lore. Home: 55 Fernwood Rd., Summit, N.J.

MARVIN, Walter S(ands), banker, broker; b. Brooklyn, N.Y., June 24, 1889; s. Charles A. and Mabel S. (Metcalf) M.; student, Williams Coll., 1913; m. Jean Murray, May 26, 1917; children—Murray Sands, John Howland, Matthew. Reporter New York Sun, 1911-1915; stock salesman Am. Philippine Co., 1915-16; bond salesman Hemphill, Noyes & Co., 1916-22, partner, 1922-29; pres. Curtiss-Wright Airports Corpn., 1928-29; partner Foster, McConnell & Co., 1931, Foster, Marvin & Co. since 1932. Served as 1st lieutenant General Staff, U.S. Army, Washington, D.C., 1917-19. Trustee Montclair Art. Mus.; mem. budget com. Montclair Community Chest. Mem. Pilgrims Soc., S.A.R., Chi Psi. Republican. Conglist. Clubs: Williams, Broad Street (New York); Montclair Golf; Aviation Country. Home: 184 Upper Mountain Av., Montclair, N.J. Office: 2 Wall St., New York, N.Y.

MARVIN, Walter Taylor, coll. prof.; b. New York, Apr. 28, 1872; s. Walter Taylor and Eliza Rowland (Jarvis) M.; A.B., Columbia, 1893, grad. student, 1895-97; student U. of Jena, 1893-94, Gen. Theol. Sem., New York, 1894-95, univs. of Halle and Bonn, 1897-98; Ph.D., Bonn, 1898; m. Adelaide Camilla Hoffman, Apr. 14, 1903; children—Dorothy Hope, Hoffman. Asst. in Columbia, 1898-99; instr. and asst. prof., Adelbert Coll., Cleveland, 1899-1905; preceptor, Princeton, 1905-10; prof. philosophy, Rutgers U., since July 1, 1910, dean of faculty, 1921-25, dean Coll. of Arts and Sciences since 1925. Member of American Philosophical Society, Am. Psychological Association. Club: Century. Author: Die Giltigkeit unserer Erkenntnis der objektiven Welt, 1898; Syllabus of an Introduction to Philosophy, 1899; Introduction to Systematic Philosophy, 1903; A First Book in Metaphysics, 1912; The History of European Philosophy, 1917. Co-Author: The New Realism, 1912. Address: New Brunswick, N.J.

MARX, Harry S., lawyer; b. Coshocton, O., Aug. 16, 1878; s. Henry and Frances P. (Stockman) M.; student Northwestern U. Law Sch., 1902; m. Grace A. McGowen, 1906. Began practice at Chicago; moved to New York, 1909, to enter law dept. Wells Fargo & Co., express; gen. atty. same, 1914 until organization, 1918, of Am. Ry. Express Co. of which was gen. counsel, 1923-29; v.p. and gen. counsel Ry. Express Agency, Inc., of Delaware; vice-pres., gen. counsel and dir. Ry. Express Agency, Inc., of Calif. and of Va., Railway Express Motor Transport, Inc.; v.p. and dir. Citizens First Nat. Bank & Trust Co., Ridgewood, N.J.; trustee Fidelity Liquidating Trust, Ridgewood; dir. and mem. exec. and finance coms. Expressmen's Mutual Life Insurance Co. (New York). Mem. Am. Bar Assn., New York Law Inst., Assn. Practitioners before Interstate Commerce Commn., Ohio Soc., Chamber of Commerce, state of N.Y. Republican. Christian Scientist. Clubs: Traffic, Economic (New York); Ridgewood Country. Home: Ridgewood, N.J. Address: 230 Park Av., New York, N.Y.

MARZULLI, Olindo, journalist; b. Italy, Sept. 29, 1882; s. Frank R. and Filomena (Napoliello) M.; came to U.S. 1887, naturalized 1905; A.B., Sessa Aurunca, Caserta, Italy, 1905; ed. L.I. Med. Coll., Brooklyn, 1905-08, N.J. Law Sch., Newark, 1910-11; m. Maria Maccarrone, Apr. 27, 1916; children—Francis Nicholas, Olindo Quentin, Jr. Engaged in pub. Il Tribuno, 1908-10; pub. La Tribuna, 1916-22; pub. New Jersey Italian-American since 1928; pres. Italian-American Pub. Co., Liberal Pub. Co. Served as mem. N.J. Ho. of Assembly, 1918. Mem. and pres. Newark Tax Bd., 1933-37. Pres. Italian-American Civic Union; mem. Dante Alighieri Soc. Republican. Home: 408 Clifton Av. Office: 157 Verona Av., Newark, N.J.

MASLAND, Frank Elmer, Jr., pres. C. H. Masland & Sons; b. Phila., Pa., Dec. 8, 1895; s. Frank E. and Mary E. (Gossler) M.; student Dickinson Coll., Carlisle, Pa.; m. Mary Virginia Sharp, Jan. 2, 1918; children—Frank Elmer III, David S. Pres. C. H. Masland & Sons, Carlisle, Pa.; pres. Carlisle (Pa.) Homes Co. Dir. Carlisle Hosp., Carlisle and Pa. State Y.M.C.A. Com. Mem. Nat. Assn. of Mfrs. of U.S.A. Clubs: Kiwanis (Carlisle, Pa.); Penn Athletic. Home: R.D. 6. Office: Spring Rd., Carlisle, Pa.

MASON, Alpheus Thomas, univ. prof.; b. Snow Hill, Md., Sept. 18, 1899; s. Herbert William and Emma Leslie (Hancock) M.; A.B., Dickinson Coll., Carlisle, Pa., 1920; A.M., Princeton, 1921, Ph.D., 1923; m. Christine Este Gibbons, June 12, 1934; 1 dau., Louise Este, Proctor fellow Princeton U., 1922-23; asst. prof. polit. science, Trinity Coll. (now Duke U.), 1923-25; asst. prof. politics, Princeton U., 1925-30, asso. prof., 1930-36, prof. since 1936; lecturer in constl. law, Mercer Beasley Sch. of Law, Newark, N.J., 1928-32; lecturer Liberal Summer Sch., Cambridge, England, 1935; mem. of Inst. for Advanced Study, Princeton, N.J., 1938. Mem. bd. of editors Am. Polit. Science Rev. since 1937. Mem. com. of experts to make survey of adminstrn. and expenditures of State of N.J. govt., 1932. Mem. Am. Polit. Science Assn., Eugene Field Literary Soc., Sigma Alpha Epsilon. Awarded grants-in-aid by Social Science Research Council for study of Mr. Justice Brandeis, 1933, and for study of trade unions and the state in London, 1935. Presbyterian. Clubs: Nassau (Princeton); Princeton (N.Y. City); Authors (London, England). Author: Organized Labor and the Law, 1925; Brandeis: Lawyer and Judge in the Modern State, 1933; The Brandeis Way: A Case Study in the Workings of Democracy, 1938. Contbr. polit. and legal articles to jours. Home: 8 Edgehill St., Princeton, N.J.

MASON, Clarence Eugene, Jr., clergyman; b. Charlotte, N. C., Nov. 12, 1904; s. Clarence E. and Blonde (Capps) M.; A.B., Wheaton Coll., Ill., 1924; ed. Moody Bible Inst., summer 1925; Th.B., Dallas (Tex.) Theol. Sem., 1927, Th.M., same, 1927; m. Lois J. McShane, Aug. 1, 1928. Engaged as summer supply and in gospel quartet work, summers 1924-26; ordained to ministry Bapt. Ch., 1928; pastor, Weston Memorial Bapt. Ch., Phila., Pa., 1927-34; prof., Phila. Sch. of the Bible since 1928; pastor Chelsea Bapt. Ch. since 1934; prof. and dean, Atlantic City Bible Inst. since 1935; dir. Boardwalk Bible Confs. in Atlantic City, Ocean City, and Wildwood, summers, since 1935; Mem. Council, China Inland Mission. Dir. Phila. Fundamentalists since 1932. Mem. Wheaton Coll. Alumni Assn., Dallas Theol. Sem. Alumni Assn. Baptist. Home: 49 N. Jackson Av., Atlantic City, N.J.

MASON, Edgar Dwight, advertising; b. Pullman, Ill., July 27, 1888; s. Clayton C. and Carrie Elizabeth (Richards) M.; student law, LaSalle U., student sales and advertising, Scranton Correspondence Sch.; m. Norma Belle Kimberlin, Oct. 1908; children—John Edgar, Edgar Dwight, Jr., Norma Dorothy. Began as sec. with Westinghouse Electric Co., Pittsburgh, 1907, later with Carnegie Steel Co.; independent sales counsel; asst. dir. of sales Trans-continental Oil Co., vice-pres. and dir. Albert P. Hill Co., Inc., since 1923; author of books and articles on planned selling and advertising. Home: 1024 Davis Av. Office: 233 Oliver Av., Pittsburgh, Pa.

MASON, Francis Claiborne, author, asso. prof. of English; b. Onancock, Va., Oct. 4, 1900; s. Crowder W. and Emma L. (Boggs) M.; A.B., U. of Va., 1921, A.M., same, 1922, Ph.D., same, 1929; A.M., Harvard U., 1924; m. Eloise Copper, Sept. 12, 1925. Instr. Maury High Sch., Norfolk, Va., 1922-23, summers at William and Mary Coll. and U. of Va.; asst. prof. of English, Gettysburg Coll., 1925-35, asso. prof. since 1935. Mem. Tau Kappa Epsilon, Phi Beta Kappa. Author: (verse) This Unchanging Mask, 1929. Contbr. verse to lit. mags. Home: Gettysburg, Pa.

MASON, F(rancis) van Wyck, novelist; b. Boston, Mass., Nov. 11, 1901; s. Francis Payne and Ermengarde Arville (Coffin) M.; student Berkshire Sch., Sheffield, Mass., 1919-20; B.S., Harvard, 1924; m. Dorothy Louise Macready, of New York City, Nov. 26, 1927; children—F. van Wyck, II, Robert Ashton. Began as importer, 1925; pres. and treas. Van Wyck Inc.; pres. Van Wyck Mason & Co., Inc.; author since 1928. Served as 2d lt. of Interpreters, U.S. Army, with A.E.F. 1918-19; sergt. Squadron A, 101st Cav., N.Y. Nat. Guard, 1925-29; 1st lt. F.A., Md. Nat. Guard, 1930-33. Decorated Medaille de Sauvetage. Mem. Loyal Legion. Republican. Clubs: Harvard (New York); Maryland (Baltimore); Royal Bermuda Yacht (Hamilton, Bermuda). Author: Seeds of Murder, Yellow Arrow Murders, 1930; Vesper Service Murders, Shanghai Bund Murders, 1931; Sulu Sea Murders, Budapest Parade Murders, 1932; Washington Legation Murders, 1934; Seven Seas Murders, Murder in the Senate (under name of Goffrey Coffin); co-author Helen Brawner), 1935; Spider House, Captain Nemesis, Forgotten Fleet Mystery (with A.H. Young O'Brien), 1936; Castle Island Case, Hong Kong Airbase Murders, 1937; Caird Carter Murders, Singapore Exile Murders, Three Harbours, 1938. Contbr. to Writer Mag. Home: Riderwood, Md.; (summer) Nantucket, Mass.

MASON, George Marvin, lawyer; b. Grand Valley, Pa., Jan. 14, 1875; s. Benjamin and Martha Jane (Lobdell) M.; student Springbord (Pa.) High Sch., 1891-94; m. Mary L. Gross, Mar. 12, 1910; 1 son, John B. Admitted to Pa. bar, 1898, and since practiced at Erie; referee in bankruptcy, 1922-26; dep. atty. gen., Pa., 1931-35. Mem. Perry Memorial Commn. since 1931. Mem. Y.M.C.A., Erie Social Hygiene Assn. Republican. Methodist. Mason (32°, Scottish Rite). Home: 471 Arlington Rd. Office: 412 Marine Bank Bldg., Erie, Pa.

MASON, James Henry III, surgeon; b. Atlantic City, N. J., Nov. 14, 1893; s. James Henry and Lizzie (Frambes) M.; student Atlantic City (N.J.) High Sch., 1908-12; M.D., Jefferson Med. Coll., Phila., Pa., 1918; m. Violet Shreve, Dec. 27, 1920; children—James Henry IV, Richard French, Barbara Jane, Joseph Shreve. Began practice as physician and surgeon, Atlantic City, N.J., 1918; interne Atlantic City Hosp., 1918-20, asst. surgeon, 1920-31, chief surg. staff since 1932; v.p. Mason Co., Inc., wholesale grocers, Atlantic City, since 1925. Served as private, M.C., U.S. Army, 1918. Fellow Am. Coll. Surgeons; mem. Founders Group of Am. Bd. of Surgery, Atlantic Co. Med. Soc. (pres. since 1938), Phi Alpha Sigma, Alpha Omega Alpha. Republican. Methodist. Mason (32°). Club: Kiwanis (Atlantic City, N.J.). Home: 5501 Atlantic Av. Office: 1616 Pacific Av., Atlantic City, N.J.

MASON, J(ohn) Alden, anthropologist; b. Germantown, Phila., Pa., Jan. 14, 1885; s. William Albert and Ellen Louise (Shaw) M.; A.B., Central High Sch., Phila., 1903, U. of Pa., 1907; post-grad. work U. of Pa., 1907-10; Ph.D., U. of Calif., 1910-11, research fellow, 1916; m. Florence Roberts, Dec. 23, 1921; 1 son, John Alden. Asst. curator of Mexican and S. Am. archæology, Field Mus. of Natural History, Chicago, 1917-24, Mexican archæology, Am. Mus. of Natural History, New York, 1924-25; curator sect. Am. archæology and ethnology, Univ. Mus., Phila., since 1926. Del. from U. of Pa. to Internat. Sch. of Mexican Archæology and Ethnology, 1911-13; mem. Porto Rican Insular Survey, 1914-15; mem. ethnol. and archæol. expdn. to Utah, Calif., Mexico, Can., Porto Rico, Ariz., Colombia, Tex., Guatemala. Fellow A.A.A.S.; mem. Am. Anthrop. Assn. (council), Am. Ethnol. Assn., Am. Folk-Lore Soc. (council), Soc. Am. Archæalogy (vice-pres. 1938), Société des Américanistes (Paris), Soc. Pa. Archæology (pres. 1929, 30), Archæol. Soc. of Del., Phila. Anthropol. Soc., Am. Mus. Natural History, Sigma Xi; hon. mem. Sociedad de Geografia e Historia de Guatemala. Club: Explorers' (New York). Author: The Ethnology of the Salinan Indians, 1912; The Mutsun Dialect of Costanoan, 1916; The Language of the Salinan Indians, 1917; Tepecano, a Language of Western Mexico, 1918; Archæology of Santa Marta, Colombia, 1931, 1936; etc. Home: Berwyn, Pa. Address: University Museum, Philadelphia, Pa.

MASON, Lois McShane (Mrs. Clarence E. Mason, Jr.), religious edn.; b. Kansas City, Mo., May 24, 1904; d. Lewis L. and Lorena (Ellis) McShane; A.B., Wheaton (Ill.) Coll., 1925; student Moody Bible Inst., Chicago, 1925-27, U. of Chicago Grad. Sch., summer 1927; m. Clarence E. Mason, Jr., Aug. 1, 1928. Prof. of history, Wheaton Coll., 1927-28; served with husband in his pastorates; prof. of Christian edn., Phila. Sch. of the Bible since 1931, Atlantic City Bible Inst. since 1937; speaker; councillor various young people's conferences in East. Mem. Wheaton Coll. Alumni Assn. Baptist. Home: 49 N. Jackson Av., Atlantic City, N.J.

MASON, Mary Stuard Townsend, artist; b. Zanesville, O., Mar. 21, 1886; d. Charles Edwin and Jessie Fremont (Easton) M.; ed. Leachwood Sch., Norfolk, Va., Md. Inst. of Art, and Pa. Acad. of Fine Arts; m. William Clark Mason, Dec. 22, 1909; children—Mary Kathleen (Mrs. Henry Lea Hudson), William Douglas. Works: "Blue and Gold," permanent collection, Fellowship Pa. Acad. Fine Arts, 1934. Mem. bd. dirs. Norfolk Mus. of Arts and Sciences. Fellow Pa. Acad. of Fine Arts; mem. Southern States Art League, Phila. Art Alliance. Republican. Episcopalian. Clubs: Cosmopolitan (New York); Cosmopolitan, Phila. Cricket (Phila.); Phila. Country. Home: Valley Spring House, Chestnut Hill, Philadelphia, Pa.

MASON, S. Blount, Jr., ins. exec.; b. Richmond, Va., Oct. 23, 1881; s. S. Blount and Amanda Gregory (Enders) M.; student Woodbury Forest, Orange, Va., 1898-1900, Washington and Lee U., Lexington, Va., 1902; m. Mary Montgomery Wylie, Nov. 15, 1911. File clk. U.S. Fidelity & Guaranty Co., Baltimore, Md., 1903-04, and successively asst. supt. burglary claims, asst. supt casualty claims; supt. casualty claims, 1919-23, v.p. since 1923. Mem. Order of Cincinnati, S.R., Sigma Chi. Democrat. Episcopalian. Clubs: Maryland, Elkridge Hunt (Baltimore, Md.). Home: 4306 Rugby Rd. Office: U.S. Fidelity & Guaranty Co., Baltimore, Md.

MASON, Thomas William, asso. prof. chemistry; b. Wilkes-Barre, Pa., Jan. 30, 1884; s. George E. and Elizabeth R. (Frear) M.; B.S., Pa. State Coll., 1908, M.S., same, 1912; m. Ruth E. Carrel, Sept. 9, 1909; children—George Morton, Thomas William, Jr. Instr. chemistry, Mich. State Coll., 1908-09; prof. chemistry, St. Olaf Coll., 1909-10; instr. chemistry, Pa. State Coll., 1911-15, asst. prof. chemistry, 1915-21, asso. prof. analytical chemistry since 1921. Served in Pa. N.G. Fellow Am. Inst. of Chemists, Inst. of Am. Genealogy; mem. Am. Chem. Soc., Am. Philatelic Soc., Am. Mus. Natural History, Delta Upsilon, Alpha Chi Sigma, Phi Lambda Upsilon. Republican. Baptist. Mason (K.T.). Home: 135 W. Prospect Av., State College, Pa.

MASON, W. H.; pres. Keystone Mfg. Co. Address: Elkins, W.Va.

MASON, Warren Perry, physicist; b. Colorado Springs, Colo., Sept. 28, 1900; s. Edward Luther and Kate (Sagendorph) M.; B.S. in E.E., U. of Kan., Lawrence, Kan., 1921; M.A., Columbia U., 1924, Ph.D., 1928; m. Evelyn Stuart McNally, May 10, 1929; 1 dau., Penelope Evelyn. Engr., Bell Telephone Labs., since 1921; physicist and supervisor specializing in sound and elec. wave propagation and piezoelectric crystals and their industrial applications, Bell Telephone Labs., New York, since 1927. Served as private, U.S. Marine Corps, Aug.-Nov. 1918. Fellow Acoustical Soc. of America; mem. Phys. Soc. of America, Inst. Radio Engrs., Sigma Xi, Tau Beta Pi. Clubs: Torch of America (Essex Branch, Newark, N.J.); Deer Lake Assn. (Boonton, N.J.); East Orange Badminton, (pres. since 1936), East Orange Tennis (East Orange, N.J.). Author 12 scientific papers dealing with sound and elec. wave propagation and piezoelectric crystals. Holder over 50 patents on telephone apparatus, equipment. Home: 50 Gilbert Pl., West Orange, N.J. Office: 463 West St., New York, N.Y.

MASSA, Frank, electro-acoustic engr.; b. Boston, Mass., April 10, 1906; s. Ernest A. and Mary R. (Onorati) M.; B.S., Mass. Inst. Tech., 1927, M.Sc., same, 1928; m. Georgiana M. Galbraith, June 27, 1936; 1 son, Frank, Jr. Began as jr. engr., General Electric Co., Lynn, Mass., 1927; engr. in research and development on phonographs and loud speakers, Victor Talking Machine Co., Camden, N.J., 1928-29; electro-acoustic engr., RCA Mfg. Co. since 1930; developed many instruments and apparatus in field electro-acoustics; holder various patents and applications; qualified acoustic expert in ct. patent litigation. Fellow Acous. Soc. America. Asso. mem. Inst. Radio Engrs. Swope Fellow at Mass. Inst. Tech., 1927. Roman Catholic. Club: Technology (Philadelphia). Co-author (with H. F. Olsen), Applied Acoustics, 1934, 2d edit., 1939 (first Am. engring. textbook on sound). Contbr. many articles to sci. jours. Home: 111 Chestnut St., Audubon, N.J. Office: RCA Mfg. Co., Inc., Camden, N.J.

MASSINGHAM, Sherman, wholesale; b. Pittsburgh, Pa., Sept. 1, 1867; s. William A. and Rebecca M.; grad. Pittsburgh High Sch., 1861; m. Agnes Boyce, Apr. 23, 1898; children—Sherman 2d, Richard, Ruth, Betty, Esther. With George A. Kelly Co., wholesale druggists, 1881-1901, beginning as office boy with Shipley, Massingham Co., wholesale druggists since 1901, now pres; pres. Refrigeration and Equipment Co. Democrat. Episcopalian. Mason. Club: Rotary of Pittsburgh. Home: 1743 Crafton Boul. Office: 951 Penn Av., Pittsburgh, Pa.

MASSOL, Merwin Browne, magazine publishing; b. Los Gatos, Calif., Nov. 6, 1892; s. Fenelon and Angelia (Maynard) M.; student Santa Clara (Calif.) High Sch., 1908-11; m. Edith Larson, June 7, 1919; 1 son, John Fenelon. With Oral Hygiene, Inc., pubs. dental jours., since Aug. 1, 1916, successively as service mgr., business mgr., publisher, and since 1937 pres.; pres. and dir. Oral Hygiene Internat., Inc., Dental Digest, Inc. Democrat. Club:

Pittsburgh Athletic Assn. Home: Comanche Rd., Brookside Farms. Office: 1005 Liberty Av., Pittsburgh, Pa.

MAST, Samuel Ottmar, biologist; b. Washtenaw Co., Mich., Oct. 5, 1871; s. G. F. and Beata (Staebler) M.; certificate, State Normal Coll., Ypsilanti, Mich., 1897, M.Pd., 1912; B.S., U. of Mich., 1899; Ph.D., Harvard, 1906; investigator, Johns Hopkins, 1907-08; m. Grace Rebecca Tennent, 1908; children—Louise Rebecca, Elisabeth Tennent, Margaret Tennent. Instr. and prof. biology, Hope Coll., 1899-1908; asso. prof. biology and prof. botany, Goucher Coll., Baltimore, 1908-11; asso. prof. and prof. zoölogy, Johns Hopkins, since 1911, head of dept. of zoölogy and dir. zoöl. lab. since 1938. Cartwright prize, Columbia, 1909. Fellow A.A. A.S.; mem. Am. Soc. Zoölogists, Am. Physiol. Soc., Am. Soc. Naturalists, Academy of Science, Philadelphia, Phi Beta Kappa, Sigma Xi. Author: The Structure and Physiology of Flowering Plants, 1907; Light and the Behavior of Organisms, 1911; Motor Response to Light in the Invertebrate Animals, 1936; Factors Involved in the Process of Orientation of Lower Organisms in Light; also numerous papers in scientific jours. Home: 415 Woodlawn Rd., Roland Park, Baltimore, Md.

MASTEN, Fred Church; b. Canfield, O., Feb. 20, 1873; s. Landon and Harriet (Santee) M.; grad. Canfield High Sch., 1888; student North Eastern Ohio Normal Coll., 1888-92; m. Lulu Bell Ryan, Mar. 23, 1898; children—Mary Isabel (Mrs. Charles Love Ridall), Jean Santee (Mrs. William Brown Paul), Fred Church. Railroad clerk C.C.C.&St.L. R.R., 1893-98; with A. E. Masten & Co., mems. N.Y. Stock Exchange, Pittsburgh, 1894-34, successively as clerk, 1898-1906, junior partner, 1906-22, senior partner, 1922-34; retired May 23, 1934; dir. Washington Oil Co., Taylorstown Natural Gas Co. Mem. Am. Inst. Mining and Metall. Engrs. Republican. Mason (K.T.). Address: 723 Hastings St., Pittsburgh, Pa.

MASTER, Henry Buck, church moderator; b. Elizabeth, N.J., Oct. 28, 1871; s. George Buck and Esther Maria (Coxe) M.; A.B., Princeton, 1895, A.M., 1897; B.D., Princeton Theol. Sem., 1898; D.D., Hanover Coll., 1917, Lafayette Coll., 1930; LL.D., James Millikin U. and Dubuque univs., 1922; Litt.D., Coll. of Emporia, Kan., 1928; m. Lucy Olmsted, Oct. 21, 1902; children—William Olmsted, John Redman Coxe, Henry B., George Olmsted (dec.). Ordained Presbyn. ministry, 1898; pastor's asst., 1st Ch., Buffalo, N.Y., 1898-1900; acting pastor, same, 1900-03; pastor 1st Ch., Ft. Wayne Ind., 1905-19; gen. sec. Board of Pensions, Presbyterian Ch. in U.S.A., 1919-37, mem. of Board and chairman of investment committee since 1937. Initiated creation and operation of Service Pension Plan in Presbyn. Chs. in U.S.A.; mem. Layman's Com. which raised $15,000,000 fund to cover accrued liabilities. Moderator Gen. Assembly of the Presbyn. Ch. in U.S.A., Syracuse, N.Y., 1936. Y.M.C.A. sec. in France, 1918; in charge hut at Gievres 4 mos.; transferred to entertainment work; attached to Field Hosp. 3, during St. Mihiel drive. American secretary Alliance Ref. Chs. Throughout the World Holding the Presbyterian System; v.p. Alumni Assn., Princeton Theol. Sem.; hon. mem. Lawton-Wayne Post Spanish War Veterans. Republican. Mason (32°, past grand master Emanuel Chapter Rose Croix). Clubs: Princeton, University, Union League, Midday (Phila.); Princeton, City (New York); Nassau (Princeton). Home: Devon, Pa.

MASTERS, Frank M., consulting engr.; b. Meyersdale, Pa., June 18, 1883; s. Clarendon G. and Eliza (Beachley) M.; student Mercersburg (Pa.) Acad. and Cornell U.; m. Margaret Wilson, Feb. 14, 1925; children—Frank M., III, Margaret Ann. Asst. engr. with Ralph Modjeski, 1904-14; cons. engr. in pvt. practice, 1914-17; partner Modjeski & Masters, Harrisburg, since 1919; dir. Pa. Power and Light Co. Served as maj., U.S. Army, in charge Phila. Ordnance Dist., 1917-19. Dir. Harrisburg Symphony Soc. Mem. Am. Soc. for Testing Materials, Am. Soc. C.E., Am. Ry. Engring. Assn.,

Am. Inst. Steel Constrn., Engrs. Soc. of Pa., Am. Concrete Inst., Franklin Inst., A.A.A.S., Chamber of Commerce, Pa. Soc. of N.Y. Clubs: Engrs. and Architects' of Louisville (hon. mem.); Harrisburg Country, Pendennis (Louisville, Ky.); Boston (New Orleans). Wrote several tech. articles. Home: River Rd., R.D. 2. Office: State St. Bldg., Harrisburg, Pa.

MASTERS, Harry Gail, dir. elementary edn.; b. Fayette City, Pa., Mar. 11, 1881; s. George Downer and Jane (Sherman) M.; ed. Southwestern State Normal Sch., California, Pa., 1904-07; B.Sc., U. of Pittsburgh, 1923, A.M., 1930; student Columbia U., 1920; m. Elizabeth Perry, Nov. 24, 1909. Employed as prin., Pittsburgh, Pa., 1907-30, asst. in personnel dept. Bd. Edn., 1930-32, dir. elementary edn., Pittsburgh, Pa., since 1932. Life mem. Nat. Edn. Assn., Pa. State Edn. Assn.; mem. Am. Assn. Sch. Adminstrs., Phi Delta Kappa. Republican. Methodist. Mason (32°). Home: 2717 Broadway Av., Pittsburgh, Pa. Office: Board of Edn. Bldg., Pittsburgh, Pa.

MASTERS, Harry V(ictor), college pres.; b. Warren, O., Dec. 2, 1902; s. Heman Wesley and Anna (Summers) M.; A.B., Western Union Coll., LeMars, Ia., 1924; A.M., Ia. State U., 1925, Ph.D., same, 1927; m. Veerah Jones, Dec. 20, 1926; children—Thomas Lee, Jane Kathryn. Supervisor intermediate grades and jr. high schs., Hibbing, Minn., 1927-29; prof. edn. and asso. dir. Bur. of Research, Washington State Normal Sch., Bellingham, Wash., 1929-33; supt. Training Sch., O. Univ. 1933-36; dean Coll. of Edn., Drake U., 1936-38; pres. Albright Coll., Reading, Pa., since 1938. Mem. council local chapter Boy Scouts. Mem. 1939 Community Chest Finance Com. Mem. Council W.P.A. Emergency Adult Edn. for Berks Co. Div. Mem. Nat. Edn. Assn., Nat. Soc. for Study of Edn., Am. Edn. Research Assn., Kappa Delta Pi, Phi Delta Kappa. Republican. Mem. Evang. Ch. Mason (32°). Clubs: Rotary, Wyomissing, Torch. Contbr. ednl. journs. Home: 1601 Palm Av., Reading, Pa.

MATES, James Wilson, educator; b. Butler, Pa., Jan. 21, 1892; s. James Buhl and Nordena (Wilson) M.; A.B., Allegheny Coll., 1913; M.A., U. of Pittsburgh, 1925, Ed.D., 1935; m. Laverna Gregg, May 6, 1916; 1 dau., Helen Barbara. Instr. of science East Liberty Acad., Pittsburgh, 1913-17; teacher of science, Wilkinsburg (Pa.) High Sch., 1917-23; teacher with Pittsburgh Pub. Schs. since 1923, teacher, 1923-26, prin. Burgwin School since 1935. Mem. Phi Delta Kappa, Kappa Phi Kappa, Delta Tau Delta. Republican. Mem. United Presbyn. Ch. Mason (32°). Home: 1124 Chelton Av., Pittsburgh, Pa.

MATHER, Frank Jewett, Jr., professor art; b. Deep River, Conn., July 6, 1868; s. Frank Jewett and Caroline Arms (Graves) M.; A.B., Williams, 1889, L.H.D., 1923; Ph.D., Johns Hopkins, 1892; studied U. of Berlin, École des Hautes Études, Paris; m. Ellen Suydam Mills, Feb. 20, 1905; children—Margaret (Mrs. Louis A. Turner), Frank J. Instructor and assistant professor English and Romance languages, Williams College, 1893-1900; editorial writer New York Evening Post, asst. editor the Nation, 1901-06; art critic New York Evening Post, 1905-06, 1910-11; Am. editor Burlington Mag., 1904-06; joint editor Art Studies since 1923; prof. art and archæology, Princeton, 1910-33 (emeritus); dir. U. Art Mus. Socialist. Mem. Nat. Inst. Arts and Letters, Am. Acad. of Arts and Sciences, Am. Acad. of Arts and Letters, Hispanic Soc. America (corr. member), Dante Society, Delta Psi. Ensign U.S.N. Res. Force, 1917. Clubs: Century, Authors (New York). Author: Homer Martin, Poet in Landscape, 1912; The Collectors (short stories), 1912; Estimates in Art, 1916; The Portraits of Dante, 1921; A History of Italian Painting, 1923; Ulysses in Ithaca, 1926; Modern Painting, 1927; The American Spirit in Art, in The Pageant of America, 1927; Estimates in Art, series 2, 1931; Concerning Beauty, 1935; Venetian Painters, 1936; also several lit. and philol. monographs. Home: Washington Crossing, Pa.

MATHER, Thomas Ray, univ. prof.; b. Rohrsburg, Pa., May 24, 1890; s. John J. and Ella May (Black) M.; grad. Bloomsburg State Normal Sch., 1909; A.B., Williams Coll., 1913; A.M., Harvard, 1914; fellow Princeton, 1914-15; grad. study Harvard, 1920-21; m. Ruth Evelyn Hutchins, Nov. 27, 1916; children—Thomas John, Merrilie. Instr. history and English, Meadville Theol. Sch., 1915-18; instr. rhetoric, U. of Minn., 1918-20; instr. English, U.S. Naval Acad., 1921-22; instr. English, Boston U., 1922-23, asst. prof., 1923-28, prof. and chmn. dept. since 1928; vice-pres. and sec. Benton Roller Mills, Benton, Pa. Served as teacher S.A.T.C., U. of Minn., during World War. Mem. Modern Lang. Assn. of America, Am. Assn. Univ. Profs., Phi Beta Kappa. Republican. Unitarian. Mason. Home: 216 Prospect St., Belmont, Mass; also Benton, Pa. Office: 688 Boylston St., Boston, Mass.

MATHESIUS, Walther Emil Ludwig, vice-pres., operations, U.S. Steel Corpn. of Del.; b. Hoerde, Germany, Aug. 20, 1886; s. Walther and Emmy (von der Heyde) M.; came to U.S., 1911, naturalized, 1919; grad. metallurgy, Inst. Tech., Berlin, Germany, 1910, D.Engring., same, 1911; m. Ebba W. J. af Ekstroem, of Stockholm, Sweden, Oct. 28, 1912; children—Walther Herman, Herman Robert. Employed intermittently at various German works learning profession, 1904-11; instr. and asst. dept. metallurgy, Inst. Tech., Berlin, 1910-11; metallurgist, Am. Steel & Wire Co., Worcester, Mass., 1911-12; employed in various positions, Blast Furnace Dept., South Works, Ill. Steel Co., Chicago, 1912-17, supt., 1917-25, asst. gen. supt. South Works, 1925-35, gen. supt., 1935; mgr. operations, Chicago Dist., Carnegie-Ill. Steel Corpn., 1935-37; vice-pres., operations, U.S. Steel Corpn. of Del., Pittsburgh, Pa., since 1938 and dir. corpn. In compulsory mil. service Imperial German Army, heavy arty., 1905; lt. Res., resigned 1913. Mem. Am. Iron & Steel Inst., Am. Inst. Mining & Metall. Engrs., Am. Soc. for Metals. Republican. Clubs: Duquesne, Pittsburgh Athletic, Field (Pittsburgh); University, South Shore Country (Chicago). Home: 1060 Morewood Av., Pittsburgh, Pa. Office: 436 7th Av., Pittsburgh, Pa.

MATHEUS, John Frederick, coll. prof.; b. Keyser, W.Va., Sept. 10, 1887; s. John William and Mary Susan (Brown) M.; student Steubenville (O.) High Sch., 1902-05; A.B., cum laude, Western Reserve U., 1910; studied Columbia U., summers, 1914, 16, 20 and 21, A.M., 1921; student U. of Paris, 1925, U. of Chicago, 1927; m. Maude A. Roberts, 1909. Prof. Latin, Fla. A. & M. Coll., 1911-13, prof. modern langs., 1913-22; prof. and head dept. Romance langs., W.Va. State Coll., since 1922. Traveled in Cuba and Haiti. Sec. to Am. mem. Internat. Commn. to Liberia, 1930. Mem. Modern Lang. Assn., Am. Assn Teachers Spanish, French, Italian, Am. Teachers Assn., Alpha Phi Alpha. Mason. Club: El Cubo (Institute, W. Va.). Writer short stories, poems, articles, translations, 1-act plays and libretto for opera "Ouanga" (in collaboration with Clarence Cameron White, composer). Editor: (with Dr. N. B. Rivers) "Georges" by Dumas père. Address: West Virginia State Coll., Institute, W.Va.

MATHEWS, Charles Henry, Jr., railroad exec.; b. Phila., Pa., May 31, 1882; s. Charles Henry and Harriet Selina (Black) M.; A.B., Princeton U., 1905; m. Winifred Barker Munroe, Apr. 21, 1910; 1 dau., Winifred Barker (Mrs. Raymer W. Brown). With the Pennsylvania R.R. since Nov. 8, 1905, successively as clerk, Phila., 1905-13, passenger solicitor, Phila., 1913-20, asst. gen. passenger agt., Pittsburgh, Mar.-April 1920, gen. passenger agt., Pittsburgh, 1920-26, same, Phila., 1926-32, passenger traffic mgr., Phila., since June 1932; dir. Nat. Ry. Publ. Co., N.Y. Republican. Presbyterian. Clubs: Racquet (Phila.); Princeton, Nassau, Colonial (Princeton, N.J.); Princeton (New York). Home: Paoli, Pa. Office: Broad St. Station, Philadelphia, Pa.

MATHEWS, Edward Bennett, geologist; b. Portland, Me., Aug. 16, 1869; s. of Jonathan Bennett and Sophia Lucinda (Shailer) M.; A.B., Colby Coll., 1891, D.Sc., 1927; Ph. D., Johns Hopkins Univ., 1894; m. Helen Louise Whitman, Sept. 12, 1900; children—William Whitman (dec.), Margaret (Mrs. Richard W. Thorpe), John B. (dec.), Roger H. (dec.) Field asst. U.S. Geol. Survey, seasons of 1891-94; instr. mineralogy and petrography, 1894-95, asso., 1895-99, asso. prof., 1899-1904, prof. since 1904, chmn. geol. dept. since 1917, Johns Hopkins. Asst. state geologist of Md., 1898-1917, state geologist since 1917; mem. Md. State Bd. of Forestry; dir. Maryland Weather Service; chmn. div. geology and geography, Nat. Research Council, 1919-22, and mem. advisory com. since 1933; v.p. Internat. Geol. Congress, 1922, 1926, and 1929, treas., 1933; chmn. advisory council U.S. Bd. of Surveys and Maps, 1920-26, 1929—; mem. Md. State Development Commn. since 1929, Md. Water Resources Commission since 1933. Commr. Md.-Va. Boundary, 1927-31. Fellow Geol. Soc. America (treas. since 1917), Washington Acad. of Sciences, Am. Acad. of Arts and Sciences, A.A.A.S.; mem. Econ. Geologists, Mineralogical Soc., Am. Inst. Mining and Metall. Engrs., Am. Geog. Soc., Assn. of Am. State Geologists (pres. 1920-23), Md. Hist. Soc., Soc. Colonial Wars. Author: Bibliography and Cartography of Md.; Maps and Map-Makers of Md.; Building Stones of Md.; Limestones of Md.; History of Mason-Dixon Line; Boundary Line Between Virginia and Maryland (with W. A. Nelson); Physical Features of Md.; Water Resources of Md.; Catalogue Published Bibliographies in Geology; and other geol. and hist. papers. Home: Lombardy Apt., Baltimore, Md.

MATHEWS, Frank Asbury Jr., lawyer; b. Phila., Pa., Aug. 3, 1890; s. Frank Asbury and Mary Isabelle M.; student Palmyra (N.J.) grade and high sch., 1906-07, 1909-11, Phila. Business Coll., 1906, U. of Pa. Law Sch., 1911-12; LL.B., Temple U. Law Sch., Phila., 1920; m. Carol Judd Becker, Aug. 20, 1919; children—John Barry, William George, Pauline Mary, Francis Charles, Carol Ann. Admitted to N.J. bar as atty., 1919, as counsellor, 1922; mem. of firm Waddington & Mathews, Camden, N.J., since 1921. Served successively as pvt., sergt., sergt. 1st class, ordnance sergt., Ordnance Dept., U.S. Army, with A.E.F., 1917-19; 1st lt., Judge Advocate Gen's. Dept., U.S.O.R.C., 1923-26; 1st lt., Inf., N.J.N.G., 1926, serving on staff as S-2, 57th Brig., 1926-32; maj. Judge Advocate Gen's. Dept., N.J.N.G., serving on State Staff Corps, div. judge advocate, 44th Div., and lt. col., 1932-37; lt. col., Judge Advocate Gen's. Dept., N.G. of U.S., since 1937. Dist. court judge, 1st judicial dist. of Co. of Burlington (N.J.), 1929-33; asst. counsel N.J. Highway Dept., since 1934. Mem. Camden, Burlington Co., N.J. State bar assns.; Am. Legion (mem. post Frederick M. Rodgers 156, Palmyra, N.J.; Burlington Co. commdr., 1922-23; N.J. State commdr., 1925-26; nat. exec. committeeman from N.J.; chmn. Nat. Vets. Preference Com. since 1936), Kent Law Club (U. of Pa.; hon.). Republican. Episcopalian. Artisans Order Mutual Protection, Patriotic Order Sons of America. Clubs: Union League, Phila. Art Alliance, Plays and Players (Phila.); Delran Yacht (Riverton, N.J.). Home: 212 Thomas Av., Riverton, N.J. Office: 500 Broadway, Camden, N.J.

MATHEWS, William Burdette, asso. clk. Supreme Ct. of Appeals, W.Va.; b. Marshall Co., W.Va., Aug. 27, 1866; s. Christopher C. and Esther J. (Scott) M.; A.M., Waynesburg (Pa.) Coll., 1889; LL.B., George Washington U., 1891; LL.M., 1892; LL.D., Waynesburg College, 1926; m. Elizabeth Blundon, Oct. 25, 1900; children—Mrs. Sarah Esther Gilchrist, Mrs. Elisabeth Mathews Wallace, John Ingram and Edgar Blundon (twins, both dec.). Admitted to bar, 1891; teacher, 1882-89; examiner public school teachers, Marshall Co., W.Va., 1889-90; clk. 11th U.S. Census, 1890-95; sec. to speaker Ho. of Dels., W.Va., 1897; chief clk., office of auditor of W.Va., 1897-1902; Rep. presdl. elector, 1901; asst. atty.-gen. W.Va., 1902; clk. Supreme Ct. of Appeals, W.Va., 1902-37, asso. clk. since 1937; sec. W.Va. Bd. of Law Examiners since 1920. State dir. "Four Minute Men" under Com. of Pub. Information during World War. Dir. Virginia Joint Stock Land Bank of Charleston, Bank of Dunbar (W.Va.), Empire Savings & Loan Co., Empire Federal Savings & Loan Assn., Charleston Bldg. & Loan Assn., Title Trust & Mortgage Co., Virginian Savings & Loan Co.; sec.-treas. Roane Co. Development Co. Dir. Kanawha Co. Pub. Library, Union Mission Settlement; trustee emeritus W.Va. Wesleyan College; trustee 1st Methodist Episcopal Church, Charleston. Appointed, 1931, by Gov. Conley, mem. W.Va. com. for celebration of 200th anniversary of birth of George Washington; mem. President's Conf. on Home Bldg. and Home Ownership, 1931. Charter and life member American Law Inst.; mem. Am., W.Va. and Charleston bar assns., W.Va. Hist. Soc., S.R. in W.Va. (ex-pres.). Republican. Methodist. Mem. Gen. Conf. M.E. Ch., 1900, 04; mem. Gen. Bd. Control Epworth League, 1904-08; del. 4th Ecumenical Meth. Conf., 1911. Mason (32° K.C.C.H., K.T., Shriner); life mem. Elks. Clubs: Grandparents, Rotary (Charleston); W.Va. Soc. (Washington). Home: 1501 Quarrier St. Office: State Capitol, P.O. Box 1406, Charleston, W.Va.

MATHIAS, Charles McC(urdy), lawyer; b. Baltimore, Md., Dec. 16, 1886; s. John P. T. and Elizabeth A. (McCurdy) M.; A.B., Johns Hopkins U., 1908; LL.B., U. of Md. Law Sch., Baltimore, 1911; m. Theresa McE. Trail, Oct. 26, 1921; children—Charles McC., Jr., Theresa T., Edward Trail. Admitted to Md. bar, 1911 and engaged in gen. practice of law at Frederick, 1911-22, and since 1930; vice-pres. Central Trust Co., Frederick, Md., 1922-30; dir. Frederick County Products, Inc. since 1927, Frederick Brick Works, Staley Motor Co.; sec., dir. and atty. Union Mfg. Co., Frederick, since 1930; sec. and dir. Frederick Hotel Co. Served as capt. Ordnance Dept., U.S.A., 1917-19. Mem. Frederick Planning Commn., Frederick Housing Authority. Treas. Md. State Sch. for Deaf. Mem. Frederick County Bar Assn., Am. Legion, Beta Theta Pi. Republican. Episcopalian. Mason (K.T.). Club: Catoctin Country. Home: 103 Council St. Office: 25 Court St., Frederick, Md.

MATHIESEN, Anna, univ. prof.; b. Harlan, Ia., Oct. 10, 1893; d. Niels and Ane Margrethe (Nielsen) Mathiesen; student Evanston (Ill.) Acad., 1916-18, State U. of Iowa, Iowa City, 1918-20, Ph.D., 1929; A.B., Wellesley Coll., 1923, A.M., 1926; unmarried. Asst. in psychology, Wellesley Coll., 1923-26, State U. of Ia., 1926-29; instructor in psychology, Goucher Coll., 1929-32, asst. prof., 1932-36, asso. prof. since 1936, chmn. dept. of psychology since 1938; visiting lecturer psychology, Wellesley Coll., 1933-34. Asso. mem. Am. Psychol. Assn.; mem. Southern Soc. for Philosophy and Psychology, Eastern branch Am. Psychol. Assn., Washington-Baltimore branch Am. Psychol. Assn. (v.p. 1936-37), Am. Assn. Univ. Profs., Sigma Xi. Home: 2905 N. Charles St., Baltimore, Md.

MATLOCK, Isaiah, lawyer; b. Elizabeth, N.J., July 5, 1895; s. William Carroll and Bernadine G. (Martin) M.; student Newton (N.J.) pub. schs., 1901-07, St. Joseph Coll. High Sch., 1907-11, St. Joseph Coll., Phila., 1911-13; LL.B., Catholic U. of America, Washington, D.C., 1917; m. Ethel M. Mullan, Sept. 10, 1919; children—Margaret Louise, Robert Isaiah, Ethel Marie. Admitted to D.C. bar, 1917, N.J. bar, 1918; practiced in Newton, N.J., 1918-21, in Asbury Park, N.J., since 1921; mem. firm Matlock & Thautman, Asbury Park, N.J. Served as pvt., Judge Advocate's Div., U.S. Army. Asst. U.S. atty., 1919-21. Mem. Am. Bar Assn., N.J. Bar Assn. Democrat. Roman Catholic. Club: Kiwanis (Asbury Park, N.J.). Home: 10 Westra St., Interlaken, N.J. Office: 603 Mattison Av., Asbury Park, N.J.

MATRÉ, Joseph Boucard, lawyer; b. Cincinnati, O., Nov. 23, 1888; s. John and Josephine (Zuleger) M.; A.B., U. of Cincinnati, 1912; LL.B., Cincinnati (O.) Law Sch., 1913; m. Elwine Jewell Junkerman, July 14, 1917. Admitted to O. bar, 1913; atty. Union Central Life Ins. Co., Cincinnati, O., 1913-15; sec. to Alfred G. Allen, M.C., 1915-17; in practice of law asso. with Alfred G. Allen, Cincinnati, O.,

1917-18; trustee and prof. dental jurisprudence, Cincinnati Coll. Dental Surgery, 1917-18; asst. to legal adviser, Dept. of State, Washington, D.C., since 1918. Served as sergt. inf., U.S.A., 1918. Vice-pres. Montgomery County Civic Fed. Mem. Am. Soc. Internat. Law, Delta Tau Delta, Phi Delta Phi. Democrat. Mason. Club: Manor Country (Norbeck, Md.). Home: 1111 Summerfield Rd., Silver Spring, Md.

MATT, C(alman) David, rabbi; b. Kovno, Lithuania, June 24, 1887; s. Isaac and Sarah Z. (Sorinkes) M.; brought to U.S., 1891, and naturalized citizen, 1905; A.B., U. of Pa., 1909; Rabbi Jewish Theol. Sem., New York City, 1912; grad. study Dropsie Coll., 1930-36; m. Lena Friedman, Sept. 16, 1913; children—Joshua Leonard, Joseph Zalman, Hershel Jonas, Beulah and Zeldah (twins). Rabbi, Minneapolis, Minn., 1912-27, Buffalo, N.Y., 1927-29; rabbi West Phila. Jewish Community Center since 1929. Served as vol. worker for Jewish Welfare Bd., Minneapolis, Minn., during World War. Dir. Asso. Talmud Torahs of Phila., Zionist Orgn. Mem. U. of Pa. and Gratz Coll. alumni assns., Rabbinical Assn. of America, Phila. Bd. Jewish Ministers (v.p.). Jewish religion. Mem. B'nai B'rith, B'rith Sholom, Dorshe Daath, Brith Abraham. Asso. editor Am. Jewish World. Contbr. verse, reviews, interviews, sermons, articles to Anglo-Jewish press. Some poems included in various Jewish anthologies. Hóme: 271 S. 63d St., Philadelphia, Pa.

MATTAS, Clyde Leslie, physician; b. Altoona, Pa., Aug. 3, 1896; M.D., Jefferson Med. Coll., 1920; m. Margaret Grace Musser, Apr. 17, 1928; children—Margaret Grace, Jane Pettit. After usual interneships engaged in practice of medicine at Scranton; pathologist Scranton State Hosp. since 1922, Moses Taylor Hosp. since 1925; cons. pathologist Fairview State Mental Hosp., St. Mary's Mater Misericordiae Hosp. since 1938. Fellow Am. Coll. of Physicians. Home: 833 Taylor Av. Office: 1104 Union Nat. Bank Bldg., Scranton, Pa.

MATTE, Hubert Peter, cons. engr.; b. Lewiston, Me., Nov. 12, 1889; s. Napoleon and Alice (Bourque) M.; ed. Worcester Poly. Inst., 1906-10; m. Ethelyn Stickney, Sept. 5, 1912; children—Norma Alice, Natalie Bertha. Engr. and asst. supt., Southbridge Water Supply Co., Mass., 1910-12; engr. Pitometer Co., N.Y. City, 1912-14; chief engr. and mgr. Water Dept. Oak Park, Ill., 1914-18; chief engr. Ill. State Dept. Pub. Health, Springfield, Ill., 1918-20; engr. with Worthington Pump and Machinery Corpn., Harrison, N.J., 1920-27, mgr. meter division, 1927-32; cons. engr., Worthington-Gamon Meter Co., Harrison, N.J., since 1932; specialist on metering and methods of measuring flow of liquids for industrial use. Mem. Nat. Soc. Professional Engrs., N.J. Soc. Professional Engrs., Am. Water Works Assn., N.E. Water Works Assn., Essex Co. Engring. Soc. (sec.). Republican. Catholic. Club: Orange Camera (East Orange). Contbr. sci. article to tech. mags. and jours. Home: 96 Boyden Av., Maplewood. Office: Harrison, N.J.

MATTERN, Johannes, writer; b. Duisburg-Meiderich, Germany, Jan. 19, 1882; s. Carl Theodor and Maria (Denzer) M.; student U. of Münster and U. of Bonn, 1904-07; Ph.D., Johns Hopkins University, 1922; m. Carola Glaser, Aug. 2, 1919; children—John, Carl Frederick Theodore. Came to U.S., 1907, naturalized citizen, 1914. Instr. in language and mathematics, Chevy Chase (Md.) Coll. and Sem., 1907-09; asst., Library of Congress, Washington, D.C., 1909-10; reorganizer Library of Bur. Statistics, U.S. Dept. of Commerce and Labor, 1910-11; asst. librarian Johns Hopkins since 1911, also asso. prof. of political science; visiting prof. internat. law, Georgetown Univ. Law Sch., winter 1930-31; visiting prof. in history and polit. science, Tulane University, second semester 1937-38. Member American Society International Law, American Political Science Assn., American Acad. Polit. and Social Science, Phi Beta Kappa. Club: Johns Hopkins. Author: Employment of the Plebiscite in the Determination of Sovereignty, 1920; Bavaria and the Reich, 1923; Concepts of State, Sovereignty and International Law, 1928; Principles of Constitutional Jurisprudence of the German National Republic, 1928. Contbr. on polit. science, internat. law and relations. Home: 606 Evesham Av. Address: Johns Hopkins University, Baltimore, Md.

MATTES, Philip V., lawyer; b. Scranton, Pa., Oct. 14, 1887; s. Wm. Frederick and Mary (Van Cleef) M.; student Princeton U., 1906-08; A.B., Cornell U., 1910; m. Gertrude E. Russ, Apr. 22, 1914; children—Gertrude Elizabeth (Mrs. Thomas Lawson Kelly), Philip (dec.), Marion, Marjorie (dec.), Roger. Admitted to Pa. bar, 1912, and since engaged in gen. practice of law at Scranton; city solicitor of Scranton, 1922-26; county solicitor Lackawanna Co. since 1936; Dem. city chmn., 1917; Dem. nominee for judge, 1937. Served as chmn. legislative com. Chamber of Commerce, 1931. Donated site for Mattes Community Center. Mem. Am., Pa., and Lackawanna Co. (sec.) bar assns., Seal and Serpent Soc. of Cornell, Am. Legion. Democrat. Presbyn. Mason. Clubs: Kiwanis (pres., 1939), Canoe, Green Ridge. Home: 1105 Woodlawn St. Office: 705 Mears Bldg., Scranton, Pa.

MATTHAI, Joseph Fleming, v.p. U.S. Fidelity & Guaranty Co. Home: 403 Marlow Road. Office: Calvert & Redwood Sts., Baltimore, Md.

MATTHAI, William Henry, mfr.; b. Baltimore, Md., July 26, 1856; s. John Christopher and Theresa (Jackins) M.; ed. Newton Acad., Baltimore; m. Alice Bancroft Jones, Nov. 15, 1883; children—William Howard, John Clarke, Albert Dilworth, Joseph Fleming, Alice Bancroft (Mrs. Albert Dawson Williams), Margaret (Mrs. Joseph Porter Harris). Began in employ of Matthai & Ingram, mfrs. tinware, Baltimore, 1872; admitted as mem. firm Matthai-Ingram & Co., 1880; business merged, 1899, with Nat. Enameling & Stamping Co., mem. exec. com. and mgr. 2 factories in Baltimore, became v.p., 1919, resigned, 1935; vice-pres. Homeland Mfg. Co., Baltimore; mem. exec. com. U.S. Fidelity & Guaranty Co.; dir. Savings Bank of Baltimore; pres. Beaver Dam Marble Co. Mem. Am. Hardware Mfrs.' Assn. (pres., 1915), Merchants & Mfrs.' Assn. of Baltimore (pres., 1918, 19), Baltimore Assn. Commerce. Trustee Md. Gen. Hosp. Mem. Municipal Art Soc. Methodist. Club: Merchants. Home: "Lexington," 6901 Reistertown Rd., Baltimore Co., Md. Office: 415 E. Oliver St., Baltimore, Md.

MATTHEWS, Archibald Morgan, lawyer; b. Johnstown, Pa., Mar. 27, 1902; s. James M. and Eleanor (Morgan) M.; grad. Johnstown High Sch., 1919; A.B., Washington and Jefferson Coll., 1923; grad. student Harvard Law Sch., 1923-24; LL.B., Pitt Law Sch., Pittsburgh, 1927; m. Elizabeth Vivian Zoner, July 15, 1936; 1 dau., Millie Eleanor. Admitted to Pa. bar, 1927, and since in practice at Somerset; dist. atty. Somerset Co. since 1936; solicitor for Somerset Chamber of Commerce, Central City Borough, Middlecreek Twp. Mem. Somerset Co. Bar Assn. (sec.-treas.), Pa. Bar Assn., Am. Bar Assn., Alpha Tau Omega, Phi Alpha Delta, Delta Sigma Rho, Sons Am. Revolution. Republican. Presbyterian (trustee St. Paul's Ch.). Eagle. Club: Somerset Country. Address: Somerset, Pa.

MATTHEWS, Arthur Pascoe, pres. Matthews Bros. Inc.; b. Scranton, Pa., Apr. 17, 1887; s. Charles Winton and Emilie (Pascoe) M.; prep. edn., Sch. of Lackawanna, 1897-1904; Ph.G., Columbia U., 1909; m. Ruth Lowthaine Steell, June 13, 1917; children—Kathryn, Charles, Emilie. Pres. Matthews Bros., Inc., Scranton, Pa., 1909-15, mgr., 1915-27, v.p., 1927-32, pres. since 1932, dir. since 1922; dir. Third Nat. Bank & Trust Co. of Scranton. Mem. Scranton Assn. of Credit Men (v.p., and dir. since 1932), Chamber of Commerce (dir., 1937), Commercial Assn. of Scranton (dir. since 1930); past pres. Pa. Rexall Clubs. Republican. Presbyterian (trustee). Clubs: Rotary (Scranton; dir., 1935-36); Elkview Country (Carbondale, Pa.); Clemo Hunting and Fishing (Hoadleys, Pa.); Sugar Hill (Greentown, Pa.). Home: 533 Monroe Av. Office: 320 Lackawanna Av., Scranton, Pa.

MATTHEWS, Frank Edward, transit exec.; b. Salem, Mo., Feb. 12, 1885; s. William J. and Anna F. (Cawley) M.; student Deerfield Twp. High Sch., Highland Park, Ill., 1898-99, also student Gregg Shorthand & Business Coll. (Chicago) and Rutgers U. (New Brunswick, N.J.); m. Alice M. Neitman, Aug. 13, 1912; 1 son, Edward F. Began as office boy Postal Telegraph Cable Co., Chicago, 1903; served as treas. Trenton (N.J.) Transit Co., now acting treas. for receivers; sec. and dir. Terminal Cab Co., Yellow Cab Co. Mem. Trenton (N.J.) Chamber of Commerce (vice chmn. sales and advertising mgr. group). Republican. Catholic. K.C. Clubs: Civitan (Trenton, N.J.); Hopewell Valley Golf (Hopewell, N.J.). Home: 203 Buckingham Av. Office: 132 Perry St., Trenton, N.J.

MATTHEWS, Fred Elwood, cons. engr.; b. Templeton, Mass., Mar. 11, 1875; s. Albert H. and Mary E. (Marden) M.; ancestors came to America about 1800; B.S., Kan. State U., 1899, E.E., same, 1908; M.E., Brooklyn Inst. Tech., 1905; m. Alberta Cory, June 3, 1908. Employed in gen. elec. constrn. work, E. M. Reed & Co., Kansas City, Mo., 1899-1900, engr., Swift & Co., Kansas City, 1900-02, Eastern plants, Phila., Boston, and others, 1903-05; adv. mgr., De La Vergne Machine Co., N.Y. City, 1905-06; mgr. Automatic Refrigerating Co., N.Y. City and Hartford, Conn., 1907-08, placed on market first mechanically and financially successful, completely automatic refrigerating system; independent cons. refrigerating engr., N.Y. City and Leonia, N.J., 1908-28; retired since 1928. Served as specialist in refrigeration for U.S. Army for A.E.F., Washington, D.C., 1918-19. Mem. N.J. Soc. Professional Engrs., Am. Soc. Refrigerating Engrs. (charter mem. past pres.), Am. Soc. Mech. Engrs. Republican. Mason. Author: Mechanical Refrigeration. Contbr. papers to engring. socs. and articles to tech. jours. Home: 216 Leonia Av., Leonia, N.J.

MATTHEWS, H(arry) Alexander, organist, composer; b. Cheltenham, Eng., Mar. 26, 1879; s. John A. and Clara (Woods) M.; studied music with father; Mus.D., Muhlenberg Coll., 1920, U. of Pa., 1924; m. May Gwendolyn Davis, Aug. 1906; 1 dau., Phyllis Mary. Came to U.S., 1899; teacher, Phila., since 1900; organist and choirmaster St. Stephen's Church, Philadelphia. Conductor of the Philadelphia Music Club Chorus and the University Glee Club; head of theoretical dept. Clarke Conservatory of Music and Eastern Baptist Theol. Sem. Asso. Am. Guild Organist. Mem. Am. Soc. Composers, Authors and Publishers. Wrote over 200 compositions in music, including sacred and secular cantatas, anthems, duets, solos, secular songs, piano and organ pieces, etc. Prin. works: (cantatas) Life Everlasting; The Conversion; The Story of Christmas; The Triumph of the Cross; The City of God (in commemoration of Quadri-Centennial Celebration of Luth. Ch. in America); The Slave's Dream; The Lake of the Dismal Swamp; The Song of the Silent Land. Home: 3905 Vaux St. Studio: Presser Bldg., Philadelphia, Pa.

MATTHEWS, Howard Dimmitt, lawyer; b. Greeley, Ia., July 25, 1892; s. John Coleman and Helen (Dimmitt) M.; student Upper Iowa U., 1909-11; LL.B., State U. of Ia. Law Coll., 1917; m. Frances Cochran, Oct. 27, 1917 (dec.); children—Frances Meals, John Cochran, Helen Dorothy, Joseph George; m. 2d, Sara McKown, Nov. 10, 1928; 1 son, Don Bernard. Admitted to Iowa bar, 1917, W.Va. bar, 1919; practiced law, Parkersburg, W.Va., 1919-24; asst. U.S. atty., 1922-24; partner law firm Handlan, Garden & Matthews, Wheeling, W.Va., since May 1, 1925. Entered 1st O.T.C., Ft. Snelling, Minn., May 1917; overseas Aug. 1918-Feb. 1919; hon. discharged as capt. F.A., Camp Lee, Va., Mar. 11, 1919. Mem. Bd. of Edn., Triadelphia Dist., 6 yrs. Mem. Am. Bar Assn., W.Va. Bar Assn., Ohio County Bar Assn. (ex-pres.), Phi Delta Phi, Legion of Honor, Royal Order of Jesters. Republican. Presbyn. Mason (32°), Elk (past exhalted ruler, No. 28). Clubs: Parkersburg and Wheeling Kiwanis (past pres. of each); Fort Henry; Wheeling Country. Home: 21 Hamilton Av. Office: 1226 Chapline St., Wheeling, W.Va.

MATTHEWS, Isaac George, clergyman; b. Middleville, Ont., Can., May 29, 1871; s. Jacob and Jeanette (Anderson) M.; A.B., McMaster U., Ont., 1897, A.M., 1898; B.Th., McMaster Theol. Sem., 1903; Ph.D., U. of Chicago, 1912; studied Marburg U., Germany; m. Nina Blanche Foreman, Sept. 4, 1905; children—Jean Doris, Jackson Kenneth. Ordained Bapt. ministry, 1898; pastor Jackson Av. Ch., Vancouver, 1898-1900, New Westminster, B.C., 1900-03; prof. O.T. lang. and lit., McMaster U., 1904-19; pastor 1st Bapt. Ch., New Haven, Conn., 1919-20; lecturer Yale Div. Sch., 1919-20; prof. O.T. lang. and lit., Crozer Theol. Sem., since 1920; prof. history Christian Ch., Bapt. Inst., Phila., 1921-26; annual prof. Am. Sch. Oriental Research, Jerusalem, 1930-31. Mem. Soc. Bibl. Lit. and Exegesis, Am. Oriental Soc., Oriental Club of Phila. Republican. Author: The Jewish Apologetic to the Grecian World in the Apocryphal and Pseudepigraphical Literature, 1914; How to Interpret Old Testament Prophecy, 1919; Old Testament Life and Literature, 1923, revised, 1934; Commentary I and II Samuel, 1929; Commentary Haggai and Malachi, 1935; Commentary Ezechiel, 1937. Address: Crozer Theological Seminary, Chester, Pa.

MATTHEWS, John C.; mem. staff Guthrie, Huntington Memorial and St. Mary's hosps. Address: 902 Fourth Av., Huntington, W.Va.

MATTHEWS, Joshua Marsh, lawyer; b. Brookwood, Dulanys Valley, Md., Oct. 21, 1881; s. Dennis Marsh and Harriet West (Aldridge) M.; B.S., U. of Md., 1903; LL.B., U. of Md. Law Sch., 1907; m. Mary Hester Waters, Nov. 15, 1910; 1 dau., Fanny-Scott (Mrs. J. Sawyer Wilson 3d). Admitted to Md. bar, 1907 and since engaged in gen. practice of law at Baltimore; vice-pres. and dir. North American Oil Co.; dir. Standard Wholesale Phosphate & Acid Works, Inc. Served as sr. capt. Md. N.G.; 1st lt. in Ordnance Dept. during World War. Democrat. Episcopalian. Clubs: Maryland, Baltimore Country (Baltimore). Home: Marshmont, Dulanys Valley, Phoenix, Md. Office: 1108 Fidelity Bldg., Baltimore, Md.

MATTHEWS, Paul, bishop; b. Glendale, O., Dec. 25, 1866; s. Stanley and Mary Ann (Black) M.; A.B., Princeton, 1887; B.D., Gen. Theol. Sem., New York, 1890, D.D., 1916; D.D., Seabury Div. Sch., 1915, Princeton U., 1916; m. Elsie Procter, May 11, 1896; children—Charlotte Elizabeth (Mrs. H. S. van Buren), Thomas Stanley, Mary Ann (Mrs. William Mode Spackman), Harriet Procter (dec.), Margaret (Mrs. Walter Flinsch), Dorothea (Mrs. John Dooling). Deacon, 1890, priest, 1891, Protestant Episcopal Church; assistant Ch. of Advent, Walnut Hills, Cincinnati, 1890-91; entered Associate Mission, Omaha, in charge St. Paul's and St. John's chs., 1891-95; rector St. Luke's, Cincinnati, 1896-1904; dean St. Paul's Cathedral, Cincinnati, 1904-13; elected bishop coadjutor of Milwaukee, Sept. 20, 1905, but declined; dean of Cathedral, Faribault, Minn., and prof., Seabury Div. Sch., 1913-15; consecrated bishop of N.J., Jan. 25, 1915; retired as bishop of N.J., Nov. 1, 1937. Home: Merwick, Princeton, N.J.

MATTHEWS, Thomas Stockton, investment banker; b. Baltimore Co., Md.; s. Charles T. and Margaret (Woolston) M.; prep. edn. pub. sch. and Friends Sch., Baltimore; B.S., Swarthmore (Pa.) Coll., 1902; unmarried. Clk. Baker, Watts & Co., Baltimore, 1902-16; exec. Robert Garrett & Sons, investment bankers, Baltimore, 1916-18, mem. of firm since 1918; dir. and mem. exec. com. Commercial Credit Co., Md. Dry Dock Co., Charleston Transit Co., Roland Park Co. Trustee Swarthmore Coll., Sheppard and Enoch Pratt Hosp., Baltimore. Mem. Delta Upsilon. Republican. Soc. of Friends. Clubs: Maryland, Merchants (Baltimore, Md.); Howard (Md.) County Hunt. Also engaged in farming and raising live-stock. Home: Ellicott City, Md. Office: Garrett Bldg., Baltimore, Md.

MATTHEWS, William Frederick, physician; b. New Church, Va., Feb. 12, 1898; s. Samuel James and Elizabeth (Kelly) M.; A.B., U. of Richmond, Richmond, Va., 1920; M.D., Med. Coll. of Va., Richmond, Va., 1924; m. Iola Marie Marin, Nov. 11, 1927; children—William Frederick, Jr., Ann Charlotte. Interne St. Francis Hosp., Jersey City, N.J., 1924-25, N.Y. Foundling Hosp., New York, 1925-26; engaged in gen. practice of medicine and pediatrics at Allentown, Pa., 1926-27, Ernest, Pa., 1927-28, Montclair, N.J., 1928-29, pediatrics exclusively since 1929; asst. attending pediatrician Mountainside Hosp., Montclair, N.J., Essex County Isolation Hosp., Belleville, N.J.; asso. attending pediatrician New York Post Grad. Med. Sch. and Dispensary. Mem. bd. of dirs. Bur. Pub. Health Nursing, Montclair, N.J.; mem. med. adv. com. to mayor Montclair. Served in S.A.T.C., 1918. Licentiate Am. Bd. Pediatrics. Mem. Am. Acad. Pediatrics, A.M.A., N.J. State and Essex Co. med. socs., Asso. Physicians of Montclair and Vicinity, Phi Delta Omega, Phi Chi. Democrat. Baptist. Home: 280 Upper Mountain Av. Office: 61 S. Fullerton Av., Montclair, N.J.

MATTHEWS, William R(obinson), engr. and bldr.; b. Phila., Pa., July 18, 1874; s. Thomas and Margaret (Moore) M.; ed. pub. schs. and high sch., Phila., Spring Garden Inst., Phila., Pa., 1892-94; hon. M.Engring., Princeton U., 1928; m. Mary E. Hendrickson, Oct. 26, 1898. Employed as constrn. supt., 1897-1902; organized own co., 1902 and active in management since orgn., Matthews Construction Co., Inc., engrs. and bldrs., Princeton, N.J. and New York, N.Y., now chmn. of bd. since 1933; pres. First Nat. Bank of Princeton since 1933. Trustee Thomson Hall, Princeton; mem. bd. mgrs., N.J. State Hosp., Trenton, N.J. Republican. Presbyn. Mason. Clubs: Nassau, Tiger Inn (Princeton); Architectural League, Princeton (New York). Home: 177 Library Pl., Princeton, N.J.

MATTOON, Wilbur Reed, forestry; b. Harwich, Mass., Aug. 14, 1875; s. Virgil Wadhams and Mary Frances (Reed) M.; A.B., Wesleyan U., Middletown, Conn., 1899; student Cornell U., 1902-03; M.F., Yale U. Sch. of Forestry, 1904; m. Kate VanLiew, Aug. 28, 1909; children—Richard Wilbur, Martha Ellen (Mrs. George C. Hastings), Catherine VanLiew, Laura Isabell. Student forester in employ U.S. (temporary), 1903; forester in employ U.S. Forest Service since 1904, inspr. Region 3, Albuquerque, N.M., 1907-09, supervisor, 1909-12, sr. forester, Washington, D.C., since 1912; authority on farm forestry in the Southern states; first to develop value of slash pine as a profitable tree for forest management. Sr. mem. Soc. Am. Foresters. Mem. Am. Forestry Assn., Delta Kappa Epsilon. Mem. Citizens Assn., Horticultural Club. Presbyterian. Writer numerous publs. of U.S. and (few) state govts. on management of forests, planting forest trees and measuring and marketing forest products. Home: 101 Cedar Av., Takoma Park, Md. Office: U.S. Forest Service, Washington, D.C.

MATTOX, Edgar Ellsworth, physician; b. Irwin, Pa., Apr. 20, 1879; s. John Howell and Harriet (Foster) M.; ed. high sch. and bus. coll.; M.D., Md. Med. Coll., Baltimore, 1912; m. Gertrude Lillian Deitrich, June 16, 1915. Interne Society Lying-In Hosp., New York City, July-Aug. 1910, Md. Gen. Hosp., Baltimore, 1911-12; engaged in gen. practice of medicine and surgery at Pittsburgh, Pa., since 1913; surgeon at C. G. Hussey & Co. Copper Mills, Pittsburgh. Served as pres. Oakland Bd. of Trade, 1937-38. Mem. Allegheny Co. and Pa. State med. socs., Phi Chi. Mem. and trustee South Hills Sportsmens Assn. Republican. Presbyterian. Mason (K.T., 32°, Shriner). Summer home near Bellefonte, Pa. Address: 3600 Fifth Av., Pittsburgh, Pa.

MATZ, Robert Luke, prof. econs.; b. Albertis, Pa., Jan. 21, 1886; s. Davilla and Sarah (Cook) M.; Diploma, Bloomsburg State Normal Sch., 1909; A.B., Ursinus Coll., 1912; A.M., N.Y. Univ., 1919, M.B.A., 1926, Ph.D., 1928; m. Bessie B. Mapes, Oct. 25, 1893; 1 dau., Barbara. Engaged in teaching, various sch., high sch. and coll., Pa., N.J., and W.Va., 1906-23; with Winfield H. Mapes Co., New York City, 1923-25; instr. economics and political science, Bucknell U., 1925-27; asst. prof. economics, N.Y. Univ. Sch. Commerce, 1927-28; prof. of business administration and economics, Bucknell U., Lewisburg, Pa., since 1928; dir. Lewisburg Nat. Bank. Mem. Am. Econs. Assn., Polit. Sci. Assn., Lambda Chi Alpha. Democrat. Methodist. I.O.O.F. Home: 140 S. Second St., Lewisburg, Pa.

MATZAL, Leopold Charles, artist and teacher; b. Vienna, Austria, Aug. 13, 1890; s. Charles and Elenora (Pröglhöf) M.; came to U.S., 1921, naturalized, 1927; ed. art, Univ., Vienna; m. Bertha Ramer, Dec. 21, 1917 (died 1924); m. 2d, Elsa Grasme, Aug. 28, 1929; 1 son, Edmund Otto. Studied at Vienna Acad. Fine Arts, 8 yrs. and 3 yrs. in Munich and Karlsruhe, Germany; portrait and mural painter in Vienna until 1921; assisted in founding Hoboken Art and Industrial Sch.; instr. Newark Sch. of Fine and Industrial Arts since 1929; exhibited at Nat. Acad. Design, Am. Fed. of Art and various important exhbns.; represented in Pub. Library Jersey City, also Hoboken, murals at schs. in Newark, Library Jersey City; awarded various prizes at exhbns. Served in Austrian Army during World War as 1st lt. Mem. Am. Artists Professional League. Former mem. Salmagundi Club. Home: 882 S. 19th St. Studio: 550 High St., Newark, N.J.

MAURER, Charles Lewis, educator; b. Columbia County, Pa., Apr. 27, 1884; s. John and Hannah (Stine) M.; B.Pd., Bloomsburg (Pa.) State Teachers Coll., 1909, M.Pd., 1910; A.B., Ursinus Coll., 1912; A.M., U. of Pa., 1913; Ed.D., Temple U., 1931; m. Besse Helwig, Dec. 28, 1912; children—Charles Lewis, Sarah Matilda. Prin. Roaring Creek Twp. High Sch., Columbia County, Pa., 1908-10; prin. Plymouth Meeting (Pa.) Schools, 1912-13; vice headmaster Conway Hall, Carlisle, Pa., 1913-15; teacher Camden (N.J.) High Sch. since 1915, dir. of Guidance since 1933; dean and mem. bd. trustees, Coll. of South Jersey, since 1927; pres. and mem. exec. com. Bibl. Inst. of South Jersey since 1937. Mem. curriculum com. N.J. State Bd. of Edn.; formerly mem. Bd. of Edn., Collingswood, N.J. Mem. N.J. State Teachers Assn., N.E.A., Acad. Polit. and Social Science. Ind. Republican. Presbyn. (elder). Author: Early Lutheran Education in Pennsylvania, 1932. Contbr. to newspapers. Home: 130 E. Linden Av. Office: 224 Federal St., Camden, N.J.

MAURER, Felix O.; banker; b. Trevorton, Pa., Jan. 25, 1869; s. Charles Donald and Mary (Schlegel) M.; student Bloomsburg (Pa.) Coll. and Lafayette Coll., Easton, Pa.; m. Agnes W. Mackie, June 30, 1923. In gen. store business, Mahanoy Plane, Pa., Aug. 1889-Apr. 1935; pres. and dir. First Nat. Bank in Frackville, Pa., since 1934. Mem. Boy Scouts of America. Mason (Frackville Lodge; Consistory; Shriner, Rajah Shrine). Clubs: Rotary (Frackville, Pa.); Craftsmans. Home: 27 S. Third St. Office: Lehigh Av., Frackville, Pa.

MAURER, James Hudson, labor official; b. Reading, Pa., Apr. 15, 1864; s. James D. and Sarah (Lorah) M.; ed. pub. schs., 14 mos.; m. Mary J. Missimer, Apr. 15, 1886; children—Charles H., Martha M. (Mrs. Ralph Dundore). Newsboy, farm hand, factory worker, and at 15 machinist's apprentice; joined Knights of Labor, 1880, Socialist Labor Party, 1898, Socialist Party, 1902; candidate of Socialist Party for gov. of Pa., 1906; mem. Nat. Exec. Com., same party, 10 yrs.; mem. Pa. Ho. of Rep., 3 terms, 1910, 14, 16, introducing Workmen's Compensation Act, and other labor measures; pres. Pa. Federation of Labor, 1912-28; pres. Labor Age Monthly, Workers Ednl. Bur. of America; dir. Brookwood Coll., Katonah, N.Y. Became chmn. Old Age Assistance Commn. of Pa., 1917. Mem. Am. Commn. on Conditions in Ireland, 1920; made tour of Europe with Am. Seminar, 1923; mem. of Am. Fact-finding Commn. to Russia, 1927; mem. City Council, Reading, 1928-32. Socialist candidate for v.p. of U.S., 1928 and 1932, also for U.S. Senate, 1934. Author: The Far East, 1910; It Can Be Done, 1938. Home: 1355 N. 11th St., Reading, Pa.*

MAURICE, Arthur Bartlett, author; b. Rahway, N.J., Apr. 10, 1873; student Princeton. Asso. editor The Bookman, 1899-1907, editor, 1907-16; with Am. Relief for Belgium and North of France, behind German lines, 1916 to withdrawal. Author: New York in Fiction, 1901; History of the 19th Century in Caricature (with F. T. Cooper), 1934; The New York of the Novelists, 1916; Bottled Up in Belgium, 1917; Fifth Avenue, 1918; The Paris of the Novelists, 1919; A Child's Story of American Literature (with Algernon Tassin), 1923; O. Henry (for O. Henry Memorial, Asheville, N.C.); The Caliph of Bagdad (with Robert H. Davis), 1931; Magical City (text for drawings of Vernon Howe Bailey), 1935. Translator of The Flaming Crucible, and America and the Race for World Dominion. Lit. editor New York Herald, 1922-24, N.Y. Sun, 1924. Clubs: Players, Princeton (New York); Nassau (Princeton, N.J.); Savage (London). Home: 436 Cherry St., Elizabeth, N.J.*

MAVEETY, Donald John, chemist; b. Hillsdale, Mich., Aug. 23, 1894; s. Patrick J. Maveety and Susan (Hare) M.; B.S. in Chem. Engring., Purdue U., Lafayette, Ind., 1917, Chem. E., 1922; student Yale, 1917-18; m. Theodosia Williams, Sept. 25, 1917; 1 son, Donald John. Chem. engr. Bur. of Air Production, War Dept., Pittsburgh, Pa., 1917-18, Utah Copper Co., Garfield, Utah, 1918-19; chemist Nat. Biscuit Co., New York, since 1919, chief chemist since 1934. Mem. Am. Chem. Soc., Sigma Alpha Epsilon. Republican. Methodist. Home: Brooklawn Drive, Millburn, N.J. Office: 449 W. 14th St., New York, N.Y.

MAXCY, Charles Josiah, dir. of accounting; b. Minneapolis, Minn., Dec. 2, 1887; s. Charles Herbert and Kate Rebecca (Mitchell) M.; grad. DeWitt Clinton High Sch., N.Y. City, 1906, Pace Inst. of Accountancy, 1910; registered as C.P.A., N.Y. State, 1915; m. Marion E. Cooper, Jan. 21, 1918; 1 son, Donald Cooper. Began as ry. clk., 1907; practiced as pub. accountant, N.Y. City, 1909-18 and 1919-33; chief accountant Rock Island (Ill.) Arsenal, 1918-19; chief of bur. of municipal investigation and statistics, N.Y. City, 1934; became dir. div. of accounts, Federal Emergency Administration of Pub. Works, Washington, D.C., Feb. 6, 1935; now dir. finance and accounts U.S. Housing Authority. Mem. N.Y. State Soc. C.P.A., N.J. State Soc. C.P.A., Am. Inst. of Accountants, Soc. for the Advancement of Management, Am. Pub. Works Assn., Municipal Finance Officers Assn., S.A.R., Washington (D.C.) Bd. of Trade. Protestant. Mason. Contbr. tech. articles. Home: 107 W. Passaic Av., Rutherford, N.J. Office: Interior Dept. Bldg., Washington, D.C.

MAXCY, Kenneth Fuller, M.D., educator; b. Saco, Me., July 27, 1889; s. Frederick Edward and Estelle Abbey (Gilpatrick) M.; A.B., George Washington U., 1911; M.D., Johns Hopkins, 1915, D.P.H., 1921; m. Gertrude Helene McClellan, of Peterborough, Ont., Can., June 22, 1918; children—Kenneth Fuller, Frederick Reynolds, Selina Gilpatrick. Resident house officer, Johns Hopkins Hosp., 1915-16, asst. resident pediatrician, 1916-17; asst. in medicine, Henry Ford Hosp., Detroit, Mich., 1917; fellow Johns Hopkins Sch. of Hygiene and Pub. Health, 1919-21; asst. surgeon, passed asst. surgeon and surgeon U.S. Pub. Health Service, 1921-29; prof. of bacteriology and preventive medicine, U. of Va., 1929-36; prof. of pub. health and preventive medicine, U. of Minn., 1936-37; prof. of bacteriology, Sch. of Hygiene and Pub. Health, Johns Hopkins, 1937-38, prof. of epidemiology since 1938; scientific dir. Internat. Health Div., Rockefeller Foundation, 1937-39. Served as lt. Med. Corps, U.S.A., 1917, capt., 1918. Represented U.S. Pub. Health Service at Malaria Conf., League of Nations, Geneva, 1928. Mem. A.M.A., Am. Soc. Epidemiologists, Pithotomy Club, Raven Soc., Phi Beta Kappa, Sigma Xi, Alpha Omega Alpha, Delta Omega, Theta Delta Chi, Phi Beta Pi. Episcopalian. Contbr. to knowledge of endemic typhus in U.S. Mem. editorial bd. Am. Jour. Pub. Health and Am. Jour. Hygiene. Home: 700 St. Georges Rd., Baltimore, Md.

MAXEY, George Wendell, justice; b. Forest City, Pa., Feb. 14, 1878; s. Benjamin and Margaret (Evans) M.; ed. Mansfield (Pa.) State Normal Sch., 1894-97; A.B., U. of Mich., 1902; LL.B., U. of Pa., 1906; m. Lillian Danvers, Jan. 22, 1916; children—Mary D., Dorothy, Lillian Louise. Admitted to Pa. bar, 1906; in practice at Scranton, 1906-20; dist. atty. Lackawanna Co., 1914-20; judge 45th Dist., 1920-30; apptd. Nov. 24, 1930, justice Supreme Court of Pa., to fill vacancy for 6 weeks, elected, Nov. 4, 1930, for term, 1931-52. Republican. Clubs: Scranton, Scranton Country. Home: 520 Monroe Av., Scranton. Office: First Nat. Bank Bldg., Scranton, Pa.; and 362 City Hall, Philadelphia, Pa.*

MAXEY, Paul Harold, lawyer; b. Forest City, Pa., Sept. 28, 1899; s. William John and Rebecca (Brown) M.; grad. Forest City High Sch., 1916; A.B., Pa. State Coll., 1920; LL.B., U. of Pa., 1923; m. Margaret Walker, Dec. 28, 1932; children—David Walker, Thomas Fleming. Admitted to Pa. bar, 1924, and since in practice at Scranton; asst. dist. atty. of Lackawanna Co., 1930-33; examiner Pa. State Bd. of Law Examiners since 1935. Served in infantry, U.S. Army, during World War. Mem. Pa. Bar Assn., Delta Upsilon, Phi Delta Phi. Republican. Methodist. Mason. Home: 2446 N. Washington Av. Office: Lincoln Bldg., Scranton, Pa.

MAXFIELD, Ezra Kempton, prof. English; b. Winthrop, Me., Apr. 23, 1881; s. Benjamin Horace and Laverna (Kempton) M.; grad. Coburn Classical Inst., Waterville, Me., 1900; A.B., Colby Coll., Waterville, 1905; spl. study U. of Pa., 1907-08; A.M., Harvard, 1911, Ph.D., 1920; m. Jane Ernisse Crowe, July 24, 1912; children—David Kempton, Susan Ernisse. Prin. high schs., Waldoboro, Me., 1905-06; teacher of science, Friends Central High Sch., Philadelphia, Pa., 1906-08; instr. in English, Del. State U., 1909-10, Haverford (Pa.) Coll., 1911, Simmons Coll., Boston, Mass., 1911-12; asst. prof. English, Colby Coll., 1912-16, U. of Rochester, 1916-17; prof. English, Northeastern Coll., Boston, 1917-18; asst. in English, Harvard, 1919-20; prof. and head of dept. English, Washington and Jefferson Coll., since 1920. Pres. Men's Club, First Presbyn. Ch., 1937-38; chmn. dist. com. Boy Scouts, 1934-38; exec. sec. Fortnightly Club, 1931-38, pres., 1930-31. Mem. Modern Lang. Assn. America, Linguistic Soc. America, A.A.A.S., Am. Assn. Univ. Profs., Editorial Committee on Coll. Reading of Nat. Council of Teachers of English (1932-39), Modern Humanities Assn. (England), Delta Upsilon. Republican. Quaker. Club: Rotary of Washington, Pa. (v.p. 1937-38, pres. 1938-39). Contbr. articles and reviews to lit. and professional publs. Home: 311 E. Beau St., Washington, Pa.

MAXFIELD, Jane Crowe (Mrs. Ezra Kempton Maxfield), sch. principal; b. Baltimore, Md., Mar. 11, 1882; d. Alfred Dean and Susan Augusta (Ernisse) Crowe; diploma, Rochester Free Acad., 1901; A.B., U. of Rochester, 1905, A.M., same, 1909; A.M., Columbia U., 1910; grad. study, Boston U., 1917-18; m. Ezra Kempton Maxfield, July 24, 1912; children—David Kempton, Susan Ernisse. Employed as teacher high sch. Fairport, 1905-06; instr. modern langs., Geneva Coll., 1907-08; instr. English, Simmons Coll., 1910-12; prin. Washington Sem., Washington, Pa., since 1932. Mem. Am. Assn. Univ. Women, Assn. Deans of Women of Western Pa., Jr. Coll. Council of Middle Atlantic States, Middle States Assn. of Colls. and Secondary Schs., Theta Eta, Phi Beta Kappa. Republican. Presbyn. Club: Current Events. Home: 311 E. Beau St., Washington, Pa.

MAXFIELD, J(oseph) P(ease), engineer; b. San Francisco, Calif., Dec. 28, 1887; s. Joseph Elwin and Harriett Whitemore (Mansfield) M.; S.B., Mass. Inst. Tech., 1910; m. Milicent Arnold Harrison, June 20, 1914; children—Katherine Hayward, Eleanor Taylor. Instr. physics and electro-chemistry, Mass. Inst. Tech., 1910-14; research physicist, Western Electric Co., at New York, 1914-19, dept. head (later Bell Telephone Labs.), 1919-26; mgr. engring. and research Victor Talking Machine Co., Camden, N.J., 1926-29; cons. engr. Electrical Research Products, Inc., New York, N.Y., 1929-33, staff engr., 1933-36, dir. commercial engring. since 1936; dir. Nichols Products Co., Moorestown, N.J. Fellow Am. Inst. Elec. Engrs., Am. Phys. Soc., Acoustical Soc. of America, American Geographic Society. Mem. Society of Friends. Club: Wyoming Field (Milburn, New Jersey). Author: (with Douglas Stanley) The Voice, Its Production and Reproduction, 1933. Home: R.F.D. 1, Madison, N.J. Office: 195 Broadway, New York, N.Y.

MAXSON, Charles W., chief dept. surgery, South Baltimore Gen. Hosp.; visiting surgeon, West Baltimore Gen. and Union Memorial hosps. and Hosp. for Women of Md.; asst. surgeon Mercy Hosp. Address: 827 N. Charles St., Baltimore, Md.

MAXWELL, Charles Frederick, sch. supt.; b. Greensburg, Pa., Mar. 17, 1885; s. Andrew Joseph and Angeline Reamer (Baker) M.; student Greensburg (Pa.) Sem.; A.B., Lafayette Coll., Easton, Pa.; M.A., U. of Pittsburgh; m. Eva Elmira Hertzog, June 21, 1911; children—Ruth Elmira, Charles Frederick, Jr. Successively teacher, prin. and supervising prin., Youngwood (Pa.) Borough Schs., 1909-16; asst. supt. schs., Westmoreland County, Pa., 1916-30, supt. since 1930. Organizer and sponsor Parent-Teacher Assn. in Westmoreland Co.; mem. exec. bd. Greensburg (Pa.) Y.M.C.A.; mem. exec. com. Boy Scouts of America. Mem. Pa. State Edn. Assn. (mem. professional ethics commn.; life mem.; pres. 1937), N.E.A. (state del. 1935), Westmoreland Co. Schoolmen's Assn., Phi Delta Kappa. Lutheran. Mason (32°, K.T., Tall Cedars of Lebanon). Club: Rotary of Greensburg (past pres.). Home: 525 Plymouth St. Office: 3d Floor, Court House, Greensburg, Pa.

MAXWELL, Charles Pomp, lawyer; b. Easton, Pa., Mar. 13, 1887; s. John and Sue Mixsell (Pomp) M.; A.B., Lafayette Coll., 1908; studied in law office, 1908-11; m. Katharine Stewart Vigelius, June 8, 1929; 1 son, Peter. Admitted to Pa. bar, 1911, and since engaged in gen. practice of law at Easton; served as asst. dist. atty., Northampton Co., Pa., 1920-24; instr. in law, Lafayette Coll., 1919-29; mem. Northampton Co. Bd. Benchers and Law Examiners since 1922; examiner Pa. State Bd. of Law Examiners since 1924. Served as capt. inf. O.R.C. and maj. inf. U.S.A., 1917-19. Mem. Am., Pa. State, and Northampton Co. (past pres.) bar assns., Zeta Psi, Mil. Order Fgn. Wars, Pennsylvania Society. Republican. Episcopalian. Clubs: Pomfret (Easton); Northampton County Country. Home: 322 Spring Garden St. Office: Northampton Nat. Bank Bldg., Easton, Pa.

MAXWELL, Earl L., lawyer; b. St. George, W.Va., Sept. 5, 1888; s. W. B. and Carrie (Lindsey) M.; student Davis and Elkins Coll., 1904-07, W.Va. Univ. Law Sch., 1907-09; m. Nellie E. Rexstrew, Nov. 25, 1919; 1 son, Robert Earl. Admitted to W.Va. bar, 1909, and engaged in gen. practice of law at Elkins; served as city atty. Elkins, and pros. atty. Randolph Co., W.Va. Served as chmn. Randolph Co. Dem. Com. several terms. Democrat. Home: 122 S. Randolph Av. Office: Scott Bldg., Elkins, W.Va.

MAXWELL, Frank Jarvis, postmaster; b. Clarksburg, W.Va., Nov. 11, 1897; s. W. Brent and Lillie (Jarvis) M.; student W.Va. Univ., Morgantown, W.Va., 1916-20; m. Clara Gibson, Oct. 12, 1920; children—Franklin Jarvis, Jr., William Brent 3d. In employ Union Nat. Bank, Clarksburg, W.Va., 1920-28; agt. W.B. Maxwell Estate, 1930-34; postmaster of Clarksburg, W.Va., since 1934; dir. Union Nat. Bank since 1930; vice-pres. and dir. Mountain State Brewing Co., Clarksburg, W.Va. Served in Ambulance Corps, U.S.A., 1917-19, with A.E.F. in Italy; awarded War Medal (Italy). Served as chmn. Dem. Co. Com., 1932-34, treas., 1930-32. Mem. W.Va. Athletic Commn., 1931-33. Mem. Phi Kappa Psi. Democrat. Episcopalian. Elk. Club: Clarksburg Country. Home: 355 Buckhannon Av., Clarksburg, W.Va.

MAXWELL, George Ralph, physician; b. Denver, Colo., Jan. 16, 1898; s. Cyrus Haymond and Melvina Jane (Adams) M.; B.S., W.Va. University, 1921; M.D., University of Cincinnati Coll. of Medicine, 1923; grad. student Harvard U. Med. Sch., 1929, 1938; m. Florence Lucille Sutphen, Sept. 10, 1926; children—Mary, George Ralph II. Interne, Grant Hosp., Columbus, O., 1923-24; instr. phys. diagnosis, W.Va. Univ. Med. Sch., 1926-35, asst. prof. since 1935. Served in C.O.T.S., Camp Gordon, Ga., 1918. Fellow Am. Coll. Physicians. Certified by Am. Bd. of Internal Medicine. Pres. W.Va. Tuberculosis and Health Assn., 1935. Mem. W.Va. State Med. Assn. (council 1932-36), Monongalia Co. Med. Soc. (sec. 1926-38), Sigma Nu, Alpha Kappa Kappa. Democrat. Methodist. Mason. Club: Lions of Morgantown. Home: 330 Woodland Rd. Office: 364 High St., Morgantown, W.Va.

MAXWELL, Haymond, judge; b. Clarksburg, W.Va., Oct. 24, 1879; s. Edwin and Loretta (Shuttleworth) M.; A.B., W.Va. Univ., 1900, LL.B., 1901; m. Carrie V. Maxwell, June 28, 1905; children—Edwin, Haymond, Virginia, Emily, Porter W. Admitted to W.Va. bar, 1901 and began practice with father at Clarksburg under title of Maxwell & Maxwell; mem. Ho. of Delegates, W.Va., 1904-06; judge Criminal Court of Harrison County, W.Va., 1909-12; judge Circuit Court, 15th Jud. Circuit, 1913-25; practiced 1925-28, apptd. judge Supreme Court of Appeals of W.Va., Aug. 1928, and elected to same office in Nov. 1928 for term of 12 yrs. Mem. Phi Sigma Kappa, Phi Alpha Delta, Phi Beta Kappa. Republican. Methodist. Mason. Home: 1511 Lee St. Address: State Capitol, Charleston, W.Va.

MAY, Edwin Charles, retired business exec.; b. Phila., Pa., Mar. 22, 1880; s. Barney and Pauline (Fleishman) M.; ed. pub. schs., Phila. and Pittsburgh, 1886-94, business coll., Pittsburgh, 1897-98; m. Gertrude Brilles, Apr. 17, 1905. Vice-pres. and treas. May Drug Co., Pittsburgh, Pa., 1903-29; retired. Chmn. laws and enforcement branch Mayor's Better Traffic Com., Pittsburgh, 1925-30; chmn. Pittsburgh advisory com. Federal Housing Adminstrn., 1935-37. Mem. bd. Western State Penitentiary, Pittsburgh, since 1924, pres. since 1927; v.p. Montefiore Hosp., Pittsburgh, 1929-36; dir. Allegheny Co. Council, Boy Scouts of America, since 1918, treas., 1923-30. Mem. Pittsburgh Housing Assn. (dir. since 1928, pres. since 1935), Urban League of Pittsburgh (dir., 1921-37, pres. 1924-27), Rotary Internat. (gov. 6th dist. 1919-20). Club: Rotary (Pittsburgh; pres. 1913-14, dir. 1910-16). Home: 6300 Beacon St. Office: May Bldg., Pittsburgh, Pa.

MAY, Herbert Arthur, mfg. exec.; b. Watertown, Wis., June 27, 1892; s. Edward and Helena (Mulberger) M.; student Staunton (Va.) Mil. Acad., 1908-10; m. Sara Norton Davidson, Aug. 10, 1918; children—Herbert Arthur, Philip Davidson, Edward James, Sara Margot. Salesman Atlantic Refining Co., Pittsburgh, 1918-21; bond dept. Union Trust Co., Pittsburgh, 1921-23; v.p. and treas. Standard Gauge Steel Co., Beaver Falls, Pa., 1923-25; v.p. and asst. treas. Union Drawn Steel Co., Beaver Falls, Pa., 1925-30; asst. to pres. Westinghouse Electric & Mfg. Co., East Pittsburgh, Pa., 1931-33; v.p. Safety Car Heating & Lighting Co., Pittsburgh, 1933-36; v.p. Union Switch & Signal Co., Pittsburgh, Pa., since 1936; dir. Pittsburgh & West Va. Ry., Pennroad Corpn., Safety Car Heating & Lighting Co., Wheeling & Lake Erie R.R., Forbes Nat. Bank, Mackintosh-Hemphill Co., Pittsburgh Steel Foundry Corpn., Davidson Ore Mining Co. Dir. Civic Club, Tuberculosis League of Pittsburgh, Travelers Aid Soc. Republican. Presbyterian. Clubs: Duquesne, Pittsburgh, Rolling Rock, Rolling Rock Hunt (Pittsburgh); Cloud, Terrace (New York); Racquet (Phila.); Allegheny Country (Sewickley, Pa.). Home: 6530 Beacon St. Office: 3605 Gulf Bldg., Pittsburgh, Pa.

MAY, Kenneth Floyd, insurance exec.; b. Bridgeport, Conn., Jan. 16, 1898; s. Frank Kenneth and Lillian Jessie (Long) M.; grad. High Sch., Erie, Pa., 1916; m. Mary Isabel Tenney, Aug. 10, 1935. Began as ins. agt., 1917; examiner Ins. Co. of N. America, Phila., 1919-20, special agt., 1920-29, supt. of agencies, Chicago, 1929-31; asst. sec. Nat. Union Fire Ins. Co., Pittsburgh, since 1931; sec. Birmingham Fire Ins. Co., Pittsburgh, since 1932; pres. Pittsburgh Marine Sales Co. Republican. Methodist. Mason (32°, Shriner). Clubs: Pittsburgh Athletic Assn., Insurance of Pittsburgh (dir.), Automobile Superintendents (Chicago); Automobile Underwriters (New York). Home: 5260 Centre Av. Office: 139 University Place, Pittsburgh, Pa.

MAY, Peter H.; v.p. and comptroller Md. Casualty Co. Home: 1304 E. 33d St. Office: 701 W. 40th St., Baltimore, Md.

MAYER, Edward Everett, psychiatrist; b. Allegheny, Pa., June 18, 1876; s. Lippman and Elise (Hecht) M.; B.A., U. of Pittsburgh, 1895, M.A., 1899, M.D., 1897; studied U. of Wuerzberg, Germany, 1897-98, U. of Paris, 1898-99; m. Rose Mae Lamm, June 16, 1902; 1 dau., Catherine (Mrs. Norman J. De Roy). Practiced at Pittsburgh, Pa., since 1900; apptd. Bd. of Health physician, 1900; asso. prof. neurology, U. of Pittsburgh, 1902-1910, professor psychiatry since 1910; dir. Mental Health Clinic, Dept. Pub. Welfare, Pittsburgh, since 1922; also served as psychiatrist to Montefiore, South Side and Presbyn. hosps.; med. dir. Fairview Sanatorium. Mem. Am. Med. Assn., Am. Psychiatric Assn., Assn. for Research on Nervous and Mental Diseases, Am. Psychopathol. Assn., Central Neuropsychiatric Assn., Am. Orthopsychiatric Assn. and other med. soc. Ind. Republican. Reformed Jewish religion. Clubs: Concordia, South Hills Golf. Editor: Oppenheim's Diseases of the Nervous System, 1900; (with others) Tice's Practice of Medicine, 1914; (with others) Graham's Surgical Diagnosis, 1931. Home: 5562 Hobart St. Office: 3401 5th Av., Pittsburgh, Pa.

MAYER, Erwin Emanuel, physician; b. Karlsruhe, Germany, June 21, 1892; s. Alfred H.A. and Ida (Schnadig) M. citizens of U.S.; M.D., Coll. Phys. and Surgeons of U. of Md., 1914; m. Miriam Lustig, Aug. 22, 1918; children—Jane Ida, Erwin Emanuel, Jr. Interne Mercy Hosp., Baltimore, Md., 1914-15, res. phys., 1915-17; instr. medicine, U. of Md. Coll. Phys. and Surgs., 1919-25; on vis. staffs following hosps., Union Memorial, Women of Md., Sinai, West Baltimore, Mercy, Ch. Home and Infirmary. Served as 1st lt. then capt. Med. Corps, U.S.A., 1917-19, diagnostician receiving ward, Camp Meade, Md. Fellow Am. Coll. Phys. Diplomate Am. Bd. Internal Medicine. Mem. A.M.A., Southern Med. Assn., Med. & Chirurg. Soc. Md., Baltimore City Med. Soc. Democrat. Jewish religion. Mason. Club: Suburban of Baltimore County (dir.). Home: The Esplanade, Baltimore, Md.

MAYER, Fred Sidney, clergyman; pres. General Conv. of the New Jerusalem in U.S. (Swedenborgian). Address: 3812 Barrington Rd., Baltimore, Md.*

MAYERBERG, Emil R.; chief eye, ear, nose and throat dept. Homeopathic, Wilmington Gen. and Delaware hosps.; mem. courtesy staff St. Francis Hosp.; consultant Babies Hosp., Wilmington, and Kent Gen. Hosp., Dover. Address: 601 Delaware Av., Wilmington, Del.

MAYES, William Harrison, insurance; b. May 5, 1888; s. John G. and Adella Alwilda (Lyle) M.; grad. Clarion (Pa.) State Teachers Coll., 1910; m. Charlotte Belle Glenn, Jan. 14, 1915 (died Jan. 12, 1919); 1 son, William Glenn; m. 2d, Grace Abigail Gayton, Sept. 27, 1920; 1 son, Carl Gayton. Teachers rural sch., 1906-07; teacher mathematics and commercial subjects, Brookville (Pa.) High Sch., 1910-13; with Brookville Title & Trust Co., 1913-20, beginning as bookkeeper and advancing to teller; cashier and dir. First Nat. Bank, Brockway, Pa., 1920-31; First Nat. of Brockway taken over by Deposit Nat. Bank, DuBois, Pa., Oct. 1931, asso. with them until 1932; agt. Conn. Mutual Life Ins. Co. and gen. insurance lines since 1933; an organizer and sec.-treas. and dir. Brockway Macaroni & Supply Co.; trustee J. G. Mayes Estate. Sch. dir. Brockway Borough, 8 yrs.; former chmn. Boy Scout troop com.; Sunday Sch. supt., Brookville M.E. Ch., 1916-19, Brockway M.E. Ch., 1924-39; choir dir. 1930-39. Republican. Methodist. Mason (32°, Shriner), Odd Fellow. Club: Acacia. Address: 901 Main St., Brockway, Pa.

MAYHAM, Ray Edwin, banker; b. Jersey City, N.J., Apr. 3, 1882; s. Rev. Thomas Creighton and Mary Adaline (Lawyer) M.; grad. Centenary Collegiate Inst., Hackettstown, N.J., 1899; student Am. Inst. Banking, New York, N.Y., 1900-03; m. Grace Helen Terrill, June 28, 1911; children—Grace, Ray Edwin, Robert Terrill. Clk. Equitable Trust Co., N.Y. City, 1899-1910; asst. treas. Union Trust Co., Jersey City, N.J., 1910-12; state bank examiner, N.J., 1912-20; comptroller W. Side Trust Co., Newark, N.J., 1920-24, v.p., 1924-28, became pres., 1928; v.p. S. Side Nat. Bank and Trust Co., Newark, 1925-28, pres. 1928-34; v.p. Peoples Nat. Bank, Newark, 1926-28, pres., 1928-34 (bank merged with S. Side Nat. Bank & Trust Co. and W. Side Trust Co.); pres. W. Side Securities Co., 1929-33; mem. loan com. sub. dist. 11 of 2d Federal Reserve Dist., Nat. Credit Corpn., 1931-36; treas. Newark Clearing House Assn., 1924-31, v.p. since 1938, mem. clearing house com. since 1931. Vice-pres. bd. trustees Centenary Collegiate Inst. Pres. League of Dem. Clubs of N.J., 1910-12; mem. Union County (N.J.) Dem. Com., 1909-11 and 1922-36; pres. Rahway Democratic Club, 1909-11; president Westfield Democratic Club, 1922-36. Served as capt., C.W.S., U.S.A., World War. Mem. N.J. State Chamber Commerce (dir.), Essex Co. Bankers Assn. (treas. 1931-32, v.p. 1932-34, pres. since 1934-35), N.J. Bankers Assn. (chmn. com. on federal reserve relations since 1935), Am. Inst. of Banking, Am. Acad. Polit. and Social Science, S.A.R. (historian Westfield chapter since 1921, pres. 1928, treas. N.J. soc., 1929-32 and since 1935), N.J. Hist. Soc., S.C. Hist. Soc., Union Co. Hist. Soc., Am. Legion (comdr. Martin Wallberg Post, Westfield, N.J., 1922), U.S. Reserve Officers Assn., Westfield Dem. Club. Mason, Elk, mem. Royal Arcanum. Club: Down Town (Newark). Contbr. to banking jours.; speaker before banking and business orgns. Home: 414 Lenox Av., Westfield, N.J. Office: 59 Springfield Av., Newark, N.J.

MAYNARD, Edward Washburn, mfg. exec.; b. Newport, R.I., Sept. 13, 1875; s. Washburn and Elizabeth (Brooks) M.; B.S., Worcester (Mass.) Poly. Inst., 18—; m. Harriet L. Harrington, Oct. 4, 1907; children—Robert H., Bessie M. (Mrs. William Anderson Henry). Asst. supt. Marquette Works, E. I. du Pont de Nemours & Co., Wilmington, Del, 1904-07, Louviers Works, 1908-10, Senter Works, 1910-11; supt. of Senter Atlas Powder Co., Wilmington, Del., 1911-16, Giant Works, 1916-20, gen. supt. high explosive dept., 1920-27, dir. since 1927, v.p. since 1930; v.p. and dir. Darco Corpn., Wilmington; dir. Wilmington Suburban Water Co., Del. Trust Co., Wilmington Savings Fund. Clubs: Rotary, Wilmington Country (Wilmington, Del.); Chemists (New York). Home: R.D. 3. Office: care Atlas Powder Co., Wilmington, Del.

MAYNARD, Theodore, author, univ. prof.; b. Madras, India, Nov. 3, 1890; s. Rev. Thomas Henry and Elizabeth Anthony (Teague) M.; in U.S., 1909-11, and since 1920; A.B., Fordham University; A.M., Georgetown University; Litt. D., Marquette U.; Ph.D., Catholic U. of America; m. Sarah Katherine Casey, June 8, 1918; children—Michael Felix Antony, Rosemary Joan, Paul Francis, Philip Austin Theodore, Christine Mary, Mary Theodore Clare, Kevin Peter Desmond. While studying for the Congregational ministry preached a sermon in Vermont on "Fools" that resulted in demand for his resignation; returned to England, 1911, as "hand" on a cattle boat; received in Roman Catholic Ch., 1913; spent 7 months novitiate with the Dominicans; laid aside monastic habit and engaged in lit. work; prof. English lit., Dominican Coll., San Rafael, Calif., 1921-25, at St. John's Coll., Brooklyn, N.Y., 1925-27, at Grad. Sch., Fordham U., New York, 1927-29, Georgetown U., 1929-34, Mt. St. Mary's Coll., Emmitsburg, Md., since 1934. Vice-pres. Catholic Poetry Society of America. Author: Laughs and Whifts of Song, 1915; Drums of Defeat, 1916; Folly and Other Poems, 1918; Carven from the Laurel Tree, 1918; Poems, 1919; A Tankard of Ale, 1919; The Last Knight, 1921; The Divine Adventure, 1921; Our Best Poets, 1922; The Book of Modern Catholic Verse, 1926; The Book of Modern Catholic Prose, 1927; Exile and Other Poems, 1928; De Soto and the Conquistadores, 1930; Preface to Poetry, 1933; The Connection between the ballade, Chaucer's Modification of it, Rime Royal and the Spenserian Stanza, 1934; Man and Beast, 1936; The Odyssey of Francis Xavier, 1936; The World I Saw, 1938; Apostle of Charity, 1939; also many articles in mags. Lecturer on lit. and other topics. Address: Westminster, Md.

MAYS, Jacob Henry, wholesale seed mcht.; b. Weiser Park, Pa., Feb. 16, 1879; s. Henry Jacob and Susan Mary (Deppen) M.; ed. Womelsdorf (Pa.) Pub. Sch., Albright Coll., Myerstown, Pa., Stoner's Business Sch., Reading, Pa.; m. Minnie M. Bickel, Nov. 12, 1904; children—Margaret Elizabeth (Mrs. Sidney McIlvain) Evelyn Gertrude (Mrs. Burns Sinclair Ryan). Partner with father in Mays Seed Co.; wholesale seed mchts., Weiser Park, Pa., 1900-04, owner since 1904. Justice of the peace, Borough of Womelsdorf, Pa., 1901-07; del. Dem. Co. Conv., Reading, Pa., 1901-02, Dem. Nat. Conv., Baltimore, Md., 1912; mem. Dem. Exec. State Com., 1916-22; nat. del.-at-large Dem. Nat. Conv., New York, 1924; treas. Dem. State Com., 1924-26; state mgr. Home Owners' Loan Corpn., Pa., 1933-34; mem. Pa. Bd. of Arbitration of Claims, 1937-38. V.p. and dir. Womelsdorf (Pa.) Bank & Trust Co.; dir. Laureldale Cemetery Co. Dir. Reading (Pa.) Fair Assn., Reading Hosp.; charter mem. Conrad Weiser Memorial Park Assn.; mem. Com. on Property, Weiser Park, Pa., (chmn., 1922-30). Mem. S.A.R., Pennsylvania German Society. Democrat. Reformed Church. Mason (Royal Arch Chapter, K.T.). Club: Wyomissing (Reading, Pa.). Address: Weiser Park, Pa.

MAYS, Paul Kirtland, artist; b. Cheswick, Pa., Oct. 4, 1888; s. Dallas and Lucy Hall (Kirtland) M.; student Art Students League, 1907-10, Hawthorne Sch. of Provincetown, Mass., 1911; studied at Newlyn Sch. of Painting, London and Colarossi Acad., Paris, 1923-24; m. Eleanor Moore, 1916; 1 dau., Lucy Kirtland; m. 2d, Margaret Pendleton Cooper, 1926. Represented by painting "Monterey," Cleveland Women's Club; "Jungle," White House; "Taos," U. of Pa.; "Harvest," Oberlin Coll.; murals, "Indian Legends," Gallery of Contemporary Art (Phila.); also murals in U.S. Post Office, Norristown, Pa., Grauman's Theatre, and Paramount Theatre, Los Angeles. Mem. Nat. Soc. of Mural Painters. Home: Bryn Athyn, Pa.; and Monterey, Calif.

MAYSER, Charles William, coll. prof.; b. Buffalo, N.Y., June 3, 1876; s. Charles W. and Katherine (Lang) M.; student Buffalo pub. schs., 1882-92, New Haven Normal Sch. Gymnastics, 1899-1901, Chautauqua Sch. of Physical Edn., 1900-04; m. Ana M. Farnsworth, Sept. 6, 1905. Asso. gymnasium, Yale, 1899-1900; football coach and athletic dir. Williston Acad., Easthampton, Mass., 1901-02; athletic dir., Newark Acad., Newark, N.J., 1902-09, Tome Sch., Port Deposit, Md., 1910-12; football coach and athletic dir. Franklin and Marshall Coll., Lancaster, Pa., 1913-14, Iowa State Coll., 1915-23; prof. physical edn., Franklin and Marshall Coll., since 1923. Owner and dir. Camp Sunapee Boys Camp, New London, N.H. Mem. Am. Wrestling Coaches Assn. (pres.). Republican. Mem. German Reformed Ch. Mason. Club: Rotary. Home: R.D. 3, Lancaster, Pa.

MAYWOOD, Armour Ames, clergyman; b. AuSable, Mich., Jan. 22, 1873; s. William P. and Martha J. (Wigle) M.; A.B., Albion Coll., 1896; student Boston U. Sch. of Theology, 1896-97; hon. D.D., Albion Coll., 1906; m. Pearl Field, Aug. 10, 1897; children—Dorothy Field (Mrs. John Wendell Bird), Eleanor Elizabeth (Mrs. Kenneth Carlson). Ordained to ministry M.E. Ch., 1898; pastor at various chs. in Mich., 1897-1925; pastor at Jamestown, N.Y., 1925-34; pastor Mt. Lebanon M.E. Ch., Pittsburgh, Pa., since 1934. Republican. Mem. M.E. Ch. Mason (K.T., 32°). Home: 3243 Gaylord Av., Pittsburgh, Pa.

MAZER, Charles, surgeon; b. Province of Kiev, Russia, Nov. 1, 1881; s. Emanuel and Rose (Hankin) M.; came to U.S., 1893, naturalized, 1913; student Brown Coll. Prep. Sch., Phila., 1903-04; M.D., Medico-Chirurgical Coll., Phila., 1908; m. Rose Spector, 1903; children—Anna Frances (Mrs. Morris Weisman), Beatrice Martha (Mrs. Ralph Sollot), Morton Leonard (M.D.), Lorna Ruth (Mrs. Samuel Blasky). Began as physician, Phila., 1908; asst. gynecologist, Mt. Sinai Hosp., 1917-23, chief in gynecology since 1923; asst. prof. in gynecology and obstetrics, Grad. Sch., U. of Pa., since 1928. Mem. Socialist Party since 1900; candidate for various offices on Socialist ticket including mayor of Phila., 1935. Fellow Am. Coll. Surgeons; diplomate Am. Bd. Obstetrics; mem. Pa. Med. Soc., A.M.A., A.A.A.S., Sigma Xi. Author: Clinical Endocrinology of the Female. Contbr. to med. jours. Address: 2047 Spruce St., Philadelphia, Pa.

McADAMS, Laura Jean; prof. French and German, Davis & Elkins Coll. Address: Davis & Elkins College, Elkins, W.Va.

McADAMS, Thomas Branch, banker; b. Richmond, Va., Nov. 12, 1879; s. George Brockenbrough and Sarah Reed (Branch) M.; desc. Christopher Branch, from Eng. to Chesterfield Co., Va., 1620; B.A. from Richmond College (now U. of Richmond), 1897, M.A., 1898; LL.D., U. of Richmond, 1924; m. Edna Harris McLure, Oct. 9, 1906; children—Sarah Reed (dec.), Edna Wylie, Louise Brockenbrough, Thomas Branch (dec.), Juliet Gill, George Brockenbrough. Began as clk. Merchants Nat. Bank, 1898; with Thomas Branch & Co., 1899-1904; with Merchants Nat. Bank, 1904, sr. v.p. until 1925, also partner Scott & Stringfellow until 1925; exec. v.p. State & City Bank & Trust Co., 1925-26; exec. mgr. State-Planters Bank & Trust Co., 1926-33; pres. Union Trust Co., Baltimore, since 1933; dir. Johnson Pub. Co., U.S. Fidelity & Guaranty Co., Baltimore, Spotless Co., Inc. Was col. on staffs Govs. Swanson and Mann; state dir. Nat. War Savings Campaign, and mem. Liberty Loan Exec. Co., World War. Trustee U. of Richmond. Mem. Am. Bankers Assn. (pres., 1921-22), Va. Bankers Assn. (pres., 1912), Assn. Reserve City Bankers (pres., 1918), Richmond Clearing House Assn. (pres., 1921), Am. Acceptance Council (exec. com., 1921-24). Phi Beta Kappa, Phi Kappa Sigma (grand alpha, 1926), etc. Mason (K.T., 32°, Shriner), Elk. etc. Democrat. Episcopalian. Clubs: Maryland, Elkridge Hunt, Merchants; Commonwealth, Rotary (ex-pres.), Country of Va. (ex-pres.); Bankers (New York). Home: 237 Lambeth Rd. Office: Baltimore and St. Paul Sts., Baltimore, Md.

McADOO, Henry Molseed, pres. U. S. Leather Co.; b. Phila., Pa., June 7, 1880; s. William and Margaret Anne (Campbell) McA.; grad. Friends Central Sch., Phila., 1898; m. Margaret Gaulbert Nice, of Phila., Apr. 26, 1911; children—William Nice, Henry Molseed, Richard Budd. Began as clerk, 1898; partner McAdoo & Allen, leather, Phila., since 1906; pres. Peabody Leather Co. since 1923; pres. U. S. Leather Co. since 1935; dir. C. C. Collings & Co., Nice Ball Bearing Co. Served as capt. Q. M. Dept., U. S. Army, during World War. Republican. Episcopalian. Clubs: Union League, Phila. Cricket, Bachelors' Barge (Phila.). Home: Skippack Pike, Fort Washington, Pa. Office: 27 Spruce St., New York, N.Y.

McAFEE, Joseph Ernest, community service; b. Louisiana, Mo., Apr. 4, 1870; s. John Armstrong and Anna Waddle (Bailey) M.; A.B., Park Coll., Mo., 1889; Union Theol. Sem., 1889-90; Auburn Theol. Sem., 1891-93 (certificate of graduation); Princeton Theol. Sem., Princeton U., 1895-96, B.D., 1896; m. Adah Elizabeth Brokaw, July 26, 1898; 1 dau., Janet Brokaw. Asst., 1890-91, and 1893-96, prof. Greek, 1896-1900, chaplain and prof. history of religion and ethics, 1900-00, Park Coll.; asso. sec. Bd. of Home Missions Presbyn. Ch. in U.S.A., 1906-14, sec., 1914-17; sec. Am. Missionary Assn., 1918-20; community counselor extension div., U. of Okla., 1921-23; dir. community service, Community Ch., New York, 1924-32. Author: Missions Striking Home, 1908; World Missions, from the Home Base, 1911; Religion and the New American Democracy, 1917; A Mid-West Adventure in Education, 1937; College Pioneering, 1938; (booklets) Community Types and Programs; Religion Without a Church; Organizing the Community for Good Will; You Are a McAfee; historical papers of Park College; also bulls. on community extension, community house, town govt., beautification, etc. Contbr. on social and religious subjects. Home: 94 Prospect Hill Av., Summit, N.J.

McAFEE, W(illiam) Keith, manufacturer; b. Pittsburgh, Pa., Jan. 26, 1893; s. James and Winifred (Harrington) McA.; ed. Allegheny Prep. Sch., grad. U. of Pa., 1915; m. Katharine Kirk, Sept. 11, 1920; children—Robert Keith, William Keith. With Westinghouse Electric & Mfg. Co., 1915-20, successively as student apprentice, 1915-16, design engr., 1916-17, production clerk, 1918-19, traveling engr., 1919-20; foreman engine house Pa. R.R., 1920-22; chief engr. Universal Sanitary Mfg. Co., 1922-23; vice-pres. Cambridge Sanitary Mfg. Co., 1923-30; pres. Universal Sanitary Mfg. Co. since 1928. Fellow Am. Ceramic Soc. (past pres.), A.A.A.S.; mem. Ohio Ceramic Industries Assn. (past pres.), Am. Soc. Sanitary Engring. (dir.), Am. Soc. Mech. Engrs., Vitreous China Plumbing Assn. (chmn.), Am. Inst. Elec. Engrs., Soc. of Rheology, Ceramic Assn. of N.J., Nat. Soc. Professional Engrs., Pa. Soc. Professional Engrs., Army Ordnance Assn. Mem. New Castle Chest Bd., Greater New Castle Assn. Bd. Clubs: University (Pittsburgh); Castle, New Castle Field (dir.). Home: 235 Hazelcroft Av. Address: Box 391, New Castle, Pa.

McALISTER, David Irons, lawyer; b. McDonald, Pa., Feb. 21, 1896; s. Charles B. and Minnie (Campbell) McA.; A.B., Washington and Jefferson Coll., 1918, A.M. 1920; LL.B., U. of Pittsburgh, 1922; m. Mary Eleanor Woodard, Oct. 5, 1928; 1 dau., Patricia Maebelle. Admitted to Pa. bar, 1922, and since practiced in Washington, Pa.; asso. with Hughes & Hughes; later mem. firm Hughes & McAlister, now Hughes, McAlister & Zelt; dir. Washington Burial Vault Co.; pres. Vaultite Corpn. Served in Signal Corps and in Aviation Service, U.S. Army, 1918. Mem. Am., Pa. State and Washington Co. bar assns., Internat. Assn. Ins. Counsel, Alpha Tau Omega, Delta Sigma Rho, Phi Delta Phi. Republican. Mem. United Presbyn. Ch. Elk. Clubs: University (Pittsburgh); Washington County Golf and Country (Washington). Home: 165 LeMoyne Av. Office: 63 S. Main St., Washington, Pa.

McALISTER, John Barr, M.D.; b. Carroll Co., Md., Jan. 31, 1864; s. James and Jane A. (Barr) M.; A.B., Pa. Coll., Gettysburg, 1884; M.D., U. of Pa., 1887; m. Helen Motter, Jan. 20, 1909. Practiced in Harrisburg, Pa., since 1887; med. dir. Harrisburg Hosp. Trustee Pa. Coll., Gettysburg Coll. (pres. bd.). Mem. A.M.A., Am. Coll. Physicians, Med. Soc. State of Pa. (pres. 1915-16), Dauphin Co. Med. Soc. (ex-pres.), Harrisburg Acad. Medicine (ex-pres.), Phi Beta Kappa. Republican. Presbyn. Clubs: Harrisburg, Country. Home: 232 N. 3d St. Office: 234 N. 3d St., Harrisburg, Pa.

McANDREW, Mary Bonaventure, supt. schs.; b. Carbondale, Pa.; d. James T. and Bridget (Nealon) McA.; grad. East Stroudsburg State Teachers Coll., 1909; A.B., Marywood Coll., Scranton, Pa., 1923; A.M., Teachers Coll., Columbia U., 1936. Engaged as teacher pub. schs., Carbondale to 1934, supt. schs., Carbondale, since 1934. Served as sec. Carbondale Community Service, 1922-33. Mem. State Adv. Council of Nat. Youth Adminstrn. Mem. Nat. Council to Fight Infantile Paralysis. Formerly trustee East Stroudsburg State Teachers Coll. Mem. N.E.A., American Assn. Sch. Adminstrs., Pa. State Edn. Assn. (pres. 1936), Northeastern Dist. Pa. State Edn. Assn. (pres. 1934), Pa. Hist. Assn., Carbondale Teachers Assn. (pres. 1922-26). Democrat. Roman Catholic. Home: 6 Wayne St., Carbondale, Pa.

McANDREW, Paul Clark, physician; b. Archbald, Pa., May 8, 1905; s. John Joseph and Celia (Clark) McA.; B.S., St. Bonaventure's Coll., 1927; M.D., Georgetown Med. Coll., 1931; m. Mary L. Brennan, Jan. 18, 1936; 1 dau., Pauline Mary. Resident phys., Fairview State Hosp., 1932-34; 1st lt. Med. Res. Corps, U.S.A., 1934-35; in pvt. practice of medicine at Scranton, Pa., since 1935; med. dir. Lackawanna Co. Tuberculosis Hosp. since 1936; consultant in chest diseases, St. Mary's Hosp. since 1937; mem. staff Scranton State Hosp. Mem. A.M.A., Pa. State and Lackawanna Co. med.

McBRIDE, F(rancis) Scott, Anti-Saloon League superintendent; b. Carroll Co., O., July 29, 1872; s. Frank and Harriet (Miller) McB.; B.S. Muskingum Coll., New Concord, Ohio, 1898, D.D. from the same, 1915; grad. Pittsburgh Theol. Sem., 1901; m. Geraldine Van Fossen, July 10, 1901; children—Christine Harriet (Mrs. Lewis Watt), Geralda Pearl (Mrs. Arthur R. Armstrong), John Van Fossen (dec.). Ordained ministry U.P. Ch., 1901; pastor Kittanning, Pa., 1901-09, 9th Av. Ch., Monmouth, Ill., 1909-11; dist. supt. Anti-Saloon League of Ill., 1911-12; Springfield state supt. Ill. Anti-Saloon League, Chicago, 1912-24; gen. supt. Anti-Saloon League of America, 1924-36; now mem. exec. and administrative coms. of Anti-Saloon League of America; supt. Pa. Anti-Saloon League since 1936. Mem. World League against Alcoholism (exec. com.). Vice moderator United Presbyn. Church, 1934-35. Mem. Federal Council Chs. of America (exec. com.), Pi Gamma Mu. Editor Ill. Issue, 1912-15, Pennsylvania Issue since 1936. Home: 1346 Foulkrod St. Office: 504 Wesley Bldg., Philadelphia, Pa.

McBRIDE, John Bavington, lawyer; b. Canonsburg, Pa., Sept. 8, 1876; s. John B. and Almira Jane (Scott) McB.; grad. Jefferson Acad., Canonsburg, 1894; A.B., Washington and Jefferson Coll., 1898, A.M., 1902; LL.B., U. of Pittsburgh, 1902; unmarried. Admitted to Pa. bar, 1902, and since practiced in Pittsburgh; dir. First Nat. Bank, Canonsburg, since 1933, vice-pres. since 1934. Trustee of Trustees of Gen. Assembly of United Presbyn. Ch. of N. America. Mem. Allegheny Co. Bar Assn. Republican. Mem. First United Presbyn. Ch. of Pittsburgh (elder). Home: Route 1, Canonsburg, Pa. Office: 720 Bakewell Bldg., Pittsburgh, Pa.

McBRIDE, Lois Mary, judge; student Grove City (Pa.) Coll., Vassar Coll. (Poughkeepsie, N.Y.), and U. of Pittsburgh Law Sch.; m. George McBride, Apr. 25, 1924. Judge Allegheny County Ct., Pittsburgh, since 1933. Home: Elm Rd., Bradford Woods, Pa. Office: Room 509, Court House, Pittsburgh, Pa.

McBRIDE, Milford Lawrence, lawyer; b. Mercer Co., Pa., Feb. 17, 1889; s. George W. and Margaret Jane (McCoy) McB.; Ph.B., Grove City (Pa.) Coll., 1909; LL.B., U. of Pa., 1914; m. Elizabeth Bartley Douthett, Apr. 18, 1917; children—Katherine Douthett, Milford Lawrence. Admitted to Mercer Co. bar, 1914, Pa. Supreme Court, 1914, U.S. Supreme Ct., 1932; practiced law at Grove City, Pa. since 1914; dir. First Nat. Bank, Grove City, Pa. Served as 2d lt., F.A. Central Officers Training Sch., Camp Taylor, Ky., 1918. Dir. Grove City Hosp. Mem. Mercer Co. Bar Assn. (pres. 1935-36), Pa. Bar Assn., Am. Bar Assn. Republican. Presbyterian. Mason (Past Master). Home: 418 Stewart St. Office: First National Bank Bldg., Grove City, Pa.

McBRIDE, William, v.p. Pittsburgh Steel Foundry Corpn.; b. Troy, N.Y., Oct. 28, 1874; s. John and Elizabeth (Blakeley) M.; student pub. schs. and Rensselaer Poly. Inst., Troy, N.Y.; m. Emma M. Boggs, Apr. 12, 1905; 1 dau., Mrs. V.L.P. Shriver, Jr. Asst. engr. signals N.Y.C. & Hudson River R.R., Albany, N.Y.; U.S. govt. engr. on river and harbor constrn.; sales agt. Standard Underground Cable Co., Pittsburgh, 1902-06; organized, 1906, Fort Pitt Spring & Mfg. Co., McKees Rocks, Pa., pres. to 1928, when sold interests and devoted self to travel; v.p. in charge sales and dir. Pittsburgh Steel Foundry Corpn. since Apr. 1936. Clubs: Duquesne (Pittsburgh); Edgeworth (Sewickley); Lotos (New York). Home: Sewickley, Pa. Office: 1801 Union Bank Bldg., Pittsburgh, Pa.

McBRIDE, William Kervin, surgeon; b. Harrisburg, Pa., Aug. 13, 1901; s. William K. and Sarah K. (Hopple) M.; student Harrisburg Central High Sch., 1915-19, Dickinson Coll., 1919-21; A.B., U. of Pa., 1922; M.D., U. of Pa. Med. Sch., 1926; post grad. study, Allegemeines Krankenhaus, Vienna, Austria, 1934; Cook Co. Hosp., Chicago, 1938; unmarried. Interne Hosp. of P.E. Ch., Phila., 1926-28; chief resident Harrisburg Polyclinic Hosp., 1928-29; in gen. practice of medicine since 1929; asso. surgeon Harrisburg Polyclinic Hospital; dir. Allison-East End Trust Co. Dir. Harrisburg Sch. Dist., 1931-35, pres., 1933-35. City treas., Harrisburg, Pa., 1936-40. Mem. A.M.A., Pa. State Med. Soc., Harrisburg Acad. Medicine, Dauphin Co. Med. Soc., Patriotic Order Sons of America. Republican. Methodist. Mason (Scottish Rite, K.T., Shriner, Tall Cedars), Elk, Moose. Club: Kiwanis (Harrisburg). Home and Office: 52 N. 18th St., Harrisburg, Pa.

McBRIDE, William Manley, newspaper editor; b. Paterson, N.J., Dec. 1, 1894; s. Andrew and Catherine (Manley) McB.; grad. high sch., Paterson, 1913; m. Mary Cecilia Meade, June 10, 1918; children—Eileen Therese, Marilyn. Began as reporter Passaic Daily Herald, 1913, mng. editor, 1918-25, editor, 1925-32; exec. editor of Herald-News since Apr. 1932. Pres. N.J. Unit, Associated Press; dir. The Passaic Daily News, Passaic Community Chest, Passaic Chamber of Commerce. Mem. Psychol. Examining Bd. of Med. Corps, U.S.A., Camp Dix, N.J., World War. Mem. N.J. State Press Assn., Am. Legion. Clubs: Pica, Passaic City. Home: 155 Albion St. Address: 140 Prospect St., Passaic, N.J.

McBURNEY, James Howard, milling exec.; b. Midway, Pa., Nov. 2, 1860; s. John R. and Lizzie K. (Ross) McB.; student Ingleside Acad. and Duff's Coll.; m. Sara B. Scott, July 12, 1893; children—Lois, John R., J. Glenn, Elizabeth, Jean. Partner Canonsburg (Pa.) Milling Co. since orgn., 1891; pres. bd. dirs. Chartiers Bldg. & Loan Assn. since 1920. Pres. bd. dirs. Canonsburg Gen. Hosp. since 1908; dir. Geneva Coll., Beaver Falls, Pa., since 1909; mem. Synod's bd. trustees Ref. Presbyn. Ch. of North America since 1906. Presbyn. Home: West Pike St. Office: 1-19 N. Central Av., Canonsburg, Pa.

McBURNEY, John White, research structural materials; b. Sumner, Wash., May 30, 1890; s. Elmer J. and Lena (McBurney) White; name changed to McBurney when adopted by maternal grandparents; ed. public schools, Cambridge, O.; A.B., Ohio State U., 1913; student George Washington U., 1916-17; m. Mary Theresa Marshall, June 6, 1913; 1 son, John Taggart. Sanitary bacteriologist U.S. Pub. Health Service, 1913-18; chemist Youngstown Sheet Tube Co., 1918-21; engr. tests Cleveland Bd. Edn., 1921-24; tech. service dept. Standard Paint Co. 1924-26; research asso. at Nat. Bur. Standards for Brick Mfrs. Assn., 1926-32, for Asphalt Tile Mfrs. Assn., 1932-34; rep. Am. Standards Assn. at Nat. Bur. Standards, 1934-35; sr. technologist Nat. Bur. Standards since 1935. Fellow A.A.A.S., Am. Inst. Chemists; mem. Rheological Soc., Am. Soc. Mech. Engrs., Am. Concrete Inst., Am. Ceramic Soc., Soc. Chem. Industry, Washington Acad. Science, Washington Philos. Soc., Am. Soc. Testing Materials (chmn. com. on mortar since 1937), Am. Standards Assn. (sec. com. on masonry since 1934; sec. com. on plastering since 1935), Phi Kappa Tau. Club: Cosmos (Washington, D.C.). Contbr. articles to tech. jours. and reports to professional socs. Home: 414 Taylor St., Chevy Chase, Md. Office: National Bureau of Standards, Washington, D.C.

McCABE, David Aloysius, economist; b. Providence, R.I., Mar. 8, 1883; s. James and Anna Rebecca (Bradley) M.; A.B., Harvard, 1904; Ph.D., Johns Hopkins U., 1909; m. Irene Louise Duntlin, June 21, 1929; children—Anne Lucie, Patricia Alice. Special agent of Department of Agriculture and Tech. Instruction for Ireland, 1904-05; instr. economics, Catholic U. of America, 1905-08; fellow in polit. economy, Johns Hopkins, 1908-09; instr. economics, 1909-10, asst. prof., 1910-19, prof., 1919—, Joseph Douglas Green, 1895, prof. of Economics, 1938—. Princeton U. Spl. agt. U.S. Commn. on Industrial Relations, 1914, 15; chmn. Newark Regional Labor Board, 1933-34. Entered Signal R.C., Aviation Sect., Oct. 12, 1917; capt., A.S.A.; Oct. 9-Dec. 16, 1918. Catholic. Author: The Standard Rate in American Trade Unions, 1912; (with G. E. Barnett) Mediation, Investigation and Arbitration in Industrial Disputes, 1916; National Collective Bargaining in the Pottery Industry, 1932; Labor and Social Organization (with R. A. Lester), 1939. Home: Princeton, N.J.

McCABE, Thomas Bayard, banker, pres. Scott Paper Co.; b. Whaleyville, Md., July 11, 1893; s. William Robbins and Beulah (Whaley) McC.; student Wilmington Conf. Acad., Dover, Del., 1907-10; A.B., Swarthmore Coll., 1915; m. Jeannette Everett Laws, Feb. 28, 1924; children—Thomas Bayard, Richard Whaley. With Scott Paper Co., Chester, Pa., since 1916, as salesman, 1916-17, asst. sales mgr., 1919-20, sales mgr., 1920-22, dir. since 1921, sec. and sales mgr., 1922-27, v.p., 1927, pres. since 1927; dir. Nova Scotia Wood Pulp & Paper Co., Ltd., Brunswick Pulp & Paper Co.; dir. Federal Reserve Bank of Phila. since 1938, chmn. of bd. since 1939. Served as private, advancing to capt., U.S. Army, 1917-19. Former chmn. Men's Alumni Council of Swarthmore Coll.; former pres. Phila. Sales Mgrs. Club. Mem. bd. mgrs. Swarthmore Coll. Mem. Delta Upsilon. Republican. Presbyn. (trustee). Clubs: Rittenhouse, Union League, Sunday Breakfast (Phila.); Rolling Green Golf, Springhaven (Media, Pa.). Home: 607 N. Chester Rd., Swarthmore, Pa. Office: Scott Paper Co., Chester, Pa.; Federal Reserve Bank, Philadelphia, Pa.

McCABE, Warren Lee, prof. chem. engring.; b. Bay City, Mich., Aug. 7, 1899; s. James C. and Frances (Cooke) McC.; B.S., U. of Mich., 1922, M.S., same, 1923, Ph.D., 1928; m. Lillian F. Hoag, July 28, 1924; children—Warren Lee, Barbara Louise. Instr. chem. engring., M.I.T., 1923-25; lecturer chem. engring. Worcester Poly. Inst., 1925; successively, instr., asst. prof., and asso. prof. chem. engring., U. of Mich., 1925-36; prof. chem. engring., Carnegie Inst. Tech. since 1936, head of chem. engring. dept. since 1937. Served in S.A.T.C., 1918. Mem. Am. Chem. Soc., Am. Inst. Chem. Engrs., Sigma Xi, Tau Beta Pi, Phi Lambda Upsilon. Republican. Presbyterian. Home: 223 Morrison Drive, Mt. Lebanon, Pittsburgh, Pa.

McCAFFERTY, Ernest D(air), v.p. H. J. Heinz Co.; b. Harrison, O., Nov. 9, 1870; s. Theodore B. and Emily (Dair) McC.; Ph.B., Adrian (Mich.) Coll., 1893; LL.B., Cincinnati Law Sch., 1895; m. Florence Emma Bowles, July 21, 1897; children—Thomas Bowles, Ruth (wife of Dr. C. W. Skinner). Admitted to Ohio bar, 1895, and began practice in Harrison; with H. J. Heinz Co. since 1897, successively as atty. in legal dept. since 1897, private sec. to H. J. Heinz, 1899-1919, asst. sec., 1907-23, sec. since 1923, vice-pres. since 1938, and dir. since 1913; sec. and dir. H. J. Heinz Corpn.; dir. H. J. Heinz Co. of Mass., H. J. Heinz Co., Ltd., London, Eng.; sec. and dir. Lake Charles Products Corpn. Mem. Sigma Alpha Epsilon. Republican. Presbyterian. Mason. Club: Duquesne. Author: Biography of H. J. Heinz. Home: Mt. Royal Boul., Allison Park, Pa. Office: H. J. Heinz Co., Pittsburgh, Pa.

McCAFFREY, Thomas, Jr., pres. Thomas McCaffrey Co.; b. Pittsburgh, Pa., Apr. 2, 1902; s. Thomas and Rose (O'Donnell) McC.; B.A., Holy Cross Coll., Worcester, Mass., 19—; m. Lillian Stocker, Nov. 24, 1926; children—Thomas III, Richard, William. Pres. Thomas McCaffrey Co., real estate, Pittsburgh, Pa., since 1928; pres. Foster Federal Savings & Loan Assn. since 1928. Mem. bd. govs. Pittsburgh Real Estate Bd. since 1935. Mem. Squirrel Hill Bd. of Trade (treas. since 1938), Fox Chapel Dist. Assn. Catholic. Club: Pittsburgh Athletic. Home: 4106 Butler St. Office: 7039 Meade Pl., Pittsburgh, Pa.

McCAGUE, Robert Harshe, banker; b. Edgeworth, Pa., May 21, 1895; s. George E. and Georgie Marie (Smith) McC.; grad. Hill Sch., Pottstown, Pa., 1914; Litt.B., Princeton U., 1918; m. Dorothea Lundeen Cooper, Oct. 3, 1921; children—Barbara Cooper, Alice Graham. Inspr. Carnegie Steel Co., 1919-21; with Dillon, Read & Co., 1921-28; with Union Nat. Bank of Pittsburgh since 1928, vice-pres. since 1931. Served in the Rainbow Div., U.S. Army, with A.E.F., 1918-19. Trustee Valley Hosp., Sewickley, Pa. Republican. Presbyterian. Clubs:

Duquesne, Harvard-Yale-Princeton (Pittsburgh); Allegheny Country, Edgeworth (Sewickley, Pa.). Mem. Am. Radio Relay League, Station W8KBJ. Home: 625 Pine Rd., Sewickley, Pa. Office: 4th Av. at Wood St., Pittsburgh, Pa.

McCAHAN, David, prof. of insurance; b. Huntingdon, Pa., Aug. 26, 1897; s. Albert Johnson and Amanda Mabel (Settle) McC.; B.Sc. in Econ., U. of Pa., 1920, M.A., 1922, Ph.D. 1928; post-grad. work, George Washington U., 1922-26; C.L.U., Am. Coll. Life Underwriters, 1929; m. Rebekah Finley Morse, June 22, 1927; children—Patricia Morse, David, Elizabeth, John Finley. Instr. statistics, Wharton Sch. (U. of Pa.), 1920-22, asst. prof. of ins., 1926-34, asso. prof., 1934-36, professor since 1936; asst. mgr. ins. dept. Chamber Commerce of U.S., 1922-26; sec., asst. dean Am. Coll. Life Underwriters, 1929-34, dean since 1934 (trustee). Member Board of Corporators of the Presbyterian Ministers Fund since 1936; mem. Hygiene Reference Board of the Life Extension Institute since 1936. Served as ensign United States Naval Flying Corps during World War. Member Am. Acad. Polit. and Social Science, Am. Assn. Univ. Profs., Am. Assn. U. Teachers of Ins., Am. Econ. Assn., Nat. Chapter-Chartered Life Underwriters (sec. since 1931), Beta Gamma Sigma, Lambda Chi Alpha. Republican. Presbyn. (elder Swarthmore Presbyn. Ch.). Author: State Insurance in the United States, 1929; Life Insurance as Investment (with S. S. Huebner), 1933. Editor Chartered Life Underwriters Sect. of Life Association News; spl. ins: editor latest revision Webster's New International Dictionary. Contbr. professional articles. Home: 607 Strath Haven Av., Swarthmore, Pa. Office: Logan Hall, U. of Pa., Philadelphia, Pa.

McCAHILL, David Ignatius Bartholomew, lawyer, ry. official; b. Warren County, Ia., Feb. 25, 1884; s. Matthew and Catherine Josephine (Donovan) McC.; LL.B., Drake Univ., 1907, LL.D., 1931; LL.M., Yale, 1908; grad. study U. of Pittsburgh, 1914; m. Marie Eleanor Kaye, Sept. 9, 1909; children—David Ignatius Bartholomew, Marie Kaye and Margurite Katherine (twins). Admitted to Ia. bar, 1907, and began practice at Des Moines; moved to San Francisco, Calif., 1908, to Pittsburgh, Pa., 1913; mem. firm David I. McCahill; pres. Harmony Short Line Ry., Land & Bus Company, Harmony Realty Company, Harmony Short Line Motor Transportation Company, Ellwood-Koppel Bridge Co.; counsel Associated Gas & Electric Co. and subsidiaries. Served as apprentice and master at arms U.S.N., 1898-1904; capt. inf., Calif. N.G., 1911-13. Trustee Drake U. since 1923; trustee Western Penitentiary of Pa., 1924-25, treas., 1924, chmn. bd., 1924-25; dir. Boys' Club Federation Internat.; founder, pres. emeritus and dir. Boys' Club of Pittsburgh; mem. White House Conf. on Child Health and Protection, 1930. Mem. Pittsburgh Symphony Soc. (v.p.; mem. exec. bd.). Mem. Delta Theta Phi, Chi Delta. Republican. K.C. Clubs: Duquesne, Rotary, Pittsburgh Athletic Assn., Pittsburgh Field (life), Pittsburgh Polo. Home: 5078 Warwick Terrace. Office: 714 Frick Bldg., Pittsburgh, Pa.

McCAIN, C(harles) Curtice, ry. official; b. at Minneapolis, Minn., Sept. 18, 1856; s. John Curtice and Sarah Ann (Dailey) M.; pub. sch. edn.; m. Maria Bradley Shaw, Apr. 8, 1886; children—Curtice Shaw, H. Berrien. Clerk and chief clerk Trunk Lines Association, New York, 1877-87; auditor Interstate Commerce Commission, Washington, 1887-95; commr. Assn. of Lake Lines, Buffalo, 1895-1907; chmn. Trunk Line Assn., Oct. 1, 1907-May 1918; sec. Eastern Freight Traffic Com. U.S. R.R. Administration, May 1918-Mar. 31, 1919; appointed mgr. Eastern Freight Inspection Bur., Apr. 1, 1919; mem. Official Classification Com., 1920-34 (retired on account of ill health). Republican. Episcopalian. Author: Compendium of Transportation Theories, 1890; (pamphlet) Changes in Freight Rates for Fifty Years, 1894; (pamphlet) Diminished Purchasing Power of Railway Earnings, 1908. Home: East Orange, N.J.

McCAIN, Samuel Howard, lawyer; b. Freeport, Pa., Apr. 27, 1875; s. William Gibson and Nancy Jane (Rowland) McC.; student Chambersburg (Pa.) Acad., Pa. State Coll.; LL.B., Yale, 1900; m. M. E. Adele Gilpin, Jan. 18, 1908; children—Samuel Howard, John Gilpin. Admitted to Pa. bar, 1900, and since practiced at Kittanning, Pa.; dir. Armstrong Co. Trust Co., Kittanning Telephone Co., Kittanning Thrift Co. Mem. Book and Gavel Soc. (Yale). Republican. Presbyterian. Club: Rotary of Kittanning (past pres.). Home: 324 N. McKean St. Office: Keystone Bldg., Kittanning, Pa.

McCALL, Arthur G(illett), soil scientist; b. Buena Vista, O., Nov. 11, 1874; s. Moses D. and Alice (Gillett) McC.; B.S., Ohio State U., 1900; Ph.D., Johns Hopkins, 1916; m. Harriett M. Flower, Dec. 1896; children—Herbert F., Elizabeth L., Dorothy H., Harriett A. Scientist, Bur. of Soils, U.S. Dept. Agr., 1901-04; prof. agronomy and head of dept., Ohio State U., 1904-16; prof. geology and soils, U. of Md., 1916-27; in charge soil investigations, Md. Expt. Sta., 1916-27; chief of soil investigations, U.S. Dept. Agriculture, 1927-36; with Soil Conservation Service since 1936. Served with Army Ednl. Corps, U.S.A., France, 1919. Exec. sec. 1st Internat. Congress Soil Science. Fellow Am. Assn. Advancement Science, Am. Soc. Agronomy (ex-pres.); mem. Assn. Official Agrl. Chemists, Sigma Xi, Alpha Zeta, Phi Kappa Phi, Gamma Sigma Delta, Alpha Gamma Rho; corr. mem. Czechoslovakian Academy Soil Science. Congregationalist. Club: Cosmos. Author: Physical Properties of the Soil, 1908; Broom Corn Culture, 1912; Studies of Soils, 1915; Studies of Crops, 1916. Home: College Park, Md. Address: U.S. Dept. of Agriculture, Washington, D.C.

McCALL, Max Adams, agronomist; b. Jamestown, Kan., Oct. 20, 1888; s. Andrew Rogers and Mary Pamelia (McKee) McC.; B.S.A., Ore. Agrl. Coll., 1910; M.S., Wash. State Coll., 1922; Ph.D., U. of Wis., 1932; m. Marjorie Sellers, Nov. 14, 1914 (died 1918); 1 dau., Marjorie Sellers; m. 2d, Bernadine Haller, Dec. 27, 1920; 1 dau., Maxine Adams. Instr. high sch., Davenport, Wash., 1910-11, Ore. Agrl. Coll., 1911-12, high sch. of Klamath County, Ore., 1912-14; county agrl. agt. Klamath County, 1914; dry farm specialist Wash. Agrl. Expt. Station and supt. Adams Branch Station, Lind, Wash., 1914-24; agronomist, sr. agronomist, prin. agronomist in charge cereal agronomy, div. of cereal crops and diseases, Bur. Plant Industry, U.S. Dept. Agr., Washington, D.C., 1924-29, in charge of div. since 1929, asst. chief of Bur. since 1935. Fellow A.A.A.S., Am. Soc. Agronomy (ex-pres.), Am. Soc. Plant Physiology, Wash. Bot. Soc., Wash. Acad. Science, Gamma Sigma Delta, Phi Kappa Phi, Sigma Xi, Kappa Sigma. Club: Cosmos. Author official bulls. Home: 209 Taylor St., Chevy Chase, Md. Office: The Mall, Washington, D.C.

McCAMEY, Harold Emerson, lawyer; b. East Orange, N.J., Oct. 28, 1894; s. John Albert and Harriet (Fallis) McC.; prep. edn. pub. schs., Sheffield, Pa.; A.B., Grove City Coll., 1916; LL.B., U. of Pittsburgh, 1918; m. Adelaide Burnap, Feb. 3, 1928; 1 dau., Patricia Lou; m. 2d, Dorothy Trowbridge, Dec. 28, 1935. Admitted to Pa. bar, 1922, and since practiced in Pittsburgh; mem. firm Dickie, Robinson & McCamey. Mem. Allegheny Co., Pa. State and Am. bar assns., Phi Gamma Delta, Delta Theta Phi. Republican. Methodist. Clubs: Oakmont Country (Oakmont, Pa.); Longue Vue Country (Verona, Pa.); Pittsburgh Athletic Assn., The Fellows (Pittsburgh). Home: Waldheim Rd., Fox Chapel, Pa. Office: Grant Bldg., Pittsburgh, Pa.

McCAMIC, Charles, lawyer; b. Wellsburg, W.Va., Dec. 4, 1874; s. Nathan Stanton and Frances (Dowden) M.; LL.B., Yale, 1899; LL.D., West Va. Wesleyan U., 1925; m. Anna F. Smith, Apr. 9, 1902; 1 dau., Frances Smith (Mrs. W. R. Tinker, Jr.). Admitted to the W.Va. bar, 1899, and to the Supreme Court of U.S., 1911; practiced Moundsville 8 yrs., Wheeling since 1907; mem. McCamic & Clarke. Mem. W.Va. Ho. of Rep., 1905. Served as capt. World War, 1917-18; now lt. col. J.A.G., Res. Mem. Am. Bar Assn., W.Va. Bar Assn. (sec. 10 yrs.), Am. Law Inst., Am. Legion, (1st adj. State orgn.), Mil. Order Fgn. Wars of U.S., 27th Div. Assn., Kappa Alpha, Phi Alpha Delta, Phi Beta Kappa, (pres. Northern W.Va. Phi Beta Kappa Alumni Assn.), Scabbard and Blade, Order of the Coif. Episcopalian. Mason, Sojourners. Clubs: Nat. Arts, Grolier, Yale (New York); Ft. Henry, Wheeling Country; Metropolitan, Army and Navy (Washington, D.C.). Author: Doctor Samuel Johnson and the American Colonies, 1925. Also operates a farm near Bethany, W.Va. Home: Moundsville, W.Va. Office: Wheeling, W.Va.

McCAMIC, Jay Thomas, lawyer; b. Wellsburg, W.Va., July 1, 1894; s. Nathan Stanton and Frances Priscilla (Dowden) McC.; A.B., summa cum laude, Washington and Jefferson Coll., Washington, Pa., 1919; grad. study London Sch. Econs., London, Eng., 1919; LL.B., Yale U. Law Coll., 1922; m. Joan Whitehead, May 20, 1926 (died 1937); children—Jeremy Charles, Jolyon Whitehead. Admitted to W.Va. bar, 1922 and engaged in gen. practice of law at Wheeling since 1922; mem. firm McCamic and Clarke since 1933; admitted to practice before all state cts. and U.S. Dist. Ct.; admitted to practice before Supreme Ct. of U.S., 1934; city solicitor of Wheeling, W.Va., since 1935; dir. Morris Plan Savings & Loan Co., Wheeling since 1930. Served as 2d lt. inf., U.S.A., 1917-19; with A.E.F. in France. Mem. Am. Law Inst., Ohio Co. Bar Assn. (pres.), Phi Tau Gamma, Beta Theta Pi, Phi Alpha Delta. Republican. Home: 13 Romney Rd. Office: Nat. Bank of W.Va. Bldg., Wheeling, W.Va.

McCANCE, Pressly Hodge, business exec., lawyer; b. Edgewood, Pa., June 29, 1893; s. William James and Nancy (Hodge) McC.; student Edgewood (Pa.) High Sch., 1907 to 1911; Litt.B., Princeton U., 1915; LL.B., U. of Pittsburgh Law Sch., 1920; m. Ruth Lenhart, Dec. 15, 1926; children—James, Pressly, Edward. Atty. in law dept. Transcontinental Oil Co., Pittsburgh, 1919-23; atty. in law dept. Phila. Co. and subsidiary cos., public utilities, Pittsburgh, Pa., 1923-29, dir. of personnel, 1929-37, asst. to pres., 1937-38, v.p. since 1938, dir. since 1938; dir. Equitable Gas Co., Pittsburgh Rys. Co. Served as lt., 57th Arty., A.E.F., 1917-19. Pres. Children's Aid Soc. of Allegheny Co. since 1935; v.p. Pittsburgh Assn. for Improvement of the Poor since 1938. Mem. Better Business Bur. of Pittsburgh (treas. since 1937), Pittsburgh Personnel Assn. (dir.), Western Pa. Safety Council, Pittsburgh Chamber of Commerce (dir.). Republican. Presbyterian. Clubs: Harvard-Yale-Princeton, Longue Vue Country, Duquesne (Pittsburgh, Pa.). Home: 115 Yorkshire Rd. Office: 435 6th Av., Pittsburgh, Pa.

McCANDLESS, James Frank; b. Huntington, Pa.; s. John Alexander and Sarah (Livermore) McC.; ed. pub. schs. of Mercer, Pa.; unmarried. With Boggs & Buhl, dept. store, 1883-1926, beginning as clerk and advancing to vice-pres. and treas.; retired 1926; dir. Boggs & Buhl, Peoples Pittsburgh Trust Co., Dollar Branch Peoples Pittsburgh Trust Co., First Nat. Bank, Rex-Hide, Inc., A. M. Fruit Growers, Inc., D. L. Clark Co. Republican. Presbyterian. Clubs: Duquesne, Longue Vue, Pittsburgh Athletic (Pittsburgh). Address: Boggs & Buhl, Pittsburgh, Pa.

McCANDLESS, Lee Campbell, lawyer; b. Butler Co., Pa., Mar. 7, 1902; s. William B. and Mary Elizabeth (Campbell) McC.; prep. edn., Butler Co. pub. schs.; A.B., Grove City Coll., 1923, A.M., 1924; LL.B., U. of Pittsburgh, 1929; m. Zella Josephine White, June 11, 1925; 1 son, Richard Lee. Teacher pub. schs. of Pa. 4 yrs.; admitted to Pa. bar 1929, and since practiced in Butler; mem. firm Marshall & McCandless; dist. atty. Butler Co. since 1936. Active in community and church work, community chest, Y.M.C.A. and Boy Scouts. Mem. Butler Co., Pa. State and Am. bar assns., United Commercial Travelers. Rpublican. Presbyterian. Mason (Shriner), Elk. Clubs: Lions, Elks (Butler). Home Route 5. Office: Butler County Nat. Bank Bldg., Butler, Pa.

McCANDLESS, Milton Lowrie, physician; b. Butler Co., Pa.; s. William Harrison and Harriett (Glenn) McC.; M.D., Western Reserve U., 1895; m. Gertrude Lyon, June 16, 1897; children—Lyon, Milton Lowrie, Helen. Engaged in gen. practice of medicine at Rochester, Pa., since 1905; dir. Rochester Gen. Hosp. since 1905. Served as pres. Rochester Bd. Health since 1912. Mem. Beaver Co. Med. Soc. Republican. Presbyn. (elder First Ch.). Mason (32°). Club: Beaver Valley Country. Home: 351 Jefferson St., Rochester, Pa.

McCANDLISS, Lester C., univ. prof.; b. Anderson, Ind., June 16, 1886; s. Harry E. and Harriet (Barr) McC.; B.S. in C.E., Purdue U., Lafayette, Ind.; m. Abby McNamee, Oct. 12, 1910; children—Alfred Neal, John Harry. With C.,B.&Q. R.R., 1909-10; Carmichael Constrn. Co., Akron, O., 1910-12; became instr. civil engring. dept., U. of Pittsburgh, 1912, prof. and head dept. civil engring. since 1933. Served as capt. Engrs. Corps, U.S. Army, 1917-19. Mem. bd. dirs. Pittsburgh Motor Club; mem. Better Traffic Com., City of Pittsburgh. Mem. Soc. for Promotion of Engring. Edn. (chmn. Allegheny sect. 1938), Am. Soc. Civil Engrs. Club: Faculty (U. of Pittsburgh). Home: 741 S. Linden Av. Office: 306 State Hall, U. of Pittsburgh, Pittsburgh, Pa.

McCANN, Minnie Almack, (Mrs. Charles Robert McCann), prin. business sch.; b. Coshocton, O., Mar. 8, 1888; d. John William and Sarah (Preston) Almack; A.B., Goucher Coll., 1909; student Peabody Conservatory, Baltimore, Md., 1906-07; diploma, McCann Sch. of Bus., Hazleton, Pa., 1926; m. Charles Robert McCann, Aug. 4, 1921; children—John William, Margery Jane. Employed as teacher English, high sch., Coshocton, O., 1909-15, 1918-21; prin. McCann Sch. of Business, Reading, Pa., since 1931 and joint owner. Mem. Nat. Commercial Teachers Fed., Eastern Commercial Teachers Assn., Parent Teachers Assn., Am. Assn. Univ. Women, Nat. Fed. Bus. & Professional Womens Clubs, Y.W.C.A., Am. Legion Auxiliary, Alpha Gamma Delta, Alpha Iota. Republican. Methodist. O.E.S. Clubs: Woman's, College, Business and Professional Woman's (Reading). Lecturer on literary topics. Home: 435 Greenwich St. Office: 546 Court St., Reading, Pa.

McCARDELL, Adrian LeRoy, banking; b. Frederick, Md., Mar. 12, 1873; s. Adrian Ceolfrid and Alforetta Rebecca (Stonebraker) McC.; A.B., Franklin and Marshall Coll. 1893; m. Eleanor Clingan, Oct. 1, 1903; children—Claire, Adrian LeRoy, Jr., Robert Clingan, John Malcolm. Began as clk. Frederick Co. Nat. Bank, Frederick, Md., 1893, later asst. cashier, vice-pres., and pres. since 1924; dir. and treas. West End Realty Co. since 1908; pres. and dir. Community Finance Co.; dir. Frederick Co. Nat. Bank, Mutual Ins. Co.; pres. Frederick Clearing House Assn. Served as chmn. Y.M.C.A. and U. War Work drives in Frederick Co. during World War. Mem. exec. com. Frederick Co. Chapter Red Cross. Pres. Parent Teachers Assn., 1920; Bd. Edn. Frederick Co., 1920-26. Mem. Md. Senate, 1926-30, State Tax Commn. Md., 1930-37. Dir. Y.M.C.A.; treas. and mem. exec. com. Frederick Playground Commn. Dir. and treas. Trustees of Home for Aged. Mem. S.A.R., Chi Phi, Md. Masonic Vets. Assn., Trustees Md. Masonic Homes, K.T. Ednl. Foundation (chmn. and treas. Md. Div.), Trustees Masonic Temple Assn., Frederick. Democrat. Evang. Ref. Ch. Mason (K.T., 33°, Shriner). Clubs: Monocacy, Red Fez (Frederick). Home: 301 Rockwell Terrace. Office: 1 N. Market St., Frederick, Md.

McCARTER, Henry, artist, illustrator; b. at Norristown, Pa., July 5, 1866; ed. Philadelphia, and Paris, France, under Thos. Eakin, late Puvis de Chavannes, Alexander Harrison, Rixens, Toulouse, Lautrec, Léon Bonnât. Illustrated for Scribner's, Century, Collier's, and other mags. Instr. Pa. Acad. Fine Arts, Phila., Art Students' League, New York. Bronze medal, Buffalo Expn., 1905; silver medal, St. Louis Expn., 1904; gold medals San Francisco Expn., 1915; Beck prize, Pa. Acad. Fine Arts, 1906; 1st prize, Phila. Art Week, 1924; Joseph Pennell gold medal, Pa. Acad. Fine Arts, 1930; gold medal, Art Club of Phila., 1936. Represented in permanent exhibits: Pa. Acad. Fine Arts, Pa. Art Museum. Address: Pa. Academy of Fine Arts, Philadelphia, Pa.

McCARTER, Robert Harris, lawyer; b. Newton, Sussex Co., N.J., Apr. 28, 1859; s. Thomas N. and Mary Louise (Haggerty) M.; A.B., Princeton, 1879, LL.D. honoris causa, 1904; LL.B., Columbia, 1882; LL.D. honoris causa, N.J. Law Sch., 1935; m. Mary Bouvier Peterson, Oct. 12, 1886; children—George W. C., Mrs. Eleanor Young. Admitted to bar, 1882, since practicing at Newark, N.J.; sr. mem. firm of McCarter & English. Atty.-gen. of N.J., 1903-08. Ex-pres. N.J. State Bar Assn.; trustee Newark Museum Assn. Republican. Presbyn. Clubs: University (New York); Rumson (N.J.); Essex (Newark, N.J.). Home: Rumson (P.O. Red Bank), N.J. Office: Raymond-Commerce Bldg., Newark, N.J.

McCARTER, Thomas Nesbitt, corpn. mgr.; b. Newark, N.J., Oct. 20, 1867; s. Thomas Nesbitt and Mary Louise (Haggerty) McC.; A.B., Princeton, 1888, A.M., 1891; LL.D., Rutgers U., 1937, Newark U., 1938, John Marshall College, 1938; studied law in father's office, and at Columbia U., 1889-90; m. Madeleine G. Barker, Feb. 9, 1897; children—Mrs. Nelson Doubleday, Thomas N., Uzal H., Mrs. Carlos D. Kelly. Member law firm of McCarter, Williamson & McCarter, 1891-99, then practiced alone; judge 1st Dist. Court of Newark, 1896-99 (resigned); member N.J. Senate from Essex Co., 1899-1902; chairman executive com. Rep. State Com., during campaign of 1901; apptd. by Governor Murphy atty. gen. of N.J., 1902, for term of 5 yrs.; resigned, 1903, to become pres. of Public Service Corpn. of N.J., of which was the principal organizer (this corpn., through its subsidiaries, controls and operates nearly all the important gas, electric and transportation utilities of the state), continued as pres. to 1939, chmn. of bd. since Apr. 1939, also sr. exec. officer Pub. Service Corpn. and all subsidiaries; chmn. bd. and mem. exec. com. Fidelity Union Trust Co., Newark; dir. and mem. exec. com. Chase Nat. Bank; dir. N.Y. & Long Branch R.R. Co. Pres. Am. Electric Ry. Assn., 1911-12. Trustee Edison Electric Inst. (pres. 1934-36), Newark Coll. Engring. since 1929; life trustee Rutgers U. since 1938. Clubs: Essex, Newark Athletic, Down Town (Newark); Links, Princeton, Recess (N.Y. City); Ivy, Nassau (Princeton); Rumson Country, Deal Golf, Seabright Beach; Seaview Golf (Absecon, N.J.); Rolling Rock (Pittsburgh); Boca Raton, Mountain Lake (Fla.). Author: District Court Practice of New Jersey, 1898; One Phase of a Jerseyman's Activities, 1933, supplementary vol., 1939. Home: Rumson, N.J.; (winter) Mountain Lake, Lake Wales, Fla.; also 277 Park Av., New York, N.Y. Office: 80 Park Place, Newark, N.J.

McCARTHY, Anna Loretto, supervising prin. of schools; b. Clinton, Wayne Co., Pa., Apr. 12, 1879; d. John and Anna (McGowan) McCarthy; grad. Mayfield High Sch., 1896; grad. East Stroudsburg Normal Sch., 1898; A.B., Marywood Coll., 1925, A.M., 1927; student summers, Pa. State Coll., Cornell U., Mount Gretna Chautauqua; unmarried. Teacher of elementary grades, Mayfield, Pa., Schools, 1898-1903, vice prin., 1903-13, supervising prin. since 1913; supt. Sacred Heart Sunday Sch., 1913-29. Mem. Safety Council of Pa.; active in Red Cross, Boy Scout and other civic organizations. Mem. Pa. State Edn. Assn., Supervising Prins. Assn. of Lackawanna Co., Secondary Sch. Prins. of N.E.A., Marywood Coll. Alumnæ Assn. (mem. bd. dirs.). Democrat. Roman Catholic. Home: 820 Lackawanna Av., Mayfield, Pa.

McCARTHY, Daniel J., neurologist; b. Phila., Pa., June 22, 1874; s. Daniel and Rebecca M.; M.D., U. of Pa., 1895; married. Practiced in Phila. since 1899; prof. med. jurisprudence, U. of Pa.; neurologist to Phila. Gen. Hosp. (Blockley), and St. Agnes Hospital; consulting neurologist, State Hosp. for Insane, Norristown. Trustee Drexel Inst. Mem. A.M.A., Med. Soc. State of Pa., Phila. Med. Soc., Am. Neurol. Assn., Phila. Neurol. Soc., Am. Medico-Psychol. Assn., Pathol. Soc. Phila. Catholic. Editor: Reese's Medical Jurisprudence and Toxicology (8th edit.). Author: The Prisoner of War in Germany, 1917. Home: 2025 Walnut St., Phila., Pa.*

McCARTHY, Louise Faber, lawyer; b. Ridley Park, Pa., May 8, 1902; d. Henry A. and Louise (Faber) McC.; A.B., Trinity Coll., 1923; LL.B., U. of Pa. Law Sch., 1926, LL.M., same, 1929. Admitted to Pa. bar, 1926, and since engaged in gen. practice of law; asso. with office of Clark, Clark, McCarthy and Wagner, Phila., 1927-33; atty. with Pub. Works Adminstrn., Washington, D.C., 1933-35, transferred to Harrisburg, Pa., as chief counsel for Pa., 1935-38, transferred to New York, N.Y., as regional counsel, Region No. 1 comprising 6 New England states and N.Y., Pa., N.J., Del. and Md. since 1938. Mem. Am. Bar Assn., Federal Bar Assn., Pa. State and Phila. Co. bar assns., Order of the Coif, Kappa Beta Pi. Democrat. Roman Catholic. Home: Ingleside, Ridley Park, Pa Office: 2 Lafayette St., New York, N.Y.

McCARTNEY, James Lincoln, physician; b. Chunking, China, July 24, 1898; s. James Henry and Saddie (Kisseck) McC.; came to U.S., 1900, born Am. citizen; student Ohio Wesleyan U., Delaware, O., 1916-18; B.S., U. of Chicago, 1921; M.D., Rush Med. Coll., Chicago, Ill., 1923; student Columbia U., 1928-29; diplomate Nat. Bd. of Med. Examiners, 1927; m. Edith Muriel Tufts, Dec. 27, 1924; children—Helen Catherine, Joan Elizabeth, James Robert. Interne, Brooklyn Hosp., New York, 1923-24; pvt. practice at Hankow, China, 1924-27; govt. physician, St. Elizabeth's Hosp., Washington, D.C., 1927-28; physician, Inst. for Child Guidance, New York, 1928-29, Conn. State Dept. of Health, 1929-31, N.Y. State Dept. of Correction, 1931-34, 1935-38; pvt. practice at Portland, Ore., 1934; physician Battle Creek (Mich.) Sanitarium, 1935; asso. dir. med. dept. Sharpe & Dohme, pharmaceutical biological mfrs., Phila., since 1938. Served in S.A.T.C., 1918; with Am. volunteers in China, 1925-27; now lt. commdr., M.C., as Volunteer Specialist, U.S.N.R. Fellow Am. Coll. of Physicians, Am. Psychiat. Assn. (sec., sect. on forensic psychiatry, 1937-39); mem. A.M.A., N.Y. State Med. Soc., Greene Co. Med. Soc., Assn. of Mil. Surgeons, Phi Chi. Awarded Freer Med. Medal, Rush Med. Coll., Chicago, Ill., 1923; Fiske prize, R.I. State Med. Soc., 1924; Commonwealth fellowship, New York, 1928; research grant by Salmon Memorial Com. of N.Y. Acad. of Medicine, 1933. Unitarian. Mason. Clubs: Shardo, China Club of Philadelphia (organizer and first pres.). Sent to China by Rockefeller Foundation to teach at Peking Union Med. Coll., 1920-21; lecturer Elmira Women's Coll., 1931-32. Columnist Hankow Herald and Shanghai Times, "Your Health," 1924-27. Author of numerous tech. articles and monographs; editor Sharpe & Dohme Seminar. Home: 502 Arbutus St. Office: 640 N. Broad St., Philadelphia, Pa.

McCARTY, Harriet Duncan, librarian; b. Allegheny City, Pa., Nov. 16, 1875; d. Ambrose Augustine and Sallie (Duncan) McC.; A.B., Pa. Coll. for Women, 1897; ed. Pratt Inst. Sch. Library Sci., 1898. Employed as cataloger Carnegie Library of Pittsburgh, 1898-1907; librarian Pub. Library, Sewickley, Pa., 1907-20; branch librarian Carnegie Pub. Library of Pittsburgh, 1920-26; librarian Pa. Coll. For Women, Pittsburgh, Pa., since 1926. Mem. Am. Library Assn., Spl. Libraries Assn., Pa. Library Assn. Democrat. Home: 5758 Howe St., Pittsburgh, Pa.

McCARTY, Roy Anderson, mgr. steam and stoker divs. Westinghouse Electric & Mfg. Co.; b. Galbraith Springs, Tenn., Oct. 2, 1882; s. Isaac Anderson and Addie Sarah (Galbraith) M.; B.S. in E.E., U. of Tenn., Knoxville; m. Jennie Cornelia Creamer, 1906; m. 2d, Emily Elizabeth Wischmeyer, 1926; children—Richard, Marion, Audrey. Student training course Westinghouse Electric & Mfg. Co., 1903-05, tester, 1905-06, design engr., 1906-09, insulation engr., 1909-11, sect. engr., 1911-28, div. engr., 1928-30, mgr. generator engring. dept., 1930-35, mgr. generator operating div., 1935-37, mgr. small motor plant, Lima, O., 1937-38, mgr. steam apparatus plant, Lester, Phila., Pa., and stoker

McCASLAND

plant, Attica, N.Y., since 1938. Mem. Am. Inst. E.E., Am. Soc. M.E., Am. Management Assn., Nat. Elec. Mfrs. Assn., Chamber of Commerce. Presbyn. Clubs: Phila. Automobile, Art (Phila.); University (Pittsburgh); Aronimink Golf. Home: 827 Lindale Av., Drexel Hill, Pa. Office: care Westinghouse Electric & Mfg. Co., Lester, Phila., Pa.

McCASLAND, Selby Vernon; prof. of religion, Goucher Coll. Home: 4132 Westview Road, Baltimore, Md.

McCASLIN, Murray Frew, physician; b. Lawrence Co., Pa., Feb. 21, 1904; s. D. Scott and Elizabeth (Frew) McC.; B.S., U. of Pittsburgh, 1926; M.D., U. of Pittsburgh Med. Sch., 1929; grad. student, U. of Minn. Grad. Sch., Mayo Clinic, 1930-31; m. Harriet Elizabeth Wilson, Oct. 3, 1936. Engaged in practice limited to ophthalmology at Pittsburgh, Pa., since 1931; mem. staff, dept. of ophthalmology, Eye & Ear Hosp., Falk Clinic, both Pittsburgh, U. of Pittsburgh Med. Sch., Columbus Hosp., Wilkinsburg. Fellow Am. Coll. Surgeons; mem. Am. Med. Assn., Pa. State and Allegheny Co. med. socs., Pittsburgh Ophthal. Soc., Phi Rho Sigma. Republican. United Presbyn. Mason (32°), Shriner. Home: 6016 Hampton St. Office: Union Trust Bldg., Pittsburgh, Pa.

McCAULEY, Thomas Augustine, educator; b. Newton, Mass., Jan. 10, 1897; s. Bartholomew and Julia (Minihan) McC.; student Boston Coll. High Sch., 1910-14, St. Mary's Junior Coll., North East, Pa., 1914-17, St. Alphonsus Sem. Esopus, N.Y., 1918-1924; A.M., Catholic U. of America, Washington, D.C., 1931. Roman Catholic priest in Redemptorist Order since June 17, 1923; prof. of English lit. and poetry, St. Mary's Coll., North East, Pa., 1925-30, 1931-36; rector St. Mary's Coll., North East, Pa., since June 1936. Address: N. Lake St., North East, Pa.

McCAULEY, William Deles, lawyer; b. Moorefield, W.Va., July 3, 1900; s. Geo. Wm. and Eleanor (O'Donohue) McC.; LL.B., W.Va. Univ. Law Sch., 1924; m. Blanche White, 1924. Admitted to W.Va. bar, 1924, and since engaged in gen. practice of law at Moorefield; mem. firm McCauley & McCauley; also dist. mgr. for Fidelity Investment Assn. of Wheeling, W.Va.; served as town recorder, Moorefield, W.Va., 1926; prosecuting atty. of Hardy Co., 1928-32. Served in S.A.T.C., 1918. Organizer and past pres. Vol. Fire Co., 1934-38. Mem. W.Va. Bar Assn., Phi Delta Phi. Democrat. Presbyn. Mason. Modern Woodman. Club: Lions of Moorefield. Office: Moorefield, W.Va.

McCLAIN, Harry Clement, M.D., med. dir.; b. Huntingdon Co., Pa., May 30, 1880; s. Frank C. and Margaret A. (Shrader) McC.; student Juniata Coll., Huntingdon, Pa., 1895; M.D., Medico-Chirurgical Coll., Phila., Pa., 1902; m. Lena B. Laidig, Sept. 20, 1905; 1 dau., Pauline M. (dec.). In practice medicine in Hustontown, Pa., since 1902; co. med. dir., Fulton Co., Pa., since 1935. Mem. Post Graduate Interstate Assembly of America, Franklin Co. Med. Soc., Patriotic Order Sons of America. Methodist. Mason (32°, Shriner). Address: Hustontown, Pa.

McCLEAN, Lee Dudley, coll. prof.; b. Denver, Ill., May 31, 1886; s. Louis Baldwin and Laura (Green) McC.; A.B., Culker-Stockton Coll., Canton, Mo., 1909; A.M., Yale, 1912; m. Jennie L. McRoberts, Sept. 10, 1914; children—Laura Miriam, Jane Elizabeth. Instr. history and social sci., high sch., East St. Louis, Ill., 1910-11; instr. econs. and sociology, Bowdoin Coll., 1913-14, asst. prof., 1914-20; prof. econs. and sociology and head of dept., Allegheny Coll. since 1920. Mem. Am. Sociol. Soc., Am. Assn. Univ. Profs., Pa. Conf. Social Work, Pa. Charities Assn., Delta Tau Delta. Republican. Conglist. Home: 388 N. Main St., Meadville, Pa.

McCLEARY, Thomas Galbraith, supt. pub. schs., retired; b. New Castle, Pa., May 18, 1874; s. Samuel E. and Asenath (Braham) McC.; ed. Geneva Coll., 1891-94; A.B., U. of Chicago, 1902; (hon.) Ped.D., West Minster Coll., New Wilmington, Pa., 1930; (hon.)

572

Ped.D., Geneva Coll., Beaver Falls, Pa., 1937; m. Agnes M. Fetterman, Aug. 25, 1904 (dec. 1938); children—Samuel B., Charles F., Thomas G. Began as teacher pub. schs., New Castle, Pa., 1894; supt. schs., Kane, Pa., 1908-11, Washington, Pa., 1911-20, Braddock, Pa., 1920-37, retired from active work, 1937. Republican. Mem. United Presbyterian Ch. (elder). Home: 438 Second St., Braddock, Pa.; Kranghurst Hotel, St. Petersburg, Fla.

McCLELLAN, George Edwin, r.r. exec.; b. Bellefonte, Pa., June 4, 1903; s. Charles Benton and E. Armina (Haupt) McC.; ed. pub. sch. and high sch., Bellefonte, Pa.; m. Mildred Jane Watson, Aug. 29, 1931; children—Charity Louise, George Edwin. Began as locomotive fireman on Pa. R.R., 1921; clk. Bellefonte Central R.R., 1923, and advanced through various positions to vice-pres., treas., gen. mgr. and dir. since 1937; dir. Bellefonte Trust Co. Democrat. Episcopalian. Mason (K.T., Shriner). Club: Kiwanis. Home: 155 E. Linn St. Office: 12 N. Spring St., Bellefonte, Pa.

McCLELLAN, Robert Price, chmn. of bd. First National Bank of Irwin; b. in Fayette County, Pa., Dec. 13, 1862; s. Robert Price and Margaret (Matthews) McC.; student pub. schs., Fayette Co., Pa., 1868-79, pvt. study, 1879-88; m. Mary Fullerton Larimer, Jan. 2, 1890; children—John Price, Robert Hamilton, Clara (Mrs. Earle B. Beacham). In practice medicine at Irwin, Pa., since 1888; chmn. of bd. First Nat. Bank of Irwin since 1909; president Jersey Cereal Co., Chicago, Ill., since 1923. Presbyterian. Mason. Club: Kiwanis (Irwin, Pa.). Home: 805 Pennsylvania Av. Office: 405 Main St., Irwin, Pa.

McCLELLAN, William Smith, business exec.; b. York, Pa., Feb. 3, 1887; s. William Henry and Mary Ellen (Smith) McC.; student Worcester (Mass.) Acad., 1902-04; A.B., Williams Coll., Williamstown, Mass., 1908; m. Josephine Niles, Apr. 14, 1917; children—Josephine, Catharine, Bruce, Mary Hamilton. With P. H. Glatfelter Co., paper mfrs., Spring Grove, Pa., since 1908, v.p. and dir. since 1928; dir. S. G. Water Co. Pres. Spring Grove Sch. Bd. since 1925. Republican. Presbyterian. Clubs: Union League, Williams (New York); Lafayette (York, Pa.); York (Pa.) Country. Author: Smuggling in the America Colonies, 1912. Address: Spring Grove, Pa.

McCLELLAND, Clark Russell, coll. dean; b. Blairsville, Pa., May 25, 1882; s. John and Nancy Jane (Gormley) McC.; A.B., Grove City Coll., 1915; A.M., U. of Pittsburgh, 1924; Ph.D., N.Y. Univ., 1931; m. Olive Malone, Aug. 9, 1917; 1 dau. Mary Malone. Engaged as teacher rural schs., 1900-10; teacher high sch., Monessen, Pa., 1915-17, prin., 1917-24, city supt. schs., 1924-30; student and instr. N.Y. Univ., 1930-31; prof. edn., Kutztown State Teachers Coll., 1931-35, dean of instrn. since 1935; instr., Grove City Coll. summers, 1915, 18, 19. Life mem. N.E.A. Republican. Presbyn. Home: College Hill, Kutztown, Pa.

McCLELLAND, Ellwood Hunter, technology librarian; b. Rockdale Mills, Pa., May 23, 1878; s. John M. and Reba (Tedlie) McC.; Ph.B., Lafayette Coll., 1905; m. Grace E. Windsor, June 3, 1924. Engaged as asst., Carnegie Library of Pittsburgh, 1904-07, technology librarian continuously since 1908; also editor, Proceedings of Engrs. Soc. of Western Pa., 1917-38, Technical Book Review Index, 1917-28; abstract editor, Fuels and Furnaces, 1923-24, Rolling Mill Journal, 1928-30. Fellow A.A.A.S. Mem. Am. Chem. Soc., Am. Foundrymen's Assn., Am. Soc. for Testing Materials, Am. Library Assn., Inst. of Metals, Iron and Steel Inst., Soc. of Rheologists, Soc. for Promotion Engring. Edn., Bot. Soc. of Western Pa., N.Y. Library Assn., Sigma Nu. Republican. Has compiled and published many bibliographies on tech. subjects; Literature of the Coal Industry (annually) 1918-25; Review of Iron and Steel Literature (annually) since 1917. Home: 1375 Cordova Rd., Pittsburgh, Pa. Office: Carnegie Library of Pittsburgh, Pittsburgh, Pa.

McCLELLAND, George William, vice-pres. Univ. of Pa.; b. Dobbs Ferry, N.Y., June 18,

McCLINTOCK

1880; s. Charles Paul and Meta Janet (Babcock) McC.; grad. Westminster Sch., Simsbury, Conn., 1898; A.B., University of Pa., 1903, Ph.D., 1916, LL.D. from the same university, 1931; m. Mildred I. Child, Nov. 4, 1916; children—George Bryant, Marion Child. Instr. English and Latin, Coll. City of New York, 1905-11; instr. English, U. of Pa., 1911-17, asst. prof., 1917-25, prof. since 1925, dir. admissions, 1921-26, vice-pres., 1925-39, provost since 1939. Mem. Assn. Coll. and Secondary Schs. of Middle States and Md. (sec. since 1912), Modern Lang. Assn. America, St. Andrews Soc., Kappa Sigma, Phi Beta Kappa, Beta Gamma Sigma. Presbyterian. Clubs: Rittenhouse (Phila.); University of Pa. (New York). Home: 730 South Latches Lane, Merion, Pa. Office: College Hall, Univ. of Pa., Philadelphia, Pa.

McCLINTIC, Clifton F., M.D., penitentiary warden; b. Williamsburg, W.Va., Aug. 9, 1884; s. Michael L. and Laura Jane (Lynch) McC.; diploma Randolph-Macon Acad., 1902; student Randolph-Macon Coll., 1902-06; M.D., U. of Cincinnati, 1919; studied in Europe, 1928; unmarried. Prin. high sch., Anoka, Minn., 1907-09; instr. East High Sch., Minneapolis, 1909-11; instr. in anatomy, U. of Minn., 1910-11; prof. anatomy and physiology, U. of S.D., 1911-12; asso. prof. anatomy, Emory U., Atlanta, Ga., 1912-13; prof. physiology and pharmacology, Southern Methodist U., Dallas, Tex., 1913-14; prof. anatomy, Baylor U., 1914-15; prof. anatomy and histology, Ohio Coll. Dental Surgery, Cincinnati, 1915-16; exec. sec. U. of Cincinnati Med. Sch. and instr. in anatomy, 1917-19; prof. anatomy and head of dept., Detroit Coll. of Medicine (now Wayne U. Med. Sch.), 1919-31, also chief of staff Eloise Hosp., etc.; warden W.Va. Penitentiary since 1933; dir. Greenbrier Valley Bank, Lewisburg, W.Va. Mem. W.Va. legislature, 1921-23 and 1933-35. Pres. Wild Life League of W.Va., 1935-36. Mem. A.M.A., Am. Soc. Neurology and Psychiatry, Internat. Neurol. Congress, Kappa Sigma, Nu Sigma Nu. Democrat. Mason (K.T.). Clubs: Grosse Ile Golf (Detroit); Fort Henry (Wheeling, W.Va.); Batchawana Hunting and Fishing (Oontario, Can.). Research work on gangrene in Raynaud's Disease and Buerger's Disease, on epilepsy and sleeping sickness, and revised method for treatment of such conditions. Contbr. to med. jours. Home: Williamsburg, W.Va.

McCLINTIC, George Warwick, judge; b. Pocahontas Co., W.Va., Jan. 14, 1866; s. William H. and Mary (Mathews) McC.; A.B., Roanoke Coll., Salem, Va., 1883, LL.D., 1928; LL.B., University of Virginia, 1886; m. Mary Ethel Knight, Oct. 17, 1907; 1 dau., Elizabeth K. Practiced at Charleston, 1888-1921; mem. Ho. of Delegates, W.Va., 1919-21; judge U.S. Dist. Court, Southern Dist., W.Va., by apptmt. of Pres. Harding, since Aug. 4, 1921. Republican. Presbyn. Mason (K.T., Shriner); Grand Master Grand Lodge of Masons of W.Va., 1905-06. Home: 1598 Kanawha St. Office: Federal Bldg., Charleston, W.Va.

McCLINTIC, Robert Hofferd, coal and gas exec.; b. Pittsburgh, Pa., July 3, 1901; s. Howard Hale and Margaret Wallick (McCulloch) McC.; student Hill Sch., Pottstown, Pa., 1915-19, Milford Sch., Milford, Conn., 1919-20, Hun's Sch., Princeton, N.J., 1920-21; unmarried. Served from laborer to asst. mgr. Leetsdale Shop, McClintic-Marshall Steel Corpn., Leetsdale, Pa., 1921-27; v.p. Steel Frame House Co. (subsidiary of McClintic-Marshall), Pittsburgh, 1927-31; sales promotion dept. Koppers Co., producers coal, oil, gas, etc., Pittsburgh, Pa., 1931-36, asst. to pres. since 1937; trustee and mem. of exec. com. Koppers United Co.; trustee Dollar Savings Bank. Mem. and exec. Community Fund, Pittsburgh. Republican. Episcopalian. Clubs: Duquesne, Pittsburgh, Pittsburgh Golf, Rolling Rock, Fox Chapel Golf (Pittsburgh, Pa.). Home: 1130 Beechwood Boul. Office: Koppers Bldg., Pittsburgh, Pa.

McCLINTOCK, Charles Arbuthnot, banker; b. Pittsburgh, Pa., June 15, 1883; s. Jonas Roup and Elizabeth (Arbuthnot) McC; A.B., Princeton U., 1907; unmarried. Vice-pres. and dir.

McCLINTOCK, Colonial Trust Co., Pittsburgh, Pa.; dir. Darby Petroleum Corpn. Served as maj., Inf., U.S. Army, during World War. Mem. Carnegie Hero Fund Commn.; trustee West Pa. Hosp.; mem. bd. mgrs., Thorn Hill Sch. for Boys. Presbyterian. Mason (Lodge 679, Consistory, Shriner). Clubs: Duquesne, Pittsburgh Athletic Assn., Harvard-Yale-Princeton (Pittsburgh); Fox Chapel Golf (Pittsburgh); Rolling Rock (Ligonier, Pa.). Home: 6425 5th Av. Office: 414 Wood St., Pittsburgh, Pa.

McCLINTOCK, Gilbert Stuart, lawyer; b. Wilkes-Barre, Pa., Dec. 27, 1886; s. Andrew Hamilton and Eleanor (Welles) McC.; prep. edn., Lawrenceville (N.J.) Sch.; A.B., Princeton, 1908; unmarried. Began practice of law at Wilkes-Barre, 1912; dir. Glen Alden Coal Co., Miners Nat. Bank of Wilkes-Barre, Lehigh & Wilkes-Barre Coal Co., Delaware, Lackawanna & Western Coal Company. Pres. Wyoming Valley Council Boy Scouts of America, 1916-25, Wyoming Valley Welfare Fed., 1927-30, Wyoming Valley Soc. Arts and Sciences since 1923; dir. Osterhout Free Library, Children's Home of Wilkes-Barre; trustee Bucknell U.; mem. visiting com. Dept. of Art and Archæology, Princeton U. Mem. Am. and Pa. State bar assns., Am. Museum Natural History, College Art Soc. Presbyterian. Clubs: Westmoreland (Wilkes-Barre); University (New York); Metropolitan (Washington, D.C.). Home: 44 S. River St. Office: 34 S. River St., Wilkes-Barre, Pa.

McCLINTOCK, Walter, ethnologist; b. Pittsburgh, Pa., Apr. 25, 1870; s. Oliver and Clara C. (Childs) M.; B.A., Yale, 1891, hon. M.A., 1911; unmarried. Spent 1896-1909 with Blackfeet tribe of Indians, in Mont.; adopted as son of Chief Mad Wolf and collected many valuable ethnol. materials, especially photographs, moving pictures, songs, legends, etc.; made a mem. of Blackfeet tribe by ceremonials. McClintock Peak, Glacier Nat. Park, named by nat. govt., Feb. 7, 1912. Lectured before scientific and educational institutes in U.S., Great Britain and Germany, 1907-13; fellow in ethnology, Southwest Museum, Los Angeles; curator Yale University Library. Author: The Old North Trail; Leben, Bräuche, Legenden der Schwarzfuss-Indianer; Medizinal und Nutsflanzen der Schwarzfuss-Indianer; Old Indian Trails; Tragedy of the Blackfoot; Blackfoot Culture. Contbr. to mags. Address: The Ruskin, Pittsburgh, Pa.

McCLINTOCK, Walter John, lawyer; b. Meadville, Pa., July 9, 1885; s. John Oliver and Harriet Elizabeth (Coburn) McC.; prep. edn. Meadville Pub. Schs.; A.B., Allegheny Coll., Meadville, 1907; LL.B., Dickinson Sch. of Law, Carlisle, Pa., 1910, A.M., Dickinson Coll., 1910; m. Dorothy Alexander Kennedy, Aug. 29, 1922 (died Jan. 4, 1924); m. 2d, Grace Wheeler Smith, Apr. 10, 1930. Admitted to Pa. bar, 1910, and since practiced in Meadville; dir. Meadville Merchants Nat. Bank & Trust Co. Sec. and trustee Meadville Theol. Sch., Chicago, Ill. Republican. Unitarian. Mason, Odd Fellow. Clubs: Country, University, Iroquois Boating and Fishing (Meadville). Home: 515 Walnut St. Office: 359 Center St., Meadville, Pa.

McCLOSKEY, Edward William, physician; b. Chestnut Hill, Phila., Pa., Mar. 25, 1885; s. John and Anna (Lawless) McC.; B.S., U. of Pa., 1908; M.D., U. of Pa. Med. Sch., 1911; (hon.) A.M., Villanova Coll., 1912; m. Katharine Richards, Aug. 21, 1921. Resident phys., St. Joseph's Hosp., Phila., 1911-12; phys., Chestnut Hill Hosp., 1912-17, chief of staff, 1933-37; in pvt. practice of medicine at Phila. since 1912. Served as 1st lt., capt. then maj. Med. Corps Res., U.S.A., 1917-19; now lt. col. Fellow Am. Coll. Physicians; mem. Phila. Coll. Phys., Nu Sigma Nu. Democrat. Roman Catholic. Club: Philadelphia Cricket (St. Martins). Home: 7 East Chestnut Hill Av., Philadelphia, Pa.

McCLOSKEY, Robert Francis, vice-pres. Blaw Knox Co.; b. Pittsburgh, Pa., Dec. 9, 1888; s. George A. and Mary B. (Martin) McC.; ed. Pittsburgh High Sch. and Alexander Hamilton Inst., m. Ruth McVeigh, Aug. 15, 1909; children—Robert, Ruth, Lawrence, John, James, Mildred. Began as office boy, 1901; mgr. North Side plant Riter, Conley Co., 1909-13, gen. supt., 1913-18; with Blaw Knox Co. since 1919, production mgr., 1919-34, vice-pres. since 1934; pres. Hoboken Land Co.; vice-pres. Blaw Knox Internat. Co. Trustee Sacred Heart Ch.; dir. Boys Club of Pittsburgh. Clubs: Pittsburgh Athletic, Pittsburgh Field; Bankers (New York). Home: 938 N. Highland Av., Pittsburgh, Pa. Office: Blawnox, Pa.

McCLOSKEY, Thomas David, lawyer, corpn. official; b. Somerville, Mass., Jan. 7, 1873; s. Thomas and Abigail (Warnock) McC.; A.B., Geneva Coll., Beaver Falls, Pa., 1893; LL.B., Harvard, 1899; m. Grace P. Moorhead, Nov. 4, 1904 (died Dec. 27, 1925); m. 2d, Elizabeth Wood Lilley, Apr. 20, 1933. Admitted to Mass. bar, 1899, Pa. bar, 1902; in practice, Pittsburgh, since 1901; mem. firm McCloskey, Best & Leslie; vice chmn. bd. Firth-Sterling Steel Co.; pres. Wolf-Tongue Mining Co.; dir. Thompson & Co., Western Savings & Deposit Bank. Presbyn. Club: Duquesne. Home: 1311 Squirrel Hill Av. Office: Oliver Bldg., Pittsburgh, Pa.

McCLOY, John, lt. U.S.N., retired; b. Brewster, N.Y., Jan. 30, 1876; s. James and Margret (McCann) McC.; ed. pub. and parochial schs., N.Y. City; m. Sarah F. Higgens, Apr. 17, 1907. Enlisted with rate of seaman, U.S. N., 1898, served in Cuba and Puerto Rico campaigns; in Phillipines and China campaigns, 1899-1902; boatswain, 1903; helped to extinguish fire on U.S.S. Pawnee loaded with powder and shell alongside magazine; beach master for landing force in occupation of Vera Cruz, 1914; commanded U.S.S. Curlew in mine sweeping in North Sea, 1919; promoted to lt., 1918; retired 1928 after 30 yrs. and 6 mos. active service. Awarded Congressional Medal of Honor, relief expdn. to Peking, 1900; Medal of Honor for extraordinary heroism and distinguished conduct in battles in occupation Vera Cruz, 1914; Navy Cross for operations while in command U.S.S. Curlew, 1919; Letter of Commendation from sec. of navy for skillful navigation in ice, 1917-18; campaign decorations for W. I., Spanish War, 1898, Phillipines, 1899-1902, China, 1900, Panama, 1903-04, Mexico, 1914, World War, 1917-19. Mem. Naval Order, Am. Irish Hist. Soc., Am. Legion, Vets. Fgn. Wars, Roamers, Army and Navy Legion of Valor. Democrat. Roman Catholic. Club: Adventurers (New York). Home: 128 Sylvan Av., Leonia, N.J.

McCLUE, Arthur Eugene, M.D.; b. Horton, W.Va., June 26, 1898; s. Arthur M. and Blanche M. (Stotler) McC.; B.S., W.Va. U., 1922; M.D., U. of Louisville, 1925; m. Wilma Householder, Feb. 7, 1931. Began practice at New Cumberland, W.Va., 1925; state health commr. of W.Va., since June 1933. Served as 1st lt. U.S. Army, World War. Mem. A.M.A., Phi Beta Pi. Democrat. Episcopalian. Mason, Odd Fellow, K.P. Address: State Capitol, Charleston, W.Va.

McCLUNG, Clarence Erwin, zoölogist; b. Clayton, Calif., Apr. 5, 1870; s. Charles Livingston and Annie Howard (Mackey) M.; Ph.G., U. of Kan., 1892, A.B., 1896; A.M., 1898, Ph.D., 1902; grad. student, Columbia, 1897, U. of Chicago, 1899; m. Anna Adelia Drake, Aug. 31, 1899; children—Ruth Cromwell, Della Elizabeth. Asst. prof. zoölogy, 1897-1900, asso. prof., 1900-06, head of dept. and curator vertebrate paleontol. collections, 1902-12, acting dean, School of Medicine, 1902-06, U. of Kan.; prof. zoölogy and dir. zoöl. lab., University of Pa., 1912; visiting professor Keio Univ., Tokyo, 1933-34. Member embryol. staff, Woods Hole, Mass., 1893, 1914— (trustee); head of scientific expdns. to Ore., Wash. and Western Kan. Chmn. div. biology and agr., Nat. Research Council, Washington, 1919-21 (fellowship bd.); mem. advisory bd., Wistar Inst., Morris Arboretum. Republican. Conglist. Fellow A.A.A.S. (v.p. sect. F, 1926); mem. Am. Zoöl. Soc. (pres. 1910, 14), Am. Philos. Soc., Am. Soc. Naturalists (pres. 1927), Acad. Natural Sciences Phila., Nat., Washington and Kan. acads. of science, Am. Assn. of Anatomists, Union of Am. Biol. Socs. (pres. 1922-30), Sigma Xi (pres. 1919-21), Tri Beta (pres. 1936, 38). Author of Microscopical Technique, Chromosome Theory of Heredity (general cytology); also tech, papers on cytology, sex-determination, paleontology, etc. Mng. editor Journal of Morphology; pres. bd. trustees and seci-editor Biol. Abstracts. Clubs: Cosmos, Lenape. Home: Wallingford, Pa.*

McCLUNG, Frank Arthur, pres. Union Trust Co. of Butler; b. West Sunbury, Pa., Feb. 2, 1882; s. Charles Hultz and Hannah Jane (Guinn) McC.; student West Sunbury (Pa.) Acad., 1896-1900, Grove City (Pa.) Coll., 1904-06; m. Mary Anetta Goehring, June 5, 1912; children—Richard Goehring, Robert Marshall, Frank Arthur, Mary Ann. Teacher common and high schs., Penn Twp., 1906-08; principal Zelienople (Pa.) Pub. Schs., 1908-11; co. supt. schs., Butler Co., Pa., 1911-20; trust officer Union Trust Co. of Butler, Pa., 1920-33, pres. and trust officer since 1933; dir. Peoples Telephone Corpn. of Butler, Suburban Telephone Co., West Winfield R.R. Co. Pres. bd. edn., Butler, Pa., since 1926; pres. and dir. Y.M.C.A. since 1934. Mem. Butler Chamber of Commerce (dir.). Republican. United Presbyterian. Club: Rotary (Butler, Pa.). Home: 324 W. Penn St. Office: 101 N. Main St., Butler, Pa.

McCLUNG, James, M.D.; b. Rupert, W.Va., Sept. 29, 1874; s. Joseph E. and Kathrin (Murry) McC.; student W.Va. U., 1896-97; M.D., U. of Md., 1901; m. Maude Weaver, 1902; children—Beatrice, Marion (Mrs. Harold Sargent), Kathryn (Mrs. Lavis Welch), Margaret, James E., Bill Dennis, Ruth Roe. Practice as physician and surgeon, Richmond, W.Va., since 1901; established The McClung Hosp., Richmond, 1905, and since owned and conducted same; dir. Cherry River Nat. Bank; farmer and stockman. Mem. State Senate, 1913-17. Pres. W.Va. Hosp. Assn.; mem. W.Va. Med. Soc.; dir. Farm Bureau; pres. Nat. "Ramp" Club, Richmond. Republican. Baptist. Mason, Odd Fellow, Elk. Now owns family estate "Glencoe," owned by family for many years. Address: Richwood, W.Va.

McCLURE, Charles Freeman Williams, anatomist; b. Cambridge, Mass., Mar. 6, 1865; s. Charles Franklin and Joan Elizabeth (Blake) M.; A.B., Princeton, 1888, A.M., 1892; Coll. Phys. and Surg. (Columbia), 1890-91; univs. of Berlin, 1893, Kiel, 1895, Würzburg, 1897; hon. Sc.D., Columbia, 1908; m. Grace Latimer Jones, Aug. 25, 1921. Instr. biology, 1891-95, asst. prof., 1895-1901, prof. comparative anatomy, 1901-34, Princeton U., now prof. emeritus. Mem. Peary Relief Expdn., 1899. Mem. Am. Soc., Naturalists, Am. Zoöl. Soc., Assn. Am. Anatomists (v.p., 1910-11, exec. com., 1912-16, pres., 1920-21), Am. Philos. Soc., Anatomische Gesellschaft, Phi Beta Kappa, Sigma Xi; fellow A.A.A.S. Clubs: Ivy, Nassau (Princeton); Columbus (Columbus, O.). Author of numerous papers on the anatomy and development of the vascular system, oedema, etc. Formerly editor Anatomical Record. Home: Princeton, N.J.

McCLURE, George William, lawyer; b. Braddock, Pa., Nov. 9, 1902; s. Samuel Richard and Jennie (Hamill) McC.; grad. North Braddock High Sch., 1920; student, Pa. State Coll. 1920-21; A.B., Coll. of Wooster (O.), 1924; LL.B., U. of Pittsburgh, 1928; m. Lucile Jackson, June 28, 1929; children—Samuel Richard, II, Jane Evelyn, George William, Walter Jackson. Mathematics teacher, Swissvale (Pa.) High Sch., 1924-25; admitted to Pa. bar, 1928, and practiced in Pittsburgh; mem. firm McClure & McClure. Mem. North Braddock Bd. of Edn. 1935-37; mem. bd. mgrs. Carnegie Library of Braddock; mem. council Allegheny County Community Fund. Mem. Allegheny Co. Bar Assn., Delta Theta Phi. Republican. Presbyterian. Mason, Knight of Pythias. Club: Braddock Rotary. Home: 819 Bell Av., Braddock, Pa. Office: 429 4th Av., Pittsburgh, Pa.

McCLURE, Grace Latimer Jones (Mrs. Charles F. W. McClure), educator; b. Columbus, O., Apr. 3, 1879; d. George Dudley and Eva Jane (Latimer) Jones; A.B., Bryn Mawr, 1900, A.M., 1902; studied Ohio State U., Harvard, Dartmouth; m. Charles Freeman Williams McClure, of Princeton U., Aug. 25, 1921. Head mistress Columbus School for Girls, 1904-38, also sec. of board; organizer and ednl. adviser to bd. of Old Trail School, Akron, O., 1920-22. Originator of Head-Mistresses Assn. Middle West, sec., 1912-14, pres., 1922-24, 1930-33, and rep. on Coll. Entrance Exam. Bd., 1922-24, 29-33; originator, pres., Ohio Bryn Mawr Club, 1916-21; pres. Columbus Br. Assn. Collegiate Alumnæ, 1911-14, and state rep., 1918-21; mem. com. of revision of Coll. Entrance Examination Bd., 1924-34. Member N.J. Soc. Colonial Dames of America, Am. Order of the Crown, Princeton Chapter Garden Club of America. Author: The Columbus School for Girls Grammars, 1910, 4th edit., 1925; What Makes Christmas Christmas, and other plays for children; also pamphlets and articles. Home: Princeton, N.J.

McCLURE, James Focht, lawyer; b. Lewisburg, Pa., Jan. 9, 1892; s. Harold Murray and Margaret (Focht) McC.; grad. Bucknell Acad., Lewisburg, 1909; student Bucknell U., 1909-11; A.B., Amherst (Mass.) Coll., 1913; student U. of Pa. Law Sch., 1913-15; m. Florence K. Fowler, June 28, 1924; children—Richard Fowler, James Focht. Admitted to Pa. bar, 1920; vice-pres. Middle Creek Valley Telephone Co. since 1917; treas. Selingsgrove Water Supply Co. since 1917, and also sec. since 1925; dir. Buffalo Valley Telephone Co. since 1920; dir. Lewisburg Nat. Bank, 1920-27; solicitor and dir. Lewisburg Trust & Safe Deposit Co. since 1927; dir. Watsontown & Paxton Brick Co. Served as ordnance sergt. Ordnance Dept., U.S. Army, 1917-19. Mem. Pa. House of Reps., 1925, 26; dir. and sec. Lewisburg Sch. Dist.; dir. Lewisburg Cemetery Assn. Mem. Patriotic Order Sons of America, Sigma Chi. Republican. Presbyterian. Club: Lewisburg Rotary. Home: 63 University Av. Office: 224 St. Louis St., Lewisburg, Pa.

McCLURE, John James, insurance broker; b. Chester, Pa., Sept. 24, 1886; s. William J. and Sabina (McClay) McC.; student Swarthmore (Pa.) Prep. Sch. and Swarthmore Coll.; m. Alice V. Jennings, Feb. 8, 1930; children—John James, William J., Marjorie Holmes Garrison, Sabina Elizabeth. Ins. broker, Chester, Pa.; pres. Chester Materials Co., Consumers Ice & Coal Co., McClure & Co., Chester, Pa. State senator 9th Senatorial Dist. of Pa., 1929-37. Mason (Shriner), Elk, Moose. Clubs: Penn Athletic, Springhaven Country, Aronomink Country. Home: 20th and Providence Av. Office: 802 Crozer Bldg., Chester, Pa.

McCLURE, Norman Egbert, coll. pres.; b. Norristown, Pa., Nov. 19, 1893; s. Linwood Dunham and Bertha Emily (Egbert) M.; A.B., Ursinus Coll., 1915; A.M., Pa. State Coll., 1916; Ph.D., U. of Pa., 1925; Litt.D., Pa. Mil. Coll., 1936; m. Doris Myers, June 26, 1924; children—Elizabeth Anne, Barbara. Instr. in English, Pa. State Coll., 1915-17; prof. of English, Ursinus Coll., 1928-36, pres. since 1936. Republican. Episcopalian. Editor: Essays Toward Living (with Albert Croll Baugh), 1929; Letters and Epigrams of Sir John Harrington, 1930; Selected Plays of Shakespeare (with Karl J. Holzknecht), vol. 1, 1936, vol. 2, 1937, vol. 3, 1937. Address: Ursinus College, Collegeville, Pa.

McCLURE, Walter Hudson, mfg. glass jars; b. Wheeling, W.Va., July 1, 1882; s. James Hunter and Belle Frances (Chambers) McC.; student Linsley Inst., Wheeling, W.Va., 1896-99, Washington and Jefferson Coll., Washington, Pa.; 1899-1900; m. Besse Reppetto, Nov. 17, 1908; children—Frances (Mrs. Evan L. Webster, Jr.), Olive R., James G., Barbara A. Began as office boy in wholesale grocery co., 1900; asso. with Hazel-Atlas Glass Co., mfr. glassware, Wheeling, W.Va., since 1903, now v.p. and gen. sales mgr. Republican. Presbyn. Clubs: Fort Henry (Wheeling); Cloud (New York). Home: 5 Rockledge Rd. Office: Hazel-Atlas Glass Co., Wheeling, W.Va.

McCLUSKEY, Frank P., judge; b. West Easton, Pa., Jan. 21, 1878; s. John and Susan (Martin) McC.; student Lafayette Coll., Easton, Pa.; m. Alice M. Riddle, Nov. 21, 1908; children—Frank P., Edward S., Donald, Alice May. Asst. dist. atty., Northampton Co., Pa., 1912-16, dist. atty., 1916-20; judge of Third Judicial Dist., Pa., since 1934, pres. judge since 1938. Mason (Rajah Temple, Lehigh Consistory), Moose, K.P. Clubs: Pomfret, Jacksonian, Northampton Country (Easton, Pa.). Home: 130 Pennsylvania Av. Office: Northampton Bank Bldg., Easton, Pa.

McCOLLIN, Frances, composer; b. Phila., Pa., Oct. 24, 1892; d. Edward Garrett and Alice Graham (Lanigan) McCollin; ed. Pa. Inst. for the Blind, Overbrook, Pa., and Miss Wright's Sch., Bryn Mawr, Pa.; unmarried. Conducted choruses, Burd Sch., Phila., 1922-33, Swarthmore Coll., 1923-24; lecturer on musical topics, Baltimore, Md., 1932-35, Phila. since 1924; composer since 1907; works include (orchestral) Adagio, 1927; (chorals for women's voices) Spring in Heaven, 1929; The Coming of June, 1935; The Singing Leaves, 1917; (chorals for mixed voices) The Nights O' Spring, 1918; Then Shall the Righteous Shine Forth, 1920; What Care I, 1923; Come Hither Ye Faithful, 1925; Now the Day is Over, 1925; also many compositions published and in manuscript form for voice, organ, and orchestra; her works have been performed by Phila. Orchestra, Peoples Symphony Orchestra of Boston, Indianapolis Symphony Orchestra, Phila. Chamber String Simfonietta, Robin Hood Dell Orchestra. Awarded prizes by Am. Guild of Organists, 1918, Chicago Madrigal Club, 1918, 23, Matinee Musical Club of Phila., 1918. Hon. mem. Nat. Fed. of Music Clubs, New Century Club of Phila.; mem. Am. Composers' Alliance, Phila. Music Club, Art Alliance of Phila. Socialist. Episcopalian. Home: 2128 De Lancey Place, Philadelphia, Pa.

McCOLLOUGH, A. E.; editor Intelligencer-Journal. Address: 8 W. King St., Lancaster, Pa.

McCOLLUM, Elmer Verner, physiological chemist; b. nr. Ft. Scott, Kan., Mar. 3, 1879; s. Cornelius Armstrong and Martha Catherine (Kidwell) M.; B.A., University of Kansas, 1903, M.A., 1904; Ph.D., Yale, 1906; Sc.D., University of Cincinnati, 1920; LL.D., University of Manitoba, 1938. Instr. agrl. chemistry, 1907-08, asst. prof., 1908-11, asso. prof., 1911-13, prof., 1913-17, U. of Wis.; prof. biochemistry, Sch. of Hygiene and Pub. Health, Johns Hopkins, since 1917. Mem. internat. com. on vitamin standards of League of Nations, 1931, and international and mixed commns. on nutrition, 1935. Del. 10th Pan-Am. Sanitary Conf., Bogota, 1938; chmn. nutrition sect. Pan-Am. Sanitary Bur. since 1939. Mem. A.A.A.S., Am. Soc. Biol. Chemists (pres., 1927-29), Am. Chem. Soc., Am. Public Health Association, Am. Assn. Univ. Profs., Harvey Soc. (hon.), Am. Home Economics Assn. (hon.), Am. Acad. Political and Social Science, Nat. Academy Sciences, Des Moines Academy Medicine (hon.), Kaiserlich Deutsche Academie der Naturforscher zu Halle, Royal Academy of Medicine (Belgium), National Advisory Council of U.S. Public Health Service, Phi Beta Kappa. Received Howard N. Potts gold medal, Franklin Inst., "for distinguished scientific work," 1921, John Scott medal from the City of Phila., 1924, Newell Sill Jenkins medal from Conn. State Dental Soc., 1927, gold medal of Am. Inst. of N.Y., 1934, Callahan medal of Ohio State Dental Soc., 1935. Writer on nutrition and relation of diet to growth and to disease. Author: Text Book of Organic Chemistry for Medical Students, 1916; The Newer Knowledge of Nutrition, 1918, 5th edit., 1939; The American Home Diet, 1919; Foods, Nutrition and Health, 4th edit., 1937. Home: 2510 Talbot Rd. Address: School of Hygiene and Public Health, Johns Hopkins Univ., Baltimore, Md.

McCOMAS, Henry Clay, psychologist; b. Baltimore, Md., Dec. 21, 1875; s. Henry Clay and Mary (Parker) M.; A.B., Johns Hopkins, 1897; A.M., Columbia, 1898; grad. Union Theol. Sem., New York, 1900; Ph.D., Harvard, 1910; m. Edith R. Gates, Oct. 20, 1897. Ordained Congl. ministry, 1900; pastor North Attleboro, Mass., 1900-03, Cadillac, Mich., 1903-07; instr. psychology, Princeton, 1909-12, asst. prof., 1912-21, asso. prof., 1921; pres. H. C. McComas Coal Company since 1927; pres. Baltimore Coal Exchange since 1930; lecturer in psychology, Johns Hopkins Univ., since 1928. Collaborator on Psychol. Index, 1909-11; sec. Psychological Review Pub. Co. Capt. Sanitary Corps, U.S.A., 1918-19. Fellow A.A.A.S.; mem. Am. Psychol. Assn., Phi Gamma Delta. Author: Some Types of Attention, 1911; The Psychology of Religious Sects, 1912; The Aviator, 1921; Ghosts I Have Talked With, 1935. Home: 320 Hawthorne Rd., Roland Park, Md.

McCONATHY, Osbourne, prof. music; b. Bullitt Co., Ky., Jan. 15, 1875; s. William Jacob and Cynthia (Osbourne) McC.; ed. pub. schs.; studied music under pvt. teachers; Mus.D., Am. Conservatory Music, Chicago, 1937; m. Alice Mary Brown, July 9, 1907; children—Osbourne William, Elizabeth, James Stewart. Supervisor of music, pub. schs., Louisville, 1893-1903, Chelsea, Mass., 1903-13; prof. music methods and dir. dept. of pub. sch. and community music, Northwestern U., 1913-25; editor music publs. of Silver, Burdett & Co., Newark. Supt. Eastern session Am. Inst. of Normal Methods, Boston, 1909—. Mem. N.E.A. (pres. music sect. 3 terms), Music Supervisors' National Conference (president 1919; member educational council), Music Teachers' Nat. Assn. (pres. 1922), Ill. State Music Teachers' Assn. (pres. 1924, 25), New York Southern Society. Music dir. Louisville annual music festivals, 1900-03; asso. conductor North Shore music festivals, 1914-25. Mem. Ky. N.G. 3 yrs. Democrat. Episcopalian. Mason. Clubs: University (Evanston); Collegiate (Chicago); Town Hall, Southern (New York). Co-Author: The Progressive Music Series (14 books issued), 1914; Music in Secondary Schools, 1917; A Book of Choruses, 1923; The Symphony Series, 1925; The Music Hour Series, 1927; The Oxford Piano Course, 1927; An Approach to Harmony, 1927; Ditson School and Community Band Series, 1928; The Catholic Music Hour, 1929; Music in the Jr. High School, 1930; The Junior Band Series, 1931; Music of Many Lands and Peoples, 1932; Music in Rural Education, 1933; Pieces We Like to Play, 1934; Gregorian Chant Manual, 1935; Music Highways and Byways, 1936. Editor: The School Song Book, 1909. Home: Glen Ridge, N.J.

McCONNELL, Alexander, lawyer; b. Greensburg, Pa., May 4, 1883; s. Alexander D. and Ella McC.; student Greensburg, Pa., High Sch., 1901-05, Washington and Jefferson Coll., Washington, Pa., 1905-06; LL.B., U. of Pa., 1909; m. Henrietta A. Hershey, May 14, 1914; children—Henrietta Josephine (Mrs. Vincent E. Williams), Alexander Daniel, David Turney. Admitted to Pa. bar, 1910, and since practiced at Greensburg; mem. of firm, Portser, Gregg & McConnell, Greensburg, Pa., since 1938. Mem. Phi Kappa Sigma. Presbyterian. Home: 409 N. Maple Av. Office: First Nat. Bank Bldg., Greensburg, Pa.

McCONNELL, John Cumming, banker; b. Youngstown, O., Jan. 28, 1900; s. Lemuel C. and Clara (Cumming) M.; grad. Rayen Sch., Youngstown, O., 1918; A.B., Adelbert Coll., Western Reserve U., 1922; LL.B., Law Sch., same, 1924; Sch. of Commerce, U. of Wis., summer, 1921; m. Mildred M. Mahon, Mar. 12, 1925. Admitted to Ohio bar, 1924; atty. for Union Trust Co., Cleveland, 1924-33; trust agent of Supt. of Banks of Ohio in charge of liquidation of trust depts. of Union Trust Co., 1933-37; spl. counsel for atty. gen. of Ohio, 1937-38; exec. v.p. Nat. Bank of W.Va., Wheeling, since 1938. Served in the U.S. Army, 1918. Trustee Oglebay Inst.; dir. Tri-State Music Assn. Mem. Ohio State Bar Assn., Am. Bankers Assn., W.Va. Bankers Assn., Delta Tau Delta, Phi Delta Phi. Republican. Clubs: Fort Henry, Wheeling Country (Wheeling). Home: R.D. 2, Triadelphia, W.Va. Office: Nat. Bank of W.Va., Wheeling, W.Va.

McCONNELL, Malcolm Findley, gen. supt. Homestead Steel Works, Carnegie-Illinois Steel Corpn.; b. New Castle, Pa., Nov. 3, 1880; s. Malcolm and Emma Frances (Findley) M.; student mech. engring. U. of Pittsburgh, Sc.D. (hon.), 1937; m. Jean Norris, Apr. 16, 1908; 1 son,

Malcolm Findley. Draftsman Sharon (Pa.) Works, Nat. Steel Co., Mar.-Nov. 1900; constrn. engr. LaBelle Iron Works, Steubenville, O., 1902-04; steam engr. New Castle (Pa.) Works, Carnegie Steel Co., 1905-06, engr. gen. offices, Pittsburgh, 1907-09, asst. gen. supt. Mingo and Bellaire Works, 1909-26, gen. supt. Mingo Works, 1926-33, gen. supt. Homestead Steel Works, 1933-35; gen. supt. Homestead Steel Works, Carnegie-Ill. Steel Corpn., since 1935. Pres. bd. dirs. Homestead (Pa.) Hosp.; pres. Carnegie Library of Homestead; dir. The Community Fund, Pittsburgh. Mem. Eastern States Blast Furnace and Coke Oven Assn., Am. Iron and Steel Inst., Engrs. Soc. of Western Pa. Clubs: University, Duquesne Golf Assn. (Pittsburgh); Oakmont (Pa.) Country. Home: 610 Tenth Av. Office: Carnegie-Illinois Steel Corpn., Munhall, Pa.

McCONNELL, Robert Steffan, ex-asst. chief engr. Baldwin Locomotive Works; b. Phila., Sept. 10, 1870; s. Robert and Sara Ann (Steffan) M.; student Phila. schs.; B.S., Swarthmore (Pa.) Coll., 1890; m. Vera Blanchard, Mar. 21, 1934. Asso. in architecture with Theophilus P. Chandler and Rankin and Kellogg, Phila., to 1896; with Baldwin Locomotive Works, Phila., 1897-1939. Mem. Canadian Soc. of Phila., Am. Soc. of M.E., A.A.A.S., Am. Philatelic Soc., Phi Kappa Psi. Clubs: Art, Penn Athletic (Phila.). Home: The Chatham, 20th and Walnut Sts., Philadelphia, Pa.

McCONNELL, William Calder, corpn. official; b. Halifax, Pa., Apr. 4, 1860; s. George Washington and Sarah (Marsh) M.; student Franklin and Marshall Coll., Lancaster, Pa.; m. Ida V. Martz, June 9, 1881 (dec.); 1 dau., Katharine. Entered partnership of Kulp, McWilliams & Co., dealers in lumber, brick and ice, Jan. 1, 1882; when partnership dissolved, 1886, formed with Mr. McWilliams partnership of McWilliams & McConnell, and in ice and brick trade until firm's dissolution, 1903; one of incorporators of Roaring Creek Water Co., Shamokin, Pa., and Anthracite, Bear Gap, and Shamokin Water Co.; pres. Shamokin Banking Co. (now Shamokin Banking & Trust Co.) for several yrs., Shamokin Light, Heat & Power Co. (now Pa. Power & Light Co.), Northumberland Water Co. (now White Deer Mountain Water Co.); treas. and dir. Roaring Creek Water Co.; v.p. and dir. Kulpmont Water Co.; Shamokin & Trevorton Bus Line Co.; dir. Consumers Water Co., Girardville, Pa. Represented 17th Pa. Congl. Dist. in Rep. Nat. Conv. which renominated Benjamin Harrison for the Presidency, Minneapolis, 1892; state senator, 27th Senatorial Dist., 1908-12, elected 1914 to Senate to fill vacancy caused by death of Hon. John T. Fisher and served 1914-24. Chmn. commn. for selection of site (a large portion of which was donated by him and his wife) and erection of State Hosp. for Injured Persons of Trevorton, Shamokin and Mount Carmel coal fields, which has been open for patients since 1911, chmn. bd. trustees for several yrs. Mason (K.T.), Odd Fellow, Elk. Clubs: Union League (Phila.); Pennsylvania Soc. (New York); Shamokin Valley Country. Home: 157 East Sunbury St. Office: McConnell Bldg., Shamokin, Pa.

McCORD, Frederick Albert, investment banker; b. Wilkes-Barre, Pa., Mar. 23, 1886; s. James and Hattie B. (Adams) McC.; grad. Wilkes-Barre High Sch., 1902; Ph.B., Syracuse (N.Y.) U., 1910; m. Elisabeth Adah Brooks, June 18, 1913; children—Jane Elisabeth (Mrs. Edward Rhoads Potts), Martha Brooks. Began as life ins. clerk, 1906; successively life ins. solicitor, life ins. mgr., bond salesman, and sales mgr.; vice-pres., treas. and dir. Frederick Peirce & Co., investment bankers, Phila., since 1928; vice-pres., treas. and dir. Pub. Investing Co., Foresight Foundation, Inc.; treas. and dir. Norfolk-Portsmouth Bridge Inc. Mem. Hist. Soc. of Pa., Phi Beta Kappa, Delta Tau Delta. Republican. Mem. Soc. of Friends. Home: Wayne, Pa. Office: 225 S. 15th St., Philadelphia, Pa.

McCORD, John Lewis Earl, prof. farm management and agrl. economics; b. Berwinsdale, Pa., Nov. 9, 1892; s. John Newton and Irene Dinesha (Hurd) McC.; grad. Lock Haven Normal Sch., 1910; B.S., Pa. State Coll., 1915; M.S., Cornell U., 1920; grad. study Cornell U., 1928, 1931, 1939; m. Helen May Miller, June 5, 1917; children—Robert Earl, Richard Newton, Ruth Elizabeth. Employed as co. agrl. extension agt., Jefferson Co., Pa., 1916-20; asst. prof. farm management and agrl. economics., Pa. State Coll., 1920-24, asso. prof., 1924-28, prof. farm management and agrl. economics, 1928-34, 1935-36, and since 1936; head dept. agrl. economics, U. of Puerto Rico, 1934-35, and Feb.-May 1936. em. Am. Farm Econs. Assn., Delta Sigma Rho, Pi Gamma Mu, Lambda Chi Alpha. Republican. Presbyn. Mason. (32°). Home: 414 Locust Lane, State College, Pa.

McCORD, Joseph, author; b. Moline, Ill., July 21, 1880; s. Joseph Smith and Sara Anna (Christy) McC.; prep. edn. Ia. City Acad., Iowa City, Ia., 1894-98; A.B., State. U. of Ia., 1901; m. Clara Kingswell Wheeler, Sept. 4, 1907; 1 son, Joseph. Began as draftsman, 1901; mineral explorations, Mich. and Minn. Iron Ranges, Mich. Copper Country, 1902-11; rep. of Gulland of London, diamonds, 1911-14; steel mfg. Phila. and Baltimore, 1914-26; newspaper work with Baltimore News, Baltimore American, Baltimore Post, Brooklyn Daily Eagle, 1926-32; author since 1932. Mem. Authors Guild, Authors League of America. Republican. Mason. Author: Silver Linings, 1932; Bugles Going By, 1933; Dream's End, 1934; Dawns Delayed, Heart's Heritage, With All My Heart, 1935; One Way Street, Dotted Line Honeymoon, Magnolia Square, 1936; Flanders' Folly, The Prodigal Moll, The Return of Joan, 1937; The Piper's Tune, Redhouse on the Hill, 1938; A Husband for Hiliary, Sweet for a Season, 1939. Home: Boonsboro, Washington County, Md. Address: Care M. S. Mill, Agent, 286 5th Av., New York, N.Y.

McCORD, Ralph Bemus, county treas.; b. North East, Pa., May 30, 1890; s. William F. and Florence Elizabeth (Bemus) McC.; student High Sch., North East, Pa., 1906-10; D.V.M., Cornell U., 1913; m. Mary Elizabeth Lyons, May 10, 1918. General veterinary practice, North East, Pa., 1913-17; postmaster, North East, Pa., 1924-33; with Pa. Dept. Mil. Affairs, Harrisburg, 1934-35; treas. Erie Co., Pa., since 1935. Commd. 2d lt., U.S. Army, 1917; participated in all major engagements overseas and served with army of occupation in Germany, 1917-19; hon. disch. from 4th Div., U.S. Army, as capt., August 1919. Comdr. Lake Shore Post, Am. Legion, since 1920, 29th Dist., 1925-28; western vice comdr., Dept. of Pa. Am. Legion, 1929. Mem. Vets. Fgn. Wars. Republican. Presbyterian. Mason, Elk, Eagle, I.O.O.F. Moose. Club: Erie (Pa.) Press. Home: 14 Grant St., North East, Pa. Office: Court House, W. 6th St., Erie, Pa.

McCORMACK, Frederick O.; v.p. Emerson Drug Co.; b. Dallas Ferry, N.Y., Aug. 11, 1897; s. Frederick Clarke and Anne (Preston) M.; student Princeton U.; m. Margaretta McNeal, May 10, 1934; children—Margaret Emerson, Kim. First v.p., sec. and dir. Emerson Drug Co. since 1933. Home: Brooklandville, Baltimore County, Md. Office: Eutaw and Lombard Sts., Baltimore, Md.

McCORMACK, William Joseph, lawyer; b. West Orange, N.J., July 12, 1902; s. Thomas Joseph and Anne (Hoare) McC.; student Our Lady of the Valley Sch., Orange, N.J., 1909-17, St. Benedict's Prep. Sch., Newark, N.J., 1917-21; LL.B., N.J. Law Sch., Newark, 1922-25; m. Loretta Vreeland, Oct. 3, 1929; children—Grace, Jean. Began as caddy when boy; in factory T. A. Edison Co., West Orange, N.J., summers 1918, 1919, 1920; clk. Knauthe, Nachod, and Kuhn, New York, 1921-22, asst. dept. mgr., 1922-22; clk. in law office, Newark, while at law sch., 1922-25; admitted to N.J. bar, 1925, and since 1927 practiced at Newark and Orange, N.J.; settlement officer Fidelity Union Title and Mortgage Guarantee Co., Newark, Essex Title Guarantee and Trust Co., Montclair, N.J., 1925-27; mem. firm McCormack and O'Keefe, Orange, N.J., since 1938. Asst. atty. gen. of N.J., assigned as trial counsel to highway dept., since 1934; Dem. Chmn., West Orange, N.J., since 1933; municipal chmn. Nat. Foundation for Infantile Paralysis, Inc., since 1938. Mem. Essex County Bar Assn., Orange Bar Assn., St. Benedict's Alumni Assn., Kelly Pilgrims, Joel Parker Assn., N.J. State Elks Assn., Kings Bench, Delta Theta Phi. Awarded scholarship key from Kings Bench and Delta Theta Phi, 1925. Democrat. Roman Catholic. Elk (Orange Lodge 135), K.C. (Orange Council 235). Clubs: West Orange (N.J.) Democratic; Gold Bee Track (St. Benedict's Prep. Sch., Newark, N.J.). Home: 19 Dartmouth Rd., West Orange, N.J. Office: 308 Main St., Orange, N.J.

McCORMICK, Arthur Burd, clergyman; b. Mercer, Pa., Sept. 12, 1872; s. William A. and Martha (Burd) McC.; A.B., D.D., Westminster Coll., New Wilmington, Pa.; student Western Theol. Sem., 1893-95, 1906-07; m. Mary E. Olsen, Sept. 19, 1900; 1 dau., Martha Caroline (Mrs. Thomas Smyth). Ordained Presbyn. ministry, 1897; pastor North Clarendon and Irvine, Pa., 1897-98, North Warren, 1899-1907, Central Ch., New Castle, 1907-14, West Presbyn. Ch., Binghamton, N.Y., 1914-26, Eastern dist. sec. General Council of Presbyn. Ch. in U.S.A., 1926-29; pastor Second Ch., Oil City, Pa., 1929—. Regular writer for Presbyn. Bd. of Publn. since 1922. Acting editor of Presbyn. Banner, Pittsburgh, 1927. Mem. S.A.R.; actively interested in Boy Scouts of America. Republican. Feature writer, "The World as I See It," for The Presbyterian, Phila. Mem. Rotary and Wanango Clubs. Pres. Civic Educational Forum; pres. Community Concert Assn.; chmn. Nat. Missions Com. of Erie Presbytery. Home: Oil City, Pa.

McCORMICK, Charles Perry, pres. McCormick & Co., Inc.; b. Morelia, Mexico (of Am. parents) June 9, 1896; s. Rev. Hugh Pendleton and Anne Pauline (Perry) McC.; ed. schools in Puerto Rico, Birmingham, Ala., Paris, France, Lincoln High School, Va.; grad. Baltimore City Coll., 1915, Johns Hopkins, 1919; m. Marion Andrew Hinds, Sept. 14, 1921; children—Rosalie Anne, Charles Perry, Jr. Joined U.S. Navy, April 17, 1917; naval athletic dir. 5th Naval Dist. for 9 months; served overseas on S.S. Edgar F. Luckenbach; hon. disch. 1919. Began working for McCormick & Co., Inc., importers, exporters, grinders, Baltimore, during vacations in 1912; dir. since 1926, v.p. 1928-32, pres. since 1932 (at death of W. M. McCormick, founder); pres. The McCormick Sales Co.; pres. Better Business Bureau of Baltimore; chmn. bd. Baltimore Branch of Federal Reserve Bank, 1939; dir. The McCormick Warehouse Co., Baltimore Steam Packet Co. (Old Bay Line), Equitable Trust Company, Eutaw Savings Bank. Mem. bd. of dirs. Chamber of Commerce of the U.S.A., Baltimore Assn. of Commerce. Nat. councillor Am. Spice Trade Assn., 1927, Mayonnaise Assn., 1928-31, Nat. Assn. Insecticide and Disinfectant Mfrs., 1932, 36, Tea Assn., 1933; Asso. Grocery Mfrs. of America, 1934-35, 37, Am. Spice Trade Assn., 1938, Flavoring Extract Mfrs. Assn., 1939. Pres. Baltimore Export Mgrs. Club, 1928; pres. Mayonnaise Products Mfg. Assn. of America, Inc., 1928-32; pres. Nat. Assn. Insecticide and Disinfectant Mfrs., 1935; dir. Associated Grocery Manufacturers of America, 1935-37. Mem. Baltimore Criminal Justice Commn., advisory Council Md. State Employment Service, Phi Gamma Delta. Mem. University Bapt. Ch. Mason (K.T., Shriners, Jesters). Clubs: Baltimore Country, Maryland Yacht (Baltimore); Gibson Island Yacht (Md.); Rotary; Merchants. Author: Multiple Management, 1938. Contbr. many articles on management, the McCormick System, etc., to jours. Home: 7 East 39th St. Office: McCormick Building, Baltimore, Md.

McCORMICK, Howard, artist; b. Hillsboro, Ind., Aug. 19, 1875; s. Isaac Newton and Sarah Elizabeth (Bryce) McC.; ed. pub. schs., Newcastle and Indianapolis, Indiana; art education, Indianapolis School of Art, New York School of Art and Julian Acad., Paris, France; m. Josephine Newell, May 16, 1911; children—Newell, Sally, Nancy. Painter and wood engraver. Prin. works: Habitat Indian groups (Hopi, Apache, Navajo), Am. Mus., N.Y. City; New Jersey Indians, N.J. State Mus., Trenton; Am. Red Cross war models, at Washington, D.C., hdqrs.; Gesso painting, prize purchase, John Herron Inst., Indianapolis; mural decorations, Museum of Science and Industry, N.Y. City, and 6 murals at Trenton, also mural decorations for George W. Perkins, Riverdale, N.Y., and Frank J. Marion, Stamford, Conn. A.N.A. (engraver), 1928. Club: Salmagundi. Home: 165 Leonia Av., Leonia, N.J.*

McCORMICK, John Hays, pres. J. H. McCormick & Co.; b. Williamsport, Pa., July 12, 1879; s. Henry Clay and Ida (Hays) McC.; student U. of Pa., Yale Law Sch., 1938; m. Martha Allen Foresman, Apr. 18, 1906; children—Ida Hays (Mrs. Jay Clark, III), Henry Clay. Pres. J. H. McCormick & Co., mfg., Williamsport, Pa., since 1931. Dir. or trustee J. O. Brown Library, Williamsport Hosp., Williamsport Dickinson Sem. Republican. Presbyterian. Clubs: Ross, Williamsport Country. Home: 1024 First Av. Office: 25 Susquehanna St., Williamsport, Pa.

McCORMICK, Louis Provance, physician; b. Connellsville, Pa., Aug. 7, 1866; s. Joseph Trevor and Susan (Newmeyer) McC.; M.D., Jefferson Med. Coll., Phila., 1891; m. Kathryn Felsinger, Feb. 1, 1906; children—Helen L. (Mrs. Daniel Dugger), Martha P., Kathryn F. Began practice of medicine, 1891; mem. staff Connellsville (Pa.) State Hosp.; dir. Second Nat. Bank. Served as surgeon in Philippine Islands during Spanish-Am. War and Philippine Insurrections, U.S. Vols., 1898-99. Life trustee Carnegie Free Library, Connellsville. Mem. A.M.A. Mason (32°, Shriner). Home: 508 Vine St. Office: 110 N. Pittsburgh St., Connellsville, Pa.

McCORMICK, Seth Thomas, Jr., lawyer; b. Montoursville, Pa., Sept. 14, 1880; s. Horace G. and Margaretta (Hill) McC.; student pub. schs., Williamsport, 1886-98; Ph.B., Lafayette Coll., Easton, Pa., 1902; m. Esther Thompson, June 29, 1910; children—Esther (Mrs. S. Dale Furst, Jr.), Dorothy (Mrs. Stephen C. Husted). Admitted to Pa. bar, 1906; practiced in Williamsport in association with Seth T. McCormick, 1906-16, alone 1916-36; mem. firm McCormick, Herdic & Furst, Williamsport, Pa., since 1936; dir. Pa. Power & Light Co., West Branch Bank and Trust Co., Darling Valve & Mfg. Co., Milton Mfg. Co. Mem. State Bd. Charities, 1926-30. Pres. bd. mgrs. Williamsport (Pa.) Hosp. Mem. Lycoming Law Assn. (pres. 1921-22), Pa. Bar Assn. (v.p. 1929-30), Williamsport Foundation (dir.). Republican. Presbyterian. Clubs: Ross, Williamsport Country (Williamsport, Pa.); Grays Run (Williamsport). Home: Oak Ridge Pl. Office: 429 Pine St., Williamsport, Pa.

McCORMICK, Vance Criswell, newspaper pub.; b. Harrisburg, Pa., June 19, 1872; s. of Henry and Annie (Criswell) M.; Ph.B., Yale, 1893, M.A., 1907; LL.D., Dickinson College, 1934; m. Gertrude Howard Olmsted, Jan. 5, 1925. Publisher The Patriot (morning newspaper) and Evening News, Harrisburg. Mem. City Council, Harrisburg, 1900-02; mayor, 1902-05; Dem. candidate for gov. of Pa., 1914; chmn. Dem. Nat. Campaign Com., 1916. Chmn. War Trade Bd., 1917-19; mem. war mission to Great Britain and France, 1917; adviser to the President, Am. Commn. to Negotiate Peace, Paris, 1919. Dir. Federal Reserve Bank. Member Yale corpn., 1913-36; trustee, mem. exec. com. Pa. State Coll.; pres. bd. Harrisburg Acad. Mem. Delta Psi. Presbyn. Clubs: Philadelphia (Phila.); University, Yale, St. Anthony (New York); Metropolitan (Washington, D.C.); Yeaman's Hall (Charleston, S.C.). Home: Harrisburg, Pa.

McCORMICK, William Wallace, assoc. prof. physics; b. Marissa, Ill., Aug. 30, 1906; s. James Harvey and Bessie Mae (Cowden) McC.; B.S., Geneva Coll., Beaver Falls, Pa., 1927; M.S., U. of Mich., 1932, Ph.D., same, 1936; grad. study, U. of Wis., summer 1934; m. Beulah Mae Ewing, Dec. 24, 1938. Engaged as prin. high sch., 1927-29; instr. physics, Geneva Coll., Beaver Falls, Pa., 1929-33, asst. prof. physics, 1933-38, assoc. prof. physics since 1938. Mem. Am. Phys. Soc., Am. Physics Teachers Assn., Sigma Xi. Mem. United Presbyn. Ch. Contbr. to Physical Review. Home: 3406 7th Av., Beaver Falls, Pa.

McCOUCH, Grayson Prevost, neurophysiologist; b. Chestnut Hill, Phila., Pa., Sept. 9, 1888; s. Harry Gordon and Virginia (Mallet-Prevost) McC.; A.B., Harvard, 1911; M.D., U. of Pa. Med. Sch., 1915; student Oxford, 1920; m. Cecile Louise Kievits, Mar. 26, 1919; 1 son, Gordon Prevost. Interne U. of Pa. Hosp., 1915-17; studied neuropathology, Pa. Hosp. for Mental and Nervous Diseases, 1919; instr. physiology, U. of Pa. Med. Sch., 1920-28, asst. prof. since 1928. Served as neuropsychiatrist, U.S. Navy Base Hosp. No. 5, Brest, France, 1917-18. Mem. A.A.A.S., Am. Physiol. Soc., Coll. of Phys. of Phila., Phila. Physiol. Soc., Phila. Neurological Soc. Home: Rose Tree Rd., Media, Pa.

McCOWN, Edward C., clergyman; b. Fayetteville, Tenn., Feb. 10, 1875; s. Samuel S. and Margaret Jane (Wyatt) McC.; student Muskingum Coll. (New Concord, O.), Cedarville (O.) Coll.; A.B., Westminster Coll., New Wilmington, Pa.; grad. Pittsburgh Theol. Sem., 1904; D.D., Sterling (Kan.) Coll.; m. Pearl Neely, Oct. 11, 1904; children—Mary Margaret, Joseph Neely, Virginia. Ordained ministry U.P. Ch., 1904; pastor Mt. Lebanon Ch., Pittsburgh, since 1904 (congregation grown from 176 to 2250). Trustee Westminster Coll. Mem. Home Mission Bd., U.P. Ch., also of Evangelistic Com. and Com. on Union of All Presbyn. Bodies; elected moderator Gen. Assembly U.P. Ch., 1935. Republican. Home: 243 Washington Rd., South Hills Branch, Pittsburgh, Pa.

McCOY, Frank Ross, army officer; b. Lewistown, Pa., Oct. 29, 1874; s. Gen. Thomas Franklin and Margaret Eleanor (Ross) M.; grad. U.S. Mil. Acad., 1897; grad. Army War Coll., 1908; m. Frances Field Judson, Jan. 26, 1924. Commd. 2d lt. cav., June 11, 1897; promoted through grades to brig. gen., Dec. 4, 1922; brig. gen. (temp.), August 26, 1918-Mar. 15, 1920; promoted major general, September 3, 1929. Served on western frontier, Cuba and Philippines, Santiago campaign, Moro expdns., Mindanao and Jolo; comdd. Datu Ali expdn., 1905; a.d.c. to Maj. Gen. Leonard Wood, in Cuba and P.I.; to President Roosevelt, 1902, 1906-08; sec. Moro Province, 1905; engr. same, 1905-06; a.d.c. to Secretary of War William Howard Taft, 2d intervention to Cuba, and while he was provisional gov.; Gen. Staff, 1911-14; comd. cav. patrol dist. on Rio Grande border and in actions at Cavazas Crossing and Ojo de Agua against Mexican bandits, 1915-16; mil. attaché, Mexica, 1917; Gen. Staff A.E.F., Gen. Hdqrs., 1917-18; col. 165th Inf., May 1-Aug. 16, 1918; brig. gen. comdg. 63d Inf. Brig., Aug.-Nov. 1918; dir. Army Transport Service, dep. dir. gen., and dir. gen. of transportation, A.E.F., 1918-19. Chief of staff Am. Mil. Mission to Armenia, 1919, and of spl. mission to Philippines, 1921; asst. to gov. gen. of P.I., 1921-25; dir. gen. Red Cross, and comdr. Am. Relief Mission to Japan, 1923; apptd. by President Coolidge to supervise presidential election of Nicaragua, 1928; chmn. Commn. of Inquiry and Conciliation (Bolivia-Paraguay), Jan.-Sept. 1929, at Washington, D.C.; comdg. gen. 4th Corps Area, Cavalry Div., and 7th Corps Area, 1929-33; apptd. Am. mem. Commn. of Inquiry (Manchuria), League of Nations (Lytton Commn.), 1932; commanding 6th Corps Area, 1935, 2d Corps Area, 1936-38; retired Nov. 1, 1938. Awarded D.S.M. with oak leaf cluster. Presbyn. Fellow Royal Geog. Soc., London. Clubs: Knickerbocker, Boone and Crockett (New York); Rittenhouse (Phila.); Metropolitan, Army and Navy, Chevy Chase (Washington). Author: Principles of Military Training, 1918. Home: Lewistown, Pa.

McCRACKEN, Charles Chester, educator; b. Bellefontaine, O., June 27, 1882; s. James Erskine and Mary Linda (Cooke) McC.; A.B., Monmouth (Ill.) Coll., 1908; A.M., Harvard, 1911, Austin fellow, 1914-15, Ph.D., 1916; m. Frances Cleo Fulton, August 15, 1911; children—Janet May, Charles William, Mary Ruth, James Edward. Teacher country and village schs., Ohio, 1901-04; head of science dept. high sch., Monmouth, Ill., 1906-07; head of mathematics dept., high sch., Lancaster, O., 1908-10; dean of Normal Coll., Ohio Northern U., 1911-14; prof. psychology and edn., Western Coll. for Women, 1915-17; prof. sch. administration, Ohio State U., summers 1913, 14, 15; prof. sch. administration, same univ., 1917-30; sec. Coll. of Edn., same univ., 1917-20, asst. dean, 1920-22; research counselor, coll. dept., Bd. of Christian Edn., Presbyn. Ch. in U.S.A., 1928-29, 1929-30 (half-time; on leave from Ohio State U.); pres. Conn. State Coll., Storrs, Conn., 1930-35; gen. dir. college dept. Bd. of Christian Edn., Presbyn. Church in U.S.A., since October 1, 1935. Has made many surveys of county school systems, Ohio and Fla.; mem. com. of 6, U.S. Bur. Edn., in survey of negro colls. and univs. of U.S., 1926-27; spl. investigator for joint legislative com. on economy and taxation for Ohio Gen. Assembly, 1926-27; mem. exec. com. Am. Council on Edn., 1929-32; specialist, land grant college survey, U.S. Bur. of Edn., 1929-30. Mem. Phi Delta Kappa. Republican. Presbyn. Author: Community Interests and School Consolidation of Logan County, Ohio, 1921-27; Survey of Logan County and Bellefontaine, Ohio, Schools, 1923; Local School District Boundaries Within the County School Districts of the State of Ohio (with Glen Drummond), 1929. Contbr. articles on higher edn. to mags. Home: 209 Kent Rd., Ardmore, Pa. Office: Witherspoon Bldg., Philadelphia, Pa.

McCRACKEN, Lee Alexander, judge; b. Cornplanter Twp., Pa., May 3, 1880; s. J. P. and Odelia (Dodds) McC.; LL.B., U. of Mich. Law Dept., Ann Arbor, Mich.; m. Georgia Vaughn French, Oct. 1, 1913; 1 son, Robert Alexander. Dist. atty., Venango Co., Pa., 1914-26; appointed pres. judge, Cts. of Venango Co., Pa., 1932, to fill vacancy caused by advancement of Hon. William M. Parker, elected to 10-yr. term, 1933, and since pres. judge. Dir. Red Cross. Club: Kiwanis (Oil City, Pa.). Home: 122 Cowell Av., Oil City, Pa. Office: Court House, Franklin, Pa.

McCRACKEN, Robert Thompson, lawyer; b. Philadelphia, July 15, 1883; s. James S. and Josephine (Thompson) M.; A.B., Central High Sch., Phila., 1900; B.S., U. of Pa., 1905, LL.B., 1908; m. Anna M. Erdman, June 1, 1909 (died 1934); 1 dau., Matilda. Admitted to Pa. bar, 1908, and since practiced in Phila.; partner Montgomery & McCracken, of which firm U.S. Supreme Court Justice Owen J. Roberts was formerly member; dir. Pa. R.R. Co.; trustee Penn Mutual Life Ins. Co.; trustee U. of Pa. Apptd. chmn. on professional ethics and grievances, Am. Bar Assn., 1935; pres. Pa. Bar Assn., 1938-39; mem. Phila. Law Assn. (v.p.). Home: 1009 Westview St. Office: Morris Bldg., Philadelphia, Pa.

McCRACKEN, Samuel, banker; b. Scranton, Pa., Nov. 12, 1876; s. Leroy and Charlotte (Little)) McC.; student pub. sch., Scranton, Pa., 1886-93; m. Phebe Englert, June 4, 1902; children—George Englert, Elizabeth Jane. Clk. Traders Nat. Bank, Scranton, Pa., 1893-1903; treas. Union Savings & Trust Co., Pittston, Pa., 1903-07; asst. cashier Peoples Bank of Wilkes-Barre, Pa., 1907-09, cashier, 1909-15; cashier Miners' Nat. Bank of Wilkes-Barre, Pa., 1915-1923, v.p., 1923-24, exec. v.p. since 1924, dir. since 1921; dir. Lehigh Valley Coal Sales Co., Lehigh Valley Coal Co. Dir and treas. Wilkes-Barre Y.M.C.A.; mem. exec. com. Boy Scouts of America, Wilkes-Barre; mem. exec. and budget com. Community Welfare Fed. Republican. Methodist. Home: 98 Academy St. Office: Miners' Nat. Bank, Wilkes-Barre, Pa.

McCRADY, Edward, Jr., bldg. materials; b. North Braddock, Pa., Dec. 10, 1902; s. Edward and Margaret Jane (Baldrige) McC.; B.S., Pa. State Coll., 1924; m. Ruth Rodgers, Dec. 1, 1928; children—Nancy, Edward IV, Richard Clay. Began as civil engr., McCrady Brothers Co., 1924; dir. and mgr. yards McCrady Rodgers Co. since 1928; v.p. and dir. McCrady Construction Co.; treas. and dir. Milliken Brick Co., Van Ormer Brick Co. Mem. Transportation Research Commn., Pittsburgh. Mem. Phi Gamma Delta. Republican. Presbyterian. Mason (A.A.O.N.M.S., A.A.S.R.). Clubs: Pittsburgh Athletic Assn.; Braddock Rotary. Home: Logi Road, R.D. 1, Wilkinsburg, Pa. Office: 308 Sixth St., Braddock, Pa.

McCRADY, John Baldrige, bldg. materials; b. North Braddock, Pa., Nov. 15, 1905; s. Edward and Margaret (Baldrige) McC.; grad. Edgewood High Sch., 1923; B.S. in Industrial Engring., U. of Pittsburgh, 1927; m. Eleanore C. Watson, Jan. 1, 1930; children—Howard C., II, Margaret C., John B. Began as salesman McCrady-Rodgers Co., 1927, now dir., sales mgr., v.p. and asst. treas.; dir. Milliken Brick Co. Mem. Phi Gamma Delta, Omicron Delta Kappa. Presbyterian. Mason. Home: R.D. Wm. Penn Highway, Wilkinsburg, Pa. Office: 239 Fourth Av., Pittsburgh, Pa.

McCREA, Lowrain Edward, surgeon; b. Lamar, Mo., June 7, 1896; s. Edward Lee and Eliza Lenora (Wade) McC.; grad. Table Rock (Neb.) High Sch., 1914; M.D., Jefferson Med. Coll., 1919; m. May McGregor Cooper, Dec. 31, 1924; adopted dau., Sybil Ewart (Mrs. DeWitt Norton McClumpha). Chief resident St. Agnes Hosp., Phila., 1920-21; resident physician in urology Long Island Coll. Hosp., 1923-24; asst. urologist, Grad. Hosp., Temple U. Hosp., Phila. Gen. Hosp., 1928-32; instr., U. of Pa., 1928-31; demonstrator of pathology, Temple U. Med. Sch., 1928-31; asst. urologist Phila. Gen. Hosp since 1932; asso. in urology, Temple U. Med. Sch., 1932-38, asst. prof. since 1938. Mem. A.M.A., Phila. Co. Med. Soc., Am. Urol. Assn., Phila. Coll. of Physicians, Phi Beta Pi, Theta Nu Epsilon. Protestant. Mason. Home: 341 Llandrillo Rd., Bala-Cynwyd, Pa. Office: 1930 Chestnut St., Philadelphia, Pa.

McCREADY, J. Homer, otolaryngologist; b. Wellsville, O.; s. James Campbell and Mary Ann (MacIntosh) M.; student Jefferson Med. Coll., 1906, U. of Vienna, 1908-09; m. Jean Brown, Dec. 3, 1912; children—James H., William B., Emily Jean. Prof. otolaryngology, U. of Pittsburgh. Fellow Am. Coll. Surgeons; mem. Am. Laryngol., Rhinol. and Otol. Soc., Am. Acad. Ophthalmology and Otolaryngology, Am. Bd. Otolaryngology, A.M.A., Pa. State Med. Soc., Allegheny Co. Med. Soc., Pittsburgh Otol. Soc., Pittsburgh Acad. Medicine. Clubs: Faculty, University, Pittsburgh Field. Home: 5521 Aylesboro Av., Pittsburgh, Pa.

McCREADY, Robert Thompson Miller, lawyer; b. Sewickley, Pa.; s. Robert (M.D.) and Rachel Catharine (Miller) McC.; ed. prep. dept. Allegheny Coll., Meadville, Pa., and at Ohio Wesleyan U.; A.B., Princeton, 1890; LL.B., New York Law Sch., 1893; m. Margaret Courtney, Mar. 14, 1900; children—Robert, Mary Courtney, James Miller, Margaret, Rachel Catharine. Admitted to Pa. bar, 1893, and since practiced at Pittsburgh. Mem. Am. Bar Assn., Phi Beta Kappa, Phi Delta Theta. Clubs: Keystone Athletic (Pittsburgh); Edgeworth Club; Princeton (New York). Home: Sewickley Heights, Pa. Office: Union Bank Bldg., Pittsburgh, Pa.

McCREARY, George Boone, clergyman, educator; b. New Concord, O., Dec. 9, 1875; s. Henry (M.D.) and Samantha Ann (Stevenson) McC.; B.A., Muskingum Coll., New Concord, O., 1895; M.A., 1902, D.D., 1924; Ph.D., Grove City (Pa.) Coll., 1914; grad. Pittsburgh Theol. Sem., 1898; student U. of Chicago, 1901; m. Lova Ruth Fowler, Sept. 24, 1901; children—Dorothy, Jane Elizabeth, Robert Henry. Ordained ministry U.P. Ch., 1900; pastor Pretty Prairie, Kan., 1900-01; teacher Ingleside Acad., Burgettstown, Pa., 1902-03; pastor Hobart, Okla., 1903-05; prof. Greek, Bible and philosophy, Epworth U., Oklahoma City, Okla., 1905-08; prof. Bible and philosophy, also registrar Sterling Coll., 1908-14; prof. Bible and philosophy, Hope Coll., Holland, Mich., 1914-17; prof. Greek, Muskingum Coll., 1917-20, also acting prof. Bible, 1917-19; prof. philosophy, same coll., 1920-24; prof. philosophy of religion and applied Christianity, Xenia Theol. Sem. (now Pittsburgh-Xenia Theol. Sem.), since 1924. Lecturer on war aims, S.A.T.C., World War. Mem. S.A.R. Address: 206 Ridge Av., Ben Avon, Pittsburgh, Pa.

McCREARY, Lewis Ward, clergyman; b. Fredericktown, O., Dec. 25, 1876; s. Abraham Cyrenus and Rhoda Ellen (Martin) McC.; Ph. B., Hiram Coll., 1903; m. Inez Downs, Aug. 9, 1905. Ordained to ministry Christian Ch., 1903; minister, Hamilton Av. Ch., St. Louis, Mo., 1905-19; exec. sec., Baltimore Fed. Chs., 1919-25; minister, Park Av. Ch. Disciples of Christ, East Orange, N.J., since 1925; mem. exec. com. Federal Council Chs. in America since 1922. Trustee Ward Coll., Buenos Aires, Argentina, S.A. Mem. Theta Phi. Mem. Disciples of Christ Ch. Home: 89 Lafayette Av., East Orange, N.J.

McCREARY, Robert Emmett, lawyer; b. Monaca, Pa., Aug. 24, 1897; s. Thomas William and Mary Rose (Ganley) McC.; grad. Monaca Pub. Sch., 1911; studied Fostoria (O.) High Sch., 1911-13, Monaca High Sch., 1913-14; A.B., Allegheny Coll., Meadville, Pa., 1918; LL.B., U. of Pittsburgh Law Sch., 1922; m. Ellen Cain, July 9, 1935; children—Robert Emmett, Charles Cain. Admitted to bar, 1922; since in gen. practice of law; mem. law firm Bradshaw, McCreary & Reed; solicitor Boro of Monaca since 1923, Monaca Sch. Dist. since 1935; dist. atty. Beaver County since 1936. Enlisted as seaman, U.S. Navy, Apr. 30, 1918; hon. discharged as ensign, May 9, 1919. Mem. Delta Tau Delta, Delta Sigma Rho, Phi Delta Phi, Order of the Coif, Am. Legion. Republican. K.C., Elk. Clubs : Monaca Turn Verein, Monaca Cornet Band. Home: 1127 Indiana Av., Monaca, Pa. Office: Beaver Trust Bldg., Beaver, Pa.

McCREATH, Lesley, analytical and cons. chemist; b. Harrisburg, Pa., Feb. 15, 1881; s. Andrew S. and Eliza (Berghaus) McC.; studied Harrisburg (Pa.) Acad.; Ph.B., Yale U., 1901; m. Margaret Elmer Bailey, Nov. 23, 1907; children—Andrew S. III (dec.), Margaret (dec.), Lesley, James II (dec.). Chemist Magnolia Sugar R.R. Co., Lawrence, La., 1901-03; field work in coal property of Ky. and W.Va., 1904; associated with father under name of Andrew S. McCreath & Son, analytical and cons. chemists, Harrisburg, Pa., since 1905; dir. Harrisburg Nat. Bank, Harrisburg Rys. Co. Pres. and dir. Harrisburg Cemetery Assn.; pres. Harrisburg Hosp.; mem. exec. com. Harrisburg Welfare Foundation; sec.-treas. Diocese of Harrisburg, P.E. Ch. Clubs: Harrisburg (Pa.) Country; Graduate (New Haven, Conn.); Gibson Island (Gibson Island, Md.). Home: N. River Road. Office: 236-242 Liberty St., Harrisburg, Pa.

McCREIGHT, Israel (Major), retired banker; b. Jefferson Co., Pa., Apr. 22, 1865; s. John and Eliza (Uncapher) McC.; ed. McCreight country sch.; grad. Eastman Business Coll., 1882; m. Alice B. Humphrey, of Jeff Co., Pa., July 20, 1887; children—Donald, Jim and Jack (twins), Catherine (wife of Rev. R. N. Stumpf), Martha (Mrs. Floyd Swisher), Major I., Jr., Rembrandt (dec.). Began as clerk in gen. store, 1882; clerk in private bank, 1883; moved to Dakota Territory, 1885, successively cashier Moore & Dodd (live stock store), supplying Indians, schs. and garrison Ft. Totten and shipping buffalo bones and live stock; became asst. cashier First Nat. Bank, DuBois, 1886; bought DuBois Deposit, 1888, enlarging same to present $4,-000,000 bank, cashier and pres. 40 yrs., now dir.; was treas. James J. Hill Fat Stock Show when they were planning extension of St.P., M.&M. R.R. to west; active, 1892-1910, in buying of coal, developing mines and building two railroads into district; organized Cook Forest State Park Project (now largest in state). Mem. sch. bd., 20 yrs. One of first drafted to form Local Bd., donating services as sec. throughout World War. Mem. two conservation congresses, peace confs., etc. Received letter from U.S. War Dept. in praise of his work; awarded medal by State Bankers' Assn., loving cup by pub. schs. Pres. DuBois Hist. Assn. Republican. Mason, Elk (Master, twice Ruler). Clubs: Kiwanis, Acorn. Author: Chief Flying Hawk's Tales, 1936; Cook Forest History, 1936; History of DuBois, 1938. Wrote Theodore Roosevelt's Conservation Policy, 1906; History of Local Draft Board, 1918; also numerous financial articles in mags. and newspapers. Home: DuBois, Pa.

McCRORY, William Bruce, lawyer; b. Norwood, Ill., Aug. 7, 1878; s. James T. and Ann (Horne) McC.; ed. Pittsburgh pub. and high schs.; A.B., Westminster Coll., New Wilmington, Pa., 1901; LL.B., U. of Pittsburgh Law Sch., 1908; m. Mrs. Adelaide S. Holt Irwin, Nov. 11, 1920. With Crucible Steel Co. of America, 1901-05; admitted to Allegheny County (Pa.) bar, 1908; admitted Supreme Court (Pa.), 1909; mem. law firm Ache and Wassell, 1910-16, Ache and McCrory, 1916-26, individually since 1926; v.p. and dir. Cretestone Co.; dir. General Cement Products Corpn. Mem. bd. Pittsburgh Florence Crittenton Home. Mem. Am. Bar Assn., Pa. State Bar Assn., Allegheny County Bar Assn., Am. Judicature Soc., Pi Rho Phi. Mason (32°, Shriner). Republican. United Presbyterian. Clubs: University (Pittsburgh); Wildwood Country (Allison Park, Pa.). Home: 732 Summerlea St. Office: 400 Standard Life Bldg., Pittsburgh, Pa.

McCRUM, Arlington Bliss, lawyer; b. Feb. 17, 1880; s. Lloyd Logan and Emma (Shaffer) McC.; A.B., W.Va. Univ.; LL.B., W.Va. Univ. Law Sch.; m. Madeline Broderick, 1927; children—Sara Patten, A. Bliss, Jr. Admitted to W.Va. bar, 1901, and since engaged in gen. practice of law at Charleston; served as mem. W.Va. Ho. of Dels., 1907-10; mem. W.Va. Senate, 1912-15; mem. State Bd. of Control, 1915-17; sec., dir. and gen. atty. Atlantic Greyhound Corpn.; exec. sec. Pub. Utilities Assn. W.Va. Served as 1st lt. Q.M.C. during World War. Mem. Phi Kappa Sigma. Republican. Mem. M.E. Ch. Clubs: Edgewood Country, Kanawha Country (Charleston). Home: 828 Chestnut Rd. Office: Charleston Nat. Bank Bldg., Charleston, W.Va.

McCUE, C(harles) A(ndrews), agrl. educator; b. Cass City, Mich., May 29, 1879; s. Charles E. and Catherine Sariah (Campbell) McC.; grad. high sch., Cass City, 1897; B.S., Mich. Agrl. Coll., 1901; post-grad. work, same coll., 1903-04, U. of Pa., 1910-12, 1913-14; m. Florence E. Beebee, June, 1906 (died Nov. 1907); 1 son, John Beebee; m. 2d, Essie B. Willis, of Newark, Del., March 1912. With U.S. Forest Service, 1901-03; instr. horticulture, Mich. Agrl. Coll., 1904-07; with U. of Del. since 1907, prof. horticulture until 1920; director of the Delaware Agricultural Experiment Station since 1920, also director Agricultural Extension and dean Sch. of Agr., U. of Del. Fellow A.A.A.S.; mem. Am. Soc. Hort. Science. Republican. Methodist. Mason (32°). Editor of Proceedings of Association of Land-Grant Colleges and Universities, 1928-34. Contbr. on original investigations in horticulture. Home: Newark, Del.

McCULLOCH, Duncan, Jr., educator; b. Baltimore, Md., Sept. 14, 1898; s. Rev. Duncan and Mary Sterett (Carroll) McC.; preparatory edn., Univ. School for Boys, Baltimore, 1910-15; A.B., Princeton, 1919; m. Sarah Ludington Humphreys, May 26, 1923; children—Sarah Ludington, Mary Sterett Carroll, Duncan III, Richard Sears. Mgr. research bureau of A. W. Shaw Co., 1919-20; merchandise counsel War Dept., sales of surplus war equipment and supplies, 1921; pres. Gen. Purchasing Agts., Inc., 1922; business mgr. Oldfields Sch. (for girls), 1923-26, v.p. Oldfields Sch., Inc. (founded by grandmother in 1866), 1926-32, pres. since 1932, also trustee. Mem. U.S. Naval Res. Force, 1917-21. Mem. Nat. Assn. Principals of Schs. for Girls, Pvt. Sch. Assn. of Baltimore, Progressive Edn. Assn., Princeton Alumni Assn. of Md., St. Andrew's Soc. Republican. Episcopalian. Home: "Hillside," Glencoe, Md. Address: Oldfields School, Glencoe, Md.

McCULLOCH, James Edward, sociologist; b. Montgomery Co., Va., July 29, 1873; s. Benjamin and Elizabeth (McDonald) M.; A.B., Randolph-Macon College, Va., 1898; B.D. from Vanderbilt University, Nashville, 1901; m. Minerva Annette Clyce, Sept. 3, 1903; children—Elizabeth Allen, Donella Margaret, Edith Isabelle. Missionary sec. Young People's Socs. M.E. Ch., S., 1901-02; Southern sec. Student Vol. Movement for Foreign Missions, 1902-03; studied instns. in Europe engaged in the training of religious and social workers, 1903-04; pres. Methodist Training Sch. for Religious Workers, 1905-11; gen. sec. Southern Sociol. Congress, 1911-19; ednl. sec. Am. Sociol. Congress, 1920—; gen. sec. Southern Coöperative League for Edn.

and Social Service, 1921; dir. Home Betterment League, 1925; executive secretary Vanderbilt University School of Religion, 1927-1933; was organizer and exec. secretary of the Charleston Educational Center. Author: The Open Church for the Unchurched, 1905; Mastery of Love, 1910; Home—The Savior of Civilization, 1923. Editor: Call of the New South, 1912; Challenge of Social Service, 1913; Human Way, 1913; South Mobilizing for Social Service, 1913; Battling for Social Betterment, 1914; The New Chivalry—Health, 1915; Democracy in Earnest, 1918; Distinguished Service Citizenship, 1920. Contbr. to mags. on social subjects; inventor of an original design for aircraft. Home: Silver Spring, Md.*

McCULLOCH, John H.; mem. surg. staff Beckley and Oak Hill hosps. Address: Beckley Hosp., Beckley, W.Va.

McCULLOCH, Joseph Paul, oil production; b. Greason, Pa., Feb. 13, 1894; s. Christian Tritt and Mary (Paul) McC.; student Mercersburg Acad., 1911-13; B.S., Pa. State Coll., 1917; m. Elizabeth Ashfield Walker, Feb. 1929. Geologist with Neely Clover Co., Ky., 1917; geologist Sinclair Exploration Co., 1919-25, mgr. in Colombia, S.A., 1931; geologist with Gulf Oil Co., 1925-26; consultant geological work, 1931-34; rep. production dept., Texas Corpn., in Europe, 1934-36; exec. Calif. Standard Oil Co., Ltd., London, Eng., 1937-38; dir. Indian Oil Concessions, Calcutta, India, 1939. Served as 1st lt. Field Arty., U.S. Army, with A.E.F. in France and Germany, 1917-19. Mem. Am. Assn. Petroleum Geologists, Am. Inst. of Mining and Metall. Engrs., Inst. of Petroleum Technologists (England), Phi Delta Theta. Presbyterian. Clubs: Cosmos (Washington, D.C.); Explorers (New York); Sind, (Karachi, India). Home: Newville, Pa. Office: 8, Clive Row, Calcutta, India.

McCULLOUGH, Clarence Joseph, M.D., surgeon; b. Beaver County, Pa., June 30, 1890; s. Samuel Logan (M.D.) and Margaret Stockton (Proudfit) M.; grad. Carnegie (Pa.) High Sch., 1907; student Pa. State Coll., 1907-10; M.D., U. of Pa., 1914; m. Dorothea Dupras Larkin, Dec. 8, 1923. Interne Methodist and Episcopal Hosps., Phila. and Cincinnati Gen. Hosp., 1914-16; practice limited to ophthalmology and otolaryngology, Washington, Pa., since 1914; mem. staff Washington Hosp., Washington, Pa. Served as capt. Med. Corps, U.S. Army, 1918-19; with A.E.F. in France and Army of Occupation in Germany. Mem. Am. Acad. Ophthalmology and Otolaryngology, A.M.A., Pa. State Med. Soc., Washington Co. Med. Soc. (trustee and 1st v.p.), Phi Rho Sigma. Republican. Presbyterian. Mason. Clubs: University (Pittsburgh); Washington (Pa.) Golf; American Legion, Internat. Lions (hon. mem.). Home: 64 Watson Av. Office: 628-38 Washington Trust Bldg., Washington, Pa.

McCULLOUGH, F(rank) Witcher, sec. Nat. Bituminous Coal Commn.; b. Huntington, W.Va., May 3, 1889; s. Frank Fenton and Alice Valeria (Witcher) McC.; prep. edn. Bingam Mil. Sch., Asheville, N.C.; grad. of Law Sch., W.Va. U., 1910; m. Kathleen Guthrie, Jan. 30, 1912; children—Witcher Guthrie, Frank Witcher. Admitted to W.Va. bar, 1910, and began practice in Huntington; 1st asst. U.S. atty., Southern Dist., W.Va., 1913-21; treas. State Bd. of Control, W.Va., 1926-31; mem. legal staff Pub. Works Adminstrn., Washington, D.C., 1933; dir. NRA for W.Va., 1934; dir. Nat. Emergency Council, W.Va., 1934-37; dir. for W.Va. Works Progress Administrn., 1935-37; sec. Nat. Bituminous Coal Commn., Washington, D.C., since May 1937. Mem. Am. Bar Assn., W.Va. Bar Assn., Cabell County Bar Assn., Phi Kappa Psi, The Mountain (W.Va. U.). Democrat. Episcopalian. Mason, Elk. Clubs: Nat. Press, Cosmos (Washington, D.C.); Edgewood Country (Charleston, W.Va.). Home: Huntington, W.Va. (legal); Wardman Park Hotel, Washington, D.C. Office: 734 15th St., N.W., Washington, D.C.

McCUNE, Joseph Condit, mech. engr. and inventor; b. Brilliant, O., Jan. 9, 1890; s. Samuel James and Elizabeth Ann (Purdy) McC.; ed. Washington and Jefferson Coll., 1906-07; M.E., Cornell U., 1911; m. Lucie Clay Brown, Oct. 22, 1919; children—Samuel Knox, Thompson Brown. Began as apprentice, Cutler-Hammer Mfg. Co., 1911-12; with Pittsburgh Rys. Co., 1912-13; asso. with Westinghouse Air Brake Co. continuously since 1913, successively, asst. to chief engr., mech. expert, asst. to dist. engr., asst. dist. engr., dist. engr., asst. dir. of engring., dir. of research since 1937. Served with 7th Regt. N.Y.N.G., Mexican border, 1916; 1st lt. engrs., U.S.A., 1917-19, with A.E.F. Mem. Pittsburgh Chamber of Commerce. Mem. Am. Soc. Mech. Engrs., Am. Welding Soc., Engring. Soc. Western Pa., Air Brake Assn., Pittsburgh Ry. Club, Soc. Automotive Engrs., Army Ordnance Assn., Alpha Tau Omega, Tau Beta Pi. Awarded First Sibley Prize, Cornell U. Republican. Presbyn. Clubs: Edgewood, Country (Edgewood). Home: 420 Locust St., Edgewood, Pa. Office: Wilmerding, Pa.

McCURDY, Alexander, Jr., organist; b. Eureka, Calif., Aug. 18, 1905; s. Alexander and Lillie May (Ervin) McC.; studied piano, organ, harmony and counterpoint with Wallace A. Sabin, Berkeley, Calif., 1919-24, piano with Edwin Hughes, and organ with Lynnwood Farnam, N.Y. City, 1924-27; grad. Curtis Institute of Music, Philadelphia (scholarship), 1934; Mus.D., Susquehanna University, 1936; m. Flora Bruce Greenwood (harpist Philadelphia Orchestra 1931-32), June 6, 1932; 1 dau., Xandra. Organist Trinity Episcopal Ch., Oakland, Calif., 1919-21, First Congl. Ch., 1921-23; choirmaster and organist St. Luke's Episcopal Ch., San Francisco, 1923-24, Ch. of the Redeemer, Morristown, N.J., 1924-27; dir. music Morristown Prep. Sch., 1925-27; debut as concert organist at Town Hall, N.Y. City, 1926; choirmaster and organist 2d Presbyn. Ch., Phila., since 1927; condr. Trenton Choral Art Soc., 1928-35; head of organ dept. Curtis Inst. of Music since 1935; headmaster St. James Choir Sch. for Boys since 1937; head music dept., Episcopal Acad., Overbrook, Pa., since 1937; soloist for Am. Guild of Organist's convs., 1930, 32, 35, 37; recitals at San Diego Expn., 1935; spl. recitalist Swarthmore Coll. since 1933. Dir. Am. Organ Players Club. Republican. Presbyn. (elder). Mason. Club: University. Home: 2031 Locust St. Studio: 21st and Walnut St., Philadelphia, Pa.

McCURDY, Ralph Gordon, elec. engr.; b. Eureka, Calif., Jan. 29, 1891; s. Alexander and Lillie May (Ervin) McC.; B.S., U. of Calif., Berkeley, Calif., 1913; m. Leila Margaret Ruffner, June 10, 1914; children—Margaret Switzler (Mrs. William A. Holliday), Mary Elizabeth, Ruth Katherine, Ervin Ruffner, Davis Wilson, Ralph Gordon, Sanford Alexander. Elec. engr. Pacific Gas & Electric Co., Oakland, Calif., 1913; mem. engring. staff Joint Com. on Inductive Interference, Calif. R.R. Commn., engaged in investigations of elec. interference between power and telephone systems, 1913-16; mem. staff transmission and protection engr., Am. Telephone & Telegraph Co., New York, 1916-19, elec. engr. in dept. development and research, 1919-34, noise prevention engr., 1930-34; noise prevention engr. Bell Telephone Labs., New York, 1934-37, asst. dir. transmission development in charge dept. prevention noise and crosstalk, transmission rating and local transmission, since 1937. Fellow Am. Inst. E.E.; mem. Joint Com. on Plant Coordination of Edison Electric Inst. and Bell Telephone System, Am. Standards Assn. (chmn. tech. com. on sound levels and sound level meters), Acoustical Soc. America, Tau Beta Pi, Sigma Xi, Alpha Kappa Lambda. Republican. Presbyterian. Author tech. articles in professional jours. Holder 15 patents. Home: 11 Brownes Terr., Englewood, N.J. Office: 463 West St., New York, N.Y.

McCUSKEY, Roy, clergyman, educator; b. Cameron, Marshall Co., W.Va., June 19, 1883; s. John Henry and Margaret Jane (Manning) McC.; grad. W.Va. Conf. Sem., Buckhannon, 1905; A.B., W.Va. Wesleyan Coll., 1908, D.D., 1922; S.T.B., Boston U. Sch. of Theology, 1911; m. Jessie B. Fulton, Sept. 9, 1908; children—John Fulton, Paul Livingstone, Leah Rachel. Ordained ministry M.E. Ch., 1905; successively pastor Cameron Circuit and Holly Grove, W.Va., Hingham, Mass., Shinnston, W.Va., North Street Ch., Wheeling, Seventh Av. Ch., Huntington, until 1920; supt. Parkersburg Dist., W.Va., 1920-26; pastor St. Andrews Ch., Parkersburg, and Thomson Ch., Wheeling, until 1931; pres. W.Va. Wesleyan Coll. since July 1, 1931. Mason. Clubs: Rotary (Buckhannon); Kiwanis (Wheeling). Home: Buckhannon, W.Va.

McCUSKEY, William C. D., urologist; b. Wheeling, W.Va.; s. Samuel Vergil and Ella Mae (Williams) M.; A.B., W.Va. Wesleyan Coll., 1922; M.D., Jefferson Med. Coll., 1928; M.Sc., Pa. Post-Grad. Sch. of Medicine, 1931; m. Florence M. Kuneke, Jan. 28, 1930; children—Bradford Mann, Barbara Ann. Interne Govt. Hosp., Fitzsimmons Gen. Hosp., Denver, 1928-30; practiced urology, Wheeling, since 1931. Mem. S.A.T.C., 1918. Trustee State Crippled Children's Assn. Certified by Am. Bd. Urology; fellow Am. Coll. Surgeons; mem. Am. Urol. Soc., Ohio County Med. Soc. (pres.), State Bd. Med. Examiners, State Bd. Pub. Health, Nu Sigma Nu. Democrat. Mason (Shriner), Elk. Clubs: Wheeling Country, Fort Henry (Wheeling); Belmont Country (St. Clairsville, O.). Home: Hazlett Court. Office: 60 14th St., Wheeling, W.Va.

McCUTCHEN, Robert Tarrant, chaplain; b. Beloit, Wis., Nov. 4, 1881; s. John Corbly and Adela Murilla (Hull) McC.; ed. Lewis Inst., Chicago, Hobart Coll., Geneva, N.Y., Nashotah (Wis.) Theol. Sem.; m. Frances O. Heyer, June 5, 1907; children—Frederic Meredith, Barbara. Ordained deacon and priest P.E. Ch., 1907; missionary in Philippine Islands, 1910-21; founder and dir. Moro uplift work in Sulu Archipelago, Philippine Islands, ministering to the only Mohammedans under the American flag; rector Trinity Ch., Victoria, Tex., 1921-26, Trinity Ch., Mattiesburg, Miss., 1926-29, Trinity Ch., Shamokin, Pa., 1929-36; Episcopalian chaplain, Mont Alto State Tubercular Sanatorium, South Mountain, Pa., since 1936; also chaplain, State Forestry Sch. of Pa. State Coll. at Mont Alto, Pa., since 1936. Mem. Kappa Alpha. Address: The Rectory, South Mountain, Pa.

McCUTCHEON, Thomas P., Jr.; prof. of chemistry, Univ. of Pa. Address: University of Pa., Philadelphia, Pa.

McDANIEL, Leon Sayre, coll. pres.; b. Meadowbrook, W.Va., Mar. 25, 1887; s. John Abraham and Lorena Ann (Coffman) M.; A.B., Bethany Coll., 1914; M.A., Columbia U., 1918; Ed.D., U. of Calif., Berkeley, 1928; m. Edna Hardin, Sept. 11, 1915; children—Everts, Ernest, Lorene, Darl. Began as teacher 1-room rural sch., 1905; teacher pub. and private schs., many yrs.; engaged in social settlement and instnl. ch. work, New York, 1916-23; dir. relig. edn. Coll. Av. Methodist Ch., Berkeley, Calif., 1926-28; mem. faculty Ariz. State Teachers Coll., Tempe, Ariz., 1928-30; visiting prof., W.Va. U., summer, 1930; head dept. edn., Ark. State Teachers Coll., Conway, 1930-32; founder, 1932, and since pres. Kanawha Coll. (accredited jr. coll.). Mem. bd. trustees State Dental Hygienists Training Sch. for Negroes. Mem. Am. Assn. Univ. Profs. Baptist. Elk. Home: 4 Grosscup Road, Charleston, W.Va.

McDANIEL, Walton Brooks, prof. Latin; b. Cambridge, Mass., Mar. 4, 1871; s. Samuel Walton and Georgiana Frances (Brooks) McD.; A.B., Harvard, 1893; A.M., Harvard Grad. Sch., 1894, Ph.D., same, 1899; grad. study, U. of Berlin, Germany, 1897-98; also study, Paris and Rome; m. Alice Corinne Garlichs, Aug. 2, 1899. Asst. in Greek and Latin, Harvard, 1896-97, instr., 1899-1901; instr. Greek and Latin, Radcliffe, 1900-1901; instr. Latin, U. of Pa., 1901-03, asst. prof., 1903-09, prof., 1909-37, prof. emeritus of Latin language and literature and engaged in research and writing since 1937; on leave of absence, prof. Am. Acad. in Rome, Italy, 1920-21. Fellow A.A.A.S. Mem. Am. Philos. Soc., Am. Philol. Assn. (past pres.), Classical Assn. of Eng. and Wales, Société des Etudes Latines de France, Mediæval Acad. of America, Archæol. Inst. of America, Classical Assn. of Atlantic States, Phi Beta Kappa. Democrat. Author: Roman Private Life and its Survivals, 1924; Guide for the Study of English Books on Roman Private Life (booklet) 1926. Contbr. to Am. and fgn. philol. and archæol. journs. Home: (winter) 4082 Malaga Av., Coconut Grove, Fla.; (summer) "Silvamere," Oak Bluffs, Mass. Office: College Hall, University of Pa., Philadelphia, Pa.

McDAVID, John Edwin, pres. Nat. Bank of Commerce of Charleston; b. Grayson, Ky., Feb. 16, 1900; s. John Edwin and Mildred (Black) McD.; student pub. schs., Grayson, Ky.; m. Elizabeth Rodgers, Oct. 2, 1924; children—John Edwin, William Rodgers. Certified pub. accountant, W.Va. and Ky.; pres. Nat. Bank of Commerce of Charleston, W.Va., since 1935. Republican. Presbyterian. Mason (Shriner), Elk, Moose. Home: 934 Greendale Drive. Office: National Bank of Commerce, Charleston, W.Va.

McDERMOTT, Frank Alexander, chem. supt.; b. Washington, D.C., Aug. 3, 1885; s. Frank Paine and Anna Virginia (McKeever) McD.; student George Washington U., Washington, D.C., 1906-09; B.S., U. of Pittsburgh, 1913, M.S., 1914; m. Mary E. Tallentire, Oct. 20, 1909; children—Frances Virginia, Margaret. Attendant hygienic lab., U.S. Pub. Health Service, Washington, D.C., 1906-11; research fellow, Mellon Inst., Pittsburgh, Pa., 1911-15; research chemist Corby Co., Washington, D.C., 1915-18; chemist exptl. sta. E.I. du Pont de Nemours & Co., Wilmington, Del., 1918-26, chem. supt. Deepwater Alcohol Plant, since 1926. Mem. Am. Chem. Soc., A.A.A.S., Am. Inst. Chemists, Soc. Am. Bacteriologists, Del. Soc. Natural History, Soc. Chem. Industry. Episcopalian. Home: 815 W. 32d St. Office: P.O. Box 746, Wilmington, Del.

McDERMOTT, John Joseph, pres. Lebanon Steel & Iron Co.; b. New York, N.Y., Mar. 12, 1892; s. Henry and Winifred (Harris) McD.; student N.Y. pub. schs., Pace Inst., New York; m. Catherine K. Herbertson, Aug. 9, 1920; 1 dau., Kay. Accountant Naylor & Co., N.Y., 1912-17; asst. auditor W. R. Grace & Co., N.Y., 1919-21; sec. Naylor & Co., 1921-24; sec. and treas. Lebanon (Pa.) Iron Co., 1924-28; sec. and treas. Wrought Iron Co. of America, Lebanon, Pa., 1928-35; president Lebanon Steel & Iron Co. (successor to Wrought Iron Company) since 1935. Served as chief petty officer, U.S. Navy, 1917-19. Member Lebanon Chamber of Commerce, American Legion. Republican. Roman Catholic. Elk. Clubs: Lebanon Country, Quentin Riding (Lebanon, Pa.). Home: 238 S. First Av. Office: East Cumberland St., Lebanon, Pa.

McDIVITT, Michael Myers, clergyman; b. Clearfield Co., Pa., Sept. 8, 1882; s. John Turner and Rachel Catherine (Myers) McD.; A.B., Washington and Jefferson Coll., 1904; S.T.M., Western Theol. Sem., 1907; B.D., Free Church Coll., Glasgow, Scotland, 1909; (hon.) A.M., Washington and Jefferson Coll., 1910; (hon.) D.D., Washington and Jefferson Coll., 1923; m. Maude Estella Ashbrook, Sept. 15, 1908; 1 son, Marcus Denney. Ordained to ministry Presbyn. Ch., 1907; minister, Canonsburg, Pa., 1907-11, Blairsville, Pa., 1911-19, Knoxville Presbyn. Ch., Pittsburgh, Pa., 1919-36, First Ch., Kittanning, Pa. since 1936; mem. bd. trustees Western Theol. Sem., Presbytery of Pittsburgh, Johnson C. Smith University; moderator Blairsville Presbytery, Pittsburgh Presbytery; pres. Synod of Pa. Republican. Presbyn. Mason. Clubs: Country (Kittanning); The Circle, South Hills Country (Pittsburgh). Contbr. to religious journs. Home: 411 N. McKean St., Kittanning, Pa.

McDONALD, Edward, banker; b. McDonald, Pa., Jan. 11, 1864; s. John N. and Elizabeth Mary (Lee) McD.; A.B., Washington & Jefferson Coll., 1884; unmarried. Pres. First Nat. Bank, McDonald, Pa., since 1892. President bd. trustees Washington and Jefferson Coll. Republican. Presbyterian. Club: Duquesne (Pittsburgh). Home: McDonald, Pa.

McDONALD, Ellice, bio-chemist, pathologist; b. Fort Ellice, Manitoba, Can., Oct. 27, 1876; s. Archibald and Ellen (Inkster) McD.; ed. St. John's Coll., Winnipeg, Can., McGill U. (M.D. 1901), Montreal, P.Q.; m. Ann Heebner, Oct. 15, 1907; children—Vicomtess Diane de Branges de Bourica, Ellice. Successively resident surgeon Kensington Hosp. and New York Lying-in Hosp., asst. in pathology, Albany Med. Sch., instr. Columbia U. Coll. of Pharmacy and Science, 1901-07; instr. surgery, N.Y. Post-Grad. Med. Sch. and Hosp., 1907-16; asst. prof. of gynecology, Grad. Sch. of Medicine U. of Pa., 1922-35; dir. Cancer Research Fund, 1928-35; dir. Biochemical Research Foundation of Franklin Inst. since 1935. Served with Canadian Army Med. Service, 1916-19. Awarded gold medal, Internat. Faculty of Sciences, London, 1938. Fellow Am. Coll. Surgeons; mem. Am. Inst. of City of New York, Biochem. Soc., Faraday Soc., Assn. for Study Internal Secretions, Pathol. Soc. Phila., Deutschen Chemischen Gesellschaft, Franklin Inst. of Pa., Soc. Chem. Industry, Am. Assn. Cancer Research, Am. Phys. Soc., Am. Chem. Soc., A.A.A.S., Internat. Soc. Exptl. Cytology, N.Y. Pathol. Soc. (life), Gen. Alumni Soc. U. of Pa., Phila. County Med. Soc., Grad. Soc. McGill U., Pa. Hort. Soc. Clubs: University; Merion Cricket (Haverford, Pa.); Concord Country (Concordsville, Pa.). Author: Studies in Gynecology and Obstetrics, 1914; Ectopic Pregnancy, 1919. Editor: Reports of the Cancer Research Labs. of U. of Pa., Vol. 1, 1930-31, Vol. 2, 1932-33; Reports of the Biochemical Research Foundation of Franklin Inst., Vol. 3, 1934-35, Vol. 4, 1936-37. Contributor many articles on cancer and bio-chemical research to med. jours. Home: 901 Harvard Av., Swarthmore, Pa. Office: 133 S. 36th St., Philadelphia, Pa.

McDONALD, Harl, composer and prof. music: b. nr. Boulder, Colo., July 27, 1899; s. Willis Burr and Floy (Van Taffelmire) McD.; Mus.B., U. of So. Calif., 1917; diploma Leipzig Cons., 1922, student U. of Leipzig, 1921-22; (hon.) Mus.D., Coll. of Pacific, 1920; (hon.) Mus.D., Phila. Mus. Acad., 1934; m. Eleanor Gosling, Dec. 19, 1925; children—Charlotte Burr, Frances Tabor. Instr. in conservatory, U. of Calif., Los Angeles, 1920-21; two tours, U.S.A. and Europe as concert pianist, 1921, 1924; head music dept., Sayward Sch., 1924-26; lecturer music, U. of Pa., 1926, asst. prof., 1927-30, prof. and dir. music since 1934; dir. Phila. Orchestra Assn. Mem. Am. Musicol. Soc., Sigma Xi. Republican. Episcopalian. Composer 4 symphonies, 3 concertos, 4 orchestral suites, and many other works for instruments and voice. Home: St. Davids, Pa.

McDONALD, John Nesbit, banker; b. McDonald, Pa., Mar. 7, 1875; s. John Noble and Elizabeth Mary (Lee) McD.; studied Kiskiminetas Springs Sch., Saltsburg, Pa., 1891-93; A.B., Washington & Jefferson Coll., 1897; m. Pauline Elizabeth Wilson, Sept. 24, 1913; children—John Nesbit, Jr., Anne, Joseph Wilson. Vice-pres. and dir. First Nat. Bank, McDonald, Pa., since 1902. Republican. Presbyterian. Club: Montour Heights Country (Coraopolis, Pa.). Home: McDonald, Pa.

McDONALD, Michael F(rancis), lawyer, judge; b. Sugar Notch, Pa., Aug. 10, 1880; s. Anthony and Sarah (Carlin) McD.; ed. pub. sch. and high sch., Sugar Notch, Pa., 1886-97; m. Sallie M. McGowan, Aug. 21, 1912; children—Michael F., Jr. John L., Joseph M. Engaged in teaching, 1897-1904; studied law in office of John T. Lenahan; admitted to Pa. bar, 1904, and since engaged in gen. practice of law at Wilkes-Barre; judge of Ct. of Common Pleas of Luzerne Co. since Dec. 1, 1938; dir. First Nat. Bank of Ashley, Pa., Wilkes-Barre & Hazleton Ice Co., Smith-Bennett Corpn. Mem. Wilkes-Barre Law and Library Assn., Am. Bar Assn., Pa. Bar Assn. Democrat. Roman Catholic. Club: Wyoming Valley Country (Hanover Twp., Pa.). Home: 6 Brown St., Ashley, Pa. Address: Court House, Wilkes-Barre, Pa.

McDONALD, Orville Lowe, lawyer; b. Bridgeport, W.Va., Dec. 7, 1888; s. Mordecai S. and Emma V. (Roe) McD.; student Potomac State Coll., Keyser, W.Va., 1907-08, 1909-10, W.Va. Univ., Morgantown, 1908-09; LL.B., Washington & Lee Univ., Lexington, Va., 1912; m. Nelle Winona Reese, Oct. 17, 1916; children—Robert O., Richard R. Admitted to W.Va. bar, 1912 and since engaged in gen. practice of law at Clarksburg; mem. firm Strother & McDonald since 1913; served as municipal judge City of Clarksburg, 1922-27; city atty., 1931 and 1933-35; commr. of accts. county ct. Harrison Co., 1930-37; divorce commr. circuit ct. since 1937; sec. West Va. Mine Supply Co., Clarksburg since 1938; sec.-treas. Potomac Improvement Co., Clarksburg, since 1923. Served as pres. Clarksburg Area of Boy Scouts of America. Mem. Am., W.Va. State and Harrison Co. bar assns. Democrat. Baptist. Mason (Shriner), Elk. Clubs: Elks, Lions, Potomac Hunting & Fishing (Clarksburg). Home: 401 E. Main St. Office: Lowndes Bank Bldg., Clarksburg, W.Va.

McDONALD, Peter, pres. Keystone Lumber Co.; b. Ireland, Nov. 7, 1874; s. Peter and Mary M.; student high sch.; m. Catherine Collins, June 6, 1906; 1 dau., Marie H. Pres. Keystone Lumber Co., Phila., since 1922; pres. Keystone Masons Supply Co., Keystone Half Time Bldg. & Loan Assn., Young Mens Bldg. & Loan Assn., Over The Top Bldg. & Loan Assn., Advance Mortgage & Finance Co.; v.p. Belmont Half Time Bldg. & Loan Assn. No. 2, Belmont Half Time Bldg. & Loan Assn., Empire Trust Co.; dir. Am. Union Bldg. & Loan Assn., Empire Half Time Bldg. & Loan Assn., Park Half Time Bldg. & Loan Assn., Farhill Coal Co. Club: Bankers Country. Home: 6145 Nassau St. Office: 1431-1447 N. 52d St., Philadelphia, Pa.

McDONNELL, Frank Joseph, lawyer; b. Scranton, Pa., Apr. 6, 1899; s. Frank Joseph and Mary Anne (Brown) McD.; A.B., St. Thomas Coll., 1917; M.A., Catholic U., Washington, D.C., 1918; LL.B., U. of Pa., 1922; unmarried. Began practice at Scranton, 1922; tax collector Scranton Dunmore Poor Dist., 1929-30; became U.S. atty. Middle Dist. of Pa., Mar. 24, 1934. Served as 2d lt. U.S. Army, World War. Mem. Am. and Pa. State bar assns., Lackawanna Bar Assn. (dir. 1928-32), Phi Delta Phi, Hare Law Club (U. of Pa.). Democrat. Catholic. Clubs: Scranton, Elks, Scranton Country. Home: 504 Monroe Av. Office: Lincoln Trust Bldg., Scranton, Pa.*

McDONNELL, John William, physician; b. Locust Gap, Pa., July 26, 1891; s. Peter A. and Mary A. (Grathwohl) McD.; grad. Sunbury (Pa.) Pub. Schs., 1909; M.D., U. of Pa., 1917; m. Laura I. Nevin, Apr. 10, 1917; children—John Nevin, Jane Marie. Interne Scranton (Pa.) State Hosp., 1917-18; in practice of medicine, Sunbury, Pa., since 1919; sec. of staff Mary M. Packer Hosp. Served in U.S. Army, Columbus, O., Barracks, 1918; disch. on account phys. disability from accident injury, 1908. Mem. Northumberland Co. Med. Soc. (past pres.), Pa. Med. Soc. A.M.A. Democrat. Catholic. Elk. Clubs: Susquehanna Valley Country (Sunbury); Sunbury Grouse (Barbours, Pa.). Home: 217 Race St. Office: 21 S. 4th St., Sunbury, Pa.

McDONNELL, Patrick Joseph, physician; b. Archbald, Pa., Dec. 17, 1879; s. Patrick Joseph and Catherine (Healey) McD.; Ph.B., Wesleyan U., Middletown, Conn., 1904; M.D., Johns Hopkins Med. Sch., Baltimore, Md., 1908, post-grad. work, 1917; m. Elizabeth Fitzgerald, Sept. 21, 1921; children—Thomas, John, Ann. Interne, Providence Hosp. (Washington, D.C.), Manhattan Maternity Hosp. (New York), 1908-10; in gen. practice medicine, Tonopah, Nev., 1910-15, Archbald, Pa., 1915-17, Scranton, Pa., since 1919; chief of med. service Scranton State Hosp. since 1936, Mercy Hosp. (Scranton) since 1923; consultant Keller Memorial Hosp. (Scranton) since 1938. Commd. capt., M.C., U.S. Army, Nov. 1917, sent to base hosp., Camp Taylor, Louisville, Ky.; chief of medicine Base Hosp. 79, France, 1918-19; commd. maj., Sept. 1918; hon. disch., July 1919. Dir. Oral Sch. of Northeastern Pa. Mem. Alpha Delta Phi. Club: Scranton (Pa.) Country. Played varsity baseball (capt. 1903) and football, Wesleyan U., 1900-04; coach Johns Hopkins U. football team, 1906. Home: 616 Taylor Av. Office: Medical Arts Bldg., Scranton, Pa.

McDONOUGH, Andrew L., lawyer; b. South Plainfield, N.J., Jan. 29, 1894; s. Peter J.

and Anne M. McD.; LL.B., U. of Notre Dame, South Bend, Ind., 1919; m. Winifred Allan, Sept. 18, 1920; children—Winifred J., Marion A., Andrew L., Jr. Admitted to N.J. bar as atty., 1920; engaged in gen. practice of law at Plainfield, N.J. since 1920; mem. firm McDonough & McDonough since 1921; served as asst. atty. gen. N.J., 1929-32; dir. Plainfield Lumber & Supply Co., Queen City Home Bldg. & Loan Assn. Served as pvt. to 2d lt. (pilot) A.S., U.S.A., 1917-19. Mem. Plainfield Bar Assn., Am. Legion. Republican. Roman Catholic. K.C. Home: 1021 Kenyon Av. Office: 119 W. Front St., Plainfield, N.J.

McDONOUGH, John E., judge; b. Phila., Pa., Dec. 25, 1873; s. Hugh J. and Mary Jane (Bailey) McD.; student pub. schs.; m. Julia C. Holl, Sept. 14, 1916; children—Mary, Anna, Julia, Frances. Pres. judge, Orphans' Ct., Delaware (Pa.) Co., since 1937. Author: Idyls of the Old South Ward. Home: Bullen's Lane, Ridley Twp., Delaware Co., Pa. Office: Court House, Media, Pa.

McDONOUGH, Roger Henry, librarian; b. Trenton, N.J., Feb. 24, 1909; s. Michael and Margaret (Finn) McD.; A.B., Rutgers U., 1934; B.S. in Library Science, Columbia U., 1936; unmarried. Employed as student asst., Rutgers Univ. Library, 1930-34, reference librarian, 1934-37; librarian New Brunswick Free Pub. Library since 1937. Mem. Am. Library Assn., N.J. Library Assn., Special Libraries Assn. Club: Rotary of New Brunswick. Home: 376 George St., New Brunswick, N.J.

McDOUALL, Leslie Gates, banking; b. Buffalo, N.Y., Feb. 16, 1892; s. Rev. James W. and Margaret (Brown) McD.; ed. pub. schs. and high sch., Paterson, N.J.; m. Florence E. Gebert, June 16, 1915; children—Virginia Gebert (Mrs. Paul A. Ward), Douglas Brown. Began as clk. in Bank of Pittsburgh, 1908-10; accountant in Trust Dept., Fidelity Union Trust Co., Newark, N.J., 1910-21, asst. trust officer, 1921-29, asso. trust officer, 1929-34, trust officer, 1934-36, vice-pres. and trust officer since 1936; vice-pres., treas. and dir. Groebe-McGovern Co.; dir. Leo Schloss, Inc., Dun & Bradstreet, Inc., R. G. Dun-Bradstreet Corpn. Trustee Home for Incurables & Convalescents, Newark, Centenary Jr. Coll. Mem. exec. council and finance com. Am. Bankers Assn.; mem. exec. com. and past pres. N.J. Bankers Assn. Republican. Episcopalian. Mason. Clubs: Essex, Downtown (Newark); Baltusrol Golf (Springfield). Home: 85 N. 18th St., East Orange. Office: 755 Broad St., Newark, N.J.

McDOUGLE, Ivan Eugene, coll. prof.; b. Huntington, Tenn., July 17, 1892; s. Ernest Clifton and Linna Alice (Caldwell) McD.; grad. Ky. State Normal Sch., 1910; A.B., Clark Coll., Worcester, Mass., 1915; A.M., Clark U., 1916, Ph.D., 1918; m. Hazel Agnes Montague, Dec. 28, 1918; 1 dau., Jean Caldwell. Asst. in history, Clark Coll., 1915-18; prof. economics and sociology, Sweet Briar (Va.) Coll., 1919-24; asso. prof. economics and sociology, Goucher Coll., 1924-31, prof., 1931—; prof. sociology, summer sessions, Coll. of William and Mary, 1925-30. Mem. Md. Commn. on Higher Edn. of Negroes, 1935-37; chmn. Md. Commn. on Scholarships since 1937; chmn. Advisory Bd. Recreation, Baltimore, since 1936. Mem. Am. Sociol. Soc., Am. Assn. of University Profs., Population Association America. Member Disciples of Christ. Author: An Economic Study of Lexington, Ky. (1800-1820), 1916; Slavery in Kentucky (1792-1865), 1918; Mongrel Virginians (with Arthur H. Estabrook), 1926. Also articles in mags. Home: 1219 Roundhill Rd. Address: Goucher College, Baltimore, Md.

McDOWELL, Harry Bleakley, banker; b. Sharon, Pa., Apr. 19, 1882; s. Alexander and Clara (Bleakley) McD.; student Trinity Hall, Washington, Pa., 1898-1900; B.S., Washington and Jefferson Coll., Washington, Pa., 1904; student Harvard Law Sch., 1905-06; m. Grace Osborne, Nov. 22, 1911; children—Mary (Mrs. George S. Warren, Jr.), Margaret, Elizabeth, Harry Bleakley, Alexander (dec.). Began as banker, 1904; cashier McDowell Nat. Bank, Sharon, Pa., 1907-19, v.p., 1919-33, pres. since 1933; pres. and dir. Sharon Coal and Ice Co.; v.p. and dir. Shenango Valley Water Co.; treas. and dir. First Federal Savings & Loan Assn.; dir. Federal Res. Bank of Cleveland. Dir. Liberty Loan Campaign, Mercer Co., Pa., World War. Trustee F. H. Buhl Club Fund; dir. Pa. State Chamber of Commerce. Mem. Econ. Policy Commn.; Am. Bankers Assn., Phi Gamma Delta. Republican. Presbyterian. Mason (Sharon Lodge 250; New Castle Consistory 32°; Shriner; Royal Order Jesters, Pittsburgh; K.T., Sharon); Elk (Sharon Lodge 103). Clubs: Duquesne (Pittsburgh); Shrine (Erie, Pa.); Sharon Country. Home: 1109 State St. Office: 62-66 E. State St., Sharon, Pa.

McDOWELL, Milton Speer, dir. agrl. extension; b. Milroy, Pa., Jan. 13, 1872; s. William Elliott and Louisa (McGuire) McD.; B.S., M.S., Pa. State Coll.; m. Mabel Gertrude Snyder, June 28, 1900; children—Milton S., Jr., Louise, Elizabeth, Henrietta. Employed as agrl. chemist with large mfg. corpns., 1892-98; chemist, Pa. Agrl. Expt. Sta., 1898-1910, asst. dir. agrl. extension, 1910-12, dir. agrl. extension, Pa. State Coll. since 1912. Mem. Pa. State Farm Show Commn. Mem. Kappa Sigma, Alpha Zeta, Gamma Sigma Delta. Presbyn. Mason (K.T., 32°). Club: Kiwanis. Home: 112 W. Beaver Av., State College, Pa.

McDOWELL, Samuel John, ceramic engr.; b. Bloomingburg, O., Sept. 4, 1894; s. Frank and Kate (Millikan) McD.; B. of Cer. Engring., O. State U., 1917, Cer. Engr., same, 1933; m. Caroline Zentmyer, Jan. 28, 1919; 1 son, Robert Bruce. Began as ceramic engr. Detroit Star Grinding Wheel Co., Detroit, Mich., 1917; ceramic engr. A. C. Spark Plug Co., Flint, Mich., 1917-25, Columbus, O., Sta. U.S. Bur. Mines, 1925-26; supt. Columbus Branch Nat. Bur. Standards, 1926-27; supt. Corning Terra Cotta Co., Corning, N.Y., 1927-32; ceramic engr. A. C. Spark Plug Co., Flint, Mich., 1933-35; factory mgr. Plant No. 3, General Ceramics Co., Keasbey, N.J., since 1935. Fellow A.A A.S., Am. Ceramic Soc.; mem. Am. Inst. Ceramic Engrs. (sec. 1939-40), N.J. Ceramic Soc., Beta Theta Pi, Sigma Xi. Democrat. Presbyn. Club: Golf and Country (Metuchen, N.J.). Contbr. tech. articles to mags. and journs. Home: Oak Hills, Metuchen, N.J. Office: General Ceramics Co., Keasbey, N.J.

McDOWELL, Ted Gaylor, newspaper editor; b. Silerville, Ky., Nov. 13, 1902; s. Joseph and Cora (Barnett) McD.; A.B., U. of Ky., Lexington, 1926; m. Katherine Bird, June 1, 1933. Began as editor Harlan (Ky) Enterprise, weekly, Harlan, Ky., 1926; reporter, Lexington (Ky.) Herald, 1926-28; reporter, rewrite man, Louisville (Ky.) Courier-Journal, 1928-30; editor Beckley Post-Herald, Beckley, W.Va., since 1930. Commd. 2d lt. M.I. Res., O.R.C., 1930. Past pres. Beckley Chamber of Commerce, pres. Rotary Club, sec. Police Civil Service Commn. Served as nat. committeeman, Young Rep. League of W.Va. Mem. W.Va. Newspaper Council, Nat. Editorial Assn., Sigma Delta Chi, Omicron Delta Kappa, Res. Officers Assn. (past pres. local). Republican. Presbyn. Mason. Moose. Club: Black Knight Country. Home: 21 Williams St. Office: 73 Prince St., Beckley, W.Va.

McELFISH, A. G., pres. Cumberland Savings Bank. Address: Cumberland, Md.

McELLROY, William Swindler, college prof. and pastor; b. Edgewood, Pa., Sept. 26, 1893; s. John Moss and Ida May (Sheffler) McE.; B.S., U. of Pittsburgh, 1916, M.D., Sch. of Medicine, 1917; post-grad. work Harvard Med. Sch., 1917; m. Ellenore Hambly, June 10, 1917. Began as student asst. in physiology, U. of Pittsburgh, 1915; instr. in phys. chemistry, U. of Pittsburgh, 1917-19, asst. prof. of phys. chemistry, 1919-20, prof. of phys. chemistry since 1920; asst. dean, Sch. of Medicine, U. of Pittsburgh, 1921-38, acting dean during 1938, dean since Jan. 1939; chemist to Elizabeth Steel Magee Hosp., Pittsburgh, since 1925, to Children's Hosp., Pittsburgh, since 1925, to Presbyn. Hosp., Pittsburgh, since 1925, to St. Francis Hosp., Pittsburgh, since 1920. Lt., j.g., M.C., U.S.N.R.F. Fellow Am. Coll. of Physicians; mem. Am. Soc. for Exptl. Biology and Medicine, Am. Soc. for Biol. Chemists, Allegheny Co. Med. Soc., Alpha Omega Alpha, Sigma Xi, Sigma Chi. Republican. Presbyterian. Mason. Clubs: Pittsburgh Athletic Assn. & Faculty Club (Pittsburgh); Edgewood (Pa.); Chesapeake Yacht (Easton, Md.); Miles River Yacht (St. Michaels, Md.). Home: King Edward Apts. Office: School of Medicine, U. of Pittsburgh, Pittsburgh, Pa.

McELROY, George, lawyer; b. Brooklyn, N.Y., Dec. 28, 1893; s. William and Margaret (Scheidt) McE.; grad. Pratt Inst., 1914, Casino Tech. Night Sch., E. Pittsburgh, 1915; grad. study, Carnegie Tech., 1916; LL.B., N.J. Law Sch., Newark, 1928; grad. study, Columbia U. Law Sch., 1929; m. Esther V. Schmeelk, Aug. 17, 1914; children—George H., LeRoy, Mary (Mrs. Sigfrid Hauck), Ellen. Employed in various positions with L.I. R.R. Co., Brooklyn, N.Y., 1911-14; cadet signal engr., Brooklyn Rapid Transit, 1914; asso. with Westinghouse Electric & Mfg. Co., tester, E. Pittsburgh, Pa., 1915-16, erection engr., N.Y. City, 1916-19, sales engr., 1919-24, mgr., Bridgeport, Conn., 1924-28, syndicate rep., N.Y. City, 1928-33; sec.-treas. Utilities Engring. & Equipment Corpn., N.Y. City, 1933-34; admitted to N.J. bar, 1929 and engaged in gen. law practice, Elizabeth, 1934-36; chief clk. Chancery Ct., Trenton, N.J., since 1936; registered professional engr., N.Y. State; registered elec. and mech. engr., N.J. Dem. candidate for Assembly in 1931, for Co. Register, 1932; ward leader. Former mem. A.I.E.E. Mem. Am. Bar Assn., Union City Bar Assn., Delta Theta Phi. Democrat. Methodist. Mason (32°, Shriner). Elk. Home: 749 Linden Av., Elizabeth, N.J. Office: State House Annex, Trenton, N.J.

McELROY, Margaret Julia, author; b. Newton, Ia., July 27, 1880; d. William Owen and Julia Maria (Cavanagh) McE.; student Ia. State Coll.; grad. Cornell U. Training Sch. for Supervisors of Pub. Sch. Music, 1912; A.B., Cornell U., 1913; grad. study, State U. of Ia. Formerly teacher of English, pub. schs., Doylestown, Pa., then teacher of English and reading in pub. schs., Ithaca, N.Y.; devoting time to writing and revision of children's books since 1923. Member American Library Association, National Council of Teachers of English, Phi Beta Kappa, Alpha Delta Pi. Republican. Author: Adventures of Johnny T. Bear, 1926; A Child's First Book in Reading, also Teachers' Manual of same, 1927. Co-Author: (with J. O. Younge) The Squirrel Tree, 1927; Tatters, 1929; (with J. O. Younge) Toby Chipmunk, 1930; also reader manuals, and teaching equipment. Home: Doylestown, Pa.

McELROY, Samuel Fremont, pres. and gen. mgr. Latrobe Die-Casting Co.; b. Sharpsburg, Pa., Nov. 13, 1892; s. Samuel Wilson and Ella Harrington (Laufman) McElroy; m. Alice Margaret Paulin, Oct. 9, 1920; children—Mary Virginia, Barbara Ann, Antoinette Paulin. With Mich. Smelting & Refining Co., Detroit, 1916-20, Doehler Die Casting Co., Phila., 1920-32; pres., gen. mgr. and dir. Latrobe (Pa.) Die-Casting Co. since 1932. Served as lt. U.S. Army, 1918-19. Republican. Home: 741 Walnut St. Office: North and Unity Sts., Latrobe, Pa.

McELWAIN, Howard Byer; asso. in surgery, U. of Md.; surgeon St. Joseph's, Mercy and South Baltimore Gen. hosps. Address: 31 E. North Av., Baltimore, Md.

McELWEE, William, Jr., county solicitor; b. Edenburg, Pa., Aug. 16, 1874; s. William and Emeline (Cooper) McE.; student New Wilmington (Pa.) Union Sch. 1887 to 1890, Westminster Coll., New Wilmington, Pa., 1893 to 1897; m. Cora Belle Marshall, Sept. 28, 1905; 1 dau., Mareline. Principal, Path Valley Acad., Dry Run, Franklin Co., Pa., 1897-99, Eau Claire (Pa.) Acad., 1899-1900; prof. mathematics, Amity Coll., College Springs, Ia., 1900-01; admitted to Lawrence Co. bar, 1905; gen. practice, 1905-12; co. solicitor, Lawrence Co., Pa., 1912-20, since 1934; mem. Pa. Ho. of Reps., 1930-34. Active in ch. and philanthropic activities, New Wilmington, Pa., since 1908. Republican. Presbyterian. Club: Rotary of New Wilmington, Pa. (pres. 1929-30). Home: 335 Waugh Av., New Wilmington, Pa. Office: 601 Lawrence Savings & Trust Bldg., New Castle, Pa.

McENTIRE, Lloyd, civil engr.; b. Erwinna, Pa., Sept. 10, 1887; s. Howell and Lucinda (George) M.; student Frenchtown High Sch. and Lerch Prep. Sch.; C.E., Lehigh U., Bethlehem, Pa.; unmarried. Draftsman Pa. R.R., 1909; draftsman Am. Bridge Co., 1909-13, bridge engr., 1913-16, principal asst. engr., 1916-17, inspector, 1920, draftsman, 1921; civil engr., Saylorsburg, Pa., since 1921. Served as pvt., Inf., U.S. Army, 1918. Mem. Am. Soc. for Testing Materials, Nat. Geog. Soc. Mason (K.T.; Shriner, Scottish Rite). Clubs: Acacia, Harvard. Wrote reports on bridge engring. Address: Church Rd., R.F.D. 3 Route, Saylorsburg, Pa.

McFALL, John Monteith, lawyer; b. Greenville, S.C., Sept. 3, 1885; s. Andrew Calhoun and Lillian Duncan (McCullough) McF.; A.B., Coll. of Charleston, S.C., 1904; M.A., Columbia U., 1906; LL.B., George Washington U. Law Sch., Washington, D.C., 1915; m. Eulalie McLeod, Aug. 31, 1929; 1 dau., Eulalie Swinton. Began as teacher, San Antonio, Tex., 1906; headmaster Peacock Mil. Acad., San Antonio, 1907-08, Donaldson Mil. Acad., Fayetteville, N.C., 1908-11; prof. law, George Washington U. Law Sch., Washington, D.C., 1918-20; admitted to Ga. bar, 1915, and practiced at Atlanta, Ga., 1915-16; v.p. and chief atty. U.S. Fidelity & Guaranty Co., Baltimore, Md., since 1928; pres. Allied Mortgage Cos., Inc., Asso. Mortgage Cos., Inc., Baltimore, since 1935; lecturer ins. law, U. of Md. Law Sch., Baltimore, since 1926. Mem. Am. Bar Assn., The Benchers, Phi Delta Phi, Phi Kappa Sigma. Episcopalian. Clubs: Elkridge (Baltimore, Md.). Home: Ruxton, Md. Office: U.S. Fidelity & Guaranty Co., Baltimore, Md.

McFALL, William Bailey, lawyer, banker; b. Pittsburgh, Pa., Oct. 11, 1890; s. William Bailey and Martha (Ramage) McF.; A.B., Washington & Jefferson Coll., 1912; LL.B., U. of Pittsburgh, 1915; m. Ruth McKee, Sept. 23, 1919; children—Martha Frances, Sara Jane. Admitted to Pa. bar, 1915; since in gen. practice of law; mem. firm Dalzell, McFall & Pringle since 1922; pres. Commonwealth Trust Co., Pittsburgh, since 1938. Dir. Legal Aid Soc., Pittsburgh. V.p. Allegheny Co. Bar Assn. Republican. United Presbyterian. Home: 420 Parker Drive, Mt. Lebanon Twp., Allegheny County, Pa. Address: Commonwealth Trust Co., Pittsburgh, Pa.

McFARLAND, Archie J.; exec. v.p. and dir. Wheeling Steel Corpn. Office: care Wheeling Steel Corpn., Wheeling, W.Va.

McFARLAND, Frieda Wiegand, (Mrs. Paul Boyton McF.), univ. prof.; b. Grand Forks, N.D., Oct. 31, 1887; d. Rev. F. J. and Susan A. (Smith) Wiegand; A.B., Ind. Univ., Bloomington, Ind., 1919; A.M., George Washington U., Washington, D.C., 1927; student Columbia U., 1918; m. Paul Boyton McFarland, June 16, 1923. Engaged in teaching, pub. schs. in Minn. and Ind., 1907-17; instr. in physiology and geography, Jr. High Sch., Bedford, Ind., 1913-17; teacher of art, Jr. High Sch., Bloomington, Ind., 1917-19; head of dept. of textiles, clothing and art, U. of Md., College Park, Md. since 1919. Mem. Am., State and D.C. home econs. assns., Am. Assn. Univ. Profs., Omicron Nu, Alpha Lambda Delta, Alpha Omicron Pi, Campus Club. Episcopalian. Club: Progress (College Park). Author: Good Taste in Dress, 1936. Home: 15 Wine Av., Hyattsville, Md.

McFARLAND, J(ohn) Horace, masterprinter; b. McAlisterville, Juniata Co., Pa., Sept. 24, 1859; s. Col. George F. and Adeline D. (Griesemer) M.; ed. pvt. sch., Harrisburg, 1867-71; further edn. in printing office and continued pvt. reading and study; L.H.D., Dickinson Col., 1924; m. Lydia S. Walters, May 22, 1884; children—Helen Louise, Katharine Sieg (dec.), Robert Bruce. After learning printing business, established for self, Jan. 1, 1878; moved and established Mt. Pleasant Press, 1889, inc., 1891, as J. Horace McFarland Co. of which is now president; also pres. McFarland Publicity Service. Printer of and contbr. to American Gardening, 1890-93; printer of and contbg. photographs and articles to Country Life in America, 1901-04, and to Country Calendar, Suburban Life and Countryside mags. during their existence. Editor "Beautiful America" dept. of the Ladies Home Journal, 1904-07. Lecturer on civic, scenic and horticultural topics, especially on roses. Sec. Municipal League of Harrisburg, 1901—; mem. Harrisburg Park Commn., 1905-13; pres. Harrisburg Board of Trade, 1912-13, Am. League for Civic Improvement, 1902-04, Am. Civic Assn., 1904-24, v.p. Nat. Municipal League, 1912-28. Conducted campaign for preservation Niagara Falls, 1905—, for preserving and developing national parks, 1911—, and for roadside development, 1925—. Am. mem. Internat. Niagara Control Bd., 1926—; apptd. by President Franklin D. Roosevelt mem. Nat. Park Trust Fund Bd., 1935. Treas. commn. on living conditions of war workers, Dept. of Labor, 1918-19; mem. com. on zoning, Dept. of Commerce, 1921—; chmn. State Art Commn. of Pa., 1927—. Pres. Central Pa. Typothetæ, 1921-22; pres. American Rose Society, 1930-32, Harrisburg Music Foundation, 1929-33; trustee Dickinson College. Mem. Am. Assn. Nurserymen (chmn. Am. joint com. on hort. nomenclature, 1916—; chmn. com. on hort. quarantine, 1920—), Garden Club of America, Royal Hort. Soc. (London), Council Pa. Hort. Soc. and other tech. and philanthropic socs. Methodist. Republican. Clubs: City (New York); Cosmos (Washington). Author: Photographing Flowers and Trees, 1902; Getting Acquainted with the Trees, 1904; Laying Out the Home Grounds, 1915; My Growing Garden, 1915; The Rose in America, 1923; Roses of the World in Color, 1936. Joint Author: How to Grow Roses, 1930 (rev. 1937); What Every Rose Grower Should Know, 1931. Editor: The American Rose Annual, 1916—; The American Rose Magazine, 1933—; Pennsylvania Gardens, 1937—; assisted in illustrating, as well as printing, also contbr. Bailey's Standard Cyclopedia of Horticulture, Taylor's Garden Dictionary. Contbr. to N.Y. Times, The Flower Grower, Horticulture and other periodicals. Developed Breeze Hill Gardens for testing roses and other ornamental plants, 1912—. Awarded George Robert White medal of honor for horticulture by Mass. Hort. Soc., 1933; Cornelius Amory Pugsley medal by Am. Scenic and Historic Preservation Soc., 1938. Home: Breeze Hill, 2101 Bellevue Rd. Office: Mt. Pleasant Press, Harrisburg, Pa.

McFARLAND, Joseph, pathologist; b. Phila., Pa., Feb. 9, 1868; s. Joseph and Susan E. (Grim) M.; acad. edn. Lauderbach Acad., Phila.; M.D., U. of Pa., 1889, Medico-Chirurg. Coll., 1898; studied Heidelberg and Vienna, 1890, Berlin and Halle, summer of 1895, Pasteur Inst., Paris, summer of 1903; Sc.D., Ursinus Coll., Pa., 1913; m. Virginia E., d. Gen. William B. Kinsey, Sept. 14, 1892; children—Helen Josephine, Katharine A., Ruth, Joseph. Prof. pathology and bacteriology, Medico-Chirurg. Coll., 1896-1916; prof. pathology, Woman's Med. Coll. Pa., 1911-13; prof. pathology and bacteriology, U. of Pa., 1916—. Maj., M.C.U.S.A.; chief of lab. service, Base Hosp., Camp Beauregard, Alexandria, La., Jan.-Mar. 1918, at Gen. Hosp. 9, Lakewood, N.J., Apr.-Nov. 1918, General Hospital 14, Ft. Oglethorpe, Ga., Nov. 1918; director laboratory instruction in M.O.T.C. at Camp Greenleaf, Nov. 1918. Fellow Am. Coll. of Physicians, Coll. Physicians of Phila., A.M.A., Acad. of Natural Sciences Phila., Acad. of Stomatology; mem. Med. Soc. State Pa., Phila. County Med. Soc., Am. Assn. Pathologists and Bacteriologists, Soc. Clin. Pathologists. Author: Pathogenic Bacteria, 9 edits., 1896-1919; Text-book of Pathology, 2 edits., 1904, 09; Biology, General and Medical, 5 edits., 1910-1926; The Breast (with Dr. John B. Deaver), 1917; Fighting Foes Too Small to See, 1923; Surgical Pathology, 1924; also many contbns. to med. lit. in English and German. Home: 542 W. Hortter St., Mt. Airy, Philadelphia, Pa.

McFARLAND, William West, M.D., med. dir.; b. Pittsburgh, Pa., Dec. 10, 1878; s. William and Ada (West) McF.; student East Liberty (Pa.) Acad., 1895-98; M.D., U. of Pa., 1902; m. Rosa Minear, June 12, 1907; 1 son, Robert West. Med. insp. Bur. of Child Welfare, City of Pittsburgh, Pa., 1910-29, supervisor, 1929-32, dir. of pub. health, 1933; exec. dir. Gen. Health Council of Allegheny Co., Pittsburgh, Pa., since 1934; med. columnist Pittsburgh Sun Telegraph since 1935. Mem. Pa. Pub. Health Assn. (pres. 1938-39), Allegheny Co. Med. Soc., Pa. State Med. Soc., A.M.A., Pittsburgh Acad. of Medicine, Venereal Disease Control Com. of Allegheny Co. (chmn. since 1935), Blindness Prevention Assn., Mental Hygiene Assn., Diphtheria Prevention Assn., Am. Pub. Health Assn., Am. Social Hygiene Assn., Civic Club of Allegheny Co., Pittsburgh Community Fund. Republican. Protestant. Club: Ligonier (Pa.) Country. Author articles on health conditions. Home: Arlington Apts. Office: 519 Smithfield St., Pittsburgh, Pa.

McFEELY, Percy Ralph, physician; b. Baltimore, Md., Nov. 3, 1891; s. Percy Thomas and Miriam (Usilton) McF.; M.D., N.Y. Med. Coll., N.Y. City, 1914; m. Agnes Demott, June 14, 1916; children—Elizabeth, Dorothy. Interne Flower Hosp., N.Y. City, 1914-15; engaged in gen. practice of medicine at Bogota, N.J., since 1915; mem. med. staff Hackensack Hosp., Holy Name Hosp.; sch. physician, Bogota bd. edn. since 1932. Served as 1st lt. Med. Corps, U.S.A., 1917-19. Mem. bd. Health. Mem. Bergen County Med. Soc., N.J. Med. Soc., A.M.A. Mem. Reformed Ch. Mason. Royal Arcanum. Club: Masonic. Home: 242 Palisade Av., Bogota, N.J.

McGALLIARD, David Cubberley, elec. engr.; b. Hamilton Twp., Mercer Co., N.J., Jan. 24, 1895; s. William Vannest and Mary Anna (West) McG.; student Trenton (N.J.) High Sch., 1909-14; E.E., Lehigh U., Bethlehem, Pa., 1919; m. Helen Elizabeth Howard, June 10, 1922; children—William Vannest, David Howard. Telephone engring. Bell Telephone Labs., New York, 1919-26; engring. assignments Elec. Research Products, Inc., New York, 1926-33, operating mgr., 1933-36, service mgr., 1936-37; industrial engring. Western Electric Co., New York, since 1937. Served as elec. sergt., 75th Coast Arty. Corps, U.S. Army, during World War. Presbyterian. Home: 217 Wheaton Pl., Rutherford, N.J. Office: 195 Broadway, New York, N.Y.

McGARRAH, Albert Franklin, clergyman; b. West Monterey, Pa., Feb. 23, 1878; s. James S. and Amanda (Wilson) M.; B.S., Grove City (Pa.) Coll., 1898, B.A., 1901, D.D., 1923; grad. Western Theol. Sem., 1903; m. Alice M. Kiskaddon, Nov. 30, 1903; children—George Robert (dec.), Donald, Mary Elizabeth. Teacher and salesman, 1893-1900; ordained Presbyn. ministry, 1904; pastor Big Oak, Calif., 1904-06; spl. field rep. Presbyn. Home Mission Bd., 1906-09, on finance and methods, Presbyn. Gen. Assembly, 1909-12; supt. home missions and ch. extension, St. Louis, 1912-13; sec. Ch. Efficiency Bur., Chicago, 1914-18; asso. field dir. Presbyn. New Era Movement, 1919-24; director campaigns department of Presbyterian Ch., U.S.A., 1924-31; dir. Ch. Campaigns Bur. of Home Missions Council since 1931. Spl. lecturer on ch. administration, various theol. schools. Author: A Modern Church Program, 1915; Modern Church Finance, 1916; Modern Church Management, 1917; Practical Inter-Church Methods, 1919; Money Talks, 1922; also booklets and pamphlets on similar topics. Home: Swarthmore, Pa. Office: Granite Bldg., Pittsburgh, Pa.

McGARVEY, Robert James, newspaper editor; b. Elizabeth, N.J., Sept. 15, 1911; s. Robert and Mary (McGovern) McG.; student Battin High Sch., Elizabeth, N.J.; unmarried. Began as reporter, radio commentator Sta. WHBI, Newark, N.J., 1938-39; pub. Plainfield (N.J.) Post since 1938; editor Union Co. Home News, Elizabeth, N.J., since 1939; asso. editor Westfield (N.J.) Standard since 1939. Mem. Am. Newspaper Guild. Elk. Home: 627 Jackson Av. Office: 251 N. Broad St., Elizabeth, N.J.

McGEARY, William Roy, clergyman; b. Leechburg, Pa., Sept. 18, 1895; s. George W. and Lettie (Leech) McG.; A.B., Muskingum Coll., New Concord, O., 1918; Th.B., Pittsburgh Theol. Sem., 1924; Th.M., Pittsburgh-Xenia Sem., 1932; (hon.) D.D., Muskingum Coll., 1935; (hon.) D.D., Sterling Coll., Sterling, Kan., 1935; m. Carrie Gatts, Nov. 29, 1917; children—William Roy, Jr., Hunter Alvin. Engaged as teacher and prin. high schs., 1918-21; ordained to ministry U. Presbyn. Ch., Oct. 9, 1924; asst. pastor, Pittsburgh, 1921-22, 1922-24; pastor, McKeesport, Pa., 1924-28, Second U.P. Ch., Pittsburgh, 1928-30, Knoxville United Presbyn. Ch., Pittsburgh, since 1930. Served in U.S.N.R.F., 1917-19. Dir. Board of Publication and Bible Sch. Work, Sabbath Assn. of Western Pa. Republican. United Presbyn. Club: South Hills Rotary (Pittsburgh). Home: 226 Charles St., Pittsburgh, Pa.

McGEE, Lemuel Clyde, physician; b. New Boston, Tex., Aug. 2, 1904; s. Thos. Lemuel and Sarah Elizabeth (Murrell) McG.; A.B., Baylor Univ., Waco, Tex., 1924; student Baylor U. Coll. of Medicine, Dallas, Tex., 1924-25; Ph.D. in Biochemistry, U. of Chicago, 1927; M.D., Rush Med. Coll. of U. of Chicago, 1929; m. Mary Virginia Provence, May 29, 1933; 1 dau., Lenore. Biochemist in Inst. for Juvenile Research of State of Ill., Chicago, 1928-29; interne Baylor Univ. Hosp., Dallas, Tex., 1930, Presbyn. Hosp., Chicago, 1931; instr. physiology and pharmacology, Baylor U. Coll. of Medicine, Dallas, Tex., (half time) 1932-34, attdg. physician, Parkland Hosp. (part time) 1933-34, med. clinics once each week, Baylor U. Coll. Medicine, 1934; mem. staff Davis Memorial Hosp., Elkins, W.Va. since 1935, chief physician dept. medicine, Golden Clinic since 1935. Served as 1st lt. Med. Corps Res. U.S.A., 1934-38; lt. M.C.-S(V), U.S.N.R. since 1938. Fellow Am. Coll. Physicians. Certified by Am. Bd. Internal Medicine. Diplomate Nat. Bd. Med. Examiners. Mem. A.M.A., Am. Heart Assn., Southern and W.Va. State Med. assns., W.Va. Heart Assn., Randolph County Hist. Soc., Sigma Xi, Alpha Omega Alpha. Club: Kiwanis. Contbr. articles to med. journs. Home: 240 Boundary Av. Office: Davis Memorial Hosp., Elkins, W.Va.

McGEE, William Lewis, banking; b. Upland, Pa., Mar. 15, 1887; s. Rev. Benjamin Franklin Gould (D.D.) and Frances Roop (Lewis) McG.; A.B., Princeton U., 1909; m. Elizabeth Crozer Lewis, Oct. 31, 1916; children—Ralph Lewis, Elizabeth Lewis, Eleanore Lewis. Began as jr. accountant with Lybrand, Ross Bros. & Montgomery, 1910; successively accountant and credit mgr., Scott Paper Co., spl. inspr. Dept. Pub. Works, Phila., traveling auditor, Firestone Tire & Rubber Co., sr. accountant, Lybrand, Ross Bros. & Montgomery, accountant U.S. Food Adminstrn., accountant and auditor, own company, Wm. Lewis McGee & Co., 1919-31; spl. dept. sec. of banking of Pa., 1931-35; vice-pres. and treas. Real Estate Trust Co., Phila., Pa., 1935-39, exec. vice-pres. since 1939. Mem. Pa. Inst. Certified Pub. Accountants, Robert Morris Assos., Phila. Credit Men's Assn. Republican. Episcopalian. Mason (K.T., Shriner) Clubs: Union League, Princeton (Philadelphia); Rolling Green Golf (Springfield, Pa.). Home: Bent Rd., Bowling Green, Media, Pa. Office: S.E. Cor. Broad & Chestnut Sts., Philadelphia, Pa.

McGILL, Earl William, pres. Crawford County Trust Co.; b. Crawford Co., Pa., Sept. 4, 1880; s. William R. and Caroline A. (Harkins) McG.; student pub. schs.; m. Julia Thaxter, Jan. 25, 1923; children—Ben T., Robert E. Began with Lamberton Nat. Bank, Franklin, Pa., 1900; teller Dollar Savings and Trust Co., of Youngstown, O. 1901-03; cashier First Nat. Bank of Conneaut Lake, 1903-05; asst. treas. Electric Mfg. and Power Co., Spartansburg, S.C., 1908-11; pres. Crawford County Trust Co., Meadville, Pa., since 1911; dir. Meadville Telephone Co., Meadville Terminals Co., McCrosky Tool Corpn., Yost Mfg. Co., Jamestown (N.Y.) Telephone Corpn., Pa. Engring. Corpn., Peoples Telephone Corpn. of Butler (Pa.), Champion DeArment Tool Co., Meadville Bldg. & Loan Assn., Keystone View Co., Meadville Housing Corpn.; treas. and dir. Raybould Coupling Co. Trustee Park Av. Congl. Ch., Meadville, Pa.; dir. Meadville City Hosp. Mem. Meadville Chamber of Commerce (ex-pres.). Clubs: Rotary (ex-pres.); Iroquois, Meadville Country (Meadville, Pa.). Home: 560 Walnut St. Office: Chestnut and Market Sts., Meadville, Pa.

McGILLICUDY, Cornelius. See Mack, Connie.

McGINLEY, Thomas Atterbury, pres. The Duff-Norton Mfg. Co.; b. Pittsburgh, Pa., July 18, 1880; s. John Rainey and Jennie (Atterbury) McG.; Ph.B., Yale, 1901; m. Estelle Schnable Floyd, Nov. 22, 1924; children—John R., II, Elizabeth McGinley Borden, Gertrude McGinley Jay; step-children—Mary Floyd Brown, Walter I. Floyd. Treas. Eaglis Corpn. (Del.) since 1932; pres. The Duff-Norton Mfg. Co., Pittsbugh, The Canadian Duff-Norton Co., Coaticook, P.Q., Can., since 1928; dir. Westinghouse Air Brake Co., Union Switch & Signal Co., Western Allegheny R.R. Co., Fidelity Trust Co. (Pittsburgh), Pittsburgh Screw & Bolt Corpn. Burgess of Borough of Sewickley Heights, Pa., since 1935. Dir. Allegheny Gen. Hosp. Republican. Presbyterian. Clubs: Duquesne, Pittsburgh, Allegheny Country (life), Rolling Rock (Ligonier, Pa.); Sewickley Hunt (Sewickley Heights, Pa.). Home: Sewickley Heights, Pa. Office: 2709 Preble Av., Pittsburgh, Pa.

McGINNESS, Samuel Wilson, lawyer; b. Allegheny City, Pa., Aug. 28, 1881; s. Joseph Wilson and Agnes Jane (Gibson) McG.; studied Park Inst., Pittsburgh, 1895-98; Litt.B., Westminster Coll., New Wilmington, Pa., 1901; LL.B., U. of Pittsburgh, 1909; unmarried. Accountant Westinghouse Interests, 1902-05; admitted to Allegheny County bar, 1909; since in gen. practice of law. Mem. Pittsburgh Chamber of Commerce, Theta Upsilon Omega (past nat. pres), Sigma Phi Epsilon. Republican. United Presbyterian. Mason (32°, Knights Templar, Shriner). Club: University (Pittsburgh). Has spoken many times before fraternal organizations, men's clubs and churches; principal address: "The Cross Fitchee" (over 50 appearances in Pa., O., W.Va. and N.Y.). Contbr. to fraternal mags., etc. Home: King Edward Apts. Office: 3106 Grant Bldg., Pittsburgh, Pa.

McGINNIS, Bernard Benedict, state senator; b. Genesee, Pa., Dec. 1, 1879; s. Bryan and Ellen (Moran) McG.; A.B., Cornell U., 1905; unmarried. Federal appraiser of customs, 1913-16; asst. U.S. atty., 1916-19; spl. asst. to atty. gen., 1919-20; asst. county solicitor, 1923-31; Pa. state senator since 1934. City chmn. Dem. Party, Pittsburgh, Pa., since 1935. Home: 12 E. North Av. Office: 908 Park Bldg., Pittsburgh, Pa.

McGINNIS, Bernard Carlton, banking; b. Wayne Co., W.Va., Nov. 29, 1888; s. Grant and Florence (Bing) McG.; student rural schs. Wayne Co., W.Va.; m. Gladys Smith, July 3, 1911; children—Harold Smith, Maxine (Mrs. William Lee Ramsey), Bernard Carlton, Jr., Rupert Carey, Karleen, Kermit Eldridge. Began as carpenter foreman, later gen. bldg. contractor; now pres. and treas. McGinnis Company, Inc., Huntington, W.Va.; pres. Twentieth Street Bank; chmn. bd. Industrial Savings & Loan Co.; mem. firm Gerchow & McGinnis. Pres. Huntington Regional Clearing House Assn. Republican. Methodist. Mason. Home: 333 11th Av. Office: 825 Second Av., Huntington, W.Va.

McGINNIS, Claude Stonecliffe, prof. physics; b. Indianapolis, Ind., Oct. 12, 1881; s. Robt. Henry and Alice (Stonecliffe) McG.; B.S., Mass. Inst. Tech., 1906; Ph.D., U. of Pa., 1911; m. Margaret Elizabeth Enman, April 9, 1909 (dec.); children—Robert Enman, Arthur Tiffin. Asst. in physics, M.I.T., 1906-08; instr. physics, U. of Pa., 1908-11; prof. physics, U. of N.B., Fredericton, N.B., Can., 1911-20; prof. physics and head of dept., Temple U., since 1920. Mem. A.A.A.S, Am. Assn. Physics Teachers, Am. Assn. Univ. Profs., Sigma Xi. Home: 129 Washington Lane, Wyncote, Pa.

McGINNIS, J. H.; mem. law firm McGinnis & Mann. Address: Beckley, W.Va.

McGLANNAN, Alexius, surgeon; b. Baltimore, July 24, 1872; s. Alexius W. and Agnes Veronica (Gallagher) McG.; A.B., Calvert Hall, Baltimore, 1887; Ph.G., Md. Coll. Pharmacy, 1890; M.D., Coll. Phys. and Surg., Baltimore, 1895; LL.D., Loyola Coll., 1924; m. Sally Porter Law, July 2, 1910. Prof, surgery, U. of Md. Med. Sch., and Coll. Physician and Surgeons, Baltimore. Consulting surgeon Mercy Hosp. Mem. Med. and Chirurg. Faculty of Md. (pres. 1929), A.M.A., Am. Surg. Assn., Southern Surg. Assn., Am. Gastro-Enterol. Assn.; fellow Am. Coll. Surgeons. Club: Maryland. Author: Laboratory Manual of Physiological Chemistry, 1900; Simon's Chemistry (collaborator), 1901; Manual of Physics and Inorganic Chemistry, 1903; Manual of Organic and Physiological Chemistry, 1903. Collaborator, Kelly-Musser Therapeutics, also of Tice's System and Lewis' System of Surgery. Contbr. articles on surg. subjects to medical jours. Address: 115 W. Franklin St., Baltimore, Md.

McGOVERN, Edward Francis, lawyer; b. Wilkes-Barre, Pa., Oct. 25, 1891; s. Edward Francis and Ellen E. (Murphy) McG.; grad. Wilkes-Barre High Sch., 1909; student Hillman Acad., 1910-11; LL.B., U. of Pa., 1914; unmarried. Admitted to Pa. bar, 1914, and since practiced in Wilkes-Barre; dir. and atty. Susquehanna Bldg. & Loan Assn. Mem. Am. Bar Assn., Luzerne Co. Bar Assn. Democrat. Roman Catholic. Elk, Owl, Eagle, K. of C. Club: Fox Hill Country. Home: 239 N. Main St. Office: 526 Second Nat. Bank Bldg., Wilkes-Barre, Pa.

McGOVERN, John Francis, Jr., surgeon; b. Hoboken, N.J., April 14,1889; s. John Francis and Mary A. (McGrath) McG.; B.S., Rutgers U., 1912; student Cornell U. Med. Coll., 1912-15; M.D., Albany Med. Coll., 1917; m. Ann McCormick, Sept. 10, 1924; 1 dau., Nancy Frances. Interne Hudson St. Hosp., 1917-18; 1st. lt. Med. Corps, U.S. Army. Evacuation Hosp., No. 31, 1918-19; in practice of medicine at New Brunswick, N.J., since 1919, specializing in surgery; city phys., City of New Brunswick, 1926-30; co. phys., Middlesex Co., N.J., 1930-33; attdg. surg., St. Peter's Hosp., New Brunswick, since 1919; asst. attdg. surg., Middlesex Hosp., New Brunswick, since 1930. Fellow Am. Coll. Surgs.; mem. N.J. State Med. Soc., Med. Sect. of Rutgers Club (New Brunswick), Zeta Psi. Democrat. Roman Catholic. Clubs: Rutgers Alumni; Cornell (New York); Lawrence Brook Country. Home: 24 Livingston Av., New Brunswick, N.J.

McGOWAN, James, Jr., corporation official; b. in Scotland, February 8, 1886; s. James and Janet Hunter (Donald) McG.; S.B., Mass. Inst. Tech., 1908; m. Elizabeth Perce, 1919. Dir. Campbell Soup Co. since 1931; v.p. Campbell Soup Co. (Central Division), Campbell Soup Co., Ltd. Home: Beach Haven, N.J. Office: Campbell Soup Co., Camden, N.J.

McGRANERY, James Patrick, congressman; b. Philadelphia, Pa., July 8, 1895; s. Patrick and Bridget (Gallagher) McG.; grad Temple U. Law Sch., 1928; unmarried. Admitted to bar, 1928; mem. law firm Masterson & McGranery; mem. 75th and 76th Congresses (1937-41) 2d Pa. Dist. Served as chmn. Registration Commn., Philadelphia. Pilot observed, duration of World War; also served as adjutant 111th Inf. Democrat. Catholic. Clubs: Whitemarsh Valley (Pa.) Country; Art, Penn Athletic, Philopatrian Literary Inst. (Philadelphia). Home: 1137 S. 23d St., Philadelphia, Pa. Office: 1703 Finance Bldg., Philadelphia, Pa.

McGRATH, John Bernard, lawyer; b. Cresson, Pa., July 5, 1854; s. John and Margaret (McHugh) McG.; ed. pub. schs., Dudley, Pa.; m. Lydia Ingram Marmion, July 18, 1888; children—Margaret (Mrs. J. F. Clark), John J., George H. Admitted to Pa. bar, 1899, and since practiced at Houtzdale; mem. firm McGrath & Smith since 1937; pres. Anda Coal Co., Houtzdale, Chestnut Hill Coal Co.; sec. and treas. Greenwood Coal Co. since 1925. Mem. council for Draft Bd., chmn. Minute Men, active in Liberty Loan movement during World War. Solicitor for borough councils and sch. dists.; chmn. Dem. Co. Com., 1900-03 (2 terms); Congressional Senatorial Referee; mem.

McGRAW, sch. bd., and borough council, Houtzdale. Mem. Houtzdale Chamber of Commerce, Clearfield Co. Law Assn., Pa. State Bar Assn., Am. Bar Assn., Co. Hist. Assn., Co. Tubercular Soc. Democrat. K.C. Home: 505 Good St. Office: 719 Hannah St., Houtzdale, Pa.

McGRAW, James Henry, Jr., publisher; b. Madison, N.J., May 9, 1893; s. James Henry and Mildred (Whittlesey) McG.; A.B., Princeton U., 1915; m. Lois Durand Scheerer; children—Barbara W., James Henry III. Successively sec.-treas., v.p. and treas., exec. v.p., McGraw-Hill Pub. Co., chmn. of bd. since 1935, pres. since 1937; chmn. bd. and dir. McGraw-Hill Bldg. Corpn., McGraw-Hill Book Co.; dir. Business Pubs. Internat. Corpn.; trustee Franklin Savings Bank. Mem. Nat. Industrial Conf. Bd.; mem. Army Ordnance Assn. Republican. Presbyn. Clubs: University, Engineers, Princeton (N.Y. City). Home: Madison, N.J. Office: 330 W. 42d St., New York, N.Y.

McGRAW, Thomas Henry, Jr., steel exec.; b. Bay City, Mich., Sept. 18, 1877; s. Thomas Henry and Pauline (Uberhorst) McG.; ed. private schs., Ithaca, N.Y.; M.E., Cornell U. 1899; m. Mary Evans, Pittsburgh, Pa., June 29, 1904; children—David Evans, John Sears, Durban Alexander. District sales mgr. Erie (Pa.) City Iron Works, 1902-27; sec. Standard Seamless Tube Co., 1914-28; gen. mgr. Carbon Steel Co., 1924-26; pres. and chmn. bd. Braeburn Alloy Steel Corpn. since 1926. Mem. Am., Iron & Steel Inst., Am. Soc. for Metals, Kappa Alpha. Republican. Clubs: Duquesne, Oakmont Country, Longue Vue Country, University (Pittsburgh); Engineers (New York, N.Y.), Everglades (Palm Beach, Fla.). Awarded several patents pertaining to water tube boilers. Home: Oakmont, Pa.; (winter) Pinehurst, N.C. Office: Braeburn, Pa.

McGREGOR, James Clyde, coll. prof.; b. Wheeling, W.Va., July 10, 1883; s. Harlan Page and Lucy (Baggs) M.; student U. of Va., 1901; B.S., Washington and Jefferson Coll. 1905, A.M., 1908; Ph.D., U. of Pa., 1913; studied constl. law, Columbia, 1916; m. Grace N. Gilleland, July 10, 1917; children—Robert Harlan, Eleanor Lucy, Margaret Nancy. Prof. history and polit. science, Washington and Jefferson Coll., 1913—. Mem. Am. Hist. Assn., Am. Polit. Science Assn., Kappa Sigma. Clubs: University, Twilight (Washington, D.C.); University (Pittsburgh). Author: The Disruption of Virginia, 1922; also articles on history and government in New Century Book of Facts. Home: Washington, Pa.*

McGREW, Dallas Dayton Lore; b. of Am. parentage, Cawnpore, Ind., Aug. 20, 1881; s. George Harrison (D.D.) and Anna Julia (Lore) M.; A.B., Harvard, 1903; m. Dorothea deKay Gilder, May 19, 1916 (died Mar. 10, 1920); m. 2d, Elizabeth Wright Barber, of Englewood, N.J., Sept. 27, 1921; children—Helena D., John R., Sarah E. Assistant to consulting architect to the Philippine Commn., 1905-06; asst. supt. St. Joseph Lead Co., 1906-11; financial editor and tr. to publisher Boston Journal, 1913-16; with International Banking Corpn. in China, Japan, France, 1916-21; Am. counsellor to ministry of foreign affairs, Japan, 1921-29 (retired); asso. architect Nat. Park Service since Jan. 1, 1939. In France with Am. Field Service, attached to 2d and 7th French armies, Jan.-July 1915. Clubs: Chevy Chase (Washington, D.C.); Tokyo Club, Tokyo Golf (Tokyo, Japan). Address: Edgemoor Lane, Bethesda, Md.

McGUIRE, Hugh Edward, M.D.; b. North Side, Pittsburgh, Pa., Oct. 16, 1872; s. Hugh and Annie E. (Reel) M.; student Piersol Acad., West Bridgewater, 1894 and 95; M.D., U. of Western Pa. (now U. of Pittsburgh), 1900; m. Mayme Duddy, Apr. 15, 1913 (died May 15, 1923); 1 dau., Mary Louise. Interne Western Pa. Hosp., Pittsburgh, 1900-01; asst. in surgery South Side Hosp., Pittsburgh, 1905-09, surgeon since 1909; chief surgeon Jones & Laughlin Steel Corpn., Pittsburgh, since 1912. Pres. Allegheny Co. Med. Soc., 1926, Pittsburgh Surg. Soc., 1934 and 35; mem. Phi Beta Phi. Republican. Catholic. Clubs: Pittsburgh Athletic Assn., South Hills Country (Pittsburgh). Home: 5651 Darlington Road. Office: 320 Jenkins Bldg., Pittsburgh, Pa.

McGUIRE, Patrick Joseph, lawyer; b. Webster Springs, W.Va., Sept. 29, 1894; s. Peter Joseph and Mary McG.; LL.B., W.Va. Univ. Law Sch.; m. Edith M. Loughtin, Sept. 27, 1914; children—Marjorie Anne, Ruth Virginia. Admitted to W.Va. bar, and engaged in gen. practice of law at Wellsburg; served as mem. W.Va. Ho. of Reps. 1931-33; prosecuting atty. of Brooke Co. Mem. Phi Alpha Delta. Democrat. Elk. Home: 915 Main St. Office: City Bldg., Wellsburg, W.Va.

McGUIRE, Thomas Wilcox, civil and mining engr.; b. Ironton, O., Aug. 13, 1902; s. John Milton and Effie (Wilcox) McG.; ed. W.Va. U., 1921-23, U. of Cincinnati, 1923-25, Wilson Engineering Sch., 1925-26; m. Vesta Casto, Dec. 31, 1926; children—Betty Lou, Thomas Wilcox, II, Mary Carolyn. Began as rodman on engring. corps, 1923; chief engr. Winfrede (W.Va.) Coal Co., 1926-28; area engr. E. I. duPont de Nemours & Co., installing pipe line, Belle, W.Va., 1928-31; asst. engr., U.S. Govt. (charge of drilling and grouting locks and dams), Huntington Dist., W.Va., 1931-36; chief engr. Carbon Fuel Co. (engring. work for 6 mines, 2 all-mechanical; engaged in mining domestic coal and mfr. by-products), Carbon, W.Va., since 1937. Registered civil engr. State of W.Va. Republican. Presbyterian. Home: Carbon, W.Va.

McGURL, John B., lawyer; b. Ashland, Pa., Sept. 25, 1879; s. M. J. and Margaret (Breslin) McG.; student Pa. Teachers Coll.; m. Laura Quinn, Aug. 4, 1908; children—Blanche M., John B., Mary M. Admitted to bar; pres. and dir. First Nat. Bank of Minersville, Pa. First dist. atty., Schuylkill Co., Pa., 1932-38. Active in local philanthropic movements for many years. Mem. Am. Red Cross (mem. Schuylkill Co. exec. bd.), Am. Bar Assn., Pa. Bar Assn., Schuylkill Co. Law Assn., Bd. of Censors, Bd. of Examiners. K.C. (Schuylkill Council, Pottsville, Pa.). Clubs: Pottsville Country, Schuylkill Country (Pottsville, Pa.). Home: 452 Sunbury St., Minersville, Pa. Office: 110 Center St., Pottsville, Pa.

McHENRY, Donald Barton, med. dir.; b. Stillwater, Pa., Feb. 25, 1891; s. William L. and Leila I. (Edgar) McH.; student State Normal Sch., Bloomsburg, Pa., 1907-11; M.D., Jefferson Med. Coll., Phila., Pa., 1915; postgrad. work in obstetrics and gynecology, U. of Pa., 1928-29; m. Bertha M. Ferguson, Feb. 9, 1918. Interne South Side Hosp., Pittsburgh, Pa., 1915-16; 1st asst. physician Wernersville (Pa.) State Hosp., 1916-17; specialist in obstetrics and gynecology, Danville, Pa., since 1929; registrar vital statistics and med. dir., Montour Co. Pa., since 1935; mem. staff Bloomsburg (Pa.) Hosp. since 1929; 2d v.p. and dir. Montour County Trust Co., Danville, Pa., since 1932. Served as lt., M.R.C., U.S. Army, 1917-18. Mem. Danville (Pa.) Chamber of Commerce, Am. Legion, Nu Sigma Nu, Alpha Omega Alpha. Mem. Christian Ch. Address: Bloom Rd., Danville, Pa. Died June 4, 1939.

McHENRY, Jesse Parsons, supt. schs.; b. Woodlands, W.Va., July 5, 1895; s. John R. and Stella V. M.; grad. West Liberty State Teachers Coll., 1918; B.S. in Edn., W.Va. U., 1929; M.Edn., U. of Pittsburgh, 1936; m. Beryl M. Black, June 22, 1921; children—Wilbur L., Jess P. Became teacher, 1912; supt. schs., Ohio Co. Bd. of Edn. since 1929. Served in U.S. Army, 1918-19. Methodist. Club: Civitan (Wheeling). Home: Warwood, Wheeling, W.Va.

McILHATTAN, William Hamilton, supt. of schools; b. Knox, Pa., May 30, 1890; s. Edwin Stanton and Margaret Anna (Pickens) McI.; student Edinburgh (Pa.) High Sch., 1906-09, Clarion State Normal Sch., 1909-12; A.B., U. of Pittsburgh, 1922, A.B. in edn., 1922; A.M., Teachers Coll., Columbia, 1927; grad. student U. of Pittsburgh, 1938—; m. Katherine Stewart, Mar. 10, 1922; children—Patricia Jean, Edwin Stewart. Teacher rural school, Knox, Pa., 1909-10; teacher, East Brady, Pa., 1912-13; science teacher, Leechburg (Pa.) High Sch., 1913-15; supervising prin., East Brady, 1915-17, 1919-22, Brookville, Pa., 1922-29; supervising prin., Somerset, Pa., 1929-34; supt. of schools, Greensburg, Pa., since 1934; teacher Clarion State Teachers Coll., summers 1922, 23, 28. Attended Second O.T.C., 1917; served as 2d lt. Field Arty., U.S. Army, Fort Sill, Okla., and with A.E.F., France, 1918-19. Mem. Pa. State Edn. Assn., N.E.A., Am. Assn. of Sch. Adminstrs., Phi Delta Kappa. Republican. Presbyterian. Mason (32°). Club: Rotary of Greensburg. Home: 227 Tremont Av. Office: 122 N. Maple Av., Greensburg, Pa.

McILVAIN, Greer, pres. Nat. Fireproofing Corpn.; b. Monongahela, Pa., June 10, 1898; s. Charles Greer and Nancy May (Donaldson) G.; student Lafayette Coll., Easton, Pa., 1918-20; LL.B., Duquesne U., Pittsburgh, 1924; m. Josephine Claire Dowling, Nov. 10, 1926; children—Nancy May, Mary Elizabeth, Jane, Greer, Josephine Lou. Admitted to Allegheny Co. bar, 1924; exec. v.p. Nat. Fireproofing Corpn., 1932, pres. since 1933. In Air Service, U.S.N. World War. Mem. Phi Kappa Psi. Republican. Presbyterian. Mason. Home: 1140 S. Negley Av. Office: Republic Bldg., Pittsburgh, Pa.

McILVAINE, William Alexander Hamilton, lawyer; b. Vanceville, Pa., Mar. 1, 1871; s. William Robert and Sarah E. (Hamilton) McI.; A.B., Washington and Jefferson Coll., 1894; m. Annie Gertrude Wilson, Nov. 10, 1902; children—Alexander, John Wilson, Elizabeth Hamilton (Mrs. William M. Cooper); m. 2d, Florence Hook Sturgis, Apr. 3, 1923. Admitted to Pa. bar, 1898, and since practiced in Washington, Pa.; mem. firm McIlvaine & Williams until 1937; mem. firm McIlvaine & McIlvaine since 1937; vice-pres. and dir. Washington Union Trust Co., George Washington Hotel Corpn. Trustee Washington and Jefferson Coll. Mem. Delta Tau Delta, Phi Tau Gamma. Republican. Presbyterian (elder Second Presbyterian Ch. since 1913). Club: Bassett (Washington, Pa.). Home: 47 N. Wade Av. Office: Washington Trust Bldg., Washington, Pa.

McILWAIN, Knox, elec. engring.; b. Phila., Pa., Sept. 4, 1897; s. George Knox and Mary Scofield (Cowell) McI.; ed. Kent (Conn.) Sch., 1908-14; B.S., Princeton, 1918; B.S. in E.E., U. of Pa., 1921, E.E., same, 1930; m. Viola Beale Homer, June 20, 1922 (div.); children—Elizabeth Starr, Constance Beale, Cintra Crosby. Engring. asst., Bell Telephone Co. of Pa., 1921-24; asso. with Moore Sch. Elec. Engring. of U. of Pa. continuously since 1924, instr. elec. engring., 1924-28, asst. prof. 1928-37, asso. prof. since 1937. Served as ensign U.S.N.R.F., 1917-19. Mem. Inst. Radio Engrs., Soc. for Promotion Engring. Edn., Phi Beta Kappa, Sigma Xi, Eta Kappa Nu, Tau Beta Pi, Delta Phi. Episcopalian. Clubs: Princeton of Philadelphia, St. Elmo. Co-author (with J. G. Brainerd): High Frequency Alternating Currents, 1931, 2d edit., 1939; (with Harold Pender) asso. editor in chief, Electrical Engineers Handbook, 3d edit., 1936. Contrbr. tech. articles to mags. Home: 2117 Pine St. Office: 200 S. 33d St., Philadelphia, Pa.

McINERNEY, William Ignatius, mill supt.; b. Phila., Pa., June 10, 1890; s. Dennis Francis and Mary Ann (Mother's maiden name Leach); student Gesu Parochial Sch. (Phila.), 1896-1902, Phila. Central Evening High Sch., 1909-16, Franklin Inst., Phila., 1916-18; m. Helen Joseph Thompson, Sept. 8, 1920; children—Mary, Joan, William Thompson. Supervisor mfr. armor plate, ordnance, etc., Midvale Steel Co. (Phila), 1904-20; supt. armor plate dept. U.S. Naval Ordnance Plant (S. Charleston, W.Va.), 1920-22; mill supt. Pittsburgh Crucible Steel Co., Midland, Pa., since 1922; also supt. Nat. Drawn Steel Co., East Liverpool, Pa., since 1936. Burgess Borough of Midland, Beaver Co., Pa., since Jan. 1, 1938; Mem. Am. Inst. Mining and Metall. Engrs., Am. Soc. for Metals, Assn. of Iron & Steel Engrs. Republican. Roman Catholic. Mem. K.C. Clubs: Penn Athletic of Phila. (life mem. rowing assn.); East Liverpool (Pa.) Country (pres. since 1938). Home: 78 Park Pl. Office: Pittsburgh Crucible Steel Co., Midland, Pa.

McINTIRE, Carl, clergyman; b. Ypsilanti, Mich., May 17, 1906; s. Charles Curtis and Hettie (Hotchkin) McI.; ed. Southeastern State Teachers Coll., Durant, Okla., 1923-26; A.B., Park Coll., Parkville, Mo., 1927; ed. Princeton Theol. Sem., 1928-29; B.D., Westminster Theol. Sem., 1931; m. Fairy Eunice Davis, May 27, 1931; children—Marianna Hotchkin, Sally Celeste. Ordained to ministry Presbyn. Ch., 1931; pastor Atlantic City, N.J., 1931-33; pastor Collingswood Presbyn. Ch., 1933-38, Bible Presbyn. Ch., Collingswood, N.J. since 1938; sec. and mem. Ind. Bd. Presbyn. Fgn. Missions; pres. bd. dirs. Faith Theol. Sem., Wilmington, Del. Mem. Phi Kappa Delta. Presbyterian. Editor and pub. religious news weekly The Christian Beacon. Author: A Cloud of Witnesses, 1938. Home: 426 Collins Av., Collingswood, N.J.

McINTYRE, George Imbrie, banker; b. Allegheny Co., Pa., June 26, 1881; s. Hercules and Christine (Stirling) McI.; ed. Pittsburgh (Pa.) Acad.; m. Helen Ridgeway, of West Park, Pa., Sept. 12, 1917; children—Helen Louise, Stuart R. Bookkeeper Ohio Valley Trust Co., 1902-10; asst. sec. and treas. Ohio Valley Trust Co., 1910-25; sec.-treas. Beaver Trust Co. since July 15, 1925; v.p. and dir. Midland (Pa.) Bank; sec.-treas. Beaver (Pa.) Bldg. Co. Dir. Beaver Borough Sch. Dist., 1 term, 1935-36. Republican. Presbyterian. Mason. Clubs: Fort McIntosh (Beaver); Beaver Valley Country (Beaver Falls, Pa.). Home: 355 Second St. Office: care Beaver Trust Co., Beaver, Pa.

McINTYRE, John T(homas), dramatist author; b. Phila., Pa., Nov. 26, 1871; s. Patrick and Sarah (Walker) M. Author: The Ragged Edge, 1902; Blowing Weather, 1923; A Young Man's Fancy, 1925; Shot Towers, 1926; Slag, 1927; Stained Sails, 1928; Drums in the Dawn, 1932; Steps Going Down, 1936; Ferment, 1937; Signing Off, 1938. Home: 259 S. 17th St., Philadelphia, Pa.

McINTYRE, Joseph Daniel, pres. Dr. D. Jayne & Son, Inc.; b. Washington, D.C., Feb. 13, 1894; s. John T. and Marie (Bowers) McI.; B.S. in chemistry, George Washington U., 1920; m. Mabel Elizabeth Passau, Nov. 21, 1915; 1 dau., Catherine Elizabeth. Jr. chemist drug and poisonous plant dept., U.S. Dept. of Agr., Washington, D.C., 1913-15, chemist, 1915-17; chemist U.S. Bur. Internal Revenue, Treasury Dept., Washington, D.C., 1919-24; asso. with Dr. D. Jayne & Son, Inc., Phila., since 1924, pres. since 1932; cons. chemist representing pharm. and med. mfrs., 1926-28. Served as sergt. Master Hosp., U.S. Army, during World War; at Army Med. Sch., Washington, D.C., 1917; sergt. in charge bacteriol. and serological labs., U. of D'John, France, 1918. Mem. Am. Chem. Soc., Am. Pharm. Assn. Republican. Protestant. Elk. Club: Cosmos (Washington, D.C.). Author numerous articles on scientific subjects. Home: 1108 Wilde Av., Drexel Hill. Office: Delaware Av. and Vine St., Philadelphia, Pa.

McIVER, Joseph, neuro-psychiatry; b. Madison Co., Tex., Sept. 27, 1886; s. Walter and Jennie (Searcy) McI.; grad. high sch., Rogers Prairie, Tex., 1906; M.D., U. of Tex., 1912; m. Regina McManus, September 2, 1916 (died March 22, 1932). Began practice at Phila., 1913; chief of visiting staff Phila. General Hosp.; neurologist to Misericordia Hosp. Served in U.S.N.R.F., U.S. Naval Hosp., League Island, Phila., 1917-19. Fellow A.M.A.; mem. Phila. County Med. Soc., Phila. Neurol. Soc., Phila. Psychiatric Soc., Coll. of Physicians of Phila., Am. Neurol. Assn. Republican. Catholic. Home: Garden Court Plaza, 47th and Pine Sts. Office: 255 S. 17th St., Philadelphia, Pa.

McKAIG, Edgar Stanley, lawyer; b. Philadelphia, Pa., Nov. 1, 1886; s. William and Susan Campbell (MacFarlane) McK.; A.B., Central High Sch., Philadelphia, 1904; Litt.B., Princeton U., 1908; LL.B., U. of Pa. Law Sch., 1911; m. Annah Colket French, Oct. 15, 1914; children—Annah Colket (Mrs. W. Penn-Gaskell Hall, III), Marjorie French. Admitted to bar, 1911; associated with law firm Porter, Foulkrod & McCullagh, 1911-16; in private practice, 1916-34; mem. firm Adams, Childs, McKaig & Lukens since 1934; pres. and dir. Samuel H. French & Co., Samuel H. French Paint Co. Asst. city solicitor, Philadelphia, 1916-20; mem. Philadelphia Zoning Commn. Served in U.S. Field Arty., Camp Zachary Taylor, Louisville, O.T.C., World War. Pres. Home Missionary Society of Philadelphia; pres. and trustee Philadelphia Commercial Museum, Exhibition and Convention Halls; dir. Mercantile Library; mem. exec. com. U.S. Figure Skating Assn. Mem. Am. Bar Assn., Pennsylvania Bar Assn., Philadelphia Bar Assn., Phi Delta Phi. Republican. Episcopalian. Clubs: Union League, Princeton, Penn (Philadelphia); Shanswood; Merion Cricket (Haverford); Radnor (Pa.) Hunt; pres. Philadelphia Skating Club and Humane Soc., Ardmore, Pa. (oldest skating club in North America) where 1938 U.S. figure skating championships were held. Home: Radnor, Pa. Office: 700 Integrity Bldg., Philadelphia, Pa.

McKAY, John J., investments; b. Next, W. Va., 1880; s. Joseph and Mary C. (Archer) McK.; student country sch. and commercial course; m. Mabel Grass, 1908; children—Betty G. (Mrs. F. W. Bules), Jean. Began as bank clk., 1897; now pres. First-Tyler Bank & Trust Co., Sistersville, W.Va.; also pres. W. A. Sniffen Co., Joseph McKay & Sons (Sistersville, W.Va.), Arthur Oil Co., Adkay Petroleum Co., Chase Gasoline Co.; v.p. and dir. Gen. Petroleum Engrs.; sec.-treas. and dir. Paden City Glass Co.; sec. and dir. Wells Hotel Corpn. Sec.-treas. and dir. Sistersville (W.Va.) Cemetery Assn. Republican. Presbyterian. Mason. Club: Kiwanis (Sistersville, W.Va.). Home: 714 Main St. Office: Thistle Bldg., Sistersville, W.Va.

McKAY, Leo Hugh, lawyer; b. Black Ash, Crawford Co., Pa., Feb. 12, 1895; s. Hugh Gilliau and Florence Ida (Ross) McK.; grad. Sharon (Pa.) High Sch., 1912; A.B., Allegheny Coll., 1916; LL.B., U. of Pa., 1922; m. Ruth Moore Ellis, Sept. 14, 1918; children—Ellis Hugh, Margaret Adelia, Donald Ross, Florence Ross. Admitted to Mercer Co. bar, 1921, Pa. Supreme Court, 1922; practiced with father, Hugh G. McKay, as mem. firm McKay & McKay, 1922-30 (father died Dec. 6, 1930); practiced alone, 1930-33; mem. firm Brockway, Whitla & McKay since 1933; dist. atty., Mercer Co., Pa., 1928-31. Pres. Erie Lay Conf. of M.E. Ch. since 1935; del. to Gen. Conf. of M.E. Ch., 1932; mem. Uniting Conf. of Methodist Ch., 1939; v.p. Pa. State Sabbath Sch. Assn. since 1937; pres. Pa. Fed. of Organized Bible Classes, 1932-35. Trustee Allegheny Coll. since 1931. Served as 2d lt. Air Service (pilot), U.S. Army, 1918. Mem. Am. Bar Assn., Pa. Bar Assn. (mem. exec. com.), Mercer Co. Bar Assn. (vice-pres., 1939), Phi Gamma Delta, Phi Beta Kappa, Order of Coif. Republican. Methodist. Mason (K.T.). Home: Route 2, Sharon, Pa. Office: First Nat. Bank Bldg., Sharon, Pa.

McKAY, Marion K., prof. economics; b. Delaware Co., O., Jan. 5, 1885; s. George and Letitia (Huddleston) McK.; B.S., O. Northern U., 1907; A.B., O. State U., 1910; A.M., Harvard U., 1912, Ph.D., same, 1917; m. Alma Bailey, Nov. 30, 1912; 1 dau., Marian Rae. Engaged in teaching in pub. schs. O. and Mich., 1900-05 and 1910-12; prof. economics, U. of N.H., 1917-20; prof. economics, U. of Pittsburgh since 1920; mem. Pres. Hoover's Com. on Taxation of Homes, Pa. Tax Com., 1924-27; mem. Spl. Finance and Taxation Com. Pa., 1935; adviser Dept. Pub. Instrn. since 1937; mem. State Council Edn. since 1936, State Sanitary Water Bd. since 1936; mem. Spl. Commn. for O. River Basin Sanitation; chmn. State Advisory Council on Unemployment Compensation since 1938. Pres. Civic Club (Allegheny Co.), 1931-35. Trustee O. Northern U. Mem. Am. Econ. Assn., Nat. Tax Assn. Democrat. Baptist. Research dir., conducting complete original city surveys of Sharon and New Castle, Pa.; sponsor of spl. sessions for business execs. Home: 3420 Iowa St., Pittsburgh, Pa.

McKAY, William Shields, real estate and ins. broker; m. Findley Twp., Mercer Co., Pa., Dec. 16, 1871; s. Alexander B. and Anna Maria (Paxton) McK.; student Grove City (Pa.) High Sch. to 1889, Grove City Coll., 1889-90; m. Lida Raymond, Oct. 22, 1902; children—Aaron Raymond, Donald Alexander, William Shields, Eleanor, Kathryn, Nancy. Janitor Grove City Banking Co. (now First Nat. Bank), 1889-90, teller and asst. cashier, 1890-1904, cashier, 1904-19; cashier Oil City (Pa.) Nat. Bank, 1919-23; pres. First Nat. Bank, Greenville, Pa., 1923-36; in real estate and insurance business, Grove City, Pa., since 1936. Dir. Community Finance Co., Turner McKay Co. Served as chmn. Mercer Co., for Liberty Loan and Red Cross drives. Sec. bd. of trustees Grove City Coll. since 1906. Mem. Pa. Bankers Assn. (chmn. agrl. com. and treas., 1925-36), Nat. Grange. Republican. Presbyterian. Mason. Clubs: Rotary, Commercial (Grove City, Pa.). Author articles on agrl. work in relation to banking. Home: 412 W. Main St. Office: 132 S. Broad St., Grove City, Pa.

McKEE, Captain William, prof. economics and business adminstrn., chmn. div. social sciences, investment and business consultant; b. Freeport, Kan., April 29, 1895; s. Benjamin Prentice and Nettie (Cooper) McK.; A.B., Ottawa U., Kan., 1920; A.M., U. of Chicago, 1924; grad. study, Harvard U. Grad. Sch. Business Adminstrn., summers 1928-29, U. of Chicago, summers 1925, 26, 37; m. Florence Chynoweth Pollard, of New Castle, Pa., June 18, 1929; children—William Pollard, Robert Cooper, Thomas Benjamin. Hotel proprietor, 1912-14; mcht. school supplies, 1921-23; prof. economics and business Adminstrn., Westminster Coll., New Wilmington, Pa., since 1924, also chmn. div. social sciences since 1937; investment and business consultant since 1929; instr. Youngstown Coll. night sessions, 1927-30; instr. in Am. Inst. of Banking, New Castle, Pa., 1924-25, Youngstown, O., 1926-30, Sharon, Pa., 1927-32, 1938-39. Held spl. session for business execs., 1936-37, 1937-38 and 1938-39. Directed city surveys, New Castle, 1936-37, Sharon, 1937-38. Served in O. T.C., U.S.A., 1918. Mem. Am. Econ. Assn., Am. Statis. Assn. Republican. Mem. Christian Ch. Mason (32°). Author of problem and question books in economics, marketing, law and finance; magazine articles on economics and business; forthcoming book on Sources and Uses of Bank Funds in Shenango and Mahoning Valleys from May 1, 1936, to May 1, 1937, for publ. in 1940. Club: Field (New Castle). Home: 212 Park St., New Wilmington, Pa.

McKEE, Edward Bernard, clergyman, asso. prof.; b. Phila., Pa., Aug. 25, 1904; s. George B. and Sarah C. (McCloskey) McK.; A.B., Villanova Coll., 1928; eccles. study, Augustinian Coll., 1928-32; A.M., Cath. U. of America, 1933; grad. student, U. of St. Louis, Mo., summer 1933, U of Pa., summers 1935-36, Catholic U. of America, summers 1937-38. Ordained priest R.C. Ch., 1931; asso. prof. religion dept., Villanova Coll., Villanova, Pa., since 1932, mem. Bd. Student Counsellors since 1932, dir. intra-mural sports program since its beginning, 1932, moderator The Villanovan, coll. weekly since 1932. Address: Villanova College, Villanova, Pa.

McKEE, Joel Stoneroad, banker; b. Fayette Co., Pa., Sept. 22, 1875; s. Finley and Eliza Ann (Harper) McK.; A.B., Ohio Northern U., Ada, O., 1899; m. Daisie Eleanor Cummings, April 2, 1903; children—William Finley, Eleanor Eliza (both dec.). Teacher country sch., 1895-96, Coll., 1897-99, also teaching various schs., 1899-1902; engaged in banking work, 1902-18; nat. bank examiner, 1918-28; cashier First Nat. Bank of Lawrence Co. since 1928, v.p. and cashier since 1931; dir. Union Trust Co. of New Castle; sec. and treas. First Securities Co.; pres. New Castle Cleaning House Assn. Republican. Presbyterian. Mason. Club: New Castle (Pa.) Field. Home: 217 E. Edison Av. Office: 101 E. Washington St., New Castle, Pa.

McKEE, Paul Harper, clergyman; b. Clarkson, O., Sept. 30, 1898; s. William Finley and Mary Leotta (White) McK.; A.B., Wooster Coll., O., 1921; Th.B., Princeton Theol. Sem., 1926; study, U. of Grenoble, France, 1925; (hon.) D.D., Beaver Coll., 1938; m. Anne McKennan

McKEE

Oliphant, June 1, 1927; children—William Finley 2d, Duncan Oliphant, Margaret McKennan (dec.). Instr. Am. Univ., Beirut, Syria, 1923-25; ordained to ministry Presbyn. Ch., 1926; asst. pastor, Steubenville, O., 1926-27, St. Paul Presbyn. Ch., Phila., Pa., 1927-28; minister, New Phila., O., 1928-32, Latrobe, Pa., since 1932. Served in S.A.T.C., 1918. Mem. S.A.R., Am. Legion. Democrat. Presbyn. Rotarian. Home: 625 E. Main St., Latrobe, Pa.

McKEE, Samuel Henry, pres. Title Guaranty Co. of Pittsburgh; b. Westmoreland Co., Pa., Sept. 15, 1851; s. Robert C. and Rachel (Henry) McK.; student Monmouth (Ill.) Coll., 1872; m. Jane A. Taggart. Pres. Title Guaranty Co. of Pittsburgh. Pres. bd. dirs. Duff's Iron City (Pa.) Coll.; mem. bd. Am. Missions, United Presbyn. Ch. of North America. Mem. Phi Delta Theta. Home: 7428 Ben Hur St. Office: Frick Bldg., Pittsburgh, Pa.

McKEEHAN, Hobart Deitrich, clergyman; b. nr. Newport, Perry Co., Pa., Apr. 26, 1897; s. Lincoln Scott and Eldorado (Mahaffy) McK.; student Valparaiso (Ind.) U., 1915-17; student 1 yr. under Prof. J. P. Mahaffy, of Dublin U.; grad. Ref. Theol. Sem., Lancaster, Pa., 1919; B.D. and S.T.M., Lincoln-Jefferson U. 1920; post-grad. work Oxford U.; D.D., Franklin and Marshall Coll., 1936; m. Verna Marie Klinepeter, Dec. 21, 1918. Ordained ministry Ref. Ch. in U.S.A., 1919; spl. preacher, Bethel Ch., High Point, N.C., summer 1918; pastor St. Paul's Ch., Dallastown, Pa., 1919-24, The Abbey Ch., Huntingdon, 1924—. Spl. preacher at Oxford (Eng.) in behalf of Anglo-Am. good will. Del. World Alliance Ref. Chs., Zürich, Switzerland, 1923, and to World Alliance of Reformed and Presbyn. Chs., Belfast, Ireland, 1933. Mem. Students' Univ. Research Assn. (ex-pres.), Pi Gamma Mu. Mem. Maccabees, Sr. Order Am. Mech. Rotarian. Author: The Patrimony of Life, 1925; Anglo-American Preaching, 1928. Contbr. to Best Sermons, 1924, also to American Reformed Pulpit, 1928. Editor: Great Modern Sermons, 1923. Contbr. Christian World Pulpit, The Minister's Annual, The Expository Times, and The Speakers Bible; also literary revs. in Am. and British jours. Lecturer. Home: 607 Church St., Huntingdon, Pa.

McKEEHAN, Joseph Parker, lawyer; b. nr. Carlisle, Pa., Nov. 20, 1876; s. Joseph Hamlin and Mary Graham (Parker) M.; A.B., Dickinson Coll., Pa., 1897, A.M., 1899, LL.B., 1902; m. Helen Wile, June 6, 1917; 1 son, Joseph Parker. Instr. Latin, 1897-99, vice prin., 1899-1900, Dickinson Preparatory Sch.; prof. law, Dickinson Sch. of Law, since 1902; spl. dep. atty. gen. Commonwealth of Pa., 1926-27. Pres. Carlisle Deposit Bank and Trust Co. Mem. Jury of Awards, Paris Expn., 1900; mem. jury and sec. departmental jury for social economy St. Louis Exposition, 1904; delegate to Universal Congress Lawyers and Jurists at St. Louis, Mo., 1904; president of Carlisle Hospital. Member Am. Bar Assn., Pa. Bar Assn., Pa. Scotch-Irish Soc., Phi Beta Kappa, Beta Theta Pi. Presbyn. Republican. Club: Carlisle Country (pres.). Contbr. numerous articles to Dickinson Law Rev. Home: 300 S. College St. Office: Public Square N.W., Carlisle, Pa.

McKELVY, Eugene Adams, v.p. General Refractories Co.; b. Pittsburgh, Pa., Oct. 4, 1880; s. James Spear and Isadore (Adams) McK.; ed. Pittsburgh High Sch. and Pa. State Coll.; B.S. Harvard Univ., 1902; m. Carolyn Woodruff Scovel, June 20, 1918; children—James Scovel, Sally Butler, Carolyn Adams, Cynthia Darragh. Began as surveyor, 1902; with Harbison Walker Refractories Co., Pittsburgh, 1903-11; v.p. and dir. General Refractories Co. since 1911. Republican. Episcopalian. Clubs: Duquesne (Pittsburgh); Racquet (Philadelphia). Home: Ardmore, Pa. Office: Real Estate Trust Bldg., Philadelphia, Pa.

McKELVY, Francis Graham, pres. Alpha Portland Cement Co.; b. Pittsburgh, Pa., Aug. 9, 1883; s. William M. and Frances (Graham) McK.; student Shady Side Acad., Pittsburgh, 1894-99, Lawrenceville (N.J.) Acad., 1899-1900; A.B., Princeton U., 1904; m. Louise Corwin, Nov. 9, 1910; children—Louise Make-peace, William Graham. Clk. Alpha Portland Cement Co., Easton, Pa., 1906-07, asst. sec., 1907-08, purchasing agent, 1908-11, sec., 1911-14, 2d v.p., 1914-17, 1st v.p., 1917-34, exec. v.p., 1934-35, pres. since 1935. Served as capt. Ordnance Dept., U.S. Army, 1917. Trustee Lafayette Coll., Easton, Pa. Mem. Am. Soc. Mech. Engrs., Am. Soc. for Testing Materials. Republican. Presbyterian. Clubs: Pomfret, Country of Northampton Co. (Easton); Fishers Island (Fishers Island, N.Y.); University, Princeton (New York, N.Y). Home: Oakhurst, High St. Office: 15 S. Third St., Easton, Pa.

McKELVY, William McKinney, stock broker; b. Braddock, Pa., May 10, 1895; s. James Percy (M.D.) and Sarah (McKinney) McK.; student Shady Side Acad., Pittsburgh, 1907-12, Haverford (Pa.) Sch., 1912-15, Lafayette Coll. Easton, Pa., 1915-19; m. Ruth Hicks Sheldon, Apr. 2, 1921; children—William Sheldon, Jane Sheldon. Began as salesman for oil co., 1921; later treas. Beaver Refining Co.; then partner R. V. Nuttall & Co. and Gammack & Co.; now partner McCutcheon, McKelvy & Durant; dir. Allegheny-Ludlum Steel Corpn. Mem. U.S. Naval Reserve. Mem. New York Stock Exchange, Pittsburgh Stock Exchange, Theta Delta Chi; asso. mem. New York Curb Exchange. Republican. United Presbyterian. Clubs:: Pittsburgh, Pittsburgh Athletic Assn.; Allegheny Country (Sewickley, Pa.); Oakmont (Pa.) Country; Seaview Golf (Absecon, N.J.). Home: 1400 Bennington Av. Office: 343 Union Trust Bldg., Pittsburgh, Pa.

McKENNA, J. Frank, lawyer; b. Pittsburgh, Pa., Mar. 8, 1877; s. Bernard and Mary (McShane) McK.; LL.B., U. of Pittsburgh Law Sch., 1902; LL.D., Duquesne U., 1917; m. Elizabeth Florence Heyl, June 12, 1906; children—Mary J. Frank, Elizabeth F. (Mrs. James L. Poth), William Heyl, Bernard, Charles F., Robert B., David G. Admitted to Allegheny Co. bar, 1902; since in gen. practice law; mem. law firm Strassburger & McKenna since 1927; mem. faculty Duquesne University Law Sch. 1912-39, lecturer and teacher in law of wills, orphans' court and equity since 1912; pres. and dir. Heyl & Patterson, Inc.; treas. and dir. Hanlon-Gregory Galvanizing Co., Carnegie Lumber Co., Tri-Lok Co.; sec. Grant Bldg., Inc. Sec. and dir. St. Joseph's Protectory for Homeless Boys; dir. Home of the Good Shepherd (Troy Hill), Pittsburgh Hosp. Catholic (mem. ch. com. Sacred Heart Ch.). Mem. K.C. Clubs: Pittsburgh Athletic Assn., Pittsburgh Field. Home: 5621 Stanton Av. Office: 2602 Grant Bldg., Pittsburgh, Pa.

McKENNA, Philip Mowry, metallurgist and mfr.; b. Pittsburgh, Pa., June 16, 1897; s. Alex G. and Elizabeth (Mowry) McK.; A.B., George Washington Univ., Washington, D.C., 1921; m. Dorothy Collins, Mar. 30, 1922; children—Sydney Edith, Philip Collins, Carol Elizabeth. Began as chem. asst., U.S. Bur. of Standards, Washington, D.C., 1914-15; invented and patented method of separating nickel and cobalt, 1913; patented process separating pure ferrotungsten, 1916; vice-pres. Chemical Products Co. refining tungsten, 1916-25; research, 1925-28; research dir. Vanadium Alloys Steel Co., 1928-38, vice-pres., 1936-38; based on series of inventions covered by 10 patents founded McKenna Metals Co., mfrs. hard carbide tool materials under trade name Kennametal for machine hard steel, Latrobe, Pa., and propr. since 1938. Fellow A.A.A.S. Mem. Am. Inst. Mining and Metall. Engrs.; Am. Soc. for Metals, Am. Chem. Soc., Am. Acad. Polit. Sci., Am. Soc. Tool Engrs., Engrs. Soc. of Western Pa. Democrat. Home: Latrobe, Pa.

McKENNA, Roy Carnegie, steel mfr.; b. Allegheny, Pa., Mar. 7, 1883; s. Thomas A. and Anna (Hogan) M.; E.E., U. of Pittsburgh, 1903; m. Mary Martin, Oct. 25, 1905; 1 dau., Jean Martin. Partner McKenna Brass & Mfg. Co., Pittsburgh, Pa., 1903-26, pres., 1926-37; pres. Vanadium-Alloys Steel Co., Colonial Steel Co., Anchor Drawn Steel Co., Pittsburgh; dir. Keystone Nat. Bank of Pittsburgh, Vulcan Iron and Mold Co., Latrobe, Pa., Pomona (Calif.) Pump Co. Dir. Pa State Chamber of Commerce, Latrobe (Pa.) Hosp., Latrobe Library; trustee U. of Pittsburgh. Clubs: Pittsburgh Athletic (charter mem.), Amen Corner (Pittsburgh); Engineers (New York). Home: High Acres, Latrobe, Pa. Office: Grant Bldg., Pittsburgh, Pa.

McKENNEY, Frederic Duncan, lawyer; b. Washington, March 11, 1863; s. James Hall and Virginia Dorcas (Walker) M.; student Columbian (now George Washington) U., 1 yr.; A.B., Princeton, 1884, A.M., 1887; LL.B., Columbian, 1886, LL.M., 1887; m. Kathleen Handley, July 10, 1899; children—Virginia, Frederica. Admitted to D.C. bar, 1886, Supreme Court of U.S., 1889; member firm McKenney & Flannery, now McKenney, Flannery & Craighill, general practice. Counsel at Washington for the Pennsylvania System; counsel for U.S. in the Orinoco Steamship Co. affair, U.S. Venezuela arbitration, The Hague, 1910. Agent and atty. for U.S. in U.S. Peruvian arbitration of Landreau Claim, London, 1922; counsel for U.S. before U.S.-British Pecuniary Claims Commn. (arbitrating the Fiji land claims), London, 1923. Mem. Am. Bar Assn., Am. Soc. Internat. Law, etc. Episcopalian. Clubs: University (New York); Metropolitan (Washington). Home: "Handleyhall," Kensington, Md. Office: Hibbs Bldg., Washington, D.C.

McKENNY, Luke Mansfield, lawyer; b. Cleveland, O., Feb. 11, 1896; s. Luke and Annie Laura (Mansfield) McK.; student pub. schs., Cleveland, O., and Trenton, N.J., 1902-11; m. Ruth Margaret Wilde, Aug. 9, 1938. Began as atty., 1923; admitted to N.J. bar as atty., 1923, counsellor at law, 1928; in pvt. practice at East Orange, N.J., since 1928. Attached to Insp. Gen's. Office, Hdqrs., Service of Supply, U.S. Army, Tours, France, 1918-19. Asst. city counsel, East Orange, N.J., since 1939. Mem. Am. Bar Assn., East Orange Legal Group, Am. Legion. Republican. Presbyterian. Mason (32°), Knights of the Golden Eagle. Club: Kiwanis (East Orange, N.J.). Home: 49 Prospect St. Office: 507 Main St., East Orange, N.J.

McKENRICK, Paul Lossing (pen name Read McKenrick), writer; b. Curwensville, Pa., Mar. 19, 1870; s. Joseph Francis and Margaret Eleanor (Read) McK.; ed. high sch. (Clearfield, Pa.), Eastman Bus. Sch., studied law with father; m. Eva Sarah Gates, June 9, 1898; children—Robert Paul, Kathryn Eleanor, Ruth Evelyn, Margaret Helen. Employed as auditor corpns. at Middlesboro, Ky., 1890-94, sec. and treas. Mingo Coal & Coke Co., same, 1894-97; mgr. McKenrick & Co., mfrs. agts., Pittsburgh, Pa., 1897-98; auditor Manufacturers Natural Gas Co., Kittanning, Pa., 1899-1907, Merchants Nat. Bank, 1900-22; cashier Merchants Nat. Bank, 1922-33, also served as dir. both corpns.; retired 1933. Served as chmn. Kittanning and mem. bd. dirs Armstrong Co. Liberty Loan drives, 1917-18. Served as burgess Applewold Borough, Pa., 1904-10; sec. Council, Applewold, 1910-30. Treas. Kittanning Presbytry, 1915-33. Mem. S.A.R. Democrat. Presbyterian. Contbr. fiction and articles to mags. and jours. specializing in fiction and history with Pa. and Ky. background. Home: 628½ Hawthorne Av., Kittanning, Pa.

McKENZIE, Carl Harry, telephone official; b. Dallas, Tex., May 1, 1900; son of H. A. and Ella E. (Mitchell) McK.; B.S., Lehigh U., Bethlehem, Pa., 1922, M.S., 1923; M.B.A., Harvard U., 1926; unmarried. Accountant Pub. Service Commn., Harrisburg, Pa., 1924-30; asst. treas. Pa. Telephone Corpn., Erie, Pa., 1930-32, sec.-treas. and dir. since 1932; sec.-treas. and dir. Ohio Associated Telephone Co., Upstate Telephone Corpn. of New York, Tri-State Associated Telephone Corpn. Served in U.S. Marine Corps, 1917-19. Mem. Erie Chamber of Commerce. Republican. Mem. Loyal Order of Moose. Clubs: Erie, Rotary, Erie Maennerchor, East Erie Turners (Erie). Home: 713 French St. Office: 20 E. Tenth St., Erie, Pa.

McKENZIE, Fayette Avery, educator; b. Montrose, Pa., July 31, 1872; s. Edwin and Gertrude (Avery) M.; B.S., Lehigh U., 1895, LL.D., 1916; Ph.D., U. of Pa., 1906; m.

Nettie T. Tressel, Apr. 26, 1915. Instr. modern langs. and social science, Juniata Coll., Huntingdon, Pa., 1897-1900; instr. modern langs., Blight Sch., Phila., 1900-03; teacher Wind River Govt. Indian Sch., 1903-04; prof. economics and sociology, Ohio State U., 1905-15; pres. Fisk U., Nashville, Tenn., 1915-26, brought the institution to full recognition as a standard college and raised an endowment of a million dollars; prof. sociology, Juniata Coll., since 1926, dean of men, 1927-29, dir. extension since 1928, developed in 1933 a complete freshman class in Altoona, Pa., as a branch of Juniata. Spl. agt. Indian census and joint author Indian Census Report, U.S. Census Bur., 1910. Pres. univ. and social settlement sect. of Ohio State Conf. Charities and Correction, 1909-15; pres. Pub. Recreation Commn., Columbus, 1910-12; mem. Indian Survey Staff of Inst. for Government Research, 1926-27. Founder Soc. of American Indians; mem. Am. Sociol. Soc., Phi Beta Kappa. Presbyn. Author: The American Indian in Relation to the White Population of the United States, 1908. Joint author of Recreation Survey of Washington, D.C., 1915. Home: Huntingdon, Pa.

McKENZIE, John E., attending surgeon Raleigh Gen. Hosp. Address: 20 Heber St., Beckley, W.Va.

McKENZIE, Kenneth, univ. prof.; b. Cambridge, Mass., July 24, 1870; s. Alexander and Ellen Holman (Eveleth) M.; A.B., Harvard, 1891, A.M., 1893, Ph.D., 1895; post-grad. work in Europe at various times; hon. Doctor, U. of Padua, 1922; m. Aimée G. Leffingwell, July 30, 1908. Instr. modern langs., Union Coll., N.Y., 1895-98; prof. Romance langs., W.Va., U., 1898-1900; instr. Romance langs., 1900-05, asst. prof. Italian, Yale, 1905-15; prof. Romance langs. and head of dept., U. of Ill., 1915-25; prof. Italian, Princeton, 1926-38, prof. emeritus since 1938; instr. at Columbia U. Summer Sch., 1914-15, University of California, summer session, 1931. Mem. Modern Lang. Assn., Assn. Mod. Lang. Teachers Central West (pres. 1918), Dante Soc., Am. Assn. Teachers of Italian (pres. 1924), Societá Filologica Romana, Beta Theta Pi, Phi Beta Kappa Fraternity. Cavaliere della Corona d'Italia; corresponding mem. R. Istituto Lombardo di Scienze e Lettere; fellow Mediaeval Acad. of America. Clubs: Nassau (Princeton); Literary (Chicago); Authors' (London). Has published Concordanza delle Rime di Francesco Petrarca, 1912; Il Ventaglio by Carlo Goldoni, transl., 1910; Il Bestiario Toscano, 1912; Symmetrical Structure of Dante's Vita Nuova, Italian Bestiaries, Italian Fables in Verse, A Sonnet Ascribed to Davanzati, in Publs. of Modern Lang. Assn.; Ysopet-Avionnet, 1921; and editions of Alfred de Musset, Victor Hugo, Sardou, Molière, La Fontaine, and Dante's Vita Nuova; Conferenze sulla letteratura americana, 1922; Elementary French Grammar (with A. Hamilton), 1923; Selections from Silvio Pellico, 1924; Antonio Pucci, Le Noie, 1931. Writer scientific articles for Modern Philology, Modern Language Notes, Annual Reports of Dante Soc., Romanic Rev., Italica, Giornale Storico d. Letteratura Ital., Yale Review, Enciclopedia Italiana, and various memorial volumes. Gen. editor Century Modern Lang. Series. Dir. Italian Br. Am. Univ. Union in Europe, 1918-19; Am. exchange prof. in Italy, 1921-22. Home: Princeton, N.J.

McKENZIE, Loratius Lucius, coll. prof.; b. Shreveport, La., Sept. 20, 1893; s. Thomas and Flavia Leontine (Spears) McK.; A.B., Paine Coll., Augusta, Ga., 1915; A.B., U. of Mich., Ann Arbor, 1922, A.M., 1923; grad. study Columbia U., 1929-30; m. Ellie M. Doss, June 2, 1924; children—Loratius Lucius, Jr., Helen Doss. Instr. chemistry and physics, Paine Coll., 1915-16, 1918-21; instr. history and physics, Tex. Coll., Tyler, Tex., 1916-17; instr. social scis., Lane Coll., Jackson, Tenn., 1923-24; prof. history and polit. sci. and head dept. history and polit. sci., W.Va. State Coll., Institute, W.Va. since 1924. Mem. Am. Teachers Assn., Am. Hist. Assn., Assn. for Study of Negro Life and History, W.Va. State Teachers Assn., Omega Psi Phi. Awarded Urban League Fellowship, 1923; Gen. Edn. Bd. Fellowship, 1929-30. Republican. Methodist. Home: Institute, W.Va.

McKENZIE, Mrs. R. Tait (Ethel O'Neil), poet, pianist, lecturer; b. Hamilton, Ont.; d. John Hamilton and Hannah (MacGowan) O'Neil; ed. Hamilton Collegiate Inst., Hamilton Conservatory of Music; studied piano with pvt. teachers, New York and Berlin; m. Dr. Robert Tait McKenzie, physician and sculptor, at Chapel Royal, Dublin, Ireland, Aug. 18, 1907 (died Apr. 28, 1938). Followed profession as concert pianist, in America and abroad; teacher and head dept. music, Science Hill Sch., Shelbyville, Ky., one of oldest schs. for girls in U.S., 1904-07; apptd. advisor to Tait McKenzie collection of bronzes, U. of Pa., 1939; lecturer on ancient musical instruments. Mem. Daughters of Brit. Empire (regent William Blake Chapter), Soc. Ancient Musical Instruments, Animal Rescue League, Art Alliance, Poetry Soc. America; hon. mem. Art, Contemporary, Faculty Clubs. Presented to Ct. St. James, 1927; King George and Queen Elizabeth, 1937, 39. Episcopalian. Clubs: Acorn, Sedgely (Philadelphia); Garden, Sesame (London). Author: Secret Snow (book of verse), 1932; Angel Musicians, 1928. Contbr. Biography of Jessie Wilcox Smith to Pa. Golden Book, 1937; Catalogue Tait McKenzie Collection, University of Pa., 1939. Contbr. verse to mags. and jours. Home: 2014 Pine St., Philadelphia, Pa.; also, summer, Mill. of Kintail, Almonte, Ont.

McKENZIE, William Raymond, physician; b. Houtzdale, Pa., Feb. 15, 1890; s. William and Jane (Wiseman) McK.; M.D., Coll. Phys. and Surgeons, Baltimore, 1915; student Grad. Sch. Medicine of U. of Pa., 1932; m. Estelle M. Bane, May 23, 1917. Instr. diseases of nose and throat, U. of Md., 1923, asst. in diseases of nose and throat since 1927; chief of nose and throat clinic, Baltimore City Health Dept., 1924-34; rhinologist and otolaryngologist on staff Mercy Hosp., 1919-35, consultant since 1935; surgeon on staff Baltimore Eye, Ear, Nose and Throat Hosp. since 1930; rhinologist, otolaryngologist and peroral endoscopist, St. Joseph's Hosp. since 1932, South Baltimore Gen. Hosp. since 1934; mem. asso. staff in rhinology and otolaryngology, Union Memorial Hosp. since 1925; mem. staff Church Home and Infirmary Hosp. since 1938. Served as lt. then capt. Med. Res. Corps, U.S.A., 1917-19, with A.E.F., 1918-19. Fellow Am. Coll. Surgeons, A.M.A. Mem. Med. & Chirurg. Faculty of Md., Baltimore City Med. Soc., Southern Med. Soc., Phi Chi. Democrat. Episcopalian. Club: Baltimore Country. Home: 3209 N. Charles St. Office: 101 W. Read St., Baltimore, Md.

McKERNAN, Frank J., elec. mfg.; b. Johnstown, Pa., 1894; s. William J. and Susannah (Campbell) McK.; m. Delilah Ling, Oct. 7, 1921; children—Zita, Betty, Joe. Industrial engr., Cambria Steel Co., 1917-21, General Electric Co., 1921-22; supt. and gen. mgr., Universal Electric & Mfg. Co., Johnstown, Pa., 1922-28, pres. since 1928. Home: 131 Fayette St. Office: 618 Elder St., Johnstown, Pa.

McKINNEY, Howard Decker, prof. of music; b. Pine Bush, N.Y., May 29, 1889; s. John Luther and Marianna (Decker) McK.; grad. Middletown (N.Y.) High Sch., 1909; Litt.B., Rutgers U., 1913; student Columbia, 1915; unmarried. Master and teacher of music, St. Paul's Sch., Garden City, N.Y., 1913—; dir. of music, Rutgers U., 1915; asst. prof. of music, N.J. Coll. for Women, 1923; prof. of music, Rutgers U., New Brunswick, N.J., since 1930; editor J. Fischer & Bro., music pubs., New York. Mem. Am. Soc. Composers and Pubs., Delta Upsilon, Phi Beta Kappa. Club: Town Hall (New York). Author: Discovering music (with W. R. Anderson), 1934; Music and the Human Spirit (with W. R. Anderson), 1939. Editor: Songs of Rutgers, 1938. Home: 66 Harrison Av., New Brunswick, N.J.

McKINNEY, James Ferguson, banker; b. Salem, N.Y., July 8, 1864; s. John and Martha (Ferguson) McK.; student Salem (N.Y.) Acad., 1870-83; grad. Troy (N.Y.) Business Coll., 1884; m. May P. McEachron, Sept. 21, 1888; 1 son, Stanley J. Began as accountant and road salesman, Troy, N.Y., 1884; asst. cashier, First Nat. Bank, Stafford, Kan., 1888-90; cashier, Anderson Co. Nat. Bank, Garnett, Kan., 1890-93, Ness Co. Bank, Ness City, Kan., 1893-97, Adrian (Minn.) Bank, 1897-1901; treas., Palisades Trust & Guaranty Co., Englewood, N.J., 1902-36, pres.-treas. since 1937, dir. since 1908, mem. exec. com. since 1912. Republican. Presbyterian. Home: 509 Engle St. Office: Palisades Trust & Guaranty Co., Park Pl., Englewood, N.J.

McKINNEY, Paul Vincent, research chemist; b. Erie, Mich., Jan. 9, 1901; s. William Thomas and Jessie Fremont (Heffelman) McK.; A.B., Wooster (O.) Coll., 1921, A.M., 1923; student Ohio State U., Columbus, O., 1921-25; Ph.D., Princeton U., 1931; m. Mathilde Christman, Sept. 1, 1927; 1 son, William Bruce. Instr. in chemistry, Millersburg (O.) High Sch., 1921-22, Celina (O.) High Sch., 1922-23, Wooster (O.) Coll., 1923-28; Baker Co. fellow, Princeton U., 1928-29; asst. in chemistry, Princeton, 1929-30, asst. instr., 1930-31; instr. in chemistry, Rutgers U., New Brunswick, N.J., 1931-33; research chemist Phillips Petroleum Co., Bartlesville, Okla., 1933-36; industrial fellow, Mellon Inst., Pittsburgh, 1936, senior industrial fellow since 1937. Mem. Am. Chem. Soc., Am. Assn. Univ. Profs., Am. Soc. Testing Materials, Sigma Xi, Phi Lambda Upsilon, Phi Beta Kappa. Presbyterian. Granted patent on process for preparation of a catalytic material. Contbr. many articles to professional jours. Home: 1015 Macon Av. Office: Mellon Institute, Pittsburgh, Pa.

McKINNEY, William Wilson, clergyman; b. Easton, Pa., May 17, 1893; s. William Glenn and Jeannette May (Malone) McK.; A.B., U. of Pittsburgh, 1913, B.S., same, 1914, A.M., same, 1916, Ph.D., same, 1936; B.S.T., Western Theol. Sem., 1919; B.T., Auburn Theol. Sem., 1926; unmarried. Engaged as prin. Cresson High Sch., 1914-16; instr. U. of Pittsburgh, 1917-19; ordained to ministry Presbyn. Ch. and pastor, Elizabeth, Pa., 1919-28 pastor, Ambridge, Pa., since 1928. Dir. Western Pa. Sabbath Assn., Nat. Reform Assn. Mem. Pi Gamma Mu, Alpha Tau Epsilon. Moderator Beaver Presbytery. Republican. Presbyterian. Mason (32°). I.O.O.F. Author: Eighteenth Century Presbyterianism in Western Pennsylvania, 1921; Early Pittsburgh Presbyterianism, 1938. Contbr. weekly S.S. lesson Presbyterian Banner, 1928-37, and many articles to religious papers. Home: 823 Maplewood Av., Ambridge, Pa.

McKINSTRY, Arthur Raymond, bishop; b. Greeley, Kan., July 26, 1895; s. Leslie Irwin and Cevilla (Surbeck), McK.; Ph.B., Kenyon Coll., Gambier, O., 1918, M.A., 1920; Bexley Hall Div. Sch., Gambier, 1917-19; S.T.B., Episcopal Theol. Sch., Cambridge, Mass., 1920; studied Harvard Grad. Sch.; D.D., Kenyon Coll., 1937, U. of the South, 1937; m. Isabelle Van Dorn, June 19, 1920; children—Isabelle Van Dorn, Margaret Adelaide, Barbara Louise, James Thomas, Arthur St. Clair. Deacon, 1919, priest 1920, Protestant Episcopal Church; on staff of St. Paul's Cathedral, Boston, Mass., 1919-20; canon Grace Cathedral, Topeka, Kan., also chaplain Bethany Coll., 1920-21; rector Ch. of the Incarnation, Cleveland, 1921-24; sec. field dept. Nat. Council P.E. Ch., N.Y. City, 1924-27, later asso. sec.; rector St. Paul's Ch., Albany, 1927-31, and pres. bd. trustees Endownment Fund same ch.; became rector St. Mark's Episcopal Ch., San Antonio, Tex., Dec. 1, 1931; now bishof of Del. Pres. Clergymen's Mut. Ins. League; mem. Bishop and Standing Com. of West Tex. Diocese; mem. Diocesan Exec. Bd., pres. standing com.; mem. Forward Movement Commn., P.E. Ch.; mem. budget and program com., com. of fifteen on social internat. questions, com. on aided dioceses in missionary dists., Gen. Conv., 1937. Served as chaplain of Assembly, N.Y. legislature. Mem. Sigma Pi. Address: "Bishopstead," Wilmington, Del.

McKINSTRY, Edwin Lincoln, newspaper editor; b. Camden, N.J., June 19, 1867; s. Charles Humphrey and Martha Morrison (Blaker) McK.; student Pa. pub. schs., 1873-78, mil.

McKNIGHT sch., Chester Springs, Pa., 1878-80, Friends Central Sch., Phila., Pa., 1885-86, State Normal Sch., West Chester, Pa., 1888-90; m. Loraine Stone, June 8, 1893; 1 son, Hugh Exton. Began as printer's devil, 1880; teacher pub. sch., 1886-88; reporter Daily Local News, West Chester, Pa., 1893-1917, asst. editor, 1917-24, editor since 1924, v.p. since 1938. Independent Republican. Presbyterian (elder First Presbyn. Ch., West Chester; Sunday Sch. teacher since 1890). Home: 140 Dean St. Office: 10 S. High St., West Chester, Pa.

McKNIGHT, Robert James George, clergyman, educator; b. Slippery Rock, Pa., July 9, 1878; s. Robert and Elizabeth (Campbell) McK.; A.B., Geneva Coll., Beaver Falls, Pa., 1896 (D.D., 1918); grad. Ref. Presbyn. Theol. Sem., Pittsburgh, Pa., 1899; B.D., Princeton Theol. Sem., 1900; studied Johns Hopkins, 1901-02, Columbia, 1903, U. of Leipzig, 1904-05; Ph.D., U. of Chicago, 1907; m. Grace Patterson, of Staunton, Ill., Sept. 20, 1905; children—Robert James George, Hugh Patterson. Ordained Ref. Presbyn. ministry, 1903; pastor Middletown, Pa., 1903-04; instr. Morgan Park (Ill.) Mil. Acad., 1907-08; pastor Wilkinsburg, Pa., 1909-16; prof. Bibl. lit., Ref. Presbyn. Sem., since 1916, pres. since 1929. Pres. Keystone Driller Co., Beaver Falls, Pa., since 1935. Moderator Ref. Presbyn. Synod, 1934. Chautauqua lecturer and Bible teacher, summers 1912-17. Home: 1311 Singer Pl., Wilkinsburg, Pa. Office: 7418 Penn Av., Pittsburgh, Pa.

McKNIGHT, Robert Wilson, advertising; b. Sewickley, Pa., Aug. 20, 1895; s. Charles and Eliza (Wilson) McK.; student Morristown (N.J.) Sch., 1912-15; A.B., Princeton U., 1915-19; attended U. of Paris (France), 1919; m. Rachel Arrott, Aug. 6, 1921; children—Anne Arrott, Mary Rachel, Charles, Harlan Baird. Began as bond salesman Dillon, Read & Co., 1920; founded, 1923, and since pres. and dir. R. W. McKnight, Inc., advertising; pres. and dir. Western Nat. Bank, Pittsburgh (assets now being liquidated under control of officers), since 1925; rep. of Alexander Film Co., in Pittsburgh Dist. (motion picture advertising since 1938. Served as 2d lt., 119th Inf., World War; now lt. col. 393d Inf., Reserve. Dir. Woods Run Settlement. Mem. Am. Legion, 40 and 8. Democrat. Presbyterian. Clubs: Edgeworth, Allegheny Country (Pittsburgh); Farmington Country (Charlottesville, Va.); Tower (Princeton U.). Home: Sewickley, Pa. Office: 605 Investment Bldg., Pittsburgh, Pa.

McKOWN, Gilbert Campbell, newspaper editor; b. Berkeley Co., W.Va., Nov. 25, 1890; s. Gilbert William and Anna McK.; student Mercersburg (Pa.) Acad., 1908-10; Litt.B., Princeton U., 1914, A.M., 1915; m. Elizabeth W. Trimble, Oct. 15, 1919. Began as instr. English, Mercersburg Acad., Mercersburg, Pa., 1915-17; editor Martinsburg World, Martinsburg, W.Va., 1919-21; editor Martinsburg Journal, daily newspaper, Martinsburg, W.Va. since 1921. Served in O.T.C., F.A., Camp Benjamin Harrison, 1917, Motor Transport Corps, Camp Joseph Johnston, 1918. Mem. Key and Seal Club (Princeton U.). Mem. W.Va. Newspaper Council (since 1921). Democrat. Mem. Ref. Church. Kiwanis. Home: 1117 W. King St. Office: The Journal, Martinsburg, W.Va.

McKOY, Thomas Hall, Jr., partner McKoy, Gaston & Page; b. Norfolk, Va., Apr. 26, 1893; s. Thomas Hall and Caroline Langley (Cooke) M.; student Gilman's and St. James Schs., Md.; m. Catharine C. Cassard, June 3, 1922; children—Thomas Hall, III, Linda Cassard. Entered employ Hambleton & Co., bankers, 1915, retiring as partner, 1931; partner McKoy, Gaston & Page, N.Y. City, since 1931; pres. and dir. New Hampshire Jockey Club, Inc.; v.p. and dir. Natural Gas Reserve Corpn.; dir. Distributors Group, Inc. Clubs: Bachelors Cotillon (Baltimore); Phila. Racquet, Phila. Cricket, Rose Tree Hunt, Radnor Hunt (Phila.). Home: "Lookafar Farm," Chestnut Hill, Pa. Office: 61 Broadway, New York, N.Y.

McLANAHAN, Austin, banker; b. Chambersburg, Pa., Oct. 31, 1871; s. Johnston and Rebecca Ann (Austin) McL.; A.B., Princeton, 1892, LL.B., U. of Md., 1897; m. Romaine Le Moyne, Nov. 6, 1902; children—Jean Romaine (Mrs. Francis C. Taliaferro), Anne Austin. With Alex Brown & Sons, 1894-1922, mem. firm, 1902-22; pres. Savings Bank of Baltimore since 1922; dir. First Nat. Bank. Pres. Export and Import Bd. of Trade, Baltimore, 1920-22. Served as maj. A.R.C., France, World War. Trustee Sheppard & Enoch Pratt Hosp. Presbyterian. Clubs: Maryland, Chesapeake (Baltimore); Elk Ridge Fox Hunting. Home: 4801 Green Spring Av. Office: Savings Bank of Baltimore, Baltimore, Md.

McLANAHAN, James Craig, judge; b. Baltimore, Md., Apr. 28, 1881; s. Samuel and Maude (Imbrie) M.; student Lawrenceville (N.J.) Sch., 1895-97; A.B., Princeton U., 1901; LL.B., U. of Md., 1903; m. Linda H. Walke, Apr. 21, 1934; children—James Craig, Linda Walke. Admitted to Md. bar, 1903, and began practice of law in Baltimore; asst. U.S. dist. atty., Dist. of Md., 1910-15; formed partnership France & McLanahan, later France, McLanahan & Rouzer, 1912; mem. latter to 1915 and 1919-38; asso. judge Supreme Bench of Baltimore City since 1938; assigned as judge Circuit Ct. No. 2, Baltimore, 1938-39, Baltimore City Ct., part III, since Jan. 9, 1939. Enlisted Md. Nat. Guard, 1915; commd. 1st lt., F.A., 1915, capt., 1917; entered Federal service, 1917; attended F.A. Sch. of Fire, Fort Sill, Okla., July-Sept. 1917; assigned as instr., Sept. 1917, later apptd. asst. dir.; commd. major, U.S. Army, 1918; commd. lt. col., Oct. 6, 1918; hon. discharged, Jan. 3, 1919, and commd. lt. col. F.A. Res.; commd. major, Md. Nat. Guard, 1922, commd. lt. col., 1923, col. 1925, brig. gen., 1931, resigned Dec. 1, 1938. Mem. Am. Bar Assn., Md. State Bar Asen., Baltimore City Bar Assn. Republican. Presbyn. Clubs: Maryland, Baltimore Country, Elkridge, Gibson Island. Home: 4414 Underwood Road. Chambers: Court House, Baltimore, Md.

McLANAHAN, Samuel, surgeon; b. Lawrenceville, N.J., July 26, 1901; s. Samuel and Mary Minor (Latane) McL.; grad. Lawrenceville (N.J.) Sch., 1919; A.B., Princeton U., 1923; M.D., Johns Hopkins, 1927; m. Evelyn Willoughby Sharp, July 2, 1937; 1 dau., Mary Sharp. Interne Johns Hopkins Hosp., 1927-28; asst. resident and resident surgeon Union Memorial Hosp., 1928-32; visiting surgeon Baltimore City Hosps.; asst. visiting surgeon Johns Hopkins Hosp.; mem. visiting staff Union Memorial Hosp., Hosp. for Women of Md., Church Home and Infirmary, Home for Incurables; cons. surgeon Provident Hosp.; instr. in surgery, Johns Hopkins Med. Sch., since 1933; asst. in surgery, U. of Md. Med. Sch., since 1935. Chmn. First Aid Com., Baltimore Chapter Am. Red Cross; mem. bd. mgrs. Egenton Home (for girls). Fellow Am. Coll. Physicians; mem. Baltimore City Med. Soc., Med. and Chirurg. Faculty of Md., A.M.A., Phi Beta Kappa, Alpha Omega Alpha. Republican. Presbyterian. Club: Johns Hopkins Faculty. Home: Cambridge Arms Apts. Office: 108 E. 33d St., Baltimore, Md.

McLAUGHLIN, Joseph Clifford, lawyer; b. Penn Twp., Butler Co., Pa., Nov. 12, 1893; s. James and Mary (Mahon) McL.; student Georgetown Prep. Sch., Washington, D.C., 1909-12, Notre Dame U., South Bend, Ind., 1912; LL.B., Georgetown Law Sch., Washington, D.C., 1916; m. Kathryn Ekas, Feb. 22, 1922; children—Mary Alice, Jane and Joan (twins), Ellen. Began as clk. in drafting room State Highway Dept., Pittsburgh, 1918; admitted to Butler Co. bar, 1922; since in gen. practice law; admitted to practice before Supreme Ct. of Pa., 1924. Served in U.S. Army, Apr. 1917-Jan. 1918, World War, as sergt. of ordnance. Democrat. Catholic. Home: 910 E. Brady St. Office: 406 Butler Co. Nat. Bank Bldg., Butler, Pa.

McLAUGHLIN, Mary Murray, chmn. Dept. of Pub. Assistance; b. Bullion, Pa., Dec. 10, 1877; d. Joseph E. and Martha E. (Leslie) Murray; student Pittsburgh Acad.; m. C. M. McLaughlin, M.D., Jan. 16, 1906; children—Charles S., Jane Ellen. Teacher pub. sch., Westmoreland Co., Pa., 1889-90, Allegheny Co., 1890-1906; mem. Mother's Assistance Fund Bd., 1934-37; chmn. Dept. Pub. Assistance, Armstrong Co., 1938-39. Republican. Protestant. Club: Freeport (Pa.) Womans (pres. 1926-27). One of the first 100 women to serve on a Federal Jury of Pa., 1935. Address: 518 High St., Freeport, Pa.

McLAUGHLIN, Thomas H., bishop; b. New York, N.Y., July 15, 1881; s. John and Margaret (Byrne) McL.; prep. edn., St. Francis Xavier High Sch.; A.B., St. Francis Xavier Coll., 1901; S.T.D., Imperial Royal U., Innsbruck, Austria, 1908. Ordained R.C. priest, 1904; chaplain Innsbruck and Fennberg, Austria; asst. St. Michael's Ch., Jersey City, N.J., 1908; prof. of philosophy and theology, Seton Hall College and Immaculate Conception Sem., S. Orange and Darlington, N.J., 1908-36; pres. Seton Hall Coll., 1922-33; became auxiliary bishop, Newark, N.J., 1935, bishop of Paterson, 1938; examiner clergy, 1910; diocesan official since 1923; became consultor Newark Diocese, 1923, vicar gen., 1933. Mem. Cath. Ednl. Assn., Cath. Philos. Assn., Cath. Hist. Assn., Irish Hist. Assn., Collectors League of N.J. Address: 178 Devrom Av., Paterson, N.J.

McLEAN, Donald H., congressman; b. Paterson, N.J., Mar. 18, 1884; s. Alexander and Annie (Thompson) McL.; LL.B., George Washington U., 1906; m. Edna H. Righter, Nov. 18, 1909; children—Donald H., Edward R. Page, U.S. Senate, 1897-1902; pvt. sec. to Senator John Kean of N.J., 1902-11; admitted to N.J. bar and began law practice at Elizabeth; mem. firm Whittemore & McLean; was spl. master in chancery of N.J., later asst. prosecutor of pleas, Union Co., N.J.; mem. 73d to 76th Congresses (1933-41), 6th New Jersey District. Formerly chairman Union County Republican Com. and sec. N.J. Rep. State Com. Mem. Phi Sigma Kappa (former nat. sec., treas., chancellor and president). Episcopalian. Mason. Elk. Clubs: University (Washington); Locust Grove Golf (pres.). Home: 65 Bauer Terrace, Hillside, N.J. Office: 125 Broad St., Elizabeth, N.J.

McLEAN, Eugene L., clergyman; b. Amity Twp., Berks Co., Pa., July 19, 1869; s. James Brewster and Mary Amanda (Lorah) M.; student Keystone State Normal Sch., 1885-87; A.B., Franklin & Marshall Coll., 1890, A.M., 1894; student Theol. Sem., Lancaster Pa., 1890-93; D.D., Ursinus Coll., 1927; m. Mary Neff, Nov. 15, 1905; children—Mary Margaret, Kathryn Virginia, Pauline Eugenia. Ordained ministry of Reformed Ch., 1893; pastor Trinity Ch., Everett, Pa., 1893-98, Grace Ch., Frederick, Md., 1898-1913, First Ch., Quakertown, Pa., 1914-16, Christ Ch., Phila., 1916-22; treas. Bd. of Ministerial Relief of Reformed Ch. in U.S. since 1920, sec. since 1938; sec.-treas. Soc. for Relief of Ministers and their Widows of Reformed Ch. in U.S. since 1927. Pres. Md. Classis Reformed Ch., 1908, Potomac Synod, Reformed Ch., 1912, Phila. Classis, Reformed Ch., 1939; mem. exec. com. Reformed Ch. in U.S., 1926-32, promotional com. of Evang. and Reformed Ch. since 1934, com. to Unite Bd. of Ministerial Relief of the Reformed Ch. and Bd. of Pension and Relief of the Evang. Synod of North America. Mem. Ministerial Assn. (Frederick, Md., and Quakertown, Pa.), Ministerial Assn., Reformed Ch., Phila.; Phi Kappa Psi. Republican. Mason. Home: 4706 Hazel Av. Office: 1505 Race St., Philadelphia, Pa.

McLEAN, Robert, newspaper executive; b. Phila., Pa., Oct. 1, 1891; s. William L. and Sarah Burd (Warden) McL.; Litt. B., Princeton, 1913; m. Clare Randolph Goode, April 28, 1919. Pres. Bulletin Co., pubs. Evening Bulletin Philadelphia; dir. Associated Press since 1924, first v.p., 1936-37, pres., 1938. Mem. First Troop Philadelphia City Cavalry, 1915; Mexican border service, 1916-17; commd. 2d lt. Cav. R.C., May 7, 1917; capt. Field Arty. R. C., 311th Regt., 79th Div., Aug. 15, 1917; maj. F.A., June 30, 1918; served at Sch. of Fire, Ft. Sill, Okla. Presbyn. Home: Ft. Washington, Pa. Office: Bulletin Bldg., Philadelphia, Pa.

McLELLAN, George Arthur, physician; b. Newark, N.J., Nov. 19, 1886; s. George Hubbard and Susan Whitehead (Sayre) McL.; M.D.,

McLELLAN, Long Island Med. Coll., 1909; m. Marjorie Haddon, Sept. 10, 1913; children—Emily Louise, George Hubbard, Arthur Sayre. Interne The Brooklyn (N.Y.) Hosp., 1910-12; engaged in gen. practice of medicine and surgery at East Orange, N.J. since 1912; junior attending surgeon Orange Memorial Hosp.; pres. East Orange Bd. Health since 1925; dir. Ampere Bank & Trust Co. Fellow Am. Coll. Surgeons; mem. Soc. Surgeons of N.J., Alpha Kappa Kappa. Republican. Baptist. Home: 19 Hawthorne Av., East Orange, N.J.

McLELLAN, Roy Davison, geologist; b. Noel Shore, Nova Scotia, Aug. 21, 1892; s. John Gilmore and Electa (O'Brien) McL.; came to U.S., 1909, naturalized, 1927; ed. Whitworth Coll., Tacoma, Wash., 1911-14; A.B., U. of Wash., 1915, B.Sc., 1916, M.Sc. 1922, Ph.D., 1927; m. Haroldine Mavis Searle, Aug. 17, 1926; children—Wilfred Dana, Lowell Gilmore, Muriel Aletha, Kelvin Roy, Jay Densmore. Engaged as teaching fellow, Dept. Geology, U. of Wash., 1920-22, instr. geology, 1922-25; petrographer, Central Research Lab. Am. Smelting & Refining Co., Perth Amboy, N.J., since 1925. Served as assayer, Dominion of Can. Assay Office, Vancouver, B.C., 1916-20. Fellow A.A.A.S. Mem. Mineral. Soc. of America, Am. Inst. Mining & Metall. Engrs., Sigma Xi. Republican. Presbyterian. Club: Plainfield Mineralogical (Plainfield). Contbr. sci. articles to tech. jours. Home: 24 Lillian Terrace, Woodbridge. Office: Am. Smelting & Refining Co., Perth Amboy, N.J.

McLEOD, Malcolm, prof. English; b. Penicuik, Scotland, June 9, 1878; s. Alexander and Margaret (Muir) McL.; came with parents to U.S., 1888; A.B., Harvard, 1904, A.M., 1906, Ph.D., 1914; m. Florence Alden Skinner, June 30, 1917; 1 dau., Margaret Alden. Asst. and instr. in English, Harvard, 1907-16, Sheldon traveling fellow, 1914-15; asst. prof. English, Carnegie Inst. Tech., 1916-21, prof. and head of dept. since 1921. Mem. Modern Lang. Assn. America, English Assn. Western Pa. (ex-pres.). Clubs: Junta (Pittsburgh); Harvard Club of Western Pa. Co-Author: The Nelson Handbook of English (with J. H. Hanford and E. C. Knowlton), 1931; The New Handbook of English (with Stith Thompson), 1936. Home: 928 Bellefonte St. Address: Carnegie Inst. of Tech., Pittsburgh, Pa.

McLURE, Norman Roosevelt, engr., mfr.; b. Phila., Pa., Jan. 20, 1880; s. Alfred D. and Eugenie (Hitchcock) McL.; student West Jersey Acad., Bridgeton, N.J.; C.E., Princeton, 1904; m. Elizabeth Meriwether, in St. Louis, April 17, 1911. Inspr. of bridges, N.Y.,O.&W. R.R., 1904; in charge of erecting Quebec Bridge, 1905-07; asst. engr., later chief engr., Phoenix Iron Co., 1911-17; successively works mgr. Phila. Roll & Machine Co., supt. Norvell Chem. Corpn., vice-pres. Keystone Screw Co.; now vice-pres. and dir. E. J. Lavino & Co., and subsidiaries, mfrs. of alloys and refractories, Phila., since 1926. Mem. Am. Soc. Civil Engrs., Am. Iron and Steel Inst., Princeton Engrs. Assn., Pa. Soc. Sons of the Revolution. Republican. Presbyterian. Clubs: Racquet, Gulph Mills Golf, Phila. Skating, Pickering Hunt (Phila.); Princeton (New York); Ivy (Princeton). Home: "Hemlock Hill," Radnor, Pa. Office: 1528 Walnut St., Philadelphia, Pa.

McMAHON, John Robert, author; b. British India, Sept. 1, 1875; s. John Todd and Sarah (Douglas) M.; mostly self taught; m. Margherita Arlina Hamm (died 1907); 1 dau. Arlina Douglas; m. 2d, Beatrice Lessey, June 17, 1913. Reporter and Sunday article writer for various New York newspapers from 1894; began writing fiction for mags., 1910; contributed to Saturday Evening Post, etc.; specialized in economics of agriculture during World War, traveling in U.S. and Can.; went abroad in 1919 for after-war survey of Europe in behalf of The Country Gentleman. Pvt. Co. D, 202d Regt. N.Y., Spanish-Am. War; 9 mos. service, including 3 mos. in Cuba. Mem. Authors' League America. Author: Toilers and Idlers, 1907; The House That Junk Built, 1915; Success in the Suburbs, 1917; Your House, 1927; The Wright Brothers—Fathers of Flight, 1930. Editor and part author of How These Farmers Succeeded, 1919. Home: Little Falls, N.J. *

McMANUS, Ambrose, pres. McManus Bros.; b. Newark, N.J., May 28, 1890; s. Walter and Delia (Mulcahy) McM.; student Newark (N.J.) Acad., 1902-05, St. Benedict's Prep. Sch., Newark, N.J., 1905-07; m. Katharine Booth Brady, April 15, 1915; children—Kathleen, John Ambrose, William Walter, Nancy Booth, Richard. Pres. McManus Bros., furniture, Elizabeth, N.J., since 1916; v.p. Central Home Trust Co., Elizabeth, N.J., since 1925; treas. of Hales Bedding Stores of N.Y., Inc., since 1939; receiver of Winfield-Scott Hotel, Elizabeth, N.J., 1933-38. Mem. Union Co. (N.J.) Park Commn. (pres., 1935-37), Elizabeth (N.J.) Bd. of Edn. (pres., 1936, 1937); mem. Sinking Fund Commn. of City of Elizabeth (N.J.). Treas. Union Co. (N.J.) Tuberculosis League since 1915; mem. Bd. of Mgrs., St. Elizabeth Hosp. Mem. Elizabeth (N.J.) Chamber of Commerce (pres., 1916-19). Democrat. Catholic. K.C., Elk. Clubs: Suburban Golf (past treas. and dir.), Rotary (pres., 1920-21; Elizabeth, N.J.). Home: 752 N. Broad St. Office: 1152 E. Jersey St., Elizabeth, N.J.

McMARLIN, John G., banker; b. Adams Twp., Butler Co., Pa., July 23, 1870; s. James A. and Emaline (Duncan) McM.; student high sch., Butler, Pa., 1885-87, Witherspoon Inst., Butler, Pa., Duffs Mercantile Coll., Pittsburgh, Pa., 1887; m. Maude Mitchell, Aug. 18, 1894; children—Harold L. (dec.), James A. (dec.). With Butler (Pa.) Savings Bank, 1890-91; with The Butler County Nat. Bank and Trust Co., Butler, Pa., since 1891, v.p., cashier and dir. since 1900. Mem. Red Cross. Clubs: Bankers (Pittsburgh), Kiwanis (Butler, Pa.). Home: 558 Third St. Office: Diamond and South Main St., Butler, Pa.

McMASTER, John Dennis, lawyer; b. Jersey City, N.J., Sept. 2, 1897; s. John Stevenson and Jane (Dennis) McM.; A.B., Princeton, 1919; study Yale Sch. of Law, 1919-21, Columbia U. Law Sch., 1921-22; m. Annette Holbrook, Nov. 9, 1921; children—Joan Holbrook, Annette Sheldon. Admitted to N.J. bar, 1922 and since engaged in gen. practice of law in Jersey City; admitted to N.Y. bar, 1930 and mem. firm Gifford, Woody, Carter & Hays, One Wall St., New York, N.Y., since 1929; served as spl. master in chancery of N.J., 1938; mem. bd. mgrs. Provident Instn. for Savings, Jersey City; dir. Colonial Life Ins. Co., Jersey City, N.J. Served as ensign, A.S., U.S.N. during World War. Trustee First Presbyn. Ch., and Family Service Assn., Jersey City, N.J. Mem. N.J. Bar Assn., Princeton Graduate Council. Democrat. Presbyn. Clubs: Princeton (New York); Arcola Country (Ridgewood, N.J.); Lawyers' (New York); Campus (Princeton, N.J.). Home: 22 Gifford Av., Jersey City, N.J. Office: One Exchange Pl., Jersey City, N.J.

McMATH, Robert Edwin, steel mfr.; b. Oct. 21, 1886; s. Edwin Augustus and Harriet C. (Lapham) McM.; studied East High Co., Rochester, N.Y., 1900-03; A.B., Harvard, 1907, LL.B., Law Sch., 1910; m. Grace E. Riehman, Sept. 9, 1914. Admitted to N.Y. bar, 1911; practiced law, 1911-18; asst. sec. Bethlehem (Pa.) Steel Corpn., 1918-19, sec., 1919-30, financial v.p. and sec. since 1930, now also dir. Republican. Clubs: Harvard, University, The Links, Inc. (New York). Home: 1019 Prospect Av. Office: 701 E. Third St., Bethlehem, Pa.

McMILLAN, William Andrew, surgeon; b. Jacquet River, N.B., Can., Apr. 2, 1875; s. Thomas and Mary (Harvey McM.); came to U.S., 1897, naturalized, 1911; M.D., Coll. Phys. and Surgs., Baltimore, Md., 1903; m. Eleanor Owen, June 24, 1903; children—William Owen, Thomas Harvey, John Osler; engaged in practice of medicine and surgery at Charleston, W.Va.; organized and built McMillan Hosp., chief surgeon and dir.; div. surgeon, N. Y. Central, B.&O. R.R. and Virginian Ry.; chief surgeon Hatfield-Campbells Creek Coal Co., Am. Rolling Mill Co.; dir. Nat. Bank of Commerce, Charleston, since 1924. Served as maj. Med. Corps, W.Va. N.G., retired. Fellow Am. Coll. Surgeons, Am. Med. Assn.; mem. W.Va. State and Kanawha Co. med. socs., Caledonian Soc. Republican. Presbyn. (elder). Mason (K.T., 32°, Shriner). Home: 1550 Virginia St., Office: McMillan Hosp., Charleston, W.Va.

McMILLEN, Clayton Lafayette, supt. of schs.; b. Meadville, Pa., May 27, 1902; s. Frank Marseillas and Katherine (Estelle) McM.; student, Allegheny Coll., Meadville, Pa., 1922-23; B.S., Thiel Coll., Greenville, Pa., 1927; M.A. in Edn., Columbia U., 1933; unmarried. Teacher mathematics and science, Harmonsburg, Pa., 1927-28; supervising prin., Saltsburg, Pa., 1928-37; supt. of schs., Etna, Pa., since 1937. Republican. Presbyterian. Mason (Past Master). Clubs: Rotary, Alcoma Country. Author ednl. articles in various mags. Home: 26 Elm Lane. Office: Hickory St., Etna, Pa.

McMILLEN, Wheeler, editor; b. near Ada, O., Jan. 27, 1893; s. Lewis D. and Ella (Wheeler) McM.; ed. country schs.; student Ohio Northern U.; m. Edna Doane, May 28, 1915; 1 son, Robert Doane. Reporter Cincinnati Post, 1912; owner Covington Republican, 1914-18; farmer, Hardin Co., O., 1918-22; asso. editor The Country Home (formerly Farm and Fireside), 1922-34, editor, 1934-37, editorial dir. 1937-39; editor-in-chief Farm Journal and Farmers Wife since 1939. Pres. Nat. Farm Chemurgic Council; pres. Am. Assn. of Agrl. Editors, 1934-38; dir. Nat. Swine Growers Assn. Mem. Grange, Am. Soc. Agri. Engrs., Am. Economic Assn., Am. Hist. Assn. Hon. mem. Kappa Tau Alpha Fraternity, U. of Mo. Republican. Clubs: Cosmos, Nat. Press (Washington, D.C.); Saddle and Sirloin, Union League (Chicago). Author: The Farming Fever, 1924; The Young Collector, 1928; Too Many Farmers, 1929. Home: Hopewell, N.J. Office: 230 S. Seventh St., Philadelphia, Pa.

McMILLION, Theodore Miller, prof. of biology; b. Williamsburg W.Va., Oct. 5, 1903; s. John Addison and Margaret (Livesay) McM.; A.B., W.Va. Univ., 1926, A.M., 1929; student U. of Pittsburgh evenings and summers, 1931-36; m. Vallie Richard, Mar. 27, 1929. Instr. in biology and chemistry, Geneva Coll., 1926-29, asst. prof. of Biology, 1929-32, asso. prof., 1932-35, prof. since 1935. Fellow A.A.A.S.; mem. Pa. Acad. of Science, Phi Beta Kappa, Sigma Xi. Republican. Presbyterian. Home: 3217 6th Av., Beaver Falls, Pa.

McMULLEN, Joshua Willard, supervising prin. schs.; b. Glasgow, Del., Oct. 1, 1897; s. James F. and Mary (Richards) McM.; A.B., U. of Del., 1921; A.M., U. of Pa., 1935; m. Irene Richards, June 30, 1923; children—Robert Willard, Joann Irene. Engaged in teaching pub. schs., 1921-23; supervising prin. schs. since 1923; supervising prin. Oxford Borough Sch. Dist. since 1923. Mem. Nat. Edn. Assn., Am. Assn. Sch. Administrs., Sigma Nu. Republican. Mason. Club: Rotary of Oxford. Home: 39 Addison St., Oxford, Pa.

McMULLEN, Richard Cann, governor; b. Glasgow, Del., Jan. 2, 1868; s. James and Sarah Louise (Boulder) McM.; ed. pub. schs. and Goldey Coll., Wilmington, Del.; m. Florence E. Hutchinson, Jan. 17, 1895; children— Laura Boulden (wife of Comdr. James W. Whitfield, U.S.N.), Richard Hutchinson, Florence Rebecca (Mrs. Irvin Spencer Taylor). In leather mfg. business since 1888, Charles Mullen, later Mullen & Pierson, Daniel Pierson, Amalgamated Leather Cos.; supt. and v.p. Standard Kid Mfg. Co., 1917-29, later Standard Div. of Allied Kid Co.; v.p. Allied Kid Co. since 1929. Served as mem. Wilmington City Council, and mem. Del. Pub. Utility Commn.; elected gov. of Del. for term, 1937-41. Mem. S.A.R. Dem. League. Democrat. Methodist. Mason, Odd Fellow, Red Man, Ancient Order United Workmen. Clubs: Kiwanis, Monarch. Home: Wilmington. Address: State House, Dover, Del.

McMURRAY, John Boyd, physician; b. West Middletown, Pa., Oct. 23, 1878; s. William Boyd and Katherine (Armstrong) McM.; stud. Ohio U., 1896-98; M.D., U. Md., 1901; grad. student U. of Pa., 1903-04, Univ. of Paris, 1928; m. Bird Hanover, 1902; m. 2d, Minnie Sehen, 1906; m. 3d, Marg. B. Galvin,

McMURRAY, July 10, 1935. Began practice as physician in Houston, Pa., 1901; in practice in Washington, Pa., since 1905; practice limited to eye, ear, nose and throat; mem. staff Washington Hosp.; pres. and dir. Washington Union Trust Co. Served as capt. Med. Corps, U. S. Army during World War. Mem. A.M.A. (vice-chmn. nose and throat sect. 1906), Pa. Med. Soc. (vice-pres. 1910; sec. eye, ear, nose and throat sect. 1928), Am. Acad. Ophthalmology and Oto-laryngology, Am. Laryngol., Rhinol. and Otol. Soc., Pittsburgh Ophthal. Soc., Pittsburgh Oto-laryngol. Soc. (past pres.). Republican. Mem. United Presbyn. Ch. Clubs: Washington Country, Nemacolm Country, University, Lions (hon.), all of Pittsburgh. Home: 400 N. Wade Av. Office: Washington Trust Bldg., Washington, Pa.

McMURRAY, Thomas Edward, physician; b. Pittsburgh, Pa., Nov. 8, 1882; s. Thomas and Charlotte (Barkley) McM.; student Pittsburgh Acad., 1898-1901; M.D., U. of Pittsburgh, 1905; m. Mary Emmert, Nov. 8, 1906; children —Thomas Edward, Stuart E. In pvt. practice medicine, Wilkinsburg, Pa., since 1906; mem. med. staff Columbia Hosp., Pittsburgh, since 1910, Pittsburgh Hosp., since 1925; mem. preceptral staff, U. of Pittsburgh, since 1930. Served as 1st lt., M.C., U.S. Army, during World War. Fellow Am. Coll. Physicians; mem. A.M.A., Pittsburgh Acad. of Medicine. Republican. Protestant. Clubs: University (Pittsburgh); Madison Golf and Country (Madison, O.); Alcoma Golf (Wilkinsburg, Pa.) Author: articles on epilepsy, poisoning, pneumonia, etc. Home: 5836 Ferree St., Pittsburgh, Pa. Office: 1017 Center St., Wilkinsburg, Pa.

McMURTRIE, Edith, artist, art teacher; b. Phila., Pa.; d. Henry and Mary Susan (Chase) McMurtrie; student Germantown Friends Sch. 1891-1900, Bryn Mawr. Coll., 1900-01; art edn. Pa. Acad. of Fine Arts and European study on Cresson scholarship; unmarried. Professional painter of portraits and landscapes since 1911; teacher of art at Moorstown Friends Acad., Stevens School, Germantown, Pa., Wilmington High Sch. and William Penn High Sch., Phila. Exhibited at Annual Exhibition Pa. Acad. of Fine Arts, Art Alliance, Art Club, Fellowship of Acad. of Fine Arts, Plastic Club, Germantown Art League (Phila.); Corcoran Biennial and Art Club (Washington, D.C.); Toledo Art Museum; also Harrisburg, Scranton, Wilkes-Barre, etc. Painting "The Circus" bought by Pa. Acad. Fine Arts for its permanent collection. Awarded Cresson European scholarship by Pa. Acad. Fine Arts; Mary Smith Prize at annual exhibition Pa. Acad., 1929; hon. mention Plastic Club Annual Oil Exhbn., 1939. Mem. Fellowship Acad. of Fine Arts (mem. bd. mgrs., 1936-37). Plastic Club (pres. since 1936), Phila. Teachers Assn., Phila. Art Teachers Assn. Republican. Episcopalian. Home: 5302 Knox St. Studio: 1714 Chestnut St., Philadelphia, Pa.

McNAIR, Harold Vane, lawyer; b. Middletown, Pa., June 13, 1893; s. Alvan and Ella F. (Melhorn) McN.; student Middletown (Pa.) High Sch., 1907-10; A.B., Gettysburg (Pa.) Coll., 1913; LL.B., LaSalle Coll.; unmarried. In practice of law at Harrisburg; formerly with R. W. Hunt & Co., cons. engrs. Councilman, Middletown, Pa.; burgess, Middletown, Pa. (third term); borough solicitor, Highspire and Royalton, Pa. Chmn. Middletown (Pa.) Welfare Com. Mem. Pa. State Bar Assn., Dauphin Co. Bar Assn., Am. Legion, Phi Gamma Delta. Democrat. Methodist. Elk. Author: Sesquicentennial Ode; Pittsburgh; also mag. and newspaper articles. Home: 8 N. Union St., Middletown, Pa. Office: 103 Market St., Harrisburg, Pa.

McNAIR, William N., ex-mayor; b. Middletown, Pa., Oct. 5, 1880; s. Alvin and Maria (Swartz) McN.; A.B., Gettysburg Coll., 1900, A.M., 1905; LL.B., U. of Mich., 1903; m. Helen Seip, Apr. 14, 1914; children—Helen, Betty. Admitted to Pa. bar, 1904; in practice at Pittsburgh; formerly mayor of Pittsburgh. Dir. Ingram Inst. of Economics, San Diego, Calif., 1930-31. Mem. Phi Gamma Delta. Democrat. Episcopalian. Odd Fellow. Wrote Pittsburgh Tax Plan, 1916. Home: 1212 Sheridan Av. Office: 725 Bakewell Bldg., Pittsburgh, Pa.

McNALL, James Morgan, physician; b. North Star, Pa., Sept. 26, 1865; s. James H. and Frances Ann (Morgan) McN.; M.D., Jefferson Med. Coll., 1890; m. Lou Emma Irvin, Aug. 29, 1895. Mem. Pittsburgh Free Dispensary, 1892-95; in charge Pa. Tuberculosis Clinic, Wilkinsburg, Pa., 1910-17; asso. with World War Vets. hosps., 1921-35, clin. dir. 1924-35; chief Hill Crest Sanitorium since 1935. Served as maj. Med. Corps, U.S.A., 1917-20, in charge Tuberculosis Examining Bd. Mem. City Council Wilkinsburg, Pa., 1905-16. Mem. Allegheny Co. Med. Soc., Pa. Med. Soc., A.M.A. Republican. Mason, Elk. Home: Hill Crest San., Woodville, Pa.

McNALLY, Thomas Francis, clergyman; b. Phila., Pa., May 9, 1887; s. Patrick J. and Sarah A. (Kelly) McN.; ed. LaSalle Coll., Phila., 1900-03, Sem. of St. Charles Borromeo, Overbrook, Pa., 1906-14; (hon.) A.M., LaSalle Coll., 1928; (hon.) LL.D., LaSalle Coll., 1938. Ordained to ministry R.C. Ch. priest, 1914; financial sec. Archdiocese of Phila., 1914-29; Diocesan Master of Ceremonies, 1918-29; rector Immaculate Conception Ch., Jenkintown, Pa., since 1929. Dir. Cath. Children's Bur., Phila., St. Mary's Inst. for the Blind, Lansdale, Pa. Elevated to the rank of Domestic Prelate to His Holiness, the Pope, 1922. Roman Catholic. K.C. Club: Huntindon Valley Country (Abington). Author: Doctrinal Sermons for Children (2 vols.), 1937 and 1938. Home: 604 West Av., Jenkintown, Pa.

McNAMARA, Edward Paul, supervisor ceramics extension; b. Troy, N.Y., Sept. 27, 1910; s. John Vincent and Josephine (McChristian) McN.; ed. Rensselaer Poly. Inst., 1929-31; B.S., Alfred U., 1935; M.S., Pa. State Coll., 1936; m. Alma May Falle, Apr. 18, 1933; children—Imelda Anne, Edward Paul, Jr., John Vincent. Engaged as part-time research worker, Glass Lab., Alfred U., 1934-35; research asst., dept. ceramics, Pa. State Coll., 1935-36, supervisor ceramics extension, Div. Mineral Industries Extension since 1936. Mem. Am. Ceramic Soc., Inst. Ceramic Engrs., Sigma Xi, Keramos, Phi Lambda Upsilon. Author: Ceramics—General Preparatory, Vol. I, 1937; Ceramics—Raw Materials, Vol. II, 1938; Ceramics—Clay Products and Whiteware, Vol. III, 1939. Contbr. papers on glass to tech. journs. Home: 515 E. Beaver St., State College, Pa.

McNARY, Carl Whittier, high school prin.; b. Steubenville, O., Aug. 6, 1887; s. Joseph Cloakey and Nancy (McLaughlin) McN.; grad. Steubenville (O.) High Sch., 1906; A.B., Westminster Coll., New Wilmington, Pa., 1910; student Duquesne U. Law Sch., Pittsburgh, 1915-18; M.Ed., U. of Pittsburgh, 1938; m. Marion Gaston Lytle, March 31, 1917 (deceased May 3, 1926); 1 son, Warren Lytle; m. 2d, Natalie Johnson, Aug. 24, 1929. Prin. Derry (Pa.) High Sch., 1910-11; teacher, La Trobe (Pa.) High Sch., 1911-12, Crafton (Pa.) High Sch., 1912-15, Latimer High Sch., Pittsburg, 1915-19; prin., East High Sch., Erie, Pa., 1919-21; prin. Academy High Sch., Erie, Pa., since 1921; admitted to Pa. bar, 1919. Mem. N.E.A., Am. Assn. of Sch. Adminstrs., Pa. Edn. Assn. Mason. Presbyterian. Home: 3215 Erie St. Office: Academy High School, Erie, Pa.

McNASH, John Harrison; pres. Hazel-Atlas Glass Co. Office: 15th and Jacob Sts., Wheeling, W.Va.

McNAUGHER, John, theologian; b. Allegheny, Pa., Dec. 30, 1857; s. Joseph and Jessie (White) M.; A.B., Westminster Coll., 1880; grad. Xenia (O.) Theol. Sem., 1884; postgrad. course Edinburgh, Scotland, D.D., Westminster, 1889; LL.D., Monmouth, 1906; Litt. D., Muskingum Coll., New Concord, O., 1937; LL.D., U. of Pittsburgh, 1938; m. Ella M. Wilson, Apr. 26, 1888. Ordained U.P. ministry, 1885; pastor Fredericksburg, O., 1885-86; professor N.T. lit. and exegesis, Pittsburgh Theol. Sem., since 1887, and pres. of faculty since 1909. Mem. Bd. of Pub., since 1898; mem. Presbyn. Alliance Commn. since 1896; del. Pan-Presbyn. Council, Liverpool, 1904, New York, 1909, Pittsburgh, 1921, Cardiff, 1925, Boston, 1929, Belfast, 1933, Montreal, 1937. Pres. Alliance of Reformed Churches Throughout World Holding the Presbyterian System, 1921-1925; chairman Committee on Confessional Statement, 1919-23; moderator General Assembly United Presbyterian Ch., 1929-1930. Author: United Presbyterian Church—Its History and Mission, 1899; The History of Theological Education in the United Presbyterian Church and Its Ancestries, 1931; (brochures) The Virgin Birth; Authorship of Hebrews; The Resurrection of Jesus; also contbr. to the religious press. Editor: The Psalms in Worship; Bible Songs, 1901; Psalter Hymns, 1911; The Psalter of the United Presbyterian Church (new version), 1912; Bible Songs, No. 4, 1917; Evangelistic Songs, No. 2, 1919; Children's Praise, No. 2, 1921; The Psalter Hymnal, 1927; Bible Songs Hymnal, 1927. Home: 321 Lafayette Av., Pittsburgh, Pa.

McNAUGHER, William Harper, judge; b. Pittsburgh, Pa., Mar. 13, 1891; s. John and Ella Mae (Wilson) McN.; A.B., Westminster Coll., New Wilmington, Pa., 1912; LL.B., U. of Pittsburgh, 1917; m. Jean Hamilton, Oct. 11, 1930. Admitted to Pa. bar, 1917; asst. dist. atty., Allegheny County, 1919-21; mem. of law firm Alter, Wright & Barron, Pittsburgh, 1921-25, 1926-30; spl. counsel for U.S. govt., Pittsburgh, 1925-26; judge, Ct. of Common Pleas, Allegheny Co., Pa., since 1930. Served as 1st lt. 320th F.A., 82d Div., A.E.F., during World War. Mem. bd. Fed. of Social Agencies, Salvation Army, Boy Scouts of America, Y.M.C.A. Mem. Am. Legion (Observatory Post 81; county comdr. 1923-24), Vets. of Fgn. Wars (Atwood Post). Republican. Protestant. Clubs: Duquesne, University (Pittsburgh). Home: Alder Ct. Apts. Office: City-County Bldg., Pittsburgh, Pa.

McNAUGHTON, Edna Belle, prof. home economics edn., U. of Md. Address: University of Md., College Park, Md.

McNAUGHTON, John, lawyer; b. New York, N.Y., June 27, 1885; s. John and Annie (O'Grady) McN.; grad. Troy (N.Y.) High Sch., 1904; LL.B., New York U., 1924; m. Grace Babcock, June 1, 1916; children—Grace Babcock, Margaret, Mary Jane, John William. With Erie R.R., 1904-25, as brakeman, conductor, trainmaster; admitted to N.J. bar, 1925, and since practiced in Pompton Lakes, N.J.; borough atty. since 1933. Assemblyman from Passaic County, N.J. State Legislature, 1935-36; mem. Wanaque, N.J., Bd. of Edn. 9 years; freeholder Passaic County since 1937; recorder Borough of Wanaque. Mem. N.J. Bar Assn., Pompton Lakes Chamber of Commerce, Passaic County Hist. Soc., Delta Chi. Episcopalian. Mason, Jr. Order of United Am. Mechanics. Club: Butler (N.J.) Rotary. Home: Meadowbrook Av., Wanaque, N.J. Office: 314 Wanaque Av., Pompton Lakes, N.J.

McNAUL, James Franklin, lawyer; b. Currensville, Pa., Sept. 9, 1862; s. Robert Way and Melessa Laurie (Wilson) McN.; student Williamsport Coll., 1883-84; m. Anna Janet Morrow, June 22, 1898; children—James Franklin, Anna Janet (Mrs. Geo. M. Leathem), Morrow. Admitted to bar, 1889; since in private practice, specializing in corpn. law; dir. Harve Coal Co. Republican. Presbyterian. Mason. Home: 749 N. Highland Av. Office: Union Trust Bldg., Pittsburgh, Pa.

McNEER, Selden Spessard, lawyer; b. Monroe Co., W.Va., Mar. 31, 1894; s. Edwin Selden and Nora (Spessard) McN.; student Hampden-Sydney Coll., Hampden-Sydney, Va., 1911-14; LL.B., Washington and Lee U. Law Sch., Lexington, Va., 1916; m. Jean Alexander Gregory, Dec. 27, 1919; children—Jean Gregory (Mrs. James Theodore Hundley), Selden Spessard, Jr., Anne Alexander, Richard Gregory. Admitted to Va. bar, 1916 and engaged in practice of law at Covington, 1916-17; admitted to W.Va. bar, 1919 and since engaged in gen. practice of law at Huntington; mem. firm Campbell & McNeer since 1935; dir. Fesenmeier Brewing Co., Huntington, W.Va. since 1933. Enlisted as private Base Hosp. 41, University, Va.; commd. 2nd lt. Inf., disch. 1919. Mem.

McNEIL, Am., W.Va. State and Cabell Co. (pres.) bar assns., Kappa Alpha, Phi Delta Phi, S.A.R. Independent Democrat. Episcopalian. Club: Guyan Country. Home: 535 13th Av. Office: First Huntington Nat. Bank Bldg., Huntington, W.Va.

McNEIL, Sister Marie Gertrude, prof. mathematics; b. Geneseo, N.Y., Jan. 3, 1893; d. Frank J. and Margaret (Rowan) McN.; A.B., Seton Hill Coll., 1922; grad. study, Notre Dame U., summers 1923-27, M.S., 1927; grad. study, Columbia U., summers 1930-37, regular attendance, 1937-38. Teacher, St. Joseph Acad., Greensburg, Pa., 1921-22; associate prof. of mathematics Seton Hill Coll., Greensburg, Pa., 1922-26, asst. prof., 1926-28, prof. of math. since 1928; absent on leave at Columbia U., 1937-38. Mem. Math. Assn. America, Am. Math. Soc. Republican. Roman Catholic. Home: Seton Hill College, Greensburg, Pa.

McNEIL, Marshall, corr.; b. San Antonio, Tex., Mar. 29, 1900; s. Clarence W. and P. Jane (Taylor) McN.; ed. pub. schs.; m. Blanche Venable, May 2, 1925; 1 son, Neil Venable. Engaged in newspaper work in San Antonio, Beaumont and Houston, Tex., until 1929, then at Pensacola and Jacksonville, Fla.; city editor Houston Press, 1926-29; mng. editor Jacksonville Journal, 1929-30; corr. for and mng. editor Scripps-Howard Newspaper Alliance, Washington, D.C., 1930-34, and 'corr. since 1937; editor Knoxville (Tenn.) News-Sentinel, 1934-37. Episcopalian. Home: Hillandale, Silver Spring, Md. Office: Scripps-Howard Newspaper Alliance, 1013 13th St. N.W., Washington, D.C.

McNEIL, Robert Lincoln, pharmaceutical mfr.; b. Phila., Pa., May 4, 1883; s. Robert and Mary Hubbard (Urwiler) McN.; B.S. in economics, U. of Pa., 1904; m. Grace Fannie Slack, of Bethel, Conn., Oct. 2, 1914; children—Robert Lincoln, Henry Slack. Began bus. career in father's drug store; formed partnership with father, 1908; established mfg. laboratory, 1914, and became exec. partner; father retired, 1925, when retail div. was discontinued; incorporated as McNeil Labs., 1933, and since pres. One of founders Kensington (Phila.) Bd. of Trade (dir. since 1908, pres. 1916-18); vice-chmn. Kensington Dist. Liberty Loan and War Chest Campaigns, 1916-18; v.p. Law Enforcement League, 1922-24; an organizer of Pharm. Contact Com. (to cooperate with U.S. Dept. of Agr. for establishing standards of nonofficial preparations), co-chmn., 1924-27. Mem. Am. Pharm. Mfrs. Assn. (dir. since 1919, pres. 1927-29, chmn. bd. directors 1929-36), Am. Drug Mfrs. Assn. (dir. 1929-36, treas. since 1936), Am. Pharm. Assn., Kappa Sigma; hon. mem. Vet. Guard of Nat. Guard of Pa. Presbyterian (elder First Ch., Germantown). Mason. Clubs: Union League, Presbyterian Social Union, Skytop (Phila.); Lake Placid. Home: "Overlcok," Chestnut Hill, Pa. Office: 2900 N. 17th St., Philadelphia, Pa.

McNETT, William Brown, painter, illustrator; b. Omaha, Neb., Nov. 8, 1896; s. Frank and Emily Wright (Brown) McN.; grad. Omaha High Sch., 1912; student Johns Hopkins Med. Sch. (dept. of art as applied to medicine), Baltimore, Md., 1920-23; m. Elizabeth Vardell, Dec. 30, 1924; children—Elizabeth Vardell, William Brown (dec.), Mary Linda. Commercial artist, portrait painter and illustrator since 1913, specializing in illustrating medical books; dir. dept. of med. art, Temple Med. Sch., since 1932. Portraits: Col. William J. Martin, former pres., for Davidson (N.C.) Coll.; Dr. Charles G. Vardell, pres. emeritus, for Flora Macdonald Coll., Red Springs, N.C. Represented in William Shoemaker Jr. High Sch., Phila., and many private collections. Med. works illustrated: Textbook of Surgery, by W. W. Babcock, 1924-28, 2d edit., 1932; Obstetrics, by P. B. Bland, 1927-28; Thyroid Gland, by E. P. Sloan, 1928-29; Surgery, by F. E. Stewart and W. E. Lee, 1930; Cleft Palate by G.M. Dorrance, 1931; Surgery, by Warren Bickham and Calvin Smyth, Jr., 1932; Endocrinology, by C. Mazor Goldstein, 1933; Proctology, by H. E. Bacon, 1932-38; Urology, by L. C. Herman, 1928-38; Hematology by Pepper-Farley, 1933; Allergy by Tufts, 1936; chapters in Nelson's Surgery, Lewis' Surgery, Encyclopedia of Medicine, Curtis Gynecology; illustrator of "Bodyscome," by Segal, New York. Served in U.S. Army, with A.E.F., 1917-19. Ind. Democrat. Presbyterian. Clubs: Graphic Sketch, Fellowship, Artists Union of Phila. (past vice-pres.), Art Alliance of Phila. Home: 128 Woodside Av., Narberth, Pa.

McNICOL, Donald Monroe, elec. engr., editor, writer; b. Hopetown, Ont., July 23, 1875; s. William and Harriet (Dunsheath) McN.; came to U.S., 1900, naturalized, 1917; ed. pub. schs., Canada; m. Helen Bauman, 1900. Employed as telegrapher with western r.r.s, 1891-1906; elec. engr., Postal Telegraph Co., New York, N.Y., 1909-18; editor Telegraph and Telephone Age mag., New York, N.Y., 1918-22; asst. to pres., Radio Corpn. of America, New York, N.Y., 1922-24; editorial dir., Radio Engineering mag., 1924-34; engaged in writing since 1934. Served in spl. engring. for Signal Corps, U.S.A., 1917-18. Mayor of Roselle Park, N.J., 1929-32. Pres. Inst. Radio Engrs., 1926. Republican. Presbyn. In addition to regular work acted as instr. Teachers Coll. of Columbia U., 1911-12, lecturer, Sheffield Sci. Sch. of Yale Univ. and at Cooper Union, N.Y., 1912, 1916. Wrote first Am. book having title Radio Telegraphy, 1906. Author: American Telegraph Practice, 1913; Telegraphie en Amerique (Paris), 1916; Morse and Printing Telegraphy, 1918; The Engineering Rise in Radio, 1928; A Chronological History of Electric Communication, 1929; The Amerindians, 1937. Home: 132 Union Rd., Roselle Park, N.J.

McNUTT, George D., pres. First Nat. Bank, Canonsburg; b. Chartiers Twp., Washington Co., Pa., Dec. 12, 1862; s. William A. and Nancy (Weaver) McN.; student Duff's Coll., Pittsburgh, Pa.; m. Alice R. Fife, 1890; children—Nancy Olive, John W., Mary Adams. Bookkeeper Canonsburg (Pa.) Bank, Ltd., 1885-90; cashier, 1890-91; became cashier First Nat. Bank, Canonsburg, Pa., 1891, dir. since 1891, pres. since 1919; treas. and dir. Canonsburg Steel & Iron Works, 1904-18; dir. Cecil Improvement Co. since 1902, pres. since 1919; dir. Chartiers Bldg. & Loan Assn. Dir. Canonsburg Sch. Bd., 1895-1901, treas. since 1920; dir. and treas. Canonsburg Gen. Hosp. since 1916. Mem. session 1st Presbyn. Ch. since 1908. Presbyterian. Club: Washington County Golf (Canonsburg, Pa.). Home: 224 W. Pike St. Office: Pike and Central Av., Canonsburg, Pa.

McNUTT, William Roy, clergyman; b. nr. Amsterdam, Bates Co., Mo., April 6, 1879; s. Andrew and Adrienne (Pahud) McN.; A.B., Ottawa (Kan.) U., 1908, D.D., 1923; A.M., U. of Pa., 1909; B.D., Crozer Theol. Sem., Chester, Pa., 1912; m. Minnie E. Willard Turner, June 27, 1911; 1 dau., Frances Athena. Teacher in Mo. pub. schs., 1899-1902; student pastor in Kan., 1902-08; ordained Baptist ministry, 1912; minister Angora Ch., Phila., 1909-12, Prospect Hill Ch., Prospect Park, Pa., 1912-16, First Ch., Worcester, Mass., 1916-28; prof. practical theology, Crozer Theol. Sem., since 1928. Acting pastor Am. Ch., Munich, part of 1935-36. Y.M.C.A. divisional sec., Blois, France, 1918. Trustee Worcester (Mass.) Poly. Inst., 1919-28; mem. bd. dirs., Mass. Bapt. Conv., 1917-23, Northern Bapt. Edn. Soc., 1920-28. Winner Kan. State Oratorical Contest, 1907, represented Kan. in interstate contest; awarded gold P by U. of Pa., 1911, as mem. winning team in Pa.-Princeton-Columbia triangular annual debate. Mem. Delta Sigma Rho. Baptist. Kiwanian. Author: Polity and Practice in Baptist Churches, 1935. Editor of the Bulletin of Crozer Theol. Sem. Home: Crozer Seminary Campus, Chester Pa.; (summer) Oak Bluffs, Martha's Vineyard, Mass.

McRAE, George Wadsworth, pub. utility exec.; b. Malden, Mass., Oct. 5, 1888; s. Colin and Ella (Rankin) McR.; B.S., Mass. Inst. Tech., 1910; m. Harriet E. Bruning, Sept. 24, 1912; 1 son, Colin. Employed as telephone engr. with Am. Telephone & Telegraph Co., 1910-22, chief engr., Ill. Bell Telephone Co., Chicago, 1922-23, N.Y. Telephone Co., 1924-25, gen. mgr., 1925-27; vice-pres. and gen. mgr. N.J. Bell Telephone Co., Newark, N.J., since 1927; dir. Nat. Newark & Essex Banking Co. Trustee Newark Coll. of Engring. Mem. Am. Inst. Elec. Engrs. Clubs: Essex, Downtown, Athletic (Newark); Essex County Country (West Orange). Home: 451 Walton Rd., Maplewood, N.J. Office: 540 Broad St., Newark, N.J.

McREYNOLDS, Frederick Wilson, lawyer; b. Delphi, Ind., Sept. 11, 1872; s. Lafayette Emerson and Mary Belle (Wilson) M.; A.B., Dartmouth; LL.B., Columbian (now George Washington) U.; m Jessie Brooks Stabler, October 9, 1894; children—George Brooke (capt. U.S. Army), Catherine (Mrs. Robert Leighton Barnes), Alice Brooke. Admitted to D.C. bar, 1896, and engaged in practice at Washington, 1896-1915; assistant professor of law and finance, Tuck School of Administration and Finance, of Dartmouth Coll., 1915-19; counsel for War Trade Bd. and Com. on Pub. Information, 1917-18; spl. atty. in charge of Internal Revenue litigation, 1919-22; private practice, 1922—. Chmn. Bd. of Pub. Welfare of D.C. Democrat. Episcopalian. Mem. Am. Econ. Assn., Sigma Chi, Soc. of the Cincinnati. Clubs: Chevy Chase, Nat. Press, Lawyers', Cosmos. Home: Ashton, Md. Office: Investment Bldg., Washington, D.C.

McSHANE, John Joseph, Jr., chmn. bd. William G. Johnston Co.; b. Pittsburgh, Pa., Sept. 27, 1881; s. John J. and Susan (Durning) McS.; ed. St. Paul's Parochial Sch. and Pittsburgh High Sch.; unmarried. With William G. Johnston Co., printers, lithographers, mfrs. sch. supplies since 1900, beginning as clerk, advanced through various positions, becoming chmn. bd., 1933, dir. of purchases, 1902. Mem. Chamber of Commerce. Republican. K.C., Elk; mem. bd. govs. and dir. North Side Lions. Home: 3109 Landis St. Office: 1130 Ridge Av., Pittsburgh, Pa.

McSHERRY, William Clinton, lawyer; b. Frederick, Md., Jan. 10, 1888; s. James and Clara Louise (McAleer) McS.; prep. edn. public schools of Frederick, Md.; A.B., Mt. St. Mary's, Emmitsburg, Md., 1908; A.M., 1910; LL.B., U. of Md., 1910; m. Mary Natalie McCarthy, April 9, 1913; children—William Clinton, James. Admitted to Md. bar, 1910, and since practiced in Frederick; pres. and counsel Western Md. Trust Co.; pres. and counsel Peoples Liquidating Coprn.; dir. and counsel Woodsboro Savings Bank; chmn. Frederick City Housing Authority; mem. Md. State License Bureau. Mem. Am. Bar Assn., Md. State Bar Assn., Frederick County Bar Assn. (former pres.). Democrat. Roman Catholic. Home: 19 E. 2d St. Office: 21 E. 2d St., Frederick, Md.

McSPADDEN, Joseph Walker, editor; b. Knoxville Tenn., May 13, 1874; s. Walker L. and Margaret J. (Porter) M.; A.B., U. of Tenn., 1897; m. Inez McCrary, Dec. 16, 1902; children—Chester Ford, Florence. Engaged in lit. work as editor since 1898. Mem. Phi Kappa Phi, Tenn. Soc., Phi Gamma Delta. Author: Shakespearan Synopses, 1902; Synopses of Dickens' Novels, 1904; Stories of Robin Hood, 1904; Stories from Wagner, 1905; Stories from Dickens, 1906; Stories from Chaucer, 1907; Famous Painters of America, 1907; Waverly Synopses, 1909; The Land of Nod, 1909; Opera Synopses, revised edit., 1935; Book of Holidays, 1917; Boys' Book of Famous Soldiers, 1919; The Story of George Washington, 1920; Abraham Lincoln, 1921; Theodore Roosevelt, 1923; Stories from Great Operas, 1923; Famous Sculptors of America, 1924; Romantic Stories of the States (12 titles), 1926-29; Indian Heroes, 1928; Pioneer Heroes, 1929; How They Carried the Mail, 1930; To the Ends of the World and Back, 1931; How They Sent the News, 1936; Light Opera and Musical Comedy, 1936; Beautiful Hawaii, 1939; How They Carried the Torch, 1939. Editor: American Statesman's Year Book, 1912, 1913; Mystery Library, 1921; Famous Dogs in Fiction, 1921. Club: National Arts (N.Y. City). Home: Montclair, N.J. Office: 15 Gramercy Park, New York, N.Y.

McSPARRAN, John Aldus, farmer; b. Lancaster County, Pennsylvania, October 22, 1873; s. James G. and Sarah Margaret (Collins) McS.;

McSWEENEY Ph.B., Lafayette Coll., 1893; m. Betty Harrison Goodwin, Dec. 2, 1902; children—Sarah Margaret (Mrs. Sam R. Long), Lucy Isabella (Mrs. George W. Buller), Charles Goodwin, John Collins; m. 3d, Laura McCullough, of Pilottown, Md., Jan. 30, 1926; children—Donald Harry, Gray Fleming. Engaged in farming since 1894; master Pa. State Grange, 1914-24; sec. Pa. State Dept. Agr., 1931-34. Candidate for gov. of Pa., Dem. Party, 1922. Mem. Patrons Husbandry. Democrat. Methodist. Home: Greene, Pa.

McSWEENEY, John Joseph, newspaper editor; b. Hanover Twp., Pa., June 28, 1902; s. Matthew Joseph and Hannah Theresa (Caverly) McS.; student Hanover Twp. (Pa.) pub. schs., 1907-19; m. Regina Chissler, Sept. 13, 1930. Began as newspaper corr., 1916; successively Plymouth rep., city reporter, city editor, mng. editor and editor, The Evening News, Wilkes-Barre, now chief editorial writer Times-Leader Evening News. Formerly pres. Bd. of Edn., Hanover Twp. Mem. Vets. Fgn. Wars (hon.). Democrat. Roman Catholic. K.C. Author: Little Studies. Home: 35 S. Regent St. Office: The Times-Leader Evening News, Wilkes-Barre, Pa.

McSWEENY, James Laurence, clergyman; b. Claremont, N.H., Sept. 17, 1865; s. James and Mary (Lawler) McS.; student pub. schs., Pittsfield, Mass., 1872-79; St. Charles Coll., Ellicott City, Md., 1887-90; A.M., St. Mary's Sem., Baltimore, Md., 1895, S.T.B., 1894. Pastor, Chestertown, Md., 1895-1902, Delaware City, Del., 1902-08, Hockessin, Del., 1908-25, St. Patrick's, Wilmington, Del., since 1925. Moderator Diocesan Conf., Del., 1916-38; official Diocese of Wilmington, Del., since 1916. Address: 1414 King St., Wilmington, Del.

McVAY, Sister Mary Stanislaus, prof. history; b. Jefferson, Pa.; d. Franklin Wallace and Anna Virginia (Bradley) McVay; ed. Duquesne U., 1912-13, Cath. Univ., summers 1913-16, U. of Pittsburgh, 1916-17; A.B., Duquesne U., 1919; grad. study Notre Dame U., summers 1924-27, A.M., same, 1927. Mem. Sisters of Charity of Seton Hill; prof. history, Seton Hill, Greensburg, Pa., since 1919. Mem. Am. Hist. Soc., Nat. Geog. Soc., Pi Gamma Mu. Democrat. Roman Catholic. Home: Seton Hill, Greensburg, Pa.

McVICAR, Nelson, judge; b. Chatham, Ont., Can., Jan. 25, 1871; s. John and Catherine (Grass) McV.; ed. pub. and high schs. of Ontario and U. of Mich.; came with parents to U.S., 1886; m. Bertha A. Woodrow, July 10, 1901; children—John Wayne, Catherine Louise Brendel. Admitted to Pa. bar, 1896, and began practice at Pittsburgh. Mem. Pa. Ho. of Rep., 1914-24; judge Court of Common Pleas of Allegheny Co., Pa., 1925-28; judge U.S. Dist. Court, Western Pa., Dist., since 1928. Republican. Presbyterian. Mason, Odd Fellow. Home: 1127 Park St., Tarentum, Pa. Office: New Federal Bldg., Pittsburgh, Pa.

McWILLIAMS, James Bruce, pres. Railway Maintenance Co.; b. Westmoreland Co., Pa., Sept. 8, 1884; s. John Flemming and Alice Mary (Davis) McW.; grad. Greensburgh (Pa.) High Sch., 1903; B.S., Pa. State Coll., 1907; m. Elizabeth Rumsey, Dec. 24, 1923; children —Jean Rumsey, Robert Bruce. With engring. corps Pa. R.R., 1907-20; works mgr. Hero Mfg. Co., Philadelphia, 1920-23; pres. Detroit (Mich.) Motor Casting Co., 1923-25, Railway Maintenance Corpn., Pittsburgh, since 1925; pres. and dir. Leechgrip Co.; dir. Stevenson & Foster Co., Star Marble & Tile Co., Allegheny Equipment Co. Republican. Episcopalian. Clubs: Duquesne, Oakmont Golf, Pittsburgh Athletic Assn. (Pittsburgh). Home: 5914 Braeburn Road. Address: P.O. Box 1888, Pittsburgh, Pa.

McWILLIAMS, William J.; mem. law firm McWilliams & Duckett. Address: Annapolis, Md.

MEAD, Douglass Sargeant, prof. English literature; b. Greenwich, Conn., Feb. 17, 1895; s. Ezekiel Close and Jennie (Bahr) M.; A.B., Dickinson Coll., 1917; A.M., Teachers Coll. of Columbia U., 1920; A.M., Princeton U., 1924, Ph.D., same, 1927; m. Mary Anna Bagenstose, Aug. 22, 1924; children—Douglass Sargeant, Jr., Marjorie Louise. Engaged as instr. English, Lafayette Coll., 1919-20; instr. English, Pa. State Coll., 1920-25, asst. prof., 1925-28, asso. prof., 1928-29, prof. English literature since 1929. Served in U.S.N. Res., 1918. Mem. Modern Lang. Assn., Shakespearean Assn., Am. Assn. Univ. Profs., Kappa Sigma. Republican. Presbyn. Home: 617 Sunset Rd., State College, Pa.

MEAD, Edward Sherwood, educator; b. Medina, O., Jan. 25, 1874; s. Giles F. and Martha A. M.; A.B., DePauw U., 1896; fellow U. of Chicago, 1896-98, U. of Pa., 1898-1901 (Ph.D., 1899); m. Emily Fogg, June 1, 1900; children—Margaret, Richard Ramsay, Katherine (dec.), Elizabeth, Priscilla. Instr. in commerce and industry, 1900-04, asst. prof. finance, 1904-07, prof., 1907—, chmn. Extension Sch. Com., 1913-14, Wharton Sch. of Finance and Commerce, U. of Pa. Dir. Evening Sch. of Accounts and Finance, 1904-13. Served as govt. rep. under NRA. Mem. Am. Econ. Assn., Am. Acad. Polit. and Social Science, Phi Beta Kappa, Delta Upsilon, Beta Gamma Sigma. Clubs: University (Phila.); University of Pa. (New York). Author: Trust Finance, 1903; Story of Gold, 1908; Corporation Finance, 1910. 7th edit., 1933; The Careful Investor, 1914; Harvey Baum—a Study of the Agricultural Revolution (with Bernhard Ostrolenk), 1928; Voluntary Allotment (with same), 1933. Contributor to economic journals and to reviews on gold and silver production, railroads, coal supply, the organization of trusts, and other topics in finance, commerce and industry. Home: 4107 Pine St., Philadelphia, Pa.

MEAD, Frank Spencer, author; b. Chatham, N.J., Jan. 15, 1898; s. Frank and Lillie (Spencer) M.; A.B., U. of Denver, 1922; student Episcopal Theol. Sem. of Va., 1922-23; B.D., Union Theol. Sem., 1927; m. Judy Duryee, Oct. 24, 1928; children—Donald Duryee, Judy Spencer. Sec. 23d Street Y.M.C.A., N.Y. City, 1923-24; asst. pastor Reformed Ch., Harlem, N.Y., 1925-27; pastor Grace M.E. Ch., Newark, N.J., 1927-31; Kearny (N.J.) Ch., 1931-34; editor Homiletic Rev., 1934; editorial staff Christian Herald. Served in U.S. Army, 1917-18. Mem. Beta Theta Pi. Author: The March of Eleven Men, 1932; 250 Bible Biographies, 1934; See These Banners Go, 1935; The Ten Decisive Battles of Christianity, 1937; Right Here at Home, 1939. Home: 45 Hillside Av., Chatham, N.J. Office: 419 4th Av., New York, N.Y.

MEAD, Gilbert Wilcox, educator; b. Pittsburgh, Pa., May 7, 1889; s. Rev. Wesley Gilbert (Ph.D.) and Carolyn Switzer (Wilcox) M.; diploma Southwestern Pa. Normal Sch., 1905; B.A., Allegheny College, 1911, Litt.D., same college, 1934; M.A., Columbia University, 1916; studied same university, 1916-18; LL.D., Birmingham-Southern Coll., 1933; traveled and studied in Eng. and France; m. Iva Madeline Clark, Aug. 18, 1914; children—John Clark, Gilbert Wilcox, Francis Hudson, Robert Wesley (dec.). Teacher county sch., Allegheny Co., Pa., 1905-07; prin. and supervisor schs., Bergenfield, N.J., 1911-15; English master Buckley Sch., New York, 1915-17; instr. in English and comparative lit., Columbia, 1917-23; spl. lecturer Hunter Coll., 1917-23; head Dept. of English, Westminster Coll., Pa., 1923-25; dean Birmingham-Southern Coll., 1925-33; pres. Washington Coll., Chestertown, Md., 1933—. Pres. Dixie Intercollegiate Athletic Con., 1930-32; mem. Md. State Library Commn., Maryland Commn. on State Mental Institutions, Chesapeake Biol. Lab. (exec. com.); chmn. district council Boy Scouts of America. Mem. Modern Language Assn. America (sec. English Victorian sect.), Southern Conf. Liberal Arts Coll. Deans sec. 1930-33), Ala. Colls. Assn. (pres.), Am. Folk-Lore Soc., Southern Intercollegiate Athletic Assn. (v.p.), Ednl. Assn. M.E. Ch., S. (v.p.), Modern Humanities Research Assn. (London), Phi Beta Kappa, Phi Gamma Delta, Tau Kappa Alpha, Omicron Delta Kappa, Sigma Upsilon, Kappa Phi Kappa (nat. pres. 1937-39). Mem. M.E. Ch., S. Clubs: Rotary, Chester Yacht and Country; University (Baltimore); Contbr. literary and critical articles. Lit. editor Birmingham News-Age Herald, 1928-33. Home: Chestertown, Md.

MEADE, DeVoe; prof. animal and dairy husbandry, U. of Md. Address: University of Maryland, College Park, Md.

MEADE, Richard Hardaway, Jr., M.D.; b. Richmond, Va., May 10, 1897; s. Richard Hardaway and Nellie Prior (Atkins) M.; student Richmond Acad., 1906-13, Va. Mil. Inst., 1913-14; Richmond Coll., 1914-15; B.S., U. of Va., 1917; M.D., Harvard U., 1921; m. Mary Frazier, June 14, 1924; children—Richard Hardaway, III, Charles Harrison Frazier, James Gardiner, David Everard. Fellow Trudeau Sanatorium, 1921; interne Willard Parker Hosp., N.Y. City, 1921-22, Presbyn. Hosp., N.Y. City, 1922-23; med. missionary in China, 1924-27; asst. prof. surgery and gynecology, U. of Va., 1927-31; asso. in surgery, U. of Pa., since 1931; asso. surgeon Episcopal Hosp., Phila.; asst. surgeon University Hosp., Phila. Gen. Hosp.; consulting surgeon Home for Consumptives. Fellow Am. Coll. Surgeons; mem. Am. Assn. Thoracic Surgery, Physiol. Soc. of Phila., Laennec Soc., A.M.A., Pa. Med. Soc., Phila. Co. Med. Soc., Southern Soc. Clin. Surgeons, Delta Psi. Democrat. Episcopalian. Home: Harts Lane, Miquon, Pa. Office: 2116 Pine St., Philadelphia, Pa.

MEADER, Stephen Warren, author; b. Providence, R.I., May 2, 1892; s. Walter Sidney and Lucy Jones (Hawkes) M.; A.B., Haverford (Pa.) Coll., 1913; m. Elizabeth White Hoyt, Dec. 16, 1916; children—Stephen Warren, Jane Annesley, John Hoyt, Margaret Lucy. Case worker, Newark, N.J., 1913-14; sec. Essex Co. Big Brother Movement, Newark, 1915; publicity dept. Reilly & Britton, Chicago, 1916; editorial work Curtis Pub. Co., Phila., 1916-21; advertising writer Holmes Press, Phila., 1921-27; copy writer N. W. Ayer & Son, Phila., since 1927. Trustee Moorestown Free Library Assn., Moorestown Friends Sch. Republican. Mem. Soc. of Friends. Author: The Black Buccaneer, 1920; Down the Big River, 1924; Longshanks, 1928; Red Horse Hill, 1930; Away to Sea, 1931; King of the Hills, 1933; Lumberjack, 1934; The Will to Win, 1936; Trap Lines North, 1936; Who Rides in the Dark, 1937; T. Model Tommy, 1938; Bat: The Story of a Bull Terrier, 1939; Boy with a Pack, 1939. Contbr. juvenile fiction to boy's mags. Home: 17 Colonial Av., Moorestown, N.J. Office: N. W. Ayer & Son, Inc., Philadelphia, Pa.

MEADOR, Palma Groves, lawyer; b. Athens, W.Va., Oct. 22, 1905; s. William Henry and Rosa (Pennington) M.; grad. Beckley (W.Va.) High Sch., 1922; LL.B., W.Va. U., 1928; m. Phoebe Lemen, Apr. 15, 1927; 1 son, John Granville. Admitted to bar, 1928; practiced at Charleston since 1928; asst. city solicitor since 1935; v.p. and treas. Patton & Meador, Inc., Bowers & Meador, Inc., Smith & Meador, Inc. Mem. exec. com. W.Va. Young Republican League since 1935; vice chmn. Kanawha County Rep. Exec. Com.; chmn. Charleston City Rep. Exec. Com. Mem. Charleston Chamber Commerce, West Side Business Men's Assn., Am. Soc. Planning Officials. Pres. W.Va. State Moose Assn., 1938-39, W.Va. League of Municipalities, 1938-39, Southern W.Va. Sigma Phi Epsilon Alumni Assn. since 1937; mem. W.Va. Bar Assn. Presbyn. Moose, Elk, K.P., Jr. Order United Am. Mechanics. Clubs: Lincoln, Union League, Lake Chaweva (Charleston). Home: 4 Grandview Drive. Office: 623 Peoples Bank Bldg., Charleston, W.Va.

MEADOWS, Clarence Watson, lawyer; b. Beckley, W.Va., Feb. 11, 1904; s. Isadore and Ida (Williams) M.; grad. Beckley (W.Va.) High Sch., 1920, Ga. Mil. Acad., College Park, Ga., 1921; student Washington and Lee U. Lexington, Va., 1921-25; LL.B., U. of Ala., Tuscaloosa, Ala., 1927; m. Nancy Massie, Apr. 27, 1935; 1 dau., Helen Watson. Admitted to Ala. bar, 1927, W.Va. bar, 1929; practiced at Beckley, W.Va., 1929-37; mem. W.Va. State Legislature, 1931-32; prosecuting atty., Raleigh County, W.Va., 1933-36; atty. gen. of W.Va., Charleston, since 1937. Served in W.Va. N.G.,

MEANOR 1922-25. Trustee Alderson-Broaddus Coll.; Phillipi, W.Va. Mem. Am. Bar Assn., W.Va. Bar Assn., Am. Judicature Soc., Pi Kappa Alpha. Democrat. Baptist. Elk, Moose. Club: Edgewood Country (Charleston, W.Va.). Home: Beckley, W.Va. Office: State Capitol, Charleston, W.Va.

MEANOR, Harold H(enderson), physician and surgeon; b. Pittsburgh, Pa., Jan. 14, 1884; s. David C. and Elizabeth (Henderson) M.; M.D., U. of Pittsburgh, Med. Sch., 1906; m. Mary Margaret Baker, June 22, 1909; children—Harold H., Eleanor Holmes, Margaret Elizabeth. Engaged in gen. practice of medicine at Coraopolis, Pa. since 1907, specializing in surgery since 1930; res. phys. Allegheny Gen. Hosp., Pittsburgh, 1906-07; mem. staff, Valley Hosp., Sewickley since 1910; dir. Coraopolis Trust Co. Fellow Am. Coll. Surgs., Am. Med. Assn., Radiol. Soc. of N.A. Mem. Pa. and Allegheny Co. med. socs. Mem. Commn. for Examining Soldiers during World War. Republican. Presbyterian. Mason (32°, Shriner); Clubs: University (Pittsburgh); Edgeworth (Sewickley); Montour Country (Coraopolis Heights). Home: 1226 State St., Coraopolis, Pa.

MECHLING, Benjamin Franklin, pres. Atlantic Elevator Co.; b. Phila., Pa., Dec. 17, 1883; s. Benjamin Franklin and Grace (Hubbs) M. student Germantown (Pa.) Acad., Cornell U.; m. Ethel Love; children—Mary Ann W., Dorothy (Mrs. Dodge). Exec. v.p. Nice Ball Bearing Co.; dir. Nat. Bank of Germantown and Trust Co., Andorra Nurseries. Mem. Pa. Soc. of Sons of Revolution, Phila. Soc. for Promoting Agr. Clubs: Automobile (dir.), Union League, Rotary (Phila.); Huntington Valley Hunt. Home: Orchard Lane Farm, Flourtown, Pa. Office: Erie Av. and "D" St., Philadelphia, Pa.

MECLUSKEY, John Franklin, physician; b. Phila., Pa., Oct. 18, 1876; s. Frank and Katherine (Herd) M.; student Medico-Chirurgical Coll. (Phila.) and Md. Med. Sch.; m. Eva Barbara Miller, June 5, 1914; children—Elaine, Eva Virginia. Became surgeon North West Hosp., Phila., 1911; mem. staff St. Agnes and Episcopal Hosps. since 1924, Women's Homeopathic Hosp., Phila., since 1930. Mem. Phila. Co. Med. Assn., Pa. State Med. Assn., A.M.A. Mason (K.T., Shriner). Clubs: Physicians Motor, Philadelphia Medical (Phila.). Address: 2622 N. 17th St., Philadelphia, Pa.

MEDER, Albert Eugene, Jr., coll. prof.; b. New York, N.Y., Mar. 19, 1903; s. Albert Eugene and Anna Marie (Sommer) M.; A.B., Columbia U., 1922, A.M., same 1924; unmarried. Asst. in mathematics, Columbia U., 1922-24, instr., 1924-26; instr. mathematics, N.J. Coll. for Women, New Brunswick, N.J., 1926-29, asst. prof., 1929-33, asso. prof. mathematics since 1933, asst. to dean of Coll., 1929-32, actg. dean, 1932-34, chmn. Com. on Admission since 1934. Fellow A.A.A.S.; mem. Am. Math. Soc., Math. Assn. America, Assn. for Symbolic Logic, Nat. Council Teachers of Mathematics, Assn. Mathematics Teachers of N.J. (pres. 1935-36), Phi Beta Kappa. Received Rutgers U. Award, Medal, 1934. Republican. Presbyn. Home: 424 St. Mark's Av., Westfield, N.J. Office: N.J. College for Women, New Brunswick, N.J.

MEDFORD, Richard Carl, art museum dir.; b. Jamestown, N.Y., Nov. 13, 1907; s. William and Anna (Hansen) M.; B.A., Johns Hopkins U., 1929, M.A. 1931; studied Md. Inst. of Fine Arts, 1931-32, Harvard U., summer, 1934, U. of Paris, France, 1933 and 38; m. Sara Mish, Dec. 2, 1937. Instr. Annapolis Prep. Sch., Annapolis, Md., 1929-30; lecturer l'Ecole Fontaine, Cannes, France, 1930-31; dir. Washington Co. Mus. of Fine Arts, Hagerstown, Md., since 1932; lecturer Teachers' Coll., Johns Hopkins U., 1935-36, Western Md. Coll., Westminster, Md., 1936-37. Mem. Coll. Art Assn., Am. Inst. for Iranian Art and Archæology. Democrat. Episcopalian. Clubs: Johns Hopkins (Baltimore); Hagerstown Assembly. Editor: Bull. of Washington Co. Mus. of Fine Arts. Contbr. to Parnassus and Am. Mag. of Art. Home: Williamsport. Md. Address: Washington County Mus. of Fine Arts, Hagerstown, Md.

MEDILL, George Lodge, banker; b. Newark, Del., 1878; s. George D. and Philena (Pennock) M.; B.A., Delaware Coll.; m. Mary Dorset Cook; children—Louisa, Daniel K., George C., Mary Augusta. With engring. party, Isthmian Canal Survey, 1901; school teacher, 1902; in various positions Security Trust Co., 1903-19; state bank commr. of Del., 1919-23; v.p. Farmers' Bank of Del., 1923-25; vice-president and later president Delaware Trust Company, 1925-28; national bank examiner, 1928-34; president and director First Nat. Bank of York, Pa., since 1934; director A. B. Farquhar Co. Clubs: Lafayette, Rotary, York Country (York, Pa.). Author: Banking Laws of Delaware, 1920. Home: Wyndham Hills. Office: First National Bank, York, Pa.

MEEK, John Henry, lawyer; b. Louisa, Ky., Sept. 8, 1877; s. Edward and Amy (Kirk) M.; prep. edn., Oakview Acad., Wayne, W.Va.; LL.B., W.Va. U., 1899; m. Charlie Burgess, Nov. 14, 1901; children—John Burgess, Amy Kirk, Howard Ferguson. Admitted to W.Va. bar, 1899, and began practice at Wayne as mem. firm Naper & Meek; pros. atty. Wayne Co., 1902-03; mem. Meek & Renslow, Huntington, W.Va., 1915-20, now Vinson, Thompson, Meek & Scherr; dir. First Huntington Nat. Bank. Mem. Cabell Co. Bar Assn. (pres. 1924-25), Am. and W. Va. bar assns. Republican. Mason. Clubs: Guyandotte, Guyan Country. Home: Huntington, W. Va.

MEDSGER, Oliver Perry, naturalist and educator; b. Jacob's Creek, Pa., Nov. 1, 1870; s. Henry Harrison and Elizabeth (Hough) M.; B.S., Ohio Northern U., Ada, 1898; student Columbia, 1904-05; m. Jennie A. Arnold, Aug. 24, 1905; children—Henry Otis, Thomas Arnold, Oliver Perry. Civil engr. Westmoreland Co., Pa., 1898-99; prin. E. Huntington Twp. Schs., 1899-1900, and 1902-04; teacher sciences, high sch. Salem, O., 1900-01; head science dept. and vice prin., Kearny (N.J.) High Sch., 1904-09; teacher science, Dickinson High Sch., Jersey City, 1909-12; head science dept., Lincoln High Sch., Jersey City, 1912-32, asst. prin., 1932-33; prof. nature edn., in charge visual instrn., Pennsylvania State Coll., 1934-37, now emeritus; writing and lecturing since 1937. Organized and directed nature study in summer camps, 1917-27; naturalist, instructor department nature education, Pa. State Coll., summer sch., 1928-33; nature study courses, Rutgers U., 1929-33. Dir. American Nature Study Society since 1936. Member Kearny Shade Tree Com., 1909-33, pres. since 1920; chmn. biology sect. N.J. State Science Teachers Assn., 1927-29, pres., 1929-31; dir. N.J. Fed. Shade Tree Commns., since 1930, hon. life mem., 1933. Fellow A.A.A.S.; mem. Torrey Botanical Club. Amateur Astronomers' Association N.Y. (vice-pres.), Phi Delta Kappa Fraternity. Republican. Methodist. Author: Nature's Secrets (Vol. 12), 1921; Nature Rambles—Spring (1931)—Summer (1932)—Autumn (1932)—Winter (1932), and awarded John Burroughs medal for same, 1933; Edible Wild Plants. Co-Author: Through Field and Woodland, 1925. Made large collections of plants for Carnegie Mus., Pittsburgh, etc.; assisted in botanical survery, San Jacinto Mtn., Calif., 1901; discovered cassia medsgeri, wild flower named in his honor. Has assembled one of best seed herbaria in U.S. Contbr. nature articles to mags.; lecturer. Address: 9 Columbia Av., Arlington, N.J.

MEEKER, George Herbert, chemist; b. Phillipsburg, N.J., Aug. 13, 1871; s. George Edward and Hannah M. (Kelly) M.; B.S. (chemistry), Lafayette Coll., Pa., 1893, M.S., 1895, Ph.D., 1898; Pharm.D., Medico-Chirurg. Coll., Phila., 1906, D.D.S., 1907; spl. chem. research in Munich, 1909-10; LL.D., Ursinus Coll., Pa., 1905, Lafayette, 1925; Sc.D., Villanova, 1913; m. Annie Uhler Hunt, 1900. Chemist for various cos., 1893-95; prof. physics, chemistry, metallurgy and toxicology, Medico-Chirurg. Coll. Phila., 1897-1916; established 1907, dean Dept. Pharm. Chemistry, same to 1916; prof. chemistry, Sch. of Medicine, since 1916, established, 1918, since dean Grad. Sch. Medicine, U. of Pa., dir. Graduate Hospital, 1924-28. Toxicologist and expert chemical witness in many prominent cases. Franklin Inst. medallist, 1906; inventor of mech., elec. and chem. devices. Fellow A.A.A.S., Am. Inst. Chemists; mem. Am. Chem. Soc., Pa. Med. Soc. (hon.), Franklin Inst., Delta Upsilon, Phi Rho Sigma, Psi Omega. Clubs: Union League, Medical, Æsculapian (hon.). Mason (K.T., Shriner). Home: 4701 Pine St., Phila., Pa.

MEEKS, Benjamin Wiltshire, clergyman; b. Chase, Md., Apr. 2, 1879; s. William Andrew and Mary Anne (Earl) M.; A.B., Johns Hopkins, 1903, grad. student, 1903-04; D.D., St. Johns Coll., Annapolis, Md., 1923; m. Lillian Eva Beall, Mar. 15, 1905; children—Miriam Gertrude (Mrs. Paul T. Frisch), Benjamin Wiltshire, Elinor Virginia (dec.). Ordained to ministry M.E. Ch., 1906; pastor at Epworth Ch., Baltimore, 1902-05, Solomons, 1905-07, Grace-Hampden Ch., Baltimore, 1907-09, Ryland Ch., Washington, D.C., 1909-12, 1st Ch., Martinsburg, W.Va., 1912-16, St. Mark's Ch., Baltimore, 1916-21, Centre St. Ch., Cumberland, Md., 1921-25, Grace Ch., Roland Park, Baltimore (united with Grace Ch., Baltimore, 1928), 1925-30; supt. Washington Dist., 1930-36; pastor Calvary Ch., Frederick, Md., since 1936. Mem. gen. confs., 1924, 32, 36; mem. Uniting Conf., 1939; mem. Book Com., 1932-40; sec. N.Y. corpn. and asst. sec. Ohio corpn., Meth. Book Concern; mem. Bd. Temperance Prohibition and Pub. Morals (exec. com.) since 1931; sec.-treas. Commn. on Conf. Claimants Endowment Fund, Baltimore Annual Conf. since 1928; edited Epworth League page in Baltimore Meth., 1921-26. Mem. Washington Fed. Chs. (dir. and v.p. 1931-35, pres. 1935); dir. Lucy Webb Hayes Nat. Training Sch., Sibley Memorial Hosp., trustee Am. Univ. (mem. exec. com.) since 1931. Republican. Clubs: Rotary of Frederick, Md.; Internat. Soc. of Theta Phi. Home: 131 W. 2d St., Frederick, Md.

MEESE, Alfred Hall, educator; b. New Philadelphia, Ohio, Feb. 1, 1887; s. Patrick and Matilda (Humrighouse) M.; A.B., Berea (Ky.) Coll., 1909; student Harvard, 1910-11; B.S. in Edn., Kent (O.) State Teachers Coll. (now Kent State U.), 1916; M.A., Columbia, 1923; m. Leslie Herron Reece, Aug. 7, 1915; children —James Alfred, Robert Gordon, David Herron. School prin., Lorain, O., 1913-16; supt. schs., Shaker Heights, O., 1916-22; asst. exec. sec. Monmouth County (N.J.) Orgn. for Social Service, 1923-25; head of psychol. dept., Montclair State Teachers Coll., 1925-27; supt. North Jersey Training Sch., Little Falls, N.J., since 1927. Mem. bd. dirs. Y.M.C.A. (Paterson). Mem. Am. Assn. on Mental Deficiency, Am. Assn. Social Workers, Ohio Soc. of New York, Phi Delta Kappa. Methodist. Mason. Rotarian. Contbr. to mags. Home: Totowa Borough, N.J. Address: Little Falls, N.J.

MEESER, Spenser Byron, theologian; b. Phila., Feb. 16, 1859; s. William Henry and Josephine Hoover (Shermer) M.; grad. Girard Coll., Phila., 1874; Ph.B., Bucknell U., Lewisburg, Pa., 1883; grad. Crozer Theol. Sem., Chester, Pa., 1886; (D.D., Brown, 1901); m. Lillian Burk, Dec. 14, 1886; children—Carol Cooke (Mrs. Eugene Edmond Ayres), Burk Shermer (dec.). Ordained Bapt. ministry, 1886; pastor 1st Ch., Paterson, N.J., 1886-93, 2d Ch., Wilmington, Del., 1893-96, 1st Ch., Worcester, Mass., 1896-1902, Woodward Av. Ch., Detroit, 1902-07; abroad 1 yr.; acting pastor Emmanuel Ch., Brooklyn, 1908-09; prof. systematic theology, Crozer Theol. Sem., 1909-30. Sec. and exec. officer Citizens' State League of N.J., 1892-93; aided in securing legislative act raising age of consent in Del.; has served as del. to many convs. and religious congresses and mem. many important coms. Coll. preacher, Vassar, 1904; univ. preacher, U. of Chicago, 1906. Corr. sec. Gen. Conv. Baptists of N.A., 1907—; retired; pres. Am. Bapt. Hist. Soc., 1916-31; editor of The Crozer Quarterly. Mem. Theol. Soc. (New York), Phi Kappa Psi. Author of many published sermons and addresses. Home: Babcock Boul., Pittsburgh, Pa.

MEGARGEE, Edwin, painter; b. Philadelphia, Pa., Dec. 8, 1883; s. Sylvester Edwin and Adelaide Conchetta (Picioli) M.; student Georgetown U., Washington, D.C., 1899-1900, Drexel Inst., Phila., 1900-04, Art Students League, N.Y. City, 1904-05; m. Jean Inglee, Apr. 25, 1936. Has specialized as animal painter in domestic animals and sporting subjects, painting many prize-winning horses, dogs and cattle, characterized by soundness in animal structure; they have appeared on mag. covers and have been exhibited in prominent galleries; also specialized in dry point and aquatint, especially cock fighting prints. Etchings of famous Am. sires include Friar Rock, Whisk Broom, Fair Play and Luke McLuke; among portraits of thoroughbreds are Little Dan, Equipoise, Cavalcade, Flamenco and Quentin Durward; among equestrian portraits: Mr. and Mrs. Harvey Gibson of New York, Terrill Van Ingen, Mr. and Mrs. W. V. P. Ruxton, and T. W. Durant; his shooting scenes have appeared in Field and Stream, for which high rank has been accorded him. An accredited judge of Am. Kennel Club. Democrat. Catholic. Club: Scottish Terrier. Home: Greenbrook Road, Dunellen, N.J. Address: 41 Union Sq., New York, N.Y.*

MEGARGEL, Harold Jefferson, textile mfr.; b. Scranton, Pa., Feb. 1, 1898; s. Willard and Matilda (Westphal) M.; student Wharton Sch., U. of Pa., 1915-19; m. Florence May Goodall, Aug. 4, 1923; 1 son, Welles Franklin. Vice-pres. in charge production Scranton (Pa.) Lace Co. since 1920. Home: 811 Olive St. Office: Scranton Lace Co., Scranton, Pa.

MEGRAW, Herbert Ashton, metallurgical engr.; b. Baltimore, Apr. 28, 1876; s. John Milton and Ellen Maria (Ryan) M.; grad. Baltimore Poly. Inst., 1894; B.S. in chemistry, Cornell U., 1898; m. Mary Bollman French, Oct. 18, 1905. Assayer, 1899-1901, mill supt. and metallurgist, 1901-03, Guanajuato Consolidated Mining & Milling Co.; staff engr. Charles Butters & Co., London, 1903; metall. engr., Iola Mining Co., 1904; mgr. Montgomery Mining Co., 1905-08; supt. Nayal Milling Co., Guanajuato, Mex., 1908-12; consulting metall. engr., Mexico City, 1912; on editorial staff Engineering and Mining Journal, 1912-17, mgr. same, 1917-18; engr. Bur. of Aircraft Production, Air Service U.S.A., Dayton, O., and Washington, 1918-19; engr. Kennedy-Van Saun Mfg. & Engring. Corpn., New York, 1919-22; v.p. and treas. Crown Oil & Wax Co. and N.C. Oil Co., Baltimore, Md., 1922-26; v.p. and gen. mgr. Corchera Internacional, Seville, Spain, 1926-35, now practicing as cons. engr. Episcopalian. Mem. Am. Inst. Mining and Metall. Engrs., Phi Sigma Kappa. Clubs: Engineers', Tablada. Author: Practical Data for the Cyanide Plant, 1910; Details of Cyanide Practice, 1914; The Flotation Process, 1916. Extensive contbr. to leading mining and metall. jours. Home: 5208 St. Albans Way, Homeland, Baltimore, Md.

MEHL, Robert F(ranklin), research metallurgist and prof.; b. Lancaster, Pa., Mar. 30, 1898; s. George H. and Sarah W. (Ward) M.; B.S., Franklin and Marshall Coll., 1919; Ph.D., Princeton U., 1924; Nat. Research fellow, Harvard U., 1925-27; m. Helen M. Charles, Dec. 27, 1923; children—Robert F., Marjorie Ward, Gretchen. Prof. chemistry, Juniata Coll., 1923-25; supt. div. phys. metallurgy Naval Research Lab., 1927-31; asst. dir. research Am. Rolling Mill Co., 1931-32; dir. Metals Research Lab., Carnegie Inst. Tech. since 1932, head dept. of metallurgy since 1935. Mem. Am. Chem. Soc., Am. Soc. for Metals, Am. Inst. of Mining and Metall. Engrs., Am. Soc. for Testing Materials, British Iron and Steel Inst., British Inst. of Metals, Verein deutscher Eisenhuttenleute. Contbr. many research articles to tech jours. Home: 215 S. Linden Av., Pittsburgh, Pa.

MEIER, Fred Campbell, plant pathologist; b. Riggston, Ill., Apr. 5, 1893; s. William Herman Dietrich and Lizzie B. (Campbell) M.; B.S., Harvard, 1916, M.S., 1917; m. Agnes Walton Eastman, Oct. 23, 1920. With U.S. Dept. Agr. since 1915, prin. pathologist, Bur. Plant Industry, 1930-34; sr. scientist Extension Service since 1934. Sec. treas. Am. Phytopathol. Soc., 1929-34 and vice-pres., 1935; business mgr. of Phytopathology (internat. jour. of Am. Phytopathol. Soc.), 1930-34; fellow A.A.A.S. Research on dissemination of micro-organisms by upper air currents with govt. aviation units and commercial airlines since 1929, Lindbergh North Atlantic flight, 1933, Century of Progress stratosphere flight, 1933, Nat. Geog. Army Air Corps stratosphere flights, 1934, 35, aerial collections over Caribbean Sea, 1935; chmn. com. on aerial dissemination of pathogens and allergens, Nat. Research Council since 1937. Writer numerous tech. and popular phytopathol. and agrl. extension papers pub. by U.S. Dept. Agr. and others. Presbyterian. Clubs: Cosmos, Harvard of Washington, Federal, Kenwood Golf and Country. Home: 6402 Beechwood Drive, Chevy Chase, Md. Address: U.S. Dept. of Agriculture, Washington, D.C.*

MEIER, Mahlon Martin, lawyer; b. Newark, N.J., Oct. 24, 1902; s. Wilbur Carl and Emma Ross (Martin) M.; student Dartmouth Coll., 1919-21; Ph.B., Brown Univ., 1924; LL.B., Columbia Univ. Law Sch., 1927; m. Grace Brown, Nov. 29, 1929. Employed as law clk. in office Lindabury, Depue & Faulks, Newark, N.J., 1927, legal asso. and mem. firm, 1935-36; admitted to N.J. bar as atty., 1928, as counselor, 1931; counsel American Home Products Corpn., Jersey City, N.J., 1936-37; in pvt. practice in Hoboken, N.J., 1937-38; gen. atty. R.F.C., in N.Y. City, 1938-39; dep. commr. and counsel N.J. Alcoholic Beverage Control, Newark, N.J., since 1939. Dir. Morristown Sch. since 1936. Mem. Lawyers Soc. of Essex Co. (pres. 1933), Delta Kappa Epsilon. Episcopalian. Home: 59 Ridgewood Av., Glen Ridge, N.J. Office: 744 Broad St., Newark, N.J.

MEIGS, Arthur Ingersoll, architect; b. Phila., Pa., June 29, 1882; s. Arthur Vincent and Mary Roberts (Browning) M.; grad. William-Penn Charter Sch., Phila., 1899; A.B., Princeton, 1903; m. Harriet Geyelin, September 13, 1935. Began practice Philadelphia, 1906; member archtl. firm Mellor & Meigs, 1906-17, Mellor, Meigs & Howe, 1917-28, Mellor & Meigs since 1928; firm architects for branch banks, Phila. Savings Fund Soc.; member board dirs. Cranberry Improvement Co. Works: chapel at Bony, France, and monument at Ypres, for Am. Battle Monuments Commn.; auditorium for Bryn Mawr Coll.; Phi Gamma Delta fraternity houses, Phila., Pa. State Coll. and Seattle residences nr. Phila. for F. S. McIlhenny, Caspar W. Morris, etc., also residences for Col. Henry Dupont, Arthur E. Newbold, Jr., and Melville G. Curtis; Gymnasium Bldg., Pa. Inst. for the Deaf; a science laboratory, Haverford Coll. Served as capt., F. A., in command Co. B, Mil. Police, 4th Div., U.S.A., 1917-19; in engagements at Aisne-Marne, St. Mihiel and Argonne. Fellow Am. Inst. Architects; mem. Hist. Soc. Phila., T Square Club. Firm awarded gold medal, Archtl. League of New York, 1925; ann. medal in architecture, Phila. chapter A.I.A., 1922. Episcopalian. Clubs: Philadelphia, Whitemarsh Valley Hunt. Author: An American Country House, 1924. Home: Radnor, Pa. Office: 205 S. Juniper St., Philadelphia, Pa.

MEIGS, Cornelia Lynde, author: b. Rock Island, Ill., Dec. 6, 1884; d. Montgomery and Grace Cornelia (Lynde) M.; A.B., Bryn Mawr, 1907. Now asso. professor of English, Bryn Mawr Coll. Republican. Episcopalian. Author: Kingdom of the Winding Road, 1915; Master Simon's Garden, 1916; The Steadfast Princess (Drama League prize play), 1916; The Pool of Stars, 1919; The Windy Hill, 1921; Helga and the White Peacock (play), 1922; The New Moon, 1924; Rain on the Roof, 1925; Trade Wind, 1927 (winner $2,000 prize of Little, Brown & Co.); As the Crow Flies, 1927; The Wonderful Locomotive, 1928; Clearing Weather, 1928; The Crooked Apple Tree, 1929; The Willow Whistle, 1931; Swift Rivers, 1932; Invincible Louisa, 1933 (winner Newberry medal, 1934); Wind in the Chimney, 1934; The Covered Bridge, 1936; Young Americans, 1937; Railroad West, 1937; The Scarlet Oak, 1938. Home: 621 Pembroke Rd., Bryn Mawr, Pa.; also Brandon Vt. (summers).

MEIGS, John, civil engr.; b. Washington, D.C., Mar. 10, 1876; s. John and Sallie (Orton) M.; prep. edn., high sch., Washington, D.C.; student Columbian (now George Washington) U., 1892-96; m. Clara Thomas Stetson, Mar. 31, 1913; children—Mary Stetson, John Vincent. U.S. asst. engr. in charge constrn. bridges over Potomac River and river and harbor improvements in Baltimore Harbor, and Delaware River and Bay, etc., various periods, 1900-11; supervising engr. Penn. Bridge Co., in charge constrn., 1905-08; dir. dept. of docks, Phila., and pres. Bd. Commrs. of Navigation, State of Pa., in charge preparation and execution of plans for improvement of Port of Phila., 1911-15; cons. practice since 1916; consultant on plans for Hog Island Shipyard; cons. on port improvements, Jersey City, N.J., Wilmington, Del., etc.; mem. firm Meigs & Long, cons. engrs.; pres. Earl-Thompson Co., bldg. constrn.; chief engr. Aqua Engineering Co., engring. constrn.; chief engr. Wilmington Tunnel Co. Chmn. Port Facilities Com. of Nat. Resources Bd.; consultant to Phila. Tri-State Regional Planning Federation. Served as mem. Bd. of Advisory Engrs on Port and Harbor Facilities and mem. Gen. Contracts Bd. of U.S. Shipping Bd. Emergency Fleet Corpn. Mem. bd. dirs. Phila. Bd. of Trade; mem. Philadelphia City Planning Commn., Philadelphia Traffic Commn. Mem. Am. Soc. C.E. (ex-pres. Phila. sect.), Nat. Soc. Terminal Engrs. (ex-pres.), Soc. Municipal Engrs. of Phila. (ex-pres.), Am. Assn. Port Authorities (v.p.). Republican. Protestant. Clubs: Engineers, City. Home: Wynnewood, Pa. Office: Liberty Trust Bldg., Philadelphia, Pa.*

MEILICKE, Carl Arthur, clergyman; b. Oak Ridge, Minn., July 1, 1872; s. Edward E. and Wilhelmina (Dittmer) M.; A.B., Moravian Coll., Bethlehem, Pa., 1896; B.D., Moravian Theol. Sem., 1898; (hon.) D.D., Moravian Coll. and Theol. Sem., 1934; m. Eugenia Strehlow, Oct. 12, 1898; children—Clement Allen, Myron M., Francis T. Ordained to ministry Moravian Ch., 1898; minister, Hector, Minn., 1898-1903; minister, Wisconsin Rapids, Wis., 1903-26; minister Central Moravian Ch., Bethlehem, Pa., since 1926. Rep. Moravian Ch. (North) U.S.A. at Gen. Synods of Moravian Ch. held at Herrnhut, Saxony, Germany, 1909 and 1931. Pres. Bd. Trustees of Moravian Coll. and Theol. Sem. Mem. Moravian Ch. Home: 63 W. Church St., Bethlehem, Pa.

MEINEL, William John, pres. Heintz Mfg. Co.; b. Phila., Pa., July 3, 1893; s. Charles August and Elizabeth (Kerchenstein) M.; ed. Phila. pub. schs.; M.E., Franklin Inst., Phila.; studied business adminstrn. (evenings) Temple U., Phila.; m. Jennie Miller, Sept. 1, 1916; 1 dau., Betty Jane; m. 2d, Martha Scattergood, Sept. 3, 1938; step-children—June and George Scattergood. Began as machinist's apprentice Richard Coreless Engine Works, 1908; supt. Nazel Engring. Co., 1914-16; held various positions from supt. tool and die dept. to v.p. in charge of operations E. G. Budd Mfg. Co., Phila., 1916-32; pres., gen. mgr. and dir. Heintz Mfg. Co., mfrs. steel stampings, auto bodies, etc., Phila., since 1932. Mem. Mayor's Labor Bd., Mayor's Advisory Finance Com. V.p. Am. Stomach Hosp.; dir. Philadelphia Coll. of Pharmacy and Science. Republican. Presbyterian. Mason. Clubs: Union League, Art (Phila.). Home: Huntingdon Pike and Susquehanna Road, Huntingdon Valley, Pa. Office: Heintz Mfg. Co., Front St. and Olney Av., Philadelphia, Pa.

MEINZER, Martin Stoetzel, M.D., surgeon; b. South Amboy, N.J., Apr. 22, 1878; s. Louis F. and Amelia (Stoetzel) M.; ed. Park Pub. Sch., South Amboy, and Rutgers Prep. Sch.; B.Sc., Rutgers U., 1901, M.Sc. 1907; M.D., U. of Columbia Med. Sch., 1905; m. Elizabeth Smock, July 6, 1905; 1 dau., Helen S. Began gen. practice medicine and surgery, 1906; mem. staff of Perth Amboy Gen. Hosp. Fellow Am. Coll. Surgeons; mem. A.M.A. Presbyn. (trustee 1st Ch.). Home: 42 Market St. Office: 147 Market St., Perth Amboy, N.J.

MEISEL, Emanuel George; prof. clin. dental pathology and radiology, U. of Pittsburgh. Address: 121 University Place, Pittsburgh, Pa.

MEISENHELDER, Edmund W., surgeon; b. York, Pa., May 9, 1876; s. Edmund W. and

Maria E. (Baughman) M.; A.B., Gettysburg Coll., Gettysburg, Pa., 1898, A.M., 1901, Sc.D., 1931; M.D., Johns Hopkins University, 1902; m. Frances Faust, May 9, 1914; children—Edmund W. III, Ruth L., Samuel F., Helen (dec.). Began practice at York, 1902; surgeon York (Pa.) Hosp., 1905-13, West Side Sanitarium since 1913; cons. surgeon Gettysburg Hosp. Fellow A.C.S.; mem. A.M.A., Pa. State and York County med. socs. Republican. Lutheran. Mason (Shriner). Home: Dover Township, York Co., Pa. Address: 1253 W. Market St., York, Pa.

MEISLE, Kathryn (Mrs. Calvin M. Franklin), contralto; b. Phila., Pa., Oct. 12, 1899; d. Adam and Isabelle (Meisle) M.; musical training in U.S.; m. Calvin M. Franklin, Nov. 9, 1917. Début as Erda, in "Siegfried," with Chicago Civic Opera Co., 1923; début as Amneris in "Aïda" with Met. Opera Assn., 1935; has appeared as soloist with Boston Symphony Orchestra, Phila. Orchestra, Chicago Symphony Orchestra, Detroit Symphony Orchestra, Minneapolis Symphony Orchestra, etc.; principal rôles: Amneris in "Aïda"; Delilah in "Samson and Delilah"; Azucena in "Il Trovatore"; Erda in "Siegfried"; Fricka in "Die Walküre"; etc. Home: 1216 Wagner Av., Phila., Pa. Address: care Arthur Judson, Inc., 113 W. 57th St., New York, N.Y.

MEISTER, Walter Frederick, chem. engr.; b. St. Louis, Mo., Sept. 25, 1891; s. Otto F. and Frieda (Schlosstein) M.; ed. St. Louis grammar and high schs., B.S., Washington U., St. Louis, 1916; m. Lucile I. Smith, Nov. 30, 1918; children—Catherine W., Charles H. Analytical chemist, rising to chief chemist, Eagle-Picher Lead Co., Joplin, Mo., Cincinnati, O., Newark, N.J., 1916-19; chief chemist St. Louis Lithopone Co., Collinsville, Ill., 1919-23, 1925-27; chief chemist Evans Lead Co., Charleston, W.Va., 1923-25; mgr. lithopone production United Color & Pigment Co., Newark, N.J., 1927-37; research chemist Nat. Lead Co., South Amboy, N.J., since 1937. Mem. Am. Chem. Soc., Sigma Nu. Republican. Presbyterian. Home: 41 Georgian Ct., Elizabeth, N.J. Office: National Lead Co., South Amboy, N.J.

MELCHER, Frederic Gershom, editor and publisher; b. Malden, Mass., Apr. 12, 1879; s. Edwin Forrest and Alice Jane (Bartlett) M.; ed. pub. schs., Newton, Mass.; m. Marguerite Fellows, June 2, 1910; children—Daniel, Nancy, Charity. With Lauriat & Co., booksellers, Boston, 1895-1913; mgr. W. K. Stewart Co., booksellers, Indianapolis, Ind., 1913-18; co-editor The Publishers' Weekly since 1918; pres. R. R. Bowker & Co. Hon. fellow Am. Booksellers' Assn. (sec. 1918-20); pres. N.Y. Library Assn., 1935-36; mem. Nat. Assn. Book Pubs. (sec. 1920-23), N.Y. Booksellers' League (pres. 1924-25), Am. Inst. Graphic Arts (pres. 1927); P.E.N. Club; mem. Authors' League America (dir.), Am. Antiquarian Soc., Grolier Club, Bibliographical Soc. of America; trustee Montclair Art Museum. Republican. Unitarian. A founder of Children's Book Week, 1919; lecturer and writer on publishing and bookselling; established John Newberry medal, awarded each yr. by A.L.A. to the most distinguished contbr. to Am. literature for children (first awarded 1921) and Caldecott medal for the best Am. picture book (first award for 1937). Home: Montclair, N.J. Office: 62 W. 45th St., New York, N.J.

MELDRUM, William Buell, prof. chemistry; b. Hull, Can., Dec. 18, 1887; s. Thomas and Isabella Thane (Wilson) M.; came to U.S., 1911, naturalized, 1918; B.A. and M.Sc., McGill U.; Ph.D., Harvard, 1914; m. Phillipa Ruth Coleman, Sept. 2, 1919; children—William Buell, Jr., Phillipa Lestella, Thomas Wilson, Donald Nicol. Demonstrator in chemistry, McGill U., 1909; instr. Montreal Tech. Inst., 1910-11; Austin Teaching Fellow, Harvard U., 1911-12, 1851 Exhbn. Scholar, 1912-14; asst. prof. chemistry, Vassar Coll., 1914-17; asst. prof. chemistry, Haverford Coll., 1917-21, prof. since 1921. Served in C.W.S., U.S.A., 1918-19, with War Trade Bd., 1919. Mem. A.A.A.S., Am. Chem. Soc., Sci. Teachers Assn., Electrochem. Soc., Assn. Harvard Chemists, Franklin Inst. Mem. Religious Soc. Friends. Author: Introduction to Theoretical Chemistry, 1936; Qualitative Analysis, 1938; Semi-Micro Qualitative Analysis, 1939. Contbr. various papers to chem. jours. Asso. editor, Journal of Franklin Inst. Home: 747 College Av., Haverford Pa.

MELHORN, Nathan R., clergyman, educator; b. Ada, O., Dec. 23, 1871; s. Michael S. and Martha (Ahlefeld) M.; A.M., Ohio Northern U., 1890; grad. Luth. Theol. Sem., Phila., 1897; D.D., Muhlenberg, 1917; Litt.D. from Carthage (Illinois) College, 1926; LL.D., Midland College, Fremont, Neb., 1938; m. Florence L. Richmond, 1901; children—Nathan R., Henry B. Ordained Luth. ministry, 1897; editor of The Lutheran since 1920. Trustee Luth. Theol. Sem. Republican. Home: 4720 Warrington Av. Office: Muhlenberg Bldg., Philadelphia, Pa.

MELIODON, Jules Andre, sculptor; b. Paris, France, June 1, 1867; s. Jules Antoine and Jeanne Francoise Catherine (Van Cutsem) M.; ed. Nat. Decorative Art Sch., Nat. Beaux Arts, Jardin des Plantes Sch., France; m. Louise Gabrielle Hugot, Feb. 3, 1904; children—Louis Edward, Andree. Came to U.S., 1904, naturalized, 1911. Works: bust of Francollin, bust of Lesueur, France; soldiers memorial, Bloomingdale, N.J.; busts of Senator Chase, Fred Stevens, Ferdinand Roebling, Simon Gratz; bronze memorial, Ch. of St. Thomas the Apostle, New York; Alpha and Omega frieze, St. Elizabeth Ch., Phila. Decorated Officer of Academy by French Govt., 1898; Officer of Public Instrn., 1904; hon. mention Salon of Artistes Français, 1902. Served as pvt. in French Army, 1891-93. Mem. Art Alliance (Phila.), Am. Artists Professional League. Address: 1840 S. Bancroft St., Philadelphia, Pa.

MELLER, Harry Bertine, research engr.; b. Altoona, Pa., May 26, 1878; s. Charles William and Annie (Adams) M.; U. of Pa., 1906-07, 1908-09; Mich. Coll. of Mines, Houghton, 1907-08, 1909; Engr. of Mines, U. of Pittsburgh, 1910; Sc.D., U. of Toledo, 1938; m. Mary Alice Rothrock, Apr. 8, 1901. Clk. Pa. R.R. Co., Altoona, Pa., 1895-1900; clk. of faculty, dept. of medicine, U. of Pa., 1900-04; sec. same, 1904-07; instr. mining, 1910-11, asst. prof., 1911-12, prof., 1912-24, vice-dean, 1912-14, dean, 1914-23, School of Mines—all of University of Pittsburgh; head of air pollution investigation, Mellon Inst., U. of Pittsburgh, since 1923; chief Bur. of Smoke Regulation of City of Pittsburgh, since 1920. Mng. dir. Air Hygiene Foundation America, 1934—. Enlisted Co. C, 5th Regt., N.G. Pa., 1897; with same company and regt. Pa. Vol. Inf., May-Oct. 1898; successively 2d lt., 1903-04, 1st lt., 1904-05, capt., 1905-07, Co. L, 3d Regt., N.G. Pa.; capt. Air Service U.S.A., 1917-19. Republican. Mem. A.A.A.S., Am. Pub. Health Assn., Phi Delta Theta, Sigma Gamma Epsilon, Alpha Omicron. Mason. Home: Anderson Rd. (Millvale Br.). Office: Mellon Institute, Pittsburgh, Pa.

MELLON, Fred Stoner, pub. utilities; b. Delmont, Pa., Jan. 2, 1900; s. Thomas and Amanda (Blose) M.; student U. of Pittsburgh; LL.B., Duquesne U. Law Sch.; m. Eleanor Nichols, Jan. 1, 1917; children—Margaret Nichols, Jo Anne Stotler, Marian Stoner. Asso. with Penn-Pittsburgh Corpn., Pittsburgh, Pa., successively clk., stenographer, atty., and sec.; sec. and treas. Hotel Henry Co., Burrell Improvement Co.; dir. Union-Fidelity Title Ins. Co.; dir., asst. sec. and treas. Indian Creek Coal & Coke Co.; sec. Ligonier Valley R.R. Co., Idlewild Management Co.; asst. sec. Idlewild Company; dir., v.p. and sec. Monongahela Light & Power Co., Pittsburgh & Birmingham Passenger R.R. Co., Birmingham, Knoxville & Allentown Traction Co., Brownsville Av. St. Ry. Co., West Liberty St. Ry. Co., Mount Oliver Incline Ry. Co., South Side Passenger Ry. Co., Pittsburgh & Birmingham Traction Co., Monongahela St. Ry. Co.; dir. and v.p., Motor Square Corpn. Republican. Episcopalian. Mason (32°). Home: Jeannette, Pa. Office: Mellon Bank Bldg., Pittsburgh, Pa.

MELLON, Ralph Robertson, physician; b. New Lisbon, O., Feb. 1, 1883; s. Thomas Donelly and Angie Ellen (Robertson) M.; B.S., Grove City (Pa.) Coll., 1901, hon. D.Sc., 1936; M.D. and M.S., U. of Mich., 1909; Dr.P.H., Harvard Med. Sch., 1916; m. Arda Jane Esten, Sept. 18, 1912; children—Miriam Hinsdale, Janet Robertson. Successively instr. in medicine, asst. and asso. prof. and dir. Lab. of Clin. Pathology, U. of Mich., 1909-15; dir. of labs., Highland Hosp., Rochester, 1916-27; dir. Inst. of Pathology, Western Pa. Hosp.; asso. with Mellon Inst. Industrial Research since 1927. Mem. Society of American Bacteriologists, Assn. of Pathologists, American Society of Immunologists, American Medical Assn. Home: 6055 Bunkerhill Drive. Office: Western Pennsylvania Hospital, Pittsburgh, Pa.

MELLON, Richard King, banker; b. Pittsburgh, Pa., June 19, 1899; s. Richard Beatty and Jennie Taylor (King) M.; student Princeton University; m. Constance Prosser, April 1936. Began as messenger Mellon National Bank, 1920, vice-pres., 1924-34, pres. since 1934; pres. and dir. Forbes Nat. Bank, Mellbank Corpn.; dir. Union Trust Co. of Pittsburgh, Pullman Inc., Pa. R.R. Co., Westinghouse Air Brake Co., Union Switch & Signal Co., Koppers Co., Gulf Oil Corpn. of Pa., Pittsburgh Plate Glass Co., Nat. Union Fire Ins. Co., Pan-Am. Airways, Inc., Aluminum Co. of America, Carborundum Co. Served as student pilot, A.C., 1918. Trustee U. of Pittsburgh, Carnegie Inst.; treas. Tuberculosis League of Pittsburgh. Republican. Presbyn. Home: 6500 5th Av., Pittsburgh, Pa.

MELLON, Thomas Alexander, corpn. official; b. Pittsburgh, Pa., Nov. 19, 1873; s. Thomas Alexander and Mary (Caldwell) M.; ed. acad. in Pittsburgh and took regular course with engring. firm; m. Helen Wightman, Nov. 15, 1899; children—Thomas Alexander (dec.), Elisabeth Wightman, Edward Purcell, Helen Sedgley. Water works constrn. since 1895, also has been largely identified with housing problems, railroad construction and building of industrial plants, bridges, office buildings. Presbyterian. Mason (32°, K.T., Shriner). Clubs: Duquesne, Pittsburgh, University, Automobile, Pittsburgh Athletic Assn., Keystone Athletic Club, Allegheny Country, Pittsburgh Field, Pittsburgh Golf, Fox Chapel Golf, Rolling Rock, Rolling Rock Hunt, Clemo Hunting and Fishing, Wilkinsburg Gun, Chamber of Commerce (all of Pittsburgh or Pa.); Railroad, Engineers', Racquet and Tennis (New York); University, Metropolitan, Congressional Country (Washington, D.C.); Duck Island Club (N.C.); Henrys Lake Club (Idaho); Ribault Corporation Club. Home: 401 N. Negley Av. Office: Oliver Bldg., Pittsburgh, Pa.*

MELLON, William Larimer, banker; b. Pittsburgh, Pa.; s. James Ross and Rachel H. (Larimer) M.; ed. Pa. Mil. Acad., Chester, Pa., LL.D., Pa. Mil. Coll., 1928; m. Miss Taylor. Began with Mellon Bros., real estate and building supplies, Pittsburgh; entered street ry. business and became pres. Monongahela St. Ry., Pittsburgh; chmn. bd. Gulf Oil Corpn. and other oil cos.; also officer or dir. many other corpns. Clubs: Pittsburgh, Duquesne, etc. Home: Darlington Rd. Office: Gulf Bldg., Pittsburgh, Pa.

MELLOR, John Henry, banker; b. Wellsville, O., May 11, 1873; s. Joseph Sikes and Jane (Moulds) M.; student Rochester High Sch., 1890-93, Piersols Acad.; m. Mary Bell Wilson, June 8, 1904 (died Jan. 25, 1931); 1 dau., Mary Bell (Mrs. Ernest H. Meyer). With First Nat. Bank, Rochester, Pa., since July 10, 1895, successively as messenger, 1895-98, teller, 1898-1900, cashier, 1900-36, vice-pres. and dir. since 1936; treas. and dir. Rochester Improvement Co., Rochester Bldg. & Loan Assn.; treas. Rochester Borough, 1903-38. Served as chmn. Liberty Loan Com. for Rochester during World War. Republican. Episcopalian. Mason (K.T., Shriner). Home: 221 Madison St., Rochester, Pa.

MELLOR, Walter, architect; b. Phila., Pa., Apr. 25, 1880; s. Alfred and Isabella (Latham) M.; grad. Haverford (Pa.) Sch., 1897; B.S., Haverford Coll., 1901; B.S. in Architecture, U. of Pa., 1904; m. Elizabeth Wharton Mendelson, Oct. 11, 1919; 1 dau., Louise. In office of T. P. Chandler, 1904-06; mem. Mellor & Meigs, 1906-17, Mellor, Meigs & Howe, 1917-28, Mellor & Meigs since 1928; firm architects for branch banks, Phila. Saving Fund Soc.; auditorium for Bryn Mawr Coll.; memorial to U.S. Coast Guard Service, Arlington, Va.; chapel at Bony, France, and monument at Ypres, for Am. Battle Monuments Commn.; Phi Gamma Delta fraternity houses, Phila., Pa. State Coll. and Seattle; Gymnasium Bldg., Pa. Inst. for the Deaf; Hilles Lab. of Applied Science and Strawbridge Observatory, Haverford Coll.; residences in Phila. for F. S. McIlhenny, Casper W. Morris, etc., also residences for Col. Henry Dupont, Arthur E. Newbold, Jr., Melville G. Curtis (Bala, Pa.), etc. Dir. Kestner Evaporator Co.; trustee The Cunningham Sch. Fellow American Institute of Architects; mem. Zoöl. Soc. of Philadelphia, Art Alliance, T Square Club, Phi Gamma Delta. Firm awarded ann. medal Phila. chapter A.I.A., 1922; gold medal, Archtl. League of New York, 1925. Republican. Quaker. Clubs: Union League, Germantown Cricket, Mask and Wig (U. of Pa.). Home: Scotforth Rd., Mount Airy P.O., Philadelphia. Office: 205 S. Juniper St., Philadelphia, Pa.

MELLOR-GILL, Margaret Webster, artist; b. Germantown, Phila., Pa., Aug. 13, 1901; d. Laurence Bancroft and Sarah Elizabeth (Webster) Mellor; studied under Miss Lucy Knight, 1908-10 and 1912-14; student Germantown (Pa.) Friends Sch., 1910-12, Stevens Sch., 1914-16, Sch. of Design for Women, 1916-17, Pa. Acad. Fine Arts, 1917-22; student art of japanning under Charles Feurer, 1932; m. Logan Blair Gill, Nov. 20, 1925. Began as portrait painter and commercial artist, 1921; painter of advertisements and magazine covers until 1929; portrait painter since 1929; also painter japanned trays, boxes, etc., since 1935. Exhibited at Denver Art Museum (1-woman exhbn., 1931), Denver Junior League House, 1932, Philadelphia Art Alliance, 1933; 1525 Locust St., 1933, Hotel Belgravia, 1933, The Claridge Hotel, 1934, Junior League House, 1935, Philadelphia Art Alliance, 1936. Invited to exhibit large tea tray (japanned), Paris Expn., 1937. Exhibited water colors in New York, Chicago, Baltimore and rotary shows in west. Dir. Women's Pa. Soc. for Prevention of Cruelty to Animals. Mem. Soc. Arts and Crafts (Boston), The Arts and Crafts Guild (Phila.), Phila. Water Color Club, Phila. Art Alliance. Address: 6626 Morris Park Road, Philadelphia, Pa.

MELONEY, Lester Foye, physician; b. Brooklyn, N.Y., June 16, 1881; s. James Wright and Elizabeth (Foye) M.; ed. Columbia U., 1900 to 1905; M.D., Coll. Phys. & Surgs. of Columbia U., 1905; m. Helen Claire Rue, June 27, 1912. Interne New York Lying-In Hosp., 1905-06, French Hosp., 1906-08, St. Bartholomew Clinic, N.Y. City, 1906-07, Sanford Hall, Flushing, L.I., 1905-06; phys. and surg. Katala Hosp. of Copper River & Northwestern R.R. Co., Alaska, 1907-08; engaged in practice of medicine at Clifton, N.J., since 1908. Mem. of Township Committee Aquackanonk Township, 1914; twp. phys., Aquackanonk Twp., N.J., 1910-14; mem. of the City Council City of Clifton, N.J.; city phys. and health officer, Clifton, N.J.; dir. Clifton Trust Co. Served on Passaic Co. Dft. Bd. No. 2, vol. med. service corps, during World War. Mem. N.J. Ho. of Rep., 1920-21; mem. Passaic County Bd. of Freeholders, 1922-25; mem. Twp. Com. Aquackanonk Twp., 1914; mem. City Council, Clifton, N.J. Mem. A.M.A., N.J. State and Passaic Co. med. socs., Am. Pub. Health Assn., N.J. Health Officers Assn. Republican. Mem. Reformed Ch. Home: 156 Second St., Clifton, N.J.

MELOY, Luella Price, sociologist; b. Phila., Pa.; d. John Calvin (D.D.) and Louise (Price) M.; grad. Pa. Coll. for Women; A.M., Columbia, 1914. Teacher coll. prep. sch. of Pa. Coll. for Women, 1888-95; teacher West Newton (Pa.) Acad., 1896-1902; social worker, Charity Orgn. Soc., N.Y. City, 1902; children's agt. State Charities Aid Assn., N.Y., 1902-07; organizer Dept. of Social Service, 1909, and prof. sociology and economics, 1910-35, Pa. College for Women. Extension teacher Pa. State Coll., 1922-32. Mem. Allegheny Co. Bd. of Visitation, 1924-31. Mem. Am. Assn. of Univ. Women, Am. Sociol. Soc., Am. Assn. of Univ. Profs., Pi Gamma Mu. Presbyn. Home: 31 North Av., Washington, Pa.

MELSON, Elwood F.; mem. law firm Melson & Killoran. Address: Citizens Bank Bldg., Wilmington, Del.

MELVIN, Ridgely Prentiss, judge; b. Denton, Md., Nov. 4, 1881; s. George Thomas and Maria Louise (Hopkins) M.; A.B., St. John's Coll., Annapolis, Md.; 1899, A.M., 1900; LL.B., U. of Md. Law Sch., 1902; m. Augusta Somervell Burwell, Oct. 24, 1914; children—Augusta Burwell, Ridgely Prentiss, Jr., Mary Burwell, Elizabeth Somervell, John Burwell. Admitted to Md. bar, 1903, and since engaged in gen. practice of law at Annapolis; city counselor of Annapolis, 1907-15; counsel to co. commrs. of Anne Arundel Co., 1910-25; mem. County Bd. Edn., 1922-30; mem. Jud. Council of Md., 1922-24; mem. Md. Ho. of Dels., 1918-20; mem. Md. Senate, 1930-38; elected asso. judge Fifth Jud. Circuit Md., 1938. Served as food adminstr. Anne Arundel Co., 1918; chmn. Red Cross Chapter. Legal adv. com., dist. gov. of Rotary, 1927-28. Mem. Am., Md. State, Anne Arundel Co. bar assns., Southern Md. Soc., Phi Kappa Sigma. Democrat. Episcopalian (vestryman, mem. exec. council Diocese Md.). Home: Annapolis, Md.

MEMINGER, James Wilbert, clergyman; b. Ickesburg, Pa., Nov. 9, 1859; s. James Galbraith and Rebecca Ellen (Rice) M.; A.B., Ursinus Coll., Collegeville, Pa., 1884, B.D., Sch. of Theology, same coll., 1886, B.O., Nat. School Oratory, Phila., 1886; D.D., Ursinus, 1905; m. Florence Hollinger of Lancaster, Pa., Nov. 4, 1891; children—Cyrus Hollinger, Elizabeth Hollinger. Ordained ministry Ref. Ch. in U.S., 1886; pastor East Coventry, Pa., 1886-87, St. Paul's Ch., Lancaster, Pa., 1887-1920. Sec.-treas. bd. of relief, Gen. Synod Ref. Ch. in U.S.A., 1920-38; organizer and pres. Clergyman's Coöperative Beneficial Assn.; pres. Teachers' Protective Union. Mem. bd. dirs. Central Theol. Sem. (Dayton, O.), Ursinus Coll.; trustee Shippen Sch. for Girls. Republican. Knight of Malta. Home: Lancaster, Pa.

MEMMING, Gerrit Hermann Rudolph, prof. German; b. St. Georgiwold, Germany, Apr. 20, 1904; s. Roelf and Tadine (Udens) M.; came to U.S., 1925, naturalized, 1933; ed. Seh. Agr., Weener, Germany, 1921-23; Diploma, Wartburg Acad., Clinton, Ia., 1929; ed. Wartburg Coll., 1929-31; A.B., U. of Ill., 1932, A.M., same, 1933, Ph.D., same, 1935; grad. study, Sorbonne, U. of Paris, summer 1935, U. of Heidelberg, summer 1938; m. Agnes Katherine Blikslager, June 24, 1938. Teaching fellow, U. of Ill., 1933-35; prof. German, head of dept., Albright Coll., Reading, Pa., since 1935. Mem. Phi Kappa Epsilon (pres., 1933-35), Delta Phi Alpha, Pi Tau Beta. Received Award of Merit for play and direction in German at the Cultural Olympics, Phila., 1938. Mem. Am. Luth. Ch. Club: Deutscher Lehrerverein von Reading und Umgegend (Reading). Contbr. articles to German and English lang. mags. Home: 1230 Linden St., Reading, Pa.

MENCKEN, August, engr.; b. Baltimore, Md., Feb. 18, 1889; s. August and Anna Margaret (Abhau) M.; student Baltimore Poly. Inst., 1903-07; unmarried. Engr. Stewart & Jones Co., in N.C., 1911; engr. in constrn. div. Southern R.R., 1912; engr. Claiborne, Johnston Co., Baltimore, 1913-23; vice-pres. T. D. Claiborne Co., Baltimore, Md., 1923-32; with American Cider & Vinegar Co., Baltimore, 1932-38; engaged in pvt. practice since 1938. Mem. The Md. Assn. of Engrs., Inc. Democrat. Club: 14 W. Hamilton St. (Baltimore). Has made many elaborate models of ships, some of which are in pub. museums. Editor (and writer of introduction) First Class Passenger, a collection of sea stories, 1938; editor (and writer of Part I) Railroad Passenger, a collection of railroad stories and history of passenger equipment, 1940. Granted patent on a method of inlaying metal in wood. Home: 1524 Hollins St., Baltimore, Md.

MENCKEN, Henry Louis, author, editor; b. Baltimore, Md., Sept. 12, 1880; s. August and Anna (Abhau) M.; ed. pvt. sch. and Baltimore Polytechnic; m. Sara Powell Haardt, Aug. 27, 1930 (died May 31, 1935). Reporter, 1899, city editor, 1903-05, Baltimore Morning Herald; editor Evening Herald, 1905-06; on staff Baltimore Sun, 1906-10; Evening Sun, 1910-16, 1918-35, both Sunpapers since 1936; lit. critic Smart Set, 1908-23; co-editor same, 1914-23; editor The American Mercury, 1924-33; contbg. editor The Nation, 1921-32. Dir. A. S. Abell Co. (publisher Baltimore Sun), Alfred A. Knopf, Inc. Author: Ventures Into Verse, 1903; George Bernard Shaw—His Plays, 1905; The Philosophy of Friedrich Nietzsche, 1908; The Artist (play), 1912; A Book of Burlesque, 1916; A Little Book in C Major, 1916; A Book of Prefaces, 1917; In Defense of Women, 1917; Damn—a Book of Calumny, 1917; The American Language, 1918, 4th revision, 1936; Prejudices —First Series, 1919, Second Series, 1920, Third Series, 1922, Fourth Series, 1924, Fifth Series, 1926, Sixth Series, 1927; Notes on Democracy, 1926; Treatise on the Gods, 1930; Making a President, 1932; Treatise on Right and Wrong, 1934. Part Author: Men vs. the Man, 1910; Europe After 8:15, 1914; The American Credo, 1920; Heliogabalus (play), 1920; The Sunpapers of Baltimore, 1937. Editor: The Players' Ibsen, 1909; The Free Lance Books, 1919; The Charlatanry of the Learned, 1937. Home: 1524 Hollins St. Office: The Sun, Baltimore, Md.

MENDENHALL, Thomas Elwood, M.D.; b. Winchester, Ind.; s. William H. and Eunice (Clark) M.; M.D., U. of Pa.; m. Florence E. Wilson, July 23, 1906; 1 son, Dr. Norman Elwood. Owner Mendenhall Hosp., Johnstown, Pa., and mem. staff since 1916; obstetric lecturer and mem. staff Memorial Hosp., Johnstown, since 1916. Club: Sunnehanna Country (Johnstown, Pa.). Home: 88 Osborne St. Office: Mendenhall Maternity Hosp., Johnstown, Pa.

MENDENHALL, Walter Curran, geologist; b. Marlboro, Stark Co., O., Feb. 20, 1871; s. William King and Emma Pierce (Garrigues) M.; B.S., Ohio Normal U., 1895; student Harvard, 1896-97, U. of Heidelberg, 1899-1900; hon. Sc.D., Colo. Sch. of Mines, 1928, U. of Wis., 1932; m. Alice May Boutell, Sept. 20, 1915; children—Margaret Boutell, Alice Curran. Geologic aid, 1894-96, asst. geologist, 1896-1901, geologist since 1901, U.S. Geol. Survey. In charge ground water investigations of U.S., 1907-10; chief of Land Classification Board, 1910-22; chief geologist, 1922-31, dir. since 1931. Fellow A.A.A.S. (v.p. sect. E, 1922), Geol. Soc. America (pres. 1936); mem. Nat. Acad. of Sciences, Am. Inst. Mining Engrs., Geol. Soc. Washington (pres. 1917), Washington Acad. Sciences. Clubs: Cosmos (Washington); Chevy Chase (Md.); Harvard (New York); Faculty (Cambridge, Mass.). Author of papers appearing mainly in the publs. of U.S. Geol. Survey. Home: 9 E. Lenox St., Chevy Chase, Md. Address: U.S. Geol. Survey, Washington, D.C.

MENGEL, Charles Henry, clergyman; b. Moyers, Pa., May 8, 1879; s. Daniel and Lucy Ann (Hehn) M.; ed. Albright Coll., 1910-13, Temple U., 1913-17; hon. Ph.B., Oskaloosa Coll., 1920; m. Stella Gehris, Apr. 29, 1902; 1 son, Charles LeRoy (M.D.). Ordained to ministry Evang. Ch., 1899, pastor various chs. in Pa., 1900-22; presiding elder, 1922-30; Bishop Evang.-Congl. Ch. since 1934; pres. Burd & Rogers Memorial Home, East Pa. Conf. Evang.-Congl. Ch. Mem. Patriotic Order Sons of America, Y.M.C.A. Republican. Mem. Evang.-Congl. Ch. Home: 2611 Washington St., Allentown, Pa.

MENGEL, Levi Walter, dir. museum; b. Reading, Pa., Sept. 27, 1868; s. Matthias and Amelia M. (Soder) M.; Pharm.D., Philadelphia Coll. of Pharmacy; Sc.D., Bucknell Univ., Lewisburg, Pa., 1932; LL.D., Albright Coll., Reading, 1934; unmarried. Teacher natural sciences, 1895-1905; chemistry teacher, 1905-15; dir. of Reading Museum since 1915. Mem. bd. trustees Reading Pub. Library; fellow A.A.A.S.; mem. Am. Acad. Natural Sciences, Am. Entomol. Soc. Awarded Kiwanis medal for local service. Republican. Quaker. Mason (33°, K.T., Shriner). Club: Wyomissing. Author: Synonymic Catalogue of the Family Erycinidæ, 1905. Contbr. scientific articles. Address: Public Museum, Reading, Pa.

MENGERT, Ulric Johnson, lawyer; b. Washington, D.C., July 19, 1895; s. Ulric T. and Margaret L. (Johnson) M.; A.B., Haverford Coll., 1916; A.M., Harvard U., 1917; LL.B., Harvard U. Law Sch., 1922; m. Eleanor B. Dillenback, June 16, 1925; 1 dau., Mary Brooks. Admitted to Pa. bar, 1923 and since engaged in gen. practice of law at Phila.; asso. with firm Roberts, Montgomery & McKeehan, 1923-25, and successor, Roberts & Montgomery, 1925-30, and successor, Montgomery & McCracken, 1930-35 and mem. said firm since 1935. Served as 1st lieut. then capt., U.S.A., 1917-19; now lieut. col. C.A., U.S.A. Res. Mem. bd. mgrs. Haverford Coll. Mem. Am., Pa. State, and Phila. bar assns., Phi Beta Kappa. Republican. Lutheran. Clubs: Union League, Philadelphia Cricket. Home: 7213 Charlton St., Mt. Airy, Philadelphia. Office: 1421 Chestnut St., Philadelphia, Pa.

MENGES, Franklin, ex-congressman; b. Menges Mills, Pa. Instr. in chemistry and physics, Gettysburg Coll., 10 yrs.; later head of science dept. York High Sch., lecturer before farmers' institutes until 1917; devoted attention largely to farming since 1917; mem. 69th to 71st Congresses (1925-31), 22d Pa. Dist. Republican. Home: York, Pa.

MENTEN, Maud Leonora, asso. prof. pathology; b. Pt. Lambton, Ont., Mar. 20, 1879; d. William and Emma (Trusler) M.; came to U.S., 1907; A.B., U. of Toronto, 1904; M.D., U. of Toronto Med. Sch., 1907; Ph.D., U. of Chicago, 1916; fellow U. of Toronto, 1909-10; grad. study U. of Berlin, Germany, 1913-14. Research worker, Western Res. U., 1911-13, 1914-15; dir. labs. Magee Hosp., Pittsburgh, 1916-18; asso. with U. of Pittsburgh, Dept. Pathology since 1918, successively instr., asst. prof., and asso. prof. since 1925. Mem. Am. Pathol. Soc., Am. Soc. Cancer Research, Am. Physiol. Soc., Soc. Exptl. Biology and Medicine, Soc. Exptl. Pathology, Sigma Psi. Club: Assoc. Artists of Pittsburgh. Contbr. various papers on research to sci. jours. Home: 702 Summerlea St., Pittsburgh, Pa.

MENZIES, Alan Wilfrid Cranbrook, prof. chemistry; b. Edinburgh, Scotland, July 31, 1877; s. Thomas Hunter and Helen Charlotte (Cranbrook) M.; M.A., Edinburgh U., 1897, B.Sc., 1898; studied univs. of Leipzig and Aberdeen; Ph.D., U. of Chicago, 1910; m. Mary Isabella Dickson, Mar. 20, 1908; 1 dau., Elizabeth Grant Cranbrook. Asst. prof. and prof. chemistry, Edinburgh and Glasgow until 1908; organizer and dir. summer courses for science teachers, Ireland, 1904-08; came to U.S., 1908; asst. prof. chemistry, U. of Chicago, 1911-12; prof. chemistry, Oberlin Coll., 1912-14; prof. chemistry, Princeton, 1914—. Mem. A.A.A.S., Sigma Xi; fellow Royal Soc. Edinburgh, Chem. Soc. London. Home: Princeton, N.J.

MERCER, Beverly Howard, surety ins. co. exec.; b. Ellicott City, Md., Feb. 23, 1894; s. Eugene Peyton and Isabelle (Saffell) M.; LL.B., U. of Md. Law Sch., Baltimore, 1924; m. Hannah Greenwood Wheatley, Nov. 1, 1919; 1 dau., Hannah Elizabeth. Asso. with Fidelity and Deposit Co. of Md., Baltimore, Md., since 1911, vice-pres. and mgr. judicial dept. since 1933; asso. with American Bonding Co. of Baltimore since 1913, vice-pres. since 1933. Mem. Gamma Eta Gamma. Democrat. Episcopalian. Home: 1006 Walnut Av., Rognel Heights, Baltimore, Md.

MERCER, Eugene LeRoy, univ. dean; b. Kennett Square, Pa., Oct. 30, 1888; s. Eugene P. and Mary Bernard (Hicks) M.; grad. Kennett (Pa.) High Sch., 1906, George Sch., 1909; M.D., U. of Pa. Sch. of Medicine, 1913; m. Emily Atkinson, Jan. 7, 1914; children—Mary Ellen, Eugene LeRoy, David Hicks, Thomas Atkinson. Dir. of phys. edn. and athletics, Swarthmore (Pa.) Coll., 1914-31; dean, dept. of phys. edn., U. of Pa., since 1931. Mem. Nat. Collegiate Athletic Assn. (mem. com. on coms.), Middle Atlantic States Collegiate Athletic Assn. (past pres.), College Phys. Edn. Assn. (past pres.), Middle Atlantic States Collegiate Athletic Conf. (sec.-treas.), Sigma Xi, Delta Upsilon, Alpha Mu Pi Omega. Clubs: Del. Valley Ornithological; Rolling Green; Varsity (U. of Pa.). Home: 630 N. Chester Rd., Swarthmore, Pa.

MERCK, George Wilhelm, mfg. chemist; b. New York, N.Y., Mar. 29, 1894; s. George and Friedrike (Schenck) M.; A.B., Harvard U., 1915; m. Serena Stevens, Nov. 24, 1926; children—George W., Jr., Albert W., Serena S., John H. C., Judith F. Asso. with Merck & Co., Inc., mfg. chemists, Rahway, N.J., since 1915, pres. and dir. since 1925; dir. Colgate-Palmolive-Peet Co., N.Y. & Long Branch R.R. Co., U.N.J. R.R. & Canal Co. Pres. bd. trustees Merck Inst. of Therapeutic Research. Was mem. Zoning Bd. Adjustment, West Orange; mem. bd. govs., Orange Memorial Hosp., Orange, N.J. Mem. exec. com. and vice-pres. Mfg. Chemists Assn.; mem. exec. com. Am. Drug Mfrs. Assn.; dir. and v.p. N.J. State Chamber of Commerce; dir. Nat. Assn. Mfrs. and Regional Plan. Assn.; dir. Nat. Conf. of Jews and Christians. Republican. Clubs: Essex County, Rock Spring Country (West Orange); University, Harvard, Chemists', Down Town, Railroad-Machinery (New York); Essex (Newark); University (St. Louis, Mo.); Jupiter Island (Hobe Sound, Fla.). Home: Prospect Av., West Orange. Office: Lincoln Av., Rahway, N.J.

MEREDITH, Albert Barrett, professor edn.; b. Gorham, N.H., Feb. 2, 1871; s. Rev. William Henry and Susan (Barrett) M.; grad. Classical High Sch., Lynn, Mass., 1899; student Boston U., 1891-93; B.A., Wesleyan U., Conn., 1895, M.A., 1916, LL.D., 1921; studied Harvard, summers, 1896,1900, 1901, Teachers Coll. (Columbia), 1910-11; Pd.D., Muhlenburg Coll., Allentown, Pa., 1918, L.H.D., Upsala Coll., East Orange, N.J., 1918; LL.D., Boston University, 1930; Litt.D., Rutgers U., New Brunswick, N.J., 1937; m. Adelaide Spencer (A.B., Wellesley), June 29, 1899; 1 son, Spencer Barrett. Teacher Holbrook Military School, Ossining, N.Y., 1895-97; vice prin. high sch., Plainfield, N.J., 1897-1901; superintendent schools, Nutley, N.J., 1901-11; county supt. schs., Essex Co., N.J., 1904-12; asst. commr. edn., N.J., in charge secondary edn., 1912-20; commr. of education, State of Conn., 1920-30; prof. of edn. and head department of school administration, New York University since 1930. Lectured at State U. of N.J., New York U., Yale U., etc. Asso. ednl. dir. Y.M.C.A., Camp Dix, N.J., 1918; mem. staff on edn. and spl. training, Plans Div. of Gen. Staff, U.S.A., Washington, D.C., 1918. Made secondary school surveys for St. Paul, St. Louis, and school surveys of Cincinnati, Niagara Falls (New York) and Buffalo, administrative and financial survey, Porto Rico, 1925; consultant National Secondary Sch. Survey, 1929, and dir. many surveys. Mem. Commn. of 7 on higher edn. in Calif., Carnegie Foundation of Teaching, 1932; mem. Ednl. Advisory Com., Fall River, Mass., 1933, Philadelphia, 1937; mem. Advisory Com., Peabody Mus. (Yale); trustee Wesleyan (Conn.) University, 1928-38, Drew University, 1935—; Centenary Junior College (Hackettstown, N.J.), 1932—, Teachers College (Columbia), 1922-24, Conn. State Coll., 1921-30. Chmn. Am. Council on Edn., Washington, D.C., 1931; ednl. advisor N.J. State Bd. of Regents, 1931-38; Bd. Edn., Hartford, Conn., 1934-35; advisory bd. National Society for Prevention of Blindness (N.Y.). Member N.E.A., Nat. Council Education, Nat. Conf. on St. and Highway Safety, Nat. Soc. for Study of Edn., Phi Beta Kappa, Theta Delta Chi. Republican. Methodist. Clubs: N.Y. Schoolmasters' (pres. 1914). Author: (with John H. Greenan) Problems of American Democracy; (with Vivian Hood) Geography, History and Civics of New Jersey; also various monographs on teaching high school subjects, and on school administration. Home: 3 Tuxedo Pl., Cranford, N.J. Address: New York University, New York, N.Y.

MEREDITH, C. H.; editor The Sun. Address: Hanover, Pa.

MEREDITH, Carey L.; pres. Farmers Nat. Bank. Home: 38 Franklin St., Annapolis, Md.

MEREDITH, James Alva, lawyer; b. Alma, Tyler Co., W.Va., Jan. 27, 1875; s. Absalom P. and Catherine (Riley) M.; Normal and Classical Acad., Buckhannon, W.Va., 1895; A.B., LL.B., W.Va. U., 1900; m. Gillian Jamison, Sept. 17, 1902; 1 son, Jamison. Began practice at Middlebourne, W.Va., 1900; moved to Fairmont, 1903; apptd. judge Supreme Court of Appeals, W.Va., to fill vacancy caused by resignation of Judge Charles W. Lynch, Jan. 2, 1922, later nominated for same office by Rep. State Conv., to fill unexpired term, but defeated in election; re-apptd. mem. Supreme Court of Appeals, Dec. 18, 1922, to fill vacancy occasioned by resignation of Judge Harold A. Ritz, term expiring Nov. 1924; now mem. firm Meredith & Bell; counsel for Monongahela West Penn Public Service Co. Member Joint Legislative Com. on Revision W.Va. Code. Mem. Am. and Marion Co. bar assns., W.Va. Bar Assn. (pres. 1932-33). Methodist. Mason (32°, K.T., Shriner). Home: Fairmont, W.Va.

MEREDITH, J(esse) Harper, lawyer; b. Fairmont, W.Va., Dec. 6, 1902; s. H. Brady and Myrtle (Hill) M.; A.B., W.Va. Univ., Morgantown, 1924; LL.B., W.Va. Univ. Law Sch., 1926; m. Elizabeth Leavitt, Oct. 27, 1928; children—Leavitt, Ann. Admitted to W.Va. bar, 1926 and since engaged in gen. practice of law at Fairmont. Mem. Marion County, W.Va. bar assns., Phi Delta Phi, Sigma Chi. Democrat. Home: Country Club Rd. Office: 227 Jefferson St., Fairmont, W.Va.

MERIAM, Lewis, statistician; b. Salem, Mass., Oct. 5, 1883; s. Horatio Cook and Edith Worcester M.; A.B., Harvard, 1905, A.M., 1906; LL.B., Nat. Law School, Washington, D.C., 1908; B.L., George Washington University Law School, 1909; Ph.D., Brookings Institution, 1936; m. Pink Wilson, Aug. 25, 1909; 1 dau., Adele Stuart. Editorial and statis. asst., U.S. Bur. of Census, Washington, 1905-07; acting chief, Div. of Revision and Results, same, 1907-12; asst. chief U.S. Children's Bur., 1912-15; mem. staff, New York Bur. Municipal Research, 1915-16; mem. sr. staff, Inst. for Govt. Research, 1916-18; production mgr. div. of planning and statistics of U.S. Shipping Bd., 1918-19; statistician Joint Congressional Commn. on Reclassification of Salaries, 1919-20; mem. sr. staff, Inst. for Govt. Research, Brookings Instn., since 1920; tech. aid U.S. Senate and House committees on civil service in matters relating to Classification Act of 1923; tech. aid to Salary and Wage Commission of North Carolina, 1925; tech. dir. survey of Indian affairs, made by Inst. for Govt. Research, at request of sec. of interior, 1926-28; mem. President's Emergency Com. for Employment, 1930-31; visiting prof. pub. adminstrn., U. of Chicago, 1935-36. Clubs: Cosmos (Washington); Harvard (New York). Author: Principles Governing the Retirement of Public Employes, 1917; (with associates) The Problem of Indian Administration, 1928, A Social Outlook on Indian Missions in Facing the Future in Indian Missions, 1932; Public Service and Special Training, 1936; Public Personnel Problems, 1938; Reorganization of the National Government (with L. F. Schmickibier), 1939; also bulls., papers on statistical subjects, personnel administration and Indian administration. Home: 23 W. Washington St., Kensington, Md.

MERITT, Benjamin Dean, univ. prof.; b. Durham, N.C., Mar. 31, 1899; s. Arthur Herbert and Cornelia Frances (Dean) M.; grad. high sch., Vernon, N.Y., 1916; A.B., Hamilton Coll., 1920, A.M., 1923, LL.D., 1937; student Am. School of Classical Studies at Athens, 1920-22; A.M., Princeton, 1923, Ph.D., 1924; D.Litt., Oxford Univ., 1936; m. Mary Elizabeth Kirkland, Dec. 22, 1923; children—James Kirkland, Benjamin Dean (dec.), Arthur Dean. Instr. Greek, U. of Vt., 1923-24, Brown U., 1924-25; asst. prof. Greek, Princeton, 1925-26; asst. dir. Am. Sch. Classical Studies at Athens, 1926-28; asso. prof. of Greek and Latin, U. of Mich., 1928-29, prof., 1929-33; visiting prof. Am. Sch. Classical Studies at Athens, 1932-33; dir. Athens Coll., 1932-33; Francis White prof. of Greek, Johns Hopkins, 1933-35; prof. Inst. for Advanced Study, Princeton, since 1935. Lec-

MERITY, Howard Edward, coll. adminstrn.; b. Jersey City, N.J., July 3, 1901; s. William J. and Ellen (Plunkett) M.; A.B., Seton Hall Coll., 1926; A.M., N.Y. Univ., 1932, Ed.D., same, 1936; m. Loretta Dalton, June 28, 1930; 1 dau., Madeleine Marie. In employ as instr. agt., N.J. Bell Telephone Co., 1923-26; teacher and adminstr., Cliffside Park Jr.-Sr. High Sch., 1927-36; head dept. edn. and dir. extension div., Seton Hall Coll., South Orange, N.J., since 1936, ednl. dir. Sch. of Nursing, dir. Summer Sch.; mem. adv. com. on curriculum revision of State Bd. Examiners of Nurses, N.J.; mem. nursing sch. com. in following hosps., St. Francis, Jersey City, St. Michaels, Newark, St. Mary's, Hoboken, St. James, Newark. Mem. Kappa Delta Pi, Phi Delta Kappa. Democrat. Roman Catholic. K.C. B.P.O.E. Home: 12 Eder Terrace, South Orange, N.J.

MERKER, Ralph K., clergyman; b. Pittsburgh, Pa., July 9, 1889; s. John A. and Mathilda (Crispens) M.; grad. Allegheny High Sch., 1908; B.Sc., Carnegie Inst. Tech., 1918; S.T.B., Western Theol. Sem., 1922, S.T.M., Grad. Sch., same, 1923; grad. study, U. of Pittsburgh; m. Rose L. Lowry. Ordained Presbyn. ministry, Presbytery of Pittsburgh, June 13, 1922; pastor Manchester Ch., Pittsburgh, 1923-26; asst. pastor Knoxville Ch., Pittsburgh, 1926-29; pastor Overbrook Ch., Pittsburgh, 1929-34, First Ch., Erie, since 1934. Instr. S.A.T.C., World War. Mem. Alpha Tau. Republican. Mason (K.T.). Club: Kiwanis (Erie). Home: 1023 W. 24th St., Erie, Pa.

MERKLE, Frederick Grover, prof. soil technology; b. Detroit, Mich., Mar. 25, 1892; s. Emil Fred and Elizabeth M.; B.Sc., Mass. State Coll., 1914, M.Sc., 1917; Ph.D., Cornell U., 1929; m. Rose Vernon Walker, June 12, 1923; 1 dau., Rose Elizabeth. Engaged as grad. asst. in agronomy, Mass. State Coll., 1914-15, instr., 1915-19; asst. prof. soil technology, Pa. State Coll., 1919-26, asso. prof., 1926-30, prof. since 1930. Fellow A.A.A.S. Mem. Gamma Sigma, Sigma Xi. Presbyn. Home: 629 Sunset Rd., State College, Pa.

MERREY, Edward F(rancis), Sr., lawyer; b. Paterson, N.J., Aug. 24, 1874; s. Patrick E. and Matilda (Magowan) M.; ed. Metropolis Law Sch.; m. Marie Fanning, June 23, 1910; 1 son, Edward F., Jr. Admitted to N.J. bar as atty., 1895, as counsellor, 1899; engaged in gen. practice of law at Paterson since 1895; served as corpn. counsel City of Paterson, 1907-16, 1923-25; mem. commn. for codification of laws of N.J. relating to municipalities, 1917-18; dir. Citizens Trust Co., Alex Hamilton Hotel Corpn. Mem. Am. Bar Assn., N.J. State Bar Assn., Passaic Co. Bar Assn. Democrat. Roman Catholic. K.C. Elk. Club: Country (Arcola). Co-author (with R. B. Eckman), New Jersey Municipalities Act, 1919. Home: 525 E. 29th St. Office: 140 Market St., Paterson, N.J.

MERRICK, Frank Anderson, vice chmn. Westinghouse Electric & Mfg. Co.; b. Lambertville, N.J.; s. Stephen W. and Mary Elizabeth (Walton) M.; E.E., Lehigh U., 1891, Engr.D., 1933; m. Louise Finney, 1893; children—John F., Lester F., Sara. With Thomson Houston Electric Co. and Gen. Electric Co., 1891-96, Blood & Hale, Boston, 1896-98; with Steel Motors Co., Johnstown, Pa., mgr. and chief engr., 1898-1902; with Westinghouse Electric & Mfg. Co., East Pittsburgh, Pa., 1902; supt. Canadian Westinghouse Co., Ltd., 1903, then mgr. works, v.p. and gen. mgr.; gen. mgr. New England Westinghouse Co., Chicopee Falls, Mass., mfg. rifles and machine guns, 1917-18; special rep. Westinghouse Internat. Co., London, Eng., 1919-21; v.p. and gen. mgr. Canadian Westinghouse Co., 1921-25; v.p. and gen. mgr. Westinghouse Electric & Mfg. Co., 1925-29, pres. 1929-38, vice chmn. since Feb. 1938. Awarded Imperial Decoration Third Order of the Rising Sun (Japan), 1935. Episcopalian. Home: 95 Arkledun Av., Hamilton, Can.; and Schenley Hotel, Pittsburgh. Office: Westinghouse Electric & Mfg. Co., Pittsburgh, Pa.

MERRICK, James Kirk, artist; b. Phila., Pa., Oct. 8, 1905; s. J. Frank and Mary Elizabeth (Bennett) M.; ed. Pa. Mus. Sch. of Industrial Art, 1924-28, Cape Sch. of Art, Provincetown, Mass., summer 1932; unmarried. Began as free lance illustrator and advertising, 1928; teacher class in drawing, 1929; teaching schedule increased and discontinued commercial work, 1930; portrait and landscape painting and teaching since 1930; has exhibited by invitation at leading art insts. and acads. over wide area and in prin. cities; dir. and sec. Phila. Art Alliance; dir., treas. and asst. sec. Phila. Water Color Club. Mem. Alumni Assn. Pa. Mus. Sch. of Industrial Art. Home: 2107 Spruce St., Philadelphia, Pa.

MERRICK, Robert Graff, pres. Equitable Trust Co.; b. Baltimore, Md., Nov. 18, 1895; s. Dr. Samuel K. and Mary Charlton (Graff) M.; A.B., Johns Hopkins U., 1917, Ph.D., 1922; m. Anne McEvoy, Jan. 27, 1923. Pres. Equitable Trust Co. since 1932; officer or dir. many companies. Home: Hurstleigh Av., Woodbrook, Baltimore County, Md. Office: Munsey Bldg., Baltimore, Md.

MERRILL, Earle Abbott, lawyer; b. Farmington, Me., Sept. 22, 1867; s. Warren and Lonia (Prescott) M.; A.B., Bowdoin Coll., Brunswick, Me., 1889; spl. student engring. Cornell U., 1891-92; LL.B., New York Law Sch., N.Y. City, 1912; A.M., Bowdoin Coll., 1892; m. Helen Wickliffe, Nov. 2, 1897 (dec.); 1 dau., Helen Virginia (Mrs. Roy F. Marsh). Successively asst. supt. Edison Electric Illuminating Co. of N.Y., asst. engr. Edison Gen. Electric Co. Central Dist., engr. and mgr. Pierce & Miller Engring. Co., N.Y. City; mgr. N.Y. Office, McIntosh, Seymour & Co.; admitted to N.J. bar as atty., 1914, as counselor, 1917; engaged in gen. practice of law at Westfield, N.J., since 1914; admitted to practice before the Supreme Ct. of the U.S. Mem. N.J. State and Union Co. bar assns., Phi Beta Kappa, Delta Kappa Epsilon, Sigma Xi. Republican. Home: 17 Stanley Oval. Office: 235 E. Broad St., Westfield, N.J.

MERRILL, Melvin Clarence, editorial adminstr.; b. Richmond, Utah, Apr. 6, 1884; s. Marriner Wood and Maria Loenza (Kingsbury) M.; B.S., Utah Agrl. Coll., Logan, Utah, 1905; student Cornell U., 1910-11; M.S., U. of Chicago, 1912; A.M., Harvard U., 1913; Ph.D., Washington Univ. St. Louis, Mo., 1915; m. Amy Lyman, Sept. 9, 1914; 1 dau., adopted, Betty Jane. Engaged as teacher and prin., high sch., Springville, Utah, 1905-06; agrl. inspr., Philippines, and supt. Baguio Expt. Sta., Philippines, 1906-10; dir. dept. of agriculture, Idaho Tech. Inst., Pocatello, Idaho, 1915-17; head dept. horticulture, Utah Agrl. Coll. and Expt. Sta., Logan, Utah, 1917-22; dean Coll. of Applied Science, Brigham Young Univ., Provo, Utah, 1922-24; dir. forestry pubs., Forest Service, Washington, D.C., 1924-25; editorial chief and chief of publs., U.S. Dept. Agr., Washington, D.C., since 1925. Fellow A.A.A.S. Mem. Bot. Soc. of America, Washington Acad. of Sci., Bot. Soc. of Washington, Sigma Xi, Phi Kappa Phi, Sigma Nu. Mormon. Clubs: Torch, Harvard, University of Chicago (Washington). Home: 800 Carroll Av., Takoma Park, Md.

MERRIMAN, Harry Morton, silk mfr.; b. Waterbury, Conn., Apr. 16, 1874; s. Henry and Mary A. (Heminway) M.; ed. Sedgwick Inst., Great Barrington, Mass., and Mt. Pleasant Mil. Acad., Ossining, N.Y.; m. Maude A. Jackson, Jan. 9, 1900; children—Harry Morton, John A., Maude Heminway (wife of Lt. Joseph Nevins, U.S.N.). Began with the Heminway Silk Co., 1890, treas., 1912, pres., 1914; merged with Belding Bros. & Co., 1926, as Belding Heminway Co., of which was elected chairman board of dirs., 1926; dir. Tunxis Estates (Tolland, Mass.); pres. 115 E. 53d Street Corpn. (New York); dir. Vera Cruz Investment Co. (Tampico, Mexico). Sec. bd. mgrs. Memorial Hosp., New York. Served in U.S. Navy, Apr. 6, 1917, until after the Armistice. Mem. Pilgrim Soc., Mil. Order Foreign Wars. Clubs: Union League, Century, Explorers, New York Yacht; Army and Navy (Washington, D.C.); Bohemian (San Francisco). Home: St. Michaels, Md. Office: 22 E. 40th St., New York, N.Y.

MERRIMAN, Robert, life ins. exec.; actuary; b. Scranton, Pa., Nov. 19, 1892; s. Edwin and Mary Eliza (Shepherd) M.; ed. Scranton High Sch. and Wharton School of Finance and Accounting, U. of Pa.; m. Elsa M. Weichel, Aug. 10, 1915; children—Robert Edwin, Eleanor Louise. With Scranton Life Ins. Co. since 1911, as clerk, 1911-18, registrar, 1918-20, actuary, 1920-23, asst. sec., 1923-32, vice-pres. since 1932; consulting actuary for fraternal societies. Episcopalian. Clubs: Scranton, Scranton Country; Philadelphia Actuaries. Home: 803 Poplar St., Clarks Summit, Pa. Office: Scranton Life Bldg., Scranton, Pa.

MERRIMAN, Roger Bigelow, Jr., headmaster; b. Cambridge, Mass., Apr. 29, 1905; s. Roger B. and Dorothea (Foote) M.; A.B., Harvard, 1927; grad. work Harvard summer school and U. of Calif., 1934-35; m. Frederika Warner, June 22, 1934; 1 dau., Frederika Warner. Teacher, Brooks School, North Andover, Mass., 1928-34, seniormaster, 1932-34; headmaster Arnold School, Pittsburgh, since 1935. Republican. Episcopalian. Clubs: Harvard (Boston); Harvard-Yale-Princeton, Fox Chapel Golf, Metropolitan (Pittsburgh). Home: North Andover, Mass. Address: 400 S. Braddock Av., Pittsburgh, Pa.

MERRITT, Carroll Bradford, publisher; b. Orange, N.J., Nov. 15, 1882; s. Samuel Wiggins and Belle (Bradford) M.; ed. public schools of Newark, N.J.; m. Jane Van Blarcom Cook, Nov. 15, 1906; children—Jane Van Blarcom (Mrs. Mortimer Hall Hait), Nancy Watson, Susan Elizabeth (Mrs. John Willard Holman), Caroline Bradford. Editor and publisher Madison (N.J.) Eagle, 1902-12; advertising dept., McGraw Pub. Co., New York, 1913; mgr. Scribners Magazine; dir. Charles Scribners Sons, pubs.; dir. Madison Trust Co., Madison Bldg. & Loan Assn.; sec. August Welte Corpn. Former mem. Common Council of Borough of Madison, N.J., chmn. Recreation Commn. and Shade Tree Commn. of Madison; mem. Morris County Shade Tree Commn.; former pres. bd. of mgrs. N.J. Reformatory for Women. Mem. Madison Hist. Soc. (dir.); vice-pres. Morris and Essex Kennel Club. Republican. Presbyterian. Mason, Elk. Clubs: Players, Sales Executives (New York). Home: 14 Pomeroy Rd., Madison, N.J. Office: 597 Fifth Av., New York, N.Y.

MERRY, Frieda Kiefer (Mrs. Ralph Vickers M.), coll. prof.; b. Dayton, O., July 20, 1897; d. Dr. Chas. A. and Caroline (Schaefer) Kiefer; A.B., Ohio State U., Columbus, 1921, Ph.D., 1927; A.M., U. of Mich., Ann Arbor, 1923; m. Ralph Vickers Merry, June 1, 1929. Engaged as research asst., U. of Mich., 1921-23; asst. ednl. psychology, Teachers Coll. Columbia U., summer 1923; psychol. examiner, pub. schs., Seattle, Wash., 1923-24; asst. prof. psychology and edn., Wittenberg Coll., Springfield, O., 1924-26; dir. dept. spl. studies sponsored by Am. Foundation for the Blind and Perkins Instn., 1927-32; clinician Child Guidance Clinic, Dayton, O., 1932-33; prof. psychology and dean of women, Alfred Holbrook Coll., Lebanon, O., 1933-34; prof. edn., Morris Harvey Coll., Charleston, W.Va., since 1934. Fellow A.A.A.S. Mem. Nat. Soc. for Study of Edn., Am. Psychol. Assn., W.Va. State Edn. Assn., W.Va. Acad. of Sci., Am. Assn. Univ. Women, Phi Beta

Kappa, Pi Lambda Theta. Lutheran. Contbr. to professional mags and journs. Home: Sherwood Apts., Charleston, W.Va.

MERRY, Ralph Vickers, coll. prof.; b. Magog, P.Q., Can., Dec. 8, 1903; s. Horace R. and Emma Kate (Vickers) M.; B.A., McGill Univ., Montreal, 1926, M.A., 1927; Ed.M., Harvard U. Grad. Sch. Edn., 1930, Ed.D., 1932; came to U.S., 1927, naturalized, 1933; m. Frieda A. Kiefer, June 1, 1929. Engaged as research asso., Perkins Instn., Watertown, Mass., 1927-28; consultant, Child Guidance Clinic, Dayton, O., 1932-33; asst. prof. edn., Alfred Holbrook Coll., Lebanon, O., 1933-34; prof. edn. and psychology, Morris Harvey Coll., Charleston, W.Va., since 1934. Fellow Royal Soc. Arts, London, Eng. Asso. Am. Psychol. Assn., W.Va. State Edn. Assn., W.Va. Acad. of Sci., Phi Delta Kappa. Methodist. Contbr. to professional mags. Home: Sherwood Apts., Charleston, W.Va.

MERSHON, Oliver Francis, ophthalmologist; b. Martins Creek, Pa., Nov. 27, 1873; s. George Middaugh and Henrietta (McFall) M.; ed. Temple U., 1900-01; M.D., Medico-Chirurg. Coll., Phila., 1904; m. Harriet A. Crater, 1893 (dec.); children—Jessie Alma (Mrs. Robert Milne), John Dressel; m. 2d, Goldie May Small, Apr. 28, 1909; children—Oliver Francis, George Small, Ray Wilbur. Began career as physician, 1904; asst. demonstrator of anatomy, instr. in refraction, Medico-Chirurg. Coll., 1905-16; instr. ophthalmology, U. of Pa. Grad. Sch., 1916-20, asst. prof. since 1920. Served as mem. Med. Adv. Bd. Red Cross Hosp. No. 1, Phila., during World War. Mem. A.M.A., Pa. State, and Phila. med. assns., Ptolomy, Phi Chi, Patriotic Sons of America. Presbyn. Mason. I.O.O.F. Clubs: Aesculapian, Medical. Home: 2110 Pine St., Philadelphia, Pa.

MERTEN, William John, cons. metall. engr.; b. Essen, Germany, June 21, 1876; s. Bernhard and Wilhelmina (Dreifort) M.; came to U.S., 1899, naturalized, 1910; student metall. engring., Carnegie Inst. Tech., 1907-12; m. Louise Frances Landsbach, Dec. 6, 1900; children—Raymond W., William F., Ralph C., Robert J. Apprentice Krupp's, Essen, Germany, 1891-95; mechanic Westinghouse Electric & Mfg. Co., East Pittsburgh, Pa., 1900-04, Westinghouse Machine Co., East Pittsburgh, 1904-06; metall. engr., Union Switch & Signal Co., Swissvale, Pa., 1906-16; metall. engr. and chem. engr., Firestone Steel Products Co., Akron, O., 1916-17; metall. engr. Twin City Forge & Foundry, Hillwater, Minn., 1917-19; chief metall. engr., Westinghouse Electric & Mfg. Co., 1919-30; metall. engr. and consultant, G. A. Lyon, Inc., Detroit, Mich., 1930-33; metall. engr. on development, Pittsburgh Rolls Corpn., 1933-38; cons. metall. engr., Babcock & Wilcox, Beaver Falls, Pa., 1919-22, Calorizing Co., Wilkinsburg, Pa., 1922-24; Titusville Forge Co., Titusville, Pa., since 1933. Mem. Am. Inst. Mining and Metall. Engrs., Am. Soc. for Metals (chmn. Pittsburgh Chapter, 1923-24), Engrs. Soc. of Western Pa. Republican. Mason (Lodge 635; Royal Arch 297; K.T. 72; Shriner, Syria Lodge). Author numerous articles in tech. pubs. Address: 416 S. Lang Av., Pittsburgh, Pa.

MERTZ, John Ernest, clergyman; b. Linfield, Pa., Feb. 8, 1895; s. Rev. John Allen and Clara M. (Reber) M.; A.B., Ursinus Coll., 1914; ed. New Brunswick Theol. Sem., 1914-17; (hon.) D.D., Franklin and Marshall Coll., 1935; m. Emily E. Wiest, June 7, 1917. Ordained to ministry Reformed Ch. in America, 1917; served as student pastor, Staten Island, N.Y., 1915-17; pastor, Freehold, N.J., 1917-20, Port Jervis, N.Y., 1920-22, Paterson, N.J., 1922-26; minister Brainerd Presbyn. Ch., Easton, Pa., since 1926; served as mem. Bd. Edn. of Reformed Ch. of America for two yrs. Mem. Bd. Childrens Aid Soc. of Northampton Co. for two yrs. Past pres. Ministers Assn. of Easton, Phillipsburg, and vicinity. Republican. Mem. Presbyn. Ch. of U.S.A. Has pub. three series of Lenten addresses. Home: 157 Shawnee Av., Easton, Pa.

MERTZ, William Franklin, newspaper publisher, printer; b. Nazareth, Pa., May 29, 1894; s. Allen and Cora Cecelia (Vogel) M.; student Nazareth (Pa.) High Sch., 1907-11, Churchman Business Coll., Easton, Pa., 1911-12; m. Jeanette Abel, 1918 (died 1926); 1 child—Mary; m. 2d, Anna Kaiser, Dec. 21, 1932; children—Katharine, William Franklin. Clk. in office Lehigh Valley R.R. Co., Easton, Pa., 1912-15; clk. main office Nazareth (Pa.) Cement Co., 1915-17; clk. Hercules Cement Co., Stockertown, Pa., 1917-18; taught country sch., Palmer Twp., Pa., 1920-21; clk. Nazareth (Pa.) Item Pub. Co., Inc., 1921-24, pres., treas. and editor since 1924. Mem. Town Council, Nazareth, 1926-32 (2 terms). Mem. Chamber of Commerce (sec. since 1929). Independent Democrat. Lutheran. Elk. Club: Democratic (Nazareth, Pa.). Home: 1 Hall Sq. Office: 48 S. Main St., Nazareth, Pa.

MERZ, August, chemist; b. New York, N.Y., Nov. 7, 1873; s. Henry and Augusta (Heller) M.; grad. New York pub. schs., 1888; attended Coll. City of N.Y., to 1892; B.S., Cornell U., 1893, grad. student, same, 1893-95; student Heidelberg U., Germany, 1895-97; D.Sc., Rutgers U., 1934; m. Florence V. Doyle, Apr. 26, 1899; children—Viola (Mrs. John King Watson), Ottilie (wife of Dr. Alfred Meurlin), Henry (dec.), August. Began as chemist Heller & Merz Co., 1897, advanced through various positions, later becoming plant mgr. in the mfr. of coal tar colors and intermediates, company absorbed by Calco Chem. Co., Inc., 1930, and since v.p.; sec. Ultramarine Co.; mem. advisory com. Ironbound Branch of Fidelity Union Trust Co. Trustee East Orange Gen. Hosp., Newark Eye & Ear Infirmary; mem. advisory bd. N.J. Coll. of Pharmacy. Mem. Am. Chem. Soc., Am. Inst. Chem. Engrs., Am. Inst. Chemists, Phi Gamma Delta, Sigma Xi. Republican. Clubs: Chemists (New York); Newark Athletic. Home: 333 Harrison St., East Orange, N.J. Office: Calco Chemical Co., Inc., Bound Brook, N.J.

MESEROLE, Clinton Vanderbilt, pres. Pacific Fire Ins. Co.; b. Brooklyn, N.Y., 1876; s. Jeremiah V. and Anne S. (Richardson) M.; Polytechnic Inst., Brooklyn; B.S., Princeton, 1898; m. Ida Lewis Brooke, May 2, 1905; children—Rhe B., Anne R., Clinton V., Jere S. In fire ins. business since 1898; pres. Pacific Fire Ins. Co., Bankers & Shippers Insurance Co. of New York. Jersey Ins. Co. of New York. Special representative of Ordnance Dept., U.S.A., World War. Republican. Presbyn. Clubs: University, Princeton, Down Town (New York); Nat. Golf Links, Knickerbocker Country, Aldecress Country, Yeamans Hall. Home: Lydecker St., Englewood, N.J. Office: 95 Maiden Lane, New York, N.Y.

MESSICK, Charles Polk, chief examiner and sec. N.J. State Civil Service Comm.; b. near Georgetown, Del., June 4, 1882; s. John T. and Julia A. (West) M.; prep. edn. Country Schools, Sussex Co., Del., 1888-99; A.B., Del. Coll. (U. of Del.), Newark, 1907, A.M., 1909, LL.D., 1932; A.M., U. of Pa., 1911; hon. Dr. of Business Adminstrn., Rutgers U., 1934; m. Maude Louise Sharpley, June 30, 1909. Teacher district schools, Del., 1899-1903; instr. Wenonah (N.J.) Mil. Acad., 1907-08; teacher, later head dept. history and social science, Trenton (N.J.) High Sch., 1908-12; examiner N.J. State Civil Service Commn., 1912-17, chief examiner and sec. since 1917; supervisor evening schools, Trenton Bd. of Edn., 1916-17; dir. Prudential Ins. Co.; farmer. Mem. Trenton Bd. of Edn., 10 years, pres. 1937-39; trustee Vineland Training Sch. Chmn. N.J. State Planning Bd. since 1934; vice-chmn. N.J. Council; mem. Civil Service Assembly of U.S. and Can. (past pres., past chmn. exec. council, etc.); organizer Bureau of Public Personnel Adminstrn.; consultant on personnel, state orgn. and administrative problems to N.J. and various states; active in N.J. in public undertakings; lecturer and public speaker. Mem. Acad. Polit. and Social Science, Phi Kappa Phi, Sigma Nu. Ind. Republican. Methodist. Mason (33°), Shriner. Co-author: The Merit System in Government, and numerous monographs on public personnel administration organization and planning. Home: 1414 W. State St. Office: State House, Trenton, N.J.

MESSLER, Eugene Lawrence, engineer; b. Pittsburgh, Apr. 6, 1873; s. Thomas D. and Maria R. (Varick) M.; B.Ph., Sheffield Scientific School (Yale), 1894; m. Elizabeth V. Long, Dec. 31, 1898; children—Thomas D., E. Lawrence. Began as pattern maker and moulder, Edgar Thompson Works of Carnegie Steel Co.; successively civ. engr., gen. supt. labor and transportation and asst. blast furnace supt., Duquesne Works, Carnegie Steel Co., Pa., 1895-99; supt. and gen. supt. Eliza Furnaces, Coke Works, Jones & Laughlin Steel Co., 1899-1911; asst. to pres. Riter-Conley Mfg. Co., 1912-15; v.p. and gen. mgr. Witherow Steel Co., 1916-18; also pres. Eureka Fire Brick Works; dir. Third Nat. Bank, Pittsburgh, Fisher Scientific Co. Commd. capt. engrs., May 20, 1918; comdg. Co. G., 21st Engrs., 1st Army A.E.F., Sept. 1918-May 1919; participated in St. Mihiel, defensive sector and Meuse-Argonne offensives; lt. col. Engr. Res. Mem. Am. Iron and Steel Inst., Am. Inst. M.E., Am. Refractories Inst., Am. Soc. Mil. Engrs., Vets. of Foreign Wars, Engring. Soc. Western Pa., British Iron and Steel Inst., S.A.R., Am. Legion, Reserve Officers Assn. Clubs: Yale (New York); Harvard-Yale-Princeton, Cloister, Pittsburgh Golf, Rolling Rock. Home: 5423 Forbes St. Office: B. F. Jones Bldg., Pittsburgh, Pa.

MESTICE, Francis Paul, clergyman; b. Tricarico, Italy, Dec. 14, 1886; s. Pasquale and Mary-Carmela (Grassi) M.; ed. Gymnasium-Lyceum Sem. of Tricarico, 1898-1906, Philosophy, Sacred Theology Interdiocesan Sem. of Matera, 1906-10, State Normal Sch., Stigliani of Matera, 1913-16; grad. student Fordham U., 1933-35, Rutgers U., 1935-38. Came to U.S., 1920, naturalized, 1927. Began as Roman Catholic pastor, Italy, 1910; teacher to disabled war veterans and war wounded, Bari, Italy, 1916-18; teacher-supervisor, Vittoria Coloma, Naples, 1918-19; teacher-censor Scuola Agraria Francesco Gigante Alberobello, 1919; prof. of Italian lang. and literature, Darlington Sem., N.J., 1928-34; pastor Immaculate Conception Ch., Newark, N.J., since 1925. Awarded war cross, 1918 (Italy); Golden Cross and diploma by Pope Pius XI, 1926. Treas. Immaculate Conception Ch., Newark, N.J., 1925; spiritual dir. Holy Name Soc. Rectory: 381 Woodside Av. Church: 796 Summer Av., Newark, N.J.

METCALF, William, Jr., retired; b. Pittsburgh, Pa., Apr. 16, 1870; s. William and Christiana (Fries) M.; student Shattuck Mil. Sch., Faribault, Minn., 1883-89; attended Mich. and Cornell univs., 1889-91; LL.B., Cornell U., 1901; m. Kate Cassidy, Jan. 4, 1893; m. 2d, Faith White, Apr. 1, 1918. With Crescent Steel Co., 1891-92, Frank-Kneeland Machine Co., 1892-98, Cornell Law Sch., 1901-09; pres. Braeburn Steel Co., 1909-18; almost entirely inactive since World War; v.p. and dir. Wyckoff Drawn Steel Co.; dir. United Engineering & Foundry Co. Served as capt., Chem. Warfare Service, A.E.F., World War. Formerly trustee Carnegie Inst., Pittsburgh, Cornell Univ., Ithaca, N.Y. Mem. Chi Psi. Republican. Episcopalian. Clubs: Duquesne (Pittsburgh); Allegheny Country (Sewickley); life mem. Congressional Country (Washington, D.C.). Home: 642 Grove St., Sewickley, Pa. Address: P.O. Box 353, Sewickley, Pa.

METHENY, C. Brainerd, life ins.; b. Pittsburgh, Pa., Dec. 30, 1889; s. David and Mary Ellen (Dodds) M.; A.B., Geneva Coll., Beaver Falls, Pa., 1911; student Carnegie Inst. Tech., Pittsburgh, 1911-12; m. Kathryn Tomasson, July 22, 1919; children—David Brainerd, Richard Tomasson, John Edgar, Kathryn. Teacher Cambridge Springs High Sch., 1912; dir. athletics, Geneva Coll., 1913-17; in life insurance business since 1919; mgr. Fidelity Mutual Life Ins. Co. since 1934; pres. and dir. Sterling Photo Mfg. Co., Beaver Falls; dir. First Nat. Bank, Beaver Falls. Served in air service, U.S. Army, 1917-18. Trustee Geneva Coll.; dir. Beaver Valley Y.M.C.A., New Brighton, Pa. Dir. Pittsburgh Life Underwriters Assn.; mem. Am. Legion, Internat. Brotherhood of Magicians, Economics Club (Geneva Coll.). Independent in politics. Reformed Presbyterian. Clubs: Beaver

Falls Kiwanis (pres.); Beaver Valley University. Home: 3123 Fifth Av., Beaver Falls, Pa. Office: Grant Bldg., Pittsburgh, Pa.

METTEN, William F., newspaper pub.; b. nr. Milford, Del., Feb. 6, 1871; s. Alexander and Elizabeth M.; ed. country sch.; m. Elizabeth Janvier Murray, Nov. 1900 (died Apr. 1910); children—W. Murray, Elizabeth; m. 2d, Meta McSorley, of Wilmington, Nov. 14, 1913; children—John F., Miriam, William. Began as reporter Every Evening, Wilmington, Del., 1895, pub. of same, 12 yrs. until 1933; now bus. mgr. News-Journal Co. (consolidated newspapers). Dir. Security Trust Co.; mem. board Artisons Savings Bank. Mem. Bd. Park Commrs. (Wilmington), State Welfare Commn. Ex-pres. Wilmington Chamber Commerce and Rotary Club. Democrat. Methodist. Clubs: Wilmington, Wilmington Country (dir.). Home: 2209 Boulevard, Wilmington, Del.

METTEN, William Murray, newspaper promotion mgr.; b. Wilmington, Del., Sept. 25, 1902; s. William Fowler and Bessie (Murray) M.; student Wilmington (Del.) Friends Sch., 1918-20; B.S., Lehigh U., Bethlehem, Pa., 1925; m. Martha Louise White, Aug. 22, 1934. Advertising mgr. Grove Investments, Asheville, N.C., 1925-27; nat. advertising mgr. Asheville (N.C) Citizen, 1927-29; advertising mgr. Morris Candy Co., Atlanta, Ga., 1930; promotion mgr. Every Evening, Wilmington, 1931-32; promotion mgr. News-Journal papers since 1933. Mem. Mayor's Traffic Advisory Com. for Wilmington since 1936; exec. mem. Del. Com. for N.Y. World's Fair since 1938. Dir. Wilmington Salvation Army, Peoples Settlement. Mem. Del.-Md.-Va. Press Assn. (pres. since Jan. 1939), Delta Tau Delta. Methodist. Clubs: Advertising (pres. 1935-37, treas. since 1937; Lehigh of Del. (Wilmington; pres. since 1938). Home: 701 Nottingham Road, Wawaset Park. Office: News-Journal, Wilmington, Del.

METZ, Charles William, biologist; b. Sundance, Wyo., Feb. 17, 1889; s. Judge William Summerfield and Jennie (Gammon) M.; B.S., Pomona Coll., Claremont, Calif., 1911; studied Stanford, 1911-12, Columbia, 1912-14, Ph.D., 1916; m. Blanche E. Stafford, Aug. 20, 1913; children—Charles Baker, William Stafford, Jane Gammon, Alburn Stafford. Mem. staff, Carnegie Instn., department of genetics, 1914-30, department of embryology since 1930; visiting prof. zoölogy, Johns Hopkins U., 1930-37. Anti-malaria work (extra-cantonment sanitation), United States P.H.S., 1917-19; has specialized in cytol. and genetical research. Fellow A.A.A.S.; member Soc. Exptl. Biology and Medicine, Am. Soc. Naturalists, Am. Soc. Zoölogists, Sigma Xi, Phi Beta Kappa. Conglist. Home: 3925 Cloverhill Rd., Baltimore, Md.

METZ, Robert Carter, supt. of schs.; b. Ashley, Pa., Sept. 21, 1889; s. James L. and Rebecca (Kugler) M.; student normal sch., Bloomsburg, Pa., 1907-10; B.A., Susquehanna U., 1927; M.S., U. of Pa., 1939; m. Ethyl Brunner, Aug. 24, 1914. Connected with pub. schs., Ashley, Pa., since 1910, as eighth grade teacher, 1910-14, prin. grade sch., 1914-22, teacher mathematics in high sch., 1922-24, prin. high sch., 1924-34; supt. of schs. since 1934. Mem. Business Men's Assn. (mem. exec. bd.), Pa. State Ednl. Assn., N.E.A., Memorial Day Assn. Am. Legion; asso. mem. Firemen's Assn. Republican. Methodist. Mason (32°). Home: 23 Manhattan St. Office: 59 Ashley St., Ashley, Pa.

METZ, Russell Kenneth, banking; b. Altoona, Pa., June 16, 1903; s. Robert G. and Anna C. (Griffin) M.; ed. pub. schs. and high sch., Altoona, Pa.; m. Vera Kenzel, of New York, N.Y., Sept. 8, 1928. Employed as clk. later teller Second Nat. Bank, Altoona, Pa., 1919-25; licensed real estate salesman in Fla., 1925-26; savings teller Citizens Bank of West Palm Beach, Fla., 1926; asst. nat. bank examiner, 1926-32; vice-pres. and dir. Hopewell Nat. Bank, Hopewell, N.J., since 1932. Served as pres. borough council, Hopewell, N.J. Mem. Pa. Soc. of N.Y. Republican. Presbyn. Mason. Club: Hopewell Valley Golf. Home: E. Prospect St., Hopewell, N.J.

METZENHEIM, Henry Herman, asso. prof. engring.; b. Hanover, Germany, Feb. 14, 1885; s. Hermann and Dora (Grobel) M.; came to U.S., 1911, naturalized, 1920; B.S. in E.E. Cooper Union Inst., 1917, E.E., same, 1920; m. Clarice Wainwright, June 30, 1923. Employed as design engr., Crocker Wheeler Elec. Mfg. Co., Ampere, N.J., 1917-22; instr. elec. engring., Newark Coll. Engring., Newark, N.J., 1922-28, asst. prof., 1928-37, asso. prof. since 1937, asst. to pres. 1932-38; comptroller Newark Coll. of Engring. since 1938; supervisor evening sch., Newark Tech. Sch. since 1938. Mem. Am. Inst. Elec. Engrs., Soc. for Promotion Engring. Edn., Nat. Soc. Professional Engrs., N.J. Assn. Professional Engrs., Nat. Geographic Soc. Republican. Presbyn. Mason. Home: 55 Hollywood Av., Hillside. Office: 367 High St., Newark, N.J.

METZEROTT, Oliver, lawyer; b. Washington, D.C., Dec. 6, 1874; s. William C. and Henrietta (Eisenbrandt) M.; grad. Emerson Inst., Washington, D.C., 1893; B.S., Princeton U., 1898; LL.B., Nat. U., Washington, D.C., 1902, LL.M., 1903; unmarried. Admitted to D.C bar, 1903; mgr. and treas. Columbia Theater Co., Washington, D.C., 1908-15; in practice law and in real estate appraisal and banking business, Washington, D.C., and Hyattsville, Md., since 1903; pres. Prince Georges County (Md.) Nat. Farm Loan Assn. since 1934; dir. and mem. exec. com. Prince George's Bank & Trust Co., Hyattsville and Mt. Rainier, Md.; dir. Suburban Nat. Bank, Silver Spring, Md. Served as capt., maj., U.S. Army, during World War. Mem. Md. House of Dels., 1908, 12, 16, 31, 33, Md. State Senate, 1918-22; chmn. D.C. Rent Commn., 1923-25; mem. various Md. Prison Commns. Mem. D.C. Bar Assn., Prince Georges County Bar Assn., Sigma Nu Phi. Republican. Unitarian. Mason, Odd Fellow. Clubs: University, Chevy Chase (Washington, D.C.); Cannon (Princeton, N.J.); Rotary, Vansville Farmers' (College Park, Md.). Address: Riggs Rd., Hyattsville, Md.

METZGER, Fraser, univ. dean and chaplain; b. Gloversville, N.Y., Oct. 25, 1872; s. Albert Henry and Catherine (Lenz) M.; B.D. Defiance (O.) Coll. Biblical Inst., 1895; B.A., Union Coll., Schenectady, N.Y., 1902, L.H.D., 1935; D.D., Middlebury (Vt.) Coll., 1920; m. Jessie Lacy, June 12, 1902; children—Albert Lacy, Roscoe Fraser, Karl Edward. Began as minister, Randolph, Vt., 1895; chaplain, Penn State Coll., 1923-25; dean of mem, Rutgers U., New Brunswick, N.J., since 1925, acting chaplain since 1933. Served in F.A., U.S. Army, 1918, at O.T.C., Camp Zachary Taylor, Louisville, Ky.; now 1st lt. and chaplain, Reserve Corps. Candidate Gov. of Vt., Progressive Ticket, 1912; mem. Vt. Legislature, 1916, state food administr., 1917. Mem. Delta Upsilon, Phi Beta Kappa, Psi Chi, Tau Kappa Alpha. Republican. Congregationalist. Address: 135 College Av., New Brunswick, N.J.

METZGER, Frederick Elder, college pres.; b. Hanover, Pa., Oct. 26, 1868; s. Henry Clay and Cora (Myley) M.; B.A., Gettysburg (Pa.) Coll., 1888, M.A., 1890; grad. study, U. of Leipzig, Germany, 1890-91, Am. Sch. Classical Studies, Athens, Greece, 1891-92; m. Martha Thomas, Sept. 9, 1896; 1 dau., Margaret Thomas (Mrs. Herbert Benjamin Williams). Began as high sch. prin., 1894; prof. Latin and Greek, Md. Coll. for Women, Lutherville, 1895-1932, pres. since 1932. Mem. Phi Delta Theta. Republican. Lutheran. Home: Lutherville, Md.

METZGER, Fritz Louis, civil engring.; b. Rutland, Vt., Dec. 22, 1881; s. William and Matilda (Haara) M.; B.S. in C.E., Norwich U., 1903; m. Elverna M. Mohler, July 1, 1909; children—Janet, Fritz, Jr., Marie, John M. Engaged in profession as civil engr. since 1903; mem. firm Metzger-Richardson Company, civil engrs., Pittsburgh, Pa., since 1919; engaged principally in design of fire-proof bldg. constrn.; erected many important structures in Pittsburgh area. Registered professional engr. in Pa. Asso. mem. Am. Soc. Civil Engrs. Republican. Methodist. Mason (K.T., 32°, Shriner). Club: Highland Country. Home: 557 Dawson Av.,

Bellevue, Pa. Office: Century Bldg., Pittsburgh, Pa.

METZGER, Irvin Dilling, M.D., opnthalmologist; b. New Enterprise, Pa., Apr. 12, 1873; s. Jacob Burket and Catherine (Dilling) M.; B.E., Juniata Coll., Huntingdon, Pa., 1894, Ed.M., 1896; M.D., Hahnemann Med. Coll. Phila., 1904, hon. A.M., 1937; Oculi et Auris Chirurgus, New York Ophthalmic Hospital College, 1910; graduate study University of Vienna and London, 1913-14; D.Sc. (hon.), University of Pittsburgh, 1936; m. Dorothy Thompson, August 6, 1919; 1 son, James Thompson. Supt. pub. schs., Hollidaysburg, Pa., 1895-1900; in gen. practice, Tyrone, Pa., 1904-09, eye, ear, nose and throat practice, 1910-13; practice confined to ophthalmology, Pittsburgh, Pa., since 1914. Served as capt., Med. Corps, U.S.A., Base Hosp., Camp Taylor, Louisville, Ky., 1918-19. Administrative officer, Pa. State Bd. Med. Edn. (pres. bd.) and insp. med. schs. and hosps. Pres. Fed. State Med. Bds. of U.S., 1935-36; member Am. Inst. Homœopathy (pres. 1929-30), Ophthal., Otol. and Laryngol. Soc. (pres. 1927-28), Pa. Homœo. Med. Soc., Philos. Soc., Fellowship Soc., Pi Epsilon Rho. Republican. Baptist. Mason (32°, Shriner). Clubs: University, Torch, Quiz, Edgewood Country. Writer of med. bulls. for State of Pa. Contbr. to Jour. Am. Inst. Homœopathy, etc. Home: 450 S. Atlantic Av. Office: 5230 Center Av., Pittsburgh, Pa.

METZGER, Jacob Elry; prof. agronomy, U. of Md.; acting dir. Expt. Station. Address: University of Maryland, College Park, Md.

METZGER, Leon Daniel, lawyer; b. Sinnemahoning, Pa., Apr. 23, 1891; s. William Howard and Ella S. (Berfield) M.; ed. Ind. State Teachers Coll., 1908-11; A.B., U. of Mich., 1914; LL.B., U. of Mich. Law Sch., 1916; m. Josephine A. Klopp, Feb. 23, 1921; children—Jo-Ann, Mary Jane. Admitted to Pa. bar, 1920 and began practice of law at Harrisburg; asst. chief, Bur. of Corpns., Dept. of State, 1919-24; asst. dep. atty. gen. of Pa., 1924-26, dep. atty. gen. 1926-29; dep. sec. of revenue, 1929-32, Sec. of Revenue, 1932-35; engaged in gen. practice of law at Harrisburg since 1935, mem. firm Snyder, Hull, Leiby and Metzger. Served as 1st lieut., U.S.A., 1917-19, with A.E.F., wounded in action on Meuse-Argonne front. Mem. Pa. State, and Dauphin Co. bar assns., Sigma Phi Epsilon, Phi Delta Phi. Republican. Methodist. Mason (32°, Shriner). Home: 107 Hillside Rd. Office: Kline Bldg., Harrisburg, Pa.

METZGER, Maurice Rutt, lawyer; b. Dauphin Co., Pa., Sept. 12, 1884; s. Martin B. and Ellen E. (Rutt) M.; A.B., Lebanon Valley Coll., Annville, Pa., LL.B., U. of Pa. Law Sch.; m. Anna M. Manning, Sept. 4, 1912; children—Bruce M., Edith M. Sch. teacher, Middletown, Pa., 1902-07; admitted to Pa. bar, 1911; law partner of Judge F. B. Wickersham, 1913-20; senior mem. firm Metzger and Wickersham, Harrisburg, Pa., since 1922. Mem. Pa. Ho. of Rep., 1925-29. Dir. Middletown Drainage Co., Farmers Trust Co., Middletown Development Co. Republican. Home: 37 N. Union St., Middletown, Pa. Office: 22 S. 3rd St., Harrisburg, Pa.

METZGER, William Fridolin, pres. H. O. Swoboda, Inc.; b. Pittsburgh, Pa., July 22, 1902; s. Ludwig George and Elizabeth (Strasser) M.; student high sch., Allegheny, Pittsburgh, 1915-18, Internat. Corr. Sch., 1920-21, Carnegie Inst. Tech., 1922-24; m. Mary Elizabeth Enright, Sept. 8, 1936. Began in engring. dept. Monongahela Div., Pa. R.R., South Side, Pittsburgh, 1918; engr. dept. Koppers Co., Pittsburgh, 1919; chief draftsman H. O. Swoboda, Inc., New Brighton, Pa. 1920-25, asst. engr., 1925-29, engr., 1929-32, dir. since 1926, pres. and engr. since 1932. Mem. Engrs. Soc. of Western Pa., Am. Welding Soc. Republican. Roman Catholic. Author numerous articles in tech. pubs. Holder several U.S. and Canadian patents. Home: 133 Chestnut St., Zelienople, Pa. Office: 13th St., New Brighton, Pa.

METZLER, Sankey Wesley, pres. Wright-Metzler Co.; b. Albrightsville, W.Va., Dec. 13, 1877;

s. Noah and Mary R. (Feather) M.; student Summer Normal Sch., Kingwood, W.Va.; m. Clare Judkins, Oct. 12, 1904; children—Mrs. Martha MacDonald, William Judkins. Began in gen. store, Hartley & Sharps, Independence, W. Va., 1893, purchased interest, 1898, continuing as Hartley & Metzler until 1904; organized Wright-Metzler Co., Connellsville, Pa., 1904, Wright-Metzler Co., Uniontown, Pa., 1907, now pres. and dir.; pres. and dir. Am. Dept. Stores Corpn. of Pa., The Caldwell Store, Inc., Washington, Pa., Metzler-Wright Co., Warren, Pa. Pres. Fayette Co. Community Trust; dir. and chmn. exec. com. Uniontown (Pa.) Hosp. Mem. Uniontown Chamber of Commerce (dir.), Pa. Retailers Assn. (dir.), S.A.R. (Fort Necessity Chapter). Methodist (trustee Asbury M.E. Ch., Uniontown). Mason (32°). Clubs: Uniontown (Pa.) Country; Duquesne (Pittsburgh). Home: 81 Pennsylvania Av. Office: 20 E. Main St., Uniontown, Pa.

MEYER, Adolf, psychiatrist, neurologist; b. Niederweningen, nr. Zürich, Switzerland, Sept. 13, 1866; s. Rudolf and Anna (Walder) M.; ed. Gymnasium, Zürich; Swiss Staatsexamen for practice of medicine, 1890; post-grad. studies at Paris, London, Edinburgh, Zürich, Vienna and Berlin, 1890-92; M.D., of Zürich, 1892; LL.D., Glasgow Univ., 1901, Clark University, 1909; Sc.D., Yale University, 1934; m. Mary Potter Brooks, Sept. 15, 1902; 1 dau., Julia Lathrop. Came to U.S., Sept. 1892. Hon. fellow and later docent in neurology, U. of Chicago, 1892-95; pathologist to Ill. Eastern Hosp. for the Insane, Kankakee, 1893-95; pathologist and later dir. of clin. and lab. work, Worcester (Mass.) Insane Hosp. and docent in psychiatry, Clark U., 1895-1902; dir. Pathol. (psychiatric) Inst., N.Y. State Hosps., 1902-10; prof. psychiatry, Cornell U. Med. Coll., 1904-09; prof. psychiatry Johns Hopkins, and dir. Henry Phipps Psychiatric Clinic, Johns Hopkins Hosp., since 1910; Salmon memorial lecturer, 1932; Maudsley lecturer, 1933. Hon. pres. of Nat. Com. for Mental Hygiene and pres. Internat. Com. for Mental Hygiene since 1937; hon. mem. Boston Soc. Neurology and Psychiatry, Royal Medico-psychological Assn., New York Psychoanalytic Institute; mem. Assn. Am. Physicians, Am. Neurol. Assn. (ex-pres.) Am. Psychiatric Assn. (pres., 1927), Academie der Naturforscher zu Halle, American Institute Criminal Law and Criminology, A.A. A.S., New York Acad. Sciences, Assn. for Research in Nervous and Mental Diseases, Am. Orthopsychiatric Assn.; ex-pres. New York Psychiatric Soc.; ex-pres. Am. Psychopathol. Assn.; corr. mem. Societé de Neurologie, Societé de Psychologie and Societé Medico-psychologique (Paris). Extensive contbr. on neurology, pathology and psychiatry, etc. Zwinglian Protestant. Clubs: Century (New York); Cosmos (Washington); Baltimore Country. Home: 4305 Rugby Rd., Guilford, Baltimore. Address: Johns Hopkins Hospital, Baltimore, Md.

MEYER, Charles Albert, mfg. exec.; b. Dallas, Tex., Nov. 5, 1884; s. Charles Albert and Annie Clara (Manner) M.; student high sch., Dallas, Tex., 1897-1901; m. Doreen Seyboth, Oct. 11, 1938 (divorced); children—Charles Boyd, Rex Thomas (adopted). Was successively asst. treas., treas., sec. and treas., Fairbanks, Morse & Co., Chicago, Ill., 1902-23; sec., treas. and dir. Nat. Supply Co., Pittsburgh, Pa., since 1923; dir. Chalfant Dock Co., The Illinois Supply Co., The Nat. Supply Co., Ltd., Nat. Supply Constrn. Corpn., Nat. Supply Corpn., Spang Chalfant, Inc., Union Tool Co., Kentucky Natural Gas Corpn., The Colonial Trust Co. Mem. Pa. Soc., Chartered Inst. of Am. Inventors. Republican. Unitarian. Clubs: Duquesne, Pittsburgh Field (Pittsburgh); Lake Placid (Lake Placid, N.Y.). Author: Mercantile Credits and Collections, 1919. Home: 4309 Parkman Av. Office: 1400 Grant Bldg., Pittsburgh, Pa.

MEYER, George Young, lawyer; b. Pittsburgh, Pa., July 26, 1891; LL.B., U. of Pittsburgh Law Sch., 1913; m. Marie Bock, Nov. 18, 1914; children—Mary E., Ruth K., Mildred I., George Young, Carl F., Ann Marie. Admitted to bar, 1913, and since practiced at Pittsburgh. Mem. Allegheny Co. Bar Assn., Pa. Bar Assn., Am. Bar Assn. K.C. (Past Grand Knight). Clubs: Pittsburgh Athletic Assn., Pittsburgh Field (Pittsburgh). Home: 4734 Bayard St. Office: 1515 Berger Bldg., Pittsburgh, Pa.

MEYER, Henry Coddington, Jr., consulting engr.; b. Orange, N.J., Nov. 28, 1870; s. Henry Coddington and Charlotte English (Seaman) M.; M.E., Stevens Inst. Tech., 1892; m. Louise G. Underhill, Nov. 18, 1896; children—Henry Coddington, Emily Louise. Engring. practice, New York, 1893-1919; now pres., Meyer, Strong & Jones, Inc., consulting mech. and elec. engrs.; dir. Architects Offices, Inc. Mem. Am. Soc. M.E., Am. Soc. Heating and Ventilating Engrs., Loyal Legion. Club: Union League. Author: Design of Steam Power Plants, 1902. Home: Montclair, N.J. Office: 101 Park Av., New York, N.Y.

MEYERS, Charles Edward, clergyman, prof. English; b. Hanover, Pa., Feb. 20, 1880; s. Anthon and Margaret (Cleer) M.; A.B., Franklin and Marshall Coll., 1902; ed. Theol. Sem. Ref. Ch. in U.S., 1902-05; A.M., U. of Pa., 1915; (hon.) Litt.D., Catawba Coll., Salisbury, N.C., 1936; m. Nellie Houser, Apr. 25, 1906. Ordained to ministry Reformed Ch. in U.S., 1905; minister, Emmanuel Ch., York, Pa., 1905-09, St. John's, Phila., 1909-15; instr. English, U. of Pa., 1911-15; prof. English, Franklin and Marshall Coll. since 1915. Mem. A.A.A.S., Am. Assn. Univ. Profs., Kappa Sigma. Awarded Schaff Prize in Ch. History, Theol. Sem. Democrat. Mem. Reformed Ch. in U.S. Mason. Clubs: Cliosophic Soc., Fortnightly (Lancaster). Home: 420 State St., Lancaster, Pa.

MEYERS, Meredith, newspaperman; b. Harrisburg, Pa., Oct. 5, 1885; s. Edwin Koontz and Mary (Meredith) M.; ed. common sch., Harrisburg; m. Margaret O'Sullivan, July 22, 1920; 1 son, Robert Meredith. With Harrisburg Star-Independent, 1898-1913, as printer's apprentice, 1898-1902, reporter, 1902-05, city editor, 1905-10, mng. editor, 1910-13; editor Lewistown Sentinel since 1913; pres. Lewistown Ice & Storage Co.; acting mgr. and vice-pres. Lewistown Housing & Development Co.; dir. Russell Nat. Bank; pres. and mgr. Overhead Door Co. of Pa.; vice-pres. Consumers Discount Co. Former pres. Lewistown Chamber of Commerce, Lewistown Kiwanis Club, Tri-County Baseball League. Active in securing new industries for Lewistown; active as Dem. leader; former treas. State Dem. Com.; now dist. chmn. 18th and 22d Dists.; mem. State Dem. Exec. Com.; political speaker. Pres. F. W. Black Community Hosp.; pres. Mifflin Co. Cooperative Concert Assn.; dir. Mifflin Co. Children's Aid Soc. Awarded Most Useful Citizen medal for 1929 by com. of representative citizens annually appointed by Lewistown Kiwanis Club. Served as chmn. Juniata Valley Chapter Red Cross and various Liberty Loan drives during World War. Mem. Pa. 300th Anniversary Commn. Episcopalian. Home: 125 W. Market St. Office: 9 S. Dorcas St., Lewistown, Pa.

MEYERS, Milton Kayton, neurologist; b. 1882; s. Sigmund and Rebecca (Kayton) M.; M.D., U. of Pa., 1902; m. Ethel K. Altshuler, 1914. Practiced in Phila. since shortly after graduation from U. of Pa. Mem. A.M.A., Med. Soc. State of Pa., Phila. Neurol. Soc., Pathol. Soc. of Philadelphia, Northern Medical Society of Phila., Anthropol. Soc., Philadelphia Psychiatric Society. Translator and editor of Falta's Endocrine Diseases, Including their Treatment; (with E. A. Strecker) H. Curschmann's Clinical Neurology; editor of Lang's German-English Medical Dictionary. Contbr. chapter on nervous diseases in Loewenberg's Diagnostic Methods in Internal Medicine. Home-Office: 1529 S. Broad St., Philadelphia, Pa.

MEYERSON, Samuel Charles, lawyer; b. Brooklyn, N.Y., Nov. 5, 1893; s. Abraham A. and Esther (Goldberg) M.; student Erasmus Hall High Sch., Brooklyn, N.Y., 1907-10; LL.B., New York U., 1916; spl. courses Mercer Beasley Law Sch., 1930-31; m. Elsa Berenberg, Apr. 5, 1917; children—Lee E., Carla R. Began as lawyer, Morristown, N.J., 1917; admitted to N.J. bar as counsellor at law, 1921; in practice for self at Dover, N.J., since 1918; counsel Randolph Bldg. & Loan Assn., Lake Hoptacong Bldg. & Loan Assn.; appointed spl. master in chancery, N.J., 1925; Supreme Court commr., N.J., 1925; corpn. counsel, Dover, N.J., since 1930. Mem. Morris Co. Bar Assn., New York U. Alumni Assn. Elk, Royal Arcanum. Club: Kiwanis (Dover, N.J.). Home: 116 Connett Pl., South Orange, N.J. Office: 10 W. Blackwell St., Dover, N.J.

MEYROWITZ, Ernest duPont, optician; b. New York, N.Y., June 7, 1884; s. Emil Bruno and Cora Evelyn (Hawley) M.; student New York Pub. Schs., 1896-98, pvt. schs., Paris, France, 1898-99; grad. Berkeley Sch., New York, 1903; Ph.B., Yale, Sheffield Scientific Sch., 1906; hon. Ph.D.; m. Kate Egberton Strange, Oct. 15, 1914 (died 1935); children—Kate Strange, Jean duPont. Pres. E. B. Meyrowitz, Inc., opticians, New York, 1906-08, asst. to v.p. and gen. mgr., 1908-10, v.p., 1910-16, pres. since 1916, pres. E. B. Meyrowitz, Minn., E. B. Meyrowitz Surgical Instruments Co., New York, since 1916, pres. E. B. Meyrowitz, Ltd., London, Eng., Etablissement E. B. Meyrowitz, Paris, France, since 1920; v.p. Gen. Optical Co., Mount Vernon, 1912-20, pres. since 1920; treas. La Toja Products Co., New York, since 1934. Mem. Nat., N.Y. Guilds of Prescription Opticians, Better Vision Inst.; Fifth Av. Assn., Merchants Assn. Republican. Episcopalian. Clubs: Yale (New York); Essex Co. Country (West Orange, N.J.); Fin, Fur and Feather (Madison, N.J.); Loantaka Skeet (Morristown, N.J.). Home: 505 Berkeley Av., S. Orange, N.J. Office: 520 5th Av., New York, N.Y.

MEZGER, Fritz, prof. Germanic philology; b. Ilsfeld, Germany, Oct. 15, 1893; s. Fritz and Elizabeth (Spinnehoern) M.; ed. univs. of Tubingen, Munich, and Geneva, 1911-13, Coll. de France, Paris, 1913-14, U. of Munich, 1919; Ph.D., U. of Berlin, 1921; m. Louise Scheuerle, Oct. 31, 1923; children—Liselotte, Rotraud, Fritz, Erik. Came to U.S., 1927 and naturalized citizen, 1936; instr. at Harvard U., 1927; asso. prof., Bryn Mawr Coll., 1928-36, prof. Germanic philology since 1936. Served in German Army during World War, three times wounded. Dec. with Iron Cross First class, Second class, and Turkish Crescent. Mem. Linguistic Soc. of America, Modern Lang. Assn. of America, Société de Linguistique de Paris. Lutheran. Author: Anglo-Saxon Names of Countries and Nations, 1921; The Irishman in English Literature, 1929; An Old English Thesaurus (manuscript), 1939. Contbr. articles on comparative philology in Am., German, Swedish, and Danish jours. Home: Oak Hill Farm, Bridgeport, Pa.

MICHAELS, Frank Balmoos, pres. Stroudsburg Security Trust Co.; b. Dingmans Ferry, Pa., Dec. 15, 1873; s. Philip Miller and Fannie May (Balmoos) M.; student pub. sch., Monroe Co. Pa., 1881-91, Scranton (Pa.) Business Coll., 1899; m. Eva Coleman Herman, Apr. 25, 1925; 1 dau., Doris Lorraine. Teacher pub. schs., Monroe Co., Pa., 1892-99; dep. register of wills and recorder of deeds, Monroe Co., Pa., 1900-08; dept. co. treas., Monroe Co., 1902-08; register of wills and recorder of deeds, Monroe Co., 1909-12; treas. Security Trust Co. of Stroudsburg, Pa., 1909-33; pres. Stroudsburg Security Trust Co. (merger of Security Trust Co. and Stroudsburg Trust Co.) since 1933; dir. Stroudsburg Security Co., Worthington Mower Co. Mem. Monroe Co. Chamber of Commerce (treas. since 1931), Monroe Co. Hist. Soc. (treas. since 1932), Malta Temple Assn. (sec. since 1906). Democrat. Lutheran. Clubs: Monroe Co. Automobile (chmn. bd. govs.), Rotary, Glen Brook Country (pres.; Stroudsburg, Pa.). Home: 238 Braeside Av., East Stroudsburg, Pa. Office: Corner of 7th and Main Sts., Stroudsburg, Pa.

MICHAELS, Urlwin Orgain, insurance; b. Richmond, Va., Nov. 22, 1875; s. Robert Edward and Lucy Orgain (Hardy) M.; ed. Richmond pub. and high schs.; m. Bernice Hillsman, Oct. 31, 1899; children—Mary Louise (wife of lt. comdr. Alvin Duke Chandler), Urlwin Orgain, Albert Hillsman. Began as clerk in ins. office, 1892; spl. agent, 1898-1904; state agent Western Assurance Co. and British America Assurance Co., 1904-14; state agent Ins.

Co. of North America, 1914-17, apptd., 1917, spl. agent and sent to South America to investigate conditions in Brazil, Argentine and Chile; returned to U.S., 1918, and removed office from Richmond to Baltimore becoming partner Manny, Donnelly & Parr; resigned, 1935, and established firm U. O. Michaels & Co. and so continues; dir. Union Federal Saving & Loan Assn. Clubs: Maryland, Virginias of Md., Sportsmans (Baltimore). Home: 100 W. University Parkway. Office: Baltimore Trust Bldg., Baltimore, Md.

MICHELS, Nicholas Aloysius, prof. of anatomy; b. St. Paul, Minn., Oct. 1, 1891; s. Jean Pierre and Katerina (Kraemer) M.; A.B., St. Thomas Coll., St. Paul, Minn., 1914; A.M., U. of Minn., 1920; Dr.Sc., Louvain Univ., Belgium, 1922; m. Martha Anna Tweeddale, June 19, 1929; children—Adelle Virginia, Horace Harvey. Postgrad. studies and research, Friday Harbor Biol. Sta., 1921, Siena Univ., Italy, 1923, Sarbonne, Paris, 1923, U. of Chicago, 1925; research fund grants, Libman fellowship (1926) and A.M.A. (1928), University and Bellevue Hosp. Med. Coll. and Mt. Sinai Hosp.; asst. prof. of biology and histology, St. Louis Univ. Med. Sch., 1926-27; asso. prof. of anatomy, Creighton U. Med. Sch., Omaha, Neb., 1927-29; asso. prof. of anatomy, Daniel Baugh Inst. of Anatomy, Jefferson Med. Coll., Phila., since 1929. Mem. A.A.A.S., Am. Soc. Anatomists, Soc. Exptl. Medicine and Biology, Phila. Physiol. Soc., Pa. Acad. of Science, Neb. Acad. of Science, Soc. Scientifique de Bruxelles, Soc. d'Anthropologie de Bruxelles, Sigma Xi. Mem. Loyal Order of Moose. Am. editor of Haematologica (Italian blood jour.); author of sect. "The Mast Cells" in Downey's Handbook of Hematology, 1938. Contbr. numerous papers on blood, blood forming organs, etc. to scientific jours. Home: Hatfield, Pa. Address: Jefferson Medical College, Philadelphia, Pa.

MICHELS, Walter Christian, physicist; b. Utica, N.Y., June 14, 1906; s. Christian A. and Anna (Haigis) M.; E.E., Rensselaer Poly. Inst., 1927; Ph.D., Calif. Inst. Tech., Pasadena, Calif., 1930; m. Lorraine Elder, June 21, 1930; 1 dau., Leslyn Jane. Began as test engr., Utica Gas and Electric Co., Utica, N.Y., 1926; teaching asst., Calif. Inst. Tech., 1927-29, teaching fellow, 1929-30; Fellow Nat. Research Council, Princeton U., 1930-32; asso. in physics, Bryn Mawr Coll., 1932-34, asso. prof. since 1934, head of dept. physics since 1936. Mem. Am. Phys. Soc., Am. Assn. Physics Teachers, Am. Assn. Univ. Profs., Franklin Inst., Sigma Xi. Co-author (with William R. Smythe), Advanced Electrical Measurements, 1932. Contbr. sci. articles to phys. jours. Home: Strafford, Pa.

MICHENER, Albert Oswald, educator; b. Phila., Pa., Dec. 24, 1879; s. Charles Albert and Lydia Ann (McMullin) M.; B.S., U. of Pa., 1900; M.S. in Edn., Temple U. Grad. Sch., 1932, grad. study, same, 1932-34, Ed.D., same, 1937; Harrison Scholar, U. of Pa. Grad. Sch., 1900-01; (hon.) Pd.D., Ursinus Coll., 1934; m. Ellen Glenn Boyd, June 19, 1920; children—William Ayers, Lydia Ann, Ellen Harding. Instr. English and history, N.E. High Sch., Phila., 1902-33, dean, 1923-33; prin. Warren G. Harding Jr. High Sch., 1933-39; prin. Benjamin Franklin High Sch. since 1939; dir. and propr. Camp Munsee for Boys, Dingman's Ferry, Pa., since 1926; organist and choirmaster, P.E. Ch. of St. Simeon, Phila. Trustee Louise Haeseler Memorial Fund, Apprentices Library (Phila.). Mem. N.E.A., Pa. State Edn. Assn., Phila. Teachers Assn., High Sch. Men's Assn., Dept. of Secondary Sch. Prins., Hist. Soc. of Pa., Phi Delta Kappa, Alpha Chi Rho. Republican. Episcopalian. Clubs: Union League, Schoolmens. Author: History of the Northeast High School of Philadelphia. Home: 2131 W. Venango St., Philadelphia, Pa.

MICHIE, Thomas Johnson, lawyer; b. Northport, N.Y., June 7, 1896; s. Thomas Johnson and Emily (Hewson) M.; B.A., U. of Va., 1917, M.A., 1919, LL.B., 1921; m. Cordelia Byrd Ruffin, Feb. 18, 1928; children—Cordelia Ruffin, Thomas Johnson, Emily Hewson. Admitted to Va. bar, 1921; in gen. practice of law, 1921-26; mem. legal dept. Koppers Co. since 1926;

dir. Brooklyn Borough Gas Co., The Virginian Corpn., The Michie Co.; asst. sec. Koppers United Co. Served as 2d lt., Air Service, World War. Mem. Am. Bar Assn. (chmn. mineral sect. 1935-36), Pa., Va. and Allegheny Co. bar assns., Am. Acad. Polit. Science, Theta Delta Chi, Am. Legion (comdr. Va. Dept. 1924-25). Democrat. Episcopalian. Clubs: Duquesne (Pittsburgh); Redland (Charlottesville, Va.). Home: 5515 Darlington Road. Office: 1138 Koppers Bldg., Pittsburgh, Pa.

MIDDENDORF, Harry Stump, investment banker; b. Baltimore Co., Md., June 6, 1893; s. John William and Alice (Stump) M.; student Univ. Sch., Baltimore, 1900-11, Worcester (Mass.) Acad., 1911-12, U. of Cleimont Ferrand, France, 1919; A.B., Harvard, 1916; m. Sara Kennedy Boone, Apr. 1, 1922 (divorced 1934); children—Harry Stump, John William, William Kennedy, Sara Boone. Clerk Canton Co., Baltimore, 1916-17; salesman Continental Co., Baltimore, 1917; v.p. Middendorf Hartmann, Inc., Baltimore, 1919-20, Brinkmann & Co., Inc., 1920-22, partner J. William Middendorf & Sons, Baltimore, 1922-32; v.p. Trail & Middendorf, Inc., investment bankers, Baltimore, since 1932; sec. and treas. Insuranshares Certificates Inc., Baltimore, since 1932. Served in Battery A, Md. N.G., 1917, at 1st O.T.C., Fort Meyer, Va., 1917, as 1st lt., 310th F.A., A.E.F., 1918-19; capt., 110th F.A., Md. N.G., since 1937. Dir. South Baltimore Gen. Hosp.; treas. Taxpayers League, Baltimore Co. Mem. Sons of the Revolution. Mem. Bond Club of Baltimore (pres. 1934-35), Investment Bankers Assn. (sec.-treas. South Eastern Group 1935-36), Asso. Harvard Clubs (eastern v.p. 1924-27). Democrat. Episcopalian. Clubs: Green Spring Valley Hunt, Batchelors Cotillion (Baltimore); Howard of Md. Home: Dulaney Valley, Baltimore County, Md. Office: 410 Keyser Bldg., Baltimore, Md.

MIDDLETON, Elliott, ins. exec.; b. Cincinnati, O., Feb. 17, 1876; s. George Atherton and Alice (Elliott) M.; ed. Cincinnati pub. schs.; m. Dorothy Whitehill Thoman, Jan. 16, 1919; children—Elizabeth, Elliott. Began in insurance business, 1898; mgr., Tenn. Inspection Bureau, 1910-16; mgr., Michigan Inspection Bureau, 1916-17; asst. mgr. Western Actuarial Bureau, 1918-20; mgr. Pacific Actuarial Bureau, 1920-21; mgr. Underwriters Bureau of the Middle and Southern States, 1922-23; mgr. Fire Underwriters Electrical Bureau, 1922-23; sec. Central Traction & Lighting Bureau, 1922-23; sec. Sun Insurance Office, Ltd., Patriotic Ins. Co. and Sun Underwriters Ins. Co. since 1923; dir. Greenbrook Realty Corpn., Swan Engring Co. Inc. Republican. Episcopalian. Club: Montclair Golf. Home: 36 Warren Place, Montclair, N.J. Office: 55 Fifth Av., New York, N.Y.

MIDDLETON, Harry Collier, coal mining exec.; b. Moorestown, N.J., June 9, 1869; s. John and Abigail Boroughs (Hollingshead) M.; student high sch., Moorestown, N.J., Coll. of Commerce, Phila., 1885; m. Mary E. Edwards, Dec. 20, 1892; children—Anna, Harry, Fred, Dorothy, John, Bruce. With The Berwind White Coal Mining Co., Phila., since 1886, beginning as bookkeeper, treas. since 1912. Republican. Episcopal. Mason. Clubs: Art, Penn Athletic. Home: Moorestown, N.J. Office: 1100 Commercial Trust Bldg., Philadelphia, Pa.

MIDDLETON, Melbourne Fletcher, Jr., business exec.; b. Camden, N.J., Feb. 22, 1877; s. Dr. Melbourne Fletcher and Emily M. (King) M.; student William Penn Charter Sch., Phila., Pa., 1892-95; m. Jessamine G. Weatherby, Oct. 25, 1900; children—Dorothy, Jessamine, Charles Barey. Dir. First Nat. Bank, Camden, N.J., 1912-22, First Camden Nat. Bank & Trust Co., 1922-30; chmn. bd. Adelphia Bank & Trust Co., Phila., 1929-30; sec. and treas. Vitagiene Labs., Phila., since 1930; pres. Greenleigh Ct. Corpn., N.J., since 1932, Sentry Safety Control Corpn., Phila., since 1935; dir. Pa. & Atlantic R.R. Co. Pres. Phila. Stock Exchange, 1921-30; dir. revenue and finance, Camden, N.J., 1923-27; treas. Bd. of Edn., Camden, 1923-27. Pres. Masonic Relief Soc., Camden, since 1932. Republican. Episcopalian

(vestryman St. Paul's P.E. Ch., Camden, since 1918). Mason (32°; K.T.; Shriner; past master Camden Lodge 15). Club: Island Heights Yacht (Island Heights, N.J.; treas.). Home: Mt. Laurel Rd., Moorestown, N.J. Office: 1518 Walnut St., Philadelphia, Pa.

MIDDLETON, William, entomologist; b. Washington, D.C., Nov. 28, 1893; s. Jonas Benjamin and Christina Muir (Logan) M.; student high schs., Washington, D.C., 1907-08; grad. Emerson Inst., Washington, D.C., 1911; A.B. with distinction, George Washington U., Washington, D.C., 1925, M.A., 1928; m. Alice Louise Browning, Mar. 2, 1916; 1 dau., Louise Browning. Student asst., U.S. Dept. Agr., 1909-12; studied biology of forest insects, 1912-22; specialist in shade tree and hardy shrub insects, 1922-37; senior administrative officer and 1st asst. to officer in charge, Div. of Dutch Elm Disease Eradication, Japanese Beetle Control and Gypsy Moth and European Corn Borer Certification, Bur. of Entomology and Plant Quarantine, U.S. Dept. of Agr., Bloomfield, N.J., since 1937; lecturer psychology, George Washington U., 1926-31. Served in M.C., U.S. Army, during World War, at Yale Army Lab. Sch., New Haven, Conn., in lab. Embarkation Hosp., Newport News, Va. Mem. Am. Assn. Econ. Entomologists, Washington Entomol. Soc., Washington Biol. Soc., Washington Biologists Field Club, Nat. Shade Tree Conf. (pres. 1933-34), Am. Legion (comdr. McGroarty-Stambaugh Post, Va., 1928-29). Mason (past master). Club: Cosmos (Washington, D.C.). Author numerous papers on entomol. subjects. Home: 157 Thomas St. Office: 266 Glenwood Av., Bloomfield, N.J.

MIEL, Charles Jan, publicity and promotion; b. Hartford, Conn., March 29, 1898; s. Rev. Ernest DeFemery and Marion (Scribner) M.; grad. Hartford Pub. High Sch., 1917; A.B., U. of Pa., 1922; m. Mary Long, Feb. 2, 1928; children—Ernest, Charles Jan, Margaret Killworth. Asst. dir. financial campaigns Tamblyn & Brown, New York, 1922-28; asst. dir. campaign $1,-000,000 Episcopal Theol. Sch., Cambridge, Mass., 1922-23; dir. campaign Ch. of Holy Communion, New York, 1923; asst. dir. $15,-000,000 building and endowment campaign Cathedral St. John the Divine, New York, 1924-25; dir. Union Bldg. Fund, Mich. State Normal Coll., Ypsilanti, 1925-26; dir. endowment campaign Berkley Divinity Sch., New Haven, Conn., 1926-27; gen. mgr. U. of Pa. Fund since 1928; sec. U. of Pa. Bicentennial Com. since 1935; sec. Univ.-Alumni Council since 1932; sec. Alumni Annual Giving Com. since 1928. Dir. Am. Alumni Council, dir. of aims and policies, former vice-pres. Served as corpl. 101st Machine Gun Bn., 26th Div., U.S. Army, with A.E.F. in Toule sector, Chateau Thiery, St. Mihiel, Meuse-Argonne (received citation for bravery, Oct. 23, 1918), 1917-19. Episcopalian. Club: University of Pennsylvania (New York). Contbr. on fund raising subjects to alumni Fund survey, 1930, Assn. of Am. Colls. Bulletin, and to "Money Raising," 1938. Home: 410 Woodland Av., Wayne, Pa. Office: 1429 Walnut St., Philadelphia, Pa.

MIESSNER, Benjamin Franklin, radio engr.; b. Huntingburg, Ind., July 27, 1890; s. Charles and Mary (Reutopohler) M.; grad. high sch., Huntingburg, 1908; grad. U.S. Navy Electrical Sch., Brooklyn, 1909; studied elec. engring., Purdue, 1913-16; m. Eleanor Marguerite Schulz, June 13, 1916; children—Jane Eleanor, Mary Elizabeth. Wireless operator U.S. Navy, 1909-11; in charge radio torpedo control invention and development with John Hays Hammond, Jr., and Dr. Fritz Lowenstein, 1911-13; expert radio aide for aviation, U.S. Navy, in charge development of radio for aircraft, Pensacola, Fla., 1916-18; radio engr. with Emil J. Simon, New York, in charge aircraft radio and transoceanic receiver developments, 1918-20; dir. acoustical research laboratory, Brunswick, Balke, Collender Co., Chicago, 1921-22; cons. engr. Wired Radio, Inc., 1922-25; pres. Miessner Radio Corpn., 1925; chief engr. Garod Corpn., Belleville, N.J., 1926-27; pres. Miessner Inventions, Inc. Granted more than 100 patents in U.S. and foreign countries; a pioneer in aircraft radio, elec. phonography, radio dynamics, elec. radio receivers, elec. musical instruments, directional microphones for aircraft or submarine location, etc. Fellow Radio Club of America, Inst. of Radio Engrs.; mem. Am. Physical Soc., A.A.A.S., Acoustical Soc. America, Veteran Wireless Operators Assn., The Benjamin Franklins (Chicago), Sigma Pi; mem. Com. of 100 (Miami Beach, Fla.). Clubs: Purdue (New York); Buffalo Canoe (Crystal Bush, Ont., Can.). Author: Radio Dynamics, 1916; Hum in All-Electric Radio Receivers, 1929. Contbr. numerous articles in scientific publs. Home: Haddonfield Road, Short Hills, N.J. Office: 18 Main St., Millburn, N.J.

MIKELL, William Ephraim, prof. law; b. Sumter, S.C., Jan. 29, 1868; s. Thomas Price and Rebecca (Moses) M.; B.S., S.C. Mil. Coll., Charleston, 1890; U. of Va. Law Sch., 1894; LL.M., U. of Pa., 1915, J.U.D., 1929; LL.D., U. of S.C., 1921; D.C.L., U. of the South, Tenn., 1921; m. Martha Turner McBee, Apr. 12, 1894; children—William E., Mary McBee, Thomas Price. Practiced at Sumter, S.C., 1895-96; prof. law, U. of Pa., 1898-1938, prof. emeritus since 1938, dean faculty, 1914-29. Democrat. Episcopalian. Mem. Am. Law Inst., Am. Inst. Criminal Law and Criminology, Kappa Alpha (Southern), Phi Delta Phi, Order of the Coif. Author: Mikell's Cases on Criminal Law, 1903; Mikell's Cases on Criminal, Procedure, 1910. Wrote: Life of Chief Justice Taney, in "Great American Lawyers"; Limitations of the Treaty-Making Power of the Federal Government, pub. in Univ. of Pa. Law Review. Editor: Third edit. Clark's Criminal Law, 1915; 2d edit. Clark's Criminal Procedure, 1917. Author of proposed Penal Code for Pennsylvania, 1917. Reporter on Code of Criminal Proc. for Am. Law Inst. Home: 209 E. Johnson St., Germantown, Philadelphia, Pa.

MILES, Clarence William, lawyer; b. Cambridge, Md., June 29, 1897; s. Alonzo Lee and Agnes (Hooper) M.; student Peddie Sch., Hightstown, N.J., 1917, U. of Md. Law Sch., 1917-20; m. Sarah Virginia Phillips, Oct. 3, 1925. Mem. of law firm Miles, Bailey & Miles, Salisbury, Md., 1920-25, Miles & O'Brien, Baltimore, Md., since 1932; gen. counsel Crescent Pub. Service Co., Monumental Radio Co. (WCQO), Eastern Shore Gas Co. City Solicitor, Salisbury, Md., 1920-25; People's Counsel of Md., 1927-29. Mem. Am., Md. State, Baltimore City bar assns., Kappa Sigma. Democrat. Episcopalian. Clubs: Maryland, Elkridge (Baltimore, Md.); Gibson Island (Md.); Bankers' (New York City). Home: Garden Apts. Office: Baltimore Trust Bldg., Baltimore, Md.

MILES, Eugene L.; pres. Baltimore Nat. Bank. Home: 206 Enfield Road. Office: Baltimore and Light Sts., Baltimore, Md.

MILES, Hooper S.; sr. partner Miles, Bailey & Williams; exec. v.p. Baltimore Nat. Bank. Address: Salisbury, Md.

MILES, L(ouis) Wardlaw, coll. prof.; b. Baltimore, Md., Mar. 23, 1873; s. Francis Turquand and Jeanie (Wardlaw) M.; grad. University Sch., Baltimore, 1891; B.A., Johns Hopkins, 1894; M.D., U. of Md., 1897, LL.D., 1919; Ph. D., Johns Hopkins, 1902; m. Katharine Wistar Stockton, Jan. 25, 1908; children —Francis Turquand, Sarah Bache, Samuel Stockton, Jeanie Wardlaw. Master in German, Country Sch. for Boys, Baltimore, 1903-04; instr. in English, Princeton U., 1905, preceptor, 1905-17; headmaster Gilman Country Sch., 1919-26; lecturer St. John's Coll., Annapolis, 1926-27; collegiate prof. of English, Coll. of Arts and Sciences, Johns Hopkins, 1927—. Served as capt. 308th Inf. 77th div., A.E.F., World War; awarded the Congressional Medal. Mem. Modern Lang. Assn. America, Poetry Soc. Maryland (pres., 1924-27), Alpha Delta Phi, Phi Beta Kappa, Omicron Delta Kappa. Democrat. Episcopalian. Clubs: Baltimore; Nassau (Princeton, N.J.). Author: History of the 308th Infantry, 1927; The Tender Realist and Other Essays, 1930. Address: 506 Woodlawn Rd., Baltimore, Md.

MILLAR, Albert S., judge; b. Phila., Pa., May 7, 1894; s. William and Margaret Jane (Elliott) M.; student LL.B., Temple U. and Law Sch., 1916; m. Marguerite Priode, Sept. 12, 1917; children—Mary Maxine, William Henry, Albert. Admitted to Pa. bar, 1916, and practiced law, Phila., 1916-33; judge of Court of Common Pleas, No. 3, Phila., since 1933. Mem. Common Council, City of Phila., 1918-19; mem. State House of Reps., 1920-33. Republican. Baptist. Clubs: Philadelphia Country, Union League (Phila.). Home: 3312 Queen Lane. Office: 392 City Hall, Philadelphia, Pa.

MILLAR, Charles Caven, clergyman; b. McKeesport, Pa., June 9, 1864; s. William John and Ellen (Caven) M.; A.B., Westminster Coll., Fulton, Mo., 1889; ed. Western Theol. Sem., Pittsburgh, 1889-92, Princeton Theol. Sem., 1892-93; (hon.) D.D., Westminster Coll., 1902; m. Margaret Montgomery Knox, Nov. 28, 1895; children—Hugh Stewart, William Martin. Ordained to ministry Presbyn. Ch., U.S.A., June 12, 1893; fgn. missionary under Bd. Fgn. Missions, Presbyn. Ch. U.S.A. in Mexico, 1893-1907; pastor, Dunbar, Pa., 1908-11, Tamaqua, 1911-21, Danville, 1921-25; pastor at large in Butler (Pa.) Presbytery, 1925-38. Republican. Presbyterian. Home: 212 E. North St., Butler, Pa.

MILLENER, William Seward, sec. Flood Control Council of Susquehanna Drainage Area; b. at Spencerport, N.Y., January 5, 1872; s. of William Seward and Lucy (Ann) Millener; Pharm.G., N.Y. Coll. of Pharmacy, 1892; m. Nellie B. Davis, Oct. 17, 1893 (dec.); children—George A. (capt. U.S.A.), William S. III, Raymond D. (lt. U.S.A.). Engaged as druggist, Holley and Spencerport, N.Y., 1892-1903; at Williamsport, Pa., 1903-23; served as sec.-mgr. Williamsport Chamber of Commerce, 1913-37; exec. sec. Flood Control Council Susquehanna Drainage Area since 1937; sec.-treas. Williamsport Hotel Co. Republican. Presbyn. Mason (32°). Home: 921 W. 4th St. Office: 153 W. 4th St., Williamsport, Pa.

MILLER, Adam Frank, lawyer; b. Richland, Pa., Sept. 1, 1889; s. Edward William and Elizabeth (Shaeffer) M.; Ph.B., Muhlenberg Coll., Allentown, Pa., 1912; A.M., Dickinson Coll., 1916; LL.B., Dickinson Law Sch., Carlisle, Pa., 1916; m. Fannie Margaret Hertzler, June 5, 1917; 1 son, Edward Hertzler. Admitted Pa. bar, 1917, and since in practice in Lebanon; asso. with father in firm of Miller & Miller; dir. and solicitor Lebanon County Trust Co. Dir. Lebanon Chamber of Commerce. Mem. Am. Bar Assn., Pa. Bar Assn., Alpha Tau Omega. Republican. Lutheran. Mason, Elk. Clubs: Lebanon Country, Quentin Riding. Home: 506 Park Place. Office: Lebanon County Trust Co. Bldg., Lebanon, Pa.

MILLER, Alten S., consulting engr.; b. Richmond, Va., Oct. 6, 1868; s. William G. and Emma H. (Wiglesworth) M.; Richmond Coll., M.E., Stevens Inst. Tech., 1888; m. Virginia Bennett, Jan. 14, 1902. Began with United Gas Improvement Co., Phila., 1888; asst. supt. Omaha Gas Co. 1888-92; mgr. Nat. Gas Light & Fuel Co., Chicago, 1892-94; engr. East River Gas Co., later New Amsterdam Gas Co.,, New York, and engr. constrn., Consolidated Gas Co. of New York, 1894-1902; v.p. and mgr. Consolidated Gas, Electric Light & Power Co., Baltimore, 1902-09; pres. Union Electric Light & Power Co., St. Louis, 1909-11; v.p. Humphreys & Miller, Inc., 1911-29; v.p. Bartlett Hayward Co., 1915-36. Engr. E. River Gas Co. when it built the first tunnel into New York. Inventoried and appraised all gas properties of N.Y. City, and gas and electric properties of Baltimore, 1919-24. Republican. Episcopalian. Fellow Am. Inst. Elec. Engrs.; pres. Am. Gas Light Assn., 1902-03; mem. Am. Gas Assn., Illuminating Engring. Soc., Soc. of Gas Lighting, Am. Soc. Mech. Engrs., Am. Inst. Consulting Engrs., Chi Phi. Lt. col. Ordnance Dept., U.S.A., stationed at Washington, in charge of design of all cannon ammunition; discharged, Dec. 15, 1918. Clubs: Engineers', Railroad (New York); Nassau, Pretty Brook Tennis (Princeton); Army and Navy (Washington). Author of papers on engring. subjects and papers relating to pub. service corpns. Has invented a number of devices, some of them patented. Address: 80 Westcott Road, Princeton, N.J.

MILLER, Anna Irene; instr. English, Goucher Coll., 1917-20; asst. prof., 1920-24, asso. prof., 1924-32, prof. since 1932. Address: Goucher College, Baltimore, Md.

MILLER, Anne Moseley Mays (Mrs. Glen Earle Miller), writer, heraldric artist, genealogist; b. near Cartersville, Bartow Co., Ga.; d., James Francis and Maud (Walton) Mays; ed. Birmingham, Ala., Public Schools and High School (grad. 1908), Normal Training School (grad. 1910), Howard Coll., Birmingham, and Peabody Coll.; m. Glen Earle Miller, June 24, 1918; children —Glen Earle, Anne Walton, Frank Arnold, John Anthony III. Instr. elementary schools and jr. high schools, 7 years; registered genealogist. Mem. D.A.R., U.D.C., Inst. Am. Genealogy. Democrat. Presbyterian. Writes short stories for children, plays for children. Author: Moseleys of Virginia; Abneys of Virginia; co-author: The Mays Family. Contbr. many short stories and verse to current mags. Home: 6 Bartol Av., Ridley Park, Pa.

MILLER, Anthony Paul Molinara, contracting; b. Atlantic City, N.J., June 8, 1896; s. James Molinara and Catherine (Costante) M.; ed. Atlantic City Pub. Schs., Evans School of Cartooning, Internat. Corrs. Sch.; m. Catherine Harriet Hand, July 25, 1917; children—Anthony Paul, Gloria Marie, Jane. Concrete engr. since 1921; pres. Anthony P. Miller, Inc., general contracting, difficult foundations, Atlantic City, N.J., since 1927. Pres. Mainland Nat. Bank, Pleasantville, N.J., since 1934; pres. Chelsea Housing Corpn., Atlantic City, N.J., since 1939; pres. Ogontz Housing Corpn., Phila., since 1939. Served as civilian inspector U.S. Army Ordnance Dept. in World War. Mem. N.J. Soc. Professional Engrs., Am. Military Engrs. Catholic. K. of C., Red Men, Elks. Home: 220 S. Franklin Av., Pleasantville, N.J. Office: 3333 Arctic Av., Atlantic City, N.J.

MILLER, Arthur Barrett, architect and civil engr.; b. Winchester, Va., Aug. 11, 1874; s. William and Adelaide Gerrish (Barrett) M.; student Stevens Sch., 1891-93, Montclair (N.J.) Mil. Acad., 1888-91; M.Eng., Stevens Inst. Tech., Hoboken, N.J., 1897; m. Edith A. Canning, Nov. 7, 1902; children—Dorothy Canning (Mrs. Holger Cahill), Alice Marion (Mrs. Reid White J.), Adelaide Francis, Arthur Barrett. Engr. Gen. Elec. Co., Schenectady, N.Y., 1897-98; engr. United Engring. & Contracting Co., New York, 1899-1902; engr. Draper Co., Hopedale, Mass., 1902-04; engr. Bush Terminal Co., New York, 1904-05; engr. Walter Kidde Constructors, Inc., New York, since 1905, dir. since 1930; registered architect, N.Y., N.J., registered professional engr., N.Y., N.J. Mem. council Montclair (N.J.) Boy Scout Assn. Mem. Am. Soc. C.E.; mem. Mayflower Soc. Republican. Congregationalist. Mason (Montclair Lodge 144). Club: Pocono Lake Preserve (Pa.). Home: 47 S. Fullerton Av., Montclair, N.J. Office: 140 Cedar St., New York, N.Y.

MILLER, Ashby, v.p., asst. sec. and asst. treas. General Mills, Inc.; officer or dir. many companies. Home: 502 Rodney Court. Office: Industrial Trust Bldg., Wilmington, Del.

MILLER, Benjamin LeRoy, geologist; b. Sabetha, Kan., Apr. 13, 1874; s. Jacob J. and Mary (Moorhead) M.; student Morrill (Kan.) Coll., 1889-90, Washburn Coll. (Topeka), 1891-92; A.B., U. of Kan., 1897; U. of Chicago, summer, 1898; Ph.D., Johns Hopkins, 1903; m. Mary A. Meredith, Sept. 15, 1904 (died May 30, 1930); children—Ruth Meredith (Mrs. Otto H. Spillman), Ralph LeRoy. Teacher pub. schs. of Kan., 1894-95; asst., Kan. U. Geol. Survey, summer, 1896; prof. biology and chemistry, Penn Coll., Oskaloosa, Ia., 1897-1900; spl. asst. Ia. Geol. Survey, summer, 1899; asso. in geology, Bryn Mawr Coll., 1903-07; prof. geology, Lehigh U., since 1907. Geologist, Md. Geol. Survey, 1900-11; asst., 1904-07, asst. geologist, 1907-13, U.S. Geol. Survey; asso. geologist, Pa. Geol. Survey, since 1919. Spl. consulting editor Engring. and Mining Jour., 1920-22. Fellow A.A.A.S., Mineralogical Soc. America, Geol. Soc. America, Ia. Acad. Sciences,

Geol. Soc. London; mem. Am. Inst. Mining and Metallurgical Engineers, Society Economic Geologists, Seismological Soc. America, American Meteorol. Soc., Am. Assn. Univ. Profs., Pa. Acad. Science (pres. 1925-26), Sigma Xi, Tau Beta Pi. Has written numerous reports on geol. survey results, pub. by U.S. Geol. Survey and state geol. surveys of Iowa, Md., Va., N.C. and Pa.; articles on econ. geology in tech. jours., especially on limestones, cement, graphite and other non-metallic products; articles on stratigraphic geology of Eastern Pa. in geol. periodicals; reviews of Am. geog. lit. in Annuelle Bibliographie, Annales de Géographie, 1902-06; also collaborator with Dr. George B. Shattuck in "Geology and Geography of the Bahama Islands," in Bahama Islands, 1905; Geology of Mining Districts of South America and Central America; Mineral Deposits of South America (with Dr. J. T. Singewald, Jr.), 1919. Rotarian. Home: 429 N. New St., Bethlehem, Pa.

MILLER, Bruce Jones, educator; b. Loganton, Pa., Apr. 1, 1904; s. Horace Grant and Permilla Ellen (Jones) M.; A.B., Bucknell U., 1927; Ph.D., U. of Chicago, 1931; m. Florence W. Beckworth, Dec. 19, 1928; children—Bruce Jones, Audrey Evelyn. Instr. chemistry, Bucknell U., 1927-29, asst. prof., 1931-35, asso. prof. and chmn. dept. chemistry since 1935. Mem. Am. Chem. Soc., German Chem. Soc., Sigma Xi, Alpha Chi Sigma. Baptist. Home: 615 Taylor St., Lewisburg, Pa.

MILLER, Carl Irvin, pres. First Nat. Bank & Trust Co. of East Pittsburgh; b. Henrietta, Pa., May 13, 1881; s. Jeremiah and Mary Ann (Thatcher) M.; ed. Martinsburg (Pa.) High Sch., Lebanon (Pa.) Coll. of Business; m. Anna Marguerite Deatrick, June 22, 1916; children—Carl Thatcher, Mary Elizabeth. Clk. East Pittsburgh Nat. Bank, Wilmerding, Pa., 1900-02; with First Nat. Bank & Trust Co. of East Pittsburgh, Pa. (formerly East Pittsburgh Savings & Trust Co.), since 1902, serving successively as asst. treas., treas., v.p., dir., and pres.; dir. First National Bank of Swissdale, First National Bank of Wilmerding, Wilkinsburg Real Estate & Trust Company, Electric Bldg. & Loan Assn. Treas. Forest Hills (Pa.) Borough and Sch. Dist. since 1919, East Pittsburgh Borough and Sch. Dist. since 1931, Chalfont (Pa.) Sch. Dist. since 1931, Chalfont Borough since 1932, Trafford Borough since 1933. Mem. East Pittsburgh Chamber of Commerce (treas.). Mason. Clubs: Rotary (East Pittsburgh, Pa; treas. since 19—); Edgewood Country (Pittsburgh). Home: 7516 Tuscarora St., Pittsburgh, Pa. Office: 663 Braddock Av., East Pittsburgh, Pa.

MILLER, Charles Haven, lawyer; b. Concord Twp., Butler Co., Pa., Nov. 15, 1873; s. Joseph S. and Sarah E. (McCall) M.; ed. Township pub. schs., 1879-85, Butler (Pa.) pub. sch., 1885-89, Butler High Sch., 1889-92; A.B., Allegheny Coll., Meadville, Pa., 1898; m. Bertha B. Donaldson, June 25, 1908; children—Catherine E., David C. Admitted to Butler Co., Pa., bar, 1901; since in gen. practice law; dist. atty. Butler Co., Pa., 1928-32; sec. and treas. Corona Cord Tire Co., Butler, Pa., 1919-22. Sec. Rep. County Com., 1906, 07, 08; sec. Butler Driving Park and Fair Assn., 1922, 23, 24. Mem. Butler Co. Bar Assn., Sigma Alpha Epsilon. Republican. Methodist. Home: 233 E. Pearl St. Office: 201 Butler Co. Nat. Bank Bldg., Butler, Pa.

MILLER, Charles Lichty, lawyer; b. Lancaster, Pa., Dec. 1, 1887; s. Charles F. and Anna Blanche (Lichty) M.; A.B., Haverford Coll., 1908; LL.B., U. of Pa., 1912; awarded Gowen Fellowship, U. of Pa. Law Sch., for years 1912-13; m. Josephine Ross, July 10, 1912; children—Edward R., Ann, Elizabeth R., Barbara, Charles L. Admitted to Supreme Court of Pa. bar, 1912; associated with law firm Coyle & Keller, 1913-16; in gen. practice under own name since 1916, specializing in corpn. and insurance law; solicitor Hamilton Watch Co., Hager & Brother, Inc.; dir. Farmers Trust Co. of Lancaster. Trustee Y.W.C.A.; trustee and treas. Shippen Sch. for Girls. Mem. Phi Kappa Psi, Phi Delta Phi, Order of the Coif. Republican. Episcopalian. Clubs: Hamilton, Lancaster Country (Lancaster); Haverford (Philadelphia). Home: 1267 Wheatland Av. Office: 53 N. Duke St., Lancaster, Pa.

MILLER, Charles Robert; b. Westminster, Md., Sept. 24, 1860; s. George Washington and Charity (Brown) M.; grad. Western Md. Coll., Westminster, 1881; studied law with Charles B. Roberts, 1882-84; m. Sadie Kneller, June 13, 1894 (died Nov. 21, 1920); m. 2d, L. Beulah McCrone, June 19, 1929. Began practice of law at Westminster, 1884; dep. register of wills, Westminster, 1885-87; served under surveyor of Port of Baltimore, 1888-90; with Fidelity & Deposit Co. of Md. since 1891, vice-pres., 1903-24, pres. since 1924; vice-pres. Fidelity Permanent Bldg. & Loan Assn.; dir. Central Savings Bank of Baltimore. Trustee Western Md. Coll. Mem. Md. State and Baltimore bar assns. Democrat. Methodist. Mason. Clubs: Maryland, Concord, Baltimore Country. Home: 2200 Roslyn Av. Office: Fidelity Bldg., Baltimore, Md.

MILLER, C(harles) Wilbur, pres. Davison Chem. Co.; b. Winchester, Va., Feb. 17, 1878; s. Durbin George and Sarah (Brosius) M.; student Johns Hopkins, 1896-98; LL.B., U. of Md., 1899; m. Edith Davison, June 14, 1905; children—Edith Wilbur, Grace Calvin, Anne Ridgely, C. Wilbur. In practice of law, mem. firm Bond & Robinson, Baltimore, 1900-04; pres. Davison Chem. Co. since 1905, now also chmn. bd.; chmn. bd. Silica Gel Corpn.; dir. Baltimore Trust Co., The Cottman Co. Mem. Troop A, Md. N.G., 1898-1904, col. on staff governor, 1915. Chmn. Baltimore County Rep. Com. Trustee Md. Gen. and South Baltimore Woman's hosps. Mem. Baltimore Chamber Commerce (dir.), Kappa Sigma. Episcopalian. Clubs: Maryland, Chesapeake, Merchants, Bachelors Cotillion, Baltimore Country, Green Spring Hounds, Elkridge Hounds, Harford Hunt (Baltimore); Bankers, Union League, Chemists (New York). Home: Pleasant Hill Farm, Cockeysville, Md. Office: Baltimore Trust Bldg., Baltimore, Md.*

MILLER, David Aaron, editor; b. Gilberts, Pa., Apr. 7, 1869; s. Dr. Edward Peter and Flora Anna M.; B.E., Keystone State Coll., Kutztown, Pa., 1891; A.B. and A.M., Muhlenberg Coll., Allentown, Pa., 1894; Litt.D., Ursinus Coll., Collegeville, Pa., 1937; m. Blanche A. Berkemeyer, Sept. 25, 1900; children—Edward L. (dec.), Robert K., Samuel W., Donald P., Paul B., Margaret B. (Mrs. John E. Phillips), Julia A., Mary E. (deceased). Began as manager Allentown (Penna.) Morning Call, 1895, mng. editor since 1934; dir. Merchants Nat. Bank, Allen Mutual Fire Ins. Co. Pres. Phoebe Home for Old Folks; sec. Allentown Hosp. and Allentown Free Library; dir. Family Welfare Assn. Mem. Sch. Bd. of Allentown (finance com.; past pres.); dir. Pa. German Soc. Republican. Mem. Reformed Ch. in U.S. Mason, Odd Fellow, Elk. Club: Torch. Contbr. series of letters to Morning Call on world trip, 1933-34. Home: 2221 Chew St. Office: 6th and Linden Sts., Allentown, Pa.*

MILLER, D(avid) Roy, artist, dir. art sch.; b. Mechanicsburg, Pa., Feb. 8, 1892; s. John F. and Jennie F. (Quigley) M.; ed. pub. schs., Mechanicsburg; student Pa. Acad. Fine Arts, 1912-16 (awarded Cresson traveling scholarship to Europe); m. Mildred B. Stern, June 14, 1916. Began as artist, 1916; organizer, 1916, Country Sch. of Pa. Acad. Fine Arts, Chester Springs, Pa., dir., 1916-34; founder, 1934, and since dir. Painters' Farm, Chester Springs (sch. for study of cultural arts). Mem. Soc. Arts and Sciences. Mem. Soc. of Friends (Quaker). Recognized for outstanding development of quality reproduction for records and radio, covering entire musical range up to frequency of 16,000 cycles. Address: Painters' Farm, Chester Springs, Pa.

MILLER, Donald Edwin, educator; b. Pittsburgh, Pa., Dec. 27, 1885; s. Joseph Edwin and Lorena (Mouck) M.; student Pittsburgh Central High Sch., 1900-04; A.B., U. of Pittsburgh, 1907; summer student Columbia U., 1927, U. of Pittsburgh, 1930-35; m. Arvilla Lane, Nov. 25, 1915; 1 son, Donald Lane. Teacher, New Brighton, Pa., 1907-08, high sch. prin., 1909-12; teacher Pittsburgh High Sch., 1912-20; vice-prin., Schenley High Sch., Pittsburgh, 1920-28; first prin. Herron Hill Jr. High Sch., Pittsburgh, 1928-29; prin. Peabody High Sch., Pittsburgh, since 1929. Mem. com. of management, East Liberty (Pa.) Y.M.C.A. since 1936; sec. Pittsburgh and Allegheny Milk and Ice Assn. Mem. Phi Delta Kappa. Republican. Mason. Club: East Liberty Lions. Home: 6343 Jackson St. Office: Peabody High Sch., Pittsburgh, Pa.

MILLER, E. Clarence, investment banker; b. Philadelphia, Pa., Mar. 22, 1867; s. J. Washington and Mary A. (Bremer) M.; A.B., Central High Sch., 1884; LL.D., Muhlenberg Coll., 1922; m. Mary Wagner, of Phila., Dec. 14, 1892; children—Doris Annesley (Mrs. Joseph T. Beardwood), E. Clarence, Mary Rebecca (Mrs. Earle M. Anderson); m. 2d, Mrs. Cornelia E. Bruegel, Jan. 2, 1928. Stock and bond broker since 1884; mem. firm Mathews, Miller & Co., 1898-99, E. C. Miller & Co., 1899-1908; partner Bioren & Co. since 1908; dir. L. C. Smith-Corona Typewriters, Inc., Mutual Fire Ins. Co. (Germantown), Altoona & Logan Valley Railway Co. Mem. Phila. Stock Exchange since 1894, New York Stock Exchange since 1899. Pres. board Lutheran Theological Seminary; director Muhlenberg College; treasurer United Lutheran Church in America. Republican. Lutheran. Clubs: Union League (Philadelphia); Old York Road Country (Jenkintown, Pa). Home: Melrose Park, Pa. Office: 1508 Walnut St., Philadelphia, Pa.

MILLER, Edgar Raymond, M.D.; b. New Freedom, Pa., Apr. 19, 1899; s. Phillip W. and Amanda (Harmon) M.; grad. New Freedom Pub. Sch., 1912, New Freedom High Sch., 1916; A.B., Dickinson Coll., 1920, A.M., 1923; M.D., U. of Md., 1925; m. Elizabeth Bucke, June 15, 1927; children—Edgar Raymond, Elizabeth Jane. Began gen. practice of medicine, 1927. Fellow Am. Coll. Physicians; mem. A.M.A., Del. State Med. Soc., New Castle Co. Med. Soc., Phi Chi. Republican. Mason (Shriner). Home: Richardson Park, Del. Office: Medical Arts Bldg., Wilmington, Del.

MILLER, Edmund W., librarian; b. N.Y. City, Jan. 28, 1872; s. Edmund B. and Harriet Z. (Smith) M.; ed. pub. schs.; m. Sadie L. Perry, 1895 (died 1921); 1 dau., Dorothy E. With Jersey City Pub. Library since 1891, asst. librarian and sec., 1895-1915, librarian and sec., 1915-28, librarian and pres. since 1928. Mem. Am. Library Assn., N.Y. Library Assn., N.J. Library Assn. (pres. 1923-24), Hudson County Hist. Soc., Jersey City Museum Assn. (pres.). Mason. Clubs: Kiwanis, Fossils, Tuesday Night, N.Y. Library Club. Author of various hist. and bibliog. brochures and pamphlets. Home: 169 Summit Av. Office: Free Public Library, Jersey City, N.J.

MILLER, Edward Frederick, clergyman; b. South Euclid, O., Feb. 11, 1898; s. John and Henriette (Schroeder) M.; ed. Concordia Sem., St. Louis, Mo., 1918-20, 1921-22; A.M., Columbia U., 1923, Ph.D., same, 1927; m. Wilhelmina Peters, July 2, 1934; children—Dorothy Esther, Grace Elizabeth Olga. Ordained to ministry Lutheran Ch., Mo. Synod, 1925; pastor Zion Luth. Ch., Maywood, N.J. since 1925; mem. Mo. Synod Bd. for European Missions since 1927. Republican. Lutheran, Mo. Synod. Author: The Influence of Gesenius on Hebrew Lexicography, 1927. Home: 37 E. Pleasant Av., Maywood, N.J.

MILLER, Edward Tylor, lawyer; b. Montgomery Co., Md., Feb. 1, 1895; s. Guion and Annie E. (Tylor) M.; A.B., Yale U., 1916; student George Washington U. Law Sch., Washington, D.C., 1917; unmarried. Admitted to Md. bar, 1920 and since engaged in gen. practice of law at Easton; served as referee in bankruptcy since 1924; atty. for town of Easton since 1929; police justice and juvenile ct. justice, 1935-39; dir. Farmers & Merchants Bank, Easton, Md., Elliott & McDaniel Co. Served as 2d lt. and capt. inf., U.S.A., 1917-19 with A.E.F.; now col. comdg. 319th Inf. Res. Mem. Md. State Bar Assn., Psi Upsilon, Phi Beta Kappa, Am. Legion. Republican. Religious Soc. Friends. K.P., Elk. Clubs: Chesapeake Bay Yacht (Easton); 14 West Hamilton Street (Baltimore); Talbot Country. Home: The Pines. Office: 121 Washington St., Easton, Md.

MILLER, Emma Guffey, Dem. nat. committeewoman; b. Guffey Sta., Westmoreland Co., Pa.; d. John and Barbaretta (Hough) Guffey; A.B., Bryn Mawr (Pa.) Coll., 1899; m. Carroll Miller, 1902; children—William Gardner, III, John Guffey, Carroll, Joseph F. Guffey. Del. to Nat. Convs., 1924, 1928, 1932 and 1936; elected nat. committeewoman, 1932, re-elected, 1936; in 1924 was first and only woman receiving vote for President in nat. nominating conv. since women were granted suffrage; seconded nomination of Alfred E. Smith, 1924 and 1928, of Franklin D. Roosevelt, 1932 and 1936. Trustee State Teachers Coll., Slippery Rock, Pa.; pres. bd. trustees Assn. of Pa. State Teachers Coll.; chmn. advisory for Pa. Nat. Youth Adminstrn.; vice-chmn. Pa. Constitution Commeration Com., Pa. Three Hundredth Anniversary Com.; mem. Mayor's Com., Pittsburgh, for 200th Anniversary Celebration of Birth of Washington; mem. nat. advisory bd. of Women's Orgn. for Nat. Prohibition Repeal, 1929-33; mem. Pa. State Council of Edn., Pa. State Welfare Commn.; mem. Pa. Bd. of League of Women Voters. Mem. D.A.R. (historian Pittsburgh Chapter). Democrat. Clubs: Twentieth Century (Pittsburgh); Women's National Democratic (Washington, D.C.). Author: The Romance of the National Pike, 1927; National Youth Administration; articles on political campaigning and life in Washington, D.C. Winter home: 2929 Benton Pl., Washington, D.C. Summer home: Wolf Creek, Slippery Rock, Pa.

MILLER, F. Dean, clergyman; b. Mamont, Pa., Apr. 8, 1876; s. Alexander and Amanda (Iddings) M.; M.E. State Teachers Coll., 1896; A.B., Grove City Coll., 1900; B.D., Western Theol. Sem., 1903; Ph.D., U. of Chicago, 1913; (hon.) D.D., Grove City Coll., 1925; m. Mary McKown, June 18, 1903; children—Ruth (Mrs. S. E. Warner), F. Dean, Jr., R. Gordon (dec.). Ordained to ministry Presbyn. Ch., 1903; pastor, Wilkinsburg, Pa., 1903-14; pastor, Altoona, Pa., 1914-19; pastor First Presbyn. Ch., Bradford, Pa., since 1919. Served as pres. Bradford Chamber of Commerce, 1922, Bradford Rotary Club, 1923, Bradford Red Cross, 1924, Boy Scout Council, 1924. Gov. 27th Dist. Rotary Internat. 1930-31. Republican. Presbyn. Mason (K.T., 32°, Shriner), I.O.O.F. Club: Pennhills Country (Bradford). Lecturer before chambers of commerce, clubs, confs. and civic bodies. Home: 54 Jackson Av., Bradford, Pa.

MILLER, Floyd Harold, newspaper editor; b. Cameron, W.Va., Aug. 23, 1890; s. George E. and Essie (Carroll) M.; A.B., Waynesburg Coll., 1912; m. Elizabeth Orndoff, Dec. 25, 1915; children—Virginia C., Richard G., Mary D., Harriett H. Employed in teaching sch., 1912-16; asso. with Democrat Messenger, Waynesburg, Pa., since 1916, serving successively as news editor then editor. Democrat. Methodist. Home: 285 E. High St. Office: 52 Church St., Waynesburg, Pa.

MILLER, Floyd Laverne, petroleum research chemist; b. Arbela, Mich., Apr. 12, 1905; s. Fred J. and Laura (Baldwin) M.; A.B., Mich. State Normal Coll., 1926; M.S., U. of Mich., 1927, Ph.D., same, 1929; m. Ruth Pound, June 19, 1926; children—Marilyn Ruth (dec.), Lois Marjean, Leighton Pound. Instr. chemistry, Mich. State Normal Coll., Ypsilanti, Mich., 1926-27; A.P.I. Fellowship, U. of Mich., 1927-29; Chem. Foundation Research Grant, U. of Mich., 1929; research chemist, Esso Labs., Standard Oil Development Co., Elizabeth, N.J., 1930-33, head of lubricants and lubrication research, 1933-37, asst. dir. Esso. Labs. since 1937. Mem. Am. Chem. Soc., Soc. of Automotive Engrs., Phi Lambda Upsilon, Sigma Xi, Kappa Delta Pi, Gamma Alpha. Chmn. sub-com. on chem., insulation com., Nat. Research Council. Democrat. Presbyn. Mason. Home: 617 Sheridan Av., Roselle Park. Office: Esso Labs., Elizabeth, N.J.

MILLER, Frank Purl, pres. McCrosky Tool Corpn.; b. nr. Conneaut Lake, Pa., Dec. 20, 1883; s. Alonzo A. and Sarah Jane (Waters) M.; ed. pub. schs. of Conneaut Lake and Sadsbury Twp.; grad. Meadville (Pa.) High Sch., 1901; A.B., Allegheny Coll., 1907; studied U. of Mich. Law Sch., 1 term; m. Florence Grauel, June 23, 1910; 1 dau., Virginia Jane. Sales engr. McCrosky Reamer Co., 1907-08, gen. mgr. and sec.-treas., 1908-20; name changed to McCrosky Tool Corpn., 1920, and since pres.; dir. First Nat. Bank, Meadville, Pa.; dir. Midwest Tool & Mfg. Co., Detroit, Mich. Patentee over 50 inventions in metal-cutting and related fields. Mem. Pa. State Senate, 1923-27; chmn. Senate Com. on Public Health and Sanitation; alternate del. Rep. Nat. Conv., Cleveland, 1936; formerly mem. Meadville Sch. Bd. Chmn. Meadville Chapter Am. Red Cross and mem. State Advisory Com., World War. Life trustee Allegheny Coll. since 1920, now also v.p. of bd. and mem. exec. and finance coms.; pres. bd. trustees Meadville Y.M.C.A.; mem. Pa. State Exec. Com. Y.M.C.A.; mem. advisory council Salvation Army; mem. Crawford Co. Emergency Relief Bd., Pa. Council Nat. Econ. League; mem. state exec. com. Republican Men of Pa.; represents Crawford Co. in Taxpayer's League of Pa.; formerly trustee Edinboro State Teachers Coll. (apptd. by gov.), pres. Meadville Commercial Coll., trustee Pa. Coll. of Music. Mem. Am. Soc. Mech. Engrs., Metal Cutting Tool Inst., U.S. Chamber of Commerce, Pa. Chamber of Commerce, Meadville Chamber of Commerce, Phi Kappa Psi, Phi Beta Kappa, Delta Sigma Rho, Omicron Delta Kappa. Republican. Methodist (pres. bd. trustees Old Stone Ch. since 1918). Mason (32°). Clubs: Meadville Rotary (1st pres.), University, Meadville Country. Frequent speaker on civic polit. and religious subjects. Address: Meadville, Pa.

MILLER, Fred J., industrial engr.; b. Yellow Springs, O., Jan. 3, 1857; s. John Z. and Elizabeth (Woodhurst) M.; ed. pub. schs.; m. Julia Kindelberger, 1876; children—Katherin C., Grace E. With Am. Machinist, 1887-1907, as editor and last 10 yrs. as editor-in-chief; gen. mgr. factories of Union Typewriter Co., 1909-18; pub. service commr. of Pa., Mar. 1924-Apr. 1925. Served as maj. Ordnance Dept., U.S.A., Jan. 4, 1918-Feb. 21, 1919. Fellow A.A.A.S.; mem. Am. Soc. Mech. Engrs. (pres. 1920); mem. Hoover Com. of Engrs. on Waste in Industry. Trustee Simplified Spelling Bd. Club: Manhattan Single Tax (New York). Contbr. to Ency. Britannica. Awarded Gantt medal, by joint action of Am. Soc. M.E. and Inst. of Management, 1929. Address: Centre Bridge via New Hope, Pa.

MILLER, George Crawford, clergyman; b. Oliveburg, Pa., Apr. 1, 1878; s. Eli and Susan Anna (McKee) M.; ed. Ind. State Normal Sch., 1896-97; Ph.E., Mo. Valley Coll., 1904; B.S. Th., Western Theol. Sem., 1907; (hon.) D.D., Mo. Valley Coll., 1922; m. Alice Newton, Sept. 12, 1907; children—Catherine Virginia (Mrs. William M. Lloyd), Sara Elizabeth (dec.), George Crawford, Jr. (dec.), Robert Newton. Ordained to ministry Cumberland Presbyn. Ch., 1905; pastor Second Presbyn. Ch., Butler, Pa., continuously since 1907. Served with Y.M.C.A. in World War; in Near East Relief Service. Republican. Presbyn. Club: Kiwanis of Butler. Home: 609 E. Pearl St., Butler, Pa.

MILLER, George Edgar, chemist; b. Abbottstown, Pa., Nov. 13, 1891; s. Edward Peter and Miriam Josephine (Baker) M.; B.S., Gettysburg Coll., Gettysburg, Pa., 1914; student U. of Pa., 1914-16; Ph.D., Johns Hopkins U., 1920; unmarried. Employed as chemist, E. I. du Pont de Nemours & Co., Inc., Wilmington, Del., 1916-18; organic research, C.W.S., U.S. Govt., Edgewood Arsenal, Md., 1920-24, chief organic dept., 1924-28, chief organic and phys. depts., 1928-30, acting chief research div., 1930-32, chief research div. since 1932; treas. W. A. Taylor & Company, Inc., colorimetric control equipment, Baltimore, since 1930. Served as maj. C.W.S. Res., U.S.A., since 1924. Mem. Am. Chem. Soc., Am. Inst. Chem. Engrs., Alpha Tau Omega. Lutheran. Home: Edgewood Arsenal, Md.

MILLER, George Julius, lawyer; b. Perth Amboy, N.J., Jan. 15, 1895; s. Julius and Lena (Markoff) M.; student Perth Amboy (N.J.) local schs., 1900-12; LL.B., N.J. Law Sch., Newark, N.J., 1915; m. Bertha Francis Sarokin, Jan. 16, 1921 (died 1930); children—Carol, David. Admitted to N.J. bar, 1912, and since practiced at Perth Amboy, N.J. Served as sergt.-maj., C.A.C. and Army Field Clk., A.E.F., during World War. Asst. atty. gen., N.J., 1936-38; dir. Hist. Records Survey of N.J., 1936-37, New York, N.Y., 1937-39. Mem. Perth Amboy, Middlesex Co., N.J. and Am. Bar Assns., N.Y. Hist. Soc., N.J. Hist. Soc. Republican. Author: (historical legal books) Ye Olde Middlesex Courts, 1932, New Jersey Court of Chancery from 1686 to 1694, 1934; David A. Borrenstein—A Bio-Bibliographical Sketch of A Princeton Printer, 1935; various articles in jours. and periodicals of a legal history nature. Home: 58 State St. Office: 176 Smith St., Perth Amboy, N.J.

MILLER, George Reich, prof. physics; b. Harrisburg, Pa., May 20, 1895; s. Edward Allen and Gertrude (Reich) M.; B.S., Gettysburg Coll., 1919, M.S., same, 1921; Ph.D., U. of Mich., 1931; m. Nell Kelly, June 9, 1921; 1 son, George Thomas. Instr. physics, Gettysburg Coll., 1919-23, asst. prof., 1923-31, asso. prof., 1931-33, prof., 1933, prof. physics and head of dept., Gettysburg Coll. since 1934. Served as pvt. inf., U.S.A., 1918. Mem. Am. Phys. Soc., Phi Kappa Psi, Kappa Phi Kappa, Sigma Xi. Awarded Research Fellowship at U. of Mich. for summer 1931. Lutheran. Mason (K.T., 32°, Shriner). Contbr. articles to sci. jours. Home: 1 West St., Gettysburg, Pa.

MILLER, Gerald Howard, physician; b. Millville, N.J., July 12, 1903; s. Ferd A. and Mary Frances (Mayhew) M.; grad. Vineland (N.J.) High Sch., 1921; student Dickinson Coll., Carlisle, Pa., 1921-24; M.D., Temple U., Phila., Pa., 1929; m. Alberta Eleanor Clayton, of Cranbury, N.J., Aug. 21, 1937; 1 son, Gerald Howard, Jr. Resident physician Mercer Hosp., Trenton, N.J., 1929-31; gen. practice of medicine, Cranbury, N.J., since 1931; physician Cranbury Twp. and Monroe Twp.; school physician Cranbury Twp.; mem. staffs Mercer Hosp., Trenton, N.J., Princeton (N.J.) Hosp., Middlesex Gen. Hosp., St. Peters Hosp., New Brunswick, N.J. Hon. mem. Cranbury Fire Co.; mem. A.M.A., N.J. State Med. Soc., Mercer County Med. Soc., Alpha Chi Rho, Phi Alpha Sigma. Republican. Presbyterian. Mason (32°, Shriner). Clubs: Cranbury Lions (charter mem., 1st pres.); Y.M.C.A. (dir.). Address: Brainerd Place, Cranbury, N.J.

MILLER, Harry Hershey, civil engring.; b. Harrisburg, Pa., Feb. 14, 1892; s. John Pope and Sarah C. (Schwab) M.; grad. Harrisburg Acad., Pa. State Coll., 19—; m. May A. Clouser, Apr. 27, 1918. Employed as civil engr., Pa. Steel Co. and Bethlehem Steel Co., 1913-16; chief materials engr., Pa. Dept. of Highways since 1919; dir. Peoples Bank, Steelton, Pa. Served as sergt. inf. Pa. N.G. on Mexican border, 1916-17; 2d lt., 1st lt., then capt. inf., U.S.A., 1917-19, with A.E.F. on Gen. Staff, Chaumont, France. Commr. Boy Scouts, Lower Dauphin Dist. Mem. Am. Soc. Civil Engrs., Nat. Research Council, Highway Research Bd., Nat. Soc. Professional Engrs., Pa. Soc. Professional Engrs., Engring. Soc. of Pa., Am. Legion. Republican. Mem. United Brethren Ch. Mason (32°, Shriner). Clubs: Steelton (Steelton); Scottish Rite (Harrisburg). Home: 517 Pine St., Steelton, Pa. Office: 1118 State St., Harrisburg, Pa.

MILLER, Henry J., steel mfr.; b. Washington, D.C.; s. William J. and Frances M.; B.S. in M.E., Cornell U., 1907; m. Katherine McCook, June 1, 1910 (deceased); children—W. McCook, Henry J., William J. In rolling mill dept. Carnegie Steel Co., Pittsburgh, 1907-10; sales agt. Pittsburgh Steel Co., 1910-20, sec., 1920-29, dir. since 1923, v.p. since 1929; v.p., sec.-treas. and dir. Grays Landing Ferry Co., Pittsburgh; v.p. and dir. Pittsburgh Steel Sales Co., Standard Land and Improvement Co., Alicia Supply Co. Clubs: Duquesne, Pittsburgh Golf, Fox Chapel Golf. (Pittsburgh). Home: 5 Von Lent Pl. Office: 1600 Grant Bldg., Pittsburgh, Pa.

MILLER, Henry Newton; emeritus prof. Bible Sch. pedagogy on Herbert Moninger Foundation,

Behany Coll. Address: Bethany College, Bethany, W.Va.

MILLER, Henry Russell, author; b. Sidney, O., May 12, 1880; s. Robert Johnson and Anna Elizabeth (Shepherd) M.; A.B., Westminster Coll., New Wilmington, Pa., 1899; m. Jean Melrose Leitch, Apr. 8, 1908; 1 dau., Helen Jean. Admitted to bar, 1903, and since in practice at Pittsburgh; pres. The Crescent Press, Pittsburgh; dir. Pittsburgh Thrift Corpn. Mem. United Presbyn. Ch. Author: The Man Higher Up, 1910; His Rise to Power, 1911; The Ambition of Mark Truitt, 1913; The House of Toys, 1914; The First Division, 1920. Home: 164 Dickson Av., Ben Avon, Pa. Office: 405 Penn Av., Pittsburgh, Pa.

MILLER, Herbert Adolphus, sociologist; b. Tuftonboro, N.H., June 5, 1875; s. William Magnus and Ellen (Thompson) M.; A.B., Dartmouth, 1899, A.M., 1902; Ph.D., Harvard, 1905; studied U. of Chicago, 1911; m. Elizabeth Northway Cravath, Aug. 22, 1903; children—Gustova C., Maurice C. Instr. Latin and Greek, Fisk U., 1899-1902; asst. prof. philosophy and sociology, Olivet (Mich.) Coll., 1905-07, prof., 1907-14; prof. sociology, Oberlin Coll., 1914-25, U. of Calif., summer 1922; prof. sociology, Ohio State U., 1924-31, Summer Sch., Northwestern Univ., 1932; lecturer on social economy, Bryn Mawr College since 1933; gave courses at Yenching U., Peiping, China, and lectured at univs. of China, India, Syria, 1929-30. Mem. bd. dir. Internat. Inst. of Phila. (pres.), National Institute for Immigrant Welfare; mem. exec. com., Masaryk Inst. Made survey of immigrant conditions and school facilities for immigrants, Cleveland, Ohio, for Russell Sage Foundation, 1915; chief of div. on immigrant heritages Carnegie Corpn. Organizer and dir. Mid. European Union. Chmn. Ohio Com. on Penal Conditions. Decorated Order of the White Lion (Czechoslovakia). Mem. Am. Sociol. Soc. (com. on internat. relations), A.A.A.S., Phi Beta Kappa (hon.). Conglist. Club: Contemporary (Phila.). Author: The School and the Immigrant, 1916; Old World Traits Transplanted (joint author), 1921; Races, Nations and Classes, 1924; The Beginnings of Tomorrow, 1933; also articles on social and national questions. Home: 229 Roberts Rd., Bryn Mawr, Pa.

MILLER, Howard Daniel, nat. park supt.; b. Summit Hill, Pa., Feb. 4, 1907; s. Frank O. and Kate (Miller) M,; Ph.B., Muhlenberg Coll., 1929; ed. Bloomsburg State Teachers Coll., summer 1931, Villanova Coll., summer 1932, N.Y.U. Sch. of Extension, 1933-34; m. Martha M. Heycook, June 10, 1928; children—Miriam Ann, Franklin Howard. Engaged in teaching in pub. schs., 1929-33; dir. adult edn., Carbon Co., 1933-34; agt. for bur. vocational rehabilitation under Dept. Labor and Industry, 1934-36; supt. of highways, Carbon Co., 1936-39; project supt. Hickory Run Nat. Park since 1939; propr., mgr. Miller's Store, gen. mdse., Summit Hill, Pa., since 1938. Served as Co. Chmn. Carbon Co. Dem. Com., Sec. Summit Hill Bus. Mens Assn., Dir. Bd. Edn. Borough Sch., Summit Hill, Pa. Mem. Phi Epsilon, Kappa Phi Kappa, Theta Kappa Nu. Democrat. Lutheran. Home: 34 W. Ludlow St., Summit Hill, Pa.

MILLER, Hugh, engineer; b. Roselle, N.J., Feb. 1, 1881; s. Charles Dexter and Julia (Hope) M.; grad. Leal's Sch., Plainfield, N.J., 1897; C.E., Princeton, 1901; post-grad. work, Harvard, summers 1910, 12; m. Clara Fay, Nov. 2, 1904; children—Donald Hope, Francis Fay; m. 2d, Izetta Jewel Brown, Apr. 16, 1927. With H. de B. Parsons; consulting engr., New York, 1902; instr. civ. engring., Princeton, 1902, pvt. tutor, 1902-03; with Centennial Copper Mining Co., 1903-09; prof. civ. engring., Clarkson Coll. of Technology, Potsdam, N.Y., 1909-15; lecturer on civ. engring., Rice Inst., Houston, Tex., 1915-17; prof. civ. engring., George Washington U., 1921-26; dean Coll. of Engring., same univ., 1922-26; became prof. civ. engring., Union Coll., 1926; state engr. for Mo. of Federal Emergency Adminstrn. of Public Works, 1933-35; chief engr. Pub. Works Adminstrn. for W.Va., 1935-Aug. 1937; now pres. Hugh Miller Associates, Inc. Capt. engrs., U.S. Army, 1917-21; lt. col. U.S. Reserve since 1926. Examiner Inst. Internat. Edn. Mem. Am. Soc. C.E., Princeton Engring. Assn., Princeton Alumni Assn. of W.Va., Sigma Xi, Sigma Tau; fellow A.A.A.S. Democrat. Episcopalian. Clubs: Colonial (Princeton); Charleston Tennis. Home: 204 Berkley St. Office: Chamber of Commerce Bldg., Charleston, W.Va.

MILLER, Irving; prof. voice, Davis & Elkins Coll. Address: Davis & Elkins College, Elkins, W.Va.

MILLER, Jacob Kopel, lawyer; b. Krivoesoer, Russia, Oct. 8, 1893; s. Philip and Anna (Abrahamson) M.; brought to U.S., 1896; naturalized citizen; B.S., Pa. State Coll., 1915; LL.B., Temple U. Law Sch., 1926; m. Mina Trallis, Apr. 17, 1916; children—Mitchell Walter, Ruth Hannah. Began career as chemist, O. Hommel Co., Pittsburgh, Pa., and Frankford Arsenal, Phila., Pa.; admitted to Pa. bar, 1926, and since engaged in gen. practice of law at Phila.; now succeeded to law practice and firm name Levi, Mandel & Miller; pres. and dir. Shoe & Leather Mercantile Agency, Inc., a nat. source of credit information for shoe and leather trade, Boston, Mass., and other cities. Mem. Am., Pa. State and Phila. bar assns., Commercial Law League of America, Am. Acad. Social & Polit. Sci., Acad. Polit. Sci., Inter Collegiate Menorah Assn. (nat. treas., 1914), Phi Epsilon Pi (nat. treas., 1918-19), Delta Sigma Rho. Jewish religion. Mason. Clubs: Penn State, Lawyers (Philadelphia). Home: 3904 Vaux St., Philadelphia, Pa. Office: North American Bldg., Philadelphia, Pa.

MILLER, James Collins, univ. prof.; b. Wellington Co., Ont., Can., June 18, 1880; s. James and Ann (Collins) M.; student U. of Calif., summers, 1905-07; B.S., Throop Coll. of Tech., Pasadena, Calif., 1907; A.M., Teachers Coll. (Columbia), 1910; Ph.D., Columbia, 1913; m. Ida B. Zener, Sept. 23, 1925. As exec. officer Govt. of Alberta, Can., established its 2d provincial normal sch.; organized and put into operation the 1st university summer session in western Can.; organized and established a system of tech. edn. for Province of Alberta; dist. vocational officer of Mil. Hosp. Commn. of Can., 1916-18; lent to Govt. of U.S., 1918, to aid in orgn. of work of vocational rehabilitation, Washington, D.C.; returned to Can., Sept. 1919, to aid in organization of tech. edn. in Ontario; prof. edn., Ind. U., 1921-25; prof. ednl. administration, U. of Pa., since Sept. 1925. Mem. Am. Acad. Polit. and Social Science, A.A.A.S., N.E.A. (dept. superintendence), Nat. Soc. for Study of Edn., Phi Delta Kappa, Delta Chi. Presbyn. Author: Rural Schools in Canada, 1913; Vocational Rehabilitation of Disabled Soldiers in Alberta, 1918. Contbr. to ednl. periodicals. Address: Bennett Hall, University of Pennsylvania, Philadelphia, Pa.

MILLER, James Hunter, clergyman; b. Frankfort Springs, Pa., Aug. 29, 1865; s. George and Margaret Ann (Hunter) M.; A.B., Muskingum Coll., New Concord, O., 1893, A.M., 1896, (hon.) D.D., 1929; B.D., Allegheny Theol. Sem. (now Pittsburgh-Xenia Theol. Sem.), 1897; m. Armitta Dales Buck, May 20, 1897; children—Margaret Hunter, Dorothy Hazen, Rev. James Kenneth, Katherine Lois. Engaged in teaching pub. schs., 1884-88; teacher, Ingleside Acad., McDonald, Pa., 1893-94; ordained to ministry United Presbyn. Ch., 1897; pastor various U. Presbyn. chs., 1897-1934, retired from active service, 1934. Republican. United Presbyterian (mem. Cleveland Presbytery). Home: 3219 Wainbell Av., Pittsburgh, Pa.

MILLER, James M., pres. Central City Nat. Bank; b. Schellsburg, Pa., Aug. 6, 1881; s. Richard H. and Mary C. (Findley) M.; student pub. schs. and Teacher's Training Normal Sch.; m. Jennie Hammer, Nov. 11, 1902; children—Robert E., Dorothy M., Joseph H., Olin J., Richard Myles, Evelyn L. Sch. teacher to 1902; clk. Berwind White Coal Mining Co., 1902-05, paymaster and payroll clk., 1905-13; chief bookkeeper Windber Trust Co., 1913-21; assisted in orgn. Central City (Pa.) Nat. Bank, 1921, and served as cashier, 1921-33, v.p., 1933-37, pres. since 1937. Has been mem. Windber (Pa.) Sch. Bd., Central City Sch. Bd. Mason (Shriner). Assisted in capture of "Jaworski" or "Flathead" gang in attempt to hold-up Central City Nat. Bank, 1929. Address: Central City Nat. Bank, Central City, Pa.

MILLER, James Sherwood, mining engr.; b. Hoosick Falls, N.Y., Aug. 22, 1892; s. James M. and Marcia Harriet (Sherwood) M.; grad. Hoosick Falls Schools, 1910; E.M., Columbia U. Sch. of Mines, 1914; m. Gwenllian Davies, Nov. 17, 1917; children—Margaret Marcia, Jean Marie, Jacqueline Davies, James Sherwood. Jr. engr. with R. V. Norris, consulting engrs., Wilkes-Barre, Pa., 1914-15; asst. supt. Nesquehoning Dist., Lehigh Navigation Coal Co., Lansford, Pa., 1915-18, dist. supt. Tamaqua Dist., 1918-19, Nesquehoning Dist., 1919-25; dist. supt. Alliance Coal Mining Co., 1925-28; dir. of research Lehigh Coal & Navigation Co., 1928-33, supt. Alliance Dist., 1933-37, also Coaldale Dist., 1936-37; div. supt. Lehigh Valley Coal Co. since Sept. 15, 1937. Pres. Lansford Sch. Bd., 1931-33. Mem. Phi Delta Theta, Theta Tau. Republican. Presbyterian. Home: 342 E. Broad St. Office: Lehigh Valley Coal Co., Hazleton, Pa.

MILLER, Jay Wilson, business sch. exec.; b. Mapleton Depot, Pa., Sept. 14, 1893; s. Abram K. and Maggie (Wilson) M.; B.E., Juniata Coll., Huntingdon, Pa., 1910; B.S. in Business, U. of Minn., Minneapolis, Minn., 1924; Ed.M., Temple U., Phila., Pa., 1936, Ed.D., 1939; m. E. Lillian Steinbach, Dec. 29, 1914. Rural sch. teacher, Carrington, N.D., 1910-12; prin., Williams Business Coll., Beaver Dam, Wis., 1912-14; instr. business, Dakota Wesleyan U., Mitchell, S.D., 1914-17; head commercial dept., Menomonie (Wis.) High Sch., 1917-18; prin. accounting dept., Goldey Coll., Wilmington, Del., 1918-23, sec.-treas. and dir. of courses since 1929; instr. accounting, U. of Minn., Minneapolis, Minn., 1923-24; v.p., The Knox Sch. of Salesmanship, Oak Park, Ill., 1924-26; sales instr., Nat. Assn. of Real Estate Bds., Chicago, 1926-29. Trustee Goldey Coll. since 1932. Mem. Phi Delta Kappa. Awarded Phi Delta Kappa Award for Honors in Research, Temple U., 1936. Republican. Methodist. Mason (Oriental Lodge 27; Past Thrice Potent Master, Wilmington Lodge of Perfection, Del. Consistory). Author: Cases in Salesmanship, 1930; A Critical Analysis of the Organization, Administration and Function of the Private Business Schools of the United States, 1939; editor: Methods in Commercial Teaching, 1925. Home: 405 W. 35th St. Office: 9th St. at Tatnall, Wilmington, Del.

MILLER, Jere Edwin, pres. The Farmers & Merchants Trust Co. of Chambersburg; b. Edenville, Pa., Apr. 24, 1868; s. Hezekiah and Susan (Beauchamp) M.; student pub. schs. and Select Sch.; m. Fannie Frymier, June 27, 1896; children—Percey Edwin, Marjorie Frymier. Pub. sch. teacher, 1888-95; wholesale grocery salesman, 1895-1911; register of wills and recorder of deeds, Franklin Co., Pa., 1912-16, dep. treas., 1917-21, magistrate, 1922-29; in real estate and ins. business, Chambersburg, Pa., since 1930; v.p. The Farmers & Merchants Trust Co. of Chambersburg, Pa., 1935-36, pres. since 1936. Home: 53 Glen St. Office: Memorial Sq., Chambersburg, Pa.

MILLER, Jesse I., lawyer; b. Lexington, Ky., July 12, 1891; s. I. J. and Jennie (Faller) M.; A.B., U. of Ky., Lexington, Ky., 1912, M.A., 1913, LL.B., 1914; m. Florence Glaser, July 15, 1923; children—Jesse I., Jane Elsie. Practice of law at Lexington, Ky., 1914-17, at Washington, D.C., 1921-33, since 1934. Served as pvt. and sergt., 38th Div., U.S. Army, 1917-18, 1st lt., 1918, capt., 1918-19, maj., Judge Advocate, 1919, aide-de-camp, Maj. Gen. E. H. Crowder, Provost Marshal Gen., 1918-19, mil. attache, Managua, Nicaragua, 1920. Asst. solicitor Bur. of Internal Revenue, Washington, D.C., 1920; umpire for Am. government, Nicaraguan presidential elections, 1920; 1st exec. dir. Nat. Labor Bd., 1933-34. Mem. Am. Bar Assn., Delta Chi. Democrat. Jewish religion. Mason. Clubs: Woodmont Country (Bethesda, Md.); London Golf and Country (Purcellville, Va.).

Co-author: Spirit of Selective Service, 1920; author numerous articles on federal taxation and labor relations. Home: 14 Oxford St., Chevy Chase, Md. Office: Woodward Bldg., Washington, D.C.

MILLER, John Anderson, editor; b. Newark, N.J., Sept. 20, 1895; s. John Anderson and Augusta Rutan (Neumann) M.; preparatory edn., Newark Acad.; Ph.B., Yale U., 1915; m. Frances Elizabeth Daggett, Sept. 2, 1931; children—Sarah Mason, John Anderson. Cadet engineer, Pub. Service Ry., Newark, 1915-16, asst. to traffic engr., 1919-22; asst. editor Electric Ry. Journal (name changed to Transit Journal), 1923, asso. editor, 1924-28, acting managing editor, January-August 1929, managing editor, 1929-30, editor since 1930; editor of Aera, official publ. Am. Transit Association, 1927-28. Served as pvt., 1st N.J. Cav., Mexican border, 1916; lt., Engr. Corps. U.S.A., 1917-19; capt., Engr. R.C., 1922-33. Member Society American Military Engineers, American Transit Association, American Soc. Civil Engineers, Union Internationale de Tramways. Awarded prize, Soc. Am. Military Engrs., for paper on officers res., 1921; Arthur M. Wellington prize, Am. Soc. C.E. 1927. Republican. Episcopalian. Clubs: Yale (New York); Graduate (New Haven). Author: Master Builders of Sixty Centuries, 1938. Home: 12 Summit St., Glen Ridge, N.J. Office: McGraw-Hill Publishing Co., New York, N.Y.

MILLER, John Andrew, corpn. official; b. Baltimore, Md., Sept. 1, 1872; s. Conrad and Margaret A. (Woerling) M.; student Lawrenceville (N.J.) Sch., 1889-90, Lafayette Coll., Easton, Pa., 1891-95; m. Mary A. Cope, June 25, 1896; children—Conrad Cope, Mary Alice (Mrs. John W. Winn); m. 2d, Emily N. Moon, July 1, 1906; 1 son, John Andrew; m. 3d, Mary F. Morrissey, Aug. 1, 1931. Began as r.r. contractor, 1896; v.p. Dexter Portland Cement Co., Nazareth, Pa., 1899-1910, pres., 1910-26; pres. Clinchfield Cement Corpn., Kingsport, Tenn., 1908-26; pres. Penn-Dixie Cement Corpn., New York, N.Y., 1926-28, chmn. bd., 1928-36, pres. since 1936; pres. Dixie Sand and Gravel Corpn., Marcem Quarries Corpn.; v.p. Nazareth (Pa.) Nat. Bank & Trust Co. since 1910. Mem. Delta Kappa Epsilon. Republican. Mem. Moravian Ch. Mason. Clubs: Lotos, University, Delta Kappa Epsilon, Uptown (New York); Saucon Valley Country (Bethlehem, Pa.); Pomfret (Easton, Pa.). Home: 7 S. New St., Nazareth, Pa. Office: 60 E. 42d St., New York, N.Y.

MILLER, John Anthony, coll. prof.; b. Greensburg, Ind., Dec. 16, 1859; s. Bruno Brunen and Katherine (Arnold) M.; A.B., Indiana University, 1890, LL.D., 1928; A.M., Stanford University, 1893; Ph.D., University of Chicago, 1899; m. Mary Catharine Goodwine, Dec. 24, 1880; children—Max B., Harry L.; m. 2d, Frances Morgan Swain, June 23, 1932. Supt. schs., Rockville, Ind., 1890-91; instr. mathematics, 1891-93, asst. prof., 1893-94, Stanford; prof. mathematics, 1894-95, mechanics and astronomy, 1895-1906, Ind. U.; prof. astronomy, and dir. Sproul Obs., Swarthmore Coll., 1906-32, v.p. Swarthmore College, 1914-29, prof. of astronomy emeritus since 1932. Chief of expedition sent by Indiana University to Spain, 1905, to observe total eclipse of the sun, and of expdn. sent by Sproul Obs. to observe total eclipse of sun in Colo., 1918, and to Mexico, 1923, by Swarthmore Coll. to observe total eclipse of sun, to New Haven, Conn., 1925, to Sumatra, 1926, 29, to Vermont, 1932; tech. dir. expdn. by Hayden Planetarium to Peru, 1937. Fellow Am. Acad. Arts and Sciences, A.A.A.S., Indiana Acad. Science, Royal Astron. Soc.; mem. Am. Math. Soc., Am. Astron. Soc., Am. Philos. Soc. (sec.), Sigma Xi, Phi Beta Kappa. Republican. Friend. Author: Trigonometry for Beginners, 1896; Analytic Mechanics, 1915 (revised 1935). Contbr. to math. and astron. publs. Home: Wallingford, Pa.

MILLER, John D., lawyer; b. Hunter, Greene Co., N.Y., Dec. 6, 1856; s. Abram D. and Lydia (Douglas) M.; ed. common and night schs.; m. Jennie M. Blandin, Jan. 20, 1882; children—Harry L. (deceased), Allan D., Myron B., Walter L. Admitted to Pa. bar, 1891, and practiced in Susquehanna Co., Pa., also operating dairy farms; assisted in organizing local cooperative marketing assns. among dairymen; gen. counsel, Dairymen's League, Inc., and Dairymen's League Co-operative Assn., Inc., since Jan. 1, 1917, v.p., 1918-35; author amendments to state anti-trust acts authorizing farmers to combine for marketing purposes; also prepared first draft and assisted in preparing Capper-Volstead Co-operative Marketing Law, 1922. Dir. and mem. exec. com. Central Bank for Coöperatives; dir. Federal Prison Industries, Inc., 1934-Mar. 1937. Mem. Nat. Co-operative Milk Producers' Federation (life dir.; pres. 1922-28), Nat. Coöperative Council (pres. since 1933), Am. Inst. of Co-operation (dir.). Del. from U.S. to World's Dairy Congress, England, 1928. Mem. Am. Bar Assn., Bar Assn. Susquehanna Co. Democrat. Methodist. Mason. Odd Fellow. Home: Thompson, Susquehanna Co., Pa. Office: 11 W. 42d St., New York, N.Y.; and 1731 I St. N.W., Washington, D.C.

MILLER, John Franklin; b. Port Perry, Pa., Feb. 28, 1859; s. George Torrence and Mary Jane (Craig) M.; student Western U. of Pa. (now U. of Pittsburgh); A.B., Wooster (O.) Coll., 1881; m. Mary Louise Paull, Sept. 22, 1887; 1 dau., Rebecca Paull (Mrs. Allen Stewart Davison); m. 2d, Mrs. Clara L. Westinghouse (widow of Henry Herman Westinghouse), Apr. 5, 1937. Began with B.&O. R.R., 1880; assistant sec. Westinghouse Air Brake Co., 1899-1902, sec., 1902-05, v.p., 1905-16, pres., 1916-19, vice chmn. bd. since 1919; chmn. bd. Pittsburgh Screw & Bolt Co.; chmn. bd. First Nat. Bank of Wilmerding; dir. Am. Brake Co., Canadian Westinghouse Co., Fidelity Trust Co., Massey Concrete Products Corpn. Mem. Air Brake Assn., Western Pennsylvania Engring. Society, Hist. Soc. Western Pa., Sigma Chi, Phi Beta Kappa. Decorated Order of Rising Sun (Japan). Presbyn. Clubs: Duquesne, Pittsburgh Field Club (Pittsburgh); Edgewood Country; Engineers, Adirondack League (New York); Bradenton (Fla.) Country. Home: Edgewood, Pittsburgh, Pa. Office: Westinghouse Air Brake Co., Wilmerding, Pa.

MILLER, John Kemper; prof. of English, Univ. of Pittsburgh. Address: University of Pittsburgh, Pittsburgh, Pa.

MILLER, John Oliver, banker; b. Somerset, Pa., Feb. 14, 1875; s. Daniel S. and Mary (Lichty) M.; grad. Law Dept. of U. of Mich., Ann Arbor, Mich., 1899; m. Lucy Kennedy, May 1, 1907; children—Julian, Eliza, Barbara. Sec.-treas. Monongahela Trust Co., Homestead, 1901-08; cashier First Nat. Bank of Homestead, Pa., 1904-08; sec.-treas. Safe Deposit Trust Co., Peoples Savings Bank, Pittsburgh, Pa., 1908-16; v.p. Peoples-Pittsburgh Trust Co., 1916-28, senior v.p. since 1929; dir. Peoples East End Real Estate Co., Pittsburgh Transportation Co. Republican. Clubs: Duquesne, University (Pittsburgh). Home: 1342 Inverness Av. Office: Fourth Av., Pittsburgh, Pa.

MILLER, John S., lawyer; b. Somerset, Pa., Sept. 4, 1875; s. Josiah and Eliza M.; grad. Gettysburg Acad. and Washington and Jefferson Coll., Washington, Pa.; m. Kathrene Holderbaum, Dec. 20, 1905; 1 dau., Virginia. Sch. teacher, Somerset Co., Pa., and Waterloo, Ia.; now engaged in gen. practice of law, Somerset, Pa.; pres. Globe Mutual Fire Ins. Co. since 1936; dir. The County Trust Co., Somerset, Pa., since 1909. Dist. atty., Somerset Co., Pa., 1908-12; Pa. State Senator, 1919-23; solicitor, Somerset Co., 1920-28; dep. atty. gen. of Pa., 1927-35. Pres. Philharmonic Soc., 1916-20; active in civic and fraternal activities. Mem. Good Roads Assn. (sec. since 1919). Edited and pub. Brief History of Yost Miller Descendants; edited for State of Pa., Supreme, Superior and Common Pleas Court, Descisions of Workmen's Compensation Law. Address: Somerset, Pa.

MILLER, John Strother, tech. adviser and chemist; b. Washington, D.C., Nov. 14, 1876; s. John Strother and Minnie (Potter) M.; student Washington (D.C.) High Sch., 1894-97, Cornell U., 1898-1900; m. Clarine Gertrude Ramage, June 4, 1902; children—John Strother III, Kenneth Ramage. Asst. chemist supervising architect's office, U.S. Treas. Dept., Washington, D.C., 1902-08; with technologic branch geol. survey, U.S. Dept. of Interior, Washington, 1908-09; prin. asst. chemist Barber Asphalt Paving Co., Barber Sta., Perth Amboy, N.J., 1909-19, chief chemist, 1919-26, dir. tech. bur., 1926-38, tech. adviser since 1938, specializing in chemistry, physics and engring, relating to asphaltic hydrocarbons, their refining, compounding and use. Mem. Inst. Chem. Engrs., Am. Chem. Soc., Am. Soc. for Testing Materials, Assn. Asphalt Paving Technologists (pres. 1937), Am. Soc. of Municipal Engrs., Phi Sigma Kappa, Chemists Club (New York). Home: 1084 Bryant St., Rahway, N.J. Office: Barber Sta., Perth Amboy, N.J.

MILLER, Joseph Randolph, supt. city schs.; b. Somerset Co., Pa., Mar. 30, 1887; s. Lorenzo Job and Mary Jane (Cable) M.; B.S., Otterbein Coll., 1914; A.M., Ohio State U., 1930; m. Hazel Lois Cornetet, Sept. 2, 1915; 1 dau., Kathryn Ann. Instr. mathematics and sci., high sch., Huntington, W.Va., 1914-20, asst. prin., 1918-22; prin. Central Jr. High Sch., Huntington, W.Va., 1922-30; prin. Jr. High Sch., Ambridge, Pa., 1930-31, supt. schs., Ambridge, since 1931; summer instr. edn., Geneva Coll., Beaver Falls, Pa., 1931-38. Mem. Bd. of Trade, Community Club. Mem. N.E.A. (life), Am. Assn. Sch. Adminstrs., Pa. State Edn. Assn., Phi Delta Kappa. Presbyterian. Mason (32°, K.C.C.H.). Club: Rotary of Ambridge (past pres.). Home: 720 Park Rd., Ambridge, Pa.

MILLER, Joshua Albert; administrative co-ordinator of practice teaching, U. of Md. Address: University of Maryland, College Park, Md.

MILLER, Joshua Hauser, clergyman; b. Appenzell, Pa., Jan. 2, 1866; s. Jacob D. and Elizabeth (Hauser) M.; A.B., Muhlenberg Coll., 1893, A.M., same, 1896, Ph.D., same, 1908; ed. Luth. Theol. Sem., 1893-96; m. Anna W. Levering, Oct. 21, 1897; children—Theodore Kenneth, Adelihe Elizabeth. Ordained to ministry Luth. Ch., 1896; pastor, New Castle, Pa., 1896-1918, Irwin, Pa., 1918-38; now emeritus; pres. Greensburg Conf. Trustee Thiel Coll., Greeneville, Pa., Luth. Theol. Sem., Phila., Pa. Mem. bd. Bethesda Orphan's Home, Meadville, Pa. Mem. S.A.R. Hon. mem. G.A.R. Eagle Scout. Republican. Lutheran. Author: Bible of Nature and Bible of Grace, 1919. Home: 324 E. Moody Av., New Castle, Pa.

MILLER, Julius French, pres. Gen. Manifold & Printing Co.; b. Franklin, Pa., Nov. 13, 1883; s. Gen. Charles and Ann Adelaide (Sibley) M.; student pvt. and pub. schs.; grad. Franklin (Pa.) High Sch., 1901; LL.B., Yale U. Law Sch., 1905; m. Ethel Helen Nicklas, July 4, 1922; 1 son, Jay French. Admitted to practice law before highest court of Conn., 1905, later before Supreme Ct. of Pa. and Supreme Ct. of U.S.; sec. Galena-Signal Oil Co. and Galena Oil Corpn. (successor), 1907-32; v.p. and dir. Gen. Manifold & Printing Co., commercial and railroad printing forms, and mfrs. duplicating, 1930-32, pres. since 1932; v.p., sec. and dir. Lake Erie, Franklin & Clarion R.R. Co. Organizer Franklin Chamber of Commerce. Republican. Baptist (trustee First Ch. of Franklin). Clubs: Rotary (ex-pres.), Franklin (Franklin, Pa.); Wanango Country (Reno, Pa.); Yale (New York). Home: Miller Park. Office: 6th & Buffalo Sts., Franklin, Pa.

MILLER, Karl Greenwood, educator; b. Salem, Va., May 25, 1893; s. Charles Armand and Mary (Sherman) M.; student Coll. of Charleston, S.C., 1911-12; A.B., U. of Pa., 1915, A.M., 1918, Ph.D., 1921; m. Verna Howell, Sept. 18, 1920; 1 son, Roger Sherman. Asst. inst. in psychology, U. of Pa., 1915-17, instr., 1917-21, asst. prof., 1921-27, prof. since 1927, dir. of admissions, 1926-36, dean of coll. of liberal arts for women since 1936. Served as 2d lt. psychol. div. Air Service, U.S.A., 1918-19. Mem. Coll. Entrance Exam. Bd. (exec. com.), Commn. on Instns. of Higher Edn., Middle States Assn. of Colls. and Secondary Schs., Am. Psychol.

Assn., Am. Assn. of Univ. Profs., Friars Soc.; Phi Beta Kappa (former pres. Delta of Pa.), Phi Delta Kappa, Alpha Tau Omega. Clubs: Contemporary, Lenape (Phila.); University of Pennsylvania (New York). Home: 7122 Penarth Av., Bywood, Upper Darby, Pa.

MILLER, Laurence M.; pres. Colonial Trust Co. Home: 217 Wendover Road, Guilford. Office: 5 W. Saratoga St., Baltimore, Md.

MILLER, Lawrence Vernon, lawyer; b. Baltimore, Md., May 29, 1884; s. Decatur Howard and Agnes (Owens) M.; student Baltimore pub. schs., 1892-1902, Marstons' Univ. Sch., Baltimore, 1902-05; A.B., Yale, 1908; LL.B., U. of Md., Baltimore, 1911; m. Katherine Baum, May 29, 1931; children—Decatur Howard III, James Hamilton, Lawrence Vernon. Admitted to Md. bar, 1911, and since practiced at Baltimore; asso. with firm Marbury & Gosnell, Baltimore, 1911-19; mem. of firm Marbury, Gosnell & Williams, Baltimore, since 1919; v.p. and dir. Curtis Bay Towing Co., Baltimore, since 1920; dir. Belvidere Hotel Corpn. Mem. Am. Bar Assn., Md. Bar Assn., Baltimore Bar Assn., Maritime Law Assn. of U.S., Psi Upsilon (Yale). Democrat. Catholic. Clubs: Maryland, Merchants, Elkridge Hunt (Baltimore, Md.). Home: 11 W. Coldspring Lane. Office: Maryland Trust Bldg., Baltimore, Md.

MILLER, Leo Henry, lawyer; b. Sharpsburg, Md., Sept. 28, 1893; s. Henry M. and Emma A. M.; grad. Sheperd Coll. State Normal Sch., Sheperdstown, W.Va., 1912; A.B., W.Va. Univ., 1917; LL.B., U. of Md., 1920; m. Margaret McKlveen, Sept. 4, 1917; children—Edwin H., Margaret Ann, Daniel L. Teacher in elementary schools, 1912-14; prin. Bunker Hill High Sch., 1917-18; prin. Martinsburg (W.Va.) High Sch., 1920-23; asst. law librarian, Ia. State Law Library, Des Moines, 1923-24; admitted to Md. bar and since in gen. practice of law at Hagerstown; treas. Hagerstown Loan & Thrift Corpn.; sec. Western Md. Supply Corpn.; vice-pres. Tri-State Elec. Supply Co., Inc. Served as sergt. Motor Transport Corps, U.S. Army, during World War. Pres. Hagerstown Chamber of Commerce; dir. Infant and Child Welfare Center. Mem. Washington County, Md. State and Am. bar assns. Republican. Methodist. Mason. Clubs: Hagerstown Kiwanis; Fountainhead Country. Home: 207 W. Irvin Av. Office: 206 Second National Bank Bldg., Hagerstown, Md.

MILLER, L(ewis) Earle, lawyer; b. nr. Indiana, Pa.; s. Jacob W. and Sarah E. (Kerr) M.; B.E., Juniata Coll., Huntingdon, Pa., 1903; B.S., Southern U. 1904; LL.B., Ind. U., 1908; m. Mary Elizabeth Fleming, June 23, 1908; children—Willis E., Donald M., Anna Louise, Paul D., Lisle F. Admitted to Ind. bar, 1908 and to bar Ind. State Supreme Ct., U.S. Dist. and U.S. Circuit cts. but did not practice; admitted to Pa. bar, 1910 and since engaged in gen. practice of law at Indiana, Pa.; served as dist. atty., Indiana Co., Pa., 1924-31; mem. council, of Indiana, Pa., since 1938. Mem. Indiana Co. Bar Assn. Republican. Presbyn. Mason (Shriner). Home: 1470 Philadelphia St. Office: Savings & Trust Co. Bldg., Indiana, Pa.

MILLER, Lewis Harrison, judge; b. Jackson Co., W.Va., Nov. 19, 1890; s. Leander and Jessie (Harrison) M.; student W.Va. Wesleyan Coll., Buckhannon, 1906-07; A.B., O. Univ. Athens, O., 1913; LL.B., W.Va. Univ. Law Sch., Morgantown, 1917; m. Freda Clare Rambow, Dec. 23, 1917; children—Ruth Lee, Jo Clare, Doris Dell. Admitted to W.Va. bar, 1917, and engaged in gen. practice of law at Ripley, 1917-29; served as mem. W.Va. Senate, 1926-28; judge 5th Judicial Circuit of W.Va. since 1929. Served in Air Corps, U.S.N., 1918. Keynoter Rep. State Conv., Huntington, 1936. Mem. W.Va. Bar Assn., Order of Coif, Sigma Pi, Am. Legion. Republican. Episcopalian. Mason (32°), K.P., Modern Woodman. Club: Camera Club (Ripley). Home: 403 North St. Office: Bank of Ripley, Ripley, W.Va.

MILLER, M(ilton) Valentine, physician; b. Middleburg, N.Y., Feb. 14, 1891; s. Rev. Edgar Grim (D.D.) and Esther A. (Valentine) M.; B.S., Gettysburg Coll., 1911; M.D., U. of Pa. Med. Sch., 1916; student U. of Pa. Grad. Sch. of Medicine, 1921-22; m. Claire R. Richards, Feb. 19, 1918; children—M(ilton) Valentine, Jr., Richards Galt, David Treat, Nancy Claire. Interne Lancaster Gen. Hosp., 1916-17; engaged in gen. practice of medicine at Phila., 1919-24, practice limited to otolaryngology since 1924; otolaryngologist, Memorial Hosp., Roxborough since 1929, chief of staff since 1934, Phila. Hosp. for Contagious Diseases since 1933, Germantown Hosp. since 1937; asst. otologist to Grad. Hosp. and asso. in otology, U. of Pa. Grad. Sch. of Medicine since 1931, chief of otology clinic since 1937; asst. otolaryngologist, Univ. Hosp. and asso. in otolaryngology, U. of Pa. Sch. of Medicine since 1935; cons. otologist, Pa. Sch. for the Deaf, Mt. Airy since 1937. Served as 1st lieut. M.C., U.S.A. then capt., 1917-19, with A.E.F., gassed in action; comd. maj. Med. Corps, Pa. N.G., 1920. Fellow A.C.S., Am. Acad. Ophthalmology and Otolaryngology, Coll. of Phys., Phila., Phila. Laryngol. Soc., A.M.A. Am. Laryngol. Rhinol. and Otol. Soc.; mem. Pa. State and Phila. Co. med. socs., Phi Gamma Delta, St. Andrews Soc. of Phila. Republican. Lutheran. Club: Philadelphia Medical. Home: 114 W. Phil-Ellena St., Mt. Airy, Philadelphia, Pa.

MILLER, Moore Rudolph, clergyman; b. Lemoyne, Pa., Jan. 31, 1904; s. Jerome Rudolph and Gertrude (Moore) M.; ed. Lafayette Coll., 1922-23; A.B., Yale, 1926; S.T.B., Western Theol. Sem., Pittsburgh, 1931; grad. study, Oxford U., Eng., 1933-34; m. Miriam Melchior Witmyer, June 16, 1926; children—Michael Rudolph, Stephen Kurt. Ordained to ministry Presbyn. Ch. U.S.A., 1931; pastor, Newell, W.Va., 1931-35; pastor, Saltsburg, Pa., since 1935; moderator Kittanning Presbytery; dir. Presbyn. Book Store, Pittsburgh. Served in Pa. N.G., 1922-25; U.S.N. Res. Summer Sch., 1920; 1st lt. U.S.A. Chaplains Res. since 1938. Mem. Church Service Soc. of Scotland, Alpha Chi Rho. Awarded Fellowship Western Theol. Sem. Republican. Presbyn. of U.S.A. Mason (32°). Club: Yale (Pittsburgh). Home: The Manse, Saltsburg, Pa.

MILLER, Nathan, prof. economics and sociology; b. New Haven, Conn., Aug. 11, 1900; s. Morris and Mollie (Machlis) M.; Ph.B., Yale, 1921, A.M., same, 1922, Ph.D., same, 1925; m. Lillian Kimball, June 12, 1929; 1 dau. Elicia Kimball. Began as instr. economics and sociology, Carnegie Inst. of Tech., prof. economics and sociology since 1925. Mem. Am. Assn. Univ. Profs., Phi Beta Kappa. Home: 5655 Beacon St., Pittsburgh, Pa.

MILLER, Norman Christian; dir. University Coll. and prof. in university extension, Rutgers University. Address: New Brunswick, N.J.

MILLER, Park Hays, editor; b. Allegheny, Pa., Dec. 21, 1879; s. Oliver Laird (M.D.) and Mary Jane (Cunningham) M.; A.B., Western University of Pa. (now U. of Pittsburgh), 1899, M.A., 1926; grad. Western Theol. Sem., 1902; D.D., Centre Coll., 1930; m. Bessie P. Crider, Aug. 7, 1907; children—Grace, Park Hays. Instr. mathematics, Stewart's Prep. Sch., Sewickley, Pa., 1902-03; ordained Presbyn. ministry, 1904; supply, First Ch., Uniontown, Pa., 1903-04; pastor Compton Hill Chapel, St. Louis, 1904-08, Ch. of the Evangel, Phila., 1908-14; asst. editor Presbyn. Bd. of Publ. and Sabbath Sch Work, May 15, 1914-23; asso. editor dept. editorial work, Bd. of Christian Education of the Presbyn. Ch., U.S.A., 1923-30, asso. editor, supervisor ednl. materials, 1930-37, editor since 1937. Mem. Ednl. Commission, International Council Religious Education. Republican. Writer First Year Intermediate Graded Lessons, 1914, Westminster Senior Quarterly, 1912-14, Westminster Senior-Intermediate Quarterly, 1916-17, Intermediate Departmental Graded Lessons, 1917-20, 1922-23; Young People's Department Graded Lessons, 1923, 35, 36. Author: The Abundant Life, 1920; Our Reasonable Faith, 1922; Heroes of the Church, 1922; The New Testament Church, Its Teaching and Its Scriptures, 1926; Some Cross Sections of Old Testament Literature, 1935; The Holy Spirit in Christian Experience, 1936. Home: 904 Lindale Av., Drexel Hill, Pa. Office: Witherspoon Bldg., Philadelphia, Pa.

MILLER, Philip Sheridan, college dean; b. Stettlersville, Pa., Oct. 19, 1896; s. Mathias and Louisa A. (Schlicher) M.; A.B., Moravian Coll., 1920; Th.B., Princeton Theol. Sem., 1924; A.M., U. of Pa., 1927; Ph.D., U. of Erlangen, Germany, 1932; m. Bertha Alice Bloy, Sept. 16, 1924; children—Oakley Bloy, Joyce Rosemary. Began career as instr. in Latin, 1924; prof. Latin, Lincoln Univ., Pa., since 1928, dean of Coll. of Liberal Arts since 1937; ordained to ministry Presbyn. Ch., 1930. Mem. Am. Philol. Assn., Am. Soc. of Ch. History. Republican. Presbyn. Home: Lincoln University, Pa.

MILLER, Raymond Clinton, clergyman; b. Allentown, Pa., July 17, 1897; s. Clinton Oliver and Lillie Anora (Moser) M.; A.B. summa cum laude, Muhlenberg Coll., Allentown, Pa., 1922; A.M., Gettysburg Coll., 1924; student Luth. Theol. Sem., Gettysburg, Pa., 1922-24; B.D., Yale Divinity Sch. (Henry W. Allis Scholar), 1925; Th.M., Princeton Theol. Sem., 1929; S.T.M., Luth. Theol. Sem., Mt. Airy, Phila., 1934; student Grad. Sch. of Theol., Temple U., 1934—; m. Grace Stengele Stermer, June 13, 1925; 1 son, Raymond John. Ordained to ministry of Lutheran Ch., June 3, 1925; pastor Riegelsville, Pa., Luth. Parish, 1925-31, Lyons-Bernville, Pa., Parish since 1931. Treas. Easton Conf. of East Pa. Synod, 1928-30; sec. Lebanon Conf., 1933-35; del. of East Pa. Synod to Conv. of United Luth. Ch. in America, Milwaukee, Wis., 1930, to Ministerium of Pa., Atlantic City, N.J., 1937; pres. Luth. Pastoral Assn. of Eastern Berks Co., Pa., 1934-35; chaplain East Pa. Synod, Lititz, Pa., 1935; instr. in New Testament and missions, Luth. Leadership Training Sch., Kutztown, Pa., 1938. Served as 2d lt., S.A.T.C., U.S. Army, during World War. Mem. Acacia, Alpha Kappa Alpha, Bibl. and Semitic Club, Cosmopolitan Club (Yale). Home: Lutheran Parsonage, Lyon Station, Berks Co., Pa.

MILLER, Roy B.; surgeon Camden Clark Memorial and St. Joseph's hosps. Address: 920 Market St., Parkersburg, W.Va.

MILLER, Samuel Wilson, lawyer; b. Wooster, O., July 19, 1873; s. Samuel W. and Salina Ledlie (Crawford) M.; grad. Saltsburg (Pa.) Common Sch., 1888, Kiskiminetas Springs Sch., 1892; A.B., Princeton U., 1896; LL.B., New York Law Sch., 1898; m. Willma Frew Graff, June 12, 1900; 1 son, Samuel Graff. Admitted to New York bar, 1898, Pa. bar, 1899, Wash. State bar, 1907; practiced at Pittsburgh, 1899-1907, Spokane, Wash., 1907-13, Blairsville, Pa., since 1913; mem. law firm Miller & Gessler since 1930; dir. Blairsville Savings & Trust Co., Westmoreland Mining Co., Wilbur Coal Co., Telford Coal Co. Pres. bd. trustees Blairsville Public Library. Mem. Indiana Co. Bar Assn. Republican. Presbyterian. Mason. Home: 304 S. Walnut St. Office: 14 E. Market St., Blairsville, Pa.

MILLER, Spencer Jr., sociologist; b. Worcester, Mass., July 2, 1891; s. Spencer and Hattie M. (Ruggles) M.; grad. Bordentown (N.J.) Mil. Inst., 1908; A.B., Amherst, 1912; student Columbia Law Sch., 1912-13, dept. polit. science, 1913-15; A.M., Columbia University, 1914; George William Curtis fellow in pub. law, Columbia, 1914-15; grad. student department mechanical engring., Columbia University, 1916-17; LL.D., Kenyon Coll., 1937; m. Margaret Montague Geer, Oct. 27, 1928; children—Ann Montague, Spencer, Sidney Geer. Division Research of U.S. Commn. Industrial Relations, 1915; asst. to warden, Sing Sing Prison, N.Y., 1915-16; with industrial dept. U.S. Navy, 1917-19; asst. and instr. in govt., Columbia, 1919-20; dir. Workers' Edn. Bur., 1921; lecturer various colleges, summer schs., etc., U.S. and Europe, since 1919; member faculty Fordham U. Sch. of Social Service, 1933-35; mem. Am. delegation to 1st World Conf. on Adult Edn., Cambridge, England, Aug. 1929, also at World Conf. on Progressive Edn., Elsinore, Denmark, World Conf. on Adult Edn., Vienna, 1931, World Social Econ. Congress, 1931; external collaborator, Internat. Labor Office, and tech. adviser Am. delegation Internat. Labor Conf., 1935; round table leader Inst. of Pub. Affairs, U. of Va., 1930-38; round table leader conf. on Politics and Public Conscience, Dartmouth Coll., 1939; asso. dir. Am. Youth Commn., 1937; tech. adviser World Youth Congress, Vassar Coll., 1938, World Conf. of Christian Youth, Amsterdam, 1939. Consultant on industrial relations, P.E. Ch. since 1928; mem. bd. mgrs. Christodora House; mem. Nat. Advisory Council on Radio in Edn.; mem. Columbia Broadcasting System Com. on Adult Edn. Received Rutgers U. award for distinguished public service in industrial relations, 1939. Mem. exec. com. Nat. Rededication, Inc., 1938. Mem. Labor Com. of New York World's Fair, 1938-39; mem. World's Conf. on Edn. in a Democracy, New York, 1939. Trustee Town Hall (New York), Village of South Orange, N.J. Officer or mem. Acad. Polit. Science, N.E.A., Am. Soc. Mech. Engrs., Am. Prison Assn., Church and Social Service Commission, Am. Assn. for Adult Edn., Progressive Edn. Assn., Nat. Com. on Prisons and Prison Labor, Boys' Brotherhood Republic, Am. Federation Teachers, Nat. Occupational Conf., Nat. Crime Prevention Inst., Tax Policy League, League of Nations Assn., Coleg Harlech (Wales), Alpha Delta Phi, Pi Gamma Mu. Episcopalian. Author: The Church and Industry. Mng. editor Workers' Education Bureau Press, Inc.; editor Workers' Education Quarterly, American Labor and the Nation, Labor Speaks for Itself, What the International Labor Organization Means to America; mem. editorial bd. Jour. of Adult Education, Social Work Year Book, New Tracts for New Times. Contbr. to numerous periodicals and newspapers. Home: South Orange, N.J. Office: 1440 Broadway and 281 4th Av., New York, N.Y.

MILLER, Sydney Robotham, physician; b. at Newark, N.J., 1883; s. Fred H. and Annie (Robotham) M.; B.S., N.Y. Univ., 1905; M.D., Johns Hopkins, 1910; m. Ella Wood, Sept. 7, 1911; children—Sydney R., Donald Barker, Walter Baetjer, Mary Ellison. Practiced at Baltimore, Md., since 1914; asso. in clin. medicine, Johns Hopkins Med. Sch., since 1916; asso. prof. medicine, U. of Md., since 1920. Mem. A.M.A., Am. Coll. Physicians (pres. 1930-31), Am. Climatol. and Clin. Assn., Southern Med. Assn., Alpha Omega Alpha, Zeta Psi, Phi Beta Kappa. Presbyn. Republican. Contbr. tc med. jours. Home: 108 St. John's Rd. Office: 1115 St. Paul St., Baltimore, Md.

MILLER, Theodore Evan, clergyman; b. Chester, Pa., Apr. 9, 1899; s. Theodore Felmey and Beatrice (Jenkins) M.; student Bridgeton (N.J.) High Sch., 1912-17; B.A., Lafayette Coll., Easton, Pa., 1921; M.A., U. of Pittsburgh, 1928; B.S.T., Western Theol. Sem., Pittsburgh, 1928; student The Theol. Sem., Princeton, N.J., 1921-22, New Coll., U. of Edinburgh, Scotland, 1931-32; m. Vera Little, Apr. 18, 1925; children—Charles Samuel, Wega Beatrice Marie. Instr. science and mathematics, Am. U., Cairo, Egypt, 1922-25; jr. minister First Baptist Ch. of Pittsburgh, 1926-32; minister First Baptist Ch. of Baltimore since 1933. Served as seaman, 2d Class, U.S. Navy, 1918. Baptist. Clubs: Interchurch, Eclectic (Baltimore). Home: 3926 Oakford Av. Office: 4200 Liberty Heights Av., Baltimore, Md.

MILLER, T(homas) Grier, physician, univ. prof.; b. Statesville, N.C., Sept. 18, 1886; s. Sidney and Cora (Templeton) M.; A.B., U. of N.C., Chapel Hill, N.C., 1906; M.D., U. of Pa., 1911; m. Sarah Fenner George, June 3, 1915. Began as interne U. of Pa. Hosp., Phila., 1911, and successively asst. ward physician, ward physician, asst. chief of med. clinic since 1913; instr., U. of Pa. Sch. of Medicine, 1913-17, asso., 1916-28, asst. prof., 1928-34, prof. clin. medicine since 1934. Fellow Am. Coll. Physicians; mem. Am. Soc. of Clin. Investigation, Assn. of Am. Physicians, Am. Gastro-Enterological Assn., Am. Clin. and Climatol. Assn. Presbyterian. Clubs: Interurban Clinical, Philadelphia Country (Philadelphia). Author 58 articles in various med. jours. Home: Bryn Mawr and Woodbine Avs., Penn Valley, Narberth. Office: 318 Maloney Bldg., University Hosp., Philadelphia, Pa.

MILLER, Victor Davis, physician; b. Mason-Dixon, Pa., Mar. 15, 1876; s. Victor Davis and Alice Jane (Rench) M.; student Princeton U., 1895-96; M.D., U. of Pa. Med. Sch., 1900; m. Nellie Baechtel Loose, June 1, 1905; children—Helen Loose (Mrs. Philip Heagy Mathias), Victor Davis, Jr., Henry Loose. Interne Germantown (Pa.) Hosp., 1900-01, King's County (N.Y.) Hosp., 1901-02; engaged in gen. practice of medicine at Hagerstown, Md., since 1902; mem. of staff, Washington County Hosp.; instr. Nurses Training Sch., Washington County Hosp.; dir. Second Nat. Bank of Hagerstown. Served as chmn. local Med. Adv. Bd. during World War. Mem. A.M.A., Md. State, Cumberland Valley and Washington County med. socs. Democrat. Mem. German Ref. Ch. Club: Fountain Head Country. Home: 135 W. Washington St. Office: 131 W. Washington St., Hagerstown, Md.

MILLER, Walter L(ewis), lawyer; b. Thompson, Pa., Dec. 29, 1896; s. John D. and Jennie May (Blandin) M.; student Wyoming Sem., Kingston, Pa., 1913-15; A.B., Cornell U., 1920, LL.B., 1922; m. Frances Susan Post, June 14, 1922; children—John Douglas, 2d, Thomas Blandin, Allan Sterling. Admitted to Pa. bar, 1922, and since in gen. practice at Susquehanna; specializes in probate work, bank law and representing clients before legislatures and govt. depts. and boards. Served in Air Service, U.S. Army, with A.E.F., as pilot with rank of 2d lt., July 1917-Dec. 1918. Mem. Susquehanna Co. Bar Assn., Am. Legion, Forty and Eight. Republican. Methodist. Mason, Odd Fellow, Patron of Husbandry. Home: 301 Universal Terrace. Office: City Nat. Bank Bldg., Susquehanna, Pa.

MILLER, William Alexander, city mgr.; b. Paterson, N.J., July 23, 1893; s. William Frederick and Mary (Marshall) M.; student pub. schs. and high sch., Clifton, N.J., Columbia U., 1917; m. Ada Hamilton, Apr. 8, 1920; children—William Hamilton, John Leslie. Passed preliminary bar examination, N.J., 1913; formerly in employ Erie R.R., Texas Oil Co., and Miller Music Co.; professional musician; vice-pres., Clifton Nat. Bank since 1925; city mgr., Clifton, N.J., since 1934; dir. Claverack Bldg. & Loan Assn. Served as lieut., U.S.A., during World War; with A.E.F. in France. Pres. N.J. State League of Municipalities. Mem. Internat. City Mgrs. Assn., Am. Legion, Vets. Fgn. Wars (past comdr.). Republican. Presbyn. Mason (past master), Elk. Club: Kiwanis of Clifton (past pres.). Home: 242 Washington Av. Office: City Hall, Clifton, N.J.

MILLER, William Booth, pres. Pihl & Miller, Inc.; b. Wallingford, Pa., May 17, 1878; s. Isaac L. and Clara (Booth) M.; B.S., Swarthmore (Pa.) Coll., 1898, C.E., 1901; M.E., Cornell U., 1899; m. Helen Campbell, Apr. 5, 1906; children—Nancy Shaw (Mrs. Robert Upjohn Redpath, Jr.), Elizabeth Booth (Mrs. Kirtland C. Gardner, Jr.), Margaret Campbell (Mrs. Robert E. S. Thompson). Pres. and treas. Pihl & Miller, Inc., contracting engrs., since 1906; pres. Rock Point Sand Co., 1914-20; dir. Midland Gas Co., Warsaw Oil & Gas Co., Consumers Gas & Heat Co., 1917-25, Tidewater Portland Cement Co., 1918-23; registered professional engr. Dir. Sewickley (Pa.) Cemetery since 1934. Member Sewickley Borough Council, 1918. Mem. Engineers Soc. of Western Pa. Republican. Presbyterian (trustee Sewickley Presbyn. Ch.). Clubs: Edgeworth (dir.), Duquesne, Allegheny Country (Pittsburgh). Home: 626 Pine Rd., Sewickley, Pa. Office: Wabash Bldg., Liberty Av., Pittsburgh, Pa.

MILLGRAM, Abraham Ezra, rabbi; b. Russia, Feb. 1, 1901; s. Israel M. and Mollie (Kreis) M.; came to U.S., 1913, and naturalized citizen; B.S., Coll. of the City of N.Y., 1924; A.M., Columbia, 1927; diploma, Teachers Inst., Jewish Theol. Sem., 1923; Rabbi, Jewish Theol. Sem., 1927; m. Ida E. Tulchinsky, July 6, 1930; 1 son, Hillel Israel. Rabbi at Wilmington, Del., 1927-30; rabbi, Beth Israel, Phila., Pa., since 1930; instr. history, Gratz Coll., 1930-37. Dir. Asso. Talmud Torahs, League for Labor Palestine. Mem. Rabbinical Assembly, Phila. Bd. of Jewish Ministers. B'nai B'rith. Judaic Union. Author: An Anthology of Mediaeval Hebrew Literature, 1935; Beth Israel Hymnal, 1937. Home: 3226 W. Clifford St. Office: 32d St. and Montgomery Av., Philadelphia, Pa.

MILLIGAN, Charles H., chemist; b. Sevierville, Tenn., Oct. 4, 1888; s. Leslie Ney and Sallie (Bales) M.; A.B., Carson and Newman Coll., Jefferson City, Tenn., 1912; B.S., U. of Chicago, 1915, Ph.D., 1919; m. Ruth Tuttle, Sept. 26, 1925; children—Marion Tuttle, Barton. Instr. biology, Ewing (Ill.) Coll., 1912-13; asst. prin., Monroe (La.) High Sch., 1913-14; asst. prof. chemistry, Alfred (N.Y.) U., 1915-17; Swift fellow, U. of Chicago, 1917-18; Grafflin fellow, Johns Hopkins U., 1919-21; research chemist Procter and Gamble, Ivorydale, O., 1921-26, Champion Coated Paper Co., Hamilton, O., 1926-29; research chemist Am. Agrl. Chem. Co., Newark, N.J., 1929-35, development mgr., New York, since 1936. Served as sergt., Chem. Warfare Service, A.E.F., Paris, 1918. Mem. Am. Chem. Soc., A.A.A.S., Sigma Xi, Gamma Alpha. Author numerous articles on chemicals, paper treatment, etc. Patentee 7 U.S. patents on paper processes and phosphate products. Home: 842 Cedar Terrace, Westfield, N.J. Office: 50 Church St., New York, N.Y.

MILLIGAN, Orlando Howard, clergyman; b. East Brady, Pa., Sept. 11, 1873; s. William M. and Anna (Swan) M.; A.B., Muskingum Coll., New Concord, O., 1895; ed. Allegheny Theol. Sem., Pittsburgh, Pa., 1895-98; (hon.) D.D., Muskingum Coll., 1916; (hon.) LL.D., Muskingum Coll., 1936; m. Ivy Pearl Moore, Sept. 7, 1898; 1 son, William Moore. Ordained to ministry U. Presbyn. Ch., 1898; pastor, Elderton and Shelocta, Pa., 1898-1903, Cedarville, O., 1903-09; pastor U. Presbyn. Ch., Avalon, Pa., continuously since 1909; served as clk. Xenia Presbytery, 1907-09; clk. Allegheny Presbytery since 1911; prin. clk. Gen. Assembly of U. Presbyn. Ch. since 1931; moderator First Synod of the West, 1932. Served in Y.M.C.A. Army camps and Navy stations, 1917. Mem. bd. trustees Muskingum Coll. since 1910. Mem. Alpha Tau Epsilon. Republican. United Presbyn. Home: 805 Taylor Av., Avalon, Pittsburgh, Pa.

MILLIGAN, Samuel Cargill, M.D.; b. Southfield, Mich., Dec. 30, 1861; s. Rev. J. S. T. and Jane Thompson (Johnston) M.; B.A., Geneva Coll., Beaver Falls, Pa.; M.D., U. of Pittsburgh; m. Annie M. Gregg, May 20, 1920. Asst. prof. diseases of nose and throat, West Penn Med. Coll., 1892-98, prof. physiology, 1898-1906; mem. surg. staff South Side Hosp., Pittsburgh, many yrs. Served as asst. surgeon, 18th Regt., Pa. N.G., 1893-98; 2d brig. surgeon with rank of maj., 1899-1907. Mem. Allegheny Co. Med. Soc., Pittsburgh Acad. of Medicine, A.M.A., Vets. of Spanish-Am. War, Nu Sigma Nu (charter mem. Delta Chapter). Editor in chief Geneva Cabinet, 1887-88. Winner first flight, City Championship Golf, Tucson, Ariz., 1934. Home: 5733 Solway St. Office: 725 Jenkins Bldg., Pittsburgh, Pa.

MILLIKEN, Howard Elliott, physician; b. Harrisburg, Pa., Apr. 14, 1896; s. James T. and Mary Jane (Elliott) M.; ed. Pa. State Coll., 1914-16; M.D., U. of Pa. Med. Sch., 1920; m. Miriam Slade Sherman, Aug. 27, 1922; 1 step-dau., Betty Slade Sherman; 1 son, Howard Elliott, Jr. Interne Presbyn. Hosp., Phila., 1920-21; practice limited to surgery and obstetrics; indoor surgeon, Polyclinic Hosp. since 1937; coroner Dauphin Co. since 1929. Served in Med. Corps, U.S.A., 1917-18. Mem. Am. Med. Assn., Pa. State Med. Soc., Dauphin Co. Med. Soc. (pres. 1937-38), Harrisburg Acad. Medicine (pres. 1939-40), Barton Cooke Hirst Obstet. Soc. U. of Pa., Am. Legion, Sigma Pi, Phi Rho Sigma, Harrisburg Republican Clubs. Republican. Presbyn. Mason (32°, Shriner, Tall Cedar, Jester), Eagle, Elk, Moose. Clubs: Zembo Golf, Colonial Golf (Harrisburg). Home: 2012 N. 3d St., Harrisburg, Pa.

MILLIKEN, Lorenzo Fremont, surgeon; b. Delphene, Pa., Dec. 25, 1877; s. Samuel and Mary Ellen (Smith) M.; ed. Waynesburg Coll., 1896-98; M.D., Jefferson Med. Coll., 1905; D.Sc., U. of Pa. Grad. Sch. of Medicine, 1924; m. Margaret Lucile Willison, Sept. 11, 1901; children—Keith Willison, Herbert Samuel; Virginia Barrett (Mrs. George Linn). Engaged in gen. practice of medicine at Graysville, Pa., 1905-17, at Blair, W.Va., 1917-21; specializing in urologic surgery at Phila. since 1924; asso. prof. urology, U. of Pa. Grad. Sch. of Medicine since 1932; on staff Grad., St. Luke's and Childrens, Am. Stomach hosps. Served as vol. Spanish-Am. War, in Philippines with U.S. A., 1898-99; civilian commissary clk., 1899-1900. Mem. Am., Pa. State, Phila. Co. med. assns., Am. Urol. Assn., Phila. Urol. Assn. (past pres.), Alpha Omega Alpha. Republican. Presbyn. Elk, I.O.O.F., K.P., Patriotic Order Sons of America. Clubs: Penn Athletic, Paxson Hollow Golf. Contbr. to med. jours. Home: 3001 Hillcrest Rd., Drexel Hill, Pa. Office: 1900 Spruce St., Philadelphia, Pa.

MILLOY, James S., newspaper man; b. at Peterboro, Can., Sept. 27, 1895; s. Peter and Katherine (Farrell) M.; ed. parochial sch., high sch. and bus. coll., Peterboro; m. Winnifred Anne Blakey, July 16, 1919; children—James S., Peter B., Kathleen Anne, Richard P., Donald F. Reporter various newspapers, 1913-21; exec. sec. Minot (N.D.) Chamber Commerce, 1921-25; exec. sec. Greater N.D. Assn., 1925-31; joined Minneapolis Tribune, Oct. 1, 1931, as northwest development editor and asst. to pub.; now personal rep. of Frederick E. Murphy, pub. of Minneapolis Tribune, in New York and Washington. Republican. Roman Catholic. K.C. Club: Nat. Press (Washington). Home: 31 Oxford St., Chevy Chase, Md. Address: Minneapolis Tribune, Minneapolis, Minn.; and Hamilton Hotel, Washington, D.C.

MILLS, Frederick Cecil, economist; b. Santa Rosa, Calif., Mar. 24, 1892; s. Robert Alexander and Lily (Nightingale) M.; B.L., U. of Calif., 1914, M.A., 1916; Ph.D., Columbia, 1917, student London Sch. of Economics, Feb.-June 1919; m. Dorothy Katherine Clarke, August 20, 1919; children—William Harold, Helen Katherine, Robert Laurence. Special agent U.S. Commn. on Industrial Relations, in study of migratory labor in Calif., 1914-15; with Columbia U. since 1919, successively instr. in economics, asst. prof. business administration, asso. prof. business statistics, prof. statistics, and since 1931, prof. economics and statistics. Chief statistician Joint Com. on Taxation and Retrenchment, State of N.Y., 1929; mem. research staff, Nat. Bur. Economic Research, since 1924. Mem. A.E.F., 1917-19; commd. 2d lt. 150th F.A.; 1st lt., 316th F.A. Fellow Am. Acad. of Arts and Sciences, Royal Econ. Soc., A.A. A.S., Am. Statis. Assn. (v.p. 1926, 33; pres. 1934); mem. Am. Economic Assn. (v.p. 1938), Econometric Soc., Acad. Polit. Science, Phi Beta Kappa, Beta Gamma Sigma. Clubs: Faculty, Century (New York); Englewood Field. Author: Contemporary Theories of Unemployment, 1917; Statistical Methods, 1924 (revised 1938); The Behavior of Prices, 1927; Economic Tendencies in the United States, 1932; Prices in Recession and Recovery, 1936. Joint Author: The Trend of Economics, 1924; Recent Economic Changes, 1929. Contbr. to mags. on economic and statis. subjects. Home: 492 Engle St., Englewood, N.J.; also Charleston, Vt.

MILLS, Gail A., univ. bursar; b. Washington, Kansas, Aug. 19, 1896; s. Pleasant and Martha Ellen (Carson) M.; B.S., U. of Ill., Urbana, 1924; C.P.A., Ill., 1928; m. Helen Taylor, Mar. 11, 1922; 1 son, Robert Gail. Clerk and teller, 1914-18, cashier, 1919-20, Farmers State Bank, Mooresville, Ind.; asst. comptroller, U. of Ill., Urbana, 1923-29; bursar, Princeton U. since 1930. Served with Aero Squadron, U.S. Army, 1918-19. Treas., Mooresville, Ind., 1919-20. Mem. N.J. Soc. of C.P.A.'s, Am. Inst. of Accountants, Am. Legion, Delta Chi, Beta Alpha Psi. Republican. Methodist. Mason. Clubs: Springdale Golf, Nassau (Princeton, N.J.); Princeton (New York). Author: Accounting Manual for Colleges, 1937. Address: 150 Prospect Av., Princeton, N.J.

MILLS, John, engineer; b. Morgan Park, Ill., Apr. 13, 1880; s. John and Sarah Elizabeth (Ten Broeke) M.; A.B., U. of Chicago, 1901; A.M., U. of Neb., 1904; B.S.; Mass. Inst. of Tech., 1909; m. Emma Gardner Moore, June 1, 1909; children—John, Marion, Theodora Ten Broeke. Fellow in physics, U. of Chicago, 1901-02, U. of Neb., 1902-03; instr. physics, Western Reserve U., 1903-07, Mass. Inst. Tech., 1907-09; prof. physics, Colo. Coll., 1909-11; with engring. dept. Am. Telephone & Telegraph Co., 1911-15; with research dept. Western Electric Co., 1915-21, asst. personnel dir., 1921-23, personnel dir., 1923-24; dir. of publ., Bell Telephone Labs., Inc. since 1925. Fellow Am. Phys. Soc., Am. Inst. Elec. Engrs., Institute Radio Engineers; mem. Phi Beta Kappa, Sigma Xi, Delta Upsilon. Author: Electricity, Sound and Light, 1907; Introduction to Thermodynamics, 1909; Alternating Currents, 1911; Radio-Communication, 1917; Realities of Modern Science, 1919; Within the Atom, 1921; Letters of a Radio Engineer to His Son, 1922; Magic of Communication, 1923; Signals and Speech in Electrical Communication, 1934; A Fugue in Cycles and Bels, 1935. Inventor of several methods for wire and radio-telephony. Home: 234 Sagamore Rd., Maplewood, N.J. Address: 463 West St., New York, N.Y.

MILLSOP, Thomas E., pres. Weirton Steel Co.; b. Sharon, Pa.; s. George and Mary (McCormick) M.; ed. pub. schs.; m. Loretta Brunswick, Dec. 1, 1916. Began as laborer in steel mills, 1912, and became salesman for Weirton (W.Va.) Steel Co., 1928, pres. since 1936. Served as combat pilot with Canadian Royal Air Force, later U.S.A. Air Service, 1916-19. Mem. Am. Iron and Steel Inst. Republican. Protestant. Clubs: Athletic, Duquesne (Pittsburgh); Mo. Athletic (St. Louis). Home: Weirton, W.Va.

MILLSPAUGH, Arthur Chester, polit. scientist; b. Augusta, Mich., Mar. 1, 1883; s. Hiram E. and Lydia H. (Abbott) M.; A.B., Albion Coll., 1908; A.M., U. of Ill., 1910; Ph.D., Johns Hopkins, 1916; m. Mary Helen MacDonnell, Sept. 9, 1923; 1 son, Abbott. Prof. polit. science, Whitman Coll., 1916-17; instr. polit. science, Johns Hopkins, 1917-18; in drafting office State Dept., 1918-21; apptd. consul class 4, and assigned to State Dept., July 1, 1921; actg. fgn. trade adviser, 1921-22; petroleum specialist in State Dept., 1920-22; administrator gen. of finances, Persia, 1922-27; financial adviser and gen. receiver, Haiti, 1927-29; mem. staff Inst. for Govt. Research, 1929-36; dir. survey staff Miss. State Research Commn., 1931. Participated in state surveys, Ala., 1931-32, N.H., 1932; directed survey, Ia., 1933; asst. dir. survey Okla., 1935; mem. Survey of Montgomery County, Md., 1939. Mem. Sigma Nu, Phi Beta Kappa. Author: Party Organization and Machinery in Michigan since 1890 (thesis), 1917; The American Task in Persia, 1925; Haiti Under American Control, 1931; Public Welfare Organization, 1935; Local Democracy and Crime Control, 1936; Crime Control by the National Government, 1937. Home: 516 Goddard Rd., Bethesda, Md. Office: 722 Jackson Place, Washington, D.C.

MILLWARD, Carl Lyon, supt. schs.; b. Mt. Pleasant, Pa., Jan. 25, 1882; s. William and Nancy (Deaver) M.; student Western Pa. Inst.; Ph.B., Bucknell U., Lewisburg, Pa., 1906, A.M., 1908, Pd.D. (hon.), 1931; student Columbia U.; m. Mary V. Kreisher, 1906; children—William, Dorothy, Kathryn. Rural sch. teacher, Union Co., Pa., 1908-10; science teacher, Milton, Pa., 1910-13; prin. high sch., 1913-17; supt. of schs., Milton, Pa., since 1917; instr., Summer Sch., Bucknell U., Lewisburg, since 1923, supervisor of teacher training, 1930-31; mem. exec. council Alumni Assn. since 1933; pres. Gen. Alumni Assn. since 1935. Chmn. Four Minute Men, Milton, Pa., during World War. Awarded Silver Beaver for service to boyhood by Boy Scouts of America. Dir. European Ednl. Tours, 1926-27; mem. Cornell Group, Internat. Understanding, 1937-38; dir. Y.M.C.A.; mem. exec. bd. Boy Scouts, Susquehanna Area, scout commr., Susquehanna Area; trustee Nat. Lutheran Home for Aged, Washington, D.C., since 1932. Mem. State Ednl. Assn., N.E.A., Acacia, Sigma Chi, Kappa Phi Kappa, Phi Sigma Pi. Mason (Williamsport Consistory, K.T., Shriner), Rotary Internat. (past dist. gov.; mem. Youth com., 1939-40. Clubs: Rotary (past pres.), Manufacturers' (Milton, Pa.). Contbr. articles to the Rotarian and newspapers. Editor several publs. Home: 526 N. Front St. Office: Center St., Milton, Pa.

MILNE, Caleb Jones, Jr.; b. Philadelphia, Pa., Mar. 6, 1861; s. Caleb Jones and Sarah Margaretta (Shea) M.; ed. pvt. schs. and Episcopal Acad., Phila.; m. Lenore Bonwill, Oct. 24, 1882; children—Caleb Jones III, Marguerite, Warren. Began with father, mfr. cotton and woolen goods, Phila., 1879; partner C. J. Milne & Sons, 1885-1924; pres. United Security Trust Co., 1921-23. Mgr. Grad. Hosp., U. of Pa. Trustee Chapin Memorial Home for Aged Blind (v.p.); pres. Howard Hosp., 1915; elected a manager Pennsylvania Retreat for Blind Mutes and Aged and Infirm Blind Persons, 1930; member of the bd. of mgrs. Pa. Working Home for Blind Men; mem. advisory bd. Phila. Home for Incurables (mem. finance com.), Hahnemann Hosp.; member of Pa. Historical Commission since 1933. Mem. Amphion Musical Soc., Zoöl. Soc., Hist. Soc. Pa., Geog. Soc. Phila. (mem. bd. mgrs.), Cloth Mfrs. Assn. (ex-pres.), Geneal. Soc. Pa., Swedish Colonial Soc., Colonial Soc. Pa. (pres. 1927), N.E. Soc. Pa., Pa. Soc. S.R., Soc. Colonial Wars, Mercantile Beneficial Assn. Phila., Merchants Fund Phila., St. Andrew's Soc. Philadelphia (ex-pres.), Drama League Phila., Art Alliance, Numismatic and Antiquarian Soc. Phila. Republican. Episcopalian. Clubs: Union League, Midday, Racquet, Plays and Players, Science and Art, Belmont Cricket, Germantown Cricket, Corinthian Yacht, Phila. Country. Home: 6611 Wissahickon Av. Office: 1030 S. 10th St., Philadelphia, Pa.

MILNE, John Leslie, actuary; b. Erie, Pa., June 3, 1902; s. John McArthur and Mary Jane (Smith) M.; B.S., U. of Pa., 1924; m. Anna Charlotte Sherwood, Sept. 25, 1923; children—John Robert, David Allen, Charlotte Anne, John William. Asso. with Presbyterian Ministers Fund, oldest life ins. co. in world, Phila., Pa. since 1924, asst. actuary, 1924-27, actuary since 1927; actuary Ministers Mutual Life Ins. Co.; sec.-treas. Kenilworth Lakes. Trustee and chmn. finance com. First Presbyn. Ch., Phila., Pa. Fellow Actuarial Soc. of America; asso. Casualty Actuarial Soc. Republican. Presbyn. Mason. Clubs: Meridian, Actuaries (Philadelphia); Actuaries (Boston). Home: 527 Gainesboro Rd., Drexel Hill, Pa. Office: 1805 Walnut St., Philadelphia, Pa.

MILNER, Byron A(lbert), lawyer; b. Phila., Pa., Aug. 25, 1884; s. Thomas James and Rose (Johnson) M.; student Central High Sch., Phila., 1899-1903; B.S. in economics, Wharton Sch. of U. of Pa., 1906, post-grad. study, 1907; LL.B., U. of Pa. Law Sch., 1910; unmarried. Lecturer constl. law and govt., U. of Pa., 1906-18; teacher Girard Coll., Phila., Phila. Evening High Sch., 1903-08; admitted to Phila. bar, 1910; receiver Phila. Mortgage & Trust Co., 1917-24; spl. dep. for sec. of banking of Pa. and receiver United Security Trust Co., United Security Life Ins. & Trust Co., 1931-34. Mem. Pa. Ho. of Rep., 1917, 1919. Mem. Boosters Assn. (Phila.), Am. Acad. Polit. and Social Science, Am., Pa., and Phila. bar assns. Republican. Presbyterian. Mason (Royal Arch; K.T.; Shriner). Clubs: Union League, Penn Athletic (Phila.); Bala Golf (Phila.). Author: Selected Cases in Constitutional Law, 1924 (7 edits.). Home: 1900 Locust St. Office: 1318 Real Estate Trust Bldg., Philadelphia, Pa.

MILNOR, Joseph Willard, telegraph engr.; b. Williamsport, Pa., Oct. 25, 1889; s. Joseph Whitefield and Jennie (Fague) M.; E.E., Lehigh Univ., Bethlehem, Pa., 1912; m. Emily Miller Cox, Mar. 28, 1923; children—Robert Cox, John Willard. In employ General Electric Co., Pittsfield, Mass., 1912-13; with engring. dept. Western Union Telegraph Co., N.Y. City continuously since 1913, research engr., 1919-36, transmission engr. since 1936, in charge of telegraph and ocean cable transmission development and carrier current systems; patentee various improvements in telegraphy and reduction of elec. interference; developed practical method for computation of telegraph currents and elec. transients generally; designer of two-way highest capacity transatlantic cable; produced system of rapid picture transmission over ocean cables, 1939. Fellow Am. Inst. Elec. Engrs. Mem. Inst. Radio Engrs. Cons. mem. Assn. Am. Rys. Asso. mem. Nat. Farm Chemurgic Council. Co-chmn. Plant Coordination Com. of Edison Electric Inst. and Western Union. Mem. Tau Beta Pi. Methodist. Club: Wire (New York). Home: 12 Clinton Av., Maplewood, N.J. Office: 60 Hudson St., New York, N.Y.

MILNOR, Mark Taylor, lawyer; b. Warrensville, Pa., Aug. 6, 1890; s. Dr. M. T. and Ada (Champion) M.; student Clarion (Pa.) State Normal Sch., 1910, Wharton Sch., U. of Pa., 1911; LL.B., U. of Pa. Law Sch., 1914; m. Mary Graber, Oct. 4, 1921. Admitted to practice of law, Lycoming Co. (Pa.) cts., 1914, Supreme Ct. of Pa. and Dauphin Co. (Pa.) cts., 1915, Superior Ct. of Pa., 1917, U.S. Dist. Ct., 1924, U.S. Supreme Ct., 1937; asst. to counsel for Pa. Pub. Service Commn., 1917-19; spl. counsel Pa. Div. of Closed Banks, 1931-35; solicitor Harrisburg (Pa.) Sch. Dist. since 1933; dir. Citizens Trust Co. of Harrisburg. Served in U.S. Army, 1917-18, hon. disch. as 2d lt. Mem. Harrisburg Sch. Bd., 1925-27. Dir. Harrisburg Y.M.C.A., v.p., 1933. Mem. Central Pa. Alumni Assn. of U. of Pa. (past pres.), Am. Legion (past comdr. and charter mem. Post 27; dist. dep. comdr., 1919-20; Dauphin Co. comdr., 1921; past vice-comdr. Pa. Dept.), Harrisburg Chamber of Commerce, Dauphin Co. Bar Assn. (v.p.), Pa. State Bar Assn. Mason (charter mem. Euclid Lodge 698; Harrisburg Consistory; Zembo Temple). Clubs: University (past pres., charter mem.), Keystone Automobile (dir.)—both of Harrisburg. Republican. Home: 3208 Valley Rd. Office: 401-2 Bergner Bldg., Harrisburg, Pa.

MILSTEAD, John Olin, lawyer; b. Washington, D.C., Dec. 5, 1902; s. Thomas Lawrence and Catherine May (McClelland) M.; LL.B., Georgetown Univ. Law Sch., Washington, D.C., 1925; m. Irene Morland, Oct. 26, 1929; 1 son, John O., Jr. Admitted to bar of D.C., 1925; admitted to N.J. bar as atty., 1927, as counselor, 1930; engaged in gen. practice of law, Ocean City, N.J., 1927-34, Vineland, N.J., since 1934; mem. firm Milstead & McElroy since 1939; solicitor for Commr. Banking and Ins. of N.J. in liquidation of Vineland Trust Co., 1935-37; solicitor for Landis Twp., 1938; solicitor Mechanics Bldg. & Loan Assn., Vineland, since 1939. Mem. bd. edn. of Landis Twp., N.J., since 1937. Mem. Cumberland Co. Bar Assn. Republican. Club: Kiwanis of Vineland (past pres.). Home: 21 S. State St. Office: 640 Landis Av., Vineland, N.J.

MILTON, John; mem. law firm of Milton, McNulty & Augelli. Office: 1 Exchange Place, Jersey City, N.J.

MILTON, William Hammond, clergyman; b. Clarke Co., Va., Oct. 17, 1868; s. William Taylor and Frances Calender (Duncan) M.; B.S., Va. Mil. Inst., Lexington, Va., 1888; Theol. Sem., Alexandria, Va., 1889-92; Johns Hopkins, 1896-97; D.D., Hampden-Sydney (Va.) Coll., 1907; m. Virginia Lee Epes, June 12, 1895; children—Virginia Lee (wife of Dr. J. M. T. Finney, Jr.), William Hammond, Ann. Asst. prof. chemistry, Va. Mil. Inst., 1888-89; deacon 1892, priest, 1893, P.E. Ch.; rector St. Luke's Ch., Blackstone, Va., 1892-94, Henshaw Memorial Ch., Baltimore, Md., 1894-99, St. John's Ch., Roanoke, Va., 1899-1909, St. James' Church, Wilmington, North Carolina, 1909-36, rector emeritus since Nov. 1, 1936. Editor Diocesan Jour., Southern Va., 1906-09. Capt. engrs., Va. N.G., 1888-89. Mem. Nat. War Commn. P.E. Ch., World War; chmn. 2d Red Cross fund campaign, Wilmington, 1918. Trustee Theol. Sem. in Va., Vorhees Sch., Am. Ch. Inst. for Negroes. Del. to Triennial Gen. Conv. P.E. Ch., 1907, 13, 16, 19, 22, 25, 28, 31, 34; mem. Bd. Missions, 1912-19, Nat. Council, 1920-37; exec. sec. Nat. Field Dept., 1920-23; asst. chmn. Nat. Commn. on Evangelism, 1928-29; vice chmn. exec. council Diocese of East Carolina, 1920-32; mem. nat. field, edn., missions and publicity dept. P.E. Ch., 1920-36. Independent Democrat. Mason (K.T.). Author: The Cure of Souls, 1908; Ventures of the Soul, 1911. Home: 8 Marwood Rd., Towson, Md.

MINAHAN, Daniel Francis, realty development; b. Springfield, O., Aug. 8, 1877; s. Daniel F. and Mary E. (Murphy) M.; student St. Benedict's Coll., Newark, N.J., 1891-92, Seton Hall Coll., South Orange, N.J., 1892-95; m. Genevieve R. Fell, Feb. 17, 1919. Engaged in contracting business in Newark, N.J., 1896; pres. Minahan Realty Co., real estate development, Newark, N.J. Served as mayor of Orange, N.J., 1914-19. Mem. 66th Congress (1919-21) and 68th Congress (1923-25), 9th N.J. Dist. Democrat. Roman Catholic. Elk. Home: 415 Fairview Av., Orange, N.J. Office: 790 Broad St., Newark, N.J.

MINARD, Duane Elmer, lawyer; b. Boonton Twp., Morris Co., N.J., Apr. 27, 1880; s. George Wesley and Mary Ella (Hayes) M.; ed. Dist. Sch., Montville Twp.; m. Sara Trego Bennett, June 22, 1904; children—Dorothy Bennett, Sara (wife of Dr. A. Lawton Bennett), Duane Elmer. Clerk in country store, Montville, N.J., 1887-99; read law in offices of Elias F. Morrow and James McC. Morrow, Newark, 1899-1902; admitted to N.J. bar, 1903; counsellor, 1909; asso. and mem. Cortlandt & Wayne Parker, 1902-12; clk. to U.S. Dist. Atty., N.J., 1903-04; mem. N.J. Legislature, 1910; asst. gen. solicitor Erie R.R. Co., 1912-20, gen. atty., 1920-25; atty. U.S.R.R. Adminstrn., 1917-20; asst. atty. gen., State of N.J., 1929-34, spl. asst. atty., since 1934; mem. law firm Hobart & Minard, 1925-37, Hobart, Minard & Cooper, since 1937; cons. on water law, U.S. Nat. Resources Com.; dir. New York, Susquehanna & Western R.R. Co., N.J. State Taxpayers Assn.; counsel N.J. Assn. of Real Estate Bds. Enlisted as private N.G. of N.J., 1st Regt. Inf., Co. A, Feb. 21, 1902; private Co. F, Dec. 17, 1902; corpl. Co. F, July 6, 1903; private Co. F, Oct. 19, 1903; major and judge advocate, Judge Advocate General's Dept., Nov. 29, 1909; capt. Co. M, Feb. 16, 1912; resigned, Dec. 2, 1912. Fellow Am. Geog. Soc.; mem. Explorers Club of N.Y.; mem. Am. Bar Assn., N.J. State Bar Assn., Morris County (N.J.) Bar Assn., Interstate Commerce Practitioners Assn. Methodist. Club: Down Town (Newark). Home: Wawonaissa Farm, Boonton Twp., Morris Co., N.J. Office: 1180 Raymond Boul., Newark, N.J.

MINDNICH, Frank C., pres. Federal Trust Co. Home: 256 Conway Court. Office: 24 Commerce St., Newark, N.J.

MINER, Charles Howard, physician; b. Wilkes-Barre, Pa., July 5, 1868; s. Charles Abbott and Eliza Ross (Atherton) M.; student Wilkes-Barre (Pa.) Acad.; B.S., Princeton U., 1890; M.D., U. of Pa., 1893; m. Grace Lea Shoemaker, June 1, 1904; children—Charles Howard, Stella Mercer Shoemaker. Sec. of Health, State Dept. of Pa., 1923-27; now attending physician Wilkes-Barre (Pa.) Gen. Hosp. Served as asst. surgeon, 1st lt., 9th Regt., Pa. Inf., during Spanish-Am. War. Mem. Bd. of Health, Wilkes-Barre, Pa. Dir. Wilkes-Barre Gen. Hosp., Kirby Memorial Health Center; pres. Osterhout Free Library; asst. vestryman St. Stephen's Ch., Wilkes-Barre. Mem. Am. Coll. Physicians, Am. Bd. of Internal Medicine, Pa. Tuberculosis Soc. (ex-pres., ex-dir.), Pa. Heart Assn. (dir.), Wyoming Valley Tuberculosis Assn. (pres.), Am. Climatol. and Clin. Soc., Am. Pub. Health Assn., A.M.A. Club: Westmoreland (Wilkes-Barre, Pa.). Address: 264 S. Franklin St., Wilkes-Barre, Pa.

MINER, Robert C(harles), milling exec.; b. Wilkes-Barre, Pa., Apr. 10, 1894; s. Gen. Asher and Hetty (Lonsdale) M.; prep. edn. Lawrenceville Sch.; B.S., Princeton U., 1915; b. Elizabeth Chace Carter, Sept. 23, 1925; children—Elizabeth Caroline, Grace Lea. Vice pres. and gen. mgr. Miner-Hillard Milling Co., Wilkes-Barre, Pa., since 1924; dir. Pa. Millers Mutual Fire Ins. Co., Wilkes-Barre, Pa., since 1924, pres., 1930-36, chmn. bd. since 1936; dir. Wyoming Nat. Bank, Wilkes-Barre. Served as capt. Battery D, 109th F.A., 28th Div., U.S. Army, 1917-19; maj. 109th F.A., 28th Div., Pa. N.G., 1919-33; resigned 1933. Trustee Wilkes-Barre Gen. Hosp. since 1928. Mem. Am. Corn Millers Fed. (pres. since 1937), Pa. Millers' and Feed Dealers' Assn. (dir.). Republican. Clubs: Princeton (New York); Westmoreland (Wilkes-Barre); Princeton Charter (Princeton, N.J.). Home: 287 S. Franklin St. Office: 826 Second Nat. Bank Bldg., Wilkes-Barre, Pa.

MINICK, James William, architect; b. Carlisle, Pa., Sept. 14, 1898; s. John Drawbaugh and Emma Grace (Baer) M.; ed. Harrisburg (Pa.) Tech. Sch., 1916-17, Pa. State Coll., 1918-20, Carnegie Inst. Tech., Pittsburgh, Pa. (A.B. in architecture), 1920-22; m. Leah Gertrude Kennedy, Oct. 16, 1924; 1 son, Dean Kennedy. Successively archtl. draftsman, chief draftsman and designer in offices at Pittsburgh, Harrisburg, Pa., and Miami, Fla., 1917-18; mem. firm Jamison & Minick, Harrisburg, 1928-32; alone since 1932. Outstanding examples of his designing are: Johnson Memorial, Millersburg, Pa.; Forester St. Y.M.C.A., Harrisburg; Gymnasium, Science Bldg., Training Sch. at State Teachers Coll., Shippenburg, Pa.; Main Infirmary Bldg. at State Sanatorium for Tuberculosis, Mont Alto, Pa. Sec. Pa. State Bd. of Examiners of Architects since 1937; chief of tech. adv. bd. Civil Works Administrn. of Pa., 1932-34. Mem. Am. Inst. of Architects (sec. Southern Pa. Chapter 1935-37, treas. 1933-35, pres. since 1938), Pa. Assn. Architects (dir.), Art Assn. of Harrisburg, Theta Xi. Democrat. Lutheran. Mason. Clubs: Harrisburg; West Shore Country (Camp Hill, Pa.). Home: Camp Hill, Pa. Office: 2d and State Sts., Harrisburg, Pa.; and 2160 Market St., Camp Hill, Pa.

MINNER, Ralph Jefferson, dentist; b. Pottstown, Pa., Nov. 23, 1895; s. Jonas R. and Emma E. (Herb) M.; D.D.S., Medico-Chirurg. Coll., Phila., Pa., 1916; m. Minnie K. Ginther, Sept. 7, 1918; children—Eunice Fay Ginther, Ardath Lois Ginther, Rodney Jay Ginther. Asso. with Dr. H. W. Tomlinson, Phila., Pa., 1916; engaged in pvt. practice of dentistry at Catasauqua, Pa., since 1916. Served as 1st lt. Dental Res. Corps, U.S.A., 1918-33. Mem. Catasauqua Sch. Bd. since 1931, pres., 1933-37. Dir. Chamber of Commerce. Mem. Am. Dental Assn., Pa. State Dental Soc., Lehigh Valley Dental Soc., Psi Omega. Democrat. Lutheran. Clubs: Catasauqua, Rotary. Home: 510 Pine St. Office: 527 Front St., Catasauqua, Pa.

MINNICK, John Harrison, teacher; b. Somerset, Ind., Oct. 26, 1877; s. David Monroe and Mary (Okley) M.; grad. Marion (Ind) Normal Sch., 1903; A.B., Ind. U., 1906, A.M., 1908; grad. student U. of Ill., U. of Chicago, Columbia; Ph.D., U. of Pa., 1918; m. Eva Smith, Aug. 8, 1908; 1 dau., Marjorie Inez. Teacher high schs., Ind. and Ill., various periods; critic teacher mathematics, Ind. U., 1911-13; instr. mathematics, Horace Mann Sch., (Columbia), 1913-15; instr. mathematics 1916-17, asst. prof. edn., 1917-20; prof. edn. since 1920, dean Sch. of Edn. since 1921, U. of Pa. Mem. N.E.A, Nat. Council Teachers of Mathematics, Nat. Assn. Coll. Teachers of Edn., Phi Delta Kappa, Pi Mu Epsilon, Phi Beta Kappa, Sigma Xi, Kappa Phi Kappa, Theta Chi. United Presbyn. Author: An Investigation of Abilities Fundamental to Geometry, 1918. Developed standardized tests in geometry. Home: 4841 Hazel Av., Philadelphia, Pa.

MINTON, Wilson Parke, clergyman; b. Covington, O., Nov. 5, 1887; s. Abram Wilson and Lauretta (Himes) M.; ed. Bible and music, Moody Bible Inst., 1907-09; A.B., Defiance (O.) Coll., 1920, student Christian Divinity Sch., Defiance, O., 1917-20; (hon.) D.D., Defiance Coll., 1922; m. Bertha Anna Siebrecht, July 17, 1910; children—Paul Wilson (dec.), Ruth Lillian (Mrs. Paul R. Martin), Mary Elizabeth (Mrs. Charles F. Dugan). Began preaching as licentiate, 1908; ordained to ministry Christian Ch., 1910; pastor Goshen and Elkhart, Ind., 1910-11, Goshen, Ind., 1911-17; pastor two rural chs. in Ind. while at sch. in Defiance, O., 1917-20; fgn. mission sec. Christian Ch., 1919-31 when merged with Am. Bd. and continued sec. until 1937; supt. Conf. of Congl. and Christian Chs. of Pa., Milroy, Pa., since 1935; also editor and asso. editor missionary mags. of ch., 1920-31; took leading part in merger Congl. and Christian Chs. in U.S., consummated, 1931. Served as sec. Y.M.

MISH, Joseph Dubbs, lawyer; b. Hagerstown, Md.; Jan. 25, 1899; s. Frank Winder and Eleanor (Dubbs) M.; A.B., Princeton U., 1921; LL.B., U. of Md. Law Sch., 1926; m. Edith Crittenden, Nov. 7, 1936; 1 son, Frederick Crittenden. Admitted to Md. bar, 1926, and since engaged in gen. practice of law at Hagerstown; asso. with firm Keedy and Lane, 1926-31; mem. firm Lane & Mish since 1931; dir. and atty. Washington Co. Nat. Bank, Williamsport, Md.; dir. Blue Ridge Fire Ins. Co. (Hagerstown), Hagerstown Shoe & Legging Co., Maryland Ribbon Co. (Hagerstown), W. D. Byron & Sons of Md. (Williamsport, Md.). Served as mem. Md. Ho. of Dels. and chmn. Washington Co. del., 1931-33; mem. Md. Senate, 1939. Served in S.A.T.C. Mem. Am. Bar Assn., Md. State and Washington Co. bar assns., Phi Kappa Sigma. Democrat. Mem. Evang. Ref. Ch. Elk, Moose. Club: Fountainhead Country. Home: 203 S. Prospect St. Office: Hagerstown Trust Bldg., Hagerstown, Md.

MISSONELLIE, William, physician; b. Hawthorne, N.J., Mar. 15, 1905; s. Canio and Catherine (Vodola) M.; student U. of Md., College Park, 1923-25; M.D., George Washington U. Med. Sch., 1929; unmarried. Interne St. Joseph's Hosp., Paterson, N.J., 1929-30; engaged in gen. practice of medicine at Hawthorne, N.J. since 1930; health officer, Hawthorne, N.J., 1930-34, sch. physician, 1930; police and fire surgeon since 1937; officer Passaic Co. Tuberculosis Assn.; asso. staff of St. Joseph's Hosp.; courtesy staffs Gen. and Barnett hosps., Paterson. Served as non-commd. officer Med. Div., R.O.T.C. Mem. Passaic County, N.J. State med. Socs., A.M.A., Alpha Kappa Kappa. Roman Catholic. Elk. Clubs: North Jersey Country (Preakness); Boat (Greenwood Lake, N.Y.). Home: 404 Lafayette Av., Hawthorne, N.J.

MITCHELL, Broadus, economist; b. Georgetown, Ky., Dec. 27, 1892; s. Samuel Chiles and Alice Virginia (Broadus) M.; A.B., U. of S.C., 1913; fellow Johns Hopkins, 1917-18, Ph.D., 1918; m. Adelaide Hammond, Sept. 1, 1923 (divorced); children—Barbara Sinclair, Sidney Hammond; m. 2d, Louise Pearson Blodget, Dec. 31, 1936. With Johns Hopkins since 1919, as instr. in polit. economy, 1919-22, asso., 1922-27, asso. prof., 1927-39. Consultant to dir. NRA Div. Review, Nov. 1935-Mar. 1936. Sgt. at Camp Dix, N.J., 1918; student Personnel Officers Training Sch., Camp Sherman, O., same yr. Formerly pres., now member bd. Baltimore Urban League; member board League for Industrial Democracy; mem. editorial council Soviet Russia Today and of Social Frontier; trustee Christian Social Justice Fund. Mem. Am. Economic Assn. (exec. com.), Phi Gamma Delta, Phi Beta Kappa. Socialist. Club: Johns Hopkins. Author: The Rise of Cotton Mills in the South, 1921; Frederick Law Olmsted, a Critic of the Old South, 1924; William Gregg, Factory Master in the Old South, 1928; The Industrial Revolution in the South (with George Sinclair Mitchell), 1930; A Preface to Economics, 1932; General Economics, 1937; Practical Problems in Economics (with Louise Pearson Mitchell), 1938. Contbr. to Palgrave's Dictionary of Polit. Economy, 1926; Ency. Britannica, 14th edit.; Dictionary of Am. Biography; Ency. of the Social Sciences; also articles on industrial history. Home: 1008 Regester Av., Baltimore, Md.

MITCHELL, Claude, supt. schs. city; b. Mifflinburg, Pa., Aug. 15, 1885; s. Charles and Mary Alice (Brouse) M.; A.B., Susquehanna U., 1912; A.M., U. of Pittsburgh, 1925, Ph.D., same, 1931; m. Rhoda V. Bowersox, July 23, 1912; children—Mary Verdilla, Dorothy LaVerna, Marian Lorena. Teacher in rural schs. and prin. twp. high schs., 1909-18; supt. schs., West Newton, Pa. since 1918; served as mem. faculty summer schs. California State Teachers Coll. and Susquehanna U.; pres. West Newton Water Co. Mem. A.A.A.S., Am. Acad. Polit. and Social Sci., Phi Delta Kappa, Phi Gamma Mu. Republican. Mem. M.E.Ch. Mason. Club: Rotary of West Newton. Contbr. articles to ednl. mags. Home: West Newton, Pa.

MITCHELL, David Eaton, lawyer, utilities exec.; b. Titusville, Pa., Jan. 15, 1876; s. Claudius Augustus and Dora (Eaton) M.; A.B., Harvard, 1897, LL.B., 1899; M. Grace Whiting, Dec. 2, 1903 (died 1919); children—George Whiting (died 1920), David Eaton; m. 2d, Grace Hauck, April 19, 1927; 1 daughter, Janet. Admitted to Pa. bar, 1900; specializing in law of oil and gas, until 1924; gen. counsel, v.p. and sec. The Mfrs. Light and Heat Co., and affiliated companies of Columbia Gas & Elec. System, Pittsburgh, since 1926. Mem. Am. Bar Assn., Pa. Bar Assn., Allegheny Co. Bar Assn. Unitarian. Clubs: Duquesne, University, Fox Chapel Golf (Pittsburgh). Home: 6107 Kentucky Av. Office: 800 Union Trust Bldg., Pittsburgh, Pa.

MITCHELL, David Ray, mining engr.; b. Bell's Landing, Pa., June 12, 1898; s. John Francis and Gertrude (Johnson) M.; ed. State Teachers Coll., Lock Haven, Pa., 1915-17; B.S., Pa. State Coll., 1924, M.S., same, 1927; E.M., U. of Ill., 1930; m. Margaret Lois Rishell, Mar. 12, 1926; children—David Ray, Jr., Mary Patricia. Began as student mining engr., Bethlehem Mines Corpn., 1924; grad. asst. in mining engring., Pa. State Coll., 1926; instr. mining engring., U. of Ill., 1927 to 1929, asso., 1929 to 1931, asst. prof. 1931 to 1937, asso. prof. mining and metall. engring., 1937; prof. mining engring. and head of dept. mining engring., Pa. State Coll. since 1938. Served as pvt. Signal Batln., U.S.A., 1918-19. Mem. Am. Inst. Mining & Metall. Engrs. (sec. Coal Div.), Sigma Xi, Sigma Gamma Epsilon. Republican. Mem. M.E. Ch. Club: University. Asso. editor, Mechanization. Contbr. many tech. papers on mining, mineral preparation and fuels. Home: State College, Pa.

MITCHELL, George W.; visiting surgeon Mercy and U.S. Marine hosps. Address: 11 E. Chase St., Baltimore, Md.

MITCHELL, Harry Luzerne, pub. utility official; b. Warren, Pa., Jan. 11, 1883; s. Willis A. and Sarah Oliphant (Gemmill) M.; ed. Warren High Sch.; m. Edith M. Davidson, Sept. 19, 1908; children—Charles D., Caroline S., Margaret D. Began as clk. with cos. of West Penn System, 1902; has held exec. position in various ry. and power operating cos. of same; pres. West Penn Power Co., West Penn Rys. Co., W.Va. Power & Transmission Co., Allegheny Pittsburgh Coal Co., Steubenville Bridge Co., Windsor Power House Coal Co.; vice president Beach Bottom Power Company, Potomac Transmission Company; director Monongahela West Penn Public Service Company. Republican. Presbyterian. Clubs: Oakmont Country, Duquesne (Pittsburgh) Pike Run Country (Mt. Pleasant, Pennsylvania); Pleasant Valley Country (Connellsville, Pennsylvania). Home: 6334 Forbes St. Office: 14 Wood St., Pittsburgh, Pa.

MITCHELL, Howard Hawks, prof. mathematics; b. Marietta, O., Jan. 14, 1885; s. Oscar Howard and Mary Hoadley (Hawks) M.; Ph.B., Marietta (O.) College, 1906; Sc.D. from same college, 1935; Ph.D., Princeton University, 1910; m. Emma Vestine White, Sept. 18, 1912. Fellow in mathematics, Princeton, 1908-10; instr. mathematics, Yale, 1910-11; instr. mathematics, 1911-14, asst. prof., 1914-21, prof. since 1921, U. of Pa. Editor Trans. Am. Math. Soc., 1925-30. Served as ballistician at Aberdeen Proving Grounds, World War, 1918. Mem. Am. Math. Soc. (v.p. 1932-33), A.A.A.S. (v.p. 1932), Am. Philos. Soc., Phi Beta Kappa, Sigma Xi, Delta Upsilon. Home: Merion, Pa.

MITCHELL, Howard Walton, lawyer; b. Pittsburgh, Pa., Apr. 5, 1867; s. Joseph and Adelaide V. (McKee) M.; B.S., Pa. State Coll. 1890; LL.D., U. of Pittsburgh, 1915; m. Anna Cameron, June 11, 1896 (died Sept. 24, 1908). Began practice of law at Pittsburgh, 1893; mem. firms Lyon, McKee & Mitchell, 1897-1907, McKee, Mitchell & Patterson, 1907-08, McKee, Mitchell & Alter, 1908-19; apptd. judge Orphans' Court, 5th Jud. Dist. of Pa., by Gov. William C. Sproul, July 10, 1919, and elected to same office, Nov. 1919, for term ending, 1929, reëlected for term ending 1939. Pres. bd. Pa. State Coll., 1914-29 (acting pres. of the coll., 1920-21); pres. trustees, Pittsburgh Y.M.C.A. and Athalia Daly Home (Pittsburgh), trustee Pittsburgh Theol. Sem., Presbyn. Hosp., Henry C. Frick Ednl. Commn. Mem. American, Pennsylvania State and Allegheny Co. bar assns., Beta Theta Pi. Republican. United Presbyn. Clubs: Duquesne, University, Oakmont Country. Home: 1090 Devon Rd., Pittsburgh, Pa.

MITCHELL, J. West, physician; b. at Charleroi, Pa., August 14, 1893; s. of James Kindall and Mary Ellen (West) M.; grad. Charleroi High Sch., 1909; student Washington and Jefferson Coll., 1909-10; Ph.B., Bethany (W.Va.) Coll., -1913; B.S., U. of Pittsburgh, 1915, M.D., 1917; m. Blanche Marie Smith, June 21, 1917; children—Richard Smith, Janet Ruth. Interne St. Francis Hosp., Pittsburgh, 1916-18; electrocardiographer, Univ. Heart Sta., St. Francis Hosp., Pittsburgh, 1917-18; ward surgeon, diabetic service, U.S. Army General Hospital, No. 9, Lakewood, N.J., 1918-19; med. dir. Psychiatric Inst., New York, 1919-21; practice of internal medicine, Sewickley, Pa., 1921-39; instr. in medicine, U. of Pittsburgh, 1930-38, asst. prof. of medicine since 1938; dir. vascular service, Skin and Cancer Foundation, Pittsburgh. Served as 1st lt. Med. Corps, U.S. Army, 1917-19. Mem. Allegheny Co. Med. Soc. (mem. bd. dirs.), Pa. State Med. Soc., Heart Assn., Commn. on Diabetes Pa. State Med. Soc., Kappa Alpha Southern, Phi Rho Sigma. Republican. Club: Faculty (U. of Pittsburgh). Home: Campmeeting Rd., Sewickley, Pa. Offices: 422 Frederick Av., Sewickley, Pa.; 500 Penn Av., Pittsburgh, Pa.

MITCHELL, James Archibald, clergyman; b. Centreville, Md., May 22, 1892; s. Rev. James Archibald and Eleanor Lux (McKenney) M.; A.B., Trinity Coll., Hartford, Conn., 1915; A.M., Yale U., 1922; B.D., Va. Theol. Sem., Alexandria, 1924; Am. Seminar in Europe, summer 1937; m. Virginia Delano Powers, Sept. 14, 1931; children—James Archibald, III, Hugh Powers. Mem. faculty, St. John's U., Shanghai, China, 1915-18; ordained to ministry P.E. Ch., deacon, 1923, priest, 1924; rector All Hallows Parish, Snow Hill, Md., 1924-25; asso. rector, Ch. of the Messiah, Baltimore, Md., 1925-27, rector, 1927-31; asso. prof. practical theology, Va. Theol. Sem., 1931-33; rector, St. Paul's Ch., Englewood, N.J. since 1933; in charge summer chapels, St. Christopher's-by-the-Sea, Gibson Island, Md., 1926-32, St. John's, Fishers Island, N.Y., since 1938. Sergt. Am. Co., Shanghai Vol. Corps, 1916-18; 2d lt. U.S. F.A. Reserve, 1918. Trustee Englewood Sch. for Boys; St. Mary's Hall, Burlington, N.J. Mem. Delta Psi. Episcopalian. Clubs: (hon. mem.) Englewood, Field, Knickerbocker Golf (Englewood); Hay Harbor and Fishers Island (Fishers Island, N.Y.). Home: 125 Engle St., Englewood, N.J.

MITCHELL, John McKenney, physician; b. Centreville, Md., Sept. 23, 1895; s. James Archibald and Eleanor Lux (McKenney) M.; A.B., Trinity Coll., Hartford, Conn., 1918; M.D., Yale U. Med. Sch., 1924; m. Eleanor Alderson Janeway, Sept. 12, 1925; children—James Andrew, Eleanor Janeway. Interne New Haven (Conn.) Hosp., 1924-25, asst. resident in pediatrics, 1925, resident, 1926; pediatrician to Bryn Mawr Hosp., Bryn Mawr, Pa. since 1932; asso. pediatrician, U. of Pa.; University Hosp., since 1933; examiner for state ins., Baltimore, 1919-20. Served as 1st lt. inf., 80th div., 1917-19. Dir. Community Health & Civic Assn., Ardmore, Pa. Licentiate Am. Bd. Pediatrics. Mem. Soc. for Pediatric Research, Am. Acad. Pediatrics, Phila. Pediatric Soc., Sigma Psi, Nu Sigma Nu, Delta Psi, Alpha Omega Alpha. Democrat. Episcopalian. Home: Cushman Rd., Rosemont, Pa.

MITCHELL, Ruth Crawford, immigrant welfare; b. Atlantic Highland, N.J., June 2, 1890; d. Hanford Crawford and M. Gertrude (Smith) M.; A.B., Vassar Coll., 1912; A.M., Washington Univ., St. Louis, 1914; grad. study Johns

Hopkins U., 1923-24. Asso. with Nat. Bd. Y.W.C.A., 1916-19; dir. survey of Prague, Czechoslovakia, 1919-21; asst. to dir. Fgn. Lang. Information Service, N.Y. City, 1922-24; lecturer dept. econs., U. of Pittsburgh, 1925-28, spl. asst. to Chancellor, 1928-31; adviser, Nationality Coms. of the Cathedral of Learning since 1931, organizer of Nationality Rooms Project in Cathedral of Learning at U. of Pittsburgh; unofficial observer, Internat. Emigration Conf., Geneva, 1923; mem. bd. Internat. Migration Service, Nat. Inst. Immigrant Welfare; mem. exec. com. Masaryk Inst. Dec. Order of White Lion (Czechoslovakia), 1920. Methodist. Clubs: Twentieth Century (Pittsburgh); Vassar (New York City). Editor, Survey of Prague, 4 vols., 1920. Contbr. articles. Home: 6106 Walnut St., Pittsburgh, Pa. Office: 1309 Cathedral of Learning, Pittsburgh, Pa.

MITCHELL, Viola, violinist; b. Pittsburgh, Pa., July 11, 1911; d. Atlee D. and Blanche (Dawson) M.; student Winchester Sch. Pittsburgh, 1921-25, Ecole Fénélon, Paris, 1925-26, Lycée, Brussels, 1926-29. Began as violinist at six yrs. of age; at the age of ten played with the Minneapolis and Cleveland orchestras; studied with Miss Margaret Horne, a pupil of Joachim, Sevcik and Leopold Auer until 14 yrs. old and with Eugene Ysaye in Brussels for 3 yrs.; made European début in Brussels, 1928; has concertized in Germany, England, France, Belgium, Italy, Holland and Switzerland, playing with all the prin. orchestras of these countries; made début in America as soloist with leading orchestras of U.S., season 1934-35. Home: 1137 Wightman St., Pittsburgh, Pa.*

MITCHELL, Walter Jenifer, judge; b. Charles Co., Md., Mar. 16, 1871; s. William Hebbard and Emily Ellen (Mitchell) M.; student Charlotte Hall Sch., 1886-88; LL.B., U. of Md., 1894; m. Florence Campbell Jenifer, Jan. 18, 1899; children—Mary Emily, Hugh Maxwell, Walter Jenifer, James Craik, Elizabeth Courtenay. Admitted to Md. bar, 1894; editor and pub. La Plata (Md.) Times Crescent, 1897-1934; mem. Md. State Senate from Charles Co., 1918-34, pres., 1931-33, also pres. spl. session, 1933; apptd. chief judge 7th Judicial Circuit Court, of Md., 1934, and elected to same for term 1935-50; also asso. judge Md. Court of Appeals since 1934. Trustee Charlotte Hall Sch. Mem. Soc. of the Cincinnati. Democrat. Episcopalian. Address: La Plata, Md.

MITCHELL, William Arthur, banking; b. Hamilton, Can., June 6, 1892; s. Robert and Janet (Ewing) M.; student Hamilton Collegiate Inst., 1904-07, Queens Univ., Kingston, Can. (extra-mural), 1912-15; LL.D., Mount Union Coll., Alliance, O., 1938; m. Georgie Linn Brown, of Lakewood, O., Nov. 2, 1920; children—David Lindsey, Robert George Byssche, Janet, Elizabeth Ann. Came to U.S., 1925, naturalized, 1936. Asso. with Traders Bank of Can. and Royal Bank of Can., 1908-25; asso. with J. P. Morgan & Co., New York, since 1925, partner since 1939; dir. and mem. exec. com. Associated Dry Goods Co. Served with Canadian Army, 1914. Former pres. Wyoming (N.J.) Assn.; chmn. bd. Buxton Country Day Sch., Short Hills, N.J.; trustee Pub. Edn. Assn., New York. Presbyn. Mason. Clubs: India House, Baltusrol Golf, Short Hills (Short Hills, N.J.); Canadian Society (New York). Home: 6 Woodcrest Av., Millburn, N.J. Office: 23 Wall St., New York, N.Y.

MITCHELL, William Reynolds Keeney, banking; b. Phila., Pa., Dec. 16, 1893; s. George Lippincott and Mary Ella (Keeney) M.; B.S., U. of Pa., 1914; m. Blanche Curet; 1 dau., June Mitchell (Mrs. Ferdinand LaMotte, 3d). Asso. with Provident Trust Co. of Phila., Pa., since starting as bank clk., 1914, successively, asst. sec., asst. treas., treas., and vice-pres. and treas. since 1932; dir. Lumbermen's Fire Ins. Co., Philadelphia Nat. Ins. Co., Williams, Brown & Earle, Inc., Pocono Manor Assn. Served as 1st lt. inf., later capt. machine gun batln., U.S.A., 1917-18. Trustee Friends Central Sch.; dir. White Haven Sanatorium Assn. Mem. Alpha Tau Omega. Republican. Mem. Religious Soc. of Friends. Clubs: University (Philadelphia);

Merion Cricket (Haverford). Home: Gulph Mills, Conshohocken. Office: 1632 Chestnut St., Philadelphia, Pa.

MITRANY, David, author, educator; b. Bucharest, Rumania, Jan. 1, 1888; Ph.D., D.Sc., London Sch. of Economics and Polit. Science; m. Ena Limebeer, June 9, 1923. Editorial staff of the Manchester Guardian, 1919-22; asst. European editor of the Carnegie Endowment's "Economic and Social History of the World War." Formerly lecturer on politics, U. of London; visiting prof. in govt., Harvard, 1931-33; Dodge lecturer, Yale, 1932; prof. Inst. for Advanced Study, Princeton, N.J. Fellow Royal Econ. Soc.; mem. Brit. coordinating com. for Internat. Study, Brit. del. to Internat. Conf. for Scientific Study Internat. Relations. Author: The Problem of International Sanctions, 1926; The Land and the Peasant in Rumania, 1930; The Progress of International Government, 1934; The Effect of the War in Southeastern Europe, 1937; and many pamphlets, articles, etc. Address: Institute for Advanced Study, Princeton, N.J.*

MITTEN, Arthur Allan, transportation, banking; b. Attica, Ind., July 29, 1888; s. Thomas Eugene and Kitty (Warner) M.; prep. edn., St. John's Mil. Acad., Delafield, Wis., St. Paul's Sch., Concord, N.H., King's Sch., Stamford, Conn.; student Sheffield Scientific Sch. (Yale), and Med. Sch., Yale; M.D., U. of Buffalo; m. Gertrude H. Lemon, Dec. 27, 1911. Pres. and chmn. bd. Mitten Management, Inc., operators of city transit corpns.; chmn. bd. Phila. Rapid Transit Co., Internat. Railway Company, Mitten Bank & Trust Co.; chmn. bd. and pres. Transit Investment Corpn. Served as captain, Med. Corps, comdg. ambulance co., World War; wounded and captured by enemy, Aug. 4, 1918, and held prisoner till end of war. Trustee Temple U. Mem. Phi Rho Sigma. Republican. Episcopalian. Home: Wise Mill Rd., Roxborough, Philadelphia. Office: Mitten Bldg., Philadelphia, Pa.

MOATS, Francis P., mem. law firm Moats, Adams & Moats. Address: Parkersburg, W.Va.

MOCK, Charles Adolphus, prof. of theology; b. Bedford Co., Pa., Aug. 7, 1873; s. David B. and Elizabeth (Colebaugh) M.; B.A., Central Pa. Coll. (now merged with Albright College, Reading, Pa.), 1898, M.A., 1905; Ph.D., Grove City, Coll., 1905; M.A., and B.D., Yale, 1911; m. Sue Elizabeth Allison, Dec. 15, 1897; children—Byron Fay, Charles Edgar, Grace Lillian. Ordained ministry Evangelical Ch., 1898; pastor Oil City, Pa., 1898-1901, Johnstown, 1901-05. prof. Greek and Latin, Dallas (Ore.) Coll., 1905-09; pres. Western Union Coll., Le Mars, Ia., 1911-30; asso. editor Evangelical Messenger, 1930-34; prof., and head of dept. of systematic theology, Evangelical School of Theology, Reading, since 1934. Republican. Address: Evangelical School of Theology, Reading, Pa.

MOCKRIDGE, John Charles Hillier, clergyman; b. in Can., Sept. 8, 1872; s. Rev. Charles Henry and Sophia Ridley (Grier) M.; King's Coll. Sch., Windsor, N.S.; B.A., U of Trinity Coll., Toronto, 1893, M.A., 1894, B.D., 1914; D.D., St. Stephen's Coll., 1913; m. Beatrice B., d. of Hon. F. Osler, 1899; children—Elisabeth, Harold C. F., Beatrice, John B. O. Deacon, 1894, priest, 1896, P.E. Ch.; asst. St. Luke's Ch., Toronto, 1894-97; rector Ch. of Messiah, Detroit, 1897-1903, St. Andrew's Memorial Ch., Detroit, 1903-07, St. Paul's Ch., Louisville, Ky., 1907-10; vicar Trinity Chapel, Trinity Parish, New York, 1910-14, Trinity Ch., New York, 1914, 15; rector St. James' Ch., Phila., since 1915, also of St. Mary's Ch., 1933. Mem. bd. overseers Phila. Divinity Sch.; mem. Gen. Conv. P.E. Ch. 4 times to 1934; pres. Episcopal Acad.; founder, 1937, St. James' Choir Sch. Chaplain Pa. Soc. Colonial Wars, 1922. Clubs: University, Union League. Address: 132 S. 22d St., Philadelphia, Pa.

MOE, Alfred Kean, lawyer; b. Buffalo, N.Y., Oct. 5, 1874; s. Alfred Myron and Sarah (Mahony) M.; prep. edn. Phillips Exeter (N.H.) Acad., 1891-93; A.B., Harvard, 1897; student Harvard Law Sch., 1896-97; M.P.L., Columbian (now George Washington) U., 1901; m. Charlotte Campbell, June 6, 1906 (died Jan. 25,

1939). Admitted to N.J. bar, 1898, and practiced law in Jersey City, 1898-1902; Am. Consul, Tegucigalpa, Honduras, 1902-04, Dublin, Ireland, 1904-09, Bordeaux, France, 1909-14; resigned Feb. 1914; law practice, Elizabeth, N.J., since 1914; special master in Chancery; Supreme Court examiner; commr. Public Works, Elizabeth, N.J., 1926-33; pres. Bd. of Standards and Appeals, Elizabeth, since 1933; dir. and sec. Collins Doan Co., Jersey City. Rep. candidate for mayor, 1938. Mem. Harvard Law Sch. Assn. Republican. Episcopalian. Clubs: Harvard (New York); Harvard of N.J. Home: 1272 Clinton Pl. Office: 286 N. Broad St., Elizabeth, N.J.

MOEHLE, Frederick Louis William, architect, consulting engr.; b. Baltimore, Md., Oct. 23, 1903; s. Frank H. and Ida E. (Smith) M.; grad. Baltimore Poly. Inst., 1921; B.E. in civil engring., Johns Hopkins, 1924, grad. student, 1924-25, also part time, 1929-32; m. Margaret V. Belzner, Oct. 1, 1927; 1 son, Frederick Louis William. Chief draftsman and engr. Mexican Petroleum Corpn., 1925-27, B.&O. R.R. and Baltimore Copper Works, 1927; designer with Davison Chem. Co., at Curtis Bay, Md., 1927-28; prin. asst. engr. and architect in office of W. S. Austin, Baltimore, 1928-31; head of firm Frederick L. W. Moehle & Associates, architects and cons. engrs., Baltimore, since 1931. Commd. 2d lt. R.O.T.C., 1921-24. Mem. Am. Soc. Civil Engrs., Md. Soc. of Architects (dir.), Baltimore Chapter of Am. Inst. Architects. Lutheran. Mem. Walther League Club, Baltimore. Home: 2325 Harlem Av. Office: 409 N. Charles St., Baltimore, Md.

MOFFAT, Barclay Wellington, orthopedic surgeon; b. Orange, N.J., July 9, 1890; s. Edgar Vietor and Edith (Wellington) M.; A.B., Harvard U., 1912; M.D., Harvard U. Med. Sch., 1916; grad. study, U. of Paris, France, 1919; m. Adeline Murdoch, July 26, 1917; 1 dau., Jean. Interne Bellevue Hosp., Jan.-Aug. 1917, Seaside Hosp., 1916-17, Hosp. for Ruptured & Crippled, 1919-20; in practice at Red Bank, N.J., since 1920; asso. attdg. orthopedic surgean Post-Grad. Hosp. since 1921; attdg. orthopedic surgeon Fitkin Memorial Hosp. since 1922 to date; cons. orthopedist hosp., Allenwood Hosp.; cons. orthopedic surgeon and med. dir. N.J. State Commn. for Crippled Children. Served as orthopedic surgeon, Med. Corps, U.S. A., 1917-19. Fellow Am. Coll. Surgeons; mem. A.M.A., Am. Orthopedic Assn., Am. Acad. Orthopedic Surgeons, Acad. of Medicine of Northern N.J. Sigma Alpha Epsilon. Clubs: Harvard (New York); Boothbay Harbor Yacht. Home: Red Bank, N.J.

MOFFATT, Earl B., railroad exec.; b. Dunmore, Pa., June 29, 1890; s. James C. and Minnie (Bishop) M.; ed. grade and high sch., Dunmore, Pa., 1897-1906; m. Norma Hughes Jones, Jan. 21, 1913; children—Margaret E. (Mrs. Wm. F. Wrightnour), Norma J. With D.L.& W. R.R. since 1906, as file clerk, 1906-08, sec. to supt., 1908-10, chief clerk to gen. supt., 1910-12, service clerk to gen. supt., 1912-17, chief clerk to vice-pres. and gen. mgr., 1917-18, asst. to Federal mgr., 1918-20, asst. to vice-pres. and gen. mgr., 1920-26, gen. supt. since 1926. Mem. bd. of dirs. Scranton Chamber of Commerce; dir. Community Chest. Methodist. Clubs: Kiwanis (dir.), Scranton, Country (Scranton); Railroad (New York). Home: 1020 Olive St. Office: D.L.& W. R.R., Scranton, Pa.

MOFFET, Horace Cleon, investment banking; b. Bellwood, Pa., Sept. 27, 1904; s. Mahlon L. and Elizabeth A. (Porter) M.; grad. high sch., Altoona, Pa., 1923; also higher edn. in special courses under coll. and univ. direction; m. Ruth M. Brehm, June 29, 1932; children—James Porter, Robert Brehm. Employed in various positions to 1928; asso. with R. E. Swart & Co., Inc., investment securities, Pittsburgh, Pa., since 1928, sales correspondent and salesman, 1928-33, mgr., 1933-35, vice-pres. since 1935; dir. Bellwood Furniture Co., O'Sullivan Rubber Co. Mem. Bond Club of Pittsburgh, Investment Bankers Assn., S.A.R., Hist. Soc. of Western Pa. (sustaining mem.), Pa. Soc. of New York. Republican. Presbyn. Mason. Club:

MOFFETT, Pittsburgh Athletic. Home: 6648 Fifth Av. Office: Union Trust Bldg., Pittsburgh, Pa.

MOFFETT, Ernest Cutter, chemist; b. Fords, N.J., Nov. 17, 1888; s. Wilbur H. and Ann F. (Voorhees) M.; B.Sc., Rutgers U., New Brunswick, N.J., 1910, M.Sc., 1931; m. Sarah C. Voorhees, Sept. 21, 1915; children—Dorothy (dec.), Grace, John Voorhees (dec.). Chemist U.S. Metals Refining Co., Chrome, N.J., 1910-11; engr. Chem. Central Testing Lab., City of N.Y., 1911-16; sec.-treas. Stillwell Labs., New York, 1916-20; cons. chemist, Woodbridge, N.J., 1920-22; in charge research labs. Am. Cyanamid Co., N.Y., 1922-26, asst. to v.p. tech. dept. since 1926. Mem. Woodbridge (N. J.) Twp. Com. 1925, Woodbridge Bd. of Edn., 1930-35. Mem. Am. Chem. Soc., Phi Beta Kappa. Republican. Mason. Home: 118 Prospect St., Woodbridge, N.J. Office: American Cyanamid Co., New York, N.Y.

MOFFETT, George Monroe, food mfr. b. Parkersburg, W.Va., 1883; A.B., Princeton, 1904; married to Madeline Buckner. Pres..Corn Products Refining Co.; dir. Commercial Solvents Corpn., Standard Ins. Co., S. Puerto Rico Sugar Co., Resinox Corpn. Home: Queenstown, Md. Office: 17 Battery Pl., New York, N.Y.

MOFFETT, Louis Burdelle; b. Swedesboro, N.J., Mar. 22, 1874; s. Biddle Reeves and Mary Emma (Eastlack) M.; grad. Peirce Sch. Business Administration, Phila., Pa., 1892; m. Mary Lewis Quinn, July 3, 1894; 1 son, Louis Burdelle. With Peirce Sch. of Business Administration since 1892, sec., 1896-1900, later dir., retired 1934; now pres. Farmers and Mechanics National Bank and pres. of Woodbury Trust Co. (both of Woodbury, N.J.). Mem. N.J. State Fuel Administration, World War. Sec., treas. Sinking Fund Commn., Woodbury, N.J. Mem. N.J. Soc. of Pa. (sec.), Geneal. Soc. of Pa. (dir.). Republican. Methodist. Mason (32°). Clubs: Rotary (pres. 1931), Union League (Phila.). Author: Money and Banking, 1915. Home: Woodbury, N.J.

MOFFITT, George R., pathologist; b. Harrisburg, Pa., Nov. 15, 1879; s. Robert H. and Rebecca C. (Witman) M.; grad., Princeton U., 1902; M.D., U. of Pa. Med. Sch., 1906; m. Lillian J. Johnston, Feb. 8, 1921; children—Charlotte, George R. Resident physician St. Christopher's Children's Hosp., Phila., 1906-07, Germantown (Pa.) Hosp., 1907-09; established clin. lab., Harrisburg, 1908; physician to woman's dept. Pa. State Tuberculosis Sanatorium, Mt. Alto, Pa., 1909-10; pathologist Harrisburg Hosp. since 1911; city bacteriologist, Harrisburg, since 1912; cons. pathologist Harrisburg State Hosp. for Insane since 1929. Entered U.S. Army, 1917; served at Rockefeller Inst., Central Dept. Lab., Ft. Leavenworth, Kan., Camp Lee, Va., 1917, C.O. Southeastern Dept. Lab., Ft. McPherson, Ga., 1918-20; lt., 1917, capt., 1918, maj., 1919. Chief, bur. of labs., A.R.C. Commn. to Poland, 1920-21; as emergency measure comd. hosp. train on front during entire Bolshevik-Polish War. Mem. Harrisburg Acad. of Medicine (pres. 1932), Am. Assn. for Study of Neoplastic Diseases, Am. Pub. Health Assn., Dauphin Co. Med. Soc., Pa. State Med. Assn., A.M.A., Am. Legion, Beaufort Hunt (field master), Pa. Water Works Assn., Harrisburg Chamber of Commerce. Clubs: Harrisburg, Rotary, Harrisburg Country (Harrisburg); University, Medical (Phila.). Author numerous med. articles. Undergrad. editor Princeton Alumni Weekly, 1900-02; asst. editor Pa. State Med. Jour., 1921-25; asso. editor, 1925-28. Home: R. D. 2. Office: Harrisburg Hospital, Harrisburg, Pa.

MOFFITT, Harold Fred, physician; b. Arch Spring, Pa., Dec. 23, 1891; s. Samuel T. and Clara B. (Lindsay) M.; ed. Pa. State Coll., 1911-13; M.D., U. of Pa. Med. Sch., 1917; m. Ethel M. Sawtelle, June 9, 1923. Engaged in gen. practice of medicine and surgery at Altoona, Pa. since 1920. Served as 1st lt. Med. Corps, U.S.A., 1917-19, with A.E.F. in France. Fellow Am. Coll. surgeons; mem. Am. Med. Assn., Delta Tau Delta. Republican. Presbyn. Mason (32°, Shriner). Clubs: Blairmont Country (Hollidaysburg); Spruce Creek Rod and Gun club of Huntingdon Co. Home: 3409 Baker Boul. Office: 1115 12th Av., Altoona, Pa.

MOGEL, Charles Luther, clergyman; b. Newport, Pa., Sept. 18, 1894; s. Jesse McKee and Malinda (Carl) M.; A.B., Gettysburg Coll., 1923; ed. Gettysburg Sem., 1923-26; B.D., Mt. Airy Sem., 1931, S.T.M., 1933; m. Jessie May Smith, June 17, 1926. Engaged in teaching pub schs., 1912-16, 1917-18; in civil service work, 1918-20; ordained to ministry Luth. Ch., 1926; pastor, Ferndale, Bucks Co., Pa., 1926-36, Millersburg, Pa., since 1936; served as pres. Luth. Conf., 1927-30; treas. East Pa. Synod, 1934-37. Trustee Tressler Orphans Home. Mem. Tau Kappa Alpha. Republican. Lutheran. Mason. Home: 265 North St. Millersburg, Pa.

MOHLER, D. N.; mem. law firm Mohler, Peters & Snyder. Address: Charleston, W.Va.

MOHLER, Roy William, physician, specialist obstetrics, gynecology; b. Mt. Holly Springs, Cumberland Co., Pa., Dec. 26, 1892; s. John Wesley and Ella (Kieffer) M.; student Conway Hall, Carlisle, Pa., 1911-13; A.B., Dickinson Coll., Carlisle, Pa., 1917; M.D., Jefferson Med. Coll., Phila., Pa., 1921; m. Isabelle Blackburn, Sept. 10, 1926; 1 dau., Barbara Blackburn. Interne Bryn Mawr and Jefferson hosps., 1921-24; in practice medicine, Phila., since 1924; asso. in gynecology, Jefferson Med. Coll., Phila., since 1930; gynecologist and obstetrician Methodist Episcopal Hosp., Phila., since 1937; asst. attending obstetrician and gynecologist Pa. Lying In Hosp., Phila., since 1930. Mem. R.O.T.C., 1918-19. Diplomate Am. Bd. Obstetrics and Gynecology; fellow Am. Coll. Surgeons; mem. Obstet. Soc., Phila. (sec. 1935-39), Jefferson Soc. for Clin. Investigation, Coll of Physicians, Phila. County Med. Soc., Beta Theta Pi, Phi Alpha Sigma. Republican. Clubs: Aesculapean, University (Phila.); Rolling Green Golf (Media, Pa.). Home: 14 Radcliffe Rd., Bala-Cynwyd, Pa. Office: 1806 Spruce St., Philadelphia, Pa.

MOHLER, Samuel Loomis, prof. Latin; b. Baltimore, Md., Mar. 29, 1895; s. John Fred and Sarah (Loomis) M.; A.B., Dickinson Coll., 1914; A.M., Harvard U., 1918; Ph.D., U. of Pa., 1926; m. Harriet Holmes Stuart, June 22, 1918; children—Mary Baird, Sarah Loomis. Instr. Greek and Latin, Wilmington Conf. Acad., Dover, Del., 1914-16, Loomis Inst., Windsor, Conn., 1918, high sch., Camden, N.J., 1919-20, high sch., Chester, Pa., 1920-21; instr. Latin, U. of Pa., 1921-26; asst. prof. Latin, Franklin and Marshall Coll., Lancaster, Pa., 1926 to 1929, asso. prof., 1929-31, prof. since 1931. Served in U.S.N.R.F., 1918. Mem. Am. Philol. Assn., Classical Assn. of Atlantic States, Am. Assn. Univ. Profs., Phi Beta Kappa, Kappa Sigma. Democrat. Methodist. Home: 520 State St., Lancaster, Pa.

MOISE, Albert Luria, sec. Phila. County Bd. of Law Examiners; b. Sumter, S.C., Jan. 9, 1872; s. Edwin Warren and Esther (Lyon) M.; student Davis Mil. Sch., N.C., Randolph-Macon Coll., Ashland, Va., and U. of Va. Law Sch., Charlottesville, Va.; m. Eva May Nathans, Apr. 12, 1904; children—Alice G., Albert Luria. Spl. atty. gen. of Pa., 1911; U.S. appraiser of merchandise, Customs Dist. 11, Phila., 1917-21; now sec. Phila. Co. Bd. of Law Examiners; dir. Protective Motor Service Co., Am. Manganese Bronze Co. Mem. Am. Bar Assn., Pa. Bar Assn., Phila. Bar Assn., Kappa Sigma. Club: Lawyers (Phila.). Managing editor: Pepper & Lewis Digest and Ency. of Pa. Law; Moise and Matlack on the Insurance Law of Pa.; Lewis Blackstone's Commentaries on the Laws of England; editor 2d edit. Rickert on Pa. Negligence Law; 2d edit. Pa. Elementary Law Problems and Answers. Home: 36 W. Phila-Ellena St., Germantown. Office: Suite 1104-05 Land Title Bldg., Philadelphia, Pa.

MOIST, Ronald Farrow, lawyer; b. Fairfield, Kanawha County, W.Va., Nov. 19, 1890; s. Jerome Clayton and Cora Ellen (Wildman) M.; prep. edn. public school, Fremont, Neb., 1897-1899, Charleston, W.Va., 1899-1909; student W.Va. Wesleyan Coll., 1910-13; A.B., W.Va. U., 1915, LL.B., 1917; student Inns of Court, London, England, 1919; m. Susan Elizabeth Gillie, Sept. 14, 1922; children—Ronald Farrow, William Gillie (deceased). Admitted to W.Va. bar, 1919; and began practice in Charleston; in charge law enforcement, W.Va. State Dept. of Health, 1919-20; law clerk W.Va. Supreme Court of Appeals, 1920-22; sec. W.Va. Revision and Codification Commn., 1922-27; gen. practice of law, Clarksburg, W.Va., since 1927; adviser to Joint Legislative Code Com. and at special session of Legislature to adopt Code, 1930-31. Enlisted U.S. Army, May 1917; went with A.E.F. as corpl. 5th Engrs. (later 15th Engrs.), July 1917; transferred to Hdqrs. 3d Corps and advanced to regtl. sergt. maj.; with A.E.F. 2 years; commd. 1st lt. O.R.C. Mem. bd. of trustees W.Va. Wesleyan Coll. Mem. Am., W.Va., Harrison County bar assns., Am. Judicature Soc., Internat. Assn. Ins. Counsel, Am. Legion, La Societe des 40 Hommes et 8 Chevaux, Beta Theta Pi (former nat. v.p. and trustee), Phi Delta Phi. Republican. Methodist. Mason (32°, Shriner). Clubs: Kiwanis (past pres.), Clarksburg Country. Home: 507 Haymond Highway. Office: Empire Bldg., Clarksburg, W.Va.

MOLARSKY, Maurice, artist and teacher; b. Kiev, Russia, May 25, 1885; s. Isaac and Fanny (Sacharenko) M.; ed. Pa. Mus. and Sch. Industrial Art, 1897-98, Acad. of Fine Arts, Phila., Pa., 1899-1904; m. Tina Margolies, Mar. 18, 1916. Has followed profession of artist since 1907; executed portraits of men in pub. life and prominent women; mural and genre painter; regular contbr. to all important exhbns. in U.S.; rep. in collections, Art Club, City Hall, Jefferson Coll., Mt. Sinai Hosp., all in Phila., Nat. Acad. of Design, Am. Acad. of Arts and Letters, New York, N.Y., murals in pub. bldgs., Phila., Haverford (Pa.) Coll., Teacher's State Coll., West Chester, Pa., and many pub. and pvt. collections. Awarded many prizes, among them, Cresson Traveling Scholarship, Pa. Acad. of Fine Arts, 1904, and Fellowship Prize, 1909; Silver medal, Panama-Pacific Expn., 1915; gold medal, Phila. Art Club, 1919; gold medal of Phila. Sketch Club, 1932; Silver Medal, Sesqui-Centennial Expn., 1926. Hebrew religion. Clubs: American Artists Professional League, Art Alliance, Fellowship of Pa. Academy of Fine Arts. Home: 2101 Spruce St., Philadelphia, Pa.

MOLBY, Fred A., prof. physics, W.Va. U. Address: West Virginia University, Morgantown, W.Va.

MOLINA, Edward Charles Dixon, telephone engring.; b. New York, N.Y., Dec. 13, 1877; s. Antonio Mariano and Terese (St. Remy) M.; ed. pub. schs. and high sch.; acquired advanced math. and sci. edn. by personal efforts in pvt. study for many years.; m. Virginia Costales, Nov. 29, 1900; children—Antonio Edward, Virginia Terese. Asso. with cos. of Bell System continuously since entering employ of Western Electric Co., 1898, with engring. dept. Am. Telephone & Telegraph Co., 1901-07 in Boston, then, New York City since 1907; switching theory engr., Bell Telephone Labs., New York City since 1934; known as expert in math. theory of probability. Fellow Inst. Math. Statistics, A.A.A.S., Royal Econ. Soc. London, Eng. Mem. Am. Math. Soc., Math. Assn. America, Am. Astron. Soc., Am. Statis. Assn., Econometrical Soc., Am. Inst. Elec. Engrs., Telephone Pioneers of America, Met. Mus. of Arts. Democrat. Club: Railroad-Machinery of New York. Home: 141 Dodd St., East Orange, N.J. Office: 463 West St., New York, N.Y.

MOLITOR, Hans, physician, dir. Merck Inst.; b. Maffersdorf, Austria, Aug. 10, 1895; s. Dr. Emil and Lydia (Schmid) M.; came to U.S., 1932, naturalized, 1938; M.D., U. of Vienna Med. Sch., 1922; unmarried. Asst. prof. pharmacology, U. of Vienna Med. Sch., 1922-26; Rockefeller Traveling Fellow, Edinburgh and London, 1924; privatdozent (lecturer) pharmacology and toxicology, U. of Vienna Med. Sch., 1927-28, asso. prof., same, 1928-32; dir. Merck Inst. of Therapeutic Research, Rahway, N.J. since 1932, now engaged in development of exptl. methods for determination of the safety and therapeutic value of new drugs. Served as med. officer in Austrian Army, 1914-18. Fellow A.A.A.S., Internat. Coll. Anesthetists. Mem. Am. Physiol. Soc., Soc. Exptl. Biology and Medicine, Phila. Physiol. Soc., Internat. Anesthesia Research Soc. Evang. A.B. (Lutheran). Clubs: Athletic (Newark); Country (Colonia). Contbr. many sci. articles to med. jours. Home: 436 Cherry St., Elizabeth. Office: 50 Lawrence St., Rahway, N.J.

MOLL, Lloyd Alexis, violinist, conductor; b. Macungie, Pa., Sept. 29, 1879; s. Charles and Hannah Rebecca (Schadler) M.; studied violin and conducting under Henry Schradieck, Combs Conservatory, Phila.; m. Elizabeth R. Gorr, Jan. 31, 1912. Concert violinist, soloist, and teacher; conductor Allentown Symphony Orchestra since 1916. Democrat. Pa.-German columnist for Chronicle and News, evening newspaper, Allentown, Pa. Contbr. prose and verse to mags. and newspapers. Home: 1032 Linden St., Allentown, Pa.

MOLLER, Mathias Peter, Jr., pipe organ mfr.; b. Hagerstown, Md., May 8, 1902; s. Mathias Peter and May Belle (Greenlund) M.; student Carl's Private Sch., Hagerstown, 1913-15, Staunton Mil. Acad., Staunton, Va., 1915-16, Carl's Private Sch., 1916-17; B.S. Susquehanna U., Selinsgrove, Pa., 1917-21; private musical instruction, Peabody Inst., Baltimore; m. Hilda Mackenzie, May 9, 1923; children—Mathias Peter, III, Kevin Mackenzie. With M. P. Moller, Inc., builders of pipe organs, since 1912, beginning as apprentice organ builder, working Saturdays and summers until 1921, dir. since 1923, v.p. and treas., 1931-37, pres. and treas. since 1937; v.p. and dir. Hagerstown Trust Co., 1933-37, pres. and dir. since 1937; pres., treas. and dir. Kinetic Engring. Co.; dir. Potomac Edison Co., Remington Putnam Co. Trustee and mem. exec. com. Susquehanna U.; trustee Tressler Orphans Home (Loysville, Pa.), Hagerstown Y.M.C.A.; mem. bd. and exec. com. Bd. Foreign Missions, United Lutheran Ch. Treas. Foreign Missions Conf. of North America (Protestant interdenominational); vice chmn. Laymens Missionary Movement; mem. exec. com. Lutheran Laymen's Movement for Stewardship; frequent del. to synods and nat. convs. of United Lutheran Ch. in America. Mem. Am. Guild Organists; past pres. Alumni Assn. of Susquehanna U. Lutheran. Mason (K.T.). Clubs: Rotary, Fountainhead Country (Hagerstown); Baltimore Country (Baltimore); Lotos (New York). Home: Elm Terrace. Office: care M. P. Moller, Inc., Hagerstown, Md.

MOLLOY, J(ohn) Carroll, real estate; b. Pineville, Bucks Co., Pa., Feb. 24, 1884; s. Harry Farrell and Anna (Leedom) M.; student Doylestown (Pa.) High Sch., 1899-1901, George Sch., 1901-02, Pierce Business Sch., 1902-03; m. Eleanor Mabel Stecker, June 6, 1906 (died Sept. 13, 1908); 1 son, John Carroll; m. 2d, Mary Florence Ely, Mar. 29, 1911; children—Gerald Leedom, Kathleen Ely, Henry Warren (deceased). Began as clerk in Recorder of Deeds office, Doylestown, Pa., Jan. 3, 1903; partner in country store, Pineville, Pa., 1906-16; in real estate and insurance since 1916. Dir. and asst. sec. of bd. Doylestown Nat. Bank & Trust Co. Justice of the peace, Wrightstown Twp., Bucks Co., Pa., since 1916; dep. recorder of deeds, Bucks Co., 1904-05. Mem. Soc. Residential Appraisers, Phila. Real Estate Bd., Bucks Country Real Estate Bd. (dir. and past pres.), Nat. Real Estate Bd. Democrat. Mem. Friends Meeting. Masop (32°), Odd Fellow, Moose. Clubs: Doylestown Rotary (past pres.); Doylestown Country. Home: Pineville, Pa. Office: 30 S. Main St., Doylestown, Pa.

MOMENT, Gairdner Bostwick, coll. prof.; b. New York, N.Y., May 4, 1905; s. Alfred Gairdner and Laura (Bostwick) M.; A.B., Princeton U., 1928; Ph.D., Yale U., 1932; m. Ann Faben, June 26, 1937; 1 son, Charles Gairdner. Instr. biology, Goucher Coll., 1932-36, asst. prof., 1936-38, chmn. dept. since 1938. Mem. corpn. Mt. Desert Island Biol. Lab., Bar Harbor, Me. Mem. A.A.A.S., Am. Soc. Zoologists, Am. Assn. Univ. Profs., Phi Beta Kappa,

Sigma Xi. Conglist. Author numerous papers on biological subjects. Home: 2316 N. Calvert St., Baltimore, Md.

MOMENT, John James, clergyman; b. Orono, Ont., Can., Feb. 1, 1875; s. Robert and Sarah Wightman (Gairdner) M.; A.B., Princeton, 1896; B.D., Hartford Theol. Sem., 1906; D.D., Washington and Jefferson Coll., 1925; m. Clara Louise Cross, May 21, 1908; children—Anne, Jean Gairdner, Robert, John. Ordained Presbyn. ministry, 1906; asst. pastor First Ch., East Orange, N.J., 1906-08; asso. pastor Bergen Ref. Ch., Jersey City, N.J.; later pastor High Street Presbyn. Ch., Newark, N.J., until 1918, Crescent Avenue Ch., Plainfield, N.J., since 1918. Mem. A.A.A.S., Phi Beta Kappa. Republican. Author: Faith in Christ, 1917; The Throne of David, 1929. Home: 815 Park Av., Plainfield, N.J.

MONAGHAN, James, lawyer; b. nr. St. Louis, Mo., Sept. 21, 1854; s. J. J. and Rebecca (Murdagh) M.; descended from first settlers of Germantown, Pa., also by tradition from Oliver Cromwell; C.E., Lafayette Coll., Pa. 1876; m. Anna Jackson, June 7, 1882; children—Florence Jackson (Mrs. Herbert S. Thatcher), Gertrude, Hanna, Darlington, James. Admitted to Pa. bar, 1878; apptd. Supreme Court reporter by Gov. Pattison, 1892; asso. librarian Pa. Supreme Court, 1921. Charter mem. Pa. State Bar Assn., Chester Co. Hist. Society; vice-pres. Phila. Ethical Society; former member Am. Acad. Political and Social Science, Phila. Browning Soc., Friends of Lafayette. Editor: Chester County Reports, 2 vols.; Monaghan's Supreme Court Reports, 2 vols.; Pa. Supreme Court Reports, 19 volumes; Appellate Practice, 1 volume; Cumulative Ann. Digest of Pennsylvania Law Reports (25 vols. combined in 7 vols.), 1899-1937. First editor Pa. County Court Reports and Pa. District Reports. Author of monographs: Lafayette at Brandywine; Falstaff's Forbears; Bayard Taylor, Poet and Patriot. Home: 3309 Baring St.; (summer) Nantucket, Mass. Office: City Hall, Philadelphia, Pa.

MONAHAN, Lawrance P., lawyer; b. Westmoreland Co., Pa., July 2, 1876; s. Daniel and Gertrude (Brandt) M.; ed. Fordham U. and U. of Pittsburgh Law Sch.; m. Nellie Wurtz Feb. 22, 1906. Admitted to Pa. bar, 1900, and since engaged in gen. practice of law at Pittsburgh; dir.: Peoples-Pittsburgh Trust Co., Cochran Coal and Coke Co., Pittsburgh Brewing Co. Mem. St. Paul's Cathedral. Clubs: Pittsburgh Athletic, Butler Country. Home: Gibsonia. Office: 1808 Union Bank Bldg., Pittsburgh, Pa.

MONES, Leon, prin. high sch.; b. New York, N.Y., Dec. 8, 1894; s. Woolf and Lena (Elswit) M.; A.B., Coll. City of N.Y., 1915; grad. study, N.Y. Univ. Grad. Sch., 1915-19; D. Religious Edn., Oskaloosa U. in Absentia, 1919; A.M., N.Y. Univ. Sch. Edn., 1932; m. Dorothy Beckelman, Aug. 21, 1921; children—Janet, Walter. Engaged in teaching, high schs., 1915-16; editor, Jewish Voice, 1919-21; dir. Social Center, Temple B'nai Abraham, 1921-23; dean N.J. Coll. of Jewish Studies, 1926-38; chmn. dept. of English, Central High Sch., Newark, 1933-36; prin. Cleveland Jr. High Sch., Newark, since 1937; pres. Zenith Bldg. & Loan Assn. Mem. Phi Delta Kappa. Jewish religion. Author: Why Be Afraid, 1931; Americans in Action (with Max J. Herzberg), 1937. Contbr. articles to ednl. jours. Home: 196 Lehigh Av. Office: 392 Bergen St., Newark, N.J.

MONG, George Luther Walker, engring.; b. Somerset, Pa., May 2, 1902; s. George Luther and Lulu Jeanette (Walker) M.; B.S. in C.E., N.C. State Coll., 1922; m. Agnes Brennan, Dec. 28, 1927; 1 dau., Natalie. Employed as draftsman and engr., E. H. Walker, registered architect, 1922-27; mem. firm Walker & Mong, registered architects, Somerset, Pa., 1927-33 and 1936-37; connected with Civil Works Adminstrn. and Works Progress Adminstrn., 1933-35; resident engr. General State Authority, Mansfield and Harrisburg, Pa., since 1937; dir. Walker Granite Co. Mem. Tau Beta Pi. Republican. Lutheran. Mason, Eagle. Club:

Somerset Country. Home: W. Fairview St., Somerset, Pa. Office: Old Y.M.C.A. Bldg., Harrisburg, Pa.

MONKS, Frederick Coston, M.D., pres. Kittanning Telephone Co.; b. Curlsville, Pa., May 31, 1860; s. Capt. Thomas B. and Emily F. (Rohrer) M.; student Allegheny Coll., Meadville, Pa., 1879-83; M.D., Univ. Med. Coll., Kansas City, Mo., 1891; m. Mabel A. Allison, May 8, 1900 (died 1937); children—Margaret, Emily, Virginia. In gen. practice medicine, Kittanning, Pa., since 1891; pres. Kittanning (Pa.) Telephone Co. since 1936. Pres. Kittanning Bd. of Health, 1930; sch. insp. Pa. Health Bur., 1900-39; sch. dir. Kittanning, 1917-37. Mem. Armstrong Co. Med. Soc. (pres. 1895). Republican. Methodist (trustee 1st M.E. Ch., Kittanning, since 1900). Mason (past master, past high priest). Home: 164 S. Water St. Office: Kittanning, Pa.

MONRAD, Carl Corydon, univ. prof.; b. Buffalo, N.Y., Jan. 15, 1905; s. Charles Olaf and Wilhelmina (Lagergren) M.; B.S.E., U. of Mich., Ann Arbor, Mich., 1927, M.S.E., 1928, Ph.D., 1930; m. Christine Clark, Sept. 27, 1930; 1 dau., Margaret Eleanor. Chem. engr., Standard Oil Co., Whiting, Ind., 1930-37; asso. prof. chemical engring., Carnegie Inst. Tech., Pittsburgh, since 1937. Mem. Am. Chem. Soc., Am. Inst. of Chem. Engrs., Sigma Xi, Alpha Chi Sigma, Phi Lambda Upsilon. Republican. Congregationalist. Home: 834 Florida Av., Mt Lebanon, Pa. Office: Carnegie Inst. Tech., Pittsburgh, Pa.

MONRO, Charles Bedell, pres. Pa.-Centra. Airlines Corpn.; b. Pittsburgh, Pa., Feb. 26, 1901; s. William L. and Violet K. (Bedell) M.; student Phillips Exeter Acad., Exeter, N.H., 1916-19; A.B., Harvard, 1923; M.A., U. of Pa., 1926; m. Marjory Boyd Hill, June 3, 1926. Instr. U. of Pittsburgh, 1924-29; sec. Pittsburgh Aviation Industries Corpn., 1928-30, dir., 1930, v.p. and sec., 1931-32, exec. v.p. and sec., 1933-34; sec.-treas., Pa. Airlines, Inc., 1930-31, dir., 1930, v.p. and sec., 1931-32, exec. v.p. and sec., 1933-34; exec. v.p. and dir. Pa. Airlines & Transport Co., 1934; pres., 1934-36; pres. and dir. Pa.-Central Airlines Corpn., Pittsburgh, Pa., since 1936. Mem. Community Fund Com. since 1938. Episcopalian. Clubs: Harvard of Western Pa. (Pittsburgh); Oakmont Country (Oakmont, Pa.). Co-author: Quest of the Moon Fish, 1925. Home: 224 S. Homewood Av. Office: Allegheny County Airport, Pittsburgh, Pa.

MONRO, Hugh Reginald, mfr., banker; b. Orangeville, Ont., Can., June 18, 1871; s. Fisher and Agnes (Crawford) M.; ed. pub. schs.; LL.D., Cumberland U., 1932; m. Florence Bean, Apr. 27, 1893; children—Hugh R., Dorothy Adelle (Mrs. Wm. L. Dill, Jr.). Organized Kaumagraph Co., 1903, pres. and chmn. bd., 1903-23; pres. Montclair (N.J.) Nat. Bank, 1928-36; pres. Pennman Realty Corpn., Montclair Printing Co.; vice-pres. Niagara Lithograph Co.; dir. Guardian Life Ins. Co. of America, Montclair Trust Co.; v.p. and dir. Watchung Title and Mortgage Guaranty Co.; mem. Nat. Service Commn., 1917-18, Montclair Sinking Fund Commn. 1926-29; chmn. Town Planning Bd. (Montclair), 1930-33. Pres. Stony Brook Sclf., Stony Brook Assembly; treas. John Milton Foundation; dir. New York Christian Home, Presbyn. Pub. Co. Mem. Acad. Polit. Science; The Pilgrims of the United States, The Monro Clan (Scotland), World's S.S. Assn. (chmn. N. Am. sect. and bus. com.), Am. Tract Soc. (pres.), Internat. Assn. Daily Vacation Bible Schs. (dir.), Pocket Testament League (pres.), Bd. of Ch. Erection Presbyn. Ch. U.S.A. Presbyn. Ministers Fund, (corporator) Chamber of Commerce State of New York. Presbyterian (elder First Presbyn. Ch., Orange, N.J.). Club: Nat. Republican. Home: 60 Lloyd Rd., Montclair. Office: 129 Grove St., Montclair, N.J.; 386 4th Av., New York, N.Y.

MONRO, William Loftus, glass mfr.; b. Pittsburgh, Pa., Oct. 20, 1866; s. George Nugent and Sarah Ann (Morgan) M.; A.B., Harvard, 1889; m. Violet Kennedy Bedell, Sept. 27,

1892; children—William Loftus, Charles Bedell, George Nugent III. Admitted to bar, 1891, practicing until 1906; pres. Pittsburgh Window Glass Co., Washington, Pa., 1903-06; became gen. mgr. Am. Window Glass Co., Pittsburgh, 1906, pres. since 1919; pres. and dir., Am. Photo Glass & Export Co., Western Pa. Natural Gas Co., also officer or dir. many other companies. Mem. bd. of govs. Children's Hosp. of Pittsburgh. Pres. Am. Tariff League, Window Glass Mfrs. Assn. Mem. Allegheny Co. Bar Assn. Republican. Episcopalian. Mason., (K. T., shriner). Clubs: Duquesne, Pittsburgh Athletic, University, Longue Vue; Oakmont Country; Harvard Club of Western Pa. Home: 5840 Wilkins Av. Office: Farmers Bank Bldg., Pittsburgh, Pa.*

MONROE, Andrew Perrine, v.p. N.J. Bell Telephone Co.; b. Phila., Pa., April 27, 1890; s. William F. and Mary Elizabeth (Perrine) M.; A.B., Princeton U., 1911; m. Elizabeth R. McCreery, April 2, 1921; 1 son, Andrew Perrine, Jr. Served successively as traffic inspr., asst. traffic supervisor, dist. traffic supt., Bell Telephone Co. of Pa., 1911-20; dist. traffic mgr. to gen. traffic supervisor Bronx-Westchester, New York Telephone Co., 1920-28; gen. traffic mgr. N.J. Bell Telephone Company, 1928-36, vice-pres., personnel and pub. relations since 1936. Served as 2d lt. to capt. Signal Corps, U.S.A., 1917-19, with A.E.F. in France. Vice-pres. and chmn. finance com., N.J. State Chamber of Commerce. Dir. N.J. Taxpayers' Assn. Dir. Newark Y.M.C.A. Mem. Cap and Gown Club, Princeton. Republican. Episcopalian. Clubs: Short Hills (Short Hills); Essex (Newark); Baltusrol Golf; Newark Athletic. Home: Taylor Rd., Short Hills. Office: 540 Broad St., Newark, N.J.

MONROE, George Karl, clergyman; b. Butler, Pa., Jan. 15, 1893; s. John Noble and Dorathea M. (Pfaff) M.; A.B., Grove City Coll., 1921; S.T.B., Western Theol. Sem., Pittsburgh, Pa., 1924, S.T.M., same, 1925; m. Helen J. Hartt, Aug. 3, 1921; children—Elizabeth Annette, George Karl. Employed in woolen mill, Craigsville, Pa., 1907-10, r.r. clk., Butler, Pa., 1910-15; ordained to ministry Presbyn. Ch. U.S.A., 1924; pastor, Tarentum, Pa., 1922-27, West Alexander, Pa., 1927-39, pastor First Presbyn. Ch., Clairton, Pa., since April 1, 1939; served as stated clk. Presbytery of Washington, 1934-39; on Permanent Judicial Commn., Synod of Pa., term, 1935-41, clk. of this commn. Served with Engrs. Corps, U.S.A., 1917-19, with A.E. F. Mem. Pi Kappa Delta, Epsilon Pi. Republican. Presbyn. Mason. Home: 511 Mitchell Av., Clairton, Pa.

MONROE, Verne, pres. The Cameron Tool & Supply Co.; b. Bolivar, N.Y., Feb. 18, 1873; s. Lewis Stillman and Isabel (Logue) M.; student country sch., nr. Bolivar, N.Y., 1878-87; m. Laura Etta Turner, Dec. 24, 1893; children —Mary Esther, Alta Isabel, Verna Mabel (wife of Dr. R. Grant Culley), Pauline Virginia (wife of Dr. Clarence E. Keefer), Edwin Turner. Began as apprentice toolmaker in father's shop, 1887; now pres. The Cameron (W.Va.) Tool & Supply Co., mfrs. and dealers in drilling tools and oil well supplies. Chmn. bd. trustees Cameron (W.Va.) Methodist Ch. Republican. Methodist. Mason. Clubs: Masonic (Cameron, W. Va.); Masonic (Wheeling, W.Va.). Address: Cameron, W.Va.

MONTAGUE, Margaret Prescott, author; b. White Sulphur Springs, W.Va., Nov. 29, 1878; d. Russell W. and Harriet A. (Cary) M.; ed. at home and in pvt. schs. Author: The Poet, Miss Kate and I, 1905; The Sowing of Alderson Cree, 1907; In Calverts Valley, 1908; Linda, 1912; Closed Doors, 1915; Home to Hines Muover, 1916; Of Water and the Spirit, 1916; Twenty Minutes of Reality, 1916; The Great Expectancy, 1918; The Gift, 1919; England to America (O. Henry prize), 1920; Uncle Sam of Freedom Ridge, 1920; Deep Channel, 1923; The Man From God's Country, 1923; Leaves From a Secret Journal, 1926; Up Eel River, 1928; The Lucky Lady, 1934. Address: White Sulphur Springs, W.Va.

MONTANYE Edwin Y(erkes) prin. high sch.; b. Phila. Pa. Aug. 23 1874; s. Nathan T. and Elizabeth (Altemus) M.; desc. Dr. Jean de la Montagne came to New Amsterdam, 1637, and Benjamin Montanye, aide to Gen. Washington; ed. Central High Sch., Phila., 1890-94, Sch. of Pedagogy, Phila., 1894-95; B.S. in Edn., U. of Pa., 1915; A.M. in sociology, same, 1918; m. Matilda Rowland, Nov. 26, 1902. Prin. elementary sch., Phila., 1895-1906, prin. Northwest Grammar Sch., 1906-14, Blaine Pub. Sch., 1914-21, Ferguson Pub. Sch., 1921-24, Harding Jr. High Sch., 1924-27, Roxborough High Sch., 1927-30; prin. Olney High Sch. since 1930. Served as Co. Mgr. of Farm Labor for Phila. Co., a Federal Govt. assignment, during 1917-18. Trustee Lower Dublin Acad., Phila. Mem. Nat. Edn. Assn., Nat. Assn. Secondary Sch. Princs., Am. Acad. Polit. and Social Sci., Phila. Teachers Assn., Artisans Order of Mutual Protection. Baptist. I.O.O.F. Clubs: Schoolmens, Philadelphia Principals. Home: 8018 Crispin St., Philadelphia, Pa.

MONTEVERDE, Louis William, real estate brokerage; b. Pittsburgh, Pa., Dec. 15, 1885; s. Peter Paul and Rose Mary (Cooney) M.; ed. Sts. Peter and Paul's Acad., 1891-98, Peabody Sch., 1898-1900; m. Mary Ella Cotton, Nov. 30, 1911; children—John Paul, Mary Beatrice. Asso. with Real Estate Co. of Pittsburgh continuously since entering their employ in 1900, pres. since 1938; dir. Isaly Dairy Co., Real Estate Improvement Co. of Pittsburgh, Real Estate Co. of Pittsburgh. Dir. Regional Plan Assn. Served as asst. mgr. Real Estate Div., Housing Corpn. of U.S., during World War. Past chmn. City Planning Commn., City Transit Commn. Pres. Real Estate Bd. of Pittsburgh, 1923, now dir. and mem. advisory bd.; pres., 1935, now dir. and mem. advisory bd. Pa. Assn. Real Estate Bds. Republican. Catholic. Home: 7000 Edgerton Av. Office: 427 4th Av., Pittsburgh, Pa.

MONTGOMERY, Edward Gerrard, agricultural specialist; b. Milan, Mo., May 10, 1878; s. Richard Shadow and Elizabeth (Mooney) M.; B.S., U. of Neb., 1906, M.A., 1909; m. Ruth Bell, June 18, 1908; 1 daughter, Nancy C. Prof. agronomy, U. of Neb., 1906-11; prof. farm crops, Cornell U., 1912-20; chief of foreign marketing, U.S. Dept. Agr., 1920-21; chief of food stuffs div., U.S. Dept. Commerce, 1921-34; exec. sec. Canning Code, 1935; research work on agrl. economics, Nat. Industries Conf. Bd. and Brookings Instn., 1936-37; research Commodity Exchange Adminstrn., U.S. Dept. Agr., since 1937. Mem. Alpha Zeta, Sigma Xi. Unitarian. Club: Cosmos. Author: Examining and Grading Grains (with T. L. Lyon), 1908; The Corn Crops, 1912; Productive Farm Crops, 1914; also numerous bulls. and mag. articles. Home: 24 W. Kirke St., Chevy Chase, Md.

MONTGOMERY, Frank Stanley, clergyman; b. New Vernon, Pa., Oct. 28, 1881; s. Samuel Griffith and Callie Belle (Uber) M.; Ph.B., Grove City Coll., 1907; S.T.B., Western Theol. Sem., 1910; m. Nettie Elloid Flair, June 29, 1910; 1 dau., Navada Grace. Ordained to ministry Presbyn. Ch., 1910; pastor, Scio, O., 1910-13, Canton, O., 1913-16, Derry, Pa., 1916-18, Clarion, Pa., 1918-24, Charleroi, Pa., since 1924. Moderator Presbytery of Clarion, 1925-26; moderator Presbytery of Pittsburgh, 1933-34; chmn. Vacancy and Supply Com. of Clarion Presbytery, 1922-23; chmn. same com. in Presbytery of Pittsburgh, 1934-36; pres. Charleroi, Ministerial Assn. Republican. Presbyn. Mason. Rotarian. I.O.O.F. Charleroi, Pa. Home: Charleroi, Pa.

MONTGOMERY, Howard D(eane), lawyer; b. Marshall Co., W.Va., July 3, 1872; s. Joseph B. and Elizabeth A. (Caswell) M.; Ph.B., O. State U., 1896; LL.B., Western U. of Pa., now U. of Pittsburgh, 1899; m. Elizabeth W. Stevenson, Apr. 21, 1908 (died Jan. 23, 1937); 1 dau., Martha (Mrs. William T. McCullough, Jr.). Admitted to Pa. bar, 1899, and since continuously engaged in practice of law at Pittsburgh, specializing in business, corpn. and decedents' estates law; admitted to practice before all the cts. of Pa., the Federal cts. and cts. of many other states. Mem. Allegheny County Bar Assn. Republican. Presbyterian. Home: King Edward Apts. Office: 1505 Law and Finance Bldg., Pittsburgh, Pa.

MONTGOMERY, James Alan, clergyman; b. Germantown, Phila., June 13, 1866; s. Thomas Harrison and Anna (Morton) M.; A.B., U. of Pa., 1887, Ph.D., 1904, S.T.D., 1908; grad. Phila. Div. Sch., 1890; univs. of Greifswald and Berlin; Grad. Sch., U. of Pa., 1904; m. Mary Frank Owen, Aug. 1, 1893 (died 1900); m. 2d, Edith Thompson, of Germantown, Phila., June 17, 1902; children—James Alan, Newcomb T., George M. Deacon, 1890, priest, 1893, P.E. Ch.; curate Ch. of Holy Communion, New York, 1892-93; rector St. Paul's, W. Phila., 1893-95, St. Peter's Phila., 1895-99. Ephiphany, Germantown, 1899-1903; asst. editor Church Standard, 1897-99; instr. and prof. O.T., Phila. Div. Sch., 1899-1935; lect. and prof. Hebrew, Grad. Sch., U. of Pa., 1909—. Dir. Am. Sch. of Oriental Research in Jerusalem, 1914-15; pres. Am. Schs. of Oriental Research, 1921-33. Editor Jour. Bibl. Lit., 1910-14; editor Jour. Am. Oriental Soc., 1916-22. Mem. Soc. Bibl. Lit. and Exegesis, Am. Oriental Soc., Archæol. Inst. America, Am. Philos. Soc., Phila. Oriental Club, Zeta Psi, Phi Beta Kappa. Author: The Samaritans, the Earliest Jewish Sect, 1907; Aramaic Incantation Texts from Nippur, 1913; Religions of the Past and Present; Commentary on Daniel, 1927; History of Yaballha III, 1927; Arabia and the Bible, 1934; Hebraic Mythological Texts from Ras Shamra, 1935. Contbr. to theol. and Oriental jours. Home: 6806 Greene St., Germantown, Philadelphia, Pa.

MONTGOMERY, James Stuart, advertising; b. Rome, Ga., Apr. 12, 1890; s. John and Frances Clyde (Stafford) M.; ed. U. of Ga., 1907-09; B.S., U. of Pa., 1911; m. Mildred Schwab, July 15, 1926. Began as clk. with Curtis Pub. Co., Phila. 1911; engaged in advertising, writing for well-known advertising agencies at Phila. Served as capt. Inf. U.S.A., 1917-19, with A.E.F. in France; wounded nr. Montfaucon. Honored by award Purple Heart (U.S.). Mem. Chi Psi. Democrat. Author: (verse) Songs for Men, 1923; (novel) Tall Men, 1927; The Virtue of this Jest, 1929. Home: 1417 Spruce St. Office: Girard Trust Bldg., Philadelphia, Pa.

MONTGOMERY, Julian Earl, v.p. and dir. Wheeling Steel Corpn.; officer or dir. many companies. Address: Wheeling Steel Corpn., Wheeling, W.Va.

MONTGOMERY, Thaddeus Lemert, physician; b. Macon, Ill., May 24, 1896; s. John A. and Addie (Lewis) M.; A.B., U. of Ill., 1916; M.D., Jefferson Med. Coll., 1920; m. Pauline Woods, Sept. 12, 1922; children—Thaddeus Lemert, Jr., John Thomas, Richard Woods. Interne Jefferson Hosp., Phila., 1920-22; in practice of medicine at Phila. since 1922; clin. prof. obstetrics, Jefferson Med. Coll. since 1937. Fellow Am. Coll. Surgeons; mem. Am. Assn. of Obstetricians and Gynecologists, Am. Gynecol. Assn., Alpha Omega Alpha, Zeta Psi. Clubs: Cynwyd (Bala). Home: 30 Bala Av., Bala-Cynwyd, Pa. Office: 2031 Locust St., Phila., Pa.

MONTGOMERY, Walter Curry, lawyer; b. Waynesburg, Pa., Sept. 5, 1879; s. Thomas Hoge and Virginia (Gordon) M.; A.B., Waynesburg (Pa.) Coll., 1903; LL.B., U. of Pa., 1906; m. Grace Fordyce Sayers, June 25, 1908; children—Virginia G., Thomas F., Walter Curry, Hugh G. Admitted to bar, 1906 and since practiced at Waynesburg, Pa.; dir. First Nat. Bank, Carmichaels, Pa., Riverside Coal Co., The Mile Coal Co., Hamilton Supply Co., Shoreline Oil and Gas Co. Enlisted in 10th Inf., Pa. N.G., 1901, advancing to capt., 1911; served in A.E.F., 1917-19; commanded orgn. under Federal Service, during Mexican Border duty, 1916. Mem. Waynesburg Bd. of Edn., 1924-30; dir. Waynesburg Chamber of Commerce, formerly pres.; acting pres. of bd., v.p. and trustee Waynesburg Coll. Mem. Green Co., Pa. and Am. bar assns. Mason (32°; Past Master, Waynesburg Lodge 153; Shriner, Elk (Waynesburg Lodge 757, Past Exalted Ruler), K.P. (Past Chancellor Comdr.). Club: Green County Country (Waynesburg, Pa.). Home: 56 S. Cumberland St. Office: Commercial Bldg., Waynesburg, Pa.

MONTGOMERY, Walter Leslie, real estate broker; b. Harrisburg, Pa., Jan. 22, 1872; s. James Buchanan and Emma Lynn (Buchecker) M.; ed. pub. schs.; m. Enneta Gross, Oct. 18, 1910 (dec.); m. 2d, Sara Beckley, June 12, 1923. Engaged in real estate business, Harrisburg, since 1902; pres. Harrisburg Coal Exchange, 1913-31. Registered real estate broker. Dir. Harrisburg Reserves, 1918; chmn. joint U.S. fuel adminstrn. com. and Dauphin Co. Coal Assn., 1918. Trustee Harrisburg Bd. of Trade, 1911-13. Organizer and charter mem. Chamber of Commerce, 1914; mem. Pa. Retail Coal Merchants Assn. (v.p. 1916, pres. 1919-23), Harrisburg Mummers Assn. (pres. 1917), Chestnut St. Merchants Assn. (pres. 1921), Nat. Coal Assn. (v.p. 1922), Harrisburgh Real Estate Bd., Dauphin Hist. Soc. (life), Friendship Fire Co. (life), Nat. Geog. Soc., Municipal League, Humane Soc. of Harrisburg, Y. M.C.A., Central Pa. Fish and Game Conservation Assn., S.A.R., Am. Legion. Presbyterian. Elk (life mem.), Odd Fellow (past grand, Lodge 160). Clubs: Kiwanis (charter), Harrisburg (sec. 1926), Harrisburg City, Harrisburg Country (Harrisburg). Home: 700 N. Third St. Office: North West Corner Third and Chestnut Sts., Harrisburg, Pa.

MOODIE, William C(armichael), manufacturer; b. Glasgow, Scotland; s. Peter and Christina (McLachlan) M.; came to U.S., 1901; B.S. in mech. engring., Tufts Coll., Mass., 1918; special courses New York U., Columbia and Rutgers U.; m. Ethel Barba, Sept. 9, 1922; children—William C., Isabelle O., Donald M. Machine designer with various companies New England and New York, 1919-26; design and management work, same, 1926-38; treas. and gen. mgr. Calculagraph Co., makers of time recorders, instruments, office equipment, New York, since 1928. Mem. Am. Soc. Mech. Engrs. (chmn. small plant management com.), Delta Upsilon. Home: 30 Stephen St., Montclair, N.J. Office: 50 Church St., New York, N.Y.

MOODY, Lewis Ferry, hydraulic engr.; b. Phila., Pa., Jan. 5, 1880; s. Carlton Montague and Elizabeth Eddy (Lewis) Moody; B.S., Towne Scientific School (University of Pennsylvania), 1901, M.S., 1902; m. Eleanor Carman Greene, June 22, 1909 (died 1937); children—Mary Elizabeth (deceased), Lewis Ferry, Arthur Maurice Greene, Eleanor Lowry. Instr. mech. engring., U. of Pa., 1902-04; engring. staff hydraulic dept. of I. P. Morris Co., Phila., 1904-08; asst. prof. mech. engring., later prof. hydraulic engring., Rensselaer Poly. Inst., 1908-16, also independent practice; consulting engr. I. P. Morris Co. (now Baldwin-Southwark Corpn.), since 1911; also consulting engr. Worthington Pump & Machinery Corpn.; prof. hydraulic engring., Princeton. Fellow A.A.A.S.; mem. Am. Society Mech. Engrs. (past chmn. Phila. sect.; past. chmn. exec. com. hydraulic div.), Franklin Inst., Soc. for Promotion Engring. Edn., Sigma Xi, Tau Beta Pi. Republican. Swedenborgian. Clubs: Nassau (Princeton); Princeton (New York City). Inventor numerous improvements in hydraulic turbines, pumps and accessories; has been awarded many patents for inventions, including spiral draft tube, Moody spreading draft tube, Moody spiral pump, new high speed turbine, etc. Author of various tech. papers read before engring. socs. and articles in tech. periodicals. Home: 146 Hodge Rd., Princeton, N.J.

MOOK, Charles Craig, geologist, univ. prof.; b. Metuchen, N.J., May 7, 1887; s. Charles Oscar and Gertrude Louisa (Martin) M.; student Metuchen (N.J.) Pub. Sch., 1894-1902, Rutgers Prep. Sch., New Brunswick, N.J., 1902-04; B.S., M.A. and Ph.D., Columbia U.; m. Ruth Weir Reader, Sept. 2, 1914; children—Gertrude Elizabeth, Ruth Weir, Caryl Craig. Became research asst. Am. Museum Natural Hist., New York, 1912, lecturer and research asso. since 1938; lecturer and instr. geology, Barnard Coll., New York, 1915-22; extension lecturer Columbia U., since 1922; acting prof. Rutgers U., New Brunswick, N.J., 1922-23; asst. prof., Hunter Coll., New York, 1926-27; became asst. prof. New York Univ., 1927, later asso. prof.; became asst. prof. Brooklyn Coll., New York, 1931, now prof. Fellow A.A.A.S., N.Y. Acad. Science, Geol. Soc. America; mem. Phi Beta Kappa, Sigma Xi. Dutch Reformed Ch. Home: 231 Chestnut Av., Metuchen, N.J.

MOOK, Harold F., lawyer; b. Saegertown, Pa., June 26, 1894; s. Wallace and Julia A. (Floyd) M.; grad. Saegertown High Sch., 1911; A.B., Allegheny Coll., 1915; LL.B., U. of Pa., 1921; m. Mildred M. McCombs, July 3, 1925; children—Nancy, Robert Matthew. Admitted to Pa. bar, 1921, and since in gen. practice at Erie; county solicitor, Erie Co., 1929-32. Served in Air Service, U.S. Army, 1917-19, disch. as 2d lt. Reserve, military aviator; now capt. Air Corps, Reserve. Mem. Erie Co. Bar Assn., Pa. Bar Assn., Am. Legion. Republican. Mason, Moose. Home: 1029 W. 10th St. Office: Marine Bank Bldg., Erie, Pa.

MOON, Seymour Boston, physician; b. Mercer, Pa., Aug. 8, 1868; s. Adam Boston and Catherine Jane (Smith) M.; M.D. Chicago Homeo. Med. Coll., 1900; O. at A. Chir., N.Y. Ophthalmic Hosp., 1909; grad. study Lariboisere Hosp., Paris, France, 1923; m. Carolyn Alford, Dec. 27, 1903 (died June 4, 1917); 1 dau., Helen Blakeslee (Mrs. Hugh Schuyler Robertson). Engaged in practice of medicine at Beaver Falls, Pa., 1901-1917, and at Pittsburgh since 1909, specializing in ophthalmology since 1909; mem. staff, Beaver Valley Hosp., 1902-07, Pittsburgh Homeopathic Hosp. since 1909. Mem. Am. Acad. Ophthalmology, Am. Med. Assn., Pa. State and Allegheny Co. med. socs., Am. Inst. of Homoeopathy. Presbyn. Mason. Home: R.F.D. No. 2, Coraopolis, Pa. Office: 200 9th St., Pittsburgh, Pa.

MOON, Virgil Holland, prof. of pathology; b. Craig, Ind., July 31, 1879; s. Wm. L. and Lida A. (Stanley) M.; ed. Kan. State Teachers Coll., 1903-07; A.B., Kan. U., 1910, M.Sc., same, 1911; M.D., Rush Med. Sch., Chicago, 1913; m. Jane Thomas, Sept. 7, 1908 (dec.); 1 dau., Gladys W. (Mrs. Harold C. Colburn); m. 2d, Beryl Kelly, Dec. 20, 1916. Employed as research pathologist, 1913; prof. of pathology and bacteriology, Indiana University Sch. of Medicine, 1914-27; prof. of pathology, Jefferson Med. Coll. since 1927, dir. of labs., Jefferson Hosp. since 1927; chief visiting pathologist, Phila. Gen. Hosp. since 1927. Mem. A.A.A.S., Am. Soc. Pathology and Bacteriology, Am. Soc. Exptl. Pathology, Am. Medico-Legal Assn., Internat. Soc. Geog. Pathology, College of Physicians of Philadelphia, American Medical Society, Sigma Xi, Alpha Omega Alpha and Phi Chi frats. Clubs: University (Philadelphia); St. Davids Golf (Wayne). Author: (monograph) Shock and Related Capillary Phenomena, 1938. Contbr. research articles to med. jours. Home: 838 Morton Rd., Bryn Mawr, Pa.

MOONEY, James Elliott, coll, pres., editor, author; b. Danville, N.Y., July 30, 1901; s. Edward S. and Ellen Jane (Massey) M.; student N.Y. State Teachers Coll., 1920-22; by recommendation of Pa. Supt. Pub. Instn., received equivalent of B.S., Duquesne U.; Ed.D., Duquesne U., 1933; L.H.D., Beaver Coll., 1938; m. Mildred Charlotte Montgomery, Aug. 8, 1932; children—Ellen Mildred, James Elliott, Richard Edward, Stewart Walter. Prin. Junior High Sch., Pen Yan, N.Y., 1922-24; dir. authorship research and articles Nat. Rep. Com. on Tariff and Immigration, 1924-26; dir. English research pub. schs., Ridgefield Park, N.J., 1927; mem. ednl. and editorial depts. Chas. Scribner's Sons, 1927-38; v.p. Beaver Coll., 1938, pres. since 1939; editor and publisher Youth's Digest since 1938; pres. Youth's Digest Assn. Editor: Courage. Founder and pres. Beaver Foundation for Advancement of Edn. Formerly advisor Nat. Aeronaut. Assn., Air League of British Empire; chmn. program com. Am. Assn. Sch. Adminstrs., 1938; now adviser Am. Acad. of Air Laws, New York U., Air Youth of America (coms. headed by Winthrop Rockefeller), H. C. Frick Ednl. Commn., Pittsburgh; dir. Religious Program Am. Youth Foundation, St. Louis. Mem. Nat. Aeronaut. Assn., N.E.A., Pi Gamma Mu., Aero Club of Pittsburgh, etc. Hon. mem. Am. Legion. Received Am. Polar Explorers award, 1938 (presented by Adm. R. E. Byrd). Republican. Mason. Clubs: Manufacturers & Bankers, Social Union, Rotary (Phila.). Author: Air Travel, 1930; In a World of Travel, 1932; Wings Away, 1937; Up Ship Adventurers, 1937; Airplanes Serve the World, 1937; Pennsylvania, A Great State (chronology), 1936; Heroes of the Air (poetry prose); also social science articles. Author of program and consultant for large school systems (including City of N.Y. upon invitation from them and recommendation of New York Times) in aeronautical education, 1928-38; delivered many lectures and papers on subject. Home: Pine Rd., Five Points, Pa. Address: Beaver College, Jenkintown, Pa.

MOONEY, Melvin, physicist; b. Kansas City, Mo., July 1, 1893; s. Lee K. and Belle (Stull) M.; student Central High Sch., Kansas City, Mo., 1908-13; A.B., U. of Mo., Columbia, Mo., 1917; Ph.D., U. of Chicago, 1923; m. Loretta Funke, Oct. 7, 1923; 1 dau., Dorothy Ruth. Began as newspaper carrier, Kansas City, Mo., 1905; asst. chemist Morris Packing Co., Kansas City, Kan., 1920-23; physicist F. E. Simpson Radium Inst., Chicago, 1920-23, Western Electric Co., Cicero, Ill., 1923-24, 1927-28; nat. research fellow in physics, U. of Chicago, 1924-27; physicist U. S. Rubber Co., Passaic, N.J., since 1928. Served as pvt., Chem. Warfare Service, U.S. Army, 1918-19. Mem. American Physical Society, Society of Rheology (pres. since 1936), New York Acad. of Science, Sigma Xi, Phi Beta Kappa. Home: 102 Iroquois Av., Lake Hiawatha, N.J. Office: U. S. Rubber Co., Passaic, N.J.

MOONEY, William Roberts, pres. Bryn Mawr Trust Co.; b. Eddington, Bicks Co., Pa., Jan. 14, 1884; s. John H. and Julia B. (Roberts) M.; student pub. schs.; m. Elsie Adele Raith, Oct. 6, 1909. Began as junior clk. Commercial Trust Co.; gen. mgr. Cassatt & Co., investment bankers, Phila.; v.p. Bryn Mawr (Pa.) Trust Co., 1934-35, pres. since 1935; dir. Diligent Bldg. and Loan Assn. of Phila., Rosemont Bldg. and Loan Assn. Pres. Bryn Mawr War Memorial and Community House Assn.; trustee Bryn Mawr Fire Co. Presbyterian (trustee Bryn Mawr Presbyn. Ch.). Clubs: Union League (Phila.); Merion Cricket (Haverford, Pa.). Office: Lancaster Rd., Rosemont, Pa. Office: Lancaster and Bryn Mawr Avs., Bryn Mawr, Pa.

MOORE, Arthur Harry, governor; b. Jersey City, N.J., July 3, 1879; s. Robert White and Martha (McCoomb) M.; ed. Cooper Union and under pvt. tutors; LL.B., New Jersey Law Sch., 1924, LL.D., 1934; LL.D., Rutgers, 1927, Seton Hall Coll., 1928; M.A., Hahnemann Med. Coll., 1928; M.C.S., Rider College, Trenton, N.J., 1928; LL.D., John Marshall Coll. of Law, 1934, Princeton, 1938; m. Jennie Hastings Stevens, March 1911. Began law practice at Jersey City, 1920; sec. to mayor of Jersey City, 1908-11; city collector, 1911-13; commr. Jersey City, under commn. form of govt., 1913-25; gov. of N.J., 1926-28, 1932-35, and since Jan. 18, 1938 (first gov. in history of state to be elected for 3d term); elected to U.S. Senate for term, 1935-41, resigned 1938; prof. of legal ethics, N.J. Law Sch.; dir. Lafayette Building & Loan Assn. A leader in civic drives; organizer boys' athletic leagues, and young men in industries; A Harry Moore Sch. for Crippled Children built and named by Jersey City in recognition of his services for physically handicapped children; built Pershing Field; an authority on playgrounds; after dinner speaker. Awarded the annual medal by Ulster-Irish Soc. of N.Y. as American of Irish descent of greatest service during the year; Silver Beaver of Boy Scouts of America, 1937. Mem. Am. Forestry Assn., Nat. Anti-Pollution League. Organized Aid Assn., Hudson Co. Hist. Soc., St. Andrews Soc. of N.Y., Ulster Irish Soc. of N.Y., N.J. Hist. Soc., Ringoes Grange, Delta Theta Phi, Beta Sigma Pi. Democrat. Mason (Shriner), Elk, Moose, Forester, Eagle; mem. Scottish Clans (McLeod). Clubs: Carteret, Masonic, N.J. Rifle, N.J. Fish and Game, Circus Saints and Sinners; Riding and Hunt, University (Washington, D.C.); Lotos (New York). Home: 350 Arlington Av. Office: 921 Bergen Av., Jersey City, N.J.

MOORE, Ben Wheeler, lawyer; b. Salyersville, Ky., Jan. 1, 1891; s. John W. and Mary E. (Wheeler) M.; student Magoffin Inst., Salyersville, Ky., 1904-06; m. Willia E. Samms, June 18, 1913 (dec.); children—Marian, Ben William. Bank Clk. Charleston, W.Va., 1907-11; auditor for st. ry., Charleston, 1911-13; auditor for land co., Dunbar, W.Va., 1913-14; studied law in office of LeRoy Allebach, Charleston, W.Va.; admitted to W.Va. bar, 1915, and since engaged in gen. practice of law at Charleston; mem. firm Townsend, Bock, Moore & Townsend since 1929; commr. in chancery, circuit ct. Kanawha Co., W.Va., since 1918; spl. judge common pleas ct., Kanawha Co., 1937-38. Organized Lions Club, Charleston, W.Va., 1921, first pres., dir. since 1921; first dist. gov. W.Va. Lions Clubs, 2 terms. Mem. W.Va. and Charleston bar assns. Democrat. Baptist. Mason (32°). Clubs: Lions, Lotos. Home: 2437 Washington St. Office: Kanawha Valley Bldg., Charleston, W.Va.

MOORE, Bruce Victor, psychology; b. nr. Kokomo, Ind., Sept. 9, 1891; s. Harles Oscar and Effie (Mariah) M.; B.A., Ind. U., 1914, M.A., 1917; grad. study, Columbia, 1917-18; Ph.D., Carnegie Inst. Tech., 1921; grad. study, U. of Berlin, 1929; m. Elsie Jeanette Kohler, Aug. 20, 1924; 1 dau., Mary Ellen. Grad. asst. in psychology, Ind. U., 1916-17; army psychologist rank of 2d lt, U.S.A., 1918-19; asst. prof. psychology, Pa. State Coll., 1920-23, asso. prof., 1923-28, prof. and head department since 1928; research asso., Personnel Research Fed., 1927-28. Mem. Am. Psychol. Assn., N.E.A., Pa. State Edn. Assn., Phi Beta Kappa, Phi Delta Kappa, Kappa Delta Pi, Psi Chi, Sigma Xi, Kappa Phi Kappa. Republican. Methodist. Co-author: How to Interview (with W. V. Bingham), 1931. Co-Editor: Readings in Industrial Psychology (with G. W. Hartmann), 1931. Contributor articles on psychology. Home: 325 W. Park Av., State College, Pa.

MOORE, Charles Sumner, lawyer; b. Mays Landing, N.J., Jan. 27, 1875; s. William and Hannah (Thompson) M.; ed. Atlantic County public schs.; L.B., Swarthmore Coll., 1895; attended law lectures, U. of Pa. Law Sch.; m. Lona Tillman, Apr. 26, 1911; children—Benjamin Tillman, Minnie Thompson. Prin. Friends High Sch., Moorestown, N.J., 1895-1900; admitted to N.J. bar, 1905; prosecutor of pleas, Atlantic County, N.J., 1913-18; mem. law firm Moore & Butler; pres. Equitable Trust Co. Served as food adminstr., Atlantic Co., during World War, 1918-19. Mem. bd. mgrs. N.J. State League of Bldg. & Loan Assns.; former dir. U.S. League of Bldg. & Loan Assns. Mem. Atlantic City Survey Commn. Mem. Am. Bar Assn., N.J. State Bar Assn., Atlantic Co. Bar Assn. Mason. Clubs: Kiwanis (Atlantic City); Atlantic City Country (Northfield, N.J.); University (Philadelphia). Home: 16 S. Plaza Pl. Office: 1421 Atlantic Av., Atlantic City, N.J.

MOORE, Darius Carrier, physician and surgeon; b. Summerville, Pa., Jan. 6, 1879; s. David Karl and Martha C. (Carrier) M.; student Allegheny Coll., Meadville, Pa., 1897-99; M.D., Jefferson Med. Coll., 1903; m. Nelle Graham Jackson, of Warren, O., Nov. 6, 1908. In gen. practice of medicine and surgery at Beaver, Pa., since 1903; vice-pres. First Nat. Bank, Monaca, Pa.; pres. and asst. sec. The Fallston Co., Fallston, Pa. Mem. Am., Pa. State and Beaver County med. assns., Sigma Alpha Epsilon. Republican. Methodist. Home: 205 Beaver St., Beaver, Pa.

MOORE, Edward Clark, iron mfg.; b. Erie, Pa., Mar. 9, 1868; s. George W. and Charlotte (Rowley) M.; ed. pub. sch. and high sch., Erie, Pa.; m. Sara B. Pressly, Aug. 20, 1896; children—Martha Pressly (Mrs. Donald L. Thomas), Charlotte Weir (Mrs. Courtney M. Dale). Asso. with Erie City Iron Works, Erie, Pa., continuously since entering their employ, Jan. 1, 1885, successively, cashier and chief accountant, treas., v.p. and treas., pres. and treas., now v.p. and treas.; chmn. Northwestern Pa. advisory bd. Liberty Mut. Ins. Co. of Boston. One of founders Erie Light Inf. later Co. A. of 15th Regt. Founder Mfrs. Assn. of Erie. Honored as Chmn. State Armory Bd., 112th Regt. Corporator Hamot Hosp. and Erie Cemetery. Now vice-pres. Mfrs. Assn. One of founders Erie Yacht Club and Country Club. Republican. Presbyn. Royal Arcanum. Clubs: Erie, Press. Home: 230 W. 7th St. Office: 14th and East Av., Erie, Pa.

MOORE, Edward Thomas, lawyer; b. Passaic, N.J., July 3, 1881; s. Thomas Martin and Sarah (Wickham) M.; student Stevens Sch., Hoboken, N.J., 1897-99, Hasbroucks Inst., Jersey City, N.J., 1899, N.Y. U., 1899-1902; B.S., Princeton U., 1903; m. Lillian Ring, 1931; 1 son, Thomas Edward. Admitted to N.J. bar, 1906, N.Y. bar, 1918; prof. law, John Marshall Coll., Jersey City, N.J., since 1932. Served as maj. judge advocate, N.J.N.G., 1910-30, lt. col. since 1930. Mem. N.J. Assembly, 1909-11; U.S. commr. from N.J. on uniform state legislation, 1935-38; advisory master, N.J. Ct. of Chancery, 1929-32; supreme ct. commr., N.J., since 1909; vice-chmn. Rep. State Com. since 1934. Mem. N.J. Bar Assn. (chmn. com. on ethics 1933-36), N.Y. Bar Assn., Am. Bar Assn. (commr. from N.J. on Nat. Conf. on Uniform State Legislation, 1935-38), Sons of the Revolution, Sons of Colonial Wars, Zeta Psi. Republican. Presbyterian. Mason (Shriner), Elks. Home: 34 Ridge Av. Office: 661 Main Av., Passaic, N.J., and 150 Broadway, New York, N.Y.

MOORE, Frank Fawcett, physician; b. Camden, N.J., Oct. 22, 1887; s. Samuel Fleming and Ella (Fawcett) M.; M.D., Hahnemann Med. Coll., Phila., Pa., 1911; m. Marion I. Kennedy, June 3, 1912; 1 dau., Frances Eleanor (Mrs. Charles F. Wright). Interne, West Jersey Hosp., Camden, N.J., 1911-12; mem. obstet. staff, 1912-22, chief obstet. dept. since 1922; engaged in pvt. practice of medicine at Woodlynne, N.J., since 1912. Served as Lt. (j.g.) Med. Corps, U.S.N., 1918-20. Mem. Am. Med. Assn., N.J. State Med. Soc., Camden Co. Med. Soc. Republican. Methodist. Home: 201 Evergreen St., Woodlynne, N.J.

MOORE, Franklin Frazee, coll. pres.; b. Trenton, N.J., July 21, 1903; s. Franklin Benjamin and Alice (Frazee) M.; student Princeton Prep. Sch., 1921-22; A.B., Princeton U., 1926; B.B.A., Rider Coll., 1928; Ed M., Rutgers, 1937; m. Barbara Katzenbach Clark, Apr. 30, 1927; children—Franklin Benjamin II. Isabelle Wyncoop. Teacher, Rider Coll., 1927-28, vocational teacher, 1928-30, registrar, 1930-34, pres. since 1934. Methodist. Clubs: Arbor Inn (Princeton); Princeton, Carteret, Rotary, Trenton Yacht (Trenton); Brielle Anglers (Brielle, N.J.). Editor: Municipal Accounting and Auditing (with J. G. Gill), 1934. Home: 97 Abernethy Drive. Office: Rider College, Trenton, N.J.

MOORE, Frederic T., pres. and treas. E. Keeler Co.; b. Watkins, N.Y., 1869; s. August H. and Mary (Townsend) M.; ed. Phila. High Sch.; m. Ida Van Fecet, 1898. With E. Keeler Co., mfr. of boilers, Williamsport, since 1899, pres., treas. and dir. since 1899; dir. Milton (Pa.) Mfg. Co., Sprout Waldron Co., Muncy, Pa., West Branch Bank & Trust Co., Williamsport, Pa. Republican. Presbyterian (trustee Covenant Central Presbyn. Ch.). Clubs: Williamsport Country, Williamsport Ross. Home: 1035 W. 4th St. Office: 238 West St., Williamsport, Pa.

MOORE, Frederick Luther, mech. engring.; b. Scranton, Pa., Nov. 10, 1883; s. Sidney Howard and Margaret (Millen) M.; ed. pub. sch. and high sch., Scranton, Pa.; m. Ethel Adeline Burns, Oct. 19, 1916; children—Bonnie (dec.), Beth. Employed as draftsman, 1901-04; construction inspr., 1904-06; designer, 1906-17; mech. engr., 1918-32; cons. practice mech. engring. since 1933; registered professional engr. in Pa. Mem. Am. Soc. Mech. Engrs. Republican. Baptist. Club: Y.M.C.A. of Scranton. Home: 916 Madison Av., Scranton, Pa.

MOORE, George Roland, civil engring.; b. Manasquan, N.J., Dec. 31, 1887; s. James Henry and Carrie (Lupton) M.; C.E., Rensselaer Poly. Inst., 1909; grad. study, U. of Pa., 1910-11, U. of Cincinnati, 1912-16; m. Beulah Mabel Haines, Sept. 11, 1912. Employed in r.r. and municipal engring., 1910-12; in engring. practice in O. while instructing at U. of Cincinnati, 1912-16; in practice municipal engring. in N.J., 1916-17; highway and gen. engring. practice in N.J., 1917-26; professional consulting engring. practice in Central N.J. since 1926; dir. Manasquan Nat. Bank, Mutual Aid Bldg. & Loan Assn. Formerly Borough Councilman of Manasquan; now chmn. Citizens Adv. Com. of Borough Council of Manasquan, N.J. Trustee Manasquan Bd. Edn.; trustee Manasquan Public Library; chmn. Am. Red Cross of Manasquan; Mem. Am. Assn. of Engrs., Tau Beta Pi. Mem. M.E. Ch., Mason (32°). Club: Bonnet of Ocean County, N.J. Home: Manasquan, N.J. Office: Asbury Park, N.J.; Manasquan, N.J.

MOORE, Harry Waters, county supt. of schs.; b. High Bridge, N.J., Apr. 12, 1891; s. John Adaline (Waters) M.; Ph.B., Lafayette Coll., Easton, Pa., 1913, A.M., 1930; grad. student Teachers Coll., Columbia; m. Marguerite M. Latimer, Aug. 6, 1921. Teacher, Springfield, N.J., 1913-14, High Bridge, N.J., 1914-16, Red Bank, N.J., 1916-17; prin. Roselle (N.J.) High Sch. 1917-18; teacher, Summit, N.J., 1919-20, supervising prin., High Bridge, N.J., 1920-28; county supt. of schools, Hunterdon County, N.J., since 1928. Served in Signal Corps, U.S. Army, 1917-19; with A.E.F., 13 months. Mem. N.J. Council of Edn., Am. Legion. Mason. Clubs: Schoolmasters (Newark); Rotary (Flemington, N.J.). Home: 35 Maple Av. Office: 59 Main St., Flemington, N.J.

MOORE, Houston Burger, educator; b. Mingo, W.Va., Apr. 30, 1879; s. William John and Ida Ella (Burger) M.; A.B., Hampden-Sydney (Va.) College, 1902, A.M., 1903; m. Ida Virginia Jasper, Aug. 1, 1912; children—Caroline Nicholas, William John, Ida Virginia (dec.), Jean Setlington, Houston Burger. Fellow Latin and Greek, Hampden-Sydney Coll., 1902-03; instr. Latin and Greek, Mil. Acad., Blackstone, Va., 1903-04, Bingham Sch., Asheville, N.C., 1904-05; prin. Greenbrier Mil. Sch. since 1906. Pres. Greenbrier Co. Nat. Farm Loan Assn.; sec. bd. Lewisburg & Ronceverte Electric Ry. Co., 1918-25; dir. Lewisburg Hotel Corpn. Dir. Union Theol. Sem. in Va., Davis Stuart Sch. for Dependent Children, in W.Va.; mem. Home Mission Com. of Synod of W.Va. Presbyn. Ch., U.S.; Gen. Assembly's advisory com. on schs. and colls.; mem. gen. com. Layman's Missionary Movement, 1916-24; v.p. Assn. Mil. Colls. and Schs., 1937-38. Democrat. Home: Lewisburg, W.Va.

MOORE, Ira C(ondit), Jr., lawyer; b. Newton, N.J., Apr. 30, 1891; s. Ira C. and Kitty Decker (Shepherd) M.; grad. Perth Amboy (N.J.) High Sch., 1908; LL.B., N.J. Law Sch., 1913; m. Mildred Adelaide Gill, June 18, 1919; children—Robert Condit, Kathryn Virginia. Admitted to N.J. bar, 1913, and became asso. with Colby & Whiting, Newark; admitted to firm as Colby, Whiting & Moore, 1915; mem. firm Whiting & Moore since 1917; atty. Millburn Twp., 1932. Mem. Millburn Twp. Com. since 1936, chm. 1937, 38; pres. Wyoming Assn., 1933-34. Trustee U. of Newark. Mem. Am., N.J. State and Essex Co. bar assns. Republican. Presbyterian. Club: Wyoming (Millburn). Home: 84 Mountain Av., Millburn, N.J. (Maplewood, N.J. Post Office). Office: Essex Bldg., Newark, N.J.

MOORE, James Clark, Jr., stocks and bonds brokerage; b. Phila., Pa. Sept. 14, 1869; s. James Clark and Hannah (Calver) M.; B.S., U. of Pa., 1893; m. Bertha Bement, Apr. 23, 1902 (dec.); 1 dau., Marion (Mrs. Le Roy Goff). Engaged as real estate broker, then builder, 1893-99; mgr. bond dept., 1899-1912; mem. firm Snowden, Barclay and Moore, 1912-13; mem. firm Barclay, Moore & Co., brokers and mems. New York and Phila. stock exchanges since 1913. Mem. Phila. Acad of Scis., Acad. of Fine Arts, Hist. Soc. of Pa., Phi Delta Theta. Republican. Presbyn. Mason (past master). Clubs: Union League, University, Bachelors Barge, Penn Athletic, Midday, Bond (Philadelphia); Bankers (New York). Home: 225 S. 18th St. Office: 123 S. Broad St., Philadelphia, Pa.

MOORE, James Milton, clergyman; b. Urbana, Ill., Feb. 10, 1876; s. John Henry and Mary Sarepta (Bishop) M.; ed. Mount Morris Coll., 1891-96; B.S.L., Bethany Bib. Sem., Chicago, 1915; m. Ella Kessler, Aug. 17, 1898; children—John Edward, Mary Alice. Engaged in printing trade while attending sch., 1892-1905; student, teacher, and financial sec., Bethany Bib. Sem., Chicago, Ill., 1905-17; ordained to ministry Ch. of Brethren, 1901, full time pastor since 1918; pastor Lanark, Ill., 1918-22, Waynesboro, Pa., 1922-30, Chicago, Ill., 1930-35, Lititz, Pa. since 1935; served as moderator Gen. Conf., Hershey, Pa., 1930; has served in ofcl. capacities in Gen. and Dist. Confs. and on various coms. Republican. Ch. of the Brethren. Contbr. verse and articles to mags. Home: 405 S. Broad St., Lititz, Pa.

MOORE, John Percy, prof. zoölogy; b. Williamsport, Pa., May 17, 1869; s. John P. and Emma (Frank) M.; A.B., Central High Sch., Phila., 1886; B.S., U. of Pa., 1892, Ph.D., 1896; m. Kathleen Carter, May 16, 1892; children—Percy Warren, Kathleen, Elinor, Caroline. Scientific asst. U.S. Fish Commn., periodically, since 1890; asst. instr. zoölogy, U.of Pa., 1890-92, instr., 1892-1907, asst. prof., 1907-12, prof., 1912-39, prof. emeritus since 1939; also asst. curator and corr. sec. Acad. Natural Sciences, Phila., since 1902. Instr. biology, Hahnemann Med. Coll., Phila., 1896-98; instr. Marine Biol. Lab., Wood's Hole, Mass., 1901-02; Ludwick Inst. lecturer since 1902. Fellow A.A.A.S.; mem. Am. Soc. Naturalists, Am. Soc. Zoölogists, Ecol. Soc. America, Am. Philos. Soc., Phila. Acad. Science, Soc. Zoöl. de France. Contbr. numerous articles to scientific jours. Address: University of Pennsylvania, Phila., Pa.

MOORE, John Turner, banking; b. Colora, Md., Nov. 25, 1878; s. George and Margaret (Turner) M.; B.S., Westminster Coll., New Wilmington, Pa., 1899; m. Leonora Seybolt, May 30, 1903; children—Marguerette S. (Mrs. Charles Sheridan), Martha Ellen (Mrs. James A. Reedy), J. Turner, Jr., Frederick McCormick. Employed as chemist and steel maker with various steel cos., 1899-1906; pres. and gen. mgr. Reading (Pa.) Steel Casting Co., 1906-20; pres. and dir. Berks County Trust Co., Reading, Pa., since 1920, also pres. and dir. Moore & Moore, Inc.; dir. American Casualty Co., Northeastern Lumber Co. Republican. Clubs: Wyomissing, Berkshire Country. Home: "Willowpool," Wernersville, Pa. Office: 35 N. Sixth St., Reading, Pa.

MOORE, Joseph Earle, M.D.; b. Phila., July 9, 1892; s. Joseph Howard and Adelaide Marie (Lovett) M.; A.B., U. of Kan., 1914; M.D., Johns Hopkins, 1916; m. Grace Douglas Barclay, May 24, 1917. Asst. in medicine, instr., and asso., Johns Hopkins, 1916-23; asst. visiting physician Johns Hopkins Hosp., 1923-29; phys. in charge syphilis div. of Med. Clinic, Johns Hopkins Med. Sch. and Hosp., since 1929; spl. consultant U.S. Pub. Health Service; consultant Md. State Dept. of Health. Served as 1st lt. and capt. Med. Corps, U.S.A., with A.E.F., 1917-19; maj. Med. Res. Corps, 1920-28. Mem. A.M.A., Assn. of Am. Physicians, Am. Soc. for Clin. Investigation, Am. Clin. and Climatol. Soc., Med. and Chirurg. Faculty of Md., Phi Beta Kappa, Sigma Xi, Phi Chi. Club: Gibson Island (Md.). Author: The Modern Treatment of Syphilis, 1933. Editor Am. Jour. Syphilis, Gonorrhea and Venereal Diseases since 1935. Contbr. articles to med. jours. Home: 4422 Underwood Rd. Office: 804 Medical Arts Bldg., Baltimore, Md.

MOORE, J(oseph) Hampton, ex-mayor, ex-congressman; b. Woodbury, N.J., Mar. 8, 1864; s. Joseph B. and Mary J. (Dorff) M.; educated, pub. schs., Camden, N.J.; LL.D., Ursinus Coll., 1920; LL.D., Hahnemann Med. Coll., 1933; m. Adelaide Stone, Jan. 16, 1889; children—Clayton F. (dec.), Dorff, Edward M., Harvey, Mark M. (dec.), Sevena C. (Mrs. H. Paul Barnes), Julia D. (Mrs. Fredk. G. Eisley), Richard O. (dec.). Court reporter; reporter and editorial writer, Phila. Public Ledger, 12 yrs.; chief clerk to city treas., Phila., 1895-97, sec. Peace Jubilee, 1898; sec. to mayor of Phila., 1898-99; sec. Citizens' Com. Nat. Rep. Conv., Phila., 1899; city treas., Phila., 1901-03; chief, Bur. of Mfrs., Dept. Commerce and Labor, Washington, Jan.-June 1905; elected to 59th Congress for an unexpired term; reëlected 60th to 66th Congresses (1907-1921), 3d Pa. Dist.; resigned from Congress, 1920 on being elected mayor of Phila., seerved as mayor, 1920-23 and 1932-35. Pres. Allied Rep. Clubs of Phila., 1900-06, Pa. State League Rep. Clubs, 1900-01, Nat. League Rep. Clubs, 1903-06; del. at large Nat. Republican Conv., 1920; Presidential elector, 1932; pres. Atlantic Deeper Waterways Assn., 1907—. Mem. N.J. Soc. of Pa., Pa. Hist. Soc.; decorated Chevalier Order of the Crown (Italy), 1921. Clubs: Five O'Clock, Union League (Phila.); National Press, Congressional Country, Alfalfa (Washington). Wrote: History of Five O'Clock Club, 1891; Fiveoclockiana (poems), 1898; Through the Tropics, 1907; Roosevelt and the Old Guard, 1925; also various polit. pamphlets. Home: 319 W. Carpenter Lane. Office: Widener Bldg., Philadelphia, Pa.

MOORE, Joseph Layton, supervising prin. schs.; b. Bishop, Md., June 4, 1899; s. Daniel A. and Melissa (Grey) M.; ed. Wesley Collegiate Inst., Dover, Del., 1916-19; A.B., Wesleyan U., 1923; ed. Columbia U., summers 1924-26, U. of Pa., summers 1927-29, Temple U., summers 1930-31; m. Rose Buckson, June 30, 1925; children—Joseph Layton, Jr., James Buckson, Melissa Anne. Instr. history and social studies, Wesley Coll. Inst., Dover, Del., 1923-24, instr. social studies and asst. prin., 1924-25; prin. Dover High Sch., 1925-27; supervising prin. Ridley Park Sch. Dist. since 1927. Served as mem. bd. health, Ridley Park, Pa. Mem. Pa. State Edn. Assn. (pres. southeastern conv. dist.), vice-pres. Suburban High Sch. Prins. Assn. of Phila. (v.p.), suburban Supervising Prins. Assn. (pres.), Delaware Co. Teachers Assn. (pres.), Kappa Phi Kappa, Beta Theta Pi. Republican. Methodist. Home: 417 Free St., Ridley Park, Pa.

MOORE, Junius Teetzel, structural engr.; b. Indianapolis, Ind., Sept. 1, 1895; s. William Evan and Emma (Miller) M.; C.E., Va. Poly. Inst., 1917; m. Helen Marshall Pugh, June 29, 1921; children—Junius Teetzel, William Evan, II. Engr. U.S. Naval Ordnance Plant, 1919-20; 1st asst. bridge engr. and designer W.Va. State Road Commn., 1920-26; pres. Fireproof Products Co. since 1926; treas. Industrial Engring. Co. Served as 1st lt., U.S. Army, commanding Mine Planter "General Ord," 1917-19. Mem. Am. Soc. Civil Engr., Am. Legion. Club: Charleston Rotary. Home: 1403 Lee St. Office: 422 Professional Bldg., Charleston, W.Va.

MOORE, Merrill Miles, clergyman; b. Northfield, Mass., Oct. 9, 1897; s. Merrill Taft and Jane (Styles) M.; B.S., Colgate U., 1921; S.T.B., Gen. Theol. Sem., 1924; m. Mildred I. Pease, Oct. 4, 1926; 1 dau., Elisabeth Miles. Ordained to ministry P.E. Ch., deacon, 1924, priest, 1924; missionary in Oneida Co., N.Y., 1924-25; curate, Grace Ch., Utica, N.Y., 1925-28; rector, Trinity Ch., Bethlehem, Pa., since 1928. Served in S.A.T.C., 1919. Mem. Bethlehem Safety Commn., Northampton Co. Adv. Council S.E.R.B. Dir. Family Welfare Assn., Community Chest, Lehigh Valley Child Guidance Clinic; mem. Northampton Co. Dept. Public Assistance Bd. Trustee Jonestown Church Home. Mem. Am. Archaeol. Soc., Alpha Tau Omega, Pi Delta Epsilon. Republican. Episcopalian. Clubs: Rotary, Saucon Valley Country. Home: 222 E. Market St., Bethlehem, Pa.

MOORE, Perry Martin, pres. and chmn. bd. Maintenance Engring. Co., Inc.; b. Bloomfield, N.J., Feb. 19, 1899; s. William Douglas and Elizabeth Martin (Brown) Moore; B.Sc. in Chemistry, Rutgers University, 1919; M.A. in Chemistry Engineering, Columbia University, 1920. Chem. engr. E. I. du Pont de Nemours Co., Wilmington, Del., 1918; plant chemist Grasselli (N.J.) Chem. Co., 1919-22; asst. to gen. mgr. Central Dyestuffs & Chem. Co., Newark, N.J., 1922-23; by-products research and sales Nat. Aniline & Chem. Co., New York and Buffalo, 1923-25; chief engr. Federated Metals Corpn., Piscataway, N.J., 1925-26; chem. broker, 50 E. 42d St., New York, 1926-27; proprietor Maintenance Engring. Co., Bloomfield, N.J., 1927-29; president Maintenance Engring. Co., Inc., Bloomfield, since 1929, pres. and chmn. bd. since 1929; pres. and chmn. bd. Maintenance Sales Corpn. since 1930; exec. v.p. Benzol Distributors, Inc., Bloomfield, N.J., since 1939. Served as 1st sergt., U.S. Army, June-Dec. 1918. Mem. Phi Gamma Delta, Phi Beta Kappa. Honored as "Best Soldier," Rutgers, 1919; awarded Gilette Wynkoop prize in chemistry, Rutgers U., 1919, Du Pont Scholarship, Rutgers U., 1919, James Suydam prize in natural science, Rutgers U., 1919. Has made spl. study of waterproofing as applied to masonry structures and holds basic patents on remedial treatments. Home: 115 S. Clinton St., East Orange, N.J. Office: 59 Willet St., Bloomfield, N.J.

MOORE, Ralph Lewis, physician; b. Swedesboro, N.J., Jan. 8, 1907; s. S. Lewis and Estella (Locke) M.; student Hahnemann Coll. of Sci., Phila., Pa., 1924-26; M.D., Hahnemann Med. Coll., Phila., Pa., 1930; m. Helen Shoemaker, June 21, 1930; children—Lois Locke (dec.), Ralph Lewis, Susan Leigh. Interne Atlantic City Hosp., 1930-31; engaged in gen. practice of mediciine at Woodbury, N.J., since 1931; dir. and mem. active staff Underwood Hosp. since 1931; coroner Gloucester Co., N.J., since 1937. Mem. Gloucester Co. and N.J. State med. socs., A.M.A., Alpha Sigma. Republican. Episcopalian. Club: Kiwanis of Woodbury. Home: 127 N. Broad St. Office: 509 N. Broad St., Woodbury, N.J.

MOORE, Robert, forester; b. Danville, Pa., Sept. 29, 1900; s. Howard Robert and Jane Berryman (McGinnes) M.; B.S.F., Pa. State Coll., 1922; grad. work at La. State U., Baton Rouge, 1931-34; m. Ruth Carleton Martin, Jan. 9, 1926; 1 son, Robert. Entered lumber bus. and employed as lumber man and forester, 1917-29; extension forester, La., 1929-34; sr. agrl. economist, U.S. Dept. Agr., 1934; forester, Northeastern Lumber Mfrs. Assn., New York City, 1934-35; chief of forest management, Pa. Dept. Forests and Waters, Harrisburg, Pa., 1935-39; consulting forester, 1939. Mem. Soc. Am. Foresters, Phi Kappa Psi, Alpha Xi Sigma. Presbyn. Home: 22 Bloom St., Danville, Pa.

MOORE, Thomas Waterman, M.D.; b. Cattlettsburg, Ky., Oct. 4, 1866; s. Vincent Morgan and Addie Marian M.; M.D., Medico-Chirurgical Coll., Philadelphia, Pa.; m. Harriet Prentice Hallock, June 28, 1899; children—Joseph Hallock, Thomas Waterman. Began practice at Everett, Pa., 1893; removed to Huntington, W.Va., 1897; specialist in eye, ear, nose and throat. Dir. First Huntington Nat. Bank. Fellow Am. Coll. Surgeons; mem. A.M.A., Southern Med. Assn. (pres. 1929), W.Va. State Med. Soc. (pres. 1910), Acad. Ophthalmology and Otolaryngology, Am. Laryngol., Rhinol. and Otol. Soc. Republican. Mason (32°, K.T.). Home: 1209 Rugby Rd. Office: 1050 5th Av., Huntington, W.Va.

MOORE, William Emmett, newspaper editor; b. La Grange, Mo.; s. William Pike and Catherine Linn (Threlkeld) Moore; educated in public schools and Whipple Acad., Jacksonville, Ill., and U. of Mo.; unmarried. Reporter Quincy (Ill).) Herald and Journal, 1899-1901, Chicago American, 1901-04; city editor Chicago Inter Ocean, 1904-07; mem. staff New York Herald, 1907-08; night editor Chicago Inter Ocean, 1909-12, mng. editor, 1912-14; editorial writer, Chicago Daily News, 1914; city editor and mng. editor New York Tribune, 1915-17; with the Baltimore Sun since 1922, managing editor and vice-pres. Private Ill. Vol. Inf. in Spanish-Am. War; capt. Signal Corps, U.S.A., in World War; served in France on General Pershing's Headquarters staff; awarded three battle clasps for Aisne-Marne, Marne-Vesle and St. Mihiel campaigns, G.H.Q. citation, and Chateau-Thierry (French) medal. Mem. Phi Delta Theta, Am. Legion, Order of the World War. Clubs: University (Baltimore); National Press, University (Washington); Authors' (London). Author: Democratic Campaign Text Book, 1920; U.S. Official Pictures of the World War, 1920. Home: 100 University Parkway West. Office: The Sun, Baltimore, Md.

MOORE, William Enoch, pres. W. E. Moore & Co.; b. Boyd, N.C., Jan. 11, 1870; s. James Wright and Emily (Branson) M.; student Trinity Coll. (now Duke U.), Durham, N.C., 1888-90; m. Ruth Dawley, Mar. 27, 1922; 1 dau., Grace. Successively erection engr. Southern Electric Light Constrn. Co., Danville, Va., and New Am. Ark Light Co., New York, and sales engr. Richmond (Va.) Locomotive Works; designing engr. Moore-Edenfield Electric Mfg. Co., Augusta, Ga., 1892-96; mgr. Augusta Electric Motor Co., Augusta, Ga., 1894-96; gen. mgr. Augusta Ry. & Electric Co., Augusta, Ga., 1896-1903; constrn. engr. Pittsburgh, McKeesport & Connellsville Ry. Co., Pittsburgh, Pa., 1903-05; v.p. and gen. mgr. West Penn Traction & Water Power Co., Pittsburgh, 1905-15; mgr. Louisville & Indianapolis Traction Co., Louisville, Ky., 1908-12; pres. Gen. Steel Co., Milwaukee, 1917-19; pres. W.E. Moore & Co., engrs., Pittsburgh, Pa., since 1916; engr. U.S. Electric Steel Co., Pittsburgh Electromelt Furnace Corpn., Pittsburgh Lectrodryer Corpn., Research Corpn. of Pittsburgh. Mem. Am. Iron and Steel Inst., Am. Soc. M.E., Am. Inst. E.E., Franklin Inst. Republican. Presbyterian. Clubs: Duquesne, Pittsburgh Athletic Assn. (Pittsburgh). Home: 1402 Browning Rd. Office: 32d St., Pittsburgh, Pa.

MOORE, William Garrett, banker; b. Haddonfield, N.J., Jan. 8, 1874; s. Henry D. and Mary J. (Smith) M.; grad. Rittenhouse Acad., 1890; B.S., U. of Pa., 1894; m. Martie Doughty, June 4, 1896; m. 2d, Emma McDevitt, June 6, 1901; children—Helen (Mrs. A. P. Ellis), and John D. (1st marriage), Katherine (Mrs. C. Franklin Fritz), Elizabeth (Mrs. Stanley W. Rusk). Pres. Guanajuato Reduction & Mines Co., Empire Lumber Co.; dir. Camden (N.J.) Safe Deposit and Trust Co. Chairman rural district Eastern section U.S. War Work Campaign. Organizer and chmn. for 15 yrs., Co. Y.M.C.A., Camden Co.; organizer and pres. Musical Club of U. of Pa. Ex-pres. Presbyn. Social Union of Phila. Mem. Bd. of Education and bd. of trustees of Gen. Assembly of the Presbyn. Ch. in U.S.A.; del. of Gen. Assembly to Alliance of Chs. holding the Presbyn. System Cardiff, Wales, 1925, Boston, 1929; formerly trustee Princeton Theol. Seminary. Chmn. and department dir. Haddonfield Unemployment Relief, 1931-33. Mem. U.S. Seniors Golf Assn.; pres. Phila. Senior's Golf Assn.; mem. N.J. S.A.R. Republican. Mason (32°, K.T., Shriner). Clubs: Union League, Orpheus (ex-pres.), Pen and Pencil (Phila.); Travistock Country. Home: 257 Kings Highway W., Haddonfield, N.J. Office: 103 N. 7th St., Camden, N.J.

MOORE, William Hanson, III, provost Md. College for Women; b. Baltimore, Md., July 11, 1900; s. William Hanson and Mary (Bond) M.; student Baltimore Poly. Inst., 1915-19; A.B., Johns Hopkins University, 1923; m. Mabelle Symington, June 3, 1931; children—William Hanson, IV, Jane Ryland. Began as newspaper writer, 1923; assistant provost Johns Hopkins University, 1924-26; assistant president St. Johns Coll., 1926-28; headmaster Marston U. Sch., 1928-29; pres. Md. Coll. for Women, Lutherville, Md., 1929-30, provost since 1930. Trustee Md. Coll. for Women, Woodbrook Sch. Received Algernon Sidney Sullivan award. Member Delta Upsilon (trustee), Omicron Delta Kappa. Democrat. Episcopalian. Clubs: University, Hopkins, Tudor and Stuart, Baltimore Country (Baltimore); Naval Academy Officers. Contbr. spl. articles for Baltimore newspapers. Editor of Lacrosse News. Home: 107 Midhurst Rd., Baltimore, Md. Office: Lutherville, Md.

MOORFIELD, Amelia Berndt (Mrs. Frank Moorfield), book pub.; b. Newport, Ky., Apr. 17, 1876; d. Gustave and Caroline (Marsh) Berndt; ed. pub. sch. and high sch., Newport, Ky., and New York U.; m. Frank Moorfield, Aug. 11, 1898; 1 dau., Hannah May (Mrs. William John Shannon). Began teaching in High School then prin. Clifton Heights, Ky., 1895-98; asso. with Moorfield & Shannon, pub. radio and motion picture textbooks, travel books, etc., Nutley, N.J., since 1934, pres. since 1934. Mem. Minute Women of N.J. (v.p.), Board of Essex Co. Rep. Club., Com. of 100 of Newark Air Port, Youth Week Celebration Com. Dir. Visiting Nurses Assn., Nat. Urban League, Silver Lake Community House, Nat. Opera Club of America (v.p.), Chmn. Mothers' Peace Day. Trustee N.Y. Women's Press Club. Mem. Diocesan Altar Guilds (v.p.), Consumers League (state treas.), Am. Womens Assn. N.Y. City, League of Women Voters of N.J., Conf. of Jews and Christians (vice chmn.), Nat. Fed. Press Womens Clubs (v.p.), Newark Bus. and Professional Womens Clubs, Womens Internat. League for Peace and Freedom (mem. nat. bd. and state pres.), Girls Friendly Soc., China Aid Council of Essex Co. (pres.). Republican. Episcopalian. Clubs: Thursday Afternoon (pres.), Contemporary (chmn. legislation). Home: 35 Columbia St., Newark, N.J.; (summer) 124 Shore Boul., Granville Park, N.J., Keansburg P.O. Office: 66 Elm Pl., Nutley, N.J.

MOORHEAD, Forest G., lawyer, banker; b. Clarion Co., Pa., 1873; s. Alexander and Mary J. (Houser) M.; student Allegheny Coll., Meadville, Pa.; LL.B., Northwestern U. Law Sch., Chicago, Ill., 1901; m. Agnes Wegener, Dec. 30, 1903; 1 son, George W. Admitted to Pa. bar, 1901, and since practiced at Beaver, Pa.; mem. firm Moorhead & Marshall since 1913; pres. and dir. Midland (Pa.) Bank since 1912, Beaver (Pa.) Bldg. Co. since 1910; dir. Beaver Trust Co. Trustee Allegheny Coll., Meadville, Pa., since 1930. Mem. Pa. Bar Assn. (pres. 1935). Republican. Protestant. Author numerous speeches. Home: 358 Iroquois Pl. Office: Beaver Trust Bldg., Beaver, Pa.

MOORHEAD, Hugh McKee, physician; b. Indiana, Pa., Nov. 20, 1879; s. Alexander T. and Margaret Anna (Speedy) M.; student State Teachers Coll., Indiana, Pa., 1899-1901; M.D., Medico-Chirurgical Coll., Phila., Pa., 1906; m. Catharine Mae Johnston, June 21, 1910 (died Oct. 22, 1935); 1 dau., Mary Margaret; m. 2d, Margaret Ann Krimmel, Apr. 14, 1939. Bacteriologist, City of Erie, Pa., 1910-20; attending obstetrician Florence Crittenton Home, Erie, Pa., 1910-37, Hamot Hosp., Erie, Pa., 1920-32; attending physician Infants Home, Erie, Pa., since 1920; acting asst. surgeon U.S. Pub. Health Service, Erie, Pa., since 1918; chief proctologist Hamot Hosp., Erie, since 1936. Served as pvt., Co. F, 5th Regt., Pa. Vol. Inf., during Spanish-Am. War. Mem. Erie Co. Med. Soc., Pa. Med. Soc., A.M.A. Republican. Protestant. Mason. Clubs: Shrine, Lake Shore Golf (Erie, Pa.). Address: 217 W. 8th St., Erie, Pa.

MOORHEAD, Stirling Walker, physician; b. Phila., Pa., Apr. 22, 1882; s. William W. and Mary R. (Combs) M.; A.B., U. of Pa., 1902; M.D., U. of Pa. Med. Sch., 1905; unmarried. Served as interne at St. Christopher's Hosp. and Hosp. of U. of Pa.; asst. surgeon, then surgeon and urologist, Howard Hosp., 1908-29; asst. urologist Polyclinic Hosp., 1911-14; asst. urologist, U. of Pa. Hosp. since 1920; urologist-in-chief, Methodist Episcopal Hosp. since 1934; has filled various teaching positions in U. of Pa. Med. Sch. and asst. prof. urology since 1933; certified as specialist in urology by Am. Bd. of Urology, 1936. Served as 1st lieut. then capt. Med. Corps, U.S.A., 1917-19, with A.E.F. in France and Germany. Fellow Phila. Coll. of Physicians, Am. Urol. Assn.; mem. Psi Upsilon. Republican. Club: Aesculapian of Philadelphia. Home: 1523 Pine St., Philadelphia, Pa.

MOORHEAD, William Singer, lawyer; b. Greensburg, Pa., Aug. 2, 1883; s. James Sharpe and Elizabeth Williams (Singer) M.; grad. Lawrenceville (N.J.) School, 1902; A.B., Yale Univ., 1906; LL.B., U. of Pittsburgh, 1909; m. Constance Barr, Feb. 10, 1915; 1 son, William Singer. Admitted to Pa. bar, 1909, and began practice at Pittsburgh; mem. firm Moorhead & Knox since 1917; lecturer, U. of Pittsburgh Sch. of Law, 1909-18; pres. Inland Coal Co.; dir. Keystone Coal & Coke Co., Forbes Nat. Bank, Pittsburgh; trustee of Schenley Estate. Chmn. U.S. Tax Simplification Bd., 1922-24; chmn. orgn. com. Pittsburgh Community Fund, 1927. Trustee Carnegie Library, Carnegie Inst., Carnegie Inst. Technology; vice-pres. Tuberculosis League of Pittsburgh; chmn. Alumni Board of Yale University, 1935-37; mem. Am., Pa. and Allegheny Co. bar assns., Delta Kappa Epsilon. Presbyn. Clubs: Duquesne, Pittsburgh Golf, Fox Chapel Golf, Allegheny Country, Rolling Rock, Misquamicut Golf (Watch Hill, R.I.). Home: 5725 Aylesboro Av. Office: Oliver Bldg., Pittsburgh, Pa.

MOOS, Jean Corrodi; emeritus prof. music, Bethany Coll. Address: Bethany, W.Va.

MORALES, Franklin E., diplomat; b. Phila., Pa., Jan. 26, 1884; s. Marcos D. and Anna Maria (Cain) M.; grad. high sch. and business coll., Atlantic City, N.J.; m. Mae E. Krauss, Feb. 26, 1906; 1 dau., Thelma. Export business; v.p. Internations Commercial Corpn., 1916-19; rep. Am. jewelry mfrs. in Latin America, 1919-21; mem. firm Riker and Morales, Mexico City, Buenos Aires, Santiago, Chile. Pres. Atlantic City Rep. Club, 1907-16; Rep. County committeeman, 1912-16; E.E. and M.P. to Honduras, 1921-25. Baptist. Mason, Odd Fellow. Clubs: Penn Athletic, International of Tegucigalpa, Lakewood Country, Atlantic City Shrine. Home: 19 Messenger St. Office: 229-31 Main St., Toms River, N.J.

MORAN, (John) Léon, artist; b. Phila., Pa., Oct. 4, 1864; s. Edward and Elizabeth (McManes) M.; ed. pub. schs., Phila.; studied art under father, and at Nat. Acad. Design, New York, and in London and Paris; returned to U.S., 1879; established studio, New York, 1883; m. Helen, d. Rev. J. N. Steele, Apr. 27, 1892. Frequent exhibitor Nat. Acad. Design, New York, and elsewhere; gold medal Phila. Art Club; gold medal, Am. Art Soc., Phila., 1904. Mem. Am. Water Color Soc., Plainfield (N.J.) Art Assn. Principal works: Waylaid; An Interrupted Conspiracy; An Amateur; The Duel; An Idyl; Eel Fishing; Intercepted Dispatches; Madonna and Child; Between Two Fires; Madonna; etc. Home: 10 Orchard Av., Plainfield, N.J.

MORDELL, Albert, lawyer and writer; b. Phila., Pa., Aug. 13, 1885; s. Phineas and Anna Jochebed (Feller) M.; A.B., Central High Sch., Phila., Pa., 1903; unmarried. Admitted to Pa. bar, 1910 and since engaged in gen. practice of law at Philadelphia, Pa.; counsel for the State Bridge and Tunnel Commission since 1938. Democrat. Author: The Shifting of Literary Values, 1912; Dante and Other Waning Classics, 1915, re-issued in blue book series, 1923; The Erotic Motive in Literature, 1919; The Literature of Ecstasy, 1921; Quaker Militant: John Greenleaf Whittier, 1933. Editor: Essays in European and Oriental Literature by Lafcadio Hearn, 1923; Notorious Literary Attacks, 1926; and many other books, essays, and writings. Contbr. to newspapers and mags. Home: 4241 Viola St. Office: 610 Commercial Trust Bldg., Philadelphia, Pa.

MOREAU, Charles Ellis, newspaper pub.; b. Freehold, N.J., Mar. 26, 1899; s. Alexander Low and Anna Augusta (Ellis) M.; B.S., Dartmouth Coll., 1921; student Pulitzer Sch. of Journalism of Columbia U., 1921-22; m. Christina Eleanor Kreag, June 27, 1931; children—Christina Kreag, Alexander Low 2d, John Adam. Employed as reporter, Hunterdon Co. Democrat, Flemington, N.J., 1923-24, Madison (N.J.) Eagle, 1924-25, Miami (Fla.) Herald, 1925-26, Freehold (N.J.) Transcript, 1926; prin. stockholder, pres. and sec. Independent Press, Inc., pub. Bloomfield Independent Press and The Glen Ridge Paper, Bloomfield, N.J., since 1926; pres. Moreau Publications, Inc., pub. Evening Transcript of the Oranges and Maplewood, Orange, N.J., since 1939; pres. Moreau Realty Co., Inc., Bloomfield, N.J., since 1933; mem. bd. mgrs. Bloomfield Savings Instn. Served in S.A.T.C. Pres. Bloomfield Civic Council; vice-pres. Bloomfield Community Chest; treas. Bloomfield Youth Commn.; dir. Bloomfield Chamber of Commerce. Mem. Nat. Editorial Assn., N.J. Press Assn., Alpha Chi Rho, Gamma Delta Chi. Awarded silver cups by Nat. and N.J. press assns. for best weekly editorial page in U.S. Republican. Presbyn. Club: Dartmouth (New York). Home: 43 Woodland Rd. Office: 266 Liberty St., Bloomfield, N.J.

MOREAU, Daniel Howard, pub. and editor; b. Freehold, N.J., July 1, 1898; s. William

Marshall and Elizabeth (Jones) M.; B.S. Middlebury (Vt.) Coll., 1920; m. Lillis Dale Simmonds, Sept. 26, 1926; children—Elizabeth Dale, Anne Clotilde, Margaret Simmonds, Janet Rhea. Began as reporter on Oneonta, N.Y. Star, 1921; with Freehold, N.J. Transcript, 1921-22; purchased Hunterdon County Democrat, Flemington, N.J. and pub. and editor since 1922; purchased Delaware Valley News, Frenchtown, N.J. and pub. since 1932; dir. Hunterdon County Nat. Bank. Served in S.A.T.C., 1918. Mem. N.J. State Bd. Edn. since 1927. Mem. Nat. Editorial Assn., N.J. Press Assn. (pres. 1938-39), Chi Psi. Independent Democrat. Presbyn. Club: Rotary of Flemington. Home: 41 Pennsylvania Av., Flemington, N.J. Office: 8 Court St., Flemington, N.J.

MOREHEAD, James Caddall, coll. prof., curator; b. Pulaski Co., Va., Mar. 25, 1877; s. James William and Catherine Barbara (Yonce) M.; B.A., Roanoke Coll., 1898, M.A., 1899; M.S., Princeton U., 1900; Ph.D., Yale U., 1905; m. Jean Dandridge White, Sept. 12, 1906; children—Clayton White, Barbara Lee, James Caddall. Instr. mathematics, Northwestern U., Evanston, Ill., 1905-09, asst. prof., 1909-12; instr. mathematics and descriptive geometry, Sch. of Applied Design, Carnegie Inst. Tech., 1915-16, asst. prof., 1916-23, asso. prof., 1923-30, prof. graphics since 1930, curator Dept. Architecture, Coll. of Fine Arts, since 1923. Fellow A.A.A.S.; mem. Am. Math. Soc., Sigma Xi. Democrat. Episcopalian. Translator (with A. M. Hiltebeitel) General Investigations of Curved Surfaces, 1902 (with notes and a bibliography of C. F. Gauss Papers of 1827 and 1825). Home: 4815 Bayard St., Pittsburgh, Pa.

MOREHOUSE, J(ulius) Stanley, prof. mech. engring., actg. dean; b. Amenia, N.Y., Nov. 19, 1894; s. Henry Stebins and Bertha (Humphreville) M.; ed. Stevens Prep. Sch., Hoboken, N.J., 1913-14, Stevens Inst. Tech., 1915-17, 1919-21, M.E., same, 1921; m. Justine Kumhera, June 30, 1930; 1 son, J. Stanley, Jr. Engaged as instr. mech. engring., Villanova Coll., Villanova, Pa., 1921-22, asst. prof., 1922-24, asso. prof., 1924-26, prof. mech. engring. since 1926, actg. dean of engring. since 1938. Mem. Am. Soc. Mech. Engrs., Am. Soc. Heating and Ventilating Engrs., Soc. for Promotion Engring. Edn., Sigma Nu. Republican. Episcopalian. Mason. Home: 102 Llandaff Rd., Upper Darby, Pa.

MOREHOUSE, Lyman Foote, telephone engr.; b. Big Rapids, Mich., Oct. 21, 1874; s. Amos Robert and Lucy P. (Foote) M.; B.S. in E.E., U. of Mich., 1897, A.M., 1904; Dr. Engring. (honorary) same school, 1934; grad. student in analyt. chemistry, U. of Chicago, and in mathematics, physics, and elec. engring., U. of Mich.; m. May Cornelia Wyman, June 25, 1904 (died Feb. 12, 1921); children—Dorothy May, Marjorie Lucellen; m. 2d, Mary Spencer Schuessler, of Baton Rouge, La., Sept. 30, 1922. Instr. in physics, Washington U., 1901; instr. in physics, U. of Mich., 1902-04, instr. and later asst. prof., elec. engring., 1904-06; transmission engr. Western Electric Co., London, Eng., 1906-09; equipment engr. Am. Telephone & Telegraph Co., New York, 1909-19; equipment development engr. same co., 1919-33; asst. dir. of systems development, Bell Telephone Labs., 1933-35; tech. rep. Am. Telephone & Telegraph Co. and Bell Telephone Labs. in Europe since 1935. Mem. N.J. State Board of Education, 1928-35. Fellow Am. Inst. E.E. (mgr. 1919-23; v.p. 1925-26); fellow A.A.A.S.; mem. British Instn. of Elec. Engrs., Sigma Xi, Tau Beta Pi. Republican. Methodist. Home: 30 Draper Terrace, Montclair, N.J.; 40 Lansdowne House, Mayfair, London, England. Office: Bush House, London, Eng.

MORENO, Manuel Enrique, dentist, consul of Chile, acting consul of Uruguay; b. Traiguen, Chile, S.A., Jan. 24, 1901; s. Enrique and Clotilde (Lajana) M.; student U. of Chile, 1917-20, B.S., 1917; D.D.S., U. of Pa., 1931; m. America P. Alvarez, June 2, 1934. Instr. U. of Chile, Dental Sch., 1920-22; engaged in practice of dentistry at Santiago, Chile, 1920-28 in Phila. since 1932; ofcl. del. of Chile to VIII Internat. Dental Cong., Paris, France, 1931; acting consul of Uruguay in Phila. since 1933; consul of Chile in Phila. since 1933. Hon. dir. Infantile Welfare League of Santiago, Chile. Mem. Am. Internat. Acad., Am. Dental Assn., Pa. Assn. of Dental Surgs., Dental Alumni Soc. of U. of Pa., Pan-Am. Dental Assn., Consular Assn. of Phila. Catholic. Home: 1626 Spruce St., Philadelphia, Pa.

MOREY, Charles Rufus, educator, author; b. Hastings, Mich., Nov. 20, 1877; s. John and Addie C. (Stone) M.; A.B., University of Michigan, 1899, A.M., 1900, Litt.D., 1938; L.H.D., Oberlin College, 1932; m. Sara Tupper, May 29, 1915; 1 son, Jonathan Tupper. Fellow American School at Rome, 1900-03; fellow Princeton University, 1903-04; Marquand professor art and archæology, Princeton, 1918—; prof. in charge Am. Sch. of Classical Studies in Rome, 1925-26. Trustee Am. Schs. of Oriental Research, 1936. Fellow Mediæval Acad.; mem. Archæol. Inst. America, Am. Assn. of Univ. Profs., Am. Philos. Soc., Soc. Antiq. de France (hon. corr.), Archæol. Inst. Germany, Coll. Art Assn., Phi Beta Kappa, Theta Delta Chi. Democrat. Club: Princeton (New York). Author: East Christian Paintings in the Freer Collection, 1914; Lost Mosaics and Frescoes of Rome, 1915; Sardis, Vol. V, 1924; (with L. W. Jones) The Miniatures of the Terence MSS., 1931; Christian Art, 1935; The Mosaics of Antioch, 1938; also various articles on art and archæology. Editor: Catalogue of Museo Sacro, Vatican Library. Decorated Ordre du Mérite Syrien, 1st class, 1935; Chevalier, Order of Crown of Belgium, 1937. Home: 114 Broadmead, Princeton, N.J.

MOREY, Frank R., supv. prin.; b. York, Pa., July 28, 1895; s. Frederick A. and Emma K. (Hamme) M.; grad. York High Sch., 1913; B.S. in Edn., Pa. State Coll., 1918; M.A., Teachers Coll., Columbia U., 1923; grad. student, same, 1922-24, summers, 1928, 1933-37, and U. of Pa., winters, 1931-32; m. Edith E. Swan, June 20, 1925; children—Frederick Richard, David Swan. Teacher rural sch., Lancaster Co., Pa., 1916-17; county supervisor vocational edn., Chester Co., Pa., 1919-20; state supervisor sch. gardening, Dept. Pub. Instrn., Harrisburg, 1920-22; supervising prin., Camp Hill, Pa., 1924-29; asst. dir. Teachers Bur., Dept. Pub. Instrn., Harrisburg, 1929-30; supervising prin., Swarthmore, Pa., since 1930. Served as private, 4th O.T.C., Camp Custer, Mich., 1918; lt. 25th Co., Central O.T.S., Camp Lee, Va., 1918. Mem. N.E.A., Pa. State Edn. Assn. (life mem.; v.p. Southeastern Conv. Dist.), Delaware Co. Teachers Assn. (pres.), Rittenhouse Astron. Soc., Dept. Secondary Sch. Prins., Pa. State Alumni Assn., Am. Legion (past comdr.), Pa. State Fish and Game Protective Assn., Phi Delta Kappa. Mason (A. A.O.N.M.S.). Republican. Presbyn. Club: Swarthmore Rotary. Home: 18 Amherst Av., Swarthmore, Pa.

MOREY, George W(ashington), chemist; b. Minneapolis, Minn., Jan. 9, 1888; s. George Washington and Celia (Murphy) M.; B.S., U. of Minn., 1909; m. Lillian Dame, Sept. 10, 1910; 1 dau., Jane Belle. Asst. in chemistry, U. of Minn., 1907-09; asst. chemist, U.S. Bur. Standards, 1909-12, physical chemist, Geophysical Lab., Carnegie Instn., Washington, D.C., since 1912. Cons. expert, Internat. Critical Tables (glass). Mfr. optical glass, War Industries Bd., 1917-18; gen. mgr. Spencer Lens Co., 1918-20. Baker lecturer, Cornell U., 1932. Fellow Soc. Glass Technology (England); mem. Am. Chem. Soc., American Optical Society, American Ceramic Soc. (chairman glass division, 1931-32), Washington Acad. Sciences, Washington Chem. Soc. (treas. 1926-28; pres. 1928), Am. Soc. Testing Materials (chmn. com. glass and glass products), Am. Orchid Soc., Alpha Chi Sigma. Mason. Club: Cosmos. Home: 6 Pinehurst Circle, Chevy Chase, Md. Office: Geophysical Lab., 2801 Upton St. N.W., Washington, D.C.*

MORFORD, James Richard, lawyer; b. Wilmington, Del., Aug. 17, 1898; s. William H. and Ella P. (Ward) M.; ed. Dickinson Coll. of Law, 1916-17; LL.B., George Washington U. Law Sch., 1921; m. Claire A. Rhoads, May 5, 1917 (divorced 1936); children—James R., Jr., Constance; m. 2d, Elizabeth E. Meigs, Apr. 19, 1939. Admitted to Del. bar, 1921 and since engaged in gen. practice of law at Wilmington; mem. firm Marvel, Morford & Logan and predecessor firms since 1925; asst. city solicitor, Wilmington, 1923-25; chief dep. atty. gen., Del., 1925-28; city solicitor, Wilmington, 1935-38; atty. gen. of Del. since 1939. Served as ensign, U.S.N.R.F., 1918-19. Mem. Am., Del. State and New Castle Co. bar assns., Am. Legion, Vets. Fgn. Wars, Nat. Aeronautic Assn. Republican. Presbyn. Mason (32°). B.P.O.E. Clubs: University, Country (Wilmington). Home: The Cedars, Marshallton. Office: Delaware Trust Bldg., Wilmington, Del.

MORGAN, Albert Thomas, lawyer, banker; b. California, Pa., Oct. 8, 1872; s. Lewis W. and Ann Jane (Gregg) M.; student Calif. (Pa.) State Teachers Coll., Washington and Jefferson Coll., Washington, Pa., and Dickinson Law Sch., Carlisle, Pa.; m. Fannie Virginia Brewster, Sept. 1, 1906; 1 son, Duncan Jerome. Was vice-prin. pub. schs., Latrobe, Pa.; admitted to all Pa. State and Federal cts., including Supreme Ct. of U.S.; v.p., atty. and dir. First Nat. Bank & Trust Co. of East Pittsburgh, First Nat. Bank of Swissvale, Pa.; atty. and dir. First Nat. Bank of Wilmerding, Pa.; dir. Wilkinsburg Real Estate and Trust Co. Trustee Allegheny Coll.; dir. and atty. M.E. Ch. Union, The Goodwill Industries, Pittsburgh, Pa.; dir. and chmn. social service com. of Pittsburgh Council of Chs. Mem. Allegheny Co. Bar Assn., Pa. State Bar Assn., Am. Bar Assn. Methodist. Home: 412 Maple Av., Edgewood. Office: 1808 Law and Finance Bldg., 429 Fourth Av., Pittsburgh, Pa.

MORGAN, Alfred Powell, electrical engr.; b. Brooklyn, Apr. 15, 1889; s. Frederick Powell and Margaret (Pattison) M.; grad. Monclair (N. J.) High Sch., 1908; student Mass. Inst. Tech.; m. 2d, Ruth Whigham Shackleford, Nov. 19, 1927; children—by 1st marriage, Merritt; by 2d marriage, Alfred Powell, Charles Shackleford, Thomas Burris. Pres. Adams-Morgan Co., Morgan-Kline, Inc., A. P. Morgan, Inc.; formerly editor mech. and elec. dept., Boys' Magazine. Mem. Radio Club America, Inst. Radio Engrs. Clubs: New York Fishing, Newark Athletic. Author: How to Build a Biplane Glider, 1909; High Power Wireless Equip., 1910; Wireless Tele. Constrn. for Amateurs, 1910; Wireless Telegraphy and Telephony, 1912; The Boy Electrician, 1913; Model Flying Machines, 1913; Lessons in Wireless Telegraphy, 1912; Wireless Construction and Installation for Beginners, 1916; Experimental Wireless Construction, 1916; Homemade Electr. Apparatus, 1917; The Boy's Home Book of Science and Construction; The Story of Skyscrapers, 1934; Tropical Fish and Home Aquaria, 1935; A First Electrical Book for Boys, 1935; An Aquarium Book for Boys and Girls, 1936; Things a Boy Can Do with Electricity, 1938; The Pageant of Electricity, 1939. Contbr. articles to tech. mags. Contributed largely to development of radio telegraphy; developed and produced the first short wave regenerative receivers, with Paul Godley; holder of U.S. patents covering radio and mech. devices. Home: 69 Brookfield Rd., Upper Montclair, N.J.

MORGAN, Angela, author; b. Washington, D.C.; d. Alwyn (lawyer) and Carol Morgan (Baldwin) M.; ed. pub. schs. and under pvt. tutors, also spl. studies Columbia, and at Chautauqua, N.Y. Began as writer newspapers, Chicago, New York and Boston; contbr. prose and verse to mags.; specialized writer and interpreter of verse; gives author's readings and interpretations. Read original poem, "The Unknown Soldier," over bier of unknown soldier in rotunda of Capitol, Washington, D.C., first woman to occupy pulpit of Chapel Royal, Savoy, London, in author's reading, also appeared at Lyceum Club, London. Mem. Woman's Internat. League, Poetry Soc. America, Poetry Soc. London (a v.p.), League of Am. Pen Women (pres. Phila. br.), English-Speaking Union; chmn. Literary Arts Com. of Phila. Art Alliance; del. to Internat. Congress of Women, The Hague.

Prize winner in contest for new Am. anthem. Clubs: MacDowell, Three Arts (hon.), both of New York. Author: The Hour Has Struck (verse), 1914; The Imprisoned Splendor (fiction), 1915; Utterance and Other Poems, 1916; God Prays (booklet), 1917; Forward March! (verse), 1918; Hail, Man! (verse), 1919; Because of Beauty (verse), 1922; Silver Clothes, 1926; Selected Poems, 1927; Creator Man, 1929; Angela Morgan's Recitals (verse); Heaven Is Happening, 1931; Awful Rainbow (novel), 1932; Crucify Me! (verse), 1933; Gold on Your Pillow, 1936; Afterwhere, 1936. Nat. Federation of Women's Clubs at meeting in Richmond, Va., 1933, voted to dedicate her poem, "When Nature Wants a Man," to Franklin D. Roosevelt; her poem, "Runaway Gold" was voted best from Pa. in interstate competition for poems celebrating lighting of World's Fair, Chicago, 1933, by a beam from Arcturus; her poem to Will Rogers broadcast at dedication of Will Rogers Memorial Shrine. Elected honor poet, of Nat. Poetry Week, 1930, and awarded gold emblem; apptd. poet laureate of Gen. Federation of Women's Clubs. Address: Ogontz School, Rydal, Montgomery Co., Pa.

MORGAN, Carl Hamilton, clergyman, prof. Greek lang. and lit.; b. Camden, N.J., March 14, 1901; s. Albert D. and Elizabeth Mary (Hamilton) M.; A.B., U. of Pa., 1926; student, U. of Oxford, Eng., 1924; Th.M., Eastern Bapt. Theol. Sem., 1929, Th.D., same, 1932; A.M., U. of Pa., 1936; m. Mary McCollum Dunphey, May 17, 1929; children— Mary Elizabeth, Carol Anne. Engaged in teaching violin, Phila. Mus. Acad., 1920-28; teacher in Sch. of Music, Eastern Bapt. Theol. Sem., 1928-32; dir. collegiate dept., and prof. Greek lang. and lit., Eastern Bapt. Theol. Sem. since 1932; ordained to ministry Bapt. Ch., 1929. Mem. Phi Beta Kappa, Phi Delta Kappa. Republican. Baptist. Home: 519 Woodland Av., Haddonfield, N.J. Office: Eastern Bapt. Theol. Sem., S. Rittenhouse Sq., Philadelphia, Pa.

MORGAN, Charles Eldridge, 3d, lawyer; b. Phila., Pa., May 27, 1876; s. Charles E. and Lillie (Merrick) M.; A.B., Harvard, 1898; LL.B., U. of Pa., 1901; m. Theresa Hamilton Fish, Oct. 28, 1916. Began practice at Phila., 1901; mem. firm Morgan, Lewis & Bockius. Mem. Soc. of the Cincinnati. Republican. Episcopalian. Home: Newtown, Bucks Co., Pa. Office: Fidelity-Philadelphia Trust Bldg., Philadelphia, Pa.

MORGAN, Edward Morris, clergyman; b. Lockhaven, Pa., Dec. 18, 1881; s. Morris and Lavina Pauline (Beck) M.; A.B., Susquehanna U., 1903, A.M., same, 1906; B.D., Selinsgrove Theol. Sem., 1906; (hon.) D.D., Susquehanna U., 1924; m. Margaret E. Arbogast, April 2, 1904; children—Morris Jonathan, Julia Pauline (Mrs. Hewitt B. McCloskey), Edward Arbogast (dec.). Ordained to ministry U. Luth. Ch., 1906; pastoral charges, Milroy, Pa., 1906-07, Tyrone, Pa., 1908-11, Mifflintown, Pa., 1911-17, Tyrone, Pa., since 1920. Served as army sec. Y.M.C.A., Camp Meade, Md., and Baltimore, Md., 1918-20. Pres. Pub. Health Assn., Ambulance Assn.; commr. Boy Scouts, Tyrone, Pa., 1917-18. Dir. Tyrone Chapter Am. Red Cross. Mem. Central Pa. Synod U. Luth Ch. Republican. Lutheran. Mason (32°, Shriner). I.O.O.F. Club: Kiwanis of Tyrone, Pa. (charter mem. past pres.). Home: 1260 Logan Av., Tyrone, Pa.

MORGAN, F(isher) Corlies, univ. treas.; b. Philadelphia, Pa., May 16, 1875; s. John Buck and Sarah Fisher (Corlies) M.; prep. edn., Friends Select Sch., Germantown, Phila.; A.B., U. of Pa., 1896; LL.B., 1900; m. Mary Newbold Welsh Frazer, Sept. 5, 1908 (now dec.); m. 2d, Lilian Bartow Smith, June 4, 1917. In gen. practice of law, Phila., 1899-1917; mem. legal dept. The United Gas Improvement Co., 1900-10; treas. U. of Pa. since 1919; dir. Germantown Trust Co., San Luis Valley Land & Cattle Co. Served in various positions including asst. mgr. Pa.-Del. Div. Am. Red Cross, 1917-19. Trustee Moore Sch. of Elec. Engring.; mgr. Grad. Hosp. of U. of Pa. Mem. Am. and Phila. bar assns., Acad. Natural Sciences, Franklin Inst., Am. Acad. Polit. and Social Science, Linguistic Soc. America, Zoöl. Soc. of Phila., Soc. Colonial Wars, S.A.R., Hist. Soc. Pa., Welcome Soc., Zeta Psi. Republican. Presbyn. Clubs: University, Rittenhouse, Lenape, Sunnybrook Golf, Germantown Cricket; Winter Harbor (Me.) Yacht; Pohoqualine Fish. Home: 8625 Montgomery Av., Chestnut Hill, Philadelphia. Office: 3446 Walnut St., Philadelphia, Pa.

MORGAN, James Henry, coll. pres.; b. Concord, Del., Jan. 21, 1857; s. Samuel Jefferson and Julia Fooks (James) M.; A.B., Dickinson Coll., 1878, A.M., 1881; Ph.D., Bucknell U., 1892; LL.D., Pa. Coll., 1916, Franklin and Marshall Coll., 1917, U. of Pittsburgh, 1919; D.D., Wesleyan U., 1917; m. Mary Rebecca Curran, Dec. 30, 1890; children—Julia, Margaret Harris, Hugh Curran. Teacher, 1878-79, vice-prin., 1879-81, Pennington (N.J.) Sem.; teacher, Rugby Acad., Phila., 1881-82; prin. Dickinson Coll. Prep. Sch., Carlisle, Pa., 1882-84; adj. prof. Greek, 1884-90, prof. Greek, 1890-1914, dean, 1903-14, acting pres., 1914-15, pres., 1915-28, 1931-32, and 1933-34, Dickinson College. Sch. dir. Carlisle, Pa., 1898-1904. Mem. Gen. Conf. M.E. Ch., 1916. Mem. A.A.A.S., Am. Philol. Assn.; sec. Pa. Anti-Saloon League Mem. M.E. Ch. Author: History of Dickinson College, 1933. Home: Carlisle, Pa.

MORGAN, Jerome John, prof. chem. engring.; b. Russell, Pa., April 22, 1880; s. Martin and Christine (Hinkle) M.; B.S., Pa. State Coll., 1905, M.S., same, 1910; Ph.D., Columbia U., 1919; m. Elizabeth Perry, Aug. 21, 1907; children—Florence (Mrs. William L. F. Hardham), Jerome Perry. Engaged as asst. prof. chemistry, U. of Md., 1906-08; prof. chemistry, Coll. of Hawaii, 1908-09; instr. and asst. prof. chemistry, Stevens Inst. Tech., 1909-19; asst. prof. chem. engring., Columbia U., 1919-26, asso. prof., 1926-37, prof. since 1937; cons. engr. and pub. Mem. A.A.A.S., Am. Chem. Soc., Am. Gas Assn., Am. Inst. Chem. Engrs., Soc. for Promotion Engring. Edn., Phi Lambda Upsilon, Phi Kappa Phi, Sigma Xi, Tau Beta Pi. Republican. Methodist. Mason. Club: Canoe Brook Country (Summit, N.J.). Author: American Gas Practice, Vol. I, Production of Manufactured Gas, 1926 and 1931, Vol. II, Distribution and Utilization of City Gas, 1928 and 1935. Contbr. sci. articles to tech. jours. Home: 67 Salter Pl., Maplewood, N.J.

MORGAN, John Davis, cons. engr.; b. nr. Atlanta, Ga., June 6, 1884; s. Thomas George and Agnes (Davis) M.; student Sheffield Scientific Sch. of Yale U., Carnegie Inst. Tech. and Royal Engrs. Sch.; m. Caroline Frommel Schaller; 1 son, John Davis. Pres. Rider Ericsson Engine Co., Green Hedge Realty Co., Power Patents Co. Served as 1st lt., capt., maj. lt. col., Engrs. Corps, U.S.A.; now col. Q.M. Corps 3d Mil. Area since 19—. Mem. Am. Soc. Mech. Engrs., Soc. Professional Engrs., N.Y. Soc. Professional Engrs., Naval Inst., Soc. Am. Mil. Engrs., Mil. Order World War, Mil. Order Fgn. Wars, Army Ordnance Assn., Quartermasters Assn., Am. Legion. Republican. Baptist. Clubs: Crestmont Country (West Orange); Essex County Country. Home: High Hickory, Wyoming Av., South Orange, N.J. Office: 60 Wall St., New York, N.Y.

MORGAN, Sister M. Sylvia, prof. of chemistry; b. Glynneath, Glamorganshire, Wales, Nov. 13, 1889; d. William Joseph and Tydfil (Morris) Morgan; brought to U.S., 1893, naturalized, 1931; B.S., Coll. of New Rochelle, 1916; M.S., Fordham U., 1920; Sc.D., American U., 1925; summer student U. of Notre Dame, 1918, Columbia, 1928. Teacher of science, St. John's High Sch., Pittston, Pa., 1909-12, Marywood Sem., Scranton, Pa., 1912-19; prof. of chemistry and dir. of science, Maywood Coll., Scranton, since 1916. Fellow A.A.A.S.; mem. Am. Chem. Soc., Pa. Acad. of Science, Museum of Natural History. Pi Gamma Mu. Roman Catholic. Author of monographs: Analysis of Various Types of Oranges; Surface Tension in Detoxication Products. Home: Marywood College, Scranton, Pa.

MORGAN, Marshall Shapleigh, banking; b. Phila., Pa., June 2, 1881; s. Randal and Anna (Shapleigh) M.; ed. Germantown Acad., De Lancey Sch.; A.B., U. of Pa., 1904; m. Louise Johnson, June 6, 1906; children—Grace Price (Mrs. Henry S. Jeanes, Jr.), Anna S. (Mrs. Edward M. Greene, Jr.), Randal 3d, Marcella L. (Mrs. William Lang Day). With United Gas Improvement Co., one year; served as officer and dir. various st. ry. and interurban cos. in Ind. and O., 1905-20; asst. to chmn. of bd., Fidelity-Phila. Trust Co., 1920-37, pres. since 1937; dir. North Pa. R.R., Phila. Saving Fund. Soc., Supplee-Biddle Hardware Co., American Briquet; Stonega Coke & Coal Co., Virginia Coal & Iron Co. Dir. Franklin Inst., Pa. Acad. Fine Arts, Southeastern Pa. Chapter Am. Red Cross, Pa. Inst. for the Deaf, Sheltering Arms of P.E. Ch., Thomas Skelton Harrison Foundation, Merchants Fund (vice-pres. and dir., sec. Phila. Foundation Com. Republican. Episcopalian. Clubs: Rittenhouse, Manufacturers and Bankers, Midday, Philadelphia, Radnor Hunt. Member, Sons of the Revolution. Home: R.F.D. No. 2, Malvern, Pa. Office: 135 S. Broad St., Philadelphia, Pa.

MORGAN, Ora Sherman, agriculturist; b. Hampshire, Ill., Aug. 11, 1877; s. Lyman Delos and Elizabeth Ann (Helmar) M.; grad. State Normal U., at Normal, Ill., 1899; A.B., U. of Ill., 1905; M.S.A., Cornell U., 1907, Ph.D., 1909; m. Rose LeVille Huff, Oct. 4, 1908. Teacher dist. and high schs., Ill. and Ia., until 1905; substitute prin. Training Sch. of Northern Ill. State Normal Coll., 1905-06; dir. N.Y. State Sch., Agr., Alfred, N.Y., 1908-12; leave of absence as teacher summer session, Columbia, 1911; prof. agrl. economics and head dept., Columbia, since 1911. Agrl. advisor for N.Y. City Draft Bd., by appmt. U.S. Dept. Agr., 1918-19; mem. Food Com. of Mchts'. Assn., New York since 1917; mem. Nat. Advisory Com. of Near East Relief; advisory dir. agrl., ednl. and reconstructional work for Am. Near East Relief since 1926; made agrl. surveys for Near East Relief, 1926 and 1927; dir. of edn. for Near East Relief in Armenia, summer 1926; trustee Michael Anasgnos Schs., Greece since 1929; a dir. Near East Foundation since 1930. Official del. from Columbia U. to XV Internat. Congress of Agr., Prague, 1931; del. to 9th Internat. Dairy Congress, Copenhagen, 1931. Editor, "Agricultural Systems of Middle Europe," Macmillan Co., 1933. Mem. exec. com. of The American Com. of the Internat. Institute of Agriculture; mem. council of Internat. Conf. of Agrl. Economists; mem. agrl. com. The Resettlement of Jews, Div. Nat. Coördinating Com. Mem. A.A.A.S., Acad. Polit. Science, Am. Acad. Polit. and Social Science, Am. Econ. Assn., Am. Farm Economic Assn., Gamma Alpha, Sigma Xi. Mason. Home: 144 Longview Av., Leonia, N.J.

MORGAN, Peto W(hittaker), banker; b. California, Pa., Dec. 27, 1862; s. Lewis W. and Ann Jane (Gregg) M.; grad. State Teachers Coll., California, Pa., 1879; m. Annie Amelia Kendig, Dec. 27, 1898; children—Lewis W., Jane Craig. Teacher at Grandville, Pa., 1880-81, Irwin, Pa., 1889-93; bookkeeper Morgan & Dixon, 1881-89; cashier F.&M. Nat. Bank, Mt. Pleasant, Pa., 1893-95; cashier First Nat. Bank, Wilmerding, Pa., 1895-1911, president since 1911; director First Nat. Bank of Swissvale; chmn. bd. First Nat. Bank and Trust Co. of East Pittsburgh, Wilkinsburg Real Estate & Trust Co.; pres. Swissvale Trust Co. Republican. Methodist. Mason. Club: Duquesne. Home: 320 Maple Av., Edgewood, Pittsburgh. Office: First National Bank, Wilmerding, Pa.

MORGAN, Philip Sidney, real estate; b. Baltimore, Dec. 31, 1876; s. DeWitt Clinton and Sarah B. (Hurst) M.; student Johns Hopkins U.; m. Caroline McCabe, Apr. 9, 1901; children—Philip S., Jr., Sarah Elizabeth Jelley. Owned and operated a large cattle ranch in Western Tex., 1900-09; mem. firm Turnbull & Morgan, real estate, Baltimore, 1909, later Philip S. Morgan & Co.; now pres. Morgan & Purnell. Served as mem. Criminal Justice Commission, Commission on Efficiency and Economy, both of Baltimore. First vice-pres. Md. Tuberculosis Assn.; sec. Endowed Sanatorium for Consumptives. Pres. Johns Hopkins Mus. Assn.

Mem. Real Estate Bd. of Baltimore (pres. twice), Phi Gamma Delta, S.A.R., S.R., Soc. Colonial Wars. Democrat. Methodist. Club: Johns Hopkins Faculty. Home: 305 Woodlawn Rd. Office: 514 St. Paul St., Baltimore, Md.

MORGAN, Sherley Warner, prof. architecture; b. Cincinnati, O., Apr. 4, 1892; s. Asa Bushnell and Lydia Eleanor (Moore) M.; A.B., Princeton U., 1913; B.Arch., Columbia U., 1917; m. Ethel Palmer, June 16, 1920; children—Eleanor Harrison, Arthur Palmer, Richard Sherley, Diana Melville. Engaged as draftsman, 1915; part-time instr., Princeton U., 1915-16, instr., 1916-17, asst. prof. architecture, 1919-25, asso. prof., 1925-31, prof. architecture since 1931; dir. Sch. of Architecture Princeton U. since 1928; practicing architect while teaching, asso. with E. A. Park, 1921-25; dir. E. R. Squibb & Sons, Inc., N.Y. City. Served as pvt. later capt. inf. U.S.A., 1917-19, with A.E.F., St. Mihiel, Meuse Argonne offensives; comdg. officer U.S.A. student detachment U. of Montpelier, France, 1919. Chmn. bd. trustees, Princeton Country Day Sch., Princeton, N.J. Mem. Assn. Coll. Schs. of Architecture (past pres.), Am. Inst. Architects, Archaeol. Inst. America, Princeton Archtl. Assn., Phi Beta Kappa, Psi Upsilon. Honored as Officier d'Academie de la Republique Francais. Republican. Presbyn. Clubs: Terrace, Nassau (Princeton); Princeton, Century (New York); Ekwanok Country (Manchester, Vt.). Home: 145 Hodge Rd., Princeton, N.J.

MORGAN, T. Frank, printing; b. Warsaw, Va., Nov. 27, 1869; s. James M. and Francis Ann (Garner) M.; LL.B., George Washington U., 1899; LL.M., Nat. U., Washington, D.C., 1890; m. Grace Lee Fisher, June 9, 1897. Employed as supt. of all production depts. in the Govt. Printing Office for many yrs. including the World War period; exec. vice-pres. Lanston Monotype Machine Co., Philadelphia, Pa., since 1931. Episcopalian. Mason (K.T., 32°, Shriner). Club: Penn Athletic. Home: Alden Park Manor. Office: 24th at Locust St., Philadelphia, Pa.

MORGAN, Tali Esen, musical author, conductor; b. Llangynwyd, Glamorganshire, S. Wales, Oct. 28, 1858; s. Thomas Llyfnwy (noted Welsh historian) and Gwen M.; studied music from childhood; came to Scranton, Pa., with the family in 1877; hon. Mus.D.; m. Mary J. Jones, Jan. 31, 1881 (died Sept. 20, 1938); children—Ethel, Oscar, Edith, Kays, Paul (dec.), Marion. Mgr. and conductor of summer music festivals at Ocean Grove for 17 yrs., directing choruses of 1,200 voices and orchestra of 100; dir. vol. ch. choir (200) at the Central Meth. Ch., Brooklyn; dir. New York Festival Chorus; founder and pres. Internat. Corr. Sch. of Music; dir. Mt. Vernon (N.Y.) Choral Club of 1st M.E. Ch. (200 voices). Founder Nat. Assn. Organists, also Musicians Club of New York. Author of a standard course of music instrn. for teachers and pub. sch. supervisors. Home: Interlaken, Asbury Park, N.J.; (summer) Thousand Island Park, N.Y. Address: Central Church, 144 St. Felix St., Brooklyn, N.Y.

MORGAN, Theophilous John, artist; b. Cincinnati, O., Nov. 1, 1872; s. Theopilous John and Laura (Finch) M.; student St. Francis Xavier Coll., 1884-90; studied Cincinnati Art Sch., pupil of Rebisso Duveneck, Meakin, Lutz, Noble; m. Helice Marie Tracy, 1925. Works: "Long Point Lighthouse," "Witchery of the Moon," "The Road to Truro," "The Path of the Moon," "In Arcadia," "Old Willows," "Town Hall," "Fishing Boats." Represented in Lessing Rosenwald Collection, Phila.; Delgado Mus. of Art, New Orleans; Univ. of Ind.; Women's Hosp., Cleveland; Springville (Utah) Art Mus.; Aurora (Ill.) Mus.; Mus. of Fine Arts, Houston; Witte Memorial Mus., San Antonio; Women's Club Galleries, Harlingen, Tex.; Montgomery (Ala.) Women's Coll. Mus.; Girl Scouts Galleries, San Antonio; Los Angeles Mus. of Fine Arts; Highland Park, Soc. of Artists, Dallas. Dir. Sears Roebuck Art Galleries, Washington, D.C., 1932, East High Sch., Salt Lake City, 1934. Awards: First prize ($2500), Tex. Wild Flower Competition, 1928; gold medal, Davis Wild Flower Competition, also hon. mention, 1929; 1st prize Springfield Art Assn., Utah, 1930; Edgar B. Davis prize, 1928-30; Pabst gold medal, 1929. Mem. San Antonio Palette Assn., Washington Soc. of Artists. San Diego Art Assn., San Antonio Art League, Southern States Art League. Clubs: Washington Art; New York Water Color; Beachcombers (Princeton, Mass.). Home: Forest Glen, Md. Studio: 456 N. St. S.W., Washington, D.C.*

MORGAN, William Leverette, lawyer; b. Madison, N.Y., Mar. 27, 1873; s. Leverette J. and Adelia D. (Babcock) M.; student Rome (N.Y.) Free Acad., 1886-90; A.B., Syracuse (N.Y.) University, 1894, A.M., 1896; post graduate work in classical philology at Harvard University, 1896; m. Clara Gere Reed, Apr. 21, 1897; children—William Leverette, Mary Elizabeth (Mrs. John M. Ellis). Latin and Greek instr., Delaware Literary Inst., Franklin, N.Y., 1894-95, Wells Coll. Prep. Sch., Aurora, N.Y., 1897-98; head of Latin and Greek dept., Newark (N.J.) High Sch., 1898-1905; asso. with law firm Pitney, Hardin & Skinner, Newark, N.J., since 1905, mem. of firm since 1908; sec. and asst. treas. Newark (N.J.) Evening News; dir. L. Bamberger & Co., Nat. Newark Essex Banking Co., La Monte Safety Paper Co. V.p. and trustee Marcus L. Ward Home for Aged and Respectable Widowers and Bachelors; pres. bd. of trustees Newark Tech. Sch., Newark Coll. of Engring.; v.p. bd. of trustees Hosp. and Home for Crippled Children, Newark; formerly trustee State Teachers Pension and Annuity Fund; trustee Presbyn. Hosp., Newark. Mem. N.J. and Am. bar assns., Psi Upsilon. Republican. Presbyterian. Mason (St. Johns Lodge No. 1). Clubs: Down Town, Essex (Newark, N.J.); Manasquan River Yacht (Brielle, N.J.); Essex County Country. Home: 83 Lincoln Av., Newark; and Brielle, N.J. Office: National Newark Bldg., Newark, N.J.

MORITZ, Theodore L., ex-congressman; b. Toledo, O., Feb. 10, 1892; s. Edward and Mary (Schneider) M.; B.A., Dayton Coll., 1914; LL.B., Duquesne U., 1923; m. Agnes M. Stevenson. Teacher in high schs., 1915-25; in law practice at Pittsburgh, 1925-33; sec. to mayor of Pittsburgh, 1933-35; mem. 74th Congress (1935-37), 32d Pa. Dist. Catholic. Home: 6057 Stanton Av., Pittsburgh, Pa.*

MORLEDGE, Joseph Scott, clergyman; b. Cumberland, O., Mar. 3, 1901; s. Howard Cassady (D.D.) and Anna (Walker) M.; A.B., Grove City Coll., 1922; Th.B., Princeton Theol. Sem., 1927; A.M., Princeton U., 1927; (hon.) D.D., Grove City Coll., 1936; m. Margaret Ellen Hodge, June 21, 1927; children—Margaret Joan, Richard Addison. Engaged in teaching high sch., 1922-24; ordained to ministry Presbyn. Ch., 1927; minister Mt. Prospect Presbyn. Ch., Hickory, Pa., 1927-30; minister Third Presbyn. Ch., Washington, Pa., 1930-34; minister Sixth Presbyn. Ch., Pittsburgh, Pa., since 1934. Republican. Presbyn. Home: 1408 Wightman St., Pittsburgh, Pa.

MORNINGSTAR, Samuel Reed, wholesale bakeries; b. Huntingdon, Pa., June 26, 1886; s. George Franklin and Mary Catherine (Reed) M.; ed. high sch., Huntingdon, Pa., 1900-03, Williamson (Pa.) Trade Sch., 1903-07, Juniata Coll., Huntingdon, Pa., 1907-09; m. Margaret Mae Stott, Aug. 7, 1913; 1 dau., Laura Catherine. Employed in various positions until 1917; propr. gen. ins. agency, 1918; asso. with Morningstar Bakeries, largest bakery in U.S. for size of town, Philipsburg, Pa., and pres. and gen. mgr. since 1918; pres. and treas. Morningstar-Schnars Coal Co. Served as mem. Town Council. Past pres. Pa. Bakers Assn., Philipsburg Rotary Club. Republican. Methodist (trustee M.E. Ch.). Rotarian. Clubs: Central Counties Golf Assn. (past pres.), Philipsburg Country (trustee). Home: 202 S. Center St. Office: 408 N. Front St., Philipsburg, Pa.

MOROSO, John Antonio, author; b. Charleston, S.C., Aug. 17, 1874; s. John Antonio and Sarah (Owens) M.; grad. S.C. Mil. Acad., 1894 (class poet); m. Virginia Osborne, June 24, 1900. Engaged in newspaper work, 1894-1907; contbr. verse to newspapers and mags., 1900-07. Mem. Authors' League America, Poetry Soc. America, Dickens Fellowship (New York). Author: The Quarry, 1913; (play) Alias Santa Claus, prod. 1917; (play) Miracle Mary, prod. 1918; The People Against Nancy Preston, 1921; The Stumbling Herd, 1923; Cap Fallon, Firefighter, 1923; The City of Silent Men, 1923; Bread Eaten in Secret, 1931; Poor Passionate Fool, 1932; Marta Christiansen, 1933. Home: Cresskill, Bergen Co., N.J.

MORREALE, Eugenio, consul; b. Palermo, Italy, Jan. 28, 1891; s. Antonino and Teresa (Ariata) M.; Ph.D., Univ. of Pavia, 1919; m. Emilia De Castro, Feb. 9, 1920; children—Margherita, Maria, Gabriella. Began career as newspaper editor, 1909; entered Royal Italian consular service; press attaché Italian legation at Vienna, 1928; Royal Italian consul at Baltimore, Md. Served in Royal Italian Army during World War. Awarded Croix de Guerre; Commendatore Corona d'Italia, Cavaliere dell' Ordine dei SS. Maurizio e Lazzaro. Office: 6 W. Mount Vernon Pl., Baltimore, Md.

MORRELL, Joseph Alan, research chemist, physiologist; b. Harriston, Ont., Nov. 9, 1897; s. Richard and Jessie (Howes) M.; brought to U.S., 1898; B.A., U. of Toronto, 1921, M.A., 1922, Ph.D., 1924; m. Muriel Eveline Berry, Mar. 29, 1919 (divorced); m. 2d, Della Wilma Beekman, Aug. 9, 1934. Research fellow and instr., U. of Toronto, 1921-24; research chemist and physiologist, E. R. Squibb & Sons Research Lab., New Brunswick, N.J., since 1924, in charge production of glandular products and development of new products. Served as sapper, later sergt. Canadian Engrs., 1916-19 with B.E.F. Mem. A.A.A.S., Am. Chem. Soc., Assn. for Study Internal Secretions, Soc. for Exptl. Biology and Medicine, Phi Lambda Psi. Republican. Episcopalian. Home: Colonial Gardens, New Brunswick, N.J.

MORRILL, Dorothy Isabella, coll. prof.; b. Auburn, Me., Dec. 27, 1891; d. John Adams and Isabella Olive (Littlefield) M.; A.B., Mount Holyoke Coll., South Hadley, Mass., 1914; A.M., U. of Mich., 1915; A.M., Radcliffe Coll., Cambridge, Mass., 1919, Ph.D., 1921. Instr. German, State Normal Sch., Bloomsburg, Pa., 1915-18; asst. prof. English, Hood Coll., Frederick, Md., 1921-22, asso. prof., 1922-24, prof. since 1924. Mem. Modern Lang. Assn., Shakespeare Assn., Am. Assn. Univ. Profs., Am. Assn. Univ. Women, Phi Beta Kappa. Democrat. Conglist. Contbr. to professional publs. Address: Hood College, Frederick, Md.

MORRIS, Charles McDowell, psychologist; b. Germantown, Phila., Pa., May 2, 1909; s. William Norman and Rebekah (McDowell) M.; student Germantown Acad., Phila., 1915-27; A.B., Bucknell U., Lewisburg, Pa., 1931, M.A., 1932; Ph.D., New York U., 1938; m. Julia Furst, April 13, 1933; 1 dau., Linda. Grad. assistant in psychology, New York U., 1932-36; alumni sec. and editor, Alumni Monthly, Bucknell Univ., Lewisburg, Pa., 1936-38; resident psychologist, Woods Sch., Langhorne, Pa., since 1938. Member Am. Psychol. Assn., Am. Assn. of Applied and Professional Psychologists, Internat. Council for Exceptional Children, Phi Kappa Psi, Psi Chi, Kappa Phi Kappa, Pi Delta Upsilon, Friars. Democrat. Episcopalian. Abstractor in field of education of exceptional children, Education Abstracts. Author: A Critical Analysis of Certain Performance Tests, 1939, Measurable Error in Entrance Requirements, 1932. Home: 250 S. State St., Newtown, Pa. Office: Woods Sch., Langhorne, Pa.

MORRIS, David, clergyman; b. Morriston, Wales, Gt. Britain, Aug. 9, 1882; s. William and Elizabeth (Davies) M.; came to U.S., 1895, naturalized, 1918; A.B., Washington and Jefferson Coll., 1910; B.D., Crozer Theol. Sem., 1915; grad. study, U. of Pa., 1914-15; A.M., Washington and Jefferson Coll., 1915; m. Daisy E. Paul, June 15, 1911; children—Daisy Miriam (Mrs. Theodore Coelho), Ruth Gwendolyn (Mrs. James Hall), Esther Priscilla, Elizabeth Mildred. Ordained to ministry Bapt. Ch., 1912; built and founded First Bapt. Ch., Canonsburg, Pa., pastor, 1906-10; pastor, Minersville, Pa., 1911-13; established and built

First Ch., Steubenville, O., pastor, 1915-20; pastor, Geneva, O., 1920-22, Youngstown, O., 1922-27; pastor Allison Av. Ch., Washington, Pa., since 1927; served on many coms. in Bapt. Ch. assns. Candidate for Congress on Prohibition ticket, 1936. Republican. Baptist. Home: 104 Maple Av., Washington, Pa.

MORRIS, Earle Hedderich, civil and valuation engr.; b. Evansville, Ind., July 23, 1887; s. James Paley and Eleanora (Hedderich) M.; B.S. in C.E., Purdue U., Lafayette, Ind., 1912; (hon.) C.E., Purdue U., 1919; m. Alice McCoy, June 3, 1912; children—John Richard, Robert Lewis, Elizabeth Jane, Gloria Ellen. Employed as asst. engr. Am. Creosoting Co., Bogalusa, La. and Trenton, Ont., 1912-14; asst. engr., C.&E.I.R.R., Evansville, Ind., 1914-16; construction engr., E.&I.R.R., Terre Haute, Ind., 1916-17; asst. engr., Pub. Service Commn. Ind., Indianapolis, Ind., 1917-20; chief engr. Bd. of R.R. Commrs., Bismarck, N.D., 1920-31; chief engr. Pub. Service Commn. of W.Va., Charleston, W.Va., since 1931. Mem. Am. Soc. Civil Engrs., Am. Inst. Elec. Engrs., W.Va. Soc. Professional Engrs., Am. Water Works Assn. Registered professional engr. in W.Va. Presbyn. Home: 843 Edgewood Drive, Charleston, W.Va.

MORRIS, Edward Allen, clergyman; b. Baltimore, Md., Dec. 4, 1897; s. John Edward and Lillie Cora (Vickers) M.; ed. James Millikin U., Decatur, Ill., 1916-18, Johns Hopkins U., 1918, 1923; A.B., Bates Coll., 1921; B.D., Yale U. Divinity Sch., 1926; m. Thelma Jacobs, July 28, 1920; children—Glenys, Edward A., Jr., Charles R., Mary E., Janice A. Ordained to ministry Congregational Ch., 1921; preaching regularly (as student pastor) since 1916; pastor Orthodox Congl. Ch., Arlington, Mass., 1926-30; minister, First Presbyn. Ch. (organized in 1712), Trenton, N.J., since 1930; chmn. Standing Com. on Nat. Missions of 150th Gen. Assembly, Presbyn. Ch., U.S.A.; sec. Com. Nat. Missions, Presbytery of New Brunswick; mem. U. Promotion Com., Presbytery of New Brunswick and Synod of N.J.; pres. Trenton Council of Churches; instr. and vesper leader, N.J. Summer School of Christian Work, Blair Acad., 1939; chmn. Com. of Synod of N.J. against Race Track Gambling Legislation, 1939. Served in S.A.T.C., 1918. Trustee Presbyn. Home of Synod of N.J.; dir. Trenton City Rescue Mission. Mem. Trenton Council of Chs., Am. Legion (past chaplain Trenton post), Delta Sigma Rho. Republican. Presbyn. Mason. Author: Truths That Abide, 1938. Hon. mem. Eugene Field Soc., Nat. Assn. Authors and Journalists. Home: 26 Richey Place, Trenton, N.J.

MORRIS, Edward Shippen, dep. atty. gen.; b. Phila., Pa., Feb. 14, 1906; s. Roland S. and Augusta Twiggs Shippen (West) M.; student Phillips Exeter Acad., Exeter, N.H., 1921-24; student Princeton U., 1928; m. Leslie Crawford Hun, Apr. 16, 1932; 1 son, Roland. Admitted to Pa. bar, 1931, and practiced as mem. firm Duane, Morris & Heckscher, Phila., 1931-35; dep. atty. gen. for Commonwealth of Pa. since Feb. 1935; consul for Japan at Phila.; dir. Gilbert Spruance Paint Co., Jenks Food Co., Octavia Hill Assn., Big Brothers Assn., Jourden Tech. School, Inc. · Sec. Phila. Democratic City Com., 1933-35. Democrat. Episcopalian. Club: Princeton (Phila.). Home: 2129 Delancey St. Office: 1617 Land Title Bldg., Philadelphia, Pa.

MORRIS, Frank Kailer, surgeon; b. Baltimore, Md., Aug. 25, 1901; s. Eugene McHale and Margaret (Maloney) M.; A.B., Loyola Coll., 1923; M.D., U. of Md. Med. Sch., 1927; unmarried. Interne Union Memorial Hosp., Baltimore, Md., 1927-28, resident in gynecology and obstetrics, 1928-29; asso. to Dr. Thomas K. Galvin, 1929-37; mem. staff Mercy, Women of Md., Union Memorial, St. Joseph, Bon Secours, University, and South Baltimore hosps. Fellow Am. Med. Assn.; mem. Md. Chirurg. Soc., Baltimore City Med. Soc., Baltimore City Obstet. and Gynecol. Soc. (sec.), U. of Md. Med. Alumni Assn. (sec.). Roman Catholic. Home: 3414 Gwynns Falls Parkway. Office: 11 E. Chase St., Baltimore, Md.

MORRIS, Galloway C., official ins. cos.; b. Chester Co., Pa., Aug. 28, 1881; s. J. Cheston (M.D.) and Mary E. (Johnson) M.; student De Lancey Sch., Haverford Coll.; m. Elise Walker, Oct. 5, 1909; children—Muriel, Sophia M., Elise. Began career as clk. in office Johnson and Higgins, Phila., Pa., 1899; asso. with fire ins. agency, marine agency and brokerage, average adjusting; vice-pres. Ins. Co. of N. America, Alliance Ins. Co. of Phila., Philadelphia Fire and Marine Ins. Co., Philadelphia Investment Co.; retired, 1939. Republican. Episcopalian. Clubs: Rittenhouse, India House, University Barge. Home: Wayne. Office: 1600 Arch St., Philadelphia, Pa.

MORRIS, George, newspaper pub.; b. Fayette Co., Tenn., Jan. 30, 1886; s. Walter and Mary Etta (Parker) M.; B.A., Union University, Jackson, Tenn., 1906; LL.D. from the same univ. in 1928; m. Karen McGehee, July 23, 1907; 1 son, George. Asso. editor Nashville Banner, 1914-16; Washington corr. same newspaper, and sec. to Senator John K. Shields, 1916-17; editor Memphis News-Scimitar, 1918-26; editor Memphis Evening Appeal, 1926; vice-pres. Memphis Commercial Appeal, Inc., 1927-30, pres. and editor, 1931-32, asst. pub., 1933-37; Washington columnist and correspondent since 1937. Mem. Kappa Sigma. Named by Carnegie Peace Foundation as one of group of editors to study conditions in Europe, 1927. Del. to Dem. Nat. Conv., 1932. Democrat. Episcopalian. Home: Etowah Farm, Harwood, Md. Address: Scripps-Howard Newspaper Alliance, Washington, D.C.

MORRIS, George Baker, pres. Bradford Motor Works, Inc.; b. Pittsburgh, Pa., Aug. 12, 1883; s. Henry Thompson and Clara (Cassel) M.; student Yale, 1900-03; m. Bertha Kavanaugh, Oct. 30, 1913; children—Chapin Kavanaugh, Henry Thompson. Clk., Carnegie Steel Co., 1904-05; in mining business, 1905-1911; mgr. in partnership of Bradford (Pa.) Motor Works, 1911-28; pres. Bradford Motor Works, Inc., since 1928, dir. since 1928. Dir. Bradford Community Chest. Republican. Clubs: Bradford, Pennhills, Valley Hunt (Bradford, Pa.). Home: 123 Kennedy St. Office: 57 Holley Av., Bradford, Pa.

MORRIS, George D(elbert), refractory exec.; b. Green Lamp, O., Oct. 31, 1885; s. Albert Byron and Matilda Jane (Rayl) M.; student Marion (O.) High Sch., 1899-1903; ceramic engr., Ohio State U., Columbus, O., 1908, professional ceramic engr. (hon.), 1933; m. Mary Ethel Wilson, Jan. 1, 1913; children—Matilda Jane, John Wilson. Supt. Am. Sewer Pipe Co., Barberton, O., 1908-14, Eastern O. Sewer Pipe Co., Irondale, O., 1914-15; mgr. Evans & Howard Fire Brick Co., St. Louis, Mo., 1915-20; v.p. New Castle (Pa.) Refractories Co. since 1920, dir. since 1928; v.p. and dir. New Castle Hot Top Co. since 1929; v.p. Corundite Refractories, Massillon, O., since 1936; trustee and dir. Universal Sanitary Mfg. Co., New Castle, Pa., 1928-38. Republican. Methodist. Mason (Consistory). Club: Kiwanis (New Castle, Pa.). Home: 229 Fairfield Av. Office: New Castle Refractories Co., New Castle, Pa.

MORRIS, George Ford, painter and sculptor of horses; b. St. Joseph, Mo.; s. Joseph Euen and Jane Abigail (Lyon) M.; ed. pub. schs., Chicago, St. Joseph, Mo., Highland Park, Ill.; student Art Inst., Chicago, 1888, Julien's Acad., Paris, France, 1925-26; m. Alice Hayden Jones, 1915; 1 dau., Jane (Mrs. Irland Davis). At 16 illustrator Chicago Horseman; at 17 illustrator five of the most prominent horse and livestock papers in America; opened pub. studio, Chicago, early nineties, and worked there until 1907, when moved studio to New York, where practiced, 1907-16; in practice at Eatontown, N.J., 1916-24, Shrewsbury, N.J., since 1926, Aiken, S.C., (winter) since 1928. Painted portraits many noted champion horses and dogs; paintings exhibited Paris, France, Howard Young Galleries, New York, Chicago, Ill., Aiken, S.C., Saratoga, N.Y., Louisville, Ky., Kansas City, Mo., Fort Worth, Tex., Oklahoma City, Okla., etc. Founder mem. Am. Animal Artists Assn. (pres. and chmn. exec. com. since 1937), and of Soc. of Am. Sporting Art. Christian Scientist. Pub. George Ford Morris Annuals (champion horses), 1934-37. Address: (winter) Aiken, S.C., and Fordacre, Shrewsbury, N.J.

MORRIS, Harold Hulett, exec. chemist; b. Racine, Wis., Mar. 12, 1889; s. Harry and Helen Louise (Hulett) M.; B.A., U. of Wis., Madison, Wis., 1911, M.A., 1916, Ph.D., 1917; m. Alene Rollo, June 14, 1917 (divorced 1923); m. 2d, Vera J. Brand, March 12, 1933. Insr. chemistry, Mich. Agrl. Coll., East Lansing, 1911-12; asst. chemist Mont. Agrl. Exptl. Sta., Bozeman, 1912-14; instr. chemistry, U. of Wis., 1914-17; research chemist Nat. Carbon Co., Cleveland, O., 1917-18, Bond Mfg. Corpn., Wilmington, Del., 1921-23; research chemist E. I. du Pont de Nemours & Co., Wilmington, Del., 1918-21, exec. chemist since 1924, mgr. tech. service Krebs Pigment & Color Corpn. (subsidiary) since 1928. Fellow A.A.A.S.; mem. Acacia, Sigma Xi, Phi Lambda Upsilon, Alpha Chi Sigma. Republican. Mason (Shriner). Home: R.D. 3 Shipley Rd. Office: Nemours Bldg., Wilmington, Del.

MORRIS, Harrison Smith, author; b. Phila., Pa., Oct. 4, 1856; s. George W. and Catharine (Harris) M.; ed. pub. and pvt. schs.; m. Anna Wharton, June 2, 1896; 1 dau., Mrs. Catharine Morris Wright. Mng. dir. Pa. Acad. Fine Arts, 1893-1905; editor Lippincott's Magazine, 1899-1905; art editor Ladies' Home Journal, 1905-07; was chmn. com. on ways and means National Academy Design, N.Y.; pres. Wharton Steel Co., 1909-17. Commr.-gen. U.S. to Roman Art Exposition, 1911. Mem. Nat. Inst. Arts and Letters (v.p., treas.), Am. Philos. Soc., Phi Beta Kappa; pres. Contemporary Club, Philadelphia, 1915; president Art Association, Newport, Rhode Island; American secretary Keats-Shelley Memorial, Rome, Italy; Trustee Wagner Inst. Elector of Hall of Fame. Clubs: Franklin Inn, Sketch (Phila.); Salmagundi, Players, Lotos (New York, N.Y.); Corinthian Yacht and Conanicut Yacht. Author: A Duet, in Lyrics, poems (with J. A. Henry) 1883; Tales from Ten Poets, 1893; Madonna and Other Poems, 1894; Lyrics and Landscapes, 1908; Masterpieces of the Sea, biography of William T. Richards, 1912; Hannah Bye (a novel), 1920; Walt Whitman (biography, pub. in Italian), 1920, also in English with additions, 1929; The Landlord's Daughter (novel), 1923; Martial Notes (verse), 1929; Confessions In Art, 1929. Editor: In the Yule Log Glow, 1892; Where Meadows Meet the Sea, 1892; also wrote a continuation and completion of Lamb's Tales from Shakespeare, 1893. Contbr. verse and prose to mags. Cavaliere di Grande Groce decorato del Grande Cordone dell'Ordine della Corona d'Italia. Home: Pear Hill, Oak Lane P.O., Philadelphia, Pa.; (summer) Horse Head, Jamestown, R.I.

MORRIS, Homer Lawrence, economist; b. Dublin, Ind., July 1, 1886; s. Albert C. and Esther J. (Lawrence) M.; A.B., Earlham Coll., 1911; A.M., Columbia, 1918, Ph.D., 1921; m. Edna E. Wright, Sept. 19, 1916; 1 son, James Haisley. Instr. history and debating, Penn Coll., 1911-15; instr. economics, Hunter Coll., 1917-18; prof. economics, Earlham Coll., 1918-28; dir. child feeding relief, Berlin, Germany, under auspices of Am. Friends Service Com., 1921; field dir. famine relief, Buzuluk, Russia, 1922, and dir. child feeding relief in bituminous coal fields, 1931-32; dir. pub. relations, Reading (Pa.) Hosp., 1928-30; prof. economics, Fisk U., 1930-34; field supervisor Subsistence Homesteads Div., U.S. Dept. Interior, 1933-35; sec. Social-Industrial sect. Am. Friends Service Com. since 1935. Trustee Earlham Coll.; mem. bd. of mgrs. Pendle Hill School. Mem. Am. Economics Assn., Pi Gamma Mu. Mem. Soc. of Friends. Author: Parliamentary Franchise Reform in England from 1885 to 1918, 1921; The Plight of the Bituminous Coal Miner, 1934. Home: Plush Mill Rd., Wallingford, Pa. Address: Am. Friends Service Com., 20 So. 12th St., Philadelphia, Pa.

MORRIS, Hugh Martin, lawyer; b. Greenwood, Del., Apr. 9, 1878; s. William Wilkinson and Mary Luther (Collison) M.; A.B., Delaware Coll., 1898; LL.D. from the University of Delaware in 1928; m. Emma Carter Smith,

Oct. 10, 1908; 1 dau., Mary Smith. Began practice at Wilmington, Del., 1903; mem. firm Saulsbury, Morris & Rodney, 1914-19; v.p. Equitable Trust Co., Wilmington, 1915-19. Apptd. by President Wilson U.S. dist. judge, Dist. of Del., Jan. 27, 1919, resigned June 30, 1930; in practice at Wilmington since 1930; dir. Wilmington Trust Co.; Delaware Power Co., Del. Light & Power Co., Philadelphia, Baltimore & Washington R.R. Co.; Mgr. Wilmington Savings Fund Soc. Trustee U. of Delaware, Tower Hill School. Mem. Soc. Colonial Wars, S.A.R. (pres. Del. Chapter 1929-31), Phi Kappa Phi. Democrat. Episcopalian. Clubs: Wilmington, Rotary, Wilmington Country. Home: Polly Drummond Hill, Newark, Del. Office: du Pont Bldg., Wilmington, Del.

MORRIS, John James, Jr., lawyer; b. Georgetown, Del., Aug. 24, 1896; s. John Johnson and Belle (Donovan) M.; student Occidental Coll., 1917-18, Delaware Coll., 1919; LL.B. U. of Va., 1922; 1 son, John James. Admitted to Del. bar, 1923, and since practiced in Wilmington; asso. with U.S. Senator Daniel O. Hastings, 1923; partner Hering, Morris, James & Hitchens; U.S. atty. for Delaware since 1935. Served as 2d lt. inf., U.S. Army, World War. Mem. Am., Del. State and Newcastle Co. bar assns., Sigma Nu, Delta Theta Phi. Democrat. Methodist. Clubs: University, Wilmington Country. Home: University Club. Office: Delaware Trust Bldg., Wilmington, Del.

MORRIS, Lawrence Johnson, ins. exec.; b. West Chester, Pa., Sept. 27, 1870; s. Dr. J(ames) Cheston and Mary Ella Stuart (Johnson) M.; student Penn Charter Sch., Phila., 1881-85; A.B., Haverford (Pa.) Coll., 1889; unmarried. Partner Lawrence Johnson & Co., fgn. merchants, Phila., 1905-33; v.p. and dir. Phila. Warehouse Co., 1920-28, Abrasive Co. of Phila., 1910-29; asst. sec. and treas. The Mutual Assurance Co. ("Green Tree"), Phila., since 1933; former dir. Nat. Bank of Chester Co. & Trust Co. of West Chester, Pa., Kittanning Coal Co., etc. Dir. Phila. Bourse since 1908. Mgr. and sec. Pa. Hosp., Phila., since 1920; pres. Phila. Dispensary since 1930, Pa. Epileptic Hosp. and Colony Farm since 1903; mgr. Phila. Lying-in Hosp. and Maternity Hosp. since 1922; warden St. James Ch., Phila., since 1937. Mem. Genealogical Soc. of Pa. (pres. since 1938), Am. Philos. Soc., Wistar Assn., Acad. of Natural Sciences, Pa. Mus., Univ. Mus., Pa. Hist. Soc., Md. Hist. Soc., Del. Hist. Soc. Republican. Episcopalian. Clubs: Phila., Rittenhouse, University, University Barge (Phila.); West Chester (Pa.) Hunt. Author: Genealogy of Johnson Family of Lincolnshire, Eng., 1932. Home: Fernbank, R.D. 5, West Chester, Pa., and 2129 St. James Pl., Philadelphia, Pa. Office: 240 S. Fourth St., Philadelphia, Pa.

MORRIS, Paul L., pres. Ellis Keystone Agrl. Works; b. Pottstown, Pa., Oct. 14, 1887; s. James Harrison and Emma (Landis) M.; m. Gertrude M. Saylor, Nov. 17, 1910; children—Marion Oster, Paul L. Served in various capacities Ellis Keystone Agrl. Works, Pottstown, Pa., 1906-09, supt., 1909-22, v.p., 1922-25, pres. and gen. mgr. since 1925. Home: R.D. 4. Office: Cross and Keim Sts., Pottstown, Pa.

MORRIS, Robert Hugh, clergyman; b. Bluffton, Ga., Aug. 9, 1876; s. Rev. William Jefferson and Iowa (Singleton) M.; Southwestern Ga. Mil. Sch., Cuthbert, Ga.; Emory Coll., Oxford, Ga., 1898; M.A., Princeton, 1905; grad. Princeton Theol. Sem., 1906; D.D., Northwestern, 1909; LL.D., Coe College, Cedar Rapids, Ia., 1929; m. Lyda Addy, Oct. 3, 1900; children—Robert Hugh, Mary, William James. Ordained Presbyn. ministry, 1901; pastor Ocala, Fla., 1901-02; stated supply Barnesville, Ga., 1902-03; pastor Elmer, N.J., 1904-06, Oak Lane Ch., Phila., 1906-08, 1st Ch., Evanston, Ill., 1908-11, Central N. Broad Ch., Phila., 1911-17; became pastor First Ch., Stamford, Conn., 1917; now pastor First Ch., Haddonfield, N.J. Declined calls to Can. and England. Mason, Odd Fellow, K.P. Club: City. Author: Good Man or God-Man, 1912; Sleeping Through the Sermon, 1916; The Fifth Horseman, 1923; Pan's Pipes and the Lyre of Orpheus, 1925;

The Prince and the Pig's Gate, and Other Tales, 1928; A Communicant's Catechism, 1936. Home: Haddonfield, N.J.

MORRIS, Robert Means, lawyer; b. Punxsutawney, Pa., July 21, 1901; s. Joseph Bowman and Ella (Means) M.; B.S., Gettysburg Coll., 1924; student U. of Pittsburgh, 1924-25; LL.B., Dickinson Law Sch., 1927; A.M., Dickinson Coll., 1927; m. Nancy Johns, of Durham, N.C., Feb. 24, 1930; 1 son, Robert Johns. Admitted to Pa. bar, 1927, and became asso. with Mitchell & Morris, 1927-30; mem. firm Morris & Morris (Walter E. and Robert M.) since 1930; dist. atty. since 1933. Mem. Phi Delta Theta. Republican. Presbyterian. Mason, Elk, Eagle. Clubs: Country, Kiwanis (Punxsutawney). Home: 110 Station St. Office: Swartz Bldg., Punxsutawney, Pa.

MORRIS, Roland Sletor, lawyer; b. Olympia, Wash., Mar. 11, 1874; s. Thomas Burnside and Sarah Arndt (Sletor) M.; grad. Lawrenceville (N.J.) Sch., 1892; A.B., Princeton, 1896; LL.B., U. of Pa., 1899; LL.D., Temple U. 1921, Princeton Univ., 1921, U. of Pa., 1932; D.C.L., Univ. of Del., 1929; D.H.L., Hobart, 1933; m. Augusta Shippen West, Apr. 20, 1903; children—Sarah Morris Machold, Edward Shippen. Began practice in Phila., 1899; mem. Duane, Morris & Heeckscher since 1904; prof. internat. law, U. of Pa., since 1924; dir. Mutual Life Insurance Company of New York, Franklin Fire Insurance Co., Ambassador E. and P. to Japan, 1917-21; on special mission to Siberia, Sept.-Nov. 1918, Jan.-Mar. 1919, and July-Oct. 1919. Trustee, Carnegie Foundation, Milbank Foundation, Brookings Instn., Temple U.; mem. Bd. of City Trusts; mem. Foreign Bondholders Protective Council; regent Smithsonian Institution. Del. to Democratic National Conventions, 1904, 08, 12, 28; chmn. Dem. Finance Com. of Pa., 1908, 16; state chmn. Dem. party in Pa., 1913-16. Elected life trustee Princeton U., 1934. Mem. Am. Philos. Soc. (pres.), Asiatic Soc. of Japan, Japan Soc., Oriental Soc., Am. and Pa. bar assns., Phila. Bar Assn. (ex-chancellor); ex-pres. Phila. br. English-Speaking Union. Episcopalian. Clubs: Philadelphia, Princeton, Contemporary, University Barge (Phila.); Century (N.Y.). Chancellor Diocese of Pa. Home: 2113 Spruce St. Office: Land Title Bldg., Philadelphia, Pa.

MORRIS, Samuel; prof. chemistry, W.Va. U. Address: West Virginia University, Morgantown, W.Va.

MORRIS, Samuel, prof. biology; b. Phila., Pa., June 12, 1896; s. George Spencer and Lydia (Ellicott) M.; B.Sc., Pa. State Coll. 1922; A.M., U. of Pa., 1930, Ph.D., same, 1935; m. Alberta S. MacLean, Dec. 28, 1922; children—Samuel, Jr., Margaret MacLean. Engaged in farming, Mt. Equity Farm, Pennsdale, Pa., 1922-25; foreman Wilson & Co., Phila., Pa., 1926; technician, H. K. Mulford & Co., Glenolden, Pa., 1927; grad. student, U. of Pa., 1928-32, also instr. zoölogy, U. of Pa., 1929-32, also instr. in biology, Temple U., 1932-37; prof. biology, Scranton-Keystone Jr. Coll., La Plume, Pa. since 1937. Served with Am. Friends Service Com., on Civilian Relief, Reconstruction of Bldgs., and Reestablishment of Agr., in France, 1918-19. Mem. A.A.A.S., Am. Soc. Parisitologists, Am. Assn. Univ. Profs., Sigma Xi. Mem. Religious Soc. Friends. Contbr. articles to sci. jours. Home: Dalton, Pa.

MORRIS, Samuel John, M.D.; b. Morgantown, W.Va., Aug. 3, 1887; s. Samuel Hall and Elizabeth (Morrison) M.; M.D., W.Va. U., 1910, U. of Md., 1912; m. Edna Leyman, June 12, 1912; children—John David, Nancy Lee, Jane Block. Instr. anatomy, U. of W.Va. Med. Sch., 1912; prof. anatomy, W.Va. U., 1912-33, asst. to dean, 1933-35, med. advisor to athletic dept., prof. physical edn. and physician to health service since 1935. Fellow Am. Coll. Physicians; mem. A.M.A., W.Va. State Med. Soc., Phi Sigma Kappa. Democrat. Methodist. Mason, Elk. Home: 205 Kingwood St., Morgantown, W.Va.

MORRIS, Sarah I., M.D., prof. of preventive medicine; b. Pittston, Pa., Apr. 25, 1879; d. Joseph Hampton and Lydia (Raife) Morris;

grad. Pittston High Sch., 1897; M.D., Woman's Med. Coll., Phila., 1910; grad. student U. of Wis., 1925, Johns Hopkins Sch. of Hygiene, 1931, U. of Pittsburgh, 1938; unmarried. Interne Women's and Children's Hosp., Phila., 1910-11; mem. med. staff State Sch. for Epileptics, Skillman, N.J., 1911; mem. Student Health Staff and successively instr., asst. prof., asso. prof. of clin. medicine, U. of Wis. Med. Sch., 1911-31; prof. of preventive medicine, dir. Student Health Service, Woman's Med. Coll. of Pa., since 1931. Fellow Am. Coll. Physicians; mem. A.M.A., Co. and State med. socs., Am. Public Health Assn., Assn. Women in Public Health, Am. Women's Med. Assn., Alpha Omega Alpha, Alpha Epsilon Iota, Sigma Delta Epsilon (charter mem.). Republican. Club: Altrusa (Phila.). Ednl. work in preventive medicine. Home: 5714 Wissahickon Av., Germantown. Office: Henry Av. and Abbottsford Rd., Philadelphia, Pa.

MORRIS, Stanley Clarence, lawyer; b. Marion County, W.Va., Mar. 7, 1893; s. Michael Lincoln and Loretta Victoria (Moore) M.; student Broaddus Inst., Clarksburg, W.Va., 1905-08, U. of Wis., 1916-17; A.B., magna cum laude, Marietta (O.) Coll., 1914; LL.B., U. of W.Va., Morgantown, W.Va., 1921; m. Mary Leota Musgrave, Dec. 26, 1917; children—Mary Lee, Stanley Clarence, Jr. Admitted to W.Va. bar, 1921; mem. firm Coffman & Morris, Clarksburg, W.Va., 1921-28, Steptoe & Johnson, Clarksburg and Charleston, W.Va., since 1928; sec. and treas. and dir. Three Cities Realty Co., Charleston, W.Va., since 1937. Served as private advancing to 2d lt., U.S. Army, 1917-19, hon. disch. as 2d lt., Air Service, 1919. Chmn. city polit. com., Clarksburg, 1927; pres. Charleston Area Council Boy Scouts, 1937; mem. City Planning Commn., Charleston, since 1938. Mem. Bar Assn. of City of Charleston, W.Va. Bar Assn., Am. Bar Assn., Am. Legion (dept. comdr., Dept. of W.Va. 1928-29), Order of the Coif, Mountain (honor soc.), Phi Beta Kappa, Delta Sigma Rho, Phi Delta Phi, Delta Upsilon. Republican. Methodist. Mason. Clubs: Kiwanis (pres. 1936), Edgewood Country (Charleston, W.Va.). Author: What Are The Privileges and Immunities of Citizens of the United States, 1921; (with James W. Simonton) Nature of Property Rights in a Separately Owned Mineral Vein, 1921. Home: 508 Linden Rd. Office: 610 Kanawha Bldg., Charleston, W.Va.

MORRIS, Vlon Neilan, research chemist; b. Colorado Springs, Colo., Apr. 1, 1901; s. Joseph Franklin and Emma Belle (Brown) M.; B.S. in Chem. Engring., Purdue U., 1922, M.S., 1924; Ph.D., U. of Minn., 1926; grad. student Mass. Inst. Tech., 1928; m. Gladys Dobelbower, 1924; children—Marjorie Ann, Marilyn Jane. Research chemist Fixed Nitrogen Research Lab., Washington, D.C., 1926-27, Firestone Tire & Rubber Co., 1927-35; reaserch supervisor Resinous Products & Chem. Co., Phila., 1935-39; colloid expert Nat. Aniline and Chem. Co., Buffalo, N.Y., since 1939; dir. Nat. Hydrolator Co., Phila. Reserve officer Chem. Warfare Service, 1922-31. Mem. Am. Chem. Soc., Am. Inst. Chemists, Delta Upsilon, Sigma Xi, Tau Beta Pi, Phi Lambda Upsilon, Scabbard and Blade. Home: Crestmont Farms, Torresdale, Philadelphia, Pa. Office: National Aniline & Chemical Co., Buffalo, N.Y.

MORRIS, Walter Edmund, lawyer; b. Punxsutawney, Pa., June 10, 1891; s. Joseph Bowman and Ella (Means) M.; B.S. Ore. State Coll. Sch. of Commerce, Corvallis, Ore., 1912; LL.B., U. of Mich. Law Sch., Ann Arbor, Mich., 1916; m. Margaret Gilliland, Sept. 29, 1920; children—Ann Louise, Margaret Jane; Teacher, Marshfield (Ore.) High Sch., 1912-13; admitted to practice before Supreme Ct. of Pa., 1917, and since practiced at Punxsutawney, Pa.; senior mem. firm Morris & Morris, Punxsutawney, since 1930. Dist. atty., Jefferson Co., Pa., 1922-34; solicitor Punxsutawney Sch. Bd. since 1935; nominated, 1936, Rep. candidate for Congress from 27th Congl. Dist. of Pa. Served as 1st lt., line officer, trial judge advocate, personnel adj., 54th Inf., 6th Div., U.S. Army, during World War; hon. disch. as capt. and

**MORRIS, ** personnel adj., 28th Div., 1919; mem. local armory bd., Troop L, 104th Cav., Pa. N.G., since 1925. Mem. Am., Pa. and Jefferson Co. bar assns., Delta Sigma Rho, Sigma Delta Kappa, Am. Legion, Vets. Fgn. Wars. Republican. Presbyterian. Mason. Elk. Clubs: Punxsutawney (Pa.) Country, Punxsutawney Hunting. Home: 209 Dinsmore Av. Office: 100 W. Mahoning St., Punxsutawney, Pa.

MORRIS, Warren Francis, lawyer; b. Wetzel Co., W.Va., Feb. 20, 1899; s. Pressley D. and Nancy V. (Barr) M.; LL.B., W.Va. Univ. Law Sch., 1925; student George Washington Univ., 1925; m. Goldia A. Moore, Mar. 21, 1921 (dec.); 1 dau., Mary Jo; m. 2d Mary Margaret Kerby, Dec. 3, 1938. Admitted to W.Va. bar, 1925 and since engaged in gen. practice of law at Wheeling; in addition to pvt. practice, counsel for Conservative Life Ins. Co., Wheeling, W.Va. since 1927. Served in S.A.T.C., 1919. Republican. Methodist. Elk. K.P. Home: Buck and Donovan Apts. Office: Conservative Life Ins. Bldg., Wheeling, W.Va.

MORRIS, William Frederick, Jr.; v.p. Weirton Steel Co.; b. Mahoning, Pa., Aug. 23, 1877; s. W. F. and Nannie E. (Hooper) M.; student pub. schs.; m. Bella R. Clark, Apr. 14, 1903; children—Jack M., Harry D. Vice-pres. Weirton Steel Co. since 1929. Home: 166 N. Dithridge St. Office: Grant Bldg., Pittsburgh, Pa.

MORRISON, Caldwell, M.D.; b. Gambier, O., Aug. 9, 1866; s. Archibald M. and Margaret Caldwell (Shapter) M.; grad. West Philadelphia Acad., 1881; A.B., Columbia U., 1886; M.D., N.Y. Homeo. Med. Coll., 1889; m. Jane S. Sieger, June 8, 1898; children—Elizabeth Caldwell (wife of Herman A. Osgood, M.D.), Jean (wife of Lee W. Hughes, M.D.). Began gen. practice medicine, Summit, N.J., 1891; now at Newark; mem. staff Essex Co. Homeopathic Hosp., 1904-38, now East Orange Gen. Hosp.; mem. arthritic staff Flower and Metropolitan hosps., N.Y. City, 2 yrs.; sr. physician Baptist Home for the Aged, Newark. Mem. med. advisory bd., Newark, World War. Mem. A.M.A., N.J. State Med. Soc., Essex Co. Med. Soc., N.J. State Homeo-Med. Soc., Am. Inst. Homeopathy; Phi Beta Kappa (Columbia). Independent Republican. Presbyn. Clubs: Forest Hill Field (Bloomfield); New Jersey Chiron (Newark and vicinity). Home and Office: 379 Seventh Av., Newark, N.J.

MORRISON, Charles Munro, newspaper editor; b. Jefferson Co., Ill., Nov. 23, 1881; s. William David and Melisse (Garrison) M.; student McKendree Coll., Lebanon, Ill., 1898-99, 1901; m. Dana Rae Maxey, Oct. 26, 1901; children—Alice Morrison, Sartori and Maxey Neal. Assistant school principal, Mt. Vernon, Ill., 1901-02; prin. high sch., Fairfield, Ill., 1902-07; successively reporter, Sunday editor, political editor, editorial writer and asst. mng. editor St. Louis (Mo.) Republic, 1909-19; asso. editor St. Louis Globe-Democrat, 1919-21; chief editorial writer, Phila. (Pa.) Pub. Ledger, 1921-26; also chief editorial writer, New York Evening Post, 1924-26; dir. of editorial pages and asso. editor Phila., Pub. Ledger and Evening Ledger, 1926-29, acting editor, 1929-30, editor since 1930; v.p. and sec. Pub. Ledger, Inc., since 1936. Mem. Am. Soc. Newspaper Editors, Am. Acad. Polit. and Social Sciences. Clubs: Union League, Down Town, Camp and Trail (Phila.); National Press, Racquet (Washington). Home: Mearns Rd., Ivyland, Pa. Address: Public Ledger, Philadelphia, Pa.

MORRISON, Frank Griffith, business mgr., The Pittsburgh Press; b. Jacksonville, Ill., June 5, 1894; s. Frank E. and Kathryn A. (Braun) M.; student Illinois Coll., Jacksonville, Ill.; m. Fern Catherine Karr, March 15, 1919; 1 son, Frank Karr. Engaged as advertising mgr. Akron Evening Times, Akron, O., 1916-25, Akron Times-Press, 1925-28; business mgr. The Indianapolis Times, Indianapolis, Ind., 1928-31 business mgr. The Pittsburgh Press, Pittsburgh, Pa., since 1931. Episcopalian. Clubs: Duquesne, Field, Metropolitan. Home: 1405 Navahoe Drive, Mt. Lebanon. Office: 52 Boul. of The Allies, Pittsburgh, Pa.

MORRISON, Robert Hugh, state dir. of teacher edn.; b. Pioneer, O., Jan. 19, 1893; s. Lyman Henry and Caroline (Seeley) M.; A.B., Mich. State Normal Coll., Ypsilanti, 1923; M.A., Colo. State Coll. of Edn., Greeley, 1926; Ph.D., Columbia U., 1933; m. Mabel Magdalene Hebeler, April 17, 1918; children—Robert Joseph, John Hebeler. Teacher of history, Centreville (Mich.) High Sch., 1915-17; prin., Durant Sch., Flint, Mich., 1918-23; prof. of edn., State Coll., Greeley, Colo., 1923-31; pres. State Teachers Coll., Paterson, N.J., 1931-37; state dir. of teacher edn., Trenton, N.J., since 1937. Served as lt. Machine Corps, U.S. Army, 1917-18. Mem. N.J. Soc. for Visual Edn. (dir.). Mem. Kappa Delta Pi, Phi Delta Kappa. Home: 32 Abernethy Drive. Office: State Dept. of Public Instruction, Trenton, N.J.

MORRISON, Theodore H., M.D.; b. Philadelphia, Pa., Feb. 6, 1891; s. Morris and Anna (Lipsitz) M.; student Baltimore Poly. Inst., 1907-11; M.D., Coll. Phys. and Surg., U. of Md., 1915; m. Matilda K. Swartz, May 28, 1917 (died Dec. 11, 1929); 1 dau., Margaret Sara. Interne Mercy Hosp., Baltimore, 1915-17; in practice at Baltimore since 1917; asso. prof. gastro-enterology, U. of Md., since 1928; visiting gastro-enterologist Mercy Hosp., Ch. Home and Infirmary, Hosp. for Women of Md., Union Memorial Hosp., Sinai Hosp., University Hosp. Fellow Am. Coll. Physicians; mem. A.M.A., Southern Med. Assn., Am. Gastro-enterological Assn., Med. and Chirurg. Faculty of Md., Baltimore City Med. Soc., Phi Delta Epsilon. Mason. Clubs: Suburban, Research, Clinical Dinner. Contbr. to med. periodicals. Home: 4206 N. Charles St. Office: 1013 N. Charles St., Baltimore, Md.

MORRISON, Thomas, steel mfr.; b. in Scotland, Dec. 5, 1861; m. Elizabeth Park. Served apprenticeship as machinist and engr. in Scotland; came to U.S., 1886; became identified with Carnegie Steel Corpn.; was made Supt. Duquesne Works, 1891, Edgar Thompson Works, 1895; resigned, 1937. Office: Highland Bldg., Pittsburgh, Pa.

MORRISSEY, Richard Vincent, prof. biology; b. Wilmerding, Pa., June 22, 1904; s. John Vincent and Mary Rebecca (Richards) M.; B.S., U. of Pittsburgh, 1927, M.S., same, 1929, Ph.D., same, 1934; unmarried. Engaged as grad. asst. and instr. botany, U. of Pittsburgh, 1927-35; substitute teacher Pub. Schs., Pittsburgh, 1935-37; asst. botanist, Soil Conservation Service, 1938; prof. biology and head dept. biology, Dickinson Jr. Coll., Williamsport, Pa., since 1938. Mem. Bot. Soc. America, Pa. Acad. Sci., Square and Compass, Kappa Phi Kappa, Phi Sigma. Republican. Methodist. Mason. Editor, Open Book, Mag. of Kappa Phi Kappa. Home: 1038 S. Braddock Av., Swissvale, Pa. Office: Dickinson Jr. College, Williamsport, Pa.

MORRISSY, Elizabeth, coll. prof.; b. Elkhorn, Wis., Mar. 2, 1887; d. John and Eliza (O'Connor) M.; grad. Elkhorn High Sch., 1904; A.B., Beloit (Wis.) Coll., 1908; student U. of Wis., summer 1916; A.M., Johns Hopkins, 1922; Ph.D., 1930; unmarried. Teacher, North Branch, Mich., 1909-10, Gilmore City (Ia.) High Sch., 1910-12, Hailey (Ida.) High Sch., 1912-16, Mason City (Ia.) High Sch., 1916-20; prof. polit. economy, Coll. of Notre Dame, Baltimore, since 1920, Catholic U., summers 1938-39; part time lecturer polit. economy Nat. Cath. Sch. of Social Service, since 1937. Mem. Pres. Roosevelt's 1st Advisory Council on Economic Security; mem. advisory council on Nat. Youth Adminstrn.; mem. com. on shoes and allied industries of Wage and Hour Div., U.S. Dept. of Labor; former mem. women in industry com. of Internat. Labor Orgn.; v.p. Nat. Catholic Industrial Conf.; v.p. Nat. Catholic Peace Assn.; mem. industrial com. Nat. Catholic Charity Refugees from Germany; mem. bd. Baltimore Br. League of Nations Assn.; trustee Coll. of Notre Dame of Md. Mem. Ladies of Charity, Am. Econ. Assn., Phi Beta Kappa, Pi Gamma Mu. Democrat. Roman Catholic. Home: 332 Paddington Rd., Baltimore, Md.

MORROW, Mrs. Dwight Whitney (Elizabeth Reeve Cutter); b. Cleveland, O., May 29, 1873; d. Charles Long and Annie E. (Spencer) Cutter; B.L., Smith College, 1896, L.H.D., 1937; grad. study, Sorbonne, Paris, 1896-97; L.H.D., Amherst College, 1933; LL.D., N.J. College for Women, 1935; m. Dwight Whitney Morrow, late ambassador to Mexico (died Oct. 5, 1931); children—Elisabeth Reeve (Mrs. Aubrey Niel Morgan, now dec.), Anne Spencer (wife of Col. Charles A. Lindbergh), Dwight Whitney, Constance Cutter (Mrs. Aubrey Niel Morgan). Trustee Smith College, Northampton, Mass.; director Association for Improving Condition of the Poor (board governors). Republican. Presbyn. Clubs: Cosmopolitan (bd. govs.), Women's University, Colony, Smith College, Creek, Women's City (New York); Knickerbocker Country, Aldecress Country (Englewood). Author: The Painted Pig, 1930; Quatrains for My Daughter, 1931; Beast, Bird and Fish, 1933. Contbr. articles and verse to magazines. Home: Lydecker St., Englewood, N.J.

MORROW, Emerson Boyd, educator; b. Harrisburg, Pa., Aug. 26, 1882; s. Herbert A. and Annie Elizabeth (Hoverter) M.; A.B., Princeton U., 1904, A.M., 1905; grad. student Johns Hopkins U., 1906-08; m. Eleanor Harriet Abbe, Dec. 23, 1918. Fellowship in mathematics, Princeton, 1904-05, instr., 1905-06; head mathematics dept., Gilman Country Sch., Baltimore, Md., 1906-26, sr. master, 1910-12, asst. head, 1912-26, headmaster since 1926; founded summer sch., Sodus Point, N.Y., 1922-24, Stony Brook, L.I., 1924-26; coached one of earliest sch. boy teams in soccer, assn. football, Baltimore, Md., 1907-08. Mem. Headmasters Assn., Country Day Sch., Headmasters Assn., Phila. Headmasters Club (pres. 1937-38), Md. and Middle States Assn. (v.p. 1936-38), Phi Beta Kappa, Alpha Delta Phi. Presbyn. Clubs: Elkridge (Baltimore); Princeton (New York). Address: Gilman Country School, Baltimore, Md.

MORROW, John D. A., coal producer; b. Campbellstown, O., June 10, 1881; s. Richard Edwin and Martha Joanna (Adams) M.; B.L., Ohio Wesleyan U., 1906; m. Jessie Lehmer Bowers, Dec. 1911; children—Richard Stevens, Alan Bowers, Nancy, John Stuart. Asst. sec. Federal Trade Commn., Washington, D.C., 1916; resigned, 1916, to organize Pittsburgh Coal Producers' Assn.; elected gen. sec. Nat. Coal Assn. Sept. 1917; apptd. gen. dir. coal and coke distribution, U.S. Fuel Administration, Feb. 1, 1918, and organized and directed the work until June 30, 1919; v.p. and active exec. Nat. Coal Assn. until Dec. 1, 1922; pres. Pittsburgh (Pa.) Coal Co. Mem. Am. Acad. Polit. and Social Science, Am. Inst. Mech. Engrs., Phi Beta Kappa. Republican. Clubs: Chevy Chase (Washington); Duquesne, Allegheny Country, Edgeworth. Home: 618 Maple Lane, Shields, Pa. Office: Oliver Bldg., Pittsburgh. Pa.

MORROW, John Sandels, securities brokerage; b. Jeannette, Pa., July 31, 1894; s. John Riddle and Gertrude (Sandels) M.; student Shadyside Acad., Pittsburgh, Pa., Tome Sch., Port Deposit, Md., U. of Pittsburgh to 1917; m. Rose Dietz, Oct. 20, 1917; children—John R., II, Robert Dietz. Special agt. Dept. of Justice of U.S., 1917-18; v.p. Continental Trust Co., Pittsburgh, Pa., 1923-27; pres. Morrow & Co., 1928-32; v.p. Continental Securities Corpn., Pittsburgh, since 1932; v.p. and dir. The Square Deal Coal Co., Cleveland, O. Capt. Mil. Intelligence Res. Mem. Sigma Alpha Epsilon. Republican. Presbyterian. Clubs: Pittsburgh Athletic (Pittsburgh); Army and Navy (Washington, D.C.); Tuna (Atlantic City, N.J.). Home: 2750 Beechwood Boul. Office: 220 Fourth Av., Pittsburgh, Pa.

MORROW, S. John, lawyer; b. Crawford Co., Pa., June 24, 1879; s. Samuel J. and Mary (Sproul) M.; A.B., Allegheny Coll., 1901; studied law privately; m. Caroline Longanecker, Mar. 24, 1915; children—(adopted) William M., Robert S., Miriam B., Ellen D. Admitted to Pa. bar, 1905, and began practice in Uniontown; judge Court of Common Pleas, Fayette Co., Pa., 1926-36. Republican. Presbyterian. Mason. Club: Duquesne (Pittsburgh). Home: 17 Charles St. Office: 59 E. Main St., Uniontown, Pa.

MORSE, Adrian Osborn, educator; b. New Haven, Conn., Mar. 3, 1895; s. Clayton William and Jennie (Osborn) M.; student Stamford (Conn.) pub. schs., 1903-13; A.B., Yale Coll., 1918; M.A., U. of N.H., 1928; m. Barbara Paine, June 15, 1918; children—Jananne, Content Douglas. Employed Nat. City Bank, New York, 1919-21; instr. English, U. of N.H., 1922-23, exec. sec., 1923-28, dean of men, 1926-28; sec. to Sec. of Agr., Washington, D.C., 1928-29; exec. sec., Pa. State Coll., 1929-35, asst. to pres. in charge resident instrn. since 1935. Justice Durham (N.H.) Municipal Ct., 1926-28. Served as 1st lt., 302d F.A., A.E.F., 1917-19. Mem. Phi Beta Kappa, Psi Upsilon. Presbyn. Home: 315 E. Hamilton Av., State College, Pa.

MORSE, Alfred Handley Chipman, clergyman; b. Bridgetown, N.S., Can., Sept. 21, 1871; s. Harris Harding and Margaret Eliza (Morse) M.; B.A., Acadia Coll., 1896, M.A., 1900; grad. Rochester Theol. Sem., 1900, B.D., 1907; D.D., Ewing Coll., 1912, Ph.D., 1913; m. Ida Maud Churchill, June 19, 1901; 1 dau., Helen Churchill (Mrs. Frank C. Wigginton). Ordained Bapt. ministry, 1896; pastor Bridgewater, N.S., 1896-97, 1st Ch., Corning, N.Y., 1900-04, Strong Place Ch., Brooklyn, 1904-12, 1st Ch., Denver, Colo., 1912-30, Bergen Ch., Jersey City, N.J., since Jan. 1930. Lecturer on Christian philosophy, Denver U., 1914-17. Naturalized citizen, 1904. Trustee Colo. Woman's Coll., 1912-22 and 1926-30. Republican. Scottish Rite Mason. Club: University. Author: Christianity and Social Questions, 1902; Modernism, 1910; The Voices of the Flowers, 1913; The System of Indulgences, 1913; Life in the Open, 1926; Eternal Contrasts, 1929; A Quiver of Sunbeams, 1939. Frequent contbr. to religious mags. and jours. Home: 626 Bergen Av. Office: 50 Clinton Av., Jersey City, N.J.

MORSE, Anson Ely, prof. history; b. Lyme, Conn., July 31, 1879; s. Anson Daniel and Margaret Duncan (Ely) M.; A.B., Amherst, 1902, A.M., 1903; grad. study, U. of Wis., 1903-05, Sorbonne, Paris, 1905-06, Harvard, 1915-16; Ph.D., Princeton, 1908; m. Ruth E. Tucker, June 21, 1905; children—Richard Ely, George Edward, Carolyn Tucker. Instr. in history, Marietta (O.) Coll., 1908-14; lecturer, Amherst, 1914-15; asst. prof., Princeton, 1917-24; prof. history, Temple U., since 1924. Y.M.C.A. service with Italian Army, 1918-19. Mem. Am. Hist. Assn., Delta Kappa Epsilon. Republican. Conglist. Author: Federalist Party in Massachusetts, 1909. Editor: Writings on American History, 1903; Colloquy on the Necessity of Clergy in Government, 1917; Civilization and the World War, by A. D. Morse, 1919. Home: Princeton, N.J. Address: Temple University, Philadelphia, Pa.

MORSE, Benjamin F., merchant; b. Jamestown, N.Y., Mar. 20, 1867; s. Benedikt and Rosina Barbara (Mayer) Morse; student public school and high school, Jamestown, N.Y.; m. Elizabeth Lauderbach, Sept. 19, 1894; children—Elizabeth Jeanette, William Lauderbach, Alice Madeline. Began as bookkeeper Standard Oil Co., 1884; with Atlantic Refining Co.; asso. with Lauderbach & Co., merchant established 1869, Hazleton, Pa.; pres. Lauderbach-Griest Co., wholesale grocers, Philipsburg, Pa., since 1923; dir. Hazleton Nat. Bank, Hazleton, Pa.; sec. and treas. Hazleton Brick Co. Vice-pres. local Y.M.C.A. Republican. Presbyn. (mem. bd. trustees). Mason. Home: 311 W. Diamond Av., Hazleton, Pa.; (country) Sugar Loaf, Pa. Office: 111 W. Broad St., Hazleton, Pa.

MORSE, David Abner, lawyer; b. New York City, May 31, 1907; s. Morris and Sara (Werblin) Moscovitz; A.B., Rutgers U., 1929; LL.B., Harvard U. Law Sch., 1932; m. Mildred Hockstader, May 13, 1937. Admitted to N.J. bar, 1932; asso. with Coult, Satz & Tomlinson, Newark, 1932-33; solicitor's staff, U.S. Dept. Interior, 1933-34; atty. Petroleum Adminstrn. Bd., Washington, D.C., 1933-34; chief counsel, Petroleum Labor Bd., 1934-35; spl. asst. U.S. atty. gen., 1934-35; regional atty., Nat. Labor Relations Bd. (second region), N.Y. City, 1935-39. Served as mem. Bd. Edn., Somerville, N.J., 1937-38; partner law firm of Coult, Satz, Tomlinson & Morse, Newark, N.J., since 1939. Mem. Am. Bar Assn., Acad. Social & Polit. Sci. Jewish religion. Club: Harvard of New York. Home: Far Hills, N.J.; and New York, N.Y. Office: Military Park Bldg., Newark, N.J.

MORSE, Edwin Kirtland, engineer; b. Poland, Mahoning Co., O., July 3, 1856; s. Henry Kirtland and Mary A. (Lynn) M.; A.B., Yale, 1881; m. Caroline U. Shields, Sept. 25, 1884; m. 2d, Elizabeth Wood, Apr. 12, 1914. In various depts. of brother's bridge works at Youngstown, O., and gen. agt. for the co. at Chicago, to 1887; went to Sydney, Australia, 1887, and contracted for erection of superstructure, under firm head of Ryland & Morse, Hawkesbury Bridge, at Dangar Island (7 spans, 415 ft. each, the largest bridge in the southern hemisphere); returned to Pittsburgh, 1889; consulting engr. since 1892. Built substructures for Buffalo, Rochester & Pittsburgh R.R. Bridge, and Carnegie's Railroad, both across Allegheny River; foundations for hot metal bridges at Port Perry and Homestead, across Monongahela River for Carnegie Steel Co., substructures for Jones & Laughlin Steel Co.'s bridge across Monongahela River; 3 suspension bridges across Ohio River with channel spans 700 to 800 ft. each; consulting engr., chmn. engr. com. of Flood Commn. Transit commr. for city of Pittsburgh, 1916-20; cons. engr. City of Pittsburgh for study of flood control, wharf walls and river terminals; apptd. mem. Water and Power Resources Bd., by Gov. John S. Fisher, Nov. 9, 1927, reapptd., 1931, by Gov. Gifford Pinchot. Mem. Am. Inst. Cons. Engrs., Inc., Am. Soc. C.E. (dir); ex-pres. Engrs. Soc. of Western Pa. Cons. engr. Allegheny County Authority. Club: Duquesne. Home: 401 S. Graham St. Office: 345 4th Av., Pittsburgh, Pa.

MORSE, Gilbert Livingston, pres. Bank of Montclair; b. Yonkers, N.Y., Feb. 8, 1888; s. Gilbert Livingston and Mary (Coles) M.; student Morris High Sch., New York, 1901-05; A.B., Williams Coll., Williamstown, Mass., 1909; B.S., Harvard, 1912, M.E., 1913; m. Marion Bottomley, Jan. 14, 1914; children—Gilbert Livingston, Robert Eaton. Mining engr. New Jersey Zinc Co., Franklin, N.J., 1913-25; asst. v.p. Chatham Phenix Nat. Bank & Trust Co., New York, 1925-32; v.p. Mfrs. Trust Co., New York, 1932-33; pres. Bant of Montclair (N.J.) since 1933; pres. and dir. Watchung Title & Mortgage Co., Montclair, N.J., since 1933. Mem. Town Council, Franklin, N.J., 1921-25, Sch. Bd., Franklin, N.J., 1922-25. Mem. Phi Gamma Delta. Republican. Congregationalist. Clubs; Upper Montclair Country, Rotary (Montclair, N.J.). Home: 7 Garden St. Office: 491 Bloomfield Av., Montclair, N.J.

MORSE, Louis Shepard, mech. engring.; b. Somersworth, N.H., Sept. 16, 1873; s. Otis Barney and Inez Jane (LeGro) M.; ed. Mass. Inst. Tech., 1892-96; m. Blanche L. Gipe, June 7, 1900; children—Louis Shepard, Jr., Inez LeGro (Mrs. Joseph Redington Chamberlain), Frances (Mrs. Paul DeVoe Sleeper), Edna Ardelle (Mrs. John W. Hertzler). Chief draftsman, York (Pa.) Mfg. Co., 1896-1912, exec. engr., 1912-17, chief engr., 1917-27; chief engr., York Ice Machinery Corpn., 1927-29, exec. engr. since 1929. Member Am. Soc. Refrigerating Engrs. (pres. 1936), Am. Soc. M.E. (chmn. Susquehanna Sect. 1934), Technology Club of Central Pa., Harrisburg (pres.). Democrat. Mem. Reformed Ch. Mason (K.T.). Club: Country of York. Home: 493 Madison Av., York, Pa. Office: York Ice Machinery Corpn., York, Pa.

MORSELL, H(erndon) Tudor, Federal official; b. Cambridge, Mass., Aug. 2, 1890; s. Herndon and Elizabeth (Burton) M.; B.S., Wesleyan U., Middletown, Conn., 1914; m. Marian Edella Preston, June 12, 1917; children—Mary-Tudor, Suzanne, Elizabeth Burton. Mfrs. rep., Washington, D.C., 1915-18; real estate business, Washington, D.C., 1919-23; realtor (own firm), 1923-30; land purchasing officer Nat. Capital Park and Planning Commn., 1930-34; chief of land acquisition housing div., Pub. Works Adminstrn., 1934-38; dir. land review div. U.S. Housing Authority since 1938; chmn. sub-com. of appraisals and purchase, of Central Housing Com.; consultant for Dist. of Columbia Airport Commn., N.C.P.&P. Commn. and other govt. depts. on real estate. Served as 2d lt. field arty., U.S.A., 1918; apptd. aide to Gov. of Ky. (Ky. col.), 1934. Mem. Wesleyan Alumni Assn. (past pres.), Am. Legion, Alpha Delta Phi. Democrat. Episcopalian. Mason. Clubs: Gridiron, Chevy Chase, Alpha Delta Phi Alumni Assn. (Washington, D.C.). Home: 6317 Connecticut Av., Chevy Chase, Md. Office: Interior Bldg., North, Washington, D.C.

MORTON, Earl Austin, banker; b. Dravosburg, Pa., Sept. 6, 1882; s. Thomas Hamilton and Ida A. (Bartholomew) M.; A.M., Bucknell U., 1908; LL.B., U. of Pittsburgh, 1911; m. Henrietta Rebecca Zimmerman, Feb. 27, 1913; children—Jean Patterson (Mrs. Clay Kenton Myers), Thomas Hamilton, Robert Whigham. Principal Braddock (Pa.) High School, 1907-10; admitted to Pa. bar, 1911; asso. with Commonwealth Trust Co., Pittsburgh, since 1922, vice-pres., trust officer and dir. since 1922; dir. Atlas Steel Barrel Corpn., Albion Land Co.; dir. and asst. treas. Galvez Oil Corpn. Trustee Addison H. Gibson Foundation, Bucknell Univ. Mem. Pa. and Allegheny County bar assns., Phi Gamma Delta. Presbyterian. Mason (K.T., 32°, Shriner). Clubs: Duquesne, University (Pittsburgh). Home: 4737 Bayard St. Office: 312 Fourth Av., Pittsburgh, Pa.

MORTON, James Ferdinand, curator; b. Littleton, Mass., Oct. 18, 1870; s. James Ferdinand and Caroline Edwards (Smith) M.; A.B., A.M., Harvard, 1892; speaker's diploma, Sch. of Expression, 1894; m. Pearl K. Merritt, Mar. 3, 1934. Field sec. New York State Single Tax League, 1916-18, for N.Y. State Farmers' Nat. Single Tax League, 1917-18; sec. Common Commercial Language Com., 1918-24; curator Paterson (N.J.) Mus. since 1925. Originator of intercollegiate debates; lectures on social and lit. topics; former mem. Home Colony, Wash., and editor The Demonstrator. Ex-pres. Nat. Amateur Press Assn.; v.p. Esperanto Assn. N. America; fellow Mineral Soc. America; mem. Science League America, Am. Assn. Museums, Am. Forestry Assn., Henry George Foundation, Passaic County Hist. Soc. (exec. council), Nat. Single Tax League, N.J. Geneal. Soc., Inst. of Am. Genealogy, Nat. Assn. for Advancement of Colored People, New York Esperanto Soc., A.A.A.S., Internat. Esperanto League, Rocks and Minerals Assn., Alumni Assn. of Curry School of Expression, National Puzzlers' League, Am. Cryptogram Assn., Phi Beta Kappa Alumni of New York (also Alpha of Mass.). Clubs: Manhattan Single Tax, Blue Pencil Club, The Fossils, Manuscript, The Riddlers, Interstate Hiking, Nat. Travel, Kalem, New York Mineralogical Club. Author: The Curse of Race Prejudice, 1906; and numerous pamphlets, poems and mag. articles; on revision staff Larned's History for Ready Reference, 1919-21. Home: 334 Summer St. Address: Paterson Museum, Paterson, N.J.

MORTON, Nellie, librarian; b. Wilmington, Del., July 11, 1888; d. William Scott and Florence B. (Forrest) M.; unmarried. In training class Wilmington Inst. Free Library, 1910-11, reference asst., 1911-16, in charge branches, 1916-28; county librarian New Castle County Free Library, Wilmington, Del., since 1928. Mem. Am. Library Assn., N.J. Library Assn. Home: 302 Marsh Rd. Office: Public Library, Wilmington, Del.

MORTON, Samuel Packwood, Jr., importer and roaster of coffee; b. Baltimore, Md., Sept. 23, 1870; s. Samuel Packwood and Margaret (Wiegel) M.; student Baltimore (Md.) City Coll., 1882-86; LL.D. (hon.), Hampden-Sydney (Va.) Coll., 1938; unmarried. Began as clerk, Baltimore, 1886; in coffee business since 1890; partner and half-owner, Merchants Coffee Co., Baltimore, 1900-21; owner Morton Coffee Co., importers and roasters, Baltimore, Md., since 1921; v.p. Gen. Utilities & Operations Co. Mem. S.R., Soc. of Colonial Wars, Omicron Delta Kappa. Ind. Democrat. Episcopalian. Clubs: Maryland, Baltimore Country; University, Baltimore, Bachelors Cotillion (Baltimore). Home: Ambassador Apts. Office: 118-120 E. Pratt St., Baltimore, Md.

MORVAY, Leonard S(amuel), dentist; b. New York, N.Y., Apr. 1, 1895; s. Samuel and Bertha (Loewenstein) M.; ed. N.Y. Univ., 1913-15; D.D.S., Coll. of Jersey City, 1916; m. Rose B. Meyer, July 15, 1919; children—Leonard Samuel, Jr., Babette Rose. Engaged in practice of dentistry at Newark, N.J.; attending dentist Beth Israel Hosp., Newark, N.J., since 1917; dental consultant Rehabilitation Commn., State Labor Dept., since 1929. Served as 1st lt. Dental Corps, 7th Inf., 3d Div., U.S. Army, with A.E.F., during World War. Dir. Lion Bldg. & Loan Assn.; prof. dentistry Nurses Training Sch., Newark Beth Israel Hosp.; mem. budget com. Newark Welfare Fed., 1929-33. Mem. bd. trustees N.J. Normal Sch. for Jewish Teachers. Former trustee local chapter Military Surgeons. Fellow Internat. Coll. of Anesthetists; mem. Am. Legion, Essex Co. Vets. Alliance (charter mem.), Vets. of Foreign Wars (comdr. Post 164, 1922-23, trustee, 1933-36), Third Div. Soc. (past pres. Newark branch), Jewish War Vets., United Am. War Vets., Am. Soc. Advancement Gen. Anesthesia in Dentistry, Am. Dental Assn. (v.p., 1934-39). Jewish religion. Past pres. Northern N.J. Chapter Sojourners Club. Clubs: Optimists Internat. (charter mem. Newark Club, pres., 1928-29; lt. gov., 1929-32), Newark Dental (pres., 1933-34), Newark Civic (mem. council). Presented papers before Am. Dental Assn., New Orleans, 1936; Internat. Congress of Anesthetists, Atlantic City, N.J., 1937. Home: 62 Baldwin Av. Office: 913 Broad St., Newark, N.J.

MOSER, Guy L., congressman; b. Berks Co., Pa., Jan. 23, 1886; s. Henry G. and Margaret (Sassaman) M.; student Keystone State Teachers Coll., 1904; unmarried. Pub. sch. teacher, 1903; railway postal clk., 1904-14; post office insp., 1914-26; investment banking, 1926-31; farming, 1931-36; mem. 75th and 76th Congresses (1937-41), 14th Pa. Dist. Democrat. Mason (K.T., 32°, Shriner). Home: Douglasville, Pa.

MOSER, Herman Meyerstein, lawyer; b. Baltimore, Md., Feb. 22, 1900; s. Jack Charles and Henrietta (Meyerstein) M.; student Baltimore City Coll., 1914-17; LL.B., U. of Md., Baltimore, 1917-20; m. Henrietta Lehmayer, Mar. 3, 1921; 1 son, Peter Martin. Admitted to Md. bar, 1921, and since practiced at Baltimore; mem. firm Lehmayer & Moser, Baltimore, since 1921; dir. Title Guarantee & Trust Co.; asst. state's atty., Md., 1923-28; people's counsel of Pub. Service Commn. of Md., 1933-34; parole commr., State of Md., since 1939. Mem. Baltimore Bar Assn. (mem. judiciary com.), Md. State Bar Assn. (mem. grievance com.), Democrat. Jewish religion. Mason, Elk. Clubs: Suburban, Phoenix (Baltimore, Md.). Lecturer appellate trial work, U. of Baltimore, since 1928. Home: 5507 Roland Av. Office: 801 Fidelity Bldg., Baltimore, Md.

MOSER, Ralph Emanuel, bldg. construction; b. Maroa, Ill., Jan. 17, 1890; s. William and Belle (Friedman) M.; ed. pub. sch. at Maroa, Ill., pub. sch., high sch., Y.M.C.A. night sch., Chicago, Ill., 1896-1907; unmarried. Engaged in contracting and bldg. construction continuously since starting in 1904; with William Grace Co., Chicago, Ill., 1904-11; Thompson-Starrett Co., Chicago, Ill., 1911-14, Pittsburgh, Pa., 1914-20; one of organizers and asso. with W. T. Grange Construction Co. since 1920, sec., treas. and dir. since 1920. Republican. Trustee and chmn. of Finance Com., East End Christian Church. Mason (32°, Shriner). Club: Metropolitan. Home: 340 S. Highland Av. Office: 1100 Keenan Bldg., Pittsburgh, Pa.

MOSER, Wallace G., lawyer; b. Coaldale, Pa., Jan. 21, 1875; s. Gideon and Clara A. (Tiffany) M.; ed. pub. sch. and high sch., Scranton, Pa., 1881-94; m. Mary Powell, June 23, 1903; children—Wallace G., Blanche Elizabeth (Mrs. Archie Thompson). Employed as newspaper reporter, 1894-1905; chief clk. to County Controller, 1905-10; sec. to Mayor of Scranton, 1910-15; admitted to Pa. bar, 1915, and since engaged in gen. practice of law at Scranton. Served as war corr. in Spanish-Am. War, 1898. Mem. Council, City of Scranton, 1905-06. Republican. Conglist. Mason (K.T., 32°, Shriner). Clubs: Craftsmen, Green Ridge-Elmhurst Country. Home: 211 N. Sumner Av. Office: 1001 Mears Bldg., Scranton, Pa.

MOSER, Walter Lysander, clergyman; b. Butler, Pa., Aug. 30, 1894; s. Thomas Jefferson and Mary (Hutchinson) M.; A.B., Grove City Coll., 1915; ed. Harvard, 1915-16, Columbia, 1917-18; B.D., Western Theol. Sem., 1921; grad. study, Edinburgh and Oxford univs., 1922-23, 1926-27, Ph.D., U. of Edinburgh, 1927; D.D., Grove City Coll., 1932; m. Ilse K. Poehlmann, June 16, 1921; children—Hugh Jefferson, John Herman, Walter Lysander, Jr. Ordained to ministry Presbyn. Ch., 1921; pastor, Mars, Pa., 1921-24, Apollo, Pa., 1924-29, Greenville, Pa., 1929-33; pastor Edgewood Community Ch. since 1933; state pastor counselor, Pa. State Christian Endeavor, 1938-40. Served in inf. and F.A.O.T.C., U.S.A., 1918; chaplain, capt., Pa. N.G. since 1930. Trustee Grove City Coll., Western Theol. Sem. Mem. S.A.R., Alpha Tau Epsilon. Presbyn. Clubs: Cleric, Edgewood Country (Pittsburgh). Home: 128 Hawthorne St., Edgewood, Pittsburgh, Pa.

MOSES, Elbert Raymond, lecturer, educator; b. Sterling, Minn., June 3, 1879; s. Abram and Minerva (Dunbar) M.; grad. Cumnock Sch. of Oratory, Evanston, Ill., 1900; student Coll. of Wooster (O.), 1903-05; grad. Muskingum Coll., New Concord, O., 1907; D.Litt., Westminster College, New Wilmington, Pa., 1929; m. Martha Miller, June 15, 1907 (now deceased); children —Elbert R., Lowell M., Jane; m. 2d, Anna Throp Welbourn, Mar. 27, 1920; 1 dau., Annette D. Instr. in pub. speaking, Huron (S.D.) Coll., 1900-02, Muskingum Coll., 1905-10; prof. pub. speaking, Westminster Coll., 1910-17, 1919-23; instr. Bible reading and pulpit oratory, Pittsburgh-Xenia Theol. Sem., 1924-29, Western Theol. Sem., 1928-33, Gettysburg Theol. Sem., 1931-34; instr. pub. speaking Westinghouse Electric and Mfg. Co. since 1929, Am. Inst. Banking since 1931, Robert Morris Sch. of Business, 1934-35; v.p. Nat. Lincoln Chautauqua, 1917-19; founder, 1924, now pres. Pittsburgh School of Speech. Mem. Internat. Lyceum Assn. (1915), Delta Sigma Rho, Tau Kappa Alpha. Republican. United Presbyn. Mason (32°). Lectures: Abraham Lincoln; James Whitcomb Riley; Born Without a Chance; Master Builders of America. Pioneer broadcaster Gems of American Literature, KDKA. Writer of When I was a Country Boy; My Kind of a Boy; Friendly Traveler. Winner Ohio state oratorical contest, 1904. Home: 820 Parkside Av., Mt. Lebanon, Pittsburgh, Pa. Office: Law & Finance Bldg., Pittsburgh, Pa.

MOSES, Harry Morgan, pres. H. C. Frick Coke Co.; b. Westville, Ill., Nov. 11, 1896; s. Thomas and Robena Hamilton (Pringle) M.; ed. pub. sch. Ill., grad. high sch., 1915, Wabash Coll., Crawfordsville, Ind., 1917; m. Ruth Cantrell, Jan. 9, 1918 (dec. 1928); children—Thomas William, Marianne Morgan, Richard Cantrell; m. 2d, Garnet Strawser, Aug. 6, 1929. Began as laborer in coal mine, 1911; successively, mine foreman and supt. phosphat co.; supt. coal mine, asst. gen. supt. coal mines, gen. supt. coal mines; pres. Midwest Supply Co., 1919-21; pres. and dir. H. C. Frick Coke Co., Pittsburgh, Pa., since 1938. U.S. Coal & Coke Co., Federal Coke Corpn., U.S. Fuel Co., Hostetter Connellsville Coke Co., Sharon Coal & Limestone Co., Cumberland Coal Co., Nat. Mining Co., Mingo Coal Co., Connellsville & Monongahela Ry. Co., Youghiogheny Northern Ry. Co., Trotter Water Co., Sewickley Water Co., Franklin Twp. Water Co., Standard Water Co. Served as 2d lieut. F.A. during World War. Mem. Am. Inst. Mining & Metall. Engrs., Iron & Steel Inst., Am. Legion, Lambda Chi Alpha, Sigma Gamma Epsilon. Republican. Episcopalian. Mason (K.T., 32°, Shriner). Clubs: Duquesne, Longue Vue, Pittsburgh Athletic. Home: 1046 Beechwood Boul. Office: Frick Bldg., Pittsburgh, Pa.

MOSES, Thomas, corpn. official; b. Audenreid, Pa., Aug. 18, 1869; s. Morgan and Elizabeth (Stradling) M.; self educated; m. Robena Hamilton Pringle, Feb. 13, 1906; children—Harry Morgan, Mabel Jean (Mrs. Harold T. Leverenz), George Thomas. Worked in coal mines, 1880-1905; sec. Ill. State Mining Bd., 1905-07, insp. 5th Mining Dist., 1907-10; supt. U.S. Fuel Co., 1910-15, gen. supt., 1915-27; pres. H. C. Frick Coke Co. since 1927; also pres. Histetter-Connellsville Coke Co., Cumberland Coal Co., Sharon Coal & Limestone Co., Nat. Mining Co., U.S. Fuel Co., Mingo Coal Co., Republic-Connellsville Coke Co., U.S. Coal & Coke Co., Trotter Water Co., Standard Water Co., Connellsville & Monongahela Ry. Co., Youghiogheny Northern Ry. Co. Mem. Am. Iron and Steel Inst., Am. Inst. Mining and Metall. Engrs., Coal Mining Inst. of America, Mines Insps. Inst. of America, Ill. Mining Inst., Pittsburgh Coal Mining Inst. Republican. Mason, Elk. Clubs: Pittsburgh Athletic, Duquesne, Longue Vue Country. Home: 123 Franklin St., Danville, Ill. Office: Frick Bldg., Pittsburgh, Pa.*

MOSES, Walter, ins. co. exec.; b. Trenton, N.J., May 10, 1872; s. John and Olivia G. (Forman) M.; student Inst., Model Sch., Trenton, N.J., 1878-85, Lawrenceville (N.J.) Sch., 1885-91; B.S., Princeton, 1895; m. Eleanor C. Jones, Nov. 19, 1908. Engaged as treas. John Moses Sons Co., Trenton, N.J., Moses, Swan & McLewee Co., then vice-pres. Standard Lamp and Glass Co.; gen. field supt. Columbian Nat. Life Ins. Co.; mgr. at Phila. for Phoenix Mutual Life Ins. Co.; pres. and dir. Pa. Indemnity Corpn. since 1915, Pa. Indemnity Fire Corpn., Pa. Indemnity Co., Premium Finance Co., Pa. Gen. Underwriters, Inc.; dir. City Nat. Bank; chmn. John F. Arndt, Inc., National Plan, Inc. Served with Y.M.C.A. with A.E.F. during World War. Republican. Episcopalian. Clubs: Art, Coin d'Or, Meridian (Philadelphia); Princeton (New York); Nassau, Tiger Inn (Princeton). Home: 29 W. Tulpehocken St. Office: 1511 Walnut St., Philadelphia, Pa.

MOSKOVITZ, Harry S., portrait artist; b. Phila., Pa., Feb. 5, 1894; s. Hyman and Esther (Kallick) M.; ed. Chas. S. Close Sch., Southern High Sch., Graphic Sketch Club Art Sch., Industrial Art Sch., all of Phila., Beaux Arts Sch., France, Hilda Schule of Art, Germany; m. Florence Sutland, June 17, 1923. Began career as newspaper artist; advertising artist; engaged in painting of murals, specialized in portrait painting and etching since 1923; has painted and etched portraits of many men and women prominent in pub. life, the arts and scis., including Pres. Franklin D. Roosevelt, His Eminence D. Cardinal Dougherty, Justice Nelson Sharpe, Justice H. Edgar Barnes, George Arliss, Governor Geo. H. Earle, Frederick H. Ecker, Samuel S. Fleisher, Ellis Gimbel, Leopold Stokowski, Col. Samuel Price Wetherill, Dr. Norris W. Vaux, P. A. B. Widener III, and others. Served as pvt., Inf., during World War, with A.E.F. in Meuse-Argonne offensive; art instr. in Army Post Sch. after Armistice. Mem. Zionist Organization of America. Jewish religion. Elk. Clubs: Graphic Sketch, Phila. Boosters, One Hundred, Optimist, B'rith Sholom. Home: 6242 Larchwood Av. Studio: 1001 Chestnut St., Philadelphia, Pa.

MOSS, Harry Joseph, physician; b. Russia, June 13, 1884; s. William and Beatrice (Golove) M.; came with parents to U.S., 1894, naturalized; M.D., Jefferson Med. Coll., 1906; m. Adeline Ephrussi Grobman, Mar. 17, 1907; children—Randolph Marshall, Beatrice Geraldine (wife of Dr. P. Paul Le Van). Asst. med. dir. Mt. Sinai Hosp., New York, 1910-15; med. dir. Mt. Sinai Hosp., Chicago, 1915-17, Sinai Hosp., Baltimore, 1917-20, Brownsville and East N.Y. Hosp., Brooklyn, 1920-21, Peoples Hosp., New York, 1921-22; in practice internal medicine, East Orange, N.J., since 1922; mem. staff Newark, N.J., Beth Israel Hosp. and Orange Memorial Hosp. since 1930. Asso. editor Hosp. Management Magazine, 1918-22; contbr. to hosp. periodicals. Mem. Md. Hosp. Assn. (organizer 1917, pres. 1917-19). Mem. B'nai B'rith (organizer Orange lodge and pres. 1926-27; pres. Council of N.J. 1928-29; vice-pres. Dist. Grand Lodge 3, 1931-33), Mason, Elk. Club: Rotary. Address: 111 S. Harrison St., East Orange, N.J.

MOSS, Randolph Marshall, violinist; b. Woodbine, N.J., June 23, 1908; s. Harry Joseph and Adeline Ephrussi (Grobman) M.; ed. Peabody Conservatory, Baltimore, Md., 1917-20; fellowship Juilliard Mus. Foundation, 1926-29, grad. 1929; studied violin under well-known masters; unmarried. Concert violinist since 1918; debut

New York City, 1935; instr. N.Y. Coll. of Music, 1932, Henry St. Settlement Sch., 1935-36; concert master, Washington Nat. Symphony under Dr. Hans Kindler, 1938; awarded first prize in contest of N.J. Fed. of Music Clubs, 1929; first prize in contest comprising states of N.Y., N.J. & Pa. (Liberty Dist.) of Nat. Fed. Music Clubs and Finalist in Boston, 1929; Walter W. Naumburg Foundation Prize, 1935. Mem. Am. Guild Mus. Artists, Am. Guild Radio Artists, Am. Fed. of Musicians. After 8 yrs. experimentation perfected "Electrifonic Violin." Home: 111 Harrison St., East Orange, N.J.; also, 180 Riverside Drive, New York, N.Y. Office: 114 E. 85th St., New York, N. Y.

MOTT, Joseph Walton, hotel propr.; b. Springville, Ia., Dec. 28, 1880; s. Thomas E. and Martha (Briggs) M.; prep. edn. Westtown (Pa.) Boarding Sch., 1900-02; B.S., Haverford (Pa.) Coll., 1906; m. Elizabeth Robinson, 1911 (died 1912); 1 son, Joseph Walton; m. 2d, Lucile Gawthrop, 1917; children — Lucile Elizabeth, Barbara Walton, Joan Halloway. Hotel clerk, Hotel Morton, Atlantic City, N.J., 1906-07; cashier Hotel Chalfont, Atlantic City, 1907-08; steward Jefferson Hosp., Phila., 1909-10, St. Charles Hotel, Atlantic City, 1911; mgr. Old Traymore Hotel, Atlantic City, 1912-13; organized company that built New Traymore Hotel, 1914, mng. dir. and sec.-treas., later pres., same company, to 1936; pres. and dir. Central Pier Co. since 1920. Alternate-at-large from N.J. to Nat. Dem. Conv., 1932; del.-at-large to N.J. State Repeal Conv., 1932; Roosevelt elector, 1936. Mem. Atlantic City Bd. of Edn. (chmn. com. on finance); mem. State Bd. of Edn. since 1931. Mem. Soc. of Friends. Clubs: Haverford (Phila.); Seaview Golf (Absecon, N.J.). Home: Greentown, Pike County, Pa. Office: Central Pier, Atlantic City, N.J.

MOTT, William Elton, civil engr.; b. Burlington, N.J., Jan. 24, 1868; s. Richard Field and Susan (Thomas) M.; U. of Pa., 1884-85; S.B. in C.E., Mass. Inst. Tech., 1889; m. Amy Coughlin, Aug. 20, 1891 (died Dec. 11, 1905); children—Margaret Burling, Katharine; m. 2d, Oli Coughlin, Dec. 26, 1911. Instr. civ. engring., Mass. Inst. Tech., 1889-90; instr. and asst. prof. civ. engring. Cornell U., 1892-1905; asso. prof. hydraulic engring., Mass. Inst. Tech., 1905-09; prof. civ. engring., 1909-17, dean and dir. Coll. of Engring., 1917-32, Carnegie Inst. Tech., Pittsburgh, Pa.; retired Jan. 1933. Asso. mem. Am. Soc. C.E.; mem. A.A.A.S., Soc. Promotion Engring. Edn., Am. Forestry Assn., Theta Xi, Sigma Xi, Tau Beta Pi. Republican. Episcopalian. Home: 315 Wood St., Burlington, N.J.

MOUL, Clayton E., legislator, pres. Spring Grove Realty Co.; b. Heidelberg Twp., York Co., Pa., May 11, 1902; s. Clinton R. and Sallie A. (Hoke) M.; student Gettysburg (Pa.) Coll., 1919-23; m. Elizabeth Shriver, Dec. 27, 1924; children—Robert, Edward, Jean, Marion. Chemist Julian Simpson's Engrs., Phila., Pa., 1923-24; science teacher, Bedford (Pa.) High Sch., 1924-26, prin., 1926-28; organized Clayton E. Moul Ins. & Real Estate Agency, Spring Grove, Pa., 1928, opening second office, York, Pa., 1935, and since in business; pres. Spring Grove (Pa.) Realty Co. since 1937; v.p. Pa. Casualty Co., Lancaster, Pa., since 1934; dir. Hartley Mutual Fire Ins. Co. Mem. Pa. Ho. of Rep. since 1935. Mem. Spring Grove (Pa.) Chamber of Commerce, Lions Internat. (regional dir., 1933-34). Democrat. Lutheran. Mason (Royal Arcanum), Tau Kappa Epsilon. Club: Lions (York, Pa.; pres., 1932-33). Home: Spring Grove, York Co., Pa. Office: 75 Hartman Bldg., York, Pa.

MOUNT, Myrl Marie; prof. home and instn. management and dean Coll. of Home Economics, U. of Md. Address: University of Maryland, College Park, Md.

MOUNT, Walter Barclay, physician; b. New York, N.Y., Feb. 3, 1880; s. James Theodore and Louise (Inslee) M.; student Lawrenceville (N.J.) Sch., 1896-97; A.B., Princeton Univ., 1901; M.D., Coll. Phys. and Surgs., Columbia, 1905; m. Frieda Charlotte Bierhals, May 2, 1910; children — Sophie Louise, Gertrude Harriet (Mrs. John S. Mekeel), Helen Claire (Mrs. Frederick C. Marston, Jr.), Wilford Russell, Nanette. Surg. interne, N.Y. Hosp., 1905-07; interne Sloane Maternity Hosp., New York, 1907; assistant physician at Vanderbilt Clinic, 1909; asst. physician out-patient dept., Mountainside Hosp., Montclair, N.J., 1909-17, asst. obstetrician, 1913-16, attending obstetrician since 1916; cons. obstetrician, St. Vincent's Hosp., Montclair, N. J., 1924-30; cons. obstetrician, Montclair (N.J.) Community Hosp., 1930-38, attending obstetrician since 1938. Served as student, Med. Mil. Camp, Plattsburg, N.Y., 1916; 1st lt., M.R.C. and M.C., U.S. Army Base Hosp., Camp Merritt, N.Y., 1918-19. Fellow Am. Coll. Surgeons, Am. Coll. Physicians (1926-33); mem. Alumni Assn. N.Y. Hosp., Soc. of Alumni Sloane Hosp. for Women (v.p. 1935-37; pres., 1937-38), Asso. Physicians of Montclair and Vicinity (sec., 1912-15; pres., 1915-16), Clin. Soc. of the Oranges (sec., 1916-17; pres., 1913-14), Essex Co. Med. Soc. (mem. council, 1933-37, 1938-40; 2d v.p., 1937-38), Med. Soc. of N.J., A.M.A., N.Y. Acad. Medicine (fellow in obstetrics and gynecology; sec., 1934-35, and chmn., 1935-36, obstetrics and gynecology sect.), Quiz Med. Soc., Essex Co. Anatomical and Path. Soc., Am. Clin. and Climatol. Assn., Acad. Medicine of Northern N.J. (chmn. sect. on obstetrics and gynecology, 1927-28; v.p., 1930-33; trustee, 1935-40), N.J. Hosp. Assn. N.Y. Obstetrical Soc. (non-resident fellow), Soc. Surgeons of N.J. (sec. since 1935), N.J. Obstetrical Travel Club, Robert McKean Med. History Club, Am. Med. Editors' and Authors' Assn., Am. Assn. of History of Medicine, N.J. Health and Sanitary Assn., A.A.A.S., N.J. Birth Control League (chmn. med. advisory bd., 1936-38), Am. Assn. Obstetricians, Gynecologists and Abdominal Surgeons, Nat. Med. Council on Birth Control, Am. Bd. of Obstetrics and Gynecology, Inc. (diplomate), Nursing Council of Essex Co. (trustee, 1937-41), William Pierson Med. Library Assn. (dissolved, 1936), Med. Assn. Greater City of N. Y. (dissolved, 1936), Med. Commn. for Maternal Welfare of Essex Co. (sec., 1925-31, 1936-37; pres., 1932-35; dissolved, 1937), Camp Merritt Base Hosp. Officers Assn. (sec., 1920-25; v.p., 1929), Am. Legion (v.p. Montclair Post 34, 1924), Montclair Art Assn., Omega Club (Coll. Phys. and Surg., Columbia U.). Republican. Baptist. Clubs: Montclair Golf, Cosmopolitan (Montclair, N.J.); Princeton (New York); Nassau (Princeton, N.J.). Author of numerous articles on obstet. and gynecol. subjects for tech. and professional jours. Address: 21 Plymouth St., Montclair, N.J.

MOUNTFORD, Leslie, clergyman; b. Springfield, O., Sept. 29, 1890; s. James William and Charlotte (Meggs) M.; A.B., Monmouth Coll. (Ill.), 1912; ed. Pittsburgh Theol. Sem., 1913-16; grad. study New Coll., Edinburgh, Scotland, 1916-17; (hon.) D.D., Monmouth Coll., Monmouth, Ill., 1935; m. Una Mary DeVinney, Aug. 15, 1916. Ordained to ministry United Presbyn. Ch., 1917; minister, 2d United Presbyn. Ch., Washington, Ia., 1917-21, 2d United Presbyn. Ch., Mercer, Pa., since 1921; prof. of Bible, Westminster Coll., New Wilmington, Pa., 1938. Rep. in Pa. Federation of Chs.; past trustee Anti-Saloon League of Pa.; has held offices and places on coms. of Mercer Presbytery, First Synod of the West, and Gen. Assembly, all of U. Presbyn. Ch. Received Jamieson Scholarship Award, year's study abroad, Pittsburgh Seminary, 1916. Republican. United Presbyn. Club: Rotary of Mercer, Pa. (past pres.). Home: 114 Venango St., Mercer, Pa.

MOWLS, John Nelson, supt. of schools; b. Carroll Co., O., Sept. 29, 1894; s. William C. and Ida Belle (Magee) M.; grad. Dellroy (O.) High Sch., 1912; B.S. in Edn., Kent (O.) State Coll., 1924; A.M., U. of Pittsburgh, 1928, Ph.D., 1937; m. Pearl Trushel, Oct. 19, 1918. Elementary sch. teacher, Rose Twp., Carroll Co., O., 1912-15; asst. prin., East Sparta (O.) Pub. Schs., 1915-17; supervising prin., Hanoverton (O.) Pub. Schs., 1917-18; supervising prin., Dellroy (O.) Pub. Schs., 1919-22; science dept., Carrollton (O.) Pub. Schs., 1922-26; prin., Bellevue (Pa.) High Sch., 1926-28; supt. of schools, Bellevue, Pa., 1928-34, Uniontown, Pa., since 1934; dir. First Nat. Bank, Carrolltown, O. Served with Physical Examining Board, U.S. Army, Camp Sherman, O., during World War. Mem. Uniontown Community Fund. Mem. Am. Assn. of Sch. Adminstrs., N.E.A., Pa. State Edn. Assn., Phi Delta Kappa. Methodist. Mason. Club: Uniontown (Pa.) Kiwanis (pres. 1939). Contbr. of articles to edni. jours. Home: 25 Wilmington Av. Office: 18 E. South St., Uniontown, Pa.

MOWREY, Raymond Guy, supt. county schs.; b. Mowersville, Pa., Apr. 12, 1886; student Shippensburg State Teachers Coll., 1903-06, Pa. State Coll., various Summer sessions, U. of Pa., Extension Courses; m. Frances Katherine Greenawalt, June 25, 1908; children—Roger Conwell, Thomas Mulford, Raymond Gerald, Julia Ione, Ella Amelia, Wayne Lytle. Engaged in teaching at various schs., 1906-12; prin. high sch. Quincy Twp., 1912-17; field sec. Quincy U.B. Orphanage and Home, and prin. Quincy Orphanage Schs., 1917-19; prin. high sch. Washington Twp., 1919-22; asst. co. supt. schs. of Franklin Co., 1922-34, co. supt. since 1934; pres. Franklin Co. S.S. Assn. since 1922; del. Quadrennial Gen. Conf. U.B. Ch. since 1923. Mem. trustees Lebanon Valley Coll. since 1924. Mem. Nat., Pa., and Franklin Co. edn. assns., Am. Assn. Sch. Adminstrs., Kittochtinny Hist. Soc., Patriotic Order Sons of America. Pres. bd. dirs. Old Brown's Mill Memorial Assn. Republican. Mem. U.B. Ch. I.O.O.F. Clubs: Commercial, Republican (Chambersburg); Odd Fellows (Waynesboro); Explorers (Pine Grove Furnace). Home: Quincy, Pa. Office: Chambersburg, Pa.

MOYER, Earl Barton, clergyman; b. Reading, Pa., Nov. 28, 1887; s. Washington Jacob and Susan Sharp (Reinhold) M.; grad. Reading High Sch., 1907; student Bucknell U., Lewisburg, Pa., 1908-09; grad. Crozer Theol. Sem., Chester, Pa., 1915, post grad. work, 1915-16; student U. of Pa. Grad. Sch., 1915-16; m. Edna Lillian Gordon, Nov. 30, 1916; children—Warren Bernard, Hazel Virginia. Ordained minister of Baptist Ch., 1915; pastor Caernarvon Bapt. Ch., Elverson, Pa., 1909-12, Beulah Bapt. Ch., Russellville, Pa., 1913-16, First Bapt. Ch., Shinnston, W.Va., 1916-23; pastor Calvary Bapt. Ch., Parkersburg, W.Va., since 1923. Rec. sec. W.Va. Bapt. State Conv. since 1927; pres. Wood County Council of Religious Edn., 1924-26; pres. Parkersburg Ministerial Alliance, 1929-30, sec.-treas., 1925-29; sec.-treas. Crozer Alumni Club of W.Va., 1930-35; asso. editor Baptist Banner (state paper of W.Va. Baptists), 1925-30, editor, 1930-34; mem. W.Va. Bapt. State Conv. Exec. Bd. since 1927 (chmn. com. on finance and promotion since 1934); mem. advisory com. to State exec. sec. since 1930. Contbr. to "Voices from Templed Hills," 1927; also editorials and articles in The Baptist Banner, 1925-34; editor of W.Va. Bapt. State Conv. Annual since 1927; state corr. The Watchman-Examiner (nat. Bapt. jour.). Mem. Am., W.Va. and Parkersburg Dahlia Socs. Home: 1911 20th St. Office: 13th and Avery Sts., Parkersburg, W.Va.

MOYER, Edward Thornbury, securities brokerage; b. Phila., Pa., Dec. 31, 1897; s. Edward Evans and Mary Wilson (Pray) M.; ed. Chestnut Hill Acad., Phila., Pa., 1906-15, U. of Pa., 1915-17; m. Beatrice Stanton, Apr. 18, 1925; children—Edward E. 2d (dec.), Frank Stanton, Dorothy Downing. Asso. with Moyer & Co., stock brokers and mem. Phila. Stock Exchange, continuously since 1917, mem. firm since 1927. Mem. Kappa Alpha. Republican. Episcopalian. Mason. Home: 805 Carpenter Lane, Mt. Airy. Office: 1500 Walnut St., Philadelphia, Pa.

MOYER, Gabriel Hocker, lawyer; b. Palmyra, Pa., Nov. 9, 1873; LL.B., Dickinson Sch. of Law, Carlisle, Pa., 1898; m. Bertha Elizabeth Smith, Nov. 28, 1901. Admitted to Pa. bar, 1902, and began practice at Lebanon; mem. Pa. Ho. of Rep., 1905-09; formerly gen. mgr. State Workmen's Ins. Fund. Republican. Lutheran. Mem. Patriotic Orders Sons of America (nat. treas.), Odd Fellows, Elk. Club: Lebanon. Home: Lebanon, Pa.

MOYER, Harry Calvin, educator; b. Lebanon Co., Pa., June 23, 1889; s. Robinson Calvin and Salinda (Dubble) M.; ed. pub. sch. and high sch., Lebanon Co., Pa., 1894-1906, diploma, State Teachers Coll., West Chester, U. of Pa. Extension, 1910-12, Pa. State Coll., summers, 1913-14; B.S. and M. Dip. Supt. Schs., Columbia, Teachers Coll., 1921; m. Anna Rex Keath, June 1, 1916; 1 dau., Georgette Keath. Engaged in teaching continuously since 1907, elementary teacher, 1907-08, instr. high sch., 1910-15, asst. supt. schs., 1915-26, supt. schs., Lebanon, Pa., since 1926; vice-pres. and dir. Lebanon Nat. Bank; dir. Lebanon Mutual Ins. Co. Mem. Am. Assn. Sch. Adminstrs., Pa. State Ed. Assn., Pa. German Soc., Phi Delta Kappa. Republican. Reformed Ch. Mason. Rotarian. Club: Rotary of Lebanon (past pres.). Home: Schaefferstown. Address: Lebanon, Pa.

MOYER, James Ambrose, educator, engineer; b. Norristown, Pa., Sept. 13, 1877; s. Isaac Kulp and Jane Hunsicker (Grater) M.; E.B., State Teachers College at Westchester, Pa., 1893; Pa., 1893; S.B., Lawrence Scientific School (Harvard University), 1899; A.M., Harvard University, 1904; m. Dorothy Tremble, May 18, 1922; 1 dau., Jane Modella. Draftsman, 1899-1900; instr. in Harvard, 1901-04, in Harvard Engring. Camp, 1902-04; mech. engr. and chief computer, Gen. Electric Co., 1905-07; gen. engr. Westinghouse, Church, Kerr & Co., New York, 1907-08; asst. prof. mech. engring. in charge mech. and hydraulic labs., U. of Mich., 1908-11; jr. prof. mech. engring., U. of Mich., 1911-12; prof. mech engring. in charge of dept., Pa. State Coll., 1912-15; dir. Pa. Engring. Expt. Sta. and of univ. extension dept. of Pa., 1913-15; dir. Univ. Extension Mass. Dept. of Edn., 1915 —. Pres. Nat. Commn. on Enrichment of Adult Life (N.E.A.); N.E. rep. U.S. Dept. of Interior, 1917-20; chmn. U.S. com. of scientists on war inventions, 1918-19. Pa. del. First Nat. Conf. on Univ. Extension; past pres. Nat. Assn. Univ. Extension; mem. advisory com. on edn., U.S. Navy; mem. commission of U.S. Dept. of Interior on education by radio broadcasting; advisory bd. Nat. Home Library Foundation; edn. advisory com. World Wide Broadcasting Corpn.; v.p. National Academy Visual Instrn., Am. Association for Adult Education; sec. Internat. Elec. Congress; mem. visiting com. University Extension, Harvard; mem. Survey Commn. on Noncollegiate Tech. Edn., 1928-31. Mem. Royal Acad. (London), Am. Acad. Polit. and Social Science, Verein deutscher Ingenieure, Franklin Inst., Am. Soc. M.E., Assn. Internationale du Froid (Paris), Nat. Council of Safety, Engrs.' Soc. Pa., Soc. Automotive Engrs. (chmn. N.E. sect. and mem. nat. council), League of Nations Association (director), Am. Association Refrigerating Engrs., Am. Inst. E.E., Soc. Promotion Engring. Edn., Assn. Harvard Engrs., Lawrence Scientific Assn., National Education Association, Pi Gamma Mu (pres. Boston chapter), Phi Sigma Kappa, etc.; fellow A.A.A.S. Presbyn. Clubs: City, Harvard, Schoolmasters (Boston); Union (Ann Arbor); Authors' (London). Author: Elements of Descriptive Geometry, 1904; Descriptive Geometry for Engineers, 1905; Internal Combustion Motors, 1905; Steam Turbines, 1905; Power Plant Testing, 1911; Engineering Thermodynamics (with J. P. Calderwood and A. A. Potter), 1915; Gasoline Automobiles, 1921; Marine Steam Turbines, 1922; Oil-burning Boilers, 1923; Practical Radio (with J. F. Wostrel), 1924; Radio Construction and Repairing, 1926; Refrigeration, 1928; Radio Receiving Tubes, 1929; Industrial Electricity, 1930; Radio Handbook, 1931; Air Conditioning, 1933; Oil Fuels and Burners, 1937. Editor Bull. of Dept. of Edn.; contbr. to ednl. and engring. jours.; asso. editor of Combustion (Chicago). Home: 382 Kenrick St., Newton, Mass. Address: State House, Boston, Mass., and Pa. Bldg., Phila, Pa.

MOYER, Tilghman Huber, pres. and gen. mgr. Tilghman Moyer Co.; b. Allentown, Pa., Feb. 8, 1889; s. Albert Llewellan and Sarah (Speer) M.; student Lafayette Coll., Easton, Pa., 1906-08; m. Bessie Fretz, Apr. 12, 1912; children—Thomas Fretz, Tilghman Huber. Structural and archtl. engr. R. S. Rathbun Co., Allentown, Pa., 1908-09, 1912-14; asst. city engr., City of Allentown, Pa., 1910-12; engr. maintenance of way, N.Y. & Queens County Ry., Long Island City, N.Y., 1909-10; county engr., Lehigh Co., Pa., 1913-17; pres. and gen. mgr. Tilghman Moyer Co., design, constrn. and equipment of bank bldgs., Allentown, Pa., since 1914; pres. Highland Dwellings Corpn., Allentown, since 1938; registered professional engr., Pa., Va.; registered architect, Pa., Del., W.Va., N.J. Lt. comdr. U.S.N.R. Mem. Am. Soc. C.E., Pa. Soc. of Professional Engrs., Am. Legion. Republican. Lutheran. Mason (K.T.). Clubs: Livingston, Knickerbocker Yacht, Chester River Yacht (Chestertown, Md.). Author: Building the Bank for Business, 1926; editor Foresight (pub. of Tilghman Moyer Co.). Home: 116 N. 15th St. Office: 141 N. 9th St., Allentown, Pa.

MUDD, Stuart, bacteriologist; b. St. Louis, Mo., Sept. 23, 1893; s. Harvey Gilmer and Margaret de la Plaux (Clark) M.; B.S., Princeton, 1916; A.M., Washington U., St. Louis, 1918; M.D., Harvard, 1920; m. Emily Borie Hartshorne, Sept. 12, 1922; children—Emily Borie, Stuart Harvey, Margaret Clark. Research fellow, Harvard, 1920-23; asso., Rockefeller Inst., 1923-25; asso. in pathology, Henry Phipps Inst., U. of Pa., 1925-31, asst. prof. exptl. pathology, 1925-31; asso. prof. bacteriology, U. of Pa., 1931-34, prof. since 1934. Dir. L.I. Biol. Assn., Am. Birth Control League. Mem. A.A.A.S., Coll. of Physicians of Phila., A.M.A., Physiol. Soc., Am. Assn. Pathologists and Bacteriologists, Am. Assn. Immunologists, Soc. Exptl. Pathology, Soc. Exptl. Biology and Medicine, Harvey Soc., Soc. Am. Bacteriologists. Phi Beta Kappa, Sigma Xi. Republican. Episcopalian. Clubs: Merion Cricket (Haverford, Pa.); Princeton, Harvard (Phila.). Contbr. articles to jours. of med. sciences. Home: 734 Millbrook Lane, Haverford, Pa.

MUDGE, Edmund Webster, mfr.; b. Phila., Pa., Jan. 12, 1870; s. Thomas Henry and Mary Emma (Shepard) M.; ed. Friends' Sch. and Woods Town (N.J.) Acad.; m. Pauline Seeley, Apr. 4, 1899; children—Mary Louise (dec.), Edmund Webster, Leonard Seeley. Engaged in mfr. of iron and steel, at Pittsburgh, since 1887; head of Edmund W. Mudge & Co.; dir., chmn. finance com. Edgewater Steel Co., Fidelity Title & Trust Co.; dir. Nat. Steel Corpn., Mudge Oil Co., Hanna Furnace Corpn., Mich. Steel Corpn., Union Fidelity Ins. Co., Stoner-Mudge, Inc. Mem. Pa. Council Nat. Defense, World War. Mem. bd. dirs. Allegheny Gen. Hosp. (exec. com.). Trustee Episcopal Diocese of Pittsburgh, Trinity Cathedral, Y.M.C.A. Republican. Clubs: Pittsburgh, Duquesne, University, Pittsburgh Athletic Assn., Longue Vue, Fox Chapel Field Club (Pittsburgh); Union (Cleveland); Union League (Phila.). Home: 1000 Morewood Av. Office: Grant Bldg., Pittsburgh, Pa.

MUDGE, Lewis Seymour, church official; b. Yonkers, N.Y., Aug. 24, 1868; s. Rev. Lewis Ward (D.D.) and Elizabeth (Seymour) M.; B.A., magna cum laude, Princeton U., 1889, fellow experimental science, 1889-90, M.A., 1890; instr. mathematics, Princeton, 1892-94; grad. Princeton Theol. Sem., 1895; D.D., Franklin and Marshall, 1910; LL.D., Lafayette Coll., and U. of Dubuque, 1923; m. Caroline Denny Paxton, Feb. 11, 1896 (died Sept. 22, 1922); m. 2d, Anne Evelyn Bolton, Dec. 17, 1925. Ordained Presbyn. ministry, 1895; pastor First Ch., Beverly, N.J., 1895-99, First Ch., Trenton, 1899-1901, First Ch., Lancaster, Pa., 1908-14, Pine Street Ch., Harrisburg, 1914-21; moderator Synod of Pa., 1913-14; mem. Bd. of Edn. of Presbyn. Ch., 1900-03; mem. Gen. Bd. of Edn., 1918-20; mem. exec. commn. Presbyn. Church, 1920-21; stated clerk of General Assembly Presbyn. Ch. U.S.A., 1921-38; stated clerk emeritus since 1938; sec. Gen. Council Presbyn. Gen. Assembly U.S.A., 1923-38; moderator Gen. Assembly, 1931-32; acting gen. sec. Bd. of Christian Edn. since 1938; lecturer on ecclesiastical theology, Princeton Theol. Sem. since 1935. Sec. Joint Com. on Organic Union of Presbyn. Ch. in U.S.A. and Presbyn. Ch. of N. America, 1930-34; sec. spl. commission appointed by Presbyterian General Assembly, 1924, for "purity, peace, unity and progress"; trustee of Presbyterian General Assembly since 1921. Speaker under Y.M.C.A. at mil. camps, World War. Member executive committee Federal Council Churches of America; trustee Princeton Theol. Seminary; trustee Wilson Coll., Chambersburg, Pa.; trustee Tennent Coll., Phila.; corporator Presbyn. Ministers' Fund for Life Ins.; mem. exec. council Presbyn. Hist. Soc.; member continuation committees of Faith and Order and of Life and Work conferences; official representative of Ch. at Lausanne, 1927, Edinburgh, 1937, Oxford, 1937, Utrecht, 1938 (when World Council of Churches was organized), and at other nat. and internat. conferences in America and Europe; mem. Gen. Council of World Alliance of Presbyn. Chs. Mem. Soc. Founders and Patriots, Phi Beta Kappa. Republican. Clubs: University, Cleric, Phi Alpha Adelphoi. Editor of The Constitution, The Digest, and The Manual, of Presbyn. Church U.S.A.; author of many pamphlets and papers on ecclesiastical law and procedure, published addresses and sermons. Home: Gulph and Pennswood Roads, Bryn Mawr, Pa. Office: Witherspoon Bldg., Philadelphia, Pa.

MUDGE, William Alvin, metallurgist; b. Schenectady, N.Y., Nov. 18, 1892; s. William Henry and Amelia (Ruhf) M.; B.S., Union Coll., Schenectady, N.Y., 1914; A.M., Columbia U., 1915, Ph.D., 1920; m. Helen Gertrude Gates, Dec. 31, 1917; children—Theodore Alvin, Virginia Emily. Engaged as prof. chemistry, Albright Coll., Myerstown, Pa., 1915-17; research physicist, General Electric Co., Schenectady, N.Y., 1917; metallurgist, Internat. Nickel Co., Inc., Huntington, W.Va., since 1920. Served as capt. 47th inf. 4th Div. (regular), U.S.A., 1917-19 with A.E.F.; lt. comdr. O-V(S), U.S. N.R. since 1938. Vice commodore, Region 4, Boy Scouts of America. Mem. Electro-chem. Soc., Am. Soc. for Metals, Iron & Steel Inst. (London), Inst. of Metals (London), Internat. Soc. for Testing Materials (London), Sigma Xi, Phi Lambda Upsilon, Chi Beta Phi. Democrat. Mason. Club: Guyan Golf and Country. Contbr. many tech. articles on nickel and its alloys. Patentee many nickel alloys and processes. Home: 304 North Boul. West. Office: Internat. Nickel Co., Inc., Huntington, W.Va.

MUELLER, Carl Frank, organist, composer, conductor; b. Sheboygan, Wis., Aug. 12, 1892; s. Berthold and Helen (Wedell) M.; ed. Elmhurst (Ill.) Coll., 1906-10, Westminster Choir Sch., Princeton, N.J., summers 1927, 1928; m. Lenore Ann Eckardt, Aug. 21, 1915; children—Carlette Lenore, Renee Suzanne. Ch. organist and choir master since 1910; with St. John's Ch., St. Louis, Mo., 1911-14, Grand Av. Congl. Ch., Milwaukee, Wis. 1916-27; organist and choirmaster Central Presbyn. Ch., Montclair, N.J., since 1927; dir. choral music, State Teachers Coll., Upper Montclair, N.J., since 1928; mem. faculty, Sch. Sacred Music, Union Theol. Sem., New York City, since 1929. Founder and conductor Montclair A Cappella Choir since 1931. Fellow Westminster Choir Sch. Asso. Am. Guild of Organists. Presbyn. Mason (K.T., 32°, Shriner). Composer over 100 published numbers for piano, organ, voice and chorus. Co-editor (with wife), The Junior Choir Anthem Book, 1932. Composer The Junior Chorister, vols. I and II, 1935. Home: 10 Overlook Park, Montclair, N.J. Office: 46 Park St., Montclair, N.J.

MUELLER, Fred William, ch. official; b. Sandusky, O., Aug. 21, 1871; s. August Fred and Anna (Wekerlin) M.; prep. edn., high sch., Marietta, O., and Acad. Marietta Coll.; grad. Baldwin Wallace Coll., Berea, O., 1893, A.B., 1900; student Sem. U.P. Ch., Pittsburgh, Pa.; D.D., Nast Theol. Sem. and Baldwin Wallace Coll., Berea, 1915; m. Ellen Mack, Sept. 11, 1899; 1 dau., Ruth Hilda. Ordained ministry M.E. Ch., 1893; pastor chs. in Ohio and Pa. until 1910; dist. supt., Ohio and Mich., 1911-20; spl. editor Christliche Apologete, Dec. 1918-Apr. 1919; asso., ch. extension dept., Bd. Home Missions and Ch. Extension, M.E. Ch., 1920-28, supt. of dept. since 1928 and assistant treas., 1931-34, comptroller since 1934; dir. Nast Theol. Sem., 1918-29; trustee Baldwin-Wallace Coll., 1927-30; chmn. exec. com., treas. and trustee Children's Home, Berea; vice-pres. Bethesda Hosp., Cincinnati; del. gen. Conf. M.E. Ch., 4 times to 1928; del. Ecumenical

Conf., Atlanta, Ga., 1931; mem. Joint Meth. Unification Commn. since 1928. Mem. Kappa Nu. Republican. Home: 219 W. Gorgas Lane. Office: Wesley Bldg., Philadelphia, Pa.

MUELLER, Harry Edward, music; b. Louisville, Ky., Jan. 28, 1894; s. Paul Max and Emma Mathilda (Weinedel) M.; student N.E. Conservatory of Music, 1912-16; Mus.B., Cincinnati Conservatory of Music, 1931, Mus.M., 1933; (hon.) Mus.D., Capitol Coll. of Music, Columbus, O., 1933; m. Grace Burtis, Mar. 2, 1924; children—Ruth Helen, Paul Henry. Has followed profession as church organist since 1909; teacher Lexington Coll. of Music, Lexington, Ky., 1916-18; dir. music, First Congl. Ch., Washington, D.C., 1919-24; concert organist, Grove Park Inn, Asheville, N.C., 1924-26; dir. music First Presbyn. Ch., Huntington, W.Va., since 1926; instr. music, Marshall Coll., Huntington, W.Va., since 1926, head of music dept. since 1937; first dir. music of Charleston (W.Va.) May Festival concerts; organizer and conductor of Madrigal Club of Marshall Coll. since 1933. Served as regtl. sergt. maj. inf., U.S.A., 1918-19 with A.E.F. Mem. Am. Assn. Univ. Profs., Am. Legion. Episcopalian. Mason (S.R.). Club: Rotary of Huntington. Home: 1725 Crestmont Drive, Huntington, W.Va.

MUELLER, William Arthur, clergyman, prof. church history; b. Luedenscheid, Germany, May 8, 1902; s. Fred Wm. and Henrietta (Vogel) M.; graduated from German Gymnasium, modern branch; came to U.S., 1923, naturalized, 1929; student Rochester Theol. Sem. and U. of Rochester, 1924-26; A.M., Canisius Coll., Buffalo, N.Y., 1927; Ph.D., N.Y. Univ., 1933; grad. study, Bibl. Sem., N.Y. City, 1930-31; m. Mary Martha Fink, Aug. 6, 1927; children—William Conrad, David Livingstone, Walter George (dec.), Gordon Herbert. Began as fgn. corr. and interpreter, Germany, 1922-23; ordained to ministry Bapt. Ch., 1927; pastor, Buffalo and Brooklyn, N.Y., 1927-36; interpreter, Bapt. World Alliance Congress, Berlin, Germany, 1934, Atlanta, Ga., 1939; del. interpreter, Oxford Conf. on Life and Work, Oxford, Eng., 1937; lecturer philosophy and psychology of religion, N.Y. Univ., 1935-36; prof. ch. history and comparative religion, Eastern Bapt. Theol. Sem., Phila., Pa., since 1936. Mem. Am. Ch. History Soc., Am. Bapt. History Soc. Baptist. Author: Amerika und das Neue Deutschland, 1935; I'm a Citizen of Three Worlds, 1939; Church and State in America, a Reaffirmation of Baptist Principles, 1939. Home: 1424 E. Kerper St., Philadelphia, Pa.

MUEND, Charles J., brass works mgr.; b. Pittsburgh, Pa., Apr. 2, 1888; s. Frank J. and Josephine (Wolff) M.; ed. Pittsburgh Acad. and Carnegie Inst. Tech.; m. Edna Sauer, Apr. 2, 1919; children—Jack, Edna. Successively gen. foreman and cost accountant, asst. supt., supt., night supt. shell plant (during World War), Standard San. Mfg. Co., Pittsburgh; then supt. Haines Jones & Cadbury, Phila.; now mgr. brass works Hajoca Corpn., Phila. Mem. Joint com. on Federal Specification since 1937; represents brass plumbing mfrs. on research asso. program at Bur. of Standards, Washington, D.C. Republican. Catholic. Author: Basic Cost System for Brass Manufacturers, 1934. Home: 1114 N. 65th St. Office: 3711 Sepviva St., Philadelphia, Pa.

MUIR, Charles Marshall, minister; b. Washington, D.C., Jan. 18, 1901; s. Charles Stothard and Carlotta (Brockett) M.; student McKinley Manual Training Sch., Washington, D.C., 1914-18, Carnegie Inst. Tech., Pittsburgh, 1918-20, U. of Cal. at Los Angeles, 1922, Union Theol. Sem., N.Y., 1928; A.B. (magna cum laude), Washington & Jefferson Coll., Washington, Pa., 1922; S.T.B., Western Theol. Sem., Pittsburgh, 1925; D.D. (hon.), U. of Pittsburgh, 1934; m. Mary Jeanette Shane, June 24, 1925; children—James Wallace, Charles Marshall (dec.), John Brockett. Asst. minister Shadyside Presbyn. Ch., Pittsburgh, 1922-23; missionary in Saskatchewan, Canadian Home Mission Bd., 1923; stated supply, West Elizabeth (Pa.) and Elrama (Pa.) Chs., 1923-25; asst. min. House of Hope Presbyn. Ch., St. Paul, Minn., 1925-26; min. First Presbyn. Ch., Van Wert, O., 1927-33; mathematics prof., Giffin Jr. Coll., Van Wert, O., 1932-33; moderator, Pittsburgh Presbytery, 1937-38; minister, Bellefield Presbyn. Ch., Pittsburgh, since 1933; mem. exec. commn., Pittsburgh Presbytery; dir. of missionary broadcasts, Bd. of Foreign Missions, Presbyn. Ch. in the U.S.A.; chmn. Pittsburgh Round Table, Nat. Conf. of Christians and Jews; chmn. Peace Com., Pittsburgh Council of Chs. Served as pvt., S.A.T.C., Carnegie Inst. Tech., Pittsburgh, 1918. Dir. Presbyn. Young People's Conf., Saltsburg, Pa., 1934. Mem. Delta Tau Delta, Phi Tau Gamma (hon.), Alpha Tau Epsilon. Awarded Gilbert Old English Prize, Washington and Jefferson Coll., 1922. Republican. Presbyterian. Clubs: Alpha Tau Epsilon, Quiz, "X" (Pittsburgh). Author: chapter, "Religion" in "In 1937"; The Scientific Genesis; The Nurseries of Heaven; Are We Crazy? (play). Contbr. to Christian Century Pulpit, Pittsburgh Catholic, Jewish Criterion. Home: 509 Roslyn Pl. Address: Bellefield Presbyterian Church, 5th and Bellefield Avs., Pittsburgh, Pa.

MUIR, Malcolm, publisher; b. Glen Ridge, N.J., July 19, 1885; s. James and Susan (Brown) M.; ed. pub. and pvt. schs.; m. Lida Kelly, May 14, 1914; children—Malcolm, Eleanor Warfield. Pres. and pub. News-Week since 1937; McGraw-Hill Pub. Co., 1905-37, v.p., 1916-28, pres., 1928-37; dep. adminstr., also div. adminstr., NRA; pres. and dir. Weekly Publs., Inc.; dir. Nat. Assn. of Mfrs., Nat. Bur. Econ. Research, Am. Arbitration Assn.; v.p. and dir. Merchants Assn. of N.Y.; mem. Nat. Industrial Conf. Bd., N.Y. State Chamber of Commerce, Am. Soc. M.E., Citizens Com. for Control of Crime in N.Y. City, Burns Soc., St. Andrews Soc.; advisory board Army Ordnance Assn. Dist. of N.Y.; exec. com. Economic Club of N.Y.; past pres. Asso. Business Papers, Inc., N.Y. Trade Press Assn. Republican. Episcopalian. Clubs: Racquet and Tennis, Union League (New York); Edgartown Yacht, Morris County Golf and Country, Short Hills (past pres.). Home: Short Hills, N.J.; and 160 E. 72d St., New York, N.Y. Office: Rockefeller Center, New York City, N.Y.

MUIR, William Wallace, pres. First Nat. Bk. of Warren; b. Apr. 10, 1851, Carbondale, Pa.; s. John and Caroline (Smith) M.; student Carbondale (Pa.) Select Sch., 1856-67; m. Martha Elizabeth Fuller, Mar. 14, 1872; children—Caroline (Mrs. M. F. Cowden), George E., Edward K., Marian (Mrs. Edward von Tacky). Bridge builder Del. & Hudson Canal Co., Carbondale, Pa., 1864-68; contracting business, 1868-75, and handled constrn., remodeling numerous refineries, 1875-88; organized, 1888, and pres., 1888-1916, Muir Oil Works, Warren, Pa.; pres. Pa. Paraffine Works, Titusville, Pa., 1890-1916, constructing new plant, 1902, pres., 1890-1916, dir. since 1890; pres. Bessemer Refining Co., Titusville, Pa., 1892-1916, building new plant, 1902, dir., 1892-1916; gen. mgr. Crew Levick Co., Phila., Pa., 1902-14, pres., 1914-18; pres. First Nat. Bank, Warren, Pa., since 1912; organized, 1924, and since pres. and dir. Mason Hotel Co. and Princess Martha Hotel (now Gulf Hotel Co.), St. Petersburg, Fla.; dir. Muir Oil Works. Mem. Oil Conservation Bd., Washington, D.C., 1914-17. Mem. Nat. Petroleum Assn. in 1904 (3d pres. and dir., 1912-16). Republican. Protestant. Odd Fellow (has held all offices). Club: Rotary (St. Petersburg, Fla.). Author several speeches on oil. Has taken active part in work for crippled children since 1932. Home: 304 Fourth Av. Office: 310 Second Av., Warren, Pa.

MULDOON, Hugh Cornelius, prof. chemistry; b. Truxton, N.Y.; s. Michael and Elizabeth (Warren) M.; Ph.G., Union U., Albany, N.Y., 1912; B.S., Valparaiso U., 1925, D.Sc., 1925; student Mass. Coll. of Pharmacy, and at Boston, Harvard, Ind. and Duquesne Univs.; unmarried. Instr. chemistry and Latin, Mass. Coll. of Pharmacy, 1912-18; prof. chemistry, Albany Coll. of Pharmacy, Union U., 1918-20, and acting dean, 1918-19; prof. chemistry and dean Sch. of Pharmacy, Valparaiso U., 1920-25, Duquesne U. since 1925. Mem. revision com. U.S. Pharmacopœia since 1930. Fellow A.A.A.S.; mem. Am. Assn. Colls. of Pharmacy (pres., 1937-38, mem. syllabus com. since 1933), Am. Chem. Soc., Am. Pharm. Assn., Pa. Pharm. Assn., Pa. Acad. Science, Am. Science Teachers Assn., Nat. Soc. for Study of Edn., Phi Delta Chi, Phi Delta Psi. Republican. Roman Catholic. Author: Lessons in Pharmaceutical Latin, 1916; Organic Chemistry for Students of the Medical Sciences, 1927; Laboratory Manual of Organic Chemistry, 1927. Editor of The Science Counselor since 1935. Contbr. to pharm. jours. Home: 5650 Forbes St., Pittsburgh, Pa.; and "Lazy M," Dushore, Pa.

MULLEN, Edward Andrew, physician; b. Pottstown, Pa., Apr. 6, 1892; s. Edward J. and Mary A. (O'Hara) M.; B.S., Central High Sch., Phila., 1910; Ph.D., Phila. Coll. of Pharmacy and Science, 1913; M.D., Jefferson Med. Coll., 1917; m. Alva D. Duff, July 24, 1935; 1 son, Edward Andre. House surgeon Lennox Hill Hosp., New York, 1921-22; asst. prof. of urology, Grad. Sch. of Medicine, U. of Pa., 1932-39; asst. prof. pharmacology, Phila. Coll. of Pharmacy and Science, 1928-39; genito-urinary surgeon Phila. Gen. Hosp.; urologist St. Christophers Hosp., Memorial Hosp.; asst. urologist Grad. Hosp. U. of Pa. Served as lt. (j.g.) U.S. Navy, 1917-20; lt. comdr. Med. Corps, U.S. Navy Reserve since 1929. Fellow Am. Coll. Surgeons, Coll. of Physicians of Phila.; mem. Am. Urol. Soc., A.M.A. Roman Catholic. Club: University (Phila.). Address: 2615 W. Somerset St., Philadelphia, Pa.

MULLEN, Philip H. R., clergyman; b. Ringgold, Md., Oct. 25, 1878; s. Amos Franklin and Hannah Sophia (Oswald) M.; student Baltimore City Coll., 1894-99; A.B., Gettysburg (Pa.) Coll., 1901, (hon.) D.D., 1929; A.M., 1904; B.D., Gettysburg (Pa.) Theol. Sem., 1904; m. Clara Walker O'Neal, Feb. 1, 1905; children—Elizabeth O'Neal (Mrs. David Fruston Edwards), John Philip Edward. Ordained to ministry Lutheran Ch., 1904; pastor, Maytown, Pa., 1904-07, Freeport, Ill., 1908-15, Swissvale, Pa., 1915-35; supt. missions, Pittsburgh Synod Luth. Ch. since 1935. Sec. Northern Ill. Synod, United Luth. Ch., 1909-13, Pittsburgh Synod, 1925-30; dir. Theol. Sem., Gettysburg, Pa., 1918-38. Lutheran. Rotarian. Editor Lutheran Monthly, 1920-25, 1935-36. Home: 536 East End Av., Pittsburgh, Pa. Office: 429 Fourth Av., Pittsburgh, Pa.

MULLER, George P., M.D., surgeon; b. Phila., Pa., June 29, 1877; s. Philip R. and Frances (Hughes) M.; A.B., Central High Sch., Phila., 1895; M.D., U. of Pa., 1899; m. Helen Ramsay, Sept. 20, 1905; children—George R., Helen R., Philip, John. Practiced at Phila. since 1899; interne Lankenau Hosp., 1899-1902; successively asst. instr. surgery, instr., asso. and prof. clin. surgery, U. of Pa. Sch. of Medicine until 1933; prof. of surgery, Grad. Sch. of Medicine, U. of Pa., 1919-33; prof. of surgery, Jefferson Med. Coll. since 1936; served as surgeon to various hosps., now to Misericordia, Lankenau and Jefferson hospitals. Contract surgeon, also mem. Advisory Bd. and of Med. Corps, U.S.A., World War; hon. discharged as maj., June 30, 1919. Fellow Am. Coll. Surgeons; mem. A.M.A., Am. Surg. Assn., Clin. Surg. Soc., Interurban Surg. Soc., Am. Assn. Thoracic Surgery, Phila. Acad. Surgery, Phila. Coll. Physicians, Phila. County Med. Soc., Alpha Mu Pi Omega. Republican. Catholic. Club: Phila. Country. Contbr. abt. 50 papers, chiefly on surg. subjects; also articles in text books. Revised Davis' Applied Anatomy. Home: 1930 Spruce St., Philadelphia, Pa.

MULLER, Julius Frederick, mfg. chemist; b. Brooklyn, N.Y., Sept. 5, 1900; s. Edward Jefferson and Julia Sadie (Lang) M.; B.Sc., Rutgers U., New Brunswick, N.J., 1922, M.Sc., 1928, Ph.D., 1930; m. Ethel Mae Johnson, June 18, 1927; children—Richard Johnson, Julius Edward, James Henry. Engaged in farming, 1922-26; chemist Walker Gordon Lab. Co., Plainsboro, N.J., 1930-31; cons. chemist at New Brunswick, N.J., 1931-32; chemist National Oil Products Co., Harrison, N.J., 1932-35; chemist and propr. The Muller Laboratories, mfg. chemists, Baltimore, Md., since 1935. Mem.

Am. Chem. Soc., Sigma Xi, Phi Lambda Upsilon, Alpha Zeta. Presbyterian. Home: 5 Fairfield Drive, Catonsville. Office: 3156 Frederick Av., Baltimore, Md.

MULLER, Valentin Kurt Richard, asso. prof. archæology; b. Berlin, Germany, Sept. 23, 1889; s. Heinrich Carl and Emma (Wittenburg) M.; came to U.S., 1931, naturalized, 1936; ed. U. of Göttingen, 1908-09, U. of Munich, 1909, U. of Bonn, 1910-12; Ph.D., U. of Berlin, 1915; unmarried. Asst. dir. archæol. inst. of U. of Berlin, 1915 to 1923, privat dozent, 1923-29, extraordinary prof., U. of Berlin, 1929; asso. prof. archæology, Bryn Mawr Coll., Pa., since 1930. Mem. Archæol. Inst. of America, Am. Anthrop. Assn., Am. Oriental Soc., Coll. Art Assn. Home: 915 Wyndon Av., Bryn Mawr, Pa.

MÜLLER-MUNK, Peter, designer and prof. industrial design; b. Berlin, Germany, June 25, 1904; s. Franz and Gertrude (Munk) M.; came to U.S., 1926 and naturalized citizen, 1936; B.A., U. of Berlin, Acad. of Fine and Applied Arts, 1926; m. Ilona Tallmer, Oct. 26, 1936. Employed by Tiffany & Co. then opened own studio for metal work and industrial design, New York, N.Y., for 9 yrs.; instr. State Normal Sch., Oswego, N.Y., N.Y. Sch. of Fine and Industrial Arts, N.Y. Evening Sch. for Industrial Art, Craft Students League; prof. Carnegie Inst. Tech., Pittsburgh, Pa., since 1935; designer for Catalin Corpn., Prophylactic Brush Co., Elgin American Co.; has designed for many well-known mfrs. Exhibited at Metropolitan Mus. of Art and other leading art mus. Permanently rep. in leading art mus. Awarded prizes for outstanding work in craft. Mem. Assn. Univ. Profs., Soc. of Designer Craftsmen, Artists Congress, Associated Artists of Pittsburgh. Contbr. articles on creative art and design to leading art mags. and illustrations of his work have appeared in rep. mags. and jours. Home: 6615 Darlington Rd. Address: Carnegie Inst. of Technology, Pittsburgh, Pa.

MULLIKIN, Addison Eugene, lawyer; b. Talbot Co., Md., Sept. 26, 1874; s. Francis Charles and Margaret Eugenia M.; A.B., St. John's Coll., 1895, A.M., 1902; LL.B., U. of Md. Law Sch., 1902; unmarried. Employed as prin. Talbot Co. High Sch., Trappe, Md., 1895-1900; admitted to Md. bar, 1902, and since engaged in gen. practice of law at Baltimore; mem. firm Mullikin and Marchant, 1902-20, Mullikin and Porter, 1920-28, Mullikin, Stockbridge & Waters since 1928; mem. First Branch City Council, Baltimore, 1907-11; mem. Liquor License Bd., 1912-16; mem. Sch. Bd. of Baltimore, 1920-26 and 1930-34; Rep. candidate for gov. Md., 1926; dir. and sec. Pennsylvania Glass Sand Corpn.; dir. Southern Hotel. Trustee Springfield State Hosp., 1935-39. Mem. Am. and Md. State bar assns., Bar Assn. Baltimore City, Assn. Bar of City of New York, Phi Kappa Sigma. Republican. Presbyn. Mason (Shriner). Clubs: University (Baltimore); Woodmont Rod & Gun (Hancock, Md.). Home: 1001 St. Paul St. Office: Baltimore Trust Bldg., Baltimore, Md.

MULLIKIN, Oliver S., lawyer; b. Easton, Md., Feb. 19, 1904; s. Clayland and Retta C. (Smith) M.; student Johns Hopkins U., 1921-23; LL.B., U. of Md. Law Sch., Baltimore, 1925; m. Lillian N. Fleckenstein, Sept. 10, 1924; children—Marjorie C., Carol B., M. Loretta. Admitted to Md. bar, 1925 and since engaged in gen. practice of law at Easton; served as state's atty. for Talbot Co., 1931-34, 1935-38; dir. and atty. Easton Nat. Bank of Md. since 1934. Mem. bd. mgrs. Eastern Shore State Hosp. Mem. Kappa Alpha. Republican. Methodist. Club: Talbot Country (Easton). Home: 221 S. Hanson St. Office: Stewart Bldg., Easton, Md.

MULLIN, Charles Earl, consulting chemist; b. Hyndman, Pa., Apr. 13, 1890; s. Albert Sidney and Charlotte Catherine (Cook) M.; student Juniata Coll., 1911-13; M.S., National Univ., 1922; student Phila. Textile Sch., 1922-25; D.Sc., Universite de Nancy, France, 1927; m. B. Margaret Foster, 1913; 1 adopted son, Joseph Withers; m. 2d, Ruth F. Corbin, Aug. 2, 1934. With Marshall & Co., Chicago, 1913-15, beginning as traveling chemist and advancing to mgr.; efficiency engr. and chemist Great Western Sugar Co., 1915-16; chief chemist and asst. supt. Chem. Pigments Corpn., 1916-17; prof. of chemistry, rayon and dyeing and head div. of textile chemistry, Clemson Coll., 1925-33; consulting chemist to textile, rayon and all related industries since 1917. Fellow Internat. Faculty of Sciences (London), Chem. Soc. (London), S.C. Acad. of Sciences, Am. Inst. of Chemists (past chmn. Pa. Chapter; nat. councillor); mem. Am. Chem. Soc., Am. Assn. Textile Chemists and Colorists (mem. research com.; past sect. Phila. Sect., past chmn. Peidmont Sect.), Soc. of Chem. Industry (London), Soc. Dyers and Colorists (England), Phi Psi. Republican. Mason (32°, Shriner). Author: Acetate Silk and Its Dyes, 1927. Mem. staff Chem. Abstracts since 1915. Contbr. over 400 technical and scientific papers to jours. in U.S. and abroad. Home: 113 4th St. Office: 111 4th St., Huntingdon, Pa.

MULLIN, James Paul, pres. James T. Mullin & Sons; b. Wilmington, Del., July 28, 1888; s. John Strickland and Martha (Harbinson) M.; student Wilmington Mil. Acad., and Phillips Exeter Acad. (Exeter, N.H.); m. Jane Smith, Mar. 15, 1910; children—Jane (Mrs. Horace E. Clark), Ann, Constance. Salesman, 1908-09; mgr. Mullin's Clothing Store, Westchester, Pa., 1909-14; mgr. custom dept. James T. Mullin & Sons, Inc., men's and boys' clothing, Wilmington, Del., 1914-16, mgr. furnishing dept. 1916-23, pres. and gen. mgr. since 1923; dir. Credit Reporting Co., Security Trust Co., New Castle Mutual Ins. Co. Dir. Wilmington (Del.) Park Bd. Episcopalian. Mason. Home: 1011 Park Pl. Office: 6th and Market Sts., Wilmington, Del.

MULLIN, John H.; chief of gynecology Delaware Hosp.; mem. courtesy staff Homeopathic, Wilmington Gen. and St. Francis hosps. Address: 601 Delaware Av., Wilmington, Del.

MULLISON, Olin R., gen. mgr. chain stores; b. Loyallville, Pa., May 7, 1882; s. Elihu Breckenbridge and Elizabeth Ann (Park) M.; ed. Pleasant Hill Acad., Sweet Valley, Pa.; m. Maude C. Rozelle, June 24, 1908; children—Marion (Mrs. Addison Ellis), Elizabeth (Mrs. Burt Lauderbaugh), Helen, Edward Olin (died in infancy). School teacher, 1899-1905; dist. mgr. Chicago Portrait Co., 1905-09; prop. chain of grocery stores, Wyoming Valley, Wilkes-Barre, 1909-24; sold out to Am. Stores Co. of N.E. Pa., 1924, and since gen. mgr.; pres. and dir. First Nat. Bank, Kingston, Pa. Republican. Methodist. Mason (K.T., 32°, Shriner). Clubs: Rotary, Craftsman (Wilkes-Barre). Home: 67 Butler St., Kingston, Pa. Office: 97 Bennett St., Wilkes-Barre, Pa.

MUMFORD, Edward Warloch, sec. of trustees of U. of Pa.; b. Phila., Pa., May 6, 1868; s. Joseph Pratt and Mary E. (Bassett) M.; Ph.B., U. of Pa., 1889; (hon.) Litt.D., U. of Pa., 1939; m. Mary E. Bines, Jan. 21, 1897; children—Jean Pratt (Mrs. James D. Sorber), Mary Eno (Mrs. Alfred Douty), Philip Sherman. Began as circulation mgr. Santa Claus, children's mag., 1889; editorial dept. Curtis Pub. Co., 1890-91; asst. sec. and registrar U. of Pa., 1891-99, bursar, 1899-1904; with Powers & Armstrong, advertising, 1904-05; editor, Penn Pub. Co., 1905-19; sec. to trustees, U. of Pa. Phila., Pa., since 1919. Mem. Am. Acad. Polit. & Social Sci., Phi Beta Kappa, Beta Theta Pi. Democrat. Episcopalian. Clubs: Franklin Inn (pres.), Contemporary of Phila. (treas.). Home: The Fairfax, 43d and Locust St., Philadelphia, Pa. Office: 3447 Walnut St., Philadelphia, Pa.

MUMMA, Anna E. Davis (Mrs. Stanley N.), lawyer; b. Lancaster, Pa., Aug. 20, 1896; d. Benjamin Franklin and Martha Louise (Quade) Davis; attended Shippen School, Lancaster, Pa.; grad. Miss Madeira's Sch., Washington, D.C., 1916; LL.B., Dickinson Coll. Sch. of Law, 1923; m. Stanley N. Mumma, tobacco buyer and packer, June 25, 1924; children—Louise Davis, Deborah Stanley. Admitted to Pa. bar, 1925 and since engaged in gen. practice of law at Lancaster; served as U.S. Commr. for Eastern Dist. Pa., 1933-38. Mem. Lancaster Co. Bar Assn., Phi Delta Delta. Democrat. Mem. Trinity Lutheran Ch., Lancaster, Pa. Clubs: Junior League of Lancaster, Lancaster Country Club, College Club of Lancaster. Home: 131 E. Orange St. Office: 33 N. Duke St., Lancaster, Pa.

MUMMART, Clarence Allen, clergyman, educator; b. Welsh Run, Franklin Co., Pa., July 14, 1874; s. William L. and Catharine A. (Kerfoot) M.; ed. Cumberland Valley State Normal Sch., Shippensburg, Pa.; preachers' normal diploma, Huntington (Ind.) Coll., 1905, teachers' normal diploma, 1906, A.B., 1907, B.D., 1908, M.A., 1909, D.D., 1912; studied U. of Mich.; Ph.D., Oskaloosa (Ia.) Coll., 1913; S.T.M., Northwestern U., 1925; m. Lillie May Zimmerman, Mar. 10, 1896; children—Cletus Byron, Charles Otterbein (dec.), Ethel May (Mrs. Herschel Holmes Griffith), Mary Katharyn (Mrs. Russell Evans Griffith). Teacher pub. schs., until 1903; ordained ministry U.B. Ch., 1901; pastor for 12 yrs. in Pa., Ind. and Ohio; presiding elder, 1905-08, 1910-12; editor Christian Conservator, 1909-11, 1917-20; head dept. of Theology, Huntington Coll., 1911-17, 1919-20, pres. Huntington Coll., 1912-15 and 1925-32, prof. philosophy, history and practical theology, 1932-33; pastor Otterbein U.B. Ch., Greencastle, Pa., since 1933. Mem. Bd. of Edn. U.B. Ch., 1913-17, 1921-32, 1937—; gen. sec. of edn. U.B. Ch., 1913-17 and 1925-32; pres. Bd. Christian Edn., U.B. Ch., 1921-25, 1937—; mem. Exec. Com. Inter.-Council Religious Edn., 1923-29; supt. sch. adminstrn., Franklin Co. S.S. Assn., 1934—; bishop U.B. Ch., 1921-25, 1937—; mem. Gen. Conf. 5 times. Prohibition-Republican. Author of monographs on religious, Bibl. and ednl. subjects. Home: 236 S. Washington St., Greencastle, Pa.

MUNCH, James Clyde, pharmacologist; b. Farmer City, Ill., Feb. 20, 1896; s. Henry and Nellie (Jackson) M.; B.S., Ill. Wesleyan U., Bloomington, 1915, M.S., 1916; Ph.D., George Washington U., 1924; m. Soula Clanton Robinson. Toxicologist, Ill. Wesleyan U., 1915-16; instr. of toxicology and chemistry, U. of Louisville Med. Sch., 1916-17; pharmacologist Bur. of Chemistry, U.S. Dept. Agr., 1917-28, Bur. of Biol. Survey since 1928; prof. of physiology and pharmacology and dir. of research, Temple U. Sch. of Pharmacy since 1931; dir. pharmacological research Sharp & Dohme, 1928-36, John Wyeth & Bro., 1936-37; consultant and lab. service in pharmacology and bio-assays since Jan. 1938. Mem. revision coms. U.S. Pharmacopœia X, XI; Nat. Formulary VI; Recipe Book III. Served as lt. Sanitary Corps, U.S.A., 1918-19. Awarded Kiwanis medal of honor. Fellow A.A. A.S.; mem. Am. Chem. Soc., Am. Pharm. Assn. (v.p.), Internat. Physiol. Soc., Md. and Pa. acads. of science, Kappa Psi, Theta Kappa Psi. Mason. Author: Bio-assays—A Handbook of Quantitative Pharmacology, 1931; Manual of Biological Assaying, 1937; Elementary Pharmacology, 1938. Contbr. many articles on scientific researches to jours. Home: 40 N. Maple Av., Lansdowne, Pa. Office: 6816 Market St., Upper Darby, Pa.

MUNGER, George A.; football coach Univ. of Pa. Address: University of Pa., Philadelphia, Pa.

MUNGER, James Speer, exec. pub. utility co.; b. Nazareth, Pa., June 6, 1895; s. Henry Barker and Sarah Ann (Speer) M.; grad. Nazareth Hall Mil. Acad., 1911; B.S., Moravian Coll. & Theol. Sem., Bethlehem, Pa., 1915; grad. study Lehigh U., 1915-17; m. Kathryn S. Munger. Began as industrial engr., State Workmens Ins. Fund, Harrisburg, Pa., 1919; vice-pres. and dir. Mohler & Co., ins. agts., Pittsburgh, 1923-38; vice-pres. and dir. Blue Mountain Consolidated Water Co., Nazareth, Pa., since 1938. Served as 2d lt., Inf., U.S. Army, 1917-18. Mem. Phi Sigma Kappa. Republican. Moravian. Home: 20 Belvidere St. Office: Nazareth, Pa.

MUNN, Matthew Gordon, clergyman; b. nr. Walton, N.Y., May 13, 1871; s. Hugh Clark and Margaret (Russell) M.: ed. Westminster Coll., New Wilmington, Pa., 1892-95; A.B., Muskingum Coll., 1896; B.D., Xenia Theol.

Sem., 1899; (hon.) D.D., Tarkio Coll., 1920; m. Elizabeth M. Jackson, Aug. 21, 1900 (dec. 1917); children—Margaret Caroline (Mrs. Arthur T. Brown), Marjorie Mary (Mrs. J. Wilson McCutchan), Genevieve Elizabeth (Mrs. Theodore E. White), Malcolm Gordon; m. 2d, Grace M. McKean, Sept. 30, 1919. Ordained to ministry U. Presbyn. Ch., 1899; pastor, Chariton, Ia., 1899-1908, Waterloo, Ia., 1908-1919, Topeka, Kan. 1919-28; pastor Brown Av. U. Presbyn. Ch., Erie, Pa., since 1928; mem. Tarkio Coll. Bd., 1914-19, Sterling Coll. Bd., 1925-28. Mem. Erie Ministerial Assn. Pres. Erie Co. Presbyn. Union; ministerial rep. on Erie Community Chest bd. Republican. United Presbyn. Home: 2712 Elmwood Av., Erie, Pa.

MUNN, Ralph, librarian; b. Aurora, Ill., Sept. 19, 1894; s. Walter Ferguson and Jennie (Wood) M.; LL.B., U. of Denver, 1916, A.B., 1917; B.L.S., N.Y. State Library Sch., 1921; m. Anne Shepard, June 6, 1922; children—Robert Ferguson, Margaret Jean. Reference librarian, Seattle (Wash.) Pub. Library, 1921-25, asst. librarian, 1925-26; librarian, Flint (Mich.) Pub. Library, 1926-28; dir. Carnegie Library and Carnegie Library Sch., Pittsburgh, Pa., since 1928. Served with U.S.A., Apr. 1917-July 1919. Mem. A.L.A. (pres. 1938-39), Pa. Library Assn. (pres. 1930-31), Sigma Pi, Phi Delta Phi. Republican. Presbyn. Rotarian. Surveyed libraries of Australia and New Zealand for Carnegie Corpn., 1934. Contbr. to Carnegie Mag. Home: 1220 Sheridan Av. Office: Carnegie Library, Pittsburgh, Pa.

MUNN, Wilbur, banker; b. East Orange, N.J., Nov. 7, 1868; s. Thompson C. and Sarah J. (Smith) M.; ed. pub. schs.; m. Marie A. Byrne, June 10, 1896. Pres. Second Nat. Bank, Orange, N.J.; v.p. Asso. Bankers Title & Mortgage Guaranty Co.; treas. N.J. Orthopædic Hosp., Red Cross Chapter of the Oranges; asst. treas. Welfare Fed. of the Oranges. Mem. N.J. Soc. of Founders and Patriots of America. Republican. Presbyterian. Club: Rotary (past pres.; Orange, N.J.). Home: 383 Fairview Av. Office: Second Nat. Bank, Orange, N.J.

MUNN, William Faitoute, chemist and perfumer; b. East Orange, N.J., Jan. 20, 1891; s. William Condit and Mary (Stroud) M.; lab. asst. Columbia U., Electrochem. Lab., 1911-13; m. Clara May Bennett, Jan. 14, 1927; 1 son, William Faitoute, Jr. Chemist, West Virginia Pulp & Paper Co., New York, N.Y., 1913-15; chem. and elec. engr., Electrical Alloy Co., 1915-16; asst. dir. research and investigation, Lederle Labs., N.Y. City, 1916-17; chief chemist, Baker & Adamson Plant of General Chem. Co., Easton, Pa., 1917-18; chief chemist, Colura Pictures Corpn., 1919-20; propr. pvt. lab. at W. Faitoute Munn, West Orange, N.J., since 1920, research, investigation, analysis and specializing in photomicrography and microscopy; pres. Faitoute, Inc., perfumers, since 1936; certified chemist for Am. Bur. of Shipping, 1922-32. Fellow and past vice-pres. N.Y. Micros. Soc. Formerly fellow Royal Micros. Soc. A.A. A.S., Am. Geographic Soc.; charter mem. and fellow Radio Club of America. Mem. First Reformed Ch. Home: 75 Walker Rd., West Orange, N.J.

MUÑOZ, Gonzalo Claudio, mfr. power transmission equipment; b. Biarritz, France, June 16, 1881; s. Adolfo and Mercedes (Poey) M.; brought to U.S., 1882, naturalized, 1904; C.E., U. of Pa., 1903; m. Vivian Watkins, Aug. 1924 (died Feb. 21, 1929); married 2d, Catharine Schuyler Chambers, Mar. 16, 1939; 1 son, Juan F. Began as surveyor with engring. corps of railroad, 1903; mgr. Las Canas Sugar Estate, Cuba, 1904-07; asst., then chief engr., Outer Harbor Dock & Wharf Co., San Pedro, Calif., 1908-12; contracting engr., Los Angeles, Calif., 1913-17; asso. with American Pulley Co., mfrs. and distributors power transmission equipment, Phila., Pa., since 1919, vice-pres., gen. mgr. since 1930. Served as maj. Ordnance Dept., U.S.A., 1917-19. Mem. bd. and treas. Family Soc. of Phila. Mem. Am. Soc. Civil Engrs., Delta Phi. Club: Army and Navy (Washington, D.C.). Home: 1530 Pine Street, Phila. Office: 4200 Wissahickon Ave., Phila., Pa.

MUNRO, Dana Gardner, university professor; b. at Providence, R.I., July 18, 1892; s. Dana Carleton and Alice Gardner (Beecher) M.; student Brown Univ., 1908-11; A.B., Univ. of Wis., 1912; A.B., Brown Univ. with class of 1912; post-grad. work, Munich, 1912-13; Ph.D., U. of Pa., 1917; m. Margaret Bennett Wiley, June 1, 1920; children—Margaret Alice, Carolyn Babcock, Gardner Wiley. Studied conditions in Central America, under the Carnegie Peace Endowment, 1914-16; research fellow in polit. science, U. of Pa., 1917; regional economist for Mexico and Caribbean region, in Foreign Trade Adviser's Office, Dept. of State, 1919-20; lecturer on Latin America, Georgetown U., 1919-20; economist consul, at Valparaiso, Chile, 1920-21; detailed to Latin Am. Div., Dept. of State, July 1921, asst. chief of Div., 1923-25; 1st sec. of Legation, Panama, 1925-27, Managua, Nicaragua, 1927-29; chief Div. of Latin-Am. Affairs, Dept. of State, 1929-30; E.E. and M.P. to Haiti, 1930-32; member of Commission of Inquiry under conciliation treaty with Finland since 1933; prof. of Latin-Am. history and affairs, Princeton U., since 1932; visiting lecturer on Latin-Am. history, Columbia, 1934-35; Carnegie visiting prof. in S.A., 1935; vice-pres. Foreign Bondholders' Protective Council since 1938; dir. Sch. of Public and Internat. Affairs, Princeton U. since 1939. Member Council on Foreign Relations. Joined Air Service, U.S. Army, 1917; trained as pilot and commd. 2d lt., Oct. 1918. Mem. Delta Phi, Phi Eta, Phi Beta Kappa. Episcopalian. Author: The Five Republics of Central America, 1918; The United States and the Caribbean Area, 1933. Home: Springdale Rd., Princeton, N.J.

MUNROE, Robert, Jr., mfr.; b. Pittsburgh, Pa., April 28, 1866; s. Col. Robert and Mary (Duncan) M.; ed. Newell Inst., Pittsburgh, Pa.; m. Clara L. Hartwell, Sept. 26, 1894, 1 dau., Marion Hartwell (Mrs. John M. Baker). Began as partner with father in R. Munroe & Sons Mfg. Co., plate steel mfrs. (business established, 1835, as West Point Boiler Works); after death of father, founded and became pres. Munroe Boiler and Constrn. Co. and R. Munroe Patents Co., 1910. Mem. Pittsburgh Chamber of Commerce, Credit Men's Assn. Republican. Episcopalian. Mason (32°, Shriner). Clubs: Rotary Internat., Pittsburgh Athletic. Home: 6308 Stanton Av. Office: 23d and Smallman St., Pittsburgh, Pa.

MUNROE, Robert III, banker; b. Pittsburgh, Pa., June 25, 1895; s. Edward Reynolds and Melinda (McKee) M.; student Kiski Prep. Sch., Saltsburg, Pa., 1909-13; A.B., Amherst (Mass.) Coll., 1917; LL.B., Harvard Law Sch., 1921; m. Eleanor Bergmann Patterson, Mar. 31, 1931; 1 son, Robert Lee. Admitted to Pa. bar, 1921, and practiced at Pittsburgh, 1921-30, as mem. firm Watson & Freeman; trust officer, The Colonial Trust Co., Pittsburgh, 1930-36, v.p. in charge trusts since 1936; dir. William G. Johnston Co. Dir. Allegheny Memorial Park. Republican. Presbyterian. Clubs: Pittsburgh Athletic, Pittsburgh Field. Home: 6017 Kentucky Av. Office: 414-16 Wood St., Pittsburgh, Pa.

MUNROE, Thomas William, banking; b. Johnstown, Pa., Aug. 18, 1896; s. William A. and Katherine (Brawley) M.; ed. pub. schs. of Johnstown, Pa., bus. coll., Am. Inst. Banking, Grad. Sch. Am. Inst. Banking Rutgers U.; m. Imogene Cameron, Apr. 5, 1920; children—William Alexander, Clark Cameron, Thomas William, Jr., Judith Thompson. Began business career with Title Trust & Guarantee Co., Johnstown, Pa., 1910; vice-pres. Fidelity Deposit Bank, Derry, Pa., since 1934. Served in U.S. Army, 1917-19; with A.E.F. in France. Republican. Office: 200 S. Chestnut St., Derry, Pa.

MUNSICK, Donald Bert, lawyer; b. Newark, N.J., Feb. 15, 1893; s. George W. and Clara M. (Nettleship) M.; student Newark (N.J.) Acad., 1907-11; LL.B., Cornell U., 1915; m. Elizabeth Blanche Anderson, Dec. 10, 1917; 1 dau., Evelyn Dorothy. Admitted to N.J. bar, 1917, and since practiced at Newark, N.J. Server as 2d lt., 305th Trench Mortar Battery, 80th Div., U.S. Army, 1917-19. Mem. Maplewood (N.J.) Twp. Com. since 1935. Mem. Essex County, N.J. State and Am. bar assns., Sigma Alpha Epsilon, Am. Legion. Republican. Methodist. Home: 42 Oakview Av., Maplewood, N.J. Office: Nat. Newark Bldg., Newark, N.J.

MUNSON, G(eorge) Kibby, lawyer; b. Rochester, N.Y., May 15, 1893; s. George W. and Lena L. (Kibby) M.; A.B., U. of Rochester, 1914; LL.B., George Washington U., 1924; m. Grace L. Bulloch, Jan. 4, 1919; 1 dau., Marion Elizabeth. Employed as sec. to A. D. Sanders, congressman from 39th N.Y. Dist., 1917-27; admitted to D.C. bar, 1924; in practice law since 1928; mem. firm Hitt & Munson since 1931, specializing in income tax law and to practice before Securities and Exchange Commission; served as special examiner in the so-called sabotage cases before Mixed Claims Commn., U.S. and Germany, assisting the umpire and two commrs, until decision reached in Hamburg, Germany, was promulgated in Nov. 1930. Served in U.S.N.R.F., 1918. Mem. D.C. and Am. bar assns., Order of Coif, Delta Upsilon, Phi Delta Phi. Republican. Presbyn. Mason. Contbr. articles to law jours. and tech. publs. Home: 6900 Meadow Lane, Chevy Chase, Md. Office: Woodward Bldg., Washington, D.C.

MURDOCH, Alexander, purchasing agt. Am. Fruit Growers, Inc.; b. Pittsburgh, Pa., Oct. 19, 1877; s. Alexander and Lydia (McMaster) M.; grad. pub. schs., Pittsburgh, Pa., 1895; m. Aimee L. Beringer, June 15, 1911. Began business career as messenger in Bank of Pittsburgh and later an officer of other banks to asst. cashier First Nat. Bank; asst. auditor Am. Water Works and Guarantee Co., West Pa. Electric Co.; treas. Orchard & Investment Co., Crutchfield and Woolfolk; purchasing agt. and dir. American Fruit Growers, Inc., since 1919; vice-pres. and dir. William Penn Trust Co.; dir., asst. sec. and asst. treas. Pittsburgh Fruit & Produce Exchange; sec. and treas. Deerfield Groves Co. Vice-pres. and trustee Johnson C. Smith Univ., Charlotte, N.C. Mem. Bd. Nat. Missions of Presbyn. Ch. of N.A. Republican. Presbyn. (elder Shadyside Ch.). Mason. Rotarian. Club: Pittsburgh Rotary. Home: 1400 Squirrel Hill Av. Office: 1400 Chamber of Commerce Bldg., Pittsburgh, Pa.

MURDOCH, William Moorhead, civil engring.; b. Pittsburgh, Pa., June 1, 1879; s. James Bissett and Jeannie Adaline (Moorhead) M.; Ph.B., Sheffield Sci. Sch. of Yale U., 1898; m. Margaret Roseburg Forsyth, Sept. 26, 1901. Asso. with engring dept. div. maintenance of way, Pa. R.R. Co. continuously since 1898, engaged in maintenance of way work at Toledo, O., Pittsburgh, Pa., Indianapolis, Ind., Columbus and Cincinnati, O., now located at Pittsburgh, Pa. Served with Yale Battery, U.S. Vols. in Spanish-Am. War; served as capt. engrs. in office Chief of Engrs., Washington, D.C. and comdr. Co. C, 120th Engrs. at Ft. Benj. Harrison, Ind., during World War. Traffic safety observer of Better Traffic Com., Pittsburgh. Mem. Soc. Am. Mil. Engrs., United Spanish War Vets., Am. Legion. Chess champion of Yale U., 1896-98. Republican. Presbyn. Mason (K.T., 32°, Shriner). Home: 6808 McPherson Boul., Pittsburgh, Pa. Office: 612 Pa. Station, Pittsburgh, Pa.

MURDOCK, D. Ray, physician; b. Waynesburg, Pa., June 22, 1887; s. Benjamin Franklin and Sarah Elizabeth (Long) M.; student Waynesburg (Pa.) Coll., 1905-08; M.D., U. of Pa., 1912; m. Katharine Grace Gallagher, Nov. 24, 1914. Began practice of medicine, Greensburg, Pa., 1914; surgeon for Pa. R.R., since 1920, Jamison Coal Co., Greensburg, since 1930, Hillmann Coal Co., Irwin, Pa., since 1934; mem. staff Westmoreland Hosp., Greensburg, since 1916. Served as capt., U.S. Army, 1917-19; overseas, 1 year. Fellow A.M.A.; mem. Pa. State Med. Soc., Westmoreland Co. Med. Soc. Republican. Presbyterian. Mason (32°, Shriner). Club: Greensburg (Pa.) Country; University (Pittsburgh). Home: 534 E. Pittsburgh St. Office: First National Bank Bldg., Greensburg, Pa.

MURDOCK, George John, inventor; b. New Berlin, N.Y., Apr. 17, 1858; s. Chester and Elizabeth (Armstrong) M.; acad. and engring. edn.; m. Jeannette P., d. Thomas W. Waterman (law author), April 23, 1883; 2 children living.

Studied mech. and elec. science, and engring.; discovering in 1879 that electric lamp carbons when isolated from atmospheric air were of much longer life, he took out in 1883 the first patent in the U.S. on the enclosed form of arc lamp which is now commonly used throughout the civilized world; prior to 1885 had developed a complete system of electric lighting, including dynamo, regulator for arc lamps, arc lamps, and other accessories; other patented inventions have followed including bolt machines, files, and holder button, and button fastener (with A.L. Lesher), an exhaust turbine, an electric surface gage, magnetic drill holder, electric ry. signal indicator, and many other tools, and instruments that have come into common use; constructed, 1903, first gasoline tank with a rubber composite cover; inventor of self sealing fuel tanks for war airplanes of the type used by the U.S. and foreign govts. in World War; since war chiefly engaged in research, and development. Elected to membership in many Am. and foreign socs. Contbr. to tech. press on subjects relating to electricity and mechanics. Address: 213 W. Market St., Newark, N.J.

MURNAGHAN, Francis D., prof. applied mathematics; b. Omagh, Co. Tyrone, Ireland, Aug. 4, 1893; s. George and Angela (Mooney) M.; B.A., Nat. U. of Ireland, 1913, M.A., 1914; Ph.D., Johns Hopkins U., 1916; m. Ada May Kimbell, June 23, 1919; children—Francis D., Mary Patricia. Came to U.S., 1914, naturalized citizen, 1928. Instr. in mathematics, Rice Inst., Houston, Tex., 1916-18; asso., Johns Hopkins, 1918-21, asso. prof. applied mathematics, 1921-28, prof. since 1928; dir. Mathematics Inst., Rutgers, 1926; visiting prof., U. of Chicago, 1928, 30, U. of Pa., 1929. Fellow Am. Physical Soc., A.A.A.S.; mem. Am. Math. Soc., Math. Assn. America, London Math. Soc., Edinburgh Math. Soc., Sigma Xi, Gamma Alpha, Phi Beta Kappa. Author: Vector Analysis and the Theory of Relativity, 1922; (with Joseph S. Ames) Theoretical Mechanics, 1929; Theory of Group Representations, 1938. Home: 6202 Sycamore Rd., Baltimore, Md.

MURPHY, Eugene C., surgeon; b. Phila., Pa., Jan. 6, 1891; s. John and Johanna (Corbit) M.; ed. Temple U., 1908-09; M.D., Medico-Chirurg. Coll., 1913; unmarried. Engaged in practice of medicine at Philadelphia, Pa., since 1914, specializing in surgery since 1915; chief surgeon, St. Agnes Hosp. since 1920; attdg. surgeon, U.S. Pub. Health Service since 1923; mem. bd. dirs. St. Agnes Hosp. since 1924. Served as 1st lieut. Med. Corps, U.S.A., 1918-19, with A.E.F. as surgeon Base Hosp. No. 67, Mesves, France, 1918. Fellow Am. Coll. Surgs. Mem. Am. Med. Assn., Pa. State and Phila. Co. med. socs., Phila. Acad. Surgery, Phila. Coll. Phys. Roman Catholic. Club: Philadelphia Medical. Home: 1841 S. Broad St., Philadelphia, Pa.

MURPHY, Frederick Vernon, architect; b. Fond du Lac, Wis., Feb. 16, 1870; s. John Vernon and Alice (McCue) M.; student Columbian (now George Washington) U., 1899-1901; Architecte Diplomé par le Gouvernement Français, École des Beaux Arts, Paris, 1909; LL.D., Canisius Coll., 1924; m. Marjorie Mary Cannon, October 4, 1936; 1 son, Frederick Vernon, Jr. Prof. of architecture and head of dept. Catholic U. of America, since 1910; mem. bd. consultants Municipal Center, Washington; asso. architect Nat. Shrine of Immaculate Conception, Washington; dir. Allied Architects, Inc.; selected as architect for New Baltimore Cathedral, Baltimore, Md. Mem. design com. Ho. of Rep. Office Bldg., New Nat. Mus., New Naval Hosp. Prin. works: St. Charles Coll. Chapel, Catonsville, Md.; Martin Maloney Chem. Lab., Sacred Heart Ch., John Kenneth Mullen Memorial Library, Papal Legation (all Washington); St. Francis de Sales Ch., Buffalo, N.Y.; St. Mary's Ch., Mobile, Ala.; etc. Fellow Am. Inst. Architects (mem. bd. of examiners, registration bd., president Washington chapter, 1936-37); member Society Beaux Arts Architects, Société des Architectes Diplomés par le Gouvernement Française, Comité Permanent International des Architects. Registered architect with Nat. Council of Architectural Registration Boards. Awarded gold medal for design of Sacred Heart Church and John Kenneth Mullen Memorial Library; decorated Chevalier Legion of Honor (France); Knight Commander Order of St. Gregory. Catholic. Clubs: Cosmos, University (Washington); Columbia Country (Chevy Chase, Md.); Union Interalliée (Paris). Author: Universal Knowledge Foundation, 1927. Home: 26 William's Lane, Chevy Chase, Md. Office: 1413 H St. N.W., Washington, D.C.

MURPHY, J. Edwin, mng. editor; b. Baltimore, Md., Apr. 16, 1876; s. John C. P. and Emily R. (Mullan) M.; A.B., Loyola Coll., Baltimore, 1893; m. Mary Julia Austin, June 16, 1908. Reporter on various Baltimore newspapers, 1894-1908; city editor, later mng. editor Baltimore News, 1908-13; mng. editor New York Press, 1913-14, Washington Times, 1915-16; news editor Baltimore Evening Sun, 1917-19, mng. editor since 1919. Vice-pres. A. S. Abell Co., pubs. The Sun and The Evening Sun, Baltimore. Home: 4305 Norwood Road, Guilford, Baltimore. Office: The Evening Sun, Baltimore, Md.

MURPHY, Louis Edward, former chmn. bd. E. F. Houghton & Co.; b. Philadelphia, Pa., Apr. 16, 1874; s. Matthew Scott and Sarah (Moore) M.; ed. pub. schs., Peirce Coll., Neff Sch. and Coll., Phila., Pa.; m. Josephine Gaw, July 2, 1900; 1 dau., Ruth Gaw (Mrs. Gilbert B. Passavant). Began career as office boy for Charles Gilpin, mayor; asso. with E. F. Houghton & Co. continuously since starting in 1888 until he retired as chmn. of bd., Dec. 31, 1936, now mem. bd. dirs.; editor of "Houghton Line," 1931-36. Home: The Warwick. Office: 240 W. Somerset St., Philadelphia, Pa.

MURPHY, Louis Sutliffe, senior forest economist; b. Boston, Mass., Aug. 10, 1876; s. Joseph Henry and Elizabeth (Atkins) M.; B.S. (Chem.), Tufts Coll., Medford, Mass., 1901; M.F., cum laude, Yale U. Sch. of Forestry, 1907; student Mass. Inst. Tech., 1902-03; m. Elizabeth Ethel Cox, May 1, 1915; 1 son, Louis Sutliffe, Jr. Clk. ins. office, Obrion and Russell, Boston, Mass., 1895-97; chemist, North Packing and Provision Co., East Cambridge, Mass., 1902-05; in employ U.S. Forest Service continuously since 1907, successively student asst. (1906), forest asst., forest examiner, then forest economist, 1922-28, sr. forest economist, U.S. Forest Service, Washington, D.C., since 1928. Fellow A.A.A.S. Mem. Soc. of Am. Foresters (treas., 1914-15), Delta Tau Delta, Soc. of Robin Hood, Sigma Xi. Republican. Unitarian. Mason. Elk. Writer bulletins and professional papers. Contbr. many articles on forestry and taxation. Home: 103 East Bradley Lane, Chevy Chase, Md.

MURPHY, Miles, educator; b. Rummel, Pa., Dec. 12, 1900; s. Scott and Mary (Rummel) M.; student Blue Ridge Coll., New Windsor, Md., 1919-22; A.B., Juniata Coll., 1923; Ph.D., U. of Pa., 1927; m. Genevieve McDermott, Aug. 11, 1928; 1 son, Scott. Instr. in psychology, U. of Pa., 1925-29, asst. prof., 1929-37, asso. prof. since 1937. Mem. Am. Psychol. Assn., A.A.A.S., Am. Assn. Applied Psychology, Pa. Assn. Clin. Psychologists, Sigma Xi. Mem. Brethren Ch. Clubs: Lenape. Home: 106 Winchester Road, Merion, Pa.

MURPHY, Raymond Edward, asso. prof. geography; b. Apple River, Ill., July 24, 1898; s. Edward and Ella (Bermingham) M.; B.S. in Mining Engring., Mo. Sch. Mines & Metallurgy, Rolla, Mo., 1923; M.S. in Geology, U. of Wis., 1926; grad. student U. of Chicago, summer 1928; Ph.D. in Geography, U. of Wis., 1930; m. Marion May Fisher, May 22, 1926; 1 son, Patrick Alan. Began as asst. engr., Roxana Petroleum Corpn., Depew, Okla., 1923; instr. dept. geology, U. of Ky., 1926-28; instr. geography, Concord State Teachers Coll., Athens, W. Va., 1930-31; asst. prof. geography, Pa. State Coll., 1931-37, asso. prof. since 1937. Mem. Assn. Am. Geographers, Sigma Xi, Tau Beta Pi, Theta Tau, Gamma Alpha. Co-author (with Marion Murphy): Pennsylvania, a Regional Geography, 1937; Pennsylvania Landscapes, 1938. Contbr. bulls. and articles in professional geographic mags. Home: Lemont, Pa.

MURRAY, Albert Francis, television engr.; b. Decatur, Ala., June 22, 1894; s. Albert Francis and Elizabeth Estelle (Hertzler) M.; A.B., Maryville Coll., 1915, D.Sc., 1939; S.B., Mass. Inst. Tech., 1918; B.S., Harvard, 1918. Radio research engr. John H. Hammond, Jr., Gloucester, Mass., 1919-24; asst. chief engr., Wireless Specialty Co., 1924-27; in charge research R.C.A. Victor Co., Camden, N.J., 1930-33; engr. in charge television Philco Radio and Television Corpn., Phila., Pa., 1933-39. Served as 1st lt., Air Service, U.S. Army, 1918. Fellow Inst. of Radio Engrs. (dir.); mem. Franklin Inst. (arts and science com.), Soc. Motion Picture Engrs.; chmn. RMA Television Com. Presbyterian. Club: Penn Athletic (Phila.). Author various lectures on television. Designed and operated first successful underwater radio controlled torpedo for U.S. Navy, 1924. Home: Haddonfield Manor, Haddonfield, N.J.

MURRAY, Alfred Lefurgy, clergyman; b. Bradalbane, Prince Edward Island, Can., Oct. 30, 1900; s. Maj. Charles G. and Christy Ann (Nicholson) M.; American-Canadian ancestry; B. Religious Edn., Boston U., 1924; grad. Newton Theol. Instn., Newton Center, Mass., 1927; B.D., Colgate-Rochester Divinity Sch., Rochester, N.Y., 1930; grad. student, U. of Rochester, 1928-29, Temple U., 1937-38; M.Th., Eastern Baptist Sem., 1937; m. Frances Bryant Hoar, June 30, 1926; children—Alfred Francis, Marilyn Alda. Served as student pastor various N.E. Bapt. chs., 1924-27; ordained Bapt. ministry, 1926; dir. religious edn. Calvary Bapt. Ch., Rochester, 1927-29; pastor Columbia Av. Ch. of Christ, Rochester, 1929-31; sec. Northern Bapt. Conv., 1931-32; pastor First Bapt. Ch., Lansdale, Pa., since Feb. 1932; chmn. com. on evangelism and bd. of mgrs. Pa. Bapt. State Conv. Dir. Elm Terrace Hosp.; moderator N. Philadelphia Assn. Bapt. Chs., 1935-36. Hon. mem. Eugene Field Literary Soc. Republican. Odd Fellow. Author: The Evangelistic Congregation, 1931; Witnessing for Christ (pamphlet), 1937; Youth's Problem No. 1, 1938; Psychology for Christian Teachers, 1938. Editor: Young Ministers' Pulpit, 1936; The Magnet Master, 1937. Rev. editor of Light. Contbr. Christian Entertainments; Sermons from the Psalms. Compiler: The Supreme Test, 1935. Contbr. articles and book reviews to religious jours. Home: 331 N. Broad St., Lansdale, Pa.

MURRAY, C. Edward, Jr., mfg. insulated wire; b. Trenton, N.J., May 7, 1891; s. C. Edward and Floy (Cornell) M.; ed. Mercersburg Acad., 1905-10, Cornell U., 1911-12; m. Louise Morrison, May 21, 1914; children—Louise (Mrs. F. W. Harper, Jr.), Helen, Gail. Employed with Empire Tire & Rubber Corpn.-Murray Rubber Co., 1912-30; vice-pres. and dir. Crescent Insulated Wire & Cable Co., mfrs. elec. wires and cables, Trenton, N.J., since 1930. Vice-pres. local Boy Scouts Chapter. Mem. Alumni Council Mercersburg Acad., Phi Kappa Psi. Republican. Mem. M.E. Ch. Clubs: Carteret, Country, Engineers, Cornell (Trenton); Manufacturers and Bankers, Racquet (Philadelphia); Railroad Machinery, New York Railroad, Metropolitan Golf Roamers (New York City). Home: Willow Gate Farm, Princeton, N.J. Office: Trenton, N.J.

MURRAY, Elsie, mus. curator; b. Athens, Pa., Sept. 17, 1878; d. Millard Page and Louise Shipman (Welles) M.; student Bryn Mawr (Pa.) Coll., 1896-97; A.B., Cornell U., 1904, Ph.D., 1907, grad. study, 1923-27; grad. study Columbia U., 1914-15. Engaged in teaching, Sans Souci, S.C., 1901-03, Vassar Coll., Poughkeepsie, N.Y., 1907-09; prof. psychology, philosophy and edn., Wilson Coll., Pa., 1909-19; prof. psychology and philosophy, Sweet Briar Coll., Va., 1919-22, Wells Coll., Aurora, N.Y., 1922-23; sec. music, Cornell U., 1927-28; asso., U. of Ill., 1928-29; lecturer social psychology, Cornell U., 1932, resident doctor since 1938; engaged in research in color blindness since 1928; dir. and curator, Tioga Point Mus., Athens, Pa., since 1935. Dir. and mem. Soc. for Pa. Archaeology. Mem. A.A.A.S., Am. Psychol. Assn., Pa. Hist. Assn., Inter-Soc. Color Council, Sigma Xi, Delta Gamma. Awarded Sage Fellowship at Cornell; Grants in aid Nat. Research Council; award by Sigma Xi for research in color vision. Republican. Club: Cornell University Women (Ithaca, N.Y.). Author hist. booklets; contbr. hist. articles to mags., tech. articles to sci. mags. Home: 105 Highland Place, Ithaca, N.Y. Office: Tioga Point Museum, Athens, Pa.

MURRAY, George Welwood, lawyer; b. Edinburgh, Scotland, Mar. 8, 1856; s. Welwood and Lily (Gourlay) M.; ed. pub. and pvt. schs.; LL.B., Columbia, 1876, LL.D., 1930; m. Caroline C. Church, July 29, 1878 (died 1917); 1 dau., Lily Sylvester (wife of Prof. Adam Leroy Jones); m. 2d, May I. Ditto, May 29, 1920. Admitted to N.Y. bar, 1877; counsel law firm of Milbank, Tweed & Hope; consulting counsel Montclair Trust Co.; dir. Montclair Trust Co., Albany & Susquehanna R.R. Co., Delaware & Hudson Co., Equitable Life Assurance Society. Mem. bd. dirs. and chmn. legal research com. The Commonwealth Fund; trustee Community Chest of Montclair. George Welwood Murray Professor in Legal History established Jan. 1938. Awarded Columbia Lion, 1937. Treasurer and member of council American Law Institute; mem. Am. Bar Assn., N.Y. State Bar Assn., Assn. Bar City of New York. Clubs: Century, Broad Street (New York); Cosmos (Washington, D.C.). Home: 77 S. Mountain Av., Montclair, N.J. Office: 15 Broad St., New York, N.Y.

MURRAY, Harold A., physician; b. Newark, N.J., July 29, 1893; s. Peter and Sara (Farrow) M.; A.B. and A.M., Seton Hall Coll., South Orange, N.J.; M.D., Columbia Coll. Physicians and Surgeons, m. Beatrice Sanders, Apr. 4, 1923; children—Harrold A. Beatrice S:, John Francis, Sara Farrow, Peter, Michael. Specialist in diseases of children, Newark, N.J.; attending pediatrician St. James Hosp.; pediatrician Newark City Hosp. Fellow Am. Coll. Physicians, Am. Acad. Pediatrics. Roman Catholic. Clubs: Essex County Practitioners, Essex County Physicians. Address: 624 Mt. Prospect Av., Newark, N.J.

MURRAY, Harry Duane; b. New Garden, O., Sept. 19, 1870; s. John Hanna and Mary (Dunn) M.; M.E., Grove City Coll., 1911; m. Lena E. Daugherty, Sept. 16, 1896; children—Donald Graham, Duane Winton, John Mandal. Engaged as mcht. and supplyer tools for oil wells, 1891-98; asso. with Bessemer Gas Engine Co. in various capacities from supt. to chief mech. engr. and dir., 1898-1928; drilling for oil and gas since 1928; vice-pres. Grove City State Bank, 1928-33. Republican. Methodist. Mason (32°, Shriner). Kiwanian. Home: 149 N. Broad St., Grove City, Pa.

MURRAY, Irvin Ludgate, chemical engr.; b. New York, N.Y., May 11, 1904; s. James Irvin and Victoria (Ludgate) M.; B.S., Coll. of City of N.Y., 1924; S.M., Mass. Inst. of Tech., 1926; m. Virginia Hoff Howard, Feb. 13, 1932. Research asst., Research Lab. of Applied Chemistry, Mass. Inst. Tech., 1926-27; with Carbide & Carbon Chemicals Corpn. since 1927, now asst. supt. of engring. Mem. Am. Inst. Chem. Engrs., Am. Assn. Variable Star Observers. Presbyn. Clubs: Edgewood Country, Kanawha Country, Charleston Rifle, Kanawha Skeet (Charleston); Hickory Lodge Hunting and Fishing (Hot Springs (Va.). Home: Upper Ridgeway Rd., Charleston, W.Va. Office: Carbide & Carbon Corpn., South Charleston, W.Va.

MURRAY, Mrs. Irvin Ludgate (Virginia Elizabeth Hoff), newspaper woman; b. Harrisville, W.Va., Dec. 25, 1901; d. Silas Marion and Minnie Cecil (Wilson) Hoff; grad. Huntington High Sch., 1914-18; B.A., Marshall Coll., 1922; student Columbia U., 1927-28, U. of Paris, France, 1929-30, N.Y. Sch. of Social Work, 1930-31; m. David Clyde Howard, Aug. 7, 1926 (died 1931); m. 2d, Irvin L. Murray, Feb. 13, 1932. Reporter Huntington Herald Dispatch, 1918-22, also social editor; teacher arts, sciences, languages, Mt. Hope (W.Va.) High Sch., 1 term, 1922; reporter and columnist Huntington Advertiser, 1923; reporter, feature writer and woman's editor Charleston Gazette, 1923-26; dir. Children's Theater Dept., Assn. Jr. League of America, 1928-29; editor Children's Theater Dept., Jr. League Mag., 1928-29; family case worker N.Y. Charity Orgn. Soc., 1930-31; society and woman's editor Charleston Gazette since 1931. Republican committee woman, Cabell County, 1924. Dir. and trustee Kanawha County Pub.: Library. Mem. N.Y. City Junior League, D.A.R., W.Va. Newspaper Women's Assn. (bd. mem.), Sigma Sigma, Sigma. Episcopalian. Clubs: Charleston Woman's, Edgewood Country, Kanawha Country, Kanawha Skeet (Charleston). Home: "40 Oaks." Office: care Charleston Gazette, Hale St., Charleston, W.Va.

MURRAY, John A., physician and surgeon; b. McKees Mills, Pa., May 26, 1858; s. John P. and Elizabeth (Winslow) M.; M.D., U. of Maryland, Baltimore, 1885; M.D., Jefferson Med. Coll., Phila., 1893; unmarried. In practice medicine, Mahaffey, Pa., 1886-92, medicine and surgery, Clearfield Pa., 1894-1902, Patton, Pa., since 1904; one of five sponsors and incorporators of Clearfield (Pa.) Hosp., 1900-01, one of chiefs surgical staff, 1901-04; one of chiefs surgical staff Miners Hosp., Spangler, Pa., 1909-32. U.S. Pension Examiner during administrn. of Grover Cleveland, William McKinley, Theodore Roosevelt. Fellow Am. Coll. Surgeons; mem. Clearfield Co. Med. Soc. (pres. 1898), Cambria Co. Med. Soc., State Med. Soc., A.M.A. (delegate to Pan Am. Med. Congress, Mexico, 1896, Internat. Med. Congress, Moscow, Russia, 1898). Republican. Protestant. Author several med. articles in med. jours. Home: 900 N. 5th Av. Office: 446 Magee Av., Patton, Pa.

MURRAY, Joseph Howard, lawyer; b. Towson, Md., Aug. 2, 1898; s. Joseph Baker and Helen D. (Warfield) M.; LL.B., U. of Md. Law Sch., 1919; m. Mary L. Burns, Aug. 12, 1925; children—Joseph Howard, Jr., Richard Charles. Admitted to Md. bar, 1919, and since engaged in gen. practice of law at Towson; Baltimore Co. counsel Federal Land Bank of Baltimore since 1927; counsel Bd. Edn. Baltimore Co., 1928-31; asst. state's atty. of Baltimore Co., 1931-35; counsel county commrs. Baltimore Co., 1939. Home: 33 Alleghany Av. Office: Reckard Bldg., Towson, Md.

MURRAY, Philip, labor leader; b. Blantyre, Scotland, May 25, 1886; s. William and Rose Ann (Layden) M.; m. Elizabeth Lavery, Sept. 7, 1910; 1 son, Joseph William. Came to U.S., 1902, naturalized citizen, 1911. Mem. Internat. Bd., United Mine Workers of America, 1912, pres. Dist. No. 5, 1916, Internat. v.p. since 1920. Mem. Pa. Regional War Labor Bd., 1917-18; mem. Nat. Bituminous Coal Production Com., 1917-18, Nat. Industrial Recovery Bd. and NRA Advisory Council, 1935. Mem. Bd of Edn., Pittsburgh, since 1918. Mem. Am. Acad. Polit. and Social Science. Republican. Mem. K.C., A.O.H. Home: 752 Berkshire Av., Pittsburgh, Pa. Office: United Mine Workers Bldg., Washington, D.C.

MURRAY, Samuel, sculptor; b. Phila., Pa., June 1870; s. William Murray and Margaretta (Hannigan) M.; pupil of Thomas Eakins; married. Awarded gold medal, 1894; hon. mention, Art Club of Phila., 1897. Exhibited at Paris Expn., 1900; hon. mention, Buffalo Expn., 1901; silver medal, St. Louis Expdn., 1904; decorated Witherspoon Bldg., Phila., with prophets; represented in Fairmount Park, Phila., Metropolitan Mus., New York. Works: statues of Commodore Barry, U.S.N. and Dr. Joseph Leidy, Phila.; Bishop Shanahan memorial, St. Patrick's Cathedral, Harrisburg, Pa.; Father Corby memorial, Notre Dame U., Ind.; statue of Admiral George W. Melville, League Island Park, Phila.; busts of Admiral George W. Melville, Archbishop Ryan; Pa. State Battlefield Monument at Gettysburg, Pa.; Father Corby statue, erected on the Gettysburg Battlefield; Deshong Memorial Chester, Pa., statue of Senator Boies Penrose, Capitol Park, Harrisburg, Pa.; portrait busts of Dr. W. W. Keen John Morton, Memorial Mus. League Island Park, Phila., Dr. James Cadwalder Wilson and Dr. William Greene, Jefferson Coll., Phila., Archbishop Pendergast, Miseracordia Hosp., West Phila., Dr. Horatio C. Wood, U. of Pa., Thomas Eakins, Phila. Mus. of Arts; etc. Address: 3324 Lancaster Av., Phila., Pa.

MURRAY, Sister Teresa Gertrude, educator; b. Dubuque, Ia., Dec. 3, 1884; d. James Joseph and Elizabeth Gertrude (Royce) Murray; B.Di., Ia. Teachers Coll., Cedar Falls, Ia., 1907; A.B., U. of Chicago, 1910; A.M., Fordham U., 1930; Ph.D., Columbia U., 1938. Mem. Order of St. Benedict. Engaged in teaching, high sch. and prin. high sch., Ia. and Neb., 1906-17; in edn. dept. and dir. edn. dept. of dept. store, 1917-19; training officer, Federal Bd. for Vocational Edn., Rehabilitation Div., later merged into U.S. Vets. Bur., Washington, D.C., 1919-24; with Nat. Council Cath. Women, Washington, D.C., 1924-25; exec. sec. Diocesan Council Cath. Women, Newark, N.J., 1926-27; with Seton Hall Coll. Extension since 1937 and St. John's U. since 1938; consultant to bd. govs. N.J. Vocational Guidance Assn.; advisor to editorial bd. of Nat. Vocational Guidance Assn. Mem. Nat. Vocational Guidance Assn., Nat. Cath. Edn. Assn., Kappa Delta Pi. Democrat. Roman Catholic. Contbr. articles on student guidance to ednl. jours. Home: Benedictine Motherhouse, 851 N. Broad St., Elizabeth, N.J.

MURRAY, William D., lawyer; b. N.Y. City, July 17, 1858; s. John W. and Mary S. (Davidson) M.; A.B., Yale, 1880; LL.B., Columbia, 1882; m. Mary E. Mosher, Dec. 28, 1893; 1 son, George M. Practiced in N.Y. City, 1882-1938; member of International Committee Y.M.C.A. since 1891; trustee National Board of Y.W.C.A. Member of board of trustees of Eastern Association School; member National Council Y.M.C.A.; a founder and member executive committee Boy Scouts America; trustee committee on work, John R. Mott, Incorporated; trustee Committee on Promotion of Friendship between America and Far East; trustee, treasurer Trustees of World Student Christian Fed. Awarded Silver Buffalo by Boy Scouts America. Mem. Psi Upsilon Fraternity. Presbyn. Author: Life and Works of Jesus; Bible Stories to Tell Children, 1910; My Three Keys, 1920; Fun with Paper Folding, 1928. As He Journeyed (biography), 1929; What Manner of Man is This?; The Message of the Prophets; History of Boy Scouts of America. Home: Plainfield, N.J. Office: 68 William St., New York, N.Y.

MURRAY, William Wallace, chemist; b. Belfast, Ireland, Aug. 21, 1873; s. James A. and Margaret Ann (Shanks) M.; came to U.S., 1883, naturalized, 1896; B.S. in Chem., U. of Vt., Burlington, Vt., 1897; m. Hattie Thompson Shaw, Oct. 28, 1898. Asst. chemist Schiefflin & Co., New York City, 1897-98; asst. chem. engr. Joslin, Schmidt & Co., 1898-1900; chem. engr. with John T. Stanley, New York City, 1900-04; research chemist Acker Process Co., Niagara Falls, N.Y., 1904; chief chemist D. B. Martin & Co., Baltimore, 1904-13; chief chemist Continental Can Co., Standard Tin Plate Co., Canonsburg, Pa., since 1913; chmn. bd. dirs. First Nat. Bank at Canonsburg, Pa., since 1933; co-inventor detinning process and spl. lacquer for preventing discoloration of foods in tin cans; developed electroplating of copper, zinc and tin on steel sheets. Mem. Electrochem. Soc. (chmn. Chicago Sect. 1927), Am. Chem. Soc., A.A.A.S., Soc. of Chem. Industry (Eng.), Am. Soc. for Testing Materials, Nat. Geog. Soc., Pa. Acad. of Science, Am. Nature Assn. Republican. Mason (K.T., 32°, Shriner). Clubs: Lake Shore Athletic (Chicago); Washington County (Pa.) Golf and Country. Home: 218 Hawthorne St. Office: Standard Tin Plate Co., Canonsburg, Pa.

MURRELLE, Harlan Gregg, legal printing; b. Towanda, Pa., Nov. 19, 1901; s. Joseph Harlan and Marietta (Gregg) M.; grad. Sayre (Pa.) High Sch., 1919; A.B., Oberlin (O.) Coll., 1923; student John Marshall Law Sch., Cleveland, O., 1924-26; m. Olive Holley, Feb. 6, 1928; children—Joseph Holley, William Harlan. Bank clerk Pearl St. Savings & Trust Co. (now Cleveland Trust Co.), Cleveland, O., 1923-25; since 1925 partner Murrelle Printing Co., Sayre, Pa., specialists in the preparation and printing of legal briefs, records and appeals to State and Federal courts. Mem. Sayre Borough Council (pres. 1935-40); mem. Bradford County Rep. Com. (sec. 1938); trustee Sayre Pub. Library; chmn. Sayre Red Cross; sec. Sayre Chamber of Commerce. Republican. Presbyterian. Mason

(K.T.). Clubs: Shepherd Hills Country (Waverly, N.Y.); Sayre Rotary. Home: 418 S. Wilbur Av. Office: 203 W. Lockhart St., Sayre, Pa.

MURRIE, William F. R., pres. Hershey Chocolate Corpn.; v.p. Hershey Nat. Bank. Address: Hershey, Pa.

MURRIN, James Albert, newspaper editor; b. Pittsburgh, Pa., Aug. 18, 1894; s. James Walter and Alice (Myers) M.; ed. pub. schs., Wilkinsburg and Pittsburgh, Pa., 1902-08; grad. with extra honors, Fifth Av. High Sch., Pittsburgh, 1912; m. Helen Wilson, July 20, 1917; children—Nita May, Ralph Calvin. Began as newspaper reporter, 1912; reporter, telegraph editor, Evening News, Franklin, Pa.; city editor, Venango Daily Herald, 1917; telegraph editor, News-Herald, Franklin, Pa., 1919-31, editor since 1931; dir. Franklin Home Bldg. & Loan Assn. Served with regtl. hdqrs. 112th inf., U.S.A., with A.E.F., 1918-19; cited for exceptional front line service in France (U.S.). An organizer Am. Legion post, Franklin, Pa., adjt. later comdr. Served as mem. Franklin City Council, now 2d term. Official clerk, Presbyn. Ch. Dir. Franklin Pub. Library. Revisited France, 1928 to participate in dedication of Pa. battlefields monument at Varennes. Republican. Presbyn. (elder). Elk (past exalted ruler), Mason. Clubs: Masonic, Elks, Rotary (sec.). Home: 1035 Liberty St. Office: Liberty and 12th Sts., Franklin, Pa.

MURRIN, James Bernard, lawyer; b. Carbondale, Pa., Nov. 30, 1874; s. John and Margaret (McGroarty) M.; ed. St. Rose Acad., Carbondale, Pa., Georgetown Coll., Washington, D.C. (Class of 1900); unmarried. Studied law and admitted to Pa. bar, 1903, and since engaged in gen. practice of law at Scranton; admitted to bar Supreme Ct. Pa. and to practice before bar of the Supreme Ct. of the U.S.; dir. and sec. Liberty Discount & Saving Bank, Carbondale, 1907-10; pres. Murrin Coal Co., 1919-29; dir. Cameron Fuel Co., Montreal, Can., 1927-29; pres. Perfection Coal Co., 1917-29; vice-pres. Inter Cities Airline, Inc.; mayor Carbondale, 1911-16; mem. sch. bd., Carbondale, 1933; served as alternate del. at large, Dem. Nat. Conv., San Francisco, 1920; Dem. nominee for Auditor Gen. Pa., 1916. Served as lt. inf. Pa. N.G. on Mexican border, 1916-17; capt., capt. Div. staff, actg. adjt. with 28th Div., also with 109th Inf. and 108th Machine Gun Batt., U.S.A., 1917-19, with A.E.F., 18 mos. in France, in all important offensives. Mem. Lackawanna Bar Assn., Am. Legion, Irish Text Soc., 28th Division Officers Society, Sons of the Revolution; hereditary mem. Order of Cincinnati of Pa. (mem. Standing Com.). Democrat. Roman Catholic. Contbr. Official History 28th Division, 5 vols., 1924. Home: 306 Quincy Av., Scranton, Pa. Office: 316 N. Washington Av., Scranton, Pa.

MURRIN, John Brady, b. at Murrinsville, Pa., July 25, 1888; s. John Zachariah and Catherine (McBride) Murrin; graduate of Butler (Pa.) Business College School of Accountancy, 1913; unmarried. In U.S. Mail Service, 1906-10; subsequently entered coll. and following graduation entered Bessemer & Lake Erie R.R., where continued until 1921; entered oil and gas producing business, 1921; mem. Pa. Ho. of Reps., 1934-38. Served with 35th U. S. Engrs., A.E.F., 1917-19. Active in Democratic party. Mem. Pa. Natural Gas Men's Assn., Ohio Oil and Gas Men's Assn., Natural Gas Assn. of W.Va., Butler (Pa.) Bd. of Commerce, Vets. Foreign Wars (past post and dist. comdr.), Am. Legion (charter mem. Butler Post). Catholic. Elk, K.C. Home: 578 2d St. Office: 203 Center St., Butler, Pa.

MURRIN, Joseph S., M.D.; b. Carbondale, Pa., Nov. 23, 1876; s. John and Margaret (McGroarty) M.; ed. St. Rose Acad., Carbondale; grad. Carbondale High Sch., 1895; M.D., Georgetown U., 1907; unmarried. Extern Children's Hosp., Washington, D.C., 1906-07; interne Georgetown U. Hosp., 1907-08; resident physician Eye, Ear and Throat Hosp., Washington, D.C., 1911-12; engaged in practice of medicine, specializing in eye, ear, nose and throat, Carbondale, since 1912. Served as 1st lt. Med. Corps, U.S. Army, during World War. Mem. A.M.A., Lackawanna Med. Soc., Am. Legion (past comdr. Carbondale post), Vol. Med. Service Corps, Alpha Omega Delta; hon. mem. G.A.R. Roman Catholic. Club: Wayne Co. Hunting and Fishing. Home: 306 Quincy Av., Scranton, Pa. Office: First National Bank Bldg., Carbondale, Pa.

MUSCHAT, Maurice, surgeon; b. Riga, Latvia, July 30, 1898; s. Joseph and Rachel (Jacobson) M.; student Gymnasium in Riga; M.D., Univ. of Heidelberg, Germany, 1923; m. Clara Muschat, Jan. 10, 1917; 1 dau., Mimi. Physician and surgeon, Phila., since 1924; J. William White fellow in urology, U. of Pa., 1925-27; chief urological surgeon Mt. Sinai Hosp., Phila., since 1934, research asso. in urology, U. of Pa. Fellow Am. Coll. Surgeons, Am. Urol. Assn., A.M.A.; founder mem. Am. Bd. of Urology; mem. Phila. Co. Med. Soc., Pa. State Med. Soc. Contbr. of many scientific articles to professional jours. Home: 4730 Pine St. Office: Medical Arts Bldg., Philadelphia, Pa.

MUSGRAVE, F. G.; mem. law firm Musgrave & Blessing. Address: Point Pleasant, W.Va.

MUSGRAVE, John Knox, med. dir.; b. Pittsburgh, Pa., Oct. 29, 1886; s. Robert Crawford and Maria (McCausland) M.; B.S., Pa. State Coll., 1909; M.D., A.M., U. of Pa., 1919; m. Elizabeth Goehring Steffen, Oct. 12, 1912; children—John Knox, Louise Marie, Homer Steffen. Instr. Allegheny High Sch., Pittsburgh, 1909-12; asst. zoölogist, Pa. Dept. of Agr., Harrisburg, Pa., 1912-15; interne Allegheny Gen. Hosp., Pittsburgh, 1919-20; dir. of anaesthesia Western Pa. Hosp., Pittsburgh, since 1921. Mem. Am. Soc. Mammalogists, Am. Ornithologists Union. Republican. Protestant. Club: Wilson Ornithological, The Agora (Pittsburgh). Home: 350 Parkway Drive. Office: The Western Pennsylvania Hospital, Pittsburgh, Pa.

MUSGROVE, Eugene Richard, educator; b. Bristol, N.H., Aug. 20, 1879; s. Richard Watson and Henrietta (Guild) M.; student Tilton (N.H.) Sch., 1897-1900; B.S., Dartmouth Coll., Hanover, N.H., 1905; M.A., Brown U., Providence, R.I., 1912; m. Eva Fling, June 30, 1909; children—Donald Eugene, Geneva Fling, Malcolm Guild. Instr. in English, Dartmouth Coll., Hanover, N.H., 1905-08, Worcester (Mass.) Acad., 1908-12, Mackenzie Sch., Dobbs Ferry, N.J., 1912-13, Horace Mann Sch., New York, N.Y., 1913-14; instr. in English, East Side High Sch., Newark, N.J., 1914-17, head of English dept. since 1917. Mem. Newark, N.J. State teachers assns., N.E.A., Poetry Soc. of Eng., Poetry Soc. of America, Phi Delta Theta. Republican. Methodist Episcopalian. Editor-in-chief of The Dartmouth, 1904-05. Author: Composition and Literature (high sch. text-book), 1917; three chapters, maps, and indices in History of Bristol, N.H., 1905; edited: Burke's Conciliation with America, 1912; Scott's Rob Roy, 1917; The White Hills in Poetry, Poems of New Jersey, and other anthologies of verse. Home: 19 Amherst St., East Orange, N.J. Office: East Side High Sch., Newark, N.J.

MUSKAT, Morris, physicist; b. Apr. 1907; s. Samuel and Celia (Class) M.; student Marietta (O.) Coll., 1922-24; A.B., O. State U., Columbus, O., 1926, A.M., 1926; student U. of Chicago, summer 1927; Ph.D., Calif. Inst. Tech., Pasadena, Calif., 1929. Engaged as instr. Physics and chemistry, Bowling Green (O.) State Normal Coll., 1926-27; teaching Fellow, Calif. Inst. Tech., Pasadena, Calif., 1927-29; physicist, Gulf Research & Development Co., Pittsburgh, Pa., 1929-35, chief of physics div. since 1935. Fellow A.A.A.S., Am. Phys. Soc.; mem. Am. Geophys. Union, Soc. of Exploration Geophysicists, Am. Petroleum Inst., Pi Mu Epsilon, Sigma Xi, Phi Beta Kappa. Author: The Flow of Homogeneous Fluids Trough Porous Media, 1937; contbr. research papers to scientific publs. Home: 300 8th St., Oakmont, Pa.

MUSSER, Alfred J., coal exec.; b. Center Co., Pa., Dec. 10, 1874; s. John and Catharine M. (Dale) M.; student business colls., Williamsport, Pa., and Phila., 1894-95; m. Esther K. Durst, Nov. 24, 1899; children—Kathryn, John D. (dec.), Fred. A., Helen E., George W., Elizabeth L. Pub. sch. teacher, Centre Co., Pa., 1892-95; stenographer and accountant, deKosenko and Hetherington Mfg. Co., Phila., 1895-97; stenographer and accountant Clearfield Bituminous Coal Corpn., Indiana, Pa.. 1897-1905, purchasing agt and auditor, 1905-21, asst. gen. mgr., 1921, gen. mgr., 1921-23, v.p. and gen. mgr., since 1923, dir. since 1923; pres. and dir. Dixon Run Land Co., Beech Creek R.R. Co., Peoples Bank of Clymer; dir. Beech Creek Extension R.R. Co., Savings & Trust Co., Clymer Hardware Co., Pres. Indiana Hosp. since 1936, director since 1927. Member Pa. Chamber of Commerce (dir. since 1937). Republican. Club: Rotary (Indiana, Pa.). Home: 225 S. Sixth St. Office: 8th and Water Sts., Indiana, Pa.

MUSSER, Benjamin Francis Blase (Benjamin Musser 5th), writer; b. Lancaster, Pa., Feb. 3, 1889; s. Willis Benjamin and Katharine Witmer (Kaufman) M.; ed. Nashotah Sem., Nashotah, Wis., 1906-08, St. Joseph's Coll., Callicoon, N.Y., 1909-10; spl. studies, Harvard U., 1914; m. Helen Cobb Laning, of Wilkes-Barre, Pa., Oct. 12, 1921; children—Benjamin Francis Louis (Benjamin 6th), Frederic Antony, Ann Clare Gardiner. Engaged as columnist, N.Y. Freeman's Journal, 1913-19; columnist Phila. Catholic Standard & Times, 1919-20; columnist and feature writer, Newark Monitor, 1919-28; mng. editor The Trend, 1920-22; propr., pub., and editor Contemporary Verse, 1927-30, also JAPM, a poetry weekly, 1928-30; on editorial staff or advisory staffs of 6 verse mags., 1927-35; lecturer on poets and poetry throughout U.S., since 1927; Poet Laureate of N.J. since 1934, ratified by U.S. Congress and approved by N.J. Gov. Mem. Poetry Soc. of America, Cath. Poetry Soc. America, Washington Cath. Poetry Soc. (past pres., hon. pres.), Poetry Soc. Eng., Poetry Soc. Ala., Poetry Soc. S.W., Order Bookfellows, Press Club St. Francis Coll., Joliet, Calvert Asso., Liturgical Arts Soc., Cath. Unity League, Chatterton-Lacy Foundation, St. Anthony's Guild. Democrat. Roman Catholic. Author, co-author, or compiler of 40 books, from Angels of the Sanctuary, 1912, to The Bird Below the Waves, 1938; these include 18 books of verse, 3 vols. prose on verse, 10 vols. essays, 4 books on St. Francis and things Franciscan, the others compilations; compiled 5 anthologies, wrote introductions to 12 books by other writers; own work represented in 112 poetry anthologies and in several prose anthologies and has appeared in nearly 400 publs. in U.S., overseas and Can. Mem. since 1909 of Third Order of St. Francis (Brother Francis, III O.S.F.). Home: 107 S. Mansfield Av., Margate, Atlantic City, N.J.

MUSSER, Florence Amelia (Mrs. Charles S. Musser); b. Lancaster Co., Pa.; d. Rev. John B. and Magdalene (Risser) Bucher; ed. schs., Millersville, Pa., spl. courses and subjects at various times; m. Charles S. Musser, Jan. 1, 1906. Served for 6 yrs. as chmn. Co. Fed. and Extension of State Fed. of Pa. Womens Clubs; vice chmn. Gen. Fed., 4 yrs.; pres. Del. Co. Fed., 4 yrs.; chmn. music study and music appreciation, Matinee Musical, 6 yrs.; art chmn. New Century Club, 8 yrs.; dir. Women's Com. of Phila. Orchestra. Active in conservation, regional planning, gardening, civic activities, art and music. Republican. Episcopalian. Clubs: New Century (dir.), Art Alliance (dir.), Print, Matinee Musical, Contemporary, Pa. Hort. Soc. (Philadelphia); Twentieth Century (Lansdowne). Author of short articles; lecturer on History and Romance of Bells (a subject of much study and research). Home: 25 Dudley Av., Lansdowne, Pa.

MUSSER, Harry Plaine, elec. engr.; b. Bonsack, Va., Sept. 11, 1888; s. Henry Clay and Ida Susan (Plaine) M.; studied Roanoke Co., Va., and Lancaster Co., Pa. grade schs.; grad. Salem (Va.) High Sch., 1907; B.S. in E.E., Va. Poly. Inst., 1910; m. Lucy T. McCue, Apr. 23, 1918; children—Mary Louise, Harry Plaine. Employed in testing dept., standardizing lab. and switchboard inspection Gen. Electric Co., Schenectady, N.Y., 1910-12; construction and operating engr. Appalachian Electric Power Co., Bluefield, W.Va., 1912-15; mem. West Virginia Engring. Co., cons. elec. engrs., Charleston, since

1915; pres. Black Diamond Power Co., Elk Power Co., Glem Co., Iager Water Works, Kimball Light & Water Co., Mullens Water Works, Union Power Co., United Light & Power Co., War Light & Water Co., W.Va. Engring. Co. Dir. Charleston Chamber of Commerce, 1933, 38 and 39; mem. Am. Inst. E.E., Am. Water Works Assn., Tau Beta Pi. Presbyn. (elder). Club: Kiwanis (Charleston). Home: 1045 Valley Road. Office: 709 Security Bldg., Charleston, W.Va.

MUSSER, Paul Howard, college dean; b. Bedford, Pa., Mar. 27, 1892; s. Cyrus John (D.D.) and Henrietta Edith (Mowry) M.; prep. edn., Mercerburg (Pa.) Acad.; Franklin and Marshall Coll., 1912-13; A.B., U. of Pa., 1916, Ph.D., 1928; m. Mary Thaddeus Carr, Aug. 19, 1925; children—John Carr, Janet Anne, Virginia Ellen. With U. of Pa. since 1916, successively reader in English, asst. in English, instr. in English, asst. prof. until 1931, prof. since 1931, also dean of the Coll., dir. coll. collateral courses since 1929. Dir. Upper Darby Free Pub. Library; mem. bd. of regents Mercersburg Acad. Mem. Assn. of Coll. Presidents of Pa. (pres. 1936), Modern Lang. Assn. America, Humanity Soc. Eng. and U.S., Nat. Council of Teachers of English, Am. Acad. Polit. and Social Science, Pa. Acad. of Fine Arts, Am. Assn. Univ. Profs., Eastern Assn. of Coll. Deans and Administrators of Men, Phi Beta Kappa, Phi Kappa Psi. Mem. Ref. Ch. of U.S. Clubs: Franklin Inn, Lenape, Philobiblon, Contemporary. Author: James Nelson Barker—Biography, 1929. Home: 937 Edmonds Av., Drexel Hill, Pa. Office: College Hall, University of Pennsylvania, Philadelphia, Pa.

MUTA, Samuel Alan, physician and surgeon; b. Bridgeton, N.J., Nov. 14, 1882; s. Charles P. and Elizabeth May M.; M.D., Jefferson Med. Coll., Phila., Pa., 1904; m. Leila Camp, Apr. 14, 1907; children—Clara Elizabeth (Mrs. Arthur Kuell), Constance Alan, Leila Theresa. Began as physician, West Orange, N.J., 1905, and since in practice; formerly senior surgical staff St. Marys Hosp.; now mem. courtesy staff Orange Memorial Hosp., Orange, N.J. Dir. Lackawanna Bldg. & Loan Assn. Served as capt. surgeon, N.J. N.G., 1905-12. Mayor, West Orange, N.J., 1910-14 (two terms); mem. Bd. of Health, West Orange, N.J. Trustee Essex Co. Isolation Hosp. Mem. Acad. of Medicine of Northern N.J., Essex Co. Med. Soc., N.J. State Med. Soc., A.M.A., Clinical Soc. of the Oranges (charter mem.), Nu Sigma Nu. Independent Democrat. Episcopalian. Mason, Elk. Club: Essex County Country (West Orange, N.J.). Address: 47 Park Av., West Orange, N.J.

MUTCH, Andrew, clergyman; b. Aberdeenshire, Scotland, Nov. 2, 1870; s. Thomas and Mary Ann (Sangster) M.; grad. Edinburgh Teachers Training Coll., 1892; M.A., Edinburgh U., 1894; grad. Div. Sch., same univ., 1897; D.D., Lafayette (Pa.) Coll.; m. Petrus Dow Young, Sept. 12, 1899; children—Thomas Sangster, Mary Dow, Jessie Margaret Ada, Petrice Young, David Andrew Gordon. Came to U.S., 1912, naturalized citizen, 1925. Ordained Presbyn. ministry, 1899; asst. minister West Ch. of St. Nicholas, Aberdeen; pastor West Ch. of Galashiels and Parish of Muthill until 1912; pastor Presbyn. Ch. of Bryn Mawr, Pa., 1912-36, emeritus since 1936. Pres. Bd. Ministerial Pensions Presbyn. Ch. of U.S. Mem. St. Andrew's Soc. of Phila. Republican. Club: Gulf Mills Golf. Contbr. sermons in mags.; one sermon in "Best Sermons of 1925" (J. Fort Newton, compiler). Home: Medford Rd., Wynnewood, Pa.

MYATT, Leslie E., surgeon; b. White Bluffs, Tenn., June 10, 1893; s. Benjamin Franklin and Sarah (Robinson) M.; student Dickson (Tenn.) Normal Coll., 1908-11, Winthrop Prep. Sch., Nashville, Tenn., 1911-12; B.S., Pharm.D., Vanderbilt U., Nashville, Tenn., 1917; M.D., Johns Hopkins, 1921; post-grad. student George Peabody Coll., Nashville, summers 1913-17, London, Eng., 1926; m. Hilda Lock, Sept. 1920; 1 dau., Barbara; m. 2d, Marion Davis, Jan. 28, 1934. Interne Hosp. Women of Md., Baltimore, Md., 1921-22; resident surgeon Palmerton (Pa.) Hosp., 1922-26. Fellow Am. Coll. Surgeons; mem. Robert McKean Hist. Med. Soc. Address: 98 N. Pearl St., Bridgeton, N.J.

MYERS, Albert Cook, historian; b. York Springs, Adams Co., Pa., Dec. 12, 1874; s. John T. and Sarah A. (Cook) M.; grad. Martin Acad., Kennett Sq., Pa., 1894; grad. Swarthmore Coll. (Bach. Letters), 1898, M.L., 1901; Litt.D., Franklin and Marshall College, 1932; unmarried. In shipping business, Philadelphia, also editor hist. dept. Literary Era, 1898-1900; made hist. researches, Brit. Isles, 1900, 03, 11, 12-13, 14-17; registrar, instructor Swarthmore Coll., 1900-02; hon. curator Friends' Hist. Library, 1924-36; grad. student in History, U. of Pa., 1901-03; Joshua Lippincott traveling fellow of Swarthmore Coll., 1903-04, at U. of Wis. (as hon. fellow in Am. history), and at Harvard. Dir. Pa. State hist. exhibit and supt. hist. exhibits, Jamestown Expn., 1907; mem. mayor's hist. com. and dir. and curator of historic industries Loan Exhibit, Founders' Celebration, Phila., 1908; mem. Pa. Com. Sch. History Text Books, 1923-24; Pa. state commr., sec., chmn. hist. com., Valley Forge Park, 1923-35; commr., sec. Pa. State Hist. Commn., 1923-27, 1932-36, erecting 37 stone and bronze markers; also dir. Wm. Penn Commemoration, 1932; editing Complete Works of William Penn since 1910, and internationally known as authority on Penn, his associates and associations. Mem. Delaware and Chester County hist. socs., Pa. Fed. Hist. Socs. (ex-pres.), Friends' Hist. Assn., Phila., Friends' Historical Society England (ex-pres.), N.E. Historical Geneal. Soc. Mem. Mayor's Committee Sesquicentennial, Phila., 1925; mem. Bushy Run Battlefield Commn., State of Pa., 1932-35. Served as officer War Camp Community Service, Phila., and chairman exec. com. Hist. Soc. Pa., entertaining soldiers and sailors, 1918-19. Mem. Society of Friends. Author (or editor): Immigration of the Irish Quakers Into Pennsylvania, 1682-1750, 1902; Sally Wister's Journal, 1902; Hannah Logan's Courtship, 1904; Narratives of Early Pennsylvania, New Jersey and Delaware, 1630-1707, 1912; For Soldiers-Sailors-Marines, What to See in Historic Philadelphia, 1918; A Relic of the Susquehanna Indians, 1922; William Penn's First Charter to Pennsylvania (1682), 1925; Memoir of Gilbert Cope, 1929; Benjamin West's Mother, 1929; William Penn—His Own Account of the Delaware Indians, 1683, 1937; The Boy, George Washington—His Own Account of an Iroquois Indian Dance, 1748, 1932; Robert Wade, First American Host of Penn (1682), 1932; Records of the Court of New Castle on Delaware (1681-1699), 1935; William Marshall Swayne, Chester County's Sculptor of Lincoln, 1936; William Penn's Early Life in Brief, 1644-1674, 1937. Editor many works on hist. subjects. Home: Moylan, Delaware Co., Pa.

MYERS, C. Randolph, lawyer; b. Ebensburg, Pa., Apr. 9, 1889; s. C. Randolph and Katherine (Rist) M.; ed. Ebensburg (Pa.) High Sch., and St. Francis Coll., Loretto, Pa.; m. Margaret McDonald, 1916; 2 children. Admitted to Cambria County, Pa., bar, 1915, and since practiced at Ebensburg; referee in bankruptcy for Cambria Co., Pa., since 1918; pres. Cambria Thrift Corpn., Ebensburg, since 1937; dir. First Nat. Bank of Ebensburg, Citizens Lumber Co. Pres. Central Cambria Dist. Boy Scouts. Mem. Cambria Co. Bar Assn. (mem. exec. com. and sec. since 1918), Pa. Bar Assn., Am. Bar Assn. Catholic. K.C. (Past Grand Knight Ebensburg Council). Club: Kiwanis (Ebensburg, Pa.; pres. 1929-30). Address: Ebensburg, Pa.

MYERS, Charles, lawyer; b. Phila., Pa., Nov. 22, 1888; s. William Heyward and Eliza (Sergeant) M.; ed. Mercersburg Acad., 1902-05; A.B., Princeton, 1909; LL.B., Harvard U. Law Sch., 1912; m. Gertrude J. Hearne, June 26, 1926; children—Eliza Sergeant, Gertrude Hearne, Charles Twiggs. Admitted to Pa. bar, 1912 and since engaged in gen. practice of law at Phila.; asso. with firm Barnes, Wintersteen and Brinton, 1912-22; mem. firm Barnes, Biddle & Morris, 1922-29, and Barnes, Biddle & Myers since 1929. Served as 2d lieut., then 1st lieut. F.A., U.S.A., 1917-19. Mem. Am., Pa., and Phila. bar assns. Democrat. Episcopalian. Clubs: Princeton, Skating (Philadelphia); Mill Dam (Devon). Home: 427 Midland Av., St. Davids. Office: 1421 Chestnut St., Philadelphia, Pa.

MYERS, Charles Augustus, mfg. aromatic chemicals; b. New York, N.Y., Jan. 26, 1889; s. Charles Augustus and Ella (Hays) M.; desc. (9th generation) Adolph Myer, who came from Westphalia, Germany, and settled in Harlem (New York), 1661; desc. (on mother's side) David Hays, one of soldiers serving under George Washington in Braddock's Defeat; student of spl. course in perfumes, extracts, and allied products, Columbia U. Coll. of Pharmacy, 1926-27; m. Harriet Horn, Apr. 5, 1913 (now dec.); m. 2d, Ruth Glenn, June 17, 1933; 1 son, Charles Augustus, Jr. Asso. with Dodge & Olcott Co., mfr. essential oils, aromatic chemicals, Bayonne, N.J., since 1907, asst. to sec., 1911-19, asst. to vice-pres., 1919-23, production mgr. factory, 1923-26, gen. mgr. factory, 1926-38, 1st vice-pres. since 1938, mem. bd. dirs. since 1928; pres. Vanillaproco, Inc. and mem. bd. dirs. since 1937. Served in U.S.N.R.F., 1917-19, chief petty officer chem. service; in U.S.N.R.F., 1919-21; contributed number of new devices to science of fuel analysis; holds navigator's license for vessels up to 15 gross tons. Awarded Victory Medal by U.S. and N.Y. State. Mem. bd. dirs. Bayonne, Chamber of Commerce. Fellow Am. Geog. Soc. Mem. N.Y. Acad. Scis., Marine Mus. City of New York, Ship-Model Soc., Am. Legion. Republican. Club: Knickerbocker Country (Englewood). Interested in constrn. and collection ship models, objects and data pertaining to the sea. Home: 99 Glenwood Rd., Englewood. Office: 69 Av. A, Bayonne, N.J.

MYERS, Charles Emory, prof. plant breeding; b. nr. Tivoli, Pa., Feb. 23, 1882; s. John Andrew and Jennie Elizabeth (Kester) M.; B.S., Pa. State Coll., 1908; M.S., Cornell U., 1911, grad. study, same, 1919-20; Ph.D., Cornell U., 1922; m. Christine Bidelspacher, Dec. 31, 1910; children—Charles Andrew, Christine Elizabeth. Engaged in teaching in rural schs., 1900-04; asst. in horticulture, Pa. State Coll., 1908-12, asso., 1912-16, asst. prof. horticulture, 1916-18, asso. prof. 1918-20, prof. of plant breeding since 1920. Mem. A.A.A.S., Soc. for Hort. Sci., Am. Genetic Assn., Sigma Xi, Gamma Sigma Delta, Alpha Zeta, Acacia. Mem. Religious Soc. Friends. Mason. Contbr. articles to hort. jours. and various Agrl. Expt. Sta. bulls. Originator of improved varieties of vegetables. Home: 316 W. Fairmount Av., State College, Pa.

MYERS, Chester G., treas. Autokraft Box Corpn.; b. York, Pa., May 24, 1887; s. Edwin and Anna P. (Iaeger) M.; student York Collegiate Inst., 1899-1903, Mercersburg (Pa.) Acad., 1903-04, St. Luke's Sch., Wayne, Pa., 1905-06; m. Leah Strayer, of York, Pa., in Colombo, Ceylon, January 6, 1933; 1 dau., Garnet Odeon. Began as propr. mfg. plant, 1907, later absorbed by Autokraft Box Corpn., of which he has been treas. since 1930; treas. Leschey Myers Mfg. Co., Remco Products Corpn.; pres. Hellam Furniture Co. Clubs: Lakewood Country; Yacht, Gulf Beach (St. Petersburg, Fla.). Home: 1311 Beach Drive, N., St. Petersburg, Fla.; (summer home), Lake Mohawk, Sparta, N.J. Office: Hellam, Pa.

MYERS, Clarence Eugene, engineer; b. McKeesport, Pa., Jan. 31, 1888; s. Harry and Mary Louise (Maynes) M.; C.E., Pa. Mil. Coll., Chester, Pa., 1909, M.S., 1926, Sc.D., 1930. Instructor in civil engring. and military science and tactics, Pa. Mil. Coll., Chester, Pa., 1909-11; various positions and dist. engr. Washington, Pittsburgh, Phila., Pa. State Highway Dept., 1911-21; engr. of constrn. and dep. chief Bur. of Highways, Phila., 1921-28; dir. Dept. of City Transit, Phila., 1928-32; mem. State Registration Bd. for Professional Engrs. in Pa., Phila., since 1932, pres. since 1936; pvt. practice as cons. engr., Phila., since 1932. Served as maj., Engrs. Corps, U.S. Army, during World War. Mem. Am. Soc. C.E. (former nat. dir.), Am. Road Builders' Assn. (nat. dir.), Nat. Council of State Bds. of Engring. Examiners (dir.), Am. Inst. Cons. Engrs., Soc. of Am. Mil. Engrs., Professional Engrs. Soc., Engrs.

Soc. of Pa. Republican. Baptist. Clubs: Union League, Engineers (Phila.). Author several articles on engring. subjects. Home: Engineers Club. Office: 1814 Lincoln-Liberty Bldg., Philadelphia, Pa.

MYERS, Frank Clayton, lawyer, welfare promotion; b. York Springs, Pa., Feb. 1, 1883; s. Clayton Franklin and Sarah Elizabeth (Menges) M.; grad. Cumberland Valley State Teachers Coll., Shippensburg, Pa., 1902, Perkiomen School, Pennsburg, Pa., 1905; A.B., Princeton, 1909; LL.B., New York Law Sch., 1918; m. Mary Leanora Harvey, June 3, 1914; children—Mary Lee, Frank Clayton. Teacher pub. schs., York Co., Pa., 1902-04; state sec. Y.M.C.A., in charge student ednl. and immigration work, N.Y., also sec. N.Y. State Immigration Commn., 1909-10; editor College World, 1910-11; sec. New York Child Welfare Committee, 1912-32, pres. since 1932; also in practice of law since 1918, now mem. firm Strange, Myers, Hinds & Wight; dir., counsel and chmn. of bd. Gotham Advertising Co.; dir. and vice-pres. Lee and Simmons, Inc., Simmons Lee Corpn., Jarvis Shipping Corpn.; vice-pres., mem. bd. of dirs. and counsel Home Playyards, Inc.; sec., dir. and counsel Thessalonica Agrl. & Industrial Inst.; dir. Nat. Motion Picture League; dir., chmn. exec. com. and counsel Children's Welfare Fed. of N.Y. City; trustee Mount Holyoke Coll.; chmn. Consolidation Commission (N.J. section of New York Met. Dist.); mem. spl. com. on health of N.Y. City sch. children. Mem. Com. on Pub. Relations, Motion Picture Producers and Distributors of America. Ex-pres. Princeton Alumni Assn. of Montclair; treas. Grover Cleveland Birthplace Memorial Assn.; treas. and dir. of Nat. Child Welfare Assn.; mem. N.Y. County Lawyers Assn. Republican. Presbyn. Clubs: Princeton (New York); Princeton Terrace. Contbr. articles on govt., civic and social problems. Home: 38 Crane St., Caldwell, N.J. Office: 165 Broadway, New York, N.Y.

MYERS, Helen Ethel, librarian; b. Mount Joy, Pa., Dec. 22, 1885; d. Reuben Jacob and Helen Louise (Brennesholtz) M.; A.B., Lebanon Valley Coll., 1907; ed. Drexel Inst. Library Sch., 1907-08. Began as asst. New York Pub. Library, 1908-10; cataloger, U. of Chicago Library, 1910-11; librarian, Pub. Library, Lancaster, Pa., 1912-21; librarian, Lebanon Valley Coll. Library since 1921. Mem. Am. Library Assn., Assn. Coll. and Reference Librarians, Pa. Library Assn., State Council Sch. Libraries, Lancaster Co. Hist. Soc., Am. Assn. Univ. Women. Republican. Mem. U. Brethren in Christ Ch. Clubs: Reading Circle, Forum (Annville). Home: 120 College Av., Annville, Pa.

MYERS, Jerome I., lawyer; b. Phila., Pa., Nov. 26, 1895; s. Morris and Anna (Liebeskind) M.; grad. Central High Sch., Scranton, Pa., 1913; LL.B., Dickinson Law Sch., Carlisle, Pa., 1919; m. Ethel Grass, Dec. 2, 1924; 1 dau., Marcia. Admitted to Pa. bar, 1919, and since in practice in Scranton; private sec. Mayor Alex T. Connell, 1919-22; U.S. commr. Middle Dist. of Pa. since 1928; city solicitor since 1934; partner in law firm with B. Fenton Tinkham, 1926, until his death, 1930; dir. and gen. counsel Green Ridge Bank, Scranton. Served as chief yeoman in naval forces during World War. Sec. Lackawanna Co. Rep. Com. 3 times. Dir. and gen. counsel Jewish Home for the Friendless, Scranton. Past pres. Scranton and Pa. State Y.M.H.A. Mem. Am. Bar Assn. (mem. municipal tort and membership coms.), Lackawanna Bar Assn. (dir.; chmn. unlawful practice com.), Nat. Inst. Municipal Law Officers (chmn. municipal tort liability com.; trustee). Mason, Elk (past exalted ruler). Home: 801 Olive St. Office: Mears Bldg., Scranton, Pa.

MYERS, John Dashiell, patent lawyer; b. Washington, D.C., Dec. 2, 1888; s. George McNeir and Elizabeth Ker (Dashiell) M.; B.L., George Washington U., 1911; m. Mary Hall Laird, Mar. 1, 1916; children—Elizabeth Dashiell (Mrs. Frederick Godfrey Corbus, Jr.), John Dashiell, Warren Powers Laird. Admitted to D.C. bar, 1912, bar of Supreme Court of U.S., 1917, Pa. Supreme Court, 1925; became mem. legal staff Victor Talking Machine Co., Camden, N.J., 1911, asst. to v.p., 1916-18, counsel in charge legal staff, 1918-24; in private practice of patent, trade mark and copyright law since 1924; mem. Sec. of Commerce's patent office advisory com. since 1937. Dir. Merion (Pa.) Civic Assn. since 1921, pres. 1928-31; trustee Pennhurst (Pa.) State Sch., 1925-27. Mem. Am. Bar. Assn. (chmn. copyright com. of patent sect. 1932-35), Am. Patent Law Assn., Phila. Patent Law Assn. (pres. 1929-30); N.Y. Patent Law Assn., Lawyers Club of Phila., Constitutional Club, Theta Delta Chi. Republican. Episcopalian. Clubs: Penn, Engineers, Art. Writer of articles on patent, copyright and gen. law topics. Home: 730 Hazelhurst Av., Merion, Pa. Office: 1420 Walnut St., Philadelphia, Pa.

MYERS, John Eyster, lawyer; b. Camp Hill, Pa., Dec. 23, 1891; s. Robert L. and Joanna (Bowman) M.; student Dickinson Coll., 1908-10; LL.B., Dickinson Coll. Sch. of Law, 1913; m. Eunice Ingham, July 8, 1916; children—Thomas Ingham, George Francis, Faith, Christine, Eunice, Jane Eyster. Admitted to Pa. bar, 1913, and since engaged in gen. practice of law at Lemoyne; mem. firm Myers and Myers since 1923; prof. of practice Dickinson Coll. Sch. of Law, 1919-23; dist. atty. of Cumberland Co., 1923-27; vice-pres. Lemoyne Trust Co. Served with 304th Engrs., U.S.A. with A.E.F., 1918-19. Mem. Delta Xi, Am. Legion, Vets. Fgn. Wars. Democrat. Episcopalian. Mason. Home: 355 Walnut St., Lemoyne, Pa.

MYERS, Lanning, supt. of schools; b. Saratoga, N.Y., Apr. 25, 1882; s. Levanus and Annie S. M.; prep. edn. South Jersey Inst., 1896-99; A.B., Brown U., 1906; m. Mabel T. Campbell, Apr. 23, 1910; children—Karl, Rosalind Caws, Elizabeth Shepherd. Teacher rural schools of N.J., 1900-02; teacher in night schools, Central Falls, R.I., 1904-06; prin. Wildwood (N.J.) High Sch., 1906-24; editor Tribune-Journal, Wildwood, N.J., 1923-38; teacher of English, Wildwood High Sch., 1936-38; supt. of schools, Wildwood, since 1938; police judge, Wildwood, 1933-38; justice of the peace since 1927. Mem. bd. dirs. Wildwood Chamber of Commerce, 1922-25; rep. State Chamber of Commerce, 1923-24; pres. Cape May County Chamber of Commerce, 1923-24. Active in establishing Cape May County Library and mem. Cape May County Library Commn., 1924-28. Organized Cape May County Interscholastic Athletic Assn., 1914, and pres., 1914-24; mem. com. to form N.J. State Interscholastic Athletic Assn. Life mem. Nat. Edn. Assn. Republican. Episcopalian. Mason (past master), Odd Fellow (past officer), Moose, Jr. Order United Am. Mechanics, Patriotic Order Sons of America. Home: 111 W. Maple Av., Wildwood, N.J.

MYERS, Paul Forrest, lawyer; b. York Springs, Pa., Aug. 9, 1887; s. Clayton Franklin and Sarah Elizabeth (Menges) M.; grad. Cumberland Valley State Normal Sch., Shippensburg, Pa., 1906, Perkiomen Sch., Pennsburg, Pa., 1907; A.B., Princeton, 1913; LL.B., George Washington U., 1916; m. Mae Claire Holt, June 14, 1913; children—Paul F., Barbara Blair, Robert Holt, John Holt, Richard Clayton. Prin. pub. sch., Quincy, Pa., 1907-08; mem. com. which drafted 1st federal income tax regulations, Oct. 1913-Apr. 1914; asst. head of income tax div., U.S. Internal Revenue Bur., Apr 1914-Apr. 1915; chief clk. and head of apptmt. div., same bur., Apr. 1915-Apr. 1917, chmn. reorgn. com. and exec. atty. of bur., Apr.-Nov. 1917; chief clk. and exec. officer U.S. Treasury Dept., Dec. 1917-Jan. 1920; asst. to commr. internal revenue, Jan. 1920-Apr. 1921; gen. law practice as mem. firm Williams, Myers & Quiggle since 1921. Pres. Bd. Ministerial Pensions and Relief, United Luth. Ch. America, 1927-33. Mem. Am. and D.C. bar assns., Delta Sigma Rho. Democrat. Lutheran. Mason (K.T., Shriner). Clubs: Cosmos, Metropolitan, Chevy Chase (Washington); Charter (Princeton); Princeton (New York). Home: 102 E. Melrose St., Chevy Chase. Office: Munsey Bldg., Washington, D.C.

MYERS, Robert Lee, Jr., lawyer; b. Camp Hill, Pa., Sept. 15, 1897; s. Robert Lee and Joanna (Bowman) M.; A.B., Dickinson Coll., 1917, A.M., 1921; LL.B., Dickinson Coll. Sch. of Law, 1921; m. Evelyn Mentzer, Oct. 16, 1926; children—Robert Lee III, Edward Howard, Philip Nicholas, Virginia Elizabeth. Engaged as instr. and athletic coach, Shippensburg Teachers Coll., 1917; football coach, Dickinson Coll., 1920-21; instr. Dickinson Sch. of Law, 1923-31; admitted to Pa. bar, 1921 and since engaged in gen. practice of law at Lemoyne and Carlisle, Pa.; mem. firm Myers and Myers since 1921; served as dep. atty. gen. of Pa., 1935-36; sec. to Gov. of Pa., 1936-37; chmn. Employment Compensation Bd. of Review of Pa., since 1937; sec.-treas. The Susquehanna Co. Served as pvt. inf., U.S.A. in World War. Dem. candidate for Judge Superior Ct. of Pa., 1935. Mem. Am. and Pa. bar assns., Sigma Alpha Epsilon. Democrat. Presbyn. Mason. Home: Camp Hill. Office: Lemoyne, Pa.

MYERS, Walter L., univ. prof.; b. Lawrence, Kan., 1888; s. John E. and Jane (Pentzer) M.; B.A., State U. of Ia., Iowa City, Ia., 1908, M.A., 1912; Austin Scholar, Harvard, 1913-14; Ph.D., U. of Chicago, 1925; m. Ruth R. Barber, 1919; children—John B., Robert L. Instr. Eng., State U. of Ia., 1910-12, asst. prof., 1912-24, on leaves of absence for research, 1913-14, 1922-23, and for military service, 1917-18; successively asst. prof., asso. prof., and prof. of English, U. of Pittsburgh since 1924. Mem. Modern Lang. Assn. of America, Am. Assn. of Univ. Profs., Nat. Council of Teachers of Eng., Sigma Alpha Epsilon, Phi Beta Kappa. Presbyterian. Author: The Later Realism, 1927; Handbook for Graduate Students in English, 1924; fiction and essays in Midland, Dial, Virginia Quarterly Review. Home: 3245 Latonia Av., Dormont, Pa. Office: University of Pittsburgh, Pittsburgh, Pa.

MYERS, William Heyward, Jr., lawyer; b. Phila., Pa., June 26, 1887; s. William Heyward and Eliza (Sergeant) M.; ed. Mercersburg (Pa.) Acad., 1902-05; A.B., Princeton, 1909; LL.B., Harvard U. of Law Sch., 1912; m. Emily Price Welsh, June 1, 1920; children—William Heyward, Katharine Welsh, Anne Welsh, John Twiggs, Polly Sears. Admitted to Pa. bar, 1912 and since engaged in gen. practice of law at Phila. asso. with firm Morgan, Lewis and Bockius and mem. of firm since 1922; vice-pres. and dir. Ridge Av. Passenger Ry. Co.; dir. Keokuk and Hamilton Bridge Co. Served as 1st lt. ordnance, U.S.A., 1918, 1st lt. Transportation Corps with A.E.F., 1918-19. Trustee Estate of J. Edgar Thomson. Mem. Am., Pa., and Phila. bar assns. Democrat. Episcopalian. Clubs: Princeton, Gulph Mills Golf (Philadelphia). Home: 408 Midland Av., St. Davids, Pa. Office: 123 S. Broad St., Philadelphia, Pa.

MYERS, William Kurtz, banker; b. Millville, N.J., Dec. 17, 1883; s. Christian and Louisa (Kurtz) M.; B.S., Pa. State Coll., 1905; m. Margaret Steinbach, June 23, 1909; draftsman Pa. Steel Co., 1905-07; engr. Chicago Traction Co., 1908-19; valuation mgr. and engr. Phila. Rapid Transit Co., and Internat. Ry. Co. of Buffalo, 1919-23, v.p. Phila. Rapid Transit Co., 1923-26, pres., 1926-27; exec. v.p. Mitten Bank Securities Corpn., 1927-29, pres. 1929-38; v.p. Mitten Management, Inc., since 1927; chmn. exec. com. and vice chmn. bd. of dirs. Phila. Rapid Transit Co., 1928-31; mem. exec. com. Internat. Ry. Co., since 1928; pres. Mitten Bank & Trust Co. since 1928. Mem. Am. Soc. of M.E., Am. Soc. C.E. Clubs: Engineers, Midday (Phila.); Athletic (Buffalo). Home: 206 Winding Way, Merion, Pa. Office: Mitten Bldg., Broad and Locust Sts., Philadelphia, Pa.

MYERS, William Starr, prof. politics; b. Baltimore, Md., June 17, 1877; s. John Norris and Laura Virginia (Starr) M.; B.A., U. of N.C., 1897; studied Johns Hopkins, 1897-1900, Ph.D., 1900; m. Margaret Barr, June 8, 1910; children—Virginia Starr, Margaret Barr. Master of history, Gilman Sch., Baltimore, Md., 1900-06; asst. prof. and preceptor in history and politics, 1906-18, prof. politics since 1918, Princeton. Instr. history, U. of Tenn., summers 1911, 12; instr. history and politics, Johns Hopkins, summers 1913-16; lecturer Army War Coll., Washington, 1920-39; Naval War Coll., Newport, R.I., 1931-39; lectured and conducted

Round Table Confs., Furman Inst. of Politics, Greenville, S.C., sessions 1924, 25, Inst. Pub. Affairs, U. of Va., session 1929. Mem. Small Loans Commn., N.J., 1931-32. Trustee Lake Placid Club Ednl. Foundation, 1929-31. Mem. Beta Theta Pi, Phi Beta Kappa. Episcopalian. Author: Socialism and American Ideals, 1919; American Democracy Today, 1924; Fifty Years of the Prudential, 1926; The Republican Party, a History, 1928; American Government of Today, 1931; General George B. McClellan, 1934; The Hoover Administration (with Walter H. Newton), 1936. Editor McClellan's Mexican War Diary, 1917; Stryker's Battle of Monmouth, 1927; Kitazawa's Government of Japan, 1929; Kraus' The Crisis of German Democracy, 1932; The State Papers of Herbert Hoover (2 vols.), 1934. On editorial staff of New York Journal of Commerce at various times. Contbr. to newspapers and mags. Lecturer on hist. and polit. subjects. Home: Princeton, N.J.

MYLREA, Thomas Douglas; prof. civil engring. and head of dept., U. of Del. Address: University of Delaware, Newark, Del.

N

NACHLAS (Israel) William, orthopedic surgeon; b. Baltimore, Md., Oct. 2, 1894; s. Hertz and Rosa (Kellman) N.; grad. Baltimore pub. schs., 1910; A.B., Johns Hopkins U., 1914; M.D., Johns Hopkins Med. Sch., 1918; unmarried. Junior interne Children's Hosp. Sch., 1917, Baltimore City Hosps., 1918; resident house officer Johns Hopkins Hosp., 1918-19, orthopaedic resident, 1919-20, dispensary surgeon in orthopaedics, since 1923, asst. visiting orthopaedic surgeon since 1927; asst. in orthopaedic surgery, Johns Hopkins Med. Sch., 1919-23, instr., 1923-29, asso. since 1929; orthopaedic surgeon Robert Garrett Hosp., 1920-23; asso. in orthopaedic surgery Sinai Hosp., 1920-21, attending in same, since 1921; orthopaedic surgeon Children's Hosp. Sch. since 1920; consultant in orthopaedic surgery, Nursery and Child's Hosp., 1921-23, Provident Hosp., 1928-29; Mt. Pleasant Hosp. for Tuberculosis, 1925-39; orthopaedic surgeon Washington Co. Gen. Hosp. since 1924; visiting orthopaedist Union Memorial Hosp., Hosp. for Women of Md., West Baltimore Gen. Hosp., Levindale Home for the Aged and Infirm. Served as 1st lt., Med. Res. Corps, 1918. Mem. Am. Orthopaedic Assn., Am. Acad. Orthopaedic Surgeons, Orthopaedic Forum, Southern Med. Assn., Baltimore City Med. Soc., Md. Med. and Chirurg. Faculty, Md. Acad. Medicine and Surgery (officer), Phi Delta Epsilon, Salernum Club; fellow A.M.A.; diplomate Am. Bd. Orthopaedic Surgery. Democrat. Hebrew religion. Clubs: Phoenix Club (Baltimore); Suburban of Baltimore County; Johns Hopkins Faculty. Home: 2312 Eutaw Place. Office: 1814 Eutaw Place, Baltimore, Md.

NADAI, Arpad Ludwig, cons. engr.; b. Budapest, Hungary, Apr. 3, 1883; M.E., Federal Swiss Tech. U., 1906; D.E., Tech. U., Berlin, 1912; m. Elisabeth Vally Justine Witte, Sept. 20, 1913. Came to U.S., 1927, naturalized, 1936. Began as mech. engr. in Germany, 1906; asst. dept. engring. mechanics, Tech. U., Berlin, 1909-12; worked on scientific publs., 1912-14; officer Austrian Army, 1915-19; asst. prof. and prof. applied mechanics, U. of Göttingen, Germany, 1919-27; research prof. U. of Pittsburgh since 1934. Cons. engr. Westinghouse Electric and Mfg. Co. Research Labs., East Pittsburgh, Pa., since 1929. Mem. Am. Soc. M.E. (chmn. Plasticity Com. since 1931), Am. Soc. for Testing Materials, Soc. of Rheology, Geophys. Union, German Math. Union, Nat. Geog. Soc., Verein deütscher Ingenieure. Catholic. Author: Die elastischen Platten, 1925, pub. in German; Plasticity (mechanics of the plastic state of metals), pub. in German and English, 1927 and 1931; also "Plasticity" chapter in Handbuch der Physik, 1927. Contbg. editor Applied Mechanics Jour.; contbr. scientific articles to jours. on applied mechanics, theory of elasticity mechanics of plastic materials, creep of metals at high temperatures, etc. Home: 113 Cherry Valley Road, Wilkinsburg, Pa. Office: Westinghouse Research Labs., East Pittsburgh, Pa.

NADELL, Harry, lawyer; b. Paterson, N.J., May 15, 1899; s. Abraham and Esther (Gordon) N.; student Paterson (N.J.) High Sch., 1913-17; A.B., Harvard U., 1922, LL.B., Harvard Law Sch., 1925; m. Gertrude Cohen, Mar. 1, 1925; 1 dau., Judith. Stenographer, New York, Susquehanna & Western R.R., Jersey City, N.J., 1917, D.L.&W. R.R., New York, U.S. Shipping Bd. Emergency Fleet Corpn., Washington and Philadelphia, 1917-18; law clk. to Arthur T. Vanderbilt and Charles L. Hedden, Newark, N.J., 1925-27; admitted to N.J. bar, 1926; in pvt. practice at Paterson, N.J., since 1927; lecturer on N.J. practice, Harvard Law Sch., 1933-38; has presented course twice a year in preparation N.J. attys'. and counsellors' exams., Newark, 1926-27, Paterson, 1927-37, Paterson and Newark since 1937. Served as apprentice seaman, Harvard Naval Unit, 1918, U.S. Navy, Oct.- Dec. 1918; mem. U.S. N.R.F., 1918-21. Dir. Y.M. & Y.W.H.A., Paterson, Family Welfare Soc. of Paterson and Vicinity; chmn. Youth Service Section, Paterson Community Chest. Mem. Passaic Co. Bar Assn., N.J. State Bar Assn., Phi Beta Kappa. Republican. Jewish religion. Independent United Jersey Verein (Paterson; pres., 1930). Home: 838 Bloomfield Av., Montclair, N.J. Office: 45 Church St., Paterson, N.J.

NADWORNEY, Devora, singer; b. New York, N.Y., May 6, 1903; d. Charles and Rosa (Englander) N.; grad. Bayonne (N.J.) High Sch.; A.B., Hunter Coll., New York; m. Herman Spingarn, 1935. Began as ch. choir singer, St. Vincent de Paul's Ch., Bayonne, N.J.; singing for Nat. Broadcasting Co., New York, since 1927, also Chicago Civic Opera Co. Life mem. Nat. Fed. Music Clubs (nat. prize winner, 1923; first N.J. State vocal winner to win nat. prize). Clubs: Women's City, 200 (New York). First voice over a radio network, Jan. 4, 1923; created roles of Sofia and Vera in Am. premiere of "Resurrection," Chicago, 1926; created roles in Tcherepnine opera, "Olol," New York, 1934; known as "Voice of Gold" on radio commercial programs. Home: Bayonne, N.J. Address: 39 W. 67th St., New York, N.Y.

NAGELL, Frank Joseph, treas. Black & Decker Mfg. Co.; b. Baltimore, Md., Feb. 4, 1894; s. William and Anna (Eirich) N.; student Baltimore pub. schs., Baltimore City Coll.; Sadlers Bryant & Stratton Business Coll., Baltimore, Johns Hopkins U., Baltimore; m. Mildred McCrea, Nov. 26, 1936. Employed by father as bookkeeper, 1914-18; cost accountant Black & Decker Mfg. Co., 1920-22, accountant, 1922-24, asst. treas., 1924-30, treas. since 1930; treas. Black & Decker Mfg. Co., Ltd., Canada; dir. Black & Decker Electric Co., Black & Decker Mfg. Co. of Towson, Md. Served in U.S. Army in France 1918-19. Mem. Controllers Inst. of America. Home: 1271 Riverside Av., Baltimore, Md. Office: care Black & Decker Mfg. Co., Towson, Md.

NAGLE, Clarence Floyd, gen. supt. Scranton Electric Co.; b. Mt. Cory, O., Aug. 3, 1882; s. John B. and Emma E. N.; E.E., Lafayette Coll., Easton, Pa., 1904; m. Elsie May Smyser, 1911; children—S. F. and J. Carlyle. Began as engr., Westinghouse Electric & Mfg. Co., East Pittsburgh, Pa., 1904-05; elec. engr. Pa. Coal Co., 1905-07; mgr. Citizens Electric Illuminating Co., 1907-18; gen. supt. The Scranton (Pa.) Electric Co. since 1918. Mem. Chamber of Commerce, Phi Beta Kappa, Tau Beta Pi. Mason (Shriner). Clubs: Scranton, Kiwanis, Scranton Country (Scranton); Shrine Country (Wilkes-Barre). Home: 930 Clay Av. Office: Scranton Electric Bldg., Scranton, Pa.

NAGLE, Edgar Charles, lawyer; b. Northampton, Pa., Nov. 3, 1874; s. William H. and Amanda (Steinmetz) N.; B.S., Bloomsburg State Normal Sch., 1893; A.B., Franklin and Marshall Coll., 1899; m. Mabel L. Laubach, Sept. 28, 1908; children—Elizabeth L., Louise L., James L. Admitted to Pa. bar, 1905, and since engaged in gen. practice of law at Northampton; solicitor Borough of Northampton, 1915-34; vice-pres. and trust officer, Cement Nat. Bank since 1925; sec. Cement Bldg. & Loan Assn.; solicitor for Sch. Dist. since 1910. Mem. Pa. State Bar Assn. Republican. German Reformed. Mason. I.O.O.F. Club: Rotary of Northampton. Home: 302 East 21st St. Office: 21st and Main Sts., Northampton, Pa.

NAGORSKI, Francis Thomas, lawyer; b. West Prussia (now Poland), Sept. 18, 1879; s. John and Frances (Klavitter) N.; came to U.S., 1888, became citizen through father's naturalization; student Central High Sch., Erie, 1895-98; LL.B., U. of Mich., Ann Arbor, Mich., 1904; m. Hedwig Dymshaw, Feb. 8, 1910; children—Francis Thomas, Robert, Hubert. Began as lawyer, 1905, and since in practice at Erie, Pa.; dir. Bank of Erie Trust Co., 1917-34; mem. Pa. State Park and Harbor Commn., 1932-37. Mem. of City Council and dir. of Accounts and Finance, Erie, Pa., 1918-19; ex-officio vice mayor of Erie, Pa. Mem. Erie Co., Pa. Bar Assn., Am. Bar Assn. Republican. Catholic. Home: 522 E. 10th St. Office: 506 Palace Hardware Bldg., Erie, Pa.

NANCE, Oran H.; pres., gen. mgr. and dir. Md.&Pa. R.R. Home: 4002 St. Paul St. Office: 135 W. North Av., Baltimore, Md.

NARY, Thomas Donaldson, lawyer; b. Reading, Pa., June 14, 1904; s. Thomas and Emma Rebecca (Donaldson) N.; grad. Asbury Park (N.J.) High Sch., 1923; student Neptune (N.J.) Twp. High Sch., 1919-22, Wesleyan Coll., Middletown, N.J., 1923-25; LL.B., Dickinson Law Sch., Carlisle, Pa., 1925-28; m. Kathryn Pinckney Young, Mar. 25, 1933. Admitted to N.J. bar, 1928; asso. with firm Patterson, Rhome & Morgan, Asbury Park, N.J., 1928-38; mem. firm Proctor & Nary, Asbury Park, as partner Senator Haydn Proctor, since 1938; counsel Seacoast Trust Co., Home Bldg. & Loan Assn., Webb Bldg. & Loan Assn., Liquidating Corpn. of Asbury Park. Mem. Monmouth Co. Bar Assn. Republican. Methodist. Club: Kiwanis (Manasquan, N.J.). Home: 302 Crescent Parkway, Sea Girt, N.J. Office: Electric Bldg., Asbury Park, N.J.

NASH, Ogden, writer; b. Rye, N.Y., Aug. 19, 1902; s. Edmund Strudwick and Mattie (Chenault) N.; student St. George's Sch., Newport, R.I., 1917-20, Harvard, 1920-21; m. Frances Rider Leonard, June 6, 1931; children—Linell Chenault, Isabel Jackson. Author: Hard Lines (verse), 1931; Free Wheeling, 1931; Happy Days, 1933; The Primrose Path (verse), 1935; The Bad Parents' Garden of Verse, 1936; I'm a Stranger Here Myself, 1938. Frequent contbr. verse to leading mags. Home: 4300 Rugby Rd., Baltimore, Md.

NAVARRO, Rocco Albert, real estate and ins. broker; b. Pittsburgh, Pa., Oct. 1, 1909; s. Pasquale and Prudence (Fralliciardi) N.; gen. English course, Bellefonte Acad., 1928; A.B., Washington and Jefferson Coll., 1933; LL.B., Duquesne U. Law Sch., 1936; m. Virginia Cattanzaro, Oct. 7, 1932; 1 dau., Camilla Donna. Asso. with brother in realty business and mgr. Broad Realty Co., Pittsburgh, Pa., 1933-36, became propr. and changed name to Navarro Realty Co., 1936; vice-pres. and dir. Navarro Corpn.; on acct. of established business has not as yet taken State Bd. of Law examination. Pres. Duquesne U. Law Club, 1935. Mem. Italian Professional Assn., Y.M.C.A., Alpha Phi Delta, Tau Delta Phi, Sons of Columbus of America. Republican. Roman Catholic. Home: 6430 Navarro St. Office: 6221 Broad St., Pittsburgh, Pa.

NAYLOR, John Albert, clergyman; b. nr. Camden, N.J., Nov. 25, 1873; s. William and Rebecca S. (Ellis) N.; student Pierce Business Coll., Phila., Pa., and Conf. Course of Study of M.E. Ch.; m. Ella May Neil, Jan. 3, 1900; 1 son, John Albert. Served as seaman apprentice U.S.N., 1891-95, gunners mate, 1896-97; bookkeeper, later office mgr., 1898-1908; supply pastor M.E. Ch., 1909-1911, admitted on trial in N.J. Conf. M.E. Ch., 1912, admitted into full membership, 1914, ordained deacon, 1914, elder, 1916; served in various chs. in N.J., 1909-34; pastor, Matawan, N.J., since 1935. Dir. Centenary Fund and Preachers Aid Soc.; nat. chaplain Nat. Assn. Regulars since 1937;

mem. staff of sec. N.J. Annual Conf. Mason (K.T.). Home: 197 Main St., Matawan, N.J.

NAYLOR, Joseph Randolph, banker, mcht.; b. Wheeling, W.Va., Aug. 27, 1878; s. John Sargent and Anna (Wendelken) N.; grad. Linsly Inst., Wheeling, W.Va., 1895; A.B., Washington and Jefferson Coll., 1898, A.M., 1901; LL.B., U. of Va., 1901; m. Reita Caldwell, June 1, 1905 (died Aug. 22, 1925); children—Joseph Randolph, Anna Elizabeth; m. 2d, Mrs. Inez Leslie Murdock, Aug. 12, 1929. Instructor Linsly Institute, 1898-99; admitted to W.Va. bar, 1901, and practiced at Wheeling until 1906; member since 1906 of firm of John S. Naylor & Co., wholesale dry goods, notions, etc., inc., 1908, as John S. Naylor Co., of which was sec.-treas., 1908-17, v.p., 1917, pres. since 1918; dir. Pittsburgh Br. Federal Reserve Bank of Cleveland, 1924-30, chmn. bd., 1926, 29; pres. Nat. Exchange Bank of Wheeling. Mem. W.Va. Ho. of Rep., 1903-07. Trustee Washington and Jefferson Coll. Mem. Wheeling Landscape Commn., W.Va. Chamber of Commerce, Wheeling Chamber Commerce, Phi Gamma Delta, Phi Delta Phi. Republican. Clubs: Rotary Internat. (ex-gov. 24th dist.), Twilight, Fort Henry; Wheeling Country. Home: Bethany Pike. Office: 1401 Main St., Wheeling, W.Va.

NAYLOR, Roy Benton; b. Wheeling, W.Va., July 22, 1871; s. John Sargent and Anna (Wendelken) N.; ed. pub. schs. and Linsly Inst., Wheeling, and Marietta (O.) Coll.; (hon. A.M. Marietta, 1912); m. Nancy Dent, Jan. 15, 1902; 1 son, John S. With Wheeling News, 1890-1902; gen. mgr. Wheeling Telegraph, 1902-04; commercial sec., city and state organizations, 1905-16; now with Travelers Ins. Co.; v.p. Community Savings & Loan Co. Dir. Y.M. C.A.; chmn. Municipal Recreation Bd.; mem. Wheeling Life Underwriters Assn.; hon. mem. Nat. Recreation Assn. Republican. Mem. Disciples of Christ. Clubs: Rotary, (pres.), Twilight. Home: Hawthorne Court. Office: Central Union Bldg., Wheeling, W.Va.

NEAL, B. T., Jr.; pres. Union Trust & Deposit Co. Address: Parkersburg, W.Va.

NEAL, George Ira, lawyer; b. Milton, W.Va.; s. Andrew Dickerson and Malinda (Newman) N.; LL.B., W.Va. U., 1888; m. Eunice Earp, Dec. 5, 1912; children—Virginia (dec.), Irene, George I. Admitted to W.Va. bar, 1889; and has since practiced at Huntington; became U.S. atty. Southern Dist. of W.Va., 1933; formerly mayor of Huntington; was Dem. nominee for Congress. Mem. Huntington Chamber of Commerce (pres.). Democrat. Baptist. Club: Rotary (pres.). Home: Fifth St. and Boul. Office: Robson-Prichard Bldg., Huntington, W.Va.

NEALE, James Ralph, clergyman and coll. prof.; b. Kimbolton, O., Sept. 12, 1885; s. John and Lucina (McConnegha) N.; ed. O. State U., 1906-07; B.S., Muskingum Coll., New Concord, O., 1910; student, Xenia Theol. Sem., 1911-14, Princeton Theol. Sem., 1919-20, Columbia U., summer 1937; (hon.) D.D., Muskingum Coll., 1930; m. Edith Carolyn Patton, May 12, 1914; children—Virginia Ruth, James Ralph, Jr., Jeanne Marie, Francis Dean. Ordained to ministry U. Presbyn. Ch., 1914 and minister, Piqua, O., 1914-18; minister, New Wilmington, Pa., since 1920; also prof. religion and ethics, Westminster Coll., New Wilmington, Pa., since 1934; short term teacher in Assiut Assiut, Egypt, 1910; mem. bd. dirs. Pittsburg-Xenia Theol. Sem.; mem. bd. mgrs. New Wilmington Missionary Conf.; nat. pres. Young People's Christian Union; moderator First Synod of West, 1936. Served as exec. sec. in Y.M. C.A. War Service, France, 1917-18. Mem. Sherwood Eddy Seminar for study social, econ., polit. and rel. conditions in Europe, 1928. Republican. U. Presbyn. Club: Rotary of New Wilmington, Pa. (past pres.). Home: 347 Vine St., New Wilmington, Pa.

NEARING, Scott, sociologist; b. Morris Run, Pa., Aug. 6, 1883; s. Louis and Minnie (Zabriskie) N.; U. of Pa. Law Sch., 1901-02; B.S., U. of Pa., 1905, Ph.D., 1909; Bach. Oratory, Temple U., Phila., 1904; m. Nellie Marguerite Seeds, June 20, 1908. Sec. Pa. Child Labor Com., 1905-07; instr. economics, 1906-14, asst. prof., 1914-15, U. of Pa.; also instr. economics, Swarthmore (Pa.) Coll., 1908-13; prof. social science and dean Coll. of Arts and Sciences, Toledo (O.) U., 1915-17; became lecturer Rand Sch. of Social Science, N.Y. City, 1916; chmn. People's Council of America, 1917-18; Socialist candidate for Congress, N.Y. City, 1919. Author: Economics (with F. D. Watson), 1908; Social Adjustment, 1911; Solution of the Child Labor Problem, 1911; Wages in the United States, 1911; (with wife) Woman and Social Progress, 1912; The Super Race, 1912; Social Religion, 1913; Social Sanity, 1913; Financing the Wage Earner's Family, 1914; Reducing the Cost of Living, 1914; Income, 1915; Anthracite, 1915; Poverty and Riches, 1916; The American Empire, 1921; (with B. A. W. Russell) Debate between Scott Nearing and Bertrand Russell, 1924; The Next Step, 1924; Educational Frontiers, 1925; Oil and the Germs of War, 1925; (with Joseph Freeman) Dollar Diplomacy, 1925; The British General Strike, 1926; Education in Soviet Russia, 1926; Where Is Civilization Going?, 1927; (with Jack Hardy) Economic Organization of the Soviet Union, 1927; Whither China?, 1927; Black America, 1929; Twilight of Empire, 1930; War, 1931; Must We Starve?, 1932; Fascism, 1933; also numerous brochures and articles. Address: Box 338, Ridgewood, N.J.

NEEL, Gregg Livingstone, realtor; b. Brownsville, Pa., Feb. 1, 1893; s. Rev. J. Thomas and Rhoda A. (Gregg) N.; A.B., Waynesburg Coll., 1912; m. Hazel Mancha, Feb. 3, 1914 (dec.); children—Helen Virginia, Ruth Gregg. Engaged in real estate business in Washington Co., Pa., 1912-19, and at Pittsburgh, Pa., since Mar. 1919. Sec. Rep. Exec. Com., Allegheny Co., Pa.; sec. Rep. Men of Western Pa. Mem. Squirrel Hill Bd. of Trade, Pittsburgh (pres. 1921-22), Chamber of Commerce, Pittsburgh (chmn. Municipal Affairs Com., mem. Lake Erie Canal, Charities and Nat. Affairs coms.). Pres. Pittsburgh Free Dispensary; dir. Allegheny Gen. Hosp., Pittsburgh; vice-pres. Hist. Soc. of Western Pa.; treas. William A. Magee Memorial Fund; mem. Pittsburgh Lyceum; mem. bd. of dirs. The Public Education and Child Labor Assn. of Pa. Mem. Pa. Real Estate Assn. (dir. and chmn. of Finance Com.) Pittsburgh Real Estate Bd. (bd. govs. and chmn. Municipal Affairs Com. and mem. Community Research Bureau and Legislative Com.), S.A.R. (life mem.), mem. Point Park Com. Hon. life mem. Delta Mu Delta (U. of Pittsburgh). Republican. Presbyn. (mem. bd. trustees Pittsburgh Presbytery, mem. Session Sixth Presbyn. Ch.). Clubs: Amen Corner (vice-pres.), Pittsburgh Athletic Assn., Duquesne, Civic, Rotary. Contbr. hist. articles and addresses to hist. mags. and real estate mags. Home: 6318 Bartlett St. Office: 1926 Farmers Bank Bldg., Pittsburgh, Pa.

NEELLEY, John Haven, prof. mathematics; b. Columbia, Tenn., Oct. 30, 1892; s. Thurston Haven and Lucile (Allison) N.; B.S., Vanderbilt, 1916, A.M., same, 1920; Ph.D., Yale, 1927; m. Kathleen McKenzie, Jan. 8, 1921; children—Richard Haven, Allison McKenzie. Instr. high sch. 1912-14, 1916-19; instr. Vanderbilt U., 1919-20; math. master and athletic dir., Memphis U. Sch., 1920-23; instr. Yale U., 1924-27; asso. prof. mathematics, Carnegie Inst. Tech., 1927-30, prof. since 1930. Mem. Am. Math. Soc., Math. Assn., Sigma Xi, Phi Beta Kappa, Gamma Alpha, Sigma Nu. Democrat. Methodist. Mason. Author: New Analytic Geometry (with Smith and Gale), 1927; Differential and Integral Calculus (with Tracey), 1932. Contbr. articles on mathematics to mags. Home: 300 Broadmoor Av., Mt. Lebanon, Pittsburgh, Pa.; (summers) "Hillsite," Oakham, Mass.

NEELY, Matthew Mansfield, senator; b. Grove, W.Va., Nov. 9, 1874; s. Alfred and Mary (Morris) N.; grad. mil. dept., W.Va. U.; A.B., W.Va. U., 1901, LL.B., 1902; m. Alberta Claire Ramage, Oct. 21, 1903. Began practice, Fairmont, 1902. Mayor of Fairmont, 1908-10; clk. W.Va. Ho. of Dels., 1911-13; mem. 63d to 66th Congresses (1913-21), 1st W.Va. Dist.; U.S. senator from W.Va., 1923-29 and since 1931 for terms 1931-43. Pvt. Co. D, 1st Inf., W.Va. Vols., Spanish-Am. War, 1898; served in W.Va. N.G. corporal to maj., 1900-11 (resigned). Mem. Phi Sigma Kappa, Delta Chi, Phi Beta Kappa. Democrat. Mason (32°), Odd Fellow, Elk, K. of P., Moose. Home: Fairmont, W.Va.

NEELY, William Hamlin, lawyer; b. Mifflintown, Pa., Feb. 2, 1896; s. John Howard and Ella (Banks) N.; student Harrisburg (Pa.) Acad., 1909-13; A.B., Princeton U., 1917; LL.B., U. of Pa. Law Sch., 1922; m. Jean Bosler Chamberlain, Sept. 6, 1924; children—William Hamlin, Jr., James Chamberlain, Jean Chamberlain, Stewart McAllister. Admitted to Pa. bar, 1922, and since engaged in gen. practice of law at Harrisburg; admitted to practice before State and Fed. appellate cts.; served as spl. counsel for State of Pa., 1927-30; dep. atty. gen. of Pa., 1931-35, counsel for Pa. Securities Commn. Served as 1st lt. Air Service, U.S.A. with A.E.F., 1917-18. Cited for bravery in Meuse-Argonne. Dir. Harrisburg Hosp. Mem. Am. and Pa. bar assns., Dauphin Co. Bar Assn. (pres. 1936-37), Am. Legion. Republican. Presbyn. (trustee Pine St. Ch.). Elk, Kiwanian. Clubs: Country, Kiwanis. Home: 323 N. Front St. Office: 403 Keystone Bldg., Harrisburg, Pa.

NEESER, Robert Wilden, author; b. Seabright, N.J., July 16, 1884; s. John G. and Josephine C. (Wilden) N.; A.B., Yale, 1906, A.M., 1909; m. May 15, 1919, Susanne Belin; children—John S. (dec.), Odile Elvine, Beatrice, Robert M., Marie-José. Asst. to Am. naval attaché, Paris, 1917-18; 1st lt. inf., attached to G-2, S.O.S., A.E.F., France, 1918-19; liaison officer to Am. naval attaché, Paris, 1920-21; mgr. in France, Western Union Telegraph-Cable System, 1921-23. Decorated Médaille de la Reconnaissance Française, 1917; French Academic Palms, 1919, and Cross Legion of Honor (French). Mem. Am. Hist. Assn., Naval Hist. Soc. of U.S., U.S. Naval Inst. (life); asso. mem. Académie de Marine. Author: Statistical and Chronological History of the United States Navy (1775-1907), 1909; A Landsman's Log, 1913; Despatches of Molyneux Shuldham (1776), 1913; Our Navy and the Next War, 1915; Our Many-Sided Navy, 1914; Cruises of Gustavus Conyngham (1777-1781), 1915; Ship-Names of the United States Navy, 1922; American Naval Songs and Ballads, 1938; also articles in periodicals on naval subjects. Home: Rumson, N.J. Address: care National City Bank of New York, 60 Av. Champs Elysées, Paris, France.

NEFF, Charles Thompson, Jr., univ. bus. officer; b. Piedmont, W.Va., Feb. 4, 1899; s. Charles Thompson and Lena Drusella (Porter) N.; A.B., W.Va. Univ., Morgantown, W.Va., 1921; m. Inez Davis, Dec. 26, 1921. Employed as supt. schs., Piedmont, W.Va., 1922-27; exec. sec. W.Va., Univ. Bd. Govs. since 1927; financial sec. W.Va. Univ., Morgantown, W.Va. since 1934. Candidate C.O.T.S., Camp Gordon, Ga., 1918. Mem. Assn. Univ. and Coll. Bus. Officers, Am. Legion, Phi Kappa Sigma, Phi Lambda Upsilon, Mountain. Methodist. Mason. Club: Rotary of Morgantown. Home: 429 Grand St., Morgantown, W.Va.

NEFF, Elmer Hartshorn, mech. engr.; b. at Vienna, Mich., Mar. 6, 1866; s. Henry Clinton and Emily Jerusha (Hartshorn) N.; B.S. in M.E., U. of Mich., 1890, M.E., same, 1901; m. Isabella Cottrell, June 28, 1894 (died 1926); 1 dau., Dorothy Isabel (Mrs. Walter Andrew Curry); m. 2d, Florence Ellen Sparks, Mar. 1, 1928 (died 1933). Employed as erecting engr., Edw. F. Allis Co., Milwaukee, Wis., 1890-91; designer, Gisholt Machine Co., Madison, Wis., 1891-92; with Westinghouse interests, Pittsburgh, 1893; instructor mech. engring., Purdue University; asso. with Brown & Sharpe Mfg. Co., Providence, R.I., continuously since 1896, mgr. N.Y. territory since 1897, embracing southeastern, N.Y., L.I., northern N.J. and N.E. Pa. Served as mem. first N.J. State Park Commn.; mem. Montclair Bd. Edn., 5 yrs. Essex Co. Republican Committee over 30 yrs. One of organizers, Machinery Club, N.Y. City, and Montclair Soc. Engrs. Mem. many sci. and ednl.

socs. Mem. Upper Montclair Rep. Club. Republican. Conglist. Mason. Clubs: Commonwealth (Upper Montclair); University of Michigan, Railroad-Machinery (New York). Home: 69 Oakwood Av., Montclair, N.J.

NEFF, Jonathan Cilley, banker, hotel official; b. Philadelphia, Pa., Aug. 22, 1866; s. John R. and Josephine M. (Cilley) Neff; student Philadelphia High Sch.; m. Mary Bell Wampole, Dec. 27, 1884; 1 dau., Josephine Cilley (Mrs. John Parker Hill). Asso. with Fidelity-Phila. Trust Co. since Jan. 1884, beginning as clerk and advancing to asst. sec., now v.p. and dir.; pres. and dir. Claridge Hotel Corpn.; dir. Little Schuylkill Navigation, R.R. & Coal Co., Altoona & Logan Valley Electric Ry. Co., Johnstown Traction Co., Metropolitan Edison Co. Became treas. Presbyn. Ministers Fund, June 1895, corporator, Jan. 1921, dir. since Dec. 1922. Clubs: Midday, Art, Manufacturers and Bankers (Phila.); Merion Cricket (Haverford, Pa.). Home: 6425 Woodbine Av., Overbrook. Office: 135 S. Broad St., Philadelphia, Pa.

NEILL, William, Jr., physician; b. Charles Town, W.Va., Apr. 1, 1890; s. William and Mary V. (Simmons) N.; A.B., St. Johns Coll., Annapolis, Md., 1908, A.M., 1922; M.D., Johns Hopkins U. Med. Sch., 1912; m. Alice L. Buckler, Apr. 7, 1923; 1 son, William 3d. Interne Church Home and Infirmary, 1912-15; engaged in practice of surgery in Baltimore since 1915; surgeon Howard A. Kelly, Hosp., Baltimore, since 1915; visiting surgeon Womans Hosp. Ch. Home; consulting pathologist U.S. Marine Hosp.; cons. surgeon Cambridge Md. Hosp.; dir. Commonwealth Bank, Baltimore; instr. surgery, Johns Hopkins Med. Sch. since 1936. Served in R.A. Med. Corps, 1917-18; with Med. Corps U.S.A., A.E.F., 1918-19. Fellow Am. Coll. Surgeons, Am. Med. Assn.; mem. Southern Med. Assn., Md. Med. and Chirurg. Faculty, Johns Hopkins Gynecol. Club, Phi Sigma Kappa. Democrat. Episcopalian. Home: 3917 Canterbury Rd. Office: 1418 Eutaw Pl., Baltimore, Md.

NEILSON, Harry Rosengarten, ins. brokerage; b. Phila., Pa., Dec. 6, 1893; s. Lewis and Clara Augusta (Rosengarten) N.; ed. Episcopal Acad., Phila., Pa., 1903-08, St. Paul's Sch., Concord, N.H., 1908-12; B.S., U. of Pa., 1916; m. Alberta P. Reath, Oct. 18, 1922 (dec.); children—Harry Rosengarten, Jr., Albert Pancoast, Benjamin Reath. Began as clk. with Powers-Weightman-Rosengarten Co., 1919, asst. sec., 1922-27; and sec. to successors, Merck & Co., Inc., 1927-28; asso. with W. H. Newbold, Son & Co., 1928-34; vice-pres. and treas. Higham-Neilson Co., ins. brokers, Phila., Pa., since 1934; dir. Merck & Co., Inc., Erie & Pittsburgh R.R. Co. Served with First Troop Phila. City Cav. on Mexican border, 1916-17; 2d then 1st lt., U.S.N.A., 1917-18. Trustee Lankenau Hosp., Episcopal Acad. Mem. Delta Psi. Republican. Episcopalian. Clubs: Philadelphia, Racquet, Gulph Mills Golf, St. Anthony (Philadelphia); St. Anthony (New York). Home: St. Davids, Pa. Office: 1369 Broad St. Sta. Bldg., Philadelphia, Pa.

NEILSON, Lewis, railway official; b. Florence, N.J., Sept. 30, 1860; s. Thomas and Sarah Claypoole (Lewis) N.; A.B., U. of Pa., 1881; m. Clara A. Rosengarten, Feb. 8, 1893; children—Harry R., Mrs. Sarah C. Madeira. Began with Pa. R.R. as weighing clk., Walnut St. Wharf, June 20, 1881; asst. receiving clk. and in cashier's dept., to 1882; stenographer to 4th v.p., Capt. J. P. Green, July 16, 1883; chief clk. in that office, Dec. 1, 1885, which he occupied under Capt. Green's several promotions to 1st v.p.; chief clk. to sec. Pa. R.R., May 1, 1897, and asst. sec. pro tem., May 26, 1897, filling both positions until apptd. asst. sec. Pa. R.R. and Phila., Wilmington & Baltimore R.R. Co., June 1, 1898; sec. Pa. R.R. Co. and Phila., Wilmington & Baltimore R.R. Co. (now Phila., Baltimore & Washington R.R. Co.), 1901-1930; also sec. W. Jersey & Seashore R.R. Co., Northern Central Ry. Co., 1910-1930; was sec. 112 corpns. associated with Pa. R.R.; pres. Elmira & Williamsport R.R., 1927-30; v.p. secretarial dept., 1929-30 (retired); dir. several ry. cos. Episcopalian. Mem. U. of Pa. Alumni Assn.; ex-dir., ex-sec., ex-treas. Athletic Assn., U. of Pa. Clubs: Rittenhouse, Merion Cricket, Gulph Mills Golf, etc. Home: St. Davids, Pa.

NEILSON, Thomas Rundle, surgeon; b. Philadelphia, Pa., Oct. 29, 1857; s. Thomas and Sarah Claypoole (Lewis) N.; A.B., U. of Pa., 1877, A.M., M.D., 1880; m. Louise Fotterall, Jan. 12, 1898. Became prof. genito-urinary surgery, U. of Pa. Sch. of Medicine, 1903, now emeritus; surgeon emeritus Hosp. of P.E. Ch.; cons. surgeon St. Christopher's Hosp. for Children. Fellow Am. Surg. Assn., Am. Coll. Surgeons, Coll. Physicians of Phila. (ex-pres.), Acad. Surgery of Phila., Am. Urol. Assn.; mem. A.M.A., Société Internat. de Chirurgie, Med. Soc. State of Pa., Phila. County Med. Soc. Republican. Episcopalian. Club: Rittenhouse. Home: 1937 Chestnut St., Philadelphia, Pa.

NEISSER, Hans Philipp, univ. prof.; b. Breslau, Germany, Sept. 3, 1895; s. Gustav and Else (Silberstein) N.; grad. High Sch., Breslau, 1913; student Universities of Breslau, Freiburg and Muenchen, 1913-16 (LL.D.); m. Charlotte Schroeter, Dec. 22, 1923; children—Mary Anne, Ulrich Gustav. Came to U.S., 1933. Sec. of various govt. commns., Germany, 1922-23; 1926-27; editor of an economic magazine, 1924-26; instr. and asst. prof. Univ. of Kiel, 1927-33; staff mem. Inst. for Internat. Economics, 1927-33; prof. of monetary theory, Wharton Sch. of Commerce and Finance, U. of Pa., since 1933. Served in German Army, 1917-18. Mem. Am. Econ. Assn., Am. Econometric Soc. Home: 227 Kenyon Av., Swarthmore, Pa.

NEISSER, Rittenhouse, educator; b. Philadelphia, Pa., Nov. 24, 1873; s. John Singleton and Emma (Rittenhouse) N.; student Central High Sch., Phila., 1887-90, Temple U., evening courses, 1893-95, evening theol. course, 1896-97, Crozer Theol. Sem., Chester, Pa., 1898-1902, grad. studies, same, 1910-15, B.D., 1914, Th.M., 1915; student U. of Pa., summer, 1924; D.D., Bucknell U., Lewisburg, Pa., 1936; m. Florence May Hubbard, Nov. 28, 1894 (died Mar. 5, 1896); m. 2d, Grace Emma Wilson, June 25, 1902; 1 son, Wilson Rittenhouse. Began as rodman Survey Bur., Phila., 1891; pastor Logan Bapt. Ch., Phila., 1899-1907, Woodland Bapt. Ch., Phila., 1907-20; sec. Edn. Bd., Pa. Baptist Conv., 1920-23; asso. dir. Crozer Extension Course, Crozer Theol. Sem., 1923-27, dir. since 1927; librarian Bucknell Library, Crozer Theol. Sem. since Jan. 5, 1937. Pres. Sch. Bd. of Upland Borough, Delaware Co., Pa., since Dec. 1935. Mem. Ministers' Council, Northern Bapt. Conv., and Ministers' Council, Pa. Bapt. Conv. Dir. Baptist Camp Federation, J. Lewis Crozer Home and Hosp., J. Lewis Crozer Pub. Library; trustee, v.p. of dir. Chester Rescue Mission. Mem. Ministerial Union, Baptist Ministers' Assn. (both of Phila.), Ministers' Assn. of Chester, Am. Library Assn., Pa. Library Assn., Photozetetics Theol. Club (Phila.). Independent Republican. Club: Rotary (Chester, Pa.). Address: Crozer Theological Seminary, Chester, Pa.

NELDEN, Robert J., banker; pres. Paterson (N.J.) Savings Instn.; v.p. Dundee Water Power & Land Co., Jersey City Water Supply Co., Paterson & Hudson River R.R.; dir. First Nat. Bank. Office: 129 Market St., Paterson, N.J.*

NELL, Raymond Boyd, educator, dean; b. Allen, Pa., Jan. 12, 1891; s. Adam and Phiana (Diller) N.; B.S., Gettysburg Coll., 1912; M.A., Thiel Coll., 1920; A.B., University of Minn., 1927; A.M., Columbia University, 1927; student, Augsburg Theol. Sem., 1918-20, U. of Minn., Harvard (scholarship), Columbia Univ. (scholarship), Pa. State Coll.; m. Daisy Irene Wentz, June 16, 1916; children—Raymond Boyd II, Anna, Catherine, Irene May. Ordained ministry, 1921; pastor First Luth. Ch., Columbia Heights, Minn., 1921-23; teacher pub. sch., Mt. Holly, Pa., 1912-13; prof. Wartburg Coll., Clinton, Ia., 1913-16; supt. Nachusa (Ill.) Orphanage, 1915; prof. edn., Augsburg Coll., 1916-23; head dept. of edn., Hamline U., St. Paul, Minn., 1923-37, dir. ednl. research, 1924-28, dean, 1928-33, chmn. div. of social studies, 1934-36; prof. MacPhail Sch. of Music, 1924-26; dean, Susquehanna U., since 1937. Mem. N.E.A., Pa. Edn. Assn., Am. Assn. Univ. Profs. (pres. Hamline chapter 1927-28), Minn. Assn. Collegiate Registrars (founder; pres. 1932-34), Assn. Minn. Colls. (sec.-treas. 1932-36), Minn. Assn. Coll. Teachers of Edn. and Psychology (pres. 1933-34), A.A.A.S., Am. Acad. Polit. and Social Science, Sigma Alpha Epsilon, Kappa Phi Kappa, Pi Gamma Mu, Phi Delta Kappa. Republican. K.P. Clubs: Oxford, Midway (ednl. com.); Rotary; pres. Columbia U. Club in Minn., 1926-27. Author: Manual of Biology, 1920; Scientific Method in Education, 1920; Manual of General Science, 1921; The Nell Family in the U.S., 1929; Foundations of Modern Education, 1933; Problem-Outline in the Social Background of Education, 1933; Problems in the Technique of High School Instruction (2d edit.), 1933; Problem Outline in Practice Teaching, 1933; Modernism in Education, 1935. Contbr. articles to jours., etc. Home: 218 W. Walnut St., Selinsgrove, Pa.

NELLEY, Thomas J., co. commr.; b. Harrisburg, Pa., Jan. 26, 1877; s. Cornelius and Sarah (Geary) N.; student parochial and pub. schs.; m. Hannah Mable Hopple, May 14, 1914. Mem. Steelton (Pa.) Borough Council, 32 yrs.; v.p. Highspire (Pa.) Knitting Co.; dir. Steelton Bank & Trust Co.; Dauphin Co. (Pa.) commr. and pres. of commn. Republican. Elk (life mem.), Moose, Royal Arcanum, Eagle (life mem.). Clubs: Steelton, Kiwanis (Steelton); Republican, West End Republican (Harrisburg). Home: 947 S. Front St., Steelton, Pa. Office: Court House, Harrisburg, Pa.

NELSON, A. A., judge; b. Lilly, Pa., June 23, 1891; s. John and Catherine (McCann) N.; student commercial course St. Francis Coll., Loretto, Pa.; m. Agnes J. Wilkinson, Jan. 14, 1926; children—James A., Jane Ann, Thomas W. Admitted to practice law, Cambria Co., Pa., Jan. 1915, and later in Appellant cts. of Pa. and U.S. Dist. Ct.; 1st asst. to dist. atty., 1932-35; with firm of Shettig (Philip N. Shettig) & Nelson, Feb. 1919-Jan. 1936; pres. judge Orphans' Ct. of Cambria Co., Pa., since Jan. 1936 (elected Nov. 1935): Mem. Am. Legion (past comdr. local post, past comdr. co. com.), 40 and 8. Elk, Moose, K.C. (Past Grand Knight). Clubs: Kiwanis, Ebensburg Country (Ebensburg, Pa.). Home: 217 Highland Av. Office: Court House, Center St., Ebensburg, Pa.

NELSON, Alexander Howard, civil engring.; b. Chambersburg, Pa., Nov. 19, 1874; s. Thomas McDowell and Anne Esther (Hollinger) N.; A.B., Princeton U., 1895; grad. study, Mass. Inst. Tech., 1895-97; m. Eliza Bartels McCandless, Jan. 25, 1902; children—Margaret McCandless (Mrs. Thomas Selby Lloyd), Alexander Kirkpatrick, Stephen McCandless. Engr. Pittsburgh Bridge Co., 1897-1900; with Am. Bridge Co., 1900-01; constrn. engr., Nelson-Merydith Co., 1901-13; engaged in pvt. practice civil engring. and engr. for Atlantic Co., N.J. since 1913; mem. South Jersey Transit Authority, Atlantic City Planning and Improvement Assn. Pres. bd. dirs. Penn Hall Sch. for Girls, Chambersburg, Pa. Mem. Am. Soc. Civil Engrs., Am. Rd. Builders Assn. Republican. Presbyn. Mason (32°). Clubs: Seaview Golf (Atlantic City); Penn Athletic, Princeton (Philadelphia). Home: 1 S. Bartram Pl. Office: Guarantee Trust Bldg., Atlantic City, N.J.

NELSON, Boyd; v.p. New Amsterdam Casualty Co., also mem. advisory bd., finance com. and exec. com. Home: 211 Goodwood Gardens. Office: 227 St. Paul St., Baltiomre, Md.

NELSON, Byron, professional golfer; b. Ft. Worth, Tex., Feb. 4, 1912. Formerly professional at Ridgewood, N.J., Texarkana (Tex.) Country Club, Glen Garden Country Club, Ft. Worth, Tex.; now professional at Reading (Pa.) Country Club; won N.J. State Open Championship, 1935, Masters' Open Championship, 1937, Belmont Match Play Tournament, 1937; finalist in Professional Golfers' Assn. Championship, 1939; won Nat. Open Championship, 1939, after two play-offs. Mem. U.S. Ryder Cup Team, 1937, 1939. Address: care Reading Country Club, Reading, Pa.

NELSON, Cyril Arthur, mathematician; b. Troy, Kan., Oct. 19, 1893; s. Nicholas L. and

Tolena (Running) N.; A.B., Midland Coll. (now at Fremont, Neb.), 1914; A.M., U. of Kan., 1916; Ph.D., U. of Chicago, 1919; m. Elise Hastings Macy, June 26, 1922; children—Guerdon Holden, Cyril Irwin, Nicholas Macy, Michael Underhill. Instr. mathematics, U. of Kan., 1919-20, Western Reserve U., 1920-21; asso. in mathematics, Johns Hopkins U., 1921-27; asso. prof. mathematics, Rutgers U., since 1927. Fellow A.A.A.S.; mem. Math. Assn. America, Am. Math. Soc., Circolo Matematico di Palermo, Italy, Phi Beta Kappa, Sigma Xi. Lutheran. Home: George St. and Landing Lane, New Brunswick, N.J.

NELSON, Elnathan Kemper, chemist; b. Cincinnati, Nov. 25, 1870; s. Henry Francis and Maria Louisa (Davis) N.; B.S. in chemistry, U. of Illinois, 1894; m. Tuley C. Wetzel, Apr. 29, 1903; children—Elnathan Kemper, Berkeley Everett; m. 2d, Blanche Kennon Parker, of Washington, D.C., November 17, 1931. Served as chief chemist, Swift & Company, Chicago, 1895-1902; with Joslin, Schmidt & Co., chem. engrs., Cincinnati, 1902-03; chemist, Nelson Morris & Co., Chicago, 1903-04; in business on own account, 1904-07; asst. chemist, 1908-12, chief essential oils lab., drug div., 1912-27, sr. chemist div. of food research, 1927—, United States Bureau of Chemistry and Soils. Researches on composition of essential oils and chem. constitution of their constituents, also analytical work on oils and pharm. preparations containing them, and their derivatives, etc. Presbyn. Mem. American Chem. Soc. Contbr. various bulls. and scientific papers. Home: Silver Spring, Md.

NELSON, Frederic Cooke, journalist; b. Windsor, Conn., Nov. 17, 1893; s. Roscoe and Harriet Louise (Cooke) N.; prep. edn., pub. schs., Windsor; A.B., Harvard, 1916; m. Sylvia Isabelle Searby, Nov. 29, 1927; 1 dau., Alice Ellen. Instr. in English, Dartmouth Coll., 1916-17; mem. editorial staff Hartford (Conn.) Times, 1920-29; editorial writer, Baltimore (Md.) Sun since 1929; London corr. for same, 1931-32. Address: The Sun, Baltimore, Md.

NELSON, George Carl Edward, librarian, coll. prof.; b. New York, N.Y., Aug. 3, 1900; s. Charles and Christina (Gustafson) N.; B.S., Coll. City of New York, 1925, M.S., 1926; Ph.D., Columbia U., 1931; library certificate, McGill U., Montreal, Can., 1932; m. Lillian Gleissner, July 5, 1935. Began as asst. N.Y. Pub. Library, 1917; fellow, Coll. of City of New York, 1920, library asst., 1921-25, instr. biol. sciences, 1925-31, asst. librarian, 1928, asso. librarian with rank of asso. prof. since 1934. Mem. Am. Assn. Univ. Profs., Am. Library Assn., Student Aid Assn. (asst. treas. since 1937), Assn. Alumni of City Coll., Phi Delta Kappa, Omega Epsilon Phi. Republican. Congregationalist. Club: City (New York). Author: Introductory Biological Sciences in the Liberal Arts College, 1931; History of the Biological Sciences in the Secondary Schools of the U.S., 1928; Relation of Visual Efficiency and Academic Standing, 1926; Test in Educational Biology, 1930; Thomas Jefferson's Garden Book and His Contributions to Botany, 1939; numerous articles on biology teaching. Compiler and editor Omega Epsilon Phi Directory. Home: 401 Wearimus Rd., Ridgewood, N.J. Office: College of City of New York, New York, N.Y.

NELSON, George Merle, pub. utility pres.; b. Crisfield, Md., Dec. 20, 1897; s. William Diggs and Anna Belle N.; B.S. in E.E., U. of Del., Newark, Del., 1920; m. Elsie Hearne, Dec. 27, 1924. Engr. electric signal dept. Pa. R.R., Altoona, Pa., 1920-21; draftsman design dept. H. T. Paiste Co., Phila., Pa., 1922-23; engr. constrn. dept. American Rys. Co., Huntington, W.Va., 1923-24; engr. in sta. constrn. dept. Phila. Electric Co., Phila., Pa., 1924-25; asst. supt. operations, Eastern Shore Pub. Service Co., Salisbury, Md., 1925-35, supt. operations, 1935-39, pres. since 1938; vice-pres. and dir. Bank of Delmar, Del., since 1930. Pres. bd. trustees Delmar, Del., High Sch. Mem. Theta Chi, Tau Beta Pi., Am. Legion. Republican. Mem. M.E. Ch. Mason. Clubs: Lions (Delmar). Home: 307 Grove St., Delmar, Del. Office: 114 N. Division St., Salisbury, Md.

NELSON, Harley Arthur, research chemist; b. Herington, Kan., Aug. 1, 1890; s. Sven August and Tilinika (Larson) N.; student Friends' Univ., Wichita, Kan., 1912-13; A.B., McPherson (Kan.) Coll., 1915; A.B., U. of Kan., 1916, A.M., 1917; m. Opal Remspear, Dec. 31, 1919; children—Pamela Doris, Selma Elizabeth, Paul Harley. Asst. chemist U.S. Bureau of Standards, Washington, D.C., 1917-19; with the technical dept. of N.J. Zinc Co., Palmerton, Pa., since 1919, successively chief of paint sect. of research div., chief of pigment research div., chief of paint and ceramic research div. and since 1937 asst. to gen. mgr. of tech. dept. Mem. Bd. of Pub. Sch. Dirs., Palmerton, since 1935. Fellow Am. Inst. Chemists; mem. Am. Chem. Soc. (chmn. Lehigh Valley Sect., 1930; chmn. paint and varnish div., 1931), Am. Soc. for Testing Materials (chmn. sub-com. on accelerated tests; mem. advisory com. D-1 on paint materials), Alpha Chi Sigma. Democrat. Lutheran. Clubs: Chemists (New York); Blue Ridge Country (Palmerton, Pa.). Address: Palmerton, Pa.

NELSON, J. Arthur, insurance pres.; b. Baltimore Co., Md., Jan. 27, 1876; s. Benjamin L. and Alice O'N. (Boyd) N.; grad. McDonogh Sch., Baltimore Co., 1892; m. Katie Leon Triplett, Oct. 7, 1895; children—Boyd, Arthur L., Alice T., Margaret E. Began as stenographer, 1892; pres. New Amsterdam Casualty Co. since 1914; pres. Am. Indemnity Co.; dir. U.S. Casualty Co. Pres. Assn. of Casualty and Surety Execs.; trustee McDonogh Sch. Democrat. Mason (Shriner), Moose. Clubs: Maryland, Press, Baltimore Country. Home: 211 Goodwood Gardens, Roland Park. Office: 227 St. Paul St., Baltimore, Md.

NELSON, James Augustus, hydraulic engr.; b. Bridgeport, Conn., Oct. 11, 1868; s. James Hugh and Sarah Emma (Barr) N.; Ph.B., Sheffield Scientific School (Yale University), 1888; married, 1st, Susan V. Diacont, 2d, Effie Callison, 3d, Ada P. Orndorff. Successively general superintendent of William R. Trigg Company, Richmond, Va., asst. supt., Fore River Shipbuilding Co., Quincy, Mass., v.p. and chief engr. East Jersey Pipe Co., New York, v.p. T. A. Gillispie Co., New York, eastern rep. Union Iron Works, San Francisco, asst. mgr. Hog Island Ship Yard, Phila., partner Nelson, Lodge & Snyder, Phila., hydraulic engr. Riter Conley Co., Pittsburgh, Pa., now hydraulic engr. Bethlehem (Pa.) Steel Co. Mem. Am. Soc. C.E., Am. Water Works Assn., Yale Engring. Soc., Nat. Soc. of Professional Engrs. Club: Engineers (New York). Home: 701 High St., Bethlehem, Pa.; and 615 N. Tremain St., Mt. Dora, Fla. Office: Bethlehem Steel Co., Bethlehem, Pa.

NELSON, James Wharton, surgeon; b. Baltimore, Md., May 21, 1896; s. Joseph Thomas and Mary Margaret (Ireland) N.; A.B., St. John's Coll., Annapolis, Md., 1918; M.D., U. of Md. Med. Sch., Baltimore, 1925; m. Beatrice Mules, June 17, 1922; children—Betty Geneva, Joan. Interne South Baltimore Gen. Hosp. and Mercy Hosp., Baltimore, 1924-27; instr. surgery and oncology, U. of Md. Med. Sch., 1932-39; adjunct surgeon South Baltimore Gen. Hosp. since 1934; asst. surgeon Mercy Hosp. since 1932; dir. Laurence Buck Tumor Clinic, South Baltimore Gen. Hosp. since 1936. Served as asst. comdt. St. John's Coll., 1917-18; Field Arty., U.S.A., 1918-19; with A.E.F. in France. Fellow Am. Coll. Surgeons; mem. Am. Med. Assn., Baltimore City Med. Soc., U. of Md. Oncology Soc., Chirurg. and Med. Acad. of Science, Phi Sigma Kappa, Nu Sigma Nu. Democrat. Mason. Clubs: Maryland Yacht (fleet surgeon, Baltimore); Gibson Island (Gibson Island, Md.). Home: 10 Sulphur Spring Rd., Arbutus. Office: 1120 St. Paul St., Baltimore, Md.

NELSON, John Brockway, bacteriologist; b. Newburyport, Mass., Dec. 9, 1894; s. William Thomas and Sarah (Piper) N.; B.S., Mass. State Coll., Amherst, Mass., 1917; student Harvard-Mass. Inst. Tech. Sch. of Pub. Health, 1917-18, A.M., Harvard U., 1923; Ph.D., U. of Mo., Columbia, Mo., 1924; m. Mary Marshall Graves, Oct. 5, 1925; children—John Brockway, Marshall Graves. Bacteriologist Ky. State Health Lab., U. of Ky., Lexington, 1919-22, dept. of microbiology, Mass. State Coll., Amherst, 1924, dept. animal and plant pathology, Rockefeller Inst., Princeton, N.J., since 1925. Served with U.S. Army Med. Dept., 1918-19. Fellow A.A.A.S.; mem. Am. Soc. Exptl. Biology, Sigma Xi. Address: Rockefeller Institute, Princeton, N.J.

NELSON, John Emil, clergyman; b. Valinge, Sweden, Dec. 2, 1884; s. Nels Anton Bertilson and Amalia Josefina (Kind) N.; came to U.S., 1909, naturalized, 1927; A.B., Upsala Coll., East Orange, N.J., 1919; B.D., Augustana Theol. Sem., Rock Island, Ill., 1922; Ed.M., U. of Pittsburgh, 1937; m. Lillie Dorothy Engdahl, June 24, 1922; children—Dorothy Elaine, Byron Emil, David Paul. Earned his way through various schs. as clk., teacher, pastor's asst. etc., 1903-22; ordained to ministry Luth. Ch., 1922; pastor, Waltham, Mass., 1922-30; pastor, Gustavus Adolphus Ch., Pittsburgh, Pa., since 1930. Served in Swedish Army, 1905-07. Park Commr., City of Waltham, Mass., 1929-30. Mem. De Nio, Vitterhetssällskapet, Theta Epsilon. Republican. Lutheran. Contbr. to various Swedish and Am. papers and mags. Home: 257 S. Evaline St., Pittsburgh, Pa.

NELSON, John Evon, treas. Gulf Oil Corpn.; b. at Helensburg, Scotland, August 30, 1879; s. Ambrose and Elizabeth (Forsythe) N.; came to U.S. with parents, 1880; prep. edn., Park Inst., Pittsburgh, 1894-97; A.B., Westminster College, Pa., 1900; m. Margaret N. Dodds, Sept. 6, 1905; children—Wenley Dodds, John Oliver, Douglas Evon, Margaret Elisabeth. Clk. Keystone Nat. Bank, Pittsburgh, 1900-02; sec. to Andrew W. Mellon, 1902-08; treas. Gulf Oil Corpn. and its subsidiaries since 1908; treas. and dir. Gulf Refining Co., Mexican Gulf Oil Co., Venezuela Gulf Oil Co., Gulf Exploration Co., Am. Internat. Fuel & Petroleum Co.; treas. Lubricating and Fuel Oils, Ltd. (London), Gulf Research and Development Co., Western Gulf Oil Co.; dir. Pittsburgh Parking Garages, Belgian Gulf Oil Company (Antwerp), Société Anonyme d'Armement d'Industrie et de Commerce, Danish Am. Prospecting Co. (treas.). Trustee Westminster Coll. (exec. com.), Ellis Sch., Inc., Pittsburgh; dir., sec. Art Soc. of Pittsburgh; dir. and mem. exec. com. Children's Hosp., Pittsburgh. Mem. Kappa Phi Lambda. Republican. Presbyn. Mason. Clubs: Pittsburgh, Duquesne, University, Longue Vue, Pittsburgh Athletic; Nassau (Princeton, N.J.); Rolling Rock Club. Home: 201 N. Murtland Av. Office: Gulf Bldg., Pittsburgh, Pa.

NELSON, John Raymond, clergyman; b. Dinwiddie Co., Va., May 31, 1899; s. Edward Rosser and Ellen (Scott) N.; A.B., Wake Forest Coll., Wake Forest, N.C., 1922; Th.M., Southern Bapt. Theol. Sem., Louisville, Ky., 1925, Ph.D., 1928; m. Elizabeth Turnley, Feb. 9, 1926; children—John Raymond, Jr., Thomas Stewart (dec.). Employed as clk. ry. ticket office, Lynchburg, Va., 1915; instr. English, Wake Forest Coll., Wake Forest, N.C., 1921-22; instr. English, Male High Sch., Louisville, Ky., 1925-27; fellow in N.T. Interpretation (Greek), Southern Bapt. Theol. Sem., Louisville, Ky., 1927-28; ordained to ministry Bapt. Ch., 1925; pastor, Alexandria, Ky., 1928, Birmingham, Ala., 1928-29; asst. pastor and ednl. dir., First and Temple Bapt. Chs., Miami, Fla., 1929-31; pastor, Druid Park Bapt. Ch., Baltimore, Md., 1932-34, Alameda Bapt. Ch., Baltimore, 1933-38; pastor, First Bapt. Ch., Bethesda, Md., since 1938. Served in S.A.T.C., 1918. Democrat. Baptist. Mason. Home: 4910 Moorland Lane, Bethesda, Md.

NELSON, Oscar, carbon black mfr.; b. Hvena, Sweden, Mar. 2, 1879; s. Eric and Sophia (Carlsson) Nilsson; ed. pub. schs., Sweden; m. Harriet Engstrom, Dec. 4, 1918; children—John Oscar, Anna Marie, Thomas Arthur, Frederik Eric. Pres. and gen. mgr. United Carbon Co. since 1925; pres. United Gas Co., United Producing Co., Reliance Carbon Co., Tex. Carbon Industries, Microid Process, Inc., Westoak Gasoline Co., Okla. Salt Industries; vice-pres. Eastern Carbon Black Co., Kosmos Carbon Co.; dir. Miss. River Fuel Corpn. Republican. Lutheran. Clubs: Edgewood Country, Kanawha Country. Home:

1557 Quarrier St. Office: Union Bldg., Charleston, W.Va.

NELSON, Robert Franklin, gen. mgr. paper mill; b. Moultrie, Ga., Mar. 13, 1897; s. G. S. and Eugenia Roberta (Greene) N.; grad. Moultrie High Sch., 1914; student U. of Ga., Athens, Ga., 1914-15; grad. U.S. Naval Acad., 1918; m. Sylvia Anthony, Feb. 19, 1921; children—Robert Franklin, Joan. Commd. ensign, U.S. Navy, 1918; resigned as lt. j.g., 1922; sales engr. Johns Manville Co., New York and Phila., 1922-25; chief engr. Glassine Paper Co., mfrs. transparent paper and specialties, West Conshocken, Pa., 1925-27, supt., 1927-30, vice-pres., gen. mgr. and dir. since 1930; dir. Milprint, Inc. Dir. Glassine Greaseproof Mfg. Assn. Mem. Kappa Sigma. Republican. Clubs: Merion Cricket (Haverford, Pa.); Army and Navy (Washington, D.C.); Pylon (flying), Norristown, Pa. Home: Bryn Mawr, Pa. Office: Glassine Paper Co., West Conshocken, Pa.

NELSON, William Linton, investment trust exec.; b. Phila., Pa., Jan. 20, 1900; s. William Robert and Ella Blanche (Johnson) N.; ed. U. of Pa., 1922-26; m. Grace E. Mehorter Solly, Feb. 8, 1934. Asso. with Fidelity-Philadelphia Trust Co. in various capacities, 1922-29; filled various exec. offices with Investment Corpn. of Phila. since 1929, now vice-pres., dir. and mem. exec. com.; dir. and vice-pres. W. S. Wasserman Co.; organized Delaware Fund, Inc., an investment trust, 1938 and now dir., vice-pres. and mem. exec. com. Served as student aviator, U.S.N.R., 1917-19, overseas ten mos. Now lt. U.S.N.R. Mem. Am. Statis. Assn. Mem. U.S. Nat. Rowing Championship quadruple scull crew, 1922, U.S. Nat. Championship doubles crew, 1924-26; winner Canadian Assn. Single Rowing Championship, 1926. Republican. Presbyn. Clubs: Art Alliance, Country (Philadelphia). Contbr. papers on econ. subjects. Home: 2031 Locust St. Office: 225 S. 15th St., Philadelphia, Pa.

NELSON, Mrs. William S. (Mary Jane Andresen Nelson), musician, concert mgr.; b. New York, N.Y., Jan. 4, 1863; d. John and Henrietta (Schlesinger) Andresen; father descendant of Vikings; mother descendant of Coxe's and Weyman's (Irish and English ancestry) who came to N.Y. about 1640; student Mrs. Mary R. Griffitt's private school, New York, 1871-1880; m. William S. Nelson, Feb. 26, 1889 (died 1896); 1 son, William Ripley. Began as singer in Presbyn. Ch., Lakewood, N.J., 1896; also sang in concerts and musicals; accompanist in studio of Arthur D. Woodruff, New York and East Orange, N.J., 1897-1901, playing for his choral socs.; established studio for teaching of singing, 1 E. 40th St., New York, 1900, Orange, N.J., 1900; taught singing in Phila. until 1912; mgr. for many concerts for orchestras and for such artists as Bispham, Louise Homer, Gabrilowitsch (also as accompanist), Florence Mulford, Frances Rogers, Edith Chapman Gould and many others; mgr. many concerts; became head of ednl. dept. Griffith Piano Co., 1924; Mrs. Wm. S. Nelson's Tuesday Morning Musicales, East Orange, since 1927, presenting many noted musicians; lecturer on music. Sec. Community Concerts of the Oranges. Charter mem. Concert Mgrs. Assn. Republican. Christian Scientist. Home: 57 W. 58th St., New York, N.Y. Office: care Mrs. John Kraus, 268 S. Centre St., Orange, N.J.

NEPRASH, Jerry Alvin, prof. of sociology; b. Cedar Rapids, Iowa, July 1, 1904; s. Daniel Joseph and Frances (Fajman) N.; grad. Cedar Rapids (Ia.) High Sch., 1921; A.B., Coe Coll., Cedar Rapids, Ia., 1925; A.M., Columbia, 1926, fellow in sociology, 1925-28, Ph.D., 1932; m. Dorothy Ready, Sept. 7, 1929. Lecturer in sociology, Columbia Univ. Extension, 1927-28; with Franklin and Marshall Coll. since 1928, as asst. prof. of sociology, 1928-32, asso. prof., 1933-36, prof. since 1937; prof. of sociology, Coe Coll., summers 1929, 34. Chmn. Social Planning Com. of Lancaster Welfare Fed. since 1935, mem. exec. com. and budget com. since 1936. Mem. Am. Sociol. Soc., Am. Statis. Assn., Eastern Sociol. Conf., Am. Assn. Univ. Profs., Chi Phi, Phi Kappa Phi, Pi Gamma Mu.

Mem. Soc. of Friends. Mem. Western Bohemian Fraternal Assn. Club: Torch (Lancaster). Author: Brookhart Campaigns in Iowa, 1920-26 (1932). Contbr. papers at Annual meeting of professional socs.; also articles on methods of research in psychological aspects of society to jours. Home: 914 Virginia Av., Lancaster, Pa.

NESBITT, Frank Watterson, lawyer; b. Wheeling, W.Va., April 4, 1870; s. Thomas Wilson and Rebecca (Watterson) N.; Ph.B., Wooster (O.) Coll., 1892; LL.B., U. of Va., 1895; m. Della M. Goodwin, Oct. 20, 1897; 1 son, Russell Goodwin. City solicitor, Wheeling, 1897-1900; pros. atty. Ohio County, W.Va., 1901-04; judge 1st Jud. Circuit of W.Va., 1905-13; sr. mem. firm Nesbitt & Nesbitt; division counsel of B.& O. R.R. since 1915; solicitor of 14th Dist. of Pa. R.R. System. Mem. Am. and W.Va. bar assns. Republican. Methodist. Mason, Elk. Clubs: Ft. Henry, Wheeling Country. Home: McLure Hotel. Office: Riley Law Bldg., Wheeling, W.Va.

NESBITT, Russell Goodwin, lawyer; b. Wheeling, W.Va., Aug. 11, 1898; s. Frank Watterson and Della (Goodwin) N.; A.B., Washington & Lee Univ., Lexington, Va., 1920; student Harvard U. Law Sch., 1920-23; m. Margaret Gerwig, Oct. 9, 1926; 1 son, William Frank. Admitted to W.Va. bar, 1923 and since engaged in gen. practice of law at Wheeling; mem. firm Nesbitt & Nesbitt since 1931; served as referee in bankruptcy, 1925-31. Served as 2d lt. F.A., U.S.A., 1918; now capt. F.A. Res. Pres. Young Rep. League of W.Va., 1938-40. Mem. Am. Bar Assn., W.Va. State and Ohio Co. bar assns., Kappa Sigma. Republican. Mem. M.E. Ch. Elk. Clubs: Fort Henry, Wheeling Country (Wheeling); Army and Navy Country (Washington, D.C.). Home: 7 Rockledge Rd., Oakmont, Wheeling. Office: Riley Law Bldg., Wheeling, W.Va.

NETTING, M(orris) Graham, herpetologist; b. Wilkinsburg, Pa., Oct. 3, 1904; s. Morris G(raham) and Martha (Scoggan) N.; B.S., U. of Pittsburgh, 1926; A.M., U. of Mich., 1929; m. Jane Roberta Smith, July 24, 1930; children—Anthony Graham, Jane Lucinda. Became lecturer on conservation for Pa. Game Commn., 1925, serving until 1928; asst. in herpetology, Carnegie Museum, Pittsburgh, 1926-28, asst. curator of herpetology, 1928-32, curator of herpetology since 1932; leader Carnegie Museum Venezuelan Expdn., 1929-30; lecturer in biology and geography, U. of Pittsburgh, since 1936. Fellow A.A.A.S.; mem. Am. Soc. Ichthyologists and Herpetologists (sec. since 1931), Am. Soc. Mammalogists, Biol. Photographic Soc., Biol. Soc. of Washington, Ecol. Soc. America, Pa. Acad. Science, W.Va. Acad. Science, W. Va. Biol. Survey, Omega Delta, Phi Sigma, Sigma Xi. Republican. Protestant. Clubs: Agora, Faculty (Pittsburgh). Contbr. many articles on herpetology and geog. distribution of animals to scientific jours. Has collected reptiles throughout the U.S., also in Panama, Trinidad, Venezuela and West Indies. Home: 5920 Elwood St. Office: Carnegie Museum, Pittsburgh, Pa.

NETTLETON, Lewis Lomax, geophysicist; b. Nampa, Ida., June 24, 1896; s. Edwin Grosvenor and Eliza (Lomax) N.; B.S., U. of Ida., 1918; M.S., U. of Wis., 1921, Ph.D., 1923; m. Marion Moore, June 24, 1924; 1 son, David Lomax. Employed as research physicist, Union Switch & Signal Co., Swissvale, Pa., 1923-28; geophysicist, Gulf Oil Corpn. since 1928; advisory prof. physics, U. of Pittsburgh. Served in Field Signal Batln., U.S.A., 1918-19. Mem. A.A.A.S., Am. Phys. Soc., Am. Assn. Petroleum Geologists, Soc. of Exploration Geophysicists, Sigma Xi, Gamma Alpha. Republican. Episcopalian. Home: 1025 Washington Av., Oakmont, Pa. Office: P.O. Box 2038, Pittsburgh, Pa.

NEUBAUER, Frank Nicholas, educator; b. College Point, N.Y., June 5, 1890; s. Frank and Elizabeth (Schwarz) N.; grad. Flushing (N.Y.) High Sch., 1909; A.B., Colgate U., Hamilton, N.Y., 1913, hon. D. Sc., 1936; A.M., New York U., 1938; m. Madeleine Anthon Noonan, Dec. 26, 1916; children—Madeleine (deceased), Louise Lott. Prin. Union Sch., Bolton Landing, N.Y., 1916-18; teacher of Latin, Westfield (N.J.) High Sch., 1918-19; prin. elementary schools, Westfield, N.J., 1919-21; prin. Sr. High Sch., Westfield, since 1921; Mem. N.E.A., Council of Edn. of N.J., Theta Chi, Phi Beta Kappa, Phi Delta Kappa. Republican. Lutheran. Mason. Home: 12 Stoneleigh Park. Office: 300 Elm St., Westfield, N.J.

NEUENSCHWANDER, Paul Wells, oil production; b. Sistersville, W.Va., Dec. 13, 1899; s. William J. and Maud (Thistle) N.; student Swarthmore Coll., Swarthmore, Pa., 1917-18; B.S. in Petroleum Engring., U. of Pittsburgh, 1922; m. Pauline Drew, Apr. 2, 1924; children—Drew, Jane. Employed in engring. dept. Petroleum Exploration, Sistersville, W.Va., 1922-23; with engring. dept. W.Va. State Rd. Commn., 1923-24; with producing dept., Petroleum Exploration, 1925-30, treas. Petroleum Exploration and Wiser Oil Co., Sistersville, W. Va. since 1930, dir. since 1935; treas. and dir. Southern Petroleum Exploration, Petroleum Purchasing Co., Sistersville, W.Va.; vice-pres. and director First Tyler Bank & Trust Company, Sistersville, W.Va. Served as Republican presdl. elector W.Va., 1932; chmn. Tyler Co. Rep. Exec. Com., 1938-39. Mem. Am. Petroleum Inst., Sigma Gamma Epsilon, Phi Kappa Psi. Republican. Presbyn. Mason. Clubs: Country (Sistersville); Duquesne (Pittsburgh). Home: "Mapledge," Chelsea St. Office: Trico Bldg., Sistersville, W.Va.

NEULEN, Leon Nelson, supt. schools; b. Northwood, Ia., Nov. 16, 1894; s. John Nelson and Mary (Dale) N.; A.B., St. Olaf Coll., 1916; M.A., Columbia University, 1922, Ph.D., 1931; hon. Pd.D., Temple U., 1937; m. Helen Snyder Kugler, Dec. 18, 1936; children—Robert Nelson, (step-children) Helen, Cordelia, and George Kugler. Principal high sch., Tyler, Minn., 1916-17, Souris, N.D., 1917-18, Oakabena, Minn., 1918-20, Ravinia, S.D., 1920-22; supervisor of teachers, Champaign, Ill., 1926-27; asst. supt. schs., Champaign, 1927-28, supt., 1928-30; supt. schs., Camden, N.J., since 1931. Mem. Nat. Bd. of Review for Motion Pictures, N.Y. City, 1923, N.J. Council of Edn. since 1931, Camden County Exec. Bd. Boy Scouts of America since 1934, Schoolmen's Week Com. of U. of Pa. 1934, 35, 39; mem. exec. com. Am. Red Cross of Camden (chmn. roll call drive, 1934, 35, 36); chmn. Camden Co. Chapter Am. Red Cross since Jan. 1937; dir. Camden Co., Tuberculosis Assn., 1936, Camden Co. Council P.T.A., 1936; mem. advisory council Biblical Inst. of South Jersey, 1936; mem. advisory bd. N.J. Citizens Com. for Prevention of Crime, 1936, 37; chmn. Advanced Sch. Alumni Com. of N.J., 1937; chmn. conf. com. 10th Annual Conf. Secondary Education, Temple U. Mem. Teachers Coll. Alumni (Columbia U.) for Phila. area (pres. 1933), N.J. State Teachers Assn. (v.p. 1933-34, pres. 1935-36 and 1936-37), N.E.A. (life; resolutions com. Dept. of Superintendence, 1937, also chmn. com. on financing ednl. research; mem. Com. to Cooperate with Natl. Assn. of Teachers in Colored Schs., 1937-38; mem. advisory com. of Legislative Commns. 1938-39; advisory com. to cooperate with Am. Teachers Assn., 1938-39), Camden Chamber Commerce, Phi Delta Kappa. Awarded Progressive Edn. scholarship, Columbia, 1922, foreign research fellowship, Internat. Inst., 1925. Lutheran, Mason. Clubs: Rotary of Camden (pres. 1934-35); Tawse (New York). Author: Problem Solving in Arithmetic, 1931. Contbr. to ednl. mags. Home: 30 S. Evergreen Av., Woodbury, N.J. Office: City Hall, Camden, N.J.

NEUMAN, Abraham Aaron, rabbi and coll. prof.; b. Austria, Sept. 23, 1890; s. Max and Rachel (Rose) N.; brought to U.S., 1899, and naturalized citizen, 1906; B.S., Columbia U., 1909, A.M., same, 1912; Rabbi, Jewish Theol. Sem. of America, 1912, H.L.D., same, 1914; m. Gladys Reed, Apr. 30, 1919 (divorced); 1 son, Cyrus Adler. Rabbi, Cong. Bnai Jeshurum, Phila., 1917-18, 1919-27; rabbi, Cong. Mikveh Israel, second oldest cong. in America, Phila. since 1927; instr. history, Dropsie Coll., Phila. 1913-23, asso. prof., 1923-34, prof.

since 1934; sec. faculty Dropsie Coll. Trustee and v.p. bd. overseers, Gratz Coll. Mem. state advisory bd. Federal Writers Project of Pa. Mem. Bd. Jewish Ministers of Phila. (past pres.), Rabbinical Assembly, United Synagogue of America (council), Jewish Publication Soc. of America (mem. publ. com.), World Ct. Proponents (Phila. Com.), Am. Jewish Hist. Soc. (recording sec.), Am. Hist. Soc., Am. Oriental Soc., Pa. Hist. Soc., Committee of One Hundred. Jewish religion. Clubs: Round Table, Philmont Country. Home: 2319 N, Park Av., Philadelphia, Pa.

NEUSCHELER, Albert W(illiam), realtor; b. Newark, N.J., Apr. 24, 1894; s. John and Katherine (Kern) N.; ed. public schools and business coll., Newark; unmarried. Clerk in real estate and insurance office, Newark, N.J., 1911-17; business in his own name for real estate, ins., property management and appraisals, Newark, since 1919; dir. Mutual, Enterprise, Downtown, Adamant, Twelfth Ward, Seventh Ward Bldg. and Loan Assns.; pres. Adam Poh, Inc. Served in Corps of Engrs., U.S. Army, during World War; disch. as sergt. Vice-pres. Newark Real Estate Bd.; mem. bd. dirs. Citizens Housing Council; mem. advisory bd. Newark Planning Commn. Mem. Ironbound Mfrs. Assn., Am. Legion, Y.M.C.A. Mem. Reformed Ch. Mason. Club: Crestmont Golf. Home: 784 High St. Office: 40 Clinton St., Newark, N.J.

NEVILLE, Harvey Alexander, prof. chemistry; b. Millwood, Va., Feb. 18, 1898; s. Harvey Alexander and Mary Moffat (Drake) N.; A.B., Randolph-Macon Coll., 1918; M.A., Princeton U., 19—, Ph.D., 1921; m. Ilda Langdon, Dec. 29, 1923; children—Robert Geoffrey, Anthony Edward, Mary Alice. Asst. in chemistry, Princeton U., 1918-21; instr. chemistry, U. of Ill., 1921-24, asso. in chemistry, 1924-27; asst. prof. chemistry, Lehigh U., 1927-30, asso. prof. 1930-38, prof. chemistry and head dept. of chemistry and chem. engring., since 1938. Mem. A.A.A.S., Am. Chem. Soc., Am. Assn. Textile Chemists and Colorists, Phi Lambda Upsilon, Alpha Chi Sigma, Sigma Xi, Phi Beta Kappa, Tau Beta Pi. Democrat. Home: R.D. 1, Bethlehem, Pa.

NEVIN, David Williamson, lawyer; b. Franklin Co., Pa., Sept. 9, 1853; s. Samuel Williamson and Harriet Macomb (Balch) N.; ed. Tuscarora Acad., Chambersburg Acad.; A.B., Lafayette Coll., 1875, A.M., 1878; m. Lillian G. Patterson, June 10, 1879; children—John Denison (maj. U.S.M.C., retired), Samuel Williamson (capt. Red Cross, retired), David Burrowes. Admitted to Pa. bar, 1877, and since engaged in gen. practice of law at Easton; sec. and treas. Nevin Land Co., Easton & South Easton Suspension Bridge Co., Lehigh Bridge Co., Easton Improvement Assn., Northampton Improvement Assn.; sec. and treas. Pa. Motor Co. Electric Ry., 1887-92, Weygadt Mountain Electric Ry., 1891-1914. Served in Selective Service of U.S., 1917. Town clk., Easton, Pa., 1879-82; sec. Bd. of Health, 1879-85; pres. Easton Common Council, 1887, Council Common, 1893-97, Select Council, 1905-09; Mayor, City of Easton, 1911-20. Pres. Easton Bd. Trade, 1923. Dir. Easton Nat. Bank, 1903-17, vice-pres., 1917. Mem. Am., Pa. State, and Northampton Co. bar assns., Sigma Chi (since 1870). Republican. Presbyn. Home: 102 Wayne Av., Easton, Pa.

NEVIN, Gordon Balch, organist, composer; b. Easton, Pa., May 19, 1892; s. George Balch and Lillias Clara (Dean) N.; studied piano under Charles Maddock (Easton), organ under J. Warren Andrews (New York), theory under J. Fred Wolle (Bethlehem, Pa.); m. Jessie Harrie Young, June 30, 1915; children—Jean Lillias, Ruth Elizabeth. Organist and teacher, Easton, Pa., 1909-14, Johnstown, 1914-15; organist, Cleveland, O., and teacher at Hiram Coll., 1915-17; musical arranger for Ernest M. Skinner Co., Boston, 1917-18; organist and teacher at Greensburg, Pa., 1918-20, at Johnstown, Pa., 1920-32; professor organ and composition, Westminster Coll., New Wilmington, since 1932. Republican. Presbyterian. Mason. Author: Primer of Organ Registration, 1919; Swell Pedal Technique, 1921; First Lessons at the Organ, 1923.

Composer of a sonata, 3 suites and about 20 single numbers for the organ, 20 songs, 10 part songs (secular); anthems, also an operetta, "Following Foster's Footsteps," "The Harp and Chimes in Organ Playing," (pedagogical work) 1938; etc. Has given over 175 recitals in Eastern cities. Home: New Wilmington, Pa.

NEVIN, William Latta, capitalist; A.B., U. of Pa., 1879, LL.B., 1880; m. Mary G. Hall; 1 dau., Francis H. Apptd. one of executors of Rodman Wanamaker's Estate; formerly pres. John Wanamaker, Philadelphia, and John Wanamaker, New York (dept. stores); v.p., trustee Wanamaker Inst. of Industries; and officer or dir. various other corpns. Mem. Am. Bar Assn. Clubs: University, Merion Cricket, Philadelphia Country. Home: 329 S. 16th St. Office: 13th and Market Sts., Philadelphia, Pa.*

NEW, Archey Cameron, lawyer; b. Baltimore, Md., Feb. 3, 1890; s. Lewis W. and Emma Frances (Cameron) N.; student Baltimore City Coll., 1903-07; LL.B., U. of Md. Law Sch., Baltimore, Md., 1910; m. Evelyn J. Gibbons, Feb. 11, 1918; children—Evelyn Jeanne, Robert Cameron. Employed as newspaper reporter and real estate broker, 1910-11; admitted to Md. bar, 1911 and since engaged in gen. practice of law at Baltimore. Republican. Episcopalian. Mason, Tall Cedars of Lebanon (past nat. head). Author and composer, book and music, two mus. comedies, "The Medicine Man" (prod. 1931) and "Cremona" (prod. 1934). Contbr. hundreds of short stories to mags. and newspapers. Home: 5308 Hamlet Av. Office: 2 E. Lexington St., Baltimore, Md.

NEWBURGER, Frank L., Jr., investments, brokerage; b. Phila., Pa., Nov. 26, 1908; s. Frank L. and Helen (Langfeld) N.; ed. Cornell U., 1925-29; unmarried. Entered business as investment broker, 1929; mem. firm Newburger, Loeb & Co., investment brokers and mem. Phila. Stock Exchange, Phila., Pa., since 1931. Dir. Jewish Hosp. of Phila., Neighborhood Center. Mem. Zeta Beta Tau. Jewish religion. Clubs: Philmont Country (dir.), Locust, Bond (Philadelphia); Spring Brook Hunt of Huntingdon Valley (dir.). Home: Elkins Park. Office: 1419 Walnut St., Philadelphia, Pa.

NEWBURY, Frank Davies, economist; b. Brooklyn, N.Y., June 9, 1880; s. Henry Fitch and Anna Eliza (McAllister) N.; M.E., Cornell U., 1901; m. Mary Grace Lincoln, Aug. 28, 1907; children—Constance Lincoln, Paul Lincoln, Marshall McAllister (dec.). With Westinghouse Electric & Mfg. Co. since 1901, beginning as apprentice, design engr., 1903-10, asst. div. engr., power div., 1910, division engr., 1911-20, mgr. power engring. dept., 1920-30, gen. mgr. machinery engring., 1930-35, asst. to v.p., 1935-37, economist since 1937, mgr. new products div. since 1938. Republican. Protestant. Club: Englewood Country. Home: 577 Briar Cliff Road, Pittsburgh, Pa. Office: Westinghouse Electric & Mfg. Co., East Pittsburgh, Pa.

NEWCOMB, Bryant B., retired pub.; b. Vineland, N.J., Aug. 23, 1867; s. Franklin H. and Annie L. Loomis; student Pub. Schs., Long Branch, N.J., 1872-85; m. Selena Warwick, May 12, 1887 (died 1897); children—Franklin T., Selena W. (Mrs. James P. Haughey), Bryant B.; m. 2d, Viola May Warwick, Feb. 5, 1903 (died 1936); children—William H., Thomas W. Bookkeeper, cashier and confidential man, Bazley & Burns, contractors, Long Branch, N.J., 1885-1902; became co. commr., Monmouth Co. (N.J.) Bd. of Chosen Freeholders, 1917, later dir. and chmn.; gen. mgr. Monmouth Co. Publishing Co., pubs. of Long Branch Daily Record, Long Branch, N.J., 1917-37; pres. and dir. Long Branch (N.J.) Bldg. & Loan Assn.; dir. Allenhurst (N.J.) Nat. Bank & Trust Co. Republican. Episcopalian (sr. warden and treas. St. James Episcopal Ch., Long Branch, N.J.). Mason (32°; pres. Masonic Temple Assn.; Royal Arch, Shriner), Elk, Odd Fellow, Tall Cedars of Lebanon. Clubs: Round Table, Long Branch Republican (Long Branch, N.J.). Address: 292 Broadway, Long Branch, N.J.

NEWCOMB, James Francis, clergyman, educator; b. Kingston, Mass., Feb. 24, 1885; s.

of Marcello and Maria Alice (Callahan) N.; grad. Boston Latin High Sch., 1903; B.L., St. Charles Coll., Ellicott City, Md., 1904; A.B., St. Mary's Sem., Baltimore, 1905; theol. course, St. Mary's Sem., Belmont, N.C.; D.C.L., Rome, May 19, 1922. Ordained priest R.C. Ch., 1908; chaplain, and teacher Latin, Greek, and ancient and medieval history, 1908-13, headmaster, 1917-23, Carlton Acad., Summit, N.J.; apptd. by Pope Pius XI, prothonotary apostolic May 23, 1923; dir. Catholic students, U. of W.Va., 1923-26; dir. of music, St. Joseph's Cathedral, Wheeling, 1926-30; rector St. Joseph's Ch., Huntington, W.Va., since Nov. 1930. Supt. parish schs., Diocese of Wheeling. Mem. Headmasters' Assn., N.J. Classical Assn., S.R., N.Y. Soc. Colonial Wars (chaplain S.R. of N.J., 1924-25). Republican. K.C. Translator from French of Abbe Laplace's "Vie de la Mere Marie de Jesus," pub. under title of "Immolation," 1926, and Abbe Grimaud's "Ma Messe," 1928; from Italian of "Un Angelo di Carmelo," "Lily of Italy—St. Theresa Margaret Redi"; from French of Abbe Grimaud's Lui et Nous; Un Seul Christ (One Only Christ), 1939. Address: 1304 6th Av., Huntington, W.Va.

NEWCOMB, Thomas Higgs, clergyman; b. Welda, Kan., Sept. 21, 1890; s. William and Martha Alice (Craig) N.; grad. Garnett (Kan.) High Sch., 1910; A.B., Monmouth (Ill.) Coll., 1916, D.D., 1933; B.D., Pittsburgh-Xenia Theol. Sem., Pittsburgh, 1920; m. Naomi Ellora Finley, Dec. 8, 1922; children—Margaret Jane, Thomas Finley. Teacher grade school, Garnett, Kan., 1910-12; prin. Carlock Twp. High Sch., Carlock, Ill., 1916-17; ordained to ministry United Presbyn. Ch., 1920, pastor U.P. Ch., Chester, W.Va., 1920-25, First U.P. Ch., Buffalo, N.Y., 1925-32; pastor Eighth U.P. Ch., Pittsburgh, since 1932. Served as 2d lt., Q.M. Corps, U.S. Army, at Camp Joseph E. Johnston, 1918. Mem. Am. Legion (chaplain Post No. 81, Pittsburgh, 1932-39), Ministerial Circle of Pittsburgh, Pi Kappa Delta. Awarded Jane Hogg Gardiner scholarship at Pittsburgh Theol. Sem., 1920. Republican. Home: 15 W. McIntyre Av., N.S. Pittsburgh, Pa.

NEWCOMER, Lester Warren, sec. chamber of commerce; b. Lancaster Co., Pa., Feb. 5, 1894; s. Tobias C. and Elizabeth J. (Dombach) N.; ed. pub. schs. and high sch., Lancaster, Pa.; m. Maud E. Stauffer, Oct. 11, 1916; 1 dau., June Marie. Employed in various capacities, office clk., office mgr., salesman, to 1927; sec. Lancaster Chamber of Commerce, Lancaster, Pa., continuously since 1927. Served in U.S.N.R.F., 1918-19, overseas, Oct. 1918 to Mar. 1919. Lutheran. Mason. Home: R.F.D. No. 3, Lancaster, Pa. Office: 45 E. Orange St., Lancaster, Pa.

NEWELL, Horatio Whitman, physician; b. Niigata, Japan, Feb. 5, 1898; s. Rev. Horatio Bannister (D.D.) and Jane (Cozad) N., citizens of U.S.; A.B., Amherst Coll., Amherst, Mass., 1922; M.D., Western Reserve U., Cleveland, O., 1926; m. Pauline H. Cozad, June 24, 1927; children—Marcia Frost, Jocelyn Hale. Training in psychiatry and child guidance, Inst. for Child Guidance, New York, 1928-29; dir. Va. State Mental Hygiene Clinic, Richmond, Va., 1929-30; dir. Mental Hygiene Clinic, Bd. Edn. Cleveland, O., 1930-33; clin. dir. Mental Hygiene Clinic, Baltimore, Md., since 1933; asst. prof. psychiatry, U. of Md. Med. Sch. since 1933; dir. Montgomery Co. Mental Hygiene Soc. Served in Ambulance Service, U.S.A., 1917-19 with A.E.F. in France; unit awarded two army citations (France). Fellow Am. Psychiatric Assn. Am. Orthopsychiatric Assn. Mem. Am. Med. Assn., Baltimore County and State med. socs., Chi Phi, Phi Rho Sigma. Certified by Am. Bd. Neurology and Psychiatry. Democrat. Conglist. Home: 7106 Wardman Rd. Office: 601 W. Lombard St., Baltimore, Md.

NEWELL, Sara Marie, pianist; b. Atlantic City, N.J., June 1, 1901; d. Thomas Elmer and Georgia (Camblos) N.; student Atlantic City (N.J.) High Sch., 1916-19, Fountainebleau Summer Sch., France, 1921, Curtis Inst. Music, Phila., 1929-32; studied with Frank LaForge and Ernesto Bernmen, New York, 1923-26; unmarried. Began as pianist, Atlantic City, 1909; gave yearly recitals, 1909-14; song writer since 1917; ch. organist since 1917, Bible Presbyterian Ch., Atlantic City, since 1938; accompanist in vocal studios and coach, N.Y. City and Atlantic City, 1917-27; pianist, New York, and accompanist for vocalists and instrumentalists since 1917; pianist for choral group, Atlantic City, 1935-37; on WABC Television Programs, 1927, New York and Atlantic City programs, Curtis Broadcasts, 1931; artists-accompanist in classes of Leopold Auer and Madame Sembrich, Curtis Inst., 1931-32; mem. two piano team, Atlantic City, since 1938; teaching, Atlantic City, since 1918. Mem. N.J. Composers (judge in state contest 1937), Y.W.C.A. Club: Crescendo (Atlantic City, N.J.). Address: 3608 Atlantic Av., Atlantic City, N.J.

NEWHALL, Blackwell, corpn. official; b. Baltimore, Md., Oct. 19, 1901; s. Thomas and Honora (Guest) B.; grad. U.S. Naval Acad., 1923; m. Mary Large Harrison, Dec. 25, 1932; children—Thomas, II, John Harrison. Ensign U.S. Navy, 1923-24; asst. power engr. Philadelphia Electric Co., 1924-27; spl. asst. to v.p. in charge finance United Gas Improvement Co., 1927-29, asst. sec., 1929-32; asst. to gen. mgr. Phila. Gas Works Co., 1932-36, asst. to pres. since 1936; mem. bd. dirs. since 1938. Chmn. Southeastern Pa. Chapter, Am. Red Cross. Republican. Episcopalian: vestryman Christ Ch.; dir. Galilee Mission. Clubs: Philadelphia, Midday, University Barge. Home: 632 Winsford Road, Bryn Mawr, Pa. Office: 1401 Arch St., Philadelphia, Pa.

NEWHALL, C. Stevenson, corpn. official; b. Phila., Pa., Apr. 10, 1877; s. Gilbert H. and Elizabeth Stevenson (Smith) N.; student Germantown Acad., Phila.; unmarried. Associated with Pa. Co. for Ins. on Lives and Granting Annuities since 1896, exec. v.p., 1929-34, pres., 1934-38, chmn. bd. since 1938. Home: Midvale Av. and Stokely St., Germantown, Philadelphia. Office: 15th and Chestnut Sts., Philadelphia, Pa.

NEWHALL, Thomas, ins. exec.; b. Philadelphia, October 17, 1876; s. Daniel Smith and Eleanor (Mercer) N.; student Haverford (Pa.) Sch., 1884-93; m. Honora Guest Blackwell, May 28, 1898; children—Blackwell, Campbell, Charles Mercer. Began with Chester (Pa.) Pipe & Tube Company, 1893; with John Wanamaker, Philadelphia, 1898; president of Newhall & Co., Baltimore, 1900-07; partner E. B. Smith & Co., Phila., 1910-20; pres. Phila. & Western Ry., 1910-22; partner Drexel & Co., Phila., 1922-36, J. P. Morgan & Co. (N.Y. City), Morgan, Grenfell & Co. (London), and Morgan & Cie (Paris), 1929-1936; financial v.p. Penn Mutual Life Ins. Co.; dir. Pa. R.R. Co., Pa. Co. Was lieut. comdr. in U.S.N.R.F. during World War, serving with mining squadron, A.E.F. Republican. Episcopalian. Clubs: Philadelphia, Rittenhouse, Union League (Phila.). Home: Green Hill Farms, Overbrook, Pa. Office: 6th and Walnut Sts., Philadelphia, Pa.

NEWKIRK, Samuel Frank, Jr., civil engr.; b. Sandy Lake, Pa., Aug. 27, 1890; s. Samuel F. and Cassie (Smith) N.; student Sandy Lake (Pa.) pub. schs., 1896-1904; B.S., Sandy Lake (Pa.) Collegiate Inst., 1908; B.S. in C.E., Pa. State Coll., 1913, C.E., 1918; m. Eleanor Nichols Bates, July 15, 1916; 1 dau., Eleanor Elizabeth. Rodman Pa. Highway Dept., Franklin, Pa., 1910, transitman-chief of party, 1911-12; rodman Erie (Pa.) Engring. Dept., 1911; rodman and chainman Mercer Iron & Coal Co., Stoneboro, Pa., 1910, transitman and draftsman, 1912, engr., 1913-14; asst. engr., L. V. Metz, civil engr., Erie, Pa., 1914-15; insp., asst. engr. Town of Montclair, N.J., 1915-17; office engr. Town of Bloomfield, N.J., 1917; asst. engr. C. H. Watson, civil engr., Great Neck, N.Y., 1917-18, Air Nitrates Corpn., Muscle Shoals, Ala., 1918-19, Nicholas S. Hill, Jr., civil engr., New York, 1919-21, Pitometer Co., New York, 1921; engr. Nat. Bd. of Fire Underwriters, New York, 1921-27; supt. and engr. Elizabethtown Water Co. Consol., Elizabeth, N.J., 1927-31; engr. and supt. Bd. of Water Commrs., Elizabeth, N.J., since 1931; licensed professional engr., N.Y. and N.J.; licensed water works and water treatment plant operator, N.J. Mem. Am. Water Works Assn. (trustee N.J. Sect. since 1935, chmn. 1935-37; dir. representing N.J. since 1938), Holland Soc. of N.Y., S.A.R., Soc. Am. Mil. Engrs., N.J. Soc. of Professional Engrs. and Land Surveyors, Montclair (N.J.) Soc. of Engrs., Geneal. Soc. of Pa., Walkers Club of America, Newfoundland Club of America, Nat. Geog. Soc., Am. Soc. C.E., New England Water Works Assn., South Jersey Assn. of Water Supts., Pa. Water Operators Assn., Acacia. Methodist. Clubs: Montclair (N.J.) Athletic; Woman's of Upper Montclair (N.J.). Home: 161 Stiles St. Office: 18 W. Jersey St., Elizabeth, N.J.

NEWLON, Homer Thomas, chemist; b. New London, Mo., May 20, 1890; s. Stephen Glasscock and Katie Elizabeth (Rissmiller) N.; A.B., U. of Mo., 1913, A.M., same, 1917; Ph.D., N.Y. Univ., 1927; m. Clara Waterstripe, Jan. 31, 1916; children—Homer Thomas, Jr., Claire Beth Marie. Employed as chemist, Denver, Colo., 1917-18; instr. chemistry, Syracuse U., 1918-19; cons. chemist, Syracuse, N.Y., 1919-23; instr. in chemistry, Coll. City of N.Y., 1923-25; instr. chemistry, N.Y. Univ., 1925-28; asst. prof. chemistry, U. of Pittsburgh, 1928-31; taught in various capacities in Pittsburgh Public Schools, since 1931, head chemistry dept. Langley High Sch. since 1938. Fellow A.A.A.S. Mem. Am. Chem. Soc., Nat. Edn. Assn., Pa. Chem. Soc., Pittsburgh Chem. Soc., Pa. State Teachers Assn., Pittsburgh Teachers Assn., Phi Delta Kappa. Republican. Mem. Christian Ch. Club: Unity (Pittsburgh). Home: 243 Chesterfield Rd., Pittsburgh, Pa. Office: Langley High Sch., Pittsburgh, Pa.

NEWMAN, Bernard J., sanitarian; b. Hoosick Falls, N.Y., Mar. 15, 1877; s. Richard and Elizabeth (McClosky) N.; student Meadville (Pa.) Theol. Sch., 1897-1901; spl. study New York Sch. of Philanthropy, 1908; spl. study municipal engring., Harvard, 1914; Certified Sanitarian, U. of Pa., 1915; m. Kate Kincaid, Oct. 5, 1905; 1 son, William Kincaid. Dir. Columbia Neighborhood House, 1902-1910; exec. sec. Phila. Housing Commn., 1911-16; dir. Pa. Sch. for Social Service and Pub. Health, 1916-18; sanitary expert, Ordnance Dept., U.S.A., 1918; sanitarian, Reserve Corps U.S. Pub. Health Service, 1919-23; chief of Research Branch, Office of Industrial Hygiene and Sanitation, 1918-20, acting sanitarian-in-charge, 1920; mng. dir. Phila. Housing Assn. since 1921. Mem. sub-com. on housing, White House Conf. on Child Health and Protection, 1930-31; chmn. committee on housing, Greater Pennsylvania Council, 1931-33; chairman committee on legislation and administration, President's Conference on Home Building and Home Ownership, 1931-32 (member correlating committees on research, committee on objectives and standards, committee on housing and the community, com. on orgn. programs); mem. commn., to codify health laws of Phila.; mem. and sec. Phila. Zoning Commn., 1916-18, mem., 1924-27. Housing consultant Pa. Housing and Town Planning Assn.; pres. Better Housing Bldg. and Loan Assn.; v.p. Regional Planning Fed. of Phila. Tri-State Dist. Fellow Am. Pub. Health Assn.; mem. Am. Acad. Polit. and Social Science, Internat. Fed. Housing and Town Planning (mem. council; mem. tech. com.); chmn. advisory com. on sites, Phila. Housing Authority; mem. Wayne (Pa.) advisory com. on housing, Public Works Administration; treas. Social Service Director of Phila.; mem. Phila. Com. on Public Affairs; mem. Sectional Com. on Light and Ventilation, Bldg. Code Correlating Com. Republican. Unitarian. Joint Author: Lead Poisoning in the Pottery Trades, 1921. Editor and Compiler: Housing in Philadelphia, ann. since 1921. Author of pamphlets and magazine articles on housing, sanitation, industrial hygiene. Home: 508 E. Washington Lane. Address: 1600 Walnut St., Philadelphia, Pa.

NEWMAN, Jacob Louis, lawyer; b. Newark, N.J., Feb. 13, 1875; s. Meier and Bella (Schwarz) N.; student Newark grammar and high schs.; B.S., New York U., 1895, LL.B., 1897 (founders day orator in sr. yr.); m. Flora Stern, June 28, 1905. Studied law in offices of Colie & Swayze; admitted to N.J. bar, 1897; became counselor, 1900; admitted to practice before U.S. Supreme Ct., 1920; apptd. Supreme Ct. Commr. of N.J., 1905, spl. master in chancery, 1912, advisory master, pro hac vice; has figured in many prominent cases; dir. Nat. State Bank, Newark. Apptd. prosecutor of the pleas for Essex Co. by Gov. Fielder, Sept. 12, 1916, to fill unexpired term of Frederick F. Guild, serving until 1917. Mem. Essex Co. Bar Assn. (ex-pres.; chmn. judiciary com.), N.J. State Bar Assn. (was chmn. spl. com. in opposition to change in U.S. Supreme Ct.), Am. Bar Assn., N. J. Hist. Soc., Jr.O.U.A.M.; hon. mem. Lambda Alpha Phi. Democrat. Pres. Congregation B'nai Jeshurun. Mason (Shriner), Elk. Clubs: Essex County Lawyers (pres. 1919-20; trustee 1918-19; formerly chmn. ethics com.), Downtown, Mountain Ridge Country, Carteret Book. Home: 529 Ridge St. Office: 810 Broad St., Newark, N.J.

NEWMAN, Jarvis Everett, lawyer; b. Asbury Park, N.J., Dec. 20, 1891; s. Timbrook and Fannie (Bastedo) N.; LL.B., N.Y. Univ. Law Sch., 1914; m. Eloise Klinefelter, Nov. 24, 1923; children—Jarvis Everett, Jr., Harcourt, Ruth Eloise, Barbara (dec.). Admitted to N.J. bar as atty., 1915, as counselor and master in chancery, 1920; engaged in gen. practice of law at Asbury Park, N.J., since 1915; served as judge dist. court First Judicial Dist., Monmouth Co., 1932-37; pres. bd. edn. Wall Twp., Monmouth Co. Served as regtl. intelligence sergt. inf., U.S.A., 1917-19. Served as sec. Asbury Park Dem. Com. and Monmouth Co. Dem. Com. Mem. Monmouth Co. Bar Assn., Asbury Park Lawyers Club, Am. Legion, Vets. Fgn. Wars, Patron of Husbandry, Grange. Democrat. Methodist. Mason. Red Man. Home: R.F.D., Belmar, N.J. Office: 601 Bangs Av., Asbury Park, N.J.

NEWMAN, John Grant, clergyman; b. nr. Dandridge, Tenn., Oct. 16, 1862; s. Samuel Blair and Nancy Elizabeth (Rankin) N.; A.B., Maryville Coll., 1888, M.A., 1894, D.D., 1908, LL.D., 1921; Litt.D. from College of Emporia, Kansas, 1927; prin. New Market (Tenn.) Acad., 1888-90; grad. Union Theol. Sem., 1893; m. Mary E. Minnis, June 28, 1893 (died Mar. 7, 1901); m. 2d, Helen I. Minnis, of New Market, Dec. 19, 1906. Ordained Presbyn. ministry, 1894; prof. Latin, Maryville Coll., 1893-1903; pastor Olivet Memorial Ch., New York, 1903-05, Wyoming Presbyn. Ch., Cincinnati, 1905-08; pres. The Western Coll. for Women, Aug. 1, 1908-Aug. 30, 1912; pastor Chambers-Wylie Memorial Presbyn. Church, Philadelphia, Sept. 1, 1912-Oct. 16, 1937, since pastor emeritus. Clubs: Union League, City. Republican. Author: An Education for You. Mem. Jud. Commn. Presbyn. Ch. U.S.A., 1914-17 (chairman 1916-17); executive commn. Synod of Pa., 1915-18. Contbr. Internat. S.S. Lessons to Saturday Phila. Inquirer since July 1, 1925. Home: 4642 Hazel Av., Philadelphia, Pa.

NEWMAN, Philip Floyd, surgeon; b. Alma, Neb., Apr. 6, 1893; B.S., Creighton U., Omaha, Neb., 1918; M.D., Jefferson Med. Coll., 1921; m. Dorothy L. Albright, Jan. 8, 1927; children—Jane, Philip. After interneship engaged in practice of medicine at Allentown, Pa., specializing in surgery; mem. surg. staff, Sacred Heart Hosp., Allentown Hosp. Served in Pa. N.G. 6 yrs.. Fellow Internat. Coll. Surgeons (Geneva, 1938), Am. Med. Assn. Mem. Lehigh Valley and Lehigh Co. med. socs., Phi Beta Phi. Republican. Lutheran. Clubs: Livingston, Lehigh Country. Home: 833 N. 27th St. Office: 1435 Houston St., Allentown, Pa.

NEWPHER, James Alfred, official dept. pub. instrn.; b. Terre Hill, Pa., Dec. 30, 1897; s. Edwin John Chambers and Sarah Ann (Eshelman) N.; A.B., Franklin and Marshall Coll., 1922; A.M., U. of Pittsburgh Night and Summer schs., 1932, Ph.D., same, 1936; (hon.) LL.D., Geneva Coll., 1936; m. Olive Myrtle Houlette, June 6, 1929; children—James Alfred, Jr., Sarah Ann. Engaged in teaching rural schs., 1915-18; instr., supervisor, head social sci. dept., high sch. Kittanning, 1922-25; prof. edn.

and psychology, and dean of men, Geneva Coll., 1925-36; dir. Bur. Professional Licensing, Dept. Pub. Instrn. of Pa. since 1936. Served in S.A. T.C. Chmn. Beaver Co. Safety Council; mem. civil service commn. Beaver Falls, Pa. Mem. N.E.A., Pa. State Edn. Assn., A.A.A.S., Am. Assn. Univ. Profs., Pa. Acad. Sci., Phi Delta Kappa, Delta Sigma Phi. Democrat. Presbyn. Mason (32°). Clubs: Am. Legion, Motor (Harrisburg). Home: 3224 N. Third St., Harrisburg, Pa.

NEWSOM, Nathan William, prof. edn.; b. Independence, Miss., June 25, 1898; s. Dr. Thomas C. and Lucina Jane (Hall) N.; ed. Webb Sch., Bell Buckle, Tenn., grad. 1916; A.B., U. of Miss., 1920; LL.B., Cumberland U., Lebanon, Tenn., 1924; A.M., Columbia U., 1929; Ph.D., N.Y.U., 1931; m. Hazel Mae Campbell, June 8, 1931. Employed as prin. schs. and prin. high sch., in Miss., 1920-23; dir. teacher training, Western State Coll. of Colo., 1929-30, head dept. edn., 1930-31; asst. prof. edn., Temple U., 1931-36, asso. prof., 1936-39, prof. since 1939. Served as pvt. then 2d lt. inf., U.S.A. during World War. Mem. Am. Assn. Sch. Adminstrs., N.E.A., Pa. State Edn. Assn., Kappa Alpha, Phi Delta Kappa. Presbyn. Author: Legal Status of the County Supt., 1932; The Small High School at Work, 1936; Standards for Thesis Writing, 1936; Comprehensive Examination in Secondary Education, 1938; Administrative Practice in Large High Schs., 1939; Problems of the Teacher in the New Secondary School, 1937. Contbr. to ednl. publs. Home: 2016 N. Broad St., Philadelphia, Pa.

NEWTON, John Earle, musician, prof. music; b. Richmond Hill, Ont., April 14, 1886; s. Andrew and Ella (Pierson) N.; came to U.S., 1923; student Toronto Conservatory of Music, 1902-08, also Univ. of Toronto and in Germany and U.S.A.; m. Georgia Boyle, July 5, 1911; children—John Pinkerton, Norman Boyle, Anson Pierson, Eric Nicholson, Emma Spragge. Began as teacher of piano, 1903, and taught in various music schs. in Ont. to 1914; mem. faculty Toronto Conservatory of Music, 1914-23; instr. music, N.J. Coll. for Women, New Brunswick, N.J., 1923-26, asst. prof., 1926, asso. prof., 1927, prof. music and head dept. of music since 1928, exec. officer div. fine arts, 1931-34; instr. piano and mus. composition, Master Inst. United Arts, N.Y. City, 1932-35; mem. faculty, Rutgers U. summer sessions, 1925-26, dir. music, summer sessions since 1934. Mem. Fed. of Music Clubs, Music Teachers Nat. Assn., Beethoven Assn. N.Y. City, Phi Beta Kappa. Home: 260 Harrison Av., Highland Park, N.J.

NEWTON, Joseph Fort, clergyman; b. Decatur, Tex.; s. Lee and Sue G. (Battle) N.; student Hardy Inst. (now defunct) and Southern Bapt. Theol. Sem., Louisville, Ky.; Litt.D., Coe Coll., Cedar Rapids, Ia., 1912; D.D., Tufts Coll., 1918; D.H.L., Hobart Coll., 1927; LL. D., Temple Univ., 1929; m. Jennie Mai Deatherage, June 14, 1900; children—Joseph Emerson, David (dec.), Josephine Kate. Ordained Bapt. ministry, 1893; pastor 1st Bapt. Ch., Paris, Tex., 1897-98; asso. pastor non-sectarian ch., St. Louis,, 1898-1900; founder, and pastor People's Ch., Dixon, Ill., 1901-08; pastor Liberal Christian Ch., Cedar Rapids, Ia., 1908-16, The City Temple, London, Eng., 1916-19, Church of the Divine Paternity, New York, 1919-25, Memorial Church of St. Paul, Overbrook, Phila., 1925-1930, St. James' Church, Philadelphia, 1930-35; spl. preacher Asso. Chs., Phila., 1936, Church of St. Luke and Epiphany, Philadelphia 1938. Associate editor Christian Century, Chicago. Served as Grand Chaplain Grand Lodge of Masons of Ia. Author: David Swing, Poet Preacher, 1909; Abraham Lincoln, 1910; Lincoln and Herndon, 1910; The Eternal Christ, 1912; Sermons and Lectures, 1912; The Builders, A Story and Study of Masonry, 1914; Wesley and Woolman, 1914; What Have the Saints to Teach Us? 1914; The Ambassador, 1916; The Mercy of Hell, 1918; The Sword of the Spirit, 1918; The Theology of Civilization, 1919; Some Living Masters of the Pulpit, 1922; Preaching in London, 1923; The Men's House, 1923; Preaching in New York, 1924; The Truth and the Life, 1925; The Religion of Masonry, 1926; God and the Golden Rule, 1927; Altar Stairs, 1928; The New Preaching, 1929; Things I Know in Religion, 1930; The Angel in the Soul, 1931; The Sermon in the Making, 1932; Living Every Day, 1937; "We Have Highly Resolve," 1939; also many pamphlets on patriotic and Masonic topics, and numerous addresses and sermons; conducts daily feature in American press. Home: 1930 Rittenhouse Square. Address: 330 S. 13th St., Philadelphia, Pa.

NEY, Grover Cleveland, physician; b. Harrisonburg, Va., Feb. 9, 1886; s. Baruch and Kattie (Wise) N.; A.B., Mount St. Joseph's Coll., Baltimore, 1903, A.M., 1904; M.D., Johns Hopkins Med. Sch., 1908; m. Selma Strauss, June 21, 1918; 1 son, Bertram. Interne Sinai Hosp., Baltimore, 1908-10, resident, 1910-12; attdg. surgeon, Sinai Hosp. since 1914; visiting surgeon, West Baltimore Gen. Hosp., Hosp. for Women of Md., St. Joseph's and Franklin Square hosps. Fellow Am. Coll. Surgeons. Mem. Am. Surg. Bd., Am. Med. Assn., Med. and Chirurg. Faculty of Md. Democrat. Jewish religion. Home: 2401 Linden Av., Baltimore, Md.

NIBLO, James Martin, clergyman; b. Conshohocken, Pa., Sept. 17, 1885; s. Howard Smith and Davanna (Donaldson) N.; ed. U. of Pa., 1907-09, Phila. Divinity Sch., 1910-13; (hon.) D.D., Ursinus Coll., 1938; children—Albert Mehrer, George Culp. Ordained to ministry P.E. Ch., deacon, 1913, priest, 1913; curate, St. George's Ch., Phila., 1913-14; vicar, St. Michael's Chapel, Phila., 1915-23; asso, rector, St. Matthias Ch., Los Angeles, Calif., 1923-25; rector, St. John's Ch., Norristown, Pa., since 1925; canon residentiary, Christ Ch. Cathedral, Phila., Pa., since 1934. Mem. bd. dirs. Montgomery Hosp., Norristown, Pa. Trustee Ursinus Coll., Collegeville, Pa. Mem. Acad. Nat. Scis., Pa. Acad. Fine Arts, Phila. Republican. Episcopalian. Rotary Club of Norristown. Clubs: Union League, Penn Athletic (Philadelphia); Plymouth Country (Montgomery Co.). Home: "Oak Knoll," Plymouth Twp. Office: 27 E. Airy St., Norristown, Pa.

NICE, Harry (Whinna), governor; b. Washington, D.C., Dec. 5, 1877; s. Henry and Drucilla (Arnold) N.; student Baltimore City Coll., 1889-93, Dickinson Coll., Carlisle, Pa., 1893-96, U. of Md., 1896-99; m. Edna Viola Amos, June 5, 1906; children—William Stone (dec.), Harry Whinna, Jr. Admitted to Md. bar, 1899, practicing in Baltimore since 1899; mem. firm Dickerson & Nice since 1920; judge of Appeal Tax Court, Baltimore, 1920-24; states atty. and asst. states atty., Baltimore, 1912-19; mem. Baltimore City Council, 1903-05; sec. to mayor of Baltimore, 1905-08; supervisor elections, Baltimore, 1908-12; elected gov. of Md., Nov. 1934 for term, 1935-39. Mem. Am., Md. State and Baltimore City bar assns., Kappa Sigma. Republican. Methodist. Mason (32°, Shriner), K.P., Odd Fellow, Elk, Moose. Clubs: Scimeter, Baltimore City (Baltimore); Md. Country, Columbia Country. Home: 5701 Oakshire Rd., Mt. Washington, Baltimore, Md. Office: Fidelity Bldg., Baltimore, Md.

NICHOLLS, Joseph Klapp, lawyer; b. Phila., Pa., Dec. 25, 1876; s. Dr. Benjamin Franklin and Elizabeth Louise (Klapp) N.; student Central High School, Phila., 1895-96, Law Dept., U. of Pa., 1901-02; m. Sarah Hearn, Nov. 24, 1917. With Girard Fire and Marine Ins. Co., Phila., 1896-1907; student of law in office of Hon. Raymond MacNeille, Phila., 1907-09; admitted to Pa. bar, 1908, and since in practice in Phila.; solicitor Market St. Bldg. & Loan Assn., Cobbs Creek Parkway Home Bldg. & Loan Assn.; dir. First Regt. Inf. of Pa. Inc. Served as private, advancing to major, 1st Regt. Inf., Nat. Guard of Pa., 1904-16; capt., later maj., Adj. Gen. Dept., and lt. col. Inf., U.S. Army, 1918-19; col. Inf. Reserve since 1923, comdg. 315th Inf. since 1926. Chmn. Gov. James' Com. in Rep. primary, 1938; mem. exec. com. in charge of Phila. Rep. War Vets, 1938. Mem. Am., Pa. State and Phila. bar assns., Law Acad. of Phila. (past pres.), Pa. Soc. Sons of Revolution, Nat. Sojourners, Mil. Order of World War, Am. Legion, Reserve Officers Assn., U.S. Inf. Assn., Vet. Corps, 1st Regt. Inf., Nat. Guard of Pa., Scabbard and Blade. Episcopalian. Mason (grand marshal, grand Holy Arch Chapter of Pa.). Club: Army and Navy (Washington, D.C.). Home: 1117 S. 61st St. Office: 908 Finance Bldg., Philadelphia, Pa.

NICHOLS, Charles Walter, mining, mfg.; b. Brooklyn, N.Y., June 19, 1875; s. William H. and Hannah (Wright) N.; ed. Poly. Inst. Brooklyn; Cornell U., 1895-97; m. Adelaide Batterman, Oct. 11, 1899; children—Kathleen (Mrs. Ralph C. Coxhead), Charles W. Began as draftsman with General Chem. Co., New York, 1898; mining and mfg. business since 1901; chmn. bd. Nichols Engineering & Research Corpn.; dir. First Nat. Bank, West Orange, Phosphate Mining Co., Title Guarantee & Trust Co., Corn Exchange Bank Trust Co. Mem. Phi Kappa Psi. Conglist. Clubs: Bankers, Down Town. Home: Pleasantdale Farm, West Orange, N.J. Office: 60 Wall Tower, New York, N.Y.

NICHOLS, Firmadge King, instr. gynecology, Johns Hopkins U.; obstetrician-in-chief and asso. in gynecology St. Agnes Hosp. Address: 2 W. Read St., Baltimore, Md.

NICHOLS, Isabel McIlhenny (Mrs. H. S. Prentiss Nichols); b. Wilmington, N.C.; d. John (pioneer gas engr., philanthropist) and Bernice (Bell) McIlhenny; ed. schs., Columbus, Ga., and Mary Baldwin Sem., Staunton, Va.; m. Henry Sargent Prentiss Nichols, lawyer, June 4, 1895. Apptd. by gov. of Pa. as mem. State Council Edn.; by mayor of Phila. as mem. Phila. Art Jury; by mayor as mem. committee to assign city scholarships to Sch. of Design; v.p. Board of Christian Education by appointment of General Assembly Presbyn. Ch. U.S.A.; dir. Southeastern Chapter Am. Red Cross; dir. Emergency Aid of Pa.; dir. Germantown and Chestnut Hill Improvement Assn.; trustee Wilson Coll. for Women, Chambersburg, Pa.; v.p. Woman's Bd. Pa. Museum Sch. Industrial Art, Germantown Hort. Soc., Law Enforcement League of Phila., Independent Rep. Com. of 35; mem. Phila. Com. of 70, Woman's Nat. Com. of 100 for Law Enforcement, Pa. League of Women Voters, Advisory Bd. Fairmount Bird Club; corr. sec. Phila. Home for Incurables; chmn. Advisory Com. for Phila. of Nat. War Work Council Y.W.C.A.; mem. English-Speaking Union-Transatlantic Soc. (bd. govs.), Hist. Soc. of Pa., Athenæum of Philadelphia; sec. Civic Safety Fund Assn. Received annual award of the Southern Soc. of New York from Mary Baldwin Coll., 1937. Clubs: Acorn, Sedgeley, New Century (pres. 1913-21), Rep. Women of Pa. (Philadelphia); Women's (Germantown); hon. mem. Modern (Philadelphia), Woman's (Narberth), and Neighbors (Hatboro). Home: 346 Pelham Rd., Germantown, Phila., Pa.; (summer) 115 S. Newton Av., Chelsea, Atlantic City, N.J.

NICHOLS, Jeannette Paddock, historian; b. Rochelle, Ill.; d. Hosea Cornish Savery and Janette (Styles) Paddock; A.B., Knox Coll.; A.M. and Ph.D., Columbia; m. Roy F. Nichols, May 27, 1920. Acting prof. of history, Wesleyan Coll., Macon, Ga., 1922-23; organized research and collected biographical material for life of N. W. Aldraich (pub. 1930); free lance writing in history and biography since 1930. Awarded Curtis Scholarship in Am. History, Columbia, 1920-21; mem. Phi Beta Kappa. Mem. Am. Hist. Assn., Miss. Valley Hist. Assn., Middle States Assn. of History Teachers, Am. Assn. Univ. Women. Sponsor, World Center for Women's Archives. Protestant. Author: History of Alaska, 1924; James Styles of Kingston and George Stuart of Schoolcraft, 1936; The Growth of American Democracy (with R. F. Nichols), 1939; "Industrial History of New Jersey" (pub. in History of New Jersey, edited by I. S. Kull), 1930; contbr. to Dictionary of Am. Biography, and to hist., econ. sociol. and polit. science mags. Home: 438 Riverview Rd., Swarthmore, Pa.

NICHOLS, Pierrepont Herrick, prof. English; b. Pataha, Wash., Jan. 27, 1893; s. John and Anna (Herrick) N.; diploma Williston Acad., 1911; B.A., Allegheny Coll., 1914; student Yale Grad. Sch., 1915; A.M., Harvard, 1921, Ph.D., 1924; m. Gladys Winslow, Sept. 9,

1921; 1 son, Thomas Gilbert. Instr. English, Pa. State Coll., 1916, Carnegie Inst. Tech., 1917; asst. prin. high sch., Pepperell, Mass., 1919; instr. English, high sch., Walpole, 1920, New York U., 1924-25; asso. prof. English, Evansville Coll., 1926-27, head of dept., 1928-30; head of English department, Lincoln Memorial University, 1931-35; professor English, Slippery Rock State Teachers Coll., since 1935. Seaman U.S.N.R.F., 1917-18. Mem. Am. Assn. Univ. Profs., Modern Lang. Assn., Phi Beta Kappa, Delta Sigma Rho, Delta Tau Delta. Congregationalist. Contbr. William Dunbar as a Scottish Lydgatian, 1931 and Lydgate's Influence on the Aureate Terms of the Scottish Chaucetrians, 1932 (in publs. Modern Lang. Assn. America). Home: Slippery Rock, Pa.

NICHOLS, Roy Franklin, univ. prof.; b. Newark, N.J., Mar. 3, 1896; s. Franklin C. and Anna (Cairns) N.; A.B., Rutgers, 1918, A.M., 1919; Columbia Univ. fellow, 1920-21, Ph.D., 1923; Litt.D., Franklin and Marshall College, 1937; m. Jeannette Paddock, 1920. Instr. history Columbia, 1922-25; asst. prof., history, U. of Pa., 1925-30, prof. since 1930. Mem. Social Science Research Council. Mem. American Hist. Assn., Middle States Assn. of History Teachers (pres. 1932-33), Pa. Hist. Assn. (pres. since 1936), Pa. Federation Hist. Socs. (v.p.), Phi Beta Kappa, Pi Gamma Mu. Clubs: University, Lenape (Phila.); Cosmos (Washington, D.C.). Author: The Democratic Machine (1850-54), 1923; Syllabus for History of Civilization (joint author), 1927; Franklin Pierce, 1931. Home: Riverview Rd., Swarthmore, Pa.

NICHOLSON, (John) Kenyon, playwright; b. Crawfordsville, Ind., May 21, 1894; s. Thomas Brown and Anne (Kenyon) N.; prep. edn., high sch., Crawfordsville, and De Witt Clinton High Sch., New York; student Columbia U.; A.B., Wabash Coll., 1917; post-grad. work, Cambridge U.; m. Lucile Nikolas (actress), Dec. 24, 1924. Instr. in dramatic composition, Columbia U. Extension, since 1921. Served as 2d lt. U.S.A., 1st Army Hdqrs., A.E.F., 18 mos. Mem. Beta Theta Pi. Presbyn. Author: Honor Bright (with Meredith Nicholson), 1923; Garden Varieties, 1924; Appleton Book of Short Plays (1st series), 1925; Sally and Company, 1925; The Meal Ticket, 1926; Revues, 1926; Appleton Book of Short Plays (2d series), 1927; Here's to Your Health (with Charles Knox), 1927; Two Weeks Off (with Thomas Barrows), 1927; Tell Me Your Troubles, 1928; Taxi, 1929; Hollywood Plays, 1930; Words and Music; The American Scene (with Barrett H. Clark), 1930; also a number of plays produced on Broadway (New York)—The Barker, Civilized People, Love Is Like That (with S. N. Behrman), Eva the Fifth (with John Golden), Before You're Twenty-five, Torch Song, Stepdaughters of War, A Place in the Sun, Sailor, Beware! (with Charles Robinson), Swing Your Lady, Dance Night. Home: R.D. 2, Stockton, N.J.

NICHOLSON, Percival, pediatrician; b. Philadelphia, Pa., Dec. 14, 1881; s. Coleman Lindsey and May Paul (Robeson) N.; ed. Haverford (Pa.) Friends Sch. and Haverford Boys Sch.; B.S., Haverford Coll., 1902; M.D., U. of Pa. Med. School, 1905; m. Nell Gray Clayton, Apr. 8, 1916; 1 son, William Percival. Began practice of pediatrics, 1911; asst. physician to dispensary Children's Hosp. of Philadelphia, 1911-22, asst. visiting physician to wards, 1915-27, physician to dispensary, 1922-31, consulting pediatrician, since 1932; pediatrician Bryn Mawr Hosp. since 1931; consulting pediatrician Chester Co. Hosp. since 1930; instr. pediatrics, Grad. Sch. of U. of Pa., 1920-22, asso. in pediatrics, 1922-34, asst. prof., 1934-37, asso. prof., 1937-39, clin. prof. since 1939. Mem. A.M.A., Tri-City Pediatric Assn., Philadelphia Pediatric Soc., Pa. Med. Assn., Montgomery Co. Med. Soc. (Main Line branch); charter mem. Am. Acad. Pediatrics. Republican. Mem. Soc. of Friends. Home and Office: 16 W. Montgomery Av., Ardmore, Pa.

NICHOLSON, William R., physician; b. Boston, Mass.; s. Wm. Rufus and Katherine Stanley (Parker) N.; A.B., Univ. of Pa., 1890, M.D., 1893; m. Celia J. Bolles, July 14, 1904. Interne, Childrens Hosp., 1893-94, Pa. Hosp., 1894-97; prof. gynecology, U. of Pa. Grad. Sch. of Medicine since 1918; cons. obstetrician Presbyterian Hosp. and Preston Retreat, in pvt. practice at Phila. since 1897 specializing in gynecology and obstetrics since 1900. Mem. Am. Gynecol. Soc., Coll. of Phys. of Phila.; diplomate of Am. Bd. Gynecology and Obstetrics. Episcopalian. Home: 252 Kent Rd., Wynnewood, Pa. Office: 2023 Spruce St., Philadelphia, Pa.

NICHOLSON, William Ramsey, Jr.; b. Philadelphia, Pa., Mar. 8, 1879; s. William Ramsey and Anna J. (Hopson) N.; ed. Hamilton Sch., Phila., 1893-99; m. Ethel W. Sutton, Jan. 22, 1903; children—William Ramsey III, Winifred S. Began as salesman for wholesale hay concern, later engaged in mining in Mexico, then asst. mgr. Hotel Lafayette, Phila.; sec. and treas. Haney-White Co., builders supplies, since 1902; treas. Glenwood Foundry Co.; dir. Textile Nat. Bank, Phila., since 1920; organizer and sec. Law Enforcement League of Phila. since 1921. Sec. Y.M.C.A., Camp Meade, Pa., World War. Mem. Phila. Real Estate Bd. Mem. Pa. State Fish and Game Protective Assn., Lumbermen's Exchange. Republican. Presbyn. Mason (Shriner), K.T. Clubs: Union League, Penn Athletic, City, Lumbermen's Golf (Phila.); Boys Club of America (dir.); Cricket, Boys of Germantown (sec. since 1925); Cedarbrook Country, Old York Road Golf, Egypt Mills Hunting and Fishing (treas.). Home: Wissahickon and Midvale Av. Address: 17th and Glenwood Av., Philadelphia, Pa.

NICK, Edwin William, mfg. boiler equipment; b. Erie, Pa., Mar. 10, 1885; s. Frederick and Anna (Brevillier) N.; B.S., Pa. State Coll., 1907, E.E. on record and thesis, 1911; grad. student Harvard U. Grad. Sch. Business Adminstrn., 1911-12; m. Mildred Scholes, Jan. 1, 1914; children—Robert Edwin, Shirley. Began as elec. engr., 1907; engr. Buffalo & Lake Erie Traction Co.; apprentice General Electric Co.; elec. engr. Isthmian Canal Commn.; asso. with Northern Equipment Co., mfrs. boiler feed control, Erie, Pa., since 1912, gen. mgr., vice-pres., then pres. since 1913; chmn. bd. dirs. Copes Regulators, Ltd., London, Eng.; dir. Security-Peoples Trust Co., Pa. Research Corpn. of State College, Pa., Erie Ins. Exchange. Served 4 yrs. as cadet-pvt. to capt. Nat. Gd., now officer U.S.A. Res. Dir. Nat. Gd. Armory Bd. Co-ordinator, Dept. of Pub. Assistance, Harrisburg, Pa. Corporator Hamot Hosp., Erie, Pa. Trustee Pa. State Coll., Erie Day Sch.; dir. Erie Cemetery Assn. Active in numerous civic affairs. Twice a mem. Com. of 100 to draft platforms for presidential campaigns. Mem. Nat. Assn. Steam and Fluid Splty. Mfrs. (dir.), Am. Boiler Mfrs. Assn., Com. of 25 on Nat. Cooperation and Coordination. Republican. Episcopalian. Clubs: Kahkwa, Rotary of Erie (dir.). Home: 2020 South Shore Drive. Office: 1945 Grove Drive, Erie, Pa.

NICKEL, James Edward, M.D.; b. York Springs, Pa., Nov. 7, 1878; s. James and Barbara (Gardner) N.; M.D., Jefferson Med. Coll., 1903; m. Clara G. Baumeister, June 28, 1904; children—Dorothy (Mrs. Kennedy B. Whitley), Margaret E., J. Edward Jr. Engaged in private practice of medicine and asst. to Prof. Dowling Benjamin (chief of Cooper Hosp.), 1904-07; with Pa. State Bd. of Health Dispensary and in charge Infirmary Hosp., Mt. Alto, Pa., 1908-10; asst. med. examiner Pa. R.R., 1910-25, med. examiner, 1925-28, regional med. examiner in charge Conway-Canton territory, 1928-30, industrial surgeon and chief examiner Buffalo Dist., since 1930. Registered physician, N.Y., Pa. and Ohio. Mem. A.M.A., Pa. State Med. Soc., Erie Co. Med. Assn., Pa. Assn. of R.R. Surgeons. Republican. Presbyterian. Mason, Odd Fellow. Home: 1717 W. Ridge Road, Erie, Pa. Office: 589 Louisiana St., Buffalo, N.Y.

NICKLAS, John B., Jr., lawyer; b. Baltimore, Md., July 27, 1899; s. John B. and Louise N.; B.S. in Econ., U. of Pittsburgh, 1920, LL.B., Law Sch., 1922; m. Dorothy E. Stewart, Mar. 14, 1925; children—Nancy Lee, Virginia Stewart. Began as lawyer, 1922, and since in practice at Pittsburgh; mem. of firm McCrady, McClure, Nicklas & Hirschfield since 1934; v.p. Perry Real Estate Co. Served in O.T.C., Plattsburg, N.Y., World War. Counsel for Pittsburgh Real Estate Bd. Mem. Allegheny Co., Pa., Am. bar assns., U. of Pittsburgh Gen. Alumni Assn. (pres.; mem. alumni council), Am. Legion (past comdr., Allegheny Co.; past dist. comdr., 36th jud. dist.; present judge advocate), Alpha Kappa Psi (northeastern dist. councilor), Lambda Chi Alpha, Delta Theta Phi, Delta Sigma Rho, Omicron Delta Kappa, Beta Gamma Sigma, Sigma Delta Chi. Republican. United Presbyterian. Mason (K.T., 32°, Shriner), past master. Clubs: University, Amen Corner (Pittsburgh); St. Clair Country (Bridgeville, Pa.) Home: 153 Main Entrance Dr., Mt. Lebanon, Pa. Office: 1913-21 Investment Bldg., Pittsburgh, Pa.

NICODEMUS, Edwin Arthur, M.D., Martinsburg, Pa., May 9, 1870; s. Frederick L. and Rebecca (Berkstresser) N.; ed. pub. schs. and Millersville State Normal Sch.; M.D., Jefferson Med. Coll., 1898; m. Helen Seibert, Apr. 27, 1903 (dec.); 1 dau., Emma S. (Mrs. W. Ira Kilhefer). Began gen. practice of medicine, 1898; became pres. of staff Harrisburg Polyclinic Hosp., 1926, now cons. surgeon. Served as cavalry officer, U.S. Army, Spanish-Am. War; divisional officer on Mexican Border, 1916, in France, 1917-19. Mem. Harrisburg Bd. of Health. Pres. Dauphin County Med. Soc., 1926, Harrisburg Acad. Medicine, 1935. Republican. Lutheran. Contbr. to professional jours. Home and Office: 1437 Derry St., Harrisburg, Pa.

NICODEMUS, Frank Milton, banking; b. Baltimore, Md., Oct. 29, 1888; s. John Jeremiah and Elizabeth Copes (Eareckson) N.; student McDonogh (Md.) Sch., 1900-05; m. Bessie Warrington Mills, May 5, 1927; children—Betty Ann, Sue Elizabeth. Became accountant, Pa. R.R. Co., 1905 now v.p. Commercial Credit Co., Baltimore; vice-pres. and dir., Manufacturers Finance Co., Commercial Equipment Co., Appomattox Land Corpn. Served in Md. N.G. Episcopalian. Clubs: Chesapeake, Maryland Yacht (Baltimore). Home: My Lady's Manor, Monkton, Md. Office: First Nat. Bank Bldg., Baltimore, Md.

NICODEMUS, Kent Cassell, corpn. exec.; b. Walkersville, Md., May 21, 1882; s. Dr. John David and Rebecca (Nelson) N.; student Dickinson Coll., Carlisle, Pa., 1901-04; m. Felisa Stauffer, June 3, 1922; children—Kent Cassell, Jr., Nancy Felisa. In employ Woodward & Lothrop, dept. store, Washington, D.C., 1904; asso. with Glade Valley Milling Co., Walkersville, Md. since 1905, treas. since 1905; with Walkersville Ice Co. since 1912, treas. since 1912; treas. Glade Valley Bakery, Inc., Walkersville, Md. since 1917; treas. Valley Supply Co. Middletown, Md., since 1920; treas. Glade Valley-Garber, Inc. since 1935; dir. Farmers & Mechanics Nat. Bank, Frederick, Md. since 1929; vice president Walkersville Bank since 1937; sec. N-R Garment Co., Walkersville, Md.; propr. Vinda Bona Hotel, Braddock Heights, Md. Mem. Sigma Alpha Epsilon. Democrat. Mem. M.E. Ch. Jr.O.U.A.M. Home: Corner Pennsylvania and Fulton Avs., Walkersville, Md.

NICODEMUS, Roy Elvin, obstetrician, surgeon; b. Barberton, O., Feb. 15, 1903; s. Wilmer C. and Lillian May (Snyder) N.; ed. Bucknell U., 1921-23; M.D., Jefferson Med. Coll., 1927; m. Anne Kathryn Townsend, Nov. 24, 1924 (dec. 1932); children—Shirley Townsend, Audrey Townsend; m. 2d, Geraldine Frances Sullivan, Aug. 3, 1934; children—Robert Sullivan, Anne Sullivan. Engaged in gen. practice of medicine in 1928, specializing in obstetrics since 1930; grad. study at N.Y. Lying-In Hosp., 1929; dir. dept. obstetrics, Geisinger Memorial Hosp., Danville, Pa. since 1930. Mem. Maternal Welfare Commn. of State of Pa. Fellow Am. Coll. Surgs. Mem. Am. Med. Assn., Pa. State and Montour Co. med. socs., Phi Chi, Lambda Chi Alpha. Republican. Mason (32°). Contbr. on obstetrics to med. jours. Home: 501 Bloom St., Danville, Pa.

NICOL, Alexander R., retired capitalist; b. Ontario, Can., Jan. 6, 1862; s. Rev. Peter and

NICOLET, Henrietta (Stewart) N.; collegiate edn.; m. Minnie Elizabeth Stewart, 1888. Began as cashier of bank in Ont., 1883; moved to Tacoma, Wash., 1891, to New York, 1898, and engaged in the banking and shipping business, becoming officer or dir. in about 30 corpns.; pres. Atlantic, Gulf & West Indies Steamship Lines, 1918-21, retired 1921. Trustee Princeton Theol. Sem., Overlook Hosp. (Summit, N.J.). Republican. Presbyterian. Mason. Clubs: India House (New York), Highland (Summit, N.J.). Home: 11 Essex Rd., Summit, N.J.

NICOLET, Ben H(arry), chemist; b. Kansas City, Mo., July 30, 1890; s. Harry Lincoln and Flora (Coombs) N.; A.B., U. of Kan., Lawrence, Kan., 1910; Ph.D., Yale U., 1913; m. Kathryn Hasley, Aug. 28, 1920; children—Jane, Nancy. Research chemist, Mellon Inst., Pittsburgh, Pa., 1913-17; asst. prof. chemistry, U. of Chicago, 1919-28; chemist and sr. chemist, U.S. Dept. Agr. since 1928, with Bur. Dairy Industry, Beltsville, Md. since 1928. Served as capt. C.W.S., U.S.A., 1917-19. Fellow A.A.A.S. Mem. Am. Chem. Soc. (councilor 1938-39), Am. Inst. of Chemists, Am. Soc. Biochemists, Washington Acad. Sciences, Sigma Xi, Alpha Chi Sigma. Republican. Club: Cosmos (Washington). Contbr. to professional jours. Home: 205 Monroe Av., Riverdale, Md.

NIEDERMEYER, Frederick David, clergyman; b. Decatur, Ill., Feb. 14, 1881; s. William and Annie Elizabeth (Jahn) N.; grad. high sch., Decatur, 1897, Ill. State Normal U., 1900; A.B., U. of Ill., 1904; studied theology, Princeton Sem., 1906-09; A.M., Princeton U., 1908; D.D., Coll. of Ozarks, 1925; m. Maude Vernon Wilcox, Oct. 1, 1913; 1 son, Cedric Wilcox (dec.). Ordained ministry Presbyn. Ch., 1908; asst. minister Central Presbyn. Ch., pastor Mizpah Chapel, N.Y. City, 1909-12; pastor Adams Memorial Presbyn. Ch., N.Y. City, 1912-19, First Presbyn. Ch., Perth Amboy, N.J., since 1919. Religious work sec. Army Y.M.C.A., Camp Gordon, Atlanta, Ga., 1917-18; speaker on Liberty Loan train, 3d Liberty Loan, Tenn., Ga., Ala., Fla., 1918. Moderator Presbytery of Elizabeth (N.J.), 1924-25; commr. Gen. Assembly Presbyn Ch., U.S.A., 1933. Pres. Adelphi Ministers Assn., 1924-26; mem. Presbyterian and Reformed Ministers Association New York (president 1923-25). Republican. Clubs: Rotary of Perth Amboy (pres. 1927-28); Illini, Clergy (New York); Benham (Princeton). Author: Palestine Pathways, 1928; The Ten Commandments Today, 1928; To Show the Mind of Christ (pageant); 1931; The Seven Words From the Cross, 1932; The Missing Cross (pageant), 1933; The Story of Our Lord (pageant), 1934; The Miracle of the Resurrection, 1937. Home: 86 Market St., Perth Amboy, N.J.

NIELDS, John P., judge; b. Wilmington, Del., Aug. 7, 1868; s. Benjamin and Gertrude (Fulton) N.; Haverford Coll., Pa.; A.B., Harvard, 1889; Harvard Law Sch., 1890, 92; m. Mary Blanchard Craven, of Salem, N.J., Jan. 23, 1907; 1 dau., Ann. In practice at Wilmington, 1892—; apptd. U.S. atty. for Dist. of Del. by President Roosevelt, 1903, reapptd. 1907, and by President Taft, 1912; U.S. dist. judge, Dist. of Delaware, since 1930. Attended Plattsburg Training Camp, 1915; capt. U.S.A., 1918. Pres. Wilmington Pub. Library, Wilmington Boys' Club. Mem. Am. Bar Assn. (v.p.). Republican. Clubs: Wilmington, Wilmington Country. Home: 1401 Broom St. Office: Post Office, Wilmington, Del.*

NIEMANN, Kenneth Edward, securities brokerage; b. Pittsburgh, Pa., July 24, 1902; s. A. Edward and Irene (Myers) N.; ed. George H. Thurston Sch., Pittsburgh, Pa., 1909-17, Hotchkiss Sch., Lakeville, Conn., 1917-19; A.B., Princeton, 1923; student U. of Pa. Law Sch., 1923-24; m. Irene Bentley, Dec. 4, 1923 (div.); 1 son, Donald Edward; m. 2d, Elizabeth Buchanan, Jan. 26, 1929; children—Kenneth Edward, Jr., Lawrence Buchanan. Employed as clk. Seaboard Nat. Bank, 1924-25; asso. in various capacities from clk. to mem. firm J. H. Holmes & Co., 1925-35, name changed to Chaplin & Co. and mem. firm as gen. partner since 1935 (firm mem. of New York Stock; mem. Pittsburgh Stock Exchange. Republican. Episcopalian (vestryman St. Andrew's Ch.). Mason (32°, Shriner). Clubs: Duquesne, Pittsburgh Athletic, Longue Vue (Pittsburgh); Princeton (New York). Home: 446 S. Dallas Av. Office: 419 Wood St., Pittsburgh, Pa.

NIESLEY, Howard Graybill, asst. dir. agr. extension; b. nr. Carlisle, Pa., Mar. 22, 1890; s. John Brubaker and Elizabeth (Graybill) N.; B.S., Pa. State Coll., 1917; M.S., U. of Wis., Madison, Wis., 1923; m. Emily Blackburn, June 16, 1934; 1 dau., Cynthia B. Engaged as prin. high sch., Palenville, N.Y., 1911-13; co. agrl. agt. Dauphin Co., Harrisburg, Pa., 1917-23; specialist agrl. econs. extension, 1923-27; asst. dir. agr. extension, Pa. State Coll. since 1927. Mem. Alpha Zeta. Republican. Presbyterian. Mason (32°). Clubs: University, Centre Hills Country (State College, Pa.). Home: 517 West Park Av., State College, Pa.

NIETZ, John Alfred, prof. education; b. nr. Toledo, O., Oct. 22, 1888; s. Gottfried and Bertha (Dietrichkeit) N.; A.B., O. Northern U., 1914, B.Pd., same, 1914; A.M., O. State U., 1919; ed. U. of Chicago, 1924-26, Ph.D., same, 1933; m. Ruby K. Sawyer, Aug. 8, 1915; 1 dau., Martha S. Successively teacher in rural schs., high sch. prin., supt. schs., Maumee, O., and supt. schs. Perrysburg, O.; dean Murphy Collegiate Inst., Sevierville, Tenn., 1921-24; asso. with Sch. Edn. of U. of Pittsburgh since 1926, asso. prof. of edn., 1929-39, prof. since 1939. Mem. Nat. Edn. Assn., Pa. State Assn. Teachers of Edn., Am. Assn. Univ. Profs., Nat. Council for Social Studies, Hist. Soc. Western Pa., Phi Delta Kappa, Kappa Phi Kappa. Republican. Methodist. Mason. Contbr. numerous articles to ednl. jours. and chapters to books. Collector sch. textbooks over 50 yrs. old; now propr. 2,500 copies of such books. Home: 2901 Shady Av., Pittsburgh, Pa.

NILES, Emory Hamilton, judge; b. Baltimore, Md., Oct. 15, 1892; s. Alfred Salem and Mary Hamilton (Waters) N.; prep. edn., Baltimore Poly. Inst., 1905-09; A.B., Johns Hopkins, 1913; Rhodes Scholar, Oxford U., Eng., 1913-16, B.A., M.A., B.C.L.; LL.B., U. of Md., 1917; m. Anne Whitridge Williams, Nov. 4, 1922; children—Anne Whitridge, Emory Hamilton, Mary Waters. Began practice at Baltimore, 1919; in practice with Niles, Wolff, Barton & Morrow, 1919, became mem. firm of Niles, Barton, Morrow & Yost, 1925; lecturer in law, U. of Md., since 1925; lecturer on law of admiralty since 1926; asso. judge of Supreme Bench of Baltimore since Nov., 1938. Mem. Judicial Council of Md., 1923-34; pres. Baltimore Criminal Justice Commn., 1933-34; trustee Goucher College since 1934, pres. bd. since 1936. Commissioned 2d lieutenant 313th F.A., U.S.A., 1917, later 1st lt. and capt.; served with same regt., 80th Div., A.E.F., 1918-19. Sec. Rhodes Scholarship Committee for Md., 1924-31. Mem. Am. and Baltimore City bar assns., Md. Bar Assn. (v.p. 1935-36), Maritime Law Assn. of U.S., Alpha Delta Phi. Democrat. Unitarian. Clubs: Gibson Island Club, Hamilton St. Founder, and editor of American Maritime Cases since 1923; United States Aviation Reports since 1928. Home: 5600 Waycrest Road. Office: Court House, Baltimore, Md.

NILES, Henry Carpenter, judge; b. Angelica, Allegheny Co., N.Y., June 17, 1858; s. Rev. Henry Edward and Jeannie Eliza (Marsh) N.; ed. York Co. Acad., 1868, York High Sch., 1870. York Collegiate Inst., 1874; LL.B., Columbia, 1880; LL.D., Franklin and Marshall Coll., 1935; m. Lillie Schall, Feb. 17, 1886. Began law practice at York, Pa., June 1880; elected judge 19th Judicial Dist. Pa., Nov. 3, 1925; Dem. nominee for judge of Superior Court of Pa., 1929, justice of Supreme Court of Pa., 1930; reëlected pres. judge 19th Judicial Dist. of Pa., 1935. Pres. Pa. Bar Assn., 1904-05; state chmn. Lincoln Party, 1905-06; mem. Am. Bar Assn., Civil Service Reform Assn., Am. Acad. Polit. and Social Science, Internat. Law Assn., Nat. Assn. for Constl. Govt.; charter mem. Inst. of Law. Presbyn. Independent Democrat. Club: University (Phila.). Occasional writer and speaker on legal and polit. subjects. Home: York, Pa.

NILES, Henry Edward, consultant in management; b. Baltimore, Md., Jan. 20, 1900; s. Alfred Salem and Mary Hamilton (Waters) N.; A.B., Johns Hopkins, 1921; student Univs. of London and Cambridge, Eng., 1921-22; m. Mary Cushing Howard, Sept. 15, 1923; children—Mary Cushing, Alice Lee. Began with Baltimore Life Ins. Co. during coll. vacations; reports dept., Federal Reserve Bank of New York, Jan.-Aug., 1923; asst. mgr. Life Ins. Sales Research Bureau, Hartford, Conn., 1923-30; partner Henry E. Niles and M. C. H. Niles, consultants in management, Baltimore and Toronto, since 1930. Mem. Inst. of Management, Am. Management Assn., Nat. Office Management Assn., Am. Statistical Assn., Alpha Delta Phi. Club: University (Hartford, Conn.). Co-author (with M. C. H. Niles), The Office Supervisor, His Relations to Persons and to Work, 1935. Address: Baltimore Life Bldg., Baltimore, Md.

NILES, John S., surgeon; b. Waymart, Pa., April 16, 1862; s. Andrew Pitcher and Margaret Ann (Dorr) N.; M.D., Jefferson Med. Coll., Phila.; m. Bertine Hunsicker, April 23, 1902; children—Rachel, John, Mary, Harry Dorr, Bertine. Surgeon-in-chief, Carbondale (Pa.) Gen. Hosp.; surgeon for Hendrick Mfg. Co., Del. and Hudson R.R., Hudson Coal Co. Dir. Y.M.C.A. Club: Elkview Country (Carbondale, Pa.; dir.). Home: 74 Lincoln Av. Office: 76 N. Main St., Carbondale, Pa.

NIMICK, Thomas Howe, securities brokerage; b. Pittsburgh, Pa., Jan. 19, 1893; s. Frank Bailey and Ella Howard (Howe) N.; ed. Shadyside Acad., Pittsburgh, Pa., 1905-11; A.B., Princeton, 1915; student Harvard U. Law Sch. 1915-16; m. Genevieve D. Murtland, June 29, 1918; children—Kathleen Murland, Thomas Howe, Jr., George A. Asso. with Colonial Steel Co. in various capacities, 1916-32; broker in securities since 1935; pres. and dir. Duquesne Inclined Plane Co.; sec., treas., and dir. Perfect Laundries of Pittsburgh, Inc. Served as capt. field arty., U.S.A., 1917-19, with A.E.F. in France, 1918-19. Dir. Shadyside Hosp., Family Soc. of Allegheny Co. Republican. Episcopalian. Mason. Clubs: Pittsburgh, Duquesne, Allegheny Country, Harvard-Yale-Princeton, Fox Chapel Golf, Pittsburgh Golf. Home: 6315 Fifth Av. Office: 1045 Union Trust Bldg., Pittsburgh, Pa.

NIMKOFF, Meyer Francis, prof. sociology; b. New York, N.Y., April 16, 1904; s. Abraham and Lena (Selwiz) N.; A.B., Boston U., 1925; A.M., U. of Southern Calif., 1926, Ph.D., same, 1928; m. Frances S. Lucas, June 25, 1929; 1 son, Peter Llewellyn. Engaged as asst. prof. sociology, Bucknell U., 1928-30; dir. Inst. for Family Guidance, lecturer Broadoaks Sch. of Child Research, Whittier Coll., 1930-31; dir. Inst. for Family Guidance, asso. prof. sociology, Bucknell U., 1931-38, prof. since 1938. Mem. Am. Sociol. Soc., Eastern Sociol. Conf., Alpha Kappa Delta, Phi Delta Kappa, Phi Beta Kappa, Phi Kappa Phi. Author: The Child, 1933; The Family, 1934; Parent Child Relations, 1935. Home: 120 S. 13th St., Lewisburg, Pa.

NIMS, Albert Armstrong, coll. prof.; b. Montague, Mass., Aug. 1, 1886; s. William Henry and Lucy Almira (Armstrong) N.; B.S., Worcester Poly. Inst., 1908; E.E., 1911; m. Viola Estelle Libby, Nov. 27, 1912; children—Roland Libby, Albert Armstrong, Jr. Instr. physics, Worcester Poly. Inst., 1909-11; tester and designer Murphy Electricity Rectifier Co., Rochester, N.Y., 1911; D.C., designer Crocker-Wheeler Co., Ampere, N.J., 1912-19; elec. engr. Siemund Wenzel Electric Welding Co., 1919-33, dir. since 1931; became instr. elec. engring. dept., Newark Coll. of Engring., Newark, N.J., 1922, now prof. elec. engring.; instr. in elec. measurements, Cooper Union Evening Sch., New York, N.Y., 1917-18; instr. in elec. engring., Newark Tech. Sch., evenings, 1918-35. Mem. Am. Inst. Elec. Engrs., Soc. for Promotion Engring. Edn., Tau Beta Pi, Sigma Xi. Republican. Presbyn. Home: 120 Ashland Av., Bloomfield, N.J. Office: 367 High St., Newark, N.J.

NISSLER, Christian William, physician and med. asso.; b. Silver Bow, Mont., Sept. 1, 1888; s. Christian W. and Christine (Konzelman) N.; M.D., Jefferson Med. Coll., Phila., Pa., 1919; m. Anna Longstreet Fitzgerald, June 2, 1921; children—Christian William III, Elizabeth Ann. Joined staff of Jefferson Med. Coll., Phila., 1921, asso. in dept. chest diseases since 1933; clin. chief Dept. of Tuberculosis City of Phila., since 1924; asst. physician dept., tuberculosis, Phila. Gen. Hosp. since 1933, physician dept. of tuberculosis since 1939. Mem. Phila. Co. Med. Soc. (chmn. com. on tuberculosis, 1938-39). Republican. Episcopalian. Mason. Club: Laennec Society (Phila.). Author of article "Nontuberculosis Lesions in Children Simulating Pulmonary Tuberculosis," 1935. Address: 1034 S. 54th St., Philadelphia, Pa.

NISSLEY, Walter Baer, prof. vegetable gardening extension; b. Florin, Pa., Feb. 23, 1885; s. Amos Reist and Frances (Baer) N.; ed. Millersville (Pa.) State Teachers Coll., 1902-05; B.S., Pa. State Coll., 1910; m. Louise A. Cox, Aug. 5, 1913; children—Frances Elaine, Robert Whitehill. Engaged as asst. in soil survey work, Pa. State Coll., 1910, mem. teaching staff in horticulture, 1911-14; organized and head dept. of horticulture, L.I. State Sch. of Agr., 1914-17; engaged in commercial vegetable growing, L.I., 1918-19; prof. vegetable gardening extension, Pa. State Coll., since 1919. Mem. Delta Tau Delta, Gamma Sigma Delta. Republican. Presbyterian. Club: University (State College, Pa.). Home: 501 W. Fairmount Av., State College, Pa.

NITCHIE, Elizabeth, coll. prof.; b. Brooklyn, N.Y., March 5, 1889; d. Henry Evertson and Elizabeth Woods (Duncklee) N.; A.B., Columbia U., 1910, Ph.D., 1918. Associated with Goucher Coll., Baltimore, since 1918, as instr. in English, 1918-20, asst. prof., 1920-23, asso. prof., 1923-30, prof. English since 1930. Pres. Md. Branch of Women's Internat. League. Mem. Modern Lang. Assn., Am. Assn. Univ. Profs., Am. Assn. Univ. Women, Pi Beta Phi, Phi Beta Kappa. Presbyn. Clubs: Hamilton Street, College. Author: Vergil and the English Poets, 1919; The Criticism of Literature, 1928; Master Vergil, 1930. Contbr. many articles to revs. and jours. Home: 2436 St. Paul St., Baltimore, Md.

NITRAUER, William Ellsworth, supervising prin. schs.; b. Middletown, Pa., Dec. 26, 1903; s. William Walter and Margaret Elizabeth (Rife) N.; A.B., Lebanon Valley Coll., 1925; A.M., Columbia U., 1930; grad. study, Columbia U. part time 1935; m. Violet Priscilla Walter, June 14, 1932. Teacher and asst. prin. high sch., Annville, Pa., 1925-27; supervising prin. borough schs., Mount Joy, Pa., since 1927. Mem. troop com., Mount Joy Boy Scouts. Served as grad. mgr. athletics, Lebanon Valley Coll., 1925-27. Mem. A.A.A.S., Nat. and Pa. State edn. assns., Progressive Edn. Assn., Soc. for Curriculum Study, Central Pa. Football Officials Assn. Republican. Lutheran. Mason (32°). Clubs: Rotary (past pres.), Richland (Mount Joy). Home: 160 New Haven St., Mount Joy, Pa.

NITZSCHE, Elsa Koenig, portrait, painter; b. Phila., Pa., Mar. 24, 1880; d. Prof. George A. and Wilhelmina Marquart Koenig; studied in Pa. Acad. and grad. Woman's Sch. of Design; in France, Germany, Switzerland and Italy, 8 yrs., under Bouveret and other eminent teachers; m. George E. Nitzsche, May 1, 1909. Has exhibited in prin. exhbns. in America and abroad; hon. mention, Paris Salon; represented in many Am. and several foreign collections. Member of Longfellow Guild (president 1927-29). Club: Woman's. Author of Dickel and the Penguin, and other juvenile illustrated stories. Awarded 1st prize in Germantown, Phila., Short Story competition. Home: "Inspiration," 1024 Westview Av., Germantown, Philadelphia, Pa.; (summer) "Elsylvania, Deer Isle, Maine.

NITZSCHE, George E., recorder Univ. of Pa.; b. Nazareth, Pa., June 3, 1874; s. August J. and Ellen (Venter) N.; LL.B., University of Pennsylvania, 1898; Litt.D., Ursinus College, 1937; admitted to all the Pennsylvania courts; m. Elsa Koenig, 1909; children—Wilhelmina Koenig, Elsa Koenig (Mrs. Jack E. K. Nitzsche James). Bursar of Law Sch., 1898-1901; recorder of University of Pa., since 1901. Founder of "Old Penn" (now the Pennsylvania Gazette), official weekly of the University, and editor, 1902-16; editor Law Memorial Vol., 1900; established, 1907, Memorial Library of U. of Pa. and Her Sons; mng. editor Med. Bull., 1808-09; pres. Am. Oncologic Hosp., 1929-31; dir. St. Luke's Hosp. since 1938. Pres. Priestly Conf. Unitarian Chs., 1929-31; organizer 1931, Priestley Home for Unitarians, pres., 1931-37, now hon. pres. Exec. sec. sanitation and medicine Pa. State Pub. Safety Com.; exec. sec. mil. service Pa. Council of Defense, 1917-18; maj. U.S.A. (R.C.) Trustee First Unitarian Ch., 1900-18; pres. Phila. Rescue Home, 1913-14. Founder and 1st pres. Acacia Club of Philadelphia and Franklin Chapter of Acacia; grad. mgr. University of Pa. Musical Club, 1922-24; mem. bd. Phila. Civic Opera Co., 1923-25, pres. 1936-37; v.p. Phila. Music League since 1925; pres. La Scala Opera Co., 1925-26; hon. pres. of Penna. Grand Opera Co., 1927-28; mgr. Phila. First Open Air Music Festival, 1925; also many open air carnivals, operas, pageants and music festivals. Awarded Nat. Order White Lion by Pres. Benes', Czechoslovakia; silver cultural medalist, Italy; Chevalier Order of Crown of Italy and other foreign decorations; good citizenship medal, Phila. Chapter S.A.R.; gave the Koenig Mineral Collection and various prizes to U. of Pa. Mem. Pa. Hist. Soc., Philadelphia City History Soc., Moravian Hist. Soc., Edgar Allan Poe Club, Layman's League of Germantown (pres. 1921-23), Anthropol. Soc. (v.p. 1912-13; pres. 1929-31), Musical Fund Soc.; Penn. German Folklore Soc. (dir. since 1935); hon. member internat. B. Franklin Soc., New Helvetic Soc., Am. Soc. of the Royal Italian Orders, Omega Tau Sigma. Mason. Clubs: Sojourners (pres. 1933), Lenape, Rotary (v.p. 1921-22), Art Alliance. Author: Philadelphia (10 edits.); University of Pennsylvania, illustrated (3 edits.); University of Pennsylvania—Its Traditions, Memorials, etc. (9 edits.); Philadelphia and Her Great University; also of numerous pamphlets, articles, etc. Editor: University Lectures (7 vols.); Historical Sketch of University of Pennsylvania, 1740-1929. Home: 1024 Westview Av., Germantown. Office: 3400 Walnut St., Philadelphia, Pa.

NIXON, Anson Benoa, chem. engr.; b. Medora, Ind., Oct. 18, 1890; s. Foster Toms and Amanda E. (Wray) N.; B.S., Purdue Univ., 1915; m. Edith Harper, Sept. 13, 1919; 1 dau., Winifred Harper. Chemist Hercules Powder Co., Kenvil, N.J., San Diego, Calif., 1915-18, asst. supt., San Diego, Calif., 1918-19, Kenvil, N.J., 1919-24, supt. Parlin, N.J., 1924-28, gen. mgr. cellulose products dept., Wilmington, Del., 1928-34, gen. mgr. naval stores dept. since 1934, dir. since 1935. Trustee Westminster Presbyn. Ch., Wilmington, Del., since 1936. Mem. Am. Inst. Chem. Engrs. Republican. Presbyterian. Clubs: Wilmington, Wilmington Country, Turf (Wilmington, Del.). Home: Hollyoak, Del. Office: care Hercules Powder Co., Wilmington, Del.

NIXON, Lewis, shipbuilder; b. Leesburg, Va., Apr. 7, 1861; s. Joel Lewis and Mary Jane (Turner) N.; early edn. Leesburg; grad. U.S. Naval Acad., 1882, at head of class, and sent to Royal Naval Coll., Greenwich, Eng., by Navy Dept.; m. Sally Lewis Wood, Jan. 29, 1891; 1 son, Stanhope Wood. Tranferred to construction corps of navy, 1884; in 1890 designed battleships Oregon, Indiana and Massachusetts, and then resigned from Navy to become superintending constructor of Cramp Shipyard, Phila.; resigned, 1895, and started Crescent Shipyard, Elizabeth, N.J., on own account, where he built 100 vessels in 6 yrs., among others the submarine torpedo-boat Holland and seven other submarines, the monitor Florida, torpedo-boat O'Brien and cruiser Chattanooga; organized Standard Motor Constrn. Co.; propr. Lewis Nixon's Shipyard; started, 1895, and pres. until 1904, Internat. Smokeless Powder Co.; now sole owner and pres. Nixon Nitration Works, Raritan River Sand Co. Apptd. by Mayor Van Wyck, pres. East River Bridge Commn., 1898; trustee and pres. Webb Inst. of Naval Architecture. Democrat; succeeded Richard Croker as leader of Tammany Hall, Nov. 1901-May 1902; chmn. finance com. Dem. Congressional Campaign Com., 1902. Mem. N.Y. State Commn. to St. Louis Expn. Commr. pub. wks. Borough of Richmond, 1914-15; supt. pub. works of State of N.Y., 1919; pub. service commr. State of N.Y., 1919-20. Mem. bd. of visitors to U.S. Naval Acad., 1902, by appmt. of President Roosevelt. Received in spl. audiences by the King of England, Popes Pius X and XI, Emperor Nicholas of Russia, King of Belgians, Premier Mussolini and presidents of Argentine, Chili, Colombia, Panama, Costa Rica and Guatemala. Del. Dem. Nat. convs., 1900, 04, 08, 12, 20, 24, 32; chmn. Dem. State Conv., Buffalo, 1906; apptd. by President Taft, del. 4th Pan-Am. Conf., Buenos Aires, 1910, and E.E. and M.P. on special mission to represent U.S. at Chilean Centenary, 1910. Clubs: Lawyers, Press, Union, Brook, N.Y. Yacht (New York); Metropolitan, Army and Navy (Washington). Home: 16 E. 79th St., New York. Office: Nixon, N.J.*

NOBLE, David Amurth, clergyman; b. Bloomsburg, Pa., June 6, 1899; s. Amurth and Susan Mabel (Geiger) N.; ed. U. of Louisville, 1922-24; B.D., Presbyn. Theol. Sem. of Ky., 1925; A.B., U. of Chattanooga, 1927; grad. study, Southern Bapt. Theol. Sem., 1929-30; Ph.D., Northwestern U., 1933; m. Christena Brightwell, June 9, 1925; children—Maynard Amurth, David Franklin. Ordained to ministry Presbyn. Ch., 1925; pastor, Louisville, Ky., 1923-25; asst. pastor, Chattanooga, Tenn., 1926-28; teacher pub. speaking and Christian ethics, Moody Bible Inst., Chicago, 1928-31; pastor Leverington Presbyn. Ch., Phila., Pa. since 1933, also teacher Bible Doctrine, Bible Inst. of Pa. since 1933; mem. Christian Edn. Com. of Presbytery of Phila. North. Mem. Pi Gamma Mu. Republican. Presbyn. Club: Union League (Philadelphia). Home: 614 E. Gates St., Roxborough, Philadelphia, Pa.

NOBLE G. Kingsley, curator, explorer; b. Yonkers, N.Y., Sept. 20, 1894; s. G. Clifford and Elizabeth (Adams) N.; grad high sch., Yonkers, 1913; A.B., Harvard, 1917, A.M., 1918; Ph.D., Columbia, 1922; m. Ruth Crosby, Aug. 13, 1921; children—G. Kingsley, Alan Crosby. Leader of Harvard expdn. to Guadeloupe, 1914, to Newfoundland, 1915; zoölogist Harvard expdn. to Peru, 1916; leader Am. Mus. expdn. to Santo Domingo, 1922; lecturer on vertebrate palæontology, Columbia; curator of herpetology, Am. Mus. Natural History, since 1919, also curator exptl. biology since 1928. Visiting prof. zoölogy, U. of Chicago, 1931. Mem. Advisory Board New York Aquarium. Ensign U.S.N.R.F. Mem. Am. Soc. Zoölogists, Am. Assn. Anatomists, Am. Soc. Naturalists, New York Acad. Science, Zoöl. Soc. London, Galton Soc., Am. Philos. Soc., Sigma Xi. Republican. Unitarian. Club: Explorers. Author: The Biology of the Amphibia, 1931. Contbr. numerous scientific articles and articles in popular mags. Asso. editor Jour. of Morphology. Home: 209 Sunset Rd., Englewood, N.J. Address: American Museum of Natural History, New York, N.Y.*

NOBLE, Urbane Alexander, banking; b. Edwards, N.Y., Nov. 16, 1877; s. David and Jurane J. (Hill) N.; ed. grade schs., Edwards, N.Y., 1888-93; Potsdam Normal Sch., 1893-99; M.D., Columbia U. Med. Sch., 1904; m. Clara J. Simpson, Apr. 19, 1906; children—John, Elizabeth (Mrs. Charles E. Scott), Jane. Engaged in teaching sch., 1895-99; in pvt. practice as physician and surgeon, 1904-09; asso. with Cleveland-Simpson Co., dept. store, Scranton, Pa., since 1909, dir. since 1909, pres. since 1936; dir. First Nat. Bank of Scranton since 1932, pres. since 1936; dir. Scranton Lackawanna Trust Co.; vice-pres. and dir. First Nat. Corpn.; chmn. bd. dirs. Simpson Real Estate Corpn. Trustee Scranton-Keystone Jr. Coll. Dir. Scranton Chamber of Commerce. Republican. Presbyn. Clubs: Scranton, Country, Rotary of Scranton. Home: 520 Clay St. Office: First Nat. Bank, Scranton, Pa.

NOBLE, William Dove, surgeon; b. Preston, Md., Aug. 5, 1891; s. Jacob Leverton and Manie Eugenia (Travers) N.; A.B., St. John's Coll., Annapolis, Md., 1914, A.M., 1919; M.D., Johns Hopkins U. Med. Sch., 1918; grad. student Army San. Sch., A.E.F., in France, 1918; m. Dorothy B. Klinefelter, Sept. 15, 1922; children—Dorothy Harcourt, Jean Leverton, Ann Cushman. Resident Church Home and Infirmary, Baltimore, Md., 1919-22; asst. in surgery, Johns Hopkins U. Med. Sch., 1922-29, U. of Md. Med. Sch., 1922-25; engaged in pvt. practice surgery at Baltimore, 1922-29, in practice at Easton, Md., since 1929. Served as 1st lt. Med. Corps, U.S.A., 1918-19, with A.E.F. in France. Fellow Am. Coll. Surgeons, Am. Bd. of Surgery. Mem. Med. and Chirurg. Faculty Md., Johns Hopkins Med. & Surg. Soc., Talbot Co. Med. Soc., Phi Sigma Kappa. Democrat. Mason. Clubs: Chesapeake Bay Yacht, Talbot Country (Easton); Pithotomy (Baltimore). Home: 219 S. Hanson St. Office: 208 Goldsborough St., Easton, Md.

NOCK, Randolph Maxwell, surgeon; b. New Church, Va., July 4, 1902; s. Edward Everett and Martha Florence (Byrd) N.; student U. of Md., 1919-21; M.D., U. of Md. Med. Sch., 1925; m. Frances Earle, Sept. 25, 1929; children—Mary Earle, Edward Everett II. Engaged in practice of surgery at Salisbury, Md. Fellow Am. Coll. Surgeons; mem. Am. Med. Assn., Southern Med. Assn., Med. & Chirurg. Faculty Md., Aero-Med. Assn., Wicomico Med. Soc. Mason. Home: 114 E. William St. Office: Professional Bldg., Salisbury, Md.

NOER, Ruth Douglas, univ. prof.; b. Menominee, Mich.; d. Peter J. and Ellen Marian (Peabody) N.; B.S. in H.E., U. of Wis., Madison, 1918; student U. of Chicago, summer 1922; M.S., U. of Minn., Minneapolis, 1925; student Teachers Coll. of Columbia U., summers 1936-37. Engaged in teaching, high sch., Wabeno, Wis., 1918-20; asst. in home economics, U. of Minn., Minneapolis, 1923, instr., 1923-25; asst. prof. home economics, W.Va. U., Morgantown, W.Va., 1925-38, dean of women, 1929-38, head div. home economics since 1938. Mem. Am. Home Economics Assn., Nat. Edn. Assn. Am. Assn. Univ. Women, W.Va. Home Economics Assn., W.Va. Edn. Assn., Phi Upsilon Omicron, Pi Lambda Theta, Alpha Phi, Mortar Board. Episcopalian. Home: 233 S. High St., Morgantown, W.Va.

NOLAN, James Bennett, lawyer and historical writer; b. Milford, N.J., Dec. 1, 1879; s. James and Katherine (Stewart) N.; grad. Reading High Sch., 1896; B.S., Cornell U., 1900; post grad. work, U. of Bonn, Germany; LL.D., Albright Coll., Reading, Pa., 1938; m. E. May Smink, Oct. 24, 1906; children—Catherine, James. Admitted to Pa. bar, 1901. Lecturer and prof. emeritus Albright Coll.; Reading; dir. Reading Trust Co., Reading Gas Co., Berks Light, Heat & Power Co. First asst. over-seas commr. for K. of C., World War; served in 5th French Army on French front, Feb.-Oct. 1918. Pres. Reading Acad. Music; dir. Reading Chamber Commerce; mem. council Cornell U., Albright Coll. Mem. many hist. and lit. socs. in America, England, France and Germany. V.p Pennsylvania Historical Association, 1937. Chmn. Internat. Lafayette Centenary Pilgrimage, 1935; archivist Am. Friends of Lafayette. Decorated Chevalier Legion of Honor. Mem. in social orgns. and clubs in New York, Phila. and London. Democrat. Catholic. Author: Early Narratives of Berks County, Pa., 1927; Foundation of the Town of Reading in Pa., 1929; Tale of Reading Town—Episode from Plot Against Washington, 1930; George Washington and The Town of Reading, 1931; Smith Family of Pennsylvania, 1932; Annals of Penn Square, Reading, 1933; Lafayette in America, Day by Day, 1934; Benjamin Franklin in Scotland and Ireland, 1938; also numerous brochures. Editor: Neddie Burd's Reading Letters (Epic of Early Berks Bar), 1927; General Benjamin Franklin. Contbr. numerous articles. Home: 432 Oley St. Office: 36 N. Sixth St., Reading, Pa.

NOLL, Charles Franklin, prof. of agronomy; b. Green Park, Pa., July 22, 1878; s. Jonas and Rosanna (Hostetter) N.; ed. Cumberland Valley State Teachers Coll., 1899-1900; B.S., Pa. State Coll., 1906; M.S., Cornell U., 1910, Ph.D., same, 1920; m. Nora Crilly, Sept. 15, 1910; children—John Jacob, Charles Joseph, William Edward, Alice Catherine. Engaged as teacher in pub. schs., 1896-99 and 1900-02; asso. with agronomy dept., Pa. State Coll., since 1908, prof. of experimental agronomy since 1920, head of dept. since 1938. Mem. Am. Soc. Agronomy, Sigma Xi, Alpha Zeta, Gamma Sigma Delta, Phi Kappa Phi. Republican. Presbyterian. Home: 313 S. Burrows St., State College, Pa.

NOLLAU, Edgar Hugo, chemist; b. St. Louis, Mo., Aug. 25, 1891; s. Louis George and Lydia Louise (Muller) N.; student elementary schs., Louisville, Ky., and St. Louis, Mo., 1899-1907, secondary sch., St. Louis, 1907-11; B.S. in chem., U. of Ky., Lexington, Ky., 1914; m. Elizabeth Morton, Apr. 9, 1917; 1 dau., Elizabeth Louise. Research chemist asst. Ky. Agrl. Exptl. Sta., Lexington, Ky., 1914-15; with U.S. Dept. Agr., Washington, D.C., 1916-17; research chemist E. I. duPont de Nemours & Co., Wilmington, Del., 1918-19, asst. div. head and div. head, exptl. sta., 1919-21, chem. supt. Fabrikoid Div., Newburgh, N.Y., 1921-33, chemist main office, Wilmington, since 1933. Mem. Am. Chem. Soc., Am. Inst. Chemists, Ky. Acad. Science, Alpha Tau Omega, Alpha Chi Sigma. Episcopalian. Home: 917 Bancroft Parkway. Office: DuPont Bldg., Wilmington, Del.

NOLTE, John Frank, civil engr.; b. Huntingdon, Pa., Aug. 27, 1888; s. John Sabastin and Laura May (Wharton) N.; student Pub. Schs., Harrisburg, Pa., Zeth's Business Coll., Altoona, Pa., 1903-04, Internat. Correspondence Schs., 1909-11, Ohio Northern Prep. Sch., Ada, O., 1912-13, Ohio Northern U., 1913-17; m. Máble Theressa Knouss, Feb. 12, 1919; 1 son, Wharton Allen. Special Messenger in chief engr's. office, Pa. R.R., Altoona, Pa., 1903-05; special helper Pa. R.R. shops, 1905-09; surveyor Pa. Coal & Coke Co., Cresson, Pa., 1909-11; asst. supt. and engr. Standard Refractories, Claysburg, Pa., 1914-15; engr. inspr. test dept. Pa. R.R., Altoona, 1920-21; constrn. engr., 1923-24; asst. engr. of constrn. Fla. Power & Light Co., Miami, Fla., 1921-23, asst. engr. of constrn., 1924; sr. highway inspr. Pa. Dept. of Highways, 1928-31; adminstr. John S. Nolte Estate, 1931-35; area inspr. and field engr. Fla. Works Progress Adminstrn., since 1935; pres. and designer The Craft Mart; dir. Dade Co. Co-operatives. Served as cadet, 1st O.R.T.C.; 2d lt., Res. U.S. Army, 1st lt., Regular Army, 16th Inf. with A.E.F., and Army of Occupation in Germany, 1917-1920; now maj., Inf. Res. Corps. Organizer and dir. Self-supporting Colonies for relief clients in rural areas. Served as 1st commr. of cubbing Blair-Bedford Scout Council, Altoona, now member executive board; Pa. Commr. of Cubbing; Dade County Scout Council, Miami, Fla. Mem. Am. Soc. Engrs., Am. Legion (past post historian), Forty and Eight (past chef de train), The Am. Vets Assn., Mil. Order of Fgn. Wars of U.S., Soc. of First Div., 16th Inf. Assn., Army and Navy Union, Res. Officers Assn. (organizer and charter mem. Miami Chapter), Jr. Order of American Mechanics (organizer and charter mem. Altoona Chapter; charter mem. Miami Chapter), Nat. Sojourners, Miami Beach Association, "N" Society (honorary letter soc., Ohio Northern University), Am. Red. Cross, Veterans Army (Area Comdr.). Republican. Presbyterian (Elder). Mason. Clubs: Montgomery (Ala.) Country; Lion Paw (O.N.U.), Engineers, Tennis, William J. Bryan's Bible Class of Miami (charter mem.), Army Officers' (Fort George Mead, Md.). Author of articles on economics, unemployment, decentralization of industry, co-operative homesteads and super-highway constrn., crime preventives and youth leadership. Varsity football mgr. and pres. varsity tennis teams, O. Northern U., 1915-17. Address: Nolte Bldg., Altoona, Pa.

NOLTING, William Greaner, architect; b. Baltimore, Md., Nov. 11, 1866; s. Adolphus William and Virginia Temperance (Higgins) N.; grad. high sch., Richmond, Va.; m. Fannie Amanda Bonn, Sept. 21, 1893; children—Wm. Wyatt, Frances. Began as mem. firm Wyatt & Nolting, Baltimore, 1887; firm architects for Baltimore City Court House; Veterans' Bureau, Washington, D.C., and many other pub. and pvt. bldgs.; pres. Algonquin Bldg. Co., St. Paul Bldg. Co., Green Spring Land Co., Dunmore Realty Company. Trustee Roland Park (Md.) Country Sch. Fellow Am. Inst. Architects. Democrat. Episcopalian. Clubs: Maryland, Elkridge Country, University; Farmington Country (Charlottesville, Va.). Home: Filston Manor, Glencoe, Baltimore Co., Md. Office: Keyser Bldg., Baltimore, Md.

NOONAN, James Paul, supt. schs.; b. Zerbe, Pa., Nov. 24, 1898; s. Joseph C. and Ellen (Heplen) N.; B.S. in Edn. and A.M., New York U.; m. Julia Kenney, June 27, 1920; children—James, Julia, Helen. Prin. Amsbry schs., 1922-24; grade teacher, Brockton, 1924-27; elementary prin., Maryd, 1927-30, Tuscarora, 1930-34; supervising prin. Schuylkill Twp., 1934-37; supt. Mahanoy Twp. Schs. since 1937. Dir. Am. Red Cross. Mem. N.E.A., Pa. State Edn. Assn. Catholic. Elk, Rotarian. Home: 416 E. Mahanoy Av. Office: 246 W. Mahanoy Av., Mahanoy City, Pa.

NOONAN, Joseph F(rancis), college pres.; b. Zerbe, Pa., June 28, 1892; s. Joseph C. and Ellen (Hepler) N.; B.Pd., Millersville (Pa.) State Normal Sch., 1909, M.Pd., 1913; Ph.B., Muhlenberg Coll., Allentown, Pa., 1923; A.M., New York U., 1925, Ph.D., 1926; m. Helene Schmidt, Aug. 18, 1920. Engaged as prin. high sch., Branchdale, Pa., 1909-10; supervising prin., Duncannon, Pa., 1910-11; instr. high sch., Rahway, N.J., 1911-14; supt. schs., Mahanoy Twp., Pa., 1914-37; supt. schs., Mahanoy City, Pa., 1935-37; pres. State Teachers Coll., Mansfield, Pa., since 1937; mem. staff, Muhlenberg Coll., State Coll., and New York U., ad interim. Served as apprentice seaman U.S.N. during World War. Mem. Nat. Ed. Assn., Pa. State Ed. Assn. (past pres.), Pa. Soc., Phi Delta Kappa. Home: 73 Academy St., Mansfield, Pa.

NOONE, Ernest Langsdorff, physician; b. Manchester, N.H., Jan. 13, 1898; s. Edward and Persis Miriam (Langsdorff) N.; A.B., U. of Pa., 1919; M.D., Jefferson Med. Coll., 1923; m. Joyce Toulmin, of Preston, England, May 12, 1938. Owner and dir. Camp Lenape for Boys, Pocono Mountains, Pa., 1920-23; interne Children's Hosp., Phila., 1924, St. Joseph's Hosp., Phila., 1923, Chicago Lying-In Hosp., 1925; began practice in pediatrics, Phila., 1926; asst. prof. in pediatrics, U. of Pa. Med. Sch.; pediatrist to Phila. Gen. Hosp., Delaware Co. Hosp., Fitzgerald-Mercy Hosp. Certified by Am. Bd. Pediatrics. Mem. Am. Acad. Pediatrics, Delaware Co. Med. Assn., Phi Chi, Sigma Phi Epsilon. Presbyterian. Mason. Home: Cedar Lane and Wilde Av., Drexel Hill, Pa.

NORCROSS, Theodore White, civil engr.; b. Medford, Mass., Jan. 25, 1883; s. John Henry and Cynthia Josephine (White) N.; B.S. in C.E., Tufts College (Mass.), 1904, honorary M.S., 1935; m. Christine Seruiah Cleveland, on Sept. 8, 1909; children—Cleveland, Barbara Elizabeth, Theodore White, David Rogers. With U.S. Geol. Survey, stream gaging and hydrographic work, 1904-07, 1909-10; installing water supply and purifying plant, Springfield, Mass., 1907-09; dist. engr., U.S. Forest Service, Denver, Colo., 1910-13; asst. chief engr., U.S. Forest Service, 1913-20, chief engr., 1920—, water power, buildings, dams, bridges, other structures, trails, roads and land surveying, Washington, D.C.; mem. Federal Bd. of Surveys and Maps. Mem. Delta Upsilon, Am. Soc. C.E., Soc. Am. Foresters, Am. Forestry Assn. Conglist. Mason. Home: 407 Raymond St., Chevy Chase, Md.

NORCROSS, Wilbur Harrington, coll. prof.; b. Ralston, Pa., June 28, 1882; s. William Harrington and Martha Jane (Rees) N.; A.B., Dickinson Sem., 1902; A.B., Dickinson Coll., 1907; A.M., same, 1913; Ph.D., Johns Hopkins U., 1920; m. Agnes Frysinger, Dec. 23, 1911 (died 1917); m. 2d, Helen Burns, Aug.

9, 1918; 1 dau., Isabel Mullin. Ordained to ministry M.E. Ch., 1907; preacher Viva, Pa., 1904-07, Duncannon, Pa., 1907-08; mem. Central Pa. Conf., 1907; teacher Greek and Latin, Dickinson Sem., 1908-14, dean 1912-14; instr. psychology, Dickinson Coll., Carlisle, Pa., 1916-17, asso. prof., 1917-23, prof. since 1923, dean jr. class since 1929; prof. psychology and head of dept. Summer Sch. Johns Hopkins U. since 1928. Served as 1st lt. San. Corps., U.S.A. attached to Med. Research Lab., 1918-19; maj. Res. Corps. Dir. Carlisle Y.M.C.A. Trustee Todd Memorial Home; M.E. Home for Children. Mem. A.A.A.S., Southern Soc. Philosophy and Psychology, Kappa Delta Pi, Phi Kappa Sigma, Phi Beta Kappa, Omicron Delta Kappa (nat. v.p. 1938-39, nat. pres. 1939-41). Democrat. Mem. M.E. Ch. Mason (K.T.). Club: Johns Hopkins (Baltimore); Kiwanis (dist. gov. of Pa. 1923). Home: 111 S. College St., Carlisle, Pa.

NORDEN, N(orris) Lindsay, organist, condr.; b. Phila., Pa., Apr. 24, 1887; s. Norris Harkness and Helen Eugenia (Freas) N.; B.S., Columbia, 1909, Mus.B., 1910, A.M., 1911; m. Grace R. Vandiver, June 25, 1919 (now deceased); children—Helen Virginia (dec.), Grace Elise, Warren Everett; m. 2d, A. Barbara Matz, June 20, 1938. Asst. organist St. Bartholomew's Ch., N.Y. City, and mus. dir. parish house, 1902-04; organist and choirmaster, St. Mary's Episcopal Ch., Brooklyn, 1906-15, All Saints' Ch., Brooklyn, 1915-17; organist 2d Presbyn. Ch., Phila., 1917-27, Synagogue Rodelph Shalom, Phila., since 1922; organizer, 1912, condr., 1912-17, Aeolian Choir; condr. Mendelssohn Club, Phila., 1916-26, Reading (Pa.) Choral Soc. since 1920, Pottsville Choral Soc., 1923-25, Brahms Chorus of Phila., 1927-35; organizer, 1935, and since conductor Germantown Orchestra. Musical dir. First Presbyterian Ch., Germantown; instr. in music, High Sch. of Commerce, N.Y. City, 1909-18, Episcopal Acad., Phila., 1918-21, Curtis Institute, Phila., 1924-26, Germantown Acad., 1929-1933; guest conductor Fairmount Park Dell Concerts, 1931, 33; conductor Germantown "Pop" Concerts, 1932-33; instr. Cape Cod Inst. of Music, 1937. Composer of choral works, anthems orchestral pieces, etc., also 125 arrangements of Russian choral music. Mem. Beethoven Assn., N.Y. City, since 1936; mem. Am. Musicological Soc. Contbr. to Musical Quarterly, Christian Science Monitor. Home: 7211 Emlen St. Address: 615 N. Broad St., Philadelphia, Pa.

NORDGAARD, Martin Andrew, coll. prof.; b. Northwood, Ia., Jan. 29, 1882; s. Asmund and Helga (Mandt) N.; A.B., St. Olaf Coll., Northfield, Minn., 1903; student U. of Chicago, 1912-13, U. of Pa., 1917-18; Ph.D., Columbia U., 1922; unmarried. Teacher mathematics, acad. and high sch., Wis. and Minn., 1903-09; head mathematics dept., Columbia Lutheran Coll., Everett, Wash., 1909-12; instr. mathematics, U. of Me., 1913-16; asst. prof mathematics, Grinnell Coll., Grinnell, Ia., 1918-21; prof. mathematics and head dept., Antioch Coll., 1922-24, St. Olaf Coll., 1924-29, Upsala Coll., East Orange, N.J. since 1932; on mathematics staff, Columbia U., 1921-22, Hunter Coll., 1929-31. Mem. A.A.A.S., Math. Assn. of America, Nat. Council Teachers of Mathematics, Am.-Scandinavian Foundation. Republican. Lutheran. Home: 339 Prospect St., East Orange, N.J.

NORDSTROM, John A., pres. Machine Shop Equipment Co.; b. Stockholm, Sweden, July 10, 1883; brought to U.S., 1900; s. Frederick and Matalda (Peterson) N.; ed. pub. schs.; m. Josephine Berkquist, May 1, 1903; children—Edwin, Helen, Frederick, William, David, Lucille. Became foreman U.S. Steel Corpn., 1903, Johnson Bronze Co., 1910, Bessemer Gas Engine Co., 1912; pres. and dir. Machine Shop Equipment Co. since 1918. Republican. Lutheran. Clubs: Grove City Country (dir.), Kiwanis (pres. 1934-35), Grove City Commercial (v.p. 1938). Home: 121 Edgewood Av. Office: Third St., Grove City, Pa. Died Feb. 28, 1939.

NORMAN, George M(iller), mfg. chemist; b. Wallingford, Pa., Dec. 9, 1877; s. E. R. and Jemima Esbin (Miller) N.; B.S., Pa. State Coll., 1899; grad. study, U. of Wis., 1903-05; m. Grace G. Gutterson, of Owatomma, Minn., Feb. 14, 1916; children—Elizabeth Miller, Margaret Jean. Employed as chemist, Illinois Steel Co., Chicago, Ill., 1899-1900; with Tenn. Coal, Iron & R.R. Co. and General Chem. Co.; chemist with E. I. Du Pont de Nemours Co., 1905-13; asso. with Hercules Powder Co., Wilmington, Del., continuously since 1913, dir. since 1928. Republican. Unitarian. Clubs: Wilmington Country (Wilmington); Chemists (New York City). Home: Fairville, Pa. Office: Chester Co., Wilmington, Del.

NORMENT, William Meredith, clergyman; b. Bowling Green, Va., Oct. 28, 1886; s. Thomas Julian and Maria Hartwell (Taliaferro) N.; ed. Lynchburg (Va.) Coll., 1907-08, Richmond (Va.) Coll., 1908-09, Bethany (W.Va.) Coll., 1909-13; m. Margaret Beatrice Cox, Dec. 28, 1909; children—William Meredith, Woodford Taliaferro, Edward Cox, Paul Julian. Ordained to ministry of Disciples of Christ Ch., 1911; pastor, Indiana, Pa., 1913, Piqua, O., 1913-15, Louisville, Ky., 1915-18; pastor, Hagerstown, Md., since 1918. Pres. Capital Area Missionary Soc.; pres. Capital Area Conv.; mem. bd. mgrs. United Christian Missionary Soc. Trustee Lynchburg (Va.) Coll. Mem. Sigma Nu. Democrat. Mason. Home: 225 S. Potomac St., Hagerstown, Md.

NORRIS, Charles Camblos, physician; b. Phila., Pa., June 1, 1876; s. William Pepper and Laura (Camblos) N.; M.D., U. of Pa. Med. Sch., 1898; m. Helen E. Walsh, of Phila., Pa., Jan. 12, 1928. Interne, Pa. Hosp., 1898, U. of Pa. Hosp., 1899, Johns Hopkins Hosp., 1900; gynecologic anesthetist, U. of Pa. Hosp., 1900-03; instr. clin. gynecology, U. of Pa. Med. Sch., 1902-11, asst. in gynecologic pathology, 1907-21, instr. gynecology, 1911-22, asst. prof., 1922-27, prof. obstetrics and gynecology and dir. dept. since 1927; dir. Gynecean Hosp. Inst. Gynecol. Research of U. of Pa. since 1926; prof. gynecology, U. of Pa. Grad. Sch. of Medicine since 1927; attdg. obstetrician and gynecologist, U. of Pa. Hosp. since 1927; asso. obstetrician and gynecologist in chief, Pa. Hosp. since 1935; hon. cons. gynecologists, Phila. Gen. Hosp. since 1930; cons. obstetrician and gynecologist, Henry Phipps Inst. and Children's Hosp., Phila. Served as lt., U.S.N., 1916-18. Fellow Am. Coll. Surgs., Phila. Coll. Phys. Mem. Am. Gynecol. Soc. (pres. 1930), Am. Neisserian Med. Soc. (pres. 1937), Am. Bd. Obstetrics and Gynecology, Am. Radium Soc., Am. Gynecol. Club, Am. Soc. for Control of Cancer (dir. 1929-38), A.M.A., Pa. State and Phila. Co. med. socs., Phila. Obstet. Soc. (pres. 1929-30), Pathol. Soc. of Phila., Delta Psi. Republican. Episcopalian. Club: Philadelphia. Author: Gonorrhea in Women, 1913; Gynecological and Obstetrical Tuberculosis, 1921, rev., 1931; Uterine Tumors, 1930. Co-author (with Dr. John G. Clark), Radium in Gynecology, 1927. Contbr. about 100 articles and papers on obstetrics and gynecology. Home: Bryn Mawr, Pa. Office: 133 S. 36th St., Philadelphia, Pa.

NORRIS, George Washington, lawyer, banker; b. San Francisco, Calif., July 5, 1864; s. Joseph Parker and Mary Elizabeth (Garesche) N.; student U. of Pa., 1 yr.; m. Sarah Fox, June 10, 1891. Law practice in Phila., 1886-94; mem. Edward B. Smith & Co., bankers, 1894-1911; dir. Dept. Wharves, Docks and Ferries, Phila., 1911-15; v.-chmn. Federal Reserve Bank, Phila., 1916; Federal Farm Loan commr., 1916-20; gov. Federal Reserve Bank, Philadelphia, 1920-36; mem. bd. mgrs. Girard Trust Co., Beneficial Saving Fund Soc. (chmn.); dir. Edward G. Budd Manufacturing Co., Philadelphia Belt Line R.R. Co. Member American Academy Polit. and Social Science (dir.), Am. Econ. League (nat. council), Philadelphia Criminal Justice Assn. (pres.). Trustee The American Foundation. Democrat. Clubs: Philadelphia, Manufacturers and Bankers, Corinthian Yacht. Home: Gwynedd Valley, Montgomery Co., Pa. Office: Land Title Bldg., Philadelphia, Pa.

NORRIS, George William, M.D.; b. Phila., Jan. 1, 1875; s. William Fisher (M.D.) and Rosa Clara (Buchmann) N.; B.A., U. of Pa., 1895, M.D., 1899; unmarried. Practiced, Phila., 1899-1932, was prof. clin. medicine U. of Pa.; chief of medical service "A," Pennsylvania Hospital. Colonel Med. Corps, U.S.A., World War, later col. Med. O.R.C. Trustee of Mutual Assurance Co. of Phila. Fellow Coll. Physicians of Phila.; mem. Am. Philos. Soc., Assn. Am. Physicians, A.M.A., Phila. Pathol. Soc., Acad. Natural Sciences, Phi Kappa Sigma Fraternity. Club: Philadelphia. Author: Studies in Cardiac Pathology; Blood Pressure, Its Clinical Applications; also articles on "Pneumonia," in Osler's Modern Medicine, and numerous contbns. in med. jours. Co-author of Norris & Landis Diseases of the Chest and the Principles of Physical Diagnosis. Address: Dimock, Pa.

NORRIS, Henry; b. Phila., Pa., May 27, 1875; s. Joseph Parker and Isabel Nevins (Fry) N.; student pvt. schs., Episcopal Acad., William Blight Sch.; M.D., U. of Pa., 1896; studied in Germany, 1898-99; m. Ethel Bowman Wheeler, Aug. 3, 1898; children—Susan Wheeler, Henry, Ethel Stuart (Mrs. W. J. Robinson), Charles (dec.). Interne Univ. Hosp., Phila., 1896-98; instr. surgery, U. of Pa., 1899-1905; mem. staff Children's Hosp., St. Agnes Hosp., Howard Hosp., founder Waverly Mills (S.C.) Hosp. for Colored People, 1928; co-founder, with Dr. M. H. Briggs, of Rutherford Hosp., Rutherfordton, N.C.; retired from active work, 1925. Served with N.G. of North Carolina on Mexican Border, 1916; served in 30th Div., A.E.F., World War, had operating team and later became div. surgeon. Fellow Am. Coll. Physicians; former mem. Southern Surg. Tri-State Soc., etc. Contbr. to med. publs. Address: Bryn Mawr, Pa.; (winter) Pawleys Island, S.C.

NORRIS, Walter Blake, educator; b. Chelsea, Mass., Sept. 4, 1879; s. Edwin Somerby and Lois Florida (Clement) N.; A.B., Harvard, 1901; studied Johns Hopkins, 1908-09; m. Frances Harrison Hollyday, June 6, 1911; 1 dau., Elizabeth Hollyday. Prin. Hubbardston (Mass.) High Sch., 1901-02; instr. Attleboro (Mass.) High Sch., 1902-03; prof. English, Bridgewater (Va.) Coll., 1903-05; instr. Wenonah (N.J.) Mil. Acad., 1905-07; instructor English, 1907-19, assistant prof., 1919, asso. prof., 1919-1926, professor since 1926, United States Naval Academy. Member Williamstown Institute of Politics, 1924. Editor: (with M. E. Speare) World War Issues and Ideals, 1918; (with M. E. Speare) Vital Forces in Current Events, 1920. Author: (with H. F. Krafft) Sea Power in American History. 1920; Annapolis: Its Colonial and Naval Story, 1925; History of St. Anne's Parish, Annapolis, 1935. Contbr. on ednl., lit. and naval history topics to mags. and revs. Address: Wardour, Annapolis, Md.

NORTH, Charles Edward, sanitarian; b. Scarborough, N.Y., July 28, 1869; s. Charles Randolph and Anna Mary (Haight) N.; A.B., Wesleyan U., Conn., 1893; M.D., Coll. Phys. and Surg. (Columbia), 1900; post-grad. work in bacteriology, Columbia, 1905, in pub. health, Harvard, 1909-10; m. Amelia Potter Palmer, 1903; children—Anna P., Jean P., Amelia P., Charlotte P., Charles E. Apptd., 1908, by Dept. of Health, N.Y. City, dir. of research on value of bacterial vaccines and Opsonic Index; consulting bacteriologist Jersey City Water Dept., 1908-10; established clean milk supply for infant milk stations of New York Milk Com., 1910; cons. expert on part of N.Y. State in litigation with State of N.J. on pollution of New York Harbor by Passaic Valley Sewer, 1913; apptd. chmn. Mayor Mitchel Com. on Milk, 1917; drew plans for municipal milk plant, Jamestown, N.Y., 1918; survey milk supply City of Rochester, N.Y., 1919; expert for Montclair, N.J., in water supply litigation, 1919; survey of milk supply of Kansas City, Mo., 1921. Sec. Nat. Commn. on Milk Standards; sec. Grade A Milk Assn. Mem. A.M.A., New York Co. Med. Soc., Am. Pub. Health Assn., New York Milk Com. Author numerous reports and papers on bacteriology, pub. health, and sanitation. Home: 147 Park St., Montclair, N.J. Office: 23 E. 26th St., New York, N.Y.

NORTH, Eric McCoy, gen. sec. Am. Bible Soc.; b. Middletown, Conn., June 22, 1888; s.

Frank Mason and Louise J. (McCoy) N.; B.A., Wesleyan U., Conn., 1909, M.A., 1910, D.D., 1931; M.A., Columbia, 1910, Ph.D., 1914; grad. Union Theol. Sem., 1913; m. Gladys Haven, April 17, 1920; children—Theodora, Louise Haven, William Haven. Asst. in systematic theology, Union Theol. Sem., 1913-14; asst. prof. history of Christianity, Ohio Wesleyan U., 1915-17; asso. editor S.S. Publs., M.E. Ch., 1917-26; ordained ministry M.E. Ch., 1918; dept. sec. Bd. of Foreign Missions, M.E. Ch., 1919-26; lecturer Drew Theol. Sem., 1919-24; sec. China Union Univs., 1924-27; asso. sec. Am. Bible Soc., 1927-28, sec. since 1928. Asst. sec. Gen. War-Time Commn. of the Chs., 1918; chaplain, 1st lieutenant U.S. Army, 1918-19. Trustee Yenching University, Harvard-Yenching Institute and Drew University. Member Phi Nu Theta, Sigma Chi, Phi Beta Kappa. Author: Early Methodist Philanthropy, 1915; Organization and Administration of the Sunday School (with J. L. Cuninggim), 1917; The Kingdom and the Nations, 1921; The Worker and His Church (with Louise M. North), 1921. Editor: The Book of a Thousand Tongues, 1939. Home: 32 Badeau Av., Summit, N.J. Address: Bible House, Park Av. at 57th St., New York, N.Y.

NORTH, Henry Briggs, mfr. chemicals; b. Janesville, Wis., Jan. 14, 1879; s. Crossman and Ida M. (Briggs) N.; Ph.G., U. of Wis., Madison, Wis., 1902, B.S., 1904, A.M., 1906; grad. study, Swiss Poly. Inst., Zurich, 1907-08; D.Sc., U. of Paris, 1909; m. Harriett E. Clark, Sept. 3, 1908; 1 dau., Helen Clark (Mrs. Fred C. Fay). Asst. in chemistry, U. of Wis., Madison, Wis., 1902-04, instr., 1904-07; asso. prof. chemistry, Rutgers Coll., New Brunswick, N.Y., 1910-17; research chemist, York Metal and Alloy Co., 1917-21; organized North Metal and Chem. Co. mfr. tungsten and molybdenum compounds, York, Pa., and pres.-treas. since 1921; organized York Bleachery and Dye Works, bleaching and dyeing cotton tape and yarn, York, Pa., and pres. since 1926. Served as pres. Bd. Edn., York, Pa., since 1935. Vice-pres. Bd. Trustees Millersville State Teachers Coll. Mem. Am. Chem. Soc., Alpha Chi Sigma, Phi Gamma Delta, Phi Beta Kappa. Baptist. Elk. Clubs: Country (York, Pa.); Chemists, Phi Gamma Delta (New York). Home: 159 E. Springettsbury St., York, Pa. Office: 640 E. Mason Ave., York, Pa.

NORTHART, Paul Raymond, civil engr.; b. Chicago, Ill., Mar. 11, 1886; s. John and Mary (Schonter) N.; B.S. and C.E., Carnegie Inst. Tech.; spl. course U. of Chicago; 3-yr. course in stresses and strains in structures, Mass. Inst. Tech.; m. Mildred Schauer, Oct. 10, 1910; children—Paul Raymond, Blanche Patricia. Asst. chief field engr. Am. Steel & Wire Co., 1907; design engr. Heyl & Patterson, Inc., Pittsburgh, 1908; asst. chief design engr. bridge and retort gas plant, Riter Conley Mfg. Co., 1909; in charge design and constrn. various water supply, water coagulation and power plants for Allegheny County, 1915; assisted E. K. Morris in design 1,100 ft. suspension bridge on Ohio River nr. McKees Rocks, 1915; chief of design bldg. dept. Koppers Co., Pittsburgh, 1916-20; in charge layout certain ry. work Nat. Tube Co., 1920-21; in pvt. practice as cons., designing and constrn. engr. on large mercantile bldgs., etc., 1922-26; chief bldg. valuation appraiser, Allegheny County, Pa., 1933-36, chief valuation appraiser and assessor in charge all spl. appraisals of land, bldgs., etc. since 1936; also in pvt. practice as cons. engr. K.C. (Bellevue, Pa., Council). Club: Planners of Pittsburgh (mem. bd. govs.). Wrote articles of tech. and ednl. nature. Home: 581 Crystal Drive, Mt. Lebanon, Pa. Office: 415 County Office Bldg., Pittsburgh, Pa.

NORTHCOTT, Elliott, judge; b. Clarksburg, W.Va., Apr. 26, 1869; s. Gen. Robert Saunders and Mary (Cunningham) N.; ed. Northwestern Acad. (Clarksburg), McCabe's Univ. Sch. (Petersburg, Va.), Law Sch., U. of Mich., spl. course, 1890-91; m. Lola Beardsley, Sept. 1, 1893; 1 son, Gustavus Andrew. Admitted to bar, 1891; city atty., Huntington, 1897-98; asst. U.S. atty., Southern Dist. of W.Va., 1898-1905; U.S. atty. same, 1905-09; E.E. and M.P. to Colombia, 1909-11, to Nicaragua, Feb.-Dec. 1911, to Venezuela, 1911-13; again apptd. U.S. dist. atty. Southern Dist. of W.Va., 1922; judge U.S. Circuit Court of Appeals, 4th Circuit, since Apr. 6, 1927. Member Republican State Executive and Central Committees, 1900-08; chairman speakers' bureau Republican State Committee, 1900; chairman Republican State Committee campaign of 1904. Mem. Bd. of Regents, W.Va. Normal Schs., 1905-09. Apptd. mem. Pub. Service Commn. of W.Va., 1915, and later chmn. same. Mason (33°). Club: Guyandotte. Home: Le Sage, W.Va.*

NORTHEY, E(lmore) H(athaway), pharm. chemist; b. Stillwater, Minn., July 31, 1905; s. John Burnham and Effie (Hathaway) N.; student Stillwater (Minn.) High Sch., 1919-22; B.A., U. of Minn., Minneapolis, 1927, Ph.D., 1930; m. Alberta Vivian Oakley, July 31, 1936. Chemist E. I. duPont de Nemours & Co., Wilmington, Del., 1930-32; chemist Calco Chem. Co., Bound Brook, N.J., 1932-35, chem. supervisor for pharmaceuticals since 1935. Served as 2d. lt., O.R.C., U.S. Army, 1927-32. Mem. Am. Chem. Soc., Am. Inst. Chemists, Sigma Xi, Gamma Alpha, Phi Lambda Upsilon. Home: Shepherd Av. Office: Calco Chemical Co., Bound Brook, N.J.

NORTHROP, John Howard, scientist; b. Yonkers, N.Y., July 5, 1891; s. John I. and Alice Belle (Rich) N.; B.S., Columbia Univ., 1912, M.A., 1913, Ph.D., 1915; D.Sc., Harvard, 1936, Columbia, 1937, Yale, 1937; LL.D., U. of Calif., 1939; m. Louise Walker, June 1918; children—Alice Havemeyer, John. W.B. Cutting traveling fellow, Columbia, 1915; apptd. asst. Rockfeller Inst. for Med. Research, 1916, asso. mem., 1922, mem. of Inst. since 1924; mem. editorial bd. Jour. of Gen. Physiology and Exptl. Biology Monographs. Capt. C.W.S., U.S. Army, 1918-19. Awarded Chandler medal, Columbia, 1937. Mem. Nat. Academy of Science, A.A.A.S., Soc. for Exptl. Biology and Medicine, Harvey Soc., Am. Philos. Soc., Sigma Xi (research fellowship com.), Phi Lambda Upsilon, Kais. Deutch. Akad. der Naturforscher, D.K.E. Awarded Stevens prize, Coll. Phys. and Surg. (Columbia), 1930. Clubs: Wilderness, Nassau Gun, Century Assn. Contbr. to Jour. Gen. Physiology, Crystalline enzymes (book). Address: Rockefeller Inst. for Medical Research, Princeton, N.J.

NORTHRUP, Edwin Fitch, electrothermic engr.; b. Syracuse, N.Y., Feb. 23, 1866; s. Ansel Judd and Eliza Sophia (Fitch) N.; A.B., Amherst, 1891; Cornell University last half of 1891; fellow and Ph.D. in physics, Johns Hopkins, 1895; hon. D.Sc., Lehigh University, 1932; m. Margaret Jane Stewart, Oct. 9, 1900. In practical elec. work in the West, 1895-96; prof. physics, U. of Tex., 1896-97; became asst. to Prof. H. A. Rowland, Baltimore, 1898, in development of his multiplex printing telegraph system, and later chief constructing engr. Rowland Printing Telegraph Co. until 1902; sec. Leeds & Northrup Co., mfrs. of elec. instruments, Phila., 1903-10; mem. physics faculty, Princeton U., 1910-20; v.p. and tech. adviser Ajax Electrothermic Corpn., Trenton, N.J. Has been granted a number of U.S. patents for new instruments and methods of producing and measuring high temperatures. Fellow Am. Inst. Elec. Engrs., Am. Assn. for Advancement Science; mem. Am. Electrochem. Soc., Inventors' Guild, Franklin Inst. Author: Methods of Measuring Electrical Resistance, 1912; Laws of Physical Science, 1917; Zero to Eighty, 1937. Contbr. to scientific lit. Extended research upon elec. conductivity and properties of matter at elevated temperatures. Inventor of Ajax-Northrup high frequency induction furnace; patentee of methods and numerous devices for inductive heating used throughout the world. Médaille de bronze, Paris Expn., 1900; Edward Longstreth medal, 1912; Eliott Cresson medal, 1916; Edward Goodrich Acheson gold medal and $1,000, 1931. Home: Princeton, N.J. Office: Ajax Park, Trenton, N.J.

NORTHRUP, Harry Benedict, metallurgist; b. Akron, O., Aug. 27, 1886; s. George Willard and Laura Minerva (Benedict) N.; ed. O. State U., 1905-07, 1908-11, E.M., 1911; m. Eva Pearl Hughes, of Osceola Mills, Pa., May 5, 1913; children—Harry Hughes, Jean Benedict (Mrs. C.P. William Fisher). Employed as miner, Gogebic Range, 1907-08; instr. metallurgy, Pa. State Coll., 1911-20; chief metallurgist, Diamond Chain & Mfg. Co., Indianapolis, Ind., 1920-25; metall. sales and cons. metallurgist, mem. firm, The J. W. Kelley Co., Cleveland, O., 1925-31; dir. Mineral Industries Extension, Pa. State Coll. since 1931. Served as metallurgist, engineering division, machine gun and small arm sect. U.S.A. Ordnance Dept., Bridgeport, Conn., ordnance office, 1918-19. Mem. Am. Soc. for Metals, Acacia, Sigma Gamma Epsilon. Republican. Methodist. Mason. Home: 410 S. Gill St., State College, Pa.

NORTHWOOD, Arthur, minister; b. Franklin, N.J., June 18, 1886; s. Albert A. and Carolyn E. (Brown) N.; student Trenton (N.J. High Sch., 1900-04; A.B., Princeton U., 1909, A.M., 1911; grad. Princeton Theol. Sem., 1912; D.D., Maryville (Tenn.) Coll., 1921; m. Louanne Conover, Oct. 23, 1912; children—Arthur, Conover, Louanne, Carol (dec.), Mary (dec.). Pastor Chestnut Level Presbyterian Ch., Quarryville, Pa., 1912-20, Elizabeth Av. Presbyn. Ch., Newark, N.J., since 1920; moderator Donegal Presbytery, Pa., 1916-17, Newark (N.J.) Presbytery, 1928-29; vice-moderator Synod of N.J., 1936-37; chmn. com. on Christian Edn., Presbytery of Newark, 1930-39. Trustee Belvidere (N.J.) Home. Mem. South End Ministers' Assn. (pres. 1926), Benham Club. Presbyterian. Mason. Address: 92 Chancellor Av., Newark, N.J.

NORTON, Albert Reeves, organist, teacher; b. Newcastle, Pa., Jan. 7, 1870; s. Joseph W. and Laura W. (Reeves) N.; ed. pub. schs. and grad. high sch., New Castle, Pa.; mus. edn. N.E. Conservatory of Music, Boston, Mass., 1888-94, grad. 1894; m. E. Grace Wood, of Pittsfield, Mass., Sept. 3, 1902; children—Idalaura (Mrs. J. Harold Noble); m. 2d, Gladys E. Bebout; children—William Carmont, Alberta Muriel (Mrs. Andrew Lennox), Alice Virginia. Has followed profession as organist, choir dir. and teacher since 1895; organist and teacher, New Castle, Pa., 1895-99, at Brooklyn, N.Y., 1899-1919; at Pittsburgh, Pa., since 1920; mem. faculty in piano and organ, Pittsburgh Mus. Inst. since 1920; organist and mus. dir., Homewood Presbyn. Ch., 1920-30, Ch. U. Brethren in Christ, Greensburg, Pa., since 1931. His choir broadcast programs over KDKA a number of times. Executive Com. Asso. Am. Guild of Organists. Mem. Musicians Club of Pittsburgh. Republican. Presbyn. Home: 5112 Bayard St. Office: 131 Bellefield Av., Pittsburgh, Pa.

NORTON, John B. S.; prof. botany, U. of Md. Address: University of Maryland, College Park, Md.

NORTON, Mary Teresa, congresswoman; b. Jersey City, N.J., Mar. 7, 1875; d. Thomas and Marie (Shea) Hopkins; ed. pub. schs. and business coll.; LL.D., St. Elizabeths Coll., 1930, Rider Coll., 1937; m. Robert Francis Norton (dec.); 1 son, Robert Francis (dec.). Apptd. to represent Hudson County on Dem. State Com., 1920; vice chmn. Dem. State Com., N.J., 1921-39; elected freeholder, 1923; del. at large Dem. Nat. Conv., New York, 1924, Houston, Tex., 1928; mem. 69th to 72d Congresses (1925-33), 12th N.J. Dist., and 73d to 76th Congresses 1933-39, 13th N.J. Dist.; chmn. Ho. of Rep. Dist of Columbia Com., 72d and 73d Congresses; chmn. Com. on Labor, Ho. of Rep.; Del. at large Dem. Nat. Com., 1932-36; chmn. N.J. Dem. State Com., 1932-35. Pres. Day Nursery Assn. of Jersey City. Catholic. Mem. Nat. Business and Professional Women's League, Queen's Daughters, Catholic Daughters of America. Clubs: Democratic, Jersey City Woman's; Nat. Democratic (Washington, D.C.). Home: 2600 Boulevard, Jersey City, N.J.

NORTON, Theodore Eli, librarian; b. Tacoma, Wash., May 29, 1899; s. Eli Porter and Jessie (Bachman) N.; A.B., U. of Wash., Seattle, Wash., 1923; A.M., U. of Mich., Ann Arbor, Mich., 1929; m. Daphne Todd, May 3, 1924; 1 dau., Mary. Librarian, Wash. State Normal Sch., Cheney, Wash., 1924-27; sr. classifier, U. of Mich. Library, Ann Arbor, Mich., 1928-

30; librarian, Lafayette Coll. Library, Easton, Pa., since 1930. Served as pvt., Arty., U.S. Army, 1917-18. Sec.-treas. Am. Friends of Lafayette; chmn. Am. League for Peace and Democracy, Easton (Pa.) Branch. Mem. Am. Library Assn., Delta Tau Delta. Decorated as Officer of the Acad. of Ministry of Edn. (France). Democrat. Congregationalist. Home: 136 Wayne Av. Office: Lafayette Coll. Library, Easton, Pa.

NORTON, Warren Perham, supt. of schools; b. near Waymart, Pa., Sept. 9, 1889; s. Warren Myron and Lydia (Perham) N.; grad. Clinton Twp. High Sch., Aldenville, Wayne Co., Pa., 1907; student Keystone Acad., Factoryville, Pa., 1908-11; A.B., Brown U., 1915; A.M., Teachers Coll., Columbia, 1923; m. Helen Miles Davison, July 5, 1922; 1 son, David Warren (b. Sept. 22, 1929). Teacher in rural school, Wayne Co., Pa., 1907-08; teacher of English, Cook Acad., Montour Falls, N.Y., 1916-17, Northwestern Mil. and Naval Acad., Lake Geneva, Wis., 1917-18, Rochester (Pa.) High Sch., 1919; prin. Public Schools, Girard, Pa., 1919-22; supervising prin., Sharpsville, Pa., 1922-28; supt. of schools, Meadville, Pa., since 1928. Served as corpl. Hdqrs. Co., 17th Inf., July-Dec. 1918; 2d lt. Inf., Reserve Corps, 1918-24. Pres. bd. dirs. Meadville Y.M.C.A.; mem. bd. dirs. Meadville Library, Art and Hist. Soc.; dir. Meadville Pub. Library; chmn. Meadville chapter Am. Red Cross; dir. N.W. Sect., Pa. Forensic Music League; dir. Crawford Co. Tuberculosis and Health Soc. Mem. N.E.A., Am. Assn. Sch. Adminstrs., Dept. of Secondary Sch. Prins., Alden Kindred of America, Am. Legion (comdr. Sharpsville Post 1924-27), Meadville Round Table, Meadville Literary Union, Delta Upsilon, Kappa Phi Kappa. Baptist (pres. bd. of trustees First Bapt. Ch.). Club: Kiwanis of Meadville (vice-pres.). Home: 434 Park Av. Office: High School Bldg., Meadville, Pa.

NORVELL, George W., pres. Perry-Norvell Co.; b. Charleston, W.Va., Feb. 13, 1885; s. William Gaston and Ruth Ann (Smithers) N.; student Charleston pub. schs., 1891-1901; m. Mary Whelan, Aug. 30, 1911; children—Martha, George W. Began as clk. in coal co. office and store, Monarch, W.Va., June 1901; shipping clk. Frank Payne Co., Charleston, 1905-06, buyer, 1906-10; buyer Norvell-Chambers Shoe Co., Huntington, W.Va., 1910-13; pres. and treas. Perry-Norvell Co., shoe mfrs., Huntington, W.Va., since 1913; director G. R. Kinney Co., Inc. Member City Council, Huntington, W.Va., since 1939. Episcopalian (vestryman Trinity Episcopal Ch.). Club: Guyan Country (Huntington, W.Va.). Home: 1608 5th Av. Office: Guyan Av. and 25th St., Huntington, W.Va.

NOSS, John Boyer, coll. prof.; b. of Am. parents, Sendai, Japan, Oct. 5, 1896; s. Christopher (missionary to Japan) and Lura (Boyer) N.; A.B., Franklin & Marshall Coll., 1916; B.D., Reformed Theol. Sem., Lancaster, Pa., 1922; Ph.D., U. of Edinburgh, Scotland, 1928; m. Mary Williamson Bell, June 14, 1922. Ordained to ministry of Evang. and Reformed Ch. in the U.S., 1922; pastor, Ephrata, Pa., 1922-26, Maybole, Scotland, 1927-28; asst. prof. philosophy, Franklin & Marshall Coll., 1928-31, prof. religion since 1931. Dir. Lancaster Co. Soc. for Crippled Children, Lancaster Law and Order Soc.; pres. Lancaster Peace Council. Mem. Am. Assn. Univ. profs., Phi Beta Kappa, Sigma Pi. Republican. Mem. Evangelical and Reformed Ch. in the U.S. Club: Torch (Lancaster). Home: 509 N. President Av., Lancaster, Pa.

NOURSE, Edwin Griswold, economist; b. Lockport, N.Y., May 20, 1883; s. Edwin Henry and Harriet Augusta (Beaman) N.; grad. Lewis Inst., Chicago, 1904; A.B., Cornell U., 1906; Ph.D., U. of Chicago, 1915; m. Ray Marie Tyler, Aug. 17, 1910; 1 son, John Tyler. Instr. in finance, Wharton Sch. of Finance and Commerce (U. of Pa.), 1909-10; prof. and head dept. economics and sociology, U. of S.D., 1910-12; same, U. of Ark., 1915-18; prof. agrl. economics, Ia. State Coll., and chief of agrl. economics sect., Ia. Expt. Sta., 1918-23; chief of agrl. div., 1923-29, dir., 1929—, Inst. of Economics of the Brookings Instn., Washington. Mem. Am. Econ. Assn., Am. Acad. Arts and Sciences, Council on Foreign Relations, Am. Farm Econ. Assn. (pres. 1924), Social Science Research Council, League of Nations Com. on Nutrition, 1935-37, Alpha Zeta, Phi Kappa Phi, Gamma Sigma Delta. Author: Agricultural Economics, 1916; Chicago Produce Market (Hart, Schaffner & Marx prize), 1918; American Agriculture and the European Market, 1924; The Legal Status of Agricultural Co-operation, 1927; The Co-operative Marketing of Livestock (with J. G. Knapp), 1931; America's Capacity to Produce (with associates), 1934; Marketing Agreements Under the Agricultural Adjustment Act, 1935; 3 yrs. of the Agricultural Adjustment Administration (with J. S. Davis and J. D. Black), 1937; Industrial Price Policies and Economic Progress (with H. B. Drury, 1938. Editor Journal Farm Economics, 1925-27. Contbr. to revs. and economic journals. Home: 3802 Jocelyn St., Chevy Chase, D.C. Office: 722 Jackson Pl., Washington, D.C.

NOVAK, Emil, surgeon; b. Baltimore, Md., Mar. 8, 1884; s. Joseph and Mary (Hajek) N.; M.D. magna cum laude, U. of Md. Med. Sch., Baltimore, 1904; A.B., Loyola Coll., 1912; hon. D.Sc., Trinity Coll., Univ. of Dublin, Ire.; m. Elizabeth Grace Rogers, Mar. 24, 1913; children—Edmund Rogers, Mary Elizabeth (Mrs. Wm. F. Schmick, Jr.), Thomas Emil. Resident surgeon Md. Gen. Hosp., Baltimore, Md., 1904-05; asso. prof. gynecology, Baltimore Med. Coll., 1905-09; asso. prof. gynecology, Coll. of Physicians & Surgeons, 1909-15; asso. in gynecology, Johns Hopkins Med. Sch. since 1915. Served as mem. vol. med. service corps during World War. Fellow Am. Coll. Surgeons, Am. Gynecol. Soc., Am. Assn. Abdominal Surgeons, Gynecologists and Obstetricians; mem. A.M.A., Am. Assn. for Study Internal Secretions, Southern Surg. Assn. Hon. fellow Soc. Reg. Med., Budapest, Soc. of Obstetrics and Gynecology, Buenos Aires, Central Assn. Obstetrics and Gynecology, Tex. State Med. Assn., Phi Beta Pi. Democrat. Clubs: University (Baltimore); Gibson Island (Gibson Island, Md.). Author: Menstruation and Its Disorders; The Woman Asks The Doctor. Contbr. to various textbooks and about 300 articles to med. jours. Home: 5223 Springlake Way. Office: 26 E. Preston St., Baltimore, Md.

NOVEY, M. Alexander; asst. prof. obstetrics and instr. pathology, U. of Md.; lecturer pub. health adminstrn., John Hopkins U.; asso. obstetrician U. of Md. Hosp.; adjunct obstetrician Sinai Hosp.; adjunct attending obstetrician South Baltimore Gen. Hosp.; attending obstetrician Provident Hosp. and Free Dispensary; chief div. of maternity hygiene, Baltimore City Health Dept., Diplomate of Am. Bd. of Ostetrics and Gynecology; fellow Am. Coll. Surgeons. Address: 2424 Eutaw Pl., Baltimore, Md.

NOVOTNY, E(mil) E(rnest), research chemist, mfr.; b. Tisch Mills, Wis., Jan. 12, 1883; s. Frank L. and Theresia (Mosic) N.; student pub. schs. and high sch. In employ Ill. Leather Co., 1900-04, Griffin Wheel Co., 1904-05; head development div. Western Electric Co., 1905-15; organized Durite Plastics, mfg. synthetic resins, producing products of his inventions, Phila., Pa., vice-pres. and gen. mgr. since 1915; has taken out over 200 patents issued and pending in connection with furfural, furfural resins and synthetic resins. Mem. Am. Chem. Soc. Mason. Club: Manufacturers and Bankers (Philadelphia). Home: Waelma Farm, Prospectville, Pa. (P. O., R.D. 65A, North Wales, Pa.). Office: Frankford Sta. P.O., Philadelphia, Pa.

NOVOTNY, Joseph, theologian; b. Prague, Czechoslovakia, Feb. 27, 1886; s. Rev. Henry and Anna (Kostomlatsky) N.; student Univ. Coll., Nottingham, Eng., 1906-08, U. of Vienna, Austria, 1908-09, U. of Geneva, Switzerland, 1909, U. of Prague, Czechoslovakia, 1909-12; D.D., Acadia U., Canada, 1935; came to U.S., 1928, naturalized, 1934; m. Dagmar Mladejovsky, Feb. 16, 1922; children—Anna, Zdenek. Began as Baptist minister, Prague, 1909; minister First Baptist Ch., Prague, 1909-19; pres. Czechoslovak Baptist Union, 1919; sec. Czechoslovak Y.M.C.A., 1920; gen. sec. Union of Constanz (union of all Protestants in Czechoslovakia), 1921-28; prof. New Testament, Internat. Baptist Sem., East Orange, N.J., since 1928. Served as chaplain, Czechoslovak Army, Siberia, 1918-20. Mem. Czechoslovak Baptist Union (hon. pres. since 1928), Czechoslovak Baptist Conv. in America and Canada (pres. since 1937), Fed. of Chs. in Czechoslovakia (mem. presiding bd.), Masaryk's Inst. (Prague), Am. Inst. in Prague (corr.), New England Soc. (East Orange, N.J.). Awarded Revolutionary Medal by Czechoslovak Govt., 1920. Baptist. Club: Clergy (N.Y.). Editor 4 revs.; author 35 books and booklets; contbr. scientific and theol. revs. Address: 64 S. Munn Av., East Orange, N.J.

NOWLAND, Otho, banker; b. Cecil Co., Md., Aug. 16, 1850; s. Otho and Eliza (Warburton) N.; ed. country sch.; m. Lottie L. Jennings, Mar. 31, 1886 (dec.). Sec., treas. and later v.p. Equitable Trust Co., 1889-1903, pres., 1903-27, chmn. bd. since 1927. Home: 2405 Willard St. Office: 9th and Market Sts., Wilmington, Del.

NOWLIN, Robert Aldridge, mining engr.; b. Lynchburg, Va., Nov. 19, 1888; s. Greenwood Hopkins and Lelia (Pendleton) N.; B.S. in C.E., Va. Mil. Inst., 1910; student Mass. Inst. Tech., 1911-12; m. Georgia J. Bonham, Oct. 20, 1920; children—Ann Pendleton, Robert A., Susan Shepherd. Began as rodman and advanced to chief engr. in Thacker, Pocahontas Tug River coal fields, and Winding Gulf, 1910-32; employed by Glen Alum Coal Co., Pocahontas Consolidated Collieries Co., Turkey Gap, Gilliam, Arlington, Shawnee, Black Wolfe Coal & Coke cos. and others, 1910-14; mining engr. Crozer Land Assn., Upland Coal & Coke Co., Crozer Coal & Coke Co., Page Coal & Coke Co. since 1914; v.p. Green H. Nowlin Corpn. since 1914. Served as lt., Engring. Corps, U.S. Army, World War. Mem. Am. Inst. Mining and Metall. Engrs.; asso. mem. Am. Soc. Civil Engrs. Democrat. Episcopalian. Club: Employees Country (Gary, W.Va.). Address: Elkhorn, W.Va.

NOYES, Arthur Percy, physician; b. Enfield, N.H., Nov. 26, 1880; s. David and Eliza J. (Howe) N.; ed. Dartmouth Coll., 1899-1902; M.D., U. of Pa. Med. Sch., 1906; m. Mary A. Dwinell, of Calais, Vt., Sept. 9, 1902 (dec.), m. 2d, Esther A. Dwinell, of Calais, Vt., Sept. 12, 1936; 1 son, David Noyes. Engaged in gen. practice of medicine in New York and Connecticut, 1906-15; post grad. study, U. of Pa., 1915-16; asst. phys., Boston Psychopathic Hosp., 1916-17, chief exec. officer, 1917-20; first asst. phys., St. Elizabeth's Hosp., Washington, D.C., 1920-29; supt. R.I. State Hosp. for Mental Diseases, 1929-36; supt. Norristown State Hosp., Norristown, Pa. since 1936. Fellow Am. Med. Assn., Am. Psychiatric Assn. Mem. N.E. Soc. of Psychiatry, Pa. Med. Soc., Alpha Omega Alpha. Independent. Home: Norristown State Hosp., Norristown, Pa.

NOYES, Morgan Phelps, clergyman; b. Warren, Pa., Mar. 29, 1891; s. Charles Henry and Effie (Morgan) N.; prep. edn., Phillips Exeter (N.H.) Acad.; B.A., Yale, 1914, D.D. 1938; Union Theol. Sem., N.Y. City, 1915-17, 1919-20; Columbia, 1915-17, 1919-20, M.A. 1922; m. Marjorie Bradford Clarke, July 24, 1926; children—Sarah Clarke, William Morgan. Asst. minister Madison Av. Presbyn. Ch., N.Y. City, 1919-20; minister Presbyn. Ch., Dobbs Ferry, N.Y., 1920-25, First Presbyn. Ch., Brooklyn, N.Y., 1925-1932, Central Presbyn. Ch., Montclair, N.J., since 1932; lecturer on pub. worship, Union Theol. Sem., 1930-32. Mem. administrative bd. Com. on Friendly Relations Among Foreign Students; mem. exec. com. Central Bur. for Relief of the Evangelical Chs. of Europe; mem. Am. Sect. Universal Christian Council for Life and Work; mem. Commn. on Worship, Federal Council of Churches of Christ in America; v.p. Montclair Council of Social Agencies; mem. Council of Soc. of Descendants of Colonial Clergy. Y.M.C.A. work with Russian and Czechoslovakian armies, 1917-19. Director

NUGENT, Union Theol. Sem. Member Psi Upsilon. Club: Montclair Athletic. Editor: Prayers for Services—a Manual for Leaders of Worship, 1934. Contbr. of chapter in "The Younger Churchmen Look at the Church," 1935. Home: 181 Wildwood Av., Upper Montclair, N.J.

NUGENT, Arthur William, cartoonist, puzzles; b. Wallingford, Conn., Feb. 20, 1891; s. Edward and Lena (Barton) N.; ed. Fawcett Art Sch., Newark, N.J., 1915-16, Soc. Illustrators Art Sch., N.Y. City, 1919-23; m. Anna Harback, Oct. 18, 1917; children—Marion Ruth, Arthur William, Jr. Engaged as puzzle cartoonist, N.Y. World, 1923-31, United Features Syndicate, 1931-32, Asso. Newspapers since 1932; known in newspaper world as "the world's leading puzzle maker." Served in A.S., U.S.N. during World War. Mem. Soc. of Illustrators (N.Y. City), Am. Legion. Undefeated Nat. A.A.U. champion tumbler, 1916-21; metropolitan champion tumbler, 1916-21. Catholic. Clubs: National Turners, Tuxedo Social (Newark). Home: 12 Tuxedo Parkway, Newark, N.J. Office: care Associated Newspapers, 247 W. 43d St., New York, N.Y.

NUGENT, Barbara Birely, librarian; b. New Haven, Conn., May 4, 1903; d. Charles William and Charlotte Ann (Bushnell) Birely; A.B., Vassar Coll., Poughkeepsie, N.Y., 1923; student Columbia U. Sch. of Library Science, 1937; m. Earl Nugent, Sept. 12, 1931. Asst. branch librarian, New Haven, Conn., 1924-25, branch librarian, 1925-30; librarian Dana Coll. Seth Boyden Sch. of Business and N.J. Law Sch., which later merged to become U. of Newark, N.J., since 1930. Mem. Am. Library Assn., Spl. Libraries assn. (sec. N.J. Chapter 1939-41), Am. Assn. of Law Librarians, Law Library Assn. of Greater N.Y. Home: 14 Jones St., New York, N.Y. Office: University of Newark, Newark, N.J.

NUGENT, Gerald P., pres. Phila. Nat. League Baseball Club; b. Phila., Pa., 1893; m. Mae Mallen, 1925; one son. Formerly business mgr. Phila. Nat. League Baseball Club, pres. since 1933. Served in 108th F.A., 28th Div., U.S. Army, in France during World War. Address: care Phila. Nat. League Baseball Club, Philadelphia, Pa.

NUGENT, James Alexander, educator; b. Jersey City, N.J., June 19, 1879; s. John and Margaret (Lynch) N.; A.B., St. Peter's Coll., Jersey City, 1898, A.M., 1899; LL.D., Seton Hall Coll., 1924; Ph.D., Fordham U., 1926; m. Eleanor Farley, Dec. 31, 1913; children—Margaret, Eleanor, Dorothy. Teacher N.Y. and N.J. schs., 1900-14; prin. schs., Jersey City, 1914-23, asst. supt., 1923-24, supt. since 1924. K.C. Clubs: N.J. Schoolmasters', N.Y. Schoolmasters', Rotary of Jersey City (pres.). Home: 269 Armstrong Av. Address 2 Harrison Av., Jersey City, N.J.

NUNGESSER, Fred L., Dr., optometrist; b. Pittsburgh, Pa., Nov., 18, 1888; s. Otto and Anna R. (Seifert) N.; ed. pub. sch. and high sch., Pittsburgh, Pa., South Bend (Ind.) Coll. of Optics; m. Theresa C. Bell, of Pittsburgh, Pa., June 8, 1911; children—Helen Anne, Virginia Loretta, Fred L., Jr., Robert Paul. Has followed profession as optometrist 30 years; started Nungesser Brothers, owner since July 7, 1933; member firm Nungesser Bros.; dir. Dormont Savings and Trust Co., Has held every office in Pittsburgh Optometric Assn., treas. Penna. Optometric Assn. for 15 yrs. Republican. Mem. St. Bernards. Home: Highland Rd. at Florida Av., Mt. Lebanon. Office: Penn Av. at Seventh St., Pittsburgh, Pa.

NUNN, William Lee, prof. econs.; b. Lee Co., Ala., Nov. 14, 1902; s. William Nathan and Rosalie (Page) N.; A.B., Oglethorpe U., 1922; A.M., Columbia U., 1927; m. Millicent Fassig, May 29, 1927; 1 dau., Elizabeth Page. Engaged as instr. econs., Oita Coll., Oita, Japan, 1922-26, U. of Pittsburgh, 1927-29, N.Y. Univ., 1929-31; prof. econs., U. of Newark, N.J. since 1931. Served as chrmn. Newark Labor Relations Bd. since 1937. Mem. Newark Adv. Planning Bd. since 1938. Dir. Commodity Distribution, Federal Surplus Relief Corpn., Washington, D.C., 1933-35. Mem. Am. Econ. Assn.,

Am. Assn. Univ. Profs., Alpha Lambda Tau. Democrat. Methodist. Mason. Clubs: Athletic (Newark). Co-author (with Spahr and others): Economic Principles and Problems, 1936. Contbr. ariteles to mags. and jours. Home: 8 Barry Pl., Radburn. Office: 40 Rector St., Newark, N.J.

NURICK, Gilbert, lawyer; b. Hickory Corners, Pa., Nov. 23, 1906; s. Charles and Anna (Katz) N.; A.B., Pa. State Coll., 1928; LL.B., Dickinson Law School, 1931; m. Sylvia Krauss, of Harrisburg, Pa., Oct. 14, 1932; 1 son, Carl Joseph. Admitted to Pa. bar, 1931, and since engaged in gen. practice of law at Harrisburg; asso. with Sterling G. McNees, 1931-35 and mem. firm McNees, Hollinger and Nurick since 1935. Dir. Jewish Community Center of Harrisburg. Mem. Pa., American and Dauphin Co. bar assns., and American Judicature Society, Beta Sigma Rho, Phi Kappa Phi, Kappa Phi Kappa, Kappa Delta Pi, Delta Sigma Rho. Author: Survey of Administrative Tribunals in Pa. Independent Republican. Jewish religion. B'nai B'rith (pres. local lodge). Royal Arcanum. Club: Blue Ridge Country (Harrisburg). Home: 2233 Green St. Office: State Street Bldg., Harrisburg, Pa.

NUSBAUM, Lee, air conditioning; b. Phila., Pa., Oct. 20, 1879; s. Isaac and Julia (Kohlberg) N.; B.S. in M.E., U. of Pa. Engring. Sch., 1900; m. Josephine Adler, June 4, 1907; children—Pauline, S. Richard. Employed in Baldwin Locomotive Works, Phila., 1901; designer Pencoyd Iron Works; asst. engr. Pennsylvania Iron Works Co.; propr. Pennsylvania Engineering Co., air conditioning and refrigeration, Phila., Pa., since 1904, Western Ice Mfg. Co. since 1909; dir. Northwestern Nat. Bank. Mem. Am. Soc. Mech. Engrs., Am. Soc. Heating and Ventilating Engrs., Am. Soc. Refrigerating Engrs., Refrigerating Machinery Mfrs. Assn. Jewish religion. Clubs: Manufacturers and Bankers, Engineers (Philadelphia); Manufacturers Golf and Country (Oreland); Philmont Country (Bethayres). Home: 315 Carpenter Lane. Office: 1119 N. Howard St., Philadelphia, Pa.

NUSBAUM, Louis, actg. supt. schs.; b. Phila., Pa., Apr. 7, 1877; s. Isaac and Julia N; B.S., Temple U., 1908; hon. Ped.D., Temple U., 1930; m. Edna Kohlberg, of San Francisco, 1906; children—Louise K. (Mrs. Nathan Cronheim), Elaine. Asst. prof. pedagogy, Central High Sch., Phila., Pa., 1900-05; prin. elementary sch., 1906-11; dist. supt. schs., Phila., Pa., 1912-15, asso. supt. schs., Phila., Pa., since 1915, actg. supt. schools, 1938-39; mem. cons. staff N.J. Training Sch., Vineland, N.J. Trustee, Nat. Farm Sch., Gratz Coll. Phila. Health Council, Mt. Sinai Hosp. Mem. Nat., Pa. State edn. assns. Jewish religion. Clubs: Manufacturers and Bankers, Schoolmens. Home: 153 W. Sharpnack St., Philadelphia, Pa.

NUSE, Roy Cleveland, artist; b. Springfield, O., Feb. 23, 1885; s. Charles Elias and Etta Virginia (Butts) N.; student Cincinnati Art Acad., 1905-12, John Herron Art Inst., Indianapolis, Ind., summer 1912, Oberlin Coll., summer 1913, home study dept., U. of Chicago, 1914-15, Pa. Acad. Fine Arts, 1915-18; m. Ellen Frances Guthrie, June 27, 1911; children—Jean Paul, Oliver William, Dorothy Virginia, Lucile Emily, Janet Frances, Robert Charles. Instr. in drawing and painting, Cincinnati Art Acad., 1910-12, Oberlin Coll., 1912-15; dir. Beechwood Sch. of Fine Arts, Jenkintown, Pa., 1915-33; instr. in drawing and painting, Pa. Acad. Fine Arts, Phila., since 1925, also head of coördinated courses between the Pa. Acad. and U. of Pa. Vice-pres. Fellowship of the Pa. Acad. of the Fine Arts. Winner of Cresson Scholarship, Pa. Acad. Fine Arts, 1917-18, Thouron prize, 1918, Toppan prize, 1918; first prize medal, Phila. Sketch Club, 1921. Home: Rushland, Pa.

NUTT, Arthur, mech. engr.; b. New Rochelle, N.Y., Feb. 6, 1895; s. Charles and Ada Sophia (Robinson) N.; B.S., Worcester (Mass.) Poly. Inst., 1916; m. Ann Dewey, Nov. 29, 1917; children—William Robinson, Jean Ann. Associated with the Curtiss interests (now Curtiss-Wright) since 1916; became chief engr. motor div., Curtiss Aeroplane & Motor Co., 1919; v.p. in charge Wright Aeronautical Corpn., since 1930. Mem. Soc. Automotive Engrs., Inst. Aeronautic Sciences, Sigma Xi, Tau Beta Pi. Home: 97 Overlook Rd., Upper Montclair, N.J. Office: Wright Aeronautical Corporation, Paterson, N.J.

NUTTER, Trevey, lawyer; b. Holbrook, W.Va., Mar. 30, 1880; s. Charles William and Cordelia Alice (Hall) N.; student W.Va. Wesleyan Coll., Buckhannon, 1898-1901; LL.B., W.Va. Univ. Law Sch., 1910; m. Etta Floy Hardesty, Oct. 10, 1912; children—Mary Elizabeth, Alice Virginia, William Trevey. Admitted to W.Va. bar, 1909; engaged in gen. practice of law at Fairmont since 1911; engaged in teaching in pub. schs. and in Fairmont Normal Sch., 1901-11; served as sec. and atty. Fairmont Bus. Mens Assn., 1912-25; Rep. candidate for W.Va. Senate, 1932; dir. and atty. First Nat. Bank in Fairmont since 1933, Community Savings & Loan Co. of Fairmont since 1917. Past pres. Fairmont Bd. of Commerce, Mountaineer Area Boy Scouts of America. Mem. Am. and W.Va. State bar assns., Marion Co. Bar Assn. (past pres.), Commercial Law League of America, W.Va. Chamber of Commerce, Phi Sigma Kappa. Republican. Methodist. Mason (K.T., 32°, Shriner). K.P. Clubs: Rotary, Field (Fairmont). Home: 1013 Locust Av. Office: Jacobs Bldg., Fairmont, W.Va.

NYBURG, Sidney Lauer, lawyer, author; b. Baltimore, Dec. 8, 1880; s. Simon S. and Rebecca (Lauer) N.; student Baltimore City Coll., 1895-98, completing coll. work under a tutor; LL.B., U. of Md., 1901; m. Henrietta L. Nyburg, Jan. 9, 1907; 1 son, Robert S. Practiced in Baltimore since 1902; member of Nyburg, Goldman & Walter. Member Bar Assn. of Baltimore City. Jewish religion. Mason. Clubs: University, Chesapeake. Author: The Final Verdict, 1915; The Conquest, 1916; The Chosen People, 1917; The Gate of Ivory, 1920; The Buried Rose, 1932. Home: 2414 Linden Av. Office: First National Bank Bldg., Baltimore, Md.

NYIRI, William Anthony, M.D.; b. Vienna, Austria, Mar. 3, 1893; s. Alexander de and Maria (Sladecek) N.; M.D., State U. of Vienna, 1916; m. Anne T. Gruich, Sept. 7, 1929; children— William, Anne Marie. Came to U.S., 1926, naturalized, 1932. Began practice medicine, 1916; asst. prof. internal diseases, U. of Vienna, 1925-27, practiced at Newark, N.J., since 1927, specializing in internal diseases; prof. pathology, Rutgers U. since 1929; attending physician (med. service) St. Michaels Hosp. since 1935, (med. and metabolic services) St. Mary's Hosp., Orange, N.J., since 1937; chief metabolic service City Hosp., Newark, since 1939. Catholic. Home and Office: 30 Van Ness Pl., Newark, N.J.

O

OAKLEY, Albert Chalmer, pres. South Hills Trust Co.; b. Glenfield, Pa., Dec. 6, 1861; s. Albert Galatin and Mary Ann (Wolf) O.; ed. Commerce Sch.; m. Ann Meyers, Oct. 18, 1894; children—Marion M., Wanda P., Albert C., Charles E. Pres. and dir. South Hills Trust Co. since 1937; treas. Duquesne Heights Bldg. & Loan Assn.; sec.-treas. and mgr. Duquesne Inclined Plane Co. Home: 232 Bigham St. Office: 1212 Grandview Av., Pittsburgh, Pa.

OAKLEY, Amy (Mrs. Thornton Oakley), author; b. Bryn Mawr, Pa., Jan. 21, 1882; d. James Hunter Ewing and Hannah Chase (Whelen) E.; ed. Baldwin Sch. (Bryn Mawr, Pa.) and Agnes Irwin Sch. (Phila.); m. Thornton Oakley, Mar. 28, 1910; children—Amy (dec.), Lansdale. Writer of travel articles for mags. since 1914. Chmn. for Phila. of Am. Unitarian Campaign, 1920; mem. Asso. Com. of Women of Pa. Mus. and Sch. Industrial Art (corr. sec. 1922-26; chmn. library com.); lit. mem. Phila. Art Alliance); mem. women's exec. com. Pa. 300th Anniversary Commn.; mem. exec. com. of Women's Com. for Am.-Swedish Hist. Mus.; mem. Pa. Chapter League of Nations Assn., Pa. Acad. Fine Arts, Phila. Orchestra Assn., Swedish

Colonial Soc., English-Speaking Union, Nat. Soc. Colonial Dames. Clubs: Alpin Français; Cosmopolitan (New York); Cosmopolitan of Phila. (mem. bd. govs.; chmn. library com.). Author: Hill-Towns of the Pyrenees, 1923; Cloud-Lands of France, 1927; Enchanted Brittany, 1930; The Heart of Provence, 1936; Scandinavia Beckons, 1938. Home: "Woodstock," Villanova, Pa.

OAKLEY, Cletus Odia, prof. matematics; b. Ranger, Tex., July 9, 1899; s. Benjamin Harrison and Tellia Ophelia (Richardson) O.; B.S. in elec. engring., U. of Tex., 1923; M.S., Brown U., 1926; Ph.D., U. of Ill., 1929; m. Louise Gladney, Oct. 22, 1922; children—Gladney, Bruce. With Bell Telephone Labs., New York, 1923-24; instr., Brown U., 1924-26, U. of Ill., 1926-29; fellow, Brown U., 1929-30, asst. prof., 1930-34; asst. prof. of mathematics, Haverford Coll., 1934-37, asso. prof. since 1937. Served in U.S. Navy, 1918-19. Mem. Phi Beta Kappa, Sigma Xi. Home: Featherbed Lane, Haverford, Pa.

OAKLEY, Thornton, illustrator, mural painter; b. Pittsburgh, 1881; s. John M. and Imogen (Brashear) O.; graduate Shady Side Academy, Pittsburgh, 1987; B.S., U. of Pa., 1901, M.S., 1902 (both in architecture); studied art with Howard Pyle, Wilmington, Del., 1902-05; m. Amy Ewing, Mar., 1910; children—Amy (dec.), Lansdale. Illustrator and writer of articles in mags., 1904—. Mem. Phila. Water Color Club (sec. 1912-38, pres. 1938); mem. jury of selection and of advisory com., dept. of fine arts, San Francisco Expn., 1915. Instr. drawing, U. of Pa., 1914-15; in charge dept. illustration, Pa. Mus. Sch. of Industrial Art., Phila., 1914-19, and 1921-36; mem. Jury of Selection and Award, Dept. of Fine Arts, Sesquicentennial Expn., Phila., 1926; spl. lecturer U. of Pa., Art Inst. Chicago, Metropolitan Museum of Art, Curtis Inst., Philadelphia, Pa., Pennsylvania Museum, etc. Chmn. of water color com. Phila. Art Alliance, 1917-36, sec., 1936-37, now dir.; mem. advisory council Art Assns. Phila. Represented in many pvt. and public collections in U.S. and in Pa. Acad of Fine Arts, Brooklyn Museum, Nat. Gallery, Library of Congress, Nat. Library of Brazil, British Mus. (London), Musée Pyrénéen (Lourdes, France), Musée de la Guerre, and Luxembourg Mus. (Paris). Chmn. com. of artists in charge of decoration of Phila. for the Victory Loan campaign. Drawings of Hog Island Shipyard adopted by U.S. Govt. for its foreign news service and reproductions sent to all parts of the world, 1918; industrial verse and drawings internationally distributed by Am. Fed. Labor. Designer and founder, 1935, of Oakley medal for achievement in Creative Art at Shady Side Acad., Pittsburgh, Sch. of Industrial Art, Phila., Sch. of Fine Arts of U. of Pa. Mem. William Penn Commemoration Com. (Phila.), 1932. Awarded Arthur Spayd Brooke memorial prize, U. of Pa., 1902; Beck prize water color, Phila. Water Color Expn., 1914; silver medal for water color, Panama Expn., 1915; 1st prize, Admiral Byrd Letter Contest by G. P. Putnam's Sons, 1931; decorated by the French Govt. with Palmes d'Officier d'Académie, 1931; Phila. water color prize, Phila. Water Color Exhbn., 1935. Hon. mem. Pa. Soc. of Miniature Painters; mem. Soc. of Illustrators, 1913-33. Fellowship Pa. Acad. Fine Arts; mem. Wilmington Soc. Fine Arts, Sigma Xi. Clubs: Contemporary (pres. 1937-39, T-Square (prize membership 1901), Alpin Française, Franklin Inn (Phila.). Illustrator: Westward Ho!, 1920; Autobiography of Benjamin Franklin, 1926; Philadelphia (by H. M. Lippincott), 1926; Folk Tales of Brittany (by Elsie Masson), 1929; Awake, America!, 1934, and Six Historic Homesteads, 1935 (both by Imogen B. Oakley); and of following works by Amy Oakley—Hill-Towns of the Pyrenees, 1923; Cloud-Lands of France, 1927; Enchanted Brittany, 1930; The Heart of Provence, 1936; Scandinavia Beckons, 1938. Murals in the Franklin Inst., Phila., depicting epochs of science from its dawn unto Franklin. Arthur: Anthem, My Wondrous Land (music by Guy Marriner). Home-Studio: "Wodstock," Villanova, Delaware Co., Pa.

OAKLEY, Violet, mural and portrait painter; b. N.Y. City; d. Arthur Edmund and Cornelia (Swain) O.; pupil Art Students' League, New York, Cecilia Beaux, Pa. Acad. Fine Arts, Howard Pyle, Aman Jean, Collin and Lazar, Paris, France. Designer of stained glass windows and mural decorations, Ch. of All Angels, New York, and mural decorations in governor's reception room, State Capitol, Harrisburg, Pa., entitled "Founding of the State of Liberty Spiritual"; also series of 9 panels in senate chamber, "Creation and Preservation of the Union"; series in Hannah Penn House, Philadelphia, "Building of the House of Wisdom"; window in house of Robert Collier, New York, "Divine Comedy of Dante Alighieri"; panel in Cuyahoga Co. Court House, Cleveland, "The Constitutional Convention, Philadelphia"; sculptor of medal for the Phila. Award founded by Edward Bok; triptych in Vassar Coll. Alumnæ House; "A Vision of the Apocalypse," Poughkeepsie, N.Y.; 16 panels, "The Opening of the Book of Law," in Supreme Court of Pa. state capitol; "Life of Moses," Graphic Sketch Club, Phila.; Library of the League of Nations, Geneva, Switzerland; represented in permanent collections of Pennsylvania Academy of Fine Arts, Philadelphia, Philadelphia Water Color Club, Victoria and Albert Museum, London, and in many libraries; also many portraits privately owned. Prizes: gold and silver medals, St. Louis Exposition, 1904; gold medal of honor, Pa. Acad. Fine Arts, 1905; medal of honor, San Francisco Expn., 1915; gold medal, Archtl. League of N.Y., 1916; Phila. prize, Pa. Acad., 1922; Joseph Pennell memorial medal, Philadelphia Water Color Club, 1932; awarded degree of Litt.D., Delaware College, 1918. N.A.; mem. women's com. of Nat. Acad. of Design, New York, Fellowship Pa. Acad. Fine Arts, Hist. Soc. Pa., Water Color Club, Phila. Art Alliance (dir.); hon. mem. A.I.A., Circulo de Bellas Artes, Madrid, Spain. Clubs: Contemporary (pres. 1925); Cosmopolitan (New York); Modern (hon.), Cosmopolitan (Phila.). Author: The Holy Experiment—A Message to the World from Pennsylvania, 1922; Law Triumphant—The Opening of the Book of the Law, The Miracle of Geneva, 1933; Divine Presence, Christ at Geneva (brochure), 1937; Samuel F. B. Morse—A Dramatic Outline of the Life of the Founder of Telegraphy and the Nat. Acad. of Design (with illustrations by the author), 1939. Address: Lower Cogslea, St. George's Rd., Philadelphia, Pa.

OATES, Theodore K., chief surgeon City Hosp.; surgeon B.& O. Ry. Co. Address: City Hospital, Martinsburg, W.Va.

OBER, Bert F(rank), physician; b. nr. Stahlstown, Pa., Mar. 16, 1874; s. Henry Saylor and Mary Rebecca (Blackburn) O.; B.Ed., California Teachers Coll. (B.E.) 1897; M.D., Medico-Chirurg. Coll., Phila., 1906; grad. study, Phila. Postgrad. Inst., 1937-39; m. Kathryn Heiser Schwartz, of Adamstown, Lancaster Co., Pa., July 5, 1908. Engaged in teaching sch., 1892-1902 and two summers normal sch.; in gen. practice of medicine and surgery at Latrobe, Pa., since 1906; has been dir. or vice-pres. in a number of local bus. orgns. in the past. Served as capt. Med. Corp., U.S.A., at Ft. Oglethorpe, Camp Wheeler and Centaur, 1917-19. Mem. Acad. Medicine, Pa. State and Westmoreland Co. med. socs., Am. Legion. Republican. Methodist. Home: 333 Main St., Latrobe, Pa.

OBER, Frank Benedict, lawyer; b. Baltimore, Md., Sept. 25, 1889; s. Albert G. and Rebecca G. (Hambleton) O.; A.B., Princeton U., 1910; LL.B., Harvard U. Law Sch., 1913; m. Margaret DeLancey Rochester, April 16, 1914; children—Richard F., DeLancey R., Frank B., Jr. Admitted to Md. bar, 1913 and since engaged in gen. practice of law at Baltimore; mem. firm Ritchie, Janney, Ober and Williams since 1915; dir. Kentucky Electric Power Co. Served as maj. F.A., U.S.A., 1917-19, with A.E.F. in France. Mem. Am. Bar Assn., Md. State Bar Assn., Baltimore City Bar Assn. Democrat. Episcopalian. Clubs: Merchants, Chesapeake. Home: 908 St. Georges Rd. Office: Baltimore Trust Bldg., Baltimore, Md.

OBER, Henry Kulp, clergyman, educator; b. nr. Mastersonville, Lancaster Co., Pa., Jan. 2, 1878; s. Michael Ruhl and Susan Baker (Kulp) O.; grad. Millersville (Pa.) State Normal Sch., 1898, B.Pd., 1910, M.Pd., 1911; B.S., Franklin and Marshall Coll., 1918, M.S., 1921; M.A. Columbia, 1922; grad. student U. of Pa., 1922-24; D.D. from Franklin and Marshall College in 1927; m. Cora Brinser Hess, May 25, 1899; children— Stanley Hess (dec.), Grace Hess, Ruth Hess, Henry K. (dec.). Teacher rural schs., Pa., 1897-1902; with Elizabethtown Coll. since 1902, pres., 1916-27; boro engr. Elizabethtown Boro since 1904; sec.-treas. Buch Mfg. Co.; etc. Licensed as minister Ch. of the Brethren, 1904, bishop, 1915; pres. Lancaster S.S. Assn.; mem Gen. Bd. Religious Edn., Edn. Com. of Pa.; v.p. Pa. State S.S. Assn.; pres. bd. trustees Elizabethtown Coll. Republican. Clubs: Columbia Univ., Rural, Rotary. Author: (with others), Training the Sunday School Teacher, 1913; Principles of Education, 1923; The Plain People of Lancaster County; Child Rights, 1934. Lecturer on ednl. and general subjects. Home: Elizabethtown, Pa.

OBER, J(ohn) Hambleton, banking; b. Baltimore, Md., Dec. 19, 1887; s. Gustavus and Bessie W. (Hambleton) O.; A.B., Princeton U., 1909, A.M., 1912; grad. study U of Munich, Germany, 1909-10; grad. study Johns Hopkins U., 1911-12; m. Charlotte C. Moseley, Feb. 25, 1933; 1 dau., Charlotte M. Asso. with father, Gustavus Ober, investment banker, Baltimore, Md., 1911-17; vice-pres. and treas. Inter-continental Trading Corpn., exporters, Baltimore, 1919-22; pres. Morris Plan Bank of Baltimore, also trustee Indiahoma Refining Co., bankrupt, 1922-26; vice-pres. Hambleton and Co., investment bankers, 1927-29; vice-pres. Baltimore Trust Co., 1929-33; vice-pres. and trust officer Baltimore Nat. Bank since 1933; also trustee in reorgn.. under 77B U.S. Dairy Products Corpn., 1936-37; dir. Public Bank of Md., Standard Gas Equipment Corpn. Served in Md. N.G., 1915-17, on Mexican border, 1916; capt. F.A., U.S.A., 1917-19 with A.E.F.; in St. Mihiel and Meuse-Argonne. Trustee Community Fund of Baltimore, Family Welfare Assn., Kernan Hosp., Happy Hills Convalescent Home, all Baltimore. Democrat. Presbyn. Clubs: Elkridge, Chesapeake, Maryland, Bachelors Cotillon (Baltimore); Lawyers, Princeton (New York). Home: 3803 St. Paul St. Office: Baltimore Nat. Bank, Baltimore, Md.

OBERDORF, Harvey Alvin, telephone Co. official; b. Columbia, Pa., Dec. 20, 1882; s. Henry F. and Mary (Gonder) O.; ed. pub. schs., Columbia, Pa., Erwin Night Sch., and business coll.; m. Ida Gallager, July 15, 1908. Asso. with Columbia Telephone Co. since 1902, vice-pres., gen. mgr. and dir. since 1912; dir. Columbia Chamber of Commerce, Keeley Stove Co., Pa. Ind. Telephone Assn. Republican. Mason. Rotarian. Clubs: Columbia Rotary (treas.); Media Heights Golf. Home: 1000 Chestnut St. Office: 22 N. Third St., Columbia, Pa.

OBERHOLSER, Robert Martin, supt. schs.; b. Cains, Pa., Sept. 18, 1891; s. Christian and Margaret (Baldwin) O.; student Franklin & Marshall Acad., 1907-08; Ph.B., Franklin & Marshall Coll., 1912; M.A., U. of Pa., 1924; m. Grace Johnson, May 8, 1918; children—Robert M. (died Sept. 16, 1926), Margaret Elizabeth, Robert M. (died July 8, 1933). Teacher Downingtown (Pa.) High Sch., 1912-15, prin., 1915-16; prin. Woodbury (N.J.) High Sch., 1916-19; supt. schs., Bordentown, N.J., since 1919. Served in U.S. Army, 1917-18. Mem. N.E.A., N.J. Edn. Assn., N.J. Council of Edn., Phi Kappa Sigma. Republican. Presbyn. Mason. Home: 600 Prince St., Bordentown, N.J. Office: High Sch., Bordentown, N.J.

OBERLY, Henry Sherman, univ. prof. and exec.; b. Decatur, Ill., Apr. 2, 1898; s. Frank C. and Addie M. (Sherman) O.; A.B., Muhlenberg, Coll., 1920; A.M., U. of Pa., 1922, Ph.D., same, 1924; m. Charlotte E. Peters, Aug. 19, 1922; children—Joan, Robert Peters. Engaged as asst. instr. psychology, U. of Pa., 1920-21, instr., 1921-27, asst. prof., 1927-38, asso. prof. psychology since 1938; asst. dir. of admissions, U. of Pa., 1926-36, asso. dir. of admissions, 1936-39, dir. of admissions since 1939; sec. Faculty Research Com. since 1931; sec. Pa. Chapter of Sigma Xi, 1928-33, pres., 1935-36. Served in Plattsburg R.O.T.C., 1918; 2d lt. F.A., U.S.A., at Camp Taylor, Ky., 1918-19. Mem. Am. Psychol. Assn., Eastern Psychol. Assn. (sec.-treas. 1937-39), Sigma Xi, Alpha Tau Omega, Phi Delta Kappa. Republican. Lutheran. Contbr. articles to tech. jours. Home: 7122 Hazel Av., Upper Darby, Pa. Office: 3435 Spruce St., Philadelphia, Pa.

OBERMANNS, Henry Frank, v.p. Hammermill Paper Co.; b. Kempten, Germany, Oct. 12, 1882; s. Heinrich and Magdalena (Steusloff) O.; ed. Technische Staatslehranstalten, Chemnitz, Germany, and Technische Hoch Schule, Vienna, Austria; m. Meta Klotz, June 25, 1907; children—Henry E., Grace, Susanna. Learned paper trade in Germany; came to U.S., 1904, naturalized, 19—; laborer Hammermill Paper Co., 1904-08, asst. supt., 1908-10; mgr. Nashua River Paper Co., East Pepperell, Mass., 1911-12; supt. Arlington Paper Co., 1912-13, Am. Writing Paper Co., Holyoke, Mass., 1913-14; gen. supt. Hammermill Paper Co., 1914-30, v.p. in charge of mfg. since 1930, now also dir. Charter mem. Tech. Assn. of Paper Industry; mem. Pulp and Paper Mill Supts. Assn. Mason. Clubs: Kahkwa, Erie. Home: 401 Hammermill Road. Office: Hammermill Paper Co., Erie, Pa.

OBERMAYER, Leon Jacob, lawyer; b. Sciota, Ill., Sept. 24, 1886; s. Hermann and Veronika (Lehmann) O.; A.B., Central High Sch., Phila., Pa., 1904; LL.B., U. of Pa., 1908; m. Julia L. Sinsheimer, May 24, 1923; children—Herman Joseph, Helen Adele, Arthur Sinsheimer. Admitted to Pa. bar, 1908; mem. firm Edmonds, Obermayer & Rebmann, Phila. Mem. Phila. Bd. of Pub. Edn.; pres. Y.M. and Y.W.H.A., Phila., 1915-26, Girls' Aid, 1921-28; mem. exec. com. Nat. Council Jewish Welfare Bd.; mem. exec. council Boy Scouts of America (Phila.). Mem. Jewish Hosp. Assn. of Phila. (gov. and solicitor), Pa. Prison Soc. (gov.), Hebrew S.S. Soc. (gov.), Gratz College—Hebrew Edn. Soc. (gov.), Am. Acad. Polit. and Social Science, Am. Social Hygiene Assn., Am. Jewish Hist. Soc., Phila. Art Mus., Am. Bar Assn., Pa. Bar Assn. (v.p.), Phila. Bar Assn. (chmn. bd. of govs.), Pa. Mus. Art, Am. Mus. Natural History (N.Y.), Acad. Natural Sciences (Phila.), U. of Pa. Mus. Republican. Jewish religion; ex-pres. Congregation Adath Jeshurun; B'nai B'rith (Joshua lodge). Clubs: Locust (gov.), Lawyers, Constitutional, Philmont Country (gov.). Home: 821 Westview Av. Office: 1418 Packard Bldg., Philadelphia, Pa.

OBERNAUER, Harold, lawyer; b. Pittsburgh, Pa., Jan. 3, 1887; s. Herman and Bertha (Dinch) O.; A.B., Yale, 1910; LL.B., U. of Pittsburgh Law Sch., 1913; unmarried. Admitted to Pa. bar, 1913; also admitted to Supreme and Superior courts of Pa. and all Federal courts. Served as chmn. legal advisory bd. Dist. No. 2, Pittsburgh, during World War. Vice chmn. bd. law examiners, Allegheny Co. since 1935. Mem. Better Traffic Com., Pittsburgh. Mem. Y.M. and W.H.A. of Pittsburgh (dir. 1929-35 and since 1939), Hebrew Free Loan Assn. (dir. 1934-37), Fed. Jewish Philanthropies of Pittsburgh (dir. 1933-36); mem. Am. Bar Assn. (com. pub. relations), Pa. State Bar Assn. (chmn. com. pub. relations), Allegheny Co. Bar Assn. (pres.), U. of Pittsburgh Alumni Assn. (pres. 1935-36), U. of Pittsburgh Law Sch. Alumni Assn. (organizer and dir.), Boy Scouts of America (vice-pres. Allegheny Co. 1917-23), Pittsburgh Charter Plan (exec. com.). Jewish Religion. Mason (past master; dist. dept. Grand Master since 1926), Elk (past exalted ruler), K.P., I.O.O.F. Clubs: Yale of Pittsburgh, Pittsburgh Athletic; Pennsylvania Soc. of New York, N.Y. Home: 906 Arlington Apt. Office: 2108 Law and Finance Bldg., Pittsburgh, Pa.

OBERRENDER, John S., pres. Freeland Mfg. Co.; b. Freeland, Pa., June 4, 1900; s. Stanley E. and Jennie (Stein) O.; ed. Cornell U., 1918-19; B.S. in Econs., U. of Pa., 1922; m. Martha E. Richards, White Haven, Pa., Oct. 6th, 1923; 1 dau., Sally Ann. Asso. with Freeland Mfg. Co., mfrs. Work, Sport and Play Clothing, Freeland, Pa., since 1922, pres. since 1930. Mem. Delta Kappa Epsilon. Presbyn. Home: White Haven, Pa. Office: Freeland, Pa.

OBERT, Josiah Edwin, surgeon; b. Asbury Park, N.J., Aug. 6, 1902; s. Budd Howard and Mary Coombs (Chafey) O.; student Asbury Park (N.J.) High Sch., 1916-20, Dartmouth Coll. Med. Sch., Hanover, N.H., 1924-25; B.S., Dartmouth Coll., Hanover, N.H., 1924; M.D., N.Y.U. Med. Coll. (Bellevue Hosp.), 1928; interneship, Bellevue Hosp., New York, 1928-30; m. Edith C. Pullen, Jan. 2, 1925; m. 2d, Margaret Templeton, May 16, 1929. Jr. surgical staff, Point Pleasant (N.J.) Hosp., 1929-31, sr. surgical staff, 1931-34, chief of staff since 1934; sr. surgical staff, Charles Hosp., Trenton, N.J., 1936, chief of staff since 1937; courtesy surg. staff, Paul Kimball Hosp., Lakewood, N.J., 1936. Served as health officer, New Hanover (N.J.) and Plumsted (N.J.) Twps. Dir. Charles Hosp. (Trenton, N.J.), Ocean Co. (N.J.) Health Assn. Fellow A.M.A.; mem. Ocean County Medical Society (pres. since May 1939), N.J. State Med. Society, Am. Pub. Health Assn., Health Officers Assn. of N.J., N.J. Health Sanitary Assn., Omega Upsilon Phi (nat. mem. 1927-29), Rotary Internat. Baptist. Elk, Mason (Scottish Rite). Clubs: Cartaret (Trenton, N.J.); Dartmouth (New York); Dartmouth (Phila.). Address: Main St., New Egypt, N.J.

O'BRIEN, Charles F., ex-congressman; b. Jersey City, N.J., Mar. 7, 1879; A.B., A.M., Fordham U.; student New York Law Sch. Admitted to N.J. bar and began practice at Jersey City; has been judge 2d Criminal Court and Dept. pub. safety, Jersey City; mem. 67th and 68th Congresses (1921-25), 12th N.J. Dist.; now mem. law firm Hershenstein, O'Brien & Tartalsky. Presented name of Gov. Edward I. Edwards of N.J., as nominee for Pres. of U.S., Dem. Nat. Conv., San Francisco, 1920. Home: 407 Bergen Av. Office: 26 Journal Square, Jersey City, N.J.

O'BRIEN, Edward J., pres. Allegheny Valley Bank; b. Pittsburgh, Pa., June 4, 1885; s. Edward and Lavinia (Whalen) O'B.; student parochial schs. and High Sch., Pittsburgh, U. of Pittsburgh; widower; children—Edward J., Thomas B. Began as messenger in bank, 1902; asso. with Allegheny Valley Bank of Pittsburgh since 1902, pres. and dir. since 1927. Mem. Council Adminstrn., Pa. Bankers Assn. Roman Catholic. K.C. Clubs: Pittsburgh Athletic, Bankers (Pittsburgh). Home: Dorsey, Dorseyville Rd., Fox Chapel, Boro, Pa. Office: 5137 Butler St., Pittsburgh, Pa.

O'BRIEN, Frank A.; mem. law firm O'Brien & O'Brien. Office: Central Union Trust Bldg., Wheeling, W.Va.

O'BRIEN, J. Charles, real estate, insurance; b. Brooklyn, N.Y., Sept. 9, 1862; s. Douglass F. and Louise (Stonenall) O.; student pub. schs., Brooklyn and N.J.; m. Minnie Vanderveer, Sept. 21, 1886 (dec.); children—Edmond V., Donald P., J. Charles, Richard A. Began as office boy Butterworth & Smalley Co., N.Y. City, 1878; in business for self as broker in paper mfg. supplies, 1884-87; agent New York Life Ins. Co., Phila., 1887-90; real estate and ins. broker since 1890; v.p. and dir. Maplewood Bank & Trust Co., Maplewood Bldg. & Loan Assn.; dir. Savings Investment & Trust Co. Republican. Methodist. Mason. Club: Shongum Fishing. Home: 131 Maplewood Av., Maplewood, N.J. Office: 10 Sloan St., South Orange, N.J.

O'BRIEN, J. J. P.; judge First Judicial Circuit of W.Va. Address: Wheeling, W.Va.

O'BRIEN, J. Vick, head dept. of music, Carnegie Inst. Tech.; b. Pittsburgh, Pa., May 26, 1876; s. John William and Kathryn (Kearns) O'B.; student Hochschule, Berlin, with Humperdinck and Carl Thiel, 1902-12; studied privately, Berlin, with Friedrich Koch, DaMotta, and Paul Juon; hon. Mus. D., Duquesne U., Pittsburgh, 1928; m. Rosalyn Scott, Oct. 4, 1926; children—Virginia Jane, James Vick, Patrichia, Coralyn. Head dept. of music, Carnegie Inst. Tech., since 1912. Mem. Phi Mu Alpha Sinfonia (hon., Beta Chapter). K.C. Club: Musicians (Pittsburgh, Pa.). Composer: fifty songs, including The Stirrup Cup and I Shot an Arrow; symphony, Duskward; incidental and ballet music for Chaplet of Pan; operas, Ye Olde Virginia, Hour Before Dawn, Roses of Mercatel. Home: 5231 Gladstone Rd. Office: Schenley Park, Pittsburgh, Pa.

O'BRIEN, James Albert, pres. DeLong Hook & Eye Co.; b. Canton, N.Y., Mar. 25, 1887; s. Michael and Jane (Burke) O'B.; student high sch., Canton, N.Y., 1901-04; B.S., St. Lawrence U., Canton, N.Y., 1908; m. Helen Knibloe, Oct. 9, 1920; children—Hugh Emmett, David Welles, George Laurence, Suzanne, Paul Douglas. In employe various cos. and in various capacities, 1908-17; pres. and dir. De Long Hook & Eye Co., manufacturers metal notions, Phila., since 1919; pres. and dir. De Long Hook & Eye Co. of Can., Trans-Continental Shares Corpn. Served as maj. U.S. Army, with A.E.F., 1917-19, asst. chief of Press Bur. of Peace Commn. at Paris. Mem. Alpha Tau Omega. Republican. Roman Catholic Club: Merion Cricket (Haverford, Pa.). Home Rosemont, Pa. Office De Long Hook & Eye Co., Philadelphia, Pa.

O'BRIEN, Patrick M., abbot; b. Manchester, N.H., Oct. 29, 1885; s. Patrick and Johanna (Cronin) O'B.; A.B., St. Anselnis Coll., 1915; student Holy Cross Coll., Worcester, Mass., 1907-09, hon. M.A., 1924. Instr. St. Joseph's High Sch., Manchester, N.B., 1909-14; noviatiate St. Vincents Arch Abbey, Latrobe, Pa., 1914-15; became Benedictine monk, July 22, 1915; ordained Benedictine priest, May 30, 1920; instr. St. Benedictine Prep. Sch., Newark, 1920-32; pastor St. Joseph's Ch., Maplewood, N.J., 1933-37; elected abbot of St. Mary's Abbey, Aug. 11, 1937; pres. St. Benedicts Prep. Sch. and Delbarton Sch., Morristown, N.J., since 1937. Address: 528 High St., Newark, N.J.

O'BRIEN, Seumas, sculptor, author; b. Glenbrook, Co. Cork, Eire, Apr. 26, 1880; s. John J. and Elizabeth Harding (Aherne) O.; ed. Presentation Brothers' Sch., Cork, Cork Sch. of Art, Cork Sch. of Music, Nat. Coll. of Art (Dublin), Royal Coll. of Art (London); unmarried. Instr. in art, Cork Sch. of Art, Mt. St. Joseph's Monastery (Cork), Queenstown Tech. Sch., Nat. Coll. of Art (Dublin), until 1912; exhibited at Royal Hibernian Acad.; awarded silver medal (sculpture), by Bd. of Edn., London, 1912. Came to U.S., 1913; instr. in art, Newark (N.J.) School of Fine and Industrial Arts. Am. rep. Irish Playwrights' Assn. Mem. Am. Irish Hist. Soc., Stephen Crane Assn. Author: Duty and Other Irish Comedies 1916; The Whale and the Grasshopper, 1916; Blind, 1918. Plays prod.: Duty; Matchmakers; Malachi Desmond; '''67''; Failure of Triumphs; Blind; The Cobbler's Den; The Black Bottle; The Wild Boar; The Bird Catcher; Well—A Play in One Act, 1937; Queen Puff-Puff, 1937. Address: 37 Hathaway Place, Glen Ridge, N.J.

O'BRIEN, Thomas George; b. Geneseo, N.Y., Oct. 28, 1874; s. Thomas and Julia (Milan) O'B.; grad. Geneseo Normal Sch., 1808, Rochester (N.Y.) Business Inst., 1901; m. Mary C. Guy, Jan. 4, 1908; children—Guy Edward, Mary Elizabeth, Thomas George. Teacher pub. schs., Cuylerville, N.Y., 1898-1901; mem. faculty Drake Business Coll., Jersey City, N.J., 1901, prin., 1902-05, v.p., 1905-25 (sent to N.Y. City, 1907, to organize Drake Business Sch., of which 8 have been established), pres. since 1925. Pres. Business Edn. Assn. of State of N.Y., 1935-36. Mem. Gregg Teachers Assn. (pres. 1926), Brooklyn Chamber Commerce. Democrat. Catholic. Elk. Club: Kiwanis (pres. 1931; lt. gov. div. 1 1933); Lotos. Home: 57 Prospect St., Jersey City, N.J. Office: 154 Nassau St., New York, N.Y.

O'BRIEN, William Aloysius, lawyer; b. Jersey City, N.J., Aug. 31, 1896; s. John M. and Jennie (Anderson) O'B.; A.B., St. John's Coll., 1920, A.M., St. Peter's Coll., 1921; LL.B., Fordham Univ. Law Sch., 1923; m. Mae Schroeder, June 19, 1928; children—William Henry,

Robert. Admitted to N.J. bar 1923; engaged in gen. practice of law at Jersey City. N.J. since 1923; counsel to commr. registration, Hudson Co., 1929-36; asst. atty. gen. of N.J. and chief counsel to N.J. State Highway Dept. since 1936. Republican. Roman Catholic. K.C. Home: 1 Emory St. Office: 50 Journal Sq., Jersey City, N.J.

O'BRIEN, William Smith, ex-congressman; b. Barbour Co., W.Va., Jan. 8, 1862; s. Emmet Jones and Martha Anne (Hall) O'B.; ed. Weston (W.Va.) Academy; LL.B., W.Va. Univ., 1891; m. Emma White, Oct. 14, 1896; children—Perry Emmet, Daniel Pitt, Mary Martha, William Talbot. Admitted to W.Va. bar, 1891, and began practice at Buckhannon; mem. firm O'Brien & Hall since 1920; secretary of State of West Virginia since 1933. Formerly capt. W.Va. N.G.; judge Twelfth Jud. Circuit, W.Va., 1913-20; mem. 70th Congress (1927-29), 3d W.Va. Dist. Democrat. Methodist. Mason, K.P. Club: Lions. Home: 2212 Washington St., Charleston, W.Va.

OCKFORD, John Wyse, lawyer; b. Revere, Mass., Sept. 27, 1885; s. George Morgan and Mary Elizabeth Laura (Horne) O.; grad. Ridgewood (N.J.) High Sch., 1902; LL.B., New York U., 1905; m. Mary Frances Vaughey, June 3, 1913; children—Elizabeth (Mrs. C. Maynard Nichols), Margaret, William. Admitted to N.Y. bar, 1907, N.J. bar, 1915; also to bars of U.S. Courts of N.Y. Southern and Eastern Dists., N.J. Dist. Court, U.S. Supreme Court; practiced in New York, 1907-15, Jersey City since 1916. Mem. Hudson County (N.J.) Bar Assn. Democrat. Roman Catholic. Home: 79 Chestnut St., Ridgewood, N.J. Office: 921 Bergen Av., Jersey City, N.J.

O'CONNELL, C(harles) Leonard, univ. prof., dean; b. Pittsburgh, Pa., Apr. 24, 1890; s. John H(enry) and Charlotte T(eresa) (Mullen) O'C.; student Irwin Av. Pub. Sch., Pittsburgh, 1896-1904, Allegheny High Sch., Pittsburgh, 1904-08; Ph.G., Coll. Pharmacy, U. of Pittsburgh, 1912, A.B., Coll. Liberal Arts, 1916, Pharm.D., U. of Pittsburgh, 1929; Pharm.M., Phila. Coll. Pharmacy & Science, 1932; m. Florence Sheridan, June 30, 1920; children—C(harles) Leonard, J(ohn) F(rancis) Regis, William S(heridan), Richard L(awrence). Apprentice in pharmacy (while attending high sch.), 1906; merchandise broker and mfrs. agent, 1916-22; instr. chemistry, U. of Pittsburgh, 1922-24, asst. prof. chemistry, 1924-26, prof. pharmacy, 1926-30, prof. pharmacy since 1930, asso. dean, 1930-32, dean since 1932. Chmn. bd. mgrs. Juvenile Detention Home, Allegheny Co., since 1935; pres. Civic Club of Allegheny Co. since 1938. Mem. A.A.A.S., Am. Pharm. Assn., Pa. Pharm. Assn., Pa. Acad. Science, Federation Internationale Pharmaceutique, Kappa Psi, Omicron Delta Kappa, Phi Kappa. Democrat. Catholic. Club: Faculty (U. of Pittsburgh). Co-author (with William Pettit); Manual on Pharmaceutical Law, 1938. Home: 101 W. Steuben St. Address: 1431 Boul. of the Allies, Pittsburgh, Pa.

O'CONNELL, James Joseph, clergyman; b. Pittsburgh, Pa., Sept. 18, 1891; s. Edward and Mary (Murphy) O.; ed. Pittsburgh High Sch. and Duquesne U. Ordained catholic priest, June 1917; apptd. to Epiphany Ch., Pittsburgh, Aug. 1917; asst. pastor St. Stephen's Ch., 1922-36; pastor St. Sebastian Ch., Belle Vernon, since July 1936. Dir. Hazelwood Bank, Pittsburgh. Dir. Belle Vernon Library Assn. Club: Rotary (dir.). Directed amateur plays, 12 yrs. Address: 615 Spear St., Belle Vernon, Pa.

O'CONNELL, John Martin, mayor; b. Chicago, Ill., Aug. 14, 1897; s. T. F. and Margaret (Martin) O.; LL.B., Duquesne Univ. Law Sch., 1923; m. Catherine Dougherty, June 12, 1928; 1 dau., Mary Margaret. Admitted to Pa. Supreme Court bar, 1923; in gen. practice of law, 1923-39; mayor, City of Jeannette, Pa., since Jan. 1, 1938; dir. Jeannette Thrift Corpn. Served with 116th Engrs., U.S. Army, with A.E.F., during World War. Mem. Am. Legion, Vets. of Foreign Wars. Democrat. Catholic. Club: Rotary. Home: 412 N. Third St. Office: 305 Clay Av., Jeannette, Pa.

O'CONNOR, Dennis Francis, physician; b. Worcester, Mass June 12, 1875; s. Denis M. and Mary (Teahan) O.; A.B., Coll. of the Holy Cross, 1893, A.M., 1899; certificate, State Normal Sch., Worcester, Mass., 1895; M.D., U. of Md. Med. Sch., 1899; grad. study, U. of Vienna, Austria, 1901-02, Clark U., 1910-11; m. Loretta Radel, of Newark, N.J., June 5, 1912. Engaged in practice of medicine specializing in opthalmology since 1903, at Newark, N.J. since 1920. Served as 1st lt., capt., then maj., Med. Res. Corps, U.S.A., 1917-19. Fellow Am. Coll. Surgeons; mem. Am. Med. Assn., Am. Acad. Ophthalmology & Otolaryngology, N.J. State Med. Soc., Essex Co. Med. Soc., Acad. Medicine of N.J. Catholic. Clubs: Maplewood Country, Practitioners (Newark). Home: 27 Kingman Rd., South Orange, N.J. Office: 671 Broad St., Newark, N.J.

O'CONNOR, James Edward, pub. utility treas.; b. Marietta, Pa., Mar. 4, 1894; s. Arthur Parke and Susan (Dunn) O'C.; student pub. schs. and high sch., Marietta, Pa., grad., 1910; m. Mary Thayer Johnson, Oct. 16, 1920; children—James Haskell, Mary Thayer. Asso. with Pennsylvania Water & Power Co. since entering its employ, 1910, employed in various capacities to 1933, treas. since 1933; asst. treas., asst. sec. Safe Harbor Water Power Corpn. since 1933. Served as pvt. to 2d lt. Air Service, U.S.A., 1917-19. Club: Rodgers Forge Country (Baltimore). Home: 6401 Pinehurst Rd. Office: Lexington Bldg., Baltimore, Md.

O'CONNOR, Johnson, psychology; b. Chicago, Jan. 22, 1891; s. John and Nellie (Johnson) O'C.; prep. edn., John Dewey Sch., Chicago, Ill.; A.B., Harvard, 1913, A.M., 1914; m. Ruth Davis, Dec. 17, 1913 (died Feb. 8, 1920); 1 son, Chadwell; m. 2d, Eleanor Manning, June 3, 1931. Astronomical mathematical research with Percival Lowell, 1911-18; metall. research with Am. Steel & Wire Co., Worcester, Mass., 1918-20; elec. engring. with Gen. Electric Co., West Lynn, Mass., 1920-22; organized Human Engring. Lab. for Gen. Electric Co. to study applicants and new employes, 1922; lecturer on psychology, Stevens Inst. Tech., 1928-31; asso. prof. and dir. of psychol. studies, Stevens Inst. Tech., since 1931; lecturer in psychology, Mass. Inst. Tech., 1928-31; asst. prof. psychology, Mass. Inst. Tech., 1931-34; organized, 1930, and since dir. the Human Engring. Laboratory (affiliated with Stevens Inst. Tech., Hoboken, N.J., Armour Inst. Tech., Chicago, and having a third permanent lab. in Boston). Awarded Wertheim Fellowship, 1927. Fellow Am. Acad. Arts and Sciences, Soc. for Promotion Engring. Edn., Am. Inst. E.E. Author: Born That Way, 1928; Psychometrics, 1934; Johnson O'Connor English Vocabulary Builder, 1937; also mag. articles and occupational brochures describing measurable characteristics found common in fields of engring., law, advertising, medicine, selling, such tech. reports as Characteristics of Graduate Nurses, Study of Vocabulary Scores of 75 Executives, Common Responses to a New Form of the Free-association Test. Home: 381 Beacon St., Boston, Mass. Address: Stevens Institute of Technology, Hoboken, N.J.

O'CONNOR, Martin J., Catholic priest; vicar gen. Diocese of Scranton. Address: 315 Wyoming Av., Scranton, Pa.

O'CONNOR, Maurice Edward, golf professional; b. Staten Island, N.Y., Oct. 13, 1905; s. Maurice J. and Elizabeth (Farley) O'C.; ed. public schools and Curtis High Sch., New York; m. Estelle Perry, Apr. 20, 1932; children—Barbara Ann, Joan Claire. Asst. golf professional, Glen Ridge (N.J.) Country Club, 1923-29; golf professional, Branch Brook Golf Club, Belleville, N.J., since Dec. 1929. Roman Catholic. Home: 18 Fairview Place, Belleville, N.J.

O'CONNOR, Robert Emmett, lawyer; b. Randolph Co., W.Va., Mar. 22, 1888; s. Michael and Mary Elizabeth (Copley) O'C.; A.B., Davis & Elkins Coll., 1914; LL.B., W.Va. Univ. Law Sch., 1917; m. Julia Elizabeth Aultz, Oct. 8, 1927; children—Barbara Aultz, Robert Emmett, Jr. and Otis Leslie (twins). Admitted to W.Va. bar, 1920, and engaged in gen. practice of law at Elkins, 1920-25, and at Charleston since 1929; served as supt. dept. pub. safety of W.Va., 1925-29; formerly mem. City Council, Charleston; Rep. candidate for Congress, 6th dist. W.Va., 1938; sergt. at arms Rep. Nat. Conv., 1936. Served as capt. C.A.C., U.S.A., 1917-19, with A.E.F. in France; now maj. C.A.C. Res. Active in work Boy Scouts. Past mem. Nat. Exec. Com. Am. Legion, past dept. comdr. W.Va. Am. Legion. Trustee Davis & Elkins Coll. Mem. W.Va. and Charleston bar assns., Phi Kappa Sigma. Republican. Presbyn. Home: 1305 Quarrier St. Office: Capital City Bldg., Charleston, W.Va.

O'CONOR, Herbert Romulus, gov. of Md.; b. Baltimore, Md., Nov. 17, 1896; s. James P. A. and Mary A. (Galvin) O'C.; A.B., Loyola Coll., Baltimore, 1917, LL.D., 1924; LL.B., U. of Md., 1920; m. M. Eugenia Byrnes, Nov. 24, 1921; children—Herbert Romulus, Mary Patricia, Eugene F., James P., Robert. Admitted to Md. bar, 1919, and since practiced in Baltimore; asst. state's atty. for Baltimore, 1921-22, state's atty., 1924-34; people's counsel to Pub. Service Commn., 1923-24; atty. gen. State of Md., 1935-39; elected gov., Nov. 4, 1938, for term 1939-43. Served in U.S. Naval Res. Dir. Spring Grove State Hosp. Mem. Am. Bar Assn. (com. on criminal justice), Md. State Bar Assn. (chmn. com. on criminal justice), Nat. Pros. Attys. Assn. (pres.), Md. State Pros. Assn., Am. Legion, Vets. Foreign Wars, Phi Kappa Sigma. Democrat. Catholic. K.C., Elk, Moose, Eagle. Clubs: Merchants, Baltimore, Athletic, Baltimore Country. Home: Government House, Annapolis, Md. Office: State House, Annapolis, Md.

ODENHEIMER, Cordelia Powell (Mrs. Frank Gilliams Odenheimer); b. Leesburg, Loudoun Co., Va.; d. Edward Burr and Cordelia S. (Armstrong) Powell; ed. pvt. schs., Leesburg, Va., and Miss Pegram's and The Misses Hall's schs., Baltimore, Md.; m. Frank Gilliams Odenheimer, Sept. 28, 1887; children—Frank Gilliams, Dorothea Sothoron (dec.). Pres. Md. Div. U.D.C., 7 yrs.; v.p. gen. U.D.C., 1911-13, pres.-gen., 1915-16, reëlected, 1916-17; dir. Arlington, Shiloh monuments; mem. Mt. Vernon Chapter D.A.R., Colonial Dames America State of Va., Civil Legion; mem. exec. coop. com. Am. Defense Soc. and woman's sect. of Am. Preparatory Com., also of woman's sect. Navy League; mem. exec. com. Woman's dept. Nat. Civic Federation; mem. com. Nat. Service Sch.; mem. Com. of 100 Women of Nat. Defense World Court League; pres. Polit. Study Club, Washington, 1923-25; pres. Southern Relief Soc., 1925-26. Episcopalian. Author many short stories. Home: The Latrobe, Charles & Read Sts., Baltimore, Md.

ODGERS, Merle Middleton, coll. pres.; b. Phila., Pa., April 21, 1900; s. David and Elizabeth (Ramsay) O.; A.B., Central (Phila.) High Sch., 1918; A.B., U. of Pa., 1922, A.M., 1924, Ph.D., 1928; L.H.D., Temple U., 1938; m. Frances Bartram Bunting, June 28, 1927; children—Eleanor Bunting, John Bartram. Instr. in Latin, U. of Pa., 1922-28, asst. prof., 1928-36, prof., 1936; asst. dir. of admissions, U. of Pa., 1926-33; dean Coll. of Liberal Arts for Women (U. of Pa.), 1933-36; pres. Girard Coll., Phila., since 1936. Served in S.A.T.C., U.S.A., 1918. Trustee Temple Univ., Presser Foundation. Pres. Soc. Alumni of College, U. of Pa. Mem. Linguistic Soc. of America (trustee), Classical Assn. of Atlantic States, Phila. Classical Soc., Am. Philol. Assn., Am. Assn. Univ. Profs., N.E.A., L'Association Guillaume Budé (Paris), Phi Beta Kappa, Pi Kappa Alpha, Phi Delta Kappa, Pi Mu Epsilon, Eta Sigma Phi. Presbyterian. Clubs: University, Contemporary, Lenape, Franklin Inn (Phila.); Univ. of Pennsylvania (New York); Philadelphia Country. Author: Latin Parens, 1929. Address: Girard College, Philadelphia, Pa.

ODLUM, Floyd B., investments; b. Union City, Mich., Mar. 30, 1892; s. Rev. George A. O.; A.B., University of Colo., also LL.B., and M.B.A.; m. Hortense McQuarrie, Apr. 1, 1915 (divorced Oct. 7, 1935); children—Stanley Arnold, Bruce Wendell. Pres. Atlas Corpn., investments; dir. Am. & Foreign Power Co., United Fruit Co., Italian Superpower Corpn. Trustee Vt. Acad. (Bellows Falls). Clubs: N.Y. Yacht; Jefferson Islands (Washington, D.C.). Home:

O'DONNELL, Francis Timothy, physician; b. Parsons, Pa., Dec. 28, 1897; s. Timothy and Catherine (Whalen) O'D.; student St. Mary's High Sch., 1912-16, U. of Scranton, 1916-19; M.D., Jefferson Med. Coll., Phila., 1922; m. Bessie Barnett, Aug. 8, 1923; children—George, Francis, Raymond, James Timothy (dec.), Robert. Interne Wilkes-Barre (Pa.) Gen. Hosp., 1922-23, pediatrist, 1925; mem. consulting staffs, Mercy, Nanticoke hosps. and Saint Stanislaus Orphanage, Wilkes-Barre, Pa., since 1926; mem. teaching staff Wilkes-Barre Gen. Hosp. Nurses Sch. since 1926. Served in S.A.T.C., 1918. Supt. Municipal Hosp. in 1935; cochmn. Emergency Child Health Com., 1935-39, Diphtheria Prevention Com., 1937. Licentiate Am. Bd. Pediatrics; mem. Am., Pa. State, Lehigh Valley, Luzerne Co. med. assns., Phila. Pediatric Soc., Am. Legion, Phi Alpha Sigma, Alpha Omega Alpha. Democrat. Roman Catholic. K.C. Home: 345 N. Main St., Wilkes-Barre, Pa.

O'DONNELL, Leo Day, surgeon; b. Cleveland, O., May 8, 1895; s. Michael James and Helen A. (Day) O'D.; B.S., U. of Notre Dame, 1917; M.D., Jefferson Med. Coll., 1921; m. Elizabeth Patterson, of Pittsburgh, Pa., Sept. 28, 1927; children—Elizabeth Patterson, Mary Day, Leo Day. Interne Mercy Hosp., Pittsburgh, Pa., 1921-22. Chief Surgical Resident, Mercy Hospital, 1922-24; engaged in practice of surgery at Pittsburgh, Pa., since 1924; staff physician, Mercy Hosp., since 1924; asst. prof. surgery, U. of Pittsburgh Med. Sch. since 1937. Served in Med. Res. Corps, U.S.A., 1917-18. Fellow Am. Coll. Surgeons; mem. Am., Pa. State, and Allegheny Co. med. assns. Republican. Roman Catholic. Clubs: University, South Hills Country. Home: 704 Maryland Av., Pittsburgh, Pa.

O'DONNELL, Raymond, univ. prof.; b. Columbia, Pa., May 13, 1886; s. John Marshall and Anna Louise (Wilson) O'D.; B.S. in C.E., Pa. State Coll., 1909; m. Olive Cora Miller, Aug. 5, 1914; 1 son, John Marshall. Successively rodman, levelman, chief of party, W.N.Y. & P. Traction Co. Lines, summers 1906, 1907, 1908; became asst. in civil engring., Pa. State Coll., 1909; now prof. hydraulic and sanitary engring. Engr. with Pa. Dept. of Health, summer 1918 and 1919-20. Served as mem. exec. com. State Coll. (Pa.) Chamber of Commerce. Asso. mem. Am. Soc. C.E.; mem. Soc. for Promotion of Engring. Edn., Pa. Sewage Works Assn., Pa. Water Works Operators Assn. Author: Bulletin on Rural Sanitation, Part II. Home: 119 S. Atherton St. Office: 205 Main Engineering Bldg., State College, Pa.

O'DONNELL, Stewart H., real estate and ins.; b. Trenton, N.J., Jan. 18, 1892; s. Michael James and Mary (Stevenson) O'D.; ed. Trenton grammar sch. and Rider Business Coll.; m. Anna Woreb; children—Edward, Miriam Joyce, Gloria Marie, Vivian June, Joan Millicent, Stewart Hubert. Began in real estate and insurance business; now pres. Stewart H. O'Donnell, Inc.; sec. Crescent Tile Co., Inc.; dir. of Public Bldg. of Mercer County Bd. of Freeholders; dir. Security Nat. Bank, Loyal Bldg. & Loan Assn.; pres. North Trenton Bldg. & Loan Assn. Served as Rep. township committeeman, Ewing Twp., 3 yrs.; mem. Bd. of Chosen Freeholders of Mercer County, 5 yrs. Dir. Charles Hosp., Trenton, N.J. Sec. Trenton Baseball Club; pres. Industrial Baseball League; pres. Industrial Basketball League; pres. and treas. Lincoln Speedway (midget auto racing). Sponsor of teams in baseball, soccer, basketball, softball, boys baseball, quoits. Republican. Presbyterian (organist West Trenton Presbyn. Ch.). Clubs: Central Y.M.C.A., Union Republican, West End Republican, Chambersburg Republican, Dover Social, Prospect Height Republican. Home: 1817 Pennington Rd., Trenton, N.J.

O'DONOGHUE, Michael Joseph, lawyer; b. Bantry, Co. Cork, Ireland, Oct. 31, 1891; s. John and Mary M. (Keohane) O'D.; came to U.S., 1918 and naturalized citizen, 1924; served at Camp Custer, Mich. and Mare Island Navy Yard during war. Member Harold Mason Post, Amer. Legion. B.A., Mungret Coll., Limerick, Ireland, 1911; B.Litt., U. of Dublin, 1912, M.A., same 1913; LL.B., U. of Minn., St. Paul Coll. of Law, 1922; (hon.) LL.B., Chicago Sch. of Law, 1922; m. Kathleen M. Hickey, of Castle Island, Co. Kerry, Ire., Aug. 12, 1935; one daughter, Patricia Maria. Served as prof. of law, St. Thomas College, St. Paul, Minn., 1921-22; prof. law and English, Columbus Coll., Sioux Falls, S.D., 1922-24; admitted to S.D. bar, 1922, and in practice of law at Sioux Falls, 1921-26; admitted to Pa. bar, 1927, and since in gen. practice of law at Phila.; prof. law and English literature, Villanova Coll., 1927-29; atty. for Home Owners Loan Corpn., 1933-35, Pa. Pub. Service Commn. 1935-37; atty. with W.P.A. since 1937. Founder and organizer Gaelic Arts Soc., Phila., 1934. Mem. Democratic Lawyers Committee. Candidate for judge on the Democratic ticket, 1939. Member Philadelphia Bar Assn. and Dublin University Club. Democrat. Roman Catholic. Member of K.C. and Laymen's Retreat League of Malvern; member Holy Name Society. Author: Men and Movements, 1919; Klan and the Politicians, 1925. Home: 2428 W. Huntingdon St. Office: 1104 City Center Bldg., Philadelphia, Pa. Rit. 2562.

O'DONOVAN, Charles, physician; b. Baltimore, Md., Dec. 14, 1902; s. Charles and Rose (Shriver) O'D.; A.B., Catholic U. of America, Washington, D.C., 1921; M.D., Johns Hopkins Med. Sch., 1925; m. Eleanora Cooper, 1935; 1 son, Charles. In practice at Baltimore since 1925; asst. in pediatrics, Yale, 1927-29; instr. in pediatrics and visiting pediatrician, Johns Hopkins Med. Sch. and Hosp. since 1931. Mem. Bd. of Sch. Commrs., Baltimore, since 1936. Trustee The Park Sch., Baltimore. Catholic. Home: 300 Wyndhurst Av. Office: 5 E. Read St., Baltimore, Md.

O'DUNNE, Eugene, judge; b. Tucson, Ariz., June 22, 1875; s. Judge Edmund F. and Josephine B. (Warner) Dunne; A.B., St. Mary's Coll., Belmont, N.C., 1892, A.M., 1894; LL.B., U. of Md. Law Sch., Baltimore, 1900; m. Elise Manning Reardon, Feb. 22, 1904 (dec. 1934); children—Elise (Mrs. E. Gittings Merryman), Eugene, Jr., Kirby (Mrs. John P. Winand), Evett (dec.), Hamilton, David. Admitted to Md. bar, 1900, and since engaged in gen. practice of law at Baltimore; dep. state's atty. Baltimore City, 1903-07; apptd. asso. judge Supreme Bench, Baltimore City, 1926, and elected Nov. 1926 for 15 yr. term, 1926-41; prof. med. jurisprudence, Johns Hopkins Med. Sch. since 1920. Democrat. Roman Catholic. Clubs: Maryland, Johns Hopkins. Home: 704 Cathedral St., Baltimore, Md.

OERLEIN, Karl F(erdinand), prof. science; b. Phila., Pa., Sept. 20, 1900; s. Frederick F. and Gertrude (Stappen) O.; student Pa. State Coll., 1920-21; B.S., U. of Pa., 1925, A.M., 1930, Ph.D., 1936; m. Helen H. Babson, June 22, 1931; children—Dorothy Louise, Frances Adele. Engaged in teaching, high schs. in Pa., 1924-35; instr. sci., State Teachers Coll., Indiana, Pa., 1935-38; prof. sci., head of dept. of sci., dir. of radio, State Teachers Coll., California, Pa., since 1938; cons. in sci. edn. Fellow A.A.A.S.; mem. Am. Assn. Physics Teachers, N.E.A., Am. Sci. Teachers Assn., Pa. Acad. Sci., Franklin Inst. of Phila., Pa. State Edn. Assn., Kappa Phi Kappa, Phi Delta Kappa, Phi Sigma Pi. Organizer of and now gen. chmn., Pa. Jr. Acad. of Science. Republican. Lutheran. Club: Lions. Contbg. editor, Science Club Service. Home: 526 Third St., California, Pa.

OESTERLE, Eric Adam, clergyman; b. Woodstown, N.J., Oct. 11, 1893; s. Adam and Freada (Gieselman) O.; student Woodstown (N.J.) High Sch., 1899-1911; Ph.B., Bucknell U., Lewisburg, Pa., 1916; B.D., Crozer Theol. Sem., Chester, Pa., 1919; M.A. (hon.), U. of Pa., 1919; m. Helen Griffin Ott, June 21, 1919; children—Mary Ellen, Eric Clark. Began as clergyman, Quinton, N.J., 1919; pastor Emmanuel Baptist. Ch., Chester, Pa., 1920-25, Olney Bapt. Ch., Phila., Pa., 1925-31, First Bapt. Ch., Collingswood, N.J., since 1931. Del. to the Bapt. World's Alliance, Berlin, Germany, in 1934. Served as Y.M.C.A. worker, Fortress Monroe, Va., during World War. Dir. relief, Borough of Collingswood, N.J., since 1939. Mem. Sigma Alpha Epsilon. Republican. Baptist. Club: Rotary (Collingswood, N.J.). Address: 23 Frazer Av., Collingswood, N.J.

OESTERLING, Adolph Louis, asst. postmaster; b. Butler, Pa., June 9, 1876; s. Adam and Elizabeth (Forcht) O.; ed. high sch., Butler, Pa., 1893-95, Butler Business Coll., 1896; m. Elizabeth Mae Mattle, Oct. 22, 1902; 1 dau., Edna Marie (Mrs. Richard P. Bauer). Asso. with postoffice, Butler, Pa., since starting as clk., 1896; local sec. U.S. Civil Service Commn., 1902-31; asst. postmaster since 1931; sec. and dir. Butler Chain Co., Inc., since inc., 1920. Republican. Lutheran. I.O.O.F., K.P., Dramatic Order Knights of Korassan. Club: Lions of Butler (past pres. and dir.). Home: 220 W. Diamond St., Butler, Pa.

OFFERMANN, Henry F., theologian; b. Hanover, Germany, July 11, 1866; s. John and Margaret (Ahlf) O.; ed. Gymnasium, Stade, Hanover, Germany; Theol. Sem., Kropp; came to U.S., 1889; post-grad. course in Semitics, U. of Pa.; D.D., Muhlenberg, 1908; m. Emily Saalmann, Feb. 13, 1890; children—Henry C., Magdalene, Emily, Irma. Ordained Luth. ministry; German sec. Evang. Luth. Ministerium of Pa., 1900-08; prof. N.T. theology, Luth. Theol. Sem., Phila., since 1910. Editor Lutherisches Kirchenblatt, 1905-10; co-editor The Lutheran Church Review. Mem. bd. dirs. Mary J. Drexel Home, Phila. Author: Introduction to the Epistles and Gospels of the Church Year; Theological Studies; The Jesus of the New Testament; The Life and Work of Paul; Commentary on Matthew. Home: 7206 Boyer St., Mt. Airy, Phila., Pa.

OFFUTT, Thiemann Scott, judge; b. Montgomery Co., Md., June 12, 1873; s. William Scott and Henrietta I. H. (Baker) O.; University of Virginia, 1891-92; LL.D., St. Johns College; m. Lydia Traill Yellott, Oct. 20, 1903; children—John Yellott, Thiemann Scott, Mary Traill. Began practice at Towson, 1898; formerly counsel to Bd. of Co. Commrs. of Baltimore Co.; apptd. chief judge 3d Jud. Circuit of Md., and mem. Court of Appeals of Md., for term ending Nov. 30, 1921, elected for term ending Dec. 1, 1936. Formerly mem. Judicial Council of Md. Active in war work; chmn. soldiers and sailors memorial com. of Md. Bar Assn.; mem. advisory com. on selection of legal advisory bds.; etc. Mem. Am. Bar Assn. (pres. of judicial section, 1927-28, also mem. gen. council same), Md. Bar Assn. (pres. 1923-24), Am. Law Inst., Md. Soc. S.A.R. (pres.), Md. Tercentenary Com. Democrat. Episcopalian. Mason, Elk. Clubs: Lawyers Round Table, Maryland, Elkridge Country. Author: (with Walter L. Clark) Civil Rights of Soldiers and Sailors (pub. by Md. Council of Defense); Offutt's Code of Baltimore Co.; also various published addresses. Compiler Baltimore County Code, 1915. Home: Towson, Md.

OGBURN, Sihon Cicero, Jr., chem. engr.; b. Winston-Salem, N.C., Oct. 8, 1900; s. Sihon Cicero and Emma A. (Kapp) O.; B.Sc., U. of N.C., Chapel Hill, N.C., 1921, Ph.D., 1926; M.Sc., Washington and Lee U., Lexington, Va., 1923; m. Bessie Mae Bell, July 2, 1921; children—Sihon Cicero, III (dec.), Hugh Bell, Jean Elizabeth. Instr. chemistry, Washington and Lee U., Lexington, Va., 1921-23, asst. prof., 1923-26; prof. and head dept. chem. engring., Bucknell U., Lewisburg, Pa., 1926-36, chmn. chm. engr., 1933-36; research mgr. Gen. Chem. Co., New York, 1936-38, project engr. since 1939. Served in S.A.T.C., Plattsburgh, N.Y., 1918. Mem. Soc. for Promotion Engring. Edn. (mem. council 1935-38), Am. Chem. Soc., Am. Inst. Chem. Engrs., A.A.A.S., Soc. Chem. Industry (London), Pi Mu Epsilon, Alpha Chi Sigma, Sigma Xi. Awarded Smith Research Prize in Natural Science, U. of N.C., 1926. Democrat. Methodist. Author numerous scientific papers in Am. and fgn. jours. on chemistry, chem. engring. and chem. edn. Home: 815 Boulevard,

Westfield, N.J. Office: 40 Rector St., New York, N.Y.

OGDEN, Chester R.; surgeon St. Mary's Hosp. Address: 203 W. Main St., Clarksburg, W.Va.

OGDEN, Harry Ford, ins. exec.; b. Baltimore, Md., Dec. 9, 1887; s. William J. and Annie J. (Ford) O; student Baltimore (Md.) Pub. Schs., 1895-1907; LL.B., U. of Md., Baltimore, Md., 1910; m. Mildred B. Byrd, Sept. 12, 1916 (died, 1935); children—Mildred Elizabeth, Jane Lee, Nancy Byrd. Practice of law at Baltimore, 1910-17; adjuster Md. Motor Car Ins. Co., Baltimore, 1918-1919, in charge of claim dept., 1919-23, v.p. and sec., 1923-26; v.p. Md. Ins. Co., Baltimore, 1926-28; v.p. Fidelity & Guaranty Fire Corpn., Baltimore, Md., since 1928. Episcopalian. Clubs: Md. Yacht, Merchants' (Baltimore, Md.). Home: Edmondson Av., Ten Hills. Office: 301 Water St., Baltimore, Md.

OGDEN, Herschel Coombs, newspaper pub.; b. Worthington, W.Va., Jan. 12, 1869; s. Presley Benjamin and Mary Ellen (Coombs) O.; grad. State Normal Sch., Fairmont, 1883; A.B., W. Va. U., Morgantown, 1887; LL.D., Bethany Coll.; D.C.L., W.Va. Wesleyan Coll.; m. Mary Frances Moorehouse, Oct. 15, 1890. Established Wheeling News, 1890, and bought Wheeling Intelligencer, 1904; pres. News Pub. Co., Intelligencer Pub. Co.; pres. Parkersburg Sentinel Co., Martinsburg Journal Co.; pres. United Newspapers, owning a chain of newspapers in W. Va. Republican. Episcopalian. Clubs: Masonic, Press, Wheeling Country, Fort Henry. Home: Wheeling, W.Va.

OGDEN, Marshall W(eldon), lawyer; b. Prospect Valley, W.Va., Jan. 26, 1873; s. Van B. and Marcy E. (Talkington) O.; student Normal Sch., Fairmont, W.Va., 1894-95; LL.B., W.Va. Univ. Law Sch., 1897; m. Lelia Hawker, June 16, 1901; 1 son, Herbert Leland. Admitted to W.Va. bar, 1897 and since engaged in gen. practice of law at Fairmont; mem. firm Ogden & Ogden since 1932; served as pros. atty., 1924-28, asst. pros. atty., 1928-32; dir. and atty. Standard Bldg. & Loan Assn. since 1924. Mem. W.Va. Bar Assn., Marion Co. Bar Assn. Republican. Methodist. Elk. Home: 303 Third St. Office: McCrory Bldg., Fairmont, W.Va.

OGDEN, Rachel Cousins, educator; b. Erie Co., Pa.; d. Yocum Tyson and Ida Estelle (Bennett) Cousins; A.B., Allegheny Coll., Meadville, Pa., 1907; M.A., W.Va. U., 1919; studied Garrett Biblical Inst., Evanston, Ill., 1923, Alliance Francaise, Paris, 1924; M.A., Columbia U., 1928; studied Sorbonne, U. of Paris, 1931-32; m. L. Wayman Ogden, Jan. 23, 1912. Teacher, Allegheny Coll. Acad., 1907, Clarksburg (W.Va.) High Sch., 1907-10, Concepcion Coll., Concepcion, Chile, 1910-12, Santiago (Chile) Coll., 1912-13, Instituto Ingles, Buenos Aires, 1913-15; asst. prin. grade schs., 1915-17, Clarksburg High Sch., 1917-23, Rehabilitation Night Sch., Clarksburg, 1921-23; dean of Women, W.Va. Wesleyan Coll., 1926-32, head of Romance Language Dept. since 1932. Mem. Am. Assn. Univ. Women, Foreign Language Assn., Student Volunteers, Womans Foreign Missionary Soc., Womans Home Missionary Soc., Instituto de las Españas. Methodist. Home: Hadley, Pa. Address: West Virginia Wesleyan College, Buckhannon, W.Va.

OGELSBY, Warwick Miller, banker; b. Harrisburg, Pa., May 26, 1866; s. Joseph Jones and Fannie (Mumma) O.; grad. high sch., Harrisburg, 1882; m. Eva M. Denney, May 8, 1888 (died Mar. 4, 1912); children—Hart Denney, Richard Bradley; m. 2d, Helen Breininger Reinoehl, of Harrisburg, Pa., Mar. 25, 1919 (died July 12, 1937). Began as clerk of the School Dist. of Harrisburg, 1882; with Commonwealth Trust Co., Harrisburg, since 1883, v.p. or trust officer, 1912-26, pres., 1926-35; v.p. W. O. Hickok Mfg. Co.; v.p. Capital Bank & Trust Co.; sec. and treas. Harrisburg Hotel Co.; dir. Great Southern Lumber Co., Inc., Gaylord Container Corpn., Central Constrn. Corpn. Mem. bd. mgrs. Harrisburg Hosp. Republican. Presbyn. Mason. Club: Colonial Country. Home: 2220 N. 2d St., Harrisburg, Pa.

O'GORMAN, William Doane, ins.; b. Newark, N.J., Nov. 14, 1888; s. William and Elizabeth Holt (Kelly) O'G.; student St. Francis Xavier Sch., New York, N.Y., 1903-05, Stevens Prep. Sch., Hoboken, N.J., 1905-07; M.E., Stevens Inst. Tech., Hoboken, N.J., 1911; student Harvard, 1911-12; m. Pauline Morison, Feb. 2, 1916; children—Elizabeth, Pauline Morison, Susan, William Doane. Engr., The Carpenter Steel Co., Reading, Pa., 1912-17, dir. since 1926; v.p. and dir. O'Gorman & Young, Inc., ins. agency, Newark, N.J., since 1920; dir. Thatcher Furnace Co., Newark, N.J., since 1937. Served as lt., U.S. Army Air Service, 1917-18; capt., 1918-19; maj. of Reserves, 1919-24, lt. col., 1924-29. Mem. Nat. Assn. Casualty & Surety Agents (v.p.), N.J. Assn. Underwriters (mem. exec. com.), Chi Psi. Catholic. Clubs: Essex, Newark Athletic (Newark, N.J.); Montclair (N.J.) Golf; Harvard (N.Y.); Carvel Islands (Barnegat Bay, N.J.). Home: 190 S. Mountain Av., Montclair, N.J., and Westhampton Beach, Long Island, N.Y. Office: 1180 Raymond Boul., Newark, N.J.

OGRODOWSKA - RIDPATH, Johanna, (Mrs. Robert F. Ridpath), musician and artist; b. Warsaw, Poland, Jan. 1, 1900; d. Joseph and Appolonia (Ungling) Ogrodowska; brought to U.S., 1907, naturalized, 1910; ed. schs. for girls, Warsaw and Phila., 1905-19, Pa. Acad. Fine Arts, 1919-21, Columbia Coll. of Music, Phila., 1915-17; m. Dr. Robert F. Ridpath, Nov. 24, 1921; 1 son, Robert Ferguson, Jr. Known for both painting and singing since 1921; exhibited as one-man show, Phila., 1924; exhibited Acad. Fine Arts, 1925-26; vocal concerts in New York City and Phila. specializing in Polish folk music in costume; recital of own compositions, Art Alliance, 1938; lectures on Poland and Polish music; singing Polish songs in costumes of various sections of Poland. Awarded fellowship Acad. Fine Arts, 1917. Mem. Art Alliance, Matinee Mus. Club, Rehearsal Club, Montgomery Singers. Democrat. Roman Catholic. Home: "Carneferne," Merion, Pa. Studio: 1620 Locust St., Philadelphia, Pa.

O'HANLON, Edward Peter, ins. inspector; b. Omeath, Ireland, Apr. 12, 1891; s. Peter Edward and Celia (O'Hagan) O.; brought to U.S., 1891; student St. Francis de Sales Primary, Brooklyn, N.Y., 1897-1901, St. Patrick's Acad., Brooklyn, 1901-02; night study Euclid Business Acad., Brooklyn, 1903-05, Pratt Inst., Brooklyn, 1906-10; m. Cora Westpfahl, Mar. 30, 1929; children—Edward Peter, Patricia. Began as office boy Brooklyn Heights R.R. Co., 1902, legal dept., 1902-05, mech. div., 1905-07; traffic dept. N.Y. Telephone Co., Brooklyn, 1907-08; mech. dept. Peerless Motor Car Co., New York, 1909-10; asst. supt. Brewster & Co., Long Island City, N.Y., 1910-14; salesman Huyler's New York, 1914-15, Edison Co., Brooklyn, 1915-16; asst. mgr. Locomobile Co. of America, New York, 1916-17; supt. Dunbar Automobile Body Co., Phila., 1917-18; estimator Cadillac Motor Car Co., New York, 1918; investigator Globe Indemnity Co., New York, 1919; mgr. underwriter N.J. Indemnity Co., Newark, N.J., 1920; asst. mgr. Motor Car Abstract Co., New York, 1920-22; insp., asst. v.p. and v.p. Hooper-Holmes Bur., New York, 1922-34; proprietor O'Hanlon Reports, character insp. of applicants for ins. in United States, since 1934; pres. and dir. Nat. Inspection Bur., Inc., Boston, Mass., since 1935. Served as chief carpenter's mate, U.S. Navy, 1918-19. Mem. Casualty & Surety Assn., N.Y. Creditmen's Assn. Catholic. Mem. Hon. Order of Blue Goose. Club: Drug and Chemical (New York). While in U.S. Navy at Curtiss Aeroplant, Buffalo, N.Y., developed electro-plating process for tipping aeroplane propellers. Home: 48 Knollwood Av., Madison, N.J. Office: 111 John St., New York, N.Y.

O'HARE, Bernard V(incent), lawyer; b. Schuylkill Co., Pa., Mar. 1, 1883; s. Michael D. and Catherine (Higgins) O'H.; student pub. sch. and high sch., Shenandoah, Pa., 1890-1901; m. Nellie H. Murphy, Aug. 20, 1918; children—Catherine M., Mary E., Bernard V., Arthur, Ellen, Ann. Admitted to Pa. bar, 1906, and since engaged in gen. practice of law at Shenandoah, Pa.; dir. and counsel, Government Bldg. & Loan Assn. Candidate on Dem. ticket for Dist. Atty. of Schuylkill Co., and mem. Congress from 13th Dist.; dep. atty. gen., State of Pa., Dept. of Labor and Industry, State Workmens Insurance Fund since Mar. 1938. Mem. Schuylkill Co. Bar Assn. Democrat. Roman Catholic. Home: 305 W. Cherry St. Office: Shenandoah Trust Co. Bldg., Shenandoah, Pa.

O'HARRA, Margaret Tustin (Mrs. I. Harrison O'Harra), social worker; b. Lewisburg, P., Jan. 23, 1866; d. Francis Wayland (Ph.D.) and Maria (Probasco) Tustin; A.B., Bucknell U., 1883; A.M., 1891; Dr. Humanities, same univ., 1935; m. I. Harrison O'Harra, 1902 (died June 1937); 2 children—Ernest Tustin, Margaret (Mrs. L. T. Koons). Teacher, Bucknell U., 1883-87. Sch. dir., West Phila., 1904-13. Vice chmn. canteen dept. Am. Red Cross and Liberty Loan Com., World War. One of founders Playground Assn. of Phila.; an incorporator of Public Edn. Assn.; v.p. State Federation of Pa. Women 4 yrs. (mem. edn. com. 4 yrs.); apptd. by gov. of Pa. vice-pres. Home and Sch. League for Phila.; mem. nat. com. on marriage and the home, Federal Council Chs. of Christ in America; apptd. by Court of Common Pleas as visitor for children, 1924-27; mem. Am. Bapt. Home Mission Bd.; mem. social service com. Northern Bapt. Conv. (mem. hist. bd.); dir. State Mission Soc. of Pa. Mem. advisory bd. Rep. Women of Phila. County. Founder Bucknell Alumnæ Club of Phila. (hon. pres., 1928; mem. Am. Assn. Univ. Women, English-Speaking Union, Trans-Atlantic Soc., D.A.R., Colonial Dames of America, Phila. Art Alliance (dir. jr. work). Republican. Clubs: Civic (v.p.), College, New Century, City, Print. Writer of biographies of Mrs. Henry W. Peabody, Mrs. Helen Barrett Montgomery, Mrs. George Coleman, etc. Home: Fairfax Apts., Locust at 43d St., Philadelphia, Pa.

OHL, Jeremiah Franklin, clergyman; b. Cherryville, Northampton Co., Pa., June 26, 1850; s. Milton and Mary Elizabeth (Schick) O.; Mercersburg (Pa.) Coll., 1866-67; A.B., Muhlenberg Coll., Pa., 1871, A.M., 1874, Mus.D., 1893; grad. Luth. Theol. Sem., Phila., 1874; D.D., Wittenberg Coll., Springfield, O., 1921; m. Olivia Elizabeth Kessler, Mar. 10, 1873 (died Jan. 16, 1919); children—Hermine Elizabeth (wife of Prof. C. Theodore Benze), Else Rebecca, Frederick William. Ordained Luth. ministry, June 3, 1874; pastor, Quakertown (Pa.) Parish, 1874-93; organizer and rector Luth. Deaconess Motherhouse, Milwaukee, and instr. Theol. Sem. Luth. Ch., Chicago, 1893-98; city missionary, Phila., 1899-1930; supt. Phila. City Mission of Evang. Luth. Ch., 1903-30. Lecturer, Luth. Theol. Sem., Phila., 1910-11; mus. editor The Helper, 1882-91; lecturer at summer schs. Frequent delegate General Council Evangelical Lutheran Church in North America (now United Luth. Ch. in America), and mem. com. on liturgy and hymn books, 1885—; mem. Inner Mission Bd. and other bds. many yrs.; long active in prison reform work, and frequent del. to Nat. Prison Congress; del. to Internat. Prison Congress, 1910. Trustee Muhlenberg Coll., 1877-93; dir. Theol. Sem. Evang. Luth. Ch., Chicago, 1894-99; hon. pres. Inner Mission Soc. of Phila. Hon. asso. Pa. Chapter Am. Guild Organists; mem. Pennsylvania Prison Society, Manuscript Music Soc. of Philadelphia, Hymn Soc. Editor: Little Children's Book (mus.), 1885; revised and enlarged edit. Church Song (with Rev. Dr. Joseph A. Seiss), 1892. Chief mus. editor and contbr. to Common Service Book of the Lutheran Church, 1917, and the Parish School Hymnal, 1926; also contbr. to the Children's Hymnal and Service Book, 1929. Author: School and Parish Hymnal (with tunes), 1892; School and Parish Service Book (with music), 1892; The Responsories of Matins and Vespers Set to Music, 1909; The Inner Mission, A Handbook for Christian Workers, 1911; also festival anthem, "I Will Extol Thee," for Quadri-Centennial of the Reformation (2d prize), 1917; "The Living Hope," Easter cantata, 1923; "The Christ Child," Christmas cantata, 1925; "The Good Shepherd," cantata for gen. use,

1927. Composer of numerous hymn tunes, carols and anthems. Contbr. to Luth. Cyclo., Ency. of Missions, to church papers and periodicals. Home: 826 S. St. Bernard St., Philadelphia, Pa.

OKESON, Walter Raleigh, treas. Lehigh Univ.; b. Port Royal, Pa., Oct. 3, 1875; s. Jonathan Black and Anna (MacAdam) O.; C.E., Lehigh U., Bethlehem, Pa.; m. Rena Dettre, 1901 (died 1904); m. 2d, Gertrude Dolton Bray, 1907; 1 dau., Mrs. Anne Butchart. Surveyor South Penn Oil Co., 1896-97; draftsman Shiffler Bridge Co., 1898-99; draftsman Phoenix Bridge Co., 1899-1901, engr., 1902-10; engr. Am. Bridge Co., 1901-02; contracting engr. Phoenix Bridge Co. and Phoenix Iron Co., 1910-17; exec. sec. Alumni Assn. of Lehigh U., 1917-26, treas. and sec. bd. trustees Lehigh U. since 1923; sec. London Mines and Milling Co., Colo., 1934-36, pres. since 1936. Commr. Eastern Intercollegiate Assn., 1927-37; chmn. Nat. Football Rules Com. since 1933. Home: Old Stone House, Old Zionsville, Pa. Office: Alumni Memorial Bldg., Bethlehem, Pa.

OKIN, Irving, physician; b. New York, N.Y., Oct. 12, 1899; s. Max and Dora (Cantor) O.; A.B., Columbia U., 1920; M.D., Coll. Phys. & Surgs. of Columbia U., 1923; m. Helen M. Johantgen, June 30, 1928; 1 son, Franklin Jay. Interne Jersey City (N.J.) Hosp., 1923-24; asst. res. Manhattan Maternity & Dispensary, 1924; engaged in gen. practice of medicine at Monroe, N.Y., 1924-27; resident in pediatrics, N.Y. Post Grad. Hosp., N.Y. City, 1927; in practice specializing in pediatrics, Passaic, N.J., since 1927; asst. attdg., N.Y. Post Grad. Hosp. Babies Ward; dir. pediatrics, St. Mary's Hosp. Fellow Am. Acad. Pediatrics. Licentiate Am. Bd. Pediatrics. Mem. N.J. State Med. Soc. (chmn. sect. of pediatrics, 1939), Passaic Co. Med. Soc. Mason. Home: 165 Passaic Av., Passaic, N.J.

OLD, Marcus Calvin, zoölogist; b. Allentown, Pa., Dec. 21, 1897; s. Orlando W. and Ellen Victoria (Decker) O.; A.B., Lehigh U., 1923, A.M., same, 1925; Ph.D., U. of Mich., 1930; m. Dorothy May Geidner, Sept. 3, 1925. Began as instr. biology, Lehigh U., 1923-25; prof. biology, Olivet Coll., Mich., 1925-26; instr. zoölogy, U. of Mich., 1926-29, fellowship in zoölogy, U. of Mich., 1929; asst. prof. biology, Ursinus Coll., Collegeville, Pa., since 1930; instr. and investigator at Chesapeake Biol. Lab., Solomons, Md., for Johns Hopkins U., summers 1935-39. Served as pvt. inf. U.S.A., 1917-19, with A.E.F. Mem. Am. Micros. Soc., Ecol. Soc., Mich. Acad. Arts and Scis., Pa. Acad. Sci., Sigma Xi, Phi Sigma, Gamma Alpha. Mem. Reformed Ch. Club: Lions of Collegeville. Spl. field in zoölogy investigations is the biology of sponges. Home: 522 Main St., Collegeville, Pa.

OLDS, Edwin Glenn, prof. of mathematics; b. Buffalo, N.Y., Apr. 20, 1898; s. Edwin Nelson and Effie Ruth (Wells) O.; A.B., Cornell U., 1918; A.M., U. of Pittsburgh, 1926, Ph.D., 1931; m. Marion McNeil Knowles, Mar. 30, 1918; children—David McNeil, Marcia Elisabeth. Teacher of mathematics, Iron River (Mich.) High Sch., 1919-20, Sault Ste. Marie (Mich.) High Sch., 1920-22; with Carnegie Inst. of Tech. since 1922, as instr. of mathematics, 1922-26, asst. prof., 1926-31, asso. prof., since 1931. Fellow A.A.A.S.; mem. Inst. of Math. Statistics, Am. Math. Soc., Math. Assn. America, Nat. Council Teachers of Mathematics, Sigma Xi. Republican. Presbyterian. Mason. Author: Vocational Mathematics (with Edgar M. Starr), 1930. Contbr. to Am. Math. Monthly, Bull. Am. Math. Soc., Annals of Math. Statistics, Mathematics Teacher, Nat. Mathematics Mag. Home: 953 La Clair Av., Pittsburgh, Pa.

O'LEARY, Patrick E., lawyer; b. Altoona, Pa., Apr. 20, 1904; s. Denis J. and Catherine (Duffy) O'L.; grad. Our Lady of Mt. Carmel High Sch., 1919; student St. Francis Coll., Loretta, Pa., 1921-22; LL.B., Duquesne U., Pittsburgh, 1927; m. Ellen Marie Lawly, Apr. 5, 1934. Clerk Pa. R.R., Altoona, 1920-21, 1922-23; title examiner Potter Title & Trust Co., Pittsburgh, 1925-28; admitted to Allegheny Co. bar, 1927, also to Supreme Court and Superior Court of Pa. and U.S. Dist. Court; admitted to Blair Co. bar, 1928; began practice in Altoona; special dep. atty. gen. of Pa., assigned to Pa. Liquor Control Bd., since 1935. Dem. leader Blair Co. since 1928; Dem. nominee for dist. atty., 1935; mem. Dem. Nat. and State Speakers Bur. Mem. Blair Co. Bar Assn., Pa. Bar Assn. Roman Catholic. K. of C. (past grand knight and dist. dep.). Home: 302 Penn St., Hollidaysburg, Pa. Office: 1321 11th Av., Altoona, Pa.

OLEWINE, James Harris; prof. organic chemistry, Pa. State Coll. Address: State College, Pa.

OLIENSIS, Abraham E., M.D.; b. Russia, Dec. 18, 1885; brought to U.S., 1893; s. Solomon and Rebecca (Rabinowitz) O.; M.D., U. of Pa. Med. Sch., 1911; m. Florence E. Berkowitz, Apr. 30, 1918; children—Betty Jane, Sheldon, Doris Sue. Lecturer in medicine, Temple U., 1914-18, asso. in medicine, 1918-22, asso. prof., 1922-30; visiting physician Temple U. Hosp., 1915-30; asst. visiting physician Philadelphia Gen. Hosp., 1924-30; visiting physician Northwestern Gen. Hosp., 1931-33; now visiting physician Skin and Cancer Hosp. Mem. Philadelphia County Med. Soc., Pa. Med. Soc., Northern Med. Soc., North-End Med. Soc., Phi Lambda Kappa. Democrat. Jewish religion. Club: Physicians Motor Club. Author: Sources of Error in Estimation of Blood Pressure, 1920; The Rationale of Acute Mercuric Chloride Poisoning, 1924; Intravenous Glucose Medication, 1927. Home: 1039 Oak Lane Av. Office: 1737 Chestnut St., Philadelphia, Pa.

OLINGER, Nathaniel Aron, dentist; b. New York, N.Y., Nov. 4, 1886; s. Barnett and Cecelia Florence (Shoyer) O.; D.D.S., Medico-Chirurgical Coll. of U. of Pa., 1910; student Columbia U., 1919, Rutgers U., New Brunswick, N.J., 1933; m. Jennie Harris, Nov. 21, 1913; children—Carolyn Yvette (Mrs. John Jacob Eisenberg), Mervin Goodman. Began practice dentistry, Bloomfield, N.J., 1911; specialist in surg. prosthetic since 1916; asst. prof. Columbia U. Dental Sch. since 1938; pres. Glenwood Bldg. & Loan Assn., Bloomfield, N.J., since 1932; v.p. and dir. Mutual Finance Corpn., Abotts Inc., Video Inc.; dir. Community Trust Co. Served as lt. comdr. U.S.N.R. Dental Corps, 1937. Dir. Shary Tefilo Temple, Bloomfield Community Chest; trustee Boy Scouts Council (Bloomfield), Youths Commn. Chmn. United Jewish Appeal, 1938-39. Fellow Am. Acad. of Diseases and Surgery of the Mouth (pres. elect); mem. N.J. Acad. of Medicine, N.Y. Dental Soc., Am. Dental Assn., N.J. State Dental Soc., Essex Co. Dental Soc., Alpha Omega, Epsilon Tau Chi. Hebrew. Mason (32°, Elk, K.P. Clubs: Newark Athletic (Newark), Rotary (pres. 1935-37; charter mem.), Progress (Bloomfield); Mt. Ridge Country (Caldwell, N.J.). Author many articles on surg. prosthetic (restoration for mouth facial defects). Home: 186 Franklin St. Office: 44 Washington St., Bloomfield, N.J.

OLIPHANT, A. Dayton, judge; b. Trenton, N.J., Oct. 28, 1887; s. Henry Duncan and Elizabeth Vande Veer (Dayton) O.; student Rand Prep. Sch., Trenton, N.J., 1900-05, Princeton U., 1905-07, U. of Pa. Law Sch., 1911; m. Marguerite Broughton, June 21, 1924. Admitted to N.J. bar, 1911, and practiced at Trenton, 1911-27; prosecutor of the pleas, Trenton, 1918-23 (one term); judge circuit ct., Trenton, since 1927. Served as capt., judge advocate's dept., N.J.N.G., 1916-18. Chmn. Mercer Co. (N.J.) Rep. Com., 1914-18, vice-chmn. Rep. State Com., 1916-21. Mem. N.J. State Bar Assn., Mercer Co. Bar Assn., Am. Bar Assn., Phi Delta Theta. Republican. Presbyterian. Mason (32°, Shriner). Clubs: Tiger Inn, Nassau, Nassau Gun (Princeton, N.J.); Carteret, Trenton Country (Trenton, N.J.). Home: 43 Cleveland Lane, Princeton, N.J. Office: Court House, Trenton, N.J.

OLIPHANT, James Orin, asso. prof. history; b. Elberton, Wash., Mar. 23, 1894; s. Samuel Bruce and Leona (Stevenson) O.; ed. Eastern Wash. Coll. of Edn., Cheney, Wash., 1911-13; A.B. magna cum laude, U. of Wash., 1916, A.M., same, 1924; Ph.D., Harvard, 1930; m. Elizabeth Louise Martin, Aug. 31, 1927. Engaged in teaching history in high schs. and newspaper editor, Cheney, Wash., 1916-21; exec. sec. Eastern Wash. Coll. of Edn., 1921-24, instr. history, same, 1924-30; asso. prof. history, Antioch Coll., Yellow Springs, O., 1930-32; asst. prof. history, Bucknell U., 1933-37, asso. prof. since 1937. Served in U.S.A. with A.E.F., 1918-19. Docket clk. Wash. Ho. of Rep., 1921-23. Mem. Am. Hist. Assn., Miss. Valley Hist. Assn., Am. Soc. Ch. History, Ore. Hist. Soc., Pa. Hist. Assn., Northumberland Co. (Pa.) Hist. Soc., Hudson's Bay Record Soc., Agrl. Hist. Soc., Am. Assn. of Univ. Profs., Am. Acad. Polit. and Social Sci., Phi Beta Kappa. Democrat. Mem. Christian Church. Author: History of the State Normal School at Cheney, Wash., 1924. Co-author (with C. S. Kingston), Outline of the History of the Pacific Northwest, With Special Reference to Washington, 1926. Editor: The Territory of Washington, 1879, by Francis H. Cook, pub., 1925. Contbr. to hist. mags. Home: College Park, Lewisburg, Pa.

OLIVER, Augustus Kountze; b. Pittsburgh, Pa., July 19, 1881; s. George Tener and Mary Dorothea (Kountze) O.; prep. edn. Shady Side Acad., Pittsburgh, and St. Paul's Sch., Concord, N.H.; A.B., Yale, 1903; m. Margaretta Wood, Nov. 12, 1907; children—Joseph Wood, Augustus K. (dec.), Margaretta Wood II, Henry William, George S. II, John Bennett, Janet. Began as reporter Pittsburgh Chronicle Telegraph (owned by father), 1903; advertising mgr. same and Pittsburgh Gazette Times, 1906-09, sec. both, 1912-20, v.p., 1910-27; pres. Commerce Bldg. Co.; dir. Pittsburgh Coal Co., Scholastic Corpn., Pittsburgh Silver Peak Gold Mining Co., Dollar Savings Bank. Mem. City Council, 1919-21. Trustee Shady Side Acad. (pres. bd.), Carnegie Inst. Tech. (sec.), Carnegie Inst. (sec.), Community Fund Pittsburgh (ex-pres.), Pittsburgh Chapter Am. Red Cross (chmn. exec. com.). Mem. Psi Upsilon, Wolf's Head Soc. (Yale). Republican. Episcopalian. Clubs: Duquesne, Pittsburgh Golf, Rolling Rock, Fox Chapel Golf (Pittsburgh); Yale (N.Y. City). Home: 5522 5th Av. Office: Chamber of Commerce Bldg., Pittsburgh, Pa.

OLIVER, Bennett, steel fabricating; b. Pittsburgh, Pa., Mar. 20, 1895; s. George Tener and Mary (Kountze) O.; ed. Shadyside Acad., Pittsburgh, Pa., 1907-09, St. Paul's Sch., Concord, N.H., 1909-13, Yale U., 1913-17; m. Amalie Craighead, July 14, 1924; 1 dau., Kathleen Craighead. Asso. with Bosch Magneto Co., Springfield, Mass., Dayton Engring. Labs., Pittsburgh Chemical Co., 1919-23; one of organizers McKee-Oliver, Inc., steel warehouse and fabrication, Pittsburgh, Pa., 1923 and pres. since 1938; sec. and treas. Commerce Building Co. Served in A.S., U.S.A. with A.E.F., 1917-19. Mem. Delta Kappa Epsilon. Republican. Episcopalian. Clubs: Duquesne, Pittsburgh Golf, Fox Chapel Golf (Pittsburgh); Yale (New York); Rolling Rock (Ligonier, Pa.); Toronto Hunt (Toronto, Can.). Home: 6220 Howe St. Office: 1326 W. Carson St., Pittsburgh, Pa.

OLIVER, George Sturges, retired newspaper pub.; b. Pittsburgh, Pa., Jan. 4, 1878; s. George Tener and Mary Dorothea (Kountze) O.; grad. Shady Side Acad., Pittsburgh; A.B., Yale, 1899; m. Laura Gilpin Smith, June 1, 1910; children—George Tener, Laura Wood, Persifor Smith, Bradley Cummings. Began in newspaper business with Pittsburgh Gazette, 1900; pub. Pittsburgh Gazette Times and Pittsburgh Chronicle Telegraph, 1919-27; vice-president Commerce Building Company. Served as regional adviser for the War Industries Bd., World War; mem. Bd. of Claims Ordnance Dept., U.S.A., Pittsburgh, 1917-18. Pres. Pittsburgh Chamber Commerce, 1918-19. Mem. Psi Upsilon. Republican. Mem. Christian (Disciples) Ch. Clubs: Duquesne, Elihu, Pittsburgh Athletic, Fox Chapel Golf, Pittsburgh Golf, Rolling Rock. Home: 5238 Ellsworth Av. Office: Chamber of Commerce Bldg., Pittsburgh, Pa.

OLIVER, John Rathbone, M.D., psychiatrist, medical historian; b. Albany, N.Y., Jan. 4, 1872; s. Gen. Robert Shaw and Marion Lucy (Rathbone) O.; A.B., Harvard Univ., 1894; grad. Gen. Theol. Sem., 1900; M.D., U. of

Innsbruck, Austria, 1910; Ph.D., Johns Hopkins, 1927; unmarried. Master at St. Paul's Sch., Concord, N.H., 1894-97; priest, P.E. Ch., 1900; curate St. Mark's Ch., Phila., Pa., 1900-03 (resigned; restored to orders 1927); surgeon, Austrian Army, 1914-15; psychiatrist, Johns Hopkins Hosp., 1915-17; chief med. officer to Supreme Bench of Baltimore, 1917-30; prof. history of medicine, U. of Md., 1927-30; asso. in history of medicine, Johns Hopkins U., since 1930; pvt. practice as psychiatrist; warden Alumni Memorial Hall, Johns Hopkins. Mem. Med. O.R.C. Mem. A.M.A., Am. Psychiatric Assn., Royal Soc. Medicine (Brit.), Phi Beta Kappa. Republican. Episcopalian (mem. clerical staff Mount Calvary Ch.). Clubs: University, Press, Harvard, Charcoal. Author: The Good Shepherd, 1915; The Six-Pointed Cross in the Dust, 1917; Fear, 1927; Victim and Victor, 1928; Foursquare, 1929; Rock and Sand, 1930; Article Thirty-two, 1931; Psychiatry and Mental Health, 1932; The Good Shepherd (reprinted and revised), 1932; Tomorrow's Faith, 1932; Priest or Pagan, 1933; The Ordinary Difficulties of Everyday People, 1935; Greater Love, 1936; Spontaneous Combustion, 1937. Contbr. to Jour. Criminal Law, Internat. Clinics, Johns Hopkins Hosp. Bull., etc. Home: 3333 N. Charles St. Office: Welch Medical Library, 1900 E. Monument St., Baltimore, Md.

OLIVER, John William, prof. history; b. nr. Jackson, Mo., Apr. 12, 1887; s. Lucius Clay and Mary Louise (Alexander) O.; B.Pd., Mo. State Teachers Coll., Cape Girardeau, Mo., 1906; A.B. and B.S. in Edn., U. of Mo., 1911, A.M., 1912; Ph.D., U. of Wis., 1915; m. Helen McClure, June 2, 1928; children—John William, Robert McClure. Scholarship in American history, University of Wisconsin, 1913-14, fellowship, 1914-15; research assistant Indiana State Library and History Commissions, 1915-16, Wisconsin State Hist. Soc., 1917-18; dir. Ind. Hist. Commn., 1919-23; prof. history and head of dept., U. of Pittsburgh, since 1923. Enlisted as pvt. F.A., Central O.T.S., Camp Taylor, Ky., Aug. 5, 1918; 2d lt. and instr. F.A., Nov. 4-Dec. 15, 1918. Mem. Am. Hist. Assn., History of Science Society, American Political Science Association, Miss. Valley Hist. Assn., Ind. Hist. Society, Western Pa. Hist. Soc., Acad. Science and Art (Pittsburgh), Am. Geog. Soc., Newcomen Soc., Phi Beta Kappa, Phi Delta Kappa, Delta Sigma Rho; fellow A.A.A.S. Presbyterian. Clubs: Junta, University, Faculty. Author: Civil War Military Pension (1861-1865), 1917; Indiana Gold Star Honor Roll, 1921; Marshal Ferdinand L. Foch, 1922. Home: 55 Hoodridge Drive, Mt. Lebanon, Pittsburgh, Pa.

OLIVER, Joseph Hayden, lawyer; b. Scranton, Pa., Apr. 14, 1882; s. Joseph and Mary Ann (Maschal) O.; grad. Scranton High Sch., 1899; M.E., Bloomsburg Teacher Coll., 1900; hon. A.M., Lafayette Coll.; m. Mary Moffat Miller, Sept. 5, 1911; children—Anne Euphemia, William Joseph. School teacher, 1900-07; admitted to Pa. bar, 1906; atty. D.L.&W. R.R. Co., 1907-12, asst. gen. atty., 1912-17, 1920-21; solicitor Pa. R.R. Adminstrn., 1917-20; with Glen Alden Coal Co., since 1921, as gen. counsel, 1921-29, vice-pres. and gen. counsel since 1930; dir. D. L. & W. Coal Co.; sec. and dir. Keystone Mining Co. Past dist. gov. of Pa. Dist., Kiwanis Internat. Mem. Pa. Bar Assn. Republican. Presbyterian. Mason. Clubs: Scranton, Country (Scranton). Home: 746 Webster Av. Office: 310 Jefferson Av., Scranton, Pa.

OLIVER, L. Stauffer, judge; b. Phila., Pa., Nov. 29, 1879; s. Jesse Hughes and Fannie C. (Meyers) O.; Cert. of Prof., U. of Pa. Wharton Sch. of Finance and Econs., 1900; LL.B., U. of Pa. Law Sch., 1903; m. Margaret Hunter Scott, May 22, 1909 (died March 1930); children—Ruth, Margaret (Mrs. Thurston Crane), Stephen; m. 2d, Mina C. Fichtel, Feb. 10, 1932. Admitted to Pa. bar, 1903, and engaged in gen. practice of law at Phila., 1903-37; senior mem. several law firms, 1924-37; state counsel of Pa. for Home Owners' Loan Corpn., 1933-37; pres. judge Ct. of Common Pleas No. 7, Phila. Co. since 1937. Mem. Am., Federal, Pa., and Phila. bar assns., Am. Acad. Polit. and Social Sci., Delta Upsilon, Pa. Soc. Mayflower Descendants, Soc. Colonial Wars, English Speaking Union, Pa. Soc. Democrat. Presbyterian. Clubs: Lawyers, Cavaet, Penn Athletic, Musical Art, Whitemarsh Valley Country, Mask and Wig, Sphinx Senior Society. Home: Kenilworth Apt., Germantown. Office: City Hall, Philadelphia, Pa.

OLIVER, Rosa Virginia, librarian; b. Yanceyville, N.C., Jan. 24, 1890; d. Daniel Lindsay and Ella Joe (Willis) O.; prep. edn. pub. schs., Person Co., N.C.; A.B., Woman's Coll. of U. of N.C., Greensboro, 1921; student N.Y. State Library Sch., summer 1924, also Marshall Coll., Huntington, W.Va.; unmarried. Teacher pub. schs., Person Co., N.C., 1913-15, 1920; asst. librarian, Woman's Coll. of U. of N.C., 1921-24; asst. in N.Y. Pub. Library, 1924-25; asst. librarian, Marshall Coll., Huntington, W.Va., 1925-33, librarian since 1933. Mem. Am. Library Assn., W.Va. Edn. Assn., Am. Assn. Univ. Women, W.Va. Library Assn. Address: 1531½ Sixth Av., Huntington, W.Va.

OLIVIER, Charles Pollard, astronomer; b. Charlottesville, Va., Apr. 10, 1884; s. George Wythe and Katharine Roy (Pollard) O.; A.B., U. of Va., 1905, A.M., 1908, Ph.D., 1911; grad. study U. of Calif., 1909-10; m. Mary Frances Pender, Oct. 18, 1919 (died 1934); children—Alice Dorsey, Elsie Pender; m. 2d, Ninuzza Seymour, Oct. 23, 1936. Began as prof. of astronomy and physics in Agnes Scott College, Decatur, Georgia, 1911-14; assistant professor astronomy, U. of Va., 1914-23, asso. prof., 1923-28; prof. astronomy and dir. Flower Obs., U. of Pa., since 1928. With ordnance dept., U.S.A., work on range-finding method for anti-aircraft arty., 1918-19. Fellow A.A.A.S., Royal Astron. Soc.; mem. Am. Astron. Soc., Internat. Astron. Union (chmn. meteor commn., 1924-34), Am. Meteor Society (founder), Am. Philosophical Society, Société Astronomique de France, Société d'Astronomie d'Anvers, Phi Beta Kappa, Sigma Xi, Sigma Alpha Epsilon. Democrat. Episcopalian. Clubs: Lenape (U. of Pa.); Colonnade (U. of Va.). Author: Meteors, 1925; Comets, 1930. Contbr. to Publs. of Leander McCormick Obs., Lick Obs. Bulls., Flower Obs. Publs. and Reprints; also numerous articles in jours. Address: Flower Observatory, U. of Pa., Upper Darby, Pa.

OLIVIER, Stuart, newspaper pub.; b. Staunton, Va., July 2, 1880; s. Warner Lewis and Martha (Statton) O.; ed. U. of Va., 1897-99; m. Sarah Reeside, June 12, 1905; children—Stuart, Ann Fox. Began as reporter on Baltimore News and advanced to pub. and gen. mgr.; later bought chain of middle west newspapers, sold them, 1934; present activity directorate of more than 20 corpns. Clubs: Maryland, Elkridge, etc. Address: 2 Wyndhurst Av., Baltimore Md.

OLMES, Mildred Young, (Mrs. Hugh H. K. Olmes), artist; b. Oil City, Pa., Feb. 12, 1906; d. William Thomas and Jessie May (Foller) Young; A.B., Coll. Fine Arts, Carnegie Inst. Tech., 1928; ed. Royal Italian Univ. for Foreigners, Perugia, Italy, summer 1930, studio of R. Pougheon, Paris, France, winter 1929-30, 1930-31, Coll. Fine Arts, Carnegie Inst. Tech., summer 1934; m. Hugh H. K. Olmes, Aug. 24, 1932. Began as artist, Canton Engraving & Electrotype Co., Canton, O., 1927-29; painter in oil for exhbns.; specializes in portraits and murals; exhibited at Carnegie Inst., Pittsburgh, Le Salon (Soc. of French Artists), Paris, France, Chicago Art Inst., Eastman and Bolton Galleries, Cleveland, O., Mus. of Arts, San Francisco, Calif., Fine Arts Center, Colorado Springs, Colo., Mus. Fine Arts, Dallas, Tex., Butler Art Inst., Youngstown, O., Wichita Art Museum, Wichita, Kan., Massillon Museum, Massillon, O., etc. Mem. Alpha Kappa Psi, Mortar Board. Awarded John Porter Prize for Progress, 1926; Founders Scholarship, 1926-27, 1927-28. Episcopalian. Home: 323 W. Walnut St., Titusville, Pa.

OLMSTEAD, Robert Herman, dairy extension specialist; b. Fairdale, Pa., Apr. 13, 1892; s. George M. and Caroline E. O.; B.S., Pa. State Coll., 1916; M.S., U. of Minn., Minneapolis, Minn., 1923; m. Harriette E. Cobb, Aug. 25, 1916 (died 1923); 1 son, Robert Herman; m. 2d, Evelyn Wilson, June 23, 1925; 1 dau., Carolyn Miller. Engaged as instr. animal husbandry, Pa. State Coll., 1916-17; co. agt., Centre Co., Pa., 1917-20; farming on own acct., 1920-21; dairy extension specialist, Pa. State Coll. since 1921, in charge dairy extension dept. since 1937. Mem. Delta Upsilon. Presbyterian. Mason. Grange. Home: 136 Ridge Av., State College, Pa.

OLMSTED, Frederick L(aw), real estate and ins. agency; b. Mead Run, Pa., Feb. 4, 1873; s. Samuel Ashbill and Fannie Frances (Welch) O.; ed. pub. schs., Brockway, Pa.; m. Charlotte B. Adams, Dec. 6, 1893; children—Willa Marie (dec.), Anna Frances (dec.). Began business career in transfer and express business, 1887; engaged in real estate business since 1905 and gen. ins. agency since 1916; one of organizers Brockway Citizens Bank and now dir. and mem. discount com.; organized Brockway Oil & Gas Co., 1910, and served as pres. and gen. mgr. Served as mem. Brockway Town Council; pres. Brockway Business Men's Exchange for several yrs. Republican. Presbyn. Home: 1101 Seventh Av. Office: 451 Main St., Brockway, Pa.

OLMSTED, George Welch, public utilities exec.; b. Ridgway, Pa., May 18, 1874; s. Samuel Ashbel and Fannie Frances (Welch) O.; ed. Brockway (Pa.) High Sch.; m. Iva Catherine Groves, June 17, 1904; children—Robert Groves, Elizabeth. Pres. Delaware Olmsted Co., United Gas & Electric Corpn.; v.p. Eastern Seaboard Securities Corpn., Empire Power Corpn., Kings County Lighting Co., Long Island Lighting Co.; sec. J. G. Curtis Leather Co.; treas. B. V. Harrison Co. Trustee Allegheny Coll., Tanners Research Lab., Cincinnati. Dir. Utilities Mutual Ins. Co. Mem. nat. exec. bd. of Boy Scouts America. Mem. Empire State Gas and Electric Assn. (exec. com.), Soc. Mayflower Descendants, Order of Founders and Patriots of America, Soc. Colonial Wars, S.A.R. and S.R. Republican. Methodist. Mason (Shriner). Clubs: Conewango, Conewango Valley Country (Warren, Pa.); Kane (Pa.) Country; Union League, Bankers (New York). Home: Ludlow, Pa.

OLSEN, Thorsten Ylhen, pres. Tinius Olsen Testing Machine Co.; b. Philadelphia, Pa., June 26, 1879; s. Tinius and Charlotta (Ylhen) O.; M.E., Cornell U., 1903; m. Margarita McKinley, Oct. 31, 1905; children—Elizabeth (Mrs. Chas. A. Gruber), Charlotta (Mrs. Willits P. Haines, Jr.), Margarita (Mrs. C. Robert Tait), Thorstina (Mrs. John J. Millane, Jr.), Tinius, II, Sophia B. Supt., later gen. mgr. Tinius Olsen Testing Machine Co., 1903-12, v.p. and treas., 1912-31, pres. since 1931. Mem. Philadelphia Bd. of Trade, Philadelphia Chamber of Commerce. Republican. Presbyterian. Clubs: Union League, Cornell, Engineers (Philadelphia). Writer numerous articles on art of testing strength of materials and on balancing of rotating parts. Home: 235 Gowen Av. Office: 500 N. 12th St., Philadelphia, Pa.

OLSON, Harry Ferdinand, physicist; b. Mt. Pleasant, Ia., Dec. 28, 1901; s. Frans and Nelly (Bengtson) O.; B.E., State U. of Ia., Ia. City, Ia., 1924, M.S., 1925, Ph.D., 1928, E.E. (hon.), 1932; m. Lorene Johnson, June 11, 1935. Engr. Bell Telephone Co., Chicago, 1924-28; physicist Radio Corpn. of America, New York, 1928-30, RCA Photophone, New York, 1930-32; physicist RCA Mfg. Co., Camden, N.J., since 1932, acoustic research dir. since 1934. Mem. Tau Beta Pi, Sigma Xi, Gamma Alpha. Lutheran. Author: Applied Acoustics, 1934; also 30 technical papers. Home: 700 Station Av., Haddon Heights, N.J. Office: RCA Mfg. Co., Camden, N.J.

OLSON, Karl John; b. Grimstad, Norway, July 28, 1885; s. Ole and Anne Johnson (Christenson) O.; ed. high sch.; m. Hilma A. Björk, June 3, 1916; children—Ethel Eunice, Karl Lloyd, Hazel Edna. Came to U.S., 1902, naturalized citizen, 1911. Pres. Noslo Realty Co., East Orange, N.J.; dir. East Orange Bldg. & Loan Assn., mem. Am. Scandinavian Foundation. Mem. reception com., East Orange, for visit of Crown Prince Gustaf of Sweden, June 1926,

O'MALLEY

Prince William of Sweden, Feb. 1927. Ex-pres. N.Y. Conf. Luth. Brotherhood; v.p. Augustana Synod Lutheran Brotherhood; dir., treas. Upsala Coll.; del. synodical meeting Augustana Synod of America, 1922-24, 32-37, also to N.E. and N.Y. confs., 1916-37; treas. and mem. exec. com. N.Y. Conf. of Lutheran Augustana Synod; mem. exec. com. of N.J. State com. for 300th anniversary of Swedish Settlement on Delaware Celebration, also mem. gen. com. of same. N.J. chmn. John Ericsson Republican Club. Councilman, City of East Orange, 1937-39. Club: Rotary (dir.). Home: 236 N. Walnut St. Office: 214 N. Clinton St., East Orange, N.J.

O'MALLEY, Charles P., lawyer; b. Olyphant, Pa., July 16, 1870; s. John and Ann (Gallagher) O.; student pub. schs.; studied law in offices of Willard & Warren; m. Myra A. Hill, Jan. 26, 1929. Admitted to Lackawanna Co. bar, 1894; since in gen. practice of law; mem. law firm O'Malley, Hill, Harris & Harris, Scranton, Pa., since 1931. Mem. Pa. Ho. of Reps., 1895. Lackawanna Bar Assn., Pa. Bar Assn. Republican. Catholic. Club: Scranton (Pa.) Country. Home: 530 Clay Av. Office: Scranton Electric Bldg., Linden St., Scranton, Pa.

ONDERDONK, Adrian Holmes, educator; b. St. James School, Washington Co., Md., July 18, 1877; s. Henry and Mary Elizabeth (Latrobe) O.; grad. St. James Sch., 1905 (father headmaster); A.B., Trinity Coll., Connecticut, 1899, A.M. from same college, 1929; m. Evelynne Richardson, Nov. 2, 1912; children—Adrian Holmes, Richardson Latrobe, Henry II. With New York Shipbuilding Co., Camden, N.J., 1899-1900; a master at Gilman Sch., Baltimore, Md., 1900-03; headmaster St. James Sch., 1903-39, headmaster emeritus and head of Latin dept. since 1939. Senior fellow Trinity College. Member Headmasters' Association, Association Coll. and Prep. Schs. of Middle States and Md., Alpha Delta Phi. Democrat. Episcopalian. Address: St. James School, Washington Co., Md.

ONDERDONK, John Clarke, Jr., ins. co. exec.; b. Highwood, N.J., Mar. 13, 1894; s. John Clarke and Susan (Ryan) O.; student N.Y. Univ., 1912-17; married, Sept. 30, 1922; children—Elizabeth Morse, Susan Jane, John Clarke 3d, Frederick Bridges. Began with Metropolitan Casualty Co., 1911; with Norwich Union Indemnity Co., 1920-29; supt. burglary dept. Royal Indemnity Co. and Eagle Indemnity Co., 1929-30; v.p. and dir. Bankers Indemnity Ins. Co., Newark, N.J., since 1930. Served in U.S.N., 1917-18. Mem. Boys Com. and mem. Hackensack Branch Y.M.C.A. Republican. Episcopalian (vestryman, treas. Ch. of Atonement, Tenafly). Club: White Beeches Golf and Country (Haworth). Home: 85 Highwood Av., Englewood, N.J. Office: 15 Washington St., Newark, N.J.

O'NEILL, Edward L., ex-congressman; b. Newark, N.J., July 10, 1903; s. Joseph Luke and Margaret Cecilia (Quinn) O'N.; ed. St. James Grammar Sch.; mem. 75th Congress (1937-39), 11th N.J. Dist. Served in U.S. Navy, 1919-23. Democrat. Roman Catholic. Home: Newark, N.J.

O'NEILL, James Lewis, banker; b. Pittsburgh, Pa., Oct. 8, 1881; s. James and Martha (Torrance) O.; ed. in pub. schs. of Pittsburgh; m. Dorothy Craig, Jan. 7, 1916; children—James Craig, Martha Torrance, Jeremy Wilson. Began as messenger for Bradstreet Co., 1895-96; with Carnegie Steel Co., Pittsburgh, 1896-1918, starting as office boy and advancing through various positions to credit mgr.; apptd. v.p. Guaranty Trust Co. of New York, May 1, 1918, now operating v.p.; served as control officer NRA, Dec. 1934-June 1935; apptd. adminstr. NRA, Washington, D.C., June, 1935; resigned Aug. 1, 1935; v.p. and dir. Fidelitas Realty Co., New York; dir. Guaranty Safe Deposit Co., W. T. Grant Co. Republican. Presbyn. Mason (Shriner). Club: Duquesne (Pittsburgh). Home: Short Hills, N.J. Office: 140 Broadway, New York, N.Y.

OOSTERLING, James; supt. Lutheran Inner Mission. Home: 4313 Arabia Av., Baltimore, Md.

OPIE, Reginald Stevenson, trust officer; b. Baltimore, Md., Nov. 27, 1884; s. Dr. Thomas and Sallie (Harman) O.; student Marston U. Sch., 1893-1901; A.B., Johns Hopkins U., 1904; LL.B., U. of Md. Law Sch., 1908; m. Ethel Lyon, Mar. 4, 1918. In gen. practice of law, 1908-11; with Am. Bonding Co. and Fidelity & Deposit Co., 1911-14; with Safe Deposit & Trust Co. of Baltimore since 1914, now v.p. Mem. Phi Kappa Psi. Clubs: Baltimore Country, Merchants. Home: Garden Apartments. Office: 13 South St., Baltimore, Md.

OPPENHEIMER, Oscar W., steel products mfg.; b. Pittsburgh, Pa., Sept. 23, 1876; s. Moses and Julia (Frank) O.; ed. pub. sch. and high sch., Pittsburgh, Pa.; m. Claude F. Siesel, Dec. 22, 1908; children—Louise (Mrs. Lehman Charles Aarons), James Siesel. Began as cashier and in employ of others; sec.-treas. Apollo Steel Co., Apollo, Pa., since 1914; pres. Keystone Drum Co., Pittsburgh, Pa.; dir. Pittsburgh Steel Drum Co., Butler, Pa., S. M. Siesel Co., Milwaukee, Wis. Mem. Engrs. Soc. of Western Pa. Reformed Jewish religion. Clubs: Concordia, Westmoreland Country. Home: 5831 Bartlett St. Office: 2244 Oliver Bldg., Pittsburgh, Pa.

ORBE, Lorenzo Francis, pres. and gen. mgr. N.J. Flour Mills Co.; b. Italy, Sept. 21, 1881; came to U.S., 1897; m. Mary G. Grosse, 1905; children—Lucille M. (wife of Dr. Mario Patella), Carmine J., Lawrence F., Wilson T., Norman J., Virginia M., Octavius A. Began as insurance salesman, 1897; insurance agent, Passaic, 1900-03; began flour jobbing business for self, 1903, built flour mill and elevator at Clifton, 1917 (present location); pres. and gen. mgr. N.J. Flour Mills Co. Democrat. Catholic. Home: 110 Passaic Av., Passaic, N.J. Office: Chester St., Clifton, N.J.

ORBEN, C(harles) Milford, real estate; b. Newark, N.J., June 28, 1898; s. Charles S. and Mabel (Scholes) O.; ed. East Orange (N.J.) High Sch. and Pa. State Coll.; m. Harriet Goulding Timpson, Oct. 23, 1926; children—Charles Milford, William Winston. Began as farmer, Whitehouse, N.J., 1920; in real estate business, Newark, N.J., since 1925; vice-pres. Mt. Arlington Lakes Development Co., Hopatcong Park & Bear Pond Land Co., Morris & Sussex Water Service, Inc. Mem. N.J. Legislature, 1938-39. Mem. Alpha Gamma Rho. Home: 26 Park Rd., Millburn, N.J. Office: 786 Broad St., Newark, N.J.

ORCHARD, William J., pres. Wallace & Tiernan Products, Inc.; b. Boston, Mass., Nov. 15, 1888; s. Edward and Elizabeth (Sayce) O.; Sanitary Engr., Mass. Inst. Tech., 1911; m. Marie Francis Singler, Feb. 1, 1913; children—John E., William, Robert, Sally, Jane. Began as sanitary engr., Metropolitan Water Bd. (Boston); became gen. sales mgr. Wallace & Tiernan Co., Inc., 1915; now pres. and dir. Wallace & Tiernan Sales Corpn.; v.p. and treas. Novadel-Agene Corpn., Industrial Appliance Corpn. Mem. Essex County Rep. Com. Mem. bd. govs. and trustee Orange Memorial Hosp.; trustee N.J. Hosp. Assn.; chmn. Maplewood Citizens' Com.; ex-pres. and dir. Maplewood Civic Assn.; v.p. and dir. Welfare Federation of the Oranges & Maplewood. Fellow Am. Pub. Health Assn.; entertainment chmn. and ex-pres. Water Works Mfrs. Assn.; mem. Am. Water Works Assn.; ex-pres. and dir. Chamber of Commerce of Oranges and Maplewood; hon. mem. Am. Water Works Assn. Clubs: Essex (Newark); Rotary of Belleville (hon.); Bay Head Yacht (vice commodore and trustee); Maplewood Country (Maplewood); Chemists' (New York). Home: 50 Sagamore Road, Maplewood, N.J. Office: 11 Mill St., Belleville, N.J.

ORCUTT, Daniel Paul, elec. engr.; b. Watertown, S.D., Jan. 9, 1881; s. Alfred Stoddard and Esmah (Shepardson) O.; B.S., Denison Univ., 1905; M.E., Cornell U., 1907; m. Ruth Pickering, Sept. 22, 1910; children—Daniel Shepardson, Ruth Margaret, Marian Pickering. Supt. Denison Univ. heating & lighting plant, 1902-05; asst. engr. Westinghouse Storage Battery Co., East Pittsburgh, Pa., and Boonton, N.J., 1907-10; sales engr. Electric Storage Battery Co., New York, N.Y., 1910-20, asst. mgr. since 1920. Mem. Am. Inst., Elec. Engrs., Cornell Engring. Soc., Ohio Soc., Beta Theta Pi. Republican. Baptist. Clubs: Cornell (New York); Mohawk (Schenectady, N.Y.). Home: 820 Carlton Av., Plainfield, N.J. Office: 25 W. 43d St., New York, N.Y.

ORCUTT, Louis Edgar, insurance; b. Villisca, Ia., Feb. 1, 1878; s. Fred Howell and Almira Amanda (Schriver) O.; grad. Council Bluffs (Ia.) High Sch., 1896; student Ia. State Coll., 1905-08; special insurance lectures, New York U., 1932; m. Mary Grace Hazelton, of Council Bluffs, June 8, 1910 (died May 30, 1938); children—Henry Hazelton, Fred Louis, Ernest Louis (dec.). Began as clerk Brown, Durrell & Co., Boston, 1897; associated with father in firm of F. H. Orcutt & Son, later F. H. Orcutt & Son Co., wholesale carpets and draperies, Chicago, Ill., and Omaha, Neb., 1899-1912; asst. editor Circle and Success Mag., New York, 1913-15; asso. editor Christian Herald, New York, 1915-19; with Interchurch World Movement, 1919-20; in general insurance business, New York, since 1920; also special agt. Provident Mutual Life Ins. Co. since 1920. Chartered life underwriter granted by Am. Coll. Life Underwriters, 1932. Mem. Nat. Chapter Chartered Life Underwriters (treas., 1938-39). Served in Ia. Nat. Guard, 1906-09. Mem. Bd. of Edn., Demarest, N.J., 12 years, mem. Common Council, 3 years. Sec. Laymen's Assn. of Newark Conf. of Meth. Ch., 12 years, v.p., 1937-39, pres. since 1939; mem. finance commn. (vice-pres.) and social service commn. of Newark Conf. of Meth. Ch. Mem. S.A.R., Phi Kappa Psi. Republican. Mason. Home: Orchard Rd., Demarest, N.J. Office: 99 John St., New York, N.Y.

ORELUP, John Wesley, mfg. chemicals, organic chemist, inventor; b. St. Paul, Minn., Apr. 29, 1897; s. Bradley Spencer and Minnie (Rogers) O.; student U. of Minn., Minneapolis, 1913-17; m. Evelyn Marzolf, Sept. 18, 1918; children—Richard Bradley, John Spencer. Research chemist, Sherwin Williams, Chicago, 1917-18; research chemist Carus Chem. Co., LaSalle, Ill., 1918-20, Rit Corpn., Cable, Wis., 1920-21; chief chemist Chemical Co. of America, Springfield, N.J., 1921-30; pres. Patent Chemicals, Inc., products for petroleum industry, Jersey City, N.J., since 1930; vice-pres. Synthetic Chemical, Inc., products for textile industries, Jersey City, N.J., since 1930; pres. Lustron Corpn. since 1938; inventor and holder more than thirty Am. and fgn. patents on chem. processes. Fellow Am. Inst. Chemists. Mem. Am. Chem. Soc., Am. Petroleum Inst., Soc. Automotive Engrs., Am. Assn. Textile Chemists and Colorists, Royal Soc. London. Republican. Roman Catholic. Clubs: Chemists (New York); Yacht (Bay Head, N.J.). Contbr. to sci. publs. Home: 1 Crossgates, Short Hills. Office: 57 Wilkinson Av., Jersey City, N.J.

ORESEK, Charles William, clergyman; b. Gelsenkirchen, Westphalia, Germany, Sept. 7, 1893; s. Karl and Auguste (Frasza) Zywek; adopted by John and Caroline Oresek; brought to U.S., 1895, naturalized, 1932; ed. Mount Union Coll., Alliance, O., 1913-15 and 1916-17, Denison U., Granville, O., 1915-16; m. Bertha Ramsey, Oct. 4, 1937. Ordained to ministry Baptist Ch., 1914 while in coll. and supplied pulpit of Bapt. Ch., Brewster, O., 1914-15, and Bapt. Ch., New London, O., 1915-16; transferred to Methodist ministry, 1918; minister Meth. chs. in Venetia, Pa., 1918-19, Jefferson-James, 1919-20, Dravosburg, 1920-24, Aliquippa, 1924-28, Rochester, 1928-34, Ambridge, 1934-37, and at South Brownsville, Pa., since 1937; built new chs. at Aliquippa and Rochester. Republican. Methodist. Home: 412 Second St., South Brownsville, Pa.

ORMANDY, Eugene, music director; b. Budapest, Hungary, Nov. 18, 1899; s. Benjamin and Rosalie (Berger) O.; boy music prodigy at age of 3½ yrs. and youngest pupil at Royal State Acad. of Music at 5½; B.A. degree from same at 14½, state diploma for art of violin playing, 2 yrs. later, state diploma as professor, 1 yr. later; also grad. Gymnasium, and student U. of Budapest 3 yrs. to 1920; Mus.D., Hamline U.,

St. Paul, 1934, U. of Pa., 1937; m. Steffy Goldner, harpist New York Philharmonic Orchestra, Aug. 8, 1922. Toured Hungary as child prodigy, later toured Central Europe; apptd. head of master classes, State Conservatorium of Music, Budapest, at age of 20; came to U.S., 1921, naturalized, 1927; concertmaster, later conductor Capital Grand Orchestra, New York; substituted for Toscanini as conductor Philharmonic and Philadelphia orchestras; comdr. Minneapolis Symphony Orchestra, 1931-36; condr. Phila. Orchestra since 1936, music director since Sept. 1938. Address: care Philadelphia Orchestra, Girard Trust Bldg., Philadelphia, Pa.

ORMSBY, Alexander F.; dean John Marshall College. Address: Trust Co. of N.J. Bldg., Jersey City, N.J.

ORNDOFF, Jessie McNay, (Mrs. John Delbert Orndoff), librarian; b. nr. Waynesburg, Pa., Nov. 17, 1887; d. Samuel James and Mary Jane (Adams) McNay; A.B., Waynesburg Coll., 1909; ed. Univ. of Grenoble, France, summer 1910, U. of Pittsburgh, 1931, Library Sch., Chautauqua, N.Y., summer 1931, Columbia U., summer 1937; m. John Delbert Orndoff, Nov. 1, 1910 (dec.); children—Mary Josephine (Mrs. Charles E. Farrell), John Delbert, Jeannette Adams (Mrs. Marvin J. Herbert), Lela Joyce. Librarian, Waynesburg Coll., Waynesburg, Pa., since 1931. Mem. Spl. Libraries Assn. (Pittsburgh Chapter). Republican. Presbyn. Clubs: Woman's, Rhodora (Waynesburg). Home: 253 Third Av., Waynesburg, Pa.

ORNSTEIN, Leo, pianist, composer; b. Krementchug, Russia, Dec. 11, 1895; s. Rev. Abram and Clara O.; began on piano under father at 3; enrolled as pupil of the Imperial Conservatory of Music, Petrograd, at 9; came to U.S., 1907; studied under Mrs. Bertha Fiering-Tapper; lit. edn., Friends Sem.; m. Pauline Mallet-Prevost, Dec. 13, 1918. First pub. concert at New Amsterdam Theatre, New York, Mar. 9, 1911; has appeared as soloist with New York Symphony Orchestra, Boston Symphony Orchestra, Phila. Orchestra, Chicago Symphony Orchestra, St. Louis Symphony Orchestra, Los Angeles Philharmonic Orchestra, etc., and has concertized throughout U.S. and Can., also appeared in Norway, Sweden, Paris and London; director Ornstein School of Music, Philadelphia. Composer: (orchestra) Impressions of Chinatown; Marche Funèbre; sonatas for piano and violin; (piano) 9 miniatures; poems of 1917; (piano and orchestra) concerto; quintette for piano and string quartette, songs; 5 songs for voice and orchestra; string quartetté Op. 99; Pantomime, for orchestra; Suite for orchestra, "Lysistrata"; "Nocturne and Dance of Fates" (orchestra), 1936. Home: North Conway, N.H. Address: 251 S. 18th St., Philadelphia, Pa.

O'ROURKE, Lawrence James, psychologist; b. Seattle, Wash., Aug. 10, 1892; s. Michael L. and Mary Ellen (O'Donnell) O'R.; B.A., Lawrence Coll., Appleton, Wis., 1915; studied U. of Wis. and Cornell U.; Ph.D., George Washington U., 1922; unmarried. Formerly instr. U. of Wis. and Cornell U.; lecturer George Washington U.; psychologist Med. Research Lab., Air Service, U.S.A., Mineola, L.I., 1918; chief of selection, A.S. enlisted personnel, 1919; psychologist, Civilian Advisory Bd., War Plans Div., Gen. Staff, 1920-22; dir. research, U.S. Civil Service Commn., since 1922; mem. advisory com. Nat. Research Council; dir. Psychol. Corpn.; dir. Nation-wide Studies in English Vocabulary and Reading; consultant in personnel administration of Tenn. Valley Authority; ex-pres., mem. bd. dirs., Personnel Research Fed. Fellow A.A.A.S.; mem. Am. Psychol. Assn., Psychol. Inst. (chmn. bd. dirs.), Civics Research Inst. (chmn. bd. dirs.), Am. Statis. Assn., A.A.A.S., Am. Management Assn., Taylor Society, N.E.A., Psychol. Corporation (dir.), Am. Edn. Research Assn.; dir. of study, under auspices of Carnegie Foundation for Advancement of Teaching, on "Rebuilding the English Curriculum to Insure Greater Mastery of Essentials." Clubs: Cosmos, National Press. Author of O'Rourke Series Placement and Guidance Tests, 1923-25, under titles: General Classification Test, Jr. Grade; Mechanical Aptitude Test, Jr. Grade; Clerical Aptitude Test, Jr. Grade; College Entrance Test, Jr. Grade; Non-Language Tests; Attainment Tests; Clerical Reasoning Test; Progress Achievement Tests in English Usage, Reading and Vocabulary; text introducing a new teaching method, entitled "Self-Aids in the Essentials of Grammatical Usage"; Junior Self-Aid Series in English for elementary grades; "You and Your Community" and "Your Government Today and Tomorrow"; "English and Everyday Life," textbooks for grades 3, 4, 5, 6; also Community Civics project; also various reports issued by Civil Service Commission and articles pub. by scientific socs. and in magazines. Contbr. chapters to University Training for Federal Service, Principles and Problems in Vocational Guidance, etc. Home: 3506 Patterson St., Chevy Chase, D.C. Address: U.S. Civil Service Commn., Washington, D.C.

ORR, George P., lawyer; b. Christiana, Pa., Sept. 22, 1884; s. Jos. M. and Martha (Pownall) O.; grad. high sch., Christiana, Pa., Gilbert Acad., Chester, Pa., 1906; LL.B., U. of Pa. Law Sch., 1909; m. Virginia Bisler, Oct. 16, 1912; children—George P., Jr., Bisler, Virginia. Admitted to Pa. bar, 1909 and since engaged in gen. practice of law at Phila.; mem. firm Orr and Hall, 1921-26, Orr, Hall and Williams since 1927; dir. John Wanamaker, Phila. and New York, A. T. Stewart Co., New York, N.Y., Warner Co., Phila., Pa., G. A. Bisler, Inc., Phila., Pa., Bethlehem Foundry & Machine Co., Bethlehem, Pa. Served as spl. counsel U.S. War Trade Bd., 1917-18. Dir. Tredyffrin Twp. Sch., Chester Co., Pa. Mem. Am. Bar Assn., Pa. Bar Assn., Phila. Bar Assn. (mem. bd. govs.). Republican. Clubs: Union League, Art, Orpheus, Lawyers', Tredyffrin Country (Philadelphia); Manhasset Bay Yacht (New York). Home: Berwyn. Office: Packard Bldg., Philadelphia, Pa.

ORR, John, clergyman and coll. prof.; b. Ulster, Ire., June 28, 1884; s. James and Margaret Jane (McLeese) O.; brought to U.S., 1891, naturalized, 1918; ed. Park Coll., Mo., 1902-04; A.B., Coll. of Wooster (O.), 1907; A.M., Princeton U., 1909; B.D., Princeton Theol. Sem., 1910; grad. study, U. of Berlin, Germany, 1911-13; Ph.D., U. of Pittsburgh, 1931; m. Anna Mary Sauer, Dec. 29, 1919; children—Mary Martha, Margaret Elizabeth, John William. Ordained to ministry Presbyn. Ch. in U.S.A., 1913; pastor, Middleport, O., 1913-19, Howell, Mich., 1920-28; asst. prof. Bible, Westminster Coll., 1928-31, prof. Bible and head of Bible dept. since 1931, actg. dean 1938. Mem. A.A.A.S., Am. Assn. Univ. Profs., Nat. Assn. Bible Instrs., Pi Gamma Mu. Republican. Presbyn. Ch. U.S.A. Clubs: Clio, Calvin (Princeton, N.J.). Author: English Deism; Its Roots and Its Fruits, 1934. Traveled extensively in Europe, 1911-13. Home: 139 Beechwood Rd., New Wilmington, Pa.

ORR, John Alvin, minister; b. Cedarville, O., Sept. 7, 1874; s. James Renwick and Josephine (Little) O.; student Wooster (O.) U.; A.B., Cedarville Coll., 1897; A.B., U. of Pa., 1898, A.M., 1900; grad. Pittsburgh Theol. Sem., 1901; m. Imo Jean Roadarmer, June 4, 1902; children—J. Alvin, James R., Lois Marjorie, Eleanor P. Ordained ministry U.P. Ch., 1901; pastor Norris Sq. Ch., Phila., 1901-13, First Ch., Pittsburgh (North Side), since Nov. 1913; built community house at cost of $465,000 and head of same. President of the board of trustees of Cedarville College; chairman New World Movement; pres. bd. Colored Rescue Mission, Pittsburgh; mem. bd. Consumers' League; chairman, North Side Ministers' Assn.; president Citizens' League of Pittsburgh and Allegheny County; member Pittsburgh Council of Churches. Republican. Author: Saving the Home, 1908; How to Know Christ is God, 1921; Chains We Wear, 1921; Things Missing in Heaven; What Comes After Death. Home: 3440 Perrysville Av., Pittsburgh, Pa.

ORTMANN, Otto Rudolph, musical edn; b. Baltimore, Md., Jan. 25, 1889; s. Richard and Elizabeth (Krüger) O.; student Johns Hopkins, 1918-20; teacher's certificate, Peabody Conservatory of Music, 1913, diploma, 1917; m. Margaret Donoho; children—Arnold Arduin, Dorothea Constance. Teacher of piano and harmony, Baltimore, 1913-28; instr., Johns Hopkins, 1920-24; dir. Peabody Conservatory of Music since 1928. Mem. art museum com. of Ednl. Soc., Baltimore. Mem. Internat. Soc. of Musicology; Am. Musicological Soc., Com. of Musicology of Am. Council of Learned Socs. Composer numerous pedogogical works for piano. Author: Physical Basis of Piano Touch and Tone, 1925; Physiological Mechanics of Piano Technique, 1929. Contbr. to psychol. jours. Has made research in psychology of musical talent and music education. Home: 3034 St. Paul St., Baltimore, Md.

ORTNER, Elmer A., clergyman; b. Buffalo, N.Y., Aug. 29, 1899; s. John and Mary Louise (Venator) O.; A.B., Thiel Coll.; B.D., Philadelphia Theol. Sem.; grad. work, U. of Pittsburgh; m. Dorothy Frances Cooke, Aug. 22, 1928; children—Rosemary, Carol Louise. Ordained Lutheran ministry; pastor Saxonburg Parish, 1926-30, Trinity Ch., McKeesport, Pa., 1930-34, Christ's Ch., Pittsburgh, since 1934. Dir. Thiel Coll., John Legum Memorial (v.p. 1937-38); pres. Rogers' Parent Teachers Assn. since 1938. Mem. Delta Sigma Phi. Club: Pittsburgh Thiel (pres. 1933-34). Staff corr. The Lutheran Monthly. Home: 1108 Duffield St. Office: Margaretta and N. Beatty Sts., Pittsburgh, Pa.

ORTON, Clayton Roberts, plant pathologist; b. East Hardwick, Vt., Apr. 1, 1885; s. Lyman Squire and Ellen Mandana (Stevens) O.; prep. edn., Essex Classical Inst., Essex Center, Vt., 1901-03, Hardwick Academy, 1904-05; B.S., Univ. of Vt., 1909; M.S., Purdue, 1915; Ph.D., Columbia, 1924; m. Ethel M. Chapman, Sept. 22, 1911; children—Jean, Gardner Chapman, Patricia. Spl. agt. U.S. Dept. Agr., June 1909-Jan. 1910; asst. plant pathologist, U. of Wis., Feb.-Sept. 1910; asst. botanist, Ind. Agrl. Expt. Sta., 1910-12; asst. prof. botany, Pa. State Coll., 1913-16, asso. prof., 1916-19, also asso. prof. plant pathology, 1917-19, prof., 1919-27; plant pathologist, Pa. Agrl. Expt. Sta., 1913-27; also collaborator, Bureau Plant Industry of the United States Department of Agriculture, 1913-25 and since 1930; plant pathologist, in charge research and extension, agrl. dept. The Bayer Co., Inc., 1925-28, Bayer-Semesan Co., Inc., 1928-29; prof. plant pathology and head dept., W.Va., Univ., 1929-33; plant pathologist W.Va. Agrl. Expt. Sta., 1929—; head department of biology, W.Va. Univ., 1933-36, head dept. plant pathology and forestry, 1936-38; dean, Coll. Agrl. Forestry and Home Economics since 1938; dir. Agrl. Exp. Sta. since 1938. Sec. Advisory Bd. Am. Plant Pathologists, 1918-21; chmn., 1922-23; mem. Nat. Research Council (div. biology and agr., 1922-24; liaison mem. div. states relations, 1923-24); mem. bd. govs. Crop Protection Inst., 1920-25, 1935—; mem. W.Va. Planning Board since 1935; chairman Land-Use Commn. of W. Va. since 1934. Fellow A.A.A.S. (pres. State Coll. br., 1923); mem. Am. Phytopathological Soc. (pres. 1939), Mycological Soc. America, S. Appalachian Bot. Club, Pa. Acad. Science, Ind. Acad. Sciences, Sigma Xi, Kappa Sigma, Alpha Zeta, Gamma Sigma Delta. Episcopalian. Home: Morgantown, W.Va.

OSBORN, Albert Sherman, author; b. Sharon, Mich., Mar. 26, 1858; s. William B. and Jane (Cole) O.; ed. pub. schs.; D.Sc., Colby Coll., 1938; m. Beth Dunbar, 1888. Examiner of questioned documents since 1887. Mem. Phi Delta Theta. Republican. Unitarian. Mason. Author: Questioned Documents, 1910, 2d edit., 1929; The Problem of Proof, 1922; The Mind of the Juror, 1937. Home: 215 Midland Av., Montclair, N.J. Office: 233 Broadway, New York, N.Y.

OSBORN, George Augustus, librarian; b. Jersey City, N.J., Aug. 18, 1874; s. Walter Scott and Mary Jane (Baldwin) O.; student elementary and pub. schs., Toledo, O., Brooklyn, N.Y., and Asbury Park, N.J., also Pennington Sem., 1880-93; B.Sc., Rutgers U., 1897, A.M. (hon.), 1922; m. Edith Octavia Tye, of Haysville, Ontario, Can., Dec. 29, 1903; children—Mrs. Agnes Tye Crawford, Gertrude Elizabeth (Mrs. Samuel Carleton Stevens). Student library asst., Rutgers U., New Brunswick, N.J., 1893-97, asst. in active charge, 1897-1906, acting librarian, 1906-07, librarian since 1907. Mem. Am. Library Assn., N.J. Hist. Soc. (trustee; chmn. library com., 1931-32), N.J. Library Assn. (pres. 1928), N.J. Archæol. Soc., New Brunswick Hist. Club, Phi Beta Kappa (hon.), Beta Theta Pi.; asso. mem. N.Y. Hist. Soc. Received Rutgers Award of Merit, 1935. Republican. Episcopalian. Home: 317 Grant Av. Address: Rutgers University, New Brunswick, N.J.

OSBORN, Robert Randolph, aeronautical engr.; b. Phila., Pa., Nov. 19, 1900; s. William Harvey and Jessie Elizabeth (Byrne) O.; B.S., U. of Pa., 1925; unmarried. Began as draftsman Curtiss Aeroplane & Motor Co., Buffalo, N.Y., 1925, aerodynamics and flight test engr., 1926, designer, 1928, asst. dir. of engring., 1933, chief engr., 1934-35; consulting engr. since 1936; designer of the Curtiss "Tanager," winner of $100,000 prize in Guggenheim Safe-Aircraft Competition, 1929; made basic designs for fighter, scouting, observation, and dive-bombing airplanes built for U.S. Navy, single-engine attack airplane for U.S. Army, and twin-engine attack airplane, first of its type developed, also for U.S. Army; in charge of organization which designed and built present standard pursuit, attack, scouting, observation, and bombing airplanes for U.S. Army and Navy. Awarded A. Atwater Kent prize, Merrick Memorial prize. Fellow Inst. of Aeronautical Sciences (New York); asso. fellow Royal Aeronautical Soc. (London); mem. Sigma Alpha Epsilon, Sigma Tau, Eta Kappa Nu. Republican. Presbyterian. Regular contbr. to "Aviation" mag. since 1926. Home: 7060 City Line Av., Philadelphia, Pa.

OSBORNE, Harold Smith, engr.; b. Fayetteville, N.Y., Aug. 1, 1887; s. Cyrus Pearl and Ella Sophia (Smith) O.; B.S., Mass. Inst. Tech., 1908, Engring. D., 1910; m. Mary Agnes Wilson, Aug. 14, 1918 (died 1932); children—Margaret Ellen, Mary Agnes Wilson; m. 2d, Dorothy Brockway, Mar. 24, 1938. Engr. in transmission and protection dept., Am. Telephone & Telegraph Co., New York 1910-14, asst. to transmission and protection engr., 1914-20, Transmission Engr., 1920-1939, operating results engr. since 1939. Chmn. town planning bd., Montclair, N.J., since 1934, joint council of municipal planning bds. in Essex Co., N.J., 1937-39. Trustee Agnes Wilson Osborne World Friendship Fund. Fellow Am. Inst. E.E. (dir.; chmn. standards com., 1923-26, com. on communication, 1931-34, spl. com. on inst. activities, 1936-37, tech. program com., 1936-39, finance com. since 1939, com. on award of inst. prizes, 1936-39, publ. com., 1936-39, Edison Medal com. since 1936, committee on model registration law since 1937, coordination com. since 1938, inst. policy com. since 1938), A.A.A.S. (Am. Inst. E.E. rep. on council), Am. Phys. Soc., Acoustical Soc. of Am.; mem. Montclair Soc. of Engrs. (pres. 1928-30), U.S. Nat. Com. of Internat. Electrotech. Commn. (v.p. since 1926), Regional Plan Assn., (dir.), N.J. State Chamber of Commerce, Am. Assn. of Planning Officials (vice chmn. since 1939), Institute of Radio Engineers, Soc. for Promotion of Engring. Edn., Elec. Standards Com. (mem. com. on scope), Am. Standards Assn. (mem. standards council), Alfred Noble Prize Com. Received Austin Research Fellowship, Mass. Inst. Tech., 1908-10. Congregationalist. Clubs: Downtown Athletic, Technology (New York); Upper Montclair (N.J.) Country; Deer Lake (N.J.). Home: 379 Highland Av., Upper Montelair, N.J. Office: 195 Broadway, New York, N.Y.

OSBORNE, William Hamilton, lawyer, author; b. Newark, N.J., Jan. 7, 1873; s. Joseph P. and Kate (Hamilton) O.; grad. Newark High Sch., 1890; degree of LL.B., New York Law Sch., 1892; m. Lydia Gelston Spring, June 1, 1898; children—William H., Frederick S. Admitted to N.Y. and N.J. bars, 1894, Washington, 1918, practicing N.Y. and N.J.; counsel for Authors' League of America and Am. Dramatists. Republican. Author: The Red Mouse, 1909; The Running Fight, 1910; Catspaw, 1911; Blue Buckle, 1914; Boomerang, 1915; Neal of the Navy (moving picture serial), 1915; How to Make Your Will, 1917; also contbr. short stories to mags. Home: 213 Highland Av., Newark, N.J. Office: 744 Broad St., Newark, N.J.; also 6 E. 39th St., New York, N.Y.

OSBOURN, Samuel Edmund, educator; b. Shenandoah Junction, W.Va., June 2, 1875; s. James Burr and Nancy Alice (Link) O.; grad. Shepherd Coll. State Normal Sch., Shepherdstown, W.Va., 1894; A.B. and B.S., Hampden-Sydney (Va.) Coll., 1901, LL.D., 1930; A.M., Princeton, 1904; grad. study, Harvard, summer 1915; hon. A.M., U. of Pa., 1926; m. Mary Day Poore, June 18, 1912; children—James Poore, Samuel Edmund, Jr., Elizabeth Day. Teacher, pub. schs., W.Va., 1894-97; teacher of mathematics, Fredericksburg (Va.) Coll., 1901-03, Lawrenceville (N.J.) Sch., 1904-09, Tome Sch., Port Deposit, Md., 1909-15; headmaster Germantown Acad. since 1915. Mem. Germantown Community Council. Trustee Y.M.C.A., Germantown, Whosoever Gospel Mission, American Bible Soc. Mem. Assn. Colls. and Prep. Schs. Middle States and Md., Headmasters Assn. N.E., Kappa Sigma. Democrat. Presbyn. (elder). Clubs: University, Princeton, Science and Art. Home: 7103 Greene St., Mt. Airy, Philadelphia, Pa.

OSBOURNE, Alfred Slack, barge line exec.; b. Pittsburgh, Pa., Sept. 28, 1886; s. Walter J. and Elizabeth (Barrows) O.; ed. Williamsport Dickinson Sem., Bethlehem Prep. Sch.; M.E., Lehigh U., 1909; m. Ruth Donnan, Oct. 7, 1913; children—Alfred Slack, Jr. (dec.), Alvan Donnan, Edmund Donnan, Margaret Barrows. Employed as draftsman, then mech. engr. Pittsburgh Water Heater Co., 1910-13; mech. engr. Pittsburgh Power Reverse Gear Co., mfg. his patented device, 1914-24; chief engr. Pittsburgh Terminal Coal Co., 1924-30; vice pres. gen. mgr., and dir. Union Barge Line Corpn. since 1930; vice-pres., gen. mgr., and dir. Southern Transfer Co., Memphis, Tenn.; dir. Dravo Corpn., Inland Rivers Wharf Co. Mem. Pittsburgh Chamber of Commerce. Mem. Phi Gamma Delta. Republican. United Presbyn. Clubs: Traffic, Propeller, Traffic and Transportation, Pittsburgh Lehigh, St. Clair Country. Home: Murdstone Road, Pittsburgh (16), Pa., R.D. 9. Office: 300 Penn Av., Pittsburgh, Pa.

OSGOOD, Charles Grosvenor, educator; b. Wellsboro, Pa., May 4, 1871; s. Charles Grosvenor and Mary Josephine (Todd) O.; B.A., Yale, 1894, Ph.D., 1899; m. Isabella Sheldon Owen, Jan. 29, 1910. Asst. prof. English, U. of Colo., 1899; instr. English, Yale, 1899-1905; preceptor in English, 1905-13, prof., 1913-37, chmn. of department of English, 1918-26, professor emeritus and lecturer since 1937, Princeton Univ. Mem. Modern Lang. Assn. America. Presbyn. Author: The Classical Mythology of Milton's English Poems, 1900; Boccaccio on Poetry, 1930; Vergil and the English Mind, 1930; An Unfading Country, 1930; The Voice of England, 1935. Editor: The Pearl (Middle English poem), 1906; Selections from the Works of Samuel Johnson, 1909; Concordance to the Poems of Edmund Spenser, 1915; Boswell's Johnson, 1917; Variorem edition of the Works of Edmund Spenser, Vol. 1, 1932, Vol. 2, 1933, Vol. 3, 1934, Vol. 4, 1935, Vol. 5, 1936, Vol. 6, 1938. Translator: The Pearl (in prose), 1907. Contbr. of articles on Spenser, Milton and other subjects to philol. jours. Address: Princeton, N.J.

OSGOOD, Harlow S. chemist; b. Bradford, Pa., Apr. 16, 1902; s. Harry Warner and Mildred (McBride) O.; B.S., Westminster Coll., New Wilmington, Pa., 1927; M.S., Pa. State Coll., 1929; Ph.D., Cornell U., 1934; m. Dorothy Bradshaw Wilson, June 14, 1928; children—James Bradshaw, Charles Freeman. Began as asst. in chemistry, Expt. Sta., College Station, Tex., 1928-29; instr. chemistry, Westminster Coll., New Wilmington, Pa., 1929-31, asst. prof., 1931-38, asso. prof. chemistry since 1938. Mem. Am. Chem. Soc., Sigma Xi. United Presbyterian. Home: 540 W. Neshannock Av., New Wilmington, Pa.

OSOL, Arthur, prof. of chemistry; b. Riga, Latvia, Dec. 1, 1905; s. Peter and Caroline (Irbit) O.; brought to U.S., 1906, naturalized, 1915; grad. Northeast High Sch., Phila., 1923; Ph.G., Phila. Coll. of Pharmacy and Science, 1925, B.S. in chemistry, 1928; M.S. in chemistry, U. of Pa., 1931, Ph.D., 1933; m. Amelia Virginia Lebo, Dec. 28, 1928. With Phila. Coll. of Pharmacy and Science since 1928, as asst. in chemistry, 1928-30, instr., 1930-33, asst. prof., 1933-34, asso. prof., 1934-37, prof. since 1937, dir. of chem. labs. since 1937, asst. dean of science since 1935; scientific dir. and mem. bd. dirs. of Raymer Pharmacal Co., Phila., since 1931; prescription editor Am. Druggist Mag., New York, since 1933. Pres., Phila. Section, Am. Pharm. Assn., 1939. Chmn. com. on physical chemistry, Nat. Conf. on Pharm. Research since 1934; auxiliary mem. revision com. U.S. Pharmacopoeia and Nat. Formulary; collaborating research worker for League of Nations health com. investigating methods of analysis of opium and coca. Fellow Am. Inst. Chemists; mem. A.A.A.S.; Pa. Pharm. Assn. (pres. Phila. Sect., 1939), Am. Chem. Soc., Am. Electrochem. Soc., Am. Pharm. Assn., Franklin Inst., Sigma Xi. Republican. Baptist. Asso. editor U.S. Dispensatory, 8th edit.; asso. editor Remington's Practice of Pharm., 22d edit.; contbr. of over 100 articles to scientific jours. Home: Garden Court. Office: 43d St. and Kingsessing Av., Philadelphia, Pa.

OSTERMAYER, Robert William, pres. Pa. Industrial Chem. Corpn.; b. Camden, N.J., Nov. 26, 1895; s. Lawrence John and Anna Marie (Boehringer) O.; B.S., Pa. State Coll., 1917; m. Marguerite Morris Paschall, Sept. 1, 1920; children—Robert W., Lawrence J., Arta. Chemist DuPont Co., 1917-22; pres. and dir. Pa. Industrial Chem. Corpn. since 1922, Clairton Thrift Corpn. since 1932. Mayor, Clairton, Pa., 1934-38. Republican. Presbyterian. Home: 525 Mitchell Av. Office: 120 State St., Clairton, Pa.

OSTHAUS, Carl Edward, banker; b. Overton, Pa., Nov. 8, 1866; s. Francis and Jenny (Francke) O.; ed. pub. and commercial schs.; m. Mary A. Molyneaux, Nov. 28, 1899. Engaged in retail mercantile business, Overton, Pa., since 1890; became v.p. and dir. First Nat. Bank of New Albany upon organization, 1908, pres. since 1931; operator of home farm since 1911. Democrat. Mem. Reformed Ch. Home: Overton, Pa.

OSTHEIMER, Maurice, physician, retired; b. Phila., Pa., Apr. 3, 1873; s. Alfred J. and Ellen (Hackes) O.; A.B., Harvard, 1894; M.D., U. of Pa. Med. Sch., 1897; m. Martha Gibson McIlvain, Apr. 18, 1906; 1 son, Alfred J. III. After internships became asst. instr. pediatrics, U. of Pa. Med. Sch., 1900, asst. prof., 1922-25, resigned and retired, 1925; asst. med. inspr. Phila. Dept. Health and advanced to head diagnostician, resigned, 1920; chief children's ward, University Hosp. and also in charge out-patient clinic, diseases of children, 1900-25; at Children's and Municipal hosps. for some yrs. Held commn. in U.S.A. during World War but Health Dept. declined to release and had him continue as head diagnostician. Former mem. leading med. assns. and socs. Republican. Episcopalian. Clubs: Union League (Philadelphia); Harvard (New York). Home: Grinmet, Whitford, Pa.

OSTROLENK, Bernhard, educator, economist; b. Warsaw, Poland, May 14, 1887; s. Abraham A. and Rachel (Cherniakow) O.; B.Sc., Mass. Agr. Coll., 1911; A.B., Boston U., 1911; studied U. of Minn., summers 1912-15; A.M., U. of Pa., 1919, Ph.D., 1922; hon. academic award, Mass. State Coll., 1936; m. Esther Weinstein, Oct. 10, 1918. Dir. agr., Canby (Minn.) State High Sch., 1913-16, and organizer of several community and coöperative assns.; dir. Nat. Farm Sch., at Farm Sch., Pa., 1916-27; lecturer on agrl. finance, U. of Pa., 1923-26; mem. editorial board The Annalist, 1929-31; dir. Madison House, 1930-31; prof. economics, Coll. City New York, since 1930; economist The Business Week, 1933-34; dir. bibliographical project on coöperation for Works Progress Adminstrn., 1937-38. Mem. Am. Econ. Assn., Am. Country Life Assn., Am. Farm Economics Assn., Inst. of Coöperation. Club: Doylestown Country. Author: Social Aspects of the Food

OSWALD

Surplus; Harvey Baum—A Study of the Agricultural Revolution (with E. S. Mead); Economics of Branch Banking; The Surplus Farmer; How Banks Buy Bonds (with A. M. Massie); Voluntary Allotment (with E. S. Mead); Electricity —for Use or for Profit. Contbr. to Current History, Annalist, Atlantic Monthly, Annals of Acad. Polit. and Social Science, New York Times, etc. Home: Solebury, Pa. Office: 17 Lexington Av., New York, N.Y.

OSWALD, Charles Samuel; b. Lynnport, Pa., Feb. 9, 1871; s. Lewis H. and Mary A. (Faust) O.; ed. pub. schs., Lynnport, Pa., 1877-89; m. Messena K. Smith, Nov. 9, 1890; children —Ida May (Mrs. Frank A. Jones), George Francis, Howard James, Florence Edna (widow of Paul H. Smith, dec., and 2d wife of Ezra B. Treler), Elwood Roosevelt (dec.). Worked on father's farm, 1887-96, and gathered farm produce by huckster team, 1887-1915; bought two farms of 125 acres, including gen. mdse. store and hotel, and propr. same, 1897-1924; served as postmaster, Lynnport, Pa., continuously since 1897; third vice-pres. New Tripoli Nat. Bank and dir. same since 1917; treas. and dir. Berks & Lehigh Telephone & Telegraph Co. since 1910; treas. Jacobs Union Cemetery Assn.; an organizer and dir. Berks & Lehigh Electric Co., 1922-27 until sold. Republican. Mem. Reformed Ch. I.O.O.F. Home: Lynnport, Pa.

OSWALD, Edward, Jr.; mem. law firm Oswald & Oswald. Address: Hagerstown, Md.

OTEY, Ernest Glenwood, banking; b. Pulaski, Va., Feb. 5, 1895; s. Leonard Clyde and Flora Alice (Bishop) O.; grad. high sch. and specialized in accounting; m. Mary T. Sizer, Sept. 28, 1920; 1 dau., Mary Martha. Employed as cashier Peoples Milling Co., Pulaski, Va., 1914-16; teller, asst. cashier, then cashier, Pulaski Nat. Bank, 1917-25; cashier and dir. Bluefield (W.Va.) Nat. Bank, 1926-28; asst. nat. bank examiner at Washington, D.C., 1928-29; cashier Merchants Nat. Bank & Trust Co., Meadville, Pa., 1929-30; exec. v.p. and dir. McDowell County Nat. Bank, Welch, W.Va., 1930-33; exec. v.p First Nat. Bank of Bluefield, W.Va., 1933-35, pres. and dir. since 1935; v.p. and dir. Emory River Lumber Co., Lancing, Tenn.; dir. Bradley Boul. Development Corpn., Washington, D.C. Served with U.S.A. on Mexican border, 1916. Dir. and mem. exec. com. W.Va. Chamber of Commerce; past pres. W.Va. Bankers Assn. Democrat. Methodist. Mason (K.T., Shriner). Clubs: Rotary (past pres.), Bluefield Country (past pres.). Home: 1234 Whitethorn St. Office: 504 Princeton Av., Bluefield, W.Va.

OTHMER, Donald Frederick, chemical engr.; b. Omaha, Neb., May 11, 1904; s. Frederick George and Fredericka Darling (Snider) O.; student Armour Inst., Chicago, 1921-23; B.S., U. of Neb., 1924; M.S., U. of Mich., 1925, Ph.D., 1927; m. Marcia Mary Imray, Aug. 17, 1932. Development eng. Eastman Kodak Co. and Tenn. Eastman Corpn., 1927-30; cons. chem. engr. since 1931; instr. Poly. Inst., Brooklyn, N.Y., 1932-33, prof. since 1933, head of dept. of chem. engring. since 1937; licensed chem. engr. in N.Y., O., Pa.; cons. engr. to Duffy Mott Corpn., Rochester Mechanics Inst., Am. Chem. Products Corpn., Eastman Kodak Co., Hercules Powder Co., Electric Development Corpn., Tenn. Eastman Corpn., Vulcan Copper & Supply Co., Gray Chem. Co., Cellutate Corpn., Northwood Chem. Co., Steel Bros. (London), Insular Govt. of Puerto Rico, etc. Fellow A.A.A.S.; mem. Am. Inst. Chem. Engrs., Am. Chem. Soc., Soc. Promotion Engring. Edn., Sigma Xi, Tau Beta Pi, Phi Lambda Upsilon, Iota Alpha, Alpha Chi Sigma, Theta Kappa Nu. Club: Chemists (New York). Holder of many patents on methods, processes and engring. equipment in mfg. of rayon, plastics, wood distillation, etc. Contbr. to tech. jours. Home: Coudersport, Pa.; 202 Columbia Heights, Brooklyn, N.Y.

OTT, Frank Henry, photographer; b. Phila., Pa., June 28, 1866; s. Aaron and Bertha (Tryon) O.; ed. high sch., Towanda, Pa., Susquehanna Collegiate Inst., Towanda, Pa.; m. Harriet M. Bull, Sept. 20, 1893. Engaged in bus. of photography since 1885; propr. Ott Studio, portraiture and commercial photography, Towanda, Pa., since 1893. Served Towanda High Sch. as dir., vice-pres. and pres. bd. Republican. Presbyn. (supt. S.S. 25 yrs., elder since 1904). Mason. I.O.O.F. Club: Masonic (Towanda). Home: 506 Third St., Towanda, Pa. Office: Citizens Bank Bldg., Towanda, Pa.

OTT, Mary Castle, coll. prof.; b. Frederick, Md., Dec. 20, 1876; d. George Michael and Jennie (Hiteschew) O.; student Boston Univ., Boston, Mass., 1909-10, U. of Calif., summer 1915; A.B., Hood Coll., Frederick, Md., 1920; student U. of Chicago, 1920, 1922; A.M., Johns Hopkins U., 1925; student Harvard U., summers, 1913, 1919. Engaged in teaching, pub. schs., 1893-1903; teacher, boys high sch. Frederick, Md., 1911-24; instr. in history State Teachers Coll., Towson, Md., 1924-25; instr. of history, Hood Coll., Frederick, Md., 1919-20, asso. prof., 1925-30, prof. of history since 1930. Mem. Frederick Playground Commn., 1929-39. Mem. Dem. County Central Com. Awarded medal from Red Cross for World War work; citation from adjt. gen. of Md. for vol. war work, 1917-18. Mem. Am. Hist. Assn., Nat. Council Social Studies, Hist. Assn. Middle States, Am. Assn. Univ. Profs., Am. Assn. Univ. Women, Alumni Assn. U. of Calif., Pi Gamma Mu., Md. State Fed. Women's Clubs, U.D.C., Frederick Co. Hist. Soc., Alumnae Assn. Hood Coll. Democrat. Lutheran. Clubs: Civic, Art (Frederick). Home: 19 Rosemont Av., Frederick, Md.

OTTO, Henry H., mining engr.; b. Phila., Pa., Sept. 25, 1886; s. William F. and Catherine (Brust) O.; student Harry Hillman Acad., Wilkes-Barre, and Lehigh U.; m. Sarah Fatzinger, Oct. 30, 1916; children—William H., Henry H. Successively insp. of equipment, div. engr. and chief mining engr. Lehigh Valley Coal Co. and Coxe Bros. & Co., Inc., 1912-20; chief mining engr. Lehigh Coal and Navigation Co., Alliance Coal Mining Co. and Cranberry Creek Coal Co., 1920-25; mining engr. Hudson Coal Co., Scranton, since 1925. Mem. Am. Inst. Mining and Metall. Engrs. (chmn. anthracite sect.; exec. com. coal div.), Sigma Xi. Mason (Shriner). Clubs: Westmoreland (Wilkes-Barre); Irem Temple Country. Wrote articles on anthracite coal mining for Am. Inst. Mining and Metall. Engrs., and (with J. F. K. Brown) underground water in anthracite fields for Am. Mining Congress. Home: 1805 Vine St. Office: 424 Wyoming Av., Scranton, Pa.

OTTO, Louisa Ruisz (Mrs. Emil E. Otto), contralto, teaching; b. Allentown, Pa., Feb. 24, 1904; d. John and Theresa (Scherman) Ruisz; ed. pub. schs. and high sch., Allentown, Pa.; music with Mrs. Mae D. Miller, Frank LaForge, from N.Y. City, Percy Rector Stevens, N.Y. City, Errol K. Peters, Allentown; m. Emil E. Otto, pres. Municipal Opera Co., Allentown, Pa., Dec. 25, 1926; children—Emil Henry (dec.), Louisa Arlene. Engaged in solo parts and concert work in leading ch., schs., and clubs in E. Pa. at an early age; concerts and solo appearances in R.I., Pa., N.J., and Chicago; contralto in opera, mus. comedy and oratorio; repertoire includes Elijah, Golden Legend, Cavalleria Rusticana, Mikado, Wildflower, Naughty Marietta, Sweethearts, Merry Widow, Blossom Time, May Time, Pinafore; radio artiste in over 600 performances; teacher of voice at Pa. Conservatory of Music, Allentown, Pa., since 1932; contralto soloist Christ Luth. Ch. Mem. Allentown Mus. Club, Eastern Assn. Vocal Teachers, Allentown Municipal Opera Co. Lutheran. Home: 122 N. 14th St., Allentown, Pa. Office: 709 Hamilton St., Allentown, Pa.

OURBACKER, George Julian, investment securities; b. Louisville, Ky., Sept. 5, 1896; s. George Andrew and Pearl (Tucker) O.; ed. Louisville (Ky.) Male High Sch., 1912-16; B.S. in Econs., U. of Pa., 1920; student Oxford U., Eng., 1919; m. Eleanor Cummings, Nov. 29, 1924; 1 dau., Nancy T. Employed as bond salesman with various houses, 1921-30; mem. firm J. Lewis Henry & Co., Phila., Pa., 1930, until merged with W. C. Langley & Co. and represented them 1930-33; vice-pres. F. J. Young & Co., Inc., investment securities, Phila., Pa., since 1933. Served in U.S.A. with A.E.F., 1918-19, in Eng., 1919. Former treas. now vice-pres. Wynnewood Civic Assn. Mem. Assn. of Security Salesmen, Phi Delta Theta. Republican. Episcopalian. Clubs: Penn Athletic, Bond, Phi Delta Theta Alumni (Philadelphia); Merion Cricket (Haverford). Home: 306 Kent Rd., Wynnewood, Pa. Office: 1616 Walnut St., Philadelphia, Pa.

OVERBERGER, Edwin Wilfred, supervising prin. schs.; b. Patton, Pa., May 6, 1891; s. John B. and Helena (Hoover) O.; diploma West Chester State Teachers Coll., 1917; A.B., U. of Pittsburgh, 1928, M.Ed., same, 1936; ed. Pa. State Coll., U. of Pa., summers; m. Bertha E. Christoff, Aug. 12, 1930; 1 son, John Edward. Engaged in teaching rural schs., 1910-13, teaching elementary pub. schs., 1913-15; teacher and prin. high sch., Gallitzin, Pa., 1917-22; asst. co. supt., Cambria Co., 1922-23; supervising prin. schs., Cresson, Pa. since 1924. Trustee Cresson Pub. Library, 1929-35. Mem. Nat. Edn. Assn., Am. Assn. Sch. Adminstrs., Cambria Co. Supervising Prins. Assn. (pres. 1939), U. of Pittsburgh Glee Club. Democrat. Roman Catholic. Club: Rotary of Cresson (past pres.). Home: 227 Laurel Av., Cresson, Pa.

OVERDEER, Frank N., pres. W. D. Haddock Constrn. Co.; b. Gettysburg, Pa., May 3, 1866; s. Peter and Lucinda M. Overdeer; ed. pub. schs., 1872-82; m. Sarah E. Lysinger, Nov. 2, 1898; 1 dau., Margaret F. Began as contractor, 1901; pres. W. D. Haddock Constrn. Co., Wilmington, Del., since 1929; v.p. Security Trust Co., Wilmington, since 1939; dir. Good Will Industries. Pres. bd. trustees Hanover Presbyn. Ch. since 1929. Republican. Presbyterian. Mason (32°), Odd Fellow (Past Grand Officer). Club: Rotary (Wilmington, Del.; vice-pres. since 1938). Home: 1701 West St. Office: 804 Orange St., Wilmington, Del.

OVERHOLTS, Lee Oras, prof. of botany; b. Camden, O., June 23, 1890; s. Winfield Scott and Martha Wilmore (Kinsey) O.; grad. West Elkton High Sch., 1907; A.B., Miami U., Oxford, O., 1912; Ph.D., Washington U., St. Louis, Mo., 1915; m. Flora Mae Conarroe, July 8, 1915; children—Martha Elizabeth (Mrs. Charles Rick, Jr.), Benjamin Bruce, Ruby, Robert Winfield. Inst. in botany, Pa. State Coll., 1915-17, asst. prof., 1917-20, asso. prof., 1920-25, prof. of botany since 1925. Mem. Mycol. Soc. America (vice-pres. 1937, pres. 1938, councilor 1939), Pa. Acad. of Science, Torrey Botanical Club, Phi Beta Kappa, Sigma Xi, Phi Eta Sigma, Gamma Sigma Delta, Alpha Zeta, Phi Kappa Tau. Republican. Asso. editor Mycologia, 1926-32. Home: 143 Hartswick Av., State College, Pa.

OVREBO, Paul Johannes, prof. physics; b. Summit, S.D., Aug. 3, 1901; s. Rev. Ole Johannes and Mina (Mortenson) O.; A.B., St. Olaf Coll., Northfield, Minn., 1923; Ph.D., U. of Chicago, 1928; m. Luella Venette Jacobson, July 31, 1926; 1 son, Julian Paul. Engaged in teaching and supt. sch., N.D. and Minn., 1920-25; instr. physics, W.Va. Univ., 1928-29, asst. prof., 1929-30; prof. physics, Susquehanna U., Selinsgrove, Pa., since 1930, dir. Summer Sch., 1937, faculty mgr. Susquehanna Motet Choir since 1934, faculty adviser Student Christian Assn. since 1934. Mem. Am. Phys. Soc., Am. Assn. of Univ. Profs., Pa. Physics Teachers Conf., Sigma Xi. Republican. Lutheran. Home: 210 W. Chestnut St., Selinsgrove, Pa.

OWEN, Hubley Raborg, surgeon; b. Pensacola, Fla., May 8, 1883; s. Alfred and Mary (Hubley) O.; ed. Friends Sch., Washington, D.C., Episcopal High Sch., Alexandria, Va.; M.D., U. of Pa. Med. Sch., 1905; M.D., Jefferson Med. Coll., 1915; m. Maude Smith, at Haverhill, Mass., July 28, 1907; children—Dorothy Q. (dec.), Edgar R. After usual internship engaged in practice of medicine and surgery, Phila., since 1907; chief surgeon Med. Div., Dept. Pub. Safety, City of Phila., since 1907; prof. clin. surgery, Woman's Med. Coll. of Pa.; surgeon, Phila. Gen. Hosp. and Woman's Coll. Hosp.; instr. surgery, Jefferson Med. Coll. since 1915. Served as capt. Med. Corps, U.S.A., 1917-19, with A.E.F., Base Hosp., Nantes, France; now lt. col. Med. Res. Corps, U.S.A. Fellow Am. Coll. Surgeons, Phila. Coll. Phys., Phila. Acad. Surgery. Mem. Am. Bd. Surgery, Am. Assn. for Traumatic Surgery, Phila. County Med. Soc., Delta Psi. Episcopalian (vestryman Washington Memorial Chapel, Valley Forge, Pa.). Clubs: Racquet (Philadelphia); Pickering Hunt (Valley Forge); Phila. Aviation Country (Ambler). Home: 319 S. 16th St. Office: Broad and Spruce Sts., Philadelphia, Pa.

OWEN, Ralph Dornfeld, prof. education; b. Watertown, Wis., July 2, 1884; s. Sylvester Albert and Sophia (Dornfeld) O.; grad. high sch., Watertown, 1901; B.A., Northwestern Coll., Watertown, 1905; M.A., U. of Wis., 1909, Ph.D., 1922; M.A., Harvard, 1911; studied Teachers Coll., Columbia, 1922-23; Pd.D., Muhlenberg Coll., Allentown, Pa., 1935; m. Ada Cecile Hillemann, Sept. 27, 1910; children —Ralf Hillemann, Ruth Ada. Asst. prin. high sch., Princeton, Wis., 1905-06; supervising prin. schs., Almond, Wis., 1906-08; prof. English, Carthage (Ill.) Coll., 1911-13; head dept. of English, Milwaukee Univ. Sch. and prof. English methods, Nat. Teachers' Sem., Milwaukee, Wis., 1913-19; supt. schs., Mayville, Wis., 1919-22; head dept. edn., Bryn Mawr, 1923-25; prof. edn., grad. sch., Teachers Coll., Temple U., since 1925. Cooperated with Pa. Econ. Council in making study of cost of public edn. in state, 1936; mem. Philadelphia Survey Commn. to study pub. sch. system, 1937. Chmn. English Language Congress of Sesquicentennial Expn., Phila., 1926; Mem. Bd. of Edn. of United Lutheran Ch. of America, 1926-38; mem. N. E.A. (life), Nat. Soc. for Study of Edn., Order of Founders and Patriots of America, Soc. of Mayflower Descendants, Phi Delta Kappa. Author: Christian Bunsen and Liberal English Theology, 1922; Learning Religion from Famous Americans, 1927; Adolescent Education, 1928; Cost of Public Education, 1933-34, in Pennsylvania, 1938. Contbr. to Yearbook of School Law since 1935. Home: Llandaff Rd., Llanerch, Pa.

OWEN, W. B., editor Simpson's Leader Times. Address: Kittanning, Pa.

OWENS, Charles Allen, stock broker; b. Jersey City, N.J., July 8, 1876; s. Charles D. and Mary (Hadde) O.; student Crowther Sch., Savannah, Ga., 1885-91, Mt. Pleasant Acad., Ossining, N.Y., 1891-94; m. Mattie Payne, Dec. 27, 1902; children—Charles Allen, Marion (Mrs. Thomas B. Davidson), William Brooke. Salesman Tide Water Oil Co., 1894-97, Standard Oil Co., 1897-1910; v.p. Calif. Mineral Water Co., 1910-14; with Laird & Co., Wilmington, Del., 1914-17; organized firm Owens, Anderson & Rumford, Wilmington, 1917, bought seat N.Y. Stock Exchange; consolidated with Laird, Bissell & Meeds, Wilmington, Del., 1924, and since gen. partner; dir. Prudential Investors, Inc. Formerly mem. bd. of Harbor Commrs., Wilmington. Episcopalian. Clubs: Wilmington, Wilmington Whist, Wilmington Country (Wilmington, Del.); Brokers of America (New York). Home: 1301 Gilpen Av. Office: du Pont Bldg., Wilmington, Del.

OWENS, Edith Hunter, pub. assistance; b. Cochranville, Pa., July 12, 1881; d. Dr. George M. Dallas and Anna Deborah (McClellan) Hunter; student Cochranville (Pa.) Pub. Sch. and Fernwood Acad.; m. John Ross Owens, Sept. 17, 1902; children—Charles Ross, Edith Margaret, Caroline Elizabeth. Contralto soloist Faggs Manor Presbyn. Ch. Choir, 1896-1902, Parkesburg (Pa.) Presbyn. Choir, 1904-35, Coatesville (Pa.) Choir, 1916-18; dir. Parkesburg (Pa.) Bd. of Edn. since 1923, treas. since 1925; chmn. Chester Co. (Pa.) Pub. Assistance Bd. since Dec. 1937. Served as inspector of garments for Southeastern Chapter of Am. Red Cross for Parkesburg Branch, 1917-19. Dem. committeewoman, Parkesburg, 14 yrs. Chmn. bd. of trustees Mother's Assistance Fund, 1935-37; mem. bd. dirs. Parkesburg Free Library. Democrat. Presbyterian. Clubs: Women's Democratic of Chester County; Women's Civil and Literary (Parkesburg, Pa.). Address: 439 First Av., Parkesburg, Pa.

OWENS, Frederick William, prof. mathematics; b. Rockwell City, Ia., Nov. 18, 1880; s. James and Nancy Minerva (Terrill) O.; B.S., U. of Kan., 1902, M.S., same, 1902; Ph.D., U. of Chicago, 1907; m. Helen Barten Brewster, June 22, 1904; children—Helen Brewster (dec.), Clara Brewster (Mrs. Thomas Brigham Aitcheson, Jr.). Instr. mathematics, Evanston Acad. of Northwestern U., 1905-07; instr. mathematics, Cornell U., 1907-15, asst. prof., 1915-26; prof. mathematics and head dept. mathematics, Pa. State Coll. since 1926. Mem. A.A.A.S., Am. Math. Soc., Math. Assn. America, Assn. for Symbolic Logic, Am. Assn. Univ. Profs., Seal and Serpent, Pi Mu Epsilon (dir. gen. 1933-36), Sigma Xi, Circolo Matematico di Palermo. Republican. Conglist. Home: 462 E. Foster Av., State College, Pa.

OWENS, (James) Hamilton, editor; b. Baltimore, Md., Aug. 8, 1888; s. Gwinn Fardon and Arabella Pierpoint (Smith) O.; student Baltimore City Coll.; A.B., Johns Hopkins, 1909; m. Olga von Hartz, March 6, 1913; children— James Hamilton, Lydia Gwinn, Gwinn F., II, Olga, Lloyd. Began as reporter Baltimore News, 1909-13; with New York Press, 1913, dramatic critic, 1914-15; with Guaranty Trust Co. of New York, 1920-22, asst. mgr. London office, 1922; became editor Baltimore Evening Sun, 1922; editor The Sun since 1938. Sec. New York Com. on Nat. Defense, 1917; mng. editor Foreign Press Bur., Com. on Pub. Information, 1918. Mem. Delta Phi; hon. mem. Baltimore chapter Am. Inst. Architects. Democrat. Club: 14 W. Hamilton St. Contbr. to Ency. Britannica, 14th edit. Home: Riderwood, Md. Office: The Sun, Baltimore, Md.

OWENS, John Whitefield, newspaper editor; b. Anne Arundel Co., Md., Nov. 2, 1884; s. Cyrus Whitefield and Eliza Providence (Brashears) O.; ed. pub. schs. and night and summer courses Johns Hopkins; m. Virginia Dashiell, Sept. 16, 1918 (died May 30, 1926); children—Elizabeth Dashiell, John Whitefield. Began newspaper work with Baltimore Evening Sun, 1911; political reporter Baltimore Sun, 1913-20, mem. Washington bur. of same, 1920-24, London corr., 1924-26, editorial writer, 1926-27, editor, 1927-38; editor-in-chief The Sun and The Evening Sun since 1938. Home: 103 Goodale Rd., Homeland, Baltimore. Office: The Sun, Baltimore, Md.

OWENS, William Gundy, prof. chemistry; b. Lewisburg, Pa., May 14, 1858; s. John A. and Lucinda (Gundy) O.; ed. Univ. at Lewisburg, now Bucknell U., A.B., 1880, A.M., same, 1883; (hon.) D.Sc., Bucknell U., 1935; m. Jeannette Waffle, Aug. 25, 1885; children— Elsie (wife of Wm. W. Long, M.D.), Albert W., Jeannette (Mrs. Thos. S. Fogarty), Kathrine (Mrs. Herbert L. Hayden). Engaged in teaching continuously since 1880; instr. Bucknell Acad., 1880-85; instr. of chemistry advancing to prof., Bucknell U. since 1885; prof. of chemistry, U. of Shanghai, China, 1935-36. Mem. Am. Chem. Soc., Phi Kappa Psi. Republican. Baptist. Home: Lewisburg, Pa.

OWINGS, Capers B., physician; b. Columbia, S.C., Feb. 21, 1896; s. James and Pauline (McDowell) O.; B.S., Presbyterian Coll. of S.C., 1917; M.D., Jefferson Med. Coll., 1923; m. Maude Rich, Sept. 14, 1922; children— Robert Baxter, Franklin Fell. In practice as physician, Phila., since 1925. Served in U.S. Navy, 1917-18. Fellow Am. Coll. Surgeons; mem. Phila. Laryngol. Soc., A.M.A., Theta Kappa Psi. Presbyterian. Home: 121 W. Tulpehocken St. Office: 100 W. Coulter St., Philadelphia, Pa.

OWLETT, Gilbert Mason, Rep. Nat. committeeman; b. Wellsboro, Pa., June 13, 1892; s. Edward Howland and Ida (Wells) O.; B.S., Princeton, 1914; student U. of Pa. Law Sch., 1915-17; m. Sue Elizabeth Berkey, June 20, 1918; children—Anna Mary, Edward H. Admitted to Pa. bar, 1917, since practiced in Wellsboro, Pa.; mem. firm Crichton & Owlett, 1918-32; state senator since 1932; Rep. nat. committeeman since 1936; sec.-treas. Highland Milk Condensing Co.; vice-pres. Tioga Co. Bell Telephone Co.; dir. Tioga Co. Savings and Trust Co., Hubbell Realty Co. Mem. Am. and Pa. bar assns., Phi Delta Theta. Republican. Presbyterian. Mason, Odd Fellow. Clubs: Arch (Princeton); Ross (Williamsport); Tioga Country (Wellsboro). Home: 12 West Av. Office: Owlett Bldg., Wellsboro, Pa.

OXLEY, John Edgar, lawyer; b. White's Ferry, Md., Nov. 27, 1899; s. Charles W. and Annie (Wambler) O.; student Poolesville pub. sch., 1907-18, Bryant & Stratton Business Coll., 1919-20, Army and Navy Prep. Sch., 1920-21; LL.B., U. of Md. Law Sch., 1921-24; m. Anne Branson, June 10, 1933; children—John Edgar, Virginia Anne. Began as clerk in gen. store, 1918; in gen. practice of law, Baltimore, 1924, Rockville since 1925; owner and operator Oxley Office Bldg.; gen. counsel and dir. First Nat. Bank elected county commr., Nov. 1938; apptd. police commr., Dec. 1938, mem. Montgomery Co. Welfare Bd., Jan. 1939; now mem. Bd. Zoning Appeals, Town of Rockville. Mem. Md. State Bar Assn., Montgomery Co. Bar Assn., Delta Theta Phi. Democrat. Episcopalian. Mason (Past Master Poolesville Lodge No. 214). Clubs: Lions (pres.), Upper Montgomery County. Past pres. Poolesville Community League. Address: Rockville, Md.

OYLER, Richard Skyles, clergyman; b. Manns Choice, Pa., June 15, 1873; s. William and Elizabeth (Miller) O.; B.S., Dickinson Sem., 1898; ed. Harvard U., 1904, 1906, Emerson Coll. of Oratory, Boston, 1904, 1906; Ph.D., Grove City Pa. Spl. Sch. Philosophy, 1914; m. Mary Ardella Phoenix, Nov. 12, 1898; children —Vincent McKinley, Helen Elvira (Mrs. Joseph Locatelli), Evelyn Gertrude (Mrs. T. Stuart Williams), Mary Elizabeth (Mrs. Russel Wharton Lambert), Richard Skyles, John Wesley H., J. William. Ordained to ministry M.E. Ch., 1898; mem. Central Pa. Conf., asst. sec., 1919-27, press rep., 1917-18; dist. sec. of Stewardship, 1922-28, of Evangelism, 1922-23; dist. editor Washington Christian Advocate, 1918-21, 1925-27; del. State Conv. Pa. Council Chs., 1929-38; dean Community Standard Training Sch., Mt. Union, Pa., 1935-36; pres. World Service Council, Central Pa. Conf. and sec. bd. Philanthropies since 1936. Mem. Kappa Delta Pi. Republican. Methodist. Delivered the annual Memorial Day oration, Nat. Cemetery, Gettysburg, Pa., May 1926. Home: 2212 6th Av., Altoona, Pa.

P

PACKARD, Francis Randolph, M.D.; b. Phila., Pa., Mar. 23, 1870; s. John Hooker and Elisabeth (Wood) P.; grad. biol. dept. U. of Pa., 1889; M.D., U. of Pa., 1892; m. 1st, Christine B. Curwen (died 1901); m. 2d, Margaret Horstman, Feb. 10, 1906; children—Margaret, Ann, Elisabeth, Frances Randolph. Resident phys., Pa. Hosp., 1894-95; ex-prof. otology, Post-Grad. Sch., U. of Pa.; chief laryngologist, otologist, Pa. Hosp.; pres. Coll. of Phys. of Phila., 1931-33. Served as 1st lt. asst. surgeon, 2d Pa. Vol. Inf., Spanish-Am. War; commd. 1st lt. M.C. U.S.A., May 16, 1917; capt., Sept. 1, 1917; maj., Oct. 1, 1918; sailed for France, May 18, 1917; with Base Hosp. 10, chief centre consultant in oto-laryngology, Dist. of Paris, Oct. 1918-Jan. 1919. Pres. Am. Laryngol. Assn., 1931, Am. Otol. Soc., 1935; pres. Coll. of Physicians of Phila. 1931-34; pres. Library Co. of Phila. since 1936; mem. Am. Philos. Soc., Delta Psi. Republican. Episcopalian. Clubs: Philadelphia, University Barge, Rose Tree Hunt. Author: History of Medicine in the United States, 1901, 2d edit., 1919; Diseases of the Ear, Nose and Throat, 1909; The School of Salerno, 1920; The Life and Times of Ambroise Paré, 1921; Some Account of the Pennsylvania Hospital. Editor: The Gold-Headed Cane, 1915. Editor Annals of Medical History. Home: 304 S. 19th St., Phila., Pa.

PACKARD, John Hooker, 3d, life ins. co. exec.; b. Phila., Pa., May 4, 1884; s. Charles Stewart Wood and Eliza Gilpin (McLean) P.; student Acad. of P.E.Ch., 1898-1900, U. of Pa., 1901-03; m. Mildred Benson, Oct. 8, 1907; 1 dau., Mildred (Mrs. Charles Randolph Snowden). Employed as clk. Stokes and Packard, 1903-07; with banking house Cramp, Mitchell and Slover, 1907-09; mem. firm Benson and Packard, securities, 1909-17; treas. and dir. John Farnum Co., cotton textile mfrs., 1919-24; pres. Finance Corpn. of America, motor financing, 1924-30; vice-pres. and dir. The Pennsylvania Co. for Ins. on Lives and Granting Annuities since 1930; dir. Little Schuylkill R.R., Navigation and Coal Co. Served as maj. A.S., U.S.A. in World War. Trustee Chestnut Hill Hosp. Mem. S.R., Mil. Order World War, Delta Psi. Republican. Episcopalian. Mason. Clubs: Philadelphia, Racquet, State in Schuylkill, Sunnybrook Golf (Philadelphia); The Brook, St. Anthony (New York); Boca Raton (Florida). Home: Chestnut Hill. Office: 517 Chestnut St., Philadelphia, Pa.

PACKARD, Kent, ins. exec.; b. Reading, Mass., Dec. 19, 1886; s. Rev. George Thomas and Anna Jane (Sprague) P.; student Episcopal Acad., 1900-04, Harvard Coll., 1904-05; m. Edna Sproat Darrach, June 12, 1915; children—Kent, Henry Darrach. Engaged in newspaper work, Boston and Philadelphia, 1908-11; in advertising work, 1911-14; in gen. ins. business since 1914, now with Stokes, Packard & Smith, Inc. Genealogist Pa. Soc. Founders and Patriots of America; mem. Soc. Indian Wars, Soc. War of 1812, Psi Upsilon; dir. Walnut Street Assn., Philadelphia. Republican. Episcopalian. Mason. Club: Harvard Tredyffrin Country. Writer of articles and verses. Home: Leopard Road, Paoli, Pa. Office: 1608 Walnut St., Philadelphia, Pa.

PACSU, Eugene, univ. prof.; b. Budapest, Hungary, July 13, 1891; s. George and Anna (Lahm) P.; higher certificate, Gymnasium of the Teaching Order of the Piarists, Budapest, Hungary, 1910; Ph.D., Royal Hungarian U., Budapest, 1914; m. Martha Gergely of Budapest, Hungary, June 5, 1926; children—Anne Gregory, Margaret Gregory. Came to U.S., 1928, naturalized, 1936. Univ. asst., Royal Hungarian U., Budapest, 1919-20, adj. prof., 1920-30, private docent (life) since 1926; Rockefeller research fellow, Bur. of Standards and Nat. Inst. of Health, Washington, D.C., 1928-29; asst. prof. organic chemistry, Princeton U., 1930-34, asso. prof. since 1934. Served as 1st lt., Arty., Austro-Hungarian Army, 1914-18. Received 3 war decorations on Russian front, 1916-17. Mem. Am. and German chem. socs., Sigma Xi. Republican. Catholic. Address: Wihant Rd., Princeton, N.J.

PADDEN, John Francis, contractor plumbing, heating; b. Scranton, Pa., Sept. 28, 1894; s. John F. and Catherine (Haggerty) P.; ed. Holy Rosary Sch. (parochial), 1900-1911; m. Sylvia Moran, Nov. 21, 1916; children—John F., Jr., Leo F. Donald Joseph. Began as plumber's apprentice, 1911; became supt. Gaylord & Butler Co., Scranton, Pa.; entered bus. on own acct. as contractor plumbing, heating and ventilation, and propr. Scranton Heating Co. since 1920; served as sch. dir. City of Scranton since 1933, pres. Scranton Sch. Bd. since 1937; regional dir. Pa. State Sch. Dirs. Assn. since 1937. Served as treas. and mem. finance com. Democratic Party, Lackawanna Co. Mem. Recreation Commn. City of Scranton; dir. Cath. Mens and Boys Club; dir. Welfare Dept. Scranton Community Chest; municipal examiner for Dept. Internal Affairs, State of Pa. Mem. exec. com. Irish-Am. Soc., Lackawanna Co. Democrat. Roman Catholic. Club: Purple (Scranton). Home: 433 Cayuga St. Office: 425 W. Washington Av., Scranton, Pa.

PADDOCK, Frank, univ. prof.; b. Prairie Creek, Ind., Nov. 12, 1890; s. Scot and Ida (Hicks) P.; A.B., Ind. State Teachers Coll., Terre Haute, Ind., 1916; Ph.D., U. of Wis., Madison, Wis., 1925; m. Louise Jensen, June 23, 1925; 1 dau., Marie Louise. Engaged in teaching, pub. schs. and high sch., Ind.; instr. St. John's Mil. Acad., Delafield, Wis., 1920-22; instr. O. State U., Columbus, O., 1925-28; asst. prof. polit. science, Temple U., Phila., 1928-32, asso. prof. polit. science, 1932-39. Mem. Am. Polit. Sci. Assn. Home: 6124 N. 7th St., Philadelphia, Pa.

PADGETT, Frederick, prin. high sch.; b. Thornville, O., Feb. 10, 1903; s. Benjamin F. and Jessie M. (Steiner) P.; A.B., Heidelberg Coll., Tiffin, O., 1925; A.M. in Edn., Bucknell U., 1938; m. Margaret O. Ossman, June 1929; children—Virginia Caroline, Constance Cathleen, Margaret Elizabeth, Sandra. Teacher, Shore High Sch., Cleveland, O., 1925-26; supt. pub. schs., Pataskala, O., 1926-30; prin. jr. high sch., Sunbury, Pa., 1930-35, prin. sr. high sch., Sunbury, Pa., since 1936. Served as 2d lt. Pa. N.G., 1937-38. Kappa Phi Kappa. Republican. Mem. Reformed Ch. Mason. Home: 457 Chestnut St., Sunbury, Pa.

PAGE, Basil L.; chief of staff St. Joseph's Hosp. Address: Central Exchange Bldg., Buckhannon, W.Va.

PAGE, Charles Greenleaf, lawyer; b. Fortress Monroe, Va., Mar. 30, 1902; s. Col. Henry and Edith Longfellow Greenleaf P.; student Boys High Sch., Atlanta, Ga., 1914-17, Sewanee Mil. Acad., 1917-18; A.B., Princeton U., 1922; LL.B., Harvard Law Sch., 1925; m. Jeannette Markell, Dec. 18, 1937. Admitted to Md. bar, 1925; associated with law firm Bowie & Clark, 1925-28; asst. supt. law dept. U.S. Fidelity & Guaranty Co., 1928-31; asst. U.S. atty. for Md., 1931-34; in private practice of law at Baltimore since 1934; part time lecturer U. of Md. Law Sch., 1930-36. Mem. Am. Bar Assn., Md. State Bar Assn., Baltimore City Bar Assn. Republican. Episcopalian. Clubs: Maryland, Baltimore Country (Baltimore). Home: Allston Apts., 32d and Charles Sts. Office: Central Savings Bank Bldg., Baltimore, Md.

PAGE, Robert Powel, Jr., pres. The Autocar Co.; b. Boyce, Va., Jan. 30, 1879; s. Robert Powel and Agnes (Burwell) P.; m. Helen Hamilton, June 1908; children—Robert Powel III, Hamilton, Peter Mayo. Successively salesman, Boston mgr., New Eng. dist. mgr., gen. sales mgr., The Autocar Co., Ardmore, Pa., now pres. Home: 250 Golf View Rd. Office: The Autocar Co., Ardmore, Pa.

PAGE, William C., banker; b. Frederick Co., Md.; s. John White and Ellen (West) P.; student pub. and private schs. and Frederick City Coll.; m. Rosalie B. Williams. Pres. Calvert Bank since organization, 1900. Home: Ruxton, Baltimore County, Md. Office: Howard and Saratoga Sts., Baltimore, Md.

PAGE, William Tyler, retired clk. House of Rep.; b. Frederick, Md., Oct. 19, 1868; s. Walker Yates and Nannie (Tyler) P.; lineal descendant of Carter Braxton, signer of Declaration of Independence; collateral desc. of Pres. John Tyler; ed. acad. and pub. schs.; m. Mary Anna Weigandt, July 25, 1895 (now dec.); children—Nannie Tyler (wife of H. W. Pierce, U.S.N.), John Caspar, Eleanor L'Hommedieu (Mrs. Gordon F. Fox), Mary Addison (wife of J. H. Cronin, U.S.N.), Catherine L'Hommedieu (dec.), William Tyler. Apptd. page in clk.'s office, U.S. Ho. of Rep., 1881, and in continuous service of the House, elected clk., May 19, 1919, and reëlected in each succeeding Congress until 1931. Clk. to the minority, U.S. Ho. of Rep., since 1931. Exec. sec. U.S. Commn. for Celebration of 200th Anniversary of Birth of George Washington. Rep. nominee for Congress, 2d Md. Dist., 1902. Pres. Rep. State Voters' Assn. Episcopalian. Author: Page's Congressional Handbook, 1913. Wrote "The American's Creed," 1917. Home: Friendship Hts., Chevy Chase, Md.*

PAGON, W(illiam) Watters, cons. engr.; b. Baltimore, Md., June 3, 1885; s. William Henry and Caroline Hooper (Pattison) P.; A.B., Johns Hopkins U., 1905; B.S., Mass. Inst. Tech., Cambridge, 1907; M.C.E., Harvard U., 1910; m. Katharine Wright Dunn, June 22, 1916; children—Garrett Dunn, Hugh Breckenridge, Karen Bligh. Employed as draftsman Baltimore Bridge Co., 1907-09; in employ J. E. Greiner, also mem. firm J. E. Greiner & Co., Baltimore, 1910-16; cons. engr. in bus. on own acct. at Baltimore, Md., since 1917; dir. Industrial Corpn., Baltimore, since 1922. Served as capt. Constrn. Div., U.S.A., 1918-19. Has held many pub. and semi-pub. positions. Mem. Charter Revision Commn., Baltimore, 1930; chmn. City Plan Com., 1937-39. Mem. Am. Soc. Civil Engrs., Inst. of the Aero Sci., Engrs. Club of Baltimore. Democrat. Episcopalian. Author: Pressure Airships, 1926. Contbr. to sci. jours. Home: 114 St. Johns Rd. Office: Lexington Bldg., Baltimore, Md.

PAINE, Harold William, chem. dir; b. Warwick, R.I., July 27, 1886; s. Andrew Jackson and Ruth Emma (Wilcox) P.; student English High Sch., Providence, R.I., 1898-1903; Ph.B., Brown U., Providence, R.I., 1907; C.E., Mass. Inst. Tech., 1909; m. Beatrice Anna Sturdy, Nov. 14, 1910; children—Cecile Beatrice (Mrs. John D. Simmons), Rolf Sturdy, Harold William. Instr. in organic chemistry lab., 1909-10; job mgr., electro-plating shop, Providence, R.I., 1910-15; chemist in control lab., Nonnabo Nitrating Corpn., Providence, R.I., 1915, night supt., 1915; research chemist, Fiberloid Corpn., Springfield, Mass., 1915-17, night supt., 1917-18, asst. supt., 1918-19; research chemist, Viscoloid Co., Leominster, Mass., 1919-26, chem. supt. in charge of research and chem. control, 1926-29; asst. chem. dir. Du Pont Viscoloid Co., Arlington, N.J., 1929-37, chem. dir. plastics dept. since 1937. Mem. A.A.A.S., Am. Chem. Soc., Am. Inst. Chem. Engrs., Am. Soc. for Testing Materials, Inst. of Plastics Industry, Soc. of Rheology, Kolloid Gesellschaft, Societe Suisse de Chemie, Societe Chim. Industrielle, Verein deutscher Chemiker, Chi Phi. Congregationalist. Mason (Master; K.T.; Shriner). Club: Upper Montclair (N.J.) Country. Home: 14 Elston Rd., Upper Montclair, N.J. Office: 626 Schuyler Av., Arlington, N.J.

PAINTER, Clark Howard, lawyer; b. Butler, Pa., Aug. 15, 1905; s. Howard I. and Ella (Robb) P.; A.B., U. of Pittsburgh, 1929; LL.B., Dickinson Coll. Law Sch., 1933; m. Blanche Neyman, Aug. 16, 1926; 1 son, James Allan. Admitted to Pa. bar, 1934, and since engaged in gen. practice of law at Butler; mem. firm Painter and Painter. Serving as capt. 523 C.A., U.S.A. Res. Mem. Butler Co. Bar Assn. Republican. Protestant. Elk. Home: Butler, Pa.

PAINTER, Frank H., co. supt. schs.; b. Muncy, Pa., July 2, 1885; s. George L. and Sally C. (Rogers) P.; ed. Lycoming Co. Normal Sch., 1903-05; Ph.B., Bucknell U., 1910, A.M., same, 1916; m. Mary F. Sebring, Dec. 18, 1915; children—Sarah Catherine, Helen Wilson (dec.), Mary Anna, Robert Sebring. Employed as teacher rural schs., 1903-06; prin. high sch., Jersey Shore, Pa., 1910-23, supervising prin., 1923-27, supt. schs., Jersey Shore, Pa., 1927-35; asst. county supt., 1935-36, county supt. schs. since 1936; dir. Union Nat. Bank of Jersey Shore. Dir. Boy Scouts, Tuberculosis Soc., Childrens Aid Soc. Mem. Nat. Edn. Assn., Pa. State Edn. Assn., Grange, Sigma Alpha Epsilon. Republican. Episcopalian (vestryman, sr. warden). Mason (32°). Club: Commercial (Jersey Shore). Home: Jersey Shore, Pa. Office: Court House, Williamsport, Pa.

PAINTER, George Edward, v.p. Union Storage Co.; b. Pittsburgh, Pa., Aug. 30, 1862; s. Byron Hays and Mary S. (Lothrop) P.; student Columbia U. Sch. of Mines, class of 1883; m. Agnes Clarke, Apr. 22, 1884; children—Mildred, Clarke, Alden L.; m. 2d, Maude Una McKain, Jan. 29, 1930. With J. Painter & Sons, 1883-99, sec., 1888-99; v.p. Union Storage Co. since 1926; dir. Western Allegheny R.R. Co., First Nat. Bank, Peoples Pittsburgh Trust Co. Republican. Presbyterian. Clubs: Duquesne, Pittsburgh, Allegheny Country, St. Clair (Pittsburgh). Home: 60 Longue Vue Drive, Mt. Lebanon, Pa. Office: First National Bank, Wood St., Pittsburgh, Pa.

PAINTER, Howard I., lawyer; b. Clay Twp., Butler Co., Pa.; s. Simon P. and Loas (Sutton) P.; student West Sunbury Acad.; m. Ella R. Robb; children—Dale B., Donald R., Clark H. Engaged as sch. teacher for 18 yrs.; supt. schs. of Butler Co., two terms; admitted to Pa. bar and since engaged in gen. practice of law at Butler; mem. firm (with son) Painter and Painter; served as dist. atty., Butler Co., one term; formerly mem. Pa. Senate; now dir. Saxonburg Telephone Co. Republican. Presbyn. I.O.O.F.

Woodmen of World. Grange. Home: 221 W. Fulton St. Office: Butler Co. Nat. Bank Bldg., Butler, Pa.

PAINTER, Sidney, univ. prof.; b. New York, N.Y., Sept. 23, 1902; s. Henry McMahon and Carrie (Stevens) P.; A.B., Yale U., 1925, Ph.D., 1930; m. Nivea Elizabeth Forbes, Aug. 17, 1927; children—Mary Abigail, Ann Forbes, Julie Elizabeth. Instr. history, Yale U., 1927-30, asst. prof. history, 1930-31; asso. in history, Johns Hopkins U., 1931-36, asso. prof. history since 1936. Mem. Am. Hist. Assn., Mediaeval Acad. of America, Am. Assn. Univ. Profs. Republican. Clubs: 16 West Hamilton Street, Johns Hopkins (Baltimore). Author: William Marshal, knighterrant, baron, and regent of England, 1933; The Scourge of the Clergy, Peter of Dreux, duke of Brittany, 1937. Contbr. to hist. mags. Home: 4827 Keswick Rd., Baltimore, Md.

PAIST, Theresa Wilbur (Mrs. Frederic M. Paist); b. Boone, Ia., June 6, 1880; d. Dwight Locke and Edna (Lyman) Wilbur; A.B., Stanford U.; Litt.D., Beaver Coll.; m. Frederic M. Paist, Jan. 31, 1912; children—Gertrude Wilbur, Frances Helen, Theresa Wilbur, Frederic Mack (dec.), Horace Curtis. Teacher of mathematics, Pasadena High Sch., 1903-04; traveling sec. State Com. Y.W.C.A. of Calif. and Nev., 1904-06; traveling sec. Nat. Bd. Y.W.C.A., most of time at state univs., 1907-11; pres. Y.W.C.A. of U.S., 1921-26; mem. Nat. Bd. Y.W.C.A. (pres., 1932-38). Trustee Tennent Coll. Republican. Presbyn. Home: Wayne, Pa.

PALMER, Albert Robert, lawyer; b. East Orange, N.J., Apr. 15, 1880; s. Albert William and Susan Logan (Hansell) P.; A.B., Yale, 1901; grad. student N.Y. Law Sch., 1901-03; m. Florence M. Decker, Oct. 5, 1904 (now deceased); children—Robert Caton, Jean; m. 2d, Anna M. Vass, September 26, 1936. Admitted to New York bar, 1903, and since partner firm of Palmer & Serles; dir. and gen. counsel United Wall Paper Factories, Inc., vice-pres. Madison Trust Co.; dir. Starrett Corpn., Starrett Investing Corpn., Charles Pfizer & Co., Pacific Coast Borax Co., Washburn Wire Co. Councilman, Madison, N.J., 4 yrs., pres. Borough Council, 2 yrs. Trustee Kent Place Sch., Summit, N.J. Mem. Am. Bar Assn., Assn. Bar City of N.Y.. Republican. Mason, K.T. Clubs: Yale, Bankers, (New York); Graduate (New Haven); Wannamoisett (Providence); Baltusrol Golf (Summit, N.J.). Home: Midwood Rd., Madison, N.J. Office: 46 Cedar St., New York, N.Y.

PALMER, Avery Ray, supervising prin. of schools; b. La Fayette, N.Y., Nov. 30, 1889; s. Jirah D. and Marion (Van Antwerp) P.; grad. La Fayette (N.Y.) High Sch., 1907, State Normal Sch., Cortland, N.Y., 1911; B.S. in edn., Teachers Coll., Columbia, 1928, A.M., 1931; m. Laura Everingham, Sept. 1, 1915; children—William Ray, Jean. Teaching prin., Mumford, N.Y., 1911-13; prin. La Fayette (N.Y.) High Sch., 1912-13; prin. elementary school, Ridgefield Park, N.J., 1913-18, supervising prin. since 1918. Mem. N.E.A., Am. Assn. Sch. Adminstrs., N.J. State Edn. Assn., N.J. Schoolmasters Club, Ridgefield Park Teachers Assn., Phi Delta Kappa. Republican. Methodist. Mason (Royal Arch). Home: Ridgefield Park, N.J.

PALMER, Charles Conger, univ. prof.; b. Canton, O., July 20, 1892; s. Charles Curtis and Julia Ludlow (Conger) P.; student pub. schs., Dayton, O., 1897-1908, U. of Chicago, 1913; D.V.M., Ohio State U., Columbus, O., 1912; M.S., U. of Minn., Minneapolis, Minn., 1916; m. Lucille Hamilton Long, Sept. 4, 1913. Began as practitioner veterinary medicine, Pleasant Hill, O., 1912; instr. veterinary medicine, U. of Minn., Minneapolis, Minn., 1913-16, asst. prof. physiology and hygiene, 1916-17; prof. bacteriology and hygiene, U. of Del., Newark, Del., since 1917, head dept. animal industry, 1922-39, dir. Haskell Fund for Bacteriol. Research since 1938; dir. Mutual Bldg. & Loan Assn. Served as lt., Vet. Corps, U.S. Army, 1918, instr. Med. Officers Training Camp, Camp Greenleaf, Chickamauga Park, Ga., 1918-19. Mem. Am. Vet. Medicine Assn. (sec. sect. on research, 1932-33), Alpha Psi, Sigma Phi Epsilon, Phi Kappa Phi. Address: 85 W. Park Pl., Newark, Del.

PALMER, Charles Edwin, banking; b. Hutton, Md., Aug. 3, 1902; s. Ulysses Grant and Carrie Amelia (Jennings) P.; student Bethany Coll., Bethany, W.Va., 1918-19; A.B., U. of Ark., 1924; m. Ella M. Weaver, Sept. 16, 1929; children—Katherine Joan, Patricia. In employ Allegheny Valley Trust Co., Verona, Pa., 1925-26, Bank of Aspinwall, 1926-27; employed as an examiner by Pa. State Banking Dept., 1927-29; auditor Peoples City Bank, McKeesport, Pa., 1929-36, vice-pres. and dir. since 1936. Mem. Sigma Nu. Republican. Mem. M.E. Ch. (trustee First M.E. Ch., McKeesport). Mason (32°, Shriner). Clubs: Youghiogheny Country (McKeesport); Bankers (Pittsburgh). Home: 1411 Manor Av. Office: 301 Fifth Av., McKeesport, Pa.

PALMER, Charles Skeele, chemist; b. Danville, Ill., Aug. 4, 1858; s. Rev. William Randall and Clara E. (Skeele) P.; A.B., Amherst, 1879, A.M., 1882; Ph.D., Johns Hopkins University, 1886; University of Leipzig, Germany, 1892-93; m. Harriet B. Warner, Sept. 30, 1886 (died Dec. 11, 1932); children—Mrs. Helen W. P. Bissell, Leigh W., Mrs. Winifred W. P. Bennett. Prof. chemistry, U. of Colo., 1887-1902; pres. Colo. Sch. of Mines, 1902-03; chief chemist Washoe Smelter, Anaconda, Mont., 1903-04; asso. editor Engineering and Mining Journal, 1904-06; chem. engr. for large textile mills; fellow, Mellon Inst. of Industrial Research, U. of Pittsburgh, Nov. 1915-17. Consulting chemist United Fuel Gas Co., Charleston, W.Va., 1920. Mem. American Chemical Society (chmn. of Pittsburgh section 1934), Am. Inst. Chem. Engrs., N.E.A., A.A.A.S., Am. Electrochem. Soc. Episcopalian. Mason. Defined chemical terms in Webster's International Dictionary, 1890 edition. Translated 1st edition Nernst's "Theoretical Chemistry," 1895. Invented, 1900, and patented, 1907, basic process for cracking oils to gasoline, sold to Standard Oil Co. of Ind., 1916. Author: Chemical Oxidation Tables, 1897; A Possible Approach to the Shakespeare Question (paper in Johns Hopkins Alumni Mag.), June 1937; also many other papers on edn. and chemistry. Home: 4333 Dakota St., Oakland Station, Pittsburgh, Pa.

PALMER, Dwight R. G., pres. Gen. Cable Corpn.; b. St. Louis, Mo., June 1, 1886; s. Everett E. and Laura (Creighton) P.; student Smith Acad.; m. Helen Bannister, 1916; children—Helen, Jean, Dwight, Patricia. Pres. Gen. Cable Corpn.; also pres. Detroit Insulated Wire Co.; Dudlo Mfg. Co., Peerless Insulated Wire & Cable Co., Phillips Wire Co., Rome Elec. Co., Inc., Rome Wire Co., Inc., Safety Cable Co., Southern States Cable Co., Standard Underground Cable Co.; dir. Revere Copper & Brass, Inc., Canada Wire & Cable Co., Ltd. Clubs: Bankers, Union League, Engineers (New York); Essex County Country. Home: 154 Ralston Av., S. Orange, N.J. Office: 420 Lexington Av., New York, N.Y.

PALMER, Edgar, chmn. bd. New Jersey Zinc Co.; b. N.Y. City, Nov. 12, 1880; s. Stephen Squires and Susan Flanders (Price) P.; B.S., Princeton, 1903, E.E., 1905; m. Zilph Hayes, Nov. 22, 1910. Pres. New Jersey Zinc Co., 1912-27, now chairman of board; also chairman of the board Bertha Mineral Co., Mineral Point Zinc Company, Empire Zinc Co. of Colo., Empire Zinc Co. of Mo., New Jersey Zinc Co. of Pa., Palmer Land Co., Palmer Water Co., Master Painter's Supply Co., N.J. Zinc Sales Co., Chestnut Ridge Ry. Co., The Franklin Water Company, The Franklin General Stores, Inc.; president Smith Valley Realty Corpn., Princeton Municipal Improvement, Inc., Princeton Inn Co., Palmerton Hospital, Franklin Hospital; vice-president Annapee & Western Ry. Co., Green Bay & Western R.R. Co., Kewanee, Green Bay & Western R.R. Co.; dir. Cayuga & Susquehanna R.R. Co., Fidelity-Phenix Fire Ins. Co., Bankers & Shippers Insurance Co., Detroit, Hillsdale & Southwestern R.R. Co., Ft. Wayne & Jackson R.R. Co., New York & Queens Electric Light & Power Co., Palmerton Co., Palmerton Disposal Co., Palmerton Lighting Co., Palmerton Telephone Co., 111 Main St. Corpn., Ward Baking Corpn., Marine Basin Co., Inc., Nassau Bldg. & Loan Assn., Saucon Valley Iron & R.R. Co., Ward Baking Co.; limited partner Henderson & Co.; trustee Central Hanover Bank & Trust Co., Consol. Edison Co. of N.Y., Inc., Princeton U., Stevens Inst. Technology. Men. Am. Inst. Mining and Metall. Engrs., Princeton Engineering Assn. Republican. Episcopalian. Clubs: Metropolitan (Washington); University, Jekyl Island, Union League, Blind Brook, Apawamis, New York Yacht, Eastern Yacht, American Yacht, Manursing Island, Nassau, Princeton, Down Town Assn.; Country Club (Havana); American (London). Home: 1 Bayard Lane, Princeton, N.J. Office: 20 Exchange Pl., New York, N.Y.

PALMER, Frederic, Jr., prof. physics; b. Brookline, Mass., Oct. 17, 1878; s. Frederic and Mary (Towle) P.; A.B., Harvard, 1900, A.M., 1904, Ph.D., 1913; m. Helen Wallace, June 19, 1907; children—Frederic, Helen Wallace. Teacher Asheville (N.C.) Sch., 1900-01, Worcester (Mass.) Acad., 1901-03; instr., 1904-08, dean, 1908-29, asso. prof. physics, 1909-16, prof. physics since 1916, Haverford Coll. Mem. exec. com. Am. Inst. of Physics, 1931; v.p. Am. Assn. of Physics Teachers, 1932, pres., 1933 and 1934; mem. Commn. on Science of Coll. Entrance Examination Bd., 1935; mem. com. on physic since 1936. Fellow A.A.A.S., Am. Physical Soc.; mem. Physics Club of Phila., Franklin Inst., Phi Beta Kappa, Sigma Xi, Delta Upsilon. Democrat. Episcopalian. Ednl. sec. Y.M.C.A., Newport, R.I., 1918; lecturer physics, Harvard, 1918-19. Home: Haverford, Pa.

PALMER, Gordon, pres. theol. sem.; b. Coveney, Cambridgeshire, England, June 2, 1888; s. James Chapman and Louisa Bews (Pearson) P.; B.D., Berkeley (Calif.) Divinity Sch., 1916; Ph.B., U. of Redlands (Calif.), 1916, D.D., 1925; student Rochester (N.Y.) Theol. Sem., 1916-17; m. Mila Hakes Treat, Sept. 9, 1919; children—Gordon, Robert Hakes, Janet Treat. Came to U.S., 1909, naturalized, 1916. Student pastor Winters and Azusa, Calif., and Mumford, N.Y., 1909-17; ordained to ministry Baptist Ch., 1910; pastor 1st Ch., Mason, Mich., 1917-18, South Park Ch., Los Angeles, 1919-28, 1st Ch., Pomona, Calif., 1928-36; pres. Eastern Baptist Theol. Sem., Phila., since 1936. Vice-pres. Northern Baptist Conv., 1935-36; pres. Southern Calif. Baptist Conv., 1936; mem. bd. mgrs. Am. Baptist Home Missions Soc., Watchman-Examiner Corpn. Y.M.C.A. religious work sec., 1917; chaplain-1st lt. U.S.A., 1917-19; now chaplain-1st lt. O.R.C. Trustee U. of Redlands, 1927-34, Pomona Council Boy Scouts of America, since 1934. Dept. chaplain Am. Legion, state of Calif., 1927. Mem. Phi Kappa Delta. Mason. Author: What's Right With the World, 1939. Contbr. to religious jours. Home: 1305 Medford Rd., Wynnewood, Pa. Office: 1814 S. Rittenhouse St., Philadelphia, Pa.

PALMER, John Campbell, Jr., lawyer; b. Brooke Co., W.Va., Sept. 30, 1868; s. John Campbell and Frances Tarr (Waugh) P.; B.S., Washington and Jefferson Coll., Washington, Pa., 1890, M.S., 1893; Ph.D., Univ. of Wooster, O., 1902; m. Jeanette Ostrander, Aug. 1, 1902; children—John Campbell, III, Kathleen (Mrs. Jas. D. Sparkman), Gertrude (Mrs. Philip H. R. Whitehead), David Waugh. Admitted to W.Va. bar, 1891; engaged in gen. practice of law at Wheeling and Wellsburg since 1891; mem. firm Erskine, Palmer & Curl, Wheeling, W.Va., since 1913; pres. Wellsburg Nat. Bank, 1905-30; sec. Harvey Paper Co., 1904-29; pres. Oriental Oil Co., 1906-09; city solicitor Wellsburg, W.Va., 1898-99; sec. bd. edn. Wellsburg, 1910-11; editor Daily Leader, 1910-11. Maker of Palmer's Farm Maps of Brooke Co., W.Va., 1904, 2nd edit., 1911. Dir. Asso. Charities, Wheeling, 1919-31; mem. Red Cross, Community Chest, Y.M.C.A. Pres. Ohio County, W.Va., Bar Assn., 1920. Mem. Am. and W.Va. bar assns., W.Va. Acad. Sci., W.Va. Poetry Soc., W.Va. Nature Assn., Wheeling Math. Soc., Am. Soc. Polit. Science, Ohio Co. Hist. Soc., Phi Beta Kappa. Democrat. Presbyn. Clubs: Twilight, Oglebay Rhymers (Wheeling). Editor four annual vols. poetry of Oglebay Rhymers Club. Author of "The Class of '90" (Washington and Jefferson Coll.), 1901; A Century of Sonnets,

PALMER, John Campbell, III, lawyer; b. Wellsburg, W.Va., July 23, 1903; s. John Campbell, Jr., and Jeanette (Ostrander) P.; student U.S. Mil. Acad., 1921-23; B.S., Washington and Jefferson Coll., 1925; LL.B., Harvard U. Law Sch., 1929; m. Louise Heyman, Mar. 4, 1932. Admitted to W.Va. bar, 1929, and since engaged in gen. practice of law at Wheeling; mem. firm Erskine, Palmer & Curl since 1930; dir. and atty. Blue Ribbon Paint Co. Mem. Beta Theta Pi, Phi Tau Gamma, Theta Nu Epsilon, Sigma Delta Rho. Republican. Elk. Club: Wheeling Country. Home: 859 National Rd. Office: Riley Law Bldg., Wheeling, W.Va.

PALMER, Philip Mason, college dean; b. Westbrook, Me., May 8, 1880; s. Frederick Merrill and Clara (Parker) P.; A.B., Bowdoin, 1900, Harvard, 1902; grad. study, U of Heidelberg, 1906, 11, 13, U. of Zurich, 1921-22; Doctor, honoris causa, U. of Padua, 1922; m. Mary Frost Hodgdon, Aug. 4, 1903 (died 1911); 1 son, Philip Motley; m. 2d, Anne-Marie Bauer, June 16, 1914; children—Carl Pfeiffer, Parker, Robert, Richard, John. Instr. in modern langs., Lehigh U., 1902-05, asst. prof., 1905-06, prof., 1906-10, prof. German since 1910, dir. Coll. Arts and Sciences, 1921-36, dean since 1936. Mem. bd. pub. schs., Bethlehem, 1916-18, Pub. Library, 1918-21. Mem. Modern Lang. Assn. America, Am. Assn. Univ. Professors, Kleistgesellschaft, Goethegesellschaft, Phi Beta Kappa, Theta Delta Chi, Omicron Delta Kappa. Republican. Mem. Evang. Ch. Author: (with R. P. Moore) Sources of the Faust Tradition. Contbr. articles on ednl. subjects. Home: Lehigh Univ. Campus, Bethlehem, Pa.

PALMER, Samuel Copeland, coll. prof.; b. Concord, Pa., Apr. 27, 1874; s. Lewis and Hannah H. (Pancoast) P.; A.B., Swarthmore (Pa.) Coll., 1895, A.M., 1907; A.M., Harvard, 1909, Ph.D., 1912; m. Margaret Bancroft Swayne, Aug. 6, 1902 (died 1932); children—Samuel Copeland, Katharine, Lawrence Benjamin. Lab. asst., Radcliffe Coll., Cambridge, Mass., 1909-10; asst. prof. biology, Swarthmore (Pa.) Coll., 1911-23, asso. prof., 1924-32, prof. botany since 1932; grad. mgr. athletics, Swarthmore Coll., 1912-27, and since 1930; mem. N.C.A.A. Olympic Com. one yr. Mem. council Nat. Collegiate Athletic Assn. since 1937. Mem. Nat. Acad. of Natural Sciences, Phila., Sigma Xi (pres. Swarthmore Chapter 1938-39). Republican. Mem. Soc. of Friends. Clubs: Botanical (Phila.); Delaware Valley Ornithological (Phila.; past pres.); Rolling Green Golf (Swarthmore, Pa.). Author: Numerical Relations of the Histological Elements of the Retina in Necturus. Home: 435 Riverview Rd. Office: Swarthmore Coll., Swarthmore, Pa.

PALMER, V. Claude; judge Circuit Court of N.J. Home: Mount Holly, N.J.

PALMER, Walter, mfg. natural dyestuffs; b. Media, Pa., Mar. 30, 1888; s. Thomas Chalkley and Hannah Jane (Walter) P.; ed. Media Friends Sch., Friends Select Sch., Haverford (Pa.) Coll., 1906-10, Mass. Inst. Tech., 1911-12; m. Sara Frances Pennock, Oct. 11, 1913; children—Laura (Mrs. Charles W. Crouse), Margaret Walter, Ann Aldrich. Employed as draftsman with Walker Electric Co.; 1910; asso. with American Dyewood Co., mfrs. natural dyestuffs, Chester, Pa., continuously since 1912, successively, engr., purchasing agt., asst. mgr., then mgr. and dir. since 1919. Dir. Chester Hosp. Elwyn Training Sch. Mem. Del. Co. Inst. Sci. (pres.), Franklin Inst., Acad. of Natural Sci., Leidy Micros. Club (sec.), Aero Club of Pa. Republican. Mem. Religious Soc. of Friends. Club: Chester. Home: R.F.D. No. 2, Media, Pa. Office: Foot of Lamokin St., Chester, Pa.

PALMER, William Neavitt; surgeon Easton Emergency Hosp., Easton, Md.

PALMISANO, Vincent L., ex-congressman; b. Termini Imenese, Italy, June 13, 1883; s. Cosimo and Anna Marie (Sanzone) P.; brought to U.S. 1887; ed. parochial Schools, East Baltimore, Md.; student U. of Md.; m. Mary Fermes, Dec. 1919. Admitted to Md. bar, 1909, and began practice at Baltimore; mem. Md. Ho. of Rep., 1914; mem. city council, Baltimore, 1915-23; mem. Dem. State Central Com., Md., 1923; police examiner, Baltimore, 1925; mem. 70th to 75th Congresses (1927-39), 3d Md. Dist. Catholic. Heptasoph, Forester; mem. Federal Fraternal Assn. Home: 320 S. High St. Office: Calvert Bldg., Baltimore, Md.

PALMQUIST, Elim Arthur Eugene, exec. sec. Phila. Fed. of Churches; b. Oakland, Neb., Aug. 16, 1873; s. Andrew and Ellen (Olson) P.; prep. edn. Oakland (Neb.) High Sch., 1891-92, Morgan Park (Ill.) Acad., 1892-95; A.B., U. of Chicago, 1899; B.D., Divinity Sch., U. of Chicago, 1904; D.D., Bucknell U., Lewisburg, Pa., 1926; m. Marie Estelle Coon, June 27, 1901; m. 2d, Susie Homes Welles, Oct. 9, 1907; children—Mary Estelle (Mrs. Guy Constant Holbrook, Jr.), Charles Welles. Ordained to ministry of Baptist Ch., 1900; pastor First Bapt. Ch., Momence, Ill., 1900-05, First Bapt. Ch., Connellsville, Pa., 1906-12, North Av. Bapt. Ch., Cambridge, Mass., 1912-18; Y.M. C.A. war sec., Mass. Inst. Tech., 1918-19; field dir. for New England of Interchurch World Movement, 1919-20; exec. sec. Phila. Fed. of Churches since Nov. 1920. Dir. Phila. and Suburban Town Meeting of the Air; dir. Armstrong Assn.; sec. Mayor's Crime Commn. Mem. Delta Tau Delta. Republican. Mason. Club: Merion Cricket (Merion, Pa.). Home: 37 Norbrook Park, Narbrook, Pa. Office: Land Title Bldg., Philadelphia, Pa.

PANCOAST, Elinor, coll. prof.; b. Ottawa, Kan., May 21, 1893; d. George Lucas and Anna Marie (Nielsen) P.; student U. of Tex., Austin, Tex., 1911-13; Ph.B., U. of Chicago, 1917, A.M., 1922, Ph.D., 1927; student Bryn Mawr Coll., Pa., 1918-19. Engaged in teaching, high sch., Henrietta, Tex., 1913-16, Wichita Falls, Tex., 1917-18; editorial work, A. M. Collins Co., Phila., Pa., 1919-20; instr. econs., Goucher Coll., 1924-25, asst. prof., 1925-29, asso. prof., 1929-32, prof. and chmn. dept. of econs. and sociology since 1932; chmn. com. of Summer Sch. for Office Workers, hdqrs. N.Y. City; chmn. Workers' Edn. Com., Baltimore. Mem. Am. Econ. Assn., Am. Assn. Univ. Profs. Democrat. Episcopalian. Club: Hamilton Street (Baltimore). Home: 5108 Springlake Way, Baltimore, Md.

PANCOAST, Henry Khunrath, M.D.; b. Phila., Pa., Feb. 26, 1875; s. Seth and Susan George (Osborn) P.; grad. Friends' Central Sch., Phila., 1892; M.D., U. of Pa., 1898; m. Clara Louise Boggs, Apr. 7, 1903. Resident phys., U. of Pa. Hosp., 1898-1900; asst. instr. in clin. surgery and asst. demonstrator in surgery, U. of Pa., 1901-04; lecturer on skiagraphy, U. of Pa., and skiagrapher to Univ. Hosp. 1905-11; prof. Röntgenology, U. of Pa., and Röntgenologist to Univ. Hosp., 1912—; consulting Röntgenologist, Bryn Mawr Hosp., 1923; consulting physiologist U.S. Bur. Mines, 1923-28; consultant radiol. clinic, Phila. Gen. Hosp.; radiologist Chestnut Hill Hospital, Phila., 1931-35. Pres. First Am. Congress of Radiologists, 1933. Trustee-treas. Tabernacle Presbyn. Ch., Phila., 1911-19. Med. Corps U.S. N.R.F., 1918, grade of asst. surgeon, rank lt. (j.g.); inactive list 1919, grade of passed asst. surgeon, rank lt. Republican. Mem. Am. Röntgen Ray Soc. (sec. 1912, pres. 1913), A.M.A. (chmn. sect. on Radiology 1932), Pa. State Med. Soc., Phila. Co. Med. Soc., Pathol. Soc. Phila., Coll. of Physicians, Phila. Med. Club, Am. Radium Soc. (sec. 1917-18, pres. 1919), Radiol. Soc. N.A., Am. Coll. Radiology (pres. 1933-34), Phi Kappa Psi, Phi Alpha Sigma, first pres. Am. Bd. Radiology, 1934; dir. and mem. exec. com. Am. Soc. for Control of Cancer, 1930-36. Home: Merion, Pa. Address: University Hospital, Phila., Pa.

PANGBORN, Thomas W., machinery mfg.; b. Brooklyn, N.Y., May 29, 1880; s. Chas. T. and Ann P.; student pub. schs., LeRoy, Minn.; m. Elsie E. Schumann, June 14, 1906. Employed as mech. asst., and sales agent, Bellville Copper Rolling Mills, Soho, N.J., 1900-04; founder, 1904, and since dir. and pres. Pangborn Corpn., mfrs. blast cleaning and dust control equipment, Hagerstown, Md.; vice-pres. and dir. Pittsburgh Crushed Steel Co., Pittsburg, Pa., since 1936; dir. Equitable Trust Co., Baltimore, The Catholic Review, Baltimore; state dir. Liberty Mutual Ins. Co., Boston, Mass. Trustee, St. Mary's Industrial Sch., Good Samaritan Hosp., both Baltimore. Past pres. (3 terms) Nat. Founders Assn., Chicago, and (2 terms) Foundry Equipment Mfrs. Assn., Cleveland, O. Democrat. Roman Catholic. Club: Fountain Head Country. Home: Journeys End, Hagerstown, Md.

PANOFSKY, Erwin, prof. history of art; b. Hanover (Germany), Mar. 30, 1892; s. Arnold and Caecilie (Solling) P.; ed. Gymnasium, Berlin, 1901-10; student at universities of Berlin and Munich, 1910-14; Ph.D., University of Freiburg, 1914, University of Utrecht, 1936; m. Dora Mosse, Apr. 9, 1916; children—Hans Arnold Albert, Wolfgang Kurt Hermann. Came to America, 1934. Teacher and prof. history of art, U. of Hamburg, 1921-33; visiting prof. fine arts, N.Y. Univ., 1931-35; visiting lecturer Princeton, 1934-35, prof. Inst. for Advanced Study (Princeton), since 1935. Mem. Com. Internationale Permanente d'Histoire de l'Art; fellow Mediæval Acad. of America. Club: Princeton (New York). Author of several books and many articles pub. in Germany, Austria, England and America. Home: 97 Battle Road, Princeton, N.J.

PANTALEONE, Joseph, physician; b. Sicily, Italy, July 30, 1900; s. Dr. Raphael Charles and Angelina (Mulè) P.; brought to U.S., 1907, naturalized, 1921; A.B., U. of Pa., 1923; student Columbia U. Coll. Phys. & Surgs., 1923-25; M.D., Boston U. Med. Sch., 1928; m. Lucy Anne Polito, Sept. 28, 1931; children—Angela Florence, Raphael Joseph. Interne Waterbury (Conn.) Hosp., 1928-29; in practice of medicine at Trenton, N.J., since 1931; physician med. and obstet. dept., St. Francis Hosp. since 1934. Served in R.O.T.C., 1918-19. Dir. Italian Dept. Internat. Inst. Founder and pres. Boston U. Med. Club; founder Nat. Unico Clubs, Italian Fed. of Mercer Co. (past pres.), Trenton Philos. Soc. (sec.). Mem. Italian Business and Professional Men's Club, Med. Journal Club, A.M.A., N.J. Med. Soc., Mercer Co. Component Med. Soc., Lambda Phi Mu, Monteleonese Soc., Rosicrucian Order. Roman Catholic. L.O.O.M. Contbr. many articles to Italian-Am. papers and jours. Lecturer to civic orgns. and clubs. Composer over 100 numbers for piano. Composer more than 100 poems. Home: 504 Hamilton Av., Trenton, N.J.

PAPÁNEK, Dr. Ján, consul; b. Brezova, Czechoslovakia, Oct. 24, 1896; s. Stefan and Alzbeta (Palanska) P.; LL.D., U. of Paris, 1923, Charles' U., Prague, 1928; student L'Ecole des Sciences Politiques, Paris, 1919-21; m. Betka Papánek, Feb. 13, 1926. Officer Czechoslovak Legions in Italy during World War, 1916-18; editor V Boj, 1919; in office of Ministry of Foreign Affairs, Praha, 1922-24; commercial attaché Czechoslovak Legation, Budapest, 1925-26, Washington, D.C., 1927-31; in office of Ministry of Foreign Affairs, Praha, 1932-35; consul Czechoslovakia, Pittsburgh, since 1936. Author: La Tchécoslovaquie, 1923. Home: 43 Mt. Lebanon Boul. Office: 239 Fourth Av., Pittsburgh, Pa.

PAQUIN, Samuel Savil, newspaperman; b. Tripoli, Ia., Aug. 29, 1868; s. Cyril O. and Anne E. (Fitts) P.; A.B., U. of Minn., 1894; m. at Chicago, Helen A. Peck, Dec. 30, 1896 (died 1914); m. 2d, Josephine Frances O'Hara, Aug. 29, 1915; children—Josephine Elizabeth, Marjorie Genevieve, Samuel Savil. Editorial staff Minneapolis Tribune, 1894-96, Chicago Tribune, 1896-1900, Chicago American, 1900-07, New York Evening Journal, 1907-09; asst. gen. mgr., Internat. News Service, 1909-16; service mgr. Internat. Feature Service, 1916; service mgr. King Features Syndicate, Inc., 1921-30, daily editor, 1931-38, research dir. since 1938. Councilman, Teaneck Tp., since 1930. Mem. Psi Upsilon. Catholic. Author: Garden Fairies, 1908. Home: Teaneck, N.J. Office: 235 E. 45th St., New York, N.Y.

PARCELL, Malcolm Stevens, artist; b. Claysville, Pa., Jan. 1, 1896; s. Steven Lee and Emma (Minor) P.; grad. Carnegie Inst. Tech., Pittsburgh, 1918; m. Helen Louine Gallagher, Aug. 14, 1937. Awarded 1st prize, Associated Artists, for "Trinity Hall," 1918; Saltus gold medal, Nat. Acad. Design, for painting "Louine," 1919; Logan medal, Art Inst. Chicago, for "Jim McKee," 1924; Harris prize for "Portrait of My Mother," 1924; popularity prize winner Internat. Art Exhibit, Pittsburgh, 2 yrs. Mem. Associated Artists of Pittsburgh. Republican. Baptist. Clubs: Bassett (Washington, Pa.); Coffee House (New York). Sketches, reproductions in oils, etc., have apeared in Internat. Studio, Harper's, Art and Archæology, Vanity Fair, etc. Home: 11 N. Main St., Washington, Pa.

PARDEE, C. Marvin, banking; b. Stanhope, N.J., Mar. 1, 1894; s. Israel Platt and Alice (Lee) P.; student Hill Sch., Pottstown, Pa., 1908-13; A.B., Lafayette Coll., Easton, Pa., 1917; m. Margaret Mallory, Dec. 1, 1917 (div.); children—Margaret, Patricia. Began as runner in Wall St., New York City, 1919; asso. with Hazleton Nat. Bank since 1934, vice-pres. and dir. since 1934; dir. Altamont Hotel Co. Served as 1st lieut. A.S., U.S.A., 1917-19. Mem. Theta Delta Chi. Mem. Pa. Soc. of New York. Republican. Presbyn. Club: Valley Country. Home: 338 W. Green St. Address: Hazleton Nat. Bank, Hazleton, Pa.

PARDOE, William Sprague; prof. hydraulic engring., University of Pa. Address: University of Pa., Philadelphia, Pa.

PARENTE, Antonio, foreign exchange dealer; b. San Giovanni, Benevento, Italy, Jan. 22, 1882; s. Giovanni and Elisabetta Lepore; student Collegio Germanico Romano, Rome, Italy, 1895-99, Am. Coll., Allentown, Pa., 1903-04; m. Felicia Maio, Nov. 7, 1907; children—Hugo J., Dora E. (Mrs. Gene Deblasio). Came to U.S. Mar. 1902. Mgr. foreign Dept. Monessen (Pa.) Trust Co., 1905-1927, mgr. foreign dept. First Nat. Bank & Trust Co., Monessen, 1927-31; owner and mgr. Bureau of Foreign Affairs, foreign exchange and steamship agent since 1931. Life hon. pres. Assistenza al Reduce (Assn. of Veterans of World War), San Giovanni, Italy; corr. of Progresso Italo Americano, New York; corr. of Royal Italian Consulate, Pittsburgh, Pa. Author of 3 volumes of prose and poetry, published both in Italy and in the U.S. Contbr. to many publs., including "Roma Letteraria," "Noi e il Mondo," "Il Carroccio," "l'Araldo, l'Italia Letteraria," etc. Address: 213 Fourth St., Monessen, Pa.

PARGNY, Eugene W(illiams), past pres. Am. Sheet & Tin Plate Co.; b. Louisville, Ky., June 5, 1866; s. Joseph and Louise (Bennier) P.; ed. pub. and pvt. schs.; m. Emilie Tuman, June 28, 1893. In ins. business, 1884-86; sec. Belle of Nelson Distillery Company, 1886-1890; successively purchasing agent, sales agt., mgr. Apollo Iron & Steel Co., Pittsburgh, 1890-1901; mgr., in charge all plants in Pittsburgh dist., Am. Sheet Steel Co., 1901-04; v.p. Am. Sheet & Tin Plate Co., 1904-09, pres., 1909-32 (retired). Republican. Protestant. Clubs: Pittsburgh, Duquesne, Allegheny Country, Fox Chapelle, Golf, Rolling Rock. Home: 1054 Beechwood Boul., Pittsburgh, Pa.*

PARIS, Auguste Jean, Jr., engineer, inventor; b. N.Y. City, Jan. 31, 1874; s. Auguste Jean and Anne (Mercer) P. de Bourgogne; ed. under pvt. tutors; hon. Sc.D., St. John's Coll., Annapolis, 1921; m. Gertrude Eugenie van Ness d'Moore, 1900. Began as research-chem. engr., at Bradford, Pa., 1900; has served as dir. and consulting engr. of many chem. and mfg. cos.; inventor of many processes, covered by patents. Upon entry of U.S. into the World War, offered his entire pvt. income and his services to War Dept., also the use of his inventions for the period of the war, to U.S., Great Britain, France and Italy; associated with brother, Capt. W. Francklyn Paris, in erection of plant at Charleston, W.Va., without govt. subsidy; work carried on under general direction of Nat. Advisory Com. for Aeronautics; now operating research laboratories at Bradford and Charleston, mainly on processes relating to petroleum and chem. industries. Apptd. by gov. of W.Va. del. to Yorktown (Va.) Sesquicentennial Expn., 1931. Mem. Am. Gas Assn., Soc. Am. Mil. Engrs., etc. Officer French Acad., 1930. Club: University (Washington, D.C.). Home: Charleston, W.Va.*

PARISH, Benjamin Dores, M.D., surgeon; b. Philadelphia, Pa., July 8, 1877; s. William Henry and Isabel N. (De La Motta) P.; grad. Delancy Sch., 1895; B.S., U. of Pa., 1899, M.D., 1902; m. Helen Griffith, Nov. 16, 1904; children—Benjamin D. (M.D.), Warren G. (M.D.). Interne St. Agnes Hosp., Philadelphia, 1902, chief surg. out-patient dept., 1903-04, otologist and laryngologist, 1906-31, pres. of staff, 1934-35, now consultant in oto-laryngology; instr. otology, U. of Pa., 1906-17; asso. prof. U. of Pa. Grad Sch., 1920-27; spl. examiner U.S. Pub. Health Service; consultant Kensington Hosp. for Women, Oncologic Hosp., Norristown State Asylum, Naval Hosp., (Phila.); former pres. med. staff and oto-laryngologist Chestnut Hill Hosp. With Med. Corps, U.S.N., Naval Hosp., Phila., 1917-19. Fellow Am. Coll. Surgeons, Philadelphia Coll. Physicians; mem. A.M.A., Pa. State Med. Soc., Phila. Co. Med. Soc., Phila. Laryngol. Soc., Phi Alpha Sigma. Unitarian. Mason. Club: Medical (Philadelphia). Home: Edann Road, North Hills. Office: 1927 Spruce St., and 8033 Germantown Av., Philadelphia, Pa.

PARK, Edwards Albert, pediatrician; b. Gloversville, N.Y., Dec. 30, 1877; s. William Edwards and Sara Billings (Edwards) P.; grad. Phillips Acad., Andover, Mass., 1896; A.B., Yale, 1900, hon. A.M., 1922; M.D., Coll. Phys. and Surg. (Columbia), N.Y. City, 1905; hon. D.Sc., U. of Rochester, 1936; m. Agnes Bevan, Aug. 2, 1913; children—Sara Bevan, Charles Rawlinson, David Chapman. Interne, Roosevelt Hosp., N.Y. City, 1906-08, New York Foundling Hosp., 1908-09; Proudfit fellow in medicine and instr. in medicine, Coll. Phys. and Surg., 1909-12; instr. in pediatrics, Johns Hopkins, 1912-15, asso. prof., 1915-21; Sterling prof. pediatrics, Yale U. Sch. Medicine, 1921-27; prof. pediatrics, Johns Hopkins, and pediatrician, Johns Hopkins Hosp., since 1927. Editor Medicine, Revue Française de Pediatrie. Jahsbuch für Kinderheilkunde. Major Am. Red Cross World War. Mem. Assn. of Am. Physicians, Am. Pediatric Soc., Acad. of Pediatrics, Soc. Clin. Investigation, A.A.A.S., Am. Soc. Exptl. Pathology, Soc. Exptl. Biology and Medicine, Interurban Clin. Club, Brit. Pediatric Assn., Alpha Delta Phi. Decorated Order of Leopold (Belgium), 1919; Reconnaissance Française (France), 1919. Contbr. on rickets, deformities of the skull, physiology of the thymus gland. Home: York Road, Towson, Md. Office: Johns Hopkins Hosp., Baltimore, Md.

PARK, Marion Edwards, coll. pres.; b. Andover, Mass., Dec. 31, 1875; d. William Edwards and Sara Billings (Edwards) P.; high sch. Gloversville, N.Y.; A.B., Bryn Mawr Coll., 1898, Ph.D., 1918; studied U. of Chicago, 1900; Am. Sch. Classical Studies, Athens, Greece, 1901-02. Instr. and asst. prof. classics, Colorado Coll., Colorado Springs, Colo., 1902-06; dean of Simmons Coll., 1918-21, of Radcliffe Coll., 1921-22; pres. Bryn Mawr Coll. since Oct. 4, 1922. Mem. Am. Philol. Assn. Conglist. Home: Bryn Mawr, Pa.

PARK, (James) Theodore, prof. of mathematics; b. Sunbury, Pa., Oct. 7, 1883; s. John Minard and Clara Huntingdon (Noss) P.; B.S., Bucknell U., Lewisburg, Pa., 1906; A.M., Susquehanna U., Selinsgrove, Pa., 1927; grad. student U. of Pa., 1931-33; m. Lucie Cathryne Coons, June 24, 1915; 1 dau., Mary Cathryne. Prin., Pine Grove Mills (Pa.) High Sch., 1906-07; organized and first prin., Farnett Twp. (Pa.) High Sch., 1907-08; supervising prin. Pine Grove (Pa.) Schs., 1908-10; asst. to pres., Dickinson Sem., Williamsport, Pa., 1910-11; teacher chemistry Stamford (Conn.) High Sch., 1915-18; teacher mathematics and chemistry, Sch. of the Lackawanna, Scranton, Pa., 1911-15; teacher mathematics, Coraopolis (Pa.) High Sch., 1924-25, Chester (Pa.) High Sch., 1931-33; prof. of physics and phys. chemistry, Susquehanna U., Selinsgrove, Pa., 1925-30; prof. of calculus, Inst. of Science, Chester, Pa., since 1936; dir. of edn. Sun Ship Building and Dry Dock Co., Chester; lecturer at teachers institutes, associations, etc. Vice-pres. Snyder Co. Republican Club, 1928-30. Hon. mem. Del. Co. Inst. of Science; mem. Pa. State Teachers Assn., N.E.A., Pa. Acad. Science, Delaware Co. Inst. of Science, A.A.A.S., Royal Soc. of Arts (London), Bond and Key. Republican. Methodist. Mason (32°). Home: 610 E. 14th St., Chester, Pa.

PARKE, Francis Neal, judge; b. Westminster, Md., Jan. 6, 1871; s. George Motter and Mary White (Neal) Parke; ed. private and parochial schs. and Western Md. Coll. (Westminster, Md.); student U.S. Mil. Acad., 1889-91; unmarried. Admitted to Md. bar, 1893; practiced at Westminster and throughout State of Md.; div. counsel B.&O. R.R. Co.; apptd. asso. judge Court of Appeals of Md. (Supreme Ct.), 1924, elected for 15 yr. term, 1926. Pres. Md. State Bar Assn., 1924. Home: Westminster, Md.

PARKER, Andrew McClean ("Mac Parker"), radio commentator, advertising exec.; b. New York, N.Y., Dec. 6, 1890; s. Andrew McClean and Kate (deRosset) P.; student Plainfield (N.J.) High Sch., Phillips Exeter Acad. (Exeter, N.H.), and Lafayette Coll. (Easton, Pa.); m. Florence Mae Smith, Aug. 28, 1915; children—Andrew McClean, Katherine deRosset, Florence Lida, James, Adelaide Mears, Mary Louise, John Forbes, Peter Isaac, Gertrude Van Cortland, Richard Wayne, Charles Graham, Dedie. Began as reporter City Press Assn., Chicago, Ill., 1914; spl. writer Phila. Record, 1928-36; radio commentator, Phila., since 1929; dir. pub. relations Al Paul Lefton Co., Inc., advertising, Phila., since 1936. Mem. Chi Phi. Episcopalian. Home: 329 Chestnut Rd., Glenside, Pa. Office: 1617 Pennsylvania Boul., Philadelphia, Pa.

PARKER, Charles Wolcott, jurist; b. Newark, N.J., Oct. 22, 1862; s. Hon. Cortlandt and Elisabeth Wolcott (Stites) P.; A.B., Princeton, 1882, A.M., 1885, LL.D., 1919; LL.B., Columbia, 1885; m. Emily Fuller, Nov. 22, 1893; children—Charles W. (dec.), Dudley F., Philip M., Elinor M., Robert M. Practiced at Newark, 1885-90, later at Bayonne City and Jersey City, N.J., judge 2d Dist. Court, Jersey City, 1898-1903; judge N.J. Circuit Court, 1903-07; justice Supreme Court of N.J. 5 terms, 1907-42. Supervising editor N.J. Digest, 1907. Republican. Private, corporal and sergt. Essex Troop, of Newark, 1890-99; 1st lt. and capt. 4th N.J. Regt., 1899-1902; lt. col. and a.-a.-g. of N.J., 1902-07; a.-d.-c. on staff of Gov. Franklin Murphy. Episcopalian; chancellor P.E. Diocese of Newark. Pres. emeritus N.J. Hist. Soc.; ex-gov. Soc. Colonial Wars; mem. S.R., Founders and Patriots, N.J. State Bar Assn. Clubs: University, Princeton (New York); Essex (Newark). Morris County Golf. Home: 63 Macculloch Av. Address: 19 South St., Morristown, N.J.

PARKER, Dorothy Rothschild (Mrs. Alan Campbell), writer; b. West End, N.J., Aug. 22, 1893; d. Jacob Henry and Eliza (Marston) Rothschild; student Miss Dana's Sch., Morristown, N.J., Blessed Sacrament Convent, New York; m. Edwin Pond Parker, 1917 (dec.); m. 2d, Alan Campbell, 1934. Began as editorial worker, later on editorial bd., Vogue, Vanity Fair, and New Yorker; employed as motion-picture writer in collaboration with Alan Campbell by various studios. Mem. Screen Writers' Guild, Hollywood Anti-Nazi League, Am. League for Peace and Democracy, League of Women Shoppers, Spanish Children's Milk Fund (chmn.), N.A. Com. for Defense of Spanish Democracy (chmn. women's com.). Democrat. Author: Enough Rope, Sunset Gun, Death and Taxes, Not So Deep as a Well (verse); Sonnets for the Swing, After Such Pleasures (short stories); (play, with Elmer Rice) Close Harmony. Contbr. verse, criticism, articles, stories, to mags. Home: Pipersville, Pa.

PARKER, Edward Cary, in charge federal grain supervision; b. St. Paul, Minn., Aug. 4, 1881; s. Charles Delavan and Frances Abigail (Comings) P.; student Minn. Agr. Sch., 1899-1901; B.S.,

U. of Minn., 1905; m. Edith Carter, Feb. 11, 1908; 1 son, Ward Follett. Asst. agriculturalist, Minn. Agril. Expt. Station, 1905-08; agrl. adviser to Manchurian Govt., 1908-12; ranching and land development, Mont., 1913-23; marketing specialist U.S. Dept. Agr., 1923-33, in charge federal grain supervision, Bur. Agrl. Economics, U.S., since 1933. Sec. Mont. Ranches Co., 1915-19; pres. Treasure State Ranches Co., 1919-23. Mem. Phi Delta Theta, Sigma Xi. Unitarian. Author: Field Management and Crop Rotation, 1915; also U.S. Dept. Agr. bulls. on grain, 1932-34. Home: 120 West Woodbine St., Chevy Chase, Md. Address: U.S. Bur. Agrl. Economics, Washington, D.C.

PARKER, Edward Wheeler, statistician; b. Pt. Deposit, Md., June 16, 1860; s. William Price and Henrietta Hyde (Donnell) P.; ed. schs. there and at Baltimore, and in City Coll., Baltimore; m. Laura Harrison Bryan, Apr. 29, 1891. Apptd. statistician U.S. Geol. Survey, 1891; in charge Div. of Mineral Resources, 1907-15, dir. Anthracite Bur. of Information, Phila., 1915-37. Expert special agent 12th U.S. Census; mem. Anthracite Coal Strike Commn., 1902. Mem. Am. Inst. Mining and Metall. Engrs., Washington Acad. Sciences, Geol. Soc. Washington, Washington Soc. Engrs., Coal Mining Inst. America, Acad. Polit. Science. Clubs: Cosmos (Washington); Engineers (New York); Westmoreland; Engineers, Midday, Merion Cricket (Phila.). Author: Annual Reports on Production of Coal in United States; Production of Coke in United States, and other chapters in annual vols. U.S. Geol. Survey; also reports on coal mining, coke mfg. and petroleum refining for U.S. Census. Home: 136 W. Upsal St., Mount Airy, Phila. Office: 225 S. 15th St., Philadelphia, Pa.

PARKER, Frank; prof. of finance, University of Pa. Address: University of Pa., Philadelphia, Pa.

PARKER, Frank Claveloux, ophthalmologist; b. Norristown, Pa., Nov. 3, 1878; s. Albert Bean and Mary (Hess) P.; grad. Norristown High Sch.; M.D., U. of Pa., 1899; m. Mabel H. Craft; children—Mary Louise (Mrs. Daniel Sinclair, 3d), Clement C., Frank C. Resident surgeon Wills Hosp., Phila., 1899—; later clin. asst. Wills Hosp., Howard Hosp., Polyclinic Hosp., Children's Hosp., Phila.; ophthalmologist State Hosp., Norristown, Pa., since 1902, Charity Hosp., Norristown, since 1908; asst. surgeon Wills Hosp., 1903-22; ophthalmologist Montgomery Hosp. and State Hosp., Norristown, since 1902; attending surgeon and pres. of staff Wills Hosp.; pres. of staff Montgomery Hosp.; cons. ophthalmologist Memorial Hosp. Served as mem. advisory bd., Selective Service, during World War. Fellow Am. Coll. Surgeons; mem. Montgomery Co. Med. Soc. (pres. 19—), Pa. State Med. Soc., A.M.A., Sigma Alpha Epsilon. Republican. Mason. Clubs: Schuylkill Valley Medical, Phila. Medical, Rotary (past pres.). Home: 42 N. Whitehall Rd. Office: 1 W. Main St., Norristown, Pa.

PARKER, Frank Wilson, agronomist; b. Hamilton, Ill., Aug. 23, 1897; s. Sanford R. and Victoria (Wilson) P.; B.S., Ala. Poly. Inst., Auburn, Ala., 1918; Ph.D., U. of Wis., Madison, Wis., 1921; m. Ruth M. Talbot, 1922; children—Jean Talbot, Robert Wilson, Victoria Ann. Asst. prof. Ala. Poly. Inst., Auburn, Ala., 1922-25, asso. prof., 1925-27, prof., 1927-29; agronomist E. I. du Pont de Nemours & Co., Wilmington, Del., since 1929. Baptist. Home: Phila. Pike and Ridge Rd. Office: E. I. du Pont de Nemours & Co., Wilmington, Del.

PARKER, Henry Griffith, banker; b. New Brunswick, N.J., Sept. 2, 1866; s. William and Ann (Griffith) P.; ed. high sch. New Brunswick; hon. A.M., Rutgers U., 1920; m. Alice Florence Parker, 1896; 1 son, Henry Griffith. Chmn. bd. Nat. Bank of N.J., Interwoven Stocking Co.; v.p. New Brunswick Savings Instn.; dir. Prudential Ins. Co. of America (finance com.), New Brunswick Fire Ins. Co. (exec. com.); pres. Middlesex County (N.J.) Sinking Fund Commn. Trustee Rutgers Univ. (chmn. finance com.), N.J. Bankers Assn. Republican. Episcopalian. Home: 165 College Av. Office: 390 George St., New Brunswick, N.J.

PARKER, J. Brooks B., aviation and gen. insurance; b. Phila., Pa., Dec. 25, 1889; s. Alvin Afflick and Annie Catherine (Bloodgood) P.; prep. edn. The Haverford (Pa.) Sch., St. Luke's Sch., Wayne, Pa.; B.S., U. of Pa., 1911; unmarried. With Chubb & Son, marine ins., New York, 1911-14; asst. dir. War Risks Ins. Treas. Dept., Washington, D.C., 1914-16; asst. sec.-gen. Pan. Am. Financial Conf., Washington, D.C., 1915; asst. sec. of Am. del. of Internat. High Commn. of Uniformity of Laws Conf., Buenos Aires, 1916; asst. sec. Am.-Mexican Joint Commn. on Arbitration for State Dept., 1916; insurance, own company, Phila., 1919-20; partner Parker, Rulon-Miller & Co., insurance, Phila., 1922-25; pres. and owner Parker & Co., aviation and gen. ins., Phila. and New York, since 1925; dir. Jacobs Aircraft Engine Co. Served as 1st lt. and pilot, Air Service, U.S. Army, 1917-18. Assisted in formation of Nat. Air Transport, 1925. and in merger forming Transcontinental & Western Air, Inc., 1930; effected separation of Eastern Air Lines from North American Aviation Corpn.; ins. brokers for many of the large aviation companies; apptd. tech. adviser to U.S. Delegation 4th Diplomatic Conf. on Air Law, Brussels, Sept. 1938. Mem. bd. of govs. Seamen's Ch. Inst., Phila.; mem. bd. Geneal. Soc. Pa. Mem. Inst. of Aeronautical Sciences, Nat. Fire Protection Assn., Aeronautical Chamber of Commerce, Aviation Com. of Phila., Pa. Soc. of Colonial Wars, Sons of the Revolution, Colonial Soc. of Pa., Soc. of War 1812, Mil. Order of Foreign Wars, Mil. Order Loyal Legion, Netherlands Soc., Friars (U. of Pa.). Decorated Comdr. Shereefian Order of Ouissam Alaouite (France); medal of City of Paris. Republican. Episcopalian. Clubs: Racquet, Merion Cricket, Radnor Hunt (Phila.); Down Town, Uptown (New York). Mem. U.S. Olympic Fencing Team in foil, duelling sword and saber, 1920, in sabers, 1924; mem. Am. Team in Brit.-Am. fencing matches, 1921. Home: Strafford, Delaware County, Pa. Office: 1616 Walnut St., Philadelphia, Pa.; 100 E. 42d St., New York, N.Y.

PARKER, Roswell James, engr.; b. Williamsport, Pa., Feb. 9, 1903; s. Roy W. and Fanny (Roosa) P.; ed. Ga. Inst. Tech. and Pa. State Coll.; m. Margery Thomas, July 30, 1938. Chief inspector highway construction, Pa. Dept. Highways, 1925-31; engr.-supt. Sweeney Bros. Scranton (all branches bldg. construction), 1931-35; head WPA projects survey sewers, boundaries, etc., 1935-37; engr. Moosic Boro (Pa.) Sewer Construction since 1937; pres. and dir. Parmac Oil Transmitting Condenser Co.; dir. Scranton Radio & Television Supply Co. Mem. Am. Radio Relay League. Republican. Presbyterian. Mason. Club: Electric City Radio. Home: 1217 Linden St., Scranton, Pa.

PARKER, Terry, lawyer; b. Atchison, Kan., Nov. 1, 1870; s. James Williams and Ann Amelia (Terry) P.; student Atchison Latin and Atchison pub. schs.; attended Yale Coll., 1889-91; LL.B., Columbia Law Sch., 1894; m. Cora Whittingham, Apr. 20, 1920. Admitted to N.Y. bar, 1894, N.J. bar, 1902; became counsellor and Master in Chancery, 1909, Supreme Court Examiner, 1913; admitted to practice before Federal cts. in N.Y., 1899, U.S. Supreme Ct., 1926; now also practices as patent atty., etc. Mem. Essex Troop (now First Troop), 1903-09; 2d lt. 1st Regt. Inf., N.J.N.G., 1919, 1st lt. and batt. adj., 1910-16; Mexican Border duty, 1916, Ordnance officer; police duty Jersey City Heights, Sept. 1917; first trial judge advocate, gen. ct. martial, Camp McClellan, Anniston, Ala., Nov. 5, 1917; promoted to major and asst. div. judge advocate; hon. discharged, Nov. 2, 1918. Mem. Essex Co. Republican Com. Mem. N.Y. State Bar Assn. Mason. Home: 43 N. Walnut St., East Orange, N.J. Office: 60 Beaver St., New York, N.Y.

PARKER, William Ainsworth; mem. law firm Parker & Doub. Office: First Nat. Bank Bldg., Baltimore, Md.

PARKER, William Alden, engr.; b. Middletown, Del., Aug. 22, 1901; s. William Reese and Helen York (Slaughter) P.; ed. Lehigh U.; married. Began as draftsman Baldwin Locomotive Works, 1918; machinist Heller & Brightly, 1918, Wilcox & Gibbs, 1918-19; draftsman Baldwin Locomotive Works, summer, 1919; inspector Western Electric Co., 1921; machinist H. S. Ayers, 1921; draftsman H. C. Jesnick, 1921; designer Jackquard Knitting Machine Co., 1922; draftsman David Lupton Sons Co., 1923; designer Smith Drum Co., 1924; with Collins & Aikman Corpn. since Aug. 1924, chief engr. since 1932. Registered professional engr. in Pa., 1934. Republican. Protestant. Club: Bala Golf. Contbr. to Industrial Power. Home: 2495 N. 50th St. Office: 51st and Parkside Av., West Philadelphia, Pa.

PARKER, William M., judge; b. Oil City, Pa., Dec. 19, 1870; s. George N. and Rebecca (McCready) P.; grad. Oil City High Sch., 1886; A.B., Princeton, 1891; LL.D., Grove City Coll.; m. Helen Innis, Apr. 21, 1898; children—Helen Elizabeth (dec.), Marian (Mrs. John H. Johnson), Warren I., Rebecca M. (Mrs. Harry E. Cummins), William M. Admitted to Pennsylvania bar, 1895, and in general practice, 1895-1926; judge Common Pleas Court, Senango Co., 1926-32; judge Superior Court of Pa. since 1932. Republican. Presbyterian. Home: 305 W. 4th St., Oil City, Pa.

PARKER, William Newman, clergyman; b. Chattanooga, Tenn., Mar. 4, 1878; s. Robert Humphrey and Elizabeth (Newman) P.; A.B., Duke Univ., 1899; B.D., Drew Theol. Sem., 1905; study Phila. Divinity Sch., 1905-06; m. Mary Roberts Chester, Nov. 28, 1905. Ordained to ministry P.E. Ch., deacon, 1906, priest, 1906; rector Ch. of the Epiphany, Sherwood, Phila., Pa., continuously since 1906. Democrat. Episcopalian. Home: 826 S. 60th St., Philadelphia, Pa.

PARKIN, Francis Rogers, banking; b. Flushing, N.Y., Aug. 25, 1893; s. H. Grenville and Louisa (Ford) P.; student Peddie Sch., Hightstown, N.J., 1911-12, Princeton U., 1912-14; m. Effie M. Miller, Feb. 3, 1916; children—Emily Miller (Mrs. Frank B. Martin, Jr.), Bettine Winthrop. In employ Irving Savings Bank, N.Y. City, 1914-15; clerk Union Trust Co., N.Y. City, 1915-17, Mercantile Trust Co., N.Y. City, 1917-22; asst. cashier Seaboard Nat. Bank, N.Y. City, 1922-27; vice-pres. Equitable Trust Co., N.Y. City, 1927-30; vice-pres. Chase Nat. Bank, N.Y. City, since 1930; vice-pres. and dir. First Nat. Bank, Bound Brook, N.J., since 1929. Mem. Key and Seal, Princeton. Conglist. Clubs: Lawyers (New York); Raritan Valley Country (Somerville). Home: Canal Rd., Bound Brook, N.J. Office: 115 Broadway, New York, N.Y.

PARKIN, William (Metcalf), chem. engr.; b. Pittsburgh, Pa., Dec. 25, 1877; s. Charles and Anna (Dravo) P.; student Kisky Sch.; A.B., Stanford (Calif.) U., 1901; A.M. and E.M., Columbia U., 1902; m. Jessie Haskell, June 21, 1905; children—William Metcalf, Fred H. Engaged as steel maker, later chemist and salesman; organized The Wm. M. Parkin Company, chem. engrs., Pittsburgh. Mem. Am. Soc. for Metals, Wire Assn. Engring. Soc. of Pa., Sigma Alpha Epsilon. Republican. Methodist. Mason (32°, Shriner). Clubs: Duquesne, Pittsburgh Field (Pittsburgh). Home: 5577 Hampton St. Office: 1102 Highland Bldg., Pittsburgh, Pa.

PARKINS, George Victor, steel mfr.; pres. McKeesport Tin Plate Corpn.; dir. Potter-McCune Co., Pittsburgh & W.Va. Ry. Co. Home: Mt. Vernon Rd., Elizabeth Township, Pa. Office: McKeesport, Pa.

PARKINSON, Chauncey Wiley, mgr. Huffman Furniture & Undertaking Co.; b. Ninevah, Pa., July 20, 1886; s. John L. and Carolyn (Simpson) P.; student California (Pa.) State Teachers Coll. and Waynesburg (Pa.) Coll.; m. Inez N. Huffman, Sept. 29, 1909; children—Helen, Tom, Carolyn, Jo, Martha. Mgr. Huffman Furniture & Undertaking Co., Waynesburg, Pa., since 1915. Mem. Pa. Gen. Assembly, 1922-26, Pa. State Senate, 1926-34. Dir. Waynesburg Sch. Bd. Trustee Waynesburg Coll. Mem. Chamber of Commerce. Odd Fellow, Mason, Elk. Clubs: Green County Country. Home: 61 N. Richhill. Office: 146 E. High St., Waynesburg, Pa.

PARKINSON, William Nimon, surgeon; b. Philadelphia, Pa., Sept. 17, 1886; s. Walter and Sarah (Nimon) P.; B.S., Villanova (Pa.) Coll., 1907; M.D., Temple U., 1911; M.S., in Medicine, U. of Pa., 1925; unmarried. Asst. surgeon Joseph Price Hosp., Philadelphia, 1912-17; surgeon Montgomery Hosp., Norristown, Pa., 1922-25; chief surgeon Fla. East Coast Hosp., St. Augustine, Fla., 1926-28; prof. clin. surgery, Temple U. since 1928, dean of med. dept. since 1928 and v.p. of the university since 1937; medical director Temple U. Hosps. since 1928. Capt. Med. Corps, U.S.A., World War. Fellow Am. Coll. Surgeons; mem. A.M.A., Pa. State and Philadelphia Co. med. socs., Phi Chi. Republican. Baptist. Clubs: Phila. Country, Union League. Home: Cambridge Apts., Germantown, Philadelphia, Pa.

PARKS, Joseph Walter, propr. J. W. Parks & Sons; b. Keyser, W.Va., May 20, 1881; s. Joseph Reuben and Alice Caroline P.; student pub. schs., Altoona Business Coll. and Kings Sch., Pittsburgh; m. Viola Elnora Moore, Feb. 9, 1908; children—Robert Richard, Raymond Walter, Betty Joanne. Propr. J. W. Parks & Sons, poultry farms; chmn. First Nat. Bank, Juniata, Pa.; dir. Security Bldg. & Loan Co. Served as twp. clk., road supervisor, and county committeeman; mem. Pa. State Legislature, 1935-36. Mem. Agrl. Extension Bd.; dir. Child Welfare Bd.; chmn. Consolidated Sch. Bldg. Com. Awarded Pa. Master Farmer gold medal. Ex-pres. Blair County Road Supervisors' Assn., Civic Assn., Pa. State Poultry Assn. Lecturer on wild life and value of healthful vacations. Adopted into Winnebago Tribe, 1931; said to be first white man taken into Thunderbird Klan. Home: Altoona, Pa.

PARKS, Lytle Raymond, prof. of chemistry and dir. of the Chem. Labs., Pa. State Coll.; b. Aurora, Ind., Apr. 13, 1890; s. Joseph Gray and Julia (Ross) P.; B.S. in chem. engring., Purdue U., 1912; M.S., Pa. State Coll., 1914; Ph.D., Cornell U. 1927; m. Mabel Pauline Boyer, Sept. 2, 1915; children—Lytle Raymond, Sara Jean, Mabel Overholt. Instr. in chemistry, Pa. State Coll., 1913-16, asst. prof., 1916-20, asso. prof., 1920-27, prof. of chemistry and dir. of chem. labs. since 1927; pres. Park Dairies, processors and distributors of dairy products, Camden, N.J. Mem. Am. Chem. Soc., Sigma Xi, Phi Lambda Upsilon, Alpha Chi Sigma. Republican. Baptist. Mason (K.T., 32°, Shriner). Clubs: Centre Hills Country (State College, Pa.); Acacia (Williamsport). Contbr. of several articles on chemistry to scientific jours. Home: 141 E. Fairmount Av., State College, Pa.

PARKS, Samuel McLaughlin, Jr., golf professional; b. Hopedale, O., June 23, 1909; s. Samuel McLaughlin and Faye (Watson) P.; student Bellevue (Pa.) High Sch. and Pa. State Coll.; B.S., U. of Pittsburgh, 1931; m. Jean P. Davison, Dec. 31, 1936; 1 son, Harry Davison. Golf professional South Hills Country Club, Pittsburgh. Former mem. Ryder Cup Team; winner Nat. Open Golf Championship, 1936. Republican. Presbyterian. Home: 1270 Beechwood Boul., Pittsburgh, Pa.

PARLIN, Wellington A(mos), prof. physics; b. Des Moines, Ia., Jan. 19, 1899; s. Charles Wellington and Alice (Price) P.; A.B., Simpson Coll., 1921; M.S., U. of Ia., 1922, post-grad. work, 1923; post-grad work, Johns Hopkins U., 1926, Ph.D., 1929; m. Ora Mae Gerling, Aug. 27, 1924; children—Elizabeth Ann, Virginia Lee, Barbara Louise. Instr. physics, Emory U., 1923-26; tech. asst., Johns Hopkins U., 1929-30; prof. physics, Dickinson Coll., since 1930. Mem. Am. Physical Soc., Pa. Acad. Science, Phi Beta Kappa, Sigma Xi. Republican. Methodist. Author: The Torques and Forces Between Short Cylindrical Coils Carrying Alternating Currents of Radio Frequency, 1923; The Effect of Temperature on the Absorption Bands of Fused Quartz in the Infra Red, 1929; A Radiometer, 1930: A Method for Determining the Effect of Time and Temperature on the Distribution of Glycerin in a Vertical Column of Water, 1937; A Method for Determining the Ratio of the Effective and the Maximum Voltages of an A.C. Generator, 1937; A Simple Refractometer, 1938; A Device for Demonstrating the Difference in Sensitivity of the Eye to Red and Green Light, 1939. Home: 560 Walnut St., Carlisle, Pa.

PARR, Joseph Greer, banker; b. Jersey City, N.J., Dec. 11, 1881; s. James and Agnes (Greer) P.; ed. Jersey City High Sch., univ. extension courses, Am. Inst. of Banking; m. Florence Vreeland, June 12, 1913; 1 dau., Dorothy Vreeland. With Liberty Nat. Bank of N.Y., 1900-09; pres. Claremont Bank of Jersey City, 1909-29; exec. v.p. Trust Co. of N.J., Jersey City, 1929-34, pres. since 1934; pres. Park Trust Co., Weehawken, N.J.; pres. Trust Co. of N.J. in West New York (N.J.). Dir. Jersey City Chamber of Commerce (pres. 1931-34); former pres. Northern N.J. Clearing House Assn.; mem. N.J. Bankers Assn. (pres. Hudson Co. Group since 1935; mem. State exec. com.). Republican. Presbyterian. Mason (32°, Shriner). Clubs: Kiwanis (pres. 1931), Carteret (Jersey City); Rumson Country (Rumson, N.J.); Seabright Beach (Seabright, N.J.). Home: 276 Maple St., Englewood, N.J. Office: 35 Journal Square, Jersey City, N.J.

PARRISH, Herbert, clergyman; b. Grand Rapids, Mich., Sept. 13, 1867; s. Isaac Henry and Caroline (Cook) P.; A.B., Trinity Coll., Hartford, Conn., 1891, A.M., same, 1894; student, N.Y. Univ., Gen. Theol. Sem., U. of Pa., Johns Hopkins U., 1891-94; (hon.) D.D., Trinity Coll., 1928; m. Mary Sara Russell Mayo, June 20, 1911. Ordained to ministry P.E. Ch., deacon, 1894, priest, 1895; asst., St. Peter's Ch., Phila., 1894-95, St. Clement's Ch., Phila., 1895-98; rector chs. in San Francisco, Calif., 1898-1905; mission preacher, 1905-08; curate, All Saints Ch., London, Eng., 1908; rector, St. Luke's, Baltimore, Md., 1909-12; diocesan missioner of Md., 1912-14; rector, Christ Ch., New Brunswick, N.J., 1914-29; retired, 1929. Worked for Dept. of Justice during World War. Mem. Psi Upsilon. Republican. Episcopalian. Club: Union League (New York). Author: A New God for America; What is There Left to Believe? Home: 221 Graham St., New Brunswick, N.J.

PARRISH, Joseph Andrew, physician; b. Bellefonte, Pa., Mar. 14, 1904; s. Callistus Mitchell and Rose (Fox) P.; student Dickinson Coll., 1922-25; M.D., Jefferson Med. Coll.; 1929; m. Eleanor Catherine Lamb, Apr. 28, 1938. Interne Phila. Gen. Hosp., 1929-31; engaged in gen. practice of medicine at Bellefonte, Pa., since 1933, specializing in roentgenology since 1933; med. dir. Centre Co. since 1936; staff mem. Centre County Hosp. Mem. A.M.A., Pa. Med. Soc., Centre Co. Med. Soc. (pres. 1937-38), Phi Kappa Psi, Alpha Kappa Kappa, Alpha Omega Alpha. Democrat. Catholic. Clubs: Kiwanis, Nittany Country. Home: 30 W. High St., Bellefonte, Pa.

PARRISH, Morris Longstreth, securities brokerage; b. Phila., Pa., Nov. 5, 1867; s. George Dillwyn and Sarah Longstreth (Price) P.; ed. Friends Sch., Penn Charter Sch., Chase Sch., all of Phila., and Princeton U. (Class of 1888). Has been engaged in business of securities brokerage since 1888, mem. firm Parrish & Co., brokers, and mem. Phila. Stock Exchange since 1900 and New York Stock Exchange since 1910. Dir. Library Co. of Phila. Republican. Mem. Religious Soc. of Friends. Clubs: Philadelphia, Rabbit, Pine Valley Golf (Philadelphia); Knickerbocker, Grolier (New York). Home: Pine Valley, N.J. Office: 212 S. 15th St., Philadelphia, Pa.

PARROT, Raymond Townley, lawyer; b. Elizabeth, N.J., Mar. 15, 1880; s. George Townley and Ella (Tichenor) P.; student Pingry Sch., Elizabeth, N.J., 1893-98; Princeton U., 1898-1902; New York Law Sch., 1902-04; m. Madeleine Chapman, June 6, 1920; 1 dau., Jane. Admitted to N.J. bar, June 1905, counsellor, 1908; began practice in Elizabeth, N.J.; mem. firm Parrot & Parrot, now Parrot & Gidley; dir. Union County Trust Co. (Elizabeth); Citizens Trust Co. (Summit); atty. Union Co. Savings Bank; dir. Motor Finance Co. Former mem. Essex Troop, Newark, N.J.; mem. O.T.C., Camp Zachary Taylor, Ky., 1918. Former mem. Bd. of Health, Elizabeth; pres. N.J. Commn. for the Blind since 1932; mem. University Glee Club of New York City. Republican. Presbyterian. Clubs: Suburban Golf (Union, N.J.); Tuscarora (Millbrook, N.Y.). Home: 50 Ox Bow Lane, Summit, N.J. Office: 125 Broad St., Elizabeth, N.J.

PARROTT, Thomas Marc, univ. prof.; b. Dayton, O., Dec. 22, 1866; s. Col. Edwin A. and Mary May (Thomas) P.; A.B., Princeton, 1888, A.M., 1891; Ph.D., Leipzig, 1893; m. Mary Adamson, July 18, 1895; children—D'Arcy, Lindesay Marc, Frances Mary. Prin. prep. dept. Miami U., Oxford, O., 1888-90; studied 3 yrs. in Germany; apptd. English fellow, Princeton, 1893-94; taught English and German, Lawrenceville (N.J.) Sch., 1894-96; asst. prof. English, 1896-1902, prof., 1902-35, Princeton University, now emeritus; at Vanderbilt Univ., 1935-36. Mem. Phi Beta Kappa Fraternity. Presbyn. Progressive. Clubs: Princeton (New York and Phila.), Nassau (Princeton). Editor: (with introductions and notes) Macaulay's Essays on Milton and Addison, 1901; English Poems, from Chaucer to Kipling (with A. W. Long), 1902; Shakespeare's Merchant of Venice, 1903; Shakespeare's Macbeth, 1904; Pope's Rape of the Lock and Other Poems, 1906; Chapman's All Fools and The Gentleman Usher, 1907; Chapman's Tragedies, 1910; Shakespeare's Othello, 1912; Chapman's Comedies, 1914; Poetry of the Transition (with Willard Thorp); William Shakespeare—A Handbook; Shakespeare—Twenty-Threee Plays and Ten Sonnets (with general introduction and notes); A Critical Edition of Hamlet, Quarto Two (with Hardin Craig). Author: Studies of a Book-Lover, 1904. Address: Lawrenceville, N.J.

PARRY, Florence Fisher, columnist; b. Brookville, Pa., July 5, 1887; d. Jacob Livengood and Carrie Ella (Wilson) Fisher; prep. edn., Mrs. Smallwood's Select Sch., Washington, D.C., 1900-05; student Wheatcroft Dramatic Sch., N. Y. City, 1906-07; studied journalism, New York U., 1916; m. David William Parry, June 8, 1915 (died 1922); children—David Fisher, Florence Fisher. On stage as leading woman with Alla Nazimova, Walker Whiteside, Otis Skinner and others, 1907-15; actively identified with photography since 1923, now proprietor of the Parry Studio, Pittsburgh; began writing for Pittsburgh newspapers, 1925; now columnist (2 columns) daily, Pittsburgh Press, "I Dare Say," and "On With the Show," also dramatic critic; lecturer on the drama, etc.; broadcaster. Mem. League of Am. Pen Women, D.A.R. Republican. Baptist. Clubs: Woman's City, Woman's Press, Monday Luncheon. Home: 703 St. James St. Address: Parry Studio, 610 Smithfield St., Pittsburgh, Pa.

PARRY, George Gowen, judge; b. New York, N.Y., Dec. 4, 1874; s. Henry Chester and Martha Frazer (Harris) P.; student Germantown Acad. and Harvard (class of 1897); m. Flora Lockwood, Oct. 14, 1905 (died Feb. 1, 1907); 1 son, George Gowan; m. 2d, Sara Fox, April 27, 1912; children—Edward Owen, Henry Frazer, Richard, Francis Fox, John Collins, Stephen Harris. Admitted to Pa. bar, 1906; apptd. judge Court of Common Pleas, 1st Judicial Dist. of Pa., Jan. 26, 1932. Served as capt. and adjutant, 2d Pa. Nat. Guard, and major and adjutant gen., U.S. Army, 1917-19. Episcopalian. Clubs: Harvard, University (Phila.). Home: 8005 Crefeld St. Office: 242 City Hall, Philadelphia, Pa.

PARSON, Hubert Templeton, ex-pres. F. W. Woolworth Co.; b. Toronto, Sept. 18, 1872; s. Henry Edwin and Eliza S. (McGibben) P.; ed. high sch., Brooklyn, N.Y.; m. Maysie Adelaide Gasque, Oct. 1893. Began, 1892, as accountant with F. W. Woolworth Co., five and ten cent stores; advanced through various positions to sec., treas., gen. mgr., and was pres., 1919-32; retired under age limit of 60 yrs. Republican. Baptist. Club: Crescent Athletic. Home: Shadow Lawn, West End, N.J.; and 72 Av. Foch, Paris, France.

PARSON, Willard Sigsbee, physician; b. Mt. Jewett, Pa., Mar. 31, 1898; s. Elmer S. and Sarah Jane (Cisney) P.; student U. of Mich.,

Ann Arbor, 1916-18, O. Northern U., Ada, O., 1918-19, U. of Md. Med. Sch., Baltimore, 1919-22; M.D., Med. Coll. of Va., 1924; m. Mildred Welch, June 28, 1922; children—Willard Russell, James Sigsbee. Physician Gas & Electric Co., Baltimore, 1924-26; surgeon B.&O. R.R. Co. since 1927; pediatrician Robert Garrett Hosp. since 1926, St. Agnes Hosp. since 1930; on hosp. staff, Bon Secours, St. Agnes, Md. Gen., South Baltimore, West Baltimore hosps.; ins. examiner, Prudential Life Ins. Co., Acacia, Life Extension Inst. Served as private, U.S.A., 1919. Fellow Am. Med. Assn. Mem. Med. & Chirurg. Faculty of Md., Baltimore Co. Med. Soc., Phi Beta Pi, Theta Nu Epsilon, Am. Legion. Democrat. Mem. M.E. Ch. Mason. Club: Rolling Road Golf and Country (Baltimore). Home: Halethorpe, Baltimore, Md.

PARSONS, Dickson Ward, coll. prof.; b. Rich Mountain, W.Va., Aug. 21, 1881; s. Job Ward and Mary Jane (Ewing) P.; A.B., W.Va. Univ., 1905; M.S., U. of Wis., 1918; Ph.D., Cornell U., 1930; m. Ethel Vivian Parsons, June 25, 1910; children—Norman Welbec, Harold Ewing, Alice Virginia, Winona June. Began as teacher sci. and mathematics, high sch., Lake Charles, La., 1905-07, prep. sch., Montgomery, W.Va., 1907-15; supt. and prin. Kingwood, W.Va., 1915-17; co. agrl. agt. Lewis Co., W. Va., 1918-20; prin. and vocational agr., high sch., Shinnston, W.Va., 1920-23; supervisor vocational, agr., W.Va., 1923-26; teacher trainer, vocational agr., W.Va. Univ., Morgantown, 1926-33; teacher trainer and head dept. rural orgn., W.Va. Univ. Coll. Agr., Morgantown, W.Va., since 1933. Mem. A.A.A.S., Am. Vocational Assn., W.Va. State Edn. Assn., Phi Delta Kappa. Presbyn. Mason. Clubs: Cornell, Wisconsin (Morgantown). Home: 1239 College Av., Morgantown, W.Va.

PARSONS, Lewis Morgan, steel mfr.; b. Phila., Pa., Jan. 9, 1898; s. Alonzo and Romelia (Morgan) P.; student William Penn Charter Sch., Phila., 1905-15, U. of Pa., 1915-17, Mass. Inst. Tech., 1918; m. Marion Park, Nov. 8, 1921; 1 daughter, Marion. With Bethlehem Steel Corporation, 1919-38, Philadelphia manager sales, 1936-38; vice-president and gen. mgr. sales Jones & Laughlin Steel Corpn., Pittsburgh, Pa., since 1938, dir. since 1938. Republican. Baptist. Clubs: Duquesne (Pittsburgh); Union League, Racquet, Phila. Country, Germantown Cricket (Phila.); Athletic (Detroit, Mich.); Cloud (New York); Oakmont Country (Oakmont, Pa.); Pine Valley Golf (Clementon, N.J.). Home: Hillbrook Rd., Haverford, Pa. Office: Third Av. and Ross St., Pittsburgh, Pa.

PARSONS, Louis S.; surgeon Delaware Hosp.; asso. surgeon Delaware State Hosp., Farnhurst, Del. Address: 925 Jefferson St., Wilmington, Del.

PARSONS, Theodore Dwight, lawyer; b. La Crosse, Wis., May 24, 1894; s. Dwight L. and Minnie E. (Payne) P.; A.B., Princeton U., 1915; student Columbia U. Law Sch., 1918; m. Margaret Morford, Nov. 6, 1934; children—Theodore Dwight, Jr., John M. Admitted to N.J. bar as atty., 1919, counsellor, 1922; in gen. practice of law at Red Bank since 1920; now mem. firm Parsons, Labrecque & Borden; dir. Boro Buses, Inc., Investment Realty Co., Plastics, Inc. Served as 2d lt. A.S., U.S.A., 1917-19, with A.E.F. Gov. Monmouth Council Boy Scouts, Monmouth Memorial Hosp.; trustee Riverview Hosp., Shrewsbury Post Am. Legion. Mem. Am., N.J. State and Monmouth Co. bar assns., Zeta Psi. Republican. Presbyn. Mason. Elk. Clubs: Lions (Red Bank); Ice Boat (Shrewsbury); Boat (Monmouth); Golf (Norwood). Home: Branch Av., Little Silver, N.J. Office: 18 Wallace St., Red Bank, N.J.

PARTCH, Clarence Elmar, coll. dean; b. Rock Rapids, Ia., Mar. 12, 1884; s. Merritt Orville and Carrie M. (Schroeder) P.; B.S. in M.E., U. of Mich., 1909; Ed.M., Harvard, 1925, Ed.D., 1926; m. Vera Howard, July 31, 1912. Teacher, high sch., Des Moines, Ia., 1909-18; in soldier rehabilitation work, 1918-22; teacher training work, Northwest Mo. State Teachers Coll., 1922-24; instr. in edn., Grad. Sch., Harvard, 1925-26; asso. prof. edn., Rutgers, 1926-27, prof. edn., dean of Sch. of Edn. and dir. of summer session since 1927. Mem. N.E.A., Nat. Vocational Guidance Assn., Nat. Soc. Coll. Teachers of Edn., Nat. Soc. for Study of Edn., Nat. Econ. League, Eastern Coll. Personnel Officers Assn., Phi Beta Kappa, Sigma Xi, Phi Delta Kappa. Mason. Clubs: Michigan (New York); Kiwanis (New Brunswick). Author: Information for Prospective College Students, 1926; Case Studies in Educational and Vocational Guidance (with J. M. Brewer and others), 1926; Cases in the Administration of Guidance (with J. M. Brewer and others), 1929. Contbr. to Industrial Arts Mag., Survey, School and Society. Home: Stelton, N.J.

PARTRIDGE, Emelyn Newcomb (Mrs. George Everett Partridge), author, clinical psychologist; b. Black Rock, Kings Co., N.S.; d. Asaph Wallace and Marietta Wickwire (Eaton) Newcomb; ed. Northfield (Mass.) Sem. and Clark U.; fellow in psychology, Clark, 1920-21; m. George Everett Partridge, Aug. 31, 1898; children—Elaine Newcomb (dec.), Miriam Newcomb (Mrs. John Raymond Speck), Philip Newcomb. Widely known as story teller. Pvt. practice as clin. psychologist, Boston, 1921-25; classified group of feeble-minded and organized school for Phila. Hosp. Mental Diseases, 1925-26; assisted Dr. G. E. Partridge in study of drug addicts, Phila., also in survey of Md. Training Sch. for Boys; asst. in classification clinic Dept. of Special Education, Baltimore, 1930-33. Episcopalian. Author: Story Telling in School and Home (with husband), 1912 (Russian translation), Glooscap the Great Chief, 1913; Joyful Star (Indian stories for Camp Fire Girls), 1915; also brochures: A Study of Psychopathic Personality Among Delinquent Boys (with Dr. Partridge), 1928, and a Manual of Instructions for the Administration of Certain Performance Tests, 1931. Contbr. series of articles to Boston Sunday Globe on the intelligence of the preschool child. Home: Rugby Hall, Baltimore, Md.

PARTRIDGE, George Everett, psychologist; b. Worcester, Mass., May 31, 1870; s. George and Sarah Boyden (Capron) P.; Harvard, 1889-90; Ph.D., Clark U., 1899; m. Emelyn Smythe Newcomb, Aug. 31, 1898; children—Elaine Newcomb (dec.), Miriam Newcomb (Mrs. John R. Speck), Philip Newcomb. Instructor psychology, State Normal School, Mankato, Minn., 1900-1903; lecturer Clark University, 1904-06; psychologist, Pa. Hosp., Phila., 1923-26; for Phila. Com. for the Clinical Study of Opium Addiction, 1926; for Sing Sing Prison Jan.-Sept. 1927; clin. research, The Sheppard & Enoch Pratt Hosp., Baltimore, Oct. 1927-30; psychopathologist Md. Training Sch. for Boys, 1927—; psychologist Md. Penitentiary, 1930-31; dir. Classification and Clin. Service, Dept. of Prisons, Md., 1931-35; research in psychopathic personality and delinquency. Author: An Outline of Individual Study, 1910; The Nervous Life, 1911; Studies in the Psychology of Intemperance, 1912; Story-Telling in School and Home (with wife), 1912; Genetic Philosophy of Education (an epitome of ednl. writings of Pres. G. Stanley Hall), 1912 (Japanese transl.); A Reading Book in Modern Philosophy, 1913; The Psychology of Nations, 1919. Contbr. to scientific jours. Address: 526 W. University Parkway, Roland Park, Baltimore, Md.

PASMA, Henry Kay, clergyman, author; b. Oosterbierum, Friesland, Netherlands; s. Claus Peter and Clarissa (Nauta) P.; student Rutgers Coll., New Brunswick, N.J.; A.B., Hope Coll., Holland, Mich., 1910, A.M., 1913; grad. Western Theol. Sem., Holland, Mich., 1913; Ph.D., George Washington University, 1929; m. Olive Lucy Barnaby, May 21, 1913; children—Miriam Clarissa, Theodore Kay, Timothy Worden, Harriet Blanche (dec.). Came to U.S., 1899, naturalized citizen, 1913. Ordained ministry Ref. Ch. in America, 1913; pastor Oostburg, Wis., and Lynden, Wash., until 1922, Southern Presbyn. Ch., Charleston, Miss., 1922-27, Presbyn. Ch., Rockville, Md., since 1927. Mem. bd. dirs. Wis. Memorial Acad., Cedar Grove, Wis., 1915-17; mem. Council of Hope Coll., 1921-22; stated clk. Classis of Cascades, Ref. Ch. of America, 1920-22; moderator Presbytery of Potomac, 1936. Fellow Am. Geog. Soc.; mem. Pi Gamma Mu. Mason. Club: Rockville Rotary (pres. 1937-38). Author: Things a Nation Lives By, 1925; God's Picked Young Men, 1926; Close-Hauled, 1930; The Enchanted Sword, 1932; also articles in mags. and religious periodicals. Home: Rockville, Md.

PATCH, James Bradford, chem. engr.; b. Boston, Mass., Apr. 1, 1887; s. James Edwin and Ellen Amelia (Davis) P.; B.S., Worcester Poly. Inst., 1910; m. Helen M. Gillette, June 19, 1914; children—James Bradford, Jr., Arthur Herbert, Carol Lee. Chemist in glass factory, 1910-15; abstractor of fgn. jours. (French and German) for Chemical Abstracts pub. by Am. Chem. Soc., 1912-22; chemist and chem. engr., Whitall, Tatum Co., 1915-38, Armstrong Cork Co., Millville, N.J., since 1938. Served in Home Guards and State Militia during World War. Pres. Good Govt. League. Treas. and past pres. Millville Public Library. Officer various capacities Cumberland Council Boy Scouts of America, scoutmaster, 1911-12. Pres. Cumberland Co. Christian Endeavor Union, 1913-14. Mem. A.A. A.S., Am. Chem. Soc., Am. Ceramics Soc. Republican. Presbyn. Mason (K.T.; Master, Past High Priest and Trustee of York Rite). Clubs: Millville Racquet, Shekinah Glee (Millville); Engineers, Worcester Tech. (Philadelphia). Home: 206 Howard St. Office: care Armstrong Cork Co., S. 2d St., Millville, N.J.

PATCH, Richard Harkness, mfg. oils and leathers; b. Fitchburg, Mass., Apr. 15, 1888; s. Arthur and Jennie M. (Connor) P.; A.B., Harvard, 1910, Ph.D., Harvard, 1914; m. Elizabeth W. Remsen, Sept. 7, 1918; children—Elizabeth A., Priscilla R. Employed as chemist with R. L. Emerson Labs., Boston, 1909-10; Austin Teaching Fellow, Harvard, 1910-14; with Midvale Steel Co., Phila., Pa., in various capacities, 1914-26; asso. with E. F. Houghton & Co., mfrs. oils and leathers, Phila., Pa., continuously since 1926, dir. of plants since 1929, treas. since 1934, vice-pres. since 1936; vice-pres. E. F. Houghton & Co. of Can., Ltd.; vice-pres., treas. Anglo-American Chemical Corpn.; dir. Lubri-Zol Sales Co. Mem. Am. Chem. Soc., Am. Soc. for Metals. Republican. Episcopalian. Clubs: Harvard, Old York Road Country. Home: 435 Newbold Rd., Jenkintown. Office: 240 W. Somerset St., Philadelphia, Pa.

PATERNOSTRO, Francis Harry, physician; b. Williamsport, Pa., Oct. 3, 1902; s. Domenick and Filomena (Floria) P.; B.S., Pa. State Coll., 1926; M.D., Temple U. Med. Sch., 1930; m. Alice R. Sullivan, Nov. 16, 1932; 1 son, Robert Francis. Interne, Williamsport Hosp., 1930-31; mem. staff Williamsport Hosp., Williamsport, Pa., since 1931. Served as 1st lt. Med. Corps Res., U.S.A., since 1926. Mem. Am. Med. Assn., Pa. State Med. Soc., Lycoming Med. Soc., Inter Collegiate Alumni Assn., Temple Alumni Assn., Pa. State Alumni Assn., Phi Chi. Republican. Roman Catholic. K.C., B.P. O.E. Clubs: Exchange, Booster, Wheel. Home: 807 Grampian Boul. Office: 3 W. Third St., Williamsport, Pa.

PATERSON, John, univ. prof.; b. Eskdalemuir, Scotland, Sept. 20, 1887; s. John and Jane (Jack) P.; M.A. (1st class honors), Glasgow (Scotland) U., 1910, Ph.D., 1931; B.D., Trinity Coll., Glasgow, 1914; came to U.S., 1931; m. Jane Wilson Wiseman, Aug. 22, 1914; children—John Christie, Anne Wilson, Arthur Renwick, Walter David. Minister, Penpont Ch., Dumfriesshire, Scotland, 1915-24, Bridgend Ch., Dumbarton, Scotland, 1924-31; prof. of Hebrew and Old Testament Exegesis, Drew U., Madison, N.J., since 1931. Mem. Am. Sch. Oriental Research, Am. Oriental Soc., Soc. Biblical Lit. and Exegesis. Presbyn. Mason. Address: 29 Academy Rd., Madison, N.J.

PATERSON, Robert, editor, author, lecturer; b. Bellefontaine, O., Nov. 1885; s. Robert and (Anne) Virginia (Sharpe) P.; ed. Charlotte Hall Mil. Acad., 1901-02, Maplewood Classical Sch., 1903-04, Ohio State U., 1905-06 and 1908; m. Eleanor de Bevoise Tunison, Oct. 27, 1926. Reporter Wilmington (Del.) Morning News, later Oklahoma City Oklahoman, 1909-10; sports editor, city editor Fargo (N.D.)

Forum, 1910-14; editor Atlanta (Ga.) branch Western Newspaper Union, 1914-15; became war corr. for several newspapers, 1915; Y.M.C.A. lecturer in France, 1918; successively research editor Searchlight Library Pub. Co., asst. to editor Current Opinion, asso. editor McClure Newspaper Syndicate, legislative corr. New York Herald Tribune and asst. to Bernarr Macfadden; lecturer since 1936; editor Our State, Newark, N.J., since 1939. Vice chmn. bd. mgrs. Army Y.M.C.A., Fort Jay, Governor's Island, N.Y., 1925-31; mem. Mayor's Com. to Welcome Distinguished Guests, New York, 1928-33. Served as private Tank Corps, U.S. Army, 1918; 2d lt. 244th C.A., N.Y. Nat. Guard, 1929-32. Mem. Am. Legion (county comdr. New York County 1924-25). Conservative Democrat. Episcopalian. Mason. Club: Lambs (New York). Author: Gas Buggy, 1933; Land of the Pilgrim's Pride, 1936. Contbr. to jours. and articles on North Dakota to These United States, 1924. Home: 299 Clinton Av. Office: 1060 Broad St., Newark, N.J.

PATON, Stewart, M.D.; b. N.Y. City, 1865; s. William and Anne Stavely (Agnew) P.; A.B., Princeton, 1886, A.M., 1889; M.D., Coll. Phys. and Surg. (Columbia), 1889; post-grad. study Germany and Italy; m. F. Margaret Halsey, 1892; children—F. Evelyn, William, R. Townley. Formerly asso. in psychiatry, Johns Hopkins, and dir. of lab., Sheppard and Enoch Pratt Hosp., Baltimore; lec. in neurobiology, Princeton U., in psychiatry, Columbia; consultant in mental hygiene and lecturer in psychiatry, Yale, 1926-28. Trustee Carnegie Instn., Washington. Fellow A.A.A.S.; mem. Am. Philos. Soc., Am. Neurol. Assn., N.Y. Acad. Medicine, Eugenics Research Assn. (pres. 1919). Club: Century (New York). Author: Text-Book of Psychiatry for Use of Students and Practitioners of Medicine; Education in Peace and War, 1919; Human Behavior, 1921; Signs of Sanity and the Principles of Mental Hygiene, 1922; Prohibiting Minds, 1932. Home: 208 Stratford Rd., Baltimore, Md.

PATON, William Kennell, banker; b. Paterson, N.J., Mar. 6, 1894; s. Dr. Thomas Lloyd and Katherine (Kennell) P.; grad. Phillips Exeter Acad., Exeter, N.H., 1911; B.A., Williams Coll., Williamstown, Mass., 1915; ensign, Res. Officers Sch., U.S. Naval Acad., 1918; m. Mary Elizabeth Bendig, Apr. 25, 1925; children—William Kennell, Frederick Bendig. Started as messenger boy Guaranty Trust Co. of N.Y., 1915, asst. to gen. mgr., 1919-21, sales mgr., Phila. Office, 1921-22, mgr., Newark (N.J.) Office, 1926-30; mgr. bond dept. Harrison, Smith & Co., Phila., 1922-26; v.p. The Paterson (N.J.) Savings Instn., 1930-38; spl. rep. B.&O. R.R. Co., New York, since 1938; vice-president and director Alexander Hamilton Hotel Corpn., Paterson, since 1933; treas., dir., and chmn. finance com. Fidelity Liquidating Trust, Ridgewood, N.J., since 1935. Served as ensign, U.S. Navy, during World War, aboard U.S.S. Louisiana with Atlantic Fleet. Treas. and dir. Y.M.C.A. of Paterson, N.J., since 1930; dir. Paterson Orphan Asylum since 1931. Mem. Theta Delta Chi. Republican. Episcopalian. Mason (Wayne Lodge 581, Pa.; Royal Arch, Montgomery Chapter, Ardmore, Pa.). Clubs: Essex, Bond of N.J. (Newark, N.J.); Williams (New York); Hamilton, The Forum, Exchange (Paterson, N. J.). Home: 659 E. 24th St., Paterson, N.J. Office: 25 Broadway, New York, N.Y.

PATRICK, Ruth (Mrs. Charles Hodge, 4th), associate curator and prof. of botany; b. Topeka, Kan., Nov. 26, 1907; d. Frank and Myrtle Maria (Jetmore) Patrick; student U. of Kan., 1925-26; B.S., Coker Coll., Harteville, S.C., 1929; M.S., U. of Va., 1931, Ph.D., 1934; m. Charles Hodge, 4th (Ph.D.), July 10, 1931. Tech. asst., Temple U., 1934-35; prof. of botany, Pa. Sch. of Horticulture, Ambler, Pa., since 1935; asso. curator Acad. of Natural Sciences, Phila., since 1938. Fellow A.A.A.S.; mem. Bot. Soc. of America, Torrey Bot. Club, Acad. Natural Sciences, Phila. Bot. Club, Geol. Soc. Phila., Leidy Microscopical Soc. (curator), Sigma Xi. Presbyterian. Asso. editor of Farmers Digest. Contbr. to professional jours. Home: 2119 Spruce St. Philadelphia, Pa.

PATRICK, W. Burton; city supt. of schs. at Orange. Address: Orange, N.J.

PATRICK, Walter Albert, prof. chemistry; b. Syracuse, N.Y., Jan. 6, 1888; s. Walter A. and Mary (Manning) P.; B.S., Syracuse U., 1910, D.Sc., 1935; Ph.D., U. of Göttingen, 1914; m. Millicent Gertrude Leech, June 15, 1915; children—Virginia Mary, Patricia, Shirley. Asst. in chemistry, Mass. Inst. Tech., 1910-12, Univ. Coll., London, 1914-15; instr. in physical chemistry, Mass. Inst. Tech., 1915-16, Syracuse U., 1916-17; asso., Johns Hopkins, 1917-24, prof. chemistry since 1924; dir. Silica Gel Corpn. Mem. Sigma Xi, Kappa Sigma. Club: Baltimore Country. Inventor of silica gel; made researches on adsorption, surface energy and colloidal phenomena. Home: The Terraces, Mt. Washington, Md.*

PATTEN, Harrison Eastman, research chemist; b. Crete, Ill., May 29, 1873; s. Amos Williams and Belle (Harrison) P.; student Englewood High Sch., Chicago, 1886-89, Northwestern U. Prep. Sch., 1889-1890; A.B., Northwestern U., Prep. Sch., 1889-90; A.B., Northwestern U., 1894, A.M., 1896, grad. work, 1900, 1901; grad. work, U. of Chicago, summers, 1895, 1896; Ph.D., U. of Wis., 1902; unmarried. Asst. chemist Alston Paint Co., Chicago, 1893; instr. high schs., 1894-95 and 1896-1900; instr. chemistry, U. of Wis., 1902-06; fellow in chemistry, Northwestern U., 1905-06; soil chemist Bur. of Soils, U.S. Dept. Agr., 1906-11; physical chemist, Bur. of Chemistry, U.S. Dept. Agr., 1911-18 and 1919-20; chief chemist, Provident Chem. Works, St. Louis, 1920-21; chemist Edgewood Arsenal, U.S. War Dept., 1921-23; cons. chemist, New York and Washington, 1923-26; chemist U.S. Dept. Agr. Fixed Nitrogen. Lab., 1926-32; cons. chemist, 1932-37, research technician, U.S. Navy since 1937, on lubrication project for Bur. of Aeronautics. Served as capt., Q.M.C., U.S. Army, 1918-29; commd. Capt., Chem. Warfare Service, U.S.A. Res., 1923, Major, 1925; now on inactive list. Mem. Am. Chem. Soc., Am. Legion. Democrat. Methodist. Club: Annapolis Roads. Home: Silver Spring, Md.

PATTERSON, Alexander Evans, vice-pres. Penn Mutual Life Ins. Co.; b. Washington, D.C., June 23, 1887; s. William Hart and Georgie Anna (Evans) P.; ed. pub. school in Middle West; LL.D., Coe Coll., Cedar Rapids, Ia., 1938; m. Eleanor Morgan, Oct. 5, 1920; children—Alexander Evans, Jr., Portia. Salesman, later mgr., Equitable Life Assurance Soc., Pittsburgh, New York, Chicago, 1908-28; gen. agent Penn Mutual Life Ins. Co., Chicago, 1928-37, vice-pres. since Jan. 1, 1937. Served 27 months in U.S. Army during World War, final rank, maj. F.A. Pres. Nat. Assn. Life Underwriters, 1936. Mem. Sigma Alpha Epsilon. Republican. Episcopalian. Clubs: Chicago (Chicago); Union League, Racquet (Phila.); Merion Cricket (Merion). Home: "Seven Acres," Paoli, Pa. Office; 6th and Walnut Sts., Philadelphia, Pa.

PATTERSON, Catherine Norris, artist; b. Phila.; d. S. Henry and Mary (Yates) Norris; ed. Miss Agnes Irwin's Sch., Phila., and Pa. Acad. Fine Arts, Phila.; m. Charles Leland Harrison, Apr. 29, 1886; children—Henry Norris Harrison, John Harrison; m. 2d, Frank Thorne Patterson, Dec. 29, 1917. Miniature painter. Has exhibited at Pa. Acad. Fine Arts, Plastic Club. Mem. Fellowship Pa. Acad. of Fine Arts, Agnes Irwin Alumnæ. Club: Acorn. Home: The Barclay, 18th and Rittenhouse Square, East, Philadelphia, Pa.

PATTERSON, Clarence Arthur, lawyer; b. New Castle, Pa., July 7, 1897; s. Wm. Clendenin and Eda (Belles) P.; B.S., Washington and Jefferson Coll., Washington, Pa., 1919; LL.B., U. of Pa. Law Sch., 1922; m. Josephine Snodgrass, Apr. 19, 1924; children—Patricia Belles, Nancy Jane, Clarence Arthur II. Admitted to Pa. bar, 1922, and since engaged in gen. practice of law at New Castle, Pa.; dir. and counsel Mahoning Finance & Loan Assn.; counsel, Workmen's Compensation Bd. of Pa. Served as 2d lt., Inf., U.S. Army, 1918. Past Dem. Co. Chmn. and Dem. State Committeeman; former mem. Bd. Viewers, Lawrence Co. Past chmn. local Am. Red Cross; mem. and trustee (and past adjt.) Am. Legion; trustee New Castle Free Pub. Library (treas.), Legion Home Assn. (sec.). Mem. Pa. State, Lawrence Co. (treas.) bar assns., Delta Tau Delta, Delta Theta Phi. Democrat. Presbyterian (former deacon, trustee). Club: Field (New Castle, Pa.). Home: 702 Wilmington Av. Office: 652 First Nat. Bank Bldg., New Castle, Pa.

PATTERSON, Clifford Scott, business exec.; b. Monongahela, Pa., May 3, 1887; s. James Scott and Alice C. (Flanigan) P.; student Ohio U.; m. Rachel L. Jones, 1915; 1 dau., Mary Louise. Vice-pres. and dir. Bebout & Yohe Co., Monongahela, Pa. Mem. Monongahela City Council, 1922-26; mem. Pa. State Legislature since 1934, during 1935 session introduced bill to create Turnpike Commn. to build all-weather highway between Pittsburgh and Harrisburg, Pa. Pres. and dir. Monongahela Asso. Charities. Mem. Monongahela Business Assn. Elk (trustee; dist. dep. Grand Exalted Ruler, Pa. South West Dist., 1926-28). Club: Monongahela (Pa.) Valley Country. Home: Marine Av. Office: 200 Chess St., Monongahela, Pa.

PATTERSON, Edwin Wilhite, prof. law; b. Kansas City, Mo., Jan. 1, 1889; s. Louis Lee and Roberta Ann (Wilhite) P.; grad. Central High Sch., Kansas City, Mo., 1906; A.B., University of Mo., 1909, LL.B., 1911, LL.D., 1936; S.J.D., Harvard University, 1920; m. Dorothy Madison Thomson, Dec. 28, 1915; children—Clifton Connell (dec.), Edwin Wilhite, Penelope. Began practice at Kansas City, 1911; with Holmes, Holmes & Page until 1913; practiced alone, 1913-15; adj. prof. law, U. of Tex., 1915-17; asst. prof. law, U. of Colo., 1917-18, prof., 1918-20; prof. law, State U. of Ia., 1920-22; editor Ia. Law Review, 1922; asso. prof. law, Columbia, 1922-24, prof. since 1924. Acting prof. law, Stanford U., summer 1933. Mem. joint com. Ency. of Social Sciences; adviser Restatement of Restitution (Am. Law Inst.), 1933-37. Dept. supt. of ins., State of N.Y., 1936; in charge Revision of New York Ins. Law, 1935-39. Mem. Mo. and Ia. State Bar, Am. Bar Assn. (chmn. com. on qualification and regulation of ins. cos., 1935-39), Am. Assn. Univ. Profs. (mem. council 1933-35), Société de Législation Comparée, Phi Delta Phi, Phi Beta Kappa, Order of the Coif, QEBH (sr. soc. Univ. of Mo.). Democrat. Author: The Insurance Commissioner in the United States, 1927; Cases and Materials on Insurance, 1932; Essentials of Insurance Law, 1935; Cases on Contracts, II (2 volumes), 1935. Contbr. on legal subjects. Home: 115 Paulin Boul., Leonia, N.J.

PATTERSON, Ernest Minor, economics; b. Cincinnati, O., July 17, 1879; s. John Paul and Henrietta Frances (Jackman) P.; A.B., Park Coll., Parkville, Mo., 1902, A.M., 1904, LL.D., 1936; grad. study Univ. of Chicago, 1909-10; Ph.D., Univ. of Pa., 1912; m. Elsie Davis Reynolds, July 3, 1906; 1 dau., Grace Frances. Prof. Latin, Henry Kendall Coll., Muskogee, Okla., 1902-05; prin. Wasatch Acad., Mt. Pleasant, Utah, 1905-08; prof. economics, Washington Coll., Tenn., 1908-09; instr. in finance, U. of Pennsylvania, 1910-15, asst. prof. economics, 1915-19, prof. since 1919; visiting prof. Institut Universitaire des Hautes Études Internationales, Geneva, Switzerland, 1929; lecturer, Acad. Internat. Law, The Hague, 1931. Member American Academy Political and Social Science (pres.), Am. Econ. Assn. (v.p. 1936), Am. Philosophical Soc., Delta Sigma Phi, Beta Gamma Sigma, Pi Gamma Mu, Phi Beta Kappa. Author: (with T. Conway, Jr.) The Operation of the New Bank Act, 1914; Financial History of Philadelphia Electric Co., 1914; Western Europe and the U.S., 1922; Europe in 1927, 1927; Tests of a Foreign Government Bond, 1928; The World's Economic Dilemma, 1930; America—World Leader or World Led. Contbr. to Annals of American Acad., Am. Econ. Review, New Republic, etc. Home: 404 S. 47th St., Philadelphia, Pa.

PATTERSON, Frank Allen, prof. English; b. Allen's Hill, Ontario Co., N.Y., Aug. 14, 1878; s. Wilson Howell and Gertrude (Allen) P.;

Genesee Wesleyan Sem., Lima, N.Y., 1897-1900; A.B., Syracuse, 1904; A.M., Columbia, 1907, Ph.D., 1911; Litt.D., Syracuse, 1938; m. Bertha Cleveland, Sept. 10, 1910; children—William Allen, Myron Cleveland. Instr. in English, Syracuse, summer 1904; same, Blees Mil. Acad., Macon, Mo., 1904-06; asso. in English, U. of Ill., 1911-12; instr. in English, Columbia, 1912-14, asst. prof., 1914-19, asso. prof., 1919-31, prof. since 1931, also asst. to dir. Univ. Extension, 1912-25, asst. to dir. Summer Session, 1913-18. Founder The Facsimile Text Soc., 1929. Mem. Modern Lang. Assn. of America, Bibliog. Soc. of England, Tudor Soc. of England. Club: Men's Faculty. Author: The Middle English Penitential Lyric, 1911. Editor: The Student's Milton, 1930; Complete Works of John Milton (18 vols.), 1931. Contbr. articles, essays and reviews. Home: 120 E. Harwood Terrace, Palisades Park, N.J.

PATTERSON, Gaylard Hawkins, coll. prof.; b. Slippery Rock, Pa., Aug. 18, 1866; s. Asa M. (M.D.) and Sara (Patterson) P.; Allegheny Coll., Pa.; A.B., Ohio Wesleyan, 1888; Ph.D., Yale, 1890; S.T.B., Boston U, 1892; A.M., Harvard, 1893; m. Helen McKellar, of Toronto, Can., 1893 (died 1896); m. 2d, Millicent Louise Webber, of Toronto, Dec. 19, 1900; 1 dau., Eunice Louise. In M.E. ministry, 1893-1907; prof. history and economics, 1907-10, dean and prof. social science, 1910-14, Coll. Liberal Arts, Willamette U.; fellow in sociology, U. of Wis., 1914-15; prof. economics and sociology, Dickinson Coll., since 1915. Mem. Am. Sociol. Soc. Author: The Social Significance of the Heaven and Hell of Islam (Old and New Testament Student); The Chief Aim of High School Education; The High School Course of Study in Relation to the Elementary Course from a Social Point of View (Proc. Ore. State Teachers' Assn., 1909). Home: Carlisle, Pa.*

PATTERSON, Gordon Derby, research chemist; b. Meadville, Pa., Dec. 7, 1897; s. Thomas McCobb and Lena Margaret (Derby) P.; student Meadville (Pa.) High Sch., 1911-15; B.S., Allegheny Coll., Meadville, Pa., 1919; M.S., Ohio State U., Columbus, O., 1920, Ph.D., 1923; m. Ethel Mae Beard, Aug. 17, 1921; children—Gordon Derby, David Alan. Grad. asst. in chemistry, Ohio State U., Columbus, O., 1919-20, asst. in chemistry, 1920-22, Grasselli Research Fellow, 1922-23; research chemist, Exptl. Sta,, E. I. duPont de Nemours & Co., Wilmington, Del., 1923-26, research group leader since 1926. Mem. Am. Chem. Soc., Phi Beta Kappa, Sigma Xi, Alpha Chi Sigma, Phi Lambda Upsilon, Alpha Chi Rho. Presbyterian. Mason. Clubs: DuPont Country (Wilmington, Del.). Home: 4503 Washington Boul., Brandywine Hills, Wilmington, Del. Office: Experimental Sta., E. I. du Pont de Nemours & Co., Wilmington, Del.

PATTERSON, Graham Creighton, publisher; b. Pittsburgh, Pa., Dec. 25, 1881; s. John Mitchell and Margaret Laird (Macfarlane) P.; A.B., Cornell U., 1904; m. Maude Dewar, May 5, 1909; children—Maude Elizabeth, John Graham. Gen. sec. Cornell U. Christian Assn., 1904-05; adv. mgr. Federal Elec. Co., Chicago, 1905-07; adv. rep. for mags., 1907-18; pres. Union Electrotype Co., Chicago, 1917-18; pub. and pres. Christian Herald, 1918-30, v.p., 1931-35; president and publisher Farm Journal, Phila., since 1935. Ex-pres. Christian Herald Children's Home, Nyack, N.Y.; ex-pres. Mayesville (S.C.) Ednl. and Industrial Inst.; ex-pres. Christian Herald Industrial Missions, China; ex-pres. Bowery Mission of New York City; vice chmn. American Committee China Famine. Chmn. Evanston Emergency Plan, 1932; mem. exec. com. Evanston Community Chest, 1932-33. Mem. Nat. Publishers' Assn. (exec. com.), Delta Upsilon. Republican. Presbyn. Clubs: University (Chicago); University (Cleveland); University (New York); Detroit Athletic; Merion Cricket (Haverford, Pa.); Evanston Country. Home: 200 Golf View Rd., Ardmore, Pa. Office: 230 S. 7th St., Philadelphia, Pa.

PATTERSON, Harry Jacob, chemist; b. Yellow Springs, Pa., Dec. 17, 1866; s. William Calvin and Adaline (Mattern) P.; B.S., Pa. State Coll., 1886; post-grad. work in chemistry there, and was asst. chemist Pa. State Agrl. Experiment Station, 1886-88; D.Sc., Maryland State Coll., 1912; m. Elizabeth Hayward Hutchinson, Oct. 25, 1895; children—Blanche Seely (Mrs. Francis T. Mack), William Calvin. Chemist and vice-dir., 1888-98, dir. and chemist, 1898, Md. Agrl. Expt. Sta.; also pres. Md. Agr. Coll., May 1913-17; dean Coll. of Agr., U. of Md., 1925; emeritus since 1937. Specialist in food, fertilizer and dairy chemistry and corn fodder products; author bulletins and articles on these subjects. Fellow A.A.A.S.; mem. Assn. Official Agrl. Chemists, Am. Chem. Soc., Soc. Chem. Industry, London. Master Md. State Grange, 1905-13; sec. Md. State Bd. of Agr., 1907-17. Home: College Park, Prince Georges Co., Md.

PATTERSON, J(ames) Milton, dir. state dept. pub. welfare; b. Moscow Mills, Md., Mar. 30, 1891; s. Thomas E. S. and Amelia (Corfield) P.; student pub. schs. and high sch., bus. coll., Cumberland, Md., 1906-07; m. Flora E. Odgers, Sept. 22, 1909; children—Ruth (Mrs. James Fleming), James Corfield, John Milton, Jr. Employed as stenographer, United Brokerage Co., Clarksburg, W.V., 1907, mgr., 1908-10; mem. firm Rogers & Patterson, 1911; organized Jobbers Brokerage Co., Cumberland, Md., 1912, formed Buley-Patterson Co., 1914 which absorbed other cos. and pres. since 1912; organized Wilson Hardware Co., Cumberland, 1919 and vice-pres. since 1925; organized Buley-Patterson Potts Co., Pittsburgh, Pa., and pres. since 1928; exec. sec. Bd. State Aid and Charities, Baltimore, 1936-39; dir. State Dept. Pub. Welfare since June 1, 1939. Pres. Cumberland Chamber of Commerce. Minority floor leader and mem. Md. Ho. of Dels., 1927. Chmn. Allegany Co. Welfare Bd.; adminstr. Civil Works Administration, Allegany Co. Pres. Cumberland Y.M.C.A. Treas. and mem. bd. regents, U. of Md., College Park, Md. Mem. adv. com. Md. Employment Service; vice pres. Md. Conf. Social Work. Republican. Methodist. Mason (32°, Shriner, Past Potentate); Odd Fellow. Clubs: Rotary, Boumi Temple Golf, Scimiter, Baltimore (Baltimore). Home: 1015 Argonne Drive. Office: 120 W. Redwood St., Baltimore, Md.

PATTERSON, John Raymond, sch. supt.; b. St. Clairsville, O., Jan. 15, 1886; s. John Francis and Laura Belle (Coss) P.; Ph.B., Wooster (O.) Coll., 1914; M.A., Columbia U., 1926; Ph.D., New York U., 1929; m. Bertha Beryl Bunker, Aug. 14, 1909; 1 son, Dr. James Earl. Teacher Ohio rural schs., 1905-07; prin. City Elementary Sch., Martins Ferry, O., 1907-09; supt. schs., Amherst, O., 1914-16, Xenia, O., 1916-19, Bucyrus, O., 1919-24, Athens, O., 1924-28, Roselle, N.J., 1929-37, Millburn, N.J., since 1937; visiting prof., summer sessions, Kent (O.) State Coll., 1921-24, Missouri U., 1927 and 28, New York U., 1930-35, N.J. State Teachers Coll., Montclair, N.J., 1936-39. Mem. N.E.A., Am. Assn. Sch. Adminstrs., N.J., Council of Edn., N.J. Schoolmasters Club, Horace Mann Soc., Phi Beta Kappa, Phi Delta Kappa. Presbyn. Mason. Club: Rotary (Millburn, N.J.). Home: Baltusrol Way, Short Hills, N.J. Office: Bd. of Edn., Millburn, N.J.

PATTERSON, Marjorie, actress, author; b. Baltimore, Md.; d. Wilson and Margaret (Sherwood) P.; desc. William Patterson, father of Madame Jerome Bonaparte, and g.g.d. John Neal, of Portland, Me.; ed. Bryn Mawr Sch., Baltimore; Madame Yeatman's Sch., Neuilly, Paris; Marquise San Carlos Sch., Bornel, France; Convent Des Sœurs de Dieu, Paris; studied for her profession with Sir Frank Benson, Jules Leitner and Sir Charles Wyndham. Played leading parts in F. R. Benson's Shakespearean Co. in England, 1910, and appeared as "Anne Page," "Perdita," "Viola," and "Queen Katherine" at Shakespeare Festival, Stratford-on-Avon; at time of coronation played in matinée given by Sir Charles Wyndham, at New Theatre; engaged New Repertory Theatre, Liverpool, winter season, 1911-12; played Jababa and Jessica at Her Majesty's Theatre, 1913; played Mary Denbigh, in "Daughters of Ishmael," Mrs. Siddons, "Georgean Review," Little Theatre, 1914; leading part in Lyceum Club prize play, "Royal Way," Haymarket Theatre, "Carrots," Haymarket Theatre; played "Jessica," Shakespeare Tercentenary performance, Drury Lane Theatre, 1916; "Phiynette," in "L'Enfant Prodigue," Court Theatre, 1916; "Pierrot," in "Pierrot Prodigal," Booth's and Little theatres, New York, 1916. Episcopalian. Mem. Colonial Dames, Incorporated Stage Soc., London. Club: Women Writers (London). Author: Fortunata, 1911; The Dust of the Road, 1913; A Woman's Man, 1919; also Pan in Ambush, play in verse, prod. Court and Strand Theatres, London, Vagabond Theatre, Baltimore. Home: 14 E. Mt. Vernon Pl., Baltimore, and Woodland House, Delhi, N.Y. Address: care Safe Deposit & Trust Co., 13 South St., Baltimore, Md.

PATTERSON, Paul Chenery, journalist; b. Jacksonville, Ill., Nov. 18, 1878; s. James March and Mary Abagail (Hamilton) P.; Rushville (Ill.) High Sch.; student U. of Chicago 1 yr.; m. Elsie Jarvis McLean, Oct. 22, 1910; children—Walter Maclean, Donald Hamilton, Paul Jarvis, James March, Polly Chenery, Malcolm Maclean. Reporter Chicago Tribune, 1899-1900; reporter, copy reader, city editor, Chicago Journal, 1900-03; night city editor Chicago Inter Ocean, 1903-04; city editor Chicago Examiner, 1904-06, Washington Herald, 1906-07; city editor, mng. editor, gen. mgr. and treas. Washington Times, 1907-11; mng. editor Baltimore Evening Sun, 1911-13; business mgr., sec. and treas. Sun and Evening Sun, 1913-19; pres. and exec. editor same since Nov. 11, 1919; pres. The A. S. Abell Co., publs.; 2d v.p. Associated Press. Mem. Am. Newspaper Pubs. Assn. (pres. 1922-24), Am. Soc. Editors. Clubs: Maryland, Gibson Island, Elkridge Hunt. Home: 219 Northway, Guilford, Baltimore. Office: The Sun, Sun Square, Baltimore, Md.

PATTERSON, S(amuel) Howard, economist; b. Philadelphia, Pa., July 23, 1892; s. Samuel A. and Sara C. (Clagett) P.; grad. Central High Sch., Phila., 1909, Phila. Sch. of Pedagogy, 1911; B.S., U. of Pa., 1914, A.M., 1916, Ph.D., 1922; m. Mae E. Griffiths, June 18, 1924. Teacher in elementary schs., Phila., 1911-14, W. Phila. High Sch., 1914-20; instr. in economics, U. of Pa., 1920-22, asst. prof., 1922-28, prof. since 1928, also chmn. Dept. of Economics, 1932-38; visiting prof. summer school, Columbia University, 1935, 36, 37, 38; consulting editor McGraw-Hill Book Co. and Farrar and Rinehart; trustee Social Science Pub. Co.; mem. bd. mgrs. Armstrong Assn., Phila. Mem. Am. Econ. Assn., Am. Assn. for Labor Legislation, Am. Acad. Polit. and Social Science, A.A.A.S., Nat. Edn. Assn., Pa. State Edn. Assn., Theta Chi (dir. Alumni Corpn. of Kappa Chapter), Pi Gamma Mu (nat. treas.), Phi Delta Kappa. Republican. Presbyterian. Mason. Clubs: Contemporary, Schoolmen's, Manufacturers and Bankers. Author: Family Desertion and Non Support, 1922; Social Aspects of Industry, 1929, 35; Readings in History of Economic Thought, 1932. Co-Author: American Social Problems (with H. R. Burch), 1918; Problems of American Democracy (with same), 1922; Economic Problems of Modern Life (with K. Scholz), 1927, 31, 37; The School in American Society (with E. A. Choate and E. de S. Brunner), 1936; Problems in American Democracy (with A. W. S. Little and H. R. Burch), 1938. Contbr. to periodicals. Home: 6401 Sherwood Rd., Philadelphia, Pa.

PATTERSON, Thomas Magill, fire ins. cos. exec.; b. Armstrong Co., Pa., July 3, 1880; s. Frank K. and Sadie (Magill) P.; student high sch. and Grove City Coll.; m. Emma B. Cox, June 30, 1909; children—Thomas M., Jr., John B., Mary E. (Mrs. John Yerkes), Harriet B., Frank K. (dec.), William C. Began as rate clk. Allegheny Bd. Fire Underwriters; spl. agt. Nat. Union Fire Ins. Co. and Girard Fire Ins. Co.; asst. sec. Girard Fire Ins. Co., Phila., Pa.; sec. Pennsylvania Fire Ins. Co.; local sec. North British & Mercantile Ins. Co., Ltd., Mercantile Ins. Co. of America, Commonwealth Ins. Co. of New York, Homeland Ins. Co. of America. Republican. Presbyn. Clubs: Union League,

Down Town (Philadelphia); Aronimick Golf (Newtown Square). Home: Windermere Court Apts., Wayne, Pa. Office: 508 Walnut St., Philadelphia, Pa.

PATTERSON, William Wallace, Jr., manufacturer; b. North Side, Pittsburgh, Pa., Feb. 5, 1882; s. William Wallace, Sr., and Katherine (Riley) P.; ed. Shadyside Acad., Pittsburg, Pa.; m. Elizabeth Turney Griffith, of Greensburg, Pa., Aug. 25, 1910; children—William Wallace III, Mary Elizabeth (Mrs. Joseph Alexander Doyle, Jr.). Propr. W. W. Patterson Co., mfrs. steamboat ratchets and tackle blocks, Pittsburgh, Pa., since 1903. Republican. Protestant. Clubs: Duquesne, Montour Heights Country. Home: 807 Beaver St., Sewickley. Office: 54 Water St., Pittsburgh, Pa.

PATTISON, John Orville, banker; b. Antrim, Pa., Oct. 17, 1880; s. Orville and Susan (Bloore) P.; ed. Bryant & Stratton Business Inst. and Elmira Coll.; m. Helen Marr Redfield, June 7, 1911; children—Helen Christine, John Redfield (dec.), Jane Redfield. Pres. and dir. Pattison Nat. Bank (Elkland) and First Nat. Bank (Knoxville, Pa.) since 1926. Mason. Club: Wellsboro. Home: Main St., Elkland, Pa.

PATTISON, John R., judge; b. nr. Cambridge, Md., Jan. 6, 1860; s. John R. and Mary A. (Burroughs) P.; pub. schs. and Cambridge Acad.; m. Lillian S. Stapleford, Sept. 18, 1888. Admitted to bar, July 1882, and practiced at Cambridge; became chief judge 1st Jud. Circuit of Md., 1909, and later served as asso. judge Ct. of Appeals. Democrat. Address: Cambridge, Md.

PATTON, Hugh McKee, lawyer and title ins.; b. Belmont Co., O., Apr. 24, 1885; s. Thomas Lee and Jennie Belmont (McKee) P.; ed. Alliance (O.) High Sch., 1899-1902; A.B., Mount Union Coll., 1908; LL.B., U. of Pa. Law Sch., 1913; m. Ethelyn Montgomery, June 20, 1914. Asso. with Union-Fidelity Title Ins. Co. continuously since starting as a clk. in 1908, title officer, 1914-28, vice-pres. since 1928; admitted to Pa. bar, 1913. Mem. Pa. State and Allegheny Co. bar assns., Sigma Alpha Epsilon. Republican. Mem. M.E. Ch. Mason. Club: Metropolitan. Home: 40 Standish Boul., South Hills Branch. Office: 336 Fourth Av., Pittsburgh, Pa.

PATTON, Katharine, artist, teacher; b. Phila., Pa.; d. Walter M. and Mary E. (Dunn) P.; grad. Drexel Inst., Phila.; studied Art Students' League New York; Pa. Acad. Fine Arts; London Sch. of Art under Frank Brangwyn, A.R.A.; also in Italy, France, etc. Had two "one man" exhbns. in Phila.; exhibited at Nat. Acad. Design, New York; Corcoran Gallery of Art, Washington, D.C.; Art Inst., Chicago; Albright Gallery, Buffalo; Boston Art Club; Pa. Academy Fine Arts; Art Club of Phila.; etc. Awarded silver medal, for water color, Knoxville, Tenn., 1913; landscape medal, Nat. Assn. Women Painters and Sculptors, New York, 1918; Mary Smith prize (oil painting), Pa. Acad. Fine Arts, 1921, etc. Water colors exhibited in many cities under direction of Am. Fed. Arts and Oil Paintings on traveling exhbns. of the Fellowship of Pa. Acad. Fine Arts, in the South and West. Represented in person collections of Pa. Acad. Fine Arts, Fellowship collection of same, Municipal collection, Trenton, N.J., gallery of Pa. State Coll., John H. Vanderpoel Art Gallery (Chicago), etc. Mem. Nat. Assn. Women Painters and Sculptors for 15 yrs.; now mem. Am. Fed. Arts, Phila. Forum, Fellowship Pa. Acad. Fine Arts, Drexel Inst. Alumni Assn., City Parks Assn., Phila. Water Color Club, Art Alliance, Phila. Orchestra Assn., Playground and Recreation assn.; asso. mem. Am. Museum of Natural History; was mem. Plastic Club over 20 years. Republican. Home and Studio: 254 S. 16th St., Philadelphia, Pa.

PATTRELL, Arthur Ellis, physician; b. Norwich, Vt., Aug. 27, 1879; s. Oscar Lyman and Eleanor (Ellis) P.; B.S., Dartmouth Coll., Hanover, N.H., 1902; M.D., Dartmouth Coll. Med. Sch., Hanover, N.H., 1905; m. Nina Goulett, June 18, 1907. Asst. physician, Grafton State Hosp., Grafton, Mass., 1905-20; exec. officer, Boston Psychopathic Hosp., Boston, Mass., 1920-24; asst. supt., Sheppard & Enoch Pratt Hosp., Towson, Md. since 1924. Mem. Am. Med. Assn., Am. Psychiatric Assn., N.E. Soc. of Psychiatry, Baltimore Co. Med. Soc. Methodist. Mason, O.E.S. Club: Kiwanis of Towson. Address: Sheppard & Enoch Pratt Hosp., Towson, Md.

PAUL, Alice; b. Moorestown, N.J., Jan. 11, 1885; d. William Mickle and Tacie (Parry) P.; B.A., Swarthmore, 1905; grad. New York Sch. of Social Work, 1906; post-grad. work universities of Birmingham and London, 1907-09; M.A., U. of Pa., 1907, Ph.D., 1912; LL.B., Washington College of Law, 1922; LL.M., American U., 1927, D.C.L., 1928. Resident New York Coll. Settlement, 1905-06, and various settlements in England, 1906-09; imprisoned in Eng. and in U.S. for activities in woman suffrage movement; chmn. Congressional Com. of Nat. Am. Woman Suffrage Assn., 1912-13; nat. chmn. Congressional Union for Woman Suffrage, from its formation, 1913, until 1917, when it was merged with the Woman's Party, forming Nat. Woman's Party; chmn. of nat. exec. com. Nat. Woman's Party, 1917-21, mem. exec. com. since 1921, also chmn. com. on internat. relations; chmn. Woman's Research Foundation, 1927-37; chmn. nationality com. Inter-American Commn. of Women, 1930-33; mem. Women's Consultative Com. on Nationality of League of Nations; mem. exec. com. Equal Rights Internat.; mem. from U.S. on laws com. Internat. Council of Women. Mem. Sons and Daughters of the Pilgrims, D.A.R., Colonial Dames of 17th Century, Ladies of G.A.R., Phi Beta Kappa, Pi Gamma Mu. Quaker. Home: Moorestown, N.J. Address: 144 B St. N.E., Washington, D.C.

PAUL, Harold Leroy, judge; b. Port Carbon, Pa., Oct. 29, 1898; s. George G. and Florence C. (May) P.; A.B., U. of Pa. Coll., 1921; LL.B., U. of Pa. Law Sch., 1924; m. Marian L. Jones, June 12, 1928; 1 son, David George. Admitted to Pa. bar, 1924; referee in bankruptcy, 1924-37; judge Ct. of Common Pleas, Schuylkill Co., Pa., since Jan. 1938. Democrat. Mem. Evangelical Ch. Mason, Odd Fellow, Son of America. Clubs: Kiwanis of Pottsville (ex-pres.); Anthracite Gun of Port Carbon. Home: 201 Pike St., Port Carbon, Pa. Office: County Court House, Pottsville, Pa.

PAUL, John Davis, M.D.; b. Philadelphia, Pa., Nov. 26, 1891; s. Harry W. and Minnie R. (Irey) P.; ed. Central High Sch.; M.D., U. of Pa., 1915; m. Edith Mae Gardner, May 26, 1920; 1 son, John Davis. Resident physician Episcopalian Hosp., Philadelphia, 1915-17; pathologist Misericordia Hosp., 1919-24, Howard Hosp., 1919-26, St. Christopher's Hosp. since 1923; asso. visiting physician Episcopal Hosp. since 1920, chief of diabetic dept. since 1922; chief diabetic dept. Christopher's Hosp. since 1930, Stetson Hosp. since 1931. Served as capt. Med. Corps, U.S. Army, 1917-19; pathologist Base Hosp., France. Fellow Philadelphia Coll. Physicians; mem. Philadelphia County Med. Soc. (chmn. sect. of clinical pathology 1938), Philadelphia Metabolic Assn. (dir.), Am. Legion, Mil. Order Foreign Wars. Republican. Episcopalian. Mason. Clubs: Aesculapian, Philadelphia Rifle. Wrote: Management of the Ambulant Diabetic; Diabetes Mortality Approaches that of Tuberculosis. Address: 3112 N. Broad St., Philadelphia, Pa.

PAUL, John Rodman, lawyer; b. Phila., Pa., Aug. 6, 1852; s. John Rodman (M.D.) and Elizabeth Duffield (Neill) P.; A.B., U. of Pa., 1872, A.M., 1875; unmarried. Admitted to bar, 1875; senior mem. firm Biddle, Paul, Dawson & Yocum, Phila.; dir. Phila. Savings Fund, Athenæum of Phila. Trustee Drexel Inst., Drexel estate; v.p. Fairmount Park Art Assn.; hon. pres. Phila. Coll. Settlement. Mem. Am. Philos. Soc., Hist. Soc. Pa., Phi Beta Kappa, Soc. Colonial Wars, etc. Author: Digest of Acts and Decisions Relating to Passenger Railways, 1884. Home: Chestnut Hill, Pa. Office: Land Title Bldg., Philadelphia, Pa.

PAUL, Joseph Clarence, lawyer; b. Phila., Pa., Nov. 9, 1894; s. Clarence A. and Nettie F. (Lowery) P.; student Atlantic City (N.J.) Pub. Schs., 1900-09, Trenton (N.J.) High Sch., 1909-13; LL.B., Dickinson Law Sch., Carlisle, Pa., 1918; m. Ada E. Browning, Nov. 9, 1922; children—Joseph Browning, Edward Lober. Admitted to bar, 1920, and since in pvt. practice of law at Newark, N.J. Served in U.S.N.R.F., 1918-19. Mem. N.J. Legislature, 1935, 1936, 1938. Mem. Am. Bar Assn., Essex Co. Bar Assn., N.J. State Bar Assn., Am. Legion, Sigma Chi. Republican. Methodist. Mason, Elk. Home: 119 Sherman Pl., South Orange, N.J. Office: 1180 Raymond Boul., Newark, N.J.

PAUL, Sarah Woodman, educator; b. Tamworth, N.H., Feb. 8, 1859; d. Samuel and Eliza A. (Hidden) Woodman; B.A., Wellesley (Mass.) Coll., 1881; studied Cambridge, Eng., 1895; m. Edward A. Paul, of Washington, D.C., June 23, 1887 (died 1888). Teacher Washington, D.C., 1883-87; instr. Wellesley (Mass.) Coll., 1888-90, sec., 1890-95; prin., Kent Pl. Sch. for Girls, Summit, N.J., 1896-1925, prin. emeritus. Mem. Headmistresses Assn. of the East. Presbyterian. Clubs: Women's Univ. (New York); Fortnightly (Summit, N.J.). Address: 160 Summit Av., Summit, N.J.

PAUL, Theodore Sedgwick, lawyer; b. Phila., Pa., Feb. 9, 1890; s. Henry Neill and Margaret Crosby (Butler) P.; ed. St. Georges Sch., Newport, R.I., 1905-07; A.B., Princeton, 1911; LL.B., U. of Pa. Law Sch., 1914; m. Adeline L. F. Pepper, June 15, 1916 (div. 1936). Admitted to Pa. bar, 1914, and since engaged in gen. practice of law at Phila.; legal asst., Fraley & Paul, 1914-17; legal asst., Pepper, Bodine & Stokes, 1919-24, mem. firm, 1924-34; in practice alone since 1934. Served as pvt. cav., Pa. N.G., 1914-17, on Mexican border, 1916; capt. inf., capt. cav., and capt F.A., U.S.A., 1917-19; capt. F.A., Pa. N.G., 1920-24, maj. since 1924. Mem. Phila. Bar Assn., Am. Bar Assn., Zeta Psi. Republican. Presbyn. Clubs: Philadelphia (Philadelphia); Princeton (New York). Home: 8619 Evergreen Place, Chestnut Hill, Philadelphia. Office: 12 S. 12th St., Philadelphia, Pa.

PAULL, Lee Cunningham, insurance exec.; b. Wheeling, W.Va., May 12, 1889; s. Alfred and Lee (Singleton) P.; ed. Linsly Inst., Wheeling, W.Va., Pa. Mil. Coll., Chester, Pa., Princeton U.; m. Mary Glessner, Apr. 6, 1910; children —Lee Cunningham, William Glessner. Propr. Lee C. Paull, Inc., insurance, Wheeling, W.Va., since 1908; v.p. and dir. Industrial Land Bldg. Corpn., Camden Coal Land Co., Jay-Lea Co., Ohio Valley Industrial Corpn.; dir. and mem. exec. com. Wheeling Steel Corpn., Hazel Atlas Glass Co., Wheeling Dollar Savings & Trust Co. Chmn. bd. Ohio Valley Gen. Hosp.; dir. Wheeling Chamber of Commerce.; treas. and chmn. bd. Linsly Inst. Republican. Presbyterian. Elk. Clubs: Wheeling Country, Fort Henry (Wheeling, W.Va.); Princeton Engring. Soc. (Princeton, N.J.). Home: Highland Park. Office: Wheeling, W.Va.

PAULSON, Moses, physician; b. Baltimore, Md., May 2, 1897; s. David and Deborah (Bogatzky) P.; B.S., U. of Md., College Park, 1917; M.D., U. of Md. Med. Sch., Baltimore, 1921; m. Helen Golden, June 9, 1926. House physician Sinai Hosp., Baltimore, 1921-22; res. physician St. Agnes Hosp., Baltimore, 1922-23; res. physician Childrens Hosp., also in charge night accident service Emergency Hosp., both Washington, D.C., 1923-24; in gen. practice, Baltimore, 1924-26; full-time research in gastroenterology, Johns Hopkins U., 1926-29, and part-time to date; asst. in medicine, Johns Hopkins U. Med. Sch., 1927-28, instr., 1927-33, asso. in medicine since 1933; asst. vis. physician Johns Hopkins Hosp. since 1930, cons. in digestive diseases, Diagnostic Clinic of Johns Hopkins Hosp. since 1934; pvt. practice internal medicine since 1929; vis. physician Church Home and Infirmary, Mercy, St. Agnes and Sinai hosps. all of Baltimore. Served as hosp. apprentice 1st class, U.S.N.R., 1917-21. Fellow Am. Coll. Physicians. Mem. Assn. Am. Bacteriologists, A.M.A., Am. Gastro-Enterol. Assn., Med. and Chirurg. Faculty of Md., Phi Delta Epsilon, Phi Alpha. Democrat. Jewish religion. Mason.

Clubs: Suburban, Phoenix, Johns Hopkins. Contbr. more than 40 articles to med. publs. Mem. editorial bd. Am. Jour. of Digestive Diseases since 1934. Home: Temple Gardens Apts. Office: Medical Arts Bldg., Baltimore, Md.; Johns Hopkins Hospital, Baltimore, Md.

PAYNE, Elisabeth Stancy, author; b. Brooklyn, N.Y.; d. John F. and Josephine (Greenwood) Magovern; ed. Packer Institute, Brooklyn; m. Edward M. Payne, June 12, 1894; 1 son, Richard M. Protestant. Club: Pen and Brush. Author: (novels) All the Way by Water, 1922; Fathoms Deep, 1923; Lights Along the Ledges, 1924; Singing Waters, 1925; Hearthstones, 1927; Painters of Dreams, 1928; Hedges, 1929; Easy Street, 1930; These Changing Years, 1931; The Quiet Place, 1932; Thou, My Beloved, 1933; Out of the Dusk, 1934; Shadow on the Brook, 1935; Something to Remember, 1936; The Tide Always Rises, 1937. Home: Lakeville, Conn.; 106 Harrison St., East Orange, N.J.

PAYNE, Frank, shoe mfr.; b. Newport, Va., Nov. 30, 1861; s. Charles H. and Kizzie Jane (Kinzer) P.; grad. Va. Poly. Inst., 1882; m. Nelle Q. Norvell, Nov. 11, 1896; children— Ruth (Mrs. Wayne S. Vetterlein), Frank N., Nelle (Mrs. Kent C. Darling), Katharine Quarrier. Engaged in farming nr. Newport, 1882-92; also mem. Miller, Bell & Payne, livestock shippers, 1884-87, and retail merchant, Newport, 1887-92; with brother engaged in wholesaling of shoes as Payne Shoe Co., 1892-1905; with Endicott Johnson Co., 1905-09, Johnson Baillie Shoe Co., 1909-26; acquired interest in Perry Norvell Co., Devine & Yungel Shoe Co., Bedford Shoe Co., Goodyear Shoe Co., Gerberich Payne Shoe Company, Lancaster Shoe Company and combined 4 of cos. with G. R. Kinney Co., N.Y. City, of which was v.p., 1920-26; treas., Devine & Yungel Shoe Co., Gerberich Payne Shoe Co.; dir. Lancaster Shoe Co. Democrat. Episcopalian. Mason. Club: Harrisburg Country. Home: 1901 N. Front St. Office: Payne-Shoemaker Bldg., Harrisburg, Pa.

PAYNE, John Grove, mayor; b. Farmdale, O., Dec. 13, 1887; s. I. N. and Cora B. (Thompson) P.; ed. high sch., 1 yr.; m. Alice Montgomery, June 15, 1909; children—Elizabeth Jeanne, Jack M., Thomas R. Began as newsboy; entered employ of Pa. R.R. in transportation dept., 1907, successively clerk, timekeeper, paymaster and chief clerk to div. supt., Allegheny Div., 1917-27; customers man Laidlaw & Co., 1927-29, asso. mgr. since 1929. Elected mayor, Oil City, Pa., 1931, re-elected, 1935, first to serve second term since incorporation of city, 1871. Dir. Oil City Community Fund; mem. bd. Salvation Army. Mem. Am. Acad. Polit. and Social Science, Nat. Econ. League, Railroad Veterans Assn., Oil City Chamber of Commerce. Republican. Episcopalian. Mason (Shriner), Odd Fellow. Clubs: Gridiron (ex-pres.), Kiwanis (ex-sec.), Acacia, Aero (Oil City). Home: Cowell Av. Office: 248 Seneca St., Oil City, Pa.

PAYNE, Lewis; pres. Eastern Shore Public Service Co. Home: Park St. Office: 114 N. Division St., Salisbury, Md.

PAYNTER, Rowland Gardiner, physician and banker; b. Georgetown, Del., June 20, 1874; s. John Henry and Sallie Custis (Wright) P.; student Wilmington Conf. Acad., Dover, Del., 1888-91; A.B., Yale, 1895; M.D., U. of Pa. Med. Sch., 1895-98; m. Leah Anderson Burton, Nov. 6, 1920. Resident physician Episcopal Hosp., Phila., Pa., 1898-1901; in pvt. practice medicine at Georgetown, Del., since 1901; pres. Farmers Bank of the State of Del., Georgetown, Del., since 1918, Kent County Mutual Ins. Co., Dover, Del., since 1934; v.p. and dir. Del., Md. & Va. R.R. Co. since 1918. Med. mem. Sussex Co. (Del.) Draft Bd. during World War. Dem. candidate for Gov. of Del., 1908 (defeated). Trustee U. of Del., Protestant Episcopal Ch. of Diocese of Del. Democrat. Episcopalian. Address: Georgetown, Del.

PEABODY, Gertrude Devitt, dean of women; b. Princeton, Me., Dec. 1, 1894; d. Stephen Leonard and Georgianna (Rose) Peabody; B.S. in edn., U. of Me., 1920; A.M., Teachers Coll., Columbia, 1925, grad. student 1934-35; unmarried. Teacher of home economics, U. of Me., 1920-22; with Temple U., Phila., since 1923, as instr. in foods and nutrition, 1923-25, dir. of nursing edn. and instr. home economics, 1925-26, head dept. of home economics, 1926-30, dean of women and asst. prof. of home economics since 1930. Mem. N.E.A., Pa. State Edn. Assn., Assn. Deans of Women, Am. Assn. Univ. Women, Phi Mu, Phi Kappa Phi, Kappa Delta Pi. Republican. Conglist. Club: Women's University (Phila.). Home: 1510 N. Broad St., Philadelphia, Pa.

PEABODY, J(oseph) Winthrop, M.D.; b. Wakefield, Mass.; s. Winthrop Melvin and Anna (Freeman) P.; ed. Wakefield (Mass.) pub. schs., Boston Coll. and Georgetown U. (M.D. 1914); m. Naomi E. Galloway, Aug. 10, 1921; children—Mary Naomi, Joseph Winthrop, Sara Ann. With Pub. Welfare and Health Dept., Dist. of Columbia, since 1914; asst. resident phys. Tuberculosis Hosp., 1914 to 1918; resident phys. 1918, supt. since 1921; attending phys. Tuberculosis Assn. Chest Clinic, 1917-18; attending phys. Health Dept. Chest Clinic, 1919-21, med. dir., 1921-36, clin. advisor since 1936; gen. supt. and phys. in charge Tuberculosis Sanatoria, Glenn Dale, Md., since 1934; med. dir. Children's Tuberculosis Summer Camp since 1921; med. examiner Devitt's Camp, Allenwood, Pa., since 1830; spl. consultant Gallinger Municipal Hosp.; chmn. med. com. to assist architect in planning Tuberculosis Sanatoria, Glenn Dale, Md.; mem. staffs Georgetown U., George Washington U., Providence, and Emergency hosps.; prof. clin. medicine George Washington Sch. of Medicine, 1924-32; instr. in medicine, Georgetown U. Sch. of Medicine, 1921-28, asso. prof., 1923-24, prof. diseases of respiratory system since 1924. A pioneer in District of Columbia in use artificial pneumothorax in the treatment of pulmonary tuberculosis, acute lung abscess, and other diseases of the lungs. Many research articles, including: "The Use of Sodium Morrhuate in Pulmonary Tuberculosis," The American Review of Tuberculosis, 1923; "Phrenicotomy", Medical Annals, 1935; "Present Day Treatment of Tuberculosis," Medical Annals, 1938; "Rehabilitation as a Phase of Tuberculosis Eradication," Quarterly Review. Diplomate Am. Bd. Internal Medicine. Fellow Am. Coll. Physicians, A.M.A.; mem. Am. Acad. Tuberculosis Physicians (charter mem.; dist. counsellor Eastern Sect. 1938), Am. Coll. Chest Physicians (charter mem.; vice-chmn. legislative com. 1937-38), Am. Hosp. Assn., Nat. Tuberculosis Assn. (bd. dirs. 1928-34 and since 1936), Tuberculosis Assn. of Washington, D.C. (bd. dirs. since 1920), Pan-Am. Med. Assn. (vice-chmn. thoracic sect. 1938), Tri State Med. Assn. of the Carolinas and Va., Dist. of Columbia Med. Soc., Clin. Club of Dist. of Columbia (v.p. 1927-28), George Washington U. Med. Soc., Am. Sanatorium Assn., Southern Med. Assn. Clubs: University, Congressional Country. Home: 12 E. Melrose St., Chevy Chase, Md. Office: 1746 K St. N.W., Washington, D.C.

PEACOCK, James Craig, lawyer; b. Philadelphia, Pa., February 29, 1888; s. Rev. John (D.D.) and Annie (Craig) P.; A.B., Central High Sch., Philadelphia, 1905; A.B., Princeton, 1909; LL.B., U. of Pa., 1912; m. Dorothy Hunt, Nov. 18, 1918; 1 son, John Hunt. Admitted to bar, Phila., 1912; mem. staff legislative drafting research fund of Columbia U., 1913-17, and took part in drafting much important federal and state legislation; examiner accounts in office of commr. of accounts, N.Y. City, 1915; successively sec. Excess Profits Advisors, Tax Reviewers, and of the Advisory Tax Bd., U.S. Treasury Dept., Washington, D.C., 1917-19; mgr. Washington office of Ernst & Ernst (accountants), 1919-20; sec. tax com. Nat. Industrial Conf. Bd., 1920; counsel for legislative com. Am. Inst. Accountants, 1921-22, for Nat. Council Am. Cotton Mfrs., 1920-27, also in practice of law in D.C., 1919-34; dir. Shipping Bd. Bur. of U.S. Dept. Commerce, 1934-36; pres. United States Shipping Bd. Merchant Fleet Corpn., 1934-36; dir. Am. Bur. Shipping, 1934-36; spl. counsel U.S. Maritime Commn., 1936-37; resumed private practice, 1937. Mem. Am. Bar. Assn., Bar Assn. D.C., Am. Law Inst. Democrat. Presbyterian; trustee Chevy Chase Ch. Clubs: Nat. Press, Congressional Country (Washington); Princeton (New York); Lake Placid Club (Essex County, N.Y.); Cottage (Princeton). Contbr. Jour. of Am. Bar Assn. Home: 12 W. Irving St., Chevy Chase, Md. Address: 817 Munsey Bldg., Washington, D.C.

PEACOCK, Ralph Wilson, lawyer; b. Greensburg, Pa., Feb. 9, 1902; s. Vance D. and Lou M. (Wilson) P.; A.B., Muskingum Coll., 1922; LL.B., U. of Pittsburgh Law Sch., 1925; m. Margaret Milligan, Sept. 3, 1925; children— William Vance, Marjorie Ann. Admitted to Pa. bar, 1925, and since engaged in gen. practice of law at Washington; mem. firm Peacock and Walker since 1936; pres. and dir. Chartiers Credit Corpn.; dir. Hickory-Penn Gas Co. Mem. Pa. Bar Assn., Washington Co. Bar Assn. (pres.) Republican. United Presbyn. Mason (K.T., Shriner). Club: Canonsburg-Houston Rotary (pres.). Home: Houston, Pa. Office: Washington Trust Bldg., Washington, Pa.

PEACOCK, Robert, lawyer; b. Conshohocken, Pa., Aug. 19, 1883; s. John and Amie (Smith) P.; ed. Florence (N.J.) Schools and Rider Coll., Trenton, N.J.; studied law S. A. Atkinson's office; m. Helen Dorothy Healy, July 15, 1919; children—John Robert, Mary Jane. Admitted to N.J. bar, atty., 1910, counsellor-at-law, 1914, Supreme Court bar, 1933; practice Mount Holly, N.J., since 1910; county auditor, 1911; county solicitor, 1916-26; asst. atty. gen. of N.J. since 1929. Served with U.S. Army, during World War. Mem. N.J. Legislature, 1912-14. Mem. Burlington County, N.J. State and Am. bar assns. Republican. Methodist. Elk. Special prosecutor in Lindbergh kidnaping and murder case. Home: 2805 Ocean Av., Brigantine, N.J. Office: 105 Main St., Mount Holly, N.J.

PEAIRS, Leonard Marion, univ. prof.; b. Lawrence, Kan., June 5, 1886; s. Chalmers Addison and Susan (Banta) P.; B.S. and M.S., Kan. State Coll., Manhattan, Kan.; student Cornell U., 1909, Ph.D., U. of Chicago, 1917; m. Edith Pennington, June 15, 1915; children— Chalmers Addison, Jr., Dorothea Janet. Asst. to state entomologist of Ill., Urbana, 1907-08; asst. prof. entomologist, Md. State Coll. and asst. entomologist Md. Agrl. Expt. Sta., 1908-10; asst. to state entomologist, and instr. entomology Kan. State Coll., Manhattan, Kan., 1910-12; entomologist W.Va. Agrl. Expt. Sta., and prof. entomology, W.Va. Univ., Morgantown, W.Va., since 1912. Mem. A.A.A.S., Am. Assn. Econ. Entomologists, Am. Entomol. Soc., Sigma Xi, Phi Kappa Phi, Alpha Zeta. Home: 104 Jones Av., Morgantown, W.Va.

PEAKE, Walter Leon, lawyer; b. Tioga Co., Pa., Mar. 7, 1883; s. Frank C. and Ella M. (Close) P.; ed. high sch. Wellsboro, Pa., 1897-1901; Ph.B., Lafayette Coll., 1905; m. Elisabeth Strang, Oct. 18, 1911; 1 son, Walter Strang. Employed as teacher high sch., 1905-09; student in law office, 1906-10; admitted to Pa. bar, 1910, and engaged in practice of law at Knoxville, 1910-12, in gen. practice at Corry since 1912; served as chmn. Rep. City Com., Corry, Pa. Republican. Presbyn. Mason. I.O.O.F. Elk. Clubs: Kiwanis, Country (Corry). Home: 327 East St. Office: 1 Cameron Bldg., Corry, Pa.

PEALE, Rembrandt, Jr., coal operator; b. Staten Island, N.Y., July 18, 1895; s. Rembrandt and Minnie Eudora (Batchelor) P.; ed. Hotchkiss Sch., Lakeville, Conn., Lehigh U.; m. Helena Daly, Feb. 25, 1920; children—Patricia, Elthea. Asso. with Peale, Peacock & Kerr, Inc., and Springfield Coal Corpn. Served as 2d lt. 107th Machine Gun Batt., U.S. Army, 1917-19. Republican. Episcopalian. Clubs: Union Club (New York); Pennsylvania Society Art Club (Phila.). Home: St. Benedict, Pa. Office: St. Benedict, Pa.; Graybar Bldg., New York, N.Y.

PEARCE, Charles Sumner, pres. International Cellucotton Products Co.; b. Walworth, Wis., Sept. 16, 1877; s. George Delavan and Emily Jane (Baker) P.; grad. high sch., Sharon, Wis., 1896; B.L., U. of Wis., 1900, LL.B., 1903;

m. Vivian Leslie Coates, June 2, 1909; children—Jane Coates (Mrs. Stuart Sherman), Charles Silsbee. Entered employ of B. J. Johnson Soap Co., manufacturers of Palmolive soap, Milwaukee, Wisconsin, 1903, and became adv. and sales manager, 1907; continued with this co. and its successor The Palmolive-Peet Co., of which was v.p., 1919-24, pres., 1924-28; pres. of its successor the Colgate-Palmolive-Peet Co., 1928-33, chmn. bd., 1933-38, dir. Palmolive Co. and subsidiaries, The Parker Pen Co., Internat. Cellucotton Products Co. Upper Avenue Bank, Arlington Race Track, and others. Mem. Wis. Soc. of Chicago, Art Inst. Chicago, Kappa Sigma. Republican. Protestant. Clubs: Chicago, Commercial, Racquet, Bob O'Link Golf, Casino, Tavern, Commonwealth, Post and Paddock, Old Elm, American National Jockey Club (Chicago); Tag-a-Long (Red Cedar Lake, Wis.). Home: 209 Lake Shore Drive, Chicago. Office: 105 Hudson St., Jersey City, N.J.; and Palmolive Bldg., Chicago, Ill.

PEARCE, Henry Arthur, clergyman; b. Stonington Twp., Conn., Oct. 28, 1879; s. Frederick Parker and Mary Augusta (Boulter) P.; student Plainfield (N.J.) High Sch., 1894-98 (valedictorian), spl. studies, Columbia U., 1903-06; A.B., Union Coll., Schenectady, N.Y., 1903; B.D., Union Theol. Sem., New York, 1906; m. Viola Walker, of Schenectady, N.Y., June 28, 1906; children—Marjorie Elizabeth, Eleanor Jean. Ordained Congl. ministry; pastor First Ch., Savannah, N.Y., 1906-09, First Ch., Bay Shore, N.Y., 1909-17, East Av. Ch., Lockport, N.Y., 1917-18, St. Cloud Presbyn. Ch., West Orange, N.J., 1919-20, Patterson Memorial Presbyn. Ch., West Orange, N.J., since 1920; stated clerk of Presbytery of Morris and Orange, N.J., since 1925; recording clerk of Synod of N.J. since 1930. Exec. sec. War Camp Community Service, Syracuse, Albany and New Rochelle, N.Y., 1918-19. Pres. Boy Scout Council of West Orange (N.J.), 1922-26. Mem. Ministers' Assn. of West Orange (pres. 1938-39), N.E. Soc. of the Oranges, Phi Beta Kappa, Delta Upsilon. Republican. Address: 55 William St., West Orange, N.J.

PEARCE, Louise, med. research; b. Winchester, Mass., Mar. 5, 1885; d. Charles Ellis and Susan Elizabeth (Hoyt) P.; prep. edn., Girls' Collegiate Sch., Los Angeles, Calif., 1900-03; A.B., Stanford, 1907; M.D., Johns Hopkins, 1912. Med. house officer, Johns Hopkins, 1912-13; with Rockefeller Inst. of Med. Research since 1913, successively as fellow, asst., associate, and since 1923 as asso. member; conducted African Sleeping Sickness Mission, Belgian Congo, 1920-21; visiting prof. medicine, Peiping Union Med. Coll., China, 1931-32. Mem. Gen. Advisory Council of Am. Social Hygiene Assn. since 1925; mem. Nat. Research Council, 1931-33; trustee New York Infirmary for Women and Children, 1921-28; mem. Exec. Bd. of Med. Women's Nat. Assn., 1935-36. Mem. A.A.A.S., N.Y. Acad. Medicine, Harvey Soc., Am. Soc. for Exptl. Pathology, Am. Assn. of Univ. Women, American Medical Women's Association, Am. Soc. for Pharmacology and Exptl. Therapeutics, Am. Assn. Pathologists and Bacteriologists, Soc. for Exptl. Biology and Medicine, Am. Assn. for Cancer Research, New York Soc. Tropical Medicine, Johns Hopkins Surg. and Med. Association, American Society Tropical Medicine, Pathol. Soc. Gt. Britain and Ireland, Royal Soc. Tropical Medicine and Hygiene, British Soc. for Study of Venereal Disease (hon.), Société belge de Médicine tropicale, Peiping Soc. Natural History, Pi Beta Phi, Phi Beta Kappa, Sigma Xi, Alpha Omega Alpha. Awarded Order of the Crown (Belgium). Club: Cosmopolitan. Author: Treatment of Human Trypanosamiasis with Tryparsamide (monograph of Rockefeller Inst.), 1930; also author or co-author of about 150 papers in med. jours. and procs. Home: 148 Hodge Rd. Address: Rockefeller Institute for Medical Research, Princeton, N.J.

PEARCE, McLeod Milligan, coll. pres.; b. Bellevue, Pa., July 16, 1874; s. William and Margaret (McKinney) P.; student Geneva Coll., Beaver Falls, Pa., 1891-96, Ref. Presbyn. Theol. Sem., Pittsburgh, Pa., 1896-99; D.D., Geneva, 1915; m. Carolyn McKaig, 1900. Ordained ministry Ref. Presbyn. Ch., 1900; pastor 1st Ch., St. Louis, Mo., 1900-11, East End Ch., Pittsburgh, 1911-13, 1st Ch., Phila., 1913-19; asst. editor Am. S.S. Union, 1919-23; pres. Geneva Coll. since Sept. 1923. Editor Olive Trees (mag.), 1916-23. Home: Beaver Falls, Pa.

PEARCE, William, bishop; b. Hayle, Cornwall, Eng., Oct. 15, 1862; s. John Richard and Ann Bawden Hosking (Thomas) P.; ed. in Eng.; m. Alma E. Knoll, May 14, 1889 (died Oct. 3, 1908); 1 son, Bernard Asbury; m. 2d, Sarah Allen Dickson, of Phila., July 21, 1915 (died Sept. 14, 1917); 1 dau., Emily Dickson; m. 3d, Mabel E. Kline, of Evanston, Ill., June 8, 1922; 1 dau., Gwendolen Elizabeth. Came to U.S., 1884; ordained Free Meth. Ch., 1888; pastor Corralitos, Calif., 1889-90, Ione, 1891, San Jose, 1892-93, Alameda, 1893-95, Ione, 1896; district elder Ione and San Jose dists., 1897-1900, Portland and Salem dists., 1901-03; pastor Jamestown, N.Y., 1904; district elder Genesee Dist., 1905-07; bishop Free Meth. Ch. since 1908. Mem. Gen. Conf., 3 times, now pres. bd. administration; del. World's Missionary Conv., Edinburgh, Scotland, 1910; missionary tour to Japan, 1927. Author: Our Incarnate Lord. Home: 316 N. Perry St., Titusville, Pa.

PEARCE, William Tudor, chemist; b. Norfolk, Va., Sept. 3, 1890; s. Samuel Ferabee and Mary Holmes (Dabney) P.; A.B., Randolph-Macon Coll., 1910; M.S., U. of Ky., 1912; Ph.D., U. of Chicago, 1916; m. Elizabeth Townes, Sept. 22, 1914; children—Mildred Dabney, Elizabeth Townes, Mary Holmes, Margery Virginia. Instr. in chemistry, Clemson (S.C.) Coll., 1912-13, asst. prof., 1913-14; asst. prof. of chemistry, N.D. State Coll., 1916-18, prof. of physical and industrial chemistry, 1918-24, dean sch. of chemistry, 1924-26; dir. of research Valentine & Co., mfr. paints and varnish, 1926-30; tech. dir. Resinous Products & Chem. Co., Phila., since 1930. Mem. Am. Chem. Soc. (sec. paint and varnish div. 1924-26, chmn. 1927), Sigma Xi. Republican. Episcopalian. Contbr. many articles to Jour. Am. Chem. Soc. and other scientific jours. Home: 512 Merwyn Rd., Narberth, Pa. Office: 222 W. Washington Square, Philadelphia, Pa.

PEARL, Raymond, biologist; b. Farmington, N.H., June 3, 1879; s. Frank and Ida May (McDuffee) P.; A.B., Dartmouth, 1899, Sc.D., 1919; Ph.D., U. of Mich., 1902; U. of Leipzig, 1905, Univ. Coll., London, 1905-06, Carnegie Instn. Table, Naples Zoöl. Station, 1906; LL.D., University of Maine, 1919; Litt.D., from St. John's College, 1935; m. Maud M. DeWitt, June 29, 1903; children—Ruth DeWitt, Penelope Mackey. Asst. in zoölogy, 1899-1902, instr., 1902-06, U. of Mich.; instr. U. of Pa., 1906-07; biologist and head of dept. biology, Maine Agrl. Expt. Sta., 1907-18; prof. biometry and vital statistics, Sch. of Hygiene and Pub. Health, Johns Hopkins, 1918-25, research professor, 1925-30, prof. biology, Medical School, Johns Hopkins, 1923—; statistician, Johns Hopkins Hospital, 1919-35; director Inst. for Biol. Research, Johns Hopkins, 1925-30, professor of biology, School of Hygiene, since 1930. Engaged in biol. researches on variation in fishes, with Biol. Survey Great Lakes (U.S. Fish Commn.), 1901-02; awarded grants for research on variation in organisms from Carnegie Inst., 1904, 05, 06; expert, poultry breeding, U.S. Dept. Agr.; non-resident lecturer Grad. Sch. of Agr., Ames, Iowa, 1910, Lansing, Mich., 1912, Washington, D.C., 1939; Lowell lecturer, Boston, Mass., 1920; special lecturer, University of London, 1927; Harrington lecturer University of Buffalo, 1928; Heath Clark lecturer University of London, 1937; Patten Foundation lecturer and visiting prof., Ind. U., 1938. Member exec. com. and chmn. agrl. com. Nat. Research Council, 1916-18, and mem. exec. board, 1919-30; chief of statis. division U.S. Food Administration, 1917-19; pres. Internat. Union for Scientific Investigation of Population Problems, 1928-30. Mem. bd. visitors and govs. St. John's Coll., 1928-34; trustee Science Service, 1929-35. Editor Quarterly Review of Biology, Human Biology; asso. editor Biometrika, 1906-10, Journal Agricultural Research, 1914-18, Genetics, 1915—, Journal Experimental Zoölogy, 1915—, Metron, 1920—, Biologia Generalis, 1923-27, Acta Biotheoretica, 1937—. Fellow A.A.A.S., Am. Academy Arts and Sciences; member Am. Assn. Phys. Anthropology (pres. 1934-36), National Acad. Sciences (council, 1919-25), Am. Philos. Soc., Am. Soc. Zoölogists (sec. Eastern branch, 1911, pres. 1913), Am. Soc. Naturalists (pres. 1916-17), Washington Acad. Sciences, Am. Statis. Assn., pres. 1939, Internat. Assn. Poultry Instrs. and Investigators, Soc. de Morphologie, Paris, Phi Kappa Psi, Phi Beta Kappa, Phi Kappa Phi, Alpha Zeta; corr. mem. Acad. Nat. Sciences, Phila.; hon. fellow Royal Statist. Soc., London. Decorated Knight of the Crown of Italy, 1920, Officer, 1929. Author: Variation and Differentiation in Ceratophyllum, 1907; Variation and Correlation in the Crayfish (with A. B. Clawson), 1907; Poultry Diseases and Their Treatment (with F. M. Surface and M. R. Curtis), 1911; Modes of Research in Genetics, 1915; Diseases of Poultry (with F. M. Surface and M. R. Curtis), 1915; The Nation's Food, 1919; The Biology of Death, 1922; Introduction to Medical Biometry and Statistics, 1923; Studies in Human Biology, 1924; The Biology of Population Growth, 1925; Alcohol and Longevity, 1926; To Begin With, 1927; The Rate of Living, 1928; Constitution and Health, 1933; The Ancestry of the Long-lived (with Ruth D. Pearl), 1934; The Natural History of Population, 1939. Contbr. numerous papers to biol. jours. Club: University (Baltimore). Home: 401 Hawthorn Rd., Roland Park. Address: Johns Hopkins University, Baltimore, Md.

PEARLMAN, Martin Mandel, merchant and metals; b. Vilna, Russia, Aug. 5, 1879; s. Heyman and Hanna (Adelman) P.; came to U.S., 1897, and naturalized citizen, 1902; ed. Vilna pub. sch. and U. of Vilna; m. Florence Friedman, Sept. 6, 1905; children—Hortense Evelyn (wife of Dr. Harold L. Goldburgh), Helen May (Mrs. Irving M. Silmore), Hazel Maxine (Mrs. Robert A. Moos), Hilda Marian (Mrs. David S. Katz). Began as scrap metal dealer, 1898; acquired zinc smelting plant at Clarksburg, W.Va., 1907; built zinc smelting plant, Moundsville, W.Va., 1916, and one at Bristol, Pa., 1926; pres. Superior Zinc Corpn.; owner M. M. Pearlman & Co.; dir. Superior Hosiery Mills, Inc.; v.p. and dir. Mercer Tube & Mfg. Co., Inc. Republican. Jewish religion. Mason (32°, Shriner). Clubs: Bankers (New York); Manufacturers and Bankers (Philadelphia). Home: 135 S. 17th St. Office: 1700 Sansom St., Philadelphia, Pa.

PEARRE, Albert Austin, physician; b. Frederick, Md., Feb. 1, 1899; s. Albert Lindsay and Nannie Estelle (Dixon) P.; grad. Frederick (Md.) High Sch., 1915; B.S., U. of Va., Charlottesville, Va., 1919, M.D., 1922; m. Mary Eleanor Gould, Oct. 17, 1928; children—Eleanor Gould, Nancy Colbert, Albert Austin. Physician, in practice internal medicine, Frederick, Md., since 1925; asso. with Drs. Smith and Thomas, Frederick. Served in S.A.T.C., U. of Va., 1918. Fellow Am. Coll. Physicians; mem. A.M.A., Southern Med. Soc., Md. State Med. Soc., Alpha Omega Alpha, Phi Kappa Sigma, Phi Beta Pi. Evang. Reformed Ch. Club: Rotary (Frederick, Md.). Address: Frederick, Md.

PEARRE, Sifford, banking; b. Baltimore, Md., July 14, 1884; s. Aubrey and Anne Josephine (Sifford) P.; A.B., Johns Hopkins U., 1904; m. Angelica Wirt Yonge, Sept. 9, 1930; children—Letitia Breckinridge, Sifford, Jr. Employed as clk. Mercantile Trust Co., Baltimore, 1906-13; sec.-treas. New Amsterdam Casualty Co., Baltimore, since 1913, dir. and mem. exec. com. since 1913; vice-pres. Equitable Trust Co., Baltimore, since 1921; dir. and mem. exec. committee Roland Park Co., Industrial Bldg., Income Foundation (chmn. bd.); dir. of Northway Apt., pres. and dir. and mem. exec. com. Insuranshares Certificates; sec., treas. and dir. American Indemnity Co., all of Baltimore; dir. and mem. exec. com. Dist. Lawyers, Wash. Title Cos.; vice-pres. and dir. Consolidated Title Co. of Washington, D.C. Served as lt. U.S.N.

during World War. Mem. Delta Phi. Democrat. Episcopalian. Clubs: Gibson Island (Gibson Island); Merchants (Baltimore). Home: Gibson Island, Anne Arundel Co. Office: Calvert & Fayette Sts., Baltimore, Md.

PEARSALL, David Edelblute, research fellow, chem. engr.; b. Brookville, Pa., Feb. 2, 1899; s. Elmer E. and Ada E. (Edelblute) P.; B.S. in Chem. Engring., U. of Pa., 1922, Chem. E., 1930; m. Flora Mary MacSweyn, Aug. 20, 1928; children—David E., II, Martha Ann, Mary Flora, Donald M. Research chem. engr. Atlas Powder Co., Tamaqua, Pa., 1922-23; chem. engr. and plant foreman Vulcan Detinning Co., Pittsburgh, 1923-26; development chem. engr. Western Electric Co., Chicago, 1926-30; research fellow and chem. engr., Mellon Inst. of Industrial Research, Pittsburgh, since 1930; specialist on blasting fuses, explosives and insulations. Mem. Am. Chem. Soc., Am. Inst. Chem. Engrs., Nat. Soc. Professional Engrs. Registered engineer in State of Pa. Republican. Congregationalist. Club: Faculty. Writer on chem. subjects. Holder 6 U.S. patents. Home: Oak Hill Farms, Allison Park, Pa.

PEARSON, George Burton, Jr., vice chancellor of the State of Delaware; b. Middletown, Del., Aug. 8, 1905; s. George Burton and Mary Estelle (Cochran) Pearson; student public schools, Middletown and Newark, Del., 1911-21, Wilmington Friends Sch., 1921-23; A.B., magna cum laude, Princeton U., 1927; LL.B., U. of Pa. Law Sch., 1931; unmarried. Law clk. of Hon. Victor B. Woolley, judge U.S. Circuit Ct. of Appeals, for the 3rd Circuit, 1930-31; admitted to Del. bar, 1931; asso. atty. in law offices of Hugh M. Morris, Wilmington, 1931-39; vice chancellor State of Del. since 1939. Mem. bd. edn. Newark (Del.) Spl. Sch. Dist. Mem. Am. Bar Assn., Del. Bar Assn., New Castle County Bar Assn., Princeton Alumni Assn. of Del., U. of Pa. Alumni Assn. of Del., Friends Sch. Alumni Assn. of Wilmington. Club: Wilmington Country. Home: 94 E. Main St., Newark, Del. Office: Court House, Wilmington, Del.

PEARSON, Gerald Hamilton Jeffrey, M.D.; b. Key West, Fla., Sept. 21, 1893; s. George Lloyd and Frances (Baxter) P.; B.A., U. of Western Ontario, Can., 1915, M.D., 1915; D.Sc., U. of Pa., 1930; m. Mary Agnes Mackenzie, July 3, 1916; children—Frances Marion, Lesle Agnes, George Robert. Asst. physician Ontario (Canada) Hosp. for Insane, 1915-16; neuro-psychiatrist Ottawa Civic Hosp., 1924-25, Phila. Child Guidance Clinic, 1928-32; asso. in psychiatry, U. of Pa. Grad. Sch. of Medicine, 1932; asso. prof. child psychiatry, Temple U., Phila., since 1938. Served as capt., Med. Corps, Canadian Expeditionary Forces, 1916-19. Mem. following professional assns.: A.M.A., Phila. Co. Med. Soc., Am. Psychiat. Assn., Am. Orthopsychiat. Assn., Phila. Psychiat. Soc., Phila. Pediatric Soc., Phila. Neurol. Soc., Toronto Acad. of Medicine, Phila. Psychoanalytic Soc. Democrat. Home: 512 Windermere Road, Drexel Hill. Office: 111 N. 49th St., Philadelphia, Pa.

PEARSON, Joseph Cleaveland, dir. research; b. Andover, Me., May 25, 1879; s. Samuel Wiggin and Mary Jane (Alexander) P.; A.B., Bowdoin Coll., 1900; A.M., Harvard U. Grad. Sch., 1903; m. Marian Hazel Strayer, Sept. 21, 1912; children—Mary Helen, Samuel Strayer, Nancy Marian. Engaged as instr. mathematics and physics, Bowdoin Coll., 1903-06; magnetic observer, Carnegie Instn. of Washington, D.C., 1906-10; asst., then, asso. physicist, U.S. Bur. Standards, 1910-24; asst. to chem. engr., Lehigh Portland Cement Co., Allentown, Pa., 1924-31, dir. of research since 1932. Mem. A.A.A.S., Am. Concrete Inst. (dir. and past pres.), Am. Soc. for Testing Materials, Alpha Delta Phi. Republican. Contbr. many papers on cement and concrete to proceedings tech. socs. Home: 2001 Pennsylvania St., Allentown, Pa. Office: 718 Hamilton St., Allentown, Pa.

PEARSON, Joseph Thurman, Jr., artist; b. Germantown, Pa., Feb. 6, 1876; s. Joseph T. and Annie V. P.; pupil Pa. Acad. Fine Arts and under J. Alden Weir; m. Emily R. Fetter, Oct. 7, 1902; children—Ruth Elizabeth, Joseph Thurman, Emily, Julian Weir, Jane, Virginia, Justin. Fellowship prize, Pa. Acad., 1910; bronze medal, Buenos Aires Expn., 1910; Sesnan gold medal, Pa. Acad., 1911; 2d Hallgarten prize, Nat. Acad., 1911; hon. mention Carnegie Inst., Pittsburgh, 1911; Inness gold medal, Nat. Acad., 1915; gold medal, San Francisco Expn., 1915; Harris silver medal, Art Inst. Chicago, 1915; Temple gold medal and Stotesbury prize, 1916, and Beck gold medal, Pa. Acad., 1917; Palmer gold medal, Art Inst. Chicago, 1918; gold medal, Sesquicentennial, Phila., 1926; Joseph Pennell medal, Phila. Water Color Exhbn., 1933; 1st award Germantown Art Assn., 1934. A.N.A., 1917. Club: T Square of Phila. (hon.). Home: Huntingdon Valley, Pa.

PEARSON, Peter Henry, coll. prof.; b. Landskrona, Sweden, Mar. 1864; s. Hans and Johanna (Nilson) P.; came to U.S. at age of 5; A.B., Roanoke Coll., Va., 1890; A.M., U. of Berlin, 1893; fellow, U. of Neb.; traveled in Eng., France and Switzerland, studying ednl. methods there; L.H.D., 1906; m. Esther Lincoln, 1898; children—Agnes, Karl G. Asst., 1887, prof. English and German, 1892, prof. and head dept. English lang. and lit., 1895, and v.p. 1917, Bethany Coll.; now professor edn., Upsala Coll., East Orange, N.J., vice-president of the college, 1928-1930. Represented Bethany Coll. at Jubileum of U. of Upsala, Sweden, Sept. 1893. Lutheran. Lecturer on Shakespeare, the Elizabethan Drama, U. of Kan., 1911. Pres. Kan. State Assn. Teachers of English, 1914-15. Mem. fgn. div. U.S. Bur. Edn., 1918. Rep. U.S. Bur. of Edn. in Europe, studying schools of Scandinavia, 1920-21. Author: Questions on Shakespeare's Hamlet, 1900; Study-Plans of English and American Classics, 1907; The Study of Literature, 1913; Prairie Vikings, 1927; Methods of Learning, 1931; Shakespeare—Plots and Studies of Chief Plays, 1935. Edited edits. of Macaulay's "Essay on Milton," 1904, Longfellow's "Evangeline," 1904, and "Courtship of Miles Standish," 1905; also bulls. on edn. in Scandinavia, Holland, Switzerland and educational articles in mags. Home: Upsala College, East Orange, N.J.

PEARSON, William Alexander, M.D., educator; b. Van Wert, O., Apr. 6, 1879; s. Richard and Mary Elizabeth (Freshour) P.; Ph.C., U. of Mich., 1900; student Ferris Inst.; M.D., Hahnemann Med. Coll., 1915; Sc.D., La Salle Coll., 1928; Ph.D., Philadelphia Coll. of Pharmacy, 1935; m. Mary Longworth, Oct. 14, 1903; 1 dau., Mary Elizabeth. Research chemist, Parke, Davis & Co., Detroit, Mich., 1900-04; prof. chemistry, Ferris Inst., 1904-06; prof. chemistry, Hahnemann Med. Coll., 1906—, dean, 1913—. Mem. Am. Inst. Homœopathy, pres. 1938-39, Am. Chem. Soc., Am. Pharm. Assn., Am. Assn. Clin. Research. Methodist. Mason (32°). Clubs: Union League (Phila.), Rotary, Cynwyd, Penn. Author: Medical Chemistry, 1911; toxicology 1931; Physiological and Clinical Chemistry 1938. Home: Narberth, Pa.

PEARTREE, Armand J., real estate and mortgage financing; b. Troy, N.Y., Sept. 19, 1906; s. Edward J. and Sophia (Janelle) P.; A.B., U. of Pa., 1928; m. Madeleine Anne Braceland, Oct. 4, 1930; 1 son, Charles Edward. With John H. McClatchy, builder, Phila., successively as clerk, salesman, asst. to sales mgr. and asst. sales mgr., 1929-32; with W. A. Clarke Co. and W. A. Clarke Mortgage Co., Phila., since 1932, successively as apt. supervisor, dist. mgr., dept. head and sales mgr. of residential properties, vice-pres. since 1935, dir. since 1937. Mem. Delta Sigma Phi, Phi Chi. Club: University (Phila.). Home: 128 Cynwyd Rd., Bala-Cynwyd, Pa. Office: 1614 Walnut St., Philadelphia, Pa.

PEASE, Henry Hildreth, coal and railroads; b. Wilkes-Barre, Pa., Jan. 2, 1878; s. Erastus Sheldon and Mary (Hildreth) P.; ed. Lawrenceville (N.J.) Sch.; B.S., Princeton, 1899; m. Mae Townsend, Feb. 27, 1906; children—Henry Hildreth, Jr., Pauline Townsend. Asso. with Lehigh Coal and Navigation Co. since 1913, vice-pres. and sec. since 1922; sec. and treas. Lehigh and New England R.R. Co.; sec. Lehigh Navigation Coal Co., Inc.; vice-pres. and sec. Greenwood Corpn.; dir. and vice-pres., sec., treas. 32 corpns. subsidiary to above; dir. Central-Penn Nat. Bank. Republican. Episcopalian. Clubs: Rittenhouse, Racquet, Midday, Philadelphia Country. Home: 2307 Delancey St. Office: 1421 Chestnut St., Philadelphia, Pa.

PEASE, Lucius Curtis (Lute Pease), cartoonist, painter; b. Winnemucca, Nev., Mar. 27, 1869; s. Lucius Curtis and Mary Isabel (Hutton) P.; grad. Malone (N.Y.) Acad., 1887; m. Nell Christmas McMullin, of Washington, D.C., June 22, 1905. Began as rancher, Santa Barbara County, Calif., 1887; prospector and gold miner including 5 yrs. in Alaska; Yukon-Nome corr. Seattle-Post-Intelligencer, 1897-1901; U.S. commr. Kotzebue Sound-Point Hope Dist., Alaska, 1901-02; political cartoonist and reporter Portland Oregonian, 1902-05; editor in chief Pacific Monthly, Portland, Ore., 1906-13; political cartoonist Newark (N.J.) Evening News since 1914; painter of portraits and landscapes. Exhibited at Nat. Acad., Nat. Arts Club, New York. Clubs: Newark Art; Art Center of the Oranges, N.J. Contbr. articles and short stories to mags. Home: 105 Durand Rd., Maplewood, N.J. Office: Newark Evening News, Newark, N.J.

PEASLEE, Amos Jenkins, lawyer; b. Clarksboro, N.J., Mar. 24, 1887; s. Gideon and Emma (Waddington) P.; A.B., Swarthmore (Pa.) Coll., 1907; studied Birmingham U., Eng.; LL.B., Columbia, 1911; m. Dorothy K. Quimby, Feb. 12, 1920; children—Dorothy Waddington, Amos Jenkins, Lucy Raynes, Richard Cutts. Practiced at N.Y. City, 1911-38; dir. First Nat. Bank & Trust Co., Woodbury, N.J.; dir. Ferargil Galleries; chmn. industrial appeals bd. of NRA, Washington, D.C., 1933-34. Director Am. Courier Service, World War, rank of major, attached to Gen. Pershing's hdqrs., France; chmn. N.Y.-European Election Commn. which held election in Army and Navy in Europe, 1917; judge advocate of Gen. Court Martial in France; associated with Am. Commn. to Negotiate Peace. Mem. Am. Bar Assn., Assn. Bar of City of New York, Am. Soc. Internat. Law, Internat. Law Assn. (pres. Am. branch 1929), Pilgrims, Académie Diplomatique Internationale (Paris), Delta Upsilon. Republican. Quaker. Clubs: Metropolitan, Army and Navy (Washington); University, Columbia University (New York); Union Interalliée (Paris); Buccaneers (Berlin). Home: Clarksboro, N.J.; and Mantoloking, N.J.

PEBLY, Harry E(ugene), supervising prin. schs.; b. Latrobe, Pa., May 24, 1894; s. Henry W. and Sara (Bossert) P.; A.B., Thiel Coll., 1917; ed. Mich. State Coll., 1920-21; M.Edn., U. of Pittsburgh, 1935; m. Esther Roth, Aug. 15, 1921; children—Harry E., Jr., Esther R., Robert R., Ruth R. Prin. high sch., Monaca, Pa., 1921-22, Sharpsville, Pa., 1922-28; supervising prin. schs., Sharpsville, Pa., since 1928. Served as 2d lt. 317th Inf., U.S.A., 1917-19, with A.E.F. in three mil. campaigns. Mem. Nat. Edn. Assn., Assn. Am. Sch. Administrs., Am. Legion. Republican. Lutheran. Club: Sharpsville Service. Home: 109 Pierce Av., Sharpsville, Pa.

PECK, Staunton Bloodgood, civil and mech. engr.; b. N.Y. City, Oct. 20, 1864; s. Thomas Bloodgood and Mary Frances (Staunton) P.; student Columbia, 1882-86, fellow in engring., 1886-87, M.E., 1886, C.E., 1887; m. Clarabelle Moberly, 1893 (died 1910); m. 2d, Lola Maurene Downin, 1914. Mech. engr. with Burr & Dodge, Phila., 1887-88; asst. chief engr., Link-Belt Engring. Co., Phila., 1880-91; chief engr. Link-Belt Machinery Co., 1891-1906; v.p. Link-Belt Co., 1906-28; retired 1928; served as pres. Dodge Steel Co., Olney Foundry Co. during World War. Mem. Alpha Delta Phi. Republican. Episcopalian. Clubs: Union League, Rittenhouse, Phila. Country, Sunnybrook Golf (Phila.); University (New York). Home: Montgomery Av., Chestnut Hill, Philadelphia, Pa.

PEDERSEN, Robert Holm, artist; b. Denmark, June 1, 1906; s. Johan and Laurine (Holm) P.; came to U.S., 1924, naturalized, 1931; ed. Borgerskole, Nyborg, 1912-20, Tekniskeskole, Horsens, Denmark, 1920-24; m. Verna Francis,

May 31, 1908; children—Robert, Richard, Sonia. Began painting as a child; exhibited Chicago Art Inst., Pa. Acad. Fine Arts, Currier Art Gallery, Conn. Acad. Fine Arts, Newark Mus., Montclair Mus., and many others. Awarded 2d prize, Newark Art Club, 1936, 1st and 3d prizes, N.J. Gallery, 1937, 1st prize, Irvington Municipal Exhbn., 1938; represented N.J. in Nat. Exhbn., New York City, 1937. Mem. Am. Artists Professional League, Asbury Park Soc. Fine Arts. Home: 523 Main St., Orange, N.J.

PEELLE, Stanton Canfield, lawyer; b. Indianapolis, Ind., July 5, 1880; s. Stanton J. (late chief justice U.S. Ct. of Claims) and Mary Arabella (Canfield) P.; student pvt. and pub. schs. Indianapolis; grad. Columbian Prep. Sch., D.C., 1895; A.B., Columbian Univ. (D.C.), 1899, LL.B., 1902; m. Julia F. Ravenel, Oct. 25, 1905; children—Stanton Canfield, Ellen duB. R. (Mrs. James Parker Nolan), Elizabeth R. (Mrs. Armistead L. Boothe), Mary Canfield (dec.), William Ravenel. Admitted to D.C. bar, 1902, and since practiced in Washington, D.C.; prof. Constitutional law, Washington Coll. of Law, 1904-06; 1st asst. U.S. Atty., D.C., 1910-11; spl. asst. U.S. Atty., 1911-12; partner firm Hoehling, Peelle & Ogilby and successors since 1913, firm now Peelle, Lesh, Drain & Barnard; di. Mayflower Hotel Corpn., Sterrett Operating Service, Capital Constrn. Co. Mem. 3 Street Ry. Co. wage arbitrations. Mem. Am. Bar Assn., D.C. Bar Assn. (ex-pres.), Mil. Order Loyal Legion, S.R., Soc. Colonial Wars, Friends of Law Library of Congress (charter mem.), Theta Delta Chi. Republican. Presbyn. Clubs: Lawyers (ex-pres.), Metropolitan, Chevy Chase (gov.), University (gov.). Home: 5900 Connecticut Av., Chevy Chase, Md. Office: 1422 F St. N.W., Washington, D.C.

PEER, Alfred J., mem. law firm Heine, Peer, Laird & Mahr. Office: 744 Broad St., Newark, N.J.

PEERY, Rob Roy, composer, music editor; b. Saga, Japan, Jan. 6, 1900; s. Rev. Rufus Benton and A. Letitia (Rich) P. (Am. missionaries); A.B., Midland Coll., Fremont, Neb., 1920, hon. Mus. D., 1938; Mus. B., Oberlin (O.) Coll., 1925; student Bush Conservatory (Chicago), School of Sacred Music, Union Theol. Sem. (New York); pupil of Rubin Goldmark, N.Y.; hon. Mus. D., Wittenberg Coll., Springfield, O., 1938; m. Dorothy Wolff, Sept. 10, 1925; children—Alfred Lee, Caroline Wolff, Shirley Rich, Robyn Jean. Began career as musician, Omaha, Neb., 1920; violinist Omaha Symphony Orchestra, 1920-21; organist, Atchison, Kan., 1916-19, Denver, Colo., 1921; Statesville, N.C., 1923; Salisbury, N.C., 1925-28, 1929-31, Brooklyn, 1928-29; organist and choirmaster St. Matthew's Luth. Ch., Phila., since 1932; mem. music faculty Lenoir-Rhyne Coll., Hickory, N.C., 1922-23, Catawba Coll., Salisbury, N.C., 1926-28, 1929-31; traveling musical dir. Metro Picture Corpn., 1922; publ. mgr. Theodore Presser Co., music pubs., Phila., since 1932. Served in S.A.T.C., 1918. Awarded Etude piano prize, 1923; Ohio State prize, 1925; Homiletic Review prize hymn, 1926; $1,000 Dartmouth prize, 1930; Franklin Memorial prize, 1938. Mem. Am. Soc. Composers, Authors and Pubs., Hymn Soc. America, Com. on Ch. Music of United Luth. Ch., Am. Guild of Organists. Composer of 250 published compositions, including works for orchestra, chorus and quartet, and solos for voice, violin, organ, piano; specializes in sacred music; hymns appear in contemporary hymnals. Major works: The Nightingale (operetta), Glory to God (Christmas cantata), String Quartet in D (manuscript), Symphonic Movement in E Minor (manuscript). Author: Fiddling for Fun, 1929; Easiest Orchestra Collection, 1932; Third Position Violin Book, 1936; Young People's Choir Book, 1937. Contbr. to musical and religious jours.; mem. editorial bd. Etude Music Mag. Home: 216 Valley Rd., Merion, Pa. Office: 1712 Chestnut St., Philadelphia, Pa.

PEERY, Thomas Benton, clergyman; b. Nagasaki, Japan, Feb. 9, 1898; s. Rev. Rufus Benton and A. Letitia (Rich) P., Am. missionaries; A.B., Midland Coll., Fremont, Neb., 1920; A.M., Gettysburg Coll., Gettysburg, Pa., 1926; diploma, Gettysburg Theol. Sem., 1926; S.T.M., Temple U., Phila., Pa., 1935, S.T.D., 1936; m. Ruth Louisa Rhonemus, June 30, 1928; children—David Benton, Patricia Ann. Ordained to ministry Luth. Ch., 1926; engaged in mus. and ednl. work, 1920-23; tenor singer; asso. pastor, First Luth. Ch., Cincinnati, O., 1926; pastor, Trinity Luth. Ch., Lakewood, Cleveland, O., 1927-30; pastor, St. Matthew's Luth. Ch., Phila., Pa., since 1930; vice-pres. East Pa. Conf. Luth. Ch.; pres. Alumni Assn. Gettysburg Theol. Sem., Gettysburg, Pa.; corr. sec. Hymn Soc. of Phila.; mem. exec. com. Luth. Student Work, Phila. Served in S.A.T.C., Fort Sheridan, Ill. and Midland Coll., Atchison, Kan., 1918. Pres. Luth. Ministerial Assn., Phila., Pa., 1935. Mem. Tau Kappa Alpha. Lutheran. Club: Lutheran Social Union (Phila). Contbr. to Luth. periodicals. Home: 5021 Schuyler St., Philadelphia, Pa.

PEET, Gerald Dayton, civil engr.; b. Fairview, Ia., Nov. 25, 1890; s. John C. and Charlotte Maria (Peck) P.; prep. edn. Cortland (N.Y.) State Normal Sch., 1905-09; C.E., Columbia, 1913; m. Marie Elizabeth Rouillot, May 26, 1915; children—Elizabeth Marie, Gerald Dayton, John Randolph. With Alexander Potter, New York, in the office and as field engr., 1913-16; supt. of constrn. reinforced concrete dam, Kingsville, Texas, Feb.-June 1916; resident engr. sewage system and plant, Piermont, N.Y., 1916-17; engr. in charge various projects, Feb.-Nov. 1917; sales engr. Wallace & Tiernan Co., Inc., mfrs., Belleville, N.J., 1917-21, chief engr. since 1921; chief engr. Wallace & Tiernan Products, Inc., since 1923, sec.-treas. and dir. since 1923; chief engr. Novadel-Agene Corpn. since 1928, sec., 1930-31, asst. sec. since 1931; pres. and dir. Wallace & Tiernan Sales Corpn.; sec. and dir. Industrial Appliance Corpn., Novadel-Agene, Ltd. (Can.); dir. Lucidol Corpn. Mem. Sigma Xi, Tau Beta Pi, Theta Delta Chi. Baptist. Clubs: Essex Fells (N.J.) Country; Montclair (N.J.) Athletic. Home: 12 Berkeley Place, Montclair, N.J. Office: 11 Mill St., Belleville, N.J.

PEETS, Orville Houghton, artist; b. Cleveland, O., Aug. 13, 1884; s. Edward Orville and Mary (Houghton) P.; studied at Academie Julian and Institut des Beaux Arts, Paris, 1903-06; m. Ethel Poyntell Canby, Sept. 23, 1914. Represented in Luxembourg Collection, Jeu de Paume, Paris, Cleveland Mus. of Art, Los Angeles Mus. of Art, Wilmington Mus. of Art, New York Pub. Library, Hispanic Soc. of America Mus., State Library of Calif. at Sacramento; 50 prints of the year, 1932-33; "Fine Prints, 1934"; Am. Graphic Art Exhbn., New York World's Fair, 1939. Awards: hon. mention Paris Salon, 1914; Internat. Printmakers Exhbn. gold Medal, 1931; Cleveland Mus. of Art intaglio class 1st prize, 1932; Medaille Commemorative Francaise de la Grande Guerre, 1918. Served as 2d lt., intelligence sect., A.E.F., U.S.A., World War. Instr. in painting, Wilmington Acad. of Art. Del. State archery champion, 1939. Home: Millsboro, Del.; (summer) Woodstock, N.Y.

PEFFLEY, William Edwin, clergyman, editor; b. Marysville, Pa., Mar. 31, 1876; s. John and Susan (Kocher) P.; A.B., Albright Coll., 1902, hon. D.D., 1933; B.D., Temple U., 1912; m. Joyce Marcella Hoch., June 9, 1904. Ordained to ministry Evang. Ch., 1902; pastor Evang. Chs., Milmont, York, Scranton, Altoona, Lewistown, 1902-1916; editor Christian Endeavor magazine, 1912-22; editor S.S. lit. since 1922. Mem. Internat. Council Religious Edn., Gen. Church Bd. Christian Edn.; trustee International Soc. Christian Endeavor; dir. Pa. Christian Endeavor Union; mem. worship com. Federal Council of Churches; dean Leadership Edn. Summer School, West Milton, Pa., since 1924; pres. Bd. of Examiners Central Pa. Conf. since 1908; sec. Conf. Missionary Soc. since 1909; pres. County Bd. of Pub. Instrn.; pres. Lemoyne School Bd. Republican. Mem. Evang. Ch., Lemoyne, Pa. Author: Teacher Training Textbook; Doctrinal Handbook; Church Finance. Home: 264 Walton St., Lemoyne, Pa. Office: 3d and Reily Sts., Harrisburg, Pa.

PEINADO VALLEJO, Juan, former Spanish consul; b. Ronda, Málaga, Spain, Mar. 6, 1896; s. Joaquin Peinado Díaz and Concepción Vallejo Gonzalez; m. Rosa Berutich Llinas, Oct. 21, 1928; children—Joaquin, Rosa, Concha, Matilde. Mayor of Ronda, Apr. 1931-May 1933; gov. Almeria Province, Spain, Feb.-Oct. 1936; consul of Spain, Philadelphia, since Feb. 1937. Home: 200 Woodside Av., Narberth, Pa.

PEIRCE, Bertha Carolyn, coll. prof.; b. Ercildown, Pa., June 7, 1885; d. Ernest Fulton and Clara (Hanway) P.; grad. West Chester (Pa.) High Sch., 1902; A.B., Swarthmore Coll., 1906; A.M., Cornell U., 1907, grad. student, 1910-11; unmarried. Instr. of Latin and Greek, Swarthmore Coll.; later head dept. of classics, Hood Coll., Frederick, Md.; head dept. of classics, Beaver Coll. since 1927. Mem. Classical Assn. of Middle and Western States, Classical Assn. of Atlantic States, Phila. Classical Soc., Phi Beta Kappa. Hon. class scholarship each year as student of Swarthmore Coll.; Lucretia Mott fellowship and Classical fellowship, Cornell U. Mem. Friends' Meeting. Home: 501 West Av., Jenkintown, Pa.

PEIRCE, Frederick, investment banker; b. Bristol, Pa., Nov. 30, 1879; s. Joshua and Mary Eloise (Thomas) P.; grad. U. of Pa. Wharton Sch. of Finance and Econ., 1902; m. Ethel Eyre Tyson, Oct. 16, 1907; children—Elizabeth T., Frederick, Jr. Asso. with N. W. Halsey & Co. in Pittsburgh and other cities, 1902-16, established Phila. office and mgr. then vice-pres. and sales mgr. 12 eastern offices, 1905-16; founded securities distributing house Frederick Peirce & Co. and pres. since 1916; pres. Foresight Foundation, Inc., Public Investing Co. Republican. Clubs: Union League, Bond (Phila.). Author: The Human Side of Business, 1916. Home: Wynnewood, Pa. Office: 225 S. 15th St., Philadelphia, Pa.

PEIRCE, Mary Bisbing, prin. The Peirce Sch.; b. Springfield, Pa., Nov. 23, 1862; d. Dr. Thomas May, Sr. and Emma Louise (Bisbing) P.; desc. George P. came from Eng. to Phila., 1684; grad. Phila. High Sch. for Girls; hon. A.M., Dickinson Coll., 1910. Served as prin. and head of The Peirce Sch. in Phila. since death of father, Dr. Thomas May Peirce, Sr., 1896; has entire charge of welfare of thousands of students from all parts of world; exec. Woman's Assn. Meth. Hosp.; active in civic organs., of Phila. art, music, pub. progress and welfare. Award: Philadelphians at Home, for distinguished service to Phila., 1939. Mem. D.A.R., Acad. Fine Arts. Republican. Methodist. Clubs: Women's City (founder), Business Women's (founder), Matinee Musical (Philadelphia). Has traveled extensively. Contbr. many articles to various mags. Lecturer and pub. speaker. Home: 1616 N. Broad St. Office: 1420 Pine St., Philadelphia, Pa.

PEIRCE, Thomas May, Jr., certified public accountant; b. Phila., Pa., Apr. 14, 1878; s. Thomas May and Ruth (Stong) P.; ed. Central Manual Training High Sch., Phila., 1892-95, U. of Pa., 1895-99 (B.S.), Peirce Sch., Phila., 1899-1901; m. Grace A. Bennett, Sept. 9, 1905; children—Thomas May 3d, Ann Bennett. Instr. Peirce Sch., 1901-02; sec.-treas. Oscar Smith & Sons Co., 1902-16, Hercules Cement Corpn., 1916-20, North Pitman Land Co., 1908-36; v.p. and dir. Honorbilt Products, Inc., since 1922; pub. accountant since 1921, C.P.A. (Pa.) since 1931; administrative exec. and partner Peirce Sch. since 1934. Served as aide-de-camp to 1st lt. and adj., 2d Pa. Vol. Inf., 1898. Mem. Pa. Inst. C.P.A.'s, Nat. Assn. Cost Accountants, Nat. Commercial Teachers Fed., N.E.A., Eastern Commercial Teachers Assn., Pa. Pvt. Business Schs., Pa. Approved Pvt. Business Schs. (chmn.), Pa. Mus., Pa. Hist. Soc., Pa. S.R., Phila. Chamber of Commerce, Delta Upsilon. Universalist. Mason. Kiwanian. Author of brochures, The Case for Guarantee of Bank Deposits, Bank Failures—Causes and Remedies. Home: 1434 Pine St. Office: 312 S. Broad St., Philadelphia, Pa.

PEIRCE, William Henry, retired engineer; b. Baltimore, Aug. 22, 1865; s. William Henry and Georgia V. (Browne) P.; M.E., Stevens

Inst. Tech., 1884, E.D., from the same institution, 1935; m. Esther Royston Belt, August 23, 1933. Apprentice with Pa. R.R., Wilmington, Delaware, 1884-87; draftsman, etc., Aurora, Ill., 1887-88, assistant master mechanic, Galesburg, 1888-89, C.,B.&Q.Ry.; supt. construction, United Edison Co., New York, 1889-90; apptd. spl. investigator, 1890, v.p. 1904; ex-pres. Baltimore Copper Smelting & Rolling Co.; ex-pres. Peirce-Smith Converter Co.; ex-v.p. Am. Smelting & Refining Co.; past dir. Revere Copper & Brass, Incorporated. Mem. Am. Soc. M.E., Am. Inst. Mining Engrs., Am. Electrochem. Soc., Sigma Chi. Republican. Episcopalian. Clubs: Merchants', Baltimore Country (Baltimore); Bankers (New York). Inventor of methods in electrolytic refining of copper, and in basic converting of copper matte to copper. James Douglas medalist, Am. Inst. Mining and Metall. Engrs., 1931. Home: 100 W. University Parkway, Baltimore, Md.

PEIRCE, Willis McGerald, research engr.; b. Buffalo, N.Y., June 20, 1896; s. Walter Merton and Frances Agnes (McGerald) P.; ed. Pa. State Coll., 1914-17; B.S., U. of Ill., 1918; M.S., Yale, 1920; m. Lotta J. Ripley, July 5, 1923; children—Frances Lillian, Donald Ripley. Began as research investigator, 1919; asso. with New Jersey Zinc Co., producers of metallic zinc and zinc pigments, Palmerton, Pa., since 1919, chief metal div., 1928-36, asst. chief research, 1936-37, chief of research since 1937. Served in C.W.S., U.S.A., 1918-19. Mem. Am. Inst. Mining & Metall. Engrs. (dir.), Soc. Automotive Engrs., Brit. Inst. Metals, Lehigh Valley Engrs. Club, Sigma Pi, Gamma Alpha. Republican. Lutheran. Home: Residence Park, Palmerton, Pa.

PEISER, Kurt, social worker; b. Breslau, Germany, Feb. 3, 1897; s. Hugo and Rosa (Peiser) P.; came to U.S., 1907; A.B., U. of Mich., 1917, A.M., same, 1918; m. Carolyn Tiefenbronner, Sept. 8, 1923. Asst. supt. Jewish Orphan Home, Cleveland, O., 1918-21; exec. dir. Abraham Lincoln House, Milwaukee, Wis., 1921-23, Federated Jewish Charities, 1923-27; exec. dir. United Jewish Social Agencies, Cincinnati, O., 1927-32; exec. dir. Jewish Welfare Federation, Detroit, Mich., 1932-37; exec. dir. Federation of Jewish Charities, Phila., Pa., since 1937; lecturer, U. of Cincinnati Grad. Sch., 1927-30; lecturer, Wayne U. Grad. Sch., 1935-36. Mem. Am. Assn. Social Workers, Nat. Conf. Jewish Social Welfare, Nat. Conf. Social Work. Jewish religion. Home: 404 S. Sterling Rd., Elkins Park, Philadelphia, Pa. Office: 1700 Walnut St., Philadelphia, Pa.

PELL, Walden II, clergyman, educator; b. Quogue, L.I., N.Y., July 3, 1902; s. Francis Livingston and Ellen Van Buren (Morris) P.; diploma, St. Mark's Sch., 1920; student Princeton University, 1920-23; Rhodes scholar, Oxford University, England, 1923-26, M.A. from same, 1930; m. Edith Minturn Bonsal, Aug. 25, 1928; children—Melissa, Stuyvesant Bonsal, Mary Leigh. Master in Lenox (Massachusetts) Sch., 1926-30; headmaster St. Andrew's Sch., Middletown, Del., since 1930. Ordained deacon P.E. Ch., 1927, priest, 1928. Democrat. Clubs: Princeton (New York); Ivy (Princeton); Cardinal, Kilcannon (Oxford). Home: Middletown, Del.

PELOUZE, Percy Starr, physician; b. Camden, N.J., July 30, 1876; s. Edward and Anna Budd (Sayrs) P.; student Waverly High Sch., Baltimore Co., Md., Baltimore City Coll., Burlington (N.J.) Acad.; M.D., Jefferson Med. Coll., 1902; post grad. study in urology, Johns Hopkins, and Harvard, 1912; m. Grace Saddlemire, Dec. 1, 1904; children—Anna Grace (Mrs. Thomas J. McClelland), Ruth (Mrs. C. Stewart Lynn, Jr.). Interne St. Barnabas Hosp., Newark, N.J., 1902-03; gen. practice of medicine, Newark, N.J., 1903-12; practice in urology, Camden, N.J., 1913-15, Phila., since 1915; cystoscopist to Jefferson Hosp., Phila., 1912-17, University Hosp., since 1917; asst. prof. of urology, U. of Pa., since 1919; special consultant U.S. Pub. Health Service. Fellow Phila. Coll. of Physicians; mem. Am. Social Hygiene Assn. (mem. bd. dirs.), Am. Neisserian Med. Soc. (mem. exec. com. and past pres.), Pa. Social Hygiene Soc. (vice-pres.), Phi Beta Pi, Sigma Psi. Clubs: Phila. Medical, Aesculapius, Penn Athletic (Phila.). Mem. editorial bd. Jour. of Syphilis, Gonorrhea and Venereal Diseases; asso. editor of Cyclopedia of Medicine. Author: Gonorrhea in the Male and Female; also many journal articles. Home: 1216 Drexel Av., Drexel Hill, Pa. Office: 1737 Chestnut St., Philadelphia, Pa.

PEMBERTON, Ralph, M.D.; b. Phila., Pa., Sept. 14, 1877; s. Henry and Agnes (Williams) P.; B.S., U. of Pa., 1898, M.S., 1899, M.D., 1903, Woodward fellow in physiol. chemistry, Pepper Lab., 1908-10; grad. study Berlin, 1911, U. of Strassburg, 1912; m. Virginia Breckenridge Miller, May 23, 1911. Began practice, Phila., 1905; instr. in medicine, U. of Pa., 1907-10, asso. prof. medicine, Grad. Sch., 1928-31, prof. since 1931; asst. visiting phys., Univ. of Pa. Hosp., 1908-10; asst. visiting neurologist, Phila. Gen. Hosp., 1905-08; visiting physician and dir. dept. clin. chemistry, Presbyterian Hosp., 1913-33; visiting physician to Abington Memorial Hosp., Bryn Mawr Hosp., consulting phys. to Chester County Hosp., Orthopedic Hosp. and Infirmary for Nervous Diseases. Served as maj. Med. Corps, U.S.A., in charge intensive study and treatment of arthritis. Mem. standing com. on preventive medicine, Dept. of Health, Phila., 1921-22; chmn. Am. Com. for Control of Rheumatism, 1927-37; president Am. Assn. for Study and Control of Rheumatic Diseases; pres. Ligue Internationale contre le Rhumatisme. Fellow Am. Coll. Physicians, Coll. Physicians Phila.; mem. A.M.A. (mem. standing council on physical therapy), Am. Soc. for Clin. Investigation, American Institute Nutrition, Acad. Natural Sciences, Franklin Inst., Sigma Xi, Delta Psi. Unitarian. Clubs: Philadelphia, Racquet, Phila. Barge, Tredyffrin Country. Author: Arthritis and Rheumatoid Conditions, 1929, transl. into French, 1933, 2d edit., 1935; (with R. B. Osgood) Medical and Orthopedic Management of Chronic Arthritis, 1934. Contbr. to Nelson Loose Leaf System of Medicine since 1922, Bedside Diagnosis (by Am. authors), 1927, Textbook of Medicine (by same), 1928, internat. Encyclopædia of Medicine, 1931, Tice System of Medicine, 1934, Relation of Trauma to Disease (article on arthritis), 1936, also to Jour. of A.M.A., Archives of Internal Medicine, Am. Jour. Med. Sciences, Annals of Clin. Medicine. Editor of vol. on Medicine in Principles and Practice of Physical Therapy, 1932. Home: Paoli, Pa. Office: 2031 Locust St., Philadelphia, Pa.

PENCE, Leland Hadley, research chemist; b. Kearney, Mo., Oct. 1, 1911; s. Samuel Anderson and Rosa Louise (Reid) P.; B.S., U. of Fla., 1932; M.S., U. of Mich., 1933, Ph.D., same, 1937; m. Mary Ellen Elliott, Aug. 6, 1938. Engaged as lecture demonstrator in organic chemistry, U. of Mich., 1933-35, teaching fellow in organic chemistry, 1935-36, teaching fellow in gen. chemistry, 1936-37; organic research chemist on staff of Biochemical Research Foundation of Franklin Inst., Phila., since 1937. Served in Res. O.T.C. Mem. Am. Chem. Soc., Junior Research Club of U. of Mich., Sigma Xi, Kappa Kappa Psi. Baptist. Club: University of Michigan Men's of Phila. Contbr. to Chem. jours. Home: 4742 Pine St., Philadelphia, Pa. Office: Biochemical Research Foundation of Franklin Inst., 133 S. 36th St., Philadelphia, Pa.

PENDER, Harold, electrical engr.; b. Tarboro, N.C., Jan. 13, 1879; s. Robert H. and Martha Wallace (Hanks) P.; A.B., Johns Hopkins, 1898, Ph.D., 1901; Sc.D. from University of Pennsylvania, 1923; m. Alice Matthews, June 28, 1905; m. 2d, Ailsa Craig MacColl, Dec. 22, 1934. Teacher, McDonogh Sch., Md., 1901-02; instr. Syracuse U., 1902-03; spent winter of 1903 at La Sorbonne, Paris, upon spl. invitation of univ. authorities where established beyond question the existence of a magnetic field around a moving electrically charged body; elec. engr. Westinghouse Electric & Mfg. Co., 1903-04, N.Y.C. R.R., 1904-05; associated with Cary T. Hutchinson, electrical engineer, New York, 1905-09; sec.-treas. McCall Ferry Power Co., 1905-09; prof. elec. engring., Mass. Inst. Tech., 1909-13; dir. research div., dept. of elec. engring., Mass. Inst. Tech., 1913-14; dir. dept. elec. engring., 1914-23, dean Moore Sch. of Elec. Engring., 1923—, U. of Pa. Member International Electrochemical Committee. Fellow Am. Acad. Arts and Sciences, Am. Inst. E.E.; mem. Am. Philos. Soc., Franklin Inst. Author: Principles of Electrical Engineering, 1911; Electricity and Magnetism for Engineers, 1918; Direct-current Machinery, 1921. Editor-in-chief American Electrical Engineering Handbook. Has written numerous scientific and technical papers. Unitarian. Clubs: University, Philadelphia Country. Home: 18 Waterman Av., Chestnut Hill, Philadelphia, Pa.

PENDERGRASS, Eugene Percival, radiologist; b. Florence, S.C., Oct. 6, 1895; s. Edward J. and E. Ethel (Smith) P.; ed. pub. schs.; student Wofford Coll., 1912-14, U. of N.C., 1914-16; M.D., U. of Pa., 1918; m. Rebecca Barker, Sept. 9, 1922; children—Henry Pancoast, Jan Barker, Margaret Bradford. Interne U. of Pa. Hosp., 1918-19; asso. dir. dept. of radiology, Philadelphia Hosp., since 1922, also asst. attending radiologist; asst. prof. U. of Pa. Grad. Sch. of Medicine, 1928-37, prof. since 1937; consultant Chestnut Hill Hosp. since 1935; prof. radiology, U. of Pa. Sch. of Medicine since 1936; dir. dept. of radiology, U. of Pa. Hosp. Fellow Philadelphia Coll. Physicians; mem. Am. Roentgen Ray Soc. (ex-sec.), Am. Coll. Radiology (sec.), Philadelphia Roentgen Ray Soc. (ex-pres., ex-sec.), Philadelphia Co. Med. Soc. (dir.), Radiol. Soc. of North America, Air Hygiene Foundation of America, Inc. Presbyterian. Club: Philadelphia Country. Writer and co-writer numerous articles on med. subjects. Home: 428 Owen Road, Wynnewood, Pa. Office: 3400 Spruce St., Philadelphia, Pa.

PENDLETON, Joseph Saxton, steel mfr.; b. Washington, D.C., Oct. 28, 1873; s. Edwin Conway (rear adm. U.S.N.) and Mary Riddle (Saxton) P.; grad. Central High Sch., Washington, 1892; B.S., George Washington U., 1897, m. Mary Yocum, of Reading, Pa., May 16, 1911; children—Edwin Conway, 2d (dec.), Joseph Saxton, Jr. Asst. chemist The Carpenter Steel Co., 1897-1906, asst. mgr., 1906-14, asst. treas., 1914-16, sec., treas. and dir. since 1916; pres. and dir. Temple (Pa.) State Bank, Reading (Pa.) Savings & Loan Assn.; dir. Reading Trust Co., Yocum Bros., Am. Mutual Liability Ins. Co., Am. Policyholders Ins. Co. Mem. Mil. Order Loyal Legion, S.A.R. Republican. Clubs: Berkshire Country, Wyomissing (Reading); University (Philadelphia). Home: Calcium, Pa. Office: care The Carpenter Steel Co., Reading, Pa.

PENDLETON, Louis (Beauregard), author; b. Tebeauville, Ga., Apr. 21, 1861; s. Philip C. and Catharine (Tebeau) Pendleton; educated in private school and two years college; a student at Sorbonne, Paris, 4 summers; unmarried. Contributing editorial writer Macon (Georgia) Daily Telegraph, 1899-1914; later in charge a syndicated editorial service. Member Authors' League of America, Va. Historical Society; hon. mem. Société Académique d'Histoire Internationale. Club: Franklin Inn of Philadelphia. Author: Life of Alexander H. Stephens (Am. Crisis Biography Series), 1908; (novels and juveniles) Bewitched, 1888; In the Wire-Grass, 1889; King Tom and the Runaways, 1890; The Wedding Garment, 1894 (translated into Swedish, German, French and Braille); The Sons of Ham, 1895; In the Okefinokee, 1895; Corona of the Nantahalas, 1895; Carita, 1898; Lost Prince Almon, 1898; In the Camp of the Creeks, 1903; A Forest Drama, 1904; In Assyrian Tents, 1904; Captain Ted, 1918; Kidnapping Clarence, 1922; The Princess Lilitu, 1924; The Invisible Police, 1932 (translated into Braille—latter and Wedding Garment pub. in Eng. 1935); Echo of Drums, 1938. Contbr. to mags. Home: Bryn Athyn, Montgomery Co., Pa.

PENFIELD, Thornton Bancroft, clergyman; b. Madura, S. India, Nov. 13, 1867; s. Thornton B. and Charlotte E. (Hubbard) P.; grad. St. Johnsbury (Vt.) Acad., 1886; B.A., Columbia, 1890; M.A., New York U., 1893; grad. Union

Theol. Sem., 1893; Ph.D., Taylor U., Upland Ind., 1903; m. Martha Mee Martin, of Grand Rapids, Mich., Sept. 12, 1894; children—Charlotte Martin (wife of Dr. Reginald M. Atwater), Rev. Thornton Bancroft, Paul Livingstone. Ordained Presbyn. ministry, 1893; asst. sec. Presbyn. Bd. Home Missions, 1893-98; sec. Brooklyn Central Y.M.C.A., 1898-1900; sec. Internat. Com. Y.M.C.A.'s, 1900-14; personnel sec. Dept. of East, War Work Council Y.M.C.A., 1914-18; same Inter-ch. World Movement, 1918-20; metropolitan sec. Gen. Council Presbyn. Ch. U.S.A., 1922-24; pastor Teaneck Ch., 1915-22, Norwood (N.J.) Ch., 1922-31; now supt. Nat. Missions for Northern N.J. (Jersey City Presbytery); pres. Bergen County Council of Churches; moderator Presbytery of Jersey City, 1938-39; pres. bd. of trustees Synod of N.J. Served as exec. sec. Camp Merritt Religious Activities Com. and sec. Food Conservation Commn., Northern N.J., World War; sec. 6 Student Volunteer convs. and of Latin-Am. Conv., Panama. Mem. bd. dirs. Eastern Assn. Training Sch. for Y.M.C.A. Secs. Mem. Hymn Soc., Delta Upsilon. Mason. Republican. Clubs: Clergy, Town Hall, Columbia Univ. Club, Union Theol. Sem. Club, Delta Upsilon. Home: 156 Maple St., Englewood, N.J.

PENN, Marion, utilities exec.; b. Humboldt, Tenn., May 5, 1890; s. George Winchester and Carrie (Jarrell) P.; student Humboldt (Tenn.) pub. schs., 1895-1905; B.S. in E.E., Purdue U., Lafayette, Ind., 1911; m. Francoise Renee Besnard, Apr. 14, 1928; children—Mary Francoise, George Marion, John Jarrell, Suzanne Fernande. Test engr. Gen. Electric Co., Schenectady, N.Y., 1911-14; asst. div. supt. Pub. Service Electric & Gas Co., Elizabeth, N.J., 1914-19; plant engr., Newark, N.J., 1919-20; supt. Essex Generating Sta., Newark, 1920-21, Marion Generating Sta., Jersey City, N.J., 1921-25, Kearny (N.J.) Generating Sta., 1925-26; gen. supt. of generation, Newark, N.J., 1926-35; gen. mgr. Electric Dept., Newark, N.J., since 1935. Served as capt., 46th Regt., C.A.C., and instr. in ballistics and orientation, Coast Arty. Sch., Fort Monroe, Va., 1917-19. Fellow Am. Inst. E.E.; mem. Am. Soc. M.E., Alpha Tau Omega. Mason. Clubs: Essex, Newark Athletic (Newark); Essex Co. Country (West Orange). Home: 333 Beech Spring Rd., South Orange, N.J. Office: 80 Park Place, Newark, N.J.

PENNELL, Edred J(oseph), lawyer; b. Mifflin, Pa., Dec. 29, 1890; s. Frank M.M. and Ida (McCauley) P.; B.S., Gettysburg Coll., 1912; LL.B., U. of Pa. Law Sch., 1916; m. Ruth Glenn, Apr. 27, 1918; children—Edred J., Richard Glenn, Mary Glenn. Admitted to Pa. bar, 1917, and engaged in gen. practice of law at Norristown, 1917-36, and at Mifflintown since 1936; admitted to Supreme and Superior cts., U.S. Dist. Ct., and to practice before the Treasury Dept. of the U.S.; pres. and dir. General Factors Corpn. Served as capt. F.A., U.S.A. during World War. A founder Bryn Mawr Am. Legion and past comdr. Active in Rep. State politics. Mem. Am., Pa., Juniata Co. and Montgomery Co. bar assns., Am. Acad. of Polit. and Social Scis., Phi Gamma Delta, Phi Delta Phi. Republican. Presbyn. (elder Ch. at Bryn Mawr). Mason. Clubs: Rotary, Walnut Hills Golf. Pa. Society N.Y. Home: Mifflintown, Pa.

PENNIMAN, George Dobbin, lawyer; b. Lawyers' Hill, Howard County, Md., June 27, 1862; s. Nicholas Griffith and Rebecca Pue (Dobbin) P.; student Baltimore City Coll., 1879-81; A.B., Johns Hopkins, 1884; LL.B., U. of Md., 1886; m. Harriet Wilson Dushane, Oct. 28, 1890 (dec.); children—John A. Dushane (deceased), George Dobbin, Harriet Wilson Dushane (Mrs. Sterling Patterson), Marian Dushane (Mrs. Francis M. Barker), Nicholas Dobbin, III. Admitted to Md. bar, 1886, and since practiced in Baltimore; sr. mem. firm Penniman & Adkins; counsel for B.&O. Ry. since 1887; counsel United Rys. & Electric Co. of Baltimore, 1886-1910; counsel United Electric Light & Power Co., 1890-1902. Trustee Roland Park Country Sch. for Girls. Mem. Md. State Game and Fish Protective Assn., Phi Kappa Psi. Democrat. Episcopalian. Home: 1003 Poplar Hill Rd., Roland Park, Baltimore, Md. Office: Baltimore & Ohio Bldg., Baltimore, Md.

PENNIMAN, Josiah Harmar, provost U. of Pa.; b. Concord, Mass., July 20, 1868; s. James Lanman and Maria Davis (Hosmer) P.; A.B., U. of Pa., 1890, Ph.D., 1895, LL.D., 1922; LL.D., U. of Alabama, 1906, Washington College, Md., 1907, Ursinus Coll., 1921, Juniata Coll., 1925; Litt.D., Swarthmore, 1924; L.H.D., Muhlenberg Coll., 1929; LL.D., Franklin and Marshall Coll., 1929, Lafayette College, 1933, Lehigh U., 1934; m. Mrs. Ida Jutte Walther, 1929. Prof. English lit. since 1896, dean faculty, 1897-1909, vice-provost, 1911-20, actg. provost, 1920-23, provost since 1923, also pres., 1923-30, U. of Pa. Trustee U. of Pa., Evans Inst. Lt. col., U.S. Army (Reserve). Fellow A.A.A.S., New York Geneal. and Biog. Soc.; mem. Am. Philos. Soc., Modern Lang. Assn. America, Am. Dialect Soc., English Assn. of Great Britain, Soc. Colonial Wars, S.R., Descendants Knights of Garter. Clubs: Contemporary, Rittenhouse (Phila.); U. of Pa., Century (New York); University (Washington); Royal Societies, Pilgrims (London). Made Chevalier de la Legion d'Honneur, 1934. Author: The War of the Theatres, 1897; A Book About the English Bible, 1919; and many articles on edln. and lit. topics. Editor of Ben Jonson's Poetaster and Thomas Dekker's Satiromastix, in the Belles Lettres Series, 1905. Home: 4037 Pine St., Philadelphia, Pa.

PENNYBACKER, Everett Bryan, judge; b. Wood Co., W.Va., Feb. 13, 1893; s. William H. and Jane (McVey) P.; student Washington and Lee U., Lexington, Va., 1916-18; m. Florence Smith, Oct. 18, 1914; children—Beatrice Virginia, Frances Louise, Charles William. Admitted to W.Va. bar, 1919, and began practice at Parkersburg; prosecuting atty., Wood County, W.Va., 1932-36; judge Fourth Judicial Circuit, W.Va., since 1936. Dir. Y.M.C.A., Union Mission, Parkersburg, W.Va., Democrat. United Brethren. Mason, Elk, K.P. Home: Vienna, W.Va. Office: Court House, Parkersburg, W.Va.

PENNYPACKER, Isaac Anderson, lawyer; b. Harford Co., Md., Aug. 29, 1879; s. Isaac Rusling and Charlotte (Whitaker) P.; B.S., U. of Pa., 1904; LL.B., U. of Pa. Law Sch., 1908; m. Louise Hardey Renehan, Oct. 6, 1914; children—Louise Ramsay, Charlotte Ellen Hall, Mary Virginia, Nathaniel Ramsay. Admitted to Pa. bar, 1906 and since engaged in gen. practice of law at Phila.; asso. with George Q. Horwitz, 1906-17, with Henry, Pepper, Bodine and Stokes, 1917-19; mem. firm Pepper, Bodine, Stokes and Schoch since 1919; admitted to all State cts. and to practice before the Supreme Ct. of the U.S. Mem. Pa. State and Phila. Co. bar assns., Assn. Practitioners before Interstate Commerce Commn., Delta Phi, Soc. Cincinnati, S.R., Soc. Colonial Wars, Colonial Soc. of Pa. (mem. council), Netherlands Soc. of Phila. (past pres.), Gen. Alumni Soc. U. of Pa. (past sec. and dir.). Republican. Episcopalian. Clubs: Union League, Rittenhouse (Philadelphia). Home: 31 S. Wyoming Av., Ardmore, Pa. Office: 2228 Land Title Bldg., Philadelphia, Pa.

PENROSE, Charles, consulting engineer; b. Philadelphia, Pa., Jan. 24, 1886; s. Walter Elliot and Emily (Thompson) Penrose; 7th generation from Bartholomew Penrose (colonial shipbuilder), Bristol, England, to Philadelphia, 1700; student Prep. Sch., Dresden, Germany, 1896-97; grad. Episcopal Acad., Phila., 1903; B.S., Princeton, 1907, E.E., 1910; m. Beatrice d'Este, June 4, 1910; children—Beatrice, John Rowan, Julian d'Este, Charles; m. 2d, Virginia Carlisle, June 11, 1930; 1 dau., Barbara. Began as asst. to elec. engr. of Phila. Electric Co., 1910; engr. in charge erection Schuylkill No. 2 Sta. for same co., 1914-15, later other power constrn. work; with Day & Zimmermann, Inc., cons. engr., Philadelphia, New York and Chicago, since 1917, asst. gen. mgr., 1920-32, vice-pres., since 1932. Progress engr. U.S. Army Supply Base, Philadelphia, 1918-19. Special consultant to United States government in Federal Housing Administration, 1934. Student of economics of power production and distribution and of industrial and transportation problems; Cyrus Fogg Brackett Lecturer before Princeton U.; served as mem. Bartol Research Foundation Com. (administering Henry C. Bartol Foundation, Phila.). Mem. Am. Soc. Mech. Engrs., Am. Inst. Elec. Engrs., Franklin Inst. (bd. mgrs.), Pa. Electric Assn., Nat. Assn. Cotton Mfrs. (Boston), Am. Cotton Mfrs.' Assn. (Charlotte, S.C.), Pa. State Chamber of Commerce (industrial relations Com.), Princeton Engring. Assn. of New York (past pres.), Maryland Acad. of Sciences, Geneal. Soc. of Pa., Hist. Soc. of Pa., Hist. Soc. of N.M., Engineers Soc. of Winston-Salem, N.C. (hon.), Constrn. Div. Assn. (U.S. Army), Newcomen Soc. of England (council, at London; Am. sr. v.p.), The Guild of Brackett Lecturers of Princeton U. (exec. com.); asso. member Am. Soc. C.E.; served as mem. administrative bd., Am. Engring. Council. Republican. Episcopalian. Clubs: Princeton, Midday (Phila.); Princeton (New York); Hope (Providence, R.I.); Charter (Princeton, N.J.). Author of "New England's Power Resources," 1922; "Power in Pennsylvania," 1925; "American Colonial Transportation (1629-1783)," (1933); "Industrial Surveys," 1935; "New England—Today!" (Boston), 1937; "Industry and The State" (Alabama), 1937; "How A Banker Views A Sales Executive" (New York), 1937; "1838 April Fourth 1938," (Atlantic Centenary Address, New York) 1938; "Initiative for Americans," (New York), 1938; and many other tech. articles in mags. and revs. Home: "Hilltop Cottage," R.F.D. 2, West Chester, Pa. Office: Packard Bldg., Philadelphia, Pa., and 165 Broadway, New York, N.Y.

PENT, Rose Marie, painter; b. St. Louis, Mo.; grad. Clinton (Ia.) High Sch.; student Acad. of Fine Arts, Phila., Pa., 1924; studied art under William M. Chase, Fred Wagner, Phila., Hugh H. Breckenridge, Phila. and Gloucester, Mass., 1927; m. Howard Franklin Pent, 1892; children—Clementine Marie, Robert Edward, Howard Franklin, Jr. Has exhibited oil paintings, water colors, miniatures, etc., at many art clubs and exhbns., Philadelphia, including following—Acad. of Fine Arts of Phila., Art Alliance of Phila., Plastic Club, Art Club, Fellowship of Acad. of Fine Arts of Phila., also miniatures in Baltimore, Md., Mem. Phila. Art Alliance. Republican. Clubs: Plastic (Phila.; v.p. 1930-32, chmn. many coms.); Women's (Wyncote, Pa.). Also writes childrens verse, which illustrates with animal cartoons. Home: 305 Wyncote Rd., Jenkintown, Pa.

PENTZ, James Garfield, dept. pub. instrn. official; b. Reynoldsville, Pa., Aug. 26, 1879; s. Joseph R. and Hannah J. (Stouffer) P.; A.B., Allegheny Coll., 1903, A.M.,, same, 1913; ed. Columbia U., summers 1921-22; hon. Ped.D., Lebanon Valley Coll., 1938. Employed as high sch. teacher, prin. and supt. schs., 1903-12; state high sch. inspr., Dept. Pub. Instrn., 1912-24, dir. field service, 1924-25, dir. and chief of credentials and examination div. since 1925. Mem. Nat. Edn. Assn., Pa. State Edn. Assn., High Sch. Insprs. Assn., Delta Tau Delta. Republican. Presbyn. Mason (32°, Shriner). Home: 2060 Whitehall St. Office: Dept. of Public Instruction, Harrisburg, Pa.

PEPPER, George Wharton, lawyer; b. Phila., March 16, 1867; s. George and Hitty Markoe (Wharton) P.; A.B., U. of Pa., 1887, LL.B., 1889, LL.D., 1907; D.C.L., U. of the South, 1908; LL.D., Yale, 1914; D.C.L., Trinity, 1918; LL.D., U. of Pittsburgh, 1921, Lafayette Coll., University of Rochester and Pennsylvania Military College, 1922, Kenyon Coll., 1924, Williams College, 1936; m. Charlotte R., d. George P. Fisher, Nov. 25, 1890; children—Mrs. Adeline Newbold, Mrs. Eleanor Newbold (deceased), George Wharton. In law practice at Phila.; mem. Pepper, Bodine, Stokes & Schoch. Appointed U.S. senator, to fill vacancy caused by death of Boies Penrose, Jan., 1922, and elected for term ending 1927. Former mem. Republican Nat. Com. Algernon Sydney Biddle prof. law, University of Pa., 1893-1910; Lyman Beecher, lecturer, Yale, 1915. Decorated Grand Officer Order of Leopold II (Belgium). Trustee

University of Pa. Fellow Am. Acad. Arts and Sciences; mem. Académie Doplimatique Internationale, Am. Philos. Soc., Franklin Institute. Author: The Borderland of Federal and State Decisions, 1889; Pleading at Common Law and Under the Codes, 1891; Digest of the Laws of Pennsylvania, 1700-1901, and Digest of Decisions and Encyclopædia of Pennsylvania Law, 1754-1898 (with William Draper Lewis); The Way, 1909; A Voice from the Crowd, 1915; Men and Issues, 1924; In the Senate, 1930; Family Quarrels, 1931. Home: Devon, Pa. Office: 2231 Land Title Bldg., Philadelphia, Pa.

PEPPER, John Oscar, asso. prof. extension entomology; b. nr. Easley, S.C., June 9, 1902; s. William Oscar and Jessie Josephine (Henderson) P.; B.S., Clemson (S.C.) Agrl. & Mech. Coll., 1923; M.S., O. State U., Columbus, O., 1925; m. Lena Mae Lafler, May 7, 1925; 1 dau., Sarah Joanne. Engaged as extension entomologist in S.C., 1925-28; asst. extension entomologist, Pa. State Coll., 1928-30; advanced entomologist, Pa. State Dept. Agr., 1930-34; asso. prof. of extension entomology, Pa. State Coll. since 1934. Mem. Am. Assn. Econ. Entomologists, Sigma Xi, Gamma Alpha. Methodist. Mason. Home: 413 Ridge Av., State College, Pa.

PEPPER, O(liver) H(azard) Perry, M.D., b. Philadelphia, Pa., Apr. 28, 1884; s. William and Frances S. (Perry) P.; B.S., U. of Pa., 1905, M.D., 1908; m. Eulalie Wilcox, Dec. 2, 1916; children—Eulalie, Oliver H.P. Interne Univ. Hosp., Philadelphia, 1908-10, assistant physician, 1913-37, physician since 1937; assistant instructor, U. of Pennsylvania, 1911-12, asso. in medicine, 1912-19, asso. in research medicine, 1913-19, asst. prof. medicine, 1922-28, prof. clinical medicine, 1928-34, professor of medicine since 1934. Served as lieut. colonel Medical Corps, U.S.A.; chief of medical service Base Hospital 69, Savenay, France, World War. Mem. A.M.A., Assn. Am. Physicians, Am. Soc. for Clin. Investigation, Am. Climatol. and Clin. Assn., Am. Coll. Physicians (bd. of regents), Coll. Physicians of Philadelphia. Republican. Episcopalian. Club: Philadelphia. Author: (with Dr. David L. Farley) Practical Hematological Diagnosis, 1933. Contbr. to med. jours. Home: Ithan, Pa. Office: 36th and Spruce Sts., Philadelphia, Pa.

PEPPER, William, M.D., educator; b. Philadelphia, Pennsylvania, May 14, 1874; s. William and Frances Sergeant (Perry) P.; A.B., University of Pa., 1894, M.D., 1897, Sc.D., 1932; m. Mary Godfrey, Dec. 31, 1904 (died Oct. 2, 1918); m. 2d, Phoebe S. (Voorhees) Drayton, Apr. 3, 1922. With med. dept., U. of Pa., 1899—; dean Sch. of Medicine, 1912—. Lieutenant colonel M.C., U.S.A., during World War; commanding officer Base Hospital 74. Fellow College Physicians of Phila., Assn. Am. Med. Colleges (pres. 1920-21); mem. A.M.A. Am. Philos. Soc., Zeta Psi. Republican. Episcopalian. Home: Prospect Av., Melrose Park, Philadelphia, Pa.

PERCIVAL, Walter Clement, forester; b. Jericho, Vt., June 25, 1901; s. Charles Eugene and Sarah Jane (Nattress) P.; B.S., N.Y. State Coll. of Forestry, Syracuse, N.Y., 1923, M.S., 1926, Ph.D., 1933; grad. student Syracuse (N.Y.) Univ., summer 1932; m. Edna Phyllis Pennington, July 14, 1928; children—Charles Leigh, Phyllis Marcia. Began as asst. instr. forestry, N.Y. State Coll. of Forestry, Syracuse, N.Y., 1924-33; successively cultural foreman, U.S. Dist. ranger; W.Va. state land planning consultant, Morgantown, W.Va., 1934; coordinator Land-Use Surveys, Morgantown, 1934-36; asst. prof. forestry, W.Va. Univ., Morgantown, 1934-37, asso. prof. forestry since 1939 and forester W.Va. Agrl. Expt. Sta. since 1939, head div. of forestry since 1939; pres. W.Va. Forest Products Assn., Inc. Mem. Soc. Am. Foresters, Am. Phytopathol. Soc., Am. Bot. Soc., W.Va. Acad. Sci., W.Va. Univ. Sci. Soc., Sigma Nu, Sigma Xi, Alpha Xi Sigma, Phi Kappa Phi, Phi Epsilon Phi. Episcopalian. Home: Devon Road, Morgantown, W.Va.

PERDEW, Frank Archibald, lawyer; b. Bedford Co., Pa., May 29, 1876; s. Elijah and Malinda (Wilson) P.; student Valparaiso (Ind.) College Normal School, 1897-1900, Valparaiso Coll. Law Sch., 1902-04; m. M. Virginia Beasley, Dec. 25, 1915; children—Wilbur Wilson, Dorothy Virginia, Robert Beasley. Engaged in farming to 1900; teacher pub. schs., 1900-02; admitted to Md. bar, 1905 and since engaged in gen. practice of law at Cumberland; state's atty. for Allegany Co., 1912-16; served as judge People's Ct., Cumberland, 1927-35; apptd. trial magistrate at large for Allegany Co., Md., by Gov. O'Conor, for term 1939-41. Mem. Md. State Bar Assn., Allegany Co. Bar Assn. Democrat. Methodist. Odd Fellow. Moose. Club: Country (Cumberland). Home: 555 Rose Hill Av. Office: Liberty Trust Bldg., Cumberland, Md.

PERHAM, Roy Gates, physician; b. Rutherford, N.J., Sept. 14, 1887; s. Calvin Page and Emily Judson (Norton) P.; grad. Rutherford (N.J.) High Sch., 1905; student Syracuse U., 1905-07; M.D., Syracuse U. Coll. of Med., 1912; post grad. work, Harvard, 1913; m. Alice Jeannette Parsons, June 28, 1913; children—Roy Gates, Catherine Alice. Interne Paterson (N.J.) Gen. Hosp., 1912-13; gen. practice of medicine, Hasbrouck Heights, N.J., since 1913. Former mem. Bd. of Edn.; borough health officer since 1913; partner in Perham Foundation (organized to give employment to men and women over 40 years of age). Mem. A.M.A., N.J. State and Bergen County med. socs., Kappa Sigma, Alpha Kappa. Liberal Republican. Mem. Reformed Ch. Mason. Clubs: Lions (past pres)., Masonic (Hasbrouck Heights). Inventor of steam water gauge; Perham guards (used to prevent dressings from touching wounds); vein holder to hold vein in intervenous puncture; transfusion splint; fractured finger splint. Co-inventor (with Charles Glabon) of Queresal (salt of quinine) used with success in treatment of pneumonia and streptococcus infection. Home: 269 Raymond St. Office: 248 Boulevard, Hasbrouck Heights, N.J.

PERHAM, Roy Gates, Jr., portrait painter; b. Paterson, N.J., Apr. 18, 1916; s. Roy Gates and Alice Jeannette (Parsons) P.; grad. Hasbrouck Heights (N.J.) High Sch., 1936; student Grand Central Art Sch., 1936-37; studied art under I. B. Beales, Frank V. Dumond and Frank J. Reilly; unmarried. Portrait painter since June, 1938. One-man shows: Hasbrouck Pub. Library, Peoples Trust Co. (Hasbrouck Heights), Little Falls Women's Club; also exhibited in Guild Hall, East Hampton, L.I., N.Y., and Pub. Library, Glen Rock, N.J. Home: 269 Raymond St., Hasbrouck Heights, N.J.

PERKINS, Edward Everett, banking; b. Springfield, Md., Oct. 24, 1857; s. James Turner and Susan Elizabeth (Travers) P.; grad. Millersville (Md.) Acad., 1877; m. Grace Caroline Thompson, Oct. 26, 1892 (dec.); children—Grace Caroline, William Turner, Edw. Everett, Jr., Hanson Travers (M.D.). Began career as sch. teacher, 1877; civil engr. B.& O. R.R. and with U.S. Govt., 1883-86; dep. treas. Prince George Co., Md., Upper Marlboro, 1886-92; dep. collector U.S. internal revenue, Baltimore and Washington, D.C., 1892-1908; pres. Bowie Bldg. Assn., 1928-36; pres. Bank of Bowie, Bowie, Md., since 1926. Republican. Methodist. Home: Springfield, Md. Office: Springfield, Md.; Bowie, Md.

PERKINS, John Douglas, physician; b. Downingtown, Pa., July 24, 1890; s. John Douglas and Mary (Ashbridge) P.; M.D., U. of Pa., 1916; m. Katharne Strawbridge, Jan. 4, 1919; children—John Douglas, Benjamin Strawbridge, George Ashbridge. Interne, Episcopal Hosp., Phila., 1917, St. Christopher's Hosp., Phila., 1916-17; asst. physician Bryn Mawr Hosp. since 1923; in practice of medicine, Conshohocken, Pa., since 1919. Served as capt., Med. Corps, U.S. Army, 1918-19. Mem. Main Line Med. and Montgomery County med. assns.. Episcopalian. Mason. Home: 316 Fayette St., Conshohocken, Pa.

PERKINS, Kenneth, author; b. of Am. parents, Kodai Kanal, India, May 16, 1890; s. James C. and Charlotte Jane (Taylor) P.; prep. edn., Lowell High Sch., San Francisco, Calif.; B.L., U. of Calif., 1914, M.A., 1915; m. Grace Bemis, Dec. 25, 1919; 1 dau., Charlotte Joan. Instr. English, Pomona Coll., Claremont, Calif., 1916-18. Served as 2d lt. Field Arty., U.S.A., Camp Taylor, Ky., and Ft. Sill Sch. of Fire, Aug. 28-Dec. 24, 1918. Republican. Presbyn. Author: The Beloved Brute, 1923; Ride Him, Cowboy, 1924; The Gunfanner, 1924; Queen of the Night, 1925; The Palm of the Hot Hand (under nom de plume, King Phillips), 1926; Wild Paradise, 1927; The Starlit Trail, 1927; (scenarios) Romanceland, 1925; Beloved Brute, 1925; The Unknown Cavalier, 1926; The Canyon of Light, 1927; The Devil's Saddle, 1927; Gold, 1929; The Mark of the Moccasin, 1929; The Discard, 1930; Desire (play), prod. 1930; Voodoo'd, 1931; Horror of the Juvenal Manse, 1931; Moccasin Murders, 1931; Better Than a Rodeo (scenario), 1932; Gold (scenario), 1933; The Cañon of Light; Desert Voices, 1934; Loretta Brodell, 1935; Dance With Your Gods (play), 1934; Fast Trailing, 1936; Gunwhipped, 1935; Strange Treasure, 1935; Buccaneer Blood, 1936. Co-Author: Creoles (play), prod. 1926. Contbr. to Collier's, Am. Mag. Mem. Authors' League America, also of Dramatists' Guild of same. Home: 23 Hooper Av., Atlantic Highlands, N.J.

PERKINS, Milo Randolph, govt. official; b. Milwaukee, Wis., Jan. 28, 1900; s. Walton Asher and Gail Miriam (Randolph) P.; grad. Riverside High Sch., Milwaukee, Wis., 1916; m. Tharon Kidd, of Houston, Tex., Aug. 21, 1919; children—Milo Randolph (deceased), George Kidd. Salesman Bemis Bro. Bag Co., Houston, Tex., 1919-23, sales mgr., 1923-26; partner King-Perkins Bag Co., Houston, 1926-35; asst. to U.S. sec. of Agr., Washington, D.C., 1935-37; asst. administr. Farm Security Adminstrn., 1937-39; asso. adminstr. A.A.A. and pres. Federal Surplus Commodities Corpn. since Jan. 1939. Mem. bd. of trustees Landon Sch. for Boys, Bethesda, Md. Democrat. Home: 5601 Edgemoor Lane, Bethesda, Md. Office: 2095 South Bldg., Washington, D.C.

PERKINS, Walter Frederick, v.p. Koppers Co.; b. Baltimore, Md., June 3, 1891; s. William C. and Ida V. (Frederick) P.; student Baltimore Poly. Inst., 1906-09; C.E., Lehigh U., 1913; m. Lucinda M. Rawley, Nov. 24, 1914; children—Doris A., Sue. Began as draftsman Chesapeake & Potomac Telephone Co., 1909; rodman B.&O.R.R., 1910-11; engr. Paving Commn. of Baltimore, 1913-15; supt., later gen. supt. Bartlett Hayward Co., 1915-27; works mgr. Worthington Pump & Machinery Corpn., Harrison, N.J., 1927-32; v.p. and gen. mgr., later pres.. Bartlett Hayward Co., 1932-36; company absorbed by Koppers Co. 1936, of which is v.p. in charge Bartlett Hayward and Am. Hammered Piston Ring divs., also subsidiary Md. Dry Dock Co.; dir. Koppers Co., Md. Dry Dock Co., Mercantile Trust Co., Standard Gas Equipment Corpn., Cottman Co. Dir. Baltimore Chapter, Am. Red Cross; mem. Bd. of Correction, State of Md.; gen. chmn. Baltimore Community Fund, 1938. Mem. Am. Soc. Mech. Engrs., Am. Gas Assn., Am. Iron & Steel Inst., Tau Beta Pi. Democrat. Methodist. Clubs: Baltimore Country, Merchants and Engineers (Baltimore); Engineers (New York). Home: 104 Tunbridge Rd. Office: 200 Scott St., Baltimore, Md.

PERKINS, William Robertson, lawyer; b. Elmington, Va., Nov. 3, 1875; s. Thomas Benjamin Moore and Judith Clough (Robertson) P.; LL.B., Washington and Lee U., 1897, LL.D., 1929; m. Mary Sarah Bell, Nov. 5, 1902; children—William Robertson, Thomas Lee, Mary Clough. Admitted to Va. bar, 1897, and began practice at Lynchburg; moved to Newport News, Va., 1901, N.Y. City, 1906; counsel for Am. Tobacco Co., 1906-11, P. Lorillard Co., 1911-13, J. B. and B. N. Duke interests since 1913; pres. Stonewall Corpn.; v.p. Duke Power Co. (counsel), and Selected Industries, Inc.; dir. and counsel Am. Cynamid Co.; counsel P. Lorillard Company, British-Am. Tobacco Co. Trustee and vice chmn. The Duke Endowment; trustee Duke Univ. Mem. Am. and N.Y. State bar assns., Am. Acad. Polit. and Social Science, Va. Soc. of New York, Southern Soc., N.C. Soc. Republican. Methodist. Mason. Clubs: New

York, Commonwealth, Uptown, Quill (New York); Upper Montclair Country. Home: 125 Lorraine Av., Upper Montclair, N.J. Office: 30 Rockefeller Plaza, New York, N.Y.

PERKINS, William Warr Cassidy, chief engr. and sec. Eastern Paving Brick Assn.; b. Philadelphia, Pa., Aug. 10, 1868; s. Jeremiah C. and Mary Ann (Cassidy) P.; ed. Philadelphia High Sch. and private sch., Williamsport, Pa.; C.E., Lehigh U., 1890; m. Maude L. E. Macklem, Sept. 12, 1895; children—J. Macklem, Gertrude, Marie, Lillian, William, Alexina (dec.), James H. Instrument man N.Y.C.R.R., Buffalo, 1890-91, Niagara Falls (N.Y.) Power Co. (power tunnel), 1891-93; mem. firm Webb & Perkins, cons. engrs., Williamsport, Pa., 1893-96; master mathematics, DeVeaux Coll., Niagara Falls, 1896-99; asst. engr. Fairmount Park Commn., Philadelphia, 1899-1906; resident engr. N.Y. State Highway Dept., Buffalo, 1906-13; chief engr. Dunn Wire-Cut Lug Brick Co., Conneaut, O., 1913-19; chief engr. and sec. Eastern Paving Brick Assn., Philadelphia and Langhorne, Pa., since 1919. Mem. Am. Soc. C.E., Am. Soc. Testing Materials, Am. Pub. Works Assn., Am. Road Builders Assn., Tau Beta Pi, Phi Gamma Delta. Republican. Episcopalian. Mason. Clubs: Engineers, Lehigh University (Philadelphia). Contbr. articles to mags. on proper construction of brick pavements. Lectured before various colls. on brick pavement construction. Home: Langhorne, Pa.

PERLEY, George Arthur, chemist; b. Goffstown, N.H., Nov. 21, 1886; s. Nathaniel Hadley and Jennie (Stinson) P.; B.S., U. of N.H., 1908; M.A., Cornell U., 1910; m. Mary Foster, Nov. 23, 1910; 1 son, James Dwight; m. 2d, Muriel Murray, Aug. 19, 1930; 1 dau., Judith Ann. Asst. instr. chemistry, Cornell U., 1909-10; chief chemist and works mgr. Albany Lubricating Co., N.Y. City, 1910-11; asso. prof. phys. chem., U. of N.H., Durham, N.H., 1911-29, also cons. chemist, 1919-29; chief research dept., chem. div., Leeds & Northrup Co., Phila., Pa., since 1929. Served as 1st lt., capt. then maj. Ordnance Dept., U.S.A., 1917-19. Health officer Town of Durham, N.H., 1915-17. Fellow Am. Inst. Chemists. Mem. Am. Chem. Soc., The Electro Chem. Soc., Am. Inst. Chem. Engrs., Sigma Xi, Alpha Chi Sigma. Republican. Conglist. Has taken out several U.S. patents on chem. inventions. Contbr. over 20 articles on electro-chem. subjects. Home: 120 Waverly Rd., Wyncote, Pa. Office: 4901 Stenton Av., Philadelphia, Pa.

PERLMAN, Samuel, rabbi; b. New York, N.Y., Oct. 18, 1905; s. Jacob and Rachel Leah (Gurin) P.; B.S.S., College of City of New York, 1926; Rabbi, Jewish Inst. of Religion, New York, 1930; grad. student Columbia; unmarried. Rabbi Temple Emanu-El, Saranac Lake, N.Y., 1930-33, Brith Sholom Community Center, Bethlehem, Pa., 1933-35; rabbi Temple Emanu-El, Bayonne, N.J., since 1935. Vicepres. Bayonne Dist. of Zionist Orgn. of America; adviser to Bayonne Youth Congress; mem. exec. com. Am. Jewish Congress. Mem. Central Conf. Am. Rabbis, Rabbinical Assn. of Jewish Inst. of Religion. Chaplain Century Lodge of New York. Author of monograph, Some Aspects of Maimonidean Ethics, 1930. Home: 661 Av. C, Bayonne, N.J.

PERMAR, Robert, writer; b. Steubenville, O., Sept. 15, 1896; s. Edwin Love and Seddie (MacFarland) P.; ed. high sch. 2 yrs. and under pvt. tutors; m. Mary Margaret Sommerville, Aug. 17, 1929. Formerly a free lance book and music reviewer; editor Wheeling Intelligencer for eight years; editor in chief of "West Virginians" (biographical), 1928; supervisor, 1930, Federal Census for 5 counties of W.Va.; apptd. dep. U.S. clerk, 1932; instr. Y.M.C.A. Junior Coll. Made nat. survey of industrial edn. in pub. schs.; founder, with Irwin Fluharty, The Newspaper Feature Bureau. Republican. Episcopalian. Mason (32°, Shriner). Author: Training in the Trades, 1923; The Juggler, 1926; Shadows That Were Cast, 1936; and The Fourth Magi, 1937; also many syndicated newspaper and magazine articles. Home: 102 14th St., Wheeling. Office: Federal Bldg., Wheeling, W.Va.

PEROT, T. Morris, Jr., malt mfr.; b. Phila., Pa., May 6, 1872; s. T. Morris and Rebecca C. (Siter) P.; grad. DeLancy Sch., Phila., 1891, Pricket's Business Coll., Phila., 1893; m. Mary Gummey, May 18, 1905; children—T. Morris III, Henry F., Mary Elizabeth. In malt mfg. business since 1893; pres. since 1903, of Francis Perot's Sons Malting Co., Phila. (oldest business house in the U.S., established in 1687). Pres. Seaside House for Invalid Women; treas. Friends Charity Fuel Assn.; manager Grandon Institution. Member Pa. Hist. Soc., Pa. Soc. S.R. Republican. Quaker. Club: Union League. Home: 132 Bethlehem Pike, Chestnut Hill, Philadelphia. Office: Lafayette Bldg., Philadelphia, Pa.

PERRIN, Oliver Winfred, life insurance executive; b. Ypsilanti, Mich.; s. Oliver J. (D.D.) and Eleanora (Graves) P.; A.B., U. of Mich. A.M., 1904; m. Reneé Barrie, 1919. Asso. with The Penn Mutual Life Ins. Co. continuously since 1904; asso. actuary since 1930. Served as mem. Draft Appeal Bd. for Phila. Dist. during World War. Mem. Alumni Adv. Council, U. of Mich. Treas. Permanent Com., Internat. Congresses of Actuaries. Treas. Actuarial Soc. America; gov. Am. Inst. Actuaries. Mem. Am. Acad. Social and Polit. Sci., Friends of U. of Pa. Library, and Pa. Soc. Sons of Revolution. Clubs: Union League, Merion Cricket, University of Michigan (Philadelphia). Home: 210 Glenn Rd., Ardmore, Pa. Office: S. E. Cor. 6th & Walnut Sts., Philadelphia, Pa.

PERRINE, Van Dearing, artist; b. Garnett, Kan., 1869. Silver medal, Charleston Expn. 1902, Panama P.I. Expn., 1915; hon. mention, Carnegie Inst., 1903. Conducting a research into abstract mobile design and instrumental color orchestration. Awarded Altman prize, 1930. Represented in many Am. collections. N.A., 1931. Mem. Prometheans, Soc. Am. Painters, Sculptors and Gravers, Grand Central Art Assn. Author: Let the Child Draw. Home: Maplewood, N.J.

PERRING, Henry Garfield, architect and engr.; b. Phila., Pa., Apr. 25, 1881; s. Henry Crewe and Annie Franklin (Allen) P.; student pub. schs., Phila., night classes Drexel Inst.; m. Catharine Boot Jenkinson, Oct. 12, 1904; 1 son, Henry Brooks. Employed as draftsman engring. depts., r.r. cos., 1898-1905; engr. Keystone Fireproofing Co., 1905-09, U.S. Gypsum Co., 1909-10; in pvt. practice as architect and engr., Jacksonville, Fla., 1911-16, cons. engr., 1916-20; chief engr., Baltimore, and supervising engr. Public Improvement Commn., 1920-28; in pvt. practice at Baltimore, as Henry G. Perring Co., architects and engrs., also Perring, Remington Co., cons. engrs. since 1928; vice-pres. and chief engr. General Realty Co.; dir. and treas. Industrial Service, Inc., Consumers Credit Service, Inc.; dir. Credit Service, Inc. Served as mem. engring. com. Adv. Com. Nat. Council of Defense during World War; now Col. Q.M. Res. Mem. Am. Soc. Civil Engrs., Am. Inst. Cons. Engrs., Nat. Soc. Professional Engrs., Md. Assn. Engrs., Md. and Fla. Assn. Architects, Quartermasters Assn., Res. Officers Assn., Urban League (dir.). Republican. Episcopalian. Mason (32°, Shriner). Elk. Clubs: Engineers, Merchants (Baltimore); Engineers (New York); Engineers (Philadelphia). Home: 3304 Hillen Rd. Office: 10 W. Chase St., Baltimore, Md.

PERRY, Arthur L., supt. of schs. at Rahway. Address: Rahway, N.J.

PERRY C(ornelius) Alfred, bacteriology; b. Bernardsville, N.J., Feb. 21, 1898; s. Cornelius and Elizabeth (Harrison) P.; B.Sc., Rutgers U., New Brunswick, N.J., 1921; D.Sc., Johns Hopkins U. Sch. Hygiene & Pub. Health, 1930; m. Grace Edna Culler, Dec. 28, 1921; children —Elizabeth Matilda, Margery Jean. Employed as jr. bacteriologist N.J. State Dept. Health, 1920-22; asst. bacteriologist Md. State Dept. Health, Hurlock, Md., 1923-30, chief bacteriologist and dir. bacteriol. labs. since 1930. Served in S.A.T.C., 1918. Fellow A.A.A.S., Am. Pub. Health Assn. Mem. Soc. Am. Bacteriologists, Delta Omega, Sigma Xi. Episcopalian. Club: Johns Hopkins (Baltimore). Home: Burnbrae Rd., Towson, Md. Office: 2411 N. Charles St., Baltimore, Md.

PERRY, David R., lawyer; b. Altoona, Pa., Oct. 16, 1896; s. Albert and Agnes (Evans) P.; ed. Susquehanna Coll., Selinsgrove, Pa., Cornell U.; LL.B., Dickinson Law Sch., Carlisle, Pa., 1921; m. Margaret Louise Hoover, Nov. 29, 1930; children—Luisa, Davida. Admitted to Pa. bar, 1922, and since in practice at Altoona; special dep. atty. gen., Div. of Unemployment Compensation, State of Pa. Mem. Pa. Ho. of Rep. since 1933; mem. legislative food relief com. Mem. Am. Red Cross. Mem. Pa. State Bar Assn. Am. Bar Assn. Am. Legion, Delta Chi. Republican. Lutheran. Mason. Club: Lions (Altoona, Pa.). Home: Pinwauld St. Office: Altoona Trust Bldg., Altoona, Pa.

PERRY, John Lester, pres. Carnegie-Illinois Steel Corpn.; b. Worcester, Mass., Mar. 11, 1881; s. Fred George and Ella Matilda (Bailey) P.; grad. Worcester (Mass.) English High Sch., 1899; m. Kathryn Thayer, Aug. 31, 1904; children—Elizabeth (Mrs. James E. Walter), John Lester. With Am. Steel & Wire Co., 1899-1935, clerical and supervisory work, 1899-1917, supt. South Works, Worcester, Mass., 1917-18, North Works, 1918-25, asst. mgr. Worcester Dist., 1925-28, mgr. Worcester Dist., 1928-32, v.p. Am. Steel & Wire Co., 1933-35; pres. Tenn. Coal, Iron & R.R. Co., Birmingham, Ala., 1935-38; pres. Carnegie-Illinois Steel Corpn. since Jan. 1, 1938. Mem. Am. Iron & Steel Inst., Newcomen Soc. (Phila.), Engrs. Soc. of Western Pa. Republican. Unitarian. Clubs: Worcester (Worcester); Pittsburgh Athletic, Rolling Rock, Railway, Duquesne (Pittsburgh). Home: 1060 Morewood Av. Office: 434 Fifth Av., Pittsburgh, Pa.

PERRY, Lawrence, journalist, author; b. Newark, N.J.; s. William Aurelius and Mary (Hayes) P.; g.s. of Hon. Nehemiah Perry; m. Larry Louise Crossman, Nov. 1, 1902; 1 son, Glen Hayes. With New York Evening Sun, 1904, Evening Journal, 1904-05, Evening Post, 1906; editor Yachting, 1906-10, New York Evening Post, 1912-20, Consolidated Press Assn., 1920-33, North American Newspaper Alliance, 1933. Mem. New York Soc. Sons of Revolution. Episcopalian. Clubs: Players, Dutch Treat, Princeton (New York); Cap and Gown (hon.), Nassau (Princeton). Author: Dan Merrithew, 1910; Prince or Chauffeur, 1911; Holton of the Navy, 1913; The Fullback, 1916; The Big Game, 1918; Our Navy in the War, 1918; The Romantic Liar, 1919; For the Game's Sake, 1921; Touchdowns, 1924; Old First, 1931; The Yorkshire Rose, 1939; Beyond the Terrace (play). Contbr. short stories and articles to mags. Home: Glen Ridge, N.J. Office: 280 Broadway, New York, N.Y.

PERRY, Lynn, civil engr.; b. Millsboro, Del., Feb. 27, 1884; s. Vandalia and Rose May (Dennis) P.; B.S., U. of Pa., 1906, M.S., 1907, C.E., 1909; m. Margaret Tice, July 8, 1918. Asst. engr., Bd. of Water Supply, New York, N.Y., 1906-07; draftsman, Belmont Iron Works, Phila., and L. F. Shoemaker & Co., Phila., summer 1907; draftsman and engr., Bureau of Surveys, Phila., 1907-11; pvt. practice civil engring., Salisbury, Md., 1911-15; san. engr. New Jersey State Bd. of Health, 1915-17; prof. civil engring. dept., Lafayette Coll., Easton, Pa., since 1919; pvt. practice, Easton, Pa., since 1919; pres. Perry-Bradley Lumber Co., Dragonville, Va., since 1922; sec. Houston Perry & Co. Served as capt., 27th div., U.S. Army, 1917-19; now major, Engr. O.R.C. Mem. Am. Soc. C.E., Soc. Am. Mil. Engrs., Soc. Promotion of Engring. Edn., Mil. Order of Foreign Wars, Sigma Xi. Received R.A. meritorious service award. Democrat. Episcopalian. Mason. Club: U. of Pa. (New York). Author: Flow of Water in Open Channels, 1914; Flow of Water through Elbows and Tees, 1924; A Branch of the Perry Family Tree, 1931; Some Letters of Major William Perry, 1935; Electro-Chemistry of Sewage Treatment, 1918. Contbr. to tech. jours. Home: 828 McCartney St. Office: Lafayette Coll., Easton, Pa.

PERRY, Thomas Doane, wood working engr.; b. Charlestown, Boston, Mass., May 27, 1877; s. David Brainerd and Helen (Doane) P.; student Doane Acad., Crete Neb., 1890-93; A.B., Doane Coll., 1897; B.S., Mass. Inst. Tech., 1900; m. Ethel Goodenough Britton, Oct. 8, 1903; children—Frances Goodenough, Bretton, Thomas Doane. Supt. maintenance dept. Library Bur., Boston, Mass., 1900-02; supt. printing dept. Macey Co., Grand Rapids, Mich., 1902-06; sec. and business mgr. Grand Rapids (Mich.) Bd. of Edn., 1906-11; v.p. and mgr. Grand Rapids (Mich.) Veneer Works, 1911-24; cons. engr. Bigelow Kent Willard & Co., Boston, Mass., 1925-29; works mgr. and engr. New Albany (Ind.) Veneering Co., 1929-34; engr. Plywood Prefabricated Housing Projects, Indiana, 1935-36; development engr. Resinous Products & Chemical Co., Phila., since 1936. Mem. City Planning Commn., Grand Rapids, Mich., 1909-10; Bd. of Edn., Grand Rapids, 1914-16. Dir. Grand Rapids Y.M.C.A., 1914-24; trustee Doane Coll., Crete, Neb., since 1912. Mem. Nat. Com. Wood Utilization, 1926-33, Plywood Mfrs. Assn. (pres. 1919-22), Am. Soc. M.E., Am. Philatelic Soc., U.S. Envelope Soc., Postal Stationery Soc. Republican. Conglist. Mason. Club: Collectors (New York). Author: tech. sect. Veneers and Plywood, 1926; wood products subjects Nat. Encyclopædia, 1936; woodworking sect. Kent's Mechanical Engineers Handbook, 1938. Editor: Handbook of United States Envelopes, 1939. Frequent contbr. to engring., trade and philatelic jours. Home: Moorestown, N.J. Office: 222 W. Washingtor Sq., Philadelphia, Pa.

PERSHING, Avra N., coal operator; b. Derry Twp., Westmoreland Co., Pa., Oct. 23, 1872; s. Rev. Justus H. (D.D.) and Mary (Maguire) P.; ed. pub. schs., business coll. and Greensburg Sem.; m. Minnie Everettt, Sept. 2, 1897; children—Avra N., Jr., Kathleen E. Began as sch. teacher, 1890; teacher Hempfield Twp. Schs., prin. South East Greensburg Borough and East Greensburg Borough Schs.; asso. with Keystone Coal and Coke Co. since 1899, vice-pres., sec. and treas. since 1920; pres. and treas. Highland Farms; vice-pres. and treas. Hempfield Supply Co.; vice-pres. and treas. Mountain Coal Co.; pres. and treas. Inland Realty Co. Served on Liberty Loan Com., Westmoreland Co. during World War. Dir. and sec. Westmoreland Hosp. Assn. Republican. United Brethren. Home: 438 W. Pittsburgh St. Office: Huff Bldg., Greensburg, Pa.

PERSHING, Louise (Mrs. J. Clifford Murdoch), artist; b. Pittsburgh, Pa. May 24, 1904; d. Daniel W. and Lillian (Clarke) Pershing; ed. Pa. Acad. Fine Arts, 1924-27, Carnegie Inst. Tech.; 1927-28, spl. class, same, 1935-36, spl. class in fresco U. of Pittsburgh, 1937; m. Datus W. Berlin, May 30, 1929 (deceased 1930); m. 2d, J. Clifford Murdoch, Nov. 4, 1932; 1 son, Thomas Pershing. Has followed profession as artist since 1930; has exhibited in Phila., New York, Cincinnati, Chicago and many other cities; one-man show in New York, 1937; awarded two prizes in Asso. Artists of Pittsburgh Annual; Cooper Prize in New York from Nat. Women Assn. Painters and Sculptors; Vera Hurd Memorial Prize, Wichita, Kan. Former mem. Nat. Women Assn. Painters & Sculptors. Mem. Pa. Acad. Fine Arts, Asso. Artists of Pittsburgh. Republican. Methodist. Home: R.F.D. No. 8, Crafton, Pa.

PERSKIE, Joseph B., judge; b. Alliance, N.J., July 20, 1885; s. Harris and Minnie (Levit) P.; student U. of Pa. Law Sch., 1904-07; m. Beatrice Maslansky, Nov. 27, 1910; children—David M., Marvin, Lawrence. Admitted to N.J. bar, 1907; counsellor at law since 1910; asst. city solicitor, Atlantic City, 1916-26, city solicitor, 1926-33, solicitor Bd. of Edn., 1916-26; justice Supreme Ct. of N.J. since 1933. Mem. Commn. for Uniform Legislation in U.S., 1930-33. Dir. Fed. of Jewish Charities, Atlantic City. Mem. N.J. and Atlantic County bar assns. Republican. Jewish religion. Mem. B'nai B'rith, Elks, Eagles, Moose. Club: Country (Linwood, N.J.). Home: 5 N. Plaza Place, Atlantic City, N.J.

PERSON, John Elmer, newspaper publisher; b. Williamsport, Pa., May 21, 1889; s. Elmer Ellsworth and Sophia (Gerstenlaver) P.; student high sch., Williamsport, Pa., 1903-07, Lehigh U., 1908-10; m. Lenna Mae Braddock, Aug. 19, 1914; children—Mary Helen, John Elmer, Nancy Jane. Began as reporter on Williamsport (Pa.) Sun, 1910, city editor, 1913-19, editor, 1919-32, gen. mgr. Sun-Gazette Co., 1932-36, pres. since 1936; dir. West Branch Bank and Trust Co., WRAK, Inc. Dir. Pa. State Chamber of Commerce; v.p. Pa. State Sabbath Sch. Assn.; mem. Pa. State Y.M.C.A. Com.; pres. Williamsport Y.M.C.A.; v.p. Brown Library; mem. bd. mgrs. Williamsport Hosp., Wildwood Cemetery Co. Dir. and treas. Dickinson Jr. Coll., Williamsport, Pa. Mem. Pa. State Newspaper Publishers' Assn. (dir.), Delta Tau Delta. Republican. Methodist. Mason (33°). Clubs: Ross (Williamsport, Pa.); Manufacturers (Milton, Pa.). Home: 856 Louisa St., Williamsport, Pa.

PESSAGNO, Daniel James, asso. prof. surgery, U. of Md.; visiting surgeon Mercy Hosp. Address: 101 W. Read St., Baltimore, Md.

PESSOLANO, Frank John, surgeon; b. San Rufo, Italy, Nov. 1, 1890; s. Louis Maria and Catherina (Marmo) P.; came to U.S., 1904, naturalized, 1918; ed. New Kensington, Pa. high sch., 1906-10; M.D., U. of Pa. Med. Sch., 1915; post grad. study in Europe, 1924; m. Marie Miller, Jan. 28, 1919; 1 son, Frank John, Jr. Engaged in gen. practice of medicine at New Kensington, Pa., 1916-24, specializing in surgery since 1925; dir. St. Anthony Orphanage since 1926; dir. Logan Nat. Bank & Trust Co. since 1929. Served as 1st lt. med. corps, U.S. A., 1918. Fellow Am. Coll. Surgs. Mem. Am. Med. Assn., Pa. State Med. Soc. Republican. Roman Catholic. Clubs: Hillcrest Country (New Kensington); University (Pittsburgh). Home: 431 Freeport Rd. Office: 876 5th Av., New Kensington, Pa.

PETER, Arthur, lawyer; b. Rockville, Md., Nov. 16, 1873; s. George and Eliza Lavinia (Gassaway) P.; prep. edn., Rittenhouse Acad., Washington, D.C., and Rockville (Md.) Acad.; LL.B., with honors, Nat. Univ. Law Sch., Washington, 1894; m. Edith Marshall, July 30, 1918; children—Humphrey Marshall, Arthur. Admitted to D.C. bar, 1894, and began practice at Washington; lecturer in law, Nat. U., 1899; prof. chmn. bd. and gen counsel Washington Loan & Trust Co.; dir. Equitable Coöperative Building Assn., Potomac Joint Stock Land Bank. Del. to Dem. Nat. Conv., 1904, 12 (vice-chmn. Md. delegation, 1912). vice-chmn., trustee George Washington U.; trustee John Dickson Home. Mem. Am. Bar Assn., Md. Bar Assn., Bar Assn. D.C., Soc. of the Cincinnati, Phi Delta Phi. Presbyn. Mason. Clubs: Metropolitan, Lawyers', Chevy Chase. Home: Bethesda, Md. Office: Washington Loan & Trust Bldg., Washington, D.C.

PETER, Luther Crouse, ophthalmologist; b. St. Clairsville, Pa., Feb. 14, 1869; s. Rev. Jacob and Harriet Jane (Crouse) P.; student Susquehanna U., 1887-88; A.B., Gettysburg Coll., 1891, A.M., 1894; M.D., U. of Pa., 1894; Sc.D., Gettysburg College and Susquehanna Univ; LL.D. Gettysburg Coll. m. Carrie Chrystine Moser, June 20, 1916. Practiced in Phila. since 1894; prof. diseases of the eye. Temple University, 1917-30; professor diseases of eye, Graduate Medical School of Univ. of Pennsylvania, 1919—; ophthalmologist to Graduate Hosp., Rush Hosp. for Consumption and Allied Diseases, and Friends' Hosp. for Mental and Nervous Diseases. Fellow Am. Coll. Surgeons, Am. Ophthal. Soc., Coll. Physicians of Phila., Oxford Congress of Ophthalmology (England); mem. Internat. Congress Ophthalmology (sec. and treas. 1922), Nat. Bd. of Ophthalmology (pres. 1929-37), A.M.A., American Acad. Ophthalmology and Oto-Laryngology (expres.), Phi Gamma Delta, Phi Beta Kappa. Republican. Lutheran. Mason (K.T., Shriner). Clubs: Union League, Old York Road Country. Author: The Principles and Practice of Perimetry, 3d edit., 1931; The Extra-Ocular Muscles, 1927, 2d edit., 1936. Home: 121 E. Mt. Pleasant Av., Mt. Airy. Office: 1930 Chestnut St., Philadelphia, Pa.

PETER, Robert, lawyer; b. Rockville, Md., Sept. 29, 1897; s. Robert B. and Helen O. (Lowry) P.; LL.B., George Washington U., 1920, LL.M., 1921; m. Mary F. Tyler, Apr. 30, 1931; children—Robert Peter, III, George Tyler. Admitted to Md. bar, 1920, and since in gen. practice at Rockville; state's atty. Montgomery Co., 1927-31; dir. Montgomery Co. Nat. Bank of Rockville. Elected mem. Md. State Senate, 1938, for term expiring, 1942. Enlisted U.S.N. Reserve Force, 1917; commd. ensign, 1919. Trustee Rockville Acad. Mem. Md. Bar Assn., Montgomery Co. Bar Assn., Kappa Alpha. Democrat. Presbyn. Mason. Clubs: Manor Country (Rockville); Chevy Chase (Chevy Chase, Md.). Home: 102 N. Adams St., Rockville, Md.

PETER, T. V.; editor The Correspondent. Office: 327 N. Gay St., Baltimore, Md.

PETER, V. J.; publisher The Correspondent. Office: 327 N. Gay St., Baltimore, Md.

PETERKIN, William Gardner, lawyer; b. Culpeper, Va., Oct. 21, 1870; s. George William and Constance Gardner (Lee) P.; LL.B., U. of Va., 1894; m. Ora Moss Martin, Apr. 18, 1912; children—Julia Moss, Constance Lee. Admitted to W.Va. bar, 1894, and since practiced in Parkersburg; atty. Parkersburg Rig & Reel Co., Parkersburg; city atty. 1926-29; mem. City Council, 1902-04; State Senate, 1910-14. Major W.Va. Nat. Guard, 1898-1909. Chmn. Draft Board, Wood Co., during World War. Del. Dem. Nat. Conv., 1924; chmn. Community Chest campaign, 1937; sec. Wood Co. Am. Red Cross; sec. and treas. Wood County Soc. for Crippled Children; treas. Henry Logan Children's Home; past pres. Kiwanis Club. Trustee Protestant Episcopal High Sch. in Va., Alexandria; del. from Diocese W.Va. to triennial Gen. Conv. of Protestant Ch. six times; mem. Nat. Council Episcopal Ch. since 1926; chmn. Bd. of Finance, Diocese of W.Va. since 1931. Mem. W.Va. State Bar Assn. (sec. 1905-07), Delta Psi. Democrat. Home: 1110 Ann St. Office: 217 4th St., Parkersburg, W.Va.

PETERS, Albert Gideon, clergyman; b. Newside, Pa., Feb. 27, 1879; s. John F. and Emma M. (Wotring) P.; A.B., Ursinus Coll., 1903; ed. Ursinus Sch. of Theology, Phila., 1903-06; B.D., Central Sem., 1917; S.T.D., Temple U., 1928; m. Xenia L. Helffrich, Aug. 8, 1906; children—Ruth Helffrich (Mrs. Richard I. Knoll), Miriam Luanna (Mrs. Elwyn Jones), Mary Elizabeth (Mrs. George Flexer), Jean Luanna (Mrs. George A. Hutter). Engaged in teaching, 1887-1889; ordained to ministry Dryland Church, Reformed in U.S., 1906; asst. pastor, Northampton Co., 1905-07; pastor, Lebanon, Pa., 1907-12, Perkasie, 1912-22; pastor St. Andrew's Reformed Ch., Phila., since 1922; stated clk. Phila. Classis since 1930; contbg. editor, Reformed Evangel, 1934. Mem. Am. Acad. of Polit. and Social Science, Ministerial Assn. of Phila. Republican. Mem. I.O.O.F. and Woodman of the World. Home: 2111 S. 21st St., Philadelphia, Pa.

PETERS, Charles Clinton, prof. education; b. Duffield, Pa., Nov. 24, 1881; s. George W. and Mary Virginia (Myers) P.; A.B., Lebanon Valley Coll., Annville, Pa., 1901-05; A.M., Harvard, 1910; Ph.D., U. of Pa., 1916; studied Columbia; m. Dixie May Stone, June 12, 1907; children—Eleanor S., G. Herbert Palmer, Max Stone. Prof. classical langs., and mathematics, Clarksburg (Mo.) Coll., 1905-07 (pres. 1906-07); prof. philosophy and edn., Westfield (Ill.) Coll., 1907-11; dean and prof. philosophy and edn., Lebanon Valley Coll., 1911-13; supt. schs. Royersford, Pa., 1913-16; instr. edn., Lehigh U., 1916-17; with Ohio Wesleyan U., 1917-27, prof. edn., 1920-27; prof. edn. and dir. of ednl. research, Pa. State Coll., since 1927; prof. edn., summers, Ohio State U., univs. of W.Va., Kan., Calif., Minn., also Stanford University. Mem. Am. Sociol. Soc., Educational Research Association, Nat. Coll. Teachers of Education, Psychometric Society, American Academy of Political and Social Science, Phi Delta Kappa,

PETERS, Charles Given, lawyer; b. Union, W. Va., Dec. 6, 1890; s. Samuel Clark and Polina (Hogsett) P.; A.B., Hampden-Sydney Coll., 1915; LL.B., Washington & Lee Univ., 1917; m. Esther Teague, Dec. 5, 1926; 1 son, Charles Given, Jr. Engaged in gen. practice of law at Charleston, specializing in ins. and corpn. law; mem. firm Mohler, Peters & Snyder; dir. and mem. exec. com. Virginian Joint Stock Land Bank, Charleston, W.Va. Served as capt. hdqrs. co. inf., U.S.A., 1917-19 with A.E.F. Awarded D.S.M. 1919. Active in Dem. politics; del. to Chicago Conv., 1932; presdl. elector from W.Va., 1936. Mem. Kappa Alpha, Phi Delta Phi. Democrat. Presbyn. Mason. Elk. Clubs: Rotary, Kanawha Country, Edgewood Country. Home: 25 Brooks St. Office: Security Bldg., Charleston, W,Va.

PETERS, Errol Kunkel, dir. music and teacher singing; b. Sandy Run, Pa., June 1, 1897; s. Nathaniel and Anna L. (Kunkel) P.; ed. Muhlenberg Coll., West Chester Teachers Coll., N.Y. Univ.; studied voice under David Bispham, Perley Dunn Aldrich, Henry Hotz, Percy Rector Stephens, Warren F. Acker; m. Florence S. Smith, June 16, 1920; children—Dorice Lovine, Ardath Yvonne. Engaged as concert baritone and prologue artist, 1920-25; teacher of singing and supervisor of pub. sch. music, Emmaus, Pa., since 1923; dir. Municipal Opera Co. since 1934; dir. various choirs and choruses; dir. Pa. Conservatory of Music since 1929; mem. Lehigh Consistory Quartet. Active in all civic drives in past, and community concerts. Mem. Reformed Ch. Mason (32°). I.O.O.F. Rotarian. Home: 1011 Tilghman St. Office: 535 Hamilton St., Allentown, Pa.

PETERS, John F., electrical engr.; b. nr. Chambersburg, Pa., Sept. 11, 1884; ed. dist. sch., and by home study; m. Annie Wormington, Aug. 18, 1909. Began with Westinghouse Electrical & Mfg. Co. as a shopman, later was made asst. foreman in construction of motors, and was appointed consulting engineer Westinghouse organization in 1925. Has been awarded more than 35 patents. Awarded Longstreth medal by Franklin Inst., Phila., 1929, for invention of an automatic device for recording strokes of lightning. Address: 405 Hutchinson Av., Pittsburgh, Pa.

PETERS, Martin Loyd, supt. pub. schs.; b. Dallastown, Pa., Mar. 26, 1886; s. William H. and Kate (Martin) P.; B.S., Gettysburg Coll., 1913; A.M., U. of Pa., 1924, grad. study, same, 1924-29; m. Charlotte Fisher, 1914; 1 son, Martin Fisher. Engaged as teacher, pub. schs., Dallastown, Pa., 1904-08; teacher pub. schs. Spring Garden Twp., 1908-09; teacher and prin. high sch. Phoenixville, Pa., 1913-24, supt. pub. schs., Phoenixville, since 1924. Dir. Phoenixville Pub. Library, Phoenixville Branch Am. Red Cross. Lutheran. Mason (K.T.). Home: 136 4th Av., Phoenixville, Pa.

PETERS, Roy Stillman, lawyer; b. Saegertown, Pa., Feb. 18, 1883; s. Preston Levi and Margaret Ann (Muckinhaupt) P.; ed. high sch. Saegertown, 1898-1902; m. Helen Elizabeth Sherman, June 27, 1916; children—Neil Sherman, Charlotte Louise. Engaged in teaching sch., 1902-04; admitted to Pa. bar, 1908 and since engaged in gen, practice of law at Meadville; mem. firm Peters and Prather since 1935. Now serving fifth term as Burgess of Saegertown. Democrat. Methodist. I.O.O.F., K.P. Home: Saegertown, Pa. Office: 915 Diamond Square, Meadville, Pa.

PETERS, Sidney Newheart, cement mfg.; b. Charlotte, N.C., Mar. 10, 1880; s. Hugh Bryan and Emma (Troy) P.; ed. pub. sch. and high sch.; m. Ella Webb, Jan. 2, 1907; children—Sidney N., Jr., Lois Webb (Mrs. R. E. Kilbourne), Hugh Griffith. Began with Odell Hardware Co., Greensboro, N.C., 1895-1905; vicepres. Guilford Plaster and Cement Co., 1905-08; with Lesley and Trinkle Co., Phila., Pa., 1908-13; asso. with Giant Portland Cement Co. since 1913, gen. sales mgr. since 1920, dir. since 1935, v.p. since 1937. Republican. Methodist. Home: Sharon Hill. Office: 603-610 Pennsylvania Bldg., Philadelphia, Pa.

PETERS, Stacy Eugene, prin. high sch.; b. Dallastown, Pa., Dec. 20, 1884; s. William H. and Kate E. (Martin) P.; A.B., Gettysburg Coll., 1908; ed. U. of Pa., 1921-27, A.M., same, 1925; (hon.) A.M., Gettysburg Coll., 1911, Pd.D., same, 1933; m. Nancy R. Kauffman, Aug. 10, 1910 (dec. 1918); m. 2d, Miriam Smith Gundaker, Aug. 4, 1920. Began as teacher in grade schs., Dallastown, Pa., 1901-04; teacher high sch., prin., then supt., Downingtown, Pa., 1908-15; supt. schs., Hershey, Pa., 1915-20; prin. Stevens High Sch., Lancaster, Pa., 1920-30, prin. Lancaster high schs., 1930-32, prin. Stevens High Sch. since 1932. Mem. Lancaster Chamber of Commerce. Mem. Nat. and Pa. State edn. assns., S.R., S.A.R., Pa. German Soc., Peters Family Reunion Assn. (past pres.), Phi Delta Kappa. Lutheran (mem. Ch. Council, Hershey and Lancaster). Mason (K.T., 32°, Shriner), B.P.O.E., Independent Order of Americans, I.O.O.F. Club: Kiwanis Internat. (past sec., past pres.). Home: 425 Charlotte St. Office: Stevens School, Chestnut and Charlotte Sts., Lancaster, Pa.

PETERS, William John, explorer; b. Oakland, Calif., Feb. 5, 1863; s. William B. and Margaret (Major) P.; ed. Oakland High Sch.; m. Beatrice Boyd, Sept. 2, 1908; 1 son, Geoffrey Lloyd. Engaged in various U.S. Govt. surveys, 1885-97; in charge explorations in Alaska made by U.S. Geol. Survey, 1898, 99, 1900, 01, 02, accounts of which appear in publs. of that bur.; apptd. official rep. Nat. Geog. Soc. on Ziegler Polar expdn. to Franz Joseph Land, 1903-05; in command Magnetic Survey ships Galilee and Carnegie, 1907-13, Hudson Bay Expdn., 1914. Mem. Philos. Soc. Washington, Am. Geophysical Union, Am. Sect. Internat. Scientific Radio Union. Clubs: Cosmos, Arts. Home: Chevy Chase, Md. Address: Dept. Terrestrial Magnetism, Washington, D.C.

PETERSEN, Max, asso. prof. physics; b. Dundee, Ill., Aug. 18, 1890; s. Heinrich and Mabel (Preston) P.; B.S., Northwestern U., 1913, A.M., 1914; Ph.D., U. of Wis., 1924; m. Margaret Baily, Aug. 17, 1922; children—Miriam, Alexander. Engaged as instr. physics, U. of Wis., 1920-24; asst. prof. physics, N.Y. Univ., 1924-27; asst. prof. physics, Lehigh U., 1927-30, asso. prof. since 1930. Mem. Am. Phys. Soc., Sigma Xi, Beta Kappa, Phi Mu Alpha. Grad. Fellow, Northwestern U., 1913-14; grad. scholar astronomy, U. of Chicago, summer 1916. Home: 349 8th Av., Bethlehem, Pa.

PETERSON, Herbert Gerhard, merchant; b. Arnot, Pa., Sept. 10, 1894; s. Alfred and Maria (Peterson) P.; grad. Elkland (Pa.) High Sch., 1912; grad. Mansfield (Pa.) State Normal Sch., 1914; B.S., Ursinus Coll., Collegeville, Pa., 1917; m. Eleanor Judge, Aug. 24, 1920; children—Mary Lee, H. Gerhard. Partner and half owner T. W. Judge Co., dept. store, Mansfield, Pa., since 1920. Entered U.S. Army, May 1917; apptd. lt. Aug. 1917, capt. Sept. 1918, and served with 10th Inf. and 77th Inf.; disch. Oct. 1919. Trustee Blossburg State Hosp., 1929-35; dir. Osceola Home for Children; trustee Smythe Park Assn.; mem. Armory Bd.; mem. Boy Scout Council; Civil Works Adminstr., Tioga Co., Pa., 1933-35; mem. Mansfield Borough Council, 1925-37, pres., 1935-37. Mem. State Chamber of Commerce, Business Men's Assn. (pres., 1926-39), Am. Legion (1st post comdr., 1920), Alumni Assn. Mansfield State Teachers Coll. (pres. since 1934). Republican. Episcopalian. Mason. Club: Corey Creek Golf of Mansfield (an organizer; dir. since 1927; pres., 1927-29). Address: Mansfield, Pa.

PETERSON, Rudolph, prof. economics; b. Landskrona, Sweden, Mar. 18, 1884; s. Charles and Elna (Anderson) P.; brought to U.S., 1889, naturalized, 1892; grad. Mansfield State Normal Sch., 1908; B.Sc., Bucknell U., 1915; student Pa. State Coll. and U. of Pa., summers 1909, 1911; A.M., State U. of Ia., 1923, Ph.D., 1925; m. Edyth O. Robbins, Aug. 16, 1911; 1 dau., Jean Elizabeth. Engaged in teaching and prin. high schs., 1908-13; prof. and head economics dept., Cornell Coll., Ia., 1925-26, Geneva Coll., Beaver Falls, Pa., 1926-30; prof. economics, Bucknell U., Lewisburg, Pa., since 1930. Mem. Am. Econ. Assn., Am. Assn. Univ. Profs., Order of Artus, Kappa Delta Rho. Presbyn. Home: 129 S. 13th St., Lewisburg, Pa.

PETRY, Howard Kistler, psychiatrist; b. Springfield, Mo., Feb. 16, 1895; s. David Henry and Annie Catherine (Kistler) P.; grad. Wilkes-Barre (Pa.) High Sch., 1911; student Lafayette Coll., 1911-12; A.B., Wesleyan U., 1915; M.D., U. of Pa., 1920, post grad. student, 1923; m. Marian Elizabeth Hughes, Dec. 15, 1923; 1 son, Robert Hughes. Interne Wilkes-Barre (Pa.) Gen. Hosp., 1920-21; in practice as psychiatrist since 1921; on staff of Warren (Pa.) State Hosp., 1921-32; clin. dir. Torrance State Hosp., 1932-34; supt. Harrisburg State Hosp. since 1934; consultant in psychiatry Polyclinic Hosp., Harrisburg, Pa. Served as private in World War. Asso. Am. Coll. of Physicians; mem. A.M.A., Pa. State Med. Soc. (chmn. com. on mental hygiene), Dauphin Co. Med. Soc., Harrisburg Acad. of Med. (vicepres.), Am. Psychiatric Assn., Phila. Psychiatric Soc., Delta Upsilon, Phi Beta Pi. Presbyterian. Mason. Clubs: Rotary, Torch International, University of Harrisburg (pres.). Address: Harrisburg State Hosp., Harrisburg, Pa.

PETRY, Walter B(ennett), lawyer; b. Trenton, N.J., Sept. 13, 1894; s. Frederick, Sr., and Bertha (Gutzmann) P.; Ph.B., Lafayette Coll., 1918; ed. U. of Pa. Law Sch., 1920-22; unmarried. Admitted to N.J. bar as atty., 1924, and engaged in gen. practice of law at Trenton, 1924-31; served as asst. U.S. atty., 1931-35; engaged in gen. practice at Trenton since 1935. Served in U.S.N.Res.F., 1918. Mem. Mercer Co. Bar Assn. Republican. Presbyn. (trustee Bethany Ch.). Club: Kiwanis of Trenton. Home: 901 Edgewood Av. Office: 28 W. State St., Trenton, N.J.

PETTERSEN, Anton Lorentz, civil and cons. engr.; b. Bergen, Norway, Apr. 12, 1867; s. Peder Gjert and Johanne (Rasmussen) P.; grad. Tank's Private Sch., Bergen, 1882; diploma as civil and mech. engr., Bergen Poly. Coll., 1887; m. May McLaughlin, Sept. 1895; children—Louise Johanne (Mrs. William Christensen), Peder Gjert, Hildur (Mrs. Carl Saxer), Hiram; m. 2d, Ida Baker, June 1926. Came to U.S., 1887, naturalized citizen, 1892. Field asst. and draftsman in chief engrs. office Lehigh Valley R.R., 1887-89; asst. and draftsman, Wise & Watson, Passaic, N.J., 1889-90; transit and level man for contemplated Dundersberg Spiral R.R., Jones Landing, N.Y., 1890; chief of office Wise & Watson, Passaic and Rutherford, N.J., 1890-97; first asst. city engr., Bergen, Norway, 1897-99; chief of office Wise & Watson, 1899-1908; established and conducted own business as civil and cons. engr., since 1908; pres. Passaic & Bergen Counties Land Co., Lodi, N.J. Mem. Passaic Bd. of Health, 1894-98; mem. N.J. State Assembly, 1902-03, Board of Freeholders, Passaic Co., 1906-07; city engr. Passaic, 1905-11; borough engr., Wallington, N.J., 1910-23; apptd. by Gov. Woodrow Wilson as mem. com. of five to ascertain feasibility of making Passaic River navigable between Passaic and Paterson; city engr., Garfield, N.J., 1912-22; cons. engr., Borough of New Providence, City of Summit, Town of S. Orange, Irvington, West Orange, Milburn and Springfield, 1916-18; city commr. in charge public works, Passaic, 1922-31. Del. to Dem. Nat. Conv. from N.J., 1924. Mem. Passaic Co. Engring. Soc., N.J. Assn. Professional Engrs. and Land Surveyors. Mason. Elk. Address: 242 Gregory Av., Passaic, N.J.

PETTIBON, Arthur Wiegmann, milk and ice cream distributor; b. Burgettstown, Pa., Sept. 10, 1898; s. Thomas A. and Wilhelmina (Wiegmann) P.; student Jefferson Twp., Washington Co., Pa., grade sch., Cross Creek (Pa.) High

PETTINGILL — Sch. and Steubenville Business Coll.; m. Hazel M. Sutherland, Sept. 18, 1919; children—LaVern A., George Thomas, Evelyn M., William Glenn, Frieda Eileen, Lee Owen (dec.). Began as bookkeeper Am. Zinc & Chem. Co., 1917; engaged in dairy industry since 1919; owner Pettibon Dairy Co., Rochester, Pa., Drinkmore Dairy Co.; pres. and dir. Pettibon Dairy Products Store, Inc., Rochester, Pa.; dir. Beaver Valley Hotel Co.; operator of a public golf course. Mem. Internat. Assn. of Milk Dealers; active in local business assns. and in regional and state milk dealers assns. Republican. Methodist. Mason (32°, Shriner). Club: Rochester (Pa.) Rotary. Home: 474 Hiller St. Office: 387 Connecticut Av., Rochester, Pa.

PETTINGILL, William LeRoy, clergyman; b. Central Square, Oswego Co., N.Y., Aug. 27, 1866; s. John Benjamin and Sarah Melissa (Yerton) P.; ed. pub. schs.; D.D., Potomac U., 1923; same from Wheaton (Ill.) Coll., 1927; m. 1890; 1 dau., Ruth Pettingill; m. 2d, Mrs. Etta Turner Dodge, 1936. Ordained ministry Baptist Church, 1899; pastor North Church, Wilmington, Del., 1903-23; dean Phila. School of the Bible, 1914-28. Author: Israel, Jehovah's Covenant People; Simple Studies in Daniel; Simple Studies in Matthew; Simple Studies in Romans, Simple Studies in The Revelation; God's Prophecies for Plain People; Bible Questions Answered; Christ in the Psalms; By Grace, Through Faith, Plus Nothing; Simple Studies in Galatians. Founder and editor Serving-and-Waiting (monthly mag.), 1911-28. Home: 616 North Clayton St., Wilmington, Del.

PETTY, David Milton, supt. service div., Bethlehem Steel Co.; b. Archdale, N.C., Mar. 2, 1885; s. John W. and Mary (Tomlinson) P.; B.S., Guilford Coll., 1907; E.E. Lehigh U., 1909; m. Marybell Thomas, Oct. 15, 1919; children—David Milton, John Stewart. With Bethlehem Steel Co. since 1909, beginning as helper in elec. dept., supt. elec. dept., 1913-29, supt. service div. since 1929. Mem. Assn. Iron and Steel Engrs., Am. Inst. Elec. Engrs., Tau Beta Pi. Awarded Gary medal by Am. Iron and Steel Inst., 1935. Ind. Democrat. Mem. Moravian Ch. Clubs: Bethlehem (past pres.), University (past pres.), Saucon Valley Country (vice pres.), all of Bethlehem. Author of several technical papers. Home: 1900 Paul Av., Bethlehem, Pa.

PETTY, Nelson Lane, lawyer; b. Cranbury, N.J., Aug. 7, 1869; s. Nelson and H. Jennie (Lane) P.; student N.J. State Model Sch., 1883-87, Princeton U., 1887-91; m. Matilda G. Patterson, Apr. 20, 1915. Admitted to N.J. bar, 1894; became asst. trust officer Trenton Trust Co., 1897, now v.p. and trust officer; v.p. and dir. Real Estate Title Co.; sec. and dir. Taylor Provision Co.; dir. Star Porcelain Co., Frenchtown Porcelain Co. Dir. Mercer Hosp. Presbyn. Club: Trenton (N.J.). Home: 301 W. State St. Office: 28 W. State St., Trenton, N.J.

PEW, J(ohn) Howard, pres. Sun Oil Co.; b. Bradford, Pa., Jan. 27, 1882; s. Joseph Newton and Mary Catherine (Anderson) P.; ed. Shadyside Acad., Pittsburgh, Pa., Grove City (Pa.) Coll., Mass. Inst. Tech.; m. Helen Jennings Thompson, of Pittsburgh, Jan. 3, 1907. Engr. Marcus Hook Refinery, Sun Oil Co., 1901, and successively asst. supt., supt., vice-pres. and since 1912, pres. Sun Oil Co.; dir. Phila. Nat. Bank, Sun Shipbuilding & Dry Dock Co., Am. Petroleum Inst. Chmn. bd. trustees Grove City Coll.; pres. trustees Gen. Assembly of Presbyn. Ch. in U.S.A. Republican. Presbyn. Clubs: Union League, Phila. Country (Phila.); Merion Cricket (Haverford, Pa.). Home: "Knollbrook," Mill Creek Rd., Ardmore, Pa. Office: 1608 Walnut St., Philadelphia, Pa.

PEYTON, Thomas West IV, lawyer; b. Huntington, W.Va., Aug. 13, 1891; s. Thomas West III and Mary T. (Hovey) P.; student Morris Harvey Coll., Barboursville, W.Va., 1905-09, W.Va. U., Morgantown, W.Va., 1909-10; m. Gay Zenith Vaughan, July 24, 1912. Admitted to W.Va. bar, 1915, and since practiced at Huntington, W.Va.; mem. firm Peyton, Winters & Hereford, gen. practice of law, Huntington, W.Va., since 1933; dir. Guyan Creamery Co. Served as capt., Inf., U.S. Army, during World War, serving in Battle of Argonne. Mayor Barboursville, W.Va., 1922-24 (2 terms); asst. prosecuting atty., Cabell Co., W.Va., since 1933. Mem. Am., and W.Va. bar assns., Cabell Co. Bar Assn. (pres. 1931-32), Department of W. Va. Res. Officers Assn. (pres. 1927-28), Huntington Chapter Res. Officers Assn. (pres. 1929-30), Am. Legion, 40 and 8. Democrat. Methodist. Mason, Elk. Clubs: Kiwanis (pres. 1931-32), Guyan Valley (Huntington, W.Va.). Home: Barboursville, W.Va. Office: Huntington, W.Va.

PFAELZER, Elsie L. (Mrs. Frank A. Pfaelzer), volunteer community service; b. Baltimore, Md., Mar. 1, 1889; d. Jacob and Bertha (Arnold) Levy; student Girls' Latin School, Baltimore, Md., 1902-06, Goucher Coll., 1906-07; m. Frank A. Pfaelzer, Nov. 6, 1907 (died Jan. 16, 1928); children—Morris, Betty Arnold (Mrs. Harry Horner), Richard, Mildred Henrietta. Volunteer worker in Juvenile Aid Soc. and dir. since 1909; dir. Jewish Welfare Soc. since 1920; dir. Southeastern Pa. Chapter Am. Red Cross, 1925-36; dir. Children's Country Week Assn. since 1920; trustee Phila. Co. Mothers' Assistance Fund, 1925-37; trustee Phila. Co. Bd. of Pub. Assistance, 1937-39; mem. Old York Road Com. of Women's Com. for the Phila. Orchestra, 1939. Mem. Goucher Coll. Alumnæ Assn. Clubs: Women's City (Phila.); Philmont Country (Philmont, Pa.). Home: 70th Av. and City Line, Oak Lane, Philadelphia, Pa.

PFAFF, Will, optometrist; b. Pittsburgh, Pa., Aug. 19, 1880; s. Adam and Elizabeth (Jahn) P.; student pub. schs. and pvt. schs., clinics and ednl. classes; Dr. Ocular Science (hon.); m. Lida Anthony, Dec. 31, 1903; children—Frances Elizabeth (dec.), Marian Lucinda (Mrs. W. J. Kittredge), Florence Jean. Followed profession of optometry, Pittsburgh, 1896-1903, at McKeesport, Pa., since 1903; dir. Community Discount & Loan Assn., McKeesport Mortgage Co. Served as pres. Chamber of Commerce of McKeesport, pres. Rotary Club. Dir. Sch. Bd. McKeesport for past 15 yrs. Mem. Am., Pa., and Pittsburgh optometric assns., Beta Sigma Kappa. Republican. Methodist. Mason (K.T., 32°, Shriner). Club: Rotary (McKeesport, Pa.). Home: 1014 Fawcett St. Office: 526 Locust St., McKeesport, Pa.

PFAFFENBACH, George Arnold, lawyer; b. Havre de Grace, Md., Sept. 22, 1904; s. George and Mary A.M. (Pearson) P.; student Beacom Coll., Wilmington, Del., 1921-22; LL.B., U. of Md. Law Sch., Baltimore, Md., 1926; unmarried. Admitted to Md. bar, 1926 and since engaged in gen. practice of law at Havre de Grace; served as mem. Md. Ho. of Dels., 1935-39; counsel Columbian Bldg. Assn. of Harford Co. Sec. Chamber of Commerce of Havre de Grace. Mem. Harford County Bar Assn., Patriotic Order Sons of America. Democrat. Mem. Ref. Episcopalian Ch. Odd Fellow. Club: Kiwanis of Havre de Grace (past pres.). Home: 622 Fountain St. Office: 317 St. John St., Havre de Grace, Md.

PFAHLER, George Edward, radiologist; b. Numidia, Pa., Jan. 29, 1874; s. William H. and Sarah A. (Stine) P.; B.E., Bloomsburg State Normal Sch. (now Teachers Coll.), 1894; M.D., Medico Chirurg. Coll., Phila., 1898; Sc.D., Ursinus Coll. Collegeville, Pa.; D.M. (Cambridge U., England, 1926; m. Muriel Bennett July 10, 1918. Interne Phila. Gen. Hosp., 1898-99, asst. chief resident physician, 1899-1902; clin. prof. roentgenology, Medico-Chirurg. Coll., 1909-12, prof., 1912-16; prof. radiology, U. of Pa., since 1916; dir. radiological dept., Misericordia Hosp., Phila. Trustee Ursinus Coll. Mem. Am. Roentgen Ray Soc. (pres. 1910), Am. Electrotherapeutic Assn. (pres. 1912), Am. Radium Soc. (pres. 1922), Am. Coll. Radiology (pres. 1923), A.M.A., Pa. State Med. Soc.; hon. mem. Brit., French, German, Austrian, Scandinavian and Russian radiological socs. Episcopalian. Clubs: Medical, Medical Literature (Phila.). Contbr. many articles to med. jours. Home: 6463 Drexel Rd. Office: 1930 Chestnut St., Philadelphia, Pa.

PFAHLER, Robert Gair, mining engr.; b. Wilkes-Barre, Pa., Jan. 8, 1896; s. Charles L. and Amanda E. (Bausch) P.; E.M., Lehigh U., 1923; m. Muriel A. Gebhard, Aug. 30, 1924; children—Ann, Barbara, Carol, Dorothy. Spl. engr. Lehigh Navigation Coal Co., 1924-25; div. engr. Berwind-White Coal Mining Co., 1926-28, asst. mining engr., 1929, mining engr. since 1930. Mem. Am. Inst. Mining and Metall. Engrs., (mem. fuel values com. and subsidence com.) Am. Soc. Testing Materials, Am. Mining Congress (mem. bd. govs. coal div.), Coal Mining Inst. America, Am. Philatelic Soc., Rocks and Minerals Assn., Pa. Soc. of Professional Engrs., Am. Legion, La Société des 40 et 8, Phi Beta Kappa, Tau Beta Pi. Republican. Presbyterian. Club: Summit Country. Home: 709 15th St. Office: The Berwind-White Coal Mining Co., Windber, Pa.

PFALTZGRAFF, George W., pottery mfr.; b. York, Pa., Feb. 21, 1871; s. George and Elizabeth (Keeney) P.; ed. New York City Business Coll.; m. Maud Owen, 1904; children—Helen, Carolyn. Began work as potter; upon completion of business course, worked as stenographer, 2 yrs.; continued father's business as pottery mfr. over 50 yrs. under name of Pfaltzgraff Pottery Co., Inc.; owner Pottery Hill; mem. finance com. and dir. York Trust Co. Treas. and trustee Prospect Hill Cemetery. Mem. Reformed Ch. Clubs: Lafayette, Country (York). Home: 607 S. George St. Office: Pottery Hill, York, Pa.

PFATTEICHER, Ernst Philip, author, clergyman; b. Easton, Pa., July 28, 1874; s. Philip and Emma (Spaeth) P.; A.B., Lafayette Coll., Easton, 1895, later A.M., Ph.D., 1901, D.D., 1918; grad. Luth. Theol. Sem., Phila., 1898; student U. of Erlangen, U. of Pa.; D.D., Muhlenberg College, 1918, LL.D., 1931; m. Helen Jacoby, June 27, 1905; children—Ernst Philip, Helen Emma. Ordained Luth. ministry, 1898; asst. to Rev. Dr. Theodore E. Schmauk, of Lebanon, Pa., 1898-1902; pastor Trinity Ch., Norristown, 1902-07, Holy Communion Ch. Phila., 1907-18, Old Trinity Ch., Reading, 1918-26. Pres. Luth. Ministerium of Pa. and Adjacent States since 1926; mem. internat. continuation com. of Stockholm Conf. on Life and Work; mem. exec. bd. of United Luth. Ch.; mem. Nat. Luth. Council; dir. Luth. Theol. Sem., Phila. Mem. Acad. Polit. and Social Science, Delta Kappa Epsilon. Republican. Club: Union League. Author: The Apostles Creed in Sonnets, 1900; King David's Earth Born Son, 1907; Think on These Things, 1917; Sermons on the Gospels, Vol. I, 1918, Vol. II, 1923; The Sunday Problem, 1923; Christian Social Science, 1933; The Man from Oxford, 1934; For Pastors Only, 1935; Youth Letters (in collaboration with his daughter), 1938. Home: 415 S. 44th St. Office: 1228 Spruce St., Philadelphia, Pa.

PFEFFERLE, George Henry, mech. engring.; b. Appleton, Wis., Feb. 22, 1900; s. Stephen and Wilhelmina (Sonner) P.; ed. Lawrence Coll., Appleton, Wis., 1918-19, U. of Cincinnati, 1919-24; m. Edith Alice Jones, June 21, 1928; 1 dau., Judith Ann. Employed as research engr., Dalton Adding Machine Co., Norwood, O., 1924-27, and when merged with Remington-Rand, Inc., became plant engr., 1927-28, development engr., 1928-29; chief engr. Dresser Mfg. Co., Bradford, Pa., since 1930. Mem. Am. Soc. Mech. Engrs., Am. Gas Assn., Tau Beta Pi, Beta Kappa. Clubs: Bradford, Camera (Bradford). Home: 2 Abbott Rd., Bradford, Pa.

PFEIFFER, Karl Erwin, forester; b. Brooklyn, N.Y., Aug. 25, 1889; s. Gustav Oscar and Lois Howell (Smith) P.; A.B., Cornell U., 1912; student Cornell U. Grad. Sch., 1913-15; m. Annie Millington Bullivant, Sept. 18, 1915; children—Oscar William, Elizabeth, Mary Clare. Employed as forest asst., Md. State Bd. Forestry, Baltimore, 1915-16, asst. forester, 1916-22; asst. state forester, Md. State Dept. Forestry, Baltimore, since 1923. Dir. State Parks, Baltimore, since 1936. Mem. exec. com. Baltimore Area Council Boy Scouts of America; awarded Silver Beaver, Boy Scouts. Former dir. Md. Classified Employees Assn. Sr. mem. Soc. Am.

Foresters (former chmn. Alleghany Sect.); hon. mem. Md. Natural History Soc., Mountain Club of Md. Mem. Am. Forestry Assn., Delta Upsilon, Md. Fish and Game Protective Assn. Presbyn. Club: Cornell of Maryland. Home: 2701 Queen Anne Rd. Office: 1411 Fidelity Bldg., Baltimore, Md.

PFEIFLE, Robert, mayor; b. Almont, Pa., Apr. 14, 1880; s. Franklin and Catharine (Headman) P.; m. Gertrude Estella Heller, Feb. 11, 1905; children—Helen (Mrs. Clyde Diehl), Robert E., Evelyn (Mrs. George Brown), Dorothy Mae (Mrs. Chester Cuddy). Messenger boy, Postal Telegraph Co., 1892; with Enterprise Laundry, 1893, Wm. D. Rogers Co., 1895-99; carpenter, 1899-1906; in gen. contracting business, Bethlehem, 1906-1930; pres. Citizens' Realty Co., 1914-20, Industrial Bldg. and Loan Assn., 1916-32, Bethlehem Nat. Bank, 1928-33; now pres. Lehigh Valley Cold Storage Co.; dir. Bethlehem Hotel Corpn. Elected to Borough Council, 1915, 2 yr. term; commr., City of Bethlehem, 1920-28; mayor of Bethlehem since 1929 (now serving third term). Received Civic Award (bronze plaque) for outstanding activities in City of Bethlehem from B'nai B'rith, 1931. Pres. Bethlehem Community Chest since 1930; chmn. Bethlehem Police Pension Fund, Bethlehem Housing Authority, Bethlehem Recreation Commn., Bethlehem Bi-Centennial Com., Bethlehem Water Authority. Mem. Bethlehem Chamber Commerce, Patriotic Order Sons of America. Trustee First Moravian Ch., 1908-25. Odd Fellow, K.P. Clubs: Jacksonian Democratic, First Ward Democratic, Fourth Ward Democratic, Grover-Cleveland Democratic Assn. Home: 424 Webster St. Office: City Hall, 53 E. Broad St., Bethlehem, Pa.

PFISTER, Joseph Clement, univ. prof.; b. Newark, N.J., Mar. 10, 1867; s. John and Barbara (Heick) P.; grad. Newark Pub. Sch., 1881, Newark High Sch., 1885; A.B., Columbia U., 1889, A.M., 1890, Ph.D., 1892 (prize fellow in science; prize scholarships in mathematics and mechanics; Alumni prize for most faithful and deserving student); also attended Coll. Physicians & Surgeons (Columbia), univs. Wuerzburg and Heidelberg; m. Emma A. C. Heim, May 15, 1891; children—Eleanor Ruth (Mrs. Frederick J. Vreeland), M. Louise (Mrs. Royal V. Randall). Asst. in higher mathematics, astronomy and mechanics, Columbia U., 1889-90, instr. in same subjects, 1890-1904, prof. math. physics, 1904-11; associated in depts. of higher mathematics, astronomy and mathematical physics, Columbia U., in research and instrn. with Dr. Wm. G. Peck, Dr. Robert S. Woodward, Dr. Richard C. Maclaurine, Dr. Ernest F. Nichols and Dr. Michael I. Pupin. Fellow Am. Assn. Sciences, N.Y. Acad. Sciences; mem. Am. Math. Soc., Nat. Geog. Soc., Phi Beta Kappa. Republican. Episcopalian. Clubs: Roseville Athletic (Newark); Columbia Alumni Assn. Compiled a bibliography of mechanics and a treatise on the nebular hypothesis. Home: 240 Sixth Av., Newark, N.J.

PFUND, A. Herman, physicist; b. Madison, Wis., Dec. 28, 1879; s. Herman and Anna (Scheibel) P.; B.S., U. of Wis., 1901; Ph.D., Johns Hopkins U., 1906; m. Nelle Fuller, Aug. 30, 1910; 1 dau., Alice Elizabeth. Carnegie research asst., 1903-05, asst. in physics, 1906-07, Johnston scholar, 1907-09, asso. in physics, 1909-10, asso. prof., 1910-27, prof. since 1927, Johns Hopkins. Mem. Am. Physical Soc., Am. Soc. for Testing Materials, Optical Soc. America, Gamma Alpha, Phi Beta Kappa. Awarded Science Club medal, U. of Wis., 1901; Longstreth medal, Franklin Inst., Phila., 1922; Dudley medal, Am. Soc. for Testing Materials, 1931. Lutheran. Home: 4404 Bedford Place, Baltimore, Md.

PFUND, Harry William, asso. prof. German; b. Phila., Pa., Jan. 3, 1900; s. William J. and Anna M. (Erb) P.; A.B., Haverford Coll., 1922; A.M., Harvard U., 1926, Ph.D., same, 1931; grad. study, U. of Munich, Germany, 1922-23, Univs. of Berlin and Heidelberg, 1927-28; m. Friederike Marie Haufe, of Leipzig, Germany, July 4, 1931; children—Peter Harry, Helga Friederike. Instr. German, Harvard U., 1924-26, Haverford Coll., 1926-27; Ottendorfer travelling fellow, N.Y. Univ., 1927-28; instr. German and tutor, Harvard U. and Radcliffe Coll., 1928-30; asst. prof. German, Haverford Coll., Haverford, Pa., 1930-36, asso. prof. since 1936; asst. sec. Carl Schurz Memorial Foundation, Phila., 1931-33. Mem. Modern Lang. Assn. America, Goethe Soc. of Weimar, German Soc. of Pa. (dir.), Phi Beta Kappa. Lutheran. Author: Studien zu Wort und Stil bei Brockes, 1935. Founder and mem. editorial bd., American-German Review since 1934. Contbr. articles to mags. Home: 3 College Lane, Haverford, Pa.

PHARR, Walter Wellington, clergyman; b. Charlotte, N.C., Mar. 12, 1888; s. William Watson (M.D.) and Ida Rowena (Query) P.; A.B., Davidson Coll., Davidson, N.C., 1908; B.D., Union Theol. Sem., Richmond, Va., 1913; grad. student Sorbonne, Paris, France, 1919; hon. D.D., Davis-Elkins Coll., Elkins, W.Va., 1929; m. Minnie Louise Moore, May 23, 1930; 1 son, Walter Wellington, Jr. Engaged in teaching sch., 1908-10; ordained to ministry Presbyn. Ch., 1913; asst. pastor, Lewisburg, 1913-17, with 3 mission points, 1915-17; pastor, White Sulphur, 1915-17, and 3 mission points also supply Salem Ch. and 1 mission, 1915-17; supply, Mt. Hope, W.Va. and 1 mission, 1917-18; pastor, Mt. Hope, W.Va. and 7 missions since 1919. Served as 1st lt. chaplain, U.S.A., 1918-19; with A.E.F. in France. Chmn. County Red Cross, 1925-34, City Community Chest, 1926-30, County Welfare Bd., 1932-33. Mem. county Council of Pub. Assistance since 1938. Mem. bd. dirs. Chamber of Commerce, Mt. Hope, W.Va., 1929-32. Trustee Davis-Elkins Coll., 1932-36; trustee Union Theol. Sem., Richmond, Va., since 1932. Democrat. Presbyn. Mason (K.T., Shriner), Eastern Star, White Shrine. Home: Forest Hills, Mt. Hope, W.Va.

PHELPS, Andrew Henry; b. Steele City, Neb., Sept. 27, 1888; s. Asa E. and Marion (Clark) P.; ed. Ga. Mil. Coll. and Accountancy and Law Inst., New York; m. Emily Brown, of Brooklyn, Dec. 14, 1912; children—Emily May (Mrs. Bertram deHeus Atwood), Andrew Henry (dec.); Sarah Elizabeth. Banking and investment business, N.Y. City, 1910-11; business mgr., Y.M.C.A., 1911-17; field mgr. Chamber of Commerce U.S.A., 1917-27; sales management and pub. relations McGraw Hill Pub. Co., 1927-36; now gen. mgr. of purchases and traffic Westinghouse Electric & Mfg. Co. Exec. sec. International Trade Conf., 1919. Rep. Methodist Ch. at organization meeting World Conf. of Chs., Utrecht, Holland, 1938. Trustee Dickinson Coll. Carlisle, Pa. Mem. Pittsburgh Chamber of Commerce. Clubs: Bankers (New York); Duquesne (Pittsburgh); University (Evanston). Home: 266 Woodhaven Drive, Mt. Lebanon, Pa. Office: Union Bank Bldg., Pittsburgh, Pa.; and 150 Broadway, New York, N.Y.

PHELPS, Harold Augustus, prof. sociology; b. Fitchburg, Mass., Jan. 30, 1898; s. Ralph L. and Emilie B. (Kendall) P.; A.B., Brown U., 19—; A.M., George Washington U., 19—; Ph.D., U. of Minn., 19—; m. Beth D. Ashenden, May 22, 1925; children—Elizabeth, Thomas. Instr. sociology, U. of Minn., 1922-25; prof. sociology, Brown U., 1925-31, U. of Pittsburgh since 1931. Mem. Am. Sociol. Soc. (sec.-treas.), Am. Econ. Assn., Am. Statis. Assn., Population Assn. America. Club: The Brown. Author: Principles and Laws of Sociology, 1936; Contemporary Social Problems, 1938. Mng. editor Am. Sociol. Review. Home: 633 Olympia Road, Pittsburgh, Pa.

PHELPS, John Jay, capitalist; b. Paris, France, Sept. 27, 1861; s. William Walter and Ellen (Sheffield) P.; brought to America in infancy; B.A., Yale, 1883; m. Rose Janet Hutchinson, Apr. 26, 1888; children—Dorothy (Mrs. Davenport West), Rose. Dir. Hackensack Trust Co., U.S. Trust Co. Acting lt. U.S.N., Spanish-Am. War and World War; comdr. Div. B, Squadron XI, World War. Republican. Episcopalian. Mem. Am. Mus. Natural History, N.J. State Chamber Commerce, Am. Geog. Soc., N.E. Soc., Founders and Patriots of America, Am. Forestry Assn., Asiatic Assn., U.S. Reserve Officers' Assn., Victory Hall Assn., Waterway League of America, Roosevelt Memorial Assn., Naval Order of U.S., Navy Relief Soc., Nat. Security League, Nat. Inst. of Efficiency, Nat. Marine League, Nat. Child Welfare Assn., Nat. Assn. of Audubon Soc., Big Brother Movement, N.J. Audubon Soc., N.Y. Zoöl. Soc., N.J. Hist. Soc., Bergen County Hist. Soc., Am. Legion, S.R., Mil. Order Foreign Wars (N.Y. and N.J.), Navy League U.S., United Spanish War Vets., Psi Upsilon (Beta Chapter), Scroll and Keys (Yale) Clubs: Union League, University, Yale, Circumnavigators, Submarine Chaser of America, Army and Navy, Motor Boat of America (New York); Graduate, Conn. Auto, N.J. Auto and Motor (New Haven); Pine Orchard Club (Conn.); Lantern League (Boston); New York Yacht, N.H. Yacht, Oritani Field, Cruising Club of America. Home: Red Towers, Hackensack, N.J., and Yoncomis Island, Stony Creek, Conn. Office: Union Banking Bldg., Hackensack, N.J.

PHELPS, Winthrop Morgan, surgeon; b. Bound Brook, N.J., Apr. 11, 1894; s. Arthur Santford and Gertrude Lindall (Tappan) P.; B.S., Princeton U., 1916; M.D., Johns Hopkins Med. Sch., 1920; hon. A.M., Yale U., 1932; m. Naomi Forsythe, Sept. 20, 1925; 1 dau., Pamela Morgan. Interne Johns Hopkins Hosp., Baltimore, 1920-21, Mass. Gen. Hosp. Boston, 1921-23; resident teaching fellow, Harvard U., 1923-25; instr. orthopedic surgery, Yale U., 1925-26, asst. prof., 1926-29, asso. prof., 1929-32, prof., 1932-36; med. dir. Babbitt Hosp., Vineland, N.J., since 1936; med. dir. Children's Rehabilitation Inst., Reisterstown, Md., since 1937, and pres. bd. dirs.; med. dir. Cerebral Palsy Project, Duke Univ., Durham, N.C., since 1938; in pvt. practice at Baltimore since 1936; advisor spl. edn. of the handicapped, Columbia Univ. Teachers Coll. Served as pvt. Med. Corps U.S.A., 1917-19. Mem. bd. dirs. Johns Hopkins U. Mus. Assn. Chmn. Crippled Children's Com., Baltimore Mus. of Art. Fellow Am. Coll. Surgeons. Mem. A.M.A., Am. Acad. Orthopedic Surgeons, Am. Orthopedic Assn., Eastern Surg. Soc., Orthopedic Forum, Internat. Soc. Orthopedic Surgeons, Phi Beta Pi. Episcopalian. Clubs: Princeton of Maryland, Graduate, Yale, Johns Hopkins, Maryland Sportsman Luncheon (Baltimore); Gibson Island. Address: 3038 St. Paul St., Baltimore, Md.

PHILBRICK, Francis Samuel, prof. law; b. Iowa City, Ia., Sept. 30, 1876; s. Philetus H. and Malah P. (Brackett) P.; B.Sc., U. of Neb., 1897, M.A., 1899; Ph.D., Harvard, 1902; LL.B., Columbia University, 1913; LL.D., University of Nebraska, 1930; m. Maria Mayer-Brun, July 1910 (died 1911); m. 2d, Edith Hoppe, Sept. 1922. Mem. Am. editorial staff, Ency. Britannica, 1904-07, 1910; asst. to gen. atty. C.&O., Hocking Valley, and M.,K.&T. rys., New York, 1913-15; prof. law, U. of Calif., 1915-19, Northwestern U., 1919-22, U. of Ill., 1922-29, U. of Pa. since 1929. Prof. law, Columbia, summer sessions, 1921 and 25, U. of Mich. summer 1923; visiting prof. U. of Pa., 1928-29. Mem. Am. Legal History Soc. (sec. 1933-37), Am., N.Y. and Ill. bar assns., Am. Hist. Assn. (chmn. com. on legal history 1934—), Am. Polit. Sci. Assn., Acad. Polit. Science (New York), Neb. State Hist. Soc., Phi Delta Phi, Phi Beta Kappa, Order of the Coif. Democrat. Unitarian. Clubs: Coin d'Or, Contemporary, Franklin Inn (Phila.). Part Author: A General Survey of Continental Legal History, 1912. Translator: Huebner's History of Germanic Private Law, 1918. Editor: Laws of Indiana Territory, 1800-09 (Vol. 21 of Collections of Ill. State Historical Library), 1930; Pope's Digest, 1815 (Vol. 28 of same), 1939. Contbr. to legal periodicals. Home: 737 Harvard Av., Swarthmore, Pa.

PHILIPS, Earle Stanton, insurance; b. Kennett Square, Pa., May 2, 1892; s. Samuel Jones and Martha (Voorhees) P.; ed. Cedarcroft Sch., 1905-09, Swarthmore Coll., 1909-12; m. Margaret Wilson, Oct. 15, 1913; 1 dau., Martha Jane. Began as farmer in 1912; in employ, successively, Good Roads Machinery Co., Inc., American Road Machinery Co., Musselman-Philips Corpn., Monarch Mfg. Co., Inc.; pres. Earle S. Philips, Inc., gen. line of ins., Kennett Square, Pa., since 1912; treas. Dealers Service, Inc. Mem. Pa. Sons of Revolution, Phi Kappa Psi. Republican. Baptist (trustee First Bapt.

Ch.). Club: Union League (Philadelphia). Home: 228 Garfield St., Kennett Square, Pa. Office: Odd Fellows Bldg., Wilmington, Del.

PHILIPS, S(amuel) Jones, retired; b. Pughtown, Pa., July 26, 1861; s. David and Thamzen (Morris) P.; ed. pub. schs.; m. Martha Voorhees, Jan. 24, 1883; children—David, Earle Stanton, Ralph J. (dec.). Worked on farm, 1875-78; clerk and bookkeeper, 1879-86; sec. and treas. Am. Road Machinery Co., 1887-1916, pres. and dir., 1916-31; retired; formerly pres., treas. and dir. Kennett Foundry, Kennett Foundry & Machine Co.; now v.p. and dir. Kennett Sq. Nat. Bank & Trust Co.; pres. and dir. Advance Pub. Co.; one of organizers and dir. Kennett Bldg. & Loan Assn. One of organizers and officer Bayard Taylor Library. Home: 228 Garfiels St., Kennett Square, Pa.

PHILLIPS, Albanus, vegetable packing; b. Golden Hill, Md., Aug. 31, 1871; s. George W. and Mary Elizabeth (Leonard) P.; student pub. schs. of Md., 1877-83; m. Daisy Alma Lewis, Oct. 10, 1900; children—Alma (Mrs. Harry Wehr), Frances (Mrs. Edgar M. Skinner, Jr.), Albanus, Jr., Theodore. On sailing schooner, 1885, capt. coasting schooner, 1892; with wholesale oyster commn. mchts., Baltimore, 1893-99; engaged in business of packing vegetables, Cambridge, Md., as A. Phillips & Co., 1899-1902; an organizer and head of Phillips Packing Co. co-partnership, 1902-29, and pres. and dir. since 1929, expanded business with other plants at Newark, Townsend and Laurel, Del., and Denton, Cordova, Willoughby and Newbridge, Md.; pres. and dir. Phillips Can Co., Phillips Hardware Co., Inc., Phillips Oil Co. Cambridge, Phillips Sales Co., Inc., Phillips Commission Co. of Md., Inc., Phillips Transport Co., Cambridge; dir. Del. R.R. Co., Baltimore & Eastern R.R. Apptd. mem. staff Gov. of Md. with rank of col., 1913. Mem. Md. State Rds. Planning Commn. Mem. Md. Commn. to represent the state at N.Y. World's Fair of 1939. Mem. bd. govs. Washington Coll., Chestertown, 1922-26. Pres. Cambridge Md. Hosp. for number of yrs. Republican. Mason (Shriner), Elk. Clubs: Yacht (Cambridge); Maryland Yacht (Baltimore); Union League (Philadelphia). Home: 202 Mill St. Office: Race St., Cambridge, Md.

PHILLIPS, Albanus, Jr., business exec.; b. Cambridge, Md., Oct. 8, 1902; s. Albanus and Daisy Alma (Lewis) P.; student Cambridge (Md.) High Sch., 1914-17, Tome Sch., Port Deposit, Md., 1918-21; m. Anita Applegarth Spedden, Nov. 20, 1929; children—Anita Spedden, II, Albanus, III. Began as employee Phillips Packing Co., Cambridge, Md., 1921, v.p. since 1929; 2d v.p. and dir. Peoples Loan Savings Deposit Bank, Cambridge, Md., since 1932; v.p. Phillips Hardware Co., Inc., Cambridge, since 1929. Republican. Methodist. Mason (Shriner). Club: Cambridge (Md.) Country. Address: Cambridge, Md.

PHILLIPS, Alexander Roy, insurance; b. Waco, Tex., Feb. 8, 1880; s. George Pierce and Florence (Minney) P.; grad. Dallas (Tex.) Acad., 1897; m. Anna Garlington, Feb. 4, 1903; children—George Garlington, Alexander Roy, Jr. (dec.), Anna Elizabeth (Mrs. Henry Hicks Hurt), Helen Moore, Martha Phillips (dec.). Clk. Tex. Dept. of Hartford Fire Ins. Co., 1898-1902; spl. agt. Springfield Fire & Marine Ins. Co., 1902-06; spl. agt. Ins. Co. of N.A., 1906-12; spl. agt. Great American Ins. Co., 1912-16, asst. sec. at home office, 1916-23; v.p. and dir. Great American and American Alliance Ins. Cos. since 1923; v.p. and dir., Rochester American Ins. Co., Mass. Fire & Marine Ins. Co., Am. Nat. Fire Ins. Co., N.C. Home Ins. Co., County Fire Ins. Co. of Phila., Detroit Fire & Marine Ins. Co., all since 1928; dir. Great American Indemnity Co.; Underwriters Salvage Co. of N.Y. Mem. S.A.R., N.Y. Southern Soc. Presbyn. Club: Drug and Chemical (New York). Home: 62 Harrison Av., Montclair, N.J. Office: 1 Liberty St., New York, N.Y.

PHILLIPS, Benjamin Dwight, vice-pres. T. W. Phillips Gas & Oil Co.; b. New Castle, Pa., Nov. 20, 1885; s. Thomas W. and Pamphila (Hardman) P.; ed. Hiram College, Hiram, Ohio; m. Undine Conant, Apr. 6, 1909; children—Stella (Mrs. Rolland L. Ehrman), Clarinda (Mrs. Ferdinand H. Diebold), Undine (Mrs. Frank L. Wiegand, Jr.), Benjamin Dwight, Victor Karl, Donald Conant. Began in natural gas and oil business, 1906, with T. W. Phillips Gas & Oil Co., vice-pres. and gen. mgr. since 1920; pres. West Penn Cement Co. (Butler, Pa.); vice-pres. and dir. Pennsylvania Investment & Real Estate Corpn.; dir. Citizens Nat. Bank (New Castle, Pa.), Butler Consolidated Coal Co., Masseth Packer & Machine Co. Mem. bd. Butler Y.M.C.A. Republican. Mem. Christian (Disciples) Ch. Clubs: Butler Country; Pittsburgh Field, Duquesne (Pittsburgh); Woodmont (Md.) Rod and Gun. Home: Elm Court. Office: 205 N. Main St., Butler, Pa.

PHILLIPS, Charles Hayden, M.D.; b. Edwardsville, Pa., Apr. 24, 1892; s. David and Margaret (Jones) P.; grad. Edwardsville High Sch., 1908; student Philadelphia Coll. of Pharmacy, 1909-10; M.D., Jefferson Med. Coll., 1914; m. Joyce Marjorie Whineray, of Neston, England, Aug. 3, 1921; children—Anne Dorice, Joan Mary, Roger Whineray (died 1937). In gen. practice of medicine since 1914; attending pediatrician Wilkes-Barre Gen. Hosp., Florence Crittenton Nursery, Wilkes-Barre Children's Home; pediatrician Children's Service Center. Mem. Luzerne Co. Med. Soc., Pa. Med. Soc., A.M.A., Phila Pediatric Soc. Republican. Protestant. Club: Irem Temple Country. Home: Trucksville, Pa. Office: 200 S. Franklin St., Wilkes-Barre, Pa.

PHILLIPS, Charles L., insurance exec.; b. Hernwood, Md., May 18, 1889; s. Charles T. and Jessie (Choate) P.; LL.B., Baltimore U. Law Sch., 1910; m. Gladys L. Runge, Birmingham, England, Nov. 20, 1924; children—Brian Hartley, Patricia Odell. Asso. with U.S. Fidelity & Guaranty Co., Baltimore, Md., since entering its employ, 1910, exec. vice-pres. since 1924, dir. since 1924; dir. Fidelity & Guaranty Fire Corpn., Union Trust Co. of Md., Fidelity Ins. Co. of Can., Security Storage Co. Dir. Baltimore Chapter Red Cross. Trustee Brown Memorial Ch. Mem. Baltimore Bar Assn. Presbyn. Clubs: Maryland, Merchants, Elkridge (Baltimore). Home: 224 Northway, Baltimore, Md.

PHILLIPS, Daniel Edward, college prof.; b. Morgantown, W.Va., July 29, 1865; s. Isaac Newton and Mary Lydia (Davis) P.; grad. Fairmont (W.Va.) State Normal Sch., 1890; Peabody Normal Coll., 1892; B.A., U. of Nashville, 1893, M.A., 1894; Ph.D., Clark Univ., 1898; studied in European Universities, 1908-09; Litt.D., U. of Denver, 1914; m. Martha Croley, Feb. 12, 1896; children—Edward Rudolph, Ruth Jean. Prof. edn. and psychology, State Normal Sch., Athens, Ga., 1895-97; prof. philosophy and edn., W.Va. U., summer 1889; prof. psychology and edn., U. of Denver, 1898-1922, head dept. of psychology, 1923-29, dir. div. of psychology and edn., 1929-30; dir. City Coll. U. of Denver, 1898-1930; also mem. grad. faculty U. of Ill. Summer Sch. Organized first summer school west of Chicago in U. of Denver, 1901; mem. Bd. of Edn. City and County of Denver, 1907-13; lecturer, U. of Washington 9 summers, U. of Ill. 5 summers; teacher, Shepherd State Coll., Shepherdstown, W.Va., since 1930. Member N.E.A., Am. Geog. Soc., Am. Psychol. Assn., Internat. Congress of Psychology, Soc. for Scientific Study of Edn., Colo. Schoolmasters' Club, Sigma Phi Epsilon, Phi Delta Kappa, Kappa Delta Pi, Delta Epsilon, Sigma Pi. Author: Elementary Psychology, 1913, 27; The New Social Civics, 1926. Contbr. more than 50 articles to mags. Home: Shepherdstown, W.Va.

PHILLIPS, Edward M.; mem. surg. staff Wheeling & Ohio Valley Gen. Hosp. Address: 61 14th St., Wheeling, W.Va.

PHILLIPS, Ethel Calvert, author; b. Jersey City, N.J.; d. George Calvert and Olive Hanks (Hitchcock) P.; ed. Hasbrouck Inst. (Jersey City), Ethical Culture Sch. (N.Y. City) and Teachers Coll. (Columbia). Formerly teacher kindergarten, N.Y. City. Mem. Internat. Kindergarten Union. Democrat. Mem. Dutch Ref. Ch. Author: (juvenile stories) Wee Ann, 1919; Little Friend Lydia, 1920; Black-Eyed Susan, 1921; Christmas Light, 1922; A Story of Nancy Hanks, 1923; Humpty Dumpty House, 1924; Pretty Polly Perkins, 1925; Little Sally Waters, 1926; The Popover Family, 1927; The Santa Claus Brownies, 1928; The Lively Adventures of Johnny Ping Wing, 1929; Little Rag Doll, 1930; Gay Madelon, 1931; Pyxie, a Little Boy of the Pines, 1932; Ride-the-Wind, 1933; Jeanne-Marie and Her Golden Bird, 1934; Marty Comes to Town, 1935; The Saucy Betsy, 1936; Calico, 1937; Belinda and the Singing Clock, 1938; Peter Peppercorn, 1939. Home: 54 Wayne Pl., Nutley, N.J.

PHILLIPS, Frank Reith, pres. Philadelphia Co.; b. Cleveland, O., Oct. 29, 1876; s. Stallham Wing and Marietta (Waite) P.; grad. Central High Sch., Cleveland, 1894; law study Adelbert Coll. (now Western Reserve U.) 3 yrs.; studied engring. Case Sch. of Applied Science; m. Stella Maud Newman, Dec. 4, 1905; children—Virginia Newman (Mrs. Charles C. Zimmerman), Martha Estelle (Mrs. Charles R. Ellicott, Jr.), Bertha Jane (Mrs. L. H. Phillips). With M. A. Hanna Co., Cleveland City Rys. Co. and Cleveland Shipbuilding Co., 1896-1903; master mechanic Cleveland City Rys. Co., 1903; mechanical engr. Cincinnati, Newport & Covington Light & Traction Co., 1904-07; design engr. Ohio Brass Co., 1907; chief engr. Mich. United Light & Traction Co., 1908-10; supt. of equipment, Pittsburgh Rys. Co., 1910-23, gen. mgr. for receivers, 1923, mech. and elec. engr., 1924-26; vice-pres. and gen. mgr. Duquesne Light Co., 1926-29, now pres.; vice-pres. Equitable Gas Co., 1928, now pres.; sr. vice-pres. Philadelphia Co., 1929, pres. since 1931; also pres. Pittsburgh Rys. Co., Pittsburgh Motor Coach Co., Allegheny County Steam Heating Co., Equitable Sales Co.; dir. Farmers Deposit Nat. Bank, Reliance Life Ins. Co. Trustee University of Pittsburgh; pres. Pittsburgh Assn. for Improvement of Poor. Mem. adv. bd. Chem. Warfare Service. Mem. Am. Institute Electrical Engineers, Engineers Society of Western Pennsylvania; past pres. Am. Transit Assn. Presbyn. Clubs: Duquesne, Fellows, Pittsburgh Athletic, Oakmont Country. Active in design of first efficient double-deck motor car, Pittsburgh, 1917; originator of low-floor street car, involving principle of small diameter wheels, since largely adopted by st. ry. mfrs. and automobile designers. Home: 190 Orchard Drive, Mt. Lebanon, Pittsburgh. Office: 435 6th Av., Pittsburgh, Pa.

PHILLIPS, George William Macpherson, chem. engring.; b. New York, N.Y., Apr. 13, 1888; s. Augustus Lyon and Janet Macpherson (Fulton) P.; A.B., Central High Sch., Phila., 1906; B.S. in Chem. Engring., U. of Pa., 1910; unmarried. Began as chemist, metallurgist, plant designer, Brady Brass Co., Jersey City, N.J., 1910-13; steel and concrete designer, City of Phila., 1913-15; thermal designer, sugar technologist, sr. engr., Honolulu Iron Works Co., New York & Havana, 1916-27; development chem. engr., E. I. Du Pont de Nemours & Co., Inc., 1928; development chem. engr., Am. Cyanamid Co., 1928-31; chem. engr. and physicist, W. M. Grosvenor Labs., N.Y. City since 1931. Fellow A.A.A.S., Am. Inst. Chemists. Mem. Am. Soc. Mech. Engrs., Am. Chem. Soc., Internat. Soc. Sugar Technologists. Awarded 4 yr. scholarship to U. of Pa. by City of Phila. Introduced thermo-compressor evaporators into cane sugar industry. Presbyn. Mason. Clubs: Elmora Country (Elizabeth); Chemists (New York). Contbr. articles on sugar industry. Mech. Engring. Editor, Facts About Sugar, 1916-17. Home: 166 Summit Rd., Elizabeth, N.J. Office: 50 E. 41st St., New York, N.Y.

PHILLIPS, Harriet Duff (Mrs. John M. Phillips); b. Pittsburgh, Pa., July 26, 1881; d. Dr. John Milton and Jane (Kirk) Duff; A.B., Pa. Coll. for Women, 1903; m. John MacFarlane Phillips, Feb. 10, 1906; children—Anna Jane, Mary Templeton (wife of Dr. John Pennington Henry), Margaret Watson (Mrs. Alexander Steele Chalfant), John MacFarlane, James Macilduff. Mem. Bd. Edn. Pittsburgh Pub. Schs., Brashear Settlement. Past pres. State Fed. of Pa. Women (1934-38). Mem. D.A.R., League Am. Pen Women. Republican. Presbyn. Clubs: Womans City, Carrick Mothers, Twen-

**PHILLIPS, **
tieth Century. Home: 2336 Brownsville Rd., Pittsburgh, Pa.

PHILLIPS, Irene Calvert, librarian; b. Jersey City, N.J.; d. George Calvert and Olive Hanks (Hitchcock) Phillips; student Hasbrouck Inst., Jersey City, N.J., Pratt Inst. Sch. of Library Science, 1910-11; unmarried. Head Bernardsville (N.J.) Pub. Library, 1912-13; organized Nutley (N.J.) Free Pub. Library, 1913, and since head librarian. Mem. Pratt Grads. Assn., N.J. Library Assn. Democrat. Dutch Reformed Ch. Address: 54 Wayne Place, Nutley, N.J.

PHILLIPS, John McFarlane, mfr.; b. Pittsburgh, Feb. 15, 1861; s. James and Anna (Provost) P.; grad. Pittsburgh High Sch., 1878, and continued studies under private tutors; m. Harriet T. Duff, Feb. 1906. Began as asst. mgr. and in 1885 was made mgr. mine and mill supply dept. of Oliver Bros. & Phillips; associated, 1889, with his uncle, John Phillips, of Oliver Bros. & Phillips Co., in organizing the Phillips Mine Supply Co., pres. since 1900; director Fourteenth Street Bank of Pittsburgh. Member Board of Game Commrs. of Pa., 1905-24; dir. South Side Hosp. Mem. nat. exec. bd. Boy Scouts of America. Republican. Presbyn. Mem. Engrs.' Soc. Western Pa., N.Y. Zoöl. Soc., Campfire Club of America (hon.), Lewis & Clark Big Game Club, also Boone & Crockett Club, Pittsburgh Chamber Commerce (director). Mason (32°), K.T.; mem. Royal Order of Jesters. Clubs: Duquesne, South Hills Country. Collaborator (with Dr. William Temple Hornaday): Campfires in the Canadian Rockies, 1906. Home: Carrick, Pa. Office: 2227 Jane St., Pittsburgh, Pa.

PHILLIPS, Leslie, engr.; b. East Lexington, Mass., Apr. 23, 1890; s. James H. and Mary E. (Wilkins) P.; grad. Gen. Electric Engring Sch., 1911, Lowell Inst. of Mass. Inst. Tech., 1917; student business administrn. U. of Pittsburgh; m. Mary M. Horne, Feb. 15, 1912; 1 son, Harrison W. Engring. apprentice Gen. Electric Co., Lynn, Mass., 1908-14, motor design engr., 1914-17; in charge elec. design and power stations Stone & Webster Engring. Corpn., 1917-25; in charge design and drafting Byllesby Engring. & Management, Corpn. and Duquesne Light Co., Pittsburgh, Pa., 1925-32, senior engr. on spl. investigation work in connection with operation of utility system since 1932. Mem. Engring. Soc. of Western Pa.; asso. mem. Am. Inst. E.E. Home: 964 Jackman Av. Office: 435 6th Av., Pittsburgh, Pa.

PHILLIPS, Levi Benjamin, banker; b. Golden Hill, Dorchester Co., Md., Nov. 21, 1868; s. George Washington and Mary Elizabeth (Leonard) P.; ed. country sch.; m. Florence T. Brannock, July 23, 1895; children—Florence Mary (Mrs. W. Fletcher Williamson), Viola Lee, Levi B. Mariner, 1882-98, last 6 yrs. as master of seagoing vessel; established firm of L. B. Phillips & Co., oyster packers, Cambridge, Md., 1898, Phillips Packing Co., 1902, Phillips Hardware Co., 1903, Phillips Can Co., 1914, retired from Phillips Packing Co., 1937; elected dir. Nat. Bank of Cambridge, 1905, pres. since 1909; dir. Baltimore Br. Federal Reserve Bank, 1927-38; dir. Town Cemetery Co. Mem. Eastern Shore Soc., Soc. War of 1812. Methodist. Mason (Shriner), Elk. Clubs: Bishops Head Fish and Gun, Cambridge Country (pres.). Dir. Eastern Shore State Hosp. Home: Cambridge, Md.

PHILLIPS, Linn Voorhees, lawyer; b. Brownsville, Pa., Dec. 10, 1885; s. Samuel Arrison and Charlotta (Linn) P.; ed. Kiskiminetas Springs Sch. (Saltsburg, Pa.) and Wesleyan U. (Middletown, Conn.); LL.B., U. of Mich., 1910; m. Doris Falding, July 19, 1912; children—Doris Falding (Mrs. Russel Spencer Bishop, Jr.), Linn Voorhees. Admitted to Pa. bar, 1910; since in gen. practice of law; deputy atty. gen. since 1932; sec. and dir. River Transit Co., Summit Hotel; dir. Pecks Run Coal Co., Blue Ridge Coal Co., Lyons Coal Co. Mem. Delta Kappa Epsilon. Episcopalian (vestryman and sec.). Clubs: Uniontown Country, Summit Golf, University, Deep Creek Yacht. Home: 416 W. Main St. Office: 97 E. Main St., Uniontown, Pa.

PHILLIPS, Marie Tello (Mrs. Charles J. Yaegle), writer; b. Louisville, Ky., Feb. 23, 1874; d. Manly and Rowena Lucinda (Scales) Tello; ed. Ursuline Coll., Nottingham, O.; A.B., Western Res. U., Cleveland, O.; m. Watson P. Phillips, Aug. 28, 1912 (dec.); m. 2d, Charles J. Yaegle, Aug. 3, 1929. Founder, 1923, and pres. Pittsburgh branch and Pa. State League of Am. Pen Women; nat. pres. Bookfellows Library Guild; pres.-gen. Pittsburgh chapter Poetry Soc. of Great Britain and America. Received citation for literary attainments as hon. corr. mem. Inst. Litteraire et Artistique de France; mem. Authors' League, Authors' Guild, Poetry Soc. of America, Nat. League of Am. Pen Women, Sigma Tau Delta, Eugene Fields Soc., Am. Acad. of Poets. Awarded Sigma Tau Delta Diamond Torch, 1927, Bookfellows Silver Torch, 1927; certificate of merit in genealogy, Inst. of Am. Genealogy, 1939. Democrat. Catholic. Clubs: Congress of Clubs (Pittsburgh); Surf (Miemi Beach, Fla.). Author: (verse) Book of Verse, 1922; A Voice from the Stars, 1929; Greetings from Father Pitt, 1929; Ten Thousand Candles, 1931; The Honeysuckle and the Rose, 1933; Mary of Scotland, and Once Upon Time, 1937; (novels) Stella Marvin, 1928; Bound in Shallows, 1930, 2d edit., 1932; There's A Divinity, 1937; (essays) More Truth Than Poetry, 1934; contbr. verse to mags. Home: 6427 Darlington Rd. Office: Box 508, Pittsburgh, Pa.

PHILLIPS, Mary Catherine, (Mrs. F. J. Schlink), writer, editor; b. Clifton, N.J., Apr. 24, 1903; d. Ozro Bertsal and Sylvia (Cox) Phillips; A.B., Wellesley Coll.; 1924; m. F. J. Schlink. Began as sales girl in book dept. R. H. Macy & Co., 1924; in circulation dept. Womans Press, 1925-27; in various positions, 1927-30; with Consumers Research, 1931-32; an editor Consumers Research Bulletin, 1932-38; editor Consumers' Digest since Sept. 1938; vice-pres. Consumers' Inst. of America, Inc. Trustee Consumers Research, Inc. Mem. D.A.R., Authors' Guild. Conglist. Author: Skin Deep, the Truth about Beauty Aids, Safe and Harmful, 1934. Home: R.F.D. No. 1. Office: Washington, N.J.

PHILLIPS, Percy Wilson, lawyer; b. Southampton, N.Y., June 2, 1892; s. Wilson Edwards and Katharine (Baird) P.; LL.B., Cornell U., 1915; m. Margaret Richards Terrell, Aug. 14, 1920; children—Margaret Terrell, Janice Terrell, Alan Terrell, Barbara Terrell. Admitted to N.Y. bar, 1915, and began practice of law with Sackett, Chapman, Brown & Cross, N.Y. City; mem. U.S. Bd. Tax Appeals, 1925-31; resigned to enter law practice in Washington, D.C.; mem. firm of Ivins, Phillips, Graves & Barker. Lecturer, U. of N.C., 1929-31, Cornell U., 1937. Served as 1st lt., F.A., U.S.A., World War; now capt. F.A., O.R.C. Mem. Am. Bar Assn., D.C. and N.Y. State Bar Assns., Cornell Law Assn. (exec. com.). Republican. Methodist. Mason. Clubs: Cornell (New York); Cornell of Washington (ex-pres.), University (Washington); Columbia Country (Chevy Chase). Joint Author: The Federal Gift Tax, and Taxation Under the A.A.A. Contbr. numerous articles on federal taxation. Home: Southampton, N.Y., and Chevy Chase, Md. Office: Southern Bldg., Washington, D.C.; 20 Exchange Place, New York, N.Y.

PHILLIPS, Ralph Wesley, physiologist; b. Parsons, W.Va., Feb. 7, 1909; s. Elijah N. and Margaret Catherine (Auvil) P.; B.S., Berea (Ky.) Coll., 1930; A.M., U. of Mo., 1933, Ph.D., 1934; m. Mary Pozzi, June 1, 1934; 1 dau., Maria Diana. Research asst., U. of Mo., 1930-33; instr. animal husbandry dept., Mass. State Coll., 1933-36; asso. animal husbandman, Bur. Animal Industry, U.S. Dept. Agr., Nat. Agrl. Research Center, Beltsville, Md., 1936-39, physiologist since 1939. Mem. A.A.A.S., Am. Soc. Animal Production, Soc. for Exptl. Biology and Medicine, Genetics Club of Washington and Vicinity, Gamma Alpha, Gamma Sigma Delta, Sigma Xi. Methodist. Club: Berea College Alumni of D.C. (pres.). Contbr. bulls., articles on phases of research in animal industry, animal physiology and genetics. Home: 7064 Eastern Av., Takoma Park, D.C. Address: Nat. Agrl. Research Center, Beltsville, Md.

PHILLIPS, Samuel Edgar, newspaper pub.; b. Charlestown, W.Va., Apr. 2, 1892; s. Marcellus Edgar and Mary Elizabeth P.; ed. high sch., Greencastle, Pa.; m. Isabel Snyder, July 28, 1917; children—Samuel Edgar, Richard Snyder, Jack Marcellus. With transportation dept. Pa. R.R. and N.&W. Ry., 1912-19; pub. Hagerstown (Md.) Herald since 1919; gen. mgr. and treas. Herald-Mail Co. Served as 1st sergt. U.S.A., 1917-19; lt. cav., U.S.R. Mem. Am. Legion. Decorated D.S.C. (U.S.), Croix de Guerre (France). Republican. Presbyn. Kiwanian. Home: Hagerstown, Md.

PHILLIPS, Samuel M., v.p. and gen. mgr. Valley Mould & Iron Corpn.; b. Sharon, Pa., Dec. 3, 1887; s. Charles F. and Mary A. (McClure) P.; grad. Sharon Pub. Sch., 1903, Sharon High Sch., 1907; student Cornell U., 1907-09; m. Laura Wallis, Dec. 7, 1912; 1 son, William Wallis. Began as mech. and civil engr., 1909; engr. Stewart Furnace Co., 1909-16, asst. to gen. mgr., 1916-24, gen. mgr., 1924-28; v.p. and gen. mgr. Valley Mould & Iron Corpn., Hubbard, O., since 1928. Republican. Presbyterian. Clubs: Sharon Country (Sharon, Pa.); Youngstown Country, Youngstown City (Youngstown, O.); Union (Cleveland, O.). Home: 290 E. State St., Sharon, Pa. Office: care Valley Mould & Iron Corpn., Hubbard, O.

PHILLIPS, Theodore, vegetable packing, can mfg.; b. Cambridge, Md., Sept. 1, 1905; s. Albanus and Daisy Alma (Lewis) P.; LL.B., Tome, Sch., Port Deposit, Md. and Univ. of Va. Law Coll., 1929; m. Elizabeth Drake Morrill, May 20, 1931. Asso. with Phillips Packing Co., Md., canning food and can mfg., Cambridge, Md., since 1929, sec. 1931, vice-pres. and sec. since 1932; vice-pres. and asst. sec. Phillips Hardware Co., Inc., Cambridge, Md., since 1939. Mem. Beta Theta Pi. Republican. Methodist. Mason (Shriner). Clubs: Yacht (Cambridge); Chesapeake Bay Yacht (Easton). Home: Riverside Drive. Office: Race St., Cambridge, Md.

PHILLIPS, Thomas Wharton, Jr., ex-congressman; b. New Castle, Pa., Nov. 21, 1874; s. Thomas W. and Pamphila (Hardman) P.; Ph.B., Sheffield Scientific Sch. (Yale), 1897; m. Alma Sherman, May 28, 1908; children—Janet (Mrs. Leander McCormick-Goodhart), Katharine (Mrs. Lucien van Hoorn), Alma (deceased), Margaret (Mrs. A. C. Succop), Thomas Wharton, III, Roger Sherman. In the petroleum and natural gas business since 1897; pres. T. W. Phillips Gas & Oil Co. since 1912; pres. Pa. Investment & Real Estate Corpn., Butler, Pa.; dir. Columbia Gas & Electric Corpn. (New York), Davonian Oil Co. Mem. 68th and 69th Congresses (1923-27), 26th Pa. Dist. Trustee Phillips Univ. (Enid, Okla.), Bethany (W.Va.) Coll., Y.W.C.A. (Butler). Republican. Mem. Ch. of Christ. Mason. Clubs: Butler Country (Butler); Duquesne, Fox Chapel Golf (Pittsburgh); Chevy Chase, Woodmon Rod and Gun (Md.). Home: Butler, Pa.

PHILLIPS, William Hopestill, business exec.; b. Bath, N.Y., July 8, 1887; s. William H. and Mary Eliza (Black) P.; M.E., Cornell U., 1912; grad. student Carnegie Inst. Tech.; m. Isabel Stewart, Sept. 30, 1906; children—William H., Elizabeth Stewart. Employed as mill supt. Jones & Laughlin Steel Co.; works mgr. and engr., Nuttall Div., Westinghouse Electric Mfg. Co.; vice-pres. Molybdenum Corpn. of America, Pittsburgh, since 1926; mem. firm Phillips, Schmertz and Co., Pittsburgh, brokers. Past pres. Am. Soc. for Metals. Republican. Presbyterian. Mason (32°, Shriner). Clubs: University, Duquesne, Wildwood (Pittsburgh). Home: R.F.D. No. 2, Glenshaw, Pa. Office: 3201 Grant Bldg., Pittsburgh, Pa.

PIATT, John Elias, supervising prin. schs.; b. Broadway, Pa., July 23, 1885; s. Edwin E. and Ellen (Tubbs) P.; ed. Bloomsburg State Normal Sch., 1905-08, Pa. State Coll., summers 1912-16; A.B., Susquehanna U., 1928; study Duke U. summer 1934; A.M., Bucknell, 1937; m. Tacie Kittle, June 24, 1916; children—Evan Hale, John Elias, Jr. Engaged in teaching in twp. schs., 1908-12; teacher borough schs., Wyoming, Pa., 1912-13, teacher high sch., 1913-15, supervising prin. borough schs.,

Wyoming, Pa., since 1915. Mem. Nat. Edn. Assn., Pa. State Edn. Assn., Supervising Prins. Assn. Luzerne Co., Kappa Phi Kappa, Wyoming Bus. Mens Club (past pres., past sec.). Republican. Mem. M.E. Ch. I.O.O.F. Club: Rotary (past pres.). Home: 48 Breese St., Wyoming, Pa.

PICARD, Henry, professional golfer; b. Plymouth, Mass., Nov. 28, 1907. Began as caddie Plymouth (Mass.) Country Club, 1918; formerly professional at Charleston (S.C.) Country Club and Plymouth (Mass.) Country Club; now professional Hershey (Pa.) Country Club, also Hershey Park Golf Club, Hotel Hershey Golf Club, Hershey Juvenile Country Club; with Johnny Revolta won Internat. Four-Ball Tournament, 1935, 1936, 1937; won Hershey Open Golf Tournament, 1936, North and South Open, 1936, Masters' Tournament, 1938, and many other open and professional tournaments; won Professional Golf Assn. Championship, 1939; second highest money winner, 1937; gives 1000 golf lessons a year. Mem. U.S. Ryder Cup Team, 1935, 1937, 1939. Address: care Hershey Country Club, Hershey, Pa.

PICKARD, Frederick William, vice-pres. E. I. du Pont de Nemours & Co.; b. Portland, Me., Sept. 2, 1871; s. Charles Weston and Henrietta Mariah (Groth) P.; grad. high sch., Portland, 1890; A.B., Bowdoin Coll., Brunswick, Me., 1894; LL.D. from same coll., 1933; m. Jane Alice Coleman, Oct. 4, 1899; 1 son, John Coleman. Mng. editor Portland Transcript, 1895-1900; sec. King Mercantile Co. and Oriental Powder Co., Cincinnati, 1900-03; asst. mgr. E. I. duPont de Nemours & Co., Cincinnati, 1903-05, mgr., 1905-07, asst. mgr., Denver, Colo., 1908-09, mgr., Pittsburgh, Pa., 1909-17, dir. sales, Wilmington, Del., 1917-18, v.p. since 1918, mem. exec. com., 1918-35, mgr. dyestuffs dept., 1922-24; pres. Brookdale Land Co. Member borough council, Thornburg, Pa., 1915-17. Trustee Bowdoin Coll. Member Synthetic Organic Chem. Mfrs. Assn. (dir. 1922-24), Nat. Foreign Trade Council, Am. Chem. Soc., Phi Beta Kappa, Theta Delta Chi. Republican. Clubs: Wilmington, Wilmington Country, DuPont Country (Wilmington); Lotos, Bankers, University, Theta Delta Chi (New York); Kedgwick Salmon (New Brunswick, Can.). Author: Sixteen British Trout Rivers, 1936; Monaco and the French Riviera, 1937; Trout and Salmon Fishing in Ireland, 1938. Donor Pickard Field to Bowdoin Coll. Home: Greenville, Del. Office: DuPont Bldg., Wilmington, Del.

PICKERING, David Bedell, retired mfg. jeweler; b. Elmira, N.Y., Jan. 18, 1873; s. Silas Wright and Annie (Bedell) P.; student Newark (N.J.) Acad., 1884-89; m. Lillian Sayre, Apr. 8, 1896; children—James Sayre, David Bedell and Silas Wright (twins), Hamilton Reeve and Reynale Timothy (twins). Began as mfg. Jeweler, Newark, N.J., 1901; with Henry Blank & Co., mfg. jewelers, Newark, N.J., 1903-26, v.p., 1913-26, dir. since 1910; retired, 1926. Served with Essex Troop, N.J. N.G., 1902-12. Received merit award from Am. Assn. Variable Star Observers, 1938. Fellow A.A.A.S., Royal Astron. Soc. (London); mem. Soc. Astron. de France (founder), Internat. Astron. Union. (commr.), Am. Assn. Variable Star Observers (1st pres. 1917-19; pres. 1928-29), Am. Astron. Soc. (life), Art Centre of the Oranges (corr. sec.). Republican. Presbyterian. Mason. Author numerous articles to astron. jours.; lecturer to museums, scientific assns., etc. Mem. visiting com. Harvard Coll. Observatory, 1930-35. Address: 171 S. Burnet St., East Orange, N.J.

PICKETT, Clarence Evan, exec. sec. Am. Friends Service Com.; b. Cissna Park, Ill., Oct. 19, 1884; s. Evan and Huldah (Macy) P.; A.B., Penn Coll., Oskaloosa, Ia., 1910; B.D., Hartford Theol. Sem., 1913; grad. student Harvard Divinity Sch., 1922-23; m. Lilly Peckham, June 25, 1913; children—Rachel Joy, Carolyn Hope. Ordained to ministry of Soc. of Friends, 1913; pastor Friends Meeting, Toronto, Can., 1913-17, Oskaloosa, Ia., 1917-19; sec. Young Friends Orgn. of America, 1919-22; prof. of Bibl. lit., Earlham Coll., Richmond, Ind., 1923-29; exec. sec. Am. Friends Service Com. since 1929; consultant Farm Security Adminstrn. Dir. Friends Service, Inc.; dir. Celo Community, Inc., of N.C. Trustee Antioch Coll., Pendle Hill Grad. Sch. Dir. Non-sectarian Com. for German Child Refugees. Received, with Dr. Rufus M. Jones, Phila. Award for services advancing best interests of the community, 1939. Club: Cosmos (Washington, D.C.). Home: Wallingford, Pa. Office: 20 S. 12th St., Philadelphia, Pa.

PICKETT, Justus C.; mem. orthopedic staff City Hosp.; mem. attending surg. staff Monongalia County Hosp. Address: 235 High St., Morgantown, W.Va.

PICKLESIMER, Hayes, banking; b. Magoffin Co., Ky., Jan. 25, 1899; s. Boyd and Mary (Williams) P.; student pub. schs., Magoffin Inst., Salyersville, Ky., Eastern Ky. State Normal, Richmond, 1915-17; m. Sarah Ruth Matthews, Jan. 8, 1919; children—Mary Janice, John. In employ Salyersville Nat. Bank, Salyersville, Ky., 1917; with Kanawha Valley Bank, Charleston, W.Va. in various capacities, 1918-23; cashier Bank of Wyoming, Mullens, W.Va., 1923-24; dep. commr. of banking, of W.Va., 1924-26; in bus. on own acct. as pub. accountant, offices at Charleston and Huntington, 1926-28; asst. cashier Kanawha Valley Bank, Charleston, W.Va., 1928-29, cashier, 1929-35, vice-pres. and cashier since 1935 and dir. since 1936; dir. Central Trust Co., Charleston, W.Va., since 1937, Barium Reduction Corpn., Logan County Coal Corpn. Treas. W.Va. Chamber of Commerce; nat. councilor Charleston Chamber of Commerce. Pres. W.Va. Bankers Assn. Republican. Presbyn. Mason. Clubs: Rotary, Kanawha Country, Edgewood Country. Home: One Grosscup Drive. Office: 300 Capital St., Charleston, W.Va.

PIEKARSKI, Frank A., judge; b. Nanticoke, Pa., Aug. 17, 1879; s. Frank and Angelina (Dropiewski) P.; student Wyoming Sem., Kingston, Pa., 1897-1901; LL.B., U. of Pa., 1905; m. Martha Spotanski, Aug. 6, 1907; children—Mary (Mrs. Blair F. Gunther), Maxine (Mrs. Joseph E. Heinrich), Irene (Mrs. James K. Everhart, Jr.). Admitted to bar, 1905; asst. city solicitor, 1909-13; atty. for auditor gen., 1914-18; apptd. judge of County Court, May 6, 1933, elected for ten-year term, Nov. 7, 1933. Decorated Chevalier of Polonia Restuta. Mem. Delta Chi. Republican. Catholic. Mem. All-America Football teams, 1903 and 1904. Home: 2057 Beechwood Boul. Address: 529 Court House, Pittsburgh, Pa.

PIELEMEIER, W(alter) H(enry), prof. of physics; b. Freelandville, Ind., Feb. 6, 1889; s. William S. and Alvina (Ritterskamp) P.; student Ind. State Normal Sch., Terre Haute, 1912-13; A.B., U. of Mich., 1916, A.M., 1919, Ph.D., 1928; m. Ethel Davidson, Aug. 24, 1917; children—Emma Elizabeth, Bertha Ruth, Mary Louise. Public school teacher, 1908-12; instr. in physics, Kan. State Coll., 1916-18, U. of Mich., 1918-20; asst. prof. of physics, Pa. State Coll., 1920-23, asso. prof., 1923-35, prof. since 1935. Mem. A.A.A.S., Am. Phys. Soc., Acoustical Soc. America, Sigma Xi, Sigma Pi Sigma. Methodist. Field of research: high frequency sound and supersonics: Home: 517 E. Foster Av., State College, Pa.

PIERCE, Appleton Howe, M.D.; b. Leominster, Mass., Oct. 4, 1870; s. George W. and Charlotte (Billings) P.; student Harvard Coll., M.D., Harvard Med. Sch., 1895; m. Marion E. Yeaton, Dec. 29, 1896; children—Arthur Jameson, Marion. House officer Worcester (Mass.) City Hosp., 1894-95; asst. physician State Hosp., Worcester, 1895-96; pvt. med. practice, Leominster, Mass., 1896-1917; sr. surgeon Leominster Hosp., 1913-17; clin. dir. U.S. Pub. Health Hosp., West Roxbury, Mass., 1920-22; commd. senior surgeon U.S.P.H.S., 1922, med. officer in charge, 1922-24; med. officer in charge U.S. Vets. Bur. Hosp., Northampton, Mass., 1924-30; med. officer in charge and mgr. Vets. Adminstrn. Hosp., Coatesville, Pa., since 1930. Commd. 1st lt., U.S. Army Med. Corps, 1917, capt., 1918; chief neuro-psychiat. dept., Base Hosp. at Camp Jackson, Columbia, S.C., 1918; chief med. service U.S. Army Base Hosp. No. 85, Paris and Angers, France; commd. major, 1919; neuropsychiatrist Presidio, San Francisco, 1919, attending surgeon until resignation, Sept. 1920; commd. surgeon U.S.P.H.S. Res., Sept. 1920. Dir. Coatesville Y.M.C.A. Fellow Am. Psychiatric Assn. (mem. com. of standards and policies; chmn. Vets. Administrn. Round Table); dir., mem. exec. com. and chmn. Statewide Com. on Mental Hygiene, Public Charities Assn. of Pa.; mem. A.M.A., Mass. Med. Soc., Pa. Med. Soc., Mass. Medico-Legal Assn., New England Psychiat. Assn., Phila. Psychiat. Soc., Assn. Mil. Surgeons (v.p. W. W. Keen Chapter), Mil. Order World War (mem. staff Phila. Chapter), Am. Legion. Writer of articles on med. subjects. Address: Veterans' Administration Facility, Coatesville, Pa.

PIERCE, Carleton Custer, lawyer; b. Rowlesburg, W.Va., Oct. 19, 1877; s. John Franklin and Amanda Elizabeth (Moore) P.; ed. Franklin Coll., Ohio, 1896-97, W.Va. U., 1899-1900; m. Mary May Buckner, Nov. 28, 1902; children—Carleton Custer, Oscar Buckner. Admitted to W.Va. bar, 1901, and began practice in Preston Co.; pros. atty., Preston County, 1904-07; asst. adj. gen., W.Va., 1907-09; adj. gen. 1929-33; mayor Town of Kingwood, 1918-20; pres. Carleton Mining & Power Co.; dir. Levels Orchard Co. Mem. W.Va. Legislature, 1914-16; pres. Bd. of Edn., Preston County, 1918-22. Served as private, later 1st lt., U.S. Vols., 1898-99, Spanish-Am. War; successively capt., 1900-05, maj., 1905-07, col., 1907-09, brig. gen., 1929-33, W.Va. Nat. Guard. Mem. Sigma Chi. Republican. Methodist. Mason, K. of P. Club: Preston Country (Kingwood, W.Va.). Address: Kingwood, W.Va.

PIERCE, Clay Arthur, corpn. exec.; b. Cote Brilliant, Mo., Dec. 25, 1873; s. Henry Clay and Minnie (Finlay) P.; ed. St. Paul's Sch., Concord, N.H.; Harvard, class of '96; m. Irene Tewksbury, Oct. 15, 1898; children—Irene (Mrs. Norvin H. Green), H. C., E. E. (dec.). Became connected with the Waters-Pierce Oil Co., 1899, pres., June 1905; pres. Pierce Oil Corpn. from 1913 until retired; pres. Pierce Petroleum Corpn., 1923-26 (voluntarily resigned); dir. Brier Hill Collieries; sole administrator of H. C. Pierce Estate. Republican. Episcopalian. Club: Rumson Country. Home: Rumson, N.J.

PIERCE, Edward Lillie, mechanical engr.; b. Milton, Mass., Mar. 28, 1866; s. Edward Lillie and Elizabeth Helen (Kingsbury) P.; S.B., Mass. Inst. Tech., 1886; A.M., Princeton; m. Mary Nelson, July 3, 1901; children—Henry Nelson (dec.), Margaret Hortense, Elizabeth Kingsbury. Began in paper mfg. business, 1886; connected with Solvay Process Co., Syracuse, N.Y., 1895-1922, pres. 1917-22 (retired). Served in Porto Rico as 1st lt. 1st U.S. Vol. Engrs., Spanish-Am. War. Clubs: Nassau (Princeton); University (New York); Union (Boston). Home: 15 Hibben Rd., Princeton, N.J.

PIERCE, Frederick Williams, prof. German lang. and lit.; b. Peabody, Kan., Aug. 1, 1873; s. Cyrus Alonzo and Amelia Elvira (Williams) P.; Ph.B., Baker U., Baldwin City, Kan., 1906; Ph.D., Yale U., 1909; m. Jennie Willard Bailey, Dec. 24, 1910; 1 dau., Marguerite Louesa (dec. wife of George S. Hume). Instr. English and German, Williston Acad., Easthampton, Mass., 1909-10; instr. English, German and Latin, Cheshire Sch., Cheshire, Conn., 1910-14; prof. German lang. and lit., Pa. State Coll. since 1914. Mem. Modern Lang. Assn., Am. Assn. Univ. Profs., Phi Sigma Iota. Republican. Presbyn. Woodman. Home: 433 W. Beaver Av., State College, Pa.

PIERCE, James Harvey, mining engr.; b. Frackville, Pa., Sept. 26, 1887; s. Edward and Annette (Garaway) P.; E.M., Lehigh, 1910; m. Sara R. Hicks, Sept. 23, 1915. Mining engr. Lehigh Valley Coal Co., June-Nov. 1910; div. engr. Consolidation Coal Co., 1910-11; mining engr. Madeira Hill & Co., 1911-12; same, Paint Creek Collieries Co., 1912-13, gen. supt., 1913-15; same, East Bear Ridge Colliery Co., 1915-19; v.p. and gen. mgr. Thorne Neale & Co., 1919-27; v.p. and dir. Stuart, James & Cooke, Inc., engrs., 1927-32; pres. James H. Pierce & Co., engrs., since 1932, changed to "Pierce Management," Feb. 1937; pres. and dir. East Bear Ridge Colliery Co., Temple Coal Co., Lackawanna Coal Co., Mount Lookout Coal Co., Yorkville Pines Realty Co., Monarch Anthracite Mining Co., Inc.; management consultant West End Coal Co., engring. consultant to Lehigh Navigation Coal Co., Inc.; dir. First Nat. Bank & Trust Co. (Frackville, Pa.), A.B.A. Corpn. (New York). Tech. adviser to administrator on anthracite and bituminous coal under NRA. Mem. Am. Inst. Mining and Metall. Engrs., Am. Mining Congress. Republican. Mem. Reformed Church. Mason (32°); mem. Ind. Order Foresters. Clubs: Scranton Club; Mink Pond Club (Bushkill, Pa.). Contbr. to Coal Age. Home: 520 Clay Av., Scranton, Pa. Office: Scranton Electric Bldg., Scranton, Pa.; and 17 Battery Pl., New York, N.Y.

PIERCE, Willis Elmore, clergyman; b. Marshall Co., W.Va., May 26, 1876; s. John and Amelia Katherine (Talbott) P.; A.B., West Liberty Teachers Coll., 1899; A.B., Bethany Coll., 1903, hon. A.M., 1904; m. Margaret Vaugn Curtis, June 22, 1904; 1 dau., Helen Elizabeth (wife of Dr. Paul N. Elbin). Engaged in teaching in pub. schs., 1897-99; ordained to ministry Ch. Disciples of Christ, 1903; pastor at Cameron, W.Va., 1903-37; pastor at Moundsville, W.Va., since 1937; dir. United Christian Missionary Soc., 1929-31; mem. com. for World's Conv., Washington, D.C., 1930; dir. W.Va. State Missionary Soc., 1903-39, pres., 1930-34. County Food Adminstr. during World War. Chmn. and dir. Marshall County Centennial Commn. commemorating 100th anniversary of orgn. of county, named for Chief Justice John Marshall. Trustee Bethany Coll. Mem. Sigma Nu. Republican. Ch. Disciples of Christ. Club: Kiwanis. Home: 704 Jefferson Av., Moundsville, W.Va.

PIERCY, Samuel Kempton, clergyman; b. New York, N.Y., Mar. 17, 1877; s. Wm. J. and Louise (Pikell) P.; student Boys' High Sch., Brooklyn, 1894; A.B., Hamilton Coll., 1898, A.M., 1901, D.D., 1923; B.D., Princeton Theol. Sem., 1901; studied Leipzig U., Germany, 1901-02; m. Florence Weaver, Mar. 6, 1907; children—Elizabeth, Mary Kempton (Mrs. Robert C. Lott). Ordained Presbyn. ministry, 1903; pastor Union Presbyn. Ch., Newburgh, N.Y., 1903-11; First Ch., Crawfordsville, Ind., 1912-15; First Ch., Waterloo, N.Y., 1915-18; First Ch., White Plains, N.Y., 1918-25; First Ch., Allentown, Pa., since 1925. Home: 1107 Walnut St., Allentown, Pa.

PIERRE, William Henry; prof. agronomy, W.Va. U. Address: West Virginia University, Morgantown, W.Va.

PIERSOL, George Morris, M.D.; b. Phila., Pa., Oct. 13, 1880; s. George A. and Anne W. (Steel) P.; grad. William Penn Charter Sch., Phila., 1898; B.S., U. of Pa., 1902, M.D., 1905; m. Helen Delano, Sept. 26, 1908; children—Helen, Anne, Geo. Morris. Resident phys. 1905-06, chief res. phys., 1906-07, Hosp. of U. of Pa.; asst. instr. medicine, 1907-09, instr., 1909-12, asso. in medicine, 1912-20, prof. medicine, Grad. Sch. Medicine, 1920—, U. of Pa.; phys. to Med. Dispensary of Univ. Hosp., 1909-11; asst. phys. Univ. Hosp., 1911-13; phys. Episcopal Hosp. of Phila., 1912-16, Phila. Gen. Hosp., 1917-31, active consultant since 1931; phys. Grad. Sch. Hosp., 1920—, M.E. Hosp., 1921-31, Presbyterian Hosp., 1929-33, Abington Memorial Hosp., 1931—; prof. medicine, Woman's Med. Coll. of Pa., 1917-23. Med. dir. Bell Telephone Co. of Pennsylvania. Editor Am. Jour. Med. Sci., 1911-22; editor in chief The Cyclopedia of Medicine since 1929; editor International Clinics since 1937. Episcopalian. Fellow American Coll. Physicians, Coll. Physicians; mem. Phila. Pathol. Soc., Pediatric Soc. Phila., State and Phila. County med. socs., A.M.A., Am. Gastro-Enterol. Assn., Am. Climatol. and Clin. Assn., Assn. of Am. Physicians, Delta Tau Delta, Alpha Mu Pi Omega, Sigma Xi, Alpha Omega Alpha. Clubs: Union League, Rittenhouse, Racquet, Huntingdon Valley Country, Corinthian Yacht, Rose Tree Fox Hunting Club, Huntingdon Valley Hunt. Home: Oak Ridge Farm, Huntingdon Valley, Pa. Office: 2031 Locust St., Philadelphia, Pa.

PIERSON, Charles J., univ. prof.; b. nr. Tippecanoe, O., Apr. 12, 1866; s. David W. and Frances (Kerr) P.; A.B., Stanford U., 1897; A.M., U. of Calif., Berkeley, 1916; hon. B. Edn., State Normal Sch., Peru, Neb., 1906; m. Myrtle E. Dever, Nov. 15, 1905; children—Bernice F., Claribel G. Engaged in teaching, pub. schs. and high sch. various yrs., in Neb., 1886-90; teacher in Philippine Islands, 1901-05; teacher and prin. high schs. in Calif., various yrs., 1906-16; instr. dept. entomology and zoölogy, State Coll., College Park, Md., 1916-19, prof. vertebrate morphology, 1919-21, head dept. zoölogy, U. of Md., College Park, Md., 1921-37. Fellow A.A.A.S.; mem. Biol. Soc. of Washington (D.C.), Beta Kappa Alpha. Awarded gold medal for collection of fishes of Philippine Islands for Louisiana Expn.; gold medal for exhibit ednl. work at same expn. Democrat. Home: 16 Ravenswood Av., Hyattsville, Md.

PIERSON, Delavan Leonard, editor; b. Waterford, N.Y., Oct. 27, 1867; s. Arthur Tappan and Sarah Frances (Benedict) P.; A.B., Princeton, 1890, A.M., 1894; grad. Princeton Theol. Sem., 1894; m. Emma Belle Dougherty, Feb. 13, 1895 (died June 18, 1937). Engaged in editorial work since 1884; mng. editor Missionary Review of the World, 1891-1911, editor-in-chief, 1911—; editor Northfield Echoes, 1894-1904; regular editorial writer for Record of Christian Work, 1905-25, Bible To-Day, Sunday School Times, 1907-35; pres. Christian Stewardship Fund, Inc.; v.p. Princeton Sem. Alumni Assn., Kwato Extension Assn., Am. Christian Lit. Soc. for Moslems; treas. Pocket Testament League; dir. Am. Tract Soc., Am. Mission to Lepers, Pacific Islanders, 1906; A Spiritual Warrior—Life of Arthur T. Pierson, 1912; Why Believe It?, 1928. Home: 184 Fernwood Av., Montclair, N.J. Office: 156 5th Av., New York, N.Y.

PIERSON, Ellis Lynford, lawyer; b. Trenton, N.J., Apr. 19, 1881; s. Leslie Cooke and Mary Frances (Jones) P.; student Lawrenceville (N.J.) Sch., 1896-99; A.B., Princeton U., 1903; LL.B., Harvard, 1906; m. Alva Crossley Trapp, Oct. 20, 1927; children—John, Pamela. Admitted to N.J. bar, 1906, and since practiced in Trenton. Trustee Mercer Hosp., Trenton. Mem. Am. Bar Assn., N.J. State Bar Assn., Tiger Inn Club (Princeton U.). Republican. Presbyterian. Clubs: Princeton (New York); Harvard (Phila.); Trenton (Trenton). Home: Pennington, N.J. Office: 143 E. State St., Trenton, N.J.

PIERSON, John C.; attending surgeon Homeopathic Hosp. Address: 601 Delaware Av., Wilmington, Del.

PIERSON, John Dawson, lawyer; b. Johnsonburg, N.J., Jan. 30, 1871; s. John W. and Eunice E. (Runyon) P.; student Blair Acad., Blairstown, N.J., 1889-92; A.B., A.M., Lafayette Coll., Easton, Pa., 1896; LL.B., N.Y. Law Sch., 1902; m. Charlotte Puls, Sept. 18, 1912; children John Dawson, George C. Admitted to N.J. bar, 1900, and since in gen. practice at Hoboken, N.J.; mem. firm Pierson & Brand, practicing attys., Hoboken, N.J., since 1933. Active in civic and religious affairs; past pres. and mem. exec. com. Hudson Co. (N.J.) Council for Religious Edn. since 1923; mem. bd. dirs. Hoboken Y.M.C.A. Mem. Hoboken Chamber of Commerce, Weehawken Home Owners Assn., Alumni Assn. of Lafayette Coll., Alumni Assn. of Blair Acad., N.Y. Alumni Phi Beta Kappa. Presbyn. (moderator 1st Presbyn. Ch., Hoboken). Mason (Past Master Euclid Lodge 136), Odd Fellow (Past Grand Columbia Lodge 63; Mt. Sinai Encampment). Home: 85 Highwood Terrace, Weehawken, N.J. Office: 84 Washington St., Hoboken, N.J.

PIERSON, Leon Dewey, utilities exec.; b. Corry, Pa., June 6, 1898; s. Gustave Frederic and Emma (Johnson) P.; B.S., Allegheny Coll., Meadville, Pa., 1920; m. Lucile Richard, June 27, 1922; 1 son, Leon Richard. Salesman Sweet, Richards & Co., New York, 1920-23, sec., 1923-24; v.p. Richards, Pierson & Co., New York, 1924-25; pres. L. D. Pierson & Co., New York, 1925-27; v.p. Yeager, Young & Pierson, New York, 1927-30, Pierson, Young & Co., New York, 1930-32; pres. Eastern Shore Gas Co., Pocomoke City, Md., since 1933, Eastern Shore Gas Co. of Va., Inc., since 1933, Eastern Shore Gas Corpn. (Del.) since 1936. U.S. Army, 1918. Mem. Am. Gas Assn., Ohio Soc. of N.Y., Delta Tau Delta, Alpha Chi Sigma. Republican. Presbyterian. Mason. Home: N. Clairmont Drive, Salisbury, Md. Office: Snow Hill, Md.

PIGGOTT, Harold William, investments brokerage; b. Parkersburg, W.Va., Sept. 11, 1892; s. William Harrison and Lillie Ione (Stewart) P.; A.B., W.Va. Univ., Morgantown, W.Va., 1926; A.M., Columbia U., 1930; m. Nelle Blanche Ruble, Dec. 17, 1916; 1 son, Harold William, Jr. Engaged in teaching, prin., and supt. various schs. in W.Va., 1914-22; prin. high sch., Parkersburg, W.Va., 1922-30, supt. pub. schs., 1930-33; mem. firm Braden-Piggott & Co., investment securities, Parkersburg, W.Va., since 1933; pres. and dir. Parkersburg Automobile Club. Past dir. Parkersburg Y.M.C.A., Red Cross, Bd. of Commerce (past pres.), Community Chest, W.Va. State Chamber of Commerce, Wood County Crippled Children's Soc., Am. Automobile Assn. Republican. Methodist. Mason (K.T., Shriner). Elk. Odd Fellow. Clubs: Rotary (past pres.), Elks. Home: 1102 5th Av., South Parkersburg. Office: 612 Market St., Parkersburg, W.Va.

PIGOSSI, Dante, M.D.; b. Italy, Sept. 10, 1891; s. Joseph and Carmelina (Benassi) P.; B.S., Ohio Northern U., Ada, O., 1917; M.D., U. of Pa., 1923; m. Catherine M. Martinette, Nov. 27, 1924; children—Adrienne Louise, Vivien Carmela, Clain Cathryn, Marita Ann. Engaged in gen. practice medicine since 1924; mem. staff Canonsburg (Pa.) Gen. Hosp.; pres. Bridgeville (Pa.) Nat. Bank since 1934. Mem. Ohio Northern U. Alumni Assn. (pres., 1934-35), U. of Pa. Alumni Assn. Pres. Cosmopolitan Club, Ohio Northern U., 1915-17, Circolo Italiano (Italian students club), U. of Pa., 1921-23. Address: 430 Washington Av., Bridgeville, Pa.

PIGOTT, Albert William, physician; b. Tylertown, Miss., Sept. 19, 1895; s. John William and Montora (Hobgood) P.; student Miss. Coll., Clinton, Miss., 1912-14; B.S., U. of Miss., Oxford, 1917; M.D., U. of Pa. Med. Sch., 1919; m. Olga Hammer, Sept. 12, 1922; children—Betty Ann, Albert William, Jr. Interne Germantown Hosp., Phila., Jan.-June 1920, resigned account poor health; in pvt. practice in Tylertown, Miss., 1924-25; radiologist and clin. pathologist, Oxford Hosp., Oxford, Miss. 1925-29; instr. clin. pathology, U. of Miss. Med. Sch., Oxford, 1925-29; clinical dir. N.J. State Village for Epileptics, Skillman, N.J., 1929-37, supt. since 1937. Served in Med. Enlisted Res. Corps, 1917-18; S.A.T.C., 1918. Chmn. local Boy Scout Com. Active in community welfare. Certified as diagnostic roentgenologist by Am. Bd. Radiology. Fellow A.M.A. Mem. N.J. State and Somerset Co. (pres.) med. socs., Am. Psychiatric Assn., Am. Branch Internat. League Against Epilepsy (v.p.), N.J. Radiol. Soc., Pi Kappa Phi, Phi Alpha Sigma. Republican. Mem. Dutch Ref. Ch. Home: Skillman, N.J.

PIGOTT, Reginald James Seymour, engring. research; b. Wellington, Shropshire, Eng., Feb. 4, 1886; s. Elphic W. S. and Lillian M. (Fance) P.; grad. DeWitt-Clinton High Sch., N.Y. City, 1902; M.E., Columbia, 1906; m. Florence L. Johnston, July 2, 1908; children—William J., Beatrice L., Elizabeth C., Patricia L. Came to U.S., 1891, naturalized citizen, 1916. Chief draftsman and asst. engr. in charge constrn., Interborough Rapid Transit Co., N.Y. City, 1906-11; supt. constrn., New England Engring. Co., 1911-12; prof. steam engring., Columbia, 1912-13; construction engr., Interborough Rapid Transit, 1913-15; cons. engr. and power supt. Remington Arms-Union Metallic Cartridge Co., 1915-17; cons. engr. Remington Arms and Sanford Riley Stoker Co., and supt. mills, Bridgeport Brass Co., 1917-19; with W. B. Lashar, cons. engr., 1919-20; works mgr. Crosby Steam Gage & Valve Co., 1920-22; chief engr. Stevens & Wood, engrs. and constructors, 1922-25; cons. mech. engr. Pub. Service Production Co., 1925-28; cons. mech. engr. with

Stevens & Wood, 1928-29; staff engr. Gulf Research & Development Co. since 1929. Mem. American Soc. Mechanical Engrs. (chmn. and mem. many coms.), Am. Gas Assn., Soc. Automotive Engrs., Theta Xi, Tau Beta Pi. Republican. Episcopalian. Mason. Clubs: Engineers, Longue Vue, Pittsburgh Athletic Assn. Contbr. to Elec. Engrs. Standard Handbook, also tech. publs. Originator of vacuum tripper for turbines and holder of several patents for valves, gages, rotary pumps and compressors, lubrication testing equipment, meters, etc. Address: Gulf Research & Development Co., Post Office Box 2038, Pittsburgh, Pa.

PIKE, Clayton Warren, consulting elec. engr.; b. Fryeburg, Maine, July 11, 1866; s. Cassius W. and Abbie J. (Barker) Pike; ed. Fryeburg Acad.; Mass. Inst. Tech., 1886-89; m. Margaret E. Rattoo, June 30, 1909; children—Helen Margaret, John Clayton (dec.). Elec. engr., Merrimack Mfg. Co., Lowell, Mass., 1889-90; instr. elec. engring., U. of Pa., 1890-92; elec. engr., Queen Co., Inc., Phila., 1893-94, Falkenau Engring. Co., 1894-1900; v.p. and gen. mgr. Keller-Pike Co., Phila., 1900-11; chief of Elec. Bur., Phila., Mar. 1, 1912—; cons. engr. City of Pittsburgh, 1919, Pub. Improvement Commn., Baltimore, 1922, Phila. Rapid Transit Co. since 1923, Ambassador Bridge (Detroit to Can.), 1929, Public Service Commission of New Hampshire, 1930, State Tax Commn. of N.H., 1931, Power Authority of State of N.Y., 1931. Mem. Park Commn., Fryeburg, Me., 1933. Trustee Fryeburg Acad. Republican. Member Am. Institute E.E., Internat. Soc. Municipal Electricians, Soc. Illuminating Engrs., Society Municipal Engrs. Clubs: Engineers' (ex-pres.), Rotary (ex-sec.). Author: Roper's Engineers' Handbook (joint author), 1899; Questions and Answers for Engineers, 1901. Commd. maj. Ordnance Dept. U.S.A., 1918; chief statis. sect., 1919. Home: Fryeburg, Me. Office: Land Title Bldg., Philadelphia, Pa.

PIKE, Wilbert Victor, lawyer; b. Moorestown, N.J., Mar. 31, 1884; s. Victor S. and Deborah A. (Haines) P.; LL.B., Temple Univ. Law Sch., 1907; m. Elsie I. Dickinson, Oct. 12, 1907; 1 son, Wilbert Victor, Jr. Admitted to N.J. bar as atty., 1906, as counselor and master in chancery, 1909; engaged in gen. practice of law at Camden since 1906; supreme ct. commr., 1931; spl. master in chancery, 1938; prof. wills and adminstrn. of estates, South Jersey Law Sch. since 1926; mem. bd. and solicitor, John Estaugh Bldg. & Loan Assn., Haddonfield, Moose Bldg. & Loan Assn., Camden, Hedding Bldg. & Loan Assn. of Hedding, Glendora Bldg. & Loan Assn., of Glendora, N.J. Mem. Camden Co. Bar Assn. (pres.), Patriotic Order Sons of America. Republican. Presbyn. Mason. L.O.O.M. Home: 129 Centre St., Haddonfield. Office: 301 Market St., Camden, N.J.

PILCHER, Lewis Frederick, architect; b. Brooklyn, N.Y.; s. Lewis Stephen and Martha S. (Phillips) P.; Ph.B., Sch. of Architecture (Columbia), 1895; LL.D., U. of Colo., 1910. In practice in New York and N.J.; state architect, N.Y., 1913-23; commr. of sites, N.Y., 1913-23, commr. new prisons, 1916-23, mil. hosps., 1920-21, Hosp. Development Commn., 1917-23; cons. architect U.S. Veterans' Bur., 1923-25; prof. art, Vassar Coll., 1900-11; vice dean Sch. of Fine Arts, and asso. prof. architecture, U. of Pa., 1926-29; professor architecture, Pennsylvania State College, 1929-37; institutional consultant Pa. State Authority, 1937-38; administrator P.W.A. school program, Departments of Public Instruction, Pennsylvania, 1935. Architect Squadron C Armory, Brooklyn; First Baptist Church, Montclair, New Jersey; Gratz Coll., Phila.; Mikveh Israel Synagogue, Philadelphia; Terminal Dormitory, Vassar College; Realty Underwriters Building, Louisville, Kentucky; Haviland Bldg., New York; Dropsie Coll., Phila.; 1st Ch. of Christ, Scientist, Glens Falls, N.Y.; armory for 8th Regt. and for 1st Cavalry, New York; architect to War Dept. in charge of installations at 9th, 13th and 8th coast arty. districts, etc.; also architect for Sing Sing Prison, Wingdale (N.Y.) Prison, Cornell U. Drill Hall; armories Squadron A, Manhattan, at Buffalo, Rochester, Albany, Orleans and Troy—all of New York; consulting architect to New York City for the County Court House; advisory architect to Capital Issues Commn., 1918, and Holland Tunnel. Consulting architect on hosps. of N.J. and Insular Prison, Porto Rico; city planner, Camden, N.J., and cons. architect on Court House, City Hall and Bus Terminal. Mem. A.I.A., Loyal Legion, Psi Upsilon, Phi Beta Kappa, Sigma Xi, Scarab. Author: Historic Types of Architecture. Am. editor in architecture for Allgemeines Lexikon Bildenden Kunstler; editor in architecture, Encyclopædia Americana. Home: 6307 Overbrook Av., Philadelphia, Pa. Office: Education Bldg., Harrisburg, Pa.

PILLING, Norman Boden, metall. engr.; b. Waterbury, Conn., Jan. 23, 1893; s. John W. and Rose E. (Boden) P.; Ph.B., Sheffield Scientific Sch. (Yale U.), 1915, M.S., 1917; m. Katherine M. Williams, Sept. 25, 1917; children—Jean Williams, Barbara DeWitt. Research metallurgist, Westinghouse Electric & Mfg. Co., East Pittsburgh, Pa., 1917-24; research metallurgist, International Nickel Co., Bayonne, N.J., 1924-32, in charge metall. research, 1932-33, mgr. Research Lab., 1933-39, dir. Research Lab. since 1939. Served in Yale Battery, 10th M.F.A. on Federal Service, 1916. Mem. Am. Inst. Mining Engrs., Am. Soc. for Metals, Am. Assn. Adv. Science, British Iron & Steel Inst., British Inst. of Metals, Sigma Xi, Alpha Sigma Phi. Republican. Presbyn. Home: 1017 Cherry Lane, Westfield, N.J. Office: care International Nickel Co., Bayonne, N.J.

PILLING, William Stockman, industrialist; b. Phila., Pa., Feb. 19, 1857; s. George Platt and Tamazine Trimble (Jenks) P.; student Central High Sch., Phila.; m. Catharine Ross, Nov. 12, 1885; children—Joseph Ross, Mrs. Mary Harrington, George Platt. Began as clk. Crane Iron Co., 1872, advanced through various positions becoming treas., gen. mgr. and acting head of co., 1885, resigned, 1888; partner (with Theron I. Crane) Pilling & Crane, dealers in iron, steel, coal and coke, Phila., 1890-1917; senior partner Pilling & Company (successor to Pilling & Crane), 1917-32; retired 1932; pres. Northern Ore Co., 1895-1918, Northern Iron Co., 1902-20. Pres. board of trustees, Drew University, Madison, N.J., since 1932; dir. Central-Penn Nat. Bank. Served as chmn. iron shipment com., War Industries Bd., during World War. V.p. Am. Bible Soc. of N.Y. Mem. Am. Iron and Steel Inst., Am. Inst. Mining and Metall. Engrs., Acad. of Natural Sciences of Phila., Phila. Mus. of Art, Pa. Hist. Soc. Methodist. Clubs: Union League (Phila.); Highland Park Florida (Lake Wales, Fla.). Donator large art collection to Phila. Mus. of Art. Home: Germantown, Philadelphia, Pa. Office: 1500 Chestnut St., Philadelphia, Pa.

PILLSBURY, Donald Marion, physician; b. Omaha, Neb., Dec. 29, 1902; s. Marion Albert and Amanda (Johnston) P.; ed. U. of Omaha, 1920-21, Creighton U., 1919-20; A.M., U. of Neb., 1924; M.D., U. of Neb. Med. Sch., 1926; m. Charlotte Denny, Sept. 3, 1929; children—Katherine Esmond, Donald Marion. Engaged in practice of medicine at Phila., Pa., since 1932; interne University Hosp., Omaha, Neb., 1926-28; instr. of dermatology, U. of Pa. Med. Sch., 1928-32, asst. prof. of dermatology, 1932-37, asso. prof. dermatology since 1937. Mem. Am. Med. Assn., Coll. of Physicians of Phila., Am. Dermatol. Assn., Phi Rho Sigma, Alpha Omega Alpha, Sigma Xi. Republican. Presbyterian. Club: Philadelphia Country. Home: 626 Moreno Rd., Narberth, Pa. Office: 133 S. 36th St., Philadelphia, Pa.

PILLSBURY, Harold Crockett; attending surgeon St. Joseph's and Mercy hosps.; surgeon South Baltimore Gen. Hosp. Address: 31 E. North Av., Baltimore, Md.

PILSBRY, Henry Augustus, zoölogist; b. Iowa City, Ia., Dec. 8, 1862; s. Dexter Robert and Elizabeth (Anderson) P.; student State U. of Ia. (hon. Sc.D., 1899); m. Adeline Bullock Avery, 1890; children—Elizabeth, Grace. Has made a life-long study of mollusks; spl. curator dept. of mollusks, Acad. Natural Sciences of Phila., since 1888. Author: The Manual of Conchology (31 vols.), 1888-1931; Marine Mollusks of Japan, 1895; Guide to the Study of Helices; Barnacles of the United States, 1907; Mollusks of the Belgian Congo, 1927; also numerous articles on conchology, geology and zoölogy. Corr. mem. Zoöl. Soc. of London; hon. mem. Société Zoölogique Royale de Belgique, Real Acad. Cien., Madrid, etc. Awarded Leidy medal, 1928. Address: Acad. of Natural Sciences, Philadelphia, Pa.*

PINCHOT, Cornelia Bryce (Mrs. Gifford Pinchot); b. Newport, R.I., August 26, 1881; d. Lloyd S. and Edith (Cooper) Bryce; m. Gifford Pinchot (gov. of Pa., 1923-27 and 1931-35), 1914; 1 son Gifford Bryce. Actively identified with public affairs. (See sketch of Gifford Pinchot.). Home: Milford, Pa.

PINCHOT, Gifford, ex-gov., forester; b. Simsbury, Conn., Aug. 11, 1865; s. James W. and Mary (Eno) P.; A.B., Yale, 1889; studied forestry France, Germany, Switzerland and Austria; hon. A.M., Yale, 1901, Princeton, 1904; Sc.D., Mich. Agrl. Coll., 1907; LL.D., McGill, 1909, Pa. Mil. Coll., 1923, Yale, 1925, Temple, 1931; m. Cornelia Elizabeth Bryce, 1914; 1 son, Gifford Bryce. First American professional forester; began first systematic forest work in U.S. at Biltmore, N.C., Jan. 1892; mem. National Forest Commission, 1896; forester and chief of div. afterward Bur. of Forestry, and now the Forest Service, U.S. Dept. Agr., 1898-1910; president National Conservation Association, 1910-25. Prof. forestry, Yale, 1903-36, professor emeritus, since 1936. Commissioner of forestry of Pa., 1920-22; gov. of Pa., 1923-27 and 1931-1935. Inspected forests of P.I., 1902, and recommended forest policy for same; mem. com. on orgn. govt. scientific work, apptd. Mar. 13, 1903, commn. on pub. lands, apptd. Oct. 22, 1903, commn. on dept. methods, apptd. June 2, 1905, Inland Waterways Commn., apptd. Mar. 14, 1907, commn. on country life, apptd. Aug. 10, 1908; chmn. Nat. Conservation Commn., apptd. June 8, 1908; chmn. Joint Com. on Conservation, apptd. by the conf. of govs. and nat. orgns. at Washington, Dec. 1908. Mem. Soc. Am. Foresters, Am. Forestry Assn., Royal English Arboricultural Soc., Am. Mus. Natural History, Washington Acad. Sciences, Am. Acad. Polit. and Social Science. Member of Commn. for Relief in Belgium, 1914-15. Mem. U.S. Food Administration, Aug. 1917-Nov. 1918. Negotiated settlement of anthracite coal strike in 1923. Clubs: Century, Yale, Explorers (New York); Cosmos of Washington (pres. 1908). Author: The White Pine (with H. S. Graves), 1896; The Adirondack Spruce, 1898; A Primer of Forestry, Part I, Bull. 24, Div. of Forestry, 1899, Part 2, 1905; The Fight for Conservation, 1909; The Country Church (with C. O. Gill), 1913; The Training of a Forester, 1914, 4th edit., 1937; Six Thousand Country Churches (with C. O. Gill), 1919; To the South Seas, 1930; Just Fishing Talk, 1936. Home: Milford, Pike Co., Pa.

PINCKARD, H. R.; editor Herald-Advertiser. Address: Huntington Publishing Co., Huntington, W.Va.

PINCOFFS, Maurice Charles, M.D.; b. Chicago, Ill., Aug. 6, 1886; s. Maurice and Louise (Henrotin) P.; B.S., U. of Chicago, 1909; M.D., Johns Hopkins, 1912; m. Katharine Randall, Mar. 1, 1919; children—Maurice C., Susan R., Peter H. Began practice at Baltimore, 1912; prof. medicine, U. of Md., since 1921. Regent Am. Coll. Physicians; mem. Assn. Am. Physicians, Am. Climatol. and Clin. Assn., Md. Mental Hygiene Soc. (v.p.), Delta Kappa Epsilon, Nu Sigma Nu. Served as capt. Med. Corps, U.S.A., 1917-19. Awarded D.S.C. (U.S.); Croix de Guerre with palm (France). Clubs: Maryland, Gibson Island. Editor Annals of Internal Medicine. Home: Frederick Av. opposite Norwood Heights, Baltimore. Address: University Hosp., Baltimore, Md.

PINOLA, Frank Lewis, lawyer and banking; b. Scranton, Pa., Jan. 27, 1893; s. Louis and Caroline P.; student Cornell U.; LL.B., U. of Pa. Law Sch.; m. Helen G. Nicholson, 1917; children—Gloria, Frank L. Admitted to Pa. bar,

1915, and since engaged in gen. practice of law at Wilkes-Barre and Pittston; served as U.S. commr., 1917-28; counsel for sec. of banking in connection with closed banks of Luzerne Co., 1931-35; pres. Liberty Nat. Bank of Pittston since 1925; treas. Independent Explosives Co. of Pa.; chmn. bd. Morea Coal Co. Served as capt. field arty., U.S.A., 1917-18. Rep. nominee for State Treas., 1936. Dir. Pittston Hosp. Mem. Am., Pa., and Luzerne Co. bar assns. Republican. Roman Catholic. Clubs: Kiwanis (Pittston); Westmoreland (Wilkes-Barre). Home: 85 James St., Kingston, Pa. Office: Wilkes-Barre, Pa.; also, Pittston, Pa.

PINTO, Salvatore, artist; b. Salerno, Italy, Jan. 4, 1905; s. Luigi and Josephine P.; student Pa. Mus. Sch. of Industrial Art, 1921-25, Pa. Acad. of Fine Arts, 1925-26; Barnes Foundation traveling scholarships, 1931-33. Represented by etchings and wood engravings in Met. Mus. of Art, Whitney Mus. of Am. Art, Art Inst. Chicago, New York Pub. Library; paintings, Pa. Mus. of Art, Barnes Foundation (Merion, Pa.); exhbns. of etchings Thorman Galleries (N.Y.), 1929, Phila. Print Club, 1930; painting, Mellon Galleries (Phila.), 1932, Bignou Galleries (Paris), 1933, Valentine Galleries (N.Y.), 1935, Art Alliance (Phila.), 1938. Awarded 1st prize Phila. Print Club, 1932, Phila. Art Club gold medal, 1934. Mem. Mus. of Modern Art, United Scenic Artists of America. Club: Phila. Print (Phila.). Designed sets and costumes for Phila. Ballet. Home: 1634 Walnut St., Philadelphia, Pa.

PIPER, James, lawyer; b. Towson, Md., Aug. 16, 1874; s. Jackson and Imogen (Shoemaker) P.; student Marstons Sch., 1888-92; A.B., Johns Hopkins, 1894, post grad. study, 1894-95; LL.B., U. of Md., 1897; m. Alice D. Pitts, Dec. 15, 1900; 1 son, James. Began practice of law, 1897; successively associated with Brown & Brune, Col. Charles Marshall, Steele, Semmes & Carey, Francis J. Carey, Carey, Piper & Hall and Piper, Carey & Hall; now sr. partner Piper, Watkins & Avirett. Served with Troop A, Md. Nat. Guard, Spanish-Am. War; head Baltimore office of Naval Intelligence, World War. Mem. Am., N.Y., Md. and Baltimore City bar assns. Democrat. Episcopalian. Clubs: Maryland, Green Spring Valley Hunt, Merchants. Home: Eccleston P.O., Md. Office: Baltimore Trust Bldg., Baltimore, Md.

PIPER, Joseph DuShane, religious exec.; b. Lockport, Pa., Sept. 18, 1887; s. Edward J. and Frances (DuShane) P.; student Derry (Pa.) High Sch., 1902-05, Alden Acad., Meadville, Pa., 1906-07; A.B., Allegheny Coll., Meadville, Pa., 1910. D.D., 1927; B.D., Drew U., Madison, N.J., 1915; m. Elizabeth Houghton, May 29, 1912; children—Marian Jane (Mrs. Charles T. Nevins), Joseph DuShane. High sch. teacher and football coach, Aspinwall, Pa., 1911-12; pastor Saltsburg (Pa.) M.E. Ch., 1915-18, Black Lick (Pa.) M.E. Ch., 1919-22, Irwin (Pa.) M.E. Ch., 1922-32, Dormont (Pa.) M.E. Ch., 1932-35; dist. supt. Pittsburgh Dist. of Methodist Ch. since 1935. Served as chaplain, 352d Inf., A.E.F., 1918-19. Mem. Gen. Conf. M.E. Ch., 1936, 1939. Trustee Allegheny Coll.; dir. Ch. Union, Pittsburgh, M.E. Hosp. and Home for Aged; mem. Community Fund. Mem. Y.M.C.A., Council of Chs. Mem. Gen. Conf. of M.E. Ch., 1936; mem. Uniting Conf. of Methodism, 1939. Mem. Phi Kappa Psi. Republican. Methodist. Clubs: Kiwanis, Rotary (Pittsburgh). Home: 327 Dixon Av., Mt. Lebanon, Pittsburgh, Pa.

PIPER, William Thomas, airplane mfg.; b. Knapps Creek, N.Y., Jan. 8, 1881; s. Thomas and Sarah (Maltby) P.; B.S., Harvard U., 1903; m. Marie Vandewater, July 30, 1910 (dec.); children—William Thomas, Jr., Mary Vandewater (Mrs. John Savage Bolles), Thomas Francis, Howard, Elizabeth Maltby. Employed as constrn. supt., Lorain, O., 1903-14; oil producer, Bradford, Pa., since 1914; pres. and dir. Piper Aircraft Corporation, manufacturer airplanes, since 1929; pres. Bradford Filling Sta.; mem. firm, Dallas Oil Co., Gridiron Oil Co. Served as pvt. Pa. Vol. Inf., 1898; capt. engrs., U.S.A., 1918-19. Republican. Club: Rotary of Lock Haven. Home: 118 W. Water St., Lock Haven, Pa.

PIRSON, Sylvain Joseph Ghislain, prof. petroleum engring.; b. Vogenée, Belgium, June 28, 1905; s. Jules and Marie (Frerotte) P.; came to U.S., 1929; M.C. Engring., U. of Louvain, Belgium, 1929; M.Sc., U. of Pittsburgh, 1930; D.Sc., Colo Sch. Mines, 1931; m. Meta Bolchert, June 28, 1933; 1 son, Richard Sylvain. Engaged as instr. geophysics, Colo. Sch. of Mines, Golden, Colo., 1933-34; geophysicist, Seismograph Service Corpn., Tulsa, Okla., 1934-36; geophysicist, Gulf Research and Development Co., Pittsburgh, Pa., Feb.-June 1936; prof. petroleum and natural gas engring., Sch. Mineral Industries, Pa. State Coll. since 1936. Mem. Am. Inst. Mining Engrs., Am. Assn. Petroleum Geologists, Soc. Petroleum Geophysicists. Home: 516 N. Atherton St., State College, Pa.

PISTOR, George Emil John, civil engr.; b. Newark, N.J., Sept. 21, 1879; s. Adolph and Elizabeth (Walz) P.; C.E., Cornell U., 1901; m. Arley Niemann, Sept. 16, 1908; children—Arley (Mrs. Olin Henry Timm), John Adolph, Herman Henry. Began as structural draftsman, 1901; with Hay Foundry & Iron Works, 1901-31, successively, structural draftsman, designing engr., chief estimator, and contracting mgr.; contracting engineer Bethlehem Steel Co. since 1931; instr. Fawcett Sch. Industrial Arts, evenings, 1901-16; cons. engr. Town of Montclair since 1921. Mem. Am. Inst. Steel Constrn. (dir. 1921-31; treas. 1926-31), Am. Soc. Civil Engrs., Montclair Soc. Engrs., N.Y. State Soc. Professional Engrs., N.Y. Sales Mgrs. Club, Cornell Soc. Engrs., Sigma Xi. Licensed professional engr., N.Y. and N.J. Republican. Mem. Reformed Ch. Mason. Clubs: Country (Upper Montclair); Engineers (New York); 100 for One; Cornell of Northern Jersey; Montclair Engineers. Home: 55 Elston Rd., Upper Montclair, N.J. Office: 25 Broadway, New York, N.Y.

PITCAIRN, Harold Frederick, aviation; b. Bryn Athyn, Pa., June 20, 1897; s. John and Gertrude (Starkey) P.; grad. Academy of the New Church, Bryn Athyn, Pensylvania, 1916; student Wharton School (U. of Pennsylvania), 1917; m. Clara Davis, June 21, 1919; children—Joel, John, Charis, Stephen, Judith, Robert, Bruce, Edward Hugh. With efficiency dept. Pittsburgh Plate Glass Co., 1919-20; pres. Owosso Sugar Co., 1921-24; interest in flying started at Curtiss Sch., Buffalo, 1915, later at Curtiss Hammondsport and Newport News schs.; renewed training at Pine Valley (N.J.) Field, 1924; began building airplanes, 1925; entered air mail operation, 1928; pres. Autogiro Co. of America since 1929; dir., treas. Pitcairn Co.; propr. Pitcairn Autogiro Co.; dir. Pittsburgh Plate Glass Co., Michigan Sugar Co., G. H. Wheeler & Co., Pittsburgh Valve & Fittings Corpn., Loyal Hanna Coal & Coke Co. Served as cadet Army Air Corps, Austin and Waco, Tex., 1917. Awarded (with associates) Collier Trophy "for the greatest achievement in aeronautics" (development of the autogiro), 1930; John Scott medal, 1931. Dir. Academy of the New Church (Bryn Athyn). Mem. General Church of the New Jerusalem. Clubs: Mid-Day, Penn Athletic, Aero Club of Pa. (Phila.). Home: Bryn Athyn, Pa. Office: 1616 Walnut St., Philadelphia, Pa.

PITCAIRN, Raymond, lawyer, architect, philanthropist; b. Phila., Pa., Apr. 18, 1885; s. John and Gertrude (Starkey) P.; grad. Acad. of New Church, 1905; LL.B., U. of Pa., 1908; m. Mildred Glenn, Dec. 29, 1910; 8 children. Pres. The Pitcairn Co.; v.p. Loyal Hanna Coal & Coke Co.; dir. Pittsburgh Plate Glass Co., Pittsburgh Valve & Fittings Co., C. H. Wheeler Mfg. Co., Cairnbrook Water Co., Equitable Supply Co. Architect Cathedral of the Bryn Athyn Ch. of the New Jerusalem. Club: Union League. Office: 1616 Walnut St., Philadelphia, Pa.

PITCHER, Charles Sidney, hosp. and institutional consultant; b. Rome, Pa., Oct. 13, 1874; s. Sidney Dunham and Kate Jane (Allen) P.; student Eastman Business Coll., Poughkeepsie, N.Y., 1893-94, Chicago (Ill.) Correspondence Sch. of Law, 1900-03, extension dept., Indianapolis (Ind.) Coll. of Law, 1900-03, N.Y. Sch. of Social Work, Columbia U., 1913-14, Teachers Coll., Columbia U., 1916-17; m. Mamie Ann Birs, June 12, 1894 (died Nov. 18, 1931); children—Charles Winfield, Mamie Elizabeth; m. 2d, Harriet Elliott (Ferguson) Mitchell, June 14, 1933. Clerk Hudson River State Hosp., Poughkeepsie, N.Y., 1892-93, asst. storekeeper 1893-96, storekeeper 1896-1900; resident steward Manhattan State Hosp., East, New York, N.Y., 1900-01; resident steward, Kings Park (N.Y.) State Hosp., 1901-06, resident steward and dep. treas., 1906-11, steward and dep. treas., 1911-20; sec. to com. on dietary and food supplies of all hosps. in Dept. of Mental Hygiene (formerly State Hosp. Commn.), Albany, N.Y., 1916-20; mem. purchasing com., N.Y. State Hosps., Albany, N.Y., 1913-16; mem. legislative com. on budget, chmn. sub-com. in charge of statistics, Dept. of Mental Hygiene, Albany, N.Y., 1916-18; supt., Presbyn. Hosp., Phila., 1920-33, sec. corpn., 1931-32, chmn. corpn., 1933; dir. course in hosp. and institutional management, Temple U., Phila., 1924-28; consultant and administrator, Hollywood (Cal.) Hosp., 1937; consultant and administrator, Presbyn. Hosp. Olmsted Memorial; leasee Hollywood Hosp., Hollywood, Cal., 1937-38, consultant since 1938. Served as 1st lt., S.C., Surgeon Gen's. Office, 1918. Dir. institutional div. U.S. Food Adminstrn., 1918; mem. joint conf. com. Hosp. Assn. of Pa. and State med. socs., 1928-29; mem. survey com. Phila. Hosp. and Health Survey, 1929; mem. Mayor Moore's Com. to study hosp. situation in Phila., 1932; expert examiner, N.Y. Civil Service Commn., Municipal Civil Service Commn. of N.Y. City, 1914-31. Charter hon. fellow Am. Coll. of Hosp. Adminstrs.; life mem. Am. Hosp. Assn. (mem. com. on training hosp. execs., 1923-24; mem. com. on public edn., 1932-33; mem. Joint Com. Nat. Hosp. Assns., 1933-37; charter life mem. and trustee Am. Protestant Hosp. Assn.; (mem. exec. com.; chmn. com. on publicity; chmn. legislative com., chmn. com. on training hosp. execs.; v.p., 1931-32; pres. elect, 1932-33; pres. 1933-34); charter mem. Pa. Hosp. Assn. (v.p.; chmn. legislative com.; mem. public relations com.; trustee, 1930-33); mem. Hosp. Assn. of Phila. (v.p.; trustee; mem. exec. com.; chmn. legislative com., 1923-33); mem. Internat. Hosp. Assn., Coll. of Hosp. Management (Marquette U., Milwaukee, Wis.; mem. advisory bd., 1923-24), Quartermaster's Assn. (Washington, D.C.). Awarded Charter Hon. Fellowship by Am. Coll. of Hosp. Adminstrs., 1934. Republican. Presbyterian. Mason (Royal Arch; K.T.; Scottish Rite). Clubs: Yorktown (Va.) Country (life mem.); Arrowhead Alpine (Alpine Glens Park, Cal.; asso. life mem.). Author: articles on hosp. management to The Modern Hospital, Hospital Management, and other hosp. publs.; addresses before Am. Coll. of Surgeons, 1923; Kitchen Organization and Administration (pamphlet), 1914. Prepared reports of Com. on Dietary and Food Supplies for N.Y. State Hosps., 1916, 1917, 1918, 1919, 1920. Editorial supervisor, Basic Quantity Food Tables (book), 1917. Author of pamphlet "Institutional Food Conservation" printed and distributed in 1918 by the United States Food Administration. Home: Rome, Pa. Office: 1521 Spruce St., Philadelphia, Pa.

PITFIELD, Robert L(ucas), physician; b. Germantown, Pa., Feb. 28, 1870; s. Benj. H. and Frances (Pleasants) P.; ed. Friends Sch. and Friends Boarding Sch., Germantown, Pa., 1876-84; M.D., U. of Pa., Med. Sch., 1892; m. Georgiana G. Starin, June 19, 1894; children—Georgiana (Mrs. Jacob Reigee), Helen C. (Mrs. Eugene S. Howell), Robert L., Jr., Grace S. (Mrs. Wm. S. Anthony). Engaged in gen. practice of medicine at Germantown, Pa., continuously since 1892; served as state bacteriologist of Pa.; on staff Germantown Hosp. since 1898; invented and perfected three important methods of diagnosis and treatment now in gen. use in med. profession. Former dir. Friends Sch., Friends Library, Germantown, Pa. Fellow Phila. Coll. Phys. Mem. Psi Upsilon. Republican. Mem. Religious Soc. Friends. Author: Text Book on Bacteriology. Contbr. over 50 essays, articles, and biog. sketches for mags. Address: 5211 Wayne Av., Germantown, Philadelphia, Pa.

PITKIN, Francis Alexander, exec. dir. Pa. State Planning Bd.; b. Akron, O., June 2, 1899; s. Stephen Henderson and Bessie H. (Alexander) P.; B.S. in M.E., Case Sch. of Applied Science, Cleveland, O.; m. Ruth E. Mason, Mar. 17, 1928; 1 son, Stephen Henderson, IV. Engr. Gen. Electric Co., Schenectady, N.Y., Pittsburgh and Phila., Pa., 1922-30; chief engr. and constrn. supt. water supply and sewage system developments, Phila., 1930-34; asst. dir. Pa. State Planning Bd., Harrisburg, 1934-35, exec. dir. since 1936. Commr. The Interstate Commn. on the Del. River Basin; planning consultant Pa. Commn. on Interstate Cooperation; consultant Ohio Valley Regional Planning Commn.; chmn. Pa. Recreational Council. Mem. Am. Soc. Planning Officials, Am. Planning and Civic Assn., Nat. Assn. Housing Officials, Am. Acad. Polit. and Social Science, Phi Delta Theta. Mason. Writer numerous articles for Pa. Planning Bd. and addresses on planning topics. Home: 3105 N. 3d St. Office: 928 N. 3d St., Harrisburg, Pa.

PITKIN, Walter Boughton, psychologist, writer; b. Ypsilanti, Mich., Feb. 6, 1878; s. Caleb S. and Lucy T. (Boughton) P.; A.B., U. of Mich., 1900; grad. study Sorbonne, Paris, U. of Berlin, U. of Munich, Hartford (Conn.) Theol. Sem., 1900-05; m. Mary B. Gray, 1903; children—Richard Gray, John Gray, David Bartholomew, Robert Bolter, Walter Boughton. Lecturer in psychology, Columbia, 1905-09, prof. journalism since 1912; mem. editorial staff New York Tribune, 1907-08, Evening Post, 1909-10, Parents' Mag. since 1927; Am. mng. editor Ency. Britannica, 1927-28; story supervisor Universal Pictures Co., 1929; founder Inst. of Life Planning, 1932; editorial dir. Farm Jour., 1935-38; cons. psychologist, tech. adviser on teaching methods. Author: The Art and Business of the Short Story, 1913; Must We Fight Japan? 1920; How to Write Stories, 1922; Seeing America—Farm and Field (with Harold Hughes), 1924; Seeing America—Mill and Factory (with Harold Hughes), 1926; The Twilight of the American Mind, 1928; The Art of Rapid Reading, 1929; The Psychology of Happiness, 1929; The Young Citizen, 1929; The Art of Sound Pictures (with William M. Marston), 1930; The Psychology of Achievement, 1930; Vocational Studies in Journalism, 1931; The Art of Learning, 1931; How We Learn, 1931; Short Introduction to History of Human Stupidity, 1932; Life Begins At Forty, 1932; More Power To You, 1933; Take It Easy! 1935; Let's Get What We Want, 1935; Capitalism Carries On, 1935; Careers after Forty, 1937; Seeing America (with Harold F. Hughes), 1939; Making Good Before Forty, 1939. Editor and contbr.: The New Realism, 1913; As We Are, 1923. Contbr. to American Mag., Country Home, etc. Home: R.F.D. 1, Dover, N.J. Office: 2960 Broadway, New York, N.Y.

PITMAN, Earle Carver, chem. engr.; b. West Boylston, Mass., Oct. 10, 1893; s. Joseph Asbury and Flora Etta (Carver) P.; A.B., Harvard U., 1914; B.S., Mass. Inst. Tech., 1916; m. Mary Gove, Oct. 10, 1917; children—Aroline, Barbara Anne, Dorothy Jane; m. 2d, Mary Vincent, Oct. 20, 1934; 1 son, John Carver. Chem. engr., Brown Co., Berlin, N.H., 1916-18; supt., Lustron Co., S. Boston, Mass., 1918-19; asst. dir. Parlin (N.J.) Lab., E. I. duPont de Nemours & Co., since 1919. Fellow A.A.A.S., Am. Inst. of Chemistry; mem. Am. Chem. Soc., Electrochem. Soc., Soc. of Chem. Industry, Phi Beta Kappa, Alpha Chi Sigma. Republican. Conglist. Club: Appalachian Mountain (Boston). Home: Riverbrook, Red Bank, N.J. Office: care E. I. duPont de Nemours & Co., Parlin, N.J.

PITMAN, John Himes, astronomer; b. Conshohocken, Pa., Apr. 7, 1890; s. George Henry and Carrie May (Himes) P.; A.B., Swarthmore Coll., 1910, A.M., 1911; student U. of Calif., 1911-13; m. Katharine Elsie Anders, June 13, 1914; children—Elsie Anders (Mrs. Carlos Alberto Avila), Katharine Lorene, Doris May, Betty Jean, John Himes (deceased), Christina Anders (deceased), Daniel James, Marianna Janet. With Swarthmore Coll. since 1913, as instr. in mathematics and astronomy, 1913-18, asst. prof., 1918-28, asso. prof. since 1928. Burgess Swarthmore Borough since 1934, re-elected 1938. Mem. Am. Astron. Soc., Royal Astron. Soc., Rittenhouse Astron. Soc., A.A.A.S., Sigma Xi. Democrat. Methodist. Rotarian. Address: Swarthmore, Pa.

PITMAN, Ralph William, banking; b. Sioux City, Ia., Apr. 24, 1898; s. Arthur Francis and Albertina S. (Poort) P.; ed. pub. sch. and high sch. and Morningside Coll., Sioux City, Ia., 1916-17; LL.B., Westminster Coll., Denver, Colo., 1925; m. Elsa Mae Dowling, June 20, 1930; 1 dau., Elsa Mae. In employ Morris Plan Bank, Denver, Colo., 1920; successively, exec. vice-pres. First Industrial Bank, Denver, Colo., Morris Plan Bankers Assn., St. Louis, Mo.; vice-pres. Industrial Savings Trust Co., St. Louis, Mo.; pres. Morris Plan Bank, Phila., Pa., since 1930; exec. vice-pres. and dir. Morris Plan Bank of Va.; vice-pres. and dir. Morris Plan Corpn. of America, New York, N.Y.; trustee Morris Plan Bank of Washington, D.C.; dir. Morris Plan Bank of Wilmington, Del., Morris Plan Bank of Knoxville, Tenn. Served as pvt. then sergt. maj. inf., U.S.A., 1917-19. Past pres. exec. com., Morris Plan Bankers Assn. Methodist. Mason (32°, Shriner). Clubs: Penn Athletic, Overbrook Country (Philadelphia); Hermitage Country (Richmond, Va.); Princess Anne Country (Virginia Beach, Va.). Home: 1505 City Line, South Ardmore. Office: 1716 Arch St., Philadelphia, Pa.

PITNEY, Shelton, lawyer; b. Morristown, N.J., Mar. 29, 1893; s. Mahlon and Florence T. (Shelton) P.; grad. Hill School, Pottstown, Pa., 1910; A.B., Princeton, 1914; LL.B., Harvard, 1917; m. Etta Carrington Brown, May 14, 1918; children—Shelton, Mary Foster, James Carrington. Admitted to N.Y. bar, 1920, N.J. bar, as atty., 1921, as counsellor, 1924; in practice since Mar. 1, 1919; mem. law firm Pitney, Harding, Skinner since 1922; dir. Morristown Trust Co., Howard Savings Inst. Served in U.S. Army, 1917-19; capt. 313th F.A., 80th Div., Sept. 1917-Feb. 1919; with A.E.F. in St. Mihiel and Argonne, wounded Oct. 2, 1918. Mem. Am. Bar Assn., N.J. Bar Assn., Essex County Bar Assn., Morris County Bar Assn. Republican. Presbyterian. Clubs: Essex, Down Town (Newark), Morris County Golf, Morristown (Morristown, N.J.); Edgartown Yacht (Edgartown, Mass.); Cap and Gown (Princeton). Home: Morristown, N.J. Office: 744 Broad St., Newark, N.J.

PITT, William Page; prof. journalism, Marshall Coll. Address: Marshall College, Huntington, W.Va.

PITTENGER, Paul Stewart, mfg. pharmaceuticals; b. Easton, Pa., Sept. 20, 1889; s. Edward Stewart and Matilda (Riedy) P.; Ph.G., Medico Chirurg. Coll., 1909, Ph. Chemist, 1910, Pharm. D., 1911; Pharm. M., Phila. Coll. Pharmacy and Sci., 1919; m. Leola Bodine Welch, Sept. 10, 1913. Engaged as dir. pharmaco-dynamic research, H. K. Mulford Co., Phila., Pa., 1910-25; dir. pharmacologic research, labs., Sharp & Dohme, 1927-28, asst. gen. supt., 1928-29, asst. to pres., 1929-30, vice-pres. since 1930. Mem. Am. Drug Mfrs. Assn., Am. Pharm. Assn. Republican. Presbyn. (trustee First Presbyn. Ch., Germantown). Clubs: Union League (Philadelphia); Philadelphia Country (Bala, Pa.). Home: Cambridge Apts., Alden Park. Office: 640 N. Broad St., Philadelphia, Pa.

PITTMAN, Hobson, artist and teacher; b. Tarboro, N.C., Jan. 14, 1900; s. Biscoe and Martha Alice (Walston) P.; ed. Carnegie Inst. Tech., 1920, Columbia U., 1921-23, Pa. State Coll., 1923-24, Graphic Sketch Club, Phila. 1929-30 (evenings); unmarried. Supervisor and teacher of art, Valley, Pa., 1924-25; teacher of art, Upper Darby, 1925-31; dir. art, Friends Central Sch., Overbrook, Pa., since 1931; instr. painting, Pa. State Coll., summer sch. since 1934; traveled in Europe to study museums and galleries, 1928, 1930, 1935; served as mem. Pa. Acad. Fine Arts Jury, 1938; represented in Metropolitan Museum, Whitney Mus. Am. Art, New York City, Pa. Acad. Fine Arts (paintings purchased by all 3, 1938-39), Brooklyn Mus., and in many pvt. collections; exhibited in all the large cities of the country and in various European cities. Hon. mention San Francisco World's Fair, 1939. Mem. Am. Artists Congress, Woodstock Art Assn., both of New York, Phila. Water Club. Presbyn. Home: 57 S. Eagle Rd. Manoa, Upper Darby, Pa.

PITZ, Henry Clarence, artist; b. Phila., Pa., June 16, 1895; s. Henry William and Anna Rosina (Stiffel) P.; student Pa. Mus. Sch. of Industrial Art, 1914-17, Spring Garden Inst., 1919-20; m. Molly Wheeler Wood, June 6, 1935; 1 dau., Julia Leaming. Illustrator of books and mags. since 1920; illustrator of over 80 books and for Saturday Evening Post, Scribners, Cosmopolitan, Country Gentleman, Good Housekeeping, etc.; in charge pictorial expression, Pa. Mus. Sch. of Industrial Art since 1932. Executed 3 murals for U.S. Govt. Bldg. in Century of Progress, Chicago, 1933. Represented in permanent exhbns. Los Angeles Mus. of Art, Congl. Library, Springfield (Mo.), State Teacher's Coll., Franklin Inst., N.Y. Pub. Library. Represented in "Fine Prints of the Year," 1937. Awarded Pa. Mus. Sch. of Industrial Art pageantry prize, 1917; John Wanamaker prize, 1917; Griscom prize for Water Color, 1932; bronze medal Internat. Print Exhbn., 1932; Dana gold medal, 1933; Denver Art Mus. purchase prize, 1934; bronze medal for water color, Pa. Mus. Sch. of Industrial Art, 1934; Southern Printmakers purchase prize, 1937; first prize for illustration, Phila. Print Club, 1937; honorable mention, Ogunquist Art Center, Ogunquist, Me., 1933. Served with A.E.F., U.S.A., 1918-19. Vice-pres. Phila. Art Alliance; mem. Am. Water Color Soc., Southern Printmakers, Soc. of Illustrators, Graphic Arts Forum. Episcopalian. Clubs: Sketch (pres.), Water Color (dir.), Print (Phila.). Author: Early American Costume, 1929. Contbr. to Am. and foreign mags. Home: Plymouth Meeting, Pa. Office: 320 S. Broad St., Philadelphia, Pa.

PITZONKA, Walter W., propr. Pitzonka's Pansy Farms; b. Bristol, Pa., Dec. 29, 1891; s. Gustav and Katharine (Schmidt) P.; student Business Coll.; m. Ruth R. Roberts, Mar. 1921; children—Louisa Roberts, Katharine Virginia, Walter William. In business with father, Bristol, Pa., to 1922; proprietor Pitzonka's Pansy Farms, Bristol, Pa., since 1922; dir. Harriman Bldg. Assn. Club: Exchange (Bristol, Pa.). Home: Box 211. Office: Oxford Valley Rd., Bristol, Pa.

PIVIROTTO, Arthur Michael, ins. and finance exec.; b. Pittsburgh, Pa., July 23, 1904; s. F. Graziano and Augustina (Monier) P.; A.B., Lafayette Coll., 1931; student Western Reserve U., 1931; m. Ruth Lillian Erhardt, July 1, 1925; children—Ruth Vernon, Arthur Michael, Richard Roy. Asso. with Automobile Finance Co., Pittsburgh, since 1923, began as collector and advanced through various positions, exec. vice-pres. and dir. since 1936; vice-pres., treas. and dir., Pittsburgh Ins. Agency, Keystone Thrift Corpn. of Pa., Keystone Discount Company of Ohio. Mem. Nat. Office Mgrs. Assn., Am. Finance Conf., Am. Soc. Management Engrs., Sigma Nu. Roman Catholic. Elk. Club: Pittsburgh Athletic. Home: 5527 Coral St. Office: 5526 Penn Av., Pittsburgh, Pa.

PLACK, William L., architect; b. Altoona, Pa., June 18, 1854; s. Louis and Elizabeth (Wehn) P.; C.E., Lafayette Coll., 1876, D. Engring., 1926; studied design and sculpture, Md. Inst., Baltimore; married; worked for 3 yrs. as architectural draughtsman and traveled in Europe. Was chief draughtsman on the State Capitol bldg., Des Moines, Ia., 1882, then opened office; practiced in Altoona, Pa., 1887-90; moved to Phila., to design the new shops for Baldwin Locomotive Works; has designed many banks, schs., chs., theatres, business blocks, county ct. houses and pub. bldgs., Phila. and Pa. Fellow Am. Inst. Architects; mem. Nat. Fire Protection Assn., Franklin Inst., Am. Civic Assn., Phila. Chamber of Commerce, Wm. Penn Highway Assn. (gov.); U.S. del. Internat. Congress of Architects, Rome, Italy, 1911, London, 1924, Pan-Am. Congress of Architects, Santiago, Chile, 1923, Buenos Aires, Argentina, 1927; accredited del. of A.I.A. to World Engring. Congress, Tokio

1929. Pres. Pa. State Assn. A.I.A., 1921-23; hon. corr. mem. Sociedad Central de Arquitectos, Uruguay, Argentina, Brazil and Chile; mem. Am. Interprofessional Inst. Clubs: Old Colony, Engineers', Art (Phila.). Home: Lenox Apts. Office: 1120 Locust St., Philadelphia, Pa.

PLANK, William Bertolette, mining engr.; b. Morgantown, Pa., June 24, 1886; s. David Heber (M.D.) and Ida Eugenie (Bertolet) P.; prep. edn., Keystone State Normal Sch.; B.S. in Mining Engring., Pa. State Coll., 1908, E.M., 1909; m. Helen Josephine Beck, Apr. 8, 1912; 1 dau., Adaline Jane. Instr. Sch. of Mines, Pa. State Coll., 1908-09; mining engr. with Phila. & Reading Coal & Iron Co., Shamokin, Pa., 1909-12, Pittsburgh Coal Co., 1912-16; with U.S. Bur. Mines, 1916-20, successively as jr. mining engr. (Pittsburgh), asst. mining engr. (Pittsburgh), mining engr. (Urbana, Ill.), dist. mining engr. (Birmingham, Ala.); head dept. mining engr. and metallurgy and John Markle professor, Lafayette Coll. since 1920, dir. Boys Engring. Conf. of Coll. since 1934. Mem. Mine Safety Com. of U.S. Commn., by apptmt. of Pres. Harding, 1923; pres. Civil Service Bd. of Easton, 1926-28; chmn. Emergency Fuel Commn. of Easton during anthracite strike, 1925-26; chmn. Smoke Abatement Commn. of Easton, 1929. Mem. Am. Inst. Mining and Metall. Engrs. (v.p. Lehigh Valley sect.; chmn. div. of mineral industries edn., 1936-38; sec., 1938—), Coal Mining Inst. America, Engineers Council for Professional Development (one of 3 reps. of Am. Inst. Mining and Metall. Engrs. and mem. com. on vocational guidance), Am. Soc. for Testing Materials (chmn. com. D-16 on slate, 1928, Soc. for Promotion Engring. Edn. (chmn. mining and metall. com., 1936), Am. College Personnel Assn., Am. Assn. Univ. Profs., Engineers' Club of Lehigh Valley, Phi Kappa Phi, Tau Beta Pi, Delta Tau Delta, Sigma Gamma Epsilon. Episcopalian. Mason. Clubs: Faculty of Lafayette Coll. (pres.; 1926-27), Rotary (pres., 1926-27), Mining Club. Contbr. tech. and ednl. articles on mineral technology field, pub. principally by Am. Inst. Mining and Metall. Engrs. Home: 246 Taylor Av., Easton, Pa.

PLANT, Albert Cookman, dentist; b. Wheeling, W.Va., Apr. 5, 1878; s. John J. and Harriet E. (Bender) P.; student Wheeling pub. sch. and business coll.; D.D.S., Western Reserve U., 1902; m. Maud A. Rood, June 11, 1902. In gen. practice of dentistry since 1902. Mem. Am. Dental Soc., W.Va. State Dental Soc. (ex-sec.; now pres.), Wheeling District Dental Soc. (ex-sec.; pres. 2 yrs.), Odontol. Dental Soc. of Western Pa. Presbyterian. Mason (Scottish Rite, Shriner). Home: 5 Locust Av. Office: 606 Wheeling Bank & Trust Bldg., Wheeling, W.Va.

PLATE, Blair, bldg. contractor; b. Wirt Co., W.Va., Jan. 18, 1890; s. Albert and Anna (Rupert) P.; student common schs., Parkersburg, W.Va., 1897-1909; m. Ethel May Gailbreath, Jan. 18, 1912; 1 son, Blair. Began as bldg. contractor, Parkersburg, 1913; owner and gen. mgr. Plate Constrn. Co., gen. bldg. contractors, Parkersburg, W.Va., since 1915; pres. Parkersburg Corrugated Box Co. since 1937; dir. Peoples Nat. Bank, Parkersburg, W.Va., since 1932, v.p., 1933-35. Pres. Parkersburg Bd. of Commerce, 1931-33, dir. since 1924. Republican. Christian. Mason, Elk. Club: Lions (Parkersburg, W.Va.). Home: 4420 Emerson Av. Office: 726-800 Jeanette St., Parkersburg, W.Va.

PLATT, Charles Alexander, prof. psychology and edn.; b. Centerville, Pa., May 14, 1884; s. Daniel A. and Emma (Baker) P.; B.S., O. Northern U., 1909; A.M., Grove City Coll., 1912, Ph.D., same, 1917; grad. study, Columbia U., 1927; m. Mary Floy Fletcher, Aug. 29, 1914; 1 dau., Martha Jean (Mrs. Nicholas R. Gulyas). Engaged in teaching high sch., W.Va., and supervising prin. schs., Pa., 1909-14; prof. psychology and edn., Mansfield State Teachers Coll., Mansfield, Pa., 1914-17; prof. psychology and edn., Grove City Coll., Grove City, Pa., continuously since 1917. Served as mem. Bd. Edn., Grove City, Pa., 1921-33. Mem. Pa. State Edn. Assn. Republican. Mem. M.E. Ch. Mason (32°, Shriner). Club: Rotary of Grove City. Also known as inst. instr., lyceum lecturer and pub. speaker. Home: 523 Stewart Av., Grove City, Pa.

PLATT, Haviland Hull, engring. exec.; b. Lakewood, N.J., Apr. 6, 1889; s. Isaac Hull and Emma (Haviland) P.; student Haverford (Pa.) Sch., 1901-05; B.Sc., U. of Pa., 1909, M.E., 1930; m. Marie-Louise Fearey, Apr. 4, 1919; children—Frederick Epenetus, Patricia Louise, Pamela Hull. Elec. tester, Wm. Cramp & Sair, shipyard, 1909; elec. engr., Fels & Co., soap mfr., 1910, independent automotive engr. work, 1910-17; with Wilkening Mfg. Co., mfrs. piston rings and motor parts, Phila., since orgn., 1917, chief engr., 1917-33, v.p. in charge engring. since 1933, dir. since 1917; v.p. Platt-LePage Aircraft Co., development of rotating wing aircraft, since 1938; dir. Lykens Valley R.R. and Coal Co. Mem. Soc. of Cincinnati, Franklin Inst., Soc. of Automotive Engrs., Inst. of Aeronautical Sciences. Author several articles on automotive and aeronautical subjects. Home: 1095 Park Av., New York, N.Y. Office: Real Estate Trust Bldg., Philadelphia, Pa.

PLATT, John, engineer; b. Gloucester, Eng., June 1, 1864; s. James and Elizabeth (Waddington) P.; engring. student Univ. Coll., London, 1886-87; m. Mary Bourne Bartlett, 1891; children—Hilda (Mrs. Wilfred H. Wolfs), John, Robert, Hugh. Came to U.S., 1888; introduced marine steam turbine into U.S. Navy and Merchant Marine. Mem. Am. Soc. M.E., Soc. Naval Architects and Marine Engrs., Instn. Civ. Engrs. (Eng.). Clubs: Engineers (New York); Army and Navy (Washington, D.C.); St. Stephen's (London). Collector early Chinese and Korean pottery. Home: 532 Woodland Av., Westfield, N.J.

PLATT, John O(sgood), insurance; b. Nyack, N.Y., June 21, 1874; s. Clayton Taylor and Martha DuBose (Lucas) P.; Ed. Ury Private Sch. and St. Luke's Acad., Phila., 1883-91; m. Katharine Biddle Leonard, July 1917 (died 1918); 1 son, John Osgood; m. 2d, Mary Cox Page, 1922; children—David Page, William, Mary Cordes. Associated with Ins. Co. of N.A. since Oct. 1891, beginning as clerk and later becoming special agt., asst. sec., 1907-10, 2d v.p., 1910-16, 1st v.p., 1916-39, dir. since 1916, pres. since 1939; pres. Alliance Ins. Co., Phila. Fire & Marine Ins. Co., Indemnity Ins. Co. of N.A. Mem. bd. mgrs. Children's Hosp., Phila.; pres. Williston Sch. Bd., Paoli, Pa. Mem. Del. Soc. of the Cincinnati. Republican. Episcopalian. Clubs: Philadelphia, University Barge (Phila.). Home: "Fairfields," Paoli, Pa. Officer: 1600 Arch St., Philadelphia, Pa.

PLEASANTS, Henry, Jr., physician; b. Radnor, Pa., May 23, 1884; s. Henry and Agnes (Spencer) P.; ed. Haverford Sch., 1895-1901; A.B., Haverford Coll., 1906; M.D., U. of Pa. Med. Sch., 1910; m. Elizabeth W. Smith, June 9, 1909 (divorced 1930); children—Henry 3d, William Wilkins, Richard Rundle, Howard Spencer, Constantia Elizabeth (Mrs. Nathaniel Bowditch), Dallas Franklin; m. 2d, Vera M. Kilhefner, Jan. 28, 1932. Engaged in gen. practice of medicine at West Chester, Pa., 1910-17 and also engaged in writing since 1919. Served in Med. Corps Res., U.S.A., 1917-19, maj., 1919; lt. col. Med. Res., 1922-34. Awarded Victory Medal and 2 stars, Order Purple Heart. Fellow American College of Physicians, Philadelphia College of Physicians; mem. American Legion (past post comdr.), Mil. Order Fgn. Wars (vice comdr. Pa.), Soc. Colonial Wars, Delta Phi. Republican. Episcopalian. Clubs: St. Elmo, University, Franklin Inn (Philadelphia. Editor of Medical World, Philadelphia, Pa., 1934-36. Author: Thomas Mason, Adventurer, 1934; Four Great Artists of Chester County, 1936; Three Scientists of Chester County, 1936; Anthony Wayne, 1936; The Tragedy of the Crater, 1938. Home: 18 W. Chestnut St. Office: 133 N. High St., West Chester, Pa.

PLEASANTS, Henry, 3d, music editor; b. Wayne, Pa., May 12, 1910; s. Henry (Jr.) and Elizabeth W. (Smith) P.; ed. Montgomery Sch., Phila., 1919-27, Curtis Inst. of Music, Phila., 1928-30; studied under Horatio Connell and Giuseppe Boghetti, Phila. (voice), Zenia Nazareivitch, Phila., Ivan Engel, Hungary (piano), Tibor Serly, Hungary (composition); m. Elizabeth A. Szilagyi, Aug. 18, 1936. Asst. music critic Evening Bulletin, Phila., 1930-35; music editor since 1935. Contbr. critical articles to Modern Music. Home: 2506 S. 22d St. Office: Evening Bulletin, Philadelphia, Pa.

PLEASANTS, J(acob) Hall, physician, retired; b. Baltimore Co., Md., Sept. 12, 1873; s. Richard H. and Elizabeth M. (Poultney) P.; A.B., Johns Hopkins U., 1895; M.D., Johns Hopkins U. Med. Sch., 1899; m. Delia Tudor Wilmer, Jan. 30, 1902; children—Skipwith Wilmer (dec.), Elizabeth Poultney (Mrs. Francis H. Jencks), Delia Tudor. Interne Johns Hopkins Hosp., 1899-1900; engaged in gen. practice of medicine at Baltimore, Md., 1901-10; instr. and asso, in medicine, Johns Hopkins U., 1902-34. Served as pres. Municipal Dept. of Charities and Corrections of City of Baltimore, 1907-21. Trustee Johns Hopkins Univ., Baltimore Mus. of Art, Municipal Mus. of Baltimore; pres. bd. trustees, Peabody Inst., Baltimore, St. Timothy's Sch., Catonsville; vice-pres. bd. trustees, Md. Hist. Soc., Baltimore. Mem. Am. Med. Assn., Med. and Chirurg. Faculty of Md., Am. Antiquarian Soc., Walpole Soc., Alpha Delta Phi. Ind. Democrat. Episcopalian. Club: Johns Hopkins. Contbr. articles to med. journs. Co-author (with Howard Sill), Maryland Silversmiths, 1715-1830, 1930. Contbr. to antiquarian journals on early American portrait painters. Editor of Archives of Maryland since 1929. Home: 201 Longwood Rd., Baltimore, Md.

PLUMER, John Shaffer, physician; b. Emsworth, Pa., Sept. 1, 1886; s. Walter Lowrie and Susan Eckert (Shaffer) P.; B.S., U. of Pittsburgh, 1910; M.D., Johns Hopkins U. Med. Sch., 1914; unmarried. Interne Allegheny Gen. Hosp., Pittsburgh, Pa., 1914-15; resident surgeon, Wills Hosp., Phila., Pa., 1924-25; mem. staff, Eye and Ear Hosp., Pittsburgh, Pa., since 1931; asst. prof. ophthalmology, U. of Pittsburgh Med. Sch. since 1931; in practice of medicine at Pittsburgh since 1915, specializing in ophthalmology since 1925. Served as 1st lt. Med. Corps, U.S.N. R.F., 1917-21. Fellow Am. Med. Assn.; mem. Am. Acad. Ophthalmology and Otolaryngology, Pittsburgh Acad. of Medicine, Pittsburgh Ophthol. Soc. Republican. Presbyn. Club: Automobile of Pittsburgh. Home: 24 Plumer Av., Emsworth, Pittsburgh, Pa. Office: 121 University Pl., Pittsburgh, Pa.

PLUMER, Richard C., lawyer; b. Whitefield, N.H., July 13, 1890; s. Henry George and Jessie (Shean) P.; A.B., Dartmouth Coll., Hanover, N.H., 1912; LL.B., Harvard, 1915; m. Louise Barnes, Nov. 30, 1916. Began practice of law, 1916; prosecutor of pleas, Ocean County, N.J., 1917-22; asst. U.S. atty. N.J. Dist., 1922-27; asst. atty. gen. in charge Securities Div., Dept. of Atty. Gen., N.J., 1927-34; associated with Hood, Lafferty & Campbell since 1934, becoming mem., 1935; spl. master N.J. Court of Chancery. Mem. bd. trustees Paul Kimball Hosp., Lakewood, N.J., 1921. Mem. N.J. Bar Assn. (chmn. com. on prosecutions 1923; chmn. com. on inter-state transactions of Nat. Assn. of Securities Commns. 1926; del. from Essex County to banking section 1939), Essex County Bar Assn., Harvard Law Sch. Assn. Presbyterian. Clubs: Essex (Newark); Dartmouth of N.Y.; Dartmouth of Northern N.J. Writer of several articles and monographs. Home: 31 Washington St., East Orange, N.J. Office: 744 Broad St., Newark, N.J.

PLUMMER, Frederick Berry, clergyman; b. Hagerstown, Md., Jan. 7, 1885; s. Charles William and Sarah Ellen (Eakle) P.; A.B., Lebanon Valley Coll., Annville, Pa., 1905; grad. study Johns Hopkins U., 1912-13; (hon.) D.D., Lebanon Valley Coll., 1921; m. Emma Edna Flook, Nov. 16, 1907. Ordained to ministry U.B. Ch., 1908; pastor, Myersville, Md. Circuit, 1905-07, Shippensburg, Pa., 1907-11, Otterbein Memorial Ch., Baltimore, Md., 1911-14, Carlisle, Pa., 1914-21; pastor, St. Paul's Ch., Hagerstown, Md., since 1921; mem. five gen. confs. U.B. Ch.; mem. bd. Christian edn. since 1921; mem. bd. adminstrn. since 1933; mem. Pa. Conf. U.B. Ch. since 1903, now mem. finance com. and benevolent fund bd.; mem. Federal Council Chs. of Christ in America since 1933. Trustee Lebanon Valley Coll. since 1911, Md. Anti-Saloon League since 1922. Ind. Republican. Mem. U.B. Ch. Club: Kiwanis of Hagerstown (past pres.; past gov. Capital Dist of Kiwanis, 1931). Home: 106 E. Franklin St., Hagerstown, Md.

PLUMMER, Wilbur Clayton, univ. prof.; b. Hagerstown, Md., July 5, 1889; s. Charles William and Sarah Ellen (Eakle) P.; A.B., Lebanon Valley Coll., 1910, LL.D., 1939; A.M., U. of Pa., 1922, Ph.D., 1924; m. Florence Braastad, Aug. 30, 1920; 1 dau., Fredericka. Instr. high schs., 1910-17 and 1919-20; instr. economics, U. of Pa., 1921-27, asst. prof., 1927-31, prof. economics since 1931. With U.S.A. Ambulance Service, with French Army, 1917-19. Chief business specialist U.S. Dept. of Commerce, 1928-33; asst. dir. planning div. Pa. State Emergency Relief Adminstrn., 1934; dir. div. of professional projects, Works Progress Adminstrn. for Pa., 1935, dep. adminstr., 1936; mem. research staff Mayor's Advisory Finance Commn., Phila., 1937-38; mem. staff Nat. Bur. of Econ. Research since 1938. Twice awarded Croix de Guerre. Author: The Road Policy of Pennsylvania, 1925; National Retail Credit Survey, 1930; article on installment buying and its consequences in annals of Am. Acad. of Polit. and Social Science, 1927, etc. Home: 7713 Parkview Rd., Upper Darby, Pa. Office: Bennett Hall, U. of Pennsylvania, Philadelphia, Pa.

PLUMMER, William Edwin, cons. radio engr.; b. Adamstown, Md., Dec. 27, 1905; s. Edwin Roland and Elizabeth Garland (Johnson) P.; B.E. in E.E., Johns Hopkins U., 1929; m. Margaret Fairchild Torsch, Sept. 29, 1933; 1 son, William Torsch. Employed on tech. staff Bell Telephone Labs., New York, 1929-32; with radio sta. WFBR, Baltimore, 1932-33; s. engr. with Glena D. Gillett, cons. radio engr., Washington, D.C., since 1933; qualified to testify before the Federal Communications Commn. as an expert regarding radio transmission phenomenon. Served in R.O.T.C., 1925-29; 2d lt. O.R.C., 1929-35, 1st lt. since 1935. Mem. Inst. Radio Engrs., Sigma Phi Epsilon. Democrat. Episcopalian. Received acknowledgment by Drs. Howard A. Kelly and Grant E. Ward in book, Electrosurgery, for assistance in preparing chapter, "Physics of High Frequency Currents." Home: 3310 Windsor Av., Baltimore, Md. Office: Nat. Press Bldg., Washington, D.C.

PLYMPTON, Frank B.; pres. Hackensack Trust Co. Address: Hackensack, N.J.

PLYMPTON, George F(ranklin), lawyer; b. Hackensack, N.J., May 29, 1895; s. Franklin B. and Alida (Schoonmaker) P.; Litt.B., Princeton, 1917; LL.B., Columbia U. Law Sch., 1921; m. Frances C. Heddell, June 12, 1918; children—Robert George, Bruce Franklin. Admitted to N.J. bar as atty., 1921, as counselor, 1925, spl. master in chancery of N.J., 1938; trust officer, The Hackensack Trust Company, Hackensack, N.J., since 1922. Served as warrant officer, pay corps, U.S.N.R.F., 1917-19. Trustee Johnson Free Pub. Library, Hackensack, N.J. Mem. Bergen County (N.J.) Bar Assn., N.J. Bar Assn., Phi Delta Phi. Republican. Mem. Ref. Ch. of America. Club: Dial Lodge of Princeton Univ. Home: 170 Prospect Av. Office: 7 E. Mercer St., Hackensack, N.J.

POE, Edgar Allan, lawyer; b. Baltimore, Sept. 15, 1871; s. John Prentiss and Anne Johnson (Hough) P.; A.B., Princeton University, 1891; LL.B., University of Md., 1893; m. Annye T. McCay, Dec. 10, 1895 (died Nov. 17, 1928); 1 son, Edgar Allan; m. 2d, Mrs. Marie Louise McIlhenny, June 27, 1932. Practiced, Baltimore, 1893—; mem. firm of John P. Poe & Sons, 1894-1909; now mem. Bartlett, Poe & Claggett. Deputy state's atty. for Baltimore City, 1900-03, state's atty., 1903; deputy city solicitor, 1904-08; city solicitor, 1908-11; atty.-gen. of Md., 1912-16. Democrat. Episcopalian. Home: Garrison, Md. Office: Calvert and Redwood Sts., Baltimore, Md.

POE, Edgar Allan, Jr., lawyer; b. Baltimore, Md., Sept. 2, 1896; s. Edgar Allan and Annye T. (McCay) P.; A.B., Princeton U., 1918; LL.B., Georgetown U. Law Sch., Georgetown, Md., 1926; m. Katharine Richards, June 24, 1922; children—Edgar Allan III, Katharine Bancroft. Admitted to Md. bar, 1927, and since in gen. practice of law at Baltimore; mem. firm Bartlett, Poe & Claggett since 1929; served as asst. atty. gen. of Md., 1935-39; spl. counsel for comptroller of Md., 1935-39; gen. counsel State Aviation Commn. of Md. since 1929; sec., treas., and dir. North American Oil Co., Baltimore, since 1937. Served as capt. U.S. Marine Corps, 1917-19, with 2d div. with A.E.F.; awarded Croix de Guerre (France), Purple Heart (U.S.). Former mem. Aviation Com. U.S. Chamber of Commerce. Mem. Baltimore City Bar Assn., Am. Bar Assn., Ivy Club (Princeton). Democrat. Episcopalian. Clubs: Merchants (Baltimore); Green Spring Valley Hunt (Garrison, Md.); Green Spring Hounds (Glyndon, Md.); Ivy (Princeton); Princeton (New York). Home: Chattolanee, Baltimore County. Office: U.S. Fidelity & Guaranty Bldg., Baltimore, Md.

POE, John Prentiss, banking; b. Baltimore, Md., Sept. 20, 1900; s. S. Johnson and Laura (Cromwell) P.; student Gilman Country Sch., Roland Park, Baltimore, 1911-16; A.B., Princeton U., 1922; m. Lydia Richmond Taber Este, Oct. 1, 1938; step-children—Eleanor Este, Marion Este. Clerk Federal Reserve Bank of N.Y., 1922-23, Nat. Bank of Commerce in N.Y. (now Guaranty Trust Co.), 1923-25; mem. nat. bank examining staff, 2d Federal Reserve Dist., 1925-27; held various positions Nat. City Bank of N.Y., 1927-35; First Nat. Bank of Princeton, 1935, exec. v.p. and dir. since 1936. Mem. S.A.T.C. 1918; mem. 51st Mounted Machine Gun Squadron (Squadron A), N.Y.N.G., 1923-25. Trustee Princeton Hosp. Democrat. Episcopalian. Clubs: Princeton (New York); Nassau, Nassau Gun (Princeton). Home: Cedar Grove Road. Office: 90 Nassau St., Princeton, N.J.

POFFENBARGER, George, judge; b. Mason Co., W.Va., Nov. 24, 1861; s. Clinton and Sarah (Lewis) P.; ed. Rio Grande (O.) Coll., 1882; taught in pub. schs., Mason Co., W.Va., 1880-87 (prin. West Columbia schs., 1883-85, and of Clifton schs., 1885-87); m. Livia Nye Simpson, May 10, 1894; children—Nathan Simpson, Perry Simpson. Admitted to bar, 1887; sheriff Mason Co., W.Va., 1889-92; judge Supreme Court of Appeals of W.Va., terms 1901-12, 1913-24; resigned Dec. 31, 1922; mem. law firm Poffenbarger, Blue & Dayton, 1923-28, now Poffenbarger & Poffenbarger. Pres. Point Pleasant Development Co.; dir. Marietta Mfg. Co. Mem. S.A.R. Club: Point Pleasant Country. Republican. Presbyn. Mason. Home: 5010 Kanawha Av. Office: National Bank of Commerce Bldg., Charleston, W.Va.

POFFENBARGER, Nathan Simpson, lawyer; b. Point Pleasant, W.Va., Aug. 4, 1898; s. George and Livia (Simpson) P.; student O. Univ., Athens, O., 1916-20; LL.B., Univ. of Va. Law Coll., Charlottesville, Va., 1926; m. Harriet Bagby Stubbs, Apr. 6, 1929; 1 son, George II. Admitted to W.Va. bar, 1926 and since engaged in gen. practice of law at Charleston; mem. firm Poffenbarger & Poffenbarger since 1928; mem. city council Charleston, 1935-39. Served in inf. Central O.T.S., Camp Grant, Ill., 1918. Mem. W.Va. State and Charleston bar assns., Phi Delta Theta, Phi Delta Phi. Republican. Episcopalian. Elk. Home: 2516 Kanawha St. Office: Nat. Bank of Commerce Bldg., Charleston, W.Va.

POHLMAN, George Gordon, univ. prof.; b. Doon, Iowa, Oct. 6, 1902; s. George S. and Margaret (Heggie) P.; B.S., Iowa State Coll., 1923, M.S., 1924, Ph.D., 1930; m. Helen Curtis, June 26, 1932; children—Margaret Jean, George Gordon. Asst. and instr. agrl. chemistry and soils, U. of Ariz., 1924-28; asst. prof. and asst. agronomist, W.Va. Univ., 1930-38; prof. and agronomist since 1938. Mem. Phi Kappa Phi, Sigma Xi, Alpha Zeta, Phi Lambda Upsilon, Gamma Sigma Delta. Baptist. Address: Morgantown, W.Va.

POINT, Walter Warren, obstetrician; b. Huntington, W.Va., July 3, 1887; s. Walter Warren and Dorothy Ann (Hazan) P.; student Marshall Coll., Huntington, 1905-06; A.B., W.Va. U., 1910; M.D., Coll. Phys. and Surgeons, Baltimore, 1913; m. Maude Lore Brown, Oct. 14, 1916; children—Walter Warren, III, Robert Beverly. Interne in surgery Mercy Hosp., Baltimore, 14 mos.; asst. supt. Sydenham Hosp., Baltimore, Md., 4 mos.; began gen. practice of medicine, 1914; in practice of obstetrics since 1923; chief of obstetrices Kanawha Valley Hosp.; cons. in obstetrics, St. Francis and McMillan hosps., all of Charleston; sec., treas. and dir. Kanawha Valley Hosp., Kanawha Valley Hosp. Co. Fellow Am. Coll. Surgeons; mem. Kanawha County Med. Soc., W.Va. State Med. Assn., Am. Congress on Obstetrics and Genecology, Am. Med. Editors' and Authors' Assn., W.Va. Obstet. and Gynecol. Soc. (pres.), W. Va. Maternal Health Federation (pres.). Served as major Med. Corps, 150th Inf., 1916-17, 9th U.S. Inf., 1918-19 (overseas 1 yr.), W.Va. Nat. Guard, 1916-26; now major Med. Reserve Corps. Democrat. Presbyterian. Mason (32°, Shriner), Elk. Clubs: Rotary (past dir.), Edgewood Country (mem. bd. govs.)—both of Charleston. Home: 2444 Kanawha St. Office: 510-514 Medical Arts Bldg., Charleston, W.Va.

POLAND, John Robert; mem. bd. govs. W.Va. U. Address: Martinsburg, W.Va.

POLING, Daniel Alfred, clergyman, editor, temperance advocate; b. Portland, Oregon, November 30, 1884; s. Charles C. and Savilla (Kring) P.; A.B., Dallas (Ore.) College, 1904, A.M. from same, 1906; student Lafayette (Ore.) Sem.; grad. work, Ohio State U., 1907-09; LL.D., Albright Coll., 1916; Litt.D., Defiance Coll., 1921; D.D., Hope Coll., 1925; S.T.D., Syracuse U., 1927; D.D., U. of Vt., 1934; LL.D., Temple U., 1937; m. Susan J. Vandersall, Sept. 25, 1906 (died July 25, 1918); m. 2d, Lillian Diebold Heingartner, Aug. 11, 1919; 7 children. Prohibition candidate for gov. of Ohio, 1912; temporary chmn. Prohibition Nat. Conv., 1916; sec. Flying Squadron America and leader in campaign covering 250 cities. Pastor Marble Collegiate Ref. Ch., New York, 1923-29, Bapt. Temple, Philadelphia, since 1936; pres. Internat. Soc. of Christian Endeavor, World's Christian Endeavor Union, editor in chief of Christian Herald, and Christian Endeavor World; dir. Presbyterian Ministers Life Insurance Fund, J. C. Penney Foundation, New York. Engaged overseas in spl. war work, in British Isles, France and Germany, 1918, 19; mem. Gen. War-Time Commn. of the Churches; maj. Chaplain Officers' Reserve. President of General Synod Reformed Church in America, 1929-30. Clubs: Mt. Crotchet Country, Union League. Author: Mothers of Men, 1914; Huts in Hell, 1918; Learn to Live, 1923; What Men Need Most, 1923; An Adventure in Evangelism, 1925; The Furnace (novel), 1925; John of Oregon (novel), 1926; Radio Talks to Young People, 1926; Dr. Poling's Radio Talks, 1927; The Heretic (novel), 1928; Youth and Life, 1929; Between Two Worlds (novel), 1930; John Barleycorn—His Life and Letters (novel), 1933; Youth Marches, 1937. Home: 2315 N. Broad St., Philadelphia, Pa. Office: Baptist Temple, Broad and Berks, Philadelphia, Pa.; also 41 Mt. Vernon St., Boston, Mass.

POLK, Albert Fawcett, ex-congressman; b. Frederica, Del., Oct. 11, 1869; s. Theodore A. and Sarah F. (Fawcett) P.; B.A., Delaware Coll., Newark, Del., 1889, M.A., 1892; m. Martilla Evans, December 29, 1897 (died March 5, 1938). Began in the practice of law at Georgetown, Del., 1892; formerly chmn. Dem. County Com., Sussex Co., and mem. Dem. State Com.; counsel for Del. Senate, 1899; a legislative atty. for Del. legislature, 1905; mem. Bd. of Edn., Georgetown 7 yrs.; mem. Town Council, 1915; mem. and sec. Sussex Co. Bd. Law Examiners; mem. 65th Congress (1917-19), Del.-at-large; U.S. commr. Dist. of Del. since 1930. Presbyn. Mason (K.T.); Grand High Priest Grand Chapter R.A.M. of Del., 1911. Home: 812 N. Adams St. Office: 209 Post Office Bldg., Wilmington, Del.

POLLITT, Levin Irving, pres. Southern Gas & Electric Corpn.; b. Salisbury, Md., Apr. 28, 1866; s. Levin Irving and Anne Maria (Ralph) P.; A.B., Western Md. Coll., Westminster, 1889, A.M., 1892, hon. A.M., 1926, LL.D.,

1939; m. Fanny L. Bertron, Dec. 27, 1894; children—Pauline Frances (Mrs. Douglas R. Morrison), Levin Irving. Teacher Western Maryland Coll., 1889-90, Chamberlain-Hunt Acad., Port Gibson, Miss., 1890-98, also editor Port Gibson (Miss.) Reveille, 1895-98; gen. mgr. Natchez (Miss.) Water & Sewer Co., 1898-1901, Pine Bluff (Ark.) Water & Light Co., 1901-04; pres. Suffolk (Va.) Gas-Electric Co., 1909-24, Bluefield (Va.) Gas & Power Co., 1911-24, Henrico County (Va.) Gas Co., 1912-20, Sumter (S.C.) Gas & Power Co., 1912-24, Gas Light Co. of Augusta, Ga., 1914-24, Husband Flint Products Co., 1918-20; v.p. and gen. mgr. Southern Gas & Electric Corpn., 1909-23, pres. since 1923. Mem. Presbytery of Baltimore (moderator, 1927-28); moderator Presbyterian Church in U.S.A., 1933-34; moderator of Synod of Baltimore, 1935. Member Am. Gas Assn., Southern Gas Assn. (pres. 1921-22), Md. Hist. Soc., St. Andrew's Soc. (mem. bd. dirs.), Eastern Shore Soc. of Baltimore (pres. 1925), S.A.R. Democrat. Helped establish 1st full time course of gas engring., Johns Hopkins U., 1924. Contbr. chapter to Colonial Eastern Shore, 1918. Home: 1715 Park Pl. Office: Munsey Bldg., Baltimore, Md.

POLLOCK, Bruce Henderson, physician; b. Swann Creek, O., May 28, 1906; s. George Campbell and Kate Arbuckle (Hannan) P.; student Marshall Coll., Huntington, W.Va., 1925-28; M.D., Med. Coll. of Va., Richmond, Va., 1932; A.B., Marshall Coll., 1933; C.P.H., Johns Hopkins Sch. Pub. Health & Hygiene, 1937; m. Elsie Virginia Kay, Apr. 28, 1933. Interne Chesapeake & Ohio Ry. Hosp., Huntington, W.Va., 1932-33; camp surgeon, Civilian Conservation Corps, 1933-34; asst. surgeon, Carbon Fuel Co., Carbon, W.Va., Jan.-June 1935; in practice of medicine at Point Pleasant, W.Va., 1935-36, also jr. med. examiner for U.S. Engrs. for O. and Kanawha River Bank Clearing Project, 1935-36; first dist. health officer W.Va. State Health Dept., 1936; health officer Jackson Health Dist. W.Va. State Health Dept. since 1937 located at Point Pleasant. Served in R.O. T.C.; 1st lt. Organized Reserve Corps. Fellow A.M.A., Am. Pub. Health Assn. Mem. W.Va. State, Cabell Co., Mason Co. med. socs., W.Va. Pub. Health Assn. (v.p.), Southern Dist. W.Va. Pub. Health Assn., Epsilon Delta, Chi Beta Phi, Phi Beta Pi. Presbyn. Club: Kiwanis (Point Pleasant). Home: 1402 Kanawha St. Office: 221 6th St., Point Pleasant, W.Va.

POLLOCK, Rebecca Luella; prof. edn. W.Va. U. Address: West Virginia University, Morgantown, W.Va.

POLLOCK, Thomas Cithcart, clergyman; b. Ligonier, Westmoreland Co., Pa., Sept. 5, 1873; s. Thomas C. and Martha (Barnett) P.; A.B., U. of Wooster (now coll.), O., 1894, A.M., 1897; grad. Pittsburgh Theol. Sem., 1897; m. Mary Clarke Heade, Oct. 23, 1900; children—Thomas Clark, Margaret Heade, Martha Barnett, Jane McCracken. Ordained ministry U.P. Ch., 1897; pastor Cambridge, O., 1897-1901, 2d Ch., Monmouth, Ill., 1901-11, Oak Park Ch., Phila., since 1911. Vice-pres. Bd. of Foreign Missions of the U.P. Ch. Trustee Pittsburgh Theol. Sem. Home: 5034 Hazel Av. Office: 51st and Pine Sts., Philadelphia, Pa.

POLLOCK, Walter William, appraisal physical properties; b. Lancaster, Wis., May 8, 1863; s. Edward and Mary Elizabeth (Raines) P.; g.s. William Pollock, of Mount Union, Huntingdon Co., Pa., col. militia, Colonial Army; ed. pub. sch. and high sch., Lancaster, Wis.; m. Elizabeth Freeman Philbrook, Oct. 18, 1906; children—Elizabeth Raines, Margaret Philbrook, Walter William, Jr., Roxane Whittier. Employed on father's newspaper; employed in various positions, Milwaukee (Wis.) Sentinel and corr. various met. newspapers, 1891-99; organized Manufacturers' Appraisal Co. for appraisal of physical properties, Milwaukee, Wis., and pres. and dir. since 1899, extending business to nat. scope; treas. and dir. United States Appraisal Co., Boston, Mass. Mem. Assn. Appraisal Execs. Unitarian. Author: The Science and Practice of Urban Land Valuation, 1928. Home: 7721 St. Martin's Lane. Office: 801 Manhattan Bldg., Philadelphia, Pa.

POLOWE, David, surgeon; b. New York, N.Y., Feb. 3, 1893; s. Phoenius and Frieda (Lichtenstein) Polowetski; ed. pub. schs. New York City, 1899-1907, New York Nautical Sch. (Training ship "Newport"), 1908-10, Columbia Coll., 1918-21, Coll. of Physicians and Surgeons, Columbia, 1921-23; M.D., U. of Louisville, 1926; m. Miriam B. Seadler, Sept. 18, 1920; children—Suzanne, Barbara. Served as deck officer in U.S. Lighthouse Service, 1911-15, deck officer and master deepsea merchant vessels, 1916-22; master mariner; pilot, Great Lakes from Detroit to Chicago to Duluth, also New York Bay; served on mechant ships running submarine blockade, 1916-18; taught navigation and piloting Columbia, 1920-22. Asso. with Barnert Memorial Hosp., Paterson, N.J., since 1926, as interne, 1926-27, asso. in medicine, 1927-28, clin. asst. in gynecology, 1928-37, adjunct asso. in gynecology since 1937; in gen. practice, Paterson, 1927-38, practice limited to surgery since 1938. Diplomate Nat. Bd. of Med. Examiners; fellow A.M.A. Jewish religion. Author: Home Book of Medicine, 1938. Contbr. to Country Home Mag., Jour. Am. Med. Assn., Archives of Surgery and other med., maritime and popular periodicals. Address: 555 E. 27th St., Paterson, N.J.

POMEROY, Daniel Eleazer, banker; b. Troy, Pa., May 13, 1868; s. Newton Merrick and Annice Amelia (Davison) P.; ed. Greylock Inst. and Rochester Business Coll.; m. Frances Morse, June 18, 1895 (dec.); m. 2d, Trevania Dallas Blair-Smith, Feb. 4, 1937. With Liberty Nat. Bank, New York, 1898; asst. treas. Bankers Trust Co., 1903-04, treas., 1904-08; elected v.p., 1908, dir., 1911; resigned as v.p., 1922, but retains directorship; dir. Am. Brake Shoe & Foundry Co., Bucyrus-Erie Co. Major Am. Red Cross, World War. Mem. Rep. Nat. Com. from N.J. Trustee Am. Mus. Natural History. Mem. Pennsylvania Soc. Presbyn. Clubs: Union League, Nat. Republican, Down Town Assn., Boone and Crockett, Aldecress Country, Wilderness, Englewood, Deepdale, Nat. Golf Links of America, Links Golf, Santee, Knickerbocker Country, Rolling Rock, Links. Home: Englewood, N.J. Office: 230 Park Ave., New York, N.Y.

POND, James B(urton); b. N.Y. City, Dec. 25, 1889; s. Maj. James B(urton) and Martha Marion (Glass) P.; ed. Hasbrouck Inst., Jersey City, N.J., and Cornell U.; m. Abbie Gregory Clarke, Aug. 20, 1919; children—Barbara Huntington, Jean Woodford, James Burton. Editor of "Program" magazine; head of Pond Lecture Bureau (which was established by father 1873) more than 30 yrs.; managed Am. Tours for Sir Rabindranath Tagore, Maurice Maeterlinck, Lord Dunsany, John Galsworthy, Philip Gibbs, John Masefield, "Ian Hay," Helen Keller, Mrs. Pankhurst, Jerome K. Jerome, W. B. Yeats, Sir George H. Reid, Ruth Draper, William Beebe, General Mitchell, Rear Admiral Byrd, Dr. Annie Besant, George W. Russell, etc. U.S. Army, attached to hdqrs., Camp Dix, N.J., 1918. Fellow Soc. American Magicians, Royal Geog. Soc.; member New York Zoölogical Society (life), Sigma Nu. Republican. Presbyn. Clubs: Nat. Arts (life), Circumnavigators (pres.), Adventurers, Dutch Treat, Town Hall. Contbr. to mags. on travel and distinguished people. Traveled extensively in the Far East. Home: "Rock Ridge," Denville, N.J. Office: 2 W. 45th St., New York, N.Y.*

PONS, Carlos A., physician; b. San Juan, Puerto Rico, Mar. 24, 1896; s. Jose and Mercedes (Escalone) P.; ed. Instituto Jose de Diego, 1914-15, Jefferson Med. Coll., (pre-med.), 1915-16; M.D., Jefferson Med. Coll., 1920; m. Dr. Sara C. de Pons, Sept. 17, 1919. Pathologist Fitkin Memorial Hosp. (Neptune, N.J.), Monmouth Memorial Hospital (Long Branch, N.J.). Fellow Am. Coll. Physicians, A.M.A., Am. Soc. Clin. Pathologists. Republican. Contbr. articles on clin. pathology to med. jours. Home: Allenhurst, N.J. Office: 501 Grand Av., Asbury Park, N.J.

PONTIUS, S. Gilmore, M.D., surgeon; b. Martinsburg, Pa., Jan. 27, 1892; s. John Wesley and Mary Ida (Apple) P.; prep. edn., Mercersburg Acad.; Ph.B., Franklin & Marshall Coll., 1914; M.D., U. of Pa., 1918; grad. work at University of Minnesota Graduate Sch.; honorary degree of Sc.D.; m. Helen Booth Holman, Apr. 5, 1924; children—John, Paul, Helen, Joseph. Began practice of surgery, 1922; surgeon Lancaster Gen. Hosp., 1922-36, chief surg. staff since 1936; consulting surgeon Cripple Children's Hosp., Elizabeth, Pa.; visiting surgeon Lancaster County Hosp., St. Joseph's Hosp.; dir. Fulton Nat. Bank, Lancaster. Trustee Franklin & Marshall Coll. Certified by Am. Bd. Surgery. Fellow Am. Coll. Surgeons; pres. Lancaster City and County Med. Soc., 1937. Mem. Reformed Ch. Clubs: Hamilton, University, Lancaster Country (Lancaster). Home: R.F.D. No. 5. Office: 320 N. Lime St., Lancaster, Pa.

PONTZER, Robert Francis, lawyer; b. Kersey, Pa., June 13, 1904; s. Peter J. and Elizabeth (Kronenwetter) P.; ed. Pa. State Coll., 1923-24, Georgetown U., 1924-25; LL.B., Georgetown U. Law Sch., 1928; A.B., George Washington U., 1929; m. Bertha Friery, Nov. 30, 1933; children—Robert Friery, Peter J. Friery. Admitted to bar of D.C., 1928 and practiced law in Washington, as mem. firm Lynch & Pontzer, 1928-29; in practice at Ridgway, Pa., since 1930; mem. firm Barbour & Pontzer since 1935; dir. Community Loan Co. of Dubois, Pa., Ridgway Nat. Bank, Elk Bldg. & Loan Assn., Peoples Bldg. & Loan Assn. Served as mem. Sch. Bd. Fox Twp., 1930-36. Chmn. Young Reps. of Elk Co., 1936-37; Rep. Co. Chmn., 1938-39. Mem. Pa. and Elk Co. bar assns., Phi Beta Gamma. Republican. Roman Catholic. K.C. B.P.O.E. Moose. Granger. Clubs: Kiwanis (pres. 1933, dir. since 1933), Elk County Country Club. Home: 524 Hyde Av. Office: Masonic Bldg., Ridgway, Pa.

POOL, Joseph Henry, III, insurance; b. Haverford, Pa., May 20, 1898; s. Sidney H. and Annie A. (Alexander) P.; student DeLancy Prep. Sch., Lower Merion High Sch. and Pa. Mil. Coll.; m. Marion Weckesser, Jan. 12, 1924; children—Joseph Henry, IV, Fred Weckesser, Nancy Eleanor. Gen. agt. The Fidelity & Casualty Co. of N.Y., Wilkes-Barre, Pa. Served as 2d lt., Inf., U.S. Army, during World War. Chmn. Luzerne Co. Rep. Com.; del. to Rep. Nat. Conv., 1936. Trustee Pa. Mil. Coll.; sch. dir. Kingston Borough (Pa.), Hillman Acad., Wilkes-Barre Female Inst. Mem. Am. Legion. Mason (Shriner, trustee Irem Temple). Clubs: Westmoreland, Irem Temple Country, Wyoming Valley Country, Brodhead Hunting and Fishing (Wilkes-Barre); Merion Cricket (Haverford); Triton, Bourbonnais (Canada). Home: 160 Butler St., Kingston, Pa. Office: 220 Brooks Bldg., Wilkes-Barre, Pa.

POOLE, DeWitt Clinton, diplomat, educator; b. Vancouver Barracks, Washington, Oct. 28, 1885; s. DeWitt Clinton and Maria Woodward (Pettes) P.; A.B., Univ. of Wis., 1906; M. Dip., George Washington University, 1910; LL. D., Univ. of Delaware, 1934; m. Mrs. Rachel Simmons Blanding, Sept. 1, 1920; stepson, Alan Cornell. Entered consular service, Dec. 20, 1910; vice-consul at Berlin, Germany, 1911-14, vice-consul, Paris, 1914-15; duty Dept. of State, 1915-17; promoted consul, July 1916, and assigned to Moscow, July 1917; apptd. spl. asst. to Am. ambassador in Russia, Oct. 1918; Am. chargé d'affaires in Russia, Nov. 1918-June 1919; apptd. chief Div. of Russian Affairs, State Dept., Oct. 1, 1919; promoted consul gen. Nov. 23, 1921. Mem. tech. staff Conf. on Limitation of Armament, 1921-22. Apptd. consul gen. at Cape Town, Oct. 1, 1923; apptd. counselor embassy, Berlin, Jan. 1926, resigned, 1930; chmn. advisory bd. Sch. of Pub. Affairs, Princeton, 1930-32, dir. since 1933. Fellow Am. Geog. Soc. Mem. Council on Foreign Relations, Inst. of Pacific Relations, Academie Diplomatique Internationale, Chi Psi, etc. Clubs: Century, Princeton (New York); Metropolitan (Washington); Nassau (Princeton). Author: Democracy and the Conduct of Foreign Relations. Editor of The Public Opinion Quarterly. Home: Princeton, N.J.

POOLE, John, banker; b. Parkersburg, W.Va., May 17, 1875; s. Nathan Algernon and Lillian Agnes (DeCamp) P.; ed. commercial coll. and

Am. Inst. of Banking, Washington, D.C.; m. Frances Barber, July 12, 1921; children—Marjorie Ann, (by previous marriage) John L., Nathan and Thomas S. Clerk and cashier United States Express Co., Washington, 1890-98; mem. firm Reeves, Poole & Co., 1898-1900; with Washington Loan & Trust Co., 1900-1908; asst. cashier Nat. City Bank, 1908-09; cashier Commercial Nat. Bank, 1909-13; pres. Federal Nat. Bank, 1913-22; pres. Federal-American National Bank, 1922-33, and past pres. Stockholders' Association, Federal Reserve Bank of Richmond; mem. Federal Advisory Council, representing Fifth Federal Reserve Dist., 1929-31; now pres. The American Co., realtors; mem. bd. dirs. Chesapeake & Potomac Telephone Company. Chmn. Liberty Loan Com., Washington, 5 campaigns; former treas. Dist. Council of Defense, Roosevelt Memorial Assn. (for Washington), European Relief Council; chmn. Nat. Budget Com. for D.C.; treas. Columbia Instn. for the Deaf, D.C. Memorial Commn., Southeastern U., Y.M.C.A.; trustee American U., Washington, D.C.; ex-pres. D.C. Bankers Assn., Washington Chapter Am. Inst. Banking. Pres. Internat. Assn. Rotary Clubs, 1918-19. Republican. Episcopalian. Mason (32°, Shriner), Odd Fellow. Clubs: Rotary (ex-pres.), Columbia Country. Home: 17 E. Woodbine St., Chevy Chase, Md. Office: 807 15th St. N.W., Washington, D.C.

POOLE, William, VI, lawyer; b. Baltimore, Md., June 12, 1908; s. Edward Gilpin and Louise Caroline (Fahnestock) P.; student Tower Hill Sch., Wilmington, Del., 1923-26; A.B. (with high honors in social sciences), Swarthmore (Pa.) Coll., 1930; A.B. in jurisprudence, Oxford U., Eng., 1932, B.C.L., 1933; m. Louise Hemstreet Hiller, Sept. 11, 1935; 1 son, William VII. Admitted to Del. bar, 1934, and since in pvt. practice at Wilmington, Del. Prothonotary, New Castle Co., Del., 1936-37; asst. city solicitor, Wilmington, Del., since 1939. Mem. Am. Bar Assn., Del. State Bar Assn., Phi Beta Kappa, Phi Delta Theta, Delta Sigma Rho. Received Rhodes Scholarship from State of Del., 1930. Republican. Presbyterian. Elk. Club: Knights of the Round Table (Wilmington, Del.). Home: 1403 N. Grant Av. Office: 320 Citizens Bank Bldg., Wilmington, Del.

POOLEY, Joseph Earle, headmaster; b. Kingston, Pa., June 13, 1889; s. Martin and Fanny (Campbell) P.; A.B., Harvard U., 1911; A.M., Drew Univ., Madison, N.J., 1934; m. Gertrude Hobbes, June 30, 1917. Engaged in teaching, high sch., Dorranceton, Pa., 1915-17, Wyoming Sem., Kingston, Pa., 1917-19; asso. with Madison Acad., Madison, N.J., since 1919, headmaster since 1919, vice-pres. and treas. since 1922; spl. lecturer in English and dir. of debate, Brothers Coll., Drew Univ. since 1934. Served as pvt. inf., U.S.A., Camp Wadsworth, S.C., 1917-19. Served on Borough Council, 1929-39, pres. council since 1937. Mem. Headmasters Assn., Tau Kappa Alpha. Republican. Methodist. Clubs: Rotary, Wranglers (Madison); Harvard of New Jersey. Home: 14 Academy Rd. Office: Madison Academy, Madison, N.J.

POORE, Henry Rankin, artist; b. Newark, N.J., Mar. 21, 1859; grad. U. of Pa., 1883. Studied art at Pa. Acad. and Nat. Acad. of Design, New York; pupil of Peter Moran, Lumenais and Bouguereau; m. Katharine Stevens, June 1896. His specialty is a combination of figures with animals; has received prizes at Nat. Acad. and Am. Art Assn.; medals, Buffalo and St. Louis expns.; gold medal, Internat. Expn., Buenos Aires; silver medal, Panama P.I. Expn., 1915; purchase prize Nat. Gallery of New Zealand. A.N.A.; mem. Internat. Soc. Arts and Letters, Delta Phi (U. of Pa.). Clubs: Salmagundi, Lotos, Nat. Arts (New York); Art (Phila.); Am. Artists Professional League, Art Center of Orange, New England Soc. (past pres.), Authors Club of North Jersey (pres.). Author: Pictorial Composition and the Critical Judgment of Pictures, 1903; The Conception of Art, 1913; The New Tendency in Art, 1915; Art Principles in Practice, 1929; Modern Art—Why, What and How, 1931; Thinking Straight on Modern Art, 1934; Arts Place in Education, 1937. Home: 61 Ridge St., Orange, N.J.

POPE, Bentley H(erbert), bond broker; b. Trenton, N.J., Oct. 7, 1881; s. John May and Matilda (Downs) P.; grad. Trenton (N.J.) High Sch., 1899; m. Madeline Kuser, Nov. 17, 1909; children—Mary Madeline (Mrs. Thomas Maddock), Eileen Charlotte. Began as clerk, Mercer Pottery Co.; successively runner in Wall St.; clerk Spery Hulchinson Co., N.J., asst. Stock Exchange House; organized Bentley H. Pope, Inc., investment securities, Trenton, N.J., 1926. Chmn. Finance Co., Trinity Cathedral, Diocese of N.J. Clubs: Trenton, Trenton Country (pres.). Home: 947 Berkley Av. Office: 28 W. State St., Trenton, N.J.

POPE, Clifford Hillhouse, explorer, naturalist, author; b. Washington, Ga., Apr. 11, 1899; s. Mark Cooper and Harriet Alexander (Hull) P.; student U. of Ga., Athens, 1916-18; B.S., U. of Va., 1921; m. Sarah Haydock Davis, Sept. 8, 1928; children—Alexander Hillhouse, Hallowell, Whitney. Herpetologist, Chinese div., Central Asiatic Expdns., Am. Museum of Natural History, New York, 1921-26, asst. dept. of herpetology, 1926-27, asst. curator, dept. of herpetology, 1928-34; engaged in writing books on natural history since 1935. Fellow A.A.A.S.; mem. Am. Soc. Icthyologists and Herpetologists (pres., 1935-36), Boy Scouts of America (hon.), Chi Phi. Author: The Reptiles of China, 1935; Snakes Alive and How They Live, 1937; Turtles of the United States and Canada, 1939; also numerous tech. and popular articles on reptiles and amphibians. Home: 15 Charles Pl., Chatham, N.J.

POPE, Francis Horton, army officer; b. Fort Leavenworth, Kan., May 7, 1876; s. John (maj. gen., U.S.A.) and Clara Pomeroy (Horton) P.; grad. U.S. Mil. Acad., 1897; grad. École de l'Intendance, Paris, 1914, Army War Coll., 1924; m. Harriet Ankeny, Oct. 20, 1908; 1 dau., Mary Ankeny; m. 2d, Blanche Wilson Hampson, Sept. 27, 1924. Commd. 2d lt. Cav., U.S.A., 1897; promoted through grades to col., July 1, 1920; apptd. asst. q.m.gen., Jan. 24, 1927, with rank of brig. gen., term of 4 yrs.; served in Cuba, Spanish-Am. War; with Army of Cuban Occupation, 1899; instr. mathematics, U.S. Mil. Acad., 1899-1903; Philippine campaigns, 1903-05; Mexican Punitive Expdn., 1916; lt. col. and col. (temp.), in France, World War, 1917-19; dir. Motor Transport Service, A.E.F., Feb.-Aug. 1918; dep. dir. Motor Transport Corps, Aug. 1918-Aug. 1919. Mem. Mil. Order World War, Soc. Army of Santiago de Cuba, Soc. Moro Campaigns, Mil. Order Loyal Legion, Am. Legion. Decorated D.S.M. (U.S.); Officer Legion of Honor (French). Episcopalian. Clubs: Metropolitan, Army and Navy, Chevy Chase. Address: Schuylkill Arsenal, Philadelphia, Pa.

POPE, Frederick Allan; dist. judge Somerset County. Address: Somerville, N.J.

POPLE, Harry Earl, real estate and mortgage counselor; b. Fairmont, W.Va., Nov. 7, 1890; s. John Stephen and Missouri (Hawkins) P.; student Fairmont State Normal Sch., 1903-06, Fairmont Business College Night School, 1906-09; m. Emma Jo Queen, Nov. 30, 1926; children—Joanne Lee, Harry Earle. Bank clerk, Fairmont, W.Va., 1906-09; in real estate and fire insurance business for himself, Fairmont, 1909-10; served in U.S. Army, 1910-13; commercial traveler, 1914-17; asst. mgr. in father's dept. store, 1917-19; partner Harrison Co. Real Estate Co., Clarksburg, W.Va., 1919-21; his own real estate business, Clarksburg, W.Va., 1921-29; mortgage and loan supervisor for Equitable Life Assurance Soc., Pittsburgh, 1929-32; in real estate and loan business since 1932; real estate and mortgage counselor to banks, etc., since 1934; pres. Swan Realty & Development Co.; pres. The B. P. B. Co., Inc.; gen. mgr. Realty Building Mart. Served with 14th Regular Cav., U.S. Army, in Philippines and Mexican border, 1910-13; drafted but not called to service during World War. Republican. Methodist. Home: Swan Acres, Allison Park, Route 1, Pittsburgh, Pa. Office: Bakewell Bldg., Grant St., Pittsburgh, Pa.

POPP, Henry William, prof. botany; b. Millvale Branch, Pittsburgh, Pa., Nov. 19, 1892; s. William and Emelie (Trautvetter) P.; ed. Carnegie Inst. Tech., 1912-14; B.S., Pa. State Coll., 1917, M.S., same, 1922; Ph.D., Univ. of Chicago, 1926; m. Margaret P. McElhaney, July 1, 1919; children—Mary Jean, Margaret Kathryn, Ruth Lilian. Employed as analyt. chemist, Crucible Steel Co., Pittsburgh, Pa., 1912-14; asst. zoölogy and entomology, Pa. State Coll., 1916-17; head dept. biology, Central State Normal Sch., Lock Haven, Pa., 1917-20; instr. botany, Pa. State Coll., 1920-23; asst. plant physiologist, Boyce Thompson Inst., Yonkers, N.Y., 1923-25; asst. prof. botany, Pa. State Coll., 1925-30, asso. prof., 1930-37, prof. botany since 1937. Served in O.T.C., Camp Custer, Mich., Camp Lee, Va., and Plattsburg, N.Y., 1918. Fellow A.A.A.S. Mem. Bot. Soc. America (vice-chmn. physiol. sect., 1937), Am. Soc. Plant Physiologists, Pa. Acad. Sci., Sigma Xi, Gamma Sigma Delta, Phi Kappa Phi. Asso. Nat. Research Council. Lutheran. Mason. Home: 417 E. Adams Av., State College, Pa.

PORKESS, William, clergyman; b. Grimsby, Eng., Dec. 31, 1876; s. Uriah and Eliza Jane (Wilkin) P.; came to U.S., 1903, naturalized, 1917; ed. New Coll., London, Eng., 1899-1900; B.A., Victoria Univ., Manchester, Eng., 1903; (hon.) D.D., U. of Pittsburgh, 1922; m. Helen Halstead Frost, Dec. 27, 1906. Ordained to ministry P.E. Ch., deacon, 1908, priest, 1909; asst. St. Andrews Ch., N.Y. City, 1908, Grace Ch., 1909; asst. St. Paul's Ch., New Haven, Conn., 1909-11, Calvary, Pittsburgh, Pa., 1912; rector, Grace Ch., Pittsburgh, Pa., 1913-19; rector, St. Stephen's Ch., Wilkinsburg, Pa., since 1919. Republican. Episcopalian. Mason. Clubs: Rotary (Wilkinsburg); Junta (Pittsburgh). Author: Handbook for Use Among Teachers of Bible Classes, 1912; Studies in Camouflage, 1919; Tithing—A Starter On The Glorious Journey of Giving, 1925; Prayer and Perspective, 1926; Man in the Remaking, 1927; Daily Lenten Thoughts, 1928-35. Home: 508 Franklin Av., Wilkinsburg, Pa.

PORTER, Frederick Stanley, lawyer; b. Princess Anne, Md., Apr. 6, 1890; s. Twilley C. and Florence (Long) P.; A.B., Washington Coll., Chestertown, Md., 1912; LL.B., Washington and Lee U. Law Sch., Lexington, Va., 1916; (hon.) A.M., Washington Coll., 1917; m. Agnes C. James, Sept. 4, 1920; 1 son, Frederick Stanley, Jr. Admitted to Md. bar, 1916, and since engaged in gen. practice of law at Baltimore; instr. U. of Baltimore Law Sch. since 1935; mem. Commrs. of Opening Streets of Baltimore since 1935. Served as sergt., U.S.A., during World War. Mem. bd. visitors and govs. of Washington Coll., Chestertown, Md. Mem. Baltimore City, Md. and Am. bar assns.; Sigma Pi Epsilon. Republican. Episcopalian. Home: 4407 Underwood Rd. Office: Calvert Bldg., Baltimore, Md.

PORTER, Henry Joshua, telephone engring.; b. Windsor Locks, Conn., Nov. 15, 1880; s. Charles Austin and Melissa E. (Denslow) P.; E.E., Cornell U., 1905; m. Inez Philippa Pheland, Sept. 14, 1907; children—Charles Irving, Daphne, Inez Philippa. Employed as student telephone engr., N.Y. & N.J. Telephone Co., 1905-06; engring. asst. N.Y. Telephone Co., 1906-27; asst. engr., N.J. Bell Telephone Co., Newark, since 1927. Served as mem. Montclair Battn., 1917-18. Active in Boy Scout work; awarded Scouters Key and Silver Beaver of Boy Scouts of America. Mem. Telephone Pioneers, Montclair Soc. Engrs. Republican. Presbyn. Clubs: Cornell of Essex County (Newark); Deer Lake (Boonton). Home: 11 Wendover Rd., Montclair, N.J. Office: 540 Broad St., Newark, N.J.

PORTER, Horace Chamberlain, cons. chem. engr.; b. Urbana, Ill., July 13, 1876; s. Jasper W. and Clara J. (Chamberlain) P.; A.B., U. of Ill., 1897, M.S., 1900; Ph.D., Harvard U., 1903; m. Helen Pickard Dana, June 16, 1909; children—Mary Pickard, Robert Chamberlain. Chemist Solvay Process Co., Syracuse, N.Y., 1903-07; chem. engr. U.S. Bur. of Mines, Pittsburgh, 1907-15; chem. engr. Koppers Co., Pittsburgh, 1915-17; chem. engr. and consultant in gas and fuels since 1919; lecturer, U. of Pa.,

1928-29. Capt., Ordnance Dept., U.S. Army, 1917-19. Mem. Am. Chem. Soc. (councillor; past. chmn. div. of gas and fuels), Am. Inst. Chem. Engrs., Phi Lambda Upsilon (co-founder, ex-pres.). Republican. Episcopalian. Clubs: Engineers (Phila.); Appalachian Mountain. Author: Coal Carbonization, 1924. Contbr. Encyclopedia Britannica, Mark's Mech. Engrs. Handbook, bulletins and papers relative to coal, gasmaking, spontaneous combustion, explosion hazards, etc. Home: 3120 W. Penn St., Germantown. Office: 1833 Chestnut St., Philadelphia, Pa.

PORTER, James Marsh, cigar mfr.; b. Malden, Mass., Jan. 27, 1886; s. Dwight and Alice C. (Marsh) P.; B.S., Dartmouth, 1910; C.E., Thayer Sch. of Civil Engring., 1911; m. Melen B. Orr, Oct. 16, 1912; children—Ruth Orr, Barbara Louise. Asso. with Waitt & Bond, Inc., cigar mfrs., Newark, N.J., continuously since 1913, supt., then vice-pres., gen. mgr., now pres. and dir.; also pres. Congress Cigar Co., Porto Rican American Tobacco Co. to 1938. Mem. Theta Delta Chi. Republican. Clubs: Golf (Montclair); Athletic (Newark). Home: 3 Russell Terrace, Montclair, N.J. Office: 310 Sherman Av., Newark, N.J.

PORTER, James Wilson, Jr., real estate business; b. Sewickley, Pa., Dec. 18, 1870; s. James Wilson and Martha (Ebbert) P.; ed. prep. sch.; grad. Princeton, 1893. Began business career in mfg. business and later changed to real estate; pres. and dir. Porter and MacDowell Co. Clubs: Duquesne (Pittsburgh); Allegheny Country (Sewickley). Home: 406 Peebles St., Sewickley, Pa. Office: 345 4th Av., Pittsburgh, Pa.

PORTER, John Jermain, mfr. cement; b. Washington, D.C., June 14, 1880; s. Jermain Gildersleeve and Emily Starrett (Snowden) P.; B.S., U. of Cincinnati, 1901; m. Edith Louise Frazer, June 10, 1908; children—Jermain Doty, Louise Snowden (Mrs. Wendell Thomas). Chemist, foreman and supt. in iron and steel industry, 1901-06; asst. prof. chemistry, U. of Cincinnati, 1907-11; cons. metall. engr., 1911-12; v.p. and gen. mgr. Security Cement & Lime Co. and North Am. Cement Corpn., 1913-32; pres. latter since 1932; dir. Porter Chem. Co., Nicodemus Nat. Bank of Hagerstown. Cons. on potash to Bur. of Mines and War Industries Bd., World War. Trustee Hagerstown Pub. Library. Mem. Md. Acad. Science. Republican. Methodist. Clubs: Engineers (New York); Fort Orange (Albany, N.Y.). Home: 1199 The Terrace, Hagerstown, Md. Office: 285 Madison Av., New York, N.Y.

PORTER, Newton H.; asso. justice Supreme Court of N.J. Home: Montclair, N.J.

PORTER, William Stuart, retired banker; b. Yonkers, N.Y., Jan. 24, 1866; s. William Dodge and Alexine Mifflin (Coulter) P.; student pub. and pvt. schs., Orange, N.J., 1876-79, Greylock Inst., S. Williamstown, Mass., 1879-80, pub. sch., Baltimore, Md., 1880-81, Baltimore City Coll., 1881-82; grad. Chautauqua Literary & Scientific Circle (home work), 1887; m. Alice Matilda Reisig, May 15, 1909. With St. John-Kirkham & Co., and St. John-Kirkham Shoe Co., New York, 1883-99, successively office boy entry clerk, asst. cashier, cashier, asst. treas. and treas.; partner Stone & Porter, wholesale shoes, New York, 1900-04; pvt. auditing, New York, 1905-06; accountant in comptroller's office, U.S. Steel Corpn., New York, 1907-13; sec.-treas. Summit (N.J.) Trust Co., 1913-24, sec. 1924-37, v.p., 1925-37; sec. Summit (N.J.) Bldg. & Loan Assn. (charter mem. 1891), 1896-1927, treas., 1928-39, dir. 1900-38; now retired. Mem. Y.M.C.A. (charter mem. 1886; dir. 1900-39). Republican. Presbyn. Address: 30 Hawthorne Pl., Summit, N.J.

PORTERFIELD, Allen Wilson, coll. prof.; b. Bedington, W.Va., Aug. 30, 1878; s. Alexander Robinson and Susan Virginia (Small) P.; A.B., W.Va. U., 1900, A.M., 1901; studied Berlin, Munich and Copenhagen; Ph.D., Columbia, 1911; m. Elsie de Valois Chesley, Sept. 7, 1915; children—Allen Wilson, Joseph Arthur, Erik Adolph. Instr. Germanic langs. and lits., U. of W.Va., 1901-05; Carl Schurz fellow in German, Columbia, 1905-06; instr. in German, Columbia, 1907-17; 1st lt. A.S.S.C., U.S.A., Sept. 10, 1917-July 1, 1919; editorial staff New York Evening Post, 1919-22; prof. German, Randolph-Macon Woman's Coll., 1922-24; prof. German, W.Va. U. since 1924. Mem. Modern Language Assn. America, Linguistic Soc. America, Society for Advancement of Scandinavian Studies, Kleist Gesellschaft, Delta Phi Alpha, Phi Beta Kappa, Phi Kappa Psi, Scabbard and Blade. Democrat. Methodist. Author: Karl Lebrecht Immermann, 1911; Outline of German Romanticism, 1914. Translator: The Goose Man, 1922; Power of a Lie, 1923; Oberlin's Three Stages and Other Stories; Wolfgang Goethe; The Soul of the Moving Picture—all 1924. Editor: Modern German Stories, 1927, Arthur Schnitzler—Stories and Plays, 1929. Contbr. to numerous mags. Home: 286 Convent Av., New York, N.Y. Address: Morgantown, W.Va.

PORTNOFF, Alexander, sculptor and artist; b. Russia, Jan. 1, 1887; s. Esaia and Edith (Schapochnik) P.; came to U.S., 1908 and naturalized citizen, 1915; A.B. in Architecture, Odessa (Russia) Sch. Fine Arts, 1906; ed. Pa. Acad. Fine Arts, 1910; travelling scholarship in Europe, 1912-13; m. Marie Florence Brustin. 1920. Engaged in sculpture and painting since 1915. Represented in Allentown (Pa.) Mus., Milwaukee Art Inst., Brooklyn Mus. of Art, Phila. Coll. of Pharmacy and Sci., Phila. Mus. of Art, South Phila. High Sch., Atlanta (Ga.) Univ., Mus. of Western Art, Moscow, U.S.S.R. Honor Award, Panama Pacific Internatl. Exposition, San Francisco, 1915. Dir. Am.-Russian Inst. Mem. Nat. Sculpture Soc. Studio: 908 Clinton St., Philadelphia, Pa.; and High Point, Long Beach Island, N.J.

PORTS, Earl George, engr.; b. Hanover, Pa., Aug. 14, 1901; s. Lloyd J. and Sallie Anne (Humbert) P.; student Hanover (Pa.) High Sch., 1915-19, Bell Telephone Labs. (out-of-hour courses), 1925-29; B.S. in E.E., Gettysburg (Pa.) Coll., 1923, M.S. in Physics, 1925; m. Virginia Hope Goldsmith, Apr. 30, 1927; 1 dau., Joan Dorothy. Undergrad. instr., Gettysburg (Pa.) Coll., 1920-23, grad. instr., 1923-25; research engr. Bell Telephone Labs., N.Y. City, 1925-29; communication engr. Internat. Communication Labs., N.Y. City, 1929-31; chief engr. Federal Telegraph Co., Newark, N.J., since 1931. Mem. R.O.T.C., 1919-23. Mem. Inst. Radio Engrs., Am. Inst. E.E., Phi Kappa Rho. Republican. Mem. Reformed Ch. Holder misc. patents of radio communication apparatus. Home: 325 E. Mt. Pleasant Av., Livingston, N.J. Office: 200 Mt. Pleasant Av., Newark, N.J.

PORTSER, Robert Kay, lawyer; b. Greensburg, Pa., Sept. 21, 1871; s. Levi and Isabella (Cochran) P.; student Greensburg (Pa.) pub. schs. and Indiana (Pa.) State Normal Sch.; A.B., Princeton U., 1894; read law in offices of Marchand & Gaither, later Marchand, Gaither & Woods, later Gaither & Woods; m. Eleanor Nevada Null, July 28, 1923. Admitted to Westmoreland Co. (Pa.) bar, July 1897; asso. with Gaither & Woods, later Gaither & Whitten; in gen. practice as mem. firm Gaither, Portser & McConnell, Greensburg, Pa., 1921-Oct. 1, 1938, when firm succeeded by Portser, Gregg & McConnell (present firm lineal successor to Marchand & Marchand, established 1840, and one of oldest continuous legal firms in Westmoreland Co.); solicitor Pa. R.R. Co.; counsel Westmoreland Coal Co., Pittsburgh Coal Co., The Peoples Natural Gas Co., Greensburg Coal & Coke Co., The Employers Group (ins. carriers). Served with Co. I, 10th Regt., Pa. N.G., during Spanish-Am. War and Philippine Insurrection, on Luzon Island, in and about Manila, participating in all engagements of regt., one yr. Dir. Greensburg (Pa.) Sch. Bd. six yrs., Y.M.C.A. eight yrs. Mem. Pa. Bar Assn., Westmoreland Law Assn., Vets. Foreign Wars, United Spanish War Vets. Presbyn. (trustee First Ch., Greensburg, Pa., five yrs.). Mason (32°; dist. dep. grand master 30th Dist., Pa., 25 yrs.). Home: The Penn Albert Hotel. Office: First Nat. Bank Bldg., Greensburg, Pa.

POSEY, Thomas Edward, coll. prof.; b. Washington, D.C., June 9, 1901; s. William and Minnie P.; A.B., Syracuse Univ., 1923, A.M., 1925; grad. student O. State U., 1935-36; m. Julia Anita Sumter, Aug. 17, 1930 (died 1932); 1 dau., Barbara Ann; m. 2d, Claudie Mae Wells, July 17, 1935; 1 dau., Thomasena Ellen. Instr. econs., W.Va. State Coll., Institute, W.Va., 1925-27, asst. prof., 1927-32, asso. prof. since 1932; instr. econs., Federal Govt. Workers Edn. Sch., summer 1935; tech. adviser, W.P.A. Research Project on negroes in W.Va., summer 1934. Sec. W.Va. Negro Welfare Assn. Mem. Am. Econ. Assn., Southern Econ. Assn., Alpha Phi Alpha, W.Va. Hist. Soc. (hon.). Democrat. Methodist. Club: Mid West Chess of Institute (sec.). Home: Institute, W.Va.

POST, A. H. S., pres. Mercantile Trust Co. Address: 200 E. Redwood St., Baltimore, Md.

POST, Claude C., mechant; b. Butler, N.J., Apr. 11, 1895; s. George R. and Emma F. (Brower) P.; grad. Butler High Sch., 1914; also extension and business courses; m. Mary B. Brautigan, Oct. 5, 1922; children—Claude C., Donald George. Began in father's store, Butler, N.J., 1914-17; war service and recovering from wound, 1917-21; partner with father as Geo. R. Post & Son, gen. market, electrical appliances, 1921-38, continuing alone since death of father, 1938. Enlisted in 5th Inf., N.J. Nat. Guard, Apr. 1917, which became 114th Inf., U.S. Army; with A.E.F. 12 months; wounded and gassed; disch. Mar. 1919. Decorated Purple Heart. Past pres. Butler-Bloomingdale Chamber of Commerce. Mgr. in Morris County of Harold G. Hoffman's campaign for gov. of N.J., 1934; apptd. mil. aide to Gov. Hoffman, rank as capt.; apptd. mem. Civil Service Commn., 1936. Active in veterans' affairs; former mem. N.J. Vets. Legislative Com. Mem. Am. Legion (past comdr. Butler post), 114th Inf. Assn. (past pres.), Morris County Rep. Vets. Assn. (pres.), Vets. of Foreign Wars, Disabled Am. War Vets., Mil. Order of Purple Heart, Forty and Eight, North Jersey Vol. Firemen's Assn., Butler Fire Dept. (exempt mem.). Republican. Methodist. Mason, Elk. Home: 11 S. Gifford St. Office: 180 Main St., Butler, N.J.

POST, Harold Francis, clergyman; b. Washington, Pa., Nov. 27, 1897; s. Frank Blair and Mary Alice (McClain) P.; A.B., Washington and Jefferson Coll., 1918; S.T.M., Western Theol. Sem., Pittsburgh, Pa., 1924; (hon.) D.D., Washington and Jefferson Coll., 1938; m. Sara Emma Deitz, July 21, 1921; children—Jarvis Harold, Dorothy. Ordained to ministry Presbyn. Ch., 1924; minister, Petersburg, O., 1924-27, Wellsville, O., 1927-33, Jeannette, Pa., 1933-36; minister First Presbyn. Ch., Greensburg, Pa., since 1936. Mem. Lambda Chi Alpha. Republican. Presbyn. Mason. Clubs: Rotary, Greensburg Country. Home: 404 N. Maple Av., Greensburg, Pa.

POST, Joseph Walter, roentgenologist; b. Trenton, N.J., May 14, 1887; s. Jerrie C. and Ida E. (Dettra) P.; grad. Trenton High Sch., 1905; M.D., Hahnemann Med. Coll. and Hosp., 1909; m. Helen Gilbert Long, June 14, 1914; 1 son, Carl Thomas. Asst. roentgenologist St. Luke's Hosp., 1919, chief roentgenologist, 1919-27; asso. roentgenologist Children's Homeopathic Hosp., 1922-27; chief roentgenologist St. Luke's and Children's Hosp. since 1927; cons. roentgenologist Wm. McKinley Memorial Hosp., Trenton, N.J., since 1922, Womens Homeopathic Hosp., Philadelphia, since 1922. Fellow Am. Coll. Physicians, Am. Coll. Chest Physicians; mem. A.M.A., Philadelphia Co. Med. Soc. (chmn. Commn. on Med. Economics 1936-38), Pa. State Med. Soc., Am. Inst. Homeopathy, Philadelphia County Homeopathic Soc. (pres. 1938), Pa. State Homeopathic Soc. (2d v.p. 1934), Radiological Soc. North America, Philadelphia Roentgen Ray Soc., Oxford Med. Club (pres. 1934-35), Germantown Med. Club (sec. 1926; pres. 1931); diplomate Am. Bd. Radiology. Republican. Episcopalian. Club: Penn Athletic. Writer scientific articles. Home: Glenview Av., Wynecote, Pa. Office: 1930 Chestnut St., Philadelphia, Pa.

POST, Levi Arnold, prof. Greek; b. Stanfordville, N.Y., July 8, 1889; s. Isaac Rushmore and Mary Lydia (Arnold) P.; prep. edn., Oakwood Sem., Union Springs, N.Y., 1903-07; A.B., A.M., Haverford (Pa.) Coll., 1911; A.M.,

Harvard, 1912; A.B., Rhodes Scholar, New Coll., Oxford U., Eng., 1916, A.M., 1922; grad. study U. of Caen, France, 1919; m. Grace Hutcheson Lickely, Oct. 4, 1919; children—Robert Lickely, Arnold Rae, Jenifer Anne. Teacher mathematics, Moses Brown School, Providence, R.I., 1912-13; with Ambulance Americaine, Neuilly-sur-Seine, France, 1915; sec. Y.M.C.A. with Brit. Expeditionary Force, Mesopotamia, 1916-17; instr. in French and German, Haverford Coll., 1917-18; served as pvt., corpl. and sergt. inf., later with Censor and Press Co., school detachment, Caen, May 1918-July 1919; instr. in Greek, Haverford Coll., 1919-22, asst. prof., 1922-28, asso. prof., 1928-33, now prof. Guggenheim fellow for year 1932. Mem. Am. Philol. Assn. (sec.-treas. 1935; editor 1935-38), Linguistic Soc. of America, Phi Beta Kappa. Democrat. Quaker. Translator: Thirteen Epistles of Plato, 1925; Menander—Three Plays, 1929. Contbr. to Quarterly Rev., Hibbert Jour., Classical Quarterly, Classical Philology, Am. Jour. of Philology, etc. Author: The Vatican Plato and its Relations, 1934. Home: 9 College Lane, Haverford, Pa.

POST, Robert Cox, pres. Post-McCord Co.; b. Jersey City, N.J., Oct. 6, 1877; s. Andrew Jackson and Margaret (Combe) P.; student Stevens Sch., Hoboken, N.J., 1889-94; M.E., Stevens Inst. Tech., Hoboken, N.J., 1898, D.Eng. (hon.), 1938; m. Elizabeth Dixon, Jan. 19, 1904; children—Robert Cox, Margaret (Mrs. William H. Pierson, Jr.). Engr. United Gas Improvement Co., Phila., Pa., and Atlanta, Ga., 1898-1900; with Am. Bridge Co., New York, 1900-04; became sec. Post-McCord Co., steel constrn., New York, 1904, pres. since 1936; dir. and v.p. Citizens Nat. Bank & Trust Co., Englewood, N.J. Served with N.J.N.G. Trustee Stevens Inst. Tech.; mem. bd. of govs. and past pres., Englewood (N.J.) Hosp. Assn. Mem. Am. Soc. Mech. Engrs., Am. Inst. Steel Construction, Credit Assn. of Bldg. Trades of N.Y. (pres.), Chi Phi. Republican. Presbyterian. Clubs: Union League (New York); Englewood (N.J.); Knickerbocker Country (Tenafly, N.J.); Oakmont (N.C.). Home: 373 Walnut St., Englewood, N.J. Office: 101 Park Av., New York, N.Y.

POST, William Stone, architect; b. New York, May 10, 1866; s. George Browne and Alice Matilda (Stone) P.; grad. St. Mark's School, Southboro, Mass., 1884; acad. course, Columbia, 2 yrs., and course in architecture 4 yrs., Ph.B., 1890; m. Lilian M., d. Gen. John B. Hood, C.S.A., June 14, 1894; children—Marion Hood (Mrs. Thos. McC. Peters), Lilian (Mrs. Catesby L. Jones), Eleanora Robertson. Practiced with father until 1904, partner George B. Post & Sons until 1930. Works: New York Stock Exchange Bldg., Coll. City of New York, and Hotel Roosevelt, New York; Wisconsin State Capitol; Prudential and Mutual Benefit Life Ins. bldgs. of Newark, N.J.; Mt. Sinai Hosp., Cleveland; hotels Statler at Cleveland, Detroit, St. Louis, Buffalo, and Boston; Wade Park Manor and Fenway Hall, Cleveland; Olympic Hotel, Seattle; etc. Republican. Presbyn. Fellow A.I.A.; mem. Architectural League New York, New York Chapter A.I.A., Delta Psi. Clubs: Century, Union, Nat. Arts. Home: Bernardsville, N.J.

POSTEN, Hale J.; mem. law firm Posten, Glasscock & Posten. Address: Morgantown, W.Va.

POTTEIGER, Clarence Reuben (Dr.), sec.-treas. Warren-Knight Co.; b. Sinking Spring, Pa., Jan. 4, 1885; s. Charles William and Ida Susan (Ruth) P.; B.S., Pa. State Coll., 1907; D.V.M., George Washington U., 1913; m. Marie I. Koch, Oct. 10, 1917; children—Bruce Koch, Adele Ruth. Asst. chemist Pa. Dept. Agr., 1907; asst. bacteriologist and asst. chemist U.S. Dept. Agr., 1907-13; city chemist in charge sewage treatment works, Reading, Pa., 1914-17; asst. engr., later office engr., Engring. Div., Pa. Dept. Health, 1920-22; sec. Pa. State Bd. for Registration Professional Engrs. and Land Surveyors, 1922-26; sec., treas. and dir. Warren-Knight Co., surveying instrument mfrs., since 1926. Served as capt. Construction Div., U.S. Army, and asst. utilities officer, Camp Meade, Md. (in charge waterworks and sewerage), 1917-20. Mem. Sigma Alpha Epsilon. Republican. Lutheran. Mason. Club: Idle Hour Tennis. Home: 251 Sagamore Road, Brookline, Upper Darby, Pa. Office: 136 N. 12th St., Philadelphia, Pa.

POTTER, Benjamin Paul, physician; b. Russia, Jan. 25, 1899; came to U.S., 1911, naturalized; student Northwestern U., 1922-25; M.D., U. of Kan. Med. Sch., 1929; m. Mary Fraser, Dec. 23, 1936. Jr. interne St. Mary's Hosp., Kansas City, Mo., 1928-29; interne West Baltimore Gen. Hosp., 1929-30; res. phys. Eudowood Sanatorium, 1930-31; asst. phys. Johns Hopkins Hosp., 1930-31; res. phys. Hudson Co. Tuberculosis Hosp., Jersey City, N.J., 1931-38, first asst. phys. since 1938; consultant Allenwood Sanatorium; mem. med. adv. bd. Deborah Sanatorium, Browns Mills. Fellow A.M.A.; mem. Nat. Tuberculosis Assn., Am. Acad. Tuberculosis Phys., Am. Sanatorium Assn., Am. Assn. for Thoracic Surgery, Am. Heart Assn., N.J. Tuberculosis League, N.J. Med. Soc., Phi Delta Epsilon. Home: 263 Merrison St., Teaneck, N.J. Office: Hudson Co. Tuberculosis Hosp., Jersey City, N.J.

POTTER, Ellen Culver, state med. officer; b. New London, Conn., Aug. 5, 1871; d. Thomas Wells and Ellen (Culver) P.; M.D., Woman's Med. Coll. of Pa., 1903; LL.D., Rutgers U., 1936. In gen. practice of medicine, 1903-18; med. dir. woman's Coll. Hosp. (Phila.), 1918-20; chief of div. of child health, Pa. Health Dept., 1920-21; dir. bur. of children, Pa. Welfare Dept., 1921-23, sec. of welfare, Pa., 1923-27; supt. N.J. Woman's Reformatory, and State Home for Girls, 1928-30; dir. of medicine N.J. State Dept. of Instns. and Agencies since 1930. Trustee Woman's Med. Coll. of Pa. Mem. A.M.A., Am. Coll. of Physicians, Am. Psychiatric Assn., Am. Assn. of Social Workers, Am. Assn. of Univ. Women, Am. Med. Women's Assn. (ex-pres.), Am. Sociol. Assn., Am. Pub. Welfare Assn., Nat. Organization of Pub. Health Nurses, Nat. Com. Mental Hygiene, Nat. Com. on Care Transients and Homeless (chmn.), Nat. Probation Assn., Nat. Recreation Assn., N.J. Welfare Council (ex-pres.), Med. Soc. of N.J. and public welfare administration. Ind. Republican. Baptist. Clubs: College (Trenton), Business and Professional (N.J.). Contbr. of articles on sociology and penology. Home: 301 W. State St. Officer: State Office Bldg., Trenton, N.J.

POTTER, Francis Marmaduke, church official; b. Brooklyn, N.Y., Mar. 10, 1888; s. Ellis Frank and Annie Eliza (Tappen) P.; A.B., Rutgers U., New Brunswick, N.J., 1911, D.D., 1939; Rhodes scholar, Oxford U., Eng., B.A., 1911; A.M., Teachers Coll. (Columbia), 1913; student New Brunswick Theol. Sem., 1911-13; L.H.D., Hope Coll., Holland, Mich., 1927; m. Elsie Mook Burroughs, June 28, 1915; children—Francis Edward, Allen Marmaduke, Elsie June. Prin. Voorhees Coll., Vellore, S. India, 1914-17; teacher, Rutgers Prep. Sch., 1917-18; asso. sec. Bd. of Foreign Missions, Ref. Ch. in America, 1918-35, treas. since 1919, corr. sec. since 1935; mem. exec. com. Foreign Missions Conf. of N. America (chmn., 1935). Mem. Delta Upsilon, Phi Beta Kappa. Republican. Home: 129 Hillside Av., Metuchen, N.J. Office: 156 E. 5th Av., New York, N.Y.

POTTER, Henry B.; v.p. and gen. mgr. Baltimore Transit Co. Home: Chestnut Hill, Washington, Md. Office: Court Square Bldg., Baltimore, Md.

POTTER, John Wesley, supt. schs.; b. Howe Twp., Perry Co., Pa., Jan. 27, 1882; s. Samuel A. and Agnes (Bair) P.; Ph.B., Dickinson Coll., 1913; A.M., Columbia U., 1923; m. Leonora B. Hartzell, Oct. 13, 1906; m. 2d, Iowna Barber, Aug. 12, 1916. Asst. Prin. Newport, Pa., 1905-06; prin. Millerstown, 1907-08; teacher mathematics, Carlisle High Sch., 1908-12; teacher mathematics and science, Wilkes-Barre High Sch., 1913-18; head academic work and curative workshop instr., Reconstruction Div., U.S. Army Gen. Hosp. No. 3, 1918-19; prin. Carlisle High Sch., 1919-27; supt. of schs., Carlisle, Pa., since 1927. Mem. N.E.A., Am. Assn. Sch. Adminstrs., Pa. State Edn. Assn. (ex-pres. South Conv. Dist.). Republican. Methodist (mem. official bd.). Odd Fellow (Past Grand Master). Club: Kiwanis (past pres., dir.). Home: 614 Walnut St. Office: Lamberton Bldg., Carlisle, Pa.

POTTER, Kenneth Gordon, insurance, travel specialist; b. Waynesboro, Pa., Feb. 6, 1888; s. John A. and Florence (Gordon) P.; student Swarthmore (Pa.) Prep. Sch., 1903-08, Lehigh U., 1908-09; m. Catherine B. Ray, June 21, 1911; m. 2d, Ruth Binkley Shoemaker, June 28, 1924. Began as fire insurance agent, Waynesboro, Pa., 1909; in addition became agent Mutual Life Ins. Co., 1916, and qualified as mem. of Quarter Million Dollar Club, 1917-30; added steamship and tourist agency to business, 1919; still active in all three lines of business. Served as private, Med. Dept., U.S. Army, Camp Greenleaf, Ga., during World War. Sec. Waynesboro Bd. of Trade, 5 years; vice-pres. Bd. of Edn., 4 years, treas., 1 year, pres. 1 year; chmn. crippled children's work of Waynesboro Rotary Club, 12 years; dir. Pa. State Soc. for Crippled Children, 2 years; pres. Waynesboro Baseball Club, 12 years; mem. Blue Ridge League of Professional Baseball Clubs. Mem. Am. Steamship and Tourists Agts. Assn., Marine Travel Club (Phila.), Nat. Assn. Mutual Ins. Agts. (dir.). Mem. Phi Delta Theta. Republican. Mem. Dutch Reformed Ch. Mason (K.T., Shriner), Elk. Mem. Rotary Club of Waynesboro (1st pres., 1919; perfect attendance record since Aug. 1924). Home: 507 Clayton Av. Office: 39 E. Main St., Waynesboro, Pa.

POTTER, Maurice Allen, lawyer; b. Rowlesburg, W.Va., Dec. 22, 1896; s. George H. and Florence E. (May) P.; student Long Branch (N.J.) Pub. Schs.; A.B., Wesleyan U., Middletown, Conn., 1919; J.D., New York Univ., 1922; m. Irene Meyers, Mar. 26, 1923; children—Allen Meyers, Barbara Ann. Admitted to bar, 1922, and since in practice at Long Branch, N.J.; mem. of firm Potter & Fisher, Long Branch, N.J.; pres.; dir. and counsel, Long Branch (N.J.) Sewer Co.; dir. and counsel Long Branch (N.J.) Banking Co., Long Branch (N.J.) Bldg. & Loan Assn. Mem. Phi Beta Kappa, Phi Nu Theta, Phi Delta Phi. Republican. Methodist. Mason. Home: 164 Atlantic Av. Office: 495 Broadway, Long Branch, N.J.

POTTER, Philip Arthur, hydraulic and sanitary engr.; b. Palmer, Mass., Jan. 18, 1878; s. Philip Henry and Clara Maria (Murdock) P.; student Springfield (Mass.) High Sch., 1893-97, Boston (Mass.) U. Law Sch., 1899-1900; B.S., Mass. Inst. Tech., 1901; m. Melania Kunst, Nov. 23, 1912 (died 1930); children—Philip Arthur, Wanda Lorraine, Dorothy Helen. Engr. Bethlehem Steel Co., Steelton, Pa., 1901-07; engr. with Nicholas S. Hill, Jr., New York, 1907-12, 1928-31; represented foreign engrs. in New York, 1912-28; engr. Hackensack Water Co., Weehawken, N.J., 1931-36; engr. Pub. Utility Commn. of N.J. since 1936. Mem. Hohokus (N.J.) Bd. of Edn. (pres., 1927-29; v.p. since 1929). Mem. Am. Soc. M.E. Republican. Episcopalian. Built water works structures and water meter improvements. Home: 156 Sheridan Av., Hohokus, N.J. Office: 50 Church St., New York, N.Y.

POTTER, Pitman Benjamin, educator, author; b. Long Branch, N.J., Jan. 1, 1892; s. Joseph Covert and Louisa Ann (Lane) P.; A.B., Harvard, 1914, A.M., 1916, Ph.D., 1918; m. Jessie Isabelle Dalton, June 22, 1914; children—Dalton, James Lane. Harvard traveling fellow, in Europe, 1914; instr. in polit. science, Harvard, 1914-16; instr. in history, Yale, 1916-17; asso. in polit. science, U. of Ill., 1919-20; asst. prof. polit. science, U. of Wis., 1920-23, asso. prof., 1923-26, prof., 1926-32; sometimes visiting prof., U. of Chicago, Harvard, U. of Tex., U. of Calif.; prof. internat. organization, Inst. Univ. de Hautes Etudes Internationales, Geneva, 1930-31, and since 1932; lecturer, Académie du Droit International, The Hague, 1930, 38; dean Inst. of World Affairs, Mondsee, Austria, 1933; dir. summer session Students International Union, Geneva, 1934, 35; lecturer Institut des Hautes Etudes Internat., Univ. of Paris, 1935-36. With U.S. Bur. of Efficiency, 1918, Div. of Internat. Law of Carnegie Endowment for Internat. Peace, 1919; Round Table sec. Inst. of Politics, Williamstown, Mass.,

1921; Round Table leader on internat. orgn.; Nat. Conf. on Science of Politics, 1923-25; legal adviser to govt. of Ethiopia, 1935; mem. Italo-Ethiopian Arbitration Commn., May-Sept. 1935. Mem. Am. Soc. Internat. Law, Am. Polit. Science Assn., Acad. Polit. Science, Conf. of Teachers Internat. Law, Advisory Com. for Research in Internat. Law, Advisory Council of Internat. Students Union (Geneva), Phi Beta Kappa, Phi Kappa Epsilon. Club: International (Geneva). Author: Introduction to the Study of International Organization, 1922, 4th edit., 1935; The Freedom of the Seas in History, Law and Politics, 1924; International Civics (with R. L. West), 1927; This World of Nations, 1929; Manual Digest of Common International Law, 1932; The Wal Wal Arbitration, 1938. Contbr. numerous articles to Am. Jour. Internat. Law, Am. Political Science Rev., Political Service Quarterly, etc. Compiler: Peace Proposals, 1916-18, 1920; Autonomy and Federation Within Empire, 1920. Mem. bd. dirs. Geneva Research Centre. Address: 132 rue de Lausanne, Geneva, Switzerland; also 702 Broadway, Long Branch, N.J.

POTTER, Raymond Thornton, physician; b. Ellenville, N.Y., Mar. 18, 1891; s. Frank J. and Elizabeth (Penny) P.; B.S., Wesleyan U., Middletown, conn. 1913; M.D., Coll. Phys. & Surg. (Columbia), 1917; m. Margaret Rachel Smiley, July 23, 1918; children—Barbara Macomber, Janet Smiley. Interne, City Hosp., New York 1917; gen. med. practice, East Orange, N.J., 1920-28, practice of obstetrics and gynecology since 1928; mem. med. staff St. Michael's Hosp., Newark, N.J., 1921-25, St. Mary's Hosp., Orange, N.J., 1924-28, Orange (N.J.) Memorial Hosp. since 1920; attending obstetrician Orange (N.J.) Memorial Hosp. since 1934, Essex Co. Isolation Hosp., Belleville, N.J., since 1935; cons. obstetrician Vets. Memorial Hosp., Ellenville, N.Y., since 1928; dir. Med. Bldg. Corpn. Served as 1st lt., M.C., U.S. Army, 1917-19; Camp Greenleaf, Ga., 1918; evacuation hosp. No. 17, Fort Sam Houston, Tex., 1918; at Vladivostok, Siberia, Russia, 1918-19; capt., M.R.C., 1919-24. Mem. med. bd., Orange (N.J.) Memorial Hosp. (sec., 1938-40). Fellow Am. Coll. Surgeons; mem. Clin. Soc. of the Oranges, Essex Co. Med. Soc., Soc. of Surgeons of N.J., A.M.A., Delta Tau Delta. Republican. Methodist. Clubs: Deer Lake (Boonton, N.J.); Essex Co. Country (W. Orange, N.J.). Author of numerous obstet. articles for med. jours. Home: 86 Harrison St., East Orange, N.J. Office: 144 Harrison St., East Orange, N.J.

POTTER, Thomas Paine, clergyman; b. Blairstown, Ia., Oct. 27, 1875; s. Ellis Wilson and Susannah Maria (Jackson) P.; A.B., Cornell Coll., Mt. Vernon, Ia., 1905; m. Alma H. Burlingame, June 27, 1900 (died Apr. 3, 1914); children—Ruth Hannah, Paul Burlingame; m. 2d, Gertrude May Campbell, May 3, 1916; 1 son, Thomas Paine. Ordained ministry M.E. Ch., 1899; various pastorates, 1899-1914; field sec. Ia. Meth. Hosp., Des Moines, 1914-16; pastor, 1916-19; with apportionment dept. World Service Com., M.E. Ch., 1919-25; asst. editor Gen. Minutes of M.E. Ch. since 1925. Historian Upper Ia. Conf. of M.E. Ch., statistician since 1909; del. to Gen. Conf., 1928, 1st reserve delegate from Upper Iowa Conference to same, 1936. Mem. Bd. Edn., Teaneck, N.J., 1934-37, v.p., 1936-37; curator of Mus., Teaneck High Sch., 1937-38; trustee Baxter (Tenn.) Sem.; dir. Negro Hospitalization Com.; sec. Meth. Hist. Soc. of City of N.Y.; treas. Nat. Assn. of Church Statisticians. Republican. Contbg. editor Americana Ency. Supplement; contbr. Internat. Ency. Supplement, Encyclopædia Britannica Year Book, Paebar Anthology of Verse, also on religious, historical and statistical subjects, prose and verse. Home: 394 Woodbine St., Teaneck, N.J. Address: 150 5th Ave., New York, N.Y.

POTTS, Louis Roberts, county schs. supt.; b. Moundsville, W.Va., May 10, 1893; s. Charles Simpson and Blanche (Stockett) P.; A.B., O. State U., Columbus, O., 1916, B.Sc. in Edn., 1916, A.M., 1936; LL.B., Columbus Coll. of Law, Columbus, O., 1925; m. Adah Egbert Ferguson, Nov. 29, 1917; children—James Charles, Wayne Ferguson. Engaged in teaching and as prin. in O., 1916-18; prin. high sch., Parnassus, Pa., 1919-20; head social sci. dept., jr. high sch., Columbus, O., 1920-31; city supt. schs., Moundsville, W.Va., 1931-33, county supt. schs. since 1933. Served as corpl. ordnance, U.S.A., 1918-19, with A.E.F. in France. Mem. Am. Assn. Sch. Adminstrs., Pi Kappa Alpha. Republican. Methodist. Mason. Club: Rotary of Moundsville. Home: 304 Tomlinson Av., Moundsville, W.Va.

POUDER, George Harry, exec. civic assn.; b. Baltimore, Md., May 11, 1896; s. George Harry and Ellen J. (Owens) P.; grad. Baltimore City Coll. 1913; B.S., Johns Hopkins U., 1926; m. Elizabeth Cabell Noland, Oct. 6, 1928. In employ Western Md. Ry., 1914-17; reporter, Baltimore Sun, 1919; spl. writer, Baltimore Sun and Baltimore Evening Sun, 1920-30; with E. C. Geyer & Co., exporters and importers, Baltimore, 1919-20; with Export and Import Bd. of Trade, 1920-26; dir. Export and Import Bur., Baltimore Assn. of Commerce since 1926; exec. vice-pres. Baltimore Assn. of Commerce since 1930; instr. at various times in foreign trade, Johns Hopkins and U. of Md., in ocean shipping, Baltimore Coll. of Commerce, in Spanish and French, Baltimore City Coll. Night Sch. Served in U.S. Army Ambulance Corps with A.E.F. as sergt. major, interpreter, 1917-1919. Sec. Citizens Emergency Relief Com. since 1931; treas. Baltimore Emergency Relief Commn., 1933-36; mem. Baltimore Municipal Aviation Commn. (exec. com.); trade advisor Nat. Foreign Trade Council; mem. Nat. Advisory Com. on the Foreign Service, 1933. Mem. Am. Assn. Port Authorities (dir.), S.A.R., Md. Acad. Scis., Charcoal Club of Baltimore (pres. 1932-33). Baptist. Clubs: Merchants, Johns Hopkins, Baltimore Country (Baltimore). Home: 2 W. 39th St. Office: 22 Light St., Baltimore, Md.

POUND, John C., chief nose and throat dept. St. Agnes and Bon Secours hosps.; cons. rhinolaryngologist Allegheny Hosp. of Sisters of Charity, Cumberland, Md. Address: 2 W. Read St., Baltimore, Md.

POWELL, Alfred Richard, chem. engr.; b. Athens, O., Feb. 1, 1891; s. William A. and Marie (Montzheimer) P.; B.S., U. of Kan., 1914; A.M., U. of Neb., 1915; Ph.D., U. of Ill., 1918; m. Maribelle Skinner, Sept. 4, 1919; children—Norma M., Virginia C., Maribelle. Research chemist U.S. Bur. of Mines, 1919-23; with Koppers Co. since 1923, chem. engr. in engring. and construction div., 1923-34, chief chem. engr. since 1934. Served as 2d lt., Chem. Warfare Service, U.S. Army, 1918-19. Mem. Am. Chem. Soc. (chmn. gas and fuel div. 1937), Am. Gas Assn., Am. Inst. Mining Engrs., Alpha Chi Sigma, Sigma Xi, Gamma Alpha, Phi Lambda Upsilon. Republican. Presbyterian. Mason. Writer numerous papers on technology of coal, coke, gas and by-products of coal. Home: 57 Altadena Drive, Mt. Lebanon, Pa. Office: Koppers Bldg., Pittsburgh, Pa.

POWELL, Alvin Leslie, elec. engr.; b. Brooklyn, N.Y., Apr. 6, 1889; s. Alvin Treadwell and Helen Frances (Loskamp) P.; student S. Side High Sch., Rockville Centre, N.Y., 1903-06; E.E., Columbia U., 1910; m. Marjorie Du Bois, June 12, 1912; m. 2d, Rita MacArthur, May 14, 1921. Illuminating engr. Edison Lamp Works, Harrison, N.J., 1910-24, mgr. engring. dept., 1925-31, spl. rep. Internat. Gen. Elec. Co. in Europe, 1924-25, supervising engr. incandescent lamp dept. since 1931. Served as 1st lt., N.J. Militia Reserve, 1917-19, Plattsburgh Training Camp, 1916. Past pres. Glen Ridge (N.J.) Civic Forum. Fellow Am. Inst. E.E. (chmn. N.Y. sect.); mem. Illuminating Engring. Soc. (past pres.), Montclair (N.J.) Soc. of Engrs. (past pres.), Internat. Commn. on Illumination (mem. U.S. Nat. Com.), Elec. Assn. of N.Y., S.A.R., Sigma Xi. Republican. Baptist. Mason. Clubs: Columbia Univ., Architectural League (New York). Lecturer Columbia U. and New York U. Registered professional engr., N.Y. Author of numerous papers and broachures on all phases of lighting. Home: 194 Forest Av., Glen Ridge, N.J. Office: Gen. Electric Co., 570 Lexington Av., New York, N.Y.

POWELL, Edith Wood (Mrs. Humbert Borton Powell), pres. Pa. Council of Rep. Women; b. Germantown, Phila., Jan. 6, 1883; d. Col. George and Emiline A. Wood; ed. Friends Sch., pub. sch., St. Mary's Hall; m. Humbert Borton Powell, June 14, 1902; children—T. Jenkins, Edith Wood, Humbert Borton. Active in Rep. politics; has made speeches in four presdl. campaigns and all local and Pa. campaigns; pres. Pa. Council Rep. Women (since 1935), Womens Rep. Club of Del. Co.; vice-pres. Womens Rep. Club of Chester Co.; mem. exec. bd. State Com. of Pa.; pres. Parents-Teachers Assn.; 1st vice-pres. Nat. Federation of Womens Rep. Clubs; sec. Flowers For Flowerless; vice-pres. local Red Cross; mem. sch. bd. Radnor Twp. Del. Co.; mem. bd. Neighborhood League of Wayne, Pa. Pub. Charities Assn., Health and Welfare Council of Chester Co. Republican. Episcopalian. Clubs: Treble Clef (pres.), Womens City (vice-pres.) Art Alliance (Philadelphia); Monday Afternoon of Malvern (pres.); Acorn (Phila.). Home: Willow Dale Farm, Devon, Pa. Office: 2d and South Sts., Harrisburg, Pa.

POWELL, Francis Warren, prof. English, Davis & Elkins Coll. Address: Davis & Elkins College, Elkins, W.Va.

POWELL, Fred Wilbur, economist; b. Three Rivers, Mass., July 21, 1881; s. Orion Alvarado and Sarah Matilda (Dunn) P.; grad. high sch., Palmer, Mass., 1899; A.B., Stanford, 1904, A.M., 1905; Ph.D., Columbia, 1918; m. Sophy Hill Hulsizer, Oct. 4, 1910 (dec.). With Haskins and Sells, certified pub. accountants, New York, 1905; successively in employ Bur. Municipal Research, New York and Phila. (dir. Phila. Bur. 1909-11), Peter White (Bridgeport, Conn., and St. Louis, Mo.), Haskins and Sells (Chicago), and again with Bur. Municipal Research (New York) until 1917 (editor, 1914-16); research asso. U. of Calif., 1917-18; trade commr. at London, Eng., 1919; chief of European Div., U. S. Bur. Foreign and Domestic Commerce, 1920; senior member of staff Institute for Govt. Research (incorporated in Brookings Institution since 1928), Washington, D.C., since 1920. Statistician U.S. Bd. of Arbitration, Conductors and Trainmen vs. Railroads, in Eastern territory, 1912; chief Div. of Tabulation and Statistics, U.S. War Trade Bd., 1918-19; mem. research staff, Federal Coördinator of Transportation, 1933; research consultant Nat. Planning Bd., 1934. Club: Cosmos. Author: Railroad Promotion and Capitalization in the United States (with F. A. Cleveland), 1909; Railroad Finance (with same), 1912; Hall Jackson Kelley, Prophet of Oregon, 1917; The Recent Movement for State Budget Reform, 1917; British Industrial Reconstruction and Commercial Policies, 1920; The Railroads of Mexico, 1921; The Bureau of Mines, 1922; The Bureau of Animal Industry, 1927; The Bureau of Plant Industry, 1927; The Coast Guard (with D. H. Smith), 1929. Editor Hall J. Kelley on Oregon, 1932. Home: 3705 McKinley St., Chevy Chase, D.C. Office: 722 Jackson Pl., Washington, D.C.

POWELL, Lyman Pierson, author, editor; b. Farmington, Del., Sept. 21, 1866; s. James Ben Ralston and Mary Anna (Redden) P.; A.B., Johns Hopkins, 1890, grad. scholar, 1890-92; grad. student, U. of Wis., 1892-93; fellow, U. of Pa., 1893-95, univ. extension lecturer, 1893-95; grad. Phila. Div. Sch., 1897; D.D., Dickinson, and LL.D., U. Rochester, 1914; m. Gertrude Wilson, June 20, 1899; children—Talcott Williams, Francis Wilson. Deacon, 1897, priest, 1898, P.E. Ch.; minister, Ambler, Pa., 1897-98; rector St. John's, Lansdowne, Pa., 1898-1903, Northampton, Mass., 1904-12; prof. business ethics, New York U., 1912-13; pres. Hobart Coll. and William Smith Coll., 1913-18; vice-pres. Assn. American Colleges 1917-18; rector St. Margaret's Ch., N.Y. City, 1926-35. Lectured 1,500 times throughout United States and Canada since 1892. Mem. Phi Delta Theta and Phi Beta Kappa fraternities. Mason. Republican. Author: The History of Education in Delaware, 1893; Family Prayers, 1905; Christian Science—The Faith and Its Founder, 1907; The

Art of Natural Sleep, 1908; The Credentials of the Church, 1908; The Emmanuel Movement in a New England Town, 1909; Heavenly Heretics, 1910; Religion in Our Colleges and Universities, 1912; Lafayette, 1918; The World and Democracy, 1919; America and the League of Nations, 1919; The Teaching of Democracy, 1919; Popular Bibles in Cambridge Library of American Literature, 1921; So This Is School, 1922; Where the Good Schools Are (with wife), 1923; The Human Touch, 1925; Mary Baker Eddy, 1930; The Better Part, 1933; The House by the Side of the Road, 1933; The Second Seventy, 1936. Editor: American Historic Towns (4 vols.), 1898-1902; Current Religious Literature, 1902; Devotional Series (3 vols.), 1905-07; The Spirit of Democracy (with wife), 1918; The World Unrest and Its Relief (2 vols.), 1919. Contbr. to mags. Home: Mountain Lakes, N.J.

POWELL, Richard Roy Belden, prof. law; b. Rochester, N.Y., Oct. 11, 1890; s. Harry Teed and Carrie Louise (Brown) P.; A.B., U. of Rochester, 1911; A.M., Columbia, 1912, LL.B., 1914; m. Anne Marie Klein, May 13, 1914; children—Margaret Ruth, Richard Gordon. Admitted to N.Y. bar, 1914, and practiced at Rochester until 1921; asst. prof. law, Columbia, 1921-23, asso. prof., 1923-24, prof. since 1924, Dwight prof. law since 1931. Reporter on property, American Law Inst. since 1929; research consultant N.J. Commn. on Consolidation of Statutes, 1929-30, N.Y. Law Revision Commn., 1935-37. Member Association Bar City of N.Y., Am. Law Inst., Phi Beta Kappa, Delta Sigma Rho, Alpha Chi Rho, Delta Theta Phi. Democrat. Presbyn. Club: Columbia University (New York). Author: Cases on Law of Agency, 1924; Tiffany on Agency, 1924; Cases and Materials on Trusts and Estates, 1932; Possessary Estates, 1933; Future Interests, 1937. Contbr. to Columbia Law Review, etc. Home: 250 Booth Av., Englewood, N.J.

POWELL, Walter Anderson, retired lawyer; b. nr. Farmington, Kent Co., Del., June 16, 1855; s. James Benn Ralston and Mary Ann (Redden) P.; student Wilmington Conf. Acad., Dover, Del., 1874-75; A.B., Dickinson Coll., Carlisle, Pa., 1878; m. Jennie Knowles, Sept. 4, 1888 (died May 26, 1913); m. 2d, Ray Heydrick, June 6, 1917. Admitted to Jackson Co. (Mo.) bar, 1880, and practiced at Kansas City, Mo., 1880-1917; mem. firm Chase & Powell, 1881-93, Powell & Powell, Kansas City, Mo., 1893-1907; retired and returned to Dover, Del., 1917. Judge Circuit Ct., Jackson Co., Mo. (Independence Div.), 1907-13. Republican. Methodist. Author: The Pilgrims and Their Intellectual, Religious and Civic Life, 1923; A History of Delaware, 1928; Fight of A Century Between the Penns and Calverts over the Three Lower Counties in Delaware, 1935; Annals of a Village in Kent County, Delaware, 1934. Address: 341 N. State St., Dover, Del.

POWELL, William Allen, business exec.; b. Philadelphia, Pa., Nov. 14, 1873; s. John W. and Catharine M. (Allen) P.; ed. pub. schs.; m. Gertrude H. Graff, Nov. 2, 1905; children—Allen G., John G. Sec. Philadelphia Warehouse Co., 1905 to 1916; treas. Union Petroleum Co., 1916-21; sec. and treas. Tiona Refining Co., 1918-1933; now v.p. and treas. Tiona Petroleum Co., Phila. V.p. Merion Civic Assn. Republican. Episcopalian. Club: Union League (Philadelphia). Home: 748 S. Highland Av., Merion, Pa. Office: 1130 Widener Bldg., Philadelphia, Pa.

POWELL, William Mennig, pres. Diamond Mfg. Co., Inc.; b. Hazleton, Pa., May 10, 1893; s. William Morgan and Mazie (Mennig) P.; student Hazleton (Pa.) High Sch.; m. Janet MacDougal Thomas, Apr. 14, 1923; children—Marion Newton, Joan Mennig. Clk. Harwood Coal Co., 1912-15; div.-chief clk. Hudson Coal Co., 1915-16, asst. chief clk., 1916-17 and 1919-20, chief clk., 1920-23; v.p. and mgr. Diamond Mfg. Co., Wyoming, Pa., 1923-25, pres. since 1925; sec.-treas. Power Engring. Corpn. With Officers Training Camp, Dartmouth Coll. and Battery D, 311 F.A., 79th Div. and 101st Ordnance Co., U.S. Army, 1917-19. Treas. Code Authority, Nat. Perforated Metal Mfrs. Industry. Mem. Nat. Assn. Perforated Metal Mfrs. (pres. 1937), Pa. Mfrs. Assn., Wilkes-Barre Chamber of Commerce, Am. Legion. Episcopalian (sec. and vestryman Grace Ch.). Mason, Elk. Clubs: United Sportman (pres.); Gatineau Rod & Gun of Quebec, Can. (sec.-treas.); Pickwick Rod & Gun (treas.); Hazleton (Pa.) Veterans'; Scranton (Scranton); Westmoreland (Wilkes-Barre); Wyoming Valley Country (Wyoming, Pa.). Home: Shrine View, Dallas, Pa. Office: 253 W. 8th St., Wyoming, Pa.

POWER, Archie Dayton, research physicist; b. Baldwin, Kan., Aug. 28, 1887; s. Nathaniel Pennington and Emily Jane (Green) P.; B.S., Baker U., 1911; A.M., U. of Kan., 1912; grad. study, Johns Hopkins U., 1914-16; Ph.D., U. of Minn., 1922; m. Florence Stouder, Apr. 14, 1929; children—Donald Wilbur, John Lymer, Merle Warren. Employed as magnetic observer, Carnegie Instn., Washington, D.C., 1912-14 and 1916-18; instr. U. of Minn., 1919-24; prof. physics, Lawrence Coll., Appleton, Wis., 1924-29; with Westinghouse Lamp Co., 1929-30; research and engring., RCA Mfg. Co., Inc., Harrison, N.J., since 1930. Served as ensign, U.S.N.R.F., 1918-19, Naval Research Sta., New London, Conn. Mem. Am. Phys. Soc., Sigma Phi Epsilon, Sigma Xi, Gamma Alpha. Home: 84 Hillside Av., Caldwell. Office: RCA Mfg. Co., Inc., Harrison, N.J.

POWER, Florence Dell Stouder, research chemist; b. Denver, Colo., Oct. 9, 1898; d. Absolom Delos and Mary Alice (Dory) Stouder; student Lakewood (Colo.) Grammar Sch., 1904-11, Wheatridge (Colo.) High Sch., 1911-15, U. of Chicago, summer 1921, U. of Mich., Ann Arbor, Mich., summer 1928; A.B., Denver (Colo.) U., 1919, M.A., 1920; Ph.D., U. of Ill., Urbana, Ill., 1925; m. Dr. Archie Dayton Power, Apr. 14, 1929; children—Donald Wilbur, John Lymer, Merle Warren. Teacher of physics and chemistry, Rocky Ford (Colo.) High Sch., 1920-22; grad. asst. chemistry dept., U. of Ill., Urbana, Ill., 1922-25; asst. prof. of chemistry, Lawrence Coll., Appleton, Wis., 1925-27, asso. prof., 1927-29; research chemist, Scott & Bowne, Bloomfield, N.J., 1929-30, in charge of research, 1931-33; research chemist, Food Research Labs., New York, 1930-31; chemist, J. W. Carnrick Co., Newark, N.J., 1931; pvt. research since 1933. Mem. Am. Chem. Soc., Sigma Xi, Iota Sigma Pi. Club: Elmwood Badminton (East Orange, N.J.). Address: 84 Hillside Av., Caldwell, N.J.

POWER, Francis Ray, educator; b. Levels, W.Va., May 3, 1898; s. Rev. Thompson and Sallie Ann (Wills) P.; grad. Shepherd State Teachers Coll., Shepherdstown, W.Va., 1920; A.B., W.Va. U., 1925; A.M., Teachers Coll., Columbia U., 1929; unmarried. Worked on farm during boyhood; teacher rural schs., Hampshire County, 1915-18; employed in steel mill, summer and fall, 1918; bank teller, summer, 1920; prin. grade sch., Grafton, W.Va., 1920-21, Shinnston pub. schs., 1921-23; prof. of edn., Glenville State Teachers Coll., summer, 1925; prin. Woodrow Wilson Jr. High Sch., Charleston, 1925-31; city and dist. supt. of schs., Princeton, 1931-33; asst. state supt. of free schs. and asst. dir. in charge vocational rehabilitation since 1933. Actively engaged in work of 4-H Club, Boy Scouts, Community Chest, Crippled Children's Work, Family Welfare Service and Forums. Mem. Nat. Rehabilitation Assn. (exec. com.), N.E.A., W.Va. State Edn. Assn., Am. Assn. Sch. Administrators, Kappa Delta Pi, Phi Beta Kappa, Tau Kappa Epsilon, Teke Club. Democrat. Episcopalian. Mason (32°, Shriner). Clubs: Rotary, University, Meadow Brook Golf (Charleston). Writer official reports and bulletins under direction of State Supt. Free Schs.; also articles on W.Va. schs. pub. in state and nat. mags. Home: 1420 Kanawha St. Address: State Dept. of Edn., Charleston, W.Va.

POWERS, David Lane, congressman; b. Philadelphia, July 29, 1896; s. Thomas Jefferson and Mary (Wagner) P.; student Central High Sch., Phila., 1909-11; C.E., Pa. Mil. Coll., Chester, 1915, hon. B.Mil. Science, 1921, M.S., 1935; m. Edna May Throop, May 7, 1918; 1 dau., Elane Charlotte. Served as pvt., advancing to 1st. lt., bn. adj. inf., U.S.A., Apr. 1917-Apr. 1919. Mem. N.J. Ho. of Rep., 1928-30; mem. 73d to 76th Congresses (1933-39), 4th N.J. Dist. Trustee Prospect Hill Pvt. Sch., Trenton. Mem. Beta Zeta Epsilon. Republican. Presbyn. Mason (Shriner), Elk, Eagle, Tall Cedar of Lebanon. Clubs: Carteret, Trenton Country; Great Sedges Fishing and Gunning (Barnegat, N.J.); Yardley (Pa.) Country. Home: 935 Bellevue Av. Office: Broad St. Bank Bldg., Trenton, N.J.

POWERS, Donald Howard, research chemist; b. Boston, Mass., Mar. 31, 1901; s. Abner Howard and Josephine (Odell) P.; A.B. Boston U., 1921; A.M., Princeton, 1923, Ph.D., same, 1924; m. Margaret L. Sale, Feb. 12, 1925; children—Beatrice Wolverton, Donald Howard, Jr., Jonathan Goble. Began as research chemist, E. I. Du Pont de Nemours Co., Wilmington, Del., 1924-29; chief chemist, United States Finishing Co., Providence, R.I., 1929-32; in charge of textile div., Rohm & Haas Co., Phila., Pa. since 1932. Mem. Am. Chem. Soc., Am. Assn. Textile Chemists & Colorists, Am. Soc. for Testing Materials, Sigma Alpha Epsilon. Ind. Republican. Presbyn. Home: 200 Oak Av., Moorestown, N.J. Office: 222 W. Washington Square, Philadelphia, Pa.

POWERS, Mary Swift, (Mrs. William Frederick Powers), artist; b. Leeds, Mass., Sept. 7, 1885; d. William Henry and Clara Armenia (Warren) Swift; Regents Teaching Certificate, N.Y. Sch. Fine & Applied Arts, 1910; m. William Frederick Powers, Jan. 6, 1915 (dec.). Artist since 1927, specializing in water colors; exhibited, one-man shows, Syracuse Mus., Macbeth Galleries, New York, Marie Sterner Gallery, New York, Grace Horn Gallery, Boston, Currier Gallery of Art, Manchester, N.H. Fleming Museum, Burlington, Vt.; represented in permanent collections, Whitney Mus., N.Y. City, Addison Gallery, Andover, Mass., Wood Mus. Montpelier, Vt., Lawrence Hall, Williams Coll., and in prvt. collections. Awarded hon. mention, Montclair Mus., 1938. Home: 76 Magnolia Av. Studio: Old Tenafly Hall, Tenafly, N.J.

POWERS, Philip Henry, vice-pres. West Penn Power Co.; b. Berryville, Va., May 7, 1893; s. Philip Henry and Mary (Grove) P.; E.E., Va. Poly. Inst., 1914; m. Margaret Scott, Apr. 17, 1920; children—Philip Henry IV, Horace Scott, Berri Grove. Began as employee in utility business in 1914; asso. with West Penn Power Company continuously since 1922, now vice-pres. and dir.; v.p. and dir. West Pa. Appliance Co. Served with 304th Field Signal Btln., 79th Div., U.S.A., 1917-19. Republican. Mason (K.T., 32°, Shriner). Clubs: University, Pittsburgh Field. Office: 14 Wood St., Pittsburgh, Pa.

POWERS, Walter Palmer, pres. Ceel Holding Corpn.; b. Proctor, Vt., Sept. 9, 1890; s. Harry Palmer and Cora Alice (Prior) P.; student Proctor (Vt.) High Sch., 1905-09, Brooklyn (N.Y.) Poly. Inst., 1917-18; N.Y. U., 1922-23; B.S., in E.E., U. of Pittsburgh, 1914; unmarried. Teacher elec. engring., U. of Pittsburgh, 1914-15, Pratt Inst., Brooklyn, N.Y., 1915-21; aircraft radio work Nat. Electric Signalling Co., Brooklyn, N.Y., 1916-21; asst. prof. elec. engring. Stevens Inst. Tech. Hoboken, N.J., 1921-24; sec. U.S. Tool Co., Ampere, N.J., since 1924; pres. Ceel Holding Corpn., Ampere, N.J., since 1935; sec. Ampere Automatic Machinery Co., Associated Mfrs., Inc., Associated Patentees, Inc. Clubs: Lake Mohawk (N.J.) Golf, Lake Mohawk (N.J.) Country. Home: 111 Tuttle Av., Spring Lake, N.J. Office: Care of U.S. Tool Co., Ampere, N.J.; also 431 E. Shore Trail, Lake Mohawk, Sparta, N.J.

PRALL, Charles Edward, educator; b. West Concord, Minn., Mar. 1, 1891; s. Oscar E. and Nellie M. (Gibbons) P.; A.B., State U. of Ia., 1912, grad. fellow in edn., 1927-28, Ph.D., 1928; A.M., U. of Chicago, 1926; m. Clara Dayle Borden, June 16, 1915; 1 son, Charles Edward. Supt. schs., Essex, Ia., 1912-14, Rock Valley, 1914-17, Clarion, 1917-22,

Charles City, 1922-27; research prof. in edn., U. of Ark., 1928-29, dean Coll. of Edn. and dir. summer sessions, 1929-34; dean Sch. of Edn., U. of Pittsburgh, since 1934. Mem. Phi Delta Kappa, Kappa Delta Pi, Delta Tau Delta. Home: 4601 Bayard St., Pittsburgh, Pa.

PRATHER, Perry Franklin, physician; b. Clear Spring, Md., Nov. 4, 1894; s. George Thomas and Mary (Bain) P.; A.B., Dickinson Coll., 1916; M.D., U. of Pa. Med. Sch., 1924; hon. A.M. Dickinson Coll., 1926; m. Jessie E. Williams, Sept. 5, 1923; children—Elizabeth Anne, Frances Jean, Charles Williams. Interne U. of Pa. Grad. Hosp., Phila., 1924-25; engaged in gen. practice of medicine, Hagerstown, Md., since 1925; editor of Current Medical Digest since 1935; consultant U.S. Pub. Health Service since 1939. Served in Med. Corps, U.S.A., 1917-19. Active in work of Boy Scouts; awarded Silver Beaver, Boy Scouts of America. Associate Am. Coll. Physicians; mem. Am. Med. Assn., Medico-Chirur. Faculty of Md. Republican. Methodist. Mason. Club: Fountain Head Country. Home: 1151 The Terrace. Office: 155 W. Washington St., Hagerstown, Md.

PRATHER, Ralph Carlyle, artist, writer; b. Franklin, Pa., Nov. 4, 1889; s. George C. and Laura Ann (Say) P.; grad. high sch. St. Petersburg, Fla., 1909, Eastman Bus. Coll., Poughkeepsie, N.Y., 1910; m. Claire McCullough, of Sidney, O., Apr. 15, 1915. Began as commercial artist with commercial studio, St. Petersburg, Fla., 1912; chief draftsman, Midwest Refining Co., Denver, Colo., 1919-22, City of Glendale, Calif., 1923-24; began as ilustrator, specializing in Animals, 1920; devoted whole time to animal illustrating as free lance artist since 1924; illustrations for Saturday Evening Post and other mags., books, covers, and work for nat. advertisers; never attended art sch. or art classes, instruction and assistance given by Charles Livingston Bull; sketch direct from animals and nature in all parts of U.S. Republican. Methodist. Contbr. (in collaboration with Claire McCullough Prather) many short stories and articles to mags. Home: Business P. O. Box 71, Drexel Hill, Philadelphia, Pa.

PRATT, Arthur Henry, cons. engr.; b. Marlborough, Mass., July 9, 1874; s. Ransom Dickinson and Annette Louise (Goss) P.; ed. Mass. pub. schs. and Brooklyn Poly. Inst.; m. Florence Gertrude Linton, Apr. 22, 1902; 1 son, Warren Abbott. Engring. asst. Met. Sewerage Commission, Boston, Mass., 1891-97; draftsman, Town Engrs. Office, Brooklyne, 1897-1902; jr. engr. U.S. Engr. Office, Phila., Pa., 1902-04, supt. 4th U.S. Light House Dist., Phila., 1904; asst. engr. N.Y. State Engr., Albany, 1905; asst. engr., Bd. Water Supply City of N.Y., 1906-14; asst. engineer, Board of Estimate City of New York, 1914-17; designing engineer North Jersey District Water Supply Commn., Newark, 1919, chief engr., 1920-29, cons. engr. since 1929. Served as capt., then maj., Engrs. U.S.A., 1917-19, water supply officer II Army A.E.F. Mem. Am. Soc. Civil Engrs., Am. Water Works Assn., Am. Assn. Engrs. Episcopalian. Home: 26 Rynda Rd., South Orange, N.J. Office: 24 Commerce St., Newark, N.J.

PRATT, Auguste G., pres. Babcock & Wilcox Co.; b. Brooklyn, N.Y., Mar. 31, 1881; s. Nat. W. and Carrie V. (Deudney) P.; Boys' High Sch., Brooklyn; M.E., Stevens Institute Tech., 1903; m. Ruth Nesmith, January 5, 1905; children—Mrs. D. C. Taylor, Mrs. D. N. Fisher, Mrs. G. W. Tully, Mrs. J. W. Todd. With Babcock & Wilcox Co., mfrs. water tube steam boilers, etc., 1903, advancing to president, 1924; chm. executive com. Babcock, Wilcox & Goldie McCulloch, Ltd.; trustee Central Hanover Bank & Trust Co.; dir. Fidelity Phenix Fire Ins. Co., Fidelity & Casualty Co., Worthington Pump & Machine Co., Babcock & Wilcox, Ltd., London. Trustee Dwight Sch., Englewood, N.J.; member National Industrial Conference Board. Member American Soc. M.E., Am. Math. Soc., Chi Psi fraternity. Clubs: Engineers', Railroad, City Midday (New York); Knickerbocker Country. Home: 345 Walnut St., Englewood, N.J. Office: 85 Liberty St., New York, N.Y.

PRATT, Carl Davis, dir. exptl. lab.; b. Phila., Pa., Feb. 21, 1897; s. Charles and Anna L. (Davis) P.; A.B., Swarthmore (Pa.) Coll., 1918; m. Emily B. Wallace, Sept. 14, 1920; children—John Marshall, Charles Edward, Anne Wallace. Research and explosives chemist Reynolds Exptl. Lab., Atlas Power Co., Tamaqua, Pa., 1918-30, in charge dynamite and black blasting powder development, 1925-30, dir. lab. since 1930. Mem. Am. Chem. Soc. (chmn. Lehigh Valley Sect. 1932), Am. Inst. Chem. Engrs., Franklin Inst., Army Ordnance Assn., Sigma Xi, Phi Delta Theta. Republican. Soc. of Friends. Mason (Past Officer Tamaqua Royal Arch Chapter). Clubs: Acacia (Tamaqua, Pa.); Valley Country (Hazleton, Pa.). Contbr. to Jour. of Am. Mining Congress. Holder 6 U.S. patents on blasting powder, dynamite and blasting explosives assemblies. Home: R.D. 2. Office: Atlas Powder Co., Tamaqua, Pa.

PRATT, Carroll Cornelius, univ. prof.; b. North Brookfield, Mass., Apr. 27, 1894; s. Dana Joseph and Sara (Nutting) P.; A.B., Clark Coll., 1915; A.M., Clark U. 1917, Ph.D. 1922; grad. study, Cambridge U. Eng., 1919, U. of Berlin, Germany, 1931; m. Marjory Bates, June 16, 1923; children—Dana Joseph, Anita Caroline. Began as instr. exptl. psychology, Clark U., 1922; instr. and asst. prof. psychology, Harvard U., 1923-37, actg. organist and choirmaster, 1925; prof. psychology, Rutgers U., since 1937, head dept. psychology since 1937, dir. Psychol. and Mental Hygiene Clinic since 1937; lecturer psychology, Princeton U., 1939-40. Served as wireless operator, Signal Corps, U.S.A., 1917-19, with A.E.F. Awarded Guggenheim Fellowship to U. of Berlin, 1931. Mem. Am. Acad. Arts & Sciences, Nat. Inst. Psychology, Soc. Exptl. Psychologists, Am. Psychol. Assn., Am. Musicol. Soc. Author: The Meaning of Music, 1932; The Logic of Modern Psychology, 1939. Contbg. editor Am. Jour. Musicology, Jour. Exptl. Psychology. Contbr. articles to scientific and tech. jours. Home: 7 Bartlett St., New Brunswick, N.J.

PRATT, Frank Randall, prof. physics; b. Warsaw, Wyoming Co., N.Y., Apr. 19, 1876; s. Addison Warren and Lucy Arlett (Lathrop) P.; grad. high sch. Warsaw, 1895, Teacher's Training Class, 1897; B.Sc., with first honor, Rutgers, 1906, M.Sc., 1908; Ph.D., Princeton, 1917; m. Lottie Emeline Morey, July 6, 1911. Teacher pub. schs. until 1903; with Rutgers Coll. since 1903, instr. physics, 1910-12, asst. prof., 1912-17, asso. prof., 1917-21, prof. since 1921; head Dept. of Physics, New Jersey Coll. for Women (Rutgers Univ.), since 1927. Teacher physics, S.A.T.C., Rutgers Coll.; World War; apptd. coöperating expert by Nat. Research Council, 1923. Fellow A.A.A.S.; mem. Am. Physical Soc., New Brunswick Scientific Soc., Alumni Assn. Rutgers Univ., Phi Beta Kappa, Sigma Xi, Pi Kappa Alpha; charter mem. Am. Assn. Physics Teachers. Republican. Baptist (deacon Livingston Av. Ch.). Mason. Contbr. exptl. articles to mags. Home: 41 N. 7th Av., New Brunswick, N.J.

PRATT, Henry Basil, chemist; b. Socorro, Columbia, S.A., Mar. 27, 1873; s. Henry Barrington and Joanna (Gildersleeve) P.; parents U.S. citizens; student Hampden Sidney Coll. (Va.), 1889-91, Pratt Inst., Brooklyn, N.Y., 1901-03; B.S., Va. Poly. Inst., Blacksburg, Va., 1894; m. Augusta Riemann, Oct. 5, 1905; children—Natalie Augusta (Mrs. Robert Heuer), Jonie Gildersleeve (wife of Rev. Roscoe Metzger), Henry Basil. Supt., Bell & Bogart Soap Co. New York, 1895-1905; v.p. B. G. Pratt Co. agrl. sprays, Hackensack, N.J., since 1905. Trustee First Presbyn. Ch., Hackensack, N.J. Mem. Phi Gamma Delta. Republican. Presbyterian. Mason, K.P., Jr. Order United Am. Mechanics. Home: 116 Clinton Place. Office: Moore and Mercer Sts., Hackensack, N.J.

PRATT, Henry Sherring, zoölogist; b. Toledo, O., Aug. 18, 1859; s. Charles and Catherine (Sherring) P.; A.B., U. of Mich., 1882; admitted to Ohio bar, 1885; Ph.D.. Leipzig, 1892; univs. of Freiburg, Geneva, and Harvard, 1888-93; Innsbruck, 1902-03; Graz, 1910-11; m. Agnes Woodbury Gray, Sept. 1, 1894; 1 dau., Anna. Instr. biology, Haverford Coll., 1893-98, asso. prof., 1898-1901, prof., 1901-29 (emeritus). Instructor comparative anatomy, Cold Spring Harbor Biol. Lab., 1896-1926. Mem. Commn. for Relief in Belgium, 1916-17. Pres. Cambridge Entomol. Club, 1896; mem. Am. Soc. Naturalists, Am. Soc. Zoölogists (sec. and treas. Eastern br., 1905-06); fellow A.A.A.S. Knight Order of the Crown (Belgium). Author: Invertebrate Zoöl., 1902; Vertebrate Zoöl., 1906, 2d edit., 1925, 3d edit., 1937; Manuel of Common Invertebrates, 1916, revised edit., 1935; Manual of Vertebrates of the U.S., 1923, 2d edit., 1935; A Course in General Zoölogy, 1927; A Course in General Biology, 1927; General Biology—an Introductory Study, 1931; also various zoöl. papers. Home: Haverford, Pa.

PRAY, Kenneth L. M., prof. social planning and adminstrn.; b. Whitewater, Wis., Sept. 27, 1882; s. Theron Brown and Ellen Frances (Moffatt) P.; A.B., U. of Wis., 1907; m. Eliza Burr Lamoreux, Dec. 31, 1910 (dec.); 1 dau., Ellen Elizabeth (Mrs. F. L. Maytag II). Engaged in newspaper work as editor and corr., 1904-13; dir. publicity Dem. State Com., Pa., 1913-14; asst. then exec. sec. Pub. Charities Assn. of Pa., 1915-22; dir. Pa. Sch. Social Work, 1922-32, prof. social planning and adminstrn. since 1932; sec. and chief of staff Pa. Com. on Pub. Assistance and Relief, 1936-37. Mem. exec. com., Pa. Prison Soc. Mem. social service adv. com., Municipal Ct. of Phila. Mem. bd. trustees Pa. Industrial Sch., Huntingdon, Pa. Mem. Am. Assn. Social Workers, Nat. Conf. Social Work. Contbr. many papers to nat. and state confs. Home: 310 Woodside Av., Narberth, Pa. Office: 311 S. Juniper St., Philadelphia, Pa.

PREINKERT, Alma Henrietta, univ. registrar; b. Boston, Mass., Oct. 22, 1895; d. John F. C. and Selma S. M. (Brandes) P.; A.B., George Washington U., Washington, D.C., 1916, grad. student, 1919-21; A.M., U. of Md., College Park, 1923; student George Washington U. Law Sch., 1926-28, Am. Univ., 1929-34. Engaged in teaching, pub. schs., El Paso, Tex., 1917; in Govt. service 1918; War Dept., U. of Md., 1919; asst. registrar, U. of Md., 1921-35, registrar since 1935. Sec. Chesapeake Beach Citizens' Assn. since 1936. Mem. Am. Assn. Collegiate Registrars (pres. Md. branch 1929, sec. Middle States Assn., 1932-34), Am. Assn. Univ. Women, Md. Fed. Women's Clubs, Phi Delta Delta, Washington Alumni Assn. (pres. 1933), Kappa Delta, Phi Delta Gamma. Lutheran. Clubs: North Beach, Progress, Columbian Women. Asso. editor Journal of Am. Assn. Collegiate Registrars since 1939, circulation mgr. since 1936. Co-author (with W. C. John), The Educational Views of George Washington, 1931. Contbr. to jours. Home: 1436 Chapin St. N. W., Washington, D.C. Office: University of Maryland, College Park, Md.

PREISLER, Kenneth LeRoi, supervising prin. schs.; b. New Bloomfield, Pa., Nov. 12, 1897; s. James Calvin and Frances Clara (Wertz) P.; grad. State Teachers College, Shippensburg, Pa., 1918; A.B., Susquehanna University, Selinsgrove, Pa., 1925; A.M., Bucknell U., Lewisburg, Pa., 1935; grad. study, Columbia U., 1928; m. Olive Janetta Garber, Aug. 17, 1920; 1 dau., Janet Garber. Engaged as prin. high sch., Yoe, Pa., 1918-21; asst. prin. Duncannon, Pa., 1921-22; teacher high sch., Watsontown, Pa., 1922-27, prin. high sch., 1927-31, supervising prin. schs. since 1931. Former scoutmaster Boy Scouts, now treas. local troop com. Treas. Northumberland Co. Teachers Inst. Mem. N.E.A., Pa. State Edn. Assn., Chamber of Commerce, Masonic Hall Assn. of Watsontown, Kappa Phi Kappa. Lutheran. Mason, Knights of Malta. Home: 419 Elm St. Office: Brimmer Av., Watsontown, Pa.

PRENDERGAST, James, pres. Susquehanna Collieries Co.; b. Columbus, O., Oct. 14, 1882; s. Frank Abel and Eugenia L. (Mix) P.; student Ohio State U., Columbus; m. Mignon Poste, Apr. 26, 1907; children—Marie, Frank,

Mignon, Ruth, James. Supt. Pittsburgh Belmont Coal Co., 1906-12, purchasing agt., 1912-15; gen. supt. Morris Coal Co., 1915-17; sales agt. Baltimore & Ohio Coal Co., 1917-19; sales agt. M. A. Hanna Co., 1919-28, v.p. and dir. since 1937; pres. and dir. Susquehanna Collieries Co., Phila., since 1937; dir. Lytle Coal Co., Gen. Stoker Co., Hanna Coal Sales Co., Trabon Engring. Co., Anthracite Inst. Clubs: Bankers (N.Y.); Racquet (Phila.); Union, Cleveland Athletic, Pepper Pike (Cleveland); Westmoreland (Wilkes-Barre). Home: 20001 S. Park Blvd., Cleveland, O. Office: 859 Broad St. Station Bldg., Philadelphia, Pa.

PRENTICE, William Kelly, prof. Greek; b. N.Y. City, Oct. 28, 1871; s. William Packer and Florence (Kelly) P.; A.B., Princeton, 1892, A.M., 1895; student Princeton Theol. Sem., 1893-94; studied U. of Marburg, Germany, 1894, U. of Halle, 1897-99, Ph.D., 1900; m. Aline Burwell Glenny, May 28, 1907 (died at Athens, Greece, July 24, 1909); 1 dau., Joan; m. 2d, Maria Baldwin Hamill, May 4, 1917. Under master, Lawrenceville (N.J.) Sch., 1892-93; instr. Greek, 1894-97, asst. prof., 1900-05, prof. since 1905, Princeton. Annual prof., Am. Sch. of Classical Studies, Athens, Greece, 1908-09; Sather professor University of California, Jan.-June 1918. Mem. bd. mgrs. N.J. Children's Home Soc.; mem. Am. Council of Learned Societies, 1921-29. Mem. Am. Philol. Assn., Archæol. Inst. America, Am. Hist. Assn., Am. Assn. Univ. Profs., Phi Beta Kappa; corr. member Austrian Archæological Institute. Clubs: Nassau (Princeton); Princeton, Century (New York). Author: Greek and Latin Inscriptions, 1908; Greek and Latin Inscriptions in Syria, 1908-22; also monographs and articles on classical subjects. Served as capt. U.S.A., Oct. 1918-Jan. 1919. Home: Cherry Grove, Princeton, N.J.

PRENTIS, Henning Webb, Jr., pres. Armstrong Cork Co.; b. St. Louis, Mo., July 11, 1884; s. Henning Webb and Mary Morton (McNutt) P.; A.B., U. of Mo., 1903; A.M., U. of Cincinnati, 1907; LL.D., Hampden-Sydney (Va.) Coll., 1932, Grove City (Pa.) Coll., 1939; m. Ida Bernice Cole, Sept. 2, 1909. Sec. to pres. U. of Mo., 1903-05; sec. U. of Cincinnati, 1905-07; with the Armstrong Cork Co., since 1907, successively asst. mgr. Insulation div., Pittsburgh, Pa., to 1911, organizer, and mgr. advertising dept. of the co., 1911-20, gen. sales mgr. of floor div., with hdqrs. at Lancaster, Pa., 1920-28, elected v.p. and mem. bd. dirs., 1926, 1st v.p., 1929, pres. since Mar. 1934. Mem. of industrial advisory com. of Federal Reserve Bank of Phila., pres. Buchanan Foundation for Preservation of Wheatland. Trustee Pa. State Coll., Lincoln Memorial U., Wilson Coll. V.p. and dir. Nat. Assn. of Mfrs.; dir. Nat. Ind. Conf. Bd., U.S. Chamber of Commerce; mem. Am. Soc. Sales Executives, Am. Acad. Polit. and Social Science, Pa. Soc. of S.R., Donegal Soc., Phi Beta Kappa, Sigma Alpha Epsilon, Omicron Delta Kappa, Alpha Delta Sigma. Republican. Presbyn. Clubs: Hamilton, Country (Lancaster); Bankers, University (New York); Art (Phila.); Ross Mountain Club (New Florence, Pa.); Rolling Rock Club (Ligonier, Pa.). Speaker on civic, merchandising and ednl. subjects. Home: "Yeardley," 151 School Lane. Office: Arstrong Cork Co., Lancaster, Pa.

PRENTIS, Morton MacNutt, banker; b. St. Louis, Mo., Jan. 2, 1887; s. Henning W. and Mary Morton (MacNutt) P.; A.B., U. of Mo., 1906; m. Frances C. Lusk, Nov. 19, 1921; children—Morton M., Garnett M. Began with 3d Nat. Bank, St. Louis, 1899; various positions with Nat. Bank of Commerce, Norfolk, Va., 1906-14; nat. bank examiner, Va., 1915-18; mng. dir. Federal Reserve Bank, Baltimore, 1918-22; v.p., later pres. Merchants Nat. Bank, Baltimore, 1922-28; pres. First Nat. Bank, Baltimore, since 1928; dir. U.S. Fidelity & Guaranty Co., Savings Bank of Baltimore, Md. Life Ins. Co., Monumental Life Ins. Company of Baltimore, Md., Industrial Corporation Baltimore, Federal Reserve Bank of Baltimore. State fiscal agent of Maryland, 1924-35; trustee Community Fund of Baltimore, Harriet Lane Home (Johns Hopkins Hosp.), Goucher Coll:, Cathedral Foundation. Mem. Sigma Alpha Epsilon, Theta Nu Epsilon. Democrat. Episcopalian. Clubs: Maryland, University, Merchants, Baltimore Country. Home: 112 Elmhurst Rd., Roland Park, Baltimore. Office: First Nat. Bank, Baltimore, Md.

PRENTISS, Harriet Doan (Mrs. Irving R. Prentiss), author; b. Cleveland, O.; d. Anthony McReynolds and Martha M. Doan; desc. John Doan, counsellor to Gov. Winslow, Mass. Bay Colony and 1st gov.; ed. Ann Arbor, Mich.; m. Irving R. Prentiss. Mem. Nat. League of Pen Women (past pres. Phila. branch, vice-pres. for Eastern Pa.). Republican. Clubs: Hannah Penn, Art Alliance (Philadelphia), Womans Forum (New York). Author: From Nature Forward; In Harmony with Life; Stars (novel). Contbr. essays, verse, and fiction to mags. and newspapers. Home: 4607 Spruce St., Philadelphia, Pa.

PRESCOTT, Amos Neal, sec. J. L. Prescott Co.; b. Passaic, N.J., June 11, 1897; s. James Edward and Rose Ann (Neal) P.; student Passaic Collegiate Sch., 1900-03, Passaic Grade Schs., 1903-11, Passaic High Sch., 1915; B.S., Mass. Inst. Tech., 1918 (class of 1919); m. Marion Drukker, Oct. 4, 1921; children—Helena Marion, Amos Neal, Edward Dow. With J. L. Prescott Co. since 1918, beginning in production dept. (company organized, 1870), sec. since 1921; pres. Prescott Bros.; v.p. Passaic Rubber Co., Lotte Chem. Co.; sec. Union Bldg. & Investment Co. Pres. Passaic Y.M.C.A. Mem. Phi Sigma Kappa. Clubs: Passaic Rotary, Upper Montclair Country. Home: 116 Aycrigg Av. Office: 27 8th St., Passaic, N.J.

PRESCOTT, Stedman, judge; b. Norbeck, Md., Aug. 30, 1896; s. A. F. and Edith Stanley (Kellogg) P.; LL.B., Georgetown U. Law Sch., 1919; m. E. Callendar Minnick, July 14, 1917; children—Edith Callendar, Stedman, Jr., Mary R., Ann Minnick. Admitted to Md. bar, 1924 and since engaged in gen. practice of law at Rockville; mem. town council of Rockville, 1926-30; states atty. for Montgomery Co., 1930-34; mem. Md. Senate, 1934-38; judge Circuit Ct. since 1938; pres. Rockville Bldg. Co. since 1935; dir. Montgomery Bus Lines. Served as pvt. to 1st lt. arty., U.S.A., 1917-18. Mem. Md. Bar Assn., Delta Theta Phi. Democrat. Episcopalian. Mason. Club: Manor Country (Rockville). Home: 304 W. Montgomery Av., Rockville, Md.

PRESSMAN, Ralph, research bacteriologist and chemist; b. Phila., Pa., May 1, 1901; s. Harry and Sarah (Selling) P.; B.Sc., Phila. Coll. of Pharm. & Sci., 1929, Ph.G., same, 1930, M.Sc., same, 1931; A.M., U. of Pa., 1934, Ph.D., same, 1936; m. Elisabeth Shorre, Jan. 30, 1927. Asst. prof. bacteriology and physiol. chemistry, Phila. Coll. of Pharm. & Sci. since 1930; dir. Dean Labs., Inc., Phila., Pa., since 1930; dir. and adviser, Zeller Labs., Reading, Pa., 1935-36; research in tuberculosis, Henry Phipps Inst., Phila., since 1935. Served in Q.M. Corps, Atlanta, Ga., 1918; C.T.C., Camp Meade, 1920-21. Mem. A.A.A.S., Am. Pharm. Assn., Phila. Diabetic Soc., Sigma Xi, Alpha Sigma, Alpha Zeta Omega. Mem. Y.M.C.A. Phila. Club: Marble Hall Golf (Conshohocken). Home: 5619 N. 12th St., Philadelphia, Pa.

PRESTON, Alfred David, lawyer; b. Lewisburg, W.Va., May 1, 1873; s. Walter Creigh and Sidnie Blakemore (Davis) P.; student Univ. of Va., Charlottesville, 1891-93; m. Blanche Preston Barger, Sept. 10, 1900 (dec.). Admitted to W.Va. bar, 1896, and engaged in gen. practice of law at Fayetteville, W.Va., 1896-1900; in practice at Beckley, W.Va., 1900-09 and since 1914; in practice in New Orleans, La., 1909-14; served as judge criminal ct., Raleigh Co., 1923-26; mem. W.Va. Ho. of Dels., 1935-36. Served as 2d lieut. La. N.G., 1911-12. Mem. Am. Bar Assn., W.Va. Bar Assn. Democrat. Mason. Home: 69 N. Kanawha St. Office: Lilly Bldg., Beckley, W.Va.

PRESTON, Frances Folsom (Cleveland); b. Buffalo, July 21, 1864; d. Oscar and Emma C. (Harmon) Folsom; (her father, a lawyer and former partner of Grover Cleveland, died in 1875); grad. Wells Coll., Aurora, Cayuga Co., N.Y., 1885; m. President Cleveland in the White House, June 2, 1886; children—Ruth (died Jan. 7, 1904), Esther (Mrs. W. S. B. Bosanquet), Marion (Mrs. John H. Amen), Richard F., Francis G.; m. 2d, Thomas Jex Preston, Jr., at Princeton, Feb. 10, 1913. Home: Westland, Princeton, N.J.

PRESTON, Howard Kent, univ. prof.; b. Trenton, N.J., May 11, 1888; s. Thomas and Rachel (Kent) P.; student Trenton (N.J.) High Sch., 1901-05; C.E., Lafayette Coll., Easton, Pa., 1909; m. Florence Earlin Snyder, Sept. 2, 1912 (died 1927); children—Howard Kent, Thomas Earlin; m. 2d, Mildred Wood Whiting, June 11, 1931. Instrument man and draughtsman D.L.&W. R.R., 1909-10; instr. mathematics and mech. drawing, Lafayette Coll., Easton, Pa., 1910-12; instr. mathematics and engring., Del. Coll., Newark, Del., 1912-15, asst. prof., 1915-18; asst. engr. du Pont Engring. Co., Wilmington, Del., 1918; resident engr. N.J. State Highway Dept., Asbury Park, N.J., 1919-20; prof. mathematics and engring., U. of Del., Newark, Del., 1920-30, prof. and head dept. theoretical and applied mechanics since 1930; dir. Newark (Del.) Bldg. & Loan Assn. Mem. Am. Soc. C.E., Phi Kappa Phi, Tau Beta Pi, Alpha Chi Rho. Republican. Presbyterian. Mason. Address: 260 Orchard Rd., Newark, Del.

PRESTON, John J. D(avis), lawyer; b. Lewisburg, W.Va., Dec. 1, 1892; s. John A. and Lillie (Davis) P.; A.B., Washington and Lee U., Lexington, Va., 1913; LL.B., Washington and Lee Law Sch., 1917; unmarried. Engaged in teaching sch., 1913-15; admitted to Va. bar, 1917, W.Va. bar, 1919 and since engaged in gen. practice of law at Charleston, W.Va.; asso. with Price, Smith & Spilman, 1919-29, mem. firm, 1930-33; mem. and chmn. Pub. Service Commn. of W.Va., since 1933. Served as 2d lt. F.A., U.S.A., 1917-19. Mem. Charleston City, W.Va., State and Am. bar assns., Phi Kappa Psi, Phi Delta Phi. Democrat. Presbyn. Mason. Club: Edgewood Country (Charleston). Home: 1536 Quarrier St. Office: Capitol Bldg., Charleston, W.Va.

PRESTON, Walter Wills, lawyer; b. Harford Co., Md., Jan. 14, 1863; s. James Bond and Mary Amelia (Wills) P.; A.B., Princeton U., 1881, A.M., 1883; m. Mary Elizabeth Hall, Nov. 2, 1892 (dec.). Admitted to Md. bar 1883 and since engaged in gen. practice of law at Bel Air; states atty. Harford Co., 1891-1900; asso. judge 3d Judicial Circuit of Md., 1920-1936; pres. Commercial Savings Bank, Bel Air, Md., since 1900. Mem. Md. Legislature, 1888-92. Democrat. Episcopalian. Mason (past master). Home: Bel Air, Md.

PRETTYMAN, Cornelius William, college prof.; b. Leipsic, Del., July 21, 1872; s. Cornelius W. and Emma (Gooding) P.; A.B., Dickinson Coll., 1891; student Johns Hopkins, 1895-97; Ph.D., U. of Pa., 1899; m. Clara Bains, June 10, 1902; m. 2d, Charlotte Hopfe, of Berlin, Germany, Jan. 3, 1912. Engaged as instr., secondary schs., 1895-97; prof. of German, Dickinson Coll., since 1900; dir. Camp Moosilauke, summer sch. for boys, Pike, N.H., 1920-30. Mem. Phi Beta Kappa, Beta Theta Pi, Omicron Delta Kappa. Republican. Methodist. Author: Higher Girls Schools of Prussia, 1910. Editor: Schiller's Dreissigjähriger, Krieg, Fulda's Das Talisman, Wildenbruch's Neid. Contbr. to ednl. jours. Home: Carlisle, Pa.

PRETTYMAN, E(lijah) Barrett, lawyer; b. Lexington, Va., Aug. 23, 1891; s. Forrest Johnston and Elizabeth Rebecca (Stonestreet) P.; A.B., Randolph-Macon Coll., Ashland, Va., 1910, A.M., 1911; LL.B., Georgetown U., 1915; m. Lucy C. Hill, Sept. 15, 1917; children—Elizabeth Courtney, Elijah Barrett. Admitted to Va. bar, 1915; mem. firm Potter, Prettyman and Fisher, Hopewell, Va., 1915-17; spl. atty. Internal Revenue Dept., Washington, D.C., and N.Y. City, 1919-20; asso. and mem. firm Butler, Lamb, Foster and Pope, Chicago, and Washington, D.C., 1920-33; gen. counsel Bur. Internal Revenue, Washington, 1933-34; corporation counsel of the District of Columbia, 1934-36; member firm Hewes, Prettyman, Awalt and Smiddy, Washington, D.C., and Hartford,

Conn.; prof. of taxation, Georgetown U. Law Sch. Served in the U.S. Army, 1917-19, advancing to capt. inf. Trustee Randolph-Macon Coll., Ashland, Va. Mem. Am. and Federal bar assns., D.C. Bar Assn. (dir.), Phi Beta Kappa, Sigma Upsilon, Kappa Sigma, Gamma Eta Gamma, Omicron Delta Kappa. Democrat. Mem. M.E. Ch., S. Clubs: Civitan Internat., Columbia Country, Burning Tree, Metropolitan. Home: 106 Woodlawn Av., Chevy Chase, Md. Address: 822 Connecticut Av., Washington, D.C.

PRETTYMAN, Forrest Johnston, clergyman; b. Brookville, Md., Apr. 7, 1860; s. Elijah B. (Ph.D.) and Lydia Forrest (Johnston) P.; student St. John's Coll. (now U. of Md.), 1876-79, Washington and Lee U., 1890-94; m. Elizabeth Rebecca Stonestreet, Oct. 17, 1888; children—Elijah Barrett, Edith S., Charles Wesley, Martha Barry. Ordained ministry M.E. Ch., S., 1888; served as pastor St. James Ch., Baltimore, Bridgewater Circuit, Va., St. Paul's Ch., Baltimore, Lexington, Va., Martinsburg, West Va., Staunton, Va., Mt. Vernon Place, Washington, D.C., Trinity Ch., Baltimore, Mt. Pleasant Ch. and Emory Ch., Washington, D.C.; served as presiding elder Washington Dist.; elected chaplain U.S. Senate for the first session of the 58th Congress, Nov. 1903 (resigned); again elected chaplain Senate, Mar. 13, 1913, and served 8 yrs. (resigned); in charge Church St. Ch., Knoxville, Tenn., to Mar. 1924, then pastor of Main Street M.E. Church, Gastonia, N.C., later of Wilson Memorial Ch., Baltimore; pastor, Fredericksburg, Va., 1930-37; retired, Oct. 1937. Mem. of Commn. on Universal Faith and Order, Commn. on War Work M.E. Ch., S., Ednl. Commn. M.E. Ch., S., Exec. Com. Francis Asbury Memorial Assn., Federal Council Churches of Christ; mem. Washington Com. of Federal Council on Army and Navy Chaplains. Mem. Ecumenical Conf. of Methodism, London, 1901, Toronto, 1911; fraternal messenger to Gen. Conf. M.P. Ch., Baltimore, 1912, to Gen. Conf. Meth. Ch. of Can., Hamilton, Can., 1918. Trustee Emory U. (Atlanta, Ga.). Home: Rockville, Md.

PREWITT, Richard H(ickman), v.p. Kellet Autogiro Corpn.; b. Lexington, Ky., Jan. 22, 1901; s. David and Mattie (Rhodes) P.; ed. Culver Mil. Acad. and Purdue U.; m. Jean Mary Simpkins, July 1, 1930; 1 son, Richard. Successively stress analysist, draftsman and aerodynamic engr. Chance Vought Corpn., 1929-31; worked on autogiro theory, stress analysis and layout Kellet Autogiro Corpn., 1931-32; project engr. Autogiro Co. of America, 1932-33; design engr., later chief engr. and exec. engr., Kellet Autogiro Corpn., 1933-38, vice-pres.-engr. since 1938. Ind. Democrat. Writer of articles relating to the autogiro. Home: 126 Lansdowne Court, Lansdowne, Pa. Office: Island Road and Laycock Av., Philadelphia, Pa.

PREYER, William Yost; pres. Vick Chem. Co. Office: 100 E. 10th St., Wilmington, Del.

PREYSZ, Louis Robert Fonss, lumber mcht.; b. Big Rapids, Mich., Oct. 27, 1878; s. Christoph and Marie (Dreyer) P.; student pub. schs., Big Rapids, Mich., 1884-94; grad. Ferris Inst., Big Rapids, 1897; m. Lucile Falardeau, May 22, 1909 (died July 20, 1916); children—Marie Lucile (Mrs. Paul Schoonover), Louise Rosalie, Marguerite Ruby, Louis Robert Fonss; m. 2d, Clara Maude Cunningham, Sept. 11, 1917; children—Lillian Rose, Josephine Oleson. Stenographer to circuit judge, Big Rapids, Mich., 1897; bookkeeper and stenographer Ward Bros., Big Rapids, 1897-1904; bookkeeper, sec. and asst. mgr. Raine Andrews Lumber Co., Evenwood, W.Va., 1904-22; in wholesale lumber business for self, Elkins, W.Va., 1922-23; chmn. bd. and treas. W.Va. Lumber Co., Elkins, pres. Meadow River Lumber Co., Rainelle, W.Va., since 1935, Bank of Rainelle since 1935, Sylvania Corpn., Charleston, W.Va., since 1935; also pres. Meadow River Coal & Land Co., Rainelle; dir. Gulland-Clarke Co., Citizens Nat. Bank, Elkins, Raine Lumber & Coal Co. Served as sergt., Mich. N.G., Co. D, 2d Inf., 1902. Republican. Presbyterian. Mason (York Rite, Scottish Rite, Shriner). Address: 300 Scott St., Elkins, W.Va.

PRICE, Frank J., editor; b. Neosho, Mo., Mar. 8, 1860; s. Thomas Potts and Martha A. (Sevier) P.; desc. Gen. John Sevier, of Revolutionary Army; ed. Neosho Collegiate Inst.; m. Anna Winifred Gorden, Apr. 3, 1881; children—Thomas Albert, Laura Caroline, Sidney Gorden (dec.), Martha Sevier, Frank John. Newspaper reporter, 1885-90; Washington corr. St. Louis Republic, 1891, 92, 93; on editorial staff St. Louis Globe Democrat, 1894-95; in magazine work, 1896-97; mng. editor Washington (D.C.) Times, 1897-98; on staff New York Times, 1898-1901; editorial writer News and Commercial, New York, 1901; editorial writer and Sunday editor New York Telegraph, 1902-08; on staff Phila. Telegraph, 1909-10, and chief editorial writer, 1910-12; asso. mng. editor Public Ledger, 1912-13; editorial and special writer New York Morning Telegraph, 1914-24; now syndicates editorials and weekly political review. Editorial dir. Van Ree Pub. Co., Queensboro, N.Y. City. Del. to Nat. Dem. Conv., 1928; Dem. candidate for Congress from 15th Pa. Dist., 1930; prothonotary of Court of Common Pleas and recorder of deeds, Pike County, Pa., 1931-36, not a candidate for reëlection. Mem. S.R. Presbyn. Clubs: St. Paul's, Newspaper, Friars, Masonic; National Press (Washington). Mason. Author: The Major's Daughter, 1891; Ruth, 1892; Industrial Defense, 1916; Diplomacy and Business, 1917; Money—Basic Values at Home and Abroad, 1920; Farmers and the Federal Reserve, 1922; Economic Reflections, 1929; also more than 200 short stories, some under nom de plume of "Faulkner Conway," and brochures, pamphlets and special articles. Home: Lackawaxen, Pa.*

PRICE, Franklin Haines, librarian; b. Phila., Pa., July 3, 1882; s. Dr. Ferris Thomas and Mary Pine (Haines) P.; student Palms Business Coll., Phila., 1898, Pa. Sch. of Industrial Arts, 1906-07 and 1912; m. Alice H. Howe, Apr. 28, 1906; children—Franklin Haines, Jr., Alison Howe, Lewis Hall. Began as asst. Free Library of Phila., 1899, head of dept., 1906-10, in charge of spl. collections, 1911-25, asst. librarian, 1926-34, librarian since 1934; librarian, Jefferson Med. Coll., 1901; supervisor A.L.A. War Service, Philadelphia dist., 1918-19, Am. Mcht. Marine Library Assn., Port of Phila., 1919-20; dir. Pa. Soc. for Promotion Arts and Sciences. Dir. Travelers Aid Soc. of Philadelphia; mem. Am. and Pa. library assns., Booksellers' Assn. of Phila., Pa. Library Club, Spl. Libraries Council of Phila. Republican. Episcopalian. Clubs: Philobiblon, Rotary. Home: 1628 Pine St. Address: The Free Library of Philadelphia, Logan Square, Philadelphia, Pa.

PRICE, John B(eadle), physician, surgeon, author; b. St. Clair, Pa., Sept. 13, 1883; s. Reuben and Emma (Beadle) P.; A.B., Ursinus Coll., 1905; A.M., U. of Pa., 1910; M.D., Medico-Chirurg. Coll., 1914; grad. study, Harvard U., New York, U. of Pa. grad schs.; m. Mary E. Shade, Dec. 23, 1908; children—Janet S. (Mrs. Eden Hood), Martha Ann. Engaged in otolaryng. at Norristown, Pa. since 1919; otolaryngological surgeon Montgomery Hosp., Norristown, Pa., Pennhurst Sch., Pennhurst, Pa.; instr. otolaryngology, U. Fla. Grad. Hosp.; phys. to Ursinus Coll., Collegeville, Pa.; consultant, Norristown State and Sacred Heart hosps. Served as 1st lt. Med. Corps, U.S.A., 1918; capt. Med. Corps, Pa. N.G., 1921-22. Fellow Am. Acad. Otolaryngology. Mem. Med. Assn., Pa. State Med. Soc. Author: Remote Symptoms in Upper Respiratory Infections; Vestibular Cerebral Pathways; Constitutional Backgrounds of Infection; etc., Ind. Republican. Mem. Reformed Ch. Mason. Contbr. tech. papers to med. journs. Home: 824 DeKalb St., Norristown, Pa.

PRICE, Miles Oscar, librarian; b. Plymouth, Ind., July 31, 1890; s. Emanuel and Mary Jane (Dickson) P.; S.B., U. of Chicago, 1914; B.L.S., U. of Ill., 1922; LL.B., Columbia U., 1938; m. Fannie J. Elliott, Jan. 3, 1915; children—Miles Macy (dec.), Mary Dunsdon. Library asst., U. of Chicago, 1910-12; dept. head U. of Chicago Library, 1912-14, U. of Ill. Library, 1914-22; librarian U.S. Patent Office, 1922-29; library rep. U.S.Personnel Classifications Bd., 1923-24; library consultant U.S. Bur. of Efficiency, 1924-29; librarian Columbia U. Law Library since 1929; instr. Sch. of Library Service, summers, since 1937. Mem. Am. Library Assn., Am. Assn. Law Librarians. Methodist. Mason. Club: Men's Faculty (Columbia U.). Home: 133 Highwood Av., Leonia, N.J.

PRICE, Paul Holland, State geologist and univ. prof.; b. Uffington, W.Va., Sept. 1, 1898; s. John Clark and Sarah (Kinkaid) P.; A.B., W.Va. Univ., 1923, M.S., 1926; Ph.D., Cornell U., 1930; m. Helen Tapp, June 11, 1923; children—Allene Helen, Joann Kinkaid, Louise Tapp, Paul Holland, Jr. Employed as field asst. and asst. geologist, W.Va. Geol. Survey, 1922-34, state geologist since 1934; instr. geology, W.Va. U., 1930-36, asso. prof., 1936-38, prof. geology and head dept. of geology, W. Va. Univ., Morgantown, W.Va. since 1938. Served as 2d lt. inf., U.S.A. 1917-19 Dir. Morgantown Chamber of Commerce, state planning Bd., Research Commn. of W.Va. University; sec. Assn. Am. State Geologists. Mem. Geol. Society of America, Am. Assn. Petroleum Geologists (dist. representative), Am. Inst., Mining and Metall. Engrs., Am. Petroleum Inst. advisory council), Am. Geophys. Union, Sigma Chi, Sigma Xi. Republican. Baptist. Mason. Club: Rotary of Morgantown, Public Affairs (W. Va. U.; pres.); Double XX. Home: The Hogback. Address: Box 879, Morgantown, W.Va.

PRICE, Samuel, lawyer; b. Greenbrier Co., W.Va., July 18, 1881; s. Samuel Lewis and Mary (McCue) P.; ed. Lee Mil. Acad., Lewesburg, W.Va., 1895-96, Washington and Lee University, Lexington, Va., 1898-99, University of Va., 1900-04; unmarried. Admitted to Georgia bar, 1905 at Augusta; in practice of law in Atlanta, 1906; admitted to W. Va. bar, 1907 and in practice in Charleston, 1907; engaged in gen. practice of law at Lewesburg, W.Va. since 1908; served as states atty. for Greenbrier Co., 1924-29; now mem. law firm Price & McWhorter; president and dir. Crab Orchard Coal & Land Co., Charleston, W.Va.; dir. Penick Stone Co. Mem. Greenbrier Bar Assn. (pres.), Sigma Nu, Phi Delta Phi. Democrat. Address: Lewisburg, W.Va.

PRICE, T. Brooke; mem. law firm Price, Smith & Spilman. Address: Charleston, W.Va.

PRICE, Thomas Brooke, v.p. and gen. counsel Western Electric Co.; b. Keyser, W.Va., Aug. 31, 1890; s. George Edmund and Sally Ann (Dorsey) P.; A.B., Johns Hopkins, 1912; LL.B., Harvard, 1915; m. Caroline Ward, of Charleston, W.Va., Jan. 24, 1920; children—Edwin Ward, Ann. Dorsey, Caroline. Admitted to N.Y. bar, 1916, W.Va. bar, 1917; asso. with law firm Winthrop & Stimson, New York, 1915-16; mem. firm Price, Smith & Spilman, Charleston, W.Va., since 1917; atty, for Am. Telephone & Telegraph Co., 1934-36; v.p. and gen. counsel and dir. Western Electric Co., Inc., New York, since 1936; gen. counsel and dir. Elec. Research Products, Inc., Teletype Corpn., Mfrs. Junction Ry., 396 Hudson St. Corpn.; gen. counsel Nassau Smelting & Refining Co. Mem. Am. Bar Assn., Chi Phi. Clubs: Harvard, Railroad-Machinery (New York); The Morristown, Morris County Golf (Convent, N.J.). Contbr. to legal jours. Home: 33 Ogden Place, Morristown, N.J. Office: 195 Broadway, New York, N.Y.

PRICE, William Gray, Jr., maj. gen., retired; b. Chester, Pa., Mar. 23, 1869; s. Wm. Gray and Jane Elizabeth (Campbell) P.; ed. pub. and private schs.; hon. Doctor Mil. Sci., Pa. Mil. Coll.; m. Sallie Pennell Eyre, June 1, 1893. National Guard of Pennsylvania, April 1886; promoted through grades to brig. gen. N.G. Pa., 1910; brig. gen. N.A., Aug. 5, 1917; maj. gen. Pa. N.G., May 16, 1919; maj. gen. U.S.R.C., Apr. 9, 1921. Served as lt. col. 3d Pa. Vols., Spanish-Am. War; apptd. cmdr. 53d Arty. Brig., Camp Hancock, Ga., Aug. 5, 1917, and comd. same throughout its service in Europe; participated in Marne, Vesle, Argonne, Leys-Scheldt operations. France and Belgium; apptd. comdg. gen. Pa. N.G. on return from France, May 15, 1919; retired Nov. 23, 1933. Awarded D.S.M. (U.S.); Croix de Guerre (Belgium and

France); Comdr. Legion of Honor (France). Republican. Episcopalian. Clubs: Union League, Corinthian Yacht (Phila); Chester (Chester); Army and Navy (Washington). Home: 900 Kerlin St., Chester, Pa.

PRICE, William N., v.p. Saving Fund Soc. of Germantown and Vicinity; b. Abington, Pa., Nov. 21, 1869; s. Joel E. and Martha Shoemaker (Nice) P.; ed. Philadelphia pub. schs.; m. Fannie Allen Smith, Mar. 12, 1924. With Saving Fund Soc. of Germantown and Vicinity since 1888, advancing through all junior offices, became asst. sec. and asst. treas., 1911, sec. and treas., 1922, v.p., 1938. Clubs: Union League, Philadelphia Cricket. Home: 6905 Chew St. Office: 5458 Germantown Av., Philadelphia, Pa.

PRICE, Winfield Scott; comdg. gen. N.J. Nat. Guard, 1936-June 1939, when retired. Address: Camden, N.J.

PRICHARD, Lucy Elizabeth; prof. Latin, Marshall Coll. Address: Marshall College, Huntington, W.Va.

PRICKETT, Clifford D.; v.p. Hercules Powder Co.; b. Hazardville, Conn., Dec. 26, 1863; s. Edward and Barbara (Law) P.; student High Sch.; m. Edith Gordon, Oct. 23, 1888; children—Stanley G., Gordon. Asst. gen. mgr. Hercules Powder Co., 1904-18, v.p. and dir., 1918. Home: 900 Franklin St. Office: 900 Market St., Wilmington, Del.

PRICKETT, William, lawyer; b. Wilmington, Del., June 9, 1894; s. William Sharp and Mary Wilson (Polk) P.; A.B., Princeton U., 1915; B.A. in jurisprudence, Oxford U., Eng., 1918; m. Elisabeth Susanne deBoeck, June 16, 1919; children—Elise, William, Henry deBoeck. Admitted to Del. bar, 1919, and since practiced at Wilmington; referee in bankruptcy, New Castle Co., Dist. of Del., since 1931. Served as 2d lt., 6th F.A., A.E.F., 1917-18; attached 1st Aero Squadron, A.E.F. Mem. Am. Bar Assn., Assn. of Bar of City of N.Y., Del. Bar Assn., New Castle Co. Bar Assn., Am. Law Inst. Republican. Presbyterian. Home: 1401 Delaware Av. Office: 404 Equitable Bldg., Wilmington, Del.

PRIDE, C. Benjamin; asst. prof. surgery, W. Va. U.; mem. staff City and Monongalia County hosps. Address: 235 High St., Morgantown, W.Va.

PRIEST, George Madison, coll. prof.; b. Henderson, Ky., Jan. 25, 1873; s. George Madison and Philura (Lambert) P.; A.B., Coll. of N.J. (now Princeton U.), 1894, A.M., 1896; studied U. of Berlin, 1894-95, Freiburg, 1899, Leipzig, Marburg and Jena, 1901-02, Jena, 1906-07, Ph.D., 1907; unmarried. Began teaching at Princeton, 1895, prof. Germanic langs. since 1912. Presbyn. Author: Ebernand von Erfurt, 1907; A Brief History of German Literature, 1909; Germany Since 1740, 1915. Translator: Goethe's Faust (parts I and II), 1932. Editor of Riehl's Spielmannskind, 1902; Sudermann's Fritzchen, 1929; Anthology of German Literature in the Eighteenth Century, 1934; Geissler's Der liebe Augustin, 1938. Home: 10 Nassau St., Princeton, N.J.

PRIESTMAN, Glyndon, real estate; b. Hull, England, July 22, 1884; s. Albert and Mabel (Taylor) P.; brought to U.S., 1891; naturalized 1905; prep. edn. Germantown Friends Sch., 1892-1901; B.S., Haverford Coll., 1905; m. Dorothy Williams, Mar. 30, 1912; children —Ruth (Mrs. Anthony Burton), Sidney Williams; m. 2d, Florence Evans, June 4, 1926. Clerk in metal and rug businesses, 1905-08; in real estate business for himself, Phila., 1908-31; pres. Priestman-Helmetag Co., real estate, Phila., since 1931; dir. Pastorius Bldg. & Loan Assn., Mutual Savings Bldg. & Loan Assn., Market Square Bldg. & Loan Assn., Highland Court, Inc. Mem. Phila. Real Estate Bd. (treas., 1928-29; 2d vice-pres., 1930; treas., 1931; pres. 1932); mem. Am. Inst. of Real Estate Appraisers; chmn. of local chapter of the Inst. of Real Estate Management, 1936-37; mem. Inst. of Real Estate Management of Nat. Assn. of Real Estate Bds. Republican. Presbyterian. Club: Union League (Phila.). Home: 7905 Winston Rd. Office: 18 W. Chelten Av., Germantown, Philadelphia, Pa.

PRINCE, Arthur Leslie, soil chemist; b. Worcester, Mass., July 4, 1894; s. Benjamin M. and Lillian F. (Bixby) P.; A.B., Clark Coll., 1916; M.Sc., Mass. State Coll., 1919; m. Jeanie Y. Allan, June 20, 1923; children—Allan Bixby, Gratia McEwen. Asst. soil chemist, N.J. Agrl. Expt. Sta., since 1919; instr. in soils, Rutgers U., 1926-30, asst. prof., 1930-35, asso. prof. soils since 1935. Served in Depot Brig. and as chemist at Base Hosp., Camp Devens, Mass., U.S.A., 1917-19. Fellow A.A.A.S., Sigma Xi. Republican. Presbyn. Mason. Contbr. many papers in field of soil chemistry and soil fertility. Home: 225 Wayne St., New Brunswick, N.J.

PRINCE, Elmer Woodward, city mgr. and city engr.; b. Charles Town, W.Va., May 8, 1897; s. Solon M. and Bertha M. (Grim) P.; B.S. in C.E., W.Va. U., Morgantown, W.Va., 1920; m. Rosetta May Reed, June 30, 1922; 1 son, Elmer Woodward, Jr. Employed as plant engr., Alpha Portland Cement Co., Manheim, W.Va., 1921-22; asst. city engr. of Morgantown, W.Va., 1923-26, city engr., 1926-33, city mgr. and city engr. since 1933. Served in R.O.T.C., 1916-18. Advisor Monongalia Co. Nat. Youth Adminstrn. Dir. Morgantown Chamber of Commerce, Morgantown Community Assn., Monongalia Co. Community Chest, Monongalia Co. Art Guild. Mem. Internat. City Mgrs. Assn., Nat. Municipal League, Soc. Am. Mil. Engrs., Upper Monongahela Valley Assn., Am. Soc. Civil Engrs., Am. Pub. Works Assn., W.Va. Soc. Professional Engrs., Monongalia Co. Soc. Professional Engrs. (past pres.), W.Va. League of Municipalities (past pres., past trustee). Awarded Scroll of All-American Aviation, Inc., for interest in aviation. Republican. Lutheran. Mason, K.P., Elk. Clubs: Lions, Cherry River Navy, Curbstone Coaches Club. Home: 310 Wilson Av. Office: 389 Spruce St., Morgantown, W.Va.

PRINCE, John Dyneley, educator; b. N.Y. City, Apr. 17, 1868; s. John Dyneley and Anne Maria (Morris) P.; A.B., Columbia, 1888; U. of Berlin, 1889-90; Ph.D., Johns Hopkins, 1892; m. Adeline, d. Dr. Alfred L. Loomis, Oct. 5, 1889; 1 son, John Dyneley. Went to Babylonia with U. of Pa.'s expdn., 1888-89, as official representative of Columbia U.; prof. Semitic langs., 1892-1902, dean of Grad. Sch., 1895-1902, New York U.; prof. Semitic langs. 1902-15, prof. Slavonic langs., 1915-21, Columbia; apptd. E.E. and M.P. to Denmark, 1921; E.E. and M.P. to Yugoslavia, 1926-33; prof. of Slavonic, Columbia U., 1933-35, prof. East European Langs., 1935-37, emeritus, 1937——. Mem. Am. Oriental Soc., Am. Philos. Soc.; fellow A.A.A.S. Mem. N.J. Assembly, 1906, 1908 (speaker, 1909), N.J. Senate, 1910-13 (leader, 1911); pres. N.J. Senate, 1912, and acting gov. of N.J., 1912; pres. N.J. Civ. Service Commn., 1917-21. Decorated with Order of St. Saba (Serbia), II Class, 1912; Grand Cordon Jugoslav Crown, 1933; Grand Cross of Dannebrog, 1933. Club: Union (New York). Author: Mene, Mene, Tekel, Upharsin, 1893; A Critical Commentary on the Book of Daniel, Leipzig, 1899; Kulóskap the Master (Algonkin poems), with Charles Godfrey Leland, 1902; Materials for a Sumerian Lexicon, 1908; Assyrian Primer, 1909; Russian Grammar, 1919; Practical Grammar of the Lettish Language (the first in English), 1925; Grammar of the Serbo-Croatian Language, 1929; Fragments from Babel, 1939. Contbr. to philol., anthrop. and scientific jours. on Assyrian subjects, on langs. of Am. Indians, on Scandinavian, and on Slavonic; writer for 11th edition of Encyclopedia Britannica and Hastings' Dictionary of Religions, etc. Home: Ringwood Manor, N.J. Address: Columbia University, New York, N.Y.

PRINCE, Sydney Rhodes, lawyer; b. Mt. Sterling, Ala., Sept. 11, 1876; s. Sydney T. and Helen (Rhodes) P.; A.B., U. of Ala., 1896; LL.B., Georgetown U., 1898; m. Hattie Beverly Smith, Nov. 23, 1904; children—Sydney Rhodes, Gregory Smith. Admitted to Ala. bar, 1898, and began practice at Mobile; atty., M.&O. R.R., 1901-08, asst. gen. counsel, 1908-11, gen. counsel, 1911-18; gen. solicitor, Southern Ry. System, 1918-31; gen. counsel Southern Ry. System since 1932. Episcopalian. Mem. Phi Delta Theta, Phi Beta Kappa. Club: Chevy Chase. Home: 5 Chevy Chase Circle, Chevy Chase, Md. Address: Southern Ry. Co., McPherson Sq., Washington, D.C.

PRINTZ, Stanley Vincent, lawyer; b. Reading, Pa., Nov. 19, 1906; s. Stewart Edgar and Florence May (Shartle) P.; Ph.B., Muhlenberg Coll., Allentown, Pa., 1930; student Harvard, 1930-31; LL.B., Dickinson Sch. of Law, Carlisle, Pa., 1934. Admitted to Pa. bar, 1934, and since engaged alone in gen. practice of law at Allentown, Pa.; admitted to bars Pa. Supreme and Superior cts. and U.S. Dist. Ct. Mem. Pa. and Lehigh Co. bar assns., Sons of the Am. Revolution, Alpha Tau Omega, Alpha Kappa Alpha, Tau Kappa Alpha, Phi Alpha Theta, Omicron Delta Kappa. Republican. Evangelical and Reformed. Home: 714 Walnut St. Office: 523 Hamilton St., Allentown, Pa.

PRINZ, Hermann, prof. dental materia medica; b. Schwittersdorf, Saxony, Germany, June 13, 1868; s. August and Friderike P.; ed. Gymnasium, Leipzig, Germany; student U. of Mich., 1893-95, D.D.S., 1896, hon. A.M., 1911; student U. of Halle, Germany, 1895-96; M.D., St. Louis (Mo.) Med. Coll., 1900; grad. study U. of Berlin, 1913-14; Sc.D., U. of Pa., 1926; D.M.D., U. of Cologne, Germany, 1929; m. Lily Koop, July 5, 1905 (died Jan. 22, 1939). Apprentice to apothecary, Germany, 1884-87; came to U.S., 1889, naturalized citizen, 1896; prof. materia medica and therapeutics, Washington U., 1899-1913; same, Evans Dental Inst., U. of Pa., 1913-38, prof. emeritus since 1938. Mem. A.M.A., Am. Acad. Arts and Sciences, Sigma Xi; fellow Kaiserlich Leopold-Carolin. Akademie der Naturforscher, Halle, Germany, 1933. Awarded gold medal, Dental Soc. State N.Y., 1923; Callahan memorial award (gold medal), Ohio State Dental Soc., 1933; Jenkins memorial medal, Conn. State Dental Assn., 1934; Alumni award, U. of Pa., 1939. Author: Dental Formulary, 1907; Dental Materia Medica and Therapeutics, 1910; Diseases of the Soft Structures of the Teeth, 1928; Diseases of the Mouth and their Treatment (with Dr. S. S. Greenbaum), 1935. Contbr. to Dental Cosmos. Home: 400 S. Lansdowne Av., Lansdowne, Pa.

PRITCHARD, John Paul, prof. Greek; b. White Lake, N.Y., Feb. 8, 1902; s. John Henderson and Jane (Du Bois) P.; A.B., Cornell U., 1922, Ph.D., same, 1925; m. Ruth Belle Smith, Aug. 19, 1926; 1 son, John Paul. Prof. ancient langs., Catawba Coll., Salisbury, N.C., 1925-28; prof. Greek and head dept. of classical langs., Washington and Jefferson Coll., since 1928; mem. com. for revision of requirements for teachers of Latin in Pa., 1931-33; dean of freshman, Washington and Jefferson Coll., 1930-32. Mem. Am. Philol. Assn., Modern Lang. Assn., Phi Beta Kappa, Eta Sigma Phi Republican. United Presbyn. Club: Fortnightly. Contributor many monographs on Am. use of classical lit. criticism in mags. Home: 34 S. Lincoln St., Washington, Pa.

PRITCHARD, Robert Howard, newspaper editor; b. Weston, W.Va., Apr. 14, 1892; s. William Lloyd and Catherine (Devaney) P.; grad. Weston High Sch., 1912; student W.Va. U., 1913-17 (3½ yrs.); m. Pauline Brewster, June 9, 1920; children—Mary Catherine, Alice Lorraine, Margaret Pauline. Began as printer's apprentice on Weston (W.Va.) Democrat, 1907; worked as printer while going to high school and university; entered 2d O.T.C., Ft. Benjamin Harrison, Ind., 1917; commd. 2d. lt., U.S. Army, and assigned to 327th Machine Gun Batt.; with A.E.F. as 1st lt., 41st Div. Reporter Western Democrat, 1920; teacher of English and French, Weston High Sch., 1920-21; with Andrew Edminston, purchased Weston Democrat, 1921, and since editor; with brother co-owner Camden and Hollywood theatres until 1938. Conducted tour of W.Va. with 400 editors 1938; pres. W.Va. Council of Journalism, 1926-27; mem. bd. of govs. W.Va. Univ. Mem. Nat. Editorial Assn. (pres. 1936-37); mem. Am.

Legion (past comdr. Weston post), Beta Theta Pi. Democrat. Methodist. Mason. Club: Rotary (pres. Weston club 1938-39). Home: 415 Court Av. Office: Main St., Weston, W.Va.

PRITT, Thaddeus, banking; b. Randolph Co., W.Va., Mar. 29, 1873; s. John Benton and Rose A. (Crickard) P.; grad. pub. schs. Randolph Co., W.Va., 1893; student pvt. schs., 1893-96; m. Mary McClellan, Sept. 15, 1915; children—Thaddeus McClellan, James Wallace (dec.). Engaged in teaching pub. schs. Randolph Co., W.Va., 1896-1901; assessor of real estate, 1900-01; dep. sheriff Randolph Co., W.Va., 1901-07, sheriff, 1908-12, clk. county court, 1915-21; cashier Elkins Nat. Bank, Elkins, W.Va., 1919-29; pres. and dir. Davis Trust Co., Elkins, since 1929; sec., treas. and dir. Upper Elk Coal Co., Elkins; dir. Morrison Gross & Co. (lumber), Elkins Bldrs. Supply Co., Inter-Mountain Coal & Lumber Co., all of Elkins; propr. two farms and part owner three grazing farms in Randolph Co., W.Va. Active in civic affairs in Elkins and Randolph Co. Treas. Davis and Elkins Coll. Democrat. Presbyterian. Odd Fellow. Elk. Club: Elkins Rotary. Home: 117 Graham St., Elkins, W.Va.

PRIZER, William Mann, printing and engraving; b. Phila., Pa., Sept. 22, 1886; s. Harry Atmore and Ida Comly (Mann) P.; ed. Episcopal Acad., Phila., Pa., 1895-1903, Phillips Exeter Acad., Exeter, N.H., 1903-05; Litt.B., Princeton, 1909; m. Margaret Dice, Oct. 21, 1913; 1 son, William Mann, Jr. Asso. with William Mann Co., bank stationers, lithographers, printers, engravers, Phila., Pa., continuously since entering employ, 1909, pres. since 1928; dir. William Mann Co., North East Pa. R.R. Co. Served in signal corps, U.S.A. with A.E.F., 1918-19. Mem. Ivy Club of Princeton. Republican. Presbyn. Home: Haverford. Office: 21 N. Fifth St., Philadelphia, Pa.

PROBST, Everett William, industrial surgeon; b. Jersey City, N.J., June 22, 1905; s. Joseph F. and Clara (Rother) P.; grad. Hoboken High Sch., 1922; B.S., Lafayette Coll., 1926; student Johns Hopkins, 1926-28; M.D., Univ. and Bellevue Hosp. Med. Coll., 1930; grad. student New York U., 1931-33; m. Bertha Dansen, Feb. 12, 1937. In gen. practice, Rutherford, N.J., since 1931; med. supt. and industrial surgeon, E. I. du Pont de Nemours Co., Plastics Div., since 1937. Commd. capt. Med. Reserve, as plans and training officer 342d Med. Regt., U.S. Army. Mem. Am. and N.J. Assns. Industrial Physicians and Surgeons, A.M.A., N.J. Med. Soc., Kappa Delta Rho, Phi Alpha Sigma, Alpha Phi Omega, Royal Arcanum. Episcopalian. Club: Officers of Army and Navy. Designer of Lucite surgical splints. Home: 14 E. Park Place, Rutherford, N.J. Office: Du Pont Co., Arlington, N.J.

PROCTOR, George Nelson, chief engr.; b. Middletown, Conn., Oct. 14, 1902; s. Isaac and Emma (Thompson) P.; student Manchester High Sch., Manchester, Conn., 1916-20, N.Y.U. Grad. Sch. of Business, 1937, 1938; B.S. in M.E., Drexel Inst. Tech., Phila., 1926; m. Florence Ann Fox, Oct. 26, 1927; children—George Nelson, Nancy Joan. Machine designer Cheney Bros. Silk Co., Manchester, Conn., 1920-22; industrial fuel rep. Pub. Service Electric & Gas Co., Newark, N.J., 1926-27; chief engr. Millbank Bleachery, Lodi, N.J., 1927-29; chief engr. Emark battery div., T. A. Edison, Inc., Kearny, N.J., since 1929; registered professional engr., State of N.Y. Served as 1st lt., 312th Inf., U.S. Army (Res.), 1926-37. Trustee Verona (N.J.) Presbyn. Ch. Mem. Am. Soc. M.E., Montclair Soc. of Engrs., Tau Beta Pi, Phi Kappa Phi. Republican. Presbyterian. Address: 15 Howard St., Verona, N.J.

PROCTOR, Haydn, lawyer; b. Asbury Park, N.J., June 16, 1903; s. Phineas and Emilie (Jones) P.; B.S., Lafayette Coll., 1926; LL.B., Yale U. Law Sch., 1929; m. Dorothy Young, Aug. 5, 1933; 1 dau., Ann Pinckney. Admitted to N.J. bar as atty., 1930; engaged in gen. practice of law at Asbury Park; mem. firm Proctor & Nary; mem. N.J. Ho. of Assembly, 1936-37; judge First Jud. Dist. Ct., Monmouth Co., 1937-38; mem. N.J. Senate for term, 1939-41. Chmn. advancement com. Monmouth & Ocean Co. Boy Scouts. Mem. Monmouth Co. Bar Assn. (treas.), Phi Delta Theta. Republican. Methodist. Mason. Elk. Grange. K.P. I.O.O.F. Kiwanian. Home: 1103 Sunset Av. Office: Electric Bldg., Asbury Park, N.J.

PROCTOR, James W(illiam), physician; b. Nova Scotia, June 13, 1863; s. William and Mary (Irons) P.; came to U.S., 1886, naturalized, 1892; M.D., U. City of N.Y. Med. Sch., 1888; m. Eva Kipp, Jan. 1, 1918. Engaged in gen. practice of medicine and surgery, Englewood, N.J., since 1892; cons. surgeon, Englewood Hosp. since 1934, Holy Name Hosp. since 1915; dir. Englewood Sewerage Co. Served as City Physician of Englewood, N.J., 1895-1900. Fellow Am. Coll. Surgeons; hon. mem. Surgeons of N.J., Bergen Co. Med. Soc. Republican. Presbyn. Mason (past master). Club: Englewood (Englewood). Home: 188 Engle St., Tenafly, N.J.

PROSCH, Frederick; prof. physical and health edn., Temple University. Address: Temple University, Philadelphia, Pa.

PROSSER, Seward, banker; b. Buffalo, N.Y., May 1, 1871; s. Henry Wilbur and Anna (Fay) P.; ed. pub. schs. and Englewood (N.J.) Sch. for Boys; m. Constance Barber, Oct. 25, 1902; children—Barbara (Mrs. John A. Gifford), Anna Fay (Mrs. Leighton H. Stevens), Constance Mary (Mrs. Richard K. Mellon). Began active career with Equitable Life Assurance Soc. of U.S., later member firm Prosser & Homans, representing same; v.p. Astor Trust Co., 1907-12; president Liberty Nat. Bank, 1912-14; president Bankers Trust Company, Oct. 6, 1914-23, now dir. chmn. bd. and mem. exec. com.; dir. and mem. exec. com. Gen. Electric Co.; dir. General Motors Corpn., Bankers Safe Deposit Co., General Motors Acceptance Corporation, Equitable Life Assurance Society, International General Electric Co., Internat. Nickel Co. of Can., Ltd., Kennecott Copper Corpn., Graphite Metallizing Corporation, Braden Copper Co., etc. Republican. Episcopalian. Clubs: Union League, Metropolitan, N.Y. Yacht. Home: Palisade Av. E., Englewood, N.J. Office: 16 Wall St., New York, N.Y.

PROTHERO, John Clements, physician; b. Indiana, Pa., Aug. 5, 1905; s. Harold Ney and Louise May (Clements) P.; student Jeannette (Pa.) High Sch., 1919-23, Culver (Ind.) Mil. Acad., summer 1921; S.B., Harvard, 1927; M.D., U. of Pittsburgh Sch. of Medicine, 1931; post grad. student, U. of Edinburgh (Scotland), post grad. med. sch., 1935; unmarried. Gen. practitioner at Jeannette, Pa., since 1932; mem. visiting staff, Westmoreland Hosp., Greensburg, Pa., since 1936; mem. of firm Arlington Studios of Interior Decoration, Pittsburgh, since 1937; Ford Motor Agency, Greensburg, Pa., since 1937. Diplomate Nat. Bd. of Med. Examiners; fellow A.M.A.; mem. Westmoreland Co., Pa. State med. socs. Republican. Presbyterian. Clubs: Harvard-Yale-Princeton, Univ. (Pittsburgh); Harvard of Western Pa. (Pittsburgh). Home: 111 Magee Av. Office: 109 Magee Av., Jeannette, Pa.

PROTHRO, James Thompson, professional baseball; b. Memphis, Tenn., July 16, 1894; s. John Rosser and Roberta Alice (Thompson) P.; ed. Castle Heights Mil. Acad., 1910-12; D.D.S., U. of Tenn. Dental Sch., 1918; m. Katherine Cates, Oct. 3, 1917; 1 son, James Thompson, Jr. Engaged in practice of dentistry, Memphis, Tenn., 1918-20; entered professional baseball due to stomach disorder, 1920; played with clubs at Memphis, Tenn., Southern Assn., Washington, D.C., Am. League, Boston, Mass., Am. League, Cincinnati, O., Nat. League, Portland Ore.; mgr. Memphis Club, seven yrs., Little Rock, Ark. Club, 4 yrs.; mgr. Phila. Nat. League Baseball Club since 1939. Served in U.S.N. at Great Lakes, Ill., 1918. Democrat. Methodist. Home: 787 West Drive, Hein Park, Memphis, Tenn. Office: 921 Packard Bldg., Philadelphia, Pa.

PRUGH, Byron Edgar Peart, prohibition worker; b. Rural Valley, Armstrong Co., Pa., Apr. 21, 1859; s. James Henry and Esther Emily (Peart) P.; A.B., Park Coll., Parkville, Mo., 1884, A.M., 1887; D.D., Westminster Coll., New Wilmington, Pa., 1901; m. Maude Lillie Christian, July 28, 1886 (died Sept. 8, 1887); 1 dau., Lillie Maude; m. 2d, Sarah Markle Boyd, of Lincoln, Neb., Mar. 6, 1889 (died Nov. 9, 1897); children—Marie Jeannette (Mrs. Samuel Hunter Davis), Sadie Blanche Estelle (Mrs. M. J. Deichert), William Boyd; m. 3d, Mrs. Emma P. Dick, of West Newton, Pa., Dec. 20, 1900 (died Mar. 11, 1922); m. 4th, Ada Marshall, of Dayton, Pa., June 24, 1926. Teacher pub. schs. at age of 14 and for 10 yrs. thereafter; ordained Presbyn. ministry, 1887; home missionary and pastor in Wis., Neb., Kan., Ind., S.D., Ohio and Pa. until 1906, last pastorate at Glenfield, Pa.; evangelistic work, 1906-13; state chmn. Prohibition Party of Pa., 1913-30; national chmn. Prohibition Party, 1924-26 (resigned); chmn. Prohibition Nat. Conv., Chicago, Aug. 1928; candidate of Prohibition Party for Congress at large from Pa., 1921. Author of many Prohibition leaflets; contbr. to Prohibition press. Editor The Index, monthly Prohibition paper. Home: 128 Walnut St., Harrisburg, Pa.

PRYOR, James Chambers, rear adm.; b. Winchester, Tenn., Mar. 13, 1871; s. James Jones and Nannie Buchanan (Brazelton) P.; A.B., U. of Nashville; M.D., Vanderbilt, 1896; spl. med. courses in clinics, Vienna, Paris and London; M.A., Johns Hopkins, 1913; grad. U.S.A. War Coll., 1928; m. Georgia Leontine Mackay, June 16, 1906 (died 1914); 1 son, James Chambers; m. 2d, Frances Pierpont Siviter, June 9, 1917; 1 dau., Frances Pierpont. Entered U.S.N. as assistant surgeon with rank of ensign, 1897; advanced through grades to rear admiral, Oct. 1, 1934; retired April 1, 1935. Served on U.S.S. Albatross during Spanish-American War; medical officer Agassiz Expdn. to South Pacific Ocean on same ship, 1898-99; served as med. attendant to Theodore Roosevelt at White House and Oyster Bay; brigade surgeon Naval forces ashore at Vera Cruz, Mexico, 1914; head dept. hygiene, U.S. Naval Med. Sch., Washington, D.C., 1917-20; prof. preventive medicine, George Washington U., 1917-19; lecturer on naval hygiene, Johns Hopkins, 1919; commanded U.S. Naval Hosps., Yokohama, Japan, Pensacola, Fla., Hampton Roads, Va., U.S. Naval Med. Sch., 1925-28; med. officer and head of dept. hygiene U.S. Naval Acad., 1928-31; comdg. Naval Med. Supply Depot, Brooklyn N.Y. Spl. commendation of sec. of Navy "for extraordinary devotion in line of duty," at Battle of Ciudad Volivar, Venezuela, 1903; service medals, Spanish-Am. War, Occupation of Vera Cruz, Mexico, and World War. Fellow Am. Coll. Surgeons; mem. Am. Med. Assn., Assn. of Mil. Surgeons of U.S. (ex-pres.), Med. Soc. of D.C.; sec. Sect. on Mil. Medicine 14th Internat. Congress on Hygiene and Demography; chmn. delegation sent by U.S. to 6th Internat. Congress on Mil. Medicine and Pharmacy, at The Hague, 1931, and delegate to 8th Congress, Brussels, 1935. Democrat. Methodist. Mason. Clubs: N.Y. Yacht (New York); Sherwood Forest (Md.); Army and Navy, Chevy Chase (Washington). Author: Naval Hygiene, 1918. Contbr. to Ency. Britannica, 14th edit., and to Johns Hopkins and U.S. Naval med. bulls. Home: 184 Columbia Heights, Brooklyn; (summer) Sherwood Forest, Md. Address: 184 Columbia Heights, Brooklyn, N.Y.

PUGH, David Benjamin, coll. prof.; b. Homestead, Pa., Sept. 29, 1891; s. Richard Oliver and Hannah Marie (Williams) P.; grad. Millersville State Teachers Coll., 1912; A.B., Lebanon Valley Coll., 1916; A.M., U. of Pittsburgh, 1928; grad. study, Pa. State Coll., 1929-33; m. Grace Emma Miles, Aug. 24, 1916; children—Grace Naomi (Mrs. Amos Austin Goss), David Miles. Engaged in teaching chemistry and mathematics, high schs. in Pa. and Philippine Islands, 1910-29; instr. edn. and psychology, Pa. State Coll., 1929-34, supervisor undergrad. centers, 1934-36, dir. arts and sci. extension and supervisor undergrad. centers, Pa. State Coll. since 1936. Mem. exec. com., Jr. Coll. Council, Middle Atlantic States since 1937. Mem. Kappa Delta Pi, Kappa Phi Kappa, Phi Delta Kappa, Psi Chi. Republican. Presbyn. Mason (32°). Club: Centre Hills Country

(State College). Author: A Problem Course in Chemistry, 1921. Home: 356 E. Foster Av., State College, Pa.

PUGH, Emerson Martindale, asso. prof. physics; b. Ogden, Utah, July 19, 1896; s. William and Hattie Fox (Martindale) P.; B.S. in E.E., Carnegie Inst. Tech., 1918; M.S. in Physics, U. of Pittsburgh, 1927; Ph.D. in Physics, Calif. Inst. Tech., 1929; Ensign U.S.N., Stevens Inst. Tech., 1918-19; m. Ruth Hazel Edgin, Sept. 18, 1920; children—George Edgin, Emerson William. Employed as cashier Vinta County State Bank, 1919-20; instr. physics, Carnegie Inst. Tech., 1920-27; Petroleum Inst. Fellow, 1927-29; Nat. Research Fellow, 1929-30, asst. prof. physics, Carnegie Inst. Tech., 1930-31, asso. prof. physics since 1931. Served as engring. officer U.S.N. Res., 1918-19. Mem. Am. Phys. Soc., Am. Assn. Univ. Profs., Soc. for Promotion Engring. Edn., Sigma Xi, Tau Beta Pi, Phi Kappa Phi, Delta Tau Delta. Mem. Christian Ch. Home: 1427 Walnut St., Pittsburgh, (18) Pa.

PUGH, James Hunter, lawyer; b. Washington, D.C., Oct. 26, 1902; s. Edward Lawrence and Anais Julia (O'Connor) P.; student Georgetown Coll., D.C. 1922-24, Georgetown U. Law Sch., 1924-26; LL.B., Nat. Univ. Law Sch., D.C., 1927; m. Kathryn Varela, June 28, 1933; children—James Hunter, jr., John Philip Sousa. Admitted to Md. bar, 1932, D.C. bar, 1930, U.S. Dist. Court, 1934; engaged in gen. practice of law at Rockville, Md., since 1932; mem. Fire Bd. Chevy Chase, Md., 1931-33; mem. Citizen Com., Chevy Chase, 1931-33; elected state's atty. Montgomery Co., 1935-39; local counsel to Federal Land Bank of Baltimore, Md.; appointed mem. State Industrial Accident Commn. of Md. by Gov. H. R. O'Conor for term 1939-44. Served in Md. N.G., 1922-29. Mem. Carroll Law Club, Georgetown Univ. Democrat. Roman Catholic. Mem. K. of C. Club: Rotary of Bethesda-Chevy Chase; Bethesda Chamber of Commerce. Home: 6902 Glendale Rd., Chevy Chase. Office: Montgomery Av., Rockville, Md.

PUGH, William Barrow, church official; b. Utica, N.Y., Jan. 20, 1889; s. William Barrow and Mary Jane (Albro) P.; A.B., Central High Sch., Phila., Pa., 1907; A.B., U. of Pa., 1910; M.A., Princeton U., 1912; student Princeton Theol. Sem., 1910-13; D.D., Coll. of the Ozarks, 1933; m. Emma Marie Schaperkotter, June 28, 1917; children—William Barrow, Donald Henry. Ordained ministry Presbyn. Ch., 1915; pastor Beacon Ch., Phila., 1915-28, First Ch., Chester, Pa., 1929-38; an asst. to stated clerk of Gen. Assembly Presbyn. Ch. U.S.A., 1922-38; stated clerk Gen. Assembly Presbyn. Ch. U.S.A. since 1938; sec. gen. council Presbyn. Gen. Assembly since 1938; sec. dept. church coöperation and union of the Presbyn. Ch. U.S.A.; trustee of Presbyn. Gen. Assembly; mem. exec. council Presbyn. Hist. Soc. Del. to Federal Council of Chs. of Christ in America, 1932, 34, 36, 38; mem. exec. com. since 1932; Am. sec. of Alliance of the Reformed Chs. throughout the world holding the Presbyn. system; del. to World Alliance of Presbyn. and Reformed Churches, 1937; mem. spl. com. on revised Book of Discipline, 1932-33; mem. spl. com. on legal procedure, 1936-38. Served as chaplain 28th Div., U.S.A., participating in Oise-Aisne, Meuse-Argonne, Ypres-Lys offensives, World War; now chaplain Pa. N.G. Mem. Am. Legion (chaplain Dept. of Pa. 1925). Trustee Princeton Theol. Sem. (sec. of bd. since 1929). Republican. Clubs: Penn Athletic (Phila.); Springhaven Country (Wallingford, Pa.). Contbr. articles on ch. law to mags. Home: Providence Rd., Wallingford, Pa. Office: Witherspoon Bldg., Philadelphia, Pa.

PUGH, William Samuel, mining engr.; b. Pottsville, Pa., June 27, 1871; s. John and Rosanna (Beidelman) P.; grad. high sch., Pottsville, 1888; grad. corr. course Internat. Corr. Schs., Scranton, Pa., 1896; m. Jennie June Edwards, Oct. 27, 1896. Private practice as civil and mining engr. since 1892; now consulting mining engr. for Schuylkill Co., Pa.; frequently called to testify before courts of Anthracite region and Public Service Commn. of Pa.; employers' rep. Federal Labor Bd., Schuylkill Co., Pa., 1917-18; pres. Schuylkill Co. Bd. of Viewers since 1933. Mem. Pa. Engrs. Soc., Am. Inst. of Mining and Metall. Engrs. Republican. Presbyn. Mason (33°, K.T., Shriner). Clubs: Pottsville, Sphinx. Home: 1816 Mahantango St., Pottsville, Pa. Office: Mortimer Bldg., Pottsville, Pa.

PUGLIESE, Sebastian Charles, lawyer; b. Punxsutawney, Pa., June 17, 1903; s. Joseph and Antoinette (Capirossi) P.; ed. Indiana State Teachers Coll., 1918-21; LL.B., Dickinson Coll. Law Sch., 1924; m. Grace Margiotti, Aug. 9, 1933; children—Sebastian Charles, Jr., Joseph Margiotti. Admitted to Pa. bar, 1924 and since engaged in gen. practice of law at Pttsburgh; mem. firm Margiotti, Pugliese, Evans and Buckley; admitted to practice before higher State cts. and Federal cts. Mem. Am. and Allegheny County bar assns. Roman Catholic. Home: 39 Ordale Boul. Office: 720 Grant Bldg., Pittsbugh, Pa.

PULLEN, Thomas Granville, Jr., educator; b. Madison Court House, Va., Feb. 4, 1898; s. Thomas Granville and Annie Brown (Hilldrup) P.; A.B., Coll. of William and Mary, Williamsburg, Va., 1917; M.A., Columbia U. Teachers Coll., 1925, grad. work summers 1930, 31, 35, 1937-38; m. Margaret Louise Rowe, July 10, 1922; 1 son (foster son). Prin., teacher of English and Latin, Dinwiddie (Va.) High Sch., 1917-18; asst. prin. and teacher of Latin, Martinsville (Va.) High Sch., 1919-20; prin. Hampton (Va.) High Sch., 1920-23; head English dept., Newport News (Va.) High Sch., 1923-26; prin. Catonsville (Md.) High Sch., 1926-32; teacher of edn., U. of N.C., (summer sch.), Chapel Hill, N.C., 1927, 28; supt. of schs. for Talbot Co., Easton, Md., 1932-34; state supervisor of high schs., Md. State Dept. of Edn., Baltimore, since 1934, asst. state supt. in adminstrn., since 1936. Served as 2d lt., U.S. Marine Corps, 1918-19. Mem. Md. Com. on Secondary Schs., Middle States Assn. of Colleges and Secondary Schs. Mem. N.E.A., Am. Assn. of Sch. Administrators, State Teachers Assn., Dept. of Secondary Sch. Prins., Theta Delta Chi, Phi Beta Kappa, Phi Delta Kappa, Kappa Phi Kappa. Democrat. Methodist. Mason. Clubs: Chesapeake (Baltimore). Home: 7 S. Beechwood Av., Catonsville, Md. Office: 1111 Lexington Bldg., Baltimore, Md.

PULLINGER, Herbert, artist; b. Phila., Pa., Aug. 5, 1878; s. Frederick A. and Jennie (Seiler) P.; art ed. Sch. Industrial Art, Phila., Drexel Inst., Acad. Fine Arts; m. Frances Rittenhouse Cooley, Sept. 22, 1924. In profession as artist since 1906; began as newspaper artist; painting in oils and water colors, later specializing in making of prints, etchings, lithographs and block prints; instr. graphic arts, Sch. Industrial Art since 1924; represented in various permanent collections; exhibited in many of the large cities at important galleries; served on many art juries. Fellowship Acad. Fine Arts. Awarded Eyre Gold Medal by Fellowship, 1925; silver medal at Sesqui-Centennial Expn., 1926; many hon. mentions. Mem. Phila. Sketch Club, Phila. Print Club. Republican. Ch. of Christ Scientist. Home: 5301 Knox St. Studio: 1430 South Penn. Sq., Philadelphia, Pa.

PULSIFER, Lawson Valentine, chemical engr.; b. Manchester, Conn., Sept. 10, 1881; s. Nathan Trowbridge and Almira Houghton (Valentine) P.; A.B., Harvard, 1903; m. Ethel Burke, June 25, 1910. Began with Valentine & Co., 1903, chief chemist, 1910-29, also v.p. in charge of all mfg., pres., 1929-31; v.p. Congoleum-Nairn, Inc., since 1931; invented first waterproof varnish, 1908. Consulting chemist Govt. depts. during World War. Mem. Soc. Chem. Industry, Am. Soc. for Testing Materials, Soc. Automotive Engrs., Delta Kappa Epsilon. Progressive Republican. Conglist. Home: Mountainville, Orange Co., N.Y. Office: Kearny, N.J.*

PURDUM, R. B.; prof. chemistry, Davis & Elkins Coll. Address: Davis & Elkins College, Elkins, W.Va.

PURDUM, Smith White, fourth asst. postmaster gen.; b. Montgomery County, Md., Dec. 12, 1876; s. Thomas Fletchall and Emma (Lewis) P.; ed. pub. and pvt. schs. and corr. schs.; m. Laura Hastings Dolan, Sept. 17, 1902; children —Smith Hastings, Elizabeth Rosalie, Dorothy Lewis (Mrs. Raymond H. Hunt), Mildred Lee, Laura S., Ruth D. (Mrs. B. Brown). Ry. postal clk., 1896-1903; special agent and rural agent Postoffice Dept., 1903-06; apptd. post office inspector, 1906, inspector in charge, Washington Div., 1918-21; again postoffice inspector, 1921-33, dep. fourth asst. postmaster gen., 1933-34, fourth asst. postmaster gen. since June, 1934. Democrat. Presbyn. Odd Fellow. Home: Hyattsville, Md. Office: Post Office Dept., Washington, D.C.

PURDY, Willard Glenn, clergyman; b. Elgin, Ill., Oct. 6, 1892; s. Edward S. and Jean Cramm (Miller) P.; student Coe Coll., Cedar Rapids, Ia., 1912-16, Princeton Theol. Sem. 1919-21; hon. D.D., Coe Coll., 1916; m. Pearl Mildred Wilson, Sept. 2, 1922; children—Ruth Mildred, Helen Lois. Employed as supt. schs. in Ia., 1916-17; Y.M.C.A., sec. Fargo, N.D., 1917-18; ordained to ministry Presbyn. Ch., 1921; pastor, Montclair, N.J., 1921-37; pastor, First and Central Ch. Wilmington, Del., since 1937. Served as co. comdr. U.S.N. Hosp. Corps, 3d Rgt. Ill. N.G., 1911-14. Moderator Newark Presbytery, 1933-34, Presbytery of New Castle, 1939-40; treas. bd. of trustees Montclair (N.J.) Library. Dir. Anti-Saloon League. Trustee Wilmington (Del.) Bible Coll., Am. Theol. Sem. Wilmington. Mem. Am. Legion, Phi Alpha Pi. Republican. Presbyn. Mason (K.T.) Odd Fellow. Clubs: Kiwanis, Masonic, Cleric (Wilmington). Home: 2108 Van Buren St., Wilmington, Del.

PURINTON, Edward Earle, author; b. Morgantown, W.Va., Apr. 24, 1878; s. Daniel Boardman and Florence Abbey (Lyon) P.; grad. Doane Acad., Granville, O., 1895; A.B., Denison U., 1899; unmarried. Instr. Doane Acad., 1900, later editorial counsel or dir. various publs., lecturer on health, psychology and efficiency, etc.; now research specialist, efficiency analyst and counsel; dean Am. Efficiency Foundation, dir. Reconstruction Ednl. Alliance, dir. National Prosperity Survey, pres. National Efficiency League, all of N.Y. City. Mem. Nat. Inst. Social Sciences, Am. Acad. Polit. and Social Science, Sigma Chi. Republican. Author: Efficient Living, 1915; The Triumph of the Man Who Acts, 1916; Pétain, the Prepared, 1917; Practical Course in Personal Efficiency, 1917; Personal Efficiency in Business, 1919; also many brochures, pamphlets, and numerous articles to mags.; formerly managing, consulting or contributing editor of the Independent Weekly, Center Monthly, Psychology Mag., Herald of Health, Office Economist and Hoggson Bank Magazine. Home: 76 Grandview Av., Morgantown, W.Va. Office: 475 Fifth Av., New York, N.Y.

PURNELL, William Childs, lawyer; b. Elkton, Md., Sept. 14, 1903; s. William Greenbury and Sarah Matilda (Childs) P.; B.Sc., St. John's Coll., Annapolis, Md., 1923; student U. of Md., Baltimore, 1923-24; LL.B., Harvard U. Law Sch., 1927; m. Charlotte Marcia Thilo, of Chicago, Feb. 4, 1928; children—George Worthington Thilo, Charlotte Eugenie. Admitted to Md. bar 1927 and since engaged in gen. practice of law at Baltimore; asst. U.S. atty., Md., 1928-30; asst. gen. atty. Western Md. Ry., Baltimore, 1931-34, gen. atty. since 1934. Capt. 5th Inf., Md. N.G. since 1929; mil. aide to gov. Md., 1935-39. Mem. bd. supervisors of elections, Baltimore, 1938-39. Mem. Baltimore Bar Assn., Am. Bar Assn., Phi Sigma Kappa, Gamma Eta Gamma. Republican. Episcopalian. Clubs: University (Baltimore); Green Spring Valley Hunt (Garrison). Home: 3020 Fendall Rd. Office: Standard Oil Bldg., Baltimore, Md.

PURVIS, Joseph Dixon, physician; b. Butler, Pa., Sept. 21, 1882; s. Joseph L. and Mary Ellen (Bailey) P.; student Washington and Jefferson Coll., and U. of Pa.; m. Clara E. Schneideman, June 20, 1912; children—Joseph Dixon, Sarah Ellen. In practice at Butler, Pa.; mem. staff Butler Co. Memorial Hosp., Butler, Pa. Mem. A.M.A., Butler Co. Med. Soc., Pa. State Med. Soc., Phi Gamma Delta,

Alpha Mu Phi Omega, Alpha Omega Alpha. Mason. Home: 229 N. McKean St. Office: Butler Saving & Trust Bldg., Butler, Pa. Died Aug. 3, 1939.

PURVIS, William Edmond, clergyman; b. Allegheny, Pa., Sept. 3, 1865; s. Samuel Anderson and Martha Ann (Pinkerton) P.; A.B., Westminster Coll., New Wilmington, Pa., 1888; grad. Pittsburgh Theol. Sem., 1891; m. Florence Clarkson Mealy, Apr. 2, 1891 (died Oct. 23, 1921); children—Rev. S. J., George M., William E., Mrs. G. H. Bray, Francis P., Julian F. Ordained ministry U.P. Ch., 1891; pastor successively at Kearney, Neb., Freeport, Pa., Grove City, Pa., until 1924, Grove City Coll. since 1924. Hon. dir. Pittsburgh-Xenia Theol. Sem. Republican. Author: Immigrant Problems and Hopes, 1912. Home: Ketler Dormitory, Grove City, Pa.

PUTMAN, Dwight Frederick, clergyman; b. Somerset, Pa., Sept. 3, 1898; s. William Bruce and Caroline Harriet (Shaulis) P.; A.B., Gettysburg (Pa.) Coll., 1920, A.M., 1923; student Gettysburg Theol. Sem., 1920-23, Union Theol. Sem., New York City, 1926-28, Columbia U., 1926-28, N.Y. Univ., 1929-30; m. Agnes Rebecca Kelly, Aug. 18, 1924; children—Dwight Frederick, Kathryn Ione. Ordained to ministry Luth. Ch. in America, 1924; minister Cairnbrook Ch., Cairnbrook, Pa., 1923-26, Hudson Heights, N.J., 1927-30; minister Coll. Luth. Ch., Gettysburg, Pa., since 1930. Mem. bd. dirs. Gettysburg Theol. Sem.; pres. West Pa. Conf. U. Luth. Ch. in America. Mem. Nat. Conf. Jews and Christians. Republican. United Luth. Ch. in America. Home: 237 Springs Av., Gettysburg, Pa.

PUTNAM, Earl Bill, retired lawyer; b. Waterville, N.Y., Dec. 31, 1855; s. George and Sarah Maria (Bill) P.; student Phillips Exeter Acad., Exeter, N.H.; A.B., Harvard U., 1879; m. Grace Williams Tower, Oct. 17, 1882; children—Amelia Tower, Grace Tower (Mrs. John Irwin Bright), Earl Bill, Sarah Elizabeth (Mrs. Seaton Schroeder), Alfred, Katharine (Mrs. William D. Crane). Admitted to N.Y. State bar, 1882, and practiced at Rochester, N.Y., privately and as mem. Shepard & Putnam and Putnam & Slocum, 1882-95; became mem. Phila. bar, 1895, and began practice there, 1895; now retired; pres. and dir. Lakeside Land Co. (a Wis. corpn.) of Duluth, Minn.; dir. Fidelity-Phila. Trust Co. Mem. Colonial Soc. of Pa., S.R., Soc. Colonial Wars. Clubs: Rittenhouse, University, Harvard (Phila.); Harvard (New York). Home: 1926 Spruce St. Office: 2012 Packard Bldg., Philadelphia, Pa.

PUTNAM, Francis Joseph; prof. of law, University of Pittsburgh. Address: University of Pittsburgh, Pittsburgh, Pa.

PUTTS, B(enjamin) Swayne, radiologist; b. Baltimore, Md., Feb. 26, 1882; s. J. W. and Mary Louise (Meredith) P.; A.B., Johns Hopkins U., 1902; M.D., Johns Hopkins Med. Sch., 1906; m. Edna M. Buhl, May 25, 1910; 1 dau., Christene Buhl. Began gen. practice of medicine, 1907; radiologist St. Vincent's Hosp. since 1917, Hamot Hosp. since 1920. Fellow Am. Coll. Radiology; diplomate Am. Bd. Radiology; mem. A.M.A., Roentgen Ray Soc. America, Radiol. Soc. North America, Pa. Radiol. Soc. (pres. 1923), Erie Co. Med. Soc. (pres. 1927). Republican. Presbyterian. Clubs: University, Erie, Kahkwa. Writer on med. subjects. Home: 447 Arlington Road. Office: 117 W. 8th St., Erie, Pa.

PYLE, Charles Sumner, pres. The Nat. Bank of Rising Sun; b. West Grove, Pa., May 12, 1862; s. Joseph and Mira M. (Conard) P.; B.S., Swarthmore (Pa.) Coll., 1883; m. Ella A. Gregg, Dec. 25, 1883; children—Helen Conard (dec.), Marian Elizabeth (Mrs. Harrison R. Febr, Jr.). Teller and bookkeeper The Nat. Bank of Rising Sun, Md., 1889-93, cashier, 1893-1903, v.p., 1903-12, pres. since 1912; dir. Mutual Fire Ins. Company of Chester Co. (Pa.). Trustee and treas. West Nottingham Acad., Colora, Md. Republican. Presbyterian. Mason (Harmony Lodge 53; Scottish Rite; 32°). Address: Rising Sun, Md.

PYLE, Milton C., banker; b. West Grove, Pa., Mar. 20, 1868; s. Joseph and Mira M. (Conard) P.; ed. Friends Select Sch. and West Grove High Sch.; m. Ella R. Heston, Oct. 2, 1889 (died 1898); m. 2d, Helen Calvert, Apr. 17, 1902; 1 dau., Dorothy Calvert. Clk. Nat. Bank of West Grove, Pa., 1883-1900; mgr. lead and zinc mine, 1900-01; cashier First Nat. Bank, Perkasie, Pa., 1901-02, Nat. Bank of West Grove, 1902-17; pres. Nat. Bank & Trust Co., West Grove, since 1917. Assisted in selling of Second, Third, Fourth and Victory liberty loans. Ex-pres. Chester Co. Bankers Assn. Republican. Presbyterian (elder West Grove Ch.). Mason (chaplain since 1908). Club: Rotary. Home: 139 Prospect Av. Office: 10 Exchange Pl., West Grove, Pa.

PYLE, Robert, pres. The Conard-Pyle Co.; b. London Grove, Pa., Mar. 7, 1877; s. Robert Lewis and Elizabeth D. (Walton) P.; ed. London Grove Friends Sch.; A.B., Swarthmore Coll., 1897; post-grad. work Woodbrooke Internat. Sch. for Social and Religious Study, England, 1907; m. Hannah Warner Cadbury, Mar. 15, 1910. Acting supt. Swarthmore Coll., 1897-98; sec. The Conard-Pyle Co., 1899-1906, pres. since 1906; trust officer Nat. Bank & Trust Co. of West Grove, 1926-30, v.p., 1928-36, dir. since 1917. Mem. bd. mgrs. Swarthmore Coll. Represented Am. Rose Soc. as judge Internat. ROSE Contest, Bagatelle, Paris, France, 1911, 25, 30, 35 and 38; national councillor U.S. Chamber of Commerce for Am. Assn. Nurserymen; chmn. com. on arboretums and botanical gardens Am. Assn. Nurserymen. Trustee Am. Rose Soc. (v.p. 1913-14; pres. 1919-23; sec. 1923-32); life mem. Religious Soc. of Friends; mem. Am. Hort. Soc. (pres. 1932-35), Pa. Hort. Soc., Mass. Hort. Soc., Philadelphia Florists Club, Royal Hort. Soc. of England, Nat. Rose Soc. of England, Amis des Roses of France, (German Rose Soc.)-Verein Deutscher Rosenfreunde (German Rose Soc.), Delta Upsilon, Pi Alpha Xi, Sigma Xi. Liberal Republican. Editor (first 16 edits.) and joint editor (last 2 edits.): How to Grow Roses. Editor: (periodical) Success with Roses and Rose News. Lecturer on roses and rose gardens. Home: Rose Hill House, West Grove, Pa.

PYLE, Wallace, M.D.; b. Jersey City, N.J., Oct. 27, 1876; s. Edwin and Harriet (Myers) P.; student Stevens Prep. Sch., 1890-93, U. of Mich., 1893-94; M.D., U. of Pa., 1897; m. Ida Jarvis, Nov. 19, 1901; children—Robert M., Janet (Mrs. Jackson A. Woodruff), Barbara. Began gen. practice of medicine, 1897; mem. staff Jersey City Med. Center, Christ Hosp., Fairmount Sanatorium; consultant Bayonne Hosp.; dir. Commercial Trust Co. of N.J. Episcopalian. Club: Orange Lawn Tennis. Home: 306 Elmwynd Drive, Orange, N.J. Office: 15 Exchange Pl., Jersey City, N.J.

Q

QUAINTANCE, Altus Lacy, entomologist; b. New Sharon, Ia., Dec. 19, 1870; s. Greenberry Plumley and Sarah Jane Q.; B.S.A., Fla. Agrl. Coll. (U. of Fla.), 1893; M.S., Ala. Poly. Inst., 1894, Sc.D., 1915; m. Nellie M. Yocum, Dec. 12, 1895; children—Leeland Charles, Howard Wilbur. Entomologist with Ala. Poly. Inst., 1894, Fla. Agrl. Coll. and Expt. Sta., 1895-98, Ga. Agrl. Expt. Sta., 1899-1901; with Md. Agrl. Coll. and Expt. Sta., and state entomologist of Md., 1901-03; spl. agt. Bur. Entomology, U.S. Dept. Agr., 1903—; entomologist in charge deciduous fruit insect investigations, 1905—; asso. chief of bur. in charge research work, 1923-31. Fellow Entomol. Soc. America, A.A.A.S.; pres. Assn. Econ. Entomologists, 1904, Entom. Soc. Washington, 1912; sec. Md. State Hort. Soc., 1902-03; chmn. sect. entomology Assn. Agrl. Colls. and Expt. Stas., 1903. Has written numerous expt. sta. bulls. and contributed to publs. U.S. Dept. Agr.; joint author Coccidæ Americanæ. Home: Silver Spring, Md.

QUIER, Edwin A.; chmn. bd. City Bank & Trust Co. Address: Reading, Pa.

QUIGLEY, Francis Patrick, elec. engring.; b. Atlantic City, N.J., July 30, 1896; s. Francis Patrick and Mary Regina (Young) Q.; B.S. in E.E., U. of Pa., 1923, E.E., same, 1936; m. Marie Frances O'Keefe, Sept. 12, 1923; children—Suzanne Marie, Laurette Edith. Employed as elec. engr. with various corpns. in N.J. and Pa., 1923-33; engr. with Power Authority of State of N.Y., Federal Power Commn., Washington, D.C.; Procurement Div., Treasury Dept.; Bur. of Yards & Docks, Navy Dept.; Suburban Resettlement Adminstrn., Dept. Agr., Washington, D.C., 1933-37; with Rural Electrification Adminstrn., Washington, D.C.; Federal Emergency Adminstrn. Pub. Works, Interior Dept., Washington, D.C., since 1937. Served in U.S.N., 1917-19; now lt. comdr., U.S.N.R. Mem. Am. Inst. Elect. Engrs. (naval mem.), Am. Soc. Naval Engrs. Democrat. Roman Catholic. Club: Engineers of Philadelphia. Home: 1317 Spruce St., Philadelphia, Pa.

QUIGLEY, Margery Closey, librarian; b. Los Angeles, Calif., Sept. 16, 1886; d. Cyrus Edwards and Elizabeth (Bryant) Q.; A.B., Vassar Coll., 1908; student N.Y. State Library Sch., 1915-16. Asst. librarian, St. Louis, Mo., 1909-18; librarian, Endicott (N.Y.) Pub. Library, 1918-24; branch librarian, pub. library, Washington, D.C., 1925-1927; librarian of Montclair (N.J.) Pub. Library since 1927; instr. training sch., St. Louis Pub. Library, 1913-18, summer sch. Mo. Library Commn., 1914-16, summer sch. N.J. Library Commn., Ocean City, 1927; instr. Sch. of Library Service, Columbia U., since 1928. Served in A.L.A. war service at Ft. Riley, Kan., 1918. Mem. Am. Library Assn. (exec. bd. since 1936), A.A.U.W., N.J. Library Assn., N.Y. State Library Assn. (pres. 1925), League of Women Voters. Received grant in aid from Carnegie Corpn. of N.Y., 1931. Republican. Presbyn. Clubs: Montclair (N.J.) Women's; Town Hall (New York). Co-author (with Mary E. Clark): Poppy Seed Cakes, 1924; Etiquette, Jr., 1926; (with William Elder Marcus) Portrait of a Library, 1936. Editor: Index to Kindergarten Songs, 1914; The Tiger's Mistake (by Walter Skeat), 1930. Home: 22 Prospect Terrace, Montclair, N.J.

QUINN, Arthur Hobson, university prof., author; b. Phila., Pa., Feb. 9, 1875; s. Michael A. and Mary (MacDonough) Q.; B.S., University of Pa., 1894, Litt.D., 1931; studied modern philology at University of Munich, 1897-98; also in grad. sch., U. of Pa., Ph.D., 1899; Litt.D., St. Joseph's College, 1918; m. Helen McKee, May 31, 1904; children—Helen Cloyd, Arthur Hobson, Kathleen Carberry, Frances Badge, James Hockley. Instr. mathematics, 1894-95, English, 1895-1904, asst. prof. English, 1904-08, prof., 1908—, dean coll. faculty, 1912-22, and dir. Summer Sch., 1904-07, Univ. of Pa. Lecturer, Univ. of Chicago summer session, 1923, Columbia, 1924, New York U., 1929, 31, U. of Calif. at Los Angeles, 1937. Mem. Phi Beta Kappa (pres. Pa. Delta Chapter, 1919-20), Beta Theta Pi; sec. Assn. of Colls. and Pres. Schs. of Middle States and Md., 1903-13, pres., 1913-14. Mem. "Four-Minute Men," 1917-19. Mem. bd. Am. Nat. Theatre, 1923—; v.p. Modern Lang. Assn. America, 1922-23; mem. joint com. on materials for research, Am. Council of Learned Socs. and Social Science Research Council, since 1930; hon. mem. Conseil Historique et Heraldique de France, 1937—. Clubs: Franklin Inn, Plays and Players, Lenape. Author: Pennsylvania Stories, 1899; The Early Drama (in Cambridge History of American Literature), 1917; History of the American Drama from the Beginning to the Civil War, 1923; History of the American Drama from the Civil War to the Present Day, 2 vols., 1927 (rev. in 1 vol. 1936); The Soul of America, 1932; American Fiction, An Historical and Critical Survey, 1936. Has also written about fifty articles, for Scribner's, Century, and Yale Rev., etc. Editor: (with introductions and notes) The Faire Maide of Bristow (reprint from quarto of 1605), 1902; Representative American Plays, 1917 (rev. 1938); Emerson's Essays, 1920; Mark Twain's Prince and Pauper, 1921; Contemporary American Plays, 1923; The Literature of America (an anthology of prose and verse, with A. C. Baugh and W. D. Howe), 2 vols., 1929 (rev. 1938); R.M. Bird's The City Looking Glass, 1933. General editor Harper's Plays and Playwrights' Series. Advisory editor of American Literature. Contbr.

QUINN

and advisor on Am. playwrights to Dictionary of Am. Biography. Home: 401 Pembroke Rd., Bala-Cynwyd, Pa.

QUINN, George Edward, elec. engr.; b. Albany, N.Y., Apr. 28, 1901; s. George T. and Sarah J. (Hutson) Q.; student Albany (N.Y.) Grammar Sch., 1906-15, Albany High Sch., 1915-19; E.E., Cornell U., 1923; m. Dorothy Thorne, June 27, 1928; children—Beverley Jean, Edith Louise, Elizabeth May. Instr. elec. engring., Cornell U., 1923-26; tester Gen. Electric Co., Schenectady, N.Y., summers 1923, 1924, 1925; instr. elec. engring. (part-time), Cooper Union, New York, since 1927; with Consol. Edison Co., New York, since 1926, successively as gen. tester, jr. engr., foreman, asst. engr., test engr., asst. div. supt. and div. engr. Served as 2d lt., Signal Corps, U.S. Army (Res.), 1923-33. Mem. Bd. of Edn., Bogota, N.J., since 1934 (v.p. 1936, 37, 38; pres. 1939). Mem. Am. Inst. E.E., Eta Kappa Nu. Republican. Episcopalian. Mason. Home: 231 Queen Anne Rd., Bogota, N.J. Office: Consolidated Edison Co., 4 Irving Pl., New York, N.Y.

QUINN, James Leland, ex-congressman; b. Venango Co., Pa., Sept. 8, 1875; s. Mark and Margaret (Gorham) Q.; student St. Thomas Sch., Braddock, Pa., 1881-88; m. Clara Elizabeth Kramer, May 24, 1900; children—James Leland, Margaret, Ruth, Clara. Began as reporter, 1891; became owner and pub. The Journal, Braddock, Pa.; mem. Pa. State Legislature, 1933-35; mem. 74th and 75th Congresses (1935-39), 31st Pa. Dist. Democrat. Catholic. K.C., Elk, Eagle. Home: Braddock, Pa.*

QUINN, John J., pres. Quinn & Boden Co., Inc.; b. Boston, Mass., Mar. 29, 1883; s. Michael F. and Elinor (Kellner) Q.; cadet on Mass. Nautical Training Ship Enterprise, 1900; student business college; m. Effie J. Cagney, June 29, 1910; 1 dau., Ruth Rita (Mrs. Thomas J. Waldron). Began as clerk and office boy, 1906; now pres. Quinn & Boden Co., Inc., Rahway, N.J. Formerly mem. Rahway (N.J.) Bd. of Edn. Republican. Roman Catholic. Elk. Clubs: Rahway Yacht, Colonia Country (Rahway, N.J.). Home: 365 Stanton St. Office: Quinn & Boden Co., Inc., Rahway, N.J.

QUINN, John Joseph, lawyer; b. Red Bank, N.J., May 15, 1892; s. John and Lenora (Reilly) Q.; grad. Red Bank High Sch., 1911, New York Law Sch., 1915; m. Isabella Olena, Mar. 17, 1920; children—Caro, Joanne. Admitted to N.J. bar, 1914, and began practice in 1915; mem. firm of Quinn & Doremus; asst. prosecutor, Monmouth Co., 1917-25, prosecutor, 1925-30; U.S. atty. for State of N.J. since 1936. Democrat. Catholic. Club: Elks. Home: 26 Caro Court. Office: 73 Broad St., Red Bank, N.J.

QUINN, Mrs. Josephine Tracy, chmn. Carbon County Bd. of Assistance; b. Wilkes-Barre, Pa., July 8, 1893; d. Hugh J. and Mary (Caffrey) T.; ed. St. Mary's High Sch. and Mercy Hosp. Training Sch.; post-grad. course, Boston Floating Hosp.; m. Dr. John J. Quinn, Nov. 9, 1918 (died 1936); children—Josephine G., John J., William B., Thomas A., Celestine M. Asst. supt. McKinley Sanatorium, Columbus, Miss., 1914-16; supervisor obstetric dept. Mercy Hosp., Wilkes-Barre, 1917-18; chmn. Carbon Co. Pa. Bd. of Assistance since Jan. 1938; chmn. Mother's Assistance Fund of Carbon Co., Apr. 1936-Dec. 1937; sec. Healing Arts Com. of Carbon Co. since Sept. 1938. Clubs: Lansford Garden (historian 1935-36, 2d v.p. 1938-39), Mahoning Valley Country. Home: 141 W. Ridge St., Lansford, Pa.

QUINN, Lawrence Ray, mfg. tubular products; b. Brantford, Ont., Can., July 21, 1885; s. Alfred Jackson and Elizabeth (de Zala) Q.; came to U.S. with parents, 1890, and naturalized citizen, 1906; ed. grade and high schs., Hamilton, O., 1891-1903, O. State U., 1904-05; m. Agnes Bostwick, Aug. 21, 1915. Employed as jr. exec. American Can Co., 1905-09; reorganizing Reed Mfg. Co., Newark, N.J., and Lisk Mfg. Co., Canandaigua, N.Y., 1909-15; with munition dept. American Can Co. 1915-17; major, U.S. Army, 1917-19; vice-pres. Enameled Metals Co. and affiliated cos. since 1919. Mem. Rigid Steel Conduit Assn., Nat. Assn. of Mfg. Republican. Methodist. Mason. Clubs: Pittsburgh Athletic Assn., Amen Corner, Bell (New York). Home: 1100 N. Highland Av. Office: 61 Bridge St., Etna, Pittsburgh, Pa.

QUINN, Mary Ann, business exec.; b. Pittsburgh, Pa., Jan. 25, 1885; d. Francis X. and Mary B. (Doran) Q.; student Park Inst., Pittsburgh, Pa., U. of Pittsburgh; unmarried. Sec. and treas. Sterling Steel Foundry Co., mfrs. steel castings, Braddock, Pa., since 1911. Has been a mem. of Civic Club of Allegheny Co. for over 25 yrs. Republican. Roman Catholic. Club: Womans City (Pittsburgh). Home: 123 Virginia Av., Aspinwall, Pa. Office: 800 Washington St., Braddock, Pa.

R

RABE, Rudolph Frederick, physician; b. Hoboken, N.J., Jan. 18, 1872; s. Rudolph F. and Elizabeth (Lusbie) R.; student Hoboken (N.J.) Acad., 1880-89, Stevens Prep Sch., Hoboken, 1889-90, Lawrenceville (N.J.) Sch., 1890-91, Dwight Sch., New York City, 1891-92, Columbia U. Sch. of Arts, 1892-93, Coll. of Physicians and Surgeons, New York, 1894, N.Y. Homeopathic Med. Coll., 1894-96, U. of Berlin, Germany, 1896-97; m. Carrie A. Meiners, May 6, 1896; children—Edith Meiners (Mrs. Edith R. Whiteside), Helen Elizabeth (formerly Mrs. Harold E. Fisher); m. 2d, Elsa Schaeffer, Dec. 31, 1929. Began as physician, New York City, 1897; now retired; prof. materia medica, N.Y. Homeopathic Med. Coll., 1908 to 1926; mem. bd. dirs. N.J. State Sanatorium for Tuberculosis Diseases, 1902-03; dir. Van Loan & Co., Inc. Mem. Am. Inst. of Homeopathy, Navy League of U.S. Address: "Stirling Hall," Basking Ridge, N.J.

RACHLIN, Israel J., pres. Albert M. Greenfield & Co.; b. New York, N.Y., May 23, 1881; s. Morris and Rebecca (Kossow) R.; M.D., N.Y.U., Bellevue Hosp. Med. Coll., 1903; m. Fannie Marx, Apr. 5, 1906; children—Florence (Mrs. Irving Hollander), Albert Cyrus. Practice of medicine, Newark, N.J., 1903-08; pres. Albert M. Greenfield & Co., real estate, Newark, N.J., since 1936; pres. Union Bldg. Co., real estate, Newark, N.J., since 1928; treas. Montefiore Bldg. & Loan Assn.; dir. Clinton Trust Co., Newark, N.J. Trustee Charles Bierman Home for the Aged, Temple B'nai Jeshurun; dir. Newark Beth Israel Hosp. Hebrew religion. Clubs: Jumping Brook Country (pres.; Asbury Park, N.J.); Progress (Newark, N.J.). Home: 10 N. Ridgewood Rd., South Orange, N.J. Office: 17 Academy St., Newark, N.J.

RADASCH, Henry Erdmann, physician; b. Keokuk, Ia., May 7, 1874; s. Ephraim Erdmann and Marie (Herrforth) R.; B.Sc., U. of Ia., 1895, M.Sc., same, 1897; M.D., Jefferson Med. Coll., 1901; m. Lucy B. Turner, Aug. 30, 1901; children—Marie Turner (Mrs. Joseph M. Simons), Margery Heath (Mrs. L. Reginald Halberstadt), Henry John. In pvt. practice of medicine at Phila., 1901-03; demonstrator histology and embryology, Jefferson Med. Coll., 1901-03, asso. 1903-11, asst. prof. histology, embryology and biology, 1911-15, asso. prof. histology and embryology, 1918-22; prof. since 1922; instr. anatomy, Pa. Acad. Fine Arts, 1913-18. Served as med. examiner, U.S.A., 1918. Mem. Anat. Bd. of Pa. Mem. Am. Assn. Anatomy, Med. Club of Phila., Nu Sigma Nu, Alpha Omega Alpha, Psi Omega. Republican. Author: Compend of Histology, 1905, 1918; Manual of Histology, 1918; Manual of Anatomy, 1917. Contbr. articles to med. mags. Home: Gladwyne, Pa. Office: 307 S. 11th St., Philadelphia, Pa.

RADCLIFFE, Amos H., ex-congressman; b. Paterson, N.J., Jan. 16, 1870; grad. high sch., Paterson, and evening course New York Trade Sch. Sec. James Radcliffe & Sons Co., structural steel mfrs.; vice-president board of trustees and treasurer of Franklin Trust Co.; mem. N.J. Assembly 5 terms, 1908-12; sheriff Passaic Co., N.J., 1912-15; mayor of Paterson 2 terms, 1916-19; mem. 66th and 67th Congresses (1919-23), 7th N.J. Dist. President Benlin Securities Co., Frankham Realty Co. Mem. Fish and Game Commn. of N.J., term 1917-22; mem. Paterson Bldg. Code Commn. Mem. New Jersey N.G. 6 yrs. Mem. Iron League of N.J. Republican. Methodist. Mason, Elk. Home: 35 18th Av. Office: 96 Prospect St., Paterson, N.J.

RADCLIFFE, George L., senator; b. Lloyds, Md., Aug. 22, 1877; s. John Anthony Le Compte and Sophie D. (Travers) R.; grad. Cambridge (Md.) Sem., 1893; A.B., Johns Hopkins, 1897, Ph.D., 1900; LL.B., U. of Md., 1903; m. Mary McKim Marriott, June 6, 1906; 1 son, George Marriott. Prin. Cambridge Sem., 1900-01; teacher Baltimore City Coll., 1901-02; admitted to Md. bar, 1903; atty. for Am. Bonding Co., 1903-04, 2d v.p., 1906-14, pres., 1914-30, now dir.; first v.p., dir. and mem. exec. com. Fidelity & Deposit Co.; dir. Fidelity Trust Co., Title Guarantee and Trust Co., Baltimore Trust Co. Mem. Baltimore Bd. Liquor License Commns., 1916-19; sec. of state of Md., 1919-20; apptd. regional adviser, 1934, of Federal Emergency Administration for states of Md., Del., Va., W.Va., N.C., Tenn., Ky. and D.C.; elected U.S. Senate, Nov. 1934, term 1935-41. Mem. Md. State Council of Defense, World War; apptd. spl. commr. to organize war work records of Md. Mem. Am., Md., and Baltimore bar assns., Am. Hist. Soc., Md. Hist. Soc. (pres., trustee), Kappa Alpha. Chmn. Md. Dem. Campaign Com., 1932 and 1934. Protestant. Clubs: University, Johns Hopkins, Maryland, Merchants, Bachelors Cotillon, Baltimore Country, Jefferson Island Club. Author: Governor Hicks of Maryland and the Civil War, 1902. Home: 12 Edgevale Rd. Office: Fidelity Bldg., Baltimore, Md.

RADENBAUGH, Frances Irvine, lawyer; b. nr. Parkersburg, W.Va., Feb. 7, 1879; d. Jacob and Philippina (Miller) R.; student pub. schs. and pvt. study; student U. of Va., Charlottesville, summer 1919; home study course U. of Chicago, 1922-23; student Northwestern U., summer 1924; studied law in pvt. office. Admitted to W.Va. bar, 1923 and since engaged in gen. practice of law at Parkersburg; commr. sch. lands for Wood Co., W.Va., 1925-35; served as mem. W.Va. Ho. of Reps. 1928-30. Mem. W.Va. Bar Assn., Wood Co. Bar Assn. Republican. O.E.S. Club: Business and Professional Women's. Home: 1621 Latrobe St. Office: 430 Juliana St., Parkersburg, W.Va.

RADER, Frank S., cigar mfg.; b. Reading, Pa., Aug. 8, 1872; s. John and Ella (Schmale) R.; student pub. and high schs., Neumanstown, Pa., 1877-90; m. Mamie O. Ibach, Jan. 25, 1895; children—Odessa, John, Frank, William, George. Began career as cigar maker; pres. A. S. Valentine & Son, cigar mfrs., Myerstown, Pa.; pres. Worrelsdorf Bank & Trust Co. Served as treas. Lebanon Co., 4 yrs. Republican. Mason. Clubs: Wyomissing (Reading); Masonic. Home: Neumanstown, Pa. Office: Myerstown, Pa.

RADITZ, Lazar, artist; b. Dvinsk, Russia, Apr. 15, 1887; s. Sholom Mendel and Mary (Denenberg) R.; came to U.S., 1903; student Pa. Acad. Fine Arts, 1903-09; Boston Sch. of Art, 1909-10; 2d Toppen prize, 1906, traveling European scholarship, 1907, 08, 1st Toppen prize (for best picture painted in school) 1909; m. Henrietta Herman, pianist, of Phila., July 25, 1910; children—Violetta Constance, Albert Herman. Awarded bronze medal, San Francisco Corpn., 1915; 2d Hallgarten prize, Nat. Acad. Design, New York, 1919. Specializes in painting of portraits. Instructor The Graphic Sketch Club, Phila. Fellow Pa. Acad. Fine Arts; mem. Art Alliance, Phila. Jewish religion. Home: 143 N. 20th St. Studio: 10 S. 18th St., Philadelphia, Pa.

RAFF, A. Raymond, customs collector; b. Phila., Pa., Apr. 27, 1865; s. William and Caroline (Hahn) R.; m. Ella Virginia Shinkle, 1899; (deceased); children—John Lloyd (deceased), A. Raymond. Became mem. Phila. Common Council, 1889, Select Council, 1901; appointed to inspect all Phila. theaters following Iroquois Fire in Chicago, and suggested many changes which have been adopted in theater constrn.; supt. U.S. Mint, Phila., 1934-35; collector of customs, Port of Phila., since 1935;

dir. Northwestern Nat. Bank. Dir. Tabor Home for Homeless Children, Doylestown, Pa. Mem. Northwestern Soup Soc. (pres.). Mason, Elk (Lodge 2). Clubs: Manufacturers and Bankers, Engineers' (Phila.); Cedarbrook Country, Manufacturers Country. Home: 1300 Oak Lane Av. Office: 1631-35 W. Thompson St., Philadelphia, Pa.

RAFFERTY, Russell, editor Wheeling News-Register. Office: 15th and Main Sts., Wheeling, W.Va.

RAFTER, Joseph L.; dir. Pa. state Library and Museum. Address: State Library, Harrisburg, Pa.

RAGATZ, Lowell Joseph, prof. history, author; b. Prairie du Sac, Wis., July 21, 1897; s. John and Anna (Tarnutzer) R.; A.B., U. of Wis., 1920, M.A., 1921, Ph.D., 1925; grad. study U. of Pa., 1921-22, U. of Grenoble, U. of Paris, Collège de France, École Libre des Sciences Politiques, 1922-23, London School of Economics, 1923; m. Mary Katheryn Parker, Apr. 21, 1930; 1 son, Robert Lowell. Teaching Fellow, U. of Wis., 1920-21, U. of Pa., 1921-22; instr. history, George Washington U., 1924-27, asst. prof., 1927-31, asso. prof., 1931-37, prof. since 1937, exec. officer of history dept. since 1934, teacher in summer schs. Johns Hopkins U., 1930, 1931, U. of Neb., 1932, Northwestern U., 1937. Editor the Am. Hist. Assn. since 1929; mem. editorial bd. Jour. of Modern History since 1937. Served as pvt. Q.M.C., U.S.A., 1918-19. Awarded Jubilee medal, by U. of Wis., 1920, Justin Winsor prize of Am. Hist. Assn., 1928, Guggenheim fellowship, 1933 and 1934. Am. del. Congress Pan-Am. Inst. Geography and History, 1935. Fellow Royal Hist. Soc., Royal Soc. of Arts; mem. Am. Hist. Assn., Am. Assn. Univ. Profs.; Société d'Histoire Moderne Société de l' Histoire des Colonies Françaises, Inter-Am. Bibliog. and Library Assn. Acacia Phi Beta Kappa, Omicron Delta Kappa, Phi Delta Epsilon, Pi Gamma Mu. Progressive. Unitarian. Mason. Clubs: Cosmos, Faculty of George Washington Univ. Author: The Question of Egypt in Anglo-French Relations (1875-1904), 1922; A Guide to the Official Correspondence of the Governors of the British West India Colonies With the Secretary of State, 1923; The Old Plantation System in the British Caribbean, 1925; Statistics for the Study of British Carribean Economic History (1763-1833), 1928; The Fall of the Planter Class in the British Caribbean, 1928; Absentee Landlordism in the British Caribbean (1750-1833), 1931; Colonial Studies in the United States during the Twentieth Century, 1932 (2 supplements 1933 and 1936), new edit., 1939; A Guide for the Study of British Caribbean History, 1932; The West Indian Approach to the Study of American Colonial History, 1935; A Bibliography of Articles on Colonies and Other Dependent Territories Appearing in American Geographical Journals Through 1934, 1935. Contbr. to Internat. Bibliography of Hist. Sciences, Dictionary of American Biography, also hist. articles to mags. Home: 5715 Midwood Road, Bethesda, Md.

RAIGUEL, George Earle, M.D., lecturer; b. Phila., Pa., Oct. 26, 1880; s. Henry Reichart and Ellen Penrose (Magee) R.; prep. edn. high sch., Phila.; M.D., Hahnemann Med. Coll., Phila., 1902; spl. studies, Harvard and Oxford U., Eng.; m. Mary Matlack, Jan. 29, 1908; children—Katherine, Eleanor (dec.). Practiced in Phila., 1902-11, specializing in ophthalmology; staff lecturer on internat. policies and current events, for Am. Soc. for Extension Univ. Teaching, League for Polit Edn., Brooklyn Inst. Arts and Sciences, Inst. Arts and Sciences of Columbia Univ., and the Philadelphia Forum. Lecturer on current history and world politics. Y.M.C.A. service in Eng., Ireland, France, Italy, Siberia. Spl. rep. of P.O. Dept. in Europe, 1923; investigated econ. and polit. conditions in Russia, summer, 1924, again, 1931, 34; official del. to Pan-Pacific Conf. on Edn., Honolulu, 1927. Mem. Pa. Hist. Soc., S.R. Contbr. Ladies' Home Journal. Clubs: Art, Contemporary (Phila.); Town Hall, Players (New York). Mason. Co-Author: (with Wm. K. Huff) This is Russia; Scarlet Valley. Address: 1909 Panama St., Phila., Pa.

RAINE, Wendell Phillips, prof. business law; b. Harrisburg, Pa., May 21, 1881; s. Charles Howard and Mary Ann (Kraber) R.; B.S. in Economics, Wharton Sch. (U. of Pa.), 1907; M.A., U. of Pa. Grad. Sch., 1911; LL.B., George Washington U. Sch. of Law, 1922, LL.M., 1926; m. Alice Elizabeth Chase, June 28, 1910. Spl. agent in timber investigations Bur. of Corpns., U.S. Dept. of Commerce and Labor, 1907-08; instr. geography, Sch. of Commerce, Central High Sch., Philadelphia, 1908-13; with Wharton Sch. since 1912, successively lecturer, instr. and asst. prof. business law, now prof. business law, chmn. business law dept., 1917-34; organized, 1914, and promoter and sec. Harrisburg br. of Extension Schs. of Accounts and Finance, 1914-17. Admitted to bar of Supreme Ct. of D.C., 1918, Dist. Ct. of Appeals, 1919, Supreme Ct., of U.S., 1922. Mem. Am. and D.C. bar assns., Am. Assn. Univ. Profs., Sigma Chi, Phi Delta Phi. Club: Union League (Philadelphia). Author: Elements of Business Law (Hayworth), 1st edit., 1922, 4th edit., 1930. Home: 817 S. St. Bernard St. Address: 36th St. and Woodland Av., Philadelphia, Pa.

RAISIN, Max, rabbi; b. Nieswiez, Poland, July 15, 1881; came to U.S.; 1893; s. Aaron S. and Taube (Slutzky) R.; B.A., U. of Cincinnati, 1903; Rabbi Hebrew Union Coll., 1903; post-grad. study, U. of Calif., 1903-04; studied Columbia U., 1915-16, Union Theol. Sem., 1915-16; LL.D., U. of Miss., 1912; m. Florence I. Steinhart, July 5, 1909; children—Beatrice, Maxime (Mrs. Ellis Rosenthal), Louise. Rabbi Congregation Reim Ahuvim, Stockton, Calif., 1903, Temple Beth Israel, Meridian, Miss., 1904-13, Temple Shaare Zedek Brooklyn, 1913-21, Barnert Memorial Temple, Patterson, N.J., since 1921. Pres. Am. Jewish Congress Branch of Paterson; 1st v.p. Assn. Reform Rabbis of N.Y. City and Vicinity. Mem. numerous professional assns. Mason, B'nai B'rith. Author: A History of the Jews in Modern Times; The Jew and His Place in the World; The Reform Movement in Neo-Hebraic Literature; Mordecai Manuel Noah (in Hebrew); John Milton, Man, Poet, Prophet (Hebrew); Israel in America (essays in Hebrew); The Flight from the Diaspora. Home: 305 17th Av., Paterson, N.J.

RAKE, Geoffrey William, med. scientist; b. Fordingbridge, Eng., Oct. 18, 1904; s. Herbert Vaughan and Rosemary (Satchell) R.; student Cliff House, Bournemouth, Eng., 1910-11, Christ Ch. Choir Sch., Oxford, Eng., 1911-19, King's Sch., Canterbury, Eng., 1919-21; M.B., Guy's Hosp. Med. Sch., London, Eng., 1922, B.S., 1928; came to U.S., 1928; m. Orpha May McNutt, July 1, 1932; 1 son, Adrian Vaughan. House officer Guy's Hosp., London, Eng., 1926-28; asst. in pathology, Johns Hopkins U., Baltimore, Md., 1928-29, instr., 1929-30; asst. in pathology and bacteriology, Rockefeller Inst., New York, 1930-32, asso., 1932-36; research asso. Connaught Labs., U. of Toronto (Can.), 1936-37; head div. of microbiology, Squibb Inst. for Med. Research, New Brunswick, N.J., since 1937. Fellow Royal Soc. of Medicine (London); licentiate Royal Coll. Physicians (London); mem. Royal Coll. Surgeons (London), Harvey Soc. Awarded Hilton prize in anatomy, 1923, Stokes prize in pathology, 1924, Beaney prize in pathology, 1927, gold medal in medicine, 1927—all Guy's Hosp.; Rettlinger prize, London, 1928, Stokes traveling scholarship in pathology, London, 1930. Episcopalian. Clubs: New York Bacteriological; Guy's '28 (London, Eng.). Home: Kingston, N.J. Office: Squibb Institute, New Brunswick, N.J.

RAKEMAN, Carl, painter, illustrator; b. Washington, D.C., Apr. 27, 1878; s. Joseph and Eva R.; pupil of Royal Acad., Munich; also at Düsseldorf and Paris; m. Linda Hineline, Dec. 12, 1919. Mural decorations in U.S. Capitol, Washington, D.C.; paintings for U.S. Govt.; portraits in pub. bldgs., also in U.S. Soldiers' Home, Tenn.; Hayes Memorial Mus., Fremont, O.; State House, Columbus, O.; Kenyon Coll., Gambier, O.; etc. Mem. Art and Archaeology League, "X" Painters of Washington. Home: North Chevy Chase, Md.

RAKER, John Henry, clergyman, supt. of Good Shepherd Home; b. Raker, Pa., Jan. 1, 1863; s. Conrad Hoffman and Susannah (Dornsife) R.; A.M., Muhlenberg Coll., Allentown, Pa., 1889, D.D., 1920; student Mt. Airy Luth. Theol. Sem., 1889-92, Sch. of Oratory, Phila., 1889-92; m. Estelle Weiser, June 5, 1899; children—Ruth Dorothea (Mrs. Herbert Brown), Roberta (Mrs. William Strauss Hudders), Conrad Weiser. Ordained to ministry Evangelical Lutheran Ch., June 1892; pastor St. Johns Evang. Luth. Ch., Pen Argyl, Pa., 1892-98; pastor Holy Trinity Luth. Ch., Lebanon, Pa., 1898-1900; supt. Luth. Orphans Home, Topton, Pa., 1900-07; pastor Grace Luth. Ch., Allentown, Pa., 1907-12; founder, Feb. 21, 1908, and since supt. The Good Shepherd Home (home for crippled children and old people); a founder and dir. Topton Nat. Bank, Topton, Pa. Democrat. Editor of Sweet Charity, official organ of The Good Shepherd Home. Home: 601 St. John St. Office: Good Shepherd Home, Allentown, Pa.

RAKER, William W(esley), educator; b. Liberty, Pa., Apr. 14, 1881; s. David and Ida Ellen (King) B.; ed. Normal Sch., Muncy, Pa., 1899-1901; B.S., Bucknell U., 1907; A.M., Teachers Coll. of Columbia U., 1921; m. Helen Virginia Tyson, June 23, 1909; children— Ned Tyson (M.D.), John William. Teacher in pub. schs. and high schs., asst. and prin. high schs., Tyrone and Bradford, Pa., 1899-1920; prin. and supt. schs., Bloomsburg, Pa., 1921-30; prof. social studies, State Teachers Coll., Kutztown, Pa., 1930-32, dir. Lab. Schs. since 1932, also supervising prin. pub. schs., Kutztown, Pa. since 1932, dir. of placement. Del. to Nat. Edn. Assn. Conv., 1938. Mem. Nat. Edn. Assn., Am. Assn. Sch. Adminstrs. Soc. for Curriculum Study, Pa. State Edn. Assn. Republican. Methodist. Home: Kutztown, Pa.

RALEIGH, George Pitts, pres. Hopkins Place Savings Bank; b. Baltimore, Md., Aug. 15, 1886; s. Walter Alfred and Kate Bond (George) R.; student Baltimore (Md.) City Coll., 1899-1904; A.B., Johns Hopkins U., Baltimore, Md., 1907, post grad. work, 1910; LL.B., U. of Md., Baltimore, Md., 1910; m. Mildred D. Warfield, Mar. 16, 1921; children—George Pitts, Richard Warfield, Alfred. Gen. practice of law, 1910-13; v.p. Maryland Title Guarantee Co., 1913-19, 1930-33, now dir. and mem. exec. com.; with Western Rep. Bankers Trust Co., New York, 1919-20; v.p. Drovers and Mechanics Nat. Bank, Baltimore, Md., 1921-30; pres. Hopkins Place Savings Bank, Baltimore, Md., since 1933; dir. and mem. exec. com. Finance Co. of America; dir Central Ins. Co. Served as capt. Ordnance Dept., U.S. Army, 1917-19. Trustee Gilman Country Sch. for Boys. Mem. Beta Theta Pi. Clubs: Maryland, Baltimore (Md.) Country; Gibson Island, Johns Hopkins, Merchants. Home: 4321 N. Charles St. Office: 7 Hopkins Pl., Baltimore, Md.

RALL, Charles Rudolph, pipe fabricating and contracting; b. Pittsburgh, Pa., Oct. 9, 1865; s. Charles Otto and Anna (Steiner) R.; ed. high sch., Hampton, Ia., 1879-82; C.E., State U. of Ia., 1886; m. Clara Hieber, Dec. 31, 1901 (died 1903); m. 2d, Elizabeth Hieber, Apr. 4, 1907; 1 son, Charles Otto. Began career as mech. engr., 1889; asso. with Pittsburgh Piping and Equipment Co., pipe fabricators and contractors, Pittsburgh, Pa., since 1903, vice-pres., treas. and dir. since 1903; treas. and dir. Piping Supply Co., Hempfield Foundries Co.; pres. and dir. Sunny View Stock Farm, Inc., Rapidan, Va. Republican. Evangelical Ch. Mason (32°). Rotarian. Club: Rotary of Pittsburgh. Home: 210 Amber St. Office: 10 43d St., Pittsburgh, Pa.

RALSTON, Cameron, lecturer, educator; b. Paisley, Scotland, Apr. 21, 1899; s. Joseph and Mary (Cameron) R.; came to U.S., 1914, naturalized, 1916; ed. schs. in Scotland, Am. Bankers Assn., Richmond, Va.; m. Ruth Elsie Johan Vaughan, Apr. 13, 1930; children— Cameron, Johan, Ruth Mary. Engaged as field sec., Presbyn. Ch. U.S.A. synod of Va., 1920-

23; regional dir. Near East Relief, N.Y. City, 1923-28; field sec., Nat. Reform Assn., Pittsburgh, Pa., 1932-35; dir. religious activities, Washington and Jefferson Coll., Washington, Pa., 1935-37; resident dir., Federal Pub. Forums, State of W.Va., U.S. Dept. Interior, Office of Edn., Washington, D.C., 1937; founder of first all-student vol. church in an Am. Coll., at Washington and Jefferson Coll., 1936. Served with Va. N.G. on Mexican border, 1916; with H.F.A., U.S.A., 1917-18 with A.E.F. in France. Mem. Am. Legion, Vets. Fgn. Wars. Ind. Republican. Quaker. Mason (32°, Shriner). Rotarian. Home: Braeside, Pt. Marion, Pa.

RALSTON, Oliver Caldwell, metallurgist; b. Colorado Springs, Colo., Sept. 6, 1887; s. Orlandus Frank and Martha Jane (Caldwell) R.; B.S., Colorado Coll., Colorado Springs, 1910; m. Lala Chrisman Bartleson, Mar. 28, 1912. Assayer, chemist, and teacher of chemistry, Leadville, Colo., 1910-12; chemist, U.S. Bur. Mines, Pittsburgh, Pa., 1912-14; metallurgist, same, Salt Lake City, Utah, 1914-17; metallurgist, Hooker Electrochem. Co., Niagara Falls, N.Y., 1917-20; asst. chief metallurgist, U.S. Bur. Mines, 1920-28; director research United Verde Copper Company, 1928-35; principal chemical engineer U.S. Bureau of Mines, New Brunswick, N.J., 1935-37; chief engr., Div. of Non-Metallics, U.S. Bureau of Mines, Washington, D.C., and College Park, Md., since 1937; v.p. Sharp Lead Co.; dir. Ariz. Minerals Corpn. Was secretary research and inventions, State Council of Defense, Utah, 1917. Mem. Am. Inst. M.E., Am. Chem. Soc., Am. Electrochem. Soc., Faraday Soc., American Ceramic Soc. Author: Flotation, 1917; Electrodeposition and Hydrometallurgy of Zinc, 1921; Zink Elektrolyse und Nassverfahrung, 1928; Iron Oxide Reduction Equilibria, 1929; also numerous bulls. U.S. Bur. Mines, 1912-37. Clubs: Engineers (San Francisco); Faculty (U. of Calif.). Home: 6 Claggett Rd., Hyattsville, Md.

RAMAGE, Chesney Macaulay, surgeon; b. W. Milford, W.Va., Mar. 28, 1884; s. Benjamin Franklin and Allie (Hefner) R.; grad. Fairmont Teachers Coll., Fairmont, W.Va., 1903; B.S., W.Va. Univ., Morgantown, 1907; M.D., Johns Hopkins U. Med. Sch., 1910; m. Blake Lemley, Sept. 18, 1912; 1 dau., Eleanor Conn (Mrs. Howard Boggess). Engaged in teaching pub. schs., 1901-02; engaged in gen. practice of medicine and surgery at Fairmont, W.Va. since 1910; city health officer, Fairmont, 1910-17; supt. and chief surgeon Fairmont Emergency Hosp., 1917-21, 1933-36 and apptd. again 1936. Served as mem. draft. bd., Fairmont, 1917. Fellow Am. Coll. Surgeons. Mem. Am. Med. Assn., W.Va. Med. Assn., Marion Co. Med. Soc., Delta Tau Delta. Democrat. Methodist. Mason. Elk. Home: 401 Guffey St. Office: Fairmount Emergency Hosp., Fairmont, W.Va.

RAMBO, Ormond, Jr., investment and ins. brokerage; b. Phila., Pa., Dec. 7, 1888; s. Ormond and Ida Louise (Kennedy) R.; ed. by pvt. tutors; m. Edna Marie Stead, Oct. 25, 1919. Began as credit mgr., 1909; in real estate brokerage, Phila., Pa., 1912-19; engaged as ins. broker on own acct. as individual since 1912; dealer in investment securities, 1919-37; mem. and dir. Battles & Co., Inc., investment securities, Phila., Pa., since 1937. Trustee Am. Swedish Hist. Mus. and treas. since 1935; dir. Geneal. Soc. of Pa. Mem. Soc. of the War of 1812 (treas. Pa. soc.), S.R., Colonial Soc. of Pa., Baronial Order of Runnemede (genealogist), St. Andrews Soc. of Phila., Swedish Colonial Soc. (v.p.), Hist. Soc. of Pa., Order of Founders and Patriots of America (dep. gov. gen., 1938-39), Library Co. of Phila., Pa. Arts and Scis. Soc. (v.p.). Fellow Royal Philatelic Soc. of London, Eng. Decorated Knight 1st class, Order of Vasa (Sweden); Royal New Sweden Tercentenary Medal of Gustav V. (Sweden). Republican. Presbyn. Clubs: Union League, Manufacturers Golf and Country (Philadelphia). Home: 312 Bowman Av., Merion Station, Pa. Office: 1518 Locust St., Philadelphia, Pa.

RAMSAY, Robert Lincoln, ex-congressman; b. Durham, Eng., Mar. 24, 1877; s. John and Elizabeth (Lumsdon) R.; brought to U.S. at age of 4; LL.B., W.Va. Univ., 1901; m. Edna Brindley, of Wellsburg, W.Va., Feb. 12, 1908; children—Charlotte, Robert. Admitted to W.Va. bar, 1901; sr. mem. firm Ramsay & Wilkin since 1917; city atty. of Follansbee, 1905-30; pros. atty. Brooks County, 1908-12 and 1916-20; mem. 73d to 75th Congresses (1933-39), 1st West Virginia District. Democrat. Mem. Christian Ch. Odd Fellow. Home: Wellsburg, W.Va.*

RAMSBURG, C(harles) J(ospeh), vice-pres. Koppers Co.; b. Washington, D.C., May 31, 1877; s. Cornelius Stille and Sarah Hassler (Nourse) R.; ed. Cornell U., 1895-98; studied coal gas production in Europe, 1910; m. Jane Heath, June 1, 1904; children—Margaret Heath (Mrs. H. G. C. Williams), Harriet Nourse (Mrs. R. Putnam Goldsbury), Charles Joseph. Began as cadet engr. United Gas Improvement Co., Phila., 1898, in various capacities from works chemist to engr. of mfr., 1898-1913; became v.p. H. Koppers Co., Chicago, Ill., 1913; v.p. Koppers Co. at Pittsburgh, Pa., since 1915; v.p. and dir. Koppers Conn. Coke Co., Phila. Coke Co.; dir. Koppers Co. and White Tar Co. of N.J. Served as toluol adviser U.S. Ordnance Dept., 1917. Vice chmn. Efficiency and Economy Commn. of Pittsburgh, 1934-38; mem. Nat. Industrial Conf. Bd.; mem. Internat. Nitrogen Conf., Adriatic Sea, 1928; mem. Guild of Brackett Lecturers, Princeton U., 1938; dir. Pittsburgh Orchestra Assn. Awarded Beal medal by Am. Gas Assn. Del. 1st Internat. Coal Conf., Pittsburgh, 1926; del. 2d World's Power Conf. Berlin, 1930. Fellow Royal Soc. Arts and Commerce, London, Eng.; mem. Franklin Inst., Am. Gas Assn., Soc. of Gas Lighting, Am. Iron and Steel Inst., Delta Upsilon; hon. mem. Princeton Engring. Soc. Republican. Episcopalian. Clubs: Duquesne (Pittsburgh); Allegheny Country (Sewickley, Pa.). Contbr. tech. articles to professional socs. and confs. Home: Sewickley, Pa. Office: Koppers Bldg., Pittsburgh, Pa.

RAMSEY, Will Wallace, high school prin.; b. Stroudsburg, Pa., July 4, 1882; s. Will Harrison and Mary Ordella (Wallace) R.; grad. Stroudsburg High Sch., 1899; A.B., Lafayette Coll., 1905; m. Laura Ernst, July 7, 1908; children—Mary Christine (Mrs. Clayton Blackburn), Emily Ernst, Doris Wallace. Teacher of mathematics, Roselle (N.J.) High Sch., 1905-06; asso. with Perth Amboy (N.J.) High Sch. since 1906, as teacher of mathematics, 1906-24, prin. since 1924. Mem. N.J. State Teachers Assn., Dept. of Secondary Sch. Prins. of N.E.A. Republican. Presbyterian. Mason (past master). Home: 129 Kearney Av., Perth Amboy, N.J.

RAMSEY, William Heines Crawford, retail fuels and builders supplies; b. Bryn Mawr, Pa., Nov. 11, 1877; s. William Horn and Mary Pechin (Crawford) R.; student Haverford Coll. Grammar Sch., 1892-95; B.S. in E.E., U. of Pa., 1899; m. Frances Augustine Morgan, Oct. 8, 1907 (died July 18, 1908); m. 2d, Adah Naomi Campbell, Sept. 15, 1915; children—Naomi Campbell, John Ellis and Thomas David (twins). Engaged as cadet engr., U. of Pa., 1899-1900; draftsman and engr. with Cambria Steel Co., 1900-02; supt. Consumers Gas Co. Johnstown, Pa., 1902-06; supt. Johnstown Water Co., 1902-15; supt. Citizens Light, Heat and Power Co., 1904-05; mgr. York Water Co., York, Pa., 1915-17; engr. of construction, Camp Meade Cantonment, U.S. Army, 1917; designing engr. housing div., Emergency Fleet Corpn., 1918-20; propr. retail coal, fuel oil, and builders' supplies, business, Bryn Mawr, Pa., since 1920. Dir. Bryn Mawr Trust Co. since 1920. Served as mem. Zoning Commn., Lower Merion Twp., 1927; pres. Bryn Mawr Business Assn., 1929-31; mem. Planning Commn., Lower Merion Twp., since 1933. Trustee Bryn Mawr War Memorial, Community House Assn. Mem. Am. Soc. Mech. Engrs., 1908-32, Pa. Gas Assn., 1902-05, Pa. Water Works Assn., 1902-17, Nat. Water Works Assn., 1910-20, Psi Upsilon. Republican. Episcopalian. Club: Union League of Phila., 1933-38. Author of articles: "Meter Records and Requirements of the Public Service Commission," "The Water Distribution System of Industrial Housing Projects for Shipbuilders," "Freight Trains on the Highways." Home: 632 Montgomery Av. Office: 763 Lancaster Av., Bryn Mawr, Pa.

RANCK, Clayton Haverstick, clergyman; b. nr. Lancaster, Pa., Jan. 14, 1876; s. Jacob Eby and Martha Bausman (Haverstick) R.; prep. edn. Franklin and Marshall Acad., Lancaster, and Deichmann's Prep. Sch., Baltimore, Md.; A.B., Franklin and Marshall Coll., Lancaster, 1898; student Union Theol. Sem., 1900-01; grad. Theol. Sem. of Ref. Ch., Lancaster, 1903; postgrad. work, Columbia and Johns Hopkins Univs.; m. Kate Ernst (A.B., Goucher Coll., 1910), June 4, 1914; children—Kathryn Ernst, Clayton Ernst. Teacher mathematics, Franklin and Marshall Acad., 1898-1900; ordained ministry Ref. Ch. in U.S., 1903; pastor Mercersburg Acad., 1903-05, 3d Ref. Ch., Baltimore, 1905-16; gen. sec. Assn. Schs., Colls. and Seminaries of Ref. Ch. in U.S., 1916-18; pastor St. John's Ch., Harrisburg, Pa., 1918-22; pastor Reformed Ch. of Oak Lane, Pa., and of the students of the U. of Pa. belonging to the Ref. Ch., 1923-28; pastor to students of Phila. belonging to the Reformed Ch. since 1928. Editor social service dept. Ref. Ch. Messenger, 1912-14. Contbr. to religious papers and mags. Lecturer to young people. Home: 212 St. Mark's Square. Office: 3601 Locust Street, Philadelphia, Pa.

RANCK, Dayton Leo, treas. Bucknell Univ.; b. Union Co., Pa., June 6, 1885; s. Samuel C. and Sara C. (Werkheiser) R.; ed. Bucknell Acad., 1910-12; A.B., Bucknell U., 1916; A.M., same, 1934; m. Irene Snyder, Aug. 2, 1916; children—Marion, Lee Snyder, Doris Charlotte. In employ dept. store, 1902-10; in employ braid manufactory, 1916-24; asso. in administrative capacity with Bucknell U. since 1924, treas. since 1932; dir. Lewisburg Nat. Bank. Mem. Lambda Chi Alpha. Republican. Baptist. Mason. Home: 35 Market St., Lewisburg, Pa.

RANCK, James Byrne, coll. prof.; b. Mechanicsburg, Pa., Mar. 18, 1898; s. Henry Haverstick (D.D.) and Mary Hill (Byrne) R.; A.B. with distinction, George Washington U., 1921; A.M., Harvard U., 1924; Ph.D., Johns Hopkins U., 1931; m. Dorothy Irene Schwieger, Aug. 18, 1927; children—James Byrne, Jr., Dorothea Chandler. Employed as prin. pub. sch., Manchester, Md., 1921; master history, Swarthmore (Pa.) Prep. Sch., 1922-23; prof. history, Western Md. Coll., Westminster, Md., 1924-29; prof. history and polit. science, Hood Coll., Frederick, Md., since 1929, also head dept. history and polit. science. Served in S.A.T.C., 1918. Mem. Am. Hist. Assn., Am. Assn. Univ. Profs., Middle States Assn. of History and Social Science Teachers. Democrat. Mem. Evang. and Ref. Ch. Author: Albert Gallatin Brown, Radical Southern Nationalist, 1937. Contbr. articles to hist. publs. Home: 313 W. College Terrace, Frederick, Md.

RANCK, Lee Russell, physician; b. New Columbia, Pa., Jan. 1, 1879; s. Levi and Charlotte R.; diploma Bucknell Acad., 1898, Williamsport Commercial Coll., 1900; Ph.B., Bucknell, 1905, Sc.M., 1906; M.D., U. of Pa., 1908; m. Carrie U. Dunkle, Nov. 11, 1908 (dec.); children—Lee Russell (dec.), S. Graydon, Harold D., Cecil L.; m. 2d, Marjorie Ditzler, Sept. 3, 1932. Engaged in gen. practice of medicine at Milton, Pa., since 1908, specialized in obstetrics; physician for Reading R.R. West Milton for over 20 yrs.; pres. and dir. West Milton State Bank. Served in Spanish-Am. War, 1898. Mem. Vol. Service Corps during World War. Mem. Am., Pa. State, and Lycoming med. assns., Ashurst Surg. Soc., Delta Theta Upsilon, Sigma Chi, Phi Rho Sigma. Republican. Presbyn. Mason (32°, Shriner). Home: 174 S. Front St., Milton, Pa.

RANCK, Than Vanneman, newspaperman; b. Philadelphia, Pa., Oct. 4, 1874; s. Isaac Winters and Harriet E. (Vanneman) R.; ed. Dickinson Coll., Carlisle, Pa.; m. May Maurer, Oct. 14, 1897; 1 dau., Doris (Mrs. Doris Ranck Rend). Began as reporter Shamokin Herald, 1896; reporter Phila. Inquirer, 1897-99; state editor and editor Sunday Magazine, Philadelphia North American, 1900-06; day city editor New York American, 1906-11; chief Washington corr. Hearst newspapers, 1911; mng. editor New York American, 1912-16; editor Chicago Herald-Examiner, 1916-18, New York American, 1918-20, reorganizer of foreign service, Hearst newspapers, 1919; organizer (for Hearst interests), Boston Daily Advertiser, 1921, and editor Daily and Sunday Advertiser until 1925; editor Chicago Herald-Examiner, 1926-28; editorial mgr. Hearst newspapers, 1928-37. (Mt. Ranck in Antarctic named for him by Sir Hubert Wilkins, 1928, because of his connection with organization of that expdn.) Methodist. Mason. Home: "Fairview," Easton, Talbot Co., Md.

RAND, Gertrude, psychologist; b. New York, N.Y., Oct. 29, 1886; d. Lyman Fiske and Mary Catherine (Moench) R.; grad. Girls' High Sch., Brooklyn, N.Y., 1904; B.A., Cornell U., 1908; M.A. and Ph.D., Bryn Mawr, 1911; m. Clarence Errol Ferree, Sept. 28, 1918. Research fellow Bryn Mawr, 1911-12, Sarah Berliner research fellow, 1912-13; demonstrator and reader in exptl. and ednl. psychology, same coll., 1913-14, and asso. in exptl. and applied psychology, 1914-25; demonstrator in exptl. psychology and research asst., Nat. Research Council's Com. on Industrial Lighting, 1925-27; asso. prof. of research ophthalmology, Johns Hopkins U. Sch. Medicine, 1928-32, asso. prof. physiol. optics 1932-36; asso. dir. Research Lab. of Physiol. Optics, Baltimore, Md., since 1936. Fellow A.A.A.S.; mem. Am. Psychological Assn., Optical Society America, Am. Assn. Univ. Profs., Johns Hopkins Surg. Soc. Republican. Presbyn. Author: The Factors Which Influence the Sensitivity of the Retina to Color, 1913; Radiometric Apparatus for Use in Psychological and Physiological Optics, 1917, Studies in Physiological Optics, 2 vols., 1934 (with C. E. Ferree). Co-inventor Ferree-Rand perimeter, light-sense tester, acuity projector, multiple-exposure tachistoscope, variable illuminator, and other optical and ophthalmol. instruments. Contbr. many articles to mags. Home: 2609 Poplar Drive. Office: Research Laboratory of Physiological Optics, Baltimore, Md.

RANDAL, Boyd, sch. prin.; b. Berkeley Co., W.Va., Jan. 1, 1888; s. John Ferdinand and Imogene Tanner (Welshance) R.; grad. Shepherd State Teachers Coll., Shepherdstown, W.Va., 1905; A.B., W.Va. U., 1909; A.M., Columbia U., 1915; grad. study, U. of Chicago, 1919; m. Anna Morehed Miller, July 19, 1916; children—Keitha Anne, Elizabeth Jane. Instr. science and mathematics, Shinnston (W.Va.) High Sch., 1909-11, Shepherd State Teachers Coll., 1911-12; prin. Harpers Ferry High Sch., Harpers Ferry, W.Va., 1912-18, Cairo High Sch., Cairo, W.Va., 1918-20; dist. supt., Salem Independent Dist., Salem, W.Va., 1920-26; engaged in insurance business, Fairmont, W.Va., 1926-31; prin. Church Dist. High Sch., Hundred, W.Va., 1931-32; instr. mathematics and science Williamson High Sch., Williamson, W.Va., 1932-35, prin. since 1935. Life mem. N.E.A.; mem. W.Va. Secondary Edn. Assn., Am. Secondary Prin. Assn., W.Va. Secondary Edn. Assn., Mingo Co. Secondary Prin. Assn. (v.p.) Democrat. Presbyn. Mason (past master). Club: Kiwanis (Williamson). Home: 19 W. Sixth Av., Williamson, W.Va.

RANDALL, Alexander, urologist; b. Annapolis, Md., Apr. 18, 1883; s. John Wirt and Hannah Parker (Parrott) R.; B.A., St. Johns Coll., Annapolis, 1902, M.A., 1907; studied Johns Hopkins, 1902-03, Johns Hopkins Med. Sch., 1903-07, M.D., 1907; m. Edith T. Kneedler, June 2, 1915; children—Alexander, Peter, Virginia. Resident German Hosp., Phila., 1907-09; pvt. asst. to Dr. H. H. Young, Baltimore, 1910; resident urologist Johns Hopkins Hosp., 1911; asst. prof. surgery U. of Pa., 1923-26, asso. prof., 1926-29, prof. urology since 1929; urologist to Hosp. of University of Pennsylvania, Chestnut Hill, and Abington hospitals; consulting urologist to Mt. Sinai Hospital. Served as lt., capt. and maj. Med. Corps, U.S. Army, 1917-19; with A.E.F., Apr. 1918-May 1919. Fellow Am. Coll. Surgeons; mem. A.M.A., Phila. Acad. Surgery, Coll. of Physicians Phila., American Surgical Association, American Urological Association (pres., 1932), Am. Assn. Genito-Urinary Surgeons (pres. 1938), Société Internationale d'Urologie. Republican. Episcopalian. Clubs: Penn Athletic, Corinthian Yacht (Phila.). Author: Surgical Pathology of Prostatic Obstructions, 1931; also articles giving results of med. research. Home: Chestnut Hill, Phila. Office: Medical Arts Bldg., Philadelphia, Pa.

RANDALL, Blanchard, merchant; b. Annapolis, Md., Nov. 12, 1856; s. Alexander and Elizabeth Philpot (Blanchard) R.; A.B., St. John's Coll., Annapolis, 1874 (hon. A.M., 1906); m. Susan Katharine Brune, 1884; children—Frederick Brune, Mrs. Susan Katharine Pincoffs, Emily Brune, Mrs. Elizabeth Blanchard Slack, Blanchard, Mrs. Evelyn Barton Hanrahan, Alexander. In mercantile business, Baltimore, since 1874; sr. mem. Gill & Fisher, 1907—; dir. Safe Deposit & Trust Co., First National Bank, Maryland Life Insurance Company, The Savings Bank of Baltimore, United City Rys., Phila., Baltimore & Washington R.R. Co. Pres. Nat. Bd. of Trade, 1902 and 1903. Trustee Johns Hopkins U., Johns Hopkins Hosp. Republican. Treas. P.E. Diocese of Md. Mem. Md. Soc. of Cincinnati. Clubs: Grolier, Nat. Arts (New York); Maryland, University, South River, Catonsville Country. Home: 8 Mount Vernon Place, Baltimore, Md. Office: Chamber of Commerce, Baltimore, Md.

RANDALL, Blanchard, Jr., mcht., banker; b. Catonsville, Md., Mar. 28, 1894; s. Blanchard and Susan Katharine (Brune) R.; A.B., Johns Hopkins, 1914, grad. study in engring., 1914-15; m. Romaine LeMoyne McIlvaine, May 14, 1918; children—Blanchard III, William Brown McIlvaine, Brian Philpot, John LeMoyne. With Robert Garrett & Sons, bankers, Baltimore, Md., 1915-17; U.S. Grain Corpn., Baltimore, 1919-20; with Gill & Fisher, grain mchts. and exporters, Baltimore, 1920-33, mem. firm 1924-33; pres. Mortgage Guarantee Co., Baltimore, since 1933; pres. Purity Paper Vessels Co.; dir. Md. Trust Co., Title Guarantee & Trust Co. Private, corpl. and sergt., Md. N.G., 1915-17; duty in Federal Service, 1916; 2d lt., 1st lt. and capt., F.A., U.S.A.; a.d.c. to comdg. generals 54th F.A. Brig. and 29th Div., France, 1918-19, participating in Defensive Sector and Meuse-Argonne Offensive. Awarded Croix de Guerre (French). Chairman Community Fund, Baltimore, 1931; pres. Baltimore Chamber of Commerce, 1929-30; Rep. candidate for mayor of Baltimore, 1935; trustee Enoch Pratt Library, Md. School for Blind, Henry Watson Children's Aid, Thomas Wilson Sanitarium for Children, Eudowood Hospital, Community Fund of Baltimore; vice-chmn. Baltimore Chapter Am. Red Cross, 1933-37. Mem. Phi Kappa Psi. Republican. Episcopalian. Club: Gibson Island, South River. Home: 4901 Greenspring Av. Office: Mortgage Guarantee Co., Baltimore, Md.

RANDALL, Roland Rodrock, realtor; b. Doylestown, Pa., Oct. 12, 1898; grad. Doylestown High Sch., 1917; B.S. in economics, Wharton Sch. U. of Pa., 1921; s. William Lacey and Anna Elizabeth (Rodrock) R.; m. Marion Burnside Heist, Dec. 5, 1922; children—Roland Rodrock, Jr., Marion Burnside. Began as securities salesman, 1921; mortgage broker and real estate business, Phila., since 1925; past pres. and gen. chmn. of appraisal com., Phila. Real Estate Bd.; dir. and mem. exec. com., Pa. Real Estate Assn.; mem. com. on metropolitan bds., Nat. Assn. of Real Estate Bds.; chmn. Pa. real estate advisory com., Dept. of Pub. Instrn., Harrisburg; vice-chmn. Phila. Housing Authority; pres. Phila. Nat. Home Show, Inc.; past pres. and dir. Real Estate Magazine, Inc.; dir. Quaker City Federal Savings & Loan Assn.; dir. and real estate officer, Underdown-Parkway Bldg. & Loan Assn.; v.p. Ludway Bldg. & Loan Assn.; pres. Aquila Apartments, Inc.; pres. 4839-43 Pine Street, Inc.; pres. City Bond & Mortgage Co.; vice-pres. Town House, Inc.; sec. Windermere Court Apts. Corpn.; sec.-treas. Twenty-second & Arch Streets, Inc.; sec.-treas. Thirteenth & Locust Streets, Inc.; treas. Lynn Regis Apts., Inc.; treas. Northwest Corner 52d & Walnut Streets, Inc.; treas. Oak Lane Towers Apts., Inc.; treas. Wood-Norton Apts., Inc.; treas. Kemble Park, Inc.; mem. home service com. Am. Red Cross; mem. The Pa. Soc.; past pres. and hon. dir. Phi Gamma Delta Club of Phila. Served as 2d lt. Inf., U.S. Army, during World War. Presbyterian. Mason, Underdown-Assembly Artisans. Home: 119 E. Gorgas Lane, Germantown, Philadelphia. Office: 1211 Chestnut St., Philadelphia, Pa.

RANDLES, Andrew J., clergyman; b. Waterman, Ill., Dec. 15, 1877; s. William John and Emily (White) R.; B.A., Monmouth (Ill.) Coll., 1902; grad. Pittsburgh Theol. Sem., 1905; D.D., Westminster Coll., New Wilmington, Pa., 1927; m. Myrtle E. Beitel, June 7, 1905; children—Emily (dec.), Elizabeth, Janet, Martha. Ordained ministry U.P. Ch., 1905; pastor New Athens, O., 1905-09, Vandergrift, Pa., 1909-15, Second Ch., New Castle, Pa., 1915-32; corr. editor The United Presbyterian, 1925-33; sec. Bible sch. work, U.P. Ch. since 1932; mem. exec. com. International Council of Christian Edn. since 1932. Dir. and mem. bd. management Pittsburgh-Xenia Theol. Sem., 1916-33; mem. Unified Staff Pa. State S.S. Assn.; mem. Council Christian Edn. United Presbyn. Ch.; mem. bd. dirs. Allegheny Co. S.S. Orgn. Pres. bd. administration U.P. Ch.; chmn. com. on pastoral settlements, Gen. Assembly, 1931-32. Republican. Home: 6946 Thomas Boul. Office: 901 Publication Bldg., Pittsburgh, Pa.

RANDOLPH, Corliss Fitz, educator; b. New Milton, W.Va., July 24, 1863; s. Franklin and Mary Elizabeth (Fox) Fitz R.; A.B., A.M., Alfred (N.Y.) U., 1888, hon. L.H.D., 1903; grad. student in classical philology, Columbia, 1896-99; Ph.D., Salem Coll., W.Va., 1904 (LL.D., 1913); m. Marion Melissa Howard, Mar. 18, 1890 (she died Feb. 21, 1921); 1 dau., Mildred; m. 2d, Mrs. Grace Dawson Bell, July 7, 1926. Teacher in public schs., New Milton, W.Va., 1879-84, Montclair (N.J.) High School, 1889-91; prin. pub. sch., Ashaway, R.I., 1888-89, Staten Island, N.Y., 1892-96, and Newark, N.J., 1899-1933. Editor Alfred U. Quarterly, 1896-98; lecturer classical philology, Alfred U., 1899-1901; editor School Exchange, Newark, 1907-11. Trustee Alfred U. Editor and contbr. to Seventh Day Baptists in Europe and America, 1910. Author: History of Seventh Day Baptists in West Virginia, 1905; Report on European Schools, 1909; History of German Seventh Day Baptists, 1910; Rogerines, 1910; Education, and not Instruction, 1913; Anniversary Addresses, 1922; The Sabbath and Seventh Day Baptists, 4th revision, 1935. Joint Author: A Manual of Seventh Day Baptist Procedure, 1923, 26. Editor: Seventh Day Baptist Year Book, 1914-28. Pres. Am. Sabbath Tract Soc.; pres. and librarian Seventh Day Baptist Historical Soc.; pres. Seventh Day Baptist Gen. Conf., 1931-32; mem. N.J. Hist. Soc., Nat. Inst. Social Sciences, Am. Acad. Polit. and Social Science, Am. Soc. of Ch. History, Am. Hist. Soc., Société Académique et Historique Internationale (Paris), Congregational Hist. Soc. (England). Club: Author's (London). Home: 83 Jefferson Av., Maplewood, N.J.

RANDOLPH, Edward Fitz, clergyman; b. Mt. Horeb, N.J., Sept. 5, 1872; s. David B. F. and Mary (Kinsey) R.; A.B., Syracuse U., 1896; hon. D.D., Syracuse U., 1928; m. Anna May Hills, Sept. 7, 1898; children—Marion F., Ethel F., Frances F. Ordained to ministry M.E. Ch., 1898; joined Phila. Conf. M.E. Ch., 1898; served chs. in Cochranville and Narberth, and three chs. in Phila.: Trinity, St. James, and Tioga, 1898-1931; pastor at 1st Ch. Lancaster Pa., 1931-39; pastor Lansdowne Pa., since 1939. Mem. Delta Upsilon. Republican. Home: 17 W. Stratford Av., Lansdowne, Pa.

RANDOLPH, Evan, banking; b. Phila., Pa., Apr. 29, 1880; s. Evan and Rachel Story (Jenks) R.; A.B., Harvard, 1903; m. Hope Carson, Nov. 7, 1906; children—Hope (Mrs. William P. Hacker), Evan, Jr., Hampton C., Rachel, David Story. Began with Edw. B. Smith & Co., later mgr. bond dept., 1903-11; established Evan Randolph & Co., 1912; vice-pres.

and dir. Girard Nat. Bank, 1914-26, and Phila.-Girard Nat. Bank, 1926-28, and Philadelphia Nat. Bank since 1928; dir. Giant Portland Cement Co., United Firemen's Ins. Co.; mgr. Western Saving Fund Soc. Served as mem. Philadelphia Authority. Republican. Episcopalian. Club: Rittenhouse. Home: Cor. Seminole and Chestnut Avs., Chestnut Hill. Office: 1416 Chestnut St., Philadelphia, Pa.

RANDOLPH, Jennings, congressman; b. Salem, W.Va., Mar. 8, 1902; s. Ernest and Idell (Bingman) R.; prep. edn., Salem Acad.; A.B., Salem Coll., 1924; m. Mary Katherine Badd, Feb. 18, 1933; children—Jennings, Frank. Member editorial staff Clarksburg (W.Va.) Daily Telegram, 1924; associate editor W.Va. Review, Charleston, 1925; head of department public speaking and journalism, Davis and Elkins College, 1926-32; prof. of public speaking, Southeastern U., Washington, D.C., since 1936. Mem. 73d and 76th Congresses (1933-41), 2d W.Va. Dist. Trustee Salem and Davis Elkins Colleges. Member West Virginia Newspaper Council, West Virginia Publicity Association (dir.), Sons Am. Revolution. Lions Clubs of W.Va. (dist. gov. 1931-32), Alpha Sigma Phi, Alpha Kappa Pi. Democrat. Seventh Day Baptist. Clubs: Newspaper (New York); Nat. Press, University (Washington). Contbr. to magazines. Home: Elkins, W.Va.

RANGER, Richard Howland, electric music; b. Indianapolis, Ind., June 13, 1889; s. John Hilliard and Emily Anthon (Gillet) R.; B.S., Mass. Inst. Tech., 1911; m. Laura Anna Lewis, Nov. 27, 1924; 1 dau. Mary Wheatley. Propr. Ranger Co., printers, Boston, 1911-17; design engr. RCA, 1920-30, transatlantic reception, ship to shore telephony, 1st RCA broadcasting, transatlantic radio pictures; pres. Rangertone, Inc., electric music, organs, chimes, phonograph records and equipment, Newark, N.J., since 1930; first electric organ, 1931, NBC electric chimes, 1932, ch. chimes, 1934. Served in F.A., U.S.A., 1917, Signal Corps, 1918-20; now maj. Signal Corps Res.; in charge Signal Corps Labs., Ft. Monmouth, 1919-20. Dir. Y.M.C.A.; pres. Ridge St. Sch. P.T.A., 1939-40. Fellow Royal Soc., Inst. Radio Engrs.; mem. A.A.A.S., Am. Inst. Elec. Engrs., Acoustical Soc. America, Optical Soc. America, Phi Beta Epsilon. Republican. Episcopalian. Clubs: MIT of Northern N.J.; MIT of New York, Downtown Athletic (New York); Radio Club of America (New York). Home: 574 Parker St. Office: 201 Verona Av., Newark, N.J.

RANKEN, Howard Benedict, civil and mech. engr.; b. Troy, N.Y., Sept. 14, 1898; s. William Hugh and Alma F. (Eichholz) R.; ed. Rensselaer Poly. Inst., 1914-18; m. Edith M. Manning, Mar. 5, 1920; children—Howard Benedict, Jr., William Allison, Doris Eleanor. Designer, Glens Falls Machine Works, Glens Falls, N.Y., 1919-21, chief engr., 1922-24; draftsman, W.C. Bliss, civil engr., Miami, Fla., 1921-22, mgr., 1924-26; various engring. positions, over period, 1922-31; sales engr., W. L. Clayton, Inc., Jersey City, N.J., 1931; asst. chief engr. Reliance Adv. Co., N.Y. City, 1933; supervising engr., N.J. Geodetic Control Survey, Newark, N.J., since 1934; licensed professional engr. and land surveyor, State N.J. Served as elec. sergt. then 2d lt. C.A.R.C., 1918. Mem. Am. Soc. Mech. Engrs., Soc. Am. Mil. Engrs., Army Ordnance Assn., Am. Legion. Democrat. Episcopalian. Home: 401 Orchard St., Cranford, N.J.

RANKIN, Edward Stevens, civil engr.; b. Newark, N.J., Mar. 6, 1861; s. William and Ellen Hope (Stevens) R.; grad. Newark (N.J.) Acad., 1878; C.E., Princeton U., 1882; m. Julie S. J. Russell, Oct. 7, 1886 (died 1928); children—Russell Bruce, Edith Joy, William (dec.), Edward Stevens (dec.). Began as civil engr., N.Y.W.S.&B.R.R., Albany, N.Y., 1882; with Engring. Dept. City of Newark (N.J.) since 1887, successively as asst. engr., engr. in charge, div. engr., div. of sewers since 1929; sec. Joint Meeting Sewer Commn. since 1915; cons. engr., 1936, sec., 1928, and treas., 1930, Second River Joint Meeting. Trustee N.J. Hist. Soc. Mem. Am. Soc. C.E. (life mem.), Am.

Pub. Works Assn. (past pres.; hon. mem.), Nat. Soc. Professional Engrs. (past pres. Newark chapter), N.J. Soc., S.A.R. Republican. Presbyterian. Author: Indian Trails and City Streets, 1927; The Running Brooks, 1930. Editor Proceedings of the N.J. Historical Society, 1932. Home: 78 Douglas Rd., Glen Ridge, N.J. Office: City Hall, Newark, N.J.

RANKIN, James Latta, lawyer; b. Chester, Pa., Dec. 20, 1890; s. George and Mary (Latta) R.; grad. Chester High Sch., 1907; student U. of Pa., 1910-12; m. Edith Entwisle, Mar. 15, 1917; children—Charles E., Richard E. Admitted to Pa. bar, 1913, and since in practice in Chester; mem. firm Geary & Rankin; pres. Ewing-Thomas Corpn.; vice-pres. Marcus Hook Nat. Bank; sec. Keystone Bldg. & Loan Assn. Served as 2d lt. Coast Arty. Corps, U.S. Army, 1918. Mem. Delaware Co. Bar Assn. Republican. Club: Rolling Green (Swarthmore, Pa.). Home: 715 E. 20th St. Office: 515 Welsh St., Chester, Pa.

RANKIN, John Hall, architect; b. Lock Haven, Pa., Sept. 23, 1868; s. William Washington and Maria Amelia (Jefferies) R.; grad. Lock Haven High Sch., 1885; spl. course in architecture, Mass. Inst. Tech., 1886-88; m. Mrs. Anne Frisbie Shepard, Aug. 20, 1907. In practice at Phila., 1891—; mem. firm of Rankin & Kellogg, 1891-1903, Rankin, Kellogg & Crane, 1903-25, Rankin & Kellogg, 1925—; designers State Asylum for Chronic Insane; Free Pub. Library, Newark, N.J.; U.S. P.O. bldgs., at Camden, N.J., and Indianapolis; bldg. U.S. Dept. Agr., Washington; Mechanic Arts High Sch., St. Paul; U.S.A. Supply Depot, Fort Mason, Cal.; Hamilton Co. Ct. House, Cincinnati; Providential Trust Bldg., Phila.; Montgomery Co. Court House Annex, Norristown, Pa.; Haddon Hall Hotel, Atlantic City; Camden (N.J.) Safe Deposit & Trust Bldg.; Camden Co. Ct. House, Camden. Second lt. and battalion adj. 2d Pa. Vol. Inf., Spanish-Am. War; capt. and regtl. adj. 6th Inf., Pa. N.G., 1900-01. Apptd. by Pres. Roosevelt, 1909, mem. Nat. Advisory Bd. on Fuels and Structural Materials; apptd., 1912, mem. Permanent Com. on Comprehensive Plans, City of Phila.; mem. and 1st pres. Pa. State Bd. Examiners of Architects; mgr. Fourth Rep. Pa. Works Progress Adminstrn. Democrat. Episcopalian. Fellow A.I.A.; past pres. Phila. Chapter A.I.A.; past pres. and hon. mem. Southern Pa. Chapter A.I.A.; mem. S.R., Soc. War of 1812, Naval and Mil. Order of Spanish-Am. War. Clubs: Rittenhouse, T-Square (Phila.); Penllyn (gov.); Cosmos (Washington). Home: Deep Run Farm, Penllyn, Pa. Office: Architects Bldg., Philadelphia, Pa.

RANKIN, John O.; mem. staff Ohio Valley Gen., Reynolds Memorial and North Wheeling hosps.; mem. surg. staff Wheeling Clinic. Address: 58 16th St., Wheeling, W.Wa.

RANKIN, Lynn McGaughey, surgeon; b. Greeneville, Tenn., Sept. 26, 1896; s. Thomas Samuel and Mary (Coile) R.; A.B., Tusculum Coll., Greeneville, Tenn., 1917; M.D., Jefferson Med. Coll., 1921; m. Helen Y. Armitage, Oct. 3, 1923; children—Thomas Lynn, Julia Armitage. Interne Jefferson Hosp., Phila., 1921-23; clin. asst. in surgery, Jefferson Hosp., 1923, asst. in surgery since 1937; asso. in surgery, Del. Co. Hosp., 1927-29, vis. chief, 1929-37, chief of service in gen. surgery since 1937; asso. in surgery, Fitzgerald-Mercy Hosp., 1933; dispensary asst. surg., Presbyn. Hosp., 1933, asst. surg. since 1934; instr. operative surgery, Jefferson Med. Coll., 1927-32, demonstrator same since 1932. Served as 1st lt. Med. Corps Res. U.S.A., 1925-35. Fellow Am. Coll. Surgs. Mem. A.M.A., Pa. State Med. Soc., Del. Co. Med. Soc. (pres. Eastern Branch), West Phila. Med. Soc., Phila. Acad. Surgs., Phi Chi. Republican. Presbyn. Clubs: Medical, Physicians Motor, Medical of Del. County. Contbr. to med. jours. Home: 200 Long Lane, Upper Darby, Pa. Office: 1930 Chestnut St., Philadelphia, Pa.

RANKIN, Matthew, lawyer; b. Chester, Pa., Jan. 26, 1901; s. George and Mary (Latta) R.; A.B., Williams Coll., 1923; LL.B., U. of Pa. Law Sch., 1926; unmarried. Admitted to

Pa. bar, 1926, and since engaged in gen. practice of law at Chester; asso. with Geary & Rankin since 1926; vice-pres. Delaware Co. Trust Co. since 1936. Served as pres. Chester Y.M.C.A., 1934-35; chmn. Chester Ch. Basketball Leagues, 1935-38; pres. Del. Co. Christian Endeavor Union, 1935-36. Mem. Delaware County Bar Assn., Phi Beta Kappa, Delta Theta Phi. Republican. Presbyn. Home: 1801 Edgemont Av. Office: 515 Welsh St., Chester, Pa.

RANKIN, Walter Mead, biologist; b. Newark, N.J., Dec. 1, 1857; s. William and Ellen Hope (Stevens) R.; A.B., Williams, 1879; M.S., Princeton, 1884; Ph.D., U. of Munich, 1889; unmarried. Instr. biology, 1889-95, asst. prof., 1895-1901, prof., 1901-23, emeritus, 1923, Princeton U. Fellow A.A.A.S.; mem. Am. Soc. Naturalists. Presbyn. Clubs: Nassau (Princeton); Williams (New York). Home: Princeton, N.J.

RANSLEY, Harry C., ex-congressman; b. Phila., Pa., Feb. 5, 1863; s. Robert H. and Mary A. (Irvin) R.; ed. pub. schs. and business coll.; m. Harrie Dilks, Mar. 31, 1902; children—Elizabeth Abigail, Harriet (dec.). Mem. Dunlap, Mellor & Co., oils and naval stores, Phila., 1899—. Mem. Ho. of Rep., Pa., 2 terms; mem. Select Council of Phila. 16 yrs. (pres. 8 yrs.); sheriff of Phila. County, 1916-20; chmn. Rep. City Com., Phila., 1916-19; elected mem. 66th Congress to fill unexpired term of J. Hampton Moore, resigned, and mem. 67th to 72d Congresses (1921-33), 3d Pa. Dist. and 73d and 74th Congresses (1933-37), 1st Pa. Dist. Republican. Episcopalian. Mason. Club: Merion Cricket. Home: 1337 Ellsworth St. Office: 126 N. Front St., Philadelphia, Pa.

RANSON, Marius, rabbi; b. Cincinnati, O., Dec. 10, 1893; s. Charles E. and Rebecca (Tutleman) R.; student U. of Chicago; A.B., Univ. of Cincinnati, 1913; B. Hebrew, Hebrew Union Coll., Cincinnati, 1909; m. Annette J. Morris, 1930; 1 dau. Joan Carol. Instr. economics, Univ. of Cincinnati, 1913; instr. in theology, Hebrew Union Coll., 1914; ordained rabbi, same coll., 1914; rabbi Paterson, N.J., 1914-20; asst. rabbi Temple Beth-El, N.Y. City, 1920-21; rabbi Albany, N.Y., 1921-29; founder, rabbi, American Synagog, New York, 1929-30; rabbi Temple Sharey Tefilo, East Orange, N.J., since 1930; also editor Suburban Jewish Digest. Pres. Essex Co. Conf. Catholics, Jews and Protestants, 1934-39; organizer and chmn. of Good Will Radio Broadcasts, conducted weekly, 1937-39; chmn. of Orange and Maplewood Round Table for Jews and Christians, 1939. Served as four-minute man, also member Minute Men of New Jersey and chaplain service, Camp Merritt, during World War. President Conf. on Social Welfare, 1922; participated in public debates with Clarence Darrow, Scott Nearing and others, 1930-33; mem. exec. bd. Central Conf. Am. Rabbis, 1933-36; dir. N.J. Citizens' League and Men's League of Mercy of U.S.; dir. Community Chest, Community Center, Albany; mem. Assn. of Reform Rabbis (exec. bd., 1935-38), Phi Beta Kappa, The Judeans (N.Y.); hon. mem. Rho Pi Phi. Apptd. official arbitrator Arbitration Assn. Am., 1927. Ref. Jewish. Author: The Removal of the World Court to Jerusalem, 1914; Bergson and Judaism, 1916; The Missionary Activities of the Ancient Israelites, 1918; The Ethics of the Bible, 1925; contbr. chapter on "Judaisme et Bergsonisme" in Anthologie Juive du moyen Age à Nos Jours, 1923; also regular contbr. to Am. Hebrew, Am. Israelite, Jewish Tribune, Jewish Criterion, Jewish Advocate. First rabbi to broadcast Jewish Holy Day services, 1921. Home: 447 Tremont Pl., Orange, N.J. Office: 57 Prospect St., East Orange, N.J.

RAPALJE, de Witt, cons. civil engr.; b. Amoy, China, Aug. 6, 1880; s. Rev. Daniel and Alice (Ostrom) R., citizens of U.S.; dir. desc. (9th generation) Joris Jansen R. who came to New Amsterdam, 1623 with 1st shipload colonist; B.Sc., Rutgers U., 1900; m. Beatrice Cameron, of Dunellen, N.J., June 16, 1923; children—Ann Vanderveer, Judith Cameron. Began as telephone engr., Western Electric Co., N.Y. City, 1900-02; fire ins. inspr., 1902-05;

chief engr. farm colony developments, Hugh MacRae & Co., Wilmington, N.C., 1905-09; cons. civil engr., mem. firm, Rapalje & Loughlin, pres. Southern Map Co., sec.-treas. Cement Products Co., all of Wilmington, N.C., 1909-18; with engring. dept. Central R.R.N.J., N.Y. City, 1918-19; gen. inspr. Fire Loss & Protection sect. U.S.R.R. Adminstrn., Washington, D.C., 1919; chief fire-prevention engr., Railroad Ins. Assn., N.Y. City, 1920-34; sales engr., Wadley & Smith, Plainfield, N.J., since 1938. Pres. Plainfield Area Safety Council, Plainfield, N.J. Associate mem. Am. Soc. Civil Engrs.; mem. Plainfield Engrs. Club (exec. com.), Holland Soc. of N.Y., Chi Psi, Cap and Skull. Republican. Southern Presbyn. Club: Rutgers (Plainfield). Author: Railroad Fire Hazards, 1925. Lecturer on fire-prevention and safety topics. Home: 982 Kenyon Av., Plainfield, N.J.

RAPELJE, Walter S(uydam), gen. supt. mfg. plants; b. Brooklyn, N.Y., Jan. 9, 1883; s. Nicholas L. and Ida S. (Vanderveer) R.; B.S., Poly. Inst., Brooklyn, N.Y., 1903, M.S., same, 1904; m. Gertrude S. Van Siclen, Dec. 15, 1908. Asst. chemist, B. T. Babbitt Co., 1904-05; asst. chemist, U.S. Navy Yard, Brooklyn, N.Y., 1905-10; successively chief chemist, asst. supt., supt., treas. Kirkman & Son, Brooklyn, N.Y., 1910-34; gen. supt. domestic plants, Colgate Palmolive Peet Co., Jersey City, N.J., since 1934. Mem. Am. Chem. Soc., Am. Inst. Chem. Engrs., Holland Soc. of N.Y., St. Nicholas Soc. of Nassau Island. Mem. Dutch Reformed Ch. Home: 8849 193d St., Hollis, L.I., N.Y. Office: Colgate Palmolive Peet Co., Jersey City, N.J.

RAPKING, Aaron Henry, clergyman; b. Hannibal, O., Apr. 15, 1886; s. Henry and Caroline (Berger) R.; A.B., Baldwin Wallace Coll., 1912; B.D., Garrett Bibl. Inst., 1914; student Oberlin Sem., 1915-16, W.Va. U., 1925; D.D., Salem Coll., 1935; m. Emma P. Poorman, Dec. 25, 1912; children—Aaron Henry, Morrell Edward, Glenn Hugh, Ella Margaret (Mrs. Paul Nay). Ordained Methodist ministry, 1910; pastor, Cleveland, O., 1910-12, Pearl City, Ill., 1912-14, Huntington, O., 1914-17, Haverhill, O., 1917-19; prof. W.Va. Wesleyan Coll., in charge Dept. Rural Sociology, 1919-21; extension sociologist in rural organization, Coll. of Agr., W.Va. U., 1921-37; supt. Dept. Town and Country Work, Bd. of Home Missions and Church Extension, M.E. Ch., since 1938. Mem. W.Va. Meth. Conf. Del. M.E. Gen. Conf., 1928; mem. W.Va. Conf. Bd. of Edn. of M.E. Ch. Mem. Am. Sociol. Soc., Am. Country Life Assn., Goethe Literary Soc. Republican. Home: Lost Creek, W.Va. Office: 1701 Arch St., Philadelphia, Pa.

RASBRIDGE, Emerson B., lawyer; b. Williamsport, Pa., Apr. 17, 1898; s. Robert B. and Inez M. (Buzzard) R.; student Cornell U., 1916-20, Dickinson Law Sch., 1920-22, A.E.F. Univ., Beaune, France, 1919; m. Christine R. Saylor, Nov. 20, 1923; 1 son, Robert B., II. Admitted to Pa. bar, 1923, and since practiced in local, Superior and Supreme Courts and U.S. Dist. Court; U.S. Commr. Eastern Dist. of Pa. since 1929. Served in Ambulance Service, U.S. Army, in Italy, 1918-19. Decorated with Italian War Cross. Mem. Am. Legion, Vets. of Foreign Wars, U.S. Army Ambulance Service Assn., Scorpion, Delta Chi. Republican. Methodist. Club: Reading Country. Home: "Woods Haven," Stony Creek Mills, Pa. Office: Berks Trust Bldg., Reading, Pa.

RASCHEN, John Frederick Louis, univ. prof.; b. Bremen, Germany, Feb. 19, 1875; s. John Henry and Caroline (Schrader) R.; came to America, 1889; A.B., Baldwin-Wallace Coll., 1895; S.T.B., Nast Theol. Sem., 1898; post-grad. work Lafayette Coll., Columbia U. and U. of Heidelberg, 1905-07; A.M., Lafayette Coll., 1905; Litt.D., Dickinson Coll., 1912; m. Jennie Louise Schmidt, July 2, 1902 (died June 23, 1929); children—Harriet F. Carolyn (Mrs. S. J. Wolff), Edith Louise (Mrs. J. C. Tibbetts); m. 2d, Leonie E. L. Zeyen-Zeller, of Hamburg, Germany, June 14, 1933. Pastor Methodist Episcopal churches, Akron, N.Y., 1898-1900, Despatch, N.Y., 1900-01; head master Greek and Latin Dickinson Sem., Pa., 1901-02; instr. modern langs., 1902-05, asst. prof., 1905-06, prof., 1906-14, Lafayette Coll.; prof. Germanic lang. and lit., 1914-21, prof. modern langs., 1921—, U. of Pittsburgh, also exec. officer grad. council, 1917-24. On leave of absence at U. of Miami, 1926-27. Personnel officer U.S.A., July 1918-Jan. 1919. Mem. A.A.A.S., Modern Lang. Assn. America, Nat. Inst. Social Sciences, Am. Dialect Soc., Pa. Modern Lang. Association (president 1920-21), Linguistic Society America, Verse Writers Guild of America, Goethe Society of America, Schiller Akademie, Munich, Franklin Society (Zurich), Otto Ludwig Society, Scabbard and Blade, Sigma Kappa Phi, Phi Gamma Delta, Pi Gamma Mu. Clubs: Authors, Polygon, Faculty. Contbr. to German secular and religious press and scientific journals; on review staff of Social Science Abstracts. Author of Modern Language texts of International Modern Language Series, 1907, 10, 32, 33, 34. Address: Ruskin Apts., Pittsburgh, Pa.

RASKIN, Moses; attending otolaryngologist South Baltimore Gen. Hosp.; asso. otolaryngologist Sinai Hosp. of Baltimore; asst. ophthalmologist and otolaryngologist Mercy Hosp. Address: 2038 Eutaw Place, Baltimore, Md.

RASKOB, John J., capitalist; b. Lockport, N.Y., Mar. 19, 1879; s. John and Anna Frances (Moran) R.; ed. pub. schs. and business coll.; m. Helena Springer Green, June 18, 1906; 12 children. Asst. treas., treas., and now v.p. and mem. finance com. E. I. du Pont de Nemours Co.; resigned as chmn. finance com. Gen. Motors Corpn., 1928, to become chmn. Democratic Nat. Com.; now director General Motors Corporation; dir. Bankers Trust Co., Lawyers County Trust Co. Member President Wilson's Industrial Conf., Washington, D.C., Oct. 1919. K.C. Clubs: Union League (Phila.); Metropolitan, Bankers, Riding and Driving, N.Y. Yacht (New York); Congressional Country (Washington, D.C.). Home: Centreville, Md. Office: Empire State Bldg., 350 5th Av., New York, N.Y.

RASKOB, William Frederick, corpn. exec.; b. Lockport, N.Y., Nov. 8, 1883; s. John and Anna Frances (Moran) R.; student grammar sch., Lockport, N.Y., 1890-1900, Bryant and Stratton Business Coll., Buffalo, N.Y., 1900-01; m. Nell Dolores Kennedy, Mar. 17, 1928. Stenographer and clk. E. I. du Pont de Nemours & Co., Wilmington, Del., 1902-03, gen. accounting, 1903-15, asst. treas., 1915-35, sec. since 1935; dir. Austin Powder Co. Roman Catholic. K.C., Elk. Clubs: Wilmington, Wilmington Country (Wilmington, Del.); New York Yacht (New York, N.Y.). Home: Kennett Pike and Montchanin Rd. Office: du Pont Bldg., Wilmington, Del.

RASMUSSEN, Torlock, high sch. prin.; b. Brooklyn, N.Y., July 3, 1896; s. Thomas and Johanna R.; B.S., W.Va. Wesleyan Coll., Buckhannon, W.Va., 1922; A.M., Columbia U., 1932; m. Gertrude Reeder, Dec. 22, 1926. Teacher high sch., Elkins, W.Va., 1922-24; teacher high sch., Grafton, W.Va., 1925-31, asst. prin., 1931-33, prin. since 1933. Served as pvt. U.S. Arty., 1918. Mem. Secondary Prins. Assn. of Nat. Edn. Assn., W.Va. State Edn. Assn., Am. Legion. Republican. Methodist. Club: Kiwanis of Grafton. Home: 218 McGraw Av., Grafton, W.Va.

RASSWEILER, Clifford Fred; dir. Central Tech. Lab., E. I. du Pont de Nemours & Co. Home: 419 Riverview Road, Swarthmore, Pa.

RATCLIFF, Thomas C.; v.p. and treas. Standard Gas Equipment Corpn.; b. Hamilton, O.; s. John R. and Minerva (Conner) R.; m. Cora C. Crum. Sec. Standard Gas Equipment Corpn., 1924-31, v.p. and treas. since 1931. Home: 4411 Liberty Heights Av. Office: Bayard and Hamburg Sts., Baltimore, Md.

RATHBONE, Henry Bailey, prof. journalism; b. Merrick, L.I., N.Y., July 3, 1871; s. John and Harriet (Crawford) R.; attended Colgate Acad. and Colgate U.; Litt.D., Colgate U., Hamilton, N.Y., 1931; m. Floy Langworthy, Dec. 25, 1897; children—Josephine Langworthy, Rosina Crawford, John Hollum. Professor of practice of journalism and chairman of department journalism, N.Y. Univ., since 1924; on staff Asso. Press, United Press, N.Y. American, N.Y. Evening Journal, Chicago American, Chicago Examiner, San Francisco Examiner, N.Y. Press, New York Morning Sun, New York Evening Sun, 1895-1924. U.S. del. 5th Triennial Congress of Internat. Soc. for Commercial Edn., London, 1932. Mem. Phi Kappa Psi, Theta Nu Epsilon, Kappa Tau Alpha, Beta Gamma Sigma. Presbyn. Home: 332 Montclair Av., Newark, N.J.

RATZLAFF, Carl Johann, prof. economics; b. Valley City, N.D., Oct. 19, 1895; s. Herman and Georgina (Pedersen) R.; student U. of N. D., 1916-17; B.S., U. of Minn., 1922, M.A., 1924; grad. study U. of Chicago, 1925; M.A., Harvard, 1928, Ph.D., 1930 (Henry Lee fellow); European scholar Bur. of Internat. Research, Rockefeller Foundation, Harvard, in Geneva, Berlin, Stockholm and London, 1930-31; m. Lydia Nelson, June 15, 1921. Instr. economics, Hamline U., St. Paul, 1922-24, asst. prof., 1924-26; instr. U. of Minn., 1925-26; instr. and tutor Harvard, 1928-31; asso. prof. economics, Lafayette Coll., Easton, Pa., 1932-33, prof. and head of dept. since 1933. Mem. Intelligence Service 1st Div. U.S. Army, France., 1917-19. Mem. Am. Internat. Labor Orgn. Com. of League of Nations; mem. Pa. Com. on Pub. Assistance and Social Security Legislation; member Pennsylvania Conference on Social Work. Member Am. Econ. Assn., Am. Assn. Univ. Profs., Pi Gamma Mu, Alpha Kappa Psi. Republican. Lutheran. Author: The Scandinavian Unemployment Relief Program, 1934; Economics, Sociology and the Modern World (co-author), 1935; The Theory of Free Competition, 1936; Planned Society—Yesterday, Today, Tomorrow (co-author), 1937. Contbr. to econ. jours. Home: 620 Parson St., Easton, Pa.

RAU, Albert George, educator; b. Bethlehem, Pa., Aug. 7, 1868; s. Robert and Caroline A. (Bussè) R.; B.S., Lehigh U., 1888, M.S., 1900; Ph.D., Moravian Coll., 1910, LL.D., 1934; Litt.D., Muhlenberg, 1927; m. Gertrude L. Brunner, Feb. 6, 1894; children—Robert Otto (dec.), Henry Brunner. Supt. Moravian Prep. Sch., 1888-1909; dean Moravian Coll. and Theol. Sem. since 1909. Lecturer rural sociology, Teachers' Coll., Columbia U., 1927. Mem. A.A. A.S., Am. Soc. Polit. and Social Science, Am. Math. Assn., Am. Math. Soc., Franklin Inst., Newcomen Soc., Phi Beta Kappa, Phi Gamma Delta, also many hist. and economic socs. Republican. Moravian Mason. Author: Formation of Modern Europe, 1898; also many monographs on Pa. colonial history. Contbr. to Am. Dictionary of Biography. Home: 38 W. Market St., Bethlehem, Pa.

RAUH, Bertha Floersheim (Mrs. Enoch Rauh), welfare worker; b. Pittsburgh, Pa., June 16, 1865; d. Samuel and Pauline (Wertheimer) Floersheim; ed. high sch., Pittsburgh; m. Enoch Rauh, Dec. 5, 1888 (now dec.); children—Helen Blanche, Richard Solomon. Dir. dept. pub. welfare, Pittsburgh, 1922-34 (said to be the first woman in U.S. to be apptd. mem. mayor's cabinet, served under 3 mayors). One of the founders of Pittsburgh Am. Red Cross, Girl Scouts, Travelers Aid Soc., Family Soc., Equal Franchise Fed. (now League of Women Voters), Penny Lunches for school children, the first free dental clinic in the city; with son, founded Pittsburgh Symphony Soc., Community Forum, Business and Professional Women's Club, Soc. for Peace and Arbitration, Drama League, Tuesday Musical Club. Mem. Acad. Science and Arts, Pittsburgh Symphony Soc., Congress of Women's Clubs. Republican. Ref. Jewish religion. Clubs: Concordia, Civic, Republican Woman's Club of Pa., Westmoreland Country. Home: 5837 Bartlett St., Pittsburgh, Pa.

RAUL, Harry Lewis, sculptor; b. Easton, Pennsylvania; s. Lewis and Jane Elinor (Morley) R.; prep. edn., Lerch's Prep. Sch., Easton, Pa., student Lafayette Coll., Easton, 1905-07; pvt. pupil of Frank Edwin Elwell, New York Sch. of Art, Art Students' League, New York, under Frank Vincent DuMond and Pa. Acad. Fine Arts, Phila., under Charles Grafly, and under William M. Chase, N.Y. Sch. of Art; m. Josephine Gesner, Dec. 12, 1918; children—Josephine Lewis, David Brush. Exhibited at Nat. Acad. Design, Architectural League, Montclair (N.J.) Art Mus.,

Newark Mus., San Francisco Expn., Pa. Acad. of Fine Arts (Phila.), Ferargil Galleries (New York), New York Water Color Club, Newark Art Club, Socpanic Soc. Museum (New York), Baltimore Museum of Art, Corcoran Gallery of Art, Washington, D.C., etc. Prin. works: Traill Green Memorial, Easton; World War Memorial, Wilson Borough, Pennsylvania; Spanish-Am. War Monument, Northampton County, Pa.; Old Glory statue, West Chester, Pa.; portrait of ex-mayor Rudolph Blankenburg, Phila.; World War Memorial statue, Englewood, N.J.; Metcalf Memorial bronze group, Rosedale Cemetery, Orange, N.J.; face of Lincoln, Lincoln Trust Co. Bldg., Scranton, Pa.; Herbermann Memorial, Sea Girt, N.J.; War Mothers Memorial, Phila.; Julia Dyckman Andrus memorial, Yonkers, N.Y.; Herbermann memorial, Jersey City, N.J.; Williams-Collidge memorial Easton, Pa.; Christus Rex statue, Morristown, N.J.; Rev. Dr. William E. Barton and Esther Treat Barton memorial tablets, First Congl. Ch., Oak Park, Chicago, Ill., and Berea Coll., Ky.; Prof. Harry Thomas Spengler memorial tablet, Easton, Pa.; Henry Pânzer Memorial, Panzer Coll., E. Orange, N.J.; portrait bas-reliefs of Justice C. E. Hughes, D. U. House (Lafayette Coll.),and Nat. Mus. Washington, D.C., Rev. G. A. Hulbert, Gov. Richard W. Leche, State Office Bldg., Baton Rouge, La., Senator Ellison D. Smith, Wofford Coll., S.C., Dr. Benjamin Hobsan Frayser, Hampden-Sydney Coll., Va., and U. of the South, Sewanee, Tenn.; designed Monclair Art Mus. medal; "Venture," bronze statuette, selected by N.J. State Fed. of Women's Clubs and awarded as First Prize to Asbury Park Women's Club for art progress. Rep. in The Nat. Museum (Washington, D.C.), Hall of Nations Mus. (Internat.), Asbury Park, N.J., Montclair (N.J.) Art Museum. Sculpture pirze, Art Centre of the Oranges, 1931; Montclair Art Mus. sculpture medal, 1931. Fellow Royal Soc. of Arts (London), 1937; mem. Am. Federation of Arts, Mystic (Conn.) Art Assn., Art Centre of the Oranges (hon. life mem.; ex-pres., dir., chmn. sculpture dept.), Montclair Art Mus. (art com.), N.J. Chapter Am. Artists Professional League (N.J. chmn. 4 terms, mem. nat. exec. com.), Delta Upsilon; asso. mem. Architectural League of New York, Nat. Sculpture Soc. Wrote preface to Sculptured Crosses of Ancient Ireland by Henry O'Neill, 1916. Served as guest lecturer on art, Lafayette Coll., Nat. Assn. Women Painters and Sculptors, N.J. State Fed. Women's Clubs, N.J. Chapter Am. Inst. Architects, Montclair Art Mus., Newark Mus. Developed new technique of diorama sculpture. Chief adjuster bur. of labor and safety at Bethlehem Steel Co., South Bethlehem, Pa., 1917; conducted special research laboratory (foundry technique), Taylor-Wharton Iron and Steel Co., Easton, Pa. Home and Studio: 1740 K St. N.W., Washington, D.C.; and 1050 Washington St., Easton, Pa.

RAUL, Josephine Gesner, artist; b. Linden, N.J., Apr. 23, 1897; d. Joshua Brush and Caroline (Blancke) Gesner; ed. Vail-Deane Sch., Elizabeth, N.J., Birmingham (Pa.) Sch., Nat. Acad. of Design, Art Students League, N.Y. City; studied painting under G. Albert Thompson; m. Harry Lewis Raul, Dec. 12, 1918 (divorced); children—Josephine Lewis, David Brush. Has followed profession as artist since 1917, specializing in painting still life; exhibited Springfield (Mass.) Museum, Montclair Museum, Newark Museum, Nat. Assn. Women Painters and Sculptors; Mystic (Conn.) Art Asso. Awards: Nat. Assn. Women Painters and Sculptors, 1930, Nat. League of Am. Pen Women, 1930, N.J. Painters, 1931, Art Center of the Oranges, 1931. Mem. Am. Fed. of Arts, Mystic Art Assn., Mystic, Conn. Republican. Ch. of Christ Sci. Home: 179 Harrison St., East Orange, N.J.; (summer), Groton Long Point, Conn.

RAUSCH, Herbert S(amuel), supervising prin. schs.; b. Berks Co., Pa., Oct. 16, 1887; s. Jacob M. and Sinorah T. (Baver) R.; ed. Keystone State Normal Sch., 1904-07; Pd.B., Post Grad State Normal Sch., 1909; B.S., Susquehanna U., 1917, A.M., same, 1919; m. Cora Mae Yoder, Aug. 5, 1909; children—Russell Herbert, Miriam Elizabeth, Helen Mae. Engaged in teaching pub. schs. since 1907; ward prin. schs., Lehighton, Pa., 1909-10; supervising prin., pub. schs., Weissport, Pa., 1910-14; prin. high sch., Conshohocken, Pa., 1914-16; head of science dept., Perkasie, Pa., 1916-19; supt. schs., Lewes, Del., 1919-21; supervising prin. pub. schs., Girardville, Pa. since 1921. Served as mgr. large area of War Gardens at Perkasie, Pa. during World War. Mem. co-exec. bd. Boy Scouts. Past sec. Carbon Co. S.S. Assn.; vice-pres. Ch. Council for yrs. Republican. Lutheran. Mason (32°), I.O.O.F. Clubs: Lions (sec.-treas. 10 yrs., now pres.), Anthracite Booster (Girardville). Home: 331 Preston Av., Girardville, Pa.

RAUTENSTRAUCH, Walter, industrial engr., educator; b. Sedalia, Mo., Sept. 7, 1880; s. Julius and Anna (Nichter) R.; B.S., U. of Mo., 1902; LL.D., 1932; M.S., U. of Me., 1903; studied Cornell U., 1903-04; m. Minerva Babb, Sept. 7, 1904. Instr. U. of Me., 1902-03; asst. prof., Cornell, 1904-06; prof. industrial engring., Columbia U., since 1906. Cons. engr. to the mfg. industries. Mem. Nat. Research Council. Fellow N.Y. Acad. Sciences, A.A.A.S.; mem. Am. Soc. Refrigerating Engrs., Am. Soc. M.E., Franklin Inst., Am. Acad. Polit. and Social Science, Tau Beta Pi, Sigma Xi. Author: Syllabus of Lectures on Machine Design, 1906; Machine Drafting, 1908. The Economics of Business Enterprise, 1939; Who Gets the Money?, 1939. Co-Author: Mechanical Engineers Handbook, 1916; The Successful Control of Profits, 1930; Tomorrow in the Making, 1939. Contbr. to mags. Home: 235 Dorin Court Rd., Palisade, N.J.

RAVDIN, I(sidor) S(chwaner), prof. surgery; b. Evansville, Ind., Oct. 10, 1894; s. Marcus and Wilhelmina (Jacobsohn) R.; B.S., U. of Ind., 1916; M.D., U. of Pa. Med. Sch., 1918; m. Elizabeth Glenn, June 2, 1921; children—Robert Glenn, Elizabeth, William Dickie. Interne Univ. of Pa. Hosp.; Harrison prof, surgery, U. of Pa. Med. Sch. since 1920; in pvt. practice at Phila. since 1920, specializing in surgery. Fellow Am. Coll. Surgeons, Am. Surg. Assn.; mem. Am. Med. Assn., Am. Physiol. Soc., Am. Soc. Exptl. Pathology, Coll. of Phys., Halsted Surg. Soc., Phi Chi. Home: 2015 Delancey Place. Office: 3400 Spruce St., Philadelphia, Pa.

RAVEN, John Howard, theologian; b. Brooklyn, Oct. 3, 1870; s. Anton A. and Gertrude (Oatman) R.; A.B., Rutgers Coll., 1891, A.M., 1894; grad. New Brunswick Theol. Sem., 1894; U. of Berlin, 1902-03; D.D., Rutgers, 1899; m. Elizabeth Grier Strong, May 29, 1894; 1 son, Anton Adolph. Ordained ministry Reformed Ch. in America, 1894; pastor at Metuchen, N.J., 1894-99; acting prof., 1898-99, prof. O.T. langs. and exegesis, 1899-1939, pres. faculty, 1922-23, pres. 1923-25, New Brunswick Theol. Sem. Lecturer on English Bible, Rutgers Coll., 1910-13; lecturer in Old Testament lit., Princeton Theol. Sem., 1926-31. Author: Old Testament Introduction, General and Special, 1906; Essentials of Hebrew Grammar, 1908; Biblical Hermeneutics, 1910; History of the Religion of Israel, 1933. Compiler of General Catalogue Rutgers College, 1766-1916; Biographical Record of New Brunswick Theological Seminary, 1784-1934. Mem. com. on versions, Am. Bible Soc., 1922—; trustee Rutgers Coll. (sec. bd. 1922—); corporator Presbyn. Ministers' Fund, Phila. Pres. Zeta Psi of North America, 1912; mem. Phi Beta Kappa. Clubs: University, Interchurch, Clergy, Zeta Psi (New York). Mem. N.J. Hist. Soc., Soc. Bibl. Lit. and Exegesis. Home: 8 Bishop Pl., New Brunswick, N.J.

RAWLS, Fletcher Hooks, foodstuffs expert; b. Deer Park, Ala., Apr. 5, 1890; s. James Benjamin and Ruth Morrison (Ray) R.; ed. St. Stephens (Ala.) Jr. Coll., 1906-08; m. Iris L. Crumpler, Feb. 11, 1917; children—Estelle Harvey, Fletcher Hooks, Iris. Engaged in banana and tropical food shipping with United Fruit Co. in Costa Rica, 1908-15; mfr. of sugar in Cuba, 1915-18; raw sugar specialist for U.S. Sugar Equalization Bd., N.Y. City, 1918; studied production of sugar and demand for sugar and other food products in Scandinavia and Russia, 1919; became connected with Gilmer's, Inc., at Winston-Salem, N.C., 1920, establishing chain of dept. stores in Southeast; entered wholesale baking business, 1922, later associating with Liberty Baking Corpn., with plants throughout the country; with brother purchased Crystal Candy Co. of Winston-Salem, 1927; chief of Foodstuff Div. of U.S. Dept. of Commerce, 1934-37, promoting export trade; asst. dir. in charge industrial divs. and district offices, Bureau of Foreign and Domestic Commerce, since 1937. Cited for meritorious service during World War. Mem. Chamber Commerce, Winston-Salem (dir.). Democrat. Methodist. Mason (32°), Odd Fellow, Elk. Clubs: Civitan (v.p.), Winston-Salem Country; Kenwood (Md.) Country. Home: R. F.D. 2, Silver Spring, Md. Office: Dept. of Commerce Bldg., Washington, D.C.

RAWLS, William Lee, lawyer; b. Greenville, N.C., May 1, 1883; s. William Stowe and Margaret Olivia (Tyson) R.; ed. public schools of Baltimore; hon. A.M., St. John's Coll., 1916; m. Anna Stump, Oct. 18, 1913; children—William Stowe, John Bordley, Richard. Studied law in office of Marbury, Gosnell & Williams; admitted to Md. bar, 1905, and since practiced in Baltimore; mem. firm Marbury, Gosnell & Williams; special master by appointment of U.S. Supreme Court in case of N.J. vs. Del.; dir. Savings Bank of Baltimore; dir. Md. Life Ins. Co. of Baltimore. Mem. Md. State Bd. of Law Examiners, 1919-27; pres. Bd. of Sch. Commrs., Baltimore, 1926-32; chmn. Commn. on Revenue and Taxation, 1938. Dir. Samuel Ready Inst. for Orphan Girls, Baltimore. Mem. Bar Assn. of Baltimore City (pres. 1919-20), Md. State Bar Assn. Democrat. Clubs: Maryland, Merchants (both Baltimore). Home: 3929 Canterbury Rd. Office: 1000 Maryland Trust Bldg., Baltimore, Md.

RAY, Charles Andrew, M.D.; b. Kanawha Co., W.Va., May 4, 1864; s. John E. and Deborah A. (Gay) R.; M.D., Coll. Phys. and Surg., Baltimore, 1887; m. Mamie A. Fisher, Feb. 15, 1891; children—John V., C. A., J. Seibert. Practiced at Charleston, W.Va., since 1888; editor W.Va. Med. Jour.; mem. Kanawha County Court since 1930; chmn. Dem. County Com. 8 yrs.; live stock farmer. Served as capt. and mem. Draft Bd., World War. Fellow A.M. A.; mem. Am. Coll. Physicians, W.Va. State Med. Assn. Home: Pocotaligo, W.Va. Address: Kanawha Valley Hosp. and Sanitarium, Charleston, W.Va.

RAY, Daniel Pattee, surgeon; b. Tyrone, Pa., Nov. 14, 1879; s. John Keim and Maria (Cadwallader) R.; A.B., Dickinson Coll., 1903; M.D., Johns Hopkins U. Med. Sch., 1907; hon. A.M., Dickinson Coll., 1908; grad. study, Johns Hopkins, 1914, Vienna, Austria, 1931; m. Mary McQuown (dec.): m. 2d, Olivia P. Canney (dec.); m. 3d, Margaret Phillips, June 3, 1918. Interne Paterson (N.J.) Gen. Hosp., 1907, McKeesport (Pa.) Hosp., 1907-08, Western Pa. Hosp., Pittsburgh, 1908; in gen. practice of medicine at Johnstown, Pa., 1908-14, specializing in urology since 1914; chief genito-urinary diseases Conemaugh Valley Memorial Hosp. since 1920. Served as 1st lt. then capt. Med. Corps, U.S.A. during World War. Mem. Southmont Borough Sch. Bd., 1929-37, pres., 1930-37. Past dist. comdr. Dept. Pa., Am. Legion. Fellow Am. Coll. Surgeons; mem. Am. Med. Assn., Am. Urol. Assn., Phi Kappa Psi, Am. Legion (past comdr. Johnstown Post). Republican. Mason (32°, Shriner). Clubs: Sunnehanna Country, Bachelors. Home: 414 State St. Office: 218 Franklin St., Johnstown, Pa.

RAY, G(eorge) J(oseph), civil engr.; b. Metamora, Ill., Mar. 24, 1876; s. Jerry and Harriett (Swallow) R.; A.B., U. of Ill., 1898, C.E., 1910; D.Sc., Lafayette Coll., Easton, Pa., 1916; m. Edna Rose Hammers (AB., U. of Ill., 1901), June 23, 1903. Rodman, transitman, asst. engr., track supervisor and roadmaster, I.C. R.R., 1898-1903; div. engr., 1903-09, chief engr., Jan. 1, 1909-Feb. 1, 1919, D.,L.& W. R.R. As chief engr., had charge of constrn. of Hopatcong Slateford cut-off, one of the heaviest pieces of constrn. work yet accomplished on any r.r.; designed and built Tunkhannock viaduct, at Nicholson, Pa., largest concrete bridge ever built (2,375 ft. long, 243 ft. high). Engring. asst. to regional director, Eastern Region, U.S. R.R. Administration, New York, Feb. 1, 1919-Feb. 1920; later chief engr. D.,L.& W. R.R., v.p. and gen. mgr. same since Jan. 1, 1934. Republican. Baptist. Home: Summit, N.J. Office: 90 West St., New York, N.Y.*

RAY, Harold, banking; b. Sussex, N.J., Oct. 21, 1900; ed. pub. schs. and high sch.; m. Cora McKeag; 1 dau., Patricia Ann. In employ Farmers Nat. Bank, Sussex, N.J., 1914-19; advanced through various depts. Mechanics Nat. Bank, Trenton, N.J., 1919-27, cashier, 1927; asso. with First-Mechanics Nat. Bank, consolidation of First Nat. and Mechanics Nat. Bank, since 1928, dir. since 1932, apptd. cashier, 1931, exec. vice-pres. since 1932. Dir. of the Teachers Pension for State of N.J. Trustee Rider Coll. Clubs: Trenton Rotary (Trenton). Home: 878 Bellevue Av. Office: 1 W. State St., Trenton, N.J.

RAY, John Vickers, lawyer; b. Winifrede, W.Va., Feb. 15, 1893; s. Charles Andrew and Mamie Alice (Fisher) R.; A.B., U. of Va., Charlottesville, 1913, LL.B., 1920; B.A., Oxford Univ., Eng., 1917; m. Marion Elizabeth Lakin, Nov. 5, 1922; children—John Lakin, Olivia. Admitted to W.Va. bar, 1920 and engaged in gen. practice of law at Charleston, W.Va., since 1920; mem. firm Payne, Minor & Bouchelle, 1921-32, Payne, Minor & Ray, 1932-37, Payne, Minor, Ray & Davis since 1937. Served in Am. Ambulance with French Army, 1915-17; capt. C.A.C., U.S.A., 1917-19. Dir. Kanawha County Pub. Library, Charleston, Morris Harvey Coll., Charleston, W.Va. Mem. Am., W.Va. State and Charleston bar assns., Chi Phi, Phi Delta Phi. Democrat. Methodist. Mason. Club: Edgewood Country (Charleston). Home: 2 Oglethorpe Rd. Office: Kanawha Valley Bldg., Charleston, W.Va.

RAY, Joseph Warren, Jr., lawyer; b. Waynesburg, Pa., Sept. 1, 1889; s. Joseph Warren and Henrietta (Iams) R.; A.B., Waynesburg (Pa.) Coll., 1910; LL.B., U. of Pa., 1913; m. Elsie Jane Cooper, Dec. 30, 1915; 1 dau., Jane Cooper. Admitted to bar of the several cts of Pa., 1913; asso. with firm McDonald & Gray, Uniontown, Pa., 1913-22; partner in law firm Shelby, Hackney & Ray, 1926-36, Shelby, Ray & Coldren, Uniontown, Pa., since 1936; dir. Penstate Amusement Co., N. Kaufman's, Inc., Fayette Fuel Co., Point Marion Bridge Co. City solicitor, City of Uniontown, 1924-30. Mem. Am. and Pa. bar assns., Am. Law Inst. Republican. Mason (Shriner). Club: Uniontown (Pa.) Country. Author: Termination of Lease by Fire (Pa. Bar Assn. Quarterly), 1932. Home: 114 N. Gallatin Av. Office: 607 Fayette Title & Trust Bldg., Uniontown, Pa.

RAY, R. H., editor The Gazette. Address: 843 Philadelphia St., Indiana, Pa.

RAYCROFT, Joseph Edward, prof. hygiene; b. Williamstown, Vt., Nov. 15, 1867; s. William and Eliza (Kelty) R.; grad. Worcester (Mass.) Acad., 1892; A.B., U. of Chicago, 1896; Northwestern Medical College, 1896-98; M.D., Rush Medical College, Chicago, 1899; m. Sarah Elizabeth Butler, June 14, 1899. Instr., Worcester Acad., 1888-92; instr. hygiene, 1892-99, asst. prof., 1899-1904, asso. prof., 1904-11, U. of Chicago; prof. hygiene, Princeton, 1911-36, retired; med. consultant N.J. Dept. Institutions and Agencies since 1936. Pres. bd. mgrs. N.J. State Hosp. for Insane; mem. New Jersey Commn. on Mental Hygiene; v.p. Camp Fire Girls America, Am. Olympic Assn. Fellow Am. Physical Edn. Assn.; mem. Nat. Inst. Social Sciences, Am. Sch. Hygiene Assn., N.J. State Med. Soc. (hon.), Alpha Delta Phi, Nu Sigma Nu, Phi Beta Kappa. Clubs: Alpha Delta Phi, Princeton (New York); Nassau (Princeton). Mem. War Dept. Commn. on Training Camp Activities, 1917-19. Address: Princeton, N.J.

RAYMOND, Walter Clemens, obstetrician and gynecologist; b. Drifting, Pa., Apr. 17, 1877; s. Joseph Henry and Catherine (Rader) R.; student Central State Normal Sch., Lockhaven, Pa., 1896-98; M.D., Jefferson Med. Coll., 1906; student U. of Pa. Grad. Sch., dept. of gynecology and obstetrics, 1920-21; m. Anna Marcella Mulqueen, June 25, 1907; children—Eugene Edward (M.D.), Joseph Wilbur (M.D.), Marian Raymond (Mrs. James F. McGettigan). Gen. practice of medicine, Lilly, Pa., 1907-20; staff obstetrician Mercy Hosp., Johnstown, Pa., since 1921. Diplomate Am. Bd. Obstetrics and Gynecology. Mem. A.M.A., Pa. Med. Soc., Pittsburgh Obstet. and Gynecol. Soc. Republican. Catholic. Home: 528 Franklin St., Johnstown, Pa.

RAYNOLDS, James Wallace, chemical engineer; b. Omaha, Neb., Feb. 18, 1899; s. James Wallace and Brownie (Baum) R.; grad. Omaha Central High Sch., 1916; Chem. E., Lafayette Coll., Easton, Pa., 1920; m. Elizabeth Whiting, Aug. 24, 1935. Research chemist Binney & Smith, Easton, Pa., 1920-26, sales engr., New York, N.Y., 1926-29; sales engr. Devoe & Raynolds Co., Inc., New York, 1929-33; specialist industrial finishes, New England, 1933-35, Ohio-Apex, Inc., Nitro, W.Va., 1935-36; Raolin industrial fellow in synthetic resins, Mellon Inst., Pittsburgh, since 1936; pres. and dir. of research and development, The Raolin Corpn., Charleston, W.Va. Served as 2d lt. Coast Arty., O.R.C., U.S. Coast Arty. Sch., Fortress Monroe, Va., 1918. Mem. Am. Inst. Chem. Engrs., Delta Kappa Epsilon. Republican. Club: University (Pittsburgh). Author of various patents on the manufacture and use of rubber chloride. Home: 740 S. Negley Av. Office: Mellon Institute, Pittsburgh, Pa.

RAYNOR, George Emil, asso. prof. mathematics; b. San Francisco, Calif., Feb. 27, 1895; s. Charles Edmund and Louise (Huptcher) R.; B.S., U. of Wash., 1917; A.M., Princeton, 1920, Ph.D., same, 1923; m. Amy Becraft, Aug. 26, 1920; 1 dau., Georgia Emily. Engaged as instr. mathematics, Princeton U., 1920-23; asst. prof. mathematics, Wesleyan U., 1923-27; asso. prof. mathematics, U. of Okla., 1927-31; asso. prof. mathematics, Lehigh U., since 1931. Served as pvt. Ordnance Dept., U.S.A., 1917-18. Mem. Am. Math. Soc., Math. Assn. of America, Sigma Xi, Phi Beta Kappa, Pi Mu Epsilon. Republican. Contbr. articles to various math. jours. Home: 530 10th Av., Bethlehem, Pa.

REA, Robert W., pres. Robin Corpn.; b. Phila., Pa., Mar. 15, 1897; s. David and Hannah (Wilson) R.; student U. of Pa.; m. Helene M. A. Curley, Jan. 19, 1922; children—Robert W., Patricia Elena. Pres. and dir. Robin Corpn. since 1928. Home: Sugartown and Fairfield Roads, Devon, Pa. Office: 200 W. 9th St., Wilmington, Del.

READ, Charles William, v.p. Shenango Pottery Co.; b. Utica, N.Y., Mar. 30, 1875; s. William Joseph and Elizabeth Chalmers (Mackenzie) R.; ed. high sch.; m. Tereśé Olivia Jenstrom, Jan. 5, 1916. Began as salesman S. P. Pierce & Sons, Syracuse, N.Y.; mgr. Central New York Pottery Co., Chittenango, 1900-03; asst. mgr. Iroquois China Co., Syracuse, 1903-09; v.p., sales mgr. and dir. Shenango Pottery Co. since 1913. Vice-pres. and dir. Margaret L. Henry Children's Home; dir. Jameson Memorial Hosp. Mem. New Castle Chamber of Commerce. Clubs: Castle, Field (New Castle). Home: 205 Hazelcroft Av. Office: W. Grant St., New Castle, Pa.

READ, Conyers, prof. history; b. Philadelphia, Pa., Apr. 25, 1881; s. William Franklin and Victoria Eliza (Conyers) R.; A.B., Harvard, 1903, A.M., 1904, Ph.D., 1908; B.Litt., Oxford U., 1909; Litt.D., U. of Wis., 1938; m. Edith Coulson Kirk, June 14, 1910; children—Elizabeth, William Franklin III, Edward C. Kirk. Instr. in history, Princeton 1909-10; same, U. of Chicago, 1910-12, asst. prof., 1912-15, asso. prof., 1915-19, prof., 1919-20, nonresident prof. since 1920; treas. Wm. F. Read & Sons Co., mfrs. textiles, Philadelphia, 1920-27, v.p. and gen. mgr., 1927-30, pres., 1930-33; exec. sec. Am. Hist. Assn., 1933—; prof. English history, U. of Pa., 1934—. Served with American Red Cross overseas, 1918. Mem. Royal Historical Society (London), American Philosophical Society, Phi Beta Kappa. Clubs: University, Merion Cricket (Philadelphia); Harvard (New York). Author: Mr. Secretary Walsingham and the Policy of Queen Elizabeth (3 vols.), 1925; The Tudors, 1936. Editor: The Bardon Papers, 1909; Bibliography of British History (1485-1603), 1933; The Constitution Reconsidered, 1938. Contbr. Am. Hist. Review, English Hist. Rev., Jour. Modern History, etc. Home: 340 Sycamore Av., Merion, Pa. Office: 226 S. 16th St., Philadelphia, Pa.

READ, Harry Malcolm, M.D.; b. Norwood, Pa., May 15, 1893; s. Harry and Anna Amelia Clara Corinne (Schaum) R.; ed. Friend's Select Sch. (Philadelphia) and York High Sch.; M.D., Hahnemann Med. Coll., 1915; m. Lydia Spahr Erwin, June 14, 1919; 1 son, Harry Malcolm. Began "gen. practice of medicine, 1917; chief Dept. of Health, York Dispensary, since 1926; consultant in tuberculosis and mem. staff York Hosp. since 1928. Served as 1st lt. U.S. Army Res. Corps, 1917-19. Pres. Pa. Homeopathic Med. Soc., 1932, mem. bd. trustees, 1933-36; sec. (since 1936) and chmn. Child Health Com., York County Med. Soc.; mem. Am. Legion, Phi Alpha Gamma (past chapter pres.). Club: York Medical. Contbr. to homeo. med. jours. Home: R.D. 7. Office: 141 E. Market St., York, Pa.

READ, William Thornton, chemist; b. College Station, Tex., Mar. 8, 1886; s. Joseph Dotson and Belle (Thornton) R.; A.B., Austin Coll., Sherman, Tex., 1905, A.M., 1908; A.M., U. of Tex., 1915; student Harvard, 1915-16; Ph.D., Yale, 1921; m. Roxie Clark, of Conway, Ark., Sept. 9, 1918; children—William Thornton, Roxana Clark. Asst. editor Lampasas (Tex.) Leader, 1905-07; sec. Austin Coll., 1907-10; instr., U. of Tex., 1914-15, 1916-18; head dept. of chemistry, Tex. Technol. Coll., Lubbock, 1925-30; dean, sch. of chemistry, Rutgers U., since 1930. Served as 1st lt. Chem. Warfare Service, U.S. Army, 1918. Mem. Am. Chem. Soc., Am. Inst. Chem. Engrs., Am. Inst. Chemists, Soc. Chemists of Md., Sigma Xi, Sigma Delta Chi, Alpha Chi Sigma, Phi Lambda Upsilon (nat. v.p.). Presbyn. Club: Chemists (New York). Author: Industrial Chemistry, 1933. Home: River Rd., New Brunswick, N.J.

READIO, Wilfred Allen, teacher, artist; b. Northampton, Mass., Nov. 27, 1895; s. Fred Walter and Louise (Roller) R.; A.B., Carnegie Inst. of Tech., 1918; m. Frances Andrews, Aug. 11, 1923; 1 son, Joel. Instr. Carnegie Inst. of Tech., 1919-20, 1921-22, asst. prof., 1922-28, asso. prof. and chmn. dept. of painting and design, since 1928; in professional practice as artist and fellow L. C. Tiffany Foundation, 1920-21; instr. Colo. State Teacher's Coll., summer 1922. Exhibited as a painter and lithographer at Internat. Exhbn. of Prints, Art Inst. of Chicago, 1934 and 1935, Internat. Exhbn. of Painting, Carnegie Inst., 1934, at Print Club of Phila., etc. Rep. in permanent collections of One Hundred Friends of Pittsburgh Art, Somerset (Pa.) High Sch.; and in pvt. collections. Mem. Asso. Artists of Pittsburgh (dir. 1925-31; awarded 1st honors in painting, annual exhbn., 1921). Mem. regional exec. com. Pub. Works of Art Projects, 1933-34. Served in Engr. Corps, U.S. Army, World War, rank of M.E. senior grade. Home: 5210 Woodlawn Place, Pittsburgh, Pa.

REARICK, Allan Chamberlain, lawyer; b. Galesburg, Ill., Dec. 18, 1874; s. Francis Herman and Helen Maria (Shaw) R.; A.B., Knox Coll., Galesburg, 1897; LL.B., Columbia, 1904; m. Ethel Rawalt, June 15, 1907; children—John Shaw, Anna Maud (Mrs. Joseph W. Allen, Jr.), Allan Chamberlain. Admitted to N.Y. bar, 1904, and since practiced at N.Y. City; member of the firm of Hines, Rearick, Dorr & Hammond; counsel M.-K.-T. R.R. Company; director C.R.I.&P. Railway Company, Summit Trust Co. Trustee Kent Place School, Summit, N.J. Mem. Assn. Bar. of the City of New York, Phi Beta Kappa, Phi Delta Phi. Republican. Conglist. Clubs: University, City Midday, Baltusrol Golf, Manasquan River Golf, Canoe Brook Country. Home: 106 Beechwood Rd., Summit, N.J. Office: 61 Broadway, New York, N.Y.

REARICK, William Matthias, clergyman; b. Beavertown, Pa., Dec. 25, 1870; ed. Missionary Inst., Selinggrove, Pa., 1890-94, Theol. Dept. Susquehanna U., 1894-97; A.M., Susquehanna U., 1907, D.D., 1919; m. Ida Mildred Burns, Aug. 26, 1896 (died 1938); children—Dorothy (Mrs. Frank A. Staib), Robert Burns. Ordained to ministry United Luth. Ch. in America; pastor Buffalo Parish, Union Co., Pa., 1897-1905, Bellefonte, Pa., 1905-06; pastor at Mifflinburg since 1906; served as sec. and pres. Central Pa. and Susquehanna Synods of Luth. Ch. Trustee Susquehanna U. since 1904, pres. bd. since 1931. Republican. Lutheran. Home: 400 Market St., Mifflinburg, Pa.

REASS, Joseph Harmon, advertising exec.; b. Wheeling, W.Va., Apr. 17, 1881; s. Joseph Frank and Margaret (Wilkinson) R.; student pub. sch., Wheeling, W.Va., 1888-90, St. James Lutheran Sch., Wheeling, 1890-95; grad. Linsly Inst., Wheeling, 1898; m. Julia Loftus, Sept. 9, 1908 (died 1915); children—Julia Margaret, Joseph Loftus, Rose Katherine (dec.); m. 2d, Viola Winter, Oct. 13, 1917; children—Viola Jeannette (Mrs. William E. Maxwell), Mary Catherine, Frieda Wilkinson, Harmon Walter, George Winter, Laura Mae, Robert Frank. Began as newsboy, Wheeling, 1891; teamster, Wheeling, 1898; traveling salesman Block Bros. tobacco, Pinkerton Tobacco, Ohio, Ind., Pa., N.J., 1900-02; sec., Jos. Reass & Son Co., transfer Co., Wheeling, 1902-12; sec.-treas., Wheeling Savings & Loan Assn., 1921-34; exec. v.p. Homeseekers Fire Ins. Co., Wheeling, 1923-35; dir. Pittsburgh Branch Federal Home Loan Bank System, 1932-34; pres. Reass Advertising Co., Wheeling, W.Va., since 1922; v.p. and dir. Huntington (W.Va.) Realty Corpn. since 1934, Am. Legion Home Corpn., Wheeling, since 1937. Served as capt., Remount Div., U.S. Army, during World War. Republican nominee for mayor, Wheeling, 1917; chmn. City of Wheeling Flood Commn., 1937-38; mem. President Hoover's Housing Conf., 1931; pres. Wheeling Real Estate Bd., 1926; committeemen U.S. Bldg. & Loan League, 1926-32. Mem. Am. Legion (sec. First Dist. Exec. Council since 1938; organized Wheeling Post 1, 1919, 2 weeks before Paris meeting; del. St. Louis caucus, 1919, comdr. Ohio Valley Council, 1930), 40 & 8, Island Community Assn. (pres. 1931-32), Trade Assn. of Advertising Distributors (nat. vice-pres., 1938-39; chmn. legislative com., 1939), U.C.T. (trustee Wheeling Council, 1924-31). Republican. Lutheran. Mason (32°, Scottish Rite, Shriner), Legion of Honor. Pres. Wheeling (W. Va.) Ad Club, 1913. Home: 41 Kentucky St. Office: 804 Market St., Wheeling, W.Va.

REATH, Theodore Wood, lawyer; b. Pittsburgh, Pa., June 7, 1866; s. Benjamin Brannan and Emma Hanna (Wood) R.; A.B., U. of Pa., 1887; m. Augusta M. Roberts, Apr. 20, 1892. Admitted to Phila. bar, 1896; apptd. gen. solicitor Norfolk & Western Ry. Co., 1907, gen. counsel, 1919-36, retired. Club: Rittenhouse. Home: Pont Reading House, Old Haverford Rd., Ardmore, Pa. Office: 318 Walnut St., Philadelphia, Pa.

REBBECK, Elmer William, surgeon; b. Pittsburgh, Pa., Oct. 6, 1901; s. William George and Clara Luella (Smith) R.; B.Sc., Ohio State U., 1923; student U. of Pittsburgh, 1920-21; M.D., Hahnemann Med. Coll., 1925; grad. study, U. of Vienna, Austria, 1927; m. Luella Matheny, 1926; children—William George, Jean Elizabeth. Asst. dept. pathology, Boston U., 1926-27; asst. to Dr. G. G. Shoemaker, 1927-28; asso. with Dr. F. S. Morris in gen. surgery at Shadyside Hosp., Pittsburgh, since 1928, now staff surgeon. Fellow Am. Coll. Surgeons; mem. Phi Rho Sigma. Republican. Mason. Home: 1863 Shaw Av., Pittsburgh, Pa.

REBERT, G. Nevin; prof. edn. and dir. teacher training, Hood Coll. Address: Hood College, Frederick, Md.

REBMANN, G. Ruhland, Jr., lawyer; b. Philadelphia, Pa., Feb. 6, 1898; s. Godfrey R. and Pauline (Cooper) R.; M.E., Cornell U.; LL.B., U. of Pa.; m. Mary H. Bull, Jan. 3, 1925; children—Ann, Beverly Mary. Mem. law firm Edmonds, Obermayer & Rebmann; dir. Am. Engring. Co. Pres. Big Brother Assn. of Philadelphia; mem. bd. Community Fund of Philadelphia and vicinity. Clubs: Rittenhouse, Union League, Racquet, Midday. Home: 729 Millbrook Lane, Haverford, Pa. Office: 1418 Packard Bldg., Philadelphia, Pa.

RECKORD, Frank Frederick Dunott, M.D.; b. Harrisburg, Pa., Sept. 15, 1886; s. James Fraser and Adaline Virginia (McKeehan) R.; M.D., U. of Pa., 1911; hon. Sc.D., Gettysburg (Pa.) Coll., 1932; unmarried. Resident phys., Hosp., U. of Pa., 1911-13; began practice at Harrisburg, 1914; dep. insp. tuberculosis dispensaries, Pa. State Health Dept., 1914-20; examiner for disease of heart and lungs, later asst. tuberculosis specialist, U.S.A., and asso. chief med. service, Base Hosp., Camp Devens, Mass., 1918-19; part-time chief med. officer Med. Div. U.S. Vets. Bur., Harrisburg, 1920-24; med. officer Pennsylvania State Police Department, 1917-36; specializes in internal medicine; attending phys. Harrisburg Gen. Hosp. Fellow A.M.A.; mem. Pa. Med. Soc., Dauphin Co. Med. Soc., Harrisburg Acad. Medicine, Sons of Vets., Am. Legion. Republican. Mem. Reformed Ch. Mason (32°, Shriner). Clubs: Zembo Luncheon, Salem Reformed Church Men's. Contbr. papers on tuberculosis, etc. Home: 2447 N. 3d St. Office: 1006 N. 2d St., Harrisburg, Pa.

RECORDS, Victor Clinton, business exec.; b. nr. Laurel, Del., Oct. 31, 1877; s. William Thomas and Virginia Selenia (Giles) R.; student Miss Mary Witherbee Pvt. Sch., Laurel, Del., 1884-89, Laurel (Del.) pub. schs., 1889-92, Wilmington Conf. Acad., Dover, Del., 1892-94, Ulrich's Prep. Sch., Bethlehem, Pa., 1894; C.E., Lehigh U., Bethlehem, Pa., 1898; m. Genevieve Sharretts, Dec. 27, 1916. Levelman engrs. corps Atlas Cement Co., Northampton, Pa., 1899; mem. constrn. corps Pa. R.R. Co., Havre de Grace, Md., 1899, maintenance of way engring. dept., 1899-1900; mem. constrn. corps of City of Phila. on constrn. filter, 1901; mem. firm W. T. Records & Son, flour mills, Laurel, Del., 1902-17, owner, 1917-34, when sold business; dir. Del. Div. of Pa. R.R. Co., Kent Co. Mutual Ins. Co. Pres. Town Council, Laurel, Del., 1913-15; del. Dem. State Conv., Del., 1916, 1920; mem. commns. for condemning property for highways, Sussex Co., Del., 1935-39. Pres. Laurel (Del.) Spl. Sch. Dist. Library Commn. since 1936; mem. standing com. P.E. Ch. Diocese of Del., 1929-39, pres. Ch. Club, 1929-30, lay dep. Provincial Synods, 1920, 1922; first pres. Laymen's League of P.E. Ch. of Sussex Co., Del., 1926-28; sr. warden and vestryman St. Philip's P.E. Ch., Laurel, Del., 1918-40. Mem. Lehigh U. Alumni Assn. Democrat. Episcopalian. Mason (Past Master Hope Lodge 4). Address: 501 Central Av., Laurel, Del.

RECTOR, Thomas M(arion), engring. research dir.; b. Warrenton, Va., Feb. 26, 1894; s. Jacquelin and Elizabeth Frances R.; grad. Western High Sch., Washington, D.C., 1911; m. Elizabeth Hall Schoenly, Feb. 22, 1919; children—Jacqueline Lee, Virginia Phoebe. Began as messenger boy, Dept. of Agr., Washington, D.C., 1911; lab. asst. and asst. chemist Inst. of Industrial Research, Washington, D.C., 1911-15; chief chemist Pompeian Olive Oil Co., Baltimore, Md., 1915-17; dir. dept. of chemistry Pease Labs., New York, 1920-22; chief chemist Franklin Baker Co., Hoboken, N.J., 1922-27; chem. engr. Gen. Foods Corpn., New York, 1927-32, dir. engring. research since 1932; v.p. Vitapack Corpn. Served as 1st lt., Chem. Warfare Service, U.S. Army, 1917-19. Mem. Am. Chem. Soc., Franklin Inst. (life). Republican. Author: Scientific Preservation of Food, 1925. Home: Washington Valley Rd., Morristown, N.J. Office: 1125 Hudson St., Hoboken, N.J.

REDDICK, Olive I.; prof. economics and sociology, Hood Coll. Address: Hood College, Frederick, Md.

REDDING, Charles Summerfield, mfg. elec. instruments; b. Phila., Pa., Nov. 20, 1883; s. Thomas Alfred and Elizabeth Lois (Kennedy) R.; ed. North East Manual Training Sch., Phila., Pa., 1898-1901; B.S. in E.E., U. of Pa., 1906; m. Luella May MacDermond, Oct. 24, 1911; children—Charles Thompson, Janet Luella, James Karcher, Andrew Compton. Began career as instrument maker for Morris E. Leeds & Co., Phila., Pa., 1901-02; instr. mech. engring., U. of Pa., 1906-08; asso. with Leeds & Northrup Co., mfrs. elec. instruments, Phila., since 1909, v.p. and dir., 1918-39, pres. since 1939; dir. Phila. Mutual Fire Ins. Co. In Nat. Guard of Pa., 1909-11. Mem. Borough Council, Jenkintown, Pa., 1921-30. Trustee Community Fund of Phila. and vicinity. Pres. Abington Library Soc., Jenkintown. Mem. A.A.A.S. Am. Inst. Elec. Engrs., Am. Phys. Soc., Franklin Inst., Kappa Sigma. Republican. Mem. M.E. Ch. Mason. Clubs: Union League, Engineers' (Philadelphia); Old York Road Country (Jenkintown). Home: Baederwood, Jenkintown. Office: 4901 Stenton Av., Philadelphia, Pa.

REDFIELD, Edward Willis, artist; b. Bridgeville, Del., 1869; s. Bradley and Frances (Gale) R.; pupil Pa. Academy of Fine Arts and under Bouguereau and Fleury, Paris, France; m. at London, England, Elise Deligant, May 11, 1893; children—Elizabeth (deceased), Laurent, Horace, Louise, George Edward, Frances. Gold medal, Art Club of Phila., 1896; bronze medal, Paris Expn., 1900, Buffalo Expn., 1901; Temple gold medal, Pa. Acad. Fine Arts, Phila., 1903; 2d Hallgarten prize, Nat. Acad., 1904; Shaw Fund prize, Soc. Am. Artists, 1904; silver medal, St. Louis Expn., 1904; Jenny Sesnan gold medal, Pa. Acad. Fine Arts, 1905; Webb prize, Soc. Am. Artists, 1905; silver medal, Carnegie Inst., Pittsburgh, 1905; Fisher prize and Corcoran bronze medal, Corcoran Gallery of Art, Washington, 1907; gold medal of honor, Pa. Acad. Fine Arts, 1907; 1st Clark prize and Corcoran gold medal, Corcoran Gallery, 1908; hon. mention Paris Salon, 1908, 3d medal, 1909; gold medal, Buenos Aires (S.A.) Expn., 1910; Walter Lippincott prize, Pa. Acad. Fine Arts, 1911; gold medal, Soc. Washington Artists, 1913; Potter Palmer gold medal and 1st prize, Art Inst. Chicago, 1913; gold medal and 1st prize, Carnegie Inst., 1914; 1st prize, Wilmington Soc. of Artists, 1915; Carnegie prize, 1917, Altman prize, 1919, N.A.D.; Stotesbury prize, Pa. Acad. Fine Arts, 1921; Carnegie prize, Nat. Acad. of Design, 1922; Brown and Bigelow competition, prize $1,500, 1925; Saltus medal, N.A.D., 1927; Heinz prize $1,000, Grand Central Art Galleries, 1928; 1st prize Springfield Soc. of Artists, Newport (R.I.) Art Assn. Represented in permanent collections of Art Inst. Chicago, Carnegie Inst., Pittsburgh, Acad. Fine Arts, Art Club of Phila., Boston Art Club, New Orleans Art Assn., Telfair Acad. Fine Arts, Savannah, Corcoran Gallery; Brooklyn Inst. Arts and Sciences, John Herron Art Inst., Indianapolis Luxembourg, Detroit Mus. Art, Nat. Gallery, Buenos Aires, Cooke Collection, Honolulu, Peabody Museum, Baltimore, Met. Mus., N.Y., Lincoln (Neb.) Art Assn., Des Moines (Ia.) Art Assn., Los Angeles Art Mus., Albright Art Gallery, Buffalo, N.Y., Butler Mus., Youngstown, O., Memorial Art Gallery, Phila., Rochester Memorial Gallery, Gary (Ind.) Pub. Sch. Collection. Memphis (Tenn.) Art Mus., Grand Rapids Art Mus., Montclair (N.J.) Art Mus. Mem. Internat. Jury of Award, Panama P.I. Expn., 1915. Mem. Nat. Academy of Design, Nat. Institute Arts and Letters, Art Club, Phila. Fellowship of Pa. Acad. Fine Arts, Paris Soc. Am. Painters. Home: Center Bridge, P.O. New Hope, Pa.

REDMAN, Lawrence V., research dir.; b. Oil Springs, Ont., Can., Sept. 1, 1880; s. Richard and Mary Jane (Monteith) L.; A.B., U. of Toronto, 1908, fellow, 1908-10, D.Sc., 1931; LL.D., U. of West Ontario, 1930; m. Ellen Blossom Corey, Dec. 22, 1909; children—Alice Blossom, Lawrence Truman. Came to U.S., 1910. Asso. prof. industrial chemistry, U. of Kan., 1910-13; pres. Redmanol Chem. Products Co. since 1914; v.p. Bakelite Corpn. since 1922, also dir. research. Dir. Industrial Research Assn.; mem. Am. Inst. Chem. Engrs., Am. Inst. Chemists, A.A.A.S., Am. Chem. Soc. (ex-pres.; chmn. Chicago sect. 1918-19, N.J. sect., 1930-31), Soc. Chem. Industry (chmn. Am. and N.Y. sects., 1926-27), Farm Chemurgic Council (plastics com.), Sigma Xi, Alpha Chi Sigma.

Awarded Grasselli medal, Soc. Chem. Industry, 1931. Methodist. Clubs: Chemists of New York (pres. 1929-30); National (Can.). Author: (with A. V. H. Mory) The Romance of Research (Century of Progress Series). Contbr. papers on tech. subjects. Home: 141 Forest Av., Caldwell, N.J. Office: 230 Grove St., Bloomfield, N.J.*

REDWOOD, John, Jr., investment banker; b. Ruxton, Md., Oct. 11, 1900; s. John and Mary Louise (Mead) R.; grad. Gilman Country Sch., Roland Park, Baltimore, 1917; m. Alice Elizabeth Downing, Apr. 26, 1930. Clerk Baltimore Dry Docks & Shipbuilding Co., 1918-21; bond salesman Baker, Watts & Co., 1922-28, gen. partner since 1929; treas. and dir. Realty Improvement Co. of Baltimore City; v.p. and dir. S. B. Sexton Stove & Mfg. Co. Trustee Gilman Country Sch. for Boys, Inc., Baltimore. Independent Democrat. Episcopalian (vestryman Ch. of Good Shepherd). Clubs: Bond, Bachelors Cotillion, Merchants (Baltimore); L'Hirondelle (Ruxton). Home: Ruxton, Md. Office: Calvert and Redwood Sts., Baltimore, Md.

REED, Alexander Preston, lawyer and banking; b. Washington, Pa., Oct. 14, 1885; s. Colin M. and Adaline (Brownlee) R.; A.B., Washington and Jefferson Coll., 1907; student Harvard U. Law Sch., 1907-08; LL.B., U. of Pittsburgh Law Sch., 1910; m. Gertrude C. Schaefer, Aug. 25, 1917; childen—Matilda Jane, Alice Dickey, Alexander Preston, Jr., Charlotte Claypool. Admitted to Pa. bar, 1910 and engaged in gen. practice of law at Washington, Pa., 1910-15; trust officer Fidelity Trust Co., Pittsburgh, Pa., since 1915, vice-pres. and dir. since 1923; dir. Chaplin-Fulton Mfg. Co. Trustee Washington and Jefferson Coll., H. C. Frick Ednl. Commn. Vice-pres. Bd. Pub. Edn. of Pittsburgh. Mem. Phi Gamma Delta, Phi Delta Phi. Republican. Presbyn. Clubs: Duquesne, University, Longue Vue Country. Home: 1269 Murrayhill Av. Office: 341 Fourth Av., Pittsburgh, Pa.

REED, David Aiken, lawyer; b. Pittsburgh, Pa., Dec. 21, 1880; s. James H. and Kate J. (Aiken) R.; grad. Shadyside Acad., Pittsburgh, 1896; B.A., Princeton, 1900, LL.D., 1925; LL.B., U. of Pittsburgh, 1903; m. Adele Wilcox, Nov. 12, 1902; children—David Aiken, Rosamond. Began practice of law at Pittsburgh, 1903; apptd. mem. U.S. Senate, by gov. of Pa., Aug. 8, 1922, to succeed William E. Crow, deceased, and elected to same office following Nov., term 1923-29; reëlected, term 1929-35. Del. to London Naval Conf., 1930. Major 311th F.A., A.E.F., World War. Trustee of Princeton Univ.; mem. Dixmont (Pa.) Hosp. Mem. Am. Battle Monuments Commn. Awarded D.S.M. (U.S.); Chevalier Legion of Honor (French). Republican. Protestant. Home: 716 Amberson Av. Office: 747 Union Trust Bldg., Pittsburgh, Pa.

REED, DeVeaux H., pres. The Realty Co.; b. Dudley, Pa., May 6, 1886; s. L. C. and Louisa (Cypher) R.; ed. Juniata Coll., Huntingdon, Pa.; m. Ruby Myer, Jan. 5, 1910; children—Findlay, John, Lois. Pres. The Realty Co. since 1931; dir. McKeesport Savings & Loan Assn. Home: 1210 Evans St. Office: 6th Av. and Walnut St., McKeesport, Pa.

REED, Donald Wells, banker, dock supt.; b. Ashtabula, O., Apr. 23, 1882; s. James and Harriet (Wells) R.; student Ashtabula (O.) Pub. Sch., 1888-1900; m. Helen Marie Kelley, Sept. 6, 1905 (died 1929); children—Donald Wells, Claire Louise (Mrs. Waldo C. Pendleton); m. 2d, Marie Moore, Sept. 3, 1932. Clerk, M. A. Hanna & Co., Ashtabula, O., 1900-10; supt. Eastern Coal Docks Co., South Amboy, N.J., 1910-30; supt. Seaboard Coal Docks Co., South Amboy, N.J., since 1930; pres. South Amboy (N.J.) Trust Co. since 1919; pres. The Augusta Co. since 19—; dir. Investors and Owners Bldg. & Loan Assn. Pres. War Camp Community Service, 1917-19; chmn. Liberty Loan Drives, South Amboy, N.J. Mem. South Amboy (N.J.) Bd. of Edn. (pres., 1926-32). Trustee South Amboy (N.J.) Memorial Hosp. Assn. Republican. Episcopalian. Mason. Club: South Amboy (N.J.) Rotary. Address: 116 Livingston Av., New Brunswick, N.J.

REED, Earl Frederick, lawyer; b. Spartansburg, Pa., Apr. 4, 1894; s. Elmer B. and Orpha J. (McCuen) R.; A.B., Washington and Jefferson Coll., 1915; legal edn., U. of Pittsburgh, 1915-18; m. Dora Belle Henderson, Oct. 12, 1921; children—Virginia Belle, Earl. Served as instr. in Washington and Jefferson Coll. and Carnegie Inst. Tech.; admitted to Pa. bar, 1919, and since practiced in Pittsburgh; mem. firm Thorp, Bostwick, Reed & Armstrong. Private in U.S. Army, 1918, World War. Mem. Am., Pa. State and Allegheny County bar assns., Lambda Chi Alpha, Delta Theta Phi. Republican. Mason. Clubs: Duquesne, Long Vue Country, Oakmont Country; Surf (Miami, Fla.). Home: 6410 Beacon St., Pittsburgh; (winters) 4558 Alton Rd., Miami Beach, Fla. Office: Grant Bldg., Pittsburgh, Pa.

REED, George Leffingwell, lawyer; b. Brooklyn, N.Y., Feb. 4, 1885; s. George Edward and Ella Frances (Leffingwell) R.; A.B., Dickinson Coll., 1904; LL.B., Dickinson Coll. Sch. of Law, 1907; m. Helen R. Moorhead, Sept. 14, 1911; 1 son, George Edward. Admitted to Pa. bar, 1908 and since engaged in gen. practice of law, individually, at Harrisburg; served as mem. Pa. Ho. of Rep., 1928-32; mem. Pa. Senate, 1932-36. Mem. Pa. Bar Assn., Dauphin County Bar Assn., Phi Kappa Sigma. Republican. Methodist. Mason (33°). Home: 1915 N. Front St. Office: 603 State Theatre Bldg., Harrisburg, Pa.

REED, Gordon Wies, mfg. brick and tile; b. Chicago, Ill., Nov. 20, 1899; s. Frank and Mary C. (Wies) R.; student pub. sch. and high sch., Chicago, Ill., 1906-17; M.E., U. of Ill., 1922; m. Naomi Bradley, Sept. 18, 1928; 1 son, Thomas Care. In employ New Florence Fire Brick Co., 1922; with Industrial Publications, 1922-25; asso. with Hanley Co., mfrs. brick and tile, Bradford, Pa., since 1925, vice-pres. since 1925; dir. National Tile Co., Bovaird & Reed Oil Co. of Bradford, Pa., Reed Oil Co., Garnett, Kan., etc. Served as pvt. inf., U.S.A., 1918. Republican. Mem. Round Hill Church. Clubs: Bradford, Valley Hunt (Bradford); Cloud (New York); Round Hill (Greenwich, Conn.). Home: Apple Jack Farm, Greenwich, Conn. Office: Bradford, Pa.

REED, Henry Douglas, insulated wire mfr.; b. Poughkeepsie, N.Y., Feb. 11, 1869; s. Henry A. and Alice A. (Boardman) R.; M.E., Stevens Inst. Tech., 1892; m. Emilie C. Currier, Dec. 15, 1904. In profession as elec. engr., 1892-99; supt. Bishop Gutta Percha Co., New York, 1899-1906, vice-pres., 1906-19, pres. and dir. since 1919; pres. and dir. Bishop Wire & Cable Corpn. since 1925, No-Slip Rubber Co. since 1925, Peters Mfg. Co. since 1930, Bishop Industries, Inc., since 1930. Served on East Orange Water Commn., 1913-22, pres. bd., 1921-22. Republican. Presbyn. Clubs: Glenwood Tennis (East Orange); Essex County Country (West Orange); Roseville Athletic (Newark); Engineers (New York); Indian River Yacht (Rockledge, Fla.). Home: 30 Eastwood St., East Orange, N.J. Office: 420 E. 25th St., New York, N.Y.

REED, Henry Morrison, manufacturer; b. Millvale Borough, Allegheny Co., Pa., Sept. 16, 1880; s. John C. and Mary (Curts) R.; grad. Pittsburgh High Sch., 1897; m. Gwendolyn Daniels, Sept. 16, 1902; children—Henry Morrison, John Curts, Mary Gwendolyn (Mrs. James Nelson Stewart), William Theodore. With Standard Sanitary Mfg. Co., 1902-38, beginning as enamel mixer became asst. mgr. Pittsburgh Works, 1907, mgr. Louisville Works, 1910, asst. gen. mgr. factories, 1913, v.p. and gen. mgr. factories, 1925, 1st v.p. and chmn. exec. com., 1928; pres., 1930, now chmn. of bd. and pres. Am. Radiator and Standard Sanitary Corpn. since 1938; dir. Detroit Lubricator Co., C. F. Church Mfg. Co., Tonawanda Iron Corpn., Heating and Plumbing Finance Corpn. Republican. Presbyn. Mason (32°, Shriner), Jesters. Clubs: Metropolitan, Engineers, Blind Brook (New York); Duquesne, Pittsburgh, Oakmont Country, Long Vue Country (Pittsburgh); Butler Country (Butler, Pa.). Home: 106 Dickson Av., Ben Avon, Pa. Office: 40 W. 40th St., New York, N.Y.

REED, James Calvin, prof. business law; b. Tuscola, Ill., Feb. 20, 1869; s. John Taylor and Anna (Walter) R.; U. of Ill., 1886-87; B.Litt., U. of Mich., 1895; LL.B., Kansas City Law Sch., 1898; post-grad. work, U. of Chicago; m. Effie Anna Howe, Sept. 13, 1893; 1 dau., Mildred (Mrs. W. A. Buck). Teacher high sch., Riverside, Calif., 1895-96, 1898-1900; practiced law Kansas City, Mo.; teacher McKinley High Sch., Chicago, 1902-13; dir. State Normal Commercial Sch., Whitewater, Wis., 1913-19; prof. and head Dept. of Business Law, U. of Pittsburgh, since 1919. Founder and editor Commercial Teachers' Magazine, 1917-21. President of National Association of Teachers of Law in Collegiate Schools of Business, 1924-29. Mem. Nat. Commercial Teachers' Fed. (pres., 1919-21), Univ. Instrs. in Accounting, Beta Gamma Sigma, Lambda Chi Alpha. Republican. Presbyn. Mason. Club: Faculty. Author: Rowe's Commercial Law, 1915; A Selection of Cases on Commercial Law, 1917. Home: 5562 Hobart St. Address: University of Pittsburgh, Pittsburgh, Pa.

REED, John Elmer, lawyer; b. Erie County, Pa., Feb. 27, 1865; s. John Grubb and Candace Eliza (Blair) R.; student Edinboro (Erie Co. Pa.) Normal Sch., 1882-83, Clark's Business Coll., Erie, Pa., 1884-85, studied law, 1892-93, in office of Emory A. Walling, Erie, Pa., who became judge and justice of Pa. Supreme Court; m. Elizabeth Cora Brown, of Hamilton, Canada, Oct. 10, 1893; children—Robert Cameron, Walter (adopted). School teacher, 1887-92; admitted to Pa. bar, 1895, and began practice in Erie, Pa.; mem. Reed, Wait & Spofford to 1932, and successors Reed & Spofford (Mr. Wait elected judge Orphans Court, Erie Co., Pa.); dep. U.S. marshal for Western Dist. of Pa., 1893-94. Sec. Pa. State Flagship Niagara Commn. (for restoration of Commodore Perry's Flagship Niagara in Battle of Lake Erie, 1813); sec. and treas. Weis Pub. Library. Mem. Am. Bar Assn., Pa. Bar Assn., Erie Co. Bar Assn. (sec.), Erie Co. Hist. Soc. (sec.) Blair Society for Geneal. Research, Nat. Society Sons of the Am. Revolution. Republican. Presbyterian. Club: Orion (Erie). Author: History of Erie County, Pa., 2 vols., 1925; Chief Cornplanter, 1926; Middlebrook, 1931; Our Niagara Region; Our French Forts and Guyasutha; The Erie Triangle; The Old Custom House at Erie, Pa.; History of Western Pennsylvania. Editor and pub. The Blair Magazine, 1925-31; editor and compiler of manuscript for History of Bench and Bar of Erie County, Pa. Home: 1942 Lakeside Drive. Office: 607 Masonic Temple, Erie, Pa.

REED, Louis, lawyer and writer; b. Elizabeth, W.Va., Oct. 1, 1899; s. George William and Emma (Black) R.; A.B., Cornell U., 1923; LL.B., W.Va. Univ. Law Sch., 1928; m. Ruth Baldwin, July 5, 1923; 1 son, William Baldwin. Admitted to W.Va. bar, 1928, and engaged in gen. practice of law as mem. firm Beckett & Reed, Winfield, W.Va., 1928-32; mem. firm Mathews & Reed, Grantsville, W.Va., since 1935; free lance writer, Sherburne, N.Y., 1932-35. Served in F.A., U.S.A., 1918-19, with A.E.F. in France and Germany, dischd. as sergt. Mem. town council Grantsville, W.Va., since 1937. Pres. bd. of trustees Davis and Elkins Coll., Elkins, W.Va., since 1939. Mem. W.Va. State Bar Assn., Sigma Delta Chi, Theta Xi, Am. Legion, Forty and Eight, U.C.T. Republican. Presbyterian. Contbr. to mags. including Atlantic Monthly, Am. Spectator. Address: Grantsville, W.Va.

REED, Louis Francis, lawyer; b. Poughkeepsie, N.Y., June 21, 1871; s. Henry A. and Alice A. (Boardman) R.; Newark High Sch., 1890; LL.B., New York U. Law Sch., 1892; LL.M., 1895; m. Virginia Kent White, II, Oct. 15, 1907; children—Louis F., Pendennis White. Admitted to N.Y. bar, 1892; since in gen. practice of law; mem. Reed & Chapman since 1934; sec.-treas. and dir. Bishop Industries, Bishop Wire & Cable Corpn., Bishop Gutta Percha Co.; v.p. and dir. Peters Mfg. Co.; dir. Eastern Terra Cotta Co., Am. Woman's Realty Co. Mem. Am. Bar Assn., N.Y. Co. Lawyers Assn., N.Y. State Bar Assn., Phi Delta Phi. Republican. Presbyn. Clubs: Essex County Country, Orange Lawn Ten-

REED, Lowell Jacob, mathematics; b. Berlin, N.H., Jan. 8, 1886; s. Jason and Lowella (Coffin) R.; B.S., U. of Me., 1907, M.S., 1912; Ph.D., U. of Pa., 1915; m. Marion Balentine, Aug. 12, 1908; children—Edith Marion, Elizabeth, Robert Balentine. Instr. in mathematics and physics, U. of Me., 1907-08, instr. in mathematics, 1908-13; instr. in mathematics, U. of Pa., 1914-15; asst. prof. mathematics, U. of Me., 1915-17; dir. Bur. of Tabulation and Statistics, War Trade Bd., Washington, D.C. 1917-18; asso. prof. biostatistics, Johns Hopkins, 1918-25, prof. since 1925, also dean School of Hygiene and Public Health. Fellow Am. Pub. Health Assn., Am. Statis. Assn., A.A.A.S.; asso. fellow Am. Med. Assn.; mem. Am. Math. Soc., Math Association America, International Union for Scientific Investigation of Population Problems, Population Association of America, Phi Beta Kappa, Sigma Xi, Delta Omega, Phi Kappa Sigma. Democrat. Contbr. scientific papers. Home: 3409 Duvall Av., Baltimore, Md.

REED, Luther Dotterer, clergyman, teacher; b. N. Wales, Pa., Mar. 21, 1873; s. Rev. Ezra L. and Annie (Linley) R.; A.B., Franklin and Marshall Coll., 1892, A.M., 1897; grad. Luth. Theol. Sem., Phila., 1895; student U. of Leipzig, 1902; D.D., Thiel, 1912, Muhlenberg, 1912; A.E.D. (Doctor of Fine Arts), Muhlenberg, 1936; m. Catharine S. Ashbridge, June 2, 1906. Pastor Allegheny, Pa., 1895-1903, Jeannette, Pa., 1903-04; dir. Krauth Memorial Library, Luth. Theol. Sem., Mt. Airy, Phila., 1906—, and prof. liturgics and church art, same, 1911—; acting pres., same, 1938—. Pres. Ch. Music and Liturgical Art Society, 1907-36; president and editor Memoirs, Luth. Liturgical Assn., 1898-1906; pres. Associated Bureaus of Church Architecture of the United States and Canada since 1930; sec., later chmn. joint committee which prepared text and music of the Common Service Book and other hymnals and liturgical books of the United Lutheran Church; conducted conferences on the liturgy, church architecture and church music in many states; archivist of the ministerium of Pennsylvania, 1909—, United Lutheran Church, 1919—. Clubs: University, Art Alliance (Philadelphia). Author: (with Harry G. Archer) Psalter and Canticles Pointed for Chanting, 1897; Choral Service Book, 1901; Music of the Responses, 1903; Season Vespers, 1905; also many articles on ch. music, liturgics, ch. art, etc. Editor: History of the First English Evangelical Lutheran Church in Pittsburgh, 1909; Philadelphia Seminary Biographical Record, 1923. Co-Editor: Phila. Seminary Bulletin, 1916-33, Lutheran Church Review, 1920-28. Chmn. United Luth. Ch. coms. on Common Service Book and on ch. architecture; mem. Federal Council's Com. on Worship; hon. asso. Am. Guild of Organists. Home: 7204 Boyer St., Mt. Airy, Philadelphia, Pa.

REED, Marjorie Edna, physician; b. Lee, Pa., July 2, 1896; d. John Elmer and Ella Davenport (Partington) R.; A.B., Hiram (O.) Coll., 1918; M.D., Womens Med. Coll. of Pa., 1923. Resident Wilkes-Barre Gen. Hosp., 1923-24, dispensary staff and med. asso., 1927-29, on pediatric staff since 1930, chief baby welfare station since 1929; chief baby welfare sta., Plymouth, since 1927; asso. State Clinic for Tuberculosis, 1930-35; sch. med. inspr., rural dists., 1927-35; mem. editorial bd. Med. Woman's Journal since 1934; asso. editor Luzerne Co. Med. Bulletin since 1931; also appointed asst. clinician in State Clinic for Tuberculosis, July 1939; mem. West Side Visiting Nurses Assn., Kingston. Fellow American College of Physicians, American Medical Assn. Member Pa. and Luzerne Co. med. socs., Med. Woman's Nat. Assn., Phila. Pediatric Soc., Wyoming Valley Tuberculosis Assn. (bd. mem.), D.A.R., Daughters of War of 1812, Am. Assn. of Univ. Women, Huguenot Soc. of Pa., Wyoming Valley Hist. and Geol. Soc., Wyoming Valley Commemorative Assn. Republican. Christian Church (pres. Woman's Council). Club: Woman's Civic (Plymouth). Home: 11 E. Hillside Av. Office: 55 E. Main St., Plymouth, Pa.

REED, Merle Roland, mem. Railroad Retirement Bd.; b. Jasper Co., Ill., June 26, 1883; s. William Grant and Ella Jane (Clark) R.; B.S., Rose Poly. Inst., 1905; m. Helen Margaret Duncan, Nov. 16, 1910; children—Frances Sussana, Jane BcBirney. With Pa. R.R., 1905-38, successively as apprentice, draftsman, chief draftsman, foreman, gen. car inspector, supervisor of car repairs, master mechanic, supt. of motive power, gen. supt. of motive power; mem. Railroad Retirement Bd. since 1938. Home: 105 Raymond St., Chevy Chase, Md. Office: Railroad Retirement Board, Washington, D.C.

REED, Perley Isaac, prof. journalism; b. Lowell, O., Sept. 28, 1887; s. Benjamin and Nellie (Hall) R.; Ph.B., Nat. Normal U., 1908; A.B., magna cum laude, Marietta Coll., 1912, A.M., 1914; fellow in English, Ohio State U., 1914-16, Ph.D., 1916; spl. work, Columbia, 1924; m. Aldia Barnett, 1909; children—Judson Wardlaw, Gloria; m. 2d, Elizabeth Frost, of Shelbyville, Tenn., 1922. Teacher, principal and supt. schs. until 1911; prof. English, Ogden Coll., Bowling Green, Ky., 1912-14; asso. prof. English, Md. State Coll., College Park, 1916-17; prof. and head dept. of English, U. of Md., 1917-20; spl. examiner U.S. Civil Service Commn., Washington, D.C., summer 1918; asst. prof. English, W.Va. Univ., 1920-22, asso. prof., 1922-24, prof., 1924-27, prof. and head dept. of journalism since 1927. Exec. sec. W.Va. State Journalism Conf. since 1922; dir. W.Va. Competition of High Sch. Periodicals since 1922; sponsor W.Va. State Inst. of Sch. Journalism since 1932; lecturer W.Va. county teachers' institutes, 1922-31. Mem. Am. Assn. Univ. Profs., Am. Assn. Teachers of Journalism, Phi Beta Kappa, Kappa Tau Alpha (mem. nat. exec. council). Presbyn. Club: XX Club (Morgantown). Author: American Characters in American Plays, 1918; Applied Writing by the Journalistic Method, 1929; Writing Journalistic Features, 1931; Applied Composition (with Elizabeth Frost Reed), 1936. Home: 232 Lebanon Av., Morgantown, W.Va.

REED, Robert J., attending surgeon Ohio Valley-Gen. Hosp.; cons. surgeon Wheeling Hosp. Address: 100 12th St., Wheeling, W.Va.

REED, Robert J., Jr., mem. surg. staff Ohio Valley Gen. Hosp. Address: 100 12th St., Wheeling, W.Va.

REED, Rufus D., educator; b. Blanchester, O., Sept. 12, 1894; s. W. B. and E. J. (Barry) R.; B.S., Wilmington (O.) Coll., 1919; M.A., O. State U., Columbus, O., 1920, Ph.D., 1928; m. Pearl Vandervort, Aug. 14, 1920; 1 son, Russell F. Teacher of chemistry, Clinton Co. (O.) rural schs., 1912-16; student asst., chemistry and biology, Wilmington (O.) Coll., 1916-19; grad. asst., chemistry and biology, O. State U., Columbus, O., 1919-20; teacher of chemistry and head of dept., Lakewood (O.) High Sch., 1920-29; asst. prof. chemistry, Montclair State Teachers Coll., Upper Montclair, N.J., since 1929. Fellow Am. Assn. of Chemists; mem. Am. Chem. Soc., N.J. Science Assn. (pres., 1937; mem. testing com., div. of chem. edn.), N.J. Teachers Assn. Northeastern O. Chemistry Teachers Assn. (pres., 1928-29), Sigma Xi, Phi Lambda Epsilon. Republican. Reformed Ch. Author: General College Chemistry for the Laboratory (with R. W. McLachlan); numerous chem. articles in tech. jours. Address: 84 McCosh Rd., Upper Montclair, N.J.

REED, Wendell Monroe, civil engring.; b. Moriah, N.Y., Dec. 28, 1864; s. Coleman Ezra and Lomira (Farr) R.; C.E., U. of Vt., Burlington, Vt., 1886; m. Margaret Ogle, May 25, 1895; children—Roy Ogle, Ruth. Employed as civil engr. in r.r. work, 1886-89; employed in irrigation and city work mostly water supply and sewers in N.M., 1889-1904; engr. with U.S. Irrigation Service, 1904-12; chief engr. U.S. Indian Irrigation Service, 1912-32, retired 1932 and moved to Welcome, Md.; assisted in organizing Southern Md. Tri-County Cooperative Assn., built power house and 200 miles of distribution electric lines, pres. and mgr., 1936-38. Mem. Am. Soc. Civil Engrs., Washington Soc. of Engrs., Lambda Iota. Republican. Mason (K.T. and Shriner). Home: Wavely, Welcome, Md.

REEDER, Benjamin Garnet, lawyer; b. Shinnston, W.Va., Aug. 15, 1899; s. Charles Avery and Bertha M. (Tucker) R.; A.B., W.Va. Univ., Morgantown, 1921; LL.B., W.Va. Univ. Law Sch., 1923; m. Angie A. Friend, Aug. 15, 1923; children—Angie Louise, Margaret Eleanor, Charles Thomas, James Benjamin. Admitted to W.Va. bar, 1923; served as law librarian W.Va. Univ., Morgantown, 1923-25; engaged in gen. practice of law at Morgantown since 1925; mem. firm Baker & Reeder since 1937; sec., asst. treas. and gen. counsel Cochran Coal & Coke Co., Morgantown, W.Va.; gen. counsel Christopher Mining Co. Served as 2d lt. inf. U.S.A. during World War. Mem. Am., W.Va. State, and Monongalia Co. bar assns., Am. Legion. Republican. Methodist. Mason. Clubs: Kiwanis, Junto (Morgantown). Home: 212 Logan Av. Office: 170 Chancery Row, Morgantown, W.Va.

REEDER, Frank, Jr., lawyer; b. Easton, Pa., May 4, 1880; s. Frank and Grace E. (Thompson) R.; grad. Easton (Pa.) Acad., 1897; Ph.B., Lafayette Coll., 1901; m. Sara F. Seitz, Apr. 12, 1909; children—Gwen F. (Mrs. Chas. H. Love), Marie Louise (Mrs. W. J. B. Stokes, 2d), Frances J. Admitted to Pa. bar, 1905 and since engaged in gen. practice of law, individually, at Easton; served as Asst. Dist. Atty. of Northampton Co., 1906-08; U.S. commr. since 1926; dir. and counsel, Easton Trust Co.; dir. Easton Cemetery Co.; sec. and treas. Horner's Addition, Inc. Served as Co. Chmn. Pub. Speakers Bur., City Chmn. 4-Minute Men, Sec. Com. Pub. Safety, during World War. Mem. Northampton County Bar Assn., Pa. State Bar Assn., Zeta Psi. Republican. Episcopalian. Club: Pomfret. Home: 128 Pierce St. Office: 416 Easton Trust Bldg., Easton, Pa.

REEDER, Franklin Harris, Jr., state registrar vital statistics; b. Phila., Pa., Dec. 29, 1900; s. Franklin Harris and Anna Rachel (Loder) R.; A.B., U. of Pa., 1925; M.B., Ch.B., U. of Edinburg, Scotland, 1932; grad. student Johns Hopkins U. Sch. Hygiene and Pub. Health, 1935; m. Doris Delbridge, July 9, 1932; 1 son, Franklin Harris III. Interne Chester County Hosp., West Chester, Pa., 1932-33, Roanoke Hosp., Roanoke, Va., Jan.-June 1934; engaged in gen. practice of medicine and surgery at Williams River, W.Va., 1934-35; acting state registrar of vital statistics W.Va. State Health Dept., Charleston, W.Va., 1935-37, state registrar of vital statistics since 1937. Served as 1st lt. Med. Res. Corps, U.S.A., since 1935. Fellow Royal Med. Soc., Edinburgh. Mem. Am. Pub. Health Assn., Kanawha Co. Med. Soc., Assn. State Registration Execs. Democrat. Presbyn. Clubs: Fencing, Chess (Charleston). Contbr. to Journ. Am. Pub. Health Assn. Home: R.F.D. 2, Charleston, W.Va.

REEDER, Harry T(hompson), realtor; b. Phila., Pa., Sept. 7, 1878; s. Willes W. and Mary L. (Craven) R.; student North East Manual Training Sch., Phila., 1896-99; m. Flora Kirk, Oct. 12, 1904; children—Willes Watson, Margaret Emma (Mrs. Joseph E. Armstrong). In real estate business, Phila., since 1915; partner Craven & Reeder, real estate and ins., Phila., since 1933. Mem. Artisans Order of Mutual Protection. Republican. Methodist. Home: 123 Lynnwood Av., Glenside, Pa. Office: 1546 N. 7th St., Philadelphia, Pa.

REEDER, J. Dawson; prof. proctology, U. of Md.; proctologist St. Agnes, University and Franklin Square hosps. Address: 30 E. Preston St., Baltimore, Md.

REES, Albert Henry, insurance; b. Trenton, N.J., May 29, 1893; s. Frederick P. and Catherine (Fritz) R.; ed. George Sch. (Pa.) and Rider Coll.; m. Helen Gallagher, Oct. 18, 1916; children—Albert Henry, Charles Gallagher, Frederick P., 2d, Geoffrey Walker. Began as contractor, 1912; engaged in gen. insurance business since 1930; treas. Fell & Moon Co.; dir. First-Mechanics Nat. Bank, Trenton Mortgage Service Co.; trustee Hanover-Capitol Trust Co. Republican. Baptist. Mason (Shriner). Clubs: Carteret, Trenton Country (Trenton). Home:

Lawrenceville, N.J. Office: Broad St. Bank Bldg., Trenton, N.J.

REES, Charles W(illiam), zoologist; b. Coalville, Utah, Mar. 22, 1886; s. Edmund and Hannah (Chappel) R.; B.S., Utah Agrl. Coll., Logan, Utah, 1913; student U. of Chicago, 1916; A.M., U. of Calif., Berkeley, 1921, Ph.D., 1922; student Yale U. Sch. of Medicine, 1925-26, Johns Hopkins U., 1926-28; m. Julia Ricks, June 18, 1924; 1 dau., Evelyn Mae. Asst. prof. zoology and entomology, Utah Agrl. Coll., 1922-24; asso. zoologist, U.S. Dept. Agr., Jeanerette La., and Beltsville, Md., 1928-38, zoologist since 1938, sr. proto-zoologist Nat. Inst. of Health since 1939. Mem. A.A.A.S., Am. Assn. Tropical Medicine, Am. Assn. Parasitologists, Wash. Helminthological Soc., Wash. Acad. of Sci., Am. Public Health Assn., Sigma Xi. Mem. Latter Day Saints Ch. Contbr. of over 30 articles to sci. publs. Home: 8613 Cedar St., Silver Spring, Md.

REES, John Gilbert, poster advertising; b. Olyphant, Pa., Apr. 11, 1864; s. John and Peninnah (Williams) R.; ed. public school, Scranton, Pa.; m. Georgiana Collins, Sept. 26, 1885; children—John Arlington, F. Austen, Lillian Elma (Mrs. E. Carson Heimbach), Helen Elila (Mrs. Vernon C. Baughn), Edith Agnes (Mrs. Arthur Evans), Stationery salesman, 1890-92; mail carrier, 1892-94; advance agent Barnum & Bailey Show, 1894-1907, Hagenback Show, 1907-09; pres. American Co., poster advertising, since 1936; pres. Rees Poster Advertising Co., Rees Outdoor Advertising Co. Former mem. Nat. Guard of Pa.; past pres. Scranton Advertising Club. Republican. Baptist (chmn. bd. trustees). Mason, Odd Fellow. Clubs: Scranton, Rotary (Scranton). Home: 1740 Wyoming Av. Office: Washington and Ash, Scranton, Pa.

REESE, Albert Moore, zoölogist; b. Lake Roland, Md., Apr. 1, 1872; s. Henry and Mary Anna (Miller) R.; A.B., Johns Hopkins University, 1892, Ph.D. from same, 1900; m. Nelle Summers, June 29, 1927; children—Mary Rebecca, Albert Moore, Jr. Teacher of science and physical culture, Friends' Elementary and High School, 1892-97; lecturer on chemistry, Southern Homœ. Medical College, Baltimore, 1893-97; lecturer on histology and embryology, Pa. Coll., 1897, prof. biology and geology, Allegheny Coll., 1901-02; asso. prof. histology and embryology, Syracuse U., 1902-07; prof. zoölogy, W.Va. State U., since Sept. 1907. Fellow A.A.A.S.; mem. Am. Soc. Zoölogists, Am. Soc. Naturalists, Am. Micros. Soc., Beta Theta Pi, Phi Beta Kappa, Sigma Xi. Quaker. Author: Introduction to Vertebrate Embryology, 1904, 2d edit., 1910; The Alligator and Its Allies, 1915; Outlines of Economic Zoölogy, 1919, 24, 30; Wanderings in the Orient, 1919. Home: Morgantown, W.Va.

REESE, Charles Lee, chemist; b. Baltimore, Md., Nov. 4, 1862; s. John S. and Arnoldina O. (Focke) R.; grad. U. of Va., 1884; Ph.D., Heidelberg, 1886; hon. Sc.D., University of Pa., 1919, Colgate U., 1919, U. of Delaware, 1928; hon. Sc.D., Wake Forest (N.C.) Coll., 1934, Heidelberg, 1936; m. Harriet S. Bent, of Baltimore, Md., April 10, 1901; children—Charles Lee, John Smith, David Meredith, Eben Bent, William Fessenden (dec.). Asst. in chemistry, Johns Hopkins, 1886-88; prof. chemistry, Wake Forest Coll., 1888, S.C. Mil. Acad., 1888-96; instr. Johns Hopkins, 1896-1900; chief chemist New Jersey Zinc Co., 1901-02, and of the Eastern Dynamite Co., and dir. Eastern Lab., 1902-06; in charge chem. div. of the high explosive operating dept. of E. I. du Pont de Nemours Powder Co., 1902-11, chem. dir. same, 1911-June 1, 1924, consultant same co. until 1931 (retired); dir. E. I. du Pont de Nemours & Co. Member American Chem. Soc. (chmn. bd. 1930—; also pres. 1934), Deutsche Chemische Gesellschaft, Soc. Chem. Industry, Chem. Metall. and Mining Soc. of South Africa (hon.), Franklin Institute, Am. Inst. Chem. Engrs. (pres. 1923-25), Mfg. Chemists' Assn. (pres. 1920-23), Am. Philos. Soc., Raven Soc. (U. of Va.), English Speaking Union, Sons of Colonial Wars, Phi Beta Kappa, Sigma Xi, Phi Lambda Upsilon; fellow A.A.A.S. Associate member Naval Consulting Board, also chairman Delaware sect.; ex-mem. Nat. Industrial Conf. Bd.; mem. advisory bd. to prohibition commr.; mem. visiting com. Bur. of Standards since 1930. V.p. Internat. Union of Pure and Applied Chemistry, 1929-34; founder and chmn. Bd. Industrial Research, chmn. emeritus, 1931; hon. mem. Institution of Chemical Engineers of Great Britain, 1928; fellow Royal Soc. of Arts; pres. ex officio Wilmington Soc. Fine Arts, 1934. Episcopalian. Clubs: Chemists' (New York); Colonnade; Wilmington Country (Del.). Contbr. to chem. jours. Home: 1600 Brinckle Av. Office: du Pont Bldg., Wilmington, Del.*

REESE, Charles Lee, Jr., editor; b. Wilmington, Del., Apr. 7, 1903; s. Charles Lee and Harriet Stedman (Bent) R.; grad. Wilmington Friends Sch., 1920; B.A., U. of Va., 1924; grad. study, Cambridge U., Eng., 1924-25; m. Harriet Hurd Curtis, of Wilmington, Del., Oct. 2, 1926; children—Charles Lee, Sara Corbit, Peter Arnold Karthaus. Editor Delano Service, Paris, France, 1925; mng. editor Popular Radio, N.Y. City, 1925-27; mem. editorial staff Time (mag.), 1927; mem. news staff, Wilmington Evening Journal, 1928-34; editor Wilmington Morning News, 1934-39; editor News-Journal papers since 1939. Pres. bd. dirs. Wilmington Music Sch., 1935-38. Mem. Soc. Colonial Wars, Pi Kappa Alpha, Alpha Chi Sigma. Episcopalian. Home: Foxchase, Old Kennett Rd. Address: News-Journal Co., Wilmington, Del.

REESE, Daniel R., lawyer; b. Wales, Sept. 16, 1868; s. William R. and Ann (Williams) R.; student Dickinson Sch. of Law; m. Catharine F. Hague, Apr. 20, 1894; children—Lenore F., Weston R., Margaret H. Gen. atty. D. L.&W. R.R. Co., 1902-29; engaged in gen. practice of law since 1929; mem. advisory bd. Pa. Underwriters Mutual Ins. Co. Mem. bd. incorporators Dickinson Sch. of Law. Mem. Lackawanna Bar Assn. Club: Lackawanna Motor (dir.). Home: 749 N. Main Av. Office: 305-7 Cornell Bldg., Scranton, Pa.

REESE, Frederick Schuyler, judge; b. Ilion, N.Y., Dec. 12, 1896; s. Fred S. and Agnes (Scott) R.; LL.B., Cornell U., 1918; m. Edith L. Rathbun, Oct. 23, 1920. Admitted to N.Y. bar, 1919, Pa. bar, 1921; prof. law, Dickinson Sch. of Law, since 1919; mem. law firm Bowman & Reese, 1926-32; dist. atty., Cumberland Co., 1928-32; president judge Ct. of Common Pleas, Cumberland Co., since 1932. Pres. Carlisle Community Chest since 1936. Mem. Am. Bar Assn., Pa. Bar Assn. Republican. Episcopalian. Club: Carlisle Country. Co-Author: Pennsylvania Common Pleas Practice (2d edit.), 1927. Home: 420 W. South St. Chambers: Court House, Carlisle, Pa.

REESE, Matthias Forney, banking; b. Baltimore, Md., May 1, 1878; s. John Evan and Alice Virginia (Gibbs) R.; student Baltimore City Coll., 1892-97, U. of Md., Law School, Baltimore, 1899-1900; m. Rena Schaut, June 25, 1908; children—Matthias Forney, Jr., William Evan, Houston Gibbs, Ann Virginia. Employed as teller, Guardian Trust Co., Baltimore, Md., 1897-1900, asst. sec., 1900-01, then clk. with successor, Md. Trust Co., 1901-04; treas. Colonial Trust Co., 1904-06; in bus. with bro. as mfrs. agts. for gas and electric lighting fixtures, 1906-16; clk. Citizens Nat. Bank, 1916-18; transit mgr. Baltimore Branch Federal Res. Bank, 1918-25, cashier, 1925-30; mgr.-sec. Baltimore Clearing House Assn. since 1930; sec. Md. Bankers Assn. since 1934. Mem. Phi Kappa Sigma. Republican. Presbyn. Clubs: Optimists, Phi Kappa Sigma Club. Home: 3312 W. North Av. Office: Baltimore Clearing House, Baltimore, Md.

REESE, Mitchell, lawyer; b. Phillipsburg, N.J., Oct. 6, 1899; s. James Mitchell and Emma J. (Scammell) R.; B.S., Lafayette Coll., Easton, Pa., 1921; LL.B., Harvard U. Law Sch., 1924; m. Marguerite Schulz, July 12, 1926; children—Mary Jane, James Mitchell 3d. Admitted to N.J. bar as atty., 1924, as counselor, 1927; engaged in gen. practice of law at Trenton, N.J., since 1924; mem. firm Scammell, Knight & Reese since 1925. Served in U.S.N.R.F., 1918. Mem. Am. Bar Assn., N.J. State Bar Assn., Mercer Co. Bar Assn., Theta Delta Chi. Republican. Presbyn. Mason (Shriner). Clubs: Trenton, Trenton Country. Home: 842 Berkeley Av. Office: 1 W. State St., Trenton, N.J.

REESE, Warren Snyder, ophthalmologist; b. Scranton, Pa., Mar. 16, 1892; s. Jenkin T. and Norma (Hughes) R.; M.D., Jefferson Med. Coll., 1915; unmarried. Physician and oculist in Phila. since 1920; chief of service in ophthalmology, Pa. Hosp.; attending surgeon, Wills Eye Hosp. Fellow Am. Coll. Surgeons, Coll. Physicians of Phila.; mem. Am. Ophthal. Soc., Am. Acad. of Ophthalmology and Otolaryngology, Phila. Co. and Pa. State Med. Soc., A.M.A., Ophthalmic Club of Phila., Assn. for Research in Ophthalmology. Republican. Clubs: Delancey Bridge, Franklin Chess. Home: 1901 Walnut St., Philadelphia, Pa.

REESER, Dick M., mayor; b. New Kensington, Pa., Aug. 2, 1904; s. Dennis A. and Leone (Miller) R.; student U. of Pittsburgh; m. Emily Irwin, May 18, 1933; 1 son, Dennis Irwin. Owner Reeser's Pharmacy, 1928-33; mem. City Council, 1934-36; mgr. Reliance Life Ins. Co., 1937; mayor, New Kensington, since 1938. Chmn. Boy Scout Troop; gen. chmn. New Kensington Boys Club and Junior Patrol. Mem. Chamber of Commerce, Izaak Walton League, Sigma Alpha Epsilon, Am. Federation Musicians, Arnold Business Men's Assn. Mason, Elk, Eagle, Moose, Minute Men. Clubs: Hillcrest Country, Kiwanis, Kensington Gun. Home: 423 Keystone Drive. Office: City Hall, New Kensington, Pa.

REESIDE, John Bernard, Jr., geologist; b. Baltimore, Md., June 24, 1889; s. John Bernard and Florence May (Feathers) R.; A.B., Johns Hopkins U., 1911, Ph.D., 1915; m. Adelaide C. Quisenberry, May 3, 1918; children—John Bernard III, Corinna. Geologist U.S. Geol. Survey since 1915, charge Sect. of Paleontology and Stratigraphy since 1932. Served as 1st lt. field arty., U.S.A., 1918. Fellow A.A.A.S., Geol. Soc. of America, Paleontological Soc.; mem. Am. Assn. Petroleum Geologists, Washington Acad. Science, Washington Geol. Soc., Biol. Soc., Phi Beta Kappa. Episcopalian. Club: Cosmos (Washington, D.C.). Contributor to geol. jours. Home: 5 Luttrell Av., Hyattsville, Md. Office: U.S. Nat. Museum, Washington, D.C.

REEVE, Charles Snyder, chemist; b. Phila., Pa., Dec. 15, 1875; s. Ebenezer Scull and Anna Jane (Snyder) R.; B.S. in Chemistry, U. of Pa., 1897; m. Elizabeth A. Gumpert, Mar. 7, 1907; children—Edward G., Elizabeth Jane. Asst. chemist Gen. Electric Co., 1897-1900; chem. engr. Industrial Water Co., 1900-03; chemist Phila. Bur. of Surveys, 1903-06; asst. inspr. asphalt and cement, Dist. of Columbia, 1906-09; asst. and chemist, Office Pub. Rds., U.S. Dept. Agr., 1909-18; research chemist, The Barrett Co., 1918-22, chief chemist development dept., 1922-32, mgr. research and development since 1932. Fellow Am. Inst. Chemists. Mem. Am. Chem. Soc., Am. Soc. for Testing Materials, Soc. Chem. Industry, Am. Wood Preservers Assn., Delta Tau Delta. Episcopalian. Mason. Club: Chemists (New York). Home: 255 Glenwood Av., Leonia. Office: Barrett Co., Edgewater, N.J.

REEVE, Irving Smith, lawyer; b. Jersey City, N.J., Feb. 21, 1894; s. Arthur L. and Alma (Smith) R.; LL.B., New York Law Sch., 1917; m. Vecina M. Wilson, Feb. 19, 1924; children—Arthur Hamilton, Jean Lennox. Engaged in gen. practice of law at Englewood, N.J.; served as mayor, Englewood, N.J., 1933-35; judge first dist. ct. of Bergen Co. since 1937; dir. and atty. Closter Nat. Bank & Trust Co., Harrington Bldg. & Loan Assn. Served as regtl. sergt. maj., judge adv. gen. dept. during World War. Pres. Republican Club. Dir. Englewood Red Cross, Salvation Army. Republican. Episcopalian. Mason (32°). Clubs: Rotary (vice-pres.), Englewood Mens, Knickerbocker Country. Home: 114 Beach Rd. Office: 1 Engle St., Englewood, N.J.

REEVE, William Foster, III, prof. of law; b. Camden, N.J., July 25, 1892; s. William Foster and Mary Joy (Grey) R.; prep. edn. Episcopal Acad., Phila., 1905-08, Gunnery Sch., Washington, Conn., 1908-10; Litt.B., Princeton U., 1914; LL.B., U. of Pa., 1917; m. Kathleen Helen Wilson, Sept. 3, 1919; children—William Foster Wilson, Mark. Admitted to Pa. bar, 1919, N.J. bar, 1920; began practice in Phila.; with firm Bell, Kendrick, Trinkle & Deeter, 1919-22; lecturer in law, U. of Pa., Law Sch., 1920-22, asst. prof. of law, 1922-24, prof. since 1924; visiting prof., summers, Cornell Law Sch., 1930, Columbia Law Sch., 1931. Served in Med. Corps, U.S. Army, 1917-19; with Base Hosp. No. 10, attached to B.E.F., Le Treport, France. Dir. Newton Twp. Sch. Dist. since 1934. Adviser on trusts to Am. Law Inst. Mem. Am. Bar Assn., Pa. Bar Assn., Sharswood Law Club, Dial Lodge, Sons of the Revolution. Republican. Clubs: Rose Tree Fox Hunting (Media, Pa.); Princeton (Phila.). Author of Pa. Annotations to the Restatement of the Law of Trusts (under auspices of Pa. State Bar Assn.). Home: Coolure, Newtown Square, Pa. Office: 3400 Chestnut St., Philadelphia, Pa.

REEVES, Francis Butler, Jr., wholesale grocer; b. Phila., Pa., May 20, 1873; s. Francis Brewster and Ellen (Thompson) R.; student Germantown Acad., 1884-89, Haverford Coll., 1889-91; m. Lillian Primrose, Baltimore, Md., Feb. 16, 1897; children—Josephine Primrose (Mrs. Henry F. Walton, Jr.), Mary Primrose (Mrs. Orval A. Wales), Francis Brewster, Johnson, Lloyd. Asso. with Reeves, Parvin & Co., wholesale grocers, Phila., Pa., since 1891, office boy, clk. and salesman, 1891-94, mem. firm, 1894-1924, pres. since inc. 1924; dir. Mercantile Beneficial Soc., Merchants Fund, Philadelphia Bourse. Treas. and dir. Florence Crittenden Home. Dir. Pennsylvania Tuberculosis Soc. Mem. Phi Kappa Sigma. Dir. and vice-pres. Huntingdon Valley Kennel Club; del. A.K.C. Kennel Club, New York. Republican. Presbyn. Home: Blue Bell. Office: 400 Chestnut St., Philadelphia, Pa.

REEVES, Hugh Laing, lawyer; b. Philadelphia, Pa., May 7, 1866; s. James Johnson and Mary Hunt (Butler) R.; ed. Bridgeton pub. schs., South Jersey Inst. and West Jersey Acad.; m. Emma Laning Mulford, May 7, 1906 (dec.). Admitted to N.J. bar, 1893; now in private practice of law. Trustee Bridgeton Hosp. Assn.; treas. of trustees Presbyn. Congregation of Bridgetown; dir. Cumberland Co. (N.J.) Hist. Soc., Johnson-Reeves Playground Assn. Republican. Clubs: Bridgeton Camera Soc., Cohanzick Country (Bridgeton). Home: 25 N. Pearl St. Office: 95 E. Commerce St., Bridgeton, N.J.

REEVES, James Aloysius Wallace, college pres.; b. Latrobe, Pa., Feb. 8, 1892; s. Patrick Joseph and Mary Theresa (Noonan) R.; A.B., St. Vincent Coll., 1914; A.M., 1916; S.T.D., St. Vincent Sem., 1922; student Columbia U., 1922, U. of Pittsburgh, 1927-32; LL.D., Duquesne U., 1933; Litt.D., St. Vincent's Coll., 1936. Ordained priest of the Roman Catholic Ch., 1918; instr. in philosophy, Seton Hill Coll., Greensburg, Pa., 1921-23, asso. prof. philosophy and psychology, 1923-26, prof. since 1926, acting pres., 1930-31, pres. and mem. bd. of trustees since 1931; summer instr. Catholic Univ. of America, Washington, D.C., 1925; visiting lecturer in psychology, Duquesne U., 1930. Vice-pres. exec. bd. Westmoreland County Council Boy Scouts of America. Decorated Chevalier of the Crown of Italy, 1936. Mem. 1939 White House Conference on Children in a Democracy. Mem. National Education Association (Am. Assn. of School Adminstrs.), Nat. Catholic Ednl. Assn. (past pres. coll. sect. mem. gen. exec. bd. since 1932), Am. Council on Edn., Am. Assn. Univ. Profs., Am. Psychol. Assn. (asso. mem.), Mediæval Acad. of America, A.A.A.S. Republican. Club: University (Pittsburgh). Address: Seton Hill College, Greensburg, Pa.

REEVES, John Mercer, commn. merchant; b. Siloam, N.C., Aug. 10, 1887; s. Micajah Coke and Mary Caroline (Mercer) R.; student Oak Ridge Inst., 1905-06; A.B., U. of N.C., 1910; student U. of Chicago, 1912; m. Virginia McKenzie, Dec. 18, 1928; children—Virginia Caroline, Ann Cecelia. Prin. Dothan (Ala.) High Sch., 1911-15; salesman Hunter Mfg. & Commn. Co., 1920; vice-pres. Reeves Brothers, Inc., cotton goods commn. merchants and mfrs., N.Y. City, since 1920, now sec. and dir.; pres. and dir. Osage Mfg. Co., Bessemer City, N.C.; v.p. Mills Mill No. 1, Greenville, S.C., and Mills Mill No. 2, Woodruff, S.C.; v.p. Fairforest Finishing Co., Spartanburg, S.C. Ensign U.S. Naval Res.; served in U.S. Navy, 1917-19, part time as mem. bd. appraisal and sale Naval Clothing Depot, Brooklyn. Mem. and pres. Summit (N.J.) Bd. of Edn., 1936-37. Mem. Delta Sigma Phi. Democrat. Methodist. Mason. Clubs: Canoe Brook Country (Summit, N.J.); Merchants (N.Y. City). Home: 14 Fernwood Road, Summit, N.J. Office: 54 Worth St., New York, N.Y.

REEVES, John Robert, geologist; b. Anderson, Ind., Mar. 17, 1896; s. James R. and Martha (Collier) R.; A.B., Ind. U., Bloomington, Ind., 1921, A.M., 1922, Ph.D., 1923; m. Ruth Miller, 1932. Cons. geologist and instr. geology, Ind. U., 1921-24; geologist, Ind. Geol. Survey, 1923-24; resident geologist, Empire Gas & Fuel Co., Kan., Mich., and Ky., 1924-30; v.p. and geologist Penn-York Natural Gas Corpn., Pa. and Buffalo, N.Y., since 1930. Served as ensign, U.S.N.R.F., 1917-19. Mem. Am. Assn. Petroleum Geologists, Am. Gas Assn., Canadian Gas Assn., Phi Beta Kappa, Sigma Psi, Phi Kappa Psi. Home: Coudersport, Pa.; 140 Linwood Av., Buffalo, N.Y. Office: Jackson Bldg., Buffalo, N.Y.

REEVES, Rufus Sargent, M.D.; b. Philadelphia, Pa., Aug. 1, 1882; s. Dr. Joseph Morgan and Josephine (Lewry) R.; ed. William Penn Charter Sch.; B.S., U. of Pa., 1906, M.D., 1912; m. Edith C. Godshall, June 7, 1917; 1 dau., Edith Mary. Pro-sector to prof. anatomy, U. of Pa., 1913-14; instr. medicine, U. of Pa. Med. Sch., 1913-19; chief med. clinic U. Settlement House, 1916-20; asso. in medicine on staff Episcopal Hosp., 1920-26; physician to women's Dept. Moyamensing Prison, 1926-30; in private practice of medicine since 1913; clinician Div. of Cancer Control, Pa. Dept. of Health since 1939. Served as lt., Med. Corps, U.S. Naval Reserve, 1918-19. First v.p. Assn. of Ex-Residents and Fellows of Robert Packer Hosp., Sayre, Pa., 1936-37, pres., 1937-38; chmn. com. on med. edn. and scientific program, 1935-38; chmn. plan to educate the public through women's auxiliaries of State of Pa. Del. to Pa. State Med. Soc., 1937-40. Fellow Am. Coll. Physicians, A.M.A., Philadelphia Coll. Physicians; mem. Philadelphia Co. Med. Soc. (1st chmn. post-grad. inst.; mem. com. on foods, drugs and beverages; pres. 1939-40; dir. 1933-38), Pa. State Med. Soc. (mem. com. on pub. relations, 1936-39; mem. com. on med. edn., 1938), Gen. Alumni Soc. and Med. Alumni of U. of Pa., Delaware Co. Med. Soc. (hon.). Republican. Episcopalian. Mason (Past Master). Clubs: Overbrook Golf, Aesculapian, Physicians Motor. Writer various papers on med. subjects. Home: 2227 Spruce St. Office: Aldine Trust Bldg., 20th and Chestnut Sts., Philadelphia, Pa.

REGER, David Bright, cons. geologist; b. Rural Dale, W.Va., Apr. 11, 1882; s. Joseph Socrates and Sirene (Bunten) R.; prep. edn., W.Va. Conf. Sem. (now W.Va. Wesleyan Coll.); A.B., W.Va. U., 1909, B.S. in civil engring., 1911; m. Ella Gertrude Mattingly, Nov. 24, 1914; children—Helen Emily, Jane, Joseph Edward. Field asst. U.S. Geol. Survey, 1903-06; hydrographic surveyor U.S. Naval Sta., Guantanamo Bay, Cuba, 1906-07; with W.Va. Geol. Survey, 1909-30, as field asst., 1909-13, asst. geologist, 1913-27, acting state geologist, 1927-29, asso. geologist, 1929-30; cons. geologist for oil, gas and coal, water supply, etc., since 1919, office in Morgantown, W.Va., since 1930; pres. Pringle Run Coal Co., 1918-38; v.p. Columbia Coal & Coke Co., 1918-22; sec.-treas. and mgr. Reger Oil Co., 1920-29. Mem. Am. Inst. Mining and Metall. Engrs., Geol. Soc. America, Soc. Econ. Geologists, A.A.A.S., W.Va. Acad. Science (v.p. 1932-33; pres. 1933-34), W.Va. Coal Mining Inst., Appalachian Geol. Soc., Phi Kappa Psi (dir. James Cochran House Assn.), Phi Beta Kappa. Republican. Methodist. Elk. Author: (Geologic Reports of W.Va. Geol. Survey) Preston County (with R. V. Hennen), 1914; Logan and Mingo Counties (with R. V. Hennen), 1914; Lewis and Gilmer Counties, 1916; Barbour and Upshur Counties and Western Portion of Randolph County, 1918; Webster County, 1920; Nicholas County, 1921; Tucker County, 1923; Mineral and Grant Counties, 1924; Mercer, Monroe and Summers Counties, 1926; Randolph County, 1931; also contg. author to other reports. Contbr. numerous articles to scientific jours. Home: 112 Wilson Av. Office: 217 High St., Morgantown, W.Va.

REGER, John F(ranklin), lawyer; b. Somerset Co., N.J., Mar. 18, 1869; s. Frederick and Mary (Amerman) R.; ed. pub. schs. and pvt. tutors; m. Mary Q. Durling, Aug. 1, 1907. Began career teaching sch., 1890; studied law and admitted to N.J. bar, 1896, and since engaged in gen. practice of law at Somerville; mem. firm Reger and Smith since 1929; served as prosecutor of the pleas, 1905-10, served as County Judge, 1930-35; vice-pres. and counsel Somerville Trust Co.; vice-pres. Somerville Savings Bank; dir. Citizens Bldg. & Loan Assn. Dir. Somerset Hosp. Republican. Mem. Dutch Reformed Ch. Mason. Club: Raritan Valley Country. Home: 100 Prospect St., Somerville, N.J. Office: 12 Maple St., Somerville, N.J.

REGESTEIN, Walter Philip, research chemist; b. Boston, Mass., June 20, 1882; s. Ernst and Emma C. (Albrecht) R.; B.S., Mass. Inst. Tech., 1904; m. Mary A. Keogh, Sept. 3, 1910; children—Virginia Mary, Marjorie Ann, Elizabeth Ann. Asst. in analyt. chemistry, New York Univ., 1904; chemist, asst. supt., Hygienic Chem. Co., Elizabethport, N.J., 1905-09; asso. with E. I. Du Pont de Nemours & Co., Inc. continuously since 1909, successively asst. chemist, asst. chief chemist, chief chemist, Haskell, N.J. Plant, 1909-18, asst. div. head, div. head. Smokeless Powder Div. Exptl. Sta., 1918-21, chief chemist and ballistics engr., Carney's Point Plant, 1921-25, asst. dir. and head Powder Div. Burnside Lab., Penns Grove, N.J., since 1925. Mem. Am. Chem. Soc. Republican. Mason. Club: DuPont Country (Wilmington, Del.). Home: 905 Edgehill Rd., Wilmington, Del. Office; Burnside Lab., Penns Grove, N.J.

REGNER, Sidney Lawrence, rabbi; b. New York, N.Y., Sept. 25, 1903; s. Martin and Kate (Lichtman) R.; A.B., U. of Cincinnati, 1924; Rabbi, Hebrew Union Coll., 1927; m. Dorothy Marcus, Aug. 18, 1931; children—Norman Martin, Babette Ellen, James David. Rabbi of Reform Cong. Oheb Sholom, Reading, Pa., since 1927. Trustee Reading and Berks Co. Welfare Fed. Mem. bd. Social Welfare League, Jewish Welfare League; chmn. Family Div. Council of Social Agencies; mem. bd. Reading Birth Control League; former pres., now mem. exec. com. Reading and Berks Co. Peace Council; mem. exec. com. Jewish Community Council of Reading. Mem. Central Conf. Am. Rabbis (corr. sec.), Hebrew Union Coll. Alumni Assn., Phi Beta Kappa. Jewish religion. B'nai B'rith. Home: 1519 Linden St., Reading, Pa.

REHM, William C., lawyer; b. Lancaster, Pa., Oct. 17, 1875; s. F. William and Wilhelmina (Hoffman) R.; ed. Lancaster High Sch.; studied law privately; m. Margaret Elizabeth Griel, Oct. 28, 1903. Admitted to Lancaster Co. bar, 1901. Supreme Ct. of Pa., 1906, Superior Ct. of Pa., 1908; engaged in gen. practice of law; v.p. and dir. Conestoga Bldg. & Loan Assn., Lancaster, Pa. Elected city solicitor, Lancaster, 1919, dist. atty., 1920, city commr., 1928. Enlisted as private Pa. Nat. Guard, 1898; served on Mexican border, 1916; capt. 109th Machine Gun Batt., Co. A., during World War, participating in 5 major engagements. Mem. 28th Div. Vets. Assn., Am. Legion (past officer), Vets. Foreign Wars, Soc. of Foreign War Vets. Elk. Clubs: Hamilton, Tucquan Fishing, West Branch Hunting, Lions (ex-pres.). Wrote: Lancaster County's Military History (pub. in Lancaster Intelligencer). Home: 353 College Av. Office: 45 N. Duke St., Lancaster, Pa.

REHN, James A(bram) G(arfield), entomologist; b. Phila., Pa., Oct. 26, 1881; s. William J. and Cornelia (Loud) R.; ed. Pa. Acad. Fine Arts, Phila., 1897-98, Acad. of Natural Scis., 1898-1904; m. Dorothy D. Holman, Oct. 24, 1906; 1 son, John W(illiam) H(olman). Asso.

with Acad. of Natural Sciences, Phila. continuously since 1900, asst. to curator, 1904-18, asst. curator, 1918-25, asso. curator insects, 1925-33, curator insects since 1933, sec., 1920-38, corr. sec. since 1938; editor pubis. Am. Entomol. Soc., 1914-26, treas. since 1929. Served in Mil. Intelligence Div., Gen. Staff, U.S.A., 1918. Fellow A.A.A.S., Entomol. Soc. of America; mem. Am. Entomol. Soc., Am. Soc. of Mammalogists, Acad. of Natural Scis. of Phila., Sigma Xi, Del. Valley Ornithol. Club (past pres.); asso. mem. Am. Ornithologists Union. Republican. Home: 6026 Walton Av., Philadelphia, Pa.

REIBER, Aaron Eli, lawyer; b. Butler, Pa., Apr. 9, 1864; s. Marten and Mary (Yetter) R.; student Washington and Jefferson Coll.; A.B., Princeton, 1882; m. Florence Smith, June 1897; children—Marten A., Mary Elizabeth (Mrs. Paul Jenkins). Admitted to Pa. bar, 1885, and since engaged in gen. practice of law at Butler; mem. firm Reiber and Reiber; served as dist. atty. of Butler Co., 1890-94; judge Common Pleas Ct. of Butler Co., 1913-23; dir. Union Trust Co., Butler Consolidated Coal Co., West Pa. Cement Co. Dir. Thiel Coll. Mem. Butler Bar Assn. (v.p.), Phi Delta Theta. Democrat. Lutheran. K.P. Club: Butler Country. Home: 351 N. Main St. Office: 2 Reiber Bldg., Butler, Pa.

REIBER, Richard H(enry), artist and instr.; b. Pittsburgh, Pa., Oct. 2, 1912; s. Harry P. and Hilda May (White) R.; ed. Cleveland Heights High Sch., Cornell U., Pittsburgh U. Has followed profession of artist, etcher, portrait painter, water colorist, and lecturer since 1934; exhibited in Pittsburgh and Pa. Acad. of Fine Arts, Cleveland Mus. of Art, Cornell U.; lectures in Pittsburgh and Carnegie Mus.; traveled to West Indies, canoe trips into Northern Can., to South America; joined staff Shadyside Acad. and field sec. for same; instr. in fine arts, coach of wrestling, track, and football, Shadyside Acad. Holds commn. in R.O.T.C. Mem. Asso. Artists of Pittsburgh, Print Club of Pittsburgh, Sigma Chi, Aleph Samach, Sphinx Head. Awarded gold seal, Nat. Collegiate Schs. of Architecture. Episcopalian. Home: 4733 Wallingford St. Address: Shadyside Acad., Pittsburgh, Pa.

REIBLICH, George Kenneth, univ. prof.; b. Baltimore, Md., May 4, 1905; s. George Winfield and Emma Grace (Rice) R.; A.B., Johns Hopkins U., 1925, Ph.D., 1928; student U. of Md. Law Sch., Baltimore, 1925-28; J.D., N.Y. Univ. Law Sch., 1929; LL.M., Columbia U. Law Sch., 1937; m. Georgiana Blanchard Tufts, Nov. 26, 1932; children—Kenneth Tufts, Anne Blanchard. Instr. govt., N.Y. Univ., 1928-30; engaged in practice of law, asso. with Jenks & Rogers, N.Y. City, 1929-30; admitted to bars of N.Y., 1930, Md., 1935; prof. of law, U. of Md. Law Sch., Baltimore, since 1930. Mem. Md. State Bar Assn., Baltimore City Bar Assn., Order of Coif. Scabbard and Blade, Phi Beta Kappa, Phi Delta Phi. Democrat. Mem. Evang. Ch. Mason. K.P. Author: A Study of Judicial Administration in Maryland, 1929; Maryland Annotations to Conflict of Laws, 1937. Annotator to Trusts Restatement for Maryland. Contbr. to legal pubis. Home: 6311 Boxwood Rd., Baltimore, Md.

REICH, Henry, surgeon; b. Newark, N.J., Apr. 1, 1900; s. Aaron (Simelson) R.; student South Side High Sch., Newark, 1913-16; B.A., New York U., 1920; M.D., Columbia U., 1924; m. Norma Goodman, June 27, 1929; children—Jane, Jill. Began as surgeon, Newark, 1925; now surgeon Newark Beth Israel Hosp., Pa. R.R.; asst. attending surgeon Newark City Hosp. Served in S.A.T.C., New York U., 1918. Fellow Am. Coll. Surgeons; mem. Phi Delta Epsilon, Alpha Omega Alpha. Home: 120 Keer Av. Office: Medical Tower, Newark, N.J.

REICH, Jerome Joseph, physician; b. New York, N.Y., Mar. 25, 1898; s. Isaac Michael and Minnie (Braun) R.; grad. Barringer High Sch., Newark, N.J., 1918; student New York U., 1919-20, Newark Jr. Coll., 1920-22; M.D., George Washington U., 1927; m. Ruth H. Klein, Oct. 24, 1936; children—Ira Merrill, Melvyn Leon. Interne Elizabeth (N.J.) Gen. Hosp., 1927-28; physician and surgeon, Hillside, N.J., since 1928; mem. clinical staff Newark Beth Israel Hosp. and St. Elizabeth Hosp., courtesy staff Irvington Gen. Hosp. and Newark Presbyterian Hosp.; dir. Midway Bldg. & Loan Assn.; formerly township physician, Hillside. Chmn. NRA, Hillside Area, 1934; dir. Union County Taxpayers Assn. Fellow A.M.A.; mem. Union County Med. Soc., Clin. Soc. Beth Israel Hosp., Phi Delta Epsilon. Mason (32°, Shriner), Tall Cedars, Elk. Club: Hillside Rotary (pres. 1934). Address: 1410 Maple Av., Hillside, N.J.

REICH, Max Isaac, minister; b. Berlin, Germany, Mar. 17, 1867; s. Adolphus and Emma Wolff; R.; ed. gymasium, Berlin, Germany, and London, England; D.D., Wheaton Coll., Wheaton, Ill., 1936; m. Esther Mary Lorenzen, Sept. 5, 1888; children—Florence, Annie, William, Edward, Esther, Alice, John, Lawrence, Joseph. Came to U.S., 1915. British subject. Apprentice printing trade, London, 1880-86; served as minister Soc. of Friends; expositor of Bible; leader among Christian Jews U.S. and Germany; a founder, 1915, pres., 1921-27, 1935-38, Hebrew Christian Alliance America, hon. pres. 5 years; a founder Internat. Hebrew Christian Alliance, 1927; extension lecturer Moody Bible Inst., Chicago. Wrote: Life and Letters of J. G. M'Vicar; Breathings After the Deeper Life; Deeper Still; The Deeper Life Spiritual Aloneness. Studies in the Psalms of Israel, How Long, etc. Home: George School, near Newtown, Pa.

REICH, Nathaniel Julius, coll. prof.; b. Sarvar, Austria-Hungary, Apr. 29, 1882; s. William and Sidonie (Summer) R.; grad. Ober-Gymnasium, Badenbei-Vienna, 1900, Tech. Coll., Vienna, 1900; Ph.D., U. of Vienna, 1904; student at Universities of Vienna, Berlin, Munich, Strasbourg and Oxford; unmarried. Came to United States, 1922, naturalized, 1928. Instr., Univ. of Prague, Czecho-Slovakia, 1913-19; instr., Univ. of Vienna, 1919-22; curator, U. of Pa. Museum, Egyptian dept., 1922-25; prof. of Egyptology and other Semitic studies, Dropsie Coll. for Hebrew and Cognate Learning, Phila., since 1925; visiting lecturer in Egyptology, Semitic studies and hist. law, Johns Hopkins U., 1926. Mem. A.A.A.S., Am. Oriental Soc., Soc. Bibl. Lit., Linguistic Soc. America, Egypt Exploration Soc., Société Francaise d' Égyptologie. Jewish religion. Clubs: Oriental, Classical (Phila.). Linguistic and archaeological research in London (British Museum), Oxford, Turin (Italy), Munich; research on papyri and stone inscriptions, Brit. Museum, 1911-12, by grant of the Academy of Sciences of Vienna; received grants by Am. Council of Learned Socs. for archaeological research in European museums, 1933, 35. Author of many articles on papyrology, Egyptology and Semitic Studies pub. in U.S. and Europe. Editor of Mizraim, jour. of papyrology, Egyptology, history of ancient laws, etc. Address: P.O. Box 337, Philadelphia, Pa.

REICHARD, Gladys Amanda, anthropologist; b. Bangor, Pa., July 17, 1893; d. Noah W. and Minerva Anna (Jordan) R.; A.B., Swarthmore (Pa.) Coll., 1919; Ph.D., Columbia, 1925; post grad. study, U. of Hamburg, Germany (Guggenheim Memorial fellowship), 1926-27; unmarried. Teacher rural schs. Northampton County, Pa., 1909-11, grade schs. Bangor, 1911-15, Robert Louis Stevenson Sch., N.Y. City, 1920-21; asst. in anthropology, Barnard Coll., N.Y. City, 1921-22; research fellow U. of Calif., 1922-23; instructor in anthropology, Barnard Coll., 1923-28, asst. prof. since 1928; supervisor Navajo lang. instruction, U.S. Dept. Indian Affairs, summer 1934. Mem. Am. Folk-Lore Soc. (sec.), Am. Ethnol. Soc. (pres.), Phi Beta Kappa, Sigma Xi. Awarded Morrison prize in natural sciences by N.Y. Acad. Sciences, 1932. Author: Wiyot Grammar and Texts, 1925; Social Life of the Navajo Indians, 1928; Melanessian Design, 1933; Spider Woman, a Story of Navajo Weavers and Chanters, 1934; Navajo Shepherd and Weaver, 1936; Sandpaintings of the Navajo Shooting Chant, 1937; Grammar of Coeur d'Alene Language, 1938. Home: 230 Franklin Av., Grantwood, N.J.

REICHEL, John, bacteriologist; b. Cincinnati, O., May 30, 1886; s. Fred and Barbetta (Rotter) R.; V.M.D., U. of Pa., 1906; m. Mary V. Ford, June 1, 1909; children—John, Jr., Marian E. Engaged as instr., U. of Pa., 1907-10; bacteriologist, Mulford Biological Lab., 1911-17, dir. same, 1917-36; tech. dir., Sharp & Dohme, Inc., Phila., Pa., since 1936. Mem. Soc. Am. Bacteriologists, Am. Vet. Med. Assn., Am. Pub. Health Assn., Physiol. Soc. Phila., Phila. Pathol. Soc., Nat. Tuberculosis Assn. Republican. Clubs: Union League, Philadelphia Country. Home: 1404 Hillside Rd., Wynnewood, Pa. Office: Glenolden, Pa.

REICHOLD, Ralph George, cartoonist; b. Pittsburgh, Pa., Nov. 3, 1894; s. William and Mary Elizabeth (Giltenboth) R.; ed. Carnegie Inst. Tech., Pittsburgh, 1914-16; m. Minnie Margaret Elizabeth Scheller, of Pittsburgh, Sept. 14, 1917; children—Roy William, Earl Ralph. Newspaper artist on Pittsburgh Press since 1914, editorial cartoonist since 1928. Republican. Lutheran. Cartoons have appeared in Editor and Publisher and other nat. mags. Home: 121 Vernon Drive, Mt. Lebanon, Pa. Office: Pittsburgh Press, Pittsburgh, Pa.

REID, A(rmour) Duncan, insurance exec.; b. Kingston, Ont., Can., Mar. 13, 1874; s. William and Mary (Allen) R.; ed. pub. schs., Kingston; m. Lily Thurston (now dec.); children—A. Lionel, Ralph T., Marjorie Eileen (Mrs. L. C. Roberts); m. 2d, Rose Miller Thompson, June 2, 1906. Came to U.S., 1900, naturalized citizen, 1918. Served as insp. London Guarantee & Accident Co.; supt. agents, Ocean Accident & Guarantee Corpn., 1895-1900, exec. supt. in U.S., 1900-11; gen. mgr. Globe Indemnity Co., 1911-19, pres., 1919-39, retired Apr. 1, 1939; formerly joint gen. attorney in U.S. of The Liverpool & London & Globe Ins. Co., also of Royal Ins. Co.; dir. Star Ins. Co. of America, Newark Fire Ins. Co., Federal Union Ins. Co., Queen Insurance Co. of America, Seaboard Ins. Co., Globe Indemnity Co., 150 William Street Corpn., Royal Indemnity Co. and Eagle Indemnity Co. Served as chmn. insurance committees, New York City, Liberty Loan and Red Cross drives, World War. Was first sec. and treas. Workmen's Compensation Information Bur. Former mem. exec. com. Assn. Casualty and Surety Executives; (former chmn.), Workmen's Compensation Reinsurance Bur. Republican. Episcopalian. Mason (K.T.). Clubs: Upper Montclair Country (Montclair, N.J.); Pilgrims of U.S. Home: 39 N. Mountain Av., Montclair, N.J.

REID, Dana Berwyn, treas. Allegheny Coll.; b. Chautauqua Twp., N.Y., Oct. 23, 1892; s. Clarence Ransom and Belle M. (McCray) R.; grad. high sch., Chautauqua, N.Y., 1910; ed. Jamestown Bus. Coll., Jamestown, N.Y., 1918-19; m. Lois King Holmes, June 22, 1919; children—Roderic Eugene, Berwyn Holmes. Employed as sec. to the pres. of Allegheny Coll., 1920-28, asst. treas., 1928-29, treas. Allegheny Coll. since 1929. Republican. Baptist. Mason (32°). Club: Round Table (Meadville). Home: 964 G. Street, Meadville, Pa. Office: Allegheny College, Meadville, Pa.

REID, E. Emmet, chemist; b. Fincastle, Va., June 27, 1872; s. Thomas Alfred and Virginia (Ammen) R.; M.A., Richmond (Va.) Coll., 1892, LL.D., 1917; Ph.D., Johns Hopkins, 1898; m. Margaret Kendall, Dec. 28, 1915; children—Emmet Kendall, Alfred Gray, Martha Bell. Teacher science, Mt. Lebanon (La.) Coll., 1892-94; prof. chemistry, Coll. of Charleston, S.C., 1898-1901, Baylor U., Waco, 1901-08; research asst. and Johnston scholar, Johns Hopkins, 1908-11; research chemist, Colgate & Co., 1911-14; asso. prof., later prof. organic chemistry, Johns Hopkins, 1914-37, prof. emeritus, 1937—; visiting prof. University of Chicago, summer 1930. Gas warfare investigations, Bur. of Mines, War Dept., May 1917-Jan. 1919; research adviser to U. of Richmond, U. of S.C., Furman U., U. of Ala., Ala. Poly., Howard Coll., Birmingham-Southern Coll. Consultant du Pont Co., Hercules Powder Co., Socony-Vacuum Oil Co., Thiokol Corpn., Chem. Warfare Service. Mem. Am. Chem. Soc.

Am. Assn. Univ. Profs., Phi Beta Kappa, Sigma Xi, Pi Gamma Mu. Democrat. Baptist. Translator of Sabatier's Catalysis in Organic Chemistry, 1921. Author: Introduction to Research in Organic Chemistry, 1924; College Organic Chemistry, 1929. Contbr. numerous papers to Am. Chem. Jour., Jour. Am. Chem. Soc., etc. Home: 203 E. 33d St., Baltimore, Md.

REID, Edgar Adolphus, banker; b. Greenup Co., Ky., Apr. 1, 1864; s. Adolphus La Fayette and Henrietta (Powell) R.; student pub. schs.; m. Kate Skees Ward, Apr. 25, 1888 (dec.); 1 dau., Edith May (dec.). Became runner and bookkeeper in bank, 1884; cashier Charleston Nat. Bank, 1886-91; cashier Kanawha Nat. Bank, Charleston, W.Va., 1892-1920, pres., 1920-30; v.p. Charleston Nat. Bank since 1930; v.p., dir. and mem. exec. com. Virginian Joint Stock Land Bank, Charleston, since 1922. Formerly city treas. of Charleston. Democrat. Presbyterian. Mason (32°, Shriner). Home: 208 Bradford St. Office: 201 Capital St., Charleston, W.Va.

REID, Harry Fielding, geologist; b. Baltimore, Md., May 18, 1859; s. Andrew and Fanny Brooke (Gwathmey) R.; A.B., Johns Hopkins, 1880; C.E., Pa. Mil. Acad., 1876; Ph.D., Johns Hopkins, 1885; studied in Germany and England, 1884-86; m. Edith Gittings, Nov. 22, 1883; children—Francis Fielding, Doris Fielding. Prof. mathematics, 1886-89, physics, 1889-94, Case School of Applied Science, Cleveland; lecturer Johns Hopkins, 1894-96; asso. prof. physical geology, U. of Chicago, 1895-96; asso. prof., 1896-1901, prof. geol. physics, 1901-11, prof. dynamical geology and geography, 1911-30, professor emeritus since 1930, Johns Hopkins University. Was chief of highway div., Md. Geol. Survey, 1898-1905; spl. expert in charge of earthquake records, U.S. Geol. Survey, 1902-14. Member Commission Internationale des Glaciers; representative of U.S. in the Internat. Seismol. Assn. since 1906; hon. mem. Société Helvétiques des Sciences Naturelles; corr. mem. Philadelphia Academy of Natural Sciences; fellow Geological Soc. America, American Physical Soc., Washington Academy Sciences; mem. Nat. Acad. Sciences, Am. Philos. Soc., Seismol. Soc. America (pres. 1913), Am. Geophys. Union (chmn. 1924-26), Phi Beta Kappa. Author: Parts vi, vii, viii of Highways of Maryland, 1899. Joint Author: (with A. N. Johnson) Second Report on the Highways of Maryland, 1902; Vol. II of Report of Calif. State Earthquake Investigation Commn., 1910; also several reports and articles on glaciers, earthquakes, etc. Mem. com. Nat. Acad. Sciences apptd. at request of the President to report on the possibility of controlling the Panama slides, 1915. Home: 608 Cathedral St., Baltimore, Md.

REID, James Johnston, bacteriologist; b. Indianapolis, Ind., Aug. 7, 1898; s. John Templeton and Elizabeth (Hamilton) R.; B.S., Purdue U., Lafayette, Ind., 1923; M.S., U. of Wis., Madison, Wis., 1933, Ph.D., 1936; m. Mildred Virginia Carter, Jan. 12, 1927; children—James Carter, Janet Templeton, Mary Ann. Asst. editor Guide Pub. Co., Huntington, Ind., 1923-24; mgr. Morgantown Packing Co., 1924-32; grad. asst. and instr., dept. of agrl. bacteriology, U. of Wis., Madison, Wis., 1932-36; asst. prof. of bacteriology, Pa. State Coll. since 1936. Served as pvt. 1st class, 150 F. A., 42d (Rainbow) Div., U.S. Army, 1917-19; with A.E.F. 19 months. Mem. Soc. Am. Bacteriologists, Am. Soc. Agronomy, Alpha Zeta, Phi Lambda Upsilon, Tau Kappa Alpha, Sigma Delta Chi, Kappa Delta Pi, Sigma Xi. Republican. Presbyterian. Home: 118 W. Prospect St., State College, Pa.

REID, Legh Wilber, mathematician; b. Alexandria, Va., Nov. 18, 1867; s. Legh Wilber and Emma Catherine (Jackson) R.; B.S., Va. Mil. Inst., 1887; A.B., Johns Hopkins, 1889, grad. student, 1892-93; M.S., Princeton U., 1896; Ph.D., U. of Göttingen, Germany, 1899; m. Elizabeth Griffith Hoxton, Nov. 27, 1894. Chemist dept. of geology, Nat. Museum, Washington, D.C., 1889; computer U.S. Coast and Geodetic Survey, 1890-92; instr. in mathematics, Princeton U., 1893-97, 1899-1900; with Haverford (Pa.) Coll. since 1900, as instr. of mathematics, 1900-01, asso. prof., 1901-07, prof. and head dept. mathematics, 1907-34, prof. emeritus since 1934. Charter mem. Am. Assn. Univ. Profs., now emeritus mem.; former mem. Am. Math. Soc., Math. Assn. America; mem. Pa. Hist. Soc., Md. Hist. Soc., Va. Hist. Soc., Soc. of Genealogists (London), Soc. of the Cincinnati (del. of Va. Soc. to triennial councils since 1923), Delta Phi, Phi Beta Kappa (sec. Haverford Chapter since 1909; del. to triennial councils since 1907; 1st pres. Phila. Assn., 1915-17). Democrat. Episcopalian. Clubs: University (Baltimore); Merion Cricket (Haverford, Pa.). Author: The Elements of the Theory of Algebraic Numbers, 1910. Home: Redeswold, Blue Ridge Summit, Md. Address: Box 44, Highfield, Md.

REID, William James, Jr., clergyman; b. Pittsburgh, Pa., July 10, 1871; s. William James (D.D., LL.D.) and Mary (Bowen) R.; A.B., Princeton, 1893; grad. Pittsburgh Theol. Sem., 1896; D.D. Monmouth (Ill.) Coll., 1909; m. Margaret Morton Thompson, July 28, 1896; children—Elizabeth Thompson (Mrs. Edward Cornell Emanuel), Mary Bowen (dec.), Margaret Anna (dec.), Janet Donaldson (Mrs. Albert Victor Crookston), Helen Louise, Frances Bryce (Mrs. Joseph Tilton). Ordained ministry United Presbyterian Church, 1896; pastor First Ch., Kittanning, Pa., 1896-1900; asso. pastor First Ch., Pittsburgh, 1900-02, pastor since 1902 (father and son have served this congregation since Apr. 7, 1862); editor Sabbath Sch. Dept. of The United Presbyterian, 1902-36; asso. editor The United Presbyterian, 1913-21, editor since 1921; dir. Murdock Kerr & Co., printers, 1902-25. Treas Synod of Pittsburgh, 1902-33; mem. Bd. of Home Missions U.P. Ch., 1910-28; mem. Board of Administration, U.P. Church, since 1931; chmn. U.P. Com. on Presbyn. Unity; pres. bd. trustees Monongahela Presbytery since 1920. Republican. Home: 920 S. Aiken Av., Pittsburgh, Pa.

REIDER, Joseph, prof. Biblical philology and librarian; m. Rozyszcze, Volyhynia, Russia, Dec. 30, 1886; s. Samuel and Chasye (Sokolovski) R.; came to U.S., 1904, and naturalized citizen, 1915; A.B., Coll. of City of N.Y., 1910; Ph.D., Dropsie Coll., 1913; m. Anna Farstej, Sept. 19, 1922; children—Raphael Benjamin, Emanuel Tobias. Began as instr. Bibl. philology, Dropsie Coll., Phila., 1913, and continued to prof. Bibl. philology since 1932, librarian since 1912. Mem. Am. Soc. of Bibl. Lit., Am. Oriental Soc., Am. Library Assn. Jewish religion. Club: Oriental of Philadelphia. Home: 5125 N. 16th St., Philadelphia, Pa.

REIER, Adam William, physician; b. Glenarm, Md., Aug. 23, 1888; s. Adam and Mary E. (Steigler) R.; M.D., U. of Md. Med. Sch., Baltimore, Md., 1916; m. Sadie E. Davis, Jan. 5, 1918. Interne Baltimore City Hosp., 1916-17, resident surgeon, 1917; engaged in gen. practice of medicine and surgery at Dundalk, Md., since 1919. Served as 1st lt. Med. Corps, U.S.A., 1917-19, with A.E.F., Evacuation Hosp. 8, France, 1918-19. Mem. Am. Med. Assn., Baltimore Co. Med. Assn. (pres.), Am. Legion, Vets. Fgn. Wars, Chi Zeta Chi. Lutheran. Clubs: Rotary (Dundalk); Confrere of Baltimore (treas.); Country (Sparrows Point). Home: North Center & Dundalk Av. Office: 2 Kinship Rd., Dundalk, Md.

REIF, Edward Clarence; prof. materia medica and biology, U. of Pittsburgh. Home: 74 N. Bryant Av., Bellevue, Pa.

REIFF, Elmer Paul, M.D.; b. Franconia, Pa., May 21, 1880; s. Allen G. and Hattie (Hartzell) R.; student Franklin & Marshall Acad.; A.B., Franklin & Marshall Coll., Lancaster, Pa., 1903; M.D., U. of Pa. Med. Sch., 1907; m. Frances M. Harris, June 30, 1909. Interne Methodist Episcopal Hosp., Phila., 1907-08, asst. in med. dispensary, 1908-10, chief med. dispensary, 1910-19, physician-in-chief since 1919. Accepted by Am. Board of Internal Medicine, 1937. Mem. A.M.A., Pa. State Med. Soc., Phila. Co. Med. Soc., Phila. Coll. Physicians, West Phila. Med. Assn. (ex-pres.), Phila. Med. Club, Phi Rho Sigma, Phi Sigma Kappa. Republican. Reformed Ch. Home: 228 Derwen Road, Merion, Pa. Office: 1927 Spruce St., Philadelphia, Pa.

REIFSCHNEIDER, Charles A.; asso. prof. surgery, U. of Md.; asst. prof. oral surgery, U. of Md. Sch. of Dentistry, Baltimore; asst. visiting surgeon Baltimore City, U. of Md. and Md. Gen. hosps. Address: 104 W. Madison St., Baltimore, Md.

REIFSNYDER, Miles Samuel, clergyman; b. Sinking Springs, Pa., Apr. 16, 1903; s. Nathaniel Milton and Emma A. (Bear) R.; A.B., Franklin and Marshall Coll., Lancaster, Pa., 1923; student Lancaster Theol. Sem., Lancaster, Pa., 1923-26; S.T.B., Meth. Protestant Sem. of Westminster, Md., 1931, S.T.D., 1933; m. Margaret A. Edris, June 30, 1926; 1 dau., Marsha Diane. Ordained to ministry Evang. and Ref. Ch., 1926; pastor, Somerset Co., Pa., 1926; pastor Emmanuel Evang. & Ref. Ch., Westminster, Md., since 1930. Dir. the Westminster Players of Little Theatre Group. Mem. Phi Upsilon Kappa. Republican. Evang. & Ref. Ch. Clubs: Kiwanis (Westminster); hon. mem. Kiwanis of Taneytown. Author: (one act play) The Up-Sign, 1937; (three act plays) Three and Thirty Angels. Contbr. articles to religious mags. Home: R.F.D. 7, Westminster, Md.

REIGHARD, John Pattison, coal operator; b. nr. Bloomsburg, Pa., Sept. 19, 1881; s. Benjamin Franklin and Susan (Sierer) R.; ed. pub. schs., 1888-96, Shamokin Bus. Coll., 1896-97; unmarried. Employed as clk. Pa. R.R. Co., 1897-1905; with Guarantee Trust and Safe Deposit Co., 1905-07; supt. Excelsior Coal Co., Shamokin, Pa., 1907-35; exec. for Excelsior Coal Co. Interest since 1935; sec., treas., dir. Monitor Coal and Coke Co., Gay Coal and Coke Co.; dir. Phila. and Reading Coal and Iron Co., Nat. Dime Bank, Shamokin, Majestic Collieries Co. Republican. Mason. Elk. Clubs: Temple, Shamokin Valley Country. Home: 117 E. Independence St. Office: McConnel Bldg., Shamokin, Pa.

REILEY, Henry Baker, editor and publisher; b. Shirleysburg, Pa., Feb. 18, 1875; s. Rev. Wm. McKendree and Fannie (Baker) R.; student pub. schs., Mifflinburg, Watsontown, and Centralia, Pa., 1884-91, Baltimore City Coll. 1891-96; m. Naomi Kessler, June 27, 1900; children—James McK. (dec.), Wm. Kessler (dec.), Henry Baker, Jr., N. Elizabeth, John E., Margaret L., Ruth. Employed in printing shop and as reporter while still in sch.; with papers at Waynesboro, Pa., Altoona, Harrisburg, Carbondale and Trenton, 1896-1908; editor-mgr. Waynesboro Herald, 1908-13, Uniontown Record, 1913-15; editor-pub. Brownsville Telegraph, 1915-28; purchased three weekly papers at Somerset; merged and propr. Somerset Daily American since 1929, and also operate gen. job printing shop. Served as dir. Brownsville Pub. Library. Mem. Pa. Newspaper Pub. Assn. Republican. Methodist. Club: Somerset Rotary. Home: 218 Rosina Av. Office: 216 W. Main St., Somerset, Pa.

REILLY, Paul, lawyer; b. Philadelphia, Pa., Feb. 9, 1878; s. Thomas E. and Lenore (McCormick) R.; ed. Philadelphia pub. schs.; studied law with Jas. Aylward Develin, Esq.; m. Kathryn Sydney, Apr. 16, 1910. Admitted to Phila. bar, 1900; since in gen. practice of law. Mem. Am., Pa. and Phila. bar assns. Democrat. Mem. Society of Friends. Clubs: Manufacturers and Bankers, Manufacturers Golf and Country. Home: 430 E. Mt. Airy Av. Office: 106 S. 16th St., Philadelphia, Pa.

REILLY, William B.; chmn. exec. com. Federal Trust Co. Address: Newark, N.J.

REILY, George W., banker; b. Harrisburg, Pa., Nov. 21, 1870; s. George W. and Elizabeth (Hummel) R.; Ph.B., Yale, 1892; m. Louise Haxall Harrison, Apr. 29, 1903 (now dec.); 1 son, George W. Clk. Harrisburg Nat. Bank, 1892-93; asst. treas. Harrisburg Trust Co., 1893-97; nat. bank examiner, 1897-1903; treas. Harrisburg Trust Co., 1903-10, v.p. and treas., 1910-18, pres. since 1918; pres. Harrisburg Nat. Bank since 1927; chmn. Harrisburg

Clearing House Assn.; pres. Harrisburg Bridge Co., Newport Home Water Co., Coudersport Consol. Water Co.; dir. Federal Reserve Bank of Phila., Harrisburg Rys. Co., Chestnut Street Market Co., Magee Carpet Co., Magee Webbing Co. Mem. Pa. State Banking Bd., Dauphin Co. Emergency Relief Commn., Harrisburg City Planning Commn.; former dir. Harrisburg Sch. Dist.; ex-pres. Harrisburg Welfare Fed.; trustee Harrisburg State Hosp., Harrisburg Y.M.C.A., Harrisburg Y.W.C.A., Wilson Coll.; dir. Harrisburg Hosp. Mem. Pa. Bankers Assn. (ex-pres.), Pa. Soc. Colonial Wars, Pa. Soc. S.R., Book and Snake Soc. (Yale). Presbyn. Clubs: Country (Harrisburg); University, Philadelphia, Yale, Racquet (Philadelphia); University, Yale (New York); Graduate (New Haven). Home: Front & Reily Sts. Office: 16 S. Market Sq., Harrisburg, Pa.*

REIMANN, Hobart Ansteth, physician; b. Buffalo, N.Y., Oct. 31, 1897; s. George and Ottillia (Ansteth) R.; M.D., U. of Buffalo, 1921; m. Dorothy M. Sampson, June 12, 1926; children—George Aylette, William Page. Asst., Rockefeller Inst., New York City, 1923-26; fellow Nat. Research Council in Prague, 1926-27; asso. prof. medicine, Peking Union Med. Coll., China, 1927-30; asso. prof. medicine, U. of Minn., 1930-36; prof. medicine, Jefferson Med. Coll. since 1936; attdg. phys., Jefferson Hosp., Phila., since 1936. Served as capt. Med. Corps, N.G., N.Y., 1923-26. Mem. Assn. Am. Physicians, Am. Med. Assn., Soc. for Clin. Investigation, Am. Soc. Exptl. Pathology, Soc. Exptl. Biology and Medicine, Coll. Phys. Phila., Sigma Xi, Alpha Omega Alpha. Author: The Pneumonias, 1938. Editor: Treatment in General Medicine, 1939. Contbr. articles on infectious diseases. Home: 333 Valley Rd., Merion, Pa.

REIMANN, Stanley P(hilip), M.D.; b. Philadelphia, Pa., Oct. 13, 1891; s. Louis Philip and Jeannette (Tag) R.; M.D., U. of Pa., 1913; m. Elsie W. Bein, Oct. 26, 1918; children—Elizabeth, Pauline. Began practice at Philadelphia, 1913; dir. research lab. Lankenau Hosp. since 1926; asso. prof. experimental pathology, U. of Pa. Grad. Sch., since 1930; prof. of oncology, Hahnemann Med. Coll. and Hosp., Phila. Mem. A.M.A., Soc. Experimental Pathology, Am. Assn. Pathology and Bacteriology. Served as 1st lt. Med. Corps, U.S.A., World War. Republican. Lutheran. Clubs: University, Skytop, Whitemarsh Valley Country. Co-Author: Excursions into Surgical Subjects (with J. B. Deaver), 1923. Translator: Pathological Physiology of Surgical Diseases, by Franz Rost, 1923; Pathology for Students and Practitioners, by Eduard Kaufmann, 1929. Home: 703 W. Phil-Ellena St. Office: The Lankenau Hosp., Philadelphia, Pa.

REIMENSNYDER, John Milton, clergyman, retired; b. Smithsburg, Md., Jan. 5, 1847; s. John Junius and Susan Margaret (Bryan) R.; A.B., Gettysburg U., 1870, A.M., 1873; (hon.) D.D., Wittenberg U., 1896; (hon.) LL.D., Susquehanna U., 1927; m. Clementine C. Creveling, Sept. 2, 1873; children—Anna Cornelia, Mary Virginia, Luther Milton, Thomas Creveling, Florence Isabel. Ordained to ministry U. Luth Ch. in America, 1871; pastor, Espy, Pa., 1873-75, Lewistown, Pa., 1875-88, Milton, Pa., 1888-1938, retired, 1938; served as pres. Susquehanna Luth. Synod, 1887-89; pres. Pa. State of S.S. Assn., 1887-89; served frequently as del. to Gen. Conv. Luth. Ch. Dir. Luth. Theol. Sem., Gettysburg, Pa., 1881-89. Lutheran. Author: Science and Religion, 1928. Frequent lecturer. Won Pa. State Oratorical Contest, Harrisburg, Pa., 1920. Home: 321 N. Front St., Milton, Pa.

REIMER, Rudolph Edward, treas. Dresser Mfg. Co.; b. Cincinnati, O., May 9, 1904; s. Frank and Bessie (Umbach) R.; ed. pub. sch. and high sch., Cincinnati, O., 1910-22; Com. Engr., U. of Cincinnati, 1928; m. Cleone M. Brooks, Sept. 1, 1934; children—J. Brooks, Ross Alan. Employed as comptroller S. R. Dresser Mfg. Co., mfrs. pipe line coupling and accessories, Bradford, Pa., 1929-32, treas. 1932-36, treas. and asst. gen. mgr. since 1936; treas. and dir. The Bryant Heater Co., Cleveland, O., since 1933; sec., treas., and dir. Dresser Mfg. Co., Ltd., Toronto, Can., since 1931; dir. Clark Bros. Co., Inc., Olean, N.Y. Mem. Pa. State Chamber of Commerce. Mem. Nat. Assn. Cost Accountants, Scabbard and Blade, Pi Kappa Alpha, Alpha Kappa Psi, Phi Mu Alpha. Republican. Methodist. Mason (32°). Clubs: Bradford, Penn Hills. Home: 11 Abbott Rd. Office: 41 Fisher Av., Bradford, Pa.

REIMERT, William D.; editor Chronicle and News. Address: 98 S. Center Sq., Allentown, Pa.

REIMOLD, Abraham Gottlob Heinrich, pres. Woburn Degreasing Co. (N.J.); b. Terre Haute, Ind., Dec. 20, 1892; s. Abraham Gottlob and Marie Katherine (Schmidheiser) R.; A.B., Yale U., 1913; m. Erica Wilhelma Eva Marie Johanna Countess von Hacke, April 28, 1937. Laborer Woburn Degreasing Co., 1913, mgr., 1914-18, gen. mgr., 1918-26, pres. since 1926; v.p. Harrison Kearny Trust Co., 1927-38; pres. Zenitherm Co., Inc., 1927-32; pres. Woburn Degreasing Co. of N.J., Woburn Degreasing Co. of Can., Ltd., Woburn, Inc. First lt., Q.M.C., U.S. Army, 1918-23. Fellow Am. Geog. Soc.; dir. Agrl. Chem. Assn. (Washington, D.C.); mem. Yale Engring. Soc. Republican. German Lutheran. Clubs: Yale (New York); Essex (Newark); Essex County (West Orange); Berkeley Tennis (Orange); Orange Lawn Tennis (South Orange). Home: 610 S. Center St., Orange, N.J. Office: 1200 Harrison Av., Harrison, N.J.

REINFELD, Abraham G., physician; b. Austria, Apr. 19, 1893; s. Morris and Ann (Schneck) R.; brought to U.S., 1895, naturalized, 1901; M.D., U. of Pa. Med. Sch., 1916; grad. study, U. of Vienna, 1921-23, U. of Bordeaux, France, 1929; m. Frieda Harris, Feb. 17, 1925. Surgeon specializing in diseases of ear, nose and throat and plastic surgery, Newark, N.J., since 1923; mem. staff Newark City, Beth Israel and Newark Eye and Ear hosps. Fellow Am. Coll. Surgeons; mem. Essex County Med. Soc. Home: 354 Clinton Av., Newark, N.J.

REINHOLD, Paul Becker, machinery and limestone; b. Marietta, Pa., May 7, 1890; s. Edwin Lesher and Isabella Hoover (Becker) R.; student Tome Sch., Port Deposit, Md., 1905-08; Lehigh U., 1913; m. Anna Pentland Stewart, Dec. 29, 1929. In employ Penn Motor Car Co., 1912; with Pittsburgh Crucible Steel Co., 1912; with Crucible Steel Co. of America, 1912-22; pres. and treas. Reinhold & Co., Inc., limestone, Pittsburgh, Pa., since 1922; pres. and treas. Atlas Equipment Corpn., machinery. Former dir. Bellefonte Central R.R.; 1st vice-pres. Am. Road Builders Assn.; sec. and treas. Pa. Stone Producers Assn. for 10 yrs. Mem. Engring. Soc. of Pa., Am. Soc. of Mil. Engrs., Phi Delta Theta. Republican. Episcopalian. Mason. Club: Pittsburgh Athletic. Home: Schenley Apts. Office: Oliver Bldg., Pittsburgh, Pa.

REITER, Howard Roland, univ. prof.; b. Philadelphia, Pa., June 8, 1871; s. Benjamin O. and Catherine (Slaw) R.; grad. Pennington Sch., 1894; A.B., Pinceton U., 1898, A.M., 1900; attended Princeton Theol. Sch., 1900-03, New York Law Sch., 1904, also Harvard U. Summer Sch.; m. Edith Louise Burt, Jan. 7, 1905; children—Dr. Benjamin Reynolds, Howard Burt. Dir. athletics and coach, Wesleyan U., Middletown, Conn., 1905-10; instr. theory and practice of football, Harvard Summer Sch., 1916-26; instr. in applied psychology, Harvard Summer Sch. of Physical Edn., 1921-24; prof. physical edn., Lehigh U., since 1910, athletic director, 1910-26. Chairman Eastern Intercollegiate Wrestling Rules Committee, 2 years. Member Omicron Delta Kappa (charter mem. at Lehigh University, 1924), Sword and Crescent. Clubs: Mafia, Cottage (Princeton); Touch-Down (New York). Speaker before clubs and churches and on radio. Home: Sayre Park, Bethlehem, Pa.

REITER, Manoah Raymond, supervising prin. schs.; b. Red Hill, Pa., Nov. 1, 1894; s. Manoah A. and Maggie C. (Weiss) R.; A.B., Muhlenberg Coll., 1927; M.S., U. of Pa., 1939; m. Sadie Harpel, July 13, 1923; children—Lucille Harpel, Kathryn Naomi. Teacher in rural schs. and borough schs., 1911-27; prin. high sch., Morrisville, Pa., 1927-29, supervising prin. pub. schs., Morrisville, Pa., since 1929. Served as sergt. arty., U.S.A., 1917-19 with A.E.F. in France. Mem. Am. Assn. Sch. Adminstrs., Phi Delta Kappa, Am. Legion. Republican. Mem. M.E. Ch. Club: Rotary of Morrisville. Home: 208 W. Franklin St., Morrisville, Pa.

REITER, Murray C(harles), clergyman; b. New Texas, Allegheny Co., Pa., July 21, 1878; s. George W. and Ida Florence (Kistler) R.; prep. edn. Oakdale Acad. and Pittsburgh Acad., 1895-96; A.B., Grove City Coll., 1900, D.D., 1931; B.D., Western Theol. Sem., 1903; m. Emma Lena Beck, June 17, 1903; children—Lois Marguerite (Mrs. Edward Gray Albright), Frederick George, Murray Charles. Ordained to ministry of Presbyterian Ch., 1903; pastor Wilson and Clairton Chs., Pittsburgh, 1903-07; pastor Chartiers Ch. (founded 1775), Pittsburgh, 1907-14; pastor Bethel Ch., Pittsburgh, since 1914 (Bethel Ch., founded 1776, has had but 5 pastors). Trustee Grove City Coll.; trustee Presbytery of Pittsburgh. Republican. Home: Route 9, Pittsburgh, Pa.

REITZ, Walter Raleigh, oil refining; b. Barnesville, O., Dec. 8, 1885; s. George Frederick and Annie (Richter) R.; ed. Marion (Ind.) high sch., Sistersville (W.Va.) high sch., West Va. U.; m. Annie Elder Stanbery, Sept. 29, 1919 (died Jan. 15, 1929); m. 2d, Dorothy Anne Brown, June 30, 1934. Employed as cashier Farmers and Producers Nat. Bank, Sistersville, W.Va., 1908-10, cashier, 1910-22; pres. Union Nat. Bank, 1922-31; sec. and treas. Reno Oil Co. since 1919; sec. and treas. Ohio Valley Refining Co., 1919-31; sec. and dir. Quaker State Oil Refining Corpn. since 1931; pres. and dir. Enterprise Oil Co.; vice-pres. and dir. Oil City Nat. Bank, Oil City, Pa., Union Nat. Bank, Sistersville, W.Va. Served as 1st lieut. Ord. Dept., World War. Mem. W.Va. Senate, 1927-31. Mem. Delta Tau Delta. Republican. Presbyn. Mason. Club: Wenango Country. Home: 1206 W. First St. Office: Oil City, Pa.

REMAK, Gustavus, Jr., insurance exec.; b. Phila., Pa., Mar. 19, 1861; s. Gustavus and Sue M. (Scott) R.; grad. Episcopal Acad., Phila., 1878; A.B., U. of Pa., 1882, LL.B., 1884; m. Caroline H. Voorhees, June 10, 1896; children—Margaret Onderdonk (Mrs. Horatio H. Morris), Caroline Voorhees (Mrs. John B. Ramsay, Jr.). Admitted to Pennsylvania bar, 1884, and practiced at Philadelphia until 1930; president The Insurance Co. of State of Pa. since 1913. Republican. Episcopalian. Clubs: Rittenhouse, Down Town. Home: Prospect Av., Chestnut Hill, Phila. Office: 308 Walnut St., Philadelphia, Pa.

REMER, Daniel Flick, physician; b. Hughesville, Pa., June 27, 1885; s. Simon Peter and Martha Alice (Flick) R.; student Central Pa. Coll., New Berlin, 1900-02, Bucknell U., 1902-04; M.D., U. of Pa., 1910; post grad. study eye, ear, nose and throat, U. of Pa., 1923-26, U. of Vienna, Austria, 1927; m. Edith Sharp Bailey, Oct. 1, 1913; 1 dau., Mary Leighton. Interne Howard Hosp., Phila., 1910-12; gen. practice of medicine, Medford, N.J., 1912-16; gen. practice, Mt. Holly, N.J., 1916-26, specialist in eye, ear, nose and throat since 1926; county pysician and adviser to prosecutor, Burlington County, N.J., 1918-30. Mem. A.M.A., Phi Alpha Sigma. Republican. Episcopalian. Mason, Elk. Clubs: Union League, Phila. Medical (Phila.); Burlington County Country (Mt. Holly). Home: 417 High St. Address: Mt. Holly, N.J.

REMICK, Walter Leigh, business exec.; b. Methuen, Mass., Jan. 19, 1883; s. George A. and Sarah E. (Pillsbury) R.; A.B., Harvard, 1909; m. Florence Erminie Ayer, Dec. 29, 1921; children—Esther Louise, Sarah Elizabeth. Chemist Western Steel Corpn., 1910-11; engr. Alaska Gold Mines, Inc., 1911-15; supt. sulphur dioxide plant Va. Smelting Co., 1916-17; metallurgist U.S. Metals Refining Co., 1917-20; test engr. Research Corpn., 1920-21; instr. mining dept., Carnegie Inst. Tech., 1921-24; editor Keystone Pub. Co., 1922-24; sec.-treas. and mgr. Hydrotator Co., Hazleton, Pa., since 1924, now also dir. Mem. Am. Inst. Mining Engrs. Republican. Presbyterian. Writer various tech. papers. Home: 80 N. Church St., Hazleton, Pa.

REMPE, P. J.; v.p. Bangor Gas Co.; officer or dir. many pub. service companies. Office: Hagerstown, Md.

REMSEN, Gerard Townsend, lawyer; b. Dobbs Ferry, N.Y., Apr. 8, 1894; s. Daniel Smith and Louise (Townsend) R.; grad. Mackenzie Sch., Dobbs Ferry, 1906, Brooklyn Poly. Prep. Sch., 1909; B.S., New York U., 1914; LL.B., New York Law Sch., 1917; m. Helen Hubbard Henze, Oct. 12, 1920; children—Eleanor, Gerard Townsend. Admitted to N.Y. bar, 1917; associated with Einstein, Townsend & Guiterman, 1915-17, Remsen & Parsons, 1917-22, Townsend & Guiterman, 1922-28; partner Remsen, Burton-Smith & Remsen, 1928-31, Remsen & Remsen since 1931. Mem. bd. mgrs. New York Kindergarten Assn. since 1930, pres., 1938, sec., 1939. Mem. Am. Bar Assn., N.Y. State Bar Assn., Delta Phi. Republican. Conglist. Co-author: Preparation of Wills and Trusts, 1930. Editor: Intestate Succession in New York (5th edit.), 1918. Home: 102 Inwood Av., Upper Montclair, N.J. Office: 1 Cedar St., New York, N.Y.

RENCH, Walter Freeman, mng. editor and field rep.; b. Catoctin, Md., Dec. 12, 1868; s. John Henry and Eleanor C. (Bartlett) R.; C.E., Lehigh U., Bethlehem, Pa., 1891; m. Mary Louise Schafer, June 15, 1898; children—Marie Julia (wife Dr. William R. Pentz), Margaret Eleanor (Mrs. Frank Lee Townsend), Anne, Clari Louise (Mrs. J. Jason Bigelow), Edna Elizabeth (Mrs. Bernard J. Douredoure), Dorothea (Mrs. William J. Mick), Elsie May (dec.). In employ engring dept. Pa. R.R., Wilmington, Del., 1892-1900, supervisor of tracks, 1900-17; resigned to engage in constrn. work incidental to War, at Camp Dix, N.J. and Hog Island, Phila., 1917-19; asso. with Simmons-Boardman Pub. Co., New York and Chicago, since 1919, mng. editor Ry. Engring. and Maintenance Cyc., 1926 and 1929 edits., now field rep. in circulation dept. Mem. Am. Ry. Engring. Assn. Republican. Methodist. Mason. Club: Philadelphia Lehigh (since inception 1892). Author: Simplified Curve and Switch Work, 1917; Roadway and Track, 1921; Practical Trackwork, 1926. Home: 1117 Marlyn Rd., Philadelphia, Pa.

RENFRO, Charles Harold, public utility mgr.; b. Guthrie, Okla., Mar. 11, 1894; s. Charles Raymond and Margaret (Mack) R.; student Worcester (Mass.) Acad., 1909-11, Rensselaer Poly. Inst., Troy, N.Y., 1911-13; B.S. in elec. engring., Ore. State Coll., Corvallis, Ore., 1916; m. Helen Louise Seward, May 1, 1920; children—Charles Seward, Richard Mack. Apprentice, line and meter work, Guthrie (Okla.) Light & Power Co., part time, 1907-09; meter testing, gen. engring., etc., Ore. Power Co., Eugene & Corvallis, Ore., part time, 1913-16; student test course Gen. Electric Co., Schenectady, N.Y., 1916-17; inspection engr. Western Electric Co., Chicago, 1919-21; power sales engr. Potomac Electric Power Co., Washington, D.C., 1921-27; power sales engr. Pa. Power & Light Co., Allentown, Pa., 1927-36, commercial mgr. since 1936. Served as 1st lt., Engr. Corps, U.S. Army, in charge production Office Chief of Engrs., 1918-19; now capt. Engr. Res. assigned to Chief of Engrs. Mem. Allentown Chamber of Commerce, Am. Legion, Res. Officers' Assn. (past sec. Dept. of Pa., now dept. historian), Mil. Order of Fgn. Wars, Delta Beta Delta, Sigma Tau. Republican. Lutheran. Mason (32°). Clubs: Four Square of Allentown (past pres.); Engrs. of Lehigh Valley; Interstate Power (New York), Kiwanis. Home: 3012 Greenleaf St. Office: 901 Hamilton St., Allentown, Pa.

RENO, Claude Trexler, lawyer; b. Lyons, Pa., Apr. 4, 1882; s. Joseph F. and Millie (Trexler) R.; student Allentown (Pa.) High Sch., 1897-1900, Muhlenberg Coll., 1900-02; LL.B., Dickinson Coll. Sch. of Law, 1905; (hon.) LL.D., Muhlenberg College, 1928, Moravian College, Bethlehem, Pa., 1939; married May G. Appel, Aug. 14, 1906. Admitted to Pa. bar, 1905, and since engaged in gen. practice at Allentown; co. solicitor of Lehigh Co., 1908-12; mem. Pa. Ho. of Rep., 1910-12; city solicitor of Allentown, 1920-21; apptd. judge 31st Dist., 1921; elected president judge and served 10 yrs. voluntarily retiring to resume practice of law; apptd. atty. gen. of Pa., Jan. 18, 1939. Trustee Allentown Hosp., Luth. Theol. Sem. at Phila. Mem. Alpha Tau Omega (nat. pres. 1930-33). Republican. Lutheran (mem. exec. bd. United Luth. Ch.). Mason. Elk. Club: Livingston. Home: 325 N. 28th St., Allentown, Pa. Office: Dept. of Justice, Harrisburg, Pa.

RENTSCHLER, Harvey Clayton, physics; b. Hamburg, Pa., Mar. 26, 1881; s. Joseph F. and Rebecca (Ritzman) R.; B.A., Princeton, 1903, M.A., 1904; Ph.D., Johns Hopkins, 1908; m. Margaret Bender, 1904; 1 son, Lawrence Bender. Instr. physics, U. of Mo., 1908-10, asst. prof., 1910-13, asso. prof., 1913-17; dir. of research lamp div. Westinghouse Electric & Mfg. Co. since 1917. Fellow A.A.A.S.; mem. Am. Optical Soc., Am. Physical Soc., New York Elec. Soc. (past pres.), Am. Inst. of Science (New York), Sigma Xi, Epsilon Chi, Sigma Pi Sigma. Presbyn. Democrat. Mason. Contbr. to tech. publs. Home: 15 Monroe Av., East Orange, N.J.

RENTZ, Frederick Loeffler, pres. New Castle News Co.; b. New Castle, Pa., Mar. 12, 1868; s. John Veit and Eva Catherine (Fehler) R.; student pub. schs.; m. Annabel Masonheimer, Sept. 5, 1889; children—Ethel Agnes (Mrs. W. E. Ferver), Jacob Frederick; m. 2d, Kate Long, June 8, 1917. With New Castle News Co. since 1882, beginning as printer's devil, later becoming foreman of composing room, then manager and one-third owner, now pres. Elected mayor, New Castle, 1923; del. Rep. Nat. Conv., 1920. Chmn. Civilian Relief Com., 1917-19; worked 1 day each week on farms during World War. First pres. New Castle Trades Assembly; chmn. at dedication Pymatuning Dam and mem. Pymatuning Dam Commn., 20 yrs.; pres. hosp. bds., 30 yrs.; presented summer camp to local Y.M.C.A., Nov. 1, 1938, and was honored as first citizen at first annual Distinguished Citizen's Day in New Castle, Pa. Mem. Red Cross and Community Chest, Lion's Club Blind Fund. V.p. Perry Highway Assn.; dir. Benjamin Franklin Highway Assn. Mem. New Castle Chamber Commerce (pres. 1929), Am. Newspaper Assn., Jameson Memorial Hosp. Assn., Typographical Union (hon.), Vets. Foreign Wars (hon.), Am. Legion (hon.), G.A.R. (hon.). Clubs: New Castle Field, Rotary (ex-pres.), New Castle Motor (dir.), Lion's (hon.). Mason (32°). Delivered first speech made in New Castle Scottish Rite Cathedral, Oct. 29, 1926. Home: 315 Edison Av. Office: New Castle News Co., New Castle, Pa.

REOCH, Alexander Ernest, elec. engring.; b. Sheffield, Eng., Apr. 27, 1884; s. John Fife and Clara (Furness) R.; E.E., Sheffield Univ., Eng., 1902; came to America, 1905, naturalized citizen, U.S.A., 1924; m. Ella Stanley Jenking, Apr. 9, 1912; children—Margaret Helen, John Jenking, William Stanley. Employed as wireless engr., English Marconi Co., 1902-05; wireless engr., treas., sec., chief engr., Canadian Marconi Co., Montreal, Can., 1905-17; research engr. American Marconi Co., New York, 1917-19; asst. chief engr. Radio Corpn. of America, 1919-26, vice-pres. in charge production and service, 1926-29; vice-pres. RCA Photophone, 1929-33; mgr. real estate, Radio-Keith-Orpheum Corpn. since 1933. Mem. Inst. Radio Engrs., The Franklin Inst. Clubs: Orange Lawn Tennis (South Orange); Braidburn Country (Madison); Engineers (New York City). Home: 485 Mayhew Ct., South Orange, N.J. Office: 1270 Sixth Av., New York, N.Y.

REPASS, Ellis Arthur, clergyman; b. Rural Retreat, Va., Aug. 21, 1874; s. Luther Kurtz and Margaret Ann (Crabtree) R.; A.B., Roanoke Coll., Salem, Va., 1897; Ph.D., Central U., Indianapolis, Ind., 1904; ed. Luth. Theol. Sem., Phila., Pa., 1897-1900; (hon.) D.D., Roanoke Coll., 1936; m. Mary Florence Burch, Aug. 28, 1900; 1 son, John Howard. Ordained to ministry Luth. Ch., 1900; pastor, Mt. Tabor, Va., 1900-03, Bethlehem, Va., 1903-07, New Market, Va., 1907-15, Harrisonburg, Va., 1915-17, Salisbury, N.C., 1917-18, Mercersburg, Pa., 1918-24, Lancaster, Pa., 1925, Columbia, Pa., since 1926. Republican. Lutheran. Contbr. verse to anthologies and mags., sermons to pub. vols., articles to Luth. Ch. mags. Home: 454 Chestnut St., Columbia, Pa.

REPLOGLE, Delbert Earl, elec. engring., mfr.; b. Douglas, Alaska, July 31, 1896; s. Charles Nathaniel and Mae (Newton) R.; A.B., Pacific Coll., Newburg, Ore., 1916, B.S., same, 1916; B.S., Mass. Inst. Tech., 1924, M.S., same, 1925; Professional Engr., Univ. State of N.Y., 1929; m. Ruth Cordis Hinshaw, Sept. 8, 1918; children—Charles Vernon, Cordis Alene, Bruce Delbert. Employed as exec. maintenance dept. Boston Edison Co., 1925-26; head development div., Raytheon Mfg. Co., 1926-29; lab. new products div., National Carbon Co., 1929-30; vice-pres. Jenkins Television Corpn., 1930-31; vice-pres. De Forest Radio Co., 1931-32; chief engr. electronic div., Hygrade Sylvania Corpn., 1932-33; pres. Electronic Mechanics, Inc., mfrs. elec. insulation, Paterson, N.J., since 1933; pres. Powrex Switch Co., Waltham, Mass., since 1929. Served as supt. reservation in Alaska, 1918-20. Fellow Radio Club of America. Mem. Radio Inst. Engrs. Republican. Mem. Religious Soc. Friends. Home: 443 Meadowbrook Av., Ridgewood. Office: 85 Hazel St., Paterson, N.J.

REPPLIER, Agnes, author; b. (of French parentage) Phila., Pa., Apr. 1, 1858; d. John George and Agnes (Mathias) R.; ed. Sacred Heart Convent, Torresdale, Pa.; Litt.D., U. of Pa., 1902; Yale U., 1925, Columbia, 1927, Princeton, 1935; unmarried. Prominent as essayist; spends much time in Europe. Catholic. Laetare medal, U. of Notre Dame, 1911; gold medal of Acad. of Arts and Letters. Author: Books and Men, 1888; Points of View, 1891; Essays in Miniature, 1892; Essays in Idleness, 1893; In the Dozy Hours, 1894; Varia, 1897; Philadelphia—The Place and the People; The Fireside Sphinx, 1901; Compromises, 1904; In Our Convent Days, 1905; A Happy Half Century, 1908; Americans and Others, 1912; The Cat, 1912; Counter Currents, 1915; Points of Friction, 1920; Under Dispute, 1924; Life of Père Marquette, 1929; Mere Marie, of the Ursulines, 1931; To Think of Tea, 1932; In Pursuit of Laughter, 1936; Decades, 1937. Compiler of A Book of Famous Verse. Clubs: The Acorn, College, Cosmopolitan. Home: 920 Clinton St., Philadelphia, Pa.

REPPLIER, Sidney J., physician; b. Reading, Pa., Jan. 5, 1881; s. J. Lancaster and Sidney T. (Berghaus) R.; ed. Princeton, 1899-1900; M.D., U. of Pa. Med. Sch., 1904; m. Charlotte W. Neall, Aug. 11, 1910; children—Sidney N., Frances N. After usual interneships engaged in practice of medicine in Phila. continuously since 1904; med. dir. Curtis Pub. Co., Phila., since 1912. Served as lieut. then capt. Med. Res. Corps, U.S.A., 1917-19. Mem. Am. Med. Assn., Coll. of Phys. Phila., Phi Kappa Psi, Phi Alpha Sigma. Republican. Club: Princeton of Philadelphia. Home: 415 Roumfort Rd. Office: Curtis Pub. Co., Philadelphia, Pa.

REQUARDT, John M.; in practice of law at Baltimore. Office: 100 St. Paul St., Baltimore, Md.

RESCIGNO, Peter John, banker; b. Paterson, N.J., Sept. 18, 1899; s. Pasquale and Mary (Frank) R.; student Paterson (N.J.) High Sch., 1914-18, Princeton U., 1918, N.Y.U., 1919; m. Catherine O'Neill, Apr. 20, 1922; 1 dau., Patricia Joan. Partner Linares & Rescigno, pvt. bankers, Paterson, N.J., 1920-33, v.p. Linares & Rescigno State Bank, Paterson, N.J., since 1933; owner and operator Peter J. Rescigno Travel Service, Paterson, N.J., since 1936; dir. Benefactor Bldg. & Loan Assn. Pres. Sinking Fund Commn., City of Paterson (N.J.). Mem. Kappa Sigma. Catholic. Elk. Club: Kiwanis (Paterson, N.J.). Home: 283 Eighth Av. Office: 208 Market St., Paterson, N.J.

RETAN, George Austin, dir. laboratory schools; b. Millerton, Pa., Oct. 15, 1886; s. Edmund Arnold and Reua Budlong (Cole) R.; Pd.M., Mansfield Normal Sch., 1904; B.F., State Forest Sch., 1909; Ph. D., N.Y. Univ., 1932; grad. study, Hochschule, Darmstadt, Germany, 1910-11 (winter); m. Edith Walters, Oct. 4, 1911; children—Edith Jeannette, George Walter. Teacher, high sch., 1904-06; forester, 1909-12; prof. forestry, State Forest Sch., 1912-18; prin. schs., 1918-26; dir. lab. schs., Mansfield State Teachers Coll. since 1926. Served as mem. Pa.

REUSSILLE, **Leon, Jr.**, lawyer; b. Red Bank, N.J., May 26, 1890; s. Leon de la and Anna (Degenring) R.; Litt.B., Princeton U., 1913; LL.B., Harvard U. Law Sch., 1916; m. Frances Truex, Sept. 20, 1920. Admitted to N.J. bar, 1917, and since engaged in gen. practice of law at Red Bank; mem. firm Applegate, Stevens, Foster & Reussille since 1927; dir. Second Nat. Bank & Trust Co. of Red Bank; atty. for Borough of Sea Bright, N.J. Served as 1st lt. inf. U.S.A. during World War. Mem. Monmouth Co. Bar Assn. Democrat. Episcopalian. Clubs: Lions, Yacht (Red Bank); Monmouth County Country (Eatontown). Home: 196 Broad St., Red Bank, N.J. Office: 34 Broad St., Red Bank, N.J.

REUTER, **Frederick Brian**, banking; b. Lewisham, Kent, Eng., Mar. 17, 1897; s. Leopold Frederick and Emma Catherine (Brown) R.; came to U.S., 1925, naturalized citizen, 1932; ed. City of London Sch., 1909-14; m. Kathryn Ellen Bernegger, July 1, 1939. Banking and commercial interests, London, and in Greece, 1919-35; in investment banking, N.Y. City, 1925-32; asst. vice-pres. Girard Trust Co., Phila., Pa., 1932-35; vice-pres. Union Trust Co., Pittsburgh, Pa., since 1935; dir. Farmers Deposit Nat. Bank, Pittsburgh, Farmers Deposit Trust Co., Pittsburgh, Reliance Life Ins. Co. of Pittsburgh. Served with inf. and machine gun corps, Gt. Britain, on Western Front, 1914-18. Republican. Roman Catholic. Clubs: Duquesne (Pittsburgh); Allegheny Country (Sewickley). Home: Shields, Sewickley, Pa. Office: The Union Trust Co. of Pittsburgh, Pittsburgh, Pa.

REUTER, **Otto K.**, newspaper editor; b. Montgomery, W.Va., Feb. 18, 1910; s. Otto Conrad and Nell (Kruthoffer) R.; A.B., New River State Coll., Montgomery, W.Va., 1931; m. Margaret Morris, Sept. 24, 1937. Engaged as editor and part propr. Upper-Kanawha Times, Montgomery, W.Va., 1932-35; city editor, Hinton Daily News, Hinton, W.Va., 1935-36, editor, 1936-37, mng. editor since 1937. Republican. Methodist. Clubs: Kiwanis, New River and Greenbrier Valley Assn. (Hinton). Home: Greenbrier Drive, Bellepoint. Office: 210 Second Av., Hinton, W.Va.

REVER, **R. Rossiter**; v.p. Equitable Trust Co. Office: Calvert and Fayette Sts., Baltimore, Md.

REVERCOMB, **William Chapman**, lawyer; b. Covington, Va., July 20, 1895; s. George Anderson and Elizabeth (Chapman) R.; student Washington and Lee U., Lexington, Va., 1914-16; LL.B., U. of Va., 1919; m. Sara V. Hughes, June 9, 1926; children—William, George, Ann, James. Admitted to Va. bar, 1919, and practiced in Covington, 1919-22; admitted to W.Va. bar, 1922, and since in gen. civil practice, Charleston; dir. Citizens Nat. Bank, Covington, Big Rock Land Co. Served as corpl. Batt. A, 35th Coast Arty., U.S. Army, during World War. Mem. Rep. State Exec. Com. 1932-36; pres. Young Rep. League of W.Va., 1934-36. Mem. Am. Bar Assn., W.Va. Bar Assn., Charleston Bar Assn. (pres. 1938), Am. Legion, Raven Soc., Phi Kappa Sigma, Phi Delta Phi, Delta Sigma Rho. Republican. Presbyterian. Elk, Moose. Club: Edgewood Country (Charleston). Home: 917 Edgewood Drive. Office: 1518 Kanawha Valley Bldg., Charleston, W.Va.

REVERE, **Clinton T.**, broker; b. San Francisco, Calif., 1873; ed. pub. schs.; married; 4 children. Admitted to bar and practiced law; in newspaper business, Washington, D.C., and N.Y. City, 1899-1903; began as broker, associated with Daniel J. Sully in cotton market, 1903; now mem. Stock Exchange firm Munds, Winslow & Potter, N.Y. City. Mem. New York Coffee & Sugar Exchange, Commodity Exchange, N.Y. Cocoa Exchange. Clubs: Commodity (v.p.), India House, Baltusrol Golf, Pine Valley Golf. Author: Representative industries (in collaboration with others), 1928; Hands as Bands (novel), 1932. Contbr. short stories and articles on econ. subjects to mags. Represented U.S. as guest speaker, Internat. Cotton Congress, Paris, 1931, Rome, 1935, Cairo, Egypt, 1938. Address on Individual Capitalism vs. Political Liberalism received internat. circulation and analyses of cotton problems attract worldwide attention. Home: Westfield, N.J. Office: 40 Wall St., New York, N.Y.*

REYNARD, **Grant**, artist; b. Grand Island, Neb., Oct. 20, 1887; s. Stephen Blackstone and Jenny (Lind) R.; student Grand Island (Neb.) High Sch., 1901-04, Art Inst., Chicago, Ill. 1906, Acad. of Fine Arts, Chicago, Ill., 1909-13, Art Students League (under Harry Wickey), New York, 1929-30; studied under Mahonri Young, New York, 1916-18; m. Gwendolen Crawford, Sept. 22, 1917; children—Barbara Ann, Mary Tyson. Began as art dir. Red Book Mag., Chicago, Ill., 1913; illustration with Charles S. Chapman and Harvey Dunn, New York, 1914-15; copying in museums, Paris and London, 1923; teacher of drawing, Grand Central Sch. of Art, New York, 1930-36; represented in Met. Mus., New York; Fogg Mus., Cambridge, Mass.; Addison Gallery of Am. Art, Andover, Mass.; De Young Memorial Mus., San Francisco, Calif.; N.J. State Mus., Trenton, N.J.; Newark (N.J.) Art Mus.; Newark (N.J.) Pub. Library; Library of Congress, Washington, D.C.; New York Pub. Library; U. of Tulsa (Okla.); one man shows: Kennedy Gallery, New York; Leonard Clayton Gallery, New York; Grand Central Gallery, New York; Addison Gallery of Am. Art, Andover, Mass.; U. of Neb., Lincoln, Neb.; Joslyn Memorial Mus., Omaha, Neb.; U. of Tulsa (Okla.); numerous art socs. and museums; lecturer on painting and etching before univs. and clubs; demonstrations at Nat. Arts Club, MacDowell Club, Art Students League, New York; teacher of art (part time), Millbrook (N.Y.) Sch. for Boys since 1937; artist in residence, Palo Duro Sch. of Art, Canyon, Tex., summers 1938, 39; work in Fifty Prints of Year, 1932, Fine Prints of the Year, 1937, 100 Prints of Am. Soc. of Etchers, 1933, 34, 35, 38; prints in Contemporary American Etching, 1930, Contemporary American Prints, 1931; invited to exhibit at Century of Progress, Chicago, Ill., 1934, New York World's Fair, 1939. Awarded scholarship for summer work at MacDowell Colony, Peterborough, N.H., 1926-34; Carrington Prize for oil painting at Salmagundi Club, 1939. Mem. Am. Water Color Soc. (life), Am. Soc. of Etchers, Phila. Soc. of Etchers, Prairie Print Soc., American Artists Professional League, N.J. Water Color Soc. Baptist. Clubs: Am. Artists Group, Salmagundi Club (New York). Address: 312 Christie Heights, Leonia, N.J.

REYNOLDS, **C. J.**; urologist Bluefield Sanitarium. Address: Bluefield Sanitarium, Bluefield, W.Va.

REYNOLDS, **Charles Bingham**, author; b. Morrisania, N.Y., 1854; s. Charles O. and Lucy W.R.; A.B., Amherst, 1876; m. Miss E. Thomas, 1879. Editor Forest and Stream, 1879-1906. Author: Old St. Augustine, A Story of Three Centuries, 1885; Standard Guide to Cuba, 1905; Standard Guide to Havana, 1905; Standard Guide to St. Augustine, East Coat of Florida and Nassau, 1905; Standard Guide to Washington, 1905; Standard Guide to New York, 1906. Compiled Game Laws in Brief, 1905; Fugitives from Fate to the Port of the Havana, 1911. Home: Mountain Lakes, N.J.

REYNOLDS, **Charles Lee**, clergyman; b. De Graff, O., May 10, 1874; s. James Irwin and Julia Elvira (Reeves) R.; A.B., Washington and Jefferson Coll., 1896; grad. McCormick Theological Seminary, 1899; D.D., Coe College, Cedar Rapids, Iowa, 1906; m. Agnes Bush Pearson, Nov. 11, 1902 (died Aug. 12, 1938); children—Mrs. Eleanor Pearson McConnell, Margaret Pearson. Ordained Presbyn. ministry, 1899; pastor Cottage Grove Av. Ch., Des Moines, Ia., 1899-1906, 2d Ch. Lexington, Ky., 1906-16, Park Ch., Newark, N.J., 1916-28; supt. ch. extension, Newark Presbytery, 1928—. Moderator Synod of Ky., 1915; dir. Bd. of Christian Edn., Gen. Board of Education and College Bd. Presbyterian Church of United States of America; former pres. Newark Fed. of Chs.; dir. N.J. Temperance Soc. (sec.), N.J. Anti-Saloon League, N.J. Council Religious Edn. (sec.), Goodwill Home and Rescue Mission; v.p. Presbyn. Hosp. Member S.A.R., Kappa Chi, Phi Delta Theta, Theta Nu Epsilon. Clubs: Clergy (New York); Rotary, Wednesday (Newark). Author: The Virgin Birth, 1907; Kentucky for Christ, 1912; Four Square Life, 1913; Our Country for the World, 1917; A Nation's Prayer for Strength, 1917; also numerous articles and poems in mags. Contributed a weekly sermon to Ky. newspapers for 3½ yrs. Gov. 3d dist., Internat. Assn. of Rotary Clubs, 1920-21. Exchange preacher in Europe, summer 1936. Home: 520. Clifton Av. Office: 909 Broad St., Newark, N.J.

REYNOLDS, **Clarence Newton**, prof. of mathematics; b. Nashua, N.H., Feb. 7, 1890; s. Clarence N. and Sarah Whitmarsh (Damon) R.; grad. Malden (Mass.) High Sch., 1909; Ph.B., Brown U., 1913, A.M., 1914; Ph.D., Harvard, 1919; m. Ada B. Compton, May 13, 1922 (died Jan. 29, 1935); 1 dau., Phyllis Damon. Instr. in mathematics, Brown U., 1913-14, Wesleyan U. (Conn.), 1916-20, Dartmouth Coll., 1920-21; with U. of W.Va. since 1921, successively asst. prof., asso. prof., 1921-31, prof. of mathematics since 1931, acting head of dept. since 1938. Fellow A.A.A.S.; mem. Am. Math. Soc., Math. Assn. of America, Phi Beta Kappa, Sigma Xi. Home: 217 McLane Av., Morgantown, W.Va.

REYNOLDS, **Frank William**, pres. First Nat. Bank of Genesee; b. Millport, Pa., May 25, 1886; s. Lamont D. and Hattie (Eastman) R.; student Ulysses (Pa.) pub. schs.; m. Ruth Madeline Clark, Sept. 16, 1916; 1 dau., Joyce Marie. Clk. Genesee (Pa.) Banking Co., 1906-10, Genesee Chem. Co., 1911-17; cashier First Nat. Bank of Genesee, Pa., 1917-32, now dir., pres. and cashier since 1932; dir. Genesee Citizens Water Co., Oswayo Chem. Co. Mason. Address: First National Bank of Genesee, Genesee, Pa.

REYNOLDS, **John Earle**, banking; b. Meadville, Pa., Feb. 25, 1864; s. William and Julia Eliza (Thorp) R.; ed. Phillips Exeter Acad., 1884; A.B., Harvard, 1888; hon. A.M., Allegheny Coll., 1934; m. Katherine A. Shryock, May 20, 1911. Admitted to Pa. bar, 1890 and engaged in gen. practice of law at Meadville; became interested in real estate and gave up practice of law and entered business; treas. Meadville Gas and Water Co., then pres.; pres. Crawford Mutual Ins. Co., Merchants Nat. Bank and Trust Co.; vice-pres. Meadville Malleable Iron Co.; sec., treas. Meadville Conneaut Lake & Linesville R.R. Co.; dir. McCroskey Tool Corpn. Served two terms as mem. Meadville City Council, two terms local Bd. Health, three terms as Mayor of Meadville. Now pres. Meadville Library, Art & Hist. Assn. Clubs: Taylor Hose, Country, Iroquois Boating and Fishing (Meadville); University (New York). Contbr. hist. arts. to papers and mags. Home: 639 The Terrace. Office: Merchants Nat. Bank & Trust Co., Meadville, Pa.

REYNOLDS, **Joseph Benson**, mathematician; b. New Castle, Pa., May 17, 1881; s. Peter Speer and Lydia Ann (Kemp) R.; grad. New Castle High Sch., 1903; A.B., Lehigh U., 1907, A.M., 1910; Ph.D., Moravian Coll., Bethlehem, Pa., 1919; m. Chloey Bessie Graham, of New Castle, Pa., July 2, 1908; children—Peter Graham, Jane Niblock (Mrs. William A. Parsons), Joseph Benson. Instr. in mathematics and astronomy, 1907-13, asst. prof., 1913-21, asso. prof. 1921-27, prof. mathematics and theoretical mechanics since 1927, acting head dept. of mathematics, 1924-25, sec. of faculty, 1924-26, Lehigh U., also supervisor in charge research Am. Soc. M.E. at Lehigh U., 1929-36. Fellow A.A. A.S.; mem. Soc. Promotion Engring. Edn., Math. Assn. America, Pi Mu Epsilon, Sigma Xi, Phi Beta Kappa. Republican. Mem. Evang. and Reformed Ch. Author: Elementary Mechanics, 1928, revised, 1934; Analytic Mechanics, 1929; Analytic Geometry and the Elements of Calculus (with Dr. F. M. Weida), 1930; Forty Lessons in Analytic Mechanics, 1939. Contbr. to professional and technical jours. Home: 721 W. Broad St., Bethlehem, Pa.

REYNOLDS, Samuel Robert Means, physiologist, coll. prof.; b. Swarthmore, Pa., Dec. 9, 1903; s. Walter Doty and Elizabeth Brown (Means) R.; A.B., Swarthmore (Pa.) Coll., 1927, M.A., 1928; student U. of Chicago, 1929; Ph.D., U. of Pa., 1931; m. Mary Elizabeth Curtis, Aug. 18, 1931; children—Nancy Tupper, Harriett Jeffers. Asst. in biology, Swarthmore (Pa.) Coll., 1927, in zoölogy, 1927-29, Hannah Leedom travelling fellow, 1929-30; asst. in physiology, U. of Pa., 1929-30, George Lieb Harrison fellow, 1930-31; nat. research fellow, med. div., Dept. Embryology, Baltimore, Md., Carnegie Inst., Washington, D.C., 1931-32; instr. physiology, Western Reserve U., Cleveland, O., 1932-33; instr. physiology, Long Island Coll. of Medicine, Brooklyn, N.Y., 1933-34, asst. prof., 1934-38, asso. prof. physiology since 1938; Guggenheim fellow, U. of Rochester (N.Y.) Sch. of Medicine and Dentistry, 1937-38. Fellow A.A.A.S.; mem. Am. Physiol. Soc., Physiol. Soc. of Phila., Am. Assn. Anatomists, Soc. for Exptl. Biology and Medicine, Sigma Xi, Phi Sigma Kappa. Presbyterian. Club: Univ. of Pennsylvania (New York). Author: Physiology of the Uterus with Clinical Correlations, 1939; contbr. articles to Physiol. Rev., Am. Physiology, Science, Endrocrinology, Anatomical Record, Nature, Jour. of Physiology, Jour. of A.M.A., Proceedings of the Soc. for Exptl. Biology and Medicine, Acta Brevia Neerl., Am. Jour. Obstetrics and Gynecology. Home: 29 Craig Pl., Cranford, N.J. Office: Long Island Coll. of Medicine, Brooklyn, N.Y.

REYNOLDS, Walter Ford, mathematician; b. Baltimore, Md., May 25, 1880; s. Robert Fuller and Catherine (Myers) R.; Baltimore City Coll., 1899; A.B., Johns Hopkins, 1902; grad. work, same univ., 1902-05; m. Ada C. Williams, June 26, 1907; children—Catherine A. Mummert, Robert W., Walter F. Instr. Baltimore City Coll., 1905-06; computer U.S. Naval Obs., Washington, D.C., Jan.-Feb. 1907; with U.S. Coast and Geodetic Survey since 1907; computer U.S. and Can. boundary survey, 1908-11; chief mathematician, 1912-24; chief sect. triangulation, div. of geodesy, since 1924. Mem. Washington Philos. Soc., Math. Assn. of America, Am. Geophysical Union, Nat. Geog. Society, Washington Acad. Sciences. Methodist. Author. Triangulation in Alabama and Mississippi, 1915; Triangulation in Maine, 1918; Relation between Plane Rectangular Co-ordinates and Geographic Positions, 1921; Manual of Triangulation Computation and Adjustment, 1927; First-Order Triangulation in Southeast Alaska, 1929; Triangulation in Missouri, 1934; Triangulation in Minnesota, 1935. Home: 848 W. 37th St., Baltimore, Md.

REYNOLDS, William Nicholas, Jr., lawyer; b. Tunkhannock, Pa., May 31, 1874; s. William Nicholas and I. Ella (Billings) R.; Ph.B., Lafayette Coll., 1897; M.S., Lafayette Coll., 1900; unmarried. Studied law, law office, 1894-97; admitted to Pa. bar, 1897 and since engaged in gen. practice of law at Wilkes-Barre; mem. firm Reynolds & Reynolds since 1898; dir. U.S. Fidelity & Guaranty Co. of Baltimore, Md. Served as maj. Pa. N.G., 1898-1900. Past chmn. Recreation Com. of Wilkes-Barre. Past vice-pres. Chamber of Commerce. Mem. Am., Pa. State, and Luzerne Co. bar assns., Phi Gamma Delta. Republican. Presbyn. Mason (Shriner). Clubs: Rotary, Westmoreland (Wilkes-Barre). Home: 59 S. Franklin St. Office: Deposit & Savings Bank Bldg., Wilkes-Barre, Pa.

REYNOLDS, William Weaver, high sch. prin.; b. Phillipsburg, N.J., Sept. 28, 1901; s. William Watkin and Christine (Weaver) R.; A.B., Lafayette Coll., Easton, Pa., 1924, A.M., 1929; student Lafayette and Pa. State grad. schs.; m. Edwina M. Trotman, June 26, 1937; 1 son, William W., Jr. Teacher pub. sch., Newton, N.J., 1924-27; instr. English, high sch., Haddonfield, N.J., 1927-30, prin. since 1930. Home: 232 Ardmore Av., Haddonfield, N.J.

REZNIKOFF, Elias Jacob, pres. The Monmouth Audit Co.; b. Elisavetgrad, Ukraine, Feb. 12, 1886; s. Jacob and Sara (Bershadskaya) R.; came to U.S., 1906, naturalized, 1911; student Elementary Parochial Schs., Ukraine, 1892-1900, under pvt. tutors, 1901-05, Samuel Joseph Prep. Sch., New York, 1906-07, N.Y.U. Sch. of Accounting, 1907-10, New York Law Sch., 1910-12; m. Pauline Rafel, June 4, 1916; children—Eda Sara (adopted; Mrs. Samuel Allen Messnick), Samuel Jacob (adopted). Began as bookkeeper, New York, 1906; exec. sec. and dir. Long Branch (N.J.) Free Loan Assn. since 1924; pres. The Monmouth Audit Co., Long Branch, N.J., since Mar. 1939; sec. Vendome-Plaza Hotel. Mem. Long Branch (N.J.) Hebrew Burial Ground Assn. (sec. since 1924). Trustee Y.M. and Y.W.H.A., Long Branch, N.J. (ex-pres.). Mem. Long Branch (N.J.) Chamber of Commerce. Mem. Monmouth County Hist. Soc. (Freehold, N.J.), Am. Acad. Polit. and Social Science, Jewish Publ. Soc. of America, Am. Jewish Congress, Zionist Organ. of America, Y.M. C.A. (Long Branch, N.J.), Boy Scouts of America, Histadruth Ivrith (society for Hebrew culture), Elisavetgrad (Ukraine) Benevolent Assn., Nat. Assn. for Advancement of Colored People, Public Welfare Soc., hon. mem. Hebrew Benevolent Soc. of Long Branch. Democrat. Hebrew religion (ex-v.p. congregation). Mason. Author: The Jews Who Stood By Washington (booklet), 1938; A Tribute to America (magazine article), 1932; numerous short stories, poems, essays. Address: 177 Union Av., Long Branch, N.J.

RHAWN, Heister Guie, newspaper editor; b. Catawissa, Pa., Aug. 10, 1892; s. William Howe and Anetta May (Partridge) R.; A.B., Franklin and Marshall Coll., Lancaster, Pa., 1915; student Dickinson Sch. of Law, Carlisle, Pa.; m. Mary Cordelia Franklin, Feb. 12, 1918; 1 dau., Harriett Virginia. Editor Clarksburg (W.Va.) Exponent since 1924. Served as pvt., World War, and as mem. staff "The Right About," pub. in New York City, by Office of Surgeon Gen. U.S.A. Mem. Am. Legion, Phi Kappa Sigma. Democrat. Episcopalian. Mason, Elk, Rotarian. Home: 260 Clay St. Address: Exponent-Telegram Bldg., Clarksburg, W.Va.

RHEAD, Frederick Hurten, potter; b. Hanley, Staffordshire, Eng., Aug. 29, 1880; s. Frederick Alfred and Adolphine (Hurten) R.; ed. Hanley Govt. Art Sch., Stoke Govt. Art Sch., Burslem Wedgwood Inst., Fenton Govt. Art Sch.; m. Lois De Humphreyville Whitcomb, Sept. 16, 1917; m. 2d, Winifred Frances Pardell, Aug. 31, 1935. Came to U.S., 1902, naturalized citizen, 1918. Art dir. Wardle Art Pottery, Hanley, 1899-1902, Roseville Potteries, Zanesville, O., 1903-08, Pottery Sch. of Peoples U., St. Louis, Mo., 1909-11, Rhead Pottery Studios, Santa Barbara, Calif., 1912-17, Am. Encaustic Tiling Co., Zanesville, 1917-27, Homer Laughlin China Co., Newell, W.Va., since 1927. Fellow Am. Ceramic Soc. (chmn. art div. 1920-25; chmn. white ware div. 1926; v.p. 1926; trustee 1926-27); mem. Archtl. League New York, U.S. Potters Association (chairman art and design com.). Awarded gold medal, San Diego Expn., 1915, Charles Fergus Binns medal, 1934. Republican. Mason. Clubs: Rotary, Country (East Liverpool). Author: Studio Pottery, 1910. Asso. editor Jour. Am. Ceramic Society; contributor weekly articles to Potters Herald; also contbr. to Collier's National Encyclopedia; lecturer and contbr. articles on ceramics. Home: 1 Forsythe Pl., East Liverpool, O. Office: Homer Laughlin China Co., Newell, W.Va.

RHEUBY, Gould G.; b. Eugene, Ind., 1868; student U. of Ind.; v.p., mem. exec. and finance coms., gen. counsel and dir. Hercules Powder Co. Home: 2413 W. 17th St. Office: Delaware Trust Bldg., Wilmington, Del.

RHINEHART, N. Porter, mining engr.; b. Bon Air, Tenn., Apr. 17, 1892; s. S. A. and Jane (Weaver) R.; prep. edn., Webb School, Bellbuckle, Tenn., 1908-11; student U. of Tenn., Knoxville, 1911-14; m. Myrtle Couts Rhinehart, Aug. 29, 1916. Mining engr. Bon Air Coal & Iron Co., 1914-16; mining engr., P. M. Snyder, coal interests, Mt. Hope, W.Va., 1916-17; cons. mining engr., Mt. Hope, 1917-33; chief W.Va. Dept. of Mines, Charleston, since 1933. Mayor, Mt. Hope, 1922-28; county commr. Fayette County, W.Va., 1933. Mem. Am. Inst. Mining Engrs., W.Va., Soc. Professional Engrs., Sigma Phi Epsilon. Democrat. Baptist. Mason. Home: 2415 Washington St. Office: State Capitol, Charleston, W.Va.

RHOAD, Hiram Franklin, clergyman; b. Lebanon Co., Pa., Mar. 14, 1878; s. Jacob and Opella (Brandt) R.; A.B., Lebanon Valley Coll., 1903, A.M., same, 1912; Ph.D., Potomac U., Washington, D.C., 1928; (hon.) D.D., Lebanon Valley Coll., 1928; m. Annie May Houser, June 21, 1901; children—William Otterbein, Luke Hiram. Ordained to ministry U. Brethren in Christ, 1902; pastor, Pine Grove, Pa., 1902-04, Lykens Circuit, 1904-07, Mannheim, Pa., 1907-09, Highspire, Pa., 1909-17, State St. Ch., Harrisburg, Pa., 1917-28, Otterbein Ch., Lancaster, Pa., since 1928. Republican. Mem. U. Brethren in Christ. Home: 113 E. Clay St., Lancaster, Pa.

RHOADS, C. Brewster, lawyer; b. Oak Lane, Phila., Pa., July 4, 1892; s. E. Clinton and Mary Gertrude (Snyder) R.; grad. William Penn Charter Sch., 1909; B.S., U. of Pa., 1912; LL.B., Harvard, 1915; m. Katherine Gage, of Phila., Apr. 5, 1920 (died Feb. 6, 1930); children—Frederic Prichett, C. Brewster, Margaret Gage; m. 2d, Priscilla Chilton Stevens of Greenwich, Conn., June 15, 1935. Admitted to Pa. bar, 1915, and was asso. with father, E. Clinton Rhoads, in Phila., 1915-17; asso. with Roberts & Montgomery (now Montgomery & McCracken) since 1919, mem. of firm since 1928; prof. of law, Temple U., 1923-30. Enlisted as private 1st Troop Phila. City Cav., May 1917; comnd. 2d lt. F.A., U.S. Army, May 1918, and assigned to 103d Ammunition Train, 28th Div.; 1st lt., Sept. 1918, and assigned to hdqrs. 53 F.A. Brig., 28th Div., as asst. operations officers; with A.E.F. in Aisne-Marne, Meuse-Argonne and Lys-Scheldt fronts; disch., May 1919. Mem. Bd. of Commrs. Abington Twp., Montgomery Co., Pa., 1932-35; apptd. State reporter of Pa. Supreme Court decisions, 1938; chmn. Phila. United Campaign for 1939 (for hospitals and charitable instns.). Mem. Am. Bar Assn., Pa. Bar Assn., Phila. Bar Assn. (mem. com. of censors, 1933-36, chmn. of com., 1935), Lawyers Club. Republican. Episcopalian. Clubs: Union League, Rittenhouse (Phila.); Huntingdon Valley Country (Abington, Pa.). Home: Washington Lane, Huntingdon Valley, Pa. Office: 1421 Chestnut St., Philadelphia, Pa.

RHOADS, Charles James; b. Germantown, Philadelphia, Oct. 4, 1872; s. James E. (1st pres. of Bryn Mawr Coll.) and Margaret Wilson (Ely) R.; grad. William Penn Charter Sch., Phila., 1889; A.B., Haverford Coll., 1893 (Phi Beta Kappa); m. Lillie Frishmuth, Nov. 9, 1912. Began as clk. Girard Trust Co., Phila., 1893; asst. treas. same, 1898-1900, treas., 1900-04, v.p., 1904-14 (resigned); gov. Federal Reserve Bank of Phila., Oct. 8, 1914-Feb. 1918; pres. Central Nat. Bank, Phila., 1920; dir. Girard Trust Co., Provident Trust Co. and Provident Mutual Life Insurance Co. (Phila.); Phila. Saving Fund Soc.; Phila. Contributionship for the Insurance of Houses from Fire; partner Brown Bros. & Co., bankers, 1921-29; commr. of Indian Affairs, 1929-Apr. 21, 1933. Chmn. Phila. Co. Relief Bd., Apr. 1934-July 1935. Acting treasurer Y.M.C.A., Feb.-May 1918; chairman Y.M.C.A. War Prisoners Aid, and chief Friends Bur., Am. Red Cross (France) for relief and reconstruction work in devastated France, May 1918-Sept. 1919. Mem. bd. mgrs., Haverford Coll., pres. bd. of trustees Bryn Mawr Coll.; trustee Am. Scandinavian Foundation; treas. Am. Acad. Polit. and Social Science; treas. Am. Council of Inst. of Pacific Relations; mem. Hist. Soc. Pa., Am. Philos. Soc.; mem. Council on Foreign Relations. Orthodox Quaker. Clubs: Philadelphia, University, University Barge, Merion Cricket, St. Davids Golf (Philadelphia); Metropolitan (Washington). Home: Bryn Mawr, Pa.

RHOADS, John S., banker; b. Jenner Twp., Pa., Nov. 30, 1878; s. Alexander and Mary (Stufft) R.; student local normal sch.; m. Sarah E. Barnett, Mar. 5, 1902; children—Mary A., David A. Taught sch., 3 terms, 1896-99; dir. Stoystown Nat. Bank since 1913, pres. since 1935; pres. Quesniahoning Telephone Co., 1930-

38; dir. Somerset Trust Co. Dir. schs. since 1916, serving as an officer and treas.; pres. Somerset Co. Sch. Bd. Dir. Jenner Fair Assn., 1930-38. Served as supt. of Sunday Sch. and officer of church council, 1904-38. Home: 6 Miles West of Stoystown. Office: Stoystown, Pa.

RHOADS, Joseph Howard, lawyer; b. Phila., Pa., June 3, 1870; s. Joseph R. and Amanda (Seal) R.; ed. Penn Charter Sch., Phila., Pa., 1880-83, Rittenhouse Acad., 1883-87; children—James Logan (dec.), Esther Lowry (Mrs. Walter E. Houghton, Jr.). Admitted to Pa. bar, 1893, and since engaged in gen. practice of law at Phila.; served as asst. dist. atty., 1900-02; solicitor legal dept. Pa. R.R. Co. Mem. Law Assn. of Phila. Republican. Club: Philadelphia Country. Home: 1904 Chestnut St. Office: 715 Otis Bldg., Philadelphia, Pa.

RHOADS, Philip Garrett, engring. exec.; b. Moorestown, N.J., Apr. 20, 1902; s. William Evans and Ruth (Evans) R.; student Moorestown (N.J.) Friends' Sch., 1906-17; grad. Westtown (Pa.) Sch., 1920; B.S., Haverford (Pa.) Coll., 1924; B.S. in M.E., Mass. Inst. Tech., 1927; m. Eugenia Eckford, July 22, 1933; children—Judith Jameson, William Evans. In engring. inspection dept. Victor Talking Machine Co., Camden, N.J., 1924-25; chief eng. J. E. Rhoads & Sons, Wilmington, Del., 1927-35, partner in charge production since 1935. Trus. Woodlawn Co., Del.; mem. advisory bd. Industrial Sch. for Colored Girls. Mem. Phi Beta Kappa, Soc. of Friends. Home: 9 Barley Mill Rd. Office: 11th and Bancroft Parkway, Wilmington, Del.

RHOADS, Samuel Nicholson; b. Philadelphia, Apr. 30, 1862; s. Charles and Anna (Nicholson) R.; ed. Friends' Sch.; 3 months' spl. course in journalism, Harvard; studies in natural science, Acad. Natural Sciences and Mus. Science and Art, Phila., and Carnegie Mus., Pittsburgh; m. Mary A. Cawley, Apr. 5, 1898; 1 son, Evan L. Since 1893 has collected museum specimens of natural history in nearly every state in the Union, Can., B.C., Cuba, Mex., Central and S. America. Life mem. Acad. Natural Sciences, Phila.; mem. Am. Philos. Soc., Am. Ornithologists' Union. Mem. of Society of Friends, Orthodox branch. Edited reprint of Ord's Zoölogy, 1894; Facsimile Reprint of Young's Catalogue of American Plants of Paris (1783). Author: The Mammals of Pennsylvania and New Jersey, 1903. Contbr. many papers on Am. and African mammals and on Am. birds, reptiles and molluss to zoöl. jours. describing about 100 new species and races of mammals and birds. Home: Haddonfield, N.J.

RHODE, William S(ylvanus), printer, publisher; b. Kutztown, Pa., Sept. 8, 1878; s. Louis Franklin and Hannah (Tyson) R.; ed. Kutztown State Teachers Coll. and by private tutors; m. Edna Gehman, Apr. 19, 1905; 1 dau., Constance Edna (wife of Rev. Karl S. Henry). Began as printer's apprentice, 1890; editor Kutztown Patriot, 1902-07; pub. Rhode's Directories of Eastern Pa. Counties, 1906-10; one of the founders and partners of the Kutztown Publishing Co., 1909-14; treas. Rhode Printing-Publishing Co. since its founding, 1914; promoted Pennsylvania Industry, a monthly commerce and industry jour. of America's workshops; now pub. and mng. editor American Travel and Transportation, quarterly mag., since 1936; for many yrs. consultant to pubs. of trade jours., books and catalogs; founded new international monthly magazine, Photographic Advertising, portraying higher standards of publicity with pictures, 1938. Pres. Bd. of Edn., Kutztown, 1922-37. Protestant. Mason. Home: Kutztown, Pa. Office: 307 Main St., Kutztown, Pa.; 220 W. 42d St., New York, N.Y.

RHODES, Chester H(ager), judge; b. Gouldsboro, Pa., Oct. 19, 1887; s. Arthur L. and Stella (Hager) R.; ed. Muhlenberg Coll., 1905-06; A.B., Lehigh U., 1910, A.M., same, 1912; hon. LL.D., Pa. Mil. Coll., 1938; m. Helen M. Hauser, Nov. 23, 1912; 1 son, John Frederick. Admitted to Pa. bar, 1913, and since engaged in gen. practice of law at Stroudsburg; served as dist. atty., Monroe Co., 1920-23; mem. Pa. Ho. of Rep., 1923-29, 1931-33; judge Superior Ct. of Pa. for term, 1935-45. Trustee Pa. Mil. Coll., Mt. Airy Luth. Theol. Sem. Mem. Am. and Pa. bar assns., Alpha Tau Omega, Phi Delta Kappa. Democrat. Lutheran. Mason. Elk. Eagle. I.O.O.F. Kiwanian. Patriotic Order Sons of America. Clubs: University, Penn Athletic (Philadelphia). Home: Stroudsburg, Pa.

RHODES, Edward Everett, actuary; b. Newark, N.J., Feb. 21, 1868; s. Wesley and Frances H. (Brodhead) R.; ed. in pub. schs. of Newark; m. Clara S. Littell, Apr. 22, 1896; children—Marion Littell (Mrs. John A. Wood III), Helen B. (Mrs. Bertrand L. Gulick, Jr.), Robert D. Rhodes. Began as actuarial student with The Mutual Benefit Life Ins. Co. of Newark, Aug. 2, 1886, and has since remained in the service of that co.; was asst. mathematician (actuary), 1902-05, mathematician (chief actuary), 1905-19, vice-pres. since 1908, mem. bd. dirs. since 1912; mem. bd. dirs. Nat. State Bank of Newark. Served as expert adviser to the N.Y. (Armstrong) legislative com. investigating life ins. cos. under leadership of Hon. Charles E. Hughes and assisted in drafting remedial legislation; mem. of com. (1909-31) of 4 actuaries and 4 medical dirs. for mortality investigation since 1909, pub. first findings in 5 vols., 1912-14, and continuing publ. of data in gen. use in ins. offices; served as chmn. of com. on taxation of Assn. of Life Ins. Presidents in early period of federal income taxation, participating in congressional hearings and the framing of tax laws. Fellow of Actuarial Soc. of America (pres., 1926-27), Am. Inst. of Actuaries, Inst. of Actuaries of Gt. Britain, and Ins. Inst. of America; mem. Am. Math. Soc., Council of Direction of Internat. Congresses of Actuaries; hon. mem. Assn. of Life Ins. Counsel, Assn. of Life Ins. Med. Dirs. Mem. of various charitable and social service organizations in Newark. Author of various papers pub. by actuarial socs. Presbyn. Clubs: Essex (Newark); West Side Tennis (Forest Hills, N.Y.); Bay Head (N.J.) Yacht. Home: 233 Elwood Av. Office: 300 Broadway, Newark, N.J.

RHODES, George Irving, engineering executive; b. Andover, Mass., Nov. 27, 1883; s. Thomas Edward and Alice (Wrigley) R.; B.S., Mass. Inst. of Tech., 1905; m. Olive Wallace, 1911; children—Barbara, Priscilla. Elec. engr. Interboro Rapid Transit Co., New York, 1906-11; cons. engr. White, Weld & Co., Boston, 1912-16; engring. mgr. Ford, Bacon & Davis, New York, 1917-23, now vice-president and director; vice-president Ford, Bacon & Davis Construction Corporation. Fellow Am. Inst. E.E.; member Am. Soc. M.E., Am. Soc. Civ. Engrs. Republican. Conglist. Mason. Club: Glen Ridge Country. Home: 239 Forest Av., Glen Ridge, N.J. Office: 39 Broadway, New York, N.Y.

RHODES, George Pearson, corporation official; b. at New Castle, Pa., Mar. 21, 1871; s. James and Elizabeth (Peebles) R.; ed. pub. schs.; m. Ellen Bower, of New Castle, Pa., Nov. 26, 1895; children—John Bower, Roberta Peebles, George Pearson. With Pa. Tube Works, 1890-1900; organizer, with brother, Pa. Casting & Machine Works, 1900, v.p. and treas., 1900-24; sec. and treas. Nat. Car Wheel Co., 1905-21, pres., 1922-24; pres. Castalia Portland Cement Co. since 1923; v.p. Colonial Steel Co., 1920-27, later pres.; dir. Keystone Nat. Bank, Am. Window Glass Co., Dollar Savings Bank, Pittsburgh Steel Co., Fidelity Trust Co., Vanadium-Alloys Steel Co. Pres. St. Barnabas Free Home; trustee St. Margaret's Memorial Hosp., Calvary P.E. Ch. Republican. Mason (32°, Shriner). Clubs: Duquesne, Pittsburgh Athletic, Pittsburgh Golf, Fox Chapel Golf (Pittsburgh). Home: 5267 Wilkins Av., Pittsburgh, Pa.

RHODES, John Cecil, chemist, bacteriologist; b. Phila., Pa., Aug. 23, 1898; s. James Herbert and Alice (Russell) R.; B.S. in Chem. Engring., U. of Pa. Towne Scientific Sch., 1919; M.S., U. of Pa. Grad. Sch., 1921; m. Eleanor Magee, 1923; children—Deirdre, Eleanor; m. 2d, Margaret Lowrey, 1932. Began as instr. organic chemistry, 1919; successively water analyst, chief chemist, asst. chief Bur. Labs., Pa. State Dept. of Health, 1921-36, reinstated as consulting asst. chief since 1939; propr. and dir. Medical Arts Laboratory, Jenkintown, Pa., chemists and bacteriologists, since 1929; pres. Popular Brands, Inc.; v.p. Arkase Co., Inc.; sec. Phila. Inspected Raw Milk Commn. since 1932. Served in U.S.A., 1918. Supervisor of Tuberculosis Div., Phila. Inst. for Med. Research; sec. Pa. Biol. Research Foundation. Mem. Am. Chem. Soc., Inst. of Biochemists and Bacteriologists, Soc. Am. Bacteriologists, Inst. of Cons. Chemists and Chem. Engrs., Phila. Inst. of Cons. Chemists and Chem. Engrs., Alembic, Alpha Chi Sigma, Sigma Tau, Sigma Xi. Republican. Home: South and Paxson Avs., Wyncote, Pa. Office: Medical Arts Bldg., Jenkintown, Pa.

RHODES, Walter Kremer, prof. elec. engring.; b. Fairplay, Pa., Oct. 2, 1874; s. David and Anna (Brown) R.; B.E., Shippensburg (Pa.) State Normal Sch., 1898; Ph.B., Bucknell U., 1903, A.M., same, 1906; B.S. in E.E., U. of Mich., 1907; grad. student U. of Mich., summers 1906-11; m. Nora Noll, July 26, 1922. Engaged in teaching pub. schs. and normal sch., 1894-99; surveying and engring. construction, 1902-05; prof. elec. engring., Bucknell U., since 1907; dir. Union Nat. Bank, Lewisburg, Pa., Citizens Electric Co. Mem. Am. Inst. Elec. Engrs., Soc. for Promotion Engring. Edn., Am. Acad. Polit. and Social Scis. Democrat. Mem. Reformed Ch. Mason (K.T., 32°, Shriner). Author: Outlines in Electrical Design, vols. I and II. Home: 101 S. 4th St., Lewisburg, Pa.

RHODES, William Warren, chem. engr. and exec.; b. Chester, Pa., Jan. 27, 1888; s. Richard Somers and Fannie (Price) R.; student Chester (Pa.) High Sch., 1902-06; B.S. in Chem., U. of Pa., 1910; m. Patricia Hart Drant, M.D., Aug. 18, 1934. Chem. engr. Security Lime & Cement Co., Hagerstown, Md., 1910-11; chem. engr. and geologist Blair Limestone Co., Martinsburg, W.Va., 1911-12; chem. engr. Woodville Lime & Cement Co., Woodville, O., 1911-13; engr. Washington Bldg. Lime Co., Woodville, O., 1913, mgr. 1914-17; mem. staff of chem. dir. E. I. du Pont de Nemours & Co., Wilmington, Del., 1917-20, in organic chemicals dept. since 1920, sales dept., 1920-30, sales mgr., 1926-30; dir. of sales Kenetic Chemicals, Inc. (owned by du Pont Co. and Gen. Motors Co.), mfrs. refrigerants, Wilmington, since 1930. Fellow A.A.A.S.; mem. Am. Inst. Chem. Engrs., Am. Chem. Soc., Am. Soc. Refrigerating Engrs., Army Ordnance Assn., Priestly Chem. Club (pres. 1910), S.R. (Pa. Soc.), S.A.R. (Del. Soc.), Netherlands Soc. of Phila., Theta Delta Chi. Republican. Episcopalian. Clubs: University, Wilmington Whist, Wilmington Country (Wilmington); Rose Tree Fox Hunting (Media, Pa.). Home: Rhodesia, Westtown, Pa. Office: Nemours Bldg., Wilmington, Del.

RHONE, Mortimer Crosthwaite, judge; b. Cambria, Pa., Mar. 18, 1871; s. Zebulon S. and Jennie M. (Crosthwaite) R.; student Williamsport (Pa.) Dickinson Sem. and Williamsport Commercial Coll.; m. Florence E. Horne, Apr. 15, 1935; 1 adopted son, Leo. City solicitor, Williamsport, Pa., 1916-18; judge of the several cts. of Lycoming County, 29th Judicial Dist. of Pa., since 1938, now judge Ct. of Common Pleas. Del. Dem. Nat. Conv., Denver, Colo., 1908, Houston, Tex., 1928; one of organizers of Com. of One Hundred of City of Williamsport, later merged with Chamber of Commerce as Community Trade Assn., pres., 1938, resigning to accept judicial appointment. Mem. Pa. Bar Assn. (v.p. 1936), Am. Bar Assn. Democrat. Elk. Home; 699 Belmont Av. Office: Court House, Williamsport, Pa.

RHYNE, Sidney White, clergyman; b. Charlotte, N.C., Jan. 25, 1894; s. Aaron Sidney and Mary Margaret (White) R.; ed. Davidson Coll., 1912-13; A.B., Roanoke Coll., Salem, Va., 1918; ed. Luth. Southern Theol. Sem., Columbia, S.C., 1919-22, Northwestern U., summers 1927, 1928; (hon.) D.D., Roanoke Coll., 1938; m. Ruth Naomi Dry, June 19, 1928; children—Sidney White, Jr., Charles Sylvanus. Ordained to ministry Lutheran Ch., 1922; sec. field missions, U. Luth. Synod. of N.C., 1922-26; field sec. of Parish and Ch. Sch. Bd., Southern States, 1926-31; exec. sec. of Parish and Ch. Sch. Bd., Phila., Pa., since 1931. Served in F.A.,

U.S.A., 1917-19, with A.E.F. in France. Democrat. Lutheran. Home: 216 E. Sedgwick St., Mt. Airy, Philadelphia, Pa. Office: 1228 Spruce St., Philadelphia, Pa.

RICE, Charles P., pres. and treas. York Corrugating Co.; b. Dover Twp., York Co., Pa., Feb. 19, 1868; s. William H. and Sarah (Julius) R.; D.D.S., U. of Md., Baltimore, Md., 1891; m. Elizabeth Gallatin, May 28, 1896; 1 son, Edward Julius. In practice dental surgery, 1891-1911; pres. and treas. York (Pa.) Corrugating Co. since 1911; pres. Community Hotel Co. (operators Yorktowne Hotel) since 1926; dir. and mem. finance com. Western Nat. Bank, York, Pa., since 1923. Pres. bd. dirs. Hood Coll., Frederick, Md., since 1937; dir. and chmn. bldg. com. York Hosp. since 1923; dir. "Homewood," Home for the Aged of Potomac Synod, Reformed Ch., since 1931. Mem. Nat. Assn. Mfrs., U.S. Chamber of Commerce, Pa. State Chamber of Commerce. Mason (32°). Clubs: Country, Lafayette (York, Pa.). Home: 533 W. Market St. Office: Adams St. and Western Md. R.R., York, Pa.

RICE, Herbert Louis, mathematician; b. Chicago, Ill., Dec. 18, 1869; s. Isaac James and Eliza (Allen) R.; Univ. of Mich., 1888-91; B.S., Columbian (now George Washington) U., 1893, M.S., 1894; m. Rose Ackley, Sept. 7, 1895; children—Alice Helen, Paul Gerrett, Miriam Ackley, Howard Vernon. Asst. in office of Nautical Almanac, Washington, 1892-1902; prof. math. astronomy, Grad. Sch., Columbian, 1897-1904; asst. astronomer, U.S. Naval Obs., 1902-07; apptd. to U.S.N., Aug. 26, 1907, as prof. mathematics, rank of lt.; rank of lt.-comdr., May 23, 1917; comdr., Sept. 18, 1918; capt., Feb. 19, 1930; retired, Jan. 1, 1934. Republican. Christian Scientist. Author: Theory and Practice of Interpolation, 1899. Home: Pikesville, Md.

RICE, John, chmn. bd. Gen. Crushed Stone Co.; b. Pollstown, Pa., Oct. 10, 1866; s. George and Isabella Hitner (Potts) R.; student Sheffield Scientific Sch. (Yale U.); m. Carrie Arndt Drake, Jan. 5, 1898; children—Virginia (Mrs. Love), John. With Gen. Crushed Stone Co. since 1900, now chmn. bd.; v.p. Easton Trust Co., 1920-37, pres. since 1937; pres. Hotel Easton Co. since 1935; also dir. of each. Chmn. County Fuel Administration, World War. Presidential elector, Theodore Roosevelt, 1912. Chmn. Co. Emergency Relief, 1932-36; pres. Children's Aid Soc., 1928-29. Mem. Nat. Crushed Stone Assn. (ex-pres., dir.), Pa. Crushed Stone Assn. (ex-pres.), N.Y. Crushed Stone Assn. (ex-pres.), Easton Anglers Assn. (v.p.), Delta Psi. Clubs: Northampton Country (dir., pres.); Yale (New York and Philadelphia); University (Philadelphia); Pomfret (v.p. 1934-38); Graduates (New Haven). Home: 426 Clinton Terrace. Office: Drake Bldg., Easton, Pa.

RICE, John Stanley, state senator, mfr.; b. Arendtsville, Pa., Jan. 28, 1899; s. Leighton H. and Florence Jane (Hartman) R.; ed. pub. schs.; Gettysburg Acad. and Gettysburg Coll.; m. Grace Luene Rogers, Nov. 10, 1934. Engaged in wholesale fruit and produce business and mfr. of fruit packing supplies since 1921; dir. Rice, Trew & Rice Co., Rice Produce Co., Gettysburg-Harrisburg Transportation Co. Mem. Pa. State Senate since 1932, majority floor leader since 1937. Served in U.S. Army, last 3 mos., World War. Chmn. 75th Anniversary, Battle of Gettysburg Commn., 1938. Mem. Phi Gamma Delta. Democrat. Lutheran. Mason (Scottish Rite), Elb. Club: Lions. Home: 60 W. Broadway, Gettysburg, Pa. Office: Biglerville, Pa.

RICE, John Winter, bacteriologist; b. Williamsport, Pa., July 4, 1891; s. William and Margaret Christiana (Winter) R.; B.S., Bucknell U., Lewisburg, Pa., 1914, M.S., 1915; A.M., Columbia, 1918, Ph.D., 1922; m. Edna Amelia Miller, Aug. 21, 1918 (died 1921); children—John Miller, Martha Jane; m. 2d, Ruth Miriam (Hoffa) Frantz, Aug. 6, 1922; children—Jasper Hoffa Frantz (stepson), Andrew Cyrus, William Floyd, Ruth Eleanor. Teacher of biology, high sch., Hazleton, Pa., 1915-16; instr. of biology, Bucknell U., 1916-18, asst. prof., 1918-23, asso. prof., 1923-24, prof. of bacteriology since 1924; instr. in bacteriology, Yale Army Lab. Sch., 1918, Columbia, summer 1922. Pres. Lewisburg Bd. of Health since 1924; pres. Milk Control Dist. 4 of Pa. since 1927; pres. Pa. Assn. of Dairy and Milk Insps., 1927-28. Served as 2d lt. Sanitary Corps, U.S. A., during World War. Mem. Am. Pub. Health Assn., Am. Social Hygiene Assn., A.A.A.S., Soc. Am. Bacteriologists (pres. Central Pa. Br. 1935-36). Republican. Methodist. Mason. Home: 610 St. George St., Lewisburg, Pa.

RICE, Lacy Isaac, lawyer; b. Berkeley Springs, W.Va., Nov. 1, 1901; s. Eli L. and Ida B. Fearnow R.; LL.B., W.Va. Univ., Morgantown, 1925; m. Anna L. Thorn, Dec. 17, 1929; 1 son, Lacy Isaac, jr. Admitted to W.Va. bar, 1925 and since engaged in gen. practice of law at Martinsburg; mem. firm Emmert & Rice, 1930-34, and since death of H. H. Emert in 1934 has continued firm name; pres. and dir. Old Nat. Bank of Martinsburg since 1935; vice-pres. Berkeley Woolen Co., Martinsburg since 1937; dir. and atty. Interwoven Stocking Co.; served as mem. W.Va. Ho. of Reps. 1930-32. Mem. W.Va. Bar Assn., Berkeley County Bar Assn., Theta Chi, Phi Delta Phi. Republican. Presbyn. Elk. Mason. Clubs: Elks, Masons (Martinsburg). Home: 118 N. Tennessee Av. Office: Old Nat. Bank Bldg., Martinsburg, W.Va.

RICE, Philip X., educator; b. Bentonville, Ark., Nov. 2, 1892; s. Charles M. and Mattie A. (Ragan) R.; E.E., U. of Ark., 1916; M.S., Pa. State Coll., 1923; m. Helene Lois Hinds, Sept. 26, 1921; children—Randall Hinds, David Ragan. Head test dept. Gen. Ry. Signal Co., 1920-21; instr. Pa. State Coll., 1921-23; elec. engr. Miller Train Control Corpn., 1923-28, chief engr., 1928-30; asst. prof. elec. engring., Pa. State Coll., 1931-34, asso. prof. since 1935. Engaged in r.r. and power plant construction, U.S. Army, France, 1917-19. Mem. Am. Inst. Elec. Engrs. (asso. mem. and counselor student branch), Soc. for Promotion Engring. Edn., Inst. Traffic Engrs., Tau Beta Pi, Sigma Xi, Eta Kappa Nu. Democrat. Mem. Ch. of Christ. Wrote: Magnetic Bridge for Control of Locomotives and Automobiles; Railroad Crossing Protection. Home: 829 N. Allen St., State College, Pa.

RICE, Stuart Arthur, univ. prof.; b. Wadena, Minn., Nov. 21, 1889; s. Edward Myron and Ida Emelin (Hicks) R.; A.B., U. of Wash., 1912, A.M., 1915; Ph.D., Columbia U., 1924; m. Sarah Alice Mayfield, May 29, 1934; 1 son, Stuart Arthur. Sec. Industrial Welfare Commn., Washington, 1913; confidential inspector, Dept. of Pub. Charities, N.Y. City, 1914-15; supt. N.Y. Municipal Lodging House, 1916-17; instr., later asst. prof. sociology, Dartmouth Coll., 1923-26; prof. sociology and later statistics, U. of Pa., since 1926. Research sec. for social statistics Social Science Research Council, 1931-32; visiting prof. sociology, U. of Chicago, 1932-33; acting chmn. Com. on Govt. Statistics and Information Services, 1933; asst. dir. Bur. of the Census, 1933-36; 1st v.chmn. Central Statistical Bd., 1933-35, acting chmn. 1935-36, chmn. since 1936; spl. investigator social statistics President's Research Com. on Social Trends, 1931-32. Mem. A.A.A.S. (v.p. 1937), Am. Statis. Assn. (pres. 1933), Am. Sociol. Soc. (dir. 1930-33), Am. Econ. Assn., Internat. Inst. Statistics (chmn. Am. Com. for 25th Biennial Session). Dir. Travelers Aid Soc., Washington; mem. research com. Welfare Council of N.Y. City. Clubs: Cosmos, National Press (Washington, D.C.). Author: Farmers and Workers in American Politics, 1924; Quantitative Methods in Politics, 1928; Communication Agencies and Social Life with M. M. Willey), 1933; Next Steps in the Development of Social Statistics, 1933; also numerous scientific articles. Editor: Statistics in Social Studies, 1930; Methods in Social Science, 1931; Social Statistics in the United States, 1933. Home: 2863 Beechwood Circle, Arlington, Va. Address: University of Pennsylvania, Philadelphia, Pa.; 1319 F St., N.W., Washington, D.C.

RICH, Benjamin Sunderland, otolaryngologist; b. at Easton, Md., Mar. 9, 1901; s. Edward L. and Mary (Sunderland) R.; student Cornell University, 1919-20; B.A., Johns Hopkins U., 1923; M.D., U. of Md., 1928; m. Helen Jackson Preston, June 15, 1935. Interne Union Memorial and Mercy hosps., Baltimore, 1928-31; specialist in ear, eye, nose and throat, Baltimore, since 1931; mem. teaching staff, U. of Md. Med. Sch., Baltimore. Mem. A.M.A., Southern Med. Assn., Baltimore City Med. Soc. (sec. ear, eye, nose and throat sect., 1936, chmn. 1937), Randolph Winslow Surg. Soc., Alpha Tau Omega, Nu Sigma Nu, Pi Delta Upsilon. Democrat. Episcopalian. Home: 4106 Loch Raven Boul. Office: Medical Arts Bldg., Baltimore, Md.

RICH, Charles S.; mem. law firm Rich & Rich. Office: Union Trust Bldg., Baltimore, Md.

RICH, Edward N.; mem. law firm Rich & Rich. Office: Union Trust Bldg., Baltimore, Md.

RICH, Robert Fleming, congressman; b. Woolrich, Pa., June 23, 1883; s. Michael B. and Ida B. R.; grad. Mercersburg Acad., 1902; student Dickinson Coll., 1903-06; m. Julia Trump, June 10, 1911; children—Elizabeth, Margaret Shaw, Catharine Ann, Julia Trump. Gen. mgr. and treas. Woolrich Woolen Mills; pres. State Bank of Avis; dir., sec., treas. Chatham Water Co.; dir., treas. Pierce Mfg. Co.; dir., sec. Oak Grove Improvement Co.; dir. Lock Haven Trust Co.; del. Rep. Nat. Conv., 1924; mem. 71st to 76th Congresses (1929-41), 16th Pa. Dist. Pres. bd. Williamsport-Dickinson Sem.; trustee Dickinson Coll., Lock Haven Hosp.; mem. alumni council Mercersburg Acad., Phi Kappa Psi. Methodist. Mason (33°). Clubs: Ross (Williamsport, Pa.); Clinton Country (Loch Haven, Pa.). Home: Woolrich, Pa.

RICH, Stephen Gottheil, publisher; b. New York, N.Y., Jan. 3, 1890; s. Joseph Salomon and Gertrude (Gottheil) R.; ed. Harvard U., 1907-09; B.S., N.Y. Univ., 1914; A.M., Cornell U., 1915; Ph.D., N.Y. Univ., 1923; m. Johanna Elizabeth Turner, Jan. 24, 1920. Engaged in teaching, normal schs., Natal Province, South Africa, 1916-18, elementary schs., Durban, South Africa, 1919-20; instr. chemistry, Concord State Teachers Coll., W.Va., 1921-22; field rep., Lyons & Carnahan, publishers, 1925-32; engaged in bus. on own acct. as Stephen G. Rich, pub. mags. and catalogs for stamp collectors, Verona, N.J., since 1933. Trustee Coll. of Paterson, Paterson, N.J. Mem. N.J. Philatelic Fed. (pres. 1929-30, treas. 1931-35), Precancel Catalog Assn. (treas. since 1934), Soc. Philatelic Americans (dir. since 1938, actg. sec. 1939), Collectors Club of N.Y. (bd. govs. 1927-34, treas. 1931-34), Phi Beta Kappa, Phi Delta Kappa. Club: Verona Rotary (pres. 1936-37). Editor, The Precancel Bee, philatelic monthly since 1933. Contbr. to ednl. jours., 1917-30, to philatelic jours. since 1921. Home: 118 Sunset Av., Verona, N.J.

RICH, Thaddeus, musical dir., violinist; b. Indianapolis, Ind., Mar. 21, 1885; s. William Shipman and Susan Blanche (Slager) R.; studied violin under Richard Schliewen and Hugh McGibney (U.S.); pupil of Arno Hilf, violin, Wendling and Von Bose, piano, Quasdorf and Jadassohn, composition, Reinicke and Hermann, ensemble, Leipzig Conservatory of Music, 1897-1902; mem. Leipzig Gewandhaus Orchestra under Arthur Nikisch, 1901-02; student Royal Hochschule der Musik, Berlin, under Josef Joachim, 1902-03; Mus.D., Temple U., 1913; m. Almyra Chandler Williams, of Phila., Oct. 1, 1910; children—Louise Chandler (wife of Dr. Blanchard William Means), Thaddeus. Concert-master Berlin-Charlottenburg opera, 1903-04; tour of Germany and Austria, 1904-05; returned to U.S. and appeared on tour, 1905-06; concert-master and asso. condr. Phila. Orchestra, 1906-26; dean Coll. of Music, Temple U., since 1913; founded Rich Quartette, 1908; conducted Phila. Festival Orchestra, 1915-26; asso. with Leopold Stokowski at Curtis Inst. of Music (Phila.), 1925-26; asso. with Nikolai Sokoloff as asst. dir. of Federal Music Project since 1935. Owner of collection of rare stringed instruments. Decorated with Order of the Crown by King Ferdinand of Rumania, 1922. Home: 1520 Spruce St., Philadelphia, Pa.

RICHARD, Irwin, mfr.; b. New Hanover, Pa., Jan. 27, 1881; s. George Washington and Emma (Houck) R.; m. Carrie Renninger; children—Mrs. Beulah Henry, Mrs. Florence Miller, Clarence, Nelson, Claude, Alice, Beatrice, Paul, Ralph. Propr. Red Hill Broom Works; dir. Schwenkville Nat. Bank; chmn. Red Hill Water Commn. Pres. Eastern Broom Mfrs. and Supply Dealers Assn., Broom Inst., Red Hill Bd. of Trade. Trustee Perkiomen Sch. Mem. Patriotic Sons of America. Lutheran. Mason (Shriner). Rotarian. A leader in orgn. of broom industry, accomplishing standardization of brooms on nat. scale in coöperation with U.S. Dept. Agr. and U.S. Dept. Commerce. Home: Red Hill, Pa.

RICHARDS, Alfred Newton, prof. pharmacology; b. Stamford, N.Y., Mar. 22, 1876; s. Rev. Leonard E. and Mary E. (Burbank) R.; B.A., Yale, 1897, M.A., 1899; Ph.D., Columbia, 1901; hon. Sc.D., U. of Pa., 1925, Western Reserve, 1931, Yale, 1933; hon. M.D., University of Pa., 1932; LL.D., University of Edinburgh (Scotland), 1935; m. Lillian L. Woody, Dec. 26, 1908; 1 son, Alfred Newton. Instr., physiol. chemistry, Columbia, 1898-1904, pharmacology, 1904-08; prof. pharmacology, Northwestern Univ., 1908-10, Univ. of Pa. since 1910; Herter lecturer New York Univ. and Bellevue Hosp. Med. Coll., 1926; Croonian lecturer Royal Soc. of London, 1938. Mem. scientific staff, British Medical Research Committee, London, 1917-18; maj. Sanitary Corps, U.S.A., attached to Chem. Warfare Service, Chaumont, France, July-Dec. 1918. Mem. Nat. Acad. of Sciences, Assn. Am. Physicians, American Philosophical Society, Am. Physiological Soc., British Physiological Soc., Am. Soc. Biol. Chemists, Am. Pharmacol. Soc., Soc. Exptl. Biology and Medicine, Harvey Soc., Physiol. Soc. Phila., Sigma Xi, Alpha Omega Alpha, Phi Beta Kappa; corr. mem. Gesellsch. der Aertze in Wien; hon. mem. Am. Urol. Soc.; fellow Am. Acad. of Arts and Sciences, A.A.A.S.; hon. fellow Coll. of Physicians of Phila. Awarded Gerhard medal, 1932; Kober medal, 1933; Keyes medal, 1933; John Scott medal, 1934; medal of the N.Y. Acad. of Medicine, 1936; Phila. award for 1937. Trustee Rockefeller Foundation. Republican. Presbyn. Author of papers dealing with action of chloroform, histamine, and the function of the kidneys. Home: 6 Rugby Rd., Bryn Mawr, Pa.

RICHARDS, Alvin S(weisford), supt. city schs.; b. Zieglerville, Pa., Oct. 30, 1899; s. Amandus M. and Elizabeth (Sweisford) R.; diploma Perkiomen Sch., 1919; B.S., Ursinus Coll., 1924; A.M., U. of Pa., 1935; m. Carolyn Bergey, Dec. 26, 1925. Engaged in teaching, high sch., Schwenksville, Pa., 1924-27, asst. prin. same, 1924-27; supt. schs., West Conshohocken, Pa., since 1927. Served as pvt. inf., U.S.A., 1918. Mem. Nat. Edn. Assn., Nat. Assn. Sch. Adminstrs., Pa. State Edn. Assn., Montgomery County Supts. Assn., Suburban Supts. Assn., Am. Legion. Mem. Reformed Ch. Mason, Rotarian. Home: 215 W. Freedley St., Norristown, Pa. Office: West Conshohocken, Pa.

RICHARDS, Charles Gorman, clergyman; b. Pittston, Pa., June 28, 1872; s. Peter K. and Rosina (Corselius) R.; grad. Susquehanna Collegiate Inst., 1893; A.B., Princeton, 1897; grad. McCormick Theol. Sem., Chicago, 1901; (D.D., Dubuque [Iowa] Coll., 1912); m. Mary Louise McKnight, June 26, 1902; children—Alexander M., Louise. Ordained Presbyn. ministry, 1901; pastor 1st Ch., Columbus, Ind., 1901-06, Sterling, Ill., 1906-11, 1st Ch., Auburn, N.Y., 1911-19; exec. sec. dept. of kingdom extension in New Era Movement of Presbyterian Church, 1919-21; pastor Rogers Park Church, 1921-29, First Ch., Verona, N.J., 1929—. Trustee Hanover Coll., 1902-05, Cayuga Presbytery, 1912-19. Mason (K.T.). Mem. Nat. Service Commn.; sec. and mem. exec. com. Social Service Commn. of Presbyn. Ch., U.S.A., 1917-19. Contbr. to religious and social periodicals. Clubs: Princeton, Rotary. Home: 38 Fairview Av., Verona, N.J.*

RICHARDS, Charles Sudler, judge; b. Georgetown, Del., Aug. 29, 1878; s. Charles Fleming and Mary Catherine (Sudler) R.; grad. Wesley Collegiate Inst., Dover, Del., 1899; law student U. of Pa.; unmarried. Admitted to Del. bar, 1904, and began practice at Georgetown; dept. atty. gen. of Del., 1907-09; sec. State of Del., 1911-13; atty. for Del. legislature, session 1919, and spl. session, 1920; dep. atty. gen. for Sussex Co., Del., Jan.-July 1921; resident judge Sussex County, term 1921-33, asso. justice Supreme Court of Del., term 1933-45. Republican. Methodist. Home: Georgetown, Del.

RICHARDS, Emerson Lewis; b. Atlantic City, N.J., July 9, 1884; s. Jacob R. and Martina (Mada) R.; grad. Atlantic City High Sch., 1902; LL.B., U. of Pa., 1906; unmarried. Admitted to N.J. bar, 1907, counsellor at law, 1910; mem. Ho. of Assembly, N.J., 3 terms, 1912-14, leader of House, 1913, 14; mem. Senate, N.J., 1917, 18, and since 1922, elected pres. of Senate, 1933. Apptd. dep. atty. gen. of N.J., 1919, and assigned as counsel N.J. Interstate Bridge and Tunnel Commn., later as counsel for Del. River Bridge Joint Commn. (resigning Sept. 1923). Served as capt., later maj., U.S.A., World War. Republican. Episcopalian. Clubs: Penn Athletic, Elks Club. Home: 1245 Boardwalk. Office: Schwehm Bldg., Atlantic City, N.J.

RICHARDS, Esther Loring, psychiatrist; b. Holliston, Mass., June 6, 1885; d. David J. and Esther C. (Loring) R.; A.B., Mount Holyoke Coll., South Hadley, Mass., 1910; M.D., Johns Hopkins U. Med. Sch., 1915; (hon.) D.Sc., Mount Holyoke Coll., 1926. Interne and asst. resident, Phipps Clinic Johns Hopkins Hosp., 1915-17; asso. prof. psychiatry, Johns Hopkins U. Med. Sch. since 1923; asso. psychiatrist, Johns Hopkins Hosp. since 1920; psychiatrist in charge of outpatient dept. Henry Phipps Psychiatric Clinic Johns Hopkins Hosp. since 1920; lecturer in mental hygiene, Sch. Hygiene and Pub. Health Johns Hopkins U. since 1920; psychiatrist in chief, Baltimore City Hosps., 1931. Fellow A.M.A., Am. Pub. Health Assn. Mem. A.A. A.S., Am. Psychopathol. Assn., Am. Assn. for Study of Feebleminded, Am. Acad. Sci., Soc. for Research in Child Development, Nat. Research Council, Am. Med. Editors and Authors Assn., Southern Med. Assn., Phi Delta Gamma, Phi Beta Kappa. Presbyn. Contbr. to jours. Home: 41 W. Preston St., Baltimore, Md.

RICHARDS, Florence Harvey, physician; b. Phila., Pa., Mar. 26, 1877; d. Joseph and Bridgett (Harvey) R.; student Biol. Dept., U. of Pa., 1894-96; M.D., Woman's Med. Coll. of Pa., 1899; unmarried. Interne Woman's Hosp., 1899-1900; practice of medicine, Phila., since 1900; med. dir. William Penn High Sch., since 1910; pub. lecturer on social hygiene since 1916; lecturer on social hygiene U.S. Army Training Camp Activities, 1916-19. Mem. A.M.A., Pa. State and Phila. Co. med. socs., Am. Social Hygiene Assn., Nat. Edn. Assn., Phila. Teachers Assn., Phila. Orchestra Assn., Alumnæ of Woman's Med. Coll. of Pa., Alumni U. of Pa. Republican. Methodist. Clubs: Phila. Art Alliance, New Century Guild (Phila.). Home: 3708 Hamilton St., Philadelphia, Pa.

RICHARDS, George Warren, clergyman; b. Farmington, Berks Co., Pa., Apr. 26, 1869; s. Milton S. and Louisa (Fritch) R.; A.B., Franklin and Marshall Coll., 1887, A.M., 1890, D.D. from same, 1902; studied at universities of Berlin and Erlanger; D.Th., Heidelberg University, Germany, 1925; D.D., Edinburgh University, 1933; m. Mary A. Mosser, Nov. 19, 1890. Ordained ministry Reformed Ch. in U.S., 1890; pastor Salem Ref. Ch., Allentown, Pa., 1890-99; prof. ch. history, since 1899, pres. Theol. Sem. of Ref. Ch. in U.S., Lancaster, Pa.; travel and study in Europe, 1890, 99, 1904, 09; lecturer Biblical Seminary, New York, 1932-33. Pres., mem. exec. com. Alliance Ref. Chs. holding Presbyn. System (Western sect.); formerly pres. Alliance of Ref. Chs. holding Presbyn. Systems throughout the World; gen. sec. Continuation Com. of Conf. of Theol. Schs. of U.S. and Can.; mem. Continuation Com. of World Conf. on Faith and Order; ex-pres. Am. Soc. Ch. History, Gen. Synod of Ref. Ch. in U.S.; pres. Gen. Synod Evang. and Ref. Ch. and v.p. Federal Council Chs. of Christ in America, 1934-36. Mem. Am. Theol. Soc. (ex-pres.), Cliosophic Soc. of Lancaster (pres.). Clubs: University (Phila.); City (New York). Author: Historical and Doctrinal Studies on the Heidelberg Catechism; Christian Ways of Salvation; Reformed, What?; Beyond Fundamentalism and Modernism?; Creative Controversies in Christianity, 1938; also various pamphlets on ch. history. Translator of sermons from the German into English, under title of "Come, Creator Spirit," and "God's Search for Man." Lecturer in Internat. Theol. Seminar, Geneva, Switzerland, 1938. Home: Lancaster, Pa.

RICHARDS, Horace Clark, prof. math. physics, emeritus; b. Phila., Pa., Jan. 4, 1868; s. Thomas Webb and Henrietta (Hadry) R.; A.B., U. of Pa., 1888, Ph.D., same, 1891; grad. study Johns Hopkins U., 1891-92; m. Annie Gardiner, June 7, 1905; children—Horace Gardiner, Marie Ann. Instr. physics, U. of Pa., 1890, Bryn Mawr Coll., 1892-93; instr. physics, U. of Pa., 1893-1903, asst. prof. physics, 1903-09, prof. math. physics, 1909-38, emeritus since 1938; dir. Randal Morgan Lab. of Physics, U. of Pa., 1931-38. Served as physicist, Nat. Bur. of Standards, Washington, D.C., 1918. Fellow A.A.A.S., Am. Phys. Soc. Mem. Am. Philos. Soc., Optical Soc. of America, Franklin Inst., Am. Assn. of Physics Teachers, Am. Assn. Univ. Profs., Société Française de Physique, Phi Beta Kappa, Sigma Xi, Pi Mu Epsilon. Republican. Club: Physics of Philadelphia. Co-author (with Charles S. Potts, M.D.): Electricity, Medical and Surgical, 1911. Author: Albert Einstein and the Theory of Relativity (in World's True History), 1932. Contbr. articles to sci. jours. Home: 509 Woodland Terrace, Philadelphia, Pa.

RICHARDS, Leonard, manufacturer; b. Bloomfield, N.J., Sept. 2, 1886; s. Leonard and Caroline (Dodd) R.; student Montclair (N.J.) Mil. Acad., 1896-99, St. Paul's Ch., Concord, N.H., 1899-1903, Yale, 1903-05; m. Anita Warren, Aug. 28, 1909; children—Leonard, Warren, R. Peter. With F. R. Masters & Co., New York, 1905-06, Zapon Co., New York, 1906-17; v.p. Atlas Powder Co., Wilmington, Del., since 1917; dir. Del. Trust Co. Republican. Episcopalian. Clubs: Wilmington, Wilmington Country (Wilmington, Del.); Yale (New York); Vicmead Hunt, (Wilmington, Del.). Home: 2601 W. 17th St. Office: Delaware Trust Bldg., Wilmington, Del.

RICHARDS, Ralph Strother, sr. partner Kay Richards & Co.; b. Evanston, Ill., Mar. 4, 1881; s. William K. and Ida Katherine (Jones) R.; student pub. schs.; m. Carolyn McClurg Snowdon, Dec. 20, 1908; children—Snowdon, Mary E., Ralph S., Jr. Clerk Pa. R.R., June 1898-May 1904; in coal brokerage business, May 1904-Oct. 1914; mem. Pittsburgh Stock Exchange, Oct. 1914-May 1919; partner Holmes, Bulkley & Wardrop, May 1919-Apr. 1922; partner Kay Richards & Co. since Apr. 1922; dir. Penn Central Airlines. Trustee Elizabeth Steel Magee Hosp.; dir. Allegheny Gen. Hosp. Pres. Pittsburgh Stock Exchange, Associated Stock Exchanges; gov. N.Y. Stock Exchange. Clubs: Duquesne, Pittsburgh, Allegheny Country, Rolling Rock, Edgeworth. Home: Woodland Road, Edgeworth, Pa. Office: Union Trust Bldg., Pittsburgh, Pa.

RICHARDS, Robert Haven, lawyer; b. Georgetown, Del., Nov. 15, 1873; s. Charles Fleming and Mary Catherine (Sudler) R.; prep. edn., Dickinson Prep. Sch.; B.A., Dickinson Coll., Carlisle, Pa., 1895, LL.D., 1923; m. Lydia Newsham Haddock, of Carlisle, June 26, 1901; children—Jane Rebecca, Charles Fleming, Robert Henry. Admitted to Del. Bar, 1897, and began practice at Georgetown; dep. atty. gen. of Del., 1901-05, atty. gen., 1905-09. Counsel State of Del. in original suit brought in Supreme Court of U.S., by State of N.J. vs. State of Del., 1905, to determine boundary between the two states, and mem. of commn. representing Del. to negotiate compact; dir. Wilmington Trust Co., Equitable Trust Co., Wilmington Morris Bank, Continental American Life Insurance Company,

Electric Hose & Rubber Co. Mem. Am., Del. and New Castle bar assns., Am. Soc. Polit. and Social Science, Am. and Del. hist. assns., Soc. Colonial Wars, S.A.R. (ex-pres. Del. Chapter), Phi Beta Kappa, Phi Kappa Sigma. Republican. Presbyn. Clubs: Wilmington, Wilmington Country; Union League (Phila.); Bankers (New York. Home: 2102 Park Drive. Office: du Pont Bldg., Wilmington, Del.

RICHARDS, Robert Henry, Jr., lawyer; b. Wilmington, Del., Nov. 14, 1905; s. Robert H. and Lydia N. (Haddock) R.; student Friends Sch., Wilmington, 1910-20, Taft Sch., Watertown, Conn., 1920-24; A.B., U. of Del., Newark, Del., 1928; LL.B., Harvard Law Sch., 1931; m. Harriett Elisabeth Kellond, Jan. 1, 1930; children—Lydia Anne, Jane Kellond, Robert Henry. Admitted to Del. bar, 1931; law sec. 3d Circuit Ct. of Appeals, U.S., 1931-32; mem. of firm Richards, Layton & Finger, Wilmington, since 1932, v.p. and dir. Claymont Trust Co., Claymont, Del., since 1936. Dep. atty. gen., New Castle County, Del., 1933; chief dept. atty. gen. of Del., 1933-37; chmn. Rep. State Conv., 1936. Dir. Homeopathic Hosp., Family Soc., Wilmington. Mem. Acad. of Polit. Sciences, New Castle County, Del. and Am. bar assns., Beta Theta Pi. Republican. Clubs: Wilmington, Wilmington Country (Wilmington); Rehoboth Country (Rehobeth Beach, Del.); Concord (Pa.) Country. Home: 1102 Broom St. Office: 4072 Du Pont Bldg., Wilmington, Del.

RICHARDS, Samuel H., lawyer; b. Bridgeport, N.J.; s. Samuel and Sarah A. (Cheesman) R.; LL.B., Columbia U. Law Sch.; m. Harriet Torbert; children—Ruth (Mrs. J. Everett Magin), H. Jerome. Admitted to N.J. bar as atty. and as counselor; engaged in gen. practice of law at Camden, N.J.; mem. firm French, Richards & Bradley. Served as mem. N.J. Commn. to Commemorate 300th Anniversary of Settlement by Swedes and Finns on the Delaware. Mem. Am. Bar Assn. (v.p. 1934-35), N.J. State and Camden bar assns. Home: Haddonfield. Office: 217 N. 6th St., Camden, N.J.

RICHARDS, Samuel McClure, architect; b. Butler Co., Pa., Sept. 11, 1881; s. Martin L. and Sarah (Patterson) R.; ed. pub. sch. and high sch.; extension course in arch., Armour Inst. Tech., 1916-19; m. Amelia M. Cooper, Oct. 30, 1902; 1 son, Clarence Lester (dec.). Learned carpenter trade with A. King & Sons, Freeport, Pa., and later mgr. same firm; licensed as architect by State of Pa., 1920 and since followed profession at Freeport. Served as Dir. of the Poor, borough of Freeport, 1916-20. Mem. bd. and treas. Freeport Pub. Schs. Treas. Armstrong County, Pa., County School Bd.; pres. bd. dirs. Jos. S. Finch Co., Credit Union. Mem. Pa. Assn. Architects. Republican. Lutheran. Royal Arcanum. Home: 209 Market St., Freeport, Pa.

RICHARDS, Thomas Lohr, lawyer; b. Boyds, Md., Dec. 1, 1894; s. Thomas Davis and Sarah Ella (Carl) R.; A.B., Wooster Coll., Wooster, O., 1916; LL.B., Harvard U. Law Sch., 1920; m. Edna W. Kuhn, Oct. 8, 1924; 1 dau., Ruth Ann. Admitted to Md. bar, 1920, and since engaged in gen. practice of law at Cumberland; dir. and counsel First Federal Savings and Loan Assn. of Cumberland since 1934; local atty. Federal Land Bank of Baltimore since 1922. Served as private, corpl., and sergt., U.S.A., 1918-19; now 1st lt. Cav. Res. Mem. Allegany Co. Bar Assn., Allegany Co. Hist. Soc. (pres.), Delta Sigma Rho. Republican. Presbyn. Club: Lions. Home: 843 Mt. Royal Av. Office: Liberty Trust Bldg., Cumberland, Md.

RICHARDS, William Allison, mining engr., coal operator; b. Wilkes-Barre, Pa., Sept. 21, 1896; s. William Joseph and Catharine (Carty) R.; E.M., Lehigh U., Bethlehem, Pa., 1917; grad. student U. of Montpellier, Montpellier, Herault, France, 1919; m. Elizabeth Cumming, Oct. 27, 1923; children—Elizabeth Wolverton, William Allison (dec.). Employed with engring. corps. P. & R. Coal & Iron Co., Pottsville, Pa., 1919-21, asst. mining engr., 1921-24; gen. mgr. Ashland Coal & Coke Co., Majestic Collieries Co., Pemberton Coal & Coke Co., all of Bluefield, W.Va., 1924, pres. same cos. since 1925; pres. Sovereign Pocahontas Co., Bluefield, since 1931; chmn. bd. Bluefield Supply Co. since 1931. Served in R.O.T.C., 2d lt. to capt. engrs. U.S.A., 1917-19, with A.E.F.; awarded citation by C.O. 505th Engrs. Pres. Winding Gulf Operators Assn., 1929-31, Operators Assn. of Williamson Field, 1930. Chmn. Bituminous Coal Operators Conf., 1937. Mem. Am. Soc. Mil. Engrs., Am. Legion, Kappa Alpha. Democrat. Presbyn. Mason. Clubs: University, Clover, Country (Bluefield); Bankers (New York); Clinker (Philadelphia); Pottsville (Pottsville, Pa.). Home: 1402 Lebanon St. Office: Peery Bldg., Bluefield, W.Va.

RICHARDS, William Joseph, mining engr.; b. Minersville, Pa., Apr. 14, 1863; s. Joseph H. and Mary Elizabeth (Weaver) R.; m. Katherine Johnson Carty, of Ashland, Pa., May 9, 1889. Mining engr. with Phila. & Reading Coal & Iron Corpn., 1883-87, with Mineral Railroad & Mining Co., 1888, again with P.&R.C.&I. Co., 1889; chief engr. Lehigh & Wilkes-Barre Coal Co., 1889-97; gen. supt. same, 1897-1902; gen. mgr. P.&R.C.&I. Co., 1903-07, v.p., 1907-14, pres., 1914-27, also pres. P.&R.C.&I. Corpn., 1924-27; chmn. bd. Sovereign-Pocahontas Co., Ashland Coal and Coke Co., Majestic Collieries Co., Pemberton Coal Co. President Patriotic League of Schuylkill Co., World War; chmn. Mine Cave Commn., State of Pa.; mem. Anthracite Conciliation Board, 1904-27. Mem. Am. Inst. Mining and Metall. Engrs. Republican. Presbyn. Clubs: Pottsville, Schuylkill Country; Union League (Phila.); Railroad (New York); Westmoreland (Wilkes-Barre). Home: 1311 Howard Av., Pottsville, Pa. Office: Whitehall Bldg., New York, N.Y.*

RICHARDSON, Channing Alonzo, clergyman; b. Milton, Wis., Oct. 20, 1876; s. Ralph and Melissa Jane (Kenyon) R.; A.B., Milton Coll., 1896, A.M., same, 1897; B.D., Garrett Bibl. Inst., 1900; (hon.) D.D., Milton Coll., 1917; hon. D.D., Garrett Bibl. Inst., 1937; m. Jessie Mae Kellogg, Oct. 29, 1901 (dec.); children—George Channing (M.D.), Rev. Ralph Huntington, Frank Kellogg (atty.). Ordained to ministry Methodist Ch., 1902; pastor, Newcastle, Modesto, Palo Alto, and Napa, Calif., 1900-17; supt. Sacramento Dist. Meth. Ch., 1917-24; pastor, San Jose, Calif., 1924-29; supt. Dept. City Work Bd. Home Missions and Ch. Extension, Methodist Ch., Phila., Pa., since 1929; chmn. Bur. Goodwill Industries since 1929. Del. to Uniting Conf. of Meth. Ch., Apr. 1939. Four-minute man during World War. Dir. Goodwill Industries in Baltimore, San Diego, San Francisco, San Jose, and Boston. Republican. Methodist. Mason (32°). Home: Robt. Morris Hotel. Office: 1701 Arch St., Philadelphia, Pa.

RICHARDSON, Charles Albert, physician; b. Jefferson, Me., Dec. 17, 1875; s. Samuel Albert and Emily Bennett (Litchfield) R.; grad. Hebron (Me.) Acad., 1898; student Colby Coll., Waterville, Me., 1898-1900; M.D., McGill Univ., Med. Sch., C.M., 1904; m. Lillian Frances Hartigan, Sept. 9, 1911; 1 son, Albert. Interne Western Gen. Hosp., Montreal, 1904-05, Kings Co. Hosp., Brooklyn, N.Y., 1905-07; attending physician in medicine and obstetrics, Englewood Hosp., 1911-28, chief of obstetrics service since 1928; dir. Closter Nat. Bank & Trust Co. since 1927. Mem. Phi Delta Theta. Republican. Baptist. Mason. Home: High St. Office: Main St., Closter, N.J.

RICHARDSON, Clarence H., prof. mathematics; b. West Plains, Mo., July 21, 1890; s. Elias F. and Nannie (Hudson) R.; B.S., U. of Ky., 1913; M.S., U. of Ill., 1918; Ph.D., U. of Mich., 1927; m. Agnes Brownfield, Nov. 7, 1913; children—Clarence H., Jr., Robert Byron, Lucile (dec.). Engaged in teaching, high sch., Marion, Ky., 1913-14; instr. mathematics, Columbia Coll., Lake City, Fla., 1914-16; prof. mathematics, Georgetown (Ky.) Coll., 1918-28; prof. mathematics, Bucknell U., Lewisburg, Pa., since 1928. Mem. Math. Assn. America, Theta Kappa Nu, Phi Delta Kappa, Pi Mu Epsilon. Baptist. Author: Statistical Analysis, 1934. Co-author (with I. L. Miller): Business Mathematics, 1939. Home: 401 S. 6th, Lewisburg, Pa. Office: Bucknell University, Lewisburg, Pa.

RICHARDSON, Edgar S., lawyer; b. Stonersville, Pa., Mar. 22, 1885; s. Charles M. and Elizabeth T. (Snyder) R.; A.B., Princeton U., 1905; LL.B., U. of Pa. Law Sch., 1910; m. Juliet U. Shearer, Jan. 20, 1917; 1 dau., Mary Elizabeth. Admitted to Pa. Supreme Ct. bar, 1910; since in gen. practice at Reading, Pa.; judge Ct. of Common Pleas, Berks Co., Pa., 1924-25; gen. counsel and dir. Berks County Trust Co., Mt. Penn Trust Co., Robesonia State Bank, Reading Automobile Club; gen. counsel and v.p. Reading Chamber of Commerce. Trustee and mem. exec. com. Reading Hosp. Mem. Am. Bar Assn., Pa. Bar Assn., Berks Co. Bar Assn., Phi Delta Phi, Delta Sigma Rho. Republican. Reformed Ch. Mason. Clubs: University, Wyomissing, Reading Country, Berkshire Country (Reading, Pa.). Home: 36th St. and Woodland Av., Reiffton, Pa. Office: Berks Co. Trust Bldg., Reading, Pa.

RICHARDSON, Edward H(enderson), surgeon; b. Farmville, Va., Nov. 13, 1877; s. Hilary Goode and Mary (Perkins) R.; Master Accounts, Eastman Business Coll., Poughkeepsie, N.Y., 1894; student Va. Poly. Inst., 1896-97; A.B., Hampden-Sydney Coll., 1900, LL.D., 1921; grad. study Johns Hopkins Univ., 1900-01, M.D., 1905, surg. apprentice, 1905-10; m. Emily Gould, June 27, 1905; children—Mary Gould (Mrs. W. A. Hosley Gantt), Edward H. Resident house officer, assistant resident gynecologist and resident gynecologist, Johns Hopkins Hosp., 1905-10, asst. visiting gynecologist since 1912; instr. in gynecology, Johns Hopkins U., 1910-12, asso. in clin. gynecology, 1912-34, asso. prof. of gynecology since 1934; visiting gynecologist, Union Memorial Hosp., Woman's Hosp., Church Home and Infirmary, Sinai Hosp., Sheppard and Enoch Pratt Hosp. Fellow Am. Coll. Surgeons; mem. A.M.A., Southern Med. Assn., Southern Surg. Assn., Am. Gynecol. Soc. (v.p., 1934-35), Baltimore City Med. Soc. (pres., 1926, 27), Kappa Sigma, Omicron Delta Kappa. Presbyn. Clubs: Maryland, Johns Hopkins, Elkridge. Originator of several surg. operative procedures. Contbr. to surg. jours. Home: 3 Whitfield Rd. Office: 9 E. Chase St., Baltimore, Md.

RICHARDSON, Ernest Cushing, librarian; b. Woburn, Mass., Feb. 9, 1860; s. James Cushing and Lydia Bartlett (Taylor) R.; A.B., Amherst, 1880, A.M., 1883; Ph.D., from Washington and Jerfferson, 1887; grad. Hartford Theol. Sem., 1883; (hon. A.M., Princeton, 1896); m. Grace Duncan, d. Z. Stiles Ely, June 30, 1891; 1 dau., Mary Ely (dec.). First asst. librarian, Amherst Coll., 1879-80; librarian Hartford Theol. Sem., 1884-90, asso. prof. bibiology, 1885-90; librarian Princeton U., 1890-1920, dir., 1920-23, hon. dir. and research prof. bibliography, 1923-25, emeritus dir. since 1925; consultant in bibliography and research, Library of Congress, since 1925. Mem. N.J. Pub. Library Commn., 1900-12; trustee Hartford Theol. Sem. Mem. A.L.A. (pres., 1904-05), Am. Library Inst. (pres., 1915-18), Am. Hist. Assn., N.J. Hist. Assn., Bibliographical Society of America, etc.; corresponding member Societa Ligure di Storia Patria; corr. mem. Preussische Akademie; honorary mem. Library Association of China. Clubs: Cosmos (Washington); Princeton, Amherst (New York); Nassau (Princeton). Author: Bibliographical Synopsis of the Ante-Nicene Fathers, 1887; Classification, Theoretical and Practical, 1901, 11, 29; Revised transls. of Eusebius' Life of Constantine, 1890; Jerome and Gennadius' Lives of Illustrious Men, 1892; critical edit. of Hieronymus u. Gennadius De Viris Illustribus, 1896; Writings on American History, 1902; Index to Periodical Articles on Religion, 1907-11; Some Old Egyptian Librarians, 1911; Collections on European History, 1912-15; The Beginnings of Libraries, 1913; Biblical Libraries, 1914; Archival Libraries in the 14th Century, B.C., 1917; Essentials of International Coöperation, 1919; American Books and Libraries (League of Nations Bull.), 1925; Special Collections in North American Libraries, 1927; Some Aspects of International Library Coöperation, 1928; Subject Headings in

RICHARDSON Theology, 1928; Princeton University Library Classification, 1900-20, 1929; General Library Coöperation and American Research Books, 1929; A.L.A. Plan for Research Library Service, 1930; Possibilities of Coöperative Cataloging, 1932; A World Catalog of Manuscript Books, 1933-1937, 6 parts; Aspects of Coöperative Cataloging, 1933; Jacopo da Varagine, 1935; The Universal Library, 1939. Home: 95 Library Place, Princeton, N.J.

RICHARDSON, Ernest Gladstone, bishop; b. St. Vincent, W.I., Feb. 24, 1874; s. Jonathan C. and Dorothea Ann (Davison) R.; B.A., Dickinson Coll., 1896; M.A., Yale, 1899; D.D., Wesleyan U., Conn., 1913; LL.D., Dickinson, 1920; m. Anna E. Isenberg, Apr. 21, 1897; children—Hallam Maxon, Marion (dec.), Winifred (dec.). Ordained M.E. Ministry, 1896; pastor Wallingford, Conn., 1896-99, N.Y. City, 1899-1910, Bristol, Conn., 1910-13, N.Y. City, 1913-29; bishop M.E. Ch. since May 1920. Mem. Phi Beta Kappa, Phi Kappa Sigma. Home: 1701 Arch St., Philadelphia, Pa.

RICHARDSON, George, Jr.; mem. law firm Richardson & Kemper. Address: Bluefield, W.Va.

RICHARDSON, George Partridge, mech. engr.; b. Duxbury, Mass., Sept. 5, 1874; s. Parker Cleaveland and Harriette (Moore) R.; student Pratt Inst. Tech. High Sch., Brooklyn, 1890-93; M.E., Stevens Inst. Tech., 1897; m. Kathleen Gill Atkinson, Jan. 19, 1903; children—George Partridge, Gill McDonald, Kathleen Moore. With Isbell-Porter Co., contracting engrs., Newark, N.J., since 1897, successively as draftsman, constrn. engr., asst. engr., mgr. of regulator dept., and chief engr., v.p. since 1937. Served as 2d lt., N.J. Militia Res., 1917-19. Mem. Twp. Com., Milburn Twp., N.J., 1919. Mem. Am. Soc. M.E., Stevens Inst. Alumni Assn., Chi Psi. Home: 441 Baldwin Rd., Maplewood, N.J. Office: 46 Bridge St., Newark, N.J.

RICHARDSON, Harry Bentley, lawyer; b. Bentleyville, Pa., June 21, 1885; s. Winfield F. and Lillian (West) R.; A.B., Washington and Jefferson Coll., 1907; student U. of Pittsburgh Law Sch., 1914-16; m. Mary Jane Holt, Sept. 23, 1908; children—Jean (Mrs. G. P. Hamilton), Harrison Holt. In shipping dept. Lackawanna Steel Co., 1907-09; supt. high sch., 1909-12; with U.S. Consular Service, Liverpool, England, and Belgrade, Serbia, 1913-14; admitted to Beaver County bar, 1917; mem. firm Holt, Richardson & West since 1936; mem. Pa. State Legislature, 1927; dir. Citizens Nat. Bank (Bentleyville), Workingmen's Bldg. & Loan Assn. of Woodlawn (Aliquippa), Aliquippa Community Loan Co. Republican. Methodist. Mason. Home: Beaver, Pa. Office: 530 Franklin Av., Aliquippa, Pa.

RICHARDSON, John Holt, lawyer; b. Baltimore, Feb. 27, 1867; s. Caleb and Mary Ann Cornelius (Hawkins) R.; ed. in pub. schs., Baltimore, and Baltimore City Coll.; 1874-81; studied law pvtly.; m. Elizabeth Nitzel, June 11, 1889; children—John, Elizabeth, Mary (dec.), Standley Leroy. Began at trade of shipwright; admitted to Md. bar, 1897, and since practiced in Baltimore; justice of peace, 1896-1900. Mem. Am., Md. State and Baltimore City bar assns., S.A.R. Republican. Episcopalian. Mason (33°, K.T., Shriner). Home: Stemmer's Run, Md. Office: Maryland Trust Bldg., Baltimore, Md.

RICHARDSON, Joseph Ablett, judge; b. Pittsburgh, Pa., July 1, 1892; s. Joseph and Ann (Ablett) R.; A.B., U. of Pittsburgh, 1915; LL.B., Duquesne U. Law Sch., 1918; m. Genevieve Loveless, Dec. 25, 1918; children—Mary Louise, Joseph Ablett, Jr. Admitted to Pa. bar, 1918, and engaged in gen. practice of law at Pittsburgh until 1934; asst. U.S. atty., 1925-29; apptd. judge Co. Ct., Jan. 1934, judge of Common Pleas Ct., June 1934; elected judge Common Pleas Ct., Nov. 1935. Served as pvt. inf., U.S.A., in World War. Mem. Am. and Pa. bar assns., Delta Tau Delta, Omicron Delta Kappa. Republican. Methodist. Mason (32°, Shriner). Home: 3102 Norwood Av. Office: 702 City-County Bldg., Pittsburgh, Pa.

RICHARDSON, Leo Duane, glass bottle mfg.; b. Knox, Pa., June 5, 1894; s. George B. and Ella M. (Yates) R.; ed. pub. sch. and high sch., Knox, Pa., 1909-12; m. Hazel A. Davis, Oct. 20, 1916; children—Georgeanna, Marlys Jean, Ruth Elizabeth, Marian Davis. Employed as telegrapher and agt., B.&O. R.R. Co., 1912-22; asso. with Knox Glass Bottle Co. since 1922, sec., treas. and dir.; treas. and dir. Knox Glass Associates; treas. and dir. Knox-Oneill Co.; dir. Oil City (Pa.) Glass Bottle Co., Knox Glass Bottle Co. (Jackson, Miss.), Canadian Knox Glass Co., Ltd. Democrat. Presbyn. Mason. K.P. Club: Knox Community. Home: Pennsylvania Av., Knox, Pa.

RICHARDSON, Lunsford; chmn. bd. Vick Chem. Co. Office: 900 Market St., Wilmington, Del.

RICHARDSON, Marion Blanchard, ednl. adviser; b. Girard, Pa., Mar. 2, 1892; s. George B. and Bertha R. (Thompson) R.; student Grove City (Pa.) pub. and high schs., 1898-1912; B.S., Pa. State Coll., 1921, M.E., 1926; student Teacher's Coll., Columbia U., summer 1936; m. Georgia V. Slater, Aug. 22, 1917; children: Marion B., Jr., Charles S. Began as machine hand, Bessemer Gas Engine Co., Grove City, Pa., 1912-13; track and storeroom laborer, Bessemer & Lake Erie R.R., Feb.-Sept. 1913; locomotive fireman, 1914-15, 1916; student, R.O.T.C., Madison Barracks, N.Y.; May-Aug. 1917; 2d lieut. Ordnance N.A., 1917-19; with A.E.F., June, 1918-July, 1919; draftsman mcch. dept., B.&L.E. R.R., 1919-20; shop draftsman, Greenville, Pa., 1921-23; asso. mech. editor, Railway Age and Asso. editor Railway Mechanical Engineer, New York, 1923-33; instr., night school, Pratt Inst., Brooklyn, N.Y., 1931-32; junior partner, Ahrens & Richardson, New York, Feb.-Nov., 1933; project engr., N.J. State Civil Works Adminstrn., 1933-34; traffic-accident dir., N.J. State Emergency Recovery Adminstrn., 1934-35; special work, U.S. Govt., Washington, D.C., May-Nov. 1935; ednl. adviser, Civilian Conservation Corps, Governors Island, N.Y., since Nov. 1935. Major Infantry Reserve since 1933. Mem. Am. Soc. of Mech. Engrs. (sec., railroad div. since 1925; advisory mem. standing com. on edn. and training for the industries since 1937), Soc. of Am. Mil. Engrs., Reserve Officers' Assn., Am. Legion, Vets. Foreign Wars, Alpha Chi Rho. Episcopalian. Mason. Contbr. chapter on "Railway-Mechanical Engineering" in Vocational Guidance in Engineering Lines, 1930; also articles to tech. jours. and socs. Home: 21 Hazel Av., Livingston, N.J.

RICHARDSON, Russell, physician; b. Brooklyn, N.Y., Mar. 19, 1882; s. John Edward and Charlotte Lenox' (Russell) R.; A.B., Princeton, 1904; ed. U. of Pa., 1906-07; A.M., Harvard Grad. Sch., 1911; M.D., Harvard Med. Sch., 1911; m. Marion Eastburn Briggs, Oct. 5, 1905; children—Russell, Jr., William Eastburn, John Eastburn, Philip Briggs. Asst. in pathology, Pa. Hosp., Phila., 1911-17; dir. lab., Abington Memorial Hosp., 1916-30; dir. lab., M.E. Hosp., Phila., Pa., since 1918; instr. medicine, U. of Pa. Med. Sch., 1923-29, asso. in medicine, 1930-36, asst. prof. medicine since 1936; asso. of Geo. S. Cox Research Inst., U. of Pa., since 1931. Served as 1st lt. Med. Corps, U.S.A., 1917-18. Fellow Am. Coll. Phys., Phila. Coll. Phys. Mem. Am. Med. Assn., Soc. for Exptl. Biology and Medicine, Am. Soc. Clin. Pathologists, Phila. Pathol. Soc. Republican. Baptist. Clubs: Art, Philobiblon. Home: 320 S. 16th St., Philadelphia, Pa.

RICHARDSON, Willard Samuel; b. Woburn, Mass., July 30, 1867; s. Jesse and Mary M. (Pearson) R.; student Denison U., Granville, O., Internat. Y.M.C.A. Coll., Springfield, Mass., U. of Rochester; A.B., Brown University, 1894; B.D., Union Theological Seminary, New York, 1897; D.C.L., Acadia Univ., 1932; Master of Humanics, Springfield College, 1935; m. Laura A. Alexander, Oct. 26, 1900; children—Alice Mary, Ruth Alexander, Elisabeth. Ordained Bapt. ministry, 1897; asst. and asso. minister 5th Av. Ch., N.Y. City, 1894-1909; head master Neighborhood House, New York, 1906-09; dir. religious activities, U. of Minn., 1909-12; staff of J. D. Rockefeller since Sept. 1912. Trustee Internat. Seminary, East Orange, N.J., since 1924, Internat. Y.M.C.A. College, Springfield, Mass., since 1925, American Institute of Christian Philosophy since 1926, Colgate-Rochester Divinity Sch. since 1933; trustee Davison Fund (New York). Mem. 7th Regt. N.Y. N.G. 2 yrs. Mem. Mil. Order Loyal Legion, Alpha Delta Phi. Author: David, 1907. Home: 119 Harrison Av., Montclair, N.J. Office: 30 Rockefeller Plaza, New York, N.Y.

RICHARDSON, William E., ex-congressman; b. Exeter Tp., Berks Co., Pa., Sept. 3, 1886; s. Charles M. and Elizabeth (Snyder) R.; A.B., Princeton, 1910; LL.B., Columbia, 1913; m. Mary Eckert Potts, Feb. 24, 1926; 3 children. In practice of law at Reading, Pa., since 1914. Served with Ambulance Americaine, Belgium and France, 1915; with Squadron A, N.Y. N.G., Mexican Border, 1916; machine gunner, U.S.A., World War, participating in major engagements. Mem. 73d and 74th Congresses (1933-37), 14th Pa. Dist. Mem. Com. Fgn. Affairs, Council of Interparliamentary Union. Democrat. Home: 1255 Perkiomen Av. Office: Berks County Trust Bldg., Reading, Pa.

RICHARDSON, William Payson; b. Farmer Center, O., Nov. 6, 1864; s. Richard and Margaret (Powell) R.; student U. of Wooster, O., 1886-88; LL.B., U. of Md., 1894; LL.D., St. Lawrence U., 1903; m. Bessie H. Albaugh, Dcc. 26, 1904; 1 son, David Albaugh. Admitted to bar, 1901, and practiced at Brooklyn; organizer, 1901, and developer, dean and prof. law, Brooklyn Law Sch. (department of law of St. Lawrence U.). Mem. com. to found a university in Brooklyn. Mem. Am., N.Y. State and Brooklyn bar assns., Bar Assn. City of New York, Academy of Political Science, Ohio Soc. Republican. Presbyn. K.P. Clubs: Crescent Athletic, Rotary, Springbrook Country, Committee of One Hundred. Author: Richardson's Commercial Law, 1900; Contracts, 1934; Bills and Notes, 1932; Guaranty and Suretyship, 1929; Bailments, 1937; Selected Cases in Evidence, 1927; The Law of Evidence, 1936. Home: Kahdena Rd., Morristown, N.J. Office: 375 Pearl St., Brooklyn, N.Y.

RICHARDSON, William Waddle, physician; b. Athens, O., Oct. 8, 1877; s. Alonzo Blair and Julia Burton (Harris) R.; B.Ph., Ohio State U., 1899; M.D., U. of Pa. Med. Sch., 1902; m. Lila MacDonald, Nov. 13, 1906 (dec.); children—Alonzo Blair, Martha, Julia Harris (Mrs. Hugh Corbin), William W., Jr., Robert King. Served as asst. physician Columbus Hosp., 1903-06; chief physician Norristown (Pa.) Hosp., 1906-12; med. dir. Mercer Sanitarium, Mercer, Pa., since 1912 and mem. firm propr. of same; dir. First Nat. Bank. Served as maj. Med. Corps, U.S.A., World War. Mem. Mercer Co. Pub. Assistance Bd., Mercer Free Library Bd. Mem. Am. Coll. Physicians, Am. Psychiatric Assn., Beta Theta Pi, Phi Beta Kappa, Sigma Xi. Republican. Presbyn. Rotarian. Home: Mercer, Pa.

RICHIE, Gustavus Adolphus, clergyman and prof.; b. Shamokin, Pa., Sept. 22, 1888; s. Simon Henry and Hannah (Shensel) R.; A.B., Lebanon Valley Coll., 1913; B.D., Bonebrake Theol. Sem., 1917; A.M., U. of Pa., 1927; grad. study Northwestern U., 1930-31; (hon.) D.D., Lebanon Valley Coll., 1927; m. Mae Belle Orris, Aug. 24, 1915; 1 dau., Alice Mary. Began as stenographer, T. A. James & Co., Phila., Pa., 1907; lay asst., Marble Collegiate Ch., New York City, 1913-14; ordained to ministry Ch. of U. Brethren in Christ, 1917; minister, Allentown, Pa., 1917-23, Phila., Pa., 1923-25; prof. Bible and Greek, Lebanon Valley Coll., Annville, Pa., since 1925. Mem. Nat. Assn. Bible Instrs. Republican. Mem. Ch. U. Brethren in Christ. Home: 466 E. Main St., Annville, Pa.

RICHLEY, John William, automobile agent; b. Carroll Twp., Pa., July 30, 1874; s. John G. F. and Elizabeth Ann (Menear) R.; ed. pub. schs. and York County Acad.; m. Katie

M. Brant, Aug. 16, 1894 (dec.); children—Paul C., Ruth V. (dec.), Miriam May, Bessie Ray. Began work in painters' trade at age of 12, continuing for 3 yrs.; apprentice machinists' trade, 3 yrs.; teacher primary, later high sch., 1892-1900; became owner of bicycle shop, 1898, and included automobile repairing, 1900; held car agency for more than 19 yrs., introducing many popular makes of automobiles in York, one dept. operated as Penn Auto Co., 1915-24, main plant as J. W. Richley Auto Co.; sales and service rooms contains 50,000 sq. ft. of floor space and new plant for large trucks and tractors contains 17,000 sq. ft.; dir. First Nat. Bank, York. Designed, built and owner York Theatre, mgr. since opening, 1934. Rep. nominee for mayor, York, 1923; campaign mgr. Gov. Pinchot's primary campaign for U.S. Senator. Trustee York Co. Acad. Methodist (teacher Young Men's Bible Class). Mason (K.T., Shriner), Knight of Malta. Winner numerous auto races, holding 39 cups, many trophies, etc. Home: 635 E. Chestnut St. Office: 525 E. Market St., York, Pa.

RICHMOND, Samuel M., pres. and gen. mgr. Anderson Automobile Co., Inc.; b. Sewickley, Pa., Dec. 17, 1889; s. William S. and Kathryn (Merton) R.; grad. Sewickley Pub. Sch., 1904; m. Hetty E. Anderson, July 21, 1915; children —Mary Roberta, Julia Fleming. Successively grocery clerk, postal clerk, salesman and railroad passenger agent; sec.-treas. Anderson Automobile Co., Inc., 1919-32, pres. and gen. mgr. since 1933. Republican. Methodist. Home: 547 Centennial Av.; Office: Broad St. and Centennial Av., Sewickley, Pa.

RICHTER, William Benson, dentist, composer, author; b. Phila., Pa., May 25, 1901; s. Philip and Hannah (Negler) R.; student Central High Sch., Phila., 1915-18, Brown Prep., Phila., 1920-21; D.D.S., Phila. Dental Coll., 1925; studied music with pvt. teachers, Phila.; unmarried. Successively violinist, salesman, orchestra leader, and since 1925, dentist, Phila. Mem. Am. Dental Assn., Acad. of Polit. Science, Am. Acad. Polit. and Social Science, Alpha Omega. Orthodox Jewish religion. Author: (novels) The Ghetto's Struggle, 1935; Humanity, 1930; Sin's Aftermath, 1937; Jackson and Jefferson, 1936; author also of poems and short stories; composer of several songs published in England, and popular song, "Refugeee," 1939. Literary editor Hungarian Weekly Independence, 1930-31. Played in numerous Phila. Symphony Student Orchestras. Home: 630 N. 7th St. Office: 7101 York Rd., Philadelphia, Pa.

RICHTER, Wilmer Siegfried, artist; b. Phila., Pa., Jan. 20, 1891; s. Herman G. and Sophie (Schneck) R.; ed. Sch. of Industrial Art, 1915, Pa. Acad. of Fine Arts, 1924; study München, Germany, summer 1927, also France, Italy, Mexico, Switzerland, Belgium; m. Caroline Cermak, June 5, 1920; children—Wilmer C., Dorrit, Carole Elaine. Engaged as free lance in advertising art and mag. covers and illustration since 1915; for past 20 yrs. has exhibited in prin. cities of East Ac. Acad. Fine Arts, Phila., New York Water Club, Sweat Memorial at Portland, Me., Corcoran Art Gallery, Washington, D.C., and Chicago Art Inst.; paintings in pub. schs. and in many pvt. collections of well known persons. Served as pvt. inf., U.S.A., 1917-19, with 28th Div., A.E.F. Republican. Clubs: Sketch, Art Alliance, Water Color (Philadelphia). Home: 1021 Pennsylvania Av., Brookline, Upper Darby, Pa.

RICKABY, Mary W., newspaper editor; b. Paterson, N.J.; d. William and Bridget (Feeney) R.; ed. St. Joseph Roman Cath. Sch., Paterson, N.J. Engaged in newspaper work continuously since 1904; society and Cath. news editor, Paterson Evening News since 1921. Democrat. Roman Catholic. Home: 400 Broadway, Paterson, N.J.

RICKARD, LeRoy R(obert), lawyer; b. Mercer Co., Pa., Jan. 15, 1885; s. William E. and Susan Jane (Seidle) R.; B.S., Fredonia Vocational Sch., 1907; m. Mabel E. Hecker, Aug. 30, 1909; children—Dwight W. (dec.), Helen E. (Mrs. David C. Lewis). Worked in steel plant as laborer then clk.; engaged in teaching sch., 1904-07; admitted to Pa. bar, 1908, and since engaged in gen. practice of law at Mercer; served as dist. atty. Mercer Co., 1919-27; county solicitor Mercer Co., 1932-35; borough solicitor Mercer, Pa., since 1919 and solicitor for several other municipalities. Awarded Distinguished Service Certificate by Am. Legion, 1935. Republican. United Presbyn. Mason (K.T., 32°, Shriner). Elk, I.O.O.F. Home: 119 W. Market St. Office: First Nat. Bank Bldg., Mercer, Pa.

RICKERT, Glennis Hartman, supt. of schs.; b. Freeland, Pa., Feb. 23, 1895; s. Ambrose and Louise (Hartman) R.; A.B., Susquehanna U., Selinsgrove, Pa., 1922; M.A., Columbia U., 1928; m. Edna Speary, Aug. 1919; children—Marian, Glennis Speary. High sch. instr., Freeland, Pa., 1915-16, Wiconisco, Pa., 1916-21; supervising prin., Halifax, Pa., 1922-26; high sch., prin., Kane, Pa., 1926-32, supt. schs. since 1932. Served as private, 314th Inf., A.E.F., 1918-19. Pres. of bd. Pub. and Sch. Library, Kane, Pa., since 1934; mem. Kane Chapter Am. Red Cross since 1920; v.p. 8 yrs., Boy Scouts of America since 1927, area chmn. of training 4 yrs., v.p. Kane dist. com. since 1936, Y.M.C.A. bd. of dirs., recording sec. since 1933; chmn. Dist. 9 State Bd. of Control of Pa. Interscholastic Athletic Assn. since 1937; mem. bd. trustees First Bapt. Ch. since 1928. Mem. Am. Legion (past comdr. Posts of Kane, Halifax, Lykens), Assn. Am. Sch. Adminstrs., N.E. A., Pa. State Edn. Assn. Awarded Order of Purple Heart, 1920. Republican. Baptist. Mason. Clubs: Rotary International (gov. 1938-39, now past dist. gov., dist. 175), Kane (Kane, Pa.). Home: 120 Pine Av. Office: Chestnut St., Kane, Pa.

RICKETSON, John Howland III, insurance; b. Pittsburgh, Pa., Sept. 21, 1902; s. John H., Jr., and Anna V. (Scaife) R.; ed. Allegheny Prep. Sch., 1909-16, Middlesex Sch., Concord, Mass., 1916-21; A.B., Harvard, 1925; m. Anne King Scott, June 9, 1930; 1 son, Scott. Asso. with Edwards, George & Co., insurance agency, Pittsburgh, Pa., since 1928, vice-pres. since 1938; dir. Peoples-Pittsburgh Trust Co., Wm. B. Scaife & Sons Co. Trustee Pa. Coll. for Women. Dir. Western Pa. Sch. for the Blind. Mem. Hasty Pudding Club, Fly Club, Delta Kappa Epsilon. Republican. Clubs: Pittsburgh, Allegheny Country, Pittsburgh Golf, Rolling Rock (Pittsburgh); Harvard, Racquet and Tennis (New York City). Home: Murrayhill Av. Office: 307 Fourth Av., Pittsburgh, Pa.

RICKETTS, George Allen, physician; b. Flinton, Pa., Aug. 17, 1873; s. John and Sarah M. (Turner) R.; M.E., Lock Haven State Normal Coll., 1897; M.D., Jefferson Med. Coll., 1908 coll., 1897; m. Martha Elizabeth McCoy, May 16, 1911; children—John A., Edward A., Harriet A., George L., Robert Bruce. Began as teacher in pub. schs., 1894-1904; after interneship engaged in practice of medicine at Smithmills, Pa., 1910-18, at Osceola Mills, Pa., since 1918; chief of med. staff, Philipsburg State Hosp. since 1924; cardiologist to Philipsburg State Hosp.; surgeon to Pa. R.R. since 1930; vice-pres. First Nat. Bank of Osceola Mills. Pres. sch. bd. of Osceola Mills, 1927-39. Fellow Am. Coll. Phys., Am. Med. Assn.; mem. Pa. Med. Society. Republican. Presbyterian. Mason (32°). Address: 510 Blanchard St., Osceola Mills, Pa.

RICKEY, James Walter, hydraulic engr.; b. Dayton, O., Nov. 10, 1871; s. James and Rosaltha Jane (Jones) R.; C.E., Rensselaer Poly. Inst., 1894; m. Lucy Amelia Mitchell, Jan. 24, 1899. Began as accountant, N.P. Ry., Minneapolis, 1894; prin. asst. engr. Lake Superior Power Corpn., Sault Ste. Marie, Mich., 1896-97, St. Anthony Falls Water Power Co., and Minneapolis Mill Co., 1897-1907; chief hydraulic engr. Aluminum Co. of America, Pittsburgh, Pa., 1907-38, now consulting engineer; has designed and constructed large dams in the states of N.C., N.Y., Tenn., also Chute a Caron Dam, 200 ft. high, and 260,000 h.p. power-house, on Saguenay River, near Kenogami, Quebec (the first stage of one of the largest hydro-electric developments in the world), 1927-30. Dir. Pittsburgh Branch, Pa. Assn. for Blind; mem. Engrs. Soc. of Western Pa. (dir.), Am. Soc. C.E., Engring. Inst. of Canada, Internat. Commn. on Large Dams (Am. Tech. Com.), Rensselaer Soc. of Engrs., Sigma Xi, Theta Nu Epsilon. Republican. Presbyn. Clubs: Duquesne, Pittsburgh Athletic. Contbr. tech. articles to mags. Home: Schenley Apts. Office: 801 Gulf Bldg., Pittsburgh, Pa.

RIDDICK, Carl W., ex-congressman; b. Wells, Minn., Feb. 25, 1872; s. Isaac Hancock and Alice (Wood) R.; student Lawrence U., Appleton, Wis., and Albion (Mich.) Coll. Owner and publisher White Pigeon (Mich.) Journal, 1897-99, Winamac (Ind.) Republican, 1899-1910; sec. Rep. Ind. State Central Com., campaigns, 1906, 08; settled on Govt. homestead in Mont., 1910; county assessor Fergus Co., Mont., 2 terms, 1915-19 inclusive; mem. 66th and 67th Congresses (1919-23), 2d Mont. Dist.; Rep. nominee for U.S. senator, 1924. Home: Riva, Md.

RIDDLE, Henry Alexander, Jr.; b. Chambersburg, Pa., Mar. 22, 1885; s. Henry A. and Martha (Hunter) R.; A.B., Washington and Jefferson Coll., 1907; S.T.B., Western Theol. Sem., 1910; (hon.) D.D., Washington and Jefferson Coll., 1932; m. Frances Ritchie, Dec. 29, 1910; children—Lindsay Ritchie, Martha Elisabeth, Henry Alexander III. Ordained to ministry Presbyn. Ch., 1910; pastor, Allen Grove, Limestone and Wolf Run, W.Va., 1910-15, West Alexander, Pa., 1915-21, Westminster Ch., Greensburg, Pa., 1921-28, First Ch., Lewistown, Pa., since 1928. Trustee Washington and Jefferson Coll., Western Theol. Sem. Mem. Phi Gamma Delta, Scotch-Irish Soc. of Pa. Republican. Presbyn. Mason. Moderator, Presbytery of Huntingdon, 1939. Home: 108 N. Brown St., Lewistown, Pa.

RIDDLE, Malcolm Graeme, pres. Shreve Steamship Agency, Inc.; b. Atlantic City, N.J., Nov. 13, 1909; s. William and Florence M. (Sailor) R.; student Pa. Mil. Coll., 1924-27, Atlantic City High Sch., 1927; m. Margaret Dorman, Sept. 22, 1933; children—Suzanne, Joanne. Pres. Shreve Steamship Agency, Inc.; v.p. and dir. Atlantic City Fire Ins. Co.; asst. treas. and dir. Mary A. Riddle Co. of Del.; dir. Trident Bldg. & Loan Assn., Neptune Mortgage & Finance Co., South Jersey Title & Finance Co. Republican. Club: Atlantic City (N.J.) Kiwanis. Home: 10 N. Swarthmore Av., Ventnor, N.J. Office: 1303 Pacific Av., Atlantic City, N.J.

RIDDLE, Melvin Watt, clergyman; b. Sarver, Pa., May 23, 1889; s. John Watt and Susan (Hemphill) R.; student Cabot Inst., Cabot, Pa., 1907-09, Indiana State Teachers Coll., Pa., 1909-10; A.B., Muskingum Coll., New Concord, O., 1917; student Pittsburgh Theol. Sem., 1919-21; m. Mary Rachel Reynolds, Aug. 2, 1921; children—Lois Margaret, Ruth Genevieve. Began as teacher pub. schs., teacher high sch., then asst. supt. pub. schs. Butler Co., Pa.; ordained to ministry Presbyn. Ch., 1921; now pastor Central Presbyn. Ch., Chambersburg, Pa. Served in O.T.C., Camp Lee, Va., 1918. Republican. Presbyn. Club: Commercial of Chambersburg. Home: 222 Fifth Av., Chambersburg, Pa.

RIDENOUR, Chauncey Owen, asso. prof. English lit.; b. Glenford, O., July 6, 1894; s. Lemuel Melancthon and Sarah Alice (Orr) R.; A.B., O. Univ., 1920; A.M., Pa. State Coll., 1925; grad. study, Columbia U., 1926-27; m. Elizabeth Leukhardt Andrews, June 12, 1923; 1 son, Owen Andrews. Engaged in teaching, pub. schs., O., 1913-16; instr. English, Pa. State Coll., 1920-25, asst. prof. English lit., 1925-33, asso. prof. English lit. since 1933. Served as 2d lt. Q.M.C., U.S.A., 1917-18; 2d lt. inf., O.N.G., 1919-20. Mem. Modern Lang. Assn. of America. Awarded President's Medal, O. Univ., 1920. Republican. Lutheran. Home: 181 Mitchell Av., State College, Pa.

RIDGELY, Charles du Pont, real estate and ins. broker; b. Dover, Del., Jan. 19, 1878; s. Daniel Mifflin and Ella (Madden) R.; ed. Camden (Del.) Pub. Sch., 1884-90. Wilmington Conf. Acad., Dover, Del., 1890-93, Newark (Del.) Acad., 1893-94; m. Helene Rudolph,

Mar. 21, 1905; children—Henry Johnson, Doris Helene. In real estate and ins. business at Camden, Del., since 1904, formed Charles du Pont Ridgely & Co., Camden, 1904; v.p. Baltimore Trust Co., Camden, Del., 1931-34; dir. Del. R.R. Co. Alderman, Camden, Del., 1904-37; Del. State Senator, 1923-24, 1925-26. Republican. Soc. of Friends. Mason (Union Lodge 7, Dover, Del.), Odd Fellow (Amity Lodge 33, Camden, Del.). Descendant of the Honorable Henry Ridgely who came from Devonshire, England, in the year 1659 and settled near Annapolis, Md. He was named after Charles I. du Pont, who was his great uncle. Address: Camden, N.J.

RIDGELY, Henry, lawyer, banker; b. Dover, Del., Jan. 19, 1869; s. Edward and Elizabeth Frazer (Comegys) R.; student Wesley Collegiate Inst., Dover, and U. of Pa.; LL.D., U. of Del., 1916; m. Mabel Lloyd Fisher of Baltimore, Md., June 1, 1893; 1 dau., Philippa Elizabeth (Mrs. Harold Wolfe Horsey). Admitted to Del. bar, 1890, and began practice at Dover; pres. Farmers Bank of State of Del. since 1917. President Delaware State Board of Education, 1914-16 and 1935-36. Trustee University of Del.; mem. Del. State Bar Assn. (pres.); chairman State Bd. of Bar Examiners since 1931; mem. Del. Bankers Assn. (pres., 1928, 29), Gen Soc. Colonial Wars (v.p.), Del. Hist. Soc. (v.p.), Am. Acad. Polit. and Social Science. Author: Ridgely's Digest of Delaware Judical Reports, 1894; also of Delaware statutes relating to public schools and public libraries. Home: The Green, Dover, Del.

RIDGELY, Irwin Oliver, surgeon; b. near New Market, Md., July 22, 1892; s. Charles Carnan and Rachel (Maynard) R.; A.B., Washington Coll., Chestertown, 1913, M.S., 1918; M.D., U. of Md. Med. Sch., Baltimore, 1918; m. Virginia Sellman, Oct. 20, 1923; 1 son, Beverly Sellman. Interne Mercy Hosp., Baltimore, 1918-21; now asso. surgeon Mercy Hosp.; mem. faculty of surgical dept. U. of Md. since 1921. Fellow Am. Coll. Surgeons. Mem. Am. Med. Assn., Southern Med. Assn., Md. State Med. Soc., Chi Zeta Chi. Democrat. Episcopalian. Club: University (Baltimore). Home: 114 Ridgewood Rd. Office: 201 W. Madison St., Baltimore, Md.

RIDGEWAY, William Wesley, clergyman; b. Boston, Mass., June 25, 1891; s. John Bentley and Annie (McLellan) R.; Ph.B., St. Stephen's Coll., Annandale, N.Y., 1914; ed. Episcopal Theol. Sch., Cambridge, Mass., 1914-16, Harvard U., 1914-16, Andover Theol. Sch., 1915-16; Ph.D., Chicago Law Sch., 1927; m. Sybil Isabel Jewers, Sept. 21, 1918; children—Sybil Isabel, Dorothea Annie, Marguerite Joan, William Wesley, Jr. Ordained to ministry P.E. Ch. deacon, 1917, priest, 1918; rector, Eastport, Me., 1917; sub-dean, St. Paul's Cathedral, Detroit, Mich., 1918-19; rector, Royal Oak, Mich., 1919-20; canon and exec. priest, St. Paul's Cathedral, Erie, Pa., 1920-22; rector, Niles, O., 1922-27; rector, Cleveland, O., 1927-28; asst. Phila., Pa., 1928-29; rector St. Wilfred's Ch., Camden, N.J. since 1930. Served as mem. Bd. Adult Edn., E.R.A., Camden, N.J.; chmn. Carrie Von Nieda Memorial Fund, Camden, N.J. Republican. Episcopalian. Author: A Solution of International Problems, 1927. Home: 83 N. Dudley St., Camden, N.J.

RIDGWAY, S. Paul; in gen. practice of law since 1921. Address: Atlantic City, N.J.

RIDGWAY, William D(eacon), banker; b. Plattsburg, N.J., Mar. 3, 1893; s. Daniel W. and Eloise Collins (Deacon) R.; ed. Abington Friends Sch., 1905-10, Pierce Sch., Phila., 1911-12; m. Alice E. Hallowell, Jan. 22, 1916; children—Alice Esther, Mary Emma, Beatrice Deacon, William Deacon, Richard Hallowell. Clerk Central Nat. Bank, Philadelphia, 1910-12 (resigned because of health); farmer, 1912-28; pres. board county commrs. Montgomery Co., Pa., 1928-37; vice-pres. Jenkintown Bank & Trust Co. since Mar. 15, 1937. Mem. Washington Park Commn., 1926-30; sec. Lower Moreland Twp. Sch. Dist., 1918-29, and since 1938; pres. Lower Moreland Twp. organization of Rep. party. Pres. Huntingdon Valley Fish and Game Protective Assn.; mem. Huntingdon Valley Riders and Drivers. Mem. Soc. of Friends. Home: Bethayres, Montgomery Co., Pa. Address: Jenkintown, Pa.

RIDGWAY, William Hance, writer, mfr.; b. Bordentown, Burlington Co., N.J., June 20, 1856; s. Craig and Susan (Hance) R.; B.Sc., Swarthmore Coll., 1875, C.E., 1878; m. Mary Graham Rambo, Feb. 28, 1884; 1 dau., Isabel Graham (Mrs. Harold Dripps). Pres. Craig Ridgway & Son Co., mfrs. steam-hydraulic machinery; treas. Mutual Fire Ins. Co. of Chester Co., Pa. Inventor Ridgway steam-hydraulic system of cranes and elevators. Mem. Am. Acad. Natural Science, Franklin Inst., Philadelphia, N.J. Soc. of Pa. (pres.). Delivered addresses at mil. camps and navy yards, World War. Writer of column in S.S. Times (weekly) since 1907 and widely known for original style in advertising. Teacher Bible class and head of mission Sunday School. Founder, and pres. Coatesville Y.M.C.A.; member National Council Y.M.C.A.; also president of Pennsylvania Y.M.C.A. Republican. Presbyn. Club: Union League (Phila.). Author of the following brochures, booklets, etc.: How They Got There, 1912; Ridgway's Religion, 1909; The Way Up, 1925; The Christian Gentleman, 1932 (enlarged edit. 1937); Always Has Rained, Hasn't It?, 1932; In God We Trust; Tales of the Sawdust Trail, 1936; Draw Up a Chair, 1938. Has notable collection of things artistic from 5 and 10-cent stores. Owns what is said to be the only collection of artistic tape measures in the world. Home: Coatesville, Pa.

RIDINGER, Charles Wesley, wholesale mcht. elec. supplies and equipment; b. Irwin, Pa., Mar. 10, 1872; s. Stephen and Catherine M. (Lauffer) R.; E.E., U. of Pittsburgh, 1893; m. Lulu M. Maxwell, Apr. 7, 1927; children—Charles W., John S. Employed as elec. engr., Westinghouse Electric and Mfg. Co., 1893-96; mem. firm Fessenden and Ridinger, 1896-1900; asso. with Iron City Electric Co., elec. supplies and equipment, Pittsburgh, Pa., continuously, 1900-39, pres., 1909-39; with Westinghouse Electric Supply Co. since 1939; pres. Iron City Engring. Co.; vice bd. of trustees, U. of Pittsburgh. Has been active in Y.M.C.A. and Boy and Girl Scout work. Mem. Phi Gamma Delta, Omicron Delta Kappa. Republican. Presbyn. Mason (K.T., Shriner). Club: Duquesne. Home: 5830 Marlborough Av. Office: 575 Sixth Av., Pittsburgh, Pa.

RIDPATH, Robert Ferguson, physician; b. Jenkintown, Pa., Apr. 3, 1876; s. John Waddell and Rachel Ann (Ferguson) R.; M.D., Medico-Chirurg. Coll., June 1899; Sc.B., Ursinus Coll., 1935; m. Johanne Ogrodowski, Nov. 22, 1922; 1 son, Robert Ferguson. Asso. prof. of rhino-laryngology, Medico-Chirurg. Coll., Sept. 1913-24; asst. prof. U. of Pa. Post Grad. Sch., 1924-30; prof., Temple U. Sch. of Medicine since 1930; also practicing physician since 1900. Consultant in rhinology at Phila. Skin & Cancer Hosp.; consultant in otology and rhinology, Seashore Home (Cape May). Served as capt. in Med. Corps, U.S.A., World War. Fellow Am. Coll. of Surgeons, Coll. of Physicians (Phila.), Am. Laryngol. Soc.; mem. A.M.A. (chmn. rhino-laryngol. sect.), Am. Acad. Ophthalmology, Otology and Laryngol., Pa. Med. Soc., Phila. Laryngol. Soc., Montgomery Co. Med. Soc. Republican. Mason. Clubs: University, Medical (Phila.). Contbr. to scientific and professional jours. Home: 280 N. Bowman Av., Merion, Pa. Office: 1737 Chestnut St., Philadelphia, Pa.

RIEFLER, Winfield William, economist; b. Buffalo, N.Y., Feb. 9, 1897; s. Philip D. and Clara (Gartner) R.; A.B., Amherst Coll., 1921; Ph.D., Brookings Grad. Sch., 1927; m. Dorothy Miles Brown, Dec. 5, 1924; children—David Winfield, Donald Brown. Fgn. trade officer Dept. of Commerce, Buenos Aires, Argentina, 1921-23; div. research and statistics Federal Reserve Bd., 1923-33, exec. sec. com. on bank reserves, 1930-32, econ. adviser to exec. council, 1933-34; chmn. Central Statis. Bd., 1933-35; econ. adviser to Nat. Emergency Council, 1934-35; prof. Sch. Economics and Politics of Inst. for Advanced Study since 1935. With A.E.F., 1917-19. Awarded Croix de Guerre (France). Mem. delegation for study of econ. depression since 1937, mem. subcommittee on financial statistics since 1938, alternate mem. finance com. since 1937, all League of Nations; dir. Foreign Policy Assn. since 1938. Trustee Inst. for Advanced Study; dir. Nat. Bur. of Economic Research. Fellow Am. Statis. Assn.; mem. Alpha Delta Phi, Phi Beta Kappa, Delta Sigma Rho. Club: Cosmos (Washington, D.C.). Author: Money Rates and Money Markets in the United States, 1930. Home: Battle Court Road. Address: Fuld Hall, Princeton, N.J.

RIEGER, Charles L. W., M.D.; b. Philadelphia, Pa., Feb. 6, 1879; s. George W. and Amelia (Murr) R.; ed. Philadelphia North East Manual Training Peirce Sch. and Temple U.; M.D., Hahnemann Coll., 1907; m. Eleanor May Arbuckle, Dec. 16, 1908. Accountant for W. W. Rorer, certified public accountant, 1904-07; began gen. practice of medicine, 1907; associate in X-ray, Hahnemann Med. Coll. and Hosp., Philadelphia, since 1925; dir. E. J. Lafferty Bldg. & Loan Assn. Fellow A.M.A.; mem. Philadelphia Roentgen Ray Soc., Pa. State and Phila. Co. med. socs.; treas. Homeopathic Med. Soc., Philadelphia, 1931-34; pres. Burholme Hort. Soc., Philadelphia, since 1932. Republican. Methodist. Mason, Artesians, Sons of America. Co-Author: Temperature of the Gastro-Intestinal Tract (Archives of Internal Medicine), 1933. Home: 249 Bickley Road, Glenside, Pa. Office: 1304 Rockland St., Philadelphia, Pa.

RIELY, Compton, surgeon; b. 1872; M.D., U. of Md. Sch. of Medicine, 1897. Practiced at Baltimore since 1899; clin. prof. orthopedic surgery, U. of Md. Sch. of Medicine. Address: 2207 St. Paul St., Baltimore, Md.

RIEMAN, Aloysius Philip, physician; b. West Hoboken, N.J., Feb. 12, 1899; s. Frank J. and Margaret (Müller) R.; grad. St. Peter's High Sch., Jersey City, N.J., 1916; student Fordham U., 1916-18; B.S., New York U., 1922; M.D., Bellevue Hosp. Med. Coll., 1922; post grad. work Columbia and U. of Pa.; m. Anna Davis, Sept. 13, 1923; children—Frank E., Peggy V. and Jane M. (twins), Aloysius Philip, Jr., Davis. Interne Jersey City Hosp., 1922-23; physician and surgeon, Jersey City, N.J., since 1934; sr. attending surgeon North Hudson Hosp., Weehawken, N.J. Served with U.S. Army, 1918. Diplomate Nat. Bd. of Med. Examiners; mem. Hudson County Med. Soc., N.J. State Med. Soc., A.M.A., Med. Soc. Northern N.J., N.Y. Phys. Therapy Soc., North Hudson Clin. Soc., Alpha Omega Alpha. Roman Catholic. Address: 3566 Hudson Boul., Jersey City, N.J.

RIEMAN, Charles Ellet, banker; b. Baltimore, Md., Dec. 4, 1870; s. Joseph Henry and Anne (Lowe) R.; A.B., Princeton, 1892; m. Elizabeth Taylor Goodwin, Feb. 8, 1899. Began in banking with Commercial and Farmers Nat. Bank, 1894; pres. Western Nat. Bank of Baltimore since 1906; dir. 5th Dist. Federal Res. Bd., Md. Life Ins. Co., Baltimore Equitable Soc., Eutaw Savings Bank, Safe Deposit & Trust Co. Pres. Presbyn. Eye, Ear and Throat Charity Hosp.; trustee Peabody Inst. Presbyn. Clubs: Merchants, Maryland (Baltimore); Ivy, Nassau (Princeton). Home: 10 E. Mt. Vernon Pl., Baltimore, Md. Office: 14 N. Eutaw St., Baltimore, Md.

RIEMAN, George Frederick, v.p. Anchor Hocking Glass Corpn.; b. Brooklyn, N.Y., Aug. 20, 1892; s. George Frederick and Pauline (Baer) R.; A.B., Colgate U., 1915; m. Winifred Goff, Feb. 1, 1919; 1 son, George Frederick. Pres. Capstan Glass Co., Connellsville, Pa., 1919-37; v.p. and gen. mgr. glass div. Anchor Cap Corpn., Long Island City, N.Y., 1929-37; v.p. Anchor Hocking Glass Corpn., Lancaster, O., since 1939; pres. and dir. Nat. Bank & Trust Co., Connellsville. Served as ensign, U.S. Navy, 1917-19. Republican. Presbyterian. Home: 1015 Isabella Road, Connellsville, Pa. Office: Lancaster, O.

RIEMER, Guido Carl Leo, educator; b. Münchenbernsdorf, Germany, Aug. 27, 1873; s. Karl Titus and Agnes (Heussler) R.; A.B., Bucknell U., Pa., 1895, A.M., 1896, LL.D., 1926; A.M., Harvard, 1900; univs. of Leipzig and Berlin, 1903-05; Ph.D., Leipzig, 1905; m. Mary Grier Youngman, Dec. 23, 1901; children —Karl, Grier, Hugo, George, Isabel, Hans. Came to U.S. 1882. Prof. German, Bucknell U., 1901-18; mem. Dept. of Public Instruction of Pa., 1918-23; pres. State Normal Sch., Bloomsburg, Pa., 1923-27; pres. State Teachers Coll., Clarion, Pa., 1928-37; prof. of speech, State Teachers Coll., Kutztown, Pa., since 1937. Mem. N.E.A., Nat. Assn. Teachers of Speech, Pa. State Ednl. Assn., Phi Gamma Delta, Phi Delta Kappa. Rotarian. Author: Die Adjektiva bei Wolfram von Eschenbach, 1906; Wöterbuch und Reimverzeichnis zu dem Armen Heinrich Hartmanns von Aue, 1912. Translator: G. Freytag's Doctor Luther, 1916. Contbr. articles on education. Home: Kutztown, Pa.

RIENHOFF, William Francis, Jr., M.D., surgeon; b. Springfield, Mo., Oct. 10, 1894; s. William Francis and Sarah Aileen (Hopkins) R.; grad. Drury Acad., Springfield, 1910; A.B., Cornell U., 1915; M.D., Johns Hopkins, 1919; m. Frances Kemper Young, June 2, 1923; children—Wm. Francis, III, Hugh Young, MacCallum, Francis Colston. Interne in medicine, Johns Hopkins Hosp., 1919-1920, in surgery, 1920; asst. resident surgeon, same hosp., 1920-23, resident surgeon, 1923-25, asst. surgeon, 1925, asst. visiting surgeon, 1926-38, visiting surgeon since 1938; also instr. in surgery, Johns Hopkins, 1922-30; instr. surgical anatomy; asso. in clin. surgery, 1931-32, asso. in surgery since 1933; asso. prof. surgery, Johns Hopkins U., 1933; attending surgeon Women's, Union Memorial, Church Home, Md. Gen., Mercy and Provident hosps. Lt. comdr. U.S. Naval Reserve. Mem. bd. of trustees Gilman County Sch. for Boys. Fellow Am. Coll. Surgeons, A.M.A.; mem. Am. Surg. Assn., Soc. Clin. Surgery, Am. Soc. Thoracic Surgeons, Am. Bronchoscopic Soc., Southern Medical Asso., Soc. Univ. Surgeons, Am. Soc. Anatomists, Southern Surgical Assn., Phi Beta Kappa, Alpha Omega Alpha, Phi Sigma Kappa, Sigma Xi, Pi Gamma Mu. Democrat. Episcopalian. Clubs: Maryland, Bachelors Cotillon, Elkridge Kennels, Gibson Island, Hamilton Street. Contbr. to bulls. Johns Hopkins, A.M.A., Archives of Surgery, Southern Med. Jour., Lewis System of Surgery. Asso. editor Jour. of Surgery, Annals of Surgery. Home: 608 Belvedere Av. Office: 1201 N. Calvert St., Baltimore, Md.

RIEPE, Harry Urias Jr., real estate exec.; b. Baltimore, Md., Mar. 21, 1897; s. Harry Urias and Alice (North) R.; student Towson High Sch. and Poly. Inst. (Baltimore); m. Marion Halford Wheildon, June 1, 1925; 1 dau., Eleanor Thomas Stump. Began as sales rep. Nat. Enameling and Stamping Co., Baltimore, 1921; later asst. sales exec. Chamberlain Metal Weather Strip Co., Detroit, Mich.; organized J. H. and H. U. Riepe Co., real estate, Baltimore, Md., 1930, and since partner; dir. and v.p. Mortgage Guarantee Co., Baltimore, Md., since 1931, Saratoga Bldg. & Land Corpn., Baltimore, Md., since 1931; dir. Wyman Park Apts. Corpn.; sec., treas. and trustee Cooper Apt. Corpn. Served as 2d lt., U.S. Army, A.E.F., 1918-20. Mem. Am. Inst. Real Estate Appraisers, Apt. House Owners Assn. (pres.). Democrat. Episcopalian. Clubs: Ice of Baltimore, Md. Badminton (Baltimore, Md.). Home: 101 W. 39th St., Baltimore, Md.; and Lorely, Baltimore Co., Md. Office: 28 E. Fayette St., Baltimore, Md.

RIES, Ferdinand August, physician; b. Baltimore, Md., June 30, 1899; s. John and Josephine (Bearsch) R.; M.D., U. of Md. Med. Sch., Baltimore, 1921; post grad. study U. of Chicago, at intervals 1929-33; m. Helen Loretta Miller, Dec. 28, 1926; children—Helen Bartgis, Ferdinand August, Jr. Interne Mercy Hosp., Baltimore, 1921-22; in practice at Baltimore since 1922, specializing in internal medicine; asso. prof. physiology, U. of Md. Med. Sch., 1928-35; mem. staff Springfield State Hosp., Sykesville, Md., 1935-36; asst. in neurology, Johns Hopkins Med. Sch. since 1937; asst. dispensary neurologist, Johns Hopkins Hosp. since 1937; dispensary neuropsychiatrist, St. Joseph's Hosp. since 1937; attdg. psychiatrist, Harlem Lodge, Catonsville, Md., since 1939. Served in S.A.T.C., U.S.A., 1918. Fellow A.A.A.S.; mem. Am. Physiol. Soc., Phi Beta Pi. Home: 300 E. North Av., Baltimore, Md.

RIESER, Jacob Leinbach, real estate broker; b. Reading, Pa., Aug. 4, 1884; s. Adam Bucks and Sallie Elizabeth (Leinbach) R.; ed. Patrick Carroll Acad., Reading, Pa., Franklin and Marshall Coll., 1903-04, U. of Pa., 1904-07; m. Mildred Williams, Sept. 25, 1918; 1 dau., Anne Williams. Engaged in real estate bus. continuously since 1907, propr. Rieser Realty Co., real estate, mortgage loans, ins. and bldg.; dir. and sec. bd., Berkshire Hotel Corpn.; dir. Reading Industrial Loan and Thrift Co.; first vice-pres. Masonic Trust Corpn. Served as Washington spl. rep. for H.O.L.C., located in Phila., liquidating loans from distressed banks, trust cos. and bldg. loans for the State of Pa. Mem. Nat. Assn. Real Estate Brokers, State Assn. Real Estate Brokers, Reading Real Estate Bd., Phi Kappa Sigma. Democrat. Reformed Ch. Mason (32°). Clubs: Wyomissing, Berkshire Country. Home: 1305 Orchard Rd., Wyomissing Park, Reading, Pa. Office: 616 Washington St., Reading, Pa.

RIESMAN, David, physician; b. in Saxe-Weimar, Germany, March 25, 1867; s. Nathan and Sophie (Eismann) R.; ed. Ducal Gymnasium, Meiningen, Germany, and pub. and high schools, Portsmouth, Ohio; M.D., U. of Pa., 1892, Sc. D.; LL.D.; m. Eleanor L. Fleisher, Jan. 20, 1908; children—David, John Penrose, Mary. Practiced at Phila. since 1893; prof. clin. medicine, Phila. Polyclinic, 1900-18; asst. prof. medicine, 1908-12, prof. clin. medicine, 1912-33 (emeritus), professor history of medicine, 1933—, U. of Pa.; prof. clin. medicine, Grad. Sch., U. of Pa., 1933—; phys. to Phila. Gen. and University hosps.; cons. phys. to Women's, Chestnut Hill, Jewish and Kensington hosps.; pres. med. bd. Phila. Gen. Hospital. First lt. Med. O.R.C., 1917; lt. col. (retired) Med. R.C.; member tuberculosis and cardiovascular bd., U.S.A.; mem. bd. mgrs., University Museum. Fellow Coll. of Phys. Phila., A.A.A.S.; ex-pres. Pathol. Soc. of Phila., Northern Med. Assn. of Phila., Phila. County Med. Soc.; mem. Assn. Am. Physicians, A.M.A., Am. Gastroenterol. Assn., Am. Society Med. History (pres.), International Graduate Assembly (pres.), Phila. Heart Assn. (v.p.), Pa. Hist. Soc., Medieval Acad. America, History of Science Soc., Franklin Institute, Acad. Natural Sciences, Phila., Société Préhistorique Française, Alpha Mu Pi Omega, Alpha Omega Alpha, Sigma Chi, British Philos. Assn., Shattuck lecturer Mass. Med. Soc., 1938. Clubs: University, Philobiblon, Franklin Inn, Art Alliance. Editor: (with Dr. Ludwig Hektoen) American Textbook of Pathology, 1901; Life of Thomas Sydenham; Medicine in the Middle Ages; High Blood Pressure and Longevity and other essays; History of Interurban Clinical Club; Medicine in Modern Society. Contbr. to Osler and McCrae's System of Medicine, Hare's Modern Treatment, Forchheimer's Therapeusis of Internal Diseases, Oxford Medicine, and other med. textbooks and jours. Address: 1520 Spruce St., Phila., Pa.

RIGGER, William L.; pres. Baltimore Acceptance Co.; officer or dir. several companies. Home: 920 University Parkway. Address: P.O. Box 987, Baltimore, Md.

RIGGINS, John A., lawyer; b. Camden, N.J., Apr. 10, 1878; s. John Porter and Martha (Stafford) R.; A.B., Johns Hopkins U., 1901; LL.B., U. of Pa. Law Sch., 1904; m. Geraldine Buzby, Nov. 6, 1912; children—Elizabeth, John, Mildred. Admitted to bar, 1904; since in gen. practice of law; mem. law firm Riggins & Davis. Pres. N.J. Utilities Assn. since 1915. Mem. Am. Acad. Polit. & Social Science, Phi Sigma Kappa. Methodist. Club: Boca Raton (Fla.). Home: Haddonfield, N.J. Office: 313 Market St., Camden, N.J.

RIGGLEMAN, Leonard, college pres.; b. Blue Springs, W.Va., Apr. 16, 1894; s. Samuel Creed and Harriet (Hamrick) R.; A.B., Morris Harvey Coll., Charleston, W.Va., 1922; A.M., Southern Methodist U., 1924; D.D., Kentucky Wesleyan Coll., Winchester, Ky., 1933; m. Pauline Steele, Aug. 16, 1922; 1 dau., Roberta. Ordained to ministry of M.E. Ch. South, 1924; pastor Milton, W.Va., and part time instr. in history, Morris Harvey Coll., 1924-28; rural life specialist with agrl. extension div., W.Va.U., 1928-30; vice-pres. and head dept. religious edn., Morris Harvey Coll., 1930-31; pres. Morris Harvey Coll. since 1931. Pres. State Ministers' Conf. for State of W.Va.; mem. Gen. Bd. of Christian Edn. and pres. of Coll. sect., Ednl. Council, Bd. of Christian Edn., M.E. Church, South, 1938; mem. W.Va. Farm Tenant Rehabilitation Com.; mem. state advisory bd. of W.Va. div. of Women's Field Army of the Am. Soc. for Control of Cancer; mem. State-Wide Com. on Blindness; mem. nat. council of Nat. Econ. League for State of W.Va. Club: Kiwanis (pres. Huntington Club, 1935; dist. gov. W.Va. Dist. 1939). Home: 3722 Staunton Av. Office: Morris Harvey Coll., Charleston, W.Va.

RIGGS, Jesse Bright, ins. exec.; b. Baltimore, Md., Feb. 3, 1870; s. Lawrason and Mary Turpin (Bright) R.; student St. Paul's Sch., Concord, N.H., 1884-87, Princeton U., 1888-92; m. Charlotte Symington, Oct. 3, 1893 (died 1938); children—Emily (Mrs. James Winslow Hundley), Marie (Mrs. Robert H. Sayre III), Charlotte (Mrs. E. Cortlandt Parker), Lawrason Riggs of J. Began as ins. broker, Baltimore, Md., 1892; pres. Riggs, Rossmann & Hunter, Inc., insurance, Baltimore, since 1936; dir. U.S. Fidelity and Guaranty Co. Democrat. Episcopalian. Mason. Clubs: Maryland, Merchants (Baltimore, Md.); Fishers Island (N.Y.). Home: 3908 N. Charles St. Office: 129 E. Redwood St., Baltimore, Md.

RIGGS, Norman Colman, mathematician; b. Bowling Green, Mo., Nov. 1, 1870; s. James William and Lucretia Smith (Jones) R.; La Grange (Mo.) Coll., 1889-90; B.S. and M.S., U. of Mo., 1895; M.S., Harvard, 1898; m. Jean Augusta Shaefer, Aug. 15, 1905; children —Philip Shaefer, Paul Flood, William Horace. Instr mathematics, Pa. State Coll., 1899-1902; asst. and asso. prof. mathematics, Armour Inst. Tech., Chicago, 1902-08; asst. mathematics, 1908-10, asst prof. and prof. mechanics, 1910—, Carnegie Inst. Tech., Pittsburgh, Pa. Mem. Am. Math. Soc., Math. Assn. America, A.A. A.S., Soc. Promotion Engring. Edn., Phi Beta Kappa, Tau Beta Pi. Author: Analytic Geometry, 1910. Reviser of Hancock's Applied Mechanics for Engineers, 1915; Applied Mechanics, 1930; Strength of Materials (with M. M. Frocht), 1938. Home: R.D. 9, So. Hills, Pittsburgh, Pa.

RIGGS, Robert, artist; b. Decatur, Ill., Feb. 5, 1896; s. Frank O. and Alice (Imboden) R.; student James Millikin U., Decatur, Ill., Art Students League, New York City, Academie Julien, Paris, France; unmarried. Employed as artist for N. W. Ayer & Son, advertising agency, Phila.; since then free-lance artist in both commercial and non-commercial art; known for water colors done in Siam and Algeria and for lithographs of the prize ring and circus; represented in Whitney Mus., Mus. of Modern Art, Brooklyn Mus., Chicago Art Inst., Copenhapen Nat. Mus. and others. Prices include Logan Prize for water color, Eyre Medal, Championship Prize, Pennell Medal, Gribbel Prize, Logan Prize for Lithograph, Art Dirs. Medal and two Art Dirs. awards for commercial work. Served with Base Hosp. 48, U.S. Army, 1917-19, with A.E.F. in France. Asso. mem. Nat. Acad. Has own collection living reptiles including large pythons and boas; collection Am. Indian material and African collection. Home: 118 Maplewood Av., Philadelphia, Pa.

RIGHTOR, Chester Edward; b. Rockford, Ill., July 7, 1884; s. Elmer Abram and Arabella Victoria (Drummond) R.; A.B., U. of Wis., 1909; m. Marguerite Wilma Bimel, July 1, 1916; children—Virginia Clare, June Drummond. Began as accountant Wis. R.R. Commn., 1909; with Ernest Reckitt & Co., Chicago, 1911-12; with Training Sch. for Pub. Service of N.Y. Bur. Municipal Research and Bur. Expert Accountants, Dept. of Finance of N.Y. City, 1912-13; asst. mgr. Standard Oil Co., Bangkok, Siam, 1913-14; accountant, later dir. Dayton (O.) Bur. Municipal Research, 1914-18; with U.S. Bur. Efficiency, Washington, D.C., 6 mos., 1918; chief accountant Detroit Bur. Governmental Research, Inc., 1918-1932; lecturer in municipal finance, U. of Mich., 1920-1933; city controller, Detroit, Dec. 1932-June 1933; director Atlantic City Survey Commn., 1934; consultant Municipal Finance Commn. of N.J., 1934; in municipal service dept. Dun & Bradstreet, N.Y. City, 1935-36; chief statistician, div. of states and cities, Bur. of Census, Dept. of Commerce, Washington, D.C., since 1936. Mem. Sigma Nu, National Municipal League, Am. Statis. Assn., Municipal Finance Officers' Assn., Govtl. Research Assn., Nat. Assn. of Assessing Officers. Conglist. Mason (32°). Author: City Manager in Dayton, 1919; Preparation of a Long-Term Financial Program, 1927; also pub. annually, 1922-35, Comparative Tax Rates of Cities over 30,000, and Comparative Bonded Debt of Cities over 30,000. Home: 520 Rolling Road, Chevy Chase, Md. Office: Bur. of the Census, Washington, D.C.

RIGLING, Alfred, librarian; b. Phila., Pa., Aug. 3, 1868; s. Fidel and Jamesena (Hienerwald) R.; ed. The German-Am. "Real" Sch. 1876-83, and the several ednl. depts. of Franklin Inst.; hon. A.M., U. of Pa., 1933; m. Pearl E. Taylor, June 22, 1909. Asso. with The Franklin Institute continuously since entering its employ as library asst., 1883, librarian since 1887, asst. sec. since 1908, also asst. editor The Journal of The Franklin Institute since 1908. Fellow A.A.A.S. Mem. Am. Library Assn., Special Libraries Assn., Special Libraries Council, Phila., Pa. Library Assn., Pa. Library Club, Hist. Soc. of Pa., City History Soc., Rittenhouse Astron. Soc., Centennial Alumni, Am. Pharm. Assn., Mercantile Beneficial Assn., Alumni Assn. Franklin Inst. Sch. of Mechanic Arts, Franklin Inst. since 1893, hon. mem. since 1933 on occasion of his 50th anniversary as librarian. Inventor of a library book support widely used. Republican. Club: University. Home: 5811 Cobbs Creek Parkway, West Philadelphia, Pa.

RIKER, Charles Ross, editor, mgr.; b. Columbus, O., Aug. 18, 1883; s. Albert Birdsall and Mary Edith (Davis) R.; A.B., M.A., Mt. Union Coll.; B.S., E.E., Armour Inst. Tech.; m. Mary Woodruff, Mar. 4, 1909; 1 dau., Elizabeth (Mrs. A. M. Plantz). With Denver Gas & Electric Co., Cincinnati, 1907-10; asst. editor The Electric Journal, 1910-14, tech. editor, 1914-29, editor since 1929, mgr. since 1932. Mem. Am. Inst. Elec. Engrs. Methodist. Clubs: Criterion, Aztec. Writer several hundred articles in The Electric Journal. Home: 101 Woodhaven Drive, Mt. Lebanon, Pa. Office: 530 Fernando St., Pittsburgh, Pa.

RILEY, James Breinig, judge; b. Wheeling, W.Va., July 26, 1894; s. Thomas Sylvester and Minnie (Breinig) R.; A.B., W.Va. Univ., 1916; student Georgetown U., 1916-17; LL.B., Columbia, 1921, A.M.; 1921; m. Frances Wood, Oct. 25, 1925; children—Frances Wood, James Breinig. Admitted to W.Va. bar, 1921; mem. law firm Riley and Riley, Wheeling, 1921-37; judge W.Va. Supreme Court of Appeals since 1937. Served as 2d lt., 1st lt. and capt. U.S.M.C., 1917-19. Mem. Am., W.Va. State, and Ohio Co. bar assns., Am. Law Inst. Democrat. Roman Catholic. Elk. Club: Fort Henry (Wheeling). Home: Wheeling, W.Va. Address: Capitol Bldg., Charleston, W.Va.

RILEY, John L., M.D.; b. Snow Hill, Md., Feb. 18, 1875; s. William S. and Emily E. (Fleming) R.; student Snow Hill High Sch. 1894-95; M.D., U. of Md., 1905; m. Beulah P. Vincent, Nov. 11, 1908; 1 dau., Virginia L. In gen. practice of medicine since 1905; pres. First Nat. Bank; dir. Snow Hill Bldg. & Loan Assn., Democratic Messenger, Inc. Mem. Draft Bd., World War. Democrat. Presbyn. Mason. Address: Snow Hill, Md.

RILEY, Mark Raymond, banking; b. Orange, N.J., Apr. 13, 1892; s. Abram Mark and Jessie Duncan (Stalker) R.; A.B., Cornell U., 1915; m. Florence Bahr, June 13, 1917; children—Mark Raymond, Jr., Gilbert Bahr. Asso. with Brown Bros. & Co., investment banking, 1916-30, and Brown Bros. Harriman & Co., 1930-33; exec. vice-pres. Orange First Nat. Bank, 1933-37, pres. and dir. since 1938. Vice-pres. and dir. Chamber of Commerce and Civics of the Oranges and Maplewood. Mem. Cornell Club of Essex Co., Phi Kappa Sigma. Republican. Methodist. Club: Orange-West Orange Kiwanis (Orange). Home: 46 Euclid Av., Maplewood, N.J. Office: 282 Main St., Orange, N.J.

RILEY, Robert Hickman, state dir. of health; b. Kenna, W.Va., Aug. 13, 1879; s. Millard Filmore and Isadora Helen (Staats) R.; B.S., U. of Okla., 1909, M.D., 1913; Dr.P.H., Johns Hopkins Sch. of Hygiene and Pub. Health, 1922; m. Willie Harris, June 8, 1911; children—Robert Hickman, Charlotte Sloan (dec.),· Barbara Harris. Asst. commr. of health, Okla., 1912-14; dep. state health officer, Md., 1914-20; chief Bur. of Communicable Diseases, State Dept. Health, Md., 1920-25; asst. dir., 1925-28, dir. of health and chmn. State Bd. of Health, Md., since 1928; lecturer in Sch. of Hygiene and Pub. Health, Johns Hopkins U. since 1928. Sec. Okla. Tuberculosis Assn. 1910-14; mem. State Planning Commn., State Bd. of Aid and Charities. Mem. Conf. of State and Provincial Health Officers of North America (del. to Royal Sanitary Inst., Scotland, 1931; del. to Birmingham, Eng., 1937); mem. Governor's Advisory Council. Fellow Am. Med. Assn. (chmn. sect. on preventive and industrial medicine and pub. health), Am. Pub. Health Assn. (chmn. health officers sect. and mem. com. on administrative practice, chmn. com. on State Health Studies), Southern Med. Assn., Baltimore Co. Med. Soc. (past pres.), Med. and Chirurg. Faculty of Md. (chmn. com. on pub. instrn.), Sigma Nu, Phi Delta Pi, Delta Omega. Consultant to Children's Bur., U.S. Dept of Labor. Pres. Conf. State and Provincial Health Authorities, N.A., 1937-38. Presbyn. Mason. Rotarian. Author of papers on med. subjects. Home: 100 Beechwood Av., Catonsville, Md. Address: 2411 N. Charles St., Baltimore, Md.

RILEY, Russell Wright, insurance; b. Phila., Pa., Aug. 30, 1890; s. Eugene and Frances Augusta (Barr) R.; grad. Northeast High Sch., Phila., 1909; m. Helen Pirsson Comer, Sept., 1916; 1 dau., Miriam Comer. Two yrs. law study, 1909-11; in ins. business since 1911; resident v.p. Loyalty Group Ins. Cos., Trenton, N.J. Republican. Mason (Council, Chapter). Clubs: Carteret, Trenton, Trenton Country (Trenton, N.J.). Home: 120 Parker Pl. Office: 237 E. Hanover St., Trenton, N.J.

RILEY, Thomas S., mem. law firm Riley & Riley. Office: Riley Law Bldg., Wheeling, W.Va.

RIMKUFSKY, Benjamin Atlas, lawyer; b. N. Y. City, Aug. 25, 1906; s. Meyer and Sarah (Atlas) R.; LL.B., N.J. Law Sch., now Newark U. Law Sch., 1927; grad. study U. of Pa., 1927; m. Elizabeth Keyser, Feb. 17, 1929; children—Sigmund S., Alfred A. Admitted to N.J. bar as atty.; 1928, as counsellor, 1931; engaged in gen. practice of law at Atlantic City since 1928; solicitor for Atlantic Co. Unit of N.J. Magistrates Assn. since 1931; asst. solicitor of State Magistrates Assn. since 1935; solicitor for Atlantic County Welfare since 1937; dir. O'Neill Coal Co. Mem. Atlantic Co. Employees Assn. Mem. Fourth Ward Rep. Orgn. Mem. Bd. Govs. Atlantic City Jewish Community Center since 1933, 3d v.p. since 1938. Mem. gen. com. Dist. Grand Lodge No. 3, B'nai B'rith, 1937-39; pres. B'nai B'rith State Council, 1938; pres. B'nai B'rith Atlantic City, 1934-38, sec. 1933. Mem. Atlantic County Bar. Assn., N.J. Approved Football Ofcls. Assn. Republican. Jewish religion. Home: 38 S. Montgomery Av. Office: Guarantee Trust Bldg., Atlantic City, N.J.

RINEAR, Earl Harmon, agrl. edn. and research; b. Brecksville, O., Sept. 9, 1892; s. Charles Cortez and Amalia Charlotte (Prehn) R.; grad. Brecksville High Sch., 1910; A.B., Oberlin (O.) Coll., 1915; M.S., U. of Wis., 1925; m. Susan Lois Taylor, Sept. 5, 1925; children—Jean Taylor, Betty Ann. Farmer, Brecksville, O., 1915-24; service mgr. for Trumbull County Farm Bureau, Warren, O., 1926-27; research specialist in marketing, 1927-36, extension marketing specialist, U. of New Hampshire, Durham, N.H., 1934-36; asso. agrl. economist and asso. prof. agrl. economics, Rutgers U., New Brunswick, N.J., since 1936. Village councilman, Brecksville, O., 1922-24. Mem. Am. Farm Econ. Assn., Square and Compass. Presbyterian. Mason. Club: Rutgers (New Brunswick). Author of several bulletins of N.H. and N.J. Expt. Stations on marketing research. Home: 425 Grant Av., Highland Park, N.J. Office: New Jersey Agricultural Experimental Station, New Brunswick, N.J.

RINEHART, Daniel, hardware merchant; b. Ringgold, Md., Sept. 14, 1866; s. John and Susan (Shockey) R.; ed. Waynesbow High Sch. and Bloomsburg State Teachers Coll.; m. Meta Walter, Aug. 13, 1900; 1 dau., Margaret W. Public school teacher, Pa., and owner general store, 1890-95; hardware merchant, Waynesboro, since 1895; pres. Waynesboro Bldg. & Loan Assn. since founding, 1908; dir. First Nat. Bank & Trust Co., Waynesboro Ice & Cold Storage Co., Franklin County Fire Ins. Co.; sec.-treas. Waynesboro Real Estate Development Co. Dir. Waynesboro Y.M.C.A., Waynesboro Hosp. Mem. Pa. and Atlantic Seaboard Hardware Assn. (dir.), Franklin Co. Hist. Soc. Mem. Evangelical Lutheran Ch. (mem. bd. since 1898). Mason (32°, Shriner). Clubs: Waynesboro Advertising (dir.), Rotary. Home: 124 N. Grant St. Address: 22 W. Main St., Waynesboro, Pa.

RINGOLD, James, banker; b. Clearmont, Mo., Dec. 28, 1879; s. George M. and Judy S. R.; student Dixon (Ill.) Coll.; m. Lavinia C. Craft, June 1906; children—Marjorie, Kathrine. Began with Jackson Bank, Clearmont, 1895; with Nat. Bank, St. Joseph, Mo., 1899-1905; with U.S. Nat. Bank, Denver, Colo., since 1905, pres., 1923-35; now pres. First-Mechanics Nat. Bank, Trenton, N.J.; dir. U.S. Nat. Bank, Denver, Colo. Mem. Liberty Loan Com., Denver, World War. Chmn. State Com. R.F.C. Clubs: Denver, Denver Country, Trenton, Trenton Country; Bankers (New York). Home: 211 W. State St. Office: First-Mechanics Nat. Bank, 1 W. State St., Trenton, N.J.

RINKENBACH, William Henry, chemist; b. Carbon Co., Pa., Mar. 17, 1894; s. Leopold and Ellamanda (Oplinger) R.; grad. Perkiomen Sch., Pennsburg, Pa., 1911; A.B., Cornell U., 1915; M.S., U. of Pittsburgh, 1922; m. Ruth M. Allender, Feb. 22, 1933. Chemist E. I. du Pont de Nemours & Co., 1915-18; asst. explosives chemist U.S. Bur. of Mines, 1918-27; lecturer industrial chemistry, U. of Pittsburgh, 1921-23; lecturer popular science and travel, 1925-27; asst. chief chemist Picatinny Arsenal, U.S. War Dept., Dover, N.J., 1927-29, chief chemist since 1929; holder of patents on explosives and chem. processes; leader Carnegie Mus. (Pittsburgh) Ichthyological Expdn. to Can., 1924-25. Fellow A.A.A.S., Am. Inst. Chemists; mem. Am. Chem. Soc., Morris Co. Engrs. (pres. 1935-36), S.A.R., Pa. German Soc., Phi Lambda Upsilon, Sigma Xi. Club: Picatinny Golf (Dover). Contbr. scientific articles on explosives to jours. and govt. bulls., also papers on ichthyology and genealogical research. Home: 144 S. Morris St., Dover, N.J.

RINTOUL, James L.; v.p. Pa. Water & Power Co.; officer or dir. many companies. Home: 2020 Greenberry Road, Mt. Washington. Office: 1611 Lexington Bldg., Baltimore, Md.

RIORDAN, Frank S., lawyer; b. Germantown, Pa., Dec. 31, 1884; s. Michael P. and Anna (Gallagher) R.; grad. State Teachers Coll., E. Stroudsburg, Pa., 1907, Perkiomen Sch., Pennsburg, 1909; ed. Dickinson Coll. Law Sch., 1914-15; m. Genevieve L. Flynn, June 15, 1915; children—Frank S., Jr., Genevieve Ann. Engaged in teaching country schs., 1909-10, high sch., 1910-12, supervising prin., 1912-14; admitted to Pa. bar, 1916, and since engaged in gen. practice of law at Lansford; adjuster in charge workmens compensation for Lehigh Navigation Coal Co., Inc., Lansford, Pa. Pres. Pa. Soc. for Crippled Children. Mem. Am. and Pa. State bar assns. Republican. Roman Catholic. Elk. Rotarian. Clubs: Rotary (Lansford); Mahoning Valley Country (Lehighton, Pa.). Home: 101 W. Abbott St. Office: 25 W. Ridge St., Lansford, Pa.

RIORDAN, Joseph A., pres. Joseph A. Riordan, Inc.; b. New York, Mar. 10, 1867; s. John and Julia R.; student St. Patricks Sch., Newark, N.J., 1880-83; N.J. Business Coll., Newark, 1884-87; m. Mary Boyle, Oct. 12, 1892; children—Edward A., William A., Joseph A. (dec.), Edna A., Jerome A. Pres. Riordan Realty Co., Harrison, N.J., since 1927, Riordan Travel Agency, Harrison, N.J., since 1887, Joseph A. Riordan, Inc., ins., Harrison, N.J., since 1887; chmn. of bd. West Hudson Co. Trust Co.; dir. People's Bldg. & Loan Assn. Freeholder, Hudson Co., N.J., 1894-1900. Mem. N.J. State Ho. of Rep., 1905-07. Catholic. Elk, K.C. Clubs: Newark (N.J.) Athletic; Crestmont Golf (West Orange, N.J.). Home: 514 Davis Av. Office: 315 Harrison Av., Harrison, N.J.

RIPLEY, Edward Warren, physician; b. Rutland, Vt., Mar. 8, 1889; s. William Thomas and Isabel (Reynolds) R.; student Norwich U., Northfield, Vt., 1905-06, Trinity Coll., Hartford, Conn., 1906-10; B.S., N.Y. Univ., 1915; M.D., Cornell U. Med. Coll., 1919; m. Nellie Duret, Sept. 12, 1912 (dec.); 1 son, William Tony; m. 2d, Olive de la M. Cary, May 8, 1920; children—Richard Brandon, Louise Cary. Interne Gouverneur Hosp., New York, 1920-21; engaged in gen. practice of medicine in New York, 1921-23; in practice in Montclair, N.J., specializing in pediatrics since 1923; attdg. pediatrician, Mountainside Hosp. since 1925, Essex Co. Isolation Hosp. since 1926; dir. Asso. Physicians' Bus. Bur., Inc. Served in Med. Res. Corps., 1917, S.A.T.C., 1918. Fellow Am. Acad. Pediatrics. Licentiate Am. Bd. Pediatrics. Mem. Alpha Mu Pi Omega, Delta Psi. Home: 9 Hightmont St. Office: 56 Church St., Montclair, N.J.

RIPPEL, Julius S., investment securities; b. Newark, N.J., Sept. 21, 1868; s. Godfred C. and Susan (Seivert) R.; ed. pub. schs. and Coleman's Bus. Coll., Newark; m. Fannie Estelle Traphagen, 1898. With Graham & Co., stock brokers and steamship agts., 1887-91; organizer J. S. Rippel & Co., investment securities, 1891; chmn. bd. Merchants & Newark Trust Co.; dir. Newark Provident Loan Assn., Guaranty Co. of N.J., Securities Co. of N.J. Republican. Mem. Ref. Ch. Clubs: Essex, Down Town, Newark Athletic. Home: 67 Johnson Av. Office: 18 Clinton St., Newark, N.J.

RIPPS, A. V.; editor The Times. Address: Bayonne, N.J.

RISTINE, Charles Scott, stock broker; b. Bryn Mawr, Pa., Feb. 11, 1887; s. George Carpenter and Susannah (Shank) R.; grad. Haverford Coll., 1910; m. Dorothy S. Haines, Jan. 17, 1925; 1 dau., Dorothy S. Asso. with F. P. Ristine & Company, stock brokers, Phila., since 1921, mem. firm since 1926; dir. S. S. White Dental Mfg. Co. Served as 1st lt., 23d Inf., 2d Div., U.S. Army, during World War. Mem. Triangle Soc. (Haverford Coll.), Mil. Order of Fgn. Wars. Republican. Baptist. Clubs: Union League, Mid-Day, St. Davids Golf. Home: Strafford, Pa. Office: 123 S. Broad St., Philadelphia, Pa.

RISTINE, Frederick Pearce, partner F. P. Ristine & Co.; b. Bryn Mawr, Pa., Nov. 11, 1871; s. George Carpenter and Susannah (Shank) R.; student Haverford (Pa.) Coll.; m. Elizabeth Bray Whetstone, Nov. 17, 1904; children—Elizabeth Anne (Mrs. James Thompson Davis, Jr.), Frederick Pearce. With Real Estate Trust Co., Phila., 1894-1902; formed partnership Ristine & Conklin, 1904, which was succeeded in 1912 by F. P. Ristine & Co. (mems. N.Y. and Phila. stock exchanges and N.Y. Curb Exchange); dir. Wayne Title & Trust Co. Gov. Phila. Stock Exchange. Republican. Baptist. Clubs: Union League, Mid-Day (Phila.); St. Davids Golf, Haverford. Home: Corner Conestoga Road and Aberdeen Av., Wayne, Pa. Office: 123 S. Broad St., Philadelphia, Pa.; 15 Broad St., New York, N.Y.

RISTON, Paul; editor Times-Mirror. Address: Warren, Pa.

RITCHIE, Charles; mem. law firm Ritchie, Hill & Thomas. Address: Charleston, W.Va.

RITCHIE, John Woodside, teacher, author; b. nr. Sparta, Ill., Dec. 6, 1871; s. John Cameron and Sarah (McKelvey) R.; A.B., Maryville (Tenn.) College, 1898, Dr. Humane Letters, from same coll., 1937; post-graduate work, 4 yrs., and fellow, Univ. of Chicago; m. Sarah Pearl Andrews, Jan. 15, 1902; children—Sara Margaret, Ruth Rathbone, Elizabeth Marshall, Mary Eleanor, John Andrews. Instr. in biology, Maryville Coll., 1899-1900; with Govt. schs. and Forestry Bur., Philippine Islands, 1902-04; prof. of biology, Coll. of William and Mary, Williamsburg, Va., 1905-19, director summer session, 1912-14; science editor World Book Company, Yonkers, N.Y., since 1915. Member A.A.A.S., American Public Health Assn., Phi Beta Kappa Fraternity. Democrat. Presbyn. Author: The Lives of Plants, 1904; Physiology and Hygiene, 1905; Human Physiology, 1908; Primer of Sanitation, 1909; Primer of Physiology, 1913; Public and Personal Health, 1916; Clearing the Way, 1917; Keeping the Laws, 1917. Joint Author: Philippine Chart Primer, 1906; First Year Book, 1906; Primer of Hygiene, 1910; Primer of Sanitation for the Tropics, 1910; Sanitation and Hygiene for the Tropics, 1916; Philippine Plant Life, 1929. Editor of New-World Health Series, New-World Science Series, and other science and mathematics texts. Home: Flemington, N.J.*

RITENBAUGH, George Frederick, manufacturer; b. Pittsburgh, Pa., Jan. 3, 1894; s. George F. and Blanche (Preston) R.; student U. of Pittsburgh Evening Sch., 1915-18, 1921-22; m. Ida Klemm, Apr. 7, 1917; 1 dau., Jane Margaret. Asso. with Heppenstall Company, mfr. steel forgings and shear knives, Pittsburgh, Pa., continuously since starting as office boy, 1909, bookkeeper, 1911-15, asst. auditor, 1915-22, asst. treas., 1922-26, corpn. sec. and dir. since 1926, also treas. since 1939; sec., treas. and dir. Heppenstall Company, Detroit, Mich. Republican. Presbyterian. Mason (32°, Shriner). Rotarian. Clubs: Rotary, Syria, Temple Automobile. Home: 1202 Denniston Av. Office: 4620 Hatfield St., Pittsburgh, Pa.

RITENOUR, Joseph Paul, physician; b. Uniontown, Pa., Sept. 1, 1879; s. Joseph Kidwell and Sarah Catherine (Rodehaver) R.; B.S., Pa. State Coll., 1901; M.D., U. of Pa. Med. Sch., 1906; m. Margaret Craig Richmond, Jan. 2, 1908; children—Anne Kathrine (Mrs. Frank M. Harbison, Jr.), Joseph Richmond, John Phillips. After usual interneships engaged in gen. practice of medicine since 1907; dir. Coll. Health Service and Coll. Phys., Pa. State Coll., State College, Pa., since 1917; dir. Peoples Nat. Bank. Served as contract surgeon U.S.A., 1918. Pres. State College Bd. Health. Dir. Pa. Tuberculosis Soc. Mem. Am., Pa., Center Co. med. assns., Am. Pub. Health Assn., Am. Student Health Assn. (vice-pres.), Kappa Sigma, Phi Alpha Sigma. Republican. Presbyn. Club: Center Hills Country (vice-pres.). Home: East Campus, State College, Pa.

RITTER, Alonzo Winchester, artist; b. Hagerstown, Md., Jan. 7, 1898; s. Edward Tilden and Martha Viola (Lesher) R.; ed. pub. schs.; studied privately under D. M. Hyde, 1 yr.; unmarried. Began as artist, 1920, doing oils, water colors, etc., of landscapes, still-life and flower subjects. Exhibited at Brooklyn (N.Y.) Museum; Soc. of Washington Artists, Corcoran Gallery of Art, Nat. Gallery of Art, Smithsonian Inst. (Washington); Marshall Field Galleries (Chicago); Baltimore (Md.) Museum of Art; Cumberland Valley Annual Exhibit; Washington County Museum of Fine Arts; 1-man show. Represented by work in public and private collections, namely "Woodland Way," (mural) in Junior High Sch.; R. Bruce Carson, Alexander Hotel Lounge, etc. Awarded hon. mention, 1931, and 1st prize, 1936, Exhbn. of Cumberland Valley Artists, Washington County Museum of Fine Arts. Chmn. Hagerstown Soc. Artists. Republican. Methodist. Home and Studio: 863 Dewey Av., Hagerstown, Md.

RITTER, Ella N., physician; b. Lycoming Co., Pa., Jan. 12, 1866; d. Jacob and Mary (Miller) R.; M.E., Mansfield State Normal Sch., 1885; M.D., Woman's Med. Coll., Phila., 1893; grad. study, Phila. Polyclinic Coll. 1903. Interne, W. Phila. Hosp. for Women, 1893-94; engaged in gen. practice of medicine and surgery at Williamsport, Pa., since 1894; propr. pvt. surg. hosp., 1912-14. Mem. Am. Med. Assn., Med. Womens Assn., Pa. State and Lycoming Co. med. socs. Republican. Lutheran. Clubs: Business and Professional Womens, College, Civic. Home: 1211 W. 4th St., Williamsport, Pa.

RITTER, Thomas E.; chmn. and pres. Second Nat. Bank. Address: Allentown, Pa.

RITTER, Verus Taggart, architect; b. Muncy, Pa., June 27, 1883; s. William L. and Amelia (Spangler) R.; ed. high sch. and pvt. sch., Bloomsburg, Pa.; archtl. training in brother's office; m. Edith E. Keller, Jan. 30, 1912 (died May 24, 1935); children—Verus Taggart, Eleanor Foster. Began practice at Williamsport, Pa., 1908, at Philadelphia, since 1917; senior partner firm Ritter and Shay since 1920. Prin. works (alone): City Hall, First Nat. Bank Bldg., High Sch. and 3 jr. high schs.—all in Huntington, W.Va.; Virginian Hotel, Lynchburg, Va.; Arena for Commonwealth of Pa., Harrisburg; firm architects for Hotel Bethlehem, Lehigh Valley Nat. Bank Bldg., and Liberty High School, Bethlehem, Pa.; American Hotel, Allentown, Pa.; Masonic Temple, Chester, Pa.; 1500 Walnut St. Bldg., Market St. Nat. Bank, Drake Hotel, U.S. Custom House—all in Philadelphia, etc. Pres. Del. River Tunnel Corpn. Firm awarded gold medal by Am. Inst. Architects for Packard Building, Phila. Republican. Presbyn. Mason (32°, K.T.). Home: 356 N. Latches Lane, Merion, Pa. Office: 1500 Walnut Street Bldg., Philadelphia, Pa.

RITTER, Walter Lowrie, clergyman; b. Phila., Pa., May 5, 1888; s. Frederick and Martha Little (Haines) R.; A.B., Central High Sch., Phila., 1906; A.B., U. of Pa., 1910; A.M., Princeton, 1912; grad. Princeton Theol. Sem., 1910-13; Ph.D., Oskaloosa Coll., 1916; m. Edith Marion Mowbray, Aug. 6, 1913; children—Walter Lowrie, Jr., Jean Mowbray, Andrew Mowbray. Ordained to ministry Presbyn. Ch., June 12, 1913; pastor, Amity, N.Y., 1913-16, New Hamburg, N.Y., 1916-18, Wyncote, Pa., 1918-23, Union Tabernacle, Phila., Pa., 1923-26, Fourth Ch., Pittsburgh, Pa., 1926-32; pastor First Presbyn. Ch., Altoona, Pa., since 1932; dir. Lord's Day Alliance of Pa.; head dept. sacred lit., Beechwood Sch. for Girls, Jenkintown, Pa., 1920-23; pres. Altoona Ministerial Assn.; pastoral counsellor Blair Co. Christian Endeavor Union. Pastoral Counsellor Allegheny County Christian Endeavor Union, Southwest Central Dist. Pa. Christian Endeavor Union. Mem. adv. council Nat. Soc. for Prevention of Crime. Presbyn. Ch. U.S.A. Mason. Patriotic Order Sons of America. Clubs: Blair County Motor (Altoona); National Travel (New York City). Home: 1123 14th Av., Altoona, Pa.

RITTER, William Henry, Jr., business exec.; b. Phila., Pa., Aug. 31, 1899; s. William Henry and Selma (Holly) R.; B.S., U. of Pa., 1921; m. Dorothy Appleton, Mar. 22, 1933. Gen. mgr. and treas. P. J. Ritter Co., Bridgeton, N.J., food products, since 1936; treas. Jos. White Co., Bridgeton, N.J., seed growers, since 1936. Clubs: Univ., Philopatrian, Germantown Cricket (Phila.); Wool (New York); Cohanzick Country (Bridgeton, N.J.). Home: 31 Franklin Drive. Office: P. J. Ritter Co., Bridgeton, N.J.

RITTMANN, Walter Frank, chem. and commercial engr.; b. Sandusky, O., Dec. 2, 1883; s. Christian A. and Louisa A. (Scheel) R.; C.E., Ohio Northern U., 1905; A.B., Swarthmore Coll., 1908, M.A., 1909, M.E., 1911, Chem. E., 1917; Ph.D., Columbia, 1914; m. Anna Frances Campbell, Sept. 11, 1913; children—Frank Sears, William Campbell, Eleanor Anne. Chemist with United Gas Improvement Co., Phila., 1908-09; consulting engr., Phila., 1909-12; chem. engr. with U.S. Bur. of Mines, 1914-21; prof. engring., Carnegie Inst. Tech., 1921-33. Cons. engr. to State of Pa., 1923-24; cons. engineer U.S. Dept. Agriculture, 1925-37. Lecturer on industrial chemistry, Swarthmore Coll., 1909-12, at Columbia U., 1913. Trustee Ohio Northern U. since 1928. Fellow A.A.A.S.; mem. Am. Chem. Soc., Am. Inst. Chem. Engrs., Nat. Highways Assn. (chmn. div. of chem. engrs.), Franklin Inst., Am. Soc. M.E., Am.

Inst. Mining and Metall. Engrs., Soc. Industrial Engrs. (nat. pres. 1925-30), Administrative Bd. Am. Engring. Council, 1925-30, Sigma Psi, Phi Lambda Upsilon, Tau Beta Pi. Sigma Phi Epsilon, etc. Clubs: Chemists, Engineers, University (New York); Union League (Chicago); Duquesne (Pittsburgh). Contbr. numerous articles dealing with application of physical chemistry to industrial processes, especially those dealing with fuel, oil and gas. Address: 5705 Solway St., Pittsburgh, Pa.

RITTS, Elias, banking; b. St. Petersburg, Pa., July 6, 1883; s. John V. and Irene C. (Blakeslee) R.; ed. Haverford Coll., 1900-05; m. Helen Herr, Dec. 29, 1909; children—Mary Irene (Mrs. Albert T. Sprankle), Susan Elizabeth (Mrs. James O. Howard), John V., Ruth Emma (dec.). Employed as cashier, Lyndora Nat. Bank, Lyndora, Pa., 1907-14; asst. cashier, Butler County Nat. Bank, Butler, Pa., 1914-19, vice-pres., 1919-36, pres. and dir. since 1936; dir. Lyndora Nat. Bank, Spaide Shirt Co., West Penn Cement Co. Dir. Butler Community Chest, Butler Chamber of Commerce, Butler Y.M.C.A. Trustee Butler County Memorial Hosp., Allegheny Coll. Democrat. Methodist. Mason (32°, Shriner). Clubs: Butler Rotary (hon.), Butler Country (dir.); Duquesne (Pittsburgh). Home: Belmont Rd. Office: Main and Diamond Sts., Butler, Pa.

RITZ, Harold A., judge; b. Wheeling, W.Va., July 25, 1873; s. James M. and Catherine (McCarthy) R.; grad. Marshall Coll., State Normal Sch., Huntington, W.Va., 1889; m. Helen J. Jackson, Apr. 30, 1913. Admitted to W.Va. bar, 1894, and practiced at Bluefield; judge Circuit Court 8th W.Va. Jud. Dist., 1906; U.S. atty. Southern Dist. of W.Va., 1909-13; justice Supreme Court of Appeals of W.Va., term 1917-29; resigned, 1922, and resumed practice as mem. firm Brown, Jackson & Knight until 1925; now gen. counsel United Fuel Gas Co. Republican. Mem. Am. Bar Assn., W.Va. Bar Assn. (pres. 1929-30); mem. Am. Museum of Natural History; fellow Am. Geog. Soc. Clubs: Bluefield Country, Edgewood Country; Lotus Club (New York). Address: Charleston, W.Va.

RITZMAN, Michael Erwin, clergyman and coll. prof.; b. Gratz, Pa., Mar. 24, 1880; s. Aaron Solomon and Amelia (Laudenslager) R.; A.B., Albright Coll., 1902; ed. Drew Theol. Sem., 1909-10, Bib. Sem., New York City, 1910-12; B.D., Drew Theol. Sem., 1913; A.M., U. of Chicago, 1923; Ph.D., U. of Chicago, 1928; m. Daisy May Shaffer, Aug. 24, 1917; children—Michael Erwin, Jr., Thelma Marie, Ruth Elizabeth, Mary Esther. Ordained to ministry Evang. Ch., 1902; missionary in China, 1903-09, 1913-22; minister, LeMars, Ia., 1902-03, Villa Park, Ill., 1924-26; prof. N.T. and Missions, Evang. Sch. of Theology, Reading, Pa., since 1926. Mem. Soc. Bib. Literature and Exegesis, Nat. Assn. Bib. Instrs. Republican. Mem. Evang. Ch. Contbr. articles to religious mags. Home: 1518 N. 15th St., Reading, Pa.

RIVAS, Damaso de, pathologist, parasitologist; b. Diria, Granada, Nicaragua, Dec. 11, 1874; s. Mauricio and Carmen (Aleman) R.; B.S., U. of Pa., 1908, M.S., 1909, M.D., and Ph.D., 1910; m. Rosa Reinish, Jan. 23, 1904; children —Carlos Theodore, Ana Rosa, Maria Luisa. Bacteriologist to filtration bur. of Phila., 1904-06, state health dept., Pa., 1907-10, pathologist since 1917; research fellow in biology, U. of Pa., 1910, asst. dir. dept. of comparative pathology and Sch. of Tropical Medicine since 1910, asst. prof. parasitology, 1917-22, prof. since 1922; pathologist to Friend's Hosp., Frankford, Pa., since 1916; also pathologist Skin and Cancer Hosp., Phila.; dir. and pathologist Pan-Am. Pasteur Inst.; asst. Koch Inst., Berlin, and student at univs. of Paris, Lille, and Heidelberg; has been mem. of scientific excursions for study of tropical diseases of Africa. Awarded medal of Inst. Pasteur, Paris. Mem. Internat. Council of World Court League and rep. to the Peace Conf. in Paris. Pa. del. to 2d Internat. Congress of Tuberculosis, Washington, 1908; pres. Nicaraguan delegation of 2d Scientific Pan-Am. Congress, Washington, 1916-17; del. from Nicaragua to Sexto Mexico Latino-Americo, Havana, 1922; mem. Am. Med. Assn., Am. Soc. of Tropical Medicine, Coll. of Phys. (Phila.), Pan-Am. Med. Assn., Société de Pathologie Exotique of Paris (corr.), Alpha Kappa Kappa. Catholic. Author: Human Parasitology, 1920; Clinical Parasitology and Tropical Medicine, 1935. Contbr. to med. jours. Home: Villa Rosa, Lansdowne, Pa.

RIVENBURG, Romeyn Henry, educator; b. Clifford, Susquehanna Co., Pa., Nov. 22, 1874; s. Henry and Charity (Scutt) R.; grad. Keystone Acad., Factoryville, Pa., 1893 (valedictorian); A.B., summa cum laude, Bucknell University, 1897, A.M., 1898; studied summers, Cornell U. and Harvard; LL.D., John B. Stetson U., 1920; m. Marian Jones, Sept. 1, 1898; children—Margaret Jones (dec.), Marjorie Josephine, Marian (dec.), Romlyn Jean. Head dept. of mathematics the Peddie School, Hightstown, N.J., 1899-1923; asst. headmaster same, 1912-23; dean Bucknell U. since 1923, v.p., 1935. Mem. bd. mgrs. and chairman com. on Sunday School publications, Am. Bapt. Publ. Coc., Phila.; pres. Bd. of Edn., Hightstown. Pres. N.J. Assn. Mathematics Teachers, 1917-18; pres. higher edn. dept. and mem. exec. council, Pa. State Edn. Assn., 1931; pres. Eastern Assn. of Coll. Deans and Advisors of Men, 1933; sec. Com. on Pub. Relations, Assn. of Coll. Presidents of Pa.; mem. Phi Gamma Delta. Republican. Author: A Review of Algebra, 1914. Home: Bucknell University, Lewisburg, Pa.

RIVKIN, Harvey, editor Home News. Office: 406 W. Redwood St., Baltimore, Md.

RIZER, Richard Theodore, high school supervisor; b. Mt. Savage, Md., Apr. 28, 1900; s. George Henry and Catherine Amelia (Kirby) R.; B.S., U. of Md., College Park, Md., 1924, A.M., 1931; grad. student Pa. State Coll. summer 1935; m. Edith Idella Sleeman, June 23, 1930; children—John Richard, Jane Ridgley. Teacher of science, Frostburg (Md.) High Sch., 1924-31; prin. Jr. High Sch., Cresaptown, Md., 1931-34; prin. Sr. High Sch., Frostburg, Md., 1934-37; high sch. supervisor, Allegany County, Md., since 1937. Chmn. organization com. Potomac Council Boy Scouts of America, 1938-39. Mem. Allegany County Teachers Assn. (pres. 1935-37), Md. State Teachers Assn. (chmn. Western Region 1939), Jr. Order Am. Mechanics, Sigma Tau Omega. Republican. Methodist. Club: Frostburg Rotary (sec. 1937, vice-pres. 1938, pres. 1939). Home: 85 Frost Av., Frostburg, Md. Office: 108 Washington St., Cumberland, Md.

ROBB, Edmond E., clergyman; b. McDonald, Pa.; s. Joseph Wallace and Rachel Caroline (Lindsey) R.; student Washington & Jefferson Acad., 1900-02; M.A., Washington & Jefferson Coll., 1905; studied law under Judge J. Franklin Taylor, 1905-08; Th.M., Pittsburgh-Xenia Theol. Sem., 1911; D.D., Washington & Jefferson Coll., 1920; m. Winona Pearl Patterson, June 17, 1908; children—Glendon Patterson, Anne Jane. Ordained Presbyn. ministry, 1911; pastor First United Presbyn. Ch., Johnstown, Pa., 1911-13, Woodlawn United Presbyn. Ch., Chicago, 1913-19, First United Presbyn. Ch., Philadelphia, 1919-27, Central Presbyn. Ch., McKeesport since 1927. Republican. Mason (32°). Home: 1511 Carnegie Av., McKeesport, Pa.

ROBB, Eugene Kline, supervising prin. schs.; b. Altoona, Pa., Mar. 3, 1902; s. George David and Cora May (Kline) R.; B.S., Franklin and Marshall Coll., 1923; M.S., Pa. State Coll., 1927, Ed.D., same, 1934; m. Josephine Tussey Moore, June 23, 1928; children—George David, II, Richard Moore. Teacher sci., high sch. Hollidaysburg, Pa., 1923-25, prin. jr.-sr. high sch., Hollidaysburg, Pa., 1925-28; supervising prin. pub. schs., Bedford, Pa., since 1928. Mem. Nat. Edn. Assn., Nat. Soc. for Study of Curriculum, Progressive Edn. Assn., Pa. State Edn. Assn., Kappa Phi Kappa, Phi Kappa Sigma. Mem. Reformed Ch. Club: Rotary of Bedford (past pres. and past sec.). Home: 227 E. John St., Bedford, Pa.

ROBB, Hunter, M.D.; b. Burlington, N.J., 1863; s. Thomas and Caroline (Woolman) R.; ed. Episcopal Acad., Phila., Burlington (N.J.) College; M.D., University of Pa., 1884; m. Isabel Adams Hampton, 1894; children—Hampton, Philip Hunter; m. 3d, Marion Wilson, May 22, 1929. Resident physician, Presbyn. and Episcopal hosps., Phila., 1884-86; asst. surgeon Kensington Hosp. for Women, 1888-89; asso. in gynecology, Johns Hopkins U. and Hosp., 1889-94; in practice at Cleveland, 1894-1914; retired from practice; was prof. gynecology, Western Reserve U.; visiting gynecologist, Lakeside Hosp., Cleveland. Member Am. Gynecol. Soc., Obstet. and Gynecological Society of Paris. Episcopalian. Republican. Author: Aseptic Surgical Technique, 1894. Contributor to Hare's System of Therapeutics, 1891; Keating & Coe's Gynecology, 1894; Jewett's System of Obstetrics, 1900; Reed's Gynecology, 1901. Has written numerous papers on surg. technique and diseases of women. Maj., M.C.U.S.A., Sept. 1918-Jan. 13, 1919; served at Camp Greenleaf, Ga., at Rockefeller Inst., New York, Camp Wheeler, Ga., and Base Hosp. Home: 320 Wood St., Burlington, N.J.

ROBB, Marshall V(an Meter), pres. pub. utilities; b. Bainbridge, O., Feb. 9, 1879; s. John W. and Virginia (McMechen) R.; ed. Wabash Coll., 1896-99; m. Virginia A. Hutchinson, June 6, 1906; children—Jane (Mrs. Francis W. Chittick), Katharine (Mrs. John E. Miller), Mary V. Treas. Sullivan Co. (Ind.) Electric Co. and Wabash Valley Electric Co., 1910-22; vice-pres. First Nat. Bank of Clinton, Ind., 1919-32, pres. 1933; vice-pres. Central Ind. Power Co., Ind. Electric Corpn. and small Ind. utilities, 1922-26; interested in small telephone utilities, Ind. and Ill., 1927-28; pres. Allentown & Reading Traction Co., 1928-30; pres. Allentown & Reading Transit Co., West Newton (Ind.) Telephone Co., Consolidated Telephone Co., Florence, Ky., Berks Utilities Co., Indianapolis, Ind., since 1928. Mem. Phi Delta Theta. Republican. Presbyterian. Clubs: Athletic (Indianapolis); Wyomissing (Reading). Office: 14 N. Fifth St., Reading, Pa.

ROBBINS, Charles Dudley, pres. C. D. Robbins & Co.; b. Worcester, Mass., Nov. 5, 1886; s. Frank Arthur and Minnie Amanda (Dudley) R.; student Bowdoin Coll., Brunswick, Me., 1907-09; m. Beulah Sylvia Prince, Jan. 31, 1910; children—Beverly Prince (Mrs. John E. Holmes), Charles Dudley; m. 2d, Helen Mildred Walker, Nov. 25, 1931; children—Faith Annabelle, John Dudley. Registrar and librarian, Hotchkiss Sch., Lakeville, Conn., 1909-10; sec. Bonbright & Co., New York, 1910-17; salesman Hemphill, Noyes & Co., New York, 1917-18; partner Sutro & Kimbley, New York, 1918-23; sr. partner Charles D. Robbins & Co., Newark, investment securities, 1923-30, pres. since 1932; mem. N. Y. Stock Exchange, 1924-1930; dir. Road Horse Assn. of N.J. Mem. official bd., Morrow Memorial Ch., Maplewood, N.J. Mem. Zeta Psi. Republican. Methodist. Club: Down Town (Newark, N.J.). Home: 77 Woodland Rd., Maplewood, N.J. Office: 810 Broad St., Newark, N.J.

ROBBINS, Edmund Yard, educator; b. Windsor, N.J., Oct. 3, 1867; s. George Randall and Anna Maria (Cubberly) R.; A.B., Princeton, 1889, A.M., 1890; studied U. of Leipzig, Germany, 1891-94; m. Emeline Place Hayward, Apr. 18, 1900. Instr. Greek, 1894, asst. prof., 1897, prof., 1902-36, Ewing prof. Greek lang. and lit., 1910-36, emeritus since 1936, Princeton. Annual prof. American School of Classical Studies, Athens, Greece, 1921-22. Mem. Am. Philol. Assn., Phi Beta Kappa. Republican. Presbyn. Translator: The Nature and Origin of the Noun Genders in the Indo-European Languages (by Karl Brugmann), 1897. Home: 144 Library Pl., Princeton, N.J.

ROBBINS, Edward Rutledge, univ. prof.; b. Somerset Co., N.J., Dec. 5, 1870; s. Sylvester and Sarah Isabel (Bird) R.; A.B., Princeton, 1894; A.M., U. of Pa., 1935; m. Helen M. Carrell, Apr. 30, 1919. Instr. in mathematics, Lawrenceville (N.J.) Sch., 1894-1900; master in mathematics, William Penn Charter Sch., Phila., 1900-15; edn. dept. John Wanamaker, Phila. 1918-22; supt. schs., Jenkintown, Pa., 1922-26; head master, Swarthmore Prep. Sch.,

Swarthmore, Pa., 1926-31; instr. in mathematics, Temple U. since Sept., 1931. Served as trustee and pres. Swarthmore Prep. Sch., 1928-31. Mem. Am. Assn. Univ. Profs., Phi Beta Kappa. Awarded J.S.K. $600 math. fellowship at Princeton, 1894. Republican. Presbyterian (elder). Author: Arithmetic for Schools, 1900; Higher Arithmetic, 1902; Elementary Algebra, 1904; Algebra Review, 1906; Complete Algebra, 1908; Exercises in Algebra, 1911; Plane Geometry, 1913; Solid Geometry, 1916; Trigonometry, 1918. Home: 6935 N. 19th St., Philadelphia, Pa.

ROBBINS, Frank A. Jr., gen. mgr. steel plant; b. Pittsfield, Mass., Mar. 7, 1881; s. Frank A. and Fanny (Goodrich) R.; student high sch., Pittsfield, Mass.; S.B., Mass. Inst. Tech., 1902; m. Lida Motter, Oct. 6, 1909; children—Elizabeth (Mrs. Robert Bruce Murrie), Frances (Mrs. S. L. Hohverstott). Employed in steel plant learning the bus., 1902-08; asst. to v.p. Pa. Steel Co., 1908-16; asst. to gen. mgr., Bethlehem Steel Co., Steelton, Pa., 1916-18, gen. mgr. since 1918. Served as pres. Steelton Welfare Assn., Sch. Bd. of Steelton, Pa., Harrisburg Council of Social Agencies; chmn. Pa. State Board of Pub. Assistance. Dir. Pub. Charities Assn. of Pa., Capital Hosp. Service, Inc.; Harrisburg; v.p. Harrisburg Hosp. Mem. Am. Iron & Steel Inst., Engrs. Soc. of Pa. Republican. Presbyterian. Clubs: Steelton, Kiwanis (Steelton, Pa.). Home: 251 Pine St., Steelton, Pa.

ROBBINS, Frederick Ross, surgeon; b. Buffalo, N.C., Oct. 17, 1897; s. John Pickens and Mary Ann (Penley) R.; B.S., U. of N.C., 1919; M.D., U. of Pa. Med. Sch., 1921; m. Alberta E. Mowitz, Sept. 24, 1930; 1 son, Frederick Ross, Jr. Resident physician, Pa. Hosp., Phila., 1921-23, chief resident physician 1923-26; asst. surgeon to Pa. and Bryn Mawr hosps.; asso. surgeon to Childrens Hosp.; instr. surgery, U. of Pa. Med. Sch., U. of Pa. Grad. Sch. of Medicine. Served as pvt. inf., U.S.A., 1918; 1st lt., U.S.A. Res., 1926-35; lt. comdr. U.S.N. Res. since 1935. Fellow Am. Coll. Surgeons, Phila. Coll. Physicians, Phila. Acad. Surgery. Mem. Am., Pa. State, and Phila. Co. med. assns. Republican. Club: Union League (Philadelphia). Home: Millbank Rd., Bryn Mawr, Pa. Office: 255 S. 17th St., Philadelphia, Pa.

ROBBINS, Harry Wolcott, prof. English; b. Vershire, Vt., Jan. 31, 1883; s. Henry Clarke and Caroline Abigail (Wolcott) R.; A.B., Brown U., 19—, A.M., 1908; student U. of Chicago, summer 1912, U. of Wis., summer 1914, U. of Grenoble, 1919; Ph.D., U. of Minn., 1923; m. Florence Bliss Lyon, Aug. 30, 1910. Asst. in English, Brown U., 1908-09; instr. in English, Marblehead (Mass.) High Sch., 1909-11, Calumet (Mich.) High Sch., 1911-14, North High Sch., Minneapolis, Minn., 1914-17; instr. in English, U. Minn., 1919-23; prof. English, Bucknell U., since 1923, chmn. English Group and Grad. Div. since 1931. Enlisted in 1st O.T.C., Ft. Snelling, Minn., 1917; commd. 2d lt. and advanced to capt.; served as adj. 804th Pioneer Inf., with A.E.F., 1918-19; capt. Inf. O.R.C. since 1920; 2d lt. Cav., Pa. Nat. Guard, 1925. Mem. Modern Lang. Assn. America, Early English Text Soc., Société des Anciens Textes Française, Am. Assn. Univ. Profs., Internat. Typographical Union, Phi. Beta Kappa, Sigma Tau Telta, Lambda Chi Alpha. Repblican. Baptist. Author: Advanced Exposition (with R. E. Parker), 1933. Editor: Le Merure de Seinte Eglise, 1925; Western World Literature (with W. H. Coleman), 1938. Translator: Le Roman de la Rose. Contbr. to jours. Home: 124 St. George St., Lewisburg, Pa.

ROBBINS, Leonard H., writer; b. Lincoln, Neb., Apr. 2, 1877; s. Leonard H. and Nannie (Cole) R.; ed. U. of Neb. and Princeton. U.; m. Lena Anthony, Oct. 28, 1901; children—Ruth, Anthony. Began newspaper work at Lincoln, 1898; wrote the "In the Air" column in Newark (N.J.) Evening News, 1901-17, New York Times since 1923. Contbr. fiction to magazines. Mem. Kappa Sigma. Mason. Presbyn. Author: Jersey Jingles, 1908; Mountains and Men, 1931; Cure It with a Garden, 1933. Home: 210 Grove St., Montclair, N.J.

ROBERTS, Austin Leonard, lawyer; b. New York, N.Y., Aug. 28, 1886; s. Charles F. and Florence M. (Pickering) R.; student pub. schs. and high sch., Bayonne, N.J., 1892-1904, N.Y. Law Sch., 1920-23; m. Loretto C. Tucker, Nov. 4, 1917; children—Charles Edward, Austin Leonard, Edmund Thomas. Began as stenographer and bookkeeper, 1905-10, with Federal Cigar Co., 1911-15; ct. stenographer in office Elmer E. Demarest, referee in bankruptcy, Jersey City, N.J., 1920-23; admitted to N.J. bar as atty., 1923, as counselor, 1927; engaged in gen. practice of law at Jersey City, N.J. since 1923. Served in U.S.N. Res. Forces, 1917-18. Mem. br. edn. Twp. of Cranford, 1931-34. Republican. Episcopalian. Mason. Home: 6 Beach St., Cranford. Office: 239 Washington, St., Jersey City, N.J.

ROBERTS, E(dmund) Weston, journalist; b. New York, N.Y., Oct. 25, 1892; s. Harvey Emmett and Adelene (Weston) R.; grad. East Orange High Sch.; m. Anna Du Bois, Nov. 4, 1916; children—Du Bois, Jean Weston (Mrs. Merritt L. Budd, Jr.). Began as subscription solicitor, Insurance Advocate, 1913-16, adv. mgr., 1916, mgr., 1917-22, pres. Roberts Pub. Corpn., pub. of Insurance Advocate since 1922; pres. Index Pub. Co.; mem. firm Convention Year Books Co.; co-publisher and business mgr. Resort World. Served as officer Wyoming Civic Assn. 2 terms. Mem. Rep. Club of Millburn. Served as sergt. N.J. Militia Res. Gen. mgr. last six yrs. "Hi Ho" annual show, Millburn. Past grand master Sigma Kappa Delta, nat. high sch. frat. Past pres. Mens Club Wyoming Ch. (3 terms). Republican. Presbyn. Mason. Clubs: Wyoming (Wyoming); Insurance Square (New York). Home: 83 Chestnut St., Wyoming, N.J. Office: 123 William St., New York, N.Y.

ROBERTS, Edward Howell, theol. sem. prof., dean of students; b. Middle Granville, N.Y., Aug. 1, 1895; s. Edward and Mary (Davis) R.; student Ripon (Wis.) Coll., 1915-17, A.B., U. of Wis., Madison, Wis., 1919, M.A., 1920; Th.B., Princeton (N.J.) Theol. Sem., 1923, Th.M., 1923; student U. of Southern Calif., Los Angeles, Calif., 1925-26, U. of Calif., Berkeley, Calif., 1925-26; m. Esther Davison Hill, Dec. 27, 1927. Asst. pastor First Presbyn. Ch., New Rochelle, N.Y., 1923; ednl. work, Los Angeles, Calif., 1926-30; instr. in systematic theology, Princeton (N.J.) Theol. Sem., 1930-37, asso. prof. homiletics since 1937, dean of students since 1937. Exec. sec. Am. Assn. of Theol. Schools. Presbyn. Address: 120 Prospect Av., Princeton, N.J.

ROBERTS, Emerson Bryan, mfg. exec.; b. Oxford, Md., Oct. 10, 1890; s. Rev. Emerson Pierce and Mary (Bryan) R.; A.B., St. John's Coll., Annapolis, Md., 1911, M.A., 1913, D.Sc., 1918; m. Helen McCain Cooley, Nov. 27, 1919; 1 dau., Mary Elizabeth. Teacher of science, Kittanning (Pa.) High School, 1913-17; supervisor technical employment and training, Westinghouse Electric & Mfg. Co., Pittsburgh, 1919-36, asst. to v.p. since 1936. Served as lieut. U.S. Army Air Service, 1917-19. Mem. Soc. for Promotion of Engring. Edn., Am. Management Assn., Pittsburgh Personnel Assn. Republican. Presbyterian. Mason. Club: University (Pittsburgh). Editor, Engring. Problems for Advanced Students, 1930. Author of numerous articles on industrial relations. Home: 327 Woodside Rd., Wilkinsburg, Pa. Office: Union National Bldg., Pittsburgh, Pa.

ROBERTS, Emmett Ephriam, coll. prof.; b. McConnelsville, O., Nov. 18, 1890; s. Geo. P. and Lucy (Sevall) R.; A.B., Ohio Univ., Athens, 1915; A.M., Ohio State U., Columbus, 1916; grad. student N.Y. Univ., 1938; m. Alice Steele, Aug. 24, 1916 (died 1927); children—Dorothy Marilynn, Richard Steele; m. 2d, Margaret Hurt, Aug. 23, 1930. Engaged as prof. speech, James Millikin Univ., Decatur, Ill., 1918-19; prof. English, Southwestern La. Inst., Lafayette, 1922-27; prof. English, now journalism, Bethany (W.Va.) Coll., since 1928. Mem. Kappa Alpha. Republican. Presbyn. Contbr. articles to professional jours. and some short fiction. Home: Pendleton Av., Bethany, W.Va.

ROBERTS, Frank Calvin, civil engring.; b. New York, N.Y., June 30, 1861; s. William and Catherine (Parry) R.; C.E., Princeton, 1883; hon. A.M., Princeton, 1908, Eng.D., same, 1924; m. Amy Paxton, of Princeton, N.J., May 27, 1886; children—Katharine (Mrs. Charles Fisher Luther), William Paxton, Frank Calvin, Harmar Denny. Instr. engring., Princeton U., 1883-84; engr. Cooper, Hewitt & Co., Trenton, N.J., 1884-86, Gordon, Strobel & Lareau, Phila., 1886-88; in practice engring. in Phila., 1888-93, mem. firm Frank C. Roberts & Co., 1893-1911; mem. firm Frank C. Roberts & Co. and Edgar V. Seeler, architects and engrs., 1897-1913, and this firm designed and supervised constrn. of many well-known bldgs.; in pvt. and independent practice at Phila. since 1913, covering civil, mech., elec., and metall. engring.; has designed more than 75 iron and steel plants and over 100 blast furnaces for well-known cos. in U.S., Great Britain, Can. and Spain. Is registered patent atty. Mem. Am. Soc. Civil Engrs., Am. Inst. Mining & Metall. Engrs., Am. Iron & Steel Inst., British Iron & Steel Inst., Phi Beta Kappa. Republican. Presbyn. Clubs: Union League, Princeton (Philadelphia); Au Sable (St. Huberts, N.Y.). Author: Figure of the Earth, 1885, pub. in France, 1911. Home: Cherry Lane, Wynnewood, Pa. Office: 1719 Real Estate Bldg., Phila., Pa.

ROBERTS, George L., county commr.; b. Falls, Pa., June 16, 1868; s. S. Tracy and Rose (McKune) R.; ed. pub. sch. and high sch.; m. Emily Beebe, Dec. 21, 1904; children—Tracy, Josephine, Alfred. Engaged in hardware bus. in Sayre, Pa., 1899-1933; pres. Sayre Bldg. & Loan Assn., 1903-32; dir. Merchants & Mechanics Bank, 1912-31; serving as co. commr. Bradford Co., Pa. for term, 1932-40; co. chmn. State Emergency Relief Assn., 1932-33. Republican. Presbyn. (trustee and sec. bd. First Ch., Sayre since 1900). Home: 201 Hayden St., Sayre, Pa. Office: Court House, Towanda, Pa.

ROBERTS, Graham, retired business exec.; b. Phila., Pa., May 3, 1885; s. Dr. A. Sydney and Caroline H. (Thomson) R.; student Hill Sch., Pottstown, Pa., 1897-1902, Yale, 1902-05; m. Elizabeth W. Meyer, June 17, 1936. Investment banker with Redmond & Co., New York City, and Henry & West, Phila., 1905-17, Blair & Co., Phila., 1920-27; pres. Graham Roberts & Co., bankers, Phila., 1923-27; pres. Buck Mountain Coal Mining Co., Hazleton, Pa., since 1925; dir. Union Improvement Co. Served as commd. officer, U.S. Army, France, 1917-18. Mem. Mil. Order of Fgn. Wars (asst. sec. since 1937), Soc. of Colonial Wars, S.R., Loyal Legion, Vets. of Fgn. Wars. Republican. Episcopalian. Clubs: The Rabbit, Philadelphia Yale (mem. scholarship com.), Philadelphia, Philadelphia Country, Racquet, Corinthian Yacht (Phila.); Racquet and Tennis (New York City); State in Schuylkill (Pa.); Graduates (New Haven, Conn.). Founder Graham Roberts Scholarships at Yale and at Hill Sch., Pottstown, Pa. Home: Monument Rd. and City Line, Bala-Cynwyd, Pa.

ROBERTS, Harold Cooper, lawyer; b. Phila., Pa., July 12, 1902; s. Charles W. and Anna C. (Melcher) R.; A.B., U. of Pa., 1923; LL.B., U. of Pa. Law Sch., 1926; unmarried. Admitted to Pa. bar, 1926, and since engaged in gen. practice of law at Phila.; mem. firm White and Staples; mem. staff The Legal Intelligencer since 1925, asso. editor, 1933-36, editor since 1936, pres. The Legal Intelligencer. Mem. Am., Pa., State, and Phila. bar assns. Order of the Coif, Phi Beta Kappa. Episcopalian. Club: University (Philadelphia). Co-editor (with others); Banking Laws of Pennsylvania, 1930. Home: R.F.D. No. 1, Norristown Rd., Ambler, Pa. Office: 1930 Land Title Bldg., Philadelphia, Pa.

ROBERTS, Helen France (Mrs. Charles I. Nadel), lawyer; b. Bayonne, N.J., June 19, 1908; d. Wm. George and Helen Mary (Kelly) Roberts; grad., valedictorian, Bayonne High Sch., 1925; A.B., cum laude, Coll. of New Rochelle (N.Y.), 1929; LL.B., Fordham U. Law Sch., New York, 1932; m. Charles I. Nadel, May 28, 1937. Began as teacher of mathematics, Bayonne Jr. High Sch., 1929; practicing atty. at Bayonne, N.J., since 1934; admitted to N.J. State Bar as atty., 1933, as counsellor, 1936. Mem. Bayonne, N.J., State, Am. bar assns., Hudson Co. Bar Assn. (mem. com. workmen's compensation), Irvington Gen. Hosp. Auxiliary (1st v.p.), Auxiliary of Essex County Med. Soc., Women's Professional Panhellenic Assn. (chmn. of publicity, 1937-39), Phi Delta Delta (asso. editor, 1930-32; asst. pub. relations dir., 1932-34; pub. relations dir., 1936-38), Kappa Gamma Pi. Catholic. Club: Zonta (pres., Bayonne, N.J.). Home: 1186 Clinton Av., Irvington, N.J. Office: 780 Broadway, Bayonne, N.J.

ROBERTS, Isaac Warner, banking exec.; b. Phila., Pa., Apr. 30, 1881; s. George B. and Miriam P. (Williams) R.; B.S., Princeton U., 1903; LL.B., U. of Pa., 1906 m. Caroline Henry, Oct. 12, 1909; children—Algernon, Bayard H., Mary, Brooke, Howard H. Vice-pres. Phila. Saving Fund Soc. Home: Bala-Cynwyd, Pa. Office: 1212 Market St., Philadelphia, Pa.

ROBERTS, John H. R., insurance exec.; b. Hanover Green, Pa., May 26, 1888; s. Rev. H. J. and Winifred (Evans) R.; ed. Palmer's Business Coll., Phila., Pa., Schuylkill Sem. (now Albright Coll.), Reading, Pa., Bucknell U.; B.E., Sc.B., LL.B.; m. Anna M. Gring, 1916; 1 dau., Marjorie. Admitted to Pa. bar; private sec. with C.&N.W. R.R. Co., 1912; chief clerk Western Union Telegraph Co., 1913-14; traveling adjuster, dist. claims mgr. with T. H. Mastin & Co., St. Louis and Chicago, 1914-18; asso. with Pennsylvania Indemnity Corpns. since 1919, successively adjuster, dist. claims mgr., claims mgr., dir. since 1931, vice-pres. in charge of claims since 1932. Served as 1st lieut. Ordnance Corps, U.S.A., 1918. Mem. Am., Pa., and Phila. bar assns., Internat. Assn. Ins. Counsel, Army Ordnance Assn., Am. Legion, Forty and Eight, Am. Vets. Assn., Phi Kappa Psi. Republican. Baptist. Mason (32°, Shriner), Elk. Clubs: Lawyers, Exchange, Le Coin d'Or. Home: Glenwood Rd., Merion Station. (Office: 1511 Walnut St., Philadelphia, Pa.

ROBERTS, John William, phytopathologist; b. Alma, Neb., July 4, 1882; s. Samuel Leonidas and Anna (McGlathery) R.; A.B., U. of Neb., Lincoln, 1904, A.M., 1909; Ph.D., George Washington U., Washington, D.C., 1917; m. Ethel Hutchins, Dec. 10, 1911. Asso. with U.S. Bur. Plant Industry since starting as sci. asst., 1909, advanced through successive grades to prin. pathologist in charge of investigation of bacterial and fungus diseases of deciduous fruit trees, Bur. of Plant Industry, U.S. Dept. Agr. at U.S. Hort. Research Sta., Beltsville, Md., since 1935; served as mem. Federal Insecticide and Fungicide Bd., 1924-27. Fellow A.A. A.S. Mem. Am. Phytopathol. Soc. (editor 1929-31), Wash. Bot. Soc. (pres. 1936), Chi Phi, Sigma Xi. Club: Cosmos (Washington, D.C.). Mem. com. on policy and mss., Jour. of Agricultural Research since 1930. Home: 1619 R St. N. W.; Washington, D.C. Address: Beltsville, Md.

ROBERTS, Kate Louise; b. Lodi, N.J.; d. James and Jane (Chippendale) R.; grad. Normal Sch., Newark, N.J.; studied art and music in Berlin and Munich. Formerly with Pub. Library, N.Y. City; later reference librarian, Newark Pub. Library, Swedenborgian. Compiler: The Club Woman's Handybook of Programs and Club Management, 1914; Hoyt's New Cyclopedia of Practical Quotations, 1922, 27. Actively identified with ednl. and economic affairs. Home: 506 Meeker St., South Orange, N.J.

ROBERTS, Kenneth (Lewis), author; b. Kennebunk, Me., Dec. 8, 1885; s. Frank Lewis and Grace Mary (Tibbets) Roberts; A.B., Cornell University, 1908; Litt.D., Dartmouth College, 1934, Colby College, 1935, Middlebury College, 1938; m. Anna S. Mosser, Feb. 14, 1911. Editor in chief, Cornell Widow, 1905-08; reporter, spl. writer and conductor of humorous column and page, Boston Post, 1909-17; editorial staff, Puck, 1916-17; staff Life, New York, 1915-18. Capt. Intelligence Sect., Siberian Expeditionary Force, 1918-19. Staff corr. Saturday Evening Post since 1919. Mem. Nat. Inst. Arts and Letters, Phi Beta Kappa. Author: Europe's Morning After, 1921; Why Europe Leaves Home, 1922; Sun Hunting, 1923; The Collector's Whatnot (with Booth Tarkington and Hugh McNair Kahler), 1923; Black Magic, 1924; Concentrated New England, 1924; Florida Loafing, 1925; Florida, 1926; Antiquamania (illustrated by Booth Tarkington), 1928; Arundel, 1930; The Lively Lady, 1931; Rabble in Arms, 1933; Captain Caution, 1934; For Authors Only and Other Gloomy Essays, 1935; It Must Be Your Tonsils, 1936; Northwest Passage, 1937; Trending into Maine, March to Quebec, 1938. Home: Kennebunk Beach, Me. Address: Saturday Evening Post, Philadelphia, Pa.

ROBERTS, Newell Wells, govt. official; b. Utica, N.Y., Nov. 14, 1885; s. James B. and Josephine I. (Combs) R.; B.S., Colgate U., 1908, M.S., 1913; m. Mary Louise Rider, Feb. 1, 1923. Asso. with Bemberger mining interests, Salt Lake City, Utah, and asst. engr. Daly West mine, 1908-11; mining engr., Durham Coal & Iron Co., Chattanooga, Tenn., 1911-12; asst. to pres. in charge operations of 26 mines, Davis Coal & Coke Co., Baltimore, 1912-13; asso. Cons. Mining Engrs., New York, 1914-15; gen. mgr. exptl. plant, New York, 1915-17; v.p. and dir. Internat. Coal Products Corpn., New York, 1917-21; reports and investigations, New York, 1921-23; engr. and rep. of chmn. of bd. and dir. The Securities Co., New York, 1923-32; dep. adminstr. Bituminous Coal Code, NRA, Washington, D.C., 1933-35; sec. Nat. Bituminous Coal Commn., Washington, D.C., 1935-36, adviser, 1937, dir. of marketing div. in charge of establishing prices since 1938. Mem. Am. Inst. Mining Engrs., Phi Beta Kappa, Delta Kappa Epsilon. Presbyn. Club: Kenwood Country (Washington, D.C.). Home: 20 Brookwood Rd., South Orange, N.J.; 6124 32d Pl., N.W., Washington, D.C. Office: 734 15th St., N.W., Washington, D.C.

ROBERTS, W. Frank; chmn. bd. Standard Gas Equipment Co.; b. Pa., Jan. 25, 1879; s. Albert W. and Eliza R.; M.E., Lehigh U., 1902; m. Laura H. Roberts, 1904. With Standard Gas Equipment Co. since 1928, now chmn. bd. and pres. Home: 4007 Greenway. Office: Bayard and Hamburg Sts., Baltimore, Md.

ROBERTS, Warren R., auditor gen. of Pa.; b. Northampton Co., Pa., Nov. 29, 1873; s. John and Sarah Ann (Hendricks) R.; ed. public and private schools in Freemansburg and Bethlehem, Pa.; m. Sadie Dreisbach, Aug. 18, 1908. Recorder of deeds, Northampton Co., Pa., 1906-11; pres., The Woodring-Roberts Corpn., Bethlehem, Pa., 1911-36; state senator, 1926-37; auditor gen. of Pa. since 1936; dir. First Nat. Bank & Trust Co. of Bethlehem (Pa.), Woodring-Roberts Corpn. Mem. Chamber of Commerce, Welfare Assn., Community Chest Assn., Business Men's Assn., Bethlehem, Pa. Democrat. Lutheran. Clubs: Bethlehem, Rotary, Northampton Co. Historical (Bethlehem, Pa.). Home: 1850 Easton Av., Bethlehem, Pa. Office: State Capitol, Harrisburg, Pa.

ROBERTSHAW, John Alfred, mfg. heat control devices; b. Pittsburgh, Pa., Mar. 22, 1894; s. Frederick William and Ida H. (Oldshue) R.; ed. Epiphany Parochial Sch., 1900-07, Central High Sch., 1907-11, Duquesne Univ., evenings, 1913-14; m. Emma Luella Ryan, Nov. 3, 1925; children—John Alfred, Jr., William Ryan, Emma Hope (dec.), Frederick Oldshue. Employed as brass finisher, 1911-13, bench metallurgist, then salesman and sales mgr.; vice-pres. and gen. mgr. Robertshaw Thermostat Co., mfr. heat control devices, Youngwood, Pa., since 1928; vice-pres. Reynolds Metals Co., Richmond, Va.; pres. Grayson Heat Control Ltd., Lynwood, Calif., American Thermometer Co., St. Louis, Mo.; pres. and gen. mgr. Coal Operators Casualty Co., Greensburg; pres. Grove Lock Corpn.; dir. Barclay Westmoreland Trust Co. Mem. U.S.N., 1918-19, ensign U.S.N.R., 1919. Dir. Westmoreland Hosp. Assn.; trustee Torrence State Hosp. Mem. Gas Appliance and Equipment Mfrs. (dir.). Republican. Roman Catholic. B.P.O.E. Clubs: Country, Westmoreland Polo and Hunt, Pike Run Country, Greensburg, Duquesne (Pittsburgh); Country (Oakmont). Home: R.F.D. No. 4, Greensburg. Office: Youngwood, Pa.

ROBERTSON, Andrew Wells, chairman board Westinghouse Electric & Mfg. Co.; b. Panama, N.Y., Feb. 7, 1880; s. David and Margaret (Ganson) R.; A.B., Allegheny Coll., 1906, also LL.D.; LL.B., U. of Pittsburgh, 1910; m. Besse Belle Montgomery, June 30, 1910 (died 1917); 1 dau., Elizabeth Montgomery; m. 2d, Agnes Shields, July 5, 1918; children—David S., William Ganson. Admitted to the bar, 1910; became title officer Guaranty Title & Trust Co., 1912; trust officer, 1913; served as atty. for the Pittsburgh Railways and the Duquesne Light Co., 1913-18; gen. atty. Phila. Co. and affiliates, 1918-26; vice-pres., 1923; pres., 1926; chmn. bd. Westinghouse Electric & Mfg. Co. and subsidiaries since 1929; dir., Westinghouse Electric & Mfg. Co., Canadian Westinghouse Co., Ltd., Westinghouse Air Brake Co., Union Switch & Signal Co., Farmers Deposit Nat. Bank of Pittsburgh, Chase Nat. Bank of New York; chmn. bd. trustees Allegheny Coll.; trustee U. of Pittsburgh; dir. Buhl Foundation, Pittsburgh, Pa. Mem. Am., Pa. and Allegheny County bar assns.; Phi Beta Kappa, Phi Delta Theta. Clubs: St. Andrews Golf, Blind Brook, City Midday, Racket and Tennis, Rockefeller Center Luncheon (New York); Duquesne, University, Longue Vue Country, South Hills Country (Pittsburgh). Home: Clairton, Pa. Office: 1304 Union Bank Bldg., Pittsburgh, Pa.

ROBERTSON, Benjamin Perry, clergyman; b. Tigerville, S.C., Jan. 22, 1863; s. William Davis and Marinda Rachel (Westmoreland) R.; A.M., Judson Coll., Hendersonville, N.C., 1889, George Washington U., 1905; Th.M., Southern Bapt. Theol. Sem., Louisville, Ky., 1892; D.D., Union U., Jackson, Tenn., 1920; Ph.D., People's Nat. U., Atlanta, 1923, LL.D., 1924; m. Mary Ida Osborne, June 7, 1892 (died June 29, 1910); children—Mary Marguerite (Mrs. Julius F. Fisher), Lila Budd (Mrs. F. M. Whiteside), Grace Love (Mrs. W. B. Hart); m. 2d, Nannie Lind Davis, of Atlanta, Ga., July 8, 1911; children—Marinda Lind (Mrs. Roger E. Settle), Benjamin Berry, Paul Sellers. Ordained Bapt. ministry, 1888; pastor First Ch., Gaffney, S.C., 1892-99, Fuller Memorial Ch., Baltimore, 1899-1905, First Ch., Arcadia, Fla., 1905-06; financial sec. Columbia Coll., Lake City, Fla., 1906-07; pastor Central Ch., Atlanta, 1908-11; supt. Bapt. Missions, Atlanta, 1911-15; pastor St. Charles Av. Ch., New Orleans, 1915-18; a founder and first pres. board trustees, later gen. sec. bd. Bapt. Bible Inst., New Orleans, 1918-19; pastor First Ch., Paducah, Ky., 1919-22; visited Bible lands, 1922; pastor First Ch., Sanatobia, Miss., 1922-25, First Ch., Hyattsville, Md., since 1925. One of the founders, and first president of the Baptist Bible Training Sch., Washington, since 1930. Mem. Southern Bapt. Conv.; del. Bapt. World Alliance, Stockholm, 1923; preaching, lecturing, studying in Eng., summer, 1927; del. Bapt. World Alliance, Toronto, Can., 1928, Atlanta, Ga., 1939. Democrat. A leader in founding North Greenville Bapt. Acad., 1891, Limestone Coll., 1894-95. Author: The Holy Spirit, 1929. Home: Hyattsville, Md.

ROBERTSON, Campbell, research chemist; b. Kalamazoo, Mich., Jan. 31, 1906; s. Peter Daniel and Margaret Helen (Cousin) R.; student Western Normal High Sch., Kalamazoo, Mich., 1917-21, U. of Mich., Ann Arbor, Mich., 1921-24; B.S., Columbia U., 1927, Ph.D., 1930 (as of Feb., 1931); m. Josephine Russell, Oct. 12, 1929; children—Philip, David. Research chemist, E. I. du Pont de Nemours & Co., Perth Amboy, N.J., 1930-31, production mgr., 1932-35, research supervisor since 1936. Mem. Am. Chem. Soc., Am. Ceramic Soc., Sigma Xi, Alpha Chi Sigma, Phi Lambda Upsilon. Republican. Author articles in Jour. of Physical Chemistry. Home: 531 Locust St., Roselle, N.J. Office: E. I. du Pont de Nemours & Co., Perth Amboy, N.J.

ROBERTSON, Charles Edward, investment securities; b. Scranton, Pa., Feb. 11, 1876; s. William George and N. Josette (Dolph) R.; ed. Sch. of the Lackawanna, Lafayette Coll., 1895-97; C.E., Princeton, 1900; m. Mary Esther Swift, June 28, 1911 (died Jan. 19, 1930). Employed as engr., 1901-02; asst. prin. Sch. of

Coal Mines, Internat. Corr. Schs. of Scranton, 1902-08, editor sch. paper, 1908-09; mgr. Fidelity Securities Co., 1910-15; in bus. own acct. as propr. Charles E. Robertson & Co., investment securities since 1915; dir. Ralph E. Weeks Corpn.; former dir. First Nat. Bank, Dunmore, Pa. Active in Liberty Loan drives during World War. Mem. Northern Pa. Princeton Alumni Assn. Republican. Mem. M.E. Ch. Author: How Money Makes Money, 1922. Home: 1205 Clay Av. Office: Connell Bldg., Scranton, Pa.

ROBERTSON, David Allan, educator; b. Chicago, Oct. 17, 1880; s. John and Christina (Mitchell) R.; A.B., U. of Chicago, 1902, grad. student, 1902-05, fellow, 1904-05; LL.D. from George Washington U., 1928; Litt.D. Bucknell U., 1929; m. Anne Victoria Knobel, Dec. 26, 1906; 1 son, David Allan. Asst. in English, 1904-05, asso., 1905-06, instr., 1906-10, asst. prof., 1910-14, asso. prof., 1914-23, U. of Chicago, also secretary to pres., 1906-20, and head of Hitchcock House; dean Coll. of Arts, Lit. and Science, same univ., 1920-23. Editor University Record, 1915-20; sec. U. of Chicago war service, 1917-18; sec. Assn. Am. Univs., 1918-23; investigated 200 Am. colleges for Assn. Am. Univs., 1924-29; asst. dir. Am. Council on Edn., 1924-30, in charge internat. relations, 1924-28; visited 50 univs. abroad 6 times between 1909 and 1926; mem. com. on Am. University Union, 1924-27; sec. Com. on Personnel Methods, 1927-30, pres. of Goucher Coll. since 1930. Member Baltimore Municipal Commn. on Employment Stabilization, 1930. Mem. Coll. Entrance Examination Bd. Elder Ch. of the Covenant, Washington, 1926-30. Brown Memorial Ch., Baltimore, 1931—; pres. Washington Federation of Chs., 1929-30; member exec. com. Baltimore Federation of Chs., 1930-36, vice-pres., 1935-36. Mem. Coll. Library Advisory Board of A.L.A. since 1937; mem. Mayor's Com. on Fine Arts, Baltimore, since 1937. Mem. Lit. Soc. (Washington), Modern Lang. Assn. America, Am. Assn. Univ. Profs. (hon.), N.E.A., and Dept. Superintendence same, Nat. Soc. Study of Edn., Religious Edn. Assn. (v.p. 1931), Middle States Assn. of Colls. and Secondary Schools (pres. 1936-37), Md. Hist. Soc., St. Andrew's Soc., Foreign Policy Assn., Am. Council Pharm. Edn. since 1932, Baltimore Assn. Commerce since 1933, League of Nations Assn. (exec. com. since 1934), Md. Commn. on Higher Edn. of Negroes, 1934, Am. Council on Edn. (chmn. com. on dictionary of ednl. terms, 1934, chmn. com. on publs.) Md. Commn. on Mandatory Old Age Pension, 1934-35, Omicron Delta Kappa (hon.), Phi Gamma Delta, Phi Beta Kappa (served as pres. Beta of Ill., and Beta of Md.; chmn. on qualifications since 1931; mem. Senate since 1931); a founder and exec. officer University Orchestral Assn., Chicago; a founder and former pres. Renaissance Soc., Chicago; hon. mem. Assn. Am. Colleges; mem. exec. com. Assn. of Am. Colleges, 1933-35; mem. exec. com. and chmn. com. on graduate instruction of Southern Univ. Conf., 1937; mem. Nat. Vocational Guidance Assn. (trustee, 1929); board dir. Westminster Foundation, 1937—; mem. of Nat. Advisory Com. of N.Y. World's Fair, 1939 for State of Md.; trustee Goucher Coll., Fisk Univ. Phi Beta Kappa Foundation; mem. of Presbyterian Eye, Ear and Throat Hospital, Baltimore; mem. bd. of the Lyric Co., Baltimore. Republican. Presbyn.; mem. Nat. Capital Presbyn. Commn. of Gen. Assembly; mem. Baltimore Presbyn. Social Union (vice-pres. 1934-35, pres. 1936-37). Clubs: Town Hall (New York); University (Baltimore); Johns Hopkins Faculty. Author: American Universities and Colleges, 1927; and repts. and articles on English lit. and higher edn. in mags. Home: 2229 N. Charles St., Baltimore, Md.

ROBERTSON, Frank Adrian, publisher; b. Delmar, Md., Mar. 5, 1885; s. Joseph W. and Catherine (Foskey) R.; grad. pub. sch., 1899; m. Mary E. Harris, Dec. 21, 1905; 1 son, John Parsons (died 1933); m. 2d, Elizabeth M. Miller, Jan. 1, 1933; 1 dau., Carolyn A. Began as newsboy, 1893; engaged as newspaper pub. and advertising man on various newspapers, 1900-19; purchased Washington Star, 1919, selling it, 1927; pub. daily paper, Canandaigua, N.Y., 1930-32; repurchased Washington Star, 1932, and since publisher; pres. Star Publishing Co., publishing and printing. Postmaster, Washington, N.J., since Aug. 27, 1935. Democrat. Presbyn. Mason. Home: 222 W. Washington Av. Office: 13 W. Church St., Washington, N.J.

ROBERTSON, Harold Frederick, physician; b. Phila., Pa., Mar. 3, 1900; s. William Egbert and Anna Gertrude (Frederick) R.; A.B., Central High Sch., 1918; B.S., Wesleyan U., 1922; M.D., U. of Pa., 1926; m. Mildred Bender Bright, Oct. 21, 1922; children—Harold Frederick, Jr., William Egbert 2d. Interne Phila. Gen. Hosp., 1926-28; engaged in gen. practice of medicine at Phila. since 1928; asso. in medicine Temple Univ. Med. Sch., 1928-33; instr. in medicine, U. of Pa. since 1933; visiting syphilologist Wills Eye Hosp., 1928-39; asst. visiting physician to Phila. Gen. Hosp. since 1928; asst. visiting physician Meth. Hosp., Phila. Fellow Am. Coll. Phys., Phila. Coll. Phys. Mem. Phila. Co. Med. Soc., Sigma Xi, Psi Upsilon, Alpha Mu, Pi Omega. Episcopalian. Home: 327 S. 17th St., Philadelphia, Pa.

ROBERTSON, John, pres. C. T. Williams & Co., Inc.; b. Glasgow, Scotland, Dec. 26, 1891; s. Duncan and Grace (Fisher) R.; ed. Hillhead Acad. and High Sch., Glasgow; m. Henrietta Hooper Thompson, Oct. 16, 1919. Asst. treas. and asst. sec. Fidelity Securities Co. of Md., 1922; v.p. and treas. C. T. Williams & Co., Inc., successors, 1922-33, pres. since 1933. Home: 4807 Norwood Av. Office: Fidelity Bldg., Baltimore, Md.

ROBERTSON, John Tabb, v.p. Fidelity & Guaranty Fire Corpn.; b. Baltimore, Md., June 25, 1879; s. William J. and Clara (Tabb) R.; ed. pub. sch.; m. Mary E. Kirkman, Nov. 4, 1904. One of organizers, 1928, Fidelity & Guaranty Fire Corpn., now v.p., sec. and dir. Home: 202 S. Athol Av. Office: 301 Water St., Baltimore, Md.

ROBERTSON, Robert Harlan, part owner Pocomoke Foundry & Machine Works; b. Quantico, Md., Dec. 15, 1877; s. Robert Greensbury and Rebecca Caroline (Bacon) R.; student Wicomico Co., Md., Elementary and high schs., 1882-96, Goldeys Business Coll., Wilmington, Del., 1896-97; m. Gertrude L. Kerns, Sept. 5, 1905; children—Julia Bacon, Annie Kerns (Mrs. Sylvester Thomas Schicktanz), R. Harlan, Jr. Began as foreman and accountant in lumber mfg. plant, Whaleyville, Va., 1897; held various positions Jackson Bros. Co., 1897-1901; employed by Atlantic Coast Lumber Co., Georgetown, S.C., 1901-03, Surry Lumber Co., Dondron, Va., 1903-07; part owner and mgr. Pocomoke Foundry & Machine Works since 1907; pres. and dir. Citizens Nat. Bank of Pocomoke City; dir. Johnson Meat Products Co. Served as del. Md. Legislature, 1918. Trustee Pocomoke High Sch. Pres. Group Six, Md. Bankers Assn., Nov. 1938-Nov. 1939. Democrat. Presbyn. (elder; supt. Sunday Sch. 27 yrs.). Mason (Past Master). Club: Rotary (Pocomoke City). Address: Pocomoke City, Md.

ROBERTSON, Sidney Hampton, dept. store mcht.; b. Roane Co., W.Va., July 3, 1877; s. George W. and Delilah E. (Melton) R.; student pub. schs. of W.Va., 1883-98; m. Gladys M. Grubb, Dec. 26, 1900; children—Guy Morgan, Ruth Lois (dec.), Inez Kathleen. Engaged in teaching pub. schs., 1894-99; traveling salesman, 1900-08; organized Robertson-Parris Co., dept. store, Clendenin, W.Va., and pres. since 1907; pres. Robertson Oil & Gas Co. since 1920; vice-pres. Farmers & Citizens State Bank, Hays Oil & Gas Co., Clendenin, W.Va., Poca Fork Oil & Gas Co., all Clendenin, W.Va. Served as mem. city council, Clendenin, 1905-15. Apptd. mem. W.Va. Senate from 8th dist., Nov. 1937, elected mem. W.Va. Senate from 8th dist., Nov. 1938. Dir. Kanawha Co. Pub. Library, Charleston, W.Va. Democrat. Southern Meth. Mason (K.T., 32°, Shriner). Active in combining the M.E. Ch. South and M.E. Ch. soon after the Gen. Confs. adopted unification; combined Clendenin ch. claims to be the first ch. in America to adopt the legal name, The Methodist Church. Address: Clendenin, W.Va.

ROBERTSON, Stuart, university prof.; b. Newark, N.J., July 9, 1892; s. William Lyall and Louise Henriette (Glorieux) R.; A.B., Princeton U., 1912, A.M., 1913, Ph.D., 1917; m. Helen Ames Farr, July 17, 1918; 1 dau., Mary Louise. Instr. in English, Temple U., 1919-23, asst. prof. 1924-29, prof. since 1929, chmn. English department, since 1936. Attended 2d O.T.C., Ft. Myer, Va., 1917; served in Air Service, U.S.A.; disch. as 1st lt., 1919. Mem. Am. Assn. Univ. Profs., Modern Lang. Assn. America, Phi Beta Kappa. Democrat. Presbyn. Club: Princeton (Phila.). Author: The Development of Modern English, 1934. Editor Familiar Essays, 1930. Contbr. to jours. Home: 913 N. 65th St., Philadelphia, Pa.

ROBERTSON, Thomas Ernest, patent lawyer; b. at Washington, D.C., May 7, 1871; s. Thomas J. W. and Jane M. (Turner) R.; LL.B., National University, Washington, 1906, LL.D., 1926; LL.D., Bates Coll., 1930; m. Mary Brackett, June 29, 1897; children—Thomas Brackett, Nathan Wood, Louis. Practiced patent law in Washington, D.C., 1906-20, as sr. mem. firm Robertson & Johnson; commr. of patents, by apptmt. of Presidents Harding, Coolidge and Hoover, 1921-33. Apptd. by President Coolidge chmn. Am. delegation to negotiate treaty concerning industrial property, The Hague, Oct. 8-Nov. 6, 1925 (duly ratified by U. S. Senate); del. to Pan-Am. Trade Mark Conv., Washington, 1929; prof. patent law, Nat. University Law Sch. Trustee Stores Coll. (Harpers Ferry). Mem. Am. Bar Assn. (chmn. patent sect. 1939), Am. Patent Law Assn. (pres. 1918-19), Gamma Eta Gamma. Republican. Episcopalian. Clubs: University, Cosmos, Torch. Home: 116 Shepherd St., Chevy Chase, Md.

ROBERTSON, William Egbert, M.D.; b. 1869; s. William and Ellen (Harding) R. M.D., U. of Pa., 1892, graduate studies 3 yrs. biol. dept., U. of Pa., one yr., Heidelberg, Vienna; m. Anna Gertrude Frederick. Practiced at Philadelphia, Pennsylvania, since 1892; formerly professor theory and practice of medicine and clin. medicine, Temple U. Dept. of Medicine; visiting physician Phila. Gen Hosp. Fellow Am. Coll. Physician, also Coll. Physicians, Phila.; mem. A.M.A., Med. Soc. State of Pa., Pathol. Soc. Phila. Address: 327 S. 17th St., Philadelphia, Pa.

ROBERTSON, William Joseph, editor; b. Fincastle, Botetourt Co., Va., Sept. 19, 1888; s. William Gordon and Anne Anthony (Breckinridge) R.; ed. high sch. and 1 yr. at Virginia Mil. Inst., Lexington, Va.; m. Susan Radford Preston, or "Greenfield," Botetourt Co., Va., Nov. 14, 1918; children—Preston Breckinridge, William Joseph, Mason Gordon, Susannah Preston. With engring. dept. Louisville & Nashville Ry. at Louisville, Ky., 1905-09; civ. engr. in mountains of Ky., Tenn., Va. and Ala., 1909-12; began newspaper work with Roanoke (Va.) Times, 1912; later with newspapers and Associated Press in South and dailies in Del. and Philadelphia; now editor Easton (Pennsylvania) Express. Commd. capt. inf. U.S.A., 1st O.T. C., Ft. McPherson, Ga., 1917; later served at Camp Gordon (Ga.), Kelly Field (Tex.) and Camp McClellan, Anniston, Ala.; honorably discharged, February 1919. Democrat. Episcopalian. Clubs: Kiwanis, Torch. Author: The Changing South, 1927; A History of du Pont Company's Relations with the American Government, 1927; contbr. to mags. Home: 726 Lafayette St. Office: Easton Express, Easton, Pa.

ROBERTSON, W(illiam) Spencer, mfr.; b. Brooklyn, N.Y., Jan. 10, 1885; s. William and Minnie Louise (Higgins) R.; ed. pub. schs., Brooklyn; m. Mabel Brooks, Oct. 16, 1906; children—Whitney Spencer, Rodney Taylor, Malcolm Brooks, Enid. With Simpson, Thacher & Bartlett, attys., N.Y. City, 1900-08; asst. to v.p. Am. Locomotive Co., 1908-15, sec., 1915-30, dir., 1919-30; pres. The Permutit Co., mfrs. water conditioning equipment, N.Y. City, since 1930. Pres. nat. council Y.M.C.A. of U.S. 1928-29, treas., 1933-37; mem. gen. bd. same since 1927. Mem. exec. com. N.J. Nat. Rep. Finance Com. Trustee Drew U. Republican. Methodist. Clubs: Union League, Bankers (New York); Morris County Golf, Nassau (Princeton).

Home: 116 Madison Av., Madison, N.J. Office: 330 W. 42d St., New York, N.Y.

ROBIE, Theodore Russell, psychiatrist and neurologist; b. Baldwinville, Mass., Jan. 28, 1900; s. Walter Franklin and Bertha E. (Little) R.; student Norwich U., Northfield, Vt., 1918-19; B.S., Dartmouth Coll., Hanover, N.H., 1922; M.D., Yale U. Sch. of Medicine, 1925; m. Elizabeth Harland, July 18, 1922; children—Margery Helen, Marian Harland, Betsy Jane. Interne, Grasslands Hosp., Valhalla, N.Y., 1925-26; asst. physician, Hudson River State Hosp., Poughkeepsie, N.Y., 1926-28; asst. psychiatrist, N.Y. State Dept. of Mental Hygiene, Albany, N.Y., 1928-30; dir. Essex Co. Mental Hygiene Clinic, Cedar Grove, N.J., 1930-33; pvt. practice as psychiatrist and neurologist at E. Orange, N.J., since 1933. Served as pvt., S.A.T.C., Norwich U., Northfield, Vt. 1918. Mem. A.M.A., Am. Psychiat. Assn., Am. Orthopsychiat. Assn., N.Y. Neurological Soc., Northern N.J. Neuro-Psychiat. Assn., N.J. State Med. Soc. Congregationalist. Clubs: Montclair (N.J.) Athletic; Osler (Essex Co., N.J.; med.). Author numerous papers for scientific journals. Home: 30 Norman Rd., Montclair, N.J. Office: 144 Harrison St., East Orange, N.J.

ROBINS, Edward, author; b. Pau, France, Mar. 2, 1862; s. Edward and Gertrude (Rodney-Fisher) R.; ed. Middletown, Conn., and mil. acad. Phila.; hon. A.M., U. of Pa., 1912; m. Emily Jewell Walton, Mar. 29, 1910. Began newspaper work, Kansas City, 1883; joined staff Philadelphia Public Ledger, 1884; asst. dramatic and mus. editor, 1888-94, dramatic and mus. editor, 1895-97, same paper; since then devoted to authorship. Author: Echoes of the Play House, 1895; Benjamin Franklin, 1898; The Palmy Days of Nance Oldfield, 1898; Twelve Great Actors, 1900; Twelve Great Actresses, 1900; Romances of Early America, 1902; Life of General Sherman, 1905. Juveniles: A Boy in Early Virginia; Chasing an Iron Horse; With Thomas in Tennessee; With Washington in Braddock's Campaign. Contbr. to newspapers and mags. on dramatic and hist. subjects. Pres. Hist. Soc. of Pa. and chmn. com. on library and collections; v.p. General Soc. Pa.; trustee Gilpin Library. Chmn. bd. Simon Gratz Collection MSS. Dir. Athenæum Phila., Welcome Soc. of Pa. Mem. Numismatic and Antiquarian Soc. of Pa., Art Alliance of Phila., Phila. Soc. for Preservation of Landmarks; Mem. adv. com. of Hist. and Patriotic Socs. for New York World's Fair, 1939. Address: Historical Society of Pa., 1300 Locust St., Philadelphia, Pa.

ROBINS, Henry Reed, pres. Commonwealth Title Co.; b. Phila, Pa., Feb. 22, 1875; s. William B. and Anne B. (Reed) R.; student Episcopal Acad. and Delancey Sch., Phila.; m. Reba T. Case, Apr. 30, 1901; 1 dau., Esther de Berdt. V.p., Land Title & Ins. Co., Phila., 1901-13, 1918-22, Real Estate Title & Ins. Co., (Phila.), 1913-18; pres. Commonwealth Title Co., Phila., since 1929; dir. Bankers Bond & Mortgage Co. Past pres. Am. Title Assn. Episcopalian (trustee, Ch. Foundation; vestryman of Old Christ Church). Mason. Clubs: Philadephia, Germantown Cricket (Phila.). Home: 505 Hansberry St., Germantown. Office: 1220-24 Sansom St., Philadelphia, Pa.

ROBINS, Stanley Godman, lawyer; b. Crisfield, Md., Sept. 20, 1900; s. John B. and Dorothy (Fiedler) R.; B.S., Washington Coll., Chestertown, Md., 1921; student U. of Md. Law Sch., Baltimore, Md., 1921-23; m. Jane Loreman, June 16, 1926; children—John B. 2d, Ann Garrett, Jane Lynne. Admitted to Md. bar, 1923 and engaged in gen. practice of law with father, John B. Robins, Crisfield, Md., 1923-25; asso. with firm Ellegood, Freeny & Wailes, Salisbury, Md., 1925-27; mem. firm Wailes & Robins, 1927-34, Long & Robins, Salisbury, Md. since 1934. Mem. Md. Bar. Assn., Wicomico Co. Bar Assn., Phi Kappa Sigma. Republican. Mason. Clubs: Tri-State Sportsmen's (Salisbury); Phi Kappa Sigma (Baltimore). Home: N. Clairmont Drive. Office: E. Main St., Salisbury, Md.

ROBINSON, Alexander Cochrane, banker; b. Ripley, N.Y., Oct. 19, 1864; s. Alexander Cochrane and Catherine Mather (Ely) R.; B.S., U. of Pittsburgh, 1882, hon. M.A., 1916; m. Emma Payne Jones, Oct. 2, 1890 (died 1909); children—Alexander Cochrane, John Noel, David (dec.). Began as clk. with Robinson Bros., bankers, Pittsburgh, 1882, partner, 1891; firm dissolved 1910; v.p. Commonwealth Trust Co., Pittsburgh, 1910-16; pres. Peoples-Pittsburgh Trust Co., 1916-33, chmn. bd. since 1933; dir. Pa. Industries, Inc., Western Allegheny R.R. Co., Am. Reinsurance Co., Pa. Bankshares, First Nat. Bank, Nat. Union Fire Ins. Co., etc. Chmn. Sewickley Valley br. Am. Red Cross, World War and was mem. exec. com. Pa. Council Nat. Defense. Treas. Community Fund of Allegheny County; pres. Sewickley Advisory Council; member Banking Board of Commonwealth of Pa.; dir. Sewickley Public Schools; trustee Western Theol. Sem.; trustee Pa. Coll. for Women, Valley Hosp. Mem. Hist. Soc. of Western Pa., Am. Bankers Assn. (ex-pres. savings bank div.). Republican. Presbyn. Clubs: Duquesne, Rolling Rock, Allegheny Country, Edgeworth. Speaker and writer on financial subjects. Home: Manada, Sewickley, Pa. Office: Peoples-Pittsburgh Trust Co., Pittsburgh, Pa.

ROBINSON, Benjamin O.; mem. staff Camden-Clark Memorial and St. Joseph's hosps. Address: 809½ Market St., Parkersburg, W.Va.

ROBINSON, Chalfant, univ. prof.; b. Cincinnati, Mar. 14, 1871; s. William Adin and Elizabeth Jane (Page) R.; grad. U. of Cincinnati, 1893; student univs. of Berlin and Freiburg, 1900-01; Ph.D., Yale, 1902; m. Anne Shaw Hamilton, May 29, 1900; children—Agnes Elizabeth (dec.), Hamilton. Lecturer on history, Yale, 1902-03, Mt. Holyoke Coll., 1903-04; asso. prof. history, Smith Coll., 1905; asst. prof. history, Yale, 1910-14; visiting prof. mediæval history, 1914-15, curator mediæval manuscripts since 1920, Princeton U. Fellow Royal Hist. Soc.; hon. mem. Institut Historique et Heraldique (France); mem. Pipe Roll Soc., Mediæval Acad. America. Republican. Clubs: Century, Yale (New York); Graduate (New Haven); Nassau (Princeton); Royal Soc. Club (London); Union Interalliée (Paris). Author: The History of Two Reciprocity Treaties, 1904; Continental Europe (1270-1598), 1916; The Great Roll of the Pipe, 1927; The Case of King Louis XI of France and Other Essays in Mediæval History, 1929; Memoranda Roll of the King's Remembrancer 1230-1, 1933. Also hist. monographs. Home: Princeton, N.J.

ROBINSON, Charles Kilbourne, lawyer; b. Cape May, N.J., June 13, 1877; s. Jesse H. and Jennie (Shaw) R.; B.S., George Washington U., 1897; LL.B., Harvard U. Law Sch., 1901; m. Mary E. Alexander, Jan. 6, 1904; children—Hamilton A., Charles E. Admitted to Pa. bar, 1903 and engaged in gen. practice of law at Pittsburgh; pvt. sec. to Hon. George Frisbee Hoar, U.S. Sen., served as clk. Judiciary Com., U.S. Senate; apptd. spl. counsel City of Pittsburgh, 1907, later first asst. City Solicitor; spl. counsel in charge all pub. utilities litigation, resigned 1921; counsel for Met. Plan Commn. for creation "Greater Pittsburgh"; mem. firm Dickie, Robinson and McCamey since 1930; vice-pres. Yellow Cab Co. of Pittsburgh, Pittsburgh Transportation Co.; dir. Rieck-McJunkin Dairy Co., Justus Mulert Co. Vice-pres. Pittsburgh Chamber of Commerce. Republican. Presbyterian. Clubs: Duquesne, University, Harvard-Yale-Princeton, Harvard of Western Pa., Golf, Oakmont Country, Pittsburgh Field; Pine Valley, N.J. Home: 1060 Morewood Av. Office: 2415 Grant Bldg., Pittsburgh, Pa.

ROBINSON, David Moore, univ. prof.; b. Auburn, N.Y., Sept. 21, 1880; s. Willard Haskell and Ella (Moore) R.; Poly. Inst., Brooklyn, 1890-94; A.B., U. of Chicago, 1898, fellow, 1898-1901, Ph.D., 1904; student Am. Sch. Classical Studies, Athens, Greece, 1901-03, fellow, 1902-03; student Halle, 1902, Berlin, 1903-04, Bonn, 1909; mem. excavating staff, Corinth, 1902-03, Sardis, 1910; LL.D., Jamestown Coll., 1915; L.H.D., Trinity Coll., 1925; Litt.D., from Syracuse U., 1933; m. Helen Haskell, Aug. 31, 1910; 1 dau., Alice Bradford. Asst. prof. Greek and head of the Classical Dept. Ill. Coll., 1904-05; asso. in classical archæology, 1905-08, asso. prof., 1908-12, prof. Greek archæology and epigraphy, 1912-13, prof. classical archæology and epigraphy, 1913-20, W.H. Collins Vickers prof. archæology and epigraphy, 1920—, lecturer in Greek lit. since 1915, Johns Hopkins U. Actg. dir. and prof. Greek lang. and lit., Am. Sch. Classical Studies in Athens, 1909-10 (now mem. mng. com.); lecturer Bryn Mawr Coll., 1911-12; prof. classical philology, summer session, Columbia U., 1919; lecturer Bur. Univ. Travel, 1922; prof. Greek, Notre Dame Coll., Md., 1921-35. Dir. of excavations at Pisidian Antioch and Sizma for U. of Mich., 1924; Charles Eliot Norton lecturer, Archæological Inst. of America, 1925, 28, Harry Wilson lecturer 1935-36; dir. excavations, Olynthus, 1928-38; C. L. Moore lecturer, Trinity Coll., Conn., 1925. Lecturer in fine arts, New York U., 1926-31; summer session, U. of Calif., 1927; on leave of absence for research in Rome and Greece, 1927-28, 1937-38; prof. Latin, Syracuse U., summers 1929, 1931-33; visiting prof. U. of Chicago, summer 1930; McBride lecturer, Western Reserve U., 1930; leader of the Augustan Pilgrimage, 1937; asso. editor Classical Weekly, 1913-35, American Jour. Philology, Internat. Humanistic Review Litteris, Supplementum Epigraphicum Græcum; editor-in-chief Johns Hopkins Studies in Archæology (29 vols.), chmn. publ. com. Art Bulletin (editor-in-chief, 1919-21); joint editor, with Hadzsits, of series Our Debt to Greece and Rome (44 vols.). Trustee Baltimore Art Museum; dir. Johns Hopkins Mus.; hon. pres. Baltimore Sch. Arts League; hon. pres. Baltimore Archæol. Soc.; sec. Johns Hopkins Philol. Assn., 1915-20, pres., 1921-22 and 1935-36; former pres. Baltimore Classical Club; pres. Classical Assn. Atlantic States, 1920-21; pres. College Art Assn. America, 1919-23; v.p.Archæol. Inst. America, 1913-36; gen. sec. 1921-23; bus. mgr. Am. Journal of Archæology, 1921-23, editor news discussions and bibliography, 1932-38, editor bibliography since 1938; mem. American Classical League, American Philological Association, Coll. Art Assn., Am. Assn. Univ. Profs., Am. History Soc., Am. Linguistic Soc., Am. Sch. Classical Studies at Rome (chmn. advisory council, 1920-21), Am. Numismatic and Antiquarian Soc., Am. Oriental Soc., Am. Federation of Arts, Classical Assn. Atlantic States, Archæol. Club, Am. Philos. Soc., S.A.R., Université Internationale, Phi Beta Kappa; hon. mem. Archæol. Society of Greece, German Archæol. Institute; fellow Am. Acad. Arts and Sciences, Am. Geog. Soc., Johns Hopkins Academic Council. Clubs: Johns Hopkins, Roland Park Country, Bachelors Cotillon, University, Coin. Author: Ancient Sinope, 1906; Inscriptions from the Cyrenica, 1913; The Songs of Sappho (with M. M. Miller), 1925; Sappho and Her Influence, 1924; The Greek Idyls, Theocritus, Bion, Moschus (with M. M. Miller), 1926; The Deeds of Augustus, 1926; Roman Sculptures from Pisidian Antioch, 1926; Greek and Latin Inscriptions from Asia Minor, 1926; Greek and Latin Inscriptions of Sardis (with W. H. Buckler), 1932; A Catalogue of the Greek Vases in the Royal Ontario Mus. of Archæology, Toronto (2 vols.), 1930; Excavations at Olynthus (Vol. II), Architecture and Sculpture, 1930; (Vol. III) Coins of Olynthus, 1931; (Vol. IV) Terra Cottas of Olynthus, found in 1928, 1931; (Vol. V) Mosaics, Vases and Lamps of Olynthus, 1933; (Vol. VI) The Coins found at Olynthus in 1931, 1933; (Vol. VII) The Terra Cottas found at Olynthus in 1931, 1933; (Vol. VIII with J. W. Graham) The Hellenic House, 1938; (Vol. IX, with P. A. Clement) The Chalcidic Mint and the Excavation Coins, 1938; The Robinson Collection, Corpus Vasorum, Baltimore, Vol. I, 1933; Vol. II, 1937, Vol. III, 1938; A Short History of Greece, 1936; Pindar—A Poet of Eternal Ideas, 1936; also some 300 philol. and archæol. articles. Address: 300 Club Rd., Baltimore, Md.

ROBINSON, Dwight Parker, engineer; b. Boston, Mass., May 1, 1869; s. Edgar and Susannah (Snelling) R.; A.B., Harvard, 1890; S.B., Mass. Inst. Tech., 1892; m. Mary Elizabeth Stearns, May 20, 1897 (died Nov. 20, 1907); m. 2d, Mary Elizabeth Dahlgren, July 25, 1912. Began with Stone & Webster, construction engrs., etc., Boston, 1893, admitted to partnership, 1911, and served as pres. Stone & Webster Engring. Corpn., Stone & Webster Constrn. Co., etc.; organized Dwight P. Robinson & Co., Inc., 1919, with headquarters in New York, and engaged in engineering and construction work in U.S. and abroad; merged, Jan. 1, 1928, with three other orgns. to form the United Engineers & Constructors, Inc. Fellow Am. Inst. E.E. Home: Eagle Rd., St. Davids, Pa. Office: 347 Madison Av., New York, N.Y., and 1401 Arch St., Philadelphia, Pa.

ROBINSON, Edmund Grubb, chem. exec.; b. Wilmington, Del., Feb. 23, 1886; s. John Craig and Elizabeth (Grubb) R.; student Wilmington (Del.) Friends' Sch., 1892-1901; A.B., Swarthmore (Pa.) Coll., 1905; m. Amy M. Oct. 12, 1909; 1 dau., Elinor (Mrs. Richard L. Chase). Began as chemist E. I. du Pont de Nemours & Co., Wilmington, Del., 1905 and various other positions; gen. mgr. organic chemicals dept. since 1925, dir. since 1937. Mem. Am. Inst. Chem. Engrs., Phi Sigma Kappa, Sigma Xi. Republican. Unitarian. Clubs: Wilmington, University, Wilmington Country (Wilmington, Del.). Home: 909 Nottingham Rd. Office: du Pont Bldg., Wilmington, Del.

ROBINSON, Edward Levi, banker; b. Lancaster Co., nr. Kilmarnock, Va., May 3, 1864; s. Edwin Orem and Martha (Cox) R.; grad. Baltimore (Md.) City Coll., 1881; m. Hester Myra Dodson, Oct. 21, 1890 (died Nov. 1, 1930); m. 2d, Elizabeth Cheever Blaser, Apr. 28, 1933. Served as entry clerk in wholesale drug house, Baltimore, 1881-82; then connected with Drovers & Mechanics Nat. Bank, 1882-89; asst. paying teller, 1889-1905, v.p., 1905-19, pres. since 1927, Eutaw Savings Bank; vice-pres. of Citizens Nat. Bank, Baltimore, 1918-27; dir. 1st Nat. Bank (Baltimore), Md. Casualty Co. Trustee Goucher Coll. (Baltimore), Md. Sch. for the Blind, Y.M.C.A. Mem. Am. Bankers Assn. (pres. savings bank sect. 1910-11). Democrat. Baptist. Clubs: University, Baltimore Country. Home: 501 Overhill Rd., Roland Park. Office: Eutaw Savings Bank, Baltimore, Md.

ROBINSON, Edward Moore, investment banker; b. N.Y. City, Feb. 3, 1894; s. Edward Moore and Ailene (Ivers) R.; grad. St. Paul's Sch., Concord, N.H., 1911; A.B., Harvard, 1915; E.M., Lehigh U., 1917; m. Elizabeth Grace Norbeck, Sept. 9, 1922; children—Edward Moore, Mary Elizabeth; m. 2d, Mary Hayne Bailey, June 15, 1937. Mining engr. and salesman, Weston, Dodson & Co., Bethlehem, Pennsylvania, 1919-22; pvt. secretary to John Markle, New York, 1922-27; pres. Atlantic & Pacific Internat. Corpn., 1928-29; partner Lew Wallace & Co., N.Y. Stock Exchange, 1932-35; Investment counsel, 1936—; dir. Morris Plan Industrial Bank of New York, Positype Corpn. of America. Served as 1st lt., U.S.A., 1917-1919. Mem. Psi Upsilon. Republican. Episcopalian. Mason. Clubs: University, Harvard, City Midday, Louisiana, Morris County Golf, Point Judith Country, Forest Lake, Anglers. Home: Convent, N.J. Office: 1 Wall St., New York, N.Y.

ROBINSON, Edwin Allin, chemist, tech. dir.; b. Denver, Colo., Nov. 17, 1907; s. Peter Jabez Edwin and Carrie Myton (Smith) R.; student East Denver High Sch., Denver, Colo., 1921-24; A.B., U. of Denver (Colo.), 1928, M.S., 1929; Ph.D., Columbia U., 1933; m. Mary Louise Bartlett, June 6, 1933; children—Jane, George Bartlett. Instr. in chemistry, U. of Denver (Colo.), 1928-29; chemist Eastman Kodak Co., Rochester, N.Y., summers 1929, 1930; asst. in chemistry, Columbia U., 1930-32; chemist Tenn. Eastman Corpn., Kingsport, Tenn., 1933-36; tech. dir. Nat. Oil Products Co., industrial div., Harrison, N.J., since 1936. Mem. Am. Chem. Soc., Am. Inst. of Chemists, Sigma Xi, Phi Lambda Upsilon, Beta Theta Pi. Awarded Du-Pont Fellowship, Columbia U., 1932-33. Republican. Methodist. Club: Chatham (N.J.) Fish and Game Protective Assn. Home: 13 Charles Pl., Chatham, N.J. Office: National Oil Products Co., Harrison, N.J.

ROBINSON, Edwin Crawford, mfg. exec.; b. Duquesne, Pa., Dec. 27, 1893; s. Benjamin F. and Ella (Herwig) R.; m. Harriet E. Smith, Nov. 17, 1924. Treas. McKeesport (Pa.) Tin Plate Corpn. since 1929. Mason. Clubs: Youghiogheny Country; Pittsburgh Country, Pittsburgh Athletic. Home: 3330 Beechwood Boul., Pittsburgh, Pa. Office: McKeesport Tin Plate Corpn., McKeesport, Pa.

ROBINSON, G(eorge) Canby, M.D., educator; b. Baltimore, Md., Nov. 4, 1878; s. Edward Ayrault and Alice (Canby) R.; A.B., Johns Hopkins University, 1899, M.D., 1903; studied U. of Munich, 1908-09; LL.D., Washington University, 1928; Sc.D., George Washington Univ., 1932; m. Marion B. Boise, December 7, 1912; children—Margaret Boise, Otis Boise. Assistant demonstrator anatomy, Cornell U., 1903-04; res. pathologist and res. phys. Pa. Hosp., Phila., 1904-08; dir. Pathol. Lab. Presbyn. Hosp., Phila., 1909-10; res. phys. Rockefeller Inst. Hosp., New York, and asso. in medicine, Rockefeller Inst., 1910-13; asso. prof. medicine, Washington U., St. Louis, 1913-20; dean med. sch., same, 1917-20; prof. medicine and dean Vanderbilt Med. Sch., 1920-28; acting prof. medicine, Johns Hopkins Med. Sch., 1921-22; dir. New York Hosp. and Cornell Med. Coll. Assn., 1928-35; prof. medicine, Cornell U. Med. Coll., 1928-35; visiting prof. of medicine, Peiping (China) Union Med. Coll., 1935; lecturer in medicine, Johns Hopkins, since 1936. Mem. A.M.A., Assn. Am. Physicians (pres.), Am. Soc. Clin. Investigation, Harvey Society (pres.), Am. Physiol. Soc., Am. Pharmacol. Soc., Alpha Delta Phi, Nu Sigma Nu, Alpha Omega Alpha; fellow A.A.A.S. Mem. Soc. of Friends. Author: Therapeutic Use of Digitalis, 1923; Patient as a Person, 1939; also numerous papers on physiology and pathology of human circulation, medical education. and social aspects of medicine. Home: 4712 Keswick Road, Baltimore, Md.

ROBINSON, George Thomas, coal operator; b. in Eng., Feb. 23, 1868; s. William and Mary Ann (Hadley) R.; came to U.S., 1882; ed. common schs., night schs. and corr. sch.; m. Laura Adela Barry, Aug. 4, 1892; 1 son, Earle Barry. Began with Cambria Steel Co. (now Bethlehem Steel Co.), 1891, and was made supt. mines same co., 1901; entered business for self, 1912, after having organized the Valley Coal Co., Central Coal Co., Citizens Coal Co., Dixonville Coal Co., and other coal companies; now pres. Cambria-Stafford Coal Co., Robinson Motor Co., Dixonville Coal Co., Citizens Coal Co.; sec.-treas. Johnstown Retail Coal Producers' Assn.; director Johnstown Savings & Loan Co. With U.S. Fuel Adminstrn., 1917-19. Mem. bd. dirs. Conemaugh Valley Memorial Hosp. (chmn. finance com.), Johnstown Y.M.C.A.; dir. Johnstown Salvation Army. Mem. Central Pa. Coal Producers' Assn., Johnstown Chamber Commerce (ex-pres.), Pa. Soc. of New York. Republican. Methodist. Mason, K.P. Clubs: Rotary (ex-pres., dir.), Sunnehama Country. Home: 143 Greene St. Office: United States Bank Bldg., Johnstown, Pa.

ROBINSON, Harold McAfee, clergyman, educator; b. Shelbyville, Mo., Mar. 1, 1881; s. Joseph Carle and Hannah Catherine (McAfee) R.; A.B., Park Coll., 1901; B.D., Princeton Theol. Sem., 1904; grad. work same, 1909-11; studied U. of Leipzig, 1904-05; D.D., Lafayette and Park colls., 1919, University of Dubuque, Ia., 1920; LL.D., Macalester College, 1933, Trinity University, Waxahachie, Texas, 1935; Dr. Relig. Edn., Waynesburg College, 1937; m. Mary Greer Wiley, June 29, 1915; children—Joseph Carle (deceased), Harold McA., John Greer. Ordained Presbyn. ministry, 1905; pastor Milroy, Pa., 1905-09; sec. Centennial Com., Princeton Theol. Sem., 1911-13; pastor Market Sq. Ch., Germantown, Phila., 1913-17; prof. Bible and coll. pastor, Lafayette Coll., 1917-19; sec. Presbyn. Bd. Publn. and S.S. Work, Phila., 1919-23; sec. div. of Christian Edn. in Home, Ch. and Community of Bd. of Christian Edn. Presbyn. Ch. U.S.A., 1923-27, administrative sec., 1927-34; gen. sec. Presbyn. Bd. of Christian Edn., 1934—; lecturer on Christian edn., Princeton Theol. Sem., 1927-30. Mem. Internat. Council of Religious Edn.; chmn. ednl. commn., Internat. Council, 1926-30, acting gen. sec., 1936-37, chmn. exec. com., 1930-38; mem. exec. com. Council of Ch. Bds. of Edn., vice-pres., 1936, pres., 1937. Mem. North Am. Administration Com. and Bd. of Mgrs. World's S.S. Assn.; mem. Nat. Council Boy Scouts of America; mem. Nat. Preaching Mission Com., Univ. Christian Mission Com.; v.p. bd. trustees Princeton Theol. Sem.; mem. bd. dirs. Presbyn. Coll. Christian Edn., Chicago; mem. Gen. Council of Presbyn. Ch. in U.S.A. Clubs: University, Down Town (Phila.). Author: How to Conduct Family Worship; The Kingdom of God is at Hand; also Sunday Sch. lessons and numerous contbns. on religious edn. Home: 7944 Pleasant Av., Chestnut Hill. Office: Witherspoon Bldg., Philadelphia, Pa.

ROBINSON, Harry Maximilian, physician; b. Cincinnati, O., Sept. 14, 1884; s. Maximilian and Rose (Band) R.; M.D., U. of Md. Med. Sch., Baltimore, 1909; m. 2d, Mary Venite Ryan, Sept. 4, 1922; children—Harry M., Jr., R. Vail. Asst. in dept. dermatology, U. of Md. Med. Sch., 1910-15; asst. in depts. dermatology and syphilis, Johns Hopkins Hosp., 1912-21; prof. dermatology and syphilis, U. of Md. Med. Sch. since 1934. Mem. Am. Med. Assn., Southern Med. Assn. (chmn. dermatol. sect. 1937), Atlantic Dermatol. Conf. Democrat. Presbyn. Author: (med.) Practical Dermatology and Syphilology, 1939; (verse) A Few Odd Fancies, 1925; When Thoughts Go Wandering, 1927; Jimmieboy, 1935. Contbr. many articles to med. jours. Home: 106 E. Chase St., Baltimore, Md.

ROBINSON, Howard Lee, lawyer; b. nr. Clarksburg, W.Va., Nov. 21, 1887; s. Joseph Blackwell and Martha Evelyn (Fox) R.; LL.B., Washington and Lee, 1913; m. Katherine Ernst, Jan. 14, 1926. Admitted to W.Va. bar, 1913, in practice at Clarksburg; mem. firm Robinson & Robinson, 1921-34; mem. firm Robinson & Stump since 1934; U.S. atty. Northern Dist. of W.Va., 1934-1938. Served as pvt. U.S.A., 1917-19. Chmn. Harrison Co. Dem. Exec. Com., 1930-32. Mem. Am., W.Va. State and Harrison Co. bar assns. Democrat. Baptist. Mason, Elk, K.P. Club: Kiwanis (pres. 1930). Home: 363 Washington Av. Address: Union Nat. Bank Bldg., Clarksburg, W.Va.

ROBINSON, Ira Ellsworth, lawyer; b. near Grafton, W.Va., Sept. 16, 1869; s. William and Mary (Sayre) R.; grad. Fairmont State Normal School, 1889; studied law at University of Va., 1890; m. Ada Sinsel, Oct. 25, 1892 (dec.); children—William Arthur (dec.), Ada May (dec.). Began practice at Grafton, 1891; pros. atty., Taylor Co., W.Va., 1896-1900; mem. W.Va. Senate, 1902-04; apptd. by gov. a judge of Supreme Court of Appeals, to fill vacancy, Oct. 1907, and elected, Nov. 8, 1908; resigned Oct. 26, 1915; pres. (chief justice) of that court, 1910, 15; Rep. nominee for gov. of W.Va., 1916; regent State Normal Schs., 1901-07; apptd. to adjudicate War Minerals Claims, Washington, 1921; mem. Federal Radio Commn., 1928-32, chmn., 1928-30. Lecturer W.Va. Univ. Coll. of Law, Northwestern U., 1920. Mem. Am. Bar Assn., Am. Law Inst., W.Va. Bar Assn.., Harrison County Bar Assn., Mem. Gen. Conf. M.E. Ch., 1912, 1916. Chmn. Draft Appeals Bd., 1917-18. Contbr. to legal periodicals. Home: "Adaland" (P.O., R.F.D., Philippi) Barbour Co., W. Va. Office: Goff Bldg., Clarksburg, W.Va.

ROBINSON, J. Ben, dental educator; b. Clarksburg, W.Va., Apr. 16, 1883; s. Joseph B. and Martha (Fox) R.; grad. Teachers Training Sch., Marshall Coll., Huntington, W.Va., 1908; D.D.S., U. of Md., 1914; m. Beulah Minor Welsh, June 27, 1917; 1 dau., Evelyn Blackwell. In part-time practice of dentistry since 1914; prof. operative dentistry, U. of Md., 1919-21, dean of Sch. of Dentistry since 1924. Pres. Am. Assn. Dental Schs., 1932-33; mem. Md. State Bd. Dental Examiners, 1922-24. Pres. Am. Coll. Dentists, 1934-35. Fellow N.Y. Acad. Dentists; mem. Am. Dental Assn. (trustee 1936-38, mem. council on edn.), Md. State Dental Assn. (pres. 1921-22), Md. Hist. Soc., S.A.R., Psi Omega (Supreme Grand Master), Phi Sigma Kappa, Omicron Kappa Upsilon. Democrat. Baptist. Clubs: University, Kiwanis (pres. 1934), Torch. Home: 3206 Elgin Av. Office: Med. Arts Bldg., Baltimore, Md.

ROBINSON, J. French, geologist; b. Elizabeth, Wirt Co., W.Va., Dec. 13, 1890; s. Jefferson Donald and Mamie (Jacobs) R.; B.S. in civil engring., W.Va. U., 1915, M.S., 1918; Ph.D., U. of Pittsburgh, 1929; m. Ethel Gertrude Board, Nov. 10, 1915; 1 son, James Donald. Asst. geologist B.&O. R.R., 1914-18; engr. Ford, Run Franklin Coal & Coke Corpn., 1918-19; geologist Seneca Hill Oil Co., 1919-20; asst. state geologist of Pa., 1920-21; geologist and engr. Peoples Natural Gas Co. and Columbia Natural Gas Co., 1923-33; mgr. N.Y. Natural Gas Corpn., Keuka Constrn. Corpn., 1930-36; v.p. Peoples Natural Gas Co., Columbia Natural Gas Co., Belmont Quadrangle Drilling Corpn., 1933-35; pres. and dir. Peoples Natural Gas Co., N.Y. State Natural Gas Corpn., Keuka Constrn. Corpn., Brave Water Co., Reserve Gas Co., Lycoming United Gas Corpn.; v.p. and dir. Belmont Quadrangle Drilling Co.; dir. Hope Constrn. and Refining Co., Gas Cos. Inc. Mem. Inst. of Mining and Metall. Engrs., Am. Gas Assn., Am. Inst. Petroleum Geologists, Am. Mining Congress, Am. Petroleum Inst., Pa. Natural Gas Men's Assn. (past pres.), Engr. Soc. of W. Pa. (past pres.), Sigma Nu. Mem. East End Christian Church (trustee). Mason (32°, Shriner), Elk. Clubs: Pittsburgh Field (dir.), Long Vue Country (dir.), Metropolitan (dir.), Duquesne (Pittsburgh); Wellsboro Hunting; Tyoga Country. Contbr. to tech. publs. Home: 516 Edgerton Place. Office: 545 William Penn Way, Pittsburgh, Pa.

ROBINSON, James Reed, pres. Robinson Ventilating Co.; b. Washington Co., Pa., Aug. 17, 1865; s. Samuel Butler and Margery (Kennedy) R.; student mech. engring., Cornell U.; m. Ella M. Baer, June, 1889; children—Paul Woods, Robert Roger, Lawrence Reed, Mayer Randolph, Margery Elizabeth, Gertrude Van Arsdalin, Ruth Winifred. Shop foreman Washington (Pa.) Mfg. Co., 1890-93; partner Abrams & Robinson, machine mfrs., 1893-1906; pres. Robinson Machine Co., 1906-10; mgr. Scottdale Foundry & Machine Co., 1910-13; in engring. business for self, 1913; obtained charter, 1913, and since pres. Robinson Ventilating Co. Author (text-book): Practical Mine Ventilation, 1922. Home: 346 New Castle St. Office: Robinson Ventilating Co., Zelienople, Pa.

ROBINSON, Jedidiah Waldo, lawyer; b. Taylor Co., W.Va., June 11, 1881; s. Franklin Pierce and Elizabeth Catherine (Hull) R.; A.B., W.Va. U., Morgantown, 1905; LL.B., W.Va. Univ. Law Coll., 1906; m. Sarah Caroline Poe, Sept. 1, 1909; children—William Waldo, James Poe, Charles Urban. Admitted to W.Va. bar, 1906 and since engaged in gen. practice of law at Grafton; mem. firm Warder & Robinson, 1907-17, Robinson, Warder & Robinson, 1918-27, in individual practice since 1927; local atty. for B.&O. R.R. Co. and other large corpns. Past pres. Chamber of Commerce, and Y.M.C.A., Grafton, W.Va.; mem. exec. com. W.Va. State Y.M.C.A. Mem. Am., W.Va. State, and Taylor Co. bar assns., Sigma Nu. Past gov. 24th dist. Rotary Internat. Republican. Methodist. Mason (K.T.), Eastern Star. Clubs: Rotary of Grafton; Scottish Rite (Grafton). Home: 212 McGraw Av. Office: First Nat. Bank Bldg., Grafton, W.Va.

ROBINSON, John Jenkins; b. Academia, Pa., Mar. 1, 1870; s. Robert A. and Elizabeth (Laird) R.; student Tuscarora Acad., Academia, Pa., 1886-89, Airy View Acad., Port Royal, Pa., 1884-86; grad. Princeton, 1894; m. Jessie F. Mumford, Dec. 22, 1898; children—John Mumford, Richard Stuart (dec.), Newton Laird (dec.). In employ Thomas Roberts & Co., 1898-1900, New York Shipbuilding Co., 1901-03; with Oliver H. Bair Co., funeral dirs., Phila., continuously since 1903, v.p. and treas. since 1923. Served as mem. bd. dirs. Chestnut St. Business Assn. Pres. Funeral Dirs. Assn. of Phila. Republican; mem. Masonic Vets. Assn. Episcopalian (vestryman Ch. of The Saviour, West Phila.). Mason (K.T., 33°, Shriner). Clubs: Penn Athletic, Union League (Phila.). Home: 5407 Gainor Rd. Office: 1820 Chestnut St., Philadelphia, Pa.

ROBINSON, Joseph Arnold, physician; b. Pittsburgh, Pa., Apr. 1, 1892; s. Joseph Harper and Fanny (Hill) R.; M.D., U. of Pittsburgh, 1913; grad. studies, U. of Buffalo, 1933; m. Catherine Wareham, Oct. 14, 1914; children—Helen May, Dorothy Grace. Engaged in gen. practice of medicine in New Bethlehem, Pa. continuously since 1914; dir. First Nat. Bank. Mem. Am. Med. Assn., U.S. Pub. Health Assn., Pa. Med. Soc., Armstrong Co. Med. Soc., Sigma Phi Epsilon, Alpha Kappa Kappa. Republican. Mem. M.E. Ch. Mason (32°, Shriner). Home: New Bethlehem, Pa.

ROBINSON, Lindsay Ellsworth, neuropsychiatrist, endocrinologist; b. Aurora, Ont., Canada, May 23, 1900; s. Henry and Mary Jane (Drewry) R.; M.B., U. of Toronto, 1925; certificate in neurology and psychiatry, U. of Vienna, 1929; spl. study in neuropathology, Royal Coll. Surgeons, Edinburgh, Scotland, 1929; m. Phyllis Francis Pointon, Oct. 10, 1937. Came to U.S., 1925, naturalized, 1936. Asst. physician, Howard, R.I., 1925-27; asst. physician State Hosp., Greystone Park, N.J., 1927-29, asst. dir. mental hygiene, 1929-34; dir. mental hygiene Trenton State Hosp., 1934-38; in private practice of neuropsychiatry and endocrinology since 1938. Home and Office: 332 Park Av., Newark, N.J.

ROBINSON, Louis Newton, economist; b. Tunkhannock, Pa., Nov. 3, 1880; s. John Marklin and Annie Elizabeth (Thacher) R.; A.B., Swarthmore (Pa.) Coll., 1905; studied Cornell U., 1905-06; Joshua Lippincott traveling fellow, Swarthmore Coll., univs. of Halle and Berlin, 1906-07; fellow in economics and statistics, Cornell, 1907-08, Ph.D., 1911; m. Caroline Hadley, June 18, 1908; children—Walter Hadley, Miles Hadley, Alice, Christine, John Mark, T. Thacher. Instr. in economics, 1908-09, asst. prof., 1909-13, professor, 1913-18, also lecturer since 1926, Swarthmore College; chief probation officer, Municipal Court Phila., 1918-21; directed survey the small loan business under auspices of Russel Sage Foundation, 1922-24; mem. and sec. Pa. State Penal Commn. of 1913; mem. Pa. Commn. to Investigate Prison System of 1917; mem. Pa. Parole Commn., 1925-27; mem. Pa. Crime Commn., 1927-29; sec. com. of Nat. Crime Commn. on Pardons, Parole, Probation, Penal Laws and Institutional Correction, 1926-28; chmn. Pa. Com. on Penal Affairs; mem. bd. trustees Eastern State Penitentiary; mem. and later chmn. bd. Prison Industries Reorganization Adminstrn. 1935-1938. Mem. Am. Inst. Criminal Law and Criminology, Am. Statis. Assn., Delta Upsilon, Phi Beta Kappa. Quaker. Author: History and Organization of Criminal Statistics (Hart Schaffner & Marx prize essay series), 1911; Penology in the United States, 1921; Should Prisoners Work?, 1931; (with Maude E. Stearns) Ten Thousand Small Loans, 1930; (with Rolf Nugent) Regulation of the Small Loan Business, 1935; also numerous articles and pamphlets on criminology and finance. Home: 411 College Av., Swarthmore, Pa.

ROBINSON, Lucius W., coal bus.; s. Lucius W. and Ruth (DeMoss); student Phillips Andover Acad.; m. Harriet Virginia Overton, June 27, 1917; children—Virginia O., Ruth DeMoss, Sarah Morgan, Lucia W. Began learning bus. at coal mines, 1913; pres. J. F. Massey & Co.; dir. Rochester and Pittsburgh Coal Co., Helvetia Coal Mining Co. Republican. Episcopalian. Clubs: Duquesne, Fox Chapel, HYP, Rolling Rock (Pittsburgh); Allegheny Country (Sewickley, Pa.). Home: 1401 Bennington Av., Pittsburgh, Pa. Office: Savings & Trust Co. Bldg., Indiana, Pa.; also Gulf Bldg., Pittsburgh, Pa.

ROBINSON, Maurice Richard, publisher; b. Wilkinsburg, Pennsylvania, December 24, 1895; s. Richard Bradley and Rachel S. C. (Calderwood) R.; A.B., Dartmouth College, 1920; m. Florence Liddell, June 2, 1934; 1 son, Richard. Founded Western Pennsylvania Scholastic, 1920, title changed to Scholastic, 1932, editor and publisher since 1922; editor and publisher Junior Scholastic since September 1937; president Scholastic Corpn; also publisher Saplings (annual volume). Served as pvt., sergt. and 2d lt. U.S. Army, 1917-19. Mem. Delta Tau Delta. United Presbyterian. Club: University (Pittsburgh). Home: 715 Wallace Av., Wilkinsburg, Pa. Office: 250 E. 43d St., New York, N.Y.; and Chamber of Commerce Bldg., Pittsburgh, Pa.

ROBINSON, Ovid Daniel, producing and refining oil; b. Titusville, Pa., Mar. 2, 1885; s. Marquis D. and Flora (MacQuarrie) R.; ed. pub. schs. and high sch.; m. Ethel Cooper, Sept. 14, 1910; children—Helen (Mrs. Wallace Ransom Persons), Ovid Daniel, Jr. Began as salesman for Canfield Oil Co.; sec. and treas. Robinson Oil Co., 1903-08; pres. Riverside Oil Co., 1908-16; v.p. Transcontinental Oil Co., 1916-25; pres. Republic Oil Co. since 1925; also pres. Republic Oil Refining Co., Republic Pipe Line Co. Mem. Chamber of Commerce, Pittsburgh. Republican. Methodist. Mason. Clubs: Montour Heights Country (Coraopolis); Duquesne (Pittsburgh). Home: 1032 Hiland Av., Coraopolis, Pa. Office: Benedum-Trees Bldg., Pittsburgh, Pa.

ROBINSON, Robert P., ex-gov.; b. nr. Wilmington, Del., Mar. 28, 1869; s. Robert L. and Frances E. (Delaplaine) R.; ed. dist. sch., and Rugby Acad., Wilmington; m. Margaret H. Fouraker, of Wilmington, June 9, 1904. Began in employ of Central National Bank, Wilmington, 1888, president since 1916; governor of Delaware for term 1925-29. Republican. Presbyn. Mem. The Grange. Clubs: Wilmington, Young Men's. Home: Christian Hundred, nr. Wilmington, Del. Office: Central Nat. Bank, Wilmington, Del.

ROBINSON, Samuel Murray, naval officer; b. Eulogy, Tex., Aug. 13, 1882; s. Michael and Susan Sinai (Linebarger) R.; grad. U.S. Naval Acad., 1903; post-grad. in elec. engring.; m. Emma Mary Burnham, Mar. 1, 1909; children—James Burnham, Murray. Midshipman U.S.N., Feb. 1903; promoted through grades to rear adm., May 1931. Chief Bur. of Engring., U.S. Navy, May 1931-June 1935; became inspector of machinery Gen. Electric Co., Schenectady, N.Y., June 1935, now senior mem. Compensation Bd. Mem. Am. Soc. Naval Engrs., U.S. Naval Inst. Democrat. Episcopalian. Clubs: University (Washington); Manor (Norbeck). Author: Electric Ship Propulsion. Home: Manor Club, Norbeck, Md. Address: Compensation Bd., Navy Dept., Washington, D.C.

ROBINSON, Stewart MacMaster, clergyman, editor; b. Clinton, N.Y., July 21, 1893; s. Rev. William Courtland and Frances Augusta (Horner) R.; A.B., Princeton, 1915, A.M., 1918, B.D., 1918; D.D., Tusculum Coll., Greenville, Tenn., 1929; m. Anne MacGregor Payne, Sept. 4, 1917; children—Stewart Payne, Anne MacGregor, James Courtland, Alexander Proudfit, Nancy Wiltsie. Ordained to ministry Presbyn. Ch., 1918; asst. pastor Ch. of the Covenant, Cleveland, O., 1919-21, 1st Ch., Lockport, N. Y., 1921-28, 2d Ch., Elizabeth, N.J., since 1929; editor The Presbyterian since 1934. Served as divisional chaplain, U.S.A., with A.E.F., 1918-19; now chaplain (capt.), R.O.C. Mem. bd. Am. Tract Soc.; dir. World Dominion, Inc., Stony Brook Assembly and Sch. Mem. Victoria Inst. of London (asso.), Princeton Univ. Rowing Assn. (bd. stewards), Army and Navy Chaplains (federal council com.), Phi Beta Kappa. Del. Pan-Presbyn. Alliance, 1937; nominated for moderator Presbyn. Ch., 1935. Republican. Contbr. to religious jours. Home: 23 Kempshall Pl. Office: 1161 E. Jersey St., Elizabeth, N.J.; and 1217 Market St., Philadelphia, Pa.

ROBINSON, Victor, medical historian, editor; b. August 16, 1886; s. William J. (M.D.) and Marie (Halper) R.; N.Y. Univ. Law Sch., 1906-08; Ph.G., N.Y. Coll. of Pharmacy, 1910; Ph.C., Columbus, 1911; M.D., Chicago Coll. Medicine and Surgery (now Loyola U.), 1917. Since 1909 active in med. history as organizer, traveler, author, editor, lecturer, and radio speaker; prof. history of medicine, Temple U. Sch. of Medicine, Philadelphia, since 1929; lecturer on history of nursing, Temple U. Sch. of Nursing since 1937. Mem. organizing com. and council, History of Science Coc. Editor of Historia Medicinae (10 vols.), Med. Review of Reviews, Med. Life (only monthly jour. of med. history in English lang.). The Modern Home Physician (a new encyclopedia of med. knowledge), 1934-38, Am. edits. of Paolo Mante gazza, 1935-36, Encyclipædia Sexualis, 1936. Author: An Essay on Hasheesh, 1912; Pathfinders in Medicine, 1912; Pioneers of Birth Control, 1919; Don Quixote of Psychiatry, 1919; Life of Jacob Henle, 1921; The Story of Medicine, 1931; Syllabus of Medical History, 1933. Contbr. of hist. chapters to George M. Piersol's The Cyclopedia of Medicine, Max Neuberger Festschrift, Scientific Monthly, Archives of Dermatology and Syphilology, Brit. Jour. of Dermatology and Syphilis, Bull. of Inst. of History of Medicine of John Hopkins U. and other professional publs. Founder of Froben Press, for publ. of medico-historical journeys to various countries in Europe, 1910, 22, 27, 32, 38, also monographs on med. history. Address: 4 Saint Luke's Place, New York, N.Y.; and Temple University Sch. of Medicine, Philadelphia, Pa.

ROBINSON, William, entomologist; b. Hamilton, Ont., Can., Sept. 7, 1890; s. James and Louise Jane (Colyer) R.; B.S.A., U. of Toronto, 1918; M.S., U. of Kan., 1924; Ph.D., U. of Minn. (Caleb Dorr Fellowship), 1926; m. Clara Beatrice Mittelberger, Sept. 28, 1921. Asst. prof. of entomology, U. of Minn., 1926-28; asst. prof. of Pathology, U. of Chicago, 1928-31; sr. entomologist U.S. Dept. of Agr. since 1931; credited with discovery of healing properties of drug "allantoin," 1935, also healing properties of drug "urea," 1936. Fellow A.A.A.S.; mem. Entomol. Soc. of America, Entomol. Soc. of Washington, Ecol. Soc. of America, Sigma Xi, Phi Sigma. Methodist. Club: Quadrangle (U. of Chicago). Home: Burnt Mills Hills, Silver Spring, Md. Office: Dept. of Agriculture Bldg., Washington, D.C.

ROBINSON, William Christopher, mfr.; b. Pittsburgh, Aug. 27, 1867; s. George Thomas and Althea (Dilworth) R.; ed. Shadyside Acad., Pittsburgh, and Mt. Washington Sch., Washington, Pa.; m. Mary McMasters Laughlin, May 21, 1902; children—Alexander Laughlin, William Christopher, Henry Holdship (dec.), Mary Franklin, Althea Dilworth. Supt. Robinson-Rea Mfg. Co., mfrs. rolling mill machinery and engines, 1902-05; founder, 1905, Nat. Metal Molding Co., mfrs. metal molding, conduit, later elec. fittings, consol., 1928, as Nat. Electric Products Corporation, of which is president; director Am. Water Works, West Penn Power Co., West Penn R.R., Monongahela West Penn Pub. Service, Jones & Laughlin Steel Corpn., Mellon Nat. Bank, Union Trust Co. of Pittsburgh. Dir. Allegheny Gen. Hosp. Episcopalian. Mason (32°). Clubs: Duquesne, Pittsburgh, Allegheny Country (pres.), Pittsburgh Golf (Pittsburgh); Racquet and Tennis, Links, New York Yacht (New York). Home: Franklin Farm, Sewickley, Pa. Office: 1200 Fulton Bldg., Pittsburgh, Pa.

ROBINSON, Wilton Howarth, orthopedic surgeon; b. Pittsburgh, Pa., Oct. 13, 1878; s. Ernest C. and Lillie (Wilton) R.; M.D., Western U. of Pa. (now U. of Pittsburgh), 1900; unmarried. Asst., dept. of orthopedic surgery, Med. Dept., Western U. of Pa., 1904-08; demonstrator, dept. of orthopedic surgery, U. of Pittsburgh Med. Sch., 1908; chief orthopedic surgeon, South Side Hosp., Pittsburgh, since 1912. Served as lt., advancing to major, div. of orthopedic surgery, U.S. Army M.C., during World War. Mem. Allegheny Co. Med. Soc. (pres., 1934-35; mem. com. on grad. edn.; chmn. President's Brace Fund Com.), Pittsburgh Orthopedic Club (sec.), Allegheny Co. Soc. for the Care of Crippled Children (dir.). Author of numerous scientific papers. Home: 6017 Stanton Av. Office: 144 S. 20th St., Pittsburgh, Pa.

ROBINSON, Winifred Josephine, coll. dean; b. Barry Co., Mich., Oct. 17, 1867; d. Walter J. and Pamelia (Wheelock) R.; B.Pd., Mich. State Normal Coll., 1892, M.Pd., 1912; B.Pd., B.S., U. of Mich., 1899; A.M., Columbia, 1904, Ph.D., 1912; unmarried. Prin. high sch., Caro, Mich., 1892; instr. Mich. State Normal Coll., training dept., 1893-95; instr. Vassar Coll., dept. of biology, 1900-07; asst. in laboratory, New York Bot. Gardens, 1908; instr. in botany, 1909-13, asst. prof., 1913, Vassar Coll.; dean Women's Coll., U. of Del., 1914-38, emerita. Adviser of women, U. of Wis., summer session, 1913-14. Has devoted much attention to bot. research; won scholarship, New York Bot. Gardens, 1903. Fellow A.A.A.S.; mem. Nat. Assn. of Deans of Women, Nat. Assn. of Personnel Appointment Officers, Nat. Assn. Collegiate Registrars, Adult Edn. Assn., Progressive Edn. Assn., N.E.A., Am. Assn. Univ. Women, Nat. Inst. Social Sciences, Del. Hist. Soc., Am. Acad. Polit. and Social Science, Alpha Phi, Pi Gamma Mu, Phi Kappa Phi, Phi Beta Kappa, Nat. Arts Club. Mem. women's com. Del. Council Defense. Contbr. research articles on plant morphology and on Pteridophyta of the Hawaiian Islands. Home: Newark, Del. and Newfane, Vt.

ROBISON, Samuel Shelburn, naval officer; b. Juanita Co., Pa., May 10, 1867; grad. U.S. Naval Acad., 1888; m. Mary Louise, d. Rear Adm. C. E. Clark, 1893. Promoted ensign, July 1, 1890; lt. jr. grade, Apr. 23, 1898; lt., Mar. 3, 1899; lt. comdr., July 1, 1905; comdr., Dec. 27, 1909; captain, July 1, 1914; rear admiral, Sept. 21, 1918. Served on Boston during Spanish-Am. War, 1898; with Bur. of Equipment, Navy Dept., 1904-06; navigator Tennessee, 1906-08; exec. officer Pennsylvania, 1908-09; with Bureau of Equipment, 1909-10, Bur. of Steam Engring., 1910-11; comd. Cincinnati, 1911-13; asst. to Bur. Steam Engring., Navy Dept., 1913-14, 1914-15; comd. Jupiter, 1914; comd. South Carolina, 1915-17; comdr. Submarine Force, Atlantic Fleet, 1917-18; mem. Naval Armistice Commn., 1918-19; comdt. Navy Yard, Boston, 1919-21; mil. gov. Santo Domingo, 1921-22; mem. Gen. Bd., Navy Dept., 6 mos., 1923; admiral in command Battle Fleet, June 30, 1923-25; admiral in command U.S. Fleet, 1925-26; comdr. 13th Naval Dist., Oct. 1, 1926-28; apptd. supt. U.S. Naval Acad., June 1928; retired, 1931; now supt. Adm. Farragut Acad., Tom's River, N.J. Home: Tom's River, N.J.; (summer) Clifton, Md.

ROCK, Katharine Howard, librarian; b. Brockton, Mass., July 27, 1897; d. Edward Thomas and Agnes (Howard) R.; ed. Phillips High Sch., Swampscott, Mass., 1911-15; B.S., Simmons Coll. Sch. of Library Sci., Boston, 1919. Asso. librarian, Skidmore Coll., Saratoga Springs, N.Y., 1919-21; librarian Pub. Library, Greenville, Pa., since 1921. Mem. Am. Library Assn., Pa. Library Assn., Nat. Fed. of Bus. and Professional Women's Clubs, Simmons Coll. Alumnae Assn. Republican. Presbyn. Clubs: Business and Professional Women's, Junior Civic League, Burbank, Coterie, Theatre Guild, Thiel Women's, Sharon College (Greenville). Home: 5 College Av., Greenville, Pa.

ROCKHOLD, Kenneth Edward, mgr. industrial dept. Careva Co.; b. Burlington, Ia., Nov. 18, 1891; s. Joseph and Emily (Moore) R.; student U. of Colo.; B.S., U. of Ill.; m. Mildred Kite Johnson Connolly, May 30, 1925; 1 son, Kenneth Edward. Draftsman, L. E. Rodgers Engineering Company, Chicago, and Zanesville, O., 1914-17; mech. engr. Steel & Tube Co. of America, Zanesville, 1917-20, Wellman-Seaver Morgan Co., Cleveland, O., 1920-21; chief draftsman Theodor Kundtz Co., 1921-23; chief mech. engr. Eastern Dist., The Austin Co., Philadelphia, 1924-30; mgr. industrial dept. Careva Co., York, Pa., since 1930; heating and ventilating engr. Registered professional engr. in Pa. Mem. York Engring. Soc. Author various articles on heating, piping and air conditioning. Home: 863 S. George St. Office: Careva Co., York, Pa.

ROCKWELL, Albert, banking, oil and ranching; b. Warren, Pa., Jan. 28, 1877; s. Franklin H. and Tamar (Gilbert) R.; grad. The Hill Sch., Pottstown, Pa., 1895; B.Sc., Harvard U., 1900; m. Helen Pendleton Cole, Sept. 12, 1918; 1 dau., Lavalette (Mrs. Edward J. Sheil). Vice-pres. Warren Nat. Bank; dir. First Nat. Bank (Warren, Pa.), Am.-Hawaiian Steamship Co. (New York). Pres. Watson Memorial Home, Warren, Pa.; trustee Sherman Ranch, Kansas. Republican. Episcopalian. Clubs: Conewango, Conewango Valley Country (Warren); Harvard (New York). Home: 504 Third Av. Office: 422 Third Av., Warren, Pa.

ROCKWELL, Edward Henry, civ. engr.; b. Worcester, Mass., Apr. 20, 1869; s. Edward Munson and Martha Josephine (Smith) R.; B.S., Worcester Polytechnic Institute, 1890, C.E., 1920; hon. D. Eng. from same inst., 1933; m. Lena Hortense Warfield, Oct. 29, 1891; children—Grace Margaret (Mrs. Stanley R. Kingman), Dorothy (Mrs. Mark A. Burns), Doris, Donald Edward, Mrs. W. W. Cheney. With George S. Morrison, cons. engr., Chicago, 1890-92; submaster high sch., Leominster, Mass., 1893-95; with Norcross Bros., bldg. steel work, Worcester, Mass., 1895-97; in charge installation of machinery, and supt. Holliston (Mass.) Yarn Co., 1897-99; draftsman Boston Bridge Works, 1899-1900, Boston Navy Yard, 1900-01; asst. engr. Boston Bridge Works, 1901-02; instr. in civ. engring., Tufts Coll., 1902-03, asst. prof., 1903-06, prof. structural engring., 1906-18, prof. civ. and structural engring., 1918-22; dean of engring. and prof. civ. engring., Rutgers U., 1922-28; Simon Cameron Long prof. civ. engring., Lafayette Coll., since 1928. With Boston Bridge Works, summer 1906; asst. engr. Boston Transit Commn., summer 1907; designing engr. Suffolk County Court House extension, Sept. 1907-June 1908, cons. engr. on constrn. same, June 1908-Jan. 1910; cons. engr. commn. on Galveston causeway reconstruction, Oct. 1916-Jan. 1917; engr. and architect in charge design, contract and construction of chem. lab., Tufts Coll., July 1921-Sept. 1922; cons. engr. Gen. Crushed Stone Co., Easton, Pa., City of Perth Amboy, N.J., Oliver Iron Mining Co., Duluth, Minn., etc. Mem. Am. Soc. Civil Engrs. (ex-pres. Lehigh Valley section), Soc. for Promotion Engring. Edn., Am. Assn. Univ. Profs. N.J. Soc. Professional Engrs. (ex-pres.), Phi Beta Kappa, Sigma Xi, Lambda Chi Alpha, Tau Beta Pi. Republican. Conglist. Club: Northampton County Country. Author: Vibrations Caused by Blasting and their Effect on Structures. Contbr. to Am. Highway Engrs. Handbook and bulls. Soc. for Promotion Engring. Edn. Home: 174 Pennsylvania Av., Easton, Pa.

ROCKWELL, Frederick Frye, author; b. Brooklyn, N.Y., Apr. 2, 1884; s. Frank Warren and Elizabeth Trowbridge (Hammill) R.; spl. student Wesleyan U., Conn., 1905-06; m. Marjorie Hughan, Sept. 5, 1910; children—Wallace, Frederick F., Donald W., Margaret E. Circulation mgr. Garden Mag., 1906-07; mgr. Wilshire Book Co., 1907-08; with New York Call, 1908-09; dir. service dept. and mgr. Burpee's Seed Farms, 1917-19; with Tuthill Adv. Agency, New York, 1919-21; mgr. nursery and bulb dept. and of publicity and advertising, Seabrook Co., Seabrook Farms, Bridgeton, N.J., 1921-25. Author: Home Vegetable Gardening, 1911; Gardening Indoors and Under Glass, 1912; Making a Fruit Garden, 1914; The Pocket Garden Guide, 1914; The Key to the Land, 1915; Around the Year on the Garden, 1916; Save It for Winter! 1918; Gardening Under Glass, 1921; The Book of Bulbs, 1926; Shrubs and Gladiolus, in Home Garden Handbooks series, 1927; Rock Gardening and Evergreens, 1928; Irises, 1928; Dahlias, 1929; Lawns, 1929; Roses, 1930; Peonies, 1933; Flower Arrangement (with E. C. Grayson), 1935; Gardening Indoors (with E. C. Grayson), 1938; Daffodils, 1938. Socialist. Quaker. Mason. Garden editor New York Sunday Times; hort. editor of McCall's Mag.; editor Whittlesey House Garden Series. Contbr. to mags. Home: Ridgefield, N.J.*

ROCKWELL, Rena Victoria (Mrs. Lynn David R.), artist and teacher; b. Peoria, Ill., Aug. 9, 1890; d. Richard and Henrietta Louise (Janssen) Colwell; ed. Bradley Poly. Inst., 1906-09; m. Lynn David Rockwell, Mar. 28, 1910; children—Sheldon Colwell, Boyd David (dec.), Wilbur Chapman. Has followed profession as artist since 1931; mem. Asso. Artists of Pittsburgh since 1931; conducts pvt. classes in studio since 1934; one-man show in Asso. Artists Club and Exbn. Rooms, 1939; represented by paintings in Forest Hill Schs.; lectures on art; directs living portrait programs; conducts art tours in exhbns. and museums. Former County Art Chmn. for State Federation of Pa. Women. Awarded First Prize, Asso. Artists of Pittsburgh, 1937. Republican. Presbyterian. Clubs: Woman's (Forest Hills); Uxority (Pittsburgh). Home: 721 Cascade Rd., Forest Hills, Pa.

ROCKWELL, Willard Frederick, pres. Timken-Detroit Axle Co.; b. Boston, Mass., Mar. 31, 1888; s. Frederick Joshua and Katharine (Herr) R.; Mechanic Arts, Mass. Inst. Tech., 1905-08; m. Clara Whitcomb Thayer, June 4, 1908; children—Katharine Thayer (Mrs. William S. Potter), Janet Ella (Mrs. James Lindsay), Willard F., Margaret Eleanor, Elizabeth Thayer. Consulting engineer since 1914; chairman of the board of Standard Steel Spring Co. since 1937; v.p. Torbensen Axle Co., Cleveland, O., 1918; pres. Wis. Axle Co., Oshkosh, Wis., since 1919, Pittsburgh Equitable Meter Co. since 1925, Merco Nordstrom Valve Co., Oakland, Calif., since 1932, Timken-Detroit Axle Co., since 1933; also pres. Timken Silent Automatic Co., H. A. Smith Machine Co., Timken-Michigan Co.; dir. Raybould Coupling since 1937. Lt. Col. U.S.A. Res. Corps. Mem. Am. Soc. M.E., Soc. of Automotive Engrs., Soc. Military Engrs., Nat. Aeronautic Assn. Clubs: Duquesne, Pittsburgh Athletic, Longue Vue Country (Pittsburgh); Detroit Athletic; Advertising, Bankers (New York). Home: 140 W. Hutchinson Av., Edgewood, Pittsburgh. Office: 400 N. Lexington Av., Pittsburgh, Pa.

ROCKWELL, William Locke, lawyer; b. Plainfield, N.J., Dec. 18, 1870; s. William and Nora Whalen (Locke) R.; student Plainfield (N.J.) pub. schs., Leal's Sch., Plainfield, 1878-89, Lehigh U., Bethlehem, Pa., 1889; certificate, Sprague Corr. Sch. of Law, Detroit, Mich., 1898; m. Lavinia Shivers, Sept. 1, 1898 (died 1935); m. 2d, Clara Dorothy Wright, Nov. 12, 1929. Admitted to N.J. bar as atty., 1898, as counsellor, 1901, and practiced at Newark, N.J., and East Orange, N.J., since 1898. Served on Montclair (N.J.) Advisory Bd., Selective Draft, during World War. Dem. candidate for mayor, Montclair, 1912 (defeated); mem. Dem. Co. Com., Essex Co., N.J., 1912-21; candidate in Montclair for commr., 1920 (defeated); mem. State Bd. Tenement House Supervision, 1917 to end of term; candidate for judge Montclair Dist. Ct., 1921 (not appointed); on resignation Dem. candidate for Congress, 10th Dist., N.J., 1926, selected to run in primaries (defeated). Democrat. Mason (Northern Lodge, Newark, N.J.). Compiled Rockwell's Notaries Manual, 1st edit., 1903; 2d edit., 1911; Landlord and Tenant, 1st edit., 1907; 2d edit., 1922. (N.J. law only). Address: 219 N. Walnut St., East Orange, N.J.

RODALE, Jerome Irving, editor and pub.; b. New York, N.Y., Aug. 16, 1898; s. Michael and Bertha (Rouda) R.; grad. DeWitt Clinton High Sch.; ed. N.Y. Univ., 1916-17, Columbia, 1917; m. Anna Andrews, Dec. 1, 1927; children—Robert, Ruth, Nina. Employed as accountant in New York, N.Y., 1916-19, in Washington, D.C., 1919-23; mgr. Rodale Mfg. Co., Inc., mfrs. elec. wiring devices, 1923-32, vice-pres. Rodale Mfg. Co., Inc., Emmaus, Pa., since 1923; pres. and mgr. Rodale Publications, Inc., since 1932, pub. five mags., Fact Digest, You're Wrong About That, Everybody's Life, Tempo, and Science Facts. Democrat. Author: The King's English on Horseback, 1938; Strengthen Your Memory, 1938; Cross-Word Puzzle Word-Finder, 1938; The Verb-Finder (with K. Badger), 1937 (pub. in London, 1938). Home: 621 N. 30th St., Allentown. Office: Emmaus, Pa.

RODDY, Harry Justin; b. Landisburg, Pa., May 25, 1856; s. William Henry and Susan Catherine (Waggoner) R.; B.S., First Pa. State Normal Sch., Millersville, 1881, M.S., 1891; Ph.D., Kansas City (Mo.) U., 1906; m. Anna Houck Graver, Dec. 21, 1891; children—Anna Mary (Mrs. Clair G. Kinter), Henry Justin. Teacher pub. schs., 1877-87; teacher, First Pa. State Normal Sch., 1887-1904, dir. geography and geology work, 1906-08, head of science work, 1908-26; curator of museum and prof. geology, Franklin and Marshall Coll., since 1926. Sec. Lancaster City Tree Commn. Dir. Nature Study Club, Lancaster. Author: Common School Geography (2 books), 1913, 15; Industrial and Commercial Geography of Lancaster County, Pa., 1916; Origin of Concretions in Streams, 1917; The Reptiles of Lancaster County and the State of Pennsylvania, 1926; The Geology and Geography of Lancaster, Co., Pa., 1920. Contbr. chapters on natural history to several books, also contbr. to newspapers; lecturer on natural history subjects. Home: Conestoga, Pa. Address: Franklin and Marshall Coll., Lancaster, Pa.*

RODEFER, Onward Allen, supervising prin. schs.; b. Shadyside, O., Apr. 1, 1892; s. Charles Wells and Nettie (Houston) R.; A.B., Bethany W.Va. Coll., 1913; A.M., U. of Pittsburgh, 1934; m. Edith Smith, Oct. 25, 1917; children—David Allen, Charles Wells, James Franklin, William Onward. Engaged in teaching in high schs., 1913-16; prin. Craig Sch., Uniontown, Pa., 1916-17; prin. Independent Sch. Dist., New Salem, Pa., 1920-24; postmaster, New Salem, Pa., 1924-25; supervising prin., Centerville Borough Schs., Washington Co., Pa., 1925-29; prin. high sch., Waynesburg, Pa., 1929-36, supervising prin. schs. since 1936. Served as ensign, U.S.N.R.F. during World War. Mem. Kappa Alpha, Phi Delta Kappa. Republican. Mem. Christian Ch. Club: Rotary of Waynesburg. Home: 102 N. Porter St., Waynesburg, Pa.

RODENBAUGH, Henry Nathan, consulting engineer; b. Norristown, Pa., Nov. 20, 1879; s. William Henry and Teresa Jane (Shanks) R.; ed. high sch., Norristown; B.Sc. in Mech. Engineering, University of Pennsylvania, 1901, M.E. from same university, 1931; Wagner Inst. Science, Phila., 1908-09; m. Caroline Pickett Bransford, Nov. 17, 1904; children—Thomas Bransford, Jean Crawford, Caroline Carrington. Draftsman for the N.&W. Ry., 1902-03; yard supt. Alan Wood, Iron & Steel Co., Conshohocken, Pa., 1903-04; asst. engr., Southern Ry., Washington, D.C., 1904-05; with Carolina, Clinchfield & Ohio Ry., Bristol, Va., 1905-06; prin. asst. engr. Va. & S.W. Ry., 1906-08; structural engr. on track elevation, Phila., Germantown & Norristown Ry. (P.&R. Ry.), 1908-09; with Southern Ry. successively as asst. engr. of bridges, 1909-11, engr. in charge terminal improvements, hdqrs. Atlanta, 1911-14, supervising engr. at Washington, D.C., Jan.-May 1914, prin. asst. engr. valuation dept., 1914-18; engring. asst. to regional dir. Southern Region, U.S. R.R. Administration at Atlanta, 1918-20; regional engr. Southern and Pocahontas regions, same administration, Mar.-July 1920; chief engr. Fla. East Coast Ry., 1920-23, gen. mgr., 1923-25, dir. and v.p. in charge operation, traffic, constrn. and valuation, Mar. 1925-June 1932; also for same period, v.p. Fla. East Coast Car Ferry, Jacksonville Terminal Co. (mem. exec. com.); dir. and mem. exec. com. Fruit Growers Express Co., 1925-32; cons. engr. and advisory counsel on transportation co. problems, 1 Wall St., New York, 1932-37; v.p. in charge ry. work Day & Zimmermann, Inc., since 1937; v.p. and dir. Surprise Store Co., St. Augustine. Trustee Fla. Normal and Industrial Inst., Flagler Memorial Hosp.; chmn. St. John's County (Fla.) Bd. Trustees of Free Dental Clinic for Children. Mem. Am. Soc. C.E. (ex-pres. Fla. sect.), Am. Soc. M.E., Ry. Guild, Soc. Am. Mil. Engrs., Am. Ry. Engring. Assn., Am. Acad. Polit. and Social Science, Montgomery County (Pa.) Hist. Soc., St. Augustine (Fla.) Hist. Soc., Sigma Alpha Epsilon. Republican. Episcopalian. Clubs: St. Augustine Yacht, Ancient City Yacht, St. Augustine Country, Boca Raton (Fla.); Seaview Golf and Country (Atlantic City, N.J.). Home: Marviento, St. Augustine, Fla.; Kent and Aubrey Roads, Wynnewood, Pa. Office: Packard Bldg., Philadelphia, Pa.

RODES, Lester Alfred, supt. city schs.; b. York, Pa., Apr. 8, 1890; s. Rufus and Annie (Flury) R.; A.B., Lebanon Valley Coll., Annville, Pa., 1914; A.M., U. of Pa., 1917; m. Lucinda Potter, Dec. 25, 1914; 1 son, Harold Potter. Engaged in teaching pub. schs., Emigsville, Pa., 1907-08, Wormleysburg, Pa., 1908-10, high sch., Moorestown, N.J., 1914-16; prin. high sch., Moorestown, N.J., 1916-19; supt. schs., Cape May, N.J., 1919-35; supt. schs., South River, N.J., since 1935. Mem. Nat. Edn. Assn. (v.p.), Am. Edn. Council, N.J. Council of Edn., N.J. Schoolmasters Club, Phi Kappa Psi. Presbyterian. Mason, O.E.S. Club: Rotary of South River. Home: 11 Virginia St., South River, N.J.

RODGERS, Charles Clinton, commercial printing; b. Lawrence Co., Pa., Jan. 20, 1869; s. John B. and Catherine (Rumstay) R.; ed. pub. schs., New Castle, Pa.; m. Hannah Hursh, Apr. 24, 1890; children—Verda Oliva (dec. wife of Charles F. Datz), John B., Helen Louise. Employed as printer in New Castle, Pa., 1882-88; came to Irwin, worked on newspaper several yrs. then bought half interest in Irwin Standard, operated it for six yrs. then sold out and worked for Irwin Republican until 1910; engaged in gen. printing business with Louis C. Siegel as Rodgers Printing Co. and mem. firm since 1910, now sec. and treas. of corpn.; dir. Irwin Savings and Trust Co., Irwin Union Cemetery Assn. Served as burgess of Irwin for six yrs. Pres. Greensburg Motor Club. Republican. Methodist. Am. Mechanic. Elk, Royal Arcanum, Knight of Malta. Home: 514 Walnut St., Irwin, Pa.

RODGERS, Frank Edward, sec.-treas. Scranton Transit Co.; b. Altoona, Pa., Sept. 14, 1896; s. John Daniel and Mary Martha (Christian) R.; ed. pub. schs., Altoona, Pa.; m. Marian I. Sellers, Nov. 1, 1919 (died Sept. 18, 1937); 1 son, Frank Edward, Jr. Asso. with Scranton Transit Co. since 1929, sec. and treas. since 1934. Served in Marine Corps, U.S., 1918-19. Mem. Scranton Chamber of Commerce. Mem. Nat. Assn. Cost Accountants, Accountants Exec. Com. Am. Transit Assn., Am. Legion, Forty and Eight, Craftsmen's Club, Fraternal Order of Police. Democrat. Lutheran. Mason (32°). Elk. Clubs: Purple, Junger Maennerchor, Elmhurst Country. Home: 1625 Clay Av. Office: 234 Lackawanna Av., Scranton, Pa.

RODGERS, Henry Clay Frick, river transportation; b. Pittsburgh, Pa., Mar. 12, 1894; s. Wm. Berlein and Alice Ophelia (Jackson) R.; ed. Bellevue. sch., Holley Prep. Sch.; unmarried. Asso. with McCrady-Rodgers Co. since 1914, successively superintendent of river transportation, and supt., now vice-pres. and dir.; dir. Allegheny Trust Co., Pittsburgh Coal Exchange. Mem. S.A.R. Democrat. Mem. M.E. Church. Clubs: Duquesne, Pittsburgh Athletic (Pittsburgh); Longue Vue Country (Verona). Home: Royal York Apts. Office: 239 Fourth Av., Pittsburgh, Pa.

RODGERS, William Berlean, contracting and builders' supplies; b. Pittsburgh, Pa., Feb. 14, 1885; s. William B. and Alice (Jackson) R.; ed. pub. schs. and high sch., Pittsburgh, Pa.; m. Flora Barr, Sept. 30, 1905; children—Ruth (Mrs. Edward McCrady, Jr.), John Norwood, Matthew Jackson, Robert Barr, Barbara, Lynn. Asso. with Rodgers Sand Co., Pittsburgh, Pa., since 1902, pres. when consolidated with McCrady Bros. Co. as McCrady-Rodgers Co., now vice-pres.; elected mem. Pa. Senate, 1935; vice-pres. Moore Enameling and Mfg. Co., W. Lafayette, O.; dir. Allegheny Trust Co., Bellevue Savings and Trust Co. Served as vice-pres. Pittsburgh Chamber of Commerce. Democrat. Mem. M.E. Church. Clubs: Duquesne, Civic, Highland Country. Home: 361 Ohio River Boul. Office: 239 4th Av., Pittsburgh, Pa.

RODMAN, John Stewart, surgeon; b. Abilene, Tex., July 21, 1883; s. William L. and Bettie Crawford (Stewart) R.; m. Eunice B. Hinman, Apr. 10, 1915; children—Eunice Russell, William Louis. Interne, Pa. Hosp., Phila., and Mayo Clinic, Rochester, Minn., 1906-08; in practice of surgery at Phila. since 1908; prof. surgery, Womens Med. Coll.; surgeon in chief Womens Coll. Hosp.; surgeon Bryn Mawr Hosp.; med. sec. Nat. Bd. Med. Examiners. Maj. Med. Corps Res., U.S.A. Mem. Am. Bd. Surgery (sec.), Phila. Acad. Surgery (pres.), Delta Psi. Clubs: Philadelphia, St. Anthony. Home: 524 Manor Rd. Office: 1726 Spruce St., Philadelphia, Pa.

RODNEY, Richard Seymour, judge; b. New Castle, Del., Oct. 10, 1882; s. John H. and Annie D. (Reeves) R.; student Delaware Coll., 1900-02; m. Eliza Cochran Green, of Middletown, Del., Jan. 21, 1917; children—Eliza, Sarah Duval. Admitted to Del. bar, 1906, and began practice at Wilmington, Del.; mayor of New Castle, 1911-17; asso. judge Supreme Court of Del., term 1922-34. Served as pvt. and 1st lt., Del. N.G., 1899-1913. Mem. Am. and Del. State bar assns., Kappa Alpha. Democrat. Episcopalian. Mason, K.P. Home: New Castle, Del. Address: Wilmington, Del.*

ROE, Dudley George, lawyer; banking; b. Sudlersville, Md., Mar. 23, 1881; s. William Dudley and Martha Neal (George) R.; A.B., Washington Coll., 1901, A.M., 1904; LL.B., Univ. of Maryland, Law School, 1905; m. Anna Jane Metcalfe, Apr. 17, 1906; children—Dudley George, Jr., Brown Metcalfe, William Medford Dudley. Entered practice of law at Sudlersville, Md., 1905; entered grain business with father and mem. firm W. D. Roe & Son, one of largest handlers cash grain wheat and corn in East at Sudlersville, Md., since 1881; pres. Sudlersville Bank of Md.; dir. Queen Anne's Record Observer Pub. Co., Centreville, Md. Mem. Md. Ho. of Dels., 1907-09, Md. Senate since 1926, Dem. floor leader, 1939. Del. to Nat. Dem. Convs., 1928, 1932. Mem. bd. trustees Washington Coll., Chestertown, Md. Active in affairs of P.E. Ch.; del. from Diocese of Easton to all gen. convs. since 1919. Democrat. Episcopalian. Mason. Home: Sudlersville, Md.

ROE, John Joseph, banking; b. Ravena, N.Y., Mar. 23, 1901; s. James F. and Theresa (Aussem) R.; ed. St. Brigid's Parochial Sch., 1906-14, St. Peter's Prep. Sch., Jersey City, N.J., 1915-19, Fordham U., 1919-21; m. Mae Rita Schwind, Nov. 26, 1926; 1 dau., Joan Mae. Began as clk. in First Nat. Bank of Union City, 1921; organized First Nat. Bank of North Bergen, N.J., 1925, vice-pres. and mem. bd. dirs.; reorganized North Bergen Trust Co., 1933, chmn. bd. dirs. since 1937; vice-pres., treas., and mem. bd. mgrs. Hudson City Savings Bank, Jersey City, N.J. since 1936; dir. West Nyack Trap Rock Co., West Nyack, N.Y. since 1935. Mem. Housing Authority Twp. North Bergen since 1938. Dir. Chamber of Commerce. Mem. Bd. Govs. North Hudson Hosp. in Weehawken since 1936. Democrat. Catholic. Club: Carteret (Jersey City). Home: 1147 3d Av. North Bergen, N.J. Office: First National Bank, North Bergen N.J.

ROEBLING, Ferdinand William, III, wire rope engr.; b. Trenton, N.J., Nov. 1, 1910; s. Ferdinand William, Jr. and Ruth (Metcalf) R.; student Pomfret Sch., 1924-25 and 1928-29; B.S., Princeton U., 1933; unmarried. Began in wire mills of J. A. Roebling's Sons Co., 1933, worked in various mills, 2 yrs., now wire rope engr., 2d v.p. and dir.; dir. First-Mechanics Nat. Bank of Trenton. Grad. Princeton U., R.O.T.C.; served with 112th F.A., N.J.N.G., 2 yrs.; now 1st lt., 307th F.A. Reserves. Mem. Am. Soc. for Metals; asso. mem. Sigma Xi (research). Republican. Episcopalian. Clubs: Princeton (New York); Rumson Country, Trenton Country (Trenton); Tiger Inn (Princeton); Manasquan River Marlin and Tuna. Home: 222 W. State St. Office: 640 S. Broad St., Trenton, N.J.

ROEDER, Arthur, corpn. executive; b. Pleasantville, N.J., June 6, 1884; s. Adolph and Marie (Bonschur) R.; student civ. engring., Cornell U., 1903-07, Dr. C.E., 1907; m. Harriet K. Pupke, Feb. 15, 1913; 1 dau., Harriet A. Jr. engr., City of Newark, N.J., 1907-10; successively salesman, asst. sales mgr., production mgr., asst. to gen. mgr., Robt. H. Ingersoll and Brother, watch mfrs., N.Y. City, 1910-18; treas., later pres. U.S. Radium Corpn., N.Y. City, 1918-26; exec. vice-pres. Am. Linseed Co., N.Y. City, 1926-29; became pres. The Colo. Fuel & Iron Co., 1929, also pres. subsidiaries of same, apptd. receiver, Aug. 1, 1933, apptd. trustee, Aug. 1, 1934, chmn. reorganized company, 1936-38, chmn. of bd. since 1938. Mem. Sigma Alpha Epsilon. Republican. Swedenborgian. Clubs: Denver (Denver); Downtown Assn., Union League (New York); Baltusrol Golf (Springfield, N.J.). Home: Short Hills, N.J. Office: Continental Oil Bldg., Denver, Colo.; and 2 Wall St., New York, N.Y.

ROEDER, Jesse Norman, supt. of schs.; b. Hosenack, Pa., June 29, 1892; s. Alfred S. and Alice (Carl) R.; A.B., Franklin and Marshall Coll., 1917; A.M., Teachers Coll. of Columbia U., 1923; Ph.D., N.Y. Univ., 1933; m. Ruth Melroy, Aug. 23, 1922; children—Jesse Norman, Jr., John Paul, Thomas Melroy, Phyllis Ann, Alfred David. Engaged in teaching various schs., 1911-21; instr. science, high sch., Palmerton, Pa., 1921-22, prin., 1922-26, supt. schs., Palmerton, Pa. since 1926. Served as regtl. observer, 146 inf., U.S.A., 1918-19, with A.E.F. in France in major offensives. Mem. Nat. Edn. Assn., Nat. Assn. Sch. Supts., Pa. State Edn. Assn., Phi Delta Kappa, Phi Kappa Tau, Patriotic Order Sons of America, Bd. of Trade, Palmerton. Democrat. Mem. Evang. and Reformed Ch. Mason (32°). Club: Blue Ridge Country. Home: 308 Columbia Av., Palmerton, Pa.

ROEMER, Charles Harold, lawyer; b. Paterson, N.J., Feb. 5, 1899; s. Samuel and Bessie (Rosenzweig) R.; student Paterson (N.J.) High Sch., 1912-16; LL.B., N.Y.U. Sch. of Law, 1919; m. Rose Birnbaum, June 21, 1922; children—Gloria Lila, Ruth, Sheila. Admitted to bar, 1920, and since in practice at Paterson, N.J.; admitted Bar of U.S. Supreme Court, 1935; city atty., Paterson, N.J., 1922-24, 1928-30; prof. of law, John Marshall Coll., Jersey City, N.J., since 1931; supreme court commr. of N.J., 1936; dir. and counsel Franklin Trust Co. of Paterson; pres. Colt Brokerage Co.; sec.-treas. Frankham Realty Corpn. Served as sergt. inf., U.S. Army, 1918. Pres. Civic Council, Coll. of Paterson (N.J.) Mem. Industrial Commn. of Paterson (pres. since 1936), Passaic Co., N.J. State and Am. bar assns. Democrat. Hebrew religion. Mason. Odd Fellow, B'nai B'rith (pres. dist. 3). Home: 460 E. 41st St. Office: 148 Market St., Paterson, N.J.

ROEMER, Henry A., steel exec.; b. Struthers, O.; s. Henry and Margaret (Hill) R.; ed. pub. schs.; m. May Ethel Sahlie, 1905; children—James A., Henry A., Margaret (Mrs. Blair), John J., Gretchen. Supt. Am. Sheet Steel Co., 1906-07; asst. supt. Youngstown (O.) Sheet & Tube Co., 1907-13; gen. supt. Canton (O.) Sheet Steel Co., 1913-16, asst. gen .mgr., 1916-19; gen. mgr. Hydraulic Steel Co., Canton, 1919; v.p., gen. mgr. Superior Sheet Steel Co., Canton, 1919-22, pres., 1922-27; pres. Continental Steel Corpn., 1927-31; pres. Youngstown Pressed Steel Co., 1931-33; chmn. and pres. Sharon (Pa.) Steel Hoop Co. since 1933; dir. First Nat. Bank (Pittsburgh), Pittsburgh Coke & Iron, Union Nat. Bk. (Youngstown). Republican. Protestant. Clubs: Youngstown, Youngstown Country; Canton, Woodmont Rod and Gun, Congress Lake (Canton); Duquesne (Pittsburgh); Gun Club (Berkeley Springs, W.Va.). Home: Woodland Rd., Pittsburgh, Pa. Office: Sharon Steel Corpn., Sharon, Pa.; and Pittsburgh Steel Co., Pittsburgh, Pa.

ROESSING, Frank Myler, dir. of public works; b. Pittsburgh, Pa.; s. George Brown and Alice (Orr) R.; C.E., U. of Pittsburgh, 1900; m. Ethel Searey Harvey, Oct. 26, 1938. V.-p. C.S. Lambie Co., Pittsburgh, 1906-09; pres. and dir. Pittsburgh Electro-Galvanizing Co. since 1919. Roessing Mfg. Co., Pittsburgh, Pa., since 1913; pres. Farmers & Merchants Bank, Sharpsburg, Pa.; dir. of public works, Pittsburgh, since 1936. Mason (Consistory, Shrine). Club: Wildwood Country (Pittsburgh, Pa.). Home: 333 S. Aiken Av. Office: Director of Public Works, Pittsburgh, Pa.

ROESSING, Mrs. Jennie Bradley, suffragist, club woman; b. Pittsburgh, Pennsylvania; d. John and Anna Marie (Friedrich) Bradley; ed. public and private schools; m. Frank Myler Roessing, of Pittsburgh, Sept. 21, 1908. Pres. Pa. Woman's Suffrage Assn., 1912-16; mem. Audubon Soc., Stanton Bird Club, League of Nations Assn.; chmn. state finance com. State Fed. Pa. Women. Unitarian. Clubs: Twentieth Century, Woman's City. Address: The Ruskin, Pittsburgh, Pa.*

ROGAN, Fred Leon, publisher; b. Bristol, Va., Nov. 21, 1880; s. John Webb and Isabel (Smith) R.; prep. edn. Hotchkiss Sch., Lakeville, Conn., and Louisville Training Sch. Belmont, Ky.; student King Coll., Bristol, 1896-98, Vanderbilt, 1899-1900; m. Clara May Taylor, Oct. 3, 1913; 1 dau., Elizabeth Taylor. With Harper & Bros., 1900-06; Chicago mgr. Good Housekeeping Mag., 1906-11; mgr. in N.Y. City for Curtis Pub. Co., 1911-21; engaged in business research, 1921-27; publisher of Judge, 1927-37; business, ednl. and welfare agency research since 1937. Mem. legal advisory bd. N.Y. State Selective Service Draft, World War. Mem. Phi Delta Theta. Clubs: Cavendish, Knickerbocker Whist (New York); Baltusrol Golf (Short Hills, N.J.). Home: 126 Gates Av., Montclair, N.J. Office: 1440 Broadway, New York, N.Y.

ROGERS, Charles Henry, curator; b. Phila., Pa., Jan. 13, 1888; s. Charles R. and Emma (Duer) R.; ed. Hamilton Inst., N.Y. City, 1900-04, Haverford Coll., 1904-05; Litt.B., Princeton U., 1909; m. Margaret E. Saville, Aug. 1, 1931; children—Charles Robertson II, William Saville. Asst. in Bird Dept., Am. Mus. Natural History, 1912-20; curator Princeton Museum of Zoölogy since 1920. Served at Plattsburg, 1915, 1916; pvt. to supply sergt. 31st Machine Gun Batln., U.S.A., 1918-19. Trustee N.J. Audubon Soc. Mem. Am. Ornithologists' Union, Am. Soc. Mammalogists, Wilson Ornithol. Club, Linnaean Soc. of N.Y., Del. Valley Ornithol. Club, N.J. Field Ornithologists' Club, Trenton Naturalists' Club. Republican. Home: 20 Haslet Av., Princeton, N.J.

ROGERS, Donald Spencer, lumber mfg.; b. Port Norris, N.J., Dec. 27, 1889; s. J. Spencer and Carrie H. (Bateman) R.; prep. edn. Peddie Sch., Hightstown, N.J., 1911-13; B.S., Cornell U., 1917; m. Nancy Irene Loucks, Sept. 12, 1918; children—Donald Morton, Ralph Loucks, Nancy Jean, Ruth Elaine. Clerical work B.& O. R.R. Co., 1919; jr. accountant Marwick, Mitchell & Co., 1919; cost accountant Am. Sheet & Tin Plate Co., 1920-24; accountant Lybrand, Ross Bros. & Montgomery, 1924-29; partner H. S. Edwards & Co., 1930-33 (all Pittsburgh); vice-pres. Chas. A. Briggs Lumber & Mfg. Co., Scottdale, Pa., mfrs. hardwood flooring, trim, woodflour, since 1935; vice-pres. and dir. U.S. Ozone Co. of America; dir. Transparent Dist. Cap & Motor Parts Co. Served as 2d lt. Aviation Sect., U.S. Army, 1918. Mem. Guernsey Breeders Assn. of Pa. (dir.), Western Pa. of Guernsey Breeders Assn. (treas.), Guernsey Breeders Assn. Westmoreland Co. (pres.). Republican. Baptist. Mason. Rotarian (Scottdale). Home: 527 N. Chestnut St. Office: 128 Pittsburgh St., Scottdale, Pa.

ROGERS, Elizabeth Frances, prof. history; b. Phila., Pa., June 29, 1892; d. Prof. Robert William (Ph.D.) and Ida V. (Ziegler) R.; A.B., Goucher Coll., Baltimore, Md., 1912; A.M., Columbia U., 1913; grad. study, U. of Bern, Switzerland, 1913-14; Ph.D., Columbia U., 1917. Engaged as instr. high sch., Haddonfield, N.J., 1916-19; instr. history, Smith Coll. 1919-23; prof. history and head of dept., Wilson Coll., Chambersburg, Pa., since 1923; sabbatical leave in England, 1931-32; twenty-four summers study and travel in Europe. Member American History Association, American Association of University Professors, American Assn. Univ. Women, Phi Beta Kappa, Pi Gamma Mu. Republican. Methodist. Mem. English Speaking union (London). Author: Peter Lombard and the Sacramental System, 1917; Calendar of Correspondence of Sir Thomas More, 1922. Home: 159 Owen Av., Lansdowne, Pa. Address: Wilson College, Chambersburg, Pa.

ROGERS, Forrest Glenn, sch. supt.; b. Nittany, Pa., July 18, 1887; s. Horace Greeley and Anna May (Crawford) R.; B.S., Bucknell U., Lewisburg, Pa., 1917, M.A., 1924; m. Mabel Eudora Tomb, May 30, 1917; children—June, Helen, Marian, Glenn. Asst. prin., Limestone Twp. High Sch., Jersey Shore, Pa., 1909-12; prin., Sheridan Elementary Sch., Williamsport, Pa., 1912-14; head mathematics dept., Oak Lane Country Day Sch., Phila., 1917-19; prin., Walker Twp. High Sch., Hublersburg, Pa., 1919-23; head mathematics dept., Lock Haven (Pa.) High Sch., 1923-26; supt. of schs. of Centre Co., Pa., since 1926. Mem. Pa. State Edn. Assn. (v.p. Co. Supts'. Group), N.E.A., Library and Hist. Assn. Republican. Lutheran. Mason. Club: Kiwanis (Bellefonte, Pa.). Home:

R.D., Howard, Pa. Office: Court House, Bellefonte, Pa.

ROGERS, Harold Frantz, coll. prof.; b. Waynesburg, Pa., Mar. 11, 1878; s. Timothy Ross and Emmiline (Frantz) R.; student pub. elementary and high schs., Moundsville, W.Va., 1885-96, Waynesburg (Pa.) Coll., 1896-97; A.B., W.Va. U., Morgantown, W.Va., 1901; A.M., Harvard, 1908; m. Lulu Shannon Hogg, Aug. 13, 1913; children—Eugene Frantz, Harriet. Began as drug clk., Moundsville, W.Va., 1901; science teacher, Fairmont (W.Va.) State Normal Sch., 1903; instr. natural science and modern lang., Glenville State Normal Sch., Glenville, W.Va., 1904-06; prof. chemistry, Fairmont (W.Va.) State Teachers Coll. since 1908 (except for 1918-19), head dept. of phys. sciences since 1925; instr. chemistry, W.Va. U., Morgantown, W.Va., 1918-19. Served in corps of cadets, W.Va. U., 1897-1901. Mem. W.Va. Acad. of Science (founding mem.; pres. 1929-30), Am. Chem. Soc., A.A.A.S., Am. Assn. Univ. Profs., N.E.A., W.Va. State Education Assn., Assn. of Harvard Chemists, Lambda Delta Lambda (founder 1925), Delta Tau Delta. Republican. Methodist. Club: Harvard (Fairmont, W.Va.). Contbr. articles in science edn. to various jours. Home: 1100 Ridgely Av., Fairmont, W.Va.

ROGERS, Harry L., asso. prof. orthopedic surgery, U. of Md.; attending orthopedic surgeon West Baltimore Gen. Hosp.; asso. orthopedic surgeon Mercy Hosp., James Lawrence Kernan Hosp. and Industrial Sch. for Crippled Children; cons. orthopedic surgeon Provident Hosp. and Free Dispensary. Address: 101 E. Preston St., Baltimore, Md.

ROGERS, Harry Lincoln, physician; b. Burlington, N.J., Dec. 20, 1892; s. Thomas Ivens and Mary Emily (Whitner) R.; grad. Burlington High Sch., 1911; student U. of Pa., 1913; M.D., U. of Pa. Med. Sch., 1917; m. Martha Tosh Grove, Apr. 8, 1920; children—Mary Whitner, John Grove. Interne Western Pa. Hosp., Pittsburgh, 1917-18; practice of medicine, Riverton, N.J., since 1919, practice limited to allergic diseases since 1938; staff mem. of Jefferson (Phila.), Germantown (Pa.), Cooper (Camden), Zurbrugg (Riverside), Burlington County (Mt. Holly) Hosps.; school physician of Riverton 12 years, of Cinnaminson Twp. 10 years. Served as 1st lt. Air Service, Med. Corps, U.S. Army, 1918. Sec. Riverton Bd. of Health; former sr. warden Christ Ch., Riverton; treas. Phila. Interhospital Bridge Whist League. Fellow Coll. Physicians of Phila.; mem. Burlington County Med. Soc. (past pres.), N.J. State Med. Soc., A.M.A., Phila. Allergy Soc. (sec., treas., 1937-39), Am. Legion (past post comdr.), Sigma Chi. Republican. Episcopalian. Artisans. Clubs: Riverton Country; Germantown Cricket (Phila.). Home: 407 Main St. Office: 408 Main St., Riverton, N.J.

ROGERS, Harvey Everett, banker; b. near Trenton, N.J., Mar. 29, 1879; s. Caleb C. and Rebecca (Allen) R.; grad. pub. schs. of Hamilton Twp. and Stewart Business Coll., Trenton; m. Mary E. Reynolds, Mar. 6, 1901. Began as bookkeeper, Bloom & Godley, 1895-99; associated with father, Millwork mfg., 1899-1912; tax collector and treas. Hamilton Twp., 1913-30 (elected to six 3-yr. terms); pres. and dir. First Nat. Bank of Hamilton Sq. since 1933. Pres. Sinking Fund Commn. and pres. Police Pension Fund Commn. (Hamilton Twp.). Republican. Baptist (trustee 1st Ch., Trenton). Mason (32°, Shriner). Was poultry show mgr. for 15 yrs., having a national reputation. Mem. Lions Club. Home: Near Trenton, N.J. Office: Hamilton Square, N.J.

ROGERS, Herbert Wesley, psychologist; b. Kennebunkport, Me., June 16, 1890; s. John Zadock and Hattie Elizabeth (Morey) R.; B.S., Columbia, 1915, A.M., 1916, Ph.D., 1921; U. of Paris, 1918-19; m. Margaret E. Cobb (Ph.D.), Apr. 8, 1922; children—Charles Morey, Virginia Elizabeth, Evertson, Prudence. Psychologist, Charles William Stores, Brooklyn, N.Y., 1916-17; instr. in psychology, Yale, 1920-23; research asst. prof. psychology, U. of Minn., 1923-24; prof. psychology, Lafayette Coll., since 1924. Served as 1st lt. C.A.C., U.S.A., 1917-19. Fellow A.A.A.S.; mem. Am. Psychol. Assn., Assn. Cons. Phychologists, Assn. Psychologists to Study Social Issues, Camp Directors Assn. of America, Am. Statis. Assn., Assn. Clin Psychologists, Children's Aid Soc. of Northampton Co. (pres.), Easton Peace Action Assn. (sec.), Lehigh Valley Child Guidance Clinic (dir.), Lehigh Valley Mental Health Conf. (sec.), Phi Gamma Delta. Club: Columbia University (New York). Author: Some Empirical Tests in Vocational Selection, 1922. Contbr. to psychol. and ednl. publs. Home: 520 McCartney St., Easton, Pa.

ROGERS, Karl H(enkels), writer; b. Phila., Pa., Feb. 8, 1886; s. John I and Elizabeth (Henkels) R.; student Friends Central Sch., Phila., 1893-1900, William Penn Charter Sch., 1900-04, Univ. of Pa., 1904-07; LL.D., Xavier University, Cincinnati, 1939; m. Florence White Rogers, October 31, 1917. With Littel River Lumber Co., Townsend, Tenn., 1907-09, Pa. R.R., 1909-12; asso. with Guy C. Whidden Advertising Agency, Phila., 1912-15, John O. Powers Advertising Agency, New York, 1915-16, N. W. Ayer & Son, Phila., 1916-19, Tracy, Parry Advertising Agency, Phila., 1919-23; partner Oswald Advertising Agency, Phila., 1923-26; mgr. his own agency, Phila., 1926-29; writer and dir. Catholic Information Soc., Narbeth, Pa., since 1929; promoter of nat. "Narberth Movement" since 1930; mem. Nat. Catholic Evidence Conf., pres. 1938-40. Home: 523 Baird Rd., Merion, Pa. Address: Box 35, Narbeth, Pa.

ROGERS, Lawrence H., physician; b. Tullytown, Pa., Aug. 30, 1883; s. Irvin W. and Ida M. (Tallman) R.; A.B., Princeton U., 1904; M.D., N.Y. Univ. Med. Sch., 1908; m. Eliza C. Thropp, Aug. 25, 1922; children—Elizabeth E., Fred B. Served on staff St. Joseph's Hosp., Paterson, N.J., 1911-12; on staff Mercer Hosp., Trenton, N.J., since 1912; city physician, Trenton, N.J., 1913-24; res. physician Municipal Hosp., Trenton, N.J., 1924-25, med. supt. since 1925. Served as 1st lt. Med. Corps, U.S.A., 1917-18. Mem. Mercer Co. Med. Soc., Am. Legion. Democrat. Presbyn. Mason. Home: Municipal Hosp., Trenton, N.J.

ROGERS, Mildred, physician and surgeon; b. Lanesboro, Pa., May 26, 1894; d. William Louis and Alice E. (Farrar) R.; A.B., Goucher Coll., Baltimore, 1916; M.D., Womens Med. Coll. of Pa., 1922. Engaged as instr. high sch., Jamesburg, N.J., 1916-18; after usual interneships engaged in practice of medicine and surgery at New Castle, Pa., since 1923. Mem. bd. dirs. New Castle Y.W.C.A. Mem. Lawrence Co. Med. Soc., Zeta Phi, Am. Assn. Univ. Women, D.A.R. Presbyn. Club: Business and Professional Womens. Home: 209 N. Mercer St., New Castle, Pa.

ROGERS, Milton Barbee, utilities exec.; b. Lebanon, Ky., Mar. 15, 1895; s. William Childs and Mary (Barbee) R.; student Washington & Lee U., Lexington, Va., 1913-15; m. Lucile Williams, Mar. 16, 1920. College training class, fgn. dept., Nat. City Bank, New York, 1916; Moscow (Russia) Branch, 1917, officer, Brussels (Belgium) Branch, 1920-23; asst. gen. mgr. Studebaker Corpn. of America, New York, 1924-28, pres. Studebaker Sales Corpn. of America, Phila., 1928-29; v.p. and dir., U.S. Lines, steamship, New York, 1930-31; exec. v.p., treas. and dir., Community Water Service Co., New York, since 1932; dir. and treas. Pa. State Water Corpn., Greenwich Water and Gas System, Inc., Ohio Cities Water Corpn.; asst. treas. Am. Water Works & Electric Co., Inc. Awarded British Mil. Cross, 1918, French Croix de Guerre, 1918, Russian Order of St. Ann, 1918. Clubs: Bankers of America, City Midday (New York). Home: 125 High St., Montclair, N.J. Office: 50 Broad St., New York, N.Y.

ROGERS, Russell David, structural engr.; b. Peoria, Ill., June 21, 1892; s. David Henry Rogers and Delilah Theresa (Bates) R.; student Pekin (Ill.) High Sch., 1908-12; B.S. in Archtl. Engring., U. of Ill., Urbana, Ill., 1916; m. Lucille Modore Neill, June 14, 1916; 1 son, Neill David (dec.). Asst. testing engr., timekeeper and paymaster, asst. chemist, structural asst. to master mechanic, Corn Products Refining Co., Pekin, Ill., 1908-14; designer and checker bldgs. and bridges, reinforced concrete, steel, wood, illumination, heating and ventilation, Elgin, Joliet & Eastern R.R., Joliet, Ill., 1916-19; chief structural engr. E. I. du Pont de Nemours & Co., Wilmington, Del., since 1919; dir. Mexican Quicksilver Co.; registered professional engr. in Pa., N.Y., N.J., Mich., Ia., La., Ill., Va. and Wis. Structural engr. Bd. of Standards and Appeals, Wilmington, Del., since 1936. Mem. Am. Concrete Inst., Am. Assn. Engrs., Del. Soc. Professional Engrs. (pres. since 1939), Del. Auto Assn. (mem. exec. com.), Radio Service of America, Radio Service Men's Assn. (N.Y.), Radio Mfrs. Service, Phila., Beta Gamma, Nat. Geog. Soc. Republican. Methodist. Mason (Shriner). Clubs: Du Pont Country, Y Stamp, Masonic (all Wilmington); Roosevelt Memorial (Oyster Bay). Home: 3115 Van Buren St. Office: 13038 Du Pont Bldg., Wilmington, Del.

ROGERS, William, Jr., prof. of chemistry; b. Nottingham, England, Jan. 17, 1900; s. William and Eliza Ellen (Kerry) R.; brought to U.S., 1905, naturalized, 1914; grad. Cheltenham High Sch., Elkins Park, Pa., 1917; B.S., Princeton U., 1921, A.M., 1922, Ph.D., 1924; m. Doris Mildred Wright, June, 1927; children—Doris Mildred, William. With Temple U. since 1924, successively instr. of chemistry and asst. prof. and now asso. prof. of chemistry. Served in U.S. Navy and U.S. Naval Reserve, 1918-22. Mem. Am. Chem. Soc., Gateway Club, Franklin Inst. Episcopalian. Club: Princeton (Phila.). Home: 300 Chandler St., Phila., Pa.

ROHLFING, Charles Carroll, prof. of polit. science; b. Baltimore, Md., Jan. 29, 1902; s. Charles F. and Emma Louise (Tieman) R.; B.S. in economics, U. of Pa., 1923, A.M., 1925, Ph.D., 1930; LL.B., Temple U., 1933; student U. of Chicago, 1930, U. of N.C., 1931; m. Ethel Olive Runk, 1932; children—Charles Carroll, James Herbert. Instr. in polit. science, U. of Pa., 1923-30, asst. prof., 1930-35, asso. prof. since 1935, chmn. polit. science dept. since 1937. Consultant Pa. Joint Legislative Com. on State Finances, 1934; mem. Governor's Com. to investigate disfranchisement in Phila., 1938; mem. Taxpayers Forum of Pa.; mem. exec. bd. Inst. of Local and State Govt. Mem. Am. Polit. Science Assn., Am. Acad. of Polit. and Social Sciences, Nat. Municipal League, Am. Assn. Univ. Profs., Lambda Chi Alpha, Pi Gamma Mu. Methodist. Club: Lenape (Phila.). Author: National Regulation of Aeronautics, 1931; A Survey of the Government of Pennsylvania, 1934; State Constitutional Amendments and Conventions, 1935; Business and Government, 1938. Editor: The State Constitution of the Future, 1935. Contbr. articles to publications of learned assns. Home: Rose Tree Road, Route 2, Media, Pa.

ROHRBACH, Quincy Alvin W., college president; b. at Mertztown, Pa., June 6, 1894; s. Alvin B. and Ella L. (Warmkessel) R.; grad. Keystone State Normal Sch., Kutztown, Pa., 1912; A.B., Franklin and Marshall Coll., Lancaster, Pa., 1922; A.M., University of Pa., 1924, Ph.D., from same university, 1925; LL.D. from University of Pittsburgh, 1934; m. Laura Minerva Dunkelberger, Sept. 1, 1929. High school teacher, Mertztown, 1912-14, Delano, Pa., 1914-16; supervising prin. schs., Ringtown, Pa., 1916-21; teacher, Keystone State Normal Sch. summer sessions, 1921-24; Harrison fellow in edn., U. of Pa., 1924-25; prof. and head dept. of history and principles of edn., 1925-31, prof. of administration, 1931-34, Sch. of Edn., U. of Pittsburgh; pres. State Teachers Coll., Kutztown, Pa., since 1934. Mem. N.E.A., Nat. Soc. Coll. Teachers of Edn., Nat. Soc. for Study of Edn., Delta Sigma Phi, Phi Delta Kappa, Kappa Phi Kappa. Author: Non-Athletic Student Activities in the Secondary School, 1925. Co-Author: An Investigation of Teachers Salaries in Pittsburgh and Eighteen Similar Cities in the United States, 1928; Masters and Doctors Theses in School Administration (1922-32)—written in American Graduate Schools, 1933. Club: Rotary. Address: State Teachers College, Kutztown, Pa.

ROHRBAUGH, Lewis Guy, coll. prof.; b. Fowblesburg, Md., Feb. 24, 1884; s. Henry and

Annie (Fowble) R.; A.B., Dickinson Coll., Carlisle, Pa., 1907; B.D., Drew U., Madison, N.J., 1910; Ph.D., State U. of Iowa, 1922; m. Mae Heffelbower, June 25, 1907; 1 son, Henry Lewis. Ordained to ministry of M.E. Ch., 1910; pastorates in Kan. and Iowa, 1910-18; dir. Wesley Foundation, State U. of Ia., 1918-21; prof. philosophy and religion, Dickinson Coll., since 1922, dean of freshmen since 1932. Former mem. edn. com. Pa. Council Religious Edn. Mem. Pa. Edn. Assn., Am. Philos. Assn., Eugene Field Soc., Alpha Chi Rho, Omicron Delta Kappa. Republican. Methodist. Rotarian. Author: Religious Philosophy, 1923; The Science of Religion, 1927; A Natural Approach to Philosophy, 1934; Grandpa Weatherby (novel), 1936. Contbr. to periodicals; lecturer before religious assemblies. Home: 504 Walnut St. Office: Dickinson Coll., Carlisle, Pa.

ROHRBECK, Edwin Herman, agrl. editor; b. Walton, Ill., Mar. 10, 1895; s. Herman Theodore and Addie Lillian (Jones) R.; B.S., U. of Wis., 1924, M.S., same, 1928; m. Ruth Ora Hyndman, Aug. 29, 1929; children—Edwin Hyndman, Charles Wesley, Mary Adeline. Asst. in agrl. journalism, U. of Wis., then agrl. writer, Milwaukee Journal, 1924; agrl. editor, The Pennsylvania State College since 1924. Served as pvt. to sergt., then field clk., U.S.A., 1918-19. Mem. Am. Assn. Agrl. Coll. Editors (past v.p.), Delta Theta Sigma (past nat. pres.), Phi Kappa Phi, Alpha Zeta, Gamma Sigma Delta, Sigma Delta Chi, Pi Delta Epsilon, Epilon Sigma Phi, Farm House. Methodist. Mason. I.O.O.F. Club: University of State Coll. (past sec.). Contbr. to agrl. mags. and journs. Editor bulls. and circulars. Lecturer. Home: 439 E. Foster Av., State College, Pa.

ROHRBOUGH, Edward Gay, college president; b. Buckhannon, W.Va.; s. William Harrison and Ann (Conley) R.; student W.Va. Wesleyan Coll., Buckhannon, 1893-95; A.B., Allegheny Coll., 1900; A.M., Harvard, 1906; grad. study U. of Chicago, 1914-15; m. Lilian M. Hartman, Aug. 28, 1907; 1 son, Edward Gay. Teacher high sch., Brookville, Pa., 1900-01, Glenville (W.Va.) State Normal Sch., 1901-05, 1906-07; asst. to pres. Fairmont (W.Va.) State Normal Sch., 1907-08; pres. Glenville State Teachers Coll. since 1908; dir. Glenville Banking & Trust Co. Chmn. Gilmer County Council of Defense, 1917-18. Mem. N.E.A., W.Va. State Edn. Assn., Sigma Alpha Epsilon. Republican. Methodist. Mason. Home: Glenville, W.Va.

ROHRER, Albert Lawrence, engineer; b. Farmersville, O., Feb. 29, 1856; s. Aaron and Elizabeth (Ozias) R.; ed. common schs., followed by spl. course in physics and mechanics, Ohio State University; m. Carrie L. Gould, April 8, 1891; 1 dau., Miriam (Mrs. Joseph Bryan Shelby). Entered employ of the Thomson-Houston Electric Company, June 1884; has been with that Co. and its successor, The Gen. Electric Company, since; elec. supt. Schenectady works, Gen. Elec. Co., 1892-1923, advisory engr., 1923-26, retired. Ex-pres. Bd. Edn.; ex-treas. Free Pub. Library, Schenectady. Mem. Am. Inst. E.E., Am. Soc. M.E., Ohio Soc. New York. Unitarian. Fifth class Order of Chia Ho (China). Home: Maplewood, N.J.

ROJAHN, Isaiah Henry, cigar mfr.; b. Dallastown, Pa., July 1, 1887; s. William Francis and Martha Elizabeth (Daugherty) R.; student Dallastown (Pa.) High Sch., 1900-04; m. Flossie Alice Sechrist, Mar. 12, 1908; children—Dr. John Robert, Philip James, Hope, Jane, Joseph Sechrist. Teacher of pub. schs., Dallastown, Pa., 1904-16; gen. mgr. A. F. Fix & Co., cigar mfrs., Dallastown, 1916-33; gen. mgr. W. H. Raab & Sons, cigar mfrs., Dallastown, since 1933. Pres. Dallastown (Pa.) Bd. of Edn. since 1916. First pres. York County Cigar Mfrs. Assn., 1920-21. Trustee Bethlehem United Brethren Ch. Mem. Dallastown (Pa.) Chamber of Commerce. Republican. United Brethren Ch. Mason (Royal Arch; Commandery; K.T.). Club: Lions (pres. 1926-27; Dallastown, Pa.). Home: 17 W. Main St. Office: 123 E. Maple St., Dallastown, Pa.

ROLFE, Alfred Grosvenor, headmaster; b. Boston, Aug. 4, 1860; s. Henry Chamberlain and Abby Frances (Winchester) R.; grad. Ayer (Mass.) High Sch., 1876, Chauncy Hall Sch., Boston, 1878; A.B., Amherst, 1882, A.M., 1885, Litt.D., 1913; traveled and studied abroad, 1889-90; unmarried. Teacher, Black Hall Sch., Lyme, Conn., 1882-84, Cushing Acad., Ashburnham, Mass., 1884-85, Williston Seminary, Easthampton, 1885-86, Graylock Inst., Williamstown, 1886-89, with The Hill Sch., Pottstown, Pa., since 1890, headmaster, 1913-14, sr. master since 1914. Mem. Delta Kappa Epsilon. Club: Amherst (New York). Author: Song of Saints and Sinners; A Little Book of Charades. Address: The Hill Sch., Pottstown, Pa.

ROLFE, John Carew, univ. prof.; b. Lawrence, Mass., Oct. 15, 1859; s. William James and Eliza Jane (Carew) R.; A.B., Harvard, 1881; A.M., Cornell University, 1884, Ph.D., 1885; Litt.D., University of Pa., 1925, Oberlin College, 1933; studied Am. Sch., Athens, 1888-89; m. Alice Griswold Bailey, Aug. 29, 1900; 1 dau., Esther (Mrs. Esther R. Giorni). Instr. Latin, Cornell, 1882-85; instr. Greek and Latin, Harvard, 1889-90; asst. prof. and prof. Latin, Univ. of Mich., 1890-1902; prof. Latin lang. and lit., Univ. of Pa., 1902-32, emeritus prof. since 1932, special lecturer in Latin, 1932-37. Annual professor American Sch. Classical Studies in Rome, 1907-08, prof. in charge, 1923-24; trustee Am. Acad. in Rome. Mem. American Philos. Soc., Phi Beta Kappa, Phi Kappa Phi. Decorated Commendatore Order of the Crown (Italy). Author: Cicero and His Influence, 1923. Editor of various text-books, and with Prof. Charles E. Bennett, Allyn & Bacon's College Latin Series. Translator Suetonius, Sallust, Gellius, Nepos, Ammianus (Loeb Class. Lib.), Gentili, De Iure Belli (Classics Internat. Law). Contbr. on philol. and archæol. topics. Home: 4014 Pine St., Philadelphia, Pa.

ROLFE, Stanley Herbert, supt. of schools; b. Nanticoke, Pa., Apr. 2, 1887; s. William and Margaret (Foster) R.; A.B., Bucknell U., Lewisburg, Pa., 1909; A.M., New York U., 1928, Ed.D., 1937; m. Blanche Margaret Whitebred, 1912; children—Doris Margaret, Hilda A. (Mrs. Robert Martin Kugler), E. Jeanne; m. 2d, Emily V. Halberstadt, 1931. Teacher of grades and high sch., Nanticoke, Pa., 1910-12; teacher and vice prin., public schs., Newark, 1912-20, prin. elementary sch., 1920-29, asst. supt. of schs., 1929-36, dept. supt., 1936-37, supt. since 1937. Mem. N.J. State Council of Edn., Phi Delta Kappa. Presbyterian. Clubs: Scholia, Kiwanis, Newark Athletic, Schoolmen's, Wednesday, N.J. Schoolmasters'. Home: 430 Ridge St. Office: 31 Green St., Newark, N.J.

ROLKER, John George, ins. cos. exec.; b. Baltimore, Md., July 16, 1865; s. Herman H. and Catherine (Sulthaus) R.; student Zion Sch. of Baltimore City; m. Anna E. Flamm, June 7, 1893; 1 son, Irving St. Clair. Began as clk. for Agricultural Ins. Co., Watertown Fire Ins. Co., Germania Fire Ins. Co.; pres. John G. Rolker, Inc., Harrison Bldg. Assn.; dir. Great Am. Ins. Co.; mgr. and gen. agt. Great Am. Indemnity Co.; dir. Rochester Am. Ins. Co. Home: 232 Homewood Terrace. Office: Franklin Bldg., Baltimore, Md.

ROLLINS, Lawrence Emsley, lawyer; b. Oceana, W.Va. Nov. 4, 1904; s. Haven and Priscilla (Lamb) R.; student Concord Normal Coll., Athens W.Va., 1921-23; B.S., U. of Chicago, 1928; J.D., Northwestern Univ. Law Sch., 1932; unmarried. Admitted to W.Va. bar, 1932 and engaged in gen. practice of law at Charleston, 1932-37; propr. and editor West Virginia Review, Charleston, 1937-38; returned to practice of law, Dec. 1938 and since engaged in gen. practice at Charleston; retained as mgr. W.Va. Automobile Dealers Assn. since 1936; pres. Jules Enterprises, Inc.; dir. Crany Land Co., Capitol Housing Co., Northwestern Development Co. (all Charleston). Republican. Baptist. Elk. Home: Ruffner Hotel. Office: Charleston Nat. Bank Bldg., Charleston, W.Va.

ROMER, Isadore Ben, mcht. dept. store; b. N.Y. City, Feb. 1, 1896; s. Samuel and Anna (Ziegler) R.; student pub. schs.; m. Ella Cohen, July 6, 1919; children—Donald Bernard, Gloria Ann, Burt Harvey. Employed in dept. store, Phila., Pa., until removed to Huntington, W.Va., 1910-14; employed as clk. and teller in bank of Huntington, 1914-15; in retail dept. store since 1915, vice-pres. and gen. mgr. Huntington Dry Goods Co., Huntington, W.Va., since 1924. Served as pvt. to corpl. inf., U.S.A., 1917-19; with A.E.F. in France; wounded in action; awarded Order of Purple Heart of U.S. Vice-pres. and dir. Huntington Y.M.C.A. Dir. Chamber of Commerce; past dir. Huntington Community Chest, Boy Scout Council. Past mem. Huntington Police Civil Service Bd. Dir. Morris Memorial Hosp. for Crippled Children. Mem. Disabled Am. Vets., Vets. Fgn. Wars, Am. Legion, Forty and Eight Soc. (past local comdr., past state chaplain). Republican. Reformed Jewish religion. Elk. B'nai B'rith (past pres. and past pres. Ohev Sholom Cong.). Clubs: Executives, Lions (past dir.), Cabell Republican, Guyan Country (Huntington). Home: 502 Tenth Av. Office: 3d Av. at 9th St., Huntington, W.Va.

ROMERA-NAVARRO, Miguel, prof. Spanish lang. and literature; b. Almeria, Spain, Sept. 29, 1888; s. Federico Romera y Martinez and Carmen Novarro de Estevan; ed. Instituto, Almeria, Spain (A.B., 1905); U. of Granada, Spain (1905-08); U. of Madrid, Spain, 1908-11 (LL.M.); U. of Pa., 1918-21 and 1924-27 (A.M., Ph.D.); m. Victoria Villacastin, July 14, 1923; children—Federico (dec.), Helen, Maria Victoria, Carmen. Came to U.S., 1912, naturalized, 1927. Began as a writer in Spain, 1908; sec. of moral and polit. sciences, Ateneo of Madrid, 1909-10; studied and lectured in France and Belgium, 1911-12; instr. of Romance langs., U. of Pa., 1916-21, asst. prof., 1921-27, prof. of Spanish since 1927; lecturer and visiting prof. at Spanish and Am. univs. Representative and lecturer of the U.S. Com. on Pub. Information in Spain, 1918-19. Awarded Jusserand Traveling Fellowship, 1922. Official del. of Spain to the Am. Library Assn., 1926. Mem. Real Academia Hispano-Americana, Real Academia de Ciencias Historicas de Toledo, Modern Lang. Assn. America. Catholic. Author: America Espanola, 1919; Manual Del Comercio, 1920; Historia de Espana, 1923; Historia de la Literatura Espanola, 1927; also several books pub. in Spain. Editor: Antologia de la Literatura Espanola, 1933; Baltasar Gracian-El Criticon, 1938. Contbr. to Spanish, Spanish-Am., French and Am. jours. Home: 4320 Chestnut St., Philadelphia, Pa.

RONEY, Harold Arthur, artist; b. Sullivan, Ill., Nov. 7, 1899; s. Hugh Lily and Josephine (Brosam) R.; ed. Chicago Acad. Fine Arts, 1919-20, Art Inst. of Chicago, 1920-23, Glenwood Sch. of Landscape Painting (Sundays), 1920-23; studied pvtly. under Aldrich, Folinsbee, Dawson-Watson, and Harry Leith-Ross; m. Nettie Taylor, June 4, 1924. Artist and landscape painter since 1924; exhibited at Southern States Art League, Washington, D.C., Artists Conn. Acad. Show, Tex. Fine Arts Assn. Show, Tex. Exhbn. at Chicago World's Fair; one man shows, Phila., San Antonio, Austin, etc.; represented by paintings in Art League, Austin, Tex., Witte Mus., San Antonio, Tex., Pub. Sch. Collections, South Bend, Ind., South West Texas Teachers Coll., San Marcos, Tex. and pvt. collections. Served as pvt. U.S.A., 3 mos., 1917-18. Mem. Southern States Art League, Texas Fine Arts Assn. Awarded Second Prize, South Bend, Ind., 1923; hon. mention, Tex. Women's Club Show, 1930. Democrat. Presbyn. Propr. Summer Art Camp and teaching landscape painting, June to Sept., Kerrville, Tex. Home: (winter) Lumberville, Pa.; s(ummer) Kerville, Tex.

RONON, Gerald, corpn. official; b. Phila., Pa., May 20, 1890; s. Andrew Thomas and Annie Mary (Fitzgerald) R.; B.S., in economics, Phila. Central High Sch., 1908; m. Isabel Greble Acker, Apr. 23, 1913; children—Anne Patricia (Mrs. James McCrea, Jr.), Gerald Patrick (dec.), Isabel Cecelia, Mary Virginia, Andrew Thomas. Admitted to Pa. bar, 1911, and became mem. firm Stradley, Ronon and Stevens; mgr. Beneficial Saving Fund Soc. of Phila.; dir. The Morris Plan Bank of Phila., The Morris

ROOK 751 ROOT

Plan Co. of Phila., General Cold Storage Co., Murphy Oil Co. of Pa., Anthracite Gas Co., Botfield Refractories Co., Andorra Nurseries, Inc., Phila., Towson (Md.) Nurseries, Inc. Trustee John J. Tyler Arboretum. Mem. Am., Pa. and Phila. bar assns., Catholic Philopatrian Literary Inst. Republican. Catholic. K.C. Clubs: Union League, Penn Athletic, Catholic (Phila.); Whitemarsh Valley Country, Seaview Golf (Absecon, N.J.). Home: 215 E. Gorgas Lane. Office: Packard Bldg., Philadelphia, Pa.

ROOK, Charles Alexander, journalist; b. Pittsburgh, Aug. 11, 1861; s. Alexander W. and Harriet L. (Beck) R.; ed. Ayers Latin Sch. and Western U. of Pa. (now U. of Pittsburgh); m. Anna B. Wilson, of Pittsburgh, Sept. 9, 1884. Became connected with Pittsburgh, Dispatch, 1880; sec., 1888-96, treas., 1896-1902, pres. and editor-in-chief same, 1902-23; dir. Dept. Pub. Safety, Pittsburgh, 1923-26. Served as dir. and mem. exec. com. Associated Press. On staff Gov. Stuart, with rank of lt. col., 1907; apptd. on staff of Gov. Brumbaugh, 1915; mem. bd. inspectors Western Penitentiary, Pa.; mem. State Prison Labor Commn., 1915; del.-at-large Rep. Nat. Conv., 1908. Apptd. by Pres. Taft E.E. and M.P. at One Hundredth Anniversary of Independence of U.S. of Mex., 1910; del. Nat. Rivers and Harbors Congress, 1907-23; del. Conf. on Conservation, The White House, 1908; rep. 31st Dist. of Pa. as elector of President and v.p., 1916; del. Rep. Nat. Conv., 1920. Episcopalian. Home: (winter) La Canáda, Calif. Office: The Dispatch Bldg., Pittsburgh, Pa.*

ROOKE, Robert Levi, mem. N.Y. Stock Exchance; b. Winfield, Pa., June 21, 1891; s. Charles Morris and Olive Susan R.; student Lewisburg (Pa.) High Sch., 1906-08, Bucknell Acad., 1908-09; B.S. in E.E., Bucknell U., 1913; m. Alice Clement Withington, Oct. 15, 1921; children—Robert Charles, Dorothy Anne, William Withington. Apprentice engr. General Electric Co., Schenectady, N.Y., 1913-15, Pub. Service Electric Co., Elizabeth, N.J., 1916-17; statistician Merrill Lynch & Co., New York, 1919-28, mem. firm, 1929; mem. firm E. A. Pierce & Co., New York, 1930-33; mem. New York Stock Exchange since 1928; dir. Westfield (N.J.) Home Bldg. & Loan Assn. Served in U.S. Navy, July 1917-Dec. 1918. Trustee Bucknell U., Y.M.C.A., Westfield, N.J. Mem. Sigma Alpha Epsilon. Presbyn. Mason. Clubs: Echo Lake Country (Westfield); Pine Valley (N.J.) Golf; Downtown Athletic (New York). Home: 929 Mt. View Circle, Westfield, N.J. Office: 40 Wall St., New York, N.Y.

ROON, Leo, pres. Roxalin Flexible Lacquer Co., Inc.; b. New York, N.Y., Aug. 6, 1892; s. Julius and Gizella (Goodman) R.; student Stuyvesant High Sch., New York, 1904-08; Ph.C., Columbia U., 1912; M.S., N.Y.U., 1916; m. Anna Marie Miesem, Oct. 24, 1917; children—Lois Anne, Donald. Began as chem. engr., New York, 1916; instr. in pharm. chemistry, Columbia U., 1912-15; instr. in chemistry, N.Y.U., 1915-16; with E. R. Squibb & Sons, Brooklyn, chief of chem. div., 1916-19; chem. consultant, 1919-24; pres. Roxalin Flexible Lacquer Co., Elizabeth, N.J., since 1924; dir. Nuodex Products Co., Nuodex Products of Can., Ltd. Mem. Am. Chem. Soc., Am. Inst. Chemists, Am. Soc. for Testing Materials, (fraternity:) Tau Epsilon Phi. Mem. Community Ch. (New York). Clubs: Chemists' (New York); Southold (N.Y.) Yacht. Home: 10 Overhill Rd., South Orange, N.J. Office: 800 Magnolia St., Elizabeth, N.J.

ROONEY, Arthur Joseph, sporting enterprises; b. Coulter, Pa., Jan. 27, 1901; s. Daniel and Margaret (Murray) R.; ed. Indiana Teachers Coll., 1918-20, Georgetown U., 1920-21, Duquesne U., 1921-25, B.C.S., 1925; m. Kathleen McNulty, June 2, 1931; children—Daniel Milton, Arthur Joseph, Timothy James and twins, Patrick Joseph and John Joseph. Played football, baseball, basketball for colls. while attdg.; had contracts with Boston Red Sox and Chicago Cubs baseball clubs! mgr. Wheeling, W.Va., club in Middle Atlantic League; held A.A.U boxing championship; coached sand lot football teams; propr. Pittsburgh Pirates, professional football club since 1933, pres. since 1933; pres. Braddock Brewing Co. since 1937; agt. for Pa. of Sika Products, and Plastiment Products; pres. Fort Pitt Waterproofing and Add Mix Co. Active in Rep. politics of North Side Mem. Phi Alpha Phi. Republican. Roman Catholic. K.C. Club: Civics. Home: 940 N. Lincoln Av. Office: Fort Pitt Hotel, Pittsburgh, Pa.

ROOP, William E., pastor, bishop; b. Meadow Branch, Md., Aug. 4, 1864; s. John D. and Mary (Senseney) R.; grad. with hon. mention, Meadow Branch Elementary Sch., 1881; A.B., Western Md. Coll., 1886, A.M., 1889; C.E., Yale U. Post Grad Sch., 1889; student Yale U. Div. Post Grad. Sch., 1889; m. Annie Bucher, June 17, 1890; children—John D., Lavenia C. (wife of Rev. Ezra Wenger), Ethel A., Earl W., Helen E. (Mrs. Harry I. Rinehart), Ruth A. (wife of Hon. Carroll S. Rinehart), Mary Elizabeth (dec.). Began as pub. sch. teacher, 1886; prof. mathematics and English, Bridgewater (Va.) Coll., 1888; city engr. Westminster City Council, 1890-1912; elected to ministry Ch. of the Brethren, headquarters at Elgin, Ill., 1893, and since in pastoral charge Meadow Branch congregations, Md.; ordained full ministry, 1910; bishop for Woodberry Congregation and Fulton Av. Congregation (now First Ch. of the Brethren), Baltimore; full charge as bishop Meadow Branch Congregation since 1925, and of Long Green Valley Congregation since 1910; elected pres. Westminster Deposit & Trust Co., 1932. First pres. Blue Ridge Coll. (now New Windsor, Md.), 1899-1902. Republican. Extensive traveller, including six months tour through Europe, Asia, Africa; also Mexico, Canada and Western U.S. Del. to Am. Bankers Assn. Convs. at Boston, 1937, Houston, Tex., 1938, Seattle, Wash., 1939. Has held revival meetings in many states. Address: Westminster, Md.

ROOSE, Robert Lisle, supervising prin. schs.; b. East Pittsburgh, Pa., Sept. 17, 1895; s. Arthur Eugene (M.D.) and Lena (Fox) R.; B.S., Otterbein Coll., Westerville, O., 1918; M.S. in Edn., Municipal U. of Akron, (O.), 1926; student O. State U., 1931; m. Vera Ann Stair, June 19, 1919; children—Robert Stair, Donald Dean. In employ Goodyear Tire & Rubber Co., Akron, O., 1919-20; foreman Diamond Match Co., Barberton, O., 1920-21; engaged in teaching pub. schs., 1921-28; sec. Portage Co. (O.) Y.M.C.A., 1928-31; supt. schs., Middlebranch, O., 1931-34; supervising prin. schs., Pitcairn, Pa., since 1934. Served as corpl. Field Signal Batln., U.S.A., 80th Div., with A.E.F., 1918-19. Awarded Eagle Scout, Boy Scouts of America. Kappa Delta Pi, Am. Legion. Republican. Mem. U. Brethren Ch. Mason. Club: Kiwanis. Home: 636 Sixth St., Pitcairn, Pa.

ROOSEVELT, Nicholas Guy, banker; b. Morristown, N.J., July 21, 1883; s. Nicholas Latrobe and Eleanor (Dean) R.; student St. Paul's Sch., Concord, N.H., 1898-1900; C.E., Princeton U., 1904; m. Emily Wharton Sinkler, June 15, 1916. Began in industrial work, 1904; engr. Dodge & Day, Phila., 1908, and successor company Day & Zimmermann Inc., v.p. from incorporation to 1928, chmn. bd. since 1929; partner W. H. Newbold's Son & Co., Phila., bankers, 1929-37, spl. partner since 1938; dir. United New Jersey R.R. & Canal Co. Trustee Univ. Hosp., Univ. Mus. Episcopalian. Clubs: Phila., Racquet, Midday (Phila.); India House (New York); Sunnybrook Golf (Whitemarsh, Pa.). Home: Ambler, Pa. Office: 1517 Locust St., Philadelphia, Pa.

ROOT, Harriet Trexler, librarian; b. Mount Joy, Lancaster Co., Pa.; d. Benjamin Mylin and Martha Elizabeth (Trexler) Root; student U. of Wis. Library Sch., Madison, Wis., 1916-17. Asst. Pottsville (Pa.) Free Pub. Library, 1915-16; 1st asst. branch librarian Carnegie Library, Pittsburgh, 1917-18, branch librarian, 1918-20; organizer Ind. State Library Commn., 1920-22; librarian Bethlehem (Pa.) Public Library since July 1923. V.p. Central Council for Social Service, 1938; mem. Community Chest Corporate Council; dir. and treas. Bethlehem Y.W.C.A. Mem. Am. Library Assn., Pa. Library Assn. (pres. 1937), Moravian Hist. Soc. Republican. Episcopalian. Clubs: Bethlehem Women's, Fortnightly Reading (Bethlehem, Pa.). Home: 30 E. Market St., Office: 11 W. Market St., Bethlehem, Pa.

ROOT, Ralph Eugene, coll. prof.; b. Grundy Co., Mo., July 18, 1879; s. Lewis Fletcher and Sarah Eleanor (Pollock) R.; B.S., Morningside Coll., Sioux City, Ia., 1905; M.S. State U. of Ia. Grad Coll., 1909; Ph.D., U. of Chicago, 1911; m. Mary K. Batcheller, Dec. 28, 1904; children—Olive M. (Mrs. Ralph Gibson Meader), Lloyd Eugene, Charlotte Marian, Ellis Pollock. Teacher high sch. Forest City, Ia., 1905-06; instr. mathematics, State U. of Ia., 1906-10; teaching fellow U. of Chicago, 1910-11; instr. mathematics, U. of Mo., 1911-13; instr. mathematics, U.S. Naval Acad., Annapolis, Md., 1913-14, prof. mathematics and mechanics, Postgrad. Sch., U.S. Naval Acad., since 1914. Mem. Am. Math. Soc., Math. Assn. of America, Soc. for Promotion Engrng. Edn. Republican. Methodist. Author: The Mathematics of Engineering, 1927; Dynamics of Engine and Shaft, 1932. Contbr. articles to math. jours. Home: 7 Franklin St., Annapolis, Md.

ROOT, Robert Kilburn, univ. dean; b. Brooklyn, Apr. 7, 1877; s. William Judson and Mary Louisa (Kilburn) R.; A.B., Yale, 1898, Douglas fellow, 1899-1900, Ph.D., 1902, hon. Litt.D., 1937; unmarried. Tutor in English 1900-03, instr., 1903-05, Yale; asst. prof. of English, 1905-16, prof. since 1916, dean of the faculty since 1933, Princeton. Actg. prof. English, Stanford U., summer, 1921. Lecturer on English, Harvard U., Feb.-June, 1927; visiting professor of English, Yale Univ., 1927-28. Mem. Modern Language Assn. America, Am. Assn. Univ. Profs.; fellow Mediæval Acad. America, Am. Acad. Arts and Sciences. Episcopalian. Democrat. Clubs: Century, Princeton (New York), Author: Classical Mythology in Shakespeare, 1903; The Poetry of Chaucer, 1906, 22; Manuscripts of Chaucer's Troilus, 1914; The Textual Tradition of Chaucer's Troilus, 1916; The Poetical Career of Alexander Pope, 1938. Translator: The Legend of St. Andrew, 1899. Editor: Ruskin's Sesame and Lilies, 1901; Specimen Extracts from the Unprinted Manuscripts of Chaucer's Troilus (with Sir William S. McCormick), 1914; Chaucer's Troilus and Criseyde, 1926; (with P. R. Lieder and R. M. Lovett) British Poetry and Prose (2 vols.), 1928, rev. 38; British Drama (with same), 1929; Letters of Lord Chesterfield to His Son, 1929; Pope's Dunciad Variorum, 1929; (with L. I. Bredvold and G. Sherburn) Eighteenth Century Prose, 1932. Contbr. to philological journals and various magazines. Commd. capt. Ordnance Dept., U.S.A., Dec. 15, 1917; aircraft armament officer, 1st Army A.E.F.; maj., Feb. 17, 1919; discharged, Mar. 17, 1919; service in France, Feb. 1918-Mar. 1919; maj. Ordnance Dept., U.S.R., 1919-29. Address: The Dean's House, Princeton, N.J.

ROOT, Thomas Scott, banking; b. Phila., Pa., June 21, 1876; s. Marcus Aurelius and Cecilia (Little) R.; A.B., Boys' Central High Sch., Phila., 1892; m. Helene Flounders, Jan. 16, 1911; 1 dau., Margaret Little (Mrs. Harvey A. Collins). Engaged in banking continuously since 1894; now v.p. First Nat. Bank of Phila. Republican. Presbyterian. Mason. Home: Somerton, Pa. Office: 315 Chestnut St., Philadelphia, Pa.

ROOT, William T(homas), psychologist; b. Concordia, Kan., June 2, 1882; s. William T. and Katherine (York) R.; grad. Los Angeles State Normal, 1905; A.B., Stanford, 1912, A.M., 1913, Ph.D., 1921; m. Ida May Nyce, June 27, 1914; 1 son, William Calvin. Instr. in psychology, Los Angeles State Normal, 1913-19; prof. psychology, U. of Pittsburgh, 1921-29, also head of dept. since 1929 and dean of the Graduate School since 1935. Trustee Western Penitentiary for Pa. Member Am. Psychol. Assn., Am. Statis. Assn., A.A.A.S., Phi Delta Kappa, Sigma Xi. Author: A Socio-Psychological Study of Fifty-three Supernormal Children, 1921; A Psychological and Educational Survey of 1916 Prisoners in the Western Penitentiary for Pa., 1927; Psychology for Life Insurance Underwriters, 1929. Contbr. articles to psychol. periodicals. Home: Valencia, Pa.*

ROPER, Lewis Murphree, clergyman; b. Laurens Co., S.C., Mar. 21, 1870; s. Levi Hudgens and Caroline (Mahaffey) R.; A.B., Furman U., S.C., 1891, A.M., 1892, D.D., 1905; A.B., Columbian (now George Washington) Univ., 1892; grad. Rochester Theological Seminary, 1896; m. Leonora Mauldin, Sept. 5, 1893; children—Leonora M. (Mrs. T. L. Harris), Helen C. (Mrs. H. M. Ferguson), Ruth Mahaffey (Mrs. J. L. Woodruff), Emily Wood (Mrs. P.B. Shamhart), William Hamilton, Lewis M. Ordained Bapt. ministry, Dec., 1888; preached to country chs. in S.C., 1888-91, while attending coll.; city missionary, Washington, 1891-92; supply pastor First Bapt. Ch., Attica, N.Y., 1892-95; pastor 1st Ch., Canton, O., 1896-1900, 1st Ch., Spartanburg, S.C., 1900-12, 1st Ch., Petersburg, Va., 1912-20, Central Bapt. Ch., Johnson City, Tenn., 1920-30, Waverly Ch., Jersey City, N.J., since 1930; also evangelical and radio service, Federated Churches of Greater New York, since 1930. Trustee Furman University, Anderson (South Carolina) Female Coll.; elected pres. Furman Univ., 1903, but declined; called to supply Met. Tabernacle, London (Spurgeon's old ch.), and accepted service for May, 1911. Frequent evangelistic services in Richmond, Baltimore, Boston and other places. Author of pamphlets and mag. articles. Lecturer before college and high sch. classes. Mem. exec. bd. Tenn. Bapt. Conv. Democrat. Mem. Sigma Alpha Epsilon. Home: 32 Booraem Av., Jersey City, N.J.*

RORER, Jonathan T(aylor), prin. high sch.; b. West Chester, Pa., Aug. 21, 1871; s. Jonathan and Helen V. (Bitting) T.; student Haverford (Pa.) Coll., 1890-92; A.B., Colo. Coll., Colorado Springs, Colo., 1895; Ph.D., U. of Pa., 1901; m. Mebel Marion Ballou, June 14, 1899. Engaged in grain bus., 1892-94; instr. English and mathematics, Colo. Coll., 1894-95; instr. mathematics, Central High School, Philadelphia, 1895-99, asst prof., 1899-1903, prof. 1903-09; head department mathematics, Wuham Penn High School, Philadelphia, 1909-39; head department mathematics, Benjamin Franklin High Sch., Phila., since 1939; prin. Central Evening High Sch., Phila., since 1921; summer sch. instr., Johns Hopkins U., 1920-22, 1926-27; liquidating trustee Lancaster Av. Bldg. & Loan Assn. Served as instr. in mathematics, S.A.T.C., U. of Pa., 1918, supt. instrn., Second Div., A.E.F., Germany, 1919. Fellow A.A.A.S. Mem. Am. Math. Soc., Am. Astron. Soc. Rittenhouse Astron. Soc. (past pres.), Franklin Inst., Phi Beta Kappa. Episcopalian. Club: Schoolmen's (Phila.). Contbr. articles to scientific and ednl. jours. Asso. editor Math. Teacher, 1908-11. Home: 333 N. 34th St. Office: Broad and Green Streets, Philadelphia, Pa.

RORER, Virgil Eugene, clergyman; b. Oak Lane, Phila., Pa., Mar. 18, 1867; s. David and Mary Felton (Bickley) R.; direct des. of George Rorer who with 5 other learned men and several rabbis assisted Martin Luther in translating the Old Testament into German; A.B., Central High Sch., Phila., 1886, A.M., 1891; LL.B., Yale, 1889; student Boston U. Sch. of Theology, Boston Sch. of Expression; D.D., Dickinson Coll., 1919; m. Nellie Minora Blakely, Feb. 11, 1892 (died Dec. 27, 1924); children—Dwight Eugene, Nelson Virgil, Adele Madelene. Taught sch. 2 yrs.; admitted to bar, 1889; entered M.E. ministry, Phila. Conf., 1890; pastor successively at Jenkintown and North Wales, Pa., St. Luke's Ch., 19th St., Wissahickon, 7th St., Grace and Arch St. chs., Phila., until 1920, Meridian St. Ch., Indianapolis, 1920-30, St. Paul's Ch., Wilmington, Del., 1930-33; retired to devote himself to writing, lecturing, travel, and preaching on special occasions. Built St. Luke's and Wissahickon chs. Republican. Clubs: Literary (Indianapolis); Yale. Address: 318 Sterling Rd., Elkins Park, Pa.

ROSANOFF, Martin André, chemist; b. Nicolaeff, Russia, Dec. 28, 1874; s. Abraham H. and Clara (Bertinskaya) R.; Imperial Classical Gymnasium, Nicolaeff, 1883-91; Ph.B., New York U., 1895; studied U. of Berlin, 1895-96, U. of Paris, 1896-98; research fellow, New York U., 1899-1900, Sc.D., 1908; m.

Louise, d. James K. Place, Feb. 2, 1901 (died Aug. 30, 1918); children—Boris Place, Elizabeth Place, Marian Place (dec.), James Keyes Place; m. 2d, Charlotte Adèle Walker, of Pittsburgh, Pa., Nov. 17, 1932. Editor for exact sciences, New Internat. Ency., 1900-03; research asst. to Thomas A. Edison, Orange, N.J., 1903-04; instr. theoretical chemistry, 1904-05, asst. prof., 1905-07, New York U.; head dept. of chemistry, and dir. chem. labs., Clark U. 1907-14; also prof. organic chemistry, Clark Coll., 1910-12; prof. chem. research, 1914-15, and head dept. of research in pure chemistry, 1915-19, Mellon Inst., U. of Pittsburgh; prof. chem. research, Duquesne U., since Sept. 1933, and dean of the graduate school since Sept. 1934; local research adminstr. office of edn., U.S. Dept. of Interior, 1936-37. Fellow Am. Acad. Arts and Sciences, A.A.A.S.; mem. Am. Chem. Soc. (Nichols medalist), Royal Soc. of Arts, Nat. Inst. Social Sciences, Phi Beta Kappa. Clubs: Chemists' (New York); Royal Societies (London). Contbr. to Jour. Am. Chem. Soc., Chem. News (London), Zeitschrift für physikalische Chemie (Leipzig). Administrative director of "Guide to the School Laws of Pennsylvania," 1938. Home: 124 Longuevue Drive, Mt. Lebanon, Pa. Office: Graduate Sch., Duquesne University, Pittsburgh, Pa.

ROSE, Albert Chatellier, highway engring.; b. Washington, D.C., Oct. 14, 1887; s. Albert Jones and Caroline Agnes (McCormick) R.; grad. Germantown Acad., Phila., Pa., 1905; B.S. in civil engring., U. of Wash., 1924, C.E., 1935; m. Ella Potts Lancaster, at Seattle, Wash., July 3, 1913; children—Elinor Katherine (Mrs. Joseph Hale Darby), Samuel Lancaster, Caroline Anne. Resident and locating engineer Wash. State Highway Dept., 1910-11; roadmaster Clatsop Co., Ore., 1914-19; highway engr. dist. office, U.S. Bur. of Public Roads, Portland, Ore., 1919-24; chief sec. of visual edn. in division of information, U.S. Bur. Pub. Roads, Washington, D.C., since 1924; engaged in preparation of exhibits, motion pictures, models, dioramas, etc., for road congresses, convs. and expns.; has designed model of Appian Way now on display Nat. Mus., Washington, D.C., also series of dioramas depicting 400 yrs. highway development in U.S. Mem. Tau Beta Pi (1913), Phi Kappa (local, now Psi Upsilon). Republican. Presbyterian. Author of govt. bulletins and reports. Home: 32 E. Woodbine St., Chevy Chase, Md. Office: Willard Bldg., Washington, D.C.

ROSE, Arthur Fisher, telephone engring.; b. Staten Island, N.Y., June 9, 1893; s. William Merson and Sarah (Fisher) R.; B.S. in E.E., cum laude, Colo. Coll., Colorado Springs, 1914; m. Edith Louise Conrad, May 21, 1917; children—Jean Louise, Alan Conrad, Neil Merson, Barbara. Asst. engr., Gen. Engring. Dept., Am. Telephone & Telegraph Co., 1914-19, engr. in Transmission Sect. of Operating & Engring. Dept. since 1919, now in charge of toll transmission matters. Mem. Am. Inst. Elec. Engrs., Inst. Radio Engrs., Acoustical Soc. America. Registered professional engr. in N.Y. State. Republican. Baptist. Clubs: Racquet (Short Hills, N.J.); Wyoming (Milburn, N.J.); Cedar Grove Beach (New Dorp, S.I.). Home: 92 Elm St., Maplewood, N.J. Office: 195 Broadway, New York, N.Y.

ROSE, Charles Bedell, asst. to pres. Baldwin Locomotive Works; b. Burton, Mich., Oct. 28, 1879; s. John Woodman and Eva Grace (Bedell) R.; student Mich. State Coll., 1899-1903; m. Lillian Love, of Detroit, Dec. 19, 1905; children—Charles B., Mary Love, Elizabeth G., Robert W. Chief draftsman Olds Motor Works, 1903-06; chief engr., v.p. and gen. mgr. Velie Motors Corpn., 1908-17; v.p. Moline Plow Co., 1919-24; v.p. and gen. mgr. Fageol Motors Co., 1924-26; pres. Am.-La. France & Foamite Corpn., 1927-36; also pres. Am.-La. France and Foamite Industries, Inc., La France-Republic Corpn.; chmn. bd. Linn Mfg. Corpn.; now v.p. Baldwin Locomotive Works. Served as capt. and lt. col. Army Air Service, 1917-19. Mem. Am. Soc. M.E., Soc. Automotive Engrs. Presbyn. Mason. Clubs: Lotos (New York); Racquet (Phila.); Merion Cricket (Haverford, Pa.); Chester (Chester, Pa.). Home: 1900 Ritten-

house Sq., Philadelphia, Pa. Office: Eddystone, Pa.

ROSE, Don, lawyer; b. Grove City, Pa., Feb. 8, 1881; s. Homer Jay and Margaret Jane (Shaw) R.; A.B., Princeton U., 1902; student U. of Pittsburgh Law Sch.; m. Jean Evans; children—John Evans, Margaret Shaw, Anne Allen (Mrs. John Kennedy Foster), Don, Jean Evans. Admitted to Pa. bar, 1905, and since practiced in Pittsburgh; partner Rose & Eichenauer; dir. Pittsburgh Coal Co. and subsidiaries, Colonial Trust Co. of Pittsburgh. Asst. dist. atty., Allegheny Co., 1910-12. Mem. Am. Bar Assn., Pa. Bar Assn., Allegheny Co. Bar Assn. Republican. Presbyterian. Mason (32°). Clubs: Duquesne, Pittsburgh, Edgeworth, Harvard-Yale-Princeton, Allegheny Country (Pittsburgh); Rolling Rock (Ligonier, Pa.). Home: 46 Beaver St., Sewickley, Pa. Office: Oliver Bldg., Pittsburgh, Pa.

ROSE, Donald Frank (Don Rose), journalist, lecturer; b. Street, Somerset, Eng., June 29, 1890; s. Frank Hodson and Mary Ann (Searle) R.; B.A., Acad. of the New Church, Bryn Athyn, Pa., 1914; student summers, Columbia U., and Oxford U., England; m. Marjorie Wells, June 13, 1914; children—Tryn, Leon Starkey, Roy Hodson, Muriel, Stanley Alan, Sylvia, John Wells, Marjorie Irene, Frank Shirley, Kenneth, Mildred Donette, Donald Leslie. Came to U.S., 1908, naturalized, 1922. Sch. teacher, 1914-25; free lance journalism and book reviewing, 1927-28; joined staff of Public Ledger, Phila., as editorial writer, 1928; daily columnist Evening Public Ledger since 1932; asso. editor North Am. Rev., 1927; contbg. editor Aero Digest, 1927-31. Author: Stuff and Nonsense—a Manual of Unimportances for the Middlebrow, 1927; Stuff and Nonsense Scrap Books (4 pamphlets); Don Rose's Hardy Perennial, 1937. Editor: Wings of Tomorrow—Story of the Autogiro (with Juan de la Cierva), 1931. Lecturer and after-dinner speaker. Home: Bryn Athyn, Pa. Address: Evening Public Ledger, Philadelphia, Pa.

ROSE, Edward, physician; b. Chattanooga, Tenn., Nov. 18, 1898; s. Edward and Minnie Lillian (Dobson) R.; M.D., U. of Pa., 1921; m. Elizabeth Kirk, July 6, 1929; children—Edward Kirk, William Elliott. Interne and res. phys., Presbyn. and U. of Pa. hosps., Phila., and Gen. Hosp., Cincinnati, O., 1921-24; engaged in practice of medicine specializing in internal medicine at Phila., Pa., since 1924; successively instr., asso. and asst. prof. clin. medicine, U. of Pa. Med. Sch.; staff phys. and chief endocrine sect., U. of Pa. Hosp.; cons. to res. and nursing staff, Children's Hosp. Served in S.A.T.C., 1918. Fellow Am. Coll. Physicians, Phila. Coll. Physicians; mem. Am., Pa. State, and Phila. Co. med. assns., Am. Clin. and Climatol. Assn., Am. Assn. for Study of Goiter, Sigma Xi, Phi Chi. Mason. Home: 426 Owen Rd., Wynnewood, Pa. Office: 255 S. 17th St., Philadelphia, Pa.

ROSE, Edward Clark, pub. service official; b. Trenton, N.J., Dec. 2, 1892; s. Burroughs S. and Stella (Skillman) R.; student Pa. State Coll.; m. Mabel E. Harper, Sept. 14, 1914; children—Jane (Mrs. James T. Wilson), Jacqueline, Edward Clark. With Brown Bros. and Edward C. Rose & Co., 1925-29; v.p., later pres. First Nat. Bank of Trenton, 1925-32; pres. and chmn. exec. com. First Mechanics Nat. Bank of Trenton, 1929-32; v.p. Pub. Service Corpn., Newark, N.J., since 1932; dir. Reading R.R. Co., Del. & Bound Brook R.R., Bucks Co. Contributionship, First Mechanics Nat. Bank. Served as capt., F.A., U.S. Army, A.E.F., 1918-19; brig. gen. commanding 69th F.A. Brig., N.J. N.G., since 1938. Mem. Phi Gamma Delta. Republican. Mason. Clubs: Trenton (N.J.); Nassau (Princeton, N.J.); Bankers (New York). Home: Harmony Hollow, Harbourton, N.J. Office: 80 Park Pl., Newark, N.J.

ROSE, Goodman Alikum, rabbi; b. Phila., Pa., Nov. 6, 1890; s. Solomon Sabthai and Esther Dinah (Jaffe) R.; grad. Central High Sch., Phila., 1908; grad. Phila. Sch. of Pedagogy, 1910; A.B., Temple U., 1917; rabbi, Jewish Theol. Sem. of America, 1921; m. Alta

Sarah Gilberg, Dec. 27, 1920; children—Pascal Benjamin, Ernest Daniel. Teacher elementary grades, 1910-17; rabbi Temple Bnai Israel, Brooklyn, N.Y., 1921-24; rabbi Congregation Beth Sholom, Pittsburgh, since 1924. Home: 5921 Hobart St., Pittsburgh, Pa.

ROSE, Grace Delphine, librarian; b. Meadville, Pa.; d. Luther A. and Viola Delphine (Sampson) R.; ed. public schs. and pvt. tutors; study in Germany, 6 mos.; ed. Drexel Inst. Library Sch., 1897-98. Asst. in Pub. Library, Buffalo, N.Y., 1898-1906; librarian Pub. Library, Davenport, Ia., 1906-20; librarian Pub. Library, Des Moines, Ia., 1920-27; librarian The Morristown Library, Morristown, N.J., since 1927; served as sec. N.Y. State Library Assn., 1902-03; pres. Ia. Library Assn., 1911-12. Served as librarian of Camp Bowie, Tex., 1918; organizer of Jr. Red Cross, Scott Co., Ia., 1917-19. Mem. Am. Library Assn., N.J. Library Assn., Morristown Bus. & Professional Woman's Club, Morristown Woman's Club, Old Colony Hist. Soc., Taunton, Mass. Republican. Presbyterian. Home: 41 Franklin St., Morristown, N.J.

ROSE, Harold J(ames), research chemist; b. Pierre, S.D., May 9, 1896; s. James Albert and Abbie Egbert (Higbee) R.; A.B., Yankton (S.D.) Coll., 1917, Sc.D., 1932; student U. of Chicago, 1916-17, Carnegie Inst. Tech., 1920-21; m. Emma Esther Lewis, Sept. 16, 1919; children—Elizabeth Cornelia, Philip Higbee, Donald Lewis, Margaret Emily, Lucile Jean, Vincent Harold, Lawrence Edward. Instr. in chemistry and physics, Yankton (S.D.) Coll., 1917; research chemist in charge of coal and coke div., The Koppers Co., Pittsburgh, 1918-25, asst. chief chemist, 1925-28, asst. dir. of research, 1928-30; dir. gen. lab. dept., Koppers Research Corpn., 1930-32; senior fellow, coke fellowship, Mellon Inst., Pittsburgh, 1930-32, industrial fellow, anthracite fellowship, since 1932. Chmn. tech. com. on coal classification, Am. Standards Assn.; chmn. tech. com. on coal classification and com. on gas coal specifications, Am. Soc. for Testing Materials; mem. American Inst. of Mining and Metallurgical Engrs., Am. Soc. of Heating and Ventilating Engrs., Am. Chem. Soc. (chmn. gas and fuel div.), Am. Gas Assn. (chmn. chemical com., com. on gas coal specifications). Congregationalist. Clubs: Chemists' (New York); Coal Research of America. Author of many tech. and scientific papers on solid fuels, coal carbonization and recovery and utilization of coal products. Granted many patents in U.S. and foreign countries. Home: 219 Lytton Av. Office: Mellon Institute, 4400 Fifth Av., Pittsburgh, Pa.

ROSE, Henry Reuben, clergyman; b. Phila., Pa., Oct. 22, 1866; s. David Henry and Emma Frances (Longaker) R.; student Tufts Coll. and Harvard; B.D., Tufts Div. Sch., 1891, S.T.D., 1935; D.D., St. Lawrence U., 1916; m. Ida Louise Jones, Apr. 4, 1893; children—Dorothy (dec.), Edith Lydia (Mrs. Andrew Wilson, Jr.), Henry Brooks, David Kenneth. Ordained ministry Universalist Ch., 1891; pastor Portsmouth, N.H. and Auburn, Me., until 1898, Newark, N.J., 1898-1929, pastor emeritus since 1929. V.p. Newark Bur. Asso. Charities 25 yrs. Trustee U. of Newark. Mem. Pa. Soc. of N.J., Delta Tau Delta. Republican. Mason; Past Grand Chaplain Grand Lodge of Masons of N.J., Odd Fellow. Clubs: Wednesday (Newark); Essex Country (East Orange, N.J.); City History Club (New York); Colony Club (Harpswell Harbor, Maine). Author: Good Sense in Religion, 1897; The Outside of the Cup, 1914; If I Were 21, 1918; Hungerings of the Human Soul, 1919; The Road to Happiness, 1920. Widely known as lecturer on psychology, the drama, travel, biography and history. Has 15,000 lantern slides. Address: Box 644, Newark, N.J.

ROSE, Howard Smith, executive; b. New York, N.Y., Feb. 11, 1887; s. William Augustus and Catherine Latham (Smith) R.; student pub. grade and high schs., New York, 1892-1901; m. Elizabeth Theresa Malloy, June 29, 1910; children—Howard Cornelius, Betty Jane (dec.), Helen (Mrs. Robert D. Jackson), Thomas Smith, Nancy. Began as messenger, 1902; held various clerkships, 1902-19; asst. treas. and asst. sec. United Natural Gas Co., Oil City, Pa., 1920-27, sec.-treas. and dir. since 1927; sec.-treas. and dir. The Mars Co., Ridgway Natural Gas Co., St. Marys Natural Gas Co., Smethport Natural Gas Co., The Sylvania Corpn; v.p., treas. and dir. Rose Ice Cream Co. Director Oil City Gen. Hosp., Venango Co. Crippled Children's Soc. Republican. Clubs: Kiwanis, Oil City Boat (Oil City, Pa.); Wanango Country (Oil City, Pa.). Home: 117 W. 3d St. Office: 308 Seneca St., Oil City, Pa.

ROSE, Ivan Murray, clergyman; b. Hebron, N.S., Canada, Dec. 29, 1888; s. Edson A. and Bessie J. Rose; A.B., Acadia Univ. (N.S.), 1911, M.A., 1915, D.D., 1929; student Rochester Theol. Sem., 1915-18; m. Mildred B. Rose, of Lake George, N.S., Sept. 3, 1912; children—Robert B., Murray L. Came to U.S., 1915, naturalized, 1925. Ordained Bapt. ministry, 1912; successively minister in N.S., 1912-15, at Malone, N.Y., 1918-22, Rome, N.Y., 1922-25, First Bapt. Ch., Phila., Pa., since 1925. Mem. Gen. Council Northern Bapt. Conv. since 1934. Republican. Club: Union League. Home: 530 Glenwood Road, Merion, Pa. Address: 17th and Sansom Sts., Philadelphia, Pa.

ROSE, Mary D. Swartz (Mrs. Anton Richard Rose), nutrition expert; b. Newark, O., Oct. 31, 1874; d. Hiram B. and Martha (Davies) Swartz; B.Litt., Denison U., Granville, O., 1901; student Mechanics Inst., Rochester, N.Y., 1902; B.S., Teachers Coll. (Columbia), 1906; Ph.D., Yale, 1909; m. Anton Richard Rose, Sept. 15, 1910. Teacher in high sch., Wooster, O., 1899-1901, Fond du Lac, Wis., 1902-05; asst. in Dept. of Nutrition, Teachers Coll., 1906-07; traveling fellow, 1907-09; instr. in nutrition, 1909-11, asst. prof., 1910-1918, associate professor, 1918-1921, professor, since 1921, Teachers College, Columbia University. Dept. dir. Bur. of Conservation, Federal Food Board and N.Y. State Commn., 1918-19. Fellow A.A.A.S.; mem. American Society Biological Chemists, American Physiol. Soc., Soc. Experimental Biology and Medicine, Institute of Nutrition, Harvey Society, Sigma Xi; fellow of American Public Health Association. Mem. Nutrition Commn. of Health Orgn. of League of Nations, 1935—, Council on Foods of A.M.A., 1933—; pres. Am. Inst. of Nutrition, 1937-38. Author: Nutrition Investigations on the Carbohydrates of Lichens, Algæ, and Related Substances, 1911; Laboratory Handbook for Dietetics, 1912, 4th edit., 1937; Feeding the Family, 1916, 3d Edit., 1929; Everyday Foods in War Time, 1918; Foundations of Nutrition, 1927, 3d edit., 1938; Teaching Nutrition to Boys and Girls, 1932. Home: Edgewater, N.J.

ROSE, Philip Sheridan, editor; b. Allendale Center, Mich., July 13, 1872; s. William and Susanna (Sheridan) R.; B.S. in Mechanical Engring., Mich. State Agrl. Coll., 1899; m. Belle Ghering, 1897; children—Donald Ghering, Douglas R., Kathryn. Became mem. engring. faculty, N.Dak. Agrl. Coll., 1900, and prof. steam and exptl. engring., 1906-09; asso. editor The American Thresherman, 1909-17, also editor Gas Review, 1909-17; asso. editor Country Gentleman, feature article writer and editorial writer, 1917-27, editor in chief since 1927. One of pioneers in agricultural engineering education, especially short practical college courses. Charter mem. Am. Soc. Agrl. Engrs.; mem. Tau Beta Pi. Republican. Congregationalist. Mason. Author: Clarke's School of Traction Engineering, 1908; The Thresher's Guide (vols. 1 and 2), 1910, 11; also article "Farm Motors" in Bailey's Cyclo. of Agr., 1906. Home: 640 Ardmore Av., Ardmore, Pa. Address: The Curtis Publishing Co., Philadelphia, Pa.

ROSE, Robert E(vstafieff), dir. tech. lab., E. I. du Pont de Nemours & Co. Office: Du Pont Bldg., Wilmington, Del.

ROSE, Roy, lawyer; b. Parkers Landing, Pa., June 16, 1885; s. Homer Jay and Margaret Jane (Shaw) R.; student Sewickley Grade and High Sch.; LL.B., U. of Pittsburgh Sch. of Law; m. Ruth Hall Richardson, Oct. 9, 1914; children—Jean Cameron, Ruth Hall, Homer Jay. Admitted to Pa. bar, and since practiced in Pittsburgh; mem. Rose, Bechman & Dunn, gen. law practice; dir. Sewickley Valley Trust Co., Miller Printing Machinery Co. Pres. Commrs. of Sewickley Water Works. Republican. Presbyterian. Mason. Clubs: Edgeworth, Allegheny Country (Pittsburgh). Home: 213 Centennial Av., Sewickley, Pa. Office: 1108 Commonwealth Bldg., Pittsburgh, Pa.

ROSE, Russell Kellogg, petroleum products exec.; b. Mountainview, N.J., Feb. 25, 1890; s. Lewis Russell and Margaret Bruce (MacIntyre) R.; student Winchester Sch., New Haven, Conn., 1895-98, Summer Av. Sch., Newark, N.J., 1899-1903, Newark (N.J.) High Sch., 1903-07; m. Ethel May Bigelow, June 1, 1916; children—Jane Eleanor (Mrs. Harry Fallows), Margaret Virginia. Began as runner, Nat. Bank of Commerce, New York, 1907; with Nat. Newark-Essex Banking Co., Newark, N.J., 1909-10; clerk Federal Trust Co., Newark, N.J., 1910-12; bookkeeper, teller, etc., First Nat. Bank of Belleville (N.J.), 1912-22, cashier, 1922-24; v.p. Peoples Nat. Bank & Trust Co. of Belleville (N.J.), 1924-36; special rep. Crown Oil Co. of Harrison (N.J.) since 1936, Reinauer Bros., Lyndhurst, N.J., since 1936; asst. treas. Central Bldg. & Loan Assn. Treas. Am. Red Cross; mem. Belleville (N.J.) Police Fire Pension Fund. Republican. Mason. Clubs: Nereid Boat, Lions (organizer; hon. mem.), Rotary (Belleville, N.J.). Home: 30 Rossmore Pl., Belleville, N.J. Office: 2 Passaic Av., Harrison, N.J.

ROSE, William Palen (Will Rose), writer, newspaper pub.; b. Woodstock, N.Y., Mar. 17, 1889; s. Abram Dubois and Mary (Palen) R.; prep. sch., Kingston (N.Y.) Acad.; A.B., Cornell U., 1911; m. Jennie Louise Lamberson, June 14, 1913; 1 dau., Jeannette Louise. Began in employ Lord & Thomas Adv. Agency, Chicago, 1911; successively with Suburban Life Mag. (New York), Erie (Pa.) Herald, Washington Post and Washington Times until 1916; pub. Cambridge Springs (Pa.) Enterprise-News since 1916, also Union City Times-Enterprise. Mem. of Greater Pa. Council, 1931-34. Winner Rep. Congl. Primary, 29th Pa. Dist., 1934, 1936. Rep. candidate for State Senate, 1926; chmn. Crawford County (Pa.) Young Rep. Com., 1935. Pres. board of trustees Cambridge Pub. Schs. Mem. Pa. Newspaper Publishers Assn. (v.p. 1935), Sigma Nu, Pi Gamma Mu and Pi Delta Epsilon fraternities. Mem. Dutch Reformed Church. Mason (32°), K.P., Elk. Clubs: Rotary (pres. 1929), University; co-founder Cornell U. Dramatic Club, 1908. Known as exponent of advantages of residence and individually owned business in American small towns. Contbr. to Scribner's and other mags. Home: Cambridge Springs, Pa.

ROSE, Willis Miley, corpn. official; b. Grand Rapids, Mich., Jan. 17, 1886; s. Henry Martin and Mary Gertrude (Miley) R.; student Howe (Ind.) Sch., 1900-04, Brown U., Providence, R.I., 1904-06; B.Arch., Cornell U., 1910; m. Hildegarde Owen, May 30, 1915; children—Gilbert White, Henry Martin III, Hildegarde Owen, Dorothy Dunham. Became constrn. foreman F. A. Jones Bldg., Co., Houston, Tex., 1910; now pres. and gen. mgr., Sun Tube Corpn. (Hillside, N.J.), Gen. Extrusion Corpn. (Hillside, N.J.), pres. Engring. Investors Corpn. (Newark, N.J.); dir. Hillside (N.J.) Nat. Bank. Mem. Delta Phi. Republican. Episcopalian. Clubs: Bay Head (N.J.) Yacht; Montclair (N. J). Home: 208 N. Mountain Av., Montclair, N.J. Office: Sun Tube Corpn., Hillside, N.J.

ROSEBORO, Francis Brown, clergyman; b. Lewisburg, W.Va., June 15, 1883; s. John William and Frances Brown (Smith) R.; A.B., Fredericksburg Coll., 1903; A.B., Johns Hopkins U., 1907; unmarried. Ordained to ministry P.E. Ch., deacon, 1911, priest, 1912; master Hoosac Sch., Hoosick, N.Y., 1907-14; Episcopal Chaplain, Yale Univ., 1914-24; asst. St. Paul's Ch., Brooklyn, N.Y., 1925-30; vicar, St. Elisabeth's Ch., Phila., Pa., since 1930. Served as chaplain, U.S.A., 1917-19. Mem. Alpha Delta Phi. Democrat. Episcopalian. Clubs: Penn Athletic (Philadelphia); Alpha Delta Phi Club (New York City). Home: 1606 Mifflin St., Philadelphia, Pa.

ROSECRANS, Egbert, lawyer; b. Hoboken, N.J., Oct. 7, 1891; s. Dr. James Hankinson and Maja (Lowell) R.; ed. Hoboken public schools, Blair Acad., Blairstown, N.J., Wesleyan U., Conn., and New York Law Sch.; m. Edith Wilson, June 4, 1914 (died July 27, 1926); 1 dau., Constance; m. 2d, Aileen Rittenhouse, Feb. 15, 1931 (divorced July 24, 1936); 1 dau., Rhonda Rittenhouse. Admitted to bars of N.J., 1913, Calif., 1923, Nev., 1923, U.S. Supreme Court, 1923; began practice in Blairstown, N.J.; county counsel Warren Co., N.J., 1917, 1921-23; municipal accountant for N.J., 1918-21; counsel and special counsel for various municipal and county govts.; counsel for N.J. commr. of banking and ins., 1931-36; pres. judge Court of Common Pleas, Warren Co., N.J., since Apr. 1, 1938; special master in chancery and N.J. Supreme Court commr.; asso. counsel in defense of Hauptman in Lindbergh Kidnaping trial, 1935, and leading counsel upon the appeals; mem. law faculty, John Marshall Coll., N.J., 1938-39. Chmn. com. of judges designated by chancellor for revision of N.J. Orphan's Court rules, 1938-39; mem. N.J.-U.S. Constitution Commn. Mem. Am. Bar Assn., N.J. State Bar Assn. (gen. council), Warren County Bar Assn. (pres. 1939, trustee), Nev. and Calif. State bar assns., Soc. Sons of Revolution. Democrat. Presbyn. Home: Highroads, Blairstown, N.J. Office: Blairstown Court House, Belvidere, N.J.

ROSEN, Ben, educator; b. Baltimore, Md., May 16, 1894; s. Solomon and Rachel (Zavadie) R.; student Baltimore, Md., City Coll., 1908-11, Johns Hopkins U. Baltimore, Md., 1911-14; student Teachers Inst. of Jewish Theol. Sem., 1915-18; B.S., Teachers Coll., Columbia U., 1915, M.A., 1918; Ed.M., Harvard, 1921; m. Susan Hurwich, Sept. 5, 1920; children—Judah Ben Zion, Joy Harriet, Miriam. Principal of Florence Marshall Girl's Sch., Bureau of Jewish Edn., New York, N.Y., 1915-19; supervisor of instrn., and lecturer in pedagogy, Bureau of Jewish Edn., Boston, Mass., 1919-21; dir. of Ednl. Group, Federation of Jewish Charities, Phila., 1921-24; director Associated Talmud Torahs since 1924; dir. of surveys of Jewish edn., New York, Cleveland, Detroit, Baltimore, Rochester, etc. Served as sergt., 1st class, Ordnance Dept., 1918-19. Mem. Nat. Edn. Assn., Nat. Council for Jewish Edn., Nat. Council of Jewish Social Welfare, Phi Delta Kappa. Jewish religion. Club: Harvard (Phila.). Supervising editor, Jewish Current News since 1927; editor in chief, Jewish Education, since 1934. Home: 8319 High School Rd., Elkins Park, Pa. Office: 330 S. 9th St., Philadelphia, Pa.

ROSEN, Theodore, judge; b. Carmel, N.J., Sept. 20, 1895; s. Isaac and Esther (Rubin) R.; B.Sc., Rutgers U., 1916; LL.B., U. of Pa. Law Sch., 1922; hon. LL.D., Phila. Coll. of Law, 1935; m. Esther Van Leer Katz (Ph.D.), Mar. 9, 1924. Admitted to Pa. bar, 1921, and since engaged in gen. practice of law at Phila.; asst. dist. atty. Phila. Co., 1926-31; apptd. judge Municipal Ct., 1931, elected full term, 1931; elected judge Ct. Common Pleas No. 2 for term beginning Jan. 1938. Served in first O.T.C., 1917; commd. 2d lieut., then 1st lieut. inf. U.S.A., served 1917-19. Comdr. post Am. Legion (comdr. Phila. County Am. Legion, 1929-30). Pres. Rutgers Alumni Assn. since 1938; trustee Rutgers Alumni Fund Council. Dec. D.S.C.; Div. Citation; Medal Merit 315th Inf.; Mil. Order Purple Heart. Vice-pres. Mt. Sinai Hosp. Dir. Crime Prevention Assn. of Phila., Legal Aid Soc., Big Brother Assn., Pa. Sch. of Social Work, Juvenile Aid Soc., Eagleville Sanatorium and Hosp., Nat. Farm Sch.; civilian aide to U.S. sec. of war for Pa., 1922-26. Mem. Am., Pa. State, and Phila. bar assns., Phi Epsilon Pi, Phi Delta Phi. Republican. Jewish religion. Elk. Moose. Clubs: Penn Athletic, Locust, Green Valley Country (Philadelphia); Ashbourne Country (Elkins Park). Home: 239 W. Allen Lane. Office: 390 City Hall, Philadelphia, Pa.

ROSENAU, William, rabbi, prof. emeritus; b. Wollstein, Germany, May 30, 1865; s. Nathan and Johanna (Braun) R.; brought to U.S., 1876; rabbi Hebrew Union Coll., Cincinnati, 1889, D.H.L., 1923; B.A., U. of Cincinnati, 1888; Ph.D., Johns Hopkins U., 1900; m. Mabel Hellman, Aug. 2, 1893 (dec.); children—Marguerite Helen (Mrs. Carl Jackson Kiefer), William Hellman (dec.); m. 2d, Myra Kraus, July 8, 1925. Rabbi Temple Israel, Omaha, Neb., 1889-92, Oheb Shalom Congregation (Eutaw Place Temple), Baltimore, since 1892; instr., Johns Hopkins U., 1902-05, associate, 1905-15, asso. prof., 1915-32, prof. emeritus since 1932. Mem. Jewish Welfare Bd., Bd. of Edn., Baltimore, Com. for Higher Edn. of Negroes of Md., Md. Commn. on State Aided Colls.; vice chancellor and chancellor Jewish Chautauqua Soc.; mem. bd. Jewish Home for Consumptives, Baltimore, Associated Jewish Charities of Baltimore, Commn. of Jewish Edn. Served as sec. and pres. Central Conf. of Am. Rabbis. Author: Hebraism in Authorized Version of Bible; Jewish Ceremonial Institutions and Customs, Jewish Biblical Commentators, The Rabbi in Action; Ancient Oriental Academies, Seder Hagadah; etc. Home: Esplanade Apts. Address: 1307 Eutaw Pl., Baltimore, Md.

ROSENBACH, Abraham S. Wolf, writer, bibliographer; b. Phila., July 22, 1876; s. Morris and Isabella (Polock) R.; B.S., University of Pennsylvania, 1898, Ph.D., 1901, hon. D.A.E. from same, 1927; unmarried. Sec. The Rosenbach Co., dealers in rare books and manuscripts. Pres. Gratz Coll.; mem. bd. govs. Dropsie Coll.; trustee Free Library, Phila.; pres. Am. Jewish Hist. Soc., Philobiblon Club, Am. Friends of Hebrew Univ. of Palestine, Pa. Library Club; asso. trustee and member of Board of Graduate Education and Research, University of Pa. Mem. Historical Society of Pa. (council), N.Y. Hist. Soc., Grolier Club, Am. Antiquarian Soc., Am. Philos. Soc., Bibliog. Soc. London, Shakespeare Assn. America (pres.). Founder fellowship in bibliography at U. of Pa., 1930. Editor: (with Austin Dobson) Dr. Johnson's Prologue, 1898. Compiler: Catalogue of the Books and Manuscripts of Robert Louis Stevenson in the Library of the Late Harry Elkins Widener, 1913; Catalogue of the Widener Memorial Library in Harvard College, 1918, etc. Contbr. various articles on lit. topics. Author: The Unpublishable Memoirs, 1917; An American Jewish Bibliography, 1926; Books and Bidders, 1927; The All-Embracing Doctor Franklin, 1932; Early American Children's Books, 1933; The Libraries of the Presidents of the U.S., 1934; A Book Hunter's Holiday, 1936. Home: 2006 De Lancey St., Philadelphia, 15 E. 51st St., New York, N.Y., and Strathmere, Corson's Inlet, N.J. Office: 1320 Walnut St., Philadelphia, Pa.*

ROSENBACH, Joseph Bernhardt, prof. of mathematics; b. New York, N.Y., Oct 5, 1897; s. Louis and Anne (Wohlgemuth) R.; student Albuquerque (N.M.) High Sch., 1911-14, Poly. Inst. of Brooklyn, 1914-15; A.B., U. of N.M., Albuquerque, N.M., 1917; grad. student U. of Colo., Boulder, Colo., summer 1917; M.S., U. of Ill., Urbana, Ill., 1919, grad. student, 1918-20; m. Florence Roberta Simon, June 3, 1924; children—Loren Marshall, Ronald Neil. Instr. of mathematics, U. of N.M., Albuquerque, N. M., 1917-18, U. of Ill., Urbana, Ill., 1918-20; instr. of mathematics, Carnegie Inst. Tech., 1920-23, asst. prof., 1923-28, asso. prof., 1928-35, prof. since 1935, in charge evening degree courses in mathematics in Coll. of Engring. since 1933; engr. of maintenance Atchison, Topeka & Santa Fe Ry., summers 1915, 16, 21. Fellow A.A.A.S.; mem. Am. Math. Soc., Math. Assn. America, Cirolo Matematico di Palmero, Sigma Xi, Phi Kappa Phi, Zeta Beta Tau; hon. mem. Beta Sigma Rho. Republican. Jewish religion. Author: College Algebra (with E. A. Whitman), 1933, rev. edit., 1939; Plane Trigonometry (with E. A. Whitman and David Moskovitz), 1937; Plane and Spherical Trigonometry (with E. A. Whitman and David Moskovitz), 1937; Mathematical Tables (with E. A. Whitman and David Moskovitz), 1937. Home: 2550 Beechwood Boul., Pittsburgh, Pa.

ROSENBAUM, Leon, retired broker; b. Phila., Pa., July 10, 1874; s. Simon and Mathilde (Rau) R.; student Central High Sch., Phila., 1886-89, Pierce Business Coll., Phila., 1889 and 1901, Palmer's Business Coll., Phila., 1889-1901; m. Josephine Buka, Sept. 26, 1916 (died 1934); children—Emilie Leona (Mrs. Lucien Katzenberg), Leon. With J. Jacob Shannon & Co., Phila., since 1889, successively as employee, sec.-treas. and pres. and treas. to 1936; retired in 1936; mem. Phila. Stock Exchange since 1914. Dir. and trustee Nat. Farm Sch. Republican. Jewish religion (dir. and trustee Reformed Congregation Keneseth Israel). Home: 6803 N. 12th St. Office: 1417 Walnut St., Philadelphia, Pa.

ROSENBAUM, Morris, pres. Rosenbaum Bros.; b. Cumberland, Md., July 5, 1880; s. Simon and Fredericka (Nathan) R.; student Allegany Co. Acad., Cumberland, Md., 1886 to 1897; B.S., Lafayette Coll., 1901; m. Esther J. Bamberger, Aug. 22, 1918; children—Ruth Lenore, Simon II, Stuart N., Esther Louise. Entered father's store immediately after graduation from Lafayette (store in family since 1848); pres. Rosenbaum Bros., Inc., department store, since 1901; dir. Community Baking Co., Liberty Trust Co. Leader in Community Chest drive; mem. War Chest; dir. Associated Charities, Memorial Hosp. Awarded Silver Beaver, Boy Scouts of America. Mem. Phi Delta Theta. Republican. Jewish religion. Clubs: Cumberland Rotary (pres.), Cumberland Country. Home: The Dingle. Office: Baltimore St., Cumberland, Md.

ROSENBAUM, Samuel Rawlins, lawyer; b. Phila., Pa., Sept. 28, 1888; s. Morris and Hannah (Rottenberg) R.; B.A., Central High Sch., Phila., 1906; B.S., U. of Pa., 1910, LL.B., Law Sch., 1913, LL.M., 1917; student Inns of Court, London, 1913-15; m. Rosamond May Rawlins, of Parkstone, Dorset, England, Oct. 8, 1913 (died 1924); children—Jack Henry Rawlins, Rosamond Margaret (Mrs. Lewis A. Riley III), Hugh Samuel (dec.), Heather May; m. 2d, Edna Phillips, of Reading, Pa., May 17, 1933; children—Joan Davies, David Hugh. Admitted to Pa. bar, 1913, and since practiced at Phila.; pres. WFIL Broadcasting Co., Phila., since 1934; v.p. and dir. Bankers Securities Corpn., Albert M. Greenfield & Co., Bankers Bond & Mortgage Co.; dir. Lit Bros.; asst. to Judge Advocate Gen., U.S. Army, 1917. Asst. U.S. atty., Phila., 1918-19; asst. city solicitor, Phila., 1920-24. Vice-pres. Phila. Orchestra Assn.; pres. Robin Hood Dell Concerts, 1939. Member Banking Bd. of Pa., 1936-39, Am., Pa. and Phila. bar assns., Ind. Radio Networks Affiliates (chmn. since 1938). Author: The Rule-Making Authority in the English Supreme Court, 1917; The English County Courts, 1916; Commercial Arbitration in England, 1916. Home: 3240 School House Lane. Office: 200 Bankers Securities Bldg., Philadelphia, Pa.

ROSENBERG, Albert S., lawyer; b. Scranton, Pa., Dec. 20, 1891; s. Louis and Deborah (Aronson) R.; ed. U. of Pa. Wharton Sch. Accts. and Finance, 1911-13; LL.B., U. of Pa. Law Sch., 1916; unmarried. Admitted to Pa. bar, 1917 and since engaged in gen. practice of law at Scranton; asst. city solicitor, Scranton, Pa., 1926-33; mem. firm Rosenberg Bros., clothiers, Scranton, Pa., since 1934. Served in 19th F.A., U.S.A., 1917-19, with A.E.F.; mem. Jewish Welfare Bd. Overseas, 1919-20. Del. Rep. Nat. Conv., Cleveland, O., 1936. Vice-chmn. legal aid com. Pa. Dept. Am. Legion. Mem. Sigma Alpha Mu, Jewish War Vets., Am. Legion, Forty and Eight, Purple Club, Y.M.H.A. Republican. Jewish religion (Conservative). Mason (32°, Shriner), Elk, Eagle, B'nai B'rith (pres. 1939). Club: Elks of Scranton (trustee). Home: 616 N. Washington Av. Office: 606 Connell Bldg., Scranton, Pa.

ROSENBERG, Jacob Ellis, chemist, ceramist; b. Cere, Russia, Oct. 28, 1897; s. Samuel and Minnie (Vishasky) R.; brought to U.S., 1905, naturalized, 1917; A.B., M.S., U. of Mich., 1921; Ph.D., U. of Pittsburgh, 1925; m. Sarah R. Saul, June 1, 1926; children—Frada Miriam, David Ellis, Marcia Esse, Joel Harry. Began as chemist, 1921; asst. in chemistry U. of Pittsburgh, 1922-25; research chemist Gas Industries Co., 1926-27, U.S. Glass Co., 1927-28; prof. of physics, Duquesne U. since 1929; dir. of research O. Hommel Co. since 1930. Trustee Zionist Organization of America. Mem. Am. Chem. Soc., Am. Phys. Soc., Am. Ceramic Soc., Kappa Nu. Hebrew religion. Specialties, porcelain enameling, ceramic colors. Home: 789 Academy Place. Office: 209 4th Av., Pittsburgh, Pa.

ROSENBERG, Milton Maurice, physician; b. Scranton, Pa., Oct. 5, 1894; s. Louis and Deborah (Aronson) R.; M.D., U. of Pa. Med. Sch., 1919; grad. study U. of Vienna, Austria, 1925-26, New York Eye & Ear Hosp., 1927, Polyclinic of New York, 1933; unmarried. Resident phys., Scranton (Pa.) State Hosp., 1919-20, chief resident phys., 1920-21; vis. chief, eye, ear, nose and throat dept., State Hosp., St. Mary's Hosp., Hahnemann Hosp., Mercy Hosp., West Side Hosp. Served in Med. Res., U.S.A., during World War. Capt. Med. Dept., 109th inf., Pa. N.G., since 1926. Mem. Lackawanna Co. Med. Soc. (sec.-treas., 1929-33, pres. 1933-34), Phi Delta Epsilon, Am. Legion, Forty and Eight, Jewish War Vets. Fellow Am. Coll. Surgs. Pres. Y.M.H.A., 1928. Republican. Jewish religion. Mason (32°, Shriner). I.O.O.F. B'nai B'rith. Elk. Home: 616 N. Washington Av. Office: 327 N. Washington Av., Scranton, Pa.

ROSENBERG, Samuel, artist; b. Phila., Pa., June 28, 1896; s. Solomon and Anna (Dickstein) R.; A.B., Carnegie Inst. Tech., 1926; m. Libbie Levin, Dec. 24, 1922; 1 son, Murray Zale. Art instr. Irene Kaufmann Settlement, Pittsburgh, Pa., 1917-27; asst. prof. art, Carnegie Inst. Tech. since 1926; art dir., Y.M.H.A., Pittsburgh, since 1926; art instr., Pa. Coll. for Women, since 1937. Exhibited: Mus. of Modern Art, N.Y.; Whitney Mus., N.Y.; Corcoran Gallery, Washington, D.C.; Art Inst., Chicago; Pa. Acad., Phila.; Albright Gallery, Buffalo, N.Y.; Carnegie International (7 yrs.); Asso. Artists of Pittsburgh (25 yrs.); Butler Art Inst., Youngstown, O.; Carnegie Inst., Pittsburgh (one-man show, 1937); New York World's Fair, San Francisco World's Fair. Prin. works: Dr. Julius Koch, U. of Pittsburgh; Judge Thompson, Pittsburgh; Dr. Carhart, U. of Pittsburgh; Dr. Davis, Davis Sch., Pittsburgh; Dr. E. J. McCague, Fox Chapel, Pa.; Isaac Seder, Pittsburgh; P. J. Byrne, Pittsburgh. Principal paintings: Man-made Desert, Gazzem's Hill, God's Chillun, Fruit Market, Conversation, Fruit and Logan Street, Circus, Watermelon Market, Monday Morning. Vice-pres. Asso. Artists of Pittsburgh since 1937. Awarded Pittsburgh Asso. Artists 2d honor, 1917, 1st honor, 1920, portrait prize, 1921; Art Soc. of Pittsburgh prize, 1928, 2d honor, 1929, 1st honor, 1936; Carnegie group prize, 1935. Jewish religion. Home: 340 Coltart Av. Office: Carnegie Inst. of Technology, Pittsburgh, Pa.

ROSENBERGER, Randle Crater, bacteriologist; b. Phila., Mar. 4, 1873; s. Levi A. and Amanda (Crater) R.; M.D., Jefferson Med. Coll., 1894; m. 2d, Sallie Slifer, June 9, 1930. Associated with Jefferson Medical College since 1894, now prof. preventive medicine and bacteriology; former pathologist, St. Joseph's Hospital, Henry Phipps Inst.; dir. Clin. Lab. of Phila. Gen. Hosp. Mem. A.M.A., Assn. Am. Bacteriologist Coll. Physician, of Phila., Phila. Pathol. Soc., Med. Club of Phila., Pa. German Soc. Republican. Home: Rahns, Montgomery Co., Pa.

ROSENBERRY, M(orris) Claude, dir. music education; b. Lower Mt. Bethel Twp., Northampton Co., Pa., Jan. 7, 1889; s. Edward Shimer (M.D.) and Gertrude (McDonald) R.; student State Normal Sch., E. Stroudsburg, Pa., 1908-10; Cornell U., summers 1912-15; B.S., New York U., 1926; honorary Mus.D., Temple University, 1937; m. Mary E. Hoffman, June 12, 1915; 1 son, Edward Hoffman. Rural school teacher, 1906-08; head dept. of English, Westerleigh Collegiate Inst., New Brighton, N.Y., 1910-11; supervisor of music, E. Stroudsburg, Pa., 1911-15, Easton, Pa., 1915-19; dir. music, Girard Coll., Phila., summers 1915-19; dir. music, Reading, Pa., 1919-26; state dir. music edn., Dept. Pub. Instrn., Harrisburg, Pa., since 1926. Member Music Educators Nat. Conf., Eastern Music Educators Conf. (pres. 1929-31), N.E.A., Pa. State Edn. Assn., Phi Mu Alpha, Sinfonia. Democrat. Lutheran. Mason (32°, Shriner). Clubs: Wednesday Music Club, Torch, West Shore Country. Contbr. articles to mags. Home: 219 N. 23rd St., Camp Hill, Pa. Address: State Dept. of Pub. Instrn., Harrisburg, Pa.

ROSENBLATT, Maurice Cohn, mech. engring.; b. Atlantic City, N.J., July 7, 1889; s. Henry and Harriet (Cohn) R.; ed. U. of Pa., 1906; M.E., Cornell U., 1911; m. Sylvia Scheff, Jan. 12, 1920; 1 dau., Doris. Employed in gen. mech. engring., 1911-15; with Sound Conditioning Co., 1915-20; with Keasbey & Mattison Co., 1920-25; pres. M. C. Rosenblatt, Inc. since 1925; pres. and gen. mgr. Acoustical Corpn. of America, mech. engrs. in acoustics of bldgs., Phila., Pa., since 1929; pres. Utility Products Corpn. Served in U.S.A., 1917-18. Fellow Royal Soc. of Arts (British). Mem. Am. Soc. Mech. Engrs. Author: The Arr Process; The Eleventh Universe. Home: Pelham Court. Office: 2402 Market St., Philadelphia, Pa.

ROSENBLATT, Samuel, rabbi; b. Bratislava, Slovakia, May 5, 1902; s. Josef and Taube (Kaufman) R.; brought to U.S., 1912, naturalized, 1917; A.B., Coll. of City of N.Y., 1921; Ph.D., Columbia U., 1927; Rabbi, Jewish Theol. Sem. of America, N.Y. City, 1925; grad. study Am. Sch. Oriental Research, and Hebrew U., Jerusalem, 1925-26; m. Claire Woloch, Oct. 3, 1926; children—David Hirsch, Judah Isser. Rabbi, Trenton, N.J., 1926-27, Beth Tfiloh Cong., Baltimore, Md., since 1927; Gustav Gottheil lecturer in Semitic Langs., Columbia U., 1926-28; lecturer Jewish lit., Johns Hopkins U. since 1930. Mem. Rabbinical Assembly Jewish Theol. Sem. of America, Am. Oriental Soc., Soc. of Bib. Lit., Am. Acad. for Jewish Research, Phi Beta Kappa, Mizrachi Orgn. of America. Hazard Fellow, Am. Sch. Oriental Research, Jerusalem, 1925-26; Rayner Fellow in Semitics, Johns Hopkins U., 1928-30. Del. 19th Zionist Cong., Lucerne Switzerland, 1935. Jewish religion. B'rith Sholom. Author: The High Ways to Perfection of Abraham Maimonides, 1927; The Interpretation of the Bible in the Mishnah, 1935; The High Ways to Perfection of Abraham Maimonides II, 1938. Contbr. reviews and articles to ednl. jours. Home: 3605 Springdale Av. Office: 3200 Garrison Boul., Baltimore, Md.

ROSENBLOOM, Benjamin Louis, ex-congressman; b. Braddock, W.Va., June 3, 1880; studied at W.Va. U.; unmarried. Admitted to bar, W. Va., 1904, to Supreme Court of U.S., 1911; mem. Senate of W.Va., 1914-18; mem. 67th and 68th Congresses (1921-25), 1st W.Va. Dist.; del. to W.Va. Conv., 1933, to ratify 21st Amendment to Constitution of U.S.; elected vice mayor of Wheeling, 1935, for term of 4 years. Democrat. Home: Wheeling, W.Va.

ROSENGARTEN, Walter Edward, civil engring.; b. Phila., Pa., Jan. 21, 1890; s. John George and Marie Elizabeth (Dehner) R.; B.S. in C.E., U. of Pa., 1911, C.E., same, 1917; m. Margaret Thomas, of Frankford, Phila., Pa., June 27, 1916; children—Elizabeth Rigler, Walter Edward, John Russell. Employed as draftsman, 1907-11; instr. civil engring., U. of Pa., 1911-12; highway engr. and engr. economist, U.S. Bur. of Pub. Rds., Washington, D.C., 1912-19; traffic engr., Asphalt Inst., New York, N.Y., 1919-29; engr. Day and Zimmerman, Inc., cons. engrs., Phila., Pa., 1929-30; twp. engr., Lower Merion Twp., Ardmore, Pa., since 1930. Dir. Am. Pub. Works Assn. (past pres. Phila. Chapter). Mem. Am. Soc. Civil Engrs., Am. Soc. for Testing Materials, Am Road Builders, Internat. Assn. Road Congresses, Sigma Xi. Chmn. troop com. local Boy Scouts. Received Meritorious Service Award, and Medal, Phila. Sect. Am. Pub. Works Assn., 1939. Protestant. Club: Rotary of Ardmore (pres. 1938-39). Home: 64 Rockglen Rd., W. Park Sta., Philadelphia, Pa. Office: Township Bldg., Ardmore, Pa.

ROSENKRANS, Carl B., physician and surgeon; b. East Stroudsburg, Pa., Nov. 5, 1886; s. Seeley and Emma (Lantz) R.; student East Stroudsburg (Pa.) State Teachers Coll., Medico-Chirurgical Coll., Phila.; unmarried. Engaged in gen. practice medicine and surgery since 1911; owner Rosenkrans Hosp., East Stroudsburg, built 1923. Served as capt. M.C., 322d Inf., A.E.F., during World War. Rep. county chmn. Monroe County, Pa., since 1934. Mem. Chamber of Commerce, Am. Legion, Forty and Eight. Mason, Elk. Clubs: Lions (East Stroudsburg, Pa.); Beaver Run, Saw Creek Hunting and Fishing Assn., Maskenozha Rod and Gun. Home: 15 Smith St. Office: 171 Washington St., East Stroudsburg, Pa.

ROSENTHAL, Albert, artist; b. Phila., Jan. 30, 1863; s. Max and Caroline (Rosenthal) R.; studied art under his father and at Pa. Acad.; studied also in Munich and in Paris under Gérôme, in the École des Beaux Arts. Painting portraits since 1893; widely known as etcher and painter of portraits of famous Americans. Medals Chicago, Buffalo and San Francisco expns. Represented in museum of Brooklyn, N.Y., Youngstown, O., Dayton, O., Los Angeles, Calif., Kansas City, Mo., Dallas, Tex., Elgin, Ill., Buffalo, St. Louis, Detroit, Atlanta, Cleveland, Acad. of Fine Arts, Phila., Art. Inst. Chicago, San Francisco Mus., Newport Art Assn., State Coll. (Pa.), New Hope (Pa.) High Sch., Salmagundi Club (New York), Hist. Society of Pa., New York Hist. Soc., U.S. Capitol, Washington, etc. Life mem. Hist. Soc. Pa., New York Hist. Soc. Clubs: Penn (Phila.); Salmagundi (New York); Interalliée (Paris). Home and Studio: New Hope, Pa.

ROSENTHAL, Arthur Gerson, retail merchant; b. Shenandoah, Pa., Dec. 26, 1887; s. Joshua Lipman and Sarah Florence (Cohn) R.; student Punxsutawney (Pa.) Pub. Schs., 1892-1903, Peterson's Business Coll., Punxsutawney, Pa., 1904-05; m. Pauline Cohen, Feb. 10, 1920; children—Natalie Jean, Janet Elaine. Gen. clerk, R. Cohen clothing store, Punxsutawney, Pa., 1903-06; sr. partner and mgr. A. G. Rosenthal, dept. store, Punxsutawney, Pa., 1906-30, owner since 1930. Dir. Y.M.C.A. Mem. Chamber of Commerce (pres., 1929-30; chmn. retail div. since 1931). Republican. Jewish Religion. Elk, K.P., B'nai B'rith (pres., Punxsutawney, Pa.). Clubs: Punxsutawney Country, Kiwanis (charter mem.; pres., 1927, 1939). Home: 203 Dinsmore Av. Office: 117 E. Mahoning St., Punxsutawney, Pa.

ROSENTHAL, Lewis Jay; asso. prof. proctology, U. of Md.; visiting surgeon Mercy Hosp., Hebrew Hosp. and Asylum and Jewish Home for Consumptives; consultant Hebrew Home for Aged and Infirm. Address: 920 St. Paul St., Baltimore, Md.

ROSENTHAL, S. Leonard, dentist; b. Phila., Pa., Aug. 19, 1899; s. Jonas S. and Claire (Nusbaum) R.; D.D.S., U. of Pa. Dental Sch., 1922; m. Constance E. Lowesgrund, Mar. 31, 1928. Engaged in pvt. practice of dentistry in Phila. since 1923; dental resident Mt. Sinai Hosp., 1922-23, chief of dental service, 1924-29; engaged in research at Thos. W. Evans Mus. and Dental Inst., U. of Pa., Sch. of Dentistry since 1935. Served as pvt. S.A.T.C., U. of Pa., 1918. Mem. Am. Dental Assn., Eastern Dental Soc., Pa. State and Phila. Co. dental socs., Acad. of Stomatology. Awarded Benjamin Lord Prize for Research for 1937 by First Dist. Dental Soc. of N.Y. State. Jewish religion. Contbr. tech. publications on bacteriological and dental subjects. Lecturer. Home: 4537 Spruce St. Office: 1220 Medical Arts Bldg., Philadelphia, Pa.

ROSENWALD, Lessing J(ulius), merchant; b. Chicago, Feb. 10, 1891; s. late Julius and Augusta (Nusbaum) R.; student Cornell U., 1909-11; m. Edith Goodkind, Nov. 6, 1913; children—Julius II, Helen A., Robert L., Joan E., Janet. Identified with Sears, Roebuck & Co. from beginning of active career, became mgr. Philadelphia plant at its opening, 1920; vice chmn. bd. dirs. and chmn. exec. com. Sears, Roebuck & Co., July 1931-Jan. 1932, chmn. bd. since Jan. 1932. Chmn. trustees Rosenwald Fund, organized to carry on philanthropic activities of father. Served as seaman, 2d class, Gt. Lakes Naval Station, World War. Jewish religion. Clubs: Locust, Cornell, Philmont Country (Philadelphia); Standard (Chicago). Home: Jenkintown, Pa. Office: Sears, Roebuck & Co., Philadelphia, Pa.

ROSEWATER, Victor, journalist; b. Omaha, Feb. 13, 1871; s. Edward and Leah (Colman) R.; Ph.B., Columbia University, 1891, A.M.,

1892, Ph.D., 1893; m. Katie Katz, Jan. 27, 1904; children—Harriet Leah (Mrs. Percival M. Sax, Jr.), Edward. Began newspaper work on Omaha Bee, 1893, managing editor, 1895, editor, 1906-20, and editor and publisher of same, 1917-1920. Regent Nebraska State U., 1896-97; del. White House Conf. on Conservation of Natural Resources, 1908; del.-at-large Rep. Nat. Conv., 1908; mem. Rep. Nat. Com., 1908-12 (chmn. 1912); mem. Advisory Com. Rep. Nat. Com., 1916; mem. advisory council Nat. Civic Federation; mem. Am. Jewish Com.; Neb. State Commn. on Workmen's Compensation, 1911. Pres. 1st home rule charter conv. for Omaha, 1913. Mem. com. on labor, Advisory Commn. of Council Nat. Defense, 1917-18; administrator for Neb. of paper and pulp sect. War Industries Bd., 1918-19; chmn. Neb. Constl. Conv. Survey Com., 1919; sec. and asst. to the pres. Sesqui-Centennial Expn. Assn., 1921-25. Mem. Am. Econ. Assn. Spl. lecturer on municipal finance, U. of Neb., 1894, U. of Wis., 1904. Leader Round Table on "The Press," in Inst. of Pub. Affairs, U. of Va., 1927-29, also at Inst. Statesmanship, Rollins Coll., 1930. Author: Special Assessments—A Study in Municipal Finance, 1898. Wrote title "Laissez Faire," Palgrave's Dictionary of Political Economy; title "Omaha," in Historic Towns of the Western States, 1901; History of the Liberty Bell, 1926; History of Co-operative News-gathering in the United States, 1930; Back Stage in 1912, 1932; also many mag. articles. Address: 1530 Locust St., Philadelphia, Pa.

ROSICA, James Vincent, rector; b. Philadelphia, Nov. 22, 1906; s. Vincent and Anna Cristina R.; student St. Joachim's Parochial Sch., 1912-20, St. Joseph's High Sch., Phila., 1920-24; A.B., St. Charles' Sem., Overbrook, Pa., 1932. Asst. rector King of Peach (Catholic) Ch., 1932-33; rector Our Lady of Mt. Carmel, Shenandoah, Jan.-July 1933, Our Lady of Consolation, Phila., since July 1933. Address: 7056 Tulip St., Philadelphia, Pa.

ROSIER, Joseph, educator; b. Wilsonburg, W.Va., Jan. 24, 1870; s. John Wesley and Rebecca (Miller) R.; B.Pd., Salem (W.Va.) Coll., 1895, A.M. from same coll., 1915; LL.D., Marshall Coll., 1933; m. Iva Randolph, August 14, 1895; children—Nellie (Mrs. Hugh Simpson), Robert, Mary Josephine (Mrs. Herndon Smith). Teacher of village sch., 1890; prin. pub. schs., Salem, 1891, 92; superintendent schs., Harrison County, West Virginia, 1893, 94; member faculty, Salem Coll., 1894-96; teacher State Normal Sch., Glenville, 1896-97; with State Normal Sch., Fairmont, 1897-1900; supt. schs., Fairmont, 1900-15; pres. State Normal Sch., Fairmont, since 1915. County food administrator, World War. Consultant on education, Works Progress Adminstrn. Life mem. N.E.A. (pres., 1932-33); mem. Am. Assn. Teachers Colls., Nat. Soc. for Study of Education. Democrat. Methodist. K.P.; mem. A.O.U.W. Rotarian. Lecturer before teachers' institutes and at ednl. gatherings. Home: Fairmont, W.Va.

ROSIN, Harry, sculptor and artist; b. Phila., Pa., Dec. 21, 1897; s. Aaron and Bertha R.; ed. Sch. of Industrial Arts, 1917-20, Pa. Acad. Fine Arts, 1923-26; m. Vilna Woolseley Spitz, at Papeete, Tahiti, South Sea Islands, Sept. 19, 1936. Began as worker in wrought iron, made iron work for Curtis Inst. of Music, Josef Hofman, pianist, and others; sculpture rep. by 20-ft. figure of Christ at Guadaloupe, Fr.W.I.; now working on figure of Duke Kahanamoku for Waikiki Beach; executed many portrait commissions; exhibited in Paris, Tahiti, New York City, Phila., Pittsburgh, Chicago and other cities; represented in Pa. Mus., Pa. Acad. of Fine Arts and many pvt. collections. Served in A.S., U.S.N., Gulfport, Miss., 1918. Mem. Am. Legion. Awarded European scholarship, Pa. Acad. Fine Arts, 1926, Stewardson Prize in Sculpture, 1928, Widener Gold Medal, 1939. Studio: 201 S. 10th St., Philadelphia, Pa.

ROSINGER, Alfred, conductor; b. Vienna, Austria, Dec. 23, 1897; s. Joseph and Anna (Stoeger) R.; studied music under pvt. teacher, Vienna, Austria, 1904-12; student Gymnasium, Vienna, 1908-16, U. of Vienna (Austria), 1916; came to U.S., 1920, naturalized, 1927; m. Rose Hartel, Feb. 11, 1922. Began as piano teacher, Paterson, N.J., 1921; founded Paterson (N.J.) Symphony Orchestra, 1923, conductor since 1923. Served as cadet-aspirant, Austrian Army on the Italian front, 1916-18. Mem. Mayor's Music Weeks Com., Paterson, N.J. Founder Friends of Music Soc., 1931. Mem. Little Opera Soc. (founder, 1935), Musical Art Soc. (founder, 1938; pres.), Austrian Soc. (founder; corr. sec.), German-Am. Non-Partisan League, Fidelio Soc. (hon.). Address: 167 Sheridan Av., Paterson, N.J.

ROSOFF, Martin Allen, life ins.; b. Phila., Pa., May 25, 1907; s. Abraham and Oldie Florence (Wessel) R.; B.S. in economics, Central High Sch., 1925; student U. of Pa. Extension Sch. Finance, 1936-38, Am. Coll. Life Underwriters, C.L.U., 1938; m. Louise Virginia Hallowell, Rocky Mount, N.C., 1939. Registered as law student in office Alexander S. Harzenstein, 1925-29; engaged in profession of life ins. since 1929, started as agt. with Jefferson Standard Life Ins. Co., 1929, unit mgr., 1931, agt. and branch office mgr., Phila., Pa., since 1933. Received Barnwell Honor Award, Central High Sch. Mem. Knights of Pythias. Home: 4728 Osage Av. Office: 1616 Walnut St., Philadelphia, Pa.

ROSS, Carmon, college pres.; b. New York City, Feb. 28, 1885; s. Michael and Angela (Guzza) R.; Ph.B., Lafayette Coll., 1905; A.M., U. of Pa., 1916, Ph.D., same, 1922; m. Emma W. Kratz, Dec. 30, 1914 (died 1937); children—Angela, Barbara, Catherine. Employed as supt. schs., Doylestown, Pa., 1906-34; dir. summer demonstration school, Pa. State Coll., 1922-33; pres. Edinboro State Teachers Coll. since 1934. Served as mem. N.J. Sch. Survey Commn., Pinchot Sch. Finance Commn. Mem. Ten Yr. Plan Pa. Edn. Commn. Mem. N.E.A., Pa. State Edn. Assn. (pres. 1934), Phi Delta Kappa, Kappa Phi Kappa. Republican. Presbyn. Mason (32°). Club: Kiwanis of Erie (lieut. gov. 1928-34). Author, "Status of County Institutes in Pa.," etc. Home: Edinboro, Pa.

ROSS, Cecil Byron, coll. athletic coach; b. Selbyville, W.Va., Nov. 22, 1901; s. Samuel and Lillie (Crites) R.; student high sch., Buckhannon, W.Va., 1915-19; A.B., W.Va. Wesleyan Coll., Buckhannon, 1923; m. Mary Lurelda Morgan, June 16, 1925; children—Alice Louise, Samuel Morgan. Served as coach athletics, high sch., Buckhannon, W.Va., 1923-25; coach of athletics, W.Va. Wesleyan Coll., since 1925. Republican. Methodist. Mason. Rotarian, Home: 10 Meade St., Buckhannon, W.Va.

ROSS, Clarence Frisbee, educator; b. at Sheakleyville, Pa., Apr. 7, 1870; s. John Seymour and Nancy Maria (Frisbee) R.; A.B., Allegheny College, Meadville, Pa., 1891, A.M., 1893, LL.D., 1932; Litt.D., Dickinson College, Carlisle, Pa., 1921; fellow U. of Chicago; studied U. of Berlin, Am. Sch. of Classical Studies, Rome; m. Etta Amelia Lenhart, Aug. 28, 1899; children—Lanora Lenhart (dec.), Julian Lenhart. Prof. Greek, Mo. Wesleyan Coll., 1891-92; prin. Allegheny Coll. Prep. Sch., 1892-1902; prof. Latin, 1902-35, sec. faculty, 1901-07, 1910-18, registrar, 1893-95, 1907-08, 1918—, dean of men, 1919-30, acting pres., 1924-26, 1930-31, v.p., 1931-38, dean of College since 1938, Allegheny College. Visiting professor Greek, University of Chicago, summer 1904, 06; director New 1st Nat. Bank, Meadville, Pa., Crawford Co. Mutual Ins. Co. Exec. sec. Crawford Co., Pub. Safety Com. of Pa., 1917-19. Ind. Republican. Methodist; mem. univ. senate, M.E. Ch., 1931-32. Mason (33°). Mem. Am. Philol. Assn., Archæol. Inst. America (Pittsburgh br.), Phi Delta Theta, Phi Beta Kappa, Kappa Phi Kappa, Pi Delta Epsilon. Home: 969 Main St., Meadville, Pa.

ROSS, Edgar Samuel, chem. engr. and industrial chemist; b. Ironwood, Mich., Apr. 18, 1893; s. Solomon and Laura (Joly) R.; B.S., U. of N.H., Durham, N.H., 1917, M.S., 1921; student Grad. Sch. of Chemistry, U. of Pittsburgh, 1924-25; m. Alyce Cadwell, Oct. 6, 1917. Research chemist, Welsbach Co., Gloucester, N.J., 1917-18; chief chemist, Charlotte Chem. Labs. and Columbite Reduction Co., Charlotte, N.C., 1918-19; rare metal research, Pa. Salt Mfg. Co., Phila., 1919-22; chemist and metallurgist, McKechnie Bros., Phila., 1922-23; sr. research fellow, Mellon Inst. of Industrial Research, Pittsburgh, 1923-28; mgr. research and development, Headley Good Roads Co., Phila., 1928-29; pres. and tech. dir., Headley Emulsified Products Co., Phila., 1929-32, chmn. of the bd. and tech. dir., 1932, consultant on manufacture of bituminous emulsions, 1932-33; sales and development engr., Sun Oil Co., Phila., since 1933. Mem. Am. Inst. Chem. Engrs., Am. Chem. Soc., Am. and Internat. socs. for testing materials, Am. Soc. of Refrigerating Engrs., Nat. Research Council, Assn. of Asphalt Paving Technologists, Alpha Chi Sigma, Kappa Sigma. Republican. Episcopalian. Mason. Clubs: Chemists (New York); Springhaven (Swarthmore, Pa.). Author of several tech. articles. Holder of various U.S. patents. Home: 103 Bentley Av., Cynwyd, Pa. Office: Sun Oil Co., Marcus Hook, Pa.

ROSS, F. Clair, state treas.; b. Sandy Lake, Pa., Jan. 3, 1895; s. Clement V. and Maud (McElwaine) R.; student Grove City (Pa.) Coll.; LL.B., Columbia U. Law Sch.; student U. of Mich. Law Sch.; m. Carie Bennett, Sept. 3, 1919; children—Marilyn, Carita. Teacher Derry (Pa.) High Sch., 1915-17; gen. practice of law, 1924-35; dep. atty. gen. of Pa., 1935-37; state treas. of Pa. since 1936. Served in Flying Div., Signal Corps, U.S. Army, during World War. Mem. Am. Legion (comdr. Butler, Pa., Post, 1930-31; comdr. 26th dist., Pa., 1932-33). Odd Fellow, Mason. Club: Butler Co. Hunting and Fishing (past pres.). Home: 2205 Market St. Office: Main Bldg., State Capitol, Harrisburg, Pa.

ROSS, Fred Ernest, pediatrician; b. Waterford, Pa., Dec. 2, 1872; s. Marvin Leroy and Nancy Jane (Lunger) R.; student Waterford (Pa.) Acad., 1888-94; M.D., U. of Buffalo (N.Y.), 1897; student Boston Childrens' Hosp., 1912; m. Myrtice F. Watson, June 20, 1901 (died 1926); children—Cecil, Everett, Robert; m. 2d, Edith Laws Matthews, Aug. 10, 1929. Chief of pediatric dept., Hamot Hosp., Erie, Pa., since 1906, St. Vincent's Hosp., Erie, Pa., since 1913; chief of staff, Erie (Pa.) Infants' Home and Hosp., since 1937. Mem. A.M.A., Erie Co. med. soc. (sec., 1904-07; pres., 1908; librarian since 1909), Pa. State Med. Soc. (chmn. pediatric sect., 1927). Republican. Protestant. Address: 501 W. 9th St., Erie, Pa.

ROSS, George, lawyer; b. Doylestown, Pa., May 28, 1879; s. George and Ellen Lyman (Phipps) R.; student Lawrenceville (N.J.) Acad., 1894-96; A.B., Princeton U., 1900; unmarried. Admitted to Bucks Co. (Pa.) bar, 1902, Pa. Supreme Ct., 1903, Phila. bar, 1904; mem. firm Thomas & George Ross, Doylestown, Pa., 1902-1919; in practice at Phila. individually since 1919; dir. Doylestown Trust Co., Doylestown Cemetery. Served as 1st lt., Mexican border, 1916-17, capt. and maj., Inf., 28th Div., A.E.F., during World War; lt. col., Inf. Res. to 1939. Dem. candidate dist. atty., Bucks Co., 1903 (not elected), state senator, 1904, (not elected); since 1936 serving as one of masters appointed by Phila. Orphans Ct. to determine heirs to $18,000,000 estate of Henriette E. Garrett. Democrat. Episcopalian. Clubs: Princeton, Rittenhouse (Phila.); Colonial (Princeton). Home: Roscommon, Doylestown, Pa. Office: 1000 Provident Trust Bldg., Philadelphia, Pa.

ROSS, McElwee, clergyman; b. Sharon, S.C., Dec. 28, 1869; s. Rev. Robt. Armstrong (D.D.) and Naomi Jane (Caldwell) R.; ed. Erskine Coll., Due West, S.C., 1886-89; B.D., Allegheny Theol. Sem., Pittsburgh, Pa. (now Pittsburgh-Xenia Sem.), 1898; (hon.) D.D., Westminster Coll., 1918; m. Lylla Boyd Ketchen, of Winnsboro, S.C., June 1, 1889 (dec. 1926); 1 dau., Marlin. Engaged as newspaper editor and pub., 1891-95; ordained to ministry U. Presbyn. Ch., 1898; pastor, Oxford, Pa., 1898-1902, Newark, N.J., 1902-06; pastor First U. Presbyn. Ch., McKeesport, Pa., 1906-36, pastor emeritus since 1936; agt. of welfare work, G. C. Murphy Five and Ten-Cent Stores; pres. and dir. Westminster Coll., New Wilmington, Pa., since 1916; dir. Pittsburgh-Xenia Sem.; pres. bd. trustees

Westmoreland Presbytery. Mem. Temple U. Assn., Kappa Alpha, Chamber of Commerce. United Presbyn. Club: Youghiogheny Country (McKeesport). Contbr. to religious jours. Home: P.O. Box 229, McKeesport, Pa.

ROSS, (Pierre) Sanford 3d, artist; b. Newark, N.J., Jan. 25, 1907; s. Pierre Sanford, Jr., and Helen (Halsey) R.; ed. Taft Sch., Watertown, Conn., 1923-25, Princeton U., 1926-27; studied art with Thomas Benton, Art Students League, 1928, George Luks, 1929; unmarried. Exhibited at Princeton University, 1932; exhibited, solo, at Macbeth Gallery, New York City, 1932-33, Reinhardt Galleries, 1934, Phila. Art Alliance, 1935, The Sporting Gallery and Bookshop, 1936, Kleemann Galleries, 1936, 1937, 1939; also Contemporary Art Exhbt. N.Y. World's Fair, 1939, and Acad. Natural Sciences of Phila., 1939; invitation exhibit Whitney Mus. of Am. Art, 1936 and 1940; rep. in collections, Newark Mus., Addison Mus., Andover, Mass., San Francisco Mus. of Fine Arts, N.Y. Pub. Library, and pvt. collections; illustrations for Fortune; wrote article for Country Life. Included in Fifty Prints of the Year, 1933; Fine Prints of the Year, 1937, 1938. Republican. Presbyn. Made trip to New Zealand for big-game fishing, research, photography and painting material; then to Kenya, East Africa, for same reasons, 1936-37. Home: Rumson, N.J.

ROSS, Thomas, lawyer; b. Doylestown, Pa., Sept. 16, 1873; s. George and Ellen Sophie Lyman (Phipps) R.; student Lawrenceville (N.J.) Sch., 1888 to 1891; A.B., Princeton U., 1895; m. May Louise Blakey, Apr. 20, 1907; children—John, Thomas, George Blaikie. Gen. practice of law at Doylestown, Pa., since 1897; asst. U.S. atty., Phila., 1916-17. Trustee, Abington Memorial Hosp. Chmn. Liberty Loan Com. for Middle Bucks Co. (Pa.) and vice-chmn. War Chest for Bucks Co. (Pa.) during World War. Mem. Bucks Co. Boy Scouts of American (mem. exec. bd.; past pres.), Bucks Co. Assn. (dir.; mem. com. of '76). Democrat. Episcopalian. Club: Princeton (Phila.). Home: Roscommon. Office: Court St. at Pine, Doylestown, Pa.

ROSS, Walter C., treas. Standard Cap & Seal Corpn.; b. Port Jervis, N.Y.; s. John and Delia (Lake) R.; ed. Port Jervis High Sch. and Columbia Coll.; m. Lilian Barnes, 1910; children—Margaret, Dorothy Jean. Accountant Touiche Niven & Co., 1915-20; treas., sec. Harrison Williams Corpn., 1920-35; treas., sec. and dir. Standard Cap & Seal Corpn. since 1934; treas. and sec. Fargo Cap Corpn. Mason. Club: Joe Jefferson (Ridgewood, N.J.). Home: 471 Fairway Road, Ridgewood, N.J. Office: 1200 Fullerton Av., Chicago, Ill.; and 150 Bay St., Jersey City, N.J.

ROSSER, Edward Morgan, banker; b. Yslrod-Rondda, S. Wales, Oct. 27, 1869; s. Morgan David and Mary (Edwards) R.; brought to U.S., 1871, naturalized through father's citizenship; student Wyoming Sem.; m. Sara Deen, Sept. 20, 1905. Began as clerk, 1888; asst. cashier Kingston (Pa.) Nat. Bank, 1897-98, cashier, 1898-1908, v.p., 1908-15, pres. since 1915; v.p. and dir. Kingston Coal Co. Trustee Wyoming Sem., Hayl Library, Nesbit Memorial Hosp. (Kingston, Pa.). Republican. Presbyterian. Elk, Odd Fellow. Club: Westmoreland (Wilkes-Barre, Pa.). Home: 26 Pierce St. Office: Kingston National Bank, Kingston, Pa.

ROSSHEIM, Irving David, stock broker; b. New York, N.Y., Sept. 26, 1887; s. David and Carrie (Simon) R.; B.A., Central High Sch., Phila., Pa., 1905; B.S. in Econ., Wharton Sch., U. of Pa., 1908, LL.B., Law Sch., 1911; m. Ellen Viola Baer, June 1, 1912; children—Richard Irving, Robert Jules. Mem. faculty of Wharton Sch., U. of Pa., 1908-18; admitted to Pa. bar, 1911, and practiced in Phila., 1911-19, asso. firm Wolf, Bloch, Schorr; auditor Stanley Co. of America, 1919-24, treas., 1924-28, pres., 1928-29; gen. partner Newburger, Loeb & Co., Phila., stock brokers, since 1930; pres. First Nat. Pictures, Inc., 1928-29; dir. Warner Bros. Pictures, Inc., 1928-29. Mem. Zeta Beta Tau. Hebrew. Clubs: Lawyers, Penn Athletic (Phila.); Philmont (Pa.) Country (treas.). Co-author: First Year Bookkeeping and Accounting, 1912. Home: Rydal, Pa. Office: 1419 Walnut St., Philadelphia, Pa.

ROSSI, Louis Mansfield, corpn. exec.; b. Flushing, L.I., N.Y., Aug. 3, 1877; s. James Camille and Caroline Alice (Frame) R.; E.M., Columbia Sch. of Mines, 1899; m. Agnes Langan, June 8, 1907 (died Apr. 2, 1939); children—Margaret Archer (Mrs. Thomas Owen Meacham), Thomas Langan. Engr. Perth Amboy Terra Cotta Co., 1900-01, Nat. Fireproofing Co., 1901-03; works mgr. Perth Amboy Chem. Works, 1903-08; research Roessler & Haselacher Chem. Co., 1908-10; works mgr. Gen. Bakelite Co., 1910-19, gen. mgr., 1919-22; with Bakelite Corpn. since 1923, as dir. mfg., 1925, v.p. and dir. of mfg. since 1924; v.p. and dir. Bakelite Corpn. of W.Va., Bakelite Bldg. Products Co., Gen. Bakelite Co.; pres. and dir. Bakelite-Rogers Co., Bakelite Corpn. of Can.; v.p., treas. and dir. Condensite Co., Halowax Corpn., Redmanol Chem. Products Co.; dir. Bakelite Gesellschaft (Berlin), Bakelite, Ltd. (London). Mem. Bd. of Edn., Perth Amboy, 1910-15, City Planning Commn., 1920-24. Mem. Am. Inst. Chem. Engrs., Am. Soc. Testing Materials, Soc. Chem. Industry (England), Plastic Mfrs. Assn., Synthetic Resin Mfrs. Assn. Republican. Catholic. Club: Forsgate Country (Jamesburg, N.J.). Home: 135 Rector St., Perth Amboy, N.J. Office: 247 Park Av., New York, N.Y.

ROSSITER, Frank Saylor, surgeon; b. Pittsburgh, Pa., Nov. 13, 1885; s. John S. and Annie (Krehan) R.; M.D., U. of Pittsburgh Med. Sch., 1908; m. Alma Gruber, 1904; 1 dau., Ruth Allyne (Mrs. Russell Rose). Served as city physician Mayview Hosp., 1908; specialized in industrial surgery since 1909 with spl. study of gas poisoning, has treated over 3,000 cases carbon monoxide poisoning; company surgeon Edgar Thomson Steel, Carnegie Steel Co., 1909; asst. co. surgeon, Duquesne Steel Co., 1909-12; co. surgeon, Carrie Furnaces since 1921; surgeon Union Switch & Signal Co., 1914-19, Kopp Glass Co., 1933-36; pres. Swissvale Bd. Health since 1937. Mem. Phi Chi. Home: 7438 Irvine St. Office: 2014 Noble St., Swissvale, Pa.

ROSSITER, James Patrick, lawyer; b. Phila., Pa., Sept. 13, 1890; s. Louis T. and Elizabeth Cecilia (Griffin) R.; student Pa. State Coll., 1910-11; LL.B., Georgetown U. Law Sch., Washington, D.C., 1916; unmarried. Admitted to Pa. bar, 1917, and since engaged in gen. practice of law at Erie, Pa.; served as asst. U.S. atty. for Western Pa., 1920-21; served as mayor, Erie, Pa., 1932-36; gen. counsel The Gen. State Authority of the Commonwealth of Pa., a pub. corpn., 1937-39. Served in U.S. Army, 1917-19. Mem. Am. Bar Assn. Democrat. Roman Catholic. K.C. Clubs: Moose, Knights of Columbus (Erie, Pa.). Home: 917 Washington Pl. Office: 603 Masonic Temple, Erie, Pa.; also Harrisburg, Pa.

ROSSKAM, William Benjamin, manufacturer confections; b. Phila., Pa., Sept. 17, 1871; s. Isaac and Bertha (Gerstley) R.; student Lauterbach Acad., Ph.B., Wharton Sch., U. of Pa., 1891; m. Florence Putzel, Jan. 15, 1903. Began as office boy, 1893; v.p. Quaker City Chocolate and Confectionery Co., Inc., Phila., Pa.; dir. Ninth Bank & Trust Co. Elector for State of Pa. during adminstrn. of Pres. Coolidge. Treas. Jewish Hosp. Republican. Jewish religion. Mason. Club: Midday (Phila.). Home: 2300 N. Broad St. Office: 2140 Germantown Av., Philadelphia, Pa.

ROSSMAN, John Guise, supt. city schs.; b. Spring Mills, Pa., Aug. 23, 1887; s. H.F. and Clara (Guise) R.; A.M., Franklin and Marshall Coll., 1911, A.M., Columbia U., 1917; m. Ann Bright, Aug. 31, 1910; children—Clara Virginia, John Guise. Engaged as instr., supt. and dir. pub. schs. in Ark., 1908-23; asst. supt. schs., Gary, Ind., 1923-29; supt. schs. East Chicago, Ind., 1929-34; supt. pub. schs., Warren, Pa., since 1934; instr. in summer sessions, U. of Ark., Wash. State Coll., U. of Mon., U. of Utah, Ind. U., summers 1917-33. Served as vice-pres. Gen. Hosp. Bd., Warren, Pa.; pres. bd. Salvation Army; mem. exec. bd. Boy Scouts. Mem. Kappa Delta Pi, Phi Delta Kappa. Methodist. Club: Warren Rotary (past pres.). Contbr. to ednl. jours. Home: 10 Henry St. Office: Second and Market Sts., Warren, Pa.

ROSSMANN, Louis, dentist; b. Baltimore, Md., Mar. 5, 1893; s. Louis and Minnie (Seipple) R.; D.D.S., Baltimore Coll. Dental Surgery, 1912; student U. of Md., 1912-15; m. Mary Quinn, June 30, 1921; 1 dau., Mary Mildred. Engaged in practice of dentistry at Baltimore, Md., since 1915. Served as 1st lt., capt., maj. inf., U.S.A., 1917-19; with 1st Div., A.E.F. in France. Fellow Am. Coll. Dentists. Pres. Md. State Bd. Dental Examiners, 1936-39. Democrat. Lutheran. Clubs: Kiwanis (dir.), Baltimore Country, Athletic. Home: 3808 Juniper Rd. Office: 829 Park Av., Baltimore, Md.

ROST, Henry Lewis, banking; b. New York, N.Y., Apr. 18, 1894; s. Henry and Freda (Weissert) R.; ed. N.Y. Univ., 1914-17; m. Elsie Christophers, Dec. 26, 1921; children—Marjorie Ann, Robert Christopher. In employ Irving Trust Co., New York, N.Y., summers, 1914-17; with Bankers Trust Co., 1919-22; asso. with Peoples Bank & Trust Co., Westfield, N.J., since 1922, dir. since 1928, pres. since 1935; dir. John F. Sarle Co., New York, N.Y. Served in Mil. Intelligence and with U.S. Shipping Bd. during World War. Commr. Sinking Funds, Westfield, N.J. Mem. Am. Bankers Assn., N.J. State and County bankers assns., Am. Inst. of Banking, N.Y. Univ. Men in Finance, N.Y. City, Photographic Soc. of America. Republican. Presbyn. Clubs: Rotary, College Mens, Community Players, Presbyterian Mens, Echo Lake Country (Westfield); New York Athletic (New York). Home: 516 Hillside Av., Westfield, N.J. Office: 1 Elm St., Westfield, N.J.

ROTAN, Ellwood Joseph, lawyer; b. Phila., Pa., May 6, 1888; s. Frederick G. and Linda S. (Weyant) R.; ed. Germantown Acad., U. of Pa. Law Sch., 1908-12; m. Isabel Gest, June 26, 1922. Admitted to Pa. bar, 1912, and since engaged in gen. practice of law at Phila., Pa.; mem. firm Burch, Rotan, McDevitt and Watters since 1938; served as asst. city solicitor of Phila., 1916-28; with legal dept. Road Bur. of Phila., 1916-19, in charge legal work of bonds and contracts dept., 1919-20, in charge municipal liens, 1920-22, ct. asst. of negligence cases, 1922-28. Served in Ambulance Corps, U.S.A., on Italian front, 1918-19. Awarded two Italian War Crosses and service strip with rank of lieut. Vets. Fgn. Wars. Mem. Am. and Phila. bar assns., Delta Theta Phi. Republican. Presbyn. Mason. Clubs: Union League, Constitutional, Penn. Home: Old Oak Farm, Valley Forge, Pa. Office: 123 S. Broad St., Philadelphia, Pa.

ROTH, Frederick George Richard, sculptor; b. Brooklyn, Apr. 28, 1872; s. Johannes and Jane Gray (Bean) R.; ed. pub. and pvt. schs., Bremen, Germany, until 1888, Acad. Fine Arts, Vienna, 1892, Acad. Fine Arts, Berlin, 1894; m. New York, Madeleine E. G. Forster, Apr. 29, 1905; children—Jack Richard, Roger Frederic. Professionally engaged as sculptor since 1890; exhibited in New York, Phila., St. Louis, Chicago, Portland, Düsseldorf. N.A., 1906; mem. Nat. Sculpture Soc. (pres., 1919-21), Archtl. League, Nat. Inst. Arts and Letters, New Soc. of Artists, Soc. of Animal Painters and Sculptors. Silver medals, St. Louis, 1904, Buenos Aires, 1910; gold medal, Panama P.I. Expn., 1915; Helen Speyer memorial prize, 1924; Nat. Arts Club prize, 1924; William Goodman prize, Grand Central Galleries, New York, 1928; Nat. Arts Club prize, 1931; Cary Ramsey memorial prize, 1931. Instr. modeling, women's class, N.A.D., 1915-18; mem. con. on monuments, N.J. State Architects, 1919. Pres. Nat. Sculpture Soc., 1919-20; mem. Grand Central Art Galleries. Chief sculptor Park Dept. of N.Y. City under Pub. Works Adminstrn., 1934-36. Address: Sherwood Pl., Englewood, N.J.

ROTH, John Ernest, banker; b. Pittsburgh, Pa., Nov. 25, 1868; s. John Jacob and Elizabeth (Young) R.; ed. high sch., Pittsburgh, and Trinity Hall, Washington, Pa.; m. Anna Margaret Rindlaub, Sept. 18, 1913. Began as messenger German Savings and Deposit Bank of Pittsburgh, 1888; pres. 14th Street Bank since 1909; pres. Homestead Valve Mfg. Co., 1910-23, chmn. bd. since 1923; sec. and treas. Phillips Mine & Mill Supply Co.; treas. Munhall Valley Land Co.; dir. Forster Mfg. Company, Kingsley House Association. Former member Central Bd. of Edn., Pittsburgh. Pres. South Side Hosp. Mem. Camp Fire Club America. Republican. Lutheran. Mason. Home: 6400 Beacon St. Office: 1401 Carson St., Pittsburgh, Pa.

ROTHERMEL, Abraham Heckman, lawyer; b. Berks Co., Pa., Mar. 8, 1863; s. Abraham and Magdalena (Heckman) R.; ed. Palatinate Coll., Myerstown, Pa., 1881-82, Franklin and Marshall Acad., 1882-83, Franklin and Marshall Coll., A.B., 1887, A.M., 1890; m. Eva McKenty, Nov. 16, 1898; children—Henry McKenty (dec.), Frederic dePeyster. Admitted to Pa. bar, 1888, and since engaged in gen. practice of law at Reading; served as county solicitor, 1890-92, dist. atty., 1900-02; dir. Berks Co. Trust Co. Trustee Franklin and Marshall Coll., Lancaster, Pa. Mem. Pa. Bar Assn., Berks Co. Bar Assn. (pres. bd. law examiners), Phi Kappa Psi. Democrat. Reformed. I.O.O.F. Maccabee. Clubs: Wyomissing, University. Home: Stony Creek Mills, Pa. Office: 226 Berks Co. Trust Bldg., Reading, Pa.

ROTHERMEL, Amos Cornelius, normal sch. prin.; b. Moselem, Pa., Jan. 6, 1864; s. Lewis W. and Lydia R.; grad. Keystone State Normal Sch., Kutztown, Pa., 1886; A.B., Franklin and Marshall Coll., 1891, A.M., 1894, Litt.D., 1910; Pd.D., Dickinson Coll., 1906; m. Ada L. Spatz, June 30, 1894. Pub. sch. teacher, 1881-85; prin. Polytechnic Acad., Gilbert, Pa., 1886-87; prof. phys. sciences, 1891-99, prin., 1899-1934, Keystone State Normal Sch. (now Kutztown State Teachers Coll.); retired. Republican. Mem. Reformed Ch. Address: Kutztown, Pa.

ROTHMAN, Maurice Maxwell, physician; b. Phila., Pa., Jan. 4, 1897; s. David and Rebecca (Heisman) R.; A.B., Central High Sch., Phila., 1915; ed. U. of Pa., Premed., 1915-17; M.D., U. of Pa. Med. Sch., 1921; m. Esther Rabinowitz, May 30, 1925. Interne St. Luke's Hosp., Bethlehem, Pa., Montefiore Hosp., Pittsburgh, 1921; resident Phila. Gen. Hosp., 1922-23; in practice of medicine at Phila. since 1923, specializing in gastro-enterology; attdg. chief of gastro-enterology, Mt. Sinai Hosp. since 1927; instr. gastro-enterology, Grad. Sch. and Hosp., U. of Pa. since 1923. Fellow A.M.A.; Phila. County Med. Soc., Phi Lambda Kappa. Republican. Jewish religion. Home: 1727 Spruce St., Philadelphia, Pa.

ROTHROCK, H. H., univ. prof.; b. Lock Haven, Pa., Mar. 17, 1897; s. Clifford T. and Matilda E. (Mason) R.; B.S. in I.E., Pa. State Coll., 1918; m. Isabel P. Neilson, June 27, 1922; children—Donald N., Richard C. Time study engr. Westinghouse Electric & Mfg. Co., 1919-25, time study supervisor in charge of training and personnel, 1925-26, supt., 1926-29, dir. of wage incentives for all plants, 1929-33; prof. and head of the dept. of industrial engring., U. of Pittsburgh, since 1933. Mem. Soc. for the Advancement of Management. Mason (32°). Clubs: Faculty of U. of Pittsburgh; Forest Hills Civic (Pittsburgh). Author of tech. articles. Home: 408 Bevington Rd., Forest Hills. Office: Univ. of Pittsburgh, Pittsburgh, Pa.

ROTHROCK, Col. William Powell, retired engr.; b. Bellefonte, Pa., Dec. 5, 1867; s. David Ramsey and Jane Catherene (Powell) R.; student Bellefonte (Pa.) Acad., 1883-85; B.S., Pa. State Coll., 1893; m. Mary Elizabeth Garner, Mar. 16, 1896; 1 son, William Garner. Taught public sch. and worked on railroad, Center County, Pa., 1886-88; engring. corps., Central R.R. of Pa., Clinton Co., Pa., 1894; teacher of higher mathematics, Indiana (Pa.) State Normal Sch., 1894-95; draftsman Carnegie Steel Co., Maryland Steel Co., King Bridge Co., 1895-97; estimator and checker on bridges and steel structures, Gillette Hertzog Mfg. Co., Minneapolis, Minn., 1897-99; squad foreman and asst. chief draftsman, North Works, Illinois Steel Co., Chicago, 1899-1900; chief draftsman, Fort Pitt Bridge Works, Pittsburgh, 1900-06, engr. of construction and mem. of firm, 1906-14; chief engr. in charge of organization and reconstruction of the Manhattan Elevated Co., New York, 1914-16; private practice as consulting and contracting engr., New York, 1916-17; engr. in charge, Smith, Ames & Chisholm, Havana, Cuba, 1919-21; chief construction engr., Tropical Radio Telegraph Co., Costa Rica, Honduras, and other C.A. countries, 1921-23; constructed sugar mill at Violeta, Cuba, 1923-24; retired, 1925. Served as capt., U.S. Army Engrs., 1917, and appointed Construction Q.M. in charge of constrn. of Camp Logan, Houston, Tex., maj., 1918-19; lt. col., U.S. Army R.C., 1929-30, col., 1930-35, col. in auxiliary res. since 1935. Burgess, borough of State Coll., Pa., 1926-30; pres. of council since 1932-36. Trustee, Pa. State Coll. Mem. Am. Soc. C.E., Kappa Sigma. Scabbard and Blade. Received military citations from the President and Sec. of War of U.S., Chief of U.S. Engrs., Chief of the Q.M., and Chief of the Constrn. Div., U.S. Army. Ind. Republican. Methodist. Elk. Address: 323 W. Fairmount St., State College, Pa.

ROTHSCHILD, Felix; v.p. Sun Life Insurance Co. Office: 109 E. Redwood St., Baltimore, Md.

ROTHSCHILD, Karl, neuro-psychiatrist; b. Kirchberg, Germany, Nov. 29, 1897; s. Julius and Albertina (Salomon) R.; came to U.S., 1924, naturalized, 1929; ed. U. of Frankfurt, Germany, 1916-19, U. of Köln (Cologne), 1919-20; M.D., U. of Heidelberg, Germany, 1921; m. Lillian B. Schwartz, June 12, 1927; children—Joanne Carol, James Herman. Physician at New Brunswick, N.J., since 1926, specializing in neuro-psychiatry; dir. dept. neuro-psychiatry, St. Peter's Gen. Hosp.; asso. attdg. phys. in charge of neurology, Middlesex Gen. Hosp., New Brunswick, N.J.; cons. neurologist, Roosevelt Hosp., Menlo Park, N.J. Fellow Am. Coll. Phys., Am. Psychiatric Assn., Am. Med. Assn. Mem. Assn. for Research in Nervous and Mental Disease, N.J. State and Middlesex Co. med. socs., N.J. Neuro-Psychiatric Assn. Club: Rutgers University. Home: 149 Livingston Av., New Brunswick, N.J.

ROTHSCHILD, Solomon; vice chmn. bd. Sun Life Insurance Co. Office: 109 E. Redwood St., Baltimore, Md.

ROTHSCHILD, Stanford Z.; pres. Sun Life Insurance Co. Office: 109 E. Redwood St., Baltimore, Md.

ROUDEBUSH, Russell Irwin; prof. edn., Marshall Coll. Address: Marshall College, Huntington, W.Va.

ROULSTON, Robert Bruce, univ. prof.; b. Baltimore, Md., Nov. 6, 1877; s. Robert and Margaret (McLean) R.; A.B., Johns Hopkins U., 1900, grad. student, 1900-04, 1905-06, Ph.D., 1906; grad. student, univs. Berlin, Leipzig, Heidelberg, 1904-05; m. Helene Holmelin, Oct. 1, 1909. Master in German and Latin, Gilman Country Day Sch., Baltimore, 1905-08; instr. German, Johns Hopkins U., 1908-11, associate, 1911-17, asso. prof., 1917-28, prof. German since 1928, dir. summer courses since 1930. Mem. Modern Lang. Assn. (pres. Middle States and Md. Sect., 1931-32), Assn. of Deans and Dirs. of Summer Courses (sec. 1936-37), Phi Beta Kappa, Omicron Delta Kappa. Clubs: University, Johns Hopkins (Baltimore). Home: 313 St. Dunstans Rd., Baltimore, Md.

ROUNDS, Charles Ralph, educator; b. Arkansaw, Wis., Aug. 3, 1877; s. Cyrus and Mary (Boyd) R.; student Florence (Wis.) High Sch., 1891-94, Stevens Point State Normal Sch., 1897-99; Ph.B., U. of Wis., 1901; grad. work, U. of Ill., 1901-03; Ed.M., Harvard Grad. Sch. of Edn., 1924; m. Mabel Willis, June 29, 1904; children—Robert Willis, David Edward, Stuart Boyd, Ben Willis, Joan Woolf. Teacher country sch., Pepin Co., Wis., 1894; instr., U. of Ill., 1901-03, Whitewater (Wis.) State Normal Sch., 1903-11; head dept. of English, West Div. High Sch., Milwaukee, 1911-13; supervisor English, Wis. State Normal Sch., Milwaukee, 1913-15; head dept. English, Milwaukee State Normal Sch., 1915-21; prin. Shorewood (Wis.) Sch., 1921-23; dir. English, Elizabeth, N.J., 1924-29; asst. prof. English, N.Y. Univ., 1929-30; head dept. English, Trenton State Teachers Coll., since 1930. Lecturer and organizer Post Schs., Army Ednl. Corps, Paris, 1919. Mem. N.E.A. (chmn. com. on grammatical nomenclation 1911-15), Nat. Council Teachers of English (dir.), N.J. Council Edn., Phi Delta Kappa, Phi Kappa Sigma. Presbyn. Clubs: Harvard of N.J.; Torch, Symposium (Trenton). Author: Twenty Short, Simple Lessons in English, 1915; Pupils' Outlines for Home Study in Grammar, 1925. Editor: Holmes Autocrat of the Breakfast Table, 1913; Wisconsin in Story and Song (with H. S. Hippensteel), 1914; Wisconsin Authors and Their Works, 1916; Ruskin's Sesame and Lilies, 1916. Contbr. to professional mags., etc. Home: 2168 Pennington Road, Trenton, N.J.

ROUSE, John Gould; b. at Baltimore, Md., April 25, 1884; s. William Chapman and Elizabeth Hyatt (Murphy) R.; grad. Univ. Sch. for Boys, Baltimore, 1901; B.S., Princeton, 1905; m. Elizabeth Baum, Nov. 1, 1911; children—John Gould, Jr., Elizabeth Anne. Partner firm of Rouse, Hempstone & Co., wholesale dry goods, Baltimore, 1906-17, v.p., 1917-21, pres. since 1921; pres. Rouse, Hempstone & Co., Inc.; dir. U.S. Fidelity & Guaranty Co., 1925-27; asst. to pres. Md. Casualty Co., 1927-35; dir. Baltimore Br. Federal Reserve Bank of Richmond, 1925-28, Md. Trust Co., 1917-35; dir. Western Nat. Bank; exec. head underwriting dept. Federal Housing Adminstrn., Baltimore Insuring Office, 1934-38, deputy adminstr. since 1938. Active in Liberty Loan campaigns and mem. Am. Protective League, World War. Dir. Baltimore Y.M.C.A., 1919-24, Baltimore Assn. Commerce, 1925-27; trustee Roland Park Country Sch., 1928-36; trustee Friendly Inn Assn. Mem. Md. Hist. Soc. Democrat. Episcopalian. Clubs: Bachelors Cotillon, Elkridge Hunt. Home: 403 Somerset Rd., Baltimore, Md. Office: Federal Housing Administration, Vermont Av. and K St., N.W., Washington, D.C.

ROUSH, Gar A., mineral economist; b. Harrisburg (now Gas City), Ind., Oct. 21, 1883; s. Isaac N. and Clementine H. (McCarty) R.; A.B., Indiana U., Bloomington, 1905; M.S., U. of Wis., 1910; m. Lillian Belle Coleman, July 16, 1911. Asst. prof. metallurgy, 1912-20, asso. prof., 1920-26, Lehigh U.; acting prof. metallurgy, Mont. Sch. Mines, 1926-27; spl. adviser to the Mus. Peaceful Arts, New York, 1927-30; editor since 1913, Mineral Industry, ann. devoted to world mineral interests. Appointed supervisor of training of the inspection division Ordnance Dept., U.S.A., June 1, 1918; commissioned capt. Ordnance Department, August 1, 1918, and appointed head of educational br., inspection div., and later chief of tests, metall. br.; hon. discharged, Mar. 13, 1919; commd. maj., Staff Specialist Reserve, U.S.A., Dec. 26, 1924, and for several years served as spl. lecturer on strategic mineral supplies, Army Industrial Coll.; now assigned to Commodities Div., Planning Branch Office of Asst. Sec. of War. Member Electrochem. Soc. (asst. sec. 1912-18), Am. Inst. Mining and Metall. Engrs. (mng. editor 1917), Society of American Mil. Engrs. Presbyterian. Contbr. more than 200 articles on electrochem. and metall. and mineral economics in the tech. press, various standard encyclos. and other works of reference. Author of the sect. on Mineral Industries in rev. edit. Van Hise's Conservation of Natural Resources; sect. on Electrochemistry and Electrometallurgy in 6th edit. Standard Handbook for Electrical Engineers; Strategic Mineral Supplies; articles on strategic mineral supplies in foreign countries in Military Engineer. Home: R.F.D. 3, Wydnor, Bethlehem, Pa.

ROUZER, Paul Charles, county supt. schs.; b. Chicago, Ill., Oct. 20, 1888; s. John C. and Carrie A. (Strow) R.; B.S. in Agr., U. of Wis., Madison, 1912; student W.Va. Univ., Morgantown, 1919-20, Cornell U., 1935-37; m. Maud Ella Ketchum, Aug. 12, 1913; children—Nancy Ellen (dec.), Charles Whitney. Engaged in teaching, high sch., St. Croix Falls, Wis., 1912-15; county agrl. agt., Tyler Co., W.Va., 1915-18; asst. prof. agrl. edn., W.Va. Univ., Morgantown, W.Va., 1918-21; state supervisor vocational agriculture, State Dept. Edn., Charleston, W.Va.,

1921-22; head agr. dept., Potomac State Sch., Keyser, W.Va., 1923-32; resident mgr. Red House Farms, Subsistence Homestead, Red House, W.Va., 1933-34; county supt. schs., Mineral Co., W.Va., at Keyser, W.Va., since 1935; sec. bd. edn. Mineral Co. since 1935. Mem. Nat. Edn. Assn., W.Va. Edn. Assn., Am. Country Life Assn. Republican. Presbyn. Club: Rotary of Keyser (past pres.). Home: Potomac Drive. Office: Court House, Keyser, W.Va.

ROWAN, Charles A., chmn. bd. Westinghouse Air Brake Company; b. Pittsburgh, Pa., Sept. 27, 1874; s. William and Mary (Elder) R.; ed. pub. schs., Pittsburgh, and Parnassus (Pa.) Acad.; m. Alma Leitch, June 2, 1915; children —Charles A., Andrew Leitch, Eleanor Ward. Bookkeeper, Logan's Planing Mills, Parnassus, 1892-94, E. Pittsburgh Improvement Co., 1894-1902; asst. cashier E. Pittsburgh Nat. Bank, 1903; with Westinghouse Air Brake Co. since 1903, asst. auditor until 1910, auditor, 1910-16, controller, 1916-19, vice-pres. and controller, 1919-30, exec. vice-pres., 1930-32, pres., 1932-36, chmn. of the boards of Westinghouse Air Brake Co. and Union Switch & Signal Co. since 1936; also dir. many subsidiaries, pres. Westinghouse Internat. Brake & Signal Co. from 1927 to its dissolution in 1936; dir. First Nat. Bank of Swissvale, First Nat. Bank of Wilmerding, Wilkinsburg (Pa.) Real Estate & Trust Co. Republican. Mason (32°, Shriner). Clubs: Duquesne, Pittsburgh Club, Longue Vue (Pittsburgh); Engineers' (New York); Edgewood Country. Home: 408 Maple Av., Edgewood, Pittsburgh, Pa. Office: Westinghouse Air Brake Co., Wilmerding, Pa.

ROWAND, Harry Hamilton; judge Court of Common Pleas since 1922. Address: City-County Bldg., Pittsburgh, Pa.

ROWE, John I.; mem. law firm Rowe & Cullen. Office: Lexington Bldg., Baltimore, Md.

ROWE, Joseph Eugene, educator, mathematician; b. Emmitsburg, Maryland, Mar. 21, 1883; s. Charles Jacob and Cora (Hoke) R.; Scotch-Irish and Huguenot ancestry; A.B., first honor, Gettysburg (Pa.) Coll., 1904, LL.D., 1930; student U. of Va., 1904-05; fellow in mathematics, Johns Hopkins, 1909-10, Ph.D., 1910; m. Nina King, Sept. 6, 1911; children—Joseph Eugene, Richard King. Instructor in mathematics, Goucher Coll., 1910-11, Haverford, 1911-12, Dartmouth, 1912-14; asst. prof., asso. prof., and prof. mathematics, Pa. State Coll., 1914-20; prof. and head dept. of mathematics, Coll. of William and Mary, 1921-28, dir. extension, 1924-28; pres. Clarkson Memorial Coll. of Technology, Potsdam, N.Y., 1928-32 (resigned); engaged in research in social sciences, Johns Hopkins U., 1932-33; apptd. mem. Bd. Veterans Appeals, Feb. 23, 1934. Asst. physicist Nat. Advisory Com., Aero, May 1917-Feb. 1918. Chief ballistician, Aberdeen Proving Ground, Ordnance Dept., U.S.A., 1920-21. Mem. S.A.R., Phi Beta Kappa, Phi Kappa Phi, Theta Chi. Democrat. Episcopalian. Club: Cosmos. Author: Introductory Mathematics. Co-Author: History of Gettysburg College, 1931. Inventor mathematical instruments. Home: 2807 St. Paul St., Baltimore, Md. Address: Arlington Bldg., Washington, D.C.

ROWLAND, Albert Lindsay, educator; b. Phila., Pa., Oct. 7, 1882; s. George Lindsay and Sarah Jones (Petty) R.; A.B., Central High Sch., Phila., 1901; grad. Phila. Sch. Pedagogy, 1904; A.B., Temple U., 1908; A.M., U. of Pa., 1911, Ph.D., 1914; m. Lillie Maria Hill, Apr. 1, 1907; 1 son, George Austin. Teacher pub. schs., Phila., 1904-10; critic teacher, Phila. Sch. of Pedagogy, 1910-11; prin. Practice Sch., same, 1911-18; supt. schs. Radnor Twp., Delaware Co., Pa., 1918-19; dir. Teacher Bur., Dept. of Pub. Instrn., Pa., 1919-25; supt. schs. Cheltenham Twp., Montgomery County, Pa., 1925-32; pres. State Teachers Coll., Shippensburg, since 1932. Organized and established modern system of teacher training in State of Pa. Life mem. N.E.A.; mem. Am. Assn. of Sch. Administrative, Pa. State Edn. Assn. (former chmn. com. of tenure problems of both organization), District Superintendents, Com. of Pa. on Improvement of Instruction (chmn.), Nat. Soc. Study of Edn., Progressive Edn. Assn. (mem. advisory board), Am. Assn. Adult Edn., Pa. State Assn. Adult Edn. (pres.), Pa. Forensic League (pres. 1929-30); pres. Southeastern Conv. Dist. of Pa. State Edn. Assn., 1928-29; mem. Governor's Commn. for Study of Ednl. Problems in Pa. (mem. exec. com.; chmn. com. on teacher preparation, 1931-35). Dir. Pa. Soc. for Crippled Children. Episcopalian; rector's warden, St. Andrew's Church, Shippensburg. Mason (32°). Clubs: University (Philadelphia), Rotary of Jenkintown (pres. 1928-29); Rotary of Shippensburg (gov. 180th Rotary Dist, 1937-38); Carlisle Country, Keystone Automobile. Author: Heroes of Early American History, 1918; (with W. D. Lewis) The Silent Readers, 1920; "England and Turkey" in Studies in English Commerce and Exploration in the Reign of Elizabeth, 1934. Address: College Campus, Shippensburg, Pa.

ROWLAND, Charles Joseph, coll. prof., pub. accountant; b. Olean, N.Y., Feb. 18, 1894; s. John Whiton and Ida Mabel (Pierce) R.; A.B., Cornell U., 1917; M.B.A., Northwestern U., 1929; m. Mazie Caroline Montgomery, Aug. 29, 1921; children—Mary Montgomery, Eleanor Whiton, John Hawley. Began as teacher, high sch., Donora, Pa., 1917; resident auditor, Income Tax Unit, Washington, D.C., 1919-21; lecturer and writer on Federal Taxation, Walton Sch. of Commerce, 1921-24; sr. accountant, Lybrand, Ross Bros. & Montgomery, Detroit office, 1924; prof. in charge accounting courses, Pa. State Coll. since 1925; has followed profession as Charles J. Rowland & Co., accountants and aditors, State College, Pa. since 1931; C.P.A. in N.C. and Pa. Served in C.W.S., U.S.A. as sergt., 1918-19. Auditor Borough of State College since 1932. Mem. Am. Inst. Accountants, Am. Accounting Assn., Municipal Finance Officers Assn., Am. Assn. Univ. Profs., Pa. Inst. of C.P.A.'s, Phi Beta Kappa, Pi Gamma Mu, Delta Sigma Pi, Phi Delta Kappa, Alpha Tau Omega. Republican. Presbyn. I.O.O.F. Clubs: University, Centre Hills Country. Home: 614 W. Fairmount Av., State College, Pa.

ROWLAND, Ewart Gladstone, mayor; b. Pittsburgh, Pa., Dec. 29, 1897; s. Walter and Kate (Phillips) R.; grad. Wilkinsburg (Pa.) pub. schs., 1911; m. Agnes Burns Stover, Apr. 8, 1924; children—Walter Burton, Nancy Lee, Agnes Joanne, Ewart Gladstone. With Mfrs. Light & Heat Co., Pittsburgh, 1911-20, beginning as clerk and advancing to mgr. dist. office; private sec. to W. McK. Smith, producer of oil and gas, since 1920. Elected councilman, Washington, Pa., 1933; dir. Accounts and Finance until 1937; mayor of Washington since 1937. Enlisted in U.S. Army, Apr. 16, 1917; served 1 yr. in France with Co. L, 111th Inf.; hon. discharged, May 16, 1919. Mem. Am. Legion, Vts. Foreign Wars, 40 and 8. Republican. Episcopalian. Mason, Elk, Moose, Eagle. Home: 267 Locust Av. Office: Municipal Bldg., Washington, Pa.

ROWLAND, James Marshall Hanna, obstetrician; b. Liberty Grove, Cecil Co., Md., Feb. 14, 1867; s. William Hopkins and Sarah Margery (Hanna) R.; prep. edn., West Nottingham Acad., Colora, Md.; M.D., Baltimore Med. Coll., 1892; m. Mary Virginia Zollikofer, Dec. 28, 1898; children—Mary Z., William M., Marjory J. Began practice at Baltimore, 1892; prof. obstetrics, Baltimore Med. Coll., 1900-13; prof. obstetrics, U. of Md., 1920-37, dean Sch. of Medicine since 1916; med. dir. Baltimore Life Ins. Co. Member bd. directors Md. Gen. Hosp. Fellow Am. Coll. Surgeons; mem. A.M.A., Med. and Chirurg. Soc. of Md. (ex-pres.), Southern Med. Assn., Baltimore City Med. Soc., Baltimore Co. Med. Soc. Democrat. Methodist. Club: University. Home: 1118 St. Paul St., Baltimore, Md.

ROWLAND, Roger Whittaker, pres. Newcastle Refractories Co.; b. Springfield, Mass., Feb. 4, 1895; s. Sleigh and Celia (Mellaly) R.; grad. Pa. State Coll., 1917; m. Altana Barnum Willis, Aug. 30, 1922; children—Natalie Willis, Roger Willis. Asso. with Newcastle Refractories Co. since 1929, pres. and dir. since 1929; pres. Corundite Refractories Co.; dir. Swindell-Dressler Co.; sec. of property and supplies Commonwealth of Pa. Served as 1st lieut. Air Service, U.S.A., 1917-19, with A.E.F. in France. Mem. Pa. Rep. Exec. Com. Mem. Am. Soc. Mech. Engrs., Am. Iron and Steel Inst., Am. Ceramic Soc., Am. Refractories Inst. Clubs: Duquesne (Pittsburgh); Union (Cleveland, O.); New Castle Field. Home: 1000 Highland Av. Office: New Castle, Pa.

ROWLAND, Theodore Sherwood, prin. high sch.; b. Greenport, N.Y., Oct. 28, 1885; s. Theodore Kimble and Lillian (Case) R.; A.B., Cornell U., 1907; A.M., U. of Pa., 1928; hon. D.Sc., Ursinus Coll., 1932; m. Florence Sherrill, Nov. 28, 1911; children—Florence Sherrill (Mrs. Charles T. Redding, Jr.), Theodore Sherwood, Jr. Began as teacher of science Bethlehem Prep. Sch.; now prin. Northeast High Sch., Phila., Pa. Dir. Phila. Y.M.C.A. Mem. Franklin Inst., Am. Soc. Coll. Teachers of Physics, Pa. State Edn. Assn., Phi Delta Kappa. Republican. Presbyn. Mason. Home: 6311 N. Camac St., Philadelphia, Pa.

ROWLAND, Wilfred Ernest, manufacturer; b. Pittsburgh, Pa., Aug. 9, 1885; s. Edward and Mary (Holbrook) R.; student Mt. Pleasant (Pa.) High Sch., 1899-1902, Pierce Sch., Phila., 1910-11; m. Ruth Helen Smith, June 12, 1928; 1 dau., Marilyn Ruth. Began learning glass making, 1905; with Bryce Bros. Glass Co., Mt. Pleasant, Pa., 1905-09; salesman Bryce Bros. Glass Co., Mt. Pleasant, Pa., 1912-13; dist. sales mgr. Aluminum Cooking Utensil Co., New Kensington, Pa., 1914-21; gen. mgr. Keystone Wire Matting Co., Beaver Falls, Pa., 1922-29, owner since 1929. Served as 2d lt., Res. Air Force, U.S. Army, during World War. Republican. United Presbyterian. Club: Pittsburgh Athletic Assn. Home: 4261 Andover Terrace, Pittsburgh, Pa. Office: P.O. Box, 166, Beaver Falls, Pa.

ROWLEY, Edith, librarian; b. Wayland, N.Y., Jan. 23, 1877; d. Herbert and Sarah Alice (Richardson) R.; grad. State Normal Sch. Fredonia, N.Y., 1897; A.B., Allegheny Coll., 1905; grad. study, State Library Sch., Albany, N.Y., 1905-06; A.M., Allegheny Coll., 1913. Engaged in teaching Stockton (N.Y.) High Sch., 1897-1900; asst. librarian, Allegheny Coll., 1906-07, librarian since 1907; editor Chautauquan Daily at Chautauqua Assembly, summers 1918-31; alumni sec. and editor Alumni Bulletin, Allegheny Coll., 1920-28; rep. Asso. Press at Chautauqua, 1922-31; corr. Chautauqua news for Jamestown Journal, summers for 10 yrs. Mem. Am. and Pa. library assns., Am. Assn. Univ. Women (pres. 1932-33, 1934-36), D.A.R., Phi Beta Kappa, Alpha Gamma Delta. In travel and study abroad, 1913-14. Republican. Mem. M.E. Ch. Clubs: Business and Professional Womens, Womans Literary Soc., Bird and Tree. Home: 390 Hamilton Av., Meadville, Pa.

ROWLEY, George H., judge; b. Greenville, Pa., Nov. 25, 1882; s. George and Margaret (McGuirl) R.; A.B., Allegheny Coll., 1905; A.B., Yale, 1906; LL.B., Yale U. Law Sch., 1908; LL.D., Thiel Coll., 1938; m. Susan Templeton, July 25, 1922; children—George, Peter. Admitted to Pa. bar, 1908, and since engaged in gen. practice of law at Greenville; served as dist. atty. Mercer Co., 1911-19; U.S. Collector of Customs, Pittsburgh, 1919-23; serving as judge Ct. of Common Pleas of Mercer Co. since 1936. Mem. Pa. Bar Assn., Mercer County Bar Assn., Alpha Chi Rho. Democrat. Home: 65 Eagle St., Greenville, Pa. Office: Mercer, Pa.

ROWLEY, Myron Elliott, lawyer, b. Culmerville, Pa., Apr. 13, 1899; s. Daniel Grant and Clara Augusta (Hazlett) R.; student Tarentum High Sch., 1912-16; A.B., Washington and Jefferson Coll., Washington, Pa., 1920; LL.B., U. of Pittsburgh Law Sch., 1926; student Yale Law Sch., summer 1923, U. of Mich. Law Sch., summer 1924, 1925; m. Ethelwyn Marie Beatty, June 10, 1925; children—James Elliott, Mary Elizabeth, Nancy Ruth. Admitted to Pa. bar, 1926, and since practiced in Beaver Co.; partner law firm Craig & Rowley since 1928. Mem. Am. Bar Assn., Pa. Bar Assn., S.A.R., Beta Theta Pi. Republican. Presbyterian. Clubs: Exchange (Aliquippa, Pa.).

ROWLEY, Thomas Josiah, merchant; b. Plum Creek Twp., Armstrong County, Pa., Nov. 26, 1875; s. John and Elizabeth (George) R.; student McKee's Sch., Plum Creek Twp., 1881-95; m. Annetta Viora Mangus, May 27, 1901; children—Velma Pearl, Lela Jemina (Mrs. Eugene C. Stitt), Paul Eugene, Gladys Viora (Mrs. Ephraim S. Coffman). On farm until 1899; started grocery and feed business without capital, Vandergrift, Pa., 1904, still in same location; sustained loss of $20,000 in Mar. 1936 flood, but restocked; dir. Vandergrift Savings & Trust Co. since 1916, vice-pres. since 1937. Democrat. Lutheran. Odd Fellow. Home: 182 Lincoln Av. Office: 12 1st St., North Vandergrift, Pa.

ROWLEY, Walter N(elson), surgeon; b. Rochester, Minn., Apr. 10, 1893; s. John Martin and Nora (Nelson) R.; student Macalester Coll., St. Paul, Minn., 1912-14; M.D., Northwestern U. Med. Sch., Chicago, 1918; m. Vivian Fitch, June 28, 1912 (dec.); children—Mary Virginia (Mrs. Verner B. Hinerman), Jeanne Patrica; m. 2d, Hilda Young, May 13, 1931. Served as med. officer, Chelsea Naval Hosp., Boston, 1918-19; asso. Mayo Clinic, Rochester, Minn., 1919-23; engaged in practice of surgery at Huntington, W.Va., 1923-29, and since 1930; surgeon to Kokomo Clinic, Kokomo, Ind., 1929-30; pres. staff St. Marys Hosp., Huntington, W.Va. Served as lt. (j.g.) U.S.N.R.M.C., 1918-22; lt. comdr. U.S.N.R., 1934. Fellow Am. Coll. Surgeons. Mem. Cabell County Med. Soc., W.Va. State Med. Soc., W.Va. Obstet. and Gynecol. Soc., Mayo Clinic Resident and Ex-resident Assn., Am. Congress of Obstetricians and Gynecologists, Alpha Kappa Kappa. Republican. Episcopalian. Mason (K.T., Shriner). Clubs: Huntington Kennel Club, Inc. (pres. and dir.); Executives; American Business. Home: 1406 Spring Valley Drive. Office: 1522 6th Av., Huntington, W.Va.

ROWNTREE, Leonard George, M.D.; b. London, Can., Apr. 10, 1883; s. George and Phoebe (Martindale) R.; M.D., Western Med. Sch., London, Can., 1905; Sc.D., Western U., London, Can., 1916; m. Katherine Campbell, July 9, 1914. Interne Victoria Hosp., 1906; vol. asst., experimental therapeutics, asst., instr., asso. and asso. prof. Johns Hopkins Med. Sch., 1907-14; asso. professor medicine, Johns Hopkins, 1914-16; prof. medicine and chief dept., U. of Minn., 1916-20; prof. medicine and chief of division of medicine, Mayo Foundation, Rochester, Minn., also senior med. consultant and dir. clin. research, Mayo Clinic, 1920-32; dir. Phila. Inst. for Med. Research and research clinician Phila. General Hospital, since 1932. Member A.M.A., A.A.A.S., Assn. American Physicians, Soc. Clin. Investigators, Phi Beta Kappa, Phi Beta Pi. Episcopalian. Devised and introduced the phenolsulphonephthalein test, now in universal use in renal disorders, and participated in establishing value of renal functional studies; also devised and introduced the dye method of determining liver function and the dye method of determining the blood volume of the body; pioneer in demonstrating the beneficial effect of cortin in Addison's disease and the role of the thymus and pineal glands in growth and development. Found by administering crude wheat germ oil made by ether extraction to rats, malignant tumors have been produced by a vegetable product at will, for the first time in history. Lt. col., M.C., U.S.A. and exec. officer Med. Research Labs., A.E.F., 1917-18; col. R.C. Home: The Touraine, 1520 Spruce St. Office: Philadelphia Institute, 34th and Pine Sts., Philadelphia, Pa.

ROXBY, John B.; prof. of anatomy and histology, Temple University. Address: Temple University, Philadelphia, Pa.

ROY, William Milton, supervising prin. schs.; b. Montrose, Pa., Mar. 16, 1891; s. Levi and Nellie R.; ed. Mansfield Teachers Coll., 1910-13, grad. 1913, Western Reserve U., 1924; A.B., Pa. State Coll., 1930; grad. study, Bucknell U., 1938; m. Beulah Merrill, Nov. 29, 1916. Engaged in teaching, rural schs., 1909-11, elementary schs., 1914-15; prin. high sch., Bradford Co., Pa., 1916-22; asst. county supt., Bradford Co., Pa., 1922-34; supervising prin. schs. Towanda Borough, Towanda, Pa., since 1934. Mem. N.E.A.; Pa. State Edn. Assn., Kappa Phi Kappa. Republican. Presbyn. Mason (K.T., Shriner). Clubs: Masonic, Chamber of Commerce. Home: 302 2d St., Towanda, Pa.

ROYAL, William Carson, clergyman; b. Johnston Co., N.C., Aug. 30, 1885; s. Richard and Jane (Barbour) R.; prep. edn., Benson (N.C.) Acad.; student Wake Forest (N.C.) Coll., 1907-09; m. Nellie Smith, June 8, 1908; children—Edna Mae, Virginia Nell, Joe Smith. Missionary pastor Bapt. State Mission Bd., N. C., 1907-09; missionary pastor Va. Bapt. Bd., Hampton, Va., 1910-12; pastor 4 rural chs., Accomack Co., Va., 1913-15; pastor First Bapt. Ch., Frederick, Md., since 1916. Pres. Md. Bapt. Union Assn., 1932-35; mem. Md. Bapt. Summer Assembly, Francis Scott Key Council of Boy Scouts, Frederick Charity Orgn., Frederick County Welfare Board. Chaplain Fitzhugh Lee Chapter, Daughters of Confederacy; chaplain House of Dels., Md. Assembly, 1939. Democrat. Mason, Odd Fellow. Club: Lions (ex-pres.). Home: 219 Dill Av., Frederick, Md.

ROYE, Harry Frederick, life ins. exec.; b. Willow Grove, Pa., June 7, 1901; s. Frederick J. and Louisa (Lyons) R.; ed. West Chester (Pa.) High Sch., 1916-20, Bucknell U., 1920-23; m. Dorothy Jones, Apr. 7, 1924; children —Jean Phyllis, Nancy Ellen, Mary Lou. Employed as retail meat salesman, 1922-27; salesman, U.S. Slicing Machine Co., 1927-30; ins. salesman, 1930-35; gen. agt. Equitable Life Ins. Co. of Ia., at Camden, N.J., since 1935; mem. firm Harry Roye Organization since 1937. Served as mem. N.J. Ho. of Assembly, 1937-38; mem. Camden Chamber of Commerce, Camden Recreational Commn. (v.p. 1937-38), Camden Co. Safety Council (pres. 1937-38), Interstate Commn. on Crime. Mem. Life Underwriters Assn. Democrat. Baptist. L.O.O.M. Club: Y's Men. Home: 249 Mountwell Av., Haddonfield. Office: 300 Broadway, Camden, N.J.

ROYER, B(enjamin) Franklin, public health; b. Mason and Dixon, Pa., Dec. 13, 1870; s. John and Elizabeth (McClannahan) R.; ed. N. Ill. Normal Sch., 1892, Mercersburg Coll. (Acad.), 1895; M.D., Jefferson Med. Coll. 1899; (hon.) D.Sc., Ursinus Coll., 1919; m. Jessie Leona Ross, of Halifax, N.S., July 19, 1923 (dec.); m. 2d, Mrs. Leslie Kauffman, Chambersburg, Pa., Dec. 24, 1936. Res. phys. Jefferson Hosp., 1899-1900, chief res. phys., 1902-03, asst. demonstrator obstetrics, 1900-03; chief res. phys. Phila. Municipal Hosp. for Contagious Diseases, 1903-08; asso. chief med. inspr., 1908-09, chief med. inspr., 1909-18, actg. state commr. health, Pa. Dept. Health, 1918-19; exec. officer Mass.-Halifax Health Commn., Halifax, N.S., 1919-23; research asso. Am. Child Health Assn., 1923-24; med. dir. Nat. Soc. for Prevention of Blindness, 1925-32; vice-chmn. Pa. Emergency Child Health Com., 1933-38; chmn. Franklin Co. Health Com., 1938-39. Served as 1st lt. Med. Corps Res., U.S.A., 1911-17, capt., 1917-27. Chmn. Med. Corps U.S.A. Examining Bd., Harrisburg, Pa., during World War. Fellow Royal Inst. of Pub. Health (Eng.), Phila. Coll. Phys., A.M. A., Am. Pub. Health Assn.; mem. Am. Child Health Assn., Am. Soc. Hygiene, Pa. State and Phila. Co. med. socs., S.R., Phi Alpha Sigma. Honorary mem. Halifax Med. Soc. President Royer Renmore Assn. since 1937. Republican. Mason. Clubs: University, Medical (Philadelphia); Army and Navy (Washington, D.C.). Contbr. chapters to books on medicine and about 150 articles to med. jours. Home: The Hall, R.F.D. No. 7, Chambersburg, Pa.; 11 Wyoming Av., Tunkhannock, Pa.

ROYER, Galen Brown, clergyman; b. Lewisburg, Pa., Sept. 8, 1862; s. John Grove and Elizabeth (Reiff) R.; student Mt. Morris (Ill.) Coll., 1883-89, Northern Ind. Bus. Coll., Valparaiso, Ind., 1887; A.B., Juniata Coll., 1920, B.D., same, 1922; m. Anna Martha Miller, Mar. 5, 1885; children—Elizabeth (dec.), Daniel Long, Kathren (wife of Rev. Quincy I. Holsopple), Neta Ruth (dec.), Josephine (Mrs. Frank A. Thomas), John Galen. Engaged in teaching, 1883-89, called to ministry, 1889, ordained to ministry Ch. of Brethren, 1907; sec. Gen. Mission Bd., 1890, treas., 1900, resigned both positions, 1918 to finish coll. edn.; pastor, Pittsburgh, 1925-30, Johnstown, 1930-36, retired, 1936; in behalf of ch. visited chs. in Europe, 1907, 1910, 1913-14, this trip including mission fields in China and India; climbed Mt. Ararat, 1913; architect and contractor for ch. on large pub. plant, Elgin, Ill. Republican. Mem. Ch. of Brethren. Author: Bible Biographies for the Young (12 vols.), 1898-1904; Thirty Three Years of Missions by the Church of the Brethren, 1913. Home: Huntingdon, Pa.

RUBENSTEIN, Frank Joseph, insurance; b. Philadelphia, Pa., Dec. 25, 1890; s. Morris and Gitel (Goudiss) R.; teacher's certificate, Gratz Coll., Phila., 1910; student U. of Baltimore, 1925-27; studied Am. Coll. Life Underwriters, 1937; m. Mary Weinberg, Aug. 4, 1918; children—Bernard W., Esther G. Successively clerk, chief clerk and sec., Dropsie Coll., 1908-18; asst. to exec. dir., later asst. sec., Jewish Welfare Bd., U.S. Army and Navy, 1918-19; mem. firm S. Weinberg, wholesale leaf tobacco dealers, Philadelphia and Lancaster, 1919-24; exec. dir. Y.M. and Y.W.H.A., Baltimore, 1924-34; spl. rep. Equitable Life Assurance Soc., 1934-37, dist. mgr. since Nov. 1937. Mem. Nat. Conf. Jewish Social Work; mem. bd. Jewish Edn., Baltimore, Jewish Pub. Soc. America, Edn. com. Y.M. and Y.W.H.A. Mem. Nat. Assn. Life Underwriters, Baltimore Life Ins. Trust Council. Democrat. Mason, B'nai B'rith (pres. Menorah Lodge; chmn. program com. Dist. Grand Lodge No. 5). Home: Seville Apt. Office: 614 Baltimore Trust Bldg., Baltimore, Md.

RUDDOCK, William McClave, lawyer; b. DuBois, Pa., Jan. 27, 1900; s. William McClave and Jennie (Byers) R.; ed. Indiana State Normal Sch., 1917-19; Lit.B., Grove City Coll., 1921; LL.B., U. of Pa. Law Sch., 1925; m. Dorothy Parker, Feb. 17, 1925; children—William Parker, Donn McClave. Admitted to Pa. bar, 1925, and since engaged in gen. practice of law at Indiana; mem. firm Fisher & Ruddock since 19—; dir. Chardon Gas & Oil Co. Served as 2d lieut. staff 55th inf. Pa. N.G. Dir. Kiskiminetas Springs Sch., Saltsburg, Pa. Mem. Am., Pa., and Indiana Co. bar assns. Republican. Presbyn. (trustee First Ch.). Club: Rotary of Indiana, Pa. Home: 694 Water St. Office: Savings & Trust Bldg., Indiana, Pa.

RUDDY, John Francis, newspaper editor; b. Scranton, Pa., Aug. 18, 1894; s. Thomas A. and Elizabeth (Corbett) R.; student pub. schs.; m. Emma Rinehardt Stiles, June 10, 1920; children—Richard, Marcia. Treas. Anthracite Steel Co., Scranton, Pa., 1922-30; pres. Barrett Constrn. Co., Scranton, Pa., since 1920; city editor The Scranton Times since 1930; asso. editor Lorenz Investors' Digest since 1934. Home: 1900 N. Washington Av. Office: Penn Av. and Spruce St., Scranton, Pa.

RUDISILL, Earl Stockslager, clergyman, educator; b. Gettysburg, Pa., Jan. 23, 1891; s. Hon. David Calvin and Clara Virginia (Stockslager) R.; A.B., Gettysburg Coll., 1912; B.D., Gettysburg Theol. Sem., 1915; student U. of Chicago, summer 1919; A.M., U. of Pittsburgh, 1921; Ph.D., U. of Pa., 1925; D.D., Gettysburg Coll., 1935; m. Lillie Grace Mehring, Aug. 20, 1915; 1 son, Fred Luther. Pastor St. Stephen's Ch., Chicago, 1915-19, Aspinwall Ch., 1919-23, Grace Ch., Phila., 1923-27, St. Luke's Ch., York, Pa., 1927-34; pres. Thiel Coll., Greenville, Pa., since 1934; served as instr. psychology, U. of Pittsburgh, 1921-23, U. of Pa., 1924-25, also instr. various religious training sch.; mem. Parish and Ch. Sch. Bd. of United Luth. Ch., term 1938-1944. Trustee (ex-officio) Thiel Coll. Mem. A.A.A.S., Am. Psychol. Assn., Child Study Assn. America, Nat. Council Parent Education, Pennsylvania State Council Parent Edn., Phi Beta Kappa. Republican. Author: The Intimate Problems of Youth, 1929. Co-Author: Clinical Psychology, 1931;

The Day's Worship, 1933. Contbr. on religious and ednl. subjects. Initiated the annual "Institute of Parenthood and Home Relations," at Thiel Coll., 1934. Home: Greenville, Pa.

RUDOLFS, Willem, educator; b. Wageningen, Holland, Feb. 13, 1886; s. Willem and Antonia (van Ewijk) R.; ed. Govt. Sch., Holland, U. of Ill.; student Rutgers Univ., 1918-21; Ph.D., Pasteur Inst., Paris, 1921; m. Cornelia G. Van Laar, Sept. 21, 1921; 1 son, Willem. Came to U.S., 1915, naturalized, 1921. Began as soil chemist, U. of Ill., 1915-18; fellow Rutgers, 1919-20, biochemist, 1921-23, chief of research since 1923; prof. of water supplies and sewage disposal, Rutgers U., since 1924; chief of research, State of N.J., since 1923. Mem. Am. Soc. C.E., Am. Chem. Soc., Am. Pub. Health Assn., Professional Engring. Soc., Am. Inst. Chemists, Professional Engring. and Land Surveyors; fellow A.A.A.S. Mem. Dutch Reformed Ch. Home: Hillcrest, New Brunswick, N.J.

RUDOLPH, Joseph, life ins.; b. Baltimore, Md., Oct. 17, 1890; s. Abraham and Leah R.; student pub. schs., Baltimore, Md.; m. Lena Matz, June 24, 1919; 1 son, Herbert Ivan. In employ Snow, Church & Co., mercantile collections, Baltimore, Md., 1912-15; office clk., Baltimore Bargain House, 1915-21; solicitor for Metropolitan Life Ins. Co., 1921-36; mgr. Baltimore office, Jefferson Standard Life Ins. Co. since 1936. Home: 2310 Mt. Royal Terrace. Office: Baltimore Trust Bldg., Baltimore, Md.

RUDOLPHY, Jay Besson, physician; b. Hoboken, N.J., Nov. 30, 1887; s. Charles Bruno and Almira Josephine (Besson) R.; ed. Columbia U., 1910-11; M.D., Coll. Phys. & Surgs. of Columbia U., 1915; m. Edith Rondinella, Feb. 20, 1930; 1 dau., Elisabeth Besson. Interne, N.Y. Post Grad. Hosp. and Med. Sch., 1915-17; post grad. student ophthalmology, U. of Pa. Grad. Sch. of Medicine, 1920, asst. prof. ophthalmology since 1930; neuro-ophthalmologist, Phila. Gen. Hosp.; ophthalmic surgeon to Pa. Industrial Home for Blind Women since 1931; ophthalmologist to hosp. and chief outpatient clinic, Pa. Hosp., since 1930; asst. ophthalmologist, Lankenau Hosp. since 1935. Served as 1st lt. then capt. Med. Corps, U.S.A., active duty, World War, 1917-19. Mem. A.M.A., Am. Acad. Ophthalmology and Otolaryngology, Coll. of Physicians of Phila., Ophthalmic Club of Phila., Phi Rho Sigma. Mem. Soc. Descs. Knights of Most Noble Order of the Garter, Pa. Soc. Mayflower Descs., Soc. Mayflower Descs. in the State of N.Y., S.R., Mil. Order Fgn. Wars of U.S., Pa. Hist. Soc. Republican. Episcopalian. Home: 4043 Walnut St. Office: 230 S. 21st St., Philadelphia, Pa.

RUE, Francis Jamison, banking; b. Phila., Pa., Nov. 2, 1896; s. Levi Lingo and Mary McCurdy (Gill) R.; ed. St. Paul's Sch., Concord, N.H., 1911-14; A.B., Princeton, 1918; m. Virginia Randolph Pelzer, Apr. 7, 1920; children—Francis J., Jr., Mary Randolph, Virginia Pelzer. Asso. with The Philadelphia National Bank continuously since entering employ as clk., 1919, asst. cashier, 1920-25, asst. vice-pres., 1925-28, vice-pres. since 1928. Served as ensign Pay Corps, U.S.N.R.F., 1918-19. Mem. Phila. Charter Commn. Trustee Chestnut Hill Hosp. Mem. S.R. Republican. Episcopalian. Clubs: Rittenhouse, Princeton, Midday, Sunnybrook Golf (Philadelphia). Home: 7305 Emlen St., Philadelphia, Pa. Office: 1416 Chestnut St., Philadelphia, Pa.

RUEHLE, Godfrey Leonard Alvin, bacteriologist; b. Stillwater, Minn., Oct. 30, 1884; s. Gustav Adolph and Mathilda (Kleps) R.; Pharm.G., Univ. of Wash., Seattle, 1906, B.S. in Chemistry, 1908, M.S., 1910; grad. student Cornell U., 1916-17, Mich. State Coll. 1920-26; m. Jane Terwilliger, Dec. 3, 1912; children—John Alvin, Jane Elizabeth (Mrs. Charles W. Haas, Jr.). Engaged as asst. bacteriologist, N.Y. Agrl. Expt. Sta., Geneva, 1911-18; asst. bacteriologist, Mich. State Coll. Expt. Sta., East Lansing, 1918-19; asso. bacteriologist and asso. prof. bacteriology, Mich. State Coll., 1919-26; prof. bacteriology, Univ. of Idaho, 1926-29; sr. bacteriologist, U.S. Dept. Agr., Food and Drug Adminstrn., Washington, D.C., since 1929.

Served in N.Y. N.G., 1918. Mem. Soc. Am. Bacteriologists, Am. Pub. Health Assn., Sigma Xi. Presbyn. Contbr. bulls. and papers in relation to bacteriology. Home: 1210 E St., Silver Spring, Md.

RUF, Casper Albert, mfg. exec.; b. Parkersburg, W.Va., Dec. 11, 1896; s. Henry Conrad and Minnie Jane (Archer) R.; student Parkersburg (W.Va.) Schs., 1901-11, night sch. and corrs. courses studying accounting, taxes, law, 1911-30; m. Marie Wright, Feb. 16, 1918. Began as telegraph messenger, Parkersburg, 1911; messenger B.&O. R.R. Co., Parkersburg, 1912-13, timekeeper and car distributor, Parkersburg, 1913-17; clk. Consolidation Coal Co., Fairmont, W.Va., 1917-18; transportation timekeeper B.& O. R.R., Gassaway, W.Va., 1918-19; mgr. cost dept. Parkersburg (W.Va.) Rig & Reel Co., 1919-20, accounting mgr., 1920-24, asst. sec., 1924-33, asst. gen. mgr., 1933-34, v.p., gen. mgr. and dir. since 1934. Active in Community Chest work, Parkersburg, 1925-35. Mem. Visitation Com. of W.Va. Wesleyan Coll. Mem. Am. Petroleum Inst. Republican. Methodist (chmn. finance com. First Methodist Ch., Parkersburg). Mason (Mount Olivet Lodge 3), Elk (Parkersburg 198). Club: Bankers of America (New York City). Home: 1810 21st St. Office: 620 Depot St., Parkersburg, W.Va.

RUFF, John Klohr, contractor, builder; b. Randallstown, Md., June 9, 1891; s. Seymour and Wilhelmina (Klohr) R.; student Baltimore Poly. Sch., 1906-10; m. Mary Grimm, July 1, 1916; children—Jane, Betty (Mrs. Henry Knoche), Mary Ellen, John K., Jr. Masonry contracting business with father under name Seymour Ruff & Son, 1910-29; pres. Seymour Ruff & Sons, Inc., Baltimore, Md., 1929-37; propr. John K. Ruff Co., contractor and building, Baltimore, since 1937; pres. Randallstown Bank since 1935; chmn. bd. mgrs. Randallstown Community Bldg. since 1927. Mem. efficiency and economy commn. to coöperate with Bd. of County Commrs. for Baltimore County since 1939—. Mem. Associated General Contractors of America, Building Congress and Exchange of Baltimore. Republican. Methodist. Mason (K.T., 32°), K.P. Club: Kiwanis (Baltimore). Home: Liberty Heights Av. at Harrisonville; post office: Randallstown, Md. Office: 100 W. 22d St., Baltimore, Md.

RUGE, Edwin Gardner Weed, univ. prof.; b. Apalachicola, Fla., July 24, 1890; s. George Henry and Elizabeth (Porter) R.; A.B., Yale U., 1912; LL.B., Harvard U. Law Sch., 1915; m. Isabelle Roberts, Apr. 24, 1920. Engaged in practice of law at Atlanta, Ga., 1915-17; cost accountant Eberhard Mfg. Co., Cleveland, O., 1919-22; in practice of law asso. with Miller & Otis, N.Y. City, 1922-25; prof. law, U. of Md. Law Sch., Baltimore, Md., since 1925. Served as 1st lt. then capt. inf., U.S.A., 1917-19, with A.E.F. in France; wounded in action in Argonne; awarded D.S.C., Order of the Purple Heart; maj. and lt. col. inf., U.S.A. Res. 1919-33. Mem. Psi Upsilon. Republican. Episcopalian. Home: 3507 N. Charles St., Baltimore, Md.

RUHE, Percy Bott, newspaper editor; b. Allentown, Pa., May 28, 1881; s. E. Lehman and Sallie (Marsteller) R.; grad. high sch., Allentown, 1897; A.B., Muhlenberg Coll., Allentown, 1901; m. Amy Sieger, Mar. 20, 1912; children—Sara Louise, David, William, Joseph, Jack, Edward, Judith, Benjamin. Began as reporter Allentown Call, 1898; editor Allentown Morning Call since 1910. Founder Allentown playground system, 1912; pres. Allentown Recreation Commn. Mem. Lehigh County Humane Soc. (pres.). Republican. Episcopalian. Mason (32°). Clubs: Kiwanis, Torch. Home: Vera Cruz, Pa. Office: 101 N. 6th St., Allentown, Pa.

RUHL, Charles Reish, lumber mfr.; b. Millmont, Pa., July 14, 1877; s. John Calvin and Jennie M. (Reish) R.; student Susquehanna U., Selinsgrove, Pa., 1898-1900 (Class of 1902); m. Anna Elizabeth Spigelmyer, Dec. 24, 1900; children—Harold Reish, Myrtle Spigelmyer, Helen Meria (Mrs. William Kerstetter), Donald Calvin. Began as mfr. shipping containers, Millmont, Pa., 1908; interested in timber and lumber operations, Marlington, W.Va., 1903-04, sole owner, T. A. Ruhl Lumber Co., Millmont, Pa., mfrs. lumber, since 1903; pres. Ruhl-Watson-Phillips, Mifflinburg, Pa., planing mill and dealers retail lumber, since 1920; pres. Mifflinburg Farmers Exchange, wholesale and retail grain, mfrs. dairy and poultry feeds, since 1925; pres. Ruhl & Watson, Inc., Ruhl & Watson Lumber Co., Millmont, Pa., since 1905; pres. Lewisburg (Pa.) Planing Mill Co. since 1925; dir. and sec. bd. Mifflinburg Bank & Trust Co.; dir. Buffalo Valley Telephone Co.; dir. and vice-pres. Buffalo Valley Fire Ins. Co. since 1925. Republican. Lutheran. Address: Millmont, Pa.

RULE, Arthur Richards, real estate; b. Goshen, Oldham Co., Ky., Dec. 6, 1876; s. Rev. John and Mary W. R.; ed. dist. and pvt. schs. and acad.; m. Elizabeth Bacon Wright, Mar. 21, 1903; children—Patricia K. (wife of Albert Kellogg Stebbins, U.S.A.), Arthur R. (ensign U.S. N.), Walter W., Mary W. (wife of Geo. B. Coale, ensign U.S.N.), Elizabeth W. (wife of Lt. D. B. Johnson, U.S.A.). With Crutchfield & Woolfolk, fruit distributors, Pittsburgh, Pa., 1898-1911; an organizer Fla. Citrus Exchange, 1908; organizer North Am. Fruit Exchange, New York, 1911; organizer Gen. Sales Agency of America, 1915; an organizer, 1922, gen. mgr., 1923-30, Federated Fruit and Vegetable Growers; chmn. orgn. com. United Growers of America since 1929; pres. Mutual Service Corpn.; owner and developer of Wychwood, Westfield, N.J. (home community, awarded 1st place by Am. Inst. Architects for archtl. standard, 1936); dir. Deerfield Groves Co.; charter mem. and dir. Am. Inst. of Coöperation. Mem. gen. organizing com., 2d Pan Am. Standardization Conf., Washington, D.C., 1927; mem. exec. com. Nat. Council of Farmers' Coöperative Marketing Assn.; mem. Am. Friends of Lafayette, Acad. Polit. Science, Am. Com. Inst. of Agr. at Rome. Presbyn. Clubs: Economic, Kentuckians, Echo Lake Country. Contbr. on coöperative marketing of fruits and vegetables. Home: Westfield, N.J. Office: 580 Fifth Av., New York, N.Y.

RUMERY, Ralph Rollins, consulting engr.; b. Portland, Me., Oct. 29, 1876; s. Samuel Dayton and Emaline Carlton (Rollins) R.; student Coll. Cantonal, Lausanne, Switzerland, 1893-94, Mass. Inst. Tech., 1894-96, Harvard, 1896-98; m. Gladys Gilbert, Aug. 3, 1910; children—John Rollins, Richard Gilbert. Constrn. work U.S. Engrs. Corps, 1898-99, Boston & Me. R.R., Boston, 1899-1900, Aguierre R.R., Puerto Rico, 1900-01, Pa. Steel Co., Steelton, Pa., 1901-02, Soeldad R.R., Cuba, 1902-03, Pa. R.R., 1903-06; chief engr. N.Y. State Tax Commn., 1907-12; cons. engr. N.Y. City, 1915-20, D.&H. R.R. since 1917, Boston & Maine R.R. since 1924, Niagara Hudson Power Corpn. since 1923; pres. George C. Frye Co., surgical supplies, Portland, Me., since 1929; treas. Gilbert Thorp Land Co., New York, since 1928; pvt. practice as cons. valuation engr., New York, since 1912. Pres. Short Hills (N.J.) Pvt. Sch., 1930-34. Mem. Am. Inst. Cons. Engrs., Am. Soc. C.E. (asst. treas.), Am. Ry. Engr. Assn., S.A.R., Theta Xi. Republican. Clubs: Harvard, N.Y. Pilgrims (New York); Royal Bermuda Yacht (Hamilton, Bermuda); Fort Orange (Albany, N.Y.); Baltusrol Golf (Short Hills, N.J.). Home: Barberry Lane, Short Hills, N.J. Office: 50 Church St., New York, N.Y.

RUMSEY, Herbert, Sr., treas. Henry Muhs Co.; b. Central Valley, N.Y., Aug. 4, 1871; s. Edwin and Electa Jane (Herbert) R.; ed. Central Valley and Arden, N.Y., pub. schs., and Wrights Business College, Brooklyn, N.Y.; married Bertha S. Muhs, daughter of Henry L. Muhs, April 19, 1897; children—Edna Ernestine (Mrs. Karl Kolbe), Herbert Henry, Clifford Edwin, Doretta Elizabeth (Mrs. Albert Vreeland). Began as clerk in gen. store, 1884; employed by M. N. Day & Co., stock brokers, 1888-90; with Henry Muhs Co. since 1890, beginning as clerk, treas. and dir. since 1898. Republican. Mem. First Reformed Ch. Mason. Club: Rotary (Passaic). Home: 238 Passaic Av. Office: 41 Central Av., Passaic, N.J.

RUNK, Louis Barcroft, lawyer; b. Philadelphia, Pa., June 13, 1873; s. William M. and Elizabeth C. (Hill) R.; ed. U. of Pa., 1889-90;

A.B., Yale, 1893, A.M., same, 1903; LL.B., U. of Pa. Law Sch., 1896; m. Mary Amelia Rankin, Oct. 23, 1907; children—Elizabeth Hill (Mrs. Howard S. McMorris), Mary Amelie (Mrs. Gerald F. Rorer), John Ten Broeck. Admitted to Pa. bar, 1896 and engaged in gen. practice of law at Phila. until 1925; mem. firm Read & Pettit, 1901-08, Read, Gill & Runk, 1908-12, Kane & Runk, 1912-17, Hunsicker & Runk, 1921-25; asst. trust officer, Commonwealth Title Ins. & Trust Co. of Phila., 1925-28 when merged with Provident Trust Co., and asst. trust offficer, Provident Trust Co., 1928-39; gen. practice of law, Phila., since 1939. Served as maj. Ordnance Dept., U.S.A., 1917-19, in Bridgeport, Conn., Washington, D.C., and at Watervliet N.Y. Arsenal; in Res. Corps, 1919-37, lt. col. since 1929; now lt. col. Inactive Res. Treas. Cathedral Church of Christ (P.E.). Mem. Phila., Pa. State and Am. bar assns., Zeta Psi, Phi Beta Kappa. Democrat. Episcopalian. Mason. Club: Yale of Philadelphia. Author: two hist. monographs and various legal articles. Home: 17 W. Upsal St. Office: 526 Stephen Girard Bldg., Philadelphia, Pa.

RUNKLE, Erwin William, psychologist; b. Lisbon, Ia., May 20, 1869; s. Adam and Malinda Barbara (Sherk) R.; B.A., Coe College, Cedar Rapids, Ia., 1890; Ph.D., Yale, 1893; hon. fellow Clark U., 1899; m. May Middlekauff, 1894; 1 son, Lawrence M. Lecturer, Yale, 1893; prof. psychology and ethics, Pa. State Coll., since 1893, also librarian Carnegie Library, 1904-24; prof. emeritus since 1938. Republican. Presbyn. Fellow A.A.A.S.; mem. Am. Psychol. Assn., Phi Kappa Phi, Pi Gamma Mu. Contbr. to psychol and ednl. jours. Home: State College, Pa.

RUNYON, Frederick Oscar, cons. engr.; b. Newark, N.J., Jan. 22, 1875; s. Fernando Crans and Ruth N. (Fearey) R.; ed. pub. sch. and high sch., Newark, 1881-89, Newark Tech. Sch., 1890-93; (hon.) D.Engring., Newark Coll. Engring., 1936; m. Hattie M. Eagles, of Newark, N.J., Jan. 17, 1900 (died 1918); children—Malcolm Eagles, Mary Fearey (dec.); m. 2d, Elizabeth Meixner, June 15, 1921. In employ various cos. as engr. and elec. engr., 1890-1901; cons. engr. on own acct., Newark, N.J., 1901-04; mem. firm, Runyon & Carey, cons. engrs., Newark, N.J., since 1904; designed and supervised many municipal plants and pub. utilities; cons. engr. for State of N.J., Essex Co. and a number municipalities; pres. Newark Dist. Telegraph Co. Pres. State Bd. of Professional Engrs. and Land Surveyors. Served in Spanish-Am. war, 1898. Trustee Presbyn. Hosp., Newark, N.J. Fellow Am. Inst. Elec. Engrs. Mem. Am. Soc. Mech. Engrs., Am. Soc. Civil Engrs. Republican. Baptist. Mason. Clubs: Essex (Newark); Little Egg Harbor Yacht, Beach Haven Yacht (Beach Haven, N.J.). Home: 26 Hickory Drive, Maplewood. Office: 33 Fulton St., Newark, N.J.

RUNYON, Harry, lawyer; b. Warren Co., N.J., Dec. 8, 1891; s. John W. and Rachael E. (Green) R.; student pub. schs. and high sch., Hackettstown, N.J.; m. Helene L. Baker, Dec. 31, 1928; 1 son, Harry, Jr. Studied law in Office of Judge J. M. Roseberry, Belvidere, N.J., 1912-15; admitted to N.J. bar as atty., 1915, as counselor, 1922, engaged in gen. practice of law at Belvidere, N.J., since 1915; mayor, Belvidere, 1920; mem. N.J. Ho. of Assembly, 1921-23, only Dem. elected to N.J. Assembly in Nov. 1920; served as judge common pleas, Warren Co., 1923-38; elected to N.J. Senate, Nov. 1938 for term, 1939-42; dir. First Nat. Bank, Belvidere. Served as enlisted pvt. regular U.S.A., 1917-19. Mem. N.J. State Bar Assn., Warren County Bar Assn., Am. Legion. Democrat. Presbyn. Mason. Elk. Home: 520 Mansfield St. Office: Nat. Bank Bldg., Belvidere, N.J.

RUNYON, Laurance, physician; b. New Brunswick, N.J., Feb. 5, 1877; s. Clarkson and Laura N. (Phillips) R.; B.Sc., Rutgers U., 1899, M.Sc., same, 1903; M.D., Coll. Phys. & Surgs. of Columbia, U., 1903; m. Katharine Neilson, Feb. 9, 1916; children—Laurance, Jr., Katharine N. Interne N.Y. Post. Grad. Hosp., 1903-06; engaged in gen. practice of medicine and surgery in New Brunswick, N.J., since 1907; chief surg. staff, Middlesex Gen. Hosp. since 1925; surg. cons., St. Peter's Gen. Hosp. Fellow Am. Coll. Surgs. Mem. Am. Med. Assn., N.J. Med. Soc., Delta Phi. Democrat. Club: Lawrence Brook Country. Home: 14 Union St. Office: 80 Somerset St., New Brunswick, N.J.

RUNYON, Malcolm Eagles, cons. engr.; b. Newark, N.J., Feb. 13, 1901; s. Frederick Oscar and Hattie May (Eagles) R.; student Columbia High Sch., South Orange, N.J., 1917-21, Packard Commercial Sch., New York, 1921-22; B.S., Newark (N.J.) Coll. of Engring., 1927, M.E., 1935; m. Fern Kingston Dill, July 9, 1929 (divorced); 1 son, David. Asso. with Runyon & Carey, cons. engrs., Newark, N.J., since 1927, jr. partner since 1936; dir. and chief engr. Newark (N.J.) Dist. Telegraph Co. since 1929. Mem. Nat. Soc. of Professional Engrs., Am. Soc. M.E., N.J. Soc. of Professional Engrs. & Land Surveyors. Club: Brooklyn Fly Fishers' (Roscoe, N.Y.). Author numerous short stories for outdoor sporting mags. Home: 26 Hickory Drive, Maplewood, N.J. Office: 33 Fulton St., Newark, N.J.

RUPERT, Frank Finch, chemist; b. Caledonia, N.Y., Oct. 18, 1883; s. William Augustus and Jennie Elizabeth (Beattie) R.; A.B., U. of Kan., 1906, A.M., same, 1908; Ph.D., Mass. Inst. Tech., 1912; m. Olive Anna Buhoup, June 29, 1912; children—Margaret Belle, Alyce Louise. Engaged as instr. chemistry, U. of Kan., 1907-09 and 1911-12; jr. phys. chemist, U.S. Bur. of Mines, Pittsburgh, Pa., 1912-13; industrial fellow, Mellon Inst. Industrial Research, Pittsburgh, Pa., since 1913. Mem. A.A.A.S., Am. Chem. Soc., Pittsburgh Chemists Club, Sigma Xi. Republican. Presbyn. Home: 1106 Kelton Av., South Hills, Pittsburgh, Pa.

RUPLEY, David B.; editor Bradford Era. Address: 15 Exchange Place, Bradford, Pa.

RUPP, Charles Andrew, prof. mathematics; b. Salem, Mass., Aug. 23, 1898; s. Frank Gordon and Nellie Alice (Jones) R.; A.B., Harvard U., 1919, A.M., same, 1921; ed. U. of Brussels, Belgium, 1921-22, U. of Minn., 1922-24, U. of Tex., 1924-26; Ph.D., U. of Chicago, 1928; m. Luella Juliaan Kratz, June 22, 1929; children—Charles Andrew, Jr., Alexander Kratz, Melicent Kratz, Susan Kratz. Engaged as instr. Harvard U., 1919-21; instr. of mathematics, Hamline U., 1922-24; adjunct prof. Mathematics, U. of Tex., 1924-26; prof. mathematics, Pa. State Coll. since 1928. Served in Ordnance Corps, U.S.A., 1918-19. Mem. Am. Math. Soc., Am. Mathematics Assn., Sigma Xi, Sigma Pi Sigma, Acacia. Mason (32°). Home: 448 E. Foster Av., State College, Pa.

RUPP, George Alvin, lawyer; b. Allentown, Pa., Aug. 29, 1902; s. John Alvin and Florence R. (Ott) R.; Ph.B., Muhlenberg Coll., 1923; A.M., Lehigh U., 1926; LL.B., Dickinson Coll. Law Sch., 1929; m. Jane Lucas, July 29, 1936. Admitted to Pa. bar, 1929, and since engaged in gen. practice of law at Allentown; mem. firm Butz, Steckel & Rupp since 1929; served as mem. Pa. Senate, 1935-39. Mem. Lehigh County Bar Assn., Chi Psi. Democrat. Mem. Reformed Ch. Elk. Club: Lehigh Valley Torch (Allentown). Home: 2431 Union St. Office: Allentown Nat. Bank Bldg., Allentown, Pa.

RUPP, Paul Bertram, army chaplain; b. Manchester, Md., Apr. 28, 1883; s. William and Emma A. (Hambright) R.; A.B., Franklin and Marshall Coll., Lancaster, Pa., 1904; grad. Eastern Theol. Sem., Lancaster, Pa., 1907, post grad. student, 1912-14, B.D., 1914; student Chaplains' Sch., Camp Taylor, Ky., 1918; student U. of Chicago, 1934-35; m. Cora B. Clever, Sept. 2, 1924. Ordained to ministry Ref. Ch., 1908; minister, Saxton, Pa., 1908 to 1911; minister McKeesport, Pa., 1911-20; served as chaplain, U.S.A., 1918-19; commd. chaplain, U.S.A., 1920, stationed at Ft. Howard, Md., since 1935; pres. Allegheny Classis, 1916-17; pres. Pittsburgh Synod, Ref. Ch. in U.S., 1920-21. Dir. and sec. bd., St. Paul's Orphans Home, Greenville, Pa., 1916-20. Evang. & Ref. Ch. Mason. Odd Fellow. Contbr. articles to religious jours. Home: Fort Howard, Md.

RUSCA, Felix St. Elmo, dentist; prof. operative dentistry, Temple University. Address: 3943 Chestnut St., Philadelphia, Pa.

RUSH, Benjamin, underwriter; b. Chestnut Hill, Pa., Nov. 28, 1869; s. Richard Henry and Susan (Yerby) R.; ed. Episcopal Acad., Phila.; m. Mary Wheeler Lockwood, June 5, 1895. In ins. business since 1885; chmn. of bd. Ins. Co. of North America since 1916; pres. Indemnity Ins. Co. of N. America, Alliance Ins. Co. of Phila., Phila. Investment Corpn., Phila. Fire & Marine Ins. Co.; dir. Phila. Savings Fund, Fidelity-Phila. Trust Co., Central-Penn Nat. Bank; trustee Penn Mut. Life Ins. Co. of Phila., Mut. Assurance Co. of Phila. Mem. Average Adjusters' assns. of U.S. and Eng., Hist. Soc. Pa., Pa. Acad. Fine Arts. Republican. Episcopalian. Club: Philadelphia. Wrote: A Treatise on Marine Cargo Insurance, and A Treatise on Marine Hull Insurance. Home: "Chesteridge," Kirkland, Pa. Office: 1600 Arch St., Philadelphia, Pa.

RUSH, Eugene, pediatrician; b. Plymouth, Pa., May 23, 1890; s. Israel and Henrietta (Rosenthal) R.; student Brooklyn (N.Y.) Coll. of Pharmacy, 1908-10; Ph.G., Jefferson Med. Coll., Phila., 1914; m. Bella Sacks, Nov. 23, 1924; 1 son, Herman Eugene. Attending pediatrician, Mt. Sinai Hosp., Phila., since 1932, Jewish Seaside Home for Invalids, Atlantic City, N.J., since 1934; dir., Foster Home for Hebrew Orphans, Phila. Fellow Am. Acad. of Pediatricians; mem. A.M.A., Pa. State and Phila. Co. med. socs., Phila. Pediatric Soc., Phi Delta Epsilon. Republican. Jewish religion. Author of numerous articles on child care and children's diseases. Home: 6654 Lincoln Drive. Office: 1832 Spruce St., Philadelphia, Pa.

RUSH, Raymond Warren, pres. Allied Barrel Corpn.; b. Oil City, Pa., Mar. 13, 1888; s. H. G. and Adda B. (Palmer) R.; student Hotchkiss Sch., Lakeville, Conn., 1905-07, Yale, 1910; m. Agnes Dale Alexander, Apr. 15, 1914; children—Addalaide, Margaret Anne, Raymond Warren. Pres. Allied Barrel Corpn., Oil City, Pa., since 1929; dir. Citizens Banking Co., Oil City, Pa. Trustee, Second Presbyn. Ch., Oil City, Pa. V.p., Oil City (Pa.) Y.M.C.A. Republican. Presbyterian. Club: Wanango Country (Reno, Pa.). Home: 402 W. 2d St. Office: Allied Barrel Corpn., Oil City, Pa.

RUSS, William Adam, Jr., prof. history; b. nr. Ligonier, Pa., Mar. 23, 1903; s. William Adam, Sr., and Margaret Pearl (Roché) R.; A.B., Ohio Wesleyan U., 1924; A.M., U. of Cincinnati, 1926; Ph.D., U. of Chicago, 1933; m. Alice King Bickerstaff, Aug. 8, 1936. Engaged as instr. history, U. of Cincinnati, 1926; instr. history, DePauw U., Greencastle, Ind., 1927-30; asst. prof. history, DePauw U., 1930-33; prof. history and polit. sci., Susquehanna Univ., Selinsgrove, Pa., since 1933. Served as mem. Bd. Review of Snyder Co., Pa. Bd. of Assistance. Mem. Am. Hist. Assn., Am. Acad. Polit. & Social Sci., Miss. Valley Hist. Assn., Southern Hist. Assn., Pa. Hist. Assn., Pi Gamma Mu, Phi Mu Delta. Lutheran. Club: Selinsgrove Rotary (past pres.). Contbr. to hist. journs. Mem. Editorial Bd., Pennsylvania History, and of Susquehanna University Studies. Home: Selinsgrove, Pa.

RUSSELL, Dallmeyer, pianist and teacher; b. Pittsburgh, Pa., Nov. 12, 1886; s. Robert and Lucretia (Matthews) R.; mus. edn. Royal Conservatory of Music, Leipzig, Germany, 1905-06; studied in Berlin under Vianna DaMotta, 1906, 07, 08, 09, in Paris under Harold Bauer, 1911; m. Romaine Smith, June 25, 1912; children—Lucretia, Murelle. Pianist and teacher of music since 1909; appeared extensively as concert pianist in Berlin, Leipzig, Hamburg, and in New York City and other cities; appeared as soloist with Minneapolis and St. Louis symphony orchestras, Pittsburgh Festival and Russian Symphony orchestras; dir. Pittsburgh Mus. Inst., Inc. Mem. The Beethoven Assn., New York City. Presbyterian. Home: 319 S. Millvale Av. Studio: 131 N. Bellefield Av., Pittsburgh, Pa.

RUSSELL, Frank Henry; b. Mansfield, O., July 17, 1878; s. Frank and Aurelia Squier (Henry) R.; student Berkeley Sch., New York, 1892-

93; A.B., Yale, 1900; m. Marcetta Ford, Dec. 31, 1901 (died 1924); children—Frank Ford, Wallace Alger, Katherine (Mrs. Edward Wright Wootton); m. 2d, Constance B. Thompson, Aug. 19, 1925. Began as transportation agt., 1900; sales mgr. Laurentide Paper Co., Grand Mere P.O., 1902; pres. Automatic Hook & Eye Co. (later Talon, Inc.), Hoboken, N.J., 1905-09; mgr. Wright Co., Dayton, O., 1909-11; v.p. Burgess Co. & Curtiss, Marblehead, Mass., 1911-15, pres., 1915-18; v.p., Curtiss Aeroplane & Motor Co., New York, 1918-31; v.p. Edward G. Budd Mfg. Co., Phila., Pa., 1931-35; pres. Mfrs. Aircraft Assn. of N.Y. since 1918. Mem. Inst. Aeronautical Sciences. Republican. Clubs: Yale, Cruising Club of America (New York). Home: Newtown, Bucks Co., Pa. Office: Suite 726, Rockefeller Plaza, New York, N.Y.

RUSSELL, Franklin Ferriss, lawyer, educator; b. Brooklyn, N.Y., Mar. 5, 1891; s. Isaac Franklin and Ruth (Ferriss) R.; B.A., cum laude, New York U., 1911; Rhodes scholar at Brasenose Coll. (Oxford U.), Eng., 1911-14, B.A., 1913, B.C.L., 1914; J.D., New York U., 1915; M.A., Oxford, 1924; m. Mildred Cutter Henry, June 25, 1917; children—Mildred, Ruth Elizabeth. Admitted to N.Y. bar, 1914; mem. firm Zabriskie, Sage, Gray & Todd, 1925-28, Russell, Shevlin & Russell since Dec. 1928; prof. law, Brooklyn Law Sch., 1920, and of post-grad. dept. same since 1921; Owen D. Young prof. internat. relations, St. Lawrence U., 1925-28; admitted to N.J. bar, 1934; prof. law, Mercer Beasley School of Law, Newark U., since 1934. Member Board of Visitors, U.S. Naval Acad., 1931. Served with First N.Y. Cav. on Mexican border, 1916-17; lt. Transp. Corps, U.S.A., with A.E.F., 1918-19. Mem. Am. Bar Assn., Am. Soc. Internat. Law, Am. Law Inst., New York Classical Club, Psi Upsilon, Phi Beta Kappa, Phi Delta Phi, Am. Legion; sec. Assn. of Am. Rhodes Scholars. Republican. Mem. Dutch Ref. Ch. Author: Outline of Legal History, 1929; also numerous articles in legal publs. Home: Cragmere Park, Mahwah, N.J. Office: 67 Wall St., New York, N.Y.

RUSSELL, Henry Moore, lawyer; b. Wheeling, W.Va., July 6, 1879; s. Henry Moore and Matilda (Heiskell) R.; A.B., Linsley Mil. Acad., Wheeling, W.Va., 1896; A.B., Andover Acad., Andover, Mass., 1898; student Yale U., 1901; LL.B., U. of Va. Law Sch., Charlottesville, Va., 1903; m. Eleanor Letitia Brice, Apr. 25, 1905 (died 1936); children—Jane Taney (dec.), Ann Heiskell (Mrs. Kempton Clark), Malcolm William. Admitted to W.Va. bar, 1903, and since engaged in gen. practice of law at Wheeling, also a registered patent atty.; awarded several patents on own inventions; dir. Wheeling & Belmont Bridge Co. Served as 2d lt. Motor Transport Corps, U.S.A., 1918. Mem. W.Va. Bar Assn. Democrat. Clubs: Blue Pencil, Drama Reading (Wheeling). Home: Y.M.C.A., 20th St. Office: Register Bldg., Wheeling, W.Va.

RUSSELL, Henry Norris, astronomer; b. Oyster Bay, N.Y., Oct. 25, 1877; s. Alexander Gatherer and Eliza Hoxie (Norris) R.; A.B., Princeton, 1897, A.M., 1898, Ph.D., 1900; research student, King's Coll., Cambridge U., Eng., 1902-03; m. Lucy May Cole, Nov. 24, 1908; children—Lucy May, Elizabeth Hoxie, Henry Norris, Emma Margaret. Research asst., Carnegie Instn., Washington, stationed at Cambridge, Eng., 1903-05; instr. astronomy, 1905-08, asst. prof., 1908-11, prof., 1911—, Princeton; dir. of obs., 1912—, research prof., 1927—, research asso. Mt. Wilson Obs., 1921—. Engr., Aircraft Service U.S.A., 1918. Mem. Nat. Acad. Sciences, Am. Philos. Soc. (president, 1931-32), American Academy Arts and Sciences, American Astronomical Society (pres., 1934-37), American Physical Society; fellow A.A.A.S. (president, 1933); foreign associate Royal Astronomical Society, London (gold medalist, 1921); foreign member Royal Society, 1937; hon. fellow Royal Soc. of Edinburgh; asso. Belgian Royal Acad.; corr. French Acad. of Sciences. Awarded Henry Draper medal, Nat. Acad. Sciences, 1922; Lalande medal, French Acad., 1922; Bruce medal, Astron. Soc. Pacific, 1925; Rumford medal, Am. Acad. Arts and Sciences, 1925; Franklin medal, 1934; Janssen medal French Acad., 1936. Presbyn. Author: Determinations of Stellar Parallax, 1911; Astronomy, 1926; Fate and Freedom, 1927; The Solar System and Its Origin, 1935. Contbr. on astron. topics to scientific jours. Address: 79 Alexander St., Princeton, N.J.

RUSSELL, James Earl, coll. prof. and dean emeritus; b. Hamden, Delaware Co., N.Y., July 1, 1864; s. Charles and Sarah (McFarlane) R.; A.B., Cornell, 1887; univs. of Jena, Leipzig, Berlin, 1893-95; Ph.D., Leipzig, 1894; LL.D., Dickinson, 1903, U. Colo., 1905, McGill, 1909, Iowa, 1923; Litt.D., Columbia, 1927, Univ. State of N.Y., 1927; m. Agnes Fletcher, Delhi, N.Y., June 19, 1889 (died 1927); children—William F., Charles, James Earl, John M.; m. 2d, Alice F. Wyckoff, of Trenton, N.J., Jan. 24, 1929. Teacher in secondary schs., 1887-90; prin. Cascadilla Sch., Ithaca, N.Y., 1890-93; European commr. Regents of the University of the State of N.Y., 1893-95; European agt. Bur. of Edn., Washington, D.C., 1893-95; prof. philosophy and pedagogy, U. of Colo., 1895-97; prof. of edn., Teachers Coll. (Columbia), 1897-1927, prof. edn. on Richard March Hoe Foundation, 1927-31; dean Teachers College, 1897-1927, dean emeritus since 1927; Barnard prof. of edn., Columbia, 1904-27. Mem. N.J. State Bd. of Health since 1932, N.J. Milk Control Bd., 1933. Pres. Am. Assn. for Adult Edn., 1926-30 (chmn. 1930—); mem. Am. Psychol. Assn., Nat. Council Edn., Nat. Council on Radio in Edn., Nat. Occupational Conf. Author: The Extension of University Teaching in England and America, 1895; German Higher Schools; The History, Organization and Methods of Secondary Education in Germany, 1899; Trend in American Education, 1922; Founding Teachers College, 1937. Editor American Teachers Series. Contbr. to ednl. jours. Home: R.F.D. 4, Trenton, N.J.

RUSSELL, Karl M., supt. of schs.; b. Guy's Mills, Pa., June 21, 1885; s. Charles F. and Zora (Monroe) R.; B.S., Pennsylvania State Coll.; M.S., Univ. of Pittsburgh; m. Orma Gray, June 25, 1913. Teacher and prin. elementary schs., Crawford County, Pa., 1903-09; prin. Erie County High Sch., 1911-13; engaged in mercantile business, Guy's Mills, Crawford Co., Pa., 1913-24; prin. East Fallowfield Consol. Sch. of Crawford County (Pa.), 1924-30; prin. Jr. and Sr. High Schs., Franklin, Pa., 1930-34; supt. of schs., Franklin, since 1934. Dir. Y.M.C.A. Mem. Chamber of Commerce, Venango County (Pa.) Red Cross; dir. Community Chest. Mason. Clubs: Kiwanis (dir.), Northwestern Schoolmen's (Franklin, Pa.; pres. 1938). Home: 840 Liberty St. Office: P.O. Box 509, Franklin, Pa.

RUSSELL, Norman Felt Shelton, pres. U.S. Pipe & Foundry Co.; b. Jersey City, New Jersey, Sept. 29, 1880; s. William Jay and Francelia (Felt) R.; A.B., Colgate, 1901; m. Ella Dewees Eisenbrey, May 15, 1920; children—Norman Felt, Louis Eisenbrey, Ella King, Grace Felt. With Colgate, Hoyt & Co., bankers and brokers, New York, 1902-09; with U.S. Pipe and Foundry Co. since 1910, salesman, 1910, purchasing agt., 1912, gen. sales mgr., 1914, v.p., 1921, pres. since 1923; dir. Pa. Company for Insurances on Lives and Granting Annuities, Mechanics Nat. Bank (Burlington, N.J.), Colgate-Palmolive-Peet Co. (Jersey City, N.J.), U.S. Sugar Corpn. (Clewiston, Fla.). Trustee Colgate Univ. Mem. Am. Water Works Assn., Am. Gas Assn., Am. Inst. of Mining and Metall. Engrs., Am. Iron and Steel Inst., Army Ordnance Assn., Royal Soc. of Arts, Gen. Soc. Colonial Wars, Delta Kappa Epsilon. Mason. Republican. Baptist. Clubs: Art of Phila.; Riverton Country, Seaview Golf, Pine Valley Golf; City Midday (New York); Boca Raton (Fla.); Mountain Brook Country (Birmingham, Ala.). Home: Neshaminy Hall, Edgewater Park, N.J. Office: Burlington, N.J.

RUSSELL, Walter Charles, prof. agrl. biochemistry; b. Bellaire, O., Oct. 1, 1892; s. Charles and Eliza Jane (Kneff) R.; B.S., Ohio Wesleyan U., 1914; student Harvard U., 1919-20; M.S., Syracuse U., 1923; Ph.D., U. of Chicago, 1927; m. Mildred Irene Stephens, Aug. 25, 1923; 1 dau., Ruth Elizabeth. Instr. chemistry, O. Wesleyan U., 1915-17; grad. fellow in biochemistry, Harvard U., 1919-20; instr. in chemistry, Syracuse U., 1920-23; Swift fellow in chemistry, U. of Chicago, 1923-25; asst. prof. agrl. biochemistry, Rutgers Univ., New Brunswick, N.J., 1925-29, asso. prof., 1929-31, prof. since 1931; biochemist in nutrition, N.J. Agrl. Expt. Sta. since 1925; exec. sec. grad. faculty, Rutgers U. since 1935. Served as pvt. then capt. san. corps, U.S.A., 1917-19. Mem. Am. Chem. Soc., Am. Inst. of Nutrition, Am. Soc. Biol. Chemists, Soc. Exptl. Biology and Medicine, Sigma Xi, Delta Tau Delta, Alpha Chi Sigma. Presbyn. Home: Oak Hills, Metuchen, N.J.

RUTH, Franklin William, clergyman, legislator; b. Quakertown, Pa., Oct. 30, 1888; s. George Allen and Emma Catherine (Deily) R.; grad. Perkiomen Sem., Pennsburg, Pa., 1915, Central Theol. Sem. of the Reformed Ch., Dayton, O., 1918; m. Florence Ursula Iobst, May 1, 1909; children—Florence, Dorothea, Franklin, Robert, Rhoda, Richard, Donald, Anna. Student pastor of Mt. Carmel Reformed Ch., Dayton, O., 1916-18; pastor, Bernville (Pa.) Reformed Church, since 1918; mgr. Community Theatre, Bernville, Pa., since 1922; mem. Pa. Ho. of Rep., from 3d Berks Co. dist., 1930-36 (majority floor leader and chaplain, 1935; chmn. Ways and Means Com., 1935); mem. Pa. State Senate, from 11th Berks Co. dist., since 1936 (chmn. com. on edn., 1937; chmn. joint legislative commn. to investigate criminal ct. procedure in Pa., 1937). Chmn. 4th Liberty Loan Drive for Bernville (Pa.) Community. Mem. Bernville Borough (Pa.) Sch. Bd. since 1919, sec. since 1925. Dir. and trustee, Home for Aged Odd Fellows, Middletown, Pa., 1928; chmn. Bernville (Pa.) Red Cross, 1918. Mem. Pa. Assn. of Sch. Bd. Secs. (mem. com.), Sch. Bd. Secs. of Berks Co. (chaplain since 1927), Order United Am. Mechanics (councillor, 1908), Patriotic Order Sons of America (pres. local camp, co. chaplain, 1925-37; state chaplain, 1934-35; nat. camp del., 1927-34; comdr., 1923), Sons of Veterans (camp comdr., 1910), Order of Independent Americans. Democrat. Reformed Ch. Mason (supreme chaplain of U.S. Tall Cedars, 1936-37), Odd Fellow (Noble Grand, 1922), Local, State and Nat. Grange. Address: Bernville, Pa.

RUTH, Stephen E.; v.p. Philadelphia Nat. Bank. Address: 421 Chestnut St., Philadelphia, Pa.

RUTHERFORD, Albert Greig, congressman; b. Watford, Ont., Can., Jan. 3, 1879; s. James and Elizabeth (Bailie) R.; brought to U.S., 1883; LL.B., U. of Pa., 1904; m. Iris Estelle Burns, Sept. 12, 1906 (now dec.); children—Ira Burns, James; m. 2d, Jessica Robinson, 1937. Admitted to Pa. bar, 1904; practiced in Scranton, Pa., 1904-18 Honesdale, Pa., since 1918; mem. 75th and 76th Congresses (1937-41), 15th Pa. Dist. Mem. Pa. Nat. Guard, advancing to maj., 1904-18; lt. col. Pa. Res. Militia, 1919. Mem. Am. and Pa. State bar assns., Delta Chi. Republican. Presbyterian. Mason, Odd Fellow, Elk, K.P., Knight of Malta, Granger, Royal Arcanum. Home: Honesdale, Pa.

RUTSTEIN, Leo, chemist and author; b. Yonkers, N.Y., Apr. 13, 1896; s. Abraham and Bertha (DeNeitz) R.; ed. Newark Tech. Sch., 1911-14, N.Y. Univ., 1919-20; m. Lillian Pine, May 1, 1917; children—Robert Louis, Carol Ann. Employed as asst. chemist Clark Thread Co. and J. & P. Coats Co., Newark, N.J., and Can., 1911-13; asso. editor, Technology Cellulose Esters, 1911-36; established Rutstein Lab. and Library, Newark, N.J., 1936; mem. firm Leo Rutstein and Assos., research, cons. and mfg. chemists, Newark, N.J., since 1937, labs. at Newark and Phila., Pa. Served as asst. chief Wing Coating Sect., Bur. Aeronautics, assigned to Signal Corps, U.S.A., 1917-19; sent to Eng., France, and Germany on spl. mission, U.S.A., 1918-19. Mem. A.A.A.S., Am. Chem. Soc., Nat. Research Council (1916-18), Pi Gamma Mu, Special Library Assn. Mason (32°, Shriner). Mem. bd. of editors of Chemical Formulary, Cosmetic Formulary, Standard Chemical and Technical Dictionary. Co-Author: Aviation Chemistry (prepared for U.S., British and French govts.), 1914-18. Contbr. to chem. publs. Editor, Cellulose Acetate, 1915, Technology Cellulose Esters, 1921, Technology Cellulose Ethers, 1933. Co-editor (with others), U.S. Chemical Patents Index, 5 vols., 1915-24. Home: 727 Prospect St., Maplewood, N.J. Office: 45 Branford Place, Newark, N.J.

RUTTER, William McMurtrie; b. Evanston, Ill., Nov. 19, 1876; s. David and Mary Elizabeth (McMurtrie) R.; grad. Lawrenceville Sch., 1895; A.B., Williams Coll., 1899; m. Lucia Osborne Ford, Mar. 13, 1913 (now deceased); children—Elizabeth, Peter, Martha, Thomas. In coal business, 1900-01; in bond business and finance since 1901; pres. The Rutter Fund, Inc. Mem. exec. com. 1st Provisional Training Regt., Plattsburg, N.Y., 1915; capt. inf. and maj. Adj. Gen. Dept., U.S.A., 1917-18. Mgr. Phila. Ind. Dem. Com., Campaign for Pres., 1928; chmn. Ind. Dem. Com., Phila., 1929. Mem. Sigma Phi. Democrat. Episcopalian. Clubs: Chicago (Chicago); Penn Athletic (Phila.). Home: Pine Forge, Pa. Office: 1500 Walnut St., Philadelphia, Pa.

RUZICKA, Charles, lawyer; b. Baltimore, Md., June 1, 1896; s. Dr. Charles and Marie (Brohmann) R.; student Baltimore Poly. Sch. and sch. in Prague, Czecho-Slovakia; student Johns Hopkins; LL.B., U. of Md. Law Sch., 1917; m. Phyllis Tutein. Admitted to Md. bar, 1919, and since engaged in gen. practice of law at Baltimore; mem. firm Brown & Brune. Served in U.S.N., 1917-19. Redrafted banking laws of Md. while mem. Banking Commn., 1934-36. Mem. Am. Bar Assn. (on gen. counsel, 1935-36, state del. Md. 1936-38), Md. State and Baltimore City bar assns., Interstate Crime Commn. (rep. Md. since 1936). Home: 5803 Roland Av. Office: First Nat. Bank Bldg., Baltimore, Md.

RYAN, Frederick Behrens, advertising; b. New York, N.Y., Aug. 21, 1883; s. Charles Edgar and Florence (Behrens) R.; prep. edn. Cheshire (Conn.) Acad.; Ph.B., Sheffield Scientific Sch., Yale, 1904; m. Elizabeth Cady, Oct. 8, 1904; children—Frederick Behrens, Quincy G., Bruce E. In engineering until 1912; in advertising business with W. B. Ruthrauff since 1912; pres. and dir. Ruthrauff & Ryan, Inc. Mem. Chi Phi. Republican. Episcopalian. Clubs: University, Yale, New York Yacht (New York); Larchmont Yacht (Larchmont, N.Y.); Baltusrol Golf of Springfield, N.J. (dir.); Morris County Golf (Convent, N.J.); National Golf Links (Southampton, L.I.); Cloud (dir.), Short Hills (dir.). Home: Highland Av., Short Hills, N.J. Office: 405 Lexington Av., New York, N.Y.*

RYAN, Heber Hinds, coll. prof.; b. Lebanon, O., Aug. 21, 1886; s. Joseph Churchill and Martha Julia (Hinds) R.; B.S., Whitman Coll., 1906; A.M., Columbia U., 1911; Ph.D., U. of Chicago, 1932; m. Julia Gertrude Smith, Aug. 21, 1913; children—Jean Elizabeth, Heber Hinds. Teacher and athletic coach, Ellensburg (Wash.) High Sch., 1906-10; head dept. edn., La. State Normal Sch., Natchitoches, 1911-12; prin. Boise (Ida.) High Sch., 1912-13; elementary sch. prin., St. Louis, Mo., 1913-15; prin. Main Av. High Sch., San Antonio, 1915-18; elementary sch. prin., St. Louis, 1918-20; prin. Ben Blewett Jr. High Sch., St. Louis, 1920-26; asso. prof. and prin. University High Sch., U. of Mich., 1926-29; asso. prof. and prin. University High Sch., U. of Wis., 1929-37; dir. integration and head dept. of edn., Montclair (N.J.) State Teachers Coll., since 1937. Mem. N.E.A., N.J. Council of Edn., N.J. Edn. Assn., Eastern States Assn. of Professional Schs. for teachers, Phi Delta Kappa, etc. Conglist. Home: 115 Mt. Hebron Road, Upper Montclair, N.J.

RYAN, Hugh James, mayor; b. Johnsonburg, Pa., Aug. 5, 1892; s. James S. and Martha (Murning) R.; grad. high sch., Dubois, Pa., 1910, U. of Pittsburgh, 1916; m. Augusta McCormick, 1917; children—Rita, Hugh, Jr., Joan, Steven, Nancy. Mayor of Bradford, Pa. Served as 1st lt. U.S.A., 1917-21, capt., 1921-25, resigned, 1925. Pres. McKean Co. Tuberculosis and Health Soc. since 1928; past pres. Bradford Dental Soc. Mem. bd. govs. Delta Sigma Phi since 1925, has been editor The Carnation, its ofcl. publ. Roman Catholic. K.C., B.P.O.E., Moose, Fraternal Order of Police. Home: 45 Melvin Av., Bradford, Pa.

RYAN, John Thomas, mfr. mine safety appliances; b. Dudley, Pa., Feb. 13, 1884; s. Daniel and Mary (Maher) R.; student Juniata Coll., Huntingdon, Pa., 1902-04; B.S., Pa. State Coll., 1908, E.M., 1934; m. Mary Gavin, Nov. 7, 1928; 1 son, John Thomas. Mine foreman, W. H. Sweet Coal Co., Dudley, Pa., 1900-02; supt. Rocky Ridge Coal Mining Co. and superintending engr. Langdon Coal Co., Hopewell, Pa., 1908-10; jr. mining engr., asst. mining engr. U.S. Bur. of Mines, Pittsburgh, Pa., 1910-13; mine engr. in charge field work for Navy Dept., investigating Matanuska Coal Field, Alaska, 1913; organized Mine Safety Appliances Co., Pittsburgh, 1914, and now pres., gen. mgr. and dir.; dir. Carbon Monoxide Eliminator Corpn. Mem. Am. Inst. Mining & Metall. Engrs., Am. Soc. Safety Engrs., Rocky Mtn. Coal Mining Inst., Nat. Safety Council, Nat. Mine Rescue Assn., Mine Inspectors Inst. of America, Coal Mining Inst. of America, Phi Kappa Phi, Sigma Gamma Epsilon. Clubs: Duquesne, Pittsburgh Athletic Assn., Longue Vue Country (Pittsburgh). Home: 120 Richland Lane. Office: 201 N. Braddock Av., Pittsburgh, Pa.

RYAN, Leon Holston, business exec.; b. Wilmington, Del., June 26, 1894; s. John W. and Dora (Holston) R.; student Wilmington (Del.) High Sch., 1909-13, Drexel Inst., Phila., Pa., 1913-16; m. Reba E. Chandler, May 16, 1916; children—Maryemm Chandler, Leon Holston. Clk. Pa. R.R. Co., Wilmington, Del., 1916-19; salesman and sales mgr. Wilmington (Del.) Fibre Co., 1919-26; gen. mgr. Del. Rayon Co., New Castle, Del., since 1926, sec.-treas. since 1926; engaged in real estate development at Newark, Del., since 1936; dir. St. George's Trust Co., Troy Laundry Co. Served as sec. Dist. Exemption Bd., 1917-19; mem. Del. Labor Commn. since 1936. Mem. Am. Chem. Soc., Nat. Assn. Mfrs. Republican. Methodist. Mason. Clubs: Newark (Del.) Country (v.p. since 1938); Rehobeth Beach (Del.) Country (dir. since 1932). Home: Newark, Del. Office: New Castle, Del.

RYAN, Michael J., lawyer; b. Philadelphia, Pa., June 13, 1862; s. James and Margaret (Howden) R.; ed. La Salle Coll., Phila.; m. Eleanor Kemper, June 9, 1886. Began practice at Phila., 1884; city solicitor (corpn. counsel), Phila., 1911-16; pub. service commn. of Pa. by apptmt. of gov. of Pa., Jan. 1916-Feb. 1919; pres. Girard Avenue Title & Trust Co., 1907-1931. Trustee Temple University, Philadelphia Dental Coll., and Samaritan Hosp., 1908-28. Mem. com. of three, representing Friends of Ireland in U.S., at World Peace Conf., Paris, 1919. Mem. Am. Bar Assn., Pa. Bar Assn., Phila. Bar Assn., Am. Acad. Polit. and Social Science, Hist. Soc. of Pa., Am. Cath. Hist. Soc. Roman Catholic. Club: Clover. Home: 4632 Larchwood Av. Office: Land Title Bldg., Philadelphia, Pa.

RYAN, Michael J., lawyer; b. Jacksons, Mahanoy Twp., Schuylkill Co., Pa., Sept. 12, 1878; s. John and Sarah R.; grad. Mahanoy (Pa.) High Sch., 1886; student Pa. State Coll., 1896-97; LL.B., Dickinson Law Sch., 1900; m. Veronica Sommers, Oct. 4, 1917; 1 son, John M. Admitted to Pa. bar, 1900, and since in practice at Mahanoy; asst. dist. atty., Schuylkill Co., 1931-37; dir. Union Nat. Bank; dir. and solicitor Guarantee Saving Fund. Republican. Eagle, Elk. Club: Mahoning Valley Country. Address: Mahanoy City, Pa.

RYAN, Will Carson, educator; b. at New York City, Mar. 4, 1885; s. Will Carson and Sarah Anne (Hobby) R.; A.B., Harvard, 1907; studied Columbia, 1907-10; Ph.D., George Washington U., 1918, LL.D., 1932; m. Isabel Van Dewater, June 20, 1908; children—Carson Van Dewater, Carl Schurz, Isabel Edith, John Walker, Flora Ruby, Chester Maupin. Instr. French and German, high sch., 1909-10; Carl Schurz fellow, Columbia, 1910-11; instr. in German, U. of Wis., 1911-12; asst. editor, 1912-14, editor, 1915-17; dir. information service, U.S. Bur. Edn., 1917-20; ednl. editor N.Y. Evening Post, 1920-21; prof. of education, Swarthmore Coll., 1921-30; dir. of education, U.S. Indian Service, 1930-34, dir. planning and research, 1934-35; mem. educational staff Commonwealth Fund, 1935-36; with Carnegie Foundation for the Advancement of Teaching since 1936; staff mem. Educational Survey of Saskatchewan, Canada, 1917-18; secretary British Educational Mission to U.S., 1918; associate editor School and Society, 1921-27. Educational surveys, Santo Domingo, 1924, Porto Rico, 1925, Friends' Schools, 1924-27, Indian Schools, 1927, Virgin Islands, 1928. Methodist Secondary Schools, 1930, also mental hygiene and education, for Commonwealth Fund, New York, 1935-36. Member N.E.A., National Vocational Guidance Assn. (pres. 1926-27), Progressive Edn. Assn. (pres. 1937-39), New Edn. Fellowship, Phi Beta Kappa, Phi Delta Kappa. Clubs: Cosmos (Washington, D.C.); Harvard (New York). Author: The Literature of American School and College Athletics; Mental Health Through Education; also bulls. pub. by U.S. Bur. Edn. Home: Nutley, N.J. Address: Carnegie Foundation for the Advancement of Teaching, 522 5th Av., New York, N.Y.

RYDEN, George Herbert, univ. prof; b. Kansas City, Mo., Jan. 26, 1884; s. August and Emma Sophia (Peterson) R.; A.B., Augustana Coll., Rock Island, Ill., 1909, Litt.D., 1938; M.A., Yale, 1911, grad. study, 1916-18 and 1926-27, Ph.D., 1928; awarded Currier fellowship, Yale, for 1911-12 (resigned). Clk., K. C.S. Ry., 1902-05; instr. history and social sciences, Bethany Coll., Lindsborg, Kan., 1911-12, prof. same, 1912-16; asst. in history, Yale, 1916-18; instr. in citizenship, Dartmouth, 1921-22; asso. prof. history and polit. science, U. of Del., 1922-28, prof. since 1928; prof. history, U. of Kan., summers 1930 and 36; prof. of history, U. of Minn., summer 1932. Mem. Delaware Dutch Tercentenary Committee, 1930-31, Del. Statutes Commission, 1931-34, Del. Swedish Tercentenary Commission, 1935-38. State archivist of Delaware, since 1930; chairman Historic Markers Commn. of Del., 1931-33. Ednl. sec. Y.M.C.A., army camps, Texas, and Italian front, Jan.-Nov. 1918, Paris until Aug. 1919; dir. South Russian Mission, Am. Red Cross, 1919-21. Mem. Am. Assn. Univ. Profs. (nat. chmn. Com. E), Am. Hist. Assn., Middle States Assn. History and Social Science Teachers (president 1937-38), Am. Polit. Science Assn., Am. Soc. Internat. Law, Soc. of Am. Archivists, Hist. Soc. Del., Hist. Soc. Pa., Swedish Colonial Soc. (Phila), Del. State Soc. of the Cincinnati, Swedish Hist. Soc. (Stockholm), Augustana Hist. Soc., Phi Kappa Tau, Phi Kappa Phi. Awarded John Addison Porter prize (Yale), 1928; Italian War Cross, 1918; Orders of St. Stanislav and St. Anne (Russia), 1920; Order of the North Star (Sweden) 1938; medal of Russian Red Cross, 1920. Clubs: Newark (Del.) Country; University (Philadelphia); Torch (Delaware); Quill and Grill (Wilmington). Author: The Foreign Policy of the United States in Relation to Samoa; Delaware, The First State in the Union. Editor of Letters to and from Cæsar Rodney. Contbr. to 13th and 14th edits. Ency. Brit. and Dictionary Am. Biography and to hist. jours. Home: 26 E. Main St., Newark, Del.

RYLAND, Alban S., M.D., surgeon; b. Cressona, Pa., Aug. 18, 1880; s. Wm. H. and Emmalina (Straub) R.; grad. Millersville State Teachers Coll., 1905; M.D., Medico-Chirurg. Coll., Philadelphia, 1912; m. Kathryn S. Bittle, Dec. 11, 1913; children—June L. (A.B., Wooster Coll., 1938), Olive E. Prin. Perry Twp. High Sch., Shoemakersville, Pa., 1905-08; in gen. practice medicine, Valley View, Pa., 1913-19; post-grad. course New York Post Grad. Med. Sch. and Hosp. and U. of Pa. Polyclinic Hosp., Philadelphia, 1918; interne Mercy Hosp., Wilkes-Barre, Pa., 1912-13; in gen. practice of medicine, Pottsville, Pa., since 1919; mem. surg. staff Pottsville Hosp., pres. of staff, 1937. Fellow A.M.A.; mem. Schuylkill Co. Med. Soc. (pres. 1926), Phi Rho Sigma. Mason (A.A.O. N.M.S.), Elk. Clubs: Kiwanis (pres. 1927), Pottsville (Pottsville). Author various publs. on med. subjects. Address: 217 Mahantongo St., Pottsville, Pa.

RYLAND, George Bertram, automobile dealer; b. Confluence, Pa., Feb. 11, 1873; s. Sylvester H. and Ella (Slicer) R.; student Garrett Co. (Md.) Pub. Sch., 1880-90, Normal Sch., 1890-92; Ph.D., Phila. Coll. of Pharmacy, 1896; m. Elizabeth Woods, 1900; 1 dau., Dorothy M. (Mrs. Harold M. Jorgensen). Began as pharmacist, 1896; pres. G. B. Ryland & Co., drugs, 1898; pres. The May Drug Co., Pittsburgh, Pa., 1930; v.p. Louis K. Liggett Co., 1929; pres. Eierman Cadillac-LaSalle Co., Pittsburgh, since 1933; dir. Diamond Nat. Bank, Electric Products Co. Republican. Presbyterian. Clubs: Duquesne, Longue Vue (Pittsburgh). Home: 6315 Beacon St. Office: 5607 Baum Boul., Pittsburgh, Pa.

RYS, C(arl) F(riedrich) W(ilhelm), metall. engr.; b. Essen, Germany, Mar. 23, 1877; s. Francis and Louise (Hausmann) R.; grad. high sch., Essen; studied mech. engring., tech. schs., Hagen, Germany, 2 yrs.; grad. Sch. of Mines, Freiberg, 1902, grad. study England, 6 mos.; Dr. Engineering, University of Freiberg, 1930; m. Helen M. Witt, of Gleiwitz, Germany, June 24, 1908; children—Louise, Frederick. Came to U.S., 1903, naturalized citizen, 1911. Began with Krupp Works, Essen; with LaBelle Iron Works, Pittsburgh, Pa., 1903-04; in metall. dept., Homestead Steel Works (Carnegie Steel Co.), 1904-08; in inspection dept., Pittsburgh office, Carnegie Steel Co., 1908-10, asst. metall. engr., 1910-11, metall. engr., in charge metall. dept. since 1911, apptd. asst. to pres. May 7, 1928, also continuing as metall. engr.; apptd. chief metall. engr. of Carnegie-Ill. Steel Corpn., Oct. 1, 1935. Mem. Am. Iron and Steel Inst., Engrs. Soc. Western Pa., Am. Soc. for Metals, Soc. Automotive Engrs., Am. Inst. Mining and Metall. Engrs., Am. Ry. Engring. Assn., Am. Transit Assn., Am. Soc. for Testing Materials, Brit. Iron and Steel Inst., Army Ordnance Assn., Verein Deutscher Eisenhuttenleute. Republican. Protestant. Mason (Shriner). Clubs: Duquesne, Railway, Pittsburgh Athletic Assn. (Pittsburgh); Edgewood Country. Home: 5463 Aylesboro Av. Office: Carnegie Bldg., Pittsburgh, Pa.

RYTINA, Anton George, urologist; b. Baltimore, Md., Feb. 3, 1882; s. Anton and Anna (Hulla) R.; A.B., Loyola Coll., Baltimore, 1901; M.D., U. of Md., 1905; grad. study, Berlin, 1911; m. Katherine M. Gier, Jan. 24, 1912; children—Anthony George, Katherine Luciene. Instr., clin. lab., U. of Md., and phys. Out-patient Clinic, Johns Hopkins Hosp., 1905; phys. Phipp's Tuberculosis Clinic, Johns Hopkins Hosp., 1906-07; mem. urol. dept., Johns Hopkins Hosp., 1908-15; chief of urology, Out-patient Clinic, Mercy Hosp., 1909-10, chief urologist, 1910 to 1923; clin. prof. urology, Coll. Phys. and Surg. (now U. of M.D.), 1910-15, prof. urology, 1915; organizer, 1919, owner and operator until 1928, Morrow (later Colonial) Hosp.; organizer Colonial Hosp. Training Sch. for Nurses, 1925; organizer, 1926, dir. until 1928, Physicians and Surgeons Casualty Clinic; organizer, 1929, since dir. med. and surg. depts. Safe Harbor (Pa.) Hosp.; visiting urologist South Baltimore Gen. Hosp., U.S. Govt. Marine Hosp., U.S. Vets. Bur. Hosp.; cons. urologist St. Joseph's Hosp. Mem. Md. State Bd. of Health since 1918 (dir. and adviser venereal disease clinics); mem. Selective Draft Bd., Baltimore, World War. Men. Bd. Supervisors of City Charities, 1912-21. Fellow Am. Coll. Surgeons; mem. A.M.A., Am. Urol. Assn., Med. Chirurg. Faculty of Md., Baltimore City Med. Soc. Democrat. Catholic. Clubs: Rotary, Baltimore Athletic, Maryland Country. Contbr. on genito-urinary surgery. Pioneer in use of salvarsan and neo-salvarsan. Home: 5003 St. Albans Way. Office: 115 E. Eager St., Baltimore, Md.

S

SAALBACH, Louis, univ. prof.; b. Pittsburgh, Pa., Dec. 14, 1874; s. August and Louise (Breuninger) S.; Pharm.D., U. of Pittsburgh Sch. of Pharmacy, 1908; m. Beatrice Brooks Walton. Instr. in chemistry, U. of Pittsburgh Sch. of Pharmacy, 1896-98, prof. of pharmacy and dir. of pharm. labs. since 1907, treas. since 1932; consulting pharmacist, McKennan Pharmacy, Pittsburgh, since 1921. Mem. Pa. Pharm. Assn. (pres., 1912-13; sec., 1919-26; treas., 1925-26), Am. Pharm. Assn., A.A.A.S., Nat. Formulary (vice-chmn. revision com. since 1929). Republican. Presbyterian. Mason. Club: Univ. of Pittsburgh Faculty (Pittsburgh). Contbr. to drug and pharm. jours. Home: 5620 Wellsley Av. Office: 1431 Boul. of the Allies, Pittsburgh, Pa.

SABATINI, Raphael, artist and teacher; b. Phila., Pa., Nov. 26, 1898; s. Ernani and Mary (Sarnese) S.; student Pa. Acad. Fine Arts, sculpture with Charles Grafly, 1914-20, sculpture with Emile Bourdelle, painting with Ferdinand Leger, both Paris, France, 1920-23; m. Theresa Knoell, Jan. 15, 1930. Has followed profession as artist at Phila. since 1923; exhibited at Paris, 1922, Phila., 1923, and since has shown in many cities of U.S.; represented in pvt. collections, paintings in Pa. Acad. of Fine Arts, Phila. Mus., Allentown Mus.; teacher of sculpture, Tyler Sch. Fine Arts of Temple U., Phila., since 1936. Fellowship of Pa. Acad. Fine Arts. Awarded travelling scholarships for European study by Pa. Acad. Fine Arts, 1919 and 1920. Home: 1016 N. 4th St. Studio: 34 S. 17th St., Philadelphia, Pa.

SABY, Rasmus, prof. econs.; b. Stavanger, Norway, Mar. 16, 1881; s. Sven R. and Anne Helene (Hovde) S.; was brought to U.S., 1882, and naturalized citizen, 1887; A.B., U. of Minn., 1907, A.M., 1908; student Cornell U., 1908-09; Ph.D., U. of Pa., 1910; m. Alma Stake, Sept. 3, 1914 (dec. 1917); 1 dau., Edna Marie; m. 2d, Maude Sanford, Dec. 20, 1919; children—John Sanford, Helen, Margaret. Instr. econs., Cornell U., 1910-12, asst. prof. in govt., 1912-24; prof. polit. sci. and econs. and head of dept., Gettysburg Coll. since 1924. Served as mem. Bd. Edn. of United Lutheran Ch., 1924-36. Mem. Am. Polit. Sci. Assn., Am. Econ. Assn., Phi Beta Kappa. Republican. Lutheran. Club: Rotary. Home: 321 Carlisle St., Gettysburg, Pa.

SACHS, Louis; instr. and asst. in clin. surgery, Johns Hopkins U.; attending surgeon and asso. dir. surg. pathology Sinai Hosp.; asst. dispensary surgeon Johns Hopkins Hosp.; consulting surgeon Provident Hosp. and Free Dispensary. Home: Marlborough Apts., Baltimore, Md.

SACKETT, Robert Lemuel, civil engr.; b. Mt. Clemens, Mich., Dec. 2, 1867; s. Lemuel Miller and Emily Lucinda (Cole) S.; B.S. in C.E., U. of Mich., 1891, C.E., 1896, Dr. Engring., 1937; m. Mary Lyon Coggeshall, July 22, 1896; children—Ralph L., Mrs. Frances L. Kramer (deceased). Prof. applied mathematics, Earlham Coll., 1891-1907; prof. sanitary and hydraulic engring., Purdue U., 1907-15; dean Sch. of Engring., Pa. State Coll., Sept. 1, 1915 to June 30, 1937; dean emeritus; also dir. Engring. Expt. Sta., and of engring. extension. Fellow A.A.A.S. (v.p., 1928); Am. Soc. C.E., Soc. for Promotion Engring. Edn. (pres., 1927-28), Engrs. Council for Professional Development, Am. Soc. M.E. (v.p.), Sigma Xi, Tau Beta Pi, Phi Kappa Phi, Phi Gamma Delta. Republican. Mem. Friends Ch. Consulting engr. to Ind. State Bd. of Health, 1910-15, and to other state commns. Author: The Engineer, His Work and His Education; also numerous technical articles. Home: State College, Pa.

SACKS, Leon, congressman; b. Phila., Oct. 1902; s. Morris and Dora (Clayman) S.; B.S., in economics, Wharton Sch., U. of Pa., 1923; LL.B., U. of Pa., 1926. Admitted to Pa. bar, 1926, and since practiced in Phila.; mem. firm Sacks & Sacks; dep. atty. gen. State of Pa., 1935-36; mem. 75th and 76th Congresses (1937-41), 1st Pa. Dist. Mem. Am., Pa. State and Phila. bar assns. Democrat. Elk, B'nai B'rith, Brith Sholom. Club: McKean Law (U. of Pa.). Home: 1329 S. 6th St., Philadelphia, Pa.

SACKS, Samuel Isaiah, lawyer, civil engr.; b. Wilmington, Del., July 8, 1892; s. Jacob and Elizabeth (Berman) S.; grad. Central Manual Training High Sch., Phila., 1909; B.S. in civil engring., U. of Pa., 1913, C.E., 1916; LL.B., Temple U., 1925; student Gratz Coll., 1914-18; m. Cecilia Linker, Oct. 12, 1915; children—Marjorie Adele, Lee Beryl. Civil engr. Dept. of City Transit, Phila., 1913-19; civil engr. Wm. Linker Co., builders, 1919-25; admitted to Pa. bar, 1925; civil engr. and lawyer since 1925; partner in firm Sacks & Piwosky, lawyers, Phila.; pres. Northampton Brewery Corpn. Served in U.S.N.R.F., Sept.-Dec., 1918. Pres. Temple Beth Israel, Phila.; dir. Phila. branch Jewish Theol. Sem.; dir. United Synagogue, Old Guard of Phila. Mem. Am. Soc. Civil Engrs., Nat. Soc. Professional Engrs. (dir.), Phila. Bar Assn., Am. Legion (past comdr., Clair Post), Sigma Xi. Democrat. Home: 1821 N. 33d St. Office: Widener Bldg., Philadelphia, Pa.

SADLER, Cornelius Robinson, v.p. Babcock & Wilcox Tube Co.; b. Montgomery, Ala., May 11, 1875; s. Claudius Earl and Helena Augusta (Frazier) S.; student Internat. Corr. Schs.; m. Rossa May Bower, June 14, 1918; 1 dau., Virginia May. Began as machinist Stirling Boiler Co., Barberton, O., 1901; company was absorbed by Babcock & Wilcox Co., New York, served in various capacities, becoming supt. Barberton Works, 1918, v.p., 1930; dir. Diescher Tube Mills, Inc., Pittsburgh. V.p. Providence Hosp., Beaver Falls, Pa. Past Pres. Barberton Chamber of Commerce. Mason (32°). Clubs: Rotary, Beaver Valley Country. Co-author (with Dr. James Campbell Hodge): Weldability and Properties of Materials for Casing Strings. Home: Patterson Heights. Office: Babcock & Wilcox Tube Co., Beaver Falls, Pa.

SADLER, John Dewey, lawyer; b. Ogdensburg, N.Y., Nov. 8, 1896; s. John Thomas and Kathryn (Ralph) S.; A.B., Mount St. Mary's Coll., Emmitsburg, Md., 1918; LL.B., Georgetown U. Law Sch., Washington, D.C., 1922; m. La Rue Mong, July 30, 1930; children—John Dewey, Kathryn Lou, Anthony Luke. Admitted to Dist. of Columbia bar, 1922, and since practiced in Md. and Washington, D.C. Served in U.S. Navy during World War. Rep. candidate from Montgomery County for Md. House of Dels., 1938. Mem. D.C. Bar Assn., Seventh Dist. Rep. Club (Montgomery County; mem. exec. com.), Am. Legion. Republican. Roman Catholic. Home: 123 Del Ray Av., Bethesda, Md. Office: 1319 F. St. N.W., Washington, D.C.

SAFFORD, Elisha, clergyman; b. Nokomis, Ill., Sept. 6, 1876; s. Edwin and Rebecca (Culbertson) S.; ed. Valparaiso Coll., 1895-97; B.D., McCormick Theol. Sem., Chicago, 1901; m. Mabel R. Fulton, Nov. 10, 1904; children—Evelyn Alice (wife of Dr. Allan P. Colburn), Robert Fulton, Elisha, Jr., George Culbertson, Grace (dec.). Ordained to ministry Presbyn. Ch., 1901; pastor, Edwardsville, Ill., 1901-12, Decatur, Ill., 1912-20, Glen Moore, Pa., 1920-22; pastor, First Presbyn. Ch., Darby, Pa., since 1923. Republican. Presbyn. Clubs: Writers, Presbyn. Ministers Social Union (Philadelphia). Contbr. articles and verse to mags. and journs. Editorial Writer, Youth's Companion, 1923-28, and Bd. Christian Edn. Presbyn. Ch., 1920-30. Home: 300 Main St., Darby, Pa.

SAFFORD, Frederick Hollister, emeritus professor of mathematics; b. Lawrence, Mass., June 20, 1866; s. Joseph H. and Sarah L. (Hollister) S.; B.S., Mass. Inst. of Tech., 1888; A.M., Harvard, 1894, Ph.D., 1897; fellow Clark Univ., Worcester, Mass., 1901-02; m. Annie Barnard Flint, Jan. 1, 1891. Instr. in mathematics, Harvard, 1895-99; asst. prof. of mathematics, U. of Cincinnati, 1899-1901; with U. of Pa. since 1907, as asst. prof. of mathematics, 1907-20, prof., 1920-36, prof. emeritus since 1936. Fellow A.A.A.S.; mem. Am. Math. Soc., Math. Assn. America, Am. Astron. Soc., Sigma Xi. Presbyterian. Home: 4527 Osage Av., Philadelphia, Pa.

SAGE, Dean, lawyer; b. Brooklyn, N.Y., Dec. 13, 1875; s. Dean and Sarah A. (Manning) S.; grad. Albany (N.Y.) Acad., 1893; A.B., Yale, 1897, hon. A.M., 1928; LL.B., Harvard, 1900; LL.D., Columbia, 1928; m. Anna Parker, June 9, 1900; children—Cornelia (Mrs. Staunton Williams), Sarah (Mrs. G. L. Stewart, Jr.), Dean. Admitted to N.Y. bar, 1900, and began practice in New York; mem. firm of Sage, Gray, Todd & Sims since 1905; dep. asst. dist. atty. New York County, 1902; trustee N.Y. Trust Co.; dir. Commonwealth Ins. Co., Sage Land & Improvement Co. Served in New York office of Army Transport Service and later New York office of real estate div. of Gen. Staff during World War. Dir. Commonwealth Fund, Josiah N. Macy, Jr. Foundation; mgr. and pres. Presbyn. Hosp., New York; trustee and chmn. bd. Atlanta Univ., Atlanta, Ga.; mem. exec. com. Prison Assn. of N.Y. Mem. Bar Assn. City of New York, New York County Lawyers Assn., N.Y. State Bar Assn., Am. Bar Assn. Republican. Episcopalian. Clubs: Yale, Racquet and Tennis, Links (New York). Home: Bernardsville, N.J. Office: 49 Wall St., New York, N.Y.

SAGEBEER, Joseph Evans, lawyer; b. Allentown, Pa., Apr. 4, 1861; s. Joseph Lybrand and Harriet (Keen) S.; grad. high sch., Conshohocken, Pa., 1879; A.B., Bucknell U., 1885; grad. Crozer Theol. Sem., 1888; Ph.D., U. of Pa., 1891; m. Catharine G. Cook, June 15, 1898; children—Richard Grafflin, Catherine Cook. Admitted to Pa. bar, 1900, began practice, Phila. Mem. Phi Kappa Psi. Republican. Author: The Bible in Court—The Method of Legal Inquiry Applied to the Study of the Scriptures; also papers in mags. Home: Berwyn, Pa.

SAGENDORPH, Frank Elijah, 2d, pres. Penn Metal Corpn. of Pa.; b. Cincinnati, O., Mar. 28, 1883; s. Longley Lewis and Catherine (Crainor) S.; ed. Phila. Pub. Schs., and Peirce Business Coll., Phila.; m. Elizabeth Hagy, Oct. 3, 1905; children—William Lloyd, Frank Elijah 3d, Suzanne. Began as apprentice Penn Metal Corpn. of Pa., Phila., 1901-03, engr. and draftsman, 1903-05, jr. exec., 1905-07, v.p., 1912-33, dir. since 1919, pres. since 1933; v.p. and gen. mgr. J. Milton Hagy Waste Works, 1907-12. Republican. Episcopalian. Clubs: Union League, Kiwanis, Meridian (Phila.). Home: 126 S. Lansdowne Av., Lansdowne, Pa. Office: Oregon Av. and Swanson St., Philadelphia, Pa.

SAINT, Lawrence (Bradford), artist in stained glass; b. Sharpsburg, Pa., Jan. 29, 1885; s. Joseph Alexander and Jennie (Bradford) S.; ed. Pa. Acad. Fine Arts, Phila., 1905-09; 5 trips abroad for spl. art and stained glass studies; m. Katharine Wright Proctor, June 10, 1910; children—Samuel Proctor, Philip, Rachel, Daniel, David, Stephen, Nathanael, Benjamin. Began career as stained glass apprentice under J. Horace Rudy, East End, Pittsburgh, Pa., 1901; in various studios and studying until 1917; designed and painted at Bryn Athyn (Pa.) Cathedral, 1917-28, under Raymond Pitcairn's patronage, discovered glass paint which approximates 13th century paint; dir. Stained Glass Dept. (located at Huntingdon Valley, Pa.) of Washington Cathedral, Mount Saint Alban, Washington, D.C., 1928-35; established studio and glass-making plant, invented furnace, worked out 1300 formulas for stained glass like mediæval glass, including striated ruby. Designed and painted under Raymond Pitcairn, 6 windows Bryn Athyn Cathedral; designed and made glass formulas for North Transept Rose and 14 other windows, Washington Cathedral; responsible for color and execution of 3 clerestory windows south side of choir, Washington Cathedral; also window McShea Mausoleum, Riverside Cemetery, Norristown, Pa.; rose window St. Paul's Ch., Willimantic, Conn. Represented in Victoria and Albert Royal Mus. (London), Carnegie Inst. (Pittsburgh), and private collection of Raymond Pitcairn, Bryn Athyn, Pa., by drawings and paintings of mediæval stained glass in England and France; 4 miniature stained glass figures, home of Edward Duff Balken, Pittsburgh; miniature figure home of J. Bertram Lippincott, Phila. Republican. Baptist. Author and illustrator of A Knight of the Cross, 1914; illustrator 50 color plates, Stained Glass of the Middle Ages in England and France, 1913. Contbr. articles on stained glass to jours. and mags.; gave nation wide radio talk on stained glass May 1937; author of Lawrence Saint's stained glass creed. Lectured at Met. Mus. of Art, American Ceramic Society (general session), and at colls. and women's clubs on stained glass. Work was made subject of a 3 reel ednl. motion picture by Met. Mus. of Art. Home: Huntingdon Valley, Pa.

SAINT-GAUDENS, Homer Schiff, dir. fine arts; b. Roxbury, Mass., Sept. 28, 1880; s. Augustus and August F. (Homer) S.; A.B., Harvard, 1903; m. Carlota Dolley, June 3, 1905 (died October 24, 1927); children—Augustus, Carlota; m. 2d, Mary Louise McBride, of Pittsburgh, Feb. 27, 1929. Asst. editor The Critic, New York, 1904; mng. editor Metropolitan Magazine, 1905; stage dir. for Maude Adams in "Legend of Leonora," "Kiss for Cinderella," etc., 1908-16; directed production of "Beyond the Horizon," "The Red Robe," etc., 1919-21; asst. dir. Fine Arts, Carnegie Inst., Pittsburgh, Pa., July 1, 1921; dir. Fine Arts, same, since July 1922. Capt. Co. A, 40th Engrs. (1st Camouflage Unit), A.E.F., in charge camouflage work on front of 2d Div., 1st Corps, 3d Corps, Second Army; honorably discharged, Feb. 5, 1919; lt. col. Engineers Reserve Corps. Officer Legion of Honor (France); Officer Crown of Italy; Chevalier Order of Leopold (Belgium). Decorated with Order of the Purple Heart (U.S.). Clubs: Century, Coffee House, Harvard (New York); Pittsburgh Golf, Fox Chapel. Author: Reminiscences of Augustus Saint-Gaudens, 1909; also short stories, spl. articles in mags. Lecturer on art subjects. Address: Dept. Fine Arts, Carnegie Institute, Pittsburgh, Pa.

SAKLATWALLA, Beram D., chmn. Alloys Development Corpn.; b. Bombay, India, July 19, 1881; s. Dorab S. and Jerbai N. (Tata) S.; B.S., U. of Bombay (India), 1901; Dipl. Chem. Eng., U. of Berlin (Germany), 1906; Dr.Engring., Royal Polytechnicum, Charlottenburg, Germany, 1908; m. Ann R. Richards, Oct. 1936. Began as process chemist, Am. Vanadium Co., Pittsburgh, Pa., 1909-10, gen. supt., 1910-19; sr. v.p. and dir. Vanadium Corpn. of America, Pittsburgh, 1919-35; pres. U.S. Rustless Steel & Iron Corpn., Pittsburgh, 1935-38; chmn. Alloys Development Corpn., Pittsburgh, since 1938; partner Saklatwalla & Foote, Pittsburgh, metall. and chem. developments, since 1938. Fellow A.A.A.S.; mem. Am. Chem. Soc., Inst. Chem. Engrs., Am. Inst. of Mining and Metall. Engrs., Am. Soc. for Metals, Am. Electrochem. Soc., Brit. Iron and Steel Inst., Brit. Inst. of Metals. Recipient Andrew Carnegie award, British Iron and Steel Inst., 1908; awarded Grasselli Medal (Soc. of Chem. Industry), 1924. Republican. Clubs: Duquesne, Pittsburgh Athletic (Pittsburgh); Chemists' (New York). Home: Ruskin Apts., Ruskin Av. Office: Gulf Bldg., Pittsburgh, Pa.

SALE, William Goodridge, Jr., lawyer; b. Wilmington, N.C., July 3, 1903; s. William Goodridge and Anna Belle (Sackett) S.; A.B. and LL.B., Washington & Lee Univ.; grad. student, Yale U., 1925-26; m. Ann Meriwether Anderson, Nov. 3, 1928; children—Ann Goodridge, Grace Wilson, Jane Lewis. Admitted to W.Va. bar, 1927, and since engaged in gen. practice of law at Welch; mem. firm Sale, St. Clair & Sale. Mem. McDowell Co. Bar Assn. (pres. 1934), Phi Beta Kappa, Omicron Delta Kappa, Phi Delta Phi, Beta Theta Pi. Republican. Presbyn. Home: 155 Maple Av. Office: First Nat. Bank Bldg., Welch, W.Va.

SALEEBY, Eli Richard, physician; b. Syria, Mar. 13, 1899; s. Rasheed Assad and Labebee G.; came to U.S., 1914, and naturalized citizen, 1920; B.S., U. of N.C., Chapel Hill, N.C., 1920; M.D., Jefferson Med. Coll., Phila., 1922; unmarried. After usual interneships engaged in practice of medicine at Phila. since 1924; mem. surg. staff Jefferson Hosp.; instr. surgery and anatomy, Jefferson Med. Coll., Phila., since 1927; asst. chief surgeon, Phila. Gen. Hosp.; cons. surgeon, Norristown State Hosp. Served in S.A.T.C., U. of N.C., 1918. Mem. Am., Pa., and Phila. Co. med. assns., Sigma Xi. Republican. Presbyterian. Mason. Club: Penn Athletic, Medical (Phila.). Author: several med. articles presented before med. assemblies and pub. in nat. med. jours. Home: Penn Athletic Club of Philadelphia. Office: 225 S. 18th St., Philadelphia, Pa.

SALKELD, Howard Bernard, pres. Tasa Coal Co.; b. Lloydsville, Pa., Sept. 1, 1880; s. Samuel Scott and Etta (Sipe) S.; student Steubenville (O.) High Sch., 1896, Steubenville Bus. Coll., 1897; m. Buena Vista Taylor, Oct. 30, 1901; children—Thelma Mae (Mrs. Carl J. Mulert), Helen Virginia (Mrs. Preston H. Vestal). Clerk Aetna Standard Iron & Steel Co., Mingo, O., 1897-98; in freight office, W.&L.E. Ry., 1898; teacher, Steubenville Bus. Coll., 1898-99; clerk and stenographer, Pa. R.R., 1899-1903; office mgr. Kirkbride Coal Co. and Fort Pitt Stone & Brick Co., Carnegie, Pa., 1903-12; office mgr. and sales agent Verner Coal & Coke Co., Pittsburgh, 1912-15, v.p. and treas., 1916-25; office mgr. Interstate Pipe and Cordage Co., Pittsburgh, 1915-16; v.p. in charge of operations Carnegie Coal Co., Pittsburgh, 1923-25; treas. and dir. Tasa Coal Co., Zelienople, Pa., since 1925, pres. since 1925; pres. and dir. Shirley Gas Coal Corpn., The Freemont Coal Co., Pocono Land Co., Beverly Heights Co. Commr. Mt. Lebanon (Pa.) Twp., 1917-25, v.p. of board, 1921-25. Republican. Presbyterian. Mason (K.T., R.A.M., A.A.O. M.M.S.). Clubs: Duquesne (Pittsburgh); Almas (Dormont, Pa.); St. Clair Country (Mt. Lebanon, Pa.). Home: Zelienople, Pa.; (summer) Conneaut Lake, Pa. Office: First Nat. Bank Bldg., Zelienople, Pa.

SALKO, Samuel, artist, mural painter; b. Russia, Feb. 12, 1888; s. Samuel and Sarah S.; came to U.S., 1916, naturalized, 1923; ed. Imperial Art School, Vilno and Odessa, Russia, The Pa. Acad. of Fine Arts, 1918-22; m. Sophia Cohen, June 15, 1912; children—Samuel, Lillian (Mrs. M. Berger), Eva, Jacob. Artist since 1924. Exhibited at Phila. Sketch Club, 1934; Phila. Y.M.H.A., 1935-38; Pa. Acad. Water Color, 1935, 36; Wanamaker's Regional Art Show, 1935; Artists Union, 1937, 38. Works exhibited permanently at Jefferson Hosp. and in private collections. Awarded scholarship of Pa. Acad. Fine Arts, 1919. Jewish religion. Home: 2107 N. 8th St., Philadelphia, Pa.

SALSBURY, Nate, writer; b. Newburgh, N.Y., Apr. 27, 1888; s. Nate and Rachel (Samuels) S.; A.B., Columbia, 1909, LL.B., 1911; m. May Schloss, Aug. 2, 1919. Practiced law, 1912-17; column conductor Chicago Evening Post, 1917-19; adv. business, 1919-20; free lance writer. Republican. Clubs: White Paper, Forty Club of Chicago (hon.). Author: Our Cat, 1934. Contbr. prose and verse to Saturday Evening Post, Harper's Mag., etc. Home: 17 Smull Av., Caldwell, N.J.

SALTER, Charles Edward Wilcox, merchant; b. Scranton, Pa., June 1, 1874; s. Charles and Emily Jane (Hellar) S.; grad. Franklin (Pa.) High Sch., 1892; m. Eliza Fassett, Sept. 14, 1914. Began as errand boy, 1893; mem. of firm Woodburn, Cone & Co., dept. store, since 1906, mgr. since 1910. Dir. and mem. discount com. Exchange Bank & Trust Co.; v.p. Community Loan Co., Franklin (Pa.) Bldg. & Loan Assn. Hon. mem. Am. Legion (awarded Certificate of Distinguished Service). Republican. Episcopalian (jr. warden St. John's Episcopal Ch.). Mason (32°), Elk, Odd Fellow, Royal Arcanum. Clubs: Franklin, Washington (Franklin, Pa.). Home: 1409 Elk St. Office: 318-322 13th St., Franklin, Pa.

SALTON, Russell A.; surgeon-in-chief Williamson Memorial Hosp. Address: Williamson, W.Va.

SALTUS, Samuel Morrison, M.D.; b. Charleston, S.C., Jan. 9, 1898; s. Samuel Phillip and Cornelia (Morrison) S.; student Northeast High Sch., Phila., 1915-19, U. of Pa., 1919-21; M.D., Temple U. Med. Sch., Phila., 1925; unmarried. Began as physician, 1925, and since in pvt. practice of medicine and surgery at Phila. Fellow, A.M.A.; mem. Phila. Co. Med. Soc., Alpha Phi Alpha. Episcopalian. Mason, Elk. Club: Pyramid (Phila.). Address: 1824 W. Norris St., Philadelphia, Pa.

SALTZMAN, Charles McKinley, army officer; b. Panora, Ia., Oct. 18, 1871; s. F. J. and Lovina Elizabeth (Lahman) S.; grad. U.S. Mil. Acad., 1896; honor grad. Signal Sch., 1906; grad. Army War Coll., 1921; m. Mary Peyton Eskridge, May 9, 1899; 1 son, Charles Eskridge. Apptd. add. 2d lt. 5th Cav., June 12, 1896; promoted through grades to col., May 15, 1917; brig. gen. N.A., July 24, 1917. A.d.c. to Brig. Gen. H. C. Merriam, 1900-01; engagements at Guasimas and San Juan, Santiago Campaign, 1898, also in Philippine Insurrection and

SALVATI — Moro campaigns; signal officer, Eastern Dept., 1913-15; signal officer, U.S. troops, Panama, C.Z., 1915-16; apptd. exec. officer, Office of Chief Signal Officer, Sept. 1, 1916; chief signal officer, rank of maj. gen., Jan. 9, 1924; retired Jan. 8, 1928; apptd. mem. Federal Radio Commn., 1929, chmn. 1930-32 (resigned); appointed vice-pres. U.S. Shipping Board Merchant Fleet Corporation, 1933. Delegate from U.S. to Internat. Radio Conf., London, 1912, to Internat. Telegraph Conference, Paris, 1925, Internat. Radio Telegraph Conf., Washington, D.C., 1927; chmn. U.S. delegation to Internat. Radio Technical Consulting Com., The Hague, 1929. Given two citations "for gallantry in action," Spanish-Am. War; awarded D.S.M., "for exceptionally meritorious and conspicuous services," World War. Address: Burnt Mills Hills, Silver Spring, Md.

SALVATI, Raymond Ernest, v.p. Pond Creek, Pocahontas Co.; b. Monongah, W.Va., May 14, 1899; s. C. and Elizabeth (Armentrout) S.; B.S. in M.E., W.Va., U., 1922; m. Pearle Charlotte Williamson, Mar. 12, 1921; children —Raymond, Timothy, Marianna. With Pond Creek Pocahontas Co. since 1926, beginning as supt. Mine No. 1, v.p. since 1933; gen. mgr. Island Creek Coal Co. since 1935, v.p. since 1938. Address: Holden, W.Va.

SALZEDO, Carlos, composer, harpist, pianist; b. Arcachon, France, Apr. 6, 1885; s. Gaston and Anna (Silva) S.; came to U.S., 1909, naturalized, 1923; premier prix in solfège, piano, harp, Paris Conservatoire, Paris, France, 1901; (hon.) Mus.D., Phila. Musical Acad., 1937; m. Marjorie Call, Apr. 21, 1938. Concertized in many parts of the world as harp soloist and with Salzedo Harp Ensemble; founder and dir. harp dept., Curtis Inst. of Music since yr. 1924. Served with French Army one yr. during World War; discharged acct. illness. Pres. Nat. Assn. of Harpists; vice-pres. Internat. Soc. for Contemporary Music; chmn. program com. Beethoven Assn. Clubs: Beethoven Assn., Bohemians. Composed for orchestra, piano and harp. Home: 270 Riverside Drive, New York, N.Y. Office: Curtis Inst., Philadelphia, Pa.

SAMMONS, William P.; mem. staff Wheeling and Ohio Valley Gen. hosps. Address: 1325 Chapline St., Wheeling, W.Va.

SAMONISKY, Harris, editor; b. Delaware City, Del., June 28, 1895; s. Max and Lena (Friedman) S.; grad. Delaware City High Sch., 1912; A.B., U. of Del., 1916; m. Mina Roberta Reinach, July 14, 1918; 1 son, Byron. Reporter Wilmington (Del.) Every Evening, 1919-21, state editor 1921-23, sports editor, 1923-27, city editor, 1927-32; city editor Journal-Every Evening since merger, 1932. Served in 1st O.T.C., Ft. Myer, Va.; commd. 2d lt. Q.M.C., 1917; mem. finance dept., later salvage and reclamation div.; disch. as 1st lt., 1918. Dir. Prisoners Aid Soc. of Del.; mem. exec. com. Del. Soc. for Control of Cancer; mem. Swedish Tercentenary Commn., 1935; mem. U.S. Valley Tercentenary Commn., 1936; mem. Del. Joint Fish Commn., 1921-27. Mem. Newspaper Guild, Am. Legion, Alumni Assn. U. of Del. Ind. Republican. Mason (32°, Shriner) dep. grand master of Del., 1934, grand master, 1935. Club: Sojourners (past pres. DuPont Chapter). Home: 606 W. 26th St. Office: Girard and Orange Sts., Wilmington, Del.

SAMPLE, Paul Lindsay, merchant; b. Manteo, N.C., Sept. 17, 1897; s. Augustus Gambrel and Ida Mae (Shaw) S.; student Elizabeth City (N.C.) Pub. High Sch., 1910-14; A.B., Trinity College (now Duke U.), Durham, N.C., 1918; m. Helen Henrietta Heinz, Oct. 31, 1929; children—Miriam Elizabeth, Dorothy Jean, Becky Ann and Mathilda Mae (twins). With G. C. Murphy Co., chain variety stores, McKeesport, Pa., since 1918, as floorman, 1918-19, asst. store mgr., 1919-20, store mgr., 1921-23, supt. of stores, 1924-27, dir. of personnel, 1926-29, asst. sales mgr., 1928-30, sales mgr., 1931-37, v.p. in charge of sales since 1938, dir. since 1929. Republican. Methodist. Mason (Shriner). Clubs: Youghiogheny Country (McKeesport, Pa.); Bankers of America (New York, N.Y.). Home: 1502 Library Av., McKeesport, Pa.; (summer) 14 Emerson Av., Chautauqua, N.Y. Office: 531 5th Av., McKeesport, Pa.

SAMPSON, Edward, geologist; b. of Am. parents, Oxford, Eng., May 31, 1891; s. Alden and M(ary) Agnes (Yarnall) S.; grad. Pomfret (Conn.) Sch., 1910; C.E., Princeton, 1914, M.Sc., 1915, D.Sc., 1920; student Mass. Inst. Tech., 1916-17; m. Alfreda Cope Lewis, June 5, 1917 (died Apr. 1, 1932); children —Edward, Harold Yarnall, Agnes. Instr. Rutgers, 1919-20; asst. geologist U.S. Geol. Survey, 1920-22, asso. geologist, 1922-34; asst. prof. geology, Princeton, 1925-28, asso. prof. since 1928, chmn. dept., 1934-36. Mem. Soc. Economic Geologists (sec. 1926-33; v.p. 1935), Geol. Soc. America, Mineral. Soc. America, Mineral Soc. (London), Am. Assn. Petroleum Geologists, Geol. Soc. Washington (sec. 1924), Am. Inst. Mining and Metal. Engrs., Canadian Inst. Mining and Metal. Engrs., Sigma Xi. Served as 1st lt. Air Service Aeronautics, 1918-19. Episcopalian. Author of numerous papers on economic geology and mineral resources. Home: Lafayette Rd., Princeton, N.J.

SAMPSON, Harry Oscar, agrl. edn.; b. Dodgeville, Wis., Apr. 21, 1879; s. William and Agnes (Shipley) S.; B.S., Iowa State Coll., 1903, B.S. Agr., 1904; A.M., Columbia, 1921; m. Hattie Louise Nairn, May 29, 1908; children—Louise Nairn (Mrs. Richard K. Warr), Harry Oscar. Teacher of agriculture, Waterford, Pa., High Sch., 1904-06; asst. in agrl. edn., U.S. Dept. of Agr., 1906-08 (furloughed part time to conduct Agrl. High Sch., Calvert, Md.); prin. Sch. of Agriculture, Internat. Corr. Schs., 1908-15; prof. of agriculture, Winthrop Coll., Rock Hill, S.C., 1915-18; state supervisor of agr., State Dept. of Pub. Instrn., and prof. agrl. edn., Rutgers U., New Brunswick, N.J., since 1918. Mem. N.E.A., Am. Vocational Assn., Phi Gamma Delta, Phi Delta Kappa, Alpha Zeta. Home: 325 Lincoln Av., Highland Park, N.J. Office: College of Agriculture, Rutgers Univ., New Brunswick, N.J.

SAMSON, Harry Gilmore, pres. H. Samson, Inc.; b. Pittsburgh, Pa., July 11, 1870; s. Hudson and Susan (Gilmore) S.; student Western U. of Pittsburgh (now U. of Pittsburgh), 1897-98; m. Elizabeth Saeger, Oct. 18, 1893; children—Howard Saeger, Hudson Gilmore. With H. Samson Co., morticians, Pittsburgh, since 1898; owner H. Samson, Inc. (formerly H. Samson) since 1903, pres. since 1921; organized Samson Motor Co., automobile distributors, Pittsburgh, 1915, pres. 1915-30; dir. Samson Sales Co. Pres. Methodist Episcopal Ch., Union of Pittsburgh; trustee Christ Meth. Ch. Mem. Pittsburgh Better Business Bur., Fed. of Social Agencies (past pres.), Pittsburgh Free Dispensary (dir. since 1904), Y.M.C.A. Mem. Sons Am. Revolution, Founders and Patriots, Plymouth Colony Descendants. Republican. Methodist. Mason (Pittsburgh Lodge No. 484; Shiloh chapter; Tancred Commandery). Clubs: Rotary, Pittsburgh Field, Pittsburgh Athletic Assn. (Pittsburgh). Author: "Mystery of Death." Home: 615 Osage Rd., Mt. Lebanon, Pittsburgh, Pa. Office: 537 Neville St., Pittsburgh, Pa.

SAMUEL, Albert Herman, elec. contractor; b. Baltimore, Md., Feb. 9, 1891; s. Herman and Jennie (Hecht) S.; student pub. schs. and Baltimore Poly. Inst.; m. Sara Swartz, June 1, 1916; 1 dau., Sara Swartz. With Kingsbury Samuel Electric Co. since 1910, beginning as stock clerk, now pres. Mem. Illuminating Engring. Soc., Inst. Elec. Contractors of Md. Jewish Religion. Mason (Past Senior Stewart; Past Junior Warden; Past Master), Elk (Past Exalted Ruler). Club: Suburban of Baltimore. Home: 932 N. Charles St. Office: 530-32 N. Calvert St., Baltimore, Md.

SAMUEL, Bunford, librarian; b. Phila., Sept. 16, 1857; s. John and Rebecca (Levy) S.; ed. classical sch. Dr. John W. Fairies; m. Ella Salomon, Mar. 2, 1882; children—Alma R. (dec.), Emma L., Dorothea (Mrs. C. Livingstone Pelton); m. 2d, Edith Lamberton, Feb. 24, 1925. Assistant librarian Library Co. of Phila., in charge of the Ridgway Branch, 1878-1932. Projected, about 1880, general index of printed portraits, and compiled in pursuance thereof an index of portraits, now covering about 150,000 subjects, and of engravers thereof, extensively used, though as yet largely in M.S. Contbr. to The Bookman, Pa. Mag. of History, Scribner's, the Supplement to 9th edit. Encyclopædia Britannica, etc. Club: Author's (London). Author: Secession and Constitutional Liberty. Home: 3114 W. Coulter St., Philadelphia, Pa.

SAMUEL, Edmund Roger, physician; b. Mt. Carmel, Pa., Sept. 25, 1889; s. Edmund William and Alice (Kiefer) S.; ed. Dickinson Coll., 1906-09; M.D., U. of Pa., 1913; m. Emily G. Snyder, June 30, 1917; children—Mary Alice, Margaret Emily, Dorothy Louise. Res. phys. Chester Co. Hosp., 1913-14; pathologist, Pa. Hosp., 1914-15; in gen. practice of medicine at Mt. Carmel, Pa., since 1915; pres. Hazel Heights Land Co. since 1935. Served as capt. Med. Corps, U.S.A., 1917-19, assigned to B.E.F.; wounded in action. Awarded Purple Cross (U.S.). Mem. Rep. State Com. Pres. Cooperative Concert Assn. Mem. Am. Med. Assn., Pa. State Med. Soc. (trustee), Chamber of Commerce (past pres.), Am. Legion (past comdr. local post), Phi Kappa Sigma, Phi Rho Sigma. Republican. Methodist (trustee). Mason (32°). Clubs: Travel (pres.), Kiwanis (past pres.), Motor (past pres.), Fraternity (Mt. Carmel, past pres.). Home: Mt. Carmel, Pa.

SAMUEL, Snowden, pres. Frank Samuel & Co.; b. Phila., Pa., Dec. 26, 1897; s. Frank and Mary Buchanan (Snowden) S.; student Protestant Episcopal Acad., Phila., 1904-12; m. Elizabeth Chattam Adams, Oct. 15, 1918; 1 dau., Mary B. Puddler, American-Sewdo Iron Co., Danville, Pa., 1912-19, sec.-treas., 1919-23; partner, Frank Samuel & Co., Inc., ores and ferro alloys, Phila., since 1923, sec.-treas., 1932-34, pres. since 1934; organized Wrought Iron Research Assn., 1928, sec.-treas., 1928-31. Served as sergt., Field Signal Corps, U.S. Army, with A.E.F. during World War. Republican. Presbyterian. Clubs: Racquet, Soc. of Colonial Wars (Phila.). Home: St. Davids Av., St. Davids, Pa. Office: 200 Harrison Bldg., 15th and Market Sts., Philadelphia, Pa.

SAMUELS, Abram; asso. clin. prof. gynecology, U. of Md.; gynecologist-in-chief Mercy and Sinai hosps. Address: 1928 Eutaw Place, Baltimore, Md.

SAMUELSON, Herman; mem. law firm Samuelson & Robinson. Office: 111 N. Charles St., Baltimore, Md.

SAMUELSON, Sidney Edgar, amusement enterprises; b. New York, N.Y., Jan. 29, 1895; s. Abraham Bernard and Rose (Goldbatt) S.; B.S., Coll. of City of N.Y., 1916; m. Dorothy Soskin, Sept. 1, 1914; children—Wallace Hart Edgar, Gloria Dorette Vivienne. Operated Park Theatre, Newton, N.J., 1919-24; pres. and dir. Newton Amusement Corpn. and mng. dir. Newton Theatre Development Corpn.; cons. buyer and booker for Hildinger Enterprises, Trenton, N.J.; bus. mgr. Allied Independent Theatre Owners of Eastern Pa., Inc. Sec.-treas. Newton Recreation Commn.; first pres. Sussex Co. Council Boy Scouts. Past sec., Sussex Co. Ch. Mission Help. Democrat. Jewish religion. Rotarian. Home: 171 High St. Office: Newton Theatre, Newton, N.J.

SAMWORTH, Fred W., ry. official; b. Wilmington, Del., Feb. 23, 1892; s. Fred and Elizabeth (Hall) S.; ed. pub. schs.; m. Alice V. Blackwell, Feb. 5, 1912. Became mgr. Ohio Valley Electric Ry. Co., 1925, pres. and chmn. bd. since 1932. Home: 103 South Boul. Office: First Huntington Nat. Bank Bldg., Huntington, W.Va.

SANBORN, G. Walter, executive; b. Norwalk, O., Dec. 9, 1883; s. George Moody Stark and Blanche Olive (Pepoon) S.; student Union Classical Inst., Schenectady, N.Y., 1899-1901, Colgate U., Hamilton, N.Y., 1902-04; m. Margaret Lewis, Aug. 28, 1909; children—Virginia Elizabeth (Mrs. William Wilbert Eversmann), George. Richard. Began as machine shop helper, 1904; storekeeper and shipping clerk, Wm. Tod Co., Youngstown, O., 1905-09, purchasing agt., 1909-

17; asst. purchasing agt., United Engring. & Foundry Co., Pittsburgh, 1917-21, purchasing agt., 1921-34, v.p. in charge of purchases and traffic since 1934. Mem. Purchasing Agts. Assn. Mason (Shriner). Clubs: Rotary, Traffic, Pittsburgh Athletic (Pittsburgh). Home: 1437 N. Highland Av. Office: 2405 First Nat. Bank Bldg., Pittsburgh, Pa.

SANBORN, Walter Lyman, newspaper pub.; b. Norway, Me., Nov. 28, 1879; s. Darius Sylvester and Adelaide (Wilson) S.; ed. high sch., Norway, Me., 1893-97; A.B., Bowdoin Coll., 1901; m. Ethel Pratt Nye, Sept. 21, 1907. Employed as steamboat purser in summers and instr. pub. sch. in winters, 1901-03; employed on editorial staff, Boston Globe; propr. half interest Lansdale Pa. Reporter, 1915-23; paper dealer, 1923-27; organized Equitable Pub. Co., Lansdale, Pa. and bought North Penn Reporter, 1927, issued as daily since 1928, sec., treas. and bus. mgr. Equitable Pub. Co. Charter mem. Newspaper Pub. Assn. of Montgomery and Bucks Cos., and sec., treas., and purchasing agt. for same. Mem. Pa. Newspaper Pub. Assn., Press League of Bucks and Montgomery Cos., Delta Upsilon. Club: Bowdoin of Philadelphia. Home: Oak Drive, Lansdale, Pa. Office: 306 Courtland St., Lansdale, Pa.

SANDER, Frank V(an Derslice), mfg. chemist; b. Wheeling, W.Va., Apr. 19, 1890; s. Christian and Ida May (Hibberd) S.; B.S., U. of W.Va., 1912; Ph.D., U. of Chicago, 1921; m. Etna B. South, Jan. 18, 1913; 1 son, Frank V., Jr. Engaged as teacher, asst. prin. and prin. high schs. in W.Va., 1913-19; instr. Rush Med. Sch. of Chicago U., 1921-22; asst. prof. U. of Wis., and dir. chem. med. research, Wis. Psychiatric Inst., 1922-24; research chemist, Tech. Research Lab. of Johnson & Johnson, mfg. hospital supplies, New Brunswick, N.J., since 1924, mem. firm since 1924. Served as mem. bd. dirs. local Boy Scouts of America. Mem. Am. Chem. Soc., Sigma Xi. Republican. Protestant. Club: Rifle (New Brunswick); Univ. of Chicago (New York). Awarded several patents. Contbr. tech. articles to sci. journs. Home: 64 Lawrence Av., New Brunswick, N.J.

SANDERS, Carlton Custer, lawyer; b. Rowlesburg, W.Va., Feb. 10, 1896; s. John Henry and Maria (Poling) S.; student Broaddus Coll., Philippi, W.Va., 1913-15; A.B., W.Va. Univ., Morgantown, W.Va., 1920; LL.B., W.Va. Univ. Law Sch., 1922; m. Thelma Elizabeth Beane, Nov. 10, 1925; children—Patricia Beane, Martha Carlton, John Woodson. Admitted to W.Va. bar, 1922, and since engaged in gen. practice of law at Beckley; asst. pros. atty. Raleigh Co., W.Va., 1925-26, asst. U.S. dist. atty., 1928-29; mem. firm Ashworth & Sanders since 1937. Served in 38th Div., U.S.A., 1917-19, at Camp Shelby, Miss. Mem. W.Va. Bar Assn., Am. Bar Assn., Phi Delta Phi, Phi Kappa Sigma. Republican. Presbyn. Mason (Shriner). Elk. Club: Black Knight Country. Home: 129 Granville Av., Beckley, W.Va.

SANDERS, Charles Finley, clergyman, educator; b. Mifflinburg, Pa., Feb. 11, 1869; s. Joseph and Eva Catharine (Miller) S.; B.A., Pa. Coll., Gettysburg, Pa., 1892; grad. Luth. Theol. Sem., Gettysburg, 1895, B.D., 1899; studied U. of Leipzig, Germany, 3 semesters, 1905-06; D.D., Lafayette, 1913; m. Harriet E. Hesson, Dec. 27, 1894. Ordained Luth. ministry, 1895; pastor Avonmore, Pa., 1895-98, Blairsville, 1898-1905; teacher Blairsville Coll. for Women, 1901-05; acting professor mental science, 1906, prof. philosophy since 1907, Pennsylvania Coll. Lecturer in war camps, 1919. Mem. Am. Sociological Society. Progressive Republican. Translator: (from the German) Introduction to Philosophy (by Prof. Jerusalem), 1910, revised edit., 1932; Brief History of Modern Philosophy (Hoffding), 1912; Problems of the Secondary Teacher (Jerusalem) 1918. Author: Freshmen Orientation, 1926; The Taproot of Religion and Its Fruitage, 1931; Freshman Orientation, 1936. Mem. Phi Beta Kappa, Kappa Phi Kappa, Pi Gamma Nu. World tour, 1928-29, studying conditions in Japan, China and India; lectures on polit. and social conditions in the Orient. Wrote The Challenge of the Trinitarian to the Neopagan, 1937. Home: 135 Broadway, Gettysburg, Pa.

SANDERS, Jos. M.; mem. law firm Sanders & Day. Address: Bluefield, W.Va.

SANDERSON, Sidney, asso. prof. psychology; b. Bath, N.Y., Dec. 27, 1893; s. Benjamin Smith and Agnes (Dibblee) S.; ed. Moravian Coll., Bethlehem, Pa., 1910-11, U. of Pa., 1911-15; A.M., U. of Pa., 1923, Ph.D., same, 1929; m. Elsie D. Dorries, Dec. 19, 1936; 1 dau., Mary. Began as salesman wholesale paper, 1915; with pub. relations dept., Victor Talking Machine Co., 1916-17; with Adams & Westlake Co., heavy hdw., Phila., Pa., 1919-21; asst. in psychology, U. of Pa., 1921-22, instr. psychology, 1922-29; asst. prof. psychology, Rutgers U., 1929-34, asso. prof. since 1934. Served as sergt. med. dept. U.S.A., 1917-19 with A.E.F. Mem. A.A.A.S., Am. Psychol. Assn., Am. Assn. Univ. Profs., N. J. Assn. of Psychologists, Phi Beta Kappa, Sigma Xi, Psi Chi, Phi Sigma Kappa. Democrat. Episcopalian. Home: 112 S. 3d Av., Highland Park, N.J.

SANDO, Edwin Milton, clergyman; b. Meckville, Pa., Nov. 23, 1876; s. Henry and Rebecca (Patsches) S.; ed. Spl. Normal Classes, Annville, Pa., 1892-95; B.Ed., Cumberland Valley State Normal Sch., 1897; A.B., Ursinus Coll., 1904, A.M., same, 1910; ed. Ursinus Sch. Theology, 1904-07; hon. D.D., Ursinus Coll., 1931; m. Martha I. Poorman, June 18, 1907; children — John Henry, Paul Edwin, Martha Rebecca (Mrs. J. Robert Menchey). Ordained to ministry Reformed Ch. in U.S., 1907; minister at Hellam, Pa., 1907-20, Hanover, Pa., since 1920; stated clk. Gettysburg Classis Ref. Ch. since 1921; pres. Potomac Synod Ref. Ch., 1938-39. Mem. Patriotic Order Sons of America. Mem. Reformed Ch. Jr. O.U.A.M. Home: Hanover, Pa.

SANDS, Alexander H., Jr., trustee; b. Richmond, Va., Apr. 25, 1891; ed. McGuire's U. Sch. (Richmond) and Richmond Coll. (now U. of Richmond); m. Ella A. Reeve; children — William Reeve, Jean Hamilton. Began in banking in Va., later in employ of firm exporting leaf tobacco; became connected with James B. and B. N. Duke, New York, 1909; new sec. and trustee The Duke Endowment, The Doris Duke Trust, trust established by will of James B. Duke for Nanaline H. Duke and Doris Duke; sec. and mem. Angier B. Duke Memorial, Incorporated; treasurer and director Pearson Investment Corporation, Linden Investment Corpn., Newton Investment Corpn.; dir. Duke Power Co. and officer or dir. various other corpns. Mem. Phi. Kappa Sigma, and Omicron Delta Kappa. Home: 1 Brunswick Rd., Montelair, N.J. Office: 49 W. 49th St., New York, N.Y.

SANDS, Harry Senseney, elec. engr.; b. Fairmont, W.Va., Aug. 3, 1867; s. Joseph Evans and Virginia (Eyster) S.; ed. Fairmont Normal Sch. and Cornell U.; m. Helen Virginia Turner, Feb. 14, 1893. Electrical engr. since 1893; elec. engr. Sands Electric & Mfg. Co. since 1896; pres. Sands Electric Co.; dir. Marsh Bros. Tobacco Co. Mem. Soc. Elec. Engrs., Phi Sigma Kappa. Episcopalian. Club: Fort Henry (Wheeling). Home: Sandscrest Farms, Wheeling, W.Va. Office: 52 18th St., Wheeling, W.Va.

SANDSTON, Leonard Mark, civil engring.; b. Christchurch, N.Z., Mar. 21, 1884; came to U.S., 1908, and naturalized citizen, 1929; B.S., Mass. Inst. Tech., 1912; A.M., Columbia U., 1916; m. Margaret Elizabeth LaRoss, Dec. 25, 1919; 1 son, William LaRoss. Engaged as staff engr. and surveyor, New Zealand and Tongan govts., 1904-08; with B.&M. R.R. and C.M.&St.P. R.R., 1909-12; in pvt. practice engring. in New York City, 1914-16; in pvt. practice in Sydney, Australia, and Christchurch, N.Z., 1916-22; spl. engr. and development engr., Am. Rolling Mill Co., and cons. engr. Armco Culvert & Flume Mfrs. Co., 1922-32; engr. Dept. Pub. Works and Dept. Pub. Health, Pittsburgh, since 1932, supt.-engr. Bur. Sanitation since 1937; mem. Advisory Health Bd. of Pa. Mem. Am. Soc. C.E., Pa. State Assn. of Professional Engrs. Presbyterian. Home: 805 Western Av., Pittsburgh, Pa.

SANDY, William Charles, psychiatrist; b. Troy, N.Y., Sept. 9, 1876; s. William Charles and Eliza (Rounsavell) S.; A.B., Columbia, 1898, M.D., Coll. Phys. and Surgs., 1901; m. Vida Dowers, Dec. 30, 1905; children—Elizabeth, William Charles. Interne, Newark (N.J.) City Hosp., 1902-03; asst. phys. N.J. State Hosp., Trenton, 1905-13, Kings Park State Hosp., N.Y., 1913-15; med. dir. S.C. State Hosp., Columbia, 1915-17; asst. supt. Conn. State Hosp., Middletown, 1917-18; psychiatrist State Com. for Mental Defectives, N.Y., 1919-21; dir. Bur. of Mental Health, State Dept. of Welfare, Pa., since 1921. Served with Med. Corps, U.S.A., 1918-19; now lt. col. Med. Res. Corps. Mem. Am. Med. Assn., Pa. and Dauphin Co. med. socs., Am. Psychiatric Assn. (sec.-treas., 1933-38, pres., 1938-39), Assn. on Mental Deficiency, Phila. Psychiatric Soc., Mental Hygiene Com., Pub. Charities Assn., Nat. Com. for Mental Hygiene. Episcopalian. Mason. Clubs: University, Torch. Contbr. articles to med. jours. Home: 1011 N. Front St. Address: Education Bldg., Harrisburg, Pa.

SANFORD, Olive Corning, civic leader; b. Palmyra, N.Y., Dec. 19, 1875; d. Joseph W. and Louisa (Newton) Corning; grad. Palmyra High Sch., 1894; student Teachers Coll., Columbia, 1894-98; m. Frederic H. Sanford, July 4, 1900 (died 1927); 1 son, Frederic Corning (1908-1928). Taught school 2 years before marriage; after marriage lived in Brazil and Bolivia where husband was in rubber buying business, also traveled abroad extensively; returned to U.S., 1914, and lived in Nutley, N.J., since 1915. Mem. Bd. of Edn., 1928-34, and since 1937; mem. N.J. Assembly, 1935, 36, 1938, 39 (chmn. com. on edn.); trustee U. of Newark; chmn. N.J. Com. on Cause and Cure of War, 1928-34. Mem. Nutley League of Women Voters (pres., 1924-28), N.J. League of Women Voters (pres., 1928-34), Acad. Polit. Science. Republican. Episcopalian. Clubs: Woman's (past pres.), Am. Assn. Univ. Women (Nutley Branch); American Women's Assn. (New York). Active in local improvements. Home: 144 Whitford Av., Nutley, N.J.

SANFORD, Raymond Laraway, scientist; b. Auburn, N.Y., Aug. 29, 1884; s. Walter Edward and Grace (Laraway) S.; B.S. in E.E., U. of Vt., 1907; m. Ailene Leffingwell, Sept. 11, 1912; children—Leora Laraway, Alton Leffingwell, Elizabeth Mae, Raymond Laraway, Jr. Instr. physics and elec. engring., U. of Vt., Burlington, 1908-10; mem. staff of Nat. Bur. of Standards, Washington, D.C., since 1910, chief of magnetic measurements sect. since 1918. Fellow A.A. A.S.; mem. Am. Soc. for Testing Materials, Washington Acad. Scis., Alpha Tau Omega. Republican. Presbyn. Contbr. several papers on magnetic measurements and magnetic properties of materials. Home: 6707 46th St., Chevy Chase, Md.

SANGSTER, Margaret Elizabeth (Mrs. Gerrit Van Deth), author; b. Brooklyn, N.Y.; d. George Munson and Ida May (Demarest) S.; ed. Miss Townsend's Sch., Newark, N.J.; m. Gerrit Van Deth. Contbg. editor Christian Herald since 1913; visited Belgium, Germany and France as correspondent for Christian Herald, 1918; editor Smart Set, 1929-30. Member Christian Herald Children's Home Board; mem. bd. Bowery Mission; mem. Authors' League of America, Nat. Arts Club, Authors Club. Congregationalist. Author: (poems and stories) Friends o' Mine, 1913; Real People and Dreams, 1914; (poems) Cross Roads, 1919; The Island of Faith (novel), 1921; Your Book and Mine, 1923; Five Thousand a Year, 1924; The Hill of Ambition, 1925; The Rugged Road, 1930; The Cheerful Convalescent, 1931; Six Women Along the Way, 1931; Love Lightly (novel), 1932; God and My Garden, 1933; The Littlest Orphan and Other Christmas Stories, 1935; Singing on the Road, 1936; The Stars Come Close (novel), 1936; Surgical Call (novel), 1937; Flower Wagon, 1937; The Terrace, 1937; Little Letter to God, 1938; All Through the Day, 1939. Contbr. poems and stories to mags. Home: 315 Engle St., Tenafly, N.J.

SANVILLE, Henry Frederick, consulting engr.; b. New York, N.Y., July 11, 1872; s. Frederick

Phillip and Hannah Sophia (Leyton) S.; student Columbia U. Sch. of Mines, 1892; m. Alice C. Walker, Jan. 12, 1912; children—Henry Frederick, Donald Walker. Engr. Gen. Electric Co., Lynn, Mass., 1892-95; engr. and sec. Morris Electric Co., New York, 1895-1902; pvt. practice as consulting engr., Phila., 1902-23 and since 1932; pres. Power Equipment Co., Phila., 1923-32. One of the founders of Southwark Neighborhood House. Mem. Am. Inst. E.E. (past chmn. Phila. sect.). Republican. Congregationalist. Clubs: Engineers (past dir.; past treas.), Columbia U. Alumni (dir.; past pres., Phila.). Home: 10 Asbury Av., Melrose Park, Pa. Office: Land Title Bldg., Philadelphia, Pa.

SAPPINGTON, Samuel Watkins, pathology; b. Philadelphia, 1874; prep. edn. Friends Central High School, Phila.; M.D., Hahnemann College and Hospital, Phila., 1897. Served as interne Hahnemann Med. Hosp.; apptd. demonstrator of pathology, Hahnemann Coll., 1900, asso. prof., 1905, prof., 1907, and has served for many yrs. as prof. pathology and bacteriology same coll., and as pathologist Hahnemann Med. Coll. Mem. Am. Inst. Homœopathy, Soc. of Immunologists, Soc. Am. Bacteriologists, etc. Address: Broad St. above Race, Philadelphia, Pa.

SARTAIN, Paul Judd, M.D.; b. Phila., Pa., Nov. 26, 1861; s. Samuel and Harriet Amelia (Judd) S.; A.B., U. of Pa., 1883, A.M. and M.D., 1886; post-grad. studies in Vienna, Berlin, Paris, etc., 1886-88, hosps. of London, 1888-89; unmarried. Practiced at Phila. since 1889. Fellow Coll. of Physicians (Phila.), Am. Acad. Ophthalmology and Oto-Laryngology; mem. A.M.A., Med. Soc. State of Pa., Phila. Co. Med. Soc., Pathol. Soc., Franklin Inst., Hist. Soc. of Pa. Zoöl. Soc. of Phila., Geog. Soc. Phila. (sec. since 1894), Med. Club of Phila. (v.p. 1925), Oxford Ophthal. Congress, Colonial Soc. of Pa., Société Française d'Ophtalmologie, Delta Phi. Republican. Unitarian. Clubs: Union League, St. Elmo; Royal Socs. Club. (London). Home: 2006 Walnut St., Philadelphia, Pa.

SASSAMAN, Ira Seebold, clergyman; b. Dry Valley X Roads, Pa., June 17, 1878; s. Abraham and Elmira (Seebold) S.; ed. Central Pa. Coll., New Berlin, 1895-98, Susquehanna U., 1904-09, Pa. State Coll., 1911-12; (hon.) D.D., Susquehanna U., 1921; m. Mary Agnes Caspar, May 12, 1909; children—Ira Caspar, Rev. Robert Seebold, Charles Herbert, Mary Agnes. Engaged as teacher pub. schs., 1898-1902, salesman, 1902-04; ordained to ministry Luth. Ch., 1908; pastor, Burnham, Pa., 1908-10, State College, 1910-13, Turtle Creek, 1913-16, Northumberland, 1916-25, at Williamsport, Pa., since 1925; pres. Susquehanna Conf., Central Pa. Synod; keyman, Lycoming Co., Pa., Council of Chs.; mem. dept. of evangelism, Pa. Council of Chs.; mem. exec. com. Central Pa. Synod; mem. Pa. Interdenominational Comity Commn. since 1935; sec. Susquehanna Synod, 1920-23, pres. 1921-23 and 1935-38. Dir. Williamsport Salvation Army; dir. Nat. Preaching and Teaching Missions for North Central Area of Pa., 1936-37. Republican. Lutheran. Mason (32°). Contbr. to religious jours. Home: 735 Pearl St., Williamsport, Pa.

SATTERLEE, Herbert Livingston, lawyer; b. New York, Oct. 31, 1863; s. George B. and Sarah S.; B.S., Ph.B., Columbia, 1883, A.M., 1884, Ph.D., LL.B., cum laude, 1885; m. Louisa Pierpont, d. J(ohn) Pierpont Morgan, Nov. 15, 1900. Pvt. sec. Senator William M. Evarts, 1885-87; navigator 1st Naval Battalion, N.Y., 1891-95; col. and a.-d.-c. to Gov. L. P. Morton, 1895-96; capt. (naval militia) and a.-d.-c. to Gov. Frank S. Black, 1897-98; lt. U.S.N. (war with Spain) and chief of staff to Capt. John R. Bartlett, U.S.N.; counsel M.,K. &T. Ry. Co., 1898-1902; asst. sec. of the Navy, Dec. 1, 1908-Mar. 6, 1909; chmn. N.Y. State Commn. for the Blind, 1914-16; now mem. firm of Satterlee & Canfield, New York. Capt. Naval Militia Reserve List. Trustee Columbia University, 1917-23; president of Wilmer Foundation, president of Naval Militia Vet. Association, 1891-1922; member Nat. Inst. Social Sciences, Soc. Colonial Wars, S.R., Soc. War 1812, Soc. Foreign Wars, Vet. Arty. Corps; a founder Navy League U.S.; comdr. gen. Naval Order U.S., 1925-28; mem. Mil. and Naval Order Spanish-Am. War, American Bar Assn., N.Y. State Bar Assn., Assn. Bar City N.Y., Am. Mus. Natural History, N.Y. Hist. Soc., Met. Mus. Art, Am. Geog. Soc., St. Nicholas Soc. (pres. 1936-38), Soc. Naval Archts., Seamen's Ch. Inst. of N.Y. (v.p.), Life Saving Benevolent Assn. (pres.), State Charities Aid Assn., Grant Monument Assn. (pres.); hon. mem. Naval Acad. Grads. Assn. of New York, Marine Museum City of N.Y. (pres.). Clubs: University, Church, Union League (pres.), Union, Century, Republican, Columbia University, New York Yacht, St. Anthony, Down Town, India House (New York); Army and Navy (Washington); Bohemian (San Francisco); Round Hill Country (Greenwich, Conn.). Home: 1 Beekman Place, New York and Sotterley, St. Marys Co., Md. Office: 49 Wall St., New York, N.Y.

SATTERTHWAITE, Linton, Jr., archæologist; b. Trenton, N.J., Feb. 8, 1897; s. Linton and Florence Willis (Hibbs) S.; B.A., Yale, 1920; post grad. study of anthropology, Univ. of Pa., 1929-35; m. Margaret Elizabeth Conway, May 21, 1930. Reporter, 1920-23; admitted to N.J. bar, 1923, and practiced, 1924-28; engaged in archæological research since 1929, principally in Maya ruins at Piedras Negras, Guatemala, also in Tex. and W.Va.; asst. curator U. of Pa. Museum, field dir. of its Guatemalan expdns. since 1933. Cadet and flying officer (2d lt.) Brit. Royal Air Force, 1918-19. Mem. Am. Anthrop. Assn., Soc. for Am. Archæology, Philadelphia Anthrop. Soc. Author reports on expdns. Home: 1716 Pine St., Philadelphia, Pa.

SATTERTHWAITE, Reuben, Jr.; mem. law firm Satterthwaite & Foulk. Office: Du Pont Bldg., Wilmington, Del.

SATTERTHWAITE, William Hallowell, Jr., lawyer; b. Montgomery Co., Pa., Aug. 13, 1883; s. William H. and Hannah P. (Hallowell) S.; ed. Friends Sch., Horsham, Pa., 1890-97, George Sch., Bucks Co., Pa., 1897-1901; LL.B., U. of Pa. Law Sch., 1906; m. Elsinore M. Giddings, Aug. 13, 1914 (died Dec. 4, 1926); children—Edwin H., Hannah E. (Mrs. Joseph W. Klein), Mary Elizabeth, William H. 3d; m. 2d, Margaretta B. Taylor, Dec. 19, 1927 (died May 19, 1931). Admitted to Pa. bar, 1906, and engaged in gen. practice of law in Phila., 1906-12, and in Doylestown, Pa., since 1912; mem. firm Bunting and Satterthwaite since 1924; pres. Doylestown Trust Co. since 1920, Doylestown Bldg. and Loan Assn. since 1937. Served as exec. sec. Bucks Co. Council of Nat. Defense during World War. Dir. and pres. Doylestown Borough Sch. Bd. since 1919. Trustee George Sch. since 1924. Trustee Yearly Meeting of Friends, Phila., Pa., since 1933. Mem. Pa. and Bucks Co. bar assns. Republican. Mem. Religious Soc. of Friends. Mason. Club: Doylestown Kiwanis (past pres.). Home: 1 Lincoln Av. Office: Lyons Bldg., Doylestown, Pa.

SATZ, David Meyer, lawyer; b. Columbus, Tex., Nov. 19, 1893; s. Abraham and Lena (Wallach) S.; B.S., Harvard U., 1914; ed. Columbia U. Law Sch., 1915-17; m. Marie Loewenberg, June 15, 1922; children—David M., Jr., Margery Ann. Admitted to N.J. bar as atty., 1917, as counsellor, 1920; engaged in gen. practice of law at Newark since 1918; mem. firm Coult, Satz, Tomlinson & Morse since 1927. Served as mem. Dft. Bd. and Four Minute Man; chief speaker for Newark Red Cross on employee drives; with J.W.B. in Army of Occupation. Served for ten yrs. on Essex Co. Dem. Publicity and Speakers' Committees. Active in philanthropic and social service drives many yrs. principally on speakers' coms. Trustee Intercollegiate Menorah Assn. Mem. Am., N.J. State and Essex Co. bar assns. Democrat. Jewish religion. Clubs: Downtown of Newark; Mountain Ridge Country. Home: 263 Walton Rd., South Orange. Office: 60 Park Pl., Newark, N.J.

SAUEREISEN, Christian Fred, owner Sauereisen Cements Co.; b. Aspinwall Station, Pittsburgh, Pa., May 5, 1884; s. Christian and Sophie (Zange) S.; student Carnegie Inst. Tech. (night sch.), 1908-09; m. Marion Mildred Phillips, Nov. 17, 1928; children—Phillips Frederick, William Phillips, Ferd James. Apprenticed as clayworking potter, Homer Laughlin China Co., East Liverpool, O., 1899-1905; established the first porcelain insulator dept. for George Westinghouse at Nernst Lamp Co., Pittsburgh, 1905-10; pioneered in the casting process of sanitary pottery, Jackson Potteries Co., Ford City, Pa., 1912-14; research work on spark plugs for Edward Schwab at Bethlehem (Pa.) Spark Plug Co. and for National Lock Co., Rockford, Ill., 1915-17; established Sauereisen Cements Co., Pittsburgh, 1919, and since pres. and sole owner. Mem. Chamber of Commerce (dir.; chmn. New Bridge Com.), Y.M.C.A. (dir.), Am. Ceramic Soc. (membership com.), Engr's. Soc. of Pa., Tech. Verein. Presbyterian. Clubs: Rotary (sec.; Sharpsburg Sta.); Advertising (Pittsburgh). Author of spl. tech. articles for trade jours. on adhesives, cements and compounds. Inventor of a spark plug insulator, now used on all spark plugs, and "Sauereisen Pour-Lay Brick," melting compound substitute for troweled cement. Home: 318 Third St., Aspinwall, Pa. Office: Sharpsburg Station, Pittsburgh, Pa.

SAUL, Maurice Bower, lawyer; b. Philadelphia, Pa., Oct. 6, 1883; s. Charles G. and Eliza B.; A.B., Central High Sch., Phila., 1902; student U. of Pa., 1905-06; LL.B., U. of Pa., 1905; m. E. Adele Scott, Oct. 30, 1911; children—Robert M., Barbara, Christopher Scott. Admitted to Pa. bar, 1906, and since practiced at Phila.; asso. with John G. Johnson, Phila., 1906-17; mem. of firm Prichard, Saul, Bayard & Evans, Phila., 1917-21; mem. of firm Saul, Ewing, Remick & Saul, since 1921. Pres. and dir. Fifteenth and Chestnut Realty Co.; dir. John B. Stetson Co., Phila. Trustee U. of Pa.; dir. The School in Rose Valley. Mem. Am., N.Y., Pa. and Phila. bar assns., Order of Coif, Alpha Chi Rho. Republican. Universalist. Clubs: Lawyers, University, Le Coin d'Or, Rose Tree Hunt, Pine Valley Golf, Aronamink Golf, Phila. Skating (Philadelphia); U. of Pa., Bankers (New York). Home: Rose Valley, Moylan, Pa. Office: 2301-17 Packard Bldg., Philadelphia, Pa.

SAUL, Walter Biddle, lawyer; b. Phila., Pa., Mar. 12, 1881; s. Charles Geisler and Lidie Collard (Bower) S.; B.S., U. of Pa., 1900; LL.B., U. of Pa. Law Sch., 1903; m. Margaret Michener, June 2, 1911; children—Marguerite (Mrs. William S. Knox), Lidie Bower (Mrs. Frederick A. Van Denbergh), Florence Louise (Mrs. Robert M. Shelly), Suzanne, Richard Marshall, Thomas Alexander. Admitted to Pa. bar, 1903, since practicing at Phila.; mem. firm Saul, Ewing, Remick and Saul. Served as mem. Bd. Edn. Trustee St. Luke's and Children's Hosp.; asso. Trustee U. of Pa. Mem. Fgn. Policy Assn., Am. Acad. Polit. and Social Science, University Mus., Franklin Inst., Acad. of Natural Sciences. Clubs: University, Contemporary (Philadelphia); University of Pa. Club (New York); Bourbonnais-Kiamika Hunting and Fishing (Canada). Home: 1017 Westview St., Germantown, Philadelphia, Pa. Office: 2301 Packard Bldg., Philadelphia, Pa.

SAUNDERS, Lawrence, medical pub.; b. Philadelphia, Pa., June 17, 1890; s. Walter Burns and Frances (Baugh) S.; B.S., Wharton Sch., U. of Pa., 1914; m. Dorothy Love, Feb. 2, 1924; children—Martha Randolph, Walter Grier, Morton Trebel, Nancy Gayle Wynne. Began with W. B. Saunders Company, med. pubs., 1914, treasurer and director, 1916-36, pres. since 1936; dir. Fidelity-Phila. Trust Co. Served as lt. (jr.g.) Pay Corps, U.S.N.R.F., World War. Vice-chmn. Planning Commn., Lower Merion Twp.; mem. com. Pa. Mus. of Art; mem. advisory bd. of Delaware and Montgomery Cos. Boy Scout Council, George S. Cox Med. Research Inst.; mem. nat. bd. Am. Youth Hostels. Mem. Zeta Psi. Episcopalian. Mason. Clubs: Rittenhouse, Franklin Inn (Phila.); Authors (London); Merion Cricket. Home: Bryn Mawr, Pa. Office: W. Washington Square, Philadelphia, Pa.

SAUNDERS, Wilbour Eddy, headmaster; b. Warwick, R.I., Sept. 20, 1894; s. Colver L. and Harriet (Robertson) S.; A.B., Brown Univ., 1916; M.A., Columbia University, 1918; graduate Union Theological Seminary, 1919; student

Cambridge University (Eng.), 1919-20; D.D., Colgate University, 1936; m. Mildred A. Paige, Sept. 22, 1919. Ordained ministry Bapt. Ch., 1920; teacher Horace Mann Sch., New York, 1920-21; asst. pastor Marcy Av. Ch., Brooklyn, 1920-23, pastor, 1927-32; pastor First Ch., Rahway, N.J., 1923-27; chaplain N.J. State Reformatory, 1924-27; exec. sec. Fed. of Chs. of Rochester and Monroe Co., N.Y., 1932-35; spl. lecturer, Colgate-Rochester Div. Sch., 1933-35; headmaster Peddie Sch., Hightstown, N.J., since 1935. Pres. Hightstown (N.J.) Y.M.C.A., N.J. Council of Religious Edn.; mem. bd. mgrs. Am. Baptist Home Mission Soc. Mem. Acad. of Polit. and Social Science, Delta Tau Delta. Baptist. Mason; mem. Jr. Order Am. Mechanics, Royal Arcanum, Patriotic Order Sons of America. Home: Peddie School, Hightstown, N.J.

SAUSSER, Irvin Earl, M.D.; b. Berrysburg, Pa., Feb. 10, 1888; s. Willoughby C. and Mary Ellen (Lentz) S.; grad. Hegins High Sch., 1907, Kutztown State Teachers Coll., 1910; premedical course Medico-Chirurgical Coll., Philadelphia, 1915; M.D., Temple U., 1919; m. Katie P. Otto, Sept. 8, 1920; children—Anna Catherine Louise Elizabeth. Interne Temple U. Hosp., 1919-20; in gen. practice medicine since 1920; mem. staff Ashland (Pa.) State Hosp., Pottsville (Pa.) Hosp.; pres. First Nat. Bank, Hegins Mfg. Co. (both of Hegins, Pa.). Served as private, U.S. Army, World War. Fellow A.M.A.; mem. Pa. State Med. Assn., Schuylkill Co. Med. Assn. Lutheran. Mason, Odd Fellow. Home: Valley View, Pa.

SAUTTER, Albert Carl, physician; b. Phila., Pa., May 3, 1878; s. Christian L. and Emily (Schwaemmle) S.; B.S., U. of Pa., 1899, M.D., 1902; m. Elizabeth E. Bowles, Nov. 23, 1915. Engaged in ophthalmology, at Germantown, Phila., since 1906; ophthalmologist, Germantown Hosp. Served in Vol. Med. Corps., U.S.A. during World War. Mem. Am. Med. Assn., Am. Ophthalmol. Soc., Coll. of Physicians of Phila., Phi Alpha Sigma, Sigma Xi. Republican. Presbyn. Club: Medical (Philadelphia). Home: Cambridge Apts., Alden Park, Philadelphia. Office: Green and Coulter Sts., Germantown, Philadelphia, Pa.

SAVAGE, Henry Lyttleton, asso. prof. of English; b. Phila., Pa., Sept. 13, 1892; s. Charles Chauncey and Anne Vandervoort (King) S.; prep. edn. Blight Sch., Philadelphia, 1902-10, De Lancy School, Philadelphia, 1910-11; A.B., Princeton U., 1915; student U. of Pa., 1915-17; Ph.D., Yale, 1924; m. Mary Radclyffe Furness, June 24, 1932; children—Caroline Wood, Charles Chauncey, III. Reader in English, U. of Pa., 1915-16, instr., 1916-17; fellow in English, Yale, 1919-20; instr. in English, Princeton U., 1923-26; asst. prof. of English, Princeton, 1926-29, asso. prof. since 1929. Entered 2d Citizens' Mil. Training Camp, Plattsburg, N.Y., 1916; 1st R.O.T.C., Ft. Niagara, N.Y., May 1917; commd. 2d lt. Q.M.C., U.S. Army, Aug. 15, 1917, 1st lt. Feb. 26, 1918; with 79th Div., Camp Meade, Md., 1917-18; Hdqrs. 7th Div., A.E.F. (Meuse-Argonne offensive); instr. A.E.F. Univ., Mar.-June 1919; disch. July 1919. Mem. Modern Lang. Assn. America, Soc. for Study Mediaeval Langs. and Lit. (Oxford, England), Phi Beta Kappa. Liberal Democrat. Presbyterian. Clubs: Princeton (Phila.); Mory's Assn. (New Haven, Conn.); University Gateway, Nassau (Princeton). Editor: Saint Erkenwald (with introduction, notes and glossary), 1926. Contbr. numerous articles to learned jours. Home: 104 Jefferson Rd., Princeton, N.J.

SAVAGE, Leona Harrington (Mrs. A. J. Savage), official State Dept. Pub. Instrn.; b. Trimills, Pa., Feb. 9, 1894; d. H. J. and Elizabeth (Hower) Harrington; ed. State Teachers Coll., Bloomsburg, Pa.; m. A. J. Savage, Dec. 26, 1917. Engaged in teaching in pub. schs. of Columbia Co., 1912-35; child accounting adviser, Dept. Pub. Instrn., Harrisburg, Pa., since 1935. Serving as mem. State Exec. Com. of Dem. Party since 1928. Mem. Nat. Edn. Assn., Pa. State Edn. Assn., Daughters of America (vice councillor), Internat. Pilot Club.

Democrat. Methodist. Rebecca. Contbr. articles to ednl. mags. Home: Benton, Pa. Office: Dept. Pub. Instrn., Harrisburg, Pa.

SAVIDGE, Myron Benjamin, banking; b. Turbotville, Pa., June 11, 1896; s. Benjamin and Sophia (Runyan) S.; ed. Bethlehem Prep. Sch., 1915; grad. Keystone Acad., 1917; ed. Bucknell U., 1921; m. Lena C. Schell, Sept. 1, 1923. Asso. with Turbotville Nat. Bank since 1920, dir. since 1921, first vice-pres., active, since 1925; sec., treas., and dir. Turbotville Cemetery Co.; treas. and dir. Turbotville Water Co. since orgn., 1931. Served as treas. Turbotville Sch. Dist. since 1921; overseer of Poor; took active part in securing new consolidated sch. for Turbotville; corr. for several newspapers. Trustee State Industrial Home for Women, Muncy, Pa. Mem. Phi Gamma Delta. Democrat. Baptist. Mason (32°, Shriner). Elk. Club: Lycoming County Automobile (mem. bd. govs.); Blue Springs Driving Club of Washingtonville, Pa. (dir.). Home: Turbotville, Pa.

SAVIGE, Laurence Duane, lawyer; b. Harford, Pa., Apr. 7, 1892; s. Wright L. and Anna M. (Carey) S.; Ped.B., Bloomsburg (Pa.) State Teachers' Coll., 1912; LL.B., Dickinson Coll. Law Sch., Carlisle, Pa., 1917; m. Ethel Holderbaum, Oct. 22, 1919; children—Harriet, Martha Cary, Catherine Elizabeth. Began as prin. high sch., 1912; admitted to Pa. bar, 1918 and since engaged in gen. practice of law at Scranton; admitted to bar Pa. Supreme Ct. and other cts.; dir. and counsel First Nat. Bank of Jessup. Served as 1st lt., then capt., Inf., U.S. Army, 1917-19, with A.E.F.; maj. inf., O.R.C., Pa. N.G., 1919-29. Solicitor Blakely Borough Sch. Dist., 1922-23; Borough Solicitor for Blakely Borough, 1924-34. First comdr. Am. Legion Post, Peckville, Pa.; mem. Bd. Scranton Red Cross. Mem. Lackawanna Bar Assn., Am. Legion, Beta Theta Pi. An organizer Scranton branch Crippled Children Soc. Republican. Presbyterian. Mason (32°). Home: 515 Main St., Peckville, Pa. Office: Mears Bldg., Scranton, Pa.

SAVILLE, Joseph Hassitt, pres. The Pyrites Co.; b. Saratoga, Wyo., Mar. 19, 1889; s. Henry and Teresa (Hughes) S.; B.S., E.M., South Dakota State Sch. of Mines, Rapid City, S.D., 1910; m. Anna Gertrude Hoagland, Dec. 21, 1913; children—Joseph Hassitt, Jr., Dorothy Gertrude. Laborer, jr. engr., mill man, supt. gold mines, Black Hills, S.D., 1910-12; mem. metall. staff Anaconda (Mont.) Copper Mining Co., 1912-17; asst. mgr. Wilmington (Del.) Works, The Pyrites Co., Inc., 1917-32, v.p., 1932-35, pres. since 1935. Dir. Del. Safety Council, Wilmington (Del.) Chamber of Commerce. Mem. Am. Inst. Mining and Metall. Engrs., Canadian Inst. Mining and Metallurgy. Republican. Catholic. K.C. Clubs: Kiwanis (pres. 1939), Wilmington Country (Wilmington, Del.); Kennett Square (Pa.) Golf and Country. Address: 2807 Franklin St., Wilmington, Del.

SAVITZ, Jerohn Joseph, educator; b. Easton, Pa.; s. Joseph Franklin and Elizabeth (Bellesfield) S.; student Keystone State Normal Sch., Kutztown, Pa., 1883-85, Lafayette Coll., Pa., 1887-89; B.S., New York U., 1896, Pd.M., 1899, Pd.D., 1902; A.M., Ursinus Coll., 1897; m. Stella Keifer, Nov. 24, 1886; children— Lindar B., Helen Elizabeth, Russel Joseph. Supt. schs., Slatington, Pa., 1889-96, Boonton, N.J., 1896-1901, Westfield, N.J., 1901-14, 1915-17, also supt. schs. Union Co., N.J., 1907-14; asst. commr. edn., N.J., 1914-15; prin. State Normal Sch., Trenton, N.J., 1917-23; principal N.J. State Normal Sch. (now the State Teachers College), Glassboro, New Jersey, 1923-37. Lecturer on sch. supervision and administration New York Univ., summer 1919. Mem. State Bd. of Examiners for Teachers, N.J. Mem. N.J. State Teachers' Assn. (ex-pres.), N.J. Council of Edn. (ex-pres.). Presbyn. Mem. com. on religious edn. Presbytery of Elizabeth, N.J., 1911-15; mem. com. on edn. Presbytery of New Brunswick, 1918-20; mem. exec. com. N.J.S.S. Assn., 1930; pres. Gloucester County Council of Religious Edn. since 1930. Scottish Rite Mason (Shriner). Author: Development of the Public School System of New Jersey (thesis), 1902;

(joint author) Composition Standards, How to Establish Them. Home: Pinemar, Wenonah, N.J.

SAWDERS, James Caleb, lecturer; b. Pittsburgh, Pa., Sept. 21, 1894; s. Francis Patrick and Mary (Reddy) S.; B.S., Carnegie Inst. Tech., 1916; m. Eunice Yasinski, June 7, 1932. Began as chem. engr. Goodyear Tire & Rubber Co., 1916; mem. firm Sawders & Fulton, chemists, Pittsburgh, 1919-23; has made 16 expdns. to various parts of Latin America, visited many sections of Mexico, Central America, the West Indies and S.A. Has lectured on Latin Am. travel and on both N. and S. Am. archæology. Travels and study in Italy, 1937, Scandinavian countries, 1938. Served as mag. O.R.C., 1917-19. Fellow Am. Geog. Soc. Mem. Alpha Tau Omega. Democrat. Catholic. Clubs: University (Pittsburgh); Town Hall (New York); hon. mem. Rotary Internat. Writer of many articles on Latin Am. travel and history, Pre-Columbian history, gen. Am. archæology, and Latin Am. economics. Home: 44 Colonial Terrace, Nutley, N.J.

SAWIN, Ellen Quigley, educator; b. Wilmington, Del., Oct. 21, 1882; d. Winfield Scott and Lola (Gould) Quigley; student The Misses Hebb Sch., Wilmington, Del., 1890-1900; B.L. Smith Coll., Northampton, Mass., 1904; M.A., U. of Del., Newark, Del., 1938; m. Sanford Wales Sawin, Oct. 17, 1905; children—Sanford Wales (dec.), Philip Quigley, Eleanor (Mrs. Robert E. Dunstan), Nancy, Marian Alice, William Sanford. Teacher of Miss Alice Sellers School, Wilmington, Del., 1904-05; headmistress Sunny Hills Sch., Wilmington, Del., since 1930. Dir. Sunny Hills Lower Sch., Sanford Prep. Sch. Republican. Club: New Century (Wilmington, Del.). Address: Sunny Hills Sch., Wilmington, Del.

SAWYER, Paul Backus, business exec.; b. Lafayette, Ind., May 8, 1879; s. Arthur Lovell and Harriet (Backus) S.; B.S. in E.E., Purdue U., 1900, E.E., 1902; m. Cecilia Sherman, Sept. 25, 1904 (divorced 1932); children —John Sherman, Paul B., Jr. Pres. Lehigh Power Securities Corpn., National Power & Light Co. Mem. Sigma Alpha Epsilon. Republican. Presbyn. Clubs: Bankers (New York); Saucon Valley Country, Pine Valley Golf. Home: Pocono Lake Preserve, Pocono Lake, Pa. Office: 2 Rector St., New York, N.Y.

SAYERS, John Curtis, physician and surgeon; b. Clarion Co., Pa., June 8, 1872; s. John E. and Mary E. (Pierce) S.; m. Jeanette E. Procious, 1901; 1 son, Darwin Lowell. Engaged in gen. practice of medicine at Reynoldsville, Pa.; co. coroner, 1909-15; sch. med. inspr., 1913-32; med. inspr. local bd. health since 1916; co-organizer Peoples Nat. Bank, 1902, dir., 1903-32, pres., 1917-32; co-organizer and dir. Reynoldsville Clay Mfg. Co. since 1901, Pittsburgh Industrial Iron Works at Reynoldsville, 1905, Reynoldsville Table Works, 1930; co-organizer and treas. Nuco Coal Co., 1929; mem. staff Adrian Hosp., Punxsutawney Hosp., Maple Av. Hosp., and DuBois Hosp., DuBois, Pa.; pres. Jefferson Co. Sch. Dirs. Assn., 1913-16. Active in Boy Scout work, 1924-30. Mem. Pa. State Med. Soc., Jefferson Co. Med. Soc. (pres. 1921). Presbyn. Mason (32°, Shriner). Home: 607 Main St., Reynoldsville, Pa.

SAYLER, J(acob) Abner, judge; b. Baltimore, Md., Oct. 15, 1880; s. Jacob Abner and Anna Maria (Scharf) S.; A.B., Johns Hopkins U., 1902; LL.B., Harvard U. Law Sch., 1905; m. Helen Primrose, Dec. 5, 1908; children— Primrose, James Abner, William Primrose. Admitted to Md. bar, 1905, and since in practice of law at Baltimore; justice of peace in criminal police ct., Baltimore, 1912-16; commr. U.S. dist. ct., 1916-19; chief judge of traffic ct., Baltimore, 1935-37; asso. judge of Supreme Bench of Baltimore since 1937, elected Nov. 1938 to serve 15-yr. term, 1937-53. Mem. Baltimore City, Md. State bar assns., Beta Theta Pi. Republican. Roman Catholic. K.C. Elk. Club: Gibson Island. Home 201 North Bend Rd., Baltimore, Md.

SAYLOR, Harold Durston, lawyer; b. Pottstown, Pa., July 18, 1892; s. Henry D. and Dora B. (Gerhard) S.; student The Hill Sch.

SAYLOR, Pottstown, Pa., 1906-1910; A.B., Yale, 1914; LL.B., U. of Pa. Law Sch., 1917; unmarried. In legal practice since June 1919; dep. atty. gen. of Pa. as counsel for banking, ins. and treasury depts., 1929-35; gen. practice of law, Phila., since 1935; dir. Chelten Av. Bldg. Corpn., Alden Park Corpn. Served as 2d lt., later 1st lt., 7th Field Arty., 1st div. (later div. staff), U.S. Army, 1917-18; with A.E.F. Pres. Broad St. Hosp. of Phila. since 1936. Solicitor of Family Soc. of Phila. since 1928. Mem. Zeta Psi, Phi Delta Phi, Phi Beta Kappa. Republican. Lutheran. Clubs: Union League, Yale, Penn Athletic, Phila. Cricket (Phila.); Yale (New York); Elizabethan (New Haven, Conn.). Home: Alden Park Manor, Germantown. Office: 1700 Girard Trust Bldg., Philadelphia, Pa.

SAYLOR, Melvin Alvin; prof. physiol. chemistry, Temple Univ. Address: Temple University, Philadelphia, Pa.

SAYLOR, Owen Webster, life. ins. salesman; b. Johnstown, Pa., Aug. 15, 1887; s. John S. and Katherine (Trexel) S.; Ph.B., Franklin and Marshall Coll., 1911, A.M., same, 1917; grad. student summer courses, Harvard, U. of Ill., Carnegie Inst. Tech.; m. Helen Cover Statler, Sept. 1, 1917; children—Elizabeth Ann, Mary Helen, Joan Statler, Janet Edna. Instr., athletic dir. and coach, high sch., Greensburg, Pa., 1911-15, same, Johnstown, Pa., 1915-16, same, Franklin and Marshall Coll., 1916-17; foreman mech. dept., Bethlehem Steel Co., 1918-19; instr. and faculty mgr. athletics, high sch., Johnstown, Pa., 1920-23; life ins. salesman since 1923. Served as pvt. to corpl. inf., U.S.A., 1918. Mem. Johnstown Sch. Bd., 1928-30. Mayor, City of Johnstown, Pa., 1930-32. Mem. Recreation commn., 1926-30. Mem. Life Underwriters Assn., Chi Phi. Republican. Mem. Reformed Ch. Mason. Home: 1087 Confer Av. Office: 400 Johnstown Bank and Trust Bldg., Johnstown, Pa.

SAYRE, Everett, ins. agency; b. Ripley, W.Va., Apr. 9, 1902; s. Sylvester Brown and Clara Ellen (Kessel) S.; A.B., W.Va. Univ., 1927; A.M., U. of Ky., Lexington, Ky., 1930; m. Anna Noggle, Oct. 1, 1932. Engaged in teaching high sch., 1928-29; asso. with Raleigh Ins. Agency, Inc., Beckley, W.Va., pres. and controlling stockholder since 1938. Mem. County Rep. Exec. Com. Treas. State Lions Conv., 1939. Mem. Sigma Nu. Republican. Methodist. K.P., Modern Woodmen. Clubs: Lions (past pres.), Black Knight Country. Home: 15 Woodlawn Av. Office: Lilly Bldg., Beckley, W.Va.

SAYRE, Floyd McKinley, lawyer; b. Ripley, W.Va., Nov. 3, 1893; s. Sylvester Brown and Clara (Kessell) S.; A.B., W.Va. Univ., 1920; LL.B., W.Va. Univ. Law Sch., 1922; m. Winifred Lynch, Oct. 1, 1924; children—Truman Lynch, Floyd McKinley, Jr., Robert Brown, Frances, Graham Everett. Admitted to W.Va. bar, 1922, and since engaged in gen. practice of law at Beckley; mem. firm Sayre & Bowers since 1929. Served as 2d lt. F.A., U.S.A., 1917-19, with A.E.F. in France. Mem. Beckley Chamber of Commerce. Mem. Am. Bar Assn., W.Va. Bar Assn., Raleigh Co. Bar Assn., Sigma Nu, Phi Delta Phi. Republican. Presbyn. Mason (Shriner), Elk. Clubs: Rotary, Black Knight Country (Beckley). Home: 75 Woodlawn Av. Office: Raleigh County Bank Bldg., Beckley, W.Va.

SAYRE, Frank G.; v.p. The Pa. Co. for Insurances on Lives and Granting Annuities. Home: 3026 Midvale Av., Germantown, Philadelphia. Office: 15th and Chestnut Sts., Philadelphia, Pa.

SAYRES, Gardner Atlee, physician; b. York, Pa., Mar. 21, 1887; s. Edwin Pinkerton and Lura May (Cocklin) S.; M.D., Hahnemann Med. Coll., Phila., 1909; m. Lillian Bertha Denlinger, June 1, 1912; children—Marion Ruth, Betty Lu. Resident physician, Metropolitan Hosp., New York, 1909-10; mem. of staff, St. Joseph's Hosp., Lancaster, Pa., since 1912; physician, Rossmere Sanitarium, Lancaster, Pa., since 1930. Served as 1st lt., U.S. Army Med. Corps, 1917-18. Dir. Bethany Orphans Home. Mem. Y.M.

C.A. (dir.), Pa. Homeopathic Med. Soc. (trustee). Republican. Reformed Ch. (Elder, St. Paul's Ch.). Mason (32°, K.T.). Author of med. papers for Hahnemannian Monthly. Home: 108 S. Ann St. Office: 18 S. Duke St., Lancaster, Pa.

SCAIFE, Alan Magee, manufacturer; b. Pittsburgh, Pa., Jan. 10, 1900; s. James Verner and Mary (Magee) S.; preparatory education, Shadyside Acad., Pittsburgh; Ph.B., Sheffield Scientific Sch. (Yale University), 1920; m. Sarah C. Mellon, Nov. 16, 1927; children—Cordelia M., Richard Mellon. With Wm. B. Scaife & Sons Co., steel tank mfrs., Pittsburgh, since 1920, now v.p. and dir.; chmn. board Pittsburgh Coal Co.; dir. Mellon Nat. Bank, Forbes Nat. Bank, Pullman Co., Pullman, Inc., Air Reduction Co., A. M. Byers Co. Mem. U.S. Naval Reserve Force, World War, Trustee Elizabeth Steele Magee Hospital, Mellon Institute of Industrial Research, Carnegie Hero Fund Commission (all of Pittsburgh, Pa.), University of Pittsburgh. Republican. Protestant. Clubs: Pittsburgh, Pittsburgh Athletic Assn., Pittsburgh Golf, Duquesne, Fox Chapel Golf, Allegheny Country (Pittsburgh); Racquet and Tennis (New York). Home: 1047 Shady Av. Office: Oliver Bldg., Pittsburgh, Pa.

SCAIFE, James Verner Jr., pres. William B. Scaife & Sons Co.; b. Pittsburgh, Pa., Oct. 14, 1903; s. James Verner and Mary (Magee) S.; B.S., Yale, 1927; m. Mary Ellen Selden, Nov. 2, 1932; 1 son, Curtis Selden. Salesman, William B. Scaife & Sons Co., Oakmont, Pa., 1927-28, treas., 1929-30, v.p., 1930-33, pres. since 1933. Trustee Elizabeth Steele Magee Hosp. Mem. Pittsburgh Chamber of Commerce. Mason. Clubs: Pittsburgh, Pittsburgh Golf, Allegheny Country, Rolling Rock (Pittsburgh); Racquet and Tennis, Yale (New York). Home: Woodland Rd., Pittsburgh, Pa. Office: 26 Anne St., Oakmont, Pa.

SCAMMELL, Frank George, surgeon; b. Trenton, N.J., July 17, 1877; s. John and Sarah Jane (Scott) S.; M.D., Medico-Chirurg. Coll., Phila., Pa., 1899; grad. study, U. of Pa. Med. Coll., 1905, U. of Edinburgh, Scotland, 1927; m. Anna Reamer, Oct. 23, 1908; 1 dau., Helen Scott (Mrs. George Howard Walton). Served as city physician, Trenton, N.J., 1900-08; county phys., 1908-24; asst. surgeon, Mercer Hosp., 1900-08, surgeon since 1908, pres. staff since 1925; consulting surgeon, N.J. State Hosp. for Insane, Trenton Orthopedic Hosp., Farmer Hosp.; sec. and dir. Scammell China Co., hotel china, clubs and dinner ware, Trenton, N.J. Served as surgeon to interned Germans of Mercer Co.; surgeon No. 1 Selected Service Mercer Co. during World War. Mem. The Civil Legion. Fellow Am. Coll. Surgs. Mem. Soc. of Surgs. of N.J. (past pres.), Mercer Co. Med. Soc. (past pres.), Sons of St. George (surgeon). Republican. Baptist. Mason (32°, Shriner). Clubs: Chamber of Commerce, Country (Trenton). Home: 40 S. Clinton Av., Trenton, N.J.

SCANLAN, LeRoy Joseph, lawyer; b. Ebensburg, Pa., Oct. 11, 1891; s. William A. and Lena (Gompers) S.; ed. high sch., Johnstown, Pa., 1908-12; LL.B., U. of Mich. Law Sch., 1916; unmarried. Admitted to Pa. bar, 1916, and since engaged in gen. practice of law at Johnstown; mem. firm Scanlan and Harkins; dir. and solicitor Johnstown Motor Club; solicitor Dale Nat. Bank, State Capital Savings & Loan Assn. (Harrisburg), Fidelity & Casualty Co. of New York. Served as 1st lieut. F.A., U.S.A., 1917-19, with A.E.F. Mem. Sigma Nu, American Legion. Roman Catholic. Elk. Home: 112 Walnut St. Office: 1101 First Nat. Bank Bldg., Johnstown, Pa.

SCARBOROUGH, Harland Jay, prof. of law; b. nr. Garysville, O., Apr. 24, 1882; s. William Thomas and Frances Letitia (Umpleby) S.; B.S., Nat. Normal Univ., Lebanon, O., 1905; A.B., Antioch Coll., Yellow Springs, O., 1908; student Youngstown Law Sch., 1915-16; LL.B., U. of Mich. Law Sch., 1918; grad. study, Univ. of Chicago, summer, 1923; m. Mary Lillian McKown, June 28, 1910; children—Ruth McKown (Mrs. Leo Lowey), Martha Alice, Dorothy Ann. Engaged in teaching, pub. schs., high sch., prin. high sch. and supt. pub. instrn. in O., 1901-15; then gen. agt. life ins.; admitted to Mich. bar, 1918, to O. bar, 1918; engaged in gen. practice at Youngstown, O., 1918-22; instr. in law, Youngstown Assn. Law Sch., 1918-22; prof. law, U. of Ky. Coll. of Law, 1922-27; prof. law, N.J. Law Sch., 1927-36 and when became part of U. of Newark, prof. law, Sch. of Law of U. of Newark since 1936. Mem. Am. Assn. Univ. Profs., Phi Delta Phi. Republican. Conglist. Mason. Clubs: Cosmopolitan (Montclair); Deer Lake (Boonton). Author: Cases on Equity, 1930; Cases on Torts, 1932; Cases on Workmen's Compensation, 1934, revised 1936. Home: 405 Park St., Upper Montclair. Office: 40 Rector St., Newark, N.J.

SCARBOROUGH, James Blaine, coll. prof.; b. Mt. Gilead, N.C., June 22, 1885; s. Isham Wilson and Jane (Haywood) S.; A.B., U. of N.C., Chapel Hill, N.C., 1913, A.M., 1914; Ph.D., Johns Hopkins U., 1923; m. Lessie Neville, June 30, 1915 (dec.); children—Lucile Elizabeth, James Blaine, Jr. (dec.), Ernest Neville; m. 2d, Julia Kauffman, Aug. 18, 1930; 1 son, William Kauffman. Instr. mathematics, N.C. State Coll., Raleigh, 1914-18; instr. mathematics, U.S. Naval Acad., Annapolis, Md., 1918-21, asst. prof. mathematics, 1921-28, asso. prof., 1928-37, prof. since 1937. Fellow A.A.A.S. Mem. Am. Math. Soc., Math. Assn. of America, Inst. Math. Statistics, Phi Beta Kappa. Awarded Cain Math. Medal, U. of N.C., 1912. Independent Republican. Presbyterian. Club: Naval Acad. Officers (Annapolis). Author: Numerical Mathematical Analysis, 1930. Contbr. papers on math. subjects. Home: Ferry Farms, Annapolis, Md.

SCARFF, Paul Brown, lawyer; b. Burlington, Ia., Aug. 9, 1871; s. Dr. John and Caroline (Chamberlain) S.; A.B., Hanover (Ind.) Coll., 1894; LL.B., Columbia, 1897; m. Edith Belle Roberts, Dec. 27, 1905; children—Dorothy Belle (Mrs. Peter Doelger), Virginia May (Mrs. Carl Hornung), Paul Brown. Admitted to N.Y. bar, 1897, and since practiced in New York; mem. firm Holm, Smith, Whitlock & Scarff (now Holm, Whitlock & Scarff) since 1903; v.p., sec., dir., mem. exec. com. and gen. counsel S. H. Kress & Co.; sr. v.p., dir. and mem. exec. com. Oakite Products, Inc.; mem. advisory bd. Chemical Bank and Trust Co.; v.p., trustee and mem. exec. com. Samuel H. Kress Foundation; v.p., sec., trustee Log Cabin Assn.; sec. and trustee Limited Price Variety Stores Assn. Served on Nat. Retail Bd. of NRA. Mem. Sigma Chi. Republican. Presbyn. Mason. Club: Echo Lake Country (Westfield, N.J.). Home: 21 Stoneleigh Park, Westfield, N.J. Office: 218 Fulton St., New York, N.Y.

SCARL, Jackson E., dep. sec. Pa. Dept. of Revenue; b. Brooklyn, N.Y., Sept. 19, 1897; s. Anna (Stadiner) Scarl; ed. pub. sch. and high sch.; m. Ellen K. Stroh, Nov. 12, 1917; 1 son, Douglas H. Served as chmn. Lehigh Co. Dem. Com. since 1934; dir. Bur. Instnl. Collections, Dept. of Revenue of Pa., 1935-37; dep. sec. Pa. Dept. of Revenue since 1937; pres. Young Dem. Clubs of Pa., 1936-38; mem. fianance com. Pa. Dem. State Com.; mem. exec. com. Young Dem. Clubs of America. Democrat. Eagle. Jr. O.A.M. Moose. Club: Rotary of Allentown. Home: 1806 W. Broad St., Bethlehem, Pa. Office: State Capitol, Harrisburg, Pa.; Colonial Bldg., Allentown, Pa.

SCATTERGOOD, Alfred Garrett, vice-pres. Provident Trust Co., Phila.; b. Moorestown, N.J., Sept. 10, 1878; s. Thomas and Sarah (Garrett) S.; student Forsythe Sch., Phila., 1887-94; A.B., Haverford (Pa.) Coll., 1898, Harvard, 1899; m. Mary Cope Emlen, Apr. 27, 1904; children—Elizabeth Cope (Mrs. A. Burns Chalmers), Eleanor (Mrs. Henry Regnery), Caroline (Mrs. John S. Lanier), Henry, Roger, Arnold. Trust and treas. dept. Provident Life & Trust Co., Phila., 1900-10, purchasing agt., 1910-17, asst. treas. 1917-22; sec.-treas., Provident Trust Co., Phila., 1922-23, v.p. since 1923; mgr. Mine Hill and Schuylkill Haven R.R. Co., Saving Fund Soc. of Germantown. Clerk, Overseers of Pub. Sch. founded by Charter in

SCATTERGOOD, J(oseph) Henry, trustee, treas.; b. Phila., Jan. 26, 1877; s. Thomas and Sarah (Garrett) S.; A.B., Haverford (Pa.) College, 1896, Harvard Univ., 1897; m. Anne Theodora Morris, June 13, 1906 (dec.); children—Mary Morris (Mrs. Robert F. Norris), Thomas, Alfred G., 2d, Ellen (Mrs. W. H. Dunwoody Zook), Evelyn (Mrs. Ralph G. Bryant, Jr.); m. 2d, Dorothy S. Deane, Nov. 20, 1937. With American Pulley Co., 1897-1900, Sharpless Dyewood Extract Co., 1900-04; secretary American Dyewood Co., 1904-06; trustee of estates, 1907—; v.p., sec. American Water Softener Co., 1907—; dir. Am. Dyewood Co., United Dyewood Corpn., First National Bank, Provident Mutual Life Ins. Co., Am. Pulley Co.; pres. Ins. Co. State of Pa., 1908-11 (now dir.); asst. commr. of Indian Affairs, 1929-33. Mem. Pub. Service Commn. of Pa., 1924-26; treas. Haverford Coll. since 1916, Bryn Mawr Coll. since 1927; pres. Pa. Working Home for Blind Men; treasurer Christiansburg Industrial Inst.; trustee Hampton Inst. (chmn.). Mem. Bd. of Registration Commrs. Phila., 1906-12; original mem. Com. of 70, Phila. First Chief of Friends Reconstruction Unit in France; mem. original Red Cross Commn. to France; mem. Am. Friends' Service Com. Mem. Hist. Soc. Pa., Acad. Natural Sciences, Pa. Geneal. Soc., Am. Philos. Soc., Numismatic and Antiq. Soc., American Alpine Club. Republican. Clubs: Union League, University, Merion Cricket, Penn (Phila.); Cosmos (Washington). Home: Villanova, Pa. Address: 1608 Walnut St., Philadelphia, Pa.

SCHAAF, Edward Oswald, M.D., composer; b. East New York, L.I., N.Y., Aug. 7, 1869; s. Rudolph Wilhelm Ludwig and Barbara (Sommer) S.; M.D., Bellevue Hosp. Med. Coll. (New York U.), 1894; spl. courses U. of Vienna, 1894-96; student Berlin, 1905-09; unmarried. Began practice in Newark, N.J., 1896. Devotes attention largely to music; hon. mem. Am. Federation of Musicians. Wrote: Analysis of the Tannhauser Score (4 vols.); Twentieth Century Harmony Manual; The Art of Player-Piano Transcription (brochure), 1914; The Fundamental Principles Involved in the Composing and Arranging of Music for the Player-Piano, 1919; The Musical Individuality of the Player-Piano, 1922; The Art of Scoring for the Military Band; Treatise on Instrumentation; A Study of Modern Operatic Art (brochure), 1929; Music and the Photoplay, 1929; Analysis of the Tristan score (1 vol.); Analysis of The Mastersingers score (1 vol.). Analysis of Beethoven's Symphony No. V; Analysis of Tschaikowsky's Symphony No. IV. Among his principal musical compositions are (operas) Cymbeline (3 acts); The Maranas (3 acts), Choosing the Bride (2 acts), and one-act operas, Lucréce, La Grande Bretéche, Little George, Cathleen Ni Hoolihan, The Merry Cuckoo, Margot; also 3 symphonies, 4 string quartets, 2 masses, and many songs; Pianoforte Concerto in F-minor; overtures, Colleoni, Festival, Weequahic, Branch Brook and overture (choral) The World War. Composer of state song, "Hail New Jersey"; tone-poems, The Masque, Pandora's Box (orchestral), The Devil in the Belfry; symphonic poem, In Memoriam. Has made 120 arrangements for the player-piano, and 50 for military band; has published many essays on music. Home: 217 S. Orange Av., Newark, N.J.

SCHAAF, Royal Albert, physician and surgeon; b. Boone, Ia., Mar. 28, 1892; s. Rudolph George and Susan Maria (Doud) S.; M.D., U. Bellevue Hosp. Med. Coll., 1913; m. Helen Devore Thomas, Jan. 1, 1917; children—Royal Sommer, Kate Coleman. Interne Bellevue Hosp., 1912-15; in pvt. practice, N.Y. City, 1915-17; in pvt. practice of medicine and surgery, Newark, N.J., since 1919; attdg. surg. Presbyn. Hosp., Newark; asso. attdg. surg., Newark City, and Babies' hosps., Newark. Served as capt. Med. Corps, U.S.A., 1917-19. Fellow Am. Coll. Surgs. Mem. A.M.A., N.J. State and Essex Co. med. socs., Soc. Surgs. of N.J., Acad. Medicine of Northern N.J., Essex Co. Anat. and Pathol. Soc., Bellevue Alumni Assn., Nu Sigma Nu. Pres. Essex Co. Med. Soc. for term, 1939-40. Protestant. Clubs: Essex, Essex County Country, Doctors', Practitioners (Newark). Home: 413 Mt. Prospect Av., Newark, N.J.

SCHABACKER, Martin John, retired merchant; b. Erie, Pa., Jan. 22, 1864; s. Peter and Catherine (Garloch) S.; grad. Erie pub. schs., 1878; m. Lydia Honecker, Sept. 30, 1891 (died May 21, 1928); children—Muriel Jordan, Henry Eric, Richard Wallace (died Sept. 7, 1935). Began assisting brother, Henry George, in retail grocery store, Erie, Pa., 1876; became jr. partner Schabacker Bros., 1885; upon death of brother name changed to Schabacker & Doll, 1893, repurchased entire interest, 1894; sold retail business, 1897, retaining wholesale fruit and produce business; purchased Schaaf & Sons, 1917; discontinued business, 1927; pres. Union Storage Co., Erie, Pa., Nov. 1931-Mar. 1937; v.p. and dir. Bury Compressor Co., Erie; dir. Security-Peoples Trust Co., Erie, Lake Erie Fruit & Vineyard Co., North East, Pa.; treas. and dir. Linwood Park Co., Cleveland; dir. Erie Bolt and Nut Co., 1913-39. Trustee Ebenezer (N.Y.) Old Peoples Home, Salem Evang. Ch.; dir. Erie City Mission; dir. Erie Y.M.C.A. 1911-34. Republican. Mason (32°), K.P. Mem. Rotary Club, 1915-35. Home: 550 W. 10th St., Erie, Pa.

SCHACTERLE, George Kyle; prof. of chemistry and hygiene, Temple Univ. Address: Temple University, Philadelphia, Pa.

SCHAEFER, Frederic, manufacturer; b. Norway, Sept. 8, 1877; s. Thomas Michelsen and Rachel Johanna (Clausen) S.; came to U.S., 1894, naturalized, 1902; M.Sc. (hon.), U. of Pittsburgh, 1909; m. Sarah Bull, Sept. 5, 1902; children—Jane, Frederic Michelson, Katharine Bubb. Began as draughtsman, 1894; now partner Schaefer Equipment Co., mfrs. ry. air brake materials. Pres. Child Guidance Center. Decorated Knight of St. Olav, Norway. Republican. Episcopalian. Mason. Clubs: Duquesne, University, Fox Chapel (Pittsburgh); Wianno (Wianno, Mass.). Home: 1045 Devon Road. Office: 2710 Koppers Bldg., Pittsburgh, Pa.

SCHAEFER, Otto; ophthalmic surgeon South Baltimore Gen. Hosp. Address: 920 St. Paul St., Baltimore, Md.

SCHAEFFER, Asa Arthur; prof. of biology, Temple Univ. Address: Temple University, Philadelphia, Pa.

SCHAEFFER, Charles Edmund, general sec.; b. nr. Fleetwood, Pa., Dec. 26, 1867; s. John S. and Magdalena (Peters) S.; Keystone State Normal Sch., Kutztown, Pa.; A.B., Franklin and Marshall Coll., 1889; grad. Theol. Sem. Reformed Ch. in U.S., Lancaster, Pa., 1892; D.D., Heidelberg U. Tiffin, O., 1910; S.T.D., U. of Hungary, 1929; m. Carrie S. Leinbach, Nov. 1, 1892; m. 2d, Alice Naomi Quillman, of Norristown, Pa., Nov. 9, 1927. Ordained Reformed Ch. ministry, 1892; pastor Macungie, Pa., 1892-96, Ch. of the Ascension, Norristown, Pa., 1896-98, St. Mark's Ch., Reading, Pa., 1898-1909; gen. sec. Bd. of Home Missions Ref. Ch. in U.S., 1908—; pres. Gen. Synod Ref. Ch., 1929-32. Dept. editor Reformed Ch. Messenger, Phila., and of Outlook of Missions, Phila.; mem. Federal Council Churches of Christ in America; sec. Commn. on Evangelism; pres. Phila. Federation of Chs., 1932-35; pres. Home Missions Council, New York, 1933-35; pres. Western Sect. Alliance of Ref. Chs., 1933-35. Author: Our Home Mission Work; Glimpses Into Hungarian Life; Beside All Waters—A Study in Home Misssions. Home: 124 S. 50th St. Address: 1505 Race St., Philadelphia, Pa.

SCHAEFFER, E(dward) Carroll, lawyer; b. Reading, Pa., Nov. 14, 1879; s. Charles H. and Amelia (McKnight) S.; student, U. of Pa., 1898-1901; m. Emma M. Endlich, Nov. 11, 1909; 1 dau., Amy S. (Mrs. Frank L. Conard). Admitted to Pa. bar, 1902, and since practiced at Reading. Dir. Reading Trust Co., S. Reading Market Co. Trustee Home for Friendless Children. Democrat. Lutheran. Mason. Clubs: Wyomissing, Berkshire Country (Reading). Address: Reading, Pa.

SCHAEFFER, Edwin E., pres. Armstrong Co. Bd. of Co. Commrs.; b. Kittanning Twp., Pa., Dec. 26, 1876; s. James and Catherine (Simpson) S.; student country schs., Armstrong Co., Pa.; m. Maria Jackson, Apr. 15, 1897; children—Rev. James F., J. Barton, Edwin E., Mary K. With James Schaeffer & Son, Kittanning, Pa., 1890-1930; mem. of council, Kittanning (Pa.) Boro, pres. to 1932; elected Co. commr. Armstrong Co., Pa., 1931, re-elected, 1935; pres. Bd. of Co. Comnrs. since 1932; dir. Merchants Nat. Bank. Pres. of Bd., Armstrong Co. Hosp. Mem. Am. Red Cross of Armstrong Co., Pa. (v.p.). Republican. Baptist. Elk, Eagle, West Franklin Grange. Club: Kittanning (Pa.) Country. Home: 703 N. McKain. Office: Market St., Court House, Kittanning, Pa.

SCHAEFFER, Harold Franklin, asso. prof. chemistry; b. Phila., Pa., Sept. 21, 1899; s. Franklin Phillips and Margaretta (Morgan) S.; B.S., Muhlenberg Coll., 1922; ed. Columbia U., 1923; M.Sc., U. of N.H., 1926; grad. study, part time, U. of Pittsburgh, 1937-39; m. Katherine Arlene Fisher, Apr. 4, 1932. Engaged as instr. sciences and French, high sch., Gallitzin, Pa., 1922-24; part time instr., U. of N.H., 1924-26; with Waynesburg Coll., Waynesburg, Pa., since 1926, successively as instr. and asst. prof. of chemistry, asso. prof. of chemistry since 1937, also faculty adviser on student publs. since 1927, one of faculty advisers on Waynesburg Coll. Y.M.C.A. since 1934. Mem. A.A.A.S., Am. Chem. Soc., Pa. Chem. Soc., Alpha Chi Sigma, Phi Lambda Theta. Lutheran. Contbr. to ednl. and photographic journs. and for two seasons a weekly column on popular chemistry; illustrated lectures on certain phases of philately. Home: 92 S. West St., Waynesburg, Pa.

SCHAEFFER, Herbert Oris, lawyer; b. McCall's Ferry, Pa., Apr. 21, 1907; s. Joseph W. Schaeffer and Annie Sara (Little) S.; student Middletown (Pa.) pub. schs., 1914-26; A.B., Pa. State Coll., 1929; LL.B., U. of Mich. Law Sch., 1932; m. Virginia Mae Forsythe, June 22, 1929; children—Sandra Mae, Joseph Herbert. Admitted to Pa. bar, 1932, and since practiced in Harrisburgh, Pa.; mem. firm Schaeffer & Nissley since 1935. Mem. Pa. Bar Assn., Dauphin Co. Bar Assn., Delta Chi. Republican. Lutheran. Moose, Royal Arcanum. Home: 112 Nisley St., Middletown, Pa. Office: State St. Bldg., Harrisburg, Pa.

SCHAEFFER, J(acob) Parsons, anatomist, M.D.; b. Shamokin Dam, Pa., Aug. 20, 1878; s. George Keyser and Elizabeth (Long) S.; Central Pa. Coll.; grad. U.S. Sch. of Embalming, 1900; B.E., Keystone State Normal, 1901, M.E., 1903; M.D., U. of Pa., 1907; A.M., Cornell U., 1909, Ph.D., 1910; hon. M.A., Yale, 1913; hon. Sc.D., Susquehanna U., 1925; m. Mary Mabel Bobb, Aug. 5, 1903; 1 son, Bobb. Supervising prin. E. Greenville Pub. Schs., 1901-03; resident physn. U. of Pa. Hosp., 1908; demonstrator med. anatomy, 1907, instr., 1908-10, asst. prof., 1910-11, Cornell U.; asst. prof. anatomy, 1911-12, prof., 1912-14, Yale U.; prof. gen. anatomy and dir. Daniel Baugh Inst. of Anatomy of Jefferson Med. Coll., Phila., 1914—. Mem. Presbyn. Ch. Mem. Assn. Am. Anatomists, A.A.A.S., Am. Genetic Association, Philadelphia Academy of Natural Sciences, Am. Philos. Soc., College of Physicians Phila., A.M.A., Med. Soc. of Pa., Sigma Xi (hon.), Alpha Omega Alpha (hon.), Omega Upsilon Phi; corr. fellow Am. Laryngol. Assn. Clubs: Graduate (New Haven), University, Medical (Phila.), Cornell, Yale. Author: The Nose and the Olfactory Organ in Man; The Nose, Paranasal Sinuses, Lacrimal Passageways and Olfactory Organ in Man; The Respiratory System, in 6th to 9th editions of Morris' Human Anatomy; The Dissection of the Human Body; Waymarks in the Legalizing of Practical Anatomy in America; Outlines and Directions for the Dissection of the Human Body. Co-Author: Roentgen Diagnosis of the Head and Neck. Contbr. to "Special Cytology," and to "The Nose, Throat and Ear and Their Diseases," also many papers and monographs on anatomy and embryology in scientific and tech. jours. and revs. Home: 4634 Spruce St. Address: Jefferson Medical College, Philadelphia, Pa.

SCHAEFFER, John Ahlum, coll. pres.; b. Kutztown, Pa., May 31, 1886; s. Nathan Christ and Anna Matilda (Ahlum) S.; A.B., Franklin and Marshall Coll., Lancaster, Pa., 1904, A.M., 1905, Sc.D., 1929; Ph.D., U. of Pa., 1908; LL.D., Dickinson Coll., Carlisle, Pa., 1937; LL.D., Muhlenberg College, Allentown, Pa., 1938; m. Alice McConomy, January 2, 1912 (now dec.); children—Elizabeth (Mrs. Francis Bennett), John Nathan, Mary Helen, William Rathfon. Instr. chemistry, Carnegie Inst. Tech., 1908-11; with Eagle-Picher Lead Co., as chief chemist, dir. of manufacture, dir. of research and vice-pres., 1911-35; pres. Franklin and Marshall Coll. since 1935. Fellow A.A.A.S., Am. Inst. of Chemists, Royal Soc. of Arts; mem. Am. Inst. Chem. Engrs., Am. Soc. for Testing Materials, Am. Ceramic Soc., Am. Chem. Soc., Phi Beta Kappa, Kappa Sigma, Phi Eta, Pi Gamma Mu, Alpha Delta Sigma. Republican. Mem. Evangelical and Reformed Ch. Mason. Author: Analysis of Paints and Painting Materials (with Henry A. Gardner), 1908; Experiments in Chemistry for Engineering Students (with Joseph H. James), 1910; The Chemical Analysis of Lead and Its Compounds (with Bernard S. White, and John H. Calbeck), 1812. Contbr. articles on industrial and engring. chemistry to jours. Address: Franklin and Marshall Coll., Lancaster, Pa.

SCHAEFFER, John Nevin, prof. classics; b. Danville, Pa., July 23, 1882; s. William C. and Mary H. (Dreisbach) S.; A.B., Franklin and Marshall Coll., 1903; B. Litt., Oxford U., Eng., 1908; hon. Litt.D., Franklin and Marshall Coll., 1935; m. Ruth Herr Frantz, June 13, 1912; children—John Nevin, Jr., Philip Bausman, William Andrew, Elizabeth Frantz, Margaret Frantz. Instr. Latin and Greek, Millersville State Normal Sch., 1903 to 1905; instr. classics, Princeton U., 1909-10; prof. classics, later prof. Greek, Franklin and Marshall Col. since 1910; visiting lecturer, U. of Pa. Summer Sch., summers 1923, 1926, 1928. Served as vice-pres. then pres. Bd. Edn., Lancaster, Pa., 1923-29. Mem. Am. Philol. Assn., Classical Assn. of Atlantic States, Kappa Sigma, Phi Beta Kappa, Tau Kappa Alpha. Awarded Rhodes Scholarship, 1905-08. Democrat. Mem. Evang. & Reformed Ch. Author: An Introduction to Greek (with H. L. Crosby), 1928. Home: 503 N. President Av., Lancaster, Pa.

SCHAEFFER, Paul Nicholas, judge; b. Reading, Pa., Aug. 11, 1884; s. D. Nicholas and Katherine (Grim) S.; grad. Boys' High Sch., Reading, 1901; A.B., Franklin and Marshall Coll., Lancaster, Pa., 1905, LL.D. 1937; LL.B., U. of Pa., 1914; LL.D., Albright Coll., 1933; m. Helen M. Burkey, Sept. 20, 1918. Admitted to Pa. bar 1914, and began practice at Reading; specialized in criminal law with spl. reference to probation and restoration of criminals; apptd. president judge Court of Common Pleas of Berks County, 1924, elected to same office, 1925, re-elected, 1935. Dir. Pa. Com. on Penal Affairs; mem. Welfare Commn. of Pa. since 1924; mem. Governor's Com. on Probation in Pa., 1934, on Pub. Assistance and Relief, 1936; pres. Pa. Conf. on Social Work, 1936; assigned by Supreme Court of Pa. to take charge of proceedings for Grand Jury Investigation in Dauphin Co., Pa., 1938. Mem. Chi Phi, Pi Gamma Mu. Mem. Ref. Ch. Democrat. Mason. Club: Wyomissing. Home: 2500 Prospect Av. Office: Court House, Reading, Pa.

SCHAEFFER, Robert L., surgeon; b. Fleetwood, Berks Co., Pa., Dec. 23, 1881; s. George S. and Catharine M. (Leibelsherger) S.; ed. Keystone State Normal Sch., 1898-1901; A.B., Franklin and Marshall Coll., 1904; M.D., U. of Pa., 1908; m. Millie Louise Ochs, Nov. 30, 1914; children—Frances Clara, Robert L., Charles David. Began as interne Allentown (Pa.) Hosp., 1908 and continued as anæsthetist, 1909-14, asst. surgeon, 1914-23, surgeon in chief since 1923; surgeon for Central R.R. Co., Reading R.R. Co.; v.p. and dir. Allentown Nat. Bank. Fellow Am. Coll. Surgeons; mem. A.M.A., Am. Bd. of Surgery, Internat. Coll. of Surgeons. Democrat. Mem. Reformed Ch. Mason, Elk. Rotarian. Address: 30 N. 8th St., Allentown, Pa.

SCHAEFFER, William B., banker; b. Lehigh Co., Pa., Aug. 5, 1865; s. Charles and Hetty (Steckel) S.; student Krouts Teachers' Acad.; m. Nellie K. Fairchild, June 2, 1886; children—Raymond, Gerald A., Gerald, Violet J., Marian R. Gen. agt. C.R.R. of N.J., and Lehigh-Lackawanna Branch, Bethlehem, Pa., 1890-1900; agt. U.S. Express Co., Bethlehem, Pa., 1890-1900; Pa. State Bank Examiner, 1900-12; v.p. and treas. Wyoming Valley Trust Co., Wilkes-Barre, Pa., 1912-27, pres., 1927-31; v.p. and dir. Bertels Metal Ware Co., Inc., since 1928; v.p. and dir. Miners Nat. Bank of Wilkes-Barre (Pa.) since 1931; pres. Walnut Park Plaza, Inc., hotel, Phila., since 1933; dir. Planters Nut & Chocolate Co., Wilkes-Barre, Pa., since 1913. Home: Mountain Top, R.F.D. 1, Luzerne Co., Pa. Office: Miners Nat. Bank of Wilkes-Barre, Wilkes-Barre, Pa.

SCHAFFER, Harry, lawyer; b. Newark, N.J., July 4, 1901; s. Louis and Soffie (Schaffer) S.; student Barringer High Sch., Newark, N.J., 1914-18, Cornell U., 1919-21; A.B., Harvard, 1923, LL.B., Law Sch., 1926; unmarried. Admitted to N.J. bar, 1927; clerk Riker & Riker, 1926; asso. with Hood, Lafferty & Campbell, Newark, 1926-38. Trustee Cardiac League of N.J. Mem. Essex Co. Bar Assn., N.J. State Bar Assn., Am. Bar Assn. Mason (Columbia Lodge 21). Clubs: Harvard of N.J (Newark); Mountain Ridge Country (West Caldwell, N.J.). Home: 36 Shephard Av. Office: 744 Broad St., Newark, N.J.

SCHAFFER, William I., judge; b. Phila., Pa., Feb. 11, 1867; s. George A. and Mary H. (Irwin) S.; pub. sch. edn.; LL.D., 1920; m. Susan A. Cross. Admitted to Pa. bar, 1888; dist. atty. Delaware Co., Pa., 1893-1900; state reporter of Pa., 1900-19; atty. gen. of Pa., 1919-21; justice Supreme Cout of Pa., 1921—. Republican. Episcopalian. Clubs: Union League, Rittenhouse, Philadelphia (Phila.). Home: Haverford, Pa. Address: City Hall, Philadelphia, Pa.

SCHAFFLE, Albert Eberhard Friedrich, prof. of edn.; b. Phila., Pa., June 6, 1892; s. Samuel Wilson Wykoff and Margaret (Hutchison) S.; grad. Phila. High Sch., 1911; B.S., in agr., U. of Del., 1915; M.S., 1923; B.S., Cornell, 1916; A.M., U. of Pa., 1925; student New York U., 1928-39; m. H. Beatrice Caley, June 29, 1923, (died June 18, 1937); 1 dau., Ellen Beatrice. Teacher of science and athletic dir. Vineland (N.J.) High Sch., 1916-17; mem. extension staff, Rutgers U., 1917-18; supervising prin. of schools, Delaware Co., Pa., 1918-20; dept. head, Rehabilitation Div., U. of Del., 1920-24; teacher of science, Wilmington (Del.) High Sch., 1924-25; dir. of guidance, public schools, Wilmington, Del., 1925-27; asst. dean, Sch. of Edn., Rutgers U., since 1927, asso. prof. of edn. since 1928. Mem. Acad. Polit. Science, Nat. Soc. Coll. Teachers of Edn., Am. Assn. Univ. Profs., Am. Acad. Polit. and Social Science, N.E.A. (life mem.), Eastern States Assn. Professional Schs. for Teachers, N.J. State Teachers Assn., Internat. Council Religious Edn. (licensed instr.), A.A.A.S., Sons Am. Revolution (charter mem. and dir. of Raritan Valley Chapter), Nat. Economic League, Bound Brook Civic Assn., Phi Delta Kappa, Kappa Phi Kappa, Epsilon Pi Tau, Alpha Kappa Pi (mem. bd. govs.). Ind. Republican. Presbyterian. Clubs: Rotary, Rutgers (New Brunswick); University (Bound Brook); Cornell of Del.; Cornellians of Raritan Valley. Editor of Rutgers U. Sch. of Edn. publs., 1927-32; contbr. to ednl. jours. Home: 11 E. Union Av., Bound Brook, N.J. Office: Rutgers University, New Brunswick, N.J.

SCHALL, R(ebecca) R(ambo), (Mrs. Andrew Y. Drysdale), executive; b. Norristown, Pa., Feb. 16, 1896; d. William and Jeannette Gordon (Bromley) S.; student Norristown (Pa.) High Sch., 1909-13, Schissler Coll. of Bus., Norristown, Pa., 1913-14; m. Capt. Andrew Young Drysdale, July 27, 1935. Stenographer Midland Valley R.R. Co., 1914-25; sec. and asst. treas. Muskogee Co., Philadelphia (holding company for railroad and coal companies), since 1925; sec. and asst. treas. Kan., Okla. & Gulf Ry Co., Okla. City-Ada-Atoka Ry. Co.; sec., treas. and dir. Garland Coal & Mining Co., Philadelphia, since 1927; dir. Osage Ry. Co. Mem. D.A.R., U.S. Daughters of 1812. Republican. Episcopalian. Home: 2232 DeKalb St., Norristown, Pa. Office: 135 Independence Square, Philadelphia, Pa.

SCHALLER, Grover Luther, clergyman, editor; b. Perrysburg, O., Nov. 3, 1884; s. Frederick and Magdalene (Disher) S.; A.B., North Central Coll., Naperville, Ill., 1912; ed. McCormick Theol. Sem., Chicago, 1913-14; B.D., Evang. Theol. Sem., Naperville, Ill., 1915; (hon.) D.D.., Evang. Theol Sem., 1932; m. Amanda L. Rippberger, Apr. 18, 1914; children—Stanley Carl, Dorothy Helen. Ordained to ministry Evang. Ch., 1914; pastor, Peoria, Ill., 1915-20; asst. editor S.S. publs. of Evang. Ch., 1920-22, asso. editor since 1922; mem. Adult Com. of Internat. Council of Religious Edn.; commr. United Christian Adult Movement. Member of Evangelical Church. Editor in charge Evangelical Bible School Teacher, Evangelical Adult Bible Class Quarterly, Evangelical Home Department Quarterly. Author several pamphlets. Home: 1027 Rolleston St., Harrisburg, Pa. Office: Evangelical Press, Harrisburg, Pa.

SCHAMBERG, Gilbert Frank, lawyer; b. Philadelphia, Pa., July 22, 1878; s. Henry and Bertha (Frank) S.; grad. Central High Sch., Philadelphia, 1896; University of Pennsylvania Coll., class of 1900, LL.B., U. of Pa. Law Sch., 1904; unmarried. Admitted to Phila. and Pa. bar, 1904; in gen. practice of law, 1904-12; head of mail order dept. N. Snellenburg & Co., Philadelphia, 1913-18; field rep. Jewish Welfare Bd., Washington, D.C., and Parris Island, S.C., Jan. 1918-May 1919; engaged in farming, 1919-22; asst. sec. Big Brother Assn., 1923-36; exec. sec. Jewish Chautauqua Soc. since Jan. 1, 1936. Mem. admissions com., Nat. Farm Sch., 1931-36. Republican. Jewish religion. Home: 2204 St. James St. Office: 1701 Walnut St., Philadelphia, Pa.

SCHANCK, Thomas Ely, banking; b. Freehold, N.J., Feb. 9, 1860; s. Kortenus H. and Rebecca M. (Ely) S.; ed. Freehold Inst., 1874-76, Rutgers U., 1876-78; m. Elizabeth Mason, Dec. 4, 1884 (dec.); 1 dau., Alta (Mrs. Alta S. Woodland); m. 2d, Sarah G. Stryker, June 14, 1913. Began as clk. First Nat. Bank, Hightstown, N.J., 1878; cashier, Farmers Nat. Bank, Allentown, N.J., 1886-87; asso. with Peoples Nat. Bank, New Brunswick, N.J., continuously since 1887, cashier, 1887-1925; pres. and dir. since 1925. Mem. Masonic Lodge and Elks. Republican. Mem. 2d Reformed Dutch Ch., New Brunswick, N.J. Home: 19 Union St., Office: Peoples Nat. Bank, New Brunswick, N.J.

SCHAPHORST, William Frederick, advertising engr., tech. writer; b. Elkton, S.D., Feb. 25, 1885; s. William Frederick and Mary Ann (Lindemann) S.; B.S., S. D. State Coll., 1905, M.E., 1909; grad. study, Columbia U., summer 1907, U. of Wis., summer 1908; m. Irene Curtin, Sept. 27, 1916 (died 1918); m. 2d, Mabel Madellon Gooch, July 20, 1926; children—William Gooch (dec.), Richard Allan. Instr. mech. engring., S. D. State Coll., 1905-07; asst. prof. mech. engring., N.M. State Coll., 1907-11; began writing engring. articles, 1908, and since has made it profession; tech. writer, A. Eugene Michel Adv. Agency, 1911-17, and Geo. H. Gibson Co., 1917-20, both N.Y. City; chief engr., New Method Utilities Co., 1920-23; engaged in bus. on own acct., engring. advertising and tech. writing, Newark, N.J., since 1923; licensed professional mech. engr. in N.J. Mem. Am. Soc. Mech. Engrs. Republican. Contbr. to tech. and bus. mags. continuously since 1908, numerous articles; developed hundreds of logarithmic computing charts, many of which are published. Home: 160 Wesley Av.,

Atlantic Highlands. Office: 45 Academy St., Newark, N.J.

SCHATZ, Harry Abraham, physician; b. Russia, June 12, 1881; s. Rev. Max and Judith Coleman (Rachmil) S.; brought to U.S., 1890 and naturalized citizen, 1895; A.B., Central High Sch. for Boys, Phila., Pa., 1901; M.D., U. of Pa. Med. Sch., 1905; m. Rosalie Miriam Abuhove, Mar. 21, 1920; children—Jules Leonard, Marion Isabelle, Carol Doris. In practice of medicine at Phila. since 1905, specializing in otolaryngology; first asst. bacteriologist, U. of Pa., 1906-14; vol. asst., ear, nose and throat clinic, German Hosp., 1907-12; instr. Phila. Polyclinic Sch. for Postgrads. since 1914; asso. prof. laryngology, Grad. Sch. of Medicine, U. of Pa., instr. otology, 1918-24. Served in hosp. corps, Pa. N.G., 1902-10; 1st lieut. Med. Res. Corps; mem. Vet. Guard. 3d Regt., N.G.Pa. Mem. Phila. Laryngol. Soc., Southeast Br. of Phila. Co. Med. Soc., Sigma Xi. Republican. Jewish religion. Mason, Knights of Pythias. Clubs: Professional Circle, Lithuanian Verband (Phila.). Home: 2010 N. Broad St., Philadelphia, Pa.

SCHATZ, William Jackson, physician; b. Sellersville, Pa., Oct. 20, 1876; s. George and Mary (Leister) S.; B.S. in Phys. Edn., Temple U., Phila., 1911, B.S., 1912, M.D., 1915; m. Mary Lizzie Meyers, Apr. 22, 1899; children—Ruth Mildred, Ralph Edward. Instr. of phys. edn., Yale, 1906-07; instr. of physical edn., Univ. Sch., Cleveland, O., 1907-09; prof. of phys. edn. and dir. of Normal Sch. of Phys. Edn., Temple U., Phila. 1909-14; prof. of phys. edn., Muhlenberg Coll., Allentown, Pa., 1916-18; pvt. practice of medicine, Allentown, Pa., since 1916. Mem. Lehigh Co., Pa. State Med. Socs., A.M.A., Internat. Congress of Physiology, Am. Therapeutic Soc., Acad. of Phys. Medicine, A.A.A.S. Republican. Lutheran. Mason (32°). Club: Kiwanis (Allentown, Pa.). Author of numerous articles on exercise and health and med. articles for professional jours. Address: 1022 Walnut St., Allentown, Pa.

SCHAUM, George Fritz, clergyman; b. Shillington, Pa., Oct. 13, 1882; s. Milton F. and Amanda (Fritz) S.; student Reading (Pa.) Acad. and Business Coll.; student Eastern Theol. Sem. Reformed Ch. in U.S., 1909-12, Bible Sem., N.Y., 1919; m. Estella Naomi Scheifley, Oct. 20, 1903 (dec.); children—Grace Anna (wife of Dr. John S. Burlew), M. Ruth (wife of Rev. C. O. Goodman); m. 2d, Mary Elizabeth Hammond, Apr. 18, 1938. Ordained to ministry Evang. Ch., 1905, elder, 1907; pastor, Port Carbon, Pa., 1905-09, Columbia, Pa., 1909-13, Harrisburg, Pa., 1913-18, Lancaster, Pa., 1918-25, Sunbury, Pa., 1925-32, Reading, Pa., 1932-34, Bethany Ch., Lancaster, Pa., since 1934; vice-pres. Conf. Bd. Christian Edn., chmn. Bd. Evang. Homes; trustee and mem. exec. com. Gen. Bd. Ch. Extension; mem. 3 gen. confs. Served as chaplain U.S. Army, 1918; chaplain, U.S. Army Res. Trustee Evang. Home for Aged, Phila. and Lewisburg, Pa. Republican. Evang. Ch. Mason. Contbr. denominational S.S. literature for 20 yrs. Home: 441 W. Chestnut St., Lancaster, Pa.

SCHEELINE, Isaiah, lawyer; b. Altoona, Pa., Mar. 10, 1878; s. Alexander and Julia (Goldschmidt) S.; student Lafayette Coll.; LL.B., Dickinson Sch. of Law; m. Julia Schoenfeld; 1 son, Isaiah, Jr. In gen. practice of law; pres. Westfall Co. since 1926; v.p. Central Trust Co. of Altoona; dir. Blair Hotel Co. Candidate for Congress, 1910; candidate for presidential elector-at-large, 1916, 28. Trustee Altoona Hosp., Altoona Foundation. Clubs: Blairmont Country, Kiwanis (Altoona). Home: Brushmead Way, R.D. 2, Hollidaysburg, Pa. Office: 408 Commerce Bldg., Altoona, Pa.

SCHEELINE, Julia Schoenfeld (Mrs. Isaiah Scheeline), social worker; b. Bellaire, O., Apr. 19, 1878; d. Alexander and Rose (Hartman) Schoenfeld; A.B., Alleghany Coll., Meadville, Pa., 1897, hon. A.M., 1915; student Woman's Med. Coll., Toronto, Can., 1898; A.M., Columbia, 1909; m. Isaiah Scheeline, Sept. 25, 1916; 1 son, Isaiah. Head resident, Columbian Settlement, Pittsburgh, 1900-03; sec. immigrant aid com. Council of Jewish Women, 1910-11; field sec. Playground Recreation Assn. America, 1911-14; dir. western div. State of Pa. Child Labor Assn., 1913-16; head resident director of the Irene Kaufman Settlement, Pittsburgh, Pennsylvania, 1914-16; county chairman, home and war relief, Woman's Com. of Council Nat. Defense, Blair County. Made investigation of amusement resources of working girls in N.Y. City which led to first dance hall regulations; investigation of after-care for tuberculosis patients discharged from New York sanitaria, which led to marked reforms. Mem. Am. Sociol. Soc., Phi Beta Kappa. Home: R.D. 2, Hollidaysburg, Pa.

SCHEER, Edward Waldemar, ry. pres.; b. Zaleski, O., Apr. 28, 1875; s. Charles and Maria Ursala (Rockenbach) S.; ed. pub. schs.; m. Alice Maude Wilkinson, Apr. 28, 1903; children—Georgia Rebecca, Margaret Stewart (Mrs. John F. Harper), Edward Waldemar. Asso. with Baltimore and Ohio Railroad Company, 1890-1932, successively as office boy, messenger, clk., stenographer, chief clk. to div. supt., sec. to v.p. and gen. mgr. B.& O.S.-W.R.R., chief clk. to gen. mgr. of same, asst. sec. and chief clk. to gen. mgr., same to gen. supt., asst. to gen. supt., asst. sec. of line, supt. Ill. and Ind. divs. same, gen. supt. in charge successively of S.W., N.W. and Md. dists., gen. mgr. B.& O. Eastern Line,; v.p. Reading Co., 1932-35, C.R.R. of N.J., 1933-35; pres. Reading Co. and C.R.R. of N.J. since 1935; pres. N.Y. and Long Branch R.R. Co., Pa.-Reading Seashore Lines; dir. and mem. exec. com. Lehigh & Hudson River Ry. Co., and Pa. Co. for Insurances on Lives and Granting Annuities; dir. Mut. Fire, Marine & Inland Ins. Co., County Fire Ins. Co. of Phila., John B. Stetson Co. and Abington Memorial Hosp. Served in U.S. Army, Spanish-Am. War. Republican. Methodist. Mason (32°, K.T., Shriner). Clubs: Union League of Phila., Huntingdon Valley Country and Marine. Home: Rydal, Pa. Office: Reading Terminal, Philadelphia, Pa.

SCHEFFEY, Lewis Cass, gynecologist; b. Stamford, Conn., Sept. 21, 1893; s. Lewis Cass and Esther Mary (Werner) S.; grad. Reading (Pa.) High Sch., 1910; P.D., Phila. Coll. of Pharmacy and Science, 1915; M.D., Jefferson Med. Coll., 1920; m. Anna Catherine Thun, Dec. 12, 1922; children—Lewis Cass, III, Julia Westkott, Andrew Jackson Werner, Hildegarde Thun. Pharmacist, Jefferson Hosp., 1915-20; resident physician Jefferson Med. Coll. Hosp. Phila., 1920-22, asst. gynecologist since 1928; asso. with dept. of gynecology, Jefferson Med. Coll. since 1923, successively as instr., asst. prof. and asso. prof., and since 1938 clin. prof. Served as private Med. Reserve Corps, 1917, S.A.T.C., 1918. Fellow Am. Coll. of Surgeons, Coll. of Physicians of Phila.; diplomate Am. Bd. Obstetricians and Gynecologists; mem. Am. Gynecol. Soc., Obstet. Soc. Phila. (past pres.), A.M.A. Pa. Med. Soc., Phila. Co. Med. Soc. (dir.), Jefferson Soc. for Clin. Investigation (past pres.), Pathol. Soc. Phila., Acad. Natural Sciences of Phila., Am. Acad. Polit. and Social Science, Pa. Museum of Art, German Soc. Pa., Pa.-German Folklore Soc. (pres. 1938-39), Carl Schurz Memorial Foundation, Hist. Soc. of Berks Co. (Pa.), Alumni Assn. of Phila. Coll. of Pharmacy and Science (past pres.), Jefferson Med. Coll. Alumni Assn. (v.p.), Phil Delta Chi, Phi Alpha Sigma. Episcopalian. Clubs: University, Art Alliance (Phila.). Home: 450 Merion Rd., Merion, Pa. Office: 255 S. 17th St., Philadelphia, Pa.

SCHEIDE, John Hinsdale, oil producing, retired; b. Tidioute, Pa., Aug. 9, 1875; s. William Taylor and Ida (Hinsdale) S.; A.B., Princeton, 1896; (hon.) LL.D., Grove City Coll., 1928; (hon.) A.M., Princeton, 1930; (hon.) L.H.D., Allegheny Coll., 1934; m. Mary A. Hewitt, Jan. 6, 1904 (died 1909); m. 2d, Harriet E. Hurd, Apr. 3, 1913; 1 son, William Hurd. Engaged in producing oil, 1896-1908; retired from oil bus., 1908; mem. firm J. H. Scheide & Co., Titusville, Pa.; since retiring, active in ch., edn., anti-tuberculosis movement and book collecting. Dir. Nat. Tuberculosis Assn. (1926-35), Pa. State and Crawford Co. tuberculosis socs. Trustee Grandview Instn., Oil City, Pa., Grove City Coll., Presbyn. Missionary Home, Chautauqua, N.Y., Princeton (N.J.) Theol. Sem. Mem. Permanent Jud. Commn., Pa. Synod, Presbyn. Ch.; mem. exec. council, Friends of Princeton Library. Mem. Am. Antiq. Soc., Pa. Hist. Soc., Princeton Bibliog. Soc. Republican. Presbyn. Clubs: Country (Titusville); Philobiblon (Philadelphia); Grolier, Princeton, Bankers (New York); Tiger Inn (Princeton). Home: 221 N. Washington St., Titusville, Pa.

SCHELL, Frank Cresson, artist, editor; b. Philadelphia, Pa., May 3, 1857; s. Frank H. and Martha A. (Carr) S.; studied Pa. Acad. Fine Arts; m. Clara V. Saylor, Feb. 18, 1880. Illustrated for mags. and periodicals until 1898; artist and corr. Leslie's Weekly, Spanish-Am. War; art editor Leslie's Weekly, 1898-1903; art editor North American, Phila., 1905, retired Jan. 1925. Exhibited in New York, Chicago, Phila., Buffalo, etc. Mem. Phila. Sketch Club, Musical Arts Club of Phila., Fellowship of Pa. Acad. Fine Arts, Art Alliance of Phila., Fairmount Park Art Assn., City Parks Assn. Home: 14 Simpson Rd., Ardmore, Pa.

SCHELLING, Felix Emanuel, educator; b. New Albany, Ind., Sept. 3, 1858; s. Felix and Rose (White) S.; A.B., U. of Pa., 1881, LL.B., 1883, A.M., 1884; Litt.D., U. of Pa., 1903, Princeton, 1934; LL.D., U. of Pa., 1909, Haverford, 1920; m. Caroline Derbyshire, Mar. 7, 1886; children—Dorothea D. (wife of Prof. Joseph Seronde), Felix D. Was John Welsh Centennial prof. English lit., U. of Pa., 1893-1929, Felix E. Schelling professor same since 1929. Mem. Nat. Inst. Arts and Letters, Am. Philos. Soc., Modern Lang. Assn. America. Author: Literary and Verse Criticism of the Reign of Elizabeth, 1891; Life and Works of George Gascoigne, 1893; A Book of Elizabethan Lyrics, 1896; A Book of Seventeenth Century Lyrics, 1899; The English Chronicle Play, 1902; The Queen's Progress and Other Elizabethan Sketches, 1904; History of Elizabethan Drama, 1908; English Literature During the Lifetime of Shakespeare, 1910; The Restoration Drama, Cambridge History of Literature, 1912; The English Lyric, 1913; A History of English Drama, 1914; Thor and Other War Verses, 1918; Appraisements and Asperities as to Some Contemporary Writers, 1922; Foreign Influences in Elizabethan Plays, 1923; Elizabethan Playwrights, 1925; Shakespeare and "Demi-Science," 1927; Pedagogically Speaking, 1929; Shakespeare Biography, 1927. Editor: Ben Jonson's Discoveries, 1892; Elizabethan Lyrics, 1895; Seventeenth Century Lyrics, 1899; Eastward Ho, and The Alchemist, 1903; The Merchant of Venice, 1903; Macbeth, 1910; Beaumont and Fletcher, 1912; Typical Elizabethan Plays, 1926. Home: Lumberville, Pa.

SCHENCK, Eunice Morgan, coll. dean; b. Brooklyn, N.Y., Dec. 8, 1884; d. Nathaniel Pendleton and Elizabeth (Morgan) Schenck; A.B., Bryn Mawr Coll., 1907, Ph.D., 1913. Asso. in French, Bryn Mawr Coll., 1913-16, dean, 1916-17, asso. prof. of French, 1917, prof. since 1925, dean of Grad. Sch. since 1929; asso. dir. under Am. Red Cross of the Jardin d'Enfants Unit, France, summers, 1920, 1921. Chmn. Com. of Bryn Mawr Alumnae that furnished Univ. of Paris with a library of Am. Literature and established a permanent fund to maintain it. Dir. Reid Hall, Paris, Baldwin Sch., Bryn Mawr. Mem. Modern Lang. Assn. America, Am. Assn. Univ. Women, Am. Assn. Univ. Profs. (mem. council); foreign corr. de l'Académie de Besancon. Officer d'Académie (France), 1929; Chevalier de la Legion d'honneur, 1934. Clubs: Cosmopolitan, Bryn Mawr (New York); Women's University, Alliance Française, Cosmopolitan (Phila.). Home: Radnor Hall, Bryn Mawr, Pa.

SCHENCK, Frederick Parmenter, lawyer; b. Newark, N.J., Oct. 12, 1872; s. William Alonzo and Margaret Matilda (Sayre) S.; A.B., Syracuse U., 1895; LL.B., Syracuse U. Law Sch., 1899; m. Maud G. Barnum, Dec. 27, 1900; 1 son, Winthrop Barnum. Admitted to N.Y. bar and engaged in practice at Syracuse, 1898-99; asst. atty. Industrial Savings & Loan Assn.,

New York, 1899-1904; in practice in New York, 1904-26; engaged in gen. practice of law in East Orange, N.J., since 1926; dir. and counsel Brick Church-Fairway Bldg. & Loan Assn. Served as mem. legal adv. bd. of East Orange, N.J., during World War. Mem. Chamber of Commerce of the Oranges and Maplewood. Mem. N.J. State Bar Assn., Essex Co. Bar Assn., Phi Delta Theta, Phi Delta Phi, Syracuse Alumni Assn. Former mem. Holland Soc. of N.Y. Republican. Ch. of Christ Sci. Mason. Clubs: Art Center of the Oranges (East Orange); Deer Lake of Boonton. Home: 528 Hillside Terrace, West Orange. Office: 28 Washington Pl., East Orange, N.J.

SCHENCK, Harry Paul, physician; b. Phila., Pa., Jan. 6, 1896; s. James Buchanan and Savilla Eaton (Fries) S.; B.S., Haverford (Pa.) Coll., 1917; M.D., U. of Pa. Med. Sch., 1923; m. Edna Manvillier Lein, June 12, 1924. Research fellow, allergy, U. of Pa., 1925-28; asso. laryngologist, grad. sch., U. of Pa., 1927-34; asst. prof. pathology, sch. of dentistry, U. of Pa., 1932-38; asst. prof. otolaryngology, Sch. of Medicine, Univ. of Pa., 1935-39, professor and head of department since 1939; curator Mutter Mus., 1925-37; otolaryngologist, Children's Hosp., 1926-33. Served in Inf., U.S. Army, 1918-19, with A.E.F. in France; comdr., M.C., U.S.N.R.F., since 1935. Fellow Am. Coll. Surgeons, A.M.A., Am. Laryngol. Assn, Am Otol Soc., Coll. of Phys. of Phila., Pan-Am. Med. Assn.; mem. Am. Assn. for Study of Asthma and Allied Conditions, Am. Assn. for Study of Allergy, Am. Acad. of Ophthalmology and Otolaryngology, Phila. Laryngol. Assn., Nu Sigma Nu, Sigma Xi. Honored by Casselberry Award, 1929. Republican. Lutheran. Clubs: University, Contemporary, Philobiblon, Philadelphia Country (Phila.). Home: 1235 Wyngate Rd., Wynnewood, Pa. Office: 1912 Spruce St., Philadelphia, Pa.

SCHERER, William J., sec. and treas. J. J. Scherer Sons Co., Inc.; b. Newark, N.J., Aug. 15, 1883; s. Jacob J. and Jennie (Leaderman) S.; ed. South Eighth St. Pub. Sch. and Coleman Business Coll. (both of Newark); m. Marie A. Funke, Jan. 9, 1907; 1 son, Clarence A. Began as clerk in lawyers office, 1901; stenographer for machine shop, 1902-03; organized with father and brother the firm of J. J. Scherer Sons Co., Inc., 1903, and since sec. and treas.; treas. Irvington Mortgage & Title Guaranty Co., Van Buren Bldg. & Loan Assn. Pres. Irvington (N.J.) Sinking Fund Commn.; trustee Irvington Community Chest; v.p. St. Vincent DePaul Soc. (ch. orgn.). Democrat. Catholic. Elk. Club: Irvington Kiwanis (ex-pres. and ex-dir.). Home: 1044 Grove St. Office: 30 Woolsey St., Irvington, N.J.

SCHERMERHORN, Richard, Jr., landscape architect; b. Brooklyn, N.Y., Oct. 17, 1877; s. Richard and Jane Agnes (Fiske) S.; ed. Brooklyn Poly. Prep. Sch. and Inst., 1888-94, Rensselaer Poly. Inst., 1894-97; m. Margaret Medbury Doane, June 2, 1930; 1 son, Derick Doane. Began as landscape architect, 1900, in pvt. practice since 1909; engaged on over 100 private estates, also cemeteries, parks, country clubs, subdivisions, college campuses; consultant Allegany and Taconic state parks; designed master plans for Great Neck, Huntington, Lawrence, in N.Y., Newark, N.J., etc.; lecturer on landscape architecture, Columbia, since 1935. Served as capt. engring. sect. Sanitary Corps, U.S.A., 1917-19; with A.E.F. 8 months, including assignment with Engring. Dept. on Commn. to Negotiate Peace. Sec. Assn. for Preservation "Lindenwald," home of President Van Buren. Fellow Am. Soc. Landscape Architects (former nat. trustee, ex-pres. New York Chapter); mem. Am. Soc. Civil Engrs., Am. Planning Inst., Holland Soc. New York, N.Y. State Hist. Assn., Soc. of Engineers, Chi Phi, Montclair Engineers. Author: Schermerhorn Genealogy and Family Chronicles, 1914. Contbr. to jours. on landscape architecture, city planning, etc. and genealogy. Home: 173 Orange Road, Montclair, N.J. Office: 342 Madison Av., New York, N.Y.

SCHERR, Harry, lawyer; b. Maysville, W.Va., June 6, 1881; s. Arnold C. and Katherine (Nickel) S.; student W.Va. Univ., 1901-05; m. Rosa Wall, June 24, 1913; children—Harry, Barbara, Betsy. Admitted to W.Va. bar, 1905, and began practice at Williamson; mem. Vinson, Thompson, Meek & Scherr, Huntington, W.Va., since 1925; v.p. and counsel Bankers Finance Corpn.; v.p. Green Bag Cement Co. of W.Va.; dir. Nat. Bank of Commerce, Williamson, W.Va., Inter-Ocean Casualty Co., Cincinnati. Pres. Sch. Bd., Williamson, 1920-25. Mem. Williamson Chamber of Commerce (pres. 1922-24), Chamber of Commerce of U.S. (dir. since 1933), Huntington Chamber Commerce (dir.), W.Va. Chamber Commerce (dir. and mem. exec. com.). Mem. Am., W.Va., and Cabell Co. bar assns., Delta Chi, Kappa Alpha. Republican. Episcopalian. Clubs: Guyandot, Guyan Country (Huntington). Home: 1655 5th Av. Office: First Huntington Bank Bldg., Huntington, W.Va.

SCHICKS, George Charles, educator; b. Munson, Mass., May 11, 1893; s. George Charles and Emma (Smith) S.; Ph.G., Mass Coll. Pharmacy, 1919; Ph.C., Valparaiso U., 1922; m. Helen M. Kull, Aug. 2, 1927; children—Barbara Lou, Carol Ann. Prof. materia medica and pharmacognosy, Valparaiso (Ind.) U., 1920-24; dean and prof. materia medica and pharmacognosy, same, 1925-27; asst. dean and prof. materia medica and dispensing pharmacy, Rutgers U. Coll. of Pharmacy since 1927. Served as 2d lt. Med. Corps, bacteriol. sect., R.O. Corps since 1922. Mem. auxiliary com. on re-agents and test solutions, U.S. Pharmacopoeia; mem. Recipe Book Com. of Am. Pharm. Assn.; chmn. professional relations com. of Am. Assn. of Colls. of Pharmacy; chmn. com. on dental pharmacy of Am. Pharm. Assn.; sec. Bds. and Colls. of Pharmacy of Dist. 2. Mem. A.A.A.S., Am. Pharm. Assn., Gamma Mu, Alpha Epsilon, Kappa Psi (grand historian since 1937). Republican. Baptist. Mason, Knight Templar. Author of Dental Drugs and Preparations. Home: 66 Dryden Rd., Upper Montclair, N.J.

SCHIEDT, Richard Conrad Francis, coll. prof.; b. Weissenfels, Prussia, Sept. 21, 1859; s. Francis and Julie (Jansen) S.; grad. Gymnasium, Zeitz, Prussia, 1878; student in mathematics, zoölogy, chemistry, univs. of Erlangen and Berlin, 1878-81; theology at Lancaster, Pa., 1885-87; post-grad. work, Univ. of Pa. and Harvard; Ph.D., U. of Pa., 1899, hon. Sc.D., 1910; m. Sophie E. Gantenbein, Aug. 23, 1888; children—Mary Madeleine Julia, Norma Ruth (Mrs. Persifor H. Smith), Richard Conrad Francis. Prof. biology and geology, Franklin and Marshall Coll., Pa., 1887-1918; prof. anatomy and embryology, U. of Tenn., 1919, prof. biology emeritus since 1927; retired, 1919. Research chemist for Armstrong Cork Co. (linoleum div.), 1924-1928. Entomologist Pa. State Bd. Agr., 1893-1900. Mem. academic council Carl Schurz Memorial Foundation. One of first members Woods Hole (Mass.) Marine Biol. Orgn.; mem. Phi Beta Kappa, Phi Kappa Sigma; fellow A.A.A.S.; mem. Am. Chem. Soc., Soc. Am. Zoölogists, Soc. Old German Students in America, Société Jean Jacques Rousseau, Geneva, Deutsche Philos. Gesellschaft, Euckenbund, Steuben Society, Concord Soc. of America, etc. Member Reformed Church in United States. Author: Principles of Zoölogy, 1893; Laboratory Guide in Zoölogy, 1898; Plant Morphology, 1900; On the Threshold of a New Century, 1900; Glimpses into the Growth of America's Art Life, 1909; American Art in the Making, 1926. Contbr. on scientific and ednl. subjects. Address: 1043 Wheatland Av., Lancaster, Pa.

SCHIFANO, Emanuel Francesco, lawyer; b. Pittsburgh, Pa., Apr. 6, 1898; s. Frank and Sofia (Leonardi) S.; A.B., Pa. State Coll., 1921; LL.B., Duquesne U. Law Sch., 1926; m. Anna Theresa Barranti, July 31, 1930. Admitted to Pa. bar, 1927 and since engaged in gen. practice of law at Pittsburgh; prof. Duquesne U., 1923-24; chief of law enforcement, Dept. Pub. Instrn., Harrisburg, Pa., since 1935. Served in Students Naval Training Corps, 1918. Vice chmn. Italian Dem. Com. of Allegheny Co. Pres. Internat. Club of Pittsburgh, 1932-35. Democrat. Roman Catholic. Club: 32d Ward Democratic, Young Democratic (Pittsburgh); Y.M.C.A. (Harrisburg). Home: 20 Ansonia St., Pittsburgh, Pa. Office: Education Bldg., Harrisburg, Pa.

SCHIFFER, Herbert Michael, prof. of marketing; b. New York, N.Y., Oct. 20, 1890; s. George Philip and Catherine Frances (Burns) S.; grad. Harlem Evening Prep. Sch., 1911; B.C.S., New York U., 1916, M.B.A., 1932; m. Anna Elizabeth Kelleher, Feb. 10, 1918 (died Mar. 17, 1932); children—Anita Maurice, Doris Marie, Herbert Michael. With S. H. Wetmore Co., mfrs. of surgical glassware and druggists sundries, New York, 1905-26, as clerk and salesman, 1905-19, sales mgr., 1919-26, vice-pres., 1920-26; lecturer on marketing, New York U., evenings, 1919-26; lecturer on salesmanship, K. of C. Vets. Sch., evenings, 1920-22; asst. prof. of marketing and asst. dir. day div. Sch. of Commerce, New York U., 1926-30, asso. prof. of marketing, 1930-34, prof. since 1934, asst. dean Sch. of Commerce since 1937; lecturer on business fundamentals, Coll. of the Sacred Heart, Manhattanville, N.Y., 1928-29; prof. of marketing, Newark (N.J.) U., since 1936. Served as chief petty officer U.S.N.R.F., 1917-19; disch. as lt. Pres. New City, Rockland County, Taxpayers Assn. Mem. Am. Acad. Polit. Science, Am. Acad. Polit. and Social Science, Am. Marketing Assn., Am. Assn. Univ. Profs., Alpha Kappa Psi, Beta Gamma Sigma, Theta Nu Epsilon, Alpha Delta Sigma, Alpha Phi Sigma, Sigma Eta Phi, Sphinx, Arch and Square. Received Alumni Meritorious Service Award, New York U., 1938. Roman Catholic. K. of C. Clubs: Catholic (New York); New York U. Men in Advertising. Home: 496 Park Av., Leonia, N.J. Office: New York Univ., New York, N.Y.

SCHIFFLER, Andrew C(harles), congressman; b. Wheeling, W.Va., Aug. 10, 1889; s. Andrew and Emma S.; student pub. schs., W. Va.; m. Emma Muldrew, Mar. 30, 1910; children—Virginia A., Robert A. Studied law and admitted to W.Va. bar, 1913, and engaged in gen. practice of law as individual at Wheeling, 1913-39; served as pros. atty. Ohio Co., W. Va., 1925-33; referee in bankruptcy northern dist. W.Va., 1918-22; mem. 76th Congress (1939-41), 1st Dist. of W.Va. Served with various govt. units during World War. Chmn. Ohio Co. Rep. Com. 2 yrs. Mem. W.Va. Bar Assn., Ohio Co. Bar Assn. Republican. Presbyterian. Odd Fellow. K.P. Elk. Clubs: Fort Henry, Elks (Wheeling). Home: 7 Rockledge Rd., Wheeling, W.Va.

SCHILDNECHT, Page M(ilburn), surgeon; b. Hagerstown, Md., Dec. 4, 1902; s. Burton Claire and Lillie Mayberry (Franks) S.; grad. Hagerstown High Sch., 1920; B.S., Gettysburg Coll., 1924; M.D., Jefferson Med. Coll., 1928; m. Abigail Susan Kettering, May 26, 1928; 1 dau., Sandra. Resident physician Jefferson Hosp., Phila., 1928-30; chief resident and resident in surgery Memorial Hosp., Worcester, Mass., 1930-31; post grad. work Mass. Gen. Hosp., Boston, 1931; practice as surgeon, Lancaster, Pa., since 1932; junior surgeon Lancaster Gen. Hosp. since 1934. First lt. Med. Officers Reserve Corps, U.S. Army, 1928-38. Mem. Bd. of Health, City of Lancaster, 1934-38. Fellow A.M.A.; mem. Pa. State Med. Society, Nat. Assn. for Study of Neoplastic Diseases. Republican. Lutheran. Mason (32°), Elk. Home: 1010 Duke St. Office: 148 E. Walnut St., Lancaster, Pa.

SCHILL, Edmund, dir. of music; b. Newark, N.J., Jan. 26, 1895; s. Willam Frederick and Elizabeth (Mauer) S.; ed. Cornell U., summers 1919-21; State Teachers Coll., West Chester, Pa., summers, 1923-24, grad. vocal music, 1923, instrumental music, 1924; B.S. in Mus. Edn., N.Y. Univ. Inst. Music Edn., 1933; m. Elsie Marion Carlson, Sept. 25, 1926. Engaged as choir dir., organist and instrumentalist since 1912; office accountant, bank teller and officer, 1910-19; dir. music, pub. schs., Johnstown, Pa., 1923-25; dist. rep. Detroit Vapor Stove Co., 1925-28; organized classes and directed bands, orchestras in various N.J. cities, 1928-32; dir. music, pub. schs., Verona, N.J. since 1932; treas. Grand Bldg. & Loan Assn., Newark, N.J. Served as asst. bandmaster U.S.N., 1919. Mem. Musicians

Mutual Protective Union, Music Educators Nat. Conf., Condr. N.J. All-State High School Symphony Orchestra, Atlantic City, 1936, Essex County High School Chorus, Newark, 1939. Verona Teachers Assn. (pres.). Republican. Lutheran. Mason. Club: Rotary of Verona (past pres.). Home: 79 Park Av., Verona, N.J.

SCHILLER, Morgan Burdett, pres. Am. Tubular Elevator Co. and Advance Insulating Co.; b. New York City, July 23, 1893; s. Henry M. and Margaret (Crosby) Burdett (stepfather, William B. Schiller); student St. Paul's Sch., and Sheffield Scientific Sch. of Yale; m. Alexina Crosson Blair (dec.); children—Margaret C., Blair; m. 2d, Elizabeth Lloyd, 1925. Treas. Am. Foundry & Constrn. Co., 1920-22, pres., 1922-25; pres. Am. Tubular Elevator Co., Pittsburgh, since 1923; treas. Pittsburgh Piping and Equipment Co., 1925-28; pres. Advance Insulating Co. Home: Sewickley, Pa. Office: 714 Magee Boul., Pittsburgh, Pa.

SCHINDEL, Jeremiah Jacob, clergyman; b. Allentown, Pa., Oct. 25, 1876; s. Jacob Daniel and Ella Catherine (Schmoyer) S.; student Muhlenberg Acad., 1888-91; A.B., Muhlenberg Coll., 1896, A.M., 1899; student Luth. Theol. Sem., Mt. Airy, 1896-99; hon. D.D., Muhlenberg Coll., 1918; m. Jessie Appel Hausman, Nov. 14, 1900; children—Isabel Hausman, Mary Hausman (Mrs. Carl Otto Berger). Ordained to ministry Luth. Ch., 1899; asst. pastor, Whitehall Parish, 1899; pastor Mickley Parish, 1908-18, St. Mark's Ch., Phila., 1918-28, Christ Ch., Chestnut Hill, Phila. since 1928. Trustee Lankenau Hosp., Mary J. Drexel Home and Mother House of Deaconesses. Mem. Alpha Tau Omega, Phi Alpha Clerical Club of Phila. Republican. Lutheran. Home: 19 W. Southampton Av., Philadelphia, Pa.

SCHINZ, Albert, univ. prof.; b. Neuchâtel, Switzerland, Mar. 9, 1870; s. Charles Emile and Ida (Diethelm) S.; A.B., U. of Neuchâtel, 1888, A.M., 1889; U. of Berlin, 1892-93; Ph.D., Tübingen, 1894; U. of Paris, 1894-96; officier d'Académie, 1906; L.H.D., 1929. Instr. philosophy, U. of Neuchâtel, 1896-97; came to America, traveled and attended Clark U., 1897-98; instr. French, U. of Minn., 1898-99; prof. of French lit., Bryn Mawr Coll., 1899-1913; prof. French lit., Smith Coll., 1913-28; prof. French, University of Pa. since 1928. Author: Anti-Pragmatism, or Intellectual Aristocracy Versus Social Democracy, 1909; J. J. Rousseau, a Forerunner of Pragmatism, 1909; Accent dans l'écriture française, 1912; La*question du contrat Social, 1913; J. J. Rousseau et Michel Rey, 1916; French Literature of the Great War, 1919; Pensée religieuse de Rousseau et ses récents interprètes, 1927; Jean-Jacques Rousseau, interprétation nouvelle, 1929. Editor: XVII Century French Texts; XVIII Century French Texts; XIX Century French Texts; Nouvelle Anthologie française; Jean J. Rousseau, Vie et Oeuvres; Victor Hugo, Selected Poems; also editor selections from Maupassant, Mérimée, Gautier, Laboulaye, etc. Contbr. to scientific revs. and to mags. and papers, Europe and America. Mem. Modern Lang. Assn. America, Soc. Hist. Lit. de France, Soc. J. J. Rousseau, Phi Beta Kappa, Gamma Mu; mem. Legion of Honor (France). Address: University of Pennsylvania, Philadelphia, Pa.

SCHLACKS, Charles Henry, corporation official; b. Chicago, Ill., Nov. 12, 1865; s. Henry and Christine (Thielen) S.; ed. pub. schs.; m. Laura N. Pierson, Jan. 18, 1893. Asst. gen. mgr. D.&R.G. R.R., 1893-1900; gen. mgr. Colo. Midland R.R., 1901-04; v.p. D.&R.G. R.R., 1904-13, Western Pacific R.R., 1910-13; pres. Hale & Kilbourn Co., Phila., 1914; gen. mgr. Eddystone Rifle Plant of Midvale Steel & Ordnance Co., 1915-19; pres. Union Oil Co., Sept. 1919-Jan. 1922; dir. Barber Asphalt Corpn., Am. Pulley Co., Keystone Watch Case Corpn., Riverside Metals Co., Baldwin Locomotive Works, Midvale Steel Co. Club: Pacific Union (San Francisco). Home: Bryn Mawr, Pa.

SCHLEGEL, Albert G(eorge) W(ashington), supervising prin. schs.; b. nr. Danielsville, Pa., Feb. 22, 1897; s. Quillas A. and Mary A. (Seip) S.; A.B., Moravian Coll., 1920; A.M.,

Pa. State Coll., 1927; grad. study, Johns Hopkins U., 1930-32; Ed.D., Pa. State Coll., 1935; m. Alice C. Hess, June 14, 1924; children—Wallace Albert, Lorie Alice. Teaching and prin. schs., 1916-17, 1920-22; supervising prin. schs., Port Carbon, Pa., 1922-27; supervising prin. schs., Red Lion, Pa. since 1927. Served on York County Bd. of Emergency Adult Edn. Pres. Red Lion dist. Boy Scouts; mem. exec. com. York-Adams Area, Boy Scouts. Mem. Bd. Trade. Mem. N.E.A., Pa. State Edn. Assn. (mem. exec. council, 1936; pres. Supervising Prins. Dept. 1936), York Co. Schoolmen's Club, Phi Delta Kappa, Kappa Phi Kappa. Republican. Mem. Reformed and Evang. Ch. Mason. I.O.O.F. Clubs: Lions of Red Lion (pres. 1938-39), Country (Red Lion). Home: 31 Henrietta St., Red Lion, Pa.

SCHLEGEL, H. Franklin, clergyman; b. at Mauch Chunk, Pennsylvania, October 25, 1867; s. William and Christena (Stahl) S.; B.E., Albright College, Pennsylvania, 1897, Ph.D., 1906, D.D., 1935; m. Jean M. Herb, Mar. 30, 1916; children—William Franklin, Franklin Kehler, Sarah Christene, Jean Elizabeth. Ordained ministry United Evang. Ch., 1893; pastor Freemansburg, Pa., 1891-94, Wilkes-Barre, 1894-95, Albright Coll., 1895-97, Williamstown, 1897-99, Harrisburg, 1899-1903, Shamokin, 1903-07, Albright Coll., 1907-11, Mt. Carmel, 1911-15, Lancaster, 1915-18; presiding elder, 1918-22; now pastor Trinity Evangelical Ch., Easton, Pa. Chairman Forward Movement; chmn. Permanent Commn. on Temperance; pres. Ednl. Aid Soc.; mem. exec. com. Nat. Service Commn., Evang. Ch.; del. Gen. Conf. 8 times to 1938; mem. Commn. on Ch. Union and Federation of Evang. Ch.; mem. Commn. on Worship, Federal Council of Chs. of Christ in America; exec. sec.-treas. Bd. of Ch. Extension of Evang. Ch. Chmn. exec. com. Albright Coll., also trustee and sec. bd. of trustees; trustee Bibl. Sem. (New York), Harrisburg State Hosp.; 1st v.p. Pa. State Anti-Saloon League. Mem. Pi Gamma Mu. Republican. Mason (32°, K.T.). Maj., chaplain Res., U.S.A. Home: 682 Northampton St., Easton, Pa.

SCHLEICHER, George Berthold, elec. engr.; b. Hamburg, Germany, Nov. 26, 1896; s. George M. and Bertha (Hempel) S.; came to U.S., 1909, naturalized; 1931; grad. Phila. Trades Sch., 1915; grad. Drexel Inst., Phila., 1919; unmarried. Lab. asst., exptl. dept. Leeds & Northrup Co., Phila., 1915-17; spl. tester, Phila. Electric Co., 1917-25, tech. asst. to dir., labs. and testing sect., 1925-29, tech. asst., meter div., since 1929. Mem. Internat. Jury of Awards, Sesqui-Centennial Expn., Phila., 1926. Mem. Am. Inst. E.E., Pa. Electric Assn., Edison Electric Inst., Nat. Dist. Heating Assn. Phila. Electric Soc. of Metermen (sec.). Author of articles on metering for tech. jours. Inventor of the compensating meter. Home: 34 Trout Av., Clementon, N.J. Office: 2301 Market St., Philadelphia, Pa.

SCHLENGER, Leo, physician; b. Bayonne, N.J., May 12, 1902; s. Jacob and Anna (Brenner) S.; B.S., N.Y. Univ., 1920; M.D., U. of Md. Med. Sch., Baltimore, 1924; m. Martha F. Thompson, Jan. 13, 1926; children—Jacques S., Robert Purnell. Resident surgeon and supt. Colonial Hosp., Baltimore, Md., 1924-26; Md. *State Venereal Clinic, 1925; Mercy Hospital Venereal Disease Clinic, 1926-29; Dermatol. Clinic, Johns Hopkins Hosp., 1929; Dermatol. Clinic, Sinai Hosp., 1931. Served in S.A.T.C. Mem. A.M.A., Southern Med. Assn., Med. and Chirurg. Faculty of Md., Baltimore City Med. Soc.; Baltimore-Washington Dermatol. Soc., Phi Delta Epsilon. Democrat. Home: 4600 Liberty Heights Av. Office: 3034 E. Baltimore St., Baltimore, Md.

SCHLESINGER, Joel Louis, real estate; b. Newark, N.J., July 1, 1896; s. Louis and Sophie (Levy) S.; ed. Newark Acad. 1909-14, Columbia U. Extension, 1924; m. Florence M. Schloss, Nov. 21, 1918; 1 dau., Barbara May. Engaged in real estate bus. at Newark, N.J., since 1914, asso. with Louis Schlesinger, Inc., since 1914, sec. and treas. since 1920; field dir. Newark Real Estate Bd. Appraisal Sch. Served in U.S.N. during World War. Trustee Newark Beth Israel Hosp. Mem. Am. Inst. Real Estate Appraisers, Real Estate Bd. of Newark (pres. 1938-39), N.J. Assn. Real Estate Bds. (exec. com.). Republican. Jewish religion. Elk. Clubs: Down Town (Newark); Mountain Ridge Country (West Caldwell). Home: 45 Beverly Rd., West Orange, N.J. Office: 31 Clinton St., Newark, N.J.

SCHLESINGER, Louis, real estate, insurance; b. Newark, N.J., Dec. 16, 1865; s. Alexander and Fanny (Fleischer) S.; ed. pub. schs. of Newark; m. Sophie Levy, Oct. 8, 1890 (died May 19, 1937); children—Alexander L. (deceased), Joel L. Began as office boy, Brown & Volk, real estate, Newark, 1880; in real estate and insurance business since 1890; pres. Louis Schlesinger, Inc. since 1911; pres. Schlesinger-Heller Agency; dir. U.S. Trust Co., Progress Bldg. & Loan Assn.; sec.-treas. Union Bldg. Co., 1904-28. Nat. chmn. state bd. dirs. Nat. Real Estate Bd., past pres. N.J. Assn. Real Estate Bds.; mem. N.Y. Real Estate Bd.; mem. exec. bd. Union of Am. Hebrew Congregations since 1913; mem. admission com. Jewish Children's Home, Newark; mem. Congregation B'nai Jeshurun (Reformed Hebrew). Mason (Shriner). Clubs: Mountain Ridge Country of West Caldwell, N.J. (charter mem.); Newark Athletic, Downtown (Newark); Advertising (New York). Home: 45 Beverly Rd., West Orange, N.J. Office: 31 Clinton St., Newark, N.J.

SCHLESMAN, Carleton Hecker, chem. engring.; b. Allentown, Pa., Nov. 20, 1901; s. Charles Henry and Mary Magdaline (Hecker) S.; Chem. E., Lehigh U., 1922; Ph.D., Johns Hopkins U., 1925; unmarried. Employed as chem. engr., Atlantic Refining Co., Phila., Pa., 1924-25; chem. engr. Gen. Labs. of Standard Oil Co. of N.Y., 1925-37; head Research and Development Div. Gen. Labs. Socony Vacuum Oil Co. located at Paulsboro, N.J., since 1937. Mem. A.A.A.S., Am. Chem. Soc., Soc. Automotive Engrs., Am. Petroleum Inst., Am. Soc. for Testing Materials, Franklin Inst., Sigma Xi, Gamma Alpha, Deutsche Chemische Gesellschaft (Germany). Republican. Mem. Reformed Ch. Club: Chemists (New York City). Home: 2938 Chew St., Allentown, Pa. Office: Socony Vacuum Oil Co., Paulsboro, N.J.

SCHLEY, Kenneth Baker; b. New York, Nov. 19, 1881; s. Grant B. and Elizabeth (Baker) S.; Ph.B., Yale, 1902; m. Ellen H. Rogers, June 11, 1912; children—Anne Caroline, Kenneth Baker. Mem. firm of Moore & Schley, bankers, New York; dir. Underwood-Elliott-Fisher Co., 1st v.p. Electric Storage Battery Co.; dir. Howe Sound Co., Permutit Co., Telautograph Co., etc. Republican. Unitarian. Clubs: Knickerbocker, The Links, Yale, New York Athletic, Racquet and Tennis. Home: Far Hills, N.J. Office: 100 Broadway, New York, N.Y.

SCHLEY, Reeve, banker; b. N.Y. City, Apr. 28, 1881; s. William T. and Mary A. (Reeve) S.; A.B., Yale Univ., 1903, A.M., same university, 1933; LL.B., Columbia Univ., 1906; m. Kate deForest Prentice, September 7, 1907; children—Reeve, Eleanor Prentice. Admitted to N.Y. bar, 1906, and began with Simpson, Thacher & Bartlett, later mem. of firm; v.p. Chase Nat. Bank of city of New York since 1919; chmn. bd. Sundstrand Corpn.; pres. One East End Av. Corpn.; v.p. Underwood Elliott Fisher Co. (chmn. finance com.), Howe Sound Co., Britannia Mining & Smelting Co.; dir. Newark Factory Sites, Inc., U.S. Guarantee Co., Somerville Trust Co., Morris & Essex R.R., Commercial Trust Company of New Jersey, El Potosi Mining Co., Electric Boat Company, Stuyvesant Ins. Co., Brooklyn Real Estate Exchange. U.S. fuel administrator, New York County, 1917-19. Mem. Corpn. Yale U.; pres. bd. trustees St. Paul's Sch., Concord, N.H. Pres. American-Russian Chamber of Commerce (dir.) Phi Delta Phi, Psi Upsilon, Wolf's Head, Nat. Golf Links of America. Member State Board of Control of Institutions and Agencies of the State of New Jersey. Republican. Episcopalian. Clubs: Knickerbocker, Recess, Links, Turf and Field, Essex Fox Hounds, Somerset Hills Country. Contbr. chapter on banking in "An Outline of

SCHLINK

Careers," 1927. Home: Far Hills, N.J. Office: 18 Pine St., New York, N.Y.

SCHLINK, Frederick John, mech. engr., physicist; b. Peoria, Ill., Oct. 26, 1891; s. Valentine Louis and Margaret (Brutcher) S.; B.S., U. of Ill., 1912, M.E., 1917; married. Asso. physicist and tech. asst. to dir., U. S. Bureau of Standards, 1913-19; physicist in charge of instruments-control dept., Firestone Tire & Rubber Co., Akron, O., 1919-20; mech. engr., physicist, Western Electric Co. (now Bell Telephone Labs.), New York), 1920-22; asst. sec. Am. Standards Assn., 1922-32; tech. dir. and mng. editor, Consumers' Research, non-profit organization supplying information on goods for ultimate consumers, Washington, N.J., since 1929, pres. since 1931. Fellow Am. Phys. Soc., A.A.A.S., Am. Soc. Mech. Engrs.; mem. Soc. Automobile Engrs., Am. Econ. Assn., Army Ordnance Assn., Sigma Xi. Awarded Edward Longstreth medal of Franklin Inst., 1919. Licensed professional engr., N.Y. Author: Your Money's Worth (with Stuart Chase), 1927; One Hundred Million Guinea Pigs (with Arthur Kallet), 1933; Eat, Drink and Be Wary, 1935. Contbr. numerous papers to tech., scientific and econ. jours. and to bulletins of Consumers' Research. Home: Washington, N.J.

SCHLOSSER, Frank G(erard), lawyer; b. Hoboken, N.J., Nov. 30, 1901; s. Frank J. and Isabelle (Thompson) S.; LL.B., Fordham U. Law Sch., 1924; m. Louise H. Droste, Aug. 9, 1930; 1 dau., Louise Isabelle. Admitted to N.J. bar as atty., 1925, as counselor, 1928; engaged in gen. practice of law as individual at Hoboken, N.J., since 1926; judge recorder's ct. of Hoboken, 1930-34; asst. prosecutor of pleas of Hudson Co. since 1934; admitted to practice before Supreme Ct. of the U.S., 1935. Mem. New Jersey State Bar Assn., Hudson Co. Bar Assn., Hoboken Lawyers Club. Democrat. Roman Catholic. Author: New Jersey Criminal Practice and Procedure (with Daniel O'Regan), 1938. Home: 1310 Garden St. Office: 68 Hudson St., Hoboken, N.J.

SCHLOSSER, Ralph Wiest, college pres.; b. Schoeneck, Pa., July 21, 1886; s. John Wesley and Emma (Wiest) S.; A.B., Elizabethtown (Pa.) Coll., 1911; A.B., Ursinus Coll., 1911, A.M., same, 1912, Litt.D., 1932; A.M., Columbia U., 1922, grad. study, same, 1929-30; study Union Theol. Sem., N.Y. City, 1921-22, Bethany Bib. Sem., Chicago; m. Elizabeth D. Souders, Aug. 19, 1909; children—Ernestine Floy (Mrs. Oliver R. Heistand), Galen Henry, Mary Elizabeth (deceased), David Eugene, Nancy Joan. Began as teacher in pub. schs., 1904; instr., Elizabethtown Coll., Elizabethtown, Pa., 1906-11, prof. English, 1911-18, dean of instrn., 1922-27, pres. since 1928. Mem. Gen. Edn. Bd. of Ch. of the Brethren. Mem. Nat. Edn. Assn., Pa. Coll. Pres. Assn., Pa. German Soc., Pa. German Folklore Soc., Tau Kappa Alpha, Rotarian. Republican. Mem. Ch. of Brethren. Home: 346 Orange St., Elizabethtown, Pa.

SCHLUDERBERG, William Frederick, pres. The Wm. Schluderberg-T. J. Kurdle Co.; b. Baltimore, Md., Apr. 16, 1894; s. George and Margaret (Maasch) S.; student Baltimore (Md.) Business Coll., 19——1910); m. Marie Margaret Kurdle, Sept. 11, 1920. Associated with William Schluderberg & Sons, 1910-20; pres. The Wm. Schluderberg-T. J. Kurdle Co., meat packers, mfrs., Baltimore, Md., since 1920; v.p. and dir. The Equitable Trust Co. of Baltimore (Md.) since 1925. Mem. bd. of govs. Md. Tuberculosis Assn.; chmn. com. on adminstrn. State Development Bur. Trustee Community Fund of Baltimore City, Inner Mission Soc. of Evang. Luth. Ch. of Baltimore and Vicinity; dir. Community Placement Bur. of Baltimore, Inc.; mem. animal husbandry adv. com., U. of Md. Mem. Baltimore Assn. of Commerce (dir.), Better Business Bur. (dir.), Inst. of Am. Meat Packers (v. chmn.; dir.), Eastern Meat Packers Assn. (pres.), Baltimore Meat Packers Assn. (pres.), Md. Livestock and Meat Council (pres.), Baltimore Livestock Show (mem. exec. com.), Md. Sales Reps. Assn. Lutheran. Mason (Scottish Rite; Buomi Temple; Order of Jesters; Elk.

777

Clubs: Kiwanis (mem. of welfare com.), Reciprocity (dir.), Baltimore Country (Baltimore, Md.); Maryland Polo (v.p.; Stevenson, Md.); Elkridge-Harford Hunt (mem. bd. govs.; Harford City, Md.). Home: 39th and Fenchurch Sts., Guilford, Baltimore. Office: 3800-4000 El Baltimore St., Baltimore, Md.

SCHLURAFF, Helen M. (Mrs. Vern L. Schluraff); b. Avonia, Pa., Nov. 6, 1886; d. George S. and Margaret (Love) stone; ed. high sch., Erie, Pa.; A.B., Wilson Coll.; m. Vern L. Schluraff, Sept. 27, 1906; children—Dorothy Jane, Robert Stone. Pres. Schluraff Floral Co. since 1015; vice-pres. Fireside Bldg. & Loan Assn., 1922-28; served as Erie Co. commr. since 1932. Served as mem. Rep. State Com., 1920-32; mem. Nat. Rep. Program Com. Mem. Chamber of Commerce. Mem. Florists Telegraph Delivery Assn. Pres. League of Women Voters, 1920-22, Zonta Club, 1920-22, Erie Bus. and Professional Women's Club (5 yrs.); pres. State Fed. Bus. and Professional Women's Clubs, 1926-28, nat. sec., 1928-30, nat. vice-pres., 1930-32. Mem. D.A.R. Republican. Presbyn. O.E.S. Grange. Club: Business and Professional Women's. Home: 2727 W. 8th St. Office: 12 W. 8th St., Erie, Pa.

SCHLUTER, Frederic Edward, industrial management; b. New York, N.Y., May 31, 1900; s. Christian L. and Anna (Van Thaden) S.; B.S., Columbia, 1922; m. Charlotte Mueller, Sept. 6, 1924. Pres. Thermoid Co. since 1935; officer or dir. many other corpns. Home: Princeton, N.J. Office: Thermoid Co., Trenton, N.J.

SCHMEHL, Luther C(leveland), lawyer; b. Reading, Pa., Oct. 22, 1895; s. Edwin T. and Laura A. (Potteiger) S.; B.S., Muhlenberg Coll., 1916; LL.B., U. of Pa. Law Sch., 1922; m. Pauline M. Illig, Oct. 8, 1930; 1 dau., Nancy Catherine. Admitted to Pa. bar, 1922, and since engaged in gen. practice of law at Reading; served as asst. dist. atty., 1928-31; served as dir. Reading Sch. Bd., 1933-39, pres. of same, 1937-39. Served as sergt. Ordnance Corps, U.S.A., 1917-19. Dir. Hope Rescue Mission. Pres. Luther League of Pa., 1932-36. Mem. Berks County Bar Assn., Delta Theta, Lambda Chi Alpha. Democrat. Lutheran. Home: 22 S. 8th St. Office: 21 N. 6th St., Reading, Pa.

SCHMICK, William Frederick, newspaper man; b. Baltimore, Md., July 30, 1883; s. William Frederick and Margaret Caroline (Gebauer) S.; ed. pub. schs. and Sadler, Bryant and Stratton Bus. Coll., Sept., 1900-01; m. Nancy Mary Reindollar, Sept. 23, 1907; children—Margaret Grimes (wife of Joseph B. H. Young, U.S.N.), William Frederick, Nancy Mary. Began in circulation dept. Baltimore World, 1899, sec. and business mgr., 1903-10; advanced through successive stages to exec. v.p. The A. S. Abell Co., pubs., and bus. mgr. Baltimore Sun Newspaper. Independent Democrat. Presbyn. Mason. Clubs: Maryland, Merchants, Chesapeake, Elkridge. Home: 4601 Millbrook Rd. Office: The Sun, Baltimore, Md.

SCHMIDT, Carl Frederic, pharmacologist; b. Lebanon, Pa., July 29, 1893; s. Jacob Charles and Mary Ellen (Greth) S.; A.B., Lebanon Valley Coll., 1914; M.D., U. of Pa. Med. Sch., 1918; m. Elizabeth Viola Gruber, June 24, 1920; children—Carl Frederic, Barbara Elizabeth. Interne Univ. Hosp., 1918-19; instr. pharmacology, U. of Pa., 1919-22; asso. in pharmacology, Union Med. Coll., Peking, China, 1922-24; asst. prof. pharmacology, U. of Pa., 1924-29, asso. prof., 1929-31, prof. since 1931. Served as 1st lieut. Med. Res. Corps, U.S.A., 1918. Mem. Am. Physiol. Soc., Am. Pharmacol. Soc., Soc. for Exptl. Biology and Medicine, Sigma Xi, Alpha Omega Alpha. Republican. Lutheran. Home: 517 Old Gulph Rd., Narberth, Pa.

SCHMIDT, Carl O., mem. law firm Schmidt, Hugas & Laas. Office: Central Union Trust Bldg., Wheeling, W.Va.

SCHMIDT, Franklin Herman, pres. Nazareth Nat. Bank & Trust Co.; b. Nazareth, Pa., Dec. 5, 1879; s. Herman and Mary (Karch) S.;

SCHMIDT

student Nazareth (Pa.) High Sch., 1893-96, State Teachers Coll., Kutztown, Pa., 1896-97; m. Anna McEntire, June 3, 1913. Teller Nazareth Nat. Bank & Trust Co., 1898-1913, cashier, 1913-33, pres. since 1933; v.p. and treas. Kraemer Hosiery Co., Nazareth, since 1906; v.p. Nazareth Bldg. & Loan Assn. since 1920; v.p. and treas. Queen City Textile Corpn., Allentown, Pa., since 1934; treas. Lehigh Spinning Co., Allentown, Pa., 1939, dir. Blue Mt. Consol. Water Co. Trustee Easton (Pa.) Hosp. Mem. Northampton Co. Banker's Assn. (v.p., 1938). Lutheran. Mason (K.T., Rajah Temple Shrine, Reading, Pa.), I.O.O.F. Clubs: Rotary (Nazareth, Pa.); Northampton Country (Easton, Pa.); Glen Brook Golf (Stroudsburg, Pa.). Home: 35 N. New St. Office: 76 S. Main St., Nazareth, Pa.

SCHMIDT, Frederick W(illiam), pub. utility exec.; b. Jersey City, N.J., Nov. 15, 1870; s. John Frederick and Catharine (Besbord) S.; ed. pub. schs. and high sch., Jersey City, N.J.; m. Georgia G. Grimes, Oct. 12, 1898; children—Mary Potter (Mrs. Harry Stanley Ferguson), John Grimes (M.D.). Bookkeeper Jersey City Gas Light Co., 1896-1901; agent Jersey City Dist., Hudson County Gas Co., 1901-03; gen. agent, gas dept., Hudson Div., Public Service Corpn., N.J., 1903-04, agent Jersey City Dist., United Electric Co., 1904-08; Hudson Div., agent Public Service Electric & Gas Co., 1908-27, gen. agent since 1927; dir. Fifth Ward Savings Bank, Jersey City. Mem. Jersey City Chamber of Commerce, Edison Electric Inst., N.J. Gas Assn., N.J. State Sr. Golf Assn. Republican. Presbyn. Clubs: Essex (Newark); Cartaret (Jersey City); Arcola Country (Hackensack); Forsgate Country. Home: 53 Bentley Av., Jersey City, N.J. Office: 80 Park Place, Newark, N.J.

SCHMIDT, George Paul, coll. prof.; b. St. Louis, Mo., Feb. 26, 1894; s. Charles C. and Marianne (Stockhart) S.; A.B., Washington U., St. Louis, Mo., 1918, A.M., 1919; Ph.D., Columbia U., 1930; m. Irma Gotch, Mar. 20, 1921; children—George Paul, Jr., Marianne. Engaged as instr., then prof., Concordia Coll., Ft. Wayne, Ind., between 1920 and 1930; asst. prof. history, N.J. Coll. for Women, New Brunswick, N.J., 1930-38, prof. and head of dept. history since 1938. Mem. Am. Hist Assn., Phi Beta Kappa. Author: The Old Time College President, 1930. Contbr. articles to hist. mags. Home: Colonial Gardens, New Brunswick, N.J.

SCHMIDT, Henry D(uncan), paper board mfg.; b. York, Pa., Aug. 25, 1892; s. John Charles and Anna M. (Small) S.; prep. edn., York County Acad., York, Pa., St. Paul's Sch., Concord, N.H., York Collegiate Inst., York, Pa., 1906-10; Ph.B., Yale, 1913; m. Margaret M. Hawkins, Feb. 10, 1927; children—Helen Margaret, John Charles. Employed as sec. Standard Chain Co., York, Pa., 1914-16; vice-pres., sec. and dir. Schmidt & Ault Paper Co., York, Pa., 1914-23, pres., treas. and dir. since 1923; pres., treas. and dir. John C. Schmidt Terminal Co. since 1923; receiver Pullman Motor Car Co., 1917; dir. York Nat. Bank & Trust Co., York Rys. Co., Edison Light & Power Co., York Steam Heating Co., York Bus Co., Glen Rock Electric Light & Power Co., Community Hotel Co.; dir. York Gas Co., 1923-25. Served as 1st lieut. U.S.N., aircraft production, 1918. Pres. Mfrs. Assn., York, 1932. Mem. Paperboard Industries Assn. (pres. 1931), Nat. Paperboard Assn. (pres. since 1936). Republican. Episcopalian. Clubs: Lafayette, Country (York); Saint Elmo (New Haven, Conn.), Rotary Club of York, York, Pa. Home: 144 Merion Rd. Office: 423 King's Mill Rd., York, Pa.

SCHMIDT, Henry Kloman, organist, prof. music; b. Pittsburgh, Pa., Apr. 18, 1881; s. Henry and Mary (Kloman) S.; ed. Leipzig Conservatory, Germany, 1900-02; pvt. pupil of Martin Krause, Berlin, 1902-07; m. Mabel M. Grine, June 30, 1910; children—Mary Jeannette (Sister M. Thecla), Beatrice Virginia (Mrs. Robert McCabe), Henry Kloman, Jr., Eugene Francis, Rita Eleanor, Edith Clare, Virginia Frances (dec.). Engaged as asst. to Martin Krause, Berlin, Germany, 1904-07; pvt. instr.

music, Pittsburgh, Pa., since 1907; mem. piano staff, Carnegie Inst. Tech. since 1914; organist and choir master, Holy Rosary Ch. since 1908; head music dept. Seton Hill Coll., Greensburg, Pa., 1932-38. Mem. Am. Guild of Organists, Musicians Club of Pittsburgh. Roman Catholic. K.C. Home: 233 Amber St., Pittsburgh, Pa.

SCHMIDT, Otto, artist and art dir.; b. Phila., Pa., Aug. 9, 1876; s. George Peter and Pauline S.; attended George B. McClellan Sch. and Industrial Art Sch., Phila.; grad. Northeast High Sch., Phila., 1894; art edn. Pa. Acad. Fine Arts, 1894-95, 1900-01, Nat. Acad. of Design, N.Y. City, 1905-06, 1907; m. Jenny May Hallman, Nov. 25, 1911; children—Mildred Jenny (dec.), Norman Otto, Doris Lorrain. Mem. art staff, Phila. Evening Bulletin, Phila. Inquirer, Phila. North American, 1900-04; on art staff Munsey's N.Y. Daily News, 1904; on art staff, J. G. Bennett's New York Herald, 1904-13; art dir., Munsey's N.Y. Press and on art staff N.Y. Sun, 1913-16; contbg. artist to Judge, 1913-16; on art staff Phila. Public Ledger, 1916-33; drawings, decorations, illustrations, in black and white and color for Curtis publs. and many other leading mags. of nat. circulation; exhibited at Pa. Acad. Fine Arts, Art Club, Art Alliance, Warwick Galleries, Newman's Art Galleries, Phila., Nat. Acad. of Design Galleries, New York City; represented in The John Vanderpoel Collection, Chicago, The Fellowship of Pa. Acad. Fine Arts, and in pvt. collections in U.S. and Can. Mem. Alumni Assn. Northeast High Sch. (exec. bd.), Fellowship Pa. Acad. of Fine Arts, New York Herald Owls. Home: 3139 Belgrade St., Philadelphia, Pa.

SCHMIDT, William Henry, med. coll. prof.; b. Wallingford, Pa., Sept. 15, 1884; s. Frank and Anna (Moore) S.; M.D., U. of Pa., 1908; m. Mary Grace Clark, Nov. 23, 1910; children—Anna Emilie, Mary Grace, William Clark, Jane Russell. Private practice in Atlantic City, N.J., until 1916; specialized in treatment of cancer with X-ray and radium and developed the use of electro-surgery in cancer since 1916; prof. of phys. therapy, Jefferson Med. Coll., Phila., since 1924, dir. of the dept. since 1924; roentgenologist, St. Mary's Hosp., Phila., since 1917. Mem. Pa. State Phys. Therapeutics Assn. (past pres.), Am. Phys. Therapeutics Assn. (past pres.), Am. Congress of Phys. Therapy (pres.), Acad. of Phys. Medicine (v.p.), A.M.A., Pa. State and Phila. Co. med. socs., Am. Radium Soc. Democrat. Roman Catholic. Club: Phila. Medical (Phila.). Author of about 50 articles on the treatment of cancer. Diplomate of the Am. Bd. of Radiology. Home: 1532 W. Erie Av. Office: Medical Arts Bldg., Philadelphia, Pa.

SCHMITT, Richard Bonaventure, coll. prof.; b. Brooklyn, N.Y., July 14, 1889; s. Charles and Mary (Severing) S.; grad. St. Francis Xavier Coll. High Sch., 1906; A.B., St. Andrew-on-Hudson Coll., 1910; M.A., Georgetown U., 1913; research work, New York U., 1932-38; unmarried. Asst. prof. chemistry, Canisius Coll., Buffalo, N.Y., 1913-18; prof. chemistry, Ateneo de Manila, Philippine Islands, 1923-26; prof. chemistry and head chemistry dept., Loyola Coll., since 1926, also prof. Micro organic chemistry. Established first micro analysis lab. in Md., 1931. Mem. A.A.A.S., Am. Chem. Soc., Md. Acad. Science, Internat. Science Acad. Catholic. Club: Germania. Home: 4501 N. Charles St., Baltimore, Md.

SCHMUCKER, Samuel Christian, biologist; b. Allentown, Pa., Dec. 18, 1860; s. Beale Melancthon and Christiana Maria (Pretz) S.; A.B., Muhlenberg Coll., 1882, A. M., 1885, M.S., 1891, Sc.D., 1913; Ph.D., U. of Pa., 1893, hon. fellow in botany, same, 1899; m. Katherine Elizabeth Weaver, Dec. 29, 1885; children—Beale M., Dorothy M. Prof. natural science, Carthage (Ill.) Coll., 1883-84, Boys' High Sch., Reading, Pa., 1884-89, State Normal Sch., Indiana, Pa., 1889-95; biology, State Teachers Coll., West Chester, 1895-1923, emeritus since 1923. Lecturer on biology, Phila. Cooking Sch., 1898-1902; dean of faculty and prof. zoölogy, Wagner Institute, Philadelphia, since 1907; also popular lecturer to schools, teachers' gatherings and chautauquas. Mem. N.E.A. Episcopalian. Independent Republican. Author: The Study of Nature, 1907; Columbia Elementary Geography, 1909; Under the Open Sky, 1910; The Meaning of Evolution, 1913; Man's Life on Earth, 1925; Heredity and Parenthood, 1929. Club: Rotary. Home: West Chester, Pa.

SCHNABEL, Walter Martin, pres. The Schnabel Co.; b. Pittsburgh, Pa., 1878; s. G. A. and Elizabeth (Woods) S.; student pub. schs.; m. Leah Michaels, Jan. 1, 1908; children—Charles Warren, B. Alleyne Blanning. Began in G. A. Schnabel's Carriage Factory, Pittsburgh, 1894; mem. of firm G. A. Schnabel & Sons (formerly G. A. Schnabel's Carriage Factory), mfrs. auto truck bodies, Pittsburgh, since 1904, pres. since 1918. Home: 210 Beltyhoover Av. Office: S. 10th and Muriel Sts., Pittsburgh, Pa.

SCHNADER, William A(braham), lawyer; b. Bowmansville, Pa., Oct. 5, 1886; s. Charles B. and Elizabeth (Renninger) S.; A.B., Franklin and Marshall Coll., 1908, LL.D., 1931; LL.B., U. of Pa., 1912; m. Ethel K. Heinitsh, June 9, 1915. Began practice of law at Philadelphia, Pa., 1913; mem. firm of Schnader & Lewis; spl. dep. atty. gen. of Pa., 1923-30, atty. gen., 1930-35. Mem. Commn. on Uniform State Laws since 1924; pres. Nat. Assn. Attorneys Gen., 1933. Trustee Franklin and Marshall Coll. (Lancaster, Pa.), Cedar Crest Coll. (Allentown, Pa.), Temple U., Phila. Mem. Phi Beta Kappa, Chi Phi, Phi Delta Phi (pres. U. of Pa. Chapter), Order of the Coif. Republican. Mem. Ref. Ch. Mason. Clubs: Union League, University, Philadelphia Cricket, Rittenhouse. Author: Pennsylvania Workmen's Compensation Law, 1915. Home: 8009 St. Martin's Lane, Chestnut Hill. Office: 1719 Packard Bldg., 15th and Chestnut Sts., Philadelphia, Pa.

SCHNAUFFER, Patrick McGill, lawyer; b. Brunswick, Md., Dec. 17, 1905; s. William and Mary Hook (West) S.; A.B., Washington Coll., Chestertown, Md., 1928; LL.B., Georgetown U., Washington, D.C., 1932; m. Clara E. Magill, June 14, 1931; children—Shirley Diana, Patrick McGill, Jr. Admitted to Md. bar, 1933, and since engaged in gen. practice of law at Frederick; justice of peace, Frederick, Md., 1934-38; state's atty. Frederick Co. for term, 1939-43. Mem. Frederick County Bar Assn., Alpha Kappa, Sigma Phi Epsilon. Republican. Episcopalian. Mason, Elk. Club: Elks (Frederick). Home: 320 West College Terrace. Office: W. Church St., Frederick, Md.

SCHNEIDERMAN, J. Jerome, ins. underwriter; b. New York, N.Y., July 25, 1889; s. Harris and Shifra (Katz) S.; ed. pub. schs. and high sch., Jersey City, N.J.; m. Phoebe Bressler, Nov. 30, 1930; children—Selma Shifra, Herbert Harris. Engaged as steamboat operator, 1907-18; ins. underwriter, mem. firm W. F. Sheehan Ins. Agency, Bayonne, N.J., since 1918. Founded Cedar Lake Camp for Boys, and Camp Nah-Jee-Wah for Girls, 1920. Treas. N.J. Fed. Y.M. H.A.'s and Y.W.H.A.'s, 1912-33; treas. Y.M. H.A. of Bayonne, 1911-16 and since 1917, pres., 1916-17; 1st v.p. Gluckman Hebrew Home for Aged, Bayonne, since 1937. Dir. Hebrew Home for Orphans and Aged of Hudson Co. since 1938. Jewish religion. Mason (32°, Shriner). Elk. Clubs: Insurance Square, Hudson County Shrine. Home: 92 W. 33d St. Office: 437 Broadway, Bayonne, N.J.

SCHNUR, George Henry, Jr., clergyman; b. Vandalia, Ill., Jan. 24, 1861; s. George Henry and Marie (Esbjoern) S.; A.B., Carthage (Ill.) Coll., 1882, A.M., 1888; Lutheran Theol. Sem., Gettysburg, Pa., 1886; D.D., Wittenberg (O.) Coll., 1920; m. Nina L. Charles, July 30, 1889; children—Faith (Mrs. Walter F. Erickson), Carl Esbjoern, Marie (Mrs. John M. Hedlund), George Luther, Rev. Paul Newton. Teacher pub. schs., 1879-83; ordained Luth. ministry, 1886; home mission work, 1886-1906, founding congregations at Omaha, Nevada, Ia., Evansville, Ind., and Chillicothe, O.; pastor St. Paul, Minn., 1906-14 (built Ch. of the Reformation), Zelienople, Pa., 1914-18, Grace Ch., Erie, 1918-38. Compiler and editor of Lutheran Parish Register, 1925; editor Luther League Topics, 1898-1917; editor Lutheran Year Book, 1926-33; chmn. Year Book and Statistical Com., United Lutheran Ch., 1922-34; sec. of statistics, Pittsburgh Synod (Luth.), 1916-39. Republican. Home: 636 Lincoln Av., Erie, Pa.

SCHNURE, William Marion, mfg. concrete burial vaults; b. Selinsgrove, Pa., May 17, 1877; s. Howard Davis and Sarah Jane (Six) S.; ed. Missionary Inst. (now Susquehanna U.), 1893-95; B.S., Pa. State Coll., 1901; m. Margaret May Pippet, of Haddon Heights, N.J., June 5, 1909; children—Howard Hopkins, Margaret Jane Selin. Pa. R.R. signal dept., 1901-12; with First Nat. Bank, Selinsgrove, Pa., 1912-26, asst. cashier, 1918, vice-pres., 1919-37, dir. since 1900; propr. Selinsgrove Air Seal Vault Works; mgr. Lewistown Concrete Vault Works, Lewistown, Pa. Mem. Snyder Co. Public Safety Com. and Home Defense Police during World War. Dir. Sch. Bd. and mem. local election bds. at various times. Treas. and mem. com. Dem. Com. Snyder Co., 1936-38; past pres. Chamber of Commerce. Chmn. Library Com., Selinsgrove Community Center since 1937. Mem. Pa. Soc. Sons of the Revolution, Kappa Sigma, Snyder Co. Hist. Soc. (sec. since 1912), Northumberland Co. Hist. Soc., Selinsgrove Philatelic Soc., Nat. Concrete Burial Vault Assn. Democrat. Lutheran. Clubs: Bond & Key (Susquehanna U.). Compiler: "Selinsgrove Pa. Chronology," 2 vols., 1918, 1929. History of Selinsgrove, Pa., 1915. Contbr. many hist. articles. Organizer Susquehanna Trail Assn., 1917; dir. Susquehanna Trails Assn., 1938. Home: 100 E. Mill St. Office: 506 N. Orange St., Selinsgrove, Pa.

SCHOBINGER, George, civil engr.; b. Chicago, Aug. 6, 1885; s. John J. and Emily (Hildebrand) S.; A.B., U. of Chicago, 1905; S.B., Mass. Inst. Tech., 1908; m. Helen Lockwood Johnson, Aug. 28, 1913; children—Elizabeth Hall, Gertrude Emily, John Edwin, Barbara Anne. Engr. insp. under bd. of supervising engrs., Chicago Traction, on constrn. Chicago River tunnels, 1908-11; asst. engr. U.S. Reclamation Service, on irrigation systems, Yuma, Ariz., and Rio Grande, N.M., and Tex. projects, 1911-17; progress engr. with Am. Internat. Shipbuilding Co., Phila., 1917-19; engr. and rep. Dwight P. Robinson & Co., Inc., erecting U.S. Embassy bldgs., etc., at Rio de Janeiro, 1919-31; engring. mgr. United Engrs. & Constructors, Inc., Phila., 1931-38; v.p. Dwight P. Robinson & Co. of Brazil, Inc., United Engrs. & Constructors of Argentina, Inc.; now exec. engr. Ulen & Co., N.Y. City. Mem. Am. Soc. C.E., Am. Chamber of Commerce of Rio de Janeiro, Phi Beta Kappa. Dir. Swarthmore Sch. Dist. Clubs: Rolling Green Golf, Swarthmore Players. Home: 301 Swarthmore Av., Swarthmore, Pa. Office: 120 Broadway, New York, N.Y.

SCHOCH, Marion Schnure, pub. newspaper; b. Selinsgrove, Pa., Sept. 8, 1886; s. Henry Harvey and Emma Catherine (Schnure) S.; B.S., Susquehanna U., Selinsgrove, Pa., 1906; hon. B.Litt., Susquehanna U., 1927; unmarried. Engaged as newspaper publisher since 1908; publisher Selinsgrove Times since 1910; exec. vice-pres. First Nat. Bank of Selinsgrove; served as postmaster of Selinsgrove under Pres. Woodrow Wilson for two terms, and serving similar commn. under Pres. Franklin D. Roosevelt. Democrat. Lutheran. Home: Selinsgrove, Pa.

SCHOCH, Silas H., fire sec. Ins. Co. of North America; b. Selinsgrove, Pa., June 22, 1883; s. H. Harvey and Emma Catherine (Schnure) S.; A.B., Bucknell U.; m. Margaret Gundy, Mar. 18, 1938. Spl. agent Nat. Fire Ins. Co., 1918-28; mgr. Ins. Co. of North America, 1928-30, asst. sec., 1930-35, fire sec. since 1935. Mem. Pa. Soc. S.R., Pa. Hist. Soc., Phi Kappa Psi. Clubs: Racquet, Penn Athletic, Downtown. Home: 20th and Walnut Sts. Office: 1600 Arch St., Philadelphia, Pa.

SCHOEN, Max, educator; b. Austria, Feb. 11, 1888; s. Elias and Rose (Rosenberg) S.; A.B., Coll. of City of N.Y., 1911; Ph.D., U. of Ia., 1921; m. Rose Jacobs, Jan. 1, 1912; 1 dau., Lillian Ruth. Came to America, 1900, naturalized, 1918. Instr. high sch., Chattanooga, Tenn., 1912-14, East Tenn. State Normal Sch., 1914-20, U. of Ia., 1920-21; with Carnegie Inst. Tech. since 1921, prof. and head dept. of edn. and psychology since 1925. Fellow A.A. A.S.; mem. Am. Psychol. Assn. Editor: The Effects of Music, 1927. Author: The Beautiful in Music, 1928; Human Nature, 1930; Art and Beauty, 1932. Home: 5821 Hobart St., Pittsburgh, Pa.

SCHOFF, Hannah Kent (Mrs. Frederic Schoff), philanthropist; b. Upper Darby, Pa.; d. Thomas and Fannie (Leonard) Kent; ed. boarding sch. and pvt. courses; m. Frederic Schoff, Oct. 23, 1873; children—Wilfred Harvey, Mrs. Edith Boericke, Mrs. Louise Ehrman, Leonard Hastings, Harold Kent, Mrs. Eunice Simmons, Albert Lawrence. First pres. Pa. Congress of Mothers, 1899-1902; v.p., 1897-1902, pres., 1902-20, now hon. pres., Nat. Congress of Mothers, which, with the aid of President Roosevelt and Dept. of State, held at the White House, Mar. 1908, the 1st Internat. Congress in America on the Welfare of the Child; held 2d International Congress on Child Welfare, Washington, 1911; chmn. com. on social service, etc., New Century Club, 1900-03; hon. pres. Nat. Congress of Parents and Teachers. Organized and led a movement to obtain juvenile ct. and probation system in Pa., passed by legislature, 1901; led movement leading to enactment of same laws, 1903, after Superior Ct. had declared the laws passed in 1901 unconstitutional because of tech. errors; chmn. com. which raised salaries and recommended for appmt. 1st probation officers in Pa.; pres. Phila. Juvenile Co. and Probation Assn., 1901-23; delegate from U.S. Dept. of State to the 3d Home Edn. Congress, Brussels, 1910. Special collaborator Home Edn. Div. Bur. of Edn., 1913-19; founder and sec. bd. United Service Club for Enlisted Men, Phila.; hon. trustee Nat. Kindergarten Coll., Chicago; dir. Nat. Kindergarten Assn. Mem. Soc. of Mayflower Descendants. Compiled: Laws of Every State in the United States Concerning Dependent and Delinquent Children, 1900. Editor Child Welfare Magazine 16 yrs., and contbr. numerous articles to mags. Author: The Wayward Child; The Evolution of the Mother's Pension; Wisdom of the Ages in Bringing Up Children, 1933. Home: 3418 Baring St., Philadelphia, Pa.

SCHOFIELD, Graham Littlewood, newspaper pub.; b. Phila., Pa., Nov. 3, 1886; s. Edwin Johns and Mary Platts (Ellison) S.; ed. Northeast Manual Training Sch., Phila., Drexel Inst.; m. Reba Sharp Turner, Oct. 14, 1911; children—Edwin J. II, John T., Jean R., Marjorie (Mrs. Laurence Huntress), Barbara (Mrs. James N. Homan). Began as clk. in store, 1903; with Phila. Inquirer, 1908, then with Bloomingdale Adv. Agency, then, Jacksonville (Fla.) Metropolis; asso. with Bridgeton Evening News, Bridgeton, N.J., since 1915, publisher since 1927, pres. and gen. mgr. Evening News Co. since 1927; interested in gardening, raising irises and propagation of new varieties. Mem. Nat. Editorial Assn., N.J. Press Assn., Am. Iris Soc. Republican. Methodist. Home: 206 N. Pearl St. Office: 74 E. Commerce St., Bridgeton, N.J.

SCHOFIELD, Samuel Biggs, coll. prof. and dean; b. Georgetown, Md., Feb. 13, 1898; s. Andrew J. and Rachel S.; A.B., Western Md. Coll., 1919; student Cornell U., summers 1920-22; A.M., Princeton U., 1925; m. Corinne Troy, June 22, 1929; 1 dau., Corinne Troy. Instr. Western Md. Coll., 1919, dean of men, 1920-22, 1923-24, prof. chemistry since 1928, dean of coll., 1929-39, dean of adminstrn. since 1939. Mem. bd. mgrs. Md. Gen. Hosp., Baltimore. Mem. Am. Chem. Soc. Home: 82 W. Green St., Westminster, Md.

SCHOFIELD, W(illiam) Richison, elec. engring.; b. Phila., Pa., Oct. 20, 1895; s. William Richison and Sarah Emma (Chew) S.; ed. U. of Pa., 1914-16; m. Marie E. McIlhenny, Aug. 30, 1916. Asso. with Leeds & Northrup Co., mfrs. electrical measuring equipment and automatic control apparatus, Phila., since 1916; successively draftsman, designer, engr. and designer, then asst. chief engr., 1925-28, chief engr. since 1928. Designed temperature control apparatus for ordnance work during World War; responsible for considerable pioneering work in automatic control field (particularly temperature) after 1918. Fellow Am. Inst. Elec. Engrs.

Mem. Am. Soc. Mech. Engrs. Republican. Episcopalian. Mason. Club: Cedarbrook Country (Philadelphia). Home: 736 E. Phil-Ellena St. Office: 4901 Stenton Av., Philadelphia, Pa.

SCHOLZ, Carl, consulting mining engr.; b. Slawentzitz, Germany, July 2, 1872; s. Paul and Nanette (Schneider) S.; ed. Royal Gymnasium, Deuthen, and under Dr. Schmiedecke, in mining engring.; came to America, 1889; m. 2d Mae A. Fleming, Mar. 4, 1917; 1 dau. (by 1st marriage), Mrs. Margaret Robinson. Mining engr. and mine operator in Kanawha Dist., W. Va., 1890-1901; with mining and fuel dept. C.,R.I.&P. Ry. Co., 1902-17; consulting mining engr. C.,B.&Q. R.R. Co. and Valier Coal Co., 1917-Dec. 31, 1922. Treas. and gen. mgr. Raleigh-Wyoming Coal Co., Charleston, W.Va. Consulting engr. U.S. Bur. Mines; sent to Europe by U.S. Bur. of Mines, 1910, to investigate and report on mining conditions. Mem. Am. Inst. Mining and Metallurgical Engineers, Am. Mining Congress (ex-pres.). Contbr. on mining subjects. Pres. Chicago Public Sch. League, 1917-19. Home: 4111 Virginia Av., Charleston, W.Va.

SCHOLZ, Karl William Henry, prof. of economics; b. Riesbrick, Schleswig-Holstein, Germany, Dec. 31, 1886; s. Karl Heinrich and Marie (Jaeschke) S.; B.S., U. of Pa., 1911, A.M., 1915, Ph.D., 1918; m. Carolyn Krusen, Apr. 9, 1928; children—Carol Frieda, Arianne Elizabeth. Came to U.S., 1892, naturalized 1915. Instr. German and mathematics, Bethlehem (Pa.) Prep. Sch., 1911-14; instr. of German, U. of Pa., 1914-15, fellow in German lit., 1915-16, instr. of German, 1916-19, instr. of economics, 1919-26, asst. prof., 1926-30, prof. since 1930; special lecturer Inst. for Internat. Relations, Bethel Coll., Kan., and Lafayette Coll., Easton, Pa., summer 1939. Mem. bd. dirs. and exec. com. Phila. Housing Assn.; mem. Phila. Com. on Pub. Affairs, chmn. 1939; mem. Advisory com. Phila. Housing Authority; consultant Nat. Housing Commn.; mem. bd. dirs. Pa. Housing and Town Planning Assn.; research asso. Inst. of Local and State Govt., U. of Pa., 1937-38; trustee Phi Sigma Kappa Endowment Fund. Awarded U. of Pa. fellowship, 1915. Mem. Am. Econ. Assn., Am. Acad. Polit. and Social Science, Nat. Assn. Housing Officials, Phi Beta Kappa, Phi Sigma Kappa. Lutheran. Club: Manufacturers and Bankers, Contemporary (Phila.). Author: Art of Translation, 1918; Science and Practice of Urban Land Valuation (with W. W. Pollock), 1925; Economic Problems of Modern Life (with S. H. Patterson), 1926; Rudiments of Business Finance (with E. S. Mead), 1926. Editor: Real Estate Problems (vol. of Annals, of Am. Acad. of Polit. and Social Science), 1930. Contbr. articles to professional jours. Home: Rose Tree and Old Orchard Rds., Media, Pa.

SCHOMP, Albert L., pres. Am. Bank Note Co.; b. Somerset Co., N.J., May 21, 1880; s. Winfield S. and Arabella (Van Derveer) S.; grad. Plainfield (N.J.) High Sch., 1900; m. Charlotte Cave, Jan. 14, 1909; 1 son, Albert L. Clk., 1904-08; with Am. Bank Note Co. since 1908, asst. treas. 1912-15, v.p., 1915-29, 1st v.p., 1929-35, pres. since 1935. Mem. N. Y. Chamber of Commerce. Republican. Presbyterian. Clubs: Union League City Midday, Bond (New York); Yeaman's Hall (Charleston, S.C.); Plainfield Country. Home: Plainfield, N.J. Office: 70 Broad St., New York, N.Y.

SCHOOLCRAFT, Arthur Allen; prof. edn. W. Va. Wesleyan College. Address: W.Va. Wesleyan College, Buckhannon, W.Va.

SCHOOLFIELD, George C.; chief med. examiner Workmen's Compensation Dept. of W. Va. Address: 1021 Quarrier St., Charleston, W.Va.

SCHOONMAKER, Frederic Palen, judge; b. Limestone, Cattaraugus Co. N.Y., Mar. 11, 1870; s. Elijah R. and Eliza (Palen) S.; student, Alfred U.; A.B., Cornell U., 1891; LL.D., Alfred, 1917; studied law under Judge James Schoonmaker, of St. Paul, Minn., and Col. W. W. Brown, of Bradford, Pa.; m. Jessie L. Brown, June 23, 1892 (died 1921); children—Susie Rae (Mrs. Walter G. Blaisdell), Fay

Lillian (Mrs. Laurent Erny), Max Van Palen; m. 2d, Virginia Elliott Taylor, Dec. 23, 1937. Mem. Brown & Schoonmaker, of Bradford, Pennsylvania, 1894-1913, then Brown, Schoonmaker & Nash; became judge of U.S. District Court, Western District of Pa., January 2, 1923. Joined Pa. N.G., 1912; capt. 16th Regt., Mexican border service, 1916-17; entered U.S. service, 1917, with regt. as 112th Inf., 28th Div., A.E.F., also served as asst. chief of staff G2, 28th Div. and 92d Div., A.E.F.; detached duty with Army Gen. Staff, Langres, France, also with 2d Can. Div., B.E.F.; hon. discharged Feb. 1919, as lt. col. inf. Mem. Psi Upsilon, Phi Beta Kappa. Mason, Odd Fellow, Elk. Republican. Baptist. Clubs: Bradford, University, Athletic (Pittsburgh, Pa.); Psi Upsilon (New York). Home: Bradford, Pa.

SCHOONMAKER, William Powell, artist; b. New York, N.Y., Nov. 14, 1890; s. William Gruen and Rachel (Kortright) S.; ed. Art Students League of New York City, 1909-13; m. Corinne Turner, Aug. 21, 1919 (dec. 1920); m. 2d, Blanche A. Weitbrec, Dec. 20, 1923. Began career as commercial artist, 1913; free lance from start, in New York City, 1913-18, in Phila. since 1918; in addition to commercial work makes etchings and block prints shown in various exhbns. throughout U.S., especially in Pa. Acad. Fine Arts Water Color Show. Mem. Art Directors Club, N.Y., also Art Dirs. Club of Phila., Phila. Graphic Arts Forum, Phila. Sketch Club, Art Alliance, Print Club. Received First Award, Phila. Chapter Art Dirs. Club, 1927; First Award and Hon. Mention, same, 1928; Second Award, same, 1931. Republican. Protestant. Ancestors came from Holland, 1659, the original Heindrich Jochem Schoonmaker, soldier and friend of Peter Stuyvesant; on maternal side desc. of Samuel Gorton who assisted Roger Williams in founding Providence Plantations now R.I. Home: Hotel Gladstone, Philadelphia, Pa. Studio: 12 S. 12th St., Philadelphia, Pa.

SCHOONOVER, Frank Earle, illustrator; b. Oxford, N.J., Aug. 19, 1877; s. John and Elizabeth (LeBar) S.; ed. 9 yrs. at Model School, Trenton, N.J., 4 yrs. art dept. Drexel Inst., Phila., under Howard Pyle; m. Martha Culbertson, Jan. 18, 1911; children—Cortlandt, Elizabeth Louise. Has illustrated for Scribner's, Harper's, Century and McClure's mags., Collier's and Harper's weeklies; also for pub. houses of Houghton, Mifflin Co., Little, Brown & Co., Boston; Longmans, Green & Co., and Doubleday, Page & Co., New York. Mem. Soc. of Illustrators. Club: Players. Has written articles on life of the Canadian trapper of the Far North in Scribner's Mag., etc. Studio: 1616 Rodney St., Wilmington, Del.*

SCHOR, Charles, lawyer; b. West Hoboken, N.J., Mar. 30, 1901; s. Abraham David and Anna (Jacobs) S.; grad. Pub. Sch. 27, Jersey City, N.J., 1914, Dickinson High Sch., Jersey City, 1918, Eagan Business Sch., 1919; LL.B., New York U., 1922; m. Fannie Leila Forster, Feb. 27, 1927; children—Sanford Morton, Allen David. Admitted to N.J. bar as atty. at law, 1922, as counsellor at law, 1926; jr. mem. firm Eichmann & Seiden, Jersey City, N.J., 1922-30; in pvt. practice at Jersey City, N.J., since 1930. Knights of Pythias (recorder to Grand Tribunal of Grand Lodge of N.J.). Home: 3829 Boulevard, North Bergen, N.J. Office: 576 Newark Av., Jersey City, N.J.

SCHOTT, Carl Peter, prof. phys. edn. and athletics; b. Carleton, Neb., Nov. 17, 1886; s. Henry and Kate (Schott) S.; B.Ed., Neb. State Normal, 1909; B.P.E., Y.M.C.A. Coll., Springfield, Mass., 1912; B.S., Teachers Coll. of Columbia U., 1925; A.M., Columbia Grad. Sch. 1926, Ph.D., 1928; m. Ivy Hall Hutchison, May 29, 1913; 1 dau., Katharine. Held various positions as prin. jr. high sch., dir. recreation, dir. phys. edn. and athletics and coach, Wis., Calif. and Mich., 1912-28; dir. phys. edn., W.Va. U., Morgantown, W.Va., 1928-37; dean of sch. phys. edn. and athletics, Pa. State Coll. since 1937; served as mem. Nat. Boxing Rules Com. since 1937. Fellow in Phys. Edn. Am. Phys. Edn. Assn. Mem. Coll. Phys. Edn. Assn., Kappa Delta Pi, Phi Delta Kappa, Phi

SCHOTT   780   **SCHREYER**

Delta Theta. Republican. Mem. Religious Soc. Friends. Club: Center Hills Country (State College). Home: 634 West Prospect Av., State College, Pa.

SCHOTT, Edwin Dilts, supervising prin. schs.; b. Sabinsville, Pa., May 14, 1895; s. Edwin B. and Flora (Gill) S.; ed. Mansfield State Normal Sch., 1916-17, 1919-20; B.S., Bucknell U., 1930; m. Victoria G. Cannon, July 26, 1923; children—Edwin Dilts, Jr., Frederick Victor, James William. Engaged as teacher in rural schs., 1914-16, and pub. schs., Ludlow Pa., 1920-21; and high sch., supv. prin. Durant City (Pa.) High Sch., 1921-32; supervising prin. high sch., Shinglehouse, Pa., 1932-36; asst. prin., high sch., Liberty, Pa., 1936-37; supervising prin. borough schs., Galeton, Pa. since 1937. Served as pvt. then sergt. 4th Supply Train, U.S.A., 1917-19, with A.E.F. in France and Germany. Mem. Pa. State Edn. Assn., Pa. Acad. Sci. Republican. Methodist. Mason. Home: 2 First St., Galeton, Pa.

SCHOTTE, Karl B., telephone official; b. Kittanning, Pa., Nov. 14, 1868; s. Gustafas Adolphas and Margaret (Crary) S.; ed. Kittanning Pub. Sch.; m. Carrie Kron, Dec. 12, 1893 (died Dec. 1923); children—Margaret Crary (Mrs. H. A. Both, deceased) Karl B.; m. 2d, Lucele Cook, June 26, 1929. Pharmacist, Kittanning, Pa., 1883-1939; sec., treas., gen. mgr. Kittanning Telephone Co., 1896-1905, vice-pres., sec. and gen. mgr. since 1905; pres. and treas. George S. Rohrer Co., Kittanning, Pa., druggists, since 1918; dir. Kittanning Thrift Co. Food adminstr. Armstrong Co., Pa., during World War. Trustee and pres. bd. Kittanning Pub. Library. Democrat. Episcopalian. Elk. Club: Rotary (Kittanning, Pa.). Home: 515 N. McKean St. Office: Arch St., Kittanning, Pa.

SCHRADER, Albert Lee, univ. prof.; b. Kaukauna, Wis., May 9, 1896; s. Albert Henry and Agnes Maria Anna (Nemoede) S.; grad. Kaukauna (Wis.) High Sch., 1914; B.S., U. of Wis., 1920, M.S., 1921; Ph.D., U. of Md., 1925; m. Gotthielde Christiana Barthel, June 17, 1924; children—Joan Barthel, Eda Barthel. Fellow, U. of Wis., 1920-21, asst. in research, summer, 1921; asst. in research, U. of Md., 1921-25, asst. pomologist, 1925-29, prof. pomology, 1929-36, prof. pomology and head dept. horticulture since 1936. Mem. U.S. Naval Reserve Force, 1917-19. Mem. A.A.A.S., Am. Soc. Plant Physiologists, Am. Soc. Horticultural Science, Washington Board of Trade, Sigma Xi, Phi Kappa Phi, Phi Sigma, Alpha Zeta, Alpha Tau Omega. Episcopalian. Home: 6319 Woodside Place, Chevy Chase, Md. Address: University of Maryland, College Park, Md.

SCHRADER, Frank Charles, geologist; b. Sterling, Ill., Oct. 6, 1860; s. Christian C. and Angeline Marie (Piepo) S.; B.S., M.S., University of Kan., 1891; A.B., Harvard University, 1893, A.M., 1894; m. Kathrine Batwell, Nov. 19, 1919. Teacher of geology, Harvard, 1895-96; geologist United States Geol. Survey, 1896-1932; retired account age limit; specialized in mining geology; has traveled widely on professional work in nearly all parts of Alaska and the U.S. Fellow Geol. Soc. Am.; mem. Am. Inst. Mining and Metallurgical Engrs., Nat. Geog. Soc., Am. Forestry Assn. Washington Acad. Sciences, A.A.A.S., Mining and Metall. Soc. America (mem. sub-com. on antimony), Soc. Econ. Geologists, Geol. and Mineral. societies, Washington Petrologists' Club, Pick and Hammer Club, Mineral. Soc. of America. Clubs: Cosmos, Midriver. Contbr. to Reports U.S. Geol. Survey, and to geog. mags. Has been chief examiner of mining properties and chief witness in important mining cases in the federal courts in many cities of U.S. Home: 20 Old Chester Rd., Bethesda, Md.

SCHRAG, William Albert, prof. business administration; b. Phila., May 10, 1906; s. S. and Elizabeth T. (Liebig) S.; B.C.S., Temple U., 1929; M.B.A., Harvard U. Grad. Sch. Bus. Adminstrn., 1931; grad. study, U. of Pa., N.Y. Univ.; m. Carolyn H. Lieb, Feb. 5, 1932. Instr. in statistics, Temple U., Phila., 1931-38; asst. prof. finance since 1938; curriculum head, Bus. Administrn. Dept., Temple U. Sch. of Commerce since 1936. Mem. Am. Statis. Soc., Am. Assn. Univ. Profs., Sch. Commerce Alumni Assn. of Temple U. (past pres.), Blue Key, Phi Delta Kappa, Pi Delta Epsilon, Theta Upsilon Omega, Sigma Phi Epsilon. Lutheran. Club: Harvard Business School Alumni of Philadelphia. Home: 7522 Walnut Lane, Philadelphia, Pa.

SCHRAMM, Gustav L., judge; b. Pittsburgh, Pa., May 11, 1898; s. Rev. Alfred and Sophie (Lorch) S.; B.S., U. of Pittsburgh, 1918, A.M., same, 1920; LL.B., U. of Pittsburgh Law Sch., 1924; Ph.D., Columbia U., 1928; m. Louise Hammel, May 9, 1931. Mem. faculty of U. of Pittsburgh, 1918-34; now engaged in gen. practice of law at Pittsburgh; atty. in charge Legal Aid Soc. of Pittsburgh, 1925-34; president judge Juvenile Ct. of Allegheny Co. since 1934. Dir. Federation of Social Agencies of Pittsburgh and Allegheny Co., Community Fund, Y.M.C.A. of Pittsburgh. Home: 37 Mt. Lebanon Boul., Mt. Lebanon, Pa. Office: 3333 Forbes St., Pittsburgh, Pa.

SCHRAMM, Henry Clyde, engineer; b. Barton, Md., Sept. 23, 1892; s. John Godfrey and J. Annette (Sommerville) S.; B.S. in E.E., W.Va. U., Morgantown, W.Va., 1915, M.E., 1933; student U.S.N.R.F. Steam Engring. Sch., Stephens Inst. Tech., Hoboken, N.J., 1918; student B. G. Coll., extension courses 1933-39, Lincoln Elect. Welding Sch., Cleveland, O., 1931; m. Ella Bradley, 1917 (died 1918); m. 2d, Marion Florence Shrewsbury, June 27, 1923; children—Marion Margaret, David Clyde. Asst. to chief engr., W.Va. Pulp & Paper Co., Piedmont, W.Va., 1917-18, 1919-30, acting chief engr., 1926-30, power engr., 1930-34, chief engr., Williamsburg (Pa.) plant, since 1934. Served as Ensign (engr.), U.S.N.R.F.-3, 1918-19. Republican. Episcopalian. Author of numerous tech. articles for trade jours. Home: 628 W. 3d St. Office: W.Va. Pulp & Paper Co., Williamsburg, Pa.

SCHRAMM, Jacob Richard, botanist; b. Cumberland, Ind., Feb. 6, 1885; s. August William and Emilie (Grummann) S.; grad. Shortridge High Sch., Indianapolis, Ind., 1902; A.B., Wabash Coll., Crawfordsville, Ind., 1910; Ph.D., Washington U., 1913; m. Mildred Webster Spargo, May 27, 1913. Lackland research fellow, Mo. Bot. Garden, St. Louis, 1910-12; asst. to dir. same, 1912-15; instr. in botany, Washington U., 1913-15; asst. prof. botany, Cornell U., 1915-17, prof., 1917-25; editor-in-chief Biological Abstracts, 1925-37. Professor of botany, Univ. of Pennsylvania, 1937—. Exec. sec. div. of biology and agr. Nat. Research Council, Washington, D.C., 1922-24. Editor-in-chief Bot. Abstracts. Fellow A.A.A.S.; mem. Bot. Soc. America (ex-sec., ex-v.p. and pres., 1925), Am. Soc. Naturalists, Phi Gamma Delta, Phi Beta Kappa, Sigma Xi. Unitarian. Contbr. on plant physiology. Address: University of Pa., Philadelphia, Pa.

SCHRAMM, William Edward, clergyman; b. Marietta, O., Mar. 18, 1869; s. Theobald and Elizabeth (Cisler) S.; D.D., Capital U., Columbus, O., 1893; grad. study, Luth. Sem., Columbus, O., 1893-96; m. Mary Alice Weisman, July 9, 1896; children—Edward Weisman, Milton Howard, Walter William, Alice Martha, Anna Louise. Employed as machinist, 1885-91; ordained to ministry Luth. Ch., 1896; pastor, St. Paul Ch., Pittsburgh, Pa., 1896-1920, St. Marks Ch., Butler, Pa., since 1920; chmn. Bd. Pub., Am. Luth. Ch. Lutheran. Club: Kiwanis of Butler (past pres.). Author: What Lutherans Believe, 1930; Our Great Salvation, 1932; A Knock at Your Door, 1927; Winning the Outsider, 1934. Home: 306 New Castle St., Butler, Pa. Study: Washington and Jefferson Sts., Butler, Pa.

SCHREINER, Oswald, chemist; b. Nassau, Germany, May 29, 1875; s. Louis and Susanne (Volkert) S.; grad. Baltimore Poly. Inst., 1892; Ph.G., Univ. of Maryland, 1894; Johns Hopkins, 1894-95; B.S., U. of Wis., 1897, M.S., 1899, Ph.D., 1902; m. Frances Rector, Oct. 11, 1902; children—Louis Rector, Oswald. U.S. Pharmacopœia research fellow, 1895-96, asst. in pharm. technique, 1896-97, instr., 1897-1902, instr. phys. chemistry, 1902-03, U. of Wis.; expert phys. chemist, summer, 1902, chemist, Bur. Soils, 1903-06, chief Div. Soil Fertility Investigations, 1906—, Dept. Agr. Counseling prof. chemistry, Am. U., 1914—. U.S. del. 1st International Congress of Soil Science, Washington, D.C., 1927, chmn. exec. com. same; U.S. del. 4th Pacific Science Congress, Java, 1929 and Congress Internat. Sugar Cane Technologists, 1929; cons. del. Inter-Am. Conf. on Agr., 1930; U.S. del. 3d Internat. Congress Soil Science, Oxford, Eng., 1935. Fellow Am. Assn. for Advancement of Science; member American Chem. Soc., Am. Soc. of Agronomy, Am. Soc. of Biol. Chemists, Assn. of Agrl. Chemists (pres. 1928), Washington Acad. Science, Bot. Soc. America, Soil Sci. Soc. of America, Internat. Soil Sci. Soc., International Sugar Cane Technologists, Sigma Xi, Phi Beta Kappa. Club: Cosmos. Author: The Sesquiterpenes, 1904; Colorimetric, Turbidity, and Titration Methods Used in Soil Investigations, 1906; The Chemistry of Soil Organic Matter, 1910, Lawn Soils, 1911; Nitrogenous Soil Constituents, 1913. Home: Primrose St., Chevy Chase, Maryland.

SCHREINER, Samuel A., lawyer; b. Mt. Lebanon, Pa., June 10, 1881; s. Cyrus B. and Myrtilla (Reed) S.; A.B., Western U. of Pa., Pittsburgh, 1900; m. Mary Martha Cort, Oct. 15, 1910; children—Cyrus Bryson, Martha C., Samuel A. Admitted to Pa. Bar, 1905, and since in practice in Pittsburgh; solicitor for Mt. Lebanon (Pa) Twp. since 1912, for Castle Shannon Borough (Pa.) since 1920, for Mt. Lebanon (Pa.) Sch. Dist. since 1915, for Union Twp. (Pa.), 1925-30; dir. Mt. Lebanon Bldg. & Loan Assn.; mem. South Hills (Pa.) Bd. of Trade (past sec.). Trustee Mt. Lebanon (Pa.) United Presbyn Ch. since 1906. Republican. United Presbyterian. Club: St. Clair Country (Allegheny County). Home: 42 St. Clair Drive, Mt. Lebanon, Pa. Office: 901 Jones Law Bldg., Pittsburgh, Pa.

SCHRENK, Helmuth Herman, toxicologist; b. Golconda, Ill., Sept. 28, 1902; s. Albert and Bertha (Hesselman) S.; A.B., U. of Wis., 1925, M.S., 1926, Ph.D., 1928; m. Helen G. Pratt, Sept. 23, 1933; 1 dau., Elizabeth Pratt. Asst. state toxicologist, Wis., 1923-28; with U.S. Bureau of Mines, Pittsburgh, since 1928, as asso. toxicologist Health Lab. Sect., 1928-30, chemist in charge toxicological and biochemical lab., 1930-33, chemist Gas Sect., 1933-36, chief chemist Health Div. since 1936. Fellow A.A.A.S.; mem. Am. Chem. Soc., Am. Pub. Health Assn., Alpha Chi Sigma, Phi Lambda Upsilon, Sigma Xi, Phi Sigma, Gamma Alpha. Mem. Chemists Club, Pittsburgh. Contbr. articles in field of industrial hygiene and toxicology to professional jours. Home: 514 Bigham Rd. Office: U.S. Bureau of Mines, Pittsburgh, Pa.

SCHREPFER, Frank Andrew, educator; b. Chicago, Ill., Sept. 4, 1896; s. Michael and Anna V. (Heider) S.; B.S., U. of Ill., 1925, M.S., 1926; student U. of Chicago, summer, 1921, Harvard U., 1921-23, U. of Heidelberg, Germany, 1932-33; m. Frieda Freiberg Grant, Sept. 27, 1922; children—Kenneth Francis, June Ann. Instr., School of Fine Arts, U. of Pa., 1926-28, asst. prof., 1928-36, asso. prof. since 1936; also taught at Vassar Coll. and Harvard U.; landscape architect; v.p. and dir. Nat. Bank of Narberth. Burgess Borough of Narberth. Served with U.S. Army, in Mexico, 1916, with A.E.F., 1917-18, wounded in action. Decorated Order of the Purple Heart; awarded medal of honor, Internat. Soc. of the Inner Eye. Mem. Am. Soc. Landscape Architects, Univ. Landscape Architects Soc., Sigma Xi, Delta Sigma Rho, Phi Sigma, Gamma Sigma Delta, etc., Mil. Order of the Purple Heart (nat. comdr. 1934), Am. Legion (comdr. John McShane Post 1919; comdr. Harold D. Speakman Post 1931). Republican. Author: Hardy Evergreens, 1928; also mag. articles. Home: 315 Grayling Av., Narberth, Pa. Office: Univ. of Pennsylvania, Philadelphia, Pa.

SCHREYER, Charles Allen, v.p. West Branch Bank & Trust Co.; b. Williamsport, Pa., May 12, 1896; s. Allen Carson and Emily Amelia

(Rissell) S.; grad. Williamsport High Sch., 1914; m. Emily Marie Martin, Sept. 1, 1925; children—Anne Marie, Jane Martin. Began as messenger boy, Northern Central Trust Co., now v.p. and trust officer West Branch Bank & Trust Co., Williamsport, Pa.; dir. Cochran Coal Co., J. K. Rishel Furniture Co., Northumberland Co. Ry. Co. Dir. and trustee James V. Brown Library, Williamsport Hosp., Ida Hays McCormick Welfare Center, Inc., Social Service Bur.; sec. Williamsport Foundation or Community Trust. Mem. Pa. Bankers' Assn. (mem. coms. on trust investments, constitution and by-laws, and costs and charges; past chmn. Group Four). Republican. Lutheran (dir. and trustee St. Mark's Ch., Williamsport, Pa.) Mason. Club: Williamsport Country. Home: 608 Highland Terrace. Office: West Branch Bank & Trust Co., Williamsport, Pa.

SCHROEDER, Elmer Andrew, lawyer; b. Phila., Pa., Feb. 25, 1898; s. Peter and Anna (Gloeckner) S.; student Northeast High Sch., Phila., 1912-16; B.S., U. of Pa., 1920, LL.B., Law Sch., 1924; unmarried. Asso. with firm of White and Wetherill, Phila., 1925-26, partner, 1926-30; partner, White, Fletcher and Schroeder, Phila., 1930-34; partner, White and Schroeder, Phila., since 1934. Served as acting sergeant, inf., U.S. Army, during World War. Mem. Phila., Pa. and Am. bar assns., Am. Olympic Com., Delta Theta Phi. Republican. Lutheran. Clubs: Lawyers, Penn Athletic, Phila. Rifle (Phila.). Home: 1944 W. 69th Av. Office: 1528 Walnut St., Philadelphia, Pa.

SCHROEDER, Elmer Frederick, chemist; b. Napoleon, O., Jan. 9, 1905; s. Charles Herman and Dora (Otte) S.; A.B., Defiance Coll., Defiance, O., 1926; M.Sc., Ohio State U., 1928, Ph.D., 1930; m. Frieda K. Thieroff, Aug. 19, 1930; children—Barbara Ann, Robert Carl. Instr. of chemistry, Ohio State U., 1926-30; Sterling research fellow, Yale, 1930-31; research chemist, Cancer Research Foundation, U. of Pa., 1931-35; chief chemist, Biochem. Research Foundation, Franklin Inst., Phila., since 1935. Mem. Am. Chem. Soc., Am. Soc. Biol. Chemists, Sigma Xi, Gamma Alpha. Lutheran. Home: 923 Foulkrod St., Philadelphia, Pa. Office: 133 S. 36th St., Philadelphia, Pa.

SCHROEDER, Lloyd Leighton, lawyer; b. New York, N.Y., Jan. 27, 1904; s. Frank and Edith (Langer) S.; LL.B., N.Y. Univ. Law Sch., 1927; m. Selma C. Rhamstrom of West Englewood, N.J., June 28, 1930; 1 dau., Marjorie Louise. Began as real estate salesman, 1919; admitted to N.J. bar as atty., 1927, as counsellor, 1931, and engaged in gen. practice of law at Hackensack since 1927; served as judge of Second Criminal Judicial Dist. Ct. of Bergen Co., 1937-38; mem. N.J. Ho. of Assembly, 1931-35, and since 1939. Mem. Lawyers Club of Bergen Co., Bergen Co. Bar Assn. Republican. Protestant. B.P.O.E. Club: Lions of Hakensack. Home: 454 Ogden Av., West Englewood. Office: 210 Main St., Hackensack, N.J.

SCHROPP, John Krause Reinoehl, pres. Lebanon News Pub. Co.; b. Lebanon, Pa., July 10, 1880; s. Jacob G. and Kathryn R. (Reinoehl) S.; student Lebanon (Pa.) High Sch.; m. Eleanore E. Kneule, Sept. 19, 1926; 1 son, John. Pres. Lebanon (Pa.) News Pub. Co. since 19—; v.p. Community Hotel Co.; dir. Peoples Nat. Bank. Mayor, City of Lebanon (Pa.), 1932-35; formerly mem. Rep. State Com. Pres. Coleman Memorial Park; pres. Salem Lutheran Ch. Men's Club. Mem. Chamber of Commerce. Republican. Lutheran. Elk, Eagle, Moose, Oriole, Owl. Home: 403 Cumberland St. Office: 24 S. Eighth St., Lebanon, Pa.

SCHUCK, Charles J(ohn), lawyer; b. Pittsburgh, Pa., Apr. 22, 1875; s. John A. and Charlotte (Dick) S.; LL.B., Univ. of Mich. Law Sch., Ann Arbor, 1896; m. Margaret S. Schaffner, Feb. 24, 1903; 1 son, Charles J., Jr. (dec.). Admitted to W.Va. bar, 1897 and since engaged in gen. practice of law at Wheeling; pros. atty. of Ohio Co., W.Va., 1905-09; spl. asst. U.S. Dist Atty., W.Va., 1921-22; spl. counsel Alien Property Custodian of U.S., 1926-29; offered post as atty. gen. of Puerto Rico by Pres. Herbert Hoover, 1931, declined; counsel in various important cases in state and federal cts. Served as del. to Rep. Nat. Convs., 1924, 1928, 1932. Chmn. State Rep. Com., 1932. Rep. Congl. candidate from first dist. W.Va., 1936. Dir. Crippled Children's Soc. of Wheeling (past pres.). Pres. Wheeling Community Forum. Mem. Am. and State bar assns. Republican. K.P. (supreme rep. from W.Va.). Club: Elks. Home: 40 Heiskell St. Office: Central Union Bldg., Wheeling, W.Va.

SCHUCKER, Paul Frederick, civil engr.; b. Lancaster, Pa., May 25, 1904; s. Morris G. and Elsie M. (Pflueger) S.; B.S in C.E., Carnegie Inst. Tech., 1924, C.E., 1928; m. Helen McBride, 1926; children—Paul Frederick, Robert McBride. Civil engr. Pa. State Highway Dept., 1924; asst. engr. with John M. Rice, cons. engr., Pittsburgh, 1925-26; engr. Ford, Bacon & Davis, Inc., New York, 1926-27, Speyer & Co., investment bankers, New York, 1927-39; pres., sec. and dir. New York & Foreign Investing Corpn., Jersey City, since 1930. Asst. treas. Museum of City of New York. Mem. S.R., Tau Beta Pi, Phi Kappa Psi, Theta Tau. Republican. Presbyn. Clubs: Bonnie Briar Country, University (Larchmont). Home: Larchmont, N.Y. Office: 15 Exchange Pl., Jersey City, N.J.; 24 Pine St., New York, N.Y.

SCHUETTE, Walter Erwin, clergyman; b. Delaware, O., Nov. 14, 1867; s. Conrad Herman Louis and Victoria Mary (Wirth) S.; grad. Capital U. Acad., Columbus, O., 1881; A.B., Capital U., 1885, D.D., 1925; grad. Lutheran Sem., Columbus, 1888; m. Clyda Pearl Helsel, June 26, 1890; children—Helen Beatrice (dec.), Faith, Jessie Ruth, Winona Emma (dec.), Conrad Herman Louis, Corine Louise (Mrs. William F. Hamman), Walter Erwin. Ordained Luth. ministry, 1888; pastor successively Detroit, Mich., Bellevue and Toledo, O., until 1914; editor The Lutheran Standard, Columbus, 1909-15, The American Lutheran Survey, 1914-17; pastor Wheeling, W.Va., 1917-22; pres. Eastern Dist. Joint Synod of Ohio and Other States, 1922-30; pres. Eastern Dist. Am. Lutheran Ch. since 1931; v.p. Am. Lutheran Ch. since 1936; commr. Nat. Luth. Council since 1936; mem. Am. Luth. Conf. Commn. on Higher Edn. since 1936; editor Pastor's Monthly, 1922-28; lecturer. Author: Her Place Assigned, 1896; The Devotional Life of the Ch. Worker, 1921; God Is Faithful, 1925; Moments with God, 1925; The Best Possible Sunday School, 1928; also 19 juvenile stories and 8 playlets. Home: 223 Bank St., Sewickley, Pa.

SCHUETZ, Frederick Faber du Faur, solicitor of patents; b. Newark, N.J., July 1, 1882; s. Frederick Alexander and Sophie Faber du Faur S.; student Newark (N.J.) Acad., 1890-99; M.E., Stevens Inst. Tech., Hoboken, N.J., 1903; A.M., Columbia U., 1904; m. Anna Schuster, Oct. 17, 1906; children—Robert Frederick, Norma Elizabeth. Solicitor of U.S. and fgn. patents, trade marks, etc., New York, since 1904; dir. F. J. Emmerich Co., New York, since 1918. Treas. The Appalachian Trail Conf. since 1935; mem. Robert Treat Council of Boy Scouts of America (25 yrs. Scouter and holder Silver Beaver Award). Mem. Am. Soc. M.E., The Electrochem. Soc., A.A.A.S., N.Y. Patent Law Assn., Am. Forestry Assn., Theta Xi, Tau Beta Pi; assoc. mem. Am. Inst. E.E. Republican. Clubs: Adirondack Mountain, Inc. (N.Y. Chapter, Inc.), Green Mountain, Inc. (N.Y. Sect., Inc.). Home: 481 Summit Av., South Orange, N.J. Office: 233 Broadway, New York, N.Y.

SCHULER, Hans, sculptor; b. Morange, Lorraine, Germany, May 25, 1874; s. Otto and Amalia (Arndt) S.; brought to U.S., 1880; grad. Md. Inst. (sch. of art and design), 1894 (first medal); grad. Rinehart Sch. of Sculpture, 1898 (winning $4,000 scholarship); grad. Julian Acad., Paris, 1900 (all honors); m. Paula M. Schneider, of Baltimore, Jan. 15, 1905; children—Charlotte Agnes, Hans Carl. Awarded 3 medals Julian Acad.; Salon gold medal, 3d class, 1900; silver medal St. Louis Expn., 1904; medal Md. Inst.; etc. Principal works: "Ariadne," Walter's Gallery, Baltimore; "Memory," "Life is but the Turning of a Leaf," and many other tomb figures; portrait statutes of Samuel Smith, Pinkney White, etc.; portrait busts of Maj. Walter Reed, Dr. Osler; Buchanan memórial, Washington, D.C.; bust and medallion of Henry Walters, 1931; "Four Horsemen of the Apocalypse," Walters Gallery, Baltimore; statue "Freedom of Conscience," St. Mary's City, Md.; Md. Tercentenary medal and half dollar; monument to Johns Hopkins; heroic statue of Martin Luther, Baltimore. Dir. Maryland Inst., 1925. Mem. Nat. Sculpture Soc., Md. Inst., Charcoal Club. Mason. Home: 5 E. Lafayette Av., Baltimore, Md.

SCHULSON, Solomon, rabbi; b. Jerusalem, Palestine, Jan. 30, 1896; s. Isaac and Florence (Freiman) S.; came to U.S., Sept. 1915, naturalized, 1921; student Yeshivath Etz Chaim, Jerusalem, 1910-13, Yeshivath Torath Chaim, Jerusalem, 1913-15, Yeshivath Hebron, Palestine, 1927-29; m. Minnie Schnitzer, July 4, 1912; children—Hyman Abraham, Solly, Florence, Evelyn. Ordained rabbi, 1914; rabbi Congregation Agudas Achim, Kingston, N.Y., 1916-19, Congregation Ahavath Achim, Bridgeport, Conn., 1919-34, Congregation Adas Kodesch, Wilmington, Del., since 1934. Pres. Zionist Dist., Wilmington, since 1934; dir. Mizrachi Zionist Orgn. of America. Mem. United Palestine Appeal, Union of Orthodox Jewish Congregations of America. Mason (Temple Lodge 127, Bridgeport, Conn.), Achvoh (Jerusalem). Address: 2315 Franklin St., Wilmington, Del.

SCHULTZ, John Richie, coll. prof.; b. Canton, Mo., Dec. 12, 1884; s. John Christian and Laura (Piner) S.; A.B., Culver-Stockton College, Canton, 1905; M.A., Yale, 1909, Ph.D., 1917; studied U. of Chicago, summer 1906, British Mus., summers 1914, 23, Huntington Library, 1933; m. Dora Nelson, Canton, Aug. 8, 1917; children—James Richie, Nelson (dec.), Laurana. Prin. high sch., Canton, 1905-08; head of English dept., E. St. Louis High Sch., 1909-11; instr. English, Yale, 1912-17; prof. of English literature Allegheny Coll., Meadville, Pa., since 1917, dean of men since 1930. Member Meadville Civil Service Commission. Mem. Nat. Assn. Deans and Advisers of Men, American Dialect Soc., Alpha Sigma Phi, Acacia, Phi Beta Kappa, Pi Delta Epsilon. Republican. Methodist. Clubs: Round Table, University. Editor: (with J. M. Berdan and H. E. Joyce) Modern Essays, 1915. Unpublished Letters of Bayard Taylor, 1937. Contbr. to professional jours. Home: 380 N. Main St., Meadville, Pa.

SCHULTZ, William Clyde, physician; b. Jerseytown, Pa., July 6, 1869; s. David A. and Sarah (Johnson) S.; student Bloomsburg (Pa.) Teachers Coll., 1898-90; M.D., Jefferson Med. Coll., Phila., 1895; m. Cora Elsie Hockenbery, 1899; 1 son, William Clyde. Began as public school teacher; physician in chief, Pa. State Chest Clinic, Waynesboro, Pa., since 1919; chief of staff, Waynesboro (Pa.) Hosp., since 1936. Fellow, A.M.A.; mem. Franklin Co. Med. Soc. (past pres), Pa. State Med. Soc., Cumberland Valley Med. Assn., Pa. Pub. Health Assn. Democrat. Methodist. Mason (K.T.). Address: 114 W. Main St., Waynesboro, Pa.

SCHULZ, Leo, musician; b. Posen, Poland, Mar. 28, 1865; s. Clemens S.; Real Gymnasum, Posen, 1872-80; studied Royal Academy High Sch. of Music, Berlin; m. Ida Bartsch, Apr. 12, 1885 (died 1935); m. 2d, Johanna Beetz, March 30, 1937. Traveled through Germany as a "child wonder," giving concerts, 1870-73; resumed concert work, 1876; became soloist and 1st 'cellist, Philharmonic Orchestra, Berlin, 1885; soloist and 'cellist, Gewandhaus Orchestra, Leipzig, 1886-89; soloist Boston Symphony Orchestra and prof. N.E. Conservatory, 1889-98; soloist and 1st 'cellist New York Philharmonic Soc., 1890-1906; prof. and conductor Nat. Conservatory Orchestra; soloist and 1st 'cellist of the New York Symphony Orchestra; soloist Philharmonic Soc., New York; now retired; pres. N.Y. Tonkuenstler Soc. Prof. music, Yale. Composer of many 'cello compositions, songs, string quartettes, overtures for orchestra, cantata for chorus and orchestra, performed in pub., but not published; 2 books, 'Cello Album, and 2 books, 'Cello Classics, published in Leipzig; also 2 books, 'Cello Compositions; for 'cello and piano—3 Polish character pieces, Butterflies, Concert Study; Theme and Variations for 4 'cellos; Amerindian Fantasy Variations for 'cello and orchestra. Retired, 1929, and pensioned by N.Y. Philharmonic Symphony Soc. after 30 yrs'. service. Author: Memories—Sixty Years in the Realm of Music. Home: Woodcliff Lake, N.J.

SCHUMAKER, Albert Jesse Ringer, educator; b. Big Rock, Ill., Nov. 23, 1882; s. Rev. Lebbeus James and Emilie Jane (Coulter) S.; B.A., Marietta (O.) Coll., 1905, M.A., 1907; B.D., Hartford Theol. Sem., 1908; studied univs. of Leipzig and Berlin, 1908-10; m. C. Agnes Donahue, Jan. 25, 1919. Prof. psychol. and edn., Grove City (Pa.) Coll., 1910-11; pastor First Ch., Coraopolis, Pa., 1912-14; ordained Bapt. ministry, 1913; asst. editor Am. Sunday Sch. Union, 1914-18; again pastor First Ch., Coraopolis, 1919; dir. religious edn., Pittsburgh, 1920-29; mgr. N.E. br. Am. Bapt. Publication Soc., Boston, 1930; dir. of leadership education, Am. Bapt. Soc., Phila., since Nov. 1, 1930; sec. Leadership Training Pub. Assn. Mem. N.E.A., Phi Beta Kappa. Home: Park Towers. Office: 1701 Chestnut St., Philadelphia, Pa.

SCHUMANN, Edward Armin, surgeon; b. Washington, D.C., July 9, 1879; s. Francis and Augusta (Jung) S.; A.B., Central High Sch., Phila., 1897; M.D., U. of Pa., 1901; m. Hazel Prince, June 8, 1910; children—Edward Armin, Francis, Robert. Practiced in Phila. since 1901, limiting to obstetrics and gynecology; interne Phila. Gen. Hosp., 1901-03; surgeon Gynecean Hosp., 1906-10; gynecologist Frankford Hosp. since 1916; gynecologist and obstetrician Phila. Gen. Hosp. since 1916; obstetrician Chestnut Hill Hosp. since 1919; lecturer obstetrics Jifferson Med. Coll., 1916-24; surgeon-in-chief Kensington Hosp. for Women since 1931; prof. obstetrics, U. of Pa., since 1935; dir. Pa. Wire Glass Co. Served as lt. comdr. U.S. Naval R.C., A.E.F., World War. Fellow Am. Coll. Surgeons, A.M.A.; mem. Am. Bd. Obstetrics and Gynecology (v.p.), Am. Gynecol. Soc., Coll. of Physicians in Phila., Delta Upsilon, Alpha Mu, Pi Omega. Republican. Clubs: University, Gynecological. Author: Ectopic Pregnancy, 1921; Gonorrhea in Women, 1928; Text Book of Obstetrics, 1936; also 5 chapters in Curtis' Obstetrics and Gynecology, 1933. Contbr. professional articles. Home: 15 Pelham Rd., Mt. Airy, Philadelphia. Office: 1814 Spruce St., Philadelphia, Pa.

SCHUMANN, John Joseph, Jr., pres. General Motors Acceptance Corpn.; b. New York City, Sept. 11, 1889; s. John Joseph and Caroline Mathilda (Fichtel) S.; grad. pub. schs., N.Y. City, 1903; attended Coll. City of N.Y., 1903, Cooper Union and New York U., 1903-08; m. Florence Ward Ford, Sept. 29, 1917; children—Caroline Fairchild, John Adams, Robert Ford, Ward Ford. Employed with N. W. Harris & Co., 1903-17; with War Loan Organization, 2d Fed. Res. Dist., as asst. exec. sec. and exec. sec. of distribution com. Liberty Loan Organization, 1917-19; with Gen. Motors Acceptance Corpn., 1919, as mgr. financial sales dept., elected v.p., 1920, dir., 1921, and pres., 1929; also chmn. bd. Gen. Exchange Insurance Corpn.; pres. and dir. Gen. Motors Acceptance Corpn. (Continental), Gen. Motors Acceptance Corpn. of Del., Gen. Motors Acceptance Corpn. of Ind., Gen. Motors Acceptance Corpn., S.A., Gen. Motors Acceptance Corpn., Mexico; dir. Gen. Motors Corpn., Gen. Exchange Corpn. of Del.; v.p. and dir. Gen. Motors Management Corpn. Protestant. Clubs: Upper Montclair Country, Montclair Golf, Knoll Associates, Metropolitan, The Recess (N.Y. City); The Recess (Detroit, Mich.); Beach, Country (Madison, Conn.). Home: 309 Upper Mountain Av., Upper Montclair, N.J. Office: 1175 Broadway, New York, N.Y.

SCHUSTER, George Lee; prof. agronomy and asst. dean, Sch. of Agr., U. of Del. Address: U. of Delaware, Newark, Del.

SCHUTT, Harold Smith, pres. C. H. Geist Co.; b. Milwaukee, Wis., Mar. 28, 1884; s. Herman and Isabelle (Smith) S.; ed. Milwaukee (Wis.) pub. schs.; m. Louise Porter, Aug. 4, 1908; children—Charles Porter, Harold Smith, Jr. Successively employee Milwaukee (Wis.) Gas Co.; chief clk. Beloit (Wis.) Electric Co.; commercial mgr. South Shore Gas & Electric Co., Hammond, Ind.; mgr. Chicago Heights (Ill.) Gas Co.; mgr. Michigan City (Ind.) Gas & Electric Co.; mgr. Wilmington (Del.) Gas Co., 1909-12; v.p. and mgr. C. H. Geist Co., Inc., Phila., Pa., 1912-39, dir. since 1938, pres. same at Wilmington, Del., since 1938; pres. Indianapolis (Ind.) Water Co.; pres. Phila. Suburban Water Co., Bryn Mawr, Pa.; pres. Am. Pipe and Constrn. Co., Amsterdam, N.Y.; pres. Indianapolis (Ind.) Water Works Securities Co.; executor and trustee Estate of Clarence H. Geist, Phila., since June 12, 1938; dir. and mem. exec. com. United Gas Improvement Co., Phila.; dir. and mem. Finance Com., Continental Am. Life Ins. Co.; pres. and dir. Dept. of Pub. Safety, Wilmington, Del., since 1936; dir. Boy Scouts of America; dir. Del. Safety Council; dir. Del. Chapter of Am. Red Cross, Wilmington. Mem. Chester Co. Guernsey Cattle Club (v.p. since 1939), Am. Guernsey Cattle Club, Del. Steeplechase and Race Assn. (dir.). Clubs: Wilmington, Delaware Turf (v.p.), Wilmington Country, Vicmead Hunt (Wilmington, Del.); Racquet, Union League, Art, Mid-day (all Phila.); Seaview Golf, Absecon, N.J. (pres. since 1938); Boca Raton, Boca Raton, Fla. (pres. and dir. since 1938). Home: Greenville, Del. Office: 904 Delaware Trust Bldg., Wilmington, Del.; 2007 Fidelity Phila. Trust Bldg., Philadelphia, Pa.

SCHUYLER, Elmer Lincoln, newspaper editor; b. Orangeville, Pa., May 2, 1863; s. William and Mary (Fisher) S.; ed. public schools, 1869-77, and Bellevue Hosp. Med. Coll., 1891-93; m. Edith Bevier, June 30, 1897; children—George Bevier, William Willard (deceased), Margaret Kirk. Began as printer's apprentice, Milton (Pa.) Economist, 1882; typesetter on Grit, Williamsport, 1885-88, reporter, 1888-89, city editor, 1889-91; medical studies, 1891-93 (depression of 1893 caused him to return to newspaper work); mng. editor Williamsport Evening News, 1894-98, and 1900-09; city Editor Grit, 1898-1900; city editor Harrisburg Telegraph, 1909-11; city desk Williamsport Gazette and Bulletin, 1911, editor since July 15, 1911. Mem. bd. dirs. Williamsport Y.M.C.A.; mem. advisory bd. Salvation Army. Republican. Baptist (hon. life deacon). Rotarian of Williamsport. Home: 723 Louisa St. Office: Sun-Gazette Co., Williamsport, Pa.

SCHUYLER, William Hilliard, prof. chemistry; b. Milton, Pa., Sept. 6, 1890; B.S. in Chem. Engring., Bucknell U., 1915; grad. study, Columbia U., 1918; M.S. in Chemistry, U. of Va., 1923; m. Mary Arbutus Harner, Oct. 30, 1920; children—Harold Harner, Charles Marion, William Hilliard. Asst. prof. chemistry, Bucknell U., 1915-18, asst. prof. chem. engring., 1918-21; research, U. of Va., 1921-23; asst. prof. of chemistry, Bucknell Univ., Lewisburg, Pa., 1923-33; head of dept. of chemistry, Bucknell U. Jr. Coll., Wilkes-Barre, Pa., since 1933. Served as sergt. C.W.S., U.S.A., 1918. Fellow A.A.A.S., Am. Inst. of Chemists; mem. Am. Chem. Soc., Am. Assn. Univ. Profs., Luzerne Co. Chem. Soc. (pres.), Alpha Chi Sigma, Sigma Phi Epsilon. Republican. Baptist. Mason (32°). Home: 12 Mallery Place, Wilkes-Barre, Pa.

SCHWAB, Charles M., steel mfr.; b. Williamsburg, Pa., Feb. 18, 1862; childhood from 5th year at Loretto, Pa.; s. John A. and Pauline (Farabaugh) S.; ed. village sch. and St. Francis Coll.; hon. Dr. Engring., Lehigh, 1914, Stevens Inst. Tech., 1921; LL.D., Lincoln Memorial U., 1917, St. Francis Coll., Loretto, Pa., 1923, Franklin and Marshall Coll., 1924, Juniata Coll., 1926; D.C.S., New York U., 1918; Sc.D., Univ. of Pa., 1927; m. Emma Eurana Dinkey, of Loretto, Pa., 1883. As a boy drove stage from Loretto to Cresson, Pa., 5 miles; entered service of Carnegie Co. as stakedriver in engring. corps of Edgar Thompson Steel Works, serving as chf. engr. and asst. mgr., 1881-87; supt. Homestead Steel Works, 1887-89; gen. supt. Edgar Thompson Steel Works, 1889-97, Homestead Works, 1892-97; pres. Carnegie Steel Co., Ltd., 1897-1901; pres. U.S. Steel Corpn., 1901-03; now chmn. bd. Bethlehem Steel Corpn., Bethlehem Steel Co.; dir. Metropolitan Life Ins. Co. Director general shipbuilding, U.S. Shipping Bd. Emergency Fleet Corpn., Apr.-Dec. 1918. Pres. Am. Iron & Steel Inst., 1926-32, chmn., 1932-34. Awarded Melchett medal (British) "for distinguished service in industry," 1932. Home: 21 Riverside Drive, New York; also Bethlehem, Pa.; and (summer) Loretto, Pa. Office: 25 Broadway, New York, N.Y.

SCHWACHA, George, Jr., artist; b. Newark, N.J., Oct. 2, 1908; s. George and Bertha (Poppele) S.; ed. pub. sch. and Irvington High Sch., 1924-27, Art Students League of N.Y. City; m. Dorothy Mulford, Sept. 5, 1932; 1 dau., Barbara Gail. Has followed profession as artist since 1918; exhibited and received awards as follows: First hon. mention, N.J. State Exhibition, 1935, hon. mention for small canvasses, same, 1936, 1st hon. mention, N.J. Gallery, 1936, hon. mention, Municipal Exhbn., Irvington, 1936, hon. mention, New Haven Paint & Clay Club, 1937, 2d award, Art Centre of the Oranges, 1937, 1st medal of award also spl. hon. mention, N.J. State Exhbn., 1937, John I. H. Downes Prize $100 for best landscape, New Haven Paint & Clay Club, 1939, 1st award, N.J. Gallery, 1939 ("Oranges" Week). Represented N.J. National Exhbn., 1938. Home: 641 Lincoln Av., Orange, N.J.

SCHWARTZ, Edwin Gehman, clothing manufacturer; b. Vera Cruz, Pa., Apr. 1, 1874; s. Francis and Susanna (Gehman) S.; student Allentown pub. schs., 1888-90, Dorney's Bus. Coll., Allentown, Pa., 1891-92; m. Clara Hawk, Aug. 31, 1897; children—Dalton Francis, Harriet Susan (wife of Dr. Gerald S. Backenstoe). Began as clothing manufacturer, 1894; partner F. Schwartz & Son, Allentown, Pa., clothing mfrs., since 1894; pres. Pine Lumber Co., New Bern, N.C., 1920-38; dir. Merchants Nat. Bank, Allentown, Pa., Allentown Paint Mfg. Co. Republican. Evangelical Congregationalist. Clubs: Rotary, Brookside Country (Allentown, Pa.). Home: 37 N. 17th St. Office: 1013-21 Linden St., Allentown, Pa.

SCHWARTZ, Joseph Benjamin, lawyer; b. Hungary, Feb. 28, 1904; s. Louis and Margaret (Klein) S.; LL.B., N.J. Law Sch., Newark, N.J., 1926; m. Belle Goldberger, June 9, 1929; children—Leonard Samuel, Barbara Ann. Admitted to N.J. bar, 1927; began practice with David T. Wilentz, Perth Amboy, N.J., 1927; asso. with George L. Burton, South River, N.J., 1928-31; partner firm Smith and Schwartz, Perth Amboy, N.J., 1931-37; in pvt. practice at Perth Amboy since 1937. Sec. and v.p. Perth Amboy Y.M.H.A., 1931-37, dir. since 1932; trustee Congregation Beth Mordecai, Perth Amboy. Mem. Middlesex Co. Bar Assn., N.J. State Bar Assn., Am. Bar Assn., Perth Amboy Bar Assn., Lambda Alpha Phi. Democrat. Jewish religion. Home: 103 Lewis St. Office: Perth Amboy National Bank Bldg., Perth Amboy, N.J.

SCHWARTZ, Walter Marshall, pres. Proctor & Schwartz, Inc.; b. Phila., Pa., June 22, 1877; s. Charles Wheeler and Sarah (Preston) S.; student Germantown Acad., Phila., 1888-94, Phillips Acad., Andover, Mass., 1894-96; m. Lillian O. Hamilton, Apr. 30, 1904; children—Walter Marshall, Olivia Phillips, Phillips Kay, Lillian Hamilton. Served apprenticeship in machine shop, Proctor and Schwartz, Inc. (formerly Phila. Textile Machinery Co.), Phila., later became salesman, pres. since 1921; pres. Proctor Electric Co., Phila., 1932-39, chmn. of bd., since 1939; dir. Am. Pulley Co., First Nat. Bank of Philadelphia, Marco Company, Inc. (Philadelphia); mem. Pa. advisory bd. Am. Mutual Liability Ins. Co., Boston, Mass., since 1934; mem. bd. of mgrs. of Saving Fund Soc. of Germantown, Phila., since 1926. Served as private, 3d Pa. Inf., U.S. Volunteers, during Spanish-Am. War; as lt. col., U.S. Army, during World War. Republican. Episcopalian. Clubs: Racquet, Sunnybrook Golf (mem. bd. of govs.; Phila.); Pine Valley (N.J.) Golf (mem. bd. of govs.); Gibson Island (Gibson Island, Md.). Home: 502 Allen Lane, Mt. Airy. Office: 7th St. and Tabor Rd., Philadelphia, Pa.

SCHWARZ, Berthold Theodore Dominic, M.D.; b. Jersey City, N.J., Aug. 21, 1899; s. Dr. Wladyslaw Josef Alfons and Virginia Hedwig (von Tobolewska) S.; student St. Dominic Acad., Jersey City, 1906-14, Wm. L. Dickinson High Sch., Jersey City, 1914-1918, St. John's Coll. of Fordham U. (pre-med.), 1918-20; M.D., Univ. & Bellevue Hosp. Med. Coll., New York U., 1924; m. Thyra Ericson, Jan. 1, 1924; children—Berthold Eric, Eric Berthold, Virginia Karen. Summer playground instructor, Jersey City Public Schools, 1918-23; interneship at New York Nursery and Child's Hospital and Jersey City Hospital, 1923-25; began practice of medicine, 1924; mem. staff Medical Center of Jersey City, Margaret Hague Maternity Hosp., Greenville Hosp. and Fairmount Hosp.; asst. med. dir. Bankers Nat. Life Ins. Co., 1928-30, med. dir. since 1930; v.p. Goodwill Industries of N.J., Inc. Served as private Inf., S.A.T.C., Fordham U. Awarded Gen. Haller's Mil. Cross—Polish Army Vet. of America. Judge District Board of Elections, 1921-24. Trustee Soc. for Relief of Widows & Orphans of Med. Men of N.J.; dir. Community Welfare Chest of Jersey City; past chmn. N.J. Dist. Vocational Guidance Com. Fellow Acad. of Medicine of Northern N.J., A.M.A.; mem. American Med. Editors and Authors Association, Hudson County Med. Soc. (past sec.), Am. Pub. Health Assn., Assn. Life Ins. Med. Dirs. of America, Jersey City Med. Soc. (v.p.), American Legion (past post adj. Mason Post; del. to 1st N.J. conv.), Pi Beta Phi (past scribe), Omega Upsilon Phi; mem. med. sect. Am. Life Conv. Catholic. Clubs: Kiwanis of Jersey City (chmn. N.J. Dist. Edn. Com.); Lake Mohawk Golf, Lake Mohawk Country (Sparta, N.J.). Dir. Weekly Vocational Guidance Radio Programs, Station WAAT, 2½ yrs. Home: 35 Godfrey Road, Montclair, N.J. Office: 26 Park St., Montclair, N.J.; and 2787 Hudson Boul., Jersey City, N.J.

SCHWARZ, Lawrence Timothy, prof. economics; b. Brooklyn, N.Y., Oct. 6, 1907; s. Jacob and Katherine (Mennig) S.; A.B., Columbia Coll., 1930; A.M., Columbia U., 1931; grad. study, Columbia U., 1931-32; unmarried. Engaged in econ. research with Prof. H. Parker Willis of Columbia U., 1932-37; prof. econs. and chmn. dept. econs., Seton Hill Coll, Greensburg, Pa., since 1937. Fellow Royal Econ. Soc. Mem. Am. Econ. Assn., Am. Statis. Assn., Delta Sigma Rho. Republican. Roman Catholic. Club: Columbia University (New York). Address: Seton Hill College, Greensburg, Pa.; (summer) 6252 60th Rd., Maspeth, L.I., N.Y.

SCHWARZ, William Tefft, artist; b. Syracuse, N.Y., July 27, 1888; s. Adolph H. and Mary Cornela (Tefft) S.; Syracuse U., 1909; art edn., Colarossi and Julian acads., France, also in Spain; pupil of Charles Hawthorne, Provincetown, Mass.; m. Mabel Elizabeth Lowther, June 11, 1913; children—Elizabeth Ann, Mary Tefft, Horace Wilkinson, Ada-May, Margaret Fairfield. Served as capt. Sanitary Corps, U.S.A., 1917-19; apptd. one of official artists of A.E.F.; head of art dept. of History of Surgery; assigned to take life masks of members of Peace Conf. Represented in official war drawings, Smithsonian Instn. and Army Med. Mus.; murals in Utica (N.Y.) Hotel, Pontiac Hotel, at Oswego, N.Y., Bancroft Hotel, at Worcester, Mass., Fulton National Bank, at Lancaster, Pa., Hotel Dennis, Atlantic City, N.J.; mural painting for British War Memorial, Paris; mural for Girl Scout headquarters (used also as internat. poster); mural for Gen. Price Hall, Valley Forge, Pa.; murals for Onondaga County Savings Bank, Syracuse, N.Y.; mural for Episcopal Acad., Overbrook, Pa.; murals for Apollo Theatre, Atlantic City, N.J.; 7 murals in Internat. Arcadia Restaurant, Philadelphia; murals for Manabar, Hotel Philadelphian and Shoemaker Sch.—all of Philadelphia; murals New Engineers Club, New York; murals Quaker Home, West Chester, Pa.; four murals for Petroleum Industry Bldg., New York World's Fair. Mem. Mil. Order Foreign Wars, Phi Gamma Delta. Republican. Episcopalian. Illustrator for numerous books, also for leading mags. Home: 343 Sycamore Ave., Merion, Pa.

SCHWARZE, William Nathaniel, clergyman, educator; b. Chaska, Minn., Jan. 2, 1875; s. Ernst N. and Wilhelmine (Moench) S.; grad high sch., Elizabeth, N.J., 1890; B.A., Moravian Coll., Bethlehem, Pa., 1894, M.A., 1904, Ph.D., 1910, B.D., Moravian Theol. Sem., 1896, D.D., 1928; m. Ethel Greider, July 19, 1905; children—Margaret, Leonore, Herbert Edwin. Ordained ministry Moravian Ch., 1896; pastor Bruederfeld and Bruederheim, Alberta Can., 1896-1900; dir. Buxton Grove Theol. Sem. for native ministers, St. John's, Antigua, B.W.I., 1900-03; prof. of philosophy and church history, Moravian Coll., since 1903; pres. Moravian Coll. and Theol. Sem. since 1928; archivist Moravian Ch., Northern Province of N.A., since 1905. Pres. Bd. Trustees Bethlehem Pub. Library; mem. Sch. Bd., Bethlehem, 1911-21; trustee Linden Hall Sem., Lititz, Pa. Mem. Am. Ch. History Soc. (ex-pres.), Moravian Hist. Soc. (pres.), Am. Philos. Soc. Republican. Clubs: Torch of Lehigh Valley, Rotary (hon.). Author: History of the Moravian College and Theological Seminary, 1910; John Huss, the Martyr of Bohemia, 1915. Translator: History of the North American Indians (by David Zeisberger), 1910; also many other manuscripts. Contbr. to "The Outline of Christianity," also of numerous articles in mags. Home: 1206 Main St., Bethlehem, Pa.

SCHWED, Irving, lawyer; b. Somerville, N.J., Nov. 4, 1890; s. Charles and Caroline (Hellman) S.; student Somerville (N.J.) High Sch., 1904-08; Ph.B., Lafayette Coll., Easton, Pa., 1912; LL.B., Columbia U. Law Sch., 1915; unmarried. Law clk. with McCarter & English, 1915; admitted to N.J. bar, 1915; atty. with McCarter & English, Newark, N.J., 1915-17; mem. firm Beekman, Schwed & Beekman, Somerville, N.J., since 1925; dir. Second Nat. Bank of Somerville. Served as pvt., Q.M.C., U.S. Army, Fort H. G. Wright, N.Y., 1917-19, hon. disch. as sergt. 1st class, 1919; 1st lt., U.S. Res., 1919-24. Clk. Somerset Co. (N.J.) Grand Jury, 1926-29. Mem. U.S. Bar Assn., N.J. State Bar Assn., Somerset Co. Bar Assn. Clubs: Bachelor, Exchange, Fireside, Raritan Valley Country (Somerville, N.J.); Lafayette (New York City). Home: 117 West End Av. Office: 27 N. Bridge St., Somerville, N.J.

SCHWEINITZ, George Edmund de, M.D.; b. Phila., Oct. 26, 1858; s. Rt. Rev. Edmund and Lydia de S.; A.B., A.M., Moravian, 1876; M.D., U. of Pa., 1881, LL.D., 1914; L.H.D., Moravian College; D.Sc., U. Mich., 1922, Harvard Univ., 1927. Prof. ophthalmology, U. of Pa. Grad Sch. of Medicine, 1902-24, now emeritus; cons. ophthalmologist Phila. Hosp. Maj. Med. R.C., 1917; active service, Sept. 29, 1917-Apr. 1, 1919; lt. col. M.C., U.S.A., in France, Oct. 1917-Mar. 1918; on duty in U.S. as officer in charge of and consultant in ophthalmology, Surgeon Gen.'s Office; now brig. gen. Aux. Med. Res.; mem. editorial bd. for med. and surg. history of the war. Vice-pres. Pa. Inst. for Instrn. of Blind; trustee U. of Pa. Mem. Phila Co. Med., Neurol. and Pathol. socs., A.M.A. (pres. 1922-23), Am. Ophthal. Soc. (pres. 1916), Am. Philos. Soc., Acad. Natural Sciences, Ophthalmol. Soc. United Kingdom, Société Française d'Ophtalmologie, Société Belge d'Ophtalmologie; ex-pres. Coll. Physicians, Phila.; hon. fellow N.Y. Acad. Medicine; hon. mem. Royal Soc. Medicine, London (sect. ophthalmology), Hungarian and Egyptian Ophthalmology Socs., U. of Pa. Club (New York). Author: Diseases of the Eye (10th edit.), 1924; Diseases of the Eye, Ear, Nose and Throat (with Dr. Randall), 1899; Toxic Amblyopias, 1896 (Alvarenga prize essay). Am. editor Haab's Ophthalmoscopy and External Diseases of the Eye and Operative Ophthalmology; Pulsating Exophthalmos (with Dr. Holloway); Ophthalmic Year Book (with Dr. Jackson), 1905-09. Contbr. numerous articles and monographs on ophthal. and neurol. subjects. Bowman lecturer, London, 1923. Awarded plaque from Soc. Française d'Ophtalmologie, 1924; Howe prize medal in ophthalmology, 1927; Huguenot Cross, 1928; Leslie Dana medal for prevention of blindness, 1930. Address: 1705 Walnut Street, Philadelphia, Pa.

SCHWEINITZ, Karl de, social worker, author; b. Northfield, Minn., Nov. 26, 1887; s. Paul and Mary Catherine (Daniel) de S.; A.B., Moravian Coll., 1906; A.B., U. of Pa., 1907; L.H.D., Moravian College, 1932; m. Jessie Logan Dickson, Oct. 4, 1911; children—Mary, Karl; m. 2d, Elizabeth McCord, Benton Harbor, Michigan, August 29, 1937. Newspaper reporter, later in publicity work, 1907-11; sec. Pa. Tuberculosis Soc., 1911-13; mem. exec. staff New York Charity Orgn. Soc., 1913; gen. sec. Family Soc. of Philadelphia, 1918-30; exec. sec. Community Council of Phila., 1930-36; sec. Phila. Com. for Unemployment Relief, 1930-32; mem. Phila. County Relief Bd., 1932-36; William T. Carter prof., U. of Pa., 1933-37; exec. dir. State Emergency Relief Bd., 1936-37; sec. of Pub. Assistance of Pa., 1937; dir. Pa. Sch. of Social Work, U. of Pa., 1933-36, and since 1938. Democrat. Moravian. Clubs: Meridian, Lenape. Author: The Art of Helping People Out of Trouble, 1924; Growing Up, 1928. Home: 2406 Pine St., Philadelphia. Office: 311 S. Juniper St., Philadelphia, Pa.

SCHWEITZER, Paul Henry, coll. prof.; b. Miskolc, Hungary, May 20, 1893; s. Henry and Hermin (Robitsek) S.; M.E., Royal Hungarian Tech. U., Budapest, Hungary, 1917; Dr. Eng., Saeschische Technische Hochschule, Dresden, Germany, 1929; came to U.S., 1920, naturalized, 1925; m. Frieda Mayer, Dec. 15, 1930. Asst. master mechanic and Diesel engine designer, De La Vergne Machine Co., New York, N.Y., 1920-22; tool designer, Oakland Motor Car Co., Pontiac, Mich., 1922-23; asst. prof., Pa. State Coll., 1923-27, asso. prof., 1927-36, prof. of engrng. research since 1936; in charge of Diesel engine lab. since 1923. Served as 1st lt., Arty. Flying Corps., Austro-Hungarian Army, 1914-18; lt. commdr., U.S.N.R., since 1937. Fellow A.A.A.S.; mem. Am. Soc. M.E., Soc. of Automotive Engrs., Soc. of Rheology, U.S. Naval Inst., Sigma Xi. Author of numerous tech. bulletins, papers and articles pub. in tech. and scientific jours. in America, Eng., and Germany. Home: 617 W. Park Av. Office: Pa. State College, State College, Pa.

SCHWEIZER, J. Otto, sculptor; b. Zürich, Switzerland, Mar. 27, 1863; s. Jacob and Carolina Elisabeth (Labhardt) S.; ed. Art Sch., Zürich; Royal Acad., Dresden; under Dr. J. Schilling, Dresden, and at Florence, Italy; m. Bertha Maria Meymen, 1902; 1 son, Antonin. Came to U.S., 1894, naturalized citizen, 1904. Exhibited at Nat. Acad. Design, New York; Nat. Sculpture Soc., New York; Acad. Fine Arts, Phila.; etc. Principal works: statue, General Peter Muhlenberg, Rayburn Plaza, North Side City Hall, Philadelphia; "Angel of Peace," Pittsburgh; statues of Abraham Lincoln, Gen. M. Gregg, Gens. Pleasanton, Humphrey, Geary, Hays, Gettysburg, Pa.; Pa. State memorial and Gen. Wells, Vermont memorial, Gettysburg, Pa.; Molly Pitcher, Carlisle, Pa. (all state memorials); statue of Abraham Lincoln, and portrait medallions of Gen. U. S. Grant and 7 other gens., Lincoln Memorial Room, Union League, Phila.; equestrian statue, Frederick W. von Steuben, Sherman Boul., Milwaukee, Wis.; Steuben statues, Valley Forge, Pa., and Utica, N.Y.; Melchior Muhlenberg, bronze groups, Germantown, Pa.; James J. Davis group, Mooseheart, Ill.; statues of Adj. Gen. Stewart and Senator G. Oliver, Capitol Bldg., Harrisburg, Pa.; statue of James B. Nicholson, Phila., Senator Clay, Marietta, Ga.; "Mother of the South," Little Rock, Ark.; Colored Soldiers State Memorial Fairmont Park, Phila., Pa.; East Germantown war memorial; Central High School war memorial; E. M. Schell memorial; Preston Retreat; Apotheosis of Emanuel Swedenborg—all in Phila.; also numerous ideal groups, portrait medallions, busts, medals, plaquettes, etc. Mem. Nat. Sculpture Soc., Am. Fed. of Art. Mason (32°). Home-Studio: 2215 W. Venango St., Philadelphia, Pa.

SCHWENK, Elwood, clergyman; b. Red Hill, Pa., Oct. 28, 1894; s. John G. and Sarah Ann (Keck) S.; A.B., Muhlenberg Coll., 1917; grad. Luth. Theol. Sem., Phila., 1921; student U. of Pa. Grad. Sch., 1919-20, Luth. Theol. Sem. Grad. Sch., 1933-36; m. Stella Tabor, Mar. 27, 1918; children—Ruth Marie,

John, Tabor (dec.), Elizabeth Ann. Ordained to ministry Luth. Ch. and pastor, Kingston, Pa., 1921-26, Lansdale, Pa., 1927-29; pastor Trinity Luth. Ch., Lebanon, Pa. since 1929. Served in 317th F.H., U.S.A. with A.E.F., 1918-19, in St. Mihiel and Meuse-Argonne offensives. Mem. Lebanon Co. Bd. Pub. Assistance, 1938-39. Chaplain local post Am. Legion. Mem. and past pres. Lebanon Ministerial Assn. Played center on Muhlenberg Coll. football team, 1914-16, and 80th Div. team in France, 1918-19; certified football ofcl. since 1917; first pres. Football Officials Assn. of Northeastern Pa., 1925-26; mem. Football Officials Assn. of Central Pa. since 1929; mem. Pa. Interscholastic Athletic Assn. Lutheran. Home: 426 N. 5th St., Lebanon, Pa.

SCHWEP, Charles Franklin; v.p. Ingersoll-Rand Co.; chmn. bd. Mid City Trust Co. Home: Plainfield, N.J. Office: 11 Broadway, New York, N.Y.

SCHWINN, Jacob; mem. staff Ohio Valley Gen. Hosp. Address: 56 14th St., Wheeling, W.Va.

SCIOTTO, Bruce Albert, lawyer; b. Walstan, Jefferson Co., Pa., Aug. 8, 1899; s. Rosario and Anna Maria (Melemi) S.; student St. Vincent Coll., Latrobe, Pa., 1914-17, Duquesne U., Pittsburgh, 1919-20; LL.B., Dickinson Sch. of Law, Carlisle, Pa., 1923; m. Evelyn Rezzolla, Aug. 4, 1930; children—Evelyn Lucile, Bruce Albert, Charles Thomas. Admitted to Pa. bar, 1923; admitted to practice before Supreme Court of U.S., Circuit Court of Appeals of U.S., Federal Dist. Court of U.S., Pa. Supreme Court, Pa. Superior Court, Cambria County Court; atty. Italian Royal Consular Agency, Johnstown, Pa.; solicitor for Johnstown Chapter of Small Business Men's Assn.; special dep. atty. gen. of Pa., assigned to Pa. Liquor Control Bd. since Jan. 1937. Mem. Pa. Bar Assn. Catholic. K. of C., Elk. Home: 402 State St. Office: Johnstown Bank & Trust Co., Johnstown, Pa.

SCOFIELD, Carl Schurz, agriculturist; b. Bloomington, Minn., Feb. 5, 1875; s. John Darius and Carolyn Samantha (Damon) S.; B.S.A., U. of Minn., 1900; spl. course in chemistry of wheat, Conservatoire des Arts et Métiers, Paris, 1901; m. Emma Theresa Scott, Sept. 8, 1903 (she died April 18, 1935); children—Francis Collins, John Darius, Marcia Ann. With the United States Dept. of Agriculture since Mar. 1900; agriculturist in charge irrigation agriculture since 1905. Mem. Bot. Soc. Washington, Washington Acad. Sciences, Am. Assn. Geographers, Am. Geophysical Union (chmn. sect. hydrology 1933-35). Club: Cosmos. Author of various bulls. pub. by Bur. of Plant Industry, U.S. Dept. of Agr., also special reports and papers on quality of irrigation water. Home: Lanham, Md.

SCOON, Robert, philosophy; b. Geneva, N.Y., Sept. 21, 1886; s. Charles Kelsey and Caroline (Maxwell) S.; B.A., Hamilton Coll., 1907; apptd. Rhodes scholar from State of N.Y., 1907; B.A., Merton Coll. (Oxford U.), 1910; Ph.D., Columbia, 1916; m. Elizabeth Grier Hibben, Nov. 23, 1915; 1 son, John Grier Hibben. Instr. classics, Princeton, 1911-14; asst. prof. classics, Washington U., 1914-15; asst. prof. classics, Princeton, 1915-23, assoc. prof. philosophy, 1923-28, prof. since 1928, chmn. dept. of philosophy since Feb. 1934, Stuart prof. of philosophy since Jan. 1936. Served as 2d lt. inf., U.S.A., 1918. Mem. Am. Philos. Assn., Am. Assn. U. Profs., Chi Psi, Phi Beta Kappa. Republican. Presbyn. Clubs: Nassau (Princeton); Princeton (New York). Author: Greek Philosophy Before Plato, 1928. Compiler and Editor: Selections from Roman Historical Literature (with C. H. Jones and C. C. Mierow), 1915. Home: 19 Cleveland Lane, Princeton, N.J.

SCOTT, Campbell, industrial engr.; b. Louisville, Ky., Apr. 14, 1869; s. Preston Brown (M.D.) and Jane E. (Campbell) S.; ed. Episcopal High Sch. of Va. and Univ. Sch., Louisville; m. Nellie Mansfield Smith, Oct. 19, 1893; children—Eleanor Preston (Mrs. Reginald W. Cauchois), Preston Henry. Mgr. Edison Gen. Electric Co., Cincinnati, 1890-92; pres. Southern Engring. Co., Louisville, 1892-94; gen. mgr. C. & C. Electric Co., N.Y. City, 1897-1905; works mgr. Otis Elevator Co., 1905-16, and v.p. Militor Corpn.; now pres. Graphite Metallizing Corpn., New York. Commr. of Police, Yonkers, N.Y., 1905-06, also chmn. Joint Water Supply Commn.; mem. War Dept. Claims Bd. and chmn. Tech. Advisory Bd., War Dept., 1919-20 (advised in settlement of over $1,000,-000,000 in war claims). Mem. Am. Soc. Mech. Engrs., Soc. of Engrs. of Montclair. Republican. Episcopalian. Club: Montclair Golf. Home: 57 Union St., Montclair, N.J. Office: 15 Park Row, New York, N.Y.

SCOTT, Charles M.; chief surgeon St. Luke's Hosp. Address: 1710 Bland St., Bluefield, W. Va.

SCOTT, Edgar, investment broker; b. Am. Embassy, Paris, France, Jan. 11, 1899; s. Edgar and Mary Howard (Sturgis) S.; student Delancey Sch., Phila., Pa., 1908-11; grad. cum laude, Groton Sch., Groton, Mass., 1916; A.B., cum laude, Harvard, 1920; m. Helen Hope Montgomery, Sept. 20, 1923; children—Edgar, Robert Montgomery. Studied playwrighting; became a newspaper reporter in 1925; magazine work, Phila., 1926-27; became mem. N.Y. Stock Exchange, Feb. 1928; with partners formed Montgomery, Scott & Co., Phila., New York, and Chester, Pa., investment brokers, Jan. 1929, and since mem. firm; dir. Central Airport, Inc., Camden, N.J. Served in Am. Field Service, France, 1916, Norton-Harjes Ambulance Service, 1917, Am. Red Cross, 1917-18; student army training corps, Harvard, Fall 1918. Commr. Radnor Twp., Delaware Co., Pa., since 1934. Dir. Bryn Mawr (Pa.) Hosp.; gov. Phila. Stock Exchange. Mem. Pa. Economy League (chmn. membership com.), Phila. Assn. of Stock Exchange Firms (pres. 1938), Shakspere Soc. of Phila., Fly Club (Harvard). Republican. Unitarian. Clubs: Phila., Merion Cricket (Philadelphia); River, Brook (N.Y.C.). Home: Villa Nova, Pa. Office: 123 S. Broad St., Philadelphia, Pa.

SCOTT, Frank Dickey, clergyman; b. Waynesburg, Pa., Nov. 17, 1888; s. James A. and Melissa (Dickey) S.; A.B., Waynesburg Coll., 1910; A.B., Yale, 1914; B.D., Auburn Theol. Sem., 1915; A.M., Columbia U., 1916; (hon.), D.D., Waynesburg Coll., 1924; m. Jane Holland Hook, Sept. 22, 1915; children—Mary Ingraham, Katharine Emily. Instr. English and argumentation, Macalester Coll., St. Paul, Minn., 1910-12; ordained to ministry Presbyn. Ch., 1916; prof. sociology, Hangchow Christian Coll., China, 1916-20; pastor Arlington Heights Ch., Pittsburgh, Pa., 1920-22, Endeavor, Pa., 1922-26; pres. Presbyn. Grad. Sch. Religious Edn., Baltimore, 1926-27; pastor, Mauch Chunk, Pa., 1927-32; prof. Bible and coll. pastor, Beaver Coll., Jenkintown, Pa., since 1932; moderator Clarion Presbytery, 1925-26, Lehigh Presbytery, 1931-32. Served as pvt. to sergt. Pa. N.G., 1905-10; chaplain, 1st lt. inf., Pa. N.G., 1923, maj. since 1938. Mem. Nat. Assn. Bib. Instrs., Pa. Edn. Assn., Phi Sigma, Alpha Kappa Alpha (nat. v.p.). Republican. Presbyn. Mason (K.T.). Home: 218 Greenwood Av., Jenkintown, Pa.

SCOTT, Garfield, lawyer; b. Phila., Pa., Sept. 25, 1881; s. William Henry and Martha Jane (Parr) S.; student Germantown (Pa.) Acad., 1889-99; A.B., Princeton U., 1903; LL.B., U. of Pa., 1906; m. Grace Louise Nevin, Aug. 13, 1925; children—Hugh Nevin, Donald Allison. Admitted to Pa. bar, 1906, and in general practice at Phila., 1906-14; legal dept. United Gas Improvement Co., Phila., 1914, gen. counsel since 1922; v.p. and dir. Conn. Ry. & Lighting Co.; dir. Conn. Gas & Coke Securities Co. Republican. Presbyterian. Clubs: Union League, Midday, Merion Cricket, Phila. Country (Phila.). Home: Gate Lane, Mt. Airy. Office: 1401 Arch St., Philadelphia, Pa.

SCOTT, George Stanley, chem. engr.; b. Long Valley, N.J., June 29, 1894; s. Alvin Arthur and Medea (Gillen) S.; grad. DeWitt Clinton High Sch., New York, 1915; student Brooklyn Poly. Inst., 1915-16; Chem.E., Lehigh U., 1920; grad. student Carnegie Inst. of Tech., 1936; m. Irene Branning, June 26, 1926. Asst. investigator N.J. Zinc Co., 1918-20; jr. chemist U.S. Bureau of Mines, Pittsburgh, 1920-22; research chemist Hudson Coal Co., Scranton, Pa., 1923-25; engr. in charge exptl. briquet plant of C. W. Sewell, Bay City, Mich., 1925; chief chemist Koppers-Rheotaveur Co., Wilkes-Barre, Pa., 1926-29; asst. in charge and mem. bd. dirs. Frost Research Lab., Inc., Norristown, Pa., 1929-31; asst. dir. dept. of scientific research, Anthracite Inst., State College, Pa., 1931-34; jr. chemist and asst. chemist U.S. Bureau of Mines since 1936. Mem. Am. Chem. Soc., Am. Inst. Mining and Metall. Engrs., Tau Beta Pi, Sigma Xi. Home: 25 Wilkins Road. Office: 4800 Forbes St., Pittsburgh, Pa.

SCOTT, Henri (Guest), basso; b. Coatesville, Pa., Apr. 8, 1876; s. John Wallace and Mary (Roney) S.; ed. pub. schs., Phila.; Mus.D., Valparaiso U., 1925; m. Alice Macmichael Jefferson, Dec. 30, 1902; children—Randolph J., Henriette G., Eunice T., Janet C., J. P. Jefferson. Intended by father for business career, but became concert singer, appearing in many cities in oratorio; sang in concert tour with Caruso, 1908; engaged by Oscar Hammerstein for 5 yrs., 1909. Leading basso Manhattan Opera Co., New York, season 1909-10, Adriano Theatre, Rome, Italy, 1910-11, Chicago Grand Opera Co., 1911-14, Met. Opera Co., New York, 1915-19. Made operatic debut as Ramfis, in "Aida." Protestant. Mason. Clubs: Art Alliance, Pa. Barge (Phila.); Bohemian (San Francisco). Home: The Courtland, 43d and Chestnut St., Philadelphia, Pa.

SCOTT, Henry D(ickerson), steel mfr.; b. Bridgeport, O., Feb. 26, 1893; s. Isaac MacBurney and Flora Belle (Dickerson) S.; student Hotchkiss Sch., Lakeville, Conn., 1907-10, Yale, 1910-14; m. Lillian Elizabeth Malone, 1919. Bookkeeper Buckeye Rolling Mill Co., Steubenville, O., 1914-15; accountant Wheeling Steel & Iron Co., 1915-17; supt. Wheeling Steel Coprn., 1919-26, asst. vice-pres., 1926-30, vice-pres. in charge operations since 1937; pres. Sharon (Pa.) Tube Co. since 1930. Entered O.T.C., 1917; commd. capt. field arty. U.S.A., 1918, with A.E.F., 1917-18. Decorated with Croix de Guerre (France). Mem. Am. Legion, Am. Iron and Steel Inst., Am. Petroleum Inst., Phi Beta Kappa, Psi Upsilon. Republican. Presbyterian. Clubs: Ft. Henry, Wheeling Country (Wheeling); Country (Youngstown); Yale (New York). Author: Iron and Steel in Wheeling, 1928. Home: 1359 National Rd. Office: Wheeling Steel Corpn., Wheeling, W.Va.

SCOTT, Herbert, clergyman; b. Athens, O., June 28, 1872; s. William Henry and Sarah (Felton) S.; B.Sc., Ohio State U., 1893; student Yale Div. Sch., 1895-97; D.D., Ohio Wesleyan U., 1909; m. Clara Esther Luse, Oct. 14, 1897; children—John Luse, Alford Herbert. Ordained ministry M.E. Ch., 1897; pastor, Alexandria, Ohio, 1897-99, North Ch., Columbus, 1899-1901, First Ch., Marietta, 1901-06, Spencer Chapel, Ironton, 1906-08; supt. Columbus Dist., 1908-12; pastor Trinity Ch., Portsmouth, Ohio, 1912-14, Grace Ch., Zanesville, Ohio, 1914-20, First Ch., Des Moines, Ia., 1920-26, First Ch., Salina, Kan., 1926-28, First Ch., Rochester, N.Y., 1928-35, Dormont Church, Pittsburgh, Pa., 1935-36, Mary S. Brown Memorial Church, Pittsburgh, Pa., since 1936. Mem. General Conference M.E. Ch., 1912, 20; mem. bd. mgrs. Methodist Brotherhood, 1908-12; mem. Freedmen's Aid Bd., 1910-20; mem. Book Com. M.E. Ch., 1912-20. Home: 4312 Saline St., Pittsburgh, Pa.

SCOTT, Hugh Briar, steel sales mgr.; b. Bridgeport, O., May 2, 1891; s. Isaac M. and Flora B. (Dickerson) S.; student Hotchkiss Sch., Lakeville, Conn., 1907-09; A.B., Yale U., 1913; m. Charlotte Thompson, June 2, 1920; children—Marjorie Thompson, Hugh MacBurney, Charlotte Everson. Asso. with Wheeling Sheet & Tin Plate Co., Wheeling, W.Va., 1913-15, successively storekeeper, shipping clk., asst. mgr. order dept., mgr. litho. sales, mgr. tinplate sales; asst. gen. mgr. sales; Wheeling Steel Corpn., Wheeling, W.Va., since 1930; vice-pres. and dir. Buckeye Rolling Mill Co., Wheeling, W.Va., since 1931; dir. Sharon Tube Co., Sharon, Pa.; dir. Nat. Bank of West Va., Wheeling, W.Va. Served as pvt. to 1st lt. F.A., U.S.A., 1917-19, with 26th Div. A.E.F. in all maj. campaigns and important engagements. Mem. Am. Iron & Steel Inst., Psi Upsilon. Republican. Presbyn. Clubs: Fort Henry, Country (Wheeling); Yale (New York). Home: 13 Oak Park. Office: Wheeling Steel Corpn., Wheeling, W.Va.

SCOTT, Isaac MacBurney, mfr.; b. Tuscarawas Co., O., Feb. 19, 1866; s. Dr. Wm. Briar and Mary (Boyd) S.; ed. pub. schs., Morristown, O.; m. Flora B. Dickerson, Jan. 1, 1890; children—Hugh Briar, Henry Dickerson, Arthur MacBurney. Began with Ætna Iron & Nail Co., Bridgeport, O., 1883; sec. Beaver Tin Plate Co., Lisbon, O., 1894-98; sec. Ætna Standard Iron & Steel Co., Bridgeport, O., 1898-1900; auditor Am. Sheet Steel Co., N.Y. City, 1900-03; sec. La Belle Iron Works, Steubenville, O., 1903-04, president, 1904-13; organized, 1913, Wheeling Sheet & Tin Plate Co., and built tin plate plant at Yorkville, O., merging with Wheeling Steel & Iron Co., 1914, and pres. latter, 1914-20; company merged, 1920, with La Belle Iron Works and Whitaker-Glessner Co., forming Wheeling Steel Corpn., of which was pres. until Oct. 31, 1930; chmn. bd. Sharon Tube Co., Scott Lumber Co., Nat. Bank of W.Va.; pres. Buckeye Rolling Mill Co.; trustee Follansbee Bros. Co. Republican. Presbyn. Clubs: Fort Henry (Wheeling); Duquesne (Pittsburgh); Ohio Soc. (New York). Home: Wheeling, W.Va.

SCOTT, James Edward, clergyman; b. Plymouth, Eng., Dec. 14, 1874; s. James and Emma (Brannon) S.; student Rutherford Coll., Newcastle-on-Tyne, Eng.; A.B., Grove City (Pa.) Coll., Ph.D.; D.D., W.Va. Wesleyan Coll.; m. Harriet Randall, 1896 (now dec.); children—Lawrence Albert, Reda Blanch; m. 2d, Wilhelmena Ortland, Apr. 5, 1934. Came to U.S., 1903, naturalized citizen, 1917. Ordained M.E. ministry, 1903; pastor successively Benwood, W.Va., St. Pauls Ch., Grafton, 1915-17, St. Andrews Ch., Parkersburg, 1917-22, First Ch., Moundsville, 1922-26; supt. Parkersburg Dist., M.E. Ch., 1926-31; pastor First Ch., Fairmont, 1931-35, Thomson Ch., Wheeling, since Oct. 1935. Trustee W.Va. Wesleyan Coll. Republican. Mason. Kiwanian. Clubs: Wheeling Country, Kiwanis. Home: 201 S. Broadway, Wheeling, W.Va.

SCOTT, James Newton, pres. South Penn Telephone Co.; b. Jefferson, Pa., Nov. 25, 1867; s. James and Mary (Spencer) S.; ed. common schools of Jefferson Twp., Greene Co., Pa.; m. Lizzie Baily, Feb. 14, 1895; children—Ralph B., Anna L. Cree, J. Paul. Road supervisor, Jefferson Twp., Pa., 1902-05, treas., 1903, sch. dir., 1905-10; pres. Greene Co. (Pa.) Telephone and Telegraph Co., Waynesburg, Pa., 1907-20; sch. dir., Cumberland Twp., Pa., 1915-28; v.p, First Nat. Bank of Carmichaels (Pa.) since 1923; pres. and gen. mgr., S. Penn Telephone Co., Waynesburg, Pa., since 1923; chmn. of Bd. of Greene Co. (Pa.) Commnrs., 1928-32; pres. and gen. mgr., S. Penn Telephone Co. of W.Va., Waynesburg, Pa., since 1932; dir. Muddy Creek Valley Cemetery Co. since 1920, Greene Co. Memorial Cemetery Co. since 1930. Treas. Greene Co. Crippled Children's Soc., 1929-35 (dir. since 1929); mem. bd. of govs., Greene Co. Memorial Hosp., since 1938; trustee, Waynesburg (Pa.) Coll., since 1938. Mem. Am. Red Cross (chmn., 1934-35), Chamber of Commerce (pres. since 1934). Democrat. Presbyterian (elder, Presbyn. Ch., Waynesburg, Pa.). East Franklin Grange. Club: Kiwanis (pres., 1932; Waynesburg, Pa.). Home: 304 W. High St. Office: 60 W. High St., Waynesburg, Pa.

SCOTT, John Calvin; prof. of physiology, hygiene and pharmacology, Temple Univ. Address: Temple University, Philadelphia, Pa.

SCOTT, Joseph Prestwich, veterinarian; b. Manchester, England, Dec. 12, 1890; s. Lawrence and Mary (Banks) S.; student Manchester Grammar Sch., 1905-07; B.S., Gymnase Scientifique, Lausanne, Suisse, 1910; D.V.M., Ohio State U., Columbus, O., 1914; student Univ. of Manchester, 1914-15; M.S., Kan. State Coll., Manhattan, Kan., 1924; student U. of Colo., Boulder, Colo., 1928-29; came to U.S., 1890, naturalized, 1918; m. Lois Mary Smith, 1918 (died 1935); children—Mary Rosanna, Lawrence William. Instr. in veterinary physiology, Vet. Coll., Cornell U., 1915-16; successively instr., asst. prof., asso. prof. and prof., vaccine dept. and dept. of pathology, Kan. State Coll., Manhattan, Kan., 1916-36; research asso. Vet. Sch. and Sch. of Animal Pathology, U. of Pa., since 1936; agt. U.S. Dept. Agr., Bureau of Animal Industry, since 1936. Mem. 1st Internat. Congress of Microbiology, Paris, 1930; mem. 12th Internat. Vet. Congress, London, 1930; reporter on anaerobic diseases, 12th Internat. Congress, New York, 1934; reporter on swine influenza and del. from Pa., 13th Internat. Vet. Congress, Zurich, 1938; reporter on blackleg, 3rd Internat. Congress of Microbiology, New York, 1939. Served as pvt. in Vet. Corps, U.S. Army, 1918. Fellow A.A.A.S.; mem. Soc. Am. Bacteriologists, Am. Vet. Med. Assn., U.S. Live Stock Sanitation Assn. (com. on poultry diseases 1928), Omega Tau Sigma, Sigma Xi, Phi Kappa Phi, Gamma Sigma Delta. Congregationalist. Mason. Developed improved methods of producing blackleg immunizing agents, 1916-36, developing Kan. blackleg filtrate, 1917. Home: Route 2, Langhorne, Pa. Office: School of Animal Pathology, Univ. of Pennsylvania, Bristol, Pa.

SCOTT, Kenneth Schurch, physician; b. Oakbourne, Pa., Feb. 28, 1902; s. James Clifford and Annabel Edwards (Schurch) S.; B.S., Haverford Coll., 1923, grad. study, 1928-29; M.D., U. of Pa. Med. Sch., 1933; m. Nancy Bockius, June 15, 1923; children—Rosalie Bockius, David Quentin. Instr. in Indian Sch., Cochiti, N.M., 1923; in elec. engring. field, San Diego, Calif., 1924-26, teaching elec. engring., 1927-28; interne Abington Memorial Hosp., 1933-34; engaged in gen. practice of medicine, Doylestown, Pa., 1934-35, at Essex, Conn., 1935-37; med. supt. Pa. Epileptic Hosp. and Colony Farm, nr. West Chester, Pa. since 1937; asst. neurologist, Chester Co. Hosp. Mem. Am. Med. Assn., Pa. State and Chester Co. med. socs. Editor County Med. Soc. Reporter. Republican. Baptist. Clubs: Lions of West Chester; Essex Yacht (Essex, Conn.). Home: Oakbourne, Pa.

SCOTT, Margaretta Morris (Mrs. Samuel Bryan S.), civic worker; b. Phila., Pa., July 17, 1878; d. Charles E. and Ella G. (Benson) Morris; A.B., Bryn Mawr, 1900; grad. study sociology and econs., Bryn Mawr, 1901-06; m. Samuel B. Scott, June 12, 1907; children—Eleanor (M.D.), Sylvia (wife of Dr. Alexander Goetz), Henrietta (Mrs. Howard M. Stuckert, Jr.). Served as registration commr. for Phila., 1931-35; at various times, vice pres., corr, sec., and rec. sec., now mem. bd. dirs., Pa. Council Rep. Women; chmn. polit. sci. com. Phila. Fed. Womens Clubs, 1933-35; mem. Com. of 70, League Women Voters, City Charter Com.; vice-pres. Rep. Women Phila. Co., Twenty-Second Ward Ind. Rep. Women; mem. bd. dirs. Rep. Womens Luncheon Club of Eastern Pa. Mem. Am. Oriental Soc. Republican. Presbyn. Clubs: Art Alliance, Contemporary, Womens University. Contbr. articles on sociology and primitive religion to Journ. Am. Oriental Soc. Home: 1 Norman Lane, Chestnut Hill, Philadelphia, Pa.

SCOTT, Merit, asso. prof. physics; b. Grahamsville, N.Y., Feb. 19, 1899; s. Reuben J. and Mary E. (Hodge) S.; A.B. Cornell U., 1920, Ph.D., same, 1924; m. Dorothy B. Barnard, Dec. 28, 1928. Engaged as asst. in physics, Cornell U., 1918-20, instr. physics, 1920-26; asst. prof. physics, Union Coll., 1926-29; Guggenheim Research Asso., Cornell U., carried out research for development aircraft de-icers for elimination ice hazard, 1929-31; asst. prof. physics, Pa. State Coll., 1931-37, asso. prof. since 1937; consultant to aeronaut. industry in various capacities since 1929; engr. various aircraft cos. in summers. Served in S.A.T.C., 1918, assigned to teaching physics. Mem. Am. Phys. Soc., Am. Meteorological Soc., Inst. Aeronaut. Sci., Sigma Xi, Gamma Alpha, Phi Beta Kappa, Phi Kappa Phi, Sigma Pi Sigma. Home: Nittany Village, State College, Pa.

SCOTT, Paul Whitten, lawyer; b. Middleport, O., Aug. 25, 1869; s. Hugh Bartlett and Anna Haddon (Whitten) S.; grad. high sch., Middleport, 1885; A.B., Marietta (O.) Coll., 1890; m. Dolores Pearl McNeill, Dec. 5, 1908; 1 dau., Anna Pauline. Admitted to W.Va. bar, 1890, and began practice at Huntington; mem. firm Williams & Scott, 1893-97, Williams, Scott & Lovett, 1897-1923, Scott, Graham & Wiswell, 1923-1938, Scott & Ducker since Jan. 1, 1939; treas. Huntington Sand & Gravel Co., Duncan-Scott-Wiswell Co. Solicitor, Huntington, 1900-07. Mem. of Judical Council of West Va., term 1934-38. Pres. Cabell County Bar Assn., 1921-22; dir. Foster Foundation. Mem. Phi Beta Kappa, Alpha Sigma Phi. Republican. Presbyn. Club: Guyandot. Home: Park Hills, South Boul. Office: First Huntington Nat. Bank Bldg., Huntington, W.Va.

SCOTT, Samuel Bryan, lawyer; b. Allegheny, Pa., Aug. 26, 1878; s. Charles Hodge and Henrietta Bryan (Logan) S.; student Shady Side Acad., Phila., 1892-96; A.B., Princeton U., 1900, M.A., 1901; m. Margaretta Morris, June 12, 1907; children—Eleanor, Sylvia, Henrietta. Pvt. practice of law at Phila. since 1905; mem. Pa. State Ho. of Rep., 1907-15. Served as maj., 310th F.A., U.S. Army, 1919-29. Mem. Phila. Com. on Pub. Affairs (past pres.), Pa. Civil Service Assn. (dir.), Phila. Charter Com., Descendants of the Signers of the Declaration of Independence (pres.-gen., 1937-39), Germantown Orchestra Assn. (pres., 1937-39. Independent Republican. Presbyterian. Clubs: Princeton, Penn Athletic (Phila.). Author: State Government in Pennsylvania (1917); Algebra for Parents (1937); various tech. legal articles. Home: 1 Norman Lane, Chestnut Hill. Office: 826 Commercial Trust Bldg., Philadelphia, Pa.

SCOTT, Samuel Horace, M.D.; b. Coatesville, Pa., Mar. 26, 1865; s. Amos Shannon and Mary Louise (McPherson) S.; ed. Cralesville, Pa., Pub. Sch., Maxwell Acad., Coatesville, Pa., West Chester (Pa.) Normal Sch.; M.D., Jefferson Med. Coll., Phila., 1889; m. Annie Chandler Scarlett, Nov. 18, 1890 (died 1928); children—Margaret (Mrs. Philip H. Powers), Jane Richards (Mrs. Charles H. Moore), Horace Scarlett. In practice of medicine, 1889-1934; retired, 1934; chief of staff Cralesville Hosp. since 1917; sec. of bd. Nat. Bank of Chester Valley; v.p. Atlantic Ice Mfg. Co., Lanndale Ice Mfg. Co., Elizabethtown Ice Mfg. Co., Newtown-Langhorn Ice Mfg. Co. Mem. Coatesville Sch. Bd. (pres. since 1903), Coatesville Chamber of Commerce (pres.); rector's warden, Coatesville. Mem. Assn. of Surgeons of Pa. R.R. (treas.), Coatesville Y.M.C.A. (v.p.). Republican. Episcopalian. Mason. (K. T., Consistory). Club: Medical (Phila.). Home: 303 Chestnut St. Address: Coatesville, Pa.

SCOTT, William Berryman, geologist; b. Cincinnati, Feb. 12, 1858; s. Rev. William M. and Mary E. (Hodge) S., g. g. d. of Benjamin Franklin; A.B., Princeton, 1877; Ph.D., Heidelberg, 1880; LL.D., U. of Pennsylvania, 1906; Sc.D., Harvard University, 1909, Oxford University, 1912, Princeton, 1930; m. Alice A. Post, Dec. 15, 1883. Asst. in geology, 1883, prof. geology and palæontology, Princeton Univ., 1884-1930, now emeritus professor. Member National Academy Sciences, Am. Philos. Soc. (pres. 1918-25), Geol. Soc. America (pres. 1924-25). Awarded E. K. Kane medal, Geog. Society Phila.; Wollaston medal, Geol. Soc., London, 1910; F. V. Hayden medal, Acad. Nat. Sci., Phila., 1926; Elizabeth Clark Thompson gold medal, Nat. Acad. Sciences, 1931. Author: An Introduction to Geology, 1897, 3d edit., 1932; A History of Land Mammals in the Western Hemisphere, 1913, 2d Edit., 1937; The Theory of Evolution, 1917; Physiography, 1922; also about 60 monographs upon geol. and palæontol. subjects. Editor and joint author of Reports Princeton University expdns. to Patagonia (9 vols.). Home: 7 Cleveland Lane, Princeton, N.J.

SCOTT, William Emmett, county supt. schs.; b. Caldwell, W.Va., June 4, 1879; s. John George and Letetia Ann (Rose) S.; A.B., W.Va. U., Morgantown, W.Va., 1904; grad. student, W.Va. U., 1907-12; m. Lawrence Maude Burns,

June 15, 1910; children — Lawrence, Maude, George Madison, William Emmett, Jr., Mary Elizabeth (dec.), James Franklin. Engaged in teaching, rural schs. White Sulphur Dist., 1897-1900, high. sch., Huntington, W.Va., 1904-05; prin. pub. schs. in various cities, 1905-18; prin. pub. schs., Lewisburg, W.Va., 1918-26, Frankford, W.Va., 1926-31; county supt. schs., Greenbrier Co., Lewisburg, W.Va., since 1931. Mem. Sigma Nu. Democrat. Presbyn. Mason. Club: Rotary of Lewisburg (also social, country, etc.). Home: Maxwelton. Office: Masonic Bldg., Lewisburg, W.Va.

SCOTT, William Russell, lawyer; b. Pittsburgh, Pa., Nov. 19, 1888; s. William and Anne Lyon (King) S.; student Shadyside Acad., Pittsburgh, 1900-03, Haverford Sch., Haverford, Pa., 1903-06; A.B., Princeton U., 1910; student Harvard Law Sch., 1912-14; m. Catharine Ann French, Sept. 18, 1917; 1 son, William Russell. Admitted to Pa. bar, 1914, and since in practice at Pittsburgh; asso. firm Gordon & Smith, 1914-17, mem. firm and successor firms Gordon, Smith, Buchanan & Scott; Smith, Buchanan, Scott & Gordon; Smith, Buchanan, Scott & Ingersoll, 1919-38; engaged individually in gen. practice law since 1938; dir. Fidelity Trust Co., A.M. Byers Co., Pittsburgh. Served as capt., Inf., U.S. Army, 1917-19; aide de camp, Div. Comdr., 79th Div. and served overseas with div. in Meuse-Argonne; hon. disch. June 1919. Pa. mem. Nat. Conf. of Commrs. on uniform state laws, 1931-35; mem. Pa. State Bd. Law Examiners, 1930-35. V.p. and dir. W.Pa. Sch. for the Blind. Mem. Am., Pa., and Allegheny Co. bar assns., Am. Law Inst. Awarded divisional citation, 79th Div. Republican. Presbyn. Clubs: Pittsburgh, Duquesne, Rolling Rock, Pittsburgh Golf, Fox Chapel Golf (Pittsburgh). Home: 5439 Northumberland St. Office: 1524 Oliver Bldg., Pittsburgh, Pa.

SCOTT, Wirt Stanley, elec. engineer; b. East Monroe, O., Oct. 30, 1879; s. John M. and Rebecca M. (Havens) S.; M.E. in E.E., Ohio State U., 1911; m. Mabel Lynne Rond, Apr. 10, 1901; children—Willard P., Wirt S. Elec. laboratorian, U.S. Navy Yard, Norfolk, Va., 1900-07; supt. light and power plant, Columbus, Ohio, 1911-12; with Westinghouse Electric & Mfg. Co., 1912-35; research in motorizing cane sugar mills, Cuba and La., 1912-15, mgr. industrial heating, 1915-25, spl. rep. 1925-35; consulting engineer, special investigator on economics of electric heating; professional E.E., Ohio State U., 1932; with Philadelphia Electric Company since 1935. Mem. Alumni Assn. Ohio State U., Acacia, Sigma Xi. Republican. Methodist. Mason. Clubs: Faculty (Ohio State Univ.), Miles River Yacht (Chesapeake Bay). Contbr. articles on elec. heating to tech. publs. and lecturer on same subject. Home: Bozman, Md. Office: 1000 Chestnut St., Philadelphia, Pa.

SCOVILLE, Samuel, Jr., lawyer, author, lecturer; b. Norwich, N.Y., June 9, 1872; s. Samuel and Harriet E. (Beecher) S.; Standard High School, 1888; A.B., Yale, 1893; LL.B., U. of State of N.Y., 1895; m. Katharine Gallaudet Trumbull, Oct. 17, 1899; children — Samuel (dec.), Gurdon Trumbull, William Beecher, Henry Ward Beecher (dec.), Alice Trumbull (Mrs. Stuyvesant Barry). Admitted to N.Y. bar, 1895; mem. law firm Beecher & Scoville, 1898; admitted to Phila. bar, 1903, and since maintained prin. office there; admitted to Supreme Ct. of U.S., 1910. Trustee Wagner Inst. Dir. of a number of charitable and civic orgns. Mem. Law Assn. Phila., Am. Ornithologists' Union, Del. Valley Ornithol. Club, Delta Kappa Epsilon. Presbyn. Clubs: Coin d'Or, Franklin Inn, University; Triplet (Philadelphia); Ends of Earth, Yale (New York). Author: Brave Deeds of Union Soldiers, 1915; Abraham Lincoln, His Story, 1918; The Out-of-Doors Club, 1919; Boy Scouts in the Wilderness, 1919; The Blue Pearl, Everyday Adventures, 1920; The Inca Emerald, Wild Folk, 1922; More Wild Folk, 1924; The Red Diamond, 1925; Man and Beast, Runaway Days, 1926; Lords of the Wild, 1928; Wild Honey, 1929; The Snakeblood Ruby, 1932; Alice in Blunderland, 1934. Contbr. to magazines. Books translated into German, Hungarian,

Norwegian and Finnish. Ex-pres. N.E. Soc. of Pa. Home: Haverford, Pa.; (summer) "Treetop," Cornwall, Conn. Offices: Pennsylvania Bldg., Phila., Pa., and Woolworth Bldg., New York, N.Y.

SCRANTON, Charles Wallace, physician; b. Oxford, N.J., Oct. 28, 1897; s. Joseph Henry and Clare Wallace (Ellis) S.; student Phillips Andover Acad., Andover, Mass., 1913-15, Mass. Inst. Tech., 1915-19; M.D., Bellevue Medical Coll., N.Y. City, 1923; m. Madeline Janett Reed, July 17, 1920; children—Charles Wallace, Jr., Mary Reed, William Henry. Interne Bellevue Hosp., 1923-25, house surgeon, 1925; engaged in gen. practice of medicine and surgery at East Orange, N.J., since 1925; mem. staff Orange Memorial Hosp. since 1926, Essex Co. Hosp. since 1929. Served in transport service, 1917-19, advanced to lt. (j.g.). Fellow Am. Coll. Surgeons. Mem. Soc. of Surgeons of N.J., Delta Tau Delta, Alpha Omega Alpha. Republican. Presbyterian. Clubs: Essex County Country (W. Orange, N.J.); Roseland Gun (Roseland, N.J.); Loantaka Skeet (Morristown); North Jersey Gun (Caldwell, N.J.); Jockey Hollow Field Trial (Jockey Hollow); Mid Jersey Field Trial (Plainfield, N.J.); Pequest Valley Rod & Gun (Great Meadows, N.J.); Carolina Game Reserve (Eldorado, N.C.). Home: 59 Washington St., East Orange, N.J.

SCRANTON, Marion Margery Warren (Mrs. Worthington Scranton), vice chairman Pa. and Nat. Rep. Com.; b. Scranton, Pa., April 2, 1884; d. Everett and Ellen (Willard) Warren; ed. Miss Porter's Sch., Farmington, Conn.; m. Worthington Scranton, of Scranton, April 11, 1907; children — Marion Margery, Katherine, Sara, William Warren. Vice chmn. Lackawanna County (Pa.) Rep. Com., 1920; member Rep. State Com. since 1920, vice chmn., 1926-28; mem. Rep. Nat. Com. since 1928, vice chmn. since 1936. Home: 300 Monroe Av., Scranton, Pa.

SCRANTON, Worthington, pres. Mountain Ice Co.; b. Scranton, Pa., August 29, 1876; s. William W. and Katherine M. (Smith) S.; A.B., Yale, 1898; LL.B., Harvard, 1901; m. Marion Margery Warren, April 11, 1907; children — Marion, Katherine, Sara, William. Pres. Scranton (Pa.) Gas & Water Co., 1916-28; pres. Mountain Ice Co., Scranton, Pa., since 1924; dir. Internat. Textbook Co., First Nat. Bank of Scranton (Pa.). Trustee Community Welfare Assn., Scranton, Pa., v.p. Family Welfare Assn., Scranton, Pa. Mem. Scranton (Pa.) Chamber of Com. (dir.). Republican. Presbyn. Clubs: Scranton, Scranton Country (Scranton, Pa.); University, Yale (New York); Graduate (New Haven, Conn.). Home: Marworth, Dalton, Pa. Office: 800 Linden St., Scranton, Pa.

SCRIBNER, Charles, publisher; b. N.Y. City, Jan. 26, 1890; s. Charles and Louise (Flagg) S.; student St. Paul's Sch., 1904-09; A.B., Princeton, 1913; m. Vera Gordon Bloodgood, May 26, 1915; children — Julia Bloodgood, Charles. With Charles Scribner's Sons since 1913, sec., 1918-26, v.p. 1926-32, pres. since 1932; also pres. Princeton Univ. Press; dir. Fulton Trust Co. First lt. Remount Service, Q.M.C., World War. Trustee Skidmore Coll. Republican. Episcopalian. Club: Racquet and Tennis. Home: Far Hills, N.J. Office: 597 5th Av., New York, N.Y.

SCRIBNER, Henry Sayre, prof. of Greek; b. Plainfield, N.J., Aug. 3, 1859; s. William and Julia (Sayre) S.; desc. of Thomas Sayre ,co-founder of South Hampton, L.I., 1640; prep. edn., Phillips Exeter Acad., 1874-77; A.B., Princeton Coll., 1881, A.M., 1886; grad. student Johns Hopkins, 1886-89, U. of Goetingen, 1889-90; hon. D.Litt., U. of Pittsburgh, 1933; m. Mary Lee Myers, Dec. 28, 1891; children—Henry Lee (deceased), Joseph Myers, Emma Tailer (deceased), Annie Lee (Mrs. King E. Fauver), Lucilla Sayre (Mrs. William Richard Jackson). Teacher Saratoga, N.Y., Great Barrington, Mass., 1881-90; associated with Western U. of Pa. (now U. of Pittsburgh) since 1890, as prof. of Greek, and head of dept., 1890-1934, prof. emeritus since 1934; taught summers at Chautauqua, N.Y., and Marthas Vineyard, Mass. Student and traveler in Greece and Italy, 1937-38. Mem. Am. Philol. Assn., Archæol. Inst. America, Classical Assn. of Atlantic States, Classical Assn. of Pittsburgh. Ind. Republican. Presbyterian (elder). Contbr. to classical journals, ednl. periodicals and to Memoirs of Carnegie Museum (Catalogue of Greek and Italian vases and Etruscan urns in Carnegie Museum, Vol. XI, No. 6). Home: 6933 Thomas Boul., Pittsburgh, Pa.

SCRIBNER, Joseph M., investment banker; b. Ben Avon, Pa., June 14, 1897; s. Henry Sayre and Mary Lee (Myers) S.; student Allegheny Prep. Sch.; m. Martha Jane Judson, Sept. 22, 1920; 1 dau., Judson. With Stout & Co., investment bankers, 1919-20; then with Imbrie & Co., 1920-25; partner Wells, Deane & Singer, Pittsburgh, since 1925 (name of co. changed to Singer, Deane & Scribner, 1928); member New York Stock Exchange; pres. and dir. Pa.-Bradford Co.; treas. and dir. Morewood Corpn.; dir. Pittsburgh Parking Garages, Sloan & Zook Co. Clubs: Duquesne, Pittsburgh Golf, Harvard-Yale-Princeton (Pittsburgh); Fox Chapel Golf. Home: Oliver Road, Sewickley, Pa. Office: 1045 Union Trust Bldg., Pittsburgh, Pa.

SCUDDER, Antoinette Quinby, artist and writer; b. Newark, N.J., Sept. 10, 1898; d. Wallace M. and Ida (Quinby) S.; ed. Columbia U., 1917-18; studied under Charles Hawthorne, N.A., Richard E. Miller, N.A., and Frederick Waugh, N.A., at Art Students League of N.Y. under George Bridgman, water color with John Frazier, Providence, enamelling and jewelry work with Julia Munson Sherman. Has lately specialized in marine painting; exhibited at Newark Art Club, Montclair Mus., Art Centre of Oranges, Provincetown Art Assn., Studio Guild of N.Y. City and is mem. of these clubs and assns.; pres. Paper Mill Playhouse, Millburn, N.J., since inc., 1934. Episcopalian. Author: Provincetown Sonnets (verse), 1925; The Maple's Bride (play), 1930; Huckleberries (verse), 1929; Out of Peony and Blade (verse), 1931; Henchman of the Moon (poetic drama), 1934; East End, West End (verse), 1934; The Cherry Tart (one-act plays), 1938. Contbr. to newspapers. Home: 49 Manchester Pl., Newark, N.J.

SCUDDER, Edward Wallace, publisher; b. Newark, N.J., Jan. 15, 1882; s. Wallace McIlvaine and Ida (Quinby) S.; grad. Newark Acad., 1899; A.B., Princeton, 1903; m. Katherine Hollifield, June 4, 1907; children—Dorothea (Mrs. Scudder Doeg), Edward W., Richard P., Katherine Ida (dec.). Pub. of Newark Evening News since 1931; pres. Evening News Pub. Co., dir. J. Middleby Co., Nat. Newark and Essex Banking Co., Nat. Newark Bldg. Co. Episcopalian. Clubs: Essex, Orange Lawn Tennis, Rumson Country, Seabright Tennis, Seabright Beach. Home: 234 Ballantine Parkway, Newark, and "The Point," Rumson, N.J. Office: 215 Market St., Newark, N.J.

SCUDDER, Frank Dyckman, physician and surgeon; b. San Antonio, Tex., Jan. 25, 1888; s. Silas D. and Sarah (Wells) S.; A.B., Yale U., 1910; M.D., Coll. of Physicians and Surgeons, Columbia U., 1914; m. Ruth E. Kellogg, Dec. 30, 1916; 1 son, Frank D., Jr. Interne St. Luke's Hosp., New York, 1914-16; engaged in practice of medicine and surgery at Montclair, N.J., since 1919; chief of staff and attdg. surg., Mountainside Hosp., Montclair, N.J.; attdg. surg., Essex Co. Isolation Hosp., Belleville, N.J.; cons. surg., Newton Memorial Hosp., Newton, N.J. Served as lit. sr. grade Med. Corps U.S.N.R.F., 1918-26. Fellow Am. Coll. Surgs., A.M.A., N.J. Soc. Surgs. Mem. Am. Bd. Surgery (founders group), Asso. Phys. of Montclair (past pres.), Alpha Delta Phi, Nu Sigma Nu, Omega Club. Conglist. Clubs: Yale (New York); Golf (Montclair); City Island Yacht of N.Y. Home: 225 N. Mountain Av. Office: 65 N. Fullerton Av., Montclair, N.J.

SCUDDER, Townsend, III, writer, educator; b. Glenwood, L.I., N.Y., Aug. 27, 1900; s. Townsend and Mary Dannat (Thayer) S.; B.A., Yale, 1923, Ph.D., 1933; m. Virginia Louise Boody, June 23, 1923; children—Townsend, Thayer. Began in book editorial dept. Doubleday, Page & Co., 1923; editorial work Rockefeller Foundation, 1924; with English Dept., Yale U., 1924-31; asst. prof. English, Swarthmore Coll., since 1931. Club: Franklin Inn (Phila.). Author: The Lonely Wayfaring Man, Emerson and Some Englishmen, 1935; Jane Welsh Carlyle, 1939; also various essays and reviews. Editor: Letters of Jane Welsh Carlyle to Joseph Neuberg, 1931. Home: 205 Elm Av., Swarthmore, Pa.

SCULLY, Cornelius Decatur, mayor; b. Pittsburgh, Pa., Nov. 30, 1878; s. John Sullivan and Mary E. (Negley) S.; B.S., U. of Pa., 1901; LL.B., U. of Pittsburgh, 1904; m. Rosalie Pendleton, June 10, 1905; children—Alice Pendleton (Mrs. John C. Fisher Motz), Elizabeth Negley (Mrs. William Sanders), Cornelius Decatur, John Pendleton. Admitted to Pa. bar, 1904; mem. firm Lee & Mackey, 1904-08, Mackey & Scully, 1908-10, Mehard, Scully & Mehard, 1912-19; solicitor City of Pittsburgh, 1934; pres. City Council, 1935-36; mayor of Pittsburgh since 1936; dir. Hope Engring. Co., Pittsburgh Tube Co. Trustee U. of Pittsburgh, Carnegie Inst. of Tech., Arnold Prep. Sch. Mem. Am. Bar Assn., Kappa Sigma. Democrat. Episcopalian. Mason, Eagle. Clubs: Duquesne, University, Junta Philosophical (Pittsburgh); Gibson Island (Baltimore). Home: 6211 Howe St. Office: City-County Bldg., Pittsburgh, Pa.

SEABROOK, Byron Miller, lawyer; b. Glassboro, N.J., Sept. 19, 1892; s. Albert M. and Mary D. (Johnson) S.; LL.B., Temple U. Law Sch., 1914; m. Alice H. Elwell, Sept. 27, 1916; 1 son, Robert Elwell. Admitted to N.J. bar, as atty, 1914, as counsellor at law, 1919; in gen. practice of law in Camden since 1914. Mem. N.J. State Bar Assn., Camden Co. Bar Assn. (past pres.), Sigma Pi. Republican. Presbyn. Mason (32°). Club: Country (Merchantville). Home: 3202 Horner Av., Merchantville. Office: 428 Market St., Camden, N.J.

SEAL, Ethel Davis (Mrs. Charles E. Carpenter), interior decoration; b. Phila., Pa.; d. George Thomas and Emma Haldeman (Davis) S.; ed. pvt. schs. and Friends Sch., Germantown, Phila.; studied art, Pennsylvania Academy of Fine Arts, Pa. Mus. and Sch. of Industrial Art, Nat. Acad. Design (New York), Drexel Inst. (Phila.), and Breckenridge Sch. of Painting (Gloucester, Mass.); m. Charles Edward Carpenter, June 4, 1917. Formerly contbr. to mags. and newspapers; house-furnishing editor Phila. North American, 1914-16; household editor The Delineator, 1915-17; editor and writer syndicated newspaper features, Periodical Pub. Co., Grand Rapids, Mich., 1916-18; chief contbr. on interior decoration to Ladies' Home Jour., 1919-29; chief contbr. on interior decoration to Country Gentleman, 1924-29; now engaged in decorating, consulting and writing. Mem. Fellowship Pennsylvania Academy Fine Arts, Philadelphia Art Alliance. Republican. Episcopalian. Author: Furnishing the Little House, 1924; The House of Simplicity, 1926. Home: 2031 Locust St., Philadelphia, Pa.

SEAMAN, Augusta Huiell (Mrs. Francis P. Freeman), author; b. N.Y. City, Apr. 3, 1879; d. John Valentine and Augusta Cheeseman (Curtis) Huiell; A.B., Hunter Coll., 1900; m. Robert Reece Seaman, Oct. 3, 1906 (died Mar. 1927); 1 dau., Helen Roberta; m. 2d, Francis Parkman Freeman, Mar. 1928. Began as contributor to magazines, 1907, and later became regular contributor juvenile serials to St. Nicholas, subsequently pub. in book form. Ind. Democrat. Presbyterian. Author: Jacqueline of the Carrier Pigeons, 1910; When a Cobbler Ruled the King, 1911; Little Mamselle of the Wilderness, 1913; The Boarded-up House, 1915; The Sapphire Signet, 1916; The Girl Next Door, 1917; Three Sides of Paradise Green, 1918; Melissa-Across-the-Fence, 1918; The Slipper Point Mystery, 1919; The Crimson Patch, 1920; The Dragon's Secret, 1921; The Mystery at Number Six, 1922; Tranquillity House, 1923; The Edge of Raven Pool, 1924; Sally Simms Adventures It, 1924; Bluebonnet Bend, 1925; The Adventure of the Seven Keyholes, 1926; The Secret of Tate's Beach, 1926; The Shadow on the Dial, 1927; The Disappearance of Anne Shaw, 1928; The Book of Mysteries, 1929; The Charlemonte Crest, 1930; The House in Hidden Lane, 1931; The Brass Keys of Kenwick, 1931; The Stars of Sabra, 1932; The Mystery of the Empty Room, 1933; The Riddle at Live Oaks, 1934; Bitsy Finds the Clue, 1934; The Figurehead of the Folly, 1935; The Strange Pettingill Puzzle, 1936; Voice in the Dark, 1937; The Pine Barrens Mystery, 1937. Address: Seaside Park, N.J.*

SEAMAN, Otis R(evoe), civil engring.; b. Long Branch, N.J., Mar. 17, 1899; s. John Wesley and Turie (Martin) S.; B.S. in C.E., Lafayette Coll., 1922, C.E., same, 1926; m. Grace Metler, Oct. 10, 1936. Engaged on own acct. in profession civil engring., 1922-28; city engr., Long Branch, N.J., 1928-32; borough engr., Sea Bright Borough, 1928-32, Monmouth Beach Borough since 1930; county engr. Monmouth Co., N.J., since 1937; mem. firm, J. W. Seaman & Son, civil engrs. and surveyors, Long Branch, N.J., since 1922. Mem. Nat. Assn. Professional Engrs., N.J. Assn. Professional Engrs., Assn. of Chosen Freeholders of N.J., Co. Engrs. Assn. of N.J. Republican. Methodist. Mason. Tall Cedars. Club: Exchange (Long Branch). Home: 393 Broadway, Long Branch. Office: Court House, Freehold, N.J.

SEAMAN, William, chemist; b. Providence, R.I., Nov. 27, 1901; s. Allen and Anna (Sugarman) S.; A.B., Brown U., 1922, M.S., same, 1922; Ph.D., Cornell U., 1929; m. Sylvia S. Bernstein, Dec. 27, 1925; children—Gideon, Jonathan. Employed as chemist in U.S. Bur. Chemistry, Dept. Agr. in Washington, D.C. and N.Y. City, and in U.S. Navy Dept., Brooklyn, N.Y., 1922-27; chemist, Standard Oil Development Co., Elizabeth, N.J., 1929-31; chemist, Internat. Paper Co., Glens Falls, N.Y., 1931-33; chemist, Calco Chem. Co., Bound Brook, N.J., since 1933; served as asso. referee for Assn. of Ofcl. Agrl. Chemists, 1923-25; awarded patents on processes for utilization of petroleum wastes and uses for products from such wastes. Fellow Am. Inst. Chemists. Mem. Am. Chem. Soc., Phi Beta Kappa, Sigma Xi. Awarded final honors in chemistry, Brown U., 1922; scholarships and fellowships at Brown and Cornell. Contbr. articles to tech. publs. and jours. Home: 40 Monroe St., New York, N.Y. Office: Calco Chemical Co., Bound Brook, N.J.

SEARLES, Thomas Mount, pres. Penn Rivet Corpn.; b. Vicksburg, Miss., Aug. 14, 1891; s. Thomas Markham and Annie (Mount) S.; B.S. in E.E., Miss. State Coll., Starksville, Miss., 1909; B.S., U.S. Naval Acad., Annapolis, Md., 1913; Master in Naval Architecture and Marine Engring., Mass. Inst. Tech., 1917; student Harvard Grad. Sch. of Business Adminstrn., 1915-17; m. Clifford Burt, June 12, 1915; children—Thomas Markham, Barbara Burt. Asst. engr. officer on battleship Louisiana, in charge of operation, maintenance and repairs of boilers, engines and auxiliary machinery, U.S. Navy, 1913-15, executive officer and commanding officer on destroyer Worden, 1915, promoted from line to constrn. corps, 1915, shop supt., 1917, in charge of naval ship construction, 1917-20; mgr. and gen. agent, Aetna Life Ins. Co., Buffalo, N.Y., 1920-24, mgr., 1924-26, gen. agt. for N.J. and New York metropolitan area, 1926-33; pres. Orange Mfg. Corpn., Newark, N.J., 1933-36; pres. Penn Rivet Corpn. and subsidiaries, Equipment Corpn. and Tack Button Co., Phila., since 1936. Methodist. Clubs: Penn Athletic, Harvard, Mass. Inst. Tech., Naval Acad. Grad. Assn. (Phila.). Author of numerous articles on training and supervision of salesmen and sales organization building. Home: 323 Montrose Av., South Orange, N.J. Office: Third and Huntingdon Sts., Philadelphia, Pa.

SEARS, Julian D., geologist; b. Baltimore, Md., June 3, 1891; s. Thomas E. (M.D.) and Julia (Ducker) S.; A.B., Johns Hopkins U., 1913, Ph.D., 1919; m. Elizabeth T. Lamdin, June 16, 1919; children—William B., Richard S. Employed as geologic aid, U.S. Geol. Survey, 1915-16; geologist, Central Am. Oil Corpn., 1917-18; asso. geologist, U.S. Geol. Survey, Washington, D.C., 1918-20, geologist, 1920-24, administrative geologist since 1924. Mem. A.A.A.S., Geol. Soc. of America, Am. Assn. Petroleum Geologists, Geol. Soc. of Washington, Phi Beta Kappa, Phi Gamma Delta, Gamma Phi, Soc. of the Cincinnati of Md. Episcopalian. Club: Kenwood Golf and Country (Bethesda). Home: 21 Kennedy Drive, Chevy Chase, Md.

SEATON, Lewis Hiram, surgeon; b. McClellandtown, Pa., Nov. 30, 1885; s. Lewis Merchant and Julia (Stacey) S.; M.D., Pittsburgh U., 1910; m. Charlotte May Bietsch, Dec. 20, 1911. Interne, Uniontown (Pa.) Hosp., 1910-11; gen. practice, Grays Landing, Pa., 1911-16, at Chambersburg, Pa., since 1916; surgeon and mem. of staff, Chambersburg (Pa.) Hosp., since 1917; dir. Chambersburg Thrift Plan. Served as med. officer, B.E.F., 1917-19, as capt., Med. O.R.C., 1917-19. Mem. Chambersburg (Pa.) Bd. of Health since 1921. Fellow A.M.A., Am. Coll. Surgeons; mem. Franklin Co. Med. Assn. (past pres.), Pa. Med. Soc., Cumberland Valley Med. Assn., Fayette Co. Med. Soc. (pres., 1915-16), Chambersburg Chamber of Commerce. Awarded British Mil. Cross, 1919. Republican. Presbyterian. Mason (32°; Zembo Shrine). Club: Rotary (Chambersburg, Pa.) Address: 236 Lincoln Way, Chambersburg, Pa.

SEBRING, Lawrence Monroe, lawyer; b. Clearfield Co., Pa., Dec. 21, 1874; s. Albert B. and Lavina Alice (Brickley) S.; B.E., Indiana (Pa.) State Normal Sch., 1896, M.E., 1898; LL.B., Dickinson Sch. of Law, Carlisle, Pa., 1900; m. Fay Wick Ellis, May 18, 1910; 1 dau., Jean Elizabeth. Taught in pub. schs., Clearfield Co., and Cambria Co., Pa., and Johnstown, Pa., 1893-97; admitted to Beaver Co. Bar, 1901, Supreme Court of Pa., 1903, Superior Court of Pa., 1904, U.S. Dist. Court of Alaska, 1905; U.S. Commnr. for Dist. of Alaska, 1904-05; sec. to Alfred S. Moore, U.S. Judge, Dist. of Alaska, 2d div., 1905-06; pvt. practice of law at Beaver, Pa., since 1907. Mem. Bd. of Examiners of Beaver Co. Bar. Republican. Home: 340 Quay St. Office: 203-204 Beaver Trust Bldg., Beaver, Pa.

SECHRIST, Elizabeth Hough, librarian, author; b. Media, Pa., Aug. 31, 1903; d. Willard Graham and Mary (Parker) Hough; grad. Media High Sch., 1922; student U. of Pittsburgh (night school), 1923-25, Carnegie Library Sch. of Carnegie Inst. of Tech., 1923-24; m. Walter Levere Sechrist, of Dallastown, Pa., Oct. 6, 1930. Asst. children's librarian, Carnegie Library, Pittsburgh, 1924-25; head children's dept., Bethlehem (Pa.) Public Library, 1925-31; children's librarian, Carnegie Library, Pittsburgh, 1937-39; free lance editorial work on juvenile publs., Phila., since 1931. Author: Christmas Everywhere, 1931, rev., 1936; A Little Book of Hallowe'en, 1934; Rufie Had Monkey, 1939. Editor: Thirteen Ghostly Yarns, 1932; Pirates and Pigeons, 1933. Contbr. to mags. Home: 668 S. Main St., Red Lion, Pa.

SECHRIST, William Clinton, forester; b. Blossburg, Pa., Feb. 26, 1909; s. Edward R. and Mary (Lindie) S.; B.S., Pa. State Coll., 1931; m. Hazel B. Lodge, July 1, 1933. Began as forester, U.S. Forest Service, Calif., 1931-32, in Colo., 1932; instr. forestry, Pa. State Coll., 1932-34; with Pa. Dept. of Forests and Waters, Mont Alto, Pa., since 1935. Served as 2d lt. inf. U.S.A.R.F. Mem. Soc. Am. Foresters, Xi Sigma Pi, Tau Phi Delta. Methodist. Home: Blossburg, Pa. Office: Mont Alto, Pa.

SEDDON, Scott, lawyer; b. St. Louis, Mo., June 9, 1892; s. Judge James A. and Louise Quarles (Scott) S.; g.s. James A. Seddon, sec. of war in Confederacy under Jefferson Davis; A.B., Yale, 1914; LL.B., Washington U. Law Sch., 1916; m. Martha Ann Seifert, July 10, 1920. Admitted to Mo. bar, 1916 and in practice at St. Louis, 1916-21; admitted to Pa. bar, 1921, and asst. counsel in charge legal dept. Phila. branch Simmons Hardware Co., 1921-23; in gen. practice of law at Phila. since 1923. Served as pvt. Marine Corps U.S., 1917; 2d lieut. F.A., U.S.A., 1917-19, with A.E.F. in France. Mem. Phila. Bar Assn., Phi Delta Phi. Republican. Episcopalian. Home: Haverford Mansions, Haverford, Pa. Office: 12 S. 12th St., Philadelphia, Pa.

SEDER, Willard James, steel constrn. supt.; b. Menomonie, Wis., May 14, 1900; s. Rev. James I. and Minnie A. (Kiskhoefer) S.; B.S. in C.E., U. of Wis., Madison, Wis., 1921; m. Lovilla Marie Anderson, Dec. 4, 1925; children—June Lovilla, Anne Florence. Began as computer U.S. Forest Products Lab., Madison, Wis., 1922; engr. McClintic-Marshall Constrn. Co., Pittsburgh, 1922-25, asst. mgr., Rankin, Pa., 1925-31; gen. supt. Bethlehem Steel Co., Rankin (Pa.) Works, since 1931. Asso. mem. Am. Soc. C.E. Home: 1107 La Clair Av., Swissvale, Pa. Office: Bethlehem Steel Co., Rankin, Pa.

SEEGAR, J. KING B. E.; gynecologist St. Agnes and Bon Secours hosps.; asso. in gynecology, Md. Gen. Hosp. Address: 2 W. Read St., Baltimore, Md.

SEEGERS, John Conrad, univ. dean; b. Richmond, Va., Dec. 1, 1893; s. John Conrad and May Erwin (Ide) S.; A.B., Muhlenberg Coll., Allentown, Pa., 1913; A.M., Columbia, 1916; student U. of S.C., 1917; Ph.D., U. of Pa., 1930; m. Hazel Jordan, Aug. 1, 1917; children—John Conrad, Dorothy Anna. Instr. English, Allentown Prep. Sch., 1913-15; prof. English, Lenoir-Rhyme Coll., Hickory, N.C., 1920-23, sch. prin., Wilmington, N.C., 1920-23, asst. supt. schs., 1923-27; instr. edn., Temple U., 1927-29, prof. and dean of men since 1930. Served as 2d lt. field arty., U.S.A., 1917-18. Mem. Bd. of Edn. of the United Luth. Ch. in America since 1938. Trustee Muhlenberg Coll., dir. Oak Lane Country Day Sch. Mem. Nat. Soc. for the Study of Edn., Nat. Conf. on Elementary Lang., N.E.A., Nat. Assn. Deans of Men, Eastern Assn. Coll. Deans and Advisers of Men, Am. Assn. of Univ. Profs., Alpha Tau Omega, Phi Delta Kappa. Lutheran. Club: Sandy Run Country. Author: Men and Women of God, 1932; An Orientation Course in Education, 1933; Workbook for Orientation Course in Education (with J. S. Butterweck), 1933; contbr. to ednl. jours. Home: 123 E. Durham St., Philadelphia, Pa.

SEELEY, Mildred Louise, social work; b. Du Bois, Pa., Nov., 26, 1901; d. Frank Wesley and Mary Ann (Seaborn) S.; A.B., Conn. Coll. for Women, New London, Conn., 1923; ed. N. Y. Sch. of Social Work, 1923-25. Engaged as social worker, Louisville and Jefferson Co. Children's Home, Louisville, Ky., 1925, later dir. field dept.; now supt. Morris Co. Children's Home, Morristown, N.J.; served on various coms. for town betterment and coms. other welfare agencies and service clubs. Mem. Am. Assn. Social Workers, Nat. Conf. of Social Work, N.J. Conf. Social Work, Conn. Coll. Alumnae Assn. Republican. Episcopalian. Clubs: Business and Professional Women's (Morristown); St. Bartholomew's Community (New York). Home: 375 Mt. Kemble Av., Morristown, N.J.

SEELY, Leslie Birchard, educator; b. Luzerne Co., Pa., Apr. 22, 1877; s. Samuel Pollock and Mary Elizabeth (Patterson) P.; student Bloomsburg (Pa.) State Normal Sch., 1896-1902, U. of Pa. (grad. work), 1907-09; A.B., Haverford (Pa.) Coll., 1905; m. Mary Louise Bogenrief, July 20, 1910; 1 son, Leslie Birchard. Teacher of ungraded school, Salem Twp., Pa., 1895-96; headmaster, Chappaqua (N.Y.) Mountain Inst., 1905-06; asst. instr. in comparative anatomy, Brooklyn (N.Y.) Inst., summer 1906; teacher of physics, Northeast High Sch., Phila., 1906-15; prin. of High Sch., Middleburg, Pa., 1907-08; lecturer in physics, Wagner Free Inst. of Science, Phila., since 1914; head of science dept., Germantown High Sch., Phila., 1915-24, prin. since 1924. Mem. Nat., Pa. State, Phila. Edn. Assns., Franklin Inst., Phi Beta Kappa (hon.). Republican. Presbyterian. Home: 5918 Pulaski Av. Office: Germantown High Sch., Philadelphia, Pa.

SEELYE, Theodore E.; b. New Orleans, La., 1887; ed. U. of Mich., 1909-12. Vice-pres. Day & Zimmerman, constrn. engrs.; dir. Gannett, Seelye & Fleming Corpn. of Harrisburg, Pine Iron Wks. (Phila.). During World War was maj. engrs. corps. Home: Ambler, Pa. Office: Packard Bldg., Philadelphia, Pa.

SEGAL, Bernard G., lawyer; born at New York, N.Y., June 11, 1907; s. Samuel I. and Rose S. (Cantor) S.; A.B., Central High Sch., Philadelphia, 1924; A.B., U. of Pa. Coll., 1928; LL.B., U. of Pa. Law Sch., 1931; Gowen fellow, U. of Pa. Law Sch., June 1931-May 1932; m. Geraldine Rosenbaum, Oct. 22 1933. Admitted to practice in Supreme and Lower cts. of Pa., 1932; in Supreme Court of U.S., 1937; deputy atty. gen., 1932-35; mem. law firm Schnader & Lewis; instr. in public finance, Grad. Sch., U. of Pennsylvania; North lecturer on Franklin & Marshall Coll.; dep. atty. gen. Commonwealth of Pa., 1932-35; counsel Milk Control Commn. of Pa., 1934-35; formerly instr. polit. science, Wharton Sch. (U. of Pa.); formerly coach univ. and freshman debating teams, U. of Pa.; formerly Am. reporter on contracts Internat. Congress of Comparative Law, The Hague. As deputy atty. gen. drafted present banking codes and bldg. and loan code of Pa. Awarded Order of the Coif. Pres. Taxpayers' Forum of Pa., Inc.; mem. operations com. Pa. Economy League; dir. Jewish Hosp., Jewish Welfare Soc., Legal Aid Soc. of Philadelphia, Associated Talmud Torahs. Mem. Am. Bar. Assn., Pa. Bar. Assn. (former chmn. Pa. Jr. Bar Assn.), Philadelphia Bar Assn., Acad. Polit. and Social Sciences, Artisans Order of Mutual Protection, Delta Sigma Rho, Socialegal Club. Republican. Editor-in-chief Pa. Banking and Building and Loan Codes Annotated (pub. 1939). Home: 257 S. 16th St. Office: 1719 Packard Bldg., Philadelphia, Pa.

SEGALL, Jacob Bernard, coll. prof.; b. Roman, Roumania, Nov. 11, 1866; s. Isaac and Esther (Nadler) S.; came to U.S., 1884, naturalized, 1890; B.L., Lycée Yassy, Roumania, 1884, B.Sc., 1884; student U. of the City of N.Y., 1885-86, Columbia U., 1886-87, Politechnikum and Univ. of Zurich, Switzerland, 1887-89, U. of Munich, Germany, 1889-90, Columbia U., 1891-93; Ph.D., Columbia Univ., 1893; grad. student, U. of Paris, France, 1896-97; unmarried. Engaged in teaching, evening sch., N.Y. City, 1891-93; univ. fellow Romance langs., Columbia U., 1892-93; instr. French, Cornell U., 1893-96 and 1897-1900; lecturer modern langs., McGill Univ., Montreal, Can., 1900-01; instr. French, Coll. of City of N.Y., 1901-03; prof. Romance langs., U. of Me., Orono, Me., 1903-28; prof. French, Northwestern U., Evanston, Ill., summer 1928; prof. Romance langs., St. John's Coll., Annapolis, Md., since 1928. Mem. Modern Lang. Assn. of America, Am. Assn. Univ. Profs., Theta Chi. Served with U.S. Food Adminstrn. Fgn. Press Information, Washington, D.C., 1918-19; with Am. Relief Adminstrn., Paris, 1919. Author: Corneille and the Spanish Drama, 1902. Editor, Corneille's Le Menteur. Translator, Roumanian Folk Tales. Contbr. to mags. Address: St. John's College, Annapolis, Md.

SEGER, George N., congressman; b. N.Y. City, Jan. 4, 1866; ed. pub. schs. Engaged in building business, Passaic, N.J.; mem. Sch. Bd., 1906-11; mem. City Commn. 3 terms, 1911-23, serving 8 yrs. as mayor and 4 yrs. dir. finance; del. Rep. Nat. Conv., 1916; mem. 68th to 72d Congresses (1923-33), 7th N.J. Dist., and 73d to 76th Congresses (1933-41), 8th N.J. Dist. Mem. Council Nat. Defense, World War. Home: Passaic, N.J.

SEGOINE, Harold Richard, pres. Highland Park Bldg. Co.; b. Point Pleasant Beach, N.J., Oct. 14, 1887; s. William and Frances (Conover) S.; ed. Point Pleasant pub. schs. and Freehold High Sch.; B.Sc., Rutgers U., 1908; m. Margaret E. Suydam, Apr. 30, 1912; children—Margaret Elizabeth, Ruth Suydam (Mrs. Richard Henry McCabe), Frances Conover, Harold Richard, Jr., Mary Combs. Civil and mining engr. Geo. E. Jenkins, civil engr., 1908-10; civil engr. and asst. to pres. Livingston Manor Corpn., 1910-14; pres. Highland Park Bldg. Co., engrs. and constructors, since 1914; pres. Cronk Mfg. Co., Raritan Valley Bldg. & Loan Assn.; v.p. Mortgage Management Corpn. Served as capt., N.J. Reserves, World War. City Engr., Highland Park, N.J., 1912-14; mem. bd. of edn., 1924-27; chmn. zoning commn., Piscataway Twp., 1935-36. Pres. Middlesex Council Boy Scouts of America; dir. New Brunswick Chapter of Am. Red Cross; trustee Rutgers Fund Council; mem. council Rutgers Prep. Sch.; ex-pres., now mem. exec. com. Rutgers Alumni Council. Awarded Rutgers Medal, Silver Beaver (Boy Scouts of America). Mem. N.J. Contractors Assn., Delta Upsilon. Republican. Mem. Reformed Ch. Clubs: Rutgers, Union (New Brunswick). Licensed real estate broker in N.J. Home: River Road. Office: 238 Cleveland Av., New Brunswick, N.J.

SEGUINE, William M., sand and gravel producer; b. Mt. Bethel, Pa., Nov. 10, 1878; s. Ezra and Matilda (Reimer) S.; A.B., State Teachers Coll., East Stroudsburg, Pa., 1898, grad. study same, 1901; E.E., Pa. State Coll., 1905; unmarried. Employed as elec. engr., Western Electric Co., 1906-10; later head of mathematics dept., State Teachers Coll., East Stroudsburg, Pa.; now pres. Seguine Bogus Co., Inc., producers sand and gravel (Kenvil, N.J.), Seguine Jersey Sand Co., Inc., Kenvil Sand & Gravel Co., Portland (Pa.) Sand & Gravel Co., Inc.; dir. Dover Trust Co., Portland (Pa.) Nat. Bank, East Stroudsburg (Pa.) Nat. Bank. Pres. Roxbury Bd. Edn. for 10 yrs., mem. bd. for 19 yrs. Served as trustee Dover Gen. Hosp. for several yrs. Republican. Mason (K.T., Shriner), I.O.O.F., B.P.O.E. Club: Country of Lake Hopatcong, N.J. (pres. 1930-35). Home: Kenvil, N.J.

SEIBEL, George, writer, lecturer; b. Pittsburgh, Pa., Sept. 13, 1872; s. Nicholas and Margaret (Eidam) S.; ed. pub. schs.; m. Helen Hiller, Sept. 6, 1894. Editor Youth's Journal, 1893, Neue Welt, 1894-95, Gazette Times, 1896-1911, Volksblatt Freiheits-Freund, 1912-25; dramatic and literary editor of the Pittsburgh Sun-Telegraph, 1927-36; now asso. editor Musical Forecast, and professor of poetry and drama in Fillion Sch. Sec. Pittsburgh Morals Efficiency Commn. Mem. Deutsche Shakespeare Gesellschaft; national pres. American Turnerbund, 1923-37. Author: The Fall, 1918, 2d edit., 1923; The Wine Bills of Omar Khayyam, 1919; The Mormon Saints, 1899, 2d edit., 1919; Bacon vs. Shakespeare, 1919; The Religion of Shakespeare, 1924; Hauptmann and Sudermann, 1925; The Concert (sonnet cycle), 1934. Wrote pageant play, "The Vision of She-Who-Knows," for 125th anniversary University of Pittsburgh, 1912; The Leper, drama, 1913, revived, 1920, 29. Delivered address at Johnstown, Pa., 1916, on "The Hyphen in American History," 32d edit., 1929; has lectured in German and British univs. and over 100 American cities; has made over 600 radio broadcasts. Home: 6612 Ridgeville St. Office: 1108 Century Bldg., Pittsburgh, Pa.

SEIBERT, Florence Barbara, asso. prof. biochemistry; b. Easton, Pa., Oct. 6, 1897; d. George Peter and Barbara (Memmert) S.; A.B., Goucher Coll., 1918; Ph.D., Yale, 1923; (hon.) LL.D., Goucher Coll., 1938. Employed as chemist, Hammersley Paper Mill, 1918-20; instr. pathology and asst., U. of Chicago, 1924-28, asst. prof. and asso., 1928-32; asst. prof. biochemistry, Henry Phipps Inst., U. of Pa., 1932-37, asso. prof. since 1937. Mem. A.A.A.S., Soc. Biol. Chemistry, Am. Chem. Soc., Tuberculosis Assn., Soc. for Exptl. Biology and Medicine, Chicago Inst. Medicine, Physiol. Soc. of Phila., Am. Assn. Univ. Women, Sigma Xi, Phi Beta Kappa. Honored by award Ricketts Prize, U. of Chicago, 1924, Trudeau Medal of Nat. Tuberculosis Assn., 1938. Fellowships: Yale, 1920, Van Meter at Yale, 1921-22; Porter of Am. Physiol. Soc. at Yale, 1922-23 and at Chicago U., 1923-24; Guggenheim Fellow to Univ. Upsala, Sweden, 1937-38. Club: Women's University of Philadelphia. Home: 2406 S. 21st St., Philadelphia, Pa.

SEIDENSTICKER, Charles Alfred, retired banker; b. Penn's Manor, Pa., Mar. 28, 1874; s. Claus John and Johanna Dorothea (Schumann) S.; ed. Penn's Manor (Pa.) Public School and Stewart Business Coll., Trenton, N.J.; m. Martha Pauline Luippold, June 25, 1901; children—Alfred John (deceased), Freda Elizabeth (Mrs. George R. Bowers). Asso. with Princeton Bank & Trust Co., Princeton, N.J., and its predecessor The Princeton Bank, since 1894, beginning as jr. clerk and bookkeeper Nov. 21, 1894, served successively in all depts., sec. and treas. (when bank became trust co.), 1916-30, vice-pres. and trust officer, 1930-39, dir. 1936; retired March 28, 1939, but continues on bd. of dirs. and as chmn. of trust com. Mem. Bd. of Edn. and dist. clerk since 1904; trustee and treas. Methodist Ch.; dir. and charter mem. Princeton Y.M.C.A.; former dir. and trustee Princeton Hosp. and its first treas.; treas. Liberty Loan Campaign, United War Work Campaign and Near East Relief during World War. Former sec. and treas. Princeton Battle Monument Commn. Republican. Methodist. Address: 8 Hamilton Av., Princeton, N.J.

SEIFERT, Edwin A(ndrew), surgeon; b. Wheeling, W.Va., Apr. 1, 1900; s. Andrew J. and Quarta (Mayer) S.; B.S., O. State U., 1918; M.D., O. State U. Med. Sch., 1924; m. Evelyn Rich, June 25, 1938. Interne, City Hosp., N.Y. City, 1924-26; spl. interneship, Hosp. for Ruptured & Crippled, N.Y. City, 1926-27; resident phys., Mountainside Hosp., Montclair, N.J., 1927-28; asso. with Dr. James T. Hanan, Montclair, N.J., 1928-31; in practice at Glen Ridge, N.J., since 1937; asst. attending physician of orthopedic surgery, Mountainside Hosp., Montclair, N.J., Essex County Isolation Hosp., Belleville, N.J.; clinical asst. Hospital for the Ruptured and Crippled, New York, N.Y.; surgeon Police and Fire Depts., Glen Ridge, N.J.; mem. Glen Ridge Bd. of Health. Served in U.S.A., 1918. Fellow Am. Coll. Surgs. Mem. Am. Med. Assn., N.J. State Med. Soc., Essex Co. Med. Soc., Asso. Phys. of Montclair, N.J., and Vicinity, Phi Chi. Republican. Conglist. Mason. Club: Kiwanis of Montclair. Home: 415 Ridgewood Av., Glen Ridge, N.J.

SEIFFERT, Morgan Roe, lawyer; b. New Brunswick, N.J., Nov. 22, 1902; s. Henry and Alice (Roe) S.; B.Sc., Rutgers U., 1923; LL.B., N.J. Law Sch., 1927; m. Eleanor A. Bagley, Dec. 10, 1928; children—Elizabeth Ann, Lois Alice. Engaged in civil engring. in N.J. and New York City, 1923-27; admitted to N.J. bar as atty., 1928, as counsellor at law, 1931; asso. in practice with Edward M. and Runyon Colie, Newark, N.J., 1927-36; in pvt. practice of law, alone, New Brunswick, N.J., since 1936; sec. W. A. Cleary Corpn.; sec. State of N.J. Del. & Raritan Canal Commn. since 1935. At present 2d lt., O.R.C. Rep. candidate for N.J. Assembly, 1931. Former recorder (criminal magistrate) Highland Park, N.J. Trustee Pub. Library Borough Highland Park. Mem. New Brunswick Chamber of Commerce, New Brunswick Jr. Chamber Commerce (trustee), Greater New Brunswick Assn. (counsel), N.J. Canal Assn. (counsel). Mem. N.J. and Middlesex Co. bar assns., N.J. Soc. Professional Engrs., Raritan Club of Rutgers U., Delta Theta Pi. Republican. Mem. Reformed Ch. Club: Officers Golf of Raritan Arsenal. Home: 304 N. 4th Av., Highland Park. Office: 390 George St., New Brunswick, N.J.

SEIFRIZ, William, prof. of botany; b. Washington, D.C., Aug. 11, 1888; s. Paul and Anna (Schmidt) S.; B.S., Johns Hopkins, 1918, Ph.D., 1920; post grad. study U. of Geneva (Switzerland), Kings Coll. (London, Eng.), Kaiser Wilhelm Inst. (Germany), 1920-22; unmarried. Instr. botany, U. of Mich., 1923-25; prof. botany, U. of Pa., since 1925. Mem. Bot. Soc. America, A.A.A.S., Phi Beta Kappa, Sigma Xi. Club: Century (New York). Asso. editor Protoplasma; writer of book on protoplasm and scientific articles. Home: Chester Springs, Pa. Address: University of Pa., Philadelphia, Pa.

SEIL, Gilbert E(dward), chem. engring.; b. Brooklyn, N.Y., Oct. 29, 1888; s. Edward and Ester (Mann) S.; ed. Rutgers, 1905-08; chemist, Columbia U., 1912; M.S., U. of Pittsburgh, 1921, Ph.D., same, 1922; m. Frances Jane Merritt, May 1, 1920. Employed as chem. dir., Metal and Thermit Corpn., New York, 1915-19; Fellow, Mellon Inst., U. of Pittsburgh, 1920-23; head, Pioneer Research Div., Koppers Co., 1923-26; tech. dir., E. J. Lavino and Co., Phila., Pa., since 1926. Mem. Am. Chem. Soc., Fellow Am. Inst. of Chemists; mem. Inst. Mining and Metall. Engrs., Am. Ceramic Soc., Am. Gas Assn., Soc. for Testing Materials. Republican. Contbr. sci. articles to chem., metall., and gas-industry jours. Home: 18 Radcliffe Rd., Bala-Cynwyd, Pa. Office: E. J. Lavino & Co., Norristown, Pa.

SEILIKOVITCH, Solomon, physician; b. Odessa, Russia, May 1, 1865; s. Moses and Rebecca (Spiro) S.; came to U.S., 1886, and naturalized citizen, 1893; ed. Gymnasium, Odessa, Russia; M.D., Medico-Chirurg. Coll., 1893; m. Fannie Blum, Sept. 4, 1894; children—Rebecca (Mrs. Michael Grossberg), Theresa, Milton Selig. Engaged in gen. practice of medicine at Phila. since 1893; sr. pediatrist, Mt. Sinai Hosp., (1900-27, lecturer, Nurses' Sch., 1905-27. Enrolled as mem. Vol. Med. Service Corps, 1918. Mem. Phila. Co. Med. Soc., Phila. Pediatric Soc. Democrat. Hebrew religion. Home: 2444 S. 5th St., Philadelphia, Pa.

SEIPP, Alice, artist; b. New York, N.Y.; d. John and Alice (Mellen) S.; grad. Art sch. of Cooper Union, New York; studied painting and etching at The Art Students' League, New York. Art editor and illustrator for Woman's Inst. Domestic Arts and Sciences. Exhibited Nat. Assn. Women Painters and Sculptors, Am. Water Color Club, New York, Philadelphia, Washington and Baltimore water color clubs. Awarded hon. mention for painting at 2d Nat. Exhbn. of Palm Beach Art Center. Member of art com. of Everhart Museum, Scranton, Pa. Mem. Nat. Assn. Women Painters and Sculptors, Pen and Brush Club, New York Water Color Club. Home: 701 Olive St. Address: Woman's Institute, Scranton, Pa.*

SEIVER, Louis Max, pres. Automobile Banking Corpn.; b. Bucharest, Rumania, Nov. 21, 1889; s. Max and Rachel (Koppel) S.; student Vienna (Austria) Bus. Acad., 1906-08; m. Ida Cahane, Nov. 15, 1914; children—Theodore Johnathan, Florence Moise; came to U.S., 1910, naturalized, 1915. Began as asst. purchasing agt., Locomobile Co. of America, Bridgeport, Conn., 1913, purchasing agt., 1914; mgr. Automobile Corpn., Phila., 1915-17; mgr. Automobile Banking Corpn., Phila., automobile sales financing, 1917-20, pres. since 1920; pres. and dir. A.B.C. Credit, Inc., Phila., A.B.C. Credit Corpn. of N.Y. Republican. Clubs: Manufacturers and Bankers, Poor Richard (Phila.); Bankers of America, Advertising (New York). Home: Drexel Park, Pa. Office: Market St. National Bank Bldg., Philadelphia, Pa.

SEKOL, Severin William, cons. engr.; b. Scranton, Pa., Sept. 28, 1888; s. William F. and Fanny S.; student Scranton (Pa.) High Sch.; married, Dec. 14, 1911; 1 son, Clinton Franklin. With Glen Alden Coal Co. to 1917, successively as dist. engr., asst. mine foreman, supt. Nat. Mine Fire; mgr. Se-Rob Coal Co., 1917-23; gen. mgr. Sun Rise & Ranson Coal Co., 1923-27; mining engr. for Scranton (Pa.) Sch. Dist., 1927-33; head of firm Severin Sekol & Son, cons. engrs., Scranton, Pa., since 1933, legal rep. of numerous coal cos.; dir. Severin Sekol & Son, East Scranton Bank. Presbyterian. Mason (Union Lodge; Consistory, 32°; Shriner). Clubs: Elmhurst Country (dir.); Scranton (Pa.) Canoe (life mem.); Hole in One. Address: 1402 Myrtle St., Scranton, Pa.

SELDEN, Edwin Van Deusen, retired oil producer; b. Pittsburgh, Pa., Dec. 23, 1858; s. George Shattuck and Elizabeth Wright (Clark) S.; ed. pub. schs. and Episcopal Acad.; m. Cornelia Fuller Earp, Jan. 2, 1901; children—John Earp, Edwin Van Deusen, Jr., Elizabeth, George Samuel, William Kirkpatrick. Mem. and pres. Oil City Oil Exchange, 1878. Del. from Diocese of Erie to Gen. Conbs. of P.E. Ch., 1913-37. Dir. Pub. Charities Assn. of Pa., 1933-38; council mem. and hon. pres. Clarion and Venango Council Boy Scouts of America, 1920-37; mem. Pa. Assn. for the Blind (trustee, 1933-38). First lt. and quartermaster, 16th Regt. Inf., Pa. Nat. Guard, 1888-95; col., commanding 21st Regt. Inf., Pa. Nat. Guard, 1898-99. Address: 408 W. 2d St., Oil City, Pa.

SELINGER, Samuel, surgeon; b. New York, N.Y., Apr. 15, 1892; s. Max and Rachel (Joseph) S.; B.C.S., N.Y. Univ., 1914; M.D., N.Y. Med. Coll. and Flower Hosp., N.Y. City, 1918; unmarried. Interne North Hudson Hosp., Weehawken, N.J., 1918-19; engaged in practice of medicine and surgery, specializing in diseases of eye, ear, nose and throat, West New York, N.J., since 1920; asso. ophthalmologist and otolaryngologist, North Hudson Hosp., Weehawken, N.J., since 1921; attending otolaryngologist and ophthalmologist, Christ Hosp., Jersey City, N.J., since 1932. Fellow Am. Coll. Surgeons, A.M.A.; mem. Am. Acad. of Ophthalmology and Otolaryngology. Home: 413 16th St., West New York, N.J.

SELL, William Drumm, civil and mining engr.; b. Lancaster, Pa., Dec. 31, 1868; s. Nathaniel Engel and Elizabeth (Kassar) S.; m. Rose Osborne, June 21, 1892; children—William Osborne, Rose Elizabeth (Mrs. James P. Warren), Anne Kathryn (dec.), John McCaskey (dec.), Robert Lee, Dorothy Donnally (Mrs. Earl A. Allen), Mary Eleanor (dec.), Frank Marion, James. Chmn. Norfolk & Western R.R., 1888-90, in charge of residency, 1891; private practice as consulting engr., Logan, W.Va., 1891-1900, Charleston, W.Va., since 1900; engaged in building railroads, developing mining properties, real estate developments, valuations and appraisals. Served as capt. Corps of Engrs., U.S. Army, 1917-18. Life mem. Am. Soc. Civil Engrs., Am. Assn. Engrs. ((sr. grade), Soc. Am. Mil. Engrs. ((charter mem.), W.Va. Soc. Engrs. Democrat. Episcopalian. Home: 814 Bridge Rd. Office: 301 Virginia Land Bank Bldg., Charleston, W.Va.

SELLERS, Coleman, III, engineer; b. Phila., Pa., Feb. 13, 1893; s. Coleman and Helen Graham (Jackson) S.; student Haverford (Pa.) Sch., 1904-10; B.S. in M.E., U. of Pa., 1915, M.E., 1928; m. Kathlyne Montgomery Shattuck, Oct. 17, 1916; children—Coleman, IV, Frank Rodman Shattuck, William Woodward, Kathlyne Jackson. Research Engr., Wm. Sellers & Co., Inc., machine tools, Phila., 1915-17, asst. supt., 1919-21, engring. dept., 1921-25, exec. engr., 1925-37, plant mgr., 1937-38, engr. since 1938; supt. of repair in machine shops, Midvale Steel Co., Nicetown, Phila., 1917-18. Mem. Franklin Inst. (mem. bd. of mgrs.), Am. Soc. M.E. (chmn. Phila. sect., 1937-38), Newcomen Soc. Republican. Episcopalian. Clubs: Mask and Wig (Phila.); Engineers (Phila.); Tredyffrin Country (Paoli, Pa.). Home: Russell Rd., Daylesford, Berwyn P.O., Pa. Office: 1600 Hamilton St., Philadelphia, Pa.

SELLERS, Monroe Deetz, banker; b. Sellersville, Pa., Apr. 1, 1861; s. Lewis J. and Sarah (Deetz) S.; ed. Sellersville Grammar Sch., 1870-77; m. Martha L. Althouse, May 21, 1896; children—James Monroe, Anna (wife of M. Vaughn Mitchell), A. Margaret (wife of Rev. Edwin W. Andrews). Began as carpenter, 1878; asso. with father, Lewis J. Sellers, began manufacture of cigar boxes, Jan. 1880, continuing alone after death of father in 1906; succeeded by son on his retirement, Dec. 31, 1920; dir. Sellersville Nat. Bank since 1921, pres. 1926 to Jan. 1938, vice-pres. since 1938. Democrat. Mem. Reformed Ch. Mason (32°, Shriner). Home: 396 N. Main St., Sellersville, Pa.

SELLERS, Montgomery Porter, prof. rhetoric; b. Allegheny, Pa., Aug. 26, 1873; s. Francis Benjamin and Martha Ann (Porter) S.; Ph.B., Dickinson Coll., Carlisle, Pa., 1893, A.M., 1894; student Heidelberg, Germany, summer, 1895, Oxford, Eng., three summers, U. of Chicago; (hon.) Litt.D., Hamline U., St. Paul, Minn., 1918; m. Grace Harlan Downes, June 8, 1936. Instr. German, Dickinson Coll., Carlisle, Pa., 1893-95, adj. prof. English, 1895-1904, prof. rhetoric and English lang. since 1904; dean Dickinson Coll., 1928-33. Phi Kappa Psi, Phi Beta Kappa. Republican. Methodist. Home: 262 West High St., Carlisle, Pa.

SELLIN, (Johan) Thorsten, prof. sociology; b. Örnsköldsvik, Sweden, Oct. 26, 1896; s. Jonas and Martha (Westman) S.; ed. high sch. and coll. in Sweden until 1913; A.B., Augustana Coll., Rock Island, Ill., 1915; A.M., U. of Pa., 1916, Ph.D., 1922; grad. study, U. of Minn. (part time), 1916-20, U. of Paris, 1924-25; m. Amy J. Anderson, June 10, 1920; children—Theodore, David, Eric. Teacher modern langs., Minnesota, Coll., Minneapolis, 1916-18, Central High Sch., Minneapolis, 1919-20; case worker,

Associated Charities, Minneapolis, Feb.-Sept. 1920; Harrison fellow in sociology, U. of Pa., 1920-21; hon. fellow Am. Scandinavian Foundation, 1921; instr. in sociology, U. of Pa., 1921-22, asst. prof., 1922-30, prof. since 1930. Lecturer at Columbia Univ. since 1935. Leave of absence, 1924-26, for study and research in Europe, and 1930-33, to serve on staff of Bur. of Social Hygiene, Inc., N.Y. City. Consultant in criminal statistics, Bur. of Census, 1931—; mem. Prison Labor Compact Authority, 1934. Editor Annals of Am. Acad. Polit. and Social Science since 1929; asso. editor Jour. Criminal Law and Criminology, since 1927. Mem. Am. Prison Assn. (dir.), Nat. Probation Assn., Am. Acad. Polit. and Social Science (chmn. fellowship com.), Am. Sociol. Soc., Am. Statis. Assn. (chmn. Com. on Criminal Statistics), Sociological Research Assn., Kriminalbiol. Gesellschaft, Society générale de prisons (Paris); corr. mem. Academie Intern. de Criminalistique (Lausanne), Masaryk Sociol. Soc. (Prague). Author: Marriage and Divorce Legislation in Sweden, 1922; (with J. P. Shalloo) A Bibliographical Manual for the Student of Criminology, 1935; Research Memorandum on Crime in the Depression, 1937; Culture Conflict and Crime, 1938. Contbr. to Ency. of Social Sciences, Dictionary of Am. Biography, also to Am. and foreign jours. Home: 4427 Osage Av., Philadelphia, Pa.

SELTZ, Harry, prof. chemistry; b. Phila., Pa., June 16, 1896; s. Jacob and Elizabeth (Snyder) S.; B.S., in Chem. Engring., U. of Pa., 1917, Ph.D., same, 1922; m. Juliana Gannon Frauenheim, Dec. 26, 1934. Engaged as instr. chemistry, U. of Pa., 1918-24; instr. chemistry, Carnegie Inst. Tech., 1924-25, asst. prof., 1925-31, asso. prof. chemistry, 1931-39, prof. of chemistry since 1939. Served in C.W.S., U.S.A., 1917-18. Mem. Am. Chem. Soc., Sigma Xi, Alpha Chi Sigma. Club: University (Pittsburgh). Author: General Chemistry, 1927, 3d edit., 1939. Contbr. over 20 articles in fields thermodynamics and kinetics to sci. jours. Home: 2747 Mount Royal Rd., Pittsburgh, Pa.

SELTZER, Albert P., physician; b. Russia, Aug. 12, 1903; s. Rabbi Penches Judah and Ida (Sunshine) S.; was brought to U.S., 1905, and naturalized, 1909; ed. Temple Coll.; M.D., Temple U. Med. Sch., 1928; (hon.) certificate otology, Univ. de Bordeaux, France, 1937; unmarried. Engaged in practice of medicine at Phila. since 1929, now limited to ear, nose and throat and plastic surgery; asst. otorhinolaryngologist, St. Luke's Hosp.; on courtesy staff, Mt. Sinai, North Liberties and Jewish hosps.; instr. communicable diseases, St. Luke's Hosp. Nurses Sch.; instr. anatomy, Temple U. Med. Sch.; asst. surgeon, St. Luke's Hosp.; surgeon to Pa. R.R. Former actg. surgeon, U.S. Pub. Health Service. Mem. Phila. County Med. Soc., Pa. State Med. Soc., Phi Delta Epsilon. Jewish religion. B'nai B'rith. Home: 1332 N. Franklin St., Philadelphia, Pa.

SEMENOW, Robert W(illiam), lawyer; b. Greensburg, Pa., Dec. 6, 1897; s. Samuel and Rose (Ruben) S.; B.S. in Econ., U. of Pa., 1919; LL.B., Duquesne U., Pittsburgh, 1921; Litt.M., U. of Pittsburgh, 1937. Instr. in business law, U. of Pittsburgh, since 1920, sec., downtown div., 1922-29; gen. practice of law at Pittsburgh since 1921; prof. of business law, U. of Texas, Austin, Tex., summer 1927; counsel, Pittsburgh Real Estate Bd., 1927-39; chief of law enforcement, Pa. State Dept. of Pub. Instrn., 1929-35. Mem. Pittsburgh Real Estate Bd. (hon. life), Nat. Assn. of License Law Officials (sec.-treas.), Delta Mu Delta (hon.). Republican. Hebrew religion. Author: Pennsylvania Law of Real Estate Brokerage; Landlord and Tenant, 1931; A Survey of Real Estate Brokers' License Laws, 1936. Address: 601 Berger Bldg., Pittsburgh, Pa.

SEMMES, John Edward; mem. law firm Semmes, Bowen & Semmes. Office: Baltimore Trust Bldg., Baltimore, Md.

SENIOR, Frank Sears, civil engring.; b. Montgomery, N.Y., Nov. 17, 1876; s. George E. and Hannah (Sears) S.; C.E., Cornell U., 1896; m. Harriet Ash, Sept. 18, 1924; children—Frank Sears, Jr., John Lemaitre. Draftsman, Hall of Records, Brooklyn, N.Y., 1896 to 1898; engr. on Govt. fortifications, Great Gull Island, N.Y., 1898-99; engr., supt., and vice-pres. Arthur McMullen Co., New York, N.Y., 1899-1929; pres. and dir. Senior & Palmer, Inc., engring. constrn., N.Y. City since 1929; specialized in pneumatic foundations for bridges, has built foundations for ten ry. and highway bridges over Passaic and Hackensack rivers and Newark Bay using pneumatic process. Served as maj. Transportation Corps, U.S.A., 1918-19, on staff dir. gen. of transportation with A.E.F.; awarded citation by the Comdr. in Chief for exceptionally meritorious and conspicuous services with A.E.F.; Officier d'Academie (France). Mem. Am. Soc. Civil Engrs., Psi Upsilon. Republican. Presbyn. (trustee Central Ch.). Clubs: Golf (Montclair); Engineers, Railroad-Machinery, Cornell (New York); Seabright Tennis. Home: 82 Myrtle Av., Montclair, N.J. Office: 50 Church St., New York, N.Y.

SENN, Alfred, educator, linguist; b. Blotzheim, Haut-Rhin, France, Mar. 19, 1899 (parents Swiss citizens); s. Alfred and Bertha (Affolter) S.; grad. with highest honors, Gymnasium, St. Gallen, Switzerland, 1918; Ph.D., U. of Fribourg, Switzerland, 1921; m. Maria Vedlugaite, of Kaunas, Lithuania, July 22, 1923; children—Marie B., Elfrieda G., Alfred Erich. Came to U.S., 1930; naturalized, May 19, 1936, in Madison, Wis. In Foreign Office, Lithuania, 1921-22; privat-docent, U. of Lithuania, Kaunas, 1922-23, asst. prof. of comparative philology, 1923-30, also prin. Lithuanian evening sch. for adults; Sterling research fellow in Germanics, Yale U., 1930-31; prof. of Germanic and Indo-European philology, U. of Wis., 1931-38, also chmn. dept. comparative philology, 1932-38; prof. Germanic philology, U. of Pa., since 1938; teacher Linguistic Inst., New York, summers 1930, 31; teacher Columbia U., summer 1939; dir. Linguistic Conf., U. of Wis., 1937. Mem. Modern Lang. Assn. of America (chmn. discussion groups Slavic, 1936, German, 1937, 38), Linguistic Soc. America (exec. com., 1939), Swiss-Am. Hist. Soc. (v.p. 1934-38, dir. since 1938), mem. Com. on Slavic Studies of Am. Council of Learned Socs. since 1939. Author: Anthologia Latina, 1923; Litauische Sprachlehre, 1929; An Introduction to Middle High German, 1937. Co-author: Lithuanian-German Dictionary, vol. I, 1932, vol. II, in press; Word-Index to Wolfram's Parzival, 1938. Contbr. of numerous articles in German, Lithuanian and English to professional jours. of Europe and U.S.; consultant to editorial bd. Publs. Modern Lang. Assn. America. Interested in the cultural relations between U.S. and Switzerland. Contbr. to Am.-Swiss newspapers. Home: 112 Penarth Rd., Bala-Cynwyd, Pa.

SENNETT, Bernard Walker, lawyer; b. North East, Pa., Dec. 18, 1898; s. William C. and Bertha L. (Walker) S.; A.B., Holy Cross Coll., Worcester, Mass., 1920; LL.B., Yale Law Sch., 1923; m. Rosanna Cooney, June 28, 1928; children—William C., Mary Ann, Jane Frances. Admitted to Pa. bar, 1923; mem. law firm Barber & Sennett, Erie, Pa., since 1936; dist. mgr. Home Owners Loan Corpn., 1934-36. Served in U.S. Army, Sept.-Dec. 1918. Mem. Pa. Bar Assn., Erie County Bar Assn., Am. Legion. Catholic. Elk. Home: 1031 W. 24th St. Office: 705 Ariel Bldg., Erie, Pa.

SENSENICH, Chester George, chmn. bd. Irwin Foundry & Mine Car Co.; b. Irwin, Pa., June 20, 1904; s. Chester David and Carrie (Boyd) S.; student Norwin Union High Sch., Irwin, Pa., 1918-22; B.S. in mining engring., Pa. State Coll., 1926; m. Isabel Warren Scull, May 7, 1927; children—Isabel Scull, Lois Victoria. Began as draftsman, 1926; salesman Irwin (Pa.) Foundry & Mine Car Co., mfrs. mining equipment and gen. castings, 1927-28, sales engr., 1928-31, sales mgr., 1931-33, v.p., 1933-34, gen. mgr., 1934-37, chmn. bd. since 1938; pres. and dir. Intra State Coal & Coke Co.; dir. First Nat. Bank of Irwin. Mem. R.O.T.C. (band); mem. Gov.'s Unemployment Bd., 1933-34, Rep. Finance Com. of Pa. Mem. Coal Mining Institute of America, Kappa Sigma, Kappa Kappa Psi. Republican. United Presbyterian. Clubs: Irwin Country, Kiwanis International (Irwin, Pa.). Home: 314 Fourth St. Office: Irwin, Pa.

SENSENICH, Louis Eaby, lawyer; b. Irwin, Pa., Aug. 31, 1906; s. Chester David and Carrie Edna (Boyd) S.; student Norwin Union High Sch., Irwin, Pa., 1921-25; B.S., U. of Pittsburgh, 1929, LL.B., 1932; m. Evelyn Margaret Harbourt, June 8, 1938. Admitted to Pa. bar, 1932, and since practiced at Greensburg, Pa.; sec. and treas. Irwin (Pa.) Foundry and Mine Car Co., mfrs. mine and foundry equipment, since 1937. Mem. Sigma Alpha Epsilon, Phi Delta Phi. Republican. United Presbyterian. Home: 625 Oak St., Irwin, Pa. Office: First National Bank Bldg., Greensburg, Pa.

SENTER, Ralph Townsend, rapid transit; b. Columbus, O., Feb. 27, 1876; s. Orestes A. B. and Mary (Townsend) S.; ed. Mich. Mil. Acad. and U. of Mich., Armour Inst. Tech. Connected with various rys., including Twin City Rapid Transit Co., Chicago City Ry. Co.; now pres. Phila. Rapid Transit Co. Mason (K.T., 32°). Office: Mitten Bldg., Philadelphia, Pa.

SERENA, John Norris, lawyer; b. McKeesport, Pa., Nov. 3, 1895; s. John Elmer and Eva (Porter) S.; Litt.B., Princeton, 1916; LL.B., U. of Pittsburgh Law Sch., 1923; unmarried. Admitted to Pa. bar, 1923, and engaged in practice at Pittsburgh, 1923-26; in gen. practice at Phila. since 1926; sec. and mem. bd. govs. Republican League of Pa. Served in Co.D. Fourth Pioneer Inf., U.S.A., 1918. Mem. Pa. and Phila. bar assns., Am. Legion, Phi Delta Phi. Republican. Presbyn. Mason. Clubs: Union League, Princeton (Philadelphia); Key and Seal (Princeton, N.J.). Home: 6320 Overbrook Av. Office: 600 Commercial Trust Bldg., Philadelphia, Pa.

SERGEANT, Edgar, retired business exec.; b. New York, N.Y., Nov. 25, 1878; s. William Roberts and Edith Matilda (Leaman) S.; student Irving Sch., New York, 1887-95, Columbia Coll., New York, 1895; m. Tacie Nairn, Mar. 4, 1914; children—Sarah Fisher, Tacie Nairn (Mrs. Briscoe B. Ranson, III), Edgar, Jr., William Roberts. Began as office boy, G. P. Cooper & Co., New York, 1896; filing clerk, E. M. Sergeant Pulp & Chem. Co., New York, 1897-98, salesman, 1898-1913, vice-pres. and dir., 1913-17, pres., 1917-29; retired, 1929, to take up study of painting; formerly dir. of Bank of Nutley; dir. Eagle Fire Ins. Co., Sussex Fire Ins. Co. Served as private, 7th Regt., Nat. Guard, State of N.Y., 7 years. Mem. Nutley (N.J.) Bd. of Edn., 1920-22; chmn. Nutley (N.J.) Planning Bd. Republican. Episcopalian. Clubs: Salmagundi, Columbia U. (New York); Yountakah Country, Nutley Field (Nutley, N.J.). Studied painting under Frank V. DuMond, Art Students League, New York, 1929-31, George Pearce Ennis and Edmond Greason, Grand Central Sch., New York, 1931-33; pictures accepted by Nat. Acad. of New York, Allied Artists of America, Montclair Museum, Salmagundi Club, N.Y. Address: 160 Satterthwaite Av., Nutley, N.J.

SEWALL, Arthur Wollaston, former pres. General Asphalt Co.; b. Mobile, Ala., Nov. 19, 1860; s. Kiah Bayley and Lucretia (Day) S.; ed. high sch.; m. Cynthia Pope Yeatman, Dec. 29, 1897. In asphalt business since 1900; became pres. Gen. Asphalt Co., 1912, now dir.; dir. Federal Reserve Bank, 3d Dist, 1926-38; dir. Ins. Co. of N. America, Mut. Assurance Co., Am. Pulley Co. Dir. Zoöl. Soc. Republican. Episcopalian. Clubs: Philadelphia, Midday. Home: (winter) 1311 Spruce St., Philadelphia, Pa.; (summer) Jaffrey, N.H.

SEXSMITH, Edgar A(dgate), clergyman; b. Clark Co., Mo., Feb. 19, 1875; s. John and Mary B. (Owings) S.; student Kahoka Normal Coll., Kahoka, Mo., 1894-95, Westminster Theol. Sem., Westminster, Md., 1897-1900, Western Md. Coll., Westminster, Md., 1898-99; (hon.) D.D., Western Md. Coll., 1925; m. Fanny Lee Williams, June 11, 1901 (died 1926); m. 2d Emma K. Hess, Oct. 9, 1928 (died 1939). Ordained to ministry Meth. Prot. Ch., 1901; held various pastorates in Mo., 1900-06; pres.

SEXTON — N.Mo. Conf., 1904-06; pastor various churches in Md. and Baltimore City since 1906; exec. sec. Bd. Young Peoples Work, 1920-24; pres. Bd. Christian Edn., Meth. Prot. Ch. since 1929; pres. Md. Annual Conf. since 1934. Democrat. Meth. Protestant Ch. Mason. Home: 3600 Copley Rd. Office: 516 N. Charles St., Baltimore, Md.

SEXTON, Roy Lyman, M.D.; b. Washington, D.C., May 15, 1894; s. Grant W. and Adore (Wardell) S.; B.S., Georgetown U., 1916, M.D., 1918; m. Frances Fry, Sept. 16, 1918; children—Jean Frances, Roy Lyman. Resident phys., Sibley Memorial Hosp., 1918-19, Georgetown U. Hosp., 1919-20; practice limited to gastro-enterology and internal medicine since 1926. Served in Med. Res. Corps, U.S.A., World War. Asso. Am. Coll. Phys.; mem. Am. Med. Assn., D.C. Med. Soc., Southern Med. Soc., Am. Therapeutic Soc. Clubs: University, Congressional Country, Corinthian Yacht (Washington). Home: 28 Primrose St., Chevy Chase, Md. Office: 1801 I St., Washington, D.C.

SEYBOLD, Roscoe, v.p. Westinghouse Electric & Mfg. Co.; b. Rockville, Ind., Feb. 9, 1884; s. J. L. and Margaret Ella (Neet) S.; B.S. in E.E., Purdue U., 1907; m. Nancy Frank, Sept. 1, 1915; children—Robert J., William V. Began as clerk Westinghouse Electric & Mfg. Co., Pittsburgh, Pa., July 1, 1907, asst. to v.p. and gen. mgr., 1926-29, asst. to pres., 1929-31, comptroller, 1931-34, v.p. and comptroller since 1934; dir. Union Nat. Bank (Pittsburgh), Wilkinsburg (Pa.) Federal Savings and Loan Assn. Mem. Controllers Inst. of America (pres. 1938-39), Phi Gamma Delta. Methodist. Mason. Clubs: Duquesne, Edgewood Country (Pittsburgh); Bankers (Pittsburgh and New York). Home: 317 Maple Av., Edgewood. Office: Westinghouse Electric & Mfg. Co., 306 Fourth Av., Pittsburgh, Pa.

SEYFERT, Stanley Sylvester, univ. prof.; b. Stranstown, Pa., Mar. 19, 1881; s. Jacob Wallace and Cassie Mahala (Reber) S.; B.S., Keystone State Normal Sch. (now Kutztown State Teachers' Coll.), 1900; E.E., Lehigh U., Bethlehem, Pa., 1904, M.S., 1909; Sc.D., Mass. Inst. Tech., 1932; m. Helen Arnold Beam, Aug. 31, 1922. Instr. in elec. engring., Lehigh U., Bethlehem, Pa., 1904-09, asst. prof., 1909-14, asso. prof., 1914-28, prof. since 1928, dir. of curriculum and head of elec. engring. dept. since 1932; engr. Blue Mountain Electric Co., Bethel, Pa., 1907-17, sec.-treas., 1917-27. Mem. Am. Inst. E.E., Inst. of Radio Engrs., Soc. for Promotion of Engring. Edn., Tau Beta Phi, Eta Kappa Nu, Sigma Xi. Republican. Reformed Ch. Clubs: Engineers' of Lehigh Valley, Torch of Lehigh Valley, Rotary (Bethlehem, Pa.). Address: 55 W. Market St., Bethlehem, Pa.

SEYMOUR, Frederick Ernest, clergyman; b. Cookham, Eng., Nov. 26, 1877; s. Richard and Eliza (Peskett) S.; came to U.S., 1890, naturalized, 1927; S.T.B., Phila. Divinity Sch., 1906; m. Louise Jane Tuke, Aug. 15, 1899; children—Frederick Edmund Tuke, Gladys Ethel (Mrs. John J. Hellewell), Wilfred Ernest, Harry Cuthbert, Edith Louise, Jack Murray. Ordained to ministry P.E. Ch., deacon, 1906, priest, 1906; rector, Wakefield, R.I., 1906-17; rector, St. Philip's, Phila., Pa., 1917-26; dir. religious edn., Diocese of Pa., 1926-32; vicar, St. George's Ch., Ardmore, Pa., since 1932. Home: St. George's Rectory, Ardmore, Pa.

SHACKLETON, Samuel Paul, engr.; b. La Porte Co., Ind., Oct. 6, 1891; s. James Munson and Mary Louise (Morehouse) S.; student Kalamazoo (Mich.) Pub. Schs., 1900-10, Kalamazoo (Mich.) Coll., 1910-12; B.S. in E.E., U. of Mich., 1915; m. Mildred Welsh, June 24, 1916; children—Joyce Evelyn, Richard James. Engr. Am. Telephone & Telegraph Co., New York, 1915-34; toll maintenance engr. Bell Telephone Labs., New York, since 1934. Mem. Am. Wyoming Assn. (past pres.). Mem. Am. Inst. E.E. (past chmn. communication group, N.Y. sect.), Inst. Radio Engrs., Am. Phys. Soc., A.A.A.S. Presbyterian. Club: Wyoming (Maplewood, N.J.). Home: 430 Wyoming Av., Maplewood, N.J. Office: 463 West St., New York, N.Y.

SHAFER, Glenn McMeen, clergyman; b. Seneca Co., O., Mar. 3, 1884; s. Alfred L. and Rachel (McMeen) S.; A.B., Heidelberg U., Tiffin, O., 1903; A.M., Princeton, 1908; student Princeton Theol. Sem., 1905-08; (hon.) D.D., Dickinson Coll., 1926; m. Helen Ann Mabery, Nov. 11, 1908. Ordained to ministry Presbyn. Ch. U.S.A., 1908; pastor, Bryan, O., 1908-11, Clarion, Pa., 1911-17; pastor Second Presbyn. Ch., Carlisle, Pa., since 1917; stated clk. Synod of Pa. since 1928. Trustee Wilson Coll., Presbyn. Home of Central Pa., Presbytery of Carlisle, Synod of Pa. Mem. Canterbury Cleric of Phila., Harrisburg Cleric. Republican. Presbyn. Mason (K.T.). Club: Rotary of Carlisle. Home: 243 S. Hanover St., Carlisle, Pa.

SHAFER, Stewart Sherman, lawyer; b. Snydersville, Pa., Nov. 3, 1864; s. Alonzo Buskirk and Emma Jane (Houck) S.; ed. pub. schs.; m. Minerva Pipher, Aug. 3, 1886 (dec.); children—Lulu Alice, Nellie. Read law in office of Judge John B. Storm and admitted to Pa. bar, 1892, and since engaged in gen. practice of law at Stroudsburg; admitted to practice before Pa. Supreme Ct. and U.S. Dist. Ct.; dep. prothonotary and dep. clk. Monroe Co. Cts., 1883-91; dep. treas. and dep. register of wills and deeds, 1892; dir. and atty. First Nat. Bank, 1895-1932, First Stroudsburg Nat. Bank since 1932. Democrat. Presbyn. Mason. Improved Order Red Men. Home: 801 Main St., Stroudsburg, Pa.; (summer) 312 Belmont St., Mt. Pocono, Pa.

SHAFFER, Elmer Lentz, pathologist; b. Phila., Apr. 29, 1892; s. Adam and Sophia (Lentz) S.; A.B., Phila. Central High Sch., 1911; B.S., Haverford Coll., 1915; A.M., Princeton, 1917, Ph.D., same, 1919; m. Lillian Epstein, June 21, 1921; children—Melvin Horace, Janice Sarah. Engaged as asst. in biology, Princeton U., 1915, research fellow in biology, 1916-17, Proctor fellow, 1919; instr. biology, Haverford Coll., 1920; pathologist, St. Francis Hosp., Trenton, N.J., since 1920; dir. Shaffer Clin. Lab. since 1920; pres. Stacy Theatre Realty Corpn. Served as pathologist, U.S. Navy Base Hosp. No. 5, Brest, France, 1917-19; now ensign U.S.N.R.F. Trustee and treas. Har Sinai Temple. Dir. Jewish Federation, Y.M.H.A. Mem. A.A.A.S., Soc. Am. Bacteriologists, N.J. Soc. Clin. Pathologists, Phi Beta Kappa. Jewish religion. Mason (32°, Shriner). Club: Greenacres Country (Lawrenceville). Home: 208 State St., Trenton, N.J.

SHAFFER, Frederick Biesecker, surgeon, banker; b. Jenners, Pa., Nov. 12, 1873; s. Aaron E. and Amanda (Biesecker) S.; A.B., Franklin & Marshall Coll., 1899; M.D., U. of Pa., 1908; m. Cynthia A. Ross, Oct. 19, 1919; 1 son, Frederick Ross. Pvt. practice of medicine at Somerset, Pa., since 1909; mem. med. staff, Somerset Co. (Pa.) Hosp.; pres. and dir. Peoples Nat. Bank, Somerset, Pa., since 1937; sec.-treas. Somerset (Pa.) Drug Co. Served as 1st lt., Pa. N.G., 1911-15, capt., 1915—; Batt. Surgeon, 110th Inf., 28th Div., U.S. Army, 1917-18. Mem. Somerset (Pa.) Bd. of Edn. since 1921. Mem. Am. Legion. Mason. Clubs: Rotary, Somerset Country (Somerset, Pa.). Address: Somerset, Pa.

SHAFFER, George Wilsen, psychologist, dir. of health and physical edn.; b. Baltimore, Md., Nov. 23, 1901; s. George Evans and Alice Mae (Wilsen) S.; A.B., Johns Hopkins, 1924, Ph.D., 1928; m. Margaret Ola Cowles, Oct. 29, 1931. Physical director, Baltimore, 1917-28; dir. phys. edn., Playground Athletic League, Baltimore, 1919-27; prof. of psychology, U. of Baltimore, 1928-34; lecturer in psychology and dir. of health and phys. edn., Johns Hopkins, since 1928. Mem. Kappa Sigma, Sigma Xi, Omicron Delta Kappa. Home: Tudor Arms Apts. Office: Johns Hopkins Univ., Baltimore, Md.

SHAFFER, Harry Gus, lawyer; b. Tunnelton, W.Va., Jan. 22, 1885; s. Gus J. and Florence (Thomas) S.; grad. W.Va. Univ. Law Coll., 1908; m. Brookie Turley, Feb. 23, 1916; children—Catherine Hester, Florence Jane, Margaret Eleanor, Harry Gus, Jr., Winfield Turley. Admitted to W.Va. bar, 1909, and since engaged in gen. practice of law at Madison; mem. firm Leftwich & Shaffer; mem. W.Va. Senate, 1921-23 and pres. Senate, 1923; now pres. Boone Nat. Bank of Madison. Republican. Baptist. Mason. Clubs: Rotary, Walhonde (Madison). Address: Madison, W.Va.

SHAFFER, Isaac Augustus, Jr., pres. First Nat. Bank of Lock Haven (Pa.); b. Lock Haven, Pa., Mar. 10, 1868; s. Isaac Aker and Mary Harriet (Maus) S.; student Pub. Schs., Lock Haven, Pa., 1874-85, Christie's Sch. of Business, Lock Haven, Pa., 1885-86; m. Martha Elizabeth Mosser, Sept. 10, 1892. Asst. cashier, State Bank of Lock Haven (Pa.), 1889-93; Pa. State Bank Examiner, 1893-95; chief clerk in lumber office of Hon. A. C. Hopkins, Lock Haven, Pa., 1895-1911, trustee Hon. A. C. Hopkins Estate, 1911-31; pres. and gen. mgr., Hopkins Coal Co., Lock Haven, Pa., 1920-31; pres. and dir. First Nat. Bank of Lock Haven, Pa., since 1923; v.p. and dir. Clark Printing and Mfg. Co., Lock Haven, Pa., since 1930; office mgr., Donold S. Hopkins, Lock Haven, Pa., since 1931; dir. Shaffer, Candor & Hopkins, Inc. Trustee Lock Haven (Pa.) Hosp., Annie Halenbake Ross Library (Lock Haven, Pa.), Susquehanna U. (Selinsgrove, Pa.), Tressler Orphans Home (Loysville, Pa.). Democrat. Protestant. Mason. Clubs: Acacia (Williamsport, Pa.); Rotary (Lock Haven, Pa.). Home: 229 N. Fairview St. Office: 146 E. Water St., Lock Haven, Pa.

SHAFFER, Laurance Frederic, univ. prof.; b. Johnstown, N.Y., Aug. 12, 1903; s. Mathew Thomas and Ines (Vaissiere) S.; B.S., Union Coll., Schenectady, N.Y., 1924; M.A., Columbia U., 1927, Ph.D., 1930; m. Dorothy Rhodes, June 24, 1931; 1 son, Warren Frederic. Teacher of mathematics, Kingsley Sch., Essex Fells, N.J., 1924-26; research asso., Inst. of Ednl. Research, Columbia U. Teachers Coll., 1926-28; asst. prof. of psychology, Carnegie Inst. Tech., 1928-35, asso. prof., 1935-37, prof. since 1937, dir. of summer session since 1935. Fellow Am. Assn. for Applied Psychology, A.A.A.S.; asso. Am. Psychol. Assn.; mem. Sigma Xi, Phi Kappa Phi, Kappa Delta Pi. Democrat. Presbyterian. Author: The Psychology of Adjustment, 1936; co-author: Child Psychology, 1937; Psychology, 1938. Home: 589 Audubon Av., Mt. Lebanon, Pa. Office: Carnegie Institute of Technology, Pittsburgh, Pa.

SHAFFER, William Walter, M.D., eye, ear, nose and throat specialist; b. Cochranton, Pa., Jan. 22, 1882; s. Daniel and Adeline (Daniels) S.; student Cochranton High Sch.; M.D., U. of Pittsburgh; post-grad. course, Cornell Med. Sch.; Manhattan Eye, Ear, Nose and Throat Sch. and U. of Pa.; m. Ethel Nesbet, May 26, 1909; children—Robert N., William N. Assisted in organizing hosp. staff Meadville City Hosp. and Spencer Hosp., and became chief eye, ear, nose and throat depts. of both hosps.; dir. Crawford County Trust Co. Dir. Meadville Y.M.C.A. Fellow A.M.A.; mem. Crawford Co. Med. Soc. (past pres.), Pa. Med. Soc., Northwestern Med. Soc. F.&A.M., Crawford Lodge No. 234, Solomon Royal Arch Chapter, Northwestern Commandery, Pittsburgh Consistory, Zem Zem Shrine. Clubs: Iroquois Boating and Fishing (past dir.), Meadville Country (past dir.), Rotary (past dir.); San Marino (Calif.). Home: 723 Walnut St. Office: Crawford County Trust Co. Bldg., Meadville, Pa.

SHALER, Charles Bunn, prescription optician; b. New Washington, Pa., Jan. 28, 1884; s. Louis John and Margaret Sarah (Bunn) S.; student Clearfield (Pa.) pub. schs., 1890-97; m. Hannah Elizabeth Aten, Nov. 2, 1912; 1 son James Bunn. Began as optician, 1908; Pres. Shaler & Crawford, Inc., Pittsburgh, Pa., guild-craft opticians since 1927. Dir. Nat. Guild of Prescription Opticians. Mem. Pa. Soc. S.A.R. Republican. Presbyterian. Mason (all bodies). Club: Aero (Pittsburgh). Home: 701 East End Av. Office: 146 Union Trust Bldg., Pittsburgh, Pa.

SHALLCROSS, Samuel Miller, v.p. Am. Lime & Stone Co.; b. Wilmington, Del., Mar. 25, 1893; s. Thomas W. and Mae (Miller) S.; B.S. in E.E., U. of Del., 1914; m. Winifred Bach, May 26, 1923; children (adopted)—Thomas Byron, William Bach. Asst. to pres. Am. Lime & Stone Co., Bellefonte, Pa., 1922-

24, v.p., gen. mgr. and dir. since 1924. Served as chief petty officer, U.S. Navy, during World War. Mem. Inst. of Mining Engrs., Am. Chem. Soc., Am. Legion, Kappa Alpha, Tau Beta Pi (Alpha chapter, Del.). Republican. Clubs: University (Pittsburgh); Nittany Country, Kiwanis (Bellefonte, Pa.). Home: 135 W. Linn St., Bellefonte, Pa. Office: American Lime & Stone Co., Bellefonte, Pa.

SHALLCROSS, Thomas, Jr., realtor; b. Byberry, Phila., Pa., Sept. 29, 1875; s. Thomas and Rachael (Comly) S.; ed. Friends' Central Sch. and Pierce Business Coll., Phila.; m. Lily A. Dungan, Oct. 19, 1898; children—Cynthia (Mrs. Ernest N. Calhoun), Ruth (Mrs. Wallace R. Linton). Office boy Peter Wright & Sons, Phila., 1892-94; teller Tacony Trust Co., Tacony, Phila., 1894-1900; mgr. then v.p. Wm. H. W. Quick & Bro., Inc., Phila., 1900-28; pres. Phila. Co. for Guaranteeing Mortgages, 1929-35; gen. partner Jackson-Cross Co., Phila., realtors, since 1936; mem. adv. com. First Nat. Bank (Centennial Office); dir. Fidelity Mutual Life Ins. Co., Girard Fire & Marine Ins. Co. Land Title Bank & Trust Co., First Trust Co. Republican. Soc. of Friends. Mason. Clubs: Union League (Phila.); Phila. Country (Bala, Pa.); Skytop (Skytop, Pa.). Home: Merion, Pa. Office: Lincoln-Liberty Bldg., Phila., Pa.

SHAMBACH, Jesse Yetter, official Dept. Pub. Instrn.; b. York, Pa., May 25, 1885; s. Joshua and Sarah Jane (Yetter) S.; grad. State Normal Sch., Bloomsburg, Pa., 1905; A.B., U. of Mich., 1913; grad. study U. of Pa., Columbia U.; m. Mary B. Lowry, June 19, 1913; children—Harold L., Arthur Y., Walter N., Lawrence R. Successively teacher rural schs., teacher graded schs., prin. high sch., supervising prin., 1901-07; instr. mathematics, Bloomsburg State Normal Sch., 1907-11; supt. of schs., Berwick, Pa., 1920; staff mem. Dept. of Pub. Instrn. of Pa., 1913-20, served as bur. dir., div. chief, and dep. sec. Pub. Sch. Employees Retirement Bd.; served as mem. various state, interstate, and nat. coms. organized to survey sch. systems, develop and review legislation, dept. policies, and ednl. procedures. Chmn. training com. Harrisburg Area Council, Boy Scouts (past v.p.). Charter mem. Rotary Club, Berwick, Pa. Mem. Phi Beta Kappa, Sigma Xi. Presbyn. Club: Torch (Harrisburg). Contbr. articles to mags. Developed and edited reports and other publs. and bulls. of the Dept. Pub. Instrn. Home: 2315 Page St., Camp Hill, Pa. Office: Education Bldg., Harrisburg, Pa.

SHANAMAN, Forrest Ritter, judge; b. Reading, Pa., Jan. 13, 1886; s. William Franklin and Laura (Ritter) S.; A.B., Harvard, 1907; LL.B., U. of Pa. Law Sch., 1910; m. Dorothy Althouse, June 19, 1924; children—Peter Althouse, Patricia Nagel. Admitted to Pa. bar, 1910, and since engaged in gen. practice of law at Reading; served as asst. city solicitor, 1920-24; borough solicitor, West Reading, 1920-28; judge Ct. Common Pleas since 1928. Mem. Pa. and Berks Co. bar assns. Republican. Mem. Reformed Ch. Mason. Royal Arcanum. Oriole. Moose. Elk. Clubs: Topics, Washington Library, University, Wyomissing (Reading). Home: 1625 Union St. Office: Court House, Reading, Pa.

SHAND, William, retail merchant; b. Lancaster, Pa., Sept. 1, 1889; s. James and Annie Weir (Jamieson) S.; student Franklin and Marshall Acad., 1902-04, Franklin and Marshall Coll., Lancaster, Pa., 1904-06; A.B., Princeton U., 1909; m. Dorothy Schaeffer, Oct. 24, 1916; children—James III, William, John Douglas, Thomas Marshall. Salesman Watt & Shand, Lancaster, Pa., 1909-12, office work, 1912-15; with Watt & Shand, Inc., Lancaster, Pa., department store since 1915, treas. since 1915; pres. Industrial Bldg. & Loan Assn., Real Estate, Inc.; partner Heidelbaugh Coal Co.; dir. Hamilton Watch Co., Farmers Bank & Trust Co. Trustee Lancaster Gen. Hosp., Franklin and Marshall Coll. Mem. Phi Beta Kappa, Phi Sigma Kappa. Republican. Presbyterian. Mason (Lodge 43). Clubs: Hamilton, Lancaster Country (Lancaster, Pa.). Home: R. 3, Lititz, Pa. Office: 2 E. King St., Lancaster, Pa.

SHANDS, Alfred Rives, Jr., orthopaedic surgeon; b. Washington, D.C., Jan. 18, 1899; s. Aurelius and Agnes (Eppes) S.; A.B., U. of Va., Charlottesville, Va., 1918, M.D., 1922; m. Elizabeth Prewitt, July 17, 1926; 1 son, Alfred Rives III, Orthopaedic surgeon, Wilmington, Del.; asso. prof. of surgery in charge of orthopaedics, Duke U. Sch. of Medicine, Durham, N.C., 1930-37; med. dir. Nemours Foundation, Wilmington, Del., since 1937. Served as pvt., U.S. Army, S.A.T.C., 1918. Mem. Am. Orthopaedic Assn., Am. Acad. of Orthopaedic Surgeons, Internat. Soc. of Orthopaedic Surgery, Southern, Am. med. assns., Southern Surg. Assn., New Castle Co., Del. State med. socs., Del. Acad. of Medicine, Alpha Omega Alpha, Omicron Delta Kappa, Sigma Nu, Nu Sigma Nu. Episcopalian. Home: Nemours, Rockland Rd. Office: 803 Delaware Trust Bldg., Wilmington, Del.

SHANKS, Carrol Meteer, lawyer, v.p. and gen. solicitor; b. Fairmont, Minn., Oct. 14, 1898; s. Edgar Beeson and Lilly (Meteer) S.; B.B.A., U. of Wash., 1921; LL.B., Columbia U. Law Sch., 1925; m. Martha S. Taylor, Apr. 7, 1921; children—Wallace Tayor, Margaret Jackson, Carrol Meteer. Lecturer law, Columbia Univ. Law School, 1925-27; admitted to N.Y. bar, 1926, engaged in gen. practice of law, New York City, asso. with firm Root, Clark, Buckner & Ballantine, 1925-29 and 1931-32; asso. prof. law, Yale U. Sch. of Law, 1929-30; admitted to N.J. bar, 1933, and asso. with The Prudential Ins. Co. of America, Newark, N.J., since 1932, gen. solicitor since 1938 and v.p. since 1939. Mem. Phi Beta Kappa, Beta Gamma Sigma, Beta Theta Pi. Methodist. Clubs: Athletic (Montclair); Essex (Newark). Home: 153 Union St., Montclair. Office: Prudential Ins. Co., Newark, N.J.

SHANKWEILER, Fred L(ewis), advertising; b. Allentown, Pa., Aug. 20, 1894; s. Llewellyn and Carrie (Sensenderfer) S.; ed. high sch., Allentown, Pa., 1908-11, Bethlehem Prep. Sch., Bethlehem, Pa., 1911-13; m. Esther L. Smith, June 30, 1920; children—Carolyn M., Fred L. Employed in newspaper business and reporter, 1913-18; adv. mgr. dept. store, 1919-22; propr. Fred L. Shankweiler Advertising Agency, gen. advertising, Allentown, Pa., since 1922; pres. Home Products Co. Served as ordnance sergt., U.S.A., with A.E.F. during World War. Lutheran. Elk. Club: Rotary of Allentown. Author: Men of Allentown, 1917, 1922. Home: 23 S. Glenwood St. Office: 546 Hamilton St., Allentown, Pa.

SHANKWEILER, John Victor, prof. biology; b. Huff's Church, Pa., July 22, 1894; s. James Valentine and Kathryn (Bittenbender) S.; ed. Kutztown State Normal Sch., 1911-15; B.S., Muhlenberg Coll., 1921; A.M., Cornell U., 1927, Ph.D., same, 1931; m. Lelah I. Shuler, Sept. 1, 1921; children—Dorothy Isbel, Grace Eileen, Bruce Everett. Began as teacher, high sch., 1915-17; instr. biology, Muhlenberg Coll., 1921-27, asst. prof., 1927-31, prof. biology since 1931. Served as pvt. inf., U.S.A., 1917-19; with A.E.F. Mem. A.A.A.S., Am. Genetical Soc., Pi Kappa Tau, Sigma Xi, Omicron Delta Kappa, Patriotic Order Sons of America. Democrat. Lutheran. Mason. Club: Oakmont Tennis (Allentown). Home: R.F.D. No. 4, Allentown, Pa.

SHANLEY, Joseph Sanford, architect; b. Newark, N.J., Mar. 22, 1894; s. Michael Robert Seton and Mary (Sanford) S.; A.B., Princeton U., 1917; M.F.A., Princeton U. Archtl. Sch., 1925; m. Agnes O'Gorman, June 14, 1922; children—J. Sanford, Elaine Seton, Anthony Graham. Has followed profession as architect at Newark, N.J., since 1925. Served as lt. (j.g.) U.S.N. R.F., 1917-18. Dir. Liturgical Arts Soc., N.Y. City. Pres. Princeton Archtl. Assn., 1929-33. Mem. Am. Inst. Architects, S.A.R. Republican. Roman Catholic. Club: Essex (Newark). Home: Rumson, N.J. Office: 33 Washington St., Newark, N.J.

SHANNON, Ernest Spence, prin. high sch.; b. Parkersburg, W.Va., Dec. 31, 1902; s. Ernest Thomas and Maude Edwina (Spence) S.; A.B., Morris Harvey Coll., Charleston, W.Va., 1923; grad. student Columbia U., summer 1925; A.M., U. of N.M., Albuquerque, N.M., 1931; m. Pearl Beatrice Hainor, June 11, 1926; 1 dau., Julia Emily. Engaged in teaching, Morris Harvey Acad., Barboursville, W.Va., 1920-21; instr. English and newswriting, high sch., Parkersburg, W.Va., 1921-23; head dept. journalism and publicity, Morris Harvey Coll., Charleston, W.Va., 1923-30; teaching fellow in English, U. of N.M., 1930-31; head dept. English, Mt. State Coll., Parkersburg, W.Va., 1931-32; prin. Guyan Valley High Sch., Branchland, W.Va., 1932-34; prin. Williamstown Sch., Williamstown, W.Va., since 1934. Sec. Williamstown Chamber of Commerce. Mem. Chi Beta Phi, Zeta Kappa. Democrat. Mem. M.E. Ch. Mason. Home: 423 Williams Av., Williamstown, W.Va.

SHANNON, Floyd Bramley, pub. relations mgr.; b. New Galillee, Pa., Aug. 11, 1903; s. Floyd William and Lola (Reynols) S.; A.B., Baldwin Wallace Coll., 1925; A.M., Columbia U., 1927; m. Ruth Hall, Nov. 21, 1927; 1 son, Roger Hall. Engaged as guidance officer, University Extension, Columbia U., 1927-29; industrial psychologist, Western Electric Co., Kearny, N.J., 1929-32, employment mgr., 1932-37, pub. relations mgr. since 1937. Served on Mayors Com. for Youth Welfare, Summit, N.J., since 1938. Vice-pres. Bd. Edn., Cranford, N.J., 1933-37. Res. officer Ordnance Dept. U.S.A., 1927-38. Dir. N.J. Welfare Council, 1937-38. Mem. Am. Psychol. Assn. Republican. Unitarian. Home: 107 Larned Rd., Summit. Office: 100 Central Av., Kearny, N.J.

SHANNON, Joseph Gilmore, banking; b. Jersey City, N.J., Mar. 7, 1878; s. John M. and Anna (Hall) S.; ed. Stevens Prep. Sch., Hoboken, N.J., 1891-94, Packard Business Sch., New York, 1894-95. Began as bank clerk, New York; pres. Guttenberg (N.J.) Bank & Trust Co.; chmn. bd. of dirs. Weehawken Trust Co., Union City, N.J.; dir. Commercial Trust Co., Jersey City, N.J. Clubs: Carteret (Jersey City); Arcola (N.J.) Country; Surf (Miami Beach, Fla.). Address: Jersey City, N.J.

SHANNON, Paul E(ugene) V(irgil), clergyman; b. Mountville, Pa., Mar. 25, 1898; s. A. Lincoln and Linnie (Erb) S.; A.B., Lebanon Valley Coll., Annville, Pa., 1918, (hon.) D.D., 1937; B.D., Bonebrake Theol. Sem., 1921; m. Josephine S. Mathias, June 25, 1919 (dec.); children—Josephine Marie, Patricia Sue; m. 2d, Katherine Higgins, Nov. 1, 1932; 1 son, Paul E. V., Jr. Ordained to ministry Ch. of U. Brethren in Christ, 1917; pastor, Hillsdale, Pa., 1917, Veedersburg, Ind., summer 1918, Dayton O., 1920-24, Liberty Heights, Baltimore, Md., 1925-27, Dallastown, Pa., 1928-35, First Ch., York, Pa., since 1935; field rep. Bonebrake Theol. Sem., summers 1919, 1920, and 1927-28. Trustee Lebanon Valley Coll. Mem. York Co. Ministerial Assn. Republican. United Brethren in Christ. Odd Fellow. Club: Lions (York, Pa.). Home: 114 N. Newberry St., York, Pa.

SHARFSIN, Joseph, city solicitor; b. Allendale, S.C., July 28, 1899; s. Moses and Rebecca S.; student Dickinson Coll. Law Sch.; unmarried. Admitted to Pa. bar and since engaged in practice of law at Phila.; spl. counsel for the city controller of Phila., 1934-36; city solicitor, City of Phila., since 1936. Mem. Nat. Lawyers Guild, Lawyers Guild of Phila. (dir.), Inst. of Municipal Law Officers. Compiled annual report of law dept. of Phila., 1937. Contbr. articles to legal jours. Home: Chateau Crillon, 19th and Locust Sts. Office: City Hall Annex, Philadelphia, Pa.

SHARP, Charles Edward, physician; b. Leesburg, N.J., Dec. 13, 1891; s. Zadok and Catherine (Rogers) S.; M.D., Jefferson Med. Coll., Phila., 1914; m. Mary Peterson, 1917 (died 1918); m. 2d, Eva Minor Robbins, Feb. 10, 1923; children—Evalena, Josephine. Interne Cooper Hosp., Camden, N.J., 1914-15; in gen. practice, Port Norris, N.J., since 1915; mem. Millville (N.J.) Hosp. staff; mem. and pres. Bridgeton Hosp. staff, Bridgton, N.J.; owner Z. C. Sharp & Sons, oyster brokers, (sole owner extensive oyster boat fleet and cultivator several

SHARP, Hugh Rodney; b. Seaford, Del., July 30, 1880; s. Eli Richard and Sallie (Brown) S.; A.B., U. of Del., 1900; m. Isabella du Pont, June 6, 1908; children—Hugh Rodney, Bayard, Anne du Pont (dec.). Trustee University of Delaware; director Wilmington Soc. Fine Arts; mem. Sigma Nu. Republican. Clubs: University, Wilmington Country. Identified with numerous civic and philanthropic activities, notably in connection with U. of Del.; donor of auditorium, Mitchell Hall, to U. of Del. Home: "Gibraltar," Wilmington. Office: du Pont Bldg., Wilmington, Del.*

SHARP, Hugh Rodney: see biographical entry above (entry continues from preceding column: hundred acres oysters in Delaware Bay), N.J.; vice-pres. Raymond Pharmacal Co., Phila.; pres. Delaware Bay Shipbuilding Co., Inc., Leesburg, N.J. Pres. Port Norris Chamber of Commerce; pres. Bridgeton (N.J.) Hosp. staff. Mem. A.M.A., N.J. State Med. Soc., Cumberland Med. Soc. (past pres.). Republican. Mason. Address: Port Norris, N.J.

SHARP, Raymond, pres. Sharp Constrn. Co., Inc.; b. Reading, Pa., June 8, 1894; s. William Addison and Ellen Nora' (Rothenberger) S.; student Reading (Pa.) High Sch., 1908-12, U. of Pa., 1912-14; m. Frances Huber Cole, Aug. 28, 1933. Pres. and treas. Sharp Constrn. Co., Inc., Reading, Pa., since 1933; pres. Berks Bldg. Block Co., S. Temple Realty Corpn.; sec. and dir. Abraham Lincoln Hotel Co.; dir. Reading Industrial Thrift & Loan Co.; v.p. Contractors and Builders Exchange of Reading. Mem. Nat. Assn. of Bldg. Exchanges (pres., 1938). Republican. Mem. Reformed Ch. Club: Kiwanis (pres., 1930-31; lt.-gov., 1931-32; Middle East Div. Pa.). Home: 4225 Seventh Av., South Temple, Pa. Office: 210 N. Fifth St., Reading, Pa.

SHARPE, Francis Robert, mathematician; b. Warrington, Eng., Jan. 23, 1870; s. Alfred and Mary (Webb) S.; A.B., Cambridge U., 1892; Manchester U., 1900-01; Ph.D., Cornell U. 1907; m. Jeannette Welch, Sept., 1900; children—Elfreda J., Frances M., Edith J. Lecturer in mathematics, Queen's U., Kingston, Can., 1901-04; instr. mathematics, 1905-10, asst prof., 1910-19, prof., 1919-38, emeritus prof. since 1938, Cornell U. Naturalized citizen of U.S., 1910. Mem. Am. Math. Soc., Sigma Xi. Republican. Presbyn. Contbr. hydrodynamics and algebraic geometry. Home: Central Av., Ocean City, N.J.

SHARPE, John C., clergyman, educator; b. Shippensburg, Pa., July 4, 1853; s. Elder W. and Elizabeth (Kelso) S.; grad. Cumberland Valley State Normal Sch., Shippensburg, 1874; A.B., U. of Wooster, 1883, A.M., 1887, D.D., 1898; D.D., Lafayette Coll., 1899; LL.D., 1915; m. Mary E. Reynolds, Dec. 24, 1885. Teacher pub. schs., Cumberland Co., Pa., 1871, 1872, Glen Mills, Delaware Co., Pa., 1874, Indiana (Pa.) State Normal Sch., 1876-78, Calif. State Normal Sch., 1878-79, U. of Wooster, 1883-84, Shady Side Acad., Pittsburgh, 1884-98; prin. Blair Acad., Blairstown, N.J., since 1898, headmaster emeritus since Aug. 1, 1927. Mem. Phi Beta Kappa. Republican. Minister of Presbyn. Ch.; moderator N.J. Synod, 1913-14. Pres. Assn. Colls. and Prep. Schs. Middle States and Md., 1914-15, Headmasters' Club N.J., Pa., Del., and Md., 1916-20; mem. Headmasters Assn. Address: Blairstown, N.J.

SHARPE, John McDowell, 3d, lawyer; b. Chambersburg, Pa., Mar. 30, 1898; s. Walter King and Helen McKeehan (Cook) S.; ed. Phillips Acad., Andover, Mass., 1913-16; A.B., Princeton, 1920; LL.B., Harvard U. Law Sch., 1923; m. Elizabeth Montgomery Reisner, Apr. 4, 1925; children—John McDowell, 4th, Rachel Montgomery. Admitted to Pa. bar, 1923, and since engaged in gen. practice of law at Chambersburg; asso. with father and mem. firm Sharpe & Sharpe, 1923-34 and since death of father in practice alone; dir. Chambersburg Lumber Co., Chambersburg Oil & Gas Co., Domestic Engine & Pump Co. Served in U.S.N.R.F., 1917-19, at Torpedo Sta. and Rose Island and on S.P. 665. Mem. Pa. State and Franklin Co. bar assns., Pa. Scotch-Irish Soc., P.A.E. Soc. Andover, Cottage Club of Princeton, Lincoln's Inn Soc., Harvard. Mem. Cum Laude Hon. Soc. at Andover. Democrat. Presbyn. Club: Rotary of Chambersburg. Home: 312 Lincoln Way East. Office: 167 Lincoln Way East, Chambersburg, Pa.

SHARPLESS, Frederic C., M.D., b. Haverford, Pa., Oct. 1, 1880; s. Isaac and Lydia (Cope) S.; A.B., Haverford Coll., 1900; M.D., U. of Pa., 1903; m. Louise Sangree, Oct. 26, 1909; children—Isaac, Louise, Marian, Winifred. In gen. practice of medicine since 1906; asst. med. dir. Bryn Mawr Hosp. Mem. bd. mgrs. Haverford Coll., Dunwoody Home. Mem. Coll. of Physicians of Phila. Quaker. Home and Office: Rosemont, Pa.

SHATTUCK, Harold Bemis, civil engring.; b. Nashua, N.H., Nov. 17, 1873; s. Gilman Conant and Estelle Maria (Barnes) S.; B.S., Dartmouth Coll., 1897; B.S., Pa. State Coll., 1904, C.E., same, 1915; m. Elizabeth Moser Stuart, July 21, 1909 (dec.). Asso. with Pa. State Coll., State College, Pa., continuously, 1901-36, successively instr., asst. prof., asso. prof. then prof. railroad engring., prof. emeritus since 1936; engaged in practice as civil engr., 1907-35; borough engr., State College, Pa., for 27 yrs.; county surveyor Centre Co., 1920-32. Mem. Am. Soc. Civil Engrs., Alpha Delta Phi, Phi Beta Kappa, Phi Kappa Phi. Democrat. Presbyn. Mason (32°, Shriner). Club: University of State College (life). Home: 122 W. Beaver Av., State College, Pa.

SHAVER, Clement Lawrence; b. Marion Co., W.Va., Jan. 22, 1867; s. John Riffle and Sarah Cordelia (Cunningham) S.; ed. Fairmont (W.Va.) State Coll.; LL.B., George Washington University; m. Catherine Upshur Neale. Teacher in country schools 10 years; admitted to W.Va. bar, 1899, and practiced at Fairmont; now engaged in farming. Served as chmn. Dem. State Com. and chmn. Dem. Nat. Com. Mem. M.E. Ch.; S. Home: Fairmont, W.Va.*

SHAW, Alfred Eugene, elec. engr.; b. Parkston, S.D., June 29, 1898; s. William Henry and Nellie Maria (Dove) S.; ed. Iowa State Coll., 1917-19; B.S. in E.E., Mass. Inst. Tech., 1922, M.S., same, 1922; m. Alma P. Arps, June 19, 1928; 1 son, Alfred Eugene, Jr. Employed as student erecting engr., General Electric Co., 1923-24; constrn. engr. and design engr. pub. utilities, Ore. and Calif., 1924-25; elec. engr., Va. Electric & Power Co., 1925-33; in govt. work and independent cons. engring., 1933-38; engr. fixed capital appraisal, Day & Zimmerman, engrs., New York City, 1938-39; engr. to Vt. Pub. Service Commn., Montpelier, since Aug. 1939. Licensed professional engineer, N.Y. and Pa. Coauthor (with Bauer and Gold), The Electric Power Industry, 1939. Home: Bartley, N.J.

SHAW, Arthur Edgar, street lighting, retired; b. Natchez, Miss., May 1, 1862; s. Henry Basil and Mary Elizabeth (Lattimore) S.; ed. pvt. schs., Natchez, Miss.; m. Anna Winston Stanton, Apr. 10, 1888; children—Anna Edgar (Mrs. Jean L. Le Gorre), Elizabeth Lattimore (dec. wife of John J. Hess), Marjorie Brandon (Mrs. Howard Day), Arthur Basil. Employed at Natchez, Miss., 1878-86; sec. and treas. Bessemer Rolling Mills, Bessemer, Ala., 1889-91; sec. and treas. Globe Light & Heat Co., Chicago, Ill., 1891-94; sec. Pennsylvania Globe Gas Light Co., Phila., Pa., 1894-96; asso. with Welsbach Street Lighting Co. of America, Phila., Pa., 1896-1934, largest street lighting co. in the world, pres., 1904 to 1934 when retired. Democrat. Episcopalian. Home: 5214 Wayne Av., Germantown, Philadelphia, Pa.

SHAW, Byron Earl, physician and surgeon; b. Poplar Run, Pa., Oct. 21, 1888; s. Oliver W. and Margaret J. (Hanna) S.; grad. Ida. Tech. Inst., Pocatello, 1912; M.D., Jefferson Med. Coll., Phila., Pa., 1917; m. Agnes M. Smith, June 15, 1921; children—Norma M., Elleene B., Anita L. Engaged in gen. practice of medicine and specializing in surgery at Springdale, Pa., since 1919; surgeon West Penn Power Co. since 1921; mem. sr. surg. staffs, Allegheny Valley Hosp., Tarentum, Pa. and Citizens Gen. Hosp., New Kensington, Pa., since 1928. Served as 1st lt. Med. Corps, U.S.A., 1918-19, with A.E.F. Fellow Am. Med. Assn. Mem. Pa. State and Allegheny Co. med. socs., Phi Beta Pi, Am. Legion, Vets. Fgn. Wars. Republican. Lutheran. Clubs: Keystone Camping (Pittsburgh); National Travel (New York City). Home: 933 Pittsburgh St., Springdale, Pa.

SHAW, Charles Bunsen, librarian; b. Toledo, O., June 5, 1894; s. Hubert Grover and Elizabeth Ann (De Quedville) S.; A.B., Clark U., 1914, A.M., 1915; N.Y. State Library Sch., Albany, 1919-20; m. Dorothy Joslyn, June 25, 1918; children—Robert Joslyn, Charles Richard, Dorothy Ruth. Instr. in English, U. of Me., 1916-17, Goucher Coll., 1917-18; asso. prof. English, Woman's Coll. of U. of N.C., Greensboro, 1918-19, dir. extension div., 1922-24, librarian same, 1920-27; librarian Swarthmore Coll. since 1927; instr. Sch. of Library Service, Columbia, summer 1930; dept. of library science, U. of Mich., summers 1932—. Consultant Carnegie Corpn. Advisory Group on Coll. Libraries. Life mem. A.L.A. (chmn. editorial com. 1931-33); mem. College Library Advisory Bd. 1933-36; mem. Pennsylvania Library Assn. (vice-pres. 1937-38), Bibliog. Soc. America, North Carolina Library Assn. (expres.), Am. Assn. Univ. Profs., Franklin Inn Club (Phila.). Compiler: Reading List of Biographies, 1922; Arm Chair Travels, 1924; American Painters, 1927; List of Books for College Libraries, 1931. Contbr. to lit. and professional jours. Home: 5 Whittier Pl., Swarthmore, Pa.

SHAW, Charles Gray, univ. prof.; b. Elizabeth, N.J., June 23, 1871; s. Horace Gray and Emma Catherine (Gouge) S.; 9th in descent from John Alden; B.L., Cornell U., 1894; Ph.D., New York U., 1897; B.D., Drew Theol. Sem., 1897; studied philosophy at Jena and Berlin, 1897-99; m. E. Belle Clarke, Sept. 21, 1897; children—Winifred Clarke, Lydia Gray. Asst. prof. philosophy, 1899, prof. ethics, 1904, prof. philosophy, 1920—, New York U. Sec. Nat. Housing Com. for Congested Areas, 1927-28. Member Am. Philos. Society, British Institute of Philosophical Studies, Soc. Mayflower Descendants, Soc. Colonial Wars, S.R., Phi Gamma Delta, Sphinx Head (Cornell). Author: Christianity and Modern Culture, 1906; The Precinct of Religion, 1908; "Schools of Philosophy," in Vol. X of Science-History of the Universe, 1909; The Value and Dignity of Human Life, 1911; The Ego and Its Place in the World, 1913; The Ground and Goal of Human Life, 1919; Short Talks on Psychology, 1920; Outline of Philosophy, 1930; The Road to Culture, 1931; The Surge and Thunder—Trends of Civilization and Culture, 1932; Logic in Theory and Practice, 1935; The Road to Happiness, 1937. Editor: The 101 World's Classics, 1937. Contbr. to Ency. of Religion and Ethics, Ency. Britannica, and various mags., etc. Pedestrian; on Sept. 13, 1916, walked from Philadelphia to New York in 23 hrs. and 40 min. Lecturer on psychology, art and education. Clubs: Andiron, Faculty, N.Y. Univ. Home: Spring Lake, N.J.*

SHAW, Craig; editor Moundsville Echo. Address: Moundsville, W.Va.

SHAW, Edward D(owns), trade assn. sec.; b. Bridgeport, Conn., June 7, 1886; s. Malcolm Ross and E. Emma (Rose) S.; ancestors on mother's side came over in Mayflower, on father's side came to America, 1632; grad. Springfield (Mass.) Coll., 1909; m. Frances J. Maracek, June 14, 1911; children—Edward Leslie, Winthrop Sargent. Asst. sec. West Side Y.M.C.A., N.Y. City, 1909-10; gen. sec., The Morris Memorial, Chatham, N.Y., 1910-12, Y.M.C.A. Little Falls, N.Y., 1912-15; scout exec., Boy Scouts of America, Phila., Pa., 1915-18, Washington, D.C., 1918-26; sec. Merchants & Mfrs. Assn., Washington, D.C., since 1926. Trustee Community Chest, Washington, D.C. Mem. adv. bd. D.C. Employment Service. Mem. Nat. Assn. Retail Secs. (vice-pres. 1937-38, pres. 1939), Am. Trade Assn. Execs., Washington Chapter Springfield Alumni Assn. (pres.). Republican. Presbyterian. Mason. Clubs: Kenwood Golf and Country (Bethesda, Md.); Kiwanis of Washington (sec. and dir.). Home: 211 W. Bradley

Lane, Chevy Chase, Md. Office: 400 Star Bldg., Washington, D.C.

SHAW, Farnham H., physician; b. Fulton, N.Y., Sept. 9, 1874; s. Augustus C. and Unicy L. (Farnham) S.; ed. Mansfield State Normal Sch., 1893-95; M.D., U. of Pa. Med. Sch., 1899; m. Adelaide T. Young, Dec. 28, 1905; children—Mary McShaw (wife of Dr. T. Arthur Ryan), James B., Farnham H. Interne Rochester Gen. Hosp., Rochester, N.Y., 1899-1901; in pvt. practice of medicine at Wellsboro, Pa., since 1901; instr., mem. staff, and trustee Blossburg State Hosp., 1916-28. Served as mem. Tioga Co. Med. Advisory Bd .and local examining bd. during World War. Mem. Am., Pa. State, and Tioga Co. med. assns. Republican. Presbyn. Mason (32°). Home: 53 West Av. Office: 4 Crafton St., Wellsboro, Pa.

SHAW, George Robert, chemist; b. Frederick, Md., Dec. 13, 1895; s. Breckenridge and Sarah Virginia (LaMotte) S.; A.B., Washington & Lee Univ., 1915, A.M., same, 1916; Ph.D., U. of Wis., 1920; m. Helen P. Churchill, Nov. 18, 1920; children—Virginia Amelia, John LaMotte, Martha Churchill, Ruth Ann. Engaged as asst. in chemistry, Washington & Lee U., 1915-16, U. of Wis., 1916-17; instr. chemistry, U. of Wis., 1919-20; chemist, General Electric Co., Nela Park, Cleveland, O., 1920-29; chief chemist, RCA Mfg. Co., Harrison, N.J., since 1930. Served as pvt. to 2d lt., C.W.S., U.S.A., 1917-19. Mem. Am. Chem. Soc., Am. Phys. Soc., Phi Beta Kappa, Sigma Xi, Alpha Chi Sigma, Phi Lambda Upsilon. Received Charles A. Coffin Award, General Electric Co., 1927. Democrat. Lutheran. Mason. Home: 9 Sylvan Rd., Verona, N.J. Office: RCA Mfg. Co., Harrison, N.J.

SHAW, Harold Nichols, consulting engr.; b. Milwaukee, Wis., Oct. 13, 1895; s. David Edward and Cora Belle (Nichols) S.; B.S. in E.E., U. of Wisconsin, Madison, Wis., 1918; m. Lillian Delde Fried, Sept. 19, 1919; children—Dorothy Lillian, Stanley Edward, Janet Ann. Engaged in arc welding research, A. O. Smith Corpn., Milwaukee, Wis., 1919-20; motor designer, Louis Allis Co., Milwaukee, Wis., 1920-22; draftsman Palm Olive Co., Milwaukee, 1922-24; chief engr., Globar Corpn., Niagara Falls, N.Y., 1924-29; sales engr., Harold E. Trent Co., Phila., 1929-31; consulting engr., Griswold Mfg. Co., Erie, Pa., and other mfrs., since 1931. Served as ensign (engring.), U.S. Navy, 1918. Mem. Am. Inst. E.E. Holds numerous patents on electric heating, including industrial process kettles, induction cooking utensils and electric furnaces. Home: 125 W. 36th St. Office: The Griswold Mfg. Co., Erie, Pa.

SHAW, John J., M.D.; apptd. sec. of health, State of Pa., 1939. Home: Philadelphia, Pa. Office: Harrisburg, Pa.

SHAW, Ralph Martin, Jr., engr., mfr. spl. machinery; b. Chicago, Ill., July 27, 1897; s. Ralph Martin and Mary (Stephens) S.; A.B., Yale U., 1919; M.S., Mass. Inst. Tech., 1922; m. Madeline Read, June 15, 1927; 1 dau., Mary Eleanor. Engaged in pub. utility engring. in Calif., 1922-25; mech. engr. U.S. Pipe & Foundry Co., 1925-34, advertising mgr. same, 1934-38; pres. and chief engr., Pedrick Tool & Machine Co., mfrs. and designers spl. machinery to order, Phila., Pa., since 1938, and propr. bus. since 1938. Served in U.S.A. Officers Sch., 1918, 2d lt. F.A., U.S.A., 1918-19. Mem. Am. Inst. Elec. Engrs. Republican. Episcopalian. Mason. Club: Yale of New York. Contbr. tech. articles and monographs. Home: 608 Riverbank, Beverly, N.J. Office: 3640 N. Lawrence St., Philadelphia, Pa.

SHAW, Reuben T(aylor), educator; b. Delaware, O., Oct. 8, 1884; s. William Bigelow and Phoebe Irene (Gardner) S.; B.S., Ohio Wesleyan U., 1905, A.M., 1908; Ph.D., U. of Pa., 1926; LL.D., Ohio Wesleyan U., 1939; m. Mary Margaret Rogers, Apr. 12, 1909; children—Robert Gardner, Henry Van Dyke, Lawrence Willard, Elizabeth Rogers (deceased). Prof. of physics and chemistry, Temple U., 1905-09; teacher of chemistry and history, Radnor Hign Sch., Wayne, Pa., 1906; prof., Ursinus Coll., summer 1910; teacher of science Phila. High Schs. since 1909, head of science dept., Northeast High Sch. since 1929; sec. Power Bldg. & Loan Assn.; trustee Penn-Central Bldg. & Loan Assn.; sec. Poor Richard Fund. Served as officer Pa. Nat. Guard, 1910-13. Del. and tour organizer Conf. of World Fed. of Edn. Assns., Tokyo, 1937, Rio de Janeiro, 1939. Life mem. N.E.A. (chmn. com. on amending charter 1934-37; mem. exec. com. 1937-38; pres. 1938-39); fellow A.A.A.S.; life mem. Pa. State Edn. Assn.; mem. Pa. Acad. Science, Am. Chem. Soc., Beta Theta Pi, Phi Delta Kappa. Republican. Presbyn. Author: Study of Adequacy and Effectiveness of Pennsylvania School Employees' Retirement System, 1927. Contbr. to Jour. of N.E.A. Organizer of city and state citizen coms. for support of public schools, 1919-31; also for use of proportional representation in election of city councils. Home: 245 S. 51st St. Office: Northeast High School, Philadelphia, Pa.

SHAWHAN, Hubbard W., dir. conservation; b. Cynthiana, Ky., Nov. 28, 1890; s. Hubbard W. and Helen (Musselman) S.; grad. Asheville (N.C.) pub. schs., 1908; student U. of Ky., 1909-10; B.F. and F.E., Biltmore Forest Sch., 1913; m. Mary Kaye Alves, Apr. 18, 1917; children—Hubbard W. 4th, Mary Helen. Engaged in forest work in Oregon 2 yrs.; engr. various lumber cos. in W.Va. to 1934; dir. of Conservation, State of W.Va., since Feb. 1934. Served with 6th Trench Mortar Batt., World War; commd. major C.A. Res. Corps. Mem. Soc. Am. Foresters, Internat. Assn. Game and Fish and Conservation Commrs., Reserve Officers Assn., Am. Legion, Kappa Alpha. Democrat. Club: Edgewood Country (Charleston). Home: 6 Swarthmore Drive. Office: State Capitol Bldg., Charleston, W.Va.

SHAWKEY, Arthur Anderson, physician; b. Sigel, Pa., Aug. 23, 1870; s. George and Anna E. (Witherspoon) S.; student O. Wesleyan U., Delaware, O., 1896-97; student Portland Me. Sch. of Medicine, 1898; M.D., Coll. Phys. & Surgs., Baltimore, Md., 1900; grad. study, N.Y. Polyclinic, 1916, Harvard U. Med. Sch., 1931, N.Y. Post Grad. Med. Sch., 1916; m. Anna Work, June 15, 1903; children—Elouise Virginia, Anabel Hope (M.D.), George Arthur. Engaged in practice of medicine at Charleston, W.Va., since 1900, gen. medical, 1900-16, specializing in pediatrics since 1916; dir. Equity Savings & Loan Co., Charleston since 1904; mem. W.Va. State Bd. of Examiners of Nurses since 1937. Dir. Charleston Chapter Red Cross, Union Mission, Y.M.C.A. Fellow Am. Coll. Physicians, Am. Acad. Pediatrics; mem. Am. Med. Assn., W.Va. State Med. Assn. (past v.p.), Phi Delta Theta. Republican. Presbyn. Mason, A.O.U.W. Home: 207 Beauregard St. Office: Professional Bldg., Charleston, W.Va.

SHAWKEY, Morris Purdy, coll. pres.; b. Sigel, Pa., Feb. 17, 1868; s. George and Elizabeth Anne (Witherspoon) S.; Oberlin Coll.; A.B., Ohio Wesleyan U., 1894, A.M., 1909, Ped.D., 1918; LL.D., West Virginia Wesleyan University, 1927; m. Elizabeth Carver; children—Morris Carver, John W., Leonard Asbury. Asst. state supt. schs., W.Va., 1897-1905; mem. W.Va. Legislature, 1902-04 (chmn. com. on edn.); supt. schs., Kanawha Co., W.Va., 1907-09 (resigned); state supt. schs., W.Va., Mar. 4, 1909-21; pres. Marshall Coll., Huntington, W.Va. until 1935; now pres. Charleston (W. Va.) Ednl. Centre. Editor W.Va. Journal and Educator. Pres. State Bd. of Edn. Mem. N.E.A. (pres. dept. superintendence, 1915-16), Rotary Club, Phi Delta Theta, Phi Beta Kappa, Kappa Delta Pi. Republican. Methodist. Author: A Geography of West Virginia, 1901; Story of West Virginia, 1913; West Virginia in History, Life, Literature and Industry, 1928. Home: Charleston, W.Va.

SHAY, Harry, physician; b. Phila., Pa., Mar. 18, 1898; s. Morris and Lena (Loss) S.; M.D., U. of Pa.; m. Bertha Shaivitz, Feb. 20, 1927; 1 son, Robert Michael. Instr. in gastro-enterology, U. of Pa. Grad. Sch. of Med., 1924-28; chief, dept. of gastro-enterology, Jewish Hosp., Phila., 1928-32; chief of gastro-intestinal clinic, Mt. Sinai Hosp., Phila., since 1935. Co-dir. of Fels Fund Lab. for Research in Medicine since 1934. Home: 1530 Locust St. Office: 255 S. 17th St., Philadelphia, Pa.

SHAY, Howell Lewis, architect; b. Washington, D.C., Dec. 24, 1884; s. Aurelius King and Julia Stanford (Lewis) S.; M.S. in Architecture, U. of Pa., 1913; m. Eunice Mabel Quinby, Sept. 27, 1909; children—Howell Lewis, William Dixon, Eunice Elizabeth. Began with W. D. Kimble, architect, Seattle, Wash., 1901; in practice at Phila., Pa., since 1921; consulting architect for Board of Education, Phila., and Phila. Housing Authority; pres. Rose Valley Swimming Co.; dir. 1512 Spruce Street Corpn., Realty Investors Corpn.; director The Drake Corpn. Prin. works: Packard Building, Independence Indemnity Bldg., Drake Aptmt. Hotel, First Nat. Bank Bldg., Pennsylvania Co. Bldg., Market Street National Bank Bldg., Phila. Custom House, Appraisers Stores Bldg. (all of Phila.), Liberty High Sch. (Bethlehem, Pa.), Americus Hotel (Allentown, Pa.), Norristown (Pa.) State Hosp. Awarded medal, Am. Inst. Architects, for designing Packard Bldg., 1925. Mem. Am. Inst. Architects. Episcopalian. Mason. Clubs: Art (past dir.), T-Square (past pres.), Orpheus (past sec.); Chester (Pa.) Masonic. Home: Rose Valley, Moylan. Office: Packard Bldg., Philadelphia, Pa.

SHAY, Samuel M.; judge Circuit Court of N.J. Address: Merchantville, N.J.

SHEA, C. Bernard, merchant; b. Pittsburgh, Pa., Dec. 25, 1893; s. Joseph B. and Clara B. (Morgan) S.; student Shady Side Acad., Pittsburgh, 1906-08; grad. Hill Sch., 1912; B.S., Princeton U., 1916; m. Miriam McDonald, June 8, 1918. Began as clerk, 1917; merchandise asst., Joseph Horne Co., Pittsburgh, department store, 1919-20, research dir., 1920-22, divisional merchandise mgr., 1923-30, asst. gen. merchandise mgr., 1930-31, v.p. since 1930, dir. since 1920. Served as instr. U.S. Sch. of Mil. Aeronautics, Princeton, N.J., Nov. 1917-Dec. 1918. Trustee Shady Side Hosp., Pittsburgh. Mem. Cannon Club (Princeton). Republican. Clubs: Harvard-Yale-Princeton, Oakmont Country, Pittsburgh Golf, Fox Chapel Golf (Pittsburgh); Princeton (New York); Nassau (Princeton, N.J.). Home: 201 Tennyson Av. Office: Joseph Horne Co., Pittsburgh, Pa.

SHEAFER, Arthur Whitcomb, mining engr.; b. Pottsville, Pa., Sept. 16, 1856; s. Peter Wenrich and Harriet Newell (Whitcomb) S.; B.S., U. of Pa., 1877, post-grad. work, 1 yr.; m. Mary Cope Russel, Apr. 20, 1904. Asst. geologist, 2d geol. survey of Pa., 1878-81; in gen. practice as mining engr. Mem. Am. Inst. Mining Engrs., A.A.A.S., N. of England Inst. of Mining Engrs., Engrs. Club of Phila., Am. Acad. Polit. and Social Science, Acad. Natural Sciences of Phila. Clubs: University (Phila.); Univ. of Pa. Club (New York). Home: Pottsville, Pa.

SHEAFER, Clinton Whitcomb, automobile dealer; b. Pottsville, Pa., Apr. 27, 1892; s. William Lesley and Ada (Green) S.; grad. Mackenzie Sch., Dobbs Ferry, N.Y., 1910; student Williams Coll., Williamstown, Mass., 1910-13; m. Olive Watson, Jan. 24, 1921; 1 son, William Lesley, II. Pres. and gen. mgr. Schuylkill Motors Corpn., distributors of Dodge and Plymouth cars, Pottsville, since 1919; pres. and dir. Pottsville Supply Co.; executor Estate of William L. Sheafer. Dir. Pottsville Hosp. Served successively as private, corporal and sergeant, 4th Inf., Pa. Nat. Guard, 1916-17, and sergt. Q.M. Corps, May-Dec. 1917; 2d lt. 103d Engrs. Train, 28th Div., U.S. Army, with A.E.F., 1917-19. Mem. Phi Delta Theta. Republican. Clubs: Lions, Schuylkill Country (Pottsville); Williams (New York). Home: 19th and Oak Rd. Office: 370 S. Centre St., Pottsville, Pa.

SHEAFER, Henry, coal land management; b. Pottsville, Pa., June 19, 1863; s. Peter Wenrich and Harriet Newell (Whitcomb) S.; student private schs., Pottsville, Pa., 1879-81, high sch., Pottsville, Pa., 1881-85; A.B., U. of Pa., 1885; unmarried. Began in office of father, P. W. Sheafer, management of anthracite coal lands, 1885, and has since remained in management of coal lands; dir. Pa. Nat. Bank & Trust Co., Pottsville, Pa. Pres. The Pottsville Hosp. and Pottsville Community Hotel Co.; v.p. Pottsville Free Pub. Library and Pottsville Community Chest. Travels extensively in Europe and United

States. Clubs: Metropolitan (New York); Racquet (Phila.); Pottsville, Schuylkill Country of Pottsville (dir.). Home: 1405 Howard Av. Office: 325 S. Centre St., Pottsville, Pa.

SHEAFFER, Charles Miller, pres. Union Transfer Co.; b. Pittsburgh, Pa., Mar. 4, 1858; s. William and Jane (Campbell) S.; student pub. and high schs.; m. Margaret Virgilia Culp, Dec. 1, 1884; children—Daniel Miller, Margaret Culp (Mrs. Wilmer M. Wood), William Paul, Joseph Guy, Jeannette Elizabeth (Mrs. Henry K. Mulford, Jr.), Charles Robert, Theodore Campbell, Charles Miller. In various positions, 1874-77; associated with Pa. R.R. continuously, 1877-1928, and retired on Honor Roll; successively messenger, telegraph operator, train despatcher, yard master, div. operator Pittsburgh Div., supt. of telegraph (Phila.), supt. passenger transportation, then gen. supt. transportation, 1911-20, chief of transportation, 1920-27, asst. v.p. in charge of operation, 1927-28; pres. and dir. Union Transfer Co. since 1928; dir. Nat. Ry. Pub. Co. of N.Y., Ry. Equipment and Pub. Co. of N.Y., Scott Bros., Inc., of Phila. Served as chmn. Com. on Car Service, Washington, D.C., cooperating with Interstate Commerce Commn., meeting emergencies in connection with car shortage, 1917-18. Republican. Presbyn. Home: 401 Audubon Av., Wayne, Pa. Office: 1004 Spring Garden St., Philadelphia, Pa.

SHEAFFER, Daniel M., ry. official; b. Pittsburgh, Pa., Sept. 20, 1885; s. Charles Miller and Margaret (Culp) S.; prep. edn. Bordentown Mil. Inst.; B.S.E., U. of Pa., 1909; m. Lucille Garber Lofland, Sept. 6, 1910. District passenger solicitor, Pa. R.R. Co., Philadelphia, 1913-17, express agent, 1917-20, express traffic agent, 1920-23, mgr. mail and express traffic, 1923-27, chief of passenger transportation, 1927-35, asst. to operating v.p. since 1935; assisted in organization of Transcontinental Air Transport, Inc. (associated with Pa. R.R.), becoming dir. and mem. exec. com., 1928, and later chmn. exec. com.; organized Transcontinental & Western Air, Inc., 1930 (absorbed certain properties of T.A.T. and W.A.E.), elected director and chmn. exec. com.; dir. Curtiss-Wright Corpn., Transcontinental Air Transport, Inc., Universal Corpn. (mem. exec. com.), Standard Capital Co., Universal Pictures Co., Inc. (mem. exec. com.). Mem. aeronautics com. Chamber of Commerce of U.S. and Aeronautical Chamber of Commerce of America. Mem. Delta Kappa Epsilon. Mason. Clubs: Pa. Scotch-Irish Society (Phila.); Pa. Society, New York; Aero of Pa., Union League of Philadelphia, Racquet, St. David's Golf, Merion Cricket, Seaview Golf, Links (New York). Home: 215 Midland Av., Wayne, Pa. Office: 1624 Broad St. Station Bldg., Philadelphia, Pa.

SHEAR, Theodore Leslie, archæologist; b. New London, N.H., Aug. 11, 1880; s. Theodore R. and Mary Louise (Quackenbos) S.; A.B., New York U., 1900, A.M., 1903; Ph.D., Johns Hopkins, 1904; studied Am. Sch. at Athens, 1904-05, U. of Bonn, 1905-06; L.H.D., Trinity Coll., Hartford, Conn., 1934; m. Nora C. Jenkins, June 29, 1907 (died Feb. 16, 1927); 1 dau., Chloe Louise; m. 2d, Josephine Platner, February 12, 1931. Instr. Greek and Latin, Barnard Coll., N.Y. City, 1906-10; asso. in Greek, Columbia, 1911-23; lecturer on art and archæology, 1921-27, prof. classical archæology since 1928, Princeton; field dir. Am. Sch. of Classical Studies, Athens, since 1929; dir. excavation of Athenian Agora. Served as 1st lieutenant Air Service, U.S.A., 1917-18. Mem. Archæological Inst. America, Am. Philol. Assn., Am. Oriental Soc., Am. Numismatic Soc., Royal Soc. of Arts (London), Hellenic Soc. (London), Assn. des études grecques (Paris), Psi Upsilon, Phi Beta Kappa; hon. mem. Greek Archæol. Soc. (Athens); mem. German Archæol. Inst.; fellow Am. Acad. Arts and Sciences. Republican. Episcopalian. Clubs: Century Assn., New York Yacht. Conducted archæol. excavations at Cnidus, 1911, Sardis, 1922, Corinth, 1925-31, Athens since 1931. Author: Influence of Plato on St. Basil, 1907; Sardis—Architectural Terracottas, 1925; Corinth—The Roman Villa, 1930; also numerous articles in archæol. periodicals. Home: Princeton, N.J.

SHEARER, J(acob) Harry, pub. utility pres.; b. Philadelphia, Pa., Nov. 2, 1868; s. Jacob J. and Alice N. (Pine) S.; ed. pub. and pvt. schs., Philadelphia; m. Lurline Elizabeth Branch, Feb. 10, 1902; 1 dau., died at birth. Began with Thompson — Houston Co., Philadelphia, 1890; in operating dept. Powellton Electric Co., 1891-92; on elec. work, Columbian Expn., Chicago, 1892-93; in constrn. work, Mexico, 1893-98; mem. Gardner & Shearer, elec. and mech. contracting, Mexico City, 1899-1907; operated under name of Shearer Electrical Construction Co., contracting, 1907-11; mem. Kelvin Engring Co., 1911-15; with Eastern Shore Gas & Electric Co., 1915-16; gen. supt. Penn Central Light & Power Co., 1916-23, v.p., 1923-29, pres. same since 1929 (name changed to Pennsylvania Edison Co., 1937); also pres. and dir. 1 subsidiary co. Served on U.S.S. New Orleans, Spanish-Am. War; col. 3d Regt. Inf., Vet. Guard. Trustee Altoona Hosp; mem. exec. com. Community Chest. Mem. Am. Soc. M.E., Soc. Am. Mil. Engrs., U.S. Spanish War Vets., Vets of Foreign Wars Post 3 (comdr, 1930-31), S.A.R., Pa. State Chamber Commerce (director), Altoona Chamber Commerce, Altoona Booster Assn. (dir.). Republican. Quaker. Clubs: Rotary, Juniata Valley Country; Engineers (Philadelphia). Home: R.F.D. 3, Rosehill Lodge, Kettle Road, E.E. Office: Penn Central Bldg., Altoona, Pa.

SHEDAN, George, lawyer, judge; b. Wheeling, W.Va., Feb. 7, 1900; s. Michael and Martha Joseph (George) S.; student Parkersburg (W. Va.) pub. schs., 1906-14, high sch., 1914-18, Marietta (O.) Coll., 1920-23; LL.B., Georgetown U., Washington, D.C., 1927; m. Margaret Ann Ruberry, Dec. 30, 1937. Reporter Parkersburg (W.Va.) News, 1920, sports editor, 1921, reporter, 1924; in retail business with father at Parkersburg, 1922-23; admitted to W.Va. bar, 1927, and since practiced at Parkersburg; Municipal judge, Parkersburg, since 1938; mem. W.Va. House of Dels., 1935-36; del. from W. Va. to Nat. Young Rep. Conv., Des Moines, Ia., 1935. Mem. Wood County Bar Assn., Butler Law Club of Washington, D.C., Y.M.C.A. Republican. Catholic. Elk, Lions (Parkersburg, W. Va.). Pres. Sr. Law Class, Georgetown U., 1927. Home: 221 13th St. Office: 318½ Juliana St., Parkersburg, W.Va.

SHEDDAN, Boyd R(obert), dir. personnel; b. Oxford, N.J., Sept. 8, 1902; s. William Boyd and Alice Jane (Montgomery) S.; student Princeton (N.J.) Prep. Sch., 1919-22; A.B., Bucknell U., Lewisburg, Pa., 1926; student Wharton Sch. of Finance and Commerce (U. of Pa.), 1933-34; m. Dora Alice McDonald, Mar. 18, 1930; 1 dau., Joann. With U.S. Rubber Co. at Williamsport, Pa., and later at Chicago and Passaic, N.J., 1927-30; free lance work, 1930-33; staff asst. of personnel Pa. Emergency Relief Administrn., 1934-36, dir. of personnel, 1936-37; dir. of personnel Dept. Pub. Assistance since 1937. Mem. Am. Acad. Polit. and Social Science, Soc. for Advancement of Management, Phila. Industrial Relation Assn., Phi Gamma Delta. Persbyn. Club: Harrisburg Bucknell. Author of articles on personnel work. Home: 3116 Green St. Office: 147 N. Cameron St., Harrisburg, Pa.

SHEDDAN, William Boyd, librarian emeritus; b. Liberty Twp., Montour Country, Pa., Apr. 8, 1867; s. John Knox and Marietta (Wilson) S.; student Potts Grove (Pa.) Acad., 1881-84, Muncy (Pa.) Normal Sch., 1885-86; Ph.B., Bucknell U., Lewisburg, Pa., 1895; student Princeton (N.J.) Theol. Sem., 1897-1900; m. Alice Montgomery, Aug. 12, 1896; children—Ralph Montgomery, Boyd Robert. Teacher public schools of Pa., 1884-97, prin. Acad., Limestoneville, Pa., 1887-88, Potts Grove, Pa., 1895-96; prin. McEwensville (Pa.) High Sch., 1896-97; asst. prin. Milton (Pa.) High Sch., 1897; pastor First Presbyn. Ch., Oxford, N.J., 1900-04; asst. librarian, Princeton Theol. Sem., 1904-31, librarian, 1931-37, librarian emeritus since 1937. Presbyterian. Address: 287 Nassau St., Princeton, N.J.

SHEDDEN, Leon Bayard, banker; b. LeRoy, Pa., Mar. 4, 1893; s. James A. and Julia (Mason) S.; student Sayre (Pa.) pub. schs.; m. Emma L. Eisenhart, Sept. 19, 1916; children—Vivienne E., Donald B. Associated with First Nat. Bank of Sayre, Pa., since 1910, successively bookkeeper, teller, asst. cashier and cashier, pres. and dir. since 1928; treas. Belle Knitting Corpn.; dir. Sayre Bldg. & Loan Assn. Served as mem. Pa. State Rep. Com. Dir. Robert Packer Hosp., Sayre, Pa. Pres. Sayre Chamber of Commerce, Valley Industries, Inc. organize Bradford Co. Bankers Assn., pres. 3 yrs. Republican. Presbyn. Mason (K.T., Shriner). Clubs: Rotary (ex-pres.), Acacia (Sayre); Shepard Hills Country of Waverly, N.Y. (dir.). Home: 210 Packer Av. Office: First Nat. Bank, Sayre, Pa.

SHEEDER, Franklin Irvin, Jr., registrar, coll. prof.; b. Spring City, Pa., May 9, 1895; s. Franklin Irvin and Mary Laurine (Tyson) S.; A.B., Ursinus Coll., 1922; B.D., Central Theol. Sem., Dayton, O., 1925; A.M., U. of Pa., 1929; grad. study, U. of Chicago, 1929-30, U. of Pa. since 1934; m. Marion Josephine Xander, July 29, 1924; children—William Xander, Jocelyn Xander (both dec.). Engaged as pvt. sec. to cos. in Phila., 1913-17; ordained to ministry Evang. and Reformed Ch., 1926; pastor, St. Paul's Reformed Church, Lionville, Pa., 1926-29; asst. to pres. and instr. religion, Ursinus Coll., 1925-30, registrar and prof. religion since 1930. Served as sergt. Med. Corps, U.S.A., 1918-19, with 311th F.A., A.E.F. Mem. Collegeville Borough Council since 1934. Mem. Religious Edn. Assn., National Assn. Bibical Instr., Phi Delta Kappa. Republican. Odd Fellow. Contbr. ednl. and religious jours. Home: 702 Main St., Collegeville, Pa.

SHEEDY, Morgan John, lawyer; b. Altoona, Pa., Sept. 25, 1896; s. John Madden, M.D., and Marcella (Young) S.; student St. John's Parochial Sch., Altoona, Pa., 1903-11, Altoona High Sch., 1911-15; LL.B., Dickinson Sch. of Law, Carlisle, Pa., 1918; m. Madelyn Kathryn Rhodes, Oct. 17, 1928; children—Mary Madelyn, Marie Eileen, Virginia Ann, Morgan Madden. Admitted to Pa. bar, and Supreme Ct. of Pa., Mar. 1920, Superior Ct. of Pa., May 1920, U.S. Dist. Ct., Dec. 1932; gen. practice of law, Altoona, Pa.; solicitor Superior Bldg. & Loan Assn., Liberty Bldg. & Loan Assn., Workingmans' Bldg. & Loan Assn., Washington Bldg. & Loan Assn., Altoona, Pa. Served as Seaman, 1st class, U.S. Navy, during World War; hon. disch. Sept. 1921. Mem. Sigma Chi. Democrat. Roman Catholic. K.C. Home: 310 Wopsononock Av. Office: 1114 15th St., Altoona, Pa.

SHEEDY, Morgan M., clergyman; b. Ireland, Oct. 8, 1853; s. Michael and Mary (Madden) S.; LL.D., Notre Dame U., 1906, Mount St. Mary's (Md.) Coll., 1908. Ordained R.C. priest, 1876; rector St. John's Ch., Altoona, Pa., since Dec. 1894. First pres. and ex-treas. Catholic Summer Sch. (dir. Reading Circle Union); v.p. Catholic Total Abstinence Union of America 4 yrs. Rector Cathedral of the Blessed Sacrament, Altoona; mem. of the Bishop's Council; dean of the Diocesan Clergy. Editor and pub. The Altoona Monthly. Popular lecturer. Author: Christian Unity, 1895; Social Problems, 1896; Briefs for Our Times, 1906; etc. Home: Altoona, Pa.

SHEELY, W(illiam) C(larence), judge; b. Gettysburg, Pa., Mar. 28, 1902; s. William Clarence and Eugenia (Hanna) S.; B.S., Gettysburg (Pa.) Coll., 1923; LL.B., Dickinson Sch. of Law, Carlisle, Pa., 1926; A.M., Dickinson Coll., 1926; m. Dorothy Bushnell, Feb. 12, 1930. Admitted to Pa. bar, 1926, and engaged in gen. practice of law at Gettysburg, Pa., 1926-35; President judge, 51st Jud. Dist., Adams and Fulton counties, since 1935. Trustee Dickinson Sch. of Law. Mem. Am. Bar Assn., Pa. Bar Assn., Sigma Chi, Phi Beta Kappa. Democrat. Presbyn. Mason (K.T., Shriner), Elk, Odd Fellow. Home: 49 Chambersburg St. Office: Court House, Gettysburg, Pa.

SHEETZ, Ralph Albert, lawyer; b. Halifax Twp., Dauphin Co., Pa., June 13, 1908; s. Harry Wesley and Manora (Enders) S.; student Enola (Pa.) Grade Sch., 1914-22, East Pennsboro Twp. High Sch., Enola, 1922-26; Ph.B., Dickinson Coll., Carlisle, Pa., 1930; student U. of Calif., Berkeley, summer 1928, U. of Michigan, summer 1932, Dickinson Sch. of Law,

1930-32; LL.B., U. of Ala. Sch. of Law, Tuscaloosa, 1933; m. Ruth Lorraine Bender, May 19, 1938. Admitted to Pa. bar, 1933, and since practiced at Harrisburg and Enola, Cumberland County, Pa. Republican. Methodist. Mason (Perry Lodge, Harrisburg Consistory, Zembo Temple, Harrisburg Forest, Tall Cedars of Lebanon, Perseverance Royal Arch Chapter, Pilgram Commandery, K.T., Harrisburg Council, Royal and Select Masters, Royal Arcanum). Home: R.D. No. 4, Mechanicsburg, Pa. Office: 222 Market St., Harrisburg, Pa.; and Enola, Cumberland County, Pa.

SHELDON, John Lewis, botanist, bacteriologist; b. Voluntown, Conn., Nov. 10, 1865; s. Samuel H. and Lucy A. (Lewis) S.; B.Sc., Ohio Northern U., 1895, M.Sc., 1899; B.Sc., U. of Neb., 1899, A.M., 1901, Ph.D., 1903; m. Clara Adams Fleming, Aug. 21, 1907; 1 son, Earl Fleming. Teacher pub. schs., Conn., 1885-90, 1895-97; instr. Mt. Hermon (Mass.) Sch., 1892-94; instr. botany, prep. sch. U. of Neb., 1898-99; acting head dept. biology, Neb. State Normal Sch., 1899-1900; instr. botany, U. of Neb., 1901-03; prof. bacteriology, W.Va. U., and bacteriologist, Agrl. Expt. Sta., 1903-07; prof. botany and bacteriology, 1907-13, prof. botany, 1913-19, W.Va. University. Fellow A.A.A.S., Bot. Soc. America; mem. Am. Phytopathol. Soc., Sullivant Moss Soc., Am. Genetic Assn., Sigma Xi, Phi Beta Kappa, Theta Kappa Psi. Republican. Contbr. to bot. and agrl. publs.; investigator in plant pathology. Home: 308 Grandview Av., Morgantown, W.Va.*

SHELLEY, Carl Bartram, lawyer; b. Steelton, Pa., Oct. 23, 1893; s. Kirk and Mary E. (Gosnell) S.; grad. Steelton High Sch., 1912, Bethlehem (Pa.) Prep. Sch., 1913; A.B., Dickinson Coll., 1917, A.M., 1921; LL.B., Dickinson School of Law, 1921; m. Dr. Lorena Welbourne, Dec. 23, 1926; children—Fitzhugh Welbourne and (twins) Mary-Edythe, Winnie-Mae. Admitted to Pa. bar, 1921, later to Supreme Court of Pa., U.S. Circuit and Supreme courts; began practice in Harrisburg; asst. dist. atty., 1932-38, dist. atty. since Jan. 1938; borough solicitor, Steelton, 1924-28, Millersburg, 1928-32; dir. Peoples Bank of Steelton. Served with U. S. Army Ambulance Corps, attached to French Army, 1917-19. Decorated with 3 Croix de Guerre (France). Mem. Am. Bar Assn., Pa. State Bar Assn., Dauphin County Bar Assn. (past pres.), District Attorneys' Assn. of Pa. (sec.-treas.), Am. Legion (past comdr. Dauphin County and Steelton Post), Vets. of Foreign Wars, Phi Kappa Psi (pres. S.E. Pa. Alumni). Republican. Lutheran. Mem. Royal Arcanum (Past Regent), Elks (Past Exalted Ruler). Clubs: Steelton; Harrisburg. Home: 302 Spruce St., Steelton, Pa. Office: 15 S. Third St., Harrisburg, Pa.

SHELLY, Percy Van Dyke, univ. prof.; b. Phila., Pa., June 2, 1883; s. William Hendrie and Annie Large (Van Dyke) S.; B.S., U. of Pa., 1905, A.M., 1907, Ph.D., 1914; m. Florence M. Hunt, Apr. 11, 1911 (dec.); children—Richard Hunt, William Stuart, Edward Rothwell; m. 2d, Anne R. Lefevre, July 15, 1935. Asst. instr. English, U. of Pa., 1905-07, instr. English, 1907-14, asst. prof. English, 1914-24, prof. since 1924. Mem. Modern Lang. Assn., Am. Assn. Univ. Profs., Alpha Chi Rho, Phi Beta Kappa. Democrat. Presbyn. Author: Essays of William Hazlitt, 1924; The Living Chaucer, 1939. Co-author (with Henry S. Pancoast): First Book in English Literature, 1910. Home: 228 E. Oakdale Av., Glenside, Pa.

SHELTON, Harry Leon, coll. athletic dir.; b. Clay, W.Va., Apr. 10, 1912; s. Robert and Mae (Stephenson) S.; B.S., Davis & Elkins Coll., Elkins, W.Va., 1934; m. M. Kathryn Watring, June 10, 1934; 1 son, Norman LeRoy. Teacher and athletic coach, high sch., Piedmont, W.Va., 1934-35; athletic dir. and coach, Davis & Elkins Coll., Elkins, W.Va. since 1935. Democrat. Methodist. Mason. Mem. Kiwanis Club. Home: Watring Apts., Elkins, W.Va.

SHELTON, Whitford Huston, univ. prof.; b. Mt. Pleasant, Ia., Mar. 31, 1885; s. Charles Eldred and Julia (Woodward) S.; Ph.B., Simpson Coll., Indianola, Ia., 1905, LL.D. (hon.), 1934; M.A., U. of Colo., Boulder, Colo., 1910; student U. of Pittsburgh, 1914-17; m. Maud Vaughan, Aug. 21, 1910; children—Mary-Julia, Charles Vaughan, Eldred Vaughan. Instr. in romance languages, U. of Colo., Boulder, Colo., 1908-11; instr. in romance languages, U. of Pittsburgh, 1912-15, asst. prof., 1915-19, prof. since 1919, chmn. of the dept. of modern languages since 1934. Mem. Pa. State Modern Language Assn. (past pres.; sec.-treas.), Nat. Fed. of Modern Language Teachers (past v.p.), Modern Language Assn. of America, Société d'Histoire Littéraire de France, Assn. of Teachers of French, Sigma Kappa Phi (past nat. pres.). Awarded membership to French Legion of Honor, 1935. Republican. Methodist. Author French grammar and reading text books. Home: 1235 Lancaster Av., Swissvale, Pa. Office: Univ. of Pittsburgh, Pittsburgh, Pa.

SHENK, Hiram Herr, historian; b. Deodate, Dauphin Co., Pa., Dec. 9, 1872; s. Cyrus Gingrich and Anna R. (Herr) S.; grad. Cumberland Valley State Normal Sch., Shippensburg, Pa., 1894; A.B., Ursinus Coll., Collegeville, Pa., 1899; A.M., Lebanon Valley Coll., Annville, Pa., 1900, LL.D., 1928; grad. study U. of Wis., 1904; m. Bertha Strickler, June 26, 1900; children—Sara Lucile, Anna Esther. Teacher rural schools, Dauphin Co., 1889-93; instr. in political science, Lebanon Valley Coll., 1899-1900, prof. history and polit. science, 1900-16, also librarian of coll., 1900-05, registrar, 1906-07, dean, 1907-11; custodian of pub. records, archivist and historian, Pa. State Library, 1916-33. Ednl. sec. Y.M.C.A., Camp Travis, Tex., 1917, 18; instr. Y.M.C.A. Summer Sch., Blue Ridge, N.C., 1916-19, Silver Bay, N.Y., 1919, Lake Geneva, Wis., 1921; instr., Summer Sch., Pa. State Coll., 1925, extension lecturer, 1925-26. Sec. Pa. Federation Hist. Socs., 1918-33; exec. sec. Pa. Hist. Commn., 1927-33; prof. Am. history Lebanon Valley Coll. and field sec. alumni, 1933—. Chmn. com. Pa. hist. exhibits, Sesquicentennial Expn., Phila., 1926. Mem. Am. Hist. Assn., Acad. Polit. Science, Pa. Hist. Assn. (council), Soc. Pa. Archæological (editorial com.). Republican. Mem. United Brethren Ch. Mason. Club: Torch. Author: History of Lebanon Valley, 1931; Encyclopædia of Pennsylvania, 1932. Joint Author: Pennsylvania History Told by Contemporaries, 1925. Contributor historical monographs, also to Dictionary of Nat. Biography. Home: Annville, Pa. Address: Lebanon Valley College, Annville, Pa.*

SHENSTONE, Allen Goodrich, prof. physics; b. Toronto, Canada, July 27, 1893; came to U.S., 1910; s. Joseph Newton and Eliza (Hara) S.; B.S., Princeton U., 1914, M.A., 1920, Ph.D., 1922; B.A., Cambridge U., 1921, M.A., 1935; m. Mildred Madeline Chadwick, July 28, 1923; 1 son, Michael. Instr. Toronto U., 1922-25; prof. physics, Princeton U., since 1925. Served with Royal Engrs., 1915-19. Awarded Military Cross, 1918. Mem. A.A.A.S., Am. Physical Soc., Deutsches Physikalisches Gesellschaft. Baptist. Home: 111 Mercer St., Princeton, N.J.

SHENTON, Edward, author, illustrator, editor; b. Pottstown, Pa., Nov. 29, 1895; s. Harry Edward and Jeanette Benner (Thomas) S.; grad. West Philadelphia High Sch., 1916; student Sch. of Industrial Art, Phila., 1916-17, Acad. Fine Arts, 1920-23; m. Barbara Heriot Webster, Mar. 29, 1929; 1 son, Edward Heriot. Editor Penn Pub. Co., Phila., 1923-25, Macrae Smith Co., pubs. since 1926, also vice-pres.; instr. in illustration, Sch. of Industrial Art, Phila., since 1932; illustrated Scribner's Mag., 1934-36; assistant Fine Arts Department, Swarthmore College since 1937. Served as corpl. Co. B, 103d Engrs., 28th Div., A.E.F., Apr. 1917-May 1919. Awarded prize, Acad. Fine Arts, 1921; 2 Cresson scholarships for study abroad, 1921-22. Clubs: Franklin Inn, Writeabout Club. Author: The Gray Beginning (novel), 1924; Lean Twilight (novel), 1928; Riders of the Wind (boys' book), 1929; Couriers of the Clouds, 1930. Contbr. stories to Scribner's, Collier's, Saturday Evening Post.

Home: Westtown Farm House, Westtown, Pa. Address: care Macrae Smith Co., Publishers, 1712 Ludlow St., Philadelphia, Pa.

SHEPARD, Donald D'Arcy, lawyer; b. Fairfax County, Va., Aug. 19, 1894; s. Charles and Florence (Summers) S.; student Georgetown U. Sch. of Foreign Service, 1918-19; LL.B., George Washington U., 1918; m. Emily Hopkinson Ross. Entered Am. Foreign Service, 1915; resigned as consul at Malaga, Spain, 1924; spl. atty. Treasury Dept., Washington, D.C., 1924-27; practicing in Washington since 1927; dir. and treas. The Coalesced Co., etc. Trustee The A. W. Mellon Ednl. and Charitable Trust, Nat. Gallery of Art. Mem. Sigma Chi, Phi Delta Phi. Republican. Clubs: University, Chevy Chase, Metropolitan (Washington, D.C.); Duquesne. Home: Silver Spring, Montgomery Co., Md. Address: Mellon Nat. Bank, Pittsburgh, Pa.; also 716 Jackson Place, Washington, D.C.

SHEPARD, Fred Earl, lawyer; b. Cherokee, Ia., Mar. 6, 1900; s. Eugene Monroe and Mary Josephine (Patty) S.; B.S., Ia. State Coll., Ames, Ia., 1923; LL.B., N.J. Law Sch., Newark, N.J., 1927; m. Miriam P. Roy, June 28, 1930; 1 son, William Eugene. In employ Western Electric Co., Chicago, Ill., 1923-24, and at Kearny, N.J., 1924-27; admitted to N.J. bar as atty., 1928, as counselor, 1931; engaged in gen. practice of law at Elizabeth, N.J., since 1928; mem. Crime Detection Lab. of N.J.; served as mem. N.J. Ho. of Assembly, 1938-39; coach of wrestling, Rutgers Univ., New Brunswick, N.J., since 1937. Served as corpl., C.A.C., U.S.A. during World War; now capt. inf. U.S.A. Res. Worker in local Y.M.C.A. and Community Chest. Mem. Union County Bar Assn., Am. Bar Assn., Delta Theta Phi, Chi Phi, Scabbard and Blade. Republican. Presbyn. Clubs: Chi Phi (Elizabeth); Ancient and Royal Order of Hyjypts. Home: 19 Sayre St. Office: 7 W. Grand St., Elizabeth, N.J.

SHEPARD, Jesse S., lawyer; b. Plymouth Centre, Pa., July 9, 1872; s. Henry S. and Mary M. (Stevens) S.; LL.B., U. of Pa. Law Sch.; m. Elizabeth L. Landes, 1897; 1 son, Henry Landes. Admitted to Pa. bar, 1896, and since engaged in gen. practice of law at Phila.; mem. firm Shepard and Shepard. Home: Alden Park, Germantown, Philadelphia, Pa. Office: Phila. Savings Fund Bldg., Philadelphia, Pa.

SHEPARD, Stanley, Jr., sch. headmaster; b. Rochester, N.Y., Aug. 12, 1903; s. Stanley and Angelena (Cobb) S.; student Phillips Exeter Acad., Exeter, N.H., 1920-23, Columbia U., 1936-37; B.S., magna cum laude, Hobart Coll., Geneva, N.Y., 1927; m. Florence Ruth Creer, June 29, 1929; 1 dau., Susan Creer. Clerk, Genesee Valley Trust Co., Rochester, N.Y., 1927-28; trust new business solicitor, Nat. Bank of Commerce, New York, 1928-29; trust new business dept., later charge trust dept. of 40th St. office, The New York Trust Co., 1929-37; headmaster, Rutgers Prep. Sch., New Brunswick, N.J., since 1937. Mem. Phi Beta Kappa, Kappa Alpha Soc., Cum Laude Soc. Republican. Dutch Reform Ch. Home: 4 Huntington St. Office: Rutgers Prep. Sch., New Brunswick, N.J.

SHEPHERD, Riley Marshall, pres. Pittsburgh & Shawmut R.R.; b. Hillsboro, O., Sept. 1, 1888; s. William Lincoln and Emma Lucy (Riley) S.; student High Sch., Bethel, O., 1900-03; m. Ethel Steed, Dec. 26, 1908; 1 dau., Virginia (Mrs. Foster E. Alter). Began as machinist apprentice, Detroit Southern R.R., Springfield, O., 1903; machinist and foreman various companies, 1906-18; asst. to Federal mgr. Toledo, St. Louis & Western R.R., Toledo, O., 1918-20; asst. to receiver, same railroad, 1920-23; asst. to sr. v.p. N.Y.,C.&St.L. R.R., Toledo, 1923-27, asst. to pres., same railroad, Cleveland, O., 1927-30; pres. and dir. Pittsburgh & Shawmut R.R., Kittanning, Pa., since 1930. Republican. Christian Scientist. Mason (32°; K.T.; Shriner). Clubs: Engineers' (New York); Duquesne (Pittsburgh). Home: R.D. 3. Office: Pittsburgh & Shawmut R.R. Co., N. McKean St., Kittanning, Pa.

SHEPHERD, Walton S.; chief of staff eye dept. Shepherd & Hawes Eye, Ear, Nose and Throat Hosp. Address: 1106 Virginia St., E., Charleston, W.Va.

SHEPPARD, Lawrence Baker, shoe mfg.; b. Baltimore, Md., Dec. 13, 1897; s. Harper Donelson and Henrietta Dawson (Ayres) S.; ed. Phillips Andover Acad., Haverford Sch.; studied law U. of Va.; m. Charlotte Newton, June 12, 1919; children—Charlotte Newton, Lawrence Baker, Jr., Alma Elizabeth, Patricia Anne. Mem. Albemarle County (Va.) bar. Asso. with The Hanover Shoe, Inc., Hanover, Pa., since 1920, vice-pres., gen. mgr. and dir. since 1924; vice-pres. and dir. Sheppard & Myers, Inc.; mem. firm and mgr. Hanover Shoe Farms; dir. Evening Sun Co. Served as ensign in A.S., U.S.N., during World War. Pres. Sch. Dist. of Hanover Borough. Pres. Hanover Gen. Hosp. Vice-pres. U.S. Trotting Assn., Hambletonian Soc.; dir. Nat. Boot & Shoe Mfrs. Assn., Nat. Council of Shoe Retailers, Inc. Mem. Am. Legion, Phi Gamma Delta. Republican. Mason (K.T., Shriner), Elk, Moose. Clubs: Country, Arcadian Social, Republican (Hanover). Home: Eichelberger St., Hanover, Pa.

SHEPPARD, Thomas Trovillo, M.D.; b. Pittsburgh, Pa., Sept. 17, 1892; s. George and Sarah Jane (Little) S.; A.B., Yale U., 1914; M.D., Coll. Phys. & Surgs. (Columbia U.), 1918; m. Margaret Martin Hochpwender, May 7, 1921; children—Margaret Louise, Virginia Ann. Interne New York Hosp., and St. Mary's Hosp. for Children, 1918-19; in pvt. practice of medicine, Pittsburgh, Pa., since 1920; asst. prof. medicine, U. of Pittsburgh, since 1934; mem. staff Western Pa., Elizabeth Steele Magee, Presbyn., and Pittsburgh Eye and Ear hosps. Served as lt. (j.g.) U.S.N.R.F. during World War; lt. comdr. Med. Corps, U.S.N.R.F., 1935-37. Trustee Renziehausen Memorial Ward and Clinic for Diabetes. Asst. fellow Am. Coll. Physicians; mem. A.M.A., Pa. State and Allegheny Co. med. assns., Soc. for Biol. Research, Clin. Pathol. Soc., Pittsburgh Acad. Medicine (treas.), Zeta Psi, Nu Sigma Nu. Republican. Episcopalian. Clubs: University (Pittsburgh); Fly Fishing (Peterborough, N.H.); Western Pennsylvania Kennel. Home: 5554 Wilkins Av. Office: Medical Arts Bldg., Pittsburgh, Pa.

SHEPPARD, Walter Lee, lawyer; b. Baltimore, Md., Dec. 20, 1880; s. Franklin Lawrence and Mary Eleanor (Lee) S.; grad. Germantown Acad., Phila., 1897; A.B., U. of Pa., 1901; LL.B., U. of Pa. Law Sch., 1904; m. Martha Houston Evans, June 1, 1910; children—Walter Lee, Charles Franklin. Admitted to bar of Phila. Co. Courts, 1904, Pa. Superior Court, 1904, U.S. Dist. and Circuit Court of Appeals (3d circuit), 1904, Pa. Supreme Court, 1905, U.S. Supreme Court, 1915; began practice at Phila. with the late William W. Porter (former judge of the Pa. Superior Court), 1904; mem. of firm Foulkrod, Sheppard, Porter & Alexander since 1927; dir. Hajoca Co.; trustee Stephen and William H. Greene Estates. Pres. bd. of trustees Germantown Acad.; v.p. bd. of corporators Woman's Med. Coll. of Pa.; trustee and counsel of the Presbytery of Phila. North, Presbyn. Ch. in U.S.A. Mem. Phila. Fed. of Chs. (dir.; past v.p.), Musical Fund Soc. (dir.), Germantown Hist. Soc. and Acad. of Polit. Science, Pa. Soc. of S.A.R., Hymn Soc., Phi Kappa Psi (past nat. atty. gen., v.p. and pres.). Independent Republican. Presbyn. Clubs: Union League, Lawyers (Phila.); Orpheus (singing mem.), Science and Art (Germantown, Phila.). Home: 7329 McCallum St. Office: 14th Floor, 1500 Walnut St., Philadelphia, Pa.

SHEPPARD, William Henry Crispin, artist, author; b. Phila., Pa., Jan. 1, 1871; s. Edwin and Lydia H. (Crispin) S.; student Pa. Acad. Fine Arts, 1886-95, Julien Acad., Paris, under Bouguereau, 1896, École des Beaux Arts, Paris, under Gerome, 1897-1901; unmarried. Has followed professions of artist and author since 1901; did much art work for Acad. of Natural Sciences, Phila., 1886-95; exhibited at Paris Salon and in Pa. Bldg., Paris Expn., 1900, Pa. Acad. Fine Arts, Nat. Acad. of Design, New York; has traveled extensively in Europe and Eastern U.S. Mem. Artists Professional League of America, Am. Newspaper Guild. Author: twenty books, including The Rambler Club Series and The Don Hale Stories. Contbr. short stories and serials to mags. and other publs. Home: 626 N. Marshall St. Office: The Evening Bulletin, Philadelphia, Pa.

SHEPPERSON, Sister Mary Fides (Isabel Shepperson), coll. prof. and vice-pres.; b. Danville, Pa., Dec. 23, 1867; d. William and Mary (Neale) Shepperson; A.B., Duquesne U., 1911, A.M., 1913; grad. study, Cath. Univ., Washington, D.C., 1917-18; Ph.D., U. of Pittsburgh, 1923. Entered the Convent of Mercy, Pittsburgh, Pa., 1888; pres. Society of St. Francis since 1929; served as Regional Peace Adviser, Student Federation, Cath. Assn. for Internat. Peace, Washington, D.C., since 1938; asso. with Mount Mercy Coll. since 1929, head of history dept. since 1929; vice-pres. Mount Mercy Coll. since 1929. Mem. Catholic Peace Assn., Catholic Ednl. Assn., Pen Women, Urban League. Democrat. Roman Catholic. Author: Harp of Milan (verse), 1897; Cloister Chords, 2 vols., 1911, 1922; Seventeen Crises in World History, 1934. Home: Mount Mercy College, Fifth Av., Pittsburgh, Pa.

SHERAW, George F., automobile dealer; b. Westmoreland Co., Pa., Aug. 21, 1893; s. John F. and Emma (Gaffney) S.; student pub. schs., Yukon, Pa.; m. Mary Jane Robertson, Sept. 10, 1914; children—Robert, Edith, Harry, Ethel, George. Began as worker in coal mine, 1908; clerk for J. V. Mummert, 1910-13; ticket clerk Pa. R.R., 1913-18; coal operator Robertson Coal Co., 1918-19 (all of Yukon, Pa.); owner, Sheraw Motor Co., Altoona, Pa., since 1919. Mem. Altoona Chamber of Commerce (dir.), Altoona Industrial Expansion Corpn. (dir.), Altoona Small Business Men's Assn. (pres.), Blair Co. (Pa.) Automobile Dealers Assn. (v.p.), Pa. Parks Assn., Altoona Community Chest. Republican. Presbyn. Mason. Club: Altoona Rotary (pres.). Home: 2211 9th St. Office: 720-730 Green Av., Altoona, Pa.

SHERBONDY, Henry Smith, pres. First Nat. Bank of Smithton; b. Normalville, Pa., Oct. 4, 1865; s. Charles C. and Sarah Jane (Smith) S.; ed. common schs.; m. Lucinda Grace Williams, Nov. 9, 1893; children—C. Roy, Ralph A., Clarence H., Irwin S., Ruth C., Bessie J. Contractor and farmer; pres. First Nat. Bank of Smithton since 1937. Democrat. Presbyterian. Home: South Huntington Twp., Pa. Office: Smithton, Pa.

SHERIDAN, John Edward, lawyer; b. Waterbury, Conn., Sept. 15, 1902; s. John P. and Mary A. (Hynes) S.; B.S., U. of Pa., 1925; LL.B., Temple U. Law Sch., 1931; unmarried. Admitted to Pa. bar, 1931, and since engaged in gen. practice of law at Phila.; counsel to coroner, Phila., 1933; deputy atty. gen. of Pa., 1934; sec. Family Ct. Phila. Co., 1937; mem. bd. for revision of taxes, 1938; counsel for Del. Bridge Commn. since 1938. Served as mem. exec. council Big Brothers Assn., Honored by annual award of Big Brothers Assn., 1937, for outstanding work among juvenile delinquents. Mem. Nat. Dem. Club. Mem. U.S. Congress, 4th Dist., Pa., 1938. Catholic. Elk. Moose. Clubs: University of Pa., Penn Athletic, Americus, Whitemarsh Country. Contbr. articles to legal and financial publs. Home: 1855 N. Park Av. Office: 1417 Land Title Bldg., Philadelphia, Pa.

SHERK, Abraham Lincoln, merchant; b. Lebanon, Pa., May 5, 1862; s. Abram and Rebecca (Huber) s.; student pub. schs., Lebanon and Chambersburg, Pa.; m. Grace Croft, Mar. 17, 1892 (died Dec. 6, 1937); children—Janet C. (dec.), Harry H. Clerk R. E. Tolbert & Son, 1876-90; partner Sherk & Solenberger, 1890-97; bought out partner, 1897, continued as A. L. Sherk, 1897-1916; since 1916 asso. with son as A. L. Sherk & Son, hardware and seeds merchants, Chambersburg; dir. Valley Nat. Bank since 1912, Mechanics Bldg. & Loan Assn. since 1892. Republican. Home: 247 Ramsey Av. Office: Main and Queen Sts., Chambersburg, Pa.

SHERK, Earl Jacob, inventory and valuation engr.; b. Grantville, Pa., Jan. 4, 1899; s. Ned M. and Elizabeth F. (Kramer) S.; C.E., Cornell U., 1921; m. Emma Bloom, Sept. 8, 1928; children—Stuart, Lois. Inventory and valuation work, Gannett, Seelye and Fleming, Inc., Harrisburg, Pa., 1917-18; bldg. construction, United States Quartermasters Depot, New Cumberland, Pa., 1919-21; steel designer, Gannett Seelye and Fleming, Inc., Harrisburg, Pa., 1922; resident engr., White Deer Mountain Water Co., Lewisburg, Pa., 1923; asst. resident engr., Genesee Valley Power Co., Wiscoy, N.Y., 1923; asst. engr., Cayuga Rock Salt Co., Ludlowville, N.Y., 1924; constrn. engr., North Penn Power Co., Blossburg, Pa., 1924-26; steel designer of power plants, W. S. Barstow & Co., Reading, Pa., 1926-28; transmission and distribution engr., Metropolitan Edison Co., Reading, Pa., 1928-37, inventory and valuation engr. since 1937. Mem. Pyramid Soc., Pi Kappa Alpha. Republican. Registered engr. in the state of Pa. Home: 500 Sherwood St., Shillington, Pa. Office: 412 Washington St., Reading, Pa.

SHERMAN, Edith Bishop (Mrs. John Seward S.), author; b. Des Moines, Ia., Dec. 25, 1889; d. Webster and Wrighta (Ford) Bishop; ed. Stuart Hall, Staunton, Va., 1907, Nat. Acad. of Design, 1908-09, N.Y. Sch. Applied Design for Women, 1910-12, grad., 1912; m. John Seward Sherman, Oct. 7, 1914; children—Elisabeth, Barbara, John Seward, Jr. Engaged as free lance feature newspaper writer, 1915; contbr. to N.Y. and N.J. newspapers, 1915-21; columnist "Thrift Stamps for Thrift Stunts," N.Y. Sunday Tribune, "Woman Who Saw," N.Y. Sun; lecturer on Am. Revolution. Mem. bd. Girl Scouts of the Oranges. Awarded Listentome medals for 9 pub. books. Mem. League Am. Pen Women. Republican. Conglist. Clubs: Listentome (Orange); Pen & Brush (New York). Author: Mistress Madcap, 1925; Mistress Madcap Surrenders, 1926; Milady At Arms, 1927; Upstairs, Downstairs, 1928; The Gay Chariot, 1936; Polly What's Her Name, 1936; Mid-Flight, 1937; Mystery At High Hedges, 1937; Fighting Muskets, 1938. Contbr. short stories to leading mags.; four juvenile short stories repub. in anthologies of short articles and in Braille mag. The Searchlight. Home: 453 Melrose Pl., South Orange, N.J.

SHERMAN, George H(azzard) W(attles), production of natural gas; b. Oil City, Pa., Feb. 5, 1880; s. Oliver C. and Elizabeth Alden (Wattles) S.; ed. pub. schs., State Teachers Coll., Edinboro, Pa., 1898-1900; m. Anne Mildred Wheelock, May 17, 1913; children—Anne Nicoline, Mary Elizabeth, Mildred Wheelock. Engaged in teaching pub. schs., 1900-02; with Oil Well Supply Co. several years and then engaged in oil business in mid-west; asso. with United Natural Gas Co. and affiliated cos. since 1912, asst. sec. and dir. since 1927. Active in work of local charities and Y.M.C.A. Republican. Presbyn. Mason (32°). Clubs: Acacia, Kiwanis, Oil City Boat, Wanango Country. Home: 126 Washington Av. Office: 308 Seneca St., Oil City, Pa.

SHERMAN, Henry John, cons. engr.; b. Mt. Holly, N.J., Nov. 21, 1869; s. John and Christianna (Stark) S.; C.E., Lehigh U., 1890; m. Alice Ethel Gordon, Dec. 17, 1901; children—Elizabeth Anne (Mrs. Paul E. Shomper), Naomi, (Mrs. Robert C. Yates). Successively asst. Engring. Dept., Dist. of Columbia, draftsman and asst. Bur. Surveys, Phila., chief engr. Dept. Inland Waterways, cons. engr., Bd. Commerce and Navigation of N.J.; now mem. firm Sherman & Sleeper, cons. engrs., Camden, N.J.; treas. and dir. Tacony-Palmyra Bridge Co.; dir. Camden & Burlington Co. R.R., Burlington Co. Trust Co. Mem. Am. Soc. Civil Engrs. (dir. 1933-35, pres. Phila. Sect.). Republican. Presbyn. Club: Engineers (Philadelphia). Home: 131 Chestnut St., Moorestown, N.J. Office: 501 Cooper St., Camden, N.J.

SHERMAN, William O'Neill, surgeon; b. Pine Grove, Pa., May 4, 1880; s. Luther Grove and Caroline S.; student Franklin and Marshall Coll., 1894-97; M.D., U. of Pa., 1901; m. Lillian Johnson, Oct. 16, 1910. Practiced at Pittsburgh since 1901; chief surgeon Carnegie-Ill. Steel Corpn. since 1909; chief surgeon H. C. Frick Coke Co. and other subsidiaries of U.S. Steel Corpn.; surgeon St. Francis, Children's and Magee hosps. Fellow Am. Coll. Surgeons; mem. A.M.A., Am. Iron and Steel Inst., Am. Pub. Health Assn., Pittsburgh Acad. Medicine,

Pa. Med. Soc. Republican. Mason. Clubs: Duquesne, Pittsburgh Athletic, Longue Vue Country, etc. Home: 4400 Center Av. Office: Carnegie Bldg., Pittsburgh, Pa.

SHERO, Lucius Rogers, prof. Greek; b. Smethport, Pa., Apr. 5, 1891; s. William Francis and Lucy Sophronia (Rogers) S.; Franklin and Marshall Coll., Lancaster, Pa., 1906-07; B.A., Haverford Coll., 1911; M.A., U. of Wis., 1912, Ph.D., 1920; B.A., 3d class, Lit.Hum., Oxford U., 1917; m. Julia Adrienne Doe, June 26, 1918; children—Gertrude Caroline, Lucy Adrienne, Frances Livia. Univ. fellow, U. of Wis., 1912-14; Rhodes scholar from Wis., at Oxford U., 1914-17; asso. prof. Latin, 1917-19, prof. Latin, 1919-20, Macalester Coll.; Hoffman prof. Greek, St. Stephen's Coll., Annandale, N.Y., 1920-28; prof. Greek, Swarthmore Coll., since 1928; visiting prof. Stanford U., 1932; annual prof., Am. Sch. of Classical Studies at Athens, 1936-37; mem. mng. com. Am. Sch. Classical Studies. Mem. Am. Philol. Assn., Classical Assn. Atlantic States, Am. Archæol. Inst., Am. Assn. Univ. Profs., Phi Beta Kappa. Episcopalian. Contbr. on classical subjects. Home: 651 N. Chester Rd., Swarthmore, Pa.

SHERO, William Francis, clergyman; b. Fredonia, N.Y., June 24, 1863; s. Lewis and Clarissa (Francis) S.; grad. State Normal Sch., Fredonia, 1882; A.B., U. of Rochester, 1887; Gen. Theol. Sem., 1887-88; M.A., Hobart, 1890; Ph.D., Franklin and Marshall Coll., Pa., 1906; m. Lucy Rogers, June 11, 1890; children —Lucius Rogers, Livia Francis. Prin. Smethport Sch., 1888-90; deacon, 1889, priest, 1891, P.E. Ch.; rector Angelica, N.Y., 1891-93; chaplain de Veaux Coll., Niagara Falls, N.Y., 1893-97, head master Yeates Sch., Lancaster, Pa., 1897-99; rector St. John's Ch., Lancaster, 1898-1908; warden Racine (Wis.) Coll., 1908-16; rector Christ Ch., Greensburg, Pa., since 1916. Sec. Standing Com. of Diocese, 1918-34; pres. same since 1934. Mem. Delta Psi, Phi Beta Kappa. Author: Instruction in Christian Religion, 1903, 1913; Implications of the Religious Experience, 1907; Instructions in Holy Scripture, 1910. Home: 444 N. Main St., Greensburg, Pa.

SHERRIFF, John Charles, lawyer; b. Pittsburgh, Pa., Feb. 1, 1874; s. Charles French and Ellen (Breedon) S.; prep. edn., Pittsburgh pub. schs. and East Liberty Acad.; A.B., Princeton U., 1896; LL.B., U. of Pittsburgh, 1900; m. Anne Jacova Bray, Dec. 23, 1905. Admitted to Pa. bar, 1900, and since practiced in Pittsburgh; specialized in insurance, surety and corporation law since 1905; senior mem. firm Sherriff, Lindsay, Weis & Hutchinson; counsel many insurance cos.; dir. and counsel Fried & Reineman Packing Co. Served as capt. Ordnance, U.S. Army, World War. Mem. Federal Social Agencies; life trustee Shadyside Hosp. Mem. Am., Pa. State and Allegheny Co. bar assns., Internat. Assn. Ins. Counsel, Am. Judicature Soc. Republican. Mason. Episcopalian; trustee and mem. standing com. P.E. Diocese of Pittsburgh; was chmn. dept. of social service and judge Ecclesiastical Court many yrs. Clubs: Duquesne, Harvard-Yale-Princeton, Oakmont Country (Pittsburgh). Home: 2053 Beechwood Boul. Office: Law and Finance Bldg., Pittsburgh, Pa.

SHERRILL, Richard Ellis, prof. of geology; b. Haskell, Tex., Nov. 12, 1899; s. Richard Ellis and Katherine (Taylor) S.; grad. Haskell (Tex.) High Sch., 1916; student U. of Tex., Austin, Tex., 1918-19, Wooster (O.) Coll., 1919-20; B.S. in chemistry, Washington and Lee U., Lexington, Va., 1922; M.S., Cornell U., 1928, Ph.D., 1933; m. Mary Lucille Taylor, Nov. 6, 1926; 1 son, Donald Taylor. Instr. in geology and physics, Washington & Lee Univ., Lexington, Va., 1922-23; mining engr. Ray (Ariz.) Consol. Copper Co., 1923-24; asst. prof. of geology, Washington and Lee U., 1924-26; field geologist Marland & Tex. Oil Cos., Tex., 1926-27; Eleanor Tatum Long research fellow, Cornell U., 1927, 1932; instr. of geology, U. of Pittsburgh, 1928-29, asst. prof., 1929-33, asso. prof., 1933-38, prof. and head of oil and gas dept. since 1938; cooperating geologist with Pa. Topographic and Geologic Survey since 1936. Served as private, U.S. Army, 1918. Mem. Am. Assn. Petroleum Geologists, Am. Inst. Mining Engrs., Am. Petroleum Inst., A.A.A.S., Sigma Tau, Sigma Xi, Phi Beta Kappa, Phi Kappa Phi. Republican. Presbyterian. Mason. Contbr. geol. articles to tech. publs. Home: 1318 S. Negley St., Pittsburgh, Pa.

SHERWIN, Robert Suthers, pharmacist; b. Scranton, Pa., May 3, 1876; s. John and Ann (Williams) S.; Ph.G., Phila. Coll. of Pharmacy and Science, 1896; hon. Ph.M., Phila. Coll. Pharm. and Science, 1929; m. Margaret Senior, 1902; children—Vera (wife of Paul S. Richards, M.D.), Roberta (Mrs. Robert Burnett), Eugenia (Mrs. George Wyllie). Engaged as pharmacist in Newark, N.J.; pres. Petty's, Inc.; pres. N.J. Wholesale Drug Co., 1919-30, dir. since orgn., 1919; dir. Union Nat. Bank. Past dir. Chamber of Commerce, Broad St. Assn. (Newark, N.J.); trustee Phila. Coll. of Pharmacy and Science. Mem. Am. Pharm. Assn., N.J. Pharm. Assn. Socialist. Home: 149 Roseville Av. Office: 833 Broad St., Newark, N.J.

SHERWOOD, Edward Leggett, cons. engr.; b. Brooklyn, N.Y., Aug. 2, 1885; s. James Calvin Ham and Mary Bleecker (Leggett) S.; ed. pub. schs., Monsey, N.Y., and Ridgewood, N.J., and Highland Park Coll. (later Des Moines U.); m. Edith Grace Perkins, Feb. 21, 1907; 1 dau., Edith Louise. With General Electric Co., Schenectady, N.Y., Harrison, N.J., and dept. mgr. San Francisco, Calif., and Cincinnati, O., 1903-13; chief engr. Merchants Engring. Corpn., New York, N.Y., 1914-15; asst. to vice-pres. Abbott Motor Car Co., Detroit, Mich., 1916-17; engaged in gen. engring. practice and industrial product research as ind. consultant, N.Y. City, since 1920; pres. E.L. Sherwood Co., engrs., since 1927; pres. Victoria Consol. Silver Mining Co., Quebec. Served as capt., then major, Ordnance, U.S.A., 1918-19; now lt. col. U.S. A. Res.; designed for army improved flash light battery, also light arty. tractor. Mem. Am. Soc. Mech. Engrs., Soc. Am. Mil. Engrs., Army Ordnance Assn. Republican. Episcopalian. Clubs: Saint Nicholas Soc., Engineers (New York); Army and Navy (Washington, D.C.). Home: 215 Prospect St., Ridgewood, N.J. Office: 24 W. 40th St., New York, N.Y.

SHETLOCK, William, educator; b. Egypt, Pa., Feb. 4, 1892; s. Andrew and Catherine (Schultz) S.; student Keystone State Teachers Coll., Kutztown, 1910-12; Ph.B., Muhlenberg Coll., 1917; A.M., Columbia U., 1922; m. Ida S. Leh, Aug. 11, 1917. Teacher pub. schs., 1912-14; supervising prin. schs., Coplay, Pa., since 1916. Dir. Lehigh Co. Chapter Am. Red Cross, Lehigh Co. Crippled Childrens Soc. Mem. N.E.A., Pa. State Edn. Assn., Phi Delta Kappa, Kappa Phi Kappa, Pi Gamma Mu, Patriotic Order Sons of America. Republican. Lutheran. Club: Coplay Booster. Home: 22 S. 4th St. Office: 4th and Center Sts., Coplay, Pa.

SHEWHART, Walter Andrew, technical engr.; b. New Canton, Ill., Mar. 18, 1891; s. Anton and Esta (Barney) S.; A.B., U. of Ill., 1913, A.M., 1914; Whiting fellow U. of Calif., 1915-16; Ph.D., U. of Calif., 1917; m. Edna Hart, Aug. 4, 1914. Engr. with Western Electric Co., 1918-25; mem. tech. staff Bell Telephone Labs. since 1925, specializing in application of statistics in engring. and theory and practice of control of quality of product; lecturer on applied statistics, Stevens Inst. of Tech., 1930, U. of London, 1932 and Grad. Sch. U.S. Dept. of Agr., 1938; consultant on ammunition specifications, War Dept., since 1935. Fellow Inst. Math. Statistics (v.p. 1935-36, pres. 1937), A.A.A.S., Am. Statis. Assn. (v.p. 1934), Royal Econ. Soc., Royal Statis. Soc.; mem. Econometric Soc., Am. Math. Soc., Math. Assn. of America, Am. Phys. Soc., American Society Testing Materials, Philosophy of Science Assn., Assn. for Symbolic Logic, Psychometric Soc., Am. Acad. Polit. and Social Science, Sigma Xi, Kappa Delta Pi, Sigma Phi Epsilon. Republican. Methodist. Author: Economic Control of Quality of Manufactured Product, 1931. Contbr. scientific and tech. articles. Home: 158 Lake Drive, Mountain Lakes, N.J. Office: 463 West St., New York, N.Y.

SHIBLI, Jabir, educator; b. Betagreen, Lebanon, Syria, Aug. 1, 1886; s. Shibli Nejm and Hannah (Semaha) Shibli; student Am. Univ. of Beirut, Syria, 1901-04; B.D., Presbyn. Theol. Sem., Chicago, 1911; A.B., Oberlin (O.) Coll., 1917; A.M., U. of N.D., 1918; A.M., U. of Wis., 1922; Ph.D., Columbia U., 1932; m. Adma Hammam, Aug. 8, 1923; children—Mona Cordelia, Raymond Nadeem, David Ralph. Came to U.S., 1908, naturalized, 1916. Teacher in American High Sch. Shweir, Lebanon, Syria, 1904-08; ordained Presbyn. ministry, 1911; pastor various chs., 1911-16; prof. mathematics, Fargo (N.D.) Coll., 1918-21; asso. prof. mathematics, Pa. State Coll., since 1921. Mem. Nat. Council Teachers of Mathematics. Republican. Mason. Author: Plane and Spherical Trigonometry, 1928, revised edit., 1936; Recent Developments in the Teaching of Geometry, 1932. Home: 525 S. Sparks St., State College, Pa.

SHICK, Robert Porter, lawyer; b. Anna, Ill., May 6, 1869; s. Cyrus and Jane (Stinson) S.; A.B., Princeton U., 1890, M.A., 1893; LL.B., Harvard Law Sch., 1895; m. Constance Ingalls, Apr. 12, 1899 (died Dec. 16, 1899); m. 2d, LaRue Dewees Thomas, Feb. 12, 1907; 1 dau., Ellen Porter. Admitted to bars of Phila. Co. Courts, 1903, Berks Co. Courts, 1895, Superior Court of Pa., 1899, Supreme Court of Pa., 1898, U. S. Courts of Eastern Dist. of Pa., 1902, U.S. Supreme Court, 1905; in gen. practice of law, Phila., since 1904; dir. Citizens Bank of Reading (Pa.), 1892-1902; pres. Reading (Pa.) Stove Works, 1899-1900. Mem. Am. Bar Assn. Pa. and Phila. Co. bar assns., Pa. Hist. Soc., Pa. German Society, St. Andrew's Society, Pa. Sons of the Revolution. Republican. Episcopalian. Mason. Clubs: Church, Princeton (Phila.). Translator: Swiss Civil Code. Home: 6625 McCallum St. Office: 718 Real Estate Trust Bldg., Phila., Pa.

SHIELDS, George Robert, lawyer; b. Pigeon Forge, Tenn., Oct. 21, 1879; s. William Jesse and Sarah Ellen (Carter) S.; B.S., Murphy Collegiate Inst., Sevierville, Tenn., 1898; student Peabody Coll. for Teachers, 1899-1900; LL.M., Nat. U. Law Sch., 1912; m. Agnes Richardson Hill, Nov. 14, 1902; children—Frederick Wyatt, Mary Elizabeth, Roger Denton. Teacher pub. schs. of Tenn., 1897-1901; admitted to bar, D.C., 1911; legal aide, Office of Comptroller U.S. Treasury, 1912-16; with King & King, attys., Washington, D.C., 1917-19, mem. of firm since 1920. Specialist in matters involving suit or claim against the Federal Government. Served as capt., United States Army, aide to Brig. Gen. Herbert M. Lord, 1918-19. Mem. Am. and D.C. bar assns., Soc. Am. Mil. Engrs. Republican. Clubs: University, Columbia Country, Essex County Country. Contbr. to Income Tax Mag., The Constructor, Engineering News-Record, etc. Home: "Grey Rocks," Silver Spring, Md. Office: 728 17th St., N.W., Washington, D.C.

SHIELDS, John Franklin, lawyer; b. Chester, Pa., June 25, 1869; s. William and Sarah Elizabeth S.; B.Sc., Pa. State Coll., 1892; U. of Pa., 1892-93; LL.B., U. of Pa., 1902; m. Lorene B. Mattern, Feb. 28, 1912 (died Apr. 3, 1938). Mem. Am. and Pa. bar assns., Hist. Soc. Pa., Pa. Acad. Fine Arts, Phi Kappa Phi, Beta Theta Pi. Chmn. exec. com., pres. bd. trustees, Pa. State College. Clubs: Union League, University, Phila. Cricket. Home: 3803 Oak Rd., Germantown, Phila. Office: Girard Trust Bldg., Philadelphia, Pa.

SHIELDS, Thomas Edgar, organist and prof. music; b. Olney, Ill., July 4, 1877; s. Elisha Ward and Maria (Wunderlig) S.; ed. Moravian Parochial Sch., Bethlehem, Pa., 1890-96; (hon.) Mus.D., Muhlenberg Coll., Allentown, Pa., 1935; m. Emilie Schultze, Sept. 5, 1906; children—Agnes Gertrude (Mrs. Leonard Colin Ward), Margaret Adelaide (Mrs. Boyd King), Adelaide Emelie. Engaged as organist, Trinity Ch., Easton, Pa., 1896-98, 1st Presbyn. Ch., Reading, Pa., 1898-1901; asst. organist Moravian Ch.,

Bethlehem, Pa., 1901-02; organist Bethlehem Bach Choir since 1901; organist and choirmaster, Pro-Cathedral Ch. of the Nativity, Bethlehem, Pa., since 1902; prof. and dir. music, Lehigh U. since 1905; prof. music, Moravian Coll. for Women since 1909; mem. exec. com. Bethlehem Bach Choir. Asso. Am. Guild of Organists. Republican. Moravian. Home: 4 E. Church St., Bethlehem, Pa.

SHIGLEY, James Fremont, veterinarian; b. Hart, Mich., June 11, 1885; s. Lafayette Fremont and Elizabeth (Pringle) S.; B.Pd., Mich. State Normal Sch., 1912; D.V.M., Cornell U., 1916; m. Jennie Bertha Kelley, Oct. 25, 1916; children—James William, Robert Fremont, Dorothy Jane, Ann Elizabeth. Employed as supt. of schs., 1908-11; instr. surgery, Cornell U., 1915-16; engaged in practice vet. medicine, Kenmarc, N.D., 1916-17; chief veterinarian, Beebe Lab., 1918-23; prof. veterinary science, Pa. State Coll. since 1923; mem. bd. trustees, chmn. med. and nursing coms. Center Co. Hosp. Served as inspr. Brit. Mission, 1917. Lt. 308th Cav. Res., 1923; capt. med. det. 104th Cav., Pa. N.G., 1927. Mem. Bd. Health, State College, Pa., since 1927. Mem. Am. Veterinary Med. Assn., Pa. Veterinary Med. Assn. (sec. since 1937), Assn. Mil. Surgeons, Internat. Veterinary Congress, Parent Teacher Assn. (pres. 1936-37), Alpha Tau Delta, Omega Tau Sigma, Delta Theta Sigma, Sigma Xi, Gamma Sigma Delta. Baptist. Club: Rotary of State College. Home: 322 S. Burrowes St., State College, Pa.

SHILLING, John, sch. supt.; b. Frankford, Del., May 3, 1884; s. Edward A. and Hester A. (Hodgson) S.; student Felton (Del.) High Sch., 1890-1900, Goldey Coll. Wilmington, Del., 1901-02; Ph.B., A.M., Dickinson Coll., Carlisle, Pa., 1908, Sc.D., 1933; A.M., Columbia U., 1925; grad. student U. of Chicago, 1929; m. Laura Dix, Aug. 26, 1909; children —John, Edward William, David. Rural sch. teacher, Kent Co., Del., 1902-04; secondary teacher, N.J. State Normal Sch., Trenton, N.J., 1908-12; teacher science Trenton (N.J.) High Sch., 1912-16, North East High Sch. for Boys, Phila., Pa., 1916-18; co. supt. schs., Kent Co., Del., 1918-19; asst. state supt. of pub. instrn. in charge secondary schs., Dover, Del., since 1919. Mem. Alpha Chi Rho, Phi Beta Kappa. Methodist. Address: State House, Dover, Del.

SHINN, Owen Louis, univ. prof.; b. Phila., Pa., July 30, 1871; s. Frederick and Anna (McCabe) S.; B.S., U. of Pa., 1893, Ph.D., 1896; m. Edith M. Stringer, 1897; children— Eleanor A., M. Elizabeth. Instr. in chemistry, U. of Pa., 1893-1905, asst. prof., 1905-13, prof. of applied chemistry since 1913; dir. of U. of Pa. Summer Sch., 1916, 1917; acting dir. of chemistry dept., U. of Pa., 1926-32. Mem. U.S. Assay Commn., 1907, 1910-15. Mem. Swarthmore (Pa.) Sch. Bd., 1924-30 (treas., 1926-30). Mem. Am. Chem. Soc. (chmn. Phila. sect., 1902; chmn. of div. of chem. edn., 1932), Franklin Inst., A.A.A.S., Alpha Chi Rho (nat. pres., 1925-26), Alpha Chi Sigma, Sigma Xi, Tau Beta Pi. Methodist. Author of articles to the Jour. of Am. Chem. Soc. Home: 314 Lafayette Av., Swarthmore, Pa. Office: Univ. of Pennsylvania, Philadelphia, Pa.

SHIPLER, Guy Emery, clergyman, editor; b. Warsaw, N.Y., July 31, 1881; s. John William Harris and Mary (Danley) S.; student Hobart Coll., Geneva, N.Y., 1902-05, Litt.D., 1925; grad. Gen. Theol. Sem., New York, 1910; m. Rebekah Schultze, 1913; children—Guy Emery, Rebekah Mary. Reporter Rochester Evening Times, 1900; compiler daily official program, Pan-Am. Expn., Buffalo, N.Y., 1901; spl. corr. St. Louis Expn., 1904; reporter Boston Traveler, 1906-07; deacon, 1910, priest, 1911, P.E. Ch.; asst. rector St. Peter's Ch., St. Louis, 1910-11; rector Ch. of the Epiphany, Cincinnati, 1911-17; mng. editor the Churchman, 1917-22, editorial chief since 1922, also rector St. Paul's Ch., Chatham, N.J. Chaplain N.J. State Militia, 1918-19. Editor Social Service News, Cincinnati, 1916-17, also Official Jour. of Cincinnati Fed. of Chs. Pres. Cincinnati br., Consumers' League, 1914-17; charter mem. Cincinnati Council of Social Agencies; dir. Inst. of Family Relations of City of N.Y., Save the Children Fund; chmn. N.Y. br., Church League for Industrial Democracy; hon. pres. Chatham Community Players; mem. Hobart Coll. Alumni Council (pres., 1930-32). Mem. deputation Am. religious press, invited by British Govt. to visit Eng. and France, 1918. Awarded medal "for distinguished service in journalism," for The Churchman, School of Journalism, Univ. of Mo., 1934. Contbr. to mags. Mem. Phi Beta Kappa, Sigma Phi. Home: Chatham, N.J. Office: 425 4th Av., New York, N.Y.*

SHIPLEY, A. Earl, lawyer; b. Harford Co., Md., Jan. 21, 1896; s. Alexander and E. May (Geary) S.; student Strayer's Bus. Coll., Baltimore, 1911-12, accounting by corr. schs., 1915, U.S. Sch. of Fire, Fort Sill, Okla., 1918, U.S.A. Sch., Morbihan, France, 1918; student law under F. Neal Parke, judge Md. Court of Appeals, 1922-25; m. Gertrude Morgan, Oct. 23, 1926. Engaged in mercantile bus. on own acct., 1919-21; employed as court clk., Westminster, Md., 1922-25; admitted to Md. bar, 1925, and since engaged in gen. practice of law at Westminster; mem. firm Brown & Shipley since 1928; mem. Md. Senate for term 1938-42. Served as 2d lt. to capt. F.A., U.S.A., 1916-19, with A.E.F. in France. Mem. Md. Bar Assn., Carroll County Bar Assn. Republican. Episcopalian. Mason. K.P. Home: near Westminster, Md. Office: Court St., Westminster, Md.

SHIPLEY, Arthur Marriott, surgeon; b. Harmans, Md., Jan. 8, 1878; s. Roderick O. and Wilhelmina (Clark) S.; prep. edn., high sch. and Friends Sch., Baltimore; M.D., U. of Md., 1902; Sc.D., St. John's Coll., Annapolis; m. Julia Armistead Joynes, May 6, 1909. Supt. U. of Md. Hosp., 1904-08; asso. prof. surgery, U. of Md., 1907-14, prof. clin. surgery, 1914-20, prof. surgery and head of dept. since 1920. Capt., later maj. and lt. col., Med. R.C., 1917-19. Mem. Am. Surg. Assn., Southern Surg. Assn., Am. Assn. Thoracic Surgery, Soc. Clin. Surgery, Surgical Research Soc. Democrat. Club: Maryland. Home: 507 Edgevale Rd., Roland Park, Baltimore. Office: University Hospital, Baltimore, Md.

SHIPLEY, Charles Raymond, merchant; b. Lisbon, Md., June 23, 1883; s. Joseph Edward and Deborah Ann (McDonald) S.; ed. public and night schools of Md.; m. Edna Gertrude Young, June 3, 1908; children—Ann McDonald (Mrs. Robert Andrew Hall), Charles Raymond. Partner in firm of Warwick, Barrett & Shipley, retail dry goods, Charleston, W.Va., 1903-13; asso. United (later associated) Dry Goods Corpn., 1913-31, as merchandise mgr. H. Batterman & Co., Brooklyn, N.Y., 1913-15, dir. and merchandise mgr. J. N. Adam & Co., Buffalo, 1915-17, 1st v.p., dir. and mem. exec. com. Lord & Taylor, New York, also dir. Asso. Dry Goods Corpn., 1917-31; joined John Wanamaker, Phila., 1931, as gen. mdse. mgr., then exec. mgr. and later vice-pres.; pres. and dir. John Wanamaker, Phila., and John Wanamaker, New York, since Nov. 22, 1937; pres. and dir. A. T. Stewart Realty Co., New York; dir. John Wanamaker, London, Ltd.; dir. Pa. Co. for Ins. on Lives and Granting Annuities, Phila. Republican. Christian Scientist. Clubs: Union League (Phila.); Merion Cricket (Merion, Pa.); Pennsylvania Society (New York). Home: "Low Walls," Montgomery and Ithan Ave., Rosemont, Pa. Office: 13th and Market Sts., Philadelphia, Pa.

SHIPLEY, George, educator; b. at Baltimore, Md., Mar. 13, 1867; s. Rev. J. Lester and Elizabeth Augusta (Gere) S.; A.B., Randolph-Macon Coll., 1887, A.M., 1888; Ph.D., Johns Hopkins, 1897; m. Dorothy, d. William B. and Anne (Tyson) Willson, Nov. 20, 1913. Editor Baltimore American, 1897-1916; asso. headmaster Boys' Latin School, Baltimore, 1914-16, and headmaster, 1917-34. Mem. Phi Beta Kappa, Modern Lang. Assn. America, Simplified Spelling Bd. Clubs: University, Baltimore Country, Johns Hopkins, Gibson Island. Author: The Genitive Case in Anglo-Saxon, 1903. Address: "Fairhaven," Easton, Md.

SHIPLEY, Grant B.; chmn. bd. and chmn. exec. com. Wood Preserving Corpn.; also officer or dir. various other corpns. Home: 5398 Hobart St. Office: Koppers Bldg., Pittsburgh, Pa.

SHIPLEY, Harold Anthony, pres. Pittsburgh Industrial Engring. Co.; b. Pittsburgh, Pa., Feb. 11, 1902; s. William James and Anna Mary (Eibbenlaus) S.; m. Eleanora Elizabeth Hepp, Oct. 26, 1925; children—Harold Anthony, Elizabeth Ann. Engr., Pittsburgh-Des Moines Steel Co., 1921-25; became chief engr., Pittsburgh Engring., Foundry & Constrn. Co., 1925, later sales mgr., 1934; organized Pittsburgh (Pa.) Industrial Engring. Co., 1934, pres. since 1934. Club: Metropolitan (Pittsburgh). Home: 1400 Jancey St. Office: Pittsburgh Industrial Engineering Co., Pittsburgh, Pa.

SHIPLEY, Richard Larkin, clergyman, editor; b. Harman, Md., June 10, 1879; s. Theodore Alexander and Cecelia (Shipley) S.; grad. Westminster (Md.) Theol. Sem., 1903; D.D., Western Md. Coll., 1924; m. Cora Belle Roberts, June 20, 1907; children—Mary Louise, Roberta Cecilia. Ordained to ministry Meth. Protestant Ch., 1905; pastor various chs. in Md., First Ch., Newark, N.J., 1926-32; editor Meth. Protestant Recorder since 1932. Trustee Western Md. Coll. Mem. Am. Fed. Arts, Interchurch Club of Baltimore. Democrat. Meth. Protestant. Mason, Jr. O.U.A.M. Contbr. weekly page to Teacher's Journal and editorials to Meth. Protestant Recorder. Lecturer Westminster Theol. Sem. Home: 4135 Forest Park Av. Office: 516 N. Charles St., Baltimore, Md.

SHIPLEY, Walter Penn, lawyer; b. Phila., Pa., June 20, 1860; s. Thomas and Eliza M. (Drinker) S.; prep. edn. Friends Select Sch., Germantown, Phila.; student Haverford Coll. Class of 1881; LL.B., U. of Pa., 1883; m. Anne Emlen, of Phila., Oct. 17, 1889; children —Thomas E., James E., Walter Penn. Admitted to Pa. bar, 1883, and since in practice at Phila.; sr. mem. Shipley & Vaux, 1887-1927; half owner Girard Shoe Mfg. Co. from 1915 until dissolution of firm; dir. John C. Winston Co. Mem. Germantown Preparative Meeting of Friends (treas. of Trustees, 1900-25); dir. and treas. Home for Aged and Infirm Colored Persons since 1893. Republican. Mem. Soc. of Friends. Clubs: Franklin Chess (pres.), University (Phila.); Manhattan Chess (New York). Home: 477 Locust Av., Germantown, Philadelphia, Pa. Office: Morris Bldg., 1421 Chestnut St., Philadelphia, Pa.

SHIPLEY, William Stewart, manufacturer; b. Jersey City, N.J., Mar. 28, 1879; s. Samuel Shipley and Eliza (McFall) S.; M.E., Cooper Inst. of N.Y.; m. Anna Elizabeth Olsen, Nov. 4, 1903; 1 dau., Ruth Anna (Mrs. Stuart Bruce McNaught). Served apprenticeship with Diehl Motor Co., Elizabethfort, N.J., and Nash Gas Engine Co., Brooklyn, N.Y.; machinist York Mfg. Co., 1900-04; salesman of York products with S. J. Shipley Co., Brooklyn, 1904-07; v.p. and gen. mgr. Shipley Constrn. and Supply Co., 1907-27; v.p. and gen. Eastern mgr. York Ice Machinery Corpn., 1927-30, pres. since 1930; pres. Canadian Ice Machine Co., York-Shipley Co. of Cuba, York-Shipley Co. of China; chmn. bd. York-Shipley, Ltd., London. Dir. Pa. State Chamber of Commerce; gen. chmn. York Welfare Fed., 1934-38; Auditorium Conditioning Corpn., New York; Masterlin & Campbell Co., Chicago; mem. advisory bd. York Co. Tuberculosis Soc.; dir. York Y.M.C.A. Pres. (1938) and mem. exec. com. Refrigerating Machinery Assn.; vice-pres. Mfrs. Assn. of York; past pres. Am. Soc. Refrigerating Engrs.; mem. Nat. Assn. Practical Refrigerating Engrs. Republican. Mason. Episcopalian. Clubs: Rotary, Country (dir.), Lafayette (York); Engineers (New York); Bellport Country (Long Island). Home: Wyndham Hills, York, Pa. Office: York, Pa.

SHIPMAN, James F., judge; b. Sunbury, Pa., Oct. 29, 1884; s. Walter and Josephine (Coldreu) S.; student Bucknell U., Lewisburg, Pa., 1900-03; A.B., Lafayette Coll., Easton, Pa., 1905; LL.B., Dickinson Sch. of Law, Carlisle, Pa., 1909; A.M., Dickinson Coll., 1909; m. Mary E. Maxwell, Sept. 20, 1911; children —Frank M., Jeanne (Mrs. Herbert Cohrt), Robert D. Admitted to Pa. bar and entered practice at Sunbury, 1909; admitted to W.Va. bar 1910 and since in gen. practice at Moundsville; city solicitor, Moundsville, W.Va., 1911-13; sec. bd. edn., Moundsville, 1914-15; city solicitor, Moundsville, 1923-25; judge 2d jud. circuit of W.Va. since 1929. Mem. W.Va. Bar Assn., Marshall Co. Bar Assn., Delta Chi. Democrat. Methodist. Mason (32°, Shriner). Elk. Kiwanis. Home: 1302 6th St. Office: Court House, Moundsville, W.Va.

SHIPMAN, Jehiel G., lawyer; b. Belvidere, Warren Co., N.J., Apr. 21, 1885; s. George M. and Annie L. (Wilson) S.; grad. pub. sch., Belvidere, N.J., 1901, Blair Acad., Blairstown, N.J., 1902; A.B., Princeton U., 1906; LL.B., New York Law Sch., 1908; m. Celine Zinkensen, Nov. 28, 1917; children—Edith Celing, Pomeroy. Admitted to N.J. bar, 1909; law clk. McCarter & English, Newark, N.J., 1908-09, asso. with firm, 1909-11; asso. with Franklin W. Fort, Newark, N.J., 1911-12; partner firm of John Franklin Fort and Franklin W. Fort, Newark, 1912-17; in pvt. practice, Newark, 1919-24; partner Child & Shipman, Newark, 1924-35, firm Child, Riker, Marsh & Shipman, Newark, since 1935. Served as 1st lt., F.A., U.S. Army, 1917-19, in France with 92d Div., 1919. Trustee Blair Acad. Mem. Essex Co. Law Assn., Am. Bar Assn., Princeton Elm Club. Republican. Presbyterian. Home: 353 Highland Av. Office: 744 Broad St., Newark, N.J.

SHIPPS, Hammell Pierce, physician; b. Delanco, N.J., Sept. 13, 1900; s. Charles C. and Clara E. (Fenimore) S.; B.S., Temple U., 1922; M.D., Jefferson Med. Coll., 1926; m. Flora B. Collings, June 28, 1928; children—Charles Collings, Elizabeth Pembrook, Gordon Thomas. Interne, The Cooper Hosp., Camden, N.J., 1926-28; engaged in gen. practice of medicine at Delanco, N.J., 1928-38, specializing in gynecology and surgery; in practice of gynecology at Camden, N.J., since 1936; asst. gynecologist, Cooper Hosp., Camden; asso. in surgery, Burlington Co. Hosp., Mt. Holly, N.J.; associate gynecologist, Zurbrugg Memorial Hosp., Riverside, N.J.; dir. Delanco Bldg. & Loan Assn., Delanco Agency, Inc. Vice-pres. Bd. Edn., Delanco, N.J. Fellow Am. Coll. Surgs. Mem. Am. Med. Assn., N.J. State and Burlington Co. med. socs., Phila. Obstet. Soc. Republican. Methodist. Home: 739 Chestnut St., Delanco. Office: 719 Cooper St., Camden, N.J.

SHIVELY, Charles Stacy, prof. mathematics; b. Peru, Ind., May 25, 1875; s. Daniel P. and Harriet (Little) S.; student Butler Coll., 1898-99; B.S.D., McPherson (Kan.) Coll., 1907, A.B., 1910; A.M., U. of Denver, 1911, Ph.D., same, 1919; grad. study U. of Chicago, summer 1925; m. Anna Rivers, Apr. 17, 1904; children—Arthur Willard, Ethel May (Mrs. H. F. Bookwalter). Engaged as teacher in pub. schs., prin. village sch., teacher mathematics, high schs., Denver, Colo.; supervising teacher, Guimaras Island, P.I., 1904-06; prof. mathematics, Laverne (Calif.) Coll., 1919-20; prof. mathematics, Juniata Coll., Huntingdon, Pa., since 1920. Democrat. Brethren Ch. Home: 1525 Moore St., Huntingdon, Pa.

SHOCKLEY, Frank William, educational administrator; b. Mooreland, Ind., Oct. 15, 1884; s. John Wesley and Emma (Rhoton) S.; A.B., Indiana U., 1917; m. Borgia Haskett, Aug. 4, 1910; children—Frank William (dec.), Maebeth. Elementary teacher, later teacher and prin. high schs.; head of Ind. U. extension center, Ft. Wayne, 1917-18; asso. dir. Ind. U. extension div., 1918-20; asst. to dean of univ. extension, U. of Wis., 1920-25; dir. extension and summer session, U. of Pittsburgh since 1925, dir. jr. colls. since 1927, dir. campus evening and Saturday courses since July 1, 1938, acting dean, Sch. of Edn. since Sept. 1938. Mem. Nat. Univ. Extension Assn. (pres. 1934-35); Am. Association Jr. Colleges, Assn. for Promotion Adult Edn., Pittsburgh Council for Adult Edn., Pittsburgh Personnel Assn., N.E.A., Pa. State Edn. Assn., Pa. Assn. for Adult Edn. (pres. univ. extension sect., 1937-38), Phi Gamma Delta. Republican. Mem. Christian (Disciples) Ch. Mason. Clubs: University, Faculty (U. of Pittsburgh). Home: 1871 Shaw Av. Address: University of Pittsburgh, Pittsburgh, Pa.

SHOCKLEY, Orlando Mack, lumberman, banker; b. Berlin, Md., Nov. 7, 1875; s. John A. and Ellen (Gordy) S.; student country pub. sch., Worcester Co., Md., 1882-98; m. Lovey Carrie Mumford, Oct. 23, 1901; 1 dau., Edith Ione (Mrs. John Palmer). Pub. sch. teacher, Worcester Co., Md., 1899-1901; clk. and mgr. branch office Bowen Lumber Co., Norfolk, Va., 1901-05; formed partnership with John M. Moore, Showell (Md.), trading as Showell Mfg. Co., lumber mfrs., tomato canners, 1905, and continuously in business to date; operated general store, 1907-11; pres. The Bishopville (Md.) Bank since 1933. Mem. Md. Ho. of Reps. 1920-21. Sunday sch. supt., Showell, Md., since 1903; rep. Sunday Schs. of Worcester Co. (Md.) at 13th Internat. Sunday Sch. Conv., San Francisco, Calif., 1911; local preacher since 1909, bible class teacher since 1915. Dir. Wesley Collegiate Inst., Dover, Del. Republican. Methodist. Mason; Jr. Order United Am. Mechanics, Red Man, Odd Fellow, Order of Eastern Star. Address: Showell, Md.

SHOEMAKER, Dacia Custer-, see Custer-Shoemaker, Dacia.

SHOEMAKER, Dora Adèle, educator: b. Philadelphia, Pa.; d. J. W. and Rachel (Hinkle) S.; grad. Friends Select Sch., Phila.; Bach. of Elocution, Nat. Sch. of Elocution and Oratory (founded by parents in 1873), Phila., 1901, Master of Oratory, 1915; studied Hawn Sch. of Oratory and U. of Pa.; M.A., Marywood Coll., Scranton, Pa., 1932. Teacher and recitalist since age of sixteen; producer of plays for schools, clubs, etc.; prin., The Shoemaker School of Speech and Drama (Nat. Sch. of Elocution and Oratory), since 1915. Mem. Nat. League Am. Pen Women (Phila. br.). Presbyn. Clubs: Plays and Players, Nat. Alumni Players. Author: Out O'Doors (verse), 1932; also plays —A Patron of Art, Girls of 1776, A Fighting Chance. Home: Bala-Cynwyd, Pa. Address: 2016 Walnut St., Philadelphia, Pa.

SHOEMAKER, Edna Cooke (Mrs. Orlando), artist; b. Phila., Pa., June 19, 1891; d. George Anderson and Elizabeth (Simon) Cooke; student pub. schs., and Pa. Acad. Fine Arts, 1909-12; m. Orlando Shoemaker, May 3, 1924; children—Winslow Cooke, Abigail Anne, Oliver Ireton. Has specialized in illustrating since 1915; illustrated many books for leading publishers, also for well-known mags. of nat. circulation including Ladies Home Journal, Delineator, McCalls, and others. Mem. Fellowship Pa. Acad. Fine Arts, U. of Pa. Mus. Fine Arts, Phila. Art Alliance. Episcopalian. Club: Garden of Rose Tree. Home: Rose Tree Rd., Media, Pa.

SHOEMAKER, Frank D(ewey), mining engring.; b. Shamokin, Pa., Mar. 5, 1898; s. Elmer and Harriet (Van Horn) S.; student pub. and high schs., Shamokin, Pa., 1904-16, Pa. State Coll. Extension, 1925-27; m. Helen V. Hetrick, Aug. 24, 1918; children—William Kay, Frank Jerry. Employed as surveyor's asst. Phila. & Reading Coal & Iron Co., 1917-19; surveyor Leggitts Creek Anthracite Co., 1919-25; asst. engr. South Penn Collieries Co., 1925-31; chief mining engr., Penn Anthracite Collieries Co. since 1931. Mem. Scranton Chamber of Commerce. Mem. Am. Inst. Mining and Metall. Engrs. Republican. Lutheran. Home: 2125 Comegys Av. Office: Bowman Bldg., Scranton, Pa.

SHOEMAKER, Henry Wharton, newspaper pub.; b. N.Y. City, Feb. 24, 1882; s. Henry Francis Blanche (Quiggle) S.; ed. pvt. tutors, at Dr. E. D. Lyon's Classical School (now under title of the Allen-Stevenson School), New York, and Columbia Univ., 1897-1900; Litt.D., Juniata Coll., Huntingdon, Pa., 1917, Franklin and Marshall Coll., 1924; m. Beatrice, d. George B. Barclay, June 12, 1907; 1 son, Henry F.; m. 2d, Mabelle Ord, May 10, 1913. In employ C.H.&D. Ry., Cincinnati and N.Y., 1900-1903; sec. Am. Legation, Lisbon, Portugal, 1904; 3d sec. Am. Embassy, Berlin, 1904-05; mem. N.Y. banking house of Shoemaker, Bates & Co., 1905-11; became publisher of daily morning and evening newspapers, Pa. and Conn., 1905; president Altoona (Pa.) Times Tribune since 1912; dir. Jersey Shore (Pa.) Herald; appointed E.E. and M.P. to Bulgaria, 1930, retired 1933. Member advisory board Associated Press for Pennsylvania. Officer, New York, later Pa., N.C., 1907-19; lt. col. N.G. Pa., 1915-19; with Gen. Staff U.S.A., 1918-19; spl. rep. N.G. Pa. in Europe, 1918; lt. col. O.R.C., 1924, col. since 1933; mem. Gov. of Pa.'s Commn. for Nat. Defense, and Com. Pub. Safety, 1917-18. Mem. State Forest Commn. of Pa., 1918-30; chmn. State Hist. Commn. of Pa., 1923-30, mem. of commn. since 1936; mem. State Geographic Bd. of Pa., 1924-30; chmn. advisory bd. Pa. State Forestry Schs. since 1929; mem. bd. dirs. Allegheny Forest Expt. Station in Pa.; dir. State Archives of Pennsylvania since May 1937. Mem. bd. of trustees, Dickinson Sem., Linden Hall Sem. Decorated Grand Officer Order of the Redeemer (Greece); Grand Cordon Order of Civil Merit (Bulgaria); Comdr. Order of the Crown (Italy); Knight Order of Nicholas II (Russia). Fellow American Geog. Society, Royal Geog. Society (London); member Society American Foresters, Netherlands Society of Philadelphia (vice pres. 1915-29), Huguenot Society of Pa. (pres. 1919-20), Waldensian Hist. Soc. of Pa. (v.p. 1925-30), Pa. Federation Hist. Socs. (pres. 1925-26), S.R., Soc. Foreign Wars, Mil. Order World War, Am. Legion, etc. Mason. Clubs: Lotos, Nat. Arts, Boone and Crockett, Ends of the Earth (New York, N.Y.); Franklin Inn (Philadelphia, Pa.). Author: (biographies) General William Sprague, 1916; Chief John Logan, 1917; Gifford Pinchot, 1922; John Brown (in Pennsylvania), 1931; also several books of verse and many books, articles and brochures on Pa. history, Indians, folklore, folksongs, proverbs, old words, zoölogy, etc. Columnist of Altoona Times-Tribune. Home: McElhattan, Pa. Office: 71 Broadway, New York, N.Y.

SHOLLENBERGER, Clarence Lewars, surgeon; b. Wilmington, Del., Oct. 18, 1895; s. Clarence L. and Suzanne (Given) S.; ed. Dickinson Coll., 1913 to 1917; M.D., Hahnemann Med. Coll., Phila., 1921; m. Gladys Swartley, Dec. 23, 1920; children—Jean Elizabeth, Gladys Suzanne, John Lewars. Chief surg. res., Hahnemann Hosp., Phila., 1922-23, lecturer and asso. prof. anatomy since 1924, asso. surgeon since 1926; asst. visiting surgeon Abington Memorial Hosp., Abington, Pa., since 1926; surgeon to Women's Homeopathic Hosp., Phila., since 1939. Served as private and sergt., U.S.A., 1916-17. Fellow Am. Coll. Surgeons; mem. American Med. Assoc., Am., Pa., Phila. Co., Pa. State med. assns., Am. Inst. Homeopathy and Phila. Co. Homeo, Med. Soc., Phi Kappa Psi. Republican. Methodist. Mason (32°). Clubs: "37", Overbrooke Golf, Medical (Phila.). Contbr. articles to med. jours. Home: 662 S. Highland Av., Merion, Pa.

SHOLLENBERGER, Darius W., pres. First Nat. Bank of Montgomery (Pa.); b. McKeensburg, Pa., July 26, 1857; s. Willoughby and Sophia (Weigle) S.; student Co. Normal Sch., Muncy, Pa., 1877-79, Commercial Coll., Williamsport, Pa., 1882; m. Hannah Mary Heilman, Oct. 4, 1880 (died Nov. 1920); children —Edmund Kennard, Martha (Mrs. Joseph P. Housel), Alma (wife of Dr. W. D. Coy), Clara Mina (dec.); m. 2d, Janet Morgan, Dec. 30, 1922. Began as worker in grist mills, 1873; worker on farm, 1874-79; teacher of public schools, Lycoming Co., Pa., 1877-81; worker in machine shop, Montgomery, Pa., summers 1880, 1881; bookkeeper in office of Levi Houston, machine works, Montgomery, Pa., 1882-86, correspondence clerk, 1886-92, mgr., 1892-1926; mem. bd. of dirs., First Nat. Bank of Montgomery (Pa.), 1900-26, pres. since 1926; treas., dir. and mgr., Montgomery (Pa.) Light, Heat & Power Co. (later Montgomery & Muncy Electric Light & Power Co.), 1890-1924; pres. West Branch Telephone Co., Muncy, Pa., since 1925; dir. and treas., Montgomery (Pa.) Store Co., from organization to sale of business; dir. Muncy Lumber Co., 1916-26. Mem. Montgomery Borough (Pa.) Sch. Bd. (treas., 3 yrs; sec. 5 years; pres. since 1893); pres. Montgomery-Clinton Joint School Bd., 1927-34; mem. Lycoming Co. (Pa.) Sch. Bd. since 1938. Mem. Lycoming Co. (Pa.) Sch. Dirs. Assn. (v.p.), Montgomery (Pa.) Business Men's Assn.; mem. Pa. Soc. of N.Y. Awarded gold medal for over 50 years service as Sunday Sch. teacher, Evangelical Lutheran Ch. Republican. Mason (Consistory; K.T.; Shriner). Home: 47 Houston Av. Office: 1 Main St., Montgomery, Pa.

SHOOK, Myron George, business exec.; b. Lima, O., Feb. 9, 1895; s. Corbin Neff and Jessie (Peltier) S.; grad. Lima (O.) High Sch., 1913; B.S. in Business Adminstrn., Ohio State U., Columbus, O., 1917; m. Harriet Alberta King, May 29, 1924; 1 dau., Yvonne Elizabeth. Began as clk. Columbus (O.) Telephone Co., 1917; gen. office clk., cost accountant, claim agt. Cleveland (O.) Provision Co., 1917-19; auditor The Steel Products Co., Cleveland, O., 1919-23; asst. treas. The Glenn L. Martin Co., Baltimore, Md., 1923-24, treas. since 1924, asst. sec. since 1939, dir. since 1924. Served as non-commd. officer, Personnel Adj's. Detachment, U.S. Army, during World War. Mem. Controllers' Inst., Sigma Pi, Alpha Kappa Psi. Christian Ch. Mason. Home: 7300 Harford Rd. Office: The Glenn L. Martin Co., Baltimore, Md.

SHOOP, Irvin Edgar, mfg. confectioner; b. Dauphin Co., Pa., Nov. 13, 1881; s. William and Elizabeth (Wise) S.; student Elizabethtown Coll. Commercial Dept., 1903-05; m. Ada M. Shiffer, Jan. 1, 1907; children—Dwight L., Grace E. (Mrs. Clarence W. Wells), Ernest A. (dec.), Helen M., Esther G., Vera Blinn. Bookkeeper Buch Mfg. Co., 1907-16; with Klein Chocolate Co., Elizabethtown, Pa., since 1916, bookkeeper, 1916-20, asst. treas., credit, collection and office mgr. since 1921. Dir. Elizabethtown (Pa.) B. of Edn. since 1921, pres. since 1929. Founder, pres. and treas. Anti-Atheistic Assn., Inc. Republican. Mem. United Brethren. Home: 101 Park St., Elizabethtown, Pa.

SHOPE, Edward Pierce Lentz, ophthalmologist; b. Lehighton, Pa., Aug. 6, 1896; s. Samuel Zimmerman and Elizabeth Esther (Lentz) S.; A.B., Dickinson Coll., Carlisle, Pa., 1916, A.M., 1920; M.S., Susquehanna U., Selinsgrove, Pa., 1917; M.D., Johns Hopkins, 1920; M. Med.Sc. in ophthalmology, U. of Pa., 1931; m. Elizabeth Louise Healy, Sept. 8, 1923; children—Samuel Pierce, Daniel Nathaniel. Interne Episcopal Hosp., Phila., 1920-21; chief resident Morristown (N.J.) Memorial Hosp., 1921-23; asst. and asst. surgeon Wills Hosp., Phila., since 1929; instr. ophthal. dept., Grad. Sch. of Medicine, U. of Pa. since 1931; formerly asst. ophthalmologist to Grad. and Meth. Hosps., Phila. Certificate of Am. Bd. of Ophthalmic Examinations, 1931. Fellow Acad. of Ophthalmology and Otolaryngology; mem. A.M.A., N.J. State Med. Soc., Camden County Med. Soc. Home: 20 Gill Rd., Haddonfield, N.J. Office: 511 Cooper St., Camden, N.J.

SHOREY, Katherine Abigail, librarian; b. Davenport, Ia., Mar. 19, 1893; d. Albourne Oliver and Ida (McCulloch) Shorey; grad. Western Reserve Univ. Sch. of Library Science, Cleveland, O., 1924; A.B., Barnard Coll., Columbia U., 1931; unmarried. Social service worker Ladies Industrial Relief Soc., Davenport, Ia., 1912-17; asst. Davenport (Ia.) Pub. Library, 1920-23, 1924-25, 1927-28; asst. Columbia U. Library, New York, 1926-27, 1928-31; librarian Greene Co. Library, Xenia, O., 1931-35; librarian Martin Memorial Library, York, Pa., since 1935. Mem. Am. Library Assn., Pa. Library Assn., Western Reserve U. Alumnae Assn., Barnard Coll. Alumnae Assn. Episcopalian. Clubs: Quota, College, Woman's (York, Pa.); Lake Placid (Lake Placid, N.Y.). Home: 333 E. Market St. Office: 159 E. Market St., York, Pa.

SHORT, Albert, insurance; b. Sussex Co., Del., 1866; ed. commercial sch. and Central High Sch., Phila. Formerly cashier Berkshire Life Ins. Co., Phila.; organizer Girard Life Ins. Co., and pres. since 1927. Home: 452 Kenwood Rd., Drexel Park, Pa. Office: 529 Chestnut St., Philadelphia, Pa.

SHORT, Oliver Clark, govt. official; b. Georgetown, Del., Aug. 15, 1883; s. Eli S. and Sarah Elizabeth (Jefferson) S.; A.B., U. of Del., 1904; A.M., U. of Pa., 1913; post grad. study in psychology, Johns Hopkins, 1924-27; m. Katharine Mae Alton, Jan. 30, 1909; children—Oliver Alton, Sarah Louise, Katharine Elizabeth. Teacher and commandant mil. corps, N.C. Mil. Acad., Red Springs, 1904-05; teacher and prin. pub. schs., Delaware City, Del., 1905-06; teacher and vice prin. high sch., Dover, Del., 1906-07; teacher mathematics, Bethlehem (Pa.) Prep. Sch., 1907-08; teacher mathematics and science, Sayre (Pa.) High Sch., 1908-10; teacher science High Sch., Trenton, N.J., 1910-17, Germantown (Phila., Pa.), High Sch., 1917-18; asst. chief examiner N.J. Civil Service Commn., 1918-20; sec. and chief examiner Md. Employment Commn., 1920-22, commr., 1922-35; personnel dir. Thos. Maddock's Sons Co., Trenton, part time 3 yrs.; exec. asst. to dir. of U.S. Census, 1935-37, asst. to dir., 1937-39; personnel dir. U.S. Dept. of Commerce since 1939; reëmployment dir. for Md., U.S. Employment Service, 1933-35; lecturer on personnel adminstrn., Johns Hopkins, U. of Md., U. of Baltimore, Am. Univ.; lecturer on organization, supervision and management, Am. Univ. Mem. Assembly of Civil Service Commns. of U.S. and Can. (ex-pres.), Personnel Adminstrn. Group, Baltimore (ex-pres.), Soc. for Personnel Administration (pres.), Y.M.C.A., Trenton Chamber Commerce, Baltimore Association of Commerce. Member Phi Kappa Phi. Democrat. Episcopalian. Mason (Shriner), K.P. (past chancellor). Clubs: Gavel (ex-pres.), Schoolmasters of Trenton (ex-pres.), Rotary Internat. (ex-pres. Baltimore; ex-gov. 34th dist.), Author: The Merit System, 1928. Home: College Park, Md. Office: Commerce Bldg., Washington, D.C.

SHORT, Samuel McClellan, clergyman, educator; b. East Waterloo, Pa., May 4, 1883; s. William John and Mary (Barton) S.; B.S., Albright Coll., Myerstown, Pa., 1912, A.M., same, 1922; ed. U. of Nanking, China, 1914-15, Pa. State Coll., part time, 1932-33; m. Rachel Brown, Aug. 18, 1917; children—William J., Robert Brown, Catharine Jane, Mabel C., Carol May. Engaged in teaching in elementary schs., 1902-08; teacher and proctor, Albright Prep. Sch., 1908-12; prin. high Sch., Academia, Pa., 1912-14; prin. Albright High Sch., Liling, China, 1915-21; served as dist. and asst. state supt. Anti-Saloon League, Pa. and N.J., 1923-33; county supt. schs. Juniata Co., Mifflintown, Pa., since 1934; ordained to ministry Evang. Ch., 1916; lectured on ednl. and moral questions; active in S.S. and church work. Mem. Pa. State and Nat. edn. assns. Republican. Mem. Evang. Ch. I.O.O.F. Grange. Club: Port Royal Civic. Home: Port Royal, Pa. Office: Mifflintown, Pa.

SHORTESS, George Seidel, coll. prof.; b. Beavertown, Pa., Jan. 17, 1897; s. Thomas Albert and Mary (Seidel) S.; A.B., Johns Hopkins U., 1922; A.M., Columbia U., 1931; student U. of Pa., 1934; grad. student Johns Hopkins U., 1936-39; m. Mary Keen, June 29, 1929; children—David Keen, George Keen. Prof. biology, Mount St. Mary's Coll., Emmitsburg, Md., 1922-30; prof. biology, Elizabethtown Coll., since 1930, also dean of men since 1938. Served in Air Service, U.S. Marine Flying Corps, 1918. Mem. Am. Genetics Assn., Sigma Xi, Sigma Zeta. Democrat. Methodist. Home: 323 Orange St., Elizabethtown, Pa.

SHORTLIDGE, Jonathan Chauncey, educator; b. Concordville, Pa., Aug. 2, 1872; s. Joseph and Caroline Bailey (Gause) S.; A.B., Swarthmore Coll., 1896; A.B., Harvard, 1898; m. Helen Wood, June 14, 1923. Prin. Friends Acad., Locust Valley, N.Y., 1896-97; teacher, Maplewood Inst., Concordville, Pa., 1898-1920; since 1920 prin. Maplewood Sch. for Boys, Chester Heights, Pa.; dir. Maplewood Summer Camp. Mem. Delta Upsilon. Mason. Home: West Chester, Pa.

SHORTRIDGE, Wilson Porter, prof. history; b. Medora, Ind., July 28, 1880; s. William Howard and Rhoda Ann (Roberts) S.; A.B., Ind. U., 1907; A.M., U. of Wis., 1911; Ph.D., U. of Minn., 1919; m. Blanche Alter, Aug. 31, 1904; children—Milford Howard (dec.), Blanche Pauline, Wilson Poole, Rhoda Mildred. Teacher pub. schs., Elkhart, Ind., 1908-11; teacher North High Sch., Minneapolis, 1911-17; asst. in history, U. of Minn., 1917-18; asst. prof. history, U. of Louisville, 1918-19, prof., 1919-22; prof. history, W.Va. U., since 1922, dean of Coll. of Arts and Sciences since 1929. Mem. Am. Hist. Assn., Phi Beta Kappa. Presbyn. Mason (32°). Author: The Transition of a Typical Frontier, 1922; The Development of the United States, 1929; also articles in hist. publs. Home: 151 Wagner Rd., Morgantown, W.Va.

SHOTT, Hugh Ike, ex-congressman; b. Staunton, Va., Sept. 3, 1866; s. Daniel Webster and Lucy Ellen Bell (Hoy) S.; ed. pub. schs.; m. Mary Kate Chisholm, Jan. 10, 1894; children—Jas. Howard, Mary Lillian (Mrs. G. C. Brant, Jr.), Hugh Ike, Jr. Learned printers trade, 1882-89; in ry. mail service, 1889-96; editor and pub. Bluefield (W.Va.) Daily Telegraph; pres. Daily Telegraph Printing Co.; v.p. Telegraph Commercial Printing Co., WHIS Radio Station. Postmaster, Bluefield, 1902-13; mem. Rep. State Com., W.Va., 1908-12; mem. 71st and 72d Congresses (1929-33), 5th W.Va. Dist. Rep. nominee for U.S. senator, 1936. Mem. W.Va. Semi-Centennial Commn., Southern Newspaper Pubs'. Assn., W.Va. Pubs'. Assn. Methodist. Knight of Pythias. Clubs: Rotary, Nat. Press. Home: Bluefield, W.Va.

SHOTWELL, Fred Calvin, supervising prin. schs.; b. near Johnsonburg, N.J., Feb. 6, 1892; s. James Joseph and Theresa (Newett) S.; grad. Pa. State Normal Sch., East Stroudsburg, 1910; Ph.B., Lafayette Coll., Easton, Pa., 1916; A.M., Columbia U., 1921; m. Nettie Rae Roberson, June 22, 1916; children—Doris Roberson, Janet E., Fred Calvin, Jr. Studied commercial courses and substitute teacher, business coll., Trenton, N.J., 1911-12; head commercial dept. N.J. Reformatory, Rahway, N.J., 1912-13; head science dept., high sch., Easton, Pa., 1916-20; prin. high sch., Woodbridge, N.J., 1920-21, North Plainfield, N.J., 1921-23; supervising prin. schs., Franklin, N.J., since 1923. Served as pres. Franklin Athletic Assn. Mem. Nat. Assn. for Study of Edn., Nat. Edn. Assn. (Dept. of Elementary Sch. Prins., Dept. Secondary Sch. Prins.), Nat. Assn. Sch. Adminstrs., N.J. Edn. Assn., N.J. Schoolmasters Club (past pres.), N.J. Council of Edn., Amateur Astronomers Assn., Junior Astronomy Club (New York). Republican. Presbyterian. Mason (32°), Tall Cedars of Lebanon. Clubs: Walkill Country; Franklin Community (pres.). Home: 1 School Plaza, Franklin, N.J.

SHOTZ, Charles Sylvester, lawyer; b. Russia, Dec. 20, 1898; s. Harry and Esther (Shusterman) S.; brought to U.S., 1899, naturalized, 1915; B.S., South Phila., High Sch., 1917; Ph.G., Temple U., Phila., 1921, LL.B., 1927; married; children—Sidney Arnold, Stanley, Esther. Pharmacist, Phila., 1921-25; admitted to Pa. bar, 1927, and began practice in Phila.; counsel Dept. of Forests and Waters, Commonwealth of Pa., since 1937. Mem. Dem. Lawyers Com., 42d Ward Dem. Com.; atty. for Dem. City Com., 1932-35. Sec. Jewish Day Nursery, Phila., 1929-33, co-chmn. 1933 drive, hon. life dir. since 1933; dir. Hebrew Immigrant Aid Soc., 1929-35, sec., 1932-34, co-chmn. 1934 drive; mem. exec. com. Am. Jewish Congress, 1931-34; chmn. Tool Campaign for Palestine Workers, 1932; trustee Deborah Consumptive Relief Soc., 1932-34, co-chmn. 1934 drive, sec., 1934. Mem. Phila. Bar Assn., Law Club of Temple U., Am. Acad. Polit. Science. Mem. Independent Order B'rith Sholom, 1930-33, Independent Order B'rith Abraham, 1928-30. Home: 5010 Boudinot St. Office: 1700 Sanson St., Philadelphia, Pa.

SHOUDY, Loyal A., surgeon; b. Ellensburgh, Wash., Sept. 23, 1880; s. John Alden and Mary Ellen (Stewart) S.; A.B., U. of Wash., Seattle, Wash., 1904; M.D., U. of Pa., 1909; unmarried. Chief surgeon, Bethlehem (Pa.) Steel Co., 1914-18, chief of med. service since 1918; mem. consulting staff, St. Luke's Hosp., Bethlehem, Pa., since 1918. Fellow Am. Coll.

Surgeons, A.M.A., Am. Assn. of Industrial Physicians & Surgeons, Am. Pub. Health Assn.; mem. Nat. Safety Council (dir.), Conf. Bd. of Physicians in Industry (dir.), Phi Gamma Delta, Phi Alpha Sigma. Clubs: Bethlehem, University, Saucon Valley Country (Bethlehem, Pa.). Author: (articles) Traumatic Surgery and the Injured Worker, 1928; The Scope of Industrial Medicine and Surgery, 1928; End Results of Fractures in Industry, 1933; Heat and Muscular Cramps (co-author), 1936. Home: Spring Valley Rd. Office: 701 E. 3d St., Bethlehem, Pa.

SHREEVE, Herbert Edward, telephone engr., retired; b. Cambridge, Eng., Aug. 1, 1873; s. William Sayer and Caroline (Ogden) S.; came to U.S., 1895, naturalized, 1917; ed. pvt. schs., spl. course elec. tech., City of London Guilds, Finsbury, London; m. Emily Loring Ames, of Dedham, Mass., May 18, 1904; 1 son, Herbert Prescott. Employed as engr., Am. Bell Telephone Co., 1895-1908; in engring. dept. Western Electric Co., 1915-17, in charge radio expts. in France, 1915, first wireless telephone tests between U.S.A. and France; staff engr., Western Electric Co., 1919-23; asst. to pres. Bell Telephone Labs., 1923-26; tech. rep. in Europe, Am. Telephone & Telegraph Co., and Bell Telephone Labs., 1926-35, retired, 1935; original development work, first commercial type telephone repeater; received about 40 U.S. patents. Served as maj. then lt. col. Signal Corps, U.S.A., 1917-19, with A.E.F. Awarded Legion d'Honneur (France), D.S.M. (U.S.). Fellow Am. Inst. Elec. Engrs. Republican. Unitarian. Clubs: Engineers, Railroad Machinery, Lotos (New York); Duck Lake (Maine). Home: 88 Linden St., Wyoming, Maplewood, N.J.

SHREINER, Charles Wesley, clergyman; b. Mount Joy, Pa., Sept. 18, 1882; s. Eli and Harriet (Huffty) S.; attended U.S. Naval Acad., 1905-07, Phila. Div. Sch., 1908-11; hon. M.A., U. of Pa., 1928; D.D., Temple U. 1931; m. Mary Cardwell, Jan. 11, 1916; children—Mary Jane, Charles Wesley. Ordained ministry P.E. Ch., 1911; headmaster Church Farm Sch., Glen Loch, Pa., since 1918; also dean Convocation of Chester, Diocese of Pa.; rector Ch. of the Atonement, Phila., 1911-18. Home: Glen Loch, Pa.

SHREVE, Francis, coll. prof.; b. Burchfield, W.Va., Feb. 10, 1880; s. Silas and Jane (Taylor) S.; A.B., W.Va. Univ., Morgantown, 1909; A.M., Ohio State U., Columbus, 1912; Ph.D., Peabody Coll., Nashville, Tenn., 1921; grad. student N.Y. Univ., summer 1916; m. Elma Ruth Cobb, June 3, 1920 (dec.); children—Irvin Cobb, Agnes Ellmore; m. 2d Anne Mabel Glass, June 16, 1934. Engaged in teaching, rural schs. of W.Va., 1900-04; prin. elementary schs., Grafton, W.Va., 1909-11; prin. high sch., Mannington, W.Va., 1911-12; prof. edn., Glenville State Normal Sch., Glenville, W.Va., 1912-13; prof. edn. and philosophy, W. Va. Wesleyan Coll., Buckhannon, W.Va., 1913-15; prof. edn. and head dept. of edn., Fairmont State Teachers Coll., Fairmont, W.Va., since 1915. Mem. Nat. Soc. for Study of Edn., Am. Assn. Univ. Profs., W.Va. State Edn. Assn., Kappa Delta Pi. Democrat. Methodist. Author: The Supervised Study Plan of Teaching, 1927. Contbr. to ednl. jours. Home: 23 Oakwood Rd., Fairmont, W.Va.

SHREVE, Lyman Cyrus, lawyer; b. Union City, Erie Co. Pa., Oct. 10, 1888; s. Milton William and Mary (Hill) S.; A.B., Bucknell U., Lewisburg, Pa., 1911; student U. of Pittsburgh Law Sch., 1911-13; m. Anna G. Hastings, Feb. 26, 1916; children—John Edward, Mary Hastings, Anna Hastings. Admitted to bar, Pa. Supreme Ct., 1913, U.S. Supreme Ct., 1920; mem. firm Shreve & Shreve, attys. at law, Erie, Pa. Served in Machine Gun Co., Pa. Res. Militia, U.S. Army, during World War. Candidate for judge Common Pleas Ct. Mem. Pa. Bar Assn., Erie Co. Bar Assn., Phi Gamma Delta, Phi Delta Phi. Republican. Presbyterian (elder Ch. of the Covenant, Erie, Pa.) Mason (Consistory, Shriner). Club: Shrine (Erie, Pa.). Home: 911 W. 6th St. Office: 607 Ariel Bldg., Erie, Pa.

SHREVE, Milton William, ex-congressman; b. Venango Co., Pa., May 3, 1858; s. Rev. Cyrus and Florella (Nourse) S.; Allegheny College, Meadville, Pa., 2 yrs.; Ph.B., Bucknell U., Lewisburg, Pa., 1884, A.M., same; m. Mary Hill, 1885. Admitted to Pa. bar, 1893; dist. atty., Erie Co., Pa., 1899-1902; mem. Pa. Ho. of Rep., 3 terms, 1906-12 (speaker 1911); member 63d Congress (1913-15), and of 66th and 67th Congresses (1919-23), 25th Pa. Dist., and 68th to 72d Congresses (1923-33), 29th Dist.; practice of law since 1933. Republican. Presbyn. Mason, K.T. Home: 512 W. 9th St. Office: Ariel Bldg., Erie, Pa.

SHRIER, Albert Franklin, physician; b. New York, N.Y., July 27, 1877; s. Frank and Leah (Drucker) S.; student Coll. of City of N.Y., 1891-95; M.D., Coll. of Physicians & Surgeons, Columbia U., 1899; m. Estelle Weiss, June 7, 1922; 1 dau., Leah. Engaged in practice of medicine at New York, 1899-1916; engaged in study of tuberculosis, 1916-19; supt. Mount Pleasant (Tuberculosis) Hosp., Reisterstown, Md., since 1919. Mem. bd. of dirs. Md. Tuberculosis Assn. Democrat. Mem. Reformed Ch. Home: 6118 Park Heights Av., Baltimore, Md.

SHRIVER, Alfred Jenkins, lawyer; b. Baltimore, June 5, 1867; s. Albert and Annie (Jenkins) S.; won intercollegiate thesis prize over 2,500 competitors in 1887; A.B., Johns Hopkins, 1891; post-grad. course same, 1892; LL.B., U. of Md., 1893; hon. A.M., Loyola Coll., 1894; unmarried. In law practice at Baltimore since 1893; has been prominently identified with many estates and will contests. Mem. Baltimore City, Md. State and Am. bar assns., Phi Beta Kappa. Author: Res Gestæ as a Rule of Evidence; Law of Wills of Personal Property in Maryland Prior to Aug. 1, 1884; Status of the Original Preferred Stock of the Baltimore & Ohio R.R. Co., and other legal publs. Mem. Soc. Colonial Wars (gov.), Soc. War of 1812. Clubs: University (New York); Maryland, Baltimore Country, Merchants, Opera, Assembly, Johns Hopkins; Bar Harbor (Bar Harbor, Me.); Everglades (Palm Beach, Fla.). Home: University Club. Office: Munsey Bldg., Baltimore, Md.

SHRIVER, George G(ehr), banking; b. Avondale, Md., July 29, 1887; s. William A. and Gertrude S.; student high sch., Westminster, Md., Easton & Burnett Bus. Coll., Baltimore; m. Mildred Augusta Seibert, Apr. 10, 1912; children—Charles A., Mildred (Peggy). Employed in various capacities, 1904-12; mem. firm H. C. Brown & Co., banking, Baltimore, 1916-31; vice-pres. then pres. Hambleton & Co., 1931-33; pres. George G. Shriver & Co., Inc., investment banking, Baltimore, since 1932; dir., Washington Properties, Inc., Washington, D.C., Isaac Benesoh & Sons, Inc., Baltimore, Grove Park Inn Corpn., Asheville, N.C. Republican. Mem. Reformed Ch. Clubs: Merchants, Baltimore Country (Baltimore); Asheville Country (Asheville, N.C.). Home: 5105 St. Albans Way. Office: Mercantile Trust Bldg., Baltimore, Md.

SHRIVER, George McLean, ry. official; b. Hightstown, N.J., 1868; s. Rev. Samuel S. and Caroline (McCluskey) S.; ed. pub. schs., Baltimore, Md.; m. Elizabeth M. Chism, June 1891 (dec.). Clerk in accounting dept. B.&O. R.R. Co., 1886; pvt. sec. to pres. same rd., 1888-1901; asst. to pres., 1901-11; 2d v.p. same road, Jan. 12, 1911, sr. v.p. same since Mar. 1, 1920. Clubs: Maryland (Baltimore); Metropolitan, Bankers, Recess (N.Y.); Art (Phila.). Home: "Alsenborn," Pikesville, Md. Office: B.&O. R.R. Co., Baltimore, Md.

SHRIVER, Henry; pres. First Nat. Bank. Address: Cumberland, Md.

SHRIVER, Samuel Henry, ins. and banking; b. Pikeville, Md., Dec. 1, 1903; s. George M. and Elizabeth M. (Chism) S.; B.S., Cornell U., 1926; m. Eleanor Howard Ringgold, Nov. 11, 1929; children—Samuel Henry, Jr., Richard Hanson. Employed as farm mgr. B. F. Shriver Co., Westminster, Md., 1926-29, gen. mgr. farms, 1929-32, vice-pres. and treas. B. F. Shriver Co., 1933; asso. with Alexander & Alexander, Inc., ins. brokerage, Baltimore, Md., since 1933; pres. and dir. Peoples Bank, Pikeville, Md., since 1934; dir. Somerset Canning Co., Somerset, Pa., Georgetown Barge Docks Elevator & Ry. Co. Mem. Sigma Phi. Democrat. Episcopalian. Clubs: Merchants (Baltimore); Cornell (New York); L'hirindle (Ruxton, Md.). Home: Pikeville. Office: 503 St. Paul Pl., Baltimore; also, Peoples Bank, Pikeville, Md.

SHRYOCK, John Knight, clergyman; b. Phila., Pa., Apr. 28, 1890; s. George Augustus and Mary H. (Chipman) S.; B.S. in C.E., U. of Pa., 1910; student Phila. Divinity Sch., 1912-16; A.M., U. of Pa., 1922, Ph.D., 1927; m. Marguerite J. Schaad, July 25, 1923; 1 son, John K. Ordained to ministry P.E. Ch., deacon, 1915, priest, 1916; chaplain, St. Paul's Sch., Anking, China, 1916-23, headmaster, 1923-27; rector Grace Ch., Phila., Pa., since 1928; asso. editor Journal of the Am. Oriental Soc. since 1929; del. to Am. Council of Learned Socs., 1934-38. Trustee Central China Coll., Wuchang, China. Mem. Am. Oriental Soc., Am. Anthrop. Assn., Am. Linguistic Soc., Royal Asiatic Soc. of Great Britain and Ireland, Phila. Oriental Club, Theta Xi, Founders and Patriots of America (chaplain Pa. soc.). Republican. Episcopalian. Clubs: Union League, Penn Athletic. Author: The Temples of Anking, 1931; The Origin and Development of the State Cult of Confucius, 1932; Desire and the Universe, 1935; The Study of Human Abilities, 1937. Home: 4509 Regent St., Philadelphia, Pa.

SHRYOCK, Joseph Grundy, structural steel; b. Haddonfield, N.J., Sept. 2, 1880; s. William Knight and Virginia Susan (Schaeffer) S.; grad. Eastburn Acad., Philadelphia, Pa., 1897; student Collège Jacques Amyotå Melun, Seine et Marne, France, 1896-97; C.E., Pa. Mil. Coll., Chester, 1900, M.C.E., 1921; m. Aimée Caroline Picolet d'Hermillon, Apr. 6, 1904; children—Joseph Richard, Raymond de Souville. Draftsman, Am. Bridge Co., 1900-03; designing engr. Va. Bridge & Iron Co., 1903-04; draftsman and checker, Belmont Iron Works, Philadelphia, 1904-06, designing engr. and salesman, 1906-22, chief engr. since 1922, also vice-pres. and dir., 1926—; inventor Belmont interlocking channel floor, 1933. Mem. Am. Soc. C.E., Am. Hist. Assn., Hist. Soc. Pa., Geneal. Soc. Pa., Nat. Geneal. Soc., Inst. Am. Genealogy, Pa. German Soc., N.E. Historic-Geneal. Soc., Md. Hist. Soc., Pa. Soc. New York, Geneal. Soc. N.J., Hist. Soc. York County, Netherlands Soc. Pa., Huguenot Soc. Pa., N.Y. Geneal. and Biog. Soc. Zoöl. Soc. Phila., Pa. Acad. Fine Arts, Welsh Soc. Phila., Colonial Soc. Pa., Colonial Sons and Daughters, Pa. Soc. S.R., Pa. Soc., Société des Ingenieurs Civils de France., S.A.R. Republican. Protestant. Clubs: Engineers, Art, Wynnefield, Philadelphia Country. Home: 2217 N. 52d St., Wynnefield, Philadelphia, Pa. Office: Belmont Iron Works, Philadelphia, Pa.*

SHRYOCK, Richard Harrison, prof. history; b. Phila., Pa., Mar. 29, 1893; s. George Augustus and Mary Harrison (Chipman) S.; B.S., Central High Sch., Phila., 1911; student Phila. Sch. of Pedagogy, 1911-13; B.S., in Edn., U. of Pa., 1917, Ph.D., 1924; m. Rheva Ott, Sept. 10, 1921; children—Barbara Ott, Richard Wallace. Teacher pub. schs., Phila., 1913-16; Harrison fellow, U. of Pa., 1919-20; instr. in history, Ohio State U., 1921-24, U. of Pa., 1924--25; asso. prof. history, Duke U., 1925-31, professor, 1931-38; prof. of Am. history, Univ. of Pa., since 1938; on leave as fellowship secretary Social Science Research Council, New York City, 1936. Served as private Field Ambulance Corps, U.S.A., 1917-18; student U.S.A. Med. Sch., 1918. Mem. Am. Hist. Assn., Am. Assn. Univ. Profs., History of Science Soc., Am. Acad. Polit. and Social Science, Société Française d'Histoire de la Medécine, Am. Assn. of History of Medicine, Delta Tau Delta. Author: Georgia and the Union in 1850, 1926; The Development of Modern Medicine, 1936. Editor: The Letters of Richard D. Arnold, M.D. 1929. Asso. editor of Miss. Valley Hist. Review, Jour. of Southern History. Contbr. on hist. subjects. Home: 317 Cherry Bend, Merion, Pa.

SHUFF, Benjamin Lee, banking; b. Smithsburg, Md., May 27, 1901; s. William H. H.

and Linnie Ellen (Barkman) S.; ed. high sch., Middletown, Md., 1917-20, C.P.A. accounting, Internat. Corr. Sch., 1920-24, Am. Inst. Banking, 1924-29; m. Elizabeth Carrie Herwig, July 31, 1933. Employed as stenographer and bookkeeper, Camp Meade, Md., 1918, Curtis Bay Copper & Iron Works, Curtis Bay, Md., 1919; asst. auditor, Poole Engring. & Machine Co., Baltimore, Md., 1920; clk. and bookkeeper, Q.M. Corps, Camp Meade, Md., 1921; clk. and stenographer, Farmers & Mechanics Nat. Bank, Frederick, Md., 1922-23, teller, 1923-30, asst. cashier, 1930-35, vice-pres. and trust officer since 1935; asst. sec., asst. treas. and dir. The G.F.S. Zimmerman Co., Inc. Served as treas. Frederick City Rep. Central Com.; treas. Frederick Co. Rep. Central Com.; mem. and past sec. G.O.P. Club of Frederick Co., Md. Sec.-treas. Group 2, Md. Bankers Assn. Republican. Lutheran. B.P.O.E. L.O.O.M. Maccabees. Home: 206 N. Market St. Office: Farmers & Mechanics Nat. Bank, Frederick, Md.

SHUFF, William Denny, banking, transportation; b. Salem, Va., Sept. 8, 1891; s. William Harman and Mary (Reed) S.; student Randolph Macon Acad., Bedford, Va., 1907-09, Randolph Macon Coll., Ashland, Va., 1909-11, Nat. Bus. Coll., Roanoke, Va., 1911-12; m. Myrtle Bowling, Dec. 3, 1919; 1 dau., Mary Elizabeth. Began as bookkeeper Honaker's Dept. Store, Bluefield, W.Va., 1912; sec. and treas. Tri City Traction Co., Princeton, W.Va., since 1916; vice-pres. and dir. Princeton Bank and Trust Co. since 1931; sec. and treas. Tri City Transit Co. since 1924; dir. Princeton Wholesale Grocery Co. since 1937. Served as pvt. inf., U.S.A., during World War. Mem. Phi Kappa Sigma. Republican. Baptist. Elk. Rotarian. Club: University (Bluefield). Home: 1707 Honaker Av., Office: 1448 Main St., Princeton, W.Va.

SHUGER, Leroy Woodrow, chemist; b. Baltimore, Md., Jan. 11, 1910; s. Morres and Sophie (Geiger) S.; B.S., Johns Hopkins U., 1930, Ph.D., 1934; unmarried. Chemist, Baltimore Paint & Color Works, mfrs. paints, varnishes and chem. specialties, Baltimore, Md., since 1935, mem. of firm since 1936. Mem. Am. Chem. Soc., Am. Soc. for Testing Materials, Federation of Paint & Varnish Production Clubs, Phi Alpha. Hebrew religion. Club: Woodhome Country. Awarded several patents on inventions and processes. Home: 1701 Ellamont St. Office: 150 S. Calverton Rd., Baltimore, Md.

SHUGERT, Stanley Pulliam, prof. of mathematics, Univ. of Pa. Address: University of Pa., Philadelphia, Pa.

SHULL, George Harrison, botanist; b. Clarke Co., O., Apr. 15, 1874; s. Harrison and Catherine (Ryman) Shull. B.S., Antioch Coll., 1901; Ph.D. (botany and zoölogy), University of Chicago, 1904; m. Ella Amanda Hollar, July 8, 1906; 1 dau., Elizabeth Ellen (dec.); m. 2d, Mary J. Nicholl, Aug. 26, 1909; children—John Coulter, Georgia Mary, Frederick Whitney, David Macaulay, Barbara Weaver, Harrison. Bot. asst. U.S. Nat. Mus., 1902; bot. expert U.S. Bur. Plant Industry, 1902-04; asst. plant physiology, U. of Chicago, 1903-04; botanical investigator, Sta. for Exptl. Evolution, Carnegie Instn. of Washington, Cold Springs Harbor, L.I., 1904-15; prof. botany and genetics, Princeton U., since 1915; visiting lecturer in genetics, Rutgers U., 1929-30, L. L. Kellogg memorial lecturer, 1931. Mem. Princeton Borough Bd. of Edn. since 1928, v.p. 1934-36, pres. since 1936; pres. Mercer Co. Assn. Bds. of Edn., 1934-37. Corr. mem. Deutsche Botanische Gesellschaft; hon. mem. Gesellschaft für Pflanzenzüchtung in Wien; hon. mem. John Torrey Club of Princeton; mem. Deutsche Gesellschaft für Vererbungswissenschaft, Société Linnéenne de Lyon, Institut Internat. d'Anthropologie (Paris), Am. Assn. Univ. Profs., Torrey Bot. Club, Botanical Soc. of America, American Soc. Naturalists (v.p. 1911, pres. 1917), Ecol. Soc. America, Am. Genetic Assn. (chmn. plant sect. 1912, advisory com. 1922—), Eugenics Research Assn., Eugenics Soc. America, Genetics Soc. America, Sigma Xi (1st pres. Princeton chapter, 1932-33), Am. Geog. Soc., Am. Soc.

Plant Physiology, Washington Acad. Sciences, Am. Philos. Soc.; fellow A.A.A.S. Lecturer and author of papers on variation, heredity and plant-breeding. Founder, and mng. editor of "Genetics" (mag.), 1916-25, asso. editor since 1925; first editor genetics sect. of Botanical Abstracts, 1918-22. Address: 60 Jefferson Rd., Princeton, N.J.

SHULL, George Stephen, pres. and treas. Safety First Supply Co.; b. Everett, Pa., Sept. 14, 1885; s. Samuel P. and Sadie R. (McGraw) S.; student pub. schs. and (nights) U. of Pittsburgh; m. Mary E. McKee, Sept. 6, 1911; children—Myra E., Mary Jane, Nora Lee. Asst. auditor Pa. Water Co., 1915-16; with Safety First Supply Co. since 1917, beginning as auditor, became sec. and dir., 1919, served as sec.-treas., 1921-25, pres. and treas. since 1925. Mem. Am. Soc. Safety Engrs., Pittsburgh Personnel Assn., Forest Hills Civic Club. Mason. Club: Metropolitan. Home: 5 Cherry Valley Road, Pittsburgh, 21, Pa. Office: 530 Fernando St., Pittsburgh, Pa.

SHULL, J(ames) Marion, artist-botanist; b. Clark Co., O., Jan. 23, 1872; s. Harrison and Catharine (Ryman) S.; ed. pub. schs., business coll., and through brief attendance at Valparaiso U. and Art Students' League, New York; m. Addie Virginia Moore, Dec. 20, 1906 (died April 2, 1937); children—Virginia Moore, Francis Marion. Student and instructor Antioch Coll. Yellow Springs, O., 1896-98; supervisor music and drawing, Boise, Ida., 1898-99; teacher pub. schools, Ohio, and commercial artist, Memphis, Tenn., 1899-1906; in U. S. Post Office Dept., 1906-07; dendrological artist U. S. Forest Service, Washington, D.C., 1907-09; bot. artist Bur. Plant Industry, 1909-25, asso. botanist same since 1925. Has made abt. 600 water color drawings and many in black and white for Dept. of Agr.; widely known as breeder of new varieties of iris. Mem. A.A.A.S., American Hort. Soc., Bot. Soc. Washington, Am. Iris Soc. (silver medal), Nat. Carillon Assn. Club: Arts. Author: Rainbow Fragments—A Garden Book of the Iris, 1931. Contbr. articles and illustrations to mags. Home: 207 Raymond St., Chevy Chase, Md.

SHULL, Samuel Eakin, judge; b. Stroudsburg, Pa., May 16, 1878; s. Joseph H. and Melissa V. (Flory) S.; grad. South Easton High Sch., 1895; student Lafayette Coll., 1895-96; grad. U. of N.C., 1900; unmarried. Admitted to Pa. bar, 1900, and began practice in Stroudsburg; pres. judge 43d Judicial Dist. of Pa. since Nov. 1917. Address: Court House, Stroudsburg, Pa.

SHULMAN, Abraham, physician; b. Mount Carmel, Pa., Dec. 19, 1896; s. Jacob and Gussie Ida (Kramer) S.; ed. N.Y. Univ., 1913-14; M.D., Univ. & Bellevue Hosp. Med. Coll., 1918; m. Minnie Alice Margolin, Feb. 15, 1920; children—Robert Barry, George Howard (dec.), Edward Mitchell. Interne, Barnert Memorial Hosp., Paterson, N.J., 1918-19; engaged in gen. practice of medicine and surgery, Paterson, N.J., 1919-28, specializing in obstetrics and gynecology since 1928; associate gynecologist, Barnert Memorial Hosp. Served as lt., j.g., U.S.N.R.F., 1918-22. Fellow Am. Coll. Surgeons; mem. Passaic Co. Med. Soc., Med. Soc. of N.J., A.M.A. Hebrew religion. Club: Preakness Hills Country (Wayne Twp., N.J.). Home: 528 E. 29th St., Paterson, N.J.

SHUMAN, Albert, lawyer; b. Bula, Monongalia Co., W.Va., Nov. 3, 1885; s. Philip and Rebecca Ann (Darrah) S.; ed. Monongalia Co. pub. schs., Fairmont (W.Va.) State Normal Sch. and W.Va. U. Law Sch.; m. Goldie Lemley, Dec. 28, 1910; children—Chester Albert, Robert Lemley, Betty Jane. Teacher pub. schs., 1903-09; admitted to Monongalia bar, 1910; practiced law at Morgantown since 1910; prosecuting atty., Monongalia Co., 1929-32. Mem. Monongalia Co., W.Va. State bar assns., Phi Kappa Sigma. Republican. Methodist. Mason (32°), K.P. Club: Kiwanis (past pres.). Home: 581 Spruce St. Office: 170 Chancery Row, Morgantown, W.Va.

SHUMAN, George Hull, ophthalmologist; b. Chambersburg, Pa., Sept. 16, 1883; s. William

Alfred and Susan Louise (Leberknight) S.; grad. Chambersburg (Pa.) High Sch., 1901, The Hotchkiss Sch. (Lakeville, Conn.), 1905; M.D., Grad. Sch. of Medicine, U. of Pa., 1910; m. Mary McLaughlin, Jan. 21, 1915; 1 dau., Mary Jane. Instr. ophthalmology, Medico-Chirurgical Coll., Philadelphia, 1912-14; ophthalmic surgeon Mesta Machine Co.; asso. ophthalmologist Western Pa. Hosp., Am. Steel & Wire Co., Bethlehem Steel Co. (Pittsburgh dist.). Dir. and sec. First Mutual Bldg. & Loan Assn., Pittsburgh. Sec. Ophthalmol. Soc. of U. of Pittsburgh, 1925-37, Pittsburgh Ophthalmol. Soc. since 1921; mem. Am. Acad. Ophthalmology and Oto-Laryngology, A.M.A., Pa. State Med. Soc., Allegheny Co. Med. Soc., Pittsburgh Acad. Medicine. Clubs: Duquesne, Pittsburgh Athletic Assn. Author: Newer Methods of Determining Employer's Liability in Eye Injuries; Biomicroscopy in Industrial Ophthalmology-Medico-Legal Aspects; Observations on Trends in Ophthalmological Practice; Controlled Versus Haphazard Methods of Applying Oblique Focal Illumination in Ophthalmology; The Paraffin-Film Method of Treating Burns of the Eyelids. Home: 1 Highland Court. Office: 351 Fifth Av., Pittsburgh, Pa.

SHUMAN, Warren Newton, physician; b. Mainville, Pa., Nov. 29, 1878; s. John W. and Hariette (John) S.; ed. Bloomsburg State Normal Sch., 1894-96; A.B., Dickinson Coll., 1902; student U. of Pa. Grad. Sch., 1903-05; M.D., U. of Pa. Med. Sch., 1909, hon. A.M., Dickinson Coll., 1906; m. Mary E. Nice, June 30, 1915. Taught Latin and Greek, high sch., Steelton, Pa., 1902-03; interne, St. Timothy Hosp., 1909-10, U. of Pa. Hosp., 1910-11; in practice medicine and surgery at Jersey Shore Pa., since 1911; pres. Jersey Shore Hosp. Co.; pres. Pine Creek Lime & Stone Co., Dirk Motor Co.; dir. Jersey Shore State Bank. Republican. Methodist. Mason. Clubs: Masonic (Jersey Shore); Acacia (Williamsport). Home: 300 Front St. Office: 219 S. Main St., Jersey Shore, Pa.

SHUMBERGER, John Calvin, president radio station WSAN; b. West Fairview, Pa., Mar. 11, 1873; s. Simon and Sarah (Eckert) S.; grad. Keystone Business Coll., Harrisburg, Pa., 1898; m. Euphemia Stein, Aug. 18, 1903 (died Oct. 8, 1920); children—John Calvin, Euphemia Stein (Mrs. Edwin Terry), Anne Read (Mrs. Alfred Ryan); m. 2d, Mary Lou Irwin, Jan. 26, 1922. Organized Lebanon (Pa.) Business Coll., 1892, prin. and prof. commercial branches until 1895; organized Carlisle (Pa.) Commercial Coll., 1895, Sch. of Commerce, Harrisburg, 1895, pres. and prof. commercial branches until 1900; pub. accountant, Harrisburg, 1900-16; controller Lehigh Portland Cement Co., Allentown, Pa., 1917-37; mem. cost com. Cement Assn. of U.S.A., 1917-37; now pres. radio sta. WSAN; v.p. and controller Allentown Call Pub. Co., Chronicle and News Pub. Co.; dir. Allentown Nat. Bank. Served in the N.G., 1897-1917, comdr. in chief 11 yrs.; corpl. in Porto Rico, Spanish-Am. War, 1898; Mexican border service, 1916. Trustee Lehigh County Memorial Endowment Fund of Pa. Masonic Grand Lodge; trustee Cedar Crest Coll.; pres. Family Welfare Orgn., pres. Boys' Haven, Inc., trustee Y.W.C.A., gen. chmn. Community Chest campaign, 1935 (all of Allentown); mem. exec. com. Pa. Synod of Presbyn. Ch. U.S.A.; pres. Controllers Inst. of America, 1935; mem. Nat. Assn. Cost Accountants, Nat. Municipal League, Nat. Tax Assn., N.Y. Acad. Polit. Science, Lehigh Co. Hist. Soc. (pres.), Family Welfare Assn. of America, United Spanish War Vets, Vets. of Foreign Wars, Pa. Commandery of Mil. Order of Foreign Wars of U.S.; Grand Officers Assn. of Grand Commandery of K.T. of Pa., Allentown Chamber of Commerce (dir.). Republican. Presbyn. (ruling elder). Mason (32°, K.T., Shriner), Elk. Clubs: Bankers of America (New York); Rotary Internat., Lehigh Valley Torch, Lehigh Valley Country; Maskonozha Rod and Gun. Home: 818 N. 27th St. Office: Call Publishing Co., Allentown, Pa.

SHUMWAY, Daniel Bussier, univ. prof.; b. Phila., Pa., May 5, 1868; s. Lowell and Anna Sarah (Bussier) S.; B.S., U. of Pa., 1889;

Ph.D., U. of Goettingen, 1894; m. Elizabeth Lotze, Aug. 22, 1895; children—Anna Elsa, Hildegarde Bussier; m. 2d, Mary Quimby, June 22, 1921. Instr. English, U. of Pa., 1889-92, instr. German, 1895-1900, asst. prof. German, 1900-09, prof. of Germanic philology, 1909-38, prof. emeritus of German since 1938. Mem. Modern Language Assn. of America, Linguistic Soc. of America. Republican. Clubs: Franklin Inn, Lenape, Philobiblon, Cosmopolitan (Phila.). Author: Das Ablautende Verbum in Hans Sachs, 1895; Helmholtz' Populäre Vorträge, 1909; Translation of the Nibelungenlied, 1909; (articles) The Verb in Thomas Murner, 1897; The Language of the Lutheran Bible of 1671, 1930; The American Students of the University of Goettingen, 1910. Address: New Gulph Rd., Bryn Mawr, Pa.

SHUMWAY, Edward A., physician; b. Phila., Pa., 1870; s. Lowell and Anna Sarah (Bussier) S.; M.D., U. of Pa. Med. Sch., 1894; m. Annie Price, Oct. 26, 1901; children—Edward A., Norman Price. Physician with Phila. Gen. Hosp., 1902-24, Univ. Hosp., Phila., 1902-23, Lankenan Hosp., Phila., 1907-36; pvt. practice of ophthalmology at Phila. since 1898. Mem. Bd. of Health, Lower Merion Twp. (Pa.), 1931-35. Mem. A.M.A., Am. Ophthal. Soc., Alpha Mu Pi Omega. Republican. Club: Medical (Phila.). Home: 341 N. Bowman Av., Merion, Pa. Office: 1737 Chestnut St., Phila., Pa.

SHURE, R(alph) Deane, composer; b. Chillisquaque, Pa., May 31, 1885; s. George Brenton and Mary Eva (Becht) S.; Mus.B., Oberlin Coll., 1907; student Royal Conservatory of Music, Dresden, Germany, 1911, 12; m. Hazel Elizabeth Towne, Apr. 3, 1909; children—Ralph George, Mary Bertha (dec.). Dir. of music Central U. of Ia., 1907-09, Clarendon (Tex.) Coll., 1909-19, State Teachers Coll., Indiana, Pa., 1919-21, Am. U., Washington, D.C., 1921-31; dir. of music, Mt. Vernon Place Meth. Ch., Washington, D.C., since 1921. Composer of over 100 pub. compositions for piano, organ, voice, chamber music, chorus, symphony orchestra; specializes in symphonic works; Premiers "Circles of Washington," Nat. Symphony Orchestra, 1934; "Berkie Symphony," Nat. Symphony Orchestra, 1935; "American Symphony," based on folk music, Rochester Symphony, 1936; "Choric Symphony," employing human voice as orchestral instrument, Harrisburg Symphony, 1938; "Damascus Vignettes," orchestral fantasy, Marine Symphony, 1939. Played "Through Palestine," organ suite, in City of Jerusalem, 1935. Democrat. Methodist. Clubs: Washington Composers, Friends of Music in Library of Congress. Home: 8 Pine Av., Takoma Park, Md.

SHURE, Ralph George, lawyer; b. Wisconisco, Pa., Aug. 8, 1910; s. R. Deane and Hazel E. (Towne) S.; grad. Central High Sch., Washington, D.C., 1928; A.B., U. of Md., 1932; special student Loyola U., Chicago, 1934-35; LL.B., Georgetown U., 1936; m. Helen L. Hilsenhoff, Aug. 1, 1936; 1 dau., Linda Mary. Began as merchant, College Park, Md., 1932; attorney Home Owners Loan Corpn., Washington, D.C. and Chicago, Ill., 1934-36; manager of claims division, Union Taxicab Assn., 1936; special claims examiner General Accounting Office, Washington, D.C., 1936-37; private law practice in Md. and D.C. since 1936; police judge Town of Takoma Park, Md., since May 1, 1939; apptd. by gov. trial magistrate for Montgomery County, Md., June 1, 1939. Mem. bars of Md. Court of Appeals, Dist. Court of U.S. for D.C., U.S. Court of Appeals. Mem. Young Men's Dem. Club of Takoma Park (v.p.; former sec.), Chamber of Commerce, Delta Sigma Phi (former president), Sigma Tau Lambda, Delta Sigma Phi Alumni Soc. of Washington, D.C. (v.p.). Democrat. Methodist. Home: 102 Hodges Lane. Office: Citizens Bank Bldg., Takoma Park, Md.

SHURTLEFF, Flavel, city planning executive; b. Boston, Mass., Nov. 27, 1879; s. Flavel and Harriett (Bent) S.; A.B., Harvard, 1901, LL.B., 1906; m. Isabel Martha Brown, June 28, 1910; children—Flavel, Ruth Brown, Martha Isabel. Practiced law in Boston, 1906-21; an organizer, 1910, and sec. Nat. Conf. on City Planning, 1910-35; sec. Am. City Planning Inst., 1918-34; counsel Am. Planning and Civic Assn. since 1935; lecturer on city planning and zoning. Republican. Conglist. Mem. Am. City Planning Inst., Boston Bar Assn., Delta Upsilon. Author: Carrying Out the City Plan, 1914; also various articles on same subject. Home: Montclair, N.J. Office: 130 E. 22d St., New York, N.Y.

SHUSTER, Benjamin Harrison, physician; b. Russia, Sept. 17, 1892; s. Abraham and Hannah (Shore) S.; came to U.S., 1902, naturalized, 1913; M.D., Medico-Chirurg. Coll., 1915; m. Rose Stein, Aug. 25, 1918; children— Anita, Allen. Mem. out-patient dept., Pa. Hosp., 1917-20; asst. otologist, Medico-Chirurg. Hosp., 1920-25, Grad. Hosp. since 1925; asso. otolaryngologist, Mt. Sinai Hosp. since 1929; laryngologist, Dept. Tuberculosis, Phila. Gen. Hosp. since 1925; asso. prof. neuro-otology, U. of Pa. Grad. Sch. of Medicine since 1932; asso. in otolaryngology, U. of Pa. Med. Sch. since 1935; otolaryngologist, St. Lukes and Childrens Hosp. since 1939. Served as lt. Med. Corps, U.S.N.R.F. during World War. Mem. Am. Acad. Ophthalmology and Ootolaryngology, Am. Med. Assn., Am. Laryngol., Rhinol. and Otol. Soc., Phila. Coll. Phys., Phila. Laryngol. Soc. (v.p.), Med. League (past pres.), Phila. Co. Med. Soc. Jewish religion. Mason. K.P. Contbr. articles to med. jours. Home: 1824 Pine St., Philadelphia, Pa.

SHUTACK, George A., lawyer; b. Nesquehoming, Pa., Aug. 21, 1900; s. John and Anna S.; grad. Mauch Chunk Twp. (Pa.) High Sch., 1918; student U. of Pa., 1918; LL.B., Georgetown U. Law Sch., Washington, D.C., 1920-23; m. Helen E. Setar, Feb. 9, 1932; 1 dau., Marianne. Admitted to Supreme Ct. of D.C., Ct. of Appeals of D.C., 1923, Gen. Accounting Office, Washington, D.C., 1925, U.S. Supreme Ct., 1926, Pa. Superior Ct., Pa. Supreme Co., Allegheny Co. bar, Carbon Co. bar, 1928; asso. with firm, William C. Sullivan, Washington, D. C., 1923-27, with firm, Weil, Christy & Weil, Pittsburgh, Pa., 1927-29; in practice under own name at Nesquehoning and Lehighton, Carbon Co., Pa., since 1929. Served as pvt., U.S. Army, during World War. Dir. Panther Valley Relief Assn., 1931-33. Mem. Pa. Bar Assn., Carbon Co. Bar Assn., Am. Legion, Rotary Internat. Moose, Eagle. Home: 401 E. Catawissa St., Nesquehoning, Pa. Office: 178 S. 1st St., Lehighton, Pa.

SIBBALD, Reginald Spalding, prof. Romance langs.; b. Canon City, Colo., June 22, 1897; s. Eliazor William and Edith (Hungerford) S.; LL.B., U. of Colo., 1921, A.B., 1922, A.M., 1926; Ph.D., U. of Pa., 1934; m. Minerva Douglas Hungerford. Instr. Romance langs., U. of Colo., 1922-27, U. of W.Va., 1927-28; instr. French, N.Y. Univ., 1928-29; instr. modern langs., Drexel Inst., 1929-30; prof. Romance langs., Ursinus Coll., Collegeville, Pa., since 1931. Served in First Canadian Tank Corps, 1917-19. Mem. Alpha Tau Omega, Phi Alpha Delta. Republican. Episcopalian. Author: Marionettes in the North of France, 1936. Home: 542 Main St., Collegeville, Pa.

SICKLES, Frederick J., supt. of schools at New Brunswick. Address: Board of Education, New Brunswick, N.J.

SICKMAN, Albert Stilley, M.D.; b. Gill Hall, Pa., Jan. 5, 1889; s. William G. and Hannah A. (Stilley) S.; student Duff's Coll., Pittsburgh, 1903-05, Pittsburgh Acad., 1905-08; M.D., U. of Pittsburgh, 1912; m. Laura Ruth Miksch, Oct. 9, 1914. Physician and surgeon, Lock No. 4, Pa., since 1913; chief surgical staff Charleroi-Monessen Hosp.; dir. Nat. Bank of Charleroi and Trust Co., Thrift Plan Corpn. Served as 1st lt. Med. Corps, U.S. Army, 1918-19. Burgess North Charleroi Borough, Pa., 14 yrs. Mem. A.M.A., Pa. Med. Assn., Washington Co. Med. Assn., Pa. R.R. Assn. of Surgeons, N.Y. and New England Assn. R.R. Surgeons, Charleroi Turn Verein, Nu Sigma Nu. Republican. Lutheran. Mason (32°), Elk, Eagle, Moose, Knight of Malta, Odd Fellow. Club: Nemacolin Country (Beallsville, Pa.). Home: 502 Liberty Av. Office: 502 Lincoln Av., Lock No. 4, Pa.

SIEBERT, Christian Ludewig, sanitary engr.; b. Pittsburgh, Pa., Aug. 13, 1888; s. Elmer Ellsworth and Emma Wilhelmina (Ludewig) S.; student Mercersburg (Pa.) Acad., 1907; B.S., Lafayette Coll., Easton, Pa., 1911; student Lehigh U., Bethlehem, Pa., 1911-12; m. Nell Evelyn Jenkins, Apr. 14, 1915; children—Christian Ludewig, Natalie Astan, Marjorie Edith. Instr. sanitary science, Lehigh U., Bethlehem, Pa., 1911-12; asst. engr. Pa. Dept. of Health, Harrisburg, Pa., 1912-17, dist. engr., 1919-28, exec. engr. and principal river survey engr., 1928-38, chief river survey engr since 1938; registered professional engr. in Pa. Served as capt., Sanitary Corps, U.S., Army, 1917-19; camp sanitary engr., Camp Dix, N.J., 1917-19. Pres. Camp Hill Borough Council. Mem. Am. Soc. C.E., Am. Legion (past commdr. Post 43), Sigma Chi. Republican. Mason (Scottish Rite). Club: West Shore Country (Camp Hill, Pa.; pres., 1932-33). Home: 222 Willow Av., Camp Hill, Pa. Office: Pa. Dept. of Health, Harrisburg, Pa.

SIEDLE, Theodore A(nthony), coll. dean; b. Erie, Pa., Nov. 19, 1902; s. Edward and Mary (Deitsch) S.; B.S., Allegheny Coll., 1924; student Pa. State Coll., summer, 1926; A.M., U. of Pittsburgh, 1930, Ph.D., 1938; m. Anne Naomi Birchard, July 2, 1927; children—Theodore Edward, Mary Anne. Newspaper reporter, Erie, Pa., 1924-26; teacher pub. schs., Erie, Pa. 1926-29; grad. asst., U. of Pittsburgh, 1929; asst. dir. Downtown (Evening) Div., and instr. edn., Sch. of Edn., U. of Pittsburgh, 1929-31; dir. teachers appointment, asst. dean, and asst. prof. edn., Sch. of Edn., U. of Pittsburgh, 1931-38; dean of instruction, State Teachers Coll., California, Pa., since 1938. Mem. N.E.A., Pa. State Edn. Assn., Am. Coll. Pub. Assn., Alpha Chi Rho, Phi Delta Kappa, Pi Delta Epsilon, Omicron Delta Kappa, Scabbard and Blade. Club: Faculty of U. of Pittsburgh. Author: Fed. ednl. bul. Contbr. to ednl. mags. Home: 456 Second St., California, Pa.

SIEGEL, Harry Louis, lawyer; b. Russia, Nov. 27, 1899; s. Max and Martha (Yaffe) S.; came to U.S., 1904, naturalized, 1919; student Lancaster, (Pa.) pub. schs. and high schs., 1905-17, Carnegie Inst. Tech., 1918-19; LL.B., Dickinson Law Sch., Carlisle, Pa., 1923; m. Miriam Wenger Loss, June 29, 1924; 1 son, Stanley Herman. Admitted to Supreme Court of Pa. bar, 1923, and since practiced in Lewistown, Mifflin Co., Pa.; mem. firm Harry L. & Robert Siegel, Lewistown, Pa., since 1937, now senior mem.; dir. and mem. exec. com. Mifflin Co. Bldg. & Loan Assn.; dir. Juniata Valley Gas & Oil Co. Served as corporal, U.S. Army, during World War. Solicitor, sheriff Mifflin Co. since 1938; solicitor Borough of Lewistown since 1932; also solicitor Boroughs of Burnham and McVeytown, sch. dists. of Burnham, McVeytown, Oliver Twp., Wayne Twp., Bratton Twp., Decatur Twp. Trustee and solicitor Lewistown Hosp., community Fund Corpn., Mifflin Co. Children's Aid Soc., Lewistown Chamber of Commerce. Mem. Am. Legion, 40 & 8, Phi Epsilon Pi. Republican. Jewish religion. Elk, B'nai B'rith, Odd Fellow, Eagle. Clubs: Kiwanis (Lewistown, Pa.; pres., 1926-27); Birch Hill Country (Burnham, Pa.). Home: 23 N. Grand St. Office: Dughi Bldg., Lewistown, Pa.

SIEGEL, Isadore Abraham, physician and surgeon; b. Baltimore, Md., Feb. 6, 1898; s. Joseph and Ida (Hazenoff) S.; A.B., Johns Hopkins U., 1919; M.D., Johns Hopkins Med. Sch., 1923; m. Sylvia Ruth Gann, Sept. 22, 1929; 1 son, Howard Paige. Interne Howard Hosp., Phila., 1923-24, Hopkins Hosp., 1924, New York Lying-In Hosp., 1924-25; engaged in practice specializing in obstetrics and gynecology, Baltimore, Md., since 1925; asso. in obstetrics, U. of Md. Med. Sch., 1927-39, asst. prof. since 1939; asso. in obstetrics, Sinai Hosp., Baltimore, Md., 1929-39; dir. obstet. dept., Franklin Square Hosp. since 1937; health officer maternal hygiene, Baltimore City Health Dept. since 1935. Served in S.A.T.C., 1918. Diplomate Am. Bd. Obstetrics and Gynecology. Mem. A.M.A., Med.-Chirurg. Faculty of Md., Baltimore City Med. Soc., Baltimore Obstet. and

Gynecol. Soc., Johns Hopkins Med. and Surg. Soc., Johns Hopkins Endocrinol. Club, The J. M.H. Rowland Obstet. Soc., Sinai Hosp. Alumni Assn., Phi Delta Epsilon, Am. Legion, Zionist Orgn. of America. Democrat. Jewish religion. Club: Walbrook Tennis (Baltimore). Home: 2309 Eutaw Pl., Baltimore, Md.

SIEGMUND, Humphreys Oliver, elec. engr.; b. St. Louis, Mo., Aug. 24, 1895; s. Henry Otto and Lissette (Koch) S.; student Garfield Sch., St. Louis, Mo., 1900-09, McKinley High Sch., St. Louis, Mo., 1909-13; B.S. in E.E., U. of Ill., Urbana, Ill., 1917, E.E., 1926; m. Leola Beth Meachum, October 5, 1917; 1 dau., Alice Elizabeth. Engr. Central Ill. Pub. Service Co., Mattoon, Ill., 1916-17; mem. academic bd., U.S. Army Sch. of Mil. Aeronautics, Urbana, Ill., 1917-18; asst. prof. of elec. engring., Drexel Inst., Phila., 1918-19; engr. Western Electric Co., New York, 1919-25; mem. tech. staff Bell Telephone Labs., New York, 1925-34, dial apparatus engr. since 1934. Served as instructor, Aviation Sect. Signal Corps, U.S. Army, 1917-18; capt. Ill. N.G., 1917-18. Mem. Am. Inst. E.E., Am. Phys. Soc., Sigma Xi, Sigma Nu, Tau Beta Pi, Phi Kappa Phi, Eta Kappa Nu, Sigma Tau, Scabbard and Blade. Mason. Inventor of improvements in telephone apparatus and circuits to furnish better operation of switching equipment and to provide quiet channels for electrical communication; in charge of the design of apparatus used in dial telephone switching systems; author of numerous tech. articles. Home: 18 Harvard Terrace, West Orange, N.J. Office: 463 West St., N.Y., N.Y.

SIELKE, Albert Victor, consulting engr.; b. Mt. Vernon, N.Y., July 9, 1894; s. Leo and Johanna (Bergman) S.; student Columbia, 1913; m. Annette M. Krygsman, Oct. 18, 1915; children—Adele Janet, Alan Leonard. Archtl. draftsman, later structural engr., with W. H. McElfatrick, 1910-12; engr. U.S. Realty and Improvement Co., New York, 1912-14; engr. Degnon Contracting Co., Inc., 1914-17; reinforced concrete engr. Turner Constrn. Co., New York, 1917-18, H. D. Best Co., New York, 1918-19; v.p. and engr. Aljon Constrn. Co., Inc., New York, 1919-20; chief draftsman and designing engr., Nugent Constrn. Corpn., New York, 1920-21; private practice as cons. engr. since 1921; expert engr. to comptroller, City of New York, 1921-26; cons. engr. Dept. of Parks, New York, 1927-33. Apptd. mem. Mayor's Com. of Architects and Engrs., 1928; mem. spl. engrs. com. on West Side Improvement, 1929. Mem. Am. Inst. Cons. Engrs., Am. Soc. Civil Engrs., Nat. Soc. Professional Engrs., N.J. Soc. Professional Engrs., The Moles (founder). Clubs: Circus, Saints, Sinners Club of America (dir.). Home: 89 Hurlbut St., Westwood, N.J. Office: 475 Fifth Av., New York, N.Y.

SIGERIST, Henry Ernest, university prof.; b. Paris, France, Apr. 7, 1891; s. Ernest Henry and Emma (Wiskemann) S.; student Gymnasium, Zurich, Switzerland, 1904-10, University Coll., London, 1911, U. of Munich, Germany, 1914; M.D., U. of Zurich, 1917; m. Emmy M. Escher, Sept. 14, 1916; children—Erica Elizabeth, Nora Beate. Came to U.S., 1931. Lecturer history of medicine, U. of Zurich, 1921 to 1923, prof., 1924; prof. history of medicine, U. of Leipzig, Germany, 1925-32; prof. and dir. of Inst. of the History of Medicine, Johns Hopkins U., since 1932; Dwight H. Terry lecturer, Yale, 1938. Fellow Coll. Physicians of Madrid; corr. fellow Mediaeval Acad. of America; mem. Internat. Acad. History of Science (Paris), Kaiserl. Deutsche Akademie der Naturforscher, Am. Assn. of the History of Medicine (pres. 1937), corr. mem. Royal Society Medicine of Budapest; hon. mem. Swiss, Rumanian, Greek socs. of med. history; mem. History of Science Soc. (pres. 1939), Am. Council of Learned Socs. (advisory bd.), Alpha Kappa Kappa, Delta Omega; hon. mem. Yugoslavian Soc. of Med. History, Sect. on Med. History of Acad. of Medicine, Richmond, Va. Awarded Karl Sudhoff medal, 1933. Clubs: University, Tudor and Stuart. Author: Studien und Texte zur fruhmittelerlichen Rezeptliteratur, 1923; Ambroise Paré, Die Behandlung der Schusswunden, 1923; The Book of Cirurgia of Hieronymus Brunschwig, 1923; Albrecht von Hallers Briefe an Johannes Gesner, 1923; Antike Heilkunde, 1927; Pseudo-Apulei Herbarius (with Ernst Howald), 1927; Man and Medicine (transl. into 6 langs.), 1932; The Great Doctors (German edit. 1932), 1933; American Medicine, 1934, German edit., 1933; Socialized Medicine in the Soviet Union, 1937. Editor of many volumes, reports and bulls. of foreign univs.; editor Bull. of the Inst. of the History of Medicine since 1933; editor publs. of the Inst. of History of Medicine since 1934. Home: 3946 Cloverhill Rd. Office: 1900 E. Monument St., Baltimore, Md.

SIGLIN, H. O., editor News-Dispatch. Address: Shamokin, Pa.

SIGMAN, James Garfield, dir. visual edn.; b. Elverson, Pa., June 13, 1881; s. Christian Kurtz and Hanna Maria (Milns) S.; Pd.B., West Chester Normal Sch., 1900; Ph.B., Lafayette Coll., 1905, A.M., 1921; Ed.D., Temple U., 1933; m. Elsie Margaret Baker, June 5, 1909; children—Clara Lucretia (Mrs. William Eugene Kirsch), James George. Vice prin. high sch., later supervising prin. pub. schs., Berwick, Pa., 1906-13; teacher history, Northeast High Sch., Phila., later head history dept., Frankford High Sch., Phila.; prin. Gillespie Jr. High Sch., Phila., 1927-29; dir. Div. of Visual Edn., Pub. Schs. of Phila. since 1929. Mem. Nat. and Pa. State edn. assns., Phila. Teachers Assn., Phi Delta Kappa, Delta Tau Delta, Phila. Alumni Club of Lafayette Coll. (pres.), Delta Tau Delta Alumni Club (Phila. Chapter). Republican. Methodist. Author: Origin and Development of Visual Education in the Philadelphia Public Schools, 1933. Co-author (with Albert K. Heckel): On the Road to Civilization, 1936. Home: 5044 Erringer Pl., Philadelphia, Pa.

SIGMUND, Benjamin J., civil engr.; b. Kalisz, Poland, Feb. 22, 1886; s. Selig and Leonore (Mirantz) S.; came to U.S., 1891, naturalized, 1907; student New York Pub. Schs., 1893-99, Coll. of the City of New York, 1899-1902; C.E., Columbia U., 1906; m. Leah Astrakhan, July 4, 1909; children—Arthur Godfrey, Robert Asher, Adele Frances. Began as draftsman, Unit Concrete Steel Frame Co., Phila., 1906; chief engr., Shear Frame Co., New York, 1907-09; chief estimator, Trussed Concrete Steel Co., Detroit, Mich., 1909-11; sales mgr. Phila. office, Truscon Steel Co., 1911-33; owner Phila. Interchange Bureau, estimating bureau for steel bldg. products, Phila., since 1933; dir. Edwin H. Vare Bldg. & Loan Assn., Lodge Bldg. & Loan Assn. Mem. Am. Soc. C.E. Jewish religion. Mason, Elk. Club: Ashbourne Country (Cheltenham, Pa.). Address: 3847 N. 17th St., Philadelphia, Pa.

SILBERMAN, David, asso. gynecologist Sinai Hosp.; mem. visiting staff Mercy, South Baltimore Gen. and West Baltimore Gen. hosps. Address: 2448 Eutaw Place, Baltimore, Md.

SILIN, Isaac Jacob, lawyer; b. Sinnemahoning, Cameron Co., Pa., June 8, 1902; s. Nathan and Sarah (Sirkin) S.; grad. Erie Central High Sch., 1914-18; A.B., U. of Pa., 1922; LL.B., Harvard Law Sch., 1925; studied U. of Paris Law Sch., Acad. of Internat. Law (The Hague) and Inner Temple (London); unmarried. Admitted to Pa. bar, 1925, New York bar, 1926; partner law firm Brooks, Curtze & Silin since 1930; v.p. and dir. Nat. Erie Corpn. Formerly atty. U.S. Agency, Gen. and Special Claims Commn., U.S. and Mexico. Awarded Pugsley Scholarship in Internat. Law, Harvard Law Sch. Dir. West Tenth St. Temple (Jewish). Mem. Am., Federal, Pa. and Erie Co. bar assns., Kappa Nu; asso. mem. Assn. Bar City of N.Y. Republican. Mason. Clubs: University (Erie); Harvard of Western Pa. (Pittsburgh). Writer of articles and book reviews in legal periodicals. Home: 952 W. 8th St. Office: 1013 Erie Trust Bldg., Erie, Pa.

SILK, Charles Isadore, physician; b. Hungary, Apr. 20, 1874; s. Samuel and Katharine (Traunstein) S.; came to U.S., 1888, naturalized, 1896; student N.Y. Univ. and Bellevue Hosp., 1897-99; M.D., Cornell U. Med. Sch., 1900; m. Cecilia Ratner, Sept. 23, 1912. Interne Austro-Hungary Hosp., New York, 4 months, 1901-1902; engaged in gen. practice of medicine at Perth Amboy, N.J., 1902-17, specializing in diseases of the chest since 1917; chmn. bd. health, Perth Amboy, N.J., 1919-24, commr., 1918-24. Served as med. examiner and consultant, dft. bd., 1917. Dir. and past pres., N.J. Tuberculosis League, Middlesex Co. Tuberculosis League, Perth Amboy Y.M.H.A. and Y.W.H.A. Past pres. Perth Amboy Chapter Red Cross. Fellow Am. Coll. Chest Physicians. Mem. Am. Med. Assn., N.J. State and Middlesex Co. med. assns., Acad. of Medicine of Northern N.J., Am. Acad. Tuberculosis Physicians. Democrat. Jewish religion. Mason. Elk. Home: 278 High St., Perth Amboy, N.J.

SILK, Joseph Meryl, real estate; b. Crafton, Pa., Feb. 16, 1895; s. Thomas J. and Adelia F. (Kasberger) S.; studied O. Wesleyan U., Mt. Union Coll. and Western Theol. Sem.; m. Vera Hilda Lorence, July 18, 1915 (died 1916); m. 2d, Mary Ellen Eakin, Sept. 12, 1919; children—Joseph Meryl, Naomi Ruth, John Wesley, Eleanor Mae, Barbara Louise, Mary Ellen. Began as office boy Am. Sheet & Tin Plate Co.; served as minister M.E. Ch. six yrs.; operated gasoline station, 3 yrs.; mem. firm Perry Real Estate Co. since 1924. Pres. Pittsburgh Real Estate Bd., 1939; v.p., later sec., Pa. Real Estate Assn. Republican. Methodist. Mason. Home: Ingomar, Pa. Office: 3884 Perrysville Av., Pittsburgh, Pa.

SILL, John Brooks, physician; b. Phila., Pa., June 27, 1892; s. Albert T. and Mary C. (Bierns) S.; B.S. in economics, Central High Sch. of Phila.; M.D., U. of Pa., 1919; m. Margaret Adele Pierson, Apr. 30, 1921; 1 son, John Brooks. In practice at Trenton, N.J.; chief on obstetrical staff Mercer Hosp. Mem. A.M.A., N.J. Med. Soc., Mercer County Med. Soc. Republican. Presbyterian. Club: Trenton Yacht. Address: 942 W. State St., Trenton, N.J.

SILLIMAN, Harry Inness, editor, pub.; b. Mahanoy Plane, Pa., Dec. 15, 1876; s. John H. and Hannah (Rhoads) S.; ed. pub. schs.; m. Argenta Fay Jones, May 10, 1913; 1 dau., Edna Kathryn. Owned Tamaqua Herald at 19; with Tamaqua Courier since 1899, now asso. editor; owner and editor Pottsville Journal; pres. Miners' Journal Newspaper Co. Corpl. Co. B, 8th Pa. Vol. Inf., Spanish-Am. War. Member Planning Commn., Pottsville. Mem. bd. dirs. Pottsville Hosp., Y.W.C.A. Republican. Presbyn. Clubs: Pottsville, Schuylkill Country. Home: 1101 Mahantonga St. Office: 213 S. Center St., Pottsville, Pa.*

SILLIMAN, Reuben Daniel, lawyer; b. Hudson, Wis., May 17, 1871; s. Dwight and Marietta (Parks) S.; grad. Central High Sch., St. Paul, 1891; LL.B., U. of Mich., 1894; m. Belle Evelyn Eddy, Aug. 3, 1898; 1 son, Sherwood Eddy. Practiced law, Duluth, 1894-98, Honolulu, 1898-99 and 1901-03, San Francisco, 1903-05, since at New York. Judge Circuit Court, 1st Circuit, H.I., Mar.-June 1900, and by apptmt. of President McKinley, June 5, 1900-01, resigning to resume law practice; formerly mem. firm Choate, Larocque & Mitchell, New York City. Has been counsel in a number of important cases tried in Honolulu, San Francisco, Boston and Washington. Republican. Home: 316 Park Av., E. Orange, N.J.; (summer) "Ravinehurst," Sheffield, Mass. Office: 57 William St., New York, N.Y.

SILSLEY, John Calvin, lawyer; b. South Huntingdon Twp., Pa., July 28, 1867; s. Adam and Jennie (Mitchell) S.; B.E., Edinboro (Pa.) Normal Sch., 1889; A.B., Waynesburg (Pa.) Coll., 1893; m. Mary Cunningham, Oct. 31, 1899; children—Eliza Jane, Anna Clyde. Admitted to Westmoreland Co. (Pa.) Bar, 1896, to practice before Pa. Supreme Court, 1900, Pa. Superior Court, 1910, U.S. District Court of Pa., 1908; in practice of law at Greensburg, Pa., since 1896; atty. for Federal Land Bank of Baltimore (Md.) since 1920; represented Commonwealth of Pa. as local attorney, Westmoreland Co., Pa., 1926-30; dir. Barclay-Westmoreland Trust Co., Greensburg, Pa. Trustee, Waynesburg (Pa.) Coll. Mem. Pa. State Sabbath Sch. Assn. (v.p. and dir.), Westmoreland

Co. Sabbath Sch. Assn. (pres., 1912-33). Republican. Presbyterian. Mason (32°; Royal Arch; Shriner; Scottish Rite; Tall Cedars of Lebanon, 77). Clubs: Greensburg (Pa.) Country, Greensburg (Pa.) Shakespeare. Home: 131 Seminary Av. Office: Huff Bldg., Greensburg, Pa.

SILVER, Arthur Elmer, cons. elec. engr.; b. Dexter, Me., Aug. 14, 1879; s. Charles Bradbury and Rebecca Evelyn (Dearth) S.; B.S. in E.E., U. of Me., 1902; m. Anna Jessie Teall, Aug. 31, 1914; children—Anna Boughton (dec.), Charles Warren and Mary (twins), Elisabeth. Engaged in expert elec. course of General Electric Co., Schenectady, N.Y., 1902-04; in charge meter dept., Raleigh Electric Co., elec. engr. and chief engr., Carolina Power & Light Co., both Raleigh, N.C., 1904-10; asso. with Electric Bond & Share Co. and subsidiary, N.Y. City continuously since 1910, elec. engr. design and constrn., 1910-14, asst. chief engr., 1914-20, cons. elec. engr., 1920-32, cons. elec. engr., Ebasco Services, Inc. (subsidiary inc. 1932 to take over all service activities for clients) since 1932. In N.J. State Militia Res., 1918. Fellow A.A.A.S., Am. Inst. Elec. Engrs. Mem. Edison Electric Inst., Montclair Soc. Engrs., Phi Kappa Sigma, Phi Kappa Phi., Me. Soc. of N.Y., Green Mt. Club, Vt. and N.Y. City. Joint recipient A.I.E.E. award for Nat. Best Paper in field Engring. for 1931-32. Republican. Clubs: Athletic (Montclair); Downtown Athletic (New York); Cosmopolitan (Montclair). Home: 360 N. Fullerton Av., Upper Montclair, N.J. Office: 2 Rector St., New York, N.Y.

SILVERBLATT, Jacob, merchant; b. Manchester, Eng., July 4, 1877; s. Aaron and Bertha (Levy) S.; student pub. sch., London, and pvt. tutors; m. Etta Menkle, June 27, 1906; children—Gladys T., Arthur, Florence, Ruth B. Came to U.S., 1897, naturalized citizen, 1902. Accountant, Manchester, England, 1895-97; traveling auditor Morris & Co., Chicago, 1898-1909; in wholesale meat and provisions business as Lehigh Beef Co., Wilkes-Barre and Pittston, Pa., since 1909; pres. Lehigh Beef Co., Pittston, Pa.; v.p. Lehigh Beef Co., Wilkes-Barre, Pa.; pres. Hebrew Loan Soc., Wilkes-Barre. Pres. Temple B'nai B'rith, Wilkes-Barre; treas. Wyoming Valley Jewish Com., Wilkes-Barre; dir. Hebrew Inst., Joint Distribution Com., New York; regional dir. Joint Distribution Com., Wilkes-Barre. Republican. Mason, B'nai B'rith. Club: Craftsman (Wilkes-Barre, Pa.). Home: 86 Academy St., Wilkes-Barre, Pa. Office: Pittston, Pa.

SILVERMAN, Alexander, chemist; b. Pittsburgh, Pa., May 2, 1881; s. Philip and Hannah (Schamberg) S.; Ph.B., Western U. of Pa. (now U. of Pittsburgh), 1902, M.S., 1907, hon. Sc.D., 1930; A.B., Cornell U., 1905; hon. Sc.D., Alfred U., 1936; m. Elrose Reizenstein, Dec. 16, 1908. Chemist, Macbeth-Evans Glass Co., Pittsburgh, 1902-04; instr. chemistry, 1905-09, asst. prof., 1909-12, prof. inorganic chemistry, 1912—, head dept. of chemistry, 1918—, U. of Pittsburgh. U.S. del. to Internat. Union of Chemistry, Liege, Belgium, 1930; Madrid, Spain, 1934; Lucerne, Switzerland, 1936, Rome, Italy, 1938. Mem. Div. Chem. and Chem. Tech., Nat. Research Council, 1938—. Fellow Am. Ceramic Soc., A.A.A.S., Chemists, Am. Inst. Ceramic Engrs., Soc. of Glass Tech. (London); mem. Soc. for Protection of Science and Learning (Eng.), Am. Inst. of Chem. Engrs., Am. Chem. Soc., Am. Assn. Univ. Profs., Pa. Acad. Sciences, Electrochem. Soc., Assn. for Scientific and Tech. Ceramics (France), Pa. Chem. Soc., Sigma Xi, Phi Lambda Upsilon, Pi Lambda Phi, Omicron Delta Kappa. Jewish religion. Clubs: Chemists' (N.Y.); Authors, Polygon (Pittsburgh). Author: Laboratory Directions in Inorganic Chemistry; Study Questions and Problems in Inorganic Chemistry. Contbr. to tech. publs.; tech. and popular lecturer on scientific subjects. Consultant on glass; researches have resulted in manufacture of important commercial glasses; inventor of numerous devices for microscopic illumination. Home: 1514 Denniston Av., Pittsburgh, Pa.

SILVERMAN, Isaac H., corpn. official; b. Pittsburgh, Pa., Apr. 14, 1862; s. Henry and Babette (Frank) S.; student pub. and high schs., Pittsburgh; m. Ida Hirsch, Jan. 12, 1893 (died 1923); children—Meyer H., Edwin H., Beatrice (Mrs. Stanley H. Hinlein), Robert H. Began as accountant, 1879; contractor electric light and ry. business, Western Pa., Eastern Ohio and W.Va., 1886-90; mgr. Edison United Mfg. Co., later Edison Gen. Electric Co. and Gen. Electric Co., 1890-93; built first high speed electric lines from Detroit and Mt. Clemens, Mich., and Dayton, O., to Cincinnati, 1893; building and operating electric light plants and electric railways since 1893; now mem. Stern & Silverman, elec. engrs. and contractors, Phila.; chmn. bd. Atlantic City & Shore Co.; pres. Atlantic City & Ocean City R.R. Co.; v.p. and treas. Chester & Phila. Ry.; dir. West Jersey & Sea Shore R.R., Pa. & Atlantic R.R. Sec. Selective Service Bd., 1915-18. Dir. and treas. Nat. Farm Sch. Mem. Edison Pioneers. Republican. Jewish religion. Mason (32°). Clubs: Bankers and Manufacturers, Locust (Phila.); Pennsylvania Railroad Golf; Philmont Golf. Home: 135 S. 17th St. Office: Land Title Bldg., Philadelphia, Pa.

SILVERMAN, Meyer H., elec. supplies; b. Phila., Pa., Oct. 30, 1893; s. Isaac H. and Ida (Hirsch) S.; grad. William Penn Charter Sch., 1911; B.S. in E.E., U. of Pa., 1915; m. Mary Jane Schloss, Apr. 15, 1925; children—Mary Ann, Dean Ida, Marc Henry. Elec. engr. with Pa. R.R. Co. on electrification of suburban lines, Phila., 1915-17; elec. engr. with Sam Eiserman & Co., New York, 1920-23; with Osterhout Electric Co., illuminating engring. and fixtures, Phila., since 1923; dir. Atlantic City & Shore R.R. Co., Atlantic City & Ocean City R.R. Co. Dir. Foster Home for Hebrew Orphans, Young Men's and Young Women's Hebrew Assn. Clubs: Philmont Country; Locust (Phila.). Home: Frog Hollow Rd., Rydal, Pa. Office: 401 N. Broad St., Philadelphia, Pa.

SILVERMAN, O. Jay, certified pub. accountant; b. Phila., Pa., July 10, 1906; s. A.B. and Ida (Buchman) S.; ed. high sch. Atlantic City, N.J., 1922-26; m. Anna Milner, June 23, 1929; 1 son, Ronald P. Has followed profession as certified public accountant since 1928 practicing under name of O. Jay Silverman & Co. with offices in Atlantic City, Phila., New York City, and Vineland, N.J.; pres. Philjay Co.; sec. Jay Realty Co. Served as mem. Atlantic Co. Dem. Com., 1930; candidate for Bd. of Freeholders, 1930. Dir. Jewish Seaside Home. Sec. Cong. Beth Judah. Mem. N.J. Soc. of C.P.A.s. Democrat. Jewish religion. Home: 57 N. Raleigh Av., Atlantic City, N.J. Office: Schwehm Bldg., Atlantic City, N.J.

SILVERMAN, Sam Maxwell, utilities exec.; b. New York, N.Y., Mar. 6, 1904; s. Leo and Jenny (Cowan) S.; student Talladega (Ala.) High Sch., 1917-20; B.S., U. of Ala., Tuscaloosa, Ala., 1924; m. Gesna Mae Allen, of Greensboro, Ala., Jan. 29, 1927. Office work Ala. Water Service Co., Birmingham, Ala., 1924-25, purchasing agt., 1925-30; v.p. Phenix Engineering Co., Birmingham, Ala., 1927-30; treas. Peoples Water Service Co., Baltimore, 1930-35; v.p., gen. mgr., treas. and dir. since 1935, also v.p., gen. mgr., treas. and dir. Peoples Water Service Co., of Fla., of Ga., of S.C., of Miss., of W.Va. Mem. Scabbard and Blade, Sigma Eta, Zeta Beta Tau. Republican. Home: 7301 Park Heights Av. Office: Gillet Bldg., Baltimore, Md.

SILVERS, Earl Reed, author; b. Jersey City, N.J., Feb. 22, 1891; s. Earl Brittin and Evelyn (Reed) S.; A.B., Rutgers Coll., 1913, hon. A.M., 1923; m. Edythe I. Terrill, Dec. 14, 1916; children—Earl Reed, Edith Evelyn, Terrill (dec.). Alumni sec., 1913-16, asst. to pres., 1916-25, dir. of public information, 1925-33, dir. of alumni, and public relations since 1933, asso. prof. of English since 1929, Rutgers Univ. Editor Rutgers Alumni Quarterly, 1914-21, Rutgers Alumni Monthly, 1921-1929, and since 1938, Univ. Extension Record, 1926-33, Alumni Council Bulletin, 1933-36; exec. sec. Rutgers University Fund Council, 1935-37; on leave of absence, 1937-38; dir. Rutgers U. Press since 1938. Mem. Am. College Publicity Assn. (pres. 1929-30), Phi Beta Kappa, Delta Phi, Theta Nu Epsilon. Presbyn. Clubs: Rutgers (New Brunswick); Delta Phi (New York); Colonia (N.J.) Country. Author: Dick Arnold of Raritan College, 1920; Dick Arnold Plays the Game, 1921; Dick Arnold of the Varsity, 1921; Ned Beals, Freshman, 1922; At Hillsdale High, 1922; Ned Beals Works His Way, 1923; Jackson of Hillsdale High, 1923; The Hillsdale High Champions, 1924; Barry the Undaunted, 1924; Barry and Budd, 1925; The Spirit of Menlo, 1926; The Menlo Mystery, 1926; Carol of Highland Camp, 1927; Team First, 1929; The Red-headed Halfback, 1929; Carol of Cranford High, 1930; The Scarlet of Avalon, 1930; The Glory of Glenwood, 1931; Code of Honor, 1932. Home: Rahway, N.J.

SILVERSTONE, Seymour Symon, lawyer; b. Chicago, Ill., Sept. 8, 1899; s. Harry and Dora (Bofsky) S.; B.S. in Economics, U. of Pa., 1921; LL.B., U. of Pa., 1925; unmarried. Admitted to Pa. bar, 1925, and since engaged in gen. practice of law at Johnstown. Served in U.S.A., 1918. Trustee Greater Johnstown Community Chest, Conemaugh Valley Memorial Hosp., Cambria Co. Branch Pa. Assn. for the Blind. Mem. Pa. and Cambria Co. bar assns., Am. Legion, Beta Gamma Sigma. Republican. Jewish religion. Club: Sunnehanna Country (Johnstown). Home: 716 Second Av. Office: 602 U.S. Nat. Bank Bldg., Johnstown, Pa.

SILZER, George S., ex-governor; b. New Brunswick, N.J., Apr. 14, 1870; s. Theodore C. and Christina (Zimmerman) S.; ed. pub. and high schs; LL.D., Rutgers, 1923; m. Henrietta T. Waite, Apr. 18, 1898. Admitted to N.J. bar, 1892; mem. Bd. of Aldermen, Brunswick, N.J., 1892-96; chmn. Dem. Co. Com., Middlesex Co., 10 yrs.; mem. N.J. Senate, 1907-12; prosecutor of pleas, Middlesex Co., 1912-14; circuit judge, by apptmt. of Gov. Fielder, later by apptmt. Gov. Edwards, 1914-22 (resigned); gov. of N.J., 1923-26. Chmn. bd. New Brunswick Trust Co.; chmn. bd. and dir. Interstate Trust Co., New York, 1929-30; trustee Central Savings Bank in the City of New York. Chmn. Port of New York Authority, 1926-28. Mem. Chamber Commerce State of N.Y. Episcopalian. Mason. Elk. Clubs: Princeton, Nat. Democratic, Bankers (New York); Plainsfield Country. Home: Metuchen, N.J. Office: 744 Broad St., Newark, N.J.

SIMEONE, Peter Anthony, physician and surgeon; b. Union Hill, N.J., Oct. 12, 1902; s. Frank and Erminia (Gallo) S.; grad. Union Hill (N.J.) High Sch., 1921; student New York U., 1921-23; M.D., Univ. and Bellevue Hosp. Med. Coll., New York, 1927; m. Isabella Schiavo, Oct. 20, 1928; children—Erminia, Peter. Interne, St. Mary's Hosp., Hoboken, N.J., 1927-28; in gen. practice of medicine, Union City, N.J., since 1928. Captain in Med. Reserve Corps, attached to 303rd Med. Regt., U.S. Army. Mem. A.M.A., N.J. Med. Soc., Hudson County Med. Soc., North Hudson Physicians Soc., Lambda Phi Mu. Catholic. Home: 138 Clark St., Jersey City, N.J. Office: 555 38th St., Union City, N.J.

SIMMONS, Charles Wellington, prof. chem. engring.; b. Kingston, Ont., Sept. 28, 1897; s. Charles C. and Annie F. (Smyth) S.; came to U.S., 1926, naturalized, 1938; B.Sc. with honors, Queen's Univ., Can., 1920; M.S., Lehigh U., 1928; m. Mary Violet Elliot, Sept. 7, 1925; children—Catherine Elliot, John Wellington. Employed as gen. foreman, British Chem. Co., Trenton, Ont., 1915, with Explosive Research Labs., same, 1916; asst. in chemistry and Douglas Tutor, Queen's Univ., 1919-20; with Deloro Research Labs., Welland, Ont., 1919-26; Byllesby Research Fellow, Lehigh U., 1926-28; instr. chem. engring., Lehigh U., Bethlehem, Pa., 1928-30, asst. prof., 1931-35, asso. prof. chem. engring. since 1935; dir. of research at Lehigh U. for Raybestos-Manhattan Co. and Chester Enameling Co. Served with C.S.E.F., 1916-18. Member American Chem. Soc. (councillor, 1938; vice chmn., 1929-30, chmn. 1937 of Lehigh Valley sect.), Am. Inst. Chem. Engrs., Canadian Inst. Chemistry, Pa. Chem. Soc. (an incorporator), Sigma Xi, Tau Beta Pi, Kappa Alpha. Republican. Presbyn. Mason. Club: Engineers of Lehigh Valley. Contbr. to tech. jours. Tech. legal expert in

SIMMONS, George Bradford, bldg. management; b. St. Ives, Cornwall, Eng., Dec. 6, 1886; s. Edward Emerson and Vesta (Shallenberger) S., citizens of U.S.; grad. St. Paul's Sch., Concord, N.H., 1902; student Browne & Nichols Sch., Cambridge, Mass., 1902-03; A.B., Harvard U., 1908; m. Georgie Swindell, Feb. 23, 1911; children—Bradford, Edward Ball, William Emmet, Julian, Sarah Alden. Employed as automobile mechanic, salesman, 1908-11; real estate salesman, sales mgr., Baltimore, 1911-18; sales mgr., dist. mgr., div. (eastern) mgr., Procter & Gamble, Cincinnati, 1918-27; vice pres. and gen. mgr., The Roland Park Co., Baltimore, 1927-35; pres. Calvert Bldg. & Constrn. Co., propr. and mgr. office bldgs., Baltimore, Md., since 1935; dir. Dunleer Co. vice-president and director Travelers Aid Soc.; treas. and dir. Council of Social Agencies; dir. Criminal Justice Commn., all of Baltimore. Dir. Real Estate Bd. of Baltimore. Democrat. Club: Harvard of Md. Home: 5417 Falls Rd. Office: Calvert Bldg., Baltimore, Md.

SIMMONS, Lucretia Van Tuyl, prof. German; b. Schenevus, N.Y., 1875; d. George W. (M.D.) and Elizabeth (Van Tuyl) S.; Ph.B., Cornell U., 1898; ed. Columbia U. and Pa. State Coll., 1900-03, A.M., 1905; study, U. of Leipzig, 1907-08; Ph.D., U. of Wis., 1913; grad. study, Sorbonne, Paris, 1903, U. of Zurich and Oxford U., Eng., 1925, U. of Strassburg, 1926, U. of Vienna, summer 1929. Instr. German, Pa. State Coll., 1903-08, asst. prof., 1908-13, asso. prof., 1913-18, prof. German and head dept. German since 1918. Mem. Mod. Lang. Assn. America, Am. Assn. Teachers of German, Am. Assn. Univ. Profs., Am. Assn. Univ. Women, Mod. Lang. Assn. Pa., Phi Kappa Phi, Phi Sigma Iota, Delta Delta Delta, D.A.R. Republican. Episcopalian. Clubs: Woman's, Drama, Dickens, Cosmopolitan (State College). Author: Goethe's Lyric Poems in English Translation, prior to 1860, (pub.) 1915. Contbr. to modern lang. jours. Home: Richmondville, N.Y. Address: Pa. State Coll., State College, Pa.

SIMMONS, Sattis, newspaper pub.; b. Kenna, W.Va., Nov. 15, 1898; s. Melvin Clark and Flora Ann (Skeen) S.; student Fairplain (W.Va.) Normal Sch., 1915-18; m. Thelma Earle Corbin, June 20, 1920; children—Helen Corbin, Keith, Joyce Ann. Pub. sch. teacher, Ripley, W.Va., 1918-21; in newspaper business since 1922; pub. The Jackson Herald, Ripley, W.Va. (judged as being outstanding weekly newspaper on America, 1937), since 1922; v.p. and dir. Bank of Ripley, W.Va., since 1929. Del. to Rep. Nat. Conv., 1932; sec. Rep. Exec. Com. of W.Va. since 1936. Republican. United Brethren, Modern Woodmen of America. Address: Ripley, W.Va.

SIMMONS, William Berlin, county supt. schs.; b. Bartow, W.Va., June 21, 1888; s. Lewis P. and Amanda Catherine (Varner) S.; A.B., Bridgewater Coll., Bridgewater, Va., 1918; A.M., W.Va. U., 1928; student W.Va. U. Law Sch., summer 1924, Cornell U. Law Sch., summer 1922; LL.B., LaSalle Extension U., Chicago, 1935; grad. student, George Washington U., Washington, D.C., 1933; m. Blanche Essex, Aug. 12, 1912 (dec.); m. 2d Mary Catherine Hidy, Sept. 1, 1919; children—Margie Elizabeth, Ruth Hidy, Darla Patricia. Engaged in teaching in rural schs., high schs. and prin. various schs. while studying, 1908-22; prin. high sch., Tunneton, W.Va., 1922-26, Paw Paw, 1926-30, Berkeley Springs, 1930-35; county supt. schs., Morgan Co., since 1935. Candidate for Congress on Rep. ticket, 1936. Mem. W.Va. State Edn. Assn. Republican. Brethren. Mason (32°, Shriner). K.P. Pythian Sisters. Jr.O.U.A.M. Club: Morgan County Kiwanis (Berkeley Springs). Public Speaker. Home: Berkeley Springs, W.Va.

SIMON, Edward Paul, architect; b. Phila., Pa., June 1, 1878; s. Fred Paul and Mary Ann (Miles) S.; grad. Central High Sch., Phila., 1896, Drexel Inst., 1900; m. Edith M. Darby, Nov. 5, 1904; children—Marion Darby, Elizabeth Esten. Draftsman, Dull & Coates, architects and engrs., 1900-03; mem. firm Caldwell & Simon, 1903-06, Edward P. Simon, 1907-08, Simon & Bassett, 1908-19; pres. and treas. Simon & Simon since 1919. Prin. works: Mfrs'. Club, Fidelity-Phila. Trust Bldg., Strawbridge & Clothier Store (all of Phila.); Meade Memorial, Washington, D.C.; First Camden (N.J.) Nat. Bank & Trust Co. Bldg.; office bldg., Baldwin Locomotive Works, Eddystone, Pa., Drexel Inst. Tech.; Van Renselaer Dormitory for Women; Curtis Hall of Engring. Trustee Drexel Institute. Member American Inst. Architects, Acad. Natural Sciences, Pa. Acad. Fine Arts. Republican. Presbyn. Mason. Clubs: Union League, Engineers', Art, T Square, Manufacturers. Home: 533 Arbutus St., Germantown, Philadelphia, Pa. Office: Fidelity-Phila. Trust Bldg., Philadelphia, Pa.

SIMON, Grant Miles, architect; b. Phila., Pa., Oct. 2, 1887; s. Frederick Paul and Mary Ann S.; student Sch. Industrial Art, 1905-06; B.S., U. of Pa., 1911, M.S., 1911; ed. T Square Atelier, 1907-09, Acad. of Fine Arts, 1907-08, Ecole des Beaux Arts, Paris, France, 1914-15; m. Jamie Holcombe Hearin, Apr. 13, 1923; 1 dau., Jane Holcombe. Engaged in profession as achitect in Phila., Pa., since 1916, mem. firm Simon & Bassett, 1916-18, Simon & Simon, 1918-27, in practice at Phila. as Grant M. Simon since 1927; architect for Gordon Meade Memorial, Washington, D.C., Municipal Stadium, Phila., Pa., also Fidelity-Philadelphia Bank & Office Bldg., and University Club, both Phila., also various banking, office, and instnl. bldgs., and residences. Served on Com. of Am. Embassy, Paris, France, 1914-15, Am. Com. for Relief of French Students, 1914-15. Mem. A.I.A., Soc. Beaux Arts Architects. Republican. Home: The Chatham, 20th & Walnut Sts. Office: 1520 Locust St., Philadelphia, Pa.

SIMON, Israel A., smelting and refining; b. Pittsburgh, Pa., July 4, 1883; s. Samuel and Mary (Carey) S.; student pub. and high schs., Pittsburgh; m. Sadie Markowitz, Aug. 6, 1919 (died 1936); 1 son, Richard Samuel; m. 2d, Virginia J. Timmins, Nov. 1, 1938. Engaged in real estate and ins. business, McKeesport, Pa., 1901-13; with Duquesne Reduction Co., smelting and metal refining, 1913-24, consolidated with others to form Federated Metals Corpn., 1924, and since v.p., gen. mgr. and dir. (now div. Am. Smelting & Refining Co.); v.p. and dir. Copperweld Steel Co.; pres. and dir. Morewood Estates, Inc., Falk Products Co.; sec., dir. Falk Foundation; dir. Home for Aged. Republican. Jewish religion. Clubs: Concordia (Pittsburgh); Westmoreland Country (Verona). Home: 1060 Morewood Av. Office: 615 Gross St., Pittsburgh, Pa.

SIMON, Joseph Alfred, personal financing; b. Lock Haven, Pa., May 1, 1881; s. Herman and Bertha (Bernheimer) S.; ed. State Normal Sch., Lock Haven Bus. Coll.; m. Mae Fickensher, July 1, 1912; children—Mary Bertha, Ruth Amelia. Employed as bookkeeper, 1897-1927; sec., treas., and mgr. Community Loan Co. since 1927, name later changed to Consumer Discount Co. of Lock Haven, Pa. Served in Pa. Res. Militia during World War. Mem. Pa. Ho. of Rep., 1929-39 (chmn. Ways and Means Com., 1939). Dir. Lock Haven Chamber of Commerce, Community Service (treas. 1939). Mem. Advisory Council 1939 Worlds Fair, New York, N.Y. Democrat. Mason (32°, Shriner). Elk. I.O.O.F., K.P., Patriotic Order Sons of America. Clubs: Lock Haven Rotary (pres., 1939); Shrine (Altoona). Home: 103 W. Church St. Office: 124 E. Main St., Lock Haven, Pa.

SIMON, Morris, merchant; b. Podu-Iloie, Roumania, Nov. 5, 1892; s. Solomon and Betty (Josephson) S.; came to U.S., 1895, naturalized, 1913; student James Campbell Sch., Phila., 1902-12, Phila. Business Coll., 1912-14; m. Mae Barros, Oct. 8, 1916; children—Corinne, Ruth, Sherie. Began as mcht., Dover, Del., 1915; owner Simon's Dept. Store, ladies and men's clothing, furnishings, houseware, etc., Dover, Del., since 1916, Sherie's Ladies Shop, Dover, Del., since 1926, Simon's Shoe Store, Dover, since 1920, Sheries Ladies Shop, Vineland, N.J., since 1938. Mem. Del. Ho. of Reps., 1933-37 (2 terms), minority floor leader, 1933-35, majority floor leader, 1935-37. Jewish religion. Mason, Odd. Fellow. Club: Rotary (Dover, Del.; pres. 1937-38). Home: 312 N. Bradford St. Office: Loockerman St., Dover, Del.

SIMONS, Erwin Winslow, manufacturer; b. New Hampton, Ia., May 12, 1880; s. Henry Alpha and Emily Antoinette (Stiles) S.; student Sidney (Ia.) High Sch., 1894-96, Boyle's Business Coll., Omaha, 1899, Des Moines (Ia.) Coll., 1901; m. Janet McRae, June 17, 1903; 1 dau., Helen (Mrs. Oscar Maurice Polhemus). Began as law stenographer, 1897; stenographer Wells & Nieman Milling Co., Schuyler, Neb., 1899-1903, and sec. and dir. of successor Wells-Abbott-Nieman Co., 1903-06; advertising mgr. and asst. sales mgr. German-American Coffee Co., N.Y. City, 1907-09; advertising mgr. Listman Mills, LaCrosse, Wis., 1909-10; advertising mgr. and dir. James Mfg. Co., Ft. Atkinson, Wis., 1910-22; vice-pres. and dir. Pittsburgh Reflector Co., silver plated glass reflectors and lighting equipment, 1922-33, pres. since 1933; dir. James Mfg. Co., Ft. Atkinson, Wis. Mem. Illuminating Engring. Soc. Ind. Republican. Methodist. Home: 721 Roselawn Av., Mt. Lebanon, Pa. Office: Oliver Bldg., Pittsburgh, Pa.

SIMONS, Frank K.; v.p. Continental Diamond Fibre Co.; b. Phila., Pa., June 12, 1885; s. George W. and Fannie (Keen) S.; ed. Drexel Inst.; m. Agnes Nichols, Nov. 12, 1918; children William G., John N., Dorothy, Caroline. With Continental Diamond Fibre Co. since 1931, v.p. in charge central sales territory, Cleveland, 1931-35, exec. v.p. since 1935. Home: 249 E. Main St. Office: 70 S. Chapel St., Newark, Del.

SIMONS, Joseph H., coll. prof.; b. Chicago, Ill., May 10, 1887; s. David and Esther S.; B.S., U. of Ill., Urbana, Ill., 1919, M.S., 1922; Ph.D., U. of Calif., Berkeley, Calif., 1923; grad. study, Cambridge U., Eng., 1929-30; m. Eleanor Whittaker, Aug. 22, 1936. Engaged as research chemist, Atmospheric Nitrogen Corpn., 1924; prof. chemistry, U. of Porto Rico., 1925-26; asst. prof. Northwestern U., Evanston, Ill., 1926-32; visiting prof. chemistry, Pa. State Coll., 1933-35, asso. prof., 1935-36, prof. since 1936. Civilian consultant, C.W.S. Mem. A.A.A.S., Am. Chem. Soc., Am. Assn. Univ. Profs., Anubis, Phi Lambda Upsilon, Sigma Xi. Home: 241 Ridge Av., State College, Pa.

SIMONTON, Fagan Hull, pres. F. H. Simonton, Inc.; b. Kansas City, Mo., Aug. 1, 1894; s. William A. and Hettie (Hull) S.; student Berkeley (Calif.) High Sch., 1909-13, U. of Calif., Berkeley, 1913-14; B.S., Wharton Sch. of U. of Pa., 1917; m. Irene Van Kirk, Oct. 9, 1919; children—William Kirk, Fagan Hull, Shirley Irene. Clk. with Gilpin, Van Trump & Montgomery, Inc., 1919-28; pres. F. H. Simonton, Inc., ins. agency, Wilmington, Del., since 1928. Served in 312th F.A., 79th Div., U.S. Army, 1918-19. Mem. Del. State Athletic Commn., 1937-39; Del. state treasurer since 1939 (2 yr. term). Mem. Am. Legion, Vets. of Fgn. Wars, Friar Sr. Soc. (U. of Pa.), Phi Delta Theta. Republican. Mason (Shriner). Clubs: Wilmington, Rotary, University, Wilmington Country (Wilmington); Concord Country. Formerly capt. U. of Pa. swimming team. Home: 2400 Willard St. Office: 2068 Du Pont Bldg., Wilmington, Del.

SIMPSON, Alexander Carson, lawyer; b. Merion, Pa., Feb. 1, 1896; s. Alex, Jr., and Mary (Carson) S.; B.S. in chemistry, Pa. Mil. Coll., 1916, B.Mil.Science, 1916; LL.B., U. of Pa. Law Sch., 1922; unmarried. Admitted to Pa. bar, 1922, and since engaged in gen. practice of law at Phila.; associated with firm Brown & Williams since 1922, leave of absence since 1933; served as asst. city solicitor, Phila., 1926-27; spl. master, Cts. of Common Pleas of Phila. since 1933; prof. pleading, Temple U. Law Sch., 1928-33. Served as pvt., later 2d lt. C.A.; instr. in orientation C.A. Sch., 1918; 2d lt. C.A. Sect., O.R.C., 1919-24. Mem. Musical Fund Soc. of Phila. (dir. since 1934, counsellor since 1937). Trustee Pa. Mil. Coll.,

Chester, Pa., since 1938. Mem. Am., Pa., and Phila. bar assns., Am. Judicature Soc., Juristic Soc., Am. Law Inst., Sharswood Law Club, Am. Numismatic Soc., Theta Xi, Phi Delta Phi. Republican. Episcopalian. Clubs: University (Philadelphia); Collectors (N.Y. City). Home: 5854 Drexel Road. Office: 196 City Hall, Philadelphia, Pa.

SIMPSON, David Waterson, pres. Indiana Lumber and Supply Company; b. Blanket Hill, Armstrong County, Pennsylvania, November 24, 1858; s. Thomas and Ann (Gray) S.; student public schools; m. Elexenia Kingsborn, Nov. 10, 1881; children—Violet H., Janet G., Alex K. Clerk in country store, 1879-86; deputy sheriff, 1886-95; managed flour mill, 1895-99; county treas., 1899-1903; organized, 1903, Indiana Lumber & Supply Co. and since pres.; pres. Indiana County Thrift Corpn.; treas. Indiana County Bldg. & Loan Assn.; dir. Farmers Bank & Trust Co. (Indiana). Active in boy scout work. Methodist (mem. official bd. and bd. trustees Indiana M.E. Ch.). Odd Fellow. Home: 352 N. 9th St. Office: 200 N. 10th St., Indiana, Pa.

SIMPSON, Edward Ridgely, lawyer; b. Baltimore, Md., Oct. 17, 1891; s. Rear Adm. Edward and Camilla (Morris) S.; student Calvert and Gilman schs., Baltimore, Md.; A.B., 1902-08; Litt.B., Princeton U., 1913; LL.B., Harvard Law Sch., 1916; m. Elizabeth White Dixon, Dec. 22, 1915; children—Elizabeth Ridgely, Mary Dixon, Camilla Ridgely. Admitted to Md. bar, 1916; associated with law firm Fisher, Bruce & Fisher, 1916-25; mem. firm Smith & Smith, Cross & Simpson, 1925-30; pres. Sun Mortgage Co. since 1929. Rep. candidate for Congress, 2d Md. Dist., 1924. Enlisted in U.S. Naval Res., 1917; commd. lt. j.g. U.S.N., June 1918; resigned Jan. 1919. Mem. Am. Bar Assn., Md. Bar Assn., Baltimore City Bar Assn. Republican. Episcopalian. Clubs: Merchants (Baltimore); L'Hirondelle (Ruxton); University Cottage (Princeton, N.J.). Home: Ruxton, Md. Office: 18 E. Lexington St., Baltimore, Md.

SIMPSON, F(rank) M(orton), univ. prof.; b. Clifford, Pa., Nov. 8, 1872; s. George and Helen (Gardner) S.; grad. Montrose (Pa.) High Sch., 1891; B.S., Bucknell U., Lewisburg, Pa., 1895, M.S., 1897; student Cold Spring Harbor, N.Y., summers, 1896, 97, Cornell U., 1898-1904; m. Mary Elizabeth Wilson, June 25, 1903 (died Feb. 12, 1937); children—Geddes Wilson, James Richardson, Helen Elizabeth. Science teacher in prep. schs., Sharon, Pa., 1895-98, Delhi, N.Y., 1899-1900, Lewisburg, Pa., 1900-03; asst. prof. physics, Bucknell U., 1903-07, prof. since 1907; pres. Union Nat. Bank of Lewisburg, Citizens Electric Co., Lewisburg; v.p. Lewisburg Gas Co. Mem. Bd. of Edn., Lewisburg, since 1924. Mem. Am. Physical Soc., Am. Soc. Univ. Profs., A.A.A.S., Am. Assn. Physics, Sigma Chi. Republican. Methodist. Mason (32°). Home: 21 S. 4th St., Lewisburg, Pa.

SIMPSON, Harold Ellis, educator; b. Columbus, O., June 16, 1903; s. Edgar Lewis and Ellen (Turner) S.; Bach. Ceramic Engring., O. State U., 1925, M.S., 1926, Ph.D., 1929, (hon.) Ceramic Engr., 1938; m. Edith Mae Miller, Sept. 22, 1931. Research fellow, U.S. Bur. of Mines, 1925-27, U.S. Bur. of Standards, 1927-28; research engr., O. State U. Engring. Expt. Sta., 1929; asst. prof. ceramic engring. and research asso., Rutgers U., 1929-30; research engr., Battelle Memorial Inst., Columbus, O., 1930-36; industrial fellow, Mellon Inst., Pittsburgh, since 1936. Served in O. State N.G., 1919-20. Mem. Am. Ceramic Soc., Inst. Ceramic Engrs. Republican. Mason. Clubs: Faculty of U. of Pittsburgh, Mendelssohn Choir, Robert Kennedy Duncan Club. Home: 429 Sulgrave Rd., Pittsburgh, Pa.

SIMPSON, Iona Jewell, asst. state supt. schs.; b. Henderson, N.C., Jan. 8, 1882; d. Dr. Shadrach and Ella (Gooch) Simpson; A.B., Western Md. Coll., Westminster, Md., 1899; A.M., Teachers Coll. Columbia U., 1924; grad. student, Johns Hopkins U., summers; Ed.D., Western Md. Coll., 1937. Engaged in teaching English and sci., high sch., Westminster, Md., 1909-16; supervisor elementary schs. in Carroll Co., Md., 1916-21; asst. dir. bur. ednl. measurements, State Dept. Edn., Baltimore, Md., 1921-23, state supervisor of elementary schs., 1923-25, asst. state supt. schs. since 1925, instr. various courses, John Hopkins U., summer sessions. Democrat. Unitarian. Co-author: (with Ehrlich Smith and Orton Lowe) Adventures in Reading, 1929; (with C. J. Anderson) Supervision of Rural Schools, 1932. Contbr. bulletins and articles. Home: Preston Apts. Office: Lexington Bldg., Baltimore, Md.

SIMPSON, John Christopher, M.D.; b. Phila., Pa., Sept. 30, 1888; s. Robert and Alice (Easler) S.; M.D., U. of Pa., 1912; m. Ruth Adele Kraus, Mar. 15, 1916; 1 son, John Christopher. Pathologist, Montgomery Hosp. since 1916, Riverview Hosp. since 1917, Sacred Heart Hosp. since 1936 (all of Norristown, Pa.); coroner's physician, Montgomery Co., Pa., since 1928. Fellow Am. Soc. Clin. Pathologists; mem. Montgomery Co. Med. Soc., A.M.A., Phila. Pathol. Soc. Republican. Episcopalian. Mason. Club: Norristown Kiwanis (organizer and first pres.). Contbr. to med. jours. Address: 920 Swede St., Norristown, Pa.

SIMPSON, John Nathan, M.D.; b. Mason, W.Va., Mar. 19, 1869; s. George Perry and Phoebe (Kennedy) S.; grad. Peabody Coll. for Teachers, Nashville, Tenn., 1891; A.B., U. of Nashville, 1893; M.D., Johns Hopkins, 1902; studied univs. of Paris, Vienna and Berlin, 1905; m. Grace Emily Donley, Dec. 20, 1906; children —John Nathan, Patricia Donley. Organized, 1902, Sch. of Medicine, W.Va. U., and dean until 1935, also prof. physiology, 1902-20, professor medicine, 1920—, dean emeritus since 1935. Director Hygiene Laboratory, Department of Health, W.Va., 1913-17; surgeon Cadet Corps, W.Va. U., 1902-27; major Med. R.C., U.S.A. Fellow Am. Acad. Medicine, Am. Coll. Physicians (gov. for W.Va.); mem. W.Va. State Med. Assn. (pres. 1923), A.M.A., A.A.A.S., Phi Beta Pi, Theta Nu Epsilon. Democrat. Presbyn. Home: Morgantown, W.Va.*

SIMPSON, John R., corporation official; b. Richmond, Ind., January 29, 1876; s. Elihu C. and Mary Elizabeth (Ralston) S.; A.B., Miami University, Oxford, Ohio, 1899; LL.D., 1919; m. Mabelle Rose Pratt, June 4, 1903; 1 dau., Mrs. Barbara Pratt Lawrence. With Western Electric Co., Chicago, 1899-1903; v.p. William Filene's Sons Co., Boston, 1903-17; col. U.S. Army, 1917-19; now pres. and chmn. exec. com. Fiduciary Trust Co. of New York; chmn. bd. Van Raalte Co.; dir. McCall Corpn., dir. Tricontinental Corpn., Gen. Am. Investment Corpn., Fire Assn. of Phila., Globe & Rutgers Fire Ins. Co., Reliance Ins. Co., Fiduciary Corpn. Dir. Metropolitan Opera Guild. Awarded D.S.M. (U.S.); Order de l'Etoile Noire (France). Mem. Beta Theta Pi, Ind. Republican. Episcopalian. Clubs: University, Down Town, Knickerbocker Country, New York Yacht (New York); Aldecress Country. Home: 207 Chestnut St., Englewood, N.J. Office: 1 Wall St., New York, N.Y.

SIMPSON, Kirke Larue, newspaper man; b. San Francisco, Calif., Aug. 14, 1880; s. Sylvester C. and Frances Marion (McFarland) S.; ed. pub. schs., Trinity Sch. and Lick Sch. of Mech. Arts, San Francisco; spl. courses, U. of Calif.; unmarried. Began newspaper work in San Francisco, 1906; now with Associated Press. Served in 1st Calif. Vol. Inf., Philippine campaigns, during Spanish-Am. War. and Philippine Insurrection, 1898-99; commd. maj. Mil. Intelligence O.R.C., U.S.A., 1921. Clubs: Nat. Press. Awarded Pulitzer prize, 1921, for article on the "Unknown Soldier." Home: 302 Leland St., Chevy Chase, Md. Address: The Associated Press, Star Bldg., Washington, D.C.

SIMPSON, Maxwell Stewart, artist; b. Elizabeth, N.J., Sept. 11, 1896; s. Maxwell Gayley and Gertrude (Moore) S.; ed. Nat. Acad. of Design, N.Y. City, 1914-18; m. Elizabeth Reed, Sept. 25, 1935. Has followed profession as artist since 1919; frequent exhibitor in nat. and internat. exhbns.; represented in Newark Museum, Nat. Gallery of Art, New York Pub. Library. Mem. Modern Artists of N.J., Chicago Soc. of Etchers. Awarded a number of prizes in art sch. Home: 1147 East Jersey St., Elizabeth, N.J.

SIMPSON, Warren Brown, lawyer; b. Huntingdon, Pa., Nov. 1, 1869; s. James Randolph and Jennie M. (Brown) S.; student Huntingdon Pub. Sch., 1877-84; m. Sue Elsie Miller, Mar. 22, 1899; children—Richard Murray, Fred Miller, Robert Brown, Helen Wilkins, Mildred (Mrs. W. K. Myers); m. 2d, Dorothy Kline, Aug. 10, 1923. Mem. Pa. Legislature, 1907, 1909; sec. and gen. mgr. Raystown Water Power Co., Huntingdon, 1907-23; sec.-treas. and dir., Mapleton Limestone Co., Huntingdon, since 1924; mem. law firm J. R. & W. B. Simpson, 1892-1931, Simpson & Simpson, Huntingdon, since 1938; mem. ins. firm of W. B. and R. M. Simpson, Huntingdon, since 1931; sec. and dir. Grocers Cash Deposit Mutual Fire Ins. Co., Huntingdon Cash Deposit Mutual Fire Ins. Co.; dir. First Nat. Bank of Huntingdon. Pres. Am. Legion Community Home. Mem. Spanish-Am. War Vets., Patriotic Order Sons of America. Republican. Presbyn. K.P. Home: 814 Washington St. Office: 521 Washington St., Huntingdon, Pa.

SIMS, Charles Abercrombie, ry. contractor; b. Memphis, Tenn., June 5, 1866; s. Clifford Stanley and Mary Josephine (Abercrombie) S.; ed. pub. and high schs., Mt. Holly, N.J.; m. Julia Watkins, Apr. 21, 1897. Filled various positions on Pa. R.R. engring. corps, 1882-86; asst. engr. in charge constrn. W.Va. Central R.R., 1886-87; asst. engr. in charge constrn. surveys, etc., Pa. R.R. Co., 1887-90. Was resident engr. in charge bldg. Pa. R.R. Co.'s stone arch bridge over Conemaugh River that stood flood of 1889 at Johnstown, Pa.; was contractor 4-track stone bridge over Delaware River at Trenton, N.J. Mem. Soc. of the Cincinnati, Loyal Legion. Episcopalian. Address: 10 S. 18th St., Philadelphia, Pa.

SIMS, Joseph Patterson, architect; b. Phila., Pa., Jan. 6, 1890; s. John Clark and Grace Ledlie (Patterson) S.; B.S. in arch., U. of Pa., 1912; m. Anne Preston Scott, Jan. 16, 1917; children—Joseph Patterson, Jr., Sanders Scott. Asso. with Furness, Evans Co., 1912-17; mem. firm Willing, Sims and Talbutt, architects, Phila., Pa., since 1919. Served as 1st lt. U.S.A., 1917-19, exec. officer, U.S. Army Courier Service with A.E.F. in France, 1918-19. Former trustee Chestnut Hill Acad. Mem. Am. Inst. Architects, Print Club of Phila. (pres.), Zeta Psi. Episcopalian. Clubs: State in Schuylkill; Orpheus (Philadelphia). Home: 319 E. Gravers Lane, Chestnut Hill, Pa. Office: Architects Bldg., Philadelphia, Pa.

SIMSOHN, Julian Stern, industrial engr.; b. Phila., Pa., Jan. 19, 1890; s. Dr. Joseph S. and Clara (Stern) S.; B.S., U. of Pa., 1911; m. Cecile A. Goldsmith, Oct. 26, 1916; children—Jean Claire (Mrs. Vincenzo Savarese), Julian Stern, Marjorie Goldsmith. Chem. engr. Electrolytic Purification Co., Phila., 1911-14; engaged in pvt. practice of engring. at Phila. since 1914; consultant on boiler water purification for Phila. Electric Co., 1916-20, Phila. Rapid Transit Co., 1916-23, Atlas Portland Cement Co., 1917-20, Midvale Steel & Ordnance Co., 1918-21, Pub. Service Corpn. of N.J., 1919-21; consulting engr. for Pa. Fuel Adminstrn., 1918-19, Consol. Cigar Corpn. since 1923, Cheltenham (Pa.) Sch. Bd. since 1933, Bryn Athyn (Pa.) Acad. of New Ch. since 1932, Congregation of Mission of St. Vincent De Paul since 1935. Mem. Franklin Inst., Am. Soc. Mil. Engrs., Zoological Soc. Ind. Republican. Mem. Reformed Ch. Holder of patents on water purification, heating and industrial processes. Home: 615 Ashbourne Rd., Elkins Park, Pa. Office: 933 N. Broad St., Philadelphia, Pa.

SINCLAIR, Archibald Gordon, clergyman; b. Alberta, Can., Dec. 31, 1875; s. Robert Gordon and Jean (MacDougall) S.; came to U.S., 1918, naturalized, 1924; B.A., U. of Toronto, 1896, M.A., 1897; ed. Knox Coll., Toronto, 1896-98, New Coll., Edinburgh, Scotland, 1898-99, U. of Berlin, Germany, 1903-04; Ph.D., U. of Heidelberg, Germany, 1907; m. Clara Anderson, of Toronto, Can., Oct. 10, 1899 (died 1900); 1 dau., Helen Jean (Mrs. Edmond E. Manhard); m. 2d, Margaret Whitelaw, of Kirkintilloch, Scotland, March 29, 1909; children—Margaret Whitelaw, Jean MacDougall (Mrs. Arthur Schade), Mary Evelyn, Phillis Whitelaw. Ordained to ministry Presbyn. Ch., 1899; minister, Port Hope, Ont., 1899-1903, Dawson City, Yukon, 1908-09, Winnipeg, Can., 1909-18; minister First Presbyn. Ch., Bloomfield, N.J., since 1918. Presbyn. Mason. Club: Glen Ridge Country. Home: 67 Park Pl., Bloomfield, N.J.

SINCLAIR, John Stephens, banker; b. Brooklyn, N.Y., Apr. 6, 1897; s. David Macowan and Alice Elizabeth (Stephens) S.; grad. Boys High Sch., Brooklyn, N.Y., 1915; A.B., Columbia U., 1920, LL.B., 1922; m. Mary Hewes Biddle, Mar. 27, 1924; children—Mary Biddle, David Macowan, Sylvia Buell, John Biddle. Admitted to Pa. bar, 1922; asso. with Williams & Sinkler, Phila., later mem. firm Williams, Brittain & Sinclair, 1922-33; dep. gov. Federal Reserve Bank, Phila., 1934-36, pres. since Mar. 15, 1936; dir. James G. Biddle Co., Phila. Served as 2d lt., Inf., U.S. Army, 1918-19. Trustee Germantown Hosp. (Phila.), Drexel Inst., Community Fund of Phila., Phila. and Cheyney (Pa.) Training Sch. for Teachers. Republican. Congregationalist. Clubs: University, Rittenhouse, Phila. Cricket (Phila.). Home: 3613 Fox St. Office: 925 Chestnut St., Philadelphia, Pa.

SINGER, Edgar Arthur, Jr., prof. philosophy; b. Phila., Pa., Nov. 13, 1873; s. Edgar Arthur and Sarah Elizabeth (Phillips) S.; B.S., U. of Pa., 1892, Ph.D., 1894; Harvard, 1894-96; m. Helen Bunker, July 5, 1905; children—Edgar Arthur, Richard Bunker. Asst. in psychol. dept., Harvard, 1895; prof. philosophy, U. of Pa., 1909-29, Adam Seybert prof. of philosophy since 1929. Sergt. First U.S. Vol. Engineers, Spanish-Am. War. Mem. Am. Philos. Assn., Am. Philos. Soc., A.A.A.S., Sigma Xi, Phi Beta Kappa. Democrat. Episcopalian. Clubs: University, Harvard. Author: Modern Thinkers and Present Problems, 1923; Mind as Behavior and Studies in Empirical Idealism, 1924; Fool's Advice, 1925; On the Contented Life, 1936. Home: 4224 Chester Av., Philadelphia, Pa.

SINGEWALD, H. Elmer; banker; b. Baltimore, Md., Mar. 2, 1888; s. Joseph T. and Magdalena (Dreyer) S.; grad. Baltimore City Coll., 1905; LL.B., U. of Md., 1910; spl. banking and accounting courses, Johns Hopkins U.; m. Charlotte Stout, Sept. 17, 1938; children (by previous marriage)—Eleanor, Ruth. Began as trust clerk Fidelity Trust Co., 1907, later becoming asst. trust officer; v.p. and sec. Real Estate Trust Co. since 1926. Mem. Plattsburg Training Camp, 1916, U.S. Naval Reserve Force, 1918. Teacher at Baltimore Business Coll., Y.M.C.A. Sch. of Accounting, U. of Md. Sch. of Business Adminstrn., Am. Inst. Banking (Baltimore Chapter). Democrat. Methodist. Clubs: Johns Hopkins, Rogers Forge Golf. Home: 4404 Atwick Road. Office: 1101 N. Charles St., Baltimore, Md.

SINGEWALD, Joseph Theophilus, Jr., geologist; b. Baltimore, Md., Sept. 25, 1884; s. Joseph Theophilus and Magdalena Julianna (Dreyer) S.; grad. Baltimore City Coll., 1903; A.B., Johns Hopkins University, 1906, Ph.D., 1909; m. Laura Page Heroy, June 14, 1934; children—Frances, Page. Fellow, 1907-08, Henry E. Johnston scholar, 1910-13, associate in economic geology, 1913-17, asso. prof., 1917-1922, prof. since 1922, Johns Hopkins U. Field asst., U.S. Geol. Survey, 1907, jr. geologist, 1910; jr. geologist U.S. Bur. Mines, 1911-20; field asst., 1906, asst. geologist, 1908-13, geologist since 1913, Md. Geol. Survey; consulting economic geologist. Mem. Am. Inst. M.E., Geol. Soc. America, A.A.A.S., Geol. Soc. Washington, Freiberger Geologische Gesellschaft, Am. Assn. Petroleum Geologists, Soc. Econ. Geologists, Mining and Metall. Soc. America, Sociedad Geolojica del Peru, Gamma Alpha, Phi Beta Kappa, Sigma Xi. Clubs: Engineers (Baltimore); Explorers (New York). Author of report on iron ores, also numerous papers in tech. publs. on geology and economic geology, on geology and mineral deposits of Latin America. Home: 213 Tunbridge Rd., Baltimore, Md.

SINGLEY, Frederick J., lawyer; b. Baltimore, Md., June 11, 1878; s. Henry and Louise (Hellweg) S.; student Baltimore City Coll., 1892-97; LL.B., U. of Md. Law Sch., Baltimore, 1900; m. Katherine M. Rice, Oct. 18, 1905 (died 1928); children—Frederick J., Jr., Anne Katherine. Admitted to Md. bar, 1900, and since practiced at Baltimore; mem. firm Hinkley, Burger & Singley, attys. at law, Baltimore, since 1908; pres. and dir. Houston Natural Gas Corpn., Baltimore, since 1933; v.p. and dir. Houston Natural Gas Co., Houston, Tex., since 1933; dir. Central Savings Bk. of Baltimore. Mem. Baltimore Bd. of Edn., 1920-24. Pres. bd. of trustees Union Memorial Hosp., Baltimore; v.p. Hosp. for Consumptives of Md. Mem. Am. Bar Assn., Md. Bar Assn., Phi Kappa Sigma. Republican. Lutheran. Home: 6208 Sycamore Rd., Cedarcroft. Office: 215 N. Charles St., Baltimore, Md.

SINGLEY, John DeVinne, M.D.; b. Blairsville, Pa., Aug. 25, 1869; s. Laiseur N. and Elizabeth (DeVinne) S.; A.B., Washington and Jefferson Coll., 1892, A.M., 1897; M.D., U. of Pa., 1895; m. Margaretta Johnston, Sept. 27, 1905; 1 son, John DeVinne. Practiced as physician and surgeon, Pittsburgh, since 1896; formerly dir. Magee Pathol. Inst., Mercy Hosp.; formerly asso. prof. surgery, U. of Pittsburgh; formerly surgeon St. Margarets Hosp., now cons. surgeon; chief surgeon Pittsburgh Hosp.; dir. Geo. S. Daugherty Co., Pittsburgh. Fellow Am. Coll. Surgeons, A.M.A.; mem. Pittsburgh Acad. Medicine; Phi Kappa Sigma. Republican. Presbyterian. Club: University (Pittsburgh). Home: 812 N. Highland Av., Pittsburgh, Pa.

SINGMASTER, Elsie (Mrs. Harold Lewars), author; b. Schuylkill Haven, Pa., Aug. 29, 1879; d. of Rev. John Alden and Caroline (Hoopes) S.; A.B., Radcliffe College, 1907; Litt.D., Pa. Coll., 1916; same, Muhlenberg Coll., Allentown, Pa., 1929; same, Wilson College, Chambersburg, Pa., 1934; member Delta Gamma, Phi Beta Kappa; m. Harold Lewars, 1912 (died 1915). Author: When Sarah Saved the Day, 1909; When Sarah Went to School, 1910; Gettysburg—Stories of the Red Harvest and the Aftermath, 1913; Katy Gaumer, 1914; Emmeline, 1916; The Long Journey, 1917; Life of Martin Luther, 1917; History of Lutheran Missions, 1917; Basil Everman, 1920; John Baring's House, 1920; Ellen Levis, 1921; Bennett Malin, 1922; The Hidden Road, 1923; A Boy at Gettysburg, 1924; Bred in the Bone, 1925; Book of the United States, 1925; Keller's Anna Ruth, 1926; Book of the Constitution, 1926; Sewing Susie, 1927; Book of the Colonies, 1927; What Everybody Wanted, 1928; Virginia's Bandit, 1929; You Make Your Own Luck, 1929; A Little Money Ahead, 1930; The Young Ravenels, 1932; Swords of Steel, 1933; The Magic Mirror, 1934; Stories of Pennsylvania, 3 vols., 1937, 1938; The Loving Heart, 1937; Rifles for Washington, 1938; also over 300 short stories in mags. Home: Gettysburg, Pa.

SINKLER, John P. B., architect; b. Phila., Pa., Sept. 10, 1875; s. Wharton and Ella (Brock) S.; grad. Episcopal Acad., De Lancey Sch., Phila.; B.S. in Architecture, U. of Pa., 1898; m. Mary P. Gadsden, June 11, 1917; children—Mary D., John P. B., Ella Brock. Began practice at Phila., 1902; mem. firm Bissell & Sinkler, 1906-32; firm architects for Confederate Memorial Inst., Richmond, Va.; Abingdon (Pa.) Memorial Hosp.; Sun Hill Village, Chester, Pa.; Noreg Village, Gloucester, N.J.; Germantown Municipal Bldg., Chestnut St. Pier, Girard Municipal Piers 3 and 5, all of Phila. City architect, Phila., 1920-24, and dir. of city architecture, Jan. 1932-Dec. 31, 1935; sec. Phila. Zoning Bd. of Adjustment, Aug. 1933-Dec. 1935. Fellow Am. Inst. Architects, Franklin Inst.; mem. Phi Kappa Sigma. Democrat. Episcopalian. Home: 26 Summit St., Chestnut Hill, Pa. Office: Architects Bldg., Phila., Pa.

SINN, Francis Peirce, corpn. official; b. Germantown, Phila., Pa., Oct. 7, 1882; s. Joseph Albert and Ella Thomas (Wise) S.; B.S., Central High Sch., Phila., 1900; E.M., Lehigh U., 1904; m. Margaret Cortright Convers, Oct. 10, 1906; 1 dau., Margaret Elizabeth (dec.). Employed as engr. with various concerns, summers 1902-05; asso. with New Jersey Zinc. Co. continuously since entering its employ, 1905, successively, chem. lab., chief spelter plant, asst. then supt. and gen. supt., all of Palmerton Works, asst. to vice-pres. in N.Y. City since 1919; vice-pres., mgr. and dir., Palmerton Lighting Co., Palmerton Telephone Co., Palmerton Disposal Co., all since 1917; dir. First Nat. Bank of Palmerton, Pa., 1914-26. Served as dir., mem. exec. com. Nat. Safety Council during World War and v.p. one yr. Trustee South Side Assn. of Montclair, N.J. Mem. Mining & Metall. Soc. America, Am. Inst. Mining & Metall. Engrs., Am. Iron & Steel Inst., Am. Zinc Inst., Montclair Soc. Engrs., Sigma Xi, Chi Psi. Republican. Unitarian. Mason. Clubs: Golf (Montclair); University, Downtown, Mining (New York); Blue Ridge Country (Palmerton, Pa.). Home: 129 Orange Rd., Montclair, N.J. Office: 160 Front St., New York, N.Y.

SINNOCK, John Ray, artist; b. Raton, N.M., July 8, 1888; s. Charles W. and Mattie (Ray) S.; ed. pub. sch. and high sch., Raton, N.M., 1906-09, Pa. Mus. Sch. of Art, 1909-14, grad. course, 1914-15. Engaged as artist, sculptor, and teacher of art since 1914; instr. art, Pa Mus. Sch. of Art, Phila., Pa., 1914-17; asst. medallist, U.S. Mint, Phila., 1917-20; instr. art and head of dept., Pa. Mus. Sch. of Art, 1920-24; designer with C. J. Connick Studios, Boston, Mass., 1924-26; chief medallist and engraver, U.S. Mint, Phila., since 1926, head engraving dept.; represented by many mural decorations in Phila. high schs., and by numerous medals, portrait medallions and memorial tablets in bas-relief. Hon. mem. Phila. Water Color Club. Mem. Nat. Sculpture Soc., Am. Artists Professional League, Am. Federation of Art, Phila. Sketch Club, Phila. Art Alliance. Home: 2022 Spring Garden St., Philadelphia, Pa. Office: U.S. Mint, Philadelphia, Pa.

SINNOTT, Arthur J., newspaper man; b. Newark, N.J., Apr. 4, 1886; s. John F. and Ellen T. (Scott) S.; ed. Cathedral School, Newark, Newark Tech. Sch.; New York U. Law Sch., 1910; m. Anne Dervin, Jan. 18, 1913. Reporter, Newark News, 1905-09, city editor, 1910-12; rep. same in Europe, 1918, Washington corr., 1912-25; became mng. editor Newark News, Nov. 1, 1925, Editor in chief Jan. 1, 1933. Clubs: Gridiron, Nat. Press, Overseas Writers, Baltusrol Golf (Short Hills); Essex (Newark). Office: Care Newark News, 215 Market St., Newark, N.J.

SIPE, Chester Hale, lawyer; b. Slate Lick, Pa., Nov. 16, 1880; s. Hiram Hill and Mary (Golden) S.; grad. Slate Lick Acad., 1900; A.B., Thiel Coll., Greenville, Pa., 1907, hon. D.Litt., 1930; studied law in office of Levi M. Wise, Butler, Pa.; m. Cleo V. McKee, Feb. 18, 1928. Admitted to Butler bar, 1909, Pittsburgh bar, 1915; taught Latin, German and science, Butler High Sch., also prin. Renfrew (Pa.) High Sch. and prin. Lyndora Night Sch. for Adult Foreigners while studying law; dep. collector internal revenue and revenue agt., Pittsburgh, 1914-20. Dem. candidate for Congress, 1928 (defeated but lead Dem. ticket); mem. Pa. Senate, 1936. Mem. Pa. Hist. Soc., Pa. German Soc., Swedish Colonial Soc., Western Pa. Hist. Soc. Democrat. Lutheran. Mason (32°). Author: Mount Vernon and the Washington Family; The Indian Chiefs of Pennsylvania; The Indian Wars of Pennsylvania; Fort Ligonier and Its Times; A History of Butler Co., Pa. Extensive lecturer on Pennsylvania history. Sponsored in Pa. Senate Pennsylvania's celebration of 300th anniversary of founding of New Sweden, 1638. Home: Route 1, Freeport, Pa. Office: Butler, Pa.

SIPES, Dwight Robert, physician and surgeon; b. Harrisonville, Pa., Aug. 28, 1893; s. R. R. and Etta (Garland) S.; ed. Temple U., 1916-17, Hahnemann Med. Sch., 1918-20, Cincinnati Med. Sch., 1920-22 (M.D. 1922), Cook Co. (Ill.) Post Grad. Sch., 1938-39; m. Thelma C. Metzler, Sept. 15, 1920; children—Kepner, Betty. Interne Sacred Heart Hosp., Allentown, Pa., 1922-23, surg. resident, 1923-25, surg. asst. to Dr. W. A. Hausman, Allentown,

1923-25; in gen. practice of medicine, Everett, Pa., 1925-30, developed Everett Hosp., 1930, and since supt., dir. and surgeon. Served in Med. Corps, U.S.A., 1917-18. Chmn. Co. Bd. of Pub. Assistance of Bedford Co., 1937-39. Mem. A.M.A., Pa., and Bedford Co. med. socs., Vets. Fgn. Wars, Am. Legion, Forty and Eight, Patriotic Sons of America. Democrat. Methodist. Mason. Home: 14 W. Main St., Everett, Pa.

SIPLE, Paul Allman, explorer, geographer, lecturer; b. Montpelier, O., Dec. 18, 1908; s. Clyde L. and Fannie Hope (Allman) S.; grad. Central High Sch., Erie, Pa., 1926; B.S., Allegheny Coll., Meadville, Pa., 1932; student Grad. Sch. of Geography, Clark University; m. Ruth I. Johannesmeyer, Dec. 1936. Youngest member Admiral Byrd's Antarctic Expdn., chosen after tests among 600,000 Boy Scouts of America; in charge of biol. and zoöl. work of the expdn., bringing back specimens of penguins and seals for the Am. Mus. of Natural History; head of biol. dept. Adm. Byrd's 2d expdn., 1933-35, and mem. Byrd's personal staff; in charge erecting and equipping the base in which Byrd lived alone 4½ mos. in 1934; leader Marie Byrd sledging party into newly discovered land; toured Europe, Asia Minor and N. Africa, off the beaten paths, 1932-33; in charge research on Antarctic problems for various instns. Fellow Am. Geog. Soc.; mem. nat. council and camping com. of Boy Scouts of America; 1st and present pres. Am. Polar Soc.; mem. Veterans Foreign Wars (hon.), Clark U. Geography Soc., Alpha Chi Rho, Omicron Delta Kappa, Phi Beta Phi, Alpha Phi Omega. Awarded Congressional medals, 1930, 1937; Heckel science prize, Hatfield award, 1931; etc. Methodist. Clubs: Exchange (Erie, Pa.); Kiwanis (Bloomington, Ill.). Author: A Boy Scout with Byrd, 1931; Exploring at Home, 1932; Scout to Explorer, 1936. Home: 1158 W. 5th St., Erie, Pa.

SIPPEL, Bettie Manroe, club woman; b. Baltimore, Md.; d. William Wesley and Melcena Elizabeth (Talbott) Oursler; ed. pub. schs. and under pvt. tutors; m. John F. Sippel, of Baltimore, Mar. 7, 1890; 1 dau., Dorothy (Mrs. Wm. H. Maltbie). Active in club work since 1903; served as v.p. and pres. Md. State Federation of Women's Clubs and as pres. Sorosis Club; also served as dir. of Md. for Gen. Fed. Women's Clubs, and as chmn. Finance Com. G.F.W.C.; elected pres. G.F.W.C., June 1928. Regent Baltimore Chapter D.A.R.; pres. Woman's Missionary Society of Brown Memorial Presbyn. Ch. Widely recognized as conductor of classes on current events. Mem. exec. com. President's Conf. on Home Building and Home Ownership; adviser, President's Orgn. on Unemployment Relief; mem. advisory com. Campaign Against Hoarding; mem. nat. council Inter-Am. Inst. of Intellectual Cooperation. Home: 307 St. Dunstan's Rd., Baltimore, Md.

SIPPLE, William Virden II, owner Wm. V. Sipple & Son; b. Milford, Del., Mar. 24, 1879; s. William Virden and Ruth Annie (Holland) S.; student Milford (Del.) Pub. Sch., 1885-96; m. Linda Ruthrup Draper, Nov. 22, 1905; children —William Virden III, Henry Draper, Ellen Gray. Marble and granite cutter with Wm. V. Sipple, Milford, Del., 1896-1900, partner Wm. V. Sipple & Son, monument and memorial mfrs., 1900-1911, owner since 1911; dir. Milford (Del.) Trust Co. since 1917, v.p., 1924-38, pres. since 1938; v.p. Kent & Sussex Bldg. & Loan Assn., Milford, Del., 1919-38, pres. and dir. since 1938; dir. L.D. Caulk Co. Trustee and pres. of bd., Avenue Episcopal Ch., Milford, Del. Mem. Del. Soc. S.A.R. Republican. Methodist. Mason (Royal Arch), Odd Fellow. Club: Rehoboth Beach (Del.) Country (mem. bd. of govs. since 1926; pres., 1928-29). Address: Milford, Del.

SISSON, Edgar Grant, editor, author; b. Alto, Wis., Dec. 23, 1875; s. Earl Truman and Lucy (Learned) S.; Northwestern U., 1894-97; m. Dixie, d. Ralph A. and Frances M. Ladd, Apr. 27, 1898; children—Mildred (Mrs. Daly King), Edgar. Coll. corr. and staff reporter Chicago Chronicle, 1895-98; reporter, 1898-99, dramatic editor, 1899-1901, Chicago Tribune; asst. city editor, 1902, city editor, 1903, Chicago American; asst. city editor, 1903-09, city editor, 1909-11, Chicago Tribune; mng. editor Collier's Weekly, 1911-14; editor Cosmopolitan Magazine, 1914-17; asso. chmn. Com. on Pub. Information, Washington, D.C., May 13, 1917-Apr. 1, 1919, and gen. dir. of fgn. sect.; organized the publication and distribution of President Wilson's speeches throughout Russia, winter of 1917-18; made to President Wilson the personal report pub. by the govt., Sept. 1918, under the title "The German-Bolshevik Conspiracy"; organized the committee's service at the Paris Peace Conf., 1918-19. Mem. Delta Upsilon. Decorated Cavalier Order of the Crown (Italy), 1919. Clubs: The Players, Dutch Treat (New York). Author: 100 Red Days, a Personal Chronicle of the Bolshevik Revolution, 1917-18, 1931. Home: Montclair, N.J. Office: 10 E. 40th St., C. Byoir & Associates, New York, N.Y.

SISSON, Nelson White, physician; b. Bedford City, Va., Dec. 31, 1899; s. Landon Sydnor and Clemmintine (Jennings) S.; ed. U. of Va., 1918-19; B.S., Coll. of William and Mary, 1920; M.D., U. of Va. Med. Sch., 1924; m. Lucile Harrison, Mar. 1, 1932. Instr. dept. otolaryngology, N.Y. Univ. Coll. of Medicine since 19—; asst. visiting surg., dept. otolaryngology, Bellevue Hosp. N.Y. City, Orange Memorial Hosp., Orange, N.J., East Orange Gen. Hosp., East Orange, N.J., Presbyn. Hosp., Newark, N.J.; adjunct laryngologist, Seaside Hosp., New Dorp Beach, N.Y.; practice limited to the diseases of the ear, nose and throat. Served in Student Army Training Corps. 1918. Fellow American College Surgeons. Mem. Am. Bd. Otolaryngology, Va. State and N.J. State med. socs., Orange Mountain Med. Soc., Phi Chi. Baptist. Home: 69 Winding Way, West Orange. Office: 144 Harrison St., East Orange, N.J.

SITTERLY, Charles Fremont, theologian; b. Liverpool, N.Y., June 4, 1861; s. Peter and Lucy Bancroft (Walker) S.; A.B., Syracuse U., 1883, A.M., 1885, Ph.D., 1886, S.T.D., 1900; B.D., Drew Theol. Sem., 1886; studied Oxford, Bonn, Heidelberg, Leipzig, Berlin, 1890-92; m. Julia Cobb Buttz, Dec. 22, 1891; children—Anson Buttz (dec.), Bancroft Walker, Alice Hoagland, Emily Buttz, Hildegarde Anne, Katharine, Julia Charlotte, Lois Elizabeth. Ordained M.E. ministry, 1887; pastor Chester, N.J., 1886-88, Cranford, 1888-89, Madison, 1889-90; adj. prof. Greek and prof. English Bible, 1892-94, prof. Bibl. lit. and English Bible, 1895-1935, Drew U. Theol. Sch. Mem. Phi Beta Kappa, Am. Philol. Assn., Soc. Bibl. Lit. and Exegesis. Author: Praxis in Manuscripts of Greek New Testament, 1898; History of English Bible (with S. G. Ayres), 1899; Canon, Text and Manuscripts of the New Testament, 1914; Jerusalem to Rome—The Acts of the Apostles, 1915; Henry Anson Buttz—His Book (Life and Writings), 2 vols., 1922; The Building of Drew University, 1937. Contbr. to religious periodicals. Address: 30 Green Av., Madison, N.J.

SKARIATINA, Irina (Mrs. Victor Franklin Blakeslee) author and lecturer; b. at St. Petersburg, Russia; d of General Wladimir and Princess Mary (Lobanov of Rostov) Skariatina; educated in St. Petersburg, Russia; graduate of St. Eugenia School of Red Cross Nursing and Medical Institute; was maid of honor to Empress of Russia; m. Count Alexander Kellar (divorced, 1916); m. 2d, Victor Franklin Blakeslee, June 14, 1926. Came to America, 1923, naturalized, 1929. Began as writer and lecturer, 1930. Hon. mem. Red Cross; v.p. Women's Patriotic Soc.; hon. mem. Booksellers Assn., Theta Sigma Phi. Russian Orthodox Ch. Author: A World Can End, 1931; A World Begins, 1932; First to Go Back, 1933; Little Era in Old Russia, 1934; New Worlds for Old (with V. F. Blakeslee), 1935. Contbr. to mags. Home: Edgewood, St. David, Pa. Address: Care of Bobbs Merrill Pub. Co., 468 4th Av., New York, N.Y.

SKELLEY, William Charles, univ. prof.; b. Cleveland, O., Mar. 18, 1896; s. James Robert and Harriet (Baldwin) S.; B.S. in Agr., Ohio State U., Columbus, 1918, M.S., 1923; unmarried. Instr. of animal husbandry, Rutgers U., 1919-20, asst. prof., 1920-22, leave of absence, 1922-23, asso. prof., 1923-27, prof. animal husbandry since 1927; animal husbandman, N.J. Agrl. Expt. Station, since 1927. Dir. New Brunswick Chamber of Commerce. Mem. Am. Soc. of Animal Production. Presbyn. Mason, Elk. Clubs: Union, Lawrence Brook Country (New Brunswick); Forsgate Country (Jamesburg); Lions. Home: 119 Livingston Av., New Brunswick, N.J.

SKELLY, Daniel J., lawyer; b. Oil City, Pa., July 2, 1892; s. Joseph G. and Bridget (Moriarty) S.; LL.B., Notre Dame U. Law Sch., 1914; m. Ruth M. Mansfield, June 27, 1928; children—Julie Ann, Joseph G. Admitted to Pa. bar, 1917 and since engaged in gen. practice of law at Oil City; served as dist. atty. of Venango Co., 1930-34; mem. firm Skelly and Mogelowitz. Mem. Am. Legion. Republican. Roman Catholic. K.C. Elk. Home: 310 Innis St. Office: Oil City Nat. Bank Bldg., Oil City, Pa.

SKILLERN, Samuel Ruff, Jr., otolaryngologist; b. Phila., Pa., Apr. 16, 1885; s. Samuel Ruff and Sarah Hall (Ross) S.; student Phila. High Sch., 1902-06; M.D., U. of Pa., 1913; m. Elizabeth Morrow Corkran, June 7, 1919; children—Virginia Adams (dec.), Sarah Adams, Nancy Ross, Elizabeth Corkran. Dispensary asst. in otolaryngology, U. of Pa. Grad. Sch., 1910-13, clin. asst., 1915-17, asst., 1919-21, asst. prof. otolaryngology, 1921-29, asso. prof. since 1930. Commd. by Presibent Wilson 1st lt., Med. Res. Corps, U.S. Army, 1916; active service, World War, 1917-19, A.E.F., 1918-19; commd. capt., 1917, maj., 1919, lt.-col., 1925, col., 1932; comdg. officer, Gen. Hosp. 20 since 1932. Mem. Am. Coll. Physicians, Phila. Laryngol. Soc. (pres., 1933-35), Pa. State Med. Soc., Phila. Co. Med. Soc., A.M.A., Acad. of Ophthalmology and Otolaryngology, Am. Laryngol., Rhinol. and Otol. Soc., Officers Fgn. Wars, Am. Legion. Republican. Episcopalian. Clubs: Medical, University, Phila. Country (Phila., Pa.); Edgewater Hunting and Fishing (N.C.). Home: Yale & Overhill Rd., Bala-Cynwyd, Pa. Office: 1734 Pine St., Philadelphia, Pa.

SKILLINGTON, James Edgar, clergyman; b. Breezewood, Pa., Dec. 2, 1878; s. Robert Martin and Elmira (McLaughlin) S.; A.B., Williamsport Dickinson Sem., 1900; A.B., Dickinson Coll., Carlisle, Pa., 1905, A.M., 1910; (hon.) D.D., 1922; ed. Drew Theol. Sem., Madison, N.J., 1905-06; m. Louetta Hartzell, Dec. 27, 1905; children—Susan Virgin (Mrs. John Louis Priebe), James Edgar. Began as teacher pub. schs., 1895; entered ministry M.E. Church as student pastor, 1900; pastor at various chs., 1900-22; pastor, Altoona, Pa., 1922-30; supt. Altoona Dist., 1930-35; pastor, Bloomsburg, Pa., since 1935; del. to Gen. Conf., 1924-36 and to Uniting Conf., 1939; sec. World Service Commn.; pres. trustees Central Pa. Annual Conf. Trustee Dickinson Jr. Coll., Wesley Foundation of Pa. State Coll. Mem. Phi Kappa Sigma. Republican. Methodist. Mason. (32°), Rotarian. Home: 311 Market St., Bloomsburg, Pa.

SKILLMAN, David B(ishop), lawyer; b. Phila., Pa., Mar. 24, 1887; s. Rev. Willis Bishop and Annie Walker (Gayley) S.; B.S. in economics, Central High Sch., Phila., 1907; A.B., Lafayette Coll., 1913; m. Frances C. Bouchette, Feb. 3, 1934; children—Judith Bouchette, David Bishop, Willis Bishop. Studied law in office E. J. & J. W. Fox, Easton, Pa.; admitted to Pa. bar, 1916, and since practiced in Easton; pres. Lafayette Silk Co., Easton; treas. John H. Hagerty Lumber Co., Phillipsburg, N.J.; treas. Haytock Silk Throwing Co., Easton; dir. Easton Trust Co., Skytop Lodges, Inc. Served as ednl. dir. S.A.T.C., 1918. Trustee Lafayette Coll., Alborz Coll. (Teheran, Iran), Moravian Sem. and Coll. for Women, Easton Hosp., Pa. Hosp Assn. Mem. Am. and Pa. State bar assns., Theta Delta Chi. Republican. Presbyterian. Clubs: Pomfret, Northampton Country (Easton); Skytop (Monroe Co.). Author: The Biography of a College (a history of Lafayette Coll.), 1932. Contbr. articles on hospital and hist. subjects. Home: 640 Lafayette St. Office: Easton Trust Bldg., Easton, Pa.

SKILLMAN, Thomas Julien, civil engr.; b. Trenton, N.J., Nov. 6, 1876; s. Luther S. and

Mary B. S.; C.E., Princeton, 1898; m. Louise E. Jenkinson, Oct. 26, 1904; children—Margaret B., Thomas J., Richard J., Charlotte L. Began as rodman Pa. R.R., Mar. 1, 1899, and continued with same rd. successively as transitman, 1902; asst. supervisor, 1902-05; supervisor, 1905-13; div. engr., N.Y., Phila. & Norfolk R.R., 1913-14, West Jersey & Seashore R.R., 1914-17, Pa. R.R., 1917-19; prin. asst. engr., Eastern Pa. Div., Pa. R.R., 1919-20; chief engr. maintenance of way, Northwestern Region, and later Western Region, Pa. R.R., Chicago, 1920-26; asst. chief engr. of constrn., Western Region, Pa. R.R., Chicago, 1926; chief engr. Long Island R.R., July 1926-Feb. 1927; chief engr. Pa. R.R., Phila., 1927-36, chief engr., consultant, since Oct. 1, 1936. Republican. Presbyterian. Clubs: Union League, Princeton (Phila); St. David's Golf (Wayne, Pa.); Nassau, Cottage (Princeton, N.J.). Home: 124 St. Georges Road, Ardmore, Pa. Office: Broad Street Station Bldg., Philadelphia, Pa.

SKINKER, Murray F(ontaine), physicist; b. Denver, Colo., Apr. 12, 1898; s. George Murray and Myrtle Estelle (Gutzler) S.; B.S. in E.E., U. of Colo., 1919, M.S. in physics, same, 1921; Ph.D. in physics, Oxford U., 1924; m. Marguerite Dorothea Miller, Apr. 2, 1926; children—Thomas Murray, Neil Gilman. Engaged as asst. research engr. Brooklyn Edison Co., 1924-26, asst. dir. research, 1926-37; asso. dir. research, Consolidated Edison Co. of N.Y. since 1937. Fellow Am. Inst. Elec. Engrs. Mem. Am. Phys. Soc., Am. Soc. for Testing Materials. Rhodes scholar from Colo. to Oxford U., 1921. Republican. Conglist. Mason. Club: Cosmopolitan (Montclair). Home: 112 North Mountain Av., Montclair, N.J. Office: 55 Johnson St., Brooklyn, N.Y.

SKINNER, Charles Edward, electrical engr.; b. Redfield, Perry Co., O., May 30, 1865; s. Thomas Peter and Harriet Newell (Brown) S.; Ohio U., Sc.D., 1927; M.E., Ohio State University, 1890; D.Eng., Ohio State University, 1935; m. Harrietta Gladys McVay (B.Ph. and B.Ped., Ohio U., 1889), Apr. 25, 1893; children—Dorothy Harriet, Anna Florence, Charles Edward, Bertha Gladys, Thomas McVay. With Columbus Cash Register Co., June-Aug. 1890; with the Westinghouse Elec. & Mfg. Co., 1890-1933; successively, insulation testing and design, and iron and steel testing, to 1902; engr. insulation div. (including phys., chem. and elec. labs.), 1902-06; engr. research div., 1906-20; mgr. research dept., 1920-21; asst. dir. engring., 1922-33. Mem. Nat. Research Council (exec. com.), 1917-18, engring. div., 1921—, engring. council, 1918-20; chmn. Am. Engring. Standards Com., 1925-27; mem. Federated Am. Eng. Soc. and Am. Engring. Council, 1923—; chmn. Am. delegation Internat. Electrotech. Commn., Brussels, 1920, Geneva, 1922; del. same, London, 1924, Hague, 1925, Amsterdam, 1926, Bellagio, 1927; del. World's Power Conf., London, 1924; spl. rep. of Am. Inst. Elec. Engrs. at Conf. on Elec. Standards bet. Can., Gt. Britain and U.S., London, Mar. 1915; chmn. orgn. com. Internat. Standards Assn., Apr. 1926, rep. for further orgn., London, Sept. 1926, U.S. mem. council since 1931. Fellow Am. Inst. E.E. (v.p. and mem. exec. com., 1919-20, standards com. since 1910; pres. 1931-32); mem. Am. Physical Soc., A.A.A.S., Am. Soc. Testing Materials, Am. Petroleum Inst., Am. Electrochem. Soc., Engring. Soc., Western Pa., Pittsburgh Acad. Science and Art, Pittsburgh Philos. Soc., Franklin Inst., Beta Theta Pi, Sigma Psi, Tau Beta Pi, Sigma Tau. Mem. John Fritz Medal Bd. of Award, 1931-34, Edison Medal Com., 1929-32. Awarded Lamme gold medal, Ohio State U., 1931. Presbyn. Iwadare Foundation lecturer, Japan, 1934. Contbr. to tech. press and engring. socs. Home: 215 Elmore Road, Wilkinsburg, Pa.

SKINNER, Charles Edward, univ. prof.; b. Newark, O., Apr. 24, 1891; s. Morris Allen and Martha Leota (Loughman) S.; B.S. in Edn., Ohio U., 1914; spl. grad. study, Cornell U., 1914, and Teachers Coll. (Columbia), 1922-23; A.M., Univ. of Chicago, 1916; Ph.D., New York U., 1923; m. Mary Ethel Shuman, Aug. 5, 1917; children—Charles Edward, William James. Teacher pub. schs., St. Louisville, O., 1909-10; instr. in psychology, Ohio U., 1914-16, asst. prof. psychology, 1916-19; prof. pholosophy and psychology, Mount Union Coll., 1919-20; prof. edn., State Teachers Coll., Indiana, Pa., 1920-22; instr. in edn., New York U., 1922-23; lecturer at the Silver Bay Conferences of Y.M.C.A. secretaries, summer of 1923; prof. education, group dir. and acting dean of summer sch., Miami University, Oxford, Ohio., 1923-25; asst. prof., ednl. psychology, New York U., 1925-28; asso. prof., 1928-30, prof. edn. since 1930; chmn. sch. edn. faculty com. on publicity and publications, 1936-27, of alumni relations and student affairs, 1927-30, of student affairs since 1930; psychologist Cowles Foundation Psychiatric Clinic, N.Y. City, 1932-33. Served as 2d lt. inf., U.S.A. at Camp Custer, U. of Pittsburgh, and S.A.T.C., Lebanon Valley (Pa.) Coll., 1917-19. Awarded New York U. Alumni Meritorious Service Medallion, 1932. Mem. Am. Psychol. Assn., A.A.A.S., Am. Assn. Univ. Professors, Soc. for Scientific Study of Education, N.E.A., College Teachers of Education, American Association of Applied Psychologists, Phi Kappa Tau, Phi Delta Kappa, Kappa Delta Pi, Kappa Phi Kappa. Co-author: Psychology for Teachers, 1926, revised edition, 1933; Story and Study Reading Series, 1928; Psychology for Religious and Social Workers, 1930; Biological Foundations for Education, 1931; Good Manners for Young Americans, 1932; Introduction to Modern Education, 1937; Psychology in Everyday Living, 1938. Editor Ednl. Service Jour., 1928-32. Co-Editor: Readings in Educational Psychology, 1926; Readings in Psychology, 1935; Educational Psychology, 1936; Readings in Educational Psychology, 1937; Mental Hygiene and the Modern Education, 1939. Contbr. to Classroom Guide to the Book of Knowledge, 1929, also articles and revs. in ednl. publs. Home: 5 Highland Av., Madison, N.J. Office: 100 Washington Sq., New York, N.Y.

SKINNER, Charles Wilbur, irrigation specialist; b. Troy, O., July 12, 1864; s. Elias and Martha Jane (Orbison) S.; ed. country schs.; m. Elena M. Dougherty, June 18, 1895; children—Ella (Mrs. Philip Clark Hanford), Charles Robert, Edna Kate, Henry Vance. Began as market gardener, 1874; constructed rude system of overhead field irrigation lines in order to save crops during period of drought, 1896; worked on improvements and perfected systems first placed on sale, 1904; founder of Skinner Irrigation Co., Troy, O., 1904; established firm of C. W. Skinner & Co., Newfield, N.J., 1912. Republican. Presbyterian. Home: Newfield, N.J.

SKINNER, Clarence Aurelius, physicist; b. Loudoun Co., Va., Jan. 6, 1871; s. John Thomas and Susanne (Tinsman) S.; B.Sc., U. of Neb., 1893, grad. student and fellow in physics, 1893-96; U. of Berlin, 1896-99, Ph.D., 1899; m. Christabel Ditchburn, 1916; 1 son, John William. Demonstrator physics, 1899-1901, adj. prof., 1901-03, asst. prof., 1903-06, prof. and head dept. physics, 1906-19, U. of Neb. Chief, optical div. U.S. Bur. of Standards, 1919—. Baptist. Mem. Am. Phys. Soc. Home: Kensington, Md.

SKINNER, Clifford Weld, M.D.; b. Ashville, Chautauqua Co., N.Y., Oct. 2, 1892; s. Aaron (M.D.) and Emma (Weld) S.; grad. Lakewood (N.Y.) High Sch., 1910; B.S., Allegheny Coll., Meadville, Pa., 1921, M.S., 1923; student Northwestern U. Med. Sch., 1924-25; M.D., U. of Chicago, 1930; studied U. of Chicago, summers, 1921, 24, 25, 26, 27; m. Ruth McCafferty, June 11, 1925; children—Ruth Ann, Clifford Weld, Frank Dair, Don Covill. Instr. biology, Allegheny Coll., 1921-24; asst. in anatomy, Northwestern U., 1924-25; asso. in anatomy and later asso. prof. anatomy and asst. dean Med. Sch., Med. Coll. of Va., Richmond, 1925-28 and 1930-31; asst. prof. biology, Allegheny Coll., 1931-33, dir. of health since 1931; specialized in anesthesia, Lahey Clinic, Boston, 1935; in private practice of medicine since 1931. Dir. and trustee (treas.) Y.M.C.A. of Meadville. Fellow A.M.A., Internat. Coll. Anesthetists; mem. Am. Soc. Anesthetists, Crawford Co. Med. Soc. (sec.), Alpha Chi Rho, Delta Sigma Rho, Phi Beta Kappa, Phi Rho Sigma, Alpha Omega Alpha. Republican. Presbyn. (elder). Mason (York and Scottish Rites). Clubs: Meadville Kiwanis, Meadville Round Table. Home and Office: 295 N. Main St., Meadville, Pa.

SKINNER, Homer Lucas, surgeon; b. May 19, 1901; s. William and Floy (Lucas) S.; A.B., U. of Ohio, 1921; M.D., U. of Cincinnati Med. Sch., 1925; m. Nina Osborn, 1924; children—Homer L., Betty Anne, Donald, Robert. Interne U.S. Marine Hosp., Norfolk, Va., 1925; asst. surgeon U.S. Marine Hosp., Ellis Island, N.Y., 1926-27; chief surgeon U.S. Marine Hosp., Savannah, Ga., 1927-32, New Orleans, 1932-35, Baltimore since 1935; surgeon U.S.P.H.S., Washington, D.C. Fellow Am. Coll. Surgeons; mem. A.M.A.; asso. mem. Baltimore City Med. Soc.; mem. Phi Kappa Tau, Phi Chi. Address: U.S. Marine Hospital, Baltimore, Md.

SKINNER, Laila, dean of women; b. Speedsville, N.Y., Mar. 19, 1898; d. Charles Drake and Alberta (Harding) S.; A.B., MacMurray Coll., Jacksonville, Ill., 1921; M.B., U. of Rochester, 1923; A.M., State U. of Ia., 1930, Ph.D., same, 1932. Teacher of piano, Eastman Sch. of Music, U. of Rochester, 1923-29; asst. dir. Cook Co. Sch. of Nursing, Chicago, Ill., 1932-35; asst. dean of women and asso. prof. psychology, Ill. State Normal U., Normal, Ill., 1935-36; dean of women and asso. prof. psychology, Allegheny Coll., since 1936. Asso. mem. Am. Psychol. Assn. Mem. A.A.A.S., Nat. Assn. Deans of Women, Am. Assn. Univ. Women, Business and Professional Womens Clubs, Mu Phi Epsilon. Methodist. Home: Hulings Hall, Meadville, Pa.

SKINNER, William A(rthur), lawyer; b. Starrucca, Pa., June 23, 1875; s. James and Eliza Josephine (Penn) S.; student N.Y. Law School, 1895-96; certificate of LL.B. from U. of State of N.Y.; m, Grace M. Burrhus, Apr. 30, 1902; children—Burrhus Frederic, Edward James (deceased). Admitted to Pa. bar, 1896, and practiced in Susquehanna and Scranton; atty. for Erie R.R. Co., 1907-22, Hudson Coal Co., 1922-26. Mem. Lackawanna Co., Pa. State and Am. bar assns. Republican. Presbyterian. Clubs: Kiwanis (Scranton); Scranton Country (Clarks Summit, Pa.). Author: Skinner's Pa. Workmen's Compensation Law, 1924, 1930, 1938. Home: 2001 N. Washington Av. Office: Scranton Life Bldg., Scranton, Pa.

SKINNER, William Sherman, clergyman; b. Gouverneur, N.Y., Feb. 3, 1906; s. William Franklin and Katharine Jane (Markwick) S.; ed. Princeton U., 1923-25; A.B., Colgate U., 1927; Th.B., Princeton Theol. Sem., 1930, Th.M., same, 1931; grad. study, Univs. of Berlin and Marburg, Germany, 1931-32; m. Helen Mildred Loetscher, June 6, 1931; children—William Franklin II, Sherman. Ordained to ministry Presbyn. Ch., 1930; pastor, Bethlehem, Pa., 1933-36; pastor First Presbyn. Ch. in Germantown, Phila., Pa., since 1936. Mem. Phi Gamma Delta. Republican. Presbyn. Home: 6012 Greene St. Office: 39 W. Chelten Av., Germantown, Philadelphia, Pa.

SKOSS, Solomon Leon, prof. of Arabic; b. Tchusovaya, Perm, Russia, May 5, 1884; s. Samuel and Blume (Teizlin) S.; came to U.S., 1907, naturalized, 1913; A.B., U. of Denver, 1913, A.M., same, 1914; grad. student U. of Pa., 1922; Ph.D., Dropsie Coll., 1926; student Université Egyptiènne, and Sch. of Oriental Studies, Cairo, Egypt, 1924-25; m. Irene C. Kapnek, Mar. 5, 1926; 1 dau., Sarah Theodora. Instr. of Arabic, Dropsie Coll., 1925-32, asso. prof., 1932-34, prof. since 1934. Fellow Am. Acad. for Jewish Research. Mem. A.A.A.S., Soc. Bib. Literature and Exegesis, Am. Oriental Soc., Sigma Phi Alpha. Awarded grants by Am. Council of Learned Socs. for research work in State Pub. Library, Leningrad, Russia, 1932, and by Am. Philos. Soc., 1939, for assistance in preparation of Vol. II of the Hebrew-Arabic Dictionary of the Bible. Democrat. Jewish religion. Club: Oriental of Philadelphia (past pres.). Author and Editor: The Arabic Commentary of Ali ben Suleiman the Karaite on the Book of Genesis, 1928; Hebrew-Arabic Dictionary of the Bible of David ben Abraham al-Fasi

(10th century), Vol. I, 1936, Vol. II in preparation. Contbr. to encyc. and sci. mags. Home: 1135 W. Wyoming Av., Philadelphia, Pa.

SKUTCH, Alexander Frank, naturalist; b. Baltimore, Md., May 20, 1904; s. Robert Frank and Rachel (Frank) S.; A.B., Johns Hopkins (U., 1925, Ph.D., 1928; unmarried. Engaged in bot. research in Panama and Honduras on fellowship of Johns Hopkins U., 1928-30, Nat. Research Council fellowship, 1930-31; instr. botany, Johns Hopkins U., 1931-32; bot. collector for Arnold Arboretum in Guatemala, 1934; engaged in bus. on own acct. in bot. collecting, also in research studies of life histories of birds chiefly in Costa Rica, Guatemala and Panama; collections of plants for sale to museums and herberia in U.S. and Europe. Served as scoutmaster, Boy Scouts of America, Garrison, Md., 1925-28. Mem. Am. Ornithologists Union. Contributed many articles on botany and ornithology to tech. jours. Home: 2210 Crest Road, Baltimore, Md.

SKUTCH, Rachel Frank (Mrs. Robert Frank Skutch), social service; b. Baltimore, Md., Oct. 25, 1880; d. Alexander and Henrietta (Walter) Frank; student Sarah Randolph Sch., Girl's Latin Sch., Baltimore, Md., 1887-98; m. Robert Frank Skutch, June 17, 1902; children —Alexander Frank, Frances Poe (Mrs. John Poe Tyler), Robert Frank, Jr., Raphael Walter. Served as presiding officer or bd. mem. in many communal orgns. on vol. basis; exec. dir. Volunteer Bureau, a social service orgn., Baltimore, Md., since 1931; past pres. Baltimore dist., Md. Fed. of Women's Clubs, Council of Jewish Women, Fed. of Jewish Women's Orgns. of Md. Democrat. Jewish religion. Club: Woman's City of Baltimore (program chmn.). Home: 2210 Crest Road. Office: 16 W. Saratoga St., Baltimore, Md.

SKWEIR, John, lawyer; b. McAdoo, Pa., May 1, 1890; s. Andrew and Eva (Yankowiczk) S.; student Bloomsburg State Teachers Coll.; A.B., U. of Pa.; J.D., U. of Chicago; unmarried. Prin. East Union Twp. High Sch., 1915-17; supervising prin. East Union Twp. Schs., 1917; admitted to bar in all courts of Schuylkill County, Superior Ct. of Pa., Supreme Ct. of Pa., Federal Ct. in Eastern Dist. of Pa., Apr. 6, 1925; postmaster McAdoo, Pa., 1924-29; apptd. atty. for receiver of closed banks, Mar. 1, 1935; dir. First Nat. Bank of McAdoo; pres. bd. trustees for Waiving Depositors of First Nat. Bank of McAdoo. Solicitor Kline Twp. Sch. Dist. and Bd. of Supervisors of Kline Twp. since 1935. Served as field clerk, U.S. Army, 1918; retired in U.S. Army Officers Res. as 1st lt. Organizer and past pres. ARUS of Schuylkill County and ARUS National; solicitor Providence Assn. of Ukrainian Catholics in America. Club: Lions of Hazelton (ex-pres.). Home: 300 S. Tamaqua St. Office: 106 S. Tamaqua St., McAdoo, Pa.

SLACK, Harry Richmond, Jr., surgeon; b. LaGrange, Ga., Nov. 29, 1888; s. Henry R. and Ruth (Bradfield) S.; A.B., U. of Ga., 1908; M.D., Johns Hopkins U. Med. Sch., 1912; grad. student U. of Berlin, 1913, U. of Vienna, 1923; m. Elizabeth Randall, June 14, 1922; children—Henry R., III, Wyatt Cameron, Elizabeth B. R. Served as house officer Johns Hopkins Hosp., 1912-16; capt. Am. Red Cross in France, 1914-15; instr. and asso. prof. otolaryngology, Johns Hopkins U. Med. Sch., 1919; visiting prof. otolaryngology, Peking, China, 1922-23; exec. surgeon, Presbyn. Eye, Ear and Throat Charity Hosp. since 1924. Served as 1st lt. and capt. Med. Corps, U.S.A., 1917-19, with A.E.F. in France. Fellow Am. Coll. Surgeons; mem. A.M.A., A.A.A.S., Phi Delta Theta. Democrat. Presbyn. Clubs: Maryland, 14 Hamilton St., Elkridge (Baltimore); Gibson Island (Gibson Island, Md.). Home: 8 E. Bishop Rd. Office: 1100 N. Charles St., Baltimore, Md.

SLACK, Henry R., Jr.; asso. in otolaryngology, Johns Hopkins U.; dispensary otolaryngologist Johns Hopkins Hosp.; surgeon Presbyn. Eye, Ear and Throat Charity Hosp.; visiting laryngologist Union Memorial, Bon Secours and Children's hosps., Church Home and Infirmary and Hosp. for Women of Md. Address: 1100 N. Charles St., Baltimore, Md.

SLACK, Norris Harlan, automobile dealer; b. Strickersville, Chester Co., Pa., Mar. 10, 1891; s. Norris B. and Mary B. (Miller) S.; grad. West Chester High Sch., 1910; B.S. in engring., Pa. State Coll., 1914; m. Sarah B. Roberts, July 25, 1917; children—Norris Harlan, Mary Virginia. Began as automobile salesman, 1914; automobile business as partner, 1915-25; propr. N. Harlan Slack, automobile sales and service, since 1925; dir. First Nat. Bank of West Chester; dir. West Chester Bldg. & Loan Assn. Served as 1st lt., later capt., Motor Transport Corps, U.S. Army, with A.E.F. in France and Germany, 1917-19. Mem. West Chester Borough Council, 1924-26, West Chester Sch. Bd. since 1932, now treas. Mem. West Chester Bd. of Trade (past pres.); West Chester Civic Assn. (pres.). Chmn. Community Chest Drive, 1938. Mem. West Chester Rotary Club (past pres.). Mem. Sigma Phi Epsilon, Tau Beta Pi, Phi Kappa Phi. Republican. Methodist. Mason (K.T.). Home: E. Ashbridge Av. Office: 116 W. Market St., West Chester, Pa.

SLADE, James Jeremiah, Jr., asso. prof. engring. mech.; b. Uruapan, Michoacan, Mexico, June 25, 1900; s. James Jeremiah and Consuelo (Faris) S., citizens of U.S.; ed. Cornell U., 1919-21; B.S. in C.E., U. of N.C. 1923, M.S., 1929; m. Margaret Emily Slack, Oct. 28, 1925; 1 son, James Jeremiah, III. Employed as engr. in Mexico, 1923-27; asst. and instr. civil engring., U. of N.C., 1929-31; asst. prof. engring. mech., Rutgers U., 1931-35, asso. prof. since 1935, head of div. since 1938; asso. engr. U.S. Geol. Survey, Miss. Valley Com., 1934. Mem. Soc. for Promotion Engring. Edn., Nat. Geophys. Union, Sigma Chi, Tau Beta Pi, Sigma Xi, Sigma Upsilon. Contbr. tech. articles to sci. jours., also short stories. Author: (novel) Jacinto Duran, serialized in Mexican Life, monthly mag., Mexico City. Home: 177 Somerset St., New Brunswick, N.J.

SLANTZ, Fred William, coll. prof.; b. Scranton, Pa., Feb. 18, 1890; s. John C. and Mary (Rice) S.; B.S. in C.E., U. of Pa., 1912, C.E., 1923; m. Mary Davis, Sept. 19, 1919; children—William, Betty, Robert. Instr. in graphics, Lafayette Coll., Easton, Pa., 1915-17, asst. prof., 1921-24, prof. since 1924, dir. James Lee Pardee Placement Bur.; field engr., Interstate Commerce Commn. R.R. Valuation, C.&O. Ry., 1915-17. Served as capt., U.S. Army Air Corps. Formerly dir. Community Chest Campaign. Mem. Parent-Teachers Assn. of Easton (ex-pres.), Am. Assn. Univ. Profs., Am. Soc. C.E., Soc. for Promotion of Engring. Edn., Theta Xi, Tau Beta Pi. Clubs: Faculty, Lehigh Valley Engrs. Address: 600 Clinton Terrace, Easton, Pa.

SLATER, John Elliot, cons. engr.; b. Somerville, Mass., Aug. 11, 1891; s. Fred Raymond and Millie Eva (Gilereast) S.; grad. Somerville Latin Sch., 1909; A.B., Harvard, 1913; grad. Sch. of Business Administration Harvard, 1913; m. Pauline Mabie Holman, June 7, 1916; children—Marilyn, Dorothy Holman, Philip Elliot. With U.P.R.R., 1913-14; in employ N.Y., N.H.&H.R. R.R., 1914-25, as statistician and analyst, and last 5 yrs. as asst. to gen. mgr.; prof. transportation, U. of Ill., 1925-26; sec. and treas. Am. Brown Boveri Electric Corpn., Riverton, N.J., 1926-29; with Coverdale & Colpitts, cons. engrs., New York, since 1929, now mem. firm; exec. v.p. Am. Export Lines, Inc., Am. Export Airlines, Inc. Served as 1st lt. engrs., U.S.A., Feb.-Oct. 1918; commd. capt. Transportation Corps, Oct. 1918; overseas, Mar. 1918-June 1919. Mem. Am. Economics Assn., Phi Beta Kappa. Episcopalian. Clubs: Harvard (New York); Graduate (New Haven, Conn.); Essex Fells Country. Home: 118 Cooper Av., Upper Montclair, N.J. Office: 120 Wall St., New York, N.Y.

SLAUGHTER, Evans Griffiths, railroad exec.; b. Rio Grande, N.J., June 7, 1873; s. Dr. James Madison and Elizabeth (Griffiths) S.; ed. Rio Grande Grade Sch. and Cape May Court House High Sch.; m. Martha Simpson Bennett, Jan. 12, 1898. Hotel owner and proprietor, 1898-1907, Aldine Apts., 1907-22; assisted in organizing and building Wildwood & Delaware Bay Short Line R.R. Co., 1910-12, v.p. and gen. mgr., 1912-32 (majority of stock sold Reading R.R. Co., 1930); assisted in organizing, 1920, and v.p. City of Wildwood Bldg. & Loan Assn. until 1930; pres. Middle Bldg. & Loan Assn., until 1937; owner and publisher Tribune-Journal, 1918-38; one of organizers, 1925, Fidelity Trust Co., pres. until 1932 (sold to Marine Nat. Bank of Wildwood); resigned as officer or dir. of all companies except as owner and promoter Wildwood Gardens (real estate developers). Mem. Gen. Assembly from Cape May County, 1932. Democrat. Baptist. Mason, Rotary Internat. Club: Wildwood (N.J.) Golf. Home: Wildwood Gardens, N.J.

SLAVEN, Lant Rader, lawyer; b. Lewisburg, W.Va., Aug. 16, 1891; s. Wilbur Decatur and Nannie (Montgomery) S.; student Jefferson Sch., Charlottesville, Va., 1907-08; A.B., U. of Va., Charlottesville, Va., 1911; LL.B., U. of Va. Law Sch., 1914; m. Rowena Rardon, Oct. 5, 1920; children—Margaret Montgomery, Nancy Waddell, Katharine Hooper. Admitted to W.Va. bar, 1914, and since engaged in gen. practice of law at Williamson; mem. firm Goodykoontz and Slaven since 1920. Served as 2d lt. A.S., U.S.A., during World War. Dir. Davis Stuart Sch., Lewisburg, W.Va., W.Va. State Y.M.C.A. Mem. Am. Bar Assn., Phi Beta Kappa, Sigma Alpha Epsilon, Phi Delta Phi. Democrat. Presbyn. Home: 707 Poplar St., Williamson, W.Va.

SLAYBAUTH, J. Paul, headmaster; b. Mont Alto, Pa., June 7; 1896; s. John Edward and Annie M. (Parker) S.; student Quincy (Pa.) High Sch., 1911-14; A.B., Dickinson Coll., Carlisle, Pa., 1921; A.M., U. of Pa., 1933; m. Mary Gertrude Lynch, Sept. 4, 1924; children— Richard Lynch (dec.), Eleanor Jane. Teacher pub. schs., Franklin Co., Pa., 1914-16; prin. schs., Rouzerville, Pa., 1917-18; instr. mathematics, Mercersburg Acad., 1921-24; headmaster West Nottingham Acad. since 1924. Pres. Sch. Bd., Mont Alto Borough, Pa., 1923-26. Served as 2d lt., Inf., 1918; personnel officer S.A.T.C., U. of Pa., 1918-19. Mem. Am. Acad. Polit. and Social Science, Supervising Principals' Assn. (Chester Co., Pa.), Nat. Assn. Bibl. Instrs., N.E.A., Dept. Secondary Sch. Principals' Hist. Soc. of Cecil Co., Md. (charter mem.), Am. Geog. 'Soc., Headmasters' Club (Phila. Dist.), Alpha Chi Rho, Pi Gamma Mu, Phi Delta Kappa. Republican. Presbyn. (elder). Mason. Club: Rising Sun Lions (pres.). Address: Colora, Md.

SLEMONS, John A(ydelotte), insurance company exec.; b. Salisbury, Md., Nov. 14, 1882; s. Francis Marion and Martha Ann (Morris) S.; grad. Wicomico High Sch., 1898, Marston's Prep. Sch., 1899; A.B., Johns Hopkins U., 1902; m. Marion H. Metzger, July 3, 1915; 1 dau., Martha Ann. Reporter Baltimore American, 1902-03, Baltimore Herald, 1903-06; reporter Phila. North American, Phila. Record, 1906-07; New York corr. Phila. Record, 1907-11, city editor, 1912-16; with Pa. Indemnity Co. since 1916, vice-pres. since 1927; vice-pres. Pa. Indemnity Corpn., Pa. Indemnity Fire Corpn., Premium Finance Co. Mem. Phi Gamma Delta. Episcopalian. Mason. Clubs: Art, Meridian (Phila.). Home: 228 W. Johnson St., Germantown, Phila. Office: 1511 Walnut St., Philadelphia, Pa.

SLEPIAN, Joseph, research engr.; b. Boston, Mass., Feb. 11, 1891; s. Barnett and Anne (Bantick) S.; A.B., Harvard, 1911, A.M., 1912, Ph.D., 1913; grad. study Göttingen, Germany, 1913-14, Sorbonne, Paris, France, 1914; m. Rose Grace Myerson, Nov. 11, 1918; children—Robert Myer, David. Instr. mathematics, Cornell U., 1914-15; engr. Westinghouse Electric & Mfg. Co., East Pittsburgh, since 1918, now asso. dir. research; developed automatic lightning arrester to protect cross country transmission lines, generating stas. and substas., the de-ion principle of de-energizing destructive arc of interrupted electric circuit and control of huge currents in electric arcs with current in pencil lead; inventor of Ignition mercury arc rectifier. Mem. Am. Inst. E.E., Am. Phys. Soc.,

Am. Electrochem. Soc., Am. Math. Soc., Phi Beta Kappa. Awarded John Scott medal, 1932, Westinghouse Order of Merit; several best paper prizes by Am. Inst. E.E. Author: Conduction of Electricity in Gases; also numerous tech. papers. Home: 1115 Lancaster St., Pittsburgh. Office: Westinghouse Electric & Mfg. Co., E. Pittsburgh, Pa.

SLESINGER, Hyman Abraham, physician; b. Windber, Pa., July 8, 1904; s. Isaac and Sarah (Zimmerman) S.; B.S., U. of Pittsburgh, 1925; M.D., U. of Pittsburgh Med. Sch., 1926; m. Rhea Robin, Dec. 5, 1937. Med. resident, Windber Hosp., 1927-28; post grad. study in pediatrics, Children's Hosp., Pittsburgh, 1928-29; in pvt. practice in Pittsburgh, 1929-32, in Windber since 1932; pediatrician to Windber Hosp. since 1932. Served as lt. Med. Corps Res., 1926-33. Fellow Am. Acad. Pediatrics, Am. Med. Assn.; asso. Am. Coll. Phys. Mem. Phi Delta Epsilon, Alpha Omega Alpha. Republican. Jewish religion. Mason. Club: North Fork Country (Johnstown). Home: 803 15th St., Windber, Pa.

SLIFER, Henry Franklin, physician; b. Zions Villes, Pa., June 15, 1852; s. John B. and Lucy Ann (Mohr) S.; M.D., U. of Pa. Med. Dept., 1876; post grad. study, U. of Berlin, Germany, 1883; m. Emma J. Sclotterer, May 20, 1891; children—Victor Galen, Ward Dietrich, Melva (dec.), Alta, Rodney Franklin. Engaged in profession as phys. and surgeon since 1876; propr. drug store, 1879-90; prof. of physiology, Medico-Chirurg. Coll., Phila., 1890-95; prof. physiology, Temple U., 1907-13, emeritus prof. since 1913. Served as dir. Pub. Schs., North Wales, Pa., for 25 yrs. Mem. Am. Med. Assn., Pa. State and Montgomery Co. med. socs. Republican. Mem. Reformed Ch. (trustee). Club: Rotary of North Wales (hon.). Home: 116 Main St., North Wales, Pa.

SLINGLUFF, Jesse, lawyer; b. Baltimore Co., Md., June 7, 1870; s. Charles Bohn and Valerie (von Dorsner) S.; LL.B., U. of Md. Law Sch., Baltimore, 1897; m. Kathleen Kernan, Sept. 3, 1902; children—Kathleen Kelso, Jesse, Jr., Silvine von Dorsner (Mrs. Charles C. Savage, Jr.), John Kernan. Admitted to Md. bar, 1897 and since engaged in gen. practice of law at Baltimore; mem. firm Marbury, Gosnell & Williams since 1904; dir. Equitable Life Assurance Soc. of U.S., New York, N.Y., since 1922, Baltimore Brick Co. since 1912; vice-pres. and dir. Cottman Co., Baltimore, since 1916. Served as 1st lt. inf., U.S. Vols. during Spanish-Am. War. Served as maj. 2d Md. Inf., 1918-21. Mem. Am. Bar Assn., Md. State Bar Assn., Bar Assn. of Baltimore City. Democrat. Roman Catholic. Clubs: Elkridge, Bachelor's Cotillon (Baltimore). Home: 2925 N. Calvert St. Office: Maryland Trust Bldg., Baltimore, Md.

SLOAN, Duncan Lindley, judge; b. Pekin, Allegany Co., Md., Apr. 3, 1874; s. James Muir and Ella (Frederick) S.; A.B., Washington and Jefferson Coll., 1892; studied law with Judge David W. Sloan, Cumberland, Md.; m. Marion DeWitt, of Frostburg, Md., Feb. 22, 1917; 1 son, James DeWitt. Admitted to Md. bar, 1895, and began practice at Cumberland; city atty. Cumberland, 1910-14; chief judge 4th Jud. Circuit, Md., and asso. judge Md. Court of Appeals since 1926, for term ending 1941. Mem. Am. Bar Assn, and Md. State Bar Assn. (pres. 1931-32), Bar Assn. Allegany Co. (ex-sec.). Republican. Presbyn. Mason, Elk. Clubs: Kiwanis (ex-pres.), Cumberland Country. Home: The Dingle, Cumberland, Md.

SLOAN, Harold Paul, editor; b. Westfield, N.J., Dec. 12, 1881; s. Theodore Reber and Miriam (Hickman) S.; student U. of Pa. and Crozer Theol. Sem., Chester, Pa.; B.D., Drew Theol. Sem., 1908; D.D., Taylor U., Upland, Ind., 1917; LL.D., Asbury Coll., Wilmore, Ky., 1931; m. Ethel Beatrice Buckwalter, Apr. 3, 1909; children—Harold Paul, Ruth Radcliffe (Mrs. Charles H. Evans). Ordained to ministry M.E. Ch., 1908, serving various churches in N.J. Conf.; mem. of Gen. Confs. since 1920, of Ecumenical Conf. of 1921; apptd. dist. supt., 1934; editor Christian Advocate since 1936. Trustee Taylor U., Asbury Coll. Am. Tract Soc. Republican. Mason. Author: The Child and the Church, 1915; Historic Christianity and the New Theology, 1921; Christ of the Ages, 1928; Apostles' Creed, 1930; Personality and the Fact of Christ, 1933. Home: 707 Bendemere Av., Interlaken, N.J. Office: 150 Fifth Av., New York, N.Y.

SLOAN, Harold Stephenson, economist; b. Brooklyn, N.Y., Nov. 23, 1887; s. Alfred Pritchard and Katharine (Mead) S.; B.S., Columbia, 1909, M.A., 1926; m. Bertha Louis Florey, Sept. 14, 1910; 1 son, Alvin Florey. Began as clk. in father's business, Bennett-Sloan & Co., 1909; treas. and gen. mgr. De Camp & Sloan, Inc., Newark, N.J., 1908-25; teacher economics, Marquand Sch., Brooklyn, 1925-27, N.J. State Normal Sch., Newark, 1927-29; asst., later asso. prof. economics, N.J. State Teachers Coll., Upper Montclair, 1929-36; v.p. and executive dir. of the Alfred P. Sloan Foundation since June, 1936. Mem. Alpha Delta Phi. Unitarian. Clubs: Nat. Arts, University (New York); Montclair Golf (Montclair, N.J.). Author: Today's Economics, 1936. Contbr. econ. articles. Home: 144 Central Av., Montclair, N.J. Office: 30 Rockefeller Plaza, New York, N.Y.

SLOAN, Marianna, artist; b. Lock Haven, Pa., d. James Dixon and Henrietta Elizabeth (Ireland) S.; ed. Girls' Normal Sch., Phila., and Phila. Sch. of Design. Exhibited in larger cities of U.S., in Manchester, Eng., and at Royal Acad. London; awarded bronze medal, St. Louis Expn., 1904. Landscape pictures on permanent display at St. Louis Club, Acad. Fine Arts, Phila., etc.; mural paintings in Ch. of the Annunciation, Phila.; six subjects and about 100 life-sized figures in chancel of St. Thomas Ch., Whitemarsh, Pa.; reredos for St. John the Baptist Ch., Germantown, Phila. Republican. Episcopalian. Home: 44 Queen Lane, Germantown, Phila. Studio: 5328 Germantown Av., Germantown, Philadelphia, Pa.

SLOAN, William Allan; prof. mech. engring., Univ. of Pa. Address: University of Pa., Philadelphia, Pa.

SLOANE, Joseph, judge; b. Phila., Pa., Feb. 22, 1898; s. Moses A. and Sara S.; ed. Phila. Sch. of Pedagogy, 1915-17; LL.B., Temple U. Law Sch., 1925; unmarried. Engaged in teaching in pub. schs. of Phila., 1917-25; admitted to Pa. bar, 1925 and since engaged in gen. practice of law at Phila., 1925-35; spl. dep. atty. gen. and sr. counsel Dept. Revenue of Pa., 1935-37; judge Common Pleas Ct. of Phila. Co. since 1937. Enlisted in U.S.N., 1918, released from active service, 1918, honorably discharged, 1922 Mem. Bd. Jewish Welfare Soc., Adv. Bd. Clearing House for Vol. Workers, Jewish Youth Council. Mem. Am., Pa. and Phila. bar assns., Am. Legion. Democrat. Jewish religion. Home: 4101 Walnut St., Philadelphia, Pa.

SLOANE, T(homas) O'Conor, scientific expert; b. New York, Nov. 24, 1851; s. Christian S. and Eliza M. (O'Conor) S.; A.B., St. Francis Xavier Coll., 1869, A.M., 1873, LL.D., 1912; E.M., Columbia, 1872, Ph.D., 1876; m. Isabel X. Mitchel, Sept. 18, 1877; 1 son, T(homas) O'Conor; m. 2d, Alice M. Eyre, Apr. 16, 1884; children—Charles O'Conor, John Eyre, Alice Mary. Prof. natural sciences, Seton Hall Coll., S. Orange, N.J., 1888-89; has given many scientific lectures and acted as expert in many lawsuits about patents. Invented Self-Recording Photometer, first instrument that ever recorded mechanically on an index card the illuminating power of gas. Described in 1877 new process for determining sulphur in illuminating gas, which was found on exhaustive trial to be scientifically accurate. Has been on editorial staff of Plumber and Sanitary Engineer, Scientific American, Youth's Companion, Everyday Engring. Practical Electrics, and mng. editor The Experimenter; editor Amazing Stories. Mem. adv. bd. N.Y. Electrical Sch. Mem. State Bd. Edn., N.J., 1905-11; Author: Home Experiments in Science, 1888; Rubber Hand Stamps and the Manipulation of India Rubber, 1891; Arithmetic of Electricity, 1891; Electricity Simplified, 1891; Standard Electrical Dictionary, 1892; Electric Toy Making for Amateurs, 1892; How to Become a Successful Electrician, 1894; Liquid Air and the Liquefaction of Gases, 1899; The Electrician's Handy Book, 1905; Elementary Electrical Calculations, 1909; Motion Picture Projection, 1921; Rapid Arithmetic, 1922. Compiler: Facts Worth Knowing, 1890. Translator: Electric Light (Alglave & Boulard), 1884; Jörgensen's Life of St. Francis of Assisi. Contbr. to many scientific and other publs., including Encyclopedia Brittannica, Mineral Industry of United States, Catholic Encyclopedia. Address: 55 Montrose Av., South Orange, N.J.

SLOAT, Charles Allen, asso. prof. chemistry; b. Cashtown, Pa., Dec. 12, 1898; s. John Walter and Clara Anna (Funt) S.; B.S., Gettysburg Coll., 1923; A.M., Haverford Coll., 1924; grad. student Princeton, 1924-27; Ph.D., 1930. Engaged as asst. prof. chemistry, Gettysburg Coll., Gettysburg, Pa., 1927-37, asso. prof. chemistry since 1937. Mem. Am. Chem. Soc., Am. Soc. For Metals, Scabbard and Blade, Kappa Delta Rho, Phi Beta Kappa, Kappa Phi Kappa. Republican. Methodist. Home: 38 E. Broadway, Gettysburg, Pa.

SLOCUM, Chester A., cons. mech. engr.; b. Long Branch, N.J., Oct. 7, 1882; s. John Howard and Rachel Louise (Price) S.; student Long Branch (N.J.) Grade and High Schs., 1889-1902; M.E., Cornell U., 1906; m. Clara Jeffrey, Jan. 1, 1918. Heating design engr. with Walter S. Timmis, cons. heating and elec. engr., 1906-09; contracting engr. of power plants, Monmouth County, N.J., 1909-12; partner with Douglas Sprague, cons. engr., New York City, 1912-30, with Charles A. Fuller, cons. engr., New York City, since 1930, specializing in design heating, elec., ventilation, air conditioning, sanitation, etc.; registered architect, N.J., registered professional engr., N.Y., N.J., Pa. Mem. N.Y. Soc. Cons. Engrs., Illuminating Engring. Soc. Republican. Methodist. Club: Old Orchard Country (Long Branch, N.J.). Home: 28 6th Av., Long Branch, N.J. Office: 18 E. 41st St., New York, N.Y.

SLOCUM, George Warren; b. Kings Ferry, N.Y., Mar. 28, 1881; s. Arthur E. and Mary E. (Brown) S.; prep. edn., high sch., Milton, Pa.; student Cornell U., 1898-1900; m. Kate Watson Schreyer, Oct. 12, 1905 (died Dec. 9, 1921); children—Charlotte Watson, Arthur Fonda. A founder, 1920, and dir. Dairymen's League Cooperative Assn.; treas. The Nat. Coöperative Milk Producers' Federation; pres. Pa. Council Farm Orgns.; dir. First Nat. Bank, Milton. Trustee Pa. State Coll. Mem. Phi Gamma Delta. Republican. Presbyn. Club: Cornell (New York). Home: Milton, Pa.

SLOCUM, Harry B(ritton), surgeon; b. Long Branch, N.J., June 16, 1876; s. J. Howard and Rachel (Price) S.; ed. Princeton U., 1894-96; M.D., Coll. Phys. & Surgs. of Columbia U., 1901; m. Clemence Cooper, Apr. 9, 1902. Engaged in gen. practice of medicine at Long Branch, N.J., since 1902, specializing in surgery since 1915; attending surgeon Monmouth Memorial Hosp., Long Branch, chief of staff, same, since 1919; attending surg., Fitkin Memorial Hosp., Neptune, N.J., since 1932. Fellow Am. Coll. Surgs., N.Y. Acad. of Medicine. Mem. N.J. State Surg. Soc. Republican. Methodist. Clubs: Princeton (New York); Rumson (Rumson, N.J.). Home: Bath and Westwood Avs., Long Branch, N.J.

SLOCUM, Stephen Elmer, cons. engineer; b. Glenville, N.J., June 5, 1875; s. William Warren and Mary E. (Conde) S.; B.E., Union Coll., N.Y., 1897; scholar and fellow, Clark U., 1897-1900, Ph.D. in mathematics and physics, 1900; m. Anna Jeannette Ware, June 25, 1902; children—Dorothy Jeannette, Walter Ware, Marianna Conde, Stephen Elmer. Instr. in civ. engring., U. of Cincinnati, 1900-01, in applied mathematics, 1901-04, asst. prof., 1904-05; asst. prof. mathematics, U. of Ill., 1905-06; prof. applied mathematics, U. of Cincinnati, 1906-20; cons. engr., Phila. and Ardmore, Pa., 1920—; specialist in marine propulsion and in noise and vibration engring. Mem. Am. Soc. C.E., Am. Soc. Naval Engrs. (hon. life), Soc. Naval Architecture and Marine Engineering, S.R. Awarded gold medal by American Society Naval Engineers, 1927, for original research in modern hydrodynamics. Presbyn. elder since 1905. Author: Strength of Materials, 1906, 11; Theory and Practice of Mechanics, 1913; Resistance of Materials, 1914; Hydraulics, 1915; Beggars of the Sea (hist. novel), 1928; Noise and Vibration Engineering, 1931; also many monographs and articles in scientific, popular and Marine publs. Address: 244 E. Montgomery Av., Ardmore, Pa.

SLOCUM, Winthrop Wallace, telephone official; b. Buffalo, N.Y., Aug. 8, 1888; s. Charles Volney and Delia Ann (Clark) S.; B.Sc., Carnegie Inst. Tech., 1912, E.E., 1915; m. Helen McCune Kimball, Sept. 7, 1912; children—Mary Kimball, Martha Clark, Mgr. mining dept., Westinghouse Electric & Mfg. Co., Pittsburgh, 1912; sec. and treas. Titan Copper Products Co., Inc., Buffalo, N.Y., 1913-14; mgr. cork tile and refrigeration depts., Johns-Manville Co., Pittsburgh, 1914-16; v.p. Gainaday Electric Co., Inc., Pittsburgh, 1917-22; mgr. Bell Telephone Co. of Pa., Pittsburgh, 1922-25, dist. mgr. 1925-30, supervisor since 1930. Served as lt. (j.g.), U.S.N.R., Elec. Officer, U.S.S. Kansas, 1917-18; lt., Elec. Insp.-in-charge, Navy Yard, N.Y., 1918-19; lt. commdr., U.S.N.R., since 1931. Mem. Naval Reserve Officers Assn. of Pittsburgh (pres.). Republican. Protestant. Club: Rotary (Warren, Pa.). Author: How to Grow Your Family Tree, 1939. Home: 1016 Old Gate Rd., Wilkinsburg, Pa. Office: 416 7th Av., Pittsburgh, Pa.

SLOMAN, Joseph, artist; b. Phila., Pa., Dec. 30, 1883; s. Moses and Miriam (Levy) S.; ed. Industrial Art Sch., 1891-95; grad. Drexel Inst., 1905; m. Martha Ethel Stein, Sept. 4, 1924; 1 dau., Miriam Rosetta. Has followed profession as artist since 1905, panel paintings, murals, stained glass for chs. and domestic purposes, portrait painting, book illustrations and commercial designing; exhibited Pa. Acad. Fine Arts, Nat. Acad. of N.Y., Am. Water Color Club, Phila. Water Color Club, Phila. Sketch Club, Phila. Art Club, N.Y. Water Color Club, Am. Fed. Arts Rotary Exbn., Montclair Mus. Fine Arts, spl. one-man exhbn., Marshall Field & Co., Chicago; represented by murals in many prominent pvt. homes in N.Y. City as well as bldgs., hotels and theatres. Awards: Frances Drexel Paul prize, 1902; Art Students League scholarship, 1904; John Wanamaker prize, 1904. Mem. Alumni of Drexel Inst. Democrat. Hebrew religion. Designed stained glass window for Union City Library, 1939. Home: 423 New York Av., Union City, N.J.

SLOSSER, Gaius Jackson, clergyman, theol. sem. prof.; b. nr. Hoytville, O., June 2, 1887; s. James Elliott and Mary Elizabeth (Jackson) S.; ed. O. Northern U., 1903-04; A.B., cum laude, O. Wesleyan U., 1912; S.T.B., Boston U. Sch. of Theology, 1915, S.T.M., same, 1921; grad. study Harvard U. Grad. Sch., 1915-16; Ph.D., King's Coll. Univ. of London, Eng., 1928; m. Marguerite Louise Holbrook, June 27, 1917 (died 1925); m. 2d, Esther Victoria Thurston, Apr. 14, 1927; children—Ruth Elouise, Gaius Jackson II. Ordained to ministry M.E. Ch., 1917; served pastorates in Lynnfield, Chicopee, Medford, Holyoke and Natick, Mass., 1917-25; prof. eccles. history and history of doctrine, Western Theol. Sem. (Presbyn. U.S.A.), Pittsburgh, Pa., since 1928; transferred to Presbyn. Ch. U.S.A., 1929. Served as chaplain capt. Mass. N.G., 1917-18, 1919-23; chaplain 1st lt. then capt. 212th Engrs. U.S.A. during World War, then U.S.A. Res., 1919-1937. Exec. sec. Pub. Safety Com., City of Chicopee, Mass., 1917. Dir. Dept. History of Presbyn. Ch. U.S.A., Phila., Pa. Fellow Royal Hist. Soc., London, Eng. Mem. O. Wesleyan Union, Delta Sigma Rho; Alpha Tau Epsilon, Theol. Circle of Pittsburgh. Republican. Presbyn. U.S.A. Mason, I.O.O.F. Del. from M.E. Ch. to First World Conf. on Faith and Order, Lausanne, Switzerland, 1927; asso. del. to Second Universal Conf. on Life and Work, Oxford, Eng., and del. Second World Conf. on Faith and Order, Edinburgh, Scotland, 1937. Mem. Am. Commn. of Fifteen Theologians which prepared study texts for the Conf. Author: History of the 212th Engineers, 1918; Christian Unity, Its History and Challenge in All Communions and in All Lands, 1929; The Communion of Saints, 1937. Home: 203 Summit Av., Bellevue, Pittsburgh, Pa.

SLOTKIN, Samuel, pres. Hygrade Food Products Corpn.; b. Minsk, Russia, July 30, 1885; came to U.S., 1900, naturalized, 1905; s. Israel and Celia (Horowitz) S.; ed. pub. and high schs., N.Y. City; m. Fannie Rivkin, Mar. 1, 1908; children—Selma, Hugo, Edward James. Entered meat packing business at age of 19; founded Hygrade Provision Co., 1914; now pres. Hygrade Food Products Corpn. Active in numerous charitable orgns. Democrat. Jewish religion. Club: Bankers. Home: 1116 Elberon Av., Elberon, N.J. Office: 30 Church St., New York, N.Y.

SMAIL, Lloyd Leroy, univ. prof.; b. Columbus, Kan., Sept. 23, 1888; s. Israel L. and Adda (Thomas) S.; A.B., U. of Wash., Seattle, Wash., 1911, M.A., 1912; Ph.D., Columbia U., 1913; m. Margaret Barton, Sept. 15, 1921; 1 dau., Arlene. Instr. of mathematics, U. of Wash., Seattle, Wash., 1913-21, asst. prof., 1921-23; asst. prof. of mathematics, U. of Ore., Eugene, Ore., 1923-25; asso. prof. of mathematics, U. of Tex., Austin, Tex., 1925-26; asso. prof. of mathematics, Lehigh U., Bethlehem, Pa., 1926-29, prof. since 1929. Mem. Am. Math. Soc., Math. Assn. of America, A.A.A.S., Soc. for Promotion of Engring. Edn., Sigma Xi. Author: Elements of the Theory of Infinite Processes, 1923; Mathematics of Finance, 1925; History and Synopsis of the Theory of Summable Infinite Processes, 1925; Plane Trigonometry, 1926; College Algebra, 1931; math. portion of Van Nostrand's Scientific Encyclopedia, 1938; numerous articles in math. jours. Address: 1131 W. North St., Bethlehem, Pa.

SMALL, Frederick Percival, pres. Am. Express Co.; b. Augusta, Me., Nov. 28, 1874; s. Alonzo Porter and Henrietta (Allen) S.; grad. Cony High Sch., Augusta; student Cornell Law School; grad. Eastman Business Coll., Poughkeepsie, N.Y.; m. Clara J. Cable, June 8, 1898; children—Frederick A., Kathryn S. (Mrs. George Conkling). Began with Merchants Dispatch Transportation Co.; with Am. Express Co. since 1896, and pres. since 1923; pres. and dir. The Am. Express Co., Inc., Nat. Express Co., Wells Fargo Cuban-Mexican Corpn.; mem. advisory bd. Am. Express Branch of Chase Nat. Bank; chmn. exec. com. and dir. Wells Fargo & Co.; dir. Wells Fargo & Co. of Cuba, Amerex Holding Corporation, Remington-Rand, Inc.; trustee American Surety Co. Mem. Me. Soc., Empire State Soc. Sons of Am. Revolution. Republican. Mem. Dutch Ref. Ch. Mason (K.T., Shriner). Clubs: Lawyers, The Recess, Metropolitan (New York); Barnegat Light Yacht (N.J.). Home: Ridgefield, N.J., and Harvey Cedars, N.J. Office: 65 Broadway, New York, N.Y.

SMALL, James Craig, M.D.; b. Greencastle, Pa., Mar. 13, 1888; s. Harry K. and Adeline (Hassler) S.; grad. Chambersburg (Pa.) Acad., 1906; B.S., Gettysburg (Pa.) Coll., 1911, Sc.D., 1928; M.D., U. of Ill., Urbana, Ill., 1917; studied Army Med. Sch., 1917-18; m. Katherine Welch, Oct. 26, 1921; 1 son, James C. Student asst. in biol. chemistry, U. of Ill., Urbana, Ill., 1913-17; instr. bacteriology, Sch. of Med., Washington U., St. Louis, Mo.; 1919; in pvt. practice of medicine as internist and rheumatologist since 1921; bacteriologist, Phila. Gen. Hosp., 1920-27, dir. labs., 1927-29; asst. prof. bacteriology, grad. Sch. of Medicine, U. of Pa., 1921-37, instr. med. since 1937. Served as 1st lt., U.S.M.C., 1917-19; mem. Pneumonia Commn., U.S. Army, 1918-19. Certified Internist Am. Board Internal Medicine. Mem. A.A. A.S., A.M.A., Am. Rheumatism Soc., Phila. Rheumatism Soc. (pres. since 1938), Am. Soc. for Exptl. Pathology, Phila. Co. Med. Soc., Am. Coll. Physicians, Physiol. Soc. of Phila., Pa. Acad. Sciences, Am. Heart Assn, Pathol. Soc. of Philadelphia, John Morgan Soc., Pa. State Med. Soc., Internat. Soc. of Med. Hydrology, Phi Delta Theta, Alpha Omega Alpha, Phi Beta Kappa, Sigma Xi, Phi Alpha Sigma. Mason. Author numerous articles on med. subjects. Home: 213 Argyle Road, Ardmore, Pa. Office: N.E. Corner 36th and Walnut Sts., Philadelphia, Pa.

SMALL, Mary L.; mem. staff Mercy Hosp. and Baltimore Eye, Ear and Throat Charity Hosp. Address: 18 W. Read St., Baltimore, Md.

SMALL, Ray Arthur, mech. engr.; b. Benzonia, Mich., Aug. 1, 1881; s. Shadrach and Angeline (Hill) S.; B.S. in mech. engring., Mich. State Coll., East Lansing, Mich., 1908; m. Ruby Delvin, Dec. 24, 1908; children—Bonnie Blanche, Ruby Pearl, Ford Delvin. Supt. of constrn. for various bridge, dam and bldg. contractors in Mich., 1912-15; designer, Semet-Solvay Co., Syracuse, N.Y., 1915-17; designer, Aluminum Co. of America, Massena, N.Y., 1919-21; ventilation engr., Industrial Commn., Madison, Wis., 1921-24; engring. consultation practice, Madison, Wis., 1924-29; design, research and supervision for govt. and private enterprises, 1929-35; engaged in pvt. development of multiwheel gearless vehicle drive since 1935. Served as asst. engr., Q.M. Dept., U.S. Army, San Francisco, Calif., 1909; C.E. and supt. of constrn., Manila, P.I., 1910-11; officer in 1st Heavy Tank Batt., A.E.F., 1917-19. Sr. mem. Am. Assn. of Engrs. Protestant. Home: 227 N. Third St., Lewisburg, Pa. Office: Box S-66, Mill Hall, Pa.

SMALLEY, Harry Clark, educator; b. Augusta, N.J., Nov. 30, 1894; s. John Edward and Isabelle Hannah S.; student Newton (N.J.) High Sch., 1909-13; B.S., Rutgers U., New Brunswick, N.J., 1918; m. Ida Frances Kirk, June 21, 1921; children—Howard Frederick, Kenneth Clark, Glendon William. Teacher of rural sch., Wykertown, N.J., 1914; teacher of science, Bridgeton (N.J.) High Sch., 1918-24, asst. prin., 1924-27, prin. since 1927. Served as 2d lt., O.R.C., 1918. Mem. Boy Scouts of America (exec. bd., Cumberland Co. Council; in charge of Advancement Program). Mem. N.J. High Sch. Prins. Assn., N.E.A. (Dept. of Secondary Sch. Prins.). Republican. Methodist. K.P. Address: 80 S. Giles St., Bridgeton, N.J.

SMATHERS, Charles Blaine, brig. gen., supt. Pa. Soldiers Orphan Sch.; b. Ringgold, Pa., June 25, 1877; s. Millard Fillmore and Margaret (Irvin) S.; Ph.D., Grove City (Pa.) Coll. 1913; m. Clara McCaskey, 1905; children—Wiley Fillmore, Robert Irvin. Began teaching in pub. schs., 1893; supt. schs., Grove City, Pa., 1902-14; mem. Bur. Professional Edn., Pa. Dept. Pub. Instrn., 1914-24; supt. Pa. Soldiers' Orphan Sch. since 1924. Served as pvt., Inf., Pa. Vols., U.S. Army, Spanish-Am. War, 1898; maj., Pa. N.G. on Mexican border, 1916-17, maj., Inf., U.S. Army, 1917-19 with A.E.F., col. U.S. Army Res.; brig. gen. U.S. Army Res. since 1937, comdg. 56th Inf. Brig., 28th Div. Mem. United Spanish War Vets., Am. Legion, Vets. Fgn. Wars, Pa. Edn. Assn. Republican. Methodist. Mason, Odd Fellow. Home: Scotland, Pa.

SMATHERS, William H(owell), U.S. senator; b. Wayneville, N.C., Jan. 7, 1891; s. Benjamin Franklin (physician) and Laura (Howell) S.; student Washington and Lee U., 1907-09, U. of N.C., 1909-11; m. 2d, Mary James Foley, Feb. 9, 1938; children by first marriage—Jayne, Billie Barbara, Polly J., B., Ben. Admitted to N.C. and N.J. bar, 1912; practicing atty. at Atlantic City, N.J. 1912-22; president judge Common Pleas Court of Atlantic Co., N.J., 1922-32; commr. N.J. Superior Court, 1923; spl. master in Chancery, 1924; 1st asst. atty. gen. of N.J., 1934, state senator, 1934-36; elected U.S. senator from N.J. for term, 1937-43; mem. law firm Smathers, Scott & Munyan. Awarded Kiwanis Club "Good Deeds" award as most useful citizen of Atlantic City, 1934. Democrat. Home: Margate City, N.J. Office: Chelsea Bank Bldg., Atlantic City, N.J.

SMELTZER, Clarence Harry, asso. prof. psychology; b. Bellefonte, Pa., Sept. 4, 1900; s. William Curtis and Sallie (Garbrick) S.; ed. Pa. State Coll., 1918-20; B.S., Teachers Coll. of Columbia U., 1922, A.M., same, 1923; Ph.D., O. State U., 1931; m. Margaret Mussina, June 22, 1927; 1 dau., Kay Margaret. Teacher and asst. prin. jr. high sch., N.Y. City, 1920-24; instr. psychology, Temple U., 1924-29; instr. psychology, O. State U. Sch. Edn., 1929-31; asst. prof. psychology, Temple U.,

1931-34, asso. prof. since 1934; teacher at summer sessions, Temple U., Pa. State Coll., Ohio State U. and Miami U.; consultant on personnel State Emergency Relief Adminstrn., Harrisburg, Pa., 1935-37; tech. consultant on State Civil Service, Dept. Labor and Industry since 1937. Mem. Am. Psychol. Assn., Am. Assn. Applied Psychologists (charter mem.), Nat. Soc. Coll. Teachers of Edn., Am. Assn. Univ. Profs., Blue Key, Sigma Phi Epsilon, Phi Delta Kappa, Alpha Psi Delta. Protestant. Mason (32°, Shriner). Contbr. about 35 articles to various tech. jours. Home: 290 Bickley Rd., Glenside, Pa.

SMELTZER, William Cyrus, banker; b. Furgeson Twp., Centre Co., Pa., June 10, 1870; s Albert and Anna (Kaup) S.; ed. pub. schs. of Spring Twp., Centre Co., Pa., and Bellefonte Acad. (1887-88); m. Sallie A. Garbrick, Aug. 23, 1899; children—Clarence Harry, Norman Harold. Taught school, Spring Twp., 1888-1902; farmer and stock dealer, 1902-22; retired and traveled, 1922-27; an organizer and dir. Farmer Nat. Bank, Bellefonte, 1927, pres. since 1931; pres. and dir. Sugar Valley Mutual Fire Ins. Co.; dir. White Rock Lime & Stone Co., Inc.; treas. and dir. Merchants Gas & Oil Co. Treas. and dir. Agr. Extension Assn.; treas. and dir. Centre Co. Sheep and Wool Growers Assn. Served in Nat. Guard of Pa., 1891-98. Served as sch. dir. Spring Twp., 6 yrs., auditor, 9 yrs. Republican. Lutheran. Active in agriculture; farm owner. Home: High St. Office: High and Spring Sts., Bellefonte, Pa.

SMELZER, Donald Campbell, physician; b. Montreal, P.Q., Jan. 7, 1896; s. John Hamilton and Lillian (Campbell) S.; came to U.S., 1922, naturalized, 1930; M.D., McGill U. 1918, C.M., same, 1918; m. Ethel Proper, Dec. 8, 1924; children—Martha Ann, Barbara Campbell, Diana Claire. Asst. supt. Montreal Gen. Hosp., 1921-23; asso. supt. Buffalo Gen. Hosp., 1923-25; dir. Charles T. Miller Hosp., St. Paul, Minn., 1925-30; dir. Grad. Hosp. of U. of Pa. since 1930. Served as lt. Med. Corps Canadian Army, 1918-19; capt. R.A. Med. Corps, 1919-21. Trustee Am. Hosp. Assn. Pres. Phila. Hosp. Assn. Charter fellow Am. Coll. Hosp. Adminstrs. Fellow A.M.A., Phila. Coll. Phys.; mem. Phila. Co. Med. Soc. Mem. Alpha Kappa Kappa, Alpha Omega Alpha. Republican. Presbyn. Club: University. Home: 422 Bryn Mawr Av., Bala-Cynwyd, Pa. Office: 19th and Lombard Sts., Philadelphia, Pa.

SMILEY, E(arl) Kenneth, dir. univ. admissions; b. Caribou, Me., Mar. 11, 1899; s. Sidney Alpha and Hattie Augusta (Norton) S.; student Dartmouth Coll., Hanover, N.H., 1917-19; A.B., Bowdoin Coll., Brunswick, Me., 1921; A.M., Lehigh U., Bethlehem, Pa., 1935; m. Gertrude M. Dunlop, June 24, 1931; children—Maureen Dunlop, Marcia Dunlop. Began as master in English, Bethlehem (Pa.) Prep. Sch., 1921; instr. English, Lehigh U., Bethlehem, 1923-24, asst. dean and registrar, 1924-26; dean of men, U. of N.D., Grand Forks, N.D., 1926-33, dean Jr. Div., 1930-33; supervisor coll. work through extension courses, Lisbon, N.D., 1933; field rep., Fed. Emergency Relief Adminstrn., 1934; asst. dir. admissions Lehigh U., Bethlehem, 1934-38, dir. admissions since 1938. Mem. Assn. Deans and Advisers of Men, Beta Theta Pi, Phi Eta Sigma. Episcopalian. Mason. Club: Rotary (Bethlehem, Pa.). Home: 431 W. 3d St., Bethlehem, Pa.

SMILEY, Helen A(gnes), univ. prof.; b. Phila., Pa., July 8, 1900; d. U. Franklin and Agnes (Macfarland) S.; ed. Pa. sch. Industrial Art, 1918-19; B.S., Temple U., 1926; grad. student, Columbia U., 1932-34. Teacher of primary art and critic teacher, Wilmington Normal Sch., Wilmington, Del., 1918-22; asso. with Temple U. since 1922, instr. industrial art, 1922-37; fine arts since 1937; established The Little Playhouse, 1936, only theatre in Phila. devoted to marionette activities and plays for children; engaged in stage and costume design, puppetry, dramatic activities. Mem. Am. Assn. Univ. Profs., Art Alliance Phila., Puppeteers of America, Marionette Guild, Delta Sigma Epsilon. Republican. Presbyn. Home: 6445 Greene St., Philadelphia, Pa.

SMILLIE, Frederick Brandon, lawyer; b. Washington, D.C., May 31, 1902; s. G. F. C. and Lily (Brandon) S.; ed. Wharton Sch. of U. of Pa., 1920 to 1924, U. of Pa. Law Sch., 1924 to 1927; m. Emma Comly Miller, Apr. 17, 1929. Admitted to Pa. bar, 1927 and since engaged in gen. practice of law at Norristown; asst. gen. solicitor Lehigh Valley R.R., 1929-32; asst. dist. atty. Montgomery Co., 1932-36, dist. atty. since 1936; mem. firm Smillie and Bean since 1932; dir. Norristown-Penn Trust Co. Served as solicitor Sch. Bd. Upper Merion Twp. Mem. Montgomery County Bar Assn., Phi Delta Phi, Beta Theta Pi. Republican. Club: Union League of Philadelphia. Home: Gulph Mills, Pa. Office: 522 Swede St., Norristown, Pa.

SMITH, Albert Herman, pres. Nat. Bank of Topton, Pa.,; b. Middleburg, Pa., Nov. 24, 1867; s. James P. and Cinderella (Graybill) S.; student Middleburg (Pa.) High Sch., 1873-85, Freeburg (Pa.) Acad., 1885-89; m. Mary Sheetz, Dec. 5, 1899; children—Mildred (Mrs. W. E. Sallade), Margaret (Mrs. C. H. Nordby), James Park, Jean. Established Elizabethville (Pa.) Weekly Echo, 1898, editor, 1898-1904; organized The Nat. Bank of Topton (Pa.), 1906, cashier, 1906-26, pres. since 1926; dir. Topton Bldg. and Loan Assn. Trustee, Wernersville, Pa., State Hosp. Mem. Pa. Bankers Assn. (agrl. com.), Topton Chamber of Commerce. Democrat. Lutheran. Mason (Shriner; Reading, Pa., Consistory). Club: Kutztown (Pa.) Rotary. Has addressed civic clubs, ch. socs. and other orgns. on the Life of Washington. Home: 228 Home Av. Office: Corner Franklin St. and Home Av., Topton, Pa.

SMITH, Albert Van Deaver, lawyer; b. Baltimore, Md., Oct. 16, 1899; s. Horace Laurence and Nannie C. (Nimmo) S.; student U.S. Naval Acad., Annapolis, Md., 1917-19; B.S. in Engring., Johns Hopkins U.; 1921; LL.B., U. of Md. Law Sch., Baltimore, 1924; m. Elizabeth Brooks Harryman, Nov. 5, 1927. Engaged as cons. engr., Baltimore, 1921-24; admitted to Md. bar and since engaged in practice at Baltimore; in pvt. practice, 1924-25; served as asst. U.S. atty., 1925-29; in gen. practice since 1929; mem. firm Smith and Cross since 1935; dir. National Sash Weight Corpn. since 1934. Served as midshipman, U.S.N., 1917-19. Mem. Am. Bar Assn., Phi Gamma Delta, Tau Beta Pi. Republican. Baptist. Clubs: Merchants, Johns Hopkins (Baltimore). Home: 693 Gladstone Av. Office: Mercantile Trust Bldg., Baltimore, Md.

SMITH, A(lfred) Burton, physician and surgeon; b. Fairmount Twp., Pa., Aug. 12, 1870; s. Ziba and Mary Ann (Blaine) S.; student pub. schs., Luzerne County, Pa., 1876-88, New Columbus Acad. Prep. Sch., Luzerne County, 1888-90, Woods' Business Coll., Scranton, Pa., 1889; M.D., Medico-Chirurgical Coll., Phila., 1905; m. Maude Snell, Oct. 11, 1893; children—Leona, Russell, Gertrude; m. 2d, Ida Parrish, Aug. 12, 1936. Bookkeeper, paymaster and purchasing agt., Exeter Machine Works, West Pittston, Pa., 1890-95, sec., 1897, auditor and sec. since 1897; merchant, gen. store, Forty Fort, Pa., 1897-1901; pvt. practice of medicine and surgery at Wyoming, Pa., since 1905; assisted in organizing West Side Hosp. (now Nesbitt Memorial Hosp.), Kingston, Pa., 1912, chief surgeon of staff, 1912-32, chief of proctological dept. since 1932; chief med. examiner, Federal Reserve Assn., Wilkes-Barre, Pa., 1907-1909; pres. Pa. Title & Security Co., Wilkes-Barre, since 1910; sec. Search Light Acetylene Gas Machine Co., Wilkes-Barre, Pa., since 1911. Served as lt., capt. and maj., U.S. Army, during World War; chief surgeon, Base Hosp. No. 112, France, 1918-19. Sch. dir., Wyoming, Pa., since 1914. Mem. Luzerne Co. (Pa.) Med. Soc. (dir.), State Vets. of Foreign Wars (surgeon). Republican. Presbyterian (elder, Presbyn. Ch., Wyoming, Pa.) Mason (past master, Blue Lodge; Commandery; Shriner). Clubs: Irem Country (Dallas, Pa.); Fox Hill Country (Pittston, Pa.). Has read several papers of scientific interest before Luzerne Co. Med. Soc. Address: 394 Wyoming Av., Wyoming, Pa.

SMITH, Arthur Francis, high sch. prin.; b. Frostburg, Md., July 4, 1874; s. John Albert and Anna Mary (McKenzie) S.; A.B., Western Md. Coll., Westminster, Md., 1892, A.M., 1897; student various summer schs.; m. Esther Jenifer Jeffries, Dec. 26, 1899; 1 dau., Mary Esther (Mrs. John Frederick Fields). Engaged as prin. Md. Av. Sch., Cumberland, Md., 1894-95; vice prin. Beall High Sch., Frostburg, Md., 1895-96; prin. Grahamtown Sch., 1896-1900; prin. Central High Sch., Lonaconing, Md., since 1900. Served in Md. N.G., 1894. Served as mem. Md. Ho. of Dels., 1916-17. Mem. Nat. Edn. Assn., Md. State Teachers Assn. (pres. 1904-05). Republican. Methodist (trustee Meth. Ch.). Mason (K.T., Shriner). Club: Lions of Lonaconing (pres. 1939-40). Home: 78 E. Main St., Lonaconing, Md.

SMITH, Bela Buck, supt. city schools; b. Belle Vernon, Pa., Nov. 29, 1880; son Joseph Houseman and Martha Jane (Rankin) S.; A.B., Lafayette Coll. 1907; Ed.M., U. of Pittsburgh, 1938; m. Sallie Fulton Cook, 1908; children—Violette Jane, Joseph Houseman, Sarah Cook, Mabel Louise. Teacher rural school, Rostraver Twp., Westmoreland Co., Pa., 1900-03; teacher and athletic coach, Charleroi (Pa.) High Sch., 1907-09, Connellsville (Pa.) High Sch., 1909-12; prin. of high school, Connellsville (Pa.) High Sch., 1912-20; supt. city schools, Connellsville, 1920-38; supt. city schools, Kingston, Pa., since 1938. Mem. Bd. of Trade, Community Chest (dir.). Mem. N.E.A., Am. Assn. Sch. Adminstrs., Pa. State Edn. Assn., Lafayette Men in Edn., Phi Delta Kappa, Kappa Phi Kappa, Phi Sigma Pi. Republican. Presbyterian (moderator Red Stone Presbytery, Presbyn. Ch., U.S.A.; vice moderator Pa. Synod). Clubs: Kiwanis, Pleasant Valley Country. Contbr. to ednl. mags. Home: 32 Reynolds St., Kingston, Pa.

SMITH, Carolin N., club woman; b. Rowlesburg, W.Va., Dec. 13; d. John W. and Carolin (Lambden) Heckman; student pub. schs., Baltimore, Md.; m. Howard Wayne Smith, June 7, 1893; 1 son, Nelson Lee. Pres. Women's Am. Baptist Fgn. Mission Soc. since 1932; pres. Fed. of Women's Bds. of Fgn. Missions of North America, 1933-36. Clubs: Woman's (Ardmore, Pa.; pres. 1921-24); former mem. Woman's City, Nature, Philomusian (Phila.). Home: 111 Walnut Av., Ardmore, Pa.

SMITH, Carroll Dunham, Jr., pharmacist; b. New York, N.Y., Mar. 19, 1907; s. Carroll Dunham and Agnes (Rostelle) S.; grad. Lincoln Sch. of Teachers Coll., 1924; ed. Columbia U., 1924-25; M.E., Stevens Inst. Tech., 1929; study Harvard Grad. Sch. Bus. Adminstrn., 1929-30; m. Jeannette Smith, May 17, 1930; children—Carroll Dunham III, Julia Lorraine. Asso. with Carroll Dunham Smith Pharmacal Co. since 1930, successively, salesman, sales supervisor, office mgr., then sec., dir. and gen. mgr. since 1934. Served in U.S.N. Res. also N.Y. State Militia. Industrial dir. Orange Y.M.C.A. Mem. Orange Chamber of Commerce. Chmn. exec. com. Executive Club. Mem. Beta Theta Pi. Club: Kiwanis of Orange. Home: Old Timbers, Essex Fells, N.J. Office: Orange, N.J.

SMITH, Charles C., supt. of schs.; b. Red Lion, Pa., Jan. 5, 1891; s. Adie and Mary (Heim) S.; A.B., Lebanon Valley Coll., Annville, Pa., 1912; M.A., Columbia U., 1919; spl. student, U. of Pa., 1933-37; m. Mary Norris, June 22, 1916; children—Charles N., Robert Lewis. Coach and instr. in history, Eldersridge (Pa.) Acad., 1912-13; coach and instr. in mathematics, Mt. Union (Pa.) High Sch., 1913-16, prin., 1916-21, supervising prin., 1921-32; supt. of schs., Bridgeport, Pa., since 1932; dir. Practice Sch., Juniata Coll., Huntingdon, Pa., 1925-32. Mem. Montgomery Co. Tuberculosis Com. (pres., 1935-39), Phi Delta Kappa. Republican. Presbyterian. Mason. Club: Norristown Lions" (pres., 1938-39). Home: 512 Rambo St. Office: 7th and Ford Sts., Bridgeport, Pa.

SMITH, Charles Howard, engr.; b. Portland, Ore., Sept. 4, 1884; s. Charles Jackson and

Elizabeth (McMillan) S.; desc. Richard Smith who came to Mass. with Rogers Williams, 1636; grad. Seattle (Wash.) High Sch., 1901; student Phillips Andover Acad., 1901-02, Yale Scientific Sch., 1902-04; m. Jane Swindell, Sept. 29, 1909; children—Frances Townley (Mrs. Orville Anderson Tyler), Charles Jackson, Robert Fulton, Betsy Jane. Engr. Western Coal & Mining Co., St. Louis, 1905; then v.p. Davis Coal & Coke Co., Baltimore, Pittsburgh Terminal Ry. & Coal Co., Western Coal & Mining Co., Consol. Coal Co., St. Louis; asst. to pres. Western Md. R.R., 1907-11; v.p. and gen. mgr. Durham Coal & Iron Co., 1911-12; expert mining engr., New York, since 1913; cons. engr. Clinchfield Coal Corpn., 1913; asso. with Blair & Co., bankers, New York, 1914-21; pres. Internat. Coal Products Corpn., Clinchfield Carbocoal Corpn., Gen. Oil Gas Corpn., Bregeat Corpn. of Am., Am. & Automotive Gas Producers Corpn., 1915-21; as cons. engr. has made valuation reports on Mo. Pacific R.R. coal properties, Chicago & Eastern Ill. R.R., Utah Fuel Co., C.,M.&St.P. Ry., etc.; organized Chenery & Smith, cons. engrs., 1921-27; chmn. bd. Gen. Waterworks & Elec. Co., 1928-29; pres. Charles H. Smith & Co., Engrs.; cons. eng. Utility Management Corpn., 1937-38; cons. engr. Federal Water Service Co.; pres. Middle States Natural Gas Co. During World War did special work for Ordnance Dept., U.S. Army, U.S. Fuel Adminstrn., War Industries Bd. Mem. Am. Mining Congress, Am. Inst. Mining and Metall. Engrs., Am. Soc. Naval Engrs. (asso.), Army Ordnance Assn. Republican. Episcopalian. Clubs: Yale, Bankers (New York); Short Hills (Short Hills, N.J.); Braidburn Country (Madison, N.J.). Inventor of process for converting bituminous coal into a smokeless fuel and also effecting recovery of by-products. Home: Coniston Rd., Short Hills, N.J. Office: 90 Broad St., New York, N.Y.

SMITH, Charles Raymond, physician; b. Wexford, Pa., May 6, 1895; s. Alvah G. and Mary (Paul) S.; ed. U. of Pittsburgh, 1914-16; M.D., U. of Mich., 1920; grad. study, Harvard U. Med. Sch., 1926; m. Eleanor Mae Williams, June 23, 1923; children—Dorothy Louise, Eleanor Janice. Interne West Pa. Hosp., Pittsburgh, 1920-22; asst. surgeon Carnegie-Illinois Steel Co., 1922-26; sch. med. inspr., Munhall Borough, 1923-31; med. inspr. Bur. of Child Welfare, City of Pittsburgh, 1934-39. Served in Med. Corps Res., U.S.A., 1917-18. Mem. Am. Med. Assn., Allegheny Co. Med. Soc., Phi Beta Pi. Democrat. Mem. M.E. Ch. Clubs: Outlook, Kiwanis (Homestead). Home; 4806 Interboro Av., Homestead, Pa. Office: 805 Ann St., Homestead, Pa.

SMITH, Charles Stephenson, writer, lecturer; b. Albia, Ia., July 18, 1877; s. Samuel Stephenson and Amelia (McBride) S.; prep. edn., Parsons Acad., Fairfield, Ia.; A.B., U. of Ia., 1897; post-grad. work, Columbia, 1904-05; unmarried. Served on editorial staffs Omaha Bee, Des Moines Capital, Washington Post, Washington Times; mng. editor Nashville Tennessean, 1907-11; in Washington, New York, South America, Europe, Asia, Africa with Associated Press, 1913-35; covered Versailles, Riga Genoa, Hague, Lausanne and other conferences, growing out of World War. In Russia, under Romanoffs, Kerensky and Bolshevist regimes; accompanied Root Mission to Russia, 1917; covered Wrangell and Denikin movements against Lenin's govt., 1920, and Russian famine, 1921-22; in charge A.P. service, Moscow, 1934-35. Has lectured before universities, clubs and political institutes, on Russian and Oriental questions, and on foreign news organization. Contbr. revs. on internat. problems to many mags.; retired from active news work in 1935; purchased Havre de Venture, the home and burial place of Thomas Stone, signer Declaration of Independence, Port Tobacco, Md. Mem. Overseas Writers, Delta Tau Delta. Master of Charles County (Md.) Pomona Grange. Clubs: Nat. Press (Washington, D.C.); Western Universities (New York); Wollasten Manor Club (Mt. Victoria, Md.). Address: Havre de Venture, Port Tobacco, Md.

SMITH, Clarence Edwin, newspaper editor; b. Fairmont, W.Va., July 11, 1885; s. Gen. Clarence Linden and Margaret Virginia (Fleming) S.; prep. edn., high sch., Fairmont, and Va. Mil. Inst.; student U. of Va., 1904-05; m. Elsie Juanita Fleming, May 25, 1909; children—Caroline Fleming, Elizabeth Randolph, Clarence Edwin. Began as reporter, Fairmont Times, 1907; editor Fairmont Times since 1917; editor Wheeling (W.Va.) Register until its merger with Wheeling News-Register, 1935. Vice-pres. Fairmont Newspaper Publishing Company, Acme Land Company. Served as 2d lt., W.Va. N.G., 1907, 1st lt., 1908-10; mem. City Council, Fairmont, 1910-12; mem. Bd. of Edn., 1910-22; U.S. marshal Northern Dist. of W.Va., 1914-22. Mem. Associated Press (chmn. W.Va.). Chmn. W.Va. del. Am. Nat. Conv., 1928 and 1932; sec. Am. Sect., Internat. Joint Commn., Washington, 1933-35; apptd. mem. Nat. Bituminous Coal Commn., Washington, D.C., 1935, reapptd. 1937. Clubs: Nat. Press (Washington, D.C.); Ft. Henry (Wheeling). Home: Hillcrest, Fairmont, W.Va. Address: Nat. Bituminous Coal Commn., Washington, D.C.

SMITH, Clarence James, newspaperman; b. Easton, Pa., July 29, 1874; s. John Jackson and Sue (Bonstein) S.; grad. high sch., Easton, 1891; m. Edith Clappison, Apr. 30, 1906; children—Jack Clappison, Clarence James. Reporter Easton Daily Argus, 1893-1904, editor, 1904-10; city editor Allentown (Pa.) Morning Call, 1910-19, owner, v.p. and mng. editor, 1920-34; founder and pub., 1919, Allentown Morning Herald. Served as 1st sergt. Pa. Inf., Spanish Am. War, capt. and regtl. q.m., 1912-17; capt. on Mexican border, 1916; organizer 103d Am. Train, 28th Div., A.E.F., serving as maj. inf. in France, 1918-19; lt. col. inf., Pa. N.G., 1920-23; col. C.A. since 1923. Mem. Pa. Editorial Assn. (ex-pres.), Interstate Circulation Mgrs. Assn. (ex-pres.), Allentown Chamber Commerce (ex-pres.), Army Assn. U.S. Mil. Order Foreign Wars, Nat. Guard Assn. Pa., Vets. Foreign Wars (past pres. Holveck post.), Am. Legion (past pres. Paul Lentz post), Officers Club of 28th Div. Republican. Episcopalian. Odd Fellow, Elk. Clubs: Rotary of Allentown (ex-pres.); Poor Richard (Philadelphia). Home: 31 N. 17th St., Allentown, Pa.*

SMITH, Claude Carroll, lawyer; b. Shelburn, Ind., Nov. 14, 1888; s. Henry Thomas and Stella (Marts) S.; B.S., Central Normal Coll. of Ind., 1911; A.B., Swarthmore Coll., 1914; LL.B., U. of Pa., 1917; m. Mary Carter Roberts, June 21, 1917; children—Richard Owen, Gene Roberts, Carter Thomas, Nancy Roberts. Rural sch. teacher, Sullivan Co., Ind., 1905-07; teacher, Hymera (Ind.) High Sch., 1908, prin., 1910; admitted to Pa. bar, 1917, and began practice as asst. with Duane, Morris & Heckscher, mem. of firm since 1923; teacher business law Swarthmore Coll., 1920-27; dir. and sec. Dallett Co.; dir. Buck Hill Falls Co., Griscom Motor Co., Swarthmore Nat. Bank; solicitor Sch. Dist., Swarthmore, since 1927. Trustee Swarthmore Coll., Friends Central Sch., Trustees of Phila. Yearly Meeting of Soc. of Friends. Mem. Am., Pa. State and Phila. bar assns., Delta Sigma Rho, Phi Delta Phi, Phi Delta Theta. Democrat. Mem. Soc. of Friends (overseer). Clubs: Midday, Lawyers, Rotary (Phila.); Rolling Green Golf (Media). Home: Swarthmore, Pa. Office: Land Title Bldg., Philadelphia, Pa.

SMITH, Daniel Clarke Wharton, physician; b. Darlington, Md., Oct. 22, 1889; s. Courtauld Wharton and Lena Stuart (Janney) S.; Ph.B., Sheffield Sci. Sch. Yale U., 1911; M.D., Johns Hopkins Med. Sch., 1915; m. Edwina Caven Hensel, June 2, 1917. Interne City Hospitals, Baltimore, Johns Hopkins Hosp., 1915-17; in practice of medicine specializing in pediatrics at Baltimore since 1919; visiting pediatrician Johns Hopkins Hosp., Union Memorial Hosp., Hosp. for Women of Md.; asso. dir. Thomas Wilson Sanitarium. Served as capt. U.S.A., 1917-19; with A.E.F. Fellow Am. Acad. of Pediatrics; mem. Southern Med. Assn. A.M.A., Med. and Chirurg. Faculty of Med.; Baltimore City Med. Soc., Delta Psi. Democrat. Presbyn. Clubs: Maryland, Elkridge (Baltimore). Home: 17 Midvale Rd. Office: 108 E. 33d St., Baltimore, Md.

SMITH, Earl Baldwin, prof. art and archæology; b. Topsham, Me., May 25, 1888; s. Frank Eugene and Nellie Frances (Baldwin) S.; grad. Pratt Inst., Brooklyn, 1906; A.B., Bowdoin, 1911, L.H.D., 1931; A.M., Princeton, 1912, Ph.D., 1915; m. Ruth Preble Hall, Jan. 27, 1917 (died 1927); children—Mary Baldwin, Lacey Baldwin; m. 2d, Helen H. Hough, June 19, 1930; 1 son, Nathaniel Baldwin. Professor art and archæology, Princeton University since 1916. Served as capt. inf., U.S.A., World War. Mem. Atheneum, Archæol. Inst. of America, Coll. Art Assn., Am. Inst. for Persian Art (dir.), Am. Council of Learned Socs., Phi Beta Kappa, Psi Upsilon. Clubs: Nassau (Princeton); Princeton (New York). Author: Early Christian Iconography, 1918; Early Churches in Syria, 1929; Egyptian Architecture, 1938. Contributor to American Journal Archæology, Art Studies, Art and Archæology, The Art Bulletin. Home: 120 Broadmead, Princeton, N.J.

SMITH, Edward Brinton, Jr., investment banker; b. Phila., Pa., Dec. 5, 1896; s. Edward Brinton and Laura (Howell) S.; student St. Paul's Sch., Concord, N.H., 1914-17; m. Kathleen F. Lawrence; 1 dau., Kathleen (Mrs. Charles A. Black); m. 2d, Frances Paul Mills; children—Frances E., David Story Jenks. Mem. firm Smith, Barney & Co., investment bankers; pres. East Sugar Loaf Coal Co.; dir. Phila. & Western Ry. Co. Served in U.S. Navy with A.E.F., 1917-19. Chmn. finance com. Children's Hosp., Phila. Clubs: Radnor Hunt, Whitemarsh Valley Hunt, Racquet, Philadelphia. Home: "Sweetwaters," Edgemont, Chester Co., Pa. Office: 1411 Chestnut St., Philadelphia, Pa.

SMITH, Edward Grandison, lawyer; b. Horse Run, Harrison Co., W.Va., Apr. 8, 1868; s. Thomas Marion and Amy Minerva (Hoff) S.; LL.B., W.Va. Univ., 1889, LL.D., 1932; LL.B., Washington and Lee, 1892; LL.D., Salem (W.Va.) Coll., 1911; m. Jessie Blackshere, Oct. 18, 1899; children—John Blackshere, A.B., W.Va. U.; m. Catharine Lee Hamilton), Jill (A.B., W.Va. U.; m. Raville Lansing Turk). In practice of law at Clarksburg, W.Va., since 1892. Dem. nominee for judge Supreme Court of Appeals, 1912; del. to Dem. Nat. Conv., 1920; spl. atty U.S. Dept. Justice, 1935-36; trial examiner Nat. Labor Relations Board in the U.S. Stamping Co., Washington Mfg. Co. and Weirton Steel Co. cases, 1937; on regular trial examiners' staff since Sept. 1, 1937; mem. Coll. of Electors of Hall of Fame, New York U., 1935, reelected for 1940. Mem. bd. govs. W.Va. U., 1927-38, pres. bd., 1927-38. Mem. W.Va. Bar Assn. (chmn. com. on legal history until 1938), Am. Law Inst., S.R., S.A.R. (pres. W.Va. Soc., 1938-40), W.Va. U. Alumni Assn. (ex-pres.), Phi Delta Theta, Phi Delta Phi, Phi Beta Kappa, Order of Coif, Scabbard and Blade. Mason, Elk (life mem.). Has written The Plutocrat, 1892; Our Judiciary (1912; Needs of the University, 1913; Power Dams in Public Waters, 1914; Liberation, 1919; Price Regulation by Legislative Power, 1921; A Stonewall Phase, 1925; Judicial Law, 1928; The Amendment (Tax Limitation of W.Va.), 1932; Incidentally Non Justiciable Constitutional Questions Involved, 1933; Our Changing Constitution, 1934; Six Reasons for Supporting the President, 1936; Federal Measure of the Constitutionality of a Statute, 1936-37; The President's Supreme Court Proposal, 1937; Fundamentals, 1938; The Sit Down, 1939; The True Measure for Proposed Amendments to the National Labor Relations Act, 1939. Home: Dixie Farm, West Milford, W.Va. Office: Goff Bldg., Clarksburg, W.Va.

SMITH, Edward Patrick; asso. in gynecology and obstetrics, U. of Md.; obstetrician in chief and attending gynecologist Mercy Hosp.; mem. surg. staff Bon Secours Hosp.; mem. staff dept. gynecology, obstetrics and female urology West Baltimore Gen. Hosp.; 1st v.p. Med. and Chirurg. Faculty of Md.; mem. bd. govs. Mercy Hosp. Address: 920 St. Paul St., Baltimore, Md.

SMITH, Eliza Kennedy, pres. Pa. League of Women Voters; b. Latrobe, Pa., Dec. 11, 1889; d. Julian and Jane Eliza (Breneman) Kennedy; student Thurston Prep. Sch., Pittsburgh, 1896-1908; B.A., Vassar Coll., Poughkeepsie, N.Y., 1912; student Mrs. Catt's Sch. for Suffrage Workers, New York, 1912; m. R. Templeton Smith, Nov. 24, 1915; children—Templeton, Kennedy. Began as worker for woman suffrage, 1912; hqrs. chmn. Equal Franchise Fed., Pittsburgh, 1912-14, treas., 1914-17; pres. League of Girls Club, Pittsburgh, 1917-19; became asso. with League of Women Voters at its inception, 1919, and has served successively as co. govt. chmn., Allegheny Co. League of Women Voters, Pittsburgh, Pa., 1919-21, sec., 1921-23, pres. since 1923, v.p. Pa. League of Women Voters, Pittsburgh, Pa., 1935-38, pres. since 1938; sec. Poland Coal Co., Lowber Gas Coal Co., Ontario Gas Coal Co. Liberty Loan worker during World War. Chmn. women's div. of Citizens' Com. which investigated Supplies Dept. of City of Pittsburgh and in 1931 indicted and convicted Mayor and head of Supplies Dept.; official budget advisor of Mayor of Pittsburgh, 1932-33. Vice-pres. Pittsburgh Housing Assn. Mem. Congress of Women's Clubs, Pittsburgh, Asso. Alumnae of Vassar Coll., Poughkeepsie, N.Y., and Pittsburgh. Republican. Clubs: Twentieth Century, College (Pittsburgh). Author: Recommendations to the Mayor on the Budget of the City of Pittsburgh for the Year 1934. Home: 1336 Shady Av. Office: 605 Peoples Bank Bldg., Pittsburgh, Pa.

SMITH, Elva Sophronia; b. Burke, Vt., 1871; d. Franklin Horatio and Hattie Lovisa (Powers) S.; grad. Lyndon Inst., 1888; grad. Vt. State Normal Sch., 1890; grad. Carnegie Library Sch., Pittsburgh, Pa., 1902. Teacher pub. schs., Vt. and Calif., until 1901; mem. staff Carnegie Library, Pittsburgh, since 1902, now head of children's dept.; teacher Carnegie Library Sch. since 1904, now asso. prof. of library science; instr. extension div., Pa. State Coll., 1922-25. Associate chmn. of home education, National Congress of Parents and Teachers since 1934. Mem. A.L.A. (exec. bd. and council, 1926-30; chmn. children's librarian's sect. book production com., 1924-29), Pa. Library Assn., Carnegie Library School Assn. (pres. 1921-28), Foreign Policy Association. Unitarian. Clubs: Authors', Library (Pittsburgh); Nat. Travel. Editor: Christmas in Legend and Story (with Alice I. Hazeltine), 1915; Mystery Tales for Boys and Girls, 1917; Good Old Stories for Boys and Girls, 1919; Peace and Patriotism, 1919; Heroines of History and Legend, 1921; More Mystery Tales for Boys and Girls, 1922; A Book of Lullabies, 1925; Subject Headings for Children's Books, 1933; The Cataloging of Children's Books, 1933. Selected contents and wrote preface of The Gold-Bug, and Other Tales and Poems, by Edgar Allan Poe, 1930, The History of Children's Literature, 1937. Compiler of numerous annotated catalogues and bibliographies. Home: Cathedral Mansions, Ellsworth Av., Pittsburgh, Pa. Office: Library, Pittsburgh, Pa.

SMITH, Ernest G(ray), newspaper pub.; b. Martin's Ferry, O.. Oct. 26, 1873; s. Hiram Wolfe and Evangeline (Lash) S.; Ph.B., Lafayette Coll., Easton, Pa., 1894, M.S., 1897; LL.B., Yale, 1896; m. Marjorie Harvey, Oct. 14, 1913; children—Harrison Harvey, Lois Gray, Andries DeWitt. Began as pub. Wilkes-Barre Times-Leader, 1905; pres. Leader Pub. Co., T. L. Printery, Inc., Wilkes-Barre Airport Co., Anthracite Broadcasting, Inc., Lafayette Press, Inc., Easton, Pa.; chmn. Pa. Div. Associated Press; dir. Second Nat. Bank, Wilkes-Barre Hotels Corpn., Audit Bur. of Circulation, Chicago. Served as pvt. inf. U.S.A., Cuba, Philippines and China, 1898-1902; maj and lt. col., World War; now col. Inf. R.C. Chmn. Pa. State Parks Commn.; mem. Pa.. State Publicity Commn. Past pres. Chamber Commerce of Wilkes-Barre; Pres. Wilkes-Barre Playgrounds and Recreation Assn., pres. Wilkes-Barre Publishers Assn.; v.p. Pa. Parks Assn.; trustee Lafayette Coll., F. M. Kirby Am. Legion Foundation. Co-author Harvey-Smith History of Wilkes-Barre. Decorated D.S.M. (U.S.), 1919; Officer Black Star (France), 1919. Author: History of Northeastern Pennsylvania. Home: 4 Riverside Drive. Address: Times-Leader Bldg., Wilkes-Barre, Pa.

SMITH, Ethelbert Walton, ry. official; b. Clarksburg, W.Va., Sept. 21, 1885; s. Mortimer W. and Lucy (Walton) S.; M.E., Virginia Polytechnic Inst., 1905; m. Frances Woodbridge Sprecher, Feb. 18, 1914; 1 son, Ethelbert Walton. Shopman Pa. R.R., 1905, advanced through various positions to gen. supt. of motive power, 1922, gen. supt., 1924-26, gen. mgr., 1926-28, regional v.p., 1928-31, v.p. at Pittsburgh since 1933; co-receiver S.A.L. Ry., 1931-32; pres., Akron & Barberton Belt R.R., Akron Union Passgr. Depot Co., Duquesne Warehouse Co., Pennsylvania-Ontario Transportation Co., Pittsburgh Joint Stock Yards Co., Waynesburg & Washington R.R., Western Allegheny R.R.; v.p. Lake Erie & Pittsburgh Ry. Co., Monongahela Ry. Co., Pittsburgh, Chartiers & Youghiogheny Ry. Co., Zanesville Terminal R.R. Co. Clubs: Pittsburgh, Longue Vue, Duquesne. Home: 5621 Northumberland St. Office: 908 Pennsylvania Station, Pittsburgh, Pa.

SMITH, F. Raymond, asso. prof. physics; b. Grand Ledge, Mich., Nov. 17, 1891; s. Byron Seth and Anna Emily (Lanning) S.; A.B., Albion (Mich.) Coll., 1914; A.M., U. of Mich., 1921, Ph.D., 1927; m. E. Donella Kinsel, Dec. 25, 1917; children—Robert Kinsel, Raymond Lanning, Richard Henry. Began as sci. teacher, high schs. in Mich., 1914-16; instr. physics, Kan. State Coll., 1916-18; engr. Western Electric Co., New York, N.Y.; asst. prof. physics, Pa. State Coll., 1919-26, asso. prof. since 1926. Fellow A.A.A.S. Mem. Am. Phys. Soc., Sigma Xi, Sigma Pi Sigma, Sigma Nu. Republican. Methodist. Mason. Home: 438 E. Foster Av., State College, Pa.

SMITH, Frank Austin, clergyman; b. Lynn, Mass., June 25, 1866; s. Herbert Austin and Helen Maria (Burrill) S.; grad. Adelphi Acad., 1885; A.B., Brown U., 1889, D.D., 1917; grad. Crozer Theol. Sem., 1892; m. Blanche A. Voorhees, Sept. 23, 1902; 1 son, Herbert Stanley (dec.). Ordained Bapt. ministry, 1892; pastor 1st Ch., Somerville, 1892-1902, 1st Ch., Haddonfield, 1902-12, Central Ch., Elizabeth, 1912-24; sec. of missions, Am. Bapt. Home Mission Soc., 1924-36, Bd. Edn. of Northern Bapt. Conv. 1936—; sec. of Edn., N.J. Bapt. Conv., 1898-1924; mem. exec. com. Internat. S.S. Assn., 1901-08; mem. Bapt. Deputation to Far East, 1907. Trustee Crozer Theol. Sem., Peddie Inst., etc. Mem. Nat. Soc. S.A.R. (chaplain gen.), Phi Delta Theta. Clubs: Quill, Clergy, Roselle Golf. Home: 219 Stiles St., Elizabeth, N.J. Address: 152 Madison Av., New York, N.Y.

SMITH, Frank Webster, educator, publicist; b. Lincoln, Mass., June 27, 1854; s. Francis and Abigail Prescott (Baker) S.; grad. Phillips Academy, Andover, 1873; A.B., Harvard, 1877, grad. study classical philology and economics, 1881-83, A.M., 1882, psychology, summer 1894; Teachers Coll. (Columbia), 1899-1900; grad. student and teacher, U. of Neb., 1901-04, Ph.D., 1904; studied in England, summer, 1902; m. Annie Noyes Sinclair, Dec. 1894 (died 1897); m. 2d, Helen Louise Moore, of Omaha, Neb., Oct. 23, 1900; children—Francis Prescott, Charles Webster. Teacher Atlanta U., 1877-81, Boston Evening Sch., 1882-83, State Normal Sch., Westfield, Mass., 1883-96; supt. pub. schs., Grand Junction, Colo., 1896-99; sec. Teachers Coll. (Columbia), 1900; prin. Gordon Acad. and Training Sch., Salt Lake City, and supt. Congl. Schs. of Utah, 1900-01, also city examiner Salt Lake City, 1900; adj. prof. edn. U. of Neb., 1903-05; prin. City Normal Sch., Paterson, N.J., 1905-23, and city examiner, Paterson, 1905-20; 1st prin. State Normal Sch., Paterson (city normal sch. adopted by state), 1923-25; pres. emeritus State Normal Sch. (later State Teachers Coll.), Paterson, N.J., since 1925; state examiner, N.J., 1923-25. Has served as pres. educational organizations; exec. sec. and treas. Municipal Normal School and Teachers Coll. Assn., 13 yrs. to 1936, now pres. emeritus; dir. Colo. state ednl. exhibit, Trans-Mississippi Expn., 1898. Member N.E.A., Paterson Teachers Association, Phi Beta Kappa (Harvard), Pythagorean Club (ex-pres.). Republican. Presbyn.; commr. Gen. Assembly, 1927. Author: The High School—a Study of Origins and Tendencies, 1916; Jesus—Teacher, Principles of Teaching for Secular and Bible School Teachers, 1916; also magazine articles on edn. and economics. Address: 65 N. Maple Av., Ridgewood, N.J., and Box 442, Winter Haven, Fla.

SMITH, Frank William, real estate and ins.; b. Corry, Pa., Apr. 6, 1872; s. Andrew J. and Margaret (Van Buskirk) S.; student high sch., Corry, Pa. and Corry Business Coll.; Ph.G., U. of Buffalo, 1897; m. Bertha Marie Wolcott, Sept. 7, 1904; children—Kenneth Wolcott, Jeanne Marie (Mrs. A. Richard Wilson), Gladys Ruth. Clerk in wholesale and retail grocery store, 1888-95; partner gen. store, Spring Creek, Pa., 1895-97; pharmacist, Buffalo, N.Y., 1897, Warren, Pa., 1898-1903; fire ins. agt. Warren, 1903-07; accountant and treas. Valvoline Oil Works, Ltd., Butler, Pa., 1907-27; real estate and insurance as owner Butler County Realty Co. since 1927. Mem. Butler Chamber cf Commerce, Butler Real Estate Bd. Republican. Presbyterian. Mason. Former Rotarian. Mem. United Commercial Travelers. Home: 435 N. Washington St. Office: 231 S. Main St., Butler, Pa.

SMITH, Fred Manning, univ. prof.; b. Charleston, W.Va., Feb. 21, 1891; s. Charles Ballard and Mary (McConihay) S.; A.B., W.Va., U., Morgantown, 1913; B.A., Queen's Coll. Oxford U., Eng., 1916, M.A., 1919; Ph.D., Cornell U., 1922; unmarried. Instr. English, Glenville (W.Va.) State Coll., Glenville, 1916-17; instr. English, Cornell U., 1917-23; asst. prof. English, Ohio State U., Columbus, 1923-27; asst. and asso. prof. English, W.Va. Univ., 1927-39, prof. since 1939. Served as corpl. inf., U.S.A., 1918. Mem. Modern Lang. Assn., S.A.R., Phi Beta Kappa, Phi Kappa Phi. Awarded Rhodes Scholarship, 1912; Cornell Fellowship in English, 1917. Republican. Presbyn. Contbr. articles to dictionary, W.Va. handbook, and publs. of Modern Lang. Assn. Home: 200 S. High St., Morgantown, W.Va.

SMITH, Frederic William, lawyer; b. Newark, N.J., Jan. 26, 1880; s. Edwin and Ella L. (Francisco) S.; B.S., Rutgers Coll., 1902, M.S., 1905; LL.B., New York U., 1904; m. Grace Harris, Nov. 12, 1913 (died Apr. 28, 1923); children—Grace Winifred, Harris Frederic. Admitted to N.J. bar, 1905; practiced alone until 1917; mem. firm Day, Day, Smith & Slingerland, 1917-18; mem. Smith & Slingerland since 1918; sec. and dir. Pocono Hotels Corpn.; also officer or dir. various other companies; dir. Maplewood Bank & Trust Co., Newark Provident Loan Association, Fidelity Union Trust Co. Became pres. Nat. Council Y.M.C.A.'s of U.S., 1933; pres. Newark Welfare Fed. (community chest), 1931-35. Pres. Centenary Fund and Preachers' Aid Soc.; pres. Newark Y.M.C.A.; trustee Florence Crittenton League; trustee of Newark Univ., Rutgers Univ. Mem. Am. Bar Assn., N.J. State and Essex Co. bar assns., Delta Upsilon. Republican. Methodist. Mason. Clubs: Essex (Newark); Shongum (N.J.); Sky Top (Pa.). Home: 38 Kendall Av., Maplewood, N.J. Office: 744 Broad St., Newark, N.J.

SMITH, Frederick Cleveland, physician, proctologist; b. Phila., Pa., June 12, 1892; s. Gustavus Monroe and Harriet Amelia (Dodge) S.; M.D., Medico Chirurg. Coll., Phila., 1913; M.Sc. (Med.), U. of Pa. Grad. Sch. of Medicine, 1922; m. Isabel Clough Wolstenholme, Sept. 10, 1912; children—Isabel Phyllis, Frederick Cleveland, Jr. Engaged in gen. practice of medicine, Halifax, Pa., 1913-17; specializing in proctology since 1922; editor The Medical World since 1935; editor F. A. Davis Pub. Co. since May 1938; med. dir., Phila. Mutual Aid Soc. and United Friends Soc. since 1920. Served as 1st lieut. Med. Res. Corps, U.S.A., then capt., 1917, maj., 1924, lieut. col. since 1930; attached to British Army in France, 1917-18, wounded July 4, 1918. Fellow A.M.A., Am. Proctologic Soc.; mem. Pa. State and Phila. Co. med. socs., Proctologic Soc. Grad. Hosp. U. of Pa. (past pres.), Phi Beta Pi. Republican. Presbyn. Mason (K.T., Shriner). I.O.O.F. Club: Aesculapian. Author: Proctology for the General Practitioner, 1939. Contbr. many articles in med. jours. Home: 6247 Haverford Av. Office: 1737 Chestnut St., Philadelphia, Pa.

SMITH, Frederick O., iron mfr.; b. Wilkes-Barre, Pa., Jan. 28, 1876; s. Frederick G. and Charlotte (Rittersbach) S.; student Wilkes-Barre Pub. Sch. and Harry Hillman Acad.; m. Maude Priscilla Nagle, Sept. 14, 1899; children—Ralph O., Alan N. Began as machinist apprentice, 1890; v.p., asst. gen. mgr. and dir. Vulcan Iron Works; pres., treas. and dir. Wilkes-Barre Iron Mfg. Co.; dir. First Nat. Bank (all of Wilkes-Barre). Mem. Am. Iron and Steel Inst. Republican. Presbyterian. Clubs: Westmoreland, Wyoming Valley Country, Franklin (Wilkes-Barre); Skytop (Skytop, Pa.). Home: 16 Riverside Drive. Office: 730 S. Main St., Wilkes-Barre, Pa.

SMITH, Geoffrey Story, lawyer; b. Phila., Pa., Jan. 31, 1901; s. Edward B. and Laura (Howell) S.; grad. St. Paul's Sch., Concord, N.H., 1918; A.B. Harvard, 1922; LL.B., U. of Pa., 1925; m. Katherine Coolidge, June 17, 1922; children—Geoffrey Story, Ann Coolidge, Kaighn, William Coolidge. Admitted to Pa. bar, 1925; asso. with law firm Drinker, Biddle & Reath, Phila., 1925-32; partner Dechert, Bok & Smith, Phila., 1932-34, Dechert, Smith & Clark since 1934; mem. bd. mgrs. Girard Trust Co.; dir. J. Edwards Co., Darby, Media & Chester St. Ry. Co., East Sugar Loaf Coal Co. Pres. Community Fund of Phila. and Vicinity. Trustee St. Paul's Sch., Thomas Skelton Harrison Foundation, Phila. Republican. Episcopalian. Clubs: Philadelphia, Racquet, White Marsh Valley, Hunt (Phila.). Home: Fort Washington, Pa. Office: Packard Bldg., Philadelphia, Pa.

SMITH, George Morris Beltzhoover, clergyman, educator; b. Strasburg, Va., May 17, 1891; s. Luther Leigh and Virginia Elizabeth (Brown) S.; grad. Franklin and Marshall Acad., Lancaster, Pa., 1907; A.B., Roanoke Coll., Salem, Va., 1911, D.D., 1928; A.M., Princeton, 1912; grad. Luth. Theol. Sem., Phila., Pa., 1919; m. Lillian Johanson, June 30, 1920; children—Elizabeth Virginia, George Morris, John Leigh. Teacher, Blair Acad., Blairstown, N.J., 1912-16; ordained ministry Luth. Ch., 1918; pastor First English Luth. Ch., Mt. Vernon, N.Y., 1918-20, Evang. Luth. Ch. of the Redeemer, Buffalo, N.Y., 1920-28; pres. Susquehanna U., Selinsgrove, Pa., since 1928. Mem. College Presidents' Association of Pennsylvania, Pi Gamma Mu. Rotarian. Contbr. to Gospel Preaching for the Day, and Epistle Messages. Home: Selinsgrove, Pa.

SMITH, George Scott, newspaperman, publisher; b. Cooperstown, N.Y., Apr. 25, 1876; s. Almon White and Martha (James) S.; ed. Lyons (N.Y.) Union Sch., 1883-95; m. Sarah Bessie Mundy, Jan. 7, 1907; children—Martha Elizabeth (Mrs. Joseph M. Harre), Adelaide Susan (Mrs. William T. Henretta), T. Scott. Reporter Williamsport (Pa.) Sun, 1898; purchased Jersey Shore (Pa.) Herald, 1902, converting it into a daily paper, May 1903; became part-owner and publisher Bradford (Pa.) Daily Record, 1907, Reading (Pa.) Times, 1908, and Bridgeport (Conn.) Telegram, 1911; owner and publisher Kane Republican since 1912; dir. and mem. exec. com. Kane Bank & Trust Co.; dir. Esther Oil Corpn. Chmn. McKean Co. Rep. Com., 1918-36; mem. Rep. State Com., 1920-38; referee for dist. of Northwestern Pa. under the state workmen's law, 1916-35. Republican. Club: Kane Country. Home: 435 Chase St. Office: Republican Bldg., Kane, Pa.

SMITH, George Theodore, executive; b. N.Y. City, Apr. 29, 1855; s. Charles Tappan and Martha Elizabeth S.; student Coll. City of New York; m. Hattie Louise Young, Apr. 25, 1882; children—Edward Young (dec.), Natalie Young (Mrs. L. Fred Bruce). Pres. Am. Graphite Co., Joseph Dixon Crucible Co.; v.p. Colonial Life Insurance Co. of America, Raritan River R.R.; mem. bd. mgrs. Provident Instn. for Savings. Home: 2652 Hudson Boul. Office: 167 Wayne St., Jersey City, N.J.

SMITH, George V(alentine), gen. insurance; b. Phila., Pa., June 24, 1883; s. William Rudolph and Elizabeth (Bailey) S.; student Episcopal Acad., Phila., 1895-1900, Univ. of Pa., 1900-03; m. Eugene Oakes Rand, Feb. 15, 1918; 1 son, George Valentine. Began as ins. clerk, 1903; mem. firm Haughton & Smith, gen. ins. agts. and brokers, 1905-12; mem. firm Stokes, Packard, Haughton & Smith, 1912-33, named changed to Stokes, Packard & Smith Inc., 1933, pres. since 1935; dir. United Firemen's Ins. Co. of Philadelphia. Mem. exec. com. Phila. Fire Underwriters Assn. Served as mem. 1st Troop, Phila. City Cav., 1904-13; capt. Air Service, U.S. Army, during World War. Mem. Sons of the Revolution, Delta Psi. Episcopalian. Clubs: Philadelphia, Racquet, St. Anthony, Gulph Mills Golf (Phila.); St. Anthony (New York). Home: Glenn Rd., Ardmore, Pa. Office: 1608 Walnut St., Philadelphia, Pa.

SMITH, Gilbert, coal operator; b. Stockton, Pa., June 15, 1879; student pub. schs. Luzerne Co., Pa. and Internat. Corr. Schs., Scranton, Pa.; m. Margaret Susan Eagenbright, June 7, 1905; children—Mary Elizabeth, Helen, Margaret Susan, Joseph Wilson, Charles Gilbert, Hugh Holt, Rebecca, Paul Willard. Employed as supt. mines, McKell Coal & Coke Co., 1904-07, Thormond Coal Co., 1907-20; gen. mgr. Fire Creek Coal & Coke Co., Mason Coal Co., Inc., Dunedin Coal Co., Inc., The Erskine Co. Inc. Mem. Am. Mining Congress, New River Coal Operators Assn. (pres.). Republican. Presbyn. Mason (32°). Home: Fayetteville, W.Va.

SMITH, H. Alexander, lawyer; b. New York, N.Y., Jan. 30, 1880; s. Abram Alexander (M.D.) and Sue Lehn (Bender) S.; A.B., Princeton, 1901; LL.B., Columbia U. Sch. of Law, 1904; LL.D., U. of Brussels, Belgium, 1930; m. Helen Dominick, June 21, 1902; children—Helen Dominick (Mrs. Samuel Moor Shoemaker, Jr.), Marian Dominick (Mrs. Herbert Kenaston Twitchell), H. Alexander. Admitted to N.Y. bar, 1904, Colo. bar, 1905; in practice at Colorado Springs, Colo., 1905-18; chmn. com. on organization of trustees and faculty, Princeton U., 1919-20, exec. sec. of Univ., 1920-27, lecturer on internat. relations, 1927-30; in practice, N.Y. City, since 1932, in association with Hines, Rearick, Dorr & Hammond. Mem. Mr. Hoover's staff, U.S. Food Adminstrn., 1918. Mem. exec. com. and dir. European Children's Fund, 1919-21; mem. exec. com. and dir. Belgian Am. Ednl. Foundation; trustee Princeton Yenching Foundation; dir. Foreign Policy Assn.; mem. visiting com., Dept. of Art and Archæology, Princeton U.; mem. N.J. exec. com. Nat. Economy League; mem. nat. council Nat. Economic League. Mem. Am. Bar Assn., Acad. Polit. and Social Science, Acad. Polit. Science, Am. Inst. Mining and Metall. Engrs., Princeton Engring. Soc., Council on Foreign Relations. Soc. Colonial Wars. Decorated Officer Order of Leopold (Belgium); Officer Order Crown of Belgium; Comdr. Order of St. Sava (Serbia); also medal of Comite Nationale (Belgium), Red Cross medal and Cross of Charity (Serbia). Republican; treas. N.J. Rep. State Com. since Aug. 1934; mem. Com. on Program, Rep. Nat. Com. since 1937. Presbyn. Clubs: University, City Midday, Princeton, Nat. Republican Club (New York); Nassau, Cap and Gown, Colonial, Springdale, Golf, Pretty Brook Tennis (Princeton, N.J.). Home: 81 Alexander St., Princeton, N.J. Office: 61 Broadway, New York, N.Y.

SMITH, H. Arthur, pres. Trenton Trust Co., 1914-37, chmn. of bd. since Jan. 1937, also pres. Real Estate Title Co. of N.J.; pres. and dir. Fitz-Gibbon & Crisp, Inc.; dir. The Autocar Co., Hotel Realty Co., The Tattersall Co., and officer or dir. various other corpns. Home: Lawrenceville, N.J. Office: 28 W. State St., Trenton, N.J.

SMITH, H. Webster, mem. law firm Smith & Cross. Office: Mercantile Trust Bldg., Baltimore, Md.

SMITH, Harold Brown, printing and office supplies; b. Conneautville, Pa., Dec. 28, 1888; s. James Harrison and Carlie (Brown) S.; A.B., Washington & Jefferson Coll., 1910; m. Eleanor Thompson, Jan. 29, 1913. Real estate and oil lease broker, Hugo, Okla., 1910-15; advertising and sales mgr. A. W. McCloy Co., office supplies, Pittsburgh, Pa., 1915-23; partner Acme Printing and Stationery Co., office supplies and printing, Pittsburgh, since 1923. Mem. Kappa Sigma. Republican. Presbyterian (trustee and treas. Fouth Presbyn. Ch.). Clubs: Wildwood (dir.), Metropolitan of Pittsburgh (dir.); Kiwanis of Pittsburgh (pres. 1934; lt. gov. Pa. Dist., 1935, 36). Home: 1233 Bellrock St. Office: Arrott Power Bldg., Pittsburgh, Pa.

SMITH Harold Calmes, lawyer and dairy farmer; b. Rockville, Maryland, January 14, 1894; s. Edwin and Lucy S. (Black) S.; student Rockville Academy, 1911, Davidson (N.C.) College, 1911-12, University of Texas, 1914-16; LL.B., George Washington University, 1921; m. Anne F. Smith, Oct. 5, 1917; children—Anne Louise, Harold Calmes, Lucey Neville. Admitted to Tex. bar, 1915; practiced in Corpus Christi and Falfurrius, 1915-18; county atty., Brooks County, Tex., 1916-17; legal sec. U.S. Veterans Bur., 1919-25; admitted to Md. bar, 1924, and practiced in Rockville since 1925; judge of police court Montgomery County, Md., since 1935. Served in Co. C, 17th Inf., 1915-18. U.S. Army, World War; commd. 2d lt. Res., 1924; capt. U.S. Marine Corps Res., 1930. A founder and sec. Rockville Chamber Commerce. Rep. candidate for Congress, 6th Congl. Dist., 1932. Mem. Montgomery County Bar Assn., Am. Legion (comdr. local post 1921; mem. State exec. com., 1921-26; comdr. State of Md. 1927-28). Presbyn. Mason (Shriner, K.T.). Author: Montgomery County Code of Local Laws, 1927. Home: 108 Forest Av., Rockville, Md.

SMITH, Harold Morrison, educator; b. Falls City, Neb., Jan. 22, 1888; s. Alvin Leroy and Annie Laurie (Campbell) S.; grad. Proctor Acad., Andover, N.H., 1909; A.B., Bates Coll., Lewiston, Me., 1914; A.M., Columbia U., 1929; m. Bessie S. Braley, Dec. 24, 1910; 1 son, Morris Wadleigh. Began as teacher in country sch., 1905; asst. and instr. dept. geology and astronomy, Bates Coll., 1914-15; prin. Norridgewock (Me.) High Sch., 1915-16, Hopkinton High Sch., Contoocook, N.H., 1916-18, New Hampton (N.H.) Sch., 1918-21; headmaster, Pembroke (N.H.) Acad., 1921-32; dean and co-principal, Bordentown (N.J.) Mil. Inst., since 1932, now also sec. of corpn. Mem. N.H. Acad. Arts and Sciences, Phila., Headmaster's Club. Baptist. A.F.& A.M. (past-master; Shriner). Speaker for civic bodies, service clubs, young people's orgns., etc., and lecturer principally upon hist. subjects for many years. Active in Y.M.C.A., Boy Scout, and Red Cross work. Home: 46 Park St., Bordentown, N.J.

SMITH, Harradon Sterling, cons. engring.; b. Wilkes-Barre, Pa., Dec. 29, 1866; s. Douglass and Mary E. (Faser) S.; ed. Wilkes-Barre Acad., 1880-84; m. Elizabeth B. Hollister, Aug. 8, 1889; children—Harradon Hollister, Douglass Lee. Employed as mining engr., 1885-96; consulting engr. on county rds. and bridges, mining, and pub. works of various boroughs, at Wilkes-Barre, Pa., since 1896; pres. S. & S. Mining Co. since 1936. Life mem. Am. Soc. Civil Engrs. Mem. Am. Philatelic Soc., Wyoming Valley Philatelic Soc. (past pres.), United Sportsmen of Pa. (pres.), North East Div. Fed. of Sportsmens Clubs of Pa. (past pres.). Republican. Presbyn. Elk. Kiwanian. Home: 40 Yeager Av., Forty Fort, Pa. Office: Bennett Bldg., Wilkes-Barre, Pa.

SMITH, Harriet Lummis (Mrs. William M. Smith), writer; b. Auburndale, Mass.; d. Henry and Jennie (Brewster) Lummis; A.B., Lawrence Coll., Appleton, Wis.; m. William M. Smith, Oct. 11, 1905. Began writing for newspapers and mags. as a girl; has contributed to McClure's, Munsey's, Harper's Bazaar. Youth's Companion, Delineator, etc. Presbyn. Clubs: Woman's Literary (Baltimore); Philomusian (Phila.). Writer of continuation of "Pollyanna" series of books begun by Eleanor Porter. Author: Girls of Friendly Terrace, 1912; Peggy Raymond's Vacation, 1913; Other People's Business, 1916; Peggy Raymond's School Days, 1916; Friendly Terrace Quartette, 1920; Agatha's Aunt, 1920; Peggy Raymond's Way, 1922; Pollyanna of the Orange Blossoms, 1924; Pollyanna's Jewels, 1925; Uncertain Glory, 1926; Pollyanna's Debt of Honor, 1927; Pat and Pal, 1928;

SMITH, Harrison Bowne, investments and ins.; b. Charleston, W.Va., Mar. 2, 1898; s. Harrison Brooks and Katharine Dana (Bowne) S.; A.B., Princeton U., 1920; m. Dorothy Thayer, June 23, 1920; children—Dorothy Bowne, Harrison Bowne, Jr. Employed as clk. in treasury dept., George Washington Life Ins., Co., Charleston, W.Va., 1920-22, asst. to treas., 1922-24, asst. to pres., 1924-28, exec. vice-pres., 1928-36, resigned, 1936 to devote to pvt. interests; sec., treas. and dir. W.Va. Coal Land Co. since 1927, treas. and dir. Kanawha Co., both investment trusts or holding cos., Charleston, W.Va.; dir. Kanawha Drug Co. and Charleston Transit Co., Charleston. Served in R.O.T.C. and F.A. O.T.C. Zachary Taylor, Ky., 1917-18. Formerly active in Charleston Community Chest. Mem. Phi Beta Kappa, Cap & Gown, Princeton. Presbyn. Club: Edgewood Country. Home: "Bougemont," South Hills. Office: 811-813 Kanawha Bank & Trust Co. Bldg., Charleston, W.Va.

SMITH, Harry Lanich, pharmacist; b. Lock Haven, Pa., Nov. 6, 1893; s. James Philip and Della (Lanich) Smith; P.D., Phila. College of Pharmacy, 1915; m. Elsie Mae Kerchner, Jan. 1, 1917; children—Thelma Estella (Mrs. William Charles Brosha), Eunice Mae. Pharmacist and propr. pharmacy at Jersey Shore, Pa., since 1915; vice-pres. and dir. Jersey Short State Bank; dir. Community Plan Co. Pres. and dir. Jersey Shore Bd. Edn. Mem. Chamber of Commerce, Commercial Club. Mem. Nat. Assn. Retail Druggists, Pa. Pharm. Assn., Zeta Delta Chi. Republican. Episcopalian. Mason (32°, Shriner). Elk. Moose. Home: 1324 Allegheny St., Jersey Shore, Pa.

SMITH, Harry Leo, dist. life ins. agent; b. Hampton, Hunterdon Co., N.J., Aug. 17, 1883; s. Mahlon Aller and Ella Frances (Aller) S.; studied Hampton (N.J.) Grade Sch., 1890-97, Washington (N.J.) High Sch., 1897-99, Mergenthaler Linotype Sch., Brooklyn, 1907; m. Mae Edith Milham, Jan. 11, 1914 (died Dec. 16, 1925); m. 2d, Rebecca Dill Hoagland, Sept. 17, 1927. Began as printer, 1899; linotype operator and machinist, 1907-17; spl. agent Northwestern Mutual Life Ins. Co., 1917-27, dist. agent since 1927; dir. First Nat. Bank, Washington, N.J. Mem. Sons and Daughters of Liberty. Republican. Presbyn. Mason (Shriner, 32°, Scottish Rite), Patriotic Order Sons of America, Elk. Clubs: Kiwanis of Washington, N.J. (past pres., dir.), Washington Athletic Assn. (ex-sec.). Address: 23 W. Stewart St., Washington, N.J.

SMITH, Harvey F(etterhoff), M.D.; b. Dauphin Co., Pa., July 24, 1871; s. John K. and Eliza (Fetterhoff) S.; student Harrisburg High Sch., 1885-88; B.S., Bucknell U., 1894, D.Sc., 1924; M.D., U. of Pa., 1897; LL.D., John B. Stetson U., Fla., 1923; m. Blanche McNeal, July 31, 1901; children—Robert McNeal, Eleanor Neal (Mrs. Thomas Toby). Interne St. Joseph Hosp., 1897-99; surgical practice in Harrisburg since 1899; dir. Harrisburg Trust Co. Trustee Bucknell U. Fellow Am. Coll. Surgeons; mem. Harrisburg Acad., Pa. State Med. Soc., Phi Kappa Psi. Republican. Methodist. Clubs: Harrisburg Country, University (Harrisburg). Home: Fort Hunter, Pa. Office: 130 State St., Harrisburg, Pa.

SMITH, Harvey H(avelock), real estate; b. Pittsburgh, Pa., Nov. 3, 1860; s. Henry and Hannah (Firth) S.; grad. Pittsburgh Central High Sch., 1877; student Holy Ghost Coll., 1879; unmarried. Pres. Mackenzie Davis Lithographing Co., 1890-1903, Eighbaum Lithgrophing & Printing Co., 1903-06, Smith-Wehner Lithograph Co., 1906-08; pres. Fidelis Realty Co., Pittsburgh, since 1908; pres. Oakland Corpn. since 1912. Mem. council com. Oakland Y.M.C.A. Episcopalian; mem. Diocesan Bd. of Trustees, P.E. Ch. since 1910; pres. Laymen's Missionary League; treas. Clergymans Life Ins. Assn.; mem. Religious Edn. Commn.; senior warden St. Peter's Parish. Republican. Mason (K.T., 32°). Home: 282 Bellefield Av. Office: 3707 5th Av., Pittsburgh, Pa.

SMITH, Henry Bradford, prof. philosophy; b. Phila., Pa., Jan. 14, 1882; s. Henry Augustus and Martha Louise (Stevenson) S.; A.B., U. of Pa., 1903, Ph.D., 1909; studied Harvard, 1904-05, Munich, 1 semester, 1906; m. Mary Follett Perkins, Sept. 13, 1915 (died Jan. 20, 1925). Harrison scholar in philosophy, U. of Pa., 1903-04, 1905-06; fellow in philosophy same univ., 1906-07, research fellow same univ., 1910; instr. mathematics, Tufts Coll., 1904-05, Carnegie Inst., Pittsburgh, 1907-10; instr. mathematics, U. of Pa., 1911, in philosophy, 1911-16, asst. prof., 1916-24, prof. since 1924; sometime acting professor philosophy, University of Delaware, University of Washington and Bryn Mawr Coll. Mem. advisory bd. Philosophy of Science (mag.). Mem. Am. Philos. Assn., Institut Artist. et Lit. de France, British Inst. of Philosophy, Am. Acad. Polit. and Social Science, N.E. Soc. of Pa., Alliance Française, Pi Mu Epsilon, Phi Beta Kappa. Author: A First Book in Logic, 1922; How the Mind Falls into Error, 1923; The Collective Mind, 1924; A System of Formal Logic, 1926; Symbolic Logic, 1927; Science of Modality, 1934; also monographs and numerous articles in jours. Address: Univ. of Pennsylvania, Philadelphia, Pa.

SMITH, Hervey Bushnell, lawyer; b. Bloomburg, Pa., Dec. 23, 1905; s. Hervey Montgomery and Harriet E. (Bushnell) S.; grad. Bloomsburg State Teachers Coll., 1922; B.S., Lafayette Coll., 1925; student Mich. Law Sch., 1925-26, Dickenson Law School, 1927-30; m. Pauline M. Leitzel, Feb. 5, 1935. Admitted to Pa. bar, 1930, and since practiced in Bloomsburg; asso. with father H. Montgomery Smith (grandfather Hervey E. Smith and great-grandfather, Arthur C. Smith, all practiced law in Bloomsburg), solicitor for the Town of Bloomsburg since 1935. Sec. Columbia Co. Dem. Exec. Com. since 1930. Commd. 2d lt. O.R.C. Mem. Pa. Bar Assn., Phi Delta Theta; hon. mem. Vets. Foreign Wars. Democrat. Presbyterian. Mason, Elk, Moose. Home: 537 Market St. Office: 158 Court House Place, Bloomsburg, Pa.

SMITH, Horace Taylor, lawyer; b. Baltimore, Md., June 30, 1884; s. Horace Laurence and Elizabeth Jervis (Nimmo) S.; student Baltimore (Md.) Poly. Inst., 1898-1902; LL.B., U. of Md., Baltimore, Md., 1906; m. Mabel Wolf Smith, Nov. 11, 1911; children—Margaret Stewart (Mrs. John Edward Schmeiser), Sarah Legare. Admitted to practice before courts of Md., 1907, before U.S. Supreme Court, 1917; instr. U. of Md. Sch. of Law, Baltimore, Md., 1911-12; in practice at Baltimore, Md., since 1907; dir. B. F. Bond Paper Co., Industrial Paper Co. Served as legal advisor under selective service law during World War. Mem. Zoning Commn. of Baltimore (Md.), 1927-29; pres. Roland Park Civic League, 1928-30, pres. Baltimore Bapt. Laymens Assn., 1928-29. Dir. Baltimore Bar Library, 1933-36; trustee Eutaw Pl. Baptist Ch., Baltimore, Md. Mem. Am. Arbitration Assn. (mem. Nat. Panel of Arbitrators), Md. State Bar Assn. (mem. com. on legal ethics, 1922), Bar Assn. of Baltimore City (chmn. com. on admissions, 1922; chmn. reorganization com., 1922-23). Republican. Baptist. Mason (Royal Arch); Royal and Select Masters). Clubs: Barristers (pres., 1934), Baltimore Model Yacht (commodore, 1937), Baldric (Baltimore). Home: 209 Edgevale Rd., Roland Park. Office: Mercantile Trust Bldg., Baltimore, Md.

SMITH, Howard Chandler, physician; b. Gate City, Va., Mar. 11, 1901; s. William Daniel and Sallie Lou (Minnich) S.; A.B., William and Mary Coll., Williamsburg, Va., 1920; M.D., Johns Hopkins U. Med. Sch., 1925; m. Mary Burnam, Apr. 26, 1934; children—Sally Burnam, Florence Overall. Interne Church Home Hosp., Baltimore, 1925-26; interne in gynecology, Johns Hopkins Hosp., 1926-27, asst. resident in urology, 1927-30, resident urol. Surgeon, 1930-31; engaged in pvt. practice in Baltimore, Md., since 1931; mem. staffs Johns Hopkins, Church Home, and Union Memorial hops.; mem. exec. com. Union Memorial Hosp. Served in S.A.T.C. Mem. Kappa Sigma, Phi Beta Kappa, Nu Sigma Nu. Democrat. Club: Elkridge (Baltimore). Home: 111 Turnbridge Rd. Office: Medical Arts Bldg., Baltimore, Md.

SMITH, Howard Wayne, clergyman; b. Phila., Pa., Oct. 9, 1870; s. William R. and Emma J. (Moore) S.; A.B., Central High Sch., 1886; ed. U. of Pa. Law Sch., 1886-87, Johns Hopkins U., 1891-92, Crozer Theol. Sem., 1892-93; hon. D.D., Temple U., 1912; m. Carrie L. Heckman, June 7, 1893; 1 son, Nelson Lee. Ordained to ministry Bapt. Ch., 1894; pastor at Blackwood, N.J., 1893-95, Fulton Av. Ch., Baltimore, Md., 1895-1902, S. Broad St. Ch., Phila., Pa., 1902-05; exec. sec. Phila. Bapt. City Mission, 1905-08; asst. sec. Am. Bapt. Pub. Soc., 1908-15; pastor Ardmore Bapt. Ch. since 1916; mng. editor The Chronicle a Bapt. hist. quarterly; recording sec. Am. Bapt. Hist. Soc. Pres. Bd. Trustees Main Line Federation Chs. Chmn. bd. mgrs. Main Line Y.M.C.A. Republican. Baptist. Mason (K.T.). Clubs: Rotary, Heilikrinites. Home: 111 Walnut Av., Ardmore, Pa.

SMITH, Jacob C., physician; b. Butler Co., Pa., Nov. 29, 1871; s. Charles F. and Mary (Shoup) S.; student Slippery Rock State Normal Sch.; M.D., Pittsburgh Med. Coll., 1901; m. Maud Parke, Nov. 28, 1905. Public school teacher, 1894-96; gen. practice of medicine, Tarentum, since 1901; mem. staff Allegheny Valley Hosp.; pres. and dir. Peoples Federal Savings and Loan Assn. since 1909; vice-pres. and dir. Tarantum, Brackenridge & Butler St. Car Co. since 1907. Mem. Brackenridge Borough Council, 1907-09. Mem. Allegheny Co. and Pa. Med. Socs. Mason. Home: 1100 Carlisle St. Office: Telegram Bldg., Tarentum, Pa.

SMITH, J(ames) Brookes, life ins. exec.; b. Lexington, Ky., Mar. 11, 1885; s. Benjamin Warfield and Lillie (Treadway) S.; student Centre Coll., Danville, Ky., 1900-02; B.A., U. of Va., Charlottesville, 1906, M.A., 1906, grad. study, 1909-10; m. Margaret Howison, Aug. 16, 1910; children—Benjamin Warfield, Graham Howison (dec.), J. Brookes, Jr., Morton Howison, Rockwell MacDonald. Adjunct prof. mathematics, Ga. Tech. Inst., Atlanta, 1906-07; head dept. mathematics, high sch., Richmond, Va., 1907-09; asso. prof. mathematics, Hampden-Sydney (Va.) Coll., 1910-11, prof., 1911-18; asst. actuary Jefferson Standard Life Ins. Co., Greensboro, N.C., 1919-22; actuary Shenandoah Life Ins. Co., Roanoke, Va., 1923-31; actuary Baltimore Life Ins. Co., Baltimore, since 1931, sec. since 1936, dir. since 1936. Served as 1st lt. Q.M.C., U.S.A., 1918-19. Mem. Am. Rose Soc., Sigma Alpha Epsilon, Raven Soc. Ind. Democrat. Presbyn. Clubs: Baltimore Camera, Middle Atlantic Actuarial. Home: 1802 Dixon Rd. Office: Charles & Saratoga Sts., Baltimore, Md.

SMITH, James Edward, educator; b. Tioga Co., Pa., Aug. 18, 1902; s. David Thomas and Ella Elizabeth (Ryan) S.; grad. Mansfield State Teachers Coll., 1925; A.B., Geneva Coll., Beaver Falls, Pa., 1927; A.M., U. of Pittsburgh, 1930; m. Ella Mae Brace, Aug. 18, 1925; children—David Thomas, James Edward, Rebecca Anne. Began as teacher in rural schs.; instr. Coll. Hill Jr. High Sch., Beaver Falls, Pa., 1925-26, instr. and prin., 1926-29; supervising prin. Coll. Hill schs., 1929-30; prin. jr. high schs., Beaver Falls, Pa., 1930-35, prin. sr. high sch. since 1935. Chmn. Regional Guidance Com. for State Wide Study; pres. Beaver Valley Secondary Sch. Prins., 1938-39. Mem. Nat. and Pa. State edn. assns., Nat. Dept. Secondary Sch. Prins., Pa. Dept. Secondary Sch. Prins., Beaver Valley Schoolmens Club, Geneva Coll. Alumni Assn. (pres. 1936-38), Phi Delta Kappa. Republican. Presbyterian (elder Coll. Hill Ch.). Rotarian. Home: 3508 8th Av., Beaver Falls, Pa.

SMITH, James Gerald, economist; b. Denver, Colo., Feb. 13, 1897; s. John G. and Sigrid (Miller) S.; A.B., Princeton, 1920, A.M., 1922, Ph.D., 1926; m. Dorothy H. Zapf, June 29, 1922; children—Barbara Jean, Leila Ann. Instr. in economics Princeton U., 1922-27, asst. prof., 1928-32, asso. prof., 1932-38, prof.,

1938—; instr. Am. Inst. Banking, Trenton, 1928-30; investigator Princeton Survey of Adminstrn. and Expenditures of State Govt. of N.J., 1932-33. Mem. Am. Econ. Assn., Am. Statis. Assn., Am. Assn. of Univ. Profs. Author: Development of Trust Companies in the United States, 1928; Facing the Facts (with others), 1932; The New York Money Market (with B. H. Beckhart), 1932; Economic Planning and the Tariff, 1934; Elementary Statistics, 1934; Introduction to Economic Analysis (with A. M. McIsaac), 1936; Money Credit and Finance (with G. F. Luthringer and D. C. Cline), 1937. Editor: Facing the Facts, 1932; Economics and Social Institutions, 1938. Contbr. articles to financial and econ. jours. Home: 80 Murray Pl., Princeton, N.J. Address: Princeton University, Princeton, N.J.

SMITH, James Lee, lawyer; b. Reedy, W.Va., Oct. 11, 1862; s. John D. and Emma D. (Ashley) S.; student Wirt Co. Summer Normal, Elizabeth, W.Va., 1883-85, Glenville (W.Va.) Normal Sch., 1886-88; m. Mary Virginia Pomroy, June 10, 1891 (died 1929); children—Virgil Elton, Denzil Austin, Walter Lee; m. 2d, Mrs. Fannie Pettit, Oct. 8, 1930. Studied law while engaged as sch. teacher, 1883-91; admitted to W.Va. bar, 1891, and since engaged in gen. practice of law at Elizabeth; served as pros. atty., Wirt Co., W.Va., 1893-97, and 1909-13; mayor of Elizabeth, 1898, and 1901-04; elected to W.Va. Ho. of Dels., 1914, and unseated; asst. prosecuting atty., Wirt Co., 1914-17, and 1920-25; served as mem. W.Va. Ho. of Dels., 1931-35; atty. town of Elizabeth since 1925. Mem. Wirt County Bar Assn. Democrat. Methodist. Mem. K.P. since 1892. Known in legislature as authority on constitutional law. Author: The Higher Plane, 1939. Home: Prunty St. Office: Court St., Elizabeth, W.Va.

SMITH, J(ames) Willison, banker; b. Philadelphia, Pa., Mar. 30, 1879; s. James and Margaret (McCorkell) S.; ed. pub. schs., Phila.; (hon.) LL.D., Washington and Jefferson College; m. Sarah Winslow Drummond, June 16, 1903; children—J. Willison, Renée L., Robert Drummond, John Winslow, David Pierson. Began with The Land Title & Trust Co.; pres. The Real Estate-Land Title & Trust Company, since Nov. 1, 1927 (now The Land Title Bank & Trust Company); dir. Corn Exchange Nat. Bank, Pennsylvania Co. for Insurance on Lives & Granting Annuities, Franklin Fire Ins. Co., Giant Portland Cement Co., Am. Surety Co. of N.Y., Phila. & Reading Coal & Iron Co., W. Phila. Passenger Ry. Co., Continental Passenger Ry. Co., Philadelphia Traction Co.; trustee Estate of Rodman Wanamaker (dec.). Asst. mgr., later mgr. div. housing and transportation, Emergency Fleet Corpn., U.S. Shipping Bd., World War. Trustee Maryville (Tenn.) Coll. Mem. Beta Gamma Sigma (hon.). Republican. Presbyn. Mason. Clubs: Union League, Manufacturers, Penn Athletic, Aronimink Golf. Home: 511 S. 48th St. Offices: 100 S. Broad St., Philadelphia, Pa.

SMITH, Joe L., congressman; b. Raleigh Co., W.Va., May 22, 1880; s. Hulett A. and Angeline (McMillion) S.; ed. pub. schs.; m. Christine Carlson, Sept. 9, 1914; children—Joseph Luther, Hulett Carlson. Publisher of Raleigh Register, weekly newspaper, Beckley, W.Va., 20 yrs.; pres. Beckley Nat. Exchange Bank since 1914; pres. South Beckley Land Co., Home Ins. Agency; pres. Beckley Hotel Co.; also in real estate business; owner of Beckley Hotel. Mayor of Beckley 4 terms, 1904-29; mem. State Senate, W.Va., 1909-13; mem. 71st to 76th Congresses (1929-41), 6th W.Va. Dist. Democrat. Presbyn. Mason (32°, K.T., Shriner), Elk. Clubs: Nat. Press (Washington); Black Knight Country. Home: Beckley, W.Va.

SMITH, John Adams, clergyman; b. Akron, Lancaster Co., Pa., June 6, 1890; s. John A. and Elvina (Adams) S.; grad. Akron High Sch., 1910; B.S., Albright Coll., 1914; m. Maude Weikel, June 6, 1917. Ordained to ministry of Evangelical Congregational Church, 1914; pastor, Lansford and White Haven, Pa., 1914-15, Pottstown, Pa. 1915-19, Grace Ch., Allentown, Pa., 1919-23, Bangor, Pa., 1923-28, Emmanuel Ch., Bethlehem, Pa., 1928-33, Shamokin, Pa., 1933-38; presiding elder Western Dist. since 1938. Home: 455 Douglass St., Reading, Pa.

SMITH, John Finnie Downie, mech. engr.; b. Scotland, Oct. 13, 1902; s. Robert and Elizabeth Jane Maxwell (Downie) S.; came to U.S., 1923, naturalized citizen, 1930; diploma Royal Tech. Coll., Glasgow, 1923; B.Sc., Glasgow U., 1923; M.S., Ga. Sch. Tech., Atlanta, 1926; M.E., Va. Poly. Inst., Blacksburg, 1928; M.S., Harvard U. Engring. Sch., 1930, D.Sc., same, 1933; m. Doris Busby, Aug. 3, 1934; 1 son, Ian Downie. Began as engring. apprentice, machine designer and machinist, Albion Motor Car Co., Glasgow, 1917-23; asst. prof. exptl. engring., Ga. Sch. Tech., Atlanta, 1924-26; asst. prof. engring. drawing, Va. Poly Inst., Blacksburg, 1926-28; asst. Harvard U. Grad. Sch. of Engring., 1928-30, Nat. Research Fellow, same, 1930-32, instr. mech. engring., 1932-36; exec. engr. of research and development, E. G. Budd Mfg. Co., Phila., Pa., since 1936. Mem. Am. Soc. Mech. Engrs., Sigma Xi, Phi Kappa Phi. Presbyterian. Club: Cedarbrook Country. Home: 7315 Pittville Av., Philadelphia, Pa. Office: Hunting Park Av., Philadelphia, Pa.

SMITH, John Philip, dir. athletics; b. Hartford, Conn., Dec. 12, 1905; s. Peter F. and Anne (Riley) S.; LL.B., Notre Dame Univ., 1928; m. Mary Ellen Cobrick, Aug. 19, 1933. Engaged as line coach Notre Dame U., 1928; coach Trinity Coll., 1929; line coach Georgetown U., 1930; head coach N.C. State U., 1931-33; coach Duquesne U., 1935, dir. of athletics and head coach since 1936; capt. Notre Dame Football Team, 1927. Roman Catholic. Home: 5260 Centre Av., Pittsburgh, Pa.

SMITH, J(ohn) Spencer (Wells), merchant; b. Sherbrooke, Can., July 7, 1880; s. John R. and Ann (McIntosh) S.; ed. pub. schs., L.I., N.Y., and Brooklyn; m. Mary L. Ewing, Sept. 28, 1910; children—Ewing, Graham. Pres. J. R. Smith Sales Co. Apptd. by Gov. Woodrow Wilson as mem. Commn. to Investigate Port Conditions of New York, 1911; apptd. mem. and served as pres. N.J. Harbor Commn., 1914; mem. Bd. Commerce and Navigation of N.J. since orgn., 1915 (pres.); apptd. by War Dept., 1917, chmn. Bd. Appraisal of Bush Terminal property; vice chmn. N.Y., N.J. Port and Harbor Development Commn., 1917-21; vice chmn. Port of New York Authority, 1921-23; v.p. First Federal Savings & Loan Assn. of New York. Treas. Bronx Federal Savings and Loan Assn., N.Y.; pres. Tenafly Trust Co. of New Jersey. Mem. Soc. Terminal Engrs. (ex-pres.), Am. Assn. Port Authorities (ex-pres.), Am. Shore and Beach Preservation Assn. (pres.), Canadian Soc. New York (ex-pres.). Member Permanent Internat. Commission of Permanent International Association of Navigation Congresses. Elected mem. Bd. of Edn., Tenafly, 1908, now pres. Treas. Inter-State Sanitation Commn. of N.J., N.Y. and Conn. Democrat. Presbyn. Mason. Clubs: Nat. Democratic, Engineers, Railroad (New York); Knickerbocker Country. Home: 24 Park St., Tenafly, N.J. Office: 60 Hudson St., New York, N.Y.

SMITH, Joseph L.; judge Circuit Court of N.J. Home: 655 Lake St., Newark, N.J.

SMITH, J(oseph) Russell, geographer; b. nr. Lincoln, Va., Feb. 3, 1874; s. Thomas R. and Ellen H. Smith; B.S., University of Pa., 1898, Ph.D., 1903; Sc.D., from Columbia University, 1929; U. of Leipzig, 1901-02; fellow in economics, U. of Pa., 1902-03; m. Henrietta Stewart, June 16, 1898; children—Newlin Russell, James Stewart, Thomas Russell. Instr. history, George Sch., Newtown, Pa., 1896-99; assisted with econ. investigations, Isthmian Canal Commn., 1899-1901; instr. commerce, 1903-06, asst. prof. geography and industry, 1906-09, prof. industry, 1909-19, Wharton Sch. of Finance and Commerce, U. of Pa.; prof. economic geography, Columbia, 1919—. Lecturer U.S. War Coll. Pres. geog. sect. World Fed. of Edn. Assns., 1929-33. Investigations for U. of Pa. in North Africa and Southern Europe as to extent and possibilities of a tree crop agriculture, 1913. Pres. Northern Nut Growers' Assn., 1916, 17. Chmn. food commn. of Phila. Home Defense Com., 1917; spl. trade expert, War Trade Bd., Washington, D.C., 1918; geog. field work, Asia, 1925-26. Member of Association of America Geographers. Mem. Soc. of Friends. Clubs: Cosmos (Washington); Franklin Inn, Rolling Green Golf (Phila.); Columbia Faculty (New York); Loudoun Golf and Country (Purcellville, Va.). Author: The Organization of Ocean Commerce, 1905; The Story of Iron and Steel, 1908; The Ocean Carrier, 1908; Industrial and Commercial Geography, 1913; Commerce and Industry, 1915; Elements of Industrial Management, 1916; Influence of the Great War on Shipping, 1918; The World's Food Resources, 1919; Human Geography (a grammar school text) Book I, Peoples and Countries, 1921, Book II, Regions and Trade, 1922; North America, 1925; Home Folks, a Geography for Beginners, 1926; Tree Crops, a Permanent Agriculture, 1929; Countries, Regions and Trade, a sixth grade geography, 1930; World Folks, an elementary geography, 1931; American Lands and Peoples, 1932; Foreign Lands and Peoples, 1933; Our Industrial World, 1934; Methods of Achieving Economic Justice, 1936; Men & Resources, a geography of North America, 1937. Editor spl. vol. of Annals of Am. Acad. Polit. and Social Science. Contbr. to mags. and agrl. econ. and geog. jours. Awarded Harmon Foundation prize, 1927. Home: Swarthmore, Pa.; (June-Sept.) Round Hill, Va.

SMITH, Lauren Howe, psychiatrist; b. Cherokee, Ia., July 28, 1901; s. Aaron C. and Mary (Howe) S.; student Cherokee (Ia.) High Sch., 1915-19; B.S., State U. of Ia., Iowa City, Ia., 1923, M.D., Med. Sch., 1925; m. Mary Frances Smith, June 10, 1925; children—Robert Lauren, Richard Ralph. Asst. physician dept. for mental and nervous diseases, Pa. Hosp., Phila., 1926-27, exec. officer, 1927-30; exec. med. officer, Inst. of the Pa. Hosp., Phila., 1930-38; physician-in-chief and administrator, Inst. and Dept. for mental and nervous diseases, Pa. Hosp., Phila., since 1938; asso. in psychiatry, U. of Pa. Grad. Sch. of Medicine, since 1932, lecturer, Sch. of Edn., since 1935; psychiatrist, Swarthmore (Pa.) Coll., since 1936, Girard Coll., Phila., since 1937. Mem. Phila. Psychiat. Soc., Phila. Neurol. Soc., Phila. and Am. Coll. Physicians, Phila. Co. Med. Soc., A.M.A., Am. Psychiat. Assn., Swiss Medico-Psychoanalytic Soc. (Zurich, Switzerland). Republican. Club: Union League (Phila.). Home: 349 Millbank Rd., Bryn Mawr, Pa. Office: 111 N. 49th St., Philadelphia, Pa.

SMITH, Laurence Douglas, v.p. McKeesport Tin Plate Corpn.; b. Alexandria, Va., Nov. 16, 1892; s. James and Sophie Anne (Nagel) S.; student George Washington U.; m. Julie Trees Coffin, Oct. 15, 1936; children—Helen Frances, John Coffin, Christine Eloise, Charles Coffin. Began as mill order clerk Jones & Laughlin Steel Corpn., Aliquippa Works, 1912; employed by The Norfolk Motorist Supply Co., Norfolk, Va., 1919-25, Everglades Motors, Inc., Miami, Fla., 1925-28, Lewis Foundry & Machine Co., Pittsburgh, 1928-36; v.p. McKeesport Tin Plate Corpn. since 1936, now also dir.; dir. Blaw-Knox Co. Mem. Assn. Iron and Steel Engrs. F.& A.M. (Shriner). Clubs: Pittsburgh Field, Pittsburgh Athletic Assn. Home: 610 Pitcairn Pl., Pittsburgh, Pa. Office: McKeesport Tin Plate Corpn., McKeesport, Pa.

SMITH, Lawrence Weld, M.D., univ. prof.; b. Newton, Mass., June 20, 1895; s. William G. and Marion (Reynolds) S.; A.B., Harvard, 1916, M.D., Med. Sch., 1920; m. Dorothy Matthews. Instr. in pathology, Harvard Med. Sch., 1920-22, asst. prof., 1924-28; prof. of pathology and bacteriology, U. of Philippines, Manila, 1922-23; dir. of lab., Boston (Mass.) Floating Hosp., 1924-28; asst. prof. of pathology, Cornell U. Sch. of Medicine, 1928-31, asso. prof., 1931-34; asso. pathologist, New York Hosp., 1928-34; pathologist, Willard Parker Hosp., New York, 1928-34; prof. of pathology, Temple U. Sch. of Medicine, Phila., since 1935; pathologist and dir. of labs., Temple U. Hosp., Phila., since 1935. Mem. Am. Assn. Pathologists and Bacteriologists, Am. Soc. Cancer Research, Am. Soc.

Tropical Medicine, Am. Soc. Exptl. Pathology, Internat. Assn. Med. Museums, Soc. Exptl. Biology and Medicine, Coll. of Physicians of Phila., A.M.A., Pa. State Med. Soc., Phila. County Med. Soc., Phila. Pathol. Soc. Republican. Protestant. Co-author: Poliomyelitis, 1934; Essentials of Pathology, 1938. Contbr. of numerous articles to med. jours. Home: Huntingdon Valley, Pa. Office: N. Broad and Ontario Sts., Philadelphia, Pa.

SMITH, Lemon Lawrence; pres. and trustee Bankers Investment Trust of America. Home: "Valleybrook," Johnstown, Pa. Office: 1212 Delaware Av., Wilmington, Del.

SMITH, Levin, lawyer; b. Wood Co., W.Va., Dec. 22, 1861; s. William Haimes and Sarah (Rector) S.; student Wood County (W.Va.) schs., 1877-81; grad. Parkersburg (W.Va.) High Sch., 1881; grad. as spl. student Harvard Law Sch., 1884; m. Nellie Marshall Williams, June 21, 1887; children—Helen (Mrs. James S. McClinton), Sarah Rector, Levin, Elizabeth Keith. Admitted to Wood County bar, 1884; mem. firm Merrick & Smith, Parkersburg, W.Va., 1885-1925, Smith & Boreman, Parkersburg, 1926-29; in pvt. practice, Parkersburg, since 1929; pres. Pike Investment Co. since 1937, Smiths, Inc., Parkersburg, since 1937. Mem. Am. Bar Assn., W.Va. Bar Assn., Wood County Bar Assn. Democrat. Methodist. Odd Fellow. Home: 118 W. 12th St. Office: 219 Seventh St., Parkersburg, W.Va.

SMITH, Lloyd Weir, pres. The Union Nat. Bank of Pittsburgh; b. Pittsburgh, Pa., May 30, 1886; s. Robert Stewart and Mary (McCaslin) S.; grad. Princeton, 1908; m. Gertrude McCormick, Jan. 27, 1914; children—Martha (Mrs. C. W. Cooper), Ann Weir. Pres. The Union Nat. Bank of Pittsburgh since 1923; dir. Pittsburgh Parking Garages. Trustee and treas. Western Pa. Sch. of the Deaf, Union Dale Cemetery. Mem. Pa. Economy League. Clubs: Duquesne, Allegheny Country, Harvard-Yale-Princeton (Pittsburgh); Bankers' (New York). Home: Coraopolis Heights, Coraopolis, Pa. Office: Fourth Av. and Wood St., Pittsburgh, Pa.

SMITH, Louis A., refractories engr.; b. New Brighton, Pa., Oct. 8, 1889; s. Perry A. and Sula G. (McLean) S.; Ceramic Engr., O. State U., Columbus, O., 1912; m. Marie F. Reilly, Nov. 11, 1919; children—Mary Lou, Louis E., Frances Claire, Perry Michael, Alice Joan, John McLean, Charles William. Supt. A. F. Smith Co., brick and clay, New Brighton, Pa., 1912-16; asst. supt., coke oven dept., Jones & Laughlin Steel Corpn., Aliquippa, Pa., 1916-20, supt., 1920-27, refractories engr. since 1927. Sec. Aliquippa (Pa.) Sch. Bd. Dir. and treas. Mt. Olivet Catholic Cemetery. Mem. Am. Ceramic Soc. Republican. Catholic. K. of C. Club: Aliquippa (Pa.) Rotary (treas.). Home: 1000 Franklin Av. Office: Jones & Laughlin Steel Corpn., Aliquippa, Pa.

SMITH, Louis C., pub. utility exec.; b. Phila., Pa., June 19, 1885; s. Louis C. and Emma F. (Nyman) S.; B.S. in M.E., U. of Pa.; m. Irene Clare Endy, Oct. 18, 1911; children—Irene C., Louis C., Daniel E., Kathryn V. Pres. and mgr. Fulton County Gas & Electric Co., 1914-28; v.p. New York Power & Light Co., 1928-30; now pres. The Harrisburg Gas Co. Home: 2517 N. 2d St. Office: 14 S. Market Sq., Harrisburg, Pa.

SMITH, Lynn Allen, manufacturer; b. Pittsburgh, Pa.; June 27, 1903; s. Wesley Linford and Louise (Allen) S.; student Shady Side Acad., 1909-18, Hotchkiss Sch., Lakeville, Conn., 1918-20; A.B., Yale, 1924; m. Mary Ogden McKenna, Sept. 14, 1927; children—Allen Ogden, Shirley Lynn. Began as chemist Lee S. Smith & Son Mfg. Co., 1924;, pres. since 1926; sec. and treas. Oral Hygiene, Inc.; vice-pres. Professional Acceptance Co. Republican. Presbyterian. Mason. Clubs: Duquesne, Longue Vue (Pittsburgh). Home: 10 Robin Rd. Office: 7325 Penn Av., Pittsburgh, Pa.

SMITH, Marshall Max, foreign commerce; b. Syracuse, N.Y., Oct. 25, 1896; s. Thomas K. and Bertha C. (Schott) S.; M.E., Syracuse U., 1918; ed. Stevens Inst. Naval Sch., 1918; m. Vera A. Nourck, Sept. 22, 1922 (dec.); m. 2d, A. Juliette LeRiche, Jan. 29, 1938. Employed as engr., Foundation Co., New Orleans, La., 1919-20; supt. engr., U.S. Shipping Bd. in Turkey, Holland, Eng., 1920-25; sales engr. Worthington Pump & Machinery Corpn., Harrison, N.J., 1925-29, rep. for Japan, 1929, European mgr., 1930-38, mgr. fgn. div. since 1939; vice-pres. Worthington, Inc.; dir. S.I.P.E.C., Milan, Italy. Served in U.S.N., 1917-19, ensign overseas transport service. Mem. Am. Soc. Mech. Engrs., Beta Theta Pi. Awarded N.Y. State Scholarship, 1914. Republican. Presbyterian. Clubs: T.N.T., American (Paris, France). Home: 106 Harrison St., East Orange, N.J.

SMITH, Matthew John Adam, supervising prin. schs.; b. Lehigh Co., Pa., Apr. 13, 1889; s. Edwin Henry and Amanda (Backenstoe) S.; M.E., Kutztown Normal Sch., 1908; student Muhlenberg Coll., 1909-10; B.S., Franklin and Marshall Coll., 1917; M.S., Lehigh U., 1922; student U. of Pa., 1919-20, Pa. State Coll., summer 1931; m. Mabel Florence Schaeffer, June 28, 1919; 1 son, Alton Matthew. Teacher and prin. various schs., while attending coll., 1908-18; supervising prin. schs., Coopersburg, Pa., 1919-20, 1922-29; head biology dept. Cheltenham Twp. High Sch., 1920-22; supervising prin. schs., Fleetwood, Pa., since 1929. Served as sergt. inf., U.S.A. during World War, and in Engrs. O.T.S., Camp Humphrey, Va. Mem. Fleetwood Chamber of Commerce. Pres. Visiting Nurses Assn. of Fleetwood and Vicinity. Mem. Nat. and Pa. State edn. assns., Berks Co. Schoolmens Club. Awarded scholarship at Cold Spring Harbor Marine Labs., L.I. Democrat. Mem. Evang. and Reformed Ch. I.O.O.F., Grange. Home: 216 N. Richmond St., Fleetwood, Pa.

SMITH, Maurice A(lexander), pres. McKee Glass Co.; b. Jeannette, Pa., June 7, 1889; s. Andrew J. and Annie (Branum) S.; student Jeannette High Sch.; grad. Mercersburg Acad., 1907; M.E., Cornell U., 1911; m. Mabelle Ely, Nov. 12, 1911; children—Maurice Alexander, Robert Louis, William Branum, Anne Catherine, Gerald Ely, Thomas McKee. With McKee Glass Co. since 1911, serving as gen. mgr., vice-pres. and since 1923 pres.; dir. Glass City Bank, Westmoreland Express Co., Westmoreland Motor Freight Co., McKee Realty Co., Jeannette Thrift Co. Republican. Clubs: Rotary, Elks, Greensburg Country. Address: Jeannette, Pa.

SMITH, Melton Aubrey, mfg. steel; b. Seaville, Va., Oct. 4, 1883; s. John M. T. and Sarah Elizabeth (Melton) S.; ed. high sch., Shenandoah, Va.; m. Myrtle L. Young, Feb. 12, 1908; children—Melton Aubrey, John Reynolds. In employ various concerns, 1895-1906; in various positions with American Sheet and Tin Plate Co., Vandergrift, Pa., 1906-17; open hearth supt. to asst. gen. mgr. Edgewater Steel Co., Oakmont, Pa., 1917-25, gen. mgr. since 1925; vice-pres. and dir. Allegheny Valley Trust Co., Verona, Pa. Republican. Presbyn. Mason (32°, Shriner). Club: Country (Oakmont). Home: 850 Eleventh St., Oakmont, Pa.

SMITH, Michael Paul, lawyer; b. Pylesville, Md., May 5, 1898; s. Martin John and Avarilla Josephine (Temple) S.; student Md. Inst., Baltimore, 1921-22; LL.B., U. of Md. Law Sch., Baltimore, 1924; m. Mary Lavania Zepp, Nov. 7, 1919; children—William Bryce, Mary Miller. Employed as stenographer, Western Md. Ry., Baltimore, 1915-16, Southern Ry., Baltimore and Washington, 1916-20; mgr. James O'Meara, Baltimore, 1920-22; sec. Eastern Builders Co., Baltimore, 1922-23; sales mgr. Cohen & Hughes, Inc., Baltimore and Washington, 1923-28; admitted to Md. bar, 1924; engaged in gen. practice of law in Baltimore since 1928; counsel to treas. Baltimore County since 1939. Mem. Md. State Bar Assn., Bar Assn. of Baltimore County, Bar Assn. of Baltimore City. Democrat. Roman Catholic. Club: Kiwanis of Reisterstown, Md. (pres.). Home: 308 Main St., Reisterstown. Office: Baltimore Trust Bldg., Baltimore, Md.

SMITH Miles Woodward, editor religious publs.; b. Cincinnati, O., Nov. 23, 1889; s. Henley Woodward and Sadie Beall (Miles) S.; A.B., William Jewell Coll., Liberty, Mo., 1911, A.M., 1912, D.D., 1935; B.D., Newton (Mass.) Theol. Instrn., 1917, M.R.E., 1930; grad. student Boston U. Sch. Religious Edn. and Social Service, 1920-28 (various terms); m. Elisabeth B. Arnold, June 25, 1913; children—Dorothy Woodward, Hugh Arnold, Marjory Kemper, Robert Miles. Ordained Bapt. ministry, 1910; pastor 1st Ch., Tarkio, Mo., 1911-12, E. Sedalia Ch., Sedalia, Mo., 1912-14, Stratford St. Ch., W. Roxbury, Boston, 1917-22, Norwood, O., 1922-24; dir. deligious edn. for Mass. Bapt. Conv. in coöperation Am. Bapt. Publ. Soc., Boston, 1924-30; dir. intermediate work and editor intermediate publs. Am. Bapt. Publ. Soc., Phila., 1930-33, editor-in-chief Dept. of S.S. Publs. of same since 1933. Y.M.C.A. worker at Camp Wentworth, Boston, 1917; asst. religious work dir. Greater Boston Dist., War Work Council, Y.M.C.A., Charlestown, Mass., 1918. Mem. Internat. Council Religious Edn. (exec. com. ednl. commn., com. on improved uniform lessons), Council of Christian Edn. of Northern Bapt. Conv. Author: Homeland of the Master, 1933; Light of the Nations, 1934; Way of Wisdom, 1935. Editor-in-chief more than 100 ch. sch. publs.; mem. com. on publ. "Missions." Contbr. editorials and articles on methods in religious edn. Home: 318 Hillside Av., Jenkintown, Pa. Office: 1703 Chestnut St., Philadelphia, Pa.

SMITH, Mortimer Wilson, Jr., civil engr.; b. Clarksburg, W.Va., Oct. 2, 1890; s. Mortimer Wilson and Emma Shrom (Bartlett) S.; ed. U. of Va., Washington and Lee U.; m. Pauline Musgrave, June 6,1917. Began as civil engr., 1914; mem. firm Osborn & Smith, 1914-17; construction engr., City of Clarksburg, W.Va., 1921-27; chief engr. W.Va. State Road Comm., 1933-37. Mem. W.Va. State Legislature, 1932-33. Served as lt. Corps of Engrs., U.S. Army, 1917-18. Dir. Clarksburg City Planning Comm. Mem. Am. Soc. Civil Engrs., Phi Kappa Sigma, Vets of Foreign Wars, Am. Legion. Democrat. Presbyn. Home: 2023 Quarrier St. Office: Capitol Bldg., Charleston, W.Va.

SMITH, Oscar Franklin, prof. of Physics; b. Perry, Me., July 25, 1884; s. Adelbert Filmore and Adalaide (Golden) S.; grad. Calais (Me.) Acad., 1903; student U. of Me., Orono, Me., 1904-07; B.S., Pa. State Coll., 1911, M.S., 1916; m. Mildred Edna Barnes, June 21, 1911; children—Oscar Franklin, Thelma Barnes (Mrs. Howard C. Peck), Dorothy Arline (Mrs. Robert L. Glenn), David Filmore, John Martz. Asst. in Physics, Pa. State Coll., 1910-11, instr., 1911-12, asst. prof., 1915-16, asso. prof. physics, 1920-28, prof. and asst. dean since 1928; instr. physics, U. of Philippines, 1912-13, asst. prof. 1913-15; lecturer, Queens U., Kingston, Ontario, 1916-17. Fellow A.A.A.S.; mem. Am. Assn. Physics Teachers, Alpha Tau Omega, Phi Kappa Phi, Alpha Epsilon Delta, Sigma Pi Sigma. Odd Fellow. Home: Boalsburg, Pa. Office: Pond Laboratory, State College, Pa.

SMITH, Paul Ely, newspaper editor; b. Goshen, Ind., Sept. 28, 1896; s. Charles Henry and Salina Mary (Ely) S.; student U. of Mich., 1914-17, M.E., in absentia, 19—; music student Janische-Short Inst. of Music, Kalamazoo, Mich., 12 yrs.; m. Elsie Mae Richardson, Oct. 2, 1920; children—Richard Paul, Dorothy Mae, Roberta Sue. Began as reporter Detroit Journal, 1917, later news editor Phila. Press; European rep. of Crown Cork Co., San Feliu de Guizols, Spain, 1917-18; city editor Phila. Enquirer, 1919; mng. editor Newark Ledger, 1920; editor Toledo News-Bee, 1921-28; editor and promotion mgr., Hearst newspapers, Boston and New York, 1929-34; city editor New Bedford (Mass.) Standard Times, 1934; editor Gannett newspapers, Plainfield (N.J.) Courier-News and Rochester (N.Y.) Times Union since 1935; dir. Essential Oils Co. of Detroit. Mem. N.J. Press Assn., Am. Soc. Newspaper Editors, Am. Soc. Mech. Engrs. Republican. Baptist. Clubs: National Press (Washington, D.C.); Fox Hills Country (Staten Island, N.Y.). Contbr. feature articles to mags. Home: 741 Kensington Av. Office: Plainfield Courier-News, Plainfield, N.J.

SMITH, Paul G.; mem. law firm Nauman, Smith & Hurlock. Address: Bergner Bldg., Harrisburg, Pa.

SMITH, Peter Anthony, treas. A. P. Smith Mfg. Co.; b. Newark, N.J., Aug. 7, 1882; s.

Anthony P. and Margaret (Pierce) S.; ed. St. Aloysius Parochial Sch. (Newark), St. Peter's Coll. (Jersey City) and Stevens Sch. (Hoboken); m. Josephine C. McCabe, Jan. 26, 1910; children—Mary E., Anthony P., Joseph F., Eugene, Peter A., Thomas G., William F. Began as clerk A. P. Smith Mfg. Co., 1901, treas. since 1910; pres. Weekly Review Newspapers since 1931; chmn. South Orange Trust Co. since 1939; dir. H. V. Walker Co. (Elizabeth, N.J.); dir. and treas. Norman Realty Co. (East Orange). Served as major Specialist Res., Ordnance Div., U.S. Army. Honored as "Distinguished Citizen of Oranges and Maplewood." Village trustee South Orange; chmn. Planning Commn., South Orange; permanent chmn. Joint Meeting (a combination of 11 municipalities for joint sewerage facilities); mem. bd. Sch. Estimate, South Orange-Maplewood Sch. Dist. Mem. N.J. State Bd. of Regents; trustee Panzer Coll. of Physical Edn. and Hygiene, East Orange; dir. South Orange Maplewood Adult Sch., St. Mary's Hosp. (Orange), Welfare Fed. of the Oranges and Maplewood, Social Welfare Council; Oranges Chapter and exec. com. Am. Red Cross; treas. N.J. Joint Council on Internat. Relations; chmn. Good Govt. Council, Citizens Forum of N.J.; trustee N.J. Hosp. Plan; Essex Co. chmn. N.J. Good Will Commn.; chmn. Local Assistance Bd., South Orange; mem. advisory bd. N.J. State League of Municipalities; mem. Newark Labor Relations Bd., employment relations com. Nat. Assn. Mfrs., N.J. State Com. on Health and Welfare (apptd. by Gov. Moore); dir. N.J. Fed. of Official Planning Bds.; vice chmn. Community Safety Council; treas. Essex Co. Conf. of Catholics, Jews and Protestants; affiliated mem. Am. Soc. Civil Engrs., Am. Soc. Safety Engrs., Am. Soc. Testing Engrs., Soc. for Advancement of Management; mem. Am. Soc. Mech. Engrs. Republican. Catholic (lay trustee Our Lady of Sorrows Ch., South Orange). Mem. K.C. (4°). Clubs: Manufacturers of Bloomfield and Vicinity (v.p. and treas.); Executives of Oranges and Bloomfield. Home: 66 Stanley Road, South Orange, N.J. Office: 545 N. Arlington Av., East Orange, N.J.

SMITH, Powell Richard, merchant; b. Salem, N.J., Sept. 23, 1881; s. Richard Thompson and Amanda (Fox) S.; student Salem (N.J.) High Sch., 1916-20, Peirce Sch. of Business Adminstrn., 1920-21; m. Sara Bunting Mitchell, Oct. 31, 1906; children—William Richard, Helen Mitchell. Began as shipping clerk, Salem (N.J.) Glass Works, 1901; owner, Brown & Smith, Inc. (formerly Carpenter-Mitchell Co.), men's clothing store, Salem, N.J., since 1907; pres. Salem Co. Mutual Fire Ins. Co., Salem, N.J.; v.p. and dir. Salem (N.J.) East View Cemetery Co.; dir. City Nat. Bank & Trust Co., Farmers Mutual Fire Ins. Co. Sec. Salem (N.J.) Bd. of Edn., 1916-32. Republican. Quaker. Mason (Commandery; K.T.). Clubs: Fenwick, Exchange (Salem, N.J.); Pennsgrove (N.J.) Country. Home: 26 Oak St. Office: 191 E. Broadway, Salem, N.J.

SMITH, Preston H.; supt. of schools at Bayonne. Address: Board of Education, Bayonne, N.J.

SMITH, Ralph Eugene, lawyer; b. Beaver Falls, Pa., July 31, 1903; s. John F. and Margaret Jane (Hershey) S.; A.B., Geneva Coll., 1924; LL.B., U. of Pittsburgh Law Sch., 1928; m. Lael Acheson, July 8, 1932; 1 son, Ralph Acheson. Admitted to Pa. bar, 1928, and since engaged in gen. practice of law at Ambridge; admitted to practice before all cts. of Pa. and Fed. cts.; mem. firm Smith & Theophilus since 1932; asst. dist. atty. Beaver Co. since 1936; vice-pres., dir. and solicitor Economy Bank of Ambridge; dir. and solicitor Ambridge Bldg. & Loan Assn. Dir. Childrens Aid Soc. of Beaver Co. Mem. Pa. State and Beaver Co. bar assns., Delta Theta Phi. Republican. Presbyn. Clubs: Country, Community (Ambridge). Home: 330 Wayne St., Baden, Pa. Office: Economy Bank Bldg. Ambridge, Pa.

SMITH, Ralph H(arry), judge; b. Pittsburgh, Pa., Jan. 8, 1899; s. Harry and Elizabeth (Brand) S.; A.B., Cornell U., 1921; LL.B.,

U. of Pittsburgh, 1924; m. Florence E. Raber, Oct. 9, 1926; children—Ralph H., Jr., Janet Terry, Sara Mae. Admitted to Pa. bar, 1924, and since engaged in gen. practice of law at Pittsburgh; asst. dist. atty., Allegheny Co., 1924-26; asst. U.S. atty. Western Dist. Pa., 1926-30; spl. dep. atty. gen. of Pa., 1931-32; elected judge Ct. Common Pleas, 1933 for 10 yr. term; served as del. Dem. Nat. Conv., Phila., 1936; candidate for lt. gov. Dem. primary, 1938. Served in U.S.A., 1918. Mem. bd. mgrs. Allegheny Y.M.C.A. Mem. North Side Chamber of Commerce. Mem. bd. trustees State Industrial Home for Women, Muncy. Mem. Am. and Allegheny Co. bar assns., Am. Judicature Soc., Am. Acad. Polit. and Social Sci., Acad. Polit. Sci., Nat. Probation Soc., Am. Labor Legislation Assn., Am. Legion. Democrat. Mem. United Presbyterian Ch. Home: 2921 Perrysville Av., N.S., Pittsburgh, Pa. Office: City-County Bldg., Pittsburgh, Pa.

SMITH, Ralph Richards, supt. city schs.; b. Overbrook, Del., Feb. 27, 1892; s. William G. and Martha E. (Swain) S.; ed. Millersville State Normal Sch., 1912-15; A.B., U. of Pa., 1924, A.M., same, 1927; m. Margaret L. Powell, Dec. 29, 1917; children—Elizabeth Ruth, Margaret Powell. Engaged as teacher and supervising prin. schs. in Del., 1910-18; supervising prin. schs., Upper Moreland Twp., Willow Grove, Pa., 1919-24; asst. co. supt. schs., Montgomery Co., 1924-26; supt. city schs., Lansdale, Pa., since 1926. Served as exec. sec. Abington Branch, Y.M.C.A. of Phila., 1918-19. Mem. Bd. Dirs. Lansdale Community Service. Vice-pres. Lansdale Pub. Library. Mem. Nat. and Pa. State edn. assns., Nat. Assn. Sch. Adminstrs., Am. Legion (past comdr. post). Republican. Methodist. Mason. Club: Kiwanis of Lansdale (past pres.). Home: 620 Columbia Av. Office: Junior High School Bldg., Lansdale, Pa.

SMITH, Rauland Prall, ins. and real estate; b. Trenton, N.J., Aug. 25, 1904; s. Walter F. and Harriett Apgar (Prall) S.; ed. Phillips Exeter Acad., 1920-22; A.B., Princeton, 1926; grad. study, Oxford U., England, 1926-27; unmarried. Asso. with Walter F. Smith & Co., insurance and real estate, Trenton, N.J., since 1927, dir. and treas. since 1927; dir. Trenton Banking Co., Mutual Bldg. & Loan Assn. Dir. Wm. McKinley Memorial Hosp. Mem. Symposium, Trenton, N.J., Phi Beta Kappa. Presbyn. Clubs: Princeton of Trenton (treas.), Rotary, Trenton (Trenton); Cloister Inn of Princeton U. (Princeton). Home: Woosamonsa Rd., Hopewell Twp., Pennington, N.J. Office: 145 Academy St., Trenton, N.J.

SMITH, Richard Paul, utilities; b. Woodsboro, Md., Jan. 25, 1889; s. Charles Edward and Florence Burnetta (Smith) S.; educated at Blue Ridge Coll., New Windsor, Md.; m. Henrietta Menges, Dec. 30, 1915; children—Jeanne Menges, Lois, Doris. Pres. and dir. Potomac Edison Co., Potomac Light & Power Co., Blue Ridge Transportation Co., Northern Va. Power Co., South Penn Power Co., Braddock Heights Water Co., Franklin Transmission Co., Blue Ridge Lines, Inc., Penn Bus Co., White Star Lines, Inc.; dir. Statton Furniture Co., Marken & Bielfeld Co. Dir. Washington County Hosp., Chamber of Commerce, Hagerstown. Mem. Christ Reformed Ch. Mason. Clubs: Rotary, Fountain Head Country, Waynesboro Country. Home: Hagerstown, Md.

SMITH, Robert Metcalf, prof. English; b. Worcester, Mass., Mar. 29, 1886; s. Edward Payson and Julia Mack (Church) S.; A.B., Amherst, 1908; A.M., Columbia Univ., 1909, fellow, 1911-12, Ph.D., 1915; m. Agnes Grace Clancy, June 28, 1912. Instr. in rhetoric, U. of Minn., 1910-11; prof. English, Westminster Coll., New Wilmington, Pa., 1912-16; instr. in English, U.S. Naval Acad., 1917-19; prof. English, Drury Coll., Springfield, Mo., 1920-21; prof. English, U. of Wyoming, Laramie, 1921-25; prof. English, Lehigh U., since 1925; summer sessions, Beloit Coll., 1920, U. of Colo., 1921-23, U. of Wyoming, 1924, Lehigh U., 1926-29, Columbia U., 1930, Northwestern U., 1931, Lehigh U., 1932-34, U. of Colo., 1935,

Lehigh U., 1936-38. Mem. Modern Lang. Assn., Shakespeare Assn. of America, Shakespeare Soc. of Phila., Columbia U. English Grad. Union, Phi Gamma Delta, Phi Kappa Phi, Eta Sigma Phi. Republican. Conglist. Author: Froissart and the English Chronicle Play, 1915. Editor: Types of Philosophic Drama; Types of World Tragedy; Types of Social Comedy; Types of Farce Comedy; Types of Romantic Comedy; Types of Historical Drama; Types of Domestic Tragedy (all 1928); Types of World Literature, 1930; Book of Biography, 1930; Troilus and Cressida, 1932. General editor, Twelve Victorian Bibliographies, 1935. Spl. research in Shakespeare and other bibliographies; author of various articles on subject. Home: Lehigh Univ. Campus, Bethlehem, Pa.

SMITH, Robert R.; pres. R.R. Smith Coal Co.; officer or dir. many companies. Office: Coal Exchange Bldg., Huntington, W.Va.

SMITH, Sidney E., lawyer; b. Phila., Pa., Jan. 26, 1879; s. Archibald and Annetta (Campbell) S.; ed. Temple U. Law Sch., 1899-1902; m. Lillian M. Lamor, Apr. 25, 1906 (died 1919); children—Sidney E., Jr., Robert Campbell; m. 2d, Lucretia M. Hays, Sept. 14, 1921; 1 dau., Lillian Lamor. Admitted to Pa. bar, 1902 and since engaged in gen. practice of law at Phila. Mem. Pa. Bar Assn., Phila. Bar Assn., Law Alumni assn. of Temple U. (vice-pres.). Republican. Episcopalian. Clubs: Union League (Philadelphia); Merion Cricket (Haverford). Home: 622 S. Bowman Av., Merion, Pa. Office: Lincoln-Liberty Bldg., Philadelphia, Pa.

SMITH, Sion Bass, prof. mining law; b. Meadville, Pa., Dec. 8, 1865; s. James Wilson and Anna E. (Salisbury) S.; A.B., Allegheny Coll., 1886, M.A., 1889; m. Anna Mae, d. late Milton B. Goff, LL.D., chancellor of Western U. of Pa., June 13, 1893. Admitted to Pa. bar, 1889; practiced in Meadville, 1889-1900, since in Pittsburgh. Ex-president Winfield Railroad Company. Mem. Phi Kappa Psi (past nat. pres.). Republican. Pres. trustees N. Presbyn. Ch., Pittsburgh. Mason (33°). Home: Bellevue, Pa. Office: Oliver Bldg., Pittsburgh, Pa.

SMITH, Theodore Fell, manufacturer; b. Meadville, Pa., Aug. 21, 1893; s. Frederick William and Clara Maria (Fell) S.; grad. Greenville (Pa.) High Sch., 1911; A.B., Allegheny Coll., Meadville, Pa., 1915; m. Marion Smith Davidson, Oct. 27, 1921; children—Marion Diane, Sally Anne, Theodore Fell and Philip James Davidson (stepson). With engring. dept. Bessemer & Lake Erie R.R., 1915-19; asso. with Harris, Forbes & Co., New York, 1919-33, dist. sales mgr. in charge Western Pa. dist., 1926-33 (company liquidated 1933); dir Western Pa. dist. Federal Housing Adminstrn., 1933-36; since 1936 with Oliver Iron & Steel Corpn., mfrs. bolts, nuts, rivets, pole line hardware, Pittsburgh, as sec. and asst. treas., June-Oct. 1936, vice-pres., 1936-38, exec. v.p., Feb.-May 1938, pres. and dir. since 1938; pres. and dir. Allegheny South Side Ry. Co.; dir. Standard Steel Specialty Co. Entered 2d O.T.C., Ft. Oglethorpe, Ga., and commd. 1st lt. Inf., U.S. Army, Nov. 24, 1917; with 6th Div., A.E.F., 1918-19. Mem. exec. com. Am. Inst. Bolt, Nut and Rivet Mfrs.; asso. mem. Am. Iron and Steel Inst.; mem. Mil. Order Foreign Wars, Sons Am. Revolution, Civic Club of Allegheny Co., Phi Delta Theta. Republican. Presbyterian. Mason (32°). Clubs: Duquesne, Pittsburgh, Rolling Rock, Fox Chapel Golf (Pittsburgh); Beaver Valley Country (Beaver Falls, Pa.). Home: 5023 Frew St. Office: 1001 Muriel St., Pittsburgh, Pa.

SMITH, Thomas Alexander Jr., ins. exec.; b. Ridgely, Md., Jan. 19, 1889; s. Thomas Alexander and Ada Clayton (Frazer) S.; Ph.B., Dickinson Coll., Carlisle, Pa., 1909, A.M., 1912; LL.B., U. of Md., Baltimore, Md., 1912; m. Jennie Short Austin, June 4, 1921; 1 dau., Susan Frazer. In judicial dept. U.S. Fidelity & Guaranty Co., Baltimore, Md., 1912-15, in charge claims for Ala., Birmingham, Ala., 1915-17; in charge ct. bond sect., Globe Indemnity Co., New York, except for war service, 1917-20, general agency same 1920-21; asso. mgr. fidelity and surety dept. Commercial Casualty Ins. Co., Newwark, N.J., 1921-24, asst. sec. and mgr. dept., 1924-29, 3d v.p. (on amalgamation with Loyalty Group), 1929-37, 2d v.p. since 1937; 3d v.p. Met. Casualty Ins. Co. of N.Y., 1929-37, 2d v.p. since 1937. Served as band sergeant, U.S. Army, during World War. Mem. Sigma Alpha Epsilon. Democrat. Affiliated Episcopalian. Home: 23 Wilson Terrace, West Caldwell, N.J. Office: 10 Park Pl., Newark, N.J.

SMITH, Thomas B., ex-mayor; b. Phila., Pa., Nov. 2, 1869; s. Thomas B. and Isabella (Cairns) S.; pub. sch. edn.; m. Bessie Barrett, Mar. 26, 1896; children—Ruth (Mrs. William S. Robertson), Davis P., Harvey B., Thomas B., Fred B., Elizabeth C. Messenger boy, main office Pa. R.R., 1881; clerk same, 1882-86; resigned; was with Adam A. Catanoch, mcht., Phila., 1886-90; entered service of Phila. Record, 1890; became connected with Nat. Surety Co., 1897, becoming v.p. Mem. Common Council, Phila., 1892-1904; mem. Pa. Ho. of Rep., 1905 and spl. session, 1906; postmaster, Phila., 1911-13; mem. Pa. Pub. Service Commn., 1915; mayor of Phila., 1916-20. Mem. Del. River Bridge Joint Commn. Republican. Episcopalian. Mem. Sons of Vets. Mason (Shriner). Clubs: Union League, Manufacturers', Clover, Penn Athletic. Address: 2341 N. 22d St., Philadelphia, Pa.

SMITH, Thomas Harris, financial sales programs; b. Colon, Panama, Mar. 13, 1899; s. Wallace Neal and Belle (Harris) S., citizens of U.S.; B.S., Richmond U., Richmond, Va., 1915; m. Elizabeth Little Warner, Dec. 30, 1937. Employed as salesman with Packard Motor Car Co., Detroit, Mich., 19— to 1923; engaged in bus. on own acct. as propr. T. Harris Smith and Associates, dir. financial selling programs, Baltimore, Md., since 1923. Mem. bd. govs. Washington Coll., Chestertown, Md. Mem. Theta Chi. Conglist. Clubs: Penn Athletic (Philadelphia); Chester River Yacht and Country (Chestertown, Md.). Home: Bellepoint on the Wye, Queenstown. Office: Court Square Bldg., Baltimore, Md.

SMITH, Valentine, merchant; b. Sistersville, W.Va., May 9, 1862; s. Valentine (capt. Civil War) and Hannah (Haines) S.; student Pub. Schs., Sistersville, 1872-78; m. Annie Moore, Feb. 9, 1888 (died 1928); children—Allan Valentine, Lesbia (Mrs. Ralph H. Beard), Madeline (Mrs. Floyd Bristow), Nell. Began as store clerk, 1875; traveling salesman, D. Holliday & Co., Baltimore, Md., 1884-95; established The Val Smith Store, Waynesboro, Pa., 1895, and since owner and mgr.; pres. Carbon Transit Co., Mauch Chunk, Pa., 1910-18; 2d v.p. and dir. The Citizens Nat. Bank and Trust Co. since 1913; dir. Frick Co., 1910-18. Trustee M.E. Ch. of Waynesboro (Pa.). Pres. Y.M.C.A. since 1915. Mem. Merchants Assn. and Commercial Club (1st pres.), Chamber of Commerce (past pres.), Franklin Co. Kittochtinny Hist. Soc. Republican. Methodist (teacher of Men's Biederwolf Bible Class since orgn. 1914). Club: Advertising (Waynesboro, Pa.; past pres.). Home: 205 Clayton Av. Office: 22-28 E. Main St., Waynesboro, Pa.

SMITH, Vann H.; supt. of schools at Burlington. Address: Burlington, N.J.

SMITH, Wade Cothran, evangelist; b. Rome, Ga., June 1, 1869; s. Edward Reed and Susan (Cothran) S.; ed. grammar sch. until 12 yrs. of age, later by pvt. study; m. Zaidee Lapsley, Jan. 26, 1897; children—Cothran Godden, James Lapsley, Zaidee Lapsley, Elizabeth Cothran. Cotton exporting business, 1892-1912; editor Missionary Survey (now Presbyn. Survey), Richmond, Va., 1912-21; called as pastor to The Church by-the-Side-of-the-Road, Greensboro, N.C., 1921; licensed to preach and ordained, under "extraordinary process," by Presbytery of Orange; field worker for extension dept. of Gen. Assembly's Training Sch., Richmond, Va., 1925-1929; specializes in training for evangelism. Lesson writer, staff of S.S. Times, Phila., since 1917, conducting "Say, Fellows" Column for boys, and "The Little Jetts" cartoons column. Democrat. Author: The Little Jetts Telling Bible Stories, 1916; Say, Fellows, 1923; On The Mark, 1925; The Testament for Fishers of Men, 1925; Come and See, 1927; Get Set, 1930; Come and See, the Second—Bringing Forward the Days of the Acts, 1930; New Testament Evangelism, 1930. "Come and See" transl. into French, 1931; rewrote "The Pilgrims Progress" in modern language—issued 1931. Address: care The Sunday School Times, Philadelphia, Pa.

SMITH, Wallace Hudson, pres. Leadclad Wire Co.; b. Benwood, W.Va., Oct. 4, 1881; s. John Wesley and Elizabeth (Wallace) S.; student grade and grammar sch., Benwood and Wheeling, W.Va., 1887-96; m. Patience Elliott Hamilton, 1902; 1 son, Wallace Elliott. Telegraph operator, 1896-99; draughtsman, 1899-1903; cost accountant, 1903-06; supt., 1906-11; gen. mgr. Wheeling Metal & Mfg. Co., Glendale, W.Va., since 1911; pres. Leadclad Wire Co., Glendale, W.Va.; inventor Leadclad Products. Mayor, Glendale (4 terms). Dir. and trustee Reynolds Memorial Hosp., Inc., Glendale. Republican. Presbyterian (elder). Mason. Advertised Leadclad Products in farm mags. and on radio, originating "Neighbor Dave" on air and in mags., 1925-30. Address: Wheeling Metal & Mfg. Co., Glendale, W.Va.

SMITH, Wilbur Fisk, univ. pres.; b. Lovettsville, Loudoun Co., Va., May 21, 1856; s. Bennett Holloway and Matilda Caroline (Janney) S.; prep. edn., high sch. and Loudoun Valley Acad.; Richmond Coll., 1876; B.L., U. of Md., 1890; spl. studies, U. of Va. and Johns Hopkins; Litt.D., St. John's Coll., Annapolis, Md., 1912; m. Margaret Pattison, of Dorchester Co., Md., Apri. 16, 1884; children—Wilbur Clarence, Margery Janney (Mrs. John McNabb), Harriet Pattison (Mrs. Harold C. Hann), Everard Pattison, Robert Hopper, Caroline Cator (dec.). Began teaching, 1873; prin. English-German Sch. No. 5, Baltimore, 1883-94; prof. English, Baltimore City Coll., 1894-1911, head of English dept., 1906-11, principal, 1911-26; president University of Baltimore, 1926-35, president emeritus since 1935. Pres. Md. State Teachers' Assn., Pub. Sch. Teachers' Assn. of Baltimore; mem. St. John's Coll. Alumni Assn., Johns Hopkins Alumni Assn., Phi Delta Theta. Grand sec. Grand Council Royal Arcanum of Md. over 20 yrs.; dir. sec. Royal Arcanum Club Bldg. Co. Democrat. Episcopalian. Clubs: Chess, Whist, Baltimore Country. Home: 3805 St. Paul St., Baltimore, Md.

SMITH, William A.; judge Circuit Court of N.J. Address: Sea Girt, N.J.

SMITH, William Hamilton, physician and surgeon; b. Washington, D.C., Mar. 25, 1883; s. William Hamilton and Florence (Hodkinson) S.; M.D., George Washington U. Med. Sch., Washington, D.C., 1906; m. Madelyn V. Cook, June 8, 1925; 1 son, William Hamilton III. In pvt. practice of medicine at Baltimore, 1909-14; resident physician Presbyn. Eye, Ear, Nose & Throat Hosp., Baltimore, 1914-15; practice limited to diseases of ear, nose and throat at Hagerstown, Md., since 1915; mem. staff Washington Co. Hosp.; courtesy staff Waynesboro, Pa., and Chambersburg, Pa., hosps.; cons. otolaryngologist Md. State Sanatorium, Sabillasville, Md. Served as maj. Med. Corps, U.S.A., 1917-19. Fellow Am. Coll. Surgeons, A.M.A. Mem. Am. Acad. Ophthalmology and Otolaryngology, Med. and Chirurg. Faculty of Md., Cumberland Valley Med. Soc. (past pres.), Washington Co. Med. Soc. (past pres.), Delta Tau Delta. Democrat. Lutheran. Mason. Club: Fountain Head Country (Hagerstown). Home: 236 E. Irvin Av. Office: Arcade Bldg., Hagerstown, Md.

SMITH, W(illiam) Hinckle, capitalist; b. Phila., Pa., June 16, 1861; s. J. Frailey and Harriet L. (Hinckle) S.; B.S., University of Pennsylvania, 1882; m. Jacqueline Harrison, Nov. 28, 1883; 1 son, Col. Hoxie Harrison. Dir. Girard Trust Company, Penn Mutual Life Insurance Co., Kennecott Copper Company, Mack Trucks Incorporated, Nevada Northern Rail Road Company, Midland Valley R.R. Co., Curtiss-Wright Corpn., Adams Express Co., Braden Copper Co., Tubize Chatillon Corpn. Trustee Univ. Museum of Phila. (v.p.), Pa. Hort. Soc., Bryn Mawr (Pa.) Hosp. Clubs: Rittenhouse, Philadelphia (Phila.); Midday (New York); Yacht Club du France. Home: Bryn Mawr, Pa. Office: Girard Trust Co. Bldg., Philadelphia, Pa.

SMITH, William M.; pres. of staff Frederick City Hosp.; surgeon B.&O. R.R. Address: 7 E. Church St., Frederick, Md.

SMITH, William Mackey, coll. prof. and registrar; b. Oxford, Pa., May 18, 1881; s. George Stephenson and Elizabeth (Mackey) S.; grad. Tome Sch., Port Deposit, Md., 1899; Ph.B., Lafayette Coll., Easton, Pa., 1903; Ph.D., Columbia U., 1912; m. Henriette Crawford, Sept. 6, 1906. Instr. in mathematics, Lafayette Coll., Easton, Pa., 1906-12, asso. prof., 1915-25, registrar since 1915, prof., 1925-35, head of mathematics dept. since 1935; prof. mathematics, U. of Ore, Eugene, Ore., 1912-15. Mem. Am. Math. Soc., Math. Assn. of America, A.A.A.S., Am. Assn. of Univ. Profs., Am. Assn. of Collegiate Registrars, Phi Delta Theta. Presbyterian. Club: Northampton Country (Easton, Pa.). Address: 2 W. Campus, Easton, Pa.

SMITH, William Nelson, mech. and elec. engr.; b. Brattleboro, Vt., June 5, 1868; s. Francis Wyman and Laura Matilda (Fay) S.; student Vt. Episcopal Inst., Burlington, Vt., 1880-81, Woodstock (Vt.) High Sch., 1884-85, Columbia Grammar Sch., New York, 1885-86; M.E. in elec. engring., Cornell U., 1890; m. Fannie Louise Tilden, Sept. 28, 1897; children—Francis Wyman, Harriet Kelsey. Asst. in elec. ry. constrn., Thomas-Houston Elec. Co., Chicago office, 1890-92; foreman electric car repairs, Chicago City Ry. Co., 1893; elec. engr. New Orleans Traction Co., 1894-97; draftsman Gen. Electric Co., Schenectady, N.Y., 1898; elec. traction engr., Westinghouse, Church, Kerr & Co., New York, 1899-1911; consulting engr., Washington & Old Dominion Ry., Washington, D.C., 1912; asst. engr. Boston Edison Co., 1913; consulting engr. San Francisco-Oakland Terminal Rys., 1914; pvt. practice, Watertown, N.Y., 1915; efficiency engr. Am. Agrl. Chem. Co., Elizabeth, N.J., 1916-17; elec. engr. S. E. Junkins Co., Vancouver, B.C., Can., 1918-1924, 1926; consulting engr. Winnipeg (Manitoba, Can.) Electric Co., 1918-24, 1925; elec. engr., Sanderson & Porter, New York, and Jackson & Moreland, Boston, 1927; elec. ry. engr. E. L. Phillips & Co., New York, on N.Y. State Rys., 1928-29; report engr. and librarian, W. S. Barstow & Co., E. M. Gilbert engring. Corpn., and Utilities Management Corpn., (engrs. for Asso. Gas & Electric System), Reading, Pa., since 1929. Served as corpl., Co. D, 1st Training Regt., U.S. Army, at 1st Plattsburg Camp, 1915; Canadian Emergency Militia, 1919. Mem. Am. Inst. E.E., Engring. Inst. of Can., Pa. Soc. Professional Engrs., Nat. Soc. Professional Engrs., Am. Acad. Polit. and Social Science; fellow Royal Soc. of Arts (England). Awarded Plummer Medal by Engring. Inst. of Can. for corrosion research papers, 1922. Democrat. Episcopalian. Club: Univ. (Reading, Pa.). Inventor of "Smith-Grip" insulator pin for overhead power lines and method of determining air resistance of electric trains, 1904; original proposer of 3-wire electric ry. distribution for electrolysis prevention, 1893; designer of several interurban electric ry. systems and several of the earlier heavy R.R. electrifications (notably the L.I. R.R.); established certainty of corrosion of cast-iron and lead structures in alkaline soils independently of stray currents, 1921. Author of six professional papers read before Am. Inst. E.E., Engring. Inst. of Can. Home: 611 N. 25th St., Pennside, Reading, Pa. Office: 412 Washington St., Reading, Pa.

SMITH, William Skeldon Adamson; b. Dundee, Scotland, June 16, 1860; s. William and Jane (Mitchell) S.; ed. pub. schs.; m. Zelma, d. Maj. Sewall S. Farwell, Oct. 22, 1895; children—Stuart F., R. Graeme. Apprentice at sea, at 14, and at 23 was comdr. in British merchant marine; came to U.S., 1897, and engaged in farming in Ia.; expert in farm practice, U.S. Dept. of Agr., 1914-16; mem. Federal Farm Loan Bd., by appmt. of President Wilson, July 26, 1916-Aug. 1922. Republican. Presbyn. Mason. Address: Connecticut General Life Insurance Co., 1000 Lincoln-Liberty Bldg., Philadelphia, Pa.

SMITH, William Thomas, industrial finance and management; b. Chicago, Ill., Feb. 5, 1884;

s. Samuel and Mary Jane (Thomas) S.; ed. grammar sch.; m. Gertrude Hammond, May 10, 1905; children—Gertrude Hammond, May Janet, William Thomas. Studied and practiced architecture under Bruce Price, N.Y. City, 1898-1905; v.p. of constrn., Thompson Starrett Co., 1909-13; pres. Industrial Service Corpn., 1913-17; operating v.p. Merchant Shipbuilding Corpn., 1917-21; partner and vice-pres. W. A. Harriman & Co., Industrial finance and management, 1921-30; pres. Harriman Industrial Corpn.; chmn. bd. Wm. Cramp & Sons Ship & Engine Bldg. Co.; also officer or dir. Am. Ship & Commerce Corpn., Marion Steam Shovel Co., Electric Shovel Coal Corpn., Bear Mountain Hudson River Bridge Co., Russian Finance & Construction Co., Georgian Manganese Co., Ltd. Modern Housing of Washington Inc., No. Washington Housing Corpn., Mt. Airy Corpn., Sligo Park Properties, Inc., M.D.D.C. Corpn., Norcastle Corpn., Sterling Iron & Ry. Co. Republican. Mason. Clubs: Whitehall, Orange Lawn Tennis. Home: 61 Duffield Drive, South Orange, N.J. Office: 39 Broadway, New York, N.Y.

SMITH, William Watson; mem. law firm Smith, Buchanan & Ingersoll. Trustee Carnegie Inst. Tech., Univ. of Pittsburgh. Address: Union Trust Bldg., Pittsburgh, Pa.

SMITH, Winford Henry, M.D.; b. West Scarboro, Me., July 11, 1877; s. George Prey and Carrie P. (Burnham) S.; A.B., Bowdoin, 1899, Sc.D., 1918; M.D., Johns Hopkins, 1903; m. Jean Maguire, June 29, 1905. Interne and resident gynecologist, Lakeside Hosp., Cleveland, 1903-05; hosp. phys. N.Y. City Health Dept., 1905-06; supt. Hartford (Conn.) Hosp., 1906-09; gen. med. supt. of Bellevue and Allied hosps., N.Y. City, 1909-11; dir. Johns Hopkins Hosp., Baltimore, since 1911. Consultant on hosp. organization and planning. Commd. colonel, M.C., U.S.A.; apptd. chief of hosp. div., staff of surgeon gen., Washington, D.C. Awarded D.S.M. (U.S.). Mem. A.M.A., Am. Hosp. Assn. (pres. 1916), Am. Assn. of Hosp. Social Workers. Republican. Episcopalian. Club: Elkridge Hunt. Author of numerous papers relating to hosp. organization, administration and management. Home: 220 Wendover Road. Address: Johns Hopkins Hospital, Baltimore, Md.

SMITHERS, Ernest Leonard, ry. official; b. St. Albans, Eng., Nov. 18, 1867; Sidney J. and Louisa B. (Faulconbridge) S.; ed. pvt. sch., Eng.; m. Edith A. Williams, July 9, 1892; children—Henry L., Horace G. (dec.), Eric F., Charles H. (dec.), Edith M., Winnie. Came to U.S., 1884; began as jr. clk. St. Louis & Cairo Ry., 1884; clk. freight office, C.,B.&Q. R.R., at Chicago, 1885; clk. Cleveland, Akron & Columbus Ry., at Akron, O., 1886; sec. to pres. L.&N. R.R., at New York, 1886-89, and continued with same rd. as clk. treasurer's office, 1889-1901, transfer agt., 1901-02, asst. sec. and asst. treas., 1902-16, v.p. since Apr. 20, 1916, retired as v.p., Jan. 1, 1937, continuing as dir. since 1926. Republican. Methodist. Club: Maplewood Country. Home: East Orange, N.J.

SMITHERS, William West, lawyer; b. at Phila,. May 5, 1864; s. William Henry and Mary J. (Reed) S.; LL.B., U. of Pa., 1887; m. Virginia Lyons, of Phila., June 4, 1889 (died Jan. 14, 1924); m. 2d, Anne C. McDonnell, May 18, 1929. Practiced, Philadelphia, 1887—, spl. attention later years to corpn., ins., negligence, probate and internat. law. Mem. Am. Bar Assn. (chmn. Comp. Law Bur. and mem. since its orgn., 1908), Am. Inst. Criminal Law and Criminology (chmn. com. on transls., pub. Criminal Science Series), Bar Assn. Philadelphia (treasurer and member board governors, 1902-23), American Society Internat. Law, Historical Society of Pa., Internat. Law Assn., Am. Foreign Law Assn. (pres.), Société de Leg. Comparée, Institut de Droit Comparé. Republican. Methodist. Clubs: University, Racquet. Author: Relation of Attorney and Client, 1887; Coaching Trip Through Delaware, 1892; Life of the Milford Bard, 1894; Executive Clemency in Pennsylvania, 1909; also many legal mag. articles, including "Code Napoleon"; "Imperial German Civil Code"; "Russian Civil Law"; "The Pardoning Power." Translator: Which Was the Greater Love? (from French of Henry Bordeaux), 1930. Speaks French and Spanish. Mason (K.T.). Home: Spring Lake, N.J. Office: Otis Bldg., Philadelphia, Pa.

SMOLEY, Constantine Kenneth, civil engr., educator; b. Dwinsk, Russia, Apr. 27, 1869; s. Ossip M. and Barbara E. (Radief) S.; C.E., Federal Polytechnicum, Zurich, Switzerland, 1893; m. Pauline B. Sagorin, Feb. 21, 1894 (died Oct. 3, 1926); m. 2d, Florence N. Wood, May 31, 1928. Came to U.S., 1895, naturalized citizen, 1901. Structural draftsman, Variety Iron Works, Cleveland, 1895-96; chief draftsman Van Dorn Iron Works, 1896-1902; structural engr. Wellman, Seaver & Morgan Engring. Co., Cleveland, 1902-04; consulting engr. German-American Portland Cement Works, La Salle, Ill., 1904-05; structural engr. Ill. Steel Co., 1905-06, N.P. Ry. Co., St. Paul, Minn., 1907-09; dir. Schs. of Civ. and Structural Engring., Internat. Correspondence Schools, Scranton, Pa., in charge instrn., also preparation textbooks, 1909-26, head of C. K. Smoley & Sons, pubs. Author: Parallel Tables of Logarithms and Squares, 1901; Five-Decimal Logarithmic-Trigonometric Tables, 1908; Handbook of Civil Engineering, 1913; Parallel Tables of Slopes and Rises, 1917; Smoley's Combined Tables, 1919; Graphic Solution of a Right Triangle, 1920; Segmental Functions, 1937. Also many I.C.S. textbooks. Home: 241 4th St. N., St. Petersburg, Fla. Address: 415 Vine St., Scranton, Pa.

SMOOT, Merrill Clayvelle, physician; b. Marydel, Md., Sept. 15, 1902; s. Truston Cannon and Fannie Josephine (Griffith) S.; B.S., Washington Coll., Chestertown, Md., 1922; M.D., U. of Md. Med. Sch., Baltimore, 1928; M.Sc. in Medicine, U. of Pa. Grad. Sch. of Medicine, 1934; m. Helen Josephine Rouse, June 22, 1930. Interne Univ. Hosp., Baltimore, Md., 1928-29; in pvt. practice gen. medicine, Westminster, Md., 1929-30, at Georgetown, Del., 1930-32, at Sykesville, Md., 1934-36; resident surgeon, Newark Eye & Ear Infirmary, Newark, N.J., 1936-37; in practice specializing in diseases of eye, ear, nose and throat, Hagerstown, Md., since 1937. Mem. A.M.A., Am. Acad. of Otolaryngology and Ophthalmology, Med. and Chirurg. Soc. of Md., Washington Co. Med. Soc., Nu Sigma Nu. Republican. Methodist. Mason. Clubs: Fountain Head Country (Hagerstown); Potomac Fish and Game (Williamsport). Home: 609 Summit Av. Office: 130 W. Washington St., Hagerstown, Md.

SMUKLER, Max Edward, ophthalmologist; b. Phila., Pa., Nov. 1, 1887; s. Harris and Bessie (Sherman) S.; student Pub. Sch., Phila, Pa., 1894-1902, Central High Sch., Phila., 1902-05; M.D., Jefferson Med. Coll., Phila., 1910; m. Anna Marks, June 22, 1915; children—Ruth, Nathan. Interne, Jewish Hosp., Phila., 1910-12, New York Lying-In Hosp., New York, 1912; 1st clin. asst. to Dr. S. Lewis Ziegler and Dr. Milton J. Griscom, Wills Eye Hosp., Phila., 1914-23; chief ophthalmologist, Northern Liberties Hosp., Phila., 1924-39; asst. ophthalmologist, Phila. Bur. of Health, 1918-36, head ophthalmologist since 1936. Mem. Phila. County Med. Soc. Zeta Beta Tau. Jewish Religion (Keneseth Israel Synagogue). Mason. Author of many articles on ophthalmology pub. in the Archives of Ophthalmology, Am. Jour. of Ophthalmology and Pa. State Med. Jour. Address: 1940 N. Broad St., Philadelphia, Pa.

SMYERS, Bertrand Hunter, lawyer; b. Marion Center, Indiana Co., Pa., Mar. 10, 1872; s. William Riddle and Mary E. (Hunter) S.; student Bucknell Acad., 1888-89; A.B., Western U. of Pa. (now U. of Pittsburgh), 1893; m. Flora B. Hays, July 20, 1898; children—Bertrand H., William H., Edward C. With Pittsburgh Trust Co., 1893-1924, successively as clerk, asst. sec., sec., vice-pres. and trust officer; admitted to Pa. bar, 1898, and since in practice of law, Pittsburgh. Mem. Allegheny Co. Bar Assn., Phi Gamma Delta. Republican. Presbyterian. Rotarian (past pres. Pittsburgh Club; past gov. 33d Dist. Rotary Internat., 1930-31). Organized original Pitt Panther football team, 1889 (then Western U. of Pa.), and played as first quarter-back on teams, 1889-92, capt., 1892. Home: 2807 Perrysville Av. Office: 323 4th Av., Pittsburgh, Pa.

SMYTH, Callender Suplee, banker, trust officer; b. Phila., Pa., Nov. 28, 1878; s. Benjamin Orne and Kate H. (Breiding) S.; student public school and Central Manual Training Sch., Phila., 1886-96; m. Emily Lyle Schoenhut, June 10, 1903; children—C. Wayne, Benjamin Burton. Asst. trust officer, Germantown Trust Co., Phila., 1910-25, trust officer, 1925-26, v.p. in charge of trusts since 1926; pres. Hood Cemetery; dir. Robert Cherry Sons, Inc. Trustee and treas. Memorial Baptist Ch. Republican. Baptist. Home: 5913 Pulaski Av. Office: 5633 Germantown Av., Philadelphia, Pa.

SMYTH, Calvin Mason, retired; b. Phila., Pa., Mar. 11, 1868; s. Isaac S. and Catherine (Mason) S.; ed. Germantown Acad.; m. Margretta Wheatley Slaughter, Oct. 19, 1893; children—Calvin Mason, Anna Hoyt, Henry Comegys, Francis Slaughter. Pres. Young, Smyth, Field Co. wholesale notions, 1907-22; pres. Red Diamond Chemical Co., 1922; pres. Cheltenham Knitting Co., 1920-36; retired; mem. bd. Chelten Trust Co. Pres. Nat. Wholesale Dry Goods Assn., 1915; former pres. Merchants and Mfrs. Assn., Phila.; former mem. of boards of Phila. Chamber of Commerce, Germantown Acad., Babies Hosp.; former vestryman St. Michaels P.E. Ch., Germantown. Home: Delmar Morris Apts., Germantown, Philadelphia, Pa.

SMYTH, Charles Phelps, prof. of chemistry; b. Clinton, N.Y., Feb. 10, 1895; s. Charles Henry and Ruth Anna (Phelps) S.; prep. edn., Lawrenceville (N.J.) Sch., 1912; A.B., Princeton U., 1916, A.M., 1917; Ph.D., Harvard, 1921; unmarried. Asst. chemist U.S. Bureau of Standards, 1917-18; instr. in chemistry, Princeton U., 1920-23, asst. prof., 1923-27, asso. prof., 1927-38, prof. of chemistry since 1938; lecturer Am. Chem. Soc. Inst. of Chemistry, 1927; asso. editor Jour. Chemical Physics, 1933-36. Served as 2d lt. Ordnance Reserve Corps, 1918; 2d lt. Chem. Service Sect., Nat. Army; 1st lt. Chem. Warfare Service, U.S. Army, 1918; lt. comdr. U.S. Naval Reserve since 1937. Fellow A.A.A.S., Am. Phys. Soc.; mem. Am. Chem. Soc., Am. Philos. Soc., N.Y. Acad. Science, Alpha Chi Sigma, Phi Beta Kappa, Sigma Xi. Democrat. Episcopalian. Club: Princeton (Phila.). Author: Dielectic Constant and Molecular Structure, 1931. Contbr. over 70 scientific papers to jours. Home: 22 Morven St. Office: Frick Chemical Laboratory, Princeton, N.J.

SMYTH, Henry DeWolf, physicist; b. Clinton, N.Y., May 1, 1898; s. Charles Henry, Jr., and Ruth Anna (Phelps) S.; grad. Lawrenceville Sch., 1914; A.B., Princeton U., 1918, A.M., 1920, Ph.D., 1921; Ph.D., Cambridge U., Eng., 1923; m. Mary de Coningh, June 30, 1936. Nat. Research Council fellow in Cambridge, Eng., 1921-23, Princeton U., 1923-24; instr. in physics, Princeton U., 1924-25, asst. prof., 1925-29 ,asso. prof., 1929-36, prof. since 1936, chmn. dept. of physics since 1935. Fellow Guggenheim Memorial Foundation, Göttingen, 1931-32. Fellow Am. Phys. Soc.; mem. Phi Beta Kappa, Sigma Xi. Author: Hatter, Motion and Electricity, 1939. Contbr. to Physical Review and other scientific jours.; asso. editor of Physical Review, 1927-30. Home: Lafayette Rd. W., Princeton, N.J.

SMYTH, Henry Field, hygienist; b. Philadelphia, Pa., Nov. 1, 1875; s. Isaac Scott and Catherine Comyges S.; prep. edn., Germantown Acad.; certificate in biology, U. of Pa., 1893, M.D., 1897, Ph.D., 1912; studied U. of Vienna, 1899-1900; m. Alice E. Bracket, 1902 (died 1929); children—Henry Field, Catherine Mason; m. 2d, Clara F. Ellis, Oct. 1931. Resident phys. Phila. Home for Incurables, July-Dec. 1897, Germantown Hosp., 1898; gen. practice until 1911; pub. health student, U. of Pa., 1911-12, Wood fellow in hygiene, 1912-13, Scott fellow in hygiene, 1913-14; mem. faculty, U. of Pa., since 1914, successively instr. in bacteriology and hygiene, asst. prof. same, asst. prof. industrial hygiene since 1921, acting dir. Lab. of Hygiene, 1917-19, dir. pro tem. since 1932; mem. firm Henry Field Smyth & Clara F. Smyth, consultation and investigation of public and industrial health problems. Mem. Pa. Commn. on Sch. Ventilation, Pa. Commn. on Occupational Disease Compensation. Past asst. surgeon U.S.P.H. Res., World War; duty in industrial hygiene control, 1917-19; mem. Radnor Twp. (Delaware County, Pa.) Bd. of Health and sec. of same, 1916-17 and since 1928, also consultant. Fellow A.M.A., Am. Pub. Health Assn. (governing council 5 yrs.), Phila. Coll. Physicians (mem. pub. health com. 4 yrs.), Am. Coll. Physicians, Am. Assn. Industrial Phys. and Surgeons (dir.); mem. Nat. Safety Council (adv. health com.), Assn. Am. Bacteriologists, Sigma Xi. Methodist. Author: (with Walter Lord Obold) Industrial Microbiology, 1930. Contbr. scientific articles. Home: 107 Owen Av., Lansdowne, Pa. Address: Laboratory of Hygiene, Univ. of Pa., Philadelphia, Pa.

SMYTH, Thomas, biologist; b. Blacksburg, Va., Oct. 15, 1898; s. Dr. Ellison A., Jr. and Grace C. (Allan) S.; B.S., Va. Poly. Inst., 1920; A.M., Cornell U., 1923, Ph.D., same, 1925; study Marine Biol. Lab., Cold Spring Harbor, L.I., N.Y., summers 1920-21; m. Martha Carolyn McCormick, June 30, 1926; children—Thomas, Jr., Martha Carolyn, Mary Catherine, Ellison Arthur. Prof. biology, Hampden-Sydney College, 1920-22; asst. in ornithology, Cornell U., 1923-25; asso. prof. zoology, U. of S.C., 1925-28; prof. biology and head sci. dept., State Teachers Coll., Indiana, Pa., since 1928; served as field zoologist N.Y. Conservation Commn., summers 1927-28, 1931. Served in S.A.T.C., 1918; lt. cav. res., 1920-25. Mem. A.A.A.S., Am. Ornithologists Union, Wildlife Soc., Pa. Acad. Sci., Sigma Xi, Phi Sigma Pi. Republican. Presbyn. Co-author (with H. C. Skinner and F. M. Wheat), Textbook in Educational Biology, 1937. Contbr. articles on birds and gen. nature topics. Home: 1050 Washington St., Indiana, Pa.

SMYTH, Thomas Lawrence, physician; b. Allentown, Pa., Nov. 2, 1890; s. James P. and Catherine (Boyle) S.; M.D., Medico-Chirurg. Coll., 1913; m. Alicia M. McConnon, Jan. 26, 1920; children—Lawrence Thomas, Thomas Lawrence, Alicia M. Interne, St. Francis Hosp., Trenton, N.J., 1913-14, Childrens Hosp., Phila., 1914, Kings Co. Hosp., Brooklyn, N.Y., 1915; in gen. practice at Allentown, Pa., 1915-17 and since 1919; med. officer Vets. Bur., Allentown, 1920-22; specializing in roentgenology since 1926; roentgenologist Sacred Heart Hosp., Allentown, Pa., 1920-34, Quakertown Community Hosp., Quakertown, Pa., 1928-33; asso. roentgenologist, St. Luke's Hosp., Bethlehem; cons. roentgenologist, Grand View Hosp., Sellersville. Served as capt. Med. Corps, U.S.A. during World War. Dir. Pa. Dept. Pub. Assistance for Lehigh Co.; mem. bd. of trustees Allentown Community Chest. Diplomate Am. Bd. Radiology. Fellow Am. Coll. Radiology. Mem. Radiol. Soc. of N.A., A.M.A., Pa. State and Lehigh Co. (past pres.) med. socs., Pa. (v.p.) and Phila. Roentgen Ray socs. Democrat. Roman Catholic. Club: Livingston. Home: 111 N. 8th St., Allentown, Pa.

SNADER, David L., prof. civil engring., cons. engr.; b. Westminster, Md., July 8, 1887; s. Henry Maurer and Sarah Catherine (Zepp) S.; Arch. E., O. Northern U., 1913, C.E., 1914; M.S., 1918; A.M., Columbia U., 1926, Ph.D., 1937; m. Lelia Rogers, Sept. 2, 1919. Engaged in various capacities in constrn. operations, until 1914; in professional archtl. and engring. practice since 1914; prof. arch. and engring. Valparaiso Univ., 1914-17, Southwestern Presbyterian Univ., 1917-19; cons. archt. and engr. for State of S.D., prof. in charge dept. civil engring., S.D. State Coll., 1919-24; prof. civil (formerly structural) engring., Stevens Inst. Tech. since 1924; for ten yrs. conducted research and investigation of condition of concrete structures in service throughout U.S. In charge engring. courses in S.A.T.C. Fellow A.A.A.S. Mem. Am. Assn. Engrs., Am. Soc. Civil Engrs., Ind. Soc. Architects, Sigma Xi, Alpha Epsilon. Licensed professional engr. Democrat. Contbr. articles and bulls. on condition concrete structures. Home: 80 Washington Place, New York, N.Y. Office: Stevens Inst. Tech., Hoboken, N.J.

SNADER, Edward Roland, Jr., physician; b. Phila., Pa., Nov. 1, 1895; s. Edward Roland and Martha (McComb) S.; B.S., Haverford Coll., 1917; M.D., Hahnemann Med. Coll., 1921; m. Margaretta Henkel Rupert, of Wilmington, Del., May 16, 1925; children—Martha Jane, Edward Roland, III. Served as jr. asst. gen. med. sect., Hahnemann Hosp. Med. Dispensary, 1924-25, clin. asst., 1925-30, sr. clin. asst., 1930-31, electrocardiographer, 1928-31; instr. medicine, Hahnemann Med. Coll., 1924-25, lecturer phys. diagnosis, 1925-29, asso. prof. medicine, 1929-31, clin. prof. medicine since 1931; engaged in practice of medicine at Phila.; consultant, Allentown State Hosp., since 1932, William McKinley Memorial Hosp., Trenton, N.J., since 1936, J. Lewis Crozer Hosp., Chester, Pa., since 1937, instr. Homeopathic Hosp. of Chester Co., West Chester, Pa., since 1938. Served with med. enlisted res. corps and Hahnemann Med. Unit, S.A.T.C. Chmn. Health & Drainage Com. Wynnewood Civic Assn. Trustee Homeo. Med. Soc. of Pa., Homeo. Med. Soc. of Phila. (past pres.). Diplomate Am. Bd. Internal Medicine, 1937. Fellow Am. Coll. Phys., A.M.A.; mem. Pa. State and Phila. Co. med. socs., Am. Inst. Homeopathy, Soc. for Study Internal Secretions, Am. Assn. History of Medicine, Germantown Homeo. Med. Soc., Phila. Heart Assn., Phila. Metabolic Assn., State Diabetic Commn., Alpha Sigma. Republican. Presbyn. Clubs: Haverford, University (Philadelphia). Contbr. to med. jours. Home: "Ogston House," 547 Sussex Rd., Wynnewood. Office: Medical Arts Bldg., Philadelphia, Pa.

SNAVELY, Benjamin Frank, pres. and mgr. Consumers Ice & Coal Co.; b. Lime Valley, Pa., Sept. 15, 1878; s. Benjamin Herr and Anna (Herr) S.; ed. high sch. and business coll.; m. Anna Blanche Lichty, Oct. 18, 1905; children—Benjamin L., Clarence L., Frank L., Harry L., Mary Elizabeth. Hardware salesman Herr & Snavely, 1897-1906; opened store for Kent Light Co., Scranton, 1906; became mgr. Consumers Ice Co. (now Consumers Ice & Coal Co.), 1907, pres. since 1932; v.p. and trustee Conestoga Transportation Co. since 1932; dir. Northern Bank & Trust Co. since 1935, Peoples Bldg. Loan & Deposit Co. since 1935, Lancaster Iron Works since 1936. Pres. Lancaster Gen. Hosp., 1933-39. Pres. Lancaster Mfrs. Assn., 1921, Lancaster Chamber of Commerce, 1935. Mem. Pa. Soc. Presbyn. (elder). Clubs: Rotary, Hamilton. Home: Lampeter, Lane Co., Pa. Office: Plum St. and Ice Av., Lancaster, Pa.

SNAVELY, Edwin Russell, coll. prof. and coach; b. Martinsville, Ill., Mar. 5, 1912; s. Chester S. and Asenath (Miller) S.; B.S., U. of Ill., 1934; A.M., Columbia U., 1938; m. Freda Johnson, June 20, 1935; 1 dau., Martha Anne. Teacher gen. sci. and coach of all sports, high sch., St. Joseph, Ill., 1934-36; teacher physiology and coach all sports, high sch., Bement, Ill., 1937; dir. health and phys. edn., instr. hygiene, and coach football and basketball, Moravian Coll., Bethlehem, Pa., 1937-39; head football coach and asst. in dept. health and phys. edn., State Teachers Coll., East Stroudsburg, Pa., since 1939. Mem. Alpha Sigma Phi, Delta Theta Epsilon. Republican. Methodist. Mason. Club: Kiwanis of Bethlehem. Home: 34 6th St., Stroudsburg, Pa.

SNEAD, Samuel Jackson, golf professional; b. Bath County, Va., May 27, 1912; s. Harry Gilmore and Laura (Dudley) S.; grad. Valley High Sch., Hot Springs, Va.; unmarried. Professional golfer since 1934, White Sulphur Springs, W.Va., since 1935. Won Oakland (Calif.) Open, Bing Crosby Tournament, St. Paul Open, Nassau Open, Miami Open, 1937; Bing Crosby Tournament, Greensboro Open, Goodall Invitational, Inverness Open, Chicago Open, Canadian Open, W.Va. Open, Westchester Open, White Sulphur Springs Open (record for winnings in open and professional tournaments), 1938; St. Petersburg Open, Internat. Four-Ball (with Guldahl), 1939; mem. Ryder Cup Team, 1937. Methodist. Address: Greenbrier Golf Club, White Sulphur Springs, W.Va.

SNEDECOR, Spencer Treadwell, M.D.; b. Blue Point, N.Y., Feb. 24, 1900; s. John Roe and Ellen R. (Hallett) S.; A.B., Dartmouth Coll., 1921; M.D., Coll. Physicians & Surgeons, Columbia U., 1923; m. Mary Overton, June 16, 1923; children—Jeanne, Spencer Treadwell. Interne Kings Co. Hosp., 1923-25; began gen. practice of medicine, 1925; now specializes in fractures and orthopedics. Served in U.S. Naval Reserve, 1918. Mem. State Relief Council, 1935-36. Fellow Am. Coll. Surgeons; mem. N.J. State Med. Soc. (pres. 1937-38), Soc. Surgeons of N.J., Sigma Alpha Epsilon. Mason. Club: Oritani (Hackensack). Home: 288 Maple Hill Drive. Office: 50 Anderson St., Hackensack, N.J.

SNELL, Henry Bayley, artist; b. Richmond, Eng., Sept. 29, 1858; s. Edward and Elizabeth S.; studied Art Students' League, New York; m. Florence Francis, 1888. Gold medal, Phila. Art Club; 1st prize, Tenn. Centennial, Nashville, 1897; hon. mention, Paris Expn. 1900; asst. dir. of Fine Arts, U.S. Commn., Paris Expn., 1900; Officier de l'Académie et de l'Instruction Publique; silver medal, Buffalo Expn., 1901, St. Louis Expn., 1904; silver and gold medals, Panama P.I. Expn., 1915. N.A., 1906; hon. life pres. New York Water Color Club; mem. Am. Water Color Soc. Clubs: Lotos, National Arts, Salmagundi (New York). Home: New Hope, Pa.

SNELLING, Walter Otheman, chemist, inventor, b. Washington, Dec. 13, 1880; s. Walter Commonfort and Alice Lee (Hornor) S.; B.S. in Chemistry, Columbian (now Goerge Washington) U., 1904; B.S. in Science, Harvard, 1905; M.S., Yale, 1906; Ph.D., George Washington U., 1907; m. Marjorie Gahring Snelling, an adopted dau., May 5, 1919; children—William Augustus, Robert Fulton, Constance Charlotte, Richard Arkwright, Marilyn Verna, Charles Darwin, Thomas Edison. Ednl. and scientific work, U.S. Bur. of Mines, 1907-12, cons. chemist, same, Jan.-Sept., 1912; now cons. chemist in connection with pvt. and corporate investigations of oils, oil products and explosives. Inventor of waterproof detonator, continuous high-pressure oil-cracking process, sand-test method of testing detonators and explosives, densimeter used in testing dynamite, improved centrifuge test for explosives, new liquid gas (gasol) made from waste natural gas (left Government service to develop this and other patents). Granted more than 100 patents covering inventions in fields of chem. products and explosives. Dir. research, Trojan Powder Co., 1917—. Gave many inventions to U.S. Govt. without reserve (estimated that the waterproof detonator saved Govt. more than $500,000 a yr. in Panama Canal work). Republican. Mem. Am. Inst. Mining and Metall. Engrs., Am. Chem. Soc., Am. Electrochem. Soc., Deutsche Chemische Gesselschaft, Soc. Chem. Industry, Franklin Inst., etc. Club: Chemists' (New York). Author of about 50 scientific papers pub. by Bur. of Mines and scientific socs. Home: 110 S. 13th St., Allentown, Pa.

SNEVILY, Robert S. (St. Clair), lawyer; b. Brooklyn, N.Y., Sept. 14, 1890; s. Mansfield B. and Wilhelmina (Creevey) S.; student Columbia U. 1908-10; LL.B., N.Y. Law Sch., 1912; m. Dorothe Van Keuren, Oct. 16, 1913; children —Jane St. Clair, Robert Van Keuren. Admitted to N.Y. bar, 1913 and engaged in practice in N.Y. City; mem. firm Baylis & Sanborn, New York, N.Y., 1919-25; admitted to N.J. bar as atty., 1925, counselor, 1926; mem. firm Nichols & Snevily, N.Y. City and Westfield, N.J., 1925-35; in practice alone at Westfield, N.J., 1935-39; mem. firm Snevily & Ely, Westfield, N.J., since 1939; vice-pres. and dir. Nat. Bank of Westfield; dir. and counsel Home Bldg. & Loan Assn.; dir. Bankers Mortgage & Realty Co. Served as 1st lt. inf., U.S.A., 1917-19; with A.E.F. in France. Mem. bd. edn., Westfield, N.J., 1922-32, pres. bd., 1928-32; chmn. Emergency Relief drive, 1934. Dir. Westfield United Campaign Com. Mem. Sigma Chi. Republican. Conglist. Mason. Clubs: Echo Lake Country (v.p.), College Mens (past pres.), Rotary (Westfield). Home: 854 Standish Av. Office: 66 Elm St., Westfield, N.J.

SNIDER, Luther Crocker, geologist; b. Mt. Summit, Ind., Sept. 13, 1882; s. John and Lou

(Leath) S.; student Rose Polytechnic Inst., 1903-04, U. of Okla., 1910-11; A.B., Ind. U., 1908, A.M., 1909; Ph.D., U. of Chicago, 1915; m. Ruth Gladys Marshall, Mar. 31, 1907; children —Hester Bernice, John Luther. Teacher common and high schs., 1901-03 and 1904-06; chemist, field geologist and asst. dir. Okla. Geol. Survey, 1909-15; field geologist Pierce Oil Corpn., Tulsa, Okla., 1915-16, Cosden Oil & Gas Co., 1916-17; asst. chief and chief geologist Empire Gas & Fuel Co., Bartlesville, Okla., 1917-25; cons. geologist Henry L. Doherty & Co., 1925-35; same, Cities Service Co., since 1935. Fellow A.A.A.S., Geol. Soc. America, Paleontol. Soc., Soc. Econ. Geology; mem. Am. Inst. Mining and Metall. Engrs., Am. Assn. of Petroleum Geologists (editor 1933-37), Sigma Xi, Phi Beta Kappa (alumnus). Republican. Methodist. Mason. Author: Petroleum and Natural Gas in Oklahoma, 1913; Oil and Gas in the Mid-Continent Fields, 1920; Earth History, 1932; also various bulls. of Okla. Geol. Survey, 1910-16. Contbr. to scientific mags. Home: Leonia, N.J. Office: 60 Wall St., New York, N.Y.

SNIVELY, Samuel Frisby, ex-mayor; b. Greencastle, Pa., Nov. 24, 1859; s. Jacob Samuel and Margaret (Snyder) S.; A.B., Dickinson Coll., Carlisle, Pa., 1882, A.M., 1885; LL.B., U. of Pa., 1885; unmarried. Began practice of law at Duluth, Minn., 1886; mem. Water and Light Bd., Duluth, 1896-1903; mayor of Duluth, 1921, fourth term expiring 1937. Unanimously chosen as member of Duluth Hall of Fame, 1938. Mem. Beta Theta Pi. Episcopalian. Address: Care Sprague F. Snively, 4735 Maripoe St., Pittsburgh, Pa.

SNOKE, James Stephen, supervising prin. pub. schs.; b. Lurgan, Pa., Apr. 27, 1908; s. J. Arthur and Emma (Craig) S.; ed. Shippensburg Normal Sch., 1921-25, Shippensburg State Teachers Coll., 1925-26, 1928-30, B.S. in Edn., same, 1930; A.M., U. of Pittsburgh, 1938; student Western Theol. Sem., 1930-31, Pa. State Coll., summer 1933; m. Mary Edwards Polk, Apr. 18, 1931; 1 son, James Thomas. Instr. mathematics, jr. high sch. and sr. high sch., Leetsdale, Pa., 1930-36, guidance counsellor and instr. history, 1936, prin. high sch., 1936, supervising prin. pub. schs., Leetsdale, Pa., since 1937. Served as scoutmaster Leetsdale Boy Scout Troop since 1932; selected as scoutmaster from Allegheny Co. for Washington Jamboree, 1935. Mem. Nat. and Pa. state edn. assns., Prins. Round Table of Allegheny Co., Phi Nu Delta. Republican. Presbyn (ordained ruling elder, 1938). Home: 185 Broad St., Leetsdale, Pa.

SNOOK, H(omer) Clyde, electrophysicist; b. Antwerp, O., Mar. 25, 1878; s. Wilson Reed and Nancy Jane (Graves) S.; A.B., Ohio Wesleyan U., 1900, M.S., 1910, Sc.D. from same university, 1926; A.M., Allegheny Coll., Meadville, Pa., 1902; post-graduate work, University of Pa., 1904-08; m. May Eusebia McKee, June 24, 1903. Prof. physics and chemistry, High Sch., Ohio Soldiers and Sailors Orphans' Home, Xenia, O., 1900-01; asst. prof. chemistry, Allegheny Coll., 1901-02; wireless teleg. expert, with Queen & Co., Phila., Pa., 1902-03; pres. Roentgen Mfg. Co., Phila., 1903-13, Snook-Roentgen Mfg. Co., Phila., 1913-16; v.p. Victor Electric Corpn., Chicago, 1916-18; elec. engr. with Western Elec. Co., 1918-25; elec. engr. with Bell Telephone Laboratories, 1925-1927; consulting engineers since 1927. Fellow Am. Inst. E.E., Am. Physical Soc.; mem. American Roentgen Ray Soc., Phila., Roentgen Society, Phi Beta Kappa, Phi Delta Theta. Awarded Edward Longstreth medal, Franklin Inst., 1919; gold medal, Radiological Soc. of North America, 1923; hon. fellowship and gold medal, Am. Coll. Radiology, 1928. Chmn. noise elimination com. Nat. Safety Council, 1930. Presbyterian. Mason. Inventor X-ray transformer; numerous patented developments in X-rays, radio, the communication art, metallurgy and optics. Home: 45 Woodland Av., Summit, N.J.

SNOW, Chester, mathematician, physicist; b. Salt Lake City, Utah, June 1, 1881; s. Willard and Dora (Pratt) S.; student Utah Agrl. Coll., 1902-03; A.B., magna cum laude, Harvard, 1906; Ph.D., U. of Wis., 1914; m. May Maughan, Aug. 22, 1906; children—Chester

Weston, Margaret, Robert Maughan. Prof. physics and head of dept., 1906-11, prof. mathematics and head of dept., 1911-12, Brigham Young U., Provo, Utah; fellow in physics, U. of Wis., 1912-14; prof. mathematics and head of dept., U. of Ida., July 1914-Mar. 1920; math. physicist Bur. of Standards, Washington, Mar. 1920—. Mem. Am. Phys. Soc., Sigma Xi, Gamma Alpha (U. of Wis.). Home: 6805 Brookville Rd., Chevy Chase, Md.

SNOWDEN, Chauncey Edgar, clergyman; b. Nanticoke, Ont., May 22, 1884; s. William and Harriet (McCarthy) S.; came to U.S., 1908, naturalized, 1921; ed. Toronto U. Wycliffe Coll., 1905-09; m. Ethel Maud Durkee, Oct. 1, 1908; children—Rev. Charles Durkee, Knight, W. Melvin (M.D.). Ordained to ministry P.E. Ch., deason, 1908, priest, 1909; rector St. John Baptist Ch., Breckenridge, Colo., 1908-10, St. Peter's Ch., Minneapolis, Kans., 1910-12. Grace Ch., Winfield, Kans., 1912-16, Christ Ch., Tyler, Tex., 1916-19, Incarnation Ch., Dallas, Tex., 1919-28, St. Paul's Ch., Overbrook, Phila., Pa., since 1930; exec. sec. Field Dept. Nat. Council P.E. Ch., 1928-30. Republican. Episcopalian. Mason. Club: Union League (Philadelphia). Home: St. Paul's Rectory, Lancaster and Sherwood Rd., Overbrook, Philadelphia, Pa.

SNOWDEN, Roy Ross, M.D.; b. Sharon, Pa., Apr. 22, 1885; s. James Henry and Mary (Ross) S.; A.B., Washington & Jefferson Coll., 1907, A.M., 1912; M.D., Johns Hopkins Med. Sch., 1911; m. Nancy Ditty, July 18, 1923 (died July 21, 1938); 1 dau., Mary Ann. Resident City Hosp., Baltimore, 1911-13; asst. in medicine, Johns Hopkins Hosp., 1913-14; asst. prof. medicine, U. of Pittsburgh, 1914-38, asso. prof. since 1938; med. dir. Pittsburgh Diagnostic Clinic since 1925; v.p. Pittsburgh Diagnostic and Consultation Clinic. Served as 1st lt., A.E.F., Aug. 1917-Aug. 1918, capt., Aug. 1918-Apr. 1919. Mem. A.A.A.S., Am. Coll. Physicians (gov. for Western Pa. 1938), Am. Clin. and Climatol. Soc., Allegheny County Med. Soc., Pittsburgh Acad. Medicine, Soc. for Biol. Research (Pittsburgh), Beta Theta Pi, Phi Beta Kappa, Nu Sigma Nu. Presbyterian. Home: 165 Jefferson Drive, Mt. Lebaron, Pa. Office: 3509 Fifth Av., Pittsburgh, Pa.

SNYDER A(aron) Cecil, lawyer; b. Baltimore, Md., Sept. 14, 1907; s. Hyman and Ida M. (Pass) S.; A.B., Johns Hopkins, 1927; LL.B., Harvard, 1930; m. Wanda Gilewicz, Feb. 4, 1938. Admitted to Md. and N.Y. bars, 1930; asso. with Hawkins, Delafield & Longfellow, N.Y. City, 1930-32, with Tydinge, Sauerwein, Levy & Archer, Baltimore, 1932-33; U.S. atty. for Dist. of Puerto Rico since 1933. Chmn. com. on criminal law, Bar Assn. of P.R.; mem. Judicial Council of P.R.; commr. on Uniform State Laws from P.R. Mem. Md. State Bar Assn., Bar Assn. of U.S. Dist. Court for Puerto Rico, Colegio de Abogados de Puerto Rico, Phi Alpha, Phi Beta Kappa. Awarded Phi Alpha's Distinguished Alumnus Award, 1936. Democrat. Club: Country (San Juan). Home: 3204 Wylie Av., Baltimore, Md. Address: Box 647, San Juan, Puerto Rico.

SNYDER, Abram Elias, physician, pres. Grange Nat. Bank of Susquehanna Co.; b. Scott Twp., Lackawanna Co., Pa., Sept. 21, 1863; s. David N. and Mary Jane (Snyder) S.; student Keystone Acad., Factoryville, Pa., 1883-84; M.D., Jefferson Med. Coll., Phila., 1889; m. Ellis E. Sterns, June 19, 1889; children—Dorothy Jean, David M., Dr. Gordon E. Med. practice at New Milford, Pa., since 1890; physician, New Milford Bd. of Health since 1918; pres. Grange Nat. Bank of Susquehanna Co., New Milford, Pa., since 1936. Pres. New Milford (Pa.) Consol. Schs., 1931. Trustee Keystone Acad., 1895-1925. Mem. Susquehanna Co. Med. Soc. (sec.-treas.). Republican. Baptist (clerk, First Baptist Ch. of New Milford, Pa., since 1890). Mason (past master, New Milford, Pa., Lodge No. 507; Royal Arch; K.T., Irem Temple); Odd Fellow (past grand, Canawacta Lodge No. 207). Address: Main and Pratt Sts., New Milford, Pa.

SNYDER, Burdette Earl, mfr.; b. Baldwinsville, N.Y., June 4, 1878; s. Charles and Eliza-

beth Ann (Lunney) S.; ed. Baldwinsville High Sch.; m. Maude Gothier, Sept. 11, 1901 (died June 7, 1927); children—Winifred (Mrs. Raymond Coward), Doreathea (dec.); m. 2d, Maude Jones Beatty, June 15, 1929. Engaged in newspaper work, 1897-1903; comptroller H. H. Franklin Mfg. Co., Syracuse, N.Y., 1903-13; sec. and treas. R. B. Davis Co. since July 1913, now also dir.; sec., treas. and dir. R. B. Davis Sales Co., Davis Jephson Finance Co., Automatic Paper Machinery Co.; treas. and dir. Associated Grocery Mfrs. of America, Inc. Congregationalist. Mason. Club: Glen Ridge Country. Home: 77 Warren Pl., Montclair, N.J. Office: 40 Jackson St., Hoboken, N.J.

SNYDER, Charles David, univ. prof.; b. Circleville, O., Apr. 30, 1871; s. Frederick and Anna (Thoma) S.; A.B., Stanford U., Palo Alto, Calif., 1896; M.S., U. of Calif., Berkeley, Calif., 1904, Ph.D., 1905; grad. student U. of Berlin, Germany, 1906-07, U. of Munich, summer 1908; m. Aleida van't Hoff, Aug. 8, 1908; children—Annaleida van't Hoff, Francina Elizabeth (Mrs. Burridge Jennings), Thoma Mees van't Hoff. Instr. physiology, Johns Hopkins U. Med. Sch., 1908-10, asso. prof., 1911-20, prof. since 1921. Fellow A.A.A.S.; mem. Am. Physiol. Soc., Am. Chem. Soc., Am. Bot. Soc., Johns Hopkins Med. Soc., Sigma Xi, Goethe Soc. Republican. Clubs: Johns Hopkins, Stanford (pres.), Germania. Home: 4709 Keswick Rd., Baltimore, Md.

SNYDER, Charles E., physician, med. dir.; b. Westmoreland Co., Pa., Nov. 3, 1863; s. Cyrus J. and Lydia (Kline) S.; A.B., Heidelberg (Germany) U.; M.D., New York Univ.; m. Eva J. Campbell, 1897; children—Helen M., Richard C. Mem. of staff, Westmoreland Co. Hosp.; med. dir., Westmoreland Co., Pa., since 1935. Mayor, City of Greensburg, Pa., 1912-16. Mem. Westmoreland Co. Med. Soc. (pres.). Home: 127 N. Main St. Office: 129 N. Main St., Greensburg, Pa.

SNYDER, Claude Edwin, surgeon; b. Palmerton, Pa., Oct. 3, 1888; s. Puriette and Ida (Seem) S.; ed. Perkiomen Sch.; M.D., Jefferson Med. Coll., 1912; m. Sara Hommer, Sept. 21, 1915; children—Jane, Anna Louise. Interne Altoona Hosp., 1912-14; engaged in gen. practice of medicine and surgery at Altoona, Pa., continuously since 1914; chief of dept. gynecology and obstetrics, Mercy Hosp. Served as 1st lt. Med. Corps, U.S.A., during World War. Mem. County Bd. Dept. Pub. Assistance. Fellow Am. Coll. Surgeons; mem. Blair Co. Med. Soc. (pres.), Pa. State Med. Soc. Republican. Presbyn. Mason (K.T., Jester, Shriner). Clubs: Kiwanis (past pres.), Blairmount Country, Spruce Creek Rod and Gun, Jefferson Luncheon. Home: 1201 6th Av., Altoona, Pa.

SNYDER, Corson Cressman, clergyman; b. Harleysville, Pa., Dec. 22, 1892; s. Edwin H. and Emma (Cressman) S.; A.B., Muhlenberg Coll., 1917; S.T.M., Luth. Theol. Sem., Phila., Pa., 1920; m. Lucy Willenbecher, May 26, 1920; 1 dau., Lucy D. Ordained to ministry Luth. Ch., 1920; pastor, Shillington, Pa., 1920-24, Slatington, Pa., 1924-38; pastor St. Peter's Ch., Bethlehem, Pa., since 1938; mem. exec. bd. Luth. Ministerium of Pa. and adjacent States; pres. Allentown Conf., 1931-36; chmn. com. on revision of constitution and bylaws of Luth. Ministerium of Pa., 1938. Mem. Am. Legion (chaplain post). Mem. bd. trustees Muhlenberg Coll. since 1935. Mem. Alpha Tau Omega. Sec. Slatington Rotary Club for 3 yrs. Democrat. Lutheran. Home: 477 Vine St., Bethlehem, Pa.

SNYDER, Daniel John, judge; b. Westmoreland Co., Pa.; s. David L. and Mary Ann (Kline) S.; A.B., Heidelberg Coll., Tiffin, O., 1892, A.M., 1895; LL.B., Yale U. Law Sch., 1895; hon. LL.D., Franklin and Marshall Coll., 1938; m. Winifred Fowles, Oct. 22, 1910; children—Eleanor G., Daniel John. Admitted to bar, 1896, and engaged in gen. practice of law at Greensburg; served as mem. Pa. Ho. of Rep., 1915-18; judge Ct. Common Pleas, 1919-20; pres. judge Orphans' Ct. of Westmoreland Co. since 1921. Trustee Theol. Sem., Lancaster,

Pa. Republican. Mem. Evang. and Reformed Ch. (vice-pres. Gen. Synod, three times). Mason. Home: 29 Division Av. Office: Court House, Greensburg, Pa.

SNYDER, Edward Douglas, prof. English; b. Middletown, Conn., Oct. 4, 1889; s. Peter Miles and Grace (Bliss) S.; A.B., Yale, 1910; A.M., Harvard, 1911, Ph.D., 1913, Bayard Cutting fellow in Europe, 1913-14; m. Edith Royce, Dec. 22, 1916; children—Caroline Burgess, Charles Royce. Instr. in English, Yale, 1914-15; asst. prof. English, Haverford (Pa.) Coll., 1915-25, asso. prof. and chairman English dept., 1925-35, prof. and chmn., 1935—. Lecturer in English, Northwestern, summers 1927, 30, 32, Harvard, summers 1928-29. Member Modern Lang. Assn. America, Am. Assn. Univ. Profs., Nat. Council Teachers of English, Beta Theta Pi, Phi Beta Kappa. Unitarian. Author: The Celtic Revival in English Literature 1760-1800, 1923; Hypnotic Poetry, 1930. Editor: (with F. B. Snyder) A Book of American Literature, 1927, revised edit., 1935. Contbr. to English jours. and mags. Home: May Place, Haverford College, Haverford, Pa.; (summer) MacMahan Island, Me.

SNYDER, Frank Emerson, mem. Pa. State Ho. of Rep.; b. Liberty, Pa., Mar. 18, 1886; s. George and Mary (Heyler) S.; student Pub. Sch., Liberty, 1892-1902; grad. Lock Haven (Pa.) State Teachers Coll., 1909; m. Margaret Roupp, June 19, 1913. Prin. Moshannon (Pa.) Schs., 1906-07, Liberty Boro (Pa.) High Sch., 1907-08; partner, Fred C. Snyder, shoe dealers, Lodi, Calif., 1910-12; established Snyder Bros., hardware, implement and lumber dealers, Liberty, Pa., 1912, and since partner; owner pure bred cattle farm. Sec. Lycoming Farms Dairy Co., Williamsport, Pa., since 1932; mem. Pa. State Ho. of Rep., 1919-21, and since 1935. Pres. Liberty Boro (Pa.) Sch. Dist. since 1913, Tioga Co. (Pa.) Farm Bureau, 1918-19; dir. Tioga Co. (Pa.) Sch. Bd. since 1937. Pres. Bd. of Trustees, Jackson-Liberty Library Assn., since 1925. Mem. Tioga Co. (Pa.) Sch. Dirs. Assn. (pres.), 1923-34. Republican. Lutheran (dir. Men's Bible Class, Liberty, Pa.). K.P. (past chancellor, Liberty Valley Lodge), Mason (past master, Bloss Lodge; Zebulun Chapter; Williamsport Consistory; Shriner), Sebring Grange. Club: Laurel Hill Game and Forestry (Liberty, Pa.). Capt. football and basketball teams, Lock Haven (Pa.) State Teachers Coll.; coach track, basketball teams, Lodi (Calif.) High Sch., 1911-12. Author of article on milk problem in Pa. Home: High and Water Sts. Office: Main St., Liberty, Pa.

SNYDER, Harmon Milton, educator; b. Beatrice, Neb., Jan. 11, 1891; s. Samuel Lichtenwalner and Margaret (Wolfe) S.; A.B., Carthage Coll., 1914, A.M., 1917; D.B., Hamma Divinity Sch., Wittenberg Coll., 1917; Ph.D., U. of Chicago, 1925; research at U. of Pa.; m. Harriet Emeline McClure, May 1, 1917; 1 dau., Janice Carolyn. Ordained to ministry of Lutheran Ch., 1917; pastor, Ch. of Reformation, Chicago, 1917-21, Trinity Luth. Ch., Hays, Kan., 1921-23; instr. in philosophy, Kan. State Teachers Coll., Hays, 1923; asst. prof. of psychology and edn., Wittenberg Coll., 1923-25; prof. of sociology, Lenoir Rhyne Coll., 1925-28; asso. prof. of sociology and edn. and field rep., Carthage Coll., 1928-29; with Temple U. since 1929, as asst. prof. of edn., Teachers Coll., acting dir. of dept. of religious edn., 1931-36, coordinator of Teachers Coll. and Sch. of Theology curriculum since 1937, teacher of edn. and religious edn. Sch. of Theology since 1931; asst. prof. of sociology, Beaver Coll., 1935-36; teacher U. of Md., summer 1938; with Phila. Museum Extension Service, 1936-37. Trustee Gethsemane Sch. of Christian Edn., Phila. Mem. N.E.A., Pa. State Edn. Assn., Am. Sociol. Soc., Nat. Assn. of Sch. Adminstrs., Depts. of Religious Edn. and Social Work, Pi Gamma Mu, Kappa Phi Kappa, Phi Delta Kappa. Contbr. articles on education and religion to jours. Home: 326 Harrison Av., Glenside, Pa. Office: Temple University, Philadelphia, Pa.

SNYDER, Harry Lambright, lawyer; b. Shepherdstown, W.Va., Dec. 29, 1900; s. Harry Lambright and Ida (Baldwin) S.; student Shepherd Coll., Shepherdstown, W.Va., 1914-18, Columbia U., 1924; A.B., W.Va. U., Morgantown, W.Va., 1923, LL.B., 1925; m. Cora Ella Houston, Sept. 10, 1925; children—Harry Lambright, Giles Dougherty Houston. Admitted to W.Va. bar, 1925, and since practiced at Charleston, W.Va.; mem. firm Mohler, Peters & Snyder, attys. at law, Charleston, since 1933. Asst. U.S. Atty., Charleston, 1934-38; mem. Kanawha County (W.Va.) Bd. Edn. since 1933; Young Dem. Nat. Committeeman, 1936-37; permanent chmn. Young Democrat Nat. Conv., 1936. Mem. Young Dem. Club of W.Va. (pres. 1934-36), Am. Acad. Polit. and Social Science, Order of the Coif., Phi Kappa Psi (pres. 1934-36), Phi Beta Kappa, Phi Delta Phi, Delta Sigma Rho. Democrat. Episcopalian. Mason (Morgantown Union Lodge 4). Club: Edgewood Country (Charleston, W.Va.). Home: 504 Linden Rd. Office: 808 Security Bldg., Charleston, W.Va.

SNYDER, Harry Owen, life ins. official; b. Arcola, Ill., Aug. 20, 1886; s. Edward and Minnie (Matters) S.; ed. St. John's Mil. Acad., Delafield, Wis., Knox Coll., Galesburg, Ill.; m. Florence Pendlum, Apr. 17, 1915. Supervisor for Mutual Life Ins. Co. of N.Y., 1909-15; gen. mgr. Guardian Life Ins. Co. of America, Pittsburgh, Pa., since 1915. Mem. Phi Delta Theta. Mason (32°, Shriner). Elk. Club: Shannopin Country (Ben Avon Heights). Home: 125 Dalzell Av., Ben Avon, Pa. Office: Suite 909 Clark Bldg., Pittsburgh, Pa.

SNYDER, Henry Steinman, steel mfr.; b. Bethlehem, Pa., May 21, 1869; s. Mifflin H. and Angeline (Steinman) S.; ed. pub. schs.; m. Mary Taylor, Nov. 21, 1892. Began with Bethlehem Steel Co., 1886, serving as sec. and treas.; v.p. Bethlehem Steel Corpn. from its organization, 1904, retired Aug. 1925. Trustee and treas. St. Luke's Hosp. Dir. Union Bank & Trust Co., Bethlehem, Pa.; Pres. Bach Choir. Mem. Am. Iron and Steel Inst., Am. Inst. Mining and Metall. Engrs. Republican. Presbyn. Clubs: Union League (Phila.); Bankers (New York). Home: Bethlehem, Pa.

SNYDER, Irvin R., supt. schs.; b. Brogueville, Pa., Feb. 14, 1889; s. George and Mary C. (Henry) S.; diploma Millersville State Teachers' Coll., 1911; B.S., Gettysburg Coll., 1927, M.S., same, 1930; grad. study U. of Pa., 1934-36; m. Anna E. Linebaugh, Nov. 28, 1916; children—Irvin R., Jr, Joe R. Teacher public schools, York County, 4 yrs., York City, 2 yrs., North York, Pa., 24 yrs.; supt. North York schs., York, Pa., since 1928. Served with U.S. Emergency Fleet Corpn., 1917-21. Mem. Schoolmen's Club of York Co., Kappa Phi Kappa. Sec.-treas. York County Interscholastic Athletic Assn. Republican. Mem. U. Brethren Ch. Mason (K.T., 32°). Home: 1419 N. George St., York, Pa.

SNYDER, James Wilson, supervising prin. schs.; b. Snow Shoe, Pa., Sept. 12, 1872; s. David and Martha Gregg (Heaton) S.; grad. Bloomsburg State Teachers Coll., 1895; A.B. magna cum laude, Bucknell U., 1902, A.M., same, 1906; grad. study Lehigh U., 1919-20; m. Gertrude Mendenhall, Oct. 8, 1908; 1 son, John Mendenhall (M.D.). Engaged in teaching rural schs., Northumberland Co., Pa., 1891-94; prin. schs., Halifax, Pa., 1895-98; supervising prin. schs., Berwick, Pa., 1902-06; supervising prin. schs., Slatington, Pa., since 1906. Served as chmn. Slatington Chapter Am. Red Cross since 1917. Treas. Slatington Welfare Assn. Mem. N.E.A., Pa. State Edn. Assn., Delta Sigma. Republican. Presbyn. (elder and trustee First Ch.). Mason (32°, Shriner), I.O.O.F. Club: Rotary of Slatington. Home: 308 E. Franklin St. Office: High School Bldg., Slatington, Pa.

SNYDER, Jeremiah G., pres. Farmers Nat. Bank, Selinsgrove, Pa.; b. Port Trevorton, Pa., Oct. 15, 1872; s. Daniel and Catharine (Geist) S.; student Pub. Sch., Port Trevorton, Pa., 1880-88, Eckels Embalming Sch., Phila., 1899-1900; m. Daisy E. Bogar, June 23, 1895; children—Mary Catharine, (Mrs. John Troutman), Carl E., Helena, Warren J., Daniel B., Rachel Elizabeth (Mrs. Robert Shadle), Pauline. Learned the cabinet-making trade after leaving school; was trained early in life by father, who was an undertaker; funeral dir., Port Trevorton, Pa., since 1893; owner of gen. mdse. store., Port Trevorton, Pa., since 1900; pres. and dir. Farmers Nat. Bank, Selinsgrove, Pa., since 1900. Trustee Evangelical Ch. Mem. Sons of Vets. Republican. Mem. Evangelical Ch. Mason (Lafayette Lodge, Selinsgrove, Pa., No. 194; Harrisburg Consistory; Scottish Rite). Home: Port Trevorton, Pa.

SNYDER, Jesse O.; chmn. bd. and pres. Second Nat. Bank. Address: Hagerstown, Md.

SNYDER, J(ohn) Buell, congressman; b. Somerset Co., Pa., July 30, 1879; grad. Lock Haven (Pa.) Teachers Coll.; student summer sessions Harvard and Columbia. Prin. various schs., 1901-12; western Pa. dist. mgr. Macmillan Co., 1912-32. Mem. 73d to 76th Congresses (1933-41), 24th Pa. Dist. Legislative rep. for Pa. School Dirs. during sessions of State Legislature, 1921-23; mem. Nat. Commn. of 100 for Study and Survey of Rural Schs. in U.S., 1922-24; mem. Bd. of Edn. of Perry Township and sec. County Sch. Dirs'. Assn., 1922-32. Co-author of Guffey-Snyder Bituminous Coal Act passed by 73d Congress. Home: Perryopolis, Pa.

SNYDER, Lewis Neiffer, supervising prin. schs.; b. Steelton, Pa., Aug. 26, 1894; s. Eli Thompson and Anna Marie (Neiffer) S.; A.B., Gettysburg (Pa.) Coll., 1916; A.M., U. of Pa., 1924; grad. study Temple U., Phila., since 1933; m. Nina V. Rudisill, Gettysburg, Pa., June 20, 1918; 1 son, Wayne Elton. Teacher mathematics and prin. schs. in N.J., 1916-24; supervising prin. schs., East Mauch Chunk, Pa., 1924-26; prin. high sch., Bangor, Pa., 1926-29; supervising prin., Sellersville-Perkasie (Pa.) Schs. since 1929; dir. and mem. exec. com. Inter-County Hospitalization Plan; dir. and treas. Grand View Hosp. Served as 2d lt., F.A., U.S. Army, 1918. Mem. N.E.A., Assn. Am. Sch. Adminstrs., Pa. State Edn. Assn., Phila. Suburban Supervising Prins. Assn. (pres.), Am. Legion, Bucks Co. Teachers Assn. (v.p.), Phi Delta Kappa, Kappa Phi Kappa. Lutheran (pres. cong.). Mason (K.T.). Home: 141 Green St., Sellersville, Pa. Office: Perkasie, Pa.

SNYDER, Luther D(aniel), manufacturer; b. Hampton, Adams Co., Pa., Jan. 20, 1892; s. William H. and Mary A. (May) S.; grad. Wrightsville (Pa.) High Sch., 1909; student Pa. Business Coll., Lancaster, 1909-10; m. Mary Bell Wambaugh, 1916; 1 son, Luther Robert. Bookkeeper C. H. A. Dissinger & Bro., Wrightsville, 1910-11; bookkeeper and clerk Farmers Fire Ins. Co., York, Pa., 1911-16; in 1916 organized with E. H. Snyder (brother) Littlestown (Pa.) Hardware and Foundry Co., Inc., mfr. hardware and castings, serves as treas. and gen. mgr.; pres. and dir. Littlestown State Bank, Littlestown Canning Co., Littonian Shoe Co. Republican. Lutheran. Mason, Odd Fellow, Eagle, Patriotic Order Sons of America. Clubs: Rotary of Littlestown (sec.); Hanover Country (Hanover, Pa.). Home: E. King St. Office: Charles St., Littlestown, Pa.

SNYDER, Melvin Claud, lawyer; b. Kingwood, W.Va., Oct. 29, 1898; s. Allison W. and Laura (Jenkins) S.; LL.B., W.Va. Univ. Law Sch., Morgantown, 1923; m. Mabel Price, July 13, 1925; children—Melvin Claud, Jr., Melita Nan, Laurella. Admitted to W.Va. bar, 1923 and engaged in gen. practice of law at Kingwood, 1923-28; pros. atty. Preston Co., W.Va. since 1929, present term expires, 1940; served as mayor town of Kingwood, 1927-28; Rep. nominee for Congress 2d dist. W.Va., 1938. Capt. inf. W.Va. N.G. since 1930. Mem. Preston County and W.Va. State bar assns., Phi Delta Phi, Theta Chi. Republican. Baptist. Mason, K.P., Moose. Club: Rotary. Home: 138 Tunnelton St. Office: Court House, Main St., Kingwood, W.Va.

SNYDER, Oscar John, osteopathic physician; b. St. Louis, Mo., Nov. 17, 1866; s. Joseph Nicholas and Catherine (Legner) S.; ed. State Normal Sch., Winona, Minn., 1884-90; B.S., Columbian (now George Washington) U., 1894, M.S., 1896; D.O., Northern Inst. of Osteopathy, Minneapolis, Minn., 1899; D.Sc., Phila. Coll.

of Osteopathy, 1929; m. Aline Cantwell, June 22, 1904; children—Joseph Cantwell, Honora, James Ayers. Lt. Engr. Corps, Washington, D.C., 1900-03; began practice, 1899; pres. Phila. Coll. of Osteopathy, 1899-1907; pres. Pa. State Bd. Osteopathic Examiners, 1909-30. Pres. Pa. Osteopathic Assn., 1900-09; pres. Associated College of Osteopathy, 1905; pres. Osteopathic Clin. Research, 1914-16; pres. Am. Osteopathic Assn., 1916-17; mem. Pa. Osteopathic Assn., Phila. Osteopathic Assn., Am. Chem. Assn., Iota Tau Sigma, Phi Sigma Gamma. Awarded Distinguished Service Certificate, Am. Osteopathic Assn., 1929. Republican. Presbyn. Author published addresses, also articles in osteopathic mags. Home: Narberth, Pa. Office: Witherspoon Bldg., Philadelphia, Pa.

SNYDER, Peter W., clergyman, presbytery exec.; b. West Monterey, Pa., Jan. 20, 1873; s. John W. and Euphemia M. (Stewart) S.; A.B., Grove City Coll., 1897, D.D., 1912; student Western Theol. Sem., 1897-1900; m. Cora E. Hutchison, June 27, 1900; children—Mabel Lucille (Mrs. Harry M. Landis, Jr.), Lois Pauline (Mrs. Tom Stine), John Paul, Clifford Hutchinson, Peter LeRoy. Ordained to ministry Presbyn. Ch.; pastor, Steubenville, O., 1900-04, South Side Ch., Pittsburgh, 1904-08, Homewood Ch., 1908-21; supt. and exec. of Presbytery of Pittsburgh since 1921; mem. bd. mgrs. Presbyn. Assn. for Care of Aged and Orphans; pres. and dir. Eastern Stokol Corpn.; dir. Snyder & Swanson, Inc. Mem. Bd. Edn. Borough of Dormont. Trustee Western Theol. Sem., Pittsburgh. Republican. Presbyn. Clubs: Metropolitan, South Hills Country (Pittsburgh); Clymer Hunting. Home: 2841 Broadway, Dormont, Pa. Office: Commonwealth Bldg., Pittsburgh, Pa.

SNYDER, Q. Sheldon, pres. Pittsburgh Rolls Div. of Blaw-Knox Co.; b. Brookville, Pa., Jan. 12, 1884; s. James Henry and Lydia Ann (Bartlett) S.; m. Mary Kellam Gee, Aug. 16, 1924. Pres. and gen. mgr. Pittsburgh Rolls Corpn., mfrs. of iron and steel rolls since 1920; pres. Pittsburgh Rolls Div., Blaw-Knox Co., iron and steel, since 1929, v.p. and dir. Blaw-Knox Co. since 1937; dir. H. K. Porter Co. Dir. Pittsburgh (Pa.) Boys' Club. Mem. Am. Iron and Steel Inst., Engrs. Soc. of Western Pa., Am. Foundrymen's Soc., Y.M.C.A. (mem. com. of management). Clubs: Duquesne, Oakmont Country, Pittsburgh Athletic Assn., Butler Country (Pittsburgh). Home: Park Mansions. Office: 41st St. and Willow St., Pittsburgh, Pa.

SNYDER, Walter J., physician; b. Erie, Pa., Oct. 7, 1879; s. Jacob M. and Louise C. (Hauger) S.; grad. Erie High Sch., 1898; student Cleveland Homeopathic Med. Coll., 1899-1901; M.D., Hahnemann Med. Coll., Phila., 1903; m. Maye Rowland, Feb. 27, 1907. Resident physician Hahnemann Med. Coll., 1903-05; now on teaching staff of Hahnemann Med. Coll. and Hosp. and staffs of Broad Street Hosp.; also on courtesy staffs of Miseriacordia Hosp., Delaware Co. Hosp., Mary Fitzgerald Hosp.; pres. Nat. Decalcomania Corpn. (mfrs. transfer products to wood, glass, etc.) since 1916. Served in Vol. Med. Reserve Corps during World War. Mem. Am. Inst. of Homeopathy, Pa. State and County Med. Socs., Phi Alpha Gamma. Republican. Protestant. Clubs: Union League, Rotary (Phila.); Merion Cricket (Haverford). Address: 418 S. 47th St., West Philadelphia, Pa.

SNYDER, Warren Paul, supt. city schs.; b. Schoenersville, Pa., Jan. 8, 1898; s. Preston Valentine and Alice Catherine (Fatzinger) S.; B.S., Muhlenberg Coll., 1920; M.S., Temple U., 1933; ed. U. of Mich., 1925, Columbia U., 1921; m. Esther F. Turner, June 22, 1929; children—Warren Paul, Jr., Martha Elizabeth. Instr. sci. and phys. edn., Woodmere, N.Y., 1920-22; head of sci. dept., high sch., Bristol, Pa., 1922-26, prin. high sch., 1924-34, supt. city schs. since 1934. Mem. Nat. Edn. Assn., Pa. State Edn. Assn., Nat. Assn. Sch. Administrs., Kappa Phi Kappa, Phi Kappa Tau. Republican. Presbyn. Mason (32°). B.P.O.E. Club: Exchange of Bristol. Home: 1202 Pond St. Office: High School Bldg., Bristol, Pa.

SNYDER, Wayne L., surgeon; b. Brookville, Pa., Mar. 13, 1881; s. John Calvin and Emma Jane (Scott) S.; M.D., Jefferson Med. Coll.; m. Ruth Luther, June 4, 1907; children—Helen Louise, Mary Ruth, Anna Claire, Pauline Inez. Resident physician Jefferson Med. Coll. Hosp., 1905-06; chief surgeon, Brookville (Pa.) Hosp. since 1919. Served as capt., M.C., U.S. Army, with A.E.F. Clubs: Kiwanis, Community (Brookville, Pa.). Home: 103 Jefferson Av. Office: 127 Franklin Av., Brookville, Pa.

SNYDER, William Cordes, Jr., pres. Lewis Foundry & Machine Co. (div. Blaw-Knox Co.), v.p. and dir. Blaw-Knox Co.; b. Snow Shoe, Pa., June 12, 1903; s. W. C. and Mary Allan (Perry) S.; ed. Harrisburg Acad. and Lehigh U.; m. Virginia Harper, June 4, 1932; children—Virginia Harper, W. Cordes, III. Metallurgist Wheeling Mold & Foundry Co., Wheeling, W.Va., 1925-27; metallurgist Lewis Foundry & Machine Co. (div. Blaw-Knox Co.), 1927-36, v.p. in charge of sales, 1936-37, pres. since 1937; v.p. Blaw-Knox Co.; also dir. of both. Mem. Iron & Steel Inst., Iron & Steel Engrs., Engrs. Soc. of Western Pa. Clubs: Duquesne, University (Pittsburgh); Castalia Trout (Castalia, O.); Wheeling Country; Allegheny County Country. Home: Pine Road, Sewickley, Pa. Office: Lewis Foundry & Machine Co., Pittsburgh, Pa.

SOBEL, Isador, lawyer; b. New York, N.Y.; s. Semel and Cecelia S.; educated at College of City of New York; m. Emma Auerhaim, of Bradford, Pa., Mar. 17, 1891. Admitted to Pa. bar, 1888 and since engaged in gen. practice of law at Erie, Pa.; mem. Erie City Council, 1891-95, pres., 1894; sec. Erie Co. Rep. Com., 1889-91, chmn., 1893-97; vice-pres. Rep. League of Clubs of Pa., 1894-95, pres. 1896-98; presdl. elector, 1896; apptd. Postmaster of Erie, 1898, reapptd., 1902, 1906, 1910; first pres. Postmaster's Assn. Pa.; 1908; pres. Nat. Assn. Postmasters of Offices of First Class of U.S., 1912, first hon. pres. of this orgn., 1913. Served as gen. chmn. Erie Community Chest Campaign, 1921-22. Hon. chmn. Erie Jewish Federation. Dir. for 12 yrs., now corporator, Hamot Hosp., Erie, Pa. One of original 50 of Am. Jewish Com. (now mem. Dist. Com.). Pres. Bd. Govs. B'nai B'rith Home for Children, Dist. No. 3 since orgn., 1912. Mem. Pa. Bar Assn., Erie Co. Bar Assn. (pres. 1931-38), Zeta Beta Tau. Republican. Jewish religion. B'nai B'rith (organizer, local, 1908, mem. Gen. Com., 1910, pres. Dist. Grand Lodge, 1911-13, now mem. Gen. Com.), Mason (32°, Shriner). I.O.O.F. Club: Temple Men's. Home: 931 W. 9th St., Erie, Pa. Office: 1402 Erie Trust Bldg., Erie, Pa.

SOBEL, Jeffrey M., lawyer; b. Erie, Pa., Jan. 22, 1892; s. Isador and Emma (Auerhaim) S.; student Amherst Coll., 1909-10; A.B., U. of Pa., 1913; LL.B., Columbia U. 1916; unmarried. Admitted to bar, 1917; since in gen. practice of law; asst. dist. atty., Erie Co., 1928-32. Served in U.S. Army, 19 mos., World War. Mem. Pa. Bar Assn., Erie Co. Bar Assn., Zeta Beta Tau. Republican. Mason, B'nai B'rith. Club: University (Erie). Home: 931 W. 9th St. Office: 504 Palace Hardware Bldg., Erie, Pa.

SOBELOFF, Simon E., lawyer; b. Mar. 3, 1893; s. Jacob and Mary (Kaplan) S.; LL.B., U. of Md., 1914; m. Irene Ehrlich, May 19, 1918; children—Evva, Ruth. Began practice at Baltimore, 1914; asst. city solicitor, Baltimore, 1919-23; dep. city solicitor, 1927-31; apptd. U.S. atty., Dist. of Md., Feb. 12, 1931; resigned Mar. 12, 1934; resumed law practice. Mem. bd. dirs. Associated Jewish Charities. Republican. Club: Chesapeake. Home: 1809 Eutaw Pl. Office: Union Trust Bldg., Baltimore, Md.

SOFFEL, Sara M., judge; b. Pittsburgh, Pa., Oct. 27, 1886; d. Jacob and Katharine (Ulrich) S.; grad. Central High Sch., Pittsburgh, 1904; A.B., Wellesley Coll., 1908; LL.B., U. of Pittsburgh, 1916 (grad. highest honors at all three); hon. LL.D., Wilson Coll., 1935; unmarried. Teacher Crafton (Pa.) High Sch.,

1908-10, Central High Sch., Pittsburgh, 1910-16, Schenley High Sch., Pittsburgh, 1916-17; admitted to Pa. bar, 1917, and practiced in Pittsburgh, 1917-30; asst. city solicitor, Pittsburgh, 1922-26; head Children's Bureau, Pa. Dept. of Labor and Industry, 1929-30; apptd. judge County Court, Allegheny Co., Pa., 1930, and elected to same office, Nov. 1931, for term 1932-42; has sat in Juvenile Court and on civil side of court since 1933. Pres. Pittsburgh Branch, Am. Assn. Univ. Women; dir. Pittsburgh Housing Assn.; dir. Fed. of Social Agencies; pres. Pittsburgh Community Forum. Republican. Presbyterian. Clubs: Twentieth Century, Woman's City, Pittsburgh College, Pittsburgh Wellesley. Home: 16 Greenbush St. Address: Court House, Pittsburgh, Pa.

SOLIDAY, David Shriver, investment securities; b. Hanover, Pa., Dec. 11, 1895; s. William R. and M. Katherine (Winebrenner) S.; prep. edn. Phillips Acad., Andover, Mass., 1910-13; A.B., Amherst Coll., 1919; m. Louise H. Kondolf, May 8, 1920; children—Frances Huntington, David Shriver, Carol Louise. Began as security salesman, 1921; partner Hopper, Soliday & Co., Phila., since 1924; dir. Peoples Light & Power Co., Kan. Pub. Service Co., Tex. Pub. Service Co., Western States Utilities Co. Served in the U.S. Army during the World War. Mem. Psi Upsilon. Republican. Episcopalian. Clubs: Phila. Country, Racquet (Phila.). Home: 328 Woodley Rd., Merion, Pa. Office: 1420 Walnut St., Philadelphia, Pa.

SOLIS-COHEN, J., Jr., real estate; b. Phila., Pa., June 26, 1890; s. Dr. (laryngologist) Jacob and Miriam (Binswanger) Solis-Cohen; ed. public schools of Phila.; m. Marion Gimbel Lape, Dec. 13, 1916; children—Mary, Ann. Newspaper man, real estate editor, Phila. North American, 1908-12; asso. with Jules E. Mastbaum and Alfred W. Fleisher in real estate business in 1912, became partner, 1925, vice-pres. Mastbaum Brothers & Fleisher, 1928-31; specialized in chain store leasing, advocating percentage form of lease; real estate appraisal and consultation work since 1931; made survey of low-priced housing in England, 1936. Sr. mem. and v.p. Phila. Chapter of Soc. of Residential Appraisers; mem. of Phila. Real Estate Bd., Phila. Bd. of Trade, Phila. Tennis Assn. (exec. com.); pres. of Jewish Publ. Soc. of America; mem. of bd. of trustees and pres. of Congregation Mikveh Israel (oldest synagogue in Phila.); mem. of board of trustees of Jewish Theological Seminary of America; hon. dir. Foster Home for Hebrew Orphans of Phila.; mem. and past pres. Joshua Lodge B'nai B'rith. Mason. Clubs: Philmont Country, Locust, Variety. Home: Ramble House, Rambler Road, Elkins Park, Pa. Office: 123 S. Broad St., Philadelphia, Pa.

SOLIS-COHEN, Myer, physician; b. Phila., Pa., May 24, 1877; s. Jacob da Silva and Miriam (Binswanger) Solis-Cohen; prep. edn., George F. Martin's Sch. for Boys, Phila., 1890-93; A.B., U. of Pa., 1897, M.D., 1900; m. Rosebud Lotta Teschner, Feb. 11, 1925; 1 dau., Kathe Teschner. Interne Jewish and Phila. Gen. Hosps., 1900; asst. physician to dispensaries, U. of Pa. Hosp., 1901-09, Children's Hosp., 1901-03; asst. gynecologist, out-patient dept., Pa. Hosp., 1902-03; asst. in nose, throat and ear dept., Howard Hosp., 1902-03; clin. asst. in throat and nose, Phila. Polyclinic Hosp., 1903-04; chief of pediatric clinic, Jewish Hosp., 1907-12, attending pediatrist since 1912; visiting physician Home for Consumptives, 1903-07, cons. physician, 1907-18; asst. visiting physician Phila. Gen. Hosp., 1903-10; visiting physician Eagleville Sanatorium for Tuberculosis, 1909-12, visiting pediatrist, 1912-38; visiting pediatrist Jewish Maternity Hosp., 1922-28; attending pediatrist Mt. Sinai Hosp., 1926-32; instr. in physical diagnosis, U. of Pa. Med. Dept., 1904-07; asst. prof. of medicine, U. of Pa. Grad. Sch. of Medicine, since 1921; lecturer on med. jurisprudence, Woman's Med. Coll. of Pa., since 1923, on toxicology, 1929-37; dir. Asso. Hosp. Service of Phila. Served as capt. Med. Corps, U.S. Army, 1917-19; with A.E.F. with Base Hosp. 59, Field Hosp. 37, and 78th F.A.; now lt. col. Med. Reserve. Mem. Aid Assn. of Phila. County Med.

Soc. (dir. since 1926), Phila. County Med. Soc. (dir. since 1937; chmn. advisory com. to Med. Relief Bd., 1934-35, 1936-38; chmn. com. on med. economics, 1938; chmn. com. on public relations since 1938), Phila. Pediatric Soc. (dir., 1937-38), Coll. of Physicians of Phila., A.M.A., Pathol. Soc. of Phila., S.A.R. (mem. bd. govs. of Continental Chapter), Mil. Order of Loyal Legion, Mil. Order of World War, Am. Legion. Republican. Jewish religion. Clubs: Medical, Pow Wow (Phila.). Author: Woman in Girlhood, Wifehood and Motherhood, 1906; The Family Health, 1910; Girl, Wife and Mother, 1911; Focal Infection, 1939. Contbr. over 75 articles to med. jours. Devised pathogen-selective culture and vaccine. Address: 2110 Spruce St., Philadelphia, Pa.

SOLLENBERGER, Michael E(tter), retired banker; b. Mercersburg, Pa., Nov. 27, 1858; s. Samuel and Mary (Etter) S.; ed. Millersville (Pa.) State Normal Sch., 1879-80; m. Lydia Ann Funk, Dec. 24, 1889 (died July 12, 1926); children—Ethel Mae (wife of Prof. James Widdowson), Orville Funk, Helen Lydia (wife of Galen Bonebrake); m. 2d, Mary Alice (Stuff) Martin, Oct. 22, 1929. Engaged as teacher pub. schs., 1880-89; in ry. mail service, 1889-95; bookkeeper Bank of Waynesboro, 1895-1900, cashier, 1900-15, bank later merged and now First Nat. Bank and Trust Co. of which is dir. and mem. several coms.; vice-pres. and dir. Peoples Nat. Bank of Lemasters, Pa.; dir., treas., and pres. Waynesboro Water Co. many years until city acquired the property in 1922; one of organizers and dir. Waynesboro, Greencastle & Chambersburg St. Ry. until sold. Served as mem. and pres. City Council; pres. several terms and dir. Pub. Sch. Bd. for 12 yrs. Republican. Mem. Ch. of the Brethren; trustee and vice-pres. Children's Aid Soc. of Ch. of the Brethren, Carlisle, Pa. Home: 204 W. Main St., Waynesboro, Pa.

SOLTER, George A.; judge Supreme Bench of Baltimore City, term expires 1941. Address: Supreme Court, Baltimore, Md.

SOMERNDIKE, John Mason, Sunday School official; b. Frankford, Phila., Pa., Oct. 29, 1887; s. John Mason and Isabella (Farr) S.; grad. Central High Sch., Phila., 1894; D.D., Coll. of Ozarks, Clarksville, Ark., 1931; and also from Waynesburg (Pa.) College; m. Lydia Moor, Nov. 8, 1900 (died July 1907); m. 2d, Edna Smith, Nov. 4, 1908; children—Isabel M. (Mrs. Frederick O. Green), Jean S. (dec.), Vira Orswell, John Mason. Identified with S.S. missions of Presbyn. Ch., U.S.A., since 1895, apptd. dir., 1912; developed the missionary extension work of the Presbyn. Ch., U.S.A. Sec. Bd. Nat. Missions Presbyn. Ch. in U.S.A. in charge of S.S. Missions, Indian, and Alaska Work. Mem. exec. com. of Internat. Council of Religious Edn. Republican. Mason. Author: On the Firing Line, 1912; By-products of the Rural Sunday School, 1916; Sunday School Missionary Exercises, 1918; Sunday School Builders, 1922; The Sunday School in Town and Country, 1924; Manual of Week Day Bible Lessons, 1925. Home: South Orange, N.J. Office: 156 Fifth Av., New York, N.Y.

SOMERVILLE, E. J.; mem. law firm Somerville & Somerville. Address: Point Pleasant, W.Va.

SOMERVILLE, G. G.; mem. law firm Somerville & Somerville. Address: Point Pleasant, W.Va.

SOMERVILLE, Thomas, III, manufacturer; b. Washington, D.C., Oct. 17, 1900; s. Thomas and Anna May (Jackson) S.; ed. Washington (D.C.) Pub. Sch., 1907-17, Business High Sch., Washington, D.C., 1917-21, George Washington U., Washington, D.C., 1921-25; m. Betty Bradford, Mar. 29, 1929; children—Betty Jane, Jacquelin, Margaret Ann, Patricia. Began as mfr., Terra Cotta, D.C., 1921; with Thomas Somerville Co., Washington, D.C., since 1921, v.p. since 1938; also pres. Washington Brick Co., Muirkirk, Md., since 1935, 1st Federal Savings & Loan Assn., Washington, D.C., since 1938, First Federal Savings & Loan Assn. since 1939; v.p. Real Estate Mortgage & Guarantee Corpn., Washington, D.C., since 1934. Mem. Am. Ceramic Soc., Delta Tau Delta. Presbyterian. Mason (Blue Lodge, Chapter, Scottish Rite, York Rite, Shriner, Royal Order of Jesters). Club: Kenwood Golf and Country (Bethesda, Md.). Home: 101 Chamberlin Av., Chevy Chase, Md. Office: Muirkirk, Md.

SOMMER, Frank Henry, prof. law; b. Newark, N.J., 1872; student Metropolis Law Sch.; LL.B., New York U., 1893, LL.M., 1900, J.D., 1903. Instr. Metropolis Law Sch., 1893-94; became prof. law, New York U., 1895, also dean law faculty; practices, Newark, N.J. Home: 156 Heller Parkway, Newark, N.J.

SOMMER, George N. J., M.D., surgeon; b. Trenton, N.J., Aug. 20, 1874; s. George and Caroline (Bender) S.; student Stewart Business Coll.; M.D., U. of Pa., 1894; married Oct. 20, 1903; children—George N. J., Thomas. Began gen. practice of medicine, 1894; now med. dir. St. Francis Hosp. Chmn. med. advisory bd., Mercer Co., World War. Fellow Am. Coll. Surgeons; mem. A.M.A., N.J. State Med. Soc., Mercer Co. Component Med. Soc., Soc. Surgeons of N.J., Philadelphia Urol. Soc., Philadelphia Med. Club, Coll. Physicians of Philadelphia, Trenton Hist. Soc., Trenton Chamber of Commerce. Democrat. Mem. Elks, K.C. Club: Symposium. Home: 120 W. State St. Office: 120 W. State St., Trenton, N.J.

SOMMER, Henry Joseph, lawyer; b. Norristown, Pa., Dec. 7, 1903; s. Henry Joseph and Emily Elizabeth (Hergesheimer) S.; Ph.B., Dickinson Coll., Carlisle, Pa., 1926, B.L., Dickinson Sch. of Law, 1928; m. Margaret Miller, July 12, 1935; 1 son, Henry Joseph. Admitted to Pa. Supreme Court and Snyder County bar, 1929, and since practiced at Selinsgrove, Pa.; dist. atty. Snyder County since 1932. Capt. Judge Advocate General's Dept., U.S.A. Res., since 1934. Mem. Pa. Bar Assn., Phi Kappa Psi. Republican. Episcopalian. Mason (Lafayette Lodge 194, Selinsgrove, Pa., and Williamsport Consistory). Club: Rotary (Selinsgrove, Pa.). Address: 28 N. Market St., Selinsgrove, Pa.

SOMMERS, Paul Bergen, ins. cos. pres.; b. Franklin, O., July 3, 1885; s. Joseph K. and Cornelia (Bergen) S.; grad. Lake Forest Univ., 1908; m. Florence Adams, Dec. 24, 1914; children—Paul A., Suzanne, Margaret, Otho Lane, Barbara. Spl. agt. Scottish Union & National Ins. Co., 1908-18; in local ins. agency on own account, Cleveland, O., 1918-20; asso. with American Ins. Co., Newark, N.J., since 1920, supt. agts., 1920-23, vice-pres., 1923-35, dir. since 1924, pres. since 1935, also pres. and dir. its affiliated cos., Columbia Fire Ins. Co., Dayton, O., Dixie Fire Ins. Co. (Greensboro, N.C.), Bankers Indemnity Ins. Co. (Newark, N.J.); dir. Mutual Benefit Life Ins. Co., Reinsurance Corpn. of N.Y., Sanborn Map Co., Nat. Newark & Essex Banking Co.; mem. bd. govs., Howard Savings Instn. Trustee Newark Mus. Assn., Ins. Execs. Assn., Am. Fgn. Ins. Assn. Dir. Underwriters Labs. Fellow Ins. Inst. of America; mem. Nat. Bd. Fire Underwriters (pres.), South-Eastern Underwriters Assn. (pres.), Eastern Underwriters Assn. (v.p.), Fire Cos. Adjustment Bur. (dir.). Home: 19 Euclid Av., Maplewood, N.J. Office: 15 Washington St., Newark, N.J.

SONES, Warren Wesley David, educator; b. Dushore, Pa., Mar. 12, 1888; s. Calvin Low and Rebecca Amanda (Young) S.; B.S., Albright Coll. (Pa.), 1908; A.M., U. of Pittsburgh, 1914; Ph.D., 1925; m. Mary Alice Kennedy, Aug. 11, 1909; children—Warren Wesley David, Jean Elizabeth (Mrs. Harry N. Hill, Jr.), Mary Alice. Teacher Pa. high schs., 1908-13, high sch., Pittsburgh, 1913-25; teacher U. of Pa., Pa. State Coll., Chautauqua Inst., summer schs. and extension lecturing, 1916-25; prof. edn., dir. practice teaching, and head, Erie Center U. of Pittsburgh, 1925-38; prof. of edn. and dir. curriculum study, U. of Pittsburgh, since 1938; consultant Pa. State Dept. Edn., Carnegie Foundation for Teachers. Mem. Pa. State Park and Harbor Commn., 1932-36. Mem. A.A.A.S., Nat. Soc. for Study of Edn., N.E.A., Pa. Edn. Assn., Am. Philatelic Soc., Phi Delta Kappa. Mason. Clubs: University (Pittsburgh); Collectors (New York). Author: Secondary School Achievement Tests, 1928. Home: King Edward Apts. Office: 2032 Cathedral of Learning, Pittsburgh, Pa.

SONNEBORN, Siegmund Bachrach, retired manufacturer; b. Breidenbach, Hesse, Germany, Apr. 14, 1872; s. Levi and Amalie (Bachrach) S.; came to U.S., 1889, naturalized, 1895; ed. folks school and college in Marburg; A.B., Johns Hopkins, 1893, post grad. student 1938-39; m. Camille K. G. Goldschmid, Feb. 12, 1895; children—John (deceased), Rudolf Goldschmid, Amalie (Mrs. M. Shakman Katz), Katherine (Mrs. Leon Falk, Jr.), Josephine (Mrs. E. Frank Ross). Began as apprentice in wholesale grocery business, Germany, 1886; associated with Henry Sonneborn & Co., clothing mfrs., Baltimore, 1893-1929, becoming managing mem. of firm, 1899, and chmn. of bd., 1914-29; treas. Alma Mfg. Co., mfrs. metal products, Baltimore, 1899-1929; dir. Consol. Gas & Electric Light Co., Baltimore, 1915-29; vice-pres. L. Sonneborn Sons, Inc., oils, chemicals, paints, New York, since 1903; pres. Sonneborn Realty Co., Baltimore. Apptd. by Gov. of Md. mem. of com. to formulate first labor liability law of State of Md., 1905; dir. Park Sch., Baltimore, 1910-29; dir. Jewish Publ. Soc. many years, resigning 1929. Mem. Johns Hopkins U. Alumni Assn. Democrat. Reformed Jewish religion. Author and pub.: The Book of the Baalshem New York, 1931; The Book of the Baalshem America, 1933. Home: Stafford Hotel, Baltimore, Md.

SONTAG, Raymond James, prof. of history; b. Chicago, Ill., Oct. 2, 1897; s. Anthony Charles and Mary Elizabeth (Walsh) S.; B.S., U. of Ill., 1920, A.M., 1921; Ph.D., U. of Pa., 1924; m. Dorothea Agar, June 17, 1927; children—John Philip, Mary Agnes, William Robert, James Anthony. Instr. in history, U. of Iowa, 1921-22; with Princeton U. since 1924, as instr. in history, 1924-25, asst. prof., 1925-30, asso. prof., 1930-39, Henry Charles Lea prof. of history and chmn. dept. of history since 1939. Served as 2d lt. Inf., U.S. Army, 1918. Mem. Council on Foreign Relations, Am. Hist. Assn. Author: The Middle Ages (with Dana C. Munro), 1928; European Diplomatic History, 1933; Germany and England, Background of Conflict, 1938. Contbr. to professional and lit. jours. Home: 287 Western Way, Princeton, N.J.

SOOY, Leslie Thomas, neurologist, psychiatrist; b. Atlantic City, N.J., Nov. 21, 1906; s. Walter C. (M.D.) and Lida H. (Thomas) S.; student Hahnemann Coll. Science, Phila., Pa., 1923-25; B.S., Hahnemann Med. Coll., 1925, M.D., 1929; m. Carrie S. Compton, June 7, 1928. Began practice of medicine at Atlantic City, N.J., 1930; teacher histology and embryology, Hahnemann Med. Coll., 1930-33, asst. in dept. neurology and psychiatry, 1930-34, instr., 1934-37, lecturer neurology and psychiatry since 1937; practiced at Pitman, N.J., since 1931; mem. dept. neurology and psychiatry Hahnemann Hosp. of Phila. since 1930; neurologist and psychiatrist Underwood Hosp., Woodbury, N.J., since 1933; lecturer in psychiatry Hahnemann Hosp. Sch. of Nurses since 1934. Fellow A.M.A.; mem. Am. Inst. Homeopathy, N.J. State Med. Soc., N.J. State Homeo. Med. Soc., Gloucester County Med. Soc., Pi Upsilon Rho. Republican. Episcopalian. Mason (32°, Consistory). Home and office: 202 W. Holly Av., Pitman, N.J.

SOOY, Walter Collins, physician; b. Absecon, Atlantic Co., N.J., Sept. 21, 1869; s. Matthew Collins and Sarah (Leeds) S.; prep. edn., Absecon Schools, 1874-87; M.D., Hahnemann Med. Coll., Phila., 1890; m. Eliza Ann Hooper Thomas, Nov. 26, 1891; children—Walter Collins (deceased), Leslie Thomas, Marguerite Thomas (Mrs. Curtis Grant Craft). Gen. practice of medicine, Atlantic City, N.J., 1890-1933; retired since 1933. Mem. Am. Inst. Homeopathy, N.J. State Homeopathic Soc. Democrat. Presbyterian. Mason, Odd Fellow. Address: Atlantic and Lakeside Av., Woodcrest, Camden Co., N.J.

SOOY, William Frank; vice chancellor N.J. Court of Chancery. Address: Atlantic City, N.J.

SOPER, Morris Ames, judge; b. Baltimore, Md., Jan. 23, 1873; s. Samuel J. and Sarah Ann (Hiss) S.; Baltimore City Coll., 1890; A.B., Johns Hopkins, 1893; LL.B., U. of Md., 1895; LL.D., St. John's Coll., 1921; m. Grace

W. A. Parker, Nov. 6, 1907. Asst. state's atty., Baltimore City, 1897-99; asst. U.S. atty. Dist. of Md., 1900-10; pres. Bd. Police Commrs., Baltimore City, 1912-13; chief judge Supreme Bench of Baltimore City, 1914-21; U.S. dist. judge Dist. of Md., 1923-31; U.S. Circuit judge, 4th Circuit, since 1931. Member Am., Md. and Baltimore City bar assns., Nat. Economic League, Phi Beta Kappa. Republican. Methodist. Clubs: Maryland, University, Baltimore Country, Elkridge Country. Home: 102 W. 39th St. Address: Post Office Bldg., Baltimore, Md.

SORENSEN, Andrew Jensen, elec. engr.; b. Skjellerup, Denmark, Nov. 10, 1887; s. Mads and Mette Kirstine (Andersen) S.; came to U.S., 1914, naturalized, 1919; student Testrup Höjskole, Testrup, Denmark, 1907-08; student Grand View Coll., Des Moines, Ia., 1914-16; A.B., Ia. State Teachers' Coll., Cedar Falls, Ia., 1921; M.S., Ph.D., State U. of Ia., Iowa City, Ia., 1924; m. Dorothea Christine Thuesen, June 1, 1925; children—Frederick Allen, Raymond Andrew. Electric engr. with Union Switch & Signal Co., Swissvale, Pa., since July 1924. Served as pvt., 1st class, 105th Field Signal Batt., U.S. Army, with A.E.F., 1918-19. Republican. Presbyterian. Author of article "Magnetic Properties of Thin Films of Ferromagnetic Metals," Phys. Review, Dec. 1924. Holds about 40 patents on railroad signalling devices and controls. Home: 1204 East End Av., Edgewood, Pa. Office: Union Switch & Signal Co., Swissvale, Pa.

SORG, John Henry, lawyer; b. Pittsburgh, Pa., July 24, 1894; s. Herman and Minna (Kaufmann) S.; grad. Bordentown (N.J.) Mil. Inst., 1914; B.S. in Economics, U. of Pittsburgh, 1918, LL.B., 1921; m. Mary Harlan McCune, Jan. 2, 1923. Admitted to Pa. bar, 1921, and since practiced in Pittsburgh; dir. Ruud Mfg. Co., S. E. Armstrong Co. Served as 1st sergt. Air Service, U.S. Army, 1918. Dir. Children's Service Bureau. Mem. advisory bd. Bordentown Mil. Inst. Mem. Allegheny Co., Pa. State and Am. bar assns. Phi Gamma Delta, Phi Delta Phi. Lutheran. Clubs: University, Pittsburgh Field, Monarch, Civic (Pittsburgh). Home: 50 Woodhaven Dr., Mt. Lebanon, Pittsburgh, Pa. Office: Grant Bldg., Pittsburgh, Pa.

SOSMAN, Robert Browning, chemist; b. Chillicothe, O., Mar. 17, 1881; s. Francis A. and Mary R. (Browning) S.; B.Sc., Ohio State U., 1903, hon. Sc.D., 1938; S.B., Mass. Inst. Tech., 1904, Ph.D., 1907; m. Sarah Gibson Noble, Sept. 30, 1911; children—Robert Noble, George Gibson, Esther Browning, Edward Carey. In lab. of A. D. Little, Boston, 1906-08; physicist, assistant dir., Geophysical Lab., Carnegie Institution, 1908-28; physical chemist, Research Laboratory U.S. Steel Corporation, 1928—. Consulting chemist, Ordnance Dept., U.S.A., 1918; lecturer on geophysics, Mass. Inst. Tech., 1925-26; nat. councilor, O. State U. Research Foundation, 1937—. Mem. A.A.A.S., Am. Chem. Soc., Am. Phys. Soc., Am. Ceramic Soc. (pres. 1937), Am. Geophys. Union, Am. Inst. Mining and Metall. Engrs., Franklin Inst., Geol. Soc. America, Nat. Research Council, Washington Acad. Sci. (pres. 1928), Ceramic Assn. N.J., N.Y. Mineral. Club, Brit. Ceramic Soc., Deutsche Keramische Gesellschaft, Sigma Xi. Club: Delta Upsilon. Author of The Properties of Silica, 1927, and papers in scientific periodicals on high-temperature thermometry, refractories, and mineral chemistry and physics. Home: 117 W. Dudley Av., Westfield, N.J. Office: Research Lab., U.S. Steel Corpn., Lincoln Highway, Kearny, N.J.

SOTTER, Alice B(ennett), (Mrs. George W. S.), artist; b. Pittsburgh, Pa., d. Leopold and Anna M. (Cassidy) Bennett; student pub. sch. and high sch., and Ursuline Acad., Pittsburgh; art edn., Sch. of Design for Women, 1904, Carnegie Inst. Tech., 1915-16; m. George W. Sotter, Feb. 11, 1907. Began career as stained glass designer with J. Horace Rudy, Pittsburgh, 1904; studied and copied stained glass in Eng. and France; exhibited paintings and stained glass in Pittsburgh and Phila.; collaborating with husband in stained glass and decorating work, 1922; mem. Delaware Valley Protective Assn. (dir.), Alumni Pittsburgh Sch. of Design for Women, Phillips Mill Community Assn. Republican. Roman Catholic. Clubs: Odds and Ends, Colonial Club of Bucks County. Home: Holicong, Bucks Co., Pa.

SOTTER, George William, artist; b. Pittsburgh, Pa., Sept. 25, 1879; s. Nicholas and Katherine (Melder) S.; ed. in art in Pittsburgh schs. and at Pa. Acad. Fine Arts; pupil of Chase, Anshutz, Henry Keller, Redfield, and in stained glass, William Willet and Horace Rudy; traveled abroad to study and copy old stained glass; m. Alice E. Bennett, Feb. 11, 1907. Has specialized in landscape and stained glass; asst. prof. painting and design, Carnegie Inst. of Tech., Pittsburgh, 1910-19. Awarded silver medal, San Francisco Expn., 1915; 1st prize Asso. Artists of Pittsburgh, 1917; Art Soc. prize, Pittsburgh, 1920; hon. mention Conn. Acad. Fine Arts, 1921; Flagg prize, same, 1923. Works: "The Hill Road," Reading (Pa.) Mus.; "Pennsylvania Country," State College, Pa.; stained glass, St. Paul's Monastery, St. Agnes, Holy Innocents, St. Helenas and Sacred Heart Church (Pittsburgh), St. Peter's (Brownsville, Pa.), St. James (Cleveland), St. Mark's (St. Paul); altar window, Kendrick Sem. (St. Louis), St. Joseph's Cathedral (Wheeling, W.Va.), St. Ann's (Scranton), St. Gabriel's (Boston), St. Michael's Monastery (West Hoboken), St. Mary's (Harrisburg); altar window, All Souls Church (Sanford, Fla.), Our Lady of Lourdes (New York), Nativity Blessed Virgin (Brockport), St. Bartholomew (Norwich, N.Y.), Lady of Mt. Carmel (Doylestown); altar windows, St. Paul's P.E. Ch. (Doylestown), 19 windows N.J. State Mus., Trenton, N.J.; hanging painted cross, Lady of Mt. Carmel (Doylestown); hanging metal cross, Sacred Heart Ch. (Pittsburgh). Mem. Asso. Artists, Pittsburgh, Conn. Acad. Fine Arts, Liturgical Arts Soc., Phillips' Mill Community Assn., Phila. Art Alliance. Home: Holicong, Bucks Co., Pa.

SOULEN, Henry James, artist; b. Milwaukee, Wis., Mar. 12, 1888; s. Henry and Elizabeth (Brown) S.; ed. Milwaukee Art Students League, 1904-07, Chicago Art Inst., 1907-11, Howard Pyle Sch., Wilmington, Del., 1911; m. Gertrude Biesel, Oct. 26, 1911; children—Henry, Robert, Elizabeth, Richard, Nancy, David. Has followed profession as artist since 1911; has made illustrations and covers for Curtis Pub. Co. and other leading mags.; murals as well as easel paintings; accompanied Dr. Fosdick on trip to Holy Land to make paintings for Ladies Home Journal; commercial work for nat. advertisers. Served as treas. local sch. bd. Mem. Am. Artists Professional League. Republican. Home: R.F.D. 2, Phoenixville, Pa.

SOUSER, Kenneth, lawyer; b. Rockwood, Pa., Oct. 21, 1905; s. Russell R. and Grace (Critchfield) S.; A.B., U. of Pa., 1927; LL.B., U. of Pa. Law Sch., 1930; m. Margaret Smith, Oct. 9, 1930. Admitted to Pa. bar, 1930, and since engaged in gen. practice of law at Phila.; asso. with firm Slocum & Ferguson and successors since 1930, mem. firm Saylor, Slocum & Ferguson, 1937-38, mem. firm Saylor, Ferguson & Souser since 1938. Mem. Phila. Bar Assn., Phila. Lawyers Club. Republican. Club: Union League. Home: 325 S. Smedley St. Office: Fidelity-Phila. Trust Bldg., Philadelphia, Pa.

SOUTH, Furman, Jr., mech. engr., mfr.; b. Pittsburgh, Pa., Jan. 13, 1891; s. Furman and Elizabeth (Nagle) S.; student Pittsburgh High Sch., 1904-05, Shady Side Acad., Pittsburgh, 1905-08; M.E., Cornell U., 1912; m. Elva Markley Cameron, Nov. 24, 1917; children—Helen Cameron, Furman, III, Richard Cameron, Marian Elva. Mech. engr. Riter-Conley Mfg. Co., 1912-14; estate mgr., 1914-16; mech. engr. Carnegie Steel Co., 1916-17, 1919-20; since 1920 with Lava Crucible Co., of Pittsburgh., mfrs. graphite crucibles and special refractories, pres. since 1928; pres. and dir. United Furnace Engring. Co., Inc., New York. Served as 1st lt., Ordnance, U.S. Army, 1917-19; capt. Ordnance Reserve, 1919-29. Mem. Am. Foundrymen's Assn., Am. Ceramic Soc., Cornell Soc. of Engrs., Am. Legion, Pa. Soc., S.A.R., Sigma Alpha Epsilon. Catholic. Club: Cornell (New York). Home: 1140 Wightman St. Office: Wabash Bldg., Pittsburgh, Pa.

SOUTHERLAND, Clarence Andrew, lawyer; b. Baltimore, Md., Apr. 10, 1889; s. Clarence and Amey (Fairbank) S.; student Friends Sch., Wilmington, Del., 1895-1905, Princeton, 1905-07; LL.B., Georgetown U., 1913; m. Katharine Virden, Jan. 11, 1923; children—Katharine Virden, Clare Amey. Admitted to Del. bar, 1914, and since practiced at Wilmington; sr. partner firm Ward & Gray; atty. gen. state of Del., 1925-29; dir. Delaware Trust Co. of Wilmington, Yilson Line, Inc. Mem. Am. and New Castle County bar assns., Del. State Bar Assn. (pres., 1933-35), Bar Assn. of City of New York. Republican. Clubs: Wilmington, Wilmington Country. Home: 1900 Woodlawn Av. Office: Delaware Trust Bldg., Wilmington, Del.

SOUTHGATE, Hugh MacLellan, retired engr.; b. St. Johnsbury, Vt., Sept. 3, 1871; s. Rev. Charles MacLellan and Elizabeth Virginia (Anderson) S.; B.S., Worcester (Mass.) Poly. Inst., 1892, post-grad. B.S. in E.E., 1893; m. Alice Austin MacLaren, Dec. 12, 1900; children—Elizabeth MacLaren (Mrs. Ellis Bowen Harrison), Isabel Frances (wife of Dr. Karl Coates Corley), Hugh MacLellan. Apprentice Westinghouse Electric & Mfg. Co., East Pittsburgh, Pa., 1893-94; commercial engr., Boston, Mass., 1895-99; held various positions, London and Manchester, Eng., 1899-1910; mgr. govt. office and gen. rep., Washington, D.C., 1911-38; retired, 1938; v.p. Carlisle & Finch Co., Cincinnati, O., since 1915. Mem. Bur. Issues Assn. (pres. since 1926), Am. Philatelic Soc. (v.p. 1937-38), Am. Soc. E.E., Newcomen Soc. of Eng. (Washington Sect. sec. since 1937), Soc. of Colonial Wars in D.C. (mem. bd. of council), Baronial Order of Runnymede, Soc. of S.R. in D.C. (mem. of bd. govs. since 1919; v.p. since 1938). Presbyterian. Clubs: Metropolitan, Army and Navy Country (Washington, D.C.); Engineers (New York City); Chevy Chase (Md.). Address: 5800 Connecticut Av., Chevy Chase, Md.

SOUTHWORTH, George Clark, research engr.; b. Little Cooley, Pa., Aug. 24, 1890; s. Freedom and Mary (Fleek) S.; B.S., Grove City Coll., 1914, M.S., same, 1916; grad. student Columbia U., 1916-17; Ph.D., Yale, 1923; (hon.) D.Sc., Grove City Coll., 1931; m. Lowene Smith, Aug. 14, 1913; children—Margaret Eleanor (Mrs. Arthur G. Pulis), George Howard. Began as teacher in rural schs., 1908; asso. physicist, U.S. Bur. of Standards, 1917-18; instr., then asst. prof. of physics, Yale Univ., 1918-23; radio research engr., Am. Telephone & Telegraph Co. and Bell Telephone Labs., New York, since 1923. Mem. Internat. Radio Telegraph Conf., 1927. Fellow A.A.A.S. Mem. Am. Phys. Soc., Inst. Radio Engrs., Sigma Xi. Awarded Morris Liebman Prize, I.R.E., 1938. Republican. Presbyn. Home: Conover Lane, Red Bank, N.J. Office: P.O. Box 107, Red Bank, N.J.

SOWDEN, Lee; pres. North Philadelphia Trust Co. Home: 3823 Oak Rd. Office: Broad St. and Germantown Av., Philadelphia, Pa.

SOYSTER, Hale Bryan, petroleum engring.; b. Minneapolis, Minn., Nov. 1, 1899; s. Charles Lloyd and Luella Witt (Hammond) S.; A.B., U. of Calif., Berkeley, Calif., 1922; m. Elizabeth Mary Castner, Mar. 30, 1924; children—Hale Bryan, Jr., Huntley Hammond, Joan Elizabeth. Petroleum engr. and geologist for pvt. corpns., Los Angeles, Calif., 1922-23; cons. petroleum engr. and geologist, 1923-24; asso. petroleum technologist, U.S. Bur. of Mines, 1924-25; petroleum engr. U.S. Geol. Survey, 1925-27, oil and gas supervisor, Mid-Continent Dist., 1927-29, Rocky Mt. Dist., 1929-31; chief, Oil and Gas Leasing Div., U.S. Geol. Survey, Washington, D.C., since 1931. Served in S.A.T.C., 1918; lieut. comdr. U.S. Naval Res. since 1937. Mem. Am. Legion, Federal Club, Alpha Delta Phi. Home: 6516 Western Av., Chevy Chase, Md.

SPAETH, Edmund Benjamin, physician; b. Webster, N.Y., Apr. 22, 1890; s. Philip George and Amelia Marie (Witzig) S.; M.D., U. of Buffalo (N.Y.), 1916; student U.S. Army Med. Sch., Washington, D.C., 1916-17; m. Lea Maria Link, June 15, 1918; children—

Edmund Benjamin, Philip George, Karl Henry, George Link. Pvt. practice of ophthalmology at Phila. since 1927; asso. prof., U. of Pa. Grad. Sch. of Medicine since 1934. Served as 1st lt., M.C., U.S. Army, 1917-18, capt., 1919-20, maj., 1920-26. Awarded ophthal. medal, U. of Buffalo (N.Y.), 1927; medalist, Army Med. Sch., 1917. Republican. Unitarian. Mason. Author: Newer Methods, Ophthalmic Surgery, 1927; Principles and Practice of Ophthalmic Surgery, 1939; numerous monographs on surgery of the eye and clinical investigations. Home: 7021 Clearview St. Office: 1930 Chestnut St., Philadelphia, Pa.

SPAETH, J(ohn) Duncan (Ernst), univ. pres.; b. Phila., Sept. 27, 1868; s. Dr. Adolph and Maria Dorothea (Duncan) S.; A.B., U. of Pa., 1888; Ph.D., U. of Leipzig, 1892; studied in France and Italy, 1912-13; Litt.D., Muhlenberg Coll., 1918, U. of Pittsburgh, 1925; LL.D., U. of Oregon, 1936, U. of Pa., 1938; m. Marie Tinette Haughton, June 19, 1902; children—Dorothea Duncan, Paul Ernest, Janet Douglas, John Duncan, Jr. Asst. prof. English, Gustavus Adolphus College, St. Peter, Minnesota, 1893-94; instr., 1894-95, prof. English philology, 1895-1905, Central High Sch., Phila.; preceptor in English, 1905-11, apptd. prof., 1911, Murray prof. English lit., 1930-35, Princeton; 1st pres. U. of Kansas City, 1936-1938, now emeritus; visiting professor of comparative lit., Reed Coll., 1926-27; visiting prof. U. of Wichita, Kan., since 1938. Lecturer for Univ. Extension Soc., Bd. Pub. Edn., New York, 1905-22, Brooklyn Inst., U. of Calif., 4 summers, U. of Ore., 9 summers, U. of Southern Calif., 4 summers, U. of Colo., 2 summers, Chautauqua Instn., 1921, 23, 32, etc. Mem. bd. mgrs. N.J. State Reformatory, 1923-29. Y.M.C.A. educational dir., Camp Wheeler and Camp Jackson, 1918; active in orgn. instrn. for illiterates in army camps during World War. Mem. Modern Lang. Assn. America, Am. Dialect Soc., Am. Acad. Polit. and Social Science, Nat. Council Nat. Econ. League, Phi Beta Kappa, Psi Upsilon; steward Am. Rowing Assn.; amateur coach of Princeton Crews, 1910-25. Clubs: Nassau (Princeton); University, Country (Kansas City); Princeton (Phila.); Princeton (New York); Mazamas (mountaineering, Ore.). Author: Christian Theology in Browning's Poetry; Camp Reader for American Soldiers (several edits.), 1918 (adopted by War Dept. for A.E.F.); Old English Poetry, 1921; American Life and Letters: A Reading List (with J. E. Brown), 1934. Editor (with Henry S. Pancoast) of Early English Poems and transl. of Anglo-Saxon poems in same, 1911. Contbr. articles on Am. Literature to Am. Year Book, 1926, 27, and to Dictionary of Am. Biography, etc. Address: Nassau Club, Princeton, N.J.

SPAHR, Boyd Lee, lawyer; b. Mechanicsburg, Pa., Apr. 18, 1880; s. Murray Hurst and Clara (Koser) S.; Ph.B., Dickinson, 1900, A.M., 1903; LL.B., U. of Pa., 1904; LL.D., Lafayette, 1933; m. Katharine Febiger, Oct. 8, 1908; children—Boyd Lee, Christian Carson Febiger, John Febiger. Admitted to Pa. bar, 1904; in practice at Phila.; mem. firm Ballard, Spahr, Andrews and Ingersoll. Served as maj. and mem. Gen. Staff, U.S.A., 1918. Trustee Dickinson Coll. since 1908, pres. bd. since 1931. Mem. Phi Kappa Sigma (nat. pres., 1920-23), Phi Beta Kappa. Episcopalian. Republican. Clubs: Rittenhouse, Racquet, Union League, University, Merion Cricket, Harrisburg, Carlisle Country. Home: Haverford, Pa. Office: Land Title Bldg., Philadelphia, Pa.

SPAHR, Murray Hurst, Jr., lawyer; b. Mechanicsburg, Pa., Mar. 12, 1891; s. Murray Hurst and Clara Alberta (Koser) S.; student Conway Hall, 1905-08; Ph.B., Dickinson Coll., 1912; LL.B., U. of Pa. Law Sch., 1915; m. Mary C. Boyd, Nov. 12, 1930. Admitted to Phila. bar, 1915; associated with law firm Simpson, Brown & Williams and successor Brown & Williams, 1915-37; mem. Clark, Hebard & Spahr since Jan. 1, 1938. Mem. R.O.T.C., Plattsburg, 1916; served at Ft. Niagara, 1917; commd. 2d lt. F.A., Aug. 1917; served with A.E.F., 2d Div., 17th F.A., Army of Occupation, 2 yrs.; hon. discharged as capt. Mem. Phi Kappa Sigma. Republican. Episcopalian. Home: Rosemont, Pa. Office: 1500 Walnut St., Philadelphia, Pa.

SPAHR, Richard Rockefeller, physician; b. Mechanicsburg, Pa., July 10, 1889; s. Murray Hurst and Clara Alberta (Koser) S.; grad. Mercersburg (Pa.) Acad., 1907; pre-med. student Dickinson Coll., Carlisle, Pa., 1907-09; M.D., U. of Pa., 1913; m. Nancy Lawrence Hanes, Apr. 1, 1918; children—Nancy Lawrence, Sarah Ellen Rockefeller. Interne Pa. Hosp., Children's Hosp., Phila., Pa., Robert Packer Hosp., Sayre, Pa., 1913-16; in practice at Wilmington, Del., 1916, 1919, Middletown, Del., 1919-23, Mechanicsburg, Pa., since 1923; mem. staff Harrisburg (Pa.) Polyclinic Hosp., Seidle Memorial Hosp., Mechanicsburg, Pa., Carlisle (Pa.) Hosp.; instr. nurses Harrisburg Polyclinic Hosp. since 1925, chief in charge pediatric service since 1927. Served as 1st lt., M.C., U.S. Army, 1917, capt. and bn. comdr., Ambulance Bn., 82d Div., 1917-18, maj., 1919, A.E.F.; maj., Med. Reserve Corps, 1919-24, lt. col., 1924-31, col. since 1931; comdr. 343d Med. Regt., Regular Army, inactive since 1931. Dir. Seidle Memorial Hosp., Mechanicsburg, Pa. Mem. Pa. State, Cumberland Co., Cumberland Valley med. socs., A.M.A., Harrisburg Acad. of Medicine, Phi Kappa Sigma, Phi Alpha Sigma. Republican. Episcopalian (vestryman and warden St. Luke's Episcopal Ch., Mechanicsburg, Pa.). Mason. Clubs: U. of Pa. (Harrisburg, Pa.); Carlisle Country (Carlisle, Pa.). Address: 19 S. Market St., Mechanicsburg, Pa.

SPANGLER, Charles Cleveland, physician, surgeon; b. Jefferson, Pa., Sept. 19, 1886; s. Hamilton Andrew and Sarah Ann (Abel) S.; ed. York County Acad. and York County Normal School, 1902-05, York Collegiate Inst., 1907-08, Jefferson Med. Coll., 1908-09; M.D., U. of Md., 1915; grad. study U. of Md., 1929, Polyclinic Post Grad. School, N.Y., 1931, Vienna, Austria and Budapest, Hungary, 1933; m. Myrtle L. Shetter, Nov. 11, 1917. Teacher public schools of North York, Pa., 1905-07; interne St. Josephs Hosp., Lancaster, Pa., 1915-16, Polyclinic Hosp., Harrisburg, Pa., 1916-17; in practice, Lancaster, Pa., 1917-18, York, Pa., since 1919; surgeon York Hosp. since 1933. Served as 1st lt. Med. Corps, U.S. Army, 1918-19. Mem. Pa. State and York Co. med. socs.; first vice-pres. York Co. Med. Soc., 1936, pres., 1937, now trustee. Mason (K.T., Shriner), K.P. Clubs: Outdoor, Tramerick, Shrine, York Co. Med., American Legion, Savage Rod and Gun. Home: 418 W. Market St., York, Pa.

SPANGLER, Cleon Perry, industrial engr.; b. Lansing, Mich., May 31, 1886; s. Perry George and Margaret (Ginter) S.; B.S. in engring., U. of Mich., Coll. of Engring., 1911; m. Cora Elizabeth Stark, Sept. 18, 1922; children—William Stark, George Perry, Robert Stark. Asst., engring. corps, Cleveland and Pittsburgh Div., Pa. R.R., 1911-15; asso., Harrington Emerson, consulting engr., 1916-17, 1920-21; industrial engr. Jones & Laughlin Steel Corpn., Pittsburgh, 1922-29, asst. chief industrial engr., Pittsburgh Works, since 1930. Served as 1st lt., 23d U.S. Army Engrs., A.E.F., 1918-19. Mem. Am. Legion (past commdr. East Liberty Post No. 5; mem. Constitutional Defense Com., Dept. of Pa.), Y.M.C.A. (com. of management, East Liberty Branch), Boy Scouts of America (Troop Com., Troop No. 89). Republican. Christian Ch. (mem. of bd., East End Christian Ch.). Mason. Has delivered many speeches before patriotic socs., ch. and sch. groups. Home: 5528 Wellesley Av. Office: 2709 Carson St., Pittsburgh, Pa.

SPANGLER, Penn Sylian, pres. business school; b. Shanksville, Somerset Co., Pa., May 8, 1875; s. Conrad D. and Marguerite (Hunter) S.; ed. Meyersdale (Pa.) Prep. Sch., Iron City Coll., Pittsburgh, Otterbein (O.) Univ.; hon. LL.D., Grove City Coll., 1937; m. Mary Watson Taggart, June 4, 1903. Pub. sch. teacher for 5 yrs.; teacher of bookkeeping Iron City Coll., Pittsburgh, later prin.; prin. and mgr. Duff's Coll., Pittsburgh, 1906-22; pres. Duff's Iron City Coll. since 1922. Mem. Pittsburgh Chamber of Commerce, Lower Downtown Business Men's Assn. Dir. Boys Club of Pittsburgh. Mem. Nat. Commercial Teachers Fed., Nat. Assn. Accredited Commercial Schs., Eastern Commercial Teachers Assn., Tri-State Commercial Edn. Assn., Pa. Private Sch. Mgrs. Assn., Nat. Edn. Assn. Mem. United Brethren Ch. Mason. Clubs: Rotary, Shannopin Country (Pittsburgh). Home: 422 Forest Av., Bellevue, Pa. Office: 424 Duquesne Way, Pittsburgh, Pa.

SPANGLER, Robert Clifton; prof. botany, W.Va. U. Address: West Virginia U., Morgantown, W.Va.

SPARE, J. E.; editor Mercury-News. Address: Pottstown, Pa.

SPARE, Ralph Henry, Jr., sec. chamber commerce; b. Pottstown, Pa., Aug. 7, 1896; s. Ralph Henry and Alice (Rinker) S.; ed. Dickinson Coll., 1915-17; B.S. in Econs., U. of Pa., 1922; m. Ruth Louise Niesley, June 19, 1926; children—Robert Henry, Richard Niesley. Began as reporter for newspaper, Pottstown, Pa., 1917-19; field auditor for constrn. co., 1922-24; sec. chamber of commerce, Milton, Pa., 1924-26; sec. Chamber of Commerce, Pottstown, Pa., since 1926. Mem. Nat. Assn. of Commercial Organization Secs., Pa. Commercial Organization Sec. (pres.). Mem. Sigma Alpha Epsilon. Methodist. Mason. Home: 858 N. Evans St. Office: Chamber of Commerce, Pottstown, Pa.

SPARGO, John Adams, supt. of schools; b. Dover, N.J., Jan. 3, 1887; s. William Charles and Irene (Davenport) S.; grad. Dover High Sch., 1906; B.S., New York U., 1918, A.M., 1932; hon. L.H.D., Upsala Coll., 1935; m. Emolyn Lena Westbrook, June 28, 1911. Teacher rural schools, Morris County, N.J., 1906-08; prin. elementary sch., Millbrook, 1908-11; with East Orange, N.J., Pub. Schs., 1912-29, as teacher, 1912-18, prin. Ashland Sch., 1918-29; asst. commr. of edn. for State of N.J., 1929-34; supt. of schools, Nutley, N.J., since 1934; owner of large modern dairy farm, Dover, N.J. Dir. Nutley Pub. Library. Pres. N.J. Elementary Prins. Assn., 1926-27. Mem. N.E.A., Am. Assn. Sch. Adminstrs., Council of Edn. of N.J., Phi Delta Kappa. Republican. Methodist. Mason. Clubs: Rotary, Schoolmasters. Home: 92 Alexander Av. Office: High School, Nutley, N.J.

SPARKS, John Bertram, manufacturer; b. St. Ives, Hunts, England, Mar. 6, 1886; s. John and Mary (Waldock) S.; student Mercers Sch., London, England, 1895-1902; diploma in elec. engring., City & Guilds Tech. Coll., U. of London, 1905; student Technische Hochschule, Karlsruhe, Germany, 1905-06; m. Dorothy Catherine Wadia, of London, Eng., July 14, 1914; children—John, Joan Betty, Anne. Came to U.S., 1924, naturalized, 1937. Began as elec. engr., 1906; asst. editor Electrical Engring., London, 1908-10; asst. to Dr. H. M. Parshall, cons. engr., London, 1910-13; chief engr. Bergwerk-u. Hüttenverwaltung Ges. Frankfurt-a-Main, Germany, 1913-14; engr. with Balfour, Beatty & Co., London, Eng., 1914-15; rep. of Dr. Parshall with Barcelona Traction, Light & Power Co., Barcelona, Spain, 1915-16; engr. with Nestlé & Anglo-Swiss Condensed Milk Co., Cham. Switzerland, 1916-20; mgr. Tutbury factory, Nestlé & Anglo-Swiss Condensed Milk Co., England, 1920-24; mgr. mfg. dept. Nestle's Milk Products, Inc., N.Y. City, 1924-37, v.p. in charge of mfr. since 1937, now also dir. Mem. Am. Chem. Soc. Presbyn. Author of ednl. charts: "Histomap" of World History and "Histomap" of Evolution. Home: 601 Belvidere Av., Plainfield, N.J. Office: 155 E. 44th St., New York, N.Y.

SPARKS, William Sheppard, b. Laurel, Md., Jan. 25, 1896; s. Ernest Aldred and Isabella (Solloway) S.; ed. schs. of Baltimore, Towson and Cumberland (all Md.); m. Elfa Diana Zehrbach, July 6, 1918; children—Marjorie Jeanne, Betty Marie, William Elmer. Began career as telegraph messenger boy; then worked in silk mill, steel car plant of B.&O. R.R. and as trucker in railroad freight house; now cashier, joint freight office of Western Md. Ry. and Pa. R.R., Cumberland, Md. Served as private Co.

F, 313th Inf., 79th Div., U.S. Army; with A.E.F., 11 months. Co-dir. Cumberland Sesquicentennial Fine Arts Exhbn., 1937; chmn. Art Week, Allegany County, 1937; active in other art exhbns. Mem. Acad. Am. Poets, Am. Sunbathing Assn., Am. Civil Liberties Union, Am. Legion, Birth Control Fed. of America, Eugene Field Soc., Nat. Assn. of Audubon Socs., Nat. Com. for Revision of Comstock Law, Soc. of Open Roaders of the World, World Narcotics Research Foundation (mem. bd. dirs.; mem. organizing com.), Wilson Ornithol. Club, Wild Flower Preservation Soc., Allegany County Hist. Society, Friends of the Library (Cumberland). Freethinker. Exhibited at annual exhibitions of Cumberland Valley Artists, Hagerstown, Md., 1934-39; Charcoal Club Galleries, Baltimore, 1933; Cumberland Sesquicentennial 1937; also at Cumberland Library, Episcopal Parish House and U. of Md. Received hon. mention for "Wind and Sunlight," Cumberland Valley Artists, 1938. Club: Green Forest (Washington, D.C.). Author: Light on the Leaves (verse; illustrated by John Wenrich, Hendrik Willem van Loon and the author), 1937. Contributing editor to The Nudist (mag.). Poems have appeared in mags., newspapers and anthologies. Home: "Twisted Trees," Cumberland, Md.

SPATOLA, Joseph, Sr., pres. Spatola Importing Co.; b. Philadelphia, Pa., Mar. 19, 1887; s. Felix and Maria S.; student pub. schs.; m. Orvilla Michelotti, Apr. 17, 1907; children—Joseph, Jr., Dorothy. Pres. J. M. Thompson Co. (wholesale grocers), Felix Spatola & Sons and Spatola Importing Co. (wines, liquors); v.p. Leroux Co. (cordial mfrs.); dir. Banca Commercial Italian Trust Co. Apptd. trustee Eastern State Penitentiary by Gov. Earle, 1936; trustee Catholic Young Men's Assn. Mem. tourist com. Chamber of Commerce. Home: Hotel Roosevelt. Office: 943 N. Second St., Philadelphia, Pa.

SPAULDING, Edward Gleason, prof. philosophy; b. Burlington, Vt., Aug. 6, 1873; s. Americus V. and Mary A. (Rice) S.; B.S., U. of Vt., 1894; LL.D. from same university in 1921; A.M., Columbia University, 1896; Ph.D. Univ. of Bonn, Germany, 1900; m. Olive Strong Miner, June 2, 1913. Instr. in philosophy, Coll. City of N.Y., 1900-05; asst. prof. philosophy, 1905-14, prof. philosophy since 1914, Princeton. Lecturer in philosophy, Marine Biol. Lab., Woods Hole, Mass., 1907—. Mem. Am. Philos. Assn. (sec., 1909-17), Phi Delta Theta. Club: Princeton (New York). Served as 1st lt. Engr. Corps, U.S.A., in Chem. Warfare Service, June 5, 1918-Jan. 1, 1919. Lecturer, Brooklyn Inst. Arts and Sciences, since 1918, also at People's Institute, New York City; lecturer at summer sessions, Washington U., Harvard, U. of Chicago, U. of Calif., U. of Mich. Pres. Am. Philosophical Assn., 1932. Author: The New Rationalism, 1918; What Am I?, 1928; A World of Chance, 1936. Co-Author: The New Realism, 1912; Roads to Knowledge, 1932. Contbr. philos. and scientific periodicals. Address: 8 Edgehill St., Princeton, N.J.

SPEAKMAN, Frank L., judge; b. Wilmington, Del., Aug. 11, 1874; s. Samuel and Anna M. (Ashbridge) S.; LL.B., Yale, 1897; unmarried. Admitted to Del. bar, 1897; engaged in independent practice at Wilmington, 1897-1935; dep. atty. gen. State of Del., 1919-21; now asso. justice Del. Supreme Court. Republican. Club: Wilmington. Address: Court House, Wilmington, Del.

SPEARE, Charles Frederic, financial editor; b. Rochester, N.Y., June 17, 1874; s. Merrill and Annie (Baxter) S.; A.B., Harvard, 1899; m. Louise Halsey Burnett, Nov. 19, 1903; children—Margaret L., Elizabeth B., Muriel F. Financial editor New York Evening Mail, 1899-1919; with Brown Brothers & Co., bankers, 1919-27; financial editor syndicate service of Consolidated Press Association, 1927-33; writer financial reviews for North American Newspaper Alliance since 1933. Contributor many articles on financial and economic subjects to Review of Reviews, North American Review, and other periodicals; author of Railroad Studies, describing physical and traffic aspects of large railway systems of U.S. and Mexico; book of Nature studies, "We Found a Farm." Presbyn. Home: Bound Brook, N.J. and Salisbury, Vt. Office: 280 Broadway, New York, N.Y.

SPECK, Frank Gouldsmith, anthropologist; b. Brooklyn, N.Y., Nov. 8, 1881; s. Frank G. and Hattie L. (Staniford) S.; A.B., Columbia, 1904, A.M., 1905; fellow U. of Pa., 1908; m. Florence Insley, Sept. 15, 1910. Asst. curator ethnology, Univ. Mus., U. of Pa., 1909-11; instr. anthropology, U. of Pa., 1909-11, asst. prof., 1911-25, prof. since 1925; lecturer in anthropology, Swarthmore Coll., since 1923. Asst. editor Am. Anthropologist since 1920, Am. Jour. Archæology, 1920-23; anthropologist with Nat. Research Council (exec. com. 1925). Mem. Am. Anthropol. Assn., Am. Ethnol. Soc., Am. Folklore Soc. (pres. 1920-22), Anthropol. Soc. Phila. (pres. 1920-22), Oriental Club Philadelphia, Sigma Xi, Sigma Phi Epsilon. Extensive field work among Indian tribes of Indian Ty., Okla., Southeastern and Northeastern U.S., Can., Newfoundland and Labrador peninsula. Author: Ethnology of Yuchi Indians, 1909; Ceremonial Songs of the Creek and Yuchi Indians, 1911; The Creek Indians of Taskigi Town, 1907; The Double Curve Motive in Northeastern Algonkian Art, 1914; Hunting Territories and Myths of the Temiskaming Algonquins, 1915; Social Life and Mythology of the Temagami Ojibwa, 1915; The Nanticoke Community of Delaware, 1915; Penobscot Shamanism, 1920; The Functions of Wampum Among the Northeastern Angonkian, 1919; Penobscot Transformer Texts, 1920; Boethuk and Micmac, 1922; The Rappahannock Indians of Virginia, 1925; The Penn Wampum Belts, 1925; Native Tribes and Dialects of Connecticut, 1926; Symbolism in Penobscot Art, 1927; also chapters in the Ethnology of the Powhatan Tribes of Virginia, 1928; Tribal Boundaries of Massachusetts and Wampanoag Indians, 1928; A Study of the Delaware Indian Big House Ceremony, 1931; Catawba Texts, 1935; Penobscot Tales and Religious Beliefs, 1935; Naskapi, Savage Hunters of the Labrador Peninsula, 1935; Oklahoma Delaware Ceremonies, Feasts and Dances, 1937; Montagnais Art in Birch-Bark, 1938. Home: Swarthmore, Pa.

SPEER, Clyde Edward, coal; b. Pittsburgh, Pa., June 20, 1892; s. Louis M. and Mille (Wood) S.; B.S. in Economics, U. of Pittsburgh, 1915; m. Virginia Morris, June 20, 1916; children—Elizabeth Millicent (Mrs. A. W. Schenck, Jr.), Virginia Morris, II, Natalie Wood. Lubricating oil salesman Atlantic Refining Co., 1915-18; salesman Certainteed Products Corpn., 1918-20; coal salesman, 1920-22; with Thomas R. Heyward Co., coal and iron brokers, 1922-24; sec. and treas. Mullholand Coal Co., Pittsburgh, since 1924; pres. and treas. Clyde E. Speer Coal Co., Inc., since 1935; partner McCutcheon-McKelvy & Durant; dir. Island Coal & Trading Co., New York. Dir. and treas. Hampton Sch. Dist., 1927-37. Mem. Delta Tau Delta. Republican. Presbyterian. Mason (Shriner). Clubs: Pittsburgh Athletic Assn.; Wildwood Country. Home: Oak Hill Farms, Allison Park, Pa. Office: Gulf Bldg., Pittsburgh, Pa.

SPEER, Hugh Brownlow, clergyman; b. Zion, Ill., Oct. 7, 1874; s. James Glass and Letitia (Ritchie) S.; A.B., Monmouth Coll., 1898; Th.B., Xenia Theol. Sem., 1901; hon. D.D., Monmouth Coll., 1919; m. Ellen Augusta Moore, June 19, 1902; children—James Robert, Hugh Brownlow, Jr., Wallace Hamilton. Ordained to ministry United Presbyn. Ch., 1901; pastor, Sunbeam, Ill., 1901-06, Bovina Center, N.Y., 1906-11, Central Ch., Omaha, Neb., 1911-17, Third Ch., Pittsburgh, Pa., 1919-23; pastor First United Presbyn. Ch., Erie, Pa., since 1923. Pres. Omaha Ch. Federation, 1914; pres. Erie Ministerial Assn., 1927; chaplain Pa. Soldiers' & Sailors, Home since 1924. Served in Y.M.C.A. War Service, 1918; chaplain 1st lt. U.S.A., 1918, Camp Zachary Taylor; capt. O.R.C., 1924. Dir. Pittsburgh-Xenia Theol. Sem., 1928-38. Republican. Presbyn. Home: 127 E. 8th St., Erie, Pa.

SPEER, J(ames) Ramsey, retired manufacturer; b. Pittsburgh, Pa., July 23, 1870; s. John Z. and Katharine (McKnight) S.; B.S., Mass. Institute Tech., 1893; m. Jeannette Lowrie Childs, 1898; children—Gertrude Childs, James Ramsey. Began with Shoenberger Steel Co., 1893, gen. mgr., 1898, v.p. and gen. mgr. for Am. Steel & Wire Co., purchasers of same, 1899-1900; v.p. S. Jarvis Adams Co., Midland, Pa., 1899-1911, pres., 1911-19, chmn. bd., 1920; an organizer and pres. until 1904, Brownsville Glass Co., an organizer, 1905, v.p. until 1911, Midland Steel Co.; pres. Mackintosh-Hemphill Co., mfrs. rolling mill machinery, Pittsburgh, 1924-29; dir. Easton (Md.) Nat. Bank. Dir. and officer for alien property custodian, World War, of Bayer Co., Hayden Chem. Works, Berlin Aniline Works, Kalli Color and Chem. Co. A founder and former trustee Arnold Sch. Democrat. Episcopalian. Clubs: Miles River Yacht, Tred Avon Yacht; Talbot Country, Chesapeake Bay Yacht. Author: Chronology of Iron and Steel, 1920. Inventor of Adamite, a high carbon nickel-chrome steel alloy, also of molybdenum nickel chrome steel alloy, and of improvements in mechanical glass, etc. Joint inventor of electric ingot stripper. Home: "Wilderness," Trappe, Talbot County, Md. Office: care W. C. Rice, William Penn Hotel, Pittsburgh, Pa.

SPEER, Joseph Andrew, clergyman; b. Hanover, Ill., Oct. 10, 1874; s. Charles and Nancy (Campbell) S.; A.B., Monmouth Coll., Monmouth, Ill., 1901; B.D., Xenia Theol. Sem., Xenia, O., 1904; (hon.) D.D., Coll. of Wooster (O.), 1924; m. Lucy Stewart Harris, Sept. 6, 1904. Ordained to ministry United Presbyn. Ch., 1904; pastor various chs. in O., 1908-19; pastor, Coshocton, O., 1919-25, Tyrone, Pa., 1925-39; pastor, 1st Presbyn., West Chester, Pa., since 1939; served several times as moderator of presbyteries; known as pub. speaker before clubs and civic orgns. and state convs. of trade assns. Served as camp pastor, Ft. Oglethorpe, Ga., during World War. Served two terms as dir. Xenia Theol. Sem., one term as dir. Pittsburgh Theol. Sem. Charter mem. Kiwanis Club, Coshocton, O. Republican. Presbyn. Club: Rotary of Tyrone, Pa. (vice-pres.). Home: 317 Miner St., West Chester, Pa.

SPEER, Talbot Taylor, pres. Baltimore Salesbook Co.; b. Pittsburgh, Pa., Jan. 7, 1895; s. John L. Dawson and Margaret (Taylor) S.; student Miss Bradshaws-Brennen's, Pittsburgh, Pa., 1900-06, Episcopal High Sch., Alexandria, Va., 1907-13, U. of Va., 1913-15, U. of Md., 1915-16; m. Mary Washington Stewart, Dec. 8, 1920 (died Oct. 1926); 1 dau., Mary Washington. Began as clerk Daniel Miller Co.; with Baltimore Salesbook Co. since Jan. 1922, beginning as asst. to pres., pres. since June 1922, chmn. bd. since 1926; pres. and chmn. bd. Capitol Gazette Press, Annapolis, Md. (publs. Evening Capitol, Md. Gazette and U.S. Coast Guard Mag.), since Jan. 1927. Served as 2d lt., 7th F.A., 1st Div., U.S.A., with A.E.F., 1917-18; 1st lt., June, 1918; Capt. July 1918; wounded in action, resigned 1920. Cited for gallantry in action. Dir. Episcopal High Sch.; mem. lay council Episcopal Pro-Cathedral of Md. Dir. Baltimore Assn. Commerce, Specialty Accounting Mfrs. Assn. Clubs: Maryland, Greenspring Valley Hunt, Baltimore Country, Elkridge, Rotary, Wednesday, St. Anthony, Wythemore Hounds (pres.), Upper Marlborough Hounds, Carrolton Hounds. Home: Mays Chapel Road at Jenifer Road, Lutherville, Md. Office: 3120-50 Frederick Av., Baltimore, Md.

SPEER, William Henry, surgeon; b. Dover, Del., Feb. 5, 1888; s. Ottomer W. and Emma (Moreland) S.; M.D., U. of Pa., 1910; m. Laura Edwards, Sept. 23, 1912. Asst. surgeon, Del. Hosp., Wilmington, Del., 1911-19, chief surg. staff since 1919; chief surg. staff, St. Francis Hosp., Wilmington, Del., since 1927. Served as 1st lt., M.C., U.S. Army, Apr.-Oct. 1917, major, 1918-19. Mayor of Wilmington, Del., 1933-35. Fellow Am. Coll. Surgeons, Internat. Coll. Surgeons; mem. New Castle Co. Med. Soc. (pres., 1927), Med. Soc. of Del. (sec., 1934-37; pres., 1933), A.M.A., Alpha Kappa Kappa. Democrat. Baptist. Mason (all bodies except 33°), Elk, Eagle. Address: 917 Washington St., Wilmington, Del.

SPEERS, James M., merchant; b. Jordanstown, White Abbey, County Antrim, Ireland, Jan. 9, 1862; s. William and Mary (Milliken) S.; came to U.S., 1880; ed. pub. schs.; m. Nellie

Carter, June 14, 1888 (died May 22, 1922); children—William E., Thomas Guthrie, Peter Carter, James M., Wallace C., Theodore C.; m. 2d, Nellie Carter Dodd, Feb. 15, 1924. With James McCutcheon & Co., linens, since 1880, pres., 1912-30, chmn. bd. since 1930; dir. Patriotic Ins. Co. of America, Sun Indemnity Co. of New York, Sun Underwriters Co. Vice-pres. Presbyterian Board Foreign Missions; treas. Student Volunteer Movement, Agrl. Missions Foundation; trustee Forman Christian Coll., Lahore, India; trustee Mt. Holyoke Coll. Presbyn. Club: Union League (New York). Home: 81 S. Mountain Av., Montclair, N.J. Office: 609 5th Av., New York, N.Y.

SPEERS, Thomas Guthrie, clergyman; b. Atlantic Highlands, N.J., Aug. 27, 1890; s. James Milliken and Nellie (Carter) S.; A.B., Princeton, 1912; student Union Theol. Sem., 1912-16; D.D., Coll. of Wooster, 1935; m. Elizabeth Thacher, May 27, 1926; children—Thomas Guthrie, Elizabeth Thacher, Ellen Carter. Ordained ministry, Presbyn. Ch., 1916; asst., later asso. minister Univ. Pl. Ch., New York, 1916-18; asso. minister First Ch., New York, 1920-28; minister Brown Memorial Ch., Baltimore, Md., since 1928. Served as 1st lt. and chaplain 102d Inf., U.S.A., in France, World War. Awarded D.S.C. (U.S.); Croix de Guerre with Palm (France). Trustee Princeton U., (1932-36), Goucher Coll., Union Memorial Hosp., Presbyn. Eye, Ear and Throat Hosp. (Baltimore); mem. Presbyn. Bd. Nat. Missions. Mem. Phi Beta Kappa. Home: 4 St. John's Road, Roland Park, Baltimore, Md. Address: 1316 Park Av., Baltimore, Md.

SPEICHER, John Wilson, lawyer; b. Bernville, Pa., Dec. 30, 1886; s. Rev. Charles C. and Ada E. (Oldt) S.; A.B., Princeton U.; A.M., Dickinson Coll.; LL.B., Dickinson Sch. of Law; m. Mary G. Stanton, Aug. 24, 1915; children—John, Frances. Asst. dist. atty., Berks County, 1928-32; city solicitor, Reading, 1932-36; now solicitor West Reading Sch. Dist., Cumru Twp., Rockland Twp. and Rockland Sch. Dist. Mem. Pa. State Bar Assn., Berks Co. Bar Assn., Endlich Law Club. Mason. Club: Rotary. Home: 1200 Centre Av. Office: 44 N. 6th St., Reading, Pa.

SPEIGHT, Francis W., artist; b. Windsor, N.C., Sept. 11, 1896; s. Rev. Thomas Trotman and Margaret Otelia (Sharrock) S.; student Wake Forest Coll., 1915-17, Corcoran Sch. of Art, 1920, Pa. Acad. of Fine Arts, 1920-25; m. Sarah Jane Blakeslee, Nov. 7, 1936. Asst. instr. in drawing, Pa. Acad. of Fine Arts, 1925-31, instr. since 1931. Represented at Met. Mus. of Art, Toronto Mus., Pa. Acad. of Fine Arts, Boston Mus. of Fine Arts. Awarded Cresson Traveling scholarship, 1923, and 1925; fellowship of Pa. Acad. of Fine Arts gold medal, 1926; Soc. of Washington Artists landscape prize, 1929; Kohnstamm prize, Art Inst. Chicago, 1930; Hallgarten prize, Nat. Acad. of Design, 1930; Pa. Acad. of Fine Arts fellowship prize, 1930; Conn. Acad. of Fine Arts landscape prize, 1932; bronze medal, and 3d Clark prize, Corcoran Gallery, 1937; gold medal, Phila. Sketch Club, 1938. Asso. Nat. Acad. of Design, 1937. Home: 259 Cinnaminson Lane, Roxborough, Philadelphia, Pa.

SPEIGHT, Harold Edwin Balme, coll. dean; b. Bradford, Eng., Apr. 21, 1887; s. Edwin and Charlotte (Hall) S.; M.A., U. of Aberdeen, 1909; studied Exeter Coll. (Oxford); D.D. Tufts College, 1925; hon. A.M., Dartmouth, 1927 (Phi Beta Kappa); m. Mabel Grant, 1911; children—Christine Ray Grant, Charlotte Frances. Asst. prof. logic and metaphysics, U. of Aberdeen, 1909-10; fellow Manchester Coll (Oxford), 1910-12; served in the ministry London, England, Victoria, B.C., Berkeley, Calif., Boston, Mass., 1912-27; prof. philosophy, Dartmouth, 1927-29, prof. biography and chmn. dept., 1929-33; dean of men, Swarthmore College, since 1933, dean of Coll. since 1938. Trustee Bradford Jr. Coll. Chaplain U.S.A., overseas, 1918-19; mem. commn. investigating religious minorities in Transylvania, 1922. Fellow Am. Geog. Soc.; mem. Am. Philos. Assn., Am. Acad. Polit. and Social Sciences. Mem. Soc. of Friends. Author: Life and Writings of John Bunyan, 1928. Editor of Week Day Sermons in King's Chapel, 1925. Contbr. to Best Sermons, Book IV, and to Boston Preachers. Editor Creative Lives (series of biographies). Literary editor Christian Leader, 1927-38. Home: Swarthmore, Pa.

SPEISER, Ephraim Avigdor, Orientalist; b. Skalat, Galicia, Jan. 24, 1902; s. Jonas and Anna (Greenberg) S.; grad. Coll. of Lemberg, Austria, 1918; M.A., Univ. of Pennsylvania, 1923; Ph.D., Dropsie Coll., Philadelphia, Pa., 1924; m. Sue Gimbel Dannenbaum, July, 1937. Came to U.S., 1920, naturalized, 1926. Harrison research fellow in Semitics, U. of Pa., 1924-26; Guggenheim fellow for study in Mesopotamia, 1926-28; annual prof. Am. Sch. Oriental Research, Baghdad, Iraq, 1926-27 (discovered ancient site of Tepe Gawra and directed preliminary excavations); visiting prof. in comparative linguistics, Hebrew University of Jerusalem, 1927; asst. prof. Semitics, University of Pa., 1928-31, prof. since 1931; part-time prof. history of the Ancient Orient, Dropsie College, since 1934; field dir. joint excavations Am. Sch. Oriental Research and Mus. of U. of Pa. in Mesopotamia, 1930-32 and, 1936-37, non-resident dir. Am. Sch. Oriental Research in Baghdad since 1932. Mem. Am. Oriental Soc. (dir. 1932-36), Am. Council of Learned Socs. (sec. of Near Eastern com.), Am. Schs. Oriental Research (exec. com. 1932-35; trustee since 1935), Archæol. Inst. America, Linguistic Soc. America, Soc. Bibl. Lit., Phi Beta Kappa. Hebrew religion. Club: Oriental. Author: Mesopotamian Origins, 1930; Excavations at Tepe Gawra (vol. 1), 1935; One Hundred New Selected Nuzi Texts (with R. H. Pfeiffer), 1937; also several monographs on archæol., philol. and hist. subjects. Joint editor vols. of Am. Oriental Series and of publs. of Am. Schs. Oriental Research; spl. editor for Webster's New Internat. Dictionary. Writer of numerous reviews and articles. Address: University of Pennsylvania, Philadelphia, Pa.

SPELLER, Frank Newman, metall. engr.; b. Toronto, Can., Jan. 1, 1875; s. Newman W. and Elizabeth (Carfrae) S.; B.A.Sc., U. of Toronto, 1894; hon. D.Sc., U. of Toronto, 1923; came to U.S., 1901, naturalized, 1911; m. Roberta T. Hughes, Feb. 20, 1906. Asst. in chem. lab. and miscellaneous mining and metall. jobs; asso. with Nat. Tube Co. continuously since 1901, metall. engr., 1905-28, head metall. and research dept., 1928-39, advisory engr. since Jan. 1, 1939. Chmn. Metall. Adv. Bd. Carnegie Inst. Tech. Mem. Am. Inst. Mech. Engrs., Am. Soc. Mech. Engrs., Am. Soc. for Testing Materials. Honored by award medal by Am. Iron and Steel Inst., Longstreth Medal by Franklin Inst. Republican. Presbyn. Clubs: University (Pittsburgh); Engineers (New York). Home: 6411 Darlington Rd. Office: Frick Bldg., Pittsburgh, Pa.

SPELLISSY, Frederic F., banker; b. Philadelphia, Pa.; s. William and Sara E. (Jones) S.; ed. Central High Sch., Philadelphia; m. Laura Roth; 1 dau., Dorothy (Mrs. Seth W. Watson). Began as office boy Market St. Nat. Bank, Philadelphia, 1888, advanced through various positions, becoming v.p., now also dir.; treas. Northern Liberties Federal Savings & Loan Assn. of Philadelphia; dir. Chestnut Hill (Pa.) Title & Trust Co. Mem. Assn. of Reserve City Bankers. Clubs: Union League, Old York Road Country (Phila.). Home: 357 Pelham Road. Address: P.O. Box 7727, Philadelphia, Pa.

SPELLMIRE, Walter Bertrand, mgr.; b. Cincinnati, O., Dec. 3, 1875; s. Joseph H. and Elizabeth (Parnell) S.; B.S. in Engring., U. of Cincinnati, 1897; m. Alice Cleveland Allen, Nov. 26, 1913; children—Marion, Gertrude, Mary Alice. Sales engr. Allis Chalmers Co., 1897-1912; sales engr. Gen. Electric Co., 1912-16, mgr. Pittsburgh office since 1916. Trustee Masonic Fund Soc., Pittsburgh. Mem. Assn. Iron and Steel Engrs., Am. Inst. Elec. Engrs., Electric League of Pittsburgh, Engrs. Soc. Western Pa. (ex-pres., dir.), U.S. Chamber of Commerce (nat. councillor), Pa. State Chamber of Commerce, Pittsburgh Chamber of Commerce (dir.), U. of Cincinnati Alumni (pres. Pittsburgh chapter). Republican. Unitarian (pres. and mem. bd. trustees First Ch.). Clubs: University of Pittsburgh, Duquesne, Longue Vue, Rolling Rock, Civic of Allegheny County. Home: 5701 Solway St. Office: 436 7th Av., Pittsburgh, Pa.

SPENCE, George Knox, chemist; b. New York, N.Y., Dec. 10, 1872; s. David and Annie (Heslip) S.; ed. 2d Ward Pub. Sch., Pittsburgh; student Pa. State Coll. Prep. Sch., 1889-91; B.S., Pa. State Coll., 1895, M.S., 1910; m. Anne Martin, May 20, 1901; children—Margaret Dale (Mrs. Henry P. Vaughan), George Roland. Asst. chemist Ohio Steel Co., 1895-98; chemist N.Y. and Pa. Co. Pulp & Paper Mills, 1898-1900; chief chemist and supt. recovery dept. N.Y. & Pa. Co., 1900-08, chief chemist and supt. electric bleach plant, 1908-12, chief engring. chemist for all mills, 1912-18; chief engring. Chemist for all mills of N.Y. & Pa. Co. and Castanea Paper Co. since 1918. Mem. Johnsonburg Borough Council, 1910-12; chief burgess, Johnsonburg, 1923-28. Sch. dir., 1929-42. Mem. Tech. Assn. Pulp & Paper Industry (pres. 1925-27, exec. com. 1921-24), Pa. Stream Improvement and Water Disposal Com., Nat. Stream Improvement Com., Stream Polution Com. of Pa. Chamber of Commerce, Sigma Chi. Republican. Episcopalian. Mason, Elk. Club: Elk County Country (Ridgway, Pa.). Wrote Paper Section of Chemical Technology (I.C.S.), 1902, rev., 1910, also many articles in paper trade jours. (many copied by English, French and German trade papers). Assisted in compiling data for Paper Technology. Invented basket type electrolytic cell for manufacture of chlorine and caustic soda. Originated with J. M. Krause the weight factor method for determining fibre content of a sheet of paper; improved many other laboratory methods for pulp, paper and raw materials testing. Home: 704 Bridge St. Office: 100 W. Centre St., Johnsonburg, Pa.

SPENCER, Edith Louise, dean of women; b. Richville, N.Y., Mar. 28, 1895; d. Clinton L. and Anabel (Spooner) S.; B.S., N.Y. State Coll. for Teachers, 1917; student Boston Lyceum Sch., 1921; A.M., Teachers Coll. of Columbia U., 1927, spl. study, 1935-36, Diploma as Adviser of Women and Girls. Began career as hosp. dietitian, 1918; teacher of music and drawing; dir. cafeteria of Y.W.C.A.; mem. light opera co. in chautauqua and lyceum circuits; professional whistler on concert stage; mem. several choirs and choral socs. in various cities; dean of women since 1927; dean of women and asst. prof. art, Juniata Coll., Huntingdon, Pa., since 1936. Registered as dietitian with Am. Red Cross, 1917-20. Mem. Nat. Assn. Deans of Women, Pa. State Assn. Deans of Women, N.E.A., Pa. State Edn. Assn., Am. Assn. Univ. Women, Teachers Coll. Alumni Assn. N.Y. State Teachers Coll. Alumni Assn., Pi Gamma Mu. Republican. Presbyterian. Clubs: Music (Huntingdon, Pa.); Civic Symphony Assn. (Altoona, Pa.). Address: Juniata College, Huntingdon, Pa.; summer, Mohican Lakes, Glen Spey, N.Y.

SPENCER, Eleanor Patterson, coll. prof.; b. Northampton, Mass., 1895; d. William H. and Mary L. (Langdon) S.; A.B., Smith Coll., 1917, A.M., 1919; grad. student, Sorbonne and Ecole du Louvre, 1920-21; Ph.D., Radcliffe Coll., 1931. Asst. in dept. of art, Smith Coll., 1917-18; instr. of fine arts, Mt. Holyoke Coll., South Hadley, Mass., 1919-20; instr. of fine arts, Pine Manor Jr. Coll., Wellesley, Mass., 1921-27; asso. prof. fine arts, Goucher Coll., Baltimore, Md., 1930-36, prof. since 1936. Mem. Coll. Art Assn., Am. Assn. Univ. Profs., Phi Beta Kappa. Awarded Sachs fellowship, Harvard, 1928-30. Republican. Episcopalian. Home: Calvert and 31st St. Address: Goucher College, Baltimore, Md.

SPENCER, Francis Erle, physician; b. Oxford, Pa., Dec. 4, 1891; s. George and Elizabeth Jane (Robinson) S.; student West Grove (Pa.) High Sch., 1907-10; M.D., Hahnemann Med. Coll., Phila., 1915; m. Margaret Weer, Nov. 1935; children—Elizabeth Jane, Richard Crowe. Began as physician, 1917, and in gen. practice, 1917-29, specializing in obstetrics and gynecology; chief obstetrics and gynecology dept., Homœopathic Hosp., Wilmington. Mem. Del. State Med. Soc., New Castle County Med. Soc. Republican. Home: Weldin Rd. Office: 1101 Delaware Av., Wilmington, Del.

SPENCER, Hazelton, univ. prof.; b. Methuen, Mass., July 7, 1893; s. George Hazelton and Rosetta Mary (Munroe) S.; Norwich U., 1910-11; A.B., Boston U., 1915; A.M., Harvard, 1920, Ph.D., 1923; m. Gladys Louise Woodward, 1917 (divorced); children—Cynthia, John Hazelton, Jane, Lydia; m. 2d, Louise Smurthwaite Cline, 1933. English teacher, secondary schools, 1915-19; assistant in English, Harvard, 1921-23; assistant prof. English, University of Minn., 1923-24; asso. prof., prof., and head dept. of English, State Coll. of Wash., 1924-28; associate professor English, Johns Hopkins, 1928-37, prof. since 1937; visiting instructor, summers, U. of Ia., 1926, Harvard, 1930, 1932, Duke University, 1937, 39, Bread Loaf School of English, 1938. Mem. Modern Lang. Assn. America, Modern Humanities Research Assn., Am. Assn. Univ. Profs., Lambda, Theta Delta Chi, Phi Beta Kappa. Independent Democrat. Clubs: Johns Hopkins, Tudor and Stuart. Author: Shakespeare Improved, 1927. Editor: Selected Poems of Vachel Lindsay, 1931; Shakespeare's King Richard III, 1933; Elizabethan Plays, 1933. Contbr. to Am. and foreign philol. and lit. jours. Co-editor of Modern Language Notes, 1930—. Address: Johns Hopkins University, Baltimore, Md.

SPENCER, Herbert Lincoln, coll. pres.; b. Whitney Point, N.Y., July 13, 1894; s. William Henry and Ida Dell (Adriance) S.; grad. Whitney Point High Sch., 1913; B.S., Carnegie Inst. Tech., 1921; M.A., Ph.D., U. of Pittsburgh, 1934; m. Mildred Louise Pollard, June 6, 1916; children—Nancy Lynn, Sally Louise. Mech. engr. various industrial orgns., 1916-21; v. prin. and teacher Latimer Jr. High Sch., Pittsburgh, 1922-27; vice prin. Henry Clay Frick Training Sch. for Teachers, Pittsburgh, 1927-28, prin., 1928-34; dean Coll. Liberal Arts and Sciences, U. of Pittsburgh, 1934-35; pres. Pa. Coll. for Women, Pittsburgh, since 1935. Served as engr. A.C., U.S. Army, World War. Dir. Pittsburgh Child Guidance Clinic, Inc., Metropolitan Y.M.C.A., Federation Social Agencies. Mem. N.E.A., A.A.A.S., Pa. State Edn. Assn., Pittsburgh Acad. Science and Art, Photographic Soc. of America, Phi Delta Kappa, Kappa Phi Kappa, Iota Lambda Sigma, Phi Sigma Pi, Delta Tau Delta, Omicron Delta Kappa, Scabbard and Blade. Presbyn. Mason (32°). Clubs: Rotary, University, University of Pittsburgh Faculty Club, Unity. Address: Pennsylvania College for Women, Woodland Rd., Pittsburgh, Pa.

SPENCER, James Herbert, Jr., surgeon; b. New Athens, O., July 13, 1899; s. James Herbert and Martha Clyde (Poppino) S.; student Westminster Coll., New Wilmington, Pa., 1917-18; B.S., Coll. of Wooster, O., 1921; student Cornell U. Med. Coll., 1922-24; M.D., U. of Pa. Med. Sch., 1926; m. Ruth Whittlesey, Dec. 29, 1927; children—James Herbert III, Robert Whittlesey. Interne Harper Hosp., Detroit, Mich., 1926-27; asst. prof. anatomy, U. of Tenn. Med. Sch., Memphis, 1927-29; surg. resident, West Penn Hosp., Pittsburgh, Pa., 1929-30, asst. surgeon, 1930-31; in pvt. practice at Newton, N.J., 1931-34 and at Franklin, N.J., since 1934; surgeon, Franklin Hosp., 1931-34, surgeon in chief since 1934; surgeon, Newton Memorial Hosp., since 1932; mem. courtesy surg. staff, Horton Memorial Hosp., Middletown, N.Y., since 1931; asso. attending surgeon, St. Anthony's Hosp., Warwick, N.Y., since 1939; surgeon N.J. Zinc Co., Franklin, N.J., since 1934. Served in inf., U.S.A., 1918; 1st lt. Med. Res. Corps, 1926-27, capt. 1928-29; capt. Med. Corps, Tenn. N.G., 1928-29. Fellow Am. Coll. Surgeons, A.M.A.; mem. Sussex County Med. Soc. (pres. 1938-39). Diplomate Nat. Bd. Med. Examiners. Republican. Presbyn. Clubs: Tennis (pres.), Camera (Franklin); Tennis (Newton). President Sussex County Medical Society, 1938-39. Home: 19 Hospital Rd. Office: 23 Hospital Rd., Franklin, N.J.

SPENCER, Jervis, Jr.; v.p. and treas. Maryland Trust Co. Office: N.W. corner Calvert and Redwood Sts., Baltimore, Md.

SPENCER, Judah Colt, banker; b. Erie, Pa., Sept. 29, 1883; s. William and Mary Richards (DuPuy) S.; grad. Hill Sch., Pottstown, Pa., 1903; A.B., Princeton U., 1907; m. Almira Durban, 1917; children—Mary, George Colt, Thomas Durban. With Erie (Pa.) Foundry Co., mfrs., 1907-08; with Fulton Mfg. Co., Erie, Pa., 1908-17; with First Nat. Bank of Erie since 1917, beginning as asst. to pres. and became pres. in 1937; pres. and dir. Lawrence Park Nat. Bank since 1930. Republican. Presbyterian. Home: R.D. No. 4, Chestnut Hill, Erie, Pa. Office: 717 State St., Erie, Pa.

SPENCER, Kenneth, pres. Globe Indemnity Co.; b. Marshall, Mo., May 26, 1888; s. Thomas Edwin and Mary Lavina (Strother) S.; student of engring., U. of Mo., 1904-08; m. Mignon Martina Grasse, of St. Louis, Mo., Oct. 24, 1910; children—Mary Lavina, Elizabeth Jane. Newspaper reporter Globe-Democrat, St. Louis, 1909-10, St. Louis Star, 1910-11; special agent Ocean Accident & Guarantee Corpn., Ltd., 1911-12; asst. Western mgr. Globe Indemnity Co., 1912-16, Pacific Coast mgr., 1916-20; Pacific Coast mgr. Norwich Union and Phoenix Ins. cos., 1920-25; asst. sec. Globe Indemnity Co., New York, 1925-27, v.p., 1927-39, pres. and dir. since 1939. Mem. Sigma Alpha Epsilon. Methodist. Mason (K.T.). Clubs: Drug and Chemical (New York); Upper Montclair Country (Montclair, N.J.); Marine Golf and Country (San Rafael, Calif.). Home: 6 Sutherland Rd., Montclair, N.J. Office: 150 William St., New York, N.Y.

SPENCER, Robert Lyle, univ. dean of engring.; b. St. Johnsburg, Vt., Mar. 7, 1887; s. Carl McClelland and Mary (Burbank) S.; student Des Moines (Ia.) Pub. Schs., 1896-1905; B.S. in M.E., Ia. State Coll., Ames, Ia., 1912; m. Gertrude Levering, July 8, 1914; children—Marion Stephens, Kathleen, Roberta Levering. Instr. mech. engring., Lehigh U., Bethlehem, Pa., 1912-14, asst. prof., 1914-18; combustion engr. Bethlehem Steel Co., Bethlehem, Pa., 1918-20; supt. of steam Standard Oil Co. of Ind., Casper, Wyo., 1920-23; chief engr. Heine Boiler Co., St. Louis, Mo., 1925-27; proposition engr., Combustion Engring. Corpn., New York, 1927-28; dean of engring., U. of Del., Newark, Del., since 1928. Dir. Del. Safety Council. Fellow A.A.A.S.; mem. Am. Soc. M.E., Soc. for Promotion Engring. Edn., Newcomen Soc. (Eng.), Phi Kappa Phi, Tau Beta Pi. Republican. Congregationalist. Author numerous articles on steam power plants and engring. edn. for tech. and ednl. jours. Holds several patents on subjects relating to steam boilers, superheaters, etc. Address: 61 Kells Av., Newark, Del.

SPENCER, Roscoe Roy, M.D.; b. King William Co., Va., Jan. 28, 1888; s. Branch Worsham and Emma Roy (Burke) S.; A.B., Richmond (Va.) Coll., 1909; M.D., Johns Hopkins, 1913; m. Mary Garland Grasty, Oct. 23, 1915; children—Nathaniel Roscoe, Mary Garland. In U.S. Pub. Health Service, 1913—, now sr. surgeon; sanitary adviser to Navy Dept., 1917-18; officer in charge bubonic plague suppressive measures, Pensacola, Fla., 1919-21; in charge investigations of Rocky Mountain spotted fever, 1922-29; asso. prof. preventive medicine, George Washington U. since 1932. Exec. asst. National Cancer Inst. since 1938. Member American Medical Association, American Soc. Bacteriologists, Assn. Mil. Surgeons of U.S., Mont. Health Officers Assn. (pres. 1928), S.A.R., Phi Chi, Phi Beta Kappa and Sigma Xi frats. Club: Cosmos. Author: (with Dr. R. R. Parker) Rocky Mountain Spotted Fever, 1929. Discoverer of a preventive vaccine for Rocky Mountain spotted fever, and awarded gold medal for same, 1930, by Am. Med. Assn. Editor of "The Health Officer," 1936-38. Home: 3917 Oliver St., Chevy Chase, Md. Office: U.S. Public Health Service, Washington, D.C.

SPERR, Frederick William, Jr., cons. chemist; b. Jefferson, O., Dec. 27, 1885; s. Frederick William and Julia (Loomis) S.; A.B., O. State U., 1906; m. Lois E. Smith, Dec. 11, 1912; children—Frederick Hugh, Julia Ina (dec.), Lois Jeanette. Employed as chemist, Westinghouse Electric & Mfg. Co., 1906-08; civil and mining engr., 1908-10; chemist By-Product Coke Dept., Illinois Steel Co., 1910-12; chief chemist By-Product Coke Plant, Tenn. Coal, Iron & R.R. Co., 1912-13; chief chemist, Coke and Blast Furnace depts., Inland Steel Co., 1913-15; chief chemist, Koppers Co., 1915-25, dir. research, 1925-30; sr. fellow Mellon Inst., 1916-30; pres. Koppers Research Corpn., 1930-31; cons. chemist, Vineland, N.J. since 1931. Mem. Am. Chem. Soc., Am. Inst. Chem. Engrs., Franklin Inst., Sigma Xi, Phi Beta Kappa. Awarded Beal Medal, Am. Gas Assn., 1920, 1926. Republican. Club: Chemists (New York). Home: Vineland, N.J.

SPERRING, William F., wholesale lumber; b. Whethan, Pa., Mar. 4, 1859; s. Henry and Jane (Twigg) S.; student Lock Haven (Pa.) pub. and high schs.; grad. Christus Business Coll., 1884 (finishing in 12 weeks); m. Rosa M. Brutzman, Mar. 10, 1887 (died 1934); 1 dau., Ada Elizabeth (dec.). Left school at age of 16 to take position as tally boy in shipping lumber on canal boats; later counted lumber at the mill and inspected stock when manufactured; for seven winters worked in woods scaling logs and looking after stocking of logs and timber rafts for Pardee & Cook, Lock Haven, Pa.; after graduation from coll. became bookkeeper for same company, holding position until company disbanded; in wholesale lumber business under name of W. F. Sperring, Lock Haven, Pa., since 1914; dir. First Nat. Bank, Lock Haven, Pa. Mayor, Lock Haven, 1901-03 and 1928-33; mem. sch. bd., 6 yrs. Democrat. Presbyterian. Elk. Home: 601 Bellefonte Av., Lock Haven, Pa.

SPERRY, Melvin G.; mem. law firm Sperry & Snider. Office: Empire Bldg., Clarksburg, W.Va.

SPIEGEL, Ernest Adolf, M.D., coll. prof.; b. Vienna, Austria, July 24, 1895; s. Dr. Ignaz and Elise (Fuchs) S.; student Gymnasium, Vienna, 1905-13, Univ. of Vienna Med. Sch., 1913-18 (M.D.); m. Anna Simona (Mona) Adolf, Aug. 8, 1925. Came to U.S., 1930, naturalized, 1936. Began as physician, 1918; asst. Neurological Inst. and Polyclinic, Univ. of Vienna, 1919-24, docent, 1924-30; prof. of exptl. neurology and head of dept., Temple U. Sch. of Medicine, Phila., since 1930. Fellow Coll. of Physicians of Phila., Am. Med. Assn.; mem. Am. Neurol. Assn., Am. Physiol. Soc., Am. Therapeutic Soc., Harvey Cushing Soc., Soc. Exptl. Biology, Phila. Neurol. Soc., Phila Physiol. Soc., Assn. Nervous and Mental Diseases. Editor of Confinia Neurologica. Author of 160 scientific articles and 4 books on nervous system and nervous diseases. Home: 6807 Lawnton Av., Oak Lane, Philadelphia, Pa.

SPIEGEL-ADOLF, Anna Simona (Mona), M.D., coll. prof.; b. Vienna, Austria, Feb. 23, 1893; d. Dr. Jacques and Hedwig (Spitzer) Adolf; student Gymnasium, Vienna, 1905-13, Univ. of Vienna, Medical Sch., 1913-18 (M.D.); m. Dr. Ernest Adolf Spiegel, Aug. 8, 1925. Came to U.S., 1930, naturalized, 1936. Began as physician, Vienna, 1918; asst., Inst. of Med. Colloid Chemistry, Univ. of Vienna, 1921-30, docent, 1930; prof. of colloid chemistry and head of dept., Temple U. Sch. of Med., Phila., since 1930. Mem. Am. Am. Soc. Biol. Chemists, Biochem. Soc. (London), Am. Chem. Soc., Soc. of Exptl. Biology and Medicine, A.A.A.S., Phila. Physiol. Soc. Club: Women's University (Phila.). Co-editor: Fundamenta Radiologica and Radiologica clinica. Author of 1 book and more than 75 papers on physio-chemistry of proteins and liquids, effect of radiations, etc. Home: 6807 Lawnton Av., Oak Lane, Philadelphia, Pa.

SPIKER, Claude Carl; prof. French and Spanish, W.Va. U. Address: West Virginia U., Morgantown, W.Va.

SPILLER, Robert Ernest, prof. English; b. Phila., Pa., Nov. 13, 1896; s. William G. and Helen Constance (Newbold) S.; B.A., U. of Pa., 1917, Harrison fellow, 1919-20, M.A., 1921, Ph.D., 1924; Guggenheim fellow for foreign study, 1928-29; m. Mary Scott, June 17, 1922; children—William Scott, Constance Newbold, Mary Miles. Instr. in English, U. of Pa., 1920-21; with Swarthmore Coll. since 1921, asso. prof. English 1930-34, prof. since 1934, chmn. Humanities Div. since 1935; prof. English, summers, Duke Univ., 1927, Harvard Univ. 1930, Columbia Univ., 1931, 1937, Univ. of Southern Calif. 1933, Univ. of Mich., 1936. Advisory editor to American Literature, 1928-31, editor since 1932. Served with A.E.F. World War. Chmn. Coll. Conf. on English of Middle States and Md., 1934. Mem. Modern Language Assn. America (chmn. Am. lit. group, 1930, 31), Am. Assn. of Univ. Profs., Phi Beta Kappa. Pres. bd. dirs. The School in Rose Valley, 1931-32, 1934-35. Clubs: Franklin Inn, Writeabout (Phila.). Author: The American in England During the First Half Century of Independence, 1926; Fenimore Cooper, Critic of His Times, 1931; The Roots of National Culture (anthology), 1933. Editor: Critical Prose of Fenimore Cooper—Vol. I, Gleanings in Europe, France, 1928, Vol. II, Gleanings in Europe, England, 1930; A Descriptive Bibliography of James Fenimore Cooper (with P. C. Blackburn), 1934; James Fenimore Cooper, Representative Selections, 1936; Satanstoe (with J. D. Coppock) 1937; Esther, by Henry Adams, 1938. Contbr. to mags. Home: Swarthmore, Pa.

SPILLER, William Gibson, neurologist; b. Baltimore, Sept. 13, 1863; s. Robert Miles and Anna Augusta (Maltby) S.; M.D., U. of Pa., 1892; Sc.D., U. of Pa., 1934; LL.D., Lafayette, 1934; m. Helen C. Newbold, Jan. 3, 1888; children—Helen Newbold (Mrs. Randolph G. Adams), Robert Ernest, William Raymond, Donald Percival. Asst. clin. prof. nervous diseases and asst. prof. neuropathology, University of Pa., 1901-03, prof. neuropathology and associate prof. neurology, 1903-15, professor of neurology, 1915-1932 (emeritus); formerly prof. nervous diseases, Phila. Polyclinic; clin. prof.; Woman's Med. Coll. of Pa., 1902-25; hon. consulting neurologist Phila. Gen. Hos. Mem. Am. Neurol. Assn. (pres. 1905); Phila. Neurol. Soc. (ex-pres.), Phila. County Med. Soc., A.M.A.; fellow Coll. Physicians, Phila.; hon. fellow Acad. of Medicine, New York; corr. member Gesellschaft deutscher Nervenärzte, Soc. de Neurologie de Paris, Verein für Psychiatrie und Neurologie, Vienna; hon. mem. Soc. Estonienne de Neurologie. Extensive contbr. on neurology. Home: 4409 Pine St., Philadelphia, Pa.

SPILMAN, Edwin A., pres. Citizens Savings Bank. Home: 3200 N. Hilton St. Office: Baltimore and Eutaw St., Baltimore, Md.

SPILMAN, Robert Scott, lawyer; b. Warrenton, Fauquier Co., Va., Mar. 22, 1876; s. William Mason and Henningham Lyons (Scott) S.; B.S., Va. Mil. Inst., Lexington 1896 (Jackson Hope medal); law student U. of Va., 1899-1900; m. Eliza Polk Dillon, Apr. 4, 1907; children— Robert Scott, Frances Polk (dec.), Edward Dillon, Lisa Polk. Comdt. Sewanee (Tenn.) Sch., 1896-97; asst. prof. English, Va. Mil. Inst., 1897-99; admitted to W.Va. bar, 1900, and practiced since at Charleston; mem. firm Price, Smith & Spilman; dir. and counsel Kanawha Banking & Trust Co., Coal Run Coal Co., etc. Pres. State Bd. Law Examiners, W. Va., 1919-34; mem. Sch. Bd., Charleston, 1914-32; pres. Charleston Open Forum, 1935-39. Mem. Am. Bar Assn., Am. Law Inst., Am. Judicature Soc., W.Va. Bar Assn. (pres. 1919-20), Kappa Alpha. Democrat. Episcopalian. Mason. Clubs: Edgewood Country, Black Knight Country, Kanawha Country, Church Club of New York. Home: South Hills, Charleston. Office: Kanawha Banking & Trust Bldg., Charleston, W.Va.

SPILMAN, Robert Scott, Jr., lawyer; b. Charleston, W.Va., Jan. 6, 1908; s. Robert Scott and Eliza Polk (Dillon) S.; A.B., Va. Mil. Inst., Lexington, Va., 1928; LL.B., Harvard U. Law Sch., 1932; unmarried. Engaged as instr. Am. history, Va. Mil. Inst., 1928-29; admitted to W.Va. bar, 1932, and since engaged in gen. practice of law at Charleston; mem. firm Price, Smith & Spilman since 1937; served as mem. City Council of Charleston, 1935-39. Second vice-pres. Charleston Community Chest since 1938. Dir. Mason Coll. of Music. Mem. Am. Bar Assn., W.Va., Bar Assn., City of Charleston Bar Assn. (v.p. 1938), Kappa Alpha. Democrat. Episcopalian. Club: Edgewood Country (Charleston). Home: Roscomon Rd. Office: Kanawha Banking & Trust Bldg., Charleston, W.Va.

SPINGARN, Samuel, lawyer; b. West Hoboken (now Union City), N.J., Aug. 11, 1895; s. Emanuel and Celia (Vogler) S.; A.B., Columbia U., 1916; student Columbia U. Law Sch., 1915-18, Univ. de Poitiers, France, 1919; unmarried. Admitted to N.J. bar as atty., 1920, as counselor, 1923; asso. with firm Treacy & Milton, Jersey City, N.J., 1920-22, in practice alone at Union City, N.J., 1923-32; mem. firm Spingarn & Sachs, Union City, N.J., since 1932; dir. and counsel Sentinel Bldg. & Loan Assn. since 1922; served as counsel bd. edn., Union City, N.J., since 1926. Served corporal inf., U.S.A., 1918-19 with A.E.F. in France. Comdr. Dept. N.J., Am. Legion, 1933-34. Dir. Hebrew Home for Orphans and Aged of Hudson County, N.J. Mem. N.J. State and Hudson Co. bar assns., North Hudson Lawyers Club (pres. 1934), Pi Lambda Phi. Democrat. Jewish religion. Mason (32°, Shriner). B'nai B'rith. Am. Legion. Home: 442 New York Av. Office: 415 32d St., Union City, N.J.

SPINKS, Lewis, corpn. exec.; b. Leesburg, Va., Nov. 10, 1879; s. Alexander and Ada (Nixon) S.; ed. pub. schs. of Leesburg, night courses, New York U. Am. Bankers Inst. and other finance schs.; m. Ila Steger, May 28, 1899 (died 1908); 1 son, Russell Dudley; m. 2d, Louise Mason, June 8, 1911; 1 dau., Orra. Began as cost accountant Crescent Shipyard, 1898; timekeeper Naughton & Co., contractors, 1900-02; cost accountant Internat. Powder Co., 1902-03; treas. Standard Motor Constrn. Co. of N.J., 1903-08, v.p. and treas., 1908-30; v.p. and mgr. Raritan River Sand Co. since 1930. Mem. State Fish and Game Commn. since 1922, term ending 1939 (treas. 8 yrs; v.p. since 1937). Mem. S.A.R. (Md. Soc.). Democrat. Home: 501 Raritan Av., Highland Park, N.J. Office: Nixon, N.J.

SPITZER, Leo, univ. prof.; b. Vienna, Austria, Feb. 7, 1887; s. Wilhelm and Adele S.; came to U.S., 1935; ed at univs. of Vienna, Paris, Leipzig, Rome; m. Emma, 1919; 1 son, Wolfgang. Engaged as prof. Romance langs. at univs. of Vienna, Bonn, Marburg, Cologne, Istanbul, 1913-35; prof. Romance langs., Johns Hopkins U. since 1935. Mem. Modern Lang. Assn. of America. Jewish religion. Home: 300 E. 30th St. Address: Johns Hopkins Univ., Baltimore, Md.

SPITZNAS, James Ernest, educator; b. Frostburg, Md., July 24, 1892; s. Albert and Sarah (Goldsworthy) S.; Ph.B., Dickinson Coll., Carlisle, Pa., 1915, A.M., 1921; student W.Va. U., Morgantown, W.Va., summer 1921, U. of Chicago, summer 1922; A.M. in Edn., Columbia U. Teachers Coll., 1928; m. Elizabeth Norris Daughtrey, June 28, 1933; children—James Ernest, Jr., Elizabeth Laney. Engaged in teaching, high sch., Cape May, N.J., 1915-16, Chester, Pa., 1916-18, Frostburg, Md., 1919-24; prin. high sch., Frostburg, Md., 1924-28; high sch. supervisor, Allegany Co., Md., 1928-31; prin. high sch., Cumberland, Md., 1931-33; state supervisor high schs., western area of state, Baltimore, Md., since 1933. Served as sergt. inf., U.S.A., 1918; with advance sch. detachment, Gondrecourt, France, 1918. Mem. Am. Assn. Sch. Adminstrs., Nat. Assn. High Sch. Supervisors and Dirs., Middle States Assn. History and Social Sci. Teachers, Phi Delta Theta. Received award in nat. achievement contest sponsored by Am. Legion, 1931. Republican. Club: Rotary of Cumberland. Contbr. bull. of dept. edn. Home: La Vale, Cumberland. Office: Lexington Bldg., Baltimore, Md.

SPIVA, William Blanchet, pres. Bank of Somerset; b. Pocomoke City, Md., Jan. 4, 1874; s. Absalom and Henrietta Matthews (Feddeman) S.; student Washington High Sch., Princess Anne, Md., 1880-89; m. Margaret Dixon, Apr. 20, 1898 (died, 1920); m. 2r, Harriet Waters Murphy, Sept. 13, 1921; children—William Blanchet, Harriet Waters, R.R. telegrapher, Pa. R.R., Princess Anne, Md., Pocomoke City, Md., 1889; with Bank of Somerset (formerly Savings bank of Somerset Co.), Princess Anne, Md., since 1889, successively as runner and clerk, asst. cashier and cashier, dir. since 1912, pres. since 1929. Chmn. Liberty Loan Com. for Somerset Co. (Md.) during World War. Mem. Bd. of Govs., Washington Coll., Chestertown, Md., 1924-31; treas. Somerset Co. (Md.) chapter Am. Red Cross, 1914-39. Democrat. Episcopalian (Vestryman, St. Andrew's P.E. Ch., Princess Anne, Md.). Club: Eastern Shore Soc. (Baltimore, Md.). Address: Princess Anne, Md.

SPOFFORD, Thomas Wright, lawyer; b. North East, Pa., Aug. 20, 1885; s. James L. and Alice (Hitchcock) S.; ed. high sch., North East, Pa., 1900-04; LL.B., U. of Mich. Law Sch., 1908; m. Isabelle Pancake, Nov. 22, 1916; 1 son, Thomas Edwin. Admitted to Utah bar and in practice at Salt Lake City, 1909 to 1910; admitted to Pa. bar, 1913 and since engaged in gen. practice of law at Erie; employed in codification of Pa. laws with Legislative Reference Bur., Harrisburg, 1913-15. Mem. Pa. State and Erie Co. bar assns. Republican. Methodist. Mason (32°, Shriner). Home: 1039 W. 24th St. Office: 607 Masonic Temple, Erie, Pa.

SPOFFORD, William Benjamin, clergyman, editor; b. Claremont, N.H., Apr. 5, 1892; s. Charles Byron and Marcia (Nourse) S.; B.S., Trinity Coll., Conn., 1914; grad. Berkeley Div. Sch., 1917; studied New York Sch. of Social Work, 1917; m. Dorothy Grace Ibbotson, Aug. 5, 1915; children—William Benjamin, Marcia Grace, Suzanne. Deacon, 1917, priest, 1918, Protestant Episcopal Church; master St. Paul's School, Concord, New Hampshire, 1917-19; rector St. George's Ch., Chicago, 1919-22; labor manager B. Kuppenheimer & Company, clothing manufacturers, Chicago, 1919-23; editor The Witness, P.E. Ch. weekly, New York, since 1919; exec. sec. Ch. League for Industrial Democracy since 1922. Rector Christ P.E. Ch., Middletown, N.J. Mem. bd. dirs. Am. Civil Liberties Union; mem. Psi Upsilon. Home: Middletown, N.J. Office: 135 Liberty St., New York, N.Y.

SPOONER, Thomas, lab. mgr.; b. Whitefield, N.H., Jan. 1, 1884; s. Thomas and Clara (Prescott) S.; A.B., Bates Coll., Lewiston, Me., 1905; B.S., Mass. Inst. Tech., 1909; m. Laura Leonard Flinn, 1916; children—Patricia Flinn, Alice Florence. Engaged in elec. construction Stone & Webster, 1905-06, paper mill design Odell Mfg. Co., Groveton, N.H., 1906-07; research engr. Westinghouse Electric & Mfg. Co., E. Pittsburgh, 1909-29, asst. to dir. of research labs., 1929-36, mgr. research labs. since 1936. Mem. Am. Inst. E.E., Am. Soc. Testing Materials, Am. Phys. Soc. Republican. Baptist. Clubs: Westinghouse (ex-pres.). Contbr. to tech. and scientific publs. Home: 1016 Trenton Av., Wilkinsburg, Pa. Office: Westinghouse Electric & Mfg. Co., East Pittsburgh, Pa.

SPOTTS, Charles Dewey, coll. prof.; b. Cambridge, Pa., Apr. 26, 1899; s. Joseph Edgar and Mary Dorothy (Gault) S.; A.B., Franklin & Marshall Coll., 1922; B.D., Theol. Sem. of Reformed Ch. 1925; A.M., U. of Pa., 1933; m. Lucy B. Musselman, June 17, 1925; children—Mary Jane, Nancy Lou. Pastor St. Peter's Reformed Ch., Lancaster, 1925-31; prof. dept. of religion, Franklin & Marshall Coll., since 1931. Mem. Lancaster Bd. of Edn. since 1933. Served as private, S.A.T.C., Oct. 8, 1918-Dec. 12, 1918. Mem. exec. bd. Lancaster County Council, Boy Scouts of America; mem. Commn. on Christian Social Action, Evangelical and Reformed Church; dir. Lancaster Law and Order Soc., Recreation and Playground Assn. Mem. Phi Kappa Tau, Phi Beta Kappa, Pi Gamma Mu, Phi Delta Kappa, Phi Upsilon Kappa. Home: 834 Buchanan Av., Lancaster, Pa.

SPRAGUE, George Clare, lawyer; b. Vermontville, Michigan, June 21, 1884; s. Ernest E. and Ezoa Frances (Potter) S.; B.A., Olivet (Michigan) Coll., 1905, LL.D. from the same college, 1934; Ph.D., New York University, 1908, LL. B., 1910; m. Laura Briscoe Selden, Sept. 1, 1908; children—Joseph S. (dec.), Elizabeth Frances, Virginia Laura, Evelyn Eleanor. Instr.

history, Prospect Heights Sch., Brooklyn, 1905-08; registrar 1908-15, instr. in law, 1911-17, asst. prof. since 1917, New York U.; spl. lecturer on admiralty law, Columbia U. Law Sch., 1929; mem. Hunt, Hill & Betts, 1920-34, Crawford & Sprague since May 1, 1934. Republican. Presbyterian. Mem. Am. Bar Assn., Assn. Bar City of N.Y. (chmn. admiralty com. since 1937), Internat. Law Assn., Maritime Law Assn. of U.S. (sec.-treas. since 1937), Japan Soc., Phi Alpha Pi (Olivet); asso. mem. Average Adjusters of U.S. (chmn. 1938-39). Candidate officer, Camp Zachary Taylor, Ky., Oct.-Nov. 1918. Club: Lawyers'. Author: (with George de Forest Lord) Cases on Admiralty, 1926; also numerous law review articles on admiralty. Home: Floyd St., Englewood, N.J.; (summer) Lake Saint Catherine, Poultney, Vt. Office: 117 Liberty St., New York, N.Y.

SPRAGUE, Harry A., coll. pres.; b. Ellington, N.Y., July 31, 1885; s. William Titus and Viola (Huntington) S.; grad. high sch., Ellington, 1902, Fredonia State Normal Sch., 1905; student Chautauqua Inst., Cornell U.; B.S., Columbia, 1915, M.A., 1917; m. Julia Meeker Conklin, Mar. 27, 1914; 1 dau., Elizabeth Conklin, Prin. Union High Sch., Farmington, N.Y., 1905-06, high and grade sch., Hinsdale, N.Y., 1906-07, Schs., No. 2 and 10, Olean, N.Y., 1907-09, City Teacher Training Sch., 1908-10; supervisor and instructor, practice and exptl. sch., Teachers Coll., Columbia, 1910-11; instr., New York U., 1915-16; supervisor and instr., City Normal Sch., Newark, N.J., 1910-14; same, N.J. State Normal Sch., Newark, 1914-18; prof. of edn. and administrator, State U. of N.J., summers 1916-23; supt. city schs., Summit, N.J., 1918-23; prin. N.J. State Normal Sch., Upper Montclair, 1924-27; pres. State Teachers Coll., Upper Montclair, since 1927. Pres. Am. Assn. of Teachers Colleges, 1935-36. Mem. A.A.A.S., N.E.A., Nat. Soc. for Scientific Study of Edn., N.J. State Teachers Assn., N.J. State Council of Edn., Council of Coll. Teachers of Edn., Supts. and Prins. Round Table Assn., Commn. on Higher Edn. of Middle States Assn., Alpha Chi Rho, Phi Delta Kappa, Kappa Delta Pi. Conglist. Clubs: Rotary, Schoolmasters'. Home: 21 Macopin Av., Upper Montclair, N.J.

SPRAGUE, Howard Bennett, prof. agronomy; b. Cortland, Neb., Dec. 11, 1898; s. Elmer Ellsworth and Lucy Kent (Manville) S.; ed. Park Coll., Parksville, Mo., 1915-17; B.S., U. of Neb., 1921, M.S., same, 1923; Ph.D., Rutgers U., 1926; m. Dorothy Silbert, Sept. 11, 1926. Engaged as asst. in agronomy, U. of Neb., 1921-23; instr. in agronomy, Rutgers U., 1923-26; asst. prof. agronomy, U. of Minn., 1926-27; asst. prof. agronomy and head dept. agronomy, Rutgers U., 1927-28, asso. prof., 1928-31, prof. agronomy since 1931; agronomist, N.J. State Agr. Expt. Sta. since 1927. Served as pvt. inf. U.S.A., 1917-19, with A.E.F. Fellow A.A.A.S. Mem. Am. Soc. Agronomy (chmn. crops sect. 1936, v.p. N.E. Sect., 1930, pres., 1935), Am. Soc. Plant Physiologists, Am. Genetics Assn., Alpha Zeta, Gamma Sigma Delta, Sigma Xi. Protestant. Club: Rutgers Faculty. Home: 119 Livingston Av., New Brunswick, N.J.

SPRAGUE, John Hanly Carroll, civil engr.; b. De Nora, Pa., Apr. 2, 1907; s. John W. and Lillian (Carroll) S.; student Marshall Coll., Huntington, W.Va., 1924-25, W.Va. Univ., 1925-26; C.E., Tri-State Coll., Angola, Ind., 1937; unmarried. Employed as engr. on constrn. and later asst. to the resident engr., N.Y. Central R.R., Buffalo, N.Y. 1926-30; asso. with U.S. Corps of Engrs. Huntington Dist. since 1930, successively chief concrete inspr. on lock and dam constrn., chief of dist. testing lab., chief of concrete and soils sect.; registered professional engr. in W.Va. Mem. W.Va. Chamber of Commerce. Asso. mem. Am. Soc. Civil Engrs. Mem. Am. Concrete Inst., Am. Soc. for Testing Materials, Nat. Soc. Professional Engrs., W.Va. Soc. Professional Engrs. Methodist. Club: Engineers (Huntington). Contbr. 13 papers and discussions to professional journs. and proceedings. Home: 637 6th St. Office: U.S. Engineers Office, Huntington, W. Va.

SPRAGUE, Wheeler S., pres. and mgr. Paper Products Mfg. Co.; b. Boonville, N. Y., Aug. 10, 1875; s. Francis I. and Malinda (Dunn) S.; student pub. schs.; unmarried. Upon graduation from sch., 1893, began work in paper mill, remaining in that business until 1900; engaged in life ins., 1900-18; organized 1918, and since pres. and dir. Paper Products Mfg. Co. Mason (K.T.; Chapter, Council, Consistory). Clubs: Springhaven Country (dir.), Turf, Craftsman's, Fox Steeplechase, Bloomsburg Golf, Art; Chester; Manufacturers and Bankers (Philadelphia). Address: Swarthmore, Pa.

SPRAY, Robb Spalding, univ. prof.; b. Omaha, Neb., Feb. 19, 1890; s. Charles Henry and Maggie Augusta (Whitcomb) S.; B.S., Purdue U., Lafayette, Ind., 1914; M.S., Pa. State Coll., 1918; Ph.D., U. of Chicago, 1923; m. Grace Meloy Stouffer, Aug. 15, 1915; 1 dau., Jean Elizabeth. Instr. botany and plant pathology, Pa. State Coll., 1915-18; asso. animal pathologist, Purdue U. Veterinary Dept., 1918-20; grad. asst., U. of Chicago Dept. of Bacteriology, 1920-21; asso. prof. bacteriology and pub. hygiene, W.Va. U. Med. Sch., Morgantown, W.Va., 1921-26, prof. since 1926, prof. and head dept. since 1937. City and County Bacteriologist, Morgantown, W.Va., 1922-35. Mem. Soc. Am. Bacteriologists, Internat. Microbiol. Cong., W.Va. Scientific Soc., Sigma Xi. Awarded Logan Fellowship, U. of Chicago, 1920. Presbyterian. Co-author: 5th edit. Bergey's Manual of Determinate Bacteriology, 1929; contbr. over 45 papers on bacteriology, particularly anaerobic bacteria. Address: Box 244, R.F.D. 4, Morgantown, W.Va.

SPRIGGS, Joseph Courtland, lawyer; b. Washington, Pa., Oct. 21, 1885; s. James Donehoo and Annie E. (Wilson) S.; B.S., Washington and Jefferson Coll., Washington, Pa., 1909; B.L., U. of Pittsburgh, 1913; m. Edna A. Ayers, Apr. 14, 1921. Admitted to Washington, Pa. bar, 1913, and since in practice under own name at Washington; dir. and solicitor Washington Union Trust Co. Mem. Washington Co. Bar Assn., Pa. Bar Assn. Republican. Presbyterian. Clubs: Bassett, Washington Co. Golf and Country (Washington, Pa.). Home: 443 E. Beau St. Office: 412-414 Washington Trust Bldg., Washington, Pa.

SPRINGER, Eva, artist, miniature painter; b. Cimarron, N.M.; d. Frank and Mary Josephine (Bishop) S.; student N.M. Normal U., Las Vegas, 4 yrs., Columbia Teachers Coll., New York, 1 yr., mem. Art Students League of N. Y., 3 yrs.; student William Chase Art Sch., New York, 1 yr., Julian's Academie, Paris, France, 3 yrs., Colarossi, Paris, 2 yrs., Grande Chaumiere, 2 yrs., Delecluse, 1 yr.; unmarried. Miniature and landscape painter, etcher and painter of portraits in oil and water colors. Has exhibited in London, Paris, Rome, New York, Boston, Phila., Chicago, Los Angeles, San Francisco, many cities in South, World's Fair (San Francisco, 1915), World's Fair (Chicago 1934). Represented by oils in Acad. in N.Y., Pa. Acad., Corcoran Art Gallery (Washington). Awarded medal by Academie Julian, Paris. Mem. Pa. Soc. Miniature Painters, Brooklyn Soc. Miniature Painters, Washington Water Color Soc. Republican. Home: Cimarron, N.M. Address: care Mrs. W. B. Davis, 2425 N. 59th St., Overbrook, Philadelphia, Pa.

SPRINGER, Harold Love, physician and surgeon; b. Del., Oct. 28, 1881; s. Willard and Etta (Frist) S.; student Wilmington High Sch., 1895-98; M.D., U. of Pa. Med. Sch., 1902; m. Carolyn W. Lobdell, Oct. 2, 1906; children—Harold Love, William Lobdell, Sarah Louise. Interne Presbyn. Hosp., Phila., 1902-04; began as surgeon, 1904; in practice at Wilmington, Del.; chief surg. Del. Hosp. (Wilmington), Del. State Hosp. (Farnhurst, Del.). Mem. Med. Advisory Bd. of Del., Vol. Med. Service, Council of Nat. Defense. Fellow Am. Coll. Surgeons; mem. A.M.A., New Castle County Med. Soc., Del. State Med. Soc., Internat. Coll. of Surgeons. Presbyn. Mason (32°). Clubs: Wilmington, Rotary, Torch, Wilmington Country (Wilmington); Art (Phila.); Rose Tree Fox Hunting. Home: Centreville, Del. Office: 1013 Washington St., Wilmington, Del.

SPRINGER, Willard, Jr., banking; b. Wilmington, Del., Apr. 8, 1886; s. Willard and Etta S.; C.E., Lafayette Coll., 1907; M.F., Yale U. Sch. of Forestry, 1909; m. Edna Martenis, Apr. 15, 1915; children—Elizabeth Anne, Marietta, Nancy. Employed as forest asst., Pa. R.R. Co., 1909-12; v.p. and treas. Charles Beadenkopf Co., mfrs. glazed kid, 1925, C. & W. Pyle Co., Inc., fancy leather, 1925-31; vice-pres. Industrial Trust Co., Wilmington, Del., 1931-34, pres. and dir. since 1934; pres. and dir. Industrial Trust Bldg. Corpn.; dir. Del. Electric Power Co. Served as Del. liquor commr. Chmn. Del. State Forestry Commn. Trustee Del. State Hosp.; chmn. bd. trustees Alfred I Du-Pont Sch. Mem. Soc. Am. Foresters, Torch Club, Delta Kappa Epsilon. Democrat. Presbyn. Mason (32°, Shriner). Clubs: Wilmington, Country. Home: Rockland, Del. Office: Industrial Trust Co., Wilmington, Del.

SPRINGER, William Moore, chem. engring.; b. Brooklyn, N.Y., Feb. 13, 1893; s. Jacob and Elmira (Fischer) S.; Chem. Engr., Columbia U., 1915; m. Elinor Jacobsen, Feb. 11, 1938. Employed on dye stuff census under direction Thos. H. Norton, Dept. Commerce, 1915; with Charles Pfizer, 1915-16; asso. with Bristol-Myers Co., Hillside, N.J., since 1916, dir. research since 1919. Mem. Am. Chem. Soc., Am. Statist. Assn., Soc. for Testing Materials, Faraday Soc., Am. Inst. Phi Lambda Upsilon. Club: Chemists (New York). Home: 60 Courter Av., Maplewood. Office: Bristol-Myers Co., Hillside, N.J.

SPROUL, John Roach, v.p. Nat. Refractories Co.; b. Chester, Pa., Jan. 30, 1895; s. William Cameron and Emeline (Roach) S.; student Mercersburg Acad., 1910-13; A.B., Swarthmore Coll., 1917; student U. of Pa. Law Sch., 1919-21; m. Hazel Hatfield, June 17, 1925; 1 dau., Caroline Hatfield. Began as helper in iron foundry, 1921; salesman General Refractories Co., 1922-25, later becoming treas., v.p. and pres.; with Harbison Walker Co., 1933-35; v.p. Nat. Refractories Co. since 1935; v.p. and dir. Keystone Wood Preserving Co.; dir. Lehigh Valley R.R. Co., Philadelphia, Baltimore & Washington R.A., Lackawanna & Wyoming Valley R.R. Successively 2d lt., 1st lt. and capt., 4th Inf., U.S. Army, 1917-19. Del. Rep. Nat. Conv., 1928. Mem. Pa. Hist. Soc., Phi Kappa Psi. Awarded Order of Purple Heart. Mason (32°). Clubs: Union League, Penn Athletic, Racquet (Philadelphia); Spring Haven Country, Rolling Green Golf; Boca Raton (Boca Raton, Fla.). Home: Lapidea Manor, Chester, Pa. Office: 1520 Locust St., Philadelphia, Pa.

SPROUL, Thomas Jay, investment broker; b. Roanoke, Va., Dec. 8, 1888; s. Samuel Everett and Carrie (Sporley) S.; A.B., Swarthmore (Pa.) Coll., 1909, M.A., 1910; m. Annabelle Boyle, Mar. 4, 1916; 1 dau., Mary Caroline. Engaged in wholesale grocery business, Chester, Pa., 1912-29; asso. with Montgomery, Scott & Co., Phila., as investment broker also ins. broker since 1938; treas. and dir. Atlantic Steel Castings Co., Chester, Pa. Served two terms as mem. Pa. Ho. of Rep. from Delaware Co., 1935-36 and 1937-38; not a candidate, 1938; commissioner Nether Providence Township, 1932-35, 1936-39, pres. since 1936. Mem. Book and Key, Phi Kappa Psi. Republican. Episcopalian. Clubs: Union League, Penn Athletic (Phila.). Home: Bowling Green, Media, Pa. Office: 123 S. Broad St., Philadelphia, Pa.

SPROWLS, Jesse William, prof. psychology; b. Claysville, Pa., Aug. 17, 1887; s. Stockdale and Cora (Wallace) S.; student Southwestern State Normal Sch., Pa., 1904-06; A.B., Valparaiso U., 1910; B.S. in Edn., U. of Pittsburgh, 1914; A.M., Clark U., 1918, Ph.D., 1919; m. Mary Smith, of Washington, Pa., Aug. 27, 1914. Prin. Scenery Hill (Pa.) High Sch., 1912-15; prof. edn., Bethany (W.Va.) Coll., 1915-17; prof. pro tem., U. of Vt., 1919-20; prof. secondary edn., U. of Tenn., 1920-23; prof. philosophy and psychology, St. John's Coll. (Annapolis, Md.), 1924-27; prof. psychology, U. of Md., since 1927. Mem. Kappa Alpha. Author: Social Psychology Interpreted, 1927; Everyday Psychology, 1933. Contbr. to ednl. and psychol. jours. Home: Riggs Rd., Hyattsville, Md. Address: College Park, Md.*

SPURGEON, Dorsett Larew, physician and surgeon; b. Redbird, Mo., Oct. 6, 1902; s. Marion E. and Martha (Licklider) S.; student Cape Girardeau (Mo.) State Teachers Coll., B.S., U. of Mo., 1927; M.D., Harvard, 1929; m. Mary Dutcher, Oct. 5, 1934. Interne Boston City Hosp. (surgical), 1929-31, Boston Lying In Hosp., 1931-32; practice as physician and surgeon, Newton, N.J., since 1932; mem. staff Newton (N.J.) Memorial Hosp.; asso. on staff Franklin (N.J.) Hosp. Mem. A.M.A., N.J. Med. Soc. Democrat. Baptist. Mason. Clubs: Newton Rotary, Sussex County Country. Address: 19 Church St., Newton, N.J.

SPURLING, Oliver Cromwell, engineer; b. St. George's Bermuda Islands, Sept. 19, 1874; s. George and Sarah (Gush) S.; matriculated 1st Div., U. of London, 1891; passed senior locals, U. of Cambridge, 1892; student Chicago Sch. of Electricity (evening classes), 1898; m. Lena May Cronk, Apr. 19, 1899; children—Alyce Ione, Ralph Everett. Came to U.S., 1893, naturalized citizen, 1906. With Western Electric Co. since 1893, at Chicago, then London, Eng., until 1905, asst. plant engr. and plant engr., Chicago, 1906-14, asst. gen. supt., 1915-22, plant engr. and administrative officer, N.Y. City, since 1923. Mem. Am. Soc. C.E., Am. Soc. M.E., Am. Inst. E.E., New York Electric Soc., Art Inst. of Chicago, Telephone Pioneers of America, Inst. Mech. Engrs. and Inst. Elec. Engrs., Eng.; asso. mem. Soc. Automotive Engrs. Republican. Conglist. Mason. Clubs: Railroad-Machinery (New York); Montclair Golf. In charge design and constrn. Western Electric Company's buildings and service systems, Hawthorne Works, Ill., Kearny Works, N.J., and Point Breeze Works, Baltimore, Md. Home: 315 Highland Av., Upper Montclair, N.J. Office: 195 Broadway, New York, N.Y.

SPURR, A. C.; pres. Monongahela West Penn Pub. Service Co. Address: Fairmont, W.Va.

SQUIER, Harold Newton, pub. utility exec.; b. New York, N.Y., Dec. 25, 1881; s. Theodore Augustus and Carrie (Ball) S.; B.S., Coll. City of N.Y., 1901; M.E., Stevens Inst. Tech., 1903; m. Martha Campbell, May 10, 1922; 1 dau., Jean Campbell. Employed as engr., United Gas Improvement Co., Phila., 1903-12; supt. Hyde Park Gas Co., Scranton, Pa., 1912-29; supt. gas div., Scranton-Spring Brook Water Service Co., Scranton, Pa., since 1929; dir. Carbondale Gas Co. Mem. Scranton Chamber of Commerce. Republican. Presbyterian. Club: Kiwanis of Scranton. Home: 1702 Delaware St. Office: 135 Jefferson Av., Scranton, Pa.

SQUIRE, Frank C(arter), civ. engr.; b. Oil City, Pa., May 16, 1885; s. Edwin and Sarah A. (Carter) S.; student Pomona Coll., Claremont, Calif.; A.B., Stanford, 1907; m. Mizae Noonan, Aug. 31, 1919; children—Edward Noonan, Frank Carter. Valuation engr. Los Angeles & Salt Lake R.R., Los Angeles, Calif., 1912-14, Ore.-Wash. R.R. & Navigation Co., Portland, Ore., 1914-23; engr. Western group, President's Conf. Com., Federal Valuation of R.R.'s, Chicago, 1923-35; valuation engr. Assn. Am. R.R.'s since 1935. Attended F.A.T.C., Camp Taylor, Louisville, Ky., 1918. Mem. Am. Soc. C.E., Am. Ry. Engring. Assn. Republican. Conglist. Home: 220 Elm St., Chevy Chase, Md. Address: Transportation Bldg., Washington, D.C.

ST. CLAIR, Otis E(ugene), lawyer; b. Tazewell Co., Va., Jan. 11, 1884; s. Alexander and Maria (Tiffany) St.C.; A.B., Univ. of Va., 1907; LL.B., Univ. of Va. Law Coll., 1908; m. Lillian B. Pryor, Oct. 25, 1923; children—Richard Otis, Charles Wade. Admitted to W.Va. bar, 1909 and engaged in gen. practice of law at Bluefield, 1909-17; in practice at Welch, W.Va., since 1921; mem. firm Strother, Sale, Curd & Tucker, 1921-29; mem. firm Strother, Sale, Curd & St. Clair, 1929-33; mem. firm Sale, St. Clair & Sale since 1933; divorce commr. for McDowell Co. since 1936. Served as 1st lt. inf., U.S.A., 1917-19, attached to M.I. Div., Washington, D.C., 1918-19. Mem. W.Va. and McDowell Co. bar assns., Phi Gamma Delta, Am. Legion, Forty and Eight. Democrat. Methodist. Mason. Home: 359 Virginia Av. Office: First National Bank Bldg., Welch, W.Va.

ST. CLAIR, Wade H.; surgeon Bluefield Sanitarium. Address: 204 Ramsey St., Bluefield, W.Va.

ST. PETER, Wilfred Napoleon, prof. physics; b. Norway, Mich., June 26, 1882; s. Michael and Rose Delia (Toutloff) St.P.; A.B., A.M. and Ph.D., U. of Mich.; m. Edith Clare Kelly, Aug. 11, 1908; children—John M., Edwin J. Teacher physics, Ferris Inst., 1905-18; instr. physics, U. of Mich., 1918-24; mem. faculty U. of Pittsburgh since 1924, now prof. physics. Mem. Am. Physical Soc., Pittsburgh Physical Soc., Sigma Xi, Gamma Alpha, Alpha Chi Rho. Co-author: Outline of Atomic Physics; Laboratory Manual for Engineering Physics. Home: 3132 Avalon St., Pittsburgh, Pa.

STAATS, J. Riley, coll. prof.; b. Sumner, Ill., Sept. 9, 1895; s. Elijah David and Catherine (Brian) S.; B.Edn., Ill. State Normal U., 1929; Ph.M., U. of Wis., 1931, Ph.D., 1933; m. Mabel Meadows, Dec. 24, 1935. Engaged in teaching rural schs. and prin. schs. in Ill., 1914-29; teaching asst., U. of Wis., 1929-35; mem. faculty Western State Teachers Coll., Tenn. Summer Sch., summers 1930-32, 1934, Ill. State Normal Univ. Summer Sch., summer 1933; prof. geography, State Teachers Coll., California, Pa., since 1935. Mem. Western Pa. Geography Club, State Council of Geography Teachers (pres.), Wis. Acad. Arts, Letters and Sciences, Pa. Acad. Arts, Letters and Sciences, Kappa Delta Pi, Gamma Theta Upsilon, Sigma Xi, Pi Gamma Mu. Republican. Methodist. Mason. Clubs: Hungry, Century (California). Contbr. articles to ednl. mags. Home: 520 Second St., California, Pa.

STABLER, Evert Fred, educator; b. Clairton, Pa., Oct. 24, 1903; s. Fred Gustave and Anna (Peterson) S.; student U. of Pittsburgh, 1921-22; Litt.B., cum laude, Grove City (Pa.) Coll., 1925; M.Ed., U. of Pittsburgh, 1932, Ph.D., 1938; m. Kathryn Evans Knepper, Apr. 17, 1930; children—Constance Ann, Kaye Evert. Engaged in teaching in pub. schs. and high sch., 1924-29; prin. Fifth St. Jr. High Sch., Clairton, Pa., 1929-38, prin. Clairton Sr. High Sch. since 1938. Served as chmn. Clairton Unit of Allegheny Co. Community Fund Drive, 1935; treas. Clairton Community Forum. Life mem. N.E.A.; mem. Pa. State Edn. Assn., Junior Western Pa. Athletic Assn. (past pres.). Republican. Presbyterian. Mason. Club: Lions (Clairton, Pa.; past pres., past regional dir.). Home: 509 Halcomb Av., Clairton, Pa.

STABLER, Walter Brooke, clergyman; b. Sandy Spring, Md., June 27, 1903; s. Caleb and Wilhelmina (Laird) S.; ed. Episcopal High Sch., Alexandria, Va., 1918-21; A.B., U. of Va., 1924; B.D., Episcopal Theol. Sem. in Va., 1928; (hon.) A.M., U. of Pa., 1936; m. Marjorie Harbison, July 2, 1928; children—Frederick Harbison, Walter Brooke. Engaged in teaching, Episcopal High Sch., Alexandria, Va., 1924-25; ordained to ministry P.E. Ch., 1928 and asst., All Saints Ch., Worcester, Mass., 1928-30; sec. for Coll. Work, P.E. Ch., New York, N.Y., 1930-32; chaplain and lecturer, U. of Pa., since 1932; pres. Church Soc. for Coll. Work, Inc. Mem. Phi Beta Kappa, Phi Kappa Sigma. Episcopalian. Club: University. Author: Creative Christian Living, 1933; Without Compromise, 1934; My Father's Business, 1935. Home: 3805 Locust St., Philadelphia, Pa.

STACE, Walter Terence, prof. philosophy; b. London, Eng., Nov. 17, 1886; s. Edward Vincent and Amy Mary (Watson) S.; student Bath (Eng.) Coll., 1896-1900, Fettes Coll., Edinburgh, Scotland, 1900-02; B.A., Trinity Coll., Dublin, Ireland, 1908, Litt.D., 1929; m. Adelaide Vaughan Cooke, 1910; 1 dau., Beryl Mary Cynthia; m. 2d, Blanche Bianca Beven, of Negombo, Ceylon, 1925; children—Noel John, Jennifer Jean. In British Civil Service, Ceylon, 1910-32, holding various positions, including pvt. sec. to gov., later mayor of Colombo, and controller of revenue; came to U.S., 1932, and since prof. philosophy at Princeton U. Mem. Am. Philos. Assn., British Inst. Philos. Studies, Mind Assn. Author: Critical History of Greek Philosophy, 1920; Philosophy of Hegel, 1924; Meaning of Beauty, 1929; Theory of Knowledge and Existence, 1932; The Concept of Morals, 1937. Home: 150 Fitz Randolph Rd., Princeton, N.J.

STACEY, Alfred Edwin, Jr., vice-pres. Buensod Stacey Air Conditioning, Inc.; b. Elbridge, N.Y., Mar. 10, 1885; s. Alfred E. and Jessie (Rowe) S.; prep. edn. Munroe Collegiate Inst., 1896-1902; M.E., Syracuse U., 1906; m. Hazel King, June 29, 1910; children—Alfred Edwin, 3d, Janet King (Mrs. Stacey Simpson), Elizabeth Rowe (deceased), John Markell. Engr. Buffalo Forge Co., Buffalo, N.Y., 1906-07; chief engr. Carrier Air Conditioning Co., New York, 1908-09; vice-pres., Elbridge (N.Y.) Chair Co., 1909-11; western mgr. and engr. Carrier Air Conditioning Co., Chicago, 1911-15, Carrier Engineering Corpn., Chicago, 1915-19; chief of research Carrier Engineering Corpn., Newark, 1928-31, vice-pres. in charge of engring., 1931-33, vice-pres. and tech. sales adviser, 1934-35; vice-pres. Buensod-Stacey Air Conditioning, Inc., New York, since 1935. Lt. comdr. U.S. Naval Reserve. Mem. Am. Soc. Heating and Ventilating Engrs., Am. Inst. of New York, Am. Soc. for Testing Materials, A.A.A.S., Acoustical Soc. of America, Archæol. Inst. of America, Am. Soc. of Naval Engrs., Delta Upsilon. Club: Fells Brook (Essex Fells, N.J.). Home: 35 Wootton Rd., Essex Fells, N.J. Office: 60 E. 42d St., New York, N.Y.

STACK, Michael J., ex-congressman; b. Ireland; came to U.S. in youth; student St. Joseph's Coll., Philadelphia; A.B., St. Mary's U., Baltimore. Engaged in real estate business in Phila.; mem. 74th and 75th Congresses (1935-39), 6th Pa. Dist. Served in 90th Div. A.E.F., wounded in action. Decorated with Order of Purple Heart. Mem. Am. Legion, Vets Foreign Wars. Democrat. Address: 422 S. 52d St., Philadelphia, Pa.

STACKHOUSE, Daniel Morrell, steel mfr.; b. Johnstown, Pa., May 5, 1866; s. Powell and Lucy (Roberts) S.; ed. Friends Central High Sch., Philadelphia; B.S., U. of Pa., 1887, Mining Engr., 1888; m. Katharine E. Benkert, Jan. 18, 1893 (died Mar. 31, 1933); children—Mary, Rebecca, Josephine, Powell, Daniel Morrell, Katharine Elizabeth (wife of Dr. Jos. W. McHugh, Jr.). Blast furnace employee Cambria Iron Co., 1888-90, asst. supt. metall. dept., 1890-93, supt. order dept., 1893-97, supt. lower open hearth dept., 1897-1901; supt. open hearth dept. Cambria Steel Co., 1901-10, asst. gen. supt., 1910-23; dir. Cambria Iron Co. since 1923, pres. since 1931; dir. U.S. Nat. Bank, Johnstown Savings Bank. Dir. Family Welfare Soc., Community Chest. Active mem. Am. Iron and Steel Inst., Am. Inst. Mining and Metallurgy. Republican. Clubs: Union League (Philadelphia); Sunnehanna Country, Bachelors (Johnstown, Pa.). Home: 145 Fayette St. Office: care Bethlehem Steel Co., Johnstown, Pa.

STACKPOLE, Albert Hummel, editor; b. Harrisburg, Pa., June 28, 1897; s. Edward James and Maria Kate (Hummel) S.; grad. Harrisburg Acad., 1908-15; student Yale, 1915-17, 19; m. Mary Creighton, Oct. 9, 1920; children—Creighton, Mary Creighton. With Harrisburg (Pa.) Telegraph Press since 1919, as reporter, 1919-25, city editor, 1925-27, columnist since 1928, editor in chief since 1933, also v.p.; treas. WHP, Inc. Served successively as private, corpl., sergt. 12th F.A., U.S. Army, 1917; 2d lt. 113th F.A., with A.E.F., 1918; successively lt., capt., maj. and now lt. col. 104th Cav., Pa. Nat. Guard. Dir. Harrisburg Welfare Federation. Republican. Presbyterian. Clubs: Yale (New York); Harrisburg Country. Home: Clarks Valley, Dauphin, Pa. Office: Telegraph Bldg., Harrisburg, Pa.

STACKPOLE, Edward James, Jr., publisher; b. Harrisburg, Pa., June 21, 1894; s. Edward James and Marie Kate (Hummel) S.; A.B., Yale U., 1915; m. Frances Bailey, Aug. 17, 1917; 1 dau., Mary Frances. Engaged in publishing business since 1915; organized, and since pres. and dir., Military Service Publishing Co.; pres. and dir. Telegraph Press, Inc., The Harrisburg Telegraph (organized 1831), radio station WHP; dir. Harrisburg Hotel Co., Penn-Harris Hotel Co., radio station WKBO. Began active duty as 2d lt. Inf., O.R.C., 1917; served overseas as capt., commanding Co. M, 110th Inf., 28th Div.; wounded in action 3 times; apptd. col. 8th Inf., P.N.G. (regt. converted to 104th Cav.), 1921; brig. gen. in command 52d Cavalry Brigade since 1933. Awarded Distinguished Service Cross, Purple Heart. Mem. bd. mgrs. Harrisburg Hosp.; mem. nat. council Boy Scouts of America. Mem. Am. Legion, Vets. Foreign Wars, Mil. Order World War. Club: Harrisburg Country. Holder private pilot's license since 1933. Home: Green Meadows Farm, Dauphin R.D., Pa. Office: 104 Telegraph Bldg., Harrisburg, Pa.

STADIE, William Christopher, research physician; b. New York, N.Y., June 15, 1886; s. Charles and Augusta (Kiseo) S.; B.S., New York U., 1907; M.D., Coll. of Phys. and Surgeons, Columbia U., 1916; m. Amanda Brugger, July 28, 1922; 1 dau., Elizabeth Ann. Interne Presbyn. Hosp., New York, N.Y., 1916-18; asso. Rockefeller Inst. Hosp., New York, N.Y., 1919-21; asst. prof. medicine, Yale U., 1921-24; asso. prof. research medicine, U. of Pa. Med. Sch. since 1924. Served as 1st lieut. Med. Corps, U.S.A., 1918-19. Mem. Assn. Am. Phys., Soc. for Clin. Investigation, Harvey Soc., Alpha Omega Alpha. Republican. Episcopalian. Home: Radnor, Pa.

STADTFELD, Joseph, judge; b. N.Y. City, Aug. 12, 1861; s. Moritz and Sophie (Spier) S.; grad. Central High Sch., Pittsburgh, 1878; m. Carrie Edmundson Herron, Jan. 31, 1895; children—Rodgers Morrow, Joseph Randolph (dec.), Harold Randolph. Admitted to Pa. bar, 1886, and began practice, Pittsburgh; apptd. solicitor City of Pittsburgh, 1914, but declined; apptd. judge Common Pleas Court of Allegheny County, June 24, 1830; apptd. judge Superior Court of Pa., Nov. 7, 1931, and so continues, having been elected to full term, 10 yrs., 1932; dir. Kaufmann Dept. Stores. Mem. Am. Bar Assn. (exec. council for Pa., 1931), Pa. State Bar Assn. (v.p. 1929), Allegheny County Bar Assn. (pres. 1928-29). Mem. B'nai B'rith. Republican. Hebrew religion. Mason. Club: Concordia. Home: 5575 Wilkins Av. Chambers: City-County Bldg., Pittsburgh, Pa.

STAFFORD, Geoffrey Wardle, clergyman; b. Birmingham, Eng., Jan. 5, 1897; s. John Thomas Wardle (formerly pres. Meth. Ch. Gt. Britain and Ireland) and Edith (Hardcastle) S.; student Scarborough Coll. (Eng.), 1907-13; B.A., Durham U. (Eng.), 1915, Wadham Coll. (Oxford U.), Eng., 1921; M.A., Oxford U., 1924; B.D., London U., 1932; Litt.D., Wesleyan Coll., Buckhannon, W.V., 1928; m. Helene, d. Bishop John W. Hamilton, Dec. 27, 1923. Came to U.S., 1921, naturalized, 1928. Began as a lay preacher in Durham U. when 17 yrs. of age; asso. pastor First M.E. Ch., Baltimore, Md., 1921-23; pastor Wesley Ch., Milwaukee, 1923-26, Court St. Ch., Rockford, Ill., 1926-32, Univ. Temple Ch., Seattle, Wash., 1932-37; prof. ecclesiastical history, Drew U., Madison, N.J., since 1937; lecturer in religion, Rockford Coll., 1928-32; univ. preacher, Stanford University, 1932-36. During World War served as a lt. Northumberland Fusiliers, British Army. Author: The Sermon on the Mount, 1927. Home: (summer) Pilgrim View, Marshfield, Mass. Address: Drew Theol. Seminary, Madison, N.J.

STAHL, K(arl) F(rederich), chemist; b. Zwiefalten, Wurttemberg, Germany, Mar. 14, 1855; s. Johann Jacob and Luise (Kurz) S.; student Inst. of Tech., Stuttgart, 1872-75; U. of Tübingen, 1875-76, D.Sc.; m. Mrs. Emma Onyx Johnson, Aug. 8, 1881 (died Nov. 14, 1924); 1 dau., Minneola Luise. Came to America, 1876, naturalized, 1888. Chemist Charles Lennig & Co., Phila., 1876-80; Northwestern Fertilizer Co., Chicago, 1880-82; supt. Nat. Fertilizer Co., Nashville, Tenn., 1882-84, Johnstown (Pa.) Chem. Works, 1884-90, James Irwin & Co., Pittsburgh, 1890-99; supt. Pittsburgh works, Gen. Chem. Co., 1899-1913; research

chemist Gen. Chem. Co. and cons. chemist since 1914. Fellow A.A.A.S.; mem. Am. Chem. Soc. (chmn. Pittsburgh sect. 1916-33, now emeritus), Engr. Soc. of Western Pa. (dir. 1895; chmn. chem. sect. 1902), Nat. Assn. German-Am. Technologists (pres. 4 terms, hon. mem. 1937), Verein Deutscher Chemiker, Soc. Chem. Industry (England). Republican. Lutheran. Home: 839 Chislett St. Office: 2318 Wharton St., Pittsburgh, Pa.

STAHL, Nicholas, elec. engring.; b. New Castle, Del., July 2, 1876; s. Nicholas F. and Mary A. (Taggart) S.; A.B. magna cum laude, Princeton, 1897, A.M., same, 1898; E.E., Princeton U. Elec. Engring. Dept., 1907; m. Anna McLeod, Oct. 14, 1908; children—Barbara (Mrs. David Scott Moulton), Gretchen, Nicholas McLeod. Engr. with Westinghouse Electric & Mfg. Co., E. Pittsburgh, Pa., 1907-18; engr., gen. engr. and supt. generation, Narragansett Electric Co., Providence, R.I., 1918-27; vice-pres. United Pub. Service Co., Chicago, Ill., 1927-38; chief engr. Pa. Power & Light Co., Allentown, Pa., since 1928. Fellow Am. Soc. Mech. Engrs.; mem. Assn. Edison Illuminating Companies, American Inst. Elec. Engrs., Engrs. Club Lehigh Valley, Princeton Cannon Club. Republican. Presbyterian. Club: Princeton (New York). Home: 40 S. 16th St., Allentown, Pa. Office: 9th & Hamilton Sts., Allentown, Pa.

STAHLER, Harry Sylvester, high sch. prin.; b. Mauch Chunk, Pa., Nov. 1, 1891; s. Charles Monroe and Anna Josephine (Brighton) S.; grad. Mauch Chunk High Sch. (salutatorian), 1910; A.B., cum laude, Bucknell U., Lewisburg, Pa., 1914, A.M., 1929; m. Bessie Walker, Dec. 27, 1914; 1 dau., Mildred Louise. Engaged as teacher, athletic coach and vice-prin. schs., Hawley, Pa., 1914-16; teacher, high sch., Mauch Chunk, Pa., 1916-17; asst. sec. Mauch Chunk Y.M.C.A. Boys' Camp, summers, 1910-17; dir. Mauch Chunk Y.M.C.A., 1917; accountant, Bethlehem Steel Corpn., Bethlehem, Pa., 1917, Milton Shell Plant, 1917-18; instr. physics, Union Hill High Sch., Union City, N.J., 1918-23; prin. Union Hill High Sch. since 1923. Mem. N.E.A., N.J. State Teachers Assn. Democrat. Episcopalian. Mason. Odd Fellow. Club: New York Schoolmasters (New York City). Home: 539 44th St., Union City, N.J..

STAHLER, Horace Crawford, pres. and treas. Robert Buist Co.; b. Philadelphia, Pa., July 7, 1888; s. Henry Clay and Caroline Ball (Crawford) S.; ed. Central Manual Training Sch. and Drexel Inst. Tech.; m. Elizabeth Rainear, Feb. 12, 1913; children—Wayne Homer, Robert Crawford, John Rainear, Henry Clay, 2d. Traveling representative United Gas Improvement Co., 1905-17; treas. and dir. Robert Buist Co. since 1919, pres. since 1930. Mem. Am. Seed Trade Assn. S.A.R. (life). Clubs: Union League, Overbrook Golf, Commodore Seaside Park Yacht. Home (legal): 20 Third Av., Seaside Park, N.J. Office: 4-5-M S. Front St., Philadelphia, Pa.

STAHLMAN, Thomas Mervin, eye, ear, nose and throat specialist; b. Sigel, Jefferson Co., Pa., Sept. 30, 1874; s. John and Elizabeth (Armstrong) S.; ed. Clarion State Teachers' Coll.; M.D., U. of Pittsburgh, 1905; m. Mildred B. Worrell, Nov. 14, 1910; children—Ruth Mildred, Nancy Worrell. Prin. Corsica (Pa.) pub. schs., 1898-1900; med. asst. Jefferson County Home, 1903; interne Reineman Maternity Hosp. and Emma Kaufman Clinic, 1904-05; pres. Dormont Bd. of Health, 1915-24; now specializes in treatment of eye, ear, nose and throat; pres. and dir. Roosevelt Coal & Coke Co. Served as capt., U.S. Med. Corps, World War. Fellow A.M.A.; mem. Allegheny Co. and Pa. State med. socs., Am. Legion. Democrat. Protestant. Odd Fellow. Home: 3315 W. Liberty Av. Office: 1111 Westinghouse Bldg., Pittsburgh, Pa.

STAHR, Henry Irvin, coll. pres.; b. Lock Haven, Pa., Nov. 6, 1880; s. Isaac Summers and Hannah Camilla (Applebach) S.; A.B., Franklin and Marshall Coll., 1901, A.M., 1904, D.D., 1926; student Theol. Sem. of Ref. Ch., 1905-08, Grad. Sch. Cornell University, 1908-09; LL.D. from Ursinus College, Pa., 1935; m. Alice Webb Stockwell, Feb. 2, 1914; children—

Sarah Louise, Martha Elizabeth, Henry Irvin. Ordained ministry Ref. Ch. in U.S., 1910; pastor Faith Ch., Reading, Pa., 1910-17, Christ Ch., Bethlehem, Pa., 1917-26, Emmanuel Ch., Hanover, Pa., 1926-30; exec. sec. Bd. of Christian Edn., 1930-34; pres. Hood Coll., Frederick, Md., since July 1, 1934. Pres. Community Chest of Frederick; mem. Commn. on Higher Ednl. Instns., Evang. and Reformed Ch.; mem. Council Ch. Bds. of Edn. (treas.), Bd. of Christian Edn. of Evangelical and Ref. Ch. and Hist. Soc. of same, Pa. Folklore Soc., Am. Acad. Polit. and Social Science, N.E.A., Md.-Del. Council of Religious Edn., Nat. Council of Boy Scouts America, A.A.A.S., Phi Sigma Kappa, Pa. German Soc., S.A.R. Republican. Mason (K.T.). Clubs: Rotary of Frederick (mem. bd. dirs.); University (Baltimore); Cosmos (Washington, D.C.). Address: Hood College, Frederick, Md.

STAINSBY, Wendell Johnson, physician; b. St. Thomas, Ont., Can., Jan. 29, 1898; s. George William and Edith Corinne (Hatch) S.; ed. Saskatoon Collegiate Inst., 1912-16; B.A., Univ. of Saskatchewan, 1920; M.D., C.M., McGill U. Med. Coll., 1925; came to U.S., 1928, naturalized, 1933; m. Edith Evelyn Nicholls, Dec. 31, 1937; 1 son, Wendell Nicholls. Interne Peiping Union Med. Coll., China, 1925-26, asst. resident in surgery, 1926-27; research fellow, Cornell U. Med. Coll., 1928-31, instr. medicine, 1931-36, asst. prof., 1936-38; asst. attdg. phys. Bellevue Hosp., New York, N.Y., 1930-32, N.Y. Hosp., 1932-38; dir. dept. medicine, George F. Geisinger Hosp., Danville, Pa., since 1938. Fellow Am. Med. Assn., N.Y. Acad. Medicine; mem. Soc. Exptl. Biology and Medicine, Soc. Am. Bacteriologists, Soc. of Immunology, Harvey Soc., Am. Rheumatism Assn., Pa. State and Montour Co. med. socs. Republican. Protestant. Home: 649 Bloom Rd. Office: George F. Geisinger Hosp., Danville, Pa.

STALFORD, Martin R., banker; b. Wyalusing, Pa., Mar. 27, 1876; s. John B. and Emma (Martin) S.; ed. Pa. State Coll.; unmarried. With Nat. Bank of Wyalusing since 1900, beginning as clerk, pres. since 1935. Served as chmn. Wyalusing Branch, Am. Red Cross during World War; apptd. mem. fuel com. for Bradford Co., by Pres. Wilson. Dir. Wyalusing Twp. Sch. Bd.; chmn. Gov. Earl's Safety Com. for Bradford Co.; trustee Robert Packer Hosp., Sayre, Pa., Wyalusing Cemetery Assn.; trustee Mansfield State Teachers Coll.; mem. Constitution Com. of Pa., Pub. Assistance Bd. of Bradford Co.; mem. exec. com. Gen. Sullivan Council, Boy Scouts of America. Pres. Bradford and Sullivan County Bankers Assn., Bradford Co. Hist. Soc., S.R. (Pa. Soc.), Phi Kappa Sigma, Theta Nu Epsilon. Democrat. Presbyterian. Elk. Club: Rainbow (pres.). Home: Chillaway Farms, Wyalusing, Pa.

STALLARD, Clint Wolfe, surgeon; b. Wise, Va., Jan. 13, 1899; s. Elbert Carson and Zuela Virginia (Wheatley) S.; student William and Mary Coll., Williamsburg, Va., 1919-21; M.D., George Washington U. Med. Sch., Washington, D.C., 1925; m. Ella Cawood, Sept. 9, 1919 (now dec.); 1 son, Clint Wolfe; m. 2d, Gertrude Helen Maurek, Oct. 19, 1927; 1 dau., Mary Virginia. Interne Emergency Hosp., Washington, D.C., 1923-27; engaged in practice of medicine and surgery at Montgomery, W.Va. since 1927; traumatic and orthopedic surgeon, Laird Memorial Hosp. and Clinic, Montgomery, W.Va., since 1927. Served in R.O.T.C. at George Washington U.; six weeks training Carlisle Barracks, Pa. Fellow Am. Coll. Surgeons. Mem. Am. Med. Assn., Southern Med. Assn., W.Va. Med. Assn., Fayette Co. Med. Soc., Alpha Kappa Kappa. Presbyn. Mason (Shriner). Moose. Club: Rotary (Montgomery); Willow Grove Country. Home: 2 Davis Court St. Office: Laird Memorial Hosp., Montgomery, W.Va.

STALNAKER, Elizabeth M., prof. psychology, W.Va. U. Address: West Virginia U., Morgantown, W.Va.

STALNAKER, John Marshall, educator; b. Duluth, Minn., Aug. 17, 1903; s. William E. and Sara (Tatham) S.; B.S., U. of Chicago, 1925, A.M., 1928; m. Ruth Culp, July 29,

1933; 1 son, John Culp. Began as teacher, 1925; instr. and asst. prof. psychology and edn., Purdue U., 1926-31; examiner, U. of Chicago, 1931-36; asst. prof. psychology, Princeton U., 1936-37, asso. prof. psychology since 1937; consultant examiner Coll. Entrance Examination Board since 1936. Mem. Am. Psychol. Assn., Sigma Xi, Phi Beta Kappa, Tau Kappa Epsilon. Home: 3 Queenston Pl., Princeton, N.J.

STALTER, Charles Cooper, lawyer; b. Paterson, N.J., June 9, 1895; s. William and Kate (Brown) S.; student N.Y. Mil. Acad., Cornwall-on-Hudson, N.Y., 1908-13; LL.B., Cornell U. Law Sch., 1918; m. Helen Banigan, Nov. 4, 1921; 1 dau., Lynn. Admitted to N.J. bar as atty., 1919, as counselor, 1923; engaged in gen. practice of law as individual at Paterson, N.J., since 1918. Served as 1st lt. F.A. and C.A.C., U.S.A., 1917-19, arty. aerial observer, with A.E.F. Trustee N.Y. Mil. Acad. Alumni Assn. Mem. Am. Bar Assn, Cornell Law Assn., N.J. State, Bergen Co., Passaic Co. bar assns., Phi Delta Phi, Kappa Sigma. Republican. Mem. Dutch Ref. Ch. Clubs: Arcola Country (Arcola); Cornell (New York). Home: Hohokus. Office: 64 Hamilton St., Paterson, N.J.

STAM, Jacob, lawyer; b. Hawthorne, N.J., Sept. 18, 1899; s. Peter and Amelia E. A. (Willems) S.; LL.B., N.Y. Law Sch., N.Y. City, 1922; spl. courses, Mercer Beasley Law Sch., Newark, N.J., 1932-34; m. Deana Bowman, Apr. 6, 1923; children—Paul Bowman, Ruth Margaret, John Edward, Mary Elizabeth, David Harry, James Henry. Employed in law office and as ct. stenographer, 1915-18; in law office and accounting work, 1919-22; admitted to N.J. bar as atty., 1922, counselor, 1928; engaged in gen. practice of law at Paterson, N.J., since 1922; sec. Empire Piece Dyeing & Finishing Co.; dir. and counsel Home Lovers Bldg. & Loan Assn. Served as army field clk. hdqrs. Port of Embarkation, Hoboken, N.J., 1918-19. Pres. and dir. Florence Crittenton Home of Paterson, N.J.; sec. and dir. Star of Hope Mission, Paterson, N.J.; vice-pres. and dir. Latin America Mission, Inc., N.Y. City; trustee and counsel D.M. Stearns Missionary Fund, Inc., Phila., Pa. Mem. Passaic Co. Bar Assn. Amateur Shorthand Champion of the N.Y. Met. Dist., 1915. Republican. Undenominational Protestant. Home: 238 Jefferson St. Office: 140 Market St., Paterson, N.J.

STAMBAUGH, Fred Minton, lawyer; b. Blaine, Ky., Oct. 2, 1890; s. John Henry and Mary Elizabeth (Holbrook) S.; LL.B., Univ. of Ill., 1914; m. Thelma S., Apr. 2, 1924 (div. 1936); 1 dau., Thelma Gene. Admitted to W.Va. bar, 1914, and since engaged in gen. practice of law in state and federal cts. at Charleston. Republican. Mem. Christian Ch. Mason (32°, Shriner). Elk. Home: 403 Ruffner Av. Office: Security Bldg., Charleston, W.Va.

STAMM, John Samuel, bishop; b. Alida, Kan., Mar. 23, 1878; s. George and Mary (Schmutz) S.; grad. Northwestern Coll. Acad., Naperville, Ill., 1906; Ph.B., Northwestern Coll., 1909, Ph.M., 1910; B.D., Evang. Theol. Sem., Naperville, 1910; M.A., U. of Chicago, 1926; D.D., Evang. Theol. Sem., Naperville, Ill., 1927; LL.D., Albright College, Reading, Pa., 1935; m. Priscilla Marie Wahl, Mar. 19, 1912. Entered ministry Evang. Ch., 1899; pastor successively Bloomington and Glasgow, Mo., until 1903, Manhattan, Ill., 1903-07, Downers Grove, Ill., 1907-12, Oak Park, 1912-19; prof. systematic theology, Evangelical Theological Seminary, 1919-27, head of dept., 1922-27; elected bishop Evangelical Church, October 1926, re-elected, 1930, 1934, 1938; senior bishop and president of board of bishops, Evangelical Church. Candidate of Prohibition Party for Illinois State Senate, 1911; camp pastor, Camp Grant, Ill., 1918. Mem. exec. com. Ill. State S.S. Assn., 1916-19; mem. gov. bd. Young People's Work Evang. Ch., 1919-22; gen. sec. of evangelism, Evang. Ch., 1927-34. Lecturer and Bible teacher at summer schs., conventions, etc. Republican. Author: Evangelical Standard of Evangelism, 1924; Evangelism and Christian Experience,

1930. Address: 3d and Reily Sts., Harrisburg, Pa.

STAMM, Raymond Thomas, theol. sem. prof.; b. Milton, Pa., Mar. 16, 1894; s. Jacob Calvin and Lydia (Long) S.; A.B., Gettysburg Coll., 1920; B.D., Luth. Theol. Sem., Gettysburg, Pa., 1923; Ph.D., Univ. of Chicago, 1926; unmarried. Began as teacher pub. schs. in Pa., 1912-15; asst. in dept. of history and Bible, Gettysburg Coll., 1920-23; fellow in Dept. N.T., Divinity Sch., U. of Chicago, 1923-26; prof. N.T. lang., lit. and theology, Luth. Theol. Sem., Gettysburg, Pa., since 1926. Served in Med. Dept. Base Hosp., U.S.A., 1918-19, dischd. as sergt. Mem. Soc. Bib. Lit. and Exegesis, Phi Beta Kappa. Republican. U. Luth. Ch. in America. Mem. editorial com. The Lutheran Church Quarterly. Contbr. The Historical Relationships of Christianity and Commentary on the Gospel according to Mark, in New Testament Commentary, edited by Herbert C. Alleman, 1936, also articles and reviews. Home: Gettysburg, Pa.

STAMP, Adele Hagner, univ. dean; b. Baltimore, Md., Aug. 9, 1893; d. Frederick and Anna Rebekah (Harken) S.; A.B., Tulane U., 1921; A.M., U. of Md., 1924. Engaged in teaching, Park Sch., Baltimore, Md., 1913-14, Miss Crosly's Sch., Catonsville, Md., 1914-17; dir. Industrial Service Center, Nat. Bd. Y.W. C.A., 1918-19; field rep. Am. Red Cross, 1920-22; dean of women, U. of Md., since 1922. Served as recreation leader Nat. Bd. Y.W.C.A. War Work Council, 1917-18. Former mem. State Bd. League of Women Voters. Mem. bd. Prince George Co. Fed. of Womens Clubs. Mem. Am. Assn. Univ. Women, Mortar Board, Alpha Lambda Delta, Delta Kappa Gamma. Democrat. Methodist. Home: College Park, Md.

STANFORD, Edward Valentine, college pres.; b. Boston, Mass., Feb. 14, 1897; s. Gorham E. and Catherine E. (Fitzpatrick) S.; student Boston Coll., 1914-16, LL.D., 1932; A.B., Villanova Coll., 1918, M.S., 1922; LL.D., Loyola U., Chicago, 1936. Ordained priest R.C. Ch.; instr. in descriptive geometry, Villanova Coll., 1920-32, chaplain, 1925-32, pres. since 1932, also trustee and treas. of bd. Mem. bd. dirs. Assn. of Am. Colleges, since 1936; vice-pres. and mem. exec. com. Catholic Edn. Assn. of Pa. (past pres. coll. sect.); v.p. and mem. exec. com. Catholic Assn. for Internat. Peace; mem. exec. com. and legislative com. Assn. Coll. Presidents of Pa.; mem. exec. com., 1933—, and chmn. eastern regional unit, 1935-38, Nat. Catholic Educational Association (college sect.); mem. Nat. Commn. of Church-related Colleges, mem. exec. com. since 1935, vice chmn., 1936, chmn., 1937; vice-pres. Middle States Assn. of Colleges and Secondary Schs., 1936; chmn. Eastern Regional Conf. on World Peace, 1935; mem. ednl. com. Phila. Chamber of Commerce since 1936; mem. exec. com. 150th Anniversary Celebration of the Constitution of U.S., Phila., 1937; mem. advisory com. Police Sch. of Eastern Pa. since 1936; mem. advisory com. Am. Catholic Hist. Soc. since 1937. Mem. Am. Catholic Philos. Soc., Catholic Library Assn., Am. Acad. Polit. and Social Science. Trustee Rosemont Coll. Mem. Order of St. Augustine. Writer on ednl. and religious subjects. Home: Villanova, Pa.

STANG, William Henry, supervisor engring. dept.; b. New Brunswick, N.J., May 25, 1894; s. Henry and Martha (Ballschmidt) S.; B.S. in E.E., Rutgers U., New Brunswick, N.J., 1915; m. Hallie M. Reinhard, Apr. 27, 1921. Cost engr. N.J. Pub. Utility Commn., 1915-16, Am. Telephone & Telegraph Co., New York, 1916-17; asst. valuation engr. Pa. Power & Light Co., Allentown, Pa., 1919-27, supervisor engring. dept. since 1927. Served as 2d lt., Engrs., U.S. Army, 1917-19. Dir. Masonic Temple Assn., Allentown. Mem. Am. Legion, Lambda Chi Alpha. Lutheran. Mason, 32° (Past Master Greenleaf Lodge No. 561, F. & A.M.; Past High Priest, Allen R.A. Chapter No. 203, R.A. M.; Past Thrice Illustrious Master Allen Council No. 23, R. & S.M.; Past Comdr. Allen Commandery No. 20, K.T. of Pa.; Herald Mary Conclave No. 5, Knights of Red Cross of Constantine; Comdr. Div. No. 9, K.T. of Pa.). Clubs: Lehigh Valley Shrine, Engineers of Lehigh Valley (Allentown, Pa.). Home: 225 N. 16th St. Office: 9th and Hamilton Sts., Allentown, Pa.

STANGE, Emile, artist and teacher; b. Jersey City, N.J., July 1, 1863; s. Adolph Augustus and Adele Frances (Caudron) S.; ed. schools Hamilton, Ont.; m. Mary Frances Kelly, Aug. 12, 1886; children—Adele (Mrs. Wm. Heitsche), Gladys (dec.), Emile Fenimore (dec.), Mary Dorothy (dec.). Apprentice in photograph gallery, Hamilton, Ont., 1879; studied painting in New York; has followed profession as artist since 1884, in N.J. since 1891, at North Hackensack since 1909; frequent exhibits at Nat. Acad. Design; also Chicago, Phila., St. Louis, and many other cities; represented in N.Y. Water Color Club, N.Y. Water Color Soc.; former mem. Salmagundi Club, Professional Art League and other socs. Mem. Allied Artists America, N.Y. Soc. Painters. Republican. Unitarian. Home: North Hackensack, N.J.

STANGER, George Harold, lawyer; b. Glassboro, N.J., Sept. 25, 1902; s. Francis Albert and Josephine (Ellis) S.; student Lafayette Coll., Easton, Pa., 1920-21; m. Ruth Jeffries, June 26, 1929. Studied law in office F. A. Stanger, Jr., Bridgeton, N.J., 1921-24, admitted to N.J. bar as atty., 1924, as counselor, 1933; spl. master in chancery, 1938; supreme ct. commr., 1939; engaged in gen. practice of law at Vineland, N.J. since 1930; served as mem. N.J. Ho. of Assembly, 1936; mem. N.J. Senate for term, 1938-41; sec. and dir. Ferro Pipe & Foundry Co., Bridgeton, N.J. Served as 2d lt. inf., N.J.N.G., 1930-34; capt. inf. on mil. staff Gov. H. G. Hoffman, 1936-37; now capt. F.A., N.J.N.G. Mem. Am. and N.J. State bar assns., Sigma Chi. Republican. Methodist. Mason. Elk. Home: 5 Howard St. Office: 538 Landis Av., Vineland, N.J.

STANIER, Elmer Samuel, banker; b. Pittsburgh, Pa., Nov. 9, 1885; s. Thomas and Mathilde (Kraft) S.; ed. high sch. and (evenings) Duquesne U.; m. Marguerite Jones, Aug. 30, 1919; children—Nancy Kraft, Richard Elmer. Began as clerk traffic dept. B.&O. R.R.; became trustee Dollar Savings Bank, Oct. 15, 1926, asst. sec., Dec. 17, 1926, sec., Apr. 14, 1927, treas., Dec. 26, 1935. Sch. dir. Mt. Lebanon Twp. Trustee Methodist Episcopal Home for the Aged. Mt. Lebanon M.E. Ch.; dir. Downtown Y.M.C.A. Republican. Mason (treas. Bellefield Royal Arch Chapter). Club: St. Clair Country. Home: 70 Lebanon Hills Drive, Mt. Lebanon, Pa. Office: 338-344 Fourth Av., Pittsburgh, Pa.

STANLEY, Clarence, banker; b. Pittsfield, Mass., Jan. 14, 1897; s. William and Lila C. (Wetmore) S.; student Berkshire Sch., Sheffield, Mass., 1909-14, Yale, 1915-17; m. Augusta G. Leovy, Jan. 9, 1929; children—William, Frank L., Lila C. Associated with Nat. Commercial Bank & Trust Co., Albany, N.Y., 1919-24; with Union Trust Co. of Pittsburgh since 1924, beginning in bond dept., pres. and dir. since 1936; trustee Koppers United Co.; dir. Gen. Electric Co., Southern Pacific Co., Superior Steel Corpn. Served with U.S. Naval Aviation Corps, 1917-18. Trustee Berkshire Sch. Republican. Episcopalian. Clubs: Duquesne, University, Pittsburgh, Harvard-Yale-Princeton (Pittsburgh). Home: 1271 Beechwood Boul. Office: Union Trust Co. of Pittsburgh, Pittsburgh, Pa.

STANLEY, Edward Otis, Jr., counsel Mutual Benefit Life Ins. Co.; b. Boston, Mass., Nov. 21, 1885; s. Edward Otis and Caroline Clinton (Durfee) S.; grad. East Orange pub. schs., 1902; B.A., Princeton U., 1906; LL.B., Columbia U., 1909; m. Mary Livingston Taylor, June 1, 1915; children—David Taylor, Edward Livingston, Emily Grant, Margaret Whitney, Mary Alden. Admitted to N.Y. bar, 1909, N.J. bar, 1910; mem. law firm Sommer, Colby & Whiting, 1910-13, Pitney, Hardin & Skinner, 1913-32; asso. counsel, later counsel, Mutual Benefit Life Ins. Co. since 1932; dir. Smith & Nichols. Served as major, judge advocate, U.S. Army, 1918-19. East Orange City Counsel,

1915-16, Essex County Bd. of Elections, 1919-20. Treas. House of the Good Shepherd, Orange. Mem. Am. Bar Assn., N.J. Bar Assn., Essex County Bar Assn., Assn. of Life Insurance Counsel, Phi Beta Kappa. Republican. Episcopalian. Clubs: Essex (Newark); Rock Spring (West Orange); Keene Valley Country (Keene Valley, N.Y.). Home: 329 Lawn Ridge Road, Orange, N.J. Office: 300 Broadway, Newark, N.J.

STANLEY, Wendell M(eredith), bio-chemist; b. Ridgeville, Ind., Aug. 16, 1904; s. James G. and Claire (Plessinger) S.; B.S., Earlham Coll., Richmond, Ind., 1926, hon. Sc.D., 1938; M.S., U. of Ill., 1927, Ph.D., 1929; hon. Sc.D., Harvard, 1938, Yale, 1938; m. Marian Staples Jay, June 15, 1929; children—Wendell Meredith, Marjorie Jean, Dorothy Claire. Research asso. and instr. in chemistry, U. of Ill., 1929; Nat. Research fellow, Munich, Germany, 1930-31; with Rockefeller Inst. for Med. Research since 1931, asso. mem. since 1937. Mem. Am. Chem. Soc., Am. Phytopathological Soc., Harvey Soc. (hon.), Am. Biol. Chemists, A.A.A.S., Sigma Xi, Alpha Omega Alpha, Gamma Alpha, Phi Lambda Upsilon, Alpha Chi Sigma, Phi Kappa Phi. Awarded A.A.A.S. prize, 1936; Isaac Adler prize of $2,000 by Med. Sch. of Harvard, 1938; Rosenberger medal by U. of Chicago, 1938; John Scott medal, certificate, and premium of $1,000 by the City of Phila., 1938. Contbr. to scientific jours. Home: 2 Ober Rd., Princeton, N.J.

STANLEY, William, lawyer; b. Laurel, Md., Mar. 17, 1891; s. Charles Harvey and Margaret (Snowden) S.; A.B., St. John's Coll., Annapolis, Md., 1911; LL.B., U. of Md., 1913; m. Mary Gilbert, Oct. 1, 1914; children—Mary Jane, Elizabeth Snowden (dec.), William, Snowden. Admitted to Md. bar, 1913, practicing in Baltimore; partner Stanley & Boss, 1913-28; Hershey, Donaldson, Williams & Stanley, 1928-33; apptd. spl. asst. to atty. gen. of U.S., Washington, D.C., Apr. 1933; the asst. to the Atty. Gen. of U.S., 1933-35. Apptd. mem. Md. Commn. on Higher Edn., 1928; chmn. com. of arrangements atty. gen.'s Conf. on Crime, Dec. 1934; mem. Atty. Gen.'s Advisory Com. to plan establishment of nat. scientific and ednl. center at Washington to train adminstrs. of criminal law, also Com. to formulate new rules for pleading, practice and procedure in civil actions in federal dist. courts. Mem. Pi Sigma Kappa. Democrat. Episcopalian (vestryman; mem. exec. council Diocese of Washington). Clubs: Metropolitan, Burning Tree (Washington); Maryland (Baltimore, Md.); Bankers (New York). Home: Laurel, Md. Office: Normandy Bldg., Washington, D.C.

STANOYEVICH, Milivoy Stoyan, author, educator; b. Koprivnitsa on Timok, Yugoslavia, Feb. 14, 1882; s. Stoyan and Kupina (Radovanovich) S.; A.B., Zayetchar Coll., 1902; M.A., U. of Belgrade, 1907; LL.M., U. of Calif., 1914; Ph.D., Columbia, 1921; spl. lit. researches univs. of Munich, Paris, Vienna and Zurich; came to America, 1908; m. Beatrice, d. William W. Stevenson, Nov. 15, 1917; 1 son, Nicholas. Assistant professor modern langs. and lits., Zayetchar Coll., 1907-08; lecturer on Slavonic instns., U. of Calif., 1916; polit. adviser in Slavonic affairs to consul gen. of Russia, at San Francisco, 1916-17; owner and editor of several Yugoslav journals in America, 1909-17; exec. sec. of Serbian War Mission to America, 1918; chief of the Slavic div. U.S. Censorship, 1918-19; editor of Yugoslav dept. in Ency. Americana, 1918-20; lecturer in Slavonic history, N. Y. Bd. Edn., 1921-24; expert adviser to State of N.Y. joint legislative com. to investigate exploitation of immigrants, 1923; lecturer in Slavonic langs. and lit., Columbia U., 1920-25; asst. actuary, Carnegie Foundation for Advancement of Teaching, 1924; dir. and editor Slavonic dept. Universal Pictures Corpn., 1925-30; pres. Universal Syndicate, 1927—. Mem. Modern Language Assn. America, Acad. Polit. Science; fellow Am. Geog. Soc. Club: Cosmopolitan (Montclair). Author: Omladina u Sadashnyosti, 1907; Figure u Pesmama (prize essay), 1907; Prevodi u Srpskim Zabavnicima (prize essay), 1908; Pessimisme et Optimisme dans la Sociologie (with brother Milosh S.), 1913; Tolstoy's Theory of Social Reform—His Doctrine of Law, Money and Property, 1914 (2d edit., 1926); Russian Foreign Policy, 1916; Early Yugoslav Literature, 1922; Modern Yugoslav Literature, 1923; Slavonic Nations of Yesterday and Today, 1925. Wrote over 300 papers relating to ednl., econ., lit., polit. and sci. subjects; also numerous essays and monographs; articles and serials in mags. Home: 110 Midland Av., Montclair, N.J. Office: 11 E. 44th St., New York, N.Y.

STANTON, Albert Hayes, clergyman; b. Ekonk, Sterling, Conn., Mar. 27, 1878; s. Avery Amos and Laura Caroline (Gallup) S.; prep. edn., Norwich (Conn.) Free Acad.; A.B., Brown U., 1904; B.D., Newton (Mass.) Theol. Inst., 1907; post grad. student Harvard and Oxford (Eng.); m. Carrie May Jordan, Mar. 16, 1910. Ordained to ministry Bapt. Ch., 1907; pastor First Bapt. Ch., Yarmouth, Me., 1907-11, First Bapt. Ch., Natick, Mass., 1911-17, Bergen Bapt. Ch., Jersey City, N.J., 1917-29; pastor at large and supt. of evangelism, N.J. Bapt. Conv., since 1929. Formerly pres. Bapt. Pastors' Conf. of N.J., North Jersey Bapt. Ministers' Conf., Bapt. Ministers' Conf. of New York City and Vicinity (twice). Mem. bd. of mgrs. Am. and Foreign Bible Soc. of New York; advisory mem. state exec. com. N.J. Christian Endeavor Union; mem. Comm. on Evangelism, Federal Council of Chs. of Christ in America. Mason. Home: 70 Oakland Rd., Maplewood. N.J. Study: 158 Washington St., Newark, N.J.

STANTON, E(lwood) Dean, county commr.; b. Tacoma, O., Aug. 20, 1880; s. William and Jane S. (Davis) S.; student pvt. schs. in Ohio, Westtown (Pa.) Sch.; m. Esther Sidney Fawcett, July 28, 1909; children—Jane D., Sidney F., Ruth E., Katherine M., Elwood Dean. Employed as electrician, Phila. Quartz Co., Phila. and Chester, Pa., 1904-06; chief engr., Westtown (Pa.) Sch., 1906-16, bus. mgr., 1916-37; county commr. Chester Co. since 1935; mem. Bd. Supervisors, Westtown Twp. Mem. bd. dirs. Chester Co. Tuberculosis Soc., West Chester Community Chest. Active in West Chester Y.M.C.A. and Boy Scouts, Community Chest. Pres. Chester Co. Supervisors and Auditors Assn. Mem. exec. com. Pa. State Assn. of Twp. Supervisors. Republican. Soc. of Friends. Clubs: Westtown (Pa.) Community (treas.); Rotary (West Chester, Pa.; pres.). Home: Westtown, Pa. Office: Court House, West Chester, Pa.

STAPLES, Philip Clayton, pres. Bell Telephone Co. of Pa.; b. Revere, Mass., Oct. 24, 1882; s. John and Josephine (Goodwin) S.; A.B., Harvard, 1904; m. Mary K. Hartman, Oct. 30, 1912; children—Philip Clayton, John Hartman. Telephone salesman, 1904-10; publicity mgr. Bell Telephone Co. of Pa., 1910-18, div. mgr., 1918-19, asst. to pres., 1919-20, vice-pres., 1920-33, pres. since 1933; pres. and dir. Diamond State Telephone Co.; dir. Pa. Co., Phila. Savings Fund Soc., Insurance Co. of N.A. Penn Mutual Life Ins. Co. Dir. Phila. Chamber of Commerce, Phila. Orchestra Assn.; mem. bd. mgrs. United Campaign, Phila. Award; mem. Phila. Co. Relief Bd.; trustee Drexel Inst. Tech.; dir. Haverford Sch.; mem. bd. U. of Pa. Hosp.; pres. Franklin Inst. Republican. Episcopalian. Clubs: Harvard (N.Y. City); Harvard, Rittenhouse, Racquet, Engineers (Phila.); Merion Cricket (Haverford, Pa.). Home: Ardmore, Pa. Office: 1835 Arch St., Philadelphia, Pa.

STARK, Lyda Arthur, oral surgeon; b. Taylor Co., W.Va., Nov. 20, 1884; s. Henry Lee and Mary (Scranage) S.; student Fairmont State Normal Sch., W.Va., 1907-10, W.Va. Univ., 1911-12; D.D.S., U. of Pittsburgh Dental Sch., 1914; grad. student Columbia U., 1925-26; m. Vera Hall, 1914; 1 son, Robert Lee. Engaged in teaching pub. schs. in W.Va., 1900; in gen. practice of dentistry, Shumiston, W.Va., 1914-25; specializing in oral surgery, Clarksburg, W.Va., since 1926. Mem. Dental Adv. Com. Harrison Co. Relief. Past pres. Chamber of Commerce. Scout master 4 yrs. Pres. W.Va. State Dental Soc., 1939. Mem. Psi Omega. Republican. Baptist. Clubs: Rotary of Shumiston (past pres.); Psychology of Clarksburg (pres. 1937). Home: 524 S. 5th St. Office: 225 Main St., Clarksburg, W.Va.

STARKE, Emory P(otter), educator; b. New York, N.Y., Jan. 31, 1896; s. Morgan Lee and Mabel (Potter) S.; grad. Brooklyn Boys' High Sch., 1913; A.B., Columbia U., 1916, M.A., 1917, Ph.D., 1926; m. Ann Cornwell, June 18, 1923; 1 dau., Patricia Ann. Teacher mathematics, Coll. City of New York, 1917-19; with Rutgers U. since 1919, becoming asso. prof. mathematics, 1930 Served as 2d lt., Coast Arty. Res. Corps, U.S. Army, June-Dec. 1918. Mem. Mathematics Syllabus Com. of N.J. State Dept. Edn. Mem. Am. Math. Soc., N.J. Assn. Math. Teachers (ex-pres.), Phi Beta Kappa, Sigma Xi. Republican. Presbyn. Asso. editor Nat. Mathematics Magazine (Baton Rouge, La.). Home: 321 Grant Av., New Brunswick, N.J.

STARR, Edward, Jr., banker; b. Philadelphia, Pa., Mar. 30, 1900; s. Isaac Tatnall and Mary T. W. (White) S.; studied Chestnut Hill Acad., 1910-14, St. Paul's Sch., Concord, N.H., 1914-18; A.B., Yale U., 1922; student U. of Pa. Law Sch., 1922-23; m. Anne Townsend, May 26, 1923; children—Edward, 3d, Ralph T., Mary Anne. Associated with Drexel & Co. since 1923, becoming partner, 1937; dir. Am. Dredging Co., Chestnut Hill R.R. Co., Franklin Co. Coal Corpn., DeBardeleben Coal Corpn., Philadelphia City Passenger Ry. Co., Philadelphia, Germantown & Norristown R.R. Co., Saving Fund Soc. of Germantown, Sharp & Dohme, Inc. Served in U.S. Navy, 1918. Treas. Philadelphia Council Boy Scouts of America, Hospital Council of Philadelphia; trustee Chestnut Hill Hosp., Episcopal Hosp. Mem. Delta Kappa Epsilon, Scroll and Key, Phi Delta Phi, Sharswood Club (U. of Pa.). Republican. Episcopalian. Clubs: Racquet, Philadelphia, Yale, Sunnybrook Golf, Bond, Wilderness, Sunday Breakfast (Philadelphia); Order of the Cincinnati, State of Deleware; Misquamicut Golf (Watch Hill, R.I.). Home: Waverly Road, Laverock, Chestnut Hill. Office: 15th and Walnut Sts., Philadelphia, Pa.

STARR, Isaac, prof. research therapeutics; b. Philadelphia, Pa., Mar. 6, 1895; s. Isaac and Mary Savage (Barclay) S.; ed. Chestnut Hill Acad., 1902-12; B.S. magna cum laude, Princeton U., 1916; M.D., U. of Pa., 1920; m. Edith Nelson Page, Apr. 22, 1922; children—Isaac, Vidal Davis, Lynford Lardner, Harold Page. House officer Mass. Gen. Hosp., Boston, 1920-22; instr. in pharmacology, U. of Pa., 1922-28, asso. in medicine, 1928-33, asst. prof. clin. pharmacology, 1928-33; Hartzell prof. research therapeutics, U. of Pa., since 1933. Mem. Med. Res. Corps, S.A.T.C., 1917-18. Mem. A. M.A., Assn. Am. Physicians, Am. Soc. Clin. Investigation (sec. 1938-39, pres. 1939-40), Am. Physiol. Soc., Am. Heart Assn., Coll. Physicians of Philadelphia, Delta Psi. Episcopalian. Clubs: Philadelphia, Princeton (Philadelphia). Writer of over 35 articles in scientific jours. on kidney physiology, cardiac output in man, peripheral vascular disease, etc. Home: 505 Cresheim Valley Road, Chestnut Hill, Pa.

STARR, James, hospital administrator; b. Germantown, Phila., Pa., Apr. 5, 1870; s. James and Mary (Emlen) S.; prep. edn. Germantown Acad. and St. Paul's Sch., Concord, N.H.; B.S., U. of Pa., 1891, E.M., 1892; m. Sarah Logan Wister, Oct. 15, 1901; 1 dau., Sarah Logan (Mrs. Daniel Blain). Sec. and dir. of Collieries Supply & Equipment Co., Phila., 1908-15, pres., 1915-20; dir. of purchases Madeira, Hill & Co., 1921-28; dir. 1921-34; administrator Hosp. of Woman's Med. Coll. of Pa. since May 1933; real estate broker since 1933. Trustee Phi Kappa Sigma Foundation, 1930-38. Served as private, later corpl., Co. D, 1st Inf., Nat. Guard Pa., 1893-96; private 1st Troop, Phila. City Cav., Nat. Guard Pa., 1896-1904, sergt., 1904-08 (served in coal strikes 1897, 1902; with troop in U.S. Vols. in Puerto Rico campaign April-November 1898); organized and recruited Troop A, Cavalry Squadron, Pennsylvania Reserve Militia and served as captain, later major and brigadier adjutant, 1918-20, command of Brigade, 1920-23. Member United Spanish War Veterans, Military Order Loyal Legion, Phi Kappa Sigma (Grand Alpha 1913-15), Royal Philatelic Soc. of London (fellow), Am. Philatelic Soc., Chinese Philatelic

STARR, Lewis Abbott, lawyer; b. Woodbury, N.J., Dec. 7, 1901; s. Lewis and Louella (Abbott) S.; A.B., Princeton U., 1924; student, U. of Pa. Law Sch., 1925-26, Temple U. Law Sch., 1926-27; m. Helen Blank, July 29, 1929; children—E. Terry, Lewis 3d. Admitted to N.J. bar as atty., 1928, as counselor, 1931; engaged in gen. practice of law at Camden; mem. firm Starr, Summerill & Lloyd; pres. and dir. Office Bldg. Co. Mem. N.J. State and Gloucester Co. bar assns., Phi Kappa Sigma, Second Ward Rep. Club (Woodbury, N.J.). Republican. Episcopalian. Clubs: Country, Little Egg Harbor Yacht (Woodbury); University Cottage (Princeton). Home: 50 S. Woodland Av., Woodbury, N.J. Office: 330 Market St., Camden, N.J.

STARRETT, C. V., asso. dir. The Buhl Foundation; b. Monaca, Pa., Sept. 15, 1898; s. Andrew Dickson and Helen (Wagner) S.; A.B., U. of Pittsburgh, 1924; special study, Beaune (A.E.F.) Univ., France, Columbia U.; m. Agnes Lynch, July 28, 1923; children—Clare Jane, David Dickson. Employed as adv. copy writer and acct. exec., Ketchum, MacLeod & Grove, Pittsburgh, Pa., 1924-29; editor Pittsburgh Record, U. of Pittsburgh, 1929-32; asso. dir. of Buhl Foundation, Pittsburgh, Pa., since 1932. Served as pvt. inf., U.S.A., 1917-19, with A.E.F. Mem. Sigma Pi, Sigma Delta Chi. Presbyn. Club: Faculty, University of Pittsburgh. Home: 434 Sulgrave Rd. Office: Farmers Bank Bldg., Pittsburgh, Pa.

STATHERS, Madison, prof. Romance langs.; b. Alma, W.Va., Aug. 29, 1877; s. George and Sophia (Furbee) S.; A.B., W.Va. U., 1901; Docteur d'Université (Ph.D.), U. of Grenoble, France, 1905; studied U. of Madrid, 1909-10, U. of Grenoble, summers 1910, 21; m. Nellie M. Dauphinee, Aug. 6, 1907; 1 son, George Dauphinee. Instr. Latin and Romance langs., W.Va. Wesleyan Coll., 1902-06; instr. Romance langs., W.Va. U., 1906-07, asst. prof., 1907-10, prof. and head of dept. since 1910, chmn. com. on grad. work, 1923-30. Mem. Modern Lang. Assn. America, Am. Assn. Teachers of Spanish, Am. Assn. Univ. Profs., Sons of Revolution, Phi Kappa Psi, Phi Beta Kappa. Democrat. Presbyn. Clubs: Faculty, Morgantown Country, Muddy Creek Recreation Club, English (hon.), Beta Pi Theta (hon.). Author: Chateaubriand et l'Amérique, 1905. Editor: La Moza de Cántaro (by Lope de Vega), 1913; Historie d'un conscrit de 1813, 1921. Home: Morgantown, W.Va.

STATHERS, William Gillespie, lawyer; b. Wheeling, W.Va., Apr. 27, 1889; s. Walter E. and H. Virginia (Whiteside) S.; student W.Va. Wesleyan Coll., 1904-07; LL.B., U. of Pa. Law Sch., 1914; m. Geraldine Wallis, July 12, 1920; children—William Gillespie, Barbara Bennett. Admitted to Lewis County bar, 1914; since in gen. practice of law; mem. law firm Stathers, Stathers & Cantrall since 1937; asst. prosecuting atty. Harrison County, 1921-32. Mem. W.Va. Ho. of Delegates, 1921-22. Served as 1st lt., 332d Inf., Regt., World War. Mem. Am. Bar Assn., Am. Law Inst., Am. Judicature Soc., W.Va. Bar Assn. (pres. 1938-39), S.R., Lions Internat. (dist. gov. 1925-26), Am. Legion (dept. comdr. 1935-36), Sigma Chi, Phi Delta Phi. Republican. Presbyterian. Mason, Elk. Clubs: Clarksburg Country, Lions (Clarksburg). Home: 259 Carr Av. Office 701 Goff Bldg., Clarksburg, W.Va.

STATON, Harry (Parker), editor and mgr. newspaper syndicate; b. Brooklyn, N.Y., Nov. 22, 1879; s. Charles Lewis Jesse and Ellen (Parker) S.; ed. pub. schs., Brooklyn; m. Mabel Lydia Quick, Mar. 9, 1904; children—Alice Mabel (Mrs. Philmon Falkenburg Conover), Grace Harvey (Mrs. Joseph Xavier Du Mond), Harry Parker. Office boy Brooklyn Times, 1894-96; reporter Brooklyn Standard Union, 1896-99, Evening World, 1899-1901, Evening Sun, 1901-04; editor and art dir. N.Y. Globe, 1904-12; editor and pub. Trend Mag., 1913-15; publicity Barnum & Bailey Circus, 1916-19, editor and mgr. N.Y. Herald Tribune Syndicate since 1920. Mem. Am. Press Soc., Soc. of Illustrators. Republican. Clubs: Players, Dutch Treat (treas.), Salmagundi (N.Y. City); Barnegat Light Yacht (Harvey Cedars, N.J.). Home: Beachwood, N.J. Office: 230 W. 41st St., New York, N.Y.

STAUB, Albert William, clergyman, educator; b. Titusville, Pa., Sept. 28, 1880; s. Albert W. and Caroline (Rickert) S.; A.B., Oberlin, 1904; A.M., Columbia, 1907; B.D., Union Theol. Sem., 1907; m. Jane Frederica McIntosh, June 9, 1908; 1 son, Albert W. Ordained Congl. ministry, 1908; ednl. missionary in China, 1908-12; exec. sec. Riverdale Neighborhood Assn., Riverdale-on-Hudson, N.Y., 1912-14; dir. Atlantic Div., Am. Red Cross, 1914-19; Am. dir. Near East Coll. Assn. since 1919; exec. sec. bd. trustees Robert Coll., Am. Univ. of Beirut, Constantinople Woman's Coll., Internat. Coll. (Beirut), Sophia Am. Sch., Athens Coll.; dir. Am. Chamber Commerce for Levant, Federated Am. Chambers Commerce of Near East, Near East Foundation, Am. Friends of Turkey, Inc.; sec. bd. trustees Am. Hosp., Istanbul; trustee Oberlin-Shansi Memorial Assn., West Side Presbyn. Church, Ridgewood. Decorated: Edith Cavell Medal, Belgian Red Cross, 1919; Cross of Officer of the Order of St. Sava (Yugo-Slavia), 1923; Cross of Comdr. Nat. Order of Civil Merit (Bulgaria), 1930. Hon. adviser to Ministry of Industries of the Nat. Govt. (China), 1932. Home: 419 Beverly Rd., Ridgewood, N.J. Office: 50 W. 50th St., New York, N.Y.

STAUB, Walter Adolph; b. Phila., Pa., Feb. 27, 1881; s. Adolph and Wilhelmine (Voegelin) S.; grad. Girard Coll., 1897; C.P.A., N.Y., Pa., N.J., Mich., D.C.; m. Ida Charlotte Flury, Apr. 12, 1904; children—Walter Richard, Ernest Flury, Edmund Arthur, Helen Elizabeth, Elmer Norman, Robert Joseph, Grace Ida. With firm of Lybrand, Ross Bros. & Montgomery since 1901, mem. of firm since 1911. Mem. Bd. of Edn., Milburn, N.J., 1924-36. Trustee Overlook Hosp., Summit, N.J. Mem. Am. Inst. Accountants, N.Y. State Soc. C.P.A. (ex-pres.), Pa. Inst. C.P.A., N.J. State Soc. C.P.A. Republican. Baptist. Clubs: Lawyers', Accountants, Quill (New York); Baltusrol Golf, and Short Hills (Short Hills, N.J.). Author: Income Tax Guide, 1913; Consolidated Returns (in federal income tax), 1921; Auditing Principles (with Robert H. Montgomery), 1923; Wills, Executors and Trustees (with W. J. Grange and E. G. Blackford), 1933. Winner prize for best paper on "Mode of Conducting an Audit," Congress of Accountants, St. Louis Expn., 1904. Home: Woodcrest Av. and Farley Rd., Short Hills, N.J. Office: 90 Broad St., New York, N.Y.

STAUDENMEIER, Charles W., lawyer; b. Ashland, Pa., Nov. 4, 1894; s. Joseph and Margaret (Lutz) S.; grad. St. Mauritius Parochial Sch., 1907, Ashland Pub. Sch., 1912, Villa Nova Coll., 1914; LL.B., Dickinson Law Sch., 1916; m. Sara E. Daley, Aug. 30, 1922; children—Margaret Marie, Charles W., James Joseph, Sara Jane. Admitted to Supreme Court of Pa. bar, 1917; since in private practice of law; solicitor of controller, Schuylkill Co., 8 yrs.; deputy dist. atty. Schuylkill Co. since 1938; dir. Citizens Nat. Bank. Mem. Pa. Ho. of Reps., 1923-32, Pa. State Senate, 1932-36. Served in U.S. Army, World War. Active in Boy Scouts of America, Am. Red Cross and Crippled Children Soc. Mem. Pa. Bar Assn. (com. on statutory Law), Schuylkill Co. Bar Assn. (bd. censors), Delta Theta Phi, Am. Legion, 40 and 8, Washington Fire Co. Republican. Catholic. Elk. Clubs: Ashland Gun and Fountain Springs Country (Ashland, Pa.). Home: 1134 Spruce St. Office: 925 Centre St., Ashland, Pa.

STAUFFEN, Ernest, Jr., banker; b. Baltimore, Md., Mar. 10, 1883; s. Ernest S.; A.B., Columbia, 1904; LL.B., New York Law Sch., 1905; m. Theodora Barber, 1 dau., Mary Brent. Admitted to N.Y. bar, 1905, and began practice with firm Kirby & Wood, N.Y. City; mem. Gould & Wilkie, 1908-14; active v.p. United Dry Goods Co., 1910-16; became v.p. Liberty Nat. Bank, 1916; now chmn. trust com. Manufacturers Trust Co.; pres. Huron Holding Corpn.; dir. Carib Syndicate, C. G. Gunther's Sons, Nash-Kelvinator Corpn., Maracaibo Corpn., Refrigeration Discount Corpn., Sharp & Dohme, Simms Petroleum Co., Internat. Products Corpn., Marine Midland Corpn., Marine Midland Trust Co., Anchor Cap Corpn., Stern Bros.; trustee Austen Riggs Foundation, Central Savings Bank. Clubs: Columbia University, Union League, Down Town Assn., Hangar, Lunch, Nat. Golf Links, Englewood Golf, Knickerbocker Country. Address Corpn. Home: 40 Lincoln St., Englewood, N.J. Office: 55 Broad St., New York, N.Y.

STAUFFEN, Frederick Charles, civil engr.; b. Baltimore, Md., July 24, 1891; s. Charles F. and Emma (Kaiser) S.; grad. Baltimore Poly. Inst., 1909; special course with F. W. Wilson, cons. engr., Boston Mass., 1917-20, Johns Hopkins U., 1920-21, with F. W. Wilson, Boston, 1926-27; m. Elsie Elnora Keitel, May 15, 1920; children—Walter William, Leonora Emma, Louise Anina. Employed as draftsman, field engr. and engr. various r.r. cos., 1909-17; plant engr., Union Shipbuilding Co., Baltimore, 1917-22; civil engr., pvt. engring., 1922-23; plant engr., Union Shipbldg. Co., Baltimore Works, 1923-25, gen. supt., 1925-32; designed, constructed and patented new type of marine railway for scrapping steel vessels, 1925; private engring., 1932-34; U.S. Govt. Dept. Labor and U.S. Army Engineer, 1935; pres. Winchester Mfg. Co., mfrs. metal specialties for drug trade, Baltimore, since 1936; commr., Arundel-on-the Bay, Md. Mem. Am. Soc. Civil Engrs., Am. Soc. Mil. Engrs., Engineers Club, Baltimore. Democrat. Lutheran. Mason. Home: 605 Somerset Rd., Roland Park, Baltimore. Office: 106 S. Howard St., Baltimore, Md.

STAUFFER, B(enjamin) Grant, mfr.; b. Lancaster, Pa., Aug. 18, 1877; s. John Forney and Clara (FonDersmith) S.; ed. Franklin and Marshall Sch.; m. Rosa A. S. Sener, Oct. 31, 1900; 1 dau., Mrs. Elizabeth Ludgate (divorced). Began as bookkeeper; organized Fidelity Electric Co., 1898, and later Lancaster Storage Co.; also engaged in real estate in Lancaster; pres. Fidelity Electric Co. since 1932; pres. Lancaster Storage Co. since 1932; dir. Northern Bank & Trust Co., Conestoga, Cotton Mills, Pa. Drug Co., Buchanan Foundation, Pa. mfrs. Casualty Ins. Co. Republican. Lutheran (trustee Trinity Ch.). Clubs: Hamilton, Lancaster Country (Lancaster, Pa.). Home: Lititz Road. Office: care Fidelity Electric Co., Lancaster, Pa.

STAUFFER, Charles Milton, wholesale grocer; b. Bethlehem, Pa., Apr. 23, 1877; s. Peter F. and Sarah (Koplin) S.; ed. Bethlehem pub. schs.; m. Anna R. A. Rapp, June 21, 1900; children—Grace Anita (Mrs. William F. Hager), Charles Richard, Sara Elizabeth (Mrs. William S. Hutchinson, Jr.), Jeanne L., Annette Eleanor. Began as office boy Eberts Grocery Co., Bethlehem, Pa., 1891; Eberts Co. merged into Davies, Strauss, Stauffer Co., wholesale grocers, of Allentown, Easton, Bangor and East Stroudsburg, Pa., 1919, became v.p. and gen. mgr., 1919, now also dir.; moved to N.M. because of ill health, 1910; part owner Santa Fe New Mexican (leading daily in state), 1910-12, which was sold to late Senator Bronson Cutting; employed as business mgr., same, 2 yrs.; v.p. and dir. First Nat. Bank & Trust Co., Bethlehem, Pa.; dir. Bethlehem Industrial Loan Co., Gen. Acceptance Corpn., Bethlehem, Pa. Dir. Family Welfare Assn., 1918-24; dir. Chamber of Commerce. Democrat. Lutheran. Mason. Clubs: Saucon Valley, Rotary (Bethlehem, Pa.). Home: 926 Prospect Av., Bethlehem, Pa. Office: 114 S. Second St., Allentown, Pa.

STAUFFER, Donald Alfred, educator; b. Denver, Colo., July 4, 1902; s. Alfred Vincent and Carrie Ella (Macdonald) S.; grad. South Denver High Sch., 1918; student U. of Colo., 1918-19; B.A., Princeton U., 1923, M.A., 1924; Ph.D., U. of Oxford (England), 1927; unmarried. Instr. English lit., Princeton U., 1927-31, asst. prof., 1931-39, asso. prof. since 1939; visiting asst. prof., U. of Colo., summer, 1938. Volunteer in S.A.T.C., U. of Colo., 1918. Rhodes scholar, 1924-27; Guggenheim Fellow, 1937. Sec. N.J. Com. for selecting Rhodes scholars. Mem. Modern Lang. Assn., Phi Beta Kappa. Club: Nassau (Princeton). Author: English Biography Before 1700, 1930. Editor: The Oxford Outlook, 1925-27. Home: 302 Henry Hall., Princeton, N.J.

STAUFFER, Edgar Eugene, clergyman; b. Treverton, Pa., May 23, 1871; s. Rev. David S. and Tamma L. (Riegner) S.; student Schuylkill Sem. (now Albright Coll.), Myerstown, Pa., 1889-1892; A.B., Lafayette Coll., Easton, Pa., 1894, A.M., 1897; A.M., Gallaudet Coll., Washington, D.C., 1895; hon. D.D., Western Union Coll., LeMars, Ia., 1923; hon. Litt.D., Albright Coll., Reading, Pa., 1938; m. Reba Feger, May 14, 1896; children—Ralph Feger, James David (dec.), R. Elizabeth (Mrs. D. R. White), Richard Edgar, Dorothy Florence, Edgar Eugene. Ordained to ministry Evang. Ch., 1896; pastor in Bangor, Norristown and Harrisburg, Pa., 1896-1903; coll. pastor and prof. Bible, Albright Coll., Reading, Pa., 1903-06, prof. English lit., 1906-20; pastor, Lebanon, Pa., and Lancaster, 1920-28; prof. English, Lebanon Valley Coll., Annville, Pa., 1923-25; dist. supt. in E. Pa. Conf. Evang. Ch. since 1928; mem. exec. com. Bd. Pub.; pres. bd. trustees E. Pa. Conf. Sec. exec. com. bd. trustees, Albright Coll. Republican. Evang. Ch. Mason, Odd Fellow. Home: 1726 Olive Av., Reading, Pa.

STAUFFER, Gertrude Frantz (Mrs. Charles F. Stauffer), mem. exec. com. Rep. State Com.; b. Rohrerstown, Pa., Dec. 28, 1883; d. Samuel O. and Emma Elizabeth (Weaver) Frantz; grad. Fontgarth Hall, West Chester, Pa., 1902; m. Charles F. Stauffer, Oct. 12, 1910 (dec.); children—Charles F., Sarah Ann. Served as vice chmn. Rep. State Com., 1928-30, mem. exec. com. since 1926; dir. Rossmere Tuberculosis Sanatorium, Lancaster, Pa. Served as chmn. Lancaster City Liberty Loan Drives during World War. Mem. bd. of dirs. Red Cross of Lancaster Co. Mem. bd. of dirs. Community Service Assn. Republican. Evangelical Lutheran. Home: 327 E. Orange St., Lancaster, Pa.

STAUFFER, Milton Theobald, clergyman, lecturer; b. Easton, Pa., Sept. 19, 1885; s. William Henry and Sybilla T. (Schneider) S.; A.B., Princeton U., 1910; grad. summer sch., U. of Chicago and Yale U., 1915-16; B.D., Union Theol. Sem., 1913; D.D., Rutgers U., 1931; m. Marjorie W. Hall, Oct. 23, 1920; children—Dwight Goddard, David Hall, Donald Gilbert. Stated supply Franklin Reformed Ch., Nutley, N.J., 1911-13, ordained Dutch Reformed ministry, 1913, pastor, 1913-15; survey sec. in China, Nat. Christian Council, 1916-22; ednl. sec. Student Volunteer Movement of North America, 1922-27; sec. Foreign Mission Conf. of North America, 1927-29; pastor Second Reformed Ch., New Brunswick, since 1929; lecturer New Brunswick Theol. Sem. since 1924. Chmn. Commn. on Pastor's Conf. (Federal Council of Churches of N.J.), Clergy Commn. of Council of Relig. Edn. of N.J.; recording sec. Foreign Mission Bd. of Reformed Ch. in America. Fellow Royal Geog. Soc. (London); mem. Alpha Delta Circle, Acacia. Club: Kiwanis, Clergy. Home: 102 College Av., New Brunswick, N.J.

STAUFFER, Nathan Pennypacker, surgeon; b. Spring City, Pa., Jan. 1, 1875; s. Granville W. and Emma (Pennypacker) S.; ed. Ursinus Coll., 1891-93; D.D.S., U. of Pa. Dental Sch., 1896; M.D., Jefferson Med. Coll., 1901; m. Anna L. Pennock, 1905 (died 1919); children—Anna P., Nathan P., Jr. Engaged as prof. hygiene, Dickinson Coll., 1896-1900; prof. phys. culture, Germantown Acad., 1903-08; prof. spl. anatomy, U. of Miss., 1909-12; in practice at Phila. since 1902, specializing in diseases of ear, nose and throat since 1913; aurist, rhinologist and laryngologist at Presbyn., Del. Co., Girard Coll., Abington, Bryn Mawr, hosps. Fellow Am. Coll. Surgs., Am. Med. Assn. Mem. Phi Kappa Psi. Republican. Presbyn. Clubs: College of Physicians, Penn Athletic, Merion Cricket. Home: Rosemont, Pa. Office: 1900 Rittenhouse Square, Philadelphia, Pa.

STAUFFER, Randolph, lawyer; b. Reading, Pa., Aug. 28, 1881; s. Abner K. and Mary High (Keim) S.; A.B., Yale U., 1903; m. Frances Dice, Apr. 19, 1911; children—Randolph (died 1919), Agnew T. Dice, George Keim, Frances Dice. Admitted to Pa. bar, 1906; since in gen. practice of law; gen. counsel and dir. Reading Iron Co.; dir. East Pa. R.R. Co., Reading & Columbia Ry. Co., Seaman Motors, Inc., Red Arrow Oil Co. Mem. Pa. Bar Assn., Alpha Delta Phi. Republican. Episcopalian. Clubs: Wyomissing, Berkshire Country, Racquet (Philadelphia); Philadelphia Gun. Home: 1515 Hill Road. Office: 529 Court St., Reading, Pa.

STAUNTON, Frederick M.; pres. Charleston Daily Mail. Home: Staunton Drive, South Hills. Office: 1001 Virginia St., Charleston, W.Va.

STAVELY, Earl Baker, coll. prof.; b. Littlestown, Pa., Mar. 5, 1892; s. Charles Henry and Alverta May (Baker) S.; B.S. in E.E., Pa. State Coll., 1912, E.E., 1915; m. Helen Amanda Markle, 1918; children—Earl Baker, James Markle, Donald Charles. Was asst. in elec. engring., Columbia U.; later design engr. Crocker-Wheeler Co.; now prof. elec. engring., Pa. State Coll. Mem. Soc. Promotion Engring. Edn., Am. Inst. E.E., Tau Beta Pi, Eta Kappa Nu, Phi Kappa Phi, Sigma Phi Sigma. Republican. Mem. Reformed Ch. Mason (Past Master State Coll. Lodge No. 700). Home: 534 W. Fairmount Av., State College, Pa.

STAVITSKY, Michael Aaron, real estate and ins. broker; b. Russia, Jan. 8, 1895; s. Isaac and Yetta (Dedov) S.; brought to U.S., 1902, naturalized, 1918; B.S., N.Y. Univ., 1916; grad. study, Columbia, 1916-17; m. Eva Levy, Sept. 7, 1919; children—Judith Ida, Ethan Simon. Engaged as field sec. of Council of Y.M.H.A. and Y.W.H.A., 1916-18; dir. field work, Jewish Welfare Bd., 1919-21; engaged in real estate and ins. brokerage on own acct. at Newark, N.J., since 1922; pres. New Empire Bldg. & Loan Assn., General-Founders Bldg. & Loan Assn.; vice-pres. Capital Securities Co., Krasner, Herman, Stavitsky Co., 60 Park Place, Inc. Served as pvt., sergt., 2d lt. Signal Corps U.S.A., 1917-19. Mem. and chmn. Newark Housing Authority, 1938. Vice-pres. N.J. Assn. Housing Ofcls. Dir. Jewish Welfare Bd., Newark Y.M.H.A. and Y.W.H.A.; pres. Welfare Council of Newark; chmn. bd. trustees Cong. B'nai Abraham; chmn. Nat. Financial Council, Jewish Welfare Bd. Mem. bd. govs. Real Estate Bd. of Newark. Jewish religion. Club: Athletic (Newark). Home: South St., Murray Hill. Office: 60 Park Pl., Newark, N.J.

STAYER, J(acob) Clyde, educator; b. New Enterprise, Pa., Sept. 25, 1890; s. Jacob C. and Lydia Jane (Brown) S.; ed. Woodbury Twp. Sch., Bedford Co.; student Juniata Acad., 1908-10; B.A., Juniata Coll., 1916; studied summers, U. of Mich. and Springfield Y.M.C.A. Coll.; M.A., U. of Pittsburgh, 1934; m. Cynthia Sloan, Aug. 28, 1919; children—Louise Sloan, John Clyde. Teacher pub. schs., 1910-12, Kiskiminetas Sch. for Boys, 1916-19; prin. Juniata Acad., 1919-23; teacher mathematics, Juniata Coll., 1923-34, asst. prof. mathematics, since 1935, dean of men since 1935. Mem. Borough Council. Mem. Mat. Assn. America, Pa. Acad. Science, Sigma Xi, Sigma Delta Psi. Republican. Mem. Ch. of the Brethren. Home: 1618 Moore St., Huntingdon, Pa.

STAYTON, William H., ocean transportation; b. Smyrna, Del., Mar. 28, 1861; s. Charles Emerson and Susan (Moffatt) S.; grad. U.S. Naval Acad., 1881; LL.B., Columbian (now George Washington) U., 1889, LL.M., 1890; m. Annie Henderson, June 2, 1887; children—Charles H., Mrs. Catharine Hulett, William H., Thomas Truxtun. Resigned from navy, 1883; with U.S.M.C., 1883-91; with Naval Militia, N.Y., 1893-98; again in navy during Spanish-Am. War, commdg. various vessels. Practiced as admiralty lawyer, gradually shifting into management steamship cos.; now pres. Balto. Steamship Co., Baltimore Trading Co.; mem. board of dirs. Baltimore Ship Supply Company. Mem. Soc. Naval Architects and Marine Engrs., Governing Council of Naval Acad. Graduates (president), U.S. Naval Academy Alumni Assn. (president). Founder and chmn. bd. Assn. Against Prohibition Amendment; chmn. bd. Repeal Associates; dir. and mem. exec. com. and administrative com. Am. Liberty League. Episcopalian. Clubs: Metropolitan (Washington, D.C.); University, Merchants', Elkridge Country, Maryland (Baltimore); Army and Navy of America, New York Yacht. Home: Smyrna, Del. Office: National Press Bldg., Washington, D.C.

STEAD, John, corpn. official; b. New York, N.Y., Mar. 11, 1885; s. Henry and Mary Ellen (Morris) Stead; ed. High Sch., New York; m. Lillian V. McCormack, Feb. 1, 1930; 1 dau., Patricia Ann. V.p. Binney & Smith Co. since 1930; pres. Indian River Refrigeration Terminal Co., Ft. Pierce, Fla., Ft. Pierce Financing & Construction Co., St. Lucie Co. Bank, Ft. Pierce; v.p. W. C. Hardesty Co., N.Y. City. Republican. Clubs: New York Athletic; Northampton Country; Pomfret. Home: R.D. No. 1, Bethlehem, Pa. Office: care Binney & Smith Co., Easton, Pa.

STEAD, Robert, architect; b. N.Y. City, Jan. 27, 1856; s. Edward Briggs and Matilda Lavinia (Hagthrop) S.; ed. Coll. City of N.Y., 1872-76; studied architecture in Atelier DeMonclos, Paris, France; m. 3d, Helen Louise Coates, June 8, 1921; children (by first marriage)—W. Force, Robert, Mary, Manning F., Edward. Practiced, Washington, Mar. 1, 1884—. Architect: Metzerott (office) Bldg.; Lovejoy Sch.; Bowen Sch.; Mt. Vernon Seminary; Epiphany Mission House; Epiphany Chapel; office bldg. at 1307 and 1309 G St. N.W.; residences of E. K. Johnson, Mrs. J. F. Barbour, W. R. Riley, etc. Rep. candidate for Md. State Senate, 1899. Episcopalian. Fellow Am. Inst. Architects; mem. Archæol. Inst. America. Mason. Clubs: Cosmos, Chevy Chase (Washington). Home: 1817 De Lancey Pl., Philadelphia, Pa.

STEARNE, Allen M., judge; b. Philadelphia, Pa., Aug. 13, 1882; s. Edwin and Alice (Morris) S.; student Central High Sch. and U. of Pa. Law Sch.; m. Mary H. Simons, June 11, 1907; 1 dau., Mrs. Dorothy Starkey. In gen. practice of law, 1905-27; appointed judge Orphans Ct., July 1, 1927, elected for 10-yr. term, Nov. 1927, re-elected, 1937. Mem. S.A.R. Pres. Frankford Soc., New Jerusalem Ch. Mason (33°). Clubs: Union League (pres.), University (Philadelphia); Torresdale-Frankford Country. Author numerous legal articles for U. of Pa., Temple U. and Legal Intelligencer; church articles for New Church Messenger. Home: 4748 Castor Av. Office: 414 City Hall, Phila., Pa.

STEARNS, Frederick Wainwright, architect; b. Pittsburgh, Pa., Oct. 5, 1902; s. Isador Jerome and Lena Louise (Stearns) S.; ed. Culver Mil. Acad., 1917-20; B.Sc. Engring., U.S. Naval Acad., Annapolis, 1924; B.Arch., U. of Pa., 1926; grad. study, Drexel Inst. of Sci., 1927-29; ed. art and painting, Carnegie Inst. Tech., summers 1924-26; m. Edna Cynthia Kauffman, Sept. 13, 1926; 1 dau., Lois Marjorie. Employed as draftsman, 1926-28; designer interiors, Wanamaker Store, Phila., 1929-31; designer for architects, 1931-33; in pvt. practice as architect since 1933; architect, U.S. Navy Dept., 1934-36; asst. architect for Panama Canal, 1936-37; asst. architect for U.S. Naval Mission to Brazil since 1937; city planner and architect on design of new city, Gamboa, C.Z.; etcher and painter, exhibited at Print Club, Phila., Acad. Fine Arts, Phila., Wyeth Galleries, Kleeman & Thorman, N.Y. City, various showings Pittsburgh, Chicago; represented in various galleries and pvt. collections. Mem. Assn. Federal Architects, Alumni Assn. U.S. Naval Acad., Alumni Assn. U. of Pa. Democrat. Episcopalian. Clubs: Penn Athletic, Rowing Assn. (Philadelphia); Camera (Panama, C. Z.). Home: 6106 Christian St., Phila., Pa. Office: Design Section, Navy Yard, Phila., Pa.

STEARNS, Harry Lee, supt. schs.; b. Harford, Pa., Apr. 5, 1900; s. George A. and Grace (Greenwood) S.; grad. Harford High Sch., 1918; A.B., Dickinson Coll., 1922; M.A., U. of Pittsburgh, 1929; Ph.D., New York U., 1936; m. Helene Rynearson, June 25, 1924; children—Charlotte Marie, Richard Harry. Prin. Meshoppen (Pa.) pub. schs., 1922-25; supv. prin. schs., Clark's Summit, Pa., 1925-29; prin. North Plainfield (N.J.) High Sch., 1929-

STEARNS 35; city supt., Woodbury, N.J., since 1935. Mem. S.A.T.C., 1918. Mem. local council Boy Scouts America. Mem. N.E.A., Am. Assn. Sch. Adminstrs., N.J. Council of Edn., N.J. Schoolmasters Club, Phi Beta Kappa, Alpha Chi Rho. Republican. Presbyterian. Mason (32°). Club: Woodbury Kiwanis (dir.). Home: 45 N. Evergreen Av. Office: High School, Woodbury, N.J.

STEARNS, Louis Agassiz, univ. prof., entomologist; b. Holden, Mass., Sept. 28, 1892; s. George Henry and Sarah Amelia (Foster) S.; student Holden (Mass.) High Sch., 1908-11; B.A., Ohio Wesleyan U., Delaware, O., 1915; M.Sc., Ohio State U., Columbus, O., 1917, Ph.D., 1928; m. Margaret Ruth Foote, Feb. 2., 1918; children—Reid Foster, Delevan Henry, Sara Frances. Asst. in zoology and entomology, Ohio State U., Columbus, O., 1915-17; prof. and acting head dept. biology, Alma (Mich.) Coll., 1917-18; asso. state entomologist, Blacksburg, Va., and asso. prof. econ. entomology, Va. Poly. Inst., Blacksburg, 1918-24; asst. entomologist, N.J. Argl. Experiment Sta., New Brunswick, N.J., 1924-27, Ohio Agrl. Experiment Sta., Wooster, O., 1927-29; prof. and head dept. entomology, U. of Del., Newark, Del., since 1929. Mem. Del. Mosquito Commn., 1933-35. Mem. Am. Assn. Econ. Entomologists (chmn. Eastern Branch, 1934, Sect. of Extension, 1932), Entomol. Soc. of America, Eastern Assn. Mosquito Control Workers, S.A.R., Sigma Phi Epsilon, Sigma Xi, Phi Kappa Phi. Republican. Mason, Odd Fellow, Lions. Club: Newark (Del.) Country. Author: 96 scientific papers. Address: 278 Orchard Rd., Newark, Del.

STEBBINS, George Edwin, lawyer; b. Shelburne Falls, Mass., Jan. 27, 1882; s. Edwin Alonzo and Anna Adella (Smith) S.; A.B., Bates Coll., 1903; Ph.D., Clark U., 1907; student George Washington U., 1908-10; LL.B., Northeastern U., 1912; m. Miriam Tenney, Dec. 31, 1911; children—Margaret, Ruth. Asst. examiner U. S. Patent Office, 1908-10; admitted to Mass. bar, 1911; specializing in patent law since 1911; mem. law firm Stebbins, Blenko & Parmelee since 1935. Mem. Am. Bar Assn., Pa. Bar Assn., Allegheny County Bar Assn., Pittsburgh Patent Law Assn., Delta Tau Delta. Republican. Mason. Clubs: Duquesne, Edgewood Country (Pittsburgh). Home: 433 Maple Av., Edgewood. Office: Farmers Bank Bldg., Pittsburgh, Pa.

STEBER, Raymond William, banker; b. Warren Pa., June 26, 1890; s. Frederick A. and Louise M. (Koebley) S.; grad. Warren High Sch., 1908; A.B., Amherst Coll., 1912; studied Rutgers U. Grad Sch. of Banking, 1936-38; m. Lalla R. Bell, July 17, 1916; 1 dau., Louise Bell. With F. A. Steber Co., cigar mfr., 1912 to 1937; treas. F. A. Steber Co., 1927-32, pres. and treas., 1932-37; with Warren Bank & Trust Co. since 1937, also dir.; dir. DeLuxe Metal Furniture Co., Consumer Discount Corpn. Burgess Boro of Warren since 1934. Mem. U.S. Naval Reserve, 1917-21. Dir. Warren Gen. Hosp., Warren Library Assn., Warren Community Chest. Mem. Phi Delta Theta. Republican. Presbn. Mason. Home: 6 Verback St. Office: Warren Bank & Trust Co., Warren, Pa.

STEDMAN, John Weiss, insurance; b. Danvers, Mass., Jan. 5, 1880; s. Henry Rust and Mabel (Weiss) S.; grad. Groton (Mass.) Sch., 1898; A.B., Harvard, 1902; m. Hilda Clifford, Oct. 14, 1905; children—John Weiss, Hilda (Mrs. Franklin W. Hobbs, Jr.), Harriet Randall, William Ellery. After about 4 yrs. in operating dept. of Pere Marquette Ry., was connected with Clark, Dodge & Co. for more than 10 yrs.; became asst. treas. Prudential Insurance Co., Oct. 1915, 2d v.p., Feb. 1918, and v.p.p in charge of investments, Jan. 1924; dir. Federal Ins. Co., P.M. Ry. Mem. advisory, chmn. finance coms. Morris County Community Chest. Clubs: Harvard, Down Town Assn. (New York); Morris County Golf; New Bedford (Mass.) Yacht. Home: 10 Headley Rd., Morristown, N.J. Office: 763 Broad St., Newark, N.J.

STEED, Robert Dennis, lawyer; b. Hamlin, W.Va., Nov. 13, 1880; s. William Henry and Margaret Jane (Snyder) S.; student Marshall Coll., Huntington, W.Va., 1898-1902, W.Va. Univ., 1905-06; studied law pvtly. and at W. Va. Univ.; m. Vivian R. Workman, June 18, 1912; children—Mary Margaret, William Hugh. Prin. Point Pleasant (W.Va.) High Sch., 1902-03; supt. Guyandotte (W.Va.) city schs., 1903-05; admitted to W.Va. bar, 1906, and since practiced at Hamlin and in Charleston; also admitted to practice before Supreme Court of U.S.; now mem. firm Lee, Blessing & Steed; pros. atty. Lincoln County, W.Va., 1908-12; mayor City of Hamlin, 1910-12; mem. W. Va. State Senate, 1912-16; atty. for W.Va. Pub. Service Commn., 1916-20; asst. atty gen. of W.Va., 1920-35. Republican. Methodist. K.P. Home: 3 Grosscup Rd. Office: Union Bldg., Charleston, W.Va.

STEEL, Charles L(eighton), Jr., prin. high sch.; b. Newton, N.J., Oct. 20, 1894; s. Charles L. and Florence (Riddel) S.; B.S., Muhlenberg Coll., 1919; grad. study, Columbia U., 1921-22, N.Y. Univ., 1926, 1932, 1938; m. Gertrude Schultz, June 2, 1918; children—Charles L. 3d, Betty Ann, John Schultz. Began as teacher in pub. schs., then vice prin., prin. high sch., Teaneck, N.J. Served as pharmacist's mate, 1st class, U.S. Navy, assigned to U.S. Marines, 1917-19; with A.E.F. in France. Mem. Nat. Edn. Assn., Progressive Edn. Assn., Secondary Prins. Assn., Am. Assn. Sch. Administrs., Alpha Tau Omega. Episcopalian. Clubs: Bergen County Schoolmen's, Rotary of Teaneck. Home: 312 Maitland Av., West Englewood, N.J. Office: High School, Teaneck, N.J.

STEELE, Charles, lumber mfr., banker; b. Port Carbon, Pa., Apr. 29, 1865; s. Amos K. and Sarah A. (Keiser) S.; grad. Sunbury High Sch., 1883; A.M., Susquehanna U., 1921; m. Mary L. Seid, Oct. 26, 1892; 1 dau., Mary G. Bookkeeper Wm. Whitmer & Sons Co., mfrs. and wholesale lumber, 1883, part traveling asst. to head of firm, 1884-89, asst. mgr., 1889-93, mem. firm, 1893-1907, company incorporated as Whitmer-Steele Co., 1907, and since pres. and treas.; pres. and treas. South River Lumber Co., Inc.; pres. Wilmer Supply Co., Inc.; pres. Northumberland Nat. Bank since organization, 1903. Served 2 terms Pa. State Senate; Councilman and chief burgess, Northumberland (Pa.) Borough. Dir. and endowment treas. Susquehanna U. Republican. Lutheran. Mason (32°); past master Eureka Lodge No. 404. Club: Kiwanis (Northumberland). Home: 80 King St. Office: 65 King St., Northumberland, Pa.

STEELE, David McConnell, clergyman; b. Pittsburgh, Pa., June 11, 1873; s. John Cameron and Margaret (McConnell) S.; B.A., Wooster, 1895; M.A., Columbia, 1899, D.D., 1916; B.D., Union Theological Seminary, 1899; m. Martha Virginia Mills, May 23, 1930. Deacon, 1899, priest, 1900, P.E. Church; assistant Holy Trinity Church, Brooklyn, N.Y., 1898-1901, St. Bartholomew Ch., New York, 1901-04; rector St. Luke and Epiphany Ch., Phila., 1904-34, rector emeritus since 1934. Author: Going Abroad Overland, 1916; Vacation Journeys, East and West, 1917; Addresses and Sermons to Students, 1918; Papers and Essays for Churchmen, 1919; After Dinner Speeches, 1920. Address: Newtown Square, Pa.

STEELE, Donald Montgomery, engring. exec.; b. Philadelphia, Pa., June 6, 1889; s. Joseph M. and Mary (Stewart) S.; student Penn Charter Sch., 1910-16; B.S. in C.E., U. of Pa., 1920; m. Alice T. Randle, 1929; 1 dau., Alice Randle, II. Engr. Wm. Steele & Sons Co., 1920-24, sales exec., 1924-35; pres. Steele Bldg. Construction Co. since 1935; v.p. Wm. Steele & Sons Co.; dir. Honorbilt Products, Inc. Mem. Sigma Alpha Epsilon, Sigma Tau. Presbyterian. Clubs: University, Elk River Yacht. Home: 430 Vernon Road, Jenkintown, Pa. Office: 1613 Sansom St., Philadelphia, Pa.

STEELE, Frank John, pharmacist; b. Crawford Co., Pa., Apr. 16, 1905; s. John and Mary (Flemming) S.; student Allegheny Coll., Meadville, Pa., 1924; Ph.G., U. of Pittsburgh College of Pharmacy, 1930; student, Pennsylvania State College, Pittsburgh, 1930; married Mildred H. Morse, June 12, 1939. Employed as pharmacy apprentice, 1921-25; scholarship U. of Pittsburgh Coll. of Pharmacy, and student asst. pharmacognosy, 1925-28; resident and asst. pharmacist, Western Pa. Hosp., 1928-30, resident pharmacist, 1930-38, in charge pharmacy and asst. to chief pharmacist since 1938; active mem. Corpn. of Phila. Coll. of Pharmacy and Science since 1934. Fellow A.A.A.S., Internat. Faculty of Science, London (hon.); mem. Nat. Assn. Drug Clerks (hon.), Nat. Conf. Pharm. Research, Science Club (pres.), Naturalist Soc. (rec. sec.), Alumni Assn. U. of Pittsburgh, Beta Kappa Psi (sec.; Pittsburgh grad. chapter historian). Republican. Baptist. Home: 708 Highland Av., Meadville, Pa. Office: 123 E. Ross St., Lancaster, Pa.

STEELE, Frederick Abbott, chemist; b. Wabash Co., Ind., Dec. 4, 1899; s. Lee Cornelius and Alice Jane (Abbott) S.; ed. U. of Ill., 1919-20; B.S., U. of Notre Dame, 1923, M.S. same, 1926; grad. student, Northwestern, 1926; Ph.D., Pa. State Coll., 1928; m. Ruth Stewart Beaton, Dec. 31, 1928; children—Jean Lee, Ann Beaton. Employed as research investigator, New Jersey Zinc Co., Palmerton, Pa., 1928-37; chief research chemist, C. K. Williams & Co., Easton, Pa., since 1937. Served in S.A.T.C., 1918. Mem. Am. Chem. Soc., Am. Phys. Soc. Tech. Assn. of the Pulp and Paper Industry, Alpha Chi Sigma, Sigma Pi Sigma, Phi Lambda Upsilon, Phi Kappa Phi, Sigma Xi. Republican. Methodist. Home: 2345 Park Av., Easton, Pa.

STEELE, John D., retired mfr.; b. Low Moor, Va., Aug. 29, 1875; s. Dewitt C. and Catherine (Mallow) S.; ed. elementary sch.; m. Carrie I. Payne, Dec. 26, 1901. Clerk Charlottesville (Va.) Post Office, 1892-1900; traveling salesman, 1900-03; broker, Charleston, W.Va., 1903-16; coal operator and head coal sales agency, 1910-16; became shoe polish mfr., 1916; moved to Baltimore, 1923; pres. or prin. owner Chieftain Mfg. Co., 1929-38; now retired from active business. Dir. Pageant for City of Baltimore, 1929, to celebrate 200th anniversary; chmn. business com. Bd. of Sch. Commrs., 5 yrs.; now chmn. Commn. on City Plan. Served with Montecello Guard, Charlottesville, Va., 2 yrs.; chmn. Council of Defense, Charleston, during World War. Pres. Charleston (W.Va.) Y.M.C.A., 1905-11; pres. W.Va. Sunday Sch. Assn., 1915-23; organized Charleston Rotary Club, 1915; mem. board Association of Commerce, Baltimore, 1927-30. Headed many campaigns for money raising, Charleston. Democrat. Clubs: Woodmont Rod and Gun (Hancock, Md.); Boiling Springs Rod and Gun (Warm Springs, Va.). Home: 922 University Parkway. Office: 407 Municipal Bldg., Baltimore, Md.

STEELE, Joseph M., building constrn.; b. Philadelphia, Pa., Feb. 5, 1865; s. William and Ellen A. (Blair) S.; ed. pub. schs. and business coll., Phila.; m. Mary J. Stewart, Jan. 15, 1889; children—William III, Mary C. (wife of Dr. Leon Clemmer), Donald M., John S. Began in bldg. constrn. business, 1886; pres. Wm. Steele & Sons Co. since 1908; v.p. Girard Life Ins. Co.; dir. Tradesmen's Nat. Bank & Trust Co., Franklin Fire Ins. Co., Warner Co. Trustee Drexel Inst., Phila., Beaver Coll., Jenkintown, Pa., Geneva Coll., Beaver Falls, Pa., Am. Univ. at Cairo. Republican. Ref. Presbyn. Club: Union League. Home: Cambridge, Germantown. Office: 1304 Arch St., Philadelphia, Pa.

STEELE, Robert McCurdy, educator; b. Jefferson Co., Pa., Mar. 21, 1882; s. Joseph and Josephine Adelaide S.; Ph.B., Bucknell U., 1908; grad. study, U. of Wis., 1912-13; A.M., and Ph.D., Columbia, 1926; honorary LL.D. from Bucknell University, 1936; m. Genevieve G. Dunkle, Aug. 23, 1916; children—Joanne, Mary W. Teacher elementary schs., 1900-04; teacher Clarion (Pa.) State Normal Sch., 1908-12; supt. schs. and prin. high sch., Latrobe, Pa., 1912-20; dir. tr. sch., State Teachers Coll., Slippery Rock, Pa., 1920-26; prin. Clarion State Normal Sch., 1926-28; president State Teachers' Coll., California, Pa., 1928—. In ednl. service, U.S.A., 1918-19. Mem. N.E.A., Delta Sigma, Kappa Delta Pi, Phi Delta Kappa. Republican. Presbyn. Mason (32°, K.T.). Club: Schoolmen's. Author: A Study of Teacher

Training in Vermont, 1926. Home: California, Pa.

STEELE, Robert Thomas S(tephen), coal operator; b. Rockingham, N.C., June 15, 1873; s. Walter L. and Mary (Little) S.; B.S., U. of N.C., 1895; M.D., U. of Md. Med. Sch., 1899; m. Margaretta S. Tinsman, Oct. 17, 1901; children—Mary Elizabeth, Anne (Mrs. George E. Joy). Engaged in pvt. practice of medicine, Rockingham, N.C., 1899-1904; treas. Cochran Coal Co., Williamsport, Pa., 1904-23, pres. and dir. since 1923; pres. Kettle Creek Coal Mining Co., 1923-29; pres. and dir. Lycoming Land Co. since 1929; vice-pres. and dir. WRAK, Inc., since 1933; dir. West Branch Bank & Trust Co. Vice-pres. and dir. Williamsport Y.M.C.A. Mem. Sigma Nu. Presbyn. Clubs: Country (Williamsport); Big Bear Creek Fishing, Texas Blockhouse Fishing (Lycoming Co.); White Birch Salmon (New Brunswick, Can). Home: 904 W. 4th St. Office: 34 W. 4th St., Williamsport, Pa.

STEELE, William, 3d, engr.; b. Philadelphia, Pa., Jan. 22, 1890; s. Joseph and Mary (Stewart) S.; student U. of Pa., 1907-11; m. Edna Welsh, Oct. 16, 1912; children—Elizabeth Welsh, Joseph M., 2d, Suzanne Alexander. Field engr. Wm. Steele & Sons Co., 1911-13, gen. supt., 1913-17 and 1919-21, 1st v.p. and dir., 1921-35; v.p. United Engrs. & Constructors, Inc., since 1935; pres. and dir. Erie Nat. Bank; v.p. and dir. The Steele Corpn.; sec. and dir. The Philadelphia Authority. Served as 1st lt., U.S. Army, 1917-18, capt., 1918-19; hon. discharged, Oct. 1919. Mem. Delta Tau Delta. Republican. Episcopalian. Clubs: Union League, Engineers (Philadelphia); Bankers of America (N.Y. City). Home: Chestnut Hill. Office: 1401 Arch St., Philadelphia, Pa.

STEEN, John William, lawyer; b. Belle Vernon, Pa., Aug. 29, 1909; s. Frank Hall and Ada Griffith (Teggart) S.; grad. Monessen (Pa.) High Sch., 1927; A.B., Juniata Coll., Huntingdon, Pa., 1931; LL.B., U. of Mich., 1934; m. Lillian Elsie Baird, July 27, 1938. With engring. corps, Pittsburgh Steel Co., Monessen, Pa., 1930-33; partner Leightty Steen & Son, real estate and insurance, Belle Vernon, Pa., since Apr. 1933; admitted to Westmoreland County bar, 1935, and since in private practice; v.p. and dir. Peoples Nat. Bank & Trust Co., Monessen. Solicitor for boroughs of Belle Vernon, North Belle Vernon and Fayette City, Pa. Sec. and dir. Belle Vernon Pub. Library Assn. Received Rensselaer Polytechnical award for math. honors. Mem. Delta Theta Phi, Barristers. Republican. Methodist. Odd Fellow. Clubs: Pleasant Valley Country (Connellsville); Belle Vernon Rotary Internat.; Fraternal Order of Police (Monessen). Home: 112 Fayette St. Office: 111 Main St., Belle Vernon, Pa.

STEERE, Douglas Van, coll. prof.; b. Harbor Beach, Mich., Aug. 31, 1901; s. Edward Morris and Ruby Edith (Monroe) S.; grad. Detroit Eastern High Sch., 1918; B.S., Mich. State Coll., 1923; A.M., Harvard U., 1925, Ph.D., 1931; B.A., Oxford U., 1928; m. Dorothy Lou MacEachron, June 12, 1929; children—Helen Weaver, Anne. Asst. prof. philosophy, Haverford Coll., 1928-31, asso. prof. since 1931. Dir. Am. Friends Service Com., Pendle Hill Sch.; trustee John Woolman Memorial Assn. Mem. Am. Philos. Assn., Am. Theol. Soc., Assn. Am. Rhodes Scholars, Phi Beta Kappa. Mem. Soc. of Friends. Author: The Open Life, 1937; Prayer and Worship, 1938. Translator: Kierkegaard's Purity of Heart, 1938. Lecturer and writer on religious and social subjects. Address: Haverford Coll., Haverford, Pa.

STEERE, Jonathan Mowry, banker; b. Harrisville, R.I., Apr. 26, 1870; s. Isaac and Avis (Battey) S.; student Providence (R.I.) High Sch., 1884-85, Moses Brown Sch., Providence, 1885-87; A.B., Haverford Coll., Haverford, Pa., 1890, A.M., 1892; m. Florence Esther Trueblood, Sept. 9, 1910; children—Jonathan Mowry, David Trueblood; m. 2d, Louise Gifford Turner, Nov. 28, 1937. Teacher Tioga Friends Sch., 1892-93; with Girard Trust Co. since 1893, beginning as clerk, trust officer, 1909-28, v.p. since 1928; v.p. and dir. Turner & Harrison Steel Pen Mfg. Co., Hotel Traymore (Atlantic City), Broadway Exchange Corpn. (N.Y. City), Conard & Pyle Co.; treas. and dir. Pa. Crusher Co.; dir. Metropolitan Edison Co., of Reading, Pa., Philadelphia & Western R.R., Minehill & Schuylkill Haven R.R., Colonial Colliery Co., Kensington Ship Yard & Dry Dock. Mgr. Haverford Coll.; mem. com. Friends Select Sch.; dir. Philadelphia Y.M.C.A.; pres. Indian Rights Assn.; treas. Philadelphia Yearly Meeting of Friends, Wistar Inst. of Anatomy and Biology. Republican. Mem. Soc. of Friends (Quaker). Clubs: University, Rittenhouse (Philadelphia); Merion Cricket (Haverford). Home: 615 Walnut Lane, Haverford, Pa. Office: Girard Trust Co., Philadelphia, Pa.

STEESE, James Gordon, civil engr.; b. Mt. Holly Springs, Pa., Jan. 21, 1882; s. James Andrew and Anna Zug (Schaeffer) S.; A.B., Dickinson College, 1902, A.M., 1906; B.S. (1st honors), U.S. Military Academy, 1907; studied U. of Calif., 1908; grad. U.S. Engr. Sch., Washington, 1910; Sc.D., U. of Alaska, 1932; unmarried. Commd. 2d lt. engrs., June 14, 1907; promoted through grades to col., June 18, 1918; brigadier general and adjutant general Alaska N.G., 1926-27; retired Oct. 1927. Asst. engr. San Diego and San Francisco bays, Calif., 1907-08; duty Panama Canal, 1908-12; chief engr. 5th (expeditionary) Brig., Tex., 1913; instr. and asst. prof. engring., U.S. Mil. Acad., 1913-17; spl. rep. of gen. mgr. West Md. Ry., June-Sept. 1916; organized O.T.C., Ft. Riley, Kan., and instr. Engr. O.T.C., Ft. Leavenworth, Kan., 1917; assistant chief of engineers, U.S.A., 1917-18; detailed on General Staff and chief of section, September, 1918-June 1920; spl. mission to Adriatic and Balkan countries, 1919; pres. Alaska Road Commn., 1920-27, also chief engr., 1924, 27; dist. and acting div. engr. for rivers and harbors, Alaska Dist., 1921-27; cons. engr. Dept. Commerce, 1921-27, also for Ty. of Alaska, 1921-23; mem. spl. commn. to investigate Russian, Japanese, and Am. fur seal rookeries, June-Sept. 1922; dir. pub. works, Alaska, 1923-27; chmn. Alaska R.R., 1923-24, also chief engr., Mar.-Oct. 1923; with Gulf Oil Corpn. as gen. mgr. foreign subsidiary co., 1927-32; chmn. bd. and pres. Guajillo Corpn. and affiliated cos. since Aug. 1932; pres. Slate Creek Placers, Inc., since Feb. 1936. Brig. gen., a.d.c., Alaska N.G., 1935-37. In charge President Harding's tour of Alaska, 1923. Trustee Dickinson College since 1919, Amelia S. Givin Free Library since 1921. Fellow Royal Geog. Soc. (London), Am. Geog. Soc., Am. Assn. for Advancement of Science; member American Society Civil Engrs., Am. Inst. Mining and Metall. Engrs., Soc. Am. Mil. Engrs., Phi Beta Kappa, Phi Kappa Sigma, Pi Gamma Mu, Am. Legion. Decorated D.S.M. (U.S.); D.S.M., 2d Class (Panamanian); Officer, later Comdr. Order of Prince Danilo I, and silver medal for bravery (Montenegrin); Croix de Guerre, 2d Class (Grecian); Officer of Public Instruction (French); Khamés de l'Ahal Saxaoul, French Sahara; specially commended in Senate and Ho. of Rep. of U.S., and salary raised by spl. act of Congress, 1926. Del. U.S. Govt. to XIV Internat. Navigation Congress, Cairo, Egypt, 1926 (sec., Am. sect.), XV Internat. Navigation Congress, Venice, Italy, 1931, XVI Congress, Brussels, Belgium, 1935; del. Internat. Geographical Congress, Paris, France, 1931; del. U.S. Government to 5th Internat. Congress of Surveyors, London, Eng., 1934 (chmn. Am. section), to Internat. Geog. Congress, Warsaw, Poland, 1934 (pres. sec. I-cartography), to 4th Internat. Congress and Expn. of Photogrammetry, Paris, France, 1934 (declined), to Second World Petroleum Congress, Paris, 1937, Internat. Geog. Congress, Amsterdam, Netherlands, 1938. Republican. Episcopalian. Mason (33°), Elk. Clubs: Army and Navy (Washington); West Point Army Mess; Strangers (Colon); Croatan Country (Norfolk); Golf (Panama); Engineers (Ft. Humphreys); University (New York); Cartagena (Columbia); Officers Mess (Ft. Sam Houston). Home: Mt. Holly Springs, Pa. Office: Alamo Nat. Bldg., San Antonio, Tex.

STEEVER, Miller D(idama), prof. of law; b. Scranton, Pa., Mar. 25, 1886; s. Edgar Zell and Julia Beaumont (Collings) S.; Ph.B., Lafayette Coll., Easton, Pa., 1909; LL.B., Harvard, 1912; m. Dorothy Gladys Inglehart, July 2, 1912; children—Andrew Beaumont, Edgar Zell, IV. Admitted to Mass. bar, 1912, and began practice in Pittsfield; city clerk of Pittsfield, 1916-19; special rep. of U.S. Sec. of War, 1919-21, in charge of War Dept. cases against Brit., French and Italian ministries of munitions, Paris and London, also counsel for U.S. Liquidation Commn., London, and mem. War Dept. Claims Bd. (chmn. standing com.), Washington, D.C.; Kirby prof. of civil rights and head dept. of govt. and law, Lafayette Coll., since 1921. Mem. bars of Mass., Dist. of Columbia, Pa. Dir. Kirby Polit. Science Library and Museum. Mem. Am. Polit. Science Assn., Am. Assn. Univ. Profs., Am. Acad. Polit. and Social Science, Phi Beta Kappa (chmn. Middle Atlantic dist. since 1934), Delta Kappa Epsilon. Republican. Club: Cosmos (Washington, D.C.). Home: 32 McCartney St., Easton, Pa.

STEGEMAN, Gebhard, physical chemistry; b. Holland, Mich., June 14, 1890; s. John and Hannah (Kamps) S.; A.B., Hope Coll., Holland, Mich., 1913; A.M., Ohio State U., 1915, Ph.D., 1917; m. Mildred Smith, June 11, 1932. Instr. in chemistry, U. of Wash., 1917-18; asst. prof. of chemistry, U. of Pittsburgh, 1919-24, prof. since 1924. Served as chemist with Chemical Warfare Service, U.S. Army, 1918-19. Mem. Am. Chem. Soc., Alpha Chi Sigma, Sigma Xi. Republican. Mem. Dutch Reformed Ch. Clubs: Pittsburgh Athletic, Shannopin Country (Pittsburgh). Contbr. to Am. Chem. Soc. Jour., Jour. Phys. Chem. Home: 6 Oxford Rd., Ben Avon Heights, Pittsburgh, Pa.

STEIDLE, Edward, college dean; b. Williamsport, Pa., June 23, 1887; s. Michael and Mary (Eck) S.; B.S., Pa. State Coll., 1911, Engr. of Mines, 1914; m. Ellen May Girsham, July 29, 1920; children—Edward, Howard. Miner and mine sampler, Nipissing Mining Co., Ltd., 1908-10; miner and millman Sicorro Mining Co., 1911-12; with U.S. Bur. Mines, 1912-17; cons. engr. U.S. Bureau Mines and Mine Safety Appliances Company, 1920-28; associate professor mining engineering, Carnegie Institute Technology, 1919; organized coöperative research program in mining, fuel technology and metallurgy; sec. mining and metall. advisory bds. to Carnegie Inst. Tech. and U.S. Bur. Mines, 1924-28; dean sch. mines and metallurgy, Pa. State Coll., 1928, dean (reorganized) Sch. Mineral Industries, same, since 1929. First lt., later capt. Co. D and comdg. officer 1st Batt., 30th Engrs. (1st Gas Regt.), A.E.F.; attached to B.E.F.; twice wounded in action. Awarded citation certificate, and Victory (six service bars) and Purple Heart medals (U.S.). Mem. Am. Inst. Mining and Metall. Engrs., Engrs.' Soc. Western Pa., Coal Mining Inst. America, Pittsburgh Coal Mining Inst., Nat. Mine Rescue Assn., Mine Rescue Veterans Pittsburgh Dist., Scabbard and Blade, Druids, Phi Delta Theta, Theta Tau, Sigma Gamma Epsilon. Clubs: University, Center Hills Country. Contbr. to technical publs. Address: 323 Hamilton Av., State College, Pa.

STEIN, Charles F., lawyer; b. Baltimore, Md., Sept. 25, 1866; s. Dr. Attila Edward and Emerald (Lawrence) S.; grad. Baltimore City Coll., 1885; LL.B., U. of Md., 1888; m. Ella W. Griffith, Mar. 24, 1897; children—Charles J., Virginia S. (Mrs. William H. Pitcher, Jr.). Began as bookkeeper Theodore Mottu & Sons, 1886; admitted to bar, 1889; in gen. practice of law, 1889-1921; judge Supreme Bench of Baltimore City, 1921-36; retired, 1936, and resumed practice of law; now mem. law firm Hennighausen & Stein; dir. Nat. Central Bank of Baltimore, Md. Title Guarantee Co. Served as mem. Advisory Draft Board, 1917-18. Dir. German Aged Peoples Home, Baltimore. Mem. Am. Bar Assn., Md. Bar Assn., Bar Assn. of Baltimore City. Democrat. Episcopalian. Home: 205 Goodwood Gardens. Office: 231 St. Paul Place, Baltimore, Md.

STEIN, James Rauch, clergyman, church official; b. Schuylkill Haven, Pa., Apr. 18, 1868; s. George W. and Caroline Henry (Rauch) S.;

STEIN

A.B., Franklin and Marshall Coll., 1893, A.M., 1896, D.D., 1921; grad. Theol. Sem. Ref. Ch. in U.S., Lancaster, Pa., 1897; m. Blanche Marie Harnish (Bryn Mawr) June 14, 1898; children—Joseph Henry, Caroline Rauch, Eleanor Robb, James Rauch and George Harnish. Ordained Ref. Ch. ministry, 1897; asst. pastor First Ch., Lebanon, Pa., 1897; pastor St. Stephen's Ch., Perkasie, 1898-1900, St. John's Ch., Harrisburg, 1900-11, Christ Ch., Bethlehem, 1911-17, First Ch., Wilkes-Barre, 1917-23, Christ Church, Philadelphia, 1923-1926. Stated clerk General Synod Ref. Ch. in U.S., 1909-34; stated clerk Gen. Synod Evang. and Ref. Ch., 1934-38; retired June 25, 1938. Continues as stated clerk Eastern Synod since 1909. Rep. Pa. Council of Chs.; mem. Phila. Fed. of Chs. Mem. Pennsylvania German Soc., Lebanon Co. Hist. Soc., Phi Beta Kappa. Republican. Editor Minutes of Eastern Synod of Ref. Ch. in U.S. (annual); Minutes of General Synod of Evang. and Ref. Ch. (biennial). Co-editor Statistical Tables Evang. and Ref. Ch. (Annual). Home: 4626 Cedar Av., Philadelphia, Pa.

STEIN, LeRoy B., trade assn. exec.; b. Newark, N.J., May 30, 1898; s. Max and Ray (LaVine) S.; LL.B., Dana Coll. of Law (Newark U.), 1919; student Grad Sch., New York U., 1919-20, Pa. State Coll., 1926-27; m. Mina Rosen, Nov. 25, 1920; children—Howard Monroe, Robert. Began as portrait photographer, 1915; admitted to N.J. bar, 1922, and since in gen. practice of law; consulting credit mgr. Moskin Chain and others, 1936-37; dir. Newark Prep. Sch., 1919-27; prin. Hudson Prep. Sch., 1927-28; prin. Essex Prep. Sch., 1928-34, dean Essex Coll., 1930; field mgr. Master Printers Assn., 1934-35; code dir. Trade Typesetting Industry, Philadelphia Met. Area, under NRA, 1935-36; mgr. Philadelphia Typesetters Assn., 1935-36; field mgr. Typothetæ of Philadelphia, 1935-36; exec. dir. Cigarette Merchandisers Assn. of N.J., Inc., since 1937; mgr. Automatic Music Assn. of N.J., Inc., since 1938. Manager Amusement Board of Trade of N.J., Inc. Mem. Am. Trade Assn. Execs., Lambda Alpha Phi; charter sec. Men's Cardiac League of N.J. Jewish religion. Mason, K.P. Club: Civic League (Newark). Editor-in-chief: The Pythian Domain. Editor: Typesetters Mold, Cigarette Smoke Rings, Changing Records. Contbr. to mags. Home: 395 Chadwick Av. Office: 1142 Broad St., Newark, N.J.

STEIN, Martin Henry, M.D.; b. Russia, Dec. 10, 1890; s. Hill and Goldie S.; M.D., Medico-Chirurg. Coll., Philadelphia, 1914; unmarried. Began gen. practice of medicine, 1916; mem. staff Elizabeth Gen. Hosp., St. Elizabeth Hosp. Served in France as 1st lt., U.S. Med. Corps, World War. Fellow Am. Coll. Surgeons; mem. A.M.A., N.J. State Med. Soc., Union Co. Med. Soc. Jewish religion. Mason. Came to U.S., 1904; naturalized citizen, 1916. Home: and office: 60 Elmora Av., Elizabeth, N.J.

STEINBACH, Jacob, Jr., lawyer; b. Long Branch, N.J., Feb. 18, 1881; s. Jacob and Mary (Hall) S.; A.B., Princeton U., 1904; LL.B., N.Y. Law Sch., 1906; m. Inez Newbold, Feb. 10, 1915. Admitted to N.J. bar and engaged in gen. practice of law at Long Branch; served as dist. ct. judge, 2d Judicial Dist., Co. of Monmouth, 1913-18; judge Monmouth Co. Common Pleas Ct., 1926-30; pres., treas., counsel, Jacob Steinbach, Inc.; dir. and counsel, Long Branch Trust Co. Home: 589 Westwood Av. Office: 178 Broadway, Long Branch, N.J.

STEINBERG, Samuel Sidney, civil engr.; b. New York, N.Y., Sept. 18, 1891; s. Harris and Anne (Smith) S.; B.Engring., Cooper Union Inst. Tech., New York, 1910, C.E., 1913; m. Kathryn Helene Dox, Dec. 18, 1916; children—Douglas Sidney, Edward Harris. Constrn. engr. N.Y. Highway Dept., 1910-13; asst. engr. Tela R.R. (United Fruit Co.), Hondoras, C.A., 1913-14; jr. engr. Public Service Commn., New York, 1914; asst. engr. N.Y. State Highway Dept., 1915-18; road expert U.S. Govt. constrn., 1918; asst. prof. of civil engring., U. of Md., 1918-20, prof. and head of dept., 1920-36, dean, coll. of engring. since 1936; consultant and summer work. U.S. Bur. Pub. Rds., 1920-23, Nat. Research Council, 1924-26, Md. State Rds. Commn., 1930-31, 38, Am. Rd. Builders Assn., 1935-37. Pres. College Park (Md.) Improvement Assn.; chmn. Commn. on Rds., Prince Georges Co. (Md.) Community Council; chmn. Com. on Uniform System of Street Names and House Numbers in Met. Area of Prince Georges Co.; chmn. Md. Highway Safety Planning Council; mem. com. on highways, Md. State Planning Commn.; dir. Md. Mapping Agency. Trustee College Park Pub. Sch. Mem. Am. Soc. Civil Engrs., Md. Assn. Engrs. (past pres.), Am. Road Builders Assn. (bd. dirs.; pres. ednl. div.), Engrs. Club of Baltimore, Permanent Internat. Road Congress, Soc. for Promotion Engring. Edn., Internat. Assn. Bridge and Structural Engring., Am. Geophys. Union, Nat. Research Council, Am. Assn. Univ. Profs., Am. Engring. Council (rep. of Md. Assn. Engrs.), Nat. Bur. Standards (rep. of Nat. Research Council); Joint Com. on Land Surveys and Titles of Am. Soc. Civil Engrs. and Am. Bar Assn., Tau Beta Pi, Sigma Phi Sigma. Episcopalian (vestryman). Clubs: Rotary of College Park. Editor of Annual Proceedings of Am. Road Builders Assn., 1937, 38. Contbr. to tech. jours. Home: College Park, Md.

STEINER, Melvin Arthur, supervising prin. schs.; b. Marshallville, O., May 7, 1884; s. Daniel T. and Mary (Musser) S.; A.B., Coll. of Wooster (O.), 1909; ed. Columbia U. Teachers Coll., summer 1921; A.M., U. of Pittsburgh, 1913, Ph.D., same, 1930; m. Grace Browne, Aug. 25, 1909; children—Waldo Arthur, Ethel Irene, Ida Ruth, Vivian Grace. Began as teacher rural schs., Wayne Co., O., 1902-06; prin. schs., Evans City, Pa., 1909-11, Hazard, Ky., 1911-12, West Middlesex, Pa., 1913-18; supervising prin. schs., Ingram, Pa., since 1918; instr. State Teachers Coll., summers 1923 and 1924; asst. prof. of education, Duquesne U. Grad. Sch. since 1939; pres. bd. dirs. Ingram Credit Union since 1933. Mem. Nat. Edn. Assn., Am. Assn. Sch. Adminstrs., Nat. Soc. for Study of Edn., Am. Edn. Research Assn., Prins. Round Table of Allegheny Co. (sec. since 1929), Phi Delta Kappa. Republican. Presbyn. Mason (32°). Club: Acacia of Ingram. Contbr. to ednl. jours. Home: 59 Danvers Av. Pittsburgh (5) Pa.

STEINER, Williams Kossuth, organist; b. Pittsburgh, Pa., June 9, 1874; s. Kossuth L. and Marie (Williams) S.; pupil of S. Bissell, F. Zitterbart, Theodor Salmon, Walter E. Hall, and Heinrich Germer (Dresden), 1894-99; m. Edna A. Steiner, July 2, 1902; children—Margaret Brown (Mrs. Charles Graham Kiskaddon), Jane Louise, Edwina Lewis, Stuart Grey, Howard Markley. Organist Grace Ref. Ch. and Trinity Luth. Ch., 1891, North Av. Meth. Ch., 1893-94, Calvary M.E. Ch., 1899-1904, all of Pittsburgh; designed organ, 1907, for Rodelph Shalom Temple, Pittsburgh, and organist same, 1904-25. Teacher of piano, organ and theory. Has given 50 recitals at Carnegie Inst.; played at Buffalo and St. Louis expns., also with various symphony orchestras. Composer anthems and organ and piano music. Dir. the Germer Piano School, Pittsburgh; musical dir. Western Pa. Sch. for the Blind, Sept. 1927—. Asso. Am. Guild Organists, by exam., 1899, local examiner, 1908—. Mem. Musicians Club of Pittsburgh, Pa. Soc. S.A.R Home: 5517 Fifth Av. Studio: 201 Bellefield Av., Pittsburgh, Pa.

STEINFURTH, Albert William, clergyman; b. Erie, Pa., Mar. 11, 1891; s. John F. and Mary (Schultz) S.; m. Hilda M. Burghart, June 6, 1917; children—Myrna K., Ruth M. Pastor St. Paul's Lutheran Ch., Cincinnati, O., 1916-17, Second Lutheran Ch., Dayton, O., 1918-20, Third Lutheran Ch., Springfield, 1921-23, Zion's Lutheran Ch., Greensburg, Pa., 1924-31, Calvary Lutheran Ch., Wilkinsburg, Pa., since 1932; sec. Southern Conf., Ohio Synod, 1918-20; pres. Central Conf. of Pittsburgh Synod since 1937; also pres. Council of Churches (Wilkinsburg, Pa.), and Lutheran Inner Mission Soc. (Pittsburgh). Sec. bd. of dirs. Thiel Coll., 1930-34; mem. bd. of mgrs., Old People's Home, Zelienople, Pa. Lutheran. Clubs: Ki-wanis. KDK Book. Home: 505 Holmes St. Office: South Av. and Center St., Wilkinsburg, Pa.

STEININGER, Cloyd, lawyer; b. Middleburg, Pa., Apr. 12, 1876; s. Alfred R. and Laura E. (Waller) S.; M.A., Bucknell Coll., Lewisburg, Pa., 1903; pvt. study in law offices; m. Minnie P. Angstadt, Mar. 28, 1907; 1 dau., Mary Ellen. Admitted to bar, 1905, and since in practice at Lewisburg, Pa.; lecturer in jurisprudence, Bucknell U., Lewisburg, Pa., 1907-23; dir. Union Nat. Bank, Citizens Electric Co. Dist. atty., 1908-16; county solicitor, 1916-20. Mem. Am., and Union Co. bar assns., Pa. State Bar Assn. (zone v.p. 1930-33; formerly mem. exec. com.), Lewisburg Bus. Men's Assn. Club: Lewisburg (Pa.; past pres.). Author of extended lecture on the Trial of Jesus and the Administration of Criminal Law. Home: 1 Buffalo Rd. Office: 233 Market St., Lewisburg, Pa.

STEININGER, Russell Frail, clergyman; b. Lewistown, Pa., Apr. 1, 1897; s. Charles Franklin and Birdie Bessie (Duck) S.; student Susquehanna Acad., Selinsgrove, Pa., 1915-17; A.B., Susquehanna U., Selinsgrove, 1921; student Susquehanna Theol. Sem., 1921-24; B.O., King's Sch. of Oratory, Pittsburgh, 1925; A.M., U. of Pittsburgh, 1927, Ph.D., 1934; m. Ruth Irene Bond, Aug. 14, 1926. Ordained to ministry United Lutheran Ch. in America, 1924; pastor St. Paul's Luth. Ch. Pitcairn, Pa., and St. Mark's Luth. Ch., Trafford, Pa., 1924-29, Mt. Olivet Luth. Ch., Pittsburgh, 1929-34, St. Paul's Luth. Ch., Monessen, Pa., since 1934. Served in O.T.C., Plattsburgh, N.Y., July-Sept. 1918; bandmaster S.A.T.C., Sept.-Dec. 1918. Mem. Phi Mu Delta. Republican. Club: Rotary (Monessen). Address: 631 McKee Av., Monessen, Pa.

STEINMAN, James Hale, newspaper pub.; b. Lancaster, Pa., Oct. 22, 1886; s. Andrew Jackson and Caroline Morgan (Hale) S.; A.B., Yale 1908; LL.B., U. of Pa., 1911; m. Louise McClure Tinsley, Feb. 2, 1922; children—Louise Tinsley, Caroline Morgan Hale, Peggy. Associated with brother as pub. Lancaster New Era, Intelligencer-Journal and Lancaster Sunday News since 1911; pres. Lancaster Newspapers, Inc., Steinman Coal Corpn., Mason-Dixon Radio Group; member Pa. State Planning Board; trustee Pennsylvania State Coll.; dir. Pennsylvania State Chamber of Commerce. Dem. county chmn., Lancaster Co., 1920-23. Admitted to Pa. bar, 1911. Served as asst. adj., div. adj. and lt. col. U.S.A., 1917-19, in France, July 1918-Aug. 1919. Mem. Lancaster Bar Assn., Psi Upsilon. Episcopalian. Clubs: Yale, Racquet, Hamilton. Home: Marietta Pike. Office: 8 W. King St., Lancaster, Pa.

STEINMAN, John Frederic, newspaper pub.; b. Lancaster, Pa., Aug. 21, 1884; s. Andrew Jackson and Caroline Morgan (Hale) S.; Ph.B. Yale, 1906; m. Blanche Lazo, June 3, 1913; 1 dau., Shirley Lazo; m. 2d, Shirley Watkins, Nov. 25, 1933. Treas. Lancaster Newspapers, Inc., pubs. Lancaster New Era, Intelligencer Journal and Sunday News; pres. Steinman Development Co.; treas. Steinman Coal Co. Served as civilian at Washington, D.C., World War. Club: St. Elmo (New Haven, Conn.). Home: 231 E. Orange St. Office: 8 W. King St., Lancaster, Pa.

STEINMETZ, Philip Justice, clergyman; b. Phila., Pa., July 31, 1874; s. Philip Justice and Mary Emma (Stewart) S.; A.B. cum laude, Harvard, 1901; S.T.B., Phila. Divini'y Sch., 1904; (hon.) S.T.D., Phila. Divinity Sch., 1918; m. Clara Ethel Humason, of Phila., Pa., June 16, 1904; children—Philip Humason, Beatrice McClellan. Ordained to ministry P.E. Ch., deacon, 1904, priest, 1905; asst. to rector Ch. of St. Luke and Epiphany, Phila., Pa., 1904-06, vicar Epiphany Chapel, same parish, 1906-12; asso. rector, Calvary Ch., Summit, N.J., 1912-14, rector, 1914-15; headmaster Episcopal Acad., Phila., Pa., 1915-20; rector, St. Paul's Ch., Elkins Park, Pa., since 1918. Republican. Episcopalian. Home: 7809 York Rd., Elkins Park, Pa.

STELLMAN, Louis M., aeronautical engr.; b. Brattleboro, Vt., June 4, 1886; s. Louis H.

and Rose (Elliott) S.; B.S., U. of Mich., 1916; m. Corinne Blodgett, Sept. 29, 1909; children—Evelyn, Barbara, Corinne, Jane, Anne, Patricia. Began as student-apprentice H. H. Franklin Mfg. Co., 1909, served in various capacities until 1919, chief engr., 1919-24; cons. engr. Skinner Auto Devices, 1924-25; operating engr. Hertz Driv-Ur-Self Co., 1925-26; mgr. Mastercraft Corpn., 1927-29; exec. engr. Wright Aeronautical Corpn., 1929-30, cons. engr. for automotive products, 1930-34; sr. aeronautical engr., Naval Aircraft Factory since 1934. Mem. Soc. Automotive Engrs. Club: University (Syracuse, N.Y.). Home: 530 Forrest Av., Drexel Hill, Pa. Office: Naval Aircraft Factory, Navy Yard, Philadelphia, Pa.

STEMPEL, Guido Hermann, Jr., chemist; b. Bloomington, Ind., Oct. 7, 1906; s. Guido Hermann and Myrtle (Emmert) S.; A.B., Indiana U., 1927, A.M., 1928, Ph.D., 1934; student U. of Chicago, summer 1929; m. Alice Menninger, June 1, 1927; 1 son, Guido Hermann, III. Asst. in chemistry, Ind. U., 1928-29; with Carnegie Inst. of Tech., Pittsburgh, since 1929, as instr. of physics, 1929-30; instr. of chemistry, 1930-36, asst. prof. of chemistry since 1936. Mem. Am. Chem. Soc., Am. Assn. Univ. Profs., Phi Kappa Psi, Sigma Xi. Democrat. Episcopalian. Author: Experimental General Chemistry (with J. C. Warner), 1934. Contbr. to tech. jours. Home: 5220 Forbes St., Pittsburgh, Pa.

STEMPLE, Forrest Wilbur, univ. prof.; b. Aurora, W.Va., Dec. 10, 1881; s. David C. and Ida (Trotter) S.; student W.Va. Wesleyan U., Buckhannon, 1898-1903, 1905-06; A.B., W.Va. U., 1908; M.S., U. of Wis., 1914; Ph.D., Cornell U., 1930; m. Grace E. Townsend, June 14, 1909; children—Alice Elizabeth (Mrs. Albert Dietz), Margaret Ida, David Townsend. Engaged in teaching, pub. schs., 1900-01; teller First Nat. Bank, Terra Alta, W.Va., 1903-05; instr. State Normal, West Liberty, W.Va., 1908-09, high sch., Morgantown, W.Va., 1909-11, prep. branch W.Va. U., 1911-13, O. State U., 1914-16, W.Va. U., 1916-19; prin. high sch., Aurora, W.Va., 1919-24; prof. edn., W.Va. Univ., Morgantown, W.Va. since 1924. Served in S.A.T.C., Plattsburgh, 1918. Organizer and sec. Northwestern Turnpike Assn. (U.S. 50) 1924-28. Past pres. Country Life Congress. Chmn. W. Va. Curriculum Revision for Elementary and Secondary Schs. Mem. Nat. Curriculum Soc., Nat. Secondary Prins. Assn., W.Va. State Edn. Assn., Phi Kappa Psi, Phi Beta Kappa, Democrat. Presbyn. Home: 10 McLane Av., Morgantown, W.Va.

STENGEL, Frederick William, clergyman, educator; b. Watertown, Wis., Oct. 18, 1874; s. Charles William and Christina (Schumacher) S.; A.B., Moravian Coll., Bethlehem, Pa., 1896, D.D., 1921; B.D., Moravian Theol. Sem., 1898 (honor man); m. Elizabeth McLean High, Nov. 20, 1898; children—George Douglas, Charles William, James Frederick, Lowell Otis. Ordained ministry Moravian Ch., 1898; pastor Carver Co., Minn., 1898-1901, Bethlehem, Pa., 1901-11, Dover, O., 1911-15; pres. Linden Hall Jr. Coll. and Sch. for Girls, Lititz, Pa. since 1915. Organizer, 1907, and mgr. Moravian Illustrated Lecture Bur., for production of missionary lectures; sec. Dept. of Missionary Edn., and chmn. Bd. Religious Edn., Moravian Ch. Home: Lititz, Pa.

STENGLE, Faber E., supt. of schs.; b. Steelton, Pa., Sept. 25, 1890; s. George Albert and Mina (Eshenour) S.; A.B., Lebanon Valley Coll., Annville, Pa., 1915, M.A., 1930; M.A., U of Pa., 1933, grad. work, 1933-39; m. Ethel Virginia Horner, Nov. 6, 1919. Science teacher Annville (Pa.) High Sch., 1914-15, Lebanon (Pa.) High Sch., 1915-16; supervising prin. Swatara Twp., Oberlin, Pa., 1916-18; history teacher and dir. of athletics Steelton (Pa.) High Sch., 1920-22; teacher Central High Sch., Harrisburg, Pa., 1922-26; mem. of firm Doutrich's, Inc., men's clothiers, Pottsville, Pa., 1926-28; prin. Hummelstown (Pa.) High Sch. 1928-29, supervising prin. 1929-34; supervising prin., Collingdale, Pa., 1934-35, supt. of schs., since 1935. Served as corpl., 312th F.A., U.S. Army, overseas, 1918-20. Mem. Pa. State Edn. Assn., N.E.A. (life mem.), Dist. Supts. of Suburban Phila., Am. Assn. of Sch. Administrators, Progressive Edn. Assn., Phi Delta Kappa, Am. Legion (Collingdale Post 669). Republican. Mem. United Brethren. Club: Kiwanis (Chester Pike, Pa.). Address: 916 Bedford Av., Collingdale, Pa.

STEPHAN, Elmer Albert, dir. of art · edn.; b. Pittsburgh, Pa., Jan. 31, 1892; s. August Daniel and Mary (Braun) S.; B.Sc., U. of Pittsburgh, 1914; New York U., 1920-21; Harvard (summer), 1924; spl. work, Carnegie Inst. Tech.; unmarried. Art teacher, Bellevue (Pa.) pub. schs., 1914-16; art supervisor Bellevue and Avalon (Pa.) schs., 1916-23; art teacher Schenley High Sch., Pittsburgh, 1923-28; dir. art edn. Pittsburgh pub. schs. since 1928; staff lecturer Carnegie Inst. Dir. Eastern Arts Assn., 1930-34. Mem. Asso. Artists of Pittsburgh, Am. Fed. of Arts, Soc. of Arts and Sciences, Phi Delta Kappa. Mason (32°), Presbyterian. Edited and illustrated 8 books on Inspirational Art; illustrated Let's Go Fishin', Practical Drawing Books. Home: 209 Gladstone Rd. Address: Bd. of Education, Pittsburgh, Pa.

STEPHANO, Constantine Stephen, cigarette mfg.; b. Phila., Pa., July 29, 1902; s. Stephen and Penelope (Pampou) S.; M.E., Colo. Sch. Mines, 1925; M.Sc. in metallurgy, Mass. Inst. Tech., 1926, D.Sc., same, 1928; m. Martha Taylor, Dec. 4, 1932; 1 son, Stephen C. S. Asso. with Stephano Bros., mfr. cigarettes, Phila., Pa. since 1928, in charge of tech. operations. Asso. mem. Am. Inst. Mining & Metall. Engrs. Mem. Tau Beta Pi, Sigma Gamma Epsilon. Republican. Mem. Greek Orthodox Ch. Home: Cheltenhouse, Elkins Park, Pa. Office: 1014 Walnut St., Philadelphia, Pa.

STEPHENS, Marsena (Marcy) Preston, merchant; b. Hackettstown, N.J., Jan. 2, 1859; s. Amzi C. and Malinda (Wolfe) S.; ed. Hackettstown pub. schs.; m. Nellie Glennie of Geneseo, N.Y., 1912 (died 1917); m. 2d, Jessie MacRae Totten, of Syracuse, N.Y., Jan. 2, 1920; 1 dau., Margaret M. Except for 2 yrs. teaching rural sch., operated farm until 1889; employed by Henry Salmon & Son, Boonton, 4 yrs., C. W. Ennis & Co., Morristown, 9 yrs., becoming v.p.; purchased with brother Augustus W., old established business D. W. Day & Son, Summit, N.J., bldg. materials and coal, 1902, incorporated as Stephens-Miller Co., 1924, and since pres.; v.p. Citizens Trust Co.; dir. Hill City Bldg. & Loan Assn. Independent Republican. Mason. Club: Rotary (Summit). Home: 41 Hobart Av. Office: 38 Russell Pl., Summit, N.J.

STEPHENS, Maynard Moody, econ. geologist; b. Connersville, Ind., Apr. 25, 1908; s. Harry L. and Nona Grace (Christman) S.; B.A., U. of Minn., 1930, M.A., 1931, Ph.D., 1934; m. Muriel Darrell, Sept. 17, 1931; children—Sally Jane, Janet Muriel. Began as research asst., U. of Minn., 1929; on geology staff, U. of Minn. and Minn. State Geol. Survey, 1929-36; dir. Minneapolis Mus. of Nature Study and Natural History, 1934-36; supervisor Petroleum, Natural Gas and Refining Extension, Sch. Mineral Industries, Pa. State Coll. since 1936; dir. and vice-pres. State Coll. Cooperative Club. Served in R.O.T.C., 1925-29, O.R.C., 1929-35. Local commr. Boy Scouts of America. Mem. Sigma Xi. Republican. Methodist. Club: University. Author: Petroleum and Natural Gas Production, 1938; Natural Gas Engineering, 1939; Petroleum Refining, 1937; Petroleum Refining, 1939. Home. 812 W. Beaver Av., State College, Pa.

STEPHENS, Stephen DeWitt, univ. prof.; b. Perry Ia., Apr. 9, 1894; s. Richard and Mary Elizabeth (Pascoe) S.; A.B., U. of Wis., Madison, 1916, M.A., 1919; Ed.M. and Ed. D., Harvard; m. Alma Veda Giles, Nov. 25, 1916; children—Stanton DeWitt (dec.), Sheldon DeWitt. Teacher, Canton (Ill.) High Sch., 1916-18; instr., Bradley Inst., Peoria, Ill., 1918-19; head of English dept. Boys' Tech. High Sch., Milwaukee, Wis., 1919-25; instr. U. of Wis., Milwaukee Branch, 1919-25; head of English Dept., Pre-Legal Div., N.J. Law Sch., 1927-30, Dana Coll., 1930-36; lecturer Rutgers U., New Brunswick, N.J., since 1927; dir. of div. of Humanities, U. of Newark (N.J.) since 1936. Mem. Modern Language Assn., Nat. Council of Teachers of English, Phi Delta Kappa. Methodist. Home: 535 Summit Av., Maplewood, N.J. Office: 40 Rector St., Newark, N.J.

STEPHENSON, David Thomas, retired clergyman; b. Monroe Co., Ind., Feb. 2, 1870; s. Francis Marion and Nancy Jane (Gillaspy) S.; A.B., Indiana U., 1893, A.M., 1895; S.T.B., Garrett Biblical Inst., 1897; also post grad. study Drew Theol. Sem.; m. Alma Lurane Carpenter, Dec. 22, 1897 (died Oct. 16, 1934); children—Francis Marion, Edwin Ambrose, Helen Mae, Donald Thomas, Alma Vi. Ordained deacon Methodist Episcopal Ch., 1896, elder, 1898; pastor various chs., Chicago, Ill. 1895-1910; pastor First Ch., Goshen, First Ch., Decatur, and High St. Ch., Muncie (all Ind.), 1910-20; pastor successively State St. Ch., Trenton, First Ch., Plainfield, First Ch., Madison, Central Ch., Newark, and First Ch., Newton (all N.J.), 1920-37; retired, 1937. Mem. Phi Gamma Delta. Mason. Home: 15 Madison Av., Madison, N.J.

STEPHENSON, Franklin William, clergyman; b. Franklin, Mich., June 29, 1882; s. Chandler W. and L. Alice (Hathaway) S.; A.B., Adrian Coll., Adrian Mich., 1906; S.T.B., Westminster (Md.) Theol. Sem. 1913; D.D., Adrian Coll., 1926; m. Jennie Mabel Darling, June 29, 1910; children—Helen Elizabeth, Dorothy Mabel, Franklin William, Jr. Ordained to ministry Meth. Prot. Ch., 1906; active pastor various chs. in Mich. and Ind., 1906-24; sec. bd. edn. Meth. Prot. Ch., Pittsburgh, Pa. since 1924. Contbr. to ch. publs. Office: 3267 W. Liberty Av., Pittsburgh, Pa.

STEPHENSON, Gilbert Thomas, banker; b. Pendleton, N.C., Dec. 17, 1884; s. James Henry and Susan Anna (Fleetwood) S.; student Severn (N.C.) High Sch., 1896-99; A.B., Wake Forest (N.C.) Coll., 1902, A.M., 1904; A.M., Harvard, 1906, LL.B., 1910; m. Grace Morris White, Dec. 19, 1912; children—Thomas Wilson, James Henry. Admitted to N.C. bar, 1910 and practiced at Winston-Salem, N.C., 1910-19; mem. firm Hastings, Stephenson and Whicker, Winston-Salem, N.C., 1916-19; successively sec.; asst. trust officer, asso. trust officer, v.p., Wachovia Bank & Trust Co. of N.C., Winston-Salem, N.C., 1919-29; v.p. in charge trust dept., Equitable Trust Co., Wilmington, Del., 1929-36, dir. since 1929; mem. faculty Grad. Sch. of Banking, Am. Bankers Assn., New York, since 1935, dir. trust research dept. since 1937; mem. firm T. B. Stephenson & Sons, farmers, Pendleton, N.C., since 1914, Stephenson and Stephenson, mchts., Pendleton, N.C., since 1938. Vice-pres. Nat. Council of Y.M.C.A.'s since 1938. Pres. trust div. Am. Bankers Assn., 1930-31; chmn. com. on trust edn. which prepared textbooks Trusts I and II, 1933 to 35. Mem. Am. Bar Assn. (vice-chmn. Sect. of Real Property, Probate and Trust Law since 1938; dir. Trust Law Div.). Ind. Democrat. Baptist. Club: Rotary (Wilmington, Del.; pres. 1933-34). Author: Race Distinctions in American Law, 1910; Guide-Posts in Preparing Wills (with A. H. Eller), 1919; The Business Relation Between God and Man—A Trusteeship, 1921; The Pastor Beloved, 1925; Living Trusts, 1928; Wills, 1928; The Life Story of a Trust Man, 1930; English Executor and Trust Business, 1930; What a Life Insurance Man Should Know About Trust Business, 1932; The American System of Trust Business, 1936; Studies in Trust Business (first series), 1938; in connection with study of trust business has studied systems in Can., Eng., Scotland, Ireland, France, Germany, Denmark, Norway and Sweden. Address: 814 N. Broome St., Wilmington, Del.; Warren Place, Pendleton, N.C.

STEPTOE, Philip P., mem. law firm Steptoe, & Johnson. Address: Charleston, W.Va.

STERLING, Ernest Albert, forester; b. Brooklyn, Pa., June 27, 1878; s. Amos Gilbert and Inez Lucia (Titus) S.; ed. Bucknell U., 1898-1900; Cold Spring Biol. Lab., 1900; F.E. (Forest Engr.), Cornell U., 1902; studied at

Forest Acad., Hann-Münden, Germany, and traveled in German and Swiss forests, 1903; m. Helen George Lee, Nov. 25, 1905; 1 dau., Mary Lee. Forester N.Y. State Forest, Fish and Game Commn., summer, 1902; forest asst. Bur. of Forestry, U.S. Dept. of Agr., 1903-05; asst. forester in charge office of Forest Extension, U.S. Forest Service, 1905-07; forester Pa. R.R., 1907-12; consulting forest and timber engineer, 1912-15; mgr. trade extension dept. Nat. Lumber Mfg. Assn., 1915-17; eastern v.p., manager, The James D. Lacey Co., New York, since 1917; also private consultant. Mem. Soc. Am. Foresters, Am. Wood Preservers' Assn. (past pres.), Am. Forestry Assn., Phi Gamma Delta. Clubs: University (Washington); Cornell (New York), Scranton Country. Writer of professional articles and papers. Home: Montrose, Pa. Address: 231 S. LaSalle St., Chicago, Ill.; and Cornell Club, New York, N.Y.

STERN, Benjamin Samuel, clergyman; b. Louisville, Ky., Nov. 14, 1864; s. Max M. and Mary M. (Bender) S.; A.B., Mission House Coll., Sheboygan Co., Wis., 1887; ed. Mission House Sem., Sheboygan Co., Wis., 1887-90; hon. D.D., Heidelberg Coll., Tiffin, O., 1907; m. Clara E. Zimmerman, Oct. 6, 1901; 1 son, Adiel Martin. Ordained to ministry Reformed Ch., July 23, 1890; pastor, Dayton, O., 1890-98; chaplain State Hosp., Dayton, O., 1893-97; Supt. Miami Valley Hosp., 1898-99; pastor New Bremen, O., 1899-1903; pastor Emanuel Reformed Ch., Phila., Pa., since 1903; trustee and sec. bd. Eastern Synod of Reformed Ch.; trustee Mission House Coll. and Sem. of Sheboygan Co., Wis., 1910-35; trustee Old People's Home, Lawndale, Phila., Pa., 1903-28, sec. corpn., 1903-38; sec. bd. trustees Fort Wayne Orphans Home, 1892-1903, trustee, 1891-1903; preacher in Old Man's Home, Phila., 1921-37. Republican. Mem. Reformed Ch. Home: 413 N. 38th St., Philadelphia, Pa.

STERN, David, 3d, journalist; b. Phila., Pa., Sept. 2, 1909; s. J. David and Juliet (Lit) S.; grad. Haddonfield (N.J.) High Sch., 1928; student U. of Pa., 1930, Harvard, 1933; m. Louise Beggs, of Merion, Pa., Mar. 11, 1935; 1 son, David Thomas. Reporter, advertising salesman, comptroller, Phila. Record, 1928-35, promotion mgr., 1936-37; dramatic critic Phila. Record under name of Peter Stirling, 1933-37; v.p. and gen. mgr. Phila. Record; sec. New York Post, Camden Courier Post; v.p. Publishers Service. Mem. Phi Epsilon Pi, Harvard Club. Home: 344 Kings Highway E., Haddonfield, N.J. Office: Philadelphia Record, Philadelphia, Pa.

STERN, Elizabeth Gertrude, author; d. Rev. Aaron and Sarah Leah (Rubenstein) Levin; B.A., University of Pittsburgh, 1910, hon. M.A., 1919; student New York Sch. of Social Work, 1910-11; m. Leon T. Stern, Sept. 26, 1911; children—Thomas Noel, Richard Stephen. Teacher night school, Pittsburgh, 1907-10; principal night school, N.Y. City, 1912; organizer and director night school, Galveston, Tex., 1913. Assistant to director Yorkville Community, East Side House Settlement, N.Y. City, 1912, Jacob Schiff Immigration Bur., Galveston, 1913; dir. welfare work, Wanamaker Store, Phila., 1919, Community Centre, N.Y. City, 1923; exec. dir. Council House, N.Y. City, 1924. Writer Phila. Sunday Press, 1914; columnist Phila. Sunday Record, 1915-19; spl. writer New York Evening World, 1925; columnist to Philadelphia Ledger under name Eleanor Morton since 1926 and to the Philadelphia Inquirer, 1933-37; adviser, programming and literature, to social service, civic, ednl., agencies and organizations. Women's activities editor to the latter since 1934. Lecturer over radio and to clubs and univ. groups since 1933. Mem. Publicity Council for Nat. Defense, Phila. Mem. Pa. Exec. Com. for Amnesty to Political Prisoners. Member Voluntary Defender Committee of Philadelphia, 1933. Member Women's International League for Peace, Phila. Art Alliance, Ethical Society. Clubs: Media Women's University. Author: My Mother and I, 1917; A Friend at Court (with Leon Stern), 1923; I Am a Woman and a Jew (pseud. Leah Morton), 1926; This Ecstasy, 1927; A Marriage Was Made, 1928; When Love Comes to Woman (pseud. Leah Morton), 1929; Gambler's Wife, 1931; Not All Laughter, 1937; also series of articles on "Women Abroad" for Philadelphia Inquirer, 1936. Contbr. to mags. Home: Rose Tree Rd., Media, Pa. Office: 311 S. Juniper St., Philadelphia, Pa.

STERN, Horace, judge; b. Phila., Pa., Aug. 7, 1878; s. Morris and Matilda (Bamberger) S.; A.B., Central High Sch., Phila., 1895; B.S., U. of Pennsylvania, 1899, LL.B., summa cum laude, 1902, LL.D., 1933; LL.D., Hahnemann Medical College, 1937; m. Henrietta Pfalzer, Feb. 12, 1906; 1 dau., Mrs. Sophie S. Friendly. Admitted to Pa. bar, 1902, and began practice in Phila.; mem. Stern & Wolf, 1903-20; apptd. judge Court of Common Pleas, by Gov. Sproul, 1920, and elected to same office, 1922, term of 10 yrs.; president judge, 1924, reëlected, 1932, term of 10 yrs.; elected justice Pa. Supreme Court, term 21 yrs., 1935; lecturer U. of Pa. Law Sch., 1902-17; vice provost Law Acad. of Phila. Trustee Dropsie Coll. (v.p.), U. of Pa., Jewish Publication Soc. America (v.p.); dir. Federation Jewish Charities of Phila. (hon. pres.), Union of Am. Hebrew Congregations (executive committee), American Jewish Com. (executive committee); chairman board trustees Wharton Sch., U. of Pa. Maj. Ordnance Dept., U.S.A., 1918-19. Mem. Am. Bar Assn., Pa. Bar Assn., Bar Assn. of Phila., Am. Judicature Soc., Am. Law Inst., Am. Acad. Polit. and Social Science, Hist. Soc. of Pa., Acad. Natural Sciences of Phila., Am. Jewish Hist. Soc., Am. Legion, Phi Beta Kappa, Order of the Coif. Republican. Mason. Clubs: Lawyers, Contemporary, Midday, Philobiblon. Home: 1830 Rittenhouse Square, Philadelphia, Pa.

STERN, Howard E., lawyer; b. Philadelphia, Pa., Aug. 6, 1895; s. Sidney M. and Rose (Goldsmith) S.; B.S., Cornell U.; LL.B., Temple U.; m. Madeline Kohn, Jan. 28, 1926; children—Babette K., Rosalie Clare. Admitted to Pa. bar, 1928; in private practice of law, Philadelphia, 1928-36; mem. law firm Taylor & Stern since 1936. Asst. city solicitor, Philadelphia, since 1930; dir. West Diamond Street Bldg. Assn., Lehman Sprayshield Co. Mem. Pa. Bar Assn., Philadelphia Bar Assn., Nat. Lawyers Guild, Artisans Order of Mutual Protection, etc. Club: Lawyers. Home: 6300 N. 13th St. Office: 1420 Chestnut St., Philadelphia, Pa.

STERN, Julius David, editor, pub.; b. Philadelphia, Pa., Apr. 1, 1886; s. David and Sophie (Muhr) S.; grad. William Penn Charter Sch., Phila., 1902; A.B., U. of Pa., 1906, LL.B., 1909; student U. of Berlin, 1907; m. Juliet Lit, Nov. 22, 1908; children—David III, Juliet, Meredith, Jonathan. Reporter Phila. Public Ledger, 1908; gen. mgr. Providence (R.I.) News, 1911; purchased New Brunswick (N.J.) Times, 1912, Springfield (Ill.) News, 1914, consolidated latter with Springfield Record as Springfield News-Record, pub. 1915-19; pres. and pub., Camden (N.J.) Evening Courier since 1919, Camden Morning Post since 1926, Phila. Record since 1928, New York Post since 1934. Clubs: Locust, Penn Athletic, Poor Richard, Philmont Country (Phila.). Home: 344 King's Highway East, Haddonfield, N.J. Address: Courier-Post Bldg., Camden, N.J., Philadelphia Record Bldg., Philadelphia, Pa.; and New York Post Bldg., 75 West St., New York, N.Y.

STERN, Leon Thomas, social worker and criminologist; b. Phila., Feb. 27, 1887; s. Richard Noel and Reva Pauline (Gould) S.; grad. Pa. Sch. Social Work, 1908; N.Y. Sch. Social Work, 1911; Temple U. Law Sch., 1916-18; A.B., U. of Pa., 1923; m. Elizabeth Gertrude Levin, Sept. 26, 1911; children—Thomas Noel, Richard Stephen. Dir. Yorkville Community, N.Y. City, 1910-11; asst. mgr. Immigrants Information Bur., Galveston, Tex., 1911-12; dir. Gen. Social Bur., Phila., 1912-14; dir. ednl. dept. Municipal Court, Phila., 1914-24, chief probation officer, 1924-25; sec. research and field studies, Pa. Com. on Penal Affairs since 1925; regional dir. U.S. Atty. General's Survey of Release Procedures, 1936-37; consultant Prison Industries Reorganization Administrn., 1937-38. Mem. Pa. Prison Soc. (acting and editorial com.), Governor's Com. on Probation, 1934, Phila. Com. on Pub. Affairs since 1918; chmn. com. on delinquency of All-Phila. Conf. on Social Work, 1929. Mem. Pa. State Chember of Commerce, Com. on Crime Reduction. Sec. Phila. Council of Nat. Defense, 1917-19. Mem. Nat. Probation Assn., Am. Prison Congress (com. on jails and com. on case work since 1934), Am. Assn. Social Workers, Phila. Ethical Soc. (a religious orgn.; trustee), Am. Acad. of Polit. and Social Science. Mem. Med. Bureau to Aid Spanish Democracy, Nat. Jail Assn. (treas.), mem. Social Service Advisory Bd. of Municipal Court, Phila. Author: A Friend at Court (with Elizabeth Stern), 1923; Study of Parole in Pennsylvania, 1927; Untried Prisoner and His Defense, 1933; Detention Homes for Children (Social Work Yearbook), 1933; Case Work Enters the Prison, 1933; Social Services in County Jails, 1936; Juvenile and Domestic Relations Courts (Social Work Yearbook), 1936. Author of survey reports on courts and prison management; contbr. articles to jours. Home: Rose Tree Rd., Media, Pa. Office: 311 S. Juniper St., Philadelphia, Pa.

STERN, Oscar I., real estate; b. Phila., Pa., Aug. 12, 1899; s. Isaac L. and Fannie S.; student Wharton Sch., U. of Pa., 1919-23; m. Edith L., Aug. 9, 1925. Realtor as partner I. L. Stern & Son, Phila., since 1921; made study of real estate assessment in 12 cities for Phila. Real Estate Bd., 1927 (report used in revision of property assessment in Phila.). Mem. Phila. Real Estate Bd. (vice-pres. since 1935), South Phila. Realty Bd. (past pres.). Liberal Democrat. Contbr. to real estate publs. Home: Concord Hall Apts. Office: 503 Pine St., Philadelphia, Pa.

STERNFELD, Harry, architect; b. Phila., Pa., Nov. 21, 1888; s. Isidor and Bertha (Daiber) S.; A.B., Central High Sch., Phila., 1907; B.S. in Architecture, U. of Pa., 1911, M.S. in Architecture, 1914; winner Paris prize scholarship, 1914; studied Ecole des Beaux Arts, Paris, 1919-20 (diploma); visiting fellow Am. Academy in Rome, 1920-21; m. Flora Maxwell, July 17, 1912. Asst. prof. architecture, Carnegie Inst. Tech., 1914-18, head dept., 1918-23, except when abroad; prof. design, U. of Pa., since 1923. Engaged in practice since 1911; prin. works (self or with others), Slovak Girls' Academy, Danville, Pa.; Harrisburg Catholic High School, Harrisburg, Pa.; City Planning of Rome, N.Y.; Pittsburgh Bldg. at Sesquicentennial Expn., Phila.; War Memorial, Audenarde, Belgium; Appomattox Memorial, marking spot of Gen. Lee's surrender; U.S. Court House, Philadelphia; Hdqrs. Bldg., Ft. Monmouth, N.J.; U.S. P.O., Milton, Pa. Student Plattsburg Training Camp, 1915, 16; enlisted in U.S. inf., 1918; commd. 2d lt. F.A. and stationed at Camp Taylor, Ky., until after Armistice. Mem. Am. Inst. Architects, Sigma Xi, Tau Sigma Delta, Scarab. Awarded diploma and medal, Montevideo, S.A., for architectural design. Republican. Presbyn. Clubs: T-Square, Phila. Sketch. Home: 6445 Greene St., Germantown, Phila. Office: Architects Bldg., Philadelphia, Pa.

STERRETT, Frank William, bishop; b. Middleport, N.Y., Jan. 21, 1885; s. William J. and Mary Elizabeth (Spalding) S.; grad. high sch., Middleport, 1901; student Hobart Coll., Geneva, N.Y., 1902-03, U. of Buffalo Law Sch., 1904-05; A.B., University of Pa., 1908; B.D., Phila. Divinity School, 1911, D.D., 1924; LL.D., Hobart College, 1924, Lehigh University, 1933; m. Fredrica Lott Haring, June 18, 1910; children—Annie Lott, Margaret Howe, Frank William. Deacon, 1911, priest, 1912, P.E. Ch.; vicar Grace Chapel, St. Stephen's Parish, Kingston, Pa., 1911-12; asst., St. Stephen's Ch., Wilkes-Barre, Pa., 1912-14; rector St. Stephen's, 1915-23; consecrated bishop coadjutor Diocese of Bethlehem, Nov. 9, 1923; bishop of Bethlehem since Feb. 27, 1928. Mem. bd. trustees Philadelphia Divinity School, Hobart College, and Lehigh University; pres. of Province of Washington. Mem. Phi Delta Phi, Phi Phi Delta. Republican. Mason, Kiwanian. Home: 825 Delaware Av., Bethlehem, Pa.

STERRETT, James Ralston, lawyer; b. Academia, Pa., Mar. 21, 1853; s. John Patterson and Annie (Kennedy) S.; A.B., Washington and Jefferson Coll., 1877; m. Emma W. McConnell, Oct. 20, 1887; children—Elenor Slagel (Mrs. Oliver Ledlie Smith), Marian Kennedy (Mrs. Philip Sheridan Chess), James Ralston. Admitted to Pa. bar, 1880, and began practice at Pittsburgh; associated in practice with uncle, John M. Kennedy, 1891-1900; mem. Patterson & Sterrett, changed to Patterson, Sterrett & Acheson, 1913, Sterrett & Acheson, and since 1929, Sterrett, Acheson & Jones. Trustee Shady Side Acad. Mem. Phi Gamma Delta. Republican. Presbyterian. Club: Duquesne. Home: 5820 Aylesboro Av. Office: Oliver Bldg., Pittsburgh, Pa.

STERRETT, Thomas Garfield, newspaper editor; b. Erie, Pa., Oct. 28, 1878; s. Andrew J. and Helen (Mar) S.; ed. pub. schs. and high sch., Erie, Pa., 1884-98; m. Grace Rockwood, Feb. 8, 1912; 1 dau., Ruth Estelle (Mrs. William J. Konnerth). Followed profession as actor, 1899-1906; in U.S. Marine Corps, 1906-19; engaged in newspaper work since 1919, pub. Sterrett's Weekly, Erie, Pa. Served as pvt. Pa. Vol. Inf., Spanish-Am. War. In full charge U.S. Marine Corps Publicity Bur. during World War with rank of maj. Served as sheriff of Erie Co., Pa., 1925-29. Democrat. Home: 726 French St., Erie, Pa.

STETSON, John Batterson, Jr., b. at Philadelphia, Pa., October 14, 1884; s. John B. and Sarah Elizabeth (Shindler) S.; prep. edn., William Penn Charter Sch., Phila.; A.B., Harvard University, 1906, as of 1907; m. Ruby F. Carlisle, June 15, 1907; children—John B., Stuart C., Thomazine, Jane B. Mem. bd. dirs. John B. Stetson Co. (mfrs. hats); founder Defiance Mfg. Co., bleachers of cotton goods, Barrowsville, Mass., 1912; associated with Anderson Galleries, New York, 1910-25; E.E. and M.P. from U.S. to Poland, 1925-30. In Air Service U.S.A., as pilot and capt., 1917-20, World War. Mem. bd. trustees John B. Stetson U., De Land, Fla.; trustee Bucknell U.; curator Portuguese lit., Harvard, also mem. com. to visit dept. of Romance langs., and com. to visit Peabody Mus. Mem. Am. Geog. Soc., Am. Anthropol. Soc.; organizer Fla. State Hist. Soc. Republican. Baptist. Clubs: Manufacturers and Bankers (past pres.), University (Philadelphia); University, Harvard (New York); Harvard (Boston). Translator: The Histories of Brazil (by Pero de Magalhaes), 2 vols., 1920. Home: Elkins Park, Pa.

STEVENS, Charles Leigh, cons. engr.; b. Muskegon, Mich., May 24, 1895; s. Clifton Delmar and Stella J. (Field) S.; student Cornell U., 1912-16; m. Jessica A. Thompson, Sept. 16, 1916; children—Clifton Delmar, Jessica Anne. Cons. engr., 1916-24; owner C. L. Stevens Co., cons. engrs., Baltimore, Md., since 1924; dir. Reed Prentice Corpn. Clubs: Duquesne (Pittsburgh, Pa.); Dedham (Mass.) Polo and Country. Office: Maryland Trust Bldg., Baltimore, Md.

STEVENS, David Harrison, educator; b. Berlin, Wis., Dec. 20, 1884; s. William Waters and Katherine (McCoy) S.; A.B., Lawrence Coll., Appleton, Wis., 1906, A.M., 1910, LL.D. from the same college in 1931; A.M., Harvard University, 1912; Ph.D., U. of Chicago, 1914; m. Ruth Frances Davis, Mar. 26, 1915; children—John, Anne Elizabeth, Barbara. Teacher Latin and English, high sch., Merrill, Wis., 1907-08; instr. English, 1908-11, registrar Coll. of Liberal Arts, 1910-11, Northwestern U.; instr. English, 1914-18, asst. prof., Oct. 1919-23, and dean in College of Arts, Literature and Science, 1920-22, associate professor, 1923-25, prof. 1925-30, asst. to pres., 1926-29, asso. dean of faculties, 1929-30, U. of Chicago; v.p. Gen. Edn. Board, 1930-38, and dir. of div. for the humanities, Rockefeller Foundation since Jan. 1932. Served as capt. Mil. Intelligence Div., U.S.A., Washington, D.C., 1918-June 1919. Mem. Modern Language Association of America, (frats.) Phi Delta Theta, Phi Beta Kappa. Congregationalist. Author: Party Politics and English Journalism, 1702-1742, 1916; The Home Guide to Good Reading, 1920; Types of English Drama, 1923; The Stevens Handbook of Punctuation, 1923; College Composition, 1927; Milton Papers, 1927; A Reference Guide to Milton from 1800 to the Present Day, 1929; also articles in various modern lang. journals. Compiler: American Patriotic Prose and Verse (with Ruth D. Stevens), 1917. Home: 160 N. Mountain Av., Montclair, N.J. Office: 49 W. 49th St., New York, N.Y.

STEVENS, Donald Read, vice-pres. and works mgr. Okonite Co.; b. Richland, Mich., May 3, 1889; s. Lester Fayette and Harriet Elizabeth (Read) S.; grad. Brookline (Mass.) High Sch., 1907; B.Sc., Mass. Inst. Tech., 1911 (sr. class pres.); m. Lois Carver, June 25, 1918; children—Lois Carver, Donald Read, Carver. Draftsman and asst. to chief engr. Peerless Motor Car Co., Cleveland, O., 1911-13, asst factory mgr., 1913-15; asst. to factory mgr. Goodyear Tire & Rubber Co., Akron, O., 1915, mgr. labor dept., 1915-21, also mgr. aeronautical dept., 1917-21; Supt. Okonite Co., Passaic, N.J., 1921-24; gen. supt. Okonite Co., Passaic, and Okonite-Callender Cable Co., Paterson, 1924-28, v.p. and works mgr. same since 1928, also Hazard Insulated Wire Works, Wilkes-Barre, Pa.; dir. Okonite Co., Okonite-Callender Cable Co., Paterson (N.J.) Nat. Bank, Community Bldg. & Loan Assn., Ridgewood. Pres. N.J. Taxpayers Assn.; mem. N.J. Unemployment Relief Commn.; mem. advisory com. on industrial relations, Nat. Industrial Conf. Bd. Mem. Phi Beta Epsilon. Independent Republican. Conglist. Club: Ridgewood (N.J.) Country. Home: 141 Woodland Av., Ridgewood, N.J. Office: The Okonite Co., Passaic, N.J.

STEVENS, Ernest, prof. music; b. Elizabeth, N.J., Dec. 15, 1894; s. John George and Clara (Randolph) S.; ed. high schs., Plainfield and Montclair, N.J.; student of Howard Case and Mark Andrews; m. Eleanor Riker, Sept. 4, 1915; children—Marjorie Elizabeth, Shirley Evelyn, Eleanor. Began recording of music rolls (Aeolian and Art Tempo), 1914; personal pianist and recording mgr. for Thomas Edison, 1922-28; teacher of The Ernest Stevens Method of Applied Harmony since 1929; pres. and treas. Ernest Stevens Studios, Inc., since 1938. Presbyn. Now compiling books for publ., 1939-40. Accompanist and mem. orchestras, WEAF, WJZ, WOR. Home: 346 Park St. Office: 630 Bloomfield Av., Montclair, N.J.

STEVENS, George M., lawyer; b. Cape May, N.J., June 14, 1900; s. Lewis T. and Grace A. (Merwin) S.; LL.B., Dickinson Coll. Law Sch., Carlisle, Pa., 1922; m. Mary Williams, June 26, 1926; children—Carolyn, Barbara. Admitted to N.J. bar as atty., 1922, as counselor, 1927; admitted to practice before Supreme Ct. of the U.S., 1933; prof. of law, South Jersey Law Sch., Camden, N.J., 1928-38; vice-pres. Citizens Nat. Bank, Collingswood, N.J., since 1936; in gen. practice of law at Collingswood, N.J., since 1936. Mem. Camden Co. Bar Assn. (sec. 1922-27), S.R., Phi Kappa Psi. Republican. Presbyn. Home: 625 Park Av., Collingswood, N.J.

STEVENS, J. Thompson, surgeon, radiologist; b. Fort Ann, N.Y., Jan. 31, 1890; s. Orley and Helen Mae (Thompson) S.; grad. Glens Falls (N.Y.) High Sch., 1910; student U. of W.Va., 1910-12; M.D., Medico-Chirurg. Coll. (U. of Pa.), 1915; m. Grace Boegert Lefferts, May 5, 1917; 1 son, J. Thompson. Began practice as surgeon and radiologist, 1916; mem. staff Montclair Community, Irvington Gen. Hosps., and others. Mem. A.M.A., New York State Med. Soc., New York Co. Med. Soc., Am. Roentgen Ray Soc., Radiol. Soc. of North America, Am. Congress of Physical Therapy, Pan-Am. Med. Soc., British Inst. of Radiology, etc. Republican. Presbyn. Clubs: New York Athletic, University of Pennsylvania (New York). Author: The Control of Goiter, 1937; also numerous articles and papers on treatment of goiter, cancer, nose and throat diseases and tumors (all papers presented before nat. and internat. med. socs.; some articles reprinted, translated or abstracted in foreign med. publs.). Home: 25 Pleasant Av., Montclair, N.J. Office: 595 Madison Av., New York, N.Y.; 55 Park St., Montclair, N.J.

STEVENS, Leslie, real estate broker; b. Franklin, N.J., Apr. 4, 1900; s. John F. and Julia F. (Corcoran) S.; grad. Newton (N.J.) High Sch., 1917; student Fordham U., 1917-19, Columbia, 1 semester; m. Marion Ledos, Feb. 21, 1935. Real estate salesman, Feist & Feist, Newark, N.J., 1919-27, 1929-32; partner E. W. McDonough, Newark, 1927-29; own business, Newark, 1932-33; pres. Abeles-Stevens, Inc., real estate and insurance, Newark, since 1933. Served in S.A.T.C., Fordham U., 1918. Clubs: Baltusrol Golf (Springfield, N.J.); Newark Athletic (Newark); Crestemont Golf (West Orange, N.J.). Home: 57 Union St., Montclair, N.J. Office: 605 Broad St., Newark, N.J.

STEVENS, Richard Kingsbury, lawyer; b. Meriden, Conn., Feb. 21, 1901; s. Frank Arthur and Harriet (Beach) S.; A.B., Princeton U., 1922; LL.B., Harvard U., 1926; m. Elizabeth H. Harris, Apr. 25, 1931; children—Nora Rhoads, Richard Kingsbury, James Harris. Admitted to Phila. Co. bar, 1926; since in gen. practice; member firm Stradley, Ronon & Stevens since 1929. Trustee Pa. Industrial Home for Blind Women; elder Second Presbyn. Church, Phila.; mem. membership com. Franklin Inst. Mem. Phi Beta Kappa. Republican. Presbyterian. Clubs: Cricket, Princeton (Philadelphia); Quadrangle (Princeton, N.J.). Home: Spring Lane. Office: 1222 Real Estate Trust Bldg., Philadelphia, Pa.

STEVENS, Wayne Mackenzie, economist; b. Des Moines, Ia., July 25, 1894; s. Edwin Luther (M.D.) and Hattie Maude (McKenzie) S.; B.S., U. of Ill.; M.B.A., Northwestern U.; Ph.D., American U.; C.P.A., Dist. of Columbia; m. Phyla Marsh, Aug. 15, 1925. Business and professional experience, 1913-28, included specialty salesman, coöp. mgr., sales mgr., investigator U.S. Bur. of Markets in fruit and vegetable marketing, retail marketing, and marketing costs, sr. auditor and pub. accountant, chain store supt. and supervisor, specialist in coöp. marketing, U.S. Bur. of Agrl. Economics, head of dept. of marketing and advertising, U. of Md., and economist, Nat. Coöp. Milk Producers' Federation; prof. marketing and financial management, La. State U., 1928-37; principal organization expert, Federal Farm Bd., 1930; visiting prof. U. of Nanking, China, 1934-36; adviser Nat. Economic Council, Nat. Gov. of Republic of China, 1934-36; chmn. economics and business adminstrn., U. of Md., 1937-38, dean Coll. of Commerce since 1938; special consultant U.S. Central Statistical Bd., 1939. Mem. Institut International d'Etudes Coöperatives, Am. Farm Econ. Assn., Am. Acad. Polit. and Social Science, Am. Marketing Assn., (vice-pres. Washington, D.C., Chapter 1939), Am. Econ. Assn., Am. Assn. Univ. Profs. (pres. La. State U. Chapter 1933-34), Phi Kappa Phi, Chi Psi Omega (supreme grand chancellor, 1928-29), Beta Gamma Sigma, Delta Sigma Pi. Mason. Methodist. Club: Rotary. Author: Financial Organization and Administration, 1934; Practical Coöperative Accounting (English and Chinese edits.), 1935; Effective Structural Organization for Coöperatives (English and Chinese edits.), 1936; Coöperative Sugar Assns. (Portuguese and Spanish edits.), 1938; also of numerous bulls., monographs and other publs. of U.S. Govt., of univs. and of trade assns. on financial, accounting, and statistical analysis of business management, marketing methods, costs of marketing, and organization problems of coöps. Contbr. to periodicals of U.S., China, and other countries. Home: 18 Beechwood Rd., College Park, Md.

STEVENS, Wilbur Applegate, lawyer; b. Trenton, N.J., Sept. 22, 1906; s. Harry Addison and Isabelle (Applegate) S.; ed. Clifton pub. and high schs.; student New York U., 1925-26, N.J. Law Sch., 1926-29; m. Alice Whitfield, June 12, 1934. Investigator Acquackanock Water Co., 1923-25; in credit dept. Botany Worsted Mills, 1925-26; law clerk Judge Forster Freeman, 1926-28, Judge J. C. Barbour, 1928-30; admitted to N.J. bar, 1930; in private practice law, Paterson, N.J., 1930-32; staff attorney, Hartford Accident & Indemnity Co., Newark, since 1932. Mem. election bd., 1931, County Com., 1932-33; organizer Young Republicans of Passaic Co., 1931; now city chmn. Republican Party (Clifton); county chmn. Young G.O.P.; pres. Clifton Passaic Co. Republican League.

Mem. Clifton Bar Assn., Essex Co. Bar Assn. Mem. DeMolay, Knights of Saladin, DeMolay Legion of Honor (past state comdr.). Home: 187 Union Av., Clifton, N.J. Office: 60 Park Pl., Newark, N.J.

STEVENSON, Charles Alexander, prof. of edn.; b. Morgantown, W.Va., June 30, 1901; s. Jesse W. and Sarah (Jolliffe) S.; A.B., W.Va. U., 1929, A.M., 1933; student U. of Chicago, 1937; m. Helen Glenn, July 31, 1926. Teacher grade school, Sabraton, W.Va., 1920-23, prin., 1923-24; supt. of schs., Cass Dist., Monongalia County, W.Va., 1924-31; prin. Osage (W.Va.) Jr. High Sch., 1931-33; head dept. of edn. Davis and Elkins Coll., Elkins, W.Va., since 1933. Mem. N.E.A., W.Va., State Educational Association, W.Va. Academy of Science, Chi Beta Phi. Republican. Methodist. Home: Morgantown, W.Va.

STEVENSON, George Bond, lawyer; b. Lock Haven, Pa., Nov. 6, 1889; s. William Hurst and Adelaide C. (Kreamer) S.; ed. Central State Normal Sch. and Dickinson Coll.; m. Mary Frances Duncan, Aug. 18, 1919. Head dept. civics and history, high sch., Lock Haven, Pa., 1912-18; admitted to Pa. bar and since engaged in gen. practice of law at Lock Haven; post master, Lock Haven, 1923-35; mayor City of Lock Haven for term 1936-40, resigned to serve as state senator; elected mem. Pa. Senate, Nov. 8, 1938, rep. 26th senatorial dist. Served as yeoman, later ensign, U.S.N., 1918-19. Mem. Bd. Edn., Lock Haven, 1920-26; first pres. Chamber of Commerce; pres. bd. dirs. Annie Halenbake Ross Library, 1922-39. Mem. Clinton Co. Bar Assn., Am. Legion (past comdr. local post), Phi Kappa Psi. Mem. M.E. Ch. Mason (K.T.). I.O.O.F. Clubs: Rotary (pres.), Clinton Country, Clinton Co. Fish & Game, Motor. Home: 114 Second St., Lock Haven, Pa.

STEVENSON, George Salvadore, M.D., child psychiatrist; b. Phila., Oct. 5, 1892; s. George Edward and Anna (Musso) S.; B.S., Bucknell U., Lewisburg, Pa., 1915, M.S., 1919; M.D., Johns Hopkins, 1919; m. Amy Llewellyn Patterson, Sept. 2, 1920; children—Anne Elizabeth, Amy Llewellyn, William Chandler. Resident house officer, Johns Hopkins Hosp., 1919-20; asst. in neuro-pathology, N.Y. State Psychiatric Inst., 1920-22; instr. nervous and mental diseases, Cornell U. Med. Sch., 1920-22, 1929-34; psychiatrist Training Sch., Vineland, N.J., 1922-24; asst. prof. nervous and mental diseases and dir psychopathic dept. Minn. Gen. Hosp., U. of Minn., 1924-26, visiting neuropsychiatrist, 1925-26; lecturer Post-Grad. Sch., Columbia, 1932-36; field consultant, prevention of delinquency, Nat. Com. for Mental Hygiene, 1926-27, dir. div. on Community Clinics, 1927-39; med. dir. Nat. Com. for Mental Hygiene, since 1939. Fellow A.M.A.; mem. Am. Orthopsychiatric Assn. (ex-sec., treas., ex-pres.); mem. bd. of dirs. National Conf. of Social Work, State Charities Aid Assn., Am. Psychiatric Assn., Phila. Neurol. Soc., Minn. Neurol. Soc., Central Neuropsychiatric Assn., Am. Assn. on Mental Deficiency, Soc. for Research in Child Development. Author: Child Guidance Clinics—A Quarter Century of Development (with G. Smith), 1934. Contbr. to professional jours. Home: Everett Rd., Red Bank, N.J. Office: 50 W. 50th St., New York, N.Y.

STEVENSON, John Alford, life ins. official; b. Cobden, Ill., Mar. 1, 1886; s. John Miles and Elizabeth Candace (Wilkins) S.; grad. high sch., Cobden, 1902, Southern Ill. Normal U., 1905; A.B., Ewing (Ill.) Coll., 1908; A.M., U. of Wis., 1912; Ph.D., U. of Ill., 1918; m. Josephine Reese, Sept. 19, 1914; 1 son, John Reese. Asst. prin. high sch., Nashville, Ill., 1905-06, prin., 1906-07; prin. high sch., Olney, Ill., 1907-09; supt. schs., Olney, 1909-11; lecturer in edn., U. of Wis., 1911-12; mgr. dept. music, drawing and manual arts, Scott, Foresman & Co., pubs., Chicago, 1912-16; lecturer in edn. and sec. appointments com., dept. of edn., U. of Ill., 1916-18, asst. prof. secondary edn. and dir. summer session, 1918-19; prof. edn. and dir. Sch. of Life Ins. Salesmanship, Carnegie Inst. Tech., Pittsburgh, 1919-20; 3d v.p. Equitable Life Assurance Soc. of U.S., 1920-21, 2d v.p., 1921-28; mgr. John A. Stevenson Agency, Penn Mutual Life Inst. Co., 1928-36, v.p., 1931-33, exec. vice-pres. since 1936 and trustee since 1938; mem. bd. mgrs. Girard Trust Company, (Phila.); dir. Lumbermen's Ins. Co., Phila. Nat. Ins. Co. Pres. Friends of the University of Pa. Library; asso. trustee University of Pa., mem. bd. teacher training and bd. grad. edn. and research. Dir. Y.M.C.A. (N.Y. City and Phila.); trustee Berea College, Nat. Hospital for Speech Disorders, Nitchie School of Lip Reading; dir. and mem. exec. com. Am. Management Assn., 1934-38; dir. Ins. Fed. of Pa., v.p., 1936, pres., 1937 and 38; pres. and mem. exec. com. Marketing Executives' Soc., 1928-38; sec., mem. bd. and exec. com. Am. Coll. of Life Underwriters; mem. board and exec. com. Ministers and Missionaries Benefit Bd. of Northern Bapt. Conv.; mem. exec. com. Sales Mgrs. Assn. of Phila. and pres., 1934-35; mem. Nat. Council of Y.M.C.A. of U.S.; chmn. advisory bd. Salvation Army of Phila.; dir. The Community Fund (Phila.); mem. bd. dirs. Phila. Fed. of Chs. Charter member American Association of University Teachers of Insurance; mem. N.E.A., Nat. Assn. Life Underwriters; Life Agency Officers Assn. (v. chmn. 1933, chmn. 1934), Nat. Soc. for Study of Edn., Nat. Inst. Social Science, Am. Acad. Polit. and Social Science, St. Andrew's Soc. of Philadelphia, Sigma Nu, Kappa Delta Pi, Phi Delta Kappa, Phi Eta, Pi Gamma Mu. Republican. Baptist. Mason, K.P. Clubs: Rittenhouse, Union League (Philadelphia); Merion Cricket (Pa.); Canadian, Grolier (New York); Com. of 100, Indian Creek (Miami Beach, Fla.); Miami Beach Bath (Fla.); Bar Harbor (Bar Harbor, Me.). Author: The Project Method of Teaching, 1921; Meeting Objections, 1921; Sales Strategy, 1921; Selling Life Insurance, 1922; Farm Projects (with Carl Colvin), 1922; Constructive Salesmanship, 1923; Problems and Projects in Salesmanship, 1923; Education and Philanthropy, 1927. Co-editor Harper's Life Insurance Library. Contbr. to mags. Home: Green Hill Farms, Overbrook, Philadelphia, Pa. Office: S.E. Cor. 6th and Walnut St., Philadelphia, Pa.

STEVENSON, J(oseph) Ross, theologian; b. Ligonier, Pa., Mar. 1, 1866; s. Rev. Ross and Martha A. (Harbison) S.; A.B., Washington and Jefferson, 1886, A.M., 1889, D.D., 1897; grad. McCormick Theol. Sem., Chicago, 1889; U. of Berlin, 1889-90; LL.D., Ursinus, 1908, Lafayette, 1915; D.D., U. of Edinburg, 1919, Presbyn. Coll., Halifax, 1920, Princeton Univ., 1936; m. Florence Day, May 16, 1899; children—William Edwards, Donald Day, Theodore Dwight. Ordained Presbyn. ministry, 1890; pastor Sedalia, Mo., 1890-94; adj. prof. eccles. history, 1894-97, prof., 1897-1902, McCormick Theol. Sem., Chicago; pastor Fifth Av. Ch., New York, 1902-09, Brown Memorial Ch., Baltimore, 1909-14; pres. Princeton Theol. Sem., 1914-36. Moderator Gen. Assembly Presbyn. Ch. U.S.A., 1915; pres. Internat. Med. Missionary Soc.; member of Com. to Revise Confession of Faith; mem. Presbyn. Bd. Foreign Missions; chmn. Assembly's Dept. on Ch. Co-operation and Union; chmn. business com. and asso. vice chmn. continuation com. World Conf. of Faith and Order; mem. Am. sect. Universal Christian Council for Life and Work; mem. constituent com. of World Council, chmn. of Churches; joint exec. com. Am. Section of Faith and Order and Life and Work. In service of Y.M.C.A. and Army Ednl. Commn., overseas, 1918-19; mem. S.R. Home: 20 Alexander St., Princeton, N.J.

STEVENSON, Olla; prof. French, Marshall Coll. Address: Marshall College, Huntington, W.Va.

STEVENSON, William Lawrie, civil engring.; b. Phila., Pa., Oct. 6, 1876; s. William Clark and Elizabeth Curtis (Hoopes) S.; student U. of Pa., 1893-95; (hon.) D.Sc., Franklin and Marshall Coll., Lancaster, Pa., 1930; m. Nellie W. Pfeiffer, Feb. 22, 1900 (dec.); children—William Clark, Beatrice Lawrie (wife of Rev. Albert O. Judd). Engr. with Dept. Pub. Works, Phila., Pa., 1898-1918; chief engr., Pa. Dept. Health, 1919-37; asso. with Metcalf and Eddy, cons. engrs., Pa., 1938-39; dir. Bur. Engring., Pa. Dept. Health, Harrisburg, Pa., since 1939. Served as engr. U.S. Shipping Bd. Emergency Fleet Corpn., 1918. Fellow Am. Pub. Health Assn.; mem. Am. Soc. Civil Engrs., Pa. Water Works Assn. Republican. Home: 2214 N. 2d St., Harrisburg, Pa.

STEWART, Arthur Bonbright, corpn. official; b. Philadelphia, Pa., Feb. 27, 1881; s. George W. and Blanche C. (Arthurs) S.; student Jarvis Hall Mil. Acad., Montclair, Colo., 1893-96; B.A., Stanford U., 1901; m. Mary M. Ross, June 16, 1910; children—Sara R., Mary B. Admitted to Pa. bar, 1904, practicing at Brookville until 1917; gen. counsel Davis Coal & Coke Co., Baltimore, Md., 1917-18, v.p., 1918-26, pres. since 1926; pres. Jenner Water Co., Buxton & Landstreet Co., Boswell Improvement Co.; dir. Union Trust Co. of Md., Eutaw Savings Bank of Baltimore. Mem. Sigma Alpha Epsilon. Republican. Episcopalian. Mason. Clubs: Baltimore Country, Merchants, Maryland. Home: 416 Woodlawn Rd. Office: Keyser Bldg., Baltimore, Md.

STEWART, David Henry, supt. schs.; b. Pittsburgh, Pa., Jan. 26, 1893; s. David and Mary (Creighton) S.; B.S., Pa. State Coll., 1915; A.M., Columbia U., 1925; Ph.D., U. of Pittsburgh, 1935; m. Jeannette Hunter, June 19, 1926; children—Jane Parnell, Maryann. Engaged in teaching pub. schs., Benton, Pa., 1915, Waynesburg, Pa., 1916-17; instr. Pa. State Coll., 1920-21; supt. schs., Beaver, Pa., 1921-36; supt. schs., Dormont, Pa., since 1936. Served as pvt. inf., U.S.A., during World War. Mem. N.E.A., Pa. State Edn. Assn., Am. Assn. Sch. Adminstrs., Phi Delta Kappa. Republican. Presbyn. Mason. Home: 1535 Tolma Av., Dormont, Pa.

STEWART, George Adolph; instr. clin. surgery, Johns Hopkins U.; attending surgeon St. Agnes and Bon Secours hosps.; asst. visiting surgeon Johns Hopkins Hosp. Address: 3301 N. Charles St., and 2 W. Read St., Baltimore, Md.

STEWART, George Albert, newspaper editor and publisher; b. Clearfield Co., Pa., July 28, 1890; s. J. Ashley and Clara (Albert) S.; student pub. schs. of Woodland, Pa.; m. Nora Gray, Aug. 23, 1913; children—Richard A. (dec.), Gretchen Anne (Mrs. L. M. Sunday), Doris Gray, Elinor Jean. Clerk and stenographer, 1906-10; paymaster Pa. Coal Co., 1912-14; mgr. woodenware mfg. plant, 1910-11; mgr. Winburne Water Co., 1911-12; with Clearfield (Pa.) Progress, daily newspaper, since 1916, successively as editor-mgr., and since 1930 publisher and principal owner. Former pres. Clearfield Chamber of Commerce; past pres. Clearfield Rotary Club; mem. Pa. Legislature, 1929-31; sec. Pa. Dept. of Forests and Waters since 1939. Republican. Presbyterian. Mason (32°), Odd Fellow, Elk, Red Men. Home: Old Town Rd. Office: 106 Locust St., Clearfield, Pa.

STEWART, Harold Andrew, lawyer; b. Claysville, Pa., Apr. 13, 1896; s. William Henry and Katherine (Gruber) S.; B.S., Bucknell U., Lewisburg, Pa., 1920; LL.B., U. of Pittsburgh Law Sch., 1923; m. Helen Louise Shaw, June 30, 1926; 1 dau., Helen Shaw. Admitted to Pa. Supreme Ct. bar, 1923; since in gen. practice of law at Latrobe and Pittsburgh since 1923; served as gen. counsel McKenna Brass & Mfg. Co., Pittsburgh, and Pearce Mfg. Co., Latrobe, Pa.; asso. counsel Vanadium-Alloys Steel Co., Latrobe; sec. and dir. Brighton Electric Steel Casting Co., Beaver Falls, Pa.; dir. Vulcan Mold & Iron Co., Latrobe, McKenna Brass & Mfg. Co. Mem. Latrobe Bd. of Edn. since 1929. Served in U.S. Army, 1917-18. One of founders and dir. Latrobe Pub. Library. Mem. Pa. Bar Assn., Westmoreland Law Assn., Am. Legion (past commdr.), Delta Sigma, Phi Delta Phi. Awarded Croix de Guerre, 1917. Republican. Presbyterian. Mason. Clubs: Latrobe Play and Players (one of founders), Lamas, Latrobe Country (Latrobe, Pa.). Home: 1006 Hamilton Av. Office: 501 First Nat. Bank Bldg., Latrobe, Pa.

STEWART, James Rowe, pres. Stewart Jordan Co.; b. Philadelphia, Pa., Nov. 5, 1876; s. Samuel Jackson and Mary A. (Walton) S.; ed. Central High Sch. and Peirce Business Coll.;

m. May Belle Diehl, Sept. 8, 1909; children John Howard, James Rowe. Advertising mgr. Philadelphia Record, 1914-23, bus. mgr., 1923-26, gen. mgr. and publisher, 1926-29; pres. Stewart Jordan Co., advertising agency, since 1929. Dir. White Williams Foundation; chmn. bd. Taxpayers Forum of Pa. V.p. Philadelphia Chamber of Commerce; ex-pres. Advertising Federation of America. Presbyterian. Clubs: Poor Richard, Philadelphia Country. Home: 652 W. Phil Ellena St., Germantown. Office: Lincoln Liberty Bldg., Philadelphia, Pa.

STEWART, John Leighton, editor, publisher; b. Bakerstown, Allegheny Co., Pa., Aug. 12, 1876; s. William Grove and Mary Jane (Wright) S.; grad. Redstone Acad., Uniontown, Pa., 1895; A.B., Washington and Jefferson Coll., Washington, Pa., 1899; studied law Harvard, 1900-02; m. Margaretta Murdoch Donnan, Apr. 20, 1904; 1 dau., Lucy Donnan (Mrs. Cecil P. Northrop). Has been editor, publisher and president Washington (Pa.) Observer and The Reporter (daily newspapers) since 1912; pres. The Tribune (Beaver Falls). Pres. Washington Sem., Washington Hosp., trustee Washington & Jefferson Coll. Republican. Presbyn. Home: Washington, Pa.

STEWART, John Quincy, physicist; b. Harrisburg, Pa., Sept. 10, 1894; s. John Quincy and Mary Caroline (Liebendorfer) S.; grad. Central High Sch., Harrisburg, 1911; B.S., Princeton U., 1915, Ph.D., 1919; m. Lilian V., d. John Howell Westcott, June 17, 1925; 1 son, John Westcott. Engineer dept. of development and research, Am. Telephone & Telegraph Co., New York, investigating speech and hearing, 1919-21; designed the first "electrical voice"; with dept. of astonomy, Princeton University, 1921—, asso. prof. astron. physics, 1927. Organized small party which successfully observed longest modern total solar eclipse, from S.S. Steelmaker in the Pacific, June 8, 1937; duration was more than seven minutes. Served with 29th Engrs., A.E.F. (sound-ranging), 1918-19. Fellow Am. Physical Soc.; mem. Am. Astron. Soc., Am. Assn. Univ. Profs. Presbyn. Author: Astronomy (with H. N. Russell and R. S. Dugan), 1927, 1938. Contbr. research results to sci. jours., including comments on philos. and social implications of the phys. sciences, also contbr. of articles in gen. mags. Address: Princeton, N.J.

STEWART, Melville, lawyer; b. Benwood, W. Va., June 14, 1894; s. Harry Melville and Flora (Morgan) S.; A.B., W.Va. U., Morgantown, 1915, LL.B., 1931; m. Lela Belle Palmer, July 20, 1918; children—Eleanor Anne, Martha Harriett, Flora Jane, Lela Jo. Engaged as dir. athletics, high sch., Triadelphia Dist., 1915-17; prin. high sch., Moundsville, W.Va., 1919-21; asst. state supervisor rural schs., 1921-23; state dir. phys. edn., 1923-29; admitted to W.Va. bar, 1931 and since engaged in gen. practice of law at Charleston. Served as 1st lt. inf. U.S.A., 1917-19, hdqrs. 1st Army. Mem. Am. Bar Assn., W.Va. State Bar Assn., Bar Assn. City of Charleston, Order of Coif, Phi Delta Phi, Beta Theta Pi, Am. Legion. Republican. Methodist. Mason. Club: Edgewood Country (Charleston). Home: 4810 Staunton Av., S.E. Office: Kanawha Valley Bldg., Charleston, W.Va.

STEWART, Paul Rich, coll. pres.; b. Spraggs, Pa., Mar. 16, 1887; s. Ezra De Garmo and Lana Margaret (Waychoff) S.; grad. Waynesburg (Pa.) Coll. Acad., 1905; A.B., Waynesburg Coll., 1909, A.M., 1910, Sc.D., 1924; A.M., Columbia, 1916; m. Dessie Knight Rush, Aug. 24, 1910; children—Ruth Harriett, Walter Alan. Prof. chemistry and geology, Waynesburg Coll., 1910-21, pres. since 1921. Mem. A.A.A.S., Pa. Acad. Sciences. Democrat. Presbyn. Mason. Home: Waynesburg, Pa.

STEWART, Percy Hamilton, ex-congressman; b. Newark, Jan. 10, 1867; s. Walter E. and Anna G. (Leeper) S.; A.B., Yale, 1890; LL.B., Columbia, 1893; m. Elinor De Witt Cochran, Jan. 11, 1899; children—Eva (Mrs. Harvey Wallace Shaffer), Elinor (Mrs. Edward Lindsley Ayers). Began practice in N.Y. City, 1893; mayor of Plainfield, 1912-13; chmn. Union County Dem. Com., 1914; chmn. Washington Rock Park Commn. of N.J., 1915-19; mem. N.J. State Bd. of Edn., 1919-21; mem. N.J. State Highway Commn., 1923-29; del. Dem. Nat. Conv., 1920, 28; elected mem. 72d Congress at spl. election, Dec. 1931 to fill vacancy, 5th N.J. Dist., for term ending Mar. 3, 1933; Dem. candidate for U.S. senator, N.J., 1932. Active in non-combatant mil. affairs, World War; served as civilian aide to adj. gen. of U.S., for N.J.; treas. and mem. exec. com. Mil. Training Camps of U.S. Mem. Delta Kappa Epsilon, Skull and Bones. Presbyn. Clubs: University, Nat. Golf Links of America (New York); Meadow, Southampton Club (Southampton N.Y.); Log Cabin Gun (Plainfield); Bath and Tennis (Palm Beach, Fla.). Home: Plainfield, N.J.

STEWART, Reid Thomas, emeritus prof. of mech. engring., Univ. of Pittsburgh. Address: University of Pittsburgh, Pittsburgh, Pa.

STEWART, Rowe, newspaper pub.; b. Phila. Pa., Nov. 5, 1876; s. Samuel Jackson and Mary Alice (Walton) S.; ed. Central High Sch. and Pierce Business Coll., Phila.; m. May Belle Diehl, Sept. 8, 1909; children—James Rowe, John Howard. Began as office boy, Phila. Record, 1895; with Phila. North American, 1904-09; adv. mgr. Phila. Evening Times, 1909; with Tracy, Parry & Stewart, adv. agts., 1910-13; adv. mgr. Phila. Record, 1913-23, gen. mgr., 1924; pres. Record Pub. Co., 1925-29; pres. Stewart-Jordan Co., advertising specialists, Phila.; vice-pres. Chamber Commerce of Philadelphia. Chmn. bd. Taxpayers Forum of Pennsylvania. Mem. Internat. Adv. Assn. (past pres.). Decorated Order of Social and Civic Merit (France). Democrat. Presbyn. Mason (Shriner). Clubs: Poor Richard, Philadelphia Country; Advertising (New York). Home: 652 W. Phil Ellena St. Office: Lincoln-Liberty Bldg., Philadelphia, Pa.

STEWART, Vernon Theodore, prof. chemistry; b. Silver Creek, N.Y., Nov. 13, 1883; s. Theodore and Antoinette (More) S.; Ph.B., Syracuse U., 1905; B.S., Mass. Inst. Tech., 1915; m. Helen L. Quale, Sept. 8, 1908; 1 son, Richard More. Chem. engr. Am. Writing Paper Co., Holyoke, Mass., 1915-17; laboratory mgr. for T. A. Edison, Bloomfield, N.J., 1917-20; associated with Carleton Ellis, Montclair, N.J., 1920-21; prof. chemistry, Newark Coll. Engring. since 1922. Mem. Am. Chem. Soc., Beta Theta Pi; asso. mem. Am. Inst. Chem. Engring. Republican. Unitarian. Club: Chemists (New York). Home: 126 Essex Av., Montclair, N.J.

STEWART, Walter W., economist; b. Manhattan, Kan., May 24, 1885; s. Albert Alexander and Ella (Winne) S.; A.B., U. of Mo., 1909; studied U. of Mich. and Columbia; LL.D., U. of Mo., 1932, Dartmouth Coll., 1933; m. Helen Wynkoop, July 1912; children—Albert W., Helen A., Walter A. Instr. economics, U. of Mo., 1910-11, U. of Mich., 1911-12; asst. prof. economics, U. of Mo., 1913-15; prof. economics, Amherst Coll., 1916-22; mem. price sect. War Industries Bd., 1918; dir. Div. of Research and Statistics, Federal Reserve Bd., 1922-25; v.p. Case, Pomeroy & Co., investment securities, 1926-27, chmn. bd. since 1930; prof. Sch. of Economics and Politics, Inst. for Advanced Study since 1938; economic adviser to Bank of England, 1928-30; apptd. Nov. 1931, Am. mem. spl. advisory com., Bank of Internat. Settlements, to investigate ability of Germany to resume reparations payments under the Young Plan. Trustee Rockefeller Foundation, General Edn. Bd., Institute for Advanced Study, Bennington Coll. Mem. Am. Econ. Assn., Am. Statis. Assn., Phi Beta Kappa. Home: Far Hills, N.J. Office: Institute for Advanced Study, Princeton, N.J.

STEWART, William Cooper, M.D.; b. Parkers Landing, Pa., Dec. 26, 1890; s. William and Sarah (Cooper) S.; student Grove City (Pa.) Coll., 1913-14, U. of Mich., 1914-15; M.D., U. of Pittsburgh, 1919; m. Rita Buente, Sept. 15, 1920; children—William Cooper, Richard Alan. In gen. practice of medicine since 1920; mem. staff Butler County Memorial Hosp.; vice-pres. and dir. Foxburg (Pa.) Bank; dir. Wightman Bottle & Glass Mfg. Co. Enlisted in Med. Reserve Corps., Dec. 21, 1917; hon. discharged, Apr. 12, 1919. Mem. A.M.A., Clarion County, Pa. State Med. Socs., Phi Rho Sigma, Alpha Omega Alpha. Republican. Presbyterian. Mason. Club: Foxburg (Pa.) Country. Home: Parkers Landing, Pa.

STICKLE, John Wesley, newspaper pub.; b. Livingston Manor, N.Y., Jan. 1, 1876; s. Andrew and Mary Elizabeth (Schoonmaker) S.; ed. pub. schs.; m. Clara Nobles, July 14, 1901 (dec.); children—Floyd Archibald, Stanley Schoonmaker, John Herbert; m. 2d, Carrie Nobles, Aug. 12, 1927. Began as printer's apprentice, Wellsville Daily Reporter, 1895; pub. successively Cuba (N.Y.) Patriot, Poughkeepsie Enterprise, Virginia (Minn.) Enterprise; later gen. mgr. Morning Astorian, Astoria, Ore.; pres. pub. and gen. mgr. Allentown (Pa.) Chronicle and News, 1922-35, retired. Trustee Children's Aid Soc. Republican. Episcopalian. Mason (32°). Clubs: Rotary, Livingston, Lehigh Country. Home: R.D. 2, Quakertown, Pa.

STICKNEY, Fernald Stanley, professional engr.; b. Brownville, Me., Nov. 3, 1900; s. Clinton Stanley and Carolyn (Billings) S.; grad. Brownville High Sch., 1919; B.S. in M.E., U. of Me., 1923; student Westinghouse Elec. Engring. Sch., 1923-24, various evening courses, 1925-27, N.Y. U. evening courses, 1928-29, Alexander Hamilton Inst., 1934-37; m. Nila May Corby, Dec. 3, 1932. Design engr. Westinghouse Electric & Mfg. Co., East Pittsburgh, Pa., 1924-27; instrument design engr. and cons. engr., Newark, N.J., since 1927. Mem. Nat. Soc. Professional Engrs., Essex County Engring. Soc., Montclair Soc. Engrs., Sigma Nu, Tau Beta Pi, Phi Kappa Phi. Mason. Home: 34 McKinley Av., West Caldwell, N.J. Office: 95 Orange St., Newark, N.J.

STICKNEY, George Hoxie, cons. illuminating engr.; b. Buffalo, N.Y., Oct. 4, 1872; s. David John and Ellen Josephine (Hoxie) S.; M.E. in E.E., Cornell U., 1896; m. Minnie M. Hasness, Sept. 21, 1908 (died 1927); children—David W., Edward Lynn (dec.), George H., Jr. Began as a student engineer with General Electric Co., 1896; now retired from General Electric Co. and cons. engr. at East Orange, N.J. Served in ord. corps, defense of Boston (Mass.) Harbor, 1898. Fellow A.A.A.S., Am. Inst. Elec. Engrs.; mem. Illuminating Engring. Soc. (pres.), 1917-18), Internat. Commn. on Illumination (president U.S. national committee 1935-36), Sigma Xi. Awarded silver medal, Panama Pacific Expn. Republican. Mem. Soc. of Friends. Club: Cornell of New York. Home: Hotel Edgemere. Office: 373 William St., East Orange, N.J.

STICKNEY, Louis R., clergyman; b. Newark, N.J., Feb. 26, 1879; s. George R. and Sylvia E. (De Wulf) S.; A.B., St. Charles Coll., Ellicott City, Md., 1896; S.T.L., North Am. Coll., Rome, 1902. Ordained priest R.C. Ch., 1902; sec. Apostolic Delegation, Ottawa, Can., 1903-04, Washington, D.C., 1904-08; sec. to Cardinal Gibbons, 1908-13; chancellor Archdiocese of Baltimore, 1913-19; apptd. consultor same, 1919; rector Cathedral, Baltimore, 1919-28; pastor Shrine of the Sacred Heart, Mount Washington, Baltimore, since 1928. Awarded medal Pro Ecclesia et Pontifice, by Pope Pius X, 1908; Chevalier Order of the Crown, Belgium, 1920; created domestic prelate by Pope Pius XI, 1922. Mem. Md. Hist. Soc. Home: Shrine of the Sacred Heart, Mt. Washington, Baltimore, Md.

STIEFEL, Ralph Charles, Jr., banker; b. Ellwood City, Pa., Dec. 26, 1901; s. Ralph Charles and Mary (Bowen) S.; student Mass. Inst. Tech., 1920-22; A.B., U. of Mich., 1928; m. Juliet Thorpe Offutt, June 26, 1929. Pres. Peoples Nat. Bank of Ellwood City since 19—. Republican. Presbyterian. Club: University (Pittsburgh). Home: 329 Fourth St. Office: care Peoples Nat. Bank of Ellwood City, Ellwood City, Pa.

STIFEL, Arthur C., textile finishing; b. Wheeling, W.Va., Dec. 11, 1882; s. Wm. Frederick and Emma (Schandein) S.; student Cornell U., 1899-1901, Phila. Textile Sch., 1901-04; m. Adelaide Flaccus, Mar. 25, 1906; children—Wm. Flaccus, Arthur C., Jr., Joan A. Asso. with J. L. Stifel & Sons Inc., finishers cotton and mixed fibre fabrics, Wheeling, W.Va., since 1903, sec.-treas. since 1920; dir. Fostoria Glass Co., Wheeling, W.Va., since 1930, Wheeling Steel Corpn. since 1930, Wheeling Tile Co. since 1933. Served as Wheeling Park commr. since 1926. Dir. Ohio Valley Gen. Hosp., Florence Crittenden Home, Home for Aged and Friendless Women. Mem. Beta Theta Pi. Republican. Episcopalian. Clubs: Fort Henry, Wheeling Country (Wheeling); Duquesne (Pittsburgh). Home: Hubbards Lane. Office: 339 Main St., Wheeling, W.Va.

STIFEL, Edward William, pres. J. L. Stifel & Sons, Inc.; b. Wheeling, W.Va., Dec. 10, 1869; s. Louis C. and Elizabeth H. (Stamm) S.; student public schools, Linsly Inst., Wheeling, W.Va. Univ., Morgantown, W.Va.; grad. study, European Labs.; m. Emily Ray Pollock, Apr. 21, 1902; children—Mary Elizabeth (Mrs. H. Dewey Quarrier), Emily Jule (Mrs. Charles B. Hart), Edward William, Jr. Asso. with J. L. Stifel & Sons, Inc., bus. founded 1835, dyers, printers and finishers cotton piece goods, Wheeling, W.Va., since 1835, pres. since 1930; dir. Gee Electric Co. and other local corpns. Mem. W.Va. Bd. Aeronautics. Pres. Wheeling-Ohio County Airport. Trustee Linsly Inst., Wheeling, W.Va. Mem. Ch. of Christ Sci. Clubs: Wheeling Country, Fort Henry, Cedar Rocks Golf, Smoke Hole (Wheeling). Home: Edemar, Pleasant Valley. Office: Main & Fourth Sts., Wheeling, W.Va.

STIFLER, Francis Carr, clergyman; b. Upland, Pa., Nov. 7, 1884; s. James Madison and Jennie Mary (Carr) S.; grad. high sch., Chester, Pa., 1902; B.A., U. of Pa., 1906; M.A., Yale, 1911, B.D., 1913; D.D. from Hillsdale (Michigan) College, 1934; m. Jean Thomson Luccock, June 24, 1913; children—Francis Carr (dec.), Carol Jean. With Western Elec. Co., Chicago, later with Union Carbide Sales Co. until 1910; ordained Bapt. ministry, 1913; pastor Mich. Av. Bapt. Ch., Saginaw, Mich., 1913-17, Wilmette, Ill., 1917-28, E. Orange, N.J., 1928-35; asso. sec. Am. Bapt. Foreign Mission Soc., 1935-36; editorial secretary American Bible Soc. since 1936. Mem. Reserve Corps, I.N.G., 1917; sec. Y.M.C.A. under Nat. War Work Council, 1917-19. Mem. bd. mgrs. Bapt. Young People's Union of America, 1919-29, Missionary Edn. Movement of America, 1920-24; mem. bd. dirs. Chicago Bapt. Exec. Council, 1919-28; mem. bd. missionary coöperation Northern Bapt. Conv., 1923-28; mem. exec. com. Bapt. Extension Soc. of Newark and Vicinity, 1929-35; mem. bd. mgrs. and exec. com. New Jersey Bapt. Conv., 1929-35, v.p., 1934-35; pres. Ministerial Assn. of the Oranges, 1932-33; pres. No. Jersey Bapt. Ministers Conf., 1933-34; mem. President's Cabinet of N. Bapt. Conv., 1933-34; trustee Internat. Bapt. Sem., 1929—. Mem. Kappa Sigma. Republican. Author: Better Baptist Churches, 1937. Home: 46 Parkview Terrace, Summit, N.J. Office: Bible House, Park Av. and 57th St., New York, N.Y.

STIFLER, Francis McIlhenny, mgr. land trust; b. Roselle, N.J., Mar. 11, 1903; s. James Madison and Lucy (Burnley) S.; ed. High Sch., Evanston, Ill., 1917-21; B.S., Haverford Coll., 1925; m. Elizabeth Blount Henson, June 28, 1930; children—Josephine Woolman, Sarah Burnley, Andrew Carr. Real estate salesman, Phila., 1925-27; editor weekly newspapers, Ardmore, Pa., 1927-30; magazine editor and pub. dir., Phila., 1930-31; corr. newspapers, free-lance writer, and publicity man, 1931-34; renting agt. in New York City, 1934; mgr. Phipps Pa. Land Trust, Pittsburgh Div. Henry Phipps Estates since 1935. Active in efforts to reduce pub. expenditures and taxes in Western Pa. Pres. Bldg. Owners & Mgrs. Assn. of Pittsburgh, 1939; gov. Nat. Assn. Bldg. Owners & Mgrs., 1939; dir. Mid. Atlantic Conf. Bldg. Owners & Mgrs. Mem. Pittsburgh Real Estate Bd., Pittsburgh Chamber Commerce. Republican. Baptist; attend P.E. Ch. Clubs: Query, of Sewickley (sec. 1939); Rolling Rock Hunt (Ligonier); Civic Club of Allegheny Co. Book reviewer: formerly for Phila. Record, then Phila. Ledger, now N.Y. Herald-Tribune, specializing on sporting books. Home: 119 Walnut S., Sewickley, Pa. Office: Bessemer Bldg., Pittsburgh, Pa.

STILLMAN, Albert Leeds, fuel research; b. Hoboken, N.J., June 14, 1883; s. Prof. Thomas Bliss and Emma Louise (Pomplitz) S.; A.B., Rutgers U., 1905; Engr. of Mines, Columbia U. School of Mines, 1909; M.Sc., Rutgers Univ., 1910; m. Virginia Brown, Sept. 18, 1919. Began as mining engr., St. Lawrence Pyrites Co., Hermon, N.Y., 1909; mgr. Industrial Supply Co., 1910-16; vice-pres. Gen. Briquetting Co. later General Fuel Briquette Corpn., Jersey City, N.J., since 1916; vice-pres. Cooperstown Corpn. of Md.; acted as power of atty., Ladenburg, Thalmann & Co., N.Y. City, 1928-35; research engr., Berwind-White Coal Mining Co. since 1935. Served as capt. inf., U.S.A., 1917-19. Civil Service commr., State of N.J., 1917. Mem. Delta Kappa Epsilon. Republican. Episcopalian. Editor: T. B. Stillman's Engineering Chemistry, 2 edits., 1916-28. Author: Briquetting, 1922; Drums Beat in Old Carolina (fiction), 1939. Contbr. Jungle Haven (fiction) to American Boy, Mar.-Sept. 1933. Home: 73 Leland Av., Plainfield. Office: 1 Exchange Pl., Jersey City, N.J.

STILLMAN, Edwin A., mfr. hydraulic machinery; b. Brooklyn, N.Y., Nov. 13, 1886; s. Francis Hill and Irene A. (Bancroft) S.; M.E., Cornell U., 1908; m. Louise Huff, Feb. 16, 1920; children—Mary Louise, William Rogers, Nancy. Began with the Watson Stillman Co., 1908, pres. from 1912; pres. Pequonnock Commercial Corpn. Mem. Am. Soc. M.E., Delta Phi, S.R. Republican. Episcopalian. Clubs: University, Railroad-Machinery, Burnt Mills Polo. Home: Gladstone, N.J. Office: Roselle, N.J.

STILLMAN, Jesse Wilbur, chemist; b. Pawcatuck, Conn., Feb. 1, 1893; s. Alberti Rodolph and Tacie Elizabeth (Larkin) S.; student Pawcatuck (Conn.) High Sch., 1906-10; B.S., Dartmouth Coll., Hanover, N.H., 1914; M.A., Columbia U., 1915, Ph.D., 1920; m. Anne Wilkins Scott, Oct. 19, 1918; children—Tacie Anne, Jean Scott. Research chemist E. I. Du Pont de Nemours & Co., Wilmington, Del., 1917-20, head analytical div., Exptl. Sta., since 1920. Dir. Council of Chs. and Christian Edn. of Md. and Del. Mem. Am. Chem. Soc., Sigma Xi, Phi Lambda Upsilon. Republican. Presbyterian. Club: Du Pont Country (Wilmington). Home: 12 Lindsey Pl. Office: Du Pont Experimental Station, Wilmington, Del.

STILLMAN, W. Paul; pres. Nat. State Bank of Newark. Address: Broad St. and Edison Pl., Newark, N.J.

STILLWELL, Lewis Buckley, electrical engr.; b. Scranton, Pa., Mar. 12, 1863; s. Richard and Margaret (Snyder) S.; student Wesleyan U., Conn., 1882-84; E.E., Lehigh U., 1885, M.S., 1907, D.Sc., 1914; Sc.D., Wesleyan, 1907; m. Mary Elizabeth Thurston, Apr. 19, 1892; 1 son, Richard. Asst. electrician, Westinghouse Elec. & Mfg. Co., 1886-90; chief elec. engr., same, 1890-97; elec. dir. Niagara Falls Power Co., 1897-1900; in practice as cons. elec. engr., New York, 1900—; cons. engr. Manhattan Elev. Ry. Co. (electrification of elevated lines in N.Y. City), 1899-1906; elec. dir. Rapid Transit Subway Constr. Co., 1900-09; cons. engr. Hudson Cos., 1905-13; mem. Erie R.R. elec. commn., 1906; cons. engr. United Rys. & Elec. Co. of Baltimore, 1906-20, Interborough Rapid Transit Co., 1909-20, N.Y.,N.H.&H. R.R. Co. (Hoosac Tunnel electrification), 1910-11, N.Y., Westchester & Boston Ry. Co., 1911-15, Lehigh Navigation Elec. Co., 1912-18; consulting engr. Holland Vehicular Tunnels, 1924-27; cons. engr. Port of New York Authority since 1927. Mem. bd. of economics and engring. Nat. Assn. Owners R.R. Securities, 1921-22; mem. Nat. Research Council, 1917-18. Mem. Am. Inst. Elec. Engrs. (pres. 1909-10), Am. Inst. Cons. Engrs. (pres. 1918-19), Am. Soc. C.E., Brit. Instn. Elec. Engrs., Fed. Am. Engring. Soc. (council 1919—), Nat. Acad. Sciences, Royal Soc. Arts (Gt. Britain), Am. Philos. Soc., Franklin Inst. (Phila.), Alpha Delta Phi. Life trustee, Princeton U., 1918—; mem. bd. dirs. Chamber of Commerce, U.S.A., 1921-23. Clubs: Century, Union League, (New York); Cosmos (Washington, D.C.). Home: Princeton, N.J.

STILLWELL, Richard, archæology; b. Niagara Falls, N.Y., Feb. 16, 1899; s. Lewis Buckley and Mary Elizabeth (Thurston) S.; prep. edn., Pomfret (Conn.) Sch., 1913-17; A.B., Princeton U., 1921, M.F.A., 1924; m. Agnes Ellen Newhall, Aug. 3, 1932; children—Richard Newhall, Theodora. Instr., dept. art and archæology, Princeton U., 1924; special fellow in architecture, Am. Sch. of Classical Studies, Athens, Greece, 1924-26, 1927-31, asst. dir. 1931-32, dir., 1932-35; asst. prof., dept. of art and archæology, Princeton U. (part time), 1927-31, 1935-38, asso. prof. (part time) since 1938; mem. Inst. for Advanced Study, Princeton, N.J., since 1936; dir. of publs., Com. for Excavation of Antioch and its Vicinity. Mem. S.A.T.C., 1918; R.O.T.C., 1919-21; 2d lt. F.A., Reserve Officers Corps, 1921-26. Corr. mem. German Archæol. Inst.; mem. Holland Soc. of N.Y., Soc. of Colonial Wars in State of N.J. Republican. Episcopalian. Clubs: Nassau (Princeton); Princeton (New York). Author: The Temple of Apollo at Corinth and Other Buildings, 1931; Upper Peirene on Acrocorinth, 1929. Contbr. to Am. Jour. Archæology. Editor: Antioch-on-the-Orontes, Vol. II, 1938. Home: 55 Battle Rd., Princeton, N.J.

STIMSON, Arthur Marston, public health officer; b. Rome, N.Y., Nov. 30, 1876; s. William Hamilton and Anna Braddock (Gallup) S.; grad. Brooklyn (N.Y.) High Sch., 1894; M.D., Long Island Coll. Hosp., 1898; m. Sarah Boyd, Dec. 9, 1903; children—Elspeth (dec.), Jean, William Hamilton, Allan Braddock. Commd. asst. surgeon Pub. Health Service of U.S., July 1902; passed asst. surgeon, Aug. 1907; surgeon, Aug. 1914; asst. dir. Hygienic Lab., Washington, D.C.; detail sanitation officer U.S. Navy, 1917-19; asst. surg. gen., Pub. Health Service, 1922, med. dir., 1930; directing studies of heart disease at Nat. Inst. of Health, Washington, D.C., since 1931. Mem. Am. Public Health Assn., A.M.A. Author: Facts and Problems of Rabies; also brief history of bacteriological investigations in Public Health Service, Communicable Diseases, and other public health writings. Home: Chevy Chase, Md.

STIMSON, Dorothy, educator; b. St. Louis, Mo., Oct. 10, 1890; d. Henry Albert and Alice Wheaton (Bartlett) S.; grad. Miss Spence's Sch., New York, 1908; A.B., Vassar, 1912; A.M., Columbia, 1913, Ph.D., 1917; Inst. of Politics, Williamstown, Mass., 1922, 23, 27. Instr. history, Vassar, Feb.-June 1917; dean women and prof. history, Transylvania Coll., Lexington, Ky., 1917-21; dean, Goucher Coll., Baltimore, since 1921, asso. prof. history, 1921-31, prof. since 1931, acting pres., 1930. Guggenheim fellow (leave of absence from Goucher Coll.), 1930-31. Councilor Aloha Camps for Girls, Vt. and New Hampshire, 5 yrs. to 1921. Mem. Am. Hist. Assn., Am. Assn. Univ. Women, History of Science Society, Nat. Assn. Deans of Women, Phi Beta Kappa. Republican. Conglist. Clubs: Baltimore College, Hamilton Street Club. Author: Gradual Acceptance of Copernican Theory of Universe, 1917. Contbr. hist. articles. Address: Goucher College, Baltimore, Md.

STINCHCOMB, James, prof. of classics; b. New York, N.Y., Mar. 2, 1898; s. Delwin and Carrie (Kelley) S.; A.B., Ohio Wesleyan U., 1918; A.M., U. of Pittsburgh, 1927, Ph.D., 1929; m. Kathryn McBride, Nov. 27, 1929; children—James Delwin, Helen Jo. Prin. high sch., New Lexington, O., 1919-23, teacher of languages, Male High Sch., Louisville, Ky., 1923-24, of Latin, high sch., McKeesport, Pa., 1924-25; asst. in Latin, U. of Pittsburgh, 1925-26, instr. in Latin, 1926-29, prof. of Classics, 1929. Served in F.A., U.S.A., 1918-19. Mem. Pittsburgh Independence Day Com. since 1933. Sec. Classical Assn. of Pittsburgh since 1926. Mem. Am. Philol. Assn., Classical Assn. of the Atlantic States, Phi Gamma Delta. Democrat. Presbyn. Editor, Classical Weekly. Home: 6617 Wilkins Av., Pittsburgh, Pa.

STINE, Charles Milton Altland, chemist; b. Norwich, Conn., Oct. 18, 1882; s. Milton Henry and Mary Jane (Altland) S.; A.B., Gettysburg (Pa.) Coll., 1901, B.S., 1903, A.M., 1904, M.S., 1905; also Sc.D. from same college, 1926; Ph.D., Johns Hopkins University, 1907; LL.D. from Cumberland University, 1932; m. Martha E. Molly, Feb. 3, 1912; children—Mary Elizabeth,

Barbara Ann. Prof. chemistry, Md. Coll. for Women, 1904-05; fellow Johns Hopkins, 1906-07; joined staff of E. I. du Pont de Nemours & Co. (Eastern Lab.), July 1, 1907; in charge organic chem. work, 1909-16; trans. to Wilmington office as head organic div., 1917, and made asst. dir. chem. dept., 1919, chem. dir., May 1, 1924-30, v.p., mem. exec. com. and dir. since 1930. Trustee Gettysburg (Pa.) Coll., Tower Hill Sch., Wilmington, Univ. of Delaware. Dir. The Academy of Natural Sciences of Phila. Mem. Directors of Industrial Research Assn., Am. Chem. Soc. (councillor; mem. com. to co-operate with Chem. Warfare Service), Am. Inst. Chem. (councillor) Engrs., Franklin Inst. (life), Phi Beta Kappa, Gamma Alpha; hon. mem. Princeton Engring. Assn.; fellow A.A.A.S. Protestant. Clubs: Wilmington Country, du Pont Country (Wilmington); Chemical (Johns Hopkins University); Union League (Phila.); Wilmington Club. Has developed numerous processes and products, many of them patented, in connection with high explosives, propellent powder, dyes, artificial leather, varnishes, paints, and other inorganic and organic chemical processes and products. Home: 1100 Greenhill Av. Address: E. I. du Pont de Nemours & Co., Wilmington, Del.

STINE, Milton Henry, clergyman; b. East Prospect, York Co., Pa., Sept. 4, 1853; s. Adam and Barbara (Schoenberger) S.; A.B., Pa. Coll., Gettysburg, 1877, A.M., 1880, Ph.D., 1896; grad. Luth. Theological Seminary, Gettysburg, 1880; state teacher's certificate, Pa., 1894; D.D., Susquehanna University, 1909; Litt.D. from Gettysburg, 1931; m. Mary Atland, June 24, 1880; children—Charles M., Walter S. Ordained Luth. ministry, 1880; pastor Lebanon, Pa., 1883-92, Los Angeles, Calif., 1892-95, Harrisburg, Pa., 1895-1904, Lebanon, Pa., 1908-15, Wilmington, Del., 1915-21, Hollywood, Calif., 1921-26, Harrisburg, since 1929. Visited British Guiana as rep. of Bd. of Foreign Missions, 1914; one of first presidents of Calif. Synod of Luth. Ch.; dir. of Theological Sem., Gettysburg, 1912-18. Author: Studies on the Religious Problem of Our Country, 1887; Winter Jaunt Through Historic Lands, 1890; The Niemans, 1897; Seven Golden Candlesticks, 1906; Baron Stiegel, 1904; The Devil's Bride, 1909; The Fortunes of a Foundling, 1921; Autobiography of Mary Jane, 1923; Man in the Making, 1930; Ancient Cities and Civilizations Modernized, 1931; also religious short stories. Lecturer on travel, fulfillment of prophecy, etc. Home: 1100 Greenhill Av., Wilmington, Del.*

STINEMAN, Oliver Morton, pres. Moxham Nat. Bank; b. South Fork, Pa., Dec. 25, 1878; s. Jacob C. and Eleanor S.; student Kiskiminetas Springs Sch.; m. Bessie W. Williams, Sept. 16, 1903; children—Dorothy E., Paul Morton. Pres. Moxham Nat. Bank (Johnstown, Pa.), Stineman Coal Mining Co., South Fork (Pa.) Water Co., South Fork (Pa.) Cemetery Assn.; dir. Cambria Printing Co.; trustee Jacob C. Stineman Estate. Mem. Sons of Union Vets. Mem. Evangelical Ch. (trustee Moxham Evang. Ch.). K.P., Knights of the Golden Eagle, Knights of Malta. Home: 426 Park Av. Office: 550 Central Av., Johnstown, Pa.

STINSON, John Wesley, Jr., surgeon; b. Gouldsboro, Me., Nov. 5, 1895; s. John Wesley and Eva (Tabbutt) S.; student Coburn Classical Inst., Waterville, Me., 1911-15, Colby Coll., 1915-17, M.A., 1939; M.D., Jefferson Med. Coll., 1921; M.S. in surgery, U. of Minn., 1926, and Mayo Clinic, 1927; m. Bertha Eble Small, June 16, 1928; children—John Wesley, III, Ann Louise, Jane Small. Interne St. Joseph's Hosp., Phila., 1921-22; surgical asst. Geisinger Memorial Hosp., Danville, Pa., 1922-23; asst. pathologist Phila. Gen. Hosp., Jan.-Apr. 1923; fellow in surgery, later asst. surgeon, Mayo Clinic, 1923-27; chief div. of surgery Pittsburgh Hosp. since 1927; surg. staff South Side Hosp. Served in S.A.T.C. and M.R.C., 1918. Fellow Am. Coll. Surgeons (sec. regional fracture com., 1938-39), A.M.A.; mem. Resident and Ex-Resident Assn. of Mayo Clinic, Pa. and Allegheny Co. med. socs., N. Central Clinic Soc., Pittsburgh Surgical Soc. (pres., 1937-38), Zeta Psi, Nu Sigma Nu. Republican. Protestant. Clubs: University (Pittsburgh); Henry Clay Rod and Gun. Home: 5645 Darlington Rd. Office: Medical Arts Bldg., Pittsburgh, Pa.

STIRLING, James S.; chmn. bd. Wilmington Morris Plan Bank. Home: 1216 Lovering Av. Office: 909 Shipley St., Wilmington, Del.

STIRLING, Warren, M.D.; prof. anatomy and histology, Temple Univ. Address: Temple University, Philadelphia, Pa.

STITT, Harry C., banking; b. Shade Gap, Pa., Nov. 30, 1883; s. John B. and Lucinda C. (Kough) S.; grad. pub. schs., Huntingdon Co., Pa., 1902; m. Viola M. Senft, June 6, 1917; children—Harry C., Jr., Lydia Ann, Martha Mae. Began as clk. in postoffice, Mount Union, Pa., 1902-04; clk. First Nat. Bank, 1904-06; cashier Peoples Nat. Bank, Spring Grove, Pa., 1906-10; cashier Industrial Nat. Bank, York, Pa., since 1910, also 1st vice-pres. since 1930; sec., treas., and dir. West York Ice & Storage Co., City Ice Co.; sec. and dir. West End Bldg. & Loan Assn.; pres. and dir. White Rose Motor Club; sec. York Co. Bankers' Assn. since 1913. Served as treas. Borough of West York, York Co., Pa., since 1918. Republican. Presbyn. Mason (K.T., 32°, Shriner). I.O.O.F. Elk. Clubs: Temple, Out Door, Exchange (past pres.). Home: 1635 W. Market St. Office: 1401 W. Market St., York, Pa.

STITZEL, Jonas Wakefield, oculist; b. McEwensville, Pa., May 13, 1868; s. Jacob and Julia (Fisher) S.; M.D., Hahnemann Med. Coll., Phila.; student N.Y. Ophthalmic Hosp.; m. Anna C. Derr, Sept. 28, 1892; 1 son, Elwood W. Began as sch. teacher, 1887; practice of medicine at Hollidaysburg, Pa., since 1896, oculist since 1904. Mem. Pa. State Med. Soc. (ex-v.p.; past chmn. Bur. of Sanitary Science; past chmn., Bur. of Ophthalmology, Otology and Laryngology), Y.M.C.A. (pres. bd. of dirs., Hollidaysburg, Pa.). Mason (Blue Lodge; K.T.; Commandery; Shriner). Clubs: Kiwanis, Blairmont Country (Hollidaysburg, Pa.). Home: 415 Wayne St. Office: 413 Wayne St., Hollidaysburg, Pa.

STIVERS, Earl Raimon, engring. research; b. Baltimore, Md., Oct. 19, 1894; s. John Hadley and Hattie Freda (Nothnaegel) S.; grad. Baltimore Poly. Inst., 1912; C.E., U. of Wis., 1915; m. Bertha Marie Spivey, Sept. 3, 1921; children—David Ray, Daniel Jay. Rodman C.B.& Q. R.R., 1915; asst. in engring. corps Pa. R.R. Lines, 1916; instr. engring., U. of Fla., 1916-17; jr. engr. of valuation Interstate Commerce Commn., 1917 and 1919-20; chief of party Ala. Highway Commn., 1920; instr. ry. engring., U. of Wis., 1920-25; asso. prof. engring., Robert Coll., Constantinople, 1925-28; research engr. Package Research Lab., 1929-31, dir. of research since 1931. Pres. Rockaway Borough Bd. of Edn., 1939. Served successively as private, sergeant and 2d lt., Engring. Corps., U.S. Army, 1917-18. Mem. Am. Soc. Testing Materials, Am. Legion; asso. mem. Am. Soc. C.E. Republican. Presbyn. (trustee 1st Ch., Rockaway, 1934-39). Mason (Shriner, Eastern Star). Home: 26 Rockaway Av. Office: Stapling Machines Co., Rockaway, N.J.

STOCK, Harry Bixler, clergyman; b. Carlisle, Pa., Sept. 3, 1871; s. Jacob C. and Mary Jane (Ziegler) S.; A.M., Dickinson Coll., 1891; ed. Luth. Theol. Sem., Gettysburg, 1893-96; hon. D.D., Dickinson Coll., 1908; unmarried. Ordained to ministry U. Luth. Ch. in America, 1896; minister St. Paul's Luth. Ch., Carlisle, Pa., since 1896. Trustee J. Herman Bosler Memorial Library, Carlisle, Pa., since 1925. Mem. Beta Theta Pi. Republican. Mem. U. Luth. Ch. in America. Club: Kiwanis of Carlisle. Home: 325 W. High St., Carlisle, Pa.

STOCK, McClean, lawyer; b. Bedford, Pa., May 8, 1881; s. Charles M. and Hannah Mary (McClean) S.; student Glenville Acad., 1894-96; A.B., Gettysburg Coll., 1900, A.M., 1902; m. Stella M. Blaney, May 15, 1908; 1 son, William B. Admitted to York Co. bar, 1904; in gen. practice of law, 1904-20 and since 1928; city solicitor, City of York, 1920-22, postmaster, 1922-26; judge Ct. of Common Pleas, York Co., 1927-28; dir. Drovers & Mechanics Nat. Bank of York, Eastern Market Co. Mem. Phi Beta Kappa, Sigma Chi. Republican. Lutheran. Clubs: Lafayette, Country (York). Home: 35 S. Duke St. Office: Central Nat. Bank Bldg., York, Pa.

STOCK, Wallace Teall, lawyer; b. Fort Covington, N.Y., Mar. 8, 1881; s. Alfred Homes and Maria Augusta (Teall) S.; student Colgate Acad., 1897-99; B.A., Colgate U., 1903, M.A., 1907; student New York Law Sch., 1909-10; LL.B., St. Lawrence U. (Brooklyn Law Sch.), 1911; m. Marion Curtis, June 23, 1904; children—Catharine Virginia (Mrs. Leslie Ernest Sutton), Wallace Curtis, Shirley Curtis; m. 2d, Pauline Patterson, Dec. 17, 1938. Teacher South Jersey Inst., Bridgeton, N.J., 1903-04, Colgate U., 1904-08, New York City Sch. System, 1908-13; admitted to New York bar, 1912; associated with Bennet & Cooley, 1913-14, Loucks & Alexander, 1914-17 (partner, 1916-17), Lewis & Kelsey, 1919-25, Lewis, Garvin & Kelsey, 1925-27; partner Lewis, Garvin & Kelsey and Lewis & Kelsey, 1927-35; in private practice since 1935; lecturer on federal practice and law, New York U., 1926-28, Brooklyn Law Sch., 1938. Four-Minute man, World War. Dir. of conservation Atlantic Div. Red Cross, N.Y. City, 1917-18. Mem. Phi Beta Kappa, Alpha Tau Omega. Independent Democrat. Conglist. Mason. Published (privately): "Some Verses," 1937. Contbr. New York U. Law Review. Home: 373 Lincoln Av., Orange, N.J. Office: 61 Broadway, New York, N.Y.

STOCKBRIDGE, Enos S., lawyer; b. Baltimore, Md., May 3, 1888; s. Henry and Helen M. (Smith) S.; A.B., Amherst Coll., 1908; LL.B., Univ. of Md. Law Sch., 1910; m. Clara V. Franklin, Dec. 29, 1914; children—Janet F., Franklin, David S., Enid. Admitted to Md. bar and since engaged in gen. practice of law at Baltimore; asso. in firm Gans & Haman, 1910-17; mem. firm France, McLanahan & Rouzer, 1917-27; mem. firm Mullikin, Stockbridge & Waters since 1927; v.p. and dir. Consolidated Feldspar Corpn., Southern Hotel Co.; dir. Everel Propeller Corpn. Mem. Chi Psi. Republican. Presbyn. Club: Elkridge. Home: Montrose Rd., Govans, Md. Office: Baltimore Trust Bldg., Baltimore, Md.

STOCKER, Frederick Paul, clergyman; b. Port Washington, O., Dec. 19, 1899; s. Benjamin Allen and Elizabeth (Rufenacht) S.; B.S., Moravian Coll. and Theol. Sem., 1920, B.D., same, 1923; A.M., Teachers Coll. of Columbia U., 1928; m. Evelyn Doster, Nov. 15, 1924; children—Frederick Doster, Patricia Ann. Ordained to ministry Moravian Ch., 1923; pastor Third Ch., N.Y. City, 1923-28, First Ch., Indianapolis, Ind., 1928-31, Third Ch., N.Y. City, 1931-33, College Hill Ch., Bethlehem, Pa., 1933-36; since 1936, vice-pres. Provincial Elders Conf. of Moravian Ch., pres. exec. bd. of Eastern Dist., and vice-pres. bd. dirs. of Soc. for Propagating the Gospel (Mission Bd.) and pres. Bd. Ch. Extension of Moravian Ch. Served in S.A.T.C., 1918. Trustee Moravian Coll. and Theol. Sem.; advisory trustee Linden Hall Sem. and Jr. Coll., Moravian Sem. and Coll. for Women. Republican. Moravian. Mason. Contbr. many articles to Moravian Ch. Jour. Home: 45 W. Church St., Bethlehem, Pa.

STOCKTON, Charles Thomas, banker; b. Mercer, Pa., May 22, 1883; s. Joseph R. and Eleanor (Barnes) S.; grad. Sharon High Sch., 1902, Washington & Jefferson Coll., 1906; m. Martha Cook, June 16, 1909; 1 dau., Mary Rea. With Merchants and Mfrs. Nat. Bank since 1906, beginning as messenger, advanced through various positions, becoming v.p. and dir., 1926, treas. and dir. Valley Savings Loan Assn.; dir. Sheago Valley Water Co. Republican. Presbyterian. Mason. Clubs: Sharon (Pa.) Country; Youngstown (O.). Home: 1378 Hall Av. Office: care Merchants and Mfrs. Nat. Bank, Sharon, Pa.

STOCKTON, Richard, VI, author, soldier; b. Rotterdam, Holland, Jan. 9, 1888; s. Richard and Clemence E. (Finch) S.; brought to U.S., 1888; grad. Bordentown (N.J.) Mil. Inst., 1905; m. Helen Beryl Gove, July 24, 1907; children—Richard Finch, Jack Potter, Robert Field, Helen Clemence Carolyn, Wilbur Chafey. Pvt. A Co. Corps of Cadets, N.G.N.J., 1901; discharged as cadet lt., 1905; 2d lt. 3d inf.,

STOCKWELL

May 22, 1906; resigned 1907; pvt. E Co., 2d Inf., May 26, 1910; 1st lt., June 23, 1910; capt., May 11, 1911; assigned regtl. q.m., Feb. 12, 1912; comd. Supply Co., 2d Inf. Jan. 5, 1915; insp. small arms practice, same regt., Feb. 1915; resigned, Sept. 6, 1916; maj., Inf. O.R.C., Oct. 26, 1916; maj., 317th U.S. Inf., Aug. 27, 1917. Overseas May 25, 1918; comd. Bn. in action attached to New Zealand Div., British Army, at Serre, Gommecourt, Huberterne, etc., July, Aug. 1918; with 80th Div. St. Mihiel drive, Sept. 1918; comdt. officers and N.C.O. schools, Blois, France, Oct. 1, 1918; post adj., Dec. 1, 1918; asst. troop movement officer, Port of Embarkation, Hoboken, N.J., Feb. 9, 1919; pres. bd. to appraise damage done to commercial ships taken over by army, Sept. 30, 1919; hon. discharged, Oct. 31, 1920; maj. Q.M.Res., Dec. 6, 1924; lt. col., Oct. 18, 1928, col., Aug. 10, 1937. Apptd. mem. bd. to write Manual for Officers of the Organized Militia and Volunteers of U.S., 1915. Instr. in mil. science, Bordentown Mil. Inst., 1912-17. Trustee Am. Defense Soc., New York; mem. bd. govs. Soc. Am. Cross of Honor; mem. U.S. Inf. Assn., Order Founders and Patriots, Soc. Colonial Wars, S.R., Soc. War of 1812, Mil. Order Fgn. Wars, Union Soc. of Civil War, United Mil. Order America; gold medalist, Mil. Service Instn. of U.S., 1912, 15, 16; Reeve Memorial prize essayist, same, 1915; hon. mention, same, 1916; decoration, Am. Cross of Honor, 1914, "for valor." Episcopalian. Author: The Guardsman's Handbook, 1908; Troops on Riot Duty (with Capt. S. M. Dickinson), 1912; Peace Insurance, 1915; Peace on Earth, 1929; Inevitable War, 1933; Judge for Yourself, the Stockton Plan to Eliminate Depression, 1935. Asso. editor Am. Defense (monthly), 1915. Contbr. on mil. and patriotic topics. Mem. Speakers' Bur. Nat. Security League. Home: Trenton, N.J. Office: Sales Analysis Inst., 1050 Broad St., Newark, N.J.*

STOCKWELL, Frank Clifford, prof. elec. engring.; b. Warwick, Mass., Apr. 22, 1883; s. Frank Perley and Leonora Hannah (Chapin) S.; A.B., Bates Coll., Lewiston, Me., 1905; B.S., Mass. Inst. Tech., 1907; m. Sara Symonds, June 30, 1911; 1 dau., Mary Leonora. Instr. in physics, Stevens Inst. Tech., Hoboken, N.J., 1907-10, and in elec. engring., 1910-17; chief instr., lab. practice courses, New York Edison Co., 1913-25, ednl. dir., 1925-32; asst. prof. elec. engring., Stevens Inst. Tech., 1917-21, asso. prof., 1921-25, prof. and head dept. since 1925, Anson Wood Burchard prof. elec. engring. since 1930, dean of the Grad. Sch., 1939. Mem. Am. Inst. E.E., Inst. Radio Engrs., Soc. for Promotion Engring. Edn., Phi Beta Kappa, Tau Beta Pi. Republican. Universalist. Author: Laboratory Practice Manual, 1915. Home: Castle Point, Hoboken, N.J.

STOCKWELL, Henry Ford, lawyer; b. Hammonton, N.J., Feb. 2, 1874; s. Elam and Hester (Ford) S.; student South Jersey Inst., 1890-92; grad. Phillips Exeter Acad., 1893; A.B., Princeton U., 1897, A.M., 1900; m. Caroline Develin, July 31, 1901; children—Henry Ford, James Develin, Aylward H. Admitted to N.J. Bar as atty. 1899, and as counsellor, 1902; partner Bleakly & Stockwell, 1901-23; partner Bleakly, Stockwell & Burling, 1923-Feb. 1939; a senior partner law firm Bleakly, Stockwell, Lewis & Zink since Feb. 1939. Mem. N.J. State exec. com. of Y.M.C.A.; trustee Burlington Co. Y.M.C.A.; trustee and pres. Camp Ockanickon for Boys and Girls (one of largest camps in East) since 1924. Republican. Presbyn. (elder). Clubs: Union League (Philadelphia); Moorestown Field (N.J.) Home: 119 E. Maple Av., Moorestown, N.J. Office: West Jersey Trust Bldg., Camden, N.J.

STOCKWELL, John Wesley, Jr., clergyman; b. Portland, Me., Mar. 24, 1873; s. John Wesley and Eliza Jane (Mathias) S.; grad. high sch., Deering, Me., 1891, high sch., Portland, 1892; grad. New Ch. Theol. Sch., Cambridge, Mass., 1903; Ph.B., U. of Chicago, 1908; B.D., U. of Chicago Div. Sch. 1911; postgrad, study, U. of Chicago and Harvard; unmarried. Began as newspaperman; ordained ministry Ch. of the New Jerusalem (Swedenborgian), 1903; pastorates in Chicago and Phila.; has specialized in social service. Building sec. and acting chaplain Camp Beauregard, La., World War. Dir. Nat. New Ch. Group Study Bureau, Nat. Methods and Results Bur.; mem. exec. com. Nat. Bd. of Missions; mem. New Ch. Lecture and Publicity Bur., New Ch. Theol. Sch. bd. mgrs., U. of Chicago Div. Sch. Alumni Assn., Pa. Assn. Ch. of New Jerusalem (v.p.), etc. Founder, 1923, First Undenominational Radio Ch. America, Phila.; founder Neo-Behaviorism and Knowledge Extension Soc.; mem. com. Nat. New Ch., for Century of Progress Expn., Chicago, 1933; chmn. Radio Com. Sesqui-Centennial Expn., Phila.; chmn. Gen. Conv. of New Jerusalem 250th Swedenborg Birthday Commemoration, 1938. Mem. Franklin Inst. Republican. Mason. Clubs: Union League, Army and Navy Union. Author: Riding the Question Mark through Life Situations and Progress, 1937. Writer brochures, poems, etc.; mgr. New Church Book Center; editor The Helper—Life News (weekly). Home: 4435 Paul St. Office: 2129 Chestnut St., Philadelphia, Pa.

STODDARD, Alice Kent, artist; b. Watertown, Conn.; d. James and Alice (Kent) S.; art edn., Sch. of Design for Women, and Acad. Fine Arts, both of Phila., Pa. Represented in collections of Pa. Acad. Fine Arts (Phila.), Reading (Pa.) Mus., Delgado Mus. (New Orleans), and in Dallas (Tex.). Awarded Mary Smith prize, Pa. Acad. Fine Arts, 1911, 13, Fellowship prize, 1916, Beck medal, 1926, Carol Beck portrait prize, 1927; gold medal, Phila. Art Club, 1916; Isador medal, Nat. Acad. Design, New York, 1917, Clark prize, 1928. Asso. Nat. Acad., 1938. Home: 108 Graver Lane, Chestnut Hill. Studio: 1822 Cherry St., Philadelphia, Pa.

STODDARD, Harold Frank, clergyman; b. Jamestown, N.Y., Aug. 9, 1896; s. Verne Wade and Bertha (Knowlton) S.; A.B., Colgate U., 1920; ed. Colgate Sem., 1920-21, Western Theol. Sem., 1934-35; m. Vivian Chase, Dec. 20, 1920; children—Lynette Janice, Harold Frank, Jr., Warren Chase. Ordained to ministry Baptist Ch., 1922; asso. pastor, Pittsfield, Mass., 1921-23; pastor, Warren, Pa., 1923-31; pastor, Bellevue Bapt. Ch., Pittsburgh, Pa., since 1931; mem. bd. mgrs. Pa. Bapt. Convention, mem. exec. com., chmn. edn. dept. Served in U.S.N. during World War. Mem. Theol. Circle of Pittsburgh, Sigma Nu. Republican. Baptist. Speaker for youth groups, edn. confs. civic orgns. and clubs. Home: 806 Taylor Av., Bellevue, Pittsburgh, Pa.

STODDARD, William B., treas. Hendrick Mfg. Co.; b. Carbondale, Pa., Jan. 15, 1894; s. Eugene A. and Charlotte E. (Dinsmore) S.; grad. Carbondale High Sch., 1912; m. Emily H. Trautwein, Dec. 28, 1923; 1 son, William B. With Hendrick Mfg. Co., Carbondale, Pa., since 1916, beginning as cost accountant, dir. since 1926, treas. since 1934; dir. First Nat. Bank, Carbondale, Pa., since 1939. Served in U.S. Army, World War. Republican. Methodist. Mason (Shriner). Clubs: Elkview Country (Carbondale); Scranton (Scranton, Pa.). Home: 55 Laurel St. Office: 75 Dundoff St., Carbondale, Pa.

STODDART, Charles William, educator; b. Boscobel, Wis., Oct. 14, 1877; s. William and Emma (Sylvester) S.; A.B., Columbia, 1900, A.M., 1901; Ph.D., U. of Wis., 1909; m. Clara Coburn Cook, June 12, 1902; children—Charles William, Harold Coburn, Robert Cook. Mining business, in Colo., 1902-04; instr. and asst. prof. of soils, U. of Wis., 1904-10; prof. agrl. chemistry, 1910-20, dean Sch. Natural Sciences, 1920-24, Pa. State Coll. Fellow A.A.A.S.; mem. Beta Theta Pi, Phi Beta Kappa, Sigma Xi, Phi Kappa Phi, Alpha Zeta. Congregationalist. Club: Centre Hills. Author: Chemistry of Agriculture, 1915. Home: State College, Pa.

STOEBER, John Bernhard, dir. phys. edn. and athletics; b. Reading, Pa., July 21, 1898; s. Bernhard and Ann Lena (Wendler) S.; B.P.E., Springfield Coll., Springfield, Mass., 1925; A.M., Columbia U., 1935; m. Louise Allison Keck,

STOKES

Dec. 11, 1928; children—Joan Louise, J. Bernhard, Nancy Allison. Engaged as prof. phys. edn., dir. and coach of athletics, Thiel Coll., Greenville, Pa., since 1925, prof. phys. edn. in summer sch., 1926-27, 1932-33, head coach in football and basketball since 1932. Served in Ordnance Corps, U.S.A., 1918. Established three playgrounds at Greenville, Pa. and supervised them, 1926-32. Sec.-treas. Tri-State Intercollegiate Athletic Conf., 1928-30, 1932-34, pres., same, 1931. Mem. Am. Phys. Edn. Assn., Pa. Edn. Assn., Am. Assn. Univ. Profs. Republican. Lutheran. B.P.O.E. Clubs: Rotary (past pres.), Elks (Greenville). Home: 246 Clinton St., Greenville, Pa.

STOFFLET, Clinton F., M.D.; b. Flicksville, Pa., Feb. 1, 1877; s. Charles H. and Emma (Ackerman) S.; student Easton (Pa.) Acad., 1893-94, Lafayette Coll., Easton, 1894-95; M.D., Medico-Chirurgical Coll., Philadelphia, 1898; m. Celia Stephens, 1904; children—Pearl (Mrs. Robert A. Harrier), Harry. In gen. practice of medicine since 1898; sec. and treas. Stephen Jackson Co.; v.p. First Nat. Bank, Pen Argyle, Pa. Mayor, Pen Argyle, 1918-22. Mem. Pa. Med. Assn., Lehigh Valley Med. Assn., Northampton Co. Med. Soc. Republican. Mason, Odd Fellow, Forester. Home: Pen Argyle, Pa.

STOKEN, Norman, newspaper editor; b. Chicago, Ill., Dec. 7, 1913; s. Ben and Esther Hilda (Kite) S.; student DePaul U., Chicago, 1932-34, Northwestern U., Evanston, Ill., 1934-36; unmarried. Reporter Newark (N.J.) Ledger, 1937; editor Local Press, Union, N.J., 1937; reporter Independent Observer, Beckley, W.Va., 1937-38, editor since 1938; sec. Independent Observer Publishing Co., Beckley, since 1938. Publicity dir. Labor's Non-Partisan League of Fayette Counties, W.Va., since 1938; del. to W.Va. Industrial Union Council, 1938. Mem. Am. Newspaper Guild. Democrat. Moose. Home: John Beckley Apts. Office: 31 McCrery St., Beckley, W.Va.

STOKES, Claude Newton, univ. prof.; b. Crossville, Ill., Aug. 17, 1890; s. James Monroe and Elma (Armstrong) S.; student McKendree Acad., Lebanon, Ill., 1908-10; B.A., McKendree Coll., 1913; M.A., U. of Ill., Urbana, 1914; Ph.D., U. of Minn., Minneapolis, 1929; m. Emilie Somer, Dec. 19, 1913 (died Jan. 29, 1918); 1 dau., Elma Gale; m. 2d, Gertrude Speed, Aug. 17, 1920; 1 son, James B. High sch. teacher, 1914-26; mem. faculty, U. of Minn., 1926-32; prof. mathematics, Temple U., since 1932. Awarded scholarship, U. of Ill., 1913-14. Mem. Am. Math. Soc., N.E. A., Am. Edn. Research Assn., Nat. Council Teachers Mathematics, Phi Delta Kappa. Methodist. Home: 6416 N. Camac St., Philadelphia, Pa.

STOKES, Edward Casper, ex-governor; b. Phila., Dec. 22, 1860; s. Edward H. and Matilda G. (Kemble) S.; A.B., Brown University, 1883; LL.D., Temple University, 1909, same from Rutgers and Dickinson; unmarried. Engaged in banking since 1883; chairman board First-Mechanics' Nat. Bank, Trenton. Supt. pub. schs., Millville, N.J., 1889-98; mem. N.J. Assembly, 1891-92, Senate, 1892-1901 (pres. 1895); vice-chmn. State Rep. Com., 1900; clerk Ct. of Chancery, 1901-05; gov. of N.J., 1905-08. First pres. N.J. Bankers Assn. Office: First-Mechanics' Nat. Bank, Trenton, N.J.

STOKES, Edward Lowber, ex-congressman; b. Phila., Pa., Sept. 29, 1880; s. Thomas and Ellen (Welsh) S.; ed. St. Paul's Sch., Concord, N.H.; m. Mary Brooke, Apr. 20, 1920. Clk. Girard Trust Co., Phila., 7 yrs.; mem. firm Edward Lowber Stokes & Co., bonds; elected mem. 72d Congress, 2d Pa. Dist., at spl. election, Nov. 3, 1931, to fill vacancy for term ending Mar. 3, 1933, and reëlected to 73d Congress (1933-35), 6th Pa. Dist. Republican. Clubs: Philadelphia, Radnor Hunt. Home: Haverford, Pa., and 1708 Locust St., Phila., Pa.

STOKES, Francis J., pres. F. J. Stokes Machine Co.; b. Germantown, Phila., Pa. Dec. 24, 1873; s. Francis and Katharine W. (Evans) S.; A.B., Haverford (Pa.) Coll., 19—; m. Lelia

Woodruff, June 28, 1912; children—Francis Joseph, Allen W., Henry W. II, Alison, David. Pres. F. J. Stokes Machine Co., Phila. Overseer Germantown Friends Sch. since 1918, Wm. Penn Charter Sch. since 1928; trustee Bryn Mawr Coll. since 1936. Mem. Soc. of Chem. Engrs., Phila. Zoöl. Soc., Phila. Acad. of Natural Sciences, Acad. of Fine Arts. Clubs: University (Phila., Pa.); Chemists' (New York City). Home: 629 Church Lane, Germantown. Office: Olney P.O., Philadelphia, Pa.

STOKES, Henry Warrington; b. Philadelphia, Pa., June 24, 1867; s. Francis and Katherine Wistar (Evans) S.; A.B., Haverford (Pa.) Coll., 1887; m. Helen B. Tyson, May 20, 1905; 1 son, James Tyson. Treas. York Haven (Pennsylvania) Company, 1889-1914, pres., 1914-29; dir. Provident Mut. Life Ins. Co. Mem. Am. Paper Pulp Assn. (pres. 1923-25), Wrapping Paper Manufacturers' Service Bur. (pres. 1918-28). Pres. Rush Hosp. for Consumptives; pres. bd. mgrs. Sleighton Farm Sch. for Girls, Darlington, Pa., and of Haverford (Pa.) Coll.; mem. bd. mgrs. Dunwoody Home for Convalescents, Newtown Sq., Pa. Republican. Club: Union League (Phila.). Home: Media, Pa.

STOKES, Howard Gale, advertising, motion pictures; b. Hermon, N.Y., June 30, 1888; s. Frank Adelbert and Carrie Adelaide (Gale) S.; A.B., Colgate, 1911, M.A., 1934; m. Ulga Ultima Muller, April 18, 1914 (marriage annulled); m. 2d, Ida Jane Bassett, Dec. 3, 1932; children—Gale, Jane Austin. Advertising copywriter, 1911-12; copy mgr. N.Y. Telephone Co., 1912-19; produc. mgr. Prizma Color Ednl. Pictures, 1919-20; editor Capitol Theater Colorland Review, 1920; v.p. Prizma, Inc., 1920-24; exec. asst. Am. Telegraph & Telephone Co., 1924-25; motion picture dir., 1925-29; development mgr. ednl. dept. Electrical Research Products, Inc., subsidiary of Western Electric Co., 1929-31; became dir. of Development Erpi Picture Consultants, Inc., 1931; advertising supervisor Am. Telephone & Telegraph Co. since 1936. Del. to Conv. Advertising Fed. America, Berlin, 1929; dir. Colgate U. Alumni Corpn., 1935-38; national chmn. Colgate U. Alumni Fund, 1935-38; trustee Colgate U., 1937-39. Mem. Advertising Federation of America, Theta Nu Epsilon, Phi Gamma Delta, Phi Beta Kappa, Skull and Scroll. Republican. Protestant. Clubs: Advertising; Essex Falls (N.J.) Country. Author: (with F. L. Devereux) The Educational Talking Picture. Wrote scenario "Golden Years of Progress" of motion picture shown by Advertising Federation of America during Century of Progress Expn., Chicago; author, dir. or production mgr. more than 200 scientific, industrial or ednl. motion pictures since 1919. Home: 177 N. Arlington Av., East Orange, N.J. Office: 195 Broadway, New York, N.Y.

STOKES, John Hinchman, dermatologist, syphilographer; b. Munich, Germany, Sept. 1, 1885; s. Henry Newlin and Wilhelmina (van den Berg) S.; A.B., U. of Mich., 1908, M.D., 1912; m. Della Bixler Lee, Sept. 25, 1908; children—John H., Frederick (dec.); m. 2d, Margaret Ann Maris, Sept. 8, 1928 (dec.); 1 dau., Johanne (dec.); m. 3d, Eleanor Heaps McGahey, August 12, 1932; children—Tawn Janice, Eleanor Anne. Instructor anatomy, 1913, resident in dermatology and syphilology, 1913-14, instr. dermatology and syphilology, 1914-15, University of Michigan; instr. same, University of Illinois, 1915-16; asst. prof. dermatology and syphilology, 1916-19, asso. prof., 1919-21, and prof. of same, 1921-24, Mayo Foundation, U. of Minn. Was organizer and chief sect. of dermatology and syphilology, Mayo Clinic; prof. dermatology and syphilology, Sch. of Medicine, U. of Pa., and prof. Grad. Sch., same, since July 1, 1924. Chmn. Com. on Research in Syphilis, 1928; mem. representing U.S. Pub. Health Service on Commn. of Experts on Syphilis, League of Nations Health Orgn., 1928-35; special consultant U.S. Public Health Service, U.S. Food and Drugs Administration. Mem. American Dermatol. Assn., American Social Hygiene Assn. (vice-pres.), Phi Beta Kappa, Sigma Xi, Alpha Omega Alpha, Alpha Kappa Kappa; corr. mem. Vienna, Argentine, Brit., French and Danish dermatol. socs. Conglist. Author: The Third Great Plague—a Discussion of Syphilis for Everyday People, 1917; Today's World Problem in Disease Prevention (non-tech. discussion of syphilis and gonorrhœa, written in behalf of govt. campaign against venereal diseases and at request of Council of Nat. Defense); Text Book, Modern Clinical Syphilology, 1926, 2d edit., 1934; Dermatology and Syphilology for Nurses, 1930; Fundamentals of Everyday Dermatology, 1931, 2d edit., 1935; also a number of articles on topics pertaining to syphilis and dermatology in med. jours. Address: 4228 Spruce St., Philadelphia, Pa.

STOKES, John Stogdell, mfr.; b. Moorestown, N.J., Feb. 26, 1870; s. Nathaniel Newlin and Martha Eastbourne (Stokes) S.; student Haverford (Pa.) Coll., 1886-89; m. May Margaret Egan, May 31, 1919; children—John Stogdell, Martha Eastbourne. Began as clk. Queen & Co., Phila., 1889; v.p. and gen. mgr. Am. Metal Edge Box Co., Phila., 1889-1900; pres. Stokes & Smith Co., Phila., mfrs. of machinery, since 1900; dir. Provident Trust Co., Pa. Salt Mfg. Co. Pres. Pa. Mus. of Art; dir. Bryn Mawr Coll.; mem. bd. dirs. Phila. Orchestra; trustee Haverford Coll., Acad. of Natural Sciences of Phila. Clubs: Philadelphia, Rittenhouse, Franklin Inn, Huntingdon Valley Country. Home: Spring Valley Farm, Huntingdon Valley, Pa. Office: Summerdale, Philadelphia, Pa.

STOKES, Joseph, physician; b. Moorestown, N.J., Apr. 8, 1862; s. N. Newlin (M.D.) and Martha E. (Stokes) S.; A.B., U. of Pa., 1880; M.D., U. of Pa. Med. Sch., 1883; m. Mary Emlen, June 19, 1890; children—Eleanor (Mrs. Robert C. Smith), Samuel Emlen (M.D.), Joseph, Jr. (M.D.). Interne Univ. Hosp., Phila. 1883-84, Childrens Hosp., Phila., 1884-85; engaged in gen. practice of medicine at Moorestown, N.J., continuously since 1885; chmn. bd. and dir. Burlington Co. Trust Co., Moorestown; served as pres. Burlington Co. Trust Co., Moorestown Nat. Bank. Trustee Moorestown Friends Sch. Mem. A.M.A., N.J. State and Burlington Co. med. socs. Republican. Mem. Soc. of Friends. Home: 220 E. Main St., Moorestown, N.J.

STOKES, Joseph, Jr., physician; b. Moorestown, N.J., Feb. 22, 1896; s. Joseph and Mary (Emlen) S.; ed. Haverford Coll., 1912-16; M.D., U. of Pa. Med. Sch., 1920; m. Frances D. Elkinton, Mar. 24, 1921; children—Jean Frances, Joseph III, Donald E., Eleanor. Instr. U. of Pa. Med. Sch., 1923-24, instr. pediatrics, 1924-28, asso. pediatrics, 1928-31, Wm. H. Bennett asst. prof., 1931-33, asst. prof. pediatrics, 1933-36, asso. prof., 1936-38, William H. Bennett prof. of pediatrics since 1939; asso. physician in chief, Children's Hosp., 1936-38, physician in chief since 1939; dir. pediatric service, Abington Hosp. since 1930; chief of pediatric service, Hosp. of Pa., since 1939. Mem. bd. and vice-pres. Pocono Lake Preserve; chmn. joint com. on public health and preventive medicine, Coll. of Physicians and the Phila. County Med. Soc., 1938; formerly chmn. Med. Relief Com. of the Phila. County Relief Bd.; mem. bd. mgrs., Germantown Friends' School; mem. bd. Phila. Official Nurses Directory; mem. Sydenham Coterie. Mem. bd. dirs., Phila. Child Guidance Clinic, Phila. Child Health Soc., Phila. Pediatric Soc. Co-chmn. for Pa., Am. Acad. of Pediatrics. Fellow Phila. Coll. Physicians; mem. A.M.A., Am. Pediatric Soc., Phila. County Med. Soc., Soc. for Pediatric Research (one of founders), John Morgan Soc., Sigma Xi, Phi Beta Kappa. Republican. Mem. Society of Friends. Contbr. articles to med. jours. Home: 159 W. Coulter St. Office: 1740 Bainbridge St., Philadelphia, Pa.

STOKES, Walter, investment banker; b. Philadelphia, Pa., May 11, 1885; s. Thomas P. C. and Ellen (Welsh) S.; student Germantown Acad., 1894-98, Blith Sch., Philadelphia, 1898-1901, Central Manual Training Sch., Philadelphia, 1901-02, St. Pauls Sch., Concord, N.H., 1902-04; m. Frances Kemble Wister, May 21, 1928; children—Mary Channing, John Welsh, II. Began as bank clerk, Phila., 1904; in investment banking business since 1905; owner Walter Stokes & Co. since 1922. Republican. Episcopalian. Club: Radnor Hunt (Malvern, Pa.). Home: St. Davids, Pa. Office: 1529 Walnut St., Philadelphia, Pa.

STOKLEY, James, museum dir.; b. Phila., Pa., May 19, 1900; s. James and Irene (Stulb) S.; B.S. in Edn., U. of Pa., 1922, A.M., same, 1924; m. Susan Assheton Doughten, Sept. 14, 1933. Staff photographer, Phila. Inquirer, summers 1919, 21; asst. in psychology, U. of Pa., 1922-23; teacher science, Phila. Central High Sch., 1923-25; staff writer and asst. treas. Science Service, Inc., Washington, D.C., 1925-31; asso. dir. Franklin Inst. and dir. Fels Planetarium, Phila., 1931-39; dir. Buhl Planetarium and Inst. Popular Science, Pittsburgh, Pa., since April 17, 1939; lecturer in astronomy, U. of Pittsburgh, since 1939. Fellow A.A.A.S., Royal Astron. Soc. Mem. Am. Assn. Museums, Am. Astron. Soc., Franklin Inst., History of Sci. Soc., Seismol. Soc. of America, Brit. Astron. Assn., Royal Photographic Soc., Société Astronomique de France. Republican. Clubs: University, Philobiblon (Philadelphia). Home: 1 School House Lane, East Liberty P.O., Pittsburgh, Pa. Office: Federal & West Ohio St., N.S., Pittsburgh, Pa.

STOLL, I(saac) V(ought), veterinarian; b. near Rome, Pa., Mar. 28, 1893; s. Stephen A. and Emer B. (Cass) S.; student Rome Acad., 1908-09, Rome High Sch., 1909-12, Mansfield State Normal Sch., 1912-13; V.M.D., U. of Pa., 1916; m. Mildred Davis, June 25, 1924; children—Ruth Emer, Robert Stephen, Elizabeth Anne. In practice of veterinary medicine, devoting considerable time to sterility work in cattle and horses, Rome, Pa., since 1916 (except during World War); half owner Nichols Hardware Co., 1924-29; treas. Towanda (Pa.) Folding Box Co. since 1929; v.p., dir. Farmers Nat. Bank; owner and operator S.A.S. Hurst Stock Farms (308 acres), shipper of high class dairy cattle, Rome, Pa. Mem. Borough Council, Rome, since 1924. Served as 2d lt. Veterinary Corps, U.S. Army, at Ft. Oglethorpe, Ga., and Mounted Service Sch., Ft. Riley, Kan., 1917-19. Mem. Alpha Psi. Republican. Methodist. Mason, Odd Fellow, Granger. Address: Rome, Pa.

STOLTZ, Glenn Edwin, mgr. metal working engring.; b. Gettysburg, O., Aug. 21, 1886; s. James Harvey and Laura Belle (Reck) S.; student Ohio State U., Columbus, O.; m. Elizabeth Kirk Donehoo, June 1, 1915; children—Esther Jane, Mabel Catherine, Dorothy Elizabeth, James Harvey. Apprentice Westinghouse Electric & Mfg. Co., East Pittsburgh, Pa., 1909-11, steel mill application work, 1911-26, mgr. industrial engring., 1926-30, mgr. metal working sales, 1930-37, mgr. metal working engring. since 1937. Mem. Am. Inst. E.E., Am. Iron and Steel Inst. Republican. Presbyterian. Mason. Clubs: Edgewood, Edgewood Country, Westinghouse. Contbr. to tech. jours. Home: 151 W. Hutchison Av., Pittsburgh 18, Pa. Office: Westinghouse Electric & Mfg. Co., East Pittsburgh, Pa.

STONE, Arthur Guy, lawyer; b. Falling Rock, W.Va., Dec. 10, 1896; s. John Newton and Melissa Jane (Getchel) S.; LL.B., W.Va. Univ. Law Coll., 1918; grad. study Harvard U., 1920-21; m. Greta Payne, Aug. 17, 1928; 1 son, John William. Admitted to W.Va. bar and engaged in gen. practice of law at Charleston; law clk. W.Va. Supreme Ct., 1921-24; city solicitor Charleston, 1926-28; mem. firm Rummel, Blagg & Stone since 1928; pres. Milo Corpn. Served as lt. field arty., U.S.A., 1918. Mem. Phi Sigma Kappa. Republican. Methodist. Mason. Club: Edgewood Country (Charleston). Home: 815 Maple Rd. Office: Security Bldg., Charleston, W.Va.

STONE, Carleton Elijah, civil engr.; b. Gallia Co., O., Feb. 1, 1875; s. James William and Joanna Louisa (Kerns) S.; ed. Rio Grande Coll. (O.), 1895; C.E., O. State Univ., 1899; m. Mabel Marion Robinson, of Coraopolis, Pa., Sept. 10, 1903; children—Marion Florence (died 1938, wife of William R. Pressler), Catherine Alice (Mrs. Clayton A. Rawson), Robert Carleton. Employed as engr. municipal work, Columbus and Gallipolis, O., 1899-1900; Govt. surveys on O. River, 1901-02; draftsman Pittsburgh & L.E. R.R., Pittsburgh, Pa., 1902-16; in pvt. practice as civil engr. and surveyor, Pittsburgh, Pa., since 1917. Served as capt. Engrs. Res., U.S.A., 1917-19, in U.S., and with 122d Engrs. in France. Mem. Sch. Bd., Coraopolis, Pa., 28 yrs., now pres. bd.; mem. Bd. of

STONE, Charles Henry, surgeon; b. Embreeville, Pa., Nov. 4, 1884; s. John and Anne Exton (Steele) S.; ed. U. of Pa., 1904-06; M.D., U. of Pa. Med. Sch., 1909; grad. student U. of Pa. Grad. Med. Sch., 1927; m. Elizabeth Comly Hoopes, July 15, 1913; children—Emma Haines (dec.), Anne Exton (Mrs. William Joseph Scarlett), Elizabeth Comly, Charles Henry III, Mary Helen. Employed as clk. Lukens Steel Co., 1903-04; engaged in gen. practice of medicine, 1909-30, and specializing in surgery since 1930; surgeon Bethlehem Steel Co., Reading R.R. Co.; surgeon Coatesville Hosp.; cons. surgeon U.S. Vets. Hosp.; pres. Fairview Cemetery Assn.; dir. Chester Co. Crippled Children's Soc. Served as mem. Council Borough South Coatesville, Pa. Fellow Am. Coll. Surgs., Am. Assn. Industrial Phys. and Surgs. Mem. A.M.A., Pa. State and Chester Co. med. socs. Republican. Episcopalian. Mason. Clubs: Coatesville Country, Rotary (Coatesville); Medical (Philadelphia). Home: West Chester Rd., South Coatesville, Pa. Office: 380 Chestnut St., Coatesville, Pa.

STONE, Charles Randolph, supt. city schs.; b. Geneva, O., Apr. 14, 1885; s. Randolph Henry and Vivian Evelyn S.; A.B., Oberlin Coll., 1907; ed. U. of Chicago, summer 1910, U. of Wis., summer 1913, U. of Mich., summer 1916; A.M., U. of Pittsburgh, 1929; hon. D.Ped., Westminster Coll., New Wilmington, Pa., 1933; m. Maude E. Fox, Aug. 31, 1914; 1 son, Charles Reynard. Employed as prin. high sch. and supt. schs. in N.D., Wash., Mich. and Ill., 1907-15; supt. schs., Munhall, Pa., since 1915. Mem. Nat. Edn. Assn. (life), Pa. State Edn. Assn. (life), Soc. for Study Edn., Phi Delta Kappa, Prins. Round Table of Allegheny Co. (past pres.). Republican. Presbyn. Mason (32°, Shriner). Club: Rotary of Homestead, Pa. (past pres.). Home: 109 22d St., Munhall, Pa.

STONE, Edmund Cushing, pub. utility official; b. Charlestown, N.H., Mar. 8, 1882; s. Livingston and Rebecca Salisbury (Cushing) S.; A.B., Harvard, 1904, B.S., same, 1905; m. Caroline Holmes, Apr. 23, 1915 (died 1934); m. 2d, Camille Pollard, June 6, 1936. Employed as elec. engr., Westinghouse Electric & Mfg. Co., East Pittsburgh, Pa., 1905-11; cable engr., Allegheny Co. Light Co., Pittsburgh, 1911-12; asso. with Duquesne Light Co., Pittsburgh, continuously since 1913, in various exec. engring. positions, 1913-26, system development mgr., 1926-31, asst. to pres., 1931-38, v.p., gen. mgr. and dir. since 1938. Served as chmn. Council of Orgns. of Allegheny Co.; sec. Pa. Economy League; vice-pres. Federation of Social Agencies; mem. Chamber of Commerce. Fellow Am. Inst. Elec. Engrs. (past vice-pres., past dir.). Mem. Engrs. Soc. Western Pa. (pres.), Pa. Electric Assn. (vice-pres.). Republican. Unitarian. Clubs: Duquesne, Rotary, Harvard-Yale-Princeton (Pittsburgh). Home: 747 Valley View Rd., Mt. Lebanon, Pa. Office: 435 6th Av., Pittsburgh, Pa.

STONE, Elinore Cowan (Mrs. C. Arthur Stone), author; b. Adrian, Mich., Mar. 2, 1884; d. John F. Cowan; A.B., Mount Holyoke Coll., 1906; grad. study, U. of Calif., 1910-11; m. C. Arthur Stone, June 8, 1915. Author: The Laughingest Lady; Fear Rides the Fog; Binks—His Dog and His Heart. Contbr. short stories to leading mags. Home: 1027 Macon Av., Pittsburgh, Pa.

STONE, Elton (Elwood), prin. high sch.; b. Lyons, Neb., May 2, 1894; s. William J. and Isabelle (Robertson) S.; A.B., U. of Neb., Lincoln, Neb., 1916; A.M., Columbia U., 1924; m. Henrietta Butler, July 30, 1919. Employed as prin. high sch., Weeping Water, Neb., 1916-17, supt. schs., 1917; prin. jr. high sch., Fairbury, Neb., 1919-23; asst. prin. high sch., Bronxville, N.Y., 1923-24; prin. high sch., Easton, Pa., since 1924. Served in U.S.N., 1917-19. Mem. N.E.A. (life), Patriotic Order Sons of America, Am. Legion, Alpha Sigma Phi. Republican. Presbyterian (elder). Mason (32°). Club: Kiwanis (Easton, Pa.). Home: Easton, Pa.

STONE, Harry Everette, educator; b. Corry, Pa., Dec. 31, 1883; s. Nathaniel and Emma (Goodell) S.; A.B., Allegheny Coll., 1905; student law dept. U. of Mich., 1907-08; spl. courses in edn., U. of Pittsburgh; A.M., Teachers Coll. (Columbia), 1922; grad. and research work Columbia University, summers 1936, 37, 38; m. Sarah Louisa Day, 1907; children—Ward Day, Eleanor Jane (Mrs. William A. Thornhill, Jr.). Began as teacher in high school, Cambridge Springs, Pa., 1905; teacher high sch., Meadville, 1909-14; dir. Americanization, and vocational counselor, pub. schs. of Erie, Pa., 1915-22; dean of men, West Virginia U., since 1922, guidance, placement, loan, service, 1936. Mem. Nat. Assn. Deans and Advisers of Men (v.p. Eastern U.S.A. Div., 1929-30); mem. exec. bd., 1930-31), National Education Assn., National Soc. for Vocational Edn., Pa. State Edn. Assn. (pres. Americanization div., 1921-22) W.Va. State Edn. Assn., Personnel Research Fed., Am. Coll. Personnel Assn. (v.p., 1937-38), Am. Numis. Assn. XX Club (ex-pres.), Phi Gamma Delta, Pi Gamma Mu, Phi Delta Kappa, etc. Republican. Presbyn. Mason (32°); mem. Scottish Rite Ednl. Assn. of W.Va. (dir.), Masonic Research Soc. of W.Va. Rotarian. Lecturer; contbr. to mags. and periodicals; author of leaflets on careers. Home: Morgantown, W.Va.*

STONE, Harvey Brinton, surgeon; b. Baltimore, Md., Nov. 22, 1882; s. John Theodore and Clara May (Brinton) S.; A.B., Johns Hopkins U., 1902; M.D., Johns Hopkins U. Med. Sch., 1906; m. Ethel Hoffman, Aug. 27, 1906; children—Brinton Harvey, Douglas Hoffman, Dorothy Anne (Mrs. George H. Yeager). Resident house officer in surgery, Johns Hopkins Hosp., 1906-07; adjunct prof. surgery, U. of Va. Med. Sch., Charlottesville, 1907-10; in practice of surgery at Baltimore, Md., since 1910; in various grades of surg. service, Johns Hopkins U. Med. Sch. since 1910, asso. prof. surgery since 1927. Served as capt. then maj., Med. Corps, U.S.A., 1917-19, with A.E.F. Fellow Am. Coll. Surgeons. Mem. A.M.A., Am. Bd. of Surgery, Am. Surg. Assn., Am. Soc. Clin. Surgery, Surg. Research Soc., Southern Surg. Assn. (past pres.), Internat. Surg. Soc., Phi Beta Kappa, Alpha Omega Alpha, Phi Gamma Delta. Mem. Med. Sect. of Nat. Research Council (1935-38). Clubs: University, Maryland. Author of numerous med. publs. Home: 203 Westway, Kernewood. Office: 18 W. Franklin St., Baltimore, Md.

STONE, Mildred Fairbanks, life ins.; b. Bloomfield, N.J., May 21, 1902; d. Franklin A. and Ida L. (Garabrant) S.; grad. Bloomfield (N.J.) High Sch., 1920; A.B., Vassar Coll., 1924; grad. Am. Coll. Life Underwriters, Washington, D.C., 1929. Teacher Bloomfield High Sch., 1924-25; with Mutual Benefit Life Ins. Co. since 1925, becoming agency field sec., 1934. Trustee Bloomfield Community Chest, League for Friendly Service. Mem. League of Ins. Women in N.Y., Phi Beta Kappa. Republican. Baptist. Clubs: Vassar (New York); Am. Assn. Univ. Women (Bloomfield branch). Home: 23 Clarendon Pl., Bloomfield, N.J. Office: Mutual Benefit Life Insurance Co., Newark, N.J.

STONE, Morris Denor, engr.; b. Cambridge, Mass., Dec. 2, 1902; s. Henry and Rose (Denor) S.; grad. Weymouth High Sch., 1919; B.S., Harvard, 1923, M.S., 1925; Ph.D., U. of Pittsburgh, 1933; student Univ. of Berlin and Techniche Hochschule, Charlottenburg, 1930-31; m. Marissa Gluckmann, June 19, 1926; children—Richard Joseph, Elinore, Eugenie, Philip Morris, Stephanie Rose. Research for Am. Soc. Mech. Engrs. Steam program, Harvard, 1923-24; research engr. Westinghouse Electric & Mfg. Co., 1925-29, supervising development engr., 1929-34; head lecturer in grad. mech. design, Westinghouse Co., 1932-34; mem. faculty, U. of Pittsburgh, 1929-33; liaison engr. in Europe, 1930-31; special engr. United Engring. & Foundry Co., 1934-36, mgr. development dept. since 1936. Lt. Ordnance Reserve, U.S. Army. Mem. Am. Soc. Mech. Engrs., Iron and Steel Engrs., Tau Beta Pi. Mem. Harvard-Yale-Princeton Club, Pittsburgh. Home: 1269 Duffield St. Office: First National Bank Bldg., Pittsburgh, Pa.

STONE, Ralph Walter, geologist; b. Camden, N.Y., Nov. 17, 1876; s. Walter Chester and Sarah Cornelia (Hosley) S.; Ph.B., Hamilton Coll., Clinton, N.Y., 1899; A.B., Harvard, 1900, A.M., 1901; honorary D.Sc., Lebanon Valley College, 1938; m. Mary Edna Bull, Nov. 16, 1910; children—Mary Elizabeth, Samuel Bull. Geologist, U.S. Geol. Survey, 1901-21, contributing 50 repts. on geol. and mineral resources; asst. state geologist Pa. Topographic and Geol. Survey since Dec. 1921; geologist on municipal water supply dam, Bogota, Colombia, Nov. 1930. Mem. Com. of Awards San Francisco Expn., 1915. Mem. Geol. Soc. America, Geol. Soc. Washington, Soc. Econ. Geologists, A.A.A.S., Alpha Delta Phi, Sigma Xi. Club: Torch. Editor Pa. Acad. Sci., 1926—. Author of 18 books, including Pa. State publs. on molding sand, feldspar, caves, building stones, and 200 articles in technical and other periodicals. Home: 3115 N. Front St., Harrisburg, Pa.

STONE, Warren Moorhead, lawyer; b. Warren, Pa., July 3, 1901; s. Ralph Warren and May (Ruland) S.; student Warren High Sch., 1916-18, Lawrenceville (N.J.) Sch., 1918-19, Haverford (Pa.) Sch., 1919-21, Amherst (Mass.) Coll., 1921-22; A.B., Haverford Coll., 1925; LL.B., Harvard Law Sch., 1928; m. Dorothy E. Allison, June 14, 1930; 1 dau., Elaine Allison. Admitted to Warren County bar, 1928; jr. partner R. W. Stone & Son, 1928-34; upon death of R. W. Stone, 1934, became sr. partner firm Stone & Flick, occupying same office originally used by Brown & Stone (1870); county solicitor, Warren Co., 1930-35; v.p. and dir. Warren Motors, Inc. Trustee Warren State Hosp., Mar. 1934-June 1935. Mem. Warren County Bar Assn., Phi Delta Theta (Mass. Beta). Republican. Presbyterian. Clubs: Warren Players, Kiwanis (sec. and dir. 1928-30). Home: 605 Conewango Av. Office: 310 Second St., Warren, Pa.

STONE, Witmer, naturalist; b. Phila., Pa., Sept. 22, 1866; s. Frederick D. and Anne E. (Witmer) S.; A.B., U. of Pa., 1887, A.M., 1891, Sc.D., 1913; m. Lillie M. Lafferty, Aug. 1, 1904. Asst. curator Acad. Natural Sciences, Phila., 1891-1908, curator, 1908-24, dir. of Museum, 1925-28, v.p., 1927, director emeritus since 1929. Fellow American Ornithologists' Union (pres. 1920-23), A.A.A.S.; member American Philosophical Society, Sigma Xi, Del. Valley Ornithol. Club (ex-pres.), Phila. Bot. Club, Am. Soc. Mammalogists (pres. 1929-31), Am. Soc. Ichthyologists and Herpetologists; hon. mem. Linnæan Soc. (N.Y.), Zoöl. Soc. Phila., Netherlands Ornithol. Club, Soc. Ornith. et Mam. de France, Hungarian Ornithol. Soc.; hon. mem. Brit. Ornithologists' Union; corr. mem. German Ornithological Society, Bavarian Ornithological Soc.; mem. Internat. Com. on Zoöl. Nomenclature. Club: Franklin Inn. Author: Birds of Eastern Pennsylvania and New Jersey, 1894; American Animals (joint author), 1902; Mammals of New Jersey, 1908; Birds of New Jersey, 1909; Flora of Southern New Jersey, 1912; Report on Birds of Yucatan and Southern Mexico; The Molting of Birds; Birds and Mammals of the McIlhenny Alaskan Expedition; The Phylogenetic Value of Color Characters in Birds; Birds of the Princeton Patagonian Expdn.; Bird Studies at Cape May, N.J.; and a number of other papers in Proc. Acad. Natural Sciences, on birds, mammals, reptiles, etc. Editor of the Auk, 1912-36. Home: 452 Church Lane, Philadelphia, Pa.

STONEBACK, Robert Samuel, banker; b. Steinsburg, Pa., Mar. 11, 1881; student Emmons High Sch. and Scranton Correspondence Sch.; m. Lillie H. Wickert, Nov. 11, 1899; 1 son, H. Walter. Became teacher, 1898; now pres. Emmons Nat. Bank, Emmons Bldg. & Loan Assn.; treas. Henry Zollinger, Inc. Vice-pres. Lehigh Co. Bankers Assn. Borough sec., Emmons, Pa., 26 yrs.; pres. Emmons Sch. Dist., 24 yrs.; pres. Lehigh Co. Prison Bd.; mem. exec. com.

Boy Scouts of America; pres. Lehigh Co. Sch. Directors Assn., 16 yrs.; v.p. Emmons Chamber of Commerce. Democrat (state committeeman). Pres. St. John's Reformed Ch. Mason, Odd Fellow, K.P. Clubs: Mercantile, Rotary, Union Fish and Game (Emmons). Home: Emmons, Pa.

STONECIPHER, Alvin Harrison Morton, prof. Latin; b. Corydon, Ind., Oct. 6, 1888; s. Levi Thomas and Margaret Ann (Patterson) S.; A.B., Vanderbilt U., 1913, A.M., 1914, Ph.D., same, 1917; grad. study George Peabody Coll. for Teachers, 1916-17; m. Blanche Marie Ritchie, June 21, 1920; children—Verna Pauline, Virginia Irene, Evelyn Marie. Prof. classical langs., Ind. Central Coll., 1917-32; prof. Latin, Lebanon Valley Coll. since 1932, dean of coll. since 1936; ordained to ministry Ch. of United Brethren in Christ, 1922. Mem. Am. Philol. Assn., Eastern Assn. Coll. Deans and Advisers of Men, Pa. State Edn. Assn., Phi Beta Kappa. Democrat. Mem. United Brethren in Christ. Club: Torch (Harrisburg). Home: 471 E. Main St., Annville, Pa.

STONECIPHER, Frank Whitmore, lawyer; b. Mercer, Pa., Aug. 18, 1878; s. John Franklin and Jennie (Micke) S.; A.B., Lafayette Coll., 1899; grad. U. of Pa. Law Sch., 1902; m. Lela H. Felver, Oct. 8, 1902. Admitted to Pa. bar, 1902 and since engaged in gen. practice of law at Pittsburgh; vice-pres. and dir. Electric Products Corpn. Mem. Am., Pa. State, and Allegheny Co. bar assns., Delta Kappa Epsilon. Republican. Presbyn. Club: Duquesne. Home: Royal York Apts. Office: 2021 Farmers Bank Bldg., Pittsburgh, Pa.

STONEHOUSE, Ned Bernard, theol. seminary prof.; b. Grand Rapids, Mich., Mar. 19, 1902; s. Bernard and Margaret (DeBoer) S.; A.B., Calvin Coll., Grand Rapids, Mich., 1924; Th.B., Princeton Theol. Sem., 1927, Th.M., 1927; Th.D., Free Reformed Univ., Amsterdam, 1929; grad. study, U. of Tübingen, Germany, 1928-29; m. Winigrace Bylsma, Sept. 1, 1927; children—Marilyn Helen, Elsie Mae, Bernard John. Instr. in N.T., Westminster Theol. Sem., Phila., Pa., 1929, asst. prof., 1930-37, prof. since 1937; editor The Presbyterian Guardian, 1936-37, mem. editorial council, same, since 1937; ordained to ministry Presbyn. Ch. in U.S.A., 1932, left that body, 1936 to join in formation of Presbyn. Ch. of America and chmn. Com. on Constitution since 1936. Trustee The Presbyterian Guardian Pub. Corpn. Mem. Soc. of Bib. Lit. and Exegesis. At Princeton Theol. Sem. received award Alumni Fellow and Archibald Robertson Scholar in N.T., 1927, for study abroad. Ind. Republican. Mem. Orthodox Presbyn. Ch. Author: The Apocalypse in the Ancient Church, 1929. Contbr. to religious mags. Home: 333 Cherry Lane, Glenside, Pa.

STONER, Edward Guy, v.p. Beckwith Machinery Co.; b. Knoxdale, Pa., Oct. 31, 1889; s. David and Agnes (Harriger) S.; ed. grammar and high schs.; m. Avis Dodd, June 17, 1913; 1 dau., Mary Louise. Began as telegraph operator B.&S. R.R., 1908; supt. Atlantic Refining Co., Pittsburgh, 1916-17; salesman Beckwith Machinery Co., 1917-18, v.p. since 1918, mgr. branch offices at Cleveland, Philadelphia, Harrisburg, Wilkes-Barre and Bradford, Pa., 1919-37, gen. sales mgr. since 1937, now also dir. Republican. Mason (Scottish Rite, 32°). Club: Oakmont (Pa.) Country. Home: 607 Kirtland St. Office: 6550 Hamilton Av., Pittsburgh, Pa.

STONER, Frank R., Jr., pres. Stoner-Mudge, Inc.; b. Sewickley, Pa., Aug. 2, 1903; s. Frank R. and Helen (McCleery) S.; student Morristown (N.J.) Sch., 1919-21, Princeton U., 1921-24; m. Jane V. Nicholson, Sept. 17, 1927; children—Frank R., III, John Thorp. With McClintic Marshall Constrn. Co., Leetsdale, Pa., 1924-27; with Gen. Cement Products Corpn., Pittsburgh, 1927-32; pres. Stoner-Mudge, Inc., lacquer and chem. mfrs., Pittsburgh, Pa., since 1932. Republican. Presbyterian. Clubs: Allegheny Country, Edgeworth, Sewickley Hunt (Sewickley, Pa.); Chemists (New York); Rolling Rock Hunt, Harvard-Yale-Princeton. Home: Edgeworth, Pa. Office: Grant Bldg., Pittsburgh, Pa.

STONER, James M., Jr., retired banker; b. Pittsburgh, Pa., Mar. 20, 1869; s. James Madison and Aurelia (Palmer) S.; ed. pub. schs. and Sewickley Acad. Employed with Sharon Steel Co. as accountant, 1885-1901, purchasing agt., 1901-03; pres. Franklin Savings & Trust Co., Pittsburgh, 1903-28, retired, 1928; dir. Ohio Forge and Machine Corpn. (Cleveland), Pittsburgh Bridge and Iron Corpn. Clubs: Edgeworth, Montour Heights Country, Sharon. Home: Ohio River Boul., Sewickley, Pa.

STONESIFER, Joseph Ross, clergyman; b. Palmyra, Pa., July 27, 1875; s. Simon Cleophas and Emily George Ann (Gilbert) S.; A.B., Dickinson Coll., 1898, A.M., 1925; ed. Princeton Theol. Sem., 1908-10; m. Blanche N. Sheibley, Oct. 31, 1901; children—Dorothy McNeal, Gilbert Ross. Ordained to ministry, 1898; pastor, Chambersburg, Pa., 1898-1901, Steelton, Pa., 1901-03, Mechanicsburg, Pa., 1903-08, First Presbyn. Ch., Wilmington, Del., 1910-19; minister First Presbyn. Ch., Stroudsburg, Pa., since 1919. Served as vol. chaplain under Nat. Service Commn. Presbyn. Ch. U.S.A. during World War. Mem. Commn. on Realignment of Presbyteries, Phila. area. Mem. Phi Delta Theta. 6th St., Stroudsburg, Pa.

STONESIFER, Paul Tobias, clergyman; b. Winchester, Va., Feb. 6, 1896; s. James B. and Martha K. (Tobias) S.; grad. Massanutten Acad., Woodstock, Va., 1913; A.B., Franklin and Marshall Coll., Lancaster, Pa., 1917; B.D., Theol. Sem. of Reformed Ch., Lancaster, Pa., 1920; m. Esther M. Wittlinger, Sept. 7, 1921; 1 son, Richard James. Ordained to ministry of Reformed Ch., 1920; pastor, First Reformed Ch., Mount Pleasant, Pa., 1920-37, Zion Reformed Ch., Chambersburg, Pa., since 1937. Served as private, Inf., U.S. Army, 1917-18. Mem. bd. dirs., Hood Coll., Frederick, Md., 1929-37; mem. bd. dirs. Theol. Sem. of Reformed Ch., Lancaster, Pa., 1935-37. Mem. Sigma Pi, Phi Beta Kappa. Mason. Address: 259 S. Main St., Chambersburg, Pa.

STORER, Norman Wilson, electrical engr.; b. Orangeville, O., Jan. 11, 1868; s. Simon Brewster and Lemira (Jones) S.; M.E. (in elec. engring.), Ohio State U., 1891; m. Elizabeth W. Perry, June 14, 1899 (died Jan. 14, 1908); children—Norman Wyman, Elizabeth Perry, Morris Brewster, Florence Treadwell; m. 2d, Ruth Esther Beyer, Dec. 7, 1911. With Westinghouse Electric & Mfg. Co., 1891-1936. For yrs. designer of direct current generators and motors; then for 10 yrs. in charge of design of all electric ry. apparatus; then cons. ry. engr., interested in all kinds of electrical transportation problems and in development of electric locomotives, oil and gasoline electric locomotives and electrification of steam rys.; retired from practice as cons. engr., Oct. 1936. Fellow Am. Inst. Elec. Engrs.; mem. Unitarian Layman's League. Home: 6818 Reynolds St., Pittsburgh, Pa.; and Winter Park, Fla.

STOREY, Douglass Doty, lawyer; b. Johnstown, Pa., Oct. 31, 1888; s. Henry Wilson and Abbie Doty (Douglass) S.; ed. Johnstown pub. schs.; A.B., Washington & Jefferson Coll., 1911; LL.B., cum laude, Univ. of Pennsylvania Law School, 1914; m. Florence Holahan, October 23, 1919; children—Helen, Julia Ann. Gowen Memorial fellow, Univ. of Pennsylvania Law School, 1914-15; admitted to Supreme Court of Pennsylvania bar, 1915; prof. law, Dickinson School of Law, 1919-22; partner law firm Hause, Evans, Storey & Lick since 1922; dir. Farmers Trust Co. (Carlisle, Pa.), Pike Co. Light & Power Co. (Milford, Pa.). Served with A.E.F., Nov. 1917-June 1919, World War. Mem. bd. trustees Dickinson Sch. of Law. Mem. Phi Kappa Psi, Phi Delta Phi. Republican. Methodist. Clubs: Art (Philadelphia); Carlisle (Pa.) Country. Author: United States Supreme Court and Rate Regulation, 1915. Co-author (with William A. Schnader), Pennsylvania Workmen's Compensation Law, 1916. Home: Oakland, Carlisle, Pa. Office: Telegraph Bldg., Harrisburg, Pa.

STOREY, Walter Rendell, critic of decorative art; b. Phila., Pa., June 22, 1881; s. Edwin Adams and Elizabeth (Rendell) S.; student Pa. Mus. Sch. Industrial Arts, Phila., 1900-02, Pa. Acad. Fine Arts, Phila., 1903-08, Academie Julian, Paris, France, under Jean Paul Laurens, 1908-09; m. Muriel Alice Flewitt, Feb. 27, 1914 (died 1918); m. 2d, Helen Edith Anderson, Jan. 1, 1925; children—Hildred Anderson, Warren Charles. Exec. sec. Nat. Bd. of Review of Motion Pictures, N.Y. City, evaluating artistic content of motion pictures, 1909-12; with govt. and social orgns., designing ednl. social exhibits, and writing on art, 1913-26; critic of decorative art, N.Y. Times, since 1926; lecturer on decorative art, N.Y. Univ. and Furniture World Ednl. Inst. Awarded silver medal for artistry in ednl. exhibit World's Fair, San Francisco, 1915. Author: Beauty in Home Furnishings, 1928; Period Influences in Interior Decoration, 1937; Chippendale: A Sketch of His Life and Works. Lecturer. Contbr. articles to nat. mags. Home: 155 Grayson Pl., Teaneck, N.J.

STORK, Charles Wharton, critic, author; b. Phila., Pa., Feb. 12, 1881; s. Theophilus Baker and Hannah (Wharton) S.; A.B., Haverford Coll., 1902; A.M., Harvard, 1903; Ph.D., U. of Pa., 1905; research work in English univs., 1905; studied U. of Munich, 1907-08; m. Elisabeth, d. Franz von Pausinger (artist), Aug. 5, 1908; children—Rosalie, Francis Wharton, George Frederick, Carl Alexander. Assistant in English, 1903-05, instructor, 1906-14, assistant professor, 1914-16, University of Pennsylvania; resigned to engage in original literary work; resumed teaching of English, Harcum Junior College, Bryn Mawr, Pa., 1935. Mem. Modern Language Association of America, Poetry Soc. America (former pres.), Friends of Roerich Museum, Phi Beta Kappa (Haverford). Clubs: Franklin Inn (Philadelphia, Pa.); Harvard (New York). Author: (verse) Day Dreams of Greece, 1908; The Queen of Orplede, 1910; Sea and Bay, 1916; Sunset Harbor, 1933. Editor: Plays of William Rowley, 1910; Contemporary Verse Anthology, 1920; In the Sky Garden, Poems by Stephen Moylan Bird, 1922; Second Contemporary Verse Anthology, 1923. Translator: (from the Swedish) Selected Poems of Gustaf Fröding, 1916; Sweden's Laureate (poems of Verner von Heidenstam), 1919; (from the German) Hofmannthal's Lyrics, 1917; Anthology of Swedish Lyrics, 1917, 30; (from the Swedish) The Charles Men of Verner von Heidenstam, 1920; Modern Swedish Masterpieces (short stories), 1923; The Motherless, of Bengt Berg, 1924; The Swedes and Their Chieftains, of Verner von Heidenstam, 1925; Anthology of Swedish Stories, 1928; The Dragon and the Foreign Devils of J. G. Andersson (a book on modern China, 1928; Martin Birck's Youth of Hjalmar Söderberg, 1930; Short Stories of Hjalmar Söderberg, 1935; Tales of Ensign Stål (by J. L. Runeberg), 1938; I Sit Alone, from Norwegian of Waldemar Ager, 1931, Arcadia Borealis (poems from the Swedish of E. A. Karlfeldt), 1938. Contbr. article on Swedish literature in Collier's Encyclopedia. Contbr. of play and numerous lyrics in transl. to The German Classics, 1914; also verse, transls., articles to Century, Harper's, Nation, New Republic, Yale Review, etc. Visited Sweden, 1920, 23, writing and lecturing on Am. poetry. Decorated Order of Gustaf Vasa, 1st class, 1922. Winner contest for original play offered by Plays and Players of Phila., 1925. Edited mag., Contemporary Verse, 1917-26. Home: 8525 Seminole Av., Chestnut Hill, Phila., Pa.

STORRS, Cleveland Hitchcock, broker; b. Orange, N.J., May 10, 1900; s. Judge Charles Bigelow and Gertrude (Cleveland) S.; ed. local schs. of N.J.; grad. with war degree, Hill Sch., 1918; A.B., Yale Coll., 1923; m. Mildred McKinley, Oct. 13, 1923; 1 dau., Katharine. Held various positions, becoming chief clerk, Casper Refinery, White Eagle Oil & Refining Co., Casper, Wyo., 1923-24; head of land, lease, pipeline and production depts. at Wichita Falls, Tex., of White Eagle Oil & Refining Co. in Southern Okla., Ark., La., Texas and N.M.; partner with J. Roy McCaldin, independent operators, 1925-26; began as salesman, 1926, Campbell, Peterson & Co., Inc., resigning as v.p. and dir. of sales, 1931; customers' man Smith, Graham & Rockwell and successors, Graham & Co., 1932-34, partner in charge investment advisory dept., 1934-37; mgr. investment advisory dept., Redmond & Co. and successors, Fuller, Rodney & Redmond, since 1938; dir. and mem. exec. com. Am. Type Founders, Inc.; dir. Am. Type Founders Sales Corpn. Served as 2d lt. F.A. Officers' Reserve Corps, U.S. Army, 1918-19. Mem. Delta Kappa Epsilon. Republican. Presbyn. Club: Bankers (New York). Home: 451 Lincoln Av., Orange, N.J. Office: 44 Wall St., New York, N.Y.

STORY, Walter Scott, author; b. Springfield, Mass., June 23, 1879; s. Benjamin Franklin and Jennie Rebecca (Turner) S.; ed. pub. schs.; m. Margaret Helena Healy, Feb. 27, 1908. Began as office boy, Mass. Mut. Life Ins. Co., 1895, later sec. to pres. of Co.; mgr. lit. dept. Mut. Life Ins. Co. of New York since Feb. 1923. Mem. Authors' League America, S.A.R. Republican. Mason. Author: Skinny Harrison, Adventurer, 1922; The Young Crusader; How Richard of Devon Served Richard the Lion-Hearted, 1923; The Uncharted Island, 1926; Boy Heroes of the Sea, 1928; The Missing Million; also about 140 novelettes and short stories. Home: 14 Burnet St., Maplewood, N.J. Office: 34 Nassau St., New York, N.Y.*

STOTZ, Edward, Jr., architectural engr.; b. Pittsburgh, Pa., Apr. 23, 1896; s. Edward and Arminda B. (Irwin) S.; C.E., Lehigh U., 1919; m. Doris Davidson, Oct. 5, 1929; children—Karen, Alice. Engaged in gen. practice as architectural engr., 1919-36; partner Charles M. & Edward Stotz, Jr., since 1936. Mem. Engineers' Soc. of Western Pa. Republican. United Presbyterian. Home: 14 Hughes Av. Office: 801 Bessemer Bldg., Pittsburgh, Pa.

STOUDT, John Baer, historian-librarian; b. Topton, Pa., Oct. 17, 1878; s. John Reppert and Amanda Carl (Baer) S.; student Keystone State Normal Sch., Pa., 1898-1901; A.B., Franklin and Marshall Coll., Lancaster, Pa., 1905; student Eastern Theol. Sem., 1905-08, U. of Chicago, 1906; D.D., U. of Montpellier, France, 1924; m. Elisabeth Agnes DeLong, Oct. 15, 1908; 1 son, John Joseph. Teacher, 1896-1902; ordained ministry Reformed Ch., 1908; pastor, Emmaus, Pa., and Northampton, Pa., 1908-22; mem. administrative com. Federal Council of Chs. of Christ in America, 1922-25; asso. to pros. Cedar Coll., Allentown, Pa., 1925-26; dir. public and private hist. activities since 1926. Hon. chaplain Belgian Army. Chmn. hist. com. Reformed Ch. in U.S.; mem. Hist. Commn. of Pa., 1927-31; dir. Allentown (Pa.) Masonic Library. Organized Huguenot Soc. of Pa., 1917 (chmn. exec. com.), Pa. German Folklore Soc., 1935 (historian, exec. com.); mem. Nat. Fed. of Huguenot Socs. of America (chmn. exec. com.), John Calvin Soc. of Geneva, Waldensian Soc. of Italy, French Protestant Hist. Soc., Huguenot Soc. of London, Huguenot Soc. of Berlin. Awarded Order of the Crown (Belgium), 1924; Legion of Honor (France), 1924. Republican. Mason. Author: Folklore of Pennsylvania Germans, 1916; Sheandoah Pottery (with A. H. Rice), 1929; Liberty Bells of Pennsylania, 1930; Nicolas Martiau (colonial ancestor of George Washington), 1932. Editor numerous hist. publs. Home: 1054 Tilghman St., Allentown, Pa.

STOUFFER, Christian S., works engr.; b. Sharpsburg, Md., Feb. 27, 1881; s. Samuel S. and Annie F. (Stoner) S.; B.S. in E.E., Lehigh U., 1906; m. Ida M. Varner, June 8, 1909; children—Samuel William, Mary Isabelle, Anne Elizabeth. Engring. apprentice Westinghouse Electric & Mfg. Co., 1906-09; successively draftsman, estimator and mech. engr. Nat. Tube Co., Kewanee (Ill.) works, 1909-17; mech. engr. and works engr. Walworth Co., Kewanee Works, 1917-26; works engr. Stanley G. Flagg & Co. since 1926; dir. Pottstown Savings & Loan Assn. Pres. bd. dirs Sch. Dist. of Borough of Pottstown. Chmn. finance com. and dir. Pottstown Y.M.C.A.; dir. Pottstown Pub. Library. Mem. Am. Soc. Mech. Engrs. Republican. Presbyterian. Club: Rotary (pres. 1930-31). Home: 1000 N. Charlotte St., Pottstown, Pa. Office: Stanley G. Flagg & Co., Stowe, Pa.

STOUFFER, Samuel Maloy, supt. of schools; b. Newville, Pa., July 5, 1892; s. Samuel Maloy and Margaretta Jane (Black) S.; grad. Cumberland Valley State Normal Sch., 1912; B.S., Susquehanna Univ., Selinsgrove, Pa., 1917; A.M., New York Univ., 1927; Pd.D., Susquehanna Univ., 1936; m. Ruth B. Stoner, July 13, 1918; 1 dau., Dorothy Jane. Teacher rural sch., 1908-10; prin. high sch., Boiling Springs, Pa., 1912-13; prin. Major Bent Bldg., Steelton, Pa., 1913-14; supervising prin. Highspire, Pa., 1914-16, Sandy Twp., DuBois, Pa., 1921-22; supt. of schs., Hanover, Pa., 1922-28, Pottstown, Pa., 1928-29, Wilmington, Del., since 1929. Commd. 2d lt. Aviation Sect., Signal Corps, World War. Mem. bd. dirs. Del. Anti-Tuberculosis Soc., Inc., since 1934; mem. advisory com. State Labor Commn.; mem. bd. dirs. Wilmington Inst. Free Library; mem. civic service com. Boy Scouts of America; mem. Coordinating com. Central Reference Com. of Delaware Citizens Assn.; mem. Del. Commn. Internat. Cooperation; mem. Delaware Safety Council, Horace Mann League, Del. Soc. for the Preservation of Antiquities, Bond and Key Club (Susquehanna U.); mem. com. for the Celebration of the President's Birthday Party; mem. advisory bd. Nat. Inst. of Parent Training; mem. Susquehanna U. Alumni Assn. Life mem. N.E.A. (mem. resolutions com. 1930-32 and various other times; v.p. 1933-34); mem. Am. Assn. of School Adminstrs. (mem. com. on lay relations, 1935-40; mem. legislative com., 1938-39); mem. Nat. Com. for Mental Hygiene, Pennsylvania State Education Assn., Del. State Edn. Assn. (pres. 1931-32), Del. Americanization Com., Del. State Soc. for Mental Hygiene, Shippensburg State Teachers Coll. Alumni Assn. (pres. 1931-32), Phi Delta Kappa; council for chief execs. of Social Agencies in Del. Lutheran. Clubs: Social Service, Torch, Kiwanis, Wilmington Country, Ninety-six. Home: Brandywine Hills, Wilmington. Office: Board of Public Education, Wilmington, Del.

STOUGHTON, Bradley, metallurgical engr.; b. New York, Dec. 6, 1873; s. Col. Charles Bradley (LL.D.) and Ada Ripley (Hooper) S.; Ph.B., Sheffield Scientific Sch., 1893; B.S., Mass. Inst. Tech., 1896; m. Grace A. Van Everen, Jan. 4, 1899 (died Jan. 15, 1905); 1 son, Philip V.; m. 2d, L. Merwin, d. E. P. and Anna P. (Sands) Roe, Nov. 1, 1911; children—Sandroe, Rosamond, Leila Roosevelt. Teacher, Mass. Inst. Tech., 1896; asst. to Prof. H. M. Howe, Columbia U., 1897; metallurgist Ill. Steel Co., S. Chicago, Ill., 1898-99; chief of cost statis. div. Am. Steel & Wire Co., Cleveland, 1900; mgr. Bessemer steel dept., Benjamin Atha & Co., Newark, N.J., 1901; in business as consulting engr., 1902-23. Instr., adj. prof. and acting head dept. of metallurgy, Sch. of Mines, Columbia U., 1902-08; prof. metallurgy, Lehigh University, 1923—, also dean of College of Engineering. Member Gen. Engring. Com., Nat. Council of Defense, 1918-19; head of metall. div., later v.-chmn. engring. div., Nat. Research Council; mem. welding com., Emergency Fleet Corpn., 1918-20. Mem. Am. Inst. Mining and Metall. Engrs. (sec. 1913-21; chmn. iron and steel com., 1922-23), Am. Electrochem. Soc. (chmn. electrothermic div. 1922; pres. 1931), Yale Engring. Assn. (pres. 1922-24), Am. Iron and Steel Inst., Iron and Steel Inst. (Eng.), American Society for Metals (treas. since 1937), Am. Soc. for Testing Materials, Am. Foundrymen's Assn., Engrs. Club of the Lehigh Valley (pres. 1928-29), etc. Inventor converter for making steel castings, and a process for oil melting in cupolas. Clubs: Engineers'; Saucon Valley Country. Author: The Metallurgy of Iron and Steel, 1908; Engineering Metallurgy (with Allison Butts), 1926. Made the field study and wrote technical report used by President Harding in his successful campaign to secure the 8-hour day in the U.S. steel industry, 1922. Awarded Grasselli medal by Soc. of Chem. Industry, 1929. Home: Route 3, Bethlehem, Pa.

STOUT, Charles Frederick Cloua, manufacturer; b. Phila., Pa., Apr. 2, 1869; s. Albert Gallatin and Mary (Robinson) S.; father desc. of Jakob Stout, who came to America from Germany, 1749; ed. public schools and Barker's Acad., Germantown, Phila.; m. Mary Ridgeway Deacon, Nov. 16, 1898; children—Frederick Sturgis, Robert Gwynne, Mary Ridgeway (Mrs. Alan Lowther Day). Began career as jr. clerk Thomas T. Lee & Co., dry goods, 1885-86; senior partner of the firm of John R. Evans & Co., mfrs. of leather, Camden, N.J., 1896-1938; now pres. John R. Evans and Co.; pres. Camden Tanning Co.; pres. John R. Evans & Co., Inc., Boston; vice-pres. Lenape Trading Co.; dir. Federal Reserve Bank of Phila. since 1927. Served as mem. Council of Nat. Defense, registered col. in Q.M. Dept., and dir. Hide, Leather and Leather Goods Div., U.S. War Industries Bd., during World War. Trustee U. of Pa.; pres. board, Graduate Hosp., Phila., 14 years, trustee Evans Dental Sch., U. of Pa. Pres. Pa. Horticultural Soc., Phila. Republican. Episcopalian. Clubs: Union League, Rittenhouse, Midday, Gulph Mills Golf, Merion Cricket. Home: 214 Glenn Rd., Ardmore, Pa. Office: 2d and Erie Sts., Camden, N.J.

STOUT, Henrietta Maria, horticulturist; b. New York, N.Y., Oct. 9, 1875; d. Francis and Lucy (Langdon) Schroeder; student Miss Jourdan's Sch., 1886-89, Brearley Sch., 1890-96; m. Charles H. Stout, May 27, 1899; children—Merrell Langdon, Virginia (adopted). Engaged in horticulture since 1900. Founder Dahlia Soc. of N.J.; v.p. Am. Dahlia Soc., Dahlia Soc. of Calif., Am. Rock Garden Soc., Am. Rose Soc., Am. Iris Soc., N.Y. Bot. Garden, Brooklyn Bot. Garden, N.Y. Hort. Soc., Am. Hort. Soc.; fellow Royal Hort. Soc. and Alpine Garden Soc. (both of England). Republican. Episcopalian. Clubs: Cosmopolitan, York (New York); Short Hills Club, Short Hills Garden, Garden of N.J., Garden of America. Author: Amateur's Book of the Dahlia; also various mag. articles on horticulture. Home: Charlecote, Short Hills, N.J.

STOUT, Oliver, physician; b. Bucks Co., Pa., Nov. 11, 1869; s. Lewis Kratz and Lovenia Mitman (Althouse) S.; grad. Phila. Coll. of Pharmacy, 1891; M.D., U. of Pa. Med. Sch., 1893; m. Gail Louise Simpkins, June 11, 1902; children—Louise Martindale (Mrs. Frank Carl Podboy), Robert Simpkins (dec.). Engaged as druggist to 1894 and since engaged in gen. practice of medicine at Phila. since 1894. Mem. Phila. County Med. Soc. Republican. Mason, Jr. O.U.A.M. Home: 3351 N. 5th St., Philadelphia, Pa.

STOUT, Wesley Winans, editor; b. Junction City, Kan., Jan. 26, 1890; s. Francis Wellington and Dora (Dougherty) S.; m. Mary Lee Starr, Sept. 15, 1923. Reporter and editor various newspapers in Kan., Mo., Tex., Calif., Wash., City of Mexico, New York and Okla., 1907-17 and 1921-22; asso. editor and writer Saturday Evening Post, 1922-37, succeeded George Horace Lorimer as editor, 1937. Enlisted man United States Naval Air Force, World War, 1917-18; at sea for U.S. Shipping Bd., 1919-21. Home: Ambler, Pa. Office: Curtis Publishing Co., Philadelphia, Pa.

STOUTENBURGH, Robert Bartholomew, real estate, insurance; b. Newark, N.J., Mar. 13, 1883; s. Frederick Dodd and Carrie (Bartholomew) S.; grad. Newark (N.J.) Acad., 1901; A.B., Princeton U., 1906; m. Ethel A. King, June 2, 1908; children—Sylvia King (Mrs. Frederick Warren Bliss), Virginia King. In clothing business, 1906-11; real estate and insurance, own business, Newark, N.J., since 1911. Mem. bd. govs. Newark Real Estate Bd.; treas. Mfrs. Bldg. and Loan Assn.; pres. Industrial Bldg. Co. when it erected first modern industrial bldg. (10 stories) in Newark, 1912. Republican. Universalist (pres. Union Universalist Soc.). Clubs: Newark Athletic, Princeton (Newark); Princeton (Montclair, N.J.). Home: 31 Lloyd Rd., Montclair, N.J. Office: 9 Clinton St., Newark, N.J.

STOVER, Ross Harrison, clergyman; b. Mechanicsburg, O., Nov. 30, 1888; s. Peter Columbus and Hattie (Mahan) S.; B.A., Wittenberg Coll., Springfield, O., 1912; B.D., Hamma Div. Sch. (Wittenberg Coll.), 1915; D.D., Gettysburg (Pa.) Coll., 1923; m. Emma Stanford, Dec. 21, 1910; 1 dau., Martha Corrine. Ordained Luth. ministry, 1915; pastor First Ch., Wapakoneta, O., 1915-19, Messiah Ch., Phila., since 1919. Camp singing master for Y.M.C.A., World War. Mem. Alpha Tau Omega. Club: Union League. Author: (booklets), On the Road to Heaven, 1927; Three

Cheers, 1928; Why Am I Living, 1929; The Christian's Rainbow, 1931. Contbr. to mags. Home: 6409 N. Sixth St., Philadelphia, Pa.

STOWE, Walter Herbert, clergyman; b. Waterville, Minn., Jan. 22, 1895; s. Herbert Hugh and Addie Jane (Tower) S.; B.A., U. of Minn., 1915; B.D., Seabury Divinity Sch., 1918; S.T.D., Seabury-Western Theol. Sem., 1938; m. Kathryn Marguerite Browne, Sept. 5, 1923; children—Harriet Harper, David Andrew. Master Shattuck Sch., Faribault, Minn., 1918; King fellow Gen. Theol. Sem., N.Y. City, 1919-21; ordained Episcopal ministry, 1919; rector Trinity Ch., Woodbridge, N.J., 1919-21, St. Luke's Ch., Willmar, Minn., 1921-25, St. Mark's Ch., Denver, 1925-29, Christ Ch., New Brunswick, since 1929. Deputy Gen. Conv. of Episcopal Ch., 1928, 34 and 37; Historiographer Diocese of N.J. (Episcopal) since 1935. Trustee St. Mary's Hall, Burlington, N.J. Mem. Church Hist. Soc. (pres. since 1936), Soc. Colonial Wars. Club: Clergy (New Brunswick). Author: Anglo-Catholicism: What It Is Not and What It Is, 1933; Importance of American Church History, 1936; Life and Letters of Bishop William White, 1937; also articles in various periodicals. Mng. editor Historical Magazine of Episcopal Church since 1934. Home: 184 College Av., New Brunswick, N.J.

STOWELL, Jay Samuel, church official; b. Orwell, N.Y., Mar. 5, 1883; s. Henry John and Sarah C. (Hollis) S.; A.B., Oberlin Coll., 1909; student Oberlin Theol. Sem., 1909-10, Union Theol. Sem., 1910-12, U. of Wis., 1917; A.M., Columbia, 1912; m. Ann Wilder Stewart, June 17, 1913; children—Stewart Jay, Elizabeth Ann, John Wilder. Sch. teacher, 1901-02 and 1904-05; ordained to ministry Congl. Ch., 1912; missionary Congl. Home Missionary Soc. and Am. S.S. Union, 1905-08; prin. Union Sch. of Religion, New York, 1911-12; teacher training sec. N.Y. City S.S. Assn., 1911-12; ednl. sec. Bd. Home Missions Presbyn. Ch., 1912-15; dir. James H. Mead Club, 1916-18; editorial writer Bd. S.S.M.E. Ch., 1918-19; asst. dir. Home Missions Survey Interch. World Movement, 1919-20; dir. publicity Centenary Conservation and Bd. Home Missions and Ch. Extension of M.E. Ch. since 1920; mem. bd. mgrs. Missionary Edn. Movement since 1912; editor Pastor's Jour. since 1929. Mem. Congl. Assn. of N.Y. City, Nat. Religious Publicity Council. Author: The Sunday School at Work (with others), 1913; The Sunday School Teacher and the Program of June (with George H. Trull); Making Missions Real (with others), 1919; Home Mission Trails, 1920; Story Worship Program for the Church School Year, 1920; Mexicans and Spanish-Speaking Americans in the United States, 1921; Near Side of the Mexican Question, 1921; Methodist Adventures in Negro Education, 1922; J. W. Thinks Black, 1922; The Child and America's Future, 1923; Methodism's New Frontier, 1924; More Story Worship Programs, 1924; Makers of a New World, 1926; Between the Americas, 1930; The Utopia of Unity, 1930; also writer of articles in religious and secular publs. Home: Rockledge Av., Fox Chase, Phila., Pa. Office: 1701 Arch St., Philadelphia, Pa.

STRADER, George Stewart, business exec.; b. Giles Co., Va., Mar. 2, 1870; s. Josiah and Barbara Caroline (Johnston) S.; ed. pub. and pvt. schs., Giles County, Va.; m. Dillie Jeter, Oct. 10, 1901; children—George Stewart, Dr. Benjamin Jeter, Dr. Wi__m Robinson. Began as clk. in store, Bramwell, W.Va., 1888; propr. gen. store, Bluefield, W.Va., 1891-94; rental and real estate, Bluefield, 5 yrs.; in coal mining and selling, Bluefield, 1900-35, also wholesale business and banking; retired 1939; dir. First Nat. Bank of Bluefield, W.Va. Del. Uniting Methodist Conv., Kansas City, Mo., 1939. Independent Democrat. Methodist. Home: 2103 Bland Rd. Office: Law and Commerce Bldg., Bluefield, W.Va.

STRADLEY, Leighton Paxton, lawyer; b. Cumberland, Md., Jan. 2, 1880; s. Lon P. and Hattie (Kettlewell) S.; B.S. in economics, Wharton Sch. (U. of Pa.), 1905, LL.B., U. of Pa., 1906; m. Kathryn Jackson Wilson, June 8, 1907; children—Leighton P., Bentham Walker,

Wilson. Admitted to Phila. bar, 1908; since in gen. practice of law; sr. partner Stradley, Ronon & Stevens since 1926; dir. Kensington Shipyard & Drydock Corpn.; asst. prof. of finance and economy, Wharton Sch., since 1917. Pres. Pa. Econ. Council, Inc.; trustee Phi Sigma Kappa. Republican. Episcopalian. Mason. Clubs: Union League, Double Six (pres.), 1880 (pres.), Philadelphia Country. Author: Finance and Investments. Home: 3831 Oak Road. Office: 1907 Packard Bldg., Philadelphia, Pa.

STRADLEY, Wilmer, pres. Diamond Ice & Coal Co.; b. Wilmington, Del., Mar. 24, 1889; s. Miller and Annie Lee (Denny) S.; ed. pub. schs.; m. Mary Morris Purcell, Oct. 4, 1910. Pres. and dir. Diamond Ice & Coal Co. since 1918; officer or dir. many companies. Home: 2200 Grant Av. Office: 827 Market St., Wilmington, Del.

STRAESSLEY, Edward Charles, physician and surgeon; b. Kersey, Pa., Aug. 8, 1889; s. Charles Herman and Margaret (Pontzer) S.; student U. of Pittsburgh, 1908-10; M.D., U. of Md., Baltimore, Md., 1912; m. Margarite Brennan, Oct. 12, 1915; children—Genevieve Brennan, Mary Margaret. Physician and surgeon, Shawmut Mining Co., Shawmut Brick Co., Shawmut Tile Co., Shawmut, Pa., 1912-18; pvt. practice as physician and surgeon at Beaver Falls, Pa., since 1919. Fellow A.M.A.; mem. Pa. Med. Soc., Sigma Phi Epsilon. Catholic. K.C. Elk. Home: 1009 6th Av. Office: 1011 6th Av., Beaver Falls, Pa.

STRAGNELL, Gregory, M.D., editor; b. Boulder, Colo., Dec. 26, 1888; s. Canon and Marie (La Fevre) S.; student U. of Denver, 1906-07, Columbia U., 1907-09; M.D., Coll. Phys. and Surg. (Columbia), 1913; m. Sylvia Canfield Jelliffe, July 1920; children—Barbara, Robert. Mil. surgeon with French Army, 1914-17; surgeon in chief mil. hosps. No. 2 and No. 81, Paris, 1916-17; editor Medical Record, N.Y. City, since 1917; associate editor Journal of Nervous and Mental Diseases; dir. med. research, Schering Corpn. Mem. Washington Psychoanalytic Assn., Am. Med. Editors Assn., Internat. Congress Med. Hygiene, Am. Assn. for Study of Epilepsy, Am. Psychopathol. Assn. Home: Millburn, N.J. Office: 86 Orange St., Bloomfield, N.J.*

STRAHORN, John S., Jr.; prof. law, U. of Md. Address: U. of Maryland, Baltimore, Md.

STRANAHAN, James A., lawyer; b. Mercer, Pa., June 11, 1881; s. Robert and Elizabeth J. (Wallace) S.; A.B., Westminster Coll., New Wilmington, Pa., 1905; student U. of Pa. Law Sch., 1907-08; m. Elizabeth Quay, Sept. 24, 1914; children—Sara Elizabeth, James A., John Q. Admitted to Pa. bar, 1908, and since engaged in gen. practice of law at Mercer. Trustee George W. Wright Student Aid Fund, Mercer, Pa. Mem. Mercer County and Pa. State bar assns. Republican. Presbyn. Clubs: Rotary (Mercer); Field (New Castle). Home: 314 W. Market St., Mercer, Pa.

STRANGE, Miriam; registrar St. John's Coll. Address: 14 McDowell Hall, Annapolis, Md.

STRANGE, Robert, lawyer; b. New York, N.Y., Sept. 21, 1888; s. Joseph Huske and Kate (Egbertson) S.; grad. Columbia Sch., South Orange, N.J., 1905; A.B., Princeton, 1909; LL.B., N.Y. Law Sch., 1911; m. Edna Holcomb Bowne, Mar. 7, 1916; children—Betty-Bowne, Nancy. Admitted to bars of N.Y., 1911, N.J., 1913; master in chancery of N.J., 1916; dir. and exec. East Coast Transportation, Inc., Norton Cross Co., Inc., and other shipping firms; organizer and atty. U.S. Ship Owners Assn.; pres. and dir. Administered Fund, Inc. (investment trust), since 1931, Administered Fund Second, Inc., 1934-37; mem. law firm Strange, Myers, Hinds & Wight since 1918. Trustee Community House, South Orange. Mem. Terrace Club (Princeton). Decorated Ritterkreuz I Klasse Zaehinger Loewen. Republican. Episcopalian. Club: Down Town Assn., Down Town Athletic (N.Y. City); Orange Lawn Tennis (South Orange, N.J.); Bay Head Yacht (Bay Head, N.J.). Home: 171 Grove Rd., South Orange, N.J. Office: 165 Broadway, New York, N.Y.

STRANGE, William W.; mem. staff Huntington Memorial Hosp.; mem. attending staff St. Mary's Hosp. Address: 1139 Fourth Av., Huntington, W.Va.

STRASSBURGER, Eugene Bonn, lawyer; b. Pittsburgh, Pa., Sept. 23, 1886; s. Samuel and Julia (Morganstern) S.; A.B., Harvard Coll., 1908; LL.B., Harvard Law Sch., 1910; LL.D. (hon.), Duquesne U., 1930; m. Constance Block, May 10, 1915; children—Eugene S., Joan C., Martha L. Admitted to Pa. bar, 1910; instr. bills and notes and suretyship, Duquesne U. Law Sch., since 1920; dir. Grant Bldg., Inc., Pittsburgh Outdoor Advertising Co., Ludwig Hommel & Co. Trustee Maurice and Laura Falk Foundation, Family Welfare Assn., Union of Am. Hebrew Congregations; v.p. Rodef Shalom Congregation. Republican. Clubs: Harvard-Yale-Princeton, Concordia, Westmoreland Country (trustee), Hundred (Pittsburgh). Home: 6515 Beacon St. Office: Grant Bldg., Pittsburgh, Pa.

STRASSBURGER, Ralph Beaver, publisher, diplomat; b. Norristown, Pa., Mar. 26, 1883; s. Jacob Andrew and Mary Jane (Beaver) S.; grad. U.S. Naval Acad., 1905; LL.D., Ursinus Coll., Collegeville, Pa., 1930; m. May Bourne, 1911; 1 son, Johann Andreas Peter. Resigned from Navy, 1909; apptd. by President Taft counsel general and secretary of Legation to Roumania, Bulgaria and Servia, 1913, later 2d sec. Embassy, Tokio; jr. and sr. lt. U.S.N., World War; owner Norristown Times Herald; owner Normandy Farm, breeder of thoroughbred and hunting horses and Ayrshire cattle; owns racing stables in America, France and England. Decorated Chevalier de la Legion d'Honneur. Active supporter Rep. party in state and nat. affairs; del. at large from Pa. to Rep. Nat. Conv., 1924. Mem. Huguenot Soc. of Pa. (pres.), Colonial Soc. of Pa. (councillor), S.R., Soc. Foreign Wars, Hist. Soc. Pa., Gen. Soc. Pennsylvania, Pa. German Soc. (pres.), American Society M.E. Decorated Knight of Legion of Honor (France). Clubs: Bryn Mawr Polo, Racquet Club, Huntingdon Valley Hunt, University, Recess, Army and Navy, Press, National Republican, Racquet and Tennis, New York Yacht (New York); Metropolitan, Army and Navy, Racquet (Washington, D.C.); Travelers (Paris); Cercle de Deauville; life mem. St. Cloud (Chantilly, France); and many others in U.S. and Europe. Author: The Strassburger Family and Allied Families of Pennsylvania, 1922; The Pennsylvania German Pioneers (3 vols.), 1934; etc. Home: Normandy Farm, Gwynedd Valley, Pa.; 3, Av. de Tourville, Paris, France; (summer) La Ferme du Coteau, Deauville, France. Office: 26 Av. des Champs-Elysées, Paris, France; Norristown Times Herald, Norristown, Pa.

STRASSBURGER, William Joseph, corpn. official; b. Pittsburgh, Pa., July 6, 1879; s. Samuel and Julia (Morganstern) S.; ed. Fifth Ward Pub. Sch., Allegheny High Sch., U. of Pittsburgh (all of Pittsburgh) and Columbia U. (N.Y. City); unmarried. Successively sec., treas. and sales mgr. Allegheny Plate Glass Co., Pittsburgh; sec. and treas. Glassmere (Pa.) Land Company; pres. Pittsburgh Model Engine Co.; Iron Trade Products Co., Pittsburgh; Big Four Fluorspar & Ore Co., Marion, Ky.; Millville Lime & Stone Co., Pittsburgh; now pres. Strasswill Corpn., Pittsburgh, Grant Bldg., Inc., Pittsburgh. Trustee Pittsburgh Hosp.; dir. Art Soc. of Pittsburgh. Mem. Am. Iron and Steel Inst., U. of Pittsburgh Alumni Assn., Columbia U. Alumni Sch. Architecture. Republican. Clubs: Concordia, Rotary, Westmoreland Country, Hundred (Pittsburgh); Columbia University (N.Y. City). Home: 5734 Aylesboro Av. Office: 420 Grant Bldg., Pittsburgh, Pa.

STRATMAN, Herman, public accountant, business adminstr.; b. Pittsburgh, Pa., Apr. 12, 1886; s. John H. and Anna M. (Rischner) S.; student Duquesne and Northwestern univs.; m. Mary Isabella McCallister, Apr. 20, 1923. Clk. bookkeeper, to 1913, auditor, 1913 to 1918; public accountant since 1918; in business under own name as business adminstr., Pittsburgh, since 1918; pres. Assets Trade Exchange; treas. Am. Steel & Iron Product Co.; controller Bernard Gloekler Co.; trustee Assets Realization Co. V.p. St. John's Gen. Hosp. Unitarian. Home:

STRATTON

153 Marshall Av., Pittsburgh; (summer) Hopewell, Pa. Office: 324 Fourth Av., Pittsburgh, Pa.

STRATTON, Alfred James, pres. Reading St. Ry. Co.; b. London, Ontario, Canada, Nov. 15, 1887; s. Alfred H. and Cornelia Janet (Johnson) S.; ed. Collegiate Inst., London; m. Gertrude Curtis, June 7, 1909; children—Norman, Janet, Ruth. Came to U.S., 1909, naturalized, 1931. In employ of private engrs. and Central R.R. of N.Y. until 1912; engr. N.Y. & Queens Co. R.R., Long Island Traction Co. and Long Island Electric Co., 1912-14; engr. Mobile Light & R.R. Co., 1914-15, Binghamton Ry. Co., 1915-16; asst. engr. way and structures dept., Brooklyn Rapid Transit Co., 1916-17; valuation engr. Metropolitan Edison Co., 1918-19; with J. G. White Management Corpn. and successor, Associated Gas & Electric Co., since 1919; pres. Reading St. Ry. Co. since 1933, now also dir.; pres. and dir. Reading Traction Co. Served with Nitrates Div., Ordnance Dept., U.S. Army Civil Engring. Div., World War. Mason, Elk, Rotarian. Home: R.D. 1, Stony Creek Mills, Pa. Office: 12 S. Fifth St., Reading, Pa.

STRATTON, John Joseph, lawyer; b. Victoria, Tex., June 3, 1877; s. Thomas and Rosa Josephine (Lucas) S.; ed. Temple Coll., 1895 and pvt. instruction; m. Mary Ethel Householder, June 29, 1912 (died Jan. 19, 1939); adopted children—Herbert Forrest, Mary Elizabeth (Mrs. A. Brinton Carson). Employed as law clk. while studying law, 1894-1905; admitted to Pa. bar, 1905 and since engaged in gen. practice of law at Phila.; active in reform politics, 1906-12. Served as Govt. Appeal Agt. attached to 9th dist. dft. bd., Phila., 1916-17. Republican. Episcopalian. Clubs: American Bar Assn., Pa. Bar Assn., Phila. Bar Assn., Law Acad. of Phila. Home: 5959 Woodbine Av., Overbrook, Philadelphia. Office: Stephen Girard Bldg., Philadelphia, Pa.

STRATTON, Leon Dupre, prof. chemistry; b. Camden, N.J., Jan. 13, 1888; s. Horatio Mulford and Maria (Miller) S.; B.S. in chemistry, U. of Pa., 1909, M.S., same, 1917; Ph.D., U. of Pa., 1925; m. Laura Whipple Bruce, July 29, 1913; children—Bruce Dupre, Stephen Miller. Instr. chemistry, Drexel Inst. Tech., Phila., 1909-18; asst. prof. chemistry, 1918-20, prof. chemistry since 1920; actg. dean of men Drexel Inst. Tech., 1929-31, dean of men since 1931. Mem. Am. Chem. Soc. (mem. council), Am. Inst. Chem. Engrs., Soc. for Promotion Engring. Edn., Alpha Chi Sigma. Republican. Presbyterian. Clubs: University. Home: 205 Penn St., Ridley Park, Pa. Office: 32d and Chestnut Sts., Philadelphia, Pa.

STRAUB, George L.; chief surgeon Grace Hosp. Address: Grace Hosp., Welch, W.Va.

STRAUB, Howard Franklin, M.D., surgeon; b. Williamstown, Pa., Jan. 15, 1894; s. James Henry and Amelia Catherine (Mace) S.; student Pa. State Coll., 1916; B.S., Hahnemann Med. Coll., 1924; M.D., Hahnemann Med. Coll., 1926; m. Helen Josephine Chervanick, July 15, 1915; 1 dau., Madaline Mae (Mrs. A. Nelson Gray). Machinist Reading Locomotive Shop, 1915-17; foreman St. Clair (Pa.) Engine House, 1917-20; began gen. practice medicine and surgery, 1926; consultant Evangelical Hosp., Lewisburg, Pa.; radiologist Selinsgrove State Colony for Epileptics; med. trainer Susquehanna U., Selinsgrove Athletic Assn.; v. p. S. F. Durst & Co., Phila., Pa., and Mifflinburg Hardware Co. Deputy coroner and med. dir. Snyder County. Nat., State, and County allopathic and homeopathic medical socs., Selinsgrove Chamber of Commerce, Pi Upsilon Rho, Phi Mu Delta. Republican. Mason, Elk, Moose, Odd Fellow, Patriotic Order Sons of America. Club: Rotary. Address: 101 N. Market St., Selinsgrove, Pa.

STRAUB, James M., pres. Electric Welding Co.; b. Pittsburgh, Pa., Apr. 22, 1899; s. Theodore A. and Tecla (Moser) S.; ed. Canonsburg (Pa.) Pub. and High Sch., 1905-16; C.E., Lehigh U., 1920; m. Jane Chester, Sept. 29, 1923; children—Jean Elise, Carol. Inspecting and expiditing in shop and later drafting and estimating Fort Pitt Bridge Works, 1920-24; sec. and treas. Electric Welding Co., 1924-35, pres. since 1935, exec. vice-pres. and dir. Fort Pitt Bridge Works, Pittsburgh, since 1939. Enlisted in Naval Aviation Corps, but not called. Mem. Phi Delta Theta. Republican. Mason. Clubs: University (Pittsburgh); Rotary (McKees Rocks, Pa.); Longue Vue (Pittsburgh). Home: 240 Lytton Av., Pittsburgh, Pa. Office: McKees Rocks, Pa.; also Pittsburgh, Pa.

STRAUB, Theodore Alfred, Jr., sec. Electric Welding Co.; b. Canonsburg, Pa., Sept. 17, 1912; s. Theodore Alfred and Tecla Helena (Moser) S.; grad. Canonsburg Grade Sch., 1926, Canonsburg High Sch., 1930; B.S. in Industrial Engring., Lehigh U., 1934; unmarried. Sec. and dir. Electric Welding Co. since 1934. Mem. R.O.T.C., 1930-32. Mem. Nat. Honor Soc. (Canonsburg High Sch.). Mem. Young Republicans, Phi Delta Theta. Clubs: University, Metropolitan (Pittsburgh). Home: 132 W. College St., Canonsburg, Pa. Office: River Road, McKees Rocks, Pa.

STRAUGHN, Clinton Clement, physician; b. Salem, Salem Co., N.J., Aug. 2, 1872; s. John Summerill and Eliza Hoffman (Burden) S.; prep. edn., public schools, Salem, N.J.; M.D., Hahnemann Coll., Phila., 1896; 0. et A. Chir., New York Ophthalmic Coll., 1904; m. Martha S. Riley, Apr. 8, 1894 (died 1896); 1 dau., Helen Budd (Mrs. Henry Longstreet Conover). Practice of medicine, Matawan, N.J., 1896-1912, Red Bank, N.J., since 1912, specializing in eye, ear, nose and throat since 1904; surgeon, eye, ear, nose and throat, Ann May Memorial Hosp., Spring Lake, N.J., 1904-31; consulting ophthalmologist and laryngologist, Fitkin Memorial Hosp., Neptune, N.J., since 1931. Mem. A.M.A., Am. Inst. Homeopathy, N.J. Med. Soc., N.J. Homoeo. Med. Soc., Monmouth County Med. Soc., Am. Acad. Ophthalmology and Oto-Laryngology. Republican. Baptist. Mason, Odd Fellow, Jr. O.U.A.M. Home: Conover Lane, Middletown Township, N.J. Office: 23 Monmouth St., Red Bank, N.J.

STRAUGHN, James Henry, bishop; b. Centreville, Md., June 1, 1877; s. James Henry and Laura (Simmons) S.; A.B., Western Md. Coll., 1899, A.M., 1901, D.D., 1921; B.D., Westminster Theol. Sem., 1901; LL.D., Adrian Coll., 1937; m. Clara Bellamy Morgan, June 1, 1904; 1 dau., Laurlene. Ordained Meth. Prot. ministry, 1903; pastor various chs., Washington, D.C., Lynchburg, Va., Laurel, Del., and Baltimore; pres. Denominational Christian Endeavor Union, 1904-08, West Lafayette Coll., 1906-10; treas. and promotional sec. Methodist Protestant Ch., 1928-32; pres. Gen. Conf., same, 1936-39; bishop Methodist Ch., 1939; mem. Bd. of Missions, Board of Christian Edn. and Bd. of Publication. Pres. bd. trustees Western Md. Coll. Mason, K.P. Lecturer and writer of religious articles. Home: Cecil Apts. Office: 516 N. Charles St., Baltimore, Md.

STRAUSBAUGH, P(erry) D(aniel), univ. prof.; b. Republic, O., Mar. 21, 1886; s. John Lafayette and Fianna (Snavely) S.; B.S., Coll. of Wooster, O., 1913; student U. of Chicago, summers 1916-17, regular course, 1918-20, Ph.D., 1920; m. Mabel Mae Ross, July 21, 1906; children—Warren Laverne, Marjorie Glee (Mrs. Robert J. Heckert). Prof. of botany, Coll. of Wooster, 1920-23; prof. of botany, W. Va. Univ., since 1923, head dept. of botany, 1923-33, head dept. of botany and zoology since 1937. Mem. A.A.A.S., Am. Assn. Univ. Profs., Am. Soc. Plant Physiologists, Ecological Soc. of America, Bot. Soc. of America, W.Va. Acad. Sciences, W.Va. State Edn. Assn., Sigma Xi, Phi Beta Kappa, Alpha Gamma Rho, Gamma Alpha. Presbyterian. Club: Kiwanis. Home: 213 McLane Av., Morgantown, W.Va.

STRAUSS, Abram, physician; b. Reynoldsville, Pa., Apr. 21, 1887; s. Joseph and Mary (Ettinger) S.; student Central High Sch., Phila., Pa., 1904-05; M.D., Jefferson Med. Coll., Phila., 1910; m. Miriam Meyers, Dec. 23, 1914; children—Daniel Joseph, Richard Edwin. Began as physician, 1910; practice limited to dermatology since 1912; asso. in dermatology, Jefferson Med. Coll., Phila., since 1925; dermatologist to Jewish Hosp. since 1930; cons. dermatologist to Eastern State Penitentary since 1918. Dir. Orphans Guardians. Mem. A.M.A., Am. Bd. Dermatology, Phila. Dermatol. Soc., Omega Upsilon Phi. Club: Philmont Country (Phila.). Home: Elkins Court Apts., Elkins Park, Pa. Office: 16th and Walnut Sts., Philadelphia, Pa.

STRAUSS, George A.; asst. prof. gynecology, U. of Md.; attending gynecologist Mercy Hosp. Address: 1800 N. Charles St., Baltimore, Md.

STRAUSS, Jerome, v.p. Vanadium Corpn. America; b. New York, N.Y., Feb. 12, 1893; s. Herman and Matilda (Neuberger) S.; ed. pub. schs. (valedictorian, Bach prize); student, Coll. City of N.Y., 1906-09; M.E., Stevens Inst. Tech. (valedictorian; Priestly Prize in chemistry, Stillman Prize in applied technology), 1913; m. Ruth Argo Bryan. Engr. metall. dept. Ill. Steel Co., 1913-14; chief research engr. Vanadium Corpn. America, 1928-35, v.p. in charge research and development since 1935. Served as 1st lt., U.S. Army, Ordnance Dept., World War. Joined U.S. Naval Gun Factory, 1919, serving successively as asst. chief chemist and metallurgist, chief chemist and material engr.; now lt. comdr. U.S. Naval Res. Mem. Am. Inst. Mining and Metall. Engrs., Am. Soc. Mech. Engrs., Am. Soc. for Testing Materials, Am. Petroleum Inst., Am. Soc. Metals, Iron and Steel Inst. (Brit.), Inst. Metals (Brit.). Contbr. to scientific jours. Holder several U.S. patents. Home: Schenley Apts., Pittsburgh, Pa. Office: Bridgeville, Pa.

STRAUSS, Myer, wholesale mcht.; b. Baltimore, Md., Aug. 18, 1879; s. Moses and Caroline (Strauss) S.; ed. Baltimore City Coll., 1892-94; m. Julia Friedenwald, Baltimore, Md., June 3, 1912; adopted children (taken from Germany, 1935-36)—Nelly Eisenberg, Sigfried Rath, Manfred Rath. Asso. with Strauss Bros., Inc., wholesale dry goods, Baltimore, Md., continuously since entering its employ as clk., 1892, now pres. and dir. Dir. Bd. Jewish Edn. Jewish religion. Club: Suburban of Baltimore County. Home: 2701 Whitney Av. Office: 109 Hopkins Pl., Baltimore, Md.

STRAWBRIDGE, Anna Estes (Mrs. Francis R. S.); b. Phila., Pa., Feb. 20, 1880; d. John Barclay and Mary Perot (Dawson) Hacker; grad. Germantown Friends Sch., 1899; m. Francis R. Strawbridge, Apr. 30, 1902; children—Mary Dawson (Mrs. Walter Penn Shipley, Jr.), Elisabeth Hacker (Mrs. Thomas Biddle Harvey), Francis R., Jr., G. Stockton. Former trustee Community Fund of Phila.; hon. chmn. Council of Social Agencies of Community Fund; pres. Phila. Co. League of Women Voters; former 1st v.p. Pa. League of Women Voters; pres. Germantown Neighborhood Council. Mem. bd. dirs. Asso Hosp. Service of Phila., Germantown Settlement, Germantown Hosp., Big Brothers Assn. Pa. Branch Shut In Soc.; mem. exec. com. Phila. City Charter, exec. com. Phila. Fng. Policy Assn., mem. bd. Phila. Com. for Prevention of Blindness; mem. exec. com. Pa. Conf. Social Work; mem. Advisory Com. of 100 for Pa. Women's Participating in N.Y. Worlds Fair. Republican. Mem. Religious Soc. of Friends. Clubs: Acorn, Cosmopolitan, Sedgeley. Mem. Pa. Soc. Colonial Dames of America, Pa. Soc. New England Women, Welcome Soc., Magna Charta Dames, Home: "Woodside" School Lane, Germantown, Philadelphia, Pa.

STRAWBRIDGE, Anne West, artist and author; b. Phila., Pa., Mar. 20, 1883; d. George (M.D.) and Alice (Welsh) S.; ed. Stevens Sch. and Pelham Sch., Pa. Acad. Fine Arts. Engaged as artist specializing in painting animals since 1908; exhibited in New York City, Philadelphia, Baltimore and other cities; has devoted much time to writing since 1925. Interested in parks and dir. Friends of the Wissahicken. Mem. of Fellowship Pa. Acad. Fine Arts. Owner and operator autogiro. Republican. Episcopalian. Clubs: American Alpine (New York City); Acorn (Philadelphia). Author: Shadows of the Matterhorn (folklore of Zermatt Valley, pub. in Switzerland), 1930; Dawn after Danger (novel), 1934; The Black Swan (novel), 1935; Above the Rainbow (novel), 1938. Home: 6701 Wissahicken Av., Mt. Airy, Philadelphia, Pa.

STRAWBRIDGE, Edward R(ichie), artist. Home: 500 West Moreland Av., Chestnut Hill, Pa.*

STRAWBRIDGE, Frederic H(eap), retired merchant; b. Phila., Pa., Aug. 24, 1866; s. Justus Clayton and Mary (Lukens) S.; ed. Friends' Preparative Meeting Sch., Germantown, Phila., 1872-83; A.B., Haverford Coll., 1887; m. Bertha Gordon Walter, June 5, 1894; children—J. Clayton, Frederic H., Anna Walter (Mrs. John Winthrop Claghorn), Gordon Weld, Edward Ritchie II. Began as clk. with Strawbridge & Clothier, dept. store, Phila., 1887, continued through various depts. and admitted to firm, 1900, now dir. Mem. Troop A, Home Defense Reserve, World War; dir. S.E. Div. Am. Red Cross Warehouse. Mem. bd. dirs. Bryn Mawr Coll., Haverford Coll. Republican. Mem. Soc. of Friends. Clubs: University, Union League, Phila. Cricket. Home: 500 W. Moreland Av., Chestnut Hill, Phila. Office: 801 Market St., Philadelphia, Pa.

STRAYER, Lloyd Winfield, civil engr.; b. Hall, York Co., Pa., Nov. 8, 1885; s. Henry Lewis and Annie M. (Lighty) S.; ed. Abbottstown and York (Pa.) grade schs., 1891-99; grad. York High and Prep. Sch., 1903; student Worcester Poly. Inst., 1903-06; B.S. in C.E., Purdue U., 1908; studied U. of Pittsburgh, 1911-12; m. Lauretta M. Good, Oct. 21, 1913; 1 son, William Good (dec.). Asst. engr., later electrician Erie R.R., 1908; extra gang foreman C.M.&St.P. R.R., 1909-10; successively rodman, chainman and transitman B.&O. R.R., Pittsburgh, 1910-13, asst. supervisor of tracks, Baltimore, 1913-14, asst. div. engr. and bridge inspector, Parkersburg, W.Va., and Garrett, Ind., 1915-18, division engr., New Castle, Pa., 1918-20; engr. Pittsburgh Limestone and Associated Cos., 1920-35; chief engr. Pittsburgh Limestone Corpn. since 1935. Registered professional engr., State of Pa. Dir. Scottish Rite Cathedral Assn. Mem. Theta Xi. Republican. Episcopalian. Mason (officer York and Scottish Rite bodies). Club: New Castle (Pa.) Field. Home: 426 Winter Av. Office: 243 E. Washington St., New Castle, Pa.

STREAMER, A. Camp, elec. engring.; b. Boulder, Colo., Nov. 23, 1885; s. Francis M. and Lula A. (Walker) S.; ed. State Prep. Sch., Boulder, Colo., 1899-1903; B.S. in E.E., U. of Colo., 1907; m. Flora E. Goldsworthy, June 1, 1911; children—Flora Ethlyn (Mrs. William A. Mechesney), Douglas Camp (dec.). Asso. with Westinghouse Electric & Mfg. Co. continuously since 1907, tech. apprentice and successively switchboard engr., headquarters sales, asst. dir. sales, mgr. diversified products dept., mgr. transportation div., and mgr. switchgear div., 1936-39, gen. mgr. Pittsburgh divs. since 1939. Presbyn. Mason. Clubs: University, Edgewood Country (Pittsburgh). Home: 5 Newport Rd., Wilkinsburg. Office: Westinghouse Electric & Mfg. Co., East Pittsburgh, Pa.

STRECKER, Edward Adam, M.D.; b. Phila., Pa., Oct. 16, 1886; s. Adam and Mary (Weiler) S.; prep. edn., St. Joseph's Coll., Philadelphia, hon. Sc.D., 1935; B.A., La Salle Coll., Philadelphia, 1907, M.A., 1911, Litt.D., 1938; M.D., Jefferson Med. Coll., 1911; m. Elizabeth Kyne Walsh, Jan. 1917. Res. phys. St. Agnes Hosp., Phila., 1911-15; asst. phys. Pa. Hosp. Dept. for Nervous and Mental Diseases, 1913-17, med. dir. since 1917 and director of clinic; staff neurologist, Pa., Philadelphia and Germantown hospitals; prof. of nervous and mental diseases, Jefferson Med. Coll., 1925-31; prof. and head dept. psychiatry, U. of Pa., 1931—; clin. prof. psychiatry and mental hygiene, Yale U., 1926-32; chief of service and consultant, Institute for Mental Hygiene, Pa. Hosp., Philadelphia; also consultant to Bryn Mawr Coll., and U.S. Veterans' Bureau; Salmon lecturer, 1939. Commd. 1st lt. M.C., U.S.A., May 1917, and served 2 yrs. as div. neuro. psychiatrist 28th Div. at Camp Hancock, Ga., and in field in France, advancing to capt. and maj. Fellow Coll. of Physicians, Phila.; mem. Am. Neurol. Assn., Am. Psychiatric Assn., Alpha Omega Alpha, Sigma Phi Epsilon, Alpha Kappa Kappa, etc. Republican. Catholic. Author: Clinical Psychiatry, 1925; Clinical Neurology, 1927; Discovering Ourselves, 1931; Practical Examination of Personality and Behavior Disorders, 1936; Alcohol One Man's Meat, 1938; also numerous articles and papers on nervous and mental disorders. Spl. researches in behavior disorder of children and normal and abnormal psychology of childhood. Home: 4401 Market St. Office: 111 N. 49th St., Philadelphia, Pa.

STREEPER, Amanda, prin. high sch.; b. Narcissa, Pa., Dec. 27, 1886; d. Thomas Shay and Maria (Taggart) S.; ed. West Chester State Normal Sch., 1902-05; A.B., U. of Mich., 1917; A.M., U. of Pa., 1927. Engaged in teaching at various pub. schs. in Pa., 1905-14, Downer Sem., Milwaukee, Wis., 1917-18, high sch., South Phila., Pa., 1918-20, 1921-27, Washington Irving High Sch., 1920-21; prin. William Penn High Sch., Phila., Pa., since 1927. Pres. Middle States Assn. of History and Social Sci. Teachers. Mem. Nat. Edn. Assn. Dept. Secondary Sch. Prins., Pa. State Edn. Assn., Phila. Teachers Assn., Montgomery Co. Hist. Soc., Phi Beta Kappa. Episcopalian. Clubs: University, Women's City (Philadelphia). Home: 632 N. 40th St. Office: William Penn High School, Philadelphia, Pa.

STREET, Edward Tatum, chief engr.; b. Cincinnati, O., Dec. 9, 1884; s. David and Eunice (Fawcett) S.; ed. Oberlin Coll.; m. C. K. MacLennan, Sept. 23, 1909; children—Katharine R., Eleanor F., David. Elec. engr. North States Power Co., St. Paul., 1908-19; supt. power M. & O. Paper Co., International Falls, Minn., 1917-19; chief engr. The Ruberoid Co., New York, 1919-29; chief engr. Downingtown Mfg. Co. since 1929. Republican. Presbyterian. Home: Exton Cross Roads. Office: Box 146, Downingtown, Pa.

STREET, Frank, illustrator and painter; b. St. Joseph, Mo., Mar. 31, 1893; s. Emory J. and Laura (Rees) S.; student Art Inst., Kansas City, Mo., 1910-15, Art Students League, N.Y. City, 1915-16, Leonia Summer Sch., Leonia, N.J., 1916-18; m. May Beaumont, Nov. 17, 1917. Has followed profession as illustrator and painter since 1917; illustrator for Saturday Evening Post, Collier's Weekly Mag., McCall's Mag. and other well-known mags. of nat. circulation; executed portraits, murals, and landscapes. Served as pvt. inf. U.S.A., 1918, at Camp McArthur, Waco, Tex. Mem. Soc. of Illustrators, Am. Legion. Republican. Home: 505 Grand Av., Leonia, N.J.

STREET, J. Fletcher, architect; b. Beverly, N.J., June 11, 1880; s. John Fletcher and Emily Virginia (Phillips) S.; student Farnum Prep. Sch., Beverly; m. Ethel Frances Parker, Apr. 28, 1910; children—Edward Parker, Phillips Borden. Draughtsman, 1898-1907; in business for self since 1907; designer chs., schs., mfg. bldgs., residences, also landscape architecture. Mem. Am. Inst. Architects, Acad. Natural Sciences of Phila., Phila. Geog. Soc. (pres.). Democrat. Clubs: Art, Franklin Inn, Botanical (Phila.), Del. Valley Ornithol. Club. Author: Brief Bird Biographies. Contbr. to scientific jours. Home: Beverly, N.J. Office: 1120 Locust St., Philadelphia, Pa.

STREETER, Donald Davis, artist, craftsman; b. Vineland, N.J., Nov. 21, 1905; s. John Josephus and Mary (Heacock) S.; student Vineland Pub. Schs., 1912-24, Bucknell U., 1924-25, Pa. Mus. Sch. of Industrial Art, 1925-28, Pa. Acad. Fine Arts, 1928-29, Art Students' League, 1929-30; unmarried. Began as sign painter's asst., 1923; now engaged in making hand forged wrought iron and decorative metalwork; also artist, illustrator of books and newspapers, wood engraver, etcher, lithographer, sculptor and teacher. Lecturer on early American wrought iron. Represented in British Museum (woodcuts in miniature edition of J. R. Lowell's "The Courtin' "), Smithsonian Instn., Philadelphia Library Collection of miniature books. Exhibited Pa. Acad. Fine Arts, Brooklyn Mus., Metropolitan Mus., Toledo Mus. of Art, Columbus Gallery Fine Arts, Richmond (Va.) Acad. Arts, U. of Neb. Sch. Fine Arts, Boulder Art Assn. Hon. mention Print Club of Philadelphia, 1933. Mem. Vineland Hist. and Antiquarian Soc., Phi Gamma Delta. Club: Print. Home: Delsea Drive, Iona, N.J.

STREETER, George Linius, anatomist; b. Johnstown, N.Y., Jan. 12, 1873; s. George Austin and Hannah Green (Anthony) S.; A.B., Union Coll., New York, 1895, D.Sc., 1930; A.M., M.D., Columbia University, 1899; D.Sc., Trinity College, Dublin, 1928; LL.D., University of Michigan, 1935; m. Julia Allen Smith, Apr. 9, 1910; children—Sarah Frances, George Allen, Mary Raymond. Asst. and instr. anatomy, Johns Hopkins, 1902-06; asst. prof. anatomy, Wistar Inst. Anatomy, Phila., 1906-07; prof. anatomy and dir. anat. lab., U. of Mich., 1907-14; research asso. Carnegie Instn. of Washington, 1914-18, dir. dept. of embryology, 1918—, chairman division animal biology since 1935. Mem. Am. Association Anatomists, Am. Soc. Zoölogists, Am. Soc. Naturalists, Nat. Acad. Sciences; corr. mem. Zoöl. Soc. London; hon. mem. Anat. Soc. Gr. Britain and Ireland. Fellow Royal Soc., Edinburgh. Home: 3707 St. Paul St., Baltimore, Md.

STREETER, Thomas Winthrop; b. Concord, N.H., July 20, 1883; s. Frank Sherwin and Lilian (Carpenter) S.; grad. St. Paul's Sch., Concord, 1900; B.L., Dartmouth, 1904; LL.B., Harvard, 1907; m. Ruth Cheney, June 23, 1917; children—Frank Sherwin, Henry Schofield, Thomas Winthrop, Lilian Carpenter. Admitted to Mass. bar, 1907, and began practice with Choate, Hall & Stewart, Boston; mem. law firm of Streeter & Holmes, 1917 to 1917; treas. Am. Internat. Corpn. of New York, 1917-19, v.p., 1919-23; chmn. bd. Simms Petroleum Co., 1923-30; engaged in liquidation of Bank of U.S., 1931-35; pres. Mortgage Certificate Loan Co., 1935-37; managing partner Ungalik Syndicate, Alaska, since 1938; president and director Prudence-Bonds Corporation; director El Paso Electric Company, Gulf States Utilities Company, Key West Electric Co., Western Public Service, First National Bank, Morristown, N.J., Gen. Pub. Service Co. Chief external relations br. Div. of Purchase, Storage and Traffic, U.S. War Dept., 1918. First chmn. N.J. Aviation Commn., 1931-32. Mem. Alumni Council of Dartmouth Coll., 1920-23, and chmn. Alumni Fund Com., 1921-23. Pres. Morris Community Chest, Morristown, N.J., 1927-30. Mem. Am. Antiquarian Soc., N.H. Hist. Soc. (trustee 1922-26), Mo. Hist. Soc., Calif. Hist. Soc., Texas Hist. Soc., Delta Kappa Epsilon, Sphinx Soc. (Dartmouth); dir. New England Soc. in N.Y. City; mem. com. on Americana for coll. libraries of Am. Hist. Assn. Republican. Clubs: Morristown, Morris County Golf (Morristown), Century, Grolier, Bankers, Dartmouth, Harvard, Midday (New York); Union (Boston). Home: Sussex Av., Morristown, N.J. Office: 100 E. 42d St., New York, N.Y.

STRICKLAND, Charles Gunnison, surgeon; b. Erie, Pa., Mar. 31, 1880; s. David Hayes and Emma (Gunnison) S.; A.B., U. of Pa., 1901; M.D., U. of Pa. Med. Sch., 1904; m. Clara Walker, Oct. 29, 1907; children—Benjamin Walker, Jane Gunnison. After interneship engaged in gen. practice of medicine at Erie, Pa., 1906-14, specializing in gynecology since 1914; chief of obstet. and gynecol. staff, Hamot Hosp. since 1930; vice-pres. and dir. Marine Nat. Bank, American Sterilizer Co., Erie Malleable Iron Co.; dir. Erie Bolt and Nut Co. Fellow Am. Coll. Surgs. Diplomate Am. Bd. Obstetrics and Gynecology. Mem. Sigma Xi, Kappa Sigma. Republican. Clubs: Erie, Kahkwa (Erie). Home: 324 W. 6th St. Office: 153 W. 7th St., Erie, Pa.

STRICKLAND, Frederick H., ins. exec.; b. nr. Oxford, Pa., Feb. 22, 1886; s. Frank T. and Anna Mary (Riley) S.; student Oxford (Pa.) pub. schs., 1892-1904, Banks Business Coll., Phila., 1904-05; m. Edith M. Dunn, Dec. 8, 1906; 1 dau., Mildred E. (Mrs. S. H. Thornton). Railroad clk., Phila., 1904-05; clerk Phila. Casualty Co., 1905-11, Fidelity & Deposit Co., Baltimore, 1911-14; with New Amsterdam Casualty Co., casualty ins., fidelity and surety bonds, Baltimore, Md., since 1914, v.p. and dir. since 1916, asst. treas. since 1914; vice-pres., U.S. Casualty Co., Baltimore, since 1932; v.p., asst. treas. and dir. Am. Indemnity Co., Baltimore, since 1916, St. Paul Investment Corpn., Baltimore, since 1925. Democrat. Methodist. Clubs: Casualty and Surety, Chesapeake, Baltimore Country (Baltimore, Md.). Home: 3700 N. Charles St. Office: 227 St. Paul St., Baltimore, Md.

STRICKLER, Daniel Bursk, lawyer; b. Columbia, Pa., May 17, 1897; s. Calvin Ruby and Harriet (Bursk) S.; LL.B., Cornell U. Law Sch., 1922; m. Caroline Grace Bolton, Oct. 11, 1924; children—Nancy Cupper, Daniel Bursk. Admitted to Pa. bar, 1923, and since engaged in gen. practice of law at Lancaster; mem. Pa. Ho. of Rep., 1931-32; county solicitor, Lancaster Co., 1933-39; admitted to practice before all cts. of Pa. and before Supreme Ct. of the U.S. Served in Pa. N.G. on Mexican border, 1916-17; capt. machine gun company, U.S.A., with A.E.F., 1918-19; wounded in action, cited for bravery; awarded Purple Heart Medal; col. inf. U.S.A. Res. Past 1st vice-pres. Dept. Pa., Am. Legion. Pres. Dept. Pa. Res. Officers Assn. of U.S. Pres. and dir. Lancaster Y.M.C.A., Lancaster Red Cross. Treas. Donegal Soc. Mem. Am. and Pa. bar assns., Kappa Sigma, Phi Delta Phi, Quill and Dagger, S.R., Am. Legion. Republican. Presbyn. Mason (K.T.). Clubs: American Business, Hamilton, Country. Home: 422 N. Duke St. Office: 47 N. Duke St., Lancaster, Pa.

STRICKLER, Homer Hummel, lawyer; b. Dauphin Co., Pa., May 6, 1886; s. Lewis M. and Elizabeth (Hummel) S.; LL.B., Blackstone Sch. of Law (corr. course), 1928, J.D., same, 1937; m. Dorothy M. Hartwell, Aug. 2, 1922; stepdau., Dorothy Jane (Mrs. George E. Schell); 1 dau., Mary Elizabeth. Employed as clk. in bank and telephone co. office, 1903-09; served as dep. prothonotary Supreme and Superior Cts. of Pa., Harrisburg, 1909-37; admitted to Pa. bar, 1928, and since 1937 actively engaged in gen. practice of law at Harrisburg and Hummelstown; mem. Com. on Workmen's Compensation Law of Pa. Bar Assn. since 1933. Mem. Am., Pa. and Dauphin Co. bar assns., Assn. Practitioners Before Interstate Commerce Commn., Commercial Law League of America, Firemens Assn. of Pa., Pa. German Soc., Pa. Soc. of N.Y. Republican. Lutheran. Elk. I.O.O.F. W.O.W. Royal Arcanum. Knights of Malta. Patriotic Sons of America. Home: 221 E. Main St., Hummelstown, Pa. Office: 205 Market Sq. Bldg., Harrisburg, Pa.

STRIDER, Robert Edward Lee, bishop; b. Lee Town, Jefferson Co., W.Va., Apr. 9, 1887; s. Isaac Henry and Sarah Elizabeth (Reich) S.; A.B., A.M., University of Virginia, 1908; B.D., Virginia Theol. Sem., Alexandria, Va., 1913, D.D., 1922; m. Mary M. Holroyd, Oct. 14, 1915 (died 1917); 1 son, Robert E. Lee; m. 2d, Eleanor Armstrong Greer, June 15, 1921 (died 1936); children—Sidney Greer, Barbara Reich. Deacon, 1911, priest, 1912, P.E. Ch.; in charge Emmanuel Ch., Keyser, W.Va., and associated missions, 1911-15; rector St. Matthew's Ch., Wheeling, 1915-23; bishop coadjutor of W.Va., 1923-39; bishop of W.Va. since Jan. 10, 1939. Trustee Theol. Sem., Alexandria, Va., and of Episcopal High Sch., Alexandria. Mem. Phi Beta Kappa. Democrat. Author: Life and Work of George William Peterkin, 1929. Home: Woodlawn. Office: 1300 Market St., Wheeling, W.Va.

STRIEBY, Maurice Edward, elec. engring.; b. Colorado Springs, Colo., May 2, 1893; s. William and Anna (Breath) S.; A.B., Colo. Coll., 1914; B.S., Harvard, 1916; B.S. in E.E. Mass. Inst. Tech., 1916; m. Frances Adams, Mar. 23, 1918; children—Ann, Michael. Employed as telephone engr., Engring. Dept. N.Y. Telephone Co., 1916-17; with Development and Research Dept. Am. Telephone & Telegraph Co., 1919-29; elec. engr., Bell Telephone Labs. since 1929; vice-pres. and treas. Engineers Royalties, Inc. Served as capt. Signal Corps, U.S.A., 1917-19, with A.E.F. in France. Mem. Am. Inst. Elec. Engrs., Am. Radio Engrs. Congregationalist. Home: 175 Sagamore Rd., Maplewood, N.J. Office: 463 West St., New York, N.Y.

STRIEGEL, John George, surgeon, owner J. G. Striegel Private Hosp.; b. Shenandoah, Pa., Aug. 27, 1885; s. Karl A. Striegel and Catharine (Hirschelman) S.; M.D., U. of Pa., 1910; post grad. work, Harvard, 1918. Mass.

Gen. Hosp., Boston, Mass., 1918; m. Morea E. Fegley, June 8, 1934; children—Karl K., Elizabeth F. McElhatten, John L., Richard A. Surgeon-in-chief, treas. and dir., A. C.Milliken Hosp., Pottsville, Pa., 1923-28, Mercy Hosp., Pottsville, Pa., 1928-30; surgeon, pathologist, Pottsville Hosp., 1919-21; owner J. G. Strigel Private Hosp., Altoona, Pa., since 1933. Served as major, Med. Corps, U.S. Army, during World War. Mem. A.M.A., Blair Co. Med. Soc., Pa. State Med. Soc., Am. Legion, Vets. Foreign Wars, Kiwanis Internat. (past pres.; mem. bd. of dirs.). Republican. Address: Altoona, Pa.

STRIKOL, Albert J.; chief eye, ear, nose and throat dept. Delaware, St. Francis and Wilmington Gen. hosps. Address: 621 Delaware Av., Wilmington, Del.

STRINGER, Arthur (John Arbuthnott), author; b. Chatham, Ont., Can., Feb. 26, 1874; educated Toronto University and University of Oxford, Eng.; m. Jobyna Howland, 1900; m. 2d, his cousin, Margaret Arbuthnott Stringer, 1914. Editorial writer, Am. Press Assn., 1898-1901; lit. editor of Success, 1903-04. Author: Watchers of Twilight, 1894; Pauline and Other Poems, 1895; Epigrams, 1896; A Study in King Lear, 1897; The Loom of Destiny, 1898; The Silver Poppy, 1899; Lonely O'Malley, 1901; Hephæstus and Other Poems, 1902; The Wire Tappers, 1906; Phantom Wires, 1907; The Occasional Offender, 1907; The Woman in the Rain, 1907; Under Groove, 1909; Irish Poems, 1911; Open Water, 1912; Gun Runner, 1912; Shadow, 1913; Prairie Wife, 1915; Hand of Peril, 1916; Door of Dread, 1917; House of Intrigue, 1918; Man Who Couldn't Sleep, 1919; Prairie Mother, 1920; The Wine of Life, 1921; Are All Men Alike?, 1921; Prairie Child, 1922; City of Peril, 1923; Diamond Thieves, 1923; Empty Hands, 1924; The Story Without a Name and Manhandled (with Russell Holman); Power, 1925; In Bad with Sinbad, 1926; White Hands, 1927; The Wolf Woman, 1928; A Woman at Dusk and Other Poems, 1928; Cristina and I, 1929; The Woman Who Couldn't Die, 1929; Out of Erin, 1930; A Lady Quite Lost, 1930; The Mud Lark, 1931; Marriage by Capture, 1932; Dark Soil, 1933; Man Lost, 1934; Wife Traders, 1936; Alexander Was Great, 1937; Heather of the High Hand, 1937; The Old Woman Remembers and Other Poems, 1938; The Lamp In The Valley, 1938; The Dark Wing, 1939; also author of many photoplay features. Contbr. to mags. Traveled in S. America, Africa and Europe. Clubs: Canadian of New York (v.p.); Macaulay, Rockaway River Country, Mountain Lakes; pres. and dir. Mountain Lakes Dramatic Guild. Home: Mountain Lakes, N.J.

STRINGFELLOW, George Edward, v.p. and div. mgr. Thomas A. Edison, Inc.; b. Reva, Va., Dec. 2, 1892; s. James W. and Elizabeth F. (Bowers) S.; ed. Va. pub. schs.; m. Carrie M. Fearnow, Dec. 31, 1912. Began as salesman Thomas A. Edison, Inc., 1918; became gen. mgr. storage battery div., 1922, v.p. and div. mgr. since 1932. Mem. banking advisory board, State of N.J.; mem. bd. of govs. Am. Mining Congress; mem. Am. Inst. of Mining Engrs. Republican. Presbyterian. Clubs: Engineers, Downtown Athletic (New York); New York Railroad; Montclair Golf; Kiwanis. Home: 162 Upper Mountain Av., Montclair, N.J. Office: Thomas A. Edison, Inc., West Orange, N.J.

STROBEL, Peyton Brown, realtor; b. Baltimore, Md., Sept. 20, 1896; s. James William and Rebecca Lee (Brown) S.; student Baltimore (Md.) Poly. Inst., 1910-14; B.S., Johns Hopkins U., Baltimore, Md., 1917; m. Leslie Page, Oct. 2, 1920; children—Dorothy Page, Virginia Lee. Entered real estate business, 1919; owner Peyton B. Strobel & Co., realtors, Baltimore, since 1920. Served as lt., 45th Arty., C.A.C., during World War. Mem. Baltimore Real Estate Bd. (pres., 1931), Delta Upsilon. Democrat. Episcopalian. Club: Johns Hopkins Faculty (Baltimore, Md.). Home: 5025 Roland Av. Office: 2206 N. Charles St., Baltimore, Md.

STROCK, Henry Blaine, clergyman; b. Harrisburg, Pa., Jan. 24, 1887; s. John Henry and Sara (Yeager) S.; student Harrisburg (Pa.) High Sch., 1902-06; A.B., Gettysburg (Pa.) Coll.,

1909; M.A., Princeton U., 1912; Th.B., Princeton Theol. Sem., 1912; D.D., Washington and Jefferson Coll., 1934; m. Katharine S. Reiley, June 15, 1912; children—John Henry, Katharine Reiley, Sara Louise, Frederick Reiley, Henry Blaine, Jr. Ordained Presbyn. ministry, 1912; pastor Presbyn. Ch., Allentown, N.J., 1912-13; asst. minister 1st Ch., Pittsburgh, 1914-18; asso. minister Westminster Ch., Minneapolis, Minn., 1918-22; pastor 1st Ch., Greensburg, Pa., 1922-35, 1st Ch., Lancaster, Pa., since 1935. Trustee Johnston Smith U., Charlotte, N.C. Mem. Sigma Alpha Epsilon. Republican. Mason (K.T.). Club: Harrisburg (Pa.) Cleric. Home: 140 E. Orange St., Lancaster, Pa.

STROD, Arvid John, mfg. exec.; b. Riga, Latvia, Sept. 10, 1899; s. Gabriel and Marie (Sproge) S.; student Imperial Inst. of Mines, Petrograd, Russia; m. Eugenia Kirchgraber, Dec. 23, 1933; 1 dau., Barbara. Engring. dept., Siemens-Schuckert Co., Berlin, Germany, 1922-24; with Westinghouse Electric & Mfg. Co., East Pittsburgh, Pa., 1924-28; v.p., sales mgr. and dir. The Vitro Mfg. Co., Pittsburgh, since 1928. Mem. Am. Ceramic Soc. Home: 75 Ordale Boul., Mt. Lebanon, Pa. Office: The Vitro Mfg. Co., Pittsburgh, Pa.

STRODACH, Paul Zeller, clergyman, editor; b. Norristown, Pa., Mar. 27, 1876; s. Henri Jean Baptiste and Mary Louise (Zeller) S.; A.B., Muhlenberg Coll., Allentown, Pa., 1896, A.M., 1899; B.D., 1918, D.D., 1922; grad. Phila. Theol. Sem., 1899; grad. work, Princeton; m. Bertha Laubach, Kleppinger Apr. 6, 1904; 1 son, George Kleppinger. Ordained ministry Evang. Luth. Ch., 1899; successively pastor Ch. of the Saviour (Trenton, N.J.); asso. pastor St. John's Ch. (Easton, Pa.); pastor First Ch. (Washington, Pa.), Trinity Ch. (Canton, O.), Grace Ch. (Roxboro, Phila.), and Ch. of the Trinity, Norristown; lit. editor United Luth. Ch. Pub. House. Mem. Common Service Book Com. of United Luth. Ch., and officer or mem. other ch. orgns. Ecclesiastical illuminator and liturgiologist. Mem. Alpha Tau Omega. Republican. Author: The Church Year, 1922; Oremus, 1925; A Manual on Worship, 1929; In the Presence, 1931; His Glorious Hour, 1932; The Road He Trod, 1932; Before the Cross, 1933; Lift Up Your Heart, 1934; also monographs and essays on liturg. and hymnol. subjects and on ch. art and music. Translator: The Jesuits, 1927. Editor: Book of Family Worship; The Children's Hymnal and Service Book. Co-editor of Luther's Works, Parish School Hymnal, Army and Navy Service Book, Hymns and Prayers, etc. Home: Gwynedd Valley, Pa. Office: 1228 Spruce St., Philadelphia, Pa.

STROH, Dorothy Elizabeth, (Mrs. Merlin Everett Tisdale), lawyer; b. West Pittston, Pa., Sept. 4, 1905; d. Charles Albert and Clara Green (Andrews) Stroh; grad. Milford (Pa.) High Sch., 1922; LL.B., Dickinson Sch. of Law, Carlisle, Pa., 1925; m. Merlin Everett Tisdale, Apr. 8, 1938. In gen. practice of law, Pike Co., Pa., since 1925; admitted to Pike Co. bar and Supreme Court of Pa., 1927, to U.S. Dist. Court, 1930; borough solicitor Milford Borough, 1934-36, dist. atty. Pike Co., 1936-38 (resigned after marriage). Mem. Am. Bar Assn., Pa. Bar Assn., D.A.R., Eastern Star, Phi Delta Delta. Republican. Episcopalian. Club: Republican of Pike Co. Author: Rain on the Rocks (poems), 1932. Poems are included in Modern American Poetry for 1932 and 1933 (anthologies). Address: Milford, Pike Co., Pa.

STROMBACH, Victor Hugo, engr., architect; b. Newark, N.J., Sept. 27, 1887; s. Hugo and Maria (Geiger) S.; grad. Newark pub. schs., 1902, Newark Business Coll., 1903; student Newark Tech. Sch., 1903-04; grad. in architecture, Newark Drawing Sch., 1906; spl. course, Pratt Inst., 1906-07, Fawcett Sch. Fine and Industrial Arts, 1907-08; C.E., Ohio Northern U., 1910; m. Anna G. Guentner, Dec. 19, 1913. Chief engr. Goeller Iron Works, Newark, 1910-13; sr. partner Strombach & Mertens, Irvington, engrs. and architects, 1913-22; in private practice as engr. and architect, under own name, since 1922; instr. mathematics, architecture and construction, Fawcett Sch. Fine &

Industrial Arts, 1914-28, head architectural dept., 1920-28; pres. Trades Securities Co., Irvington Holding Co.; v.p. Irvington Mortgage & Guaranty Title Co.; dir. Peoples Nat. Bank & Trust Co., Van Buren Bldg. & Loan Assn. Formerly dir., trustee and treas. Irvington Y.M.C.A. Mem. Am. Inst. Architects, N.J. Architects Soc., N.J. Engring. Soc., Am. Artist Professional League, Soc. Medalists, Lambda Tau Delta. Republican. Lutheran. Mason (32°, Shriner), Elk. Odd Fellow. Club: Irvington Kiwanis. Home: Pleasantville Rd., New Vernon, N.J. Office: 1243 Springfield Av., Irvington, N.J.

STRONG, George Vaughan, lawyer; b. Raleigh, N.C., Dec. 23, 1893; s. George Vaughan and Sally Hall (Smith) S.; A.B., U. of N.C., Chapel Hill, N.C., 1914; m. Ethel Meryweather Newbold, Feb. 8, 1919 (died Dec. 12, 1932); children—Virginia Newbold, Sally Hall, George Vaughan, Ethelwyn Meryweather, Newbold; m. 2d, Caroline B. Garnett (nee Barclay), March 9, 1939. Admitted to N.C. bar, 1914; teacher, Wilmington, N.C. High Sch., 1914-16; editorial staff Edward Thompson Co., Northport, L.I., N.Y., 1915-17; admitted to Pa. bar, 1919, and since in practice at Phila.; mem. firm Smith & Strong, Phila., 1920-31; practiced alone, 1931-39; mem. firm Strong, Saylor & Ferguson since 1939; instr. Wharton Sch., U. of Pa., 1920-29; prof. constl. law, Temple U., Phila., 1924-33; dir. Standard Cross Thatcher Co., Chestnut Hill Title & Trust Co., Ivey & Ellington, Inc., Pelham Bldg. & Loan Assn., Morris Starrels & Co. Served as capt., F.A., U.S. Army, 1917-19. Mem. Phi Beta Kappa, Zeta Psi. Republican. Episcopalian. Mason. Clubs: University, Phila. Cricket, Fourth Street (Phila.). Home: 530 Spring Lane, Chestnut Hill. Office: 2300 Girard Trust Co. Bldg., Philadelphia, Pa.

STRONG, Nathan L., ex-congressman; b. Summerville, Jefferson Co., Pa., Nov. 12, 1859; ed. pub. schs. Telegraph operator, 1878-94; admitted to Pa. bar, 1891; dist. atty. Jefferson Co., 1895-1900; pres. Mohawk Mining Co.; director Peoples Bank of Ford City; dir. Pittsburgh & Shawmut R.R., Brookville Title & Trust Co. Press Brookville Park Assn., Jefferson Co. Agrl. Assn.; mem. 65th to 73d Congresses (1917-35), 27th Pa. Dist. Republican. Home: Brookville, Pa.

STRONG, Solomon C.; supt. of schools at West Orange. Address: Board of Education, West Orange, N.J.

STRONG, Wendell Melville, actuary; b. Indianapolis, Ind., Feb. 6, 1871; s. Melville and Persis F. (Griffith) S.; B.A., Yale, 1893; M.A., Cornell U., 1894; fellow in mathematics, Yale, 1894-95, Ph.D., 1898; LL.B., New York U., 1903; m. Susan Hoyt Evans, 1909; 1 dau., Helen Griffith. Instr. in mathematics, Yale, 1895-1900; entered actuary's dept. Mut. Life Ins. Co. of New York, 1900, asst. actuary, 1904-11, now asso. actuary. Fellow Actuarial Soc. America, Casualty Actuarial Soc., Am. Inst. Actuaries; mem. Am. Math. Soc., London Math. Soc., Phi Beta Kappa, Sigma Xi, Phi Delta Phi, Elihu Club (Yale). Vice-pres. for U.S. and Can. of Internat. Congress Actuaries, 1930. Clubs: University, Bankers, Essex County Country. Author: (with Andrew W. Phillips) Trigonometry, 1899; Logarithmic and Trigonometric Tables, 1899. Editor Trans. of Actuarial Soc. America, 1909-16; (sec., 1916-22; v.p., 1922-24, and 1926-28; mem. council, 1928-30 and since 1932; pres., 1930-32). Contbr. to math. and actuarial publs. Home: Glen Ridge, N.J. Office: 34 Nassau St., New York, N.Y.

STRONG, William Walker, physicist; b. Good Hope, Cumberland Co., Pa., May 16, 1883; s. William Harrison and Maria (Garretson) S.; B.S. with honors, Wickinson Coll., 1905; Ph.D., Johns Hopkins, 1908; m. Mary Alberta Kirk, June 17, 1916; children—Walker Albert, Margaret Kirk. Fellow by courtesy, Johns Hopkins, 1908; research asst. Carnegie Instn. Washington, D.C., 1908-11, also asst. Johns Hopkins, 1909-11; fellow Mellon Inst., Pittsburgh, 1911-13, also prof. elec. theory, U. of Pittsburgh; pres. Scientific Instrument & Elec. Machine Co., 1912; instr. Carnegie Inst., Pittsburgh, 1914; physicist for Research Corpn., 1915, 19; consulting practice. Developed a fume mask for diphenylchlorarsin and other poisonous fumes during World War. Discovered effect of magnetic psychoanalysis, 1921. Sec. Soldiers and Sailors Memorial Park Commn. since 1936. Fellow A.A.A.S., American Physical Society; Tax Justice League of Pa. (v.p.). Democrat. Methodist. Mem. Phi Beta Kappa. Mason. Author: The Absorption Spectra of Solutions (Carnegie Instn.), 2 parts, 1910, 11; The New Science of Fundamental Physics, 1918; The New Philosophy of Modern Science, 1920; also vols. I, II, III, IV of collected papers from phys. and chem. jours.; Immortality in the Light of Modern Thought, 1923; Ourselves and Our Sciences, 1930. Home: Mechanicsburg, Pa.

STROTHER, Dan. J(ames) F(rench), lawyer; b. at Washington, Virginia, June 29, 1872; s. James French and Mary (Botts) S.; ed. pub. and pvt. schs.; studied law with father and short course in U. of Va.; m. Elizabeth Garnett Grant, Nov. 25, 1902. Admitted to Va. bar, 1893, and began practice at Washington, Va.; admitted to W.Va. bar, 1896; mem. Strother, Herndon & Berry, attys. for various pub. utility and coal corpns.; pres. Bankers Pocahontas Coal Co.; dir. and officer bank and various corpns. Mem. W. Va. State Bd. Law Examiners, W.Va. Constitutional Commn., 1930 (chmn.). Mem. W.Va. State Bar Assn. (pres. 1928-29), Am. Bar Assn. (ex-chmn. sect. mineral law; mem. com. on professional ethics and grievances 5 yrs.). Farmer. Republican. Home: Welch, W.Va.

STROUD, Clara, painter and illustrator; b. New Orleans, La.; d. George and Ida (Wells) S.; grad. East Orange (N.J.) High Sch., 1909; student Newark (N.J.) Art Sch., 1909-10, Pratt Inst., Brooklyn, N.Y., 1910-12; spl. work, Ringling Sch. of Art, Sarasota, Fla., 1932. Began as teacher, critic, writer, N.J., 1912; commercial artist since 1912; instr. East Orange (N.J.) High Sch., 1912-18, Pratt Inst., Brooklyn, N.Y., 1918-20, Newark Art Sch., 1918-21, Traphagen Sch., New York, 1919-20; window decorator since 1911; designer stage settings, magazine covers, illustrator articles since 1912. Mem. Nat. Assn. Women Painters and Sculptors, N.Y. Water Color Club, Sarasota Art Assn., Asbury Park Soc. of Fine Arts, Allied Artists of Venice, Fla. Awarded N.J. Gallery Prizes, 1936, 37, 38, 39. Specializes in water colors: work exhibited throughout U.S. and in Berlin; paintings in pvt. collections and purchased for advertising. Home: Pt. Pleasant, N.J.

STROUD, Morris Wistar, pres. American Gas Co.; b. Phila., Pa., May 14, 1860; s. William Daniel (M.D.) and Charlotte Wistar (Beesley) S.; ed. Friends Select Sch., Phila., William Penn Charter Sch.; m. Margaret Perkins Rutter, Jan. 19, 1887. Began in employ of Am. Gas Co., Phila., 1890, pres. since 1900; director American Gas & Electric Company, United Gas & Improvement Co., Huntington & Broad Top Mountain R.R. & Coal Co. Episcopalian. Home: 1011 Clinton St., Phila., and Villanova, Pa. Office: 1401 Arch St., Phila., Pa.

STROUD, William Daniel, physician; b. Villa Nova, Pa., Nov. 20, 1891; s. Morris Wistar and Margaret P. (Rutter) S.; B.S., U. of Pa., 1913; M.D., U. of Pa. Med. Sch., 1916; grad. study, U. Coll. Hosp., London, 1919-20, St. Andrew's Inst. Clin. Research, Scotland, 1920, L'Hopital de Pitie, Paris, France, 1920; m. Agnes H. Shober, Sept. 19, 1923; children—William Daniel, Jr., Samuel Shober, Agnes Hutchinson, Margaret Rutter and Charlotte Wistar (twins). Engaged in practice of medicine at Phila. since 1921; cardiologist to Pa. Hosp.; dir. Heart Sta., chief Adult and Children's Heart Clinics; phys. in charge, Childrens Heart Hosp.; cardiologist to Bryn Mawr Hosp., dir. Heart Sta., Bryn Mawr; phys. in chief cardiovascular service, Abington Memorial Hosp.; cardiologist, Montgomery and Riverview hosps., Norristown, Pa.; cons. cardiologist St. Christopher's Hosp., Phila., Norristown State Hosp., Norristown, Pa.; hon. surg. to First Troop Phila. City Cavalry; prof. cardiology, U. of Pa. Grad. Sch. of Medicine, cons. cardiologist to Grad. Hosp., dir. Heart Sta., chief of Adult and Children's Heart Clinics; asso. in medicine, U. of Pa. Med. Sch. Served as 1st lt. U.S.M.C., 1917-19. Mem. Bd. trustees Community Fund, Phila. and vicinity. Mem. bd. dirs. Phila. Health Council and Tuberculosis Com., Phila. Branch Shut-In Soc., Phila. Bur. for Handicapped, Phila. Regional Council for Physically Handicapped. Mem. Bd. Dirs. Haverford Sch., Agnes Irwin Sch. Fellow A.M.A., Phila. Coll. Phys.; mem. Assn. Am. Phys., Am. Clin. and Climatol. Assn., Interurban Clin. Club, Phila. Co. Med. Soc., Main Line Branch Montgomery Co. Med. Soc., John Morgan Soc. U. of Pa., Delta Psi, Phila. Heart Assn. (pres.), Am. Heart Assn. (pres.), Am. Coll. Phys. (treas., mem. bd. regents and exec. com.). Republican. Episcopalian. Clubs: Philadelphia, Racquet, Gulph Mills Golf, Mill Dam, Mask & Wig, St. Anthony (Philadelphia); St. Anthony (New York). Contbr. articles to med. jours. Editor of sect. on diseases of heart in med. year book since 1928. Home: County Line Rd., Villa Nova, Pa. Office: 1011 Clinton St., Philadelphia, Pa.

STROUP, Philip Trimble, metallurgist; b. Mishawaka, Ind., Feb. 17, 1904; s. Charles Clifton and Helen Ardetta (Trimble) S.; student grade and high sch., Bloomington, Ind., 1910-21; A.B., Indiana U., 1925, A.M., 1926; Ph.D., U. of Wis., Madison, 1929; m. Esther Lydia Simerman, Apr. 26, 1930; children—James Philip, Katrina Charline. Research chemist, duPont-Pathe Film Corpn., 1926-27; physical chemist Aluminum Co. of America, 1929-36, research metallurgist since 1936. Mem. Am. Chem. Soc., Am. Inst. Metall. Engrs., Am. Soc. Metals, Phi Beta Kappa, Sigma Xi, Alpha Chi Sigma, Sigma Phi Epsilon, Phi Lambda Upsilon, Sigma Gamma Epsilon. Republican. Methodist. Mason. Home: 452 Pershing Drive. Office: Aluminum Research Laboratories, New Kensington, Pa.

STROUP, Thomas Andrew, mining engr.; b. Lewistown, Md., Dec. 2, 1885; s. John Knox and Eliza (Weaver) S.; B.S., Univ. of Mo. Sch. of Mines, Columbia, Mo., 1912; student Armour Inst. of Tech., Chicago, Ill., 1912-13, McGill U., Montreal, Can., 1913; unmarried. Mech. engr. Jeffrey Mfg. Co., Columbus, O., 1912-15; mining engr. Tenn. Copper Co., Copper Hill, Tenn., 1915-16, Utah Copper Co., Salt Lake City, 1916-18; mining engr. and supt. of mines Utah Fuel Co., Salt Lake City, Utah, 1918-25; cons. engr. Consol. Coal Co., Fairmont, W.Va., 1925-26; chief engr. West Va. Coal & Coke Co., Omar, W. Va., since 1926. Mem. Am. Inst. Mining Engrs., Rocky Mountain Coal Mining Inst., W.Va. Coal Mining Inst. Democrat. Unitarian. Author numerous articles on tech. subjects. Address: Omar, W.Va.

STRUB, Henry Michael, clergyman; b. Chicago, Ill., Jan. 22, 1886; s. George John and Margareth (Mehl) S.; ed. Elmhurst Coll. (Ill.), 1901-05, Eden Theol. Sem., St. Louis, Mo., 1905-08, Western Sem., Pittsburgh, Pa., 1916; A.B., Pittsburgh U., 1918; m. Henrietta Marie Weinert, June 6, 1912; children—Henry Michael, Clara Eloise, Paul Theo. Weinert, Thelma Wilhelmina Marie, Carl George. Ordained to ministry Evang. Synod of North America (now called Evang. and Reformed Ch.), 1908; pastor Marion, Tex., 1908-11, Clarington, O., 1911-12, Spring Garden, N.S. Pittsburgh, Pa., 1912-19, Erie, Pa., 1919-24; pastor Williamsport, Pa., since May 1924; denomination v.p. Atlantic Dist., Evang. Synod of N.A.; rep. Atlantic Dist. on Gen. Council; v.p. Central Pa. Synod of Evang. and Reformed Ch. since 1939. Mem. Evang. and Reformed Ch. Mason. Club: Lions. Home: 202 E. Third St., Williamsport, Pa.

STRUBE, Gustav, conductor, composer; b. Ballenstedt, Germany, Mar. 3, 1867; s. Friedrich and Henriette (Meergarten) S.; ed. Leipzig Conservatory; studied violin with Brodsky, composition with Jadassohn and Reinicke and piano with Reckendorf; m. Martha Grosse, Jan. 29, 1894; children—Claire (Mrs. Henry Schradieck), Elfriede (Mrs. Frederick Lee). Came to U.S., 1890, naturalized, 1896. First violin, Boston Symphony Orchestra, 1890-1912, also conductor of "Pops" 10 yrs.; mem. faculty Peabody Conservatory, Baltimore, Md., since 1913; organizer and condr. Baltimore Symphony Orchestra, 1915-30. Composer: 3 symphonies; 4 overtures, 3 violin concertos; Poeme Antique, for violin and orchestra; 1 'cello concerto; 2 symphonic poems for viola and orchestra; Hymn to Eros, for male chorus and orchestra; American Rhapsody, for orchestra; Symphonic Sketch Arlequinade; Symphonic Fantasie; The Captive (grand opera); 4 preludes for orchestra; Americana for orchestra; Sonata, for violin and piano; Sonata, for viola and piano; Sonata, for 'cello and piano; string quintet (2 violas); quintet for woodwind and horn; trio for piano, violin and 'cello; 2 string quartettes; trio for clarinet, horn and piano; also many smaller pieces for violin and piano. Home: 2845 N. Calvert St. Address: Peabody Conservatory, Baltimore, Md.

STRUCK, F(erdinand) Theodore, industrial educator; b. Hamburg, Germany, Mar. 18, 1886; s. Ludwig Christian Nicholous and Bertha (Runge) S.; brought by parents to U.S., 1893; grad. high sch., Hood River, Ore., 1907; B.S., in C.E., U. of Ore., 1911; A.M., Teachers Coll. (Columbia), 1914; Ph.D., Columbia, 1920; m. Alice Clark, Nov. 25, 1915; children—Robert Theodore, John Warren, Barbara Alice. Journeyman trade experience in carpentry and drafting. Teacher shop work and drawing, high sch., Tacoma, 1911-13; dir. West Orange (N.J.) Industrial Sch., 1914-15; head teacher, Essex Co. (N.J.) Vocational Sch., 1915-18; asso. prof., later prof. agrl. edn., Pa. State Coll., 1918-20; asst. dir., later dir. vocational bur., State Dept. Pub. Instrn., Pa., 1920-26; prof. industrial edn. and head of dept., Pa. State Coll., since 1926; instr. summer sessions, Del. State Coll., N.C. State Coll., Colo. State Coll., Pa. State Coll., Ia. State Coll. Trustee Nat. Assn. of Industrial Teacher-Trainers, 1938-39. Mem. Nat. Edn. Assn., American Vocational Assn., American Association Univ. Profs., Nat. Soc. Coll. Teachers of Edn., Pa. State Education Association, Pennsylvania Vocational Education Association (sec.-treas. since 1938), Phi Delta Kappa, Kappa Phi Kappa, Kappa Delta Pi, Iota Lambda Sigma (pres. Grand Chapter 1931; nat. advisory council 1931—). Republican. Methodist. Mason. Club: Pa. School Men's. Author: Construction and Repair Work for the Farm, 1923; Methods in Industrial Education, 1929; Foundations of Industrial Education, 1930; Creative Teaching, 1938; also writer of tech. reports for Pa. State Coll. and Pa. State Dept. Pub. Instrn. Contbr. to ednl. jours. Home: 527 W. Fairmount Av., State College, Pa.

STRUMIA, Max Maurice, pathologist; b. Turin, Italy, Sept. 23, 1896; s. Giovenale and Teresa (Masera) S.; student Royal U. of Turin (Italy) Sch. of Medicine; post grad. work, U. of Pa. Sch. of Medicine; m. Florence Ferretti, Oct. 13, 1924; children—Mary Arline, Paul Victor. Asst., Univ. Clinic, Turin, Italy, 1920-21; instr. in pathology, U. of Pa. Sch. of Medicine since 1923, asst. in dermatol. research lab., 1923-24, asst. for research works, Henry Phipps Inst., 1929; pathologist, Misericordia Hosp., 1923-32; pathologist and dir. of clin. lab., Bryn Mawr (Pa.) Hosp., since 1932. Engaged in first work on pneumococcus typing done in Europe with serum furnished by Rockefeller Inst., 1919-20; results pub. in Italian med. papers. Home: 857 Bryn Mawr Av., Penn Valley, Bryn Mawr, Pa. Office: Bryn Mawr Hosp., Bryn Mawr, Pa.

STRUNK, William, univ. prof.; b. Cincinnati, O., July 1, 1869; s. William and Ella (Garretson) S.; A.B., U. of Cincinnati, 1890; Ph.D., Cornell U., 1896; studied U. of Paris, 1898-99; m. Olivia Emilie Locke, June 30, 1900; children—William Oliver, Edwin Hart, Catherine (Mrs. Frank G. Amatruda). Instructor in mathematics, Rose Polytechnic Institute, Terre Haute, Ind., 1890-91; instr. in English, Cornell U., 1891-98, fellow, 1898-99, asst. prof. English, 1899-1909, prof. 1909-37, now emeritus. Mem. Modern Lang. Assn., America, Phi Beta Kappa. Democrat. Editor: Macaulay's and Carlyle's Essays on Boswell's Johnson, 1895; Dryden's Essays on the Drama, 1898; Cooper's Last of the Mohicans, 1900; Cynewulf's Juliana, 1904; Dryden's All for Love, and The Spanish Friar, 1911; Romeo and Juliet, 1911; Julius Caesar, 1915. Joint Editor: Studies in Language and Literature, in Honor of James Morgan Hart. Author: The Elements of Style, 1918; English Metres, 1923. Officier d'Académie, France. Actg. prof. English, summer session, Ohio State U., 1920; lit. consultant for motion picture Romeo and Juliet, 1935. Home: 35 Battle Road, Princeton, N.J.

STRYKER, Goss Livingston, farming; b. Auburn, N.Y., Sept. 22, 1877; s. Melancthon Woolsey and Elizabeth (Goss) S.; A.B., Hamilton Coll., Clinton, N.Y., 1901, A.M., same, 1903; m. Harriet Daniels, Jan. 21, 1911. Served as 2d and 1st lt. in 6th, 4th, 13th Cav., U.S.A., 1901-12; resigned and engaged in farming, Derby, N.Y., 1912-17; moved to Md. and engaged in farming at Timonium since 1920; vice-pres. Towson Nat. Bank; pres. Md. State Fair, Inc. Served as maj. Remount Service, U.S.A., 1917-19. Chmn. License Commn. for Baltimore Co., 1933-38. Mem. Sigma Phi. Democrat. Clubs: Maryland (Baltimore); Army and Navy (Washington). Home: Timonium, Md.

STRYKER, Josiah, lawyer; b. Plainville, N.J., Dec. 31, 1880; s. Abram VanDeripe and Mary Gertrude (Davison) S.; m. Hazel E. Benbrook, Aug. 11, 1908; 1 dau., Dorothy Benbrook. Admitted to N.J. bar as atty., 1903, counselor, 1906; legal asst. to atty. gen. of N.J., 1904-17, second asst. atty. gen. of N.J., 1917-18; mem. law firm Lindabury, Depue & Faulks since Apr. 1918, becoming sr. partner, Nov. 1936; dir. Prudential Ins. Co. of America. Mem. Am. Bar Assn., N.J. State Bar Assn. (pres. June 1934-June 1935), Essex Co. Bar Assn. Republican. Episcopalian. Clubs: Essex (Newark); Baltusrol Golf (Springfield); Rock Spring (West Orange). Home: 280 Hartford Road, South Orange, N.J. Office: 744 Broad St., Newark, N.J.

STUART, Donald Clive, author, playwright; b. Battle Creek, Mich., Apr. 10, 1881; s. Reed and Helen (Soule) S.; A.B., U. of Mich., 1903, A.M., 1904; studied U. of Paris, 1905-06; Ph. D., Columbia, 1910; m. Hertha von Baur, June 12, 1907; children—Donald Clive, Lorna. Instr. in Romance langs. and lit., 1906-10, asst. prof., 1910-19, professor of dramatic art since 1919, Princeton U. Mem. Modern Lang. Assn. America, Phi Beta Kappa, Psi Upsilon. Clubs: Princeton (New York), Nassau (Princeton). Author: Stage Decoration in France in the Middle Ages, 1910; (plays) Sunrise, 1906; A Double Deceiver (prod. at Majestic Theatre, Grand Rapids, 1912); The Development of Dramatic Art, 1929. Contbr. articles on drama. Home: The Western Way, Princeton, N.J.

STUART, Duane Reed, univ. prof.; b. Oneida, Ill., Sept. 27, 1873; s. Reed and Helen (Soule) S.; A.B., U. of Mich., 1896, Ph.D., 1901; Am. Sch. Archæology, Athens, 1898-99; U. of Munich; m. Emilie Eugenie Meddaugh, June 25, 1898; children—Emilie Maynard (Mrs. Arthur Bliss Perry), Philip Meddaugh (dec.), Duane Reed, Douglas Edmunds, Alison Edmunds. Prof. Latin, Mich. State Normal Coll., 1899-1900; instr. in Latin, 1900-01, instr. in Greek, 1902-04, asst. prof., 1905, U. of Mich.; preceptor in classics, 1905-07, prof., 1907—, Princeton; Sather prof. classical lit., U. of Calif., 1924-25; visiting lecturer, Bryn Mawr Coll., 1927-28; visiting prof., Yale, 1931; mem. Am. Philol. Assn., A.I.A., Psi Upsilon, Phi Beta Kappa. Clubs: Century (New York); Nassau (Princeton). Author: Epochs of Greek and Roman Biography, 1928. Editor: The Agricola of Tacitus, 1909; The Germania of Tacitus, 1916. Joint Collaborator: Greek Inscriptions of Southern Syria, 1911-15. Home: Princeton, N.J.

STUART, Harry Gould, supervising prin.; b. Catasauqua, Pa., Mar. 14, 1890; s. James and Lillie R. (Wonderly) S.; grad. Allentown, Pa., pub. schs., 1903, Allentown Prep. Sch., 1907; B.S., Muhlenberg Coll., 1911; M.A., Teachers' Coll., Columbia U., 1933; m. Edna M. Bermont, June 26, 1914; children—Robert B., Dorothy E. Teacher of science Johnstown (Pa.) High Sch., 1911-12, Oakmont (Pa.) High Sch., 1912-14, Paterson (N.J.) High Sch., 1914-18; prin. Ossining (N.Y.) High Sch., 1918-22; prin. Bernards High Sch., Bernardsville, N.J., 1923-30, supervising prin. since 1930. Chmn. George Washington Bicentennial, 1932. Mem. Am. Assn. Sch. Administrs., N.E.A., N.J. Edn. Assn. Republican. Methodist. Clubs: Rotary of Bernardsville (pres. 1939-40); New Jersey Schoolmasters (Newark). Home: 61 Old Army Road, Bernardsville, N.J.

STUART, Joseph Clyde, clergyman; b. Wake Co., N.C., Oct. 4, 1889; s. Wm. Franklin and Cora Nellie (Betts) S.; A.B., Elon Coll., N.C., 1912; ed. U. of N.C., 1914, Princeton Theol. Sem., 1917-20, Princeton U., 1920; m. Alice Housenick, June 25, 1929; children—Mary Josephine, Stephen Lee. Employed as prin. high schs., 1912-17; ordained to ministry Presbyn. Ch., 1920; pastor, Berwick, Pa., 1920-30; pastor First Presbyn. Ch., Blairsville, Pa., since 1930. Republican. Presbyn. Mason (32°). Home: Blairsville, Pa.

STUART, Kenneth James, artist; b. Milwaukee, Wis., Sept. 21, 1905; s. William Pope and Jenny (Ballinger) S.; ed. pub. sch. and high sch., Milwaukee, Wis., 1919-23, Pa. Acad. Fine Arts, Phila., Pa., 1923-24, under Arthur B. Carles, 1924-25, Academie Colarassi, Paris, France, 1929-30; m. Katharine Moos, June 12, 1937. Has followed profession as artist at Phila. since 1931; started free lance art work, 1932, illustrations for advertisements for nat. advertisers in well-known mags. of wide circulation; illustrations for leading advertising agencies; also illustrator of stories and articles for Ladies Home Journal, Farm Journal, and other mags.; head of illustration dept. of Moore Inst. of Sci., Art & Industry, Phila., Pa. Home: 910 Clinton St. Studio: 700 S. Washington Sq., Philadelphia, Pa.

STUART, Milton Caleb, prof. of mech. engring.; b. Caroline Co., Md., Mar. 31, 1886; s. William J. and Sarah Dorcas (Manley) S.; B.S. in mech. engring., U. of Pa., 1909, M.E., 1926; m. Ethel Everna Hinchman, May 2, 1914. Instr. Rensselaer Poly. Inst., 1909-12; steam engr. Cambria Steel Co., 1912-15; mech. engr. U.S. Naval Engring. Expt. Station, Annapolis, 1915-20; prof. of mech. engring., U.S. Postgrad. Sch., Annapolis, 1920-26; prof. of mech. engring., Lehigh U., Bethlehem, Pa., since 1926. Registered Professional Engr., Pa. Mem. Am. Soc. Mech. Engrs. (past chmn. Baltimore Sect. and Anthracite-Lehigh Valley Sect., mem. main com. on power test codes, chmn. fan test com.); mem. Soc. for Promotion Engring. Edn., Am. Soc. Heating and Ventilating Engrs., Franklin Inst., Newcomen Soc., Sigma Xi, Tau Beta Pi. Republican. Methodist. Club: Engineers (Phila.). Author: Engineering Thermodynamics (with P. J. Kiefer), 1929. Contbr. section on "Thermodynamics" to Handbook of Engineering Fundamentals; also articles to professional jours. Home: 505 Norway Place, Bethlehem, Pa.

STUART, Robert Ladue, lawyer; b. Hokendauqua, Lehigh Co., Pa., Aug. 16, 1879; s. James and Lillie R. (Wonderly) S.; grad. high sch. and business coll.; m. Clara S. Massey, May 24, 1901; 1 dau., Jean Massey. Began as stenographer Lehigh Co., 1896; court stenographer, 1899-1903; admitted to Lehigh Co. bar, 1903, later to bars of State Appellate Courts and U.S. Courts; in gen. practice law since 1903; city solicitor, Allentown, 1921-36; referee in bankruptcy, U.S. Dept. of Justice, since 1939. Mem. Am. Rose Soc. Republican. Elk. Club: John Hay Republican. Home: 34 S. 14th St. Office: 315 Commonwealth Bldg., Allentown, Pa.

STUBBLEFIELD, Edward, clergyman; b. near Lovelaceville, Ky., May 2, 1872; s. David and Julia (Peck) S.; A.B., Clinton Coll., 1895; grad. Southern Bapt. Theol. Sem., 1898; post-grad. work U. of Chicago, 1901-03; m. Mattie B. Knott, Nov. 1, 1904. Ordained Bapt. ministry, 1899; pastor Flemingsburg, Ky., 1898-1901, Wetzel Memorial Ch., Kirkwood, Mo., 1901-04, 1st Ch., Oxford, Miss., 1904-08, 1st Ch., Galveston, Tex., 1908-18, Clarksville, Tenn., 1918-21, Covington, 1921-24, Durham, N.C., 1924-27, Princeton, W.Va., since 1927. Home: 1113 S. 9th St., Princeton, W.Va.

STUBBS, Evan Lee, prof. vet. pathology; b. Oxford, Pa., Jan. 3, 1890; s. Howard Lee and Lizzie (Reisler) S.; V.M.D., U. of Pa., 1911; m. Mary L. Carothers, July 6, 1932; 1 dau., Ruth Ann. Engaged in pvt. practice as veterinarian, 1911-13; vet. Pa. Bur. of Animal Industry, 1913-28; instr. poultry diseases, U. of Pa., since 1925; poultry disease specialist, 1923-28; dir. Div. of Labs., Pa. Bur. of Animal Industry, 1926-28; asst. prof. vet. pathology, U. of Pa., 1927-30, prof. vet. pathology since 1930. Mem. Am. Vet. Med. Assn., Internat. Vet. Congress, U.S. Livestock San. Assn., Am. Assn. Pathologists & Bacteriologists, Internat. Assn. Med. Museums, Am. Poultry Sci. Assn., Soc. Am. Bacteriologists, Pa. State Vet. Med. Assn., Keystone Vet. Soc., Phila. Pathol. Soc., Sigma Xi, Phi Zeta. Republican. Mem. Religious Soc. Friends. Home: 266 Cooper Av., Lansdowne, Pa. Office: 39th St. & Woodland Av., Philadelphia, Pa.

STUBBS, Ralph Sprengle, pres. Franklin Sugar Refining Co.; b. Ashland, O., Feb. 3, 1882; s. Joseph Edward and Ella A. (Sprengle) S.; B.S., U. of Nev., 1901; m. Leonora H. Keck, Dec. 11, 1912. Clk. in San Francisco, Chicago and San Jose, 1901-04; employed by Southern Pacific R.R., Tucson, Ariz., and N.Y. City, 1905-15; traffic mgr. Am. Sugar Refining Co., New York, 1915, gen. mgr., 1916-19, v.p. since 1919; pres. Franklin Sugar Refining Co. since 1929, now also dir.; dir. Am. Sugar Refining Co. and subsidiaries, Motor Haulage Co. Dir. New York Post-Grad. Hosp. Republican. Episcopalian. Clubs: University, Traffic of New York, Hudson River Country. Home: 1185 Park Av., New York, N.Y. Office: Public Ledger Bldg., Philadelphia, Pa.

STUCK, Harry C., pres. Millmont Box Co.; b. Sunbury, Pa., 1891; s. Henry P. and Laura P. (Stine) S.; student high sch.; m. Merna A. Chapman, 1924; 1 dau., Ruth C. Sec. Millmont (Pa.) Box Co., Inc., 1926-30, sec.-treas. and gen. mgr., 1930-37, pres. and treas. since 1937; sec. and dir. Kolltex Knitting Mills, Inc.; dir. Mifflinburg Bank & Trust Co. Mason (Consistory). Home: 257 Green St., Mifflinburg, Pa. Office: Millmont Box Co., Inc., Millmont, Pa.

STUCKERT, Howard Morris, clergyman, coll. prof.; b. Phila., Pa., Feb. 21, 1884; s. J. Franklin and Mary Seeler (Fagin) S.; A.B., U. of Pa., 1907; A.M., U. of Pa. Grad. Sch., 1913, Ph.D., 1920; student Phila. Divinity Sch., 1907-10. Ordained to ministry P.E. Ch.; rector, The House of Prayer, Phila., Pa., since 1931; prof. N.T. criticism and exegesis, Phila. Divinity Sch., since 1938; head examining chaplain to Bishop of Pa. since 1933. Republican. Episcopalian. Home: Lime Kiln Pike at Church Lane, Philadelphia, Pa.

STUHR, William S., lawyer, industrialist; b. Hoboken, N.J., Nov. 23, 1894; s. William S. and Marietta Lindsay (Miller) S.; B.A., New York U., 1914, LL.B., J.D., 1917; m. Florence E. Maddocks, Jan. 18, 1919 (died May 17, 1920); 1 son, William S.; m. 2d, M. Marie Canning, Aug. 10, 1926; children—Thomas M., Bernard C., George M. Admitted to N.J. bar, 1917; mem. law firm Stuhr & Vogt since 1919; judge Weehawken Recorder's Court, 1922; corpn. counsel, Weehawken, 1923-26; 1st v.p. United Paperboard Co., 1932-38, pres. since 1938; pres. and dir. Benton & Fairfield Ry., Upco Corpn.; elected pres. and dir. Burco, Inc., Mar. 4, 1939 (appointed by Chancery Ct.); treas. and dir. Leedsmere Corpn.; dir. Federal Trust Co. of Newark, Bankers Nat. Life Ins. Co. Mem. Am. Bar Assn., N.J. State Bar Assn., Hudson Co. Bar Assn., Kappa Sigma, Theta Nu Epsilon; dir. Nat. Paperboard Assn. Independent Democrat. Mem. Dutch Reformed Ch. Mason, Elk, Moose. Clubs: Carteret (Jersey City); Essex (Newark). Home: 1 Hamilton Av., Weehawken, N.J. Office: 68 Hudson St., Hoboken, N.J.

STULL, Arthur Maurer, supt. county schs.; b. Johnstown, Pa., June 13, 1893; s. Benjamin Franklin and Mary Jane (Maurer) S.; ed. Indiana State Normal Sch., 1911-12, U. of Mich., 1914-15; B.S., U. of Pittsburgh, 1927, A.M., same, 1929, Ed.D., same, 1934; m. Ruth Boyce Morris, Jan. 8, 1918; children—William Morris, Arthur Maurer, Jr. Teacher elementary sch., Johnstown, Pa., 1912-14, prin. elementary sch., 1914-17, teacher, high sch., 1917-18; prin. high sch., Monaca, Pa., 1918-19; supervising prin., South Fork, Pa., 1919-26, Dale Borough, Johnstown, Pa., 1926-36; supt. Cambria Co. Pub. Schs., Ebensburg, Pa., since 1936. Mem. N.E.A., Am. Assn. Sch. Adminstrs., Pa. State Edn. Assn., Phi Delta Kappa. Mem. United Brethren Ch. Mason. Club: Rotary of Johntown. Home: 30 Akers St., Johnstown, Pa. Office: Court House, Ebensburg, Pa.

STULL, Eugene Stroud, Jr., mech. engring.; b. Wyncote, Pa., Nov. 20, 1893; s. Eugene Stroud and Elizabeth Crozier (Lewis) S.; B.S., Pa. State Coll., 1917; m. Hazel Campbell Ahrens, July 28, 1919; children—Eugene Stroud 3d, Donald Campbell (dec.), Lewis Rittenhouse (dec.). Employed as asst. then chief engr. R. H. Comey Co., Brooklyn, N.Y., 1919-28; project engr. Du Pont Viscaloid Co., Arlington, N.J., 1928-29; branch engr., Hoffman Beverage Co., Newark, N.J., 1929-35; research engr., Colgate-Palmolive-Peet Co., Jersey City, N.J., since 1935; pres. and treas., A. E. Force & Co., dept. store, Plainfield, N.J., since 1938. Served as 2d lt. F.A., U.S.A., 1917-19, with A.E.F. Hon. mem. First Troop Phila. City Cavalry. Mem. Bur. Issues Assn. Nat., N.Y. Precancel Club, North Jersey Precancel Club of Newark, Phi Kappa Sigma. Republican. Christian Scientist. Club: Y.M.C.A. (Rutherford). Home: 273 Washington Av., Rutherford. Office: 105 Hudson St., Jersey City, N.J.

STULL, Howard William, ex-congressman; b. near Johnstown, Pa., April 11, 1876; s. Benjamin Franklin and Mary Jane (Maurer) S.; LL.B., George Washington U., 1908; m. Rebecca Jane McGahan, Sept. 3, 1901; children—Mary Margaret (Mrs. Boyer B. Allen), Franklin Howard (dec.), Harold Webster, Sarah Frances (dec.). Clerk in father's store, 1887, with Westinghouse Electric & Mfg. Co. and Keystone Telephone Co., Pittsburgh, 1897; clk. Johnstown (Pa.) Postoffice, 1897-99; asst. postmaster Johnstown (Pa.) Postoffice, 1899-1904; mem. auditor's office U.S. Treasury Dept., 1904-08; proof clk. U.S. Land Office, Spokane, Wash., Dec. 1908-July 1909; admitted to Wash. bar, 1909, D.C. bar, 1908, Pa. bar, 1919; in practice Colville, Wash., 1910-17, Johnstown, Pa., since 1919. Pros. atty. Stevens Co., Wash., 1911-13 and 1915-16; mem. 72d Congress (1932-33), 20th Pa. Dist.; sr. council George Washington Law Sch. Mem. Nat. Council Boy Scouts of America. Mem. Pa. State and Cambria County bar assns., Pa. Soc. of N.Y., Phi Alpha Delta. Republican. Presbyterian. Mason (32°, K.T., Shriner). Clubs: Kiwanis, Rod and Gun. Home: 728 Bedford St. Office: First Nat. Bank Bldg., Johnstown, Pa.

STULL, Philip Barton, mfg. exec.; b. Chicago, Ill., Dec. 13, 1901; s. John Walter and Dorothy Evelyn (Case) S.; student Philips Acad., Andover, Mass., 1916-18, U. of Chicago, 1918-19, U. of Pa., 1919-20; m. Florence Wilson Roper, June 6, 1923; children—Dorothy Wilson, Elizabeth Walmsley, Philip Barton. Asst. purchasing agt., Stamsocott Co., Hopewell, Va., 1920-23, sales mgr., 1923; v.p. Va. Cellulose Co., Hopewell, Va., 1923-25, pres., 1925-28; gen. mgr. Va. Cellulose Div., Hercules Powder Co., 1928-37, gen. mgr. Paper Makers Chem. Div., Wilmington, Del., since 1937. Republican. Episcopalian. Clubs: Wilmington, Wilmington Country, The Turf (Wilmington, Del.). Home: Fox Chase. Office: Delaware Trust Bldg., Wilmington, Del.

STULTZ, D. E.; v.p. Potomac Edison Co. Address: Frederick, Md.

STUMP, J. Henry, mayor; b. Reading, Pa., June 4, 1880; s. John F. and Tille (Wurst) S.; ed. Reading pub. schs.; m. Laura Mae Widmyer, Nov. 29, 1911. Pres. Federal Trades Council, 1916-27; business mgr. Reading Labor Advocate, 1918-27, pres. Peoples Printing Co., 1918-38; mgr. shoe store, 1932-36. Mayor City of Reading, 1928-31, and since 1936. Socialist. Home: 820 Douglass St. Office: City Hall, 8th and Washington Sts., Reading, Pa.

STURGEON, William E(lias), prof. chemistry; b. Alamo, Tenn., Oct. 16, 1880; s. John C. and Mollie (Stephens) S.; A.B., Tex. Christian U., 1909; Ph.D., U. of Chicago, 1929; m. Mary Anne Stricker, Sept. 17, 1925; children—Mary Elizabeth, Julia Carol, Ann Runie. Engaged in teaching pub. schs. and supt. schs., various cities in Tex., 1900-14; teacher mathematics and sci., high sch., Waco, Tex., 1914-25; asst. prof. chemistry, U. of Notre Dame, 1927-30; prof. chemistry and head of dept., Beaver Coll., Jenkintown, Pa., since 1930. Fellow A.A.A.S. Mem. Am. Chem. Soc., Nat. Geographic Soc., Sigma Xi. Republican. Mem. Christian Ch. Mason (K.T., 32°, Shriner). Home: 316 Montier Rd., Glenside, Pa.

STURGES, Gertrude Cook; registrar and asst. to dean, Women's Coll., U. of Del. Address: U. of Delaware, Newark, Del.

STURGES, Lillian, illustrator; b. Wilkes-Barre, Pa.; d. Frank Caleb and Frances (Lazarus) S.; ed. Sch. of Industrial Art and Acad. of Fine Arts, Philadelphia; A.B., Carnegie Inst. Tech., Dept. of Fine Arts, 19—; unmarried. Author and illustrator: The Runaway Toys; Child's Own Book; also health booklets used in all schs. of Allegheny County. Illustrator: Bible A.B.C. Book; Eugene Field's poems, Treasury of Myths; new editions of Little Black Sambo, Aladdin, Fairy Tale Giants, Fairy Tale Princes, Fairy Tale Princesses; also first book of stories for children in Arabic and picture-text book in Arabic used in Egyptian Schs. Contbr. School Arts Mag., The Instructor, The Grade Teacher. Paintings exhibited every year in Carnegie Art Gallery and others. Art teacher and supervisor. Republican. Presbyterian. Mem. N.E.A., Pa. State Edn. Assn., Associated Artists of Pittsburgh. Clubs: Authors, Scribblers (Pittsburgh). Home: 2956 Belrose Av., Pittsburgh, Pa.

STURGIS, Margaret Castex, gynecologist; b. Goldsboro, N.C., Feb. 22, 1885; d. Francis L. and Van (Jenkins) Castex; student Woman's Coll. of U. of N.C., 1901-04; M.D., Woman's Med. Coll., of Pa., 1915; grad. study Vienna, 1925; m. Henry S. Jones, 1907 (died 1913); m. 2d, Dr. Samuel B. Sturgis, July 6, 1916. Interne New York Infirmary, 1915-16; surgical div. resident New York Hosp., 1918-19; clin. prof. gynecology, Woman's Med. Coll., 1927; asso. gynecologist, Hosp. of Woman's Med. Coll.; chief in gynecology, Woman's Hosp., Phila., 1930; asst. obstetrician and gynecologist, Phila. Gen. Hosp. Pres. of staff Woman's Hosp., Phila., 1938-39. Fellow Am. Coll. Surgeons; mem. Am. Bd. of Obstetrics and Gynecology; mem. Phila. Coll. of Physicians, A.M.A., Pa. Med. Soc., Obstet. Soc. of Phila., Am. Med. Women's Assn., Alumnae Assn. Woman's Med. Coll. of Pa. (pres. 1928), D.A.R., United Daughters of Confederacy, Alpha Epsilon Iota, Alpha Omega Alpha. Club: Women's University (Phila.). Home: 34 W. Montgomery Av., Ardmore, Pa. Office: 1930 Chestnut St., Philadelphia, Pa.

STURGIS, Russell Davis, prof. chemistry; b. Wilmington, Del., July 9, 1897; s. Lee D. and Mary (Camperson) S.; B.S., U. of Del., 1919; ed. Mass. State Coll., 1919-20; M.S., U. of Pa., 1921, Ph.D., same, 1924; m. Olive Strickland, Nov. 27, 1923; 1 dau., Marylee C. Engaged as instr. chemistry, Franklin and Marshall Coll., 1920; asso. with Ursinus Coll., Collegeville, Pa., since 1925, prof. chemistry since 1926. Served in O.T.C., Camp Lee, Va., 1918. Sec. and sch. dir. Collegeville Schs. Mem. Am. Chem. Soc. Republican. Baptist. Home: 26 Sixth Av., Collegeville, Pa.

STURM, Rolland George, research engr. physicist; b. Riverview, Cook Co., Ill., Mar. 24, 1899; s. Michael and Louisa (Rudolph) S.; B.S., U. of Neb., 1924, C.E., 1938; M.S., U. of Ill., 1926, Ph.D., 1936; m. Mary Jorden, June 16, 1926; children—Margaret Jean, Martha Lucille, Arthur Gordon. Began as laborer and sub contractor, 1923; served half time in bridge office, Neb. State Dept. Pub. Works, while studying at U. of Neb., 1924; jr. structural engr. Dist. No. 5, U.S. Bur. Pub. Roads, 1924-25 and summer 1926; engaged in special research for Am. Soc. Civil Engrs. at U. of Ill., 1925-26; instr. theoretical and applied mechanics, U.

STURTEVANT of Ill., 1926-29; bridge designer Ill. State Div. of Highways, 1927; designer sewer system and sewage disposal plant, Collinsville, Ill., 1928; research structural engr. Aluminum Co. of America, 1929-31; research engr. physicist Aluminum Research Labs. since 1931; lecturer, U. of Pittsburgh since 1936; organized night school for Aluminum Co. of America Engineers, 1936. Dir. Camp Corbly; chmn. advisory bd. Salvation Army, New Kensington; supt. Valley Heights Mission; mem. exec. com. New Kensington Community Fund; hon. adult counselor Allegheny-Kiski Group of Baptist Young People. Mem. A.A.A.S., Am. Math. Assn., Soc. of Rheology; asso. mem. Am. Soc. C.E. Republican. Baptist. Rotary Internat. of New Kensington. Writer numerous tech. articles. Home: 460 Riverview Drive. Office: Aluminum Research Laboratories, Aluminum Co. of America, New Kensington, Pa.

STURTEVANT, Charles Northmore, physician; b. Ishpeming, Mich., Aug. 29, 1884; s. Harry Brown and Mary E. (Northmore) S.; M.D., U. of Pa. Med. Sch., 1907; m. Kathreen Irvine, June 15, 1910 (dec.); children—Mary Elizabeth (Mrs. Gilbert Lippincott Bean), Charles N., Jr., Peter Mann; m. 2d, Martha Irvine, Dec. 8, 1917. Interne St. Christopher's Hosp., and University Hosp., 1907-09; engaged in gen. practice of medicine in Phila., Pa., since 1909, specializing in pediatrics since 1915; chief dept. pediatrics Frankford Hosp. Pres. Northeast Boys Club, Phila., Pa. Fellow Am. Acad. of Pediatrics. Mem. Alpha Mu Pi Omega, Northeast Medical Club (past pres.). Republican. Episcopalian (vestryman). Club: Philobiblon. Home: 4321 Frankford Av., Philadelphia, Pa.

STURTEVANT, Percy Granville, v.p. Erie Co. Electric Co.; b. Detroit Lakes, Minn., Dec. 20, 1885; s. Charles Granville and Elizabeth Augusta (Hanson) S.; E.E., U. of Minn., 1908; m. Irene I. Hauer, Sept. 25, 1918; children—Jean Margaret, Roger Granville. Foreman Gen. Electric Co., Harrison (N.J.) Lamp Works, 1909-10; electrician Detroit Lakes (Minn.) Municipal Light Plant, 1910-11; meter expert Gen. Electric Co., West Lynn Works, 9 mos., 1911; with Erie Co. Electric Co. since 1911, becoming v.p., 1922, and asst. sec., 1936. Mem. Pa. Soc. Mayflower Descendants. Republican. Lutheran. Mason. Clubs: Erie, Kahkwa, Maennerchor. Home: 4146 Beech Av. Office: 12th and French St., Erie, Pa.

STUTESMAN, John Hale; prof. of military science and tactics, Rutgers U.; lt. col. U.S. Army. Address: New Brunswick, N.J.

STUTLER, Boyd Blynn, editor; b. Coxs Mills, W.Va., July 10, 1889; s. Daniel Elias and Emily Bird (Heckert) S.; ed. pub. schs. of Gilmer and Calhoun counties, W.Va.; m. Catheolene May Huffman, Nov. 26, 1911; children—William Morris, Warren Harding. Printer W.Va. newspapers, 1900-07; editor Grantsville News, 1907-17, Logan (W.Va.) Banner and State Gazette (Point Pleasant), 1919; chief W.Va. Div. of Pub. Printing, and asst. editor and contbr. W. Va. Handbook and Manual, 1920-28; editor Service Mag., Charleston, W.Va., 1925-26, W. Va. Legionnaire, 1928-29, mng. editor W.Va. Review, 1929-32; contbg. editor Service Mag., Pittsburgh, 1926-39; mng. editor Am. Legion Mag., since 1936. Mayor Grantsville, 1911-12; pres. Bd. Edn., Grantsville, 1915-16. Enlisted as private field arty., U.S.A., 1917; with A.E.F., 1918-19; hon. disch. as regtl. personnel sergeant, 1919; 2d lt. inf., O.R.C., 1924-34, commd. col. (hon.) Ky., 1935, N.M., 1936. Mem. Am. Legion, post comdr., 1927-28, adjt. Dept. of W.Va., 1928-29, asst. nat. publicity dir. and field sec. to nat. comdr., 1932-36; mem. 80th Div. Vets. Assn., assisted in organization in France, 1919, mem. Nat. Exec. Council, 1921-23, resident sec., 1925-26; nat. vice comdr., 1926-31, nat. comdr., 1932-33. Mem. Bibliog. Soc. of America, Ohio Archæol. and Hist. Soc., Kan. Hist. Soc. (life), S.R. Republican. Author: Captain John Brown and Harper's Ferry, 1926. Contbr. to mags. and newspapers. Home: 517 Main St., Charleston, W.Va. Office: 9 Rockefeller Plaza, New York, N.Y.

STUTSMAN, Martin B., lawyer; b. Westfield, N.J., Feb. 8, 1885; s. John Martin and Anna L. (Brown) S.; LL.B., N.Y. Univ. Law Sch., 1908; m Helen M. Whitney, Nov. 7, 1912; 1 son, John Whitney. Admitted to N.J. bar as atty., 1909, as counselor, 1912; engaged in gen. practice of law as individual at Plainfield, N.J., since 1909; served as mayor of Plainfield, 1931-32 and 1935-36; judge Fourth Jud. Dist. Ct. since 1937. Mem. Union Co. Bar Assn., Phi Delta Phi. Republican. Baptist. Mason. Elk. Home: 1236 Lenox Av. Office: 220 Park Av., Plainfield, N.J.

STUTSMAN, Rachel, (Mrs. Albert P. Ball), psychologist; b. Greencastle, Ind., Apr. 17, 1894; d. Jesse O. and Lyda (Winslow) S.; ed. Earlham Coll., 1914-15; A.B., U. of Mo., 1919; ed. Cornell U., summer 1919, Bryn Mawr Coll., 1921-22, U. of Chicago, 1920-21, 1927-28, Ph.D., 1928; m. Albert P. Ball; children—James Stutsman, Lucy Jane. Engaged as social case worker, Kansas City Provident Assn., mental testing experience in instns. and clinics in Detroit and Pa., 1916-22; psychologist, Merrill-Palmer Sch., Detroit, Mich., 1922-36; taught at summer schs. of various state univs., summers 1928-38. Mem. A.A.A.S., Psychometric Soc., Am. Assn. Applied Psychology, Am. Psychol. Assn., Nat. Assn. for Parent Edn., Assn. for Research in Child Development, Womans Internat. League for Peace and Freedom (pres. Mich. branch, 1937). Protestant. Author: Mental Measurement of Preschool Children, 1931; What of Youth Today, 1935. Contbr. popular and sci. articles to ednl. jours. Home: 27 W. Curtin St., Bellefonte, Pa.

STUTZ, George Frederick Adelbert, research chemist; b. Washington, D.C., June 3, 1900; s. George Frederick Adelbert and Wilhelmina (Fey) S.; Ch.E., Lehigh U., 1922; A.M., Johns Hopkins U., 1924, Ph.D., same, 1929; m. Madeleine Spilman, Oct. 22, 1924; children—Marjorie Ann, Eleanor Winchip, Carolyn Fey. In employ New Jersey Zinc Co., mfrs. zinc metal, pigments and related products, Palmerton, Pa., since 1922, investigator, Research Div., 1924-27, 1927-28, chief Fundamental Research Div., 1928-32, chief Pigment Research Div., 1932-37, asst. chief Research Div. since 1937. Served in O.T.C., Plattsburg, N.Y.; pvt. inf. U.S.A., 1918. Mem. Am. Chem. Soc., Am. Phys. Soc., Am. Soc. for Testing Materials, Tau Beta Pi, Sigma Xi. Republican. Lutheran. Home: 422 Edgemont Av., Palmerton, Pa. Office: Research Division, New Jersey Zinc Co., Palmerton, Pa.

STYER, Freas, lawyer; b. Whitpain Twp., Montgomery Co., Pa., June 7, 1859; s. William Augustus and Elizabeth Keely (Freas) S.; ed. Whitpain Twp. Pub. Sch.; student Centre Sq. Acad., 1874-76, Treemount Sem., Norristown, Pa., 1876-80; B.A., LaFayette Coll., Easton, Pa., 1885, M.A., 1887; m. Gertrude M. Wire, Oct. 21, 1911 (died Feb. 12, 1937). Admitted to Montgomery Co. bar, 1887; since in gen. practice of law; sec. Directors of the Poor, 1901-11, county solicitor, 1911-23; supt. U.S. Mint at Philadelphia, 1921-34; dir. Norristown-Penn Trust Co.; dir. and solicitor Norristown Box Co. Chem. Rep. County Com., 1906-21; mem. Rep. State Com., 1908-22. Mem. Montgomery County Bar Assn., Sons of America. Republican. Mem. Soc. of Friends (Quaker). Mason. Home: 1620 DeKalb St. Office: 519 Swede St., Norristown, Pa.

STYRI, Haakon, metallurgist; b. Christiania (now Oslo), Norway, Mar. 17, 1886; s. Nicolai Bernhard Hansen and Anna (Haug) S.; grad. high sch., 1903, mil. acad., 1904, both Christiania; Mech. Engr., Tech. Sch., Christiania, 1907, Chem. E., 1909 (1 yr. shop practice); fellow Am. Scandinavian Foundation, Carnegie Inst. Tech., 1910; Dr. Ing., in Metallurgy, Technische Hochschule, Aachen, Germany, 1912; unmarried. Asst. prof. metallurgy of iron, Poly. Inst., Trondhjem, Norway, 1912-16; came to U.S., 1916; asst. prof. metallurgy, Carnegie Inst. Tech., 1917-20; chief of S.K.F. Research Lab., mfrs. ball bearings, 1920-27, dir. research S. K. F. Industries, 1927—. Mem. Am. Inst. Mining and Metall. Engrs., Am. Society of Metals, Am. Soc. M.E., Franklin Inst., Iron and Steel Inst. (British). Clubs: Penn Athletic (Phila.); Norwegian (Brooklyn, N.Y.). Contbr. research papers on metallurgy of steel and ball-bearing engring. Home: 6504 Lincoln Drive, Mt. Airy, Pa. Office: S.K.F., Front St. and Erie Av., Philadelphia, Pa.

SUBIN, Harry, physician; b. Phila., Pa., July 6, 1898; s. Bores S.; student U. of Pa., 1918-20; M.D., Jeff. Med. Coll., Phila., 1924; m. Adele Kant, Feb. 1, 1931; 1 son, David Kant. Gen. practice as surgeon, Atlantic City, N.J., since 1925. Served as private inf., U.S. Army, 1918. Fellow Am. Coll. Surgeons; mem. Internat. Coll. of Surgeons, A.M.A., Mil. Surgeons of America. Jewish religion. Mason (32°). Home: 2 S. Somerset Av., Ventnor, N.J. Office: 501 Professional Arts Bldg., Atlantic City, N.J.

SUDELL, Harold, sec. and treas. Mfrs.' Appraisal Co.; b. Preston, Lancashire, England; s. Charles H. and Emma (Veevers) S.; ed. high sch.; m. Mary J. Shaefer, Sept. 9, 1884; children—Clive, Muriel, Una. Came to U.S., 1873, naturalized, 1891. Bookkeeper Morris, Tasker Co., 1883-86; chief clerk Delaware Iron Co., New Castle, Del., 1886-1900, Nat. Tube Co., Philadelphia div., 1900-07; mgr. tube mill dept. Parkesburg Iron Co., 1907-14 and 1918-22; cashier Internal Revenue Dept., Philadelphia, 1914-18; sec.-treas. and dir. Manufacturers' Appraisal Co. since 1922. An advocate of single tax, being responsible for single tax bills introduced in 1935, 1937 and 1939 Legislatures. Treas. Del. Single Tax Campaign Com., 1895-98; treas. Democratic Club of Philadelphia, 1904-17. Presbyterian. Home: 301 Kathmere Road, Brookline, Upper Darby, Pa. Office: 801 Manhattan Bldg., Philadelphia, Pa.

SUGDEN, William Herbert, clergyman; b. Wilkes-Barre, Pa., June 11, 1898; s. William and Selina (Horsefield) S.; student Harry Hillman Acad., Wilkes-Barre, Pa., 1916-17; A.B., Bucknell U., Lewisburg, Pa., 1922; B.D., Princeton Theol. Sem., 1925; student Westminster Cambridge Univ., England, 1925-26; m. Laura Grover Schobert, May 22, 1923; children—Henry Louvett, Marianne, William Alfred. Ordained to ministry of Presbyterian Ch., May 15, 1925; minister, Westminster Presbyn. Ch., Wilkes-Barre, Pa., since 1926. Served in U.S. Army, Sept.-Dec. 1918. Mem. Delta Sigma, Tau Kappa Alpha. Republican. Mason (grand chaplain, Grand Lodge of Pa., 1937). Mem. Wilkes-Barre Rotary Club. Home: 106 Hanover St., Wilkes-Barre, Pa.

SULLIVAN, Francis W., asst. U.S. atty.; b. McKeesport, Pa., Jan. 20, 1902; s. William F. and Elizabeth (Busch) S.; B.S., U. of Pa., 1925; LL.B., Temple U. Law Sch., 1930; unmarried. Legal advisor Nat. Recovery Administrn., 1934-35; counsel Works Progress Administrn., 1936-37; asst. U.S. atty., Eastern Dist. of Pa., since 1937. Mem. Am. Bar Assn., Pa. Bar Assn., Philadelphia Bar Assn., Federal Bar Assn. (president Philadelphia Chapter), National Lawyers' Guild. Clubs: Penn Athletic, Overbrook Golf, Seaview Golf, Whitemarsh Valley Country. Home: Warwick Hotel, 17th & Locust Sts. Office: Girard Trust Co. Bldg., and U.S. Attorney's Office, Custom House Bldg., Philadelphia, Pa.

SULLIVAN, Frank H., v.p. Atlantic Greyhound Corpn.; b. Bucyrus, O., May 11, 1894; s. Cornelius A. and Cora (Lamb) S.; ed. Bucyrus High Sch.; m. Vivian I. Root, Jan. 13, 1915; 1 dau., Eunice Virginia. V.p. and comptroller Atlantic Greyhound Corpn. and Predecessors since 1934. Home: 5 Grosscup Drive. Office: 1100 Kanawha Valley Bldg., Charleston, W.Va.

SULLIVAN, John J(ames), lawyer; b. Phila., Pa., June 29, 1877; s. Jeremiah J. and Ann (Patterson) S.; ed. Notre Dame Acad., Phila.; A.B., St. Joseph's Coll., Phila., 1896, A.M., 1898, LL.D., 1914; LL.B., U. of Pa., 1899; LL.D., Fordham U. 1911; Litt.D., Duquesne U., 1931; unmarried. Admitted to Pa. bar, 1899, and since practiced at Phila.; prof. corpn. law, U. of Pa., since 1915; dir. Market St. Nat. Bank, Union Traction Company of Phila. Trustee Catholic University of America, Rosemont Coll., St. Emma Industrial and Agricultural Institute. Mem. Pa. State Council of Edn. Republican. Catholic. Clubs: Union League, Merion Cricket, Radnor Hunt. Author: Pennsylvania Business Law, 1906, 12th edit., 1937; American Business Law, 1908, 4th edit., 1927; American Corporations, 1911, 2d edit., 1921. Home: 1910 Walnut St. Office: 2035 Land Title Bldg., Philadelphia, Pa.

SULLIVAN, Mark A., lawyer; b. Jersey City, N.J., Nov. 23, 1877; s. Mark and Catherine (Driscoll) S.; A.B., St. Peter's Coll., Jersey City, N.J., 1897, A.M., 1898, hon. LL.D., 1915; m. Lila V. Ward, July 11, 1906 (died 1936); children—Mark A., Lila V. (Mrs. Edward White), Winifred, Mary, Eileen (Mrs. James Cotter), Thomas W., Jeanne, Joseph. Admitted to N.J. bar, 1903, and since practiced at Jersey City; mem. bd. mgrs. Provident Inst. for Savings, Jersey City, since 1936; dir. Commercial Trust Co. of N.J.; assemblyman, New Jersey, 1907-10; judge Ct. of Errors and Appeals, N.J., 1910, 1911, Common Pleas Ct. of Hudson Co., N.J., 1913-18; pres. Hudson Co. Park Commn. since 1931. Mem. Am. Bar Assn., N.J. State Bar Assn., Hudson Co. Bar Assn. Democrat. Catholic. Club: Carteret (Jersey City, N.J.). Home: 23 Duncan Av. Office: 15 Exchange Pl., Jersey City, N.J.

SULLIVAN, William Cleary, lawyer; b. Washington, D.C., Sept. 25, 1880; s. George North and Kate (Cleary) S.; ed. parochial and pub. schs.; grad. Business High Sch., Washington, 1896; LL.B., Georgetown U. Sch. of Law, 1901; m. Ida Gabrielle Wagener, Nov. 27, 1917. Admitted to practice in Supreme Court of D.C., 1901, Court of Appeals, 1901, Supreme Court of U.S., 1904, also state and federal courts of Maryland, U.S. Treasury Department, Board of Tax Appeals and other governmental agencies; associated in practice with late Joseph J. Darlington, Washington, 1901, until his death, 1920, succeeding him in practice. Mem. faculty Georgetown U. Sch. of Law, 1910-18, and 1921-32; engaged in general practice. Mem. American Bar Assn., Bar Assn. of D.C., Soc. Natives of D.C., Columbia Hist. Soc., Catholic Hist. Soc., etc. K.C. Clubs: University, Columbia Country. Home: 27 Primrose Pl., Chevy Chase, Md. Office: Nat. Metropolitan Bank Bldg., Washington, D.C.

SULTZBACH, Daniel Isaiah, clergyman; b. Elizabethville, Pa., Oct. 24, 1879; s. Jos. Henry and Kathryn Emma (Hartman) S.; A.B., Muhlenberg Coll., Allentown, Pa., 1904, A.M., 1907; student Luth. Theol. Sem., Phila., 1904-07; grad. study Tem. U., U. of Pa., Luth. Theol. Sem., 1922-25; Ph.D., Central U., Indianapolis, 1932; m. Esther Amanda Scheirer, Oct. 23, 1923; 1 dau., Eleanor Dolores. Ordained to ministry U. Luth. Ch. America, 1907; asso. pastor, St. Stephen's, Phila., 1907-08, Ch. of Resurrection, Phila., 1908-25, Sacramento Luth. Parish since 1925; pres. West End Ministerium of Lykens Valley, 1934; chmn. Inner Missions, Pottsville Conf. Served as mem. bd. Luth. Orphans Home and Asylum for Aged and Infirm, 1927-36. Mem. faculty, Standard Leadership Training Sch., Schuylkill Co. S.S. Assn. Republican. Lutheran. Mason (32°), Rotarian. Author: Philosophy of the Christian Religion; Protestant Thought of Europe During the 19th Century. Home: Main St., Valley View, Pa.

SUMMERILL, John Morris, Jr., lawyer; b. Penns Grove, N.J., Aug. 3, 1898; s. John Morris and Eleanor W. (Jacoby) S.; B.S., Rutgers Univ., New Brunswick, N.J., 1922; m. Martha H. Mason, Feb. 11, 1939. Studied law N.J. Law Sch., Newark; admitted to N.J. bar as atty., 1926, as counselor, 1929; mem. N.J. Ho. of Assembly, 1930-31; elected to N.J. Senate, 1938 for term, 1939-41; dir. City Nat. Bank and Trust Co. of Salem, N.J. Mem. Am. Bar Assn., N.J. State Bar Assn., Kappa Sigma. Republican. Methodist. Club: Rotary of Penns Grove. Home: 18 E. Maple Av., Penns Grove. Office: Broadway & New Market Sts., Salem, N.J.

SUMMERILL, Joseph John Jr., lawyer; b. Woodbury, N.J., Aug. 8, 1891; s. Joseph John and Altha Mae (Simpers) S.; student William Penn Charter Sch., Phila., Pa., 1904-10, U. of Va., Charlottesville, Va., 1910-12; LL.B., U. of Pa. Law Sch., 1915; m. Marguerite Starr, Aug. 22, 1917; children—Kathryn, Joseph John III. Admitted to N.J. bar, 1915, and began practice with father-in-law, Lewis Starr, Camden, N.J.; partner Starr, Summerill & Lloyd, Camden, N.J., 1926-34, sr. partner since 1934; sec. and dir. Office Bldg. Co., Camden, N.J., since 1926, Manahath Cemetery Co., Woodbury, N.J., since 1924. Served as 1st lt., U.S.R.C., A.E.F., 1917-18. Prosecutor of pleas, Gloucester Co. (N.J.) and asst. atty. gen. of N.J., 1923-33. Mem. N.J. State Bar Assn. (treas. and trustee since 1934); mem. Am. Bar Assn., Camden Co. Bar Assn., Gloucester Co. Bar Assn., S.R., Phi Kappa Sigma, Phil Delta Phi. Democrat. Episcopalian. Clubs: Elk River (Md.) Yacht (commodore since 1938); Woodbury (N.J.) Country. Home: 30 N. Broad St., Woodbury, N.J. Office: 4th and Market Sts., Camden, N.J.

SUMMERILL, Thomas Carney, newspaper pub.; b. Penns Grove, N.J., July 16, 1901; s. William Austin and Kate Harris (Webber) S.; Litt.B., Rutgers U., 1923; m. Ann Sprague Zerby, Dec. 28, 1929; 1 son, Thomas Carney, Jr. Asso. with father in pub. Penns Grove (N.J.) Records, as local editor and mgr., 1923-29; adv. mgr. and business mgr. Salem (N.J.) Standard & Jerseyman since 1929; propr. and pub. Penns Grove Record since 1937. Mem. Borough Council Penns Grove, N.J., 1925-29; sec. Chamber of Commerce, Penns Grove, 1924-29; Chamber of Commerce, Salem, N.J., 1930-37; sec. Penns Grove Rotary Club, 1926-29; pres. Salem Rotary Club, 1937-38. Mem. Phi Gamma Delta. Ind. Democrat. Episcopalian. Mason. Rotarian. Home: 170 Johnson St. Office: 199 E. Broadway, Salem, N.J.

SUMNER, William Albert, lawyer; b. Haledon, N.J., July 8, 1874; s. George A. and Sarah E. (House) S.; student pvt. schs., Paterson, N.J. and Tacoma, Wash., 1882-91, Yale, 1891-92; m. Margaret J. Banister, Oct. 16, 1920 (died 1930); 1 dau., Frances Elizabeth. Admitted to N.J. bar, June 1901; mem. firm Humphreys & Sumner, Paterson, N.J., 1904-29; in pvt. practice, Paterson, since 1929. Pres. bd. mgrs. Paterson Gen. Hosp. Assn. Mem. Am. Bar Assn., N.J. Bar Assn., Passaic Co. Bar Assn., Assn. of the Bar of the City of N.Y. Republican. Presbyterian. Club: Hamilton (Paterson, N.J.). Home: Pompton Plains, N.J. Office: First National Bank Bldg., Paterson, N.J.

SUNDERMAN, F(rederick) William, M.D., chemist; b. Altoona, Pa., Oct. 23, 1898; s. William August and Elizabeth Catherine (Lehr) S.; B.S., Gettysburg Coll., 1919; M.D., U. of Pa., 1923, Ph.D., 1929; m. Clara Louise Bailey, June 2, 1925; children—Clara Louise (dec.), F(rederick) William. Instr., U. of Pa., 1923, asst. in dermatology, 1923; interne Pa. Hosp., 1924-25; instr. research medicine, U. of Pa., 1925-30, asst. prof. research medicine since 1931; chief Diabetic Clinic A, Pa. Hosp., since 1929; asso. in charge chem. div. of Pepper Laboratory, U. of Pa. Hosp., since 1933. Lt. comdr., U.S. Med. Res. Corps. Dir. Chamber Music Club, Philadelphia. Diplomat Nat. Bd.; fellow Coll. Physicians, Philadelphia; certified by Am. Bd. Internal Medicine. Fellow American Society of Clinical Pathologists, American Assn. of History of Medicine; mem. Am. Soc. Biol. Chemistry, Am. Soc. for Clin. Investigation, Physiol. Soc. Philadelphia, Philadelphia County Med. Soc., Am. Med. Assn., Phi Sigma Kappa, Alpha Kappa Kappa, Phi Beta Kappa, Sigma Xi. Independent in politics. Lutheran. Wrote more than 40 articles pertaining to biol. chemistry and internal medicine. Home: 2210 Delancey St. Address: 701 Maloney Clinic, U. of Pa., Philadelphia, Pa.

SUNDHEIM, Harry Garfield, lawyer; b. Philadelphia, Pa., Aug. 30, 1880; s. Jonas and Mina (Plash) S.; student Central High Sch. of Phila. and U. of Pa.; m. Lennie Scharff, Oct. 23, 1911; children—Harry G., John Scharff. Admitted to bar, 1903; since in gen. practice of law; mem. law firm Sundbein, Folz & Sundheim; dir. Bonwit Teller & Co., Lit Bros., Benjamin Franklin Hotel Corpn., Bankers Bond & Mortgage Co., Bankers Securities Corpn., City Stores Co. Dir. Federation of Jewish Charities. Clubs: Locust (Philadelphia); Philmont (Pa.) Country. Home: 2036 Delancey St. Office: 1632 Bankers Securities Bldg., Philadelphia, Pa.

SUNDHEIM, Joseph H., lawyer; b. Philadelphia, Pa., Dec. 11, 1878; s. Herman and Caroline (Hoffman) S.; LL.B., U. of Pa. Law Sch., 1904; m. Blanche Lang, June 15, 1908; children—Herman L., Robert G., David J., Thomas R. Admitted to Pa. bar, 1904; since in private practice of law at Philadelphia; counsel Pa. League of Bldg. & Loan Assns., 1929-38, pres., 1928. Republican. Jewish religion. Author: Law of Building and Loan Associations, 3 edits. Home: 224 W. Walnut Lane. Office: 1500 Land Title Bldg., Philadelphia, Pa.

SUPER, John Henry, prin. high sch.; b. Pottsville, Pa., Mar. 13, 1887; s. John Henry and Emma (Haeseler) S.; A.B., Dickinson Coll., 1909; A.M., U. of Pa., 1913; m. Sadie P. Rothermel, Aug. 28, 1913; 1 son, Robert Henry. Teacher French and Latin, Conway Hall, Carlisle, Pa., 1909-12; teacher French and Latin, J. M. Coughlin High Sch., Wilkes-Barre, Pa., 1913-23, asst. prin. same sch., 1923 to 1932, prin. since 1932. Mem. Nat. Edn., Pa. State Edn. Assn., Assn. Secondary Sch. Prins., Phi Kappa Sigma. Republican. Lutheran. Mason. Home: 302 Academy St., Wilkes-Barre, Pa.

SUPPLEE, Frederick Milton, ins. agt.; b. Washington, D.C., Sept. 2, 1876; s. A. I. D. and Katherine (Buckley) S.; student pub. schs., Washington, D.C.; m. Elizabeth Griffith; 1 dau., Katharine Lee (Mrs. Chase Ridgely). Engaged in business as ins. agt. and broker at Baltimore; asso. with J. Ramsay Barry & Co., Inc.; pres. Arlington Federal Savings & Loan Assn.; v.p. Sun Mortgage Co.; dir. Lincoln Service, Inc., Aetna Bldg. & Loan Assn., Homeseekers Bldg. & Loan Assn.; pres. Frank H. Creese & Co. Mem. bd. govs. Md. Tuberculosis Sanatorium. Pres. S.A.R. Mason (32°, Shriner). Club: University. Home: 3901 Greenway. Office: 15 E. Fayette St., Baltimore, Md.

SURDAM, Truman Arnold, investment banking; b. Middletown, N.Y., Dec. 24, 1878; s. Ira and Alice (Lewis) S.; ed. pub. schs.; m. May Albro, Oct. 15, 1903. Clk. Third Nat. Bank, Scranton, Pa., 1893-1900; cashier, 1st Nat. Bank, Forest City, Pa., 1900-06; engaged in Investments and insurance, 1906-19; treas. Surdam & Co., investment banking, since 1919. Served with Co. D, 13th Regt., Pa. Vol. Inf., Spanish-Am. War. Republican. Methodist. Mason (K. T.,, Shriner). Home: 919 Clay Av. Office: Mears Bldg., Scranton, Pa.

SUSMAN, Milton Kay, lawyer and editor; b. Pittsburgh, Pa., Dec. 15, 1906; s. David J. and Rebecca (Brockstein) S.; B.Litt., Harvard, 1927; A.B., U. of Pittsburgh, 1929; LL.B., U. of Pittsburgh Law Sch., 1932; m. Minnie E. Spero, Oct. 18, 1936. Admitted to Pa. bar, 1932 and since engaged in gen. practice of law at Pittsburgh; editor Jewish Criterion since 1933; ednl. dir. Edn'l. Center Young Mens and Womens Hebrew Assn. of Pittsburgh since 1934. Mem. Allegheny Co. Bar Assn. (sec. pub. relations com. since 1938), Phi Beta Kappa, Delta Sigma Rho, Tau Epsilon Rho, Sigma Delta Chi, Phi Epsilon Pi. Republican. Jewish religion (dir. jr. congregation Rodef Shalom Temple). Home: 5854 Forbes St. Office: 620 Bakewell Bldg., Pittsburgh, Pa.

SUSSMAN, Samuel, educator; b. Phila., Pa., Jan. 10, 1805; s. Louis and Libbie (Meltzer) S.; student Yeshivah Mishkan Yisrael, Phila., 1908-09, Gratz Coll., Phila., 1913-15 (grad.), Sch. of Pedagogy, Phila., 1914-16; B.S., in chemistry, U. of Pa., 1920; Ph.D., Dropsie Coll. for Hebrew and Cognate Learning, Phila., 1926; m. Jennie Derman, Dec. 14, 1920; 1 dau., F. Rebecca. Teacher, Parkside Hebrew Sch., Phila., 1918; prin. Oheb Sholom Talmud Torah, 1920-23, Shaare Zedek Sch. 1923-24, Har Zion Temple since 1924; editor Jewish Current Events, 1927-32, Jewish Current News since 1936; mng. editor Har Zion Bulletin since 1938; editor Congl. Teachers Bulletin since 1938; founder and editor The Sussmanews since 1934. Served in Engrs. Reserve Corps, U.S.

SUTCH, William Perry, collection mgr.; b. Phila., Pa., Oct. 13, 1884; s. John W. and Margaret M. (Perry) S.; student Norristown (Pa.) High Sch., 1897-1901, Pierce Sch., Phila., 1905-06; m. Emily Mae Steinhauer, Sept. 21, 1907; children—John W., William P. (dec.). Clk. Adams Express Co., Phila., 1901-05; bookkeeper in charge, Field Co., Inc., Phila., 1907; asst. bookkeeper, Supplee Hardware Co., Phila., 1908-10; asst. mgr., Engrs. Club, Phila., 1910-14; office mgr., Quaker City Sweater Mills, Phila., 1915; pres. and gen. mgr., Kresge Shoe Co., Phila., 1916-18; office mgr. and accountant in charge, Walter M. Steppacher & Bros., Phila., and Emery Shirt Factory, Phila., 1918-24; collection mgr. and asst. credit mgr., B. E. Block & Bros. Dept. Store, Norristown, Pa., since 1924; dir. Norris Bldg. and Loan Assn. Councilman and chmn. of Finance Com., Norristown, Pa., 1930-36; treas., Borough of Norristown (Pa.) Community Chest. Mem. Norristown (Pa.) Chamber of Commerce (treas. since 1926). Republican. Methodist. Moose. Home: 813 Stanbridge St. Office: 15 W. Main St., Norristown, Pa.

SUTER, Francis L., v.p. Armstrong Cork Co.; b. Pittsburgh, Pa., Jan. 9, 1877; s. John P. and Emma A. (Vickroy) S.; ed. Pittsburgh grammar and high schs.; m. Mary M. Barr, Oct. 21, 1903; 1 dau., Elizabeth M. Clk. Liberty Nat. Bank, Pittsburgh, 1893-1900; clk. Armstrong Cork Co., Pittsburgh, 1900-09, asst. gen. mgr. linoleum plant, Lancaster, Pa., 1909-29, gen. mgr., 1929-32; v.p. and treas. Armstrong Cork Co., 1932-38, 1st v.p. since 1938, dir. since 1927; dir. Farmers Bank & Trust Co., Lancaster Brick Co. (both of Lancaster). Dir. Lancaster Gen. Hosp., Lancaster Welfare Federation. Ex-pres. Lancaster Chamber of Commerce. Republican. Presbyterian. Clubs: Hamilton, Lancaster Country (Lancaster). Home: 1112 Wheatland Av. Office: care Armstrong Cork Co., Lancaster, Pa.

SUTHERLAND, Abby Ann (Mrs. William Furby Brown), educator; b. on Cape Breton, N.S., Can., Jan. 6, 1876; d. John and Mary Ann (Gwinn) S.; brought to U.S., 1892; A.B. Radcliffe Coll., 1899; hon. Ph.D., Temple U. Phila., 1916; m. William Furby Brown, Sept. 20, 1916. Teacher Bradford (Mass.) Acad., 1899-1902; instr. English, Ogontz Sch., Rydal, Pa., since 1902, prin. since 1909, pres. since 1909. Mem. Progressive Edn. Assn. of Headmistresses, Foreign Policy Assn. Republican. Presbyterian. Clubs: Wyncote Women's, New Century, Civic, Huntingdon Valley Golf. Author of pamphlets, Talks with Girls, General Information Guide, Increasing the Vocabulary. Address: Ogontz School, Pa.

SUTHERLAND, (Clarence) Hale, prof. civil engring.; b. Foxcroft, Me., May 22, 1884; s. Ira Addison and Anne Hale (Wade) S.; A.B., Harvard, 1906; S.B., Mass. Inst. Tech., 1911; m. Margaret Townsend, Sept. 14, 1920; children—John Hale, Mary Flint. Structural draftsman Corrugated Bar Co., Buffalo, N.Y., 1911-13; instr. civil engring., Mass. Inst. Tech., 1913-17, asst. prof., later asso. prof., 1919-30; prof. civil engring. and head of dept., Lehigh U. since Sept. 1930; on leave as prof. civil engring., Robert Coll., Constantinople, 1926-27. Served as 1st lt. engrs., U.S. Army, 1917-19; with A.E.F. 12 mos. in Service of Supply. Mem. American Society C.E., Pennsylvania Society of Professional Engineers, American Concrete Institute, Society for Promotion Engineering Education, Sigma Xi, Tau Beta Pi, Theta Chi. Member Society of Friends since 1927. Mason. Author: (with W. W. Clifford) Introduction to Reinforced Concrete Design, 1926; Structural Theory (with H. L. Bowman), 1930; Structural Design (with same), 1938. Home: Bethlehem, Pa.

SUTHERLAND, Howard, ex-senator; b. near Kirkwood, Mo., Sept. 8, 1865; s. John Webster and Julia P. (Reavis) S.; A.B., Westminster Coll., Fulton, Mo., 1889; studied law at Columbian (now George Washington) U., but did not complete course; m. Effie Harris, May 28, 1889. Editor Republican (daily and weekly), Fulton, Mo., 1889-90; served from clk. to chief of population div., 11th Census, 1890-93; removed to Elkins, W.Va., 1893; with Davis-Elkins coal and r.r. interests 10 yrs., becoming gen. land agt.; later coal and timber land business on own account. Member W.Va. State Senate, 1908-12; mem. 63d and 64th Congresses (1913-17), W.Va. at large; elected U.S. senator for term 1917-23; del. at large to Rep. Nat. Conv., 1924, 28, 32, 36; alien property custodian, 1925-33; pres. Fidelity Investment Assn., Wheeling, 1933-35. Republican. Presbyn. Mem. Beta Theta Pi, etc. Mason (32°), LL.D., George Washington U. Home: Elkins, W.Va.; 405 Wyoming Apts., Washington, D.C.

SUTHERLAND, John Bain, prof. physical edn.; b. Coupar, Angus, Scotland, Mar. 21, 1889; s. Archibald and Mary (Burns) S.; D.D.S. U. of Pittsburgh (Pa.), 1918; unmarried. Came to U.S., 1904, naturalized, 1914. Football coach, Lafayette Coll., Easton, Pa., 1919-23; same U. of Pittsburgh since 1924, also teacher of dentistry in the univ., 1919-33, and prof. physical edn., since 1932. Served in Med. R.C., U.S. Army, 1917-18, World War. Fellow Am. Coll. Dentists; mem. Am. Dental Soc., Druids, Scabbard and Blade, Sigma Chi, Psi Omega, Omicron Delta Kappa. Presbyn. Mason (32°, Shriner). Clubs: Rotary, Variety, Pittsburgh Athletic Assn., Pittsburgh Breakfast (pres. 1938). Home: Pittsburgh Athletic Association. Address: University of Pittsburgh, Pittsburgh, Pa.

SUTHERLAND, Robert Lee, prof. sociology; b. Clarinda, Ia., Feb. 11, 1903; s. Donald Brant and Charlotte (Cleveland) S.; A.B., Knox Coll., 1925; A.M., Oberlin Coll., 1926; Ph.D., U. of Chicago, 1930; m. Marjorie Lewis, Aug. 24, 1926; 1 dau., Elizabeth. Prof. of public speaking, Huron (S.D.) Coll., 1926-27; prof. sociology, Bucknell U., since 1930, chmn. social science div., 1934-36 and since 1938, dean of men since 1938. Research sec. Negro Youth Project of Am. Council on Edn. Mem. Am. Sociol. Soc., Nat. Council on Religion in Higher Edn. (bd. dirs.), Pa. Conf. on Social Work, Pa. Com. on Penal Affairs (mem. advisory com.), Am. Assn. Univ. Profs., Phi Beta Kappa, Delta Sigma Rho, Sigma Delta Chi, Tau Kappa Epsilon. Democrat. Presbyn. Author: Introductory Sociology (with J. L. Woodward), 1937. Contbr. to jours. Home: 40 S. Water St., Lewisburg, Pa.

SUTHERLAND, Walter Coray, wholesale grocer; b. Exeter, Pa., Nov. 7, 1862; s. Smith and Laura (Stanton) S.; ed. private sch., 1867-74, pub. schs., 1874-80, Wyoming Sem., Kingston, Pa., 1880-82; m. Grace Klotz, Apr. 17, 1889; children—Martha Chapman (wife of Major Samuel K. Mitchell), Marian Grace (wife of Allan P. Kirby), Esther Klotz (wife of Dr. J. Antrim Crellin). Began as wholesale grocery salesman Githens, Rexamer & Co., 1882; mem. firm Sutherland & McMillan, wholesale grocers, since 1892. Republican. Episcopalian. Clubs: Westmoreland, Fox Hill, Craftsmans. Home: 502 Susquehanna Av., West Pittston, Pa. Office: 10 Sutherland Place, Pittston, Pa.

SUTLIFF, Stephen Dana, M.D.; b. Luzerne Co., Pa., May 23, 1878; s. Ross and Oliva (Kingsbury) S.; student Wyoming Sem., 1898, U. of Md., 1901; M.D., 1901; m. Ruth Lamb, July 18, 1901; children—Stephen Dana, Robert Lamb. In gen. practice of medicine, Shippensburg, Pa., since 1901; mem. staff Carlisle and Chambersburg (Pa.) hosps. Mem. Cumberland Co. Med. Soc. (pres. 3 terms), A.M.A., Pa. State Medical Soc. Republican. Methodist. Mason (32°). Club: Scottish Rites. Address: 105 E. King St., Shippensburg, Pa.

SUTPHEN, William Gilbert Van Tassel, author; b. Phila., May 11, 1861; s. Rev. Morris Crater and Eleanor (Brush) S.; A.B., Princeton U., 1882; hon. A.M., 1926. Author: The Golficide, 1898; The Golfer's Alphabet, 1899; The Cardinal's Rose, 1900; The Golfer's Calendar, 1901; The Nineteenth Hole, 1901; The Gates of Chance, 1904; The Doomsman, 1906; In Jeopardy, 1922; The Sermon on the Cross, 1927; King's Champion, 1927. Ordered deacon, P.E. Ch., 1921, ordained priest, 1923. Clubs: Morristown, Morris County Golf. Home: Morristown, N.J.

SUTPHIN, William Halstead, congressman; b. Browntown, Middlesex Co., N.J., Aug. 30, 1887; s. James Taylor and Charlotte (Brown) S.; ed. pub. schs., Matawan, N.J.; m. Catharine Bonner, Oct. 19, 1922; children—Susan, William Taylor. Mayor of Matawan, 1916-19 and 1922-28; mem. 72d to 76th Congresses (1931-41), 3d N.J. Dist. Served with 1st Squadron, N.J. Cav., Mexican Border, 1916; enlisted as pvt., U.S.A., May 1917; discharged as capt., July 1919. Mem. Holland Soc., Sons of Am. Revolution. Democrat. Presbyn. Home: Matawan, N.J.

SUTTLE, Clifford B., engr. and exec; b. Lincoln, Ill., Sept. 2, 1883; s. Robert F. and Mary Alice (Stowe) S.; A.B. in civil engring., U. of Ill., Urbana, Ill., 1906; m. Lydia Cox, Sept. 14, 1910; 1 dau., Mary Elizabeth. Engr. Pitometer Co. and John A. Cole & Edward S. Cole, engrs., 1906-09; engr. Macon Gas & Water Co., to 1912, Tampa Works Co. to 1922 and R. D. Wood & Co., 1909-14; also engr. and exec. Estate of Stuart Wood since 1914; sec., treas. and dir. Cotiga Development Co. since 1925. Home: 49 Penarth Rd., Bala-Cynwyd, Pa. Office: Provident Trust Bldg., Philadelphia, Pa.

SUTTON, Erastus W., banking and telephone exec.; b. Parker, N.J., May 10, 1876; s. Aaron S. and Mary E. (Apgar) S.; student pub. schs., Parker, N.J., 1881-94; m. Angeline Rinehart, Jan. 24, 1898. Engaged in gen. merchandise bus. as propr., 1896; now in gen. advisory and personnel capacity, N.J. Telephone Co.; v.p. and dir. Hunterdon County Nat. Bank, Flemington Water Co. Mem. City Council of Lebanon, N.J.; now mayor City of Lebanon. Dem. state committeeman. Address: Lebanon, N.J.

SUTTON, George Miksch, ornithologist, bird artist; b. Bethany, Neb., May 16, 1898; s. Harry Trumbull and Lola Anna (Miksch) S.; student Tex. Christian U., Ft. Worth, 1913-14; B.S., Bethany (W.Va.) Coll., 1919; student U. of Pittsburgh, 1923-25; Ph.D., Cornell U., 1932; unmarried. Mem. staff Carnegie Mus. Pittsburgh, 1919-25; curator of birds Cornell U. since 1931; Pa. state ornithologist, 1925-29; teacher ornithology, U. of Pittsburgh, 1925; member of expdns. for Carnegie Mus. to Labrador, 1920, 28, to Hudson Bay, 1923, 26; solo expdn. to Southampton Island, Hudson Bay, 1929-30 (discovered nests of blue goose); expdn. to Churchill, Hudson Bay, 1931 (discovered eggs of Harris's sparrow); expdns. since 1930 to Saskatchewan, Southern States of U.S. (for ivory-billed woodpeckers), Western Okla., Rio Grande Valley, British Columbia and Mexica; devoted much time to painting birds from life, furnishing bird illustrations for H. H. Bailey's Birds of Florida, H. DuPuy's Bird Friends and Foes, Allen's American Bird Biographies, Roberts' Birds of Minnesota and Todd's Birds of Western Pennsylvania. Mem. Am. Ornithologists' Union, Wilson Ornithol. Club, Cooper Ornithol. Club, Sigma Xi, Phi Kappa Phi, Beta Theta Pi, Cranbrook Inst. Science. Clubs: Savage (Ithaca, N.Y.); Explorers (New York). Author: Introduction to Birds of Pennsylvania, 1928; Exploration of Southampton Island, Hudson Bay, 1932; Eskimo Year, 1934; Birds in the Wilderness, 1936. Contbr. to mags. Home: Pebble Hearths, Bethany, W.Va. Address: Fernow Hall, Cornell U., Ithaca, N.Y.

SUTTON, Isaac C., lawyer; b. Bryn Mawr, Pa., Jan. 10, 1877; s. William Henry and Hannah (Anderson) S.; student Haverford (Pa.) Sch.; Ph.B., Wesleyan U., Middletown, Conn., 1900; LL.B., U of Pa. Law Sch., 1903; m. Ruth Clark, Nov. 12, 1912; children—James A., I. Crawford. Admitted to Phila., bar, 1903;

associated with father, 1903-13, Walnut, Sutton & Faught (subsequently Sutton & Faught), 1913-38; in pvt. practice, Phila., since 1938; presiding judge Family Ct., Phila., 1937. Served in Spanish-Am. War; dir. for Southern Camps, under War Dept. Com. on Training Camp Activities, World War. Recipient Beaver Award for contribution to boys' welfare. Pa. State dir. Nat. Youth Adminstrn.; mem. staff Internat. Boy Scout Jamboree, England; chmn. bd. Community and Edn. Dept. Council Social Agencies, Phila.; chmn. com. Daniel Boone Homestead under state Hist. Commn.; chmn. Com. on Marking Graves of Signers of Constitution, 150th Anniversary of Constitution; mem. Nat. Boy Scout Council; dir. Pa. Public Edn. and Child Labor Assn., Philadelphia Emergency Com. on Pub. Edn., Indian Rights Assn. Mem. Am. Bar Assn., Pa. Bar Assn., Phi Delta Phi, Psi Upsilon. Democrat. Unitarian. Mason. Home: 5409 Overbrook Av. Office: Finance Bldg., Philadelphia, Pa.

SUTTON, John Blair, pres. Sutton Engring. Co.; b. Pittsburgh, Pa., Sept. 21, 1882; s. John Anderson and Annie (Woods) S.; ed. Pittsburgh Central High Sch.; m. Helen Murdoch, Oct. 8, 1932; children—John Blair, Mary Ormsby (Mrs. Cebra Graves). Supt. electric furnaces and rolling mills, Crucible Steel Co. of America, 1903-22; pres. Sutton Engring. Co., machinery mfrs., since 1922. Mem. Am. Iron and Steel Inst. Republican. Presbyterian. Home: 6315 Kentucky Av. Office: 1209 Park Bldg., Pittsburgh, Pa.

SUTTON, Thomas, lawyer; b. Indiana, Pa., May 3, 1854; s. John and Mary Agnes (Walker) S.; ed. Indiana Pub. Sch., 1859-70; A.B., Princeton U., 1873, A.M., 1876; student Columbia Law Sch., 1876-77; m. Ella P. Hildebrand, Oct. 22, 1878; children—Edward Hildebrand, John S. Began as atty. 1877; with Indiana Foundry Co. since 1878, becoming pres. and dir., 1918. Treas. Indiana State Teachers Coll. (formerly Indiana State Normal Sch.), 1878-83, mem. bd. trustees, 1883-1936, sec., 15 yrs., pres.; 1898-1936. Mem. Phi Sigma Pi. Republican. Presbyterian. Address: 209 S. Sixth St., Indiana, Pa.

SUYDAM, Richard Schoonmaker, paint and varnish mfr.; b. Pittsburgh, Pa., Apr. 22, 1872; s. M. Bedell and Emma (Copeland) S.; student Phillips Acad., 1887-89; Yale U., 1893; m. Mary E. Dilworth, Nov. 15, 1899; children —Elizabeth D. (Mrs. J. Stuart Brown), Louise D. (Mrs. Howard H. McClintic). Pres. M. B. Suydam Co., paint and varnish mfrs., since 1895. Republican. Presbyterian. Clubs: Pittsburgh, Duquesne, Allegheny County, Pittsburgh Golf (Pittsburgh). Home: 5416 Darlington Road. Office: Preble Av., North Side, Pittsburgh, Pa.

SWAIN, James Edgar, prof. history; b. Judson, Ind., Aug. 20, 1897; s. Daniel Miller and Lucinda Frances (Payton) S.; A.B., Ind. U., 1921, A.M., 1922; Ph.D., U. of Pa., 1925; m. Esther Wimmer, Sept. 3, 1919; 1 son, James Edgar II. Engaged as teacher high sch., Bloomington, Ind., 1921-22; asst. in history, Ind. U., 1922; instr. history, U. of Pa., 1923-25; prof. history, Muhlenberg Coll., Allentown, Pa., since 1925. Mem. Am. Hist. Assn., Pa. Hist. Assn., Phi Delta Kappa, Phi Alpha Theta, Omicron Delta Kappa, Phi Sigma Nu, Alpha Kappa Alpha, Alpha Tau Omega, Authors Club of London. Harrison Fellow U. of Pa. Democrat. Mem. Religious Soc. Friends. Club: Lehigh Country. Author: Struggle for Control of the Mediterranean, 1934; History of World Civilization, 1938. Contbr. articles on history. Home: 140 N. 28th St., Allentown, Pa.

SWAIN, James Ramsay, clergyman; b. Marlboro, N.J., Sept. 8, 1872; s. George and Ann Elizabeth (Beekman) S.; A.B., Princeton, 1894 (class orator); student Princeton Theol. Sem., 1898-1901; D.D., Coe Coll., 1927, Park Coll., 1927; m. Fanny Mulford Jessup, June 11, 1902; children—Ann Jessup (wife of Rev. Edwin O. Kennedy), Mary Louise (wife of C. Andrew Herschel), Elisabeth Ramsay. Ordained ministry Presbyn. Ch., 1901; Y.M.C.A. sec. at Princeton U., 1894-95; instr. at Am. Univ., Beyrouth, Syria, 1895-98; pastor Dutch Reformed Ch., Flushing, L.I., 1901-05; Woodland Presbyterian Ch., Phila., since 1905; dir. Young People's Dept. Montrose Bible Conf., 1908, 09; summer preacher Baptist Tabernacle, Llandudno, Wales, 1910; a leader of summer conferences at Eaglesmere, Pa., Canton, Pa., Pocono Pines, Pa., Stony Brook, N.Y., Blairstown, N.J., Martha's Vineyard, Mass., etc. Mem. of the Bd. of Pub. and S.S. Work of Presbyn. Ch., 1908-18; prof. of church history and Christian missions, 1928-36; prof. of hist. geog. of Holy Land, Bible manners and customs, Bibl. archeology, 1937-38, Temple U. Sch. of Theology; moderator of Presbytery of Phila., 1932-33; commr. to General Assembly, 1911, 21, 31. Served as vol. chaplain, Camp Upton, L.I., 1917-18. Trustee Washington Coll. (Tenn.), 1932-36. Mem. Phi Beta Kappa. Clubs: Republican, Adelphoi (Phila.); Phi Beta Kappa Soc. of Phila. and vicinity. Wrote: "The Banner of His Banqueting House," "The Mistletoe of Bethlehem," "The Cedar of Lebanon," "What Is That in Thine Hand?" "The Christian's Ministry" and contributions to church periodicals. Home: 428 S. 44th St., Philadelphia, Pa.

SWAIN, Robert Lee, state official; b. Redden, Del., Sept. 29, 1887; s. Rev. Charles Philip and Martha Hester (Messick) S.; Pharm. D., U. of Md., 1909, LL.B., 1932; Pharm. M., Phila. Coll., Pharmacy and Science, 1934; Pharm. D., Conn. Coll. of Pharmacy, New Haven, 1934; Sc.D., Washington Coll., Chestertown, Md., 1935; m. Esther Beach Sprecher, of Sykesville, Md., Oct. 3, 1910; children—Daniel B. (dec.), Robert Lee. Pharmacist, Sykesville, Md., 1909-28; mem. Md. Bd. of Pharmacy since 1920 (sec. since 1925); dep. food and drug commr. Md. Dept. of Health since 1922; lecturer pharm. law, Temple U., since 1933. Trustee U.S. Pharmacopoea since 1936, West Nottingham Acad. (Colora, Md.). Mem. Am. Pharm. Assn. (pres. 1934), Conf. of Pharm. Law Enforcement Officials (founder, and chmn. since 1929), Nat. Assn. Bds. of Pharmacy (dir. dept. edn., 1930-32, pres., 1938), Md. Hist. Soc., Theta Kappa Nu. Club: University (Baltimore). Editor of Md. Pharmacist since 1925. Home: 3507 Edgewood Rd. Office: 2411 N. Charles St., Baltimore, Md.

SWAN, Herbert S., city planner, industrial consultant; b. Shickley, Neb., Jan. 8, 1888; s. A.P. and Emma (Johnson) S.; Ph.B., U. of Chicago, 1910; grad. study Columbia, 1910-11; m. Alma Oswald, Aug. 21, 1915; children— Hugo, Herbert S. Engaged in industrial development, city planning and zoning work since 1911; consultant to cities of Newark, Paterson, Plainfield, Hoboken, Atlantic City (N.J.), New York, Albany, Troy, Yonkers, White Plains (N.Y.), Hartford, Waterbury, Danbury, Bridgeport, Norwalk, Greenwich, Bristol, New London (Conn.), Harrisburg (Pa.), Durham, Charlotte (N.C.), and many others; consultant Mid-Hudson Port Survey Com., Com. on Nat. Resources. Mem. Am. Inst. City Planning, Nat. Conf. on City Planning; mem. com. on city planning and zoning of President Hoover's Conf. on Home Bldg. and Ownership. Author or co-author of many booklets and reports on industrial development, zoning and planning of Am. cities. Contbr. to Nat. Municipal Review, Am. City, Jour. of Land and Pub. Utility Economics, Am. Architect, City Management, Engring. News Record, Archtl. Forum, Jour. Am. Inst. Architects. Homer: 338 Highland Av., Upper Montclair, N.J. Office: 15 Park Row, New York, N.Y.

SWAN, John Joseph, mech. engr., manager; b. Washington, D.C., Sept. 22 1872; s. Henry Clay and Virginia Sylvania (Rogers) S.; grad. Washington, D.C., High Sch., 1891; M.E. in elec. engring., Cornell U., Sibley Coll. Engring., 1897; m. Helen Richards Clark, Apr. 2, 1902; children—Katherine Clark (Mrs. Donald H. Webb), Virginia Rogers (Mrs. Albert Muldavin). Asst. civil engr. U.S. Army Engr. Corps, 1891; asso. editor Engineering News, New York, 1897; asst. to pres. and asst. sales engr. Ingersoll-Sergeant Drill Co., Paris, 1900, New York, 1903; successively asst. to pres. and chief engr. Longmead Iron Co., sec. W. P. Pressinger & Co.; asst. sales mgr. Keller Mfg. Co.; mgr. N.Y. office, Chicago Pneumatic Tool Co., engring. vice-pres. Am. Arms Co.; lt. col., U.S. Army, as mem. Com. on Classification Personnel; asst. mgr. Prestolite Co., engr. Business Exchange, and resident mgr. Sidney Blumenthal; comptroller Barnard Coll., Columbia U., since 1928. Capt. Engrs.; lt. col. Reserve Corps. Rep. dist. committeeman. Mem. Am. Soc. Mech. Engrs., (vice chmn. finance com. since 1936), Montclair Soc. for Engrs., N.Y. Elec. Soc., Beta Theta Pi, Sphinx Head; formerly asso. Inst. Elec. Engrs. Republican. Congregationalist. Home: 296 Claremont Av., Montclair, N.J. Office: 607 W. 119th St., New York, N.Y.

SWAN, Thomas Hadden, research chemist; b. Monmouth, Ill., July 8, 1896; s. John Nesbit and Eurilda Jane (Duffield) S.; ed. Monmouth (Ill.) and Oxford (Miss.) pub. schs., 1902-14, Monmouth Coll., 1914-15; B.S., U. of Miss., 1918; M.A., Columbia U., 1921; Ph.D., Ohio State U., 1924; m. Elizabeth Baker Kirk, Aug. 22, 1930; 1 dau., Sarah Ann. Asst. in chemistry, U. of Miss., 1916-18, Columbia U., 1919-21, Ohio State U., 1921-24; fellow Mellon Inst. of Industrial Research, 1924-34, sr. fellow since 1934. Served in U.S. Army, Chem. Warfare Service, 1918. Mem. A.A.A.S., Am. Chem. Soc., Alpha Chi Sigma, Gamma Alpha, Sigma Xi. Independent in politics. Presbyterian. Club: University (Pittsburgh). Home: 90 23d St., Troy, N.Y. Address: Mellon Inst. of Industrial Research, Pittsburgh, Pa.

SWANEY, Homer H., lawyer; b. Greene Twp., Pa., Mar. 1, 1881; s. Robert M. and Alice M. (Anderson) S.; ed. pub. schs., Hookstown Acad. and Grove City Coll.; m. Elizabeth B. Craig, May 26, 1909; 1 son, Robert L. County auditor, 1906; admitted to Beaver Co. bar, 1908; gen. counsel and dir. Ing-Rich Mfg. Co. and affiliated interests since 1933; gen. counsel Pa. Power Co. since 1934; dir. Ingram-Richardson Mfg. Co. V.p. Pa. Assn. of Boroughs, 1928-33; mem. exec. com. Pa. League of Bldg. & Loan Assn., 1929-33, elected 2d v.p. 1933, 1st v.p., 1934, pres., 1935; sec. Beaver Valley Water Co. since 1932. Mem. advisory bd. and chmn. Salvation Army of Beaver Falls. Republican. Protestant. Mason. Dist. gov. Pa. Kiwanis Dist., 1928. Home: Patterson Heights. Office: Federal Bldg., Beaver Falls, Pa.

SWANEY, Walter Glen, sec., treas. and gen. mgr. Kerotest Mfg. Co.; b. Pittsburgh, Pa., Apr. 1, 1891; s. James and Mary (Hertrick) S.; student Thaddeus Stevens Pub. Sch., 1897-1903, Iron City Coll. (both of Pittsburgh), 1903-05; m. Gertrude Belle Miller, Dec. 10, 1911 (died Aug. 14, 1914); 1 son, James Miller (died Mar. 17, 1938); m. 2d, Catherine J. Wilson, Nov. 2, 1934. Successively stenographer, bookkeeper, salesman, welder, Pittsburgh, until 1915; sec., treas. and gen. mgr. Kerotest Mfg. Co. (formerly Pittsburgh Reinforced Brazing & Mfg. Co., until 1926) since 1915; sec. and treas. Mueller & Herr, Inc., Hempfield Oil & Gas Co. Republican. Presbyterian. Mason (Scottish Rite, A.A.O.N.M.S.). Club: Pittsburgh Athletic. Home: 803 Royal York Apartment. Office: 2525 Liberty Av., Pittsburgh, Pa.

SWANK, Calvin Peter, clergyman; b. Northumberland Co., Pa., Apr. 26, 1880; s. Clarence Wesley and Cordetia Esther (Persing) S.; A.B., Susquehanna U., Selinsgrove, Pa., 1904; A.M., Susquehanna U. Theol. Sch., 1905; student Gettysburg (Pa.) Theol. Sem., 1905-07; S.T.D., Temple U. Theol. Sch., 1921; (hon.) D.D., Susquehanna U., 1929; m. Margaret Catharine Rothrock, Apr. 23, 1908; 1 son, Paul Rothrock. Ordained to ministry U. Luth. Church America, 1907; pastor Highspire, Pa., 1907-09, Camden, N.J., 1910-21, Muhlenberg Memorial, Phila., Pa., 1921-32; supt. missions of East Pa. Synod, U. Luth. Ch. America, since 1932, pres. Synod, 1927-29; chmn. com. to entertain U. Luth. Ch. America, 1932; vice chmn. com. to entertain World Conv. Luth. in Phila., 1940; dir. Phila. Federation of Chs.; vice pres. Inner Mission Soc. Republican. Lutheran. Mason. Club: The Chapter (Phila.). Home: 6303 N. Fairhill St. Office: 701 Muhlenberg Bldg., Philadelphia, Pa.

SWANN, Samuel Donovan, etcher; b. Fernandina, Fla., Feb. 22, 1889; s. Samuel Davis and Frances (Perkins) S.; student St. John's Coll., Annapolis, Md., 1904-07; m. Margherita Harrell, Feb. 23, 1910; children—Samuel Donovan, Jr., Francis Edward, Evelyn Epps. Vicepres. Standard Remedy Co., Baltimore, Md. since 1910; interested in etching since 1929; exhibited at Conn. Acad. Fine Art, Print Club, Phila., Los Angeles, Chicago, New York; represented in collections of J. P. Morgan, Mrs. J. D. Rockefeller, Jr., Mrs. Franklin Roosevelt; one of first aviators in Md.; first in world to take an amphibian plane from water, Baltimore, 1911. Served as 1st lt. A.S., U.S.A., 1918-19, with A.E.F., 11th Squadron, 1st day bombardment group. Mem. Etchcrafters Art Guild (dir. since 1928), Etchcrafters of America (sec. since 1939), Md. Hist. Soc. Home: 879 Park Av. Office: 10 W. Chase St., Baltimore, Md.

SWANN, William Francis Gray, physicist; b. Ironbridge, Shropshire, Eng., Aug. 29, 1884; s. William Francis and Anne (Evans) S.; student Brighton (Eng.) Tech. Coll., 1900-03, Royal Coll. of Science (London), Univ. Coll., Kings Coll., City and Guilds of London Inst., 1903-07; B.Sc., London, 1905, D.Sc., 1910; asso. Royal Coll. of Science, 1906; hon. M.A., Yale University, 1924; hon. D.Sc., Swarthmore College, 1929; hon. F.T.C.M., London, 1936; m. Sarah Frances Mabel Thompson, Aug. 14, 1909; children—William Francis, Charles Paul, Sylvia. Jr. demonstrator in physics, Royal Coll. Science, London, 1905-07; asst. lecturer and demonstrator in physics, U. of Sheffield, 1907-13; came to U.S., 1913; chief of physical div. Dept. Terrestrial Magnetism, Carnegie Instn. Washington, 1913-18; prof. physics, U. of Minn., 1918-23, U. of Chicago, 1923-24, Yale, 1924-27; dir. Sloane Lam., 1924-27, also chmn. advisory research com. Bartol Research Foundation of Franklin Inst., and dir. same since 1927. Fellow Physical Society, London; member British Assn., A.A.A.S. (v.p. 1923-24), Am. Philos. Soc., Am. Physical Soc. (v.p. 1929, 30; pres. 1931-33), Am. Math. Soc., Optical Soc., Washington Acad. Sciences (v.p. 1923-24), Philos. Society Washington, Am. Geophys. Union (chmn. sect. D, 1923-24), Franklin Inst., Nat. Research Council, 1921-23, Gamma Alpha, Sigma Xi. Hon. Fellow, Trinity Coll., London. Asso. editor Journal of Franklin Inst. Episcopalian. Clubs: Cosmos (Washington, D.C.); Explorers Club, N.Y., Great Chebeauge Golf, Rolling Green Golf, Philadelphia Art Alliance; Connaught (London). Author: The Architecture of the Universe, 1934. Co-author: The Story of Human Error, 1936. Contbr. to Philos. Mag., Physical Rev., Jour. of Franklin Inst., Philos. Trans. Royal Soc., Ency. Britannica, etc. Cellist; conductor Swarthmore Symphony Orchestra. Home: 609 Ogden Av. Address: Bartol Research Foundation, Whittier Pl., Swarthmore, Pa.

SWANSON, Neil Harmon, newspaper editor and author; b. Minneapolis, Minn., June 30, 1896; s. Hermon N. and Eda Caroline (Peterson) S.; student U. of Minn., Minneapolis, 1913-15; m. Katharine Heath, Aug. 24, 1917 (div. 1931); children—Neil H., Jr., Jean Patricia, Robert H., Margaret R.; m. 2d, Margaret Diana Koch, Aug. 29, 1931. Asso. with Minneapolis Journal, 1915-24, city editor, 1924-27, asst. mng. editor, 1927-28, mng. editor, 1928-30; mng. editor Pittsburgh Press, 1930-31; asst. mng. editor Baltimore Evening Sun, 1931-38, acting mng. editor since 1938. Mem. exec. com. Associated Press mng. Editors' Assn. Served as 1st lt. then capt. inf., U.S.A., 1917-19; with A.E.F. in France. Mem. Soc. Am. Hists. Methodist. Author: The Flag Is Still There, 1933; The Judas Tree, 1933; The Phantom Emperor, 1934; The First Rebel, 1937; The Forbidden Ground, 1938. Signed contract, 1939, to write 25 Am. hist. novels, each an individual unit, the whole to tell continuous story of settlement and development of Del., Pa. and Md. westward to Miss. River. Home: 614 Park Av., Baltimore, Md.

SWANSON, William Fredin, dentist, asso. prof. bacteriology; b. Arroyo, Pa., Dec. 19, 1893; s. Joseph and Anna (Lundberg) S.; B.S., Pa. State Coll., 1915; D.D.S., U. of Pittsburgh Coll. of Dentistry, 1920, M.S., 1930; m. Ida Moore, Aug. 24, 1917; children—Ruth Bernice, William F., Jr. Instr. of bacteriology, U. of Pittsburgh, 1920-25, asst. prof., 1925-36, asso. prof. bacteriology since 1936. Fellow Am. Coll. of Dentists; mem. Odontol. Soc. of Western Pa. (pres. 1938), Delta Tau Delta, Psi Omega, Omicron Delta Kappa, Omicron Kappa Upsilon, Phi Sigma. Republican. Methodist. Mason (32°). Club: Faculty of University of Pittsburgh. Home: 5326 Pocusset St., Pittsburgh, Pa.

SWARD, Keith, prof. psychology and head dept., Pa. Coll. for Women. Home: New Kensington, Pa.

SWART, Howard A., in charge orthopedic and traumatic surgery Charleston Gen. Hosp. Address: 1021 Quarrier St., Charleston, W.Va.

SWARTLEY, Stanley Simpson, coll. prof.; b. North Wales, Pa., July 2, 1884; s. Mahlon R. and Mary (Godshalk) S.; A.B., U. of Pa., 1905, Ph.D., 1917; S.T.B., Boston U., 1908, A.M., 1909; Columbia, summers 1912, 13; m. Annette Miller, Apr. 12, 1909. Master in English and Latin, Harrisburg Acad., 1908-10; Harrison fellow in Eng., U. of Pa., 1913-14, 1916-17; instr. English, 1919-14, asst. prof., 1914-20, asso. prof., 1920-21, prof. English lang., and head of dept., 1921—, Allegheny Coll.; leave of absence, 1927-28, for travel and study in Europe, also 1938-39. Mem. Modern Lang. Assn. America, Nat. Council Teachers of English, Phi Delta Theta, Phi Beta Kappa, Am. Dialect Soc., Pi Delta Epsilon. Republican. Methodist. Mason (32°). Clubs: University, Round Table, Iroquois. Author: Life and Poetry of John Cutts, 1917; Aids to Good English, 1933, rev. edits., 1936, 38. Home: 656 William St., Meadville, Pa.

SWARTWOUT, Mary Cooke, art mus. dir.; b. Cleveland, O., Dec. 19, 1876; d. William Jay and Mary (Isom) Cooke; grad. Starret Sch., Oak Park, Ill., 1897; student Oberlin (O.) Coll. Conservatory, 1897-98; grad. in home economics, Lewis Institute, Chicago, Ill., 1899; m. Leslie George Swartwout, June 28, 1900. Staff member Toledo (Ohio) Museum of Art, 1920-24; director Grand Rapids (Michigan) Art Gallery, 1924-32; director Montclair (N.J.) Art Museum since 1932. Mem. Am. Assn. of Museums, Am. Fed. Arts, Coll. Art Assn., Eastern Art Assn., Am. Artists Professional League. Republican. Congregationalist. Home: 28 Gates Av. Office: 1 S. Mountain Av., Montclair, N.J.

SWARTZ, Aaron Snyder, lawyer; b. Norristown, Pa., Aug. 20, 1887; s. Aaron S. and Anna Louise (Keller) S.; A.B., Princeton U., 1908; student U. of Pa. Law Sch.; LL.D., Washington and Jefferson Coll., 1936; m. Jean Simms Buchanan, Jan. 26, 1914; children—Aaron S., III, Clara Rosalie, Walter Buchanan. Partner law firm High, Dettla & Swartz; dir. Montgomery Trust Co., Wildman Mfg. Co. Pres. Pa. Bar Assn., 1935-36. Home: 1739 DeKalb St. Office: 40 E. Airy St., Norristown, Pa.

SWARTZ, Charles Kephart, geologist; b. Baltimore, Jan. 3, 1861; s. Joel and Adelia (Rosecrans) S.; A.B., Johns Hopkins, 1888, Ph.D., 1904; U. of Heidelberg, 1889; fellow, Clark U., 1889-90; B.D., Oberlin Theol. Sem., 1892; m. Elizabeth A. Howard, Dec. 12, 1892; children—Joel Howard, William Hamilton, Frank McKim, Howard Currier, Charles Dana. Instr. geology, 1904-05, asso., 1905-06, asso. prof. geology and palæontology, 1907-10, collegiate prof. geology, 1910-31, emeritus prof. since 1931, Johns Hopkins U. Asst. Md. Geol. Survey. Fellow Am. Geol. Soc., A.A.A.S. Pres. Paleontological Soc., 1935; v.p. Geol. Soc. of America, 1936. Home: 2601 Lyndhurst Av., Baltimore, Md.

SWARTZ, Frank McKim, paleontologist; b. Bellevue, O., May 19, 1899; s. Charles Kephart and Elizabeth (Howard) S.; A.B., Johns Hopkins U., 1921, Ph.D., same, 1926; m. Ruth Passmore Hull, Nov. 25, 1926; children—Frank McKim, Jr., Mary Elizabeth. Engaged as instr. bus. geography, U. of N.C., 1923-24; instr. Paleontology, Pa. State Coll., 1925-27, asst. prof., 1927-30, asso. prof. since 1930; asso. geologist, Pa. Topographic and Geol. Survey since 1929; aide The Journal of Paleontology, 1939. Fellow Geol. Soc. of America, Paleontol. Soc. of America. Asso. mem. Soc. of Econ. Paleontologists and Mineralogists. Mem. Sigma Gamma Epsilon, Sigma Xi. Republican. Contbr. sci. papers and articles to tech. jours. Home: 728 N. Atherton St., State College, Pa.

SWARTZ, Joel Howard, geophysicist; b. Bellevue, O., Nov. 10, 1893; s. Charles Kephart and Elizabeth (Howard) S.; A.B., Johns Hopkins U., 1915, Ph.D. in Geology, 1923; m. Virginia Markley, Dec. 28, 1920; children—Donald Markley, William Alan. Prof. chemistry, physics, and biology, McKendree Coll., Lebanon, Ill., 1915-16; geologist, Md. Geol. Survey, 1916; geologist, oil corpn., Tampico, Mexico, 1920; geologist Tenn. Geol. Survey, 1921-23, 1927; asst. in geology, Johns Hopkins U., 1920-21, instr. geology, 1921-23; asst. prof. geology, U. of N.C., 1923-26, asso. prof. geology and geophysics, 1926-30; cons. engr. U.S. Bur. of Mines, 1929, sr. geophysicist, 1930-36; sr. geophysicist U.S. Geol. Survey since 1936. Served in Ambulance Service, U.S.A., 1917-18, in A.S., U.S.A., 1918. Fellow Geol. Soc. of America; mem. Geol. Soc. of Washington. Mem. Am. Geophys. Union, Phi Beta Kappa, Sigma Xi. Methodist. Home: 2601 Lyndhurst Av. Office: Custom House, Baltimore, Md.

SWARTZ, Leon Emerson, civil engr.; b. Mechanicsburg, Pa., July 9, 1888; s. Albert H. and Helen S. (Miller) S.; B.S. in C.E., Pa. State Coll., 1911; unmarried. Engaged in profession of civil engring. and as individual contractor at Lewistown, Pa., since 1911. Served as 1st lt. U.S. Engrs. during World War. Mem. Am. Soc. Civil Engrs., Soc. Am. Mil. Engrs., Delta Tau Delta. Republican. Protestant. Home: Lewistown, Pa.

SWARTZ, Morris Emory, clergyman; b. Pine Grove Mills, Pa., Feb. 7, 1868; s. George Musser and Mary (Keen) S.; Ph.B., Dickinson Coll., 1889, A.M., 1892; B.D., Drew Theol. sem., Madison, N.J., 1892; hon. D.D., Dickinson Coll., 1910; m. Carrie Myrta Bashore, Aug. 28, 1894; children—Robert Bashore, Morris Emory, Jr. Ordained to ministry M.E. Ch., 1892; served at West Fairview, Pa., 1892-94 and various chs. in Pa., 1894-1917; dist. supt. Harrisburg Dist., 1917-18; exec. sec. Washington Area for the "Centenary," 1918-22; editor-mgr. Washington Christian Advocate, 1926-27; dist. supt. Sunbury and Harrisburg dists., 1927-33; pastor Newberry M.E. Ch., Williamsport, Pa., 1933-39; retired Apr. 15, 1939. Mem. Sigma Chi. Republican. Mem. M.E. Ch. Home: 12 S. Royal St., York, Pa.

SWARTZ, Osman Ellis, lawyer; b Newark, O., Nov 3, 1880; s. Samuel Ellis and Jane Harriet (Ellis) S.; Ph.B., Shurtleff Coll., Alton, Ill., 1899; LL.B., Washington and Lee U., 1902; m. Marion Stephenson Swartz, Feb. 17, 1929. Admitted to W.Va. bar, 1902, and began practice at Clarksburg; counsel Monongahela West Penn. Pub. Service Co., Fairmont, W.Va., 1918-23; counsel Consolidation Coal Co., Fairmont, 1918-23, gen. atty. at N.Y. City, 1923-28; gen. counsel United Carbon Co., Charleston, W. Va., since 1928; pres. Camden Natural Gas Co., Adamston Homes, Inc.; v.p. Norwood Gas Co.; sec. Washington Gas Co. Served as pvt., U.S.A., World War. Mem. W.Va. Bar Assn., New York Law Inst., Phi Kappa Psi. Democrat. Baptist. Club: Edgewood Country (Charleston). Home: 465 Linden Av. Office: Union Bldg., Charleston, W.Va.

SWARTZEL, Karl Dale, prof. of mathematics; b. Lewisburg, O., July 1, 1869; s. William and Ketura (Ozias) S.; B.S., Ohio State U., 1893, M.S., 1894; student U. of Wis., 1901, Harvard, 1902-03; m. Helen Ebersole, June 16, 1904; children—Mary Helen (wife of Dr. Wm. E. Danforth, Jr.), Frances Elizabeth (wife of Kenneth N. Monnett), Karl Dale. Fellow in mathematics Ohio State U., 1893-95, instr., 1895-99, asst. prof. 1899-1906, asso. prof., 1906-08, prof., 1908-22; prof. mathematics and head of department, University of Pittsburgh, 1922-39, professor emeritus since 1939;

special instr. Kenyon Coll., 1898-1900; entrance examiner Ohio State Med. Bd., 1915-22. Served as ednl. dir. 6th Dist., S.A.T.C., during World War. Mem. Am. Math. Assn., Math. Soc., Soc. for Promotion Engring. Edn., A.A. A.S., Sigma Alpha Epsilon, Sigma Xi. Republican. Unitarian. Club: Faculty (U. of Pittsburgh). Author: Farm Arithmetic, 1912; Pre-Science Mathematics, 1927. Contbr. articles to jours. Home: 11329 Joffre St., Los Angeles, Calif.

SWAYZE, George Ayres, lawyer; b. Harveyville, Luzerne Co., Pa., Oct. 25, 1876; s. Clarke M. and Mary L. (Ayres) S.; A.B., Central High Sch., Philadelphia, 1899; LL.B., U. of Pa., 1903; m. Emma Barr, Oct. 27, 1906; 1 son, William Barr. Admitted to the bar, 1903; since in private practice at Philadelphia; gen. counsel and dir. South Philadelphia Nat. Bank, Philadelphia. Mem. Am. Bar Assn., Pa. Bar Assn., Philadelphia Bar Assn. Republican. Presbyterian. Clubs: Lawyers, Manufacturers and Bankers (Philadelphia). Home: 3710 Huey Av., Drexel Hill, Delaware Co., Pa. Office: 816 Market St. Bank Bldg., Philadelphia, Pa.

SWEADNER, Charles Albert, editor; b. Libertytown, Frederick Co., Md., Oct. 28, 1876; s. Richard and Octavia (Beall) S.; ed. Braddock grammar and high schs., U. of Pittsburgh; m. Jessie C. Inglis (died Jan. 19, 1919); children—Catherine (Mrs. John Kinneman), Richard I. Chemist Carnegie Steel Co., 1896-1902; began in newspaper work, 1902, became financial editor Pittsburgh Leader, 1902; editor Money & Commerce (official organ Pa. and W.Va. bankers assns.), since 1903; pres. Finance Co. (owner Money & Commerce) since 1928. Burgess West Homestead Borough, 1905-08. Chmn. publication com. Pa. Bankers Assn., 22 yrs. Republican. Methodist. Home: 1028 East End Av. Office: 104 Vandergrift Bldg., Pittsburgh, Pa.

SWEENEY, Richard H., lawyer; b. Hagerstown, Md., Apr. 3, 1893; s. John Bernard and Sophie Jeanette S.; student Catholic U., 1912-14, Catholic Univ. Law Sch., 1915-17, Georgetown U. Law Sch., 1917-18; unmarried. Engaged in gen. practice of law at Hagerstown, Md.; city police magistrate, Hagerstown, 1931-35; city atty., Hagerstown, 1937-39; mayor, Hagerstown, term, 1939-41. Served in U.S.N., 1918. Mem. Am. Legion. Democrat. Roman Catholic. K.C., Elk. Home: 169 S. Prospect St., Hagerstown, Md.

SWEENEY, Stephen Binnington, univ. prof.; b. Brooklyn, N.Y., July 9, 1899; s. Vaiden Brooker and Lizzie Minor (Aiguier) S.; B.S. in Econs., U. of Pa. Wharton Sch., 1922; Ph.D., U. of Pa. Grad. Sch., 1927; m. Marion Elizabeth Meikle, Oct. 2, 1925; children—James Perry, Jean Helen. Employed as ocean steamship officer on various ships intermittently, 1919-24; instr. econs., U. of Pa. Wharton Sch. of Commerce & Finance, 1922-25, instr. in ins., 1925-27, asst. prof. of ins., 1927-37, asso. prof. since 1937, in these positions, part time since 1932; consultant in ins., Parker & Co., Phila., 1927-32; dir. workmen's compensation, Dept. Labor and Industry of Pa., 1932-35; dir. of employment, Works Progress Adminstrn. in Pa., 1935-36, asst. adminstr., 1936-37; dir. Inst. of Local and State Govt., U. of Pa., since 1937. Served as chief q.m., U.S.N., 1917-19. Dir. Phila. and Suburban Town Meetings (pres.). Mem. Am. Econ. Assn., Am. Polit. Sci. Assn., Sigma Phi Epsilon. Methodist. Club: Lenape of Univ. of Pa. (Phila.). Home: 25 Roselawn Av., Lansdowne, Pa.

SWEENEY, Thomas William, ins. broker; b. Chicago, Ill., June 6, 1899; s. Thomas M. and Edna (Ruth) S.; B.S. in Econs., U. of Pa., 1923; m. Genevieve Ellen Bloomer, Jan. 16, 1926; children—Thomas William, Jr., Robert Berrell. Employed as asst. to publicity mgr., home office, Phoenix Mutual Life Ins. Co., Hartford, Conn., 1923-25; asso. with H. Mosenthal & Son, ins. brokers established 1868, N.Y. City, since 1925, sec. and dir. since 1928. Served as q.m. 3d class, U.S.N.R.F., 1918-22. Asso. mem. Young Mens Bd. Trade N.Y., U.S. Jr. Chamber of Commerce, N.Y. State Jr. Chamber of Commerce (past pres.), N.J. Taxpayers Assn. (dir.), Essex Co. Citizens Budget Com. (chmn.), Maplewood Civic Assn. (past pres.), Maplewood Community Service (trustee), Maplewood Citizens Com. (trustee), Maplewood Community Adv. Council. Mem. official bd., Morrow Memorial M.E. Ch. Mem. Ins. Brokers Assn. of N.Y., Life Underwriters of N.Y., N.Y. Bd. of Trade, Phi Sigma Kappa, S.A.R.; Am. Legion. Republican. Methodist. Clubs: University of Pennsylvania, Suburban Pennsylvania of N.J. Home: 22 Sunset Terrace, Maplewood, N.J. Office: 1 Cedar St., New York, N.Y.

SWEENEY, William Joseph, chem. engring.; b. Boston, Mass., May 6, 1898; s. Thomas J. and Ellen (Murphy) S.; B.S., Mass. State Coll., 1919; M.S., Pa. State Coll., 1924; D.Sc., Mass. Inst. Tech., 1928; m. Louise Clarke, Aug. 20, 1930; children—William Joseph, Jr., John Francis. Successively research asst., instr. chemistry, and asst. prof., Pa. State Coll., 1919-26; research lab. applied chemistry and part time research asst., Mass. Inst. Tech., 1926-28; dir. industrial research, Pa. State Coll., 1928-29; phys. chemist and chem. engr., Standard Oil Co. of La., 1929-32, asst. dir. research and development dept., 1932-34, dir. development and research labs., 1934-36; asso. dir. Esso Labs., Standard Oil Development Co., Bayway, N.J., since 1936. Served in O.T. Schs., Plattsburg, N.Y., and Camp Lee, Va., 2d lt. inf., U.S.A.; capt. C.W.S. Res. Mem. Inst. Chemists, Am. Chem. Soc., Soc. Automotive Engrs., Am. Inst. Chem. Engrs., Am. Petroleum Inst. Awarded DuPont Fellowship, M.I.T. Democrat. Roman Catholic. Home: 38 Aberdeen Rd., Elizabeth. Office: Esso Labs., Bayway, N.J.

SWEENY, E(dward) Arthur, newspaper editor and pub.; b. Irwin, Pa., Nov. 20, 1882; s. Edward B. and Rebecca E. (Muse) S.; ed. pub. schs.; unmarried. Began as reporter on newspaper, Greensburg, Pa., 1900; served as corr. Asso. Press as well as Pittsburgh and Phila. newspapers for many yrs.; after serving in various editorial capacities, acquired interest in Greensburg Morning Review, 1909, later became owner and pub.; brought about consolidation of daily newspapers in Greensburg into Tribune Review Publishing Co., 1924 and pres. and publisher since 1924. Served as del. Rep. Nat. Convs., 1924, 1928, 1932. Unsuccessful candidate for auditor general of Pa., 1936; appointed sec. of welfare of Pa., Jan. 17, 1939. For many yrs. active in civic welfare movements in Greensburg and Westmoreland Co. Mem. Internat. Typographical Union. Republican. Methodist. Mason (32°, Shriner). Home: 430 N. Maple Av. Office: Tribune Review Bldg., Greensburg, Pa.

SWEET, Albert Whitman, state health officer; b. West Warwick, R.I., Apr. 14, 1887; s. Albert Loring and Emma Francis (Whitman) S.; student Classical High Sch., Providence, R.I., 1904-07; Ph.B., Brown U., Providence, R.I., 1911, M.A., 1912, Ph.D., 1915; m. Alice Victoria Lisk, May 26, 1916 (divorced); children—Albert Whitman, James Lisk. Grad. sch. instr. in biol. dept., Brown U., Providence, R.I., 1911-14; bacteriologist Newport (R.I.) Water Works, 1915-17; prof. bacteriology and pub. health, U. of Tenn. Coll. of Medicine, Memphis, Tenn., 1919-20; prof. hygiene and dir. of dept., U. of Fla., Gainesville, Fla., 1920-24, prof. bacteriology and biol. chemistry, dir. health dept., 1925-27; dist. health officer, N.J. State Dept. of Health, Freehold, N.J., since 1927; with R.I. State Dept. Health, 1915-16, Tenn., 1920, Fla., 1921-27; organized pub. health unit, Shelby County and City of Memphis, Tenn., 1920, branch lab., 1920; directed health program and dept. under Inter-Departmental Hygiene bd., U. of Fla., 1920-24, surveyed southern univs. and schs. for same, 1925. Served with Red Cross San. Unit 17, Greenville, S.C., Oct.-Dec. 1917. Served as 1st lt. and capt. San. Corps, U.S. Army, 1917-19; at Fort Oglethorpe, Ga., Rockefeller Inst., N.Y., Army. Med. Sch., Washington, Fort Leavenworth, Kan., 1917-18; with A.E.F., France and Germany, 1918-19; at U.S. Gen. Hosp. 41, Fox Hills, Staten Island, N.Y., Aug.-Sept. 1919; capt. San. Corps Res., 1921-25, maj., 1925-35, lt. col. since 1935; dir. and organized advanced course in mil. sanitation, Med. Field Service Sch., Carlisle, Pa., since 1934; organized, 1934, and since dir. Corps Area Service Unit, San. Sect., 2d Corps Area at Governors Island, N.Y.; originated research study upon provision of potable water supplies, Army Field Force, 1936, and study of removal and decontamination of field water supplies contaminated with chem. warfare gases, 1937; organizing by request program of protection of food supplies against contamination with chem. warfare gases since 1938. Organized, 1934, and since dir. health and safety program Monmouth Council of Boy Scouts, Monmouth Am. Red Cross since 1935. Fellow Am. Pub. Health Assn.; mem. Res. Officers Assn., Assn. Mil. Surgeons (1st v.p. N.J. Chapter since 1937), N.J. Health Officers Assn., N.J. Health and Sanitary Assn., Phi Kappa Phi, Beta Theta Pi. Episcopalian. Mason (Past Master Gainesville, Fla., Lodge; Royal Arch; Commandery; Scottish Rite, Jacksonville, Fla.). Home: 137 Hudson Av., Red Bank, N.J. Office: Court House, Freehold, N.J.

SWEET, Alfred Henry, prof. European history; b. Methuen, Mass., Sept. 8, 1890; s. Charles Elkins (D.D.) and Matilda (Hill) S.; A.B., Bowdoin, 1913; Longfellow grad. scholar same, 1913-14; A.M., Harvard, 1914; Ph.D., Cornell, 1917; research work in England, 1916-17; research work in Rome and England, 1932, 34; m. Gladys Greenleaf, June 12, 1916; 1 son, Charles Woodbury Greenleaf. Instr. in history, Hobart Coll., Geneva, N.Y., 1916; President White fellow in history, Cornell U., 1916-17; acting asst. prof. English history, same univ., 1917-20; asso. prof. history, U. of Colo., 1920-21, Washington U., 1921-22; Craig prof. history, St. Lawrence U., 1922-25; prof. European history, Washington and Jefferson Coll., since 1925; lecturer on history, summers, U. of Calif., 1922, U. of Colo., 1923, 24, 27, 31, Pa. State Coll., 1928-29, U. of Pa., 1936, Coll. City of New York, 1937, U. of Tex., 1938. Del. Dem. Nat. Conv., 1936. Fellow Royal Historical Society; member American Historical Assn., Mediæval Acad. America, Am. Assn. Univ. Profs., Asiatic Soc. of Japan (life), Am. Soc. Ch. History, Beta Theta Pi, Phi Beta Kappa. Democrat. Episcopalian. Author: History of England, 1931. Contbr. to National Encyclopedia and hist. reviews. Home: Washington, Pa.

SWEET, Ellingham Tracy, newspaper editor; b. LeRaysville, Pa., Apr. 27, 1853; s. Ambrose Spencer and Cynthia (Nichols) S.; student common schs., Montrose, Pa.; m. Fannie Foster, May 28, 1879. Learned printer's trade at Montrose, Pa.; became pub. Montrose (Pa.) Chronicle, 1885; pub. Scranton (Pa.) Cricket (weekly), 1889-90; editor The Scrantonian, Scranton, Pa., since 1889, The Scranton (Pa.) Tribune since 1938. Mem. Scranton Chamber of Commerce, New England Soc. of Northeastern Pa., Am. Press Humorists Assn. Home: 1124 Diamond Av. Office: 232 N. Washington Av., Scranton, Pa.

SWEET, William Henry, banker; b. Dudley, Pa., Jan. 9, 1889; s. John and Sarah (Edwards) S.; ed. Dudley pub. and high schs.; commercial course Juniata Coll., Huntingdon, Pa., 1905-06; studied higher accounting International Correspondence Sch., 1908-09; studied economics, commercial law and banking (nights), St. Vincents Coll., Latrobe, Pa., 1932-36; m. Catharine Gray, June 24, 1916; children—William Ray, Jane Elizabeth, Nancy Ann, Sarah Emily. Began bituminous coal mining, 1902; successively Pa. R.R. Co. payroll clerk, utility co. branch office mgr., and chief accountant for group of coal cos.; trust officer Blairsville Savings & Trust Co., 1925-30, treas. since 1930, exec. v.p. since 1930; pres. and dir. Conemaugh Bldg. & Loan Assn.; dir. Bells Mill Coal Co., Braeburn Alloy Steel Corpn., Kiskiminitas Coal Co., Eby Shoe Co., Lancaster Iron Works Co. Councilman, Blairsville Borough, 1920-28. Served as corporal, 1st Pa. Cavalry. Ex-treas. Torrance State Hosp.; industrial chmn. Blairsville Chamber of Commerce; ex-pres. Westmoreland Chapter Am. Inst. Banking, Indiana County Bankers Club. Republican. Methodist (trustee). Mason. (Shriner). Club: Monroe Hunting and Fishing (Monroe Furnace, Pa.). Home: 155 N. Spring

St. Office: Blairsville Savings & Trust Co., Blairsville, Pa.

SWENEHART, John (Henry), advertising mgr.; b. Vandervoort, Clark Co., S.D., Aug. 18, 1890; s. John Henry and Bessie Imogen (Babcock) S.; B.S., S.D. State Coll., Brookings, S.D., 1911; student U. of Wis., Madison, Wis., 1911; m. Anna Lucy Lueck, July 3, 1916 (died 1923); children—Elizabeth Anne, John Delmer; m. 2d, Florence Ellen Amadon, June 5, 1926; 1 son, Walter Gordon. Agrl. dir. Jordan (Minn.) High Sch., 1911-14; co. agrl. agt., Crandon, Wis., 1914-18; asst. agrl. engr. in charge land clearing operations and prof. agrl. engring., U. of Wis., Madison, Wis., asst. state leader co. agts., 1918-28; mgr. agrl. div. Atlas Powder Co., Wilmington, Del., 1929-33, advertising mgr. since 1933. Clubs: University (Wilmington, Del); Advertising (New York). Home: 2004 Harrison St. Office: care Atlas Powder Co., Wilmington, Del.

SWICK, Clarence Herbert, geodetic mathematician; b. Wilson, N.Y., June 1, 1883; s. Charles Edgar and Alice Maria (Dobbs) S.; C.E., Cornell U., 1907; m. Hattie May Haight, June 18, 1908; children—Edgar Haight, Helen Marjorie, Eunice Reba, Alice May, Eloise Adelaide. With U.S. Coast and Geodetic Survey since 1907; field force 2 yrs.; work since 1909 in computations of gravity isostasy, triangulation, astronomy, and in editing scientific publications of Div. of Geodesy; chief of sect. of gravity and astronomy since 1924. Mem. A.A.A.S., American Geophys. Union, Cornell Soc. Engrs., Philos. Soc. Washington, Washington Society Engrs., American Astronomical Soc., Washington Academy of Sciences, Sigma Xi. Author: Triangulation Along the West Coast of Florida, 1913; Triangulation in Georgia, 1917; Descriptions of Triangulation Stations in Georgia, 1917; Modern Methods for Measuring the Intensity of Gravity, 1921; World Longitude Determinations by the U.S. Coast and Geodetic Survey in 1926, 1931; First and Second Order Triangulation in Oregon, 1932; (co-author) Formulas and Tables for the Computation of Geodetic Positions on the International Ellipsoid, 1935—all publs. of U.S. Coast and Geodetic Survey. Home: Capitol Heights, Md.

SWICK, J. Howard, ex-congressman; b. New Brighton, Pa., Aug. 6, 1879; student Geneva Coll., Beaver Falls; M.D., Hahnemann Med. Coll., 1906, M.A., 1931; m. Esther Le Ethel Duncan, 1906; one son, J. Howard. Practiced at Beaver Falls many years; president Bur. of Health, Beaver Falls, 1907-14; pres. State Bank of Beaver Falls; 1st v.p., dir. Moltrup Steel Products Co., mem. 70th to 73d Congresses (1927-35), 26th Pa. Dist. Served in Med. Corps, U.S.A., 18 mos., World War; with A.E.F., 12 mos.; col. Med. Res. Corps. Mem. Am. Legion, Vets. Foreign Wars. Republican. Methodist. Mason (32°, K.T., Shriner), K.P. Club: Lions. Home: Beaver Falls, Pa.

SWIFT, Archie Dean, banker; b. North East, Pa., Aug. 18, 1877; s. Charles James and Josephine (Reno) S.; ed. high sch., Ridgway, Pa.; m. Maud Patterson, 1902; 1 dau., Natalie Patterson; m. 2d, Bernice M. Thompson, Sept. 2, 1909; children—Shirley Bernice, Virginia Aileen, Archie Dean, Eugene Clinton, Martin Reno. Began as clk. Ridgeway Bank, 1892; clk. Elk County Bank, Ridgway, 1893-1902; teller Citizens Nat. Bank, Warren, Pa., 1902-03; asst. cashier Elk Co. Nat. Bank, Ridgway, 1903-06, cashier, 1906-16; asst. cashier Central-Penn Nat. Bank, 1916-20, cashier, 1920-28, v.p., 1922-28, pres. since 1928; pres. Civic Bldg. & Loan Assn., Ardmore, Pa.; dir. Schlichter Jute Cordage Co., Pierce Sch. Bldg. & Loan Assn., P. & W. Ry. Republican. Presbyn. Mason. Clubs: Union League, Down Town, St. David's Golf, Pine Valley Golf. Home: Wayne, Pa. Office: Central-Penn Nat. Bank, Philadelphia, Pa.

SWIFT, Clement K(innersley), chem. engr.; b. Norwood, Delaware Co., Pa., July 20, 1890; s. Charles K. and Sarah (Pollock) S.; grad. Central Manual Training Sch., Phila., 1909; B.S. in chem. engring., U. of Pa., 1915; m. Marion Henderson, Feb. 3, 1920; 1 son, Wilbert Bruce. Began as chemist, 1915; chem. engr. MacAndrews & Forbes Co., Camden, N.J., since 1926; dir. Hartman-Ledden Co., pres. 1931-34. Mem. Am. Chem. Soc., Sigma Xi. Democrat. Episcopalian. Home: 434 Oxford Rd., Brookline, Pa. Office: Camden, N.J.

SWIFT, Raymond Walter, research in nutrition; b. East Longmeadow, Mass., June 12, 1895; s. Harry Brewster and Ida Marietta (Kibbe) S.; B.S., Mass. State Coll., 1920; M.S., Pa. State Coll., 1925; Ph.D., U. of Rochester, N.Y., 1931; m. Laura Adams Dickinson, Aug. 25, 1926; children—Raymond Emory, Elizabeth Dickinson. Analytical chemist, Mass. Expt. Sta., 1920-23; research chemist, prof. of animal nutrition, Inst. of Animal Nutrition, Pa. State Coll., since 1923; asst. in physiology, U. of Rochester, N.Y., on leave, 1930-31. Served as pvt. inf., stretcher bearer and asst. bandleader, U.S.A., 1917-19, with A.E.F. Mem. Am. Inst. Nutrition, Am. Soc. Animal Production, Kappa Gamma Psi, Phi Lambda Upsilon, Gamma Sigma Delta, Phi Kappa Tau, Sigma Xi. Republican. Conglist. Known also as musician, trumpet soloist. Home: 723 McKee St., State College, Pa.

SWIGART, Paul J., banking; b. Huntingdon, Pa., Dec. 25, 1887; s. William J. and Carrie (Miller) S.; ed. Huntingdon pub. schs. and Juniata Coll.; m. Lucile M. Summerville, June 22, 1913; children—Shelley Sanborn, William Joseph, 2d, Pauline Lucile. Began as merchant and postmaster, Towner, Colo., 1910; returned to Pa., 1920, and entered employ of Standing Stone Nat. Bank, Huntingdon, 1922; cashier and dir. First Nat. Bank, Alexandria, Pa., since 1922; pres. and dir. Alexandria Water Co. Mem. Alexandria Sch. Bd. Republican. Presbyterian. Mason (Shriner). Home: 507 Main St. Office: First Nat. Bank, Alexandria, Pa.

SWIGART, William Emmert, insurance; b. Huntingdon, Pa., June 5, 1883; s. William J. and Carrie (Miller) S.; grad. Juniata Acad., 1900; A.B., Juniata Coll., 1906; m. Eva Workman, June 6, 1907; children—John Workman, Dorothy Anne, William Emmert, Jr., Naomi Marie, Martha Joan; m. 2d, Elizabeth W. Weeks, June 15, 1936. Spl. agent Penn Mutual Life Ins. Co., 1904-07; mem. firm Swigart, Harshbarger & Co., 1907-32; in fire and casualty ins. business under own name, 1932-33, incorporated under name of Swigart Associates, Inc., 1933, and since pres.; pres. Insurance Credit Club since 1933; operated General Finance Co., automobile financing, until 1938 when incorporated as General Finance Service Corpn., since pres.; pres. Budget Plan, Inc.; pres. Mutual Benefit Fire Ins. Co. and Select Risk Mutual Fire Ins. Co., both of Huntingdon, Pa.; dir. Penn Mutual Fire Ins. Co., Am. Casualty Co., First Nat. Bank of Alexandria, Penn-Liberty Ins. Co. of West Chester, Harleysville (Pa.) Mutual Casualty Co., Mutual Auto Fire Ins. Co., Harleysville; sec. Huntingdon Savings & Loan Assn.. Formerly trustee Juniata Coll. Mem. Nat. Assn. Mutual Ins. Agents (dir.), Pa. German Soc. (dir. Norristown, Pa.), Huntingdon Co. Hist. Soc. Republican. Mem. Ch. of the Brethren. Club: Huntingdon Country. Collector Early American and Oriental items; owner large library of Early Pa. and County histories, Early Bibles and Religious Imprints, First editions, etc.; also comprehensive collections of fire marks, automobile nameplates and license tags. Home: 1810 Mifflin St. Office: 409-411 Penn St., Huntingdon, Pa.

SWINDLER, James A., prof. physics.; b. Advance, Ind., May 20, 1887; s. John Henry and Ella (Kinnear) S.; B.S., Central Norman Coll., Danville, Ind., 1908; A.B., Indiana U., Bloomington, 1913, A.M., 1915; student U. of Chicago, summers, 1917 and 18, Indiana U., summers, 1922-23, Ph.D., 1925; m. Elda McKinney, Sept. 12, 1914; children—Genevieve Lowenne, Gilbert LeRoy, Jean Marie. Instr. physics, U. of Pittsburgh, 1916-17; asst. prof. physics, Pa. State Coll., 1917-19; prof. physics and head dept., Westminster Coll., New Wilmington, Pa., since 1919, registrar, 1920-36, acting dean, 1934-35, sec. of faculty, 1921-31. Chmn. New Wilmington Pub. Sch. Bd. since 1934. Fellow A.A.A.S.; mem. Am. Assn. Physics Teachers, Am. Physical Soc., Assn. Physics Teachers of Pittsburgh (chmn. 1932-33). United Presbyn. Home: 227 N. Market St., New Wilmington, Pa.

SWINDLER, Mary Hamilton, prof. archæology; b. Bloomington, Ind., Jan. 1, 1884; d. Harrison Turley and Ida M. (Hamilton) S.; A.B., Indiana U., 1905, A.M., 1906; fellow in Greek, Bryn Mawr, 1906-09, Ph.D., 1912; Mary E. Garrett European fellow, Berlin, winter 1909, Am. Sch. of Classical Studies, Athens, spring 1910. Reader in Latin and demonstrator in art and archæology, Bryn Mawr, 1912-16, instr. in Latin and classical archæology, 1916-21, asso., 1921-25, asso. prof., 1925-31, prof. classical archæology since 1931; visiting prof., Am. Sch. of Classical Studies, Athens, 1st semester, 1938-39. Editor in chief Am. Jour. of Archæology. Com. on mem. Publication in Fine Arts, Am. Council of Learned Socs., Exec. com. Am. Sch. in Athens. Exec. com. Archæol. Inst. America, Am. Oriental Soc., Coll. Art Assn., Soc. for Promotion of Hellenic Studies (London), Am. Assn. Univ. Profs., German Archæol. Inst. (Berlin), Phi Beta Kappa, Kappa Alpha Theta; fellow Royal Soc. of Arts (London). Republican. Clubs: Cosmopolitan (New York); Art Alliance (Philadelphia). Author: Ancient Painting, 1929; also monograph, Cretan Elements in the Cult and Ritual of Apollo, 1913. Contbr. articles and reviews to Am. Jour. Archæology, etc. Lecturer. Home: Bryn Mawr, Pa.

SWING, R. Hamill Davis, dentist; emeritus prof. dental surgery, Univ. of Pa. Address: University of Pa., Philadelphia, Pa.

SWINGLE, Wilbur Willis, zoölogy; b. Warrensburg, Mo., Jan. 11, 1891; s. Jacob and Emma Lucy S.; A.B., A.M., U. of Kan., 1916; Ph.D., Princeton, 1920; m. Emily Gerken, Nov. 2, 1916 (divorced); m. 2d, Alice Sullivan, Apr. 1929; children—Stephen Grey, Philip Colin. Fellow in zoölogy, University of Kansas, 1916, instructor, 1917-18; instructor zoölogy, Yale University, 1920, asst. prof., 1921-26; prof. and head dept. of zoölogy, State U. of Ia., 1926-29; prof. biology, Princeton since 1929. Mem. Am. Soc. Zoölogists, Am. Assn. Anatomists, Am. Soc. Physiologists, Soc. Exptl. Biology and Medicine, Assn. for Study Internal Secretions (council, 1931-32), Am. Soc. Naturalists, Phila. Acad. Natural Sciences, Long Island Biol. Assn. (dir.), Am. Eugenical Soc. (advisory council), Sigma Xi, Sigma Alpha Epsilon, Phi Chi. Republican. Protestant. Author numerous papers in field of exptl. zoölogy and physiology. Asso. editor Physiological Zoölogy; editor sect. on endocrinology of Biol. Abstracts. Home: 32 Hawthorne Av., Princeton, N.J.

SWINT, Benjamin Harrison, physician and surgeon; b. Pickens, W.Va., Aug. 14, 1888; s. Peter and Caroline (Winkler) S.; student Duquesne U., Pittsburgh, 1905-06; M.D., U. of Md. Med. Coll., 1911; grad. study in surgery, St. Joseph's Hosp., Baltimore, 1911-13; m. Marcellene Smith, June 6, 1916; children—Benjamin, Caroline, Bernice, Elizabeth, John, Patricia, Marcellene. Engaged in practice of medicine and surgery at Charleston, W.Va., since 1914; chief of surg. staff St. Francis Hosp., Charleston, since 1915; chmn. med. adv. com., W.Va. Dept. Pub. Assistance, 1936-39, W.Va. Compensation Dept., 1937-39; mem. W.Va. State Health Council, 1934-39. Served as 1st lt. Med. Corps, U.S.A., 1918-19; with A.E.F. in France. Active in Boy Scout work since 1921, mem. Nat. Council, past pres. Area Council; past pres. local Red Cross; dir. Community Chest, Nursing Assn., Tuberculosis Assn. Vice-pres. Nat. Council of Catholic Men. Fellow Am. Coll. Surgeons. Mem. A.M.A., W.Va. State Med. Soc., Kanawha Co. Med. Soc. (pres. 1938), Phi Chi. Republican. Roman Catholic. K.C. Club: Rotary. Home: 920 Ridgemont Rd. Office: Bank of Commerce Bldg., Charleston, W.Va.

SWINT, John J., bishop; b. Pickens, W.Va., Dec. 15, 1879; s. Peter and Caroline (Winkler) S.; A.B., St. Charles Coll., Ellicott City, Md., 1899, A.M.,; S.T.B., St. Mary's Sem., Baltimore, Md., 1904; Apostolic Mission House, Washington, D.C., 1904-05. Ordained priest R.

C. Ch., 1904; head of Diocesan Apostolate, Wheeling, many yrs.; built ch. at Beckley, and ch. and sch. at Weston; pastor, Weston; auxiliary bishop Diocese of Wheeling, Feb. 22, 1922—. Became administrator Diocese of Wheeling on death of Bishop Donahue, Oct. 4, 1923; bishop of Wheeling since Dec. 11, 1923. Home: Cor. 13th and Byron Sts., Wheeling, W.Va.

SWIREN, David Bernard, rabbi; b. Poland, Jan. 10, 1889; s. Joseph and Ethel S.; came to U.S., 1905, naturalized, 1914; Rabbi, Yeshivah Coll., New York, N.Y. (Rabbi Isaac Elhanan Theol Sem.), 1911; m. Anna Regina Grossman (d. Rabbi Jos. G.) of Phila., Pa., Jan. 14, 1914; children—Abraham Jesse, Evelyn May, Milton Solomon, Julian Meyer. Rabbi, Waterbury, Conn., 1911-15 Montefiore Congregation, Phila., 1916-17 Wilmington, Del., 1918-20; rabbi Orthodox Jewish Community and Lenas Hazedek Synagogue of West Phila. since 1921. Founder Hebrew Inst., Waterbury, Conn., sponsor and an organizer of Keren Hayesod of Phila., and a combined vets. orgns. of West Phila. Mem. Union of Orthodox Rabbis of America (exec. com.), Union of Orthodox Congs. of America, Zionist Orgn., Am. Jewish Hist. Soc., vice-chmn. Del. Americanization Com. Author: What's in Our Names, 1920; Our Life Is Like That, 1931; We Jews, 1936; (in ms.) How to Face Life (English), Debir David (Hebrew). Contbr. to Hebrew Encyc., and verse to mags. Orator in Eng. and Yiddish. Home: 5925 Larchwood Av., Philadelphia, Pa.

SWISHER, Carl Brent, univ. prof.; b. Weston, W.Va., Apr. 28, 1897; s. James Edwin and Annie Gertrude (Reger) S.; student W.Va. Wesleyan Coll., Buckhannon, W.Va., 1918-19, A.B., Pomona Coll., Claremont, Calif., 1926, A.M., 1927; Ph.D., Brookings Grad. Sch., Washington, D.C., 1929; m. Idella Gwatkin, Aug. 19, 1929; 1 dau., Carolyn. Instr. in govt., Columbia U., 1930-35; sr. specialist in information, Resettlement Adminstrn., 1935; spl. asst. to atty. gen. of U.S., 1937-38, Thomas P. Stran prof. polit. sci. since 1938, chmn. dept. since 1937. Mem. Am. Polit. Sci. Assn., Soc. Am. Historians, Phi Beta Kappa, Delta Sigma Rho. Clubs: Political Economy, Johns Hopkins (Baltimore). Author: Motivation and Political Technique in the California Constitutional Convention of 1878-1879, 1930; Stephen J. Field: Craftsman of the Law, 1930; Roger B. Taney, 1935. Editor: Selected Papers of Homer Cummings, 1939. Home: 112 W. University Parkway, Baltimore, Md.

SWOPE, Charles Siegel, college pres.; b. Saltillo, Pa., Mar. 19, 1899; s. Bruce Hudson and Anna Elizabeth (Houck) S.; grad. West Chester State Normal Sch., 1921; A.B., Dickinson Coll., Carlisle, Pa., 1925, A.M., U. of Pa., 1929; m. Edna M. McAllister, Aug. 19, 1928; 1 son, Charles Evans. Rural sch. teacher, Beaverstown, Pa., 1916-18, teacher in pvt. sch., Pennington, N.J., 1921-23 and 1925-26; supt. schs., Everett, Pa., 1926-27; instr. West Chester State Teachers Coll., 1927-35, pres. since 1935. Mem. bd. dirs. Chester County Council Boy Scouts of America; mem. bd. Pennington (N.J.) Sch. for Boys, West Chester (Pa.) M.E. Ch., Pres. Eastern Dist. Sabbath Sch. Assn. of Chester County, 1933-36. Mem. Schoolmen's Com. Mem. Acad. Polit. and Social Science, N.E.A., (ex-officio mem. Ednl. Policy Com. 1937), Pa. State Edn. Assn., Phi Kappa Sigma. Republican. Methodist. Clubs: Rotary (dir.), Elk's Club, X Club (West Chester); Schoolmen (Philadelphia). Lecturer and author articles on social studies. Home: Rosedale Av., West Chester, Pa.

SWOPE, Guy J., ex-congressman; b. Meckville, Pa., Dec. 26, 1892; s. Jeremiah Gerhart and Mary Jane (Smith) S.; std. pub. schs. of Pa., and Keystone State Teachers Coll., Kutztown, Pa.; m. Mayme Catherine Gerberich, Oct. 23, 1909; children—Marjorie Evelyn (Mrs. Leon Guyer), Harold Wesley, Lee Frederick. Pub. sch. teacher, 1909-13; U.S. internal revenue agt., 1913-18; private accountant, 1918-19; pub. accountant, banker, dept. store comptroller, 1919-35; mem. Swope and Nichols, pub. accountants, since 1936; budget sec. State of Pa., 1935-37; mem. 75th Congress (1937-39), 19th Pa. Dist. Dem. chmn. Dauphin Co., Pa., 1934-37. Democrat. Lutheran. Mason (32°, Shriner). Home: 2510 N. 2d St. Office: 212 N. 3d St., Harrisburg, Pa.

SWOPE, Harry Forrest, banker; b. Gettysburg, Pa., June 15, 1875; s. Granville Hamilton and Emma (Buckingham) S.; student Baltimore City Coll., 1889-93; m. Helen B. Selden, Nov. 4, 1903; children—Harry Forrest, Granville Hamilton. With Western Nat. Bank, 1893-96; asst. to pres. Fidelity Trust Co., 1896-1912; partner Alex Brown & Sons since 1920. Democrat. Episcopalian. Club: Maryland (Baltimore). Home: 20 Whitfield Road, Guilford. Office: 135 E. Baltimore St., Baltimore, Md.

SWOPE, John Laughlin, transit exec.; b. Osceola Mills, Pa., Feb. 27, 1877; s. Granville Hamilton and Emma Jane (Buckingham) S.; student Baltimore pub. schs. and Baltimore City Coll.; m. Edith Baily Coale, Nov. 1, 1902; children—John Laughlin, William Ellis Coale, Carey Buckingham. Became runner Western Nat. Bank, Baltimore, Md., 1895; now v.p. and dir. The Baltimore Transit Co., The Baltimore Coach Co., The Catonsville (Md.) Short Line R.R.; dir. The Nelson Corpn., The Md. Title Securities Corpn., The Homestead Fire Ins. Co. Democrat. Episcopalian. Club: Gibson Island (Md.). Home: Roland Park, Baltimore, Md. Office: 518 Equitable Bldg., Baltimore, Md.

SWOPE, Joseph Raymond, retired; b. St. Lawrence, Cambria Co., Pa., Feb. 28, 1873; s. Joseph Philip and Louisa (Glasser) S.; ed. pub. schs., 1879-88, Peirce Business Sch., Philadelphia, Sept. 1896-Feb. 1897; m. Bessie E. Gill, Dec. 16, 1902; children—Cordelia, Carlyle, Cressida (Mrs. David Bentley), Josephine. Teacher pub. sch., 1889-92; telegraph operator Western Union Telegraph Co., 1892-96; printer, 1898-1900; in flour and feed business under name of Swope Bros., 1900-37; retired, 1937; dir. U.S. Nat. Bank, Johnstown, Pa. Democrat. Mem. Christian Ch. Home: 1124 Confer Av., Johnstown, Pa.

SWOPE, Wilbur David; prof. dairy husbandry; b. Colfax, Pa., Feb. 25, 1886; s. James Franklin and Belle (Pheasant) S.; B.S., Pa. State Coll., 1919, M.S., same, 1924; m. Maude Houck, Aug. 11, 1915; children—Caroline Louise, Margaret Jean. Reared on farm; ed. Summer Normal Sch., 3 summers; taught country sch.; ed. course in agriculture, 1910-12; farm operator, 1912-14; asst. instr. dairy husbandry, Pa. State Coll., 1914-19, instr., 1919-21, asst. prof., 1921-24, asso. prof., 1924-30, prof. dairy husbandry since 1930. Mem. Am. Dairy Sci. Assn., Tau Kappa Epsilon. Republican. Methodist. Home: 122 Sparks St., State College, Pa.

SWOYER, Alfred E.; president judge 22d Judical Dist. of Pa. since 1931. Address: Honesdale, Pa.

SYBERT, Cornelius Ferdinand, lawyer; b. Loretta, Pa., Sept. 16, 1900; s. Pius Alphonse and Anna Marie (Haid) S.; A.B., Loyola Coll., Baltimore, Md., 1922; LL.B., U. of Md. Law Sch., Balto., Md., 1925; m. Elizabeth J. Johnson, Aug. 31, 1927; children—Cornelius Ferdinand, Jr., Joan Elizabeth. Employed as newspaper reporter, 1922-25; admitted to Md. bar, 1925 and since engaged in gen. practice of law at Ellicott City; sec.-treas. State Central Com. of Howard Co., 1930-34; counsel to county commrs. of Howard Co., 1931-34; state's atty. for Howard Co. for term, 1934-42; dir. and atty. Central Bank of Howard County, Clarksville, Md., since 1938. Mem. Md. State Bar Assn. Democrat. Roman Catholic. K.C. Home: Old Washington Rd., Elkridge. Office: Court Av., Ellicott City, Md.

SYDNOR, Giles Granville, clergyman; b. Halifax Co., Va., Dec. 10, 1864; s. Giles and Rebecca Pleasant (Royster) S.; A.B., Hampden-Sydney Coll., 1887; B.D., Union Theol. Sem., Va., 1893; D.D., Presbyn. Coll. of S.C.; m. Evelyn Aiken Sackett, June 24, 1897; children—Charles Sackett, Giles Granville, Henry Mosley, Louise Leyburn, James Rawlings. Ordained ministry Presbyn. Ch. in U.S., 1893; pastor successively Academy, Ottewood and Leesville chs., Va., Greene Street Ch., Augusta, Ga., First Ch., Rome, Ga., until 1919, Charles Town, W.Va. 1919—. Moderator of the Synod of Georgia, 1910; instructor ch. music, Union Theological Sem., Richmond, Va., 1920-25, spl. lecturer on Great Hymns of the Ch., 1926. While pastor at Rome conducted funeral services of Mrs. Woodrow Wilson, formerly a member of the ch.; mem. of com. which prepared and published The Presbyterian Hymnal, 1927. Trustee Danville Mil. Inst., Massanetta Springs Conf. Mem. Sigma Chi. Democrat. Kiwanian. Home: Charles Town, W.Va.*

SYDNOR, Henry Mosely, supt. county schs.; b. Rome, Ga., Nov. 29, 1902; s. Giles Granville and Evelyn Aiken (Sackett) S.; A.B., Hampden-Sydney Coll., Hampden-Sydney, Va., 1923; A.M., U. of Va., Charlottesville, Va., 1931; grad. student U. of Pittsburgh, 1937; m. Mary Bates, June 1, 1929; children—Edward Bates, Granville Lassiter. Employed as prin. high sch., Cumberland, Va., 1923-25; employed in wholesale paint bus., Richmond, Va., 1925-30; prin. high sch., Harpers Ferry, W.Va., 1931-35; supt. county schs., Jefferson Co., at Charles Town, W.Va. since 1935. Pres. Young Dem. Club, Jefferson Co., 1933-35. Mem. Kappa Sigma, Tau Kappa Alpha. Democrat. Presbyn. Home: 426 Samuel St. Office: 116 Washington St., Charles Town, W.Va.

SYKES, Charles Henry, cartoonist; b. Athens, Ala., Nov. 12, 1882; s. William Henry and Jane Palmyra (Hayes) S.; ed. high sch.; studied art at Drexel Inst., Phila.; m. Charlotte Kennedy Hannum, Sept. 11, 1907; children—William Henry (dec.), Charles Henry, John Marshall. Illustrator, 1904-06; art dept. of Phila. North American, 1906; cartoonist Williamsport (Pa.) News, 1906-08, Nashville (Tenn.) Banner, 1909-11, Phila. Public Ledger, 1911-14, Evening Public Ledger, 1914—; political cartoonist, "Life" (New York), 1922-28. Mason. Clubs: Players, Bala Golf. Home: Bala-Cynwyd, Pa. Address: Evening Public Ledger, Philadelphia, Pa.*

SYKES, Frank Herbert, life ins.; b. Philadelphia, Pa., Dec. 30, 1879; s. James and Martha Ferguson (Russell) S.; ed. Norristown (Pa.) pub. schs.; m. Edna Price Jones, June 7, 1904; 1 son, Alexander McKnight. Began as clerk, 1897; vice-president and manager agencies Fidelity Mutual Life Ins. Co. since 1924. Served in 1st Pa. Inf., in Spanish-Am. War and as 1st lt. Pa. coal riots. Awarded Carnegie Medal, MacNeill Medal and Boy Scout Honor Medal. Ex-pres. Governing Commn. of Lower Merion Twp., Pa.; pres. Police Pension Assn., Lower Merion; one of organizers Boy Scout movement in Montgomery County. Ex-pres. Assn. of Life Agency Officers; mem. Assn. Life Underwriters, Officers Assn. 1st Regt. Inf. of Pa. Republican. Mason, Elk, Sojourners. Clubs: Union League, Poor Richard (Philadelphia); Neighborhood (Bala-Cynwyd) Cynwyd (ex-pres.). Home: 372 Trevor Lane, Bala-Cynwyd, Pa. Office: Parkway at Fairmount, Philadelphia, Pa.

SYKES, M'Cready, lawyer; b. Isleham, Va., Dec. 25, 1869; s. Rev. Charles L. and Elizabeth Beck (M'Cready) S.; A.B., Princeton, 1894; m. Beatrice M. Evans, Oct. 2, 1912; children—Patricia M'Cready (Mrs. Jean-Louis Terry), Peter M'Cready, Barbara M'Cready, Gresham M'Cready. Admitted to bar, 1891; practiced law at N.Y. City, 1894-1909; fruit grower, Boise, Ida., 1909-16; resumed practice at New York, 1917. Editorial writer Boise Daily Statesman, 1916; editorial staff Brooklyn Inst. Arts and Sciences, 1916-17. Episcopalian. Club: Players. Author: Poe's Run and Other Poems, 1904. Contbr. to mags. Asso. editor Commerce and Finance, 1920-37. Home: 1113 Putnam Av., Plainfield, N.J. Office: 45 Wall St., New York, N.Y.

SYKES, Philip Louis, judge; b. Lithuania, Feb. 17, 1884; s. David and Minnie Deborah (Jacobson) S.; brought to U.S., 1889, naturalized, 1895; A.B., Johns Hopkins U., 1908, A.M., 1916; LL.B., U. of Md. Law Sch., Baltimore, 1911; m. Sara Kline, June 26, 1921;

SYLING children—Melvin Julius, Helen Lenora. Admitted to Md. bar, 1910 and since engaged in gen. practice in Baltimore; mem. firm Baum & Sykes, 1910-23, in practice alone, 1923-28; asso. judge Orphans' ct., Baltimore, 1928-34, chief judge since 1934; mem. adv. bd. of parole of Md., 1920-23. Served as chmn. legal adv. dft. bd. 5th dist. during World War. Dir. Asso. Jewish Charities of Baltimore; dir. Baltimore Talmud Torah Soc. Mem. Md. State and Baltimore City bar assns., Johns Hopkins Alumni Assn. Awarded two prizes $100 each by U. of Md. for leading class and writing the best thesis. Democrat. Jewish religion. K.P., Moose. Contbr. legal and gen. articles to pubs. Home: 2402 E. Baltimore St. Office: Munsey Bldg., Baltimore, Md.

SYLING, John C., supt. schs.; b. New Castle, Pa., July 7, 1882; s. David and Nancy (Freed) S.; ed. Ohio Northern U.; m. Florence Edna Myers, Feb. 16, 1905 (died 1938); 1 dau., Norma Jean. Teacher rural schs., Lawrence Co., Pa., 1901-05; prin. Wampum (Pa.) High Sch., 1905-16; supervising prin. Lawrence Co., Pa., schs., 1916-18, asst. co. supt. schs., 1918-26, co supt. since 1926. Mem. Pa. State Edn. Assn., N.E.A. Republican. Mem. United Presbyterian Ch. Mason. Home: 827 Franklin Av. Office: 500 Greer Boul., New Castle, Pa.

SYLVESTER, Mildred Loring (Mrs. Ermond L. Sylvester), psychologist; b. Tacoma, Wash., May 4, 1891; d. Frank H. and Mary Ellen Loring; A.B., Univ. of Washington, 1912, M.A., 1913; grad. study, Bryn Mawr Coll., 1913-14; Ph.D., Johns Hopkins, 1916; m. Ermond L. Sylvester, Jan. 1, 1922; children—Loring Ermond, Willard Parker (dec.). Instr. psychology, U. of Wash., 1917-19; asst. in ophthalmology, Med. Research Lab., Mitchell Field, L.I., N.Y., 1919-20; professorial lecturer psychology, U. of Minn., 1920-21, asst. prof. psychology, 1921-22; exec. officer and examining psychologist, Psychol. Clinic, U. of Pa., since 1931. Mem. Am. Psychol. Assn., Eastern Psychol. Assn., Pa. Assn. Clin. Psychologists (sec. 1939-40), Alpha Omicron Pi, Phi Beta Kappa, Sigma Xi. Clubs: Womens University (Philadelphia); U. of Pa. Faculty Tea Club. Home: 3645 Locust St., Philadelphia, Pa.

SYLVIA, Sister M. Morgan; see Morgan, Sister M. Sylvia.

SYME, M. Herbert; in gen. practice of law since 1932; mem. law firm Symes & Simons. Office: Market St. Nat. Bank Bldg., Philadelphia, Pa.

SYMINGTON, Donald, corpn. official; b. Baltimer, Md., Oct. 28, 1881; s. W. Stuart and Lelia Wales (Powers) S.; prep. edn., McCabe's Univ. Sch., Richmond, Va., and high sch., Bellevue, Va.; student Amherst Coll., 1904; m. Elsie Hillen Jenkins, Apr. 19, 1909; 1 dau., Martha Skipwith (Mrs. Arthur D. Foster, Jr.). Pres. McConway & Torley Corpn.; dir. Internat. Mercantile Marine Co., U.S. Lines Co., Canton Co., Canton R.R. Dairy Farmer. Served as chief munitions officer 1st Army, A.E.F.; World War; capt. Officers Reserve Corps. Home: Darlington, Md. Office: Baltimore Trust Bldg., Baltimore, Md.

SYMMONDS, Charles Jacobs, army officer; b. Holland, Mich., Oct. 6, 1866; s. Robert and Phillis Wey (Jacobs) S.; grad. U.S. Mil. Acad., 1890; m. George Crook Thomas, Feb. 21, 1894; children—Robert Earl (killed in action, World War), Katharine Godfrew, Phillis Wey. Commissioned 2d lt. 18th Inf., June 12, 1890; promoted through grades to brig. gen. Nov. 3, 1923; served as capt. a.q.m., vols., Spanish-Am. War, 1898; comdr. Intermediate Depot, Giévres, France, the principal storage depot of A.E.F. during World War; retired, Oct. 31, 1930. Awarded D.S.M. "for exceptionally meritorious and distinguished service" at Giévres; Officer Legion of Honor (France); Officer Polonia Restituta (Poland). Home: 209 Elm St., Chevy Chase, Md.

SYMONDS, Nathaniel Gardiner, v.p. Westinghouse Electric & Mfg. Co.; b. Ossining, N.Y., Sept. 19, 1878; s. Henry Clay and Beatrice (Brandreth) S.; A.B., Stanford U.; m. Amy Irene Millberry, Dec. 25, 1901; children—Henry Gardiner, Nathaniel Millberry, Amy Irene (dec.), Cortlandt. Dist. mgr. Westinghouse Machine Co., 1912-15; division mgr. Westinghouse Electric & Mfg. Co., 1915-21, dist. mgr., 1921-28, commercial v.p., 1928-32, v.p. since 1932. V.p. and gov. Nat. Elec. Mfrs. Assn.; dir. Am. Transit Assn., Heat Exchange Inst.; mem. Kappa Sigma. Clubs: Union League (Chicago); Hinsdale (Ill.) Golf; Duquesne, University, Pittsburgh Athletic Assn. (Pittsburgh); Oakmont Country; Pine Valley (N.J.) Golf; Bankers (New York). Home: Schenley Apts. Office: 306 Fourth Av., Pittsburgh, Pa.

SYMONS, Thomas Baddeley, dir. agrl. extension; b. Easton, Md., Sept. 2, 1880; s. Robert and Susan (Baddeley) S.; B.S., Md. Agrl. Coll., 1902, M.S., 1905, D.Agr., 1918; m. Susie La Roche, Apr. 10, 1907; children—Helen (Mrs. Innis LaRoche Jenkins), Isabel (Mrs. Owen Goodwin), Josephine (Mrs. James Robert Troth). Asst. entomologist, Md. Agrl. Coll., 1902-04, state entomologist, 1904-14, dean sch. of Horticulture, 1913-14; dir. of extension, U. of Md. since 1914, acting dean Coll. of Agr., 1937; dir. Prince Georges Bank & Trust Co. Mem. A.A.A.S., Md. State Hort. Soc., Md. Agrl. Soc., Kappa Alpha, Epsilon Sigma Phi. Democrat. Episcopalian. Clubs: Chesapeake (Baltimore, Md.), Rotary. Home: College Park, Md.

SYPHERD, Wilbur Owen, prof. English; b. Zion, Md., June 28, 1877; s. Jacob Owen and Josephine (Draper) S.; A.B., Del. Coll., Newark, 1896; B.S., U. of Pa., 1900; M.S. Harvard 1901, Ph.D., 1906; unmarried. Prin. schs. Port Penn, Del., 1896-98; instr. English, U. of Wis., 1901-03; prof. English, U. of Del., since 1906; teacher summer session, N.Y. Univ., 1910, U. of Calif., 1922, Harvard, 1933. Served as sec. local bd. Newcastle County, World War. Mem. Modern Lang. Assn. America, Coll. Conf. on English in Central Atlantic States, Soc. for Promotion Engring. Edn., Nat. Council of Teachers of English, Shakespeare Assn. America, Am. Assn. Univ. Profs., Sigma Phi Epsilon, Phi Kappa Phi. Clubs: Newark Country; University (Philadelphia). Author: Studies in Chaucer's House of Fame, 1907; Handbook of English for Engineers, 1913; Manual of English for Engineers, 1935; The Literature of the English Bible, 1938. Editor: The English Bible—Selections, 1921; John Christopherson's Jephthah (with F. H. Fobes), 1928. Home: Newark, Del.

SZERLIP, Leopold, orthopedic surgeon; b. New York, N.Y., Jan. 2, 1895; s. William and Hannah (Baumbhl) S.; grad. Boys High Sch., Brooklyn, 1912; student New York U., 1912-13; M.D., Bellevue Med. Coll., 1917; m. Eva Dvorken, Nov. 30, 1919; children—Eugene Poole, Janet, Martha. Served internship, Beekman St. Hosp., New York; now sr. attending orthopedist Newark Beth Israel Hosp.; attending orthopedist Newark City Hosp., St. James Hosp.; cons. orthopedist Perth Amboy Gen. Hosp., Irvington Gen. Hosp., Passaic Beth Israel Hosp., Roosevelt Hosp., Betty Bacharach Home; chief orthopedics Clinic of Newark City Dispensary. Served as 1st lt., U.S. Army Med. Corps, Ft. McPherson, Ga., and Camp Upton, N.Y., July 1918-May 1919. Fellow Am. Acad. Orthopedic Surgeons; certified by Am. Bd. Orthopedic Surgeons; mem. A.M.A., Acad. of Medicine of N.J., Essex Co. Med. Soc., N.J. Anat. and Pathol. Soc. Mason, Elk, Rotarian. Home: 43 Shepherd Av. Office: 31 Lincoln Parkway, Newark, N.J.

SZOLD, Henrietta; b. Baltimore, Md., Dec. 21, 1860; d. Benjamin and Sophia (Schaar) S.; grad. high sch., Baltimore, 1877. Teacher in pvt. sch., Baltimore, 1878-92; editorial sec. publ. com. Jewish Publ. Soc. America, 1892-1916; associated with Zionist undertakings in U.S. and Palestine since 1916. Editor Am. Jewish Year Book (Jewish Publ. Soc.), 1904-08. Pres. (Hadassah), Women's Zionist Orgn. in U.S., 1912-26; mem. Palatine Zionist Exec., with portfolio health and education, 1927-30; mem. Exec. Ha-Waad Ha-Leumi (Jewish Gen. Council), 1931-33, dir. dept. social service since 1932. Dir. Dept. Youth Immigration of Central Bur. for Settlement of German Jews since 1935. Translator: Jewish Ethics (by Lazarus); Legends of the Jews (by Ginsberg); Hebrew Renaissance (by N. Slouschz), 1909. Home: 2104 Chelsea Terrace, Baltimore, Md. Office: care Hadassah, 1860 Broadway, New York, N.Y.; also care Ha-Waad Ha-Leumi, Jerusalem, Palestine.

SZTARK, Heliodor, diplomat consul gen. Poland; b. Konin, Poznan, Poland, Mar. 28, 1886; s. Daniel and Natalia (Peczke) S.; M.A. in C.E., Tech. Inst., Darmstadt, Germany, 1907; grad. study, Tech. Inst., Brno, Czechoslovakia, 1907-10; m. Aniela Dabrowska, of Kalisz, Poland, June 4, 1907; children—Isabelle (Mrs. Antoni Wierzbicki), Janina. Engaged in civil engring. in Poland and Russia, 1910-19; in diplomatic and consular service of Republic of Poland since 1919, served at Murmansk, Russia, Cologne, Germany, Leningrad, Russia, Stettin, Germany, and Vienna, and in Central Offices of Ministry of Fgn. Affairs, Warsaw, Poland; consul gen. of Poland at Pittsburgh, Pa., since 1939; dean of consular corps of Pittsburgh Dist. Decorations: Polonia Restituta, Medal of Independence (Poland); Coroana Romaniei (Roumania); Ordre de Leopold II (Belgium); Ordine Equestre de S. Gregoria Magno (Vatican City); SS. Maurizio at Lazzaro (Italy); Legion d'Honneur (France); White Eagle (Jugoslavia). Mem. Prehistorical Soc. at Poznan, Poland, Nat. Geographic Soc., Alumni Assn. Darmsztadt Students. Home: 4916 Wallingford St., Pittsburgh, Pa. Office: 249 N. Craig St., Pittsburgh, Pa.

T

TABAK, Israel, rabbi; b. Bucovina, Rumania, Dec. 7, 1904; s. David Hager and Zirl Pesi (Wahrman) T.; ed. Secondary Schs., Prague, Bohemia, 1916-18, Rabbinical Sch., Rzesov, Poland, 1918-21; Rabbi, Rabbinical Sch., Oberwischau, Hungary, 1923; Rabbi, Yeshiva Coll., New York, 1928; student New York U., 1928-31, Johns Hopkins since 1934 (candidate for Ph.D., 1939); m. Lilian Eskolsky, June 7, 1931; children—Malca Judith, Rachel Ruth. Came to U.S., 1924, naturalized, 1930. Asst. to Rabbi Drachman, Zichron Ephraim Congregation, New York, 1925-26; rabbi Beth Jacob Congregation, Union City, N.J., 1926-31; rabbi Shaarei Zion Congregation, Baltimore, since 1931; instr. in homiletics and public speaking Ner Israel Coll., Baltimore, since 1935. Mem. bd. of edn., Talmudical Acad., Baltimore, since 1931; mem. bd. trustees Ner Israel Rabbinical Coll. since 1934; mem. exec. com. Rabbinical Council of America since 1936, v.p. since 1937; sec. Rabbinical Com. of Baltimore since 1933; member executive commission Union of Orthodox Congregations of America and Mizrachi Zionists Orgns. since 1936; mem. exec. com. United Jewish Appeal and Palestine Pavilion at New York World's Fair. Del. to World Zionist Congress, Prague, and World Mizrachi Conf., Crakow, Poland, 1933. Club: Johns Hopkins (Baltimore.) Author: Zionists at the Cross Roads, 1934; Meimonides, Master Builder of Jewish Law, 1935; What Is Jewish Nationalism?, 1936; Jewish Influences in Ethiopia, 1936; Parochial System of Education, 1938. Home: 3700 Reisterstown Rd., Baltimore, Md.

TABER, Norman Stephen, banking; b. Providence, R.I., Sept. 3, 1891; s. Alfred Henry and Mary Abbie (Weeks) T.; grad. high sch., Providence, 1909; A.B., Brown U., 1913; Rhodes scholar, Oxford, 1913-15; m. Ottilie Rose Metzger, Dec. 2, 1916; 1 dau., Mary. Clk. Rhode Island Hosp. Trust Co., Providence, 1915-19; trustee or mgr. various private estates and trusts affiliated with John Nicholas Brown Estate, 1920-30; R.I. representative of Brookmire Economic Service, 1930-33; senior mem. Norman S. Taber & Co., consultants on municipal finance, since 1933. Trustee Brown Univ., Moses Brown School (Providence), Lincoln School. Mem. bd. of mgrs. of investments and permanent funds of Yearly Meeting of Friends for N.E. Mem. Phi Beta Kappa, Alpha Delta Phi. Republican. Quaker. Clubs: Providence Art, Rock Spring. Set new world's record of 4 minutes 12 2-5 seconds for mile run, Harvard Stadium, 1915.

Home: 108 Connett Pl., S. Orange, N.J. Office: 30 Broad St., New York, N.Y.

TABLER, Homer E., physician; b. Berkeley Co., W.Va., Apr. 25, 1881; s. E. S. and Catherine R. (Whitmore) T.; student Mercersburg (Pa.) Coll., 1898-1900, Otterbein Univ., Westerville, O., 1900-01; M.D., Univ. of Md. Med. Sch., Baltimore, 1904; m. Laura K. Jenkins, Dec. 26, 1906; 1 son, Homer E., Jr. Interne Franklin Square Hosp., Baltimore, 1903-04; engaged in gen. practice of medicine at Hancock, Md., since 1904; served as chmn. Md. State Rds. Commn., 1935-38. Mem. Am. Med. Assn., Med. and Chirurg. Faculty of Md., Am. Acad. of Science, Phi Chi. Republican. Episcopalian. Mason (K.T., 32°, Shriner, Illustrious Potentate, 1938). Odd Fellow, K.P. Forester. Jr. O.U.A.M. Woodman. Clubs: University (Baltimore), Hagerstown Country. Home: Main St., Hancock, Md.

TABOR, Edward Otto, lawyer; b. Oxford Junction, Ia., Aug. 12, 1885; s. John and Magdalena Pezl T.; A.B., Tulane U., 1905; A.M., U. of Wis., 1909; LL.B., Harvard U. Law Sch., 1916; m. Marguerite B. Kaye, of Boston, Mass., July 10, 1917; children—Edward, John, Marguerite. Engaged in teaching, high sch., New Orleans, La., 1905-08, Portland, Ore., 1909-13; instr. Harvard U., 1913-16; accepted in law office Hon. Louis D. Brandeis, Boston; admitted to Pa. bar, 1917, U.S. Supreme Court, 1925; engaged in gen. practice at Pittsburgh; counsel for West Penn Power Co., West Penn Rys. Co. and asso. corpns. Headed Americanization activities in W.Pa. during World War and after; active in work for independence of Czechoslovakia; awarded Revolutionary Medal and White Lion (Czechoslovakia). Active in city mgr. movement; dir. Civic Club; chmn. Inter-racial Com.; dir. Community Fund (campaign chmn. 1935); a founder and chmn. Masaryk Institute. Candidate Rep. ticket for Congress, 1936. Mem. Allegheny Co. Bar Assn., (dir.), Pa. Bar Assn., Am. Judicature Soc.; Phi Beta Kappa, Omicron Delta Kappa. Ind. Republican. Protestant. Contbr. legal and polit. articles, including "The Supreme Court and the N.R.A." and "The University and the New American." Lecturer. Home: 6429 Bartlett St. Office: 14 Wood St., Pittsburgh, Pa.

TAFT, Frank, organist; v.p. Aeolian-Skinner Organ Co.; b. East Bloomfield, Ontario Co., N.Y., Mar. 22, 1861; s. William Pitts and Martha A. (Cowdery) T.; grad. Genesee Wesleyan Sem., Lima, N.Y., 1877, Hershey Sch. of Musical Art, Chicago, 1881; m. Ida Estelle Halsted, Apr. 16, 1891; 1 son, William Halsted. Organist Wabash Av. M.E. Ch., Chicago, 1879-80, Trinity M.E. Church, Chicago, 1881-82, Epiphany P.E. Church, New York, 1883, St. Matthews P.E. Ch., Jersey City, N.J., 1883-84, Clinton Av. Congl. Ch., Brooklyn, N.Y., 1885-94, Temple Beth El (Jewish), New York, 1894-1903, Madison Av. Reformed Ch., New York, 1895-1900, First Congl. Ch., Montclair, N.J., 1901-12; musical dir. Madrigal Singers, New York, 1888-1890; organ recitals throughout the U.S., 1886-1901; founder and dir. Bach Festivals, Montclair, N.J., 1901-05; mem. of firm J. H. and C. S. Odell & Co., organ builders, New York, 1894-97; mem. firm Harrison & Taft, organ builders, Bloomfield, N.J., 1898-1900; art. dir. and mgr. pipe organ dept., The Aeolian Co., New York, 1901-31; vice-pres. and dir. Aeolian-Skinner Organ Co., organ builders, Boston, Mass., since 1932; dir. Internat. Holding Co. of Garwood (N.J.), The Aeolian Co. A founder of Am. Guild of Organists. Mem. Montclair Art Assn., Neuen Bachgesellschaft (Leipzig, Germany), St. Wilfred Club (New York). Republican. Congregationalist. Collector of Johann Sebastian Bach pictures and other material. Home: 152 Gates Av., Montclair, N.J. Office: 27 W. 57th St., New York, N.Y.

TAFT, Julia Jessie, asso. prof. social case work; b. Dubuque, Ia., June 24, 1882; d. Charles C. and Amanda May (Farwell) T.; A.B., Drake U., 1904; A.M., B.S., U. of Chicago, 1905, Ph.D., same, 1913; unmarried; children (adopted)—Martha Scott Taft, Everett Francis Taft. Engaged in teaching high sch., 4 yrs.; asst. supt. State Reformatory, Bedford Hills, N.Y., 1912-15; psychiatric social worker State Charities Aid Assn., New York, N.Y., 1915-18; psychologist, Mental Hygiene Clinic, Childrens Agencies, Phila., Pa., 1918-26; supervisor child placing, Childrens Aid Soc., Phila., 1927-34; asso. prof. social case work, Pa. Sch. of Social Work (affiliated with U. of Pa.) since 1934; also in pvt. practice as cons. psychologist. Mem. Am. Assn. of Social Workers, Am. Orthopsychiatric Assn. Author: The Dynamics of Therapy, 1933. Editor, The Journal of Social Work Process, 1938, 39. Translator from the German: Will Therapy by Otto Rank, 1937; Truth and Reality by Otto Rank, 1937. Contbr. articles to mags. and jours. Home: Flourtown, Pa. Office: 311 S. Juniper St., Philadelphia, Pa.

TAGGART, Marion Ames, author; b. Haverhill, Mass.; d. of Alfred Gilchrist and Sarah Porter (Ames) T.; ed. entirely at home, owing to delicate health. Contbr. since 1882 of verses, stories and articles to mags. Author: The Blissylvania Post Office, 1897; Three Girls and Especially One, 1897; By Branscome River, 1897; Aser, the Shepherd, 1899; Bezaleel, 1899; Loyal Blue and Royal Scarlet, 1899; The Wyndham Girls, 1902; Miss Lochinvar, 1902; At Aunt Anna's, 1903; The Little Grey House, 1904; Nut Brown Joan, 1905; Six Girls and Bob, 1906; Daddy's Daughters, 1906; Miss Lochinvar's Return, 1906; Pussy Cat Town, 1906; Six Girls and the Tea Room, 1907; The Daughters of the Little Grey House, 1907; The Doctor's Little Girl, 1907; Six Girls Growing Older, 1908; Six Girls and the Seventh One, 1909; Sweet Nancy (sequel to The Doctor's Little Girl), 1909; Betty Gaston, the Seventh Girl, 1910; Six Girls and Betty, 1911; Nancy, the Doctor's Little Partner, 1911; Six Girls Grown Up, 1912; Nancy Porter's Opportunity, 1912; The Little Aunt, 1913; Her Daughter Jean, 1913; Beth's Wonder Winter, 1914; Nancy and the Coggs Twins, 1914; Beth's Old Home, 1915; The Garden Girls, 1916; Captain Sylvia, 1917; A Pilgrim Maid—A Story of Plymouth Colony, 1920; The Annes, 1921; The Jack-in-the-Box Books, 4 vols., 1921; Who Is Sylvia?, 1922; No Handicap, 1922; The Cable, 1923. Home: 901 N. Front St., Harrisburg, Pa.

TAGGART, Matthew H.; insurance commr. for State of Pa. since 1939. Address: State Capitol, Harrisburg, Pa.

TAGGART, Ralph Enos, corpn. official; b. Leisenring, Pa., Apr. 17, 1887; s. John K. and Mary (Enos) T.; student Phillips Andover Academy; m. Virginia Howard Bullitt, June 14, 1910; children—Ralph Enos, Virginia (Mrs. Irving L. Geer), Daniel Reeder. Chairman board Reading Iron Company; president Enos, Virginia (Mrs. Irving L. Geer), Daniel Reeder. Chmn. bd. Reading Iron Co.; pres. Phila. & Reading Coal & Iron Corpn., Phila. & Reading Coal & Iron Co., Thomas Iron Co.; dir. Stonega Coke & Coal Co., Va. Coal & Iron Co. Clubs: Rittenhouse, Art (Phila.). Home: Radnor, Pa. Office: Reading Terminal Bldg., Philadelphia, Pa.

TAITT, Francis Marion, clergyman; b. Burlington, N.J., Jan. 3, 1862; s. James Monroe and Elizabeth Ward (Conway) T.; A.B., Central High Sch., Phila., Pa., 1880, A.M., 1885; grad. Phila. Div. School, 1883; S.T.D., U. of Pa., 1920, Phila. Div. Sch., 1930; LL.D., Temple U., 1932; Litt.D., Hahnemann Coll., 1936; unmarried. Deacon, 1883, priest, 1886, P.E. Ch.; asst., St. Peter's Ch., Phila., 1883-87; rector Trinity Ch., Southwark, 1887-93, St. Paul's Ch., Chester, Pa., 1893-1929; mem. faculty, Ch. Training and Deaconess House, 1906-29; bishop coadjutor of Pa., 1929-31, bishop of Pa. since 1931. Dean of Convocation of Chester, 1903-29; dep. to Gen. Conv., 1922-28. Trustee Pa. Mil. Coll. (pres. bd.), Crozer Hosp.; dir. Chester Hosp.; pres. bd. overseers Phila. Div. Sch. Mason (grand chaplain, Grand Holy Royal Arch chapter of Pa. and grand chaplain Grand Lodge of Pa.). Home: 300 Broad St., Chester, Pa. Office: 202 S. 19th St., Philadelphia, Pa.

TALBOT, Herbert Raymond, v.p. Columbia Protektosite Co., Inc.; b. Boston, Mass., Sept. 12, 1874; s. James Stewart and Victoria (Peck) T.; ed. Boston pub. schs.; m. Cora Belle Van-Nosdall, Sept. 19, 1899; children—Ruth Victoria (Mrs. Albert Morgan Birdsall), Alice (Mrs. Vaughn Daniel Buckley). Stock boy Pitts, Kimball & Lewis, Boston, 1890-93; with Locke, Huleat & Co., Chicago, 1893-94, Pitts, Kimball & Lewis, 1894; salesman E. P. Haff & Co., New York City, 1894-96; partner Louis A. Boettiger Co., N.Y. City, 1896-1911; v.p. Louis A. Boettiger Co., Inc., 1911-1925; pres., 1925-1932; v.p. Columbia Protektosite Co., Inc., since 1932. Republican. Methodist. Mason (past master). Club: Rutherford (N.J.) Rotary. Home: 269 Ivy Pl., Ridgewood, N.J. Office: 631 Central Av., Carlstadt, N.J.

TALBOT, S. Benton, prof. biology; Davis & Elkins Coll. Address: Davis & Elkins College, Elkins, W.Va.

TALBOT, Walter LeMar, life ins.; b. Phila. Pa., Aug. 23, 1870; ed. pub. schs.; m. Estelle Mair; 1 son, Walter LeMar. Began as office boy with Fidelity Mutual Life Ins. Co., 1882, pres. since Feb. 24, 1914; dir. Corn Exchange Nat. Bank, Real Estate Trust Co., John B. Stetson Co. Episcopalian. Mason (32°). Clubs: Manufacturers and Bankers, Union League. Home: Germantown, Pa. Office: The Parkway at Fairmont Av., Philadelphia, Pa.

TALBOTT, George Harold, clergyman; b. Marengo, Ia., Feb. 8, 1894; s. George Edward and Mary Elizabeth (Davis) T.; student Mo. Valley Coll., Marshall, Mo., 1915-17; B.A., Princeton, 1922; B.S.T., Princeton Theol. Sem., 1923, M.S.T., 1923; D.D., Mo. Valley Coll., 1930; m. Barbara Baringer Stofer, June 11, 1918; children—Mary Martha (dec.), Barbara Jane. Student pastor Blairstown and Denton (Mo.) chs., 1915-17; ordained Presbyn. ministry, 1922; pastor, Clivedon Ch., Germantown, Pa., 1919-23, 1st Ch., Passaic, N.J., since 1923; chaplain Police and Fire depts. of Passaic, N.J.; Gerald V. Carroll Post, Am. Legion. Served as 1st Lt. inf.; A.E.F., World War, 1917-19; wounded in Meuse-Argonne offensive, Oct. 20, 1918; later with 126th Inf., 32d Div. Mem. Mayor's Com. of Strike Settlement, Passaic, 1926; mem. Gen. Assembly Presbyn. Ch., U.S. A., 1933 (chmn. com. on edn.); mem. Permanent Judicial Com. Synod of N.J., 1936; sec. Princeton Theol. Sem. Alumni Assn. since 1934; gov. Passaic Gen. Hosp: since 1937; moderator Presbyn. Synod of N.J. 1937-38. Member Am. Legion. Republican. Mason (32°). Clubs: Yountakah (Nutley, N.J.); Friars Club (Princeton). Home: 372 S. Parkway, Clifton, N.J. Office: 15 Grove Terrace, Passaic, N.J.*

TALCOTT, J(ames) Frederick, merchant; b. N.Y. City, Sept. 14, 1866; s. James and Henrietta Elizabeth (Francis) T.; B.A., Princeton, 1888, M.A., 1890; Oxford Univ., 1890-91; University of Berlin, 1891; Union Theological Seminary, 1892; m. Miss Frank Vanderbilt Crawford, 1890 (died 1915); children—James, Hooker, Julia Lake (Mrs. Thomas M. McMillan, Jr.), Martha Everitt (Mrs. Marshall P. Blankarn); m. 2d, Louise Simmons, Feb. 17, 1917. Pres. James Talcott, Inc., New York; dir. Am. Hosiery Co. Dir. Am. Bible Soc., McAuley Water Street Mission. Lincoln U., Children's Welfare Fed., Bowery Branch Y.M.C.A., Union Settlement Assn., New York Bible Soc., Am. Tract Soc., St. Bartholomew's Community House, Neighborhood Music Sch., Monmouth County Y.M.C.A., Indian River Sch., Federation of Protest Welfare Agencies, Inc. (sec.), Friends of Boys, Inc. (pres.), N.Y. Soc. for Suppression of Vice, Fed. Daily Vacation Bible Schs., Ft. Valley Normal and Industrial Sch.; mem. Princeton-Yenching Foundation, Friends of Princeton Library. Mem. Chamber Commerce State N.Y., N.Y. Bd. of Trade (treas.), Am. Tariff League, Dickens Fellowship of N.Y., N. Y. Geneal. and Biog. Soc., Rumson Borough Improvement Assn., Metropolitan Mus. of Art, James Talcott Fund. (pres.), English-Speaking Union, Monmouth Country Hist. Assn., N.E. Soc. Union Theol. Sem. Alumni. Republican. Episcopalian. Clubs: Nat. Republican, Pilgrims, Union League, National Arts (pres.), Church, Clergy, Nassau Country, Emipre State, Prince-

TALIAFERRO

ton University Cottage, Monmouth County Hunt, Adirondack League, Rumson Country, Seabright Lawn Tennis and Cricket, Seabright Beach, Metropolitan. Home: Rumson, N.J., and 16 East 66th St., New York. Office: 225 Fourth Ave., New York, N.Y.

TALIAFERRO, Thomas Hardy, educator; b. Jacksonville, Fla., Mar. 22, 1871; s. Warner Throckmorton and Fannie Johnston (Hardy) T.; C.E., Va. Mil. Inst., 1890; Ph.D., Johns Hopkins, 1896; m. Janie Gambrill Smith, June 30, 1897; 1 dau., Frances Warner Throckmorton (dec.). Asst. prof. Va. Mil. Inst., 1890-91; instr. Mo. Mil. Acad., 1891-92; instr. Pa. State Coll., 1896-1901, acting prof. military science and tactics, 1899-1900; prres. Fla. Agrl. Coll. and U. of Fla., 1901-04; also dir. Fla. Agrl. Expt. Sta., 1901-04; hon. fellow in mathematics and economics, Johns Hopkins, 1904-05; asst. statis. editor Bur. of Census, 1905-07; prof. civil engring., 1907-20, prof. mathematics since 1920, dean of faculty since 1937, dean College Arts and Sciences, 1927-37, dean College Engineering, 1916-20, University of Md. Mem. A.A.A.S., Am. Math. Assn., Am. Assn. Univ. Profs., Washington Soc. of Engrs., Md. State Soc. of Washington, D.C., Kappa Alpha. First Jackson Hope medallist, Va. Mil. Inst. Episcopalian. Mason. Club: Cosmos. Home: The Concord, Washington, D.C. Address: College Park, Md.

TALL, Lida Lee, educator, principal teachers college; b. Dorchester Co., Md., November 17, 1873; d. Washington and Sarah Elizabeth (Humphreys) T.; graduate Western High School, Baltimore; student normal extension courses, Johns Hopkins; studied Univ. of Chicago, summer of 1904; Columbia summer, 1907; B.S. and bachelor's diploma in education, Teachers College, Columbia, 1914; Litt.D., University of Maryland, 1926. Served as teacher and critic teacher in Baltimore city schs., instr. in edn., literature and history, Teachers' Training Sch., Baltimore, 1904-08; supervisor of grammar grades, Baltimore Co., Md., 1908-17; asst. supt. of schs., Baltimore Co., Md., 1917-18; prin. elementary dept. Lincoln Sch., Teachers Coll., 1918-20; pres. Md. State Normal Sch. (name of school changed to Teachers College, 1934), Towson, 1920-38; retired, Sept. 1938. Instr. in edn., Johns Hopkins, summer 1912. Teachers Coll. (Columbia), summers 1907, 19. Asso. editor Atlantic Ednl. Jour., 1907-11. Alumna trustee Teachers Coll., 1915-17. Sec. dept. superintendence N.E.A., 1917-18; mem. Md. State Teachers' Assn. (pres. 1935), Am. Hist. Assn., Assn. History Teachers of Middle States and Md., Am. Assn. U. Women, English Speaking Union. Clubs: College, Quota (Balti.); Business and Professional Women's. Author: Bibliography of History for Schools and Libraries (with Charles M. Andrews and J. Montgomery Gambrill), 1910. Compiler Baltimore County Course of Study (with Albert S. Cook and Isobel Davidson), 1919; How the Old World Found the New (with Eunice Fuller Barnard), 1929. Address: Cambridge Arms Apts., Baltimore, Md.

TALL, Webster C., lawyer; b. Baltimore, Md., March 8, 1892; s. Charles G. and Julia T. (Bians) T.; student Baltimore City Coll., 1905-09; LL.D., U. of Md. Law Sch., Baltimore, 1913; m. Adele R. Donaldson, Feb. 27, 1917; 1 son, Donaldson. Admitted to Md. bar, 1913 and since engaged in gen. practice of law at Baltimore; admitted to Calif. bar, 1917. Mem. Bar Assn. Baltimore City, Republican. Baptist. Mem. Eastern Shore Soc. Home: 3429 University Pl. Office: Maryland Trust Bldg., Baltimore, Md.

TALLEY, Mabel, club woman; b. Chicago, Ill., d. George A. and Julia Emma (Perkins) T.; ed. pub. sch. in Del. and pvt. instrn.; unmarried. Editor weekly women's clubs department, "The Club Corner," Wilmington (Del.) Sunday Star, 1922-32; editor The Delaware Clubwoman, 1925-30; publicity chmn. for Del. Co. Fed. of Women's Clubs, 1924, corr. sec., 1925-27, chmn. literature div., 1934-37, mem. bd. dirs., 1935-37, chmn. fine arts dept. since 1937. Worked for organization and maintenance of Marcus Hook (Pa.) Pub. Library, Well-Baby Clinic and Pub. Playground, Marcus Hook, Pa. Republican. Methodist. Clubs: Marcus Hook Century (founder, 1920; pres., 1922-24, 1933-35); Wilmington (Del.) New Century (rec. sec., 1930-32). Home: 312 Ridge Rd., Linwood, Pa. P.O. Address: Marcus Hook, Pa.

TALLEY, Randal Earl, pres. George J. Hagan Co.; b. Overbrook, Kan., Aug. 13, 1887; s. David L. and Susan Elizabeth (Burton) T.; B.S. in E.E., Kansas State Coll., 1910; m. Ethel Grace Strong, July 29, 1910; children—Hazel Bernice (Mrs. Donald N. Howe), Reva Lucille (Mrs. William D. Parry), Ethel Grace, Randall Earl, Anna Virginia. Engr. Westinghouse Electric & Mfg. Co., 1910-19; chief engr. George J. Hagan Co., 1919-25, chmn. bd., pres. and dir. since 1925; chmn. bd., pres. and dir. Hagan Foundry Corpn. (Orrville, O.); pres. and dir. Irwin Savings & Trust Co. (Irwin, Pa.). Served as councilman, North Irwin, Pa., 8 yrs. Mem. Am. Soc. for Metals, Industrial Furnace Mfrs. Assn. (ex-pres.). Republican. Presbyterian. Mason (32°, Shriner), Moose. Club: Greensburg (Pa.) Country. Home: Brush Hill Road, Irwin, Pa. Office: 2400 E. Carson St., Pittsburgh, Pa.

TALONE, Leonard A., lawyer; b. Bryn Mawr, Pa., Dec. 22, 1905; s. Nicholas and Alice (Carey) T.; grad. Conshohocken (Pa.) High Sch., 1923; B.S., U. of Pa., 1927, LL.B., 1930; unmarried. Admitted to Pa. bar and to practice before Supreme Court of Pa., 1930, and since in practice at Montgomery County, Pa.; dep. atty. gen. of Pa. since 1933. Mem. Montgomery County Housing Authority since 1938; mem. Bd. of Edn., Conshohocken, Pa., since 1933. Mem. Montgomery County Bar Assn., Pa. Bar Assn. Club: Penn Athletic (Phila.). Address: 114 Fayette St., Conshohocken, Pa.

TANBERG, Arthur P(ercival), research dir.; b. Dubuque, Ia., June 20, 1885; s. George Edmund and Antonette (Weidemann) T.; A.B., Swarthmore (Pa.) Coll., 1910, A.M., 1913; student Johns Hopkins U., Baltimore, Md. 1910-11; Ph.D., Columbia U., 1915; m. Alice Lucie Bucher, Sept. 11, 1917; children—Eric Emile, Jerome Arthur. Instr. in chemistry, Swarthmore (Pa.) Coll., 1911-13; organic chemist E. I. Du Pont de Nemours & Co., 1915-17, head of organic div., exptl. sta., Wilmington, Del., 1917-19, asst. dir., 1919-20, dir. since 1920; mem. of corpn., Artisans' Savings Bank, Wilmington, Del. Mem. Faraday Soc., Soc. of Chem. Industry, Franklin Inst., Am. Phys. Soc., Delta Epsilon, Sigma Xi. Phi Lambda Upsilon. Republican. Clubs: Wilmington Whist, Du Pont Country (Wilmington, Del.). Home: 2302 Delaware Av. Office: Du Pont Experimental Station, Wilmington, Del.

TANGER, Jacob, prof. polit. science, Pa. State Coll. Address: Pennsylvania State College, State College, Pa.

TANGER, Landis, coll. pres.; b. Strasburg, Pa., Mar. 10, 1875; s. John G. and Mary Ann (Hoover) T.; student Millersville (Pa.) State Normal Sch., 1895-98; Ph.B., Franklin and Marshall Coll., 1905, Sc.D., 1930; A.M., U. of Pa., 1914; U. of Pittsburgh, 1913-18; Columbia, summer 1920, 29, Pd.D., Muhlenberg Coll., Allentown, Pa., 1926; m. Amanda Eby, Aug. 15, 1905; children—John B., Elizabeth M., Fredk. E. Teacher pub. schs., Lancaster Co., Pa., 1895-1900; prin. pub. schs., Millersburg, Pa., 1900-03, Bedford, Pa., 1905-09; supt. schs., Scottdale, Pa., 1909-13, Homestead, 1913-22, Reading, 1922-29; pres. Millersville State Teachers Coll. since 1929. Mem. N.E.A., Nat. Assn. Study of Edn., Nat. Acad. Polit. and Social Science, Phi Delta Kappa, Kappa Sigma. Presbyn. Mason. Clubs: Rotary, Fortnightly (Lancaster). Home: Millersville, Pa.

TANNER, Henrietta Tucker, M.D., surgeon; b. Watseka, Ill.; d. William Frederick and Wilhelmina (Niemeyer) Tucker; M.D., Bennett Med. Coll., 1900, Women's Med. Coll. of Pa., 1922; m. William Elmer Tanner, Apr. 16, 1903; children—William N., Eleanor (Mrs. Eleanor Shahmoon). Began practice of medicine in Tex., 1900; removed to Philadelphia, 1915; founded surg. dept. Clinic de Notre Dame des Malades, Philadelphia, 1927, now serving as chief surgeon;

TARBELL

1st woman to operate in old Northwestern Gen. Hosp., 1932; chief dept. of oto-laryngology, Woman's Hosp., Phila.; mem. courtesy staff Germantown and Hahnemann hosps. Mem. A.M.A., Philadelphia Co. Med. Soc., Am. Assn. Univ. Women. Republican. Protestant. Club: Business and Professional Women's (dir. and chmn. health com.). Address: 419 Chew St., Olney, Philadelphia, Pa.

TANNER, Sheldon Clark, prof. of economics; b. Farmington, Utah, May 29, 1900; s. Dr. Joseph Marion and Annie (Clark) T.; B.S. (cum laude), U. of Utah, Salt Lake City, Utah, 1923, A.M., 1925; m. Gladys Green, May 17, 1921; children—Marjorie (dec.), Marilyn, Sheldon Clark (dec.). Instr. in business, U. of Utah, Salt Lake City, Utah, 1922-25; teaching fellow in economics, U. of Calif., Berkeley, Calif., 1925-27; with Pa. State Coll. since 1927, asst. prof. of economics, 1927-33, asso. prof., 1933-36, prof. since 1936; visiting prof., Utah Agrl. Coll., summer 1938; legal technician Pa. State Workmen's Compensation Bd., 1931-35; consultant Ednl. Policies Commn. of N.E.A. and Am. Assn. Sch. Adminstrs., 1938. Mem. Am. Assn. Univ. Profs., Am. Business Law Assn. (pres. 1937), Phi Kappa Tau, Phi Kappa Phi, Pi Gamma Mu, Omicron Delta Gamma, Pi Sigma Alpha, Alpha Kappa Psi, Phi Chi Theta, Phi Mu Alpha, Kappa Gamma Psi. Republican. Presbyterian. Mason (32°, K.T.). Author: Principles of Business Law, 1934, rev. edit., 1938. Contbr. articles to law reviews and scientific jours. Home: 302 S. Patterson St., State College, Pa.

TAPPAN, Benjamin, physician; b. Rochester, Pa., Mar. 19, 1890; s. William and Sarah Elizabeth (Buchanan) T.; A.B., Johns Hopkins U., 1911; M.D., Johns Hopkins U. Med. Sch., 1915; m. Elise Gail, Nov. 18, 1916 (divorced); children—Benjamin, Jr., Elise Gail, Helen Gail; m. 2d, Edna Keyes, June 10, 1933. Interne Cincinnati (O.) Gen. Hosp. 1915-16; engaged in practice of pediatrics, Baltimore, since 1918; mem. staffs, Union Memorial, Johns Hopkins, Womans, Ch. Home, St. Josephs hosps.; med. dir. Happy Hill Convalescent Home for Children, and Babies Milk Fund Assn.; asso. med. dir. Thomas Wilson Sanitarium. Fellow A.M.A. Mem. Southern Med. Assn., Med. & Chirurg. Faculty of Md., Baltimore City Med. Assn., West Baltimore Med. Soc., Am. Pub. Health Assn., Md. Acad. Scis., Child Study Assn., Johns Hopkins Med. Soc., Pithotomy Club, Clin. Club, Zend Avesta Club. Democrat. Club: Maryland (Baltimore). Contbr. to med. jours. Home: Bellona Av., Govans P.O., Baltimore, Md. Office: 1201 N. Calvert St., Baltimore, Md.

TAPPERT, Carl Reinhold, editor, clergyman; b. Hameln, Germany, Dec. 13, 1866; s. Carl Lorenz and Alwine (Harcke) T.; ed. Theol. Sem., Kropp, Schleswig, Germany, 1883-87; came to U.S., 1887, naturalized, 1896; hon. D.D., Wittenberg Coll., Springfield, O., 1928; m. Magdalene Drach, Sept. 4, 1890; children—Johanna (Mrs. Eugene Leberecht Strack), Ruth (Mrs. Georg Fricke), Martha (Mrs. Gustav Kilthau), Reinhold, Gustav, Theodor, Johannes, Edwin, Magdalene (Mrs. Edmund Hopper). Ordained to ministry Evang. Luth. Ch., 1887; pastor various chs. in N.Y. and Ont., Can., 1887-1924; editor Luthenicher Herold, ofcl. German organ of U. Luth. Ch. in America, at Phila., Pa., since 1924; asst. prof. Theol. Sem., Waterloo, Ont. 1913-15. Author of several religious booklets. Home: 4925 Hazel Av. Office: 1228 Spruce St., Philadelphia, Pa.

TARBELL, Martha, author; d. Horace Sumner and Martha A. (Treat) T.; A.B., DePauw U., 1884, A.M., 1887; A.M., Brown, 1894, Ph.D., from same, 1897; Litt.D., DePauw University, 1933. Member Kappa Kappa Gamma, American Association of Univ. Women, Pi Gamma Mu, D.A.R. Clubs: Women's University (N.Y.); Woman's, Woman's College (Orange). Author: Tarbell's Teachers' Guide to the Internat. Sunday School Lessons, annually since 1906; Geography of Palestine in the Time of Christ, 1907; In the Master's Country, 1910; (with Horace Sumner Tarbell) a series of sch. geographies, 1896, 99, text-books in language, 1891-1903. Address: East Orange, N.J.

TARR, Frederick Courtney, prof. of Spanish; b. Baltimore, Md., May 6, 1896; s. Adam Shoop and Anne (Courtney) T.; student Baltimore City Coll., 1908-11; A.B., Johns Hopkins, 1915, A.M., 1917; Ph.D., Princeton U., 1921; m. Martha Louise Slocomb, Sept. 22, 1917 (divorced May 15, 1934); 1 dau., Martha Madeleine; m. 2d, Sofia de Yturriaga y Manzano, July 28, 1934. Asso. with Princeton U. since 1920, as instr. in Spanish, 1920-22, asst. prof., 1922-28, asso. prof., 1928-37, Emory L. Ford, prof. of Spanish since 1937; formerly teacher of Spanish, Baltimore night schools (1914-15), and summer sessions of Johns Hopkins (1915-16), U. of Va. (1922-23); visiting prof. of Spanish, U. of N.M., 1938. Enlisted U.S. Army, June 2, 1917; assigned 1st sergt. Ambulance Service; commd. 1st. lt., Sept. 1917, capt., May 1918; with A.E.F. July 1918-May 1919. Mem. Modern Langs. Assn. America, Am. Assn. Univ. Profs., Am. Assn. Teachers of Spanish. Awarded John Simon Guggenheim fellowship, 1929-30. Decorated Caballero de la Orden de Isabel la Católica, 1934. Ind. Democrat. Asso. editor Hispanic Review. Author: Prepositional Complementary Clauses in Spanish, 1922; A First Spanish Grammar (with C. C. Marden), 1926; A Graded Spanish Review Grammar (with Augusto Centeno), 1933; Impresiones de España, 1933; Shorter Spanish Review Grammar, 1937; Romanticism in Spain and Spanish Romanticism, 1939. Contbr. to learned mags. of U.S. and abroad. Home: 1 College Rd., Princeton, N.J.

TARSHISH, Allan, rabbi; b. Baltimore, Md., Oct. 12, 1907; s. Robert and Minnie (Jacobson) T.; B.A., U. of Cincinnati, 1929; B.H. and Rabbi, Hebrew Union Coll., Cincinnati, O., 1932, D.H.L., 1939; m. Miriam Grad, Jan. 7, 1934. Teaching fellow, Hebrew Union Coll., Cincinnati, O., 1932-36; served as rabbi on week-ends in Owensboro, Ky., Danville, Ill., Zanesville, O., 1932-36; rabbi Beth Israel Congregation, Hazleton, Pa., since 1936. Mem. bd. Red Cross, Salvation Army, Welfare Fed., Y.M.H.A.; chmn. Scout Troop com., 1936-38; pres. Council of Social Agencies of Hazleton and Vicinity since 1939. Mem. Central Conf. of Am. Rabbis, Hebrew Union Coll. Alumni, Phi Beta Delta. Reformed Jewish. Lions, B'nai B'rith. Author: (doctorate dissertation) The Rise of American Judaism (accepted and publication planned for 1939). Address: 127 W. Birch St., Hazleton, Pa.

TARUMIANZ, Mesrop A., neuro-psychiatrist; born in Schuscha, Caucasus, September 27, 1885; son of A. M. and Anna Tarumianz; educated in College in Elizabethpol, Caucasus; .M.D. U. of Berlin, German, 1910; M.D., U. of Moscow, 1911; came to U.S. and became naturalized, 1922; m. Sonia Rabus, Sept. 27, 1911; 1 son, Alexis M. Asst. phys. Del. State Hosp., 1918-25, supt. since 1925; dir. mental hygiene clinic and state psychiatrist since 1929; chief psychiatric service, Delaware Hosp., Wilmington; cons. psychiatrist Wilmington Gen. Hosp. Served in Russian Imperial Army, field surg., Med. Dept. later in neuropsychiatric hosps., 1914-17, dischd. as maj. Diplomate Am. Bd. of Neuro-Psychiatry. Fellow A.M.A., Am. Psychiatric Assn.; mem. Nat. Com. for Mental Hygiene (mem. scientific adminstrn. com.), Am. Hosp. Assn., Nat. Conf. of Social Work, Del. State Med. Soc., New Castle Co. Med. Soc., Phila. Psychiatric Soc., Med. Club Phila. Episcopalian. Clubs: University, Torch, Rotary, Social Service (Wilmington). Home: Farnhurst, Del.

TARUN, William, chief of clinic University Hosp.; ophthalmologist and otologist James Lawrence Kernan Hosp., Industrial Sch. for Crippled Children (Baltimore), Rosewood Training Sch. for Feeble-Minded (Owings Mills), Emergency Hosp. (Havre-de-Grace). Address: 104 W. Madison St., Baltimore, Md.

TASSMAN, Isaac Samuel, physician; b. Phila., Pa., Jan. 10, 1892; s. Samuel and Betty (Schafer) T.; B.S., Central High Sch., Phila., 1909; M.D., Medico-Chirurgical Coll., U. of Pa., 1913; m. Selma Stern, Jan. 12, 1926; 1 son, William. Interne Phila. Gen. Hosp., 1913-16; clinical asst. Wills Hosp., Phila., 1916-17; chief resident physician Polyclinic Hosp., U. of Pa., 1919-20; pvt. practice specializing in ophthalmology and teaching in Grad. School of Medicine, U. of Pa., since 1920; clinical asst. Wills Hosp., Phila., 1920-23, asst. surgeon, 1923-32; asst. prof., dept. of ophthalmology, U. of Pa. Grad. Sch. of Medicine, since 1930; staff mem. ophthal. dept., Graduate Hosp., Phila., since 1920; chief refraction dept. and orthoptics Wills Hosp., Phila., since 1926. Commd. 1st lt., Med. Corps, U.S. Army, 1917; hon. dischd., 1919. Fellow Am. Acad. of Ophthalmology and Oto-Laryngology; A.M.A.; mem. State of Pa. Med. Soc., Phila. Co. Med. Soc. Author many articles on eye diseases, contbr. to ophthal. jours. Home: 6676 Lincoln Drive. Office: Medical Arts Bldg., Philadelphia, Pa.

TATE, John Matthew, Jr., mfr.; b. Pittsburgh, Pa., May 31, 1870; s. John M. and Sarah A. (Stouffer) T.; ed. Sewickley (Pa.) Acad.; m. Ernestine Payne, Mar. 16, 1899. Entered employ of Westinghouse Electric Co., Pittsburgh, 1888, and advanced to asst. gen. supt.; resigned, 1896, to become gen. mgr. Pleasant Valley Traction Co. and asst. to pres. United Traction Co., Pittsburgh; organizer, 1898, Tate-Jones & Co., engrs. and mfrs. Republican. Presbyn. Clubs: Duquesne, Allegheny Country. Home: Pine Road, Sewickley, Pa. Office: 545 William Penn Way, Pittsburgh, Pa.

TATE, William, real estate and ins.; b. Closter, N.J., Oct. 12, 1864; s. Thomas and Debbie (Naugle) T.; ed. Hammond Inst., Closter and Closter Pub. Sch., 1870-79; m. Grace H. Wallace, Mar. 4, 1890; children—Clifford Hildebrand, Beulah Dorothea. Engaged in local ins. bus. since beginning as clk. in agency, 1884, propr. ins. agency at Closter, N.J. for over 50 yrs. and real estate bus. also since 1905; dir. Closter Nat. Bank & Trust Co. since 1907, Harrington Bldg. & Loan Assn., Closter, N.J., since 1893. Served as Rep. Leader for 18 yrs. Pres. Fire Dept., Closter, N.J., 6 yrs. Pres. Trade Improvement Assn. for 15 yrs. Republican. Affiliated with Reformed Ch. of Closter for 70 yrs. I.O.O.F. Royal Arcanum. Home: West St., Closter, N.J. Office: Bank Bldg., Closter, N.J.

TATEM, Henry Randolph, Jr., physician; b. Collingswood, N.J., Oct. 20, 1905; s. Henry R. and Kate Maldin (Wilson) T.; grad. Collingswood High Sch., 1922; student Hahnemann Premed. Coll., 1922-24; M.D., B.S., Hahnemann Med. Coll., 1928; grad. student U. of Pa. Grad. Sch. of Med., 1935-36; m. Margaret Calderhead, June 26, 1930; 1 son, Henry Randolph, 3d. Interne West Jersey Homeopathic Hosp., Camden, 1928-29, chief resident physician, 1929-30, mem. surgical staff since 1930; gen. practice of medicine and surgery, Audubon, N.J., since 1930; school physician, Oaklyn, N.J., 1931-34; Audubon, since 1936; police and fire surgeon, Audubon, since 1932; mem. Bd. of Health, 1932-36; dir. Citizens Bldg. & Loan Assn. Mem. Camden County Med. Soc., N.J. State Med. Soc., A.M.A., West Jersey Homeo. Med. Soc. (pres. 1939-40), N.J. State Homeo. Med. Soc., Am. Inst. Homeopathy, Alpha Sigma. Address: Pine and Atlantic Sts., Audubon, N.J.

TAWES, John Millard, comptroller of Treasury of Md.; b. Crisfield, Md., Apr. 8, 1895; s. James B. and Alice V. (Byrd) T.; ed. Crisfield High Sch., 1906-10, Wilmington Conf. Acad., 1910-12, Sadler's Bryant & Stratton Coll., 1912-14; m. Avalynne Gibson, Dec. 25, 1915; children—Jimmie Lee, Philip Wesley. Office mgr. for Tawes-Gibson Lumber Co., Crisfield, Md., 1914-15, asst. mgr., 1915-19; sec. and treas. Tawes Baking Co., Crisfield, Md., since 1919; clerk of Circuit Court, Somerset Co., Md., 1934-38; comptroller of Treasury of Md. since 1939; treas. Sterling Printing Co.; dir. Bank of Crisfield. Trustee McCready Memorial Hosp., Crisfield Library Assn. Democrat. Methodist. Mason, Elk, K. of P., Jr.O.U.A.M. Clubs: Crisfield Rotary (past pres.); Miles River Yacht (St. Michaels, Md.); Fox Island Rod and Gun (Crisfield, Md.). Home: Crisfield, Md. Office: Annapolis, Md.

TAYLOR, Allyn Chandler, pres. Consumers Gas Co.; b. Lawrence, Mass., June 16, 1884; s. Warren French and Mary Elizabeth (Allyn) T.; B.S., Lawrence (Mass.) High Sch., 1902; studied Mass. Inst. Tech., 1902-06; m. Florence E. Welton, June 16, 1908; children—Ruth Caroline, Allyn Chandler, Lillie Welton (Mrs. Robert H. Cook), Avard Warren. Engaged in gas engring. work in various subsidiaries of United Gas Improvement Co., Phila., 1906-12; engr. Allentown-Bethlehem Gas Co., Allentown, Pa., 1913-21; asst. mgr. Consumers Gas Co., Reading, Pa., 1922-24, mgr., 1924-28, v.p., 1928-31, president since 1931, now also dir.; dir. Union Nat. Bank of Reading. Pres. Borough of Wyomissing Hills, Welfare Fed. of Reading and Berks Co. Dir. Pa. Gas Assn., Pa. State Chamber of Commerce, Reading Chamber of Commerce. Republican. Lutheran. Mason. Clubs: Wyomissing, Reading (Pa.) Country; Iris (Wyomissing, Pa.). Home: 55 Park Road, Wyomissing Hills, West Lawn, Pa. Office: 441 Penn St., Reading, Pa.

TAYLOR, Archibald Wellington, educator; b. Linwood, Neb., Apr. 15, 1877; s. Benjamin Francis and Olive Millard (Collins) T.; A.B., Doane Coll., Neb., 1902, LL.D., 1932; A.M., U. of Wis., 1908; U. of Chicago and U. of Pa., 1909-11; D.C.S. (hon.), Oglethorpe U., 1932; m. Anna M. Ross, June 1912; children—Archibald W. (dec.), Robert Ross (dec.). Principal Puget Sound Academy, 1902-05; superintendent public schools, Ritzville, Washington, 1905-07; instructor economics, Purdue U., 1908-09, Ia. State Teachers' Coll., 1910; instr. finance, U. of Pa., 1910-11; prof. economics and head of dept. economics, science and history, Wash. State Coll., 1911-16; asst. prof. economics and dir. Wall Street div., Sch. of Commerce of New York U., 1916-18, prof., 1919—, and dean Grad. Sch. of Business Administration. Mem. Am. Econ. Assn., Chamber Commerce New York, Alpha Tau Omega, Delta Phi Epsilon, Delta Mu Delta. Conglist. Club: Meridian. Home: Westfield, N.J. Office: 90 Trinity Pl., New York, N.Y.

TAYLOR, Aubrey E., publicist; b. Washington, D.C., July 19, 1899; s. John E. and Sarah Elizabeth (West) T.; ed. Business High School, Washington, D.C.; m. Jane E. Boudwin, Sept. 29, 1927; 1 dau., Ellen Blanch. Reporter Washington Times, 1916-17; with Washington Post, 1917; as reporter, until 1925, city editor, 1925-30, asst. mng. editor, 1930, mng. editor, 1931, 32; Washington rep. Nat. Economy League, 1933; apptd. asst. dir. pub. relations, Pub. Works Administration, 1933; asst. dir. information, U.S. Dept. of the Interior, 1937-39. Club: National Press (bd. govs. 1931-33). Home: 6309 Oakridge Av., Chevy Chase, Md.

TAYLOR, Britton Payne, clergyman; b. Reform, Mo., June 1, 1871; s. Robert H. and Mary E. (Payne) T.; B.Pd., State Teachers Coll., Kirksville, Mo., 1899; A.B., Central Coll., Fayette, Mo. 1902; student London, Eng., 1906; hon. D.D., Central Coll., 1914; m. Carrie E. Turner, June 25, 1902; children—Iris Sylvia (Mrs. J. A. Parvin), Mary Carolyn (Mrs. H. C. Beers), Britton M., William Robert, George E. Engaged in teaching, pub. schs. of Mo., 1889-99; asst. cashier Bank of Portland, Mo., 1890-93; ordained to ministry M.E. Ch. South., 1904; held pastorates in Richmond, St. Joseph, Kansas City, Mo., presiding elder at St. Louis, Mo., 1927-29; pastor, Charleston, W.Va., 1920-25 and 1929-34; pastor Johnson Memorial Ch., Huntington, W.Va., since 1934; chmn. bd. Christian Edn., W.Va. Conf. since 1930; mem. Uniting Conf., Kansas City, Mo., Apr. 26, 1939, which formed The Meth. Ch. Mem. bd. trustees Morris Harvey Coll., Charleston, W.Va. Mem. Huntington Ministers Assn. Democrat. Home: 315 10th Av., Huntington, W.Va.

TAYLOR, Charles Andrew, artist; b. Phila., Pa., Dec. 15, 1910; s. Andrew John and Kathryn (Lohmiller) T.; art edn. Graphic Sketch Club, Phila., Pa., 1924-27; unmarried. Has followed profession as artist since 1927; has shown in current exhbns. since 1929; specializes mostly in subjects from horse races, shows and steeplechases; painter, etcher, water colorist; represented in collections of Graphic Sketch Club, U.S.S. Saratoga, and in pvt. collections. Mem. Da Vinci Alliance, Phila., Pa. Democrat. Home and Studio: 2038 Spruce St., Philadelphia, Pa.

TAYLOR, Charles H.; pres., dir. and chmn. finance and investment com. Home Friendly Ins. Co. Home: 2604 Poplar Drive, Larchmont. Office: Home Friendly Bldg., Baltimore, Md.

TAYLOR, Charles Trueheart, M.D., surgeon; b. Weldon, N.C., Aug. 8, 1872; s. Thomas Wallace and Marie L. (Trueheart) T.; student Huntington (W.Va.) pub. schs., 1878-91, Marshall Coll., Huntington, 1891-92, Central U., Richmond, Ky., 1892-94; M.D., Hosp. Coll. of Medicine, Louisville, Ky., 1897; m. Bernice Stevenson, Jan. 1, 1903 (dec.); children—Bernice (Mrs. John W. Long), Charles Trueheart; m. 2d, Stella A. Moore, Feb. 6, 1912; 1 dau. Jane Taylor. In gen. practice of medicine and surgery since 1898; supt. Huntington State Hosp. since 1933; mem. staff Huntington Memorial Hosp., Huntington Orthopedic Hosp., C.&O. Ry. Hosp.; pres. Sovereign Gas Co., Huntington Okla. Gas Co., Midway City Gas Co. City clerk, Huntington, W.Va., 1898-99. Mem. W.Va. Nat. Guard. Mem. A.M.A., W.Va. State Med. Soc., Co. Med. Soc. Democrat. Presbyterian. Mason (32°, Shriner), Elk (Past Exalted Ruler), Modern· Woodman, Woodman of the World. Club: Guyan Country. Home: 1655 Fifth Av. Office: Huntington Nat. Bank Bldg., Huntington, W.Va.

TAYLOR, Clement Newbold, investment broker; b. Jenkintown, Pa., Sept. 13, 1893; s. William Johnson and Emily B. (Newbold) T.; grad. Hoosac Sch., Hoosick, N.Y., 1911; A.B., U. of Pa., 1915; m. Anne W. Meirs, Aug. 19, 1918 (died July 3, 1930); children—Anne Waln, Phoebe Emlen. With W. H. Newbold's Son & Co. (mem. N.Y. and Philadelphia stock exchanges and asso. mem. N.Y. Curb Exchange) since 1915, partner since 1927; dir. Monroe Coal Mining Co. Served in Mexican border service and World War, 1916-18, commd. capt., F.A., 1918. Gov. New York Stock Exchange; mem. Loyal Legion, S.R., Delta Psi. Republican. Episcopalian. Clubs: Philadelphia (Philadelphia); Sunnybrook Golf (Flourtown, Pa.); St. Anthony (New York). Home: Chestnut Hill. Office: 1517 Locust St., Philadelphia, Pa.

TAYLOR, Clyde Chalmers, banker; b. Pittsburgh, Pa., May 11, 1879; s. Joseph M. and Luella P. (Duff) T.; ed. Pittsburgh pub. schs.; m. Blanche Wettengel, of Pittsburgh, Oct. 2, 1901; children—Dorothy May (Mrs. William B. Rodgers), Marjorie Lorraine (Mrs. George S. Fichtel). Employed in treasurer's dept. Carnegie Steel Co., 1897-1901; private sec. A. M. Moreland, 1903-04; asst. cashier First-Second Nat. Bank, Pittsburgh, 1914-18; cashier First Nat. Bank, Pittsburgh, 1918-21, v.p. and cashier, 1921-33, sr. v.p. since 1933, dir. since 1924. Mem. adv. com. Reconstruction Finance Corpn. Cleveland Loan Agency. Dir. Assn. of Reserve City Bankers. Republican. Presbyterian. Clubs: Duquesne, Oakmont Country, Pittsburgh Athletic, Longue Vue Country (Pittsburgh). Home: (summer) 4323 Parkman Boul.; (winter) Hotel Schenley. Office: First Nat. Bank, Pittsburgh, Pa.

TAYLOR, Cornelia Harper, librarian; b. Dover, Del., Aug. 30, 1910; d. Herman Carter and Elva (Collins) T.; student Dover (Del.) pub., elementary and high schs., 1916-27; B.A., Coll. of William and Mary, Williamsburg, Va., 1931; grad. student U. of Del., Newark, Del. and Temple U., Phila., 1937-39; unmarried. Teacher in pub. schs., Kent County, Del., 1931-32, Claymont (Del.) High Sch., 1932-33, Dover (Del.) High Sch., 1933-37; Del. state librarian, Dover, since 1937. Mem. Am. Assn. Univ. Women (pres. Dover Branch since 1939). Congregationalist-Christian. Club: Phila. Alumni of College of William and Mary (Phila.). Home: 223 S. State St. Office: State House, Dover, Del.

TAYLOR, Cyril Stead, physical chemist; b. Worthington, Minn., Dec. 18, 1887; s. William Clyde and Zilpha (Darling) T.; B.S., U. of Minn., 1913; M.S. in Chemistry, Carnegie Inst. Tech., Pittsburgh, 1935; unmarried. Asst. chemist Nat. Bur. of Standards, Washington, D.C., 1913-18, asso. chemist, 1918-20; physical chemist Aluminum Research Labs., 1920-29; chief physical chemist Aluminum Research Laboratories, Aluminum Co. of America, since 1929. Mem. Am. Chem. Soc., Electrochem. Soc., Pa. Chem. Soc., Alpha Chi Sigma. Republican. Methodist. Club: Pittsburgh Chemist. Home: Aluminum Club. Office: care Aluminum Research Labs., New Kensington, Pa.

TAYLOR, Earl Howard, writer, editor; b. Yates Center, Kan., Feb. 15, 1891; s. Jacob Andrew and Lillian Virginia (Powell) T.; educated at the University of Nebraska, 1911-13; m. Helen Moore Martin, June 7, 1924; 1 son, Richard Powell. With Omaha Daily News, 1913-14; feature writer Kansas City Star, 1915-16 and 1919; asso. editor The Country Gentleman, Phila., since 1920 (except for interval in 1936 as polit. aide to Gov. Alfred M. Landon). Mem. U.S. Naval Armed Guard in overseas service during World War; now honorary major Tenn. Nat. Guard. Mem. Chi Phi Fraternity. Republican. Unitarian. Clubs: Swarthmore Players, Western Univ. Club. Editorial writer and contbr. economic articles. Home: 300 Harvard Av., Swarthmore, Pa. Office: Curtis Publishing Co., Philadelphia, Pa.

TAYLOR, Elmer Bruce, lawyer; b. Harrisburg, Pa., Oct. 15, 1886; s. Samuel Nimrod and Jane (Cashman) T.; prep. edn., high sch., Adams Co., Pa.; student Sch. of Commerce, Harrisburg, 1901-02; m. Alma Euada Garverich, June 30, 1909; children—Mildred Josephine, E. Bruce. Admitted to Pa. bar, 1922, and began practice at Harrisburg; asst. city solicitor, Harrisburg, 1922-23; v.p. and trust officer, Mechanics Trust Co., 1923-26, pres., 1926-30; dir. Community Discount Co. Trustee Harrisburg Polyclinic Hosp. Democrat. Methodist. Mason. Home: 29 S. 19th St. Office: Game Commission of Pa., Harrisburg, Pa.

TAYLOR, Emily (Heyward) Drayton, miniature painter; b. Phila., Apr. 14, 1860; d. Henry Edward and Mary (Brady) Drayton; ed. by pvt. governess and abroad for several yrs.; studied painting in Paris under Cécile Ferrier, and at Pennsylvania Academy of the Fine Arts, Philadelphia; m. J(ohn) Madison Taylor, M.D., Oct. 15, 1879 (he died Oct. 3, 1931); children—Edith Moore (Mrs. Albert Mansfield Patterson), Percival Drayton, Mabel Heyward (m. Prince Hohenlohe-Schillingsfurst). Important miniatures: President and Mrs. McKinley, Dr. S. Weir Mitchell, Mrs. Eugene Hale, Emmons Blaine, Mrs. Cyrus McCormick, George Hamilton, son of John McLure Hamilton, Mr. John A. Morris, Mr. Henry Howard Houston, Mr. Frank Thomson, and Cardinal Mercier, of Malines, Belgium (1924). In 1898 assisted Miss Anne Hollingsworth Wharton with Heirlooms in Miniature and wrote part of the work. Mem. Fellowship Pa. Acad. Fine Arts; pres. Soc. Miniature Painters; mem. Phila. Plastic Club, Colonial Dames, Art Alliance, Phila. Gold medal, Earl's Court, London, 1900, Charleston Expn., 1902; silver medal, San Francisco Expn., 1915; medal, Miniature Soc. of Pa.; Medal of Honor, 1919; Charles M. Lea money prize. Acad. Fine Arts, miniature exhbn., 1920. Painted portrait of Cardinal Mercier, 1924, and awarded spl. money prize by Pa. Acad. Fine Arts for same. Home: 1504 Pine St., Philadelphia, Pa.

TAYLOR, Francis Richards, lawyer; b. Philadelphia, Pa., Dec. 31, 1884; s. Thomas B. and Elizabeth (Savery) T.; grad. Westtown (Pa.) Sch., 1902; A.B., Haverford Coll., 1906, M.A., 1910; LL.B., U. of Pa. Law Sch., 1909; m. Elizabeth B. Richie, May 30, 1911; children—Esther T. (Mrs. Edward Wayne Marshall, Jr.), Hubert Richie, Marian Phillips, Margery Scull. Admitted to Phila. bar, 1909; since in gen. practice of law at Philadelphia; member of law firm of Taylor & Hoar since 1914; pres. and dir. Cheltenham Nat. Bank; sec. and dir. Friends Fiduciary Corpn. Commr. Cheltenham Twp., Pa., 1920-24; mem. Westtown Sch. Com. Pres. and dir. Hillside Cemetery Co.; mgr. Haverford Coll.; chmn. bd. Apprentice's Library Co., Philadelphia. Pres. Philadelphia Chapter Nat. Lawyers' Guild. Democrat. Mem. Soc. of Friends (Quakers). Home: 525 Ryerss Av., Cheltenham, Pa. Office: 910 Girard Trust Co. Bldg., Philadelphia, Pa.

TAYLOR, Freeman Pearson, pres. The Taylor Sch.; b. East Carmel, O., Dec. 20, 1873; s. Howard H. and Martha Lucretia (Pearson) T.; student Mt. Hope Acad., Rogers, O., 1883-87; B.S., Volant (Pa.) Coll., 1893; Ph.B., Mt. Hope Coll., Rogers, O., 1896; professional certificate, Zanerian Art Coll., Columbus, O., 1897, Pernin Inst., Detroit, Mich., 1898; m. Nora Belle Walker, Sept. 4, 1895; children—Cyril Walker, Pernin Howard Quail, Janice LaRue (Mrs. Edward James Meloney), Adele. Began as asst. Firestone Bros. Bank, Lisbon, O., 1896; organized, 1898, The Pernin Sch., Phila., featuring Pernin shorthand; received teacher's certificate in Gregg Shorthand System, 1900, and instituted system in sch., changing name of latter to The Taylor Sch., and since pres.; inactive since 1932, sons conducting the sch. Asso. mem. Royal Photog. Soc. of Gt. Britain; former mem. Gregg Shorthand Assn. of U.S. (past pres.), Eastern Commercial Teachers Assn. (mem. exec. com.). Republican. Methodist. Mason (Blue Lodge Hamilton 274, Consistory, LuLu Temple). Club: Kiwanis (Phila.; charter mem. and former mem. exec. com.). Home: 309 Lansdowne Rd., Llanerch, Pa. Office: 1207 Chestnut St., Philadelphia, Pa.; (winter) Poulson Apartments, St. Petersburg, Fla.

TAYLOR, Garvin Porter, publisher; b. Corfu, N.Y., June 20, 1890; s. Wm. Hetherington and Anna (Garvin) T.; student S. Eighth St. Pub. Sch., Newark, 1897-1902, Newark Acad., 1902-05, Racine (Wis.) Mil. Coll., 1905-06, Lake Forest (Ill.) Acad., 1906-08, U. of Ill., 1908-09; m. Jane Hanks, June 29, 1919; 1 dau., Nancy Jane. Publisher Iron Age Pub. Co., 1909-22; treas. and sec. Forged Steel Products Co., Newport, Pa., 1922-24; pres. and treas. Montclair Times Co. since 1924. Served as capt. 312 Inf., 78 Div., U.S. Army, 13 mos. overseas. Decorated Purple Heart. Past pres. N.J. Press Assn., Montclair Chamber of Commerce; mem. Delta Kappa Epsilon. Republican. Presbyn. Mason. Clubs: Montclair Golf, Montclair Athletic, Rotary. Home: 344 Highland Av. Office: 9 Park St., Montclair, N.J.

TAYLOR, George, Jr., clergyman; b. Dudley, Eng., Feb. 22, 1879; s. George and Elizabeth (Mason) T.; brought to U.S., 1886; A.B., Western Reserve U., Cleveland, 1902; B.D., Western Theol. Sem., Pittsburgh, 1910; Ph.D., Grove City (Pa.) Coll., 1914; D.D., Coll. of Ozarks, 1924; m. Eva Irene Moore, Sept. 3, 1906 (died Aug. 16, 1922); children—George, Job, Edmund Moore; m. 2d, Blanche Irene Benner, July 29, 1924. Civ. engr. with Erie R.R., Lisbon and Zanesville, O., 1902-04; draftsman Pittsburgh Coal Co., 1904-05; asst. chief draftsman Pa. R.R., Pittsburgh, 1905-07; ordained ministry, Presbyn. Ch., 1910; pastor 2d Ch., Mercer, Pa., 1910-14, First Ch., Wilkinsburg, since 1914. Served as vol. chaplain, Camp Upton, 1918. Pres. bd. trustees Western Theol. Sem.; pres. bd. mgrs. Presbyn. Home for Aged and Orphans; mem. Bd. of Fgn. Missions, Presbyn. Ch., U.S.A. Republican. Clubs: Philosophic, Cleric, Longue Vue (Pittsburgh). Author of various brochures and pamphlets on religious subjects. Home: Wilkinsburg, Pa.

TAYLOR, George William, arbitrator, asso. prof.; b. Phila., Pa., July 10, 1901; s. Harry O. and Anna C. (Lahneman) T.; B.S. in Econs., Wharton Sch. of U. of Pa., 1923; Ph.D., Grad. Sch. U. of Pa., 1928; m. Edith S. Ayling, June 18, 1924. Engaged as instr. of industry, U. of Pa., 1923; head Dept. Bus. Adminstrn., Albright Coll., Reading, Pa., 1924-29; research asso., Industrial Research Dept., U. of Pa. since 1930; asso. prof. of labor relations, Wharton Sch. of U. of Pa. since 1937; impartial chmn. for Hosiery Industry since 1931, for Men's Clothing Industry, Phila., since 1935; actg. chmn. Regional Labor Bd. for Phila., 1934-35. Mem. Am. Acad. Polit. and Social Sci., Am. Econs. Assn., Am. Assn. for Labor Legislation, Beta Gamma Sigma. Home: 205

Holmecrest Rd., Jenkintown, Pa. Office: 3440 Walnut St., Philadelphia, Pa.

TAYLOR, Gilbert Hawthorne, prof. classics; b. Hardinsburg, Ky., July 11, 1883; s. Rev. William Irvin and Gertrude (Temple) T.; A.B., DePauw U., 1909; Ph.D., U. of Mich., 1914; grad. study, U. of Berlin, Germany, 1913, Am. Acad. in Rome, 1916-20, Johns Hopkins U., 1922-24; m. Clara Elizabeth Williams, of New Wilmington, Pa., Aug. 20, 1931. Instr. Greek and Hebrew, U. of Mich., 1914-15, instr. Latin, 1915-16; prof. Romance langs., Palmer Coll., New Albany, Mo., 1921-22, Southwestern Coll., Winfield, Kan., 1924-25; prof. ancient langs., Westminster Coll., New Wilmington, Pa. since 1925. Served as 2d lt., warehouse accountant, Am. Red Cross, 1917-19, in Italy and Greece. Mem. Am. Philol. Assn., Am. Assn. Univ. Profs., Phi Beta Kappa. Republican. United Presbyn. Rotarian. Home: 319 W. Vine St., New Wilmington, Pa.

TAYLOR, Harold Edward, ins. sales promotion mgr.; b. New York, N.Y., Jan. 1, 1892; s. Alfred Wood and Katie (Noll) T.; student New York Pub. Schs., 1905, High Sch. of Commerce, New York, 1905-06, 13th Av. Night High Sch., Newark, N.J., 1906-08, Coleman Business Coll., Newark, N.J., 1908-09, Y.M. C.A. advertising course, 1910-11; m. Evelyn Julia Haufler, Oct. 27, 1925; 1 son, Paul Harold. Began as office boy with Am. Ins. Group, Newark, N.J., 1906, office boy, loss dept., 1908-12, asst. mgr., loss dept., 1913-18, mgr. side lines dept., 1919-23, publicity mgr., 1924-25, advertising mgr., 1926-30, sales promotion mgr. since 1931. Served as Army Field Clerk, personnel div., Hdqrs. Port of Embarkation, Hoboken, 1918. Mem. N.J. Assn. of Credit Men (chmn. ins. com.), Ins. Advertising Conf. (mem. exec. com.). Clubs: Newark (N.J.) Ins. & Banking Athletic League; Newark N.J.) Athletic. Author: "Selling Tips for the Insurance Agent and Broker," 1939. Dir. Army Field Clerks Orchestra, 1918; asso. dir. Forrest Hill Little Symphony, 1920. Composed "The Newark Y March," "The American March." Home: 76 Nesbit Terrace, Irvington, N.J. Office: 15 Washington St., Newark, N.J.

TAYLOR, Harold Williams, physician and surgeon; b. Beverly, N.J., Oct. 13, 1886; s. Addison Williams and Emma Louisa (Herbert) T.; student William Penn Charter Sch., Phila., Pa., 1903-05, Columbia U., 1905-09; A.B., Coll. of Physicians and Surgeons, New York, 1915; m. Rachel Mygatt Crane, June 5, 1915; children—Thomas Slicer (dec.), Robert Williams, Alden Mygatt, Elinor Stuart. Physician N.Y. Hosp., 1915-16, Presbyn. Hosp., New York, 1916-17; attending surgeon Englewood (N.J.) Hosp. since 1925. Fellow Am. Coll. Surgeons; mem. A.M.A., Bergen Co. (N.J.) Med. Soc., Alpha Delta Phi. Republican. Unitarian. Address: 247 Mountain Rd., Englewood, N.J.

TAYLOR, H(arvey) Birchard, engineer; b. Phila., Pa., Nov. 17, 1882; s. Charles Tracy and Sophie (Davis) T.; grad. Northeast Manual Training Sch., Phila., 1901; spl. courses Towne Scientific School (University of Pa.), class of 1905 (class pres. sr. yr., center, football team 1903); m. Florence Bodine, 1908; children—Helen Louise (Mrs. George B. Clothier), Charles Tracy; m. 2d, Mrs. John McEntee Bowman, 1934; children—Anne Bowman, John McEntee Bowman. Began with I. P. Morris dept. of Cramp Shipbuilding Co., Phila., 1905, serving as draftsman, designer and engr. in mfr. large hydraulic turbine machinery; apptd. asst hydraulic engr. of the co., 1907, hydraulic engr. in charge dept., 1911, asst. to pres., 1915, v.p. Cramp Shipbuilding Co., 1917-26; pres. Cramp-Morris Industrials, Inc., Federal Steel Foundry Co., I. P. Morris & De La Vergne, Inc., Pelton Water Wheel Co., Cramp Brass & Iron Foundry Co., 1926-30; exec. v.p. Baldwin-Southwark Corpn., 1930-32; in charge of design and mfr. of turbine machinery for developments of Niagara, Keokuk, Muscle Shoals, Conowingo in U.S. and Niagara, Cedar Rapids and Shawinigan in Can. Trustee U. of Pa. Mem. Am. Soc. Mech. Engrs. (v.p. 1924-25), Am. Inst. E.E., Am. Soc. C.E., Naval Architects and Marine Engrs., Franklin Inst. Atlantic Coast Shipbuilders Assn. (pres. 1920), Gen. Alumni Soc. U. of Pa. (ex-pres.), Navy League of U.S. (pres.), Bicentennial Com. U. of Pa. (exec. dir.), Beta Theta Pi, Sphinx Sr. Soc. (U. of Pa.). Republican. Presbyn. Clubs: Union League, University, Philadelphia Country, Merion Cricket. Home: Bryn Mawr, Pa. Office: Lincoln-Liberty Bldg., Philadelphia, Pa.

TAYLOR, Henry Weston, artist; b. Chester, Pa., May 11, 1881; s. Barnard Cook and Martha Regina (Parmelee) T.; ed. Drexel Inst., 1901-02, Pa. Acad. Fine Arts, Phila., 1902-03; m. Emma Louise Pendleton, Oct. 8, 1908; children—Helena Louise (Mrs. N. Richard Nusbaum, Henry Weston, Jr. Employed in art dept. Phila. Press, 1903, with advertising agency as artist, 1904-07; free lance artist and illustrator since 1907; illustrations in all leading mags. of nat. circulation; illustrator books for well-known publishers, among them, What Will People Say? by Rupert Hughes; was sent by Maclean's Mag., Toronto, on extensive trip through N. W. Can., including 550-mile trip down Peace River in canoe; has made 12 trips through Can. for material; licensed radio operator and propr. powerful sta. with contacts throughout world. Baptist. Home: 2 Seminary Av., Chester, Pa. Studio: 2022 Walnut St., Philadelphia, Pa.

TAYLOR, Henry White, artist; b. Otisville, N.Y., Aug. 22, 1899; s. Franklin Ellsworth and Mary Agnes (White) T.; ed. Mass. Normal Art Sch., Boston, Mass., 1918-19, Pratt Inst., Brooklyn, N.Y., 1919-20, Pa. Acad. Fine Arts, Phila., Pa., 1920-23, under Daniel Garber, Lumberville, Pa., 1920, Hugh Breckenridge, Gloucester, Mass., 1925; m. Dorothy Millard, Sept. 4, 1927 (divorced 1934); 1 dau., Lois Helen; m. 2d, Dorothy Mitchell, May 9, 1938. Has followed profession as artist since 1923; with art dept. F. Wallis Armstrong Co., Phila., 1926-28; art dir. F. A. Bartlett Tree Expert Co., 1928-31; instr. pvt. classes, lectures, 1931-38; specializes in portraits; v.p. Arts in Phila. Publications, Inc. Chmn. Phila. Art Affiliation, 1938-39. Dir. Clearwater Art Mus., Mus. Sch. of Fine Arts, both of Clearwater, Fla.; pres. Fellowship of Pa. Acad. of Fine Arts, 1938-39; chmn. of Edn., Fla. Fed. of Arts, 1939-40. Mem. Phila. Art Alliance, Am. Artists Professional League. Republican. Home: White Cottage, R.F.D. No. 3, Quakertown, Pa. Studio: Clearwater, Fla.

TAYLOR, Hugh Scott, prof. chemistry; b. St. Helens, Lancashire, Eng., Feb. 6, 1890; s. James and Ellen (Stott) T.; B.Sc., Liverpool University, 1909, M.Sc., 1910, D.Sc., 1914; honorary Sc.D., from University of Louvain, Belgium, 1937; honorary LL.D., Providence Coll., 1938; studied at the Nobèl Institute, Stockholm, 1912-13; student Technische Hochschule, Hanover, 1913-14; m. Elizabeth Agnes Sawyer, June 12, 1919; children—Joan Mary, Elizabeth Sylvia. Came to U.S., 1914, and since with Princeton U., prof. chemistry since 1922, also chmn. chem. dept. since 1926; Francqui prof., U. of Louvain, Belgium, 1937. Member com. on photochemistry Nat. Research Council since 1925; mem. com. on catalysis. With British Munitions Inventions Dept., 1917-19. Fellow Royal Soc. (London), Pontifical Acad. of Sciences; hon. mem. Soc. Chem. de Belg.; mem. American Chem. Soc., American Electrochemical Soc., Am. Philos. Society, Faraday Society, Sigma Xi, Catholic. Club: Nassau. Author: (with E. K. Rideal) Catalysis in Theory and Practice, 1919, 26; Fuel Production and Utilization, 1920; Industrial Hydrogen, 1921; Elementary Physical Chemistry, 1927, rev. edit. (with H. A. Taylor), 1937; also chapters in various tech. books, and abt. 180 papers in scientific jours. Editor and part author of Treatise on Physical Chemistry, 1924. Nichols medallist, Am. Chem. Soc., 1928; Mendel medallist, Villanova Coll., 1933. Commander Order of Leopold II, 1937; Research Corpn. plaque, 1939. Home: 115 Broadmead, Princeton, N.J.

TAYLOR, James Alfred, ex-congressman; b. Lawrence Co., O., Sept. 25, 1878; s. James Clark and Malinda Ann (Bryant) T.; ed. pub. schs. and printing office; m. Bina E. Taylor, July 25, 1900; children—J(ames) Alfred, Louise, Carl Edwards, Paul Bryant, Charles Chilton, Frances Jean. Editor and publisher Alderson (West Virginia) Advertiser, 1900-05; editor Fayetteville Free Press, 1905-08, Fayetteville Sun, 1908-13; editor and propr. Fayetteville Democrat, 1913-16, Mt. Hop. Leader, 1917-19, The State Sentinel since 1920; also pub. Greenbrier Despatch, East Raimelle, W.Va., Cabin Creek Courier, Chelyan, W.Va. Corpl. and sergt. W.Va. N.G., 1908-11. Mem. W.Va. Ho. of Del., 1917, 21, 31 (speaker), 37; mem. 68th and 69th Congresses (1923-27), 6th W.Va. Dist.; Dem. nominee for gov. of W.Va., 1928; Dem. presdl. elector, 1932, serving as chmn. W.Va. Electoral Coll. Presbyn. Mason (Shriner), Moose (ex-pres. state assn.); mem. Jr. O.U.A.M., Eastern Star (past worthy grand patron, mem. bd. of govs. Eastern Star Home). Home: Fayetteville, W.Va.

TAYLOR, John Carey, educator; b. Sams Creek, Md., Apr. 22, 1896; s. John and Rosa (Wright) T.; B.S., Johns Hopkins U., 1923, A.M., 1927, Ed.D., 1930; m. Anne Howell, Aug. 16, 1924; children—Carey Howell, Donald Kaye. Engaged as teacher, jr. high sch., Baltimore, Md., 1919-23, spl. asst., 1923-26, prin. jr. high sch., 1926-30, asst. supt. since 1930. Served as corpl. Med. Corps, U.S.A., 1918-19, with A.E.F. Dir. Baltimore Y.M.C.A., Baltimore Area Boy Scouts of America. Trustee Natural History Soc. of Md. Mem. Nat. Edn. Assn., Am. Assn. Sch. Adminstrs., Ednl. Soc. of Baltimore, Phi Delta Kappa. Presbyn. Clubs: Grachur, Torch, Y.M.C.A. (Baltimore). Home: 6112 Smith Av., Mt. Washington, Baltimore, Md.

TAYLOR, John Thomas, lawyer; b. Philadelphia, June 3, 1885; s. John Barrett & Agnes Jane Taylor; A.B., Temple University; studied law, Univ. of Pa. and Inns of Court, London, Eng.; m. Louise Elizabeth Catlin, Aug. 23, 1926; children—Stewart Fraser, John Barrett, Gwendolyn H. Admitted to practice at Washington, D.C., 1911; dir. nat. legislative com. and legislative counsel Am. Legion since its formation, Apr. 15, 1919. Enlisted in U.S. Army, Apr. 6, 1917; attended O.T.C.; served in 27th and 79th divs., overseas, 17 mos.; participated in Oise-Aisne, Aisne-Marne and Argonne offensives, Verdun defensive; now col. Res.; Officier, Crown of Leopold (Belgium); Medaille Verdun (France); Officier Corona di Italia; Officer Polonia Restituta (Poland); Polska Obroncy (Poland); Officier Legion of Honor (France); Chateau Thierry medal; Order of Compassionate Heart (Russia). Mem. Am. and D.C. bar assns., Am. Soc. Mil. Engrs., Am. Legion (dir. nat. legislative com.), Reserve Officers Assn., Sigma Pi. Mason (32°, Shriner). Clubs: Army and Navy, Racquet, Congressional Country (Washington); Univ. of Pa. Club (New York). Home: 6406 Meadow Lane, Chevy Chase, Md. Office: 729 15th St. N.W., Washington, D.C.

TAYLOR, Joshua Charles, retired lawyer and banker; b. Rochdale, England, Oct. 21, 1873; brought to U.S., 1880; s. James and Martha (Stoll) T.; ed. Chester High Sch., Drexel Inst., U. of Pa.; LL.B., U. of Mich. 1899; m. Margaret E. Gilbert, Oct. 21, 1903 (dec.); m. 2d, Anne Rulon Gray, Feb. 12, 1912 (dec.); m. 3d, L. Milicent Yackey, June 13, 1931. Admitted to Pa. bar, 1899, U.S. Supreme Court, 1928; mem. law firm Taylor, Chadwick & Weeks, 1928-38; retired 1938; formerly pres. Pa. Nat. Bank and Pa. Title & Trust Co.; formerly chmn. bd. Delaware Co. Nat. Bank, Delaware Co. Trust Co.; was also atty. for each. Active in civic affairs. Formerly pres. Chester Sch. Bd. Chmn. bd. trustees Taylor Foundation, Taylor Memorial Arboretum; trustee Lindsay Law Library, Cobbs Creek Park Lands. Former mem. and del. Internat. Chamber of Commerce. Organizer and former pres. Chester Bd. of Trade, Chester Chamber of Commerce; Del. Co. Chamber of Commerce, Del. Co. Parks and Boul. Assn., etc.; pres. Del. Co. Bar Assn., 1926-32; v.p. Pa. Bar Assn., 1927-29. Republican. Episcopalian. Mason. Clubs: Chester (Chester); Union League (Philadelphia); Mountain Lake (Fla.); Spring Lake

Golf and Country (N.J.). Home: 800 E. 20th St. Office: Taylor Foundation Bldg., Chester, Pa.

TAYLOR, Katharine Haviland, author; b. Mankato, Minn.; d. Arthur Russell and Emma Louise (Haviland) Taylor; ed. at home and abroad by father. Mem. Authors' League America, Soc. of Sons and Daughters of the Clergy. Episcopalian. Author: Cecilia of the Pink Roses, 1917; Barbara of Baltimore, 1919; Yellow Soap, 1920; The Second Mrs. Clay, 1921; Natalie Page, 1921; Real Stuff, 1921; Cross Currents, 1922; A Modern Trio in an Old Town, 1922; Tony from America, 1924; Stanley John's Wife, 1926; The Secret of the Little Gods, 1927; The Youngest One, 1928; Pablito, 1929; When Men a Wooing Go, 1930; The Nine Hundred Block, 1932; Night Club Daughter, 1933; Boulevard, 1934; New Ground, 1935; Daughter of Divorce, 1939; also (plays) Keeping Him Home, 1927; The Taming of the Crew, 1928; A Mother's Influence, 1929; Mix Well and Stir, 1930; The Family Failing, 1931; Rest and Quiet, 1932; Who Can Cook?, 1934; The Failure (filmed as One Man's Journey and played by Lionel Barrymore and May Robson); other works filmed include A Man to Remember; also numerous short stories, serials, articles and poems in mags.; many short stories transcribed into Braille. Home: Route 1, York, Pa.

TAYLOR, Lily Ross, coll. prof.; b. Auburn, Ala., Aug. 12, 1886; d. William Dana and Mary Forte (Ross) T.; A.B., U. of Wis., 1906; studied Am. Acad. in Rome, 1909-10; Ph.D., Bryn Mawr, 1912; fellowship in archæology, Am. Acad. in Rome, 1917, 1919-20. Reader in Latin, Bryn Mawr, 1908-09, in archæology, 1910-12; Vassar Coll., 1912, asso. prof. Latin, 1922-24, prof., 1924-27; professor of Latin, Bryn Mawr, since 1927; acting professor in charge of School of Classical Studies, American Acad. in Rome, 1934-35; v.p. Archæol. Inst. America, 1935-37. With American Red Cross, in Italy and the Balkans, 1918-19. Mem. Am. Philol. Assn. (exec. com.), Am. Assn. Univ. Profs., Linguistic Soc. America, Am. Numismatic Soc., Soc. for Promotion of Roman Studies, Phi Beta Kappa. Author: Local Cults in Etruria (Am. Acad. in Rome), 1923; The Divinity of the Roman Emperor, 1931. Contbr. to philol. and archæol. jours., etc. Home: Bryn Mawr, Pa.

TAYLOR, Merritt Harrison, pres. Phila. Suburban Transportation Co.; b. Merion, Montgomery Co., Pa., Aug. 2, 1899; s. Abraham Merritt and Edith Page (Harrison) T.; student Haverford Sch., Ardmore, Pa., 1907-09, St. Lukes Sch., Wayne, Pa., 1909-16; B.S., Mass. Inst. Tech., 1920; m. Hester Sears Walker, Apr. 30, 1921; children—Merritt Harrison, Jr., David Walker, Peter Sears. Engr. Thomas A. Edison Laboratories, 1920-21; successively apprentice, engr., acting supt. power and maintenance and 2d v.p. Phila. & West Chester Traction Co., 1921-31, pres., 1932-36; company merged with Phila. & Garrettford St. Ry. Co. to form Phila. Suburban Transportation Co., 1936, and since pres.; pres. and dir. Aronimink Transportation Co., Eastern Securities Co., The Springfield Real Estate Co.; director Del.-Montgomery Counties Co., Peoples Light & Power Co., Realty Realization Co., Media Concrete Products Co., Tex. Pub. Service Co. Served as 2d lt. Inf., U.S. Army, World War. Mem. bd. mgrs. City Parks Assn.; mem. Soc. of Cincinnati (State of Va.), Delta Psi. Republican. Episcopalian. Home 156 Golf View Road, Ardmore, Pa. Office: 69th St. Terminal, Upper Darby, Pa.

TAYLOR, Mills James, church official; b. Reeseville, O., May 6, 1879; s. John Manlove and Columbia (Mills) T.; grad. Washington (Ia.) Acad., 1898, post-grad. study, 1899; A.B., Monmouth (Ill.) Coll., 1905; grad. Xenia (O.) Theol. Sem., 1908, D.D., Tarkio (Mo.) Coll., 1922; m. Martha Slater Dill, June 11, 1908; children—Theo Mills, John Renwick, Martha (dec.), George Dill. With U.S. mail service, 1900-03; ordained ministry U.P. Ch., 1908; pastor Ref. Presbyn. Ch., Cedarville, O., 1908-13, Second U.P. Ch., Monmouth, Ill., 1913-18; asso. sec. Bd. of Foreign Missions U.P. Ch. of N.A. since 1918; mem. editorial council The Missionary Review of the World since 1921; exec. sec. New World Movement, 1923-25; mem. bd. The United Presbyterian since 1925. Pres. Monmouth Independent Chautauqua Assn., 1914-18; trustee Cedarville Coll., 1910-13; mem. bd. mgrs. Xenia Theol. Sem., 1914-20; one of com. of two sent by U.P. Ch. to visit missions in Egypt, the Sudan, Abyssinia and India, 1921-22. Republican. Home: 619 Lawson Av., Upper Darby, Pa. Office: 1505 Race St., Philadelphia, Pa.

TAYLOR, Nelson Woodsworth, prof. of ceramics; b. Alberta, Can., Apr. 26, 1899; s. John Bristow and Emma (Donaldson) T.; B.S., U. of Saskatchewan, 1918; Ph.D., U. of Calif., 1923; m. Edith Pinnell, 1925 (divorced 1931); 1 dau., Cecily Jane; m. 2d, Miriam McIntyre, 1938. Came to U.S., 1920, naturalized, 1929. Instr. in chemistry, U. of Calif., 1923-25; asst. prof. of phys. chemistry, U. of Minn., 1925-32; Guggenheim Foundation fellow, Berlin and Gottingen, Germany, 1929-30; prof. and head dept. of ceramics, Pa. State Coll., since 1933. Served in Royal Air Force, Can., 1918. Mem. Am. Chem. Soc., Am. Ceramic Soc., Soc. Glass Technology, Sigma Xi, Phi Lambda Upsilon, Sigma Gamma Epsilon. Methodist. Home: State College, Pa.

TAYLOR, Oliver Guy, civil engr.; b. Boone Co., Ind., Oct. 28, 1883; s. Charles Andrew and Margaret Ann (Kern) T.; B.S., in civil engring., Purdue U., 1909; m. Marjorie Edwina Macdougall, Can., May 15, 1915. Topographer U.S. Geol. Survey, 1909-13, 1914-17, 1919-20; civil engr., Republic of Argentine, 1914; park engr., Yosemite Nat. Park, 1920-30; civil engr. in charge engring. Eastern Nat. Park Areas, 1930-37; chief engr. Nat. Park Service since 1937. Served as 2d lt., 1st lt. and capt., Engrs., U.S.A., with A.E.F., 1917-19. Mem. Am. Soc. Civil Engrs., Washington Soc. Engrs., Washington Sect. Am. Soc. Civil Engrs., Am. Civic and Planning Assn., Triangle. Mason. Club: Cosmos (Washington, D.C.). Home: 6313 Georgia St., Chevy Chase, Md. Office: National Park Service, Washington, D.C.

TAYLOR, Oscar Thomas, lawyer; b. Brooklyn, N.Y., Feb. 10, 1870; s. John Alonzo and Margaret (Simpson) T.; student Pub. Sch., Titusville, Pa., 1876-79, Pub. and High Sch., Olean, N.Y., 1879-86; B.S., Washington and Jefferson Coll., Washington, Pa., 1890, M.S., 1893; LL.B., U. of Buffalo (N.Y.) Sch. of Law, 1893; m. Mary Elise Calhoon, June 10, 1908; children—John Calhoun, Thomas Simpson, Robert Stevenson, William Darrington. Began as lawyer, Buffalo, N.Y., 1894; atty. for village of Depew, N.Y., 1896-98; atty. for Pan Am. Expn., Buffalo, N.Y., 1899-1904; admitted to practice in Allegheny Co., Pa., 1902; asst. dist. atty. Allegheny Co., Pa., 1911-14, co. solicitor, 1920-24; asst. city solicitor of Pittsburgh, 1930-34. Served as capt., Co. G, 202d Inf., N.Y. Vols., U.S. Army, 1898-99; lt. col., Staff of Gov. Brumbaugh, Pa., 1915-16; maj., Inf., U.S. Army, 1916; lt. col., N.G. Pa., retired, since 1921. Mem. Allegheny Co. (Pa.) Bar Assn., United Spanish War Vets. (past commdr. in chief; past dept. commdr.), Vets. of Foreign Wars, Vet. Corps of Duquesne Grays (Pa. N.G.; past pres.), Naval and Mil. Order Spanish Am. War. Awarded N.Y., Pa. and U.S. Service Medals. Republican. Methodist Episcopalian. Mason (past master), Odd Fellow (past grand), K.P. (past chancellor commdr.). Clubs: Rotary of Pittsburgh (organizer and first pres.), Mercator International (past internat. pres.). Drafted codified law and book of ceremonies and forms for United Spanish War Vets., 1910. Address: 318 S. Atlantic Av., Pittsburgh, Pa.

TAYLOR, Raymond Abbott, surgery; b. Lakewood, N.J., May 8, 1905; s. Leon Abbott and Jean Marguerite (Carstens) T.; Ph.G., Phila. Coll. of Science, 1925; A.B., U. of Pa., 1927; M.D., Jefferson Med. Coll., 1931; m. Alice Chadwick, Dec. 8, 1938. Licensed pharmacist, N.J., 1925; interne Cooper Hosp., Camden, N.J., 1931-32; surgical resident, Princeton Hosp., Princeton, N.J., 1932-33, Union Memorial Hosp. Baltimore, Md., 1933-34; physician and surgeon, specializing in surgery, Lakewood, N.J., since 1934; coroner physician, Lakewood, 1935-38; pres. and sec. Rolyat Co.; dir. Lakewood Bldg. & Loan Assn. Mem. Bd. of Health, Lakewood, since 1937; mem. Bd. of Edn., 1936-38. Mem. A.M.A., N.J. State Med. Soc., Ocean County Med. Soc., Omega Upsilon Phi, Epsilon Sigma Phi. Home: 60 Madison Av. Office: 58 Madison Av., Lakewood, N.J.

TAYLOR, Roland Leslie, banker; b. Philadelphia, Pa., July 3, 1868; s. I. J. and Ann Elisabeth (Alkins) T.; ed. Phila. High Sch.; LL.D., Maryville Coll.; m. Anita Marjory Steinmetz, Jan. 27, 1897; children—Anita Marjory (Mrs. Gordon Alyard Hardwick), Elisabeth Ann (Mrs. William Newbold Ely, Jr.), Roland Leslie (dec.). With Barker Bros. & Co., bankers, 1887-91, Real Estate Trust Co., 1891-1906; v.p. and dir. Philadelphia Trust, Safe Deposit & Ins. Co., 1906-10, pres., 1910-11; partner William A. Read & Co., 1911-21, Dillon, Read & Co. since 1921; chmn. bd. Tubize Chatillon Corpn. Served as seaman, advancing to lieut. (sr. grade), Pa. Naval Reserve, 12 yrs. Treas. Children's Seashore House (Atlantic City); pres. Fairmount Park Art Assn. Independent Republican. Episcopalian. Clubs: University (v.p.), Racquet, Penn Athletic, Corinthian Yacht. Home: Gwynedd Valley, Pa. Office: 1421 Chestnut St., Philadelphia, Pa.

TAYLOR, Samuel Alfred, engineer; b. North Versailles Twp., Allegheny Co., Pa., Oct. 24, 1863; s. Charles Thomas and Elizabeth J. (Maxwell) T.; C.E., Western U. of Pa. (now U. of Pittsburgh), 1887; Sc.D., U. of Pittsburgh, 1919; m. Anna J. Gilmore, May 17, 1893; 1 dau., Mary Elizabeth. Chief draughtsman structural iron dept., Carnegie Steel Co., 1887-88; asst. engr. of constrn., Pa. R.R., 1888-93; in private practice, 1893-1905, consulting engr., 1905—; dean Sch. of Mines, U. of Pittsburgh, 1910, 1912; dir. Carnegie Metals Co., Pittsburgh; dir. of Beaver Creek Consol. Coal Co. Trustee U. of Pittsburgh, Western Pa. Sch. for the Deaf. Member Am. Mining Congress (pres. 1912), Am. Soc. C.E., Am. Inst. Mining and Metall. Engrs. (president, 1926), Internat. Soc. Geologists, A.A.A.S., Engineers' Soc. Western Pa. (pres. 1913-14), etc. Clubs: Duquesne (Pittsburgh); Cosmos (Washington, D.C.). Acting as tech. adviser to Dr. Garfield, U.S. fuel administrator, at Washington, Sept. 18, 1917-June 30, 1919. Author of various papers in publs. of tech. assns. Home: 617 Whitney Av., Wilkinsburg, Pa. Office: Gulf Bldg., Pittsburgh, Pa.

TAYLOR, S(amuel) N(ewton), physicist; b. Farmingdale, N.Y., Apr. 24, 1858; s. Francis James and Ann (Newton) T.; Ph.B., Wesleyan U., Conn., 1887; fellow in physics, Clark U., Worcester, Mass., 1893-96, Ph.D., 1896; studied German univs., 1902-03; m. Mabel Wright Burr, Dec. 27, 1887; 1 dau., Mabel Burr. Expert electrician with Gen. Electric Co., 1887-93; instr. physics, Purdue U., 1896-99; asso. prof. physics, Syracuse U., 1899-1903; prof. physics and elec. engring., Univ. of Pittsburgh, 1903-08; in charge of astron. time service, Allegheny Obs., 1904-05; prof. elec. engring., U. of Cincinnati, 1908-11; became prof. physics, Goucher Coll., Baltimore, Sept. 18, 1911, now emeritus. Hon. fellow A.A.A.S., 1917; mem. Am. Inst. E.E., Soc. Promotion Engring. Edn., Alpha Delta Phi, Mystical Seven. Contbr. papers on elec. and tech. subjects. Methodist. Home: 2514 Maryland Av., Baltimore, Md.

TAYLOR, Thomas Gallagher, lawyer; b. New Alexandria, Pa., Sept. 30, 1889; s. Jeffery W. and Margaret McB. (Gallagher) T.; A.B., Washington and Jefferson Coll., 1911, A.M., 1914; LL.B., U. of Pittsburgh Law Sch., 1914; m. Mary L. Long, June 28, 1916; children—James Gallagher, Mary Jane. Admitted to Pa. bar, 1913, and since engaged in gen. practice of law at Greensburg; first asst. dist. atty., Westmoreland Co., Pa., 1918-26; dep. atty. gen. of Pa., 1927-35; pres. and dir. Delmont Gas Coal Co. Mem. Phi Kappa Sigma. Republican. Presbyterian. Mason (K.T., 32°, Shriner). Club: Rotary of Jeannette, Pa. Home: Hempfield Twp., Westmoreland Co., Pa. Office: 415 Safe Deposit & Trust Bldg., Greensburg, Pa.

TAYLOR, Thomas Smith, cons. physicist, teacher; b. Peoli, O., Jan. 30, 1883; s. Thomas Smith and Martha (George) T.; A.B., Nat. Normal U., Lebanon, O., 1905; A.B., Yale, 1906, Ph.D., 1909; m. Nelle M. Rietz, June 16, 1912; children—Elizabeth (Mrs. J. Guilford Moravec), Thomas Smith, Mildred Marie. Instr. physics, U. of Ill., Urbana, Ill., 1909-12; John Harling fellow, U. of Manchester, Eng., 1912; instr. physics, Yale, 1913-15, asst. prof., 1915-17; research physicist Westinghouse Electric & Mfg. Co. Co., E. Pittsburgh, Pa., 1917-19, asst. to mgrs. of research and materials and process, engring. depts., 1919-24; research physicist Mellon Inst., Pittsburgh, 1919; chief research physicist Bakelite Corpn., Bloomfield, N.J., 1924-33; cons. physicist and research worker, Boston Blacking & Chem. Co., Cambridge, Mass., 1933-34; prof. physics and head dept., Washington and Jefferson Coll., Washington, Pa., 1934-37; mgr. engring. lab., Diehl Mfg. Co., Elizabeth, N.J., 1937-38; cons. physicist, spl. teacher and lecturer, Newark (N.J.) Coll. of Engring. since 1938. Mem. Am. Soc. for Testing Materials (Marburg lecturer, 1937; chmn. com. on electric insulating materials since 1934), Alpha Chi Rho, Gamma Alpha, Phi Beta Kappa, Sigma Xi. Republican. Methodist. Address: 45 Grover Lane, Caldwell, N.J.

TAYLOR, William A(nthony), mfg. chem. equipment; b. Jarrettsville, Md., Nov. 6, 1887; s. Jesse C. and Ida V. (Jarrett) T.; A.B., Randolph Macon Coll., Ashland, Va., 1908, A.M., 1908; Ph.D., Johns Hopkins U., 1914; unmarried. Employed as chief, Sulphur Color Dept., E. I. du Pont de Nemours & Co., Wilmington, Del., 1916-21; chief, Organic Dept., Chem. Warfare Service, Edgewood Arsenal, Md., 1921-24; pres. LaMotte Chemical Products Co., Baltimore, 1924-30; pres. W. A. Taylor & Co., Inc., mfg. chlorine and phosphate control equipment and water analysis equipment, Baltimore, Md., since 1930. Mem. Am. Inst. of Chem. Engrs., Phi Gamma Delta, Sigma Xi. Democrat. Methodist. Club: Willoughby. Home: Homewood Apts. Office: 872 Linden Av., Baltimore, Md.

TAYLOR, William Francis, artist; b. Hamilton, Ont., Mar. 26, 1883; s. Thomas Elmore and Elizabeth Cooper (Hart) T.; ed. pub. schs. and Collegiate Inst., Hamilton, Ont., Art Students League, N.Y. City, 1905-07; came to U.S., 1905, naturalized, 1913; m. Mary Smyth Perkins, June 11, 1913 (died 1930); m. 2d, Minette Emelie Gundersen, Sept. 27, 1933; 1 son, William Francis, Jr. Employed as lithographer, then artist and cartoonist newspapers, Hamilton, Ont., 1898-1905; advertising art dir., New York Journal, 1908-12; artist A. G. Spalding & Bros., New York City, 1912-30; landscape and free lance artist at Lumberville, Pa., since 1930. Past pres. and sec. Del. Valley Protective Assn.; pres. Phillips Mill Community Assn., New Hope Artists and Writers. Awarded Medal for Lithography by Ontario Govt.; First hon. mention, Phila. Art Club; purchase prize Art Alliance, Phila.; Two Club Prizes, Salmagundi Club, New York. Episcopalian. Club: Salmagundi (New York). Home: Lumberville, Pa.

TAYLOR, William Rivers, clergyman; b. Phila., Sept. 28, 1856; s. Rev. William James Romeyn and Maria Louise (Cowenhoven) T.; A.B., Rutgers Coll., 1876, A.M., 1879; grad. New Brunswick Theol. Sem., 1879; D.D., U. Rochester and Rutgers; m. Annie Brown, d. James Spear, Jan. 24, 1888; children—Louise van Campen (Mrs. Wellington Hay), Anne (Mrs. John C. Case), William James Romeyn, James Spear. Ordained Reformed Ch. ministry, 1879; pastor Franklin Park, N.J., 1879-84, First Ch., Phila., 1884-88, Brick Presbyn. Ch., Rochester, N.Y., 1888-1923, emeritus, 1923—. Ex-trustee Reynolds Library, U. of Rochester; ex-dir. Auburn Theol. Sem.; ex-pres. N.Y. State Soc. of Christian Endeavor; chmn. Gen. Assembly's com. on young people; mem. com. on preparation of Book of Common Worship; Exec. Commn. and of Exec. Council Presbyn. Gen. Assembly; Mem. Phi Beta Kappa, Chi Phi Fraternity. Republican. Club: Valley Country (Keene Valley, N.Y.). Address: 516 Auburn Av., Chestnut Hill, Philadelphia, Pa.

TEAGARDEN, Florence M., prof. psychology; b. Dallas, W.Va., Sept. 5, 1887; d. William David and Sarah Ella (Braddock) T.; A.B., U. of Pa., 1915, A.M., same, 1916; Ph.D., Columbia U., 1924. Engaged in teaching in pub. schs., 1908-13; with U. of Pittsburgh since 1915, successively instr. of psychology, asst. prof., asso. prof., and prof. Mem. bd. Childrens Aid Soc., Allegheny Co. Mem. Am. Psychol. Assn., A.A.A.S., Am. Assn. Applied Psychology, Am. Assn. Univ. Profs., Pa. Assn. Clin. Psychologists (pres., 1938-39), Am. Orthopsychiatric Assn., Nat. Edn. Assn., Pa. State Edn. Assn., Sigma Xi, Pi Lambda Theta, Kappa Delta Pi, Mortar Board. Democrat. Presbyn. Club: College (Pittsburgh). Contbr. articles to prof. mags. Home: Royal York Apts., Pittsburgh, Pa.

TEAHAN, Roscoe William, surgeon; b. Charlemont, Mass., Dec. 15, 1893; s. William and Harriet E. (Hicks) T.; M.D., N.Y. Med. Coll. & Flower Hosp., 1917; grad. study, U. of Pa. Grad. Sch. of Medicine, 1923-27; m. Catherine Fraser, May 29, 1918. Engaged in gen. practice of medicine, 1919-23; med. dir. and chief surgeon, Jeanes Hosp., Phila., since 1927. Served as 1st lt. Med. Corps, U.S.A., 1918-19; roentgenologist in charge x-ray dept. U.S. Gen. Hosp., Biltmore, N.C., 1919. Fellow Am. Coll. Surgeons; certified in therapeutic radiology by Am. Bd. Radiology; mem. A.M.A., Pa. State Med. Soc., Phila. County Med. Soc. Republican. Episcopalian. Club: The Medical Club of Phila. Home: Meadowbrook, Pa. Office: 255 S. 17th St., Philadelphia, Pa.

TEAL, Harvey Don, dist. supt. schs.; b. Sycamore, O., Aug. 26, 1878; s. George W. and Alvada (Stalter) T.; A.B., Defiance Coll., 1918; A.M., O. State U., 1923; m. Jessie Case, Nov. 25, 1904; children—Betty Leah, Hal Case. Employed as dist. supt. schs., Henry Co., O., 1916-18, county supt., 1918-24; asst. co. supt., Stark Co., O., 1924-25, co. supt. schs., 1925-29; dist. supt. schs. City of Clairton, Pa., since 1929. Mem. Pa. State Edn. Assn., Supt's. Dept. N.E.A., Phi Delta Kappa. Presbyterian. Club: Rotary of Clairton. Home: 517 Halcomb Av., Clairton, Pa.

TEALL, Edna A. W., newspaper columnist; b. Essex, N.Y.; daughter of Franklin J. and Mary Dee (Webb) West; student Elizabethtown (N.Y.) Sch., 3 months; self-educated; m. Francis A. Teall, 1899; children—Frances (Mrs. Peppino Mangravite), Briseis E. B. Began as vol. community worker, Bloomfield, N.J., and New York, 1913; reporter, Newark Eve. News, Bloomfield, N.J., 1919-21, editor home page, 1921; columnist and feature story writer Newark (N.J.) Evening News since 1935, organizer and dir. Homemaking Club since 1925. Mem. Essex Co. Studio Players (mem. bd. govs.), N.Y. Home Econ. Women in Business. Universalist. Clubs: N.J. Antique (mem. bd. govs.), Newark Zonta (Newark, N.J.). Author: Batter and Spoon Fairies, 1928. Address: 31 Newell Drive, Bloomfield, N.J.

TEALL, Edward Nelson, editor; b. Brooklyn, N.Y., Mar. 23, 1880; s. F. Horace and Elizabeth (Lowry) T.; A.B., Princeton, 1902, A.M., 1905; m. Jean Christie Gillies, Feb. 18, 1905 (died Aug. 29, 1933); children—Edward N. (U.S. Navy), Robert G., William H., Archibald E. (U.S. Navy); m. 2d, Helen Hatfield, Mar. 5, 1934. On editorial staff New York Sun, 1903-17; in editorial dept. Princeton Univ. Press, 1917-19; sec. Marshall Jones Co., pubs., Boston, Mass., 1919-20; head of press dept. Chautauqua Instn., 1920-21; chief editorial writer Worcester (Mass.) Gazette, 1921-24, Camden (N.J.) Courier, 1925-28; mem. editorial staff G. & C. Merriam Co., dictionary pubs., 1928-29; editorial writing, Phila. Record, 1929-31, Pittsburgh Post-Gazette, 1932-36; specialist in compounding for Standard Dictionaries, 1936-37; editor Webster's New Illustrated Dictionary and Webster's New Handy Pocket Dictionary, 1938-39. Wrote "Watch Tower" dept. St. Nicholas Mag., 1917-27; condr. of Proofroom Dept. and contbr. of monthly article to Inland Printer since 1923. Author: Verse History of the College of New Jersey, 1915; Books and Folks, 1921; Meet Mr. Hyphen, 1937. Home: Ryers Lane, Matawan, N.J.

TEAZE, Moses Hay, cons. engr.; b. Newport, R.I., Jan. 26, 1889; s. Alexander William and Margaret (Hay) T.; B.S. in C.E., Worcester (Mass.) Poly. Inst., 1917; m. Kathryn Dodd, Sept. 24, 1921; children—Allison Dodd, David Alexander, Kathryn. Draftsman on steam powerplant design Westinghouse, Church, Kerr & Co., New York, 1906-08; draftsman, asst. supt. of constrn. Stone & Webster, Boston, 1908-09; piping designer Walter J. Jones, New York, 1909-10; draftsman Great Northern Paper Co., Millinocket, Me., 1910-11; designer Hardy S. Ferguson & Co., cons. engrs. paper and pulp industry, New York, 1911-17, project engr. 1921-28, partner since 1928; expert aide Bur. of Yards & Docks, U.S. Navy, 1918-20; power design specialist E. I. du Pont de Nemours & Co., Wilmington, Del., 1920-21. Mem. bd. of fire and police examiners, Bloomfield, N.J., since 1937. Past chmn. Bloomfield Chapter, Am. Red Cross, 10 years; past trustee Bloomfield Community Chest. Mem. Am. Soc. M.E., Am. Soc. C.E., Engring. Inst. of Can., Senior Skull (Worcester Poly. Inst.), Alpha Tau Omega, Sigma Xi, Tau Beta Pi. Independent Republican. Presbyterian. Clubs: Glen Ridge (N.J.) Country; Cedar Point Yacht (Westport, Conn.); Sky Top Lodge, Pennsylvania. Home: 31 Clarendon Pl., Bloomfield, N.J. Office: 200 Fifth Av., New York, N.Y.

TEED, Harold W(alter), minister; b. Dayton, O., Sept. 17, 1904; s. Walter Adolph and Chariene Maude (Hueber) T.; A.B., Wheaton (Ill.) Coll., 1926; Th.B., Dallas (Tex.) Theol. Sem., 1929, Th.M., 1930, Th.D., 1931; m. Margaret U. Buol, Jan. 14, 1932; children—Robert Harold, Margaret Helen. Ordained to the ministry of Presbyn. Ch., 1930; minister Emanuel Presbyn. Ch., Colorado Springs, Colo., 1930-35, First Presbyn. Ch., West Pittston, Pa., since 1935. Past pres. Beltionian Soc. Republican. Home: 211 Luzerne Av., West Pittston, Pa.

TEEL, Rolland Marshall, educator; b. Hackettstown, N.J., Nov. 7, 1885; s. Lewis Marshall and Julia Annette (Kemple) T.; Ph.B., Lafayette Coll., Easton, Pa., 1907; studied law, U. of Md., 1909-10; m. Sue B. Ashley, Sept. 20, 1911; children—Richard Ashley, Rolland Marshall. Began in dept. of entomology, Am. Mus. Natural History, N.Y. City, 1907; teacher, U.S. Naval Acad. Prep. Sch., Annapolis, 1908-14; founded Severn Sch., country boarding sch. for boys, Severna Park, Md., 1914, and has since been its active head. Mem. Naval Inst., Pvt. Sch. Assn. of Baltimore (mem. senate), Alumni Assn. Lafayette Coll. (visiting com., dept. of English), Sigma Chi. Democrat. Presbyterian. Clubs: University, in Annapolis (ex-pres.), Annapolitan (Annapolis); University (Baltimore). Home: Severna Park, Md.

TEETERS, Wilbur Oldroyd, chemist, mfr. science apparatus; b. Dover, O., May 31, 1908; s. Charles Ellis and Fanny Fern (Oldroyd) T.; B.S., Butler U., 1929; M.S., N.Y. Univ., 1931, Ph.D., same, 1935; married Dorothy Hartle, August 9, 1930; children—Nancy Jane, and Charles Ellis. Teaching fellow in chemistry, Washington Square College, New York University, 1929-34; chemist, Hoke, Inc., 1934, gen. mgr., 1935-37; development engr., Air Reduction Co., 1937-38; pres. and dir. Hoke, Inc., mfr. compressed gas equipment and sci. apparatus, N.Y. City since 1938. Mem. A.A.A.S., Am. Inst. Chemists, Am. Chem. Soc., Sigma Xi. Republican. Methodist. Home: Knickerbocker Rd., Cresskill, N.J. Office: 122 Fifth Av., New York, N.Y.

TeLINDE, Richard Wesley, gynecologist; b. Waupun, Wis., Sept. 2, 1894; s. Garret and Cora (Gerretson) TeL.; A.B., U. of Wis., 1917; M.D., Johns Hopkins U. Med. Sch., 1920; m. Catherine Davenport Long, June 1, 1927. Interne and resident Johns Hopkins Hosp., Baltimore, Md., 1920-25; engaged in practice of gynecology, Baltimore, Md. since 1925; asso. gynecology, Johns Hopkins U., 1936-39, prof. of gynecology since 1939; gynecologist in charge dispensary, Johns Hopkins Hosp. since 1930; chief gynecologist, Johns Hopkins Hosp.; visiting gynecologist at Union Memorial Hosp., Ch. Home and Infirmary, and Hosp. for the Women of Md. Served in S.A.T.C., 1918. Mem. Am. Med. Assn., Southern Med. Soc., Am. Gynecol. Soc. (sec. since 1937), Am. Gynecol. Travel Club, Gynecol. Travel Club of N.A., Baltimore City Med. Soc., Alpha Omega Alpha, Phi Beta Kappa. Presbyn. Clubs: Maryland, Elkridge Kennels (Baltimore). Contbr. many articles on gynecology, female urology and gynecol. pathology. Home: 1105 Bryn Mawr Rd. Office: Johns Hopkins Hospital, Baltimore, Md.

TELLER, Sidney A., social worker; b. Chicago, Ill., Apr. 4, 1883; s. George J. and Josephine (Zuckermann) T.; student Armour Inst. Tech., Chicago; grad. Chicago School Civics and Philanthropy (now a school of the University of Chicago), 1908; m. Julia Pines, June 27, 1916. In chem. engring. work with C.,R.I.& P. R.R., 1903-07; supt. Deborah Boys Home, Chicago, 1907-08; with United Charities of Chicago, 1908-09; dir. Stanford Park, Chicago, 1910-16; dir. Irene Kaufmann Settlement and Emma Farm Assn., Pittsburgh, since 1916. Editor Butterfly (social service mag.), 1907-17. Corr. sec. Hebrew Free Loan Assn. (Pittsburgh); dir. and mem. publicity com., Pittsburgh Fed. Social Agencies; mem. advisory council Urban League of Pittsburgh; v.p. Nat. Plant, Flower and Fruit Guild; 1st v.p. Allegheny County Scholarship Assn.; dir. Pittsburgh Dist. Dairy Council; mem. Pittsburgh Civil Liberties Union; mem. exec. com. on Parental Edn., Community Executives Round Table, Hill District Community Council, Pittsburgh Chamber Commerce, Pa. Com. on Penal Affairs, Pittsburgh Advisory Com. on Nat. Youth Adminstrn., Pittsburgh Advisory Com. on Housing, Uptown Bd. of Trade; mem. employment practices com., program com. and pub. relations com. Nat. Conf. of Jewish Social Welfare; mem. B'nai B'rith. Mem. Am. Assn. Social Workers, Am. Assn. Leisure Time Educators, Nat. Assn. for Study of Group Work. Clubs: Jewish Social Workers Club (pres.), Civic Club of Allegheny County. Address: 1835 Center Av., Pittsburgh, Pa.

TEMPLE, Charles Edward, univ. prof.; b. nr. Stanberry, Mo., Nov. 4, 1877; s. George Breckinridge and Susan Eliza (Ross) T.; Pe.B., Northwest Normal Sch., Stanberry, Mo., 1900; student U. of Mo., Columbia, Mo., 1900-03; A.B., U. of Neb., Lincoln, Neb., 1906, M.A., 1909; student U. of Mich. (part time), 1910-11, U.S. Dept. Agr. Grad Sch. (part time), 1921-22; m. Martha Gladstone, July 24, 1907 (died 1935); children—Margaret Elain (Mrs. William J. Wade), Martha Ross, Helen Dorothea (Mrs. Dale I. Hunt), Robert Gladstone; m. 2d, Bertha Robertson Marsh, 1936. Teacher in rural sch., Gentry Co., Mo., 1902-04; prin. Stanberry (Mo.) High Sch., 1904-05; instr. Beatrice (Neb.) High Sch., 1906-07, Lincoln (Neb.) High Sch., 1907-09; instr. in botany U. of Mich., Ann Arbor, Mich., 1909-11; prof. of botany U. of Ida., Moscow, Ida., 1911-14; prof. of plant pathology U. of Md., College Park, since 1914; collaborator U. S. Dept. Agr., Moscow, Ida., 1913-14, College Park, Md. since 1914; state plant pathologist, Md., since 1915. Fellow A.A.A.S.; mem. Am. Phytopathol. Soc., Am. Plant Pest Com., Nat. Shade Tree Conf., Botan. Soc. of Washington, Hyattsville Hort. Soc. (pres., 1938-39), Epsilon Sigma Phi. Mem. Grange, 7th degree. Home: Hyattsville, Md. Office: Univ. of Md., College Park, Md.

TEMPLE, Edward B., chief engr. Eastern Region, Pa. R.R. Co.; b. Swarthmore, Pa., Aug. 28, 1871; s. Charles and Philena (Marshall) T.; student private sch., Concordville, Pa.; B.S., Swarthmore Coll., 1891, Eng.D., 1923; m. Lucy T. Bartram, Oct. 17, 1895 (dec.); children—Charles, Mrs. Elizabeth Plank; m. 2d, Charlotte Evelyn Smith, Jan. 1, 1925. Began as rodman Pa. R.R., 1891, became asst. engr., 1901, asst. to chief engr. 1905, asst. chief engr., 1906; engring. asst., Allegheny Region, U.S.R.R. Adminstrn., 1918-20; asst. chief engr., Pa. R.R., 1920-27, chief engr. Eastern Region since 1927; pres. Swarthmore Nat. Bank & Trust Co. Life Mem. Hist. Soc. of Pa.. Am. Civic Assn.; mem. Am. Soc. Civil Engrs., Am. Ry. Engring. Assn., Phi Kappa Psi. Clubs: Engineers (v.p. 1923-25), Union League (Philadelphia). Home: 315 Maple Av., Swarthmore, Pa. Office: 607 Broad St. Station, Philadelphia, Pa.

TEMPLE, Henry Willson, ex-congressman; b. Belle Centre, O., Mar. 31, 1864; s. John B. and Martha (Jameson) T.; A.B., Geneva Coll., 1883, A.M., 1890; LL.D., 1913; grad. Allegheny Theol. Sem., 1887; D.D., Westminster Coll., 1902, LL.D., 1914; m. Lucy Parr, Apr. 14, 1892; children—John Parr, Martha, William Jameson, Henry Marshall, Edward Lawrence. Ordained ministry R. P. Ch., 1887; pastor Baxter, Pa., 1887-90, First U.P. Ch., Washington, Pa., 1891-1905; adj. prof. polit. science, 1898-1905, prof. history and polit. science, 1905-17, prof. international relations since Mar. 4, 1933, Washington and Jefferson College. Mem. 63d to 67th Congresses (1913-1923), 24th Pa. Dist., and 68th to 72d Congress (1923-33), 25th Dist. Republican. Editorial writer Presbyn. Banner, Pittsburgh, 1898-1900; asso. editor United Presbyn., Pittsburgh, 1903—. Mem. Am. Hist. Assn., Am. Acad. Polit. and Social Science, Am. Soc. Internat. Law (Exec. Council), Am. Polit. Science Assn., etc. Club: Cosmos (Washington, D.C.). Author: Wiliam H. Seward (in The American Secretaries of State and Their Diplomacy series); The Battle of Braddock's Field; Colonel Henry Bouquet in Western Pennsylvania in 1758-1765. Contbr. on hist. and econ. subjects. Address: Washington, Pa.

TEMPLE, William Gold, artist, educator; b. Dunn, N.C., Oct. 11, 1909; s. Delma Lathan and Florence (Collins) T.; grad. Dunn High Sch., 1929; student Pa. Acad. Fine Arts, 1929-35; m. Esther Ruth Kee, June 6, 1936. Instr. still-life painting, Pa. Acad. Fine Arts. Represented in Lambert Collection, Pa. Acad. Fine Arts. Awarded William Emlen Cresson Memorial traveling scholarship, 1933; first Charles Toppan Memorial Price, 1934; second William Emlen Cresson Memorial Traveling European Scholarship, 1935 (all Pa. Acad. Fine Arts). Chmn. publicity com. and bd. mgrs. of Fellowship of Pa. Acad. Fine Arts. Episcopalian. Home: 1718 Cherry St., Philadelphia, Pa.

TEMPLETON, Edwin Starr, lawyer; b. Bradys Bend, Pa., Apr. 23, 1854; s. Chambers and Susan (Mossman) T.; A.B., Thiel Coll., Greenville, Pa., 1875, A.M., 1878, LL.D., 1925; LL.B., George Washington U., 1877; m. Clara Shrom, July 27, 1887; children—Mary Buchanan (Mrs. Arthur Barrett), Florence Shrom (Mrs. William G. Duff), Susan Mossman (Mrs. George H. Rowley), Ruth. Admitted to bar, 1877; gen. counsel for receivers of Shenango & Allegheny R.R. and a number of the succeeding cos.; asst. gen. counsel Bessemer & Lake Erie R.R. Co., 1884-1929, gen. atty. since 1929; gen. atty. Pittsburgh & Conneaut Dock Co.; mem. law firm Templeton, Whiteman & Voorhies since 1936; pres. and dir. Creola Lumber Co.; dir. Meadville, Conneaut Lake & Linesville R.R. Co.; former pres. Ashtabula Gas Co., Greenville Gas Co.; former atty. and dir. Greenville Steel Car Co. Formerly dir. Greenville (Pa.) Schs. Decorated Order of Leopold, II (Belgian). Trustee Greenville Hosp., Shenango Valley Cemetery Assn.; was trustee Thiel Coll., 25 yrs., Edinboro State Normal Sch., 4 yrs; mem. Pa. State Board and State Council of Education, 8 yrs. Republican. Presbyterian. Mason. Clubs: Duquesne (Pittsburgh); Home: 52 Eagle St. Office: 47 Clinton St., Greenville, Pa.

TEMPLIN, Richard Jones Wagenseller, supt. schs.; b. Shamokin, Pa., Dec. 7, 1891; s. Philip S. and Mary (Newberry) T.; ed. Shamokin High Sch., Pa. Business Coll. (Lancaster) and Valparaiso U.; Sc.B., Bucknell U., 1916; A.M., 1919; m. Edith Elliott, Dec. 31, 1912; children—Richard, Evelyn, Jeanne, William, Philip, Mary, Merle, Ralph, Fred. Teacher Shamokin Twp., Northumberland Co., 1910-11; stenographer to div. engr. Pa. R.R., 1912-15; instr. of physics, Bucknell Acad., 1915-16; head dept. mathematics, Wilkes-Barre City High Sch., 1916-19; prin. Sunbury High Sch., 1919-20; instr. mathematics, Lafayette Coll., 1920-22; returned to Wilkes-Barre City High Sch., 1922; supt. schs., West Pittston, Pa., since 1923; employed by Second Nat. Bank, Wilkes-Barre, (summers) 1917-26. Mem. N.E.A., Pa. State Edn. Assn., Am. Assn. Sch. Adminstrn. Republican. Lutheran (mem. St. Paul's Ch., Shavertown). F.&A.M. (Royal Arch; K.T.; Shriner). Club: Pittston Kiwanis (past pres.). Frequent speaker before P.T.A. and service clubs. Writer various articles in Pa. State Edn. Assn. Jour. Home: Cemetery Drive, Dallas, Pa. Office: High School Bldg., West Pittston, Pa.

TEMPLIN, Richard Laurence, civ. and mech. engr.; b. Minneapolis, Kan., Jan. 20, 1893; s. Grant and Maude (Davis) T.; B.S., in C.E., U. of Kan., 1915, M.E., 1926; M.S., U. of Ill., 1917; m. Mabel Jane Harper, June 20, 1919; children—Richard Laurence, Gordon Harper. Began as rodman, A.,T.&S.F. Ry., 1915; research fellow in engring. Expt. Sta., U. of Ill., 1915-17; structural engring. detailer for Kansas City Ry. Terminal, summer 1916; asst. engr. physicist U.S. Bur. of Standards, Washington, D.C., 1917-19; chief engr. of tests Aluminum Co. of America since 1919. Mem. Nat. Advisory Com. for Aeronautics sub-com. on air craft structures. Mem. Am. Soc. for Testing Materials (Charles B. Dudley medal, 1934), Am. Soc., C.E., Am. Soc. for Metals. (Thomas Fitch Rowland prize, 1936), Engrs. Soc. of Western Pa., Acacia, Tau Beta Pi, Sigma Xi. Republican. Episcopalian; vestryman St. Andrews' Ch. Mason. Club: University (Pittsburgh). Author of scientific papers. Contbr. tech. articles to mags. Home: 354 Riverview Drive, New Kensington, Pa.

TENBROECK, Carl, bacteriologist; b. Parsons, Kan., Sept. 5, 1885; s. Andrew and Carrie (Aldrich) T.; A.B., U. of Ill., 1908; M.D., Harvard, 1913; m. Janet Rinaker, Apr. 28, 1917; children—Carlon (dec.), Jane, Nancy. Asso., Rockefeller Inst. for Med. Research, 1914-20; asso. prof. bacteriology, Peking (China) Union Med. Coll., 1920-23, prof., head of dept. pathology, 1923-27; mem. Rockefeller Inst. for Med. Research, dept. animal pathology, since 1927, dir. since 1929. Served as 1st lt., Med. Corps, U.S.A., 1917-18. Mem. A.A.A.S., Am. Assn. Pathologists and Bacteriologists, Am. Soc. Immunologists, Soc. Experimental Biology and Medicine. Research on paratyphoid bacilli, tetanus and animal diseases. Address: Rockefeller Inst., Princeton, N.J.

TENNANT, George G., lawyer; b. Jersey City, N.J., Feb. 1, 1869; s. Thomas and Hannah T.; LL.B., Columbia U. Law Sch., 1891; m. Zona McBurney; m. 2d, Anne Van Sychel, Apr. 12, 1897; children—Katharine (Mrs. Harold D. Tompkins), George G., Jean (Mrs. William D. Stubenford). Admitted to bar, 1892; mem. N.J. Assembly, 1900-02; judge Hudson Co. (N.J.) Ct. Common Pleas, 1913-18; pres. Jersey City Bd. Edn., 1908-13. Mem. Hudson Co., N.J., Am. bar assns. Democrat. Mem. Reformed Ch. Mason. Home: 613 Bergen Av. Office: 26 Journal Sq., Jersey City, N.J.

TENNANT, David Hilt, biologist; b. Janesville, Wis., May 28, 1873; s. Thomas and Mary (Hilt) T.; B.S., Olivet (Mich.) Coll., 1900; Ph.D., Johns Hopkins, 1904; m. Esther Margaret Maddux, Apr. 8, 1909; 1 son, David Maddux. Acting prof. biology and physics, Randolph-Macon Coll., Va., 1903; lecturer in biology, 1904-05, asso., 1905-06, asso. prof., 1906-12, prof., 1912-38, research prof. since 1938, Bryn Mawr Coll. Fellow A.A.A.S.; mem. Am. Soc. Naturalists (pres. 1937), Am. Soc. Zoölogists (pres. 1916), National Acad. Sciences, Am. Philos. Soc., Phi Beta Kappa, Sigma Xi. Dir. instruction in dept. of embryology, Marine Biol. Lab., Woods Hole, Mass., 1920-22; visiting prof. biology, Keio Univ., Tokyo, 1930-31; exec. officer Tortugas Marine Biol. Lab. Carnegie Instn. of Washington since 1937. Investigations in marine biology at Marine Biol. Lab., Woods Hole, Mass., Cold Spring Harbor, L.I., Bur. Fisheries Lab., Beaufort, N.C., Hopkins Marine Sta., Pacific Grove, Calif., Carnegie Inst. Washington, at Dry Tortugas, Fla., Jamaica, Naples Sta., Torres Strait, Australia, Japan. Home: Bryn Mawr, Pa.

TENNEY, Dwight, pres. Tenney Engring., inc.; b. New York, N.Y., May 20, 1889; s. Levi Sanderson and Louise Amelia (Todd) T.; student Montclair (N.J.) High Sch., 1905-09; Chem.E., Columbia U. School of Mines, 1914; m. Marietta Elizabeth Goodwin, Aug. 4, 1917; children—Mary Louise, Dwight Goodwin. Student engr. Nat. Biscuit Co., New York, 1914-19, production engr., 1919-24; chief engr. Franklin Baker Co., New York and Philippine Islands, 1919-25; engr. Continental Baking Co., New York, 1931-39; pres. and chief engr. Tenney Engring., Inc., Bloomfield, N.J., since 1932. Served as mechanic, 7th Regt., N.Y.N.G., Mexican Border, 1915; lt., sr. grade, U.S.N.R.F., during World War. Pres. bd. of health, Verona, N.J., 1934-38; mem. Rep. Co. Com., since 1936. Mem. Am. Soc. Bakery Engrs., Am. Soc. Heating and Ventilating Engrs., Am. Soc. for Testing Materials, Phi Kappa Sigma, Theta Nu Epsilon, Phi Lambda Upsilon. Republican. Episcopalian. Mason. (past master since 1937). Home: 33 Summit Rd., Verona, N.J. Office: 46 Farrand St., Bloomfield, N.J.

TERESA GERTRUDE, Sister; see Murray, Sister Teresa Gertrude.

TERHUNE, Albert Payson, author; b. Newark, N.J., Dec. 21, 1872; s. Rev. Edward Payson and Mary Virginia (Hawes) T. ("Marion Harland"); A.B., Columbia, 1893; m. Anice Morris Stockton; 1 dau., Mrs. Lorraine Stevens. Traveled on horseback through Syria and Egypt, 1893-94, investigating leper settlements, living among Bedouins of desert, etc. On staff N.Y. Evening World, 1894-1916. Park commr. State of N.J. since 1925. Clubs: Players, Adventurers, Dutch Treat, Century. Author: Syria from the Saddle, 1896; Columbia Stories, 1897; (with Marion Harland) Dr. Dale—A Story Without a Moral, 1900 (first instance of mother and son co-authors of novel); libretto of Nero, a comic opera (in collaboration with William C. de Mille), 1904; Caleb Conover, Railroader, 1907; The World's Great Events, 1908; The Fighter (novel), 1909; The New Mayor (novel), 1910; The Woman (novel), 1912; the New York World's various series of hist. articles, 1906-20; Raegan Stories (Smart Set Mag.), 1913-14; Dad, 1914; Dollars and Cents, 1915; The Locust Years, 1915; Fortune, 1918; Wonder Women of History, 1918; Lad: A Dog, 1919; Bruce, 1920; The Pest, 1920; Buff: A Collie, 1921; The Man in the Dark, 1921; Black Gold, 1921; Further Adventurers of Lad, 1922; His Dog, 1922; Black Cæsar's Clan, 1923; The Amateur Inn, 1923; Lochinvar Luck, 1923; Wolf, 1924; Treve, 1924; The Tiger's Claw, 1924; Now That I'm Fifty, 1925; The Runaway Bag, 1925; The Heart of a Dog, 1926; Treasure, 1926; Gray Dawn, 1927; Bumps, 1927; The Luck of the Laird, 1927; Lad of Sunnybank, 1928; Proving Nothing, 1929, To the Best of My Memory (autobiography), 1930; A Dog Named Chips, 1931; The Son of God, 1932; The Way of a Dog, 1934; The Book of Sunnybank, 1935; Unseen (novel), 1936; A Book of Famous Dogs, 1937; also more than 30 motion picture plays; short stories, verse in mags. Expert on physical culture topics; breeder of prize-winning collies. Received Medal of Excellence from Columbia U., 1933. Address: 67 Riverside Drive, N.Y. City, and "Sunnybank," Pompton Lakes, N.J.

TERHUNE, Anice (Morris Stockton), composer; b. Hampden, Mass.; d. John Potter and Elizabeth Morris (Olmstead) Stockton; ed. "The Elms" and the Howard School, Springfield, Mass., Conservatory of Music, Cleveland, O.; studied piano, organ and harmony under Louis Coenen, of Rotterdam, Holland, and Profs. Franklin Bassett and E. M. Bowman; m. Albert Payson Terhune; 1 dau., Mrs. Lorraine Stevens. Was several yrs. concert pianist in New York and elsewhere, and organist, Beckwith Memorial Ch., Cleveland. Presbyn. Mem. Society Descendants of Signers of the Declaration of Independence, Colonial Dames of America. Composer of more than one hundred songs; also composed music of comic opera entitled "Nero," 1904; Romance in G major, 1906; Serenade, 1907; Gaelic Lullaby, 1908; Dutch Ditties (book of 15 songs), 1909; Chinese Child's Day, 1910; Colonial Carols, 1910; "Faith," sacred song, 1910; "Song at Dusk," chorus for male voices, 1910; Barnyard Ballads, 1911; "Syrian Woman's Lament," 1911; music of operetta "The Woodland Princess," 1911; suite of six pieces for pianoforte, 1911; second suite of six pieces for pianoforte, "Songs of Summer," 1911; Schirmer's Music Spelling Book, 1912; Child's Kaleidoscope (sixteen piano pieces), 1913; The Little Dream Horse, 1913; Country Sketches (12 piano pieces), 1914; Easter Morn, 1915; Bridal Song, 1915; Our Very Own Book (songbook for children), 1916; Songs of our Street, 1916; Exaltation, When Summer Keeps the Vows of Spring, The Snow-White Gull (Eskimo Song-anthology), all 1916; In an Old Garden, and The Hill (piano), 1917; (song) The Lights of Home, 1924; (song) Shadow Fingers, 1927; Out of Doors (piano), 1927; two series of educational songs, 1932 and 1933. Author: Home Musical Education for Children, 1903; Ballade of Dead Ladies (biographic memoirs), 1917; More Superwomen (series in Ainslee's Mag.), 1917-18; Sins of the Fathers, 1918; Grey Dawn, 1919; The Story of Canada, 1919; Kings of Hearts (biog. series), 1921; The Eyes of the Village (novel), 1921; Music Study for Children (text book), 1923; The Boarder up at Em's (novel), 1925; Sunnybank Songs, 1929; (novel) The White Mouse, 1929; A Flier in Pearls, 1930; Group of Part-Songs for "The Music Hour," 1937. Contbr. fiction, verse and mus. articles to mags. Home: 67 Riverside Drive, New York, N.Y., and "Sunnybank," Pompton Lakes, N.J.

TERHUNE, Beekman Ramsey, supt. of schools; b. Saddle River, N.J., July 10, 1880; s. Herman and Eliza Jane (Ramsey) T.; grad. Paterson (N.J.) Classical and Scientific Sch., 1897; A.B., Princeton U., 1901; A.M., Columbia, 1902; m. Margaret C. Forshay, June 26, 1902 (died Jan. 30, 1920); children—Margaret Demarest (Mrs. Randolph Beebe), Elizabeth Ramsey (Mrs. Constant Watrous); m. 2d, Marie Katherine Collisi, Oct. 20, 1921; 1 son, Charles Bunnell. Teacher, Hackley Sch., Tarrytown, N.Y., 1902-03; asso. with Trenton (N.J.) schools, 1903-23, as teacher of Latin, High Sch., 1903-13, prin., Joseph Wood Sch., 1913-17, Jr. High Sch. No. 2, 1917-21, Jefferson Sch., 1921-23; supt. of schools, North Plainfield, N.J., since 1923. Dir. and mem. exec. com. Mid-City Trust Co., Plainfield; dir. and sec. Mid-City Investing Co., Plainfield. Mem. N.J. Ednl. Assn. Am. Assn. School Adminstrs., N.E.A. Presbyterian. Clubs: Plainfield Rotary (dir. and past pres.); New Jersey Schoolmasters (Newark). Home: 44 Myrtle Av. Office: 303 Somerset St., North Plainfield, N.J.

TETOR, Frederick Armit, appraiser and property analyst; b. Rome, Bradford Co., Pa., Nov. 23, 1877; s. Sterling Peter and Jennie (Weaver) T.; ed. Pittston (Pa.) High Sch. and Centremoreland (Pa.) High Sch.; private course in engring. under Prof. Cooke, Wilkes-Barre, 1895-98; m. Elizabeth V. Jones, Aug. 14, 1907; children—Virginia Elizabeth (Mrs. Donald S. Phillips), Gertrude Ailene, Frederick A., Jr. Began as machinist, 1898; construction engr. and traveling, 1902-13; construction engr., builder, Ridgewood, N.J., and vicinity, 1913-18; partner Walstrum, Gordon & Forman, real estate and insurance, 1918-37; operated as individual appraiser and property analyst, under own name, since 1929; partner Tetor & Schmults, real estate and insurance brokers, since 1937; pres. North Bergen Co.; v.p. Community Bldg. & Loan Assn. Recognized as real estate expert by courts of N.J. Pres. Hudson River Bridge Assn. and awarded medal for activity in securing Hudson River Bridge legislation. Mem. Bergen Co. Planning Bd. Mem. Am. Inst. Real Estate Appraisers, Soc. Residential Appraisers, Nat. Assn. Real Estate Boards. Republican. Presbyn. Clubs: Ridgewood Country, Lions (Ridgewood). Home: 69 Wildwood Road. Office: 9 N. Broad St., Ridgewood, N.J.

TETRICK, W(illis) Guy, newspaper pub.; b. Enterprise, W.Va., Jan. 3, 1883; s. L. Elmer and Sarah Florence (McIntire) T.; student Mountain State Business Coll., Parkersburg, W. Va., and Elliott's Business Coll., Fairmount, W.Va.; m. Virginia Anne Heavner, Feb. 9, 1910; children—Willis Guy, Catherine Virginia, Margaret Ann, James Elmer. Apptd. clk. County Court, Harrison Co., W.Va., 1907, and elected to same office for term 1908-14; pub. Clarksburg Exponent, 1915-1927; gen. mgr. Clarksburg Publishing Co. and pub. Clarksburg Exponent, Clarksburg Telegram and Sunday Exponent-Telegram since 1927; mem. firm Heavner & Tetrick. Author, compiler and pub. Census Returns of Harrison Co., (W.) Va. for 1850, Census Returns of Lewis County, (W.) Va. for 1850, Census Returns of Barbour and Taylor Cos., (W.) Va., for 1850, Census Returns of Doddridge, Ritchie and Gilmer Cos., (W.) Va., for 1850, and Calhoun County for 1860, also Obituaries from Newspapers of Northern West Virginia, Second Series, Vols. 1 to 5, covering years 1932 and 1933. Presidential elector from 3d W.Va. Dist., 1932, for Franklin D. Roosevelt; mem. W.Va. State Dem. Exec. Com. and Harrison Co. Dem. Exec. Com., 1905-1915. Mem. Associated Press (mem. Eastern advisory bd. 1925-27), Southern Newspaper Pubs. Assn. (W.Va. dir. 1922-27), W.Va. Publishers and Employing Printers Asso. (pres. since 1922), S.A.R. (pres. George Rogers Clark Chapter; registrar W.Va. State Soc.), Nat. Press Club (Washington, D. C.). Methodist. Oldd Fellow, Elk. Collector family history and genealogy of Northern W.Va. families for past 20 yrs. Home: 271 Clay St. Office: Exponent-Telegram Bldg., Clarksburg, W. Va.

TEWKSBURY, William Davis, M.D., clin. prof. medicine; b. Hutchinson, Kan., May 7, 1885; s. William Brainard and Minnie (Davis) T.; grad. high sch., Washington, D.C., 1904; M.D., George Washington U. Med. Sch., 1908; m. Susan Tidball West, Feb. 25, 1911; children —Jane West, Helen Davis. Began practice at Washington, 1908; resident physician Tuberculosis Hosp., 1908-09; physician in charge Catawba Sanatorium, Va., 1909-1911; medical supt. Tuberculosis Hosp., 1911-20; clin. prof. medicine, George Washington U. Med. Sch., since 1915; physician in charge Health Dept. Tuberculosis Clinic, 1915-21; asso. prof. medicine, Georgetown Med. Sch., 1917-19; physician in charge Tuberculosis Hosp. since 1920. Mem. Vol. Med. Service Corps. Fellow A.M.A., Am. Coll. Physicians; mem. Med. Soc. D.C., Tuberculosis Association D.C. (director), Sigma Alpha Epsilon, Phi Chi. Episcopalian. Clubs: Cosmos, Chevy Chase. Contributor of papers on pulmonary disease to Journal of A.M.A., American Review of Tuberculosis, Va. Medical Semi-Monthly, etc. Original work in use of artificial pneumothorax in treatment of acute pulmonary abscesses, 1916. Home: 101 E. Lenox St., Chevy Chase, Md. Office: Columbia Medical Bldg., Washington, D.C.

TEXTOR, Gottlieb Peffer, retail lumber; b. Butler Co., Pa., June 16, 1865; s. Christian and Mary (Peffer) T.; ed. Butler County pub. schs., 1872-84, Edinboro Normal Sch., 1887-88; m. Sarah E. Turner, June 1, 1899; children— Frederick Arthur, Wallace Marion. Began as school teacher, 1885; became clerk lumber co., 1889; organizer Brushton Lumber Co., 1894, which was incorporated as Textor Lumber Co., 1905, and since treas. and gen. mgr.; pres. and dir. First Federal Savings & Loan Assn. of Wilkinsburg. Treas. and dir. Retail Lumber Dealers Assn. of Western Pa. Republican. Episcopalian. Mason (32°). Club: Rotary. Home: 1216 Singer Place. Office: 1123 Pitt St., Wilkinsburg, Pa.

THACKRAY, George E(dward), engr., patent atty.; b. Boston, Mass., Nov. 9, 1856; s. Richard and Emma (Sterne) T.; B.S., Brooklyn Polytechnic Inst., 1874, C.E. Rensselaer Polytechnic Inst., Troy, N.Y., 1878; post-grad. student Sch. of Mines, Columbia U., 1878-80; m. Mary O'Shaughnessy, Apr. 9, 1890; children —Margaret (wife of Comdr. P. V. H. Weems) George Edward, Richard Mond. Began as designer of steel works, 1880; later worked in several steel works and rolling mills in various capacities to learn business and became supt. and chemist of various steel works; associated with Cambria Steel Co., Johnstown, Pa., 1890-98, as asst. chief engr.; then constructed structural plants for that co., and then supt. of plant, 1898-1902, structural sales engr., 1902-10; also made tech. investigations as spl. engr. for the company and served as cons. engrs. for allied interests, also handled all patent matters for the company and its successor, Midvale Steel & Ordnance Co.; became mem. exec. dept. Bethlehem Steel Co., 1923, and acted as cons. engr. and also had charge of preparation of tech. publs.; early in career, during various stoppages of work in steel operations served as U.S. engr. on Missouri River improvement, asst. div. engr. Chicago, Rock Island & Pacific R.R., engr. for N.Y. State Bd. of Commrs. (1888); registered patent atty., specializing in steel constructions, chem. and metall. apparatus and processes, etc., since 1894 for Cambria Steel Co., Johnstown, Pa. Mem. Am. Soc. Civil Engrs., Am. Inst. Mining and Metall. Engrs., Am. Soc. for Testing Materials, Am. Standards Assn. (mem. council), Am. Ry. Assn. (engring. div.), Am. Iron and Steel Inst., Chi Phi. Author: Cambria Steel (engrs. handbook), Bethlehem Structural Shapes, and other books. Home: Bethlehem Club, Bethlehem, Pa.

THADDEUS, Victor, author; b. London, Eng., Jan. 24, 1896 (Irish descent); s. Henry Jones and Mary Eva Julia (Woodward) T.; studied pvt. schs., England, France and Germany; B.S., U. of Calif., 1916; m. Elizabeth Ross, March 17, 1930; children—Patrick, Deirdre. Came to U.S., 1907, naturalized, 1917. Served 18 mos. as pvt. sergt. and 2d lt. Field Arty., U.S.A., World War. Mem. Sigma Xi. Author: Julius Cæsar—And the Grandeur That Was Rome, 1927; Voltaire—Genius of Mockery, 1928; Frederick the Great—The Philosopher King, 1930; Benvenuto Cellini and His Florentine Dagger, 1933. Contbr. to leading Am. Mags. Home: Arden, Del.*

THALHEIMER, Alvin, v.p. Am. Oil Co.; b. Baltimore, Md., July 13, 1894; s. Sam and Merla (Friedenwald) T.; A.B., Harvard, 1914; Ph.D., Johns Hopkins U., 1918; m. Fanny Blaustein, Oct. 16, 1918; 1 son, Herbert. V.p. Am. Oil Co. since 1921. Home: 5603 Roxbury Pl. Office: American Bldg., Baltimore, Md.

THATCHER, Charles Garrett, educator; b. Wilmington, Del., Oct. 20, 1891; s. Albert G. and Mary (Hibbard) T.; A.B., Swarthmore Coll., 1912; M.E., Cornell U., 1916; M.M.E., Johns Hopkins U., 1938; m. Angeline Power, Nov. 27, 1914; children—Edward Power, Albert Garrett, Edith Power. Asst. Swarthmore Coll., 1912-13; draftsman Jas. Boyd & Bro., Philadelphia, 1913-14; instr., Cornell U., 1914-16; engr. Midvale Steel & Ordnance Co., 1916-18, Philadelphia Electric Co., 1923-24; instr., later asst. prof. mech. engring., Swarthmore Coll., 1918-27, asso. prof. since 1927, chmn. Div. of Engring., 1927-36. Treas. Schofield Normal and Industrial Sch., Aiken, S.C. Mem. Am. Soc. Mech. Engrs., Am. Soc. Metals, Soc. Automotive Engrs., Soc. for Promotion Engring. Edn. Republican. Mem. Soc. of Friends. Clubs: Ozone, Rolling Green. Wrote article for Am. Soc. Mech. Engrs. annual meeting, 1938. Home: 613 Ogden Av., Swarthmore, Pa.

THATCHER, Howard Rutledge, music; b. Baltimore, Md., Sept. 17, 1878; s. Walter Caleb and Katherine (Brown) T.; student Peabody Conservatory of Music, Baltimore, Md., 1893-05, Diploma in Mus. Composition, 1906; m. Marie Amalie Kuhnel, July 3, 1907. Has followed music as a career, organist and teacher since 1899; mem. faculty, Hood Coll., Frederick, Md., 1904-06; dir. music dept., Md. Coll. for Women, Lutherville, Md., 1906-22; mem. faculty, Peabody Conservatory of Music, Baltimore, Md., since 1911; organist and choir dir., Eutaw Pl. Synagogue since 1905; organist Mt. Vernon Pl. Ch., 1902-17, Grace M. E. Ch., 1917-23, First Ch. of Christ Sci. since 1924; conductor Meyerbeer Singing Soc., 1927-29; guest conductor, Baltimore Symphony and Peabody Conservatory orchestras. Mem. Am. Soc. of Composers, Authors and Publishers. Democrat. Mason. Club: Florestan of Baltimore (bd. govs. 1909-16). Composer many mus. numbers published by leading houses and performed by Victor Herbert Orchestra, Met. Opera House Orchestra, Sousa's Band, and other famous orgns. Home: 1509 John St., Baltimore, Md.

THAWLEY, Wesley Earle, lawyer; b. Denton, Md., Oct. 13, 1895; s. Robert H. and Lena J. (Cahall) T.; LL.B., U. of Md. Law Sch., Baltimore, 1917; m. Ruthannah Gray, Dec. 28, 1920; children—Robert Hooper, Wesley E., Jr. Admitted to Md. bar, 1919, and since engaged in gen. practice of law at Denton; state's atty. for Caroline Co., Md., 1923-27; counsel Denton Nat. Bank since 1938. Served as corpl. Signal Corps, U.S.A., 1918-19. Mem. Md. State Bar Assn. Democrat. Methodist. Mason. Odd Fellow. Jr.O.U.A.M. Club: Rotary of Denton. Home: Riverton Av. Office: Law Bldg., Denton, Md.

THAYER, Frederick M., mgr. Brown, Harriman & Co., Inc.; b. Rosemont, Pa., July 17, 1896; s. John B. and Marian L. (Morris) T.; ed. Haverford (Pa.) Sch., 1904-14; A.B., causa honoris, Yale U., 1917; m. Eliza T. Talbott, Oct. 27, 1923; children—Frederick M., Marian, Harry E., Robert Thruston H., Nelson. With American Trading Corpn., New York, 1919, Sun Oil Co., 1920, Janney & Co., 1921-25; v.p. Shawmut Corpn., Boston, 1925-28; v.p. Janney & Co., Philadelphia, 1929-33; partner Graham & Co., 1933-35; mgr. Phila. office Brown, Harriman & Co., Inc., now Harriman, Ripley & Co., since 1935. Served as capt., 310th F.A., 79th Div., A.E.F., World War. Mem. Hoover Food Adminstrn., Libau, Russia, 1919. Republican. Episcopalian. Clubs: Racquet (Philadelphia); Radnor (Pa.) Hunt; Aronimink (Pa.) Golf; Commodore (P.Q., Canada). Home: Newtown Square, Pa. Office: 1529 Walnut St., Philadelphia, Pa.

THAYER, Horace Richmond, civil engr.; b. Blackstone, Mass., Sept. 3, 1877; s. Francis N. and Nancy (Paine) T.; S.B., Mass. Inst. Tech., 1898; M.S., Lehigh U., Bethlehem, Pa., 1906; m. Abby Lincoln, Sept. 27, 1899; children—Clarence R., Richard N. Engr. U.S. Navy, 1898; civil engr. Am. Bridge Co., Ambridge, Pa., 1900-03; instr. in civil engring., Lehigh U., Bethlehem, Pa., 1903-06; prof. of structural engring. Carnegie Inst. Tech., 1906-20; engr. Kopper Co., 1920-22; writer in civil engring. Internat. Correspondence Co., 1922-28; with Pa. State Coll. since 1929 as asst. prof. engring. drawing. Mem. Soc. for Promotion of Engring. Edn., Am. Soc. C.E., Triangle; hon. life mem. Authors Club of Pittsburgh. Republican. Author: Structural Design, Vol. I and II; contbr. many articles to tech. mags. Home: 521 E. Beaver Av., State College, Pa.

THEIS, Edwin Raymond, prof. chem. engring.; b. Newport, Ky., July 8, 1896; s. Edwin David and Ida Eliza (Holbrook) T.; Ch.E., U. of Cincinnati, 1921; Ph.D., U. of Cincinnati, 1926; m. Martha Celestine Pauling, July 2, 1921; children—Edwin Raymond, Richard Carl. Engaged as research asso. and dir. chem. research, Dept. Leather Research, U. of Cincinnati, 1921-27; chem. engr., Frederick Stearns & Co., Detroit, Mich., 1927; asst. prof. chem. engring., Lehigh U., Bethlehem, Pa., 1927-30, asso. prof. 1930-38, prof. chem. engring. since 1938; has served as cons. to leather and allied industries since 1927; mem. spl. U.S. Govt. com. sent to China and Japan for inspection imported skins, summer 1937. Served as 2d lt. inf. U.S.A., 1918-19; 1st lt. Ordnance Res., 1926-31, capt. since 1931. Mem. Am. Leather Chemists Assn., Am. Chem. Soc., Tech. Assn. of Fur Industry, Tau Beta Pi, Sigma Xi, Delta Sigma Phi. Republican. Methodist. Club: Lions Internat. Home: 1021 Raymond Av., Bethlehem, Pa.

THEISS, Lewis Edwin, journalist, author; b. Bermingham (now Derby), Conn., Sept. 29, 1878; s. John Henry and Anna Maria (Warren) T.; Ph.B., Bucknell U., Lewisburg, Pa., 1902, Litt. D., 1924; m. Mary Bartol, Ph.D., June 30, 1903; 1 dau., Frances Warren. Editorial staff New York Sun, 1903-12; free lance writer since 1912; editor publs. National War Garden Commn., 1918; official coöperator, U.S. Bur. Plant Industry; commercial fruit grower and horticulturist; formerly garden editor Good Housekeeping, etc.; edited publs. Pa. Department Forests and Waters, 1928-30; investigated moral situation in Americans colls. for Ladies' Home Journal; investigated for Pictorial Review, prior to passage of nat. suffrage amendment, the working of equal suffrage in all states having equal suffrage; prof. journalism, Bucknell University, since 1924; former regional dir. Regions 1 and 2, Pa. Lions Internat. (past pres. Lewisburg Club); chmn. Union County (Pa.) Chapter Am. Red Cross. Pres. Boy Scout Council, Susquehanna Valley Area. Mem. Northumberland Co., Lycoming Co., and Muncy, Pa., hist. socs., Am. Assn. Teachers of Journalism, Northern Nut Growers Assn., Pa. Nut Growers Assn., Phi Gamma Delta, Pi Delta Epsilon, Sigma Tau Delta, Pi Gamma Mu. Baptist. Awarded silver beaver for notable service to boyhood, Boy Scouts of America. Clubs: National Press (Washington, D.C.); Phi Gamma Delta (New York City). Author: In Camp at Fort Brady, 1914; His Big Brother (with wife), 1915; Lumberjack Bob, 1916; The Wireless Patrol at Camp Brady, 1917; The Secret Wireless, 1918; The Champion of the Foothills, 1918; The Hidden Aerial, 1919; The Young Wireless Operator Afloat, 1920; The Young Wireless Operator as a Fire Patrol, 1921; The Young Wireless Operator with the Oyster Fleet, 1922; The Young Wireless Operator with the U.S. Secret Service, 1923; The Wireless Operator with the U.S. Coast Guards, 1924; The Flume in the Mountains, 1925; Aloft in the Shenandoah II, 1926; Keepers of the Sea, 1927; Piloting the U.S. Air Mail, 1927; The Search for the Lost Mail Plane, 1928; Training the Air Mail Bandits, 1929; The Flying Reporter, 1930; The Pursuit of the Flying Smugglers, 1931; Wings of the Coast Guard, 1932; Flying the U.S. Mail to South America, 1933; The Mail Pilot of the Caribbean, 1934; The Flying Explorer, 1935; Guardians of the Sea, 1935; From Coast to Coast with the U.S. Air Mail, 1936; A Journey Through Pennsylvania Farm Lands, 1936; Flood Mappers Aloft, 1937; Wings Over the Pacific, 1938. Contbr. to mags. Home: Lewisburg, Pa.

THOM, William Taylor, Jr., geology; b. Roanoke, Va., June 9, 1891; s. William Taylor and Elizabeth Porter (Miller) T.; B.S., Washington and Lee University, 1913, and D.Sc., 1936; Ph.D., Johns Hopkins University, 1917; m. Rachel Trimble Hoopes, November 4, 1916; children—William Taylor, III, Judith Preston, Elizabeth Pearson. Page U.S. Senate, 1907; messenger boy Govt. Printing Office, 1908; surveyor D.C. Water Dept., 1909-10; successively geologic aide, asst. geologist, asso. geologist, geologist, sr. geologist, U.S. Geological Survey, 1913-28; chief of plan sect. Bur. of Statistics, U.S. Fuel Admn., 1918-19; in charge coal sect. U.S. Geol. Survey, 1923-24, fuel sect. (coal and oil), 1925-27; asso. prof. geology, Princeton, 1927-35, prof., 1935-36, Blair prof. of geology since 1937. Chmn. Nat. Research Council Com. on Studies in Petroleum Geology, 1931-35; chmn. Spl. Com. Geophys. and Geol. Study Continents, Am. Geophys. Union, since 1935. Spl. asst. Div. of Subsistence Homesteads, Dept. of Interior, Washington, 1933. Mem. Geol. Soc. America, Am. Geophysical Union, Yellowstone-Bighorn Research Assn., Am. Assn., Petroleum Geologists, Am. Inst. Mining & Metall. Engrs., Soc. Econ. Geologists, Washington Acad. Science, Phi Gamma Delta, Gamma Alpha, Phi Beta Kappa, Sigma Xi. Clubs: Cosmos (Washington); Princeton (New York). Author of numerous Govt. reports, also professional papers, and tech. articles. Home: 188 Prospect Av., Princeton, N.J.

THOMAS, Albert L., lawyer; b. Woodcock Twp., Crawford Co., Pa., Feb. 11, 1877; s. Washington and Sarah (Bossard) T.; student common schs. and Allegheny Coll.; m. Veda Long, Dec. 24, 1897; 1 son, T. W. Taught sch. 3 yrs. after leaving coll.; studied law and admitted to Crawford Co. bar, Dec. 1905; admitted to practice before Supreme and Superior cts. of Pa., Dist. and all Federal cts.; elected dist. atty., 1919, re-elected, 4 yrs. later; mem.

Law Examining Com. of Crawford Co. since 1909; atty. for First Nat. Bank of Meadville, Erie R.R. Co., Pa. R.R. Co., Titusville Trust Co., Springs First Nat. Bank (Cambridge Springs), Talon, Inc. (Meadville), U.S. Fidelity & Guaranty Co., Gen. Accident Fire & Life Assurance Corpn.; dir. First Nat. Bank of Meadville. Acted as spl. prosecutor, prosecuting county comrs. of Elk Co.; represented Dir. Gen. of Railroads in suit against Nat. Transit Co., subsidiary of Standard Oil Co., and recovered verdict of $249,000 (an outstanding case, there being no precedent for legal question involved); while spl. deputy atty. gen. of Pa., prosecuted and convicted the Brunos of murder (case known as Kelayres Massacre, Republican leaders shot into Democratic parade, killing five); now counsel for Legislative Com. investigating charges against Gov. Earle and other cabinet officials. Trustee State Teachers Coll. of Edinboro. Odd Fellow (mem. Cussewago Lodge No. 108). Clubs: Round Table, Kiwanis. Breeder of purebred Percheron horses and Ayrshire cattle. Home: 718 N. Main St. Office: 213-14-15 Crawford County Trust Co. Bldg., Meadville, Pa.

THOMAS, Alfred David, supt. of schs.; b. Hazleton, Pa., July 4, 1875; s. Francis and Jane (Bowlden) T.; student Bloomsburg (Pa.) Normal Sch., 1891-93; A.B., Lafayette Coll., Easton, Pa., 1905; M.A., Columbia U., 1918; hon. Ed.D., Muhlenberg, 1927; m. Hattie M. Corby, June 27, 1906. Prin., Nesquehoning (Pa.) Grammar Sch., 1896-1901; vice-prin. Hazleton (Pa.) High Sch., 1907-16, prin., 1916-20, supt. of schs. since 1920. Mem. Bd. of Charities, Hazleton, Pa.; mem. exec. bd. Hazleton (Pa.) Chapter, Am. Red Cross. Mem. Chamber of Commerce (v.p.), Y.M.C.A. (dir.), Boy Scouts of America (mem. exec. bd., Hazleton Council). Republican. Presbyterian (ruling elder and asst. supt. of Sunday Sch., Hazleton, Pa.). Club: Rotary (past pres.; Hazleton, Pa.). Home: 585 James St. Office: Green St. Sch., Hazleton, Pa.

THOMAS, Alfred Kirk, v.p. Allison-East End Trust Co.; b. Harrisburg, Pa., Oct. 24, 1874; s. Findlay Isaac and Agnes E. (Kirk) T.; grad. Harrisburgh High Sch., 1894; m. Helen B. Raysor, Oct. 9, 1907; children—Alfred Kirk, Robert Findlay. Clk. Commonwealth Trust Co., 1894-1903; cashier East End Bank, 1903-21; treas. East End Trust Co., 1921-23, pres., 1923-31; v.p. Allison-East End Trust Co. since 1931; dir. Allison Hill Real Estate Co. Dir. Humane Soc.; treas. Tuberculosis Soc. of Harrisburg and Dauphin counties. Sec. Harrisburg Clearing House Assn.; former treas. Harrisburg Chamber of Commerce. Republican. Methodist (pres. bd. trustees Stevens Memorial Ch.). Mason (Consistory, Shriner). Home: 2107 Jonestown Road. Office: Allison-East End Trust Co., Harrisburg, Pa.

THOMAS, A(llen) Russell, newspaperman; b. Lansdale, Pa., Aug. 17, 1894; s. Arthur Kitchen and Ellen Jane (Nace) T.; grad. Lansdale High Sch., 1911; student Peirce Business Coll., Phila., 1912-13; m. Helen Speirs, Apr. 29, 1922; children—Jean Skinner, Nancy Lou. Typewriter salesman, 1914-15; corr. for Phila and New York newspapers, 1916-17; sports editor Daily Intelligencer, Doylestown, Pa., since 1920; owner and mgr. North Penn News Service since 1920; corr. in Bucks Co. for Associated Press., Internat. News Service, Trans-Radio Press, and several New York, Phila., etc., newspapers. Enlisted in Air Service, U.S. Army, Dec. 13, 1917; served with A.E.F. as mem. 649th Aero Squadron and with 1st Censor and Press Co. on staff Stars and Stripes, Paris, France; disch. July 9, 1919. Mem. Phila. Sports Writers Assn. (mem. bd.), Phila. Suburban Sports Writers Assn. (past pres.), Bucks Co. Fish, Game and Forestry Assn. Republican. Baptist. Clubs: Doylestown Kiwanis (charter mem. and sec.), American Legion (charter mem.), Doylestown Maennerchor, Doylestown Country. Mason; Moose. Home: 140 E. State St. Office: Monument Square, Doylestown, Pa.

THOMAS, Donald Steadman, lawyer; b. Tidioute, Pa., Apr. 5, 1888; s. Dr. George D. and Helen (Steadman) T.; A.B., Allegheny Coll., Meadville, Pa., 1908; LL.B.; U. of Pittsburgh Law Sch., 1916; grad. work, Harvard, 1908-09; m. Eva Kanhofer, June 29, 1919; 1 dau., Helen. Admitted to Allegheny County Bar, 1916, and since in practice at Pittsburgh; mem. of firm, Campbell, Wick, Houck & Thomas, Pittsburgh, since 1931; solicitor Borough of Aspinwall (Pa.) since 1917, Borough of Blawnox (Pa.) since 1926; solicitor sch. dists. Aspinwall (Pa.) and Blawnox (Pa.) since 1926, O'Hara Twp. Sch. Dist. since 1924; dir. Mfrs. Distributing Co. Served as 2d lieut. F.A., R.C. Mem. Am. Legion (past comdr. Aspinwall, Pa., Post No. 77). Republican. Methodist. Mason (Consistory; officer, Commandery; Shriner). Club: Stanton Heights Golf (Pittsburgh). Home: 117 Lexington Av., Aspinwall, Pa. Office: 1100 Peoples Bank Bldg., Pittsburgh, Pa.

THOMAS, Edmund Wells, banker; b. Pine Forge, Pa., Aug. 18, 1889; s. Levi Griffith and Annie Eliza (Wells) T.; student Pottstown (Pa.) pub. and high schs. and Berks Co. (Pa.) country schs., 1896-1909; studied Wharton Sch. of Accounts and Finance, 1914-15; also various correspondence courses; m. Esther B. Branfield, Apr. 11, 1916; children—Edmund Wells, Richard Branfield. Advertising asst. S. F. Whitman & Sons, Sept.-Nov. 1909; clk. Nat. Iron Bank, Pottstown, Pa., 1909-13; with Penn Nat. Bk., Reading, Pa., 1913-14, asst. cashier, 1914-19; v.p. First Nat. Bank of Gettysburg, Pa., 1919-28, pres. since 1928, now also dir.; chmn. liquidating trustees Citizens Trust Co. Mem. several coms. Am., Pa. and Adams Co. bankers assns.; dir. Gettysburg Chamber of Commerce. Republican. Presbyterian. Mason, Elk. Club: Rotary (Gettysburg, Pa.); York (Pa.) Country. Teacher banking subjects York (Pa.) Chapter Am. Inst. Banking. Has made numerous speeches before banking and Rotary groups and technical addresses before honorary fraternities and classes in banking and economics, Gettysburg Coll.; writer articles on banking. Home: 131 W. Lincoln Av. Office: Center Square, Gettysburg, Pa.

THOMAS, Emma Warfield, artist; b. Phila., Pa.; d. Evan William and Martha (Gray) T.; ed. Phila. High Sch. for Girls, Phila. Normal Sch.; art edn. Pa. Acad. of Fine Arts, 1899-1905, under Cecelia Beaux, Thomas Anschutz, Hugh Breckenridge, William M. Chase, Charles Grafly. Portrait painter and illustrator since 1906; painted portraits and taught painting and sculpture, Reading, Pa., 1908-10; illustrator and portrait painter, Phila., 1910-25; created and published Fragments, a journ. for artists, 1916; art teacher, Media (Pa.) High Sch., 1917-20; painter of portraits, religious compositions and landscapes and teacher in studio residence, Phila., since 1925; exhibited in Phila., New York City, Scranton, Reading, Pa., Gloucester, Mass. Mem. of Fellowship Pa. Acad. of Fine Arts, Phila. Art Alliance. Republican. Ch. of New Jerusalem (Swedenborgian). Club: The Plastic (Phila.). Whitby Hall home of the family in Phila. for 11 generations named for Whitby, Eng.; ancestors settled in Md. and Pa. before Revolution. Studio: 3409 Hamilton St., Philadelphia, Pa.

THOMAS, Eugene Peeples, pres. Nat. Foreign Trade Council; b. Atlanta; s. Lovick Pierce and Jane (Peeples) T.; ed. high sch., Atlanta; m. Helen Ramspeck; children—Margaret (Mrs. Ralph I. Poucher), Helen (Mrs. Edward Lord Behr, Jr.). Asst. foreign mgr. Lorain Steel Co., London, Eng., 1900-04; mgr. Lorain dept. U.S. Steel Products Export Co., New York, 1904-06; asst. to pres. U.S. Steel Products Export Co., 1906-11; pres. U.S. Steel Products Co., 1911-28; v.p. U.S. Steel Corpn., 1928-32; pres. Nat. Foreign Trade Council, Inc., since 1932; pres. Nat. Foreign Trade Assn., since 1935. Chmn. Am.-Chinese Trade Council, Am.-Japanese Trade Council, Inter-Am. Advisory Com.; vice chmn. Foreign Trade Com. of Business Advisory Council, U.S. Dept. of Commerce; chmn. Exporters-Importers Advisory Com. for Export-Import Bank. Dir. Pan-Am. Soc., Am. Argentine Chamber of Commerce, Am. Arbitration Assn., Am. Exporters and Importers Assn., Foundation Co. Mem. Council on Fgn. Relations, Nat. Industrial Conf. Bd. Chevalier de la Légion d'Honneur (France); Cavaliere Ufficiale of Order Crown of Italy. Clubs: Metropolitan, India House (gov.), Plainfield Country (N.J.). Home: 749 Belvidere Av., Plainfield, N.J. Office: 26 Beaver St., New York, N.Y.*

THOMAS, Frank Andrew, wholesale gen. mdse.; b. Charleston, W.Va., Jan. 12, 1897; s. Andrew Stephen and Emma (Besserer) T.; A.B., Ohio Wesleyan U., Delaware, O., 1920; m. Josephine Royer, May 15, 1923; children—Frank Andrew, Jr., Joan L., Ruth Royer. Asso. with Thomas Field & Co., wholesale dry goods and gen. mdse., Charleston, W.Va. since 1920, vice-pres. since 1931; vice-pres. and dir. Southern Hardware Co., Charleston, since 1931; sec. and dir. Daniel Boone Hotel, Charleston, since 1931; dir. Equity Savings & Loan Co., Diamond Dept. Store, A. W. Cox Dept. Stores. Served as pvt. to 2d lt. inf., U.S.A., 1917-18. Trustee Morris Harvey Coll., Charleston. Mem. Sigma Alpha Epsilon. Methodist (trustee 1st Ch.). Mason (K.T., 32°, Shriner). Clubs: Rotary, Edgewood Country (Charleston). Home: 4 Oglethorpe Rd. Office: Virginia and Hale Sts., Charleston, W.Va.

THOMAS, Frederic Leggett, banking; b. Sandy Spring, Md., Jan. 21, 1879; s. Alban Gilpin and Susanna Haydock (Leggett) T.; B.S. in Engring., Swarthmore Coll., Swarthmore, Pa., 1898; m. Eliza Bentley, July 15, 1912; children—Sue Leggett (Mrs. Robert Chapman Turner), Kathleen (dec.), Jean Hallowell, Cornelia Hallowell. In employ credit and mercantile agency, Phila., Pittsburgh, and Louisville, Ky., 1898-1900; entered employ Savings Instn. of Sandy Spring, Md. and First Nat. Bank of Sandy Spring, 1900, promoted regularly through various positions and pres. First Nat. Bank since 1926 and pres. Savings Instn. since 1929; chmn. bd. Citizens Nat. Bank, Laurel, Md. Mem. Community Council, Sandy Spring, Md. Sr. mem. State Banking Bd. of Md. for term ending 1941. Dir. Montgomery County Gen. Hosp. Mem. Kappa Sigma, Theta Nu. Ind. Republican. Mem. Religious Soc. Friends. Home: Ashton, Md. Office: Sandy Spring, Md.

THOMAS, Frederick Lionel, lawyer; b. Lansing, W.Va., June 14, 1892; s. Ulysses Grant and Cora Alice (Calloway) T.; LL.B., W.Va. Univ. Law Coll., Morgantown, W.Va., 1917; m. Leafy Woofter, Dec. 24, 1917; children—Virginia Alice, Frederick Lionel, Jr., Robert Simpson. Admitted to W.Va. bar, 1917; with legal dept. United Fuel Gas Co., Charleston, W.Va., 1917; in practice at Charleston, W.Va., since 1919; asso. with Morton & Mohler, Charleston, 1919-20; with Price, Smith & Spilman, Charleston since 1920, mem. firm since 1930; vice-pres. and dir. Eli Smokeless Coal Co., Nuttalburg, W.Va., since 1929; sec. and dir. Vanetta Land Co., Charleston, since 1928. Served as 2d lt. F.A., U.S.A., 1917-18. Mem. Kanawha Co. Council of Pub. Assistance. Mem. Am., W.Va. bar assns., Charleston Bar Assn. (pres. 1930), Order of Coif Mountain, Phi Sigma Kappa, Phi Delta Phi. Republican. Baptist (trustee Charleston Ch.). Mason (32°, Shriner). Club: Edgewood Country. Home: Briarwood Rd. Office: Kanawha Banking & Trust Co. Bldg., Charleston, W.Va.

THOMAS, George Brinton, personnel dir.; b. Paris Twp., O., Aug. 3, 1882; s. John Robert and Hannah (Johns) T.; student Paris Twp. (O.) Grade Sch., 1887-92, Pub. Grade and High Sch., Youngstown, O., 1892-1901; M.E. in E.E., Ohio State U., Columbus, O., 1907; m. Mary Elizabeth Wright, Aug. 21, 1913; children—George Brinton, Hannah, Betty Vaiden, John Wright. Teacher of grammar grades, Youngstown Township School, O., 1901-02; elec. dept., Carnegie Steel Co., Youngstown (O.) Works, 1902-03; asst. and instr. elec. engring. dept., Mass. Inst. Tech., 1907-10; instr. and prof. elec. engring., Colo. Coll., Colo. Springs, Colo., 1910-17; conducted summer program for engring. teachers, Westinghouse Electric & Mfg. Co., E. Pittsburgh, summers 1910-16; submarine detection development, engring. dept., Western Electric Co., New York, 1917-18, dir. tech. training, 1919-24; personnel dir., Bell Telephone Labs., New York City, since 1925. Served

THOMAS, Harold Allen, prof. hydraulic and sanitary engring.; b. Ann Arbor, Mich., July 24, 1885; s. Calvin and Mary Eleanor (Allen) T.; A.B., Columbia U., 1906, C.E., 1908; m. Katherine M. Sass, Feb. 5, 1910; children—Harold A., Jr., Charles Calvin, Katherine E., Mary E. Instr. civil engring., U. of Washington, Seattle, 1909-10; prof. hydraulic engring., Rose Poly. Inst., Terre Haute, Ind., 1911-23; prof. hydraulic and sanitary engring., Carnegie Inst. Tech., since 1923. Asst. engr. Miami Conservancy Dist., Dayton, O., summer 1918; sr. engr. U.S. War Dept., Philadelphia, summer and part time 1928-29; hydraulic engr. City of Pittsburgh, part time 1927-28, Mead & Scheidenhelm, summer 1936, Westinghouse Electric & Mfg. Co., part time 1937; head hydraulic research lab. Carnegie Inst. Tech., carrying on extensive model studies of dams and other hydraulic structures in various parts of U.S. Fellow A.A.A.S.; mem. Am. Assn. Univ. Profs., Am. Soc. C.E., Soc. Promotion Engring. Edn. Author: The Hydraulics of Flood Movements in Rivers (Bull. of Carnegie Inst. Tech.); The Flood of March 1938 in the Upper Ohio Valley (Trans. of Am. Soc. C.E.), 1938. Tester of golf balls for U.S. Golf Assn. Home: 7405 Hutchinson Av. Address: Carnegie Institute of Technology, Pittsburgh, Pa.

THOMAS, Harrison McClure, banking; b. Lynn, Mass., Mar. 11, 1894; s. Elliott S. and Nora D. (McClure) T.; ed. Wesleyan Univ., 1912-13, Princeton U., 1913-16; m. Katharine Jane Black, Nov. 17, 1919 (died 1934); children—Katharine Jane, Joan; m. 2d, Mary Catherine Barton, Jan. 4, 1936; children—Henry Barton, Elisabeth McClure. Began as salesman with Harris Forbes & Co., New York and Pittsburgh, 1917-21; asst. vice-pres. Union Trust Co. of Pittsburgh, 1921-28; mem. firm Moore, Leonard & Lynch, mems. N.Y. Stock Exchange, 1928-33; asso. with Princeton Bank & Trust Co., Princeton, N.J. since 1933, asst. to the pres., 1933-34, vice-pres., 1934, pres. and dir. since 1934; dir. Trenton Mortgage Service Co., Princeton Inn Co.; pres. and trustee, N.J. Bankers Pension Fund, Inc.; mem. of exec. com., N.J. Bankers Assn. Served as pvt. to 2d lt. Ordnance Dept. U.S.A., 1918-19; 1st lt. U.S.A. Res. until 1938. Sec. Com. on the President's Program, Princeton U. Mem. Cap and Gown, Chi Psi. Republican. Presbyn. (trustee First Ch.). Clubs: Nassau, Springdale Golf (Princeton); Princeton of New York, The Lunch, Park Avenue (New York City); Yacht (Bay Head, N.J.); Triton Fish & Game (P.Q., Can.). Home: 162 Mercer St., Princeton, N.J. Office: Princeton Bank & Trust Co., Princeton, N.J.

THOMAS, Harry George, physician and surgeon; b. Hollansburg, O., May 30, 1869; s. David R. and Pherbie (Jackson) T.; B.S., Nat. Normal Univ., Lebanon, O., 1890; M.D., U. of Neb. Med. Sch., Omaha, Neb., 1896; A.B., U. of Denver, 1906, A.M., 1907; grad. study, univs. of London and Vienna, 1916, 1922-23; m. Harriet Wagner, July 30, 1890; children—Lowell Jackson (radio commentator, etc.), Hellen (dec.), Pherbie (Mrs. Raymond Thornberg; lecturer on Japan). Engaged in practice of medicine at Kirkman, Ia., 1896-1900, at Victor, Colo., 1900-16; over seas in Europe and Asia, 1916-23; Gen. Allenby's chair of medicine, adjunct prof. of pathology, Med. Dept., American Univ., Beirut, Syria, 1920-22; in practice of medicine and surgery at Asbury Park, N.J. since 1923; surgeon Hazard's Hosp., Long Branch, N.J.; mem. staff, Royal Pines Hosp., Pinewald, N.J. Served as capt. then maj. Med. Corps, U.S.A., 1917-20 with A.E.F.; in res. Med. Corps, 1921-28; lt. col. since 1928. Vice-pres. bd. edn., Asbury Park, N.J. Sec. Asbury Park Soc. of Fine Arts, Inc. Mem. A.M.A., N.J. Med. Soc., S.A.R., Vets. Fgn. Wars. Republican. Methodist. Mason. Home: 1113 Fifth Av., Asbury Park, N.J.

THOMAS, Harry V.; mem. staff Union Protestant and St. Mary's hosps. Address: 134 S. 4th St., Clarksburg, W.Va.

THOMAS, Henry Briscoe, Jr., pres. Baltimore Trust Corpn.; b. Baltimore, Md., May 2, 1893; s. Dr. Henry Briscoe and Helen (Coale) T.; student Boys Latin Sch., Baltimore and Johns Hopkins U.; m. Anne Mason Banks, June 22, 1916. V.-p. Baltimore Trust Co., 1930-33; pres. Baltimore Trust Corpn. since 1933. Home: 1124 N. Calvert St. Office: Baltimore Trust Bldg., Baltimore, Md.

THOMAS, J(acob) Earl, prof. of physiology; b. Steilacoom, Wash., Jan. 31, 1891; s. John Calvin and Nettie (Wyckoff) T.; grad. Seattle Pacific Coll., 1909; student U. of Wash., Seattle, Wash., 1910-12; M.D., St. Louis U. Med. Sch., 1918, M.S., 1924; m. Ursula May Johnson, Nov. 27, 1917; children—Jacob Earl, Marjorie Ellen. Asst. in physiology, St. Louis U. Med. Sch., 1914, instr. in physiology, 1918-20, asst. prof., 1920; asso. prof. of physiology, W. Va. U. Med. Sch., 1920-21; asso. prof., St. Louis U. Med. Sch., 1921-27; prof. of physiology, Jefferson Med. Coll., Phila., since 1927. Served in R.O.T.C. and S.A.T.C. while a med. student, 1917-19. Fellow Phila. Coll. Physicians, A.M.A., A.A.A.S.; mem. Am. Physiol. Soc., Soc. for Pharmacology and Exptl. Therapeutics, Soc. Exptl. Biology and Medicine, Phila. Co. Med. Soc., Am. Gastroenterological Assn., Phila. Physiol. Soc., Alpha Omega Alpha, Phi Chi. Contbr. articles on gastro-intestinal physiology, etc., to med. jours. Home: 619 Edmonds Av. Office: 1025 Walnut St., Philadelphia, Pa.

THOMAS, James Hooton, banker; b. Rowlesburg, W.Va., May 23, 1888; s. John and Flora (Hooton) T.; student pub. schs., Rowlesburg, W.Va.; m. Marguerite Geldbach, Dec. 3, 1910; children—John Rendle, Mary Marguerite. Began as clk., 1905; v.p. Half Dollar Trust & Savings Bank, Wheeling, W.Va.; treas. Essex Corpn., Wheeling. Republican. Methodist. Mason. Home: 10 Linden Av. Office: 1501 Market St., Wheeling, W.Va.

THOMAS, James Kay, lawyer; b. Charleston, W.Va., Feb. 23, 1902; s. George Ernest and Jean Susan (Kay) T.; student Washington and Lee U., Lexington, Va., 1920-23; LL.B., Washington and Lee Univ. Law Coll., 1926; m. Julia Lewis Roseberry, June 6, 1934; 1 dau., Julia Roseberry. Admitted to W.Va. bar, 1926 and since engaged in gen. practice of law at Charleston; mem. firm Ritchie, Hill & Thomas since 1933; served as mem. W.Va. Ho. of Dels., 1932-40, speaker of same, 1937-38, 1939-40 being first person to serve two consecutive terms as speaker of said body. Mem. Am., W.Va., City of Charleston bar assns., Am. Judicature Soc., Sigma Nu. Democrat. Methodist. Mason (K.T., Shriner). Elk. Moose. Clubs: Kanawha Country (Charleston); National Democratic (Washington, D.C.). Home: 11 Norwood Av. Office: Security Bldg., Charleston, W.Va.

THOMAS, John Charles, baritone; b. Meyersdale, Pa.; s. Reverend Milson and Anna Dorothea (Schnaebel) T.; educated high schs. and prep. sch.; student Mount Street Coll. of Homeopathy, Baltimore, Md.; studied music (scholarship), Peabody Conservatory of Music, 1910-13, voice with Blanche Sylvania Blackman and Adelin Fermin; m. Dorothy May Kaehler, Mar. 5, 1924. Début as Passion in Savage Co. of "Everywoman," London, Ont., Can., Oct. 1912; starred in "The Love Letter," "The Peasant Girl," "Apple Blossoms," "Maytime," "Alone at Last," etc.; recital début, N.Y. City, 1921; annual concert tours; operatic début Amonasro, in "Aïda," Washington, D.C., Mar. 3, 1925; has appeared with Royal Opera (Brussels), Phila. Grand Opera Co., San Francisco Opera Co., Los Angeles Opera Co.; with Chicago Civic Opera Co., 1930-31; Metropolitan Opera Co., 1933-34; various radio engagements, motion picture films. Mem. Synfonia, Phi Mu Alpha. Mason (K.T.). Clubs: Bohemian (San Francisco); Knollwood (White Plains, N.Y.); Rogers Forge (Md.); Gulf Stream (Fla.); Maryland Yacht, Talbot Country (Easton, Md.); Artists and Writers Golf Assn., New York Athletic; American Power Boat Assn., Palm Beach Yacht, Everglades, Sailfish Club of Florida; Automobile Club of America; Hillendale Country (Towson, Md.); Royal Golf (Belgium); Royal Automobile (London). Home: Easton, Md.*

THOMAS, John Frederick, mayor, state senator; b. Brookfield, O., Apr. 16, 1882; s. Evan T. and Martha Maria (Jones) T.; E. M., Ohio State U., Columbus, O., 1909; m. Jessie Olive Kelso, Sept. 1, 1938. In pvt. practice as surveyor, Sharon, Pa., since 1911; borough engr., Farrell, Pa., 1911-18; councilman, Sharon, 1926-31, mayor since 1932; surveyor Mercer County, 8 yrs.; borough engr., Wheatland, Pa., since 1936, Sharpsville, Pa., since 1934; elected mem. Pa. State Senate, 1938. Republican. Methodist. Mason, Moose, Odd Fellow, K.P. Home: 105 Logan Av. Office: 112 Chestnut Av., Sharon, Pa.

THOMAS, John Montague, insurance; b. Oxford, Ind., May 7, 1874; s. John Montague and Elizabeth (Fillius) T.; ed. Oxford Acad.; m. Grace Randol, Oct. 1, 1919; children—John Montague, 3d, Jane Randol. Clerical and field work and gen. insurance agency in West and Southwest, 1892-1917; successively sec. Fidelity Phenix Fire Ins. Co., western mgr. Fire Assn. Group (Aetna Ins. Co. group) at Chicago, 1917-27; v.p. and dir. Fire Assn. (Reliance, Victory and Constitutional Ins. cos.) at Phila., 1927-30; also v.p. several companies of Home Ins. Co., New York group; pres. and dir. Nat. Union Fire Ins. Co., Pittsburgh, Pa., since 1931; pres. and dir. Nat. Union Indemnity Co.; dir. Mellbank Surety Corpn., Fire Companies Adjustment Co. Republican. Christian Scientist. Mason. Clubs: Pittsburgh Athletic Assn., Longue Vue Country. Home: Schenley Apts. Office: 139 University Place, Pittsburgh, Pa.

THOMAS, John Parnell, congressman; b. Jersey City, N.J., Jan. 16, 1895; s. J. Parnell Feeney and Georgianna (Thomas) T.; grad. high sch. Ridgewood, N.J., student U. of Pa., 1914-17; m. Amelia Stiles, Jan. 21, 1921; children—J. Parnell, Stiles. Bond salesman with Kountze Bros., N.Y. City, 1919-20; with Paine, Webber & Co., N.Y. City, as salesman, 1920-24, as mgr. N.Y. bond dept., 1924-38; mem. 75th and 76th Congresses (1937-41), 7th N.J. Dist. Mayor of Allendale, 1926-30; mem. N.J. Assembly, 1935-37. Served as 2d and 1st lt. and capt. inf., U.S.A., with A.E.F., 1917-18. Trustee Allendale Pub. Library; dir. Allendale Bldg. and Loan Assn. Mem. Psi Upsilon. Republican. Mason. Home: Allendale, N.J.

THOMAS, John S(aunders) Ladd, clergyman; b. in South Wales, May 1, 1875; s. Thomas and Jane (Ladd) T.; pvt. schs. and Univ. Coll., London, Eng., 1892-97; came to U.S.; 1897; grad. Garrett Bibl. Inst., Evanston, Ill., 1903; m. Catherine Firman, July 1, 1897; children—Howard Wesley, Laura Mildred, Catharine Gwendolyn, Kenneth Arnold, Stuart Austin. Ordained M.E. ministry, 1902; pastor St. John's Ch., 1902-06, Centenary Ch., 1906-09, Austin Ch. (all of Chicago), 1909-22, First M.E. Ch. Germantown, Phila., since May, 1922. Chairman "Billy" Sunday Chicago Exec. Com., 1917-18; pres. trustees Chicago Training Sch.; special preacher Y.M.C.A. to American soldiers in Eng. and France, Feb.-Aug. 1919. Del. Gen. Conf. M.E. Ch., Des Moines, Ia., 1920, Atlantic City, 1932, Columbus, 1936; del. Ecumenical Conf., London, 1921; del. to World Conf. on Faith and Order, Lausanne, Switzerland, 1927, Edinburgh, 1937; del. to Ecumenical Conf. Meth. Ch., Atlanta, Ga., 1931; asso. del. World Conf. on Life and Work, Oxford, 1937; mem. Uniting Conf. for Union of Methodism in U.S.A., Kansas City, 1939. Exchange preacher Great Britain, 1927, 34; pres. Phila. Federation of Chs. 1927—; mem. Bd. Foreign Missions M.E. Ch. since 1936. Trustee Drew U. and Theol. Sem., with Meth. Hosp., Phila. Republican. Club: Union League. Contbr. to mags. and religious jours. Home: 257 High St., Germantown, Phila., Pa.

THOMAS, Lawrence Edward, v.p. and treas. Eljer Co.; b. Wickliffe, O., Jan. 17, 1895; s. Alfred L. and Mary (Clark) T.; ed. Northwestern U.; m. Veda Eisenhuth, Jan. 27, 1922; children—Virginia E., Judith L. Employed in adminstrn. office, U. of Chicago, 1912-13; with Darling & Co., Chicago, 1913-15; jr., later sr. pub. accountant Johnathan B. Cook & Co., 1915-19; v.p. and treas. Eljer Co., Ford City, Pa., since 1920, now also dir.; dir. Nat. Sanitary Co., Salem, O. Served with A.E.F., World War. Republican. Baptist. Mason. Club: Rotary (pres.). Home: 413 Highland Av., Kittanning, Pa. Office: Eljer Co., Ford City, Pa.

THOMAS, Lida Larrimore (Lida Larrimore), writer; b. Girdletree, Md., June 27, 1897; d. Henry Clay and Lida (Larrimore) Turner; student Coburn Classical Inst., Waterville, Me., 1911-14, Colby Coll., Waterville, 1914-17; A.B., Dickinson Coll., 1918; m. Charles Edwin Thomas, Feb. 21, 1931; 1 dau., Lida Larrimore. Teacher of English, high sch., Curwensville, Pa., 1918-19, Chester, Pa., 1919-26. Mem. Chi Omega. Methodist. Author: The Blossoming of Patricia the Less, 1924; Tarpaper Palace, 1928; The Wagon and the Star, 1929; Mulberry Square, 1930; The Silver Flute, 1931; Robin Hill, 1932; Jonathan's Daughter; True by the Sun, No Lovelier Spring. Author of several plays and operettas. Home: Colonial Village, Wayne, Pa.*

THOMAS, Martha Critz; prof. home economics, Hood Coll. Address: Hood College, Frederick, Md.

THOMAS, Perry Critchley, v.p. and gen. mgr. Koppers Coal Co.; b. Scranton, Pa., Jan. 28, 1888; s. Armit and Elizabeth (Edwards) T.; ed. pub. schs.; m. Lilly M. Burnette, May 17, 1914; children—Burnette Elizabeth, Perry Critchley, Griffith E. Chief engr. New River Co., MacDonald, W.Va., 1911-12, asst. gen. mgr., 1912-18; gen. mgr. East Gulf Coal Co., 1918-26; div. supt. New River & Pocahontas Consolidated Coal Co., 1926-28; v.p. and gen. mgr. Koppers Coal Co., Pittsburgh, since 1928; pres. Kimball (W.Va.) Nat. Bank. Mem. Am. Inst. Mining and Metall. Engrs., Coal Mining Inst. America. Clubs: Duquesne, Pittsburgh Field, Pittsburgh Athletic Assn. Home: 6815 Edgerton Av. Office: 1050 Koppers Bldg., Pittsburgh, Pa.

THOMAS, Ralph Llewellyn, exec. engr.; b. Marion, O., May 2, 1887; s. Rev. Welling Evan and Emma Williams (Mattoon) T.; student Bucknell Acad., Lewisburg, Pa., 1902-04, Bucknell U. 1904-05; A.B., Princeton U., 1909; B.S. in elec. engring., Mass. Inst. Tech., 1913; m. Rebekah Ober, Apr. 22, 1924; children—Ralph Llewellyn, Gustavus Ober, Rebekah Elizabeth. Student engr. Stone & Webster, 1913-15; with Pa. Water & Power Co., Baltimore, 1915-38, successively as jr. engr., efficiency engr., asst. to gen. supt., asst. gen. supt., and gen. supt.; exec. engr. Consol. Gas, Electric Light and Power Co., Baltimore, since 1938, dir. since 1939; project engr. Safe Harbor Water Power Corpn. since 1930. Served as 1st lt., capt. and adj. 302d Engrs., 77th Div., U.S. Army, 1917-19. Mem. bd. mgrs. Md. Training Sch. for Boys. Mem. Am. Inst. Elec. Engrs. (past chmn. Baltimore Sect.), Am. Soc. Mech. Engrs., Princeton Engring. Assn., Newcomen Soc. of Eng., Kappa Sigma, Phi Beta Kappa. Republican. Presbyterian. Clubs: Princeton Terrace; Baltimore Engrs. (pres. 1939-40); Gibson Island (Gibson Island, Md.). Home: 803 St. George's Rd. Office: Lexington Bldg., Baltimore, Md.

THOMAS, Richard Somers, partner Thomas and Bowker; b. Phila., Pa., Sept. 4, 1872; s. Capt. John and Theresa (Weber) T.; student Girard Coll., Phila., 1880-89, night class Drexel Inst., Phila., 1891-96, night class Spring Garden Inst., Phila., 1891-96, grad. with first prize and teachers certificate, 1896; m. Anna C. Kennedy, 1904; children—Richard A., Ella T. (Mrs. Harold A. Sholl), John W., Joseph B. Began as stone cutter apprentice, Robert D. Kelley, Phila., Pa., 1891; bldg. carver, Phila., Pa., to 1900; started in monumental cemetery works, Bordentown, N.J., 1900; formed memorial cemetery works, Bordentown, N.J., partnership of Thomas & Bowker, 1918, and since partner. Mem. Bordentown Bd. Edn. Baptist (deacon). Mason, K.P. Erected cemetery monuments throughout N.J., Pa., Del.; soldier monuments, etc., throughout country. Home: 38 Elizabeth St. Office: Crosswicks St., Bordentown, N.J.

THOMAS, Robert Benjamin, osteopathic physician; b. Boswell, Pa., Sept. 2, 1905; s. Benjamin Franklin and Bertha Verne (Jones) T.; D.O., Kirksville Coll. of Osteopathy & Surgery, Kirksville, Mo., 1928; m. Effie Mae Sadler, June 14, 1929; children—Elizabeth Carolyn, Mary Suzanne. Engaged in practice as osteopathic physician and surgeon at Huntington, W.Va. since 1928; mem. W.Va. Bd. Osteopathic Examiners since 1933, vice-pres., 1933-35, pres. for term, 1935-41. Mem Am. Osteopathic Assn., W.Va. Osteopathic Soc. (pres.), Atlas Club, Sigma Sigma Phi. Republican. Baptist. Mason. Club: Kiwanis of Huntington. Home: 1316 13th St. Office: First Huntington Nat. Bank Bldg., Huntington, W.Va.

THOMAS, Royle Price, univ. prof.; b. Sullivan, Ind., Sept. 26, 1897; s. John Moore and Eva (Price) T.; B.S., U. of Ill., Urbana, 1919; M.S., Ia. State Coll., Ames, 1925; Ph.D., U. of Wis., Madison, 1928; m. Florence Guthrie Koch, Mar. 31, 1923; 1 son, Richard Lowell. Asst. in soil exptl. fields, U. of Ill., 1919-24; instr. soils and horticulture, U. of Wis., 1925-28; asso. prof. soils, U. of Md., College Park, 1928-37, prof. soils since 1937. Served in S.A.T.C., 1918. Fellow A.A.A.S. Mem. Am. Soc. Agronomy, Soil Sci. Soc., Am. Bd. Biol. Soc., Internat. Soc. Soil Sci., Gamma Alpha, Gamma Sigma Delta, Phi Sigma, Sigma Xi. Democrat. Presbyn. Mason. Home: 16 Beechwood Rd., Calvert Hills, Hyattsville, Md.

THOMAS, Stanley Judson, bacteriologist; b. Scranton, Pa., Feb. 10, 1889; s. Daniel Judson and Adelaide (Keller) T.; B.S., Lafayette Coll., Easton, Pa., 1912; M.S., Lehigh, 1913, M.A., 1916; Ph.D., U. of Pa., 1928; m. Katharine March, Apr. 7, 1914. Asst. in biology, Lehigh, 1912-13, instr. in biology, 1913-16; research bacteriologist, H. K. Mulford Co., 1916-18, asso. dir. Mulford Labs., 1918-23; asso. prof. bacteriology, Lehigh, 1923-29, prof. since 1929, head dept. of biology since 1937. Major Sanitary R.C., U.S.A. Mem. Soc. Am. Bacteriologists, Am. Social Hygiene Assn., Am. Pub. Health Assn., Sigma Xi, Alpha Chi Rho, Alpha Epsilon Delta; fellow A.A.A.S. Republican. Club: Saucon Valley Country. Author: Bacteriology, 1925; Laboratory Manual in Bacteriology, 1930. Co-author (with R. C. Bull): Notes on Personal Hygiene, 1925; Freshman Hygiene, 1926. Contbr. to bacteriol. publs. Home: 1840 Paul Av., Bethlehem, Pa.

THOMAS, Theodore, pres. U.S. Casket Co.; b. Wilkinsburg, Pa., Dec. 2, 1885; s. Isaac S. and Adah (Sampson) T.; ed. Westminster Coll.; m. Grace Pauline McKnight, Jan. 8, 1910; children—Dorothy Grace, Theodore. With advertising dept. Westinghouse Co., 1903-05; advertising mgr. Reineke, Wilson Co., 1905-07; automobile editor Pittsburgh Post and Sun, 1907-09; advertising mgr. Kelley & Jones Co., 1909-18; vi.p. and advertising mgr. Scientific Materials Co., 1918-22; sec. and advertising mgr. Robertshaw Thermostat Co., 1922-31; pres. U.S. Casket Co. since 1931. Home: East Lincoln Highway, Greensburg, Pa. Office: Scottdale, Pa.

THOMAS, Walter, prof. plant nutrition; b. Swansea, Wales, Dec. 3, 1880; s. David Henry and Mary T.; came to America, 1908, naturalized, 1930; grad. Swansea Tech. Coll., 1900; B.Sc., U. of Wales, 1905; (hon.) D.Sc., U. of Wales, 1928; unmarried. Began as asst. in research, Univ. Coll., Wales, 1905-06; research chemist, Wellcome Chem. Research Labs., London, Eng., 1906-07; with Canadian Dept., Agr., 1908-09; asso. chemist, Pa. State Coll., 1910-15, asst. prof. agrl. chemistry, 1917-22, asso. prof., 1922-27, prof. 1927-37, prof. plant nutrition since 1937. Served in British Chem. Warfare Service, 1915-17. Mem. court of govs. Univ. Coll. of Wales. Fellow A.A.A.S.; mem. Am. Chem. Soc., Am. Soc. Agronomy, Am. Soc. Hort. Sci., Pa. Acad. Sci., Am. Soc. Plant Physiologists, Internat. Soc. Soil Sci., Sigma Xi, Phi Kappa Phi, Phi Lambda Upsilon, Gamma Sigma Delta. Democrat. Club: University (State College, Pa.). Contbr. over 40 articles and papers on various phases of mineral nutrition of plants. Home: 331 W. College Av., State College, Pa.

THOMAS, Walter Horstmann, architect; b. Philadelphia, Pa., Dec. 29, 1876; s. Richard Newton and Clara L. (Horstmann), T.; B.S. in Architecture, U. of Pa., 1899; student Ecole des Beaux Arts, Paris, 3 yrs.; m. Natalie Taylor, Oct. 1905; children—Claire, Florence; m. 2d, Ruth Sterling Boomer, Dec. 5, 1919; 1 son, Brooks. Began practice at Phila., 1906; sr. mem. Thomas & Martin; dir. city architecture, Phila., 1930-31; advisory architect, M.E. Ch. in U.S.A., 1925-33. Architect many chs., Y.M.C.A. buildings, hotels. Chmn, exec. com. City Planning Commn., Phila.; tech. dir., Phila. Housing Authority. In charge erection, maintenance and decoration of Y.M.C.A. huts, France, 1918-19. Fellow Am. Inst. Architects (v.p. Phila. chapter 1925-27, pres. 1928-30); mem. Zeta Psi. Episcopalian. Home: 47 E. Wynnewood Av., Merion, Pa. Office: Architects Bldg., Philadelphia, Pa.

THOMAS, Wesley, C.; attending urologist St. Mary's and Huntington Memorial hosps. Address: 1139 Fourth Av., Huntington, W.Va.

THOMAS, Wilbur Kelsey, humanitarian; b. Amboy, Ind., Dec. 21, 1882; s. Isaac and Eliza Jane (Shockney) T.; A.B., Friends' U., Wichita, Kan., 1904; grad. study Brown U., 1904-05; B.D., Yale, 1907; Ph.D., Boston, U., 1914; m. Elizabeth Folger, Aug. 16, 1905; children— Elizabeth Jane, Helen, Thomas Folger. Exec. dir. Am. Friends Service Com. (Quaker), 1918-29; exec. dir. Carl Schurz Memorial Foundation, Inc., since 1930; trustee John Greenleaf Whittier Homestead since 1932; dir. Am. Forestry Assn. since 1936; pres. Pa. Forestry Assn. since 1939. Home: Lansdowne, Pa. Office: 225 S. 15th St., Philadelphia, Pa.

THOMAS, Woodlief, economist; b. Brownsville, Tenn., Oct. 12, 1897; s. Spencer Farrington and Kate Pugh (Fanning) T.; U. of Tenn., 1916-18; B.S., U. of Pa., 1922; Ph.D., Brookings, 1928; m. Jean West Darrah, of Washington, D.C., Sept. 1, 1928 (dec.); children—Woodlief, Jr., Darrah; m. 2d, Mrs. Frances Marcrum Cole, Aug. 10, 1935. With Federal Reserve Bank, Phila., 1920-22; research asst. Federal Res. Bd., 1922-28; economist Transfer Com.* (office for reparations payments), Berlin, 1928-30, Federal Res. Bank of N.Y., 1930-33, Federal Res. Bd., Washington, D.C., since 1933, asst. dir. div. research and statistics since 1934. Color sergt. Engr. Corps, U.S.A., with A.E.F., 1918-19. Fellow Am. Statis. Assn.; mem. Am. Econ. Assn., Kappa Sigma. Democrat. Baptist. Club: Cosmos (Washington). Author: (with Edmund E. Day) The Growth of Manufactures, 1899-1923 (census monograph 8), 1928. Contbr. articles to bulletins and jours. Home: 26 E. Bradley Lane, Chevy Chase, Md.

THOMAS AQUINAS, Sister Mary, librarian; b. Phila., Pa., July 16, 1887; d. Daniel and Mary (McCann) Hanlon; student Villa Nova (Pa.) Coll., 1920-23; A.B., Immaculata (Pa.) Coll., 1927. Mem. Immaculate Heart of Mary Order. Teacher, Immaculate Heart Acad., Shenandoah, Pa., 1916-23; Villa Maria Acad. Immaculata, Pa., 1923-27; librarian, Immaculata (Pa.) Coll. since 1925. Mem. A.L.A., Pa. Library Assn., Catholic Library Assn. Roman Catholic. Address: Immaculata College, Immaculata, Pa.

THOMPSON, Albert Ely, surgeon; b. Washington, Pa., Nov. 16, 1874; s. William Reed (M.D.) and Margaret Agnes (Ely) T.; A.B., Washington and Jefferson Coll., Washington, Pa., 1895, A.M., 1898; M.D., U. of Pa. Med. Sch., 1898; m. Lou Helen Miller, Oct. 11, 1900; children—Helen Miller (dec.), William Reed II. Engaged in gen. practice of medicine at Washington, Pa. since 1898, specializing in surgery since 1917; chief surgeon, Washington Hosp. Served as capt. Med. Corps, U.S.A. during World War. Fellow Am. Coll. Surgeons; mem. Pa.

Med. Soc., Washington Co. Med. Soc., Phi Kappa Sigma. Republican. Presbyterian. Mason (32°, Shriner). Club: Bassett (Washington, Pa.) Home: 45 Morgan Av. Office: 644 Washington Trust Bldg., Washington, Pa.

THOMPSON, Alden Wilbur, prof. physical edn., W.Va. Address: West Virginia U., Morgantown, W.Va.

THOMPSON, Alexander Marshall, lawyer; b. Canandaigua, N.Y., Sept. 27, 1872; s. Samuel Huston and Martha Jane (McIlwain) T.; prep. edn., high sch., St. Paul, Minn.; A.B., Princeton, 1893; m. Melvina Graff, June 10, 1914. Admitted to Pa. bar, 1897 and since practiced at Pittsburgh; served as 1st asst. city solicitor, Pittsburgh; dean Law Sch., U. of Pittsburgh; judge Court of Common Pleas of Allegheny Co., Pa., since Jan. 3, 1938; pres. Scott Graff Lumber Co., Duluth, Minn. Area sec. overseas work, Y.M.C.A., at Inverness, Scotland, World War. Trustee Grove City (Pa.) Coll., Kingsley House Assn., Pittsburgh. Mem. Am. Law Inst., Philos. Soc., Polygon Club. Democrat. Presbyn. Mason (32°). Home: Wildwood Manor, Gibsonia, Pa. Office: Commonwealth Bldg., Pittsburgh, Pa.

THOMPSON, A(lfred) Paul, research engr.; b. Florence, Colo., Nov. 6, 1893; s. Western Talbot and Mary Grace (Hammond) T.; student Ia. State Coll., Ames, Ia., 1911-12; B.S., Mont. State Coll., Bozeman, Mont., 1915; M.S., U. of Ill., Urbana, Ill., 1923, Ph.D., 1925; m. Marion Leslie Hobart, Dec. 12, 1917; 1 son, Gordon Paul. Successively testing engr., research chemist and chief chemist Anaconda Copper Mining Co., Anaconda and Great Falls, Mont., 1915-22; grad. student, du Pont Fellow & asst. in chem., U. of Ill., 1922-25; research engr. Gen. Chem. Co., New York, 1925-28; research engr. and consultant Internat. Nickel Co., New York and Copper Cliff, Ont., 1928-32; research engr. and industrial fellow, Mellon Inst. of Industrial Research, Pittsburgh, since 1932. Fellow A.A. A.S.; mem. Am. Chem. Soc., Am. Ceramic Soc., Pittsburgh Chemists Club, Sigma Xi, Epsilon Chi, Phi Lambda Upsilon. Republican. Presbyterian. Holder of patents in metallurgical, chemical and ceramic fields. Contbr. articles on non-ferrous metallurgy, ceramics, chemistry to jours. Home: 4600 Bayard St., Pittsburgh, Pa.

THOMPSON, Allen D.; editor Carlisle Sentinel. Office: The Sentinel, Carlisle, Pa.

THOMPSON, Charles Impey, lawyer; b. Mont Clare, Pa., Aug. 25, 1899; s. J. Whitaker and Anna (Williamson) T.; grad. Yeates, 1917; A.B., U. of Pa., 1921, LL.B., 1924; m. Anna M. (Farnum), Apr. 5, 1926; children—Charles Impey, Joseph Whitaker 2nd, Henry F. Admitted to Pa. bar, 1924, and practiced as asso. with Ballard, Spahr, Andrews & Ingersoll, Phila., 1924-31, partner since 1931; asst. dist. atty., Phila. Co., 1925-27; lecturer and instr., U. of Pa. Law Sch., 1925-31. Served in U.S. Navy during World War; active mem. 1st Troop, Phila. City Cav., 1924-33, hon. mem. since 1933. Trustee Grad. Hosp. U. of Pa., Chestnut Hill Acad.; commr. Fairmount Park. Mem. Am., Pa. and Phila. bar assns., Order of Coif, Zeta Psi, Phi Beta Kappa. Republican. Episcopalian. Clubs: Philadelphia, Union League, Sunnybrook Golf, Whitemarsh Hunt (Phila.); Winter Harbor Yacht (Winter Harbor, Me.). Home: Spring Lane. Office: Land Title Bldg., Philadelphia, Pa.

THOMPSON, C(harles) Seymour, librarian; b. Orange, N.J., Nov. 8, 1879; s. Wilmot Haines and Laura Pamela (Garrigues) T.; B.A., Yale, 1902; m. Elizabeth Skirm Howell, June 24, 1909; 1 dau., Olive. With Pub. Library, Brooklyn, N.Y., 1903-11; asst. librarian Pub. Library, Washington, D.C., 1911-16; librarian Savannah Pub. Library, 1916-24; dir. nat. library survey made by A.L.A., 1924-27; reference and assistant librarian Univ. of Pa. Library, 1927-31, now librarian. Fellow Am. Library Inst.; mem. Hist. Soc. of Pennsylvania. Christian Scientist. Club: Yale (Phila.). Editor: A Survey of Libraries in the United States (4 vols.), 1926-27. Home: 21 President Av., Rutledge, Pa.

THOMPSON, Donald, lawyer; b. Pittsburgh, Pa., Oct. 27, 1882; s. Oliver D. and Kate Wentworth (Dresser) T.; student Shadyside Acad., Pittsburgh, 1893-99; A.B., Yale, 1903; LL.B., Pittsburgh Law Sch., 1905; m. Margaret LeRoy, July 6, 1909; children—Donald, LeRoy. Admitted to Allegheny Co. bar, 1906; since in gen. practice of law; associated with George B. Berger, Pittsburgh, since 1912; dir. H. H. Robertson Co., Crescent Brick Co., North Pole Cold Storage & Ice Co., Colonial Royalties Co., Western Allegheny R.R. Co. Served at Fortress Monroe, fall of 1918. Mem. Am., Pa. and Allegheny Co. bar assns. Republican. Presbyterian. Clubs: Pittsburgh, Duquesne (Pittsburgh); Allegheny Country (Sewickley, Pa.). Home: 605 Poia Place, Edgeworth, Pa. Office: 1220 Berger Bldg., Pittsburgh, Pa.

THOMPSON, Donald Chester, lawyer; b. Meadville, Pa., Oct. 1, 1891; s. Almon Wilson and Elizabeth (Eyeington) T.; A.B., Allegheny Coll., Meadville, Pa., 1912, A.M., 1923; m. Laura B. Roberts, Feb. 11, 1936; children—Helen Amelia, Miriam Alice and Donald Oliver. Studied law in the office of Otto Kohler, Esq., and admitted to Pennsylvania bar in 1913, and since engaged in gen. practice of law at Meadville, Pa.; admitted to bar Supreme Ct., Pa., and the Supreme Ct. of the U.S.; spl. dep. Recorder's Office, Crawford Co., 1909-20; city solicitor, Titusville, Pa., 1925-28; served as Alderman, Meadville, 1913-19; asst. in history, Allegheny Coll., 1913; lecturer commercial law, Meadville Commercial Coll., 1928-29. Served in Pa. Res. Militia, 1917, 214th Engrs. U.S. Army, 1918-19; capt. inf. O.R.C. Mem. Am. Bar Assn., Am. Legion (Nat. Defense Com.), Beta Kappa. Republican. Methodist. Mason (K.T., 32°), Grange, Patron of Husbandry. Home: Alden St. Extension. Office: 358 Cherry Lane, Meadville, Pa.

THOMPSON, Edward Jackson, lawyer; b. Philipsburg, Pa., June 2, 1901; s. Andrew Curtin and Bertha Ellen (Denning) T.; B.S. Haverford (Pa.) Coll.; LL.B., U. of Pa.; m. Harriett Barker, June 22, 1928; children—Bertha Denning, Edward Jackson. Admitted to Centre Co. bar, 1925; since in gen. practice of law; state's atty. Federal Emergency Administrn. of Pub. Works, 1933-34. Mem. Philipsburg Borough Council, 1929-37, Centre Co. Bd. of Road and Bridge Viewers, 1928-34; mem. Pa. State Senate since 1935; del. Dem. Nat. Conv., 1932-36. Mem. Am. Bar Assn. (mem. legislative com. since 1938), Pa. State Bar Assn. (mem. exec. com. 1928-37), Am. Acad. Polit. and Social Science, Patriotic Order Sons of America. Methodist. Mason, Odd Fellow, Elk, Moose, Eagle, Red Man, Grange. Club: Kiwanis (Philipsburg, Pa.). Writer articles on polit. subjects. Home: 911 Presque Isle St. Office: Moshannon Bldg., Philipsburg, Pa.

THOMPSON, Elias W., treas. Nokomis Water Co.; b. Vestal, Broome Co., N.Y., Mar. 17, 1867; s. Hamilton and Sophia R. (Winans) T.; ed. Vestal pub. schs.; m. Emma Mathewson, 1889 (now deceased); 1 dau., Ruth (wife of Dr. Edmund Thomas). Miller, 1887-1898; conducted gen. store, 1898-1903; organized Commonwealth Telephone Co., 1903, and connected with them until 1920; organized Abington Electric Co., 1920, disposing of interest, 1927; treas. and dir. Nokomis Water Co. since 1927; dir. First Nat. Bank (Nicholson), Commonwealth Telephone Co. Trustee Scranton-Keystone Jr. Coll. Republican. Elk. Home: Factoryville, Pa.

THOMPSON, Ernest, clergyman; b. Bartow Co., Ga., Nov. 10, 1867; s. Gilbert Taylor and Josephine Amanda (King) T.; A.B., Drury Coll., Springfield, Mo., 1888, A.M., 1891, D.D., 1902; grad. McCormick Theol. Sem., 1891; studied New Ch. Coll. (U. of Edinburgh), 1896-97; m. Jimmie Sawyer Graves, Oct. 15, 1891; children—Allison Garnett, Ernest Trice, Hugh Graves, Graves Haydon. Ordained Presbyn. ministry, 1891; pastor First Ch., Texarkana, Tex., 1891-95; asst. Stockbridge Free Ch., Edinburgh, 1895-96; pastor Stuart Robinson Memorial Ch., Louisville, Ky., 1897-1902, First Ch., Charleston, W. Va., since 1902. Mem. exec. com. of religious edn., Presbyn. Ch. in U.S.; chmn. home mission com. Kanawha Presbytery; moderator Gen. Assembly Presbyn. Ch. in U.S., 1933-34. Trustee Hampden-Sydney Coll., Union Theol. Sem. (Va.), Mountain Retreat Assn. (Montreat, N.C.). Democrat. Mason (32°, Shriner). Clubs: Rotary (ex-pres.), Kanawha Country. Author: Veto Power. Contbr. articles and verse to ch. papers. Home: 2006 Kanawha St., Charleston, W.Va.

THOMPSON, Eustis Henry, mech. and elec. engring.; b. Baltimore, Md., Mar. 10, 1883; s. Eustis and Elizabeth (Baker) T.; student Cornell U., 1901-05; (hon.) D.Engring., Am. Internat. Acad., Baltimore, 19—; m. Marion Ancker, Dec. 15, 1915 (divorced 1930); children—Virginia Elizabeth, Walter Ankar, Eustis Henry, Jr. In employ General Electric Co., Schenectady, N.Y., 1905-15; engring. consultant and power machinery expert, Baltimore, 1915-17; with Bartlett Hayward Co., 1917-19; elec. designer, Bethlehem Steel Co., Sparrows Point, Md., 1919-20; elec. engr. Universal Steel Co., Bridgeville, Pa., 1920-21, West Penn Power Co., Pittsburgh, Pa., 1921-22; asso. editor mag. Power, N.Y. City, 1922-25; crane supt. Baltimore Copper Smelting & Rolling Co., 1925-28; industrial research engr., 1928-32; miscellaneous engring. work, Baltimore, Md., 1932-35; with U.S. Industrial Alcohol Co., Curtis Bay, Md., 1935-38; with Glenn L. Martin Co., aircraft mfrs., Middle River, Md., since Feb. 1939. Trustee Am. Internat. Acad., Baltimore, Md. Mem. Am. Soc. Mech. Engrs., Kappa Alpha. Episcopalian. Clubs: Bachelors Cotillon, Ice Club (Baltimore). Contbr. to tech. press since 1916. Granted basic type patent on first meter for measuring maximum acceleration of harmonic vibration. Home: 1301 St. Paul St. Office: Stock Exchange Bldg., Baltimore, Md.

THOMPSON, F. Raymond, Jr. (Ray Thompson), artist, cartoonist; b. Phila., Pa., July 9, 1905; s. Francis R. and Kathryn (Mahla) T.; ed. Temple U. (journalism), 1924-27; ed. art, Pa. Acad. and Sch. Industrial Art, 1926-27, Spring Garden Inst., 1927-29; educated in advertising and journalism at Charles Morris Price School of Poor Richard Club, 1932-33; married Helen E. Macleery, September 30, 1929; children—Patricia Rae, and Elisabeth June. Free lance artist and cartoonist since 1927, working for wide variety of leading mags. including Saturday Evening Post, Colliers, and others, also newspapers and syndicates, also leading adv. agencies as well as direct with nat. advertisers; now engaged in doing continuity of nat. syndicated Sunday Page Comic "Myra North, Special Nurse," also free lance adv. cartoons and writing. Designing games and novelties. Home: 919 Melrose Av., Melrose Park, Philadelphia, Pa. Office: 1324 Walnut St., Philadelphia, Pa.

THOMPSON, Fred Charles, educator; b. New Milford, N.Y., July 23, 1876; s. Charles and Anne M. (Ferguson) T.; B.S., N.Y. Univ., 1909, A.M., same, 1911; m. Catharine M. G. Smith, July 24, 1912; 1 son, Edward Charles (M.D.). Engaged in teaching pub. schs. and as prin., 1893-1909; prin. pub. sch., Paterson, N.J., 1910-23, supervisor of schools, 1923-33; asst. supt. schs., Paterson, N.J., since 1933; vice-pres. and dir. Little Falls Nat. Bank. Served as mem. Bd. Edn., Little Falls, N.J., for 35 years. Mem. Epsilon Pi Tau, N.J. Schoolmasters Club, N.Y. Schoolmen's Club. Attends Reformed Ch. Mason. Elk. Home: 55 Ridge Av., Little Falls, N.J. Office: Paterson, N.J.

THOMPSON, French Woodville, coll. pres.; b. Monticello, Ark., Apr. 16, 1876; s. Woodville E. and Hattie Reola (McGehee) T.; A.B., Arkansas College, 1897; Union Theol. Sem., 1897-98, Louisville Theol. Sem., 1898-99; grad. McCormick Theol. Sem., Chicago, 1902; m. Helen Cain, June 30, 1908; 1 dau., Helen Reola. Ordained Presbyn. ministry, 1900; pastor 1st Ch., Hot Springs, Ark., 1902-13, 2d Ch., New Albany, Ind., 1913-16, extension sec. Presbyn. Theol. Sem., Louisville, Ky., 1917-18; war work; sec. Y.M.C.A., Camp Zachary Taylor, Ky., 1918-19; pres. Daniel Baker Coll., Brownwood, Tex., 1919-21, Tex. Presbyn. Coll., 1921-24; pres. Greenbrier Coll., Lewisburg, W.Va., since 1925. Life mem. N.E.A.; mem. Assn. of Sch. Adminstrs., Progressive Edn. Assn., W. Va. Edn. Assn., Acad. of Polit. Science, Pi

Gamma Mu. Ind. Democrat. Presbyterian. Mason (K.T.). Rotarian. Home: Lewisburg, W.Va.

THOMPSON, Hugh Graves, physician; b. Texarkana, Ark., Jan. 29, 1896; s. Ernest and Jimmie (Graves) T.; A.B., Hampden-Sydney (Va.) Coll., 1916; M.D., U. of Pa. Med. Sch. 1920; m. Frances Weimer, Sept. 24, 1927; children—Hugh Graves, Jr., Frances Weimer. Interne Lankenau Hosp., Phila., 1920-22; engaged in practice at Charleston, W.Va., since 1923, practice limited to internal medicine; dir. and med. dir. George Washington Ins. Co., W.Va., since 1937; prof. zoology, Kanawha Coll., Charleston, 1934-36; on staff at McMillan Hosp. Served as pvt. Med. Corps, U.S.A., 1916-18; Med. Res. Corps, U.S.A., 1931-36. Mem. Am. Med. Assn., W.Va. State Med. Soc., Kanawha Co. Med. Assn., Kappa Sigma, Nu Sigma Nu, Journal Club. Democrat. Presbyn. Mason. Club: Edgewood Country (Charleston). Home: 3 Thomas Drive. Office: 220 Morris St., Charleston, W.Va.

THOMPSON, James Gilfillan, banker; b. Mexico, Pa., Dec. 26, 1868; s. William Porter and Sarah Jane (Gilfillan) T.; ed. Mexico (Pa.) pub. schs., Airy View Acad. (Port Royal, Pa.) and Mifflin Acad. (Mifflintown, Pa.); m. Edna Rebecca Leisenring, Apr. 14, 1909 (died Apr. 1926); 1 son, James G., Jr.; m. 2d, Gladys Dell Marsh, Sept. 15, 1928; children—Marjorie Marsh, Nelson Gilfillan, dec.). Bookkeeper Herman & Co., Tyrone, Pa., 1886-90; bookkeeper First Nat. Bank, Mifflintown, Pa., 1890-94, asst. cashier, 1894-1902; cashier First Nat. Bank, Middleburg, Pa., 1902-17, pres. since 1917, now also dir. Mem. Loan Com. Nat. Credit Assn.; mem. Loan Agency, Reconstruction Finance Corpn., Com. on Federal Reserve Relations for 3d dist.; mem. com. for nominations of 3d Dist. Federal Reserve Dirs. Chmn. Liberty Loan Drives for Union-Snyder Dist., World War. Sch. dir., 12 yrs. Dir. Middleburg Playground Assn. Mem. Snyder County Hist. Soc. Republican. Presbyterian. Home: Middleburg, Pa.

THOMPSON, James Voorhees, religious education; b. Rock Springs, Pa., May 25, 1878; s. Johnathan MacWilliams and Anna Sara (Carpenter) T.; A.B., Wesleyan U., Conn., 1902; B.D., Drew Theol. Sem., 1905; grad. study, U. of Pittsburgh, 1912-14; Ph.D., Northwestern, 1928; m. Nora Gray, Aug. 18, 1909. Student pastor Bronxdale M.E. Ch., N.Y. City, 1903-04; asst. minister and dir. religious edn. (first recorded in U.S.), Christ M.E. Ch., Pittsburgh, 1905-07; ordained ministry M.E. Ch., 1907; teacher Shadyside Acad., Pittsburgh, 1908-12, Peabody High Sch., Pittsburgh, 1912-14; supt. young people's dept. Bd. of Sunday Schs., M.E. Ch., 1914-25; instr. dept. religious edn., Boston U., 1918; agt. World's S.S. Assn. and Bd. of Sunday Schs. M.E. Ch. in Japan, Korea and China, 1920-21; asso. minister and dir. religious edn., First M.E. Ch., Evanston, Ill., 1925-28; asst. prof. religious edn., Northwestern U., 1928-29, asso. prof., 1929-30; prof. administration in religious edn., Drew Theol. Sem., since 1930; dir. Coll. of Religious Edn. and Missions, same, 1931-35. Served as corpl. Spanish-Am. War, 1898; chaplain 325th Inf., 82d Div., A.E.F., June-Oct. 1918, sr. chaplain 2d Army Corps, Oct. 1918-19; mem. O.R.C. Decorated capt. Order of the Silver Palms (France), also Officer of Academy. Mem. Religious Edn. Assn., Internat. Council Religious Edn., Alpha Delta Phi, Phi Delta Kappa. Ind. Republican. Club: University (Evanston). Author: Handbook for Workers with Young People, 1921; The Daily Vacation Church School (with J. E. Stout), 1923; Studies in Religious Education (with Lotz and others), 1931; Orientation in Education (with Schutte and others), 1932; Great Biographies (with Lotz and others), 1938. Editor and author of "The Open Door Series" (guidance pamphlets for adolescents and their leaders). Lecturer on religious edn. Home: 11 Glendale Rd., Madison, N.J.

THOMPSON, John Vincent, paint mfr.; b. Pittsburgh, Pa., Sept. 19, 1893; s. Edward and Laura (McCulley) T.; grad. Allegheny Prep. Sch., 1911; A.B., Cornell U., 1915; m. Elizabeth Crabbe, Feb. 28, 1922. Fellow, Mellon Inst. of Industrial Research, 1915-17; supt. Thompson & Co., paint mfrs., 1919-23, treas., 1923-28, v.p., 1928-36, pres. since 1936, now also dir. Served with Pa. Nat. Guard on Mexican Border, capt., 1921-28; 1st lt. F.A., 5th Div., World War (abroad 17 mos.). Mem. Chi Phi. Republican. Presbyterian. Club: Oakmont Country. Home: 5035 Castleman St. Address: Box 6757, Pittsburgh, Pa.

THOMPSON, J(oseph) Whitaker, judge; b. Stroudsburg, Pa., Aug. 19, 1861; s. Charles Impey and Gertrude Kimber (Whitaker) T.; prep. edn., Rugby Acad.; student Univ. of Pa., 1883, LL.B., 1887; m. Anna Pennypacker Williamson, Dec. 4, 1889; children—Elisabeth Williamson, Charles Impey, Martha Josephine. Asst. U.S. atty., Eastern Dist. of Pa., 1900-04; U.S. atty., same dist., 1904-12; judge U.S. Dist. Court, same dist., 1912-31; judge U.S. Circuit Court of Appeals, 3d Circuit, 1931-38, retired Apr. 14, 1938, subject to call. Trustee State Hosp. for Insane, Eastern Pa., 1914-23 (reapptd. 1927), State Inst. for Feeble Minded and Epileptic (pres. bd.), 1913-23. Mem. Delta Psi. Clubs: Union League, Rittenhouse. Home: 2323 De Lancey St., Philadelphia, Pa.

THOMPSON, Lewis Ryers, asst. surgeon gen.; b. LaFayette, Ind., Aug. 6, 1883; s. Lewis Ryers and Laura (Steuben) T.; M.D., Louisville Med. Coll., 1905; m. Mabel Cook, Feb. 22, 1908; 1 son, Lewis Ryers. Mem. Philippine Constabulary, 1906-09; U.S. Pub. Health Service since 1910, asst. surgeon, 1910, passed asst. surgeon, 1914, surgeon, 1921, sr. surgeon, 1930, asst. surgeon gen. since 1930; director National Institute of Health, 1937. Was scientific dir. International Health Div., Rockefeller Foundation. Mem. div. of med. sciences Nat. Research Council. Fellow Am. Coll. Dentists; mem. A.M.A., Am. Pub. Health Assn., Industrial Physicians and Surgeons, Phi Chi. Episcopalian. Club: Columbia Country. Author of numerous articles and bulls. on med. subjects. Home: 17 W. Virgilia St., Chevy Chase, Md. Address: National Institute of Health, 25th and E Sts. N.W., Washington, D.C.

THOMPSON, Lloyd, judge; b. New York, N.Y., Mar. 17, 1879; s. Winfield and Anna Laura (Worman) T.; LL.B., New York Law Sch., 1900; m. Fortunita Johnston, Sept. 25, 1902; children—Alan, Marion (Mrs. Perry Jones). Admitted to N.Y. bar, 1900, and to N.J. bar, 1905 and engaged in gen. practice of law in New York City and in Westfield, N.J., to 1929; served as Judge Union Co. (N.J.) Ct. Common Pleas since 1929 and again apptd., 1939 for term 1939-44; mem. Ho. Assembly, N.J. State Legislature, 1910-11; mem. Union Co. Bd. of Taxation, 1913-29 by appointment of Gov. N.J. Mem. Am. Bar Assn., N.J. State Bar Assn., Union Co. Bar Assn. Republican. Conglist. Mason. Home: Mountainside, N.J. Office: Westfield, N.J.

THOMPSON, Lorin Hartwell, Jr., artist, mural painter, teacher; b. Pittsburgh, Pa., Mar. 19, 1911; s. Lorin H. and Daisy M. (Mullen) T.; ed. Pittsburgh pub. schs., 1917-22, Wilkinsburg (Pa.) schs., 1922-27, Fishburne Mil. Sch. (Waynesboro, Va.), 1927-29; A.B., Coll. Fine Arts, Carnegie Inst. Tech., 1933, post grad. work, same, 1935-36; m. Lorraine Walsh, Oct. 20, 1933. Artist, mural painter; teacher Ad-Art Studio, Pittsburgh. Prin. works: 4 murals, Somerset (Pa.) High Sch., 1934; murals Aluminum Co. of America for annual conv. of A.A.A.S., 1934; mural decorations in home of G. B. Ryland, Pittsburgh, 1935; 2 murals Altoona (Pa.) Post Office, 1937-38; 4 decorative mirrors Duquesne Club, Pittsburgh, 1937; commnd. by Treasury Dept., sect. of fine arts, to execute mural for Pascagoula (Miss.) Post Office. Exhibited Carnegie Inst. (Pittsburgh), Art Inst. (Chicago), William Rockhill Nelson Galleries (Kansas City, Mo.), Minneapolis Inst. Arts, U. of Ia., Corcoran Gallery of Art, Whitney Museum (New York), Bessemer Gallery (Pittsburgh), Columbus Gallery of Fine Art. Formerly dir. Sioux City (Ia.) Community Federal Art Center; formerly art dir. Manchester Ednl. Center, Pittsburgh. Mem. Associated Artists of Pittsburgh, Tau Sigma Delta; hon. mem. Architecture and Allied Arts. Home: 6405 Forbes St., Pittsburgh, Pa.

THOMPSON, Mary Wolfe (Mrs. Charles D. Thompson), author; b. Winsted, Conn., Dec. 7, 1886; d. Theodore F. (M.D.) and Gertrude (Franklin) W.; grad. N.J. State Normal Sch., Trenton, 1905, grad. study, 1906; grad. New York Sch. Fine and Applied Arts, 1915; student extension courses, Columbia, 1920-29; m. Charles D. Thompson, Sept. 11, 1915. Presbyterian. Author: Farmtown Tales, 1923; Shoemaker's Shoes, 1924; My Grandpa's Farm, 1929; The Circle of the Braves, 1931; Cherry Farm, 1932; Moccasins on the Trail, 1935; Miss Fannie's Bomb (1-act comedy), 1937; Highway Past Her Door, 1938; Shiver, the Scaredest Dog in Town, 1938. Short story writer. Home: Hohokus, N.J.

THOMPSON, Paul, banker; b. Phila., Pa.; grad. Episcopal Acad.; C.E., U. of Pa., 1885. Pres. Corn Exchange Nat. Bank and Trust Co., Phila. Clubs: Rittenhouse, Racquet, Merion Cricket, Manufacturers and Bankers; Ordinary Point (Md.) Yacht. Home: Haverford, Pa. Office: 1512 Chestnut St., Philadelphia, Pa.

THOMPSON, Richard Hardestry, ins. co. exec.; b. Baltimore, Md., July 2, 1878; s. Charles Ridgely and Sallie Virginia (Hardesty) T.; student John Hopkins U. 1897-98. In employ U.S. Fidelity & Guaranty Co., Baltimore, 1899-1902; with Maryland Casualty Co., Baltimore, Md., 1902-13, vice-pres., 1907-13; vice-pres. and dir. Md. Trust Co., 1913-14; again with Md. Casualty Co., 1914-17; exec. vice-pres. and dir. Md. Assurance Corpn., 1917-20; vice-pres. Md. Casualty Co., 1920-35, then retired, 1935; vice-pres. and dir. Security Storage Co. since 1934; introduced Christmas Savings Club idea into Baltimore, 1913; assisted in combining Md. Trust Co., Continental Trust Co., Drovers and Mechanics Nat. Bank. Past chmn. Casualty and Surety Agencies Execs. Assn. and Personal Accident and Health Underwriters Assn. Past Pres. Burglary Ins. Underwriters Assn. Chmn. Ins. Fed. of Md. since 1922. Mem. Md. Hist. Soc. Clubs: Maryland (sec. and gov. since 1921), Bachelors Cotillion, Country, Elkridge Hunt, Maryland Jockey (Baltimore); Gibson Island Yacht. Author: Around the World with a Tired Business Man, 1931; also various articles on insurance. Home: Lake and Bellona Avs., Baltimore Md.

THOMPSON, Robert Charles, vocational rehabilitation; b. Laurens, S.C., Apr. 14, 1900; s. Robert Earle and Virginia (Donaldson) T.; A.B., U. of S.C., Columbia, S.C., 1920; A.M., U. of Chicago, 1929; grad. student Johns Hopkins U., part time 1929-36; m. Pauline Clark, Oct. 29, 1924; 1 dau., Charlotte. Instr. English, Clemson Coll., S.C., 1920-21; prin. high schl., Timmonsville, S.C., 1921; training asst., U.S. Vets. Bur., Atlanta, Ga., 1922-24; dist. supervisor vocational rehabilitation, Ga. State Dept. Edn., 1924-27; state supervisor vocational rehabilitation, S.C. Dept. Edn., 1927-28; state supervisor vocational rehabilitation, Md. Dept. Edn., Baltimore, since 1929, spl. edn. since 1930, and attendance since 1933. Served as pvt. inf. U.S.A., 1918; 1st lt. inf. O.R.C. since 1922. Dir. Md. League for Crippled Children, Mental Hygiene Soc. of Md., Baltimore Goodwill Industries. Chmn. States Vocational Rehabilitation Council (1939). Dir. Nat. Rehabilitation Assn. for term 1934-42. Vice-pres. Md. Vocational Assn., 1939. Mem. Am. Legion, Forty and Eight. Democrat. Baptist. Mason (K.T.). Club: Kiwanis of Towson (dir.). Home: 513 Park Ave., Towson. Office: Lexington Bldg., Baltimore, Md.

THOMPSON, Robert Milton, pres. Citizens Trust Co. b. Lancaster Co., Pa., Feb. 15, 1901; s. Jacob G. and Clara Louise (Miller) T.; student High Sch.; m. LaFay B. Barr, Apr. 10, 1924; children—Gladys Louise, Robert Milton. Began as bookkeeper Citizens Trust Co., Harrisburg, Pa., 1920, asst. sec. and asst. treas., 1927-33, trust officer, 1933-34, treas. and sec., 1934-37, pres. since 1937. Presbyterian. Home: 1812 Park. Office: 13th and Derry Sts., Harrisburg, Pa.

THOMPSON, Russell Irvin, coll. administrator; b. Reading, Pa., Dec. 29, 1898; s. Oan Joshua and Sarah Elizabeth (Snyder) T.; student Reading (Pa.) High Sch. for Boys, 1912-16; A.B., Dickinson Coll., Carlisle, Pa., 1920; student Garrett Biblical Inst., Evanston, Ill., 1920; Ph.D., Yale, 1932; m. Ethel Mae Wright, Aug. 11, 1923. Minister Grace M.E. Ch., Reading, Pa., 1917-20; vice-principal, High Sch., Rockwood, Pa., 1921; prof. Greek and psychology, Williamsport Dickinson Sem., Williamsport, Pa., 1921-24; dir. Wesley House Settlement, New Haven, Conn., 1925-28; instr. edn. and psychology, Dickinson Coll., Carlisle, Pa., 1928-31, asso. prof. since 1931, dean, Sch. of Family Edn. since 1933, registrar of Dickinson Coll. since 1935. Served in S.A.T.C., Plattsburg, N.Y., summer 1918. Fellow A.A.A.S.; mem. Am. Assn. Collegiate Registrars, Pa. State Edn. Assn., N.E.A., Kappa Sigma. Republican. Methodist. Mason. Home: R.D. 5. Office: Dickinson Coll., Carlisle, Pa.

THOMPSON, Ruth Plumly, author; b. Philadelphia, Pa., July 27, 1895; d. George Plumly and Amanda Elton (Shuff) T.; grad. William Penn High Sch., Philadelphia. Author: The Perhappsy Chaps; The Princess of Cosytown, 1922; Kabumpo in Oz, 1922; The Wonder Book; The Cowardly Lion of Oz, 1923; Grampa in Oz, 1924; The Lost King of Oz, 1925; The Hungry Tiger of Oz, 1926; The Curious Cruise of Captain Santa, 1926; The Gnome King of Oz, 1927; The Giant Horse of Oz, 1928; Jack Pumpkinhead of Oz, 1929; The Yellow Knight of Oz, 1930; Pirates in Oz, 1931; The Purple Prince of Oz, 1932; Ojo in Oz, 1933; Speedy in Oz, 1934; The Wishing Horse of Oz, 1935; Captain Salt in Oz, 1936; Handy Mandy in Oz, 1937; The Silver Princess of Oz. King Kojo, 1938. Home: 254 S. Farragut Terrace, West Philadelphia, Pa.

THOMPSON, W. Robert, lawyer; b. Salisbury, Pa., Feb. 16, 1906; s. W. D. and Florence Keyser (Agnew) T.; A.B., Dickinson Coll., 1927; LL.B., Dickinson Law Sch., 1929; m. Anne Elizabeth Coover, Aug. 4, 1927; children—Anne Elizabeth, Patricia Jean, William Robert. Admitted to Green Co. bar, 1929, Pa. Supreme Ct., 1931; mem. law firm Waychoff & Thompson, 1929-36, Thompson & Bradley, 1936-37; dir. Arensburg Ferry Co. Chmn. Red Cross Roll Call, 1932 and 1933; mem. Childrens Aid Soc.; chmn. Greene Co. Bd. of Assistance, 1938; v.p. and dir. Greene Co. Memorial Cemetery Co., Pres. Green Co. Bar Assn., 1938; mem. Pa. State Bar Assn., Phi Kappa Psi. Mason (A.F. & A.M.). Clubs: Greene Co. Country, Rotary (pres. 1937-38). Home: Sunrise Park. Office: First Nat. Bank Bldg., Waynesburg, Pa.

THOMPSON, Willard Chandler, univ. prof.; b. Sun Prairie, Wis., Nov. 24, 1890; s. George Ezra and Frances Augusta (Chandler) T.; student Prairie (Wis.) High Sch., 1904-08; B.S. in Agr., U. of Wis., Madison, Wis., 1912; Ph.D., N.Y.U., 1934; m. Mabel Clare Bell, June 21, 1920; 1 son, Willard Chandler, Jr. Asst. in animal husbandry, U. of Ark., Fayetteville, Ark., 1912-13; instr. in poultry husbandry, Rutgers U., New Brunswick, N.J., 1913-21, prof. since 1921; poultry husbandman, N.J. Agrl. Expt. Sta., New Brunswick, N.J., since 1921; first dir. Nat. Inst. of Poultry Husbandry, Newport, Salop, England, 1924-26. Served as 2d lt., S.C., Med. Div., U.S. Army, 1918. Mem. Alpha Zeta, Sigma Xi. Republican. Dutch Reformed Ch. Mem. Rutgers Club of New Brunswick, N.J. (past pres.). Author: Egg Farming, 1936; numerous bulletins and circulars. Home: 133 N. 7th Av. H.P. Office: College Farm, New Brunswick, N.J.

THOMPSON, Wm. Cutler, prof. law; b. Chicago, Ill., Feb. 25, 1898; s. Eli Frank and Florence May (Poulson) T.; B.S., Pa. State Coll., 1919; study, Peirce Sch. Bus. Adminstrn., 1923-24; LL.B. with first honors, Temple U. Law Sch., 1927; grad. study U. of Pa. Law Sch., candidate for LL.M., 1937; m. Grace Winter, Sept. 4, 1920; children—Wm. Cutler, Jr., Carol, Robert Travis. Began as instr. high sch. and agrl. extension agt., 1920; sec. to Hon. Alex. Simpson, Jr., Justice, Supreme Ct. of Pa., 1924-27; admitted to Pa. bar, 1927, engaged in gen. practice of law, asso. with Hon. Franklin S. Edmonds, Phila., 1928-30; spl. asst. to Atty.-Gen., Dept. Justice, Washington, D.C., 1930-33; prof. law, Temple U. Sch. of Law since 1933. Served as 2d lt. inf., U.S.A. during World War; now lt. U.S.N. Res. Pres. Civic Improvement League of Ambler, Pa., 1934-35. Mem. Am. and Pa. State bar assns., Am. Assn. Univ. Profs., Alpha Zeta, Theta Chi, Phi Delta Phi, Soc. of Cincinnati. Republican. Episcopalian. Home: 8318 Roberts Road, Elkins Park, Pa. Office: Public Ledger Bldg., Philadelphia, Pa.

THOMPSON, William Phillips, real estate broker; b. Mays Landing, N.J., Nov. 10, 1879; s. Joseph and Isabella Louise (Phillips) T.; student West Jersey Mil. Acad., Bridgeton, N.J., 1897-99, Media (Pa.) Acad., 1899-1901; M.D., Md. Med. Coll., Baltimore, Md., 1905; m. Addine DeForest Smith, June 2, 1908; children—William Phillips, Charles DeForest. Resident physician, Atlantic City Hosp., 1905-06; cattle business, Silver City, N. M., 1907-17; began in real estate business, 1921, and in business for self at Atlantic City, N.J., since 1921; moving office to West Atlantic City, 1938; partner Driscoll & Thompson, insurance, West Atlantic City, since 1938; dir. and chmn. real estate com. Islanders Bldg. & Loan Assn. since 1925. Mem. twp. com., Egg Harbor, (N.J.) Twp., 1920-32; v.p. Atlantic Co. Bd. Agr., 1918-19, pres. 1920-22. Republican. Mason (Shriner). Club: Rotary (Pleasantville, N.J.); pres., 1938-39. Home: English Creek, N.J. Office: West Atlantic City, N.J.

THOMSEN, Roszel Cathcart, lawyer; b. Baltimore, Md., Aug. 17, 1900; s. William Edward and Georgie A. (Cathcart) T.; A.B., Johns Hopkins U., 1919; LL.B., U. of Md. Law Sch., 1922; m. Carol Griffing Wolf, June 1, 1929; children—George Edward, Grace Griffing, Margaret Lucille. Admitted to Md. bar, 1922 and since engaged in gen. practice of law at Baltimore; asso. with firm Soper, Bowie & Clark, 1922-23, with Bowie & Clark, 1923-26; mem. firm with Walter L. Clark since 1927; vice-pres. and dir. Thomsen Ellis Co. Served in S.A.T.C., 1918. Pres. Family Welfare Assn., Baltimore; dir. Y.M.C.A. Trustee Goucher Coll., Morgan Coll. Mem. Am. and Md. State bar assns., Bar Assn. Baltimore City (chmn. com. professional ethics), Delta Upsilon, Phi Beta Kappa, Omicron Delta Kappa, Delta Theta Phi. Republican. Methodist. Club: Chesapeake. Home: 118 Enfield Rd. Office: Baltimore Trust Bldg., Baltimore, Md.

THOMSON, John Stuart, author; b. Montreal, Can., June 6, 1869; s. F. Stuart-Douglas and Elizabeth Ryder (Ferris) T.; Presbyn. Coll., Montreal, Can., 1887-89; McGill U., 1887-89; unmarried. Jr. sec. to Sir Joseph Hickson, gen. mgr. G.T. Ry.; mgr. at N.Y. City of Can. Atlantic and Plant steamship lines; asst. to the vice-pres. of the S.F.&W. Ry., 1891-1901; Oriental mgr., Hong Kong, China, of the Pacific Mail and Toyo Kisen Kaisha trans-Pacific steamship lines, 1901-04. Fellow Am. Geog. Soc.; mem. Navy League of U.S.; mem. advisory board Geog. Players, Inc. Clubs: Transportation, Samoyede (New York); Hong Kong (China). Chmn. and asso. editor The Gateway, mag., 1919-20. "Patron" of Belgian Order of St. John of Jerusalem. Has traveled extensively in the Orient, and around the world. Leader of the successful "Clark University Movement," 1912-13, for America's and Britain's official recognition of the Chinese Republic, for which received official thanks of China, signed by President Sun Yat Sen. Author: Estabelle, 1897; A Day's Song, 1900; The Chinese, 1909; China Revolutionized, 1912; Bud and Bamboo, 1913; Fil and Filippa, 1917. Contbr. many articles on Oriental; business, and internat. topics to mags., also lecturer at colleges, churches, and science socs. Gen. committeeman, Internat. Narcotic Edn. Assn. Lit. executor of Constitutional Webster-Thomson Family (United States Senate doc. 461, 1908). Known as "Father" of revived chestnut tree of which discovered first shoots and first seed, and received thanks of U.S. Dept. Agr., 1928; also "Father" of Jersey City's zoning law. Owner of Eskimo sleddog, "Pamelus," desc. from Peary's lead dog, "Polaris," and owner of Samoyede dog "Pavlova" desc. from Nansen's and Borchgrevink's lead dog. Home: 361 Bergen Av., Jersey City, N.J., and Glen Rock, N.J.

THOMSON, McLeod, mfg. ry. rails and joints; b. Altoona, Pa., July 19, 1883; s. McLeod W. and Margaret Emma (Garver) T.; ed. Lawrenceville Sch., 1898-1902; Princeton, 1903-07; m. Irene Dorothea Dittman, Apr. 3, 1918. Engaged in development of ry. steel rails and rail joints since 1907; vice-pres. The Thomson Rail Joint Co., 1908-14; dist. rep. The Rail Joint Co., 1914-29; pres. and dir. The Thomson Rail Corpn. of N.Y. since 1929. Pres. Scotch-Irish Soc. of Pa., 1938-39. Republican. Presbyterian. Clubs: Racquet, Princeton, Merion Cricket, Seaview Golf (Philadelphia); Ivy (Princeton). Contbr. tech. articles to r.r. mags. Home: 43 S. Aberdeen Place, Atlantic City, N.J. Office: Pennsylvania Bldg., Philadelphia, Pa.

THOMSON, O(smund) R(hoads) Howard, librarian; b. London, Eng., Dec. 5, 1873; s. John (Litt.D.) and Mary Ann (Faulkner) T.; father organized Free Library of Phila.; brought to U.S., 1881; ed. under father; professional training under Tbomas L. Montgomery and John Ashhurst; Litt.D., Dickinson College, Carlisle, Pa., 1935; naturalized citizen of U.S.; m. Theodora Adelheid (Theivagt) Nice, Apr. 18, 1901. Librarian West Phila. br. Free Library of Phila., 1899-1901, Wagner Inst. br. Free Library of Phila., 1901-06; organizer, 1906, and since librarian and sec. J. V. Brown Library, Williamsport, Pa. Chmn. for Pa. for A.L.A. in United Drive; chmn. for 12 counties, A.L.A. drive; chmn. Williamsport Red Cross Book and Magazine Service (all World War). Mem. A.L.A., Pennsylvania Library Association (ex-pres.), Pennsylvania Folk Lore Society. Episcopalian. Clubs: Williamsport Chess, Kit-Kat (pres.), Williamsport Country. Author: Contribution to Classification of Prose Fiction, 1904; History of the Bucktails (with W. H. Rauch), 1906; A Normal Library Budget, 1913; Resurgam—Poems and Lyrics, 1915; Christmas, 1916; Modern Comedy and Other Poems, 1918; John Franklin Meginess, 1919; Joseph H. McMinn, 1920; Reasonable Budgets for Public Libraries (A.L.A.), 1925. Editor Lycoming Hist. Soc. publs. Lecturer on English and American poetry; contbr. poems and critical articles to mags. Address: J. V. Brown Library, Williamsport, Pa.

THOMSON, Philip Livingston, pres. Audit Bureau of Circulations; b. Schenectady, N.Y., Nov. 28, 1879; s. Alexander J. and Mary Helen (Livingston) T.; grad. Union Classical Inst., Schenectady, 1895; A.B., Union Coll., 1900, hon. A.M., 1925; A.B., Harvard, 1902; m. Dorothy Eliot Tuthill, Apr. 21, 1909; children—Donald, Dorothy, Philip Van Rensselaer. With Western Electric Co. since 1903, mgr. Pittsburgh office, 1905-11, publicity mgr., New York, 1912-29, dir. of pub. relations since 1929. Pres. Audit Bureau of Circulations since 1927; dir. Glen Ridge (N.J.) Trust Co.; mem. Association of National Advertisers (pres. 1923-24), Phi Beta Kappa, Chi Psi. Republican. Congregationalist. Clubs: Harvard, New York Advertising, Glen Ridge Country; Sachem's Head (Conn.) Yacht. Contributor to Nation's Business, Printers' Ink. Frequent speaker on advertising and public relations; delivered address at Internat. Advertising Conv., London, 1924, Berlin, 1929; awarded gold medal for distinguished service to advertising, 1939. Home: 87 Oxford St., Glen Ridge, N.J. Address: Western Electric Co., 195 Broadway, New York, N.Y.

THORINGTON, James, M.D.; b. Davenport, Ia., June 6, 1858; s. James and Mary (Parker) T.; ed. Davenport until 1874; studied Princeton, 1875-76; M.D., Jefferson Med. Coll., Phila., 1881; hon. A.M., Ursinus, 1894; m. Florence May Jennings, Sept. 15, 1885; children—James Monroe, Richard Wainwright. Surgeon of Panama R.R. Co., Colon (Aspinwall), Isthmus of Panama, 1882-89; now emeritus prof. diseases of the eye, Phila. Polyclinc and Graduates in Medicine. Mem. Am. Ophthal. Soc., A.M.A. Author: Retinoscopy, 6th edit.; Refraction and How to Refract, 7th edit., 1930; The Ophthalmoscope and How to Use It, 1906; Prisms, Their Use and Equivalents, 1913; Refraction of the Eye, 1916, 30; Methods of Refraction, translated into Chinese. Has written much in med. jours. Address: 2031 Chestnut St., Phila., Pa.

THORN, George Widmer, M.D., med. edn.; b. Buffalo, N.Y., Jan. 15, 1906; s. George W. and Fanny R. (Widmer) T.; student Wooster (O.) Coll., 1923-25; M.D., U. of Buffalo, 1929; grad. student Harvard, 1934-35, Ohio State U., 1935-36, Johns Hopkins, 1936; m. Doris Weston Huggins, June 30, 1931. Asso. in medicine and physiology, U. of Buffalo, 1932-34; Rockefeller fellow in medicine, Harvard, 1934-35; asst. prof. of physiology, Ohio State U., 1935-36; Rockefeller fellow in medicine, Johns Hopkins Med. Sch., 1936-37, asso. in medicine, 1937-38, asso. prof. in medicine since 1938. Fellow Am. Coll. Physicians; mem. Am. Soc. Clin. Investigation, Am. Phys. Soc., Alpha Omega Alpha. Contbr. numerous articles on endocrine and metabolic diseases. Home: 3 E. 33d St. Office: Johns Hopkins Hospital, Baltimore, Md.

THORNBURG, Charles Lewis, mathematician; b. Barboursville, W.Va., Apr. 17, 1859; s. James Lewis and Virginia Frances (Handley) T.; grad. Marshall Coll., Huntington, W.Va., 1876; B.S., Vanderbilt, 1881, B.E., 1882, C.E., 1883, Ph.D., 1884; LL.D., Lehigh, 1925; m. Mary Eulalia Green, Nov. 4, 1886; children—Eulalie, Charles Garland, Chesley Covington, Lewis, Marion, Richard Beaumont, Lucille Leighton, Frances Green. Fellow in mathematics, 1881-82, grad. in mathematics, 1882-84, instr. engring. dept., 1884-86, Vanderbilt; adj. prof. in engring. dept. and astronomy, 1886-95, prof. mathematics and astronomy, 1895-1925, sec. of faculty, 1900-23, Lehigh U., now prof. emeritus. Fellow A.A.A.S.; mem. Am. Math. Soc., Soc. Promotion Engring. Edn., Beta Theta Pi, Phi Beta Kappa, Tau Beta Pi. Democrat. Methodist. Author: Calculus Notes, 1906; (brochure) Elementary Differential Equations, 1914. Home: 238 E. Market St., Bethlehem, Pa.

THORNBURY, Sedgley, pres. fire ins. co.; b. Eureka, Calif., July 2, 1910; s. Delmar Leon and Alpha E. (Sedgley) T.; grad. high sch., Piedmont, Calif.; ed. Hitchcock Mil. Acad., San Rafael, Calif., Harvard U. Grad. Sch. Bus. Adminstrn.; m. Elizabeth Wildrick Bailey, of Huntingdon, Pa., July 6, 1935; 1 son, Thomas Bailey. Engaged in bus. of ins., Oakland, Calif., 1928-30, Washington, D.C., and Baltimore, 1930-33; jr. comdr. C.C.C. nr. Huntingdon, Pa., 1933-34 with rank 1st lt. U.S.A.; pres. Mercantile Mutual Underwriters; sec. State Mercantile Mutual Fire Ins. Co., both of Huntingdon, Pa.; dir. and gen. mgr. Graphic Arts Mutual Fire Ins. Co., Phila. Republican. Unitarian. DeMolay. Clubs: Rotary (Huntingdon); Maryland Yacht (Baltimore); Huntingdon Country (Huntingdon). Home: Taylor Highlands. Office: 209 5th St., Huntingdon, Pa.

THORNE, Thomas Ray, banker; b. Greenville, Pa., July 18, 1875; s. Thomas and Helen (Mandeville) T.; student high sch.; m. Areta Johnston, Sept. 12, 1907; 1 dau., Helen Areta. Cashier Greenville (Pa.) Nat. Bank, 1914-27, pres. since 1927, dir. since 1927. Pres. Greenville Bd. of Edn. since 1931. Democrat. Presbyterian. Home: 6 Columbia Av. Office: Main and Canal Sts., Greenville, Pa.

THORNTON, E(dward) Quin, M.D.; b. Merion, Alabama, 1866; s. of Prof. Edward Quin and Sallie (Cocke) T.; M.D., Jefferson Medical College, Philadelphia, 1890; m. Elizabeth Smith; 1 dau. Practiced in Philadelphia since 1890; prof. of therapeutics, Jefferson Med. Coll., emeritus since 1934; asso. visiting phys., Pa. Hosp. Member American Medical Association, Medical Soc. State of Pa., Pathol. Soc. Phila.; fellow Coll. of Physicians, Phila. Author: A Manual of Materia Medica; Dose Book and Manual of Prescription Writing; Medical Formulary, 1930. Editor: Tarrard on Treatment and Bruce on Treatment. Address: 1331 Pine St., Philadelphia, Pa.

THORNTON, Mary Bickings, physician; b. Phila., Pa., Sept. 4, 1880; d. Joseph Rex and Mary Louise (Dixon) Bickings; M.D., Woman's Med. Coll. of Pa., 1904; A.B., Temple U., 1919; m. Harold G. Thornton, Apr. 3, 1909; children—Virginia Louise, Donald Bruce. Practice of medicine and teacher since 1904; prof. of anatomy, Woman's Med. Coll. until 1936, now emeritus; formerly prof. of hygiene and physiology, Sch. of Phys. Edn., Temple U.; now lecturer on bacteriology and med. advisor, also mem. bd. mgrs., Sch. of Occupational Therapy; former clinician Woman's Hosp., Woman's Coll. Hosp., Woman's Med. Coll. Mem. Coll. Physicians of Phila., Am. Med. Assn., Pa. Med. Soc., Phila. Co. Med. Soc. Protestant. Mem. Medical Club. Address: 2703 W. Somerset St., Phila., Pa.

THORNTON, Thomas Anthony, lawyer; b. Pittsburgh, Pa., Mar. 27, 1897; s. John and Rose Gabrielle (Perry) T.; ed. Hollywood (Calif.) Sch., 1909-12, Peabody High Sch. (Pittsburgh), 1913-16; B.S. in Engring., U. of Pittsburgh, 1921; LL.B., Pittsburgh Law Sch., 1923; m. Catherine B. Bredendick, Nov. 29, 1928; 1 son, Thomas Perry. Admitted to Pa. bar, 1923; since in gen. civil practice; mem. law firm Doty & Thornton since 1923. Served in U.S. Navy 1917-18; now lt. comdr. U.S. Naval Reserve. Has managed election campaigns and headed campaign coms. Mem. oral examining bds. Dept. of Pub. Assistance, Harrisburg; dir. Boys Club, Pittsburgh; mem. bd. advisors Juvenile Ct. Mem. Allegheny County Bar Assn., Am. Legion (mem. exec. com. of Pa., 12 yrs.; dist. comdr. 34th Dist.), Veterans of Foreign Wars, Kappa Sigma, Phi Delta Phi, Omicron Delta Kappa. Republican. Catholic. Clubs: Pittsburgh Athletic Assn. (chmn. athletic com. 10 yrs.); track and field chmn. Allegheny Mountain Assn. of Amateur Athletic Union; dir. Army and Navy Club of Pittsburgh; chmn. Allegheny County Veterans Republican Club. Home: 413 N. Craig St. Office: 210 Jones Law Bldg., Pittsburgh, Pa.

THORP, Charles Monroe, lawyer; b. Hawley, Pa., Mar. 16, 1863; s. Lewis Hale and Anna Atkinson (Wise) T.; Ph.B., Cornell, 1884; m. Jessie Boulton, May 22, 1888 (died 1930); children—Margaret (Mrs. W. D. Stewart), George Boulton, Evelyn (Mrs. John R. Minter, dec.), Charles Monroe, Jessie (Mrs. E. W. Fiske, Jr.), Eleanore (Mrs. William F. Whitla); m. 2d, Goldie Donnell, Nov. 22, 1933. Admitted to Pennsylvania bar, 1886, and practiced at Pittsburgh since; member Thorp, Bostwick, Reed & Armstrong; director National Steel Corpn., Edgewater Steel Co., Blaw-Knox Co., Copperweld Steel Co. Trustee C. C. Mellor Memorial Library, Edgewood (Pittsburgh). Mem. American, Pa. State and Allegheny County bar assns., Phi Beta Kappa, Theta Delta Chi. Presbyn. Clubs: Duquesne, University, Edgewood, Longue Vue, Oakmont Country, Pittsburgh Athletic Assn. Home: 326 Maple Av., Edgewood, Pittsburgh Pa. Office: Grant Bldg., Pittsburgh, Pa.

THORPE, Merle, magazine editor; b. Brimfield, Ill., Nov. 1, 1879; s. Joseph and Mayday E. (Smith) T.; A.B., Stanford Univ., 1905; A.B., Univ. of Wash., 1908; m. Lilian Isabel Day, Aug. 17, 1909; children—George Day, Merle. Editorial work on Palo Alto (Calif.) Times, 1903-04, Washington Post, 1905-06, Havana (Cuba) Post, 1906-07, Seattle Post-Intelligencer, 1907; Adv. mgr. Washington Life, 1905; editor and mgr. The Washington Alumnus, 1907-11; editor Kansas Editor, 1913-16; prof. journalism, U. of Wash., 1907-11, U. of Kan., 1911-16; editor and pub. The Nation's Business, Washington, 1916—, former contbg. editor Collier's; dir. Nat. Metropolitan Bank, Chesapeake and Potomac Telephone Co., Capital Transit Co.; trustee Northwestern Mutual Life Insurance Co. Lecturer on journalism, U. of Calif., summers, 1914-15. Pres. Am. Assn. Journalism Teachers, 1915-16; sec. Mo. Valley Cost Congress, 1914-16; dir. Nat. Journalism Congress, 1914; asst. dir. President's Unemployment Relief Orgn.; dir. George Washington Bicentennial Commn., Nat. Publishers' Assn. Trustee George Washington U. Mem. Sigma Alpha Epsilon, Phi Delta Phi, Sigma Delta Chi. Republican. Conglist. Clubs: Chevy Chase, Metropolitan, Burning Tree, Alfalfa (Washington); Artists and Writers; The Players (N.Y.). Author: The Coming Newspaper, 1915; How's Business?, 1931; Organized Business Leadership, 1931; Neither Purse nor Sword (with James M. Beck), 1936. Contbr. short stories to nat. mags. Awarded Harvard-Bok prize for writing best individual advertisement in 1925. Home: Pook's Hill, Rockville Pike, Bethesda, Md. Office: U.S. Chamber of Commerce Bldg., Washington, D.C.

THRELKELD, Archie Loyd, supt. schools; b. Lancaster, Mo., Mar. 4, 1889; s. James Mancel and Emily Evelyn (Hounsom) T.; B.Pd., Northeast Mo. State Teachers Coll., Kirksville, Mo., 1911; studied Univ. of Wisconsin and Univ. of Chicago; B.S. in Education, U. of Mo., 1919; M.A., Columbia, 1923; LL.D.; Univ. of Denver, 1930, Colo. Coll., 1935; hon. Ed.D., Univ. of Colo., 1932; m. Anna Rebecca Miller, June 11, 1913 (died Jan. 16, 1923); children—Aubrey Miller, Richard Allen, Ellen Hounsom; m. 2d, Mary Ethel Miller, of Purdin, Mo., Aug. 12, 1925. Teacher, high sch., Kirksville, 1909-11; supt. schs., Bunceton, Mo., 1911-12, Unionville, 1912-17, Chillicothe, 1917-21; asst. supt. schs., Denver, 1921-24, dep. supt., 1924-27, supt., 1927-37; supt. schs. Montclair, N.J., since 1937. Pres. Mo. State Teachers' Assn., 1921; mem. N.E.A. (pres. Dept. Superintendence, 1936-37), Nat. Council of Edn., Nat. Soc. for Study of Edn., Phi Delta Kappa, Kappa Delta Pi. Methodist. Mason (32°). Clubs: Denver Mile High, Cactus; Montclair Rotary. Home: 198 Alexander Av. Office: 22 Valley Rd., Montclair, N.J.

THRUSH, Morris Clayton, physician and surgeon; b. Marion, Pa., Jan. 14, 1876; s. Martin W. and Emma C. (Etter) T.; Ph.G., Phila. Coll. of Pharmacy, 1896; Ph.M., U. of Buffalo (N. Y.), 1901; M.D., Medico-Chirurgical Coll., Phila., 1901; m. Edith A. Shank, Sept. 25, 1901; children—Helen A., Edith Blanche (Mrs. Meade Lorence), Gladys V. Began as pharmacist, Charlestown, W.Va., 1891; teacher of pharmacy, Medico-Chirurgical Coll., Phila., 1898-1901, asst. prof. of therapeutics since 1903. Served as lt., Med. Corps, U.S. Army, 1917-18, lt. col., 1918-39. Mem. Phila. Co., Pa. State, Am. med. assns. Presbyterian. Mason. Club: Medical (Phila.). Address: 3705 Spring Garden St., Philadelphia, Pa.

THUDIUM, William John, surgeon; b. Phila., Pa., July 26, 1894; s. John and Anna (Flammer), T.; M.D., Jefferson Med. Coll., Phila., 1917; m. Elizabeth Rommel, Oct. 15, 1932; 1 dau., Mary Elizabeth. In practice of surgery at Phila. since 1920; assoc. in gynecology, Jefferson Med. Coll., Phila., since 1936; gynecologist and obstetrician, Phila. Gen. Hosp.; gynecologist, St. Joseph's Hosp.; cons. gynecologist, Norristown State Hosp. Served as lt. U.S.N. during World War. Fellow Am. Coll. Surgs., Coll. Phys. of Phila.; mem. A.M.A., Mil. Order of Fgn. Wars, Nu Sigma Nu. Republican. Presbyterian. Mason. Clubs: Union League, University, Merion Cricket, Penn Athletic (Phila.). Home: Haverford, Pa. Office: Medical Arts Bldg., 136 S. 16th St., Philadelphia, Pa.

THUN, Ferdinand, mfr.; b. Barmen, Germany, Feb. 14, 1866; s. Ferdinand and Julia (Westkott) T.; ed. Tech. High Sch., Barmen; m. Anna N. Grebe, May 20, 1896; children—Anna C. (wife of L. C. Scheffey, M.D.), Margaret E. (Mrs. Samuel R. Fry), Wilma M. (Mrs. Charles H. Muhlenberg), Hildegard E. (Mrs. P. Erich Plehn), Ferdinand K., Louis R. Came to U.S. 1886, naturalized citizen 1892. Engaged in mfg. business at Reading, Pa., since 1892; pres. Berkshire Knitting Mills, Lehigh Structural Steel Co. (Allentown, Pa.), Carl Schurz Memorial Foundation, Delta Finance Co., Ontelaunee Orchards, Inc., Am. Nuplax Corpn., Thun Investment Co., Wyomissing Foundation; sec.-treas. Textile Machine Works, Delta Realty Corpn.; treas. Narrow Fabric Co. President Council of Wyomissing, Pa., since its orgn., 1906. Trustee Oberlaender Trust. Mem. Acad. Polit. Science. Republican. Lutheran. Clubs: Wyomissing, Berkshire Country, Reading Country; Mfrs. and Bankers (Phila.). Home: Wyomissing, Pa.

THURSTON, Alice Maud, educator; b. Pittsburgh, Pa.; d. George Henry and Mary Curry (Lewis) T.; grad. Bishop Bowman Inst.; hon. M.A., conferred by U. of Pittsburgh, 1920, in recognition of long service as an educator in the city of Pittsburgh. Organized and established Thurston Prep. Sch. for Girls; past pres. and treas. Thurston Sch. Co., operating The Thurston Prep. Day Sch. for Girls, situated 250 Shady Av., Pittsburgh; retired from sch. work, 1930. Mem. Soc. Mayflower Descendants. Episcopalian. Address: care Mrs. L. B. Stillwell, Princeton, N.J.

THURSTON, Henry Winfred, social worker; b. Barre, Vt., Feb. 28, 1861; s. Wilson and Frances Lois (Kinney) T.; A.B., Dartmouth, 1886; Ph.D., Columbia U., 1918; m. Charlotte E. Skinner, Nov. 27, 1890; children—Henry Winfred Marjorie (dec.), Charlotte Howe, Robert Ray. Supt. schs., Elk Point, Dak., 1886-87; teacher of science, Hyde Park High Sch., Chicago, 1887-88; prin. Lyons Tp. High Sch., LaGrange, Ill., 1888-93; teacher Englewood High Sch., Chicago, 1893-94; teacher civics and economics, Hyde Park High Sch., 1894-99; prin. branch, same sch., Jan.-May, 1900; head dept. of sociology, Chicago Normal Sch., 1900-05; chief probation officer, Cook Co. Juvenile Ct. (Chicago), 1905-09; state supt. Ill. Children's Home and Aid Soc., Apr. 1, 1909-12; head Children's Dept., New York Sch. of Social Work, 1912-31. Chmn. sub-com. on probation N.Y. C.O.S. Criminal Cts. Com., 1914-34. Contrbg. editor on children The Survey, 1914-17. Chmn. div. on children Nat. Conf. Social Work, 1917-20; exec. com. Child Welfare League America (chmn. 1923-26); chmn. advisory com. Dept. of Boarding Homes, N.Y. Children's Aid Soc., 1923-34; sec. Class of 1886, Dartmouth Coll. since 1936. Mem. Theta Delta Chi. Presbyn. Author: In Memoriam—W. H. Ray, 1891; Economics and Industrial History, 1899; Spare Time and Delinquency, 1918; The Dependent Child, 1930. Home: 215 Walnut St., Montclair, N.J.

THURSTON, Lee Mohrmann, prof. edn.; b. Central Lake, Mich., Aug. 7, 1895; s. George Lee and Lenore (Mohrmann) T.; A.B., U. of Mich., Ann Arbor, Mich., 1918, A.M., 1929, Ph.D., 1935; m. Jessie H. Gothro, Dec. 26, 1921; children—Jane K., Robert Lee. Engaged in teaching and supt. schs. in various cities in Mich., 1918-31; asst. supt. schs., Ann Arbor, Mich., 1931-35; dep. supt. pub. instrn. of State of Mich., Lansing, 1935-38; prof. edn., U. of Pittsburgh since 1938. Served in U.S. Marine Corps, 1918-19. Mem. N.E.A., Pa. State Edn. Assn., Am. Assn. Sch. Adminstrs., Phi Delta Kappa, Phi Kappa Phi. Contbr. to ednl. publs. Home: 612 Pennridge Rd., Pittsburgh, Pa.

THWING, Charles Burton, physicist; b. Theresa, N.Y., Mar. 9, 1860; s. Charles Grandison and Harriet (Corbin) T.; A.B., Northwestern U., 1888, A.M., 1890; A.M., Ph.D., U. of Bonn, 1894; m. Lucy Blakeslee White, Aug. 3, 1893; children—Myra, John Burton, Philip Lenard, Alice Cushing. Instr. physics, Northwestern U. Acad., 1888-93, U. of Wis., 1894-96; prof. physics, Knox Coll., 1896-1901, Syracuse U., 1901-05; research work, Western Reserve U., 1905-06; mfr. pyrometers since Nov. 1906, also mfr. paper testing apparatus; pres. Thwing-Albert Instrument Co. Has made several inventions in electricity and metallurgy. Fellow Am. Phys. Soc.; mem. Optical Soc. of America, Am. Ceramic Soc., Tech. Soc., Pulp and Paper Industry. Author: Exercises in Physical Measurement (with Louis Winslow Austin), 1896; An Elementary Physics, 1900. Contbr. to scientific jours. Home: 45 W. Tulpehocken St. Office: 3339 Lancaster Av., Phila., Pa.

THWING, John Burton, clergyman; b. Galesburg, Ill., Jan. 10, 1897; s. Charles Burton and Lucy Blakeslee (White) T.; A.B., Valparaiso U., 1920; Th.B., Princeton Theol. Sem., 1923, Th.M., same, 1927; Th.D., Eastern Bapt. Theol. Sem., 1931; m. Amber Floye Vrooman, Sept. 25, 1918; children—John Burton, Jr., Amber Floye, James Luther, Lucy Blakeslee. Ordained to ministry Presbyn. Ch. U.S.A., 1923; pastor Clement Ch., Chicago, Ill., 1923-25; pastor Braddock, Pa., 1925-27; pastor Beacon Presbyn. Ch. U.S.A., Phila., Pa., 1929-35, and Knox Presbyn. Ch. (Orthodox Presbyn) since 1935; dir. and tenor male quartettes including Cosmopolitan Male Quartette, Chicago, Ill., Princeton Sem. Male Quartette, Philadelphians, and others; radio broadcaster since 1922; dir. Grangeville Folks, WDAS since 1933. Served as sec. Y.M.C.A., 1917-20. Moderator Phila. Presbytery, 1936. Mem. Benham Club., Princeton, N.J. Contbr. many articles to ch. mags. and jours. Home: 72 E. Pastorius St., Philadelphia, Pa.

THYGESON, Phillips, prof. of ophthalmology; b. St. Paul, Minn., Mar. 28, 1903; s. Nels Marcus and Sylvie G. (Thompson) T.; A.B., Stanford U., 1925, M.D., 1928; Oph.D., U. of Colo., 1936, M.S., 1933; m. Ruth Lee Spilman, of Palo Alto, Calif., Mar. 21, 1925; children—Fritjof Peder, Kristin. Interne Colo. Gen. Hosp., Denver, 1927,-28; began practice as ophthalmologist, Denver, 1930; asst. prof. of ophthalmology, U. of Ia., Coll. of Medicine, 1932-36; with Coll. of Physicians and Surgeons, Columbia, since 1936, as asst. prof. of ophthalmology, 1936-39, prof. and head of dept. since 1939; dir. Inst. of Ophthalmology, Presbyn. Hosp., New York. Mem. A.M.A., Am. Ophthal. Soc., Am. Acad. Ophthalmology and Oto-laryngology, (Assn. for Research in Ophthalmology, Soc. Am. Bacteriologists. Contbr. to professional jours. Home: Tenafly, N.J. Office: 635 W. 165th St., New Yor, N.Y.

TIBBENS, Clyde E., M.D.; b. Franklin, Pa., Aug. 19, 1888; s. George R. and Margaret A. (Gordon) T.; B.S., Washington & Jefferson Coll., Washington, Pa., 1912, M.S., 1916; M.D., Jefferson Med. Coll., Phila., 1916; m. Nina Gertrude Whitehill, Oct. 28, 1920; children—George Filmore, Martha Anne Began gen. practice medicine, 1917; mem. staff Washington Hosp. since 1920. Served in U.S. Army Med. Corps, July 1917-June 1919; hon. discharge as maj. Mem. A.M.A., Pa. State Med. Soc., Washington Co. Med. Soc., U.S. Chamber of Commerce, Washington (Pa.) Chamber of Commerce, Phi Alpha Sigma, Alpha Tau Omega. Republican. Mason (Shriner). Clubs: Nemacolin Country, Bassett (Washington, Pa.). Home: 11 Wilmont Av. Office: 6 S. Main St., Washington, Pa.

TIBBENS, Perry McDowell, M.D.; b. Beech Creek, Pa., May 17, 1881; s. Joseph Edward and Emma Jane (McDowell) T.; grad. Beech Creek (Pa.) Common Sch., 1895; B.S., Williamsport (Pa.) Dickinson Sem., 1900; M.D., Jefferson Med. Coll., Phila., 1905; m. Grace I. Bloom, Aug. 1, 1922; 1 son, Perry McDowell II. In gen. practice of medicine with father, J. E. Tibbins, 1906-18, since in private practice at Beech Creek, Pa.; pres. and dir. Beech Creek Nat. Bank. Served as 1st lt., U.S. Gen. Hosp. No. 6, Ft. McPherson, Ga., during World War; capt.; Res. Corps, Med. Sect., Dem. County Chmn., 1936-37. Mem. Phi Alpha Sigma. Democrat. Methodist. Mason (Shriner), Elk, Odd Fellow, Grange. Club: Roosevelt Democratic. Home: Beech Creek, Pa. Died July 19, 1939.

TIBBOTT, Harve, congressman; b. Ebensburg, Pa., May 27, 1885; s. Sherman and Elizabeth (Rowland) T.; Ph.G., U. of Pittsburgh Sch. Pharmacy, 1906; m. Mary Eldora Humphreys, Sept. 16, 1908; 1 son, Rowland Humphreys. Engaged as pharmacist and propr. Tibbott's Corner Drug Store, Ebensburg, Pa. since 1906; pres. First Nat. Bank of Ebensburg since 1938; dir. Cambria Thrift Corpn. Treas. Cambria Co., 1932-36. Mem. Rep. State Com., 1936-37. Elected to U.S. Congress on Rep. ticket, Nov. 8, 1938. Pres. Ebensburg Y.M.C.A. Treas. Wm. Penn Highway Assn. Mem. Beta Phi Sigma. Republican. Mem. Christian Ch. Mason (33°, Shriner, Past Potentate). Club: Kiwanis of Ebensburg (past pres.). Home: 604 W. Horner St., Ebensburg, Pa. Office: 100 High St., Ebensburg, Pa.

TIDESWELL, Albert F., pres. Erie Coach Co.; b. Buffalo, N.Y., Dec. 19, 1885; s. Harry B. and Mina (Miller) T.; ed. Buffalo pub. schs. and Caton's Business Coll.; m. Odessa A. Smith, Oct. 14, 1908; 1 son, Albert Russell. With Erie Coach Co. and predecessors since 1906, successively purchasing agent, sec. and treas., gen. mgr. and pres. since 1927, now also dir.; dir. Erie Rys. Co., Pa. Bus. Assn. Dir. Erie Chamber of Commerce. Mason (Shriner). Clubs: Kahkwa, Motor, Erie, Shrine, Rotary. Home: Dorchester Heights. Office: 231 State St., Erie, Pa.

TIECHE, Albert U.; surgeon Beckley and Oak Hill hosps. Address: Beckley Hospital, Beckley, W.Va.

TIEMEYER, Arthur Charles, surgeon; b. Baltimore, Md., Aug. 6, 1898; s. Frederick and Gertrude (Vogt) T.; B.S., U. of Md., Baltimore, Md., 1916; M.D., U. of Md. Med. Sch., Baltimore, 1919; m. Alice Mary Henneberry, Sept. 15, 1932. Resident in obstetrics, St. Joseph's Hosp., Baltimore, 1918-19, Md. Gen. Hosp., 1919-20; post. grad. study in obstetrics and gynecology, Johns Hopkins Med. Sch., 1920-23; head dept. obstetrics and gynecology, West Baltimore Gen. Hosp. since 1924, chief of staff since 1928; visiting obstetrician and gynecologist, Hosp. for Women of Md., St. Joseph's, Md. Gen., Franklin Sq., Church Home, Sinai, and St. Agnes Hosps. Served in S.A.T.C., 1918. Dir. Md. Odd Fellows Home for Aged and Orphans. Diplomat Am. Bd. Obstetrics and Gynecology. Fellow Am. Coll. Surgeons, A.M.A. Mem. Southern Med. Assn., Med. and Chirurg. Faculty of Md., Baltimore City Med. Soc., Baltimore Obstet. and Gynecol. Soc., Phi Chi. Democrat. Mem. M.E. Ch. Mason (32°). Odd Fellow. Club: University. Home: 101 W. Monument St., Baltimore, Md.

TIFFANY, Harold Edward, cons. and analytical chemist; b. Tunkhannock, Wyo. Co., Pa., Nov. 14, 1881; s. Lewis William and Katherine (Loomis) T.; student Keytsone Acad., Factoryville, Pa., 1895-99; B.S., Bucknell U., Lewisburg, Pa., 1905, M.S., 1906; M.S., Harvard, 1906; student Columbia U., 1918-19; m. Edith Kennedy Brokaw, Apr. 12, 1911; children—Edith Elizabeth, Harold Edward. Instr. chemistry, U. of Del., Newark, Del., 1906-08, asst. prof. chemistry, mineralogy and geology, 1908-17, prof. same, 1921-23; asst. state chemist, Del., 1906-17; research chemist E. I. du Pont de Nemours & Co., Wilmington, Del., 1918-19; asst. prof. geology and mineralogy, Hunter Coll., New York City, 1919-20; organized Wilmington Testing and Research Labs., 1923, and since dir.; chemist and toxicologist to State Atty. Gen. and Coroner of New Castle County since 1925; internal revenue chemist, Wilmington, since 1926; sec. and treas. Del. Testing Labs., Inc., Wilmington, since 1938; treas. Gulf Tung Oil Industries, Inc., Wilmington, since 1938. Mem. Am. Chem. Soc., Am. Soc. for Testing Materials, Assn. of Pulp and Paper Industry, Sigma Phi Epsilon. Presbyterian. Mason (Blue Lodge; Royal Arch Chapter; K.T.; Council Royal and Select Master Masons), Modern Woodmen of America. Club: Harvard Masonic (life mem.; Cambridge, Mass.). Home: 16 Amstel Av., Newark, Del. Office: 321 Delaware Av., Wilmington, Del.

TIFFANY, Herbert Thorndike, law author and compiler; b. N.Y. City, Nov. 17, 1861; s. George Peabody and Anne Dickey (Thordike) T.; A.B., Johns Hopkins U., 1883; LL.B., U. of Md., 1885; m. Harriet F. Poultney, Apr. 21, 1908 (died 1933). State reporter Md. Court of Appeals since 1920. Mem. Am. Law Inst. Unitarian. Club: University (Baltimore). Author: Law of Real Property, 1903, enlarged edit. 1920; Law of Landlord and Tenant, 1910; Outlines of Real Property (with Herbert M. Brune, Jr.), 1929. Editor of Md. Reports, vols. 135-171. Home: 701 Cathedral St., Baltimore, Md.

TIFFANY, Joseph Edgar, testing engr.; b. Leeds, Eng., Nov. 9, 1879; s. Frank and Sarah (Watson) T.; came to U.S., 1900, naturalized, 1911; B.Sc., U. of Leeds, Eng., 1899; M.E., Sch. of Mines, Camborne, Eng., 1900; m. Elizabeth Marion Kimmell, June 22, 1904; 1 dau., Sarabelle Kimmell. Employed as engr. in various positions, 1900-12; asso. with Federal Bur. of Mines continuously since 1912; now explosives testing engr. in charge of tests on explosives and spl. investigations on application of explosives for blasting in mines. Mem. Coal Mining Inst. of America. Lutheran. Contbr. many papers and tech. articles on coal, explosives, and mining. Home: 5703 Northumberland St. Office: 4800 Forbes St., Pittsburgh, Pa.

TIFFANY, J(oseph) Raymond, corpn. lawyer; b. Ocean Grove, N.J., Sept. 4, 1888; s. Edward LeRoy and Josephine Louise (Brown) T.; grad. Hoboken (N.J.) High Sch., 1909; LL.B., N.Y. Law Sch., 1912; spl. work Columbia U.; m. Adeline Ely, Feb. 7, 1912; children—Forrest Fraser, Elizabeth Louise. Admitted to N.J. bar, 1912; also authorized to practice in various Federal Courts and U.S. Supreme Ct.; specialized in corporation law and practices before State and Federal Adminstrn. bodies and courts; sr. partner Tiffany & Massarsky, Hoboken, N.J., since 1937; gen. counsel and treas. Central Dist., Inc., Hoboken, since 1931; gen. counsel Book Mfrs. Inst., New York Roll Leaf Mfrs. Association, National Small Business Mens Assn. Judge Hoboken (N.J.) Dist. Ct., 1918-23; asst. atty. gen., N.J., 1926-34; spl. counsel N.J. State Water Policy Commn., 1927-32, N.J. State Milk Control Bd., 1928-32, Bd. of Commerce and Navigation, 1926-34, South Jersey Port Commn., 1930-34; gen. counsel Interstate Sanitation Commn. for N.Y., N.J., Connecticut since 1935; taught constitutional law, U. of Newark, Post Grad. Course, 1934-35. Mem. Hoboken Rotary Internat. Club (gov. 36th Dist., 1931-32); mem. mag. com. of Rotary Internat., "Rotarian" and "Revista Rotaria"), Am. Bar Assn., N.J. State Bar Assn., Hudson Co. Bar Assn. (former pres.), Assn. of Bar of N.Y., Interstate Commerce Commn. Practitioners Assn. Republican. Baptist. Mason (Shriner), Elk. Clubs: Advertising, Downtown Athletic, Engineers (New York); Green Brook Country (Caldwell, N.J.). Home: 110 Christopher St., Montclair, N.J. Office: 35 Newark St., Hoboken, N.J.

TILBERG, Wilbur Emanuel, coll. dean; b. Kossuth, Iowa, Dec. 13, 1884; s. Charles O. and Carrie A. (Norrbom) T.; A.B., Bethany Coll., Lindsborg, Kan., 1911; A.M., U. of Kan., Lawrence, Kan., 1912; student U. of Chicago, 1916-17; Ph. D., U. of Wis., Madison, Wis., 1927; m. Arna Vitalia Nelson, July 11, 1912; 1 son, Cedric Wilbur. Teacher of history, Okmulgee (Okla.) High Sch., 1912-13; teacher of history and dean, Midland Coll., Fremont, Neb., 1913-25; dean Gettysburg (Pa.) Coll. since 1927. Pres. Crippled Children's Soc.; pres. York-Adams Area Council of Boy Scouts of America; trustee Parish and Ch. Sch. Bd. of United Lutheran Ch. Mem. Eastern Assn. Deans and Advisers of Men, Kappa Phi Kappa, Tau Kappa Alpha. Lutheran. Club: Lions (Gettysburg, Pa.). Address: Gettysburg, Pa.

TILDEN, Marmaduke, Jr., architect; b. New York, N.Y., Feb. 18, 1883; son of Marmaduke Tilden; grad. Talmage Sch., Morristown, N.J., 1897, St. Marks Sch., Southboro, Mass., 1901; A.B., Harvard U., 1905, awarded honors in Fine Arts; m. Ellen Frazier, May 21, 1914; children—Ellen, Cornelia Sibley (Mrs. Seaman Deas Sinkler), Anne Merry. Began as draughtsman, 1907; mem. firm Bissel, Sinkler & Tilden, architects, 1914, Tilden & Register, 1915-17, Tilden, Register & Pepper, 1918-36, Tilden and Pepper since 1936. Served as lt., U.S. Air Service, World War, 1917-18. Home: Blue Bell, Pa. Office: 225 S. 15th St., Philadelphia, Pa.

TILGHMAN, George Hammond, educator; b. Johannesburg, S. Africa, Sept. 14, 1896, of Am. parents; s. Henry Ashe and Alice Tennyson (Merry) T.; B.S., Harvard University, 1919; grad. study, Columbia Univ., 1920-22, M.A., 1929; m. Ruth Slocum, Mar. 28, 1918; children—Henry Ashe, William Slocum, George Hammond, Richard Austin, Anne Ashe, Sarah Williams. Teacher of chem. and maths., Morristown (N.J.) Sch., 1920-26, headmaster since 1926. Served as 1st lt. Coast Arty. Corps, U.S.A., 1917-19. Pres. Morristown Sch. Alumni; v.p. Morris County Chapter of Am. Red Cross. Mem. Headmasters Assn., Assn. Schs. and Colls. Middle Atlantic States and Md. Republican. Episcopalian. Clubs: Harvard (New York); Lawrence Beach, Rockaway Hunt, Cedarhurst Yacht. Address: Morristown School, Morristown, N.J.

TILGHMAN, Harrison, lawyer; b. Easton, Md., Sept. 6, 1885; s. Oswald and Patty Belle (Harrison) T.; A.B., St. John's Coll., Annapolis, Md., 1903; C.E., Lehigh U., Bethlehem, Pa., 1907; LL.B., Fordham U., 1924; special student in law and finance, Columbia; unmarried. On hydro-electric power development in Calif., 1907-08; commd. 2d lt. Coast Arty., U.S. Army, 1909, and advanced through the grades to maj. (temp.) while in France, 1918; commanded group of arty. with French II Army near Verdun, spring 1918, later on Gen. Staff of Commanding Gen. Railway Arty.; resigned Oct. 1919; listed Initial Gen. Staff Eligible List, 1920; lt. col. Adj. Gen. Reserve since 1923; financial and legal employment, New York, 1919-32; admitted to N.Y. bar, 1925, Md. bar, 1933, also to Federal Courts, Southern Dist. of N.Y. and Dist. of Md. and before the S.E.C. practice from Easton, Md., since 1932, specializing in corpns. Constitutionalist. Mem. Am. Bar Assn., Soc. of Cincinnati (as successor and rep. of Lt. Col. Tench Tilghman, a.d.c. to Gen. Washington); mem. Soc. of Colonial Wars (desc. of Richard Tilghman, chancellor of Md., 1722-25); mem. Order of Stars and Bars (son of Oswald Tilghman, C.S.A.), Md. Hist. Soc., Soc. for Promotion of Engring. Edn., Sigma Phi. Clubs: Army and Navy (Washington, D.C.); Chesapeake Bay Yacht (Easton, Md.). Contbr. to newspapers and jours. Home: Foxley Hall, Easton, Md.

TILGHMAN, William Bell, mfr.; b. Salisbury, Md., Oct. 30, 1884; s. William Beauchamp and Annie Esther (Bell) T.; Eastman Coll., Poughkeepsie, N.Y., 1903; m. MaBelle Gray Sterling, June 5, 1919; children—Jean Sterling, Wm. Beauchamp, Samuel Sterling. Manufacturer fertilizers since 1908; now president W. B. Tilghman Company; dir. Salisbury National Bank, Salisbury Building & Loan Assn. Mem. staff Governor Goldsborough, rank of col. Del. Rep. Nat. Conv., 1912. Methodist. Scottish Rite Mason, Rotarian. Home: Salisbury, Md.

TILLOTSON, Edwin Ward, chemist; b. Farmington, Conn., Feb. 28, 1884; s. Edwin Ward and Mary Lewis (Root) T.; B.A., Yale, 1906, Loomis fellow, 1907-08, Silliman fellow, 1908-09, Ph.D., 1909; m. Lida Charles LeSuer, July 24, 1913; children—Mary Katherine, Edwin Ward. Research fellow dept. of industrial research, U. of Kan., 1909-13; asst. dir. Mellon Inst. Industrial Research, U. of Pittsburgh, since Apr. 1, 1913. Specialist in chemistry and technology of glass and ceramics and industrial research management. Member American Chemical Soc. (chmn. Pittsburgh sect., 1920), Am. Ceramic Soc. (sec. glass div., 1919-21; v.p. 1922; Pres. 1925; fellow, 1931), Am. Optical Soc., Soc. Glass Technology, Soc. of Rheology, Sigma Xi, Alpha Chi Sigma, Phi Lambda Upsilon. Club: University. Republican. Mason. Home: 505 S. Murtland Av., Pittsburgh, Pa.

TILTON, Elvin John, editor, publisher; b. Gibson, Ia., May 18, 1906; s. Grant and Theresa H. (Hall) T.; A.B., U. of Ia., Iowa City, Ia., 1927; m. Margaret Julia Renn, July 9, 1931; 1 dau., Jane Renn. Editor Brownsville (Pa.) Telegraph, 1928-34, publisher, 1934-38; editor and publisher Aliquippa (Pa.) Gazette since 1938; v.p. Brownsville Pub. Co.; pres. Franklin Pub. Co. Capt., 394th Inf., Organized Reserves. Republican. Methodist. Club: Rotary (Aliquippa, Pa.). Home: 2021 McMinn St. Office: 384 Franklin Av., Aliquippa, Pa.

TILTON, George Irvin, organist, choir dir.; b. Trenton, N.J., Apr. 22, 1891; s. Peter Bloom and Emily Valiska (Hartley) T.; grad. Trenton (N.J.) High Sch., 1909; studied with Sydney H. Bourne of Trenton, S. W. Sears of Phila., Clarence Dickinson of New York, H. A. Matthews of Phila., E. F. Edmunds of Phila.; m. Elinor Audrey Worth, Aug. 14, 1937. Organist and choir dir. All Saints P.E. Ch., 1909-20, Fifth Presbyn. Ch., 1920-21, Prospect Presbyn. Ch., 1921-23, Third Presbyn. Ch., since 1923, all Trenton, N.J.; teacher organ, piano, voice, choir training, theory and composition. Served as private, A.E.F., during World War. Chmn. Trenton (N.J.) Music Week Com. since 1935. Mem. Trenton Choir Assn. (pres. since 1936), Nat. Assn. Organists (pres. Central N.J. Chapter 1925-27, pres. N.J. Council 1928-30; mem. State Exec. Com. 1925-36; Nat. Exec. Com. 1928-30, Chapter Exec. Com. 1929-37), Am. Guild of Organists, Nat. Piano Teachers Guild, Am. Legion, Trenton Hist. Soc. Democrat. Episcopalian. Woodmen of the World. Club: Musicians (New York). Has given many organ recitals. Has delivered lectures on ch. musical topics, organ. Author articles for musical mags. Has organized choir festivals, Trenton, and arranged music for spl. services Trenton Council of Chs. Address: 441 Bellevue Av., Trenton, N.J.

TILY, Herbert James, merchant; b. Farnham, Eng., Feb. 3, 1866; s. James and S. Letitia (Coleman) T.; brought to U.S. in infancy; ed. pub. schs., business coll. and under pvt. tutors; hon. Mus. D., Villa Nova 1913; LL.D., Lafayette Coll., 1932; A.M., Hahnemann Med. Coll., 1932; Mus. D., Univ. of Pa., 1937; m. Lucy P. Allen, January 21, 1889; children—Harry Coleman, Lewis Herbert, Ethel Henrietta, Dorothy Osborne. Connected with Strawbridge & Clothier, Phila., since 1879, gen. mgr. since 1903, admitted to firm, 1918, v.p., 1922, pres., 1927—. Chmn. Nat. War Service Com. Dry Goods and Dept. Stores, World War. Mem. Com. on Business Ethics, NRA. Pres. Nat. Retail Dry Goods Assn., 1925-26; colleague Am. Guild Organists. Republican. Episcopalian. Mason (K.T., 32°). Clubs: Union League, Racquet, Musical Art (pres. 1922-23), Pen and Pencil, Phila. Country, Amateur Musician. Lecturer. Home: Bala-Cynwyd, Pa. Office: 801 Market St., Phila., Pa.

TINGLEY, Edrick Knox, pres. The Gilliland Labs., Inc.; b. Harford, Pa., May 7, 1887; s. Edrick M. and Clara Louise (Wilcox) T., student U. of Pa., 19— to 1913; m. Elisabeth McFadden Parker, Nov. 3, 1915. Teacher rural and twp. schs., 1905-09; instr. and demonstrator pathology, U. of Pa. Vet. Sch., 1913-14; employed by H. K. Mulford Co., 1914-18; with The Gilliland Labs., producers of pneumonia serum and other biologics, since 1918, in charge of production rabies vaccine, tuberculins, vaccines and sera, 1920-35, dir. of labs., 1920-34, sec. and treas., 1921-34, pres. since 1934; pres. Exchange Nat. Bank, Marietta, since orgn., 1934. Pres. East Donegal Twp. Bd. of Edn., 1930-36. Active in local civic affairs. Mem. Alpha Psi, Phi Zeta. Republican. Protestant. Club: Rotary, Penn Athletic, Hamilton. Address: Marietta, Pa.

TINKER, Charles Perley, clergyman; b. New London, Conn., July 26, 1864; s. George Frederick and Rebecca (Cooms) T.; student grammar and high schs., New London, Conn., 1872-84; Ph.B., Wesleyan U., Middletown, Conn., 1889, D.D., 1915; B.D., Theol. Sem., Boston, Mass., 1892; m. Mary Bragaw, June 21, 1892; children—Ann Morgan (dec.), George Frederick, Mary (dec.). Pastor 1st M.E. Ch., Ozone Park, Long Island, N.Y., 1892-94, 1st M.E. Ch., Floral Park, Long Island, 1894-97; 1st M.E. Ch., Bay Shore, Long Island, 1897-99, Cornell Memorial Ch., New York, 1899-1905; field sec. N.Y. City Ch. Extension Soc., 1907-08; chaplain and supt. N.Y.P.E. City Mission Soc., 1909-19; rector Grace Episcopal Ch., Nutley, N.J., 1919-36, rector emeritus since 1936; editor Long Island News, Floral Park, Long Island, N.Y., 1894-97, Mission News, New York, 1909-19; business mgr. Wesleyan Argus, Middletown, Conn., 1887-89. Alternate del. Gen. Conv. of Episcopal Ch., Atlantic City, N.J., 1934; pres. Newark (N.J.) Clericus, 1932-33, Paterson Clericus of Newark Diocese, 1929-30. Mem. Alpha Delta Phi. Republican. Episcopalian. Mason (chaplain Nutley, N.J., Lodge 1935-36, Madison, N.J., Lodge, 1936-37). Club: Quill (New York; v.p. 1936-37). Author articles for mags. as specialist in social welfare and founder of "Modern Method of Administrn. in Pub. Instns." Lecturer on immigration, prison reform, pub. hosps., insane, Bible study courses. Permanent sec. of Wesleyan Class of 1889 for 50 years. Address: 46 Green Village Rd., Madison, N.J.

TINKER, Wesley Rayner, Sr., sec. and treas. F. Tinker & Sons Co.; b. Pittsburgh, Pa., May 2, 1872; s. Francis and Amelia Caroline (Haller) T.; grad. Ward Sch., Pittsburgh, Pa.; student high sch., 2 yrs., passed examination but did not attend Western U.; grad. Duff's Coll., Pittsburgh; m. Pearle Elizabeth Hoagland, Feb. 3, 1898; children—Martha Elizabeth (Mrs. Guy Courtenay Blewett), Wesley Rayner, Malcolm Hoagland, Dorothy Rose, Marjorie Janet. Began as shop sweeper, 1888; later learned machinist trade; elected sec. and treas. Samuel Trethewey & Co., Ltd., 1900, and has held same position after incorporation as F. Tinker & Sons Co., 1916-39, v.p. and treas. since 1939; dir. Allegheny Valley Bank of Pittsburgh. Republican. Mason. Home: 6819 Reynolds St. Office: 5665 Butler St., Pittsburgh, Pa.

TIPPETTS, Charles Sanford, economist, university dean; b. in Glens Falls, N.Y., Jan. 16, 1893; s. of William Henry and Emily Katharine (Bell) Tippetts; graduated high school St. Petersburg, Fla., 1910; student Mercersburg (Pa.) Acad., 1910-12; Litt.B., Princeton, 1916, A.M., 1922, Ph.D., 1924; studied law, Harvard, 1916-17; m. Margaret Elizabeth Griffith, Apr. 4, 1920; children—Katherine Bell, Charles Sanford. Instr. economics, Princeton, 1919-21 and 1923-24; asst. prof. economics State U. of Ia., 1924-25, prof., 1925-28; pro. business administrn., U. of Wash., 1928-29; prof. economics U. of Buffalo, 1920-35; dean Sch. of Business Administrn., U. of Pittsburgh, since 1935; visiting prof., summer sessions, U. of Wash., 1930, W.Va. P., 1931, Ohio State U., 1932; vice chairman Federal Home Loan Bank of Pittsburgh. Director Pittsburgh Chamber of Commerce; Dir. Pittsburgh Housing Assn.; del.-at-large to Fed. of Social Agencies; mem. advisory council, Salvation Army. Served as 1st lt. 304th Inf., 76th Div., A.E.F., World War, 1917-19; capt. inf., O.R.C., 1919-34. Mem. Am. Econ. Assn., Royal Econ. Soc., Am. Assn. for Labor Legislation, Am. Assn. Univ. Profs., Scabbard and Blade, Order of Artus, Phi Beta Kappa, Beta Gamma Sigma, Delta Sigma Rho, Alpha Kappa Psi, Delta Mu Delta, Omicron Delta Kappa. Presbyn. Mason. Club: University. Author: State Banks and Federal Reserve System, 1929; Business Organization and Control (with S. Livermore), 1932. Revisor (with L. A. Froman) of Horace White's Money and Banking, 1935. Contbr. econ. articles. Home: 405 Morewood Av., Pittsburgh, Pa.

TISCHLER, Saul, lawyer; b. Newark, N.J., Feb. 16, 1903; s. Nathan and Hannah (Levy) S.; grad. Central High Sch., Newark, 1920; LL.B., New Jersey Law Sch., 1924; LL.M., New York U., 1927; unmarried. Began as fur dyer, 1921; employed by West Side Trust, Newark, 1922-23; admitted to N.J. bar, 1924; associated with law firm Levy, Fenster & McCloskey since 1924; dir. and counsel Pollak Mfg., Kearney, N.J. Mem. Am. Bar Assn., New Jersey Bar Assn., Essex County Bar Assn., Lambda Alpha Phi, Newark Y.M. & Y.W.H.A. Former editor N.J.Law Journal. Home: 323 Leslie St. Office: 868 Broad St., Newark, N.J.

TISDALE, Wendell Holmes, biologist; b. Georgianna, Ala., Jan. 5, 1892; s. William Riley and Josephine Louiza (Higdon) T.; student Bluff Springs (Fla.) High Sch., 1906-10; B.S., Ala. Polytech. Inst., Auburn, Ala., 1914; M.S., U. of Wis., Madison, Wis., 1915, Ph.D., 1917; m. Elizabeth Emma Koch, Dec. 31, 1920; children—Glenn Evan, Marilyn Elizabeth. Scientific asst. U.S. Dept. of Agriculture, 1916-18; asso. head dept. of Botany, N.C. State Coll. of Agr. and Engring., Raleigh, N.C. 1918-19, agrl. exptl. sta., 1918-19; plant pathologist, U.S. Dept. of Agr., Washington, D.C., 1919-26; plant pathologist E. I. du Pont de Nemours & Co., Wilmington, Del., 1926-36, mgr. pest control research since 1936. Mem. A.A.A.S., Phytopathological Soc., Sigma Xi, Phi Sigma, Gamma Sigma Delta. Presyterian. Mason, Elk. Home: 915 Westover Rd. Office: du Pont Experimental Station, Wilmington, Del.

TITSWORTH, William A., lawyer; b. Brooklyn, Pa., Dec. 9, 1866; s. DeWitt A. and Alice C. (Quick) T.; ed. Scranton Commercial Coll.; m. Anna Belle Boyd, Oct. 11, 1893; 1 dau., Mrs. Dorothy Ely. Served as deputy prothonotary 1887-99, prothonotary, Susquehanna County, 1904-10; chief clerk to county commrs., 1899-1904; engaged in gen. practice of law since 1910; county solicitor, 1919-24; dir. Scranton-Lackawanna Trust Co., 1922-36, South Montrose Mfg. Co. Sec. Susquehanna Agrl. Soc., 1888-1903; mem. Susquehanna Co. Bar Assn. Mason. Has taken active interest in improvement of country roads. Home: 75 Church St. Office: 24 Public Av., Montrose, Pa.

TITUS, Harry W(altner), biol. chemist; b. Laramie, Wyo., Mar. 30, 1896; s. Edward DeVillow and Emma Elizabeth (Waltner) T.; A.B., U. of Wyo., Laramie, 1918, A.M., 1925; grad. student Stockholms Högskola and The Nobel Inst., Sweden, 1919-20; Ph.D., George Washington U., 1931; m. Annie Laurie Greene, June 20, 1923; 1 son, Harry Edwin. Asst. state chemist, Laramie, Wyo., 1918-19; head dept. chemistry, Okla. Sch. Mines and Metallurgy, Wilburton, Okla., 1920-21; nutrition chemist and asst. chemist, N.M. Coll. of Agr. & Mech. Arts, State College, N.M., 1921-23, nutrition chemist and asso. prof. animal nutrition, 1923-26; asso. biol. chemist, Bur. Animal Industry, U.S. Dept. Agr., Beltsville, Md., 1926-30, biol. chemist, 1930-37, sr. biol. chemist since 1937, in charge poultry nutrition investigations since 1928. Mem. A.A.A.S., Am. Chem. Soc., Assn. Official Agrl. Chemists, Am. Soc. Biol. Chemists, Am. Inst. of Nutrition, Poultry Sci. Assn., Washington Chem. Soc., Washington Acad. Scis., Internat. Poultry Sci. Assn., Sigma Nu, Phi Kappa Phi. Home: 3705—24th St. N.E., Washington, D.C. Office: U. S. Dept. Agr., Beltsville, Md.

TITUS, Norman Edwin, surgeon; b. New York, N.Y., July 29, 1889; s. Edward C. and Fanny (Gibson) T.; Ph.B., Yale, 1910; M.D., Columbia, 1914; m. Helen A. de Witt, June 11, 1917; children—Josiah Hornblower de Witt, Norman Edwin, Nathalie Anita, William Downing. Practiced in N.Y. City since 1914; former asso. in surgery and dir. physical therapy, Columbia U., and attending surgeon and dir. physical therapy, Vanderbilt Clinic and Presbyterian Hosp., N.Y. City; ex-pres. Am. Congress of Physical Therapy, 1929-30. Fellow A.M.A. Republican. Protestant. Club: Rumson Country. Home: Rumson, N.J. Office: 730 Fifth A., New York, N.Y.

TITUS, Paul, obstetrician, gynecologist; b. Batavia, N.Y., May 6, 1885; M.D., Yale, 1908. Asst. Universitäts Frauenklinik, Heidelberg, Germany, 1908-10; asst. in obstetrics, Johns Hopkins Hosp., Baltimore, 1910-11; resident obstetrician and gynecologist, Magee Hosp., Pittsburgh, 1911-12; now obstetrician and gynecologist, St. Margaret Memorial Hosp.; cons. bostetrician and gynecologist, Pittsburgh City Homes and Hosp., Homestead Hosp. Sec., treas. and dir. Am. Bd. of Obstetrics and Gynecology; sec., treas. Advisory Bd. for Med. Specialties; mem. advisory editorial bd., Am. Jour. of Obstetrics and Gynecology. Fellow Am. Coll. Surgeons, A.M.A., Am. Assn. of Obstetricians, Gynecologists and Abdominal Surgeons (exec. council 1929-35; pres. 1937-38), Am. Gynecol. Soc.; mem. Med. Soc. State of Pa., Pittsburgh Acad. Medicine (pres. 1929-30), Allegheny Co. Med. Soc. Awarded Commanders Cross, Order of Merit, Hungary. Author: Management of Obstetric Difficulties, 1937; Diseases of Women for the General Practitioner, 1937. Writer on obstet. and gynecol. subjects. Home: 333 Devonshire St. Office: Highland Bldg., Pittsburgh, Pa.

TITUS, Robert Richard, pres. Synthane Corpn.; b. Westbury, L.I., N.Y., Feb. 4, 1894; s. Robert Franklin and Phebe (Carpenter) T.; student, Yale; m. Ann Augusta Thorne, June 10, 1920. Engr., Diamond State Fibre Co., 1914-17, engr. to v.p., 1919-28; organized Synthane Corpn., Oaks, Pa., 1928, pres. since 1928; v.p. Diamond State Fibre Co. Served as lt. (j.g.), U.S. Navy, 1917-19. Republican. Quaker. Clubs: Merion Country, Racquet. Home: Villa Nova, Pa. Office, Oaks, Pa.

TITZELL, George Graham, banker; b. Kittanning, Pa., July 1, 1857; s. Andrew and Caroline (Graham) T.; ed. Kittanning pub. schs. and Lambeth Coll.; m. Gertrude Golden, Dec. 6, 1888; children—Marguerite Gates, George Graham, Carolyn Woodward. Held position of teller Allegheny Valley Bank, 1874-86; engaged in insurance business, 1887-95; successively asst. cashier, cashier, cashier and v.p., and chmn. bd., 1895-1938; retired, 1938, retaining title with bank. Mem. bd. Armstrong County Hosp.; treas. Kittanning Cemetery Co.; mem. of Pa. Hist. Soc.; Kittanning Sch. Bd. many yrs. Republican. Episcopalian (senior warden). Clubs: Kiwanis of Kittanning, Kittanning Country (charter member). Home: 701 N. McKean St., Kittanning, Pa.

TOBEY, Franklin Joseph, physician; b. Middleborough, Mass., Mar. 10, 1886; s. John Louis and Rebecca Eleanor (Kennedy) T.; grad. Brockton (Mass.) High Sch., 1904, post grad. study, 1904-05; student Williston Acad., Easthampton, Mass., 1905-07; M.D., U. of Pa., 1911; m. Anna Helen Wood, Jan. 29, 1913; children—John Robert, Margaret Eleanor (dec.), Franklin Joseph. Interne St. Francis Hosp., Trenton, N.J., 1911-12; physician in Newark, N.J., since Dec. 7, 1912; mem. clinical staff St. Michael's Hosp., Newark, 1912-23; asso. obstetrician, St. James Hosp., Newark, 1913-18; sr. med. staff, St. Mary's Hosp., Orange, since 1924; asso. in obstetrics, Newark Presbyn. Hosp. since 1925. Mem. Newark exec. com., Boy Scouts of America. Mem. A.M.A., Acad. of Med. of Northern N.J. (sec. since 1935), Essex County Med. Soc., Alpha Kappa Kappa. Roman Catholic. Clubs: Varsity (U. of P.); Physicians' of Essex County (Newark). Address: 11 Hazelwood Av., Newark, N.J.

TOBIAS, Clarence Edwin, Jr., headmaster, clergyman; b. Phila., Pa., Mar. 24, 1903; s. Clarence E. and Rebecca C. (Gentzsch) T.; A.B., U. of Pa., 1926, study Marine Biol. Lab., 1925; A.M., Haverford Coll., 1930; ed. Divinity Sch. of P.E. Ch., Phila., 1930-37, U. of Pa. Grad. Sch., 1930-37; m. Dorothy L. McCorkle, Sept. 4, 1926; children—Gordon Larry, Joel Allan. Head dept. sci. and religion, and registrar, Friends Central Sch., Overbrook, Pa., 1926-34; sec. of coll., Guilford (N.C.) Coll., 1934-35; headmaster, Perkiomen Sch., Pennsburg, Pa., since 1935; ordained to ministry P.E. Ch., deacon, 1938, priest, 1939; asst. to rector, Christ Ch., Pottstown, Pa., since 1939; dir. Corpn. of Haverford Coll. since 1927. Trustee Perkiomen Sch. Mem. Headmasters Assn. Phila., Phi Beta Kappa, Acacia. Republican. Episcopalian-Quaker. Mason, B.P.O.E. Clubs: Penn Athletic (Philadelphia); Lehigh Country. Home: Pennsburg, Pa.

TOBIAS, William A.; v.p. and gen. mgr. Hagerstown Light & Heat Co.; officer or dir. many companies. Home: 329 N. Potomac St. Office: Public Square, Hagerstown, Md.

TODD, Chester Warren, clergyman; b. nr. Kingston, N.Y., Sept. 22, 1881; s. William Newton and Lavinia Jane (Sheridan) T.; A.B., Coll. of Wooster (O.), 1905; student Princeton Theol. Sem., 1905-08; B.D., Theol. Sch. of Susquehanna U., Selinsgrove, Pa., 1930; (hon.) S.T.M. Luth. Theol. Sem., Chicago, 1932; (hon.) S.T.D., Temple U., 1935; m. Mathilde Reidy, June 28, 1910; children—Margaret Sheridan (Mrs. William A. Kline), Virginia Knox (Mrs. James Menzies Black, Jr.), Jane Lois. Ordained to ministr Presbyn. Ch., 1908; pastor, Coudersport, Pa., 1908-10; Mount Union, Pa., 1910-19; pastor First Presbyn. Ch., Sunbury, Pa., since 1919; dir. Presbytery of Northumberland, Inc.; stated clk. Northumberland Presbytery of Presbyn. Ch. in U.S.A. since 1934. Mem. Sigma Chi, Pi Gamma Mu. Democrat. Presbyterian. Home: 203 Race St., Sunbury, Pa.

TODD, F. Phelps, life ins.; b. Salisbury, Md., Jan. 11, 1896; s. Henry S. and Agnes H. (Phelps) T.; student Tome Institute; B.S., U. of Pa., 1918; LL.B., Temple U. Law Sch.; m. Katherine R. Cooper, Dec. 1, 1917; 1 dau., Joan. Clk. Provident Mutual Life Ins. Co., 1921-24, asst. ins. supervisor, 1924-29, insurance supervisor, 1929-31, v.p. since 1931. Served as capt., U.S. Army, World War. Trustee First Presbyn. Ch.; dir. Westminster Foundation, Philadelphia. Mem. Delta Tau Delta. Club: Union League. Home: Wyncote, Pa. Office: 4601 Market St., Philadelphia, Pa.

TODD, Gordon L., chief surgeon Mercer Memorial Hosp. Address: Mercer Memorial Hosp., Princeton, W.Va.

TODD, John Reynard, engring. exec.; b. Johnstown, Wis., Oct. 27, 1867; s. Rev. James D. and Susan S. (Webster) T.; A.B., Princeton, 1889, A.M., 1891; student New York Law Sch., 1892-93; LL.D., Davidson (N.C.) Coll. 1923; m. Alice Peck Bray, July 16, 1895; children—Frances Bray (Mrs. Newell C. Bolton), Webster Bray. Admitted to bar, 1894, and practiced at New York. Republican. Presbyn. Clubs: University, Baltusrol Golf, National Golf Links. Home: Summit, N.J.; (winter) Brewton Plantation, Yemassee, S.C.; (summer) East Hampton, L.I., N.Y. Office: 420 Lexington Av., New York, N.Y.

TODD, Kirkland Wiley, investment banker; b. Wilkinsburg, Pa., Dec. 1, 1894; so. George A. T.; C.E., Cornell U., 1918; m. Kathryn Kerr, 1920; children—Kirk W., Burt Kerr. Pres. K. W. Todd Co., investment bankers, Pittsburgh, since 1921; chmn. bd. Central Ohio Steel Products Co., Jeanette, (Pa.) Glass Co.; pres. Pittsburgh Housing Corpn.; dir. Crandall, McKenzie & Henderson, Carnegie Metals Co., Pittsburgh Valve, Foundry & Const. Co. Capt. Air Service, U.S.A., World War. Republican. Presbyn. Mason (32°, Shriner). Clubs: Duquesne, Longue Vue (Pittsburgh). Home: Woodland Road. Office: Diamond Bank Bldg., Pittsburgh, Pa.

TODD, Walter Edmund Clyde, ornithologist; b. Smithfield, O., Sept. 6, 1874; s. William and Isabella (Hunter) T.; ed. Beaver (Pa.) High Sch., 1887-91; m. Leila E. Eason, Dec. 9, 1907 (died 1927). Asst. in Div. of Econ. Ornithology and Mammalogy (later Bur. of Biol. Survey), U.S. Dept. of Agr., 1891-99; curator of ornithology, Carnegie Mus., Pittsburgh, since 1899. Fellow Am. Ornithologists' Union; mem. Biol. Soc. of Washington. Methodist. Conducted numerous scientific expdns. to the east coast of Hudson Bay and to the coast and interior of Labrador, 1901-31. Awarded Brewster medal (with M. A. Carriker), 1925, by Am. Ornithol. Union, "for meritorious work on ornithology." Author: Birds of Western Pennsylvania, 1939. Contbr. numerous papers, mostly on neo-tropical birds. Home: 197 Dravo Av., Beaver, Pa. Office: Carnegie Museum, Pittsburgh, Pa.

TOLLEY, William Pearson, college pres.; b. Honesdale, Pa., Sept. 13, 1900; s. Adolphus Charles and Emma Grace (Sumner) T.; A.B., Syracuse U., 1922, A.M., 1924; B.D., Drew Theol. Sem., 1925; A.M., Columbia, 1927, Ph.D., 1930; D.D., Mt. Union College, Alliance, Ohio, 1931; LL.D., Dickinson College, Carlisle, Pa., 1933; Litt.D., Grove City (Pa.) Coll., 1938; m. Ruth Marian Canfield, July 3, 1925; children—Nelda Ruth, William Pearson. Ordained ministry M.E. Ch., 1923; alumni sec. Drew Theol. Sem., 1925-27; instr. in systematic theology, Drew Theol. Sem., 1926-28, also asst. to pres., 1927-28; acting dean Brothers Coll. and instr. in philosophy, Drew Theol. Sem., 1928-29, dean Brothers Coll., 1929-31, and prof. philosophy, 1930-31; pres. Allegheny Coll. since July 1, 1931. Served in S.A.T.C., U.S. Army, 1918. Sec.-treas. Coll. Presidents' Assn. of Pa. since 1936; mem. Univ. Senate of M.E. Ch., 1932-36, 1938—; sec.-treas. Ednl. Assn. of M.E. Ch. since 1935; dir., Meadville City Hosp., Pub. Charities Assn. of Pa. Mem. Delta Sigma Rho, Phi Beta Kappa, Phi Kappa Phi, Pi Delta Epsilon, Pi Kappa Alpha, Omicron Delta Kappa. Rotarian. Author: The Idea of God in the Philosophy of St. Augustine, 1930. Editor: Alumni Record of Drew Theological Seminary (1867-1925), 1926. Home: Meadville, Pa.

TOLMACHOFF, Innokenty Pavlovich, geologist; b. Irkutsk, Siberia, Apr. 13, 1872; s. Paul Ivanovich and Theoctista (Michaelovna) T.; ed. Classical Gymnasium, Irkutsk, 1882-93, Imperial U., St. Petersburg, Russia, 1893-97, U. of Leipzig, 1896, U. of Munich, 1899-1900; came to U.S., 1922, and naturalized citizen, 1928; m. Eugenia Alexandrovna Karpinsky, 1899; children—Pavel, Alexander; m. 2d, Eugenia Abramovna Zakharine, 1908; children—Boris, Helen; m. 3d, Marie M. McLaughlin, Nov. 22, 1934; children—Sophia, Alexandra, Innokenty. Occupied important positions with Imperial Acad. Science, St. Petersburg, and univs. in Russia and Siberia, 1897-1922; prof. paleontology, University of Pittsburgh, 1926-1933, curator Carnegie Museum since 1922; cons. work on geography and econs. Arctic countries and Siberia, and geology and paleontology. Mem. Am. Inst. Mining and Metall. Engrs., A.A.A.S., Am. Paleontol. Soc., Am. Geo. Soc., Nat. Geog. Soc., Geol. Soc. of America, Sigma Xi, Phi Sigma, Sigma Gamma Epsilon, geol. and geog. socs., Sweden, Switzerland, Germany, Russia. Russian Orthodox. Home: 7 Mawhinney St. Office: Carnegie Mus., Pittsburgh, Pa.

TOLSON, Howard Lee, urologist Memorial Hosp. Address: 122 S. Centre St., Cumberland, Md.

TOMASSENE, Raymond A., attending eye, ear, nose and throat surgeon Ohio Valley Gen. and Wheeling hosps. Address: 1144 Market St., Wheeling, W.Va.

TOMB, James Wayne, lawyer; b. Indiana, Pa., June 11, 1895; s. David Harbison and Margaret (Rankin) T.; student Indiana (Pa.) High Sch., 1908-12, Indiana (Pa.) State Normal Sch., 1912-15, Lafayette Coll., Easton, Pa., 1915-17; m. Elizabeth Wentz, Mar. 29, 1922; children—Margaret, James Wayne. Admitted to practice Nov. 9, 1923, and since in practice at Indiana, Pa.; mem. of firm Fee and Tomb, Indiana, Pa., since 1928. Served as pvt. 28th Div., U.S. Army, 1917-19. Presbyterian. Home: 315 N. 8th St. Office: Indiana Theatre Bldg., Indiana, Pa.

TOMLINSON, Charles Speaner, physician and surgeon; b. Aaronsburg, Pa., Sept. 25, 1885; s. Frank S. and Ida Minerva (Leitzel) T.; M.D., Hahnemann Med. Coll., Phila., Pa., 1909; m. Valedia Griffin, June 3, 1912; children—Margaret Jane (Mrs. Paul C. Confer), Mary Elizabeth. Engaged in gen. practice of medicine and surgery at Milton, Pa., since 1910; chief of staff, Evangelical Hosp., Lewisburg, Pa., since 1926; pres. Milton Bd. of Health. Served as pres. and dir. Community Plan Co. since 1928. Dir. Y.M.C.A. Mem. Am. Med. Assn., Am. Inst. Homeopathy, Pa. State Homeopathic Soc., Pa. State and Montour Co. med. socs. Republican. Presbyn. Mason. B.P.O.E. Club: Manufacturers. Home: 250 Broadway. Office: 108 S. Front St., Milton, Pa.

TOMLINSON, George Milton, M.D.; b. Philadelphia, Pa., May 18, 1886; s. Eden Seeley and Mary Ellen (Wright) T.; grad. Central High Sch., Philadelphia, 1904; M.D., Jefferson Med. Coll., 1908; m. Florence Elizabeth Crompton, June 28, 1911; children—Lenora May, George Milton, John Lewis, Paul Vail, Florence Elizabeth. In gen. practice of medicine since 1908; neurologist Jefferson Med. Hosp., 1918-29; neuro-psychiatrist Philadelphia Gen. Hosp., 1920-26. Pub. sch. visitor, 1915-31. Organizer, 1917, dir., 1917-18, Am. Red Cross Auxiliaries No. 193 and 391; organizer, 1933, and since pres. Phillies Knot Hole Baseball Leagues for boys under 17, Phila. Amateur Twilight League for Older Youths, 1934; organizer, 1935, and since exec. dir. Am. Youth Sponsor League, Inc.; Phila. commr. Am. Baseball Congress, 1938; mem. Philadelphia Commr. of Recreation since 1936. Mem. Philadelphia County Med. Soc. (mem. com. on social health and hygience since 1937), Sons Vets. of Civil War, The American Mechanics Order, Sons of St. George; mem. ednl. com. North East Phila. Chamber of Commerce, 1932-35. Gen. supt. East Allegheny M.E. Ch. Sch. since 1933; pres. St. George's M.E. Fellowship, 1932-37. Mason (Shriner). Writer articles on med. subjects. Address: 114 E. Allegheny Av., Philadelphia, Pa.

TOMLINSON, Norman Balderston, editor and pub.; b. Trenton, N.J., Oct. 21, 1895; s. Ernest Hibbs and Mary Briggs (Balderston) T.; student Morristown (N.J.) High Sch., 1906-10, Morris Acad., Morristown, N.J., 1910-12, Harvard Law Sch., 1916-17; Litt.B., Princeton U., 1916; m. Loretta Elizabeth Barris, June 5, 1926; children—Norman Balderston, Diane Elizabeth, Jean Elinor. Became owner Morristown (N.J.) Daily Record, 1919, and since editor and pub.; v.p. Hanover Bldg. & Loan Assn., Morristown, since 1930. Served as sergt. 1st class, U.S. Army, during World War; 1st lt., O.R.C., 1919-34. Mem. Morristown Bd. Edn., 1921-32, pres., 1930-32. Mem. Am. Legion (founder Morristown Post, 1919, and adj., 1919-21), Morristown Chamber of Commerce (dir.), Exempts of Vol. Fire Dept. Republican. Presbyterian. Clubs: Rotary (Morristown, N.J.; sec. 1926-33); Princeton Lackawanna Alumni; Spring Brook (N.J.) Country. Home: 15 Georgian Rd. Office: 55 Park Pl., Morristown, N.J.

TOMLINSON, Paul Greene, author; b. New Brunswick, N.J., Feb. 8, 1888; s. Everett Titsworth and Ann (Greene) T.; A.B., Princeton, 1909; LL.B., New York Law Sch., 1911; m. Gabriella Prout, Jan. 1917; children—Henry Prout, Ann. Financial editor McClure's Magazine, 1917-23, The Outlook, 1919-24, The Elks Magazine, 1923-31, American Legion Weekly, 1924, Harper's Magazine, 1925-36; director and secretary of Princeton U. Press, 1918-38; direction Public Opinion Quarterly. Member Princeton Borough Council, 1923; secretary Princeton Hospital, 1924-33. Baptist. Clubs: Ivy, Nassau (Princeton); Princeton (N.Y.). Author: To the Land of the Caribou, 1914; In Camp on Bass Island, 1915; The Trail of Black Hawk, 1915; The Strange Gray Canoe, 1916; The Trail of Tecumseh, 1916; A Leader of Freemen, 1917; Bob Cook and the German Spy, 1917; Bob Cook and the German Air Fleet, 1919; A Princeton Boy Under the King, 1921; A Princeton Boy in the Revolution, 1922; A History of the Trenton Banking Company, 1929; History of the Princeton Bank and Trust Co., 1934. Home: Rosedale Rd., Princeton, N.J.

TOMLINSON, Roy Everett, pres. National Biscuit Co.; b. Chicago, Dec. 4, 1877; s. Everett S. and Genevieve (Rush) T.; LL.B., U. of Wis., 1901; m. Eleanor Parsons, Dec. 25, 1905; children—Harriet, Everett. With Nat. Biscuit Co. since 1902, in legal dept. until 1917, 3d v.p., 1915-17, became pres. 1917; dir. D.L.& W. R.R. Co., Am. Can Co.; trustee Montclair Trust Company, Prudential Life Insurance Co. Republican. Conglist. Clubs: Union League (New York); Montclair Golf, Eastward Ho Golf. Home: 89 Llewellyn Rd., Montclair, N.J., and Chatham, Mass. Office: 449 W. 14th St., New York, N.Y.

TOMPKINS, Raymond Sidney, pub. utility exec.; b. Nyack, N.Y., Oct. 12, 1890; s. Charles Edgar and May Louise (McCort) T.; LL.B., Georgetown U. Law Sch., 1911; grad. student Johns Hopkins U., 1920-23; m. Emily Marie Lanning, Mar. 10, 1920; children—Raymond S., Jr., Emily Lanning. Admitted to D.C. bar, 1912 and entered practice of law in Washington; editor Post, morning daily, Frederick, Md., 1914-16; reporter, The Sun, Baltimore, 1916-18, war corr. in France, 1918-19; European corr. The Sun, 1923-24; asst. to pres. United Railways & Electric Co., Baltimore, 1925-33; dir. information and service, head pub. relations dept., Baltimore Transit Co. since 1933. Vice chmn. and mem. exec. com. Baltimore Chapter Am. Red Cross, chmn. Roll Call, 1939; v.p. Travelers Aid Soc. Chmn. pub. com. Am. Transit Assn. Mem. Sigma Nu Phi. Democrat. Episcopalian. Clubs: Twelve-Thirty, Advertising (v.p.), Mt. Washington Country (Baltimore). Author: Story of the Rainbow Division, 1920; Maryland Fighters in the Great War, 1920. Contbr. to mags. News commentator on radio since 1934. Home: 5415 Falls Rd. Terrace. Office: Equitable Bldg., Baltimore, Md.

TOOLAN, John Edward, lawyer; b. Perth Amboy, N.J., June 23, 1894; s. John and Elizabeth (McGuirk) T.; LL.B., Cornell U., 1916; m. Gertrude Maher, June 25, 1932; children—John Edward, David Stuart. Admitted to bar, 1916, and since practiced at Perth Amboy, N.J.

Served as 2d lt., 74th Inf., U.S. Army, Asst. prosecutor, Middlesex Co., N.J., 1921-26, prosector, 1926-31; state senator from Middlesex Co. since 1933. Mem. Perth Amboy Bar Assn., Middlesex Co. Bar Assn., N.J. Bar Assn., Am. Bar Assn., Gamma Eta Gamma. Democrat. Catholic. Clubs: K.C., Elk. Colonia (N.J.) Golf; Raritan Yacht (Perth Amboy, N.J.); Lake Placid (New York). Home: 134 High St. Office: 216 Smith St., Perth Amboy, N.J.

TOOLE, Thomas Aloysius, gen. ins. agency; b. Wilkes-Barre, Pa., June 24, 1901; s. James and Anna (Finn) T.; grad. Mansfield State Teachers Coll., 1923, St. Thomas' Coll., 1930; unmarried. Empld. as clk., 1923-30; propr. gen. ins. agency since 1930; elected alderman City of Wilkes-Barre, Pa., for term 6 yrs., 1933-40, resigned, 1937; mem. Pa. Ho. of Rep. since 1937; mem. city council, Wilkes-Barre, for term, 1938-42; now dir. Dept. Pub. Safety, City of Wilkes-Barre. Mem. Wilkes-Barre Republics. Democrat. Catholic. F.O.E. Club. Bohemian. Home: 32 E. Sheridan St. Office: 8 Main St., Wilkes-Barre, Pa.

TOOTHAKER, Charles Robinson, curator; b. Phila., May 4, 1873; s. Charles Everett (M.D.) and Zetta (Elder) T.; grad. Central Manual Training High Sch., Phila., 1890; spl. course in geology under E. D. Cope; other spl. courses; m. Martha Taylor McCandles, Sept. 27, 1904. Mineralogist in employ of A. E. Foote, Phila., 1890-97; asst. curator, 1898-1904, curator since 1904, Phila Commercial Museum, having charge of exhibits and ednl. work extending to schs. in all parts of Pa.; lecturer on commercial geography; lecturer U. of Pa. Commr. in charge Pa. mining exhibit, Atlanta Expn., 1895; consul of Czechoslovakia; former consul of Colombia. Decorated Officer Order of White Lion of Czechoslovakia. Mem. Geog. Soc. Phila., Pa. Soc. S.R., Schoolmen's Club, Mineralogical Club, Am. Assn. of Museums. Republican. Author: Commercial Raw Materials, 1905. Home: 4217 Pine St., Philadelphia, Pa.

TOPANELIAN, Edward, Jr., engr.; b. Worcester, Mass., Oct. 23, 1901; s. Edward and Fanny Augusta (Nichols) T.; grad. Worcester North High Sch., 1919; B.S. in E.E., Worcester Poly. Inst., 1923; E.E. (post-grad.), 1925; m. Caroline Taylor Triplett, June 29, 1929. Asst. effieiency engr. Worcester Light Co., 1921; engr. of Motor test Westinghouse Elec. & Mfg. Co., 1922; statistician with Albert S. Richey, cons. engr., 1924; research student Westinghouse Elec. & Mfg. Co., 1923-25, engr. ry. equipment, 1925-30; chief elec. engr. in charge Diesel-Electric locomotives H. K. Porter (locomotive) Co., 1930-31; consultg. engr., Climax Locomotive Co., 1931; representative Equitable Life Ins. Co. of Ia., 1932-33; engr. service station equipment tests Gulf Research & Development Co., 1933, engr. in charge rotary devices section, 1934-35, engr. in charge oil field pumping div. (rotary devices and subsurface equipment) since 1935, also ranking engr. with provisional charge of engring. dept. since 1935. Asso. mem. Am. Inst. E.E. Republican. Presbyterian. Clubs: Gulf Emclub (past pres.); Westinghouse and Gulf Tennis, Gulf Golf. Holder various patents. Engaged in research in hydraulics, supercharging, bearings, pneumatics, materials. Coach, Pittsburgh Industrial League Basketball Champions, 1938-39. Home: Riverside Heights, Verona, Pa. Office: Box 2038, Pittsburgh, Pa.

TORRENCE, Frank Miller, coll. prof.; b. Punxsutawney, Pa., Feb. 19, 1879; s. George Hugh and Virginia Caroline (Miller) T.; B.S. in M.E., Pa. State Coll., 1905, M.E., same, 1912; m. Jean Lindsay, Aug. 26, 1909; children—Joseph Lindsay (dec.), Ruth (Mrs. Harry H. Balthaser), Jean Floyd (Mrs. Clinton G. Knoll, Jr.), Barbara. Employed as printer before and while in coll.; apprentice Baldwin Locomotive Works, 1905-07; machinist, Woodward Iron Co., Birmingham, Ala., L.&N. R.R., Louisville, Ky., 1907-09; draftsman, Pa. R.R., Altoona, Pa., 1909-11; asso. with Pa. State Coll. continuously since 1911, instr. drawing and descriptive geometry, 1911-13, asst. prof., 1914-18, asso. prof. of Heatg. and Ventil. since 1919. Served as 2d sergt. Pa. Vol. Inf. in Spanish-Am. War, 1898. Former trustee Centre Co. Hosp. Former mem. Am. Soc. Mech. Engrs. Mem. Acacia. Republican. Mason. Home: 333 E. Foster Av., State College, Pa.

TORRENCE, Robert McIlvaine, v.p. Miss. Glass Co.; b. New Haven, Pa., Feb. 3, 1873; s. Thomas Rogers and Gertrude Olivia (McIlvaine) T.; student Marston's U. Sch., Baltimore, 1887-92; A.B., Johns Hopkins U., 1895; m. Helen H. Leeds, Feb. 15, 1922; 1 son, Robert Grier. Began newspaper work with Pittsburgh Chronicle Telegraph, 1895; asso. with Westinghouse Electric & Mfg. Co. until began as glass mfr., Washington, Pa.; was one of incorporators, treas. and sec. Highland Glass Co. which was merged with Western Glass Co., 1928; v.p., dir. and mem. exec. com. Miss. Glass Co., N.Y. City, since 1932. Became mem. Council of Nat. Defense at beginning of World War; transferred to Chem. and Explosive Div. upon organization of War Industries Bd. where he served as "Dollar-a-Year-Man"; chief of asbestos, magnesia, rutile, chemical glass and stoneware sects. Mem. Mil. Order Loyal Legion, Delta Phi. Republican. Episcopalian. Clubs: Elkridge, Maryland, Gibson Island (Baltimore). Author: Torrence and Allied Families. Home: 110 Edgevale Road, Baltimore, Md.

TOTH, Alexander, clergyman; b. Korosladany, Hungary, Oct. 12, 1884; s. Alexander and Janka (Borovszky) T.; come to U.S., 1909, naturalized citizen, 1925; ed. Gymnasium, Budapest and Bekes, Hungary, 1894-1902, Theol. Sem., Debrecen, Hungary, 1902-06, Theol. Sem., Geneva, Switzerland, 1907-09; (hon.) D.D., Franklin and Marshall Coll., 1925; m. Rose Nagy, of Hungary, Aug. 19, 1909 (died 1931); children—Alexander Bela, Magdalene Edith, Elizabeth Yolanda; m. 2d, Norma Henwood LeFever, June 19, 1938. Began as administrator, Karczag, Hungary, 1909; pastor, Buffalo, N.Y., 1909-11; pastor First Hungarian Reformed Ch., Cleveland, O., 1911-22; prof. Hungarian lang., lit. and history, Franklin and Marshall Coll. and instr. Theol. Sem., Lancaster, Pa., 1922-36; Hungarian Sec. Bd. Home Missions of Reformed Ch. in U.S., Phila., Pa. since 1936; editor Reformatusok Lapja, oldest Hungarian Ch. paper in America, pub. at Pittsburgh, Pa.; dir., past v.p., past treas. Hungarian Reformed Fed. of America. Mem. Reformed Ch. Home: 55 N. West End Av., Lancaster, Pa.

TOTZAUER, Josef, concert violinist, teacher; b. Trossau, Sudetenland, July 7, 1896; s. Rudolf and Catherine (Breitfelder) T.; ed. Institute of Music, Rochlitz, Germany, 1910-14, Conservatory of Music, Leipzig, Germany, 1918-22; also Trinity Coll. of Music, London; pupil of Hans Sitt, Leopold Auer, Walther Davisson, Johannes Merkel; m. Anna Falb, July 31, 1929; 1 dau., Maria Theresa. Came to U.S., 1922, naturalized, 1927. Began as vilolinist, 1914; formerly 1st violinist Symphony Orchestra, Zeitz, Germany; 1st violin Opera House, Danzig; concertmaster City Orch., Doebeln, Germany; 2d concertmaster Leipzig Philharmonic Orchestra, Germany; concert tour through U.S., 1922-24; dir. of Paterson Philharmonic Orchestra until 1930; teacher of violin and string instruments, Ridgewood, N. J., since 1930. Home: 252 Godwin Av., Ridgewood, N.J.

TOULSON, William Houston, physician; b. Chestertown, Md., July 14, 1887; s. Milbourne Asbury and Sarah Isabelle (Bordley) T.; A.B., Washington Coll., Chestertown, Md., 1908; M. D., U. of Md. Med. Sch., Baltimore, 1913; hon. M.Sc., Washington Coll., 1910; m. Helen Joynes, Oct. 21, 1921; children—Helen Isabelle, Sabra Joynes, William Houston, Jr. Interne University Hosp., Baltimore, 1913-17; asst. in urology, U. of Md. Med. Sch., Baltimore, Md., 1920-25, asso. in urology, 1925-30, prof. urology since 1930; chief of div. urology, Baltimore City Hosp. since 1923; visiting staff, Union Memorial, Church Home, Bon Secours hosps.; consultant to U.S. Marine Hosp. since 1925. Served in Med. Corps, B.E.F. in France, 1917-18, with A.E.F., 1918-19, disch. capt. Med. Corps, U.S.A. Fellow Am. Coll. Surgeons. Mem. A.M.A., Am. Assn. Genito Urinary Surgeons, Am. Urol. Assn., Internat. Soc. Urology. Democrat. Methodist. Clubs: University, Gibson Island. Home: 5403 Falls Rd. Terraces. Office: Medical Arts Bldg., Baltimore, Md.

TOWER, Carl Vernon, prof. philosophy; b. Dayton, O., Dec. 14, 1869; s. Charles Frederic and Anne Judson (Bisbee) T.; A.B., Brown U., 1893, A.M., same, 1895; Ph.D., Cornell U., 1898; grad. study Clark Univ., 1900-01; m. Emma Worman Powell, of Dayton, O., June 10, 1896 (dec.); children—Eugenie Louise (Mrs. Charles Warren Staples), Emma Powell (Mrs. Lee Carroll Messick); m. 2d, Elizabeth Burke, of Brockville, Ont., Sept. 8, 1898; 1 dau., Katharine Bisbee. Asst. in psychol. lab., Brown U., 1895-96; instr. philosophy, U. of Mich., 1898-1900; asst. to pres. Clark U., 1900-01; prof. philosophy, Knox Coll., 1901-02; prof. philosophy, U. of Vt., 1902-09; asso. prof. philosophy, U. of Mich., 1909-10; act. prof. philosophy, Trinity Coll., Hartford, 1912-13; prof. philosophy, Ursinus Coll., Collegeville, Pa. since 1913. Mem. Am. Philos. Assn., British Inst. of Philosophy, Delta Upsilon, A.A.A.S., Am. Assn. Univ. Profs., Pa. Acad. Sci. Baptist. Home: 32 Sixth Av., Collegeville, Pa.

TOWN, Charles MacLallan, life ins.; b. Philadelphia, Pa., Dec. 14, 1890; s. Henry W. and Gertrude (Eagle) T.; B. S. in Economics, St. Joseph's Coll., Philadelphia, 1907; studied U. of Pa., 1908-11; m. Julia M. Coyle, Oct. 12, 1916; 1 dau., Mary Coyle (dec.). V.p. and treas. Bell Union Coal and Mining Co., 1916-37; pres. Town Coal Co., 1917-27, Bell Union Coal Co., 1922-32; v.p. Am. Catholic Union (ins.) since 1918; dir. Pa. Mutual Life Ins. Co. since 1917, 2d v.p., 1919-30, 1st v.p., 1930-32, v.p. and treas. since 1932. Mem. Philadelphia Chapter S.A.R., S.R. Decorated Knight of the Holy Sepulchre. Mem. K.C. (4°). Club: Penn Athletic. Home: 911 N. 63d St., Philadelphia, Pa.

TOWNE, Robert Duke, editor, pub.; b. Warren, O., Jan. 4, 1866; s. Levi and Mary Ellen (Duke) T.; A.B., St. Lawrence U., Canton, N.Y., 1888; m. Maude Agnes Barackman, June 28, 1888; children—Duke (dec.), Marian Etta, Bertha Violet. Served in pulpit, Marlboro, N.H., and Lewiston, Me., 1888-98; propr. Lewiston (Me.) Daily Sun, 1898; staff Newark (N.J.) Evening News, 1900-05; editor Judge, New York, 1905, Judge and Leslie's Weekly, 1906-07; pres. Judge Co., 1907-08; propr. Scranton (Pa.) Tribune, 1908-10, Tribune-Republican, 1910-12; consolidated with Scranton Truth, 1912; founded Scranton Daily News, 1915; dir. citizenship campaign, Phila. North American, 1920; staff of Public Ledger, 1923-27; president Gazette Publishing Company and Suburban Newspapers, Incorporated, 1926-32; director and treasurer Chas. H. Ingersoll Dollar Pen Co., 1928-34. Writer of syndicated series, "The Great Awakening," appearing in various daily newspapers; editor of magazine, The Aero, since 1915. Del. at large from Pa. to Rep. Nat. Conv., 1912; a founder of Progressive Party. Lecturer on civics and economics. Home: 2029 Walnut St., Philadelphia, Pa.

TOWNSEND, G. Marshall; editor Milford Chronicle. Address: Milford, Del.

TOWNSEND, John G., Jr., senator; b. Worcester County, Md., May 31, 1871; s. John G. and Meredith (Dukes) T.; ed. country sch., Md.; LL.D., U. of Del.; m. Jennie L. Collins, July 28, 1890. Largely identified with banking, farming and business interests in Del.; pres. Baltimore Trust Co., banks at Selbyville, Bridgeville and Cambden (Del.), Selbyville Mfg. Co., Indian Swan Orchard Co., John G. Townsend, Jr. & Co., etc. Mem. Gen. Assembly of Del., 1901; del. Rep. Nat. Conv., 1908; gov. of Del., term 1917-21; mem. U.S. Senate, 2 terms 1929-42. Col. on staffs of Govs. Lea, Pennewill, and Miller. Member Mt. Rushmore Commn., Del. Gen. Conf., M.E. Church, 1912; president trustees Wilmington Conf. Acad.; member board trustees Washington College., Md., American University, Washington, D.C. and Goucher Coll. Mason, Odd Fellow, etc. Clubs: Young Men's Republican, Old Colony. Home: Selbyville, Del.

TOWNSEND, John Macdonald, v.p. and treas. Townsend Co.; b. New Brighton, Pa., Nov. 27, 1877; s. Charles C. and Juliet (Bradford) T.;

ed. U. of Mich.; m. Myrtle Myers, Jan. 28, 1904; 1 son, Edward Myers. With Townsend Co. since 1898, serving in various capacities, elected v.p. and treas., 1917, now also dir.; dir. Farmers Nat. Bank of Beaver Falls. Dir. Grove Cemetery, Beaver Valley Gen. Hosp., Am. Red Cross (Beaver County Chapter). Mem. Beaver County Mfrs. Assn. (dir.), Mil. Order Loyal Legion. Clubs: Rotary, Beaver Valley Country. Home: Patterson Heights, Beaver Falls, Pa. Office: care Townsend Co., New Brighton, Pa.

TOWNSEND, Marion Ernest, educator; b. Hammondsport, N.Y., May 16, 1889* s. (Rev.) Colwell and Lena Jane (Davis) T.; A.B., Colgate, 1912, A.M., 1922; A.M., Columbia, 1927, Ph.D., 1932; m. Blanche Buckbee, June 26, 1912; 1 dau., Agatha. Began as teacher in rural sch., 1907; prin. pub. sch., Lyndonville, N.Y., 1912-16; supervising prin., Brocton, N.Y., 1916-18; supt. schs., Walden, N.Y., 1918-21, Boonton, N.J., 1921-23, Millville, N.J., 1923-26; asst. supt. schs., Trenton, N.J., 1926-28; asst. commr. of edn., State of N.J., 1928-29; pres. N.J. State Teachers Coll., Newark, since 1929. Pres. Interstate Conf. on Teacher Training, N.J. Council on Adult Edn.; mem. exec. com. N.J. Mental Hygiene Assn.; mem. Nat. Advisory Bd. on Mental Hygiene in Edn.; mem. N.E.A., Nat. Soc. Study of Edn., Personnel Research Fed., Am. Acad. of Polit. and Social Science, Am. Council on Edn., Exploratory Com. on Emotions in Edn.; Eastern States Assn. of Professional Schs. for Teachers (pres.), Am. Ednl. Research Assn., N.J. Psychol. Council, N.J. Council of Edn., Nat. Com. on Mental Hygiene, N.J. Council of Edn. (pres.), Phi Delta Theta, Phi Beta Kappa, Phi Delta Kappa, Kappa Delta Pi. Republican. Unitarian. Mason. Clubs: Essex County Torch, N.J. Schoolmasters; Tawse (Columbia U.); Kiwanis Club of Newark (bd. dirs.); Newark Athletic Club. Author: Administration of Student Personnel Services in Teacher Training Institutions, 1932. Lecturer on mental hygiene and occupations. Home: Glen Ridge, N.J. Office: State Teachers College, Newark, N.J.

TOWNSEND, Sylvester D., banker; b. Odessa, Del., July 25, 1870; s. George L. and Cornelia (Scott) T.; ed. pub. schs.; m. Helen Price Cheairs, Oct. 16, 1902; children—Helen C., Sylvester D. Teller Delaware City Nat. Bank, 1895-1902; treas. Chambersburg Trust Co., 1902-03; with Wilmington Trust Co. since 1903, treas., later v.p., pres. since 1934; dir. Penroad Corpn., Farmers Mutual Fire Ins. Co. Dir. and treas. Wilmington Chamber of Commerce; v.p. Tri-State Regional Planning Fed.; dir. New Castle Regional Planning Bd.; dir. Wilmington Park Bd.; dir. Penn Hall Sch. Republican. Episcopalian. Clubs: Wilmington, Wilmington Country, Wilmington Whist. Home: 1304 Broome St. Office Wilmington Trust Co., Wilmington, Del.

TOWNSEND, T. C.; mem. law firm Townsend Bock, Moore & Townsend. Address: Charleston, W.Va.

TOWSON, Charles Emory, physician; b. Baltimore, Md., Nov. 28, 1891; s. Rev. Emory Shailer and Gertrud (Hugg) T.; student Princeton U., 1911-13; A.B., Whitworth Coll., Spokane, Wash., 1917; B.S., W.Va Univ., Morgantown, W.Va., 1923; M.D., U. of Pa., 1925; unmarried. Fruit ranching, Yakima Valley, Wash., 1913-14; bank clerk, Seattle, Wash., 1914; ins. salesman, Seattle, 1914-15; clerk, Spokane, Wash., 1915-16; salesman, Armour & Co., Spokane, 1917; teacher in pvt. sch., Spokane, 1917-18; real estate appraiser, Nitro, W.Va., 1919; with South Penn Oil Co., 1920-21; interne Germantown (Pa.) Hosp., 1925-27, St. Christopher's Hosp., 1927; in practice of medicine, Phila., since Mar. 1927; formerly on ear, nose and throat staffs of St. Christopher's Hosp., Phila. Hosp. for Contagious Diseases, Memorial Hosp.; now otolaryngologist Germantown Hosp.; asst. otologist Jefferson Med. Coll. Hosp., chief clin. asst. Jefferson Hosp., asso. in otology Jefferson Med. Coll., Phila. Enrolled in 1st O.T.C., Presidio, 1917, hon. disch. on account of vision; enlisted in Inf., U.S. Army, 1918; transferred to Air Service; with A.E.F. 1 year; disch. as sergt., 1919. Diplomate Am. Bd. of Otolaryngology; fellow Am. Acad. Ophthalmology and Otolaryngology, Am. Coll. Surgeons, Phila. Coll. Physicians, A.M.A.; mem. Phila. Laryngol. Soc. Club: Exchange of Germantown (pres.). Contbr. of articles to med. jours.; radio speaker on med. subjects. Home: 155 E. Walnut Lane, Germantown. Office: Medical Arts Bldg., and Germantown Professional Bldg., Philadelphia, Pa.

TRABUE, Marion Rex; b. nr. Kokomo, Ind., Apr. 30, 1890; s. Otto A. and Mary Emma (Long) T.; student DePauw U., 1907-08; A.B. Northwestern U., 1911; A.M., Columbia, 1914, Ph.D., 1915; m. Emma Wilkie Small, Apr. 20, 1913; children—Bruce McDougal, Douglas Small. Prin. high sch., Fairbury, Ill., 1911-12, Hinsdale, Ill., 1912-13; with Teachers' Coll. (Columbia), 1913-22, as research scholar, student asst., instr. and asst. prof. edn., 1917-22, dir. Bur. Ednl. Service, 1919-22; prof. ednl. administration, 1922-37, dir. Bur. Ednl. Research, 1923-37, and dir. consol. univ. div. of education, 1935-37, U. of N.C.; dean School of Education and dir. of summer sessions, Pennsylvania State College since 1937; executive secretary com. on diagnosis and training Employment Stabilization Research Inst., U. of Minn., 1931-33. Head of Diagnosis Div. of the Adjustment Service, N.Y. City, 1933; mem. Federal Council of U. S. Employment Service since 1934, tech. dir. occupational research, 1933-36; mem. staff American Youth Commn., Washington, 1936. Lt. and capt., psychol. examiner and psychologist, U.S.A., 1917-18. Mem. Personnel Research Fed., A.A.A.S., N.E.A., Am. Psychol. Association, Am. Statis. Assn., Eugenics Research Assn., Nat. Soc. Study of Education (dir., 1932-39), Soc. College Teachers of Edn. (pres. 1938-39), Am. Educational Research Assn. (pres. 1925-26), Am. Assn. for Applied Psychology, Nat. Vocational Guidance Assn., Nat. Conf. on Research in English (pres. 1926-27), Phi Beta Kappa, Phi Delta Kappa, Pi Gamma Mu, Psi Chi and Phi Kappa Phi. Club: Centre County Country. Author: (with E. L. Thorndike and J. L. Stenquist) Intellectual Status of Children Who Are Public Charges, 1915; Completion Test Language Scales, 1916; Public Education in Nassau Co., N.Y., 1917; (with F. P. Stockbridge) Measure Your Mind, 1920; Measuring Results in Education, 1924; (with B. A. Stevens) The Trabue-Stevens Spellers, 1928; (with Bessie B. Goodrich) Today's English, 1935. Editor-in-chief The North Carolina Teacher, 1924-25; asso. editor, Jour. Ednl. Research, Jour. of Experimental Edn. Home: 129 Ridge Av., State College, Pa.

TRACY, (William) Lee, actor; b. Atlanta, Ga., Apr. 14, 1898; s. William Lindsey and Ray (Griffith) T.; student Union Coll., Schenectady, N.Y., 1917-18; m. Helen I. Thomas, July 20, 1938. Began as actor, 1919; starred in play, Broadway, N.Y. City, 1926-27, Front Page, 1928; entered motion pictures, 1928; returned to stage for plays Oh Promise Me and Louder Please, 1930; starred in various talking pictures under contract to Paramount Corpn.; now under contract to RKO Radio Pictures; appeared in play The Gag Stays In, New York, 1938; starred in Idiots Delight, London, England, 1938. Served as 2d lt. inf., U.S.A, World War. Presbyn. Clubs: Green Room (New York); Masquer's (Hollywood). Home: Trucksville, Pa. Address: 7 St. James St., London, England.

TRACY, Martha, coll. prof.; b. Plainfield, N.J., Apr. 10, 1876; d. Jeremiah Evarts and Martha Sherman (Green) T.; B.A., Bryn Mawr Coll., 1898; M.D., Woman's Med. Coll. of Pa., 1904; studied Sheffield Scientific Sch. (Yale) and U. of Pa.; Dr. P.H., U. of Pa., 1917; unmarried. With Research Dept. of Experimental Pathology, Cornell U. Med. Sch., N.Y. City, 1904-07; asst. to Meningitis Commn., New York Bd. of Health, 1905; worker under Huntington Fund for Cancer Research, N.Y. City, 1907-19; prof. physiol. chemistry, 1912-20, and dean 1918-24, dean and prof. preventive medicine, 1924-31, dean since 1931, Woman's Med. Coll. of Pa. Member Phila. Board of Health, 1936. Fellow Am. Coll. Physicians, College of Physicians of Phila., A.M.A.; mem. Phila. Co. Med. Soc., Am. Assn. Univ. Women, Sigma Xi, Phi Beta Kappa (hon.), Alpha Omega Alpha. Presbyn. Clubs: Women's City, Business and Professional Woman's. Address: Woman's Medical College of Pa., East Falls, Philadelphia, Pa.

TRAGESER, Charles Alphonse, lawyer; b. Baltimore, Md., Apr. 16, 1896; s. Alphonse J. and Margaret (Kennedy) T.; student Baltimore Poly. Inst., 1910-14, Strayers Bus. Coll., Baltimore, Md., 1914-16; B.C.S., U. of Md., 1926; LL.B., U. of Md. Law Sch., Baltimore, 1922; C.P.A., U. of Md., 1928; m. Virginia B. Rhodes, June 26, 1929. Admitted to Md. bar, 1922 and since engaged in gen. practice of law at Baltimore; certified pub. accountant in practice since 1928; counsel Baltimore Transit Co.; sec., treas. and counsel Chatham Realty Co. since 1937. Served as sergt. maj., U.S.A., 1918-19; with A.E.F. in France; 1st lt. Md. N.G., 1924-27. Mem. Am. Bar Assn., Bar Assn. Baltimore City, Md. Assn. Certified Pub. Accountants, Delta Theta Pi. Democrat. Roman Catholic. Club: University (Washington, D.C.). Home: 308 Broxton Rd. Office: Equitable Bldg., Baltimore, Md.

TRAIL, Grover Cleveland, lawyer; b. Marshes, W.Va., Nov. 22, 1892; s. Harvey Washington and Narcissus (Lester) T.; student W.Va. Univ. Law Coll., 1915; m. Wilma Diehl, Sept. 17, 1919; 1 son, Grover C.; m 2d, Belma Bailey, Apr. 12, 1933; 1 son, Robert W. Admitted to W.Va. bar, 1917 and since engaged in gen. practice of law at Beckley; mem. firm Hutchinson, Crouse and Trail since 1937; served as police judge City of Beckley, 1930-31; asst. prosecuting atty. of Raleigh Co., 1925-27. Served as 2d lt. inf. U.S.A. during World War. Mem. W.Va. and Raleigh County bar assns. Phi Sigma Kappa. Republican. Elk. Home: 25 W. C St. Office: Heber and Main Sts., Beckley, W.Va.

TRAINER, G. H., developer crude oil and natural gas; b. West Union, W.Va., Mar. 27, 1861; s. William and Louisa (Hoult) T.; student High Sch., 1876 to 1880; m. V. C. Davis, Sept. 27, 1884. Merchant, about 20 yrs.; since engaged in development of oil and natural gas throughout W.Va., O. and Okla.; v.p. and dir. First Nat. Bank of Salem. V.p., dir. and trustee Salem Coll. Republican. Methodist. Club: Kiwanis (Salem). Has made many donations to help maintain Salem Coll. and to help young people attain college education. Address: Salem, W.Va.

TRAISTER, Harold Wesley, dir. of elementary edn.; b. Widnoon, Pa., June 12, 1903; s. Charles E. and Emma Mae (Shumaker) T.; grad. New Bethlehem (Pa.) High Sch., 1921; student Clarion (Pa.) State Teachers Coll., 1921-23; B.S., in edn., U. of Pittsburgh, 1926, A.M. in secondary edn., 1929, Ed.D. in elementary edn., 1939; m. Mabel Hawk, Dec. 22, 1923; 1 son, Edwin Harold. Teacher rural school, 1921-22, prin. Junior High Sch., Kitanning, Pa., 1923-26; teacher of history, McKeesport (Pa.) High Sch., 1926-29; prin. elementary edn., McKeesport West Side, 1929-30; dir. elementary edn., Beaver Falls, Pa., since 1930. Mem. Bd. of Trade, Beaver Falls, 1936-38; dir. Beaver Falls Rotary Club; mem. Pa. Curriculum Com. in Mathematics. Mem. N.E.A., Pa. Edn. Assn. (pres. council of ednl. method, pres. supervisors sec. 1938). Republican. Methodist. Mason (K.T.). Home: 1930 6th Av., Beaver Falls, Pa.

TRANSUE, Stanley F., life ins.; b. Bethlehem, Pa., Sept. 19, 1895; s. Harry U. and Anna M. (Smith) T.; ed. Bethlehem (Pa.) pub. schs.; m. Laura S. Shimer, Oct. 25, 1919. Clerk Bethlehem Steel Co., 1912-16, ordnance engr., 1916-19; owner Stanley F. Transue Agency, life ins. since 1919; pres. and dir. Hotel Bethlehem. Served with Battery A., 108th F.A., World War. Republican. Mason. Clubs: Kiwanis, Bethlehem, Sanson Valley Country (Bethlehem). Home: 1805 Kenmore Av. Office: Bethlehem Trust Bldg., Bethlehem, Pa.

TRANTER, Henry, pres. Tranter Mfg. Co.; b. Pittsburgh, Pa., Oct. 13, 1865; s. William Henry and Sarah Ann (Heaps) S.; studied Scott

(Pa.) Twp. Grade Sch., 1871-72, Union Twp. (now Green Tree Borough) Grade Sch., 1873-80, Duffs Business Coll., 1881; m. Ida Belle Hershberger, Oct. 9, 1895; children—William Parke, Edith Marjorie. Grocery clerk to 1887; clerk Allegheny County boiler inspector, 1887-91; bookkeeper J. B. Sherriff Mfg. Co., 1891-92, treas. since 1892; Tranter Davison Mfg. Co.; pres. and treas. Tranter Mfg. Co., Pittsburgh; v.p. and dir. Pittsburgh Thrift Corpn. Pres. West End Bd. of Trade, 8 yrs.; dir. Pittsburgh Chamber of Commerce since 1922 (dir. and chmn. Highways and Bridges Com.). Republican. Methodist. Mason(Royal Arch, K.T., Scottish Rite, Shriner). Clubs: Chartiers Heights Country (Crafton, Pa.); Pittsburgh Motor (dir. and v.p.); Iron City Fishing (Pittsburgh; dir.). Home: 632 Walbridge St. Office:. 105 Water St., Pittsburgh, Pa.

TRASOFF, Abraham, M.D.; b. Russia, Dec. 15, 1888; s. David and Gittel (Annof) T.; M.D., Medico-Chirurgical Coll., Phila., 1915; m. Anna Elpern, Dec. 30, 1920; children—Marjorie, Joyce. Mem. post-grad. staff Jefferson and Jewish hosps., 1916-21; consultant U.S. Vets. Bur., Phila., 1919-25; served in various depts. of medicine, 1916-26; adjunct visiting physician and head dept. allergy Mt. Sinai Hosp., 1927-33, attending visiting physician since 1933. Served as lt., later capt., U.S. Army, World War. Fellow A.M.A.; asso. mem. Am. Coll. Physicians; diplomate Am. Bd. Internal Medicine; mem. Pa. State Med. Soc., Philadelphia Co. Med. Soc., Soc. for Study Asthma and Allied Conditions. Jewish religion. Contbr. to med. jours. Home: 1710 Pine St., Philadelphia, Pa.

TRAUGH, George H., mem. eye, ear, nose and throat dept. Cook Hosp.; mem. visiting staff Fairmont Emergency Hosp. Address: 309 Cleveland Av., Fairmont, W.Va.

TRAVALINE, Frank M., Jr., lawyer; b. Phila., Pa., July 19, 1900; s. Frank M. and Antoniette (DeLecce) T.; B.S. in Econ., Wharton Sch., U. of Pa., 1923, LL.B., Law Sch., 1926; m. Winifred Stella McHugh, July 1, 1933; children—Patricia Anne, Philip Francis. Professional musician while in coll.; instr. polit. science, U. of Pa., 1926-29, lecturer, 1929-36; admitted to N.J. and Pa. bars, 1927, and since practiced at Camden, N.J., and Phila.; dir. Wythe Machine Typesetting Co., Inc. Sec. to speaker, N.J. Ho. of Reps., 1930-31 (one term); mem. N.J. Ho. of Reps. (4 terms), 1931-34. Mem. N.J. State Bar Assn., Camden Co. Bar Assn., Alpha Phi Delta (nat. pres. 1937-39). Republican. Catholic, Elk, Moose. Club: Lawyers (Phila., Pa.). Home: 1115 Stokes Av., Collingswood, N.J. Office: 528 Cooper St., Camden, N.J.; and Fox Bldg., Philadelphia, Pa.

TRAVER, Amos John, clergyman, author; b. Hartwick Seminary, N.Y., Sept. 1, 1889; s. John G. and Ettie (Tompkins) T.; A.B., Wittenberg Coll., Springfield, O., 1910; B.D., Hartwick Sem., N.Y., 1912; hon. D.D., Wittenberg Coll., 1931; m. Florence Adeline Fake, July 10, 1912; children—Katherine Florence (Mrs. Robert Barkley), Margaret Ann (dec.), Pennel. Ordained to ministry Luth. Ch., 1912; pastor, Troy, N.Y., 1912-16; pastor, St. Thomas Luth. Ch., N.Y. City, 1916-26; exec. sec. Luther League of America, 1926-31; pastor Evang. Luth. Ch., Frederick, Md., since 1931; mem. parish and ch. sch. bd., United Luth. Ch., since 1934, vice-pres. since 1938; pres. Luth. Synod of Md. since 1939. Mem. Sons of Am. Revolution. Mem. advisory council De Molay, Frederick Chapter. Republican. Lutheran. Mason. Clubs: Kiwanis of Frederick; Catoctin Country; National Travel. Author: Life Service, 1928; The Christ Who Is All, 1929; Consecrated Leadership, 1930; A Lutheran Handbook, 1936; Studies in Life Service, 1937; The Pastor's Plan-Book, 1937-38. Co-author (with Dr. Paul Heisey) Studies in Social Problems, 1938. Editor: The Luther League Review, monthly, 1926-31; Young People's Page in The Lutheran, weekly, since 1931; Lutheran Men, monthly, since 1938. Home: 33 E. Church St., Frederick, Md.

TRAYLOR, Samuel William, mfg. heavy machinery; b. Old Waverly, Tex., Feb. 6 1869; s. Simpson Elias and Cornelia Elizabeth (White) T.; student engring. U. of Kan.; m. Lottie G. Lakel, June 24, 1921; 1 son, Samuel W., Jr. Asso. engr. in installing one of first overhead st. ry. trolley systems in U.S., Laredo, Tex. about 1889; in charge of construction one of first electric light plants, Monterey, Mex., 1889; master mechanic first custom built smelter in Mexico, 1890; established Traylor Engring. & Mfg. Co. in Newark, N.J., 1906, and later at Allentown, Pa., mfg. heavy machinery for metall. installations for treatment of ores; dir. Carlton Co., Traylor Ship Bldg. Corpn., Cement Gun Co., Inc.; chmn. bd. dirs. Traylor Engring. & Mfg. Co. Trustee Mercersburg Acad. Past pres. Allentown Chamber of Commerce. Mason (32°). Clubs: Lehigh Country (Allentown); Saucon Valley Country (Bethlehem); Country (Los Angeles, Calif.). Author: Out of the Southwest, 1936. Home: Hotel Traylor, Allentown, Pa.

TRAYNOR, Harold; mgr. Pittsburgh Pirates, Nat. League baseball team. Address: Pittsburgh Nat. League Baseball Club, Pittsburgh, Pa.

TREDER, Oscar F. R., clergyman; b. Albany, N.Y.; s. Rudolph and Emma (Helvig) T.; grad. St. Stephen's Coll., Annandale, N. Y., 1901, D.D., 1917; grad. Gen. Theol. Sem., N.Y. City, 1904; m. Lillian E. Howe, Oct. 5, 1904; children—Oscar F. R., Lillian G., John Howe, Rudolph W., Alfred H. G. Ordained to ministry P.E. Ch. 1904; rector St. Luke's Ch., East Hampton, N.Y., 1904-16; dean Cathedral of the Incarnation, Garden City, N.Y., 1916-26; dean St. Stephen's Cathedral, Harrisburg, Pa., 1926-34; rector St. James' Ch., Bedford, Pa., since 1934. Mem. Sigma Alpha Epsilon. Mason (32°, K.T.). Club: Masonic (New York). Home: Harrisburg, Pa. Office: Bedford, Pa.

TREES, Joe Clifton, oil and gas operator; b. Westmoreland Co., Pa., Nov. 10, 1869; s. Isaac T. and Lucy Ann (Johnston) T.; grad Ind. Normal Sch., 1892, U. of Pittsburgh, 1895; m. Claudine Virginia Willison, Dec. 20, 1894; m. 2d, Edith Lehm, Jan. 10, 1929. Began in oil and gas business, western Pa., 1890; vice-pres. Benedum Trees Oil Co. Trustee U. of Pittsburgh. Republican. Presbyn. Mason (32°, K.T., Shriner). Clubs: Dusquesne, Pittsburgh Athletic, Field, Oakmont Country; Congressional Country (Washington, D.C.). Home: Gibsonia, Pa. Office: Benedum Trees Bldg., Pittsburgh, Pa.

TREILLE, Marguerite; prof. Romance languages, Hood Coll. Address: Hood College, Frederick, Md.

TREMAINE, Charles Milton,, musical dir.; b. Brooklyn, N. Y., June 28, 1870; s. Charles Milton and Marianna Downs (Newhall) T.; student Adelphi Acad. (now Adelphi Coll.), 1881-86, Gunnery Sch. (Washington, Conn.), 1886-88; m. Elizabeth Lyman Lord, June 7, 1900; children—Lyman Lord, Elizabeth Newhall (Mrs. William Niel Pierce). Advertising solicitor, 1897-98; advertising mgr. Aeolian Co., 1898-1903, v.p., 1903-09; pres. Bacon Piano Co., 1910-14; pres. Tremaine Piano Co., 1912-16; organizer and mng. dir. Nat. Bur. for Advancement of Music, 1916-36, pres. and chmn. Bd. of Control since 1936; organizer of Nat. Music Week, and exec. sec. Nat. Music Week Com. since 1924; organized Nat. Sch. Band Assn., 1926, Nat. Sch. Orchestra Assn., 1928, exec. sec. both assns. to 1932. Originated school music contests in 1916, held in 1600 cities and towns; promoted outdoor Christmas caroling in 2000 cities and towns and group piano instruction in over 1000; organized Nat. Sch. Music Contests. Chmn. N.Y. Music Teachers Defense Com.; mem. Music Educators Nat. Conf., S.A.R. Episcopalian. Clubs: Town Hall (chmn.), Music Round Table (New York). Home: 560 Prospect St., Westfield, N.J. Office: 30 Rockefeller Plaza, New York, N.Y.*

TREMBLY, Charles Edward, banking; b. Albright, W.Va., Apr. 14, 1873; s. George H. and Eva C. (Smith) T.; student Fairmont State Normal Sch., W.Va., 1892-94, Peabody Normal College, Univ. of Nashville, Tenn., 1895-97; A.B., W.Va. Univ., Morgantown, 1899; m. Marjorie Crane, Aug. 5, 1915; children—Gray Crane, Charles Dee. Principal high school Davis, W. Va., 1900-02; assistant cashier Terra Alta Bank, Terra Alta, W.Va., 1902-10, cashier, 1910-36, vice-president since 1936; also interested in farming, real estate and timber; vice-president Englehart Woolen Mill Co., Albright, W.Va., since 1924; treasurer Alleghany Poster Advertising Company, Terra Alta, W.Va., Terra Alta Development Co., West Va. Forest Products Assn., Terra Alta; mem. firm Tannery Lime Co., Albright, W.Va.; dir. Terra Alta Bottling Co. Served as councilman Terra Alta, several terms; city recorder several terms. Democrat. Presbyn. Mason (K.T., 32°), Odd Fellow. K.P. Clubs: Rotary (Terra Alta); Preston Country, Muddy Creek Fishing (Kingwood). Home: 101 Highland Av. Office: 219 E. Washington St., Terra Alta, W.Va.

TRENCHARD, Thomas Whitaker, judge; b. Centreton, Salem Co., N.J., Dec. 13, 1863; s. William B. and Anna M. (Golder) T.; grad. South Jersey Inst., Bridgeton, N.J., 1882; read law in office of Potter & Nixon, Bridgeton; m. Harriet Manning, Oct. 18, 1891 (she died Feb. 9, 1938). Admitted to bar of the state of New Jersey, 1886, and practiced in Bridgeton. Mem. N.J. Assembly, 1889; city solicitor, Bridgeton, 1891-99; judge Cumberland Co. Court, 1889-1906; appt. justice Supreme Court of N.J., to fill vacancy, June 8, 1906, reapptd. 5 times, present term ending 1942. Republican. Mem. Am. Bar Assn., N.J. State Bar Assn., Cumberland Co. Bar Assn. (ex-pres.), S.A.R. Baptist. Address: 816 Riverside Av., Trenton, N.J.

TRENT, William Woodson, state supt. of schools; b. nr. Summersville, W.Va., Jan. 31, 1878; s. Thomas Woodson and Mary Agnes (McClung) T.; grad. Marshall Coll. State Normal Sch., W.Va., 1902; A.B., W.Va. U., 1912; A.M., Teachers Coll., Columbia, 1921; honorary Ped.D., Salem (W.Va.) College, 1932; m. Isabel Carmichael, August 5, 1909; children—William Carmichael, Mary Bell, Nancy Agnes. Teacher, rural schs., W.Va., 1896-1900; prin. high sch., New Martinsville, W.Va., 1903-06; supt. schs., Davis, W.Va., 1910-15, Elkins, W.Va., 1915-26; pres. Broaddus College, Philippi, West Va., 1927-33; state supt. of schools of W.Va. since 1933. County food adminstr., Randolph Co., W.Va., 1917-18. Dem. nominee state supt. schs., W.Va., 1920, 24. Sec., W.Va. Edn. Assn., 1919-27 (membership increased from 1,-500 to 10,000 during term); pres. W.Va. Bapt. Conv., 1926-28. Mem. N.E.A. (life, W.Va. dir.), Assn. of Chief State Sch. Officers, Phi Beta Kappa, Kappa Delta Pi. Democrat. Kiwanian. Address: Capitol Bldg., Charleston, W. Va.

TRESCHER, Maud Byers (Mrs. John H. Trescher); b. Hempfield Twp., Pa., Dec. 28, 1876; d. William J. and Mary Elizabeth (Bair) Byers; ed. pub. sch. and high sch., Jeannette, Pa.; m. John H. Trescher, Mar. 1, 1898 (died 1917); children—John H. (M.D.), Fred B., Helen (Mrs. Harris C. Arnold), Robert L., William. Began as reporter on weekly newspaper and continued in same office, 1892-98, married the editor and asso. with same paper, 1898-1917, after death of husband paper was consolidated with another newspaper and asso. with same, 1917-33; has given practically all time to welfare work in community since 1933; served as sch. dir., two terms; mem. Pa. Ho. of Rep., 1925-27. Pres. Union Aid Assn. (charitable and welfare). Vice-pres. Westmoreland Chapter Red Cross, Womens Assn. Westmoreland Hosp. Dir. Westmoreland Childrens Aid Soc. Mem. D.A.R. Republican. Mem. Evang. and Reformed Ch. Club: Womans (Jeannette). Home: 113 S. Second St., Jeannette, Pa.

TRESS, John S., mayor, druggist; b. Beaver Falls, Pa., Jan. 31, 1895; s. Isaac and Bertha (Hofecker) T.; ed. St. Vincent Coll., Latrobe, Pa., 1909-13; Ph.G., School of Pharmacy, U. of Pittsburgh, 1916; married Feb. 18, 1928; children—Ida Patricia, John Edward, Eileen Joan, Thomas James, Helen May, Willard Joseph. Grad. pharmacist since 1916; propr. drug store, Beaver Falls, Pa. since 1919; serving as mayor of City of Beaver Falls, Pa., since 1938; dir. Beaver Falls Bldg. & Loan Assn. since 1921. Served as sergt. L.F.A., U.S.A., 1917-19, with A.E.F. in France. Mem. 323d L.F.A. Assn. (past pres., treas. since 1926). Served as mem. city council and finance officer Beaver Falls, 1932-36. In heritance Tax Investigator and Appraiser of Beaver Co., 1937-39. Democrat. Roman Catholic. Home: 2328 8th Av. Office: 24th St. and 8th Av., Beaver Falls, Pa.

TRESSLER, Frank Ellsworth, lawyer; b. New Bloomfield, Pa., July 14, 1902; s. John W. and Laura J. (Owings) T.; grad. New Bloomfield High Sch., 1920; A.B., Lafayette Coll., 1924; LL.B., Harvard, 1928; m. Hilda Virginia Bitting, Oct. 29, 1932. Admitted to Pa. bar, 1928, U.S. Dist. Court, 1928, U.S. Supreme Court, 1932; gen. practice, New Bloomfield, Pa., since 1928; dist. atty. Perry County for term 1936-40. Capt. Inf. Reserve. Trustee Carson Long Inst., New Bloomfield, since 1931. Mem. Am. Bar Assn., Pa. Bar Assn., Perry Co. Law Library, Phi Beta Kappa and Acacia. Republican. Presbyterian. Mason (32°, Shriner); past master, past high priest, past comdr.; mem. Tall Cedars, Odd Fellows, Moose, Sojourners, Lions Club. Address: New Bloomfield, Pa.

TREVORROW, Robert Johns, clergyman; b. St. Ives, Eng., May 21, 1877; s. Anthony and Dorcas Quick (Johns) T.; A.B., Coll. of Pacific, San Jose, Calif., 1898, A.M., 1901, D.D., 1913; B.D., Drew Theol. Sem., Madison, N.J., 1903; Union Theol. Sem., New York, 1911-12; m. Editha Carpenter, Oct. 25, 1905; 1 son, Robert Johns. Ordained M.E. ministry, 1898; pastor Stockton, Calif., 1898-1900, St. Paul's Ch., New York, 1900-05, Elmhurst, L.I., Carmel, Modena, Central Valley and Woodlawn Heights, 1905-13; pres. Drew Sem. for Young Women, Carmel, N.Y., 1913-17; pres. Centenary Collegiate Inst., Hackettstown, N.J., since Apr. 1917. Pres. Ednl. Assn. of M.E. Ch., 1928-29, Am. Assn. of Junior Colleges, 1935-36, Junior Council of Middle States Assn. of Colls. and Secondary Schs., 1935-37. Decorated Comdr. Order of the Crown of Roumania, 1932; Officer of the Order of the White Lion, Czechoslovakia, 1937. Clubs: Musconetcong Country, Canoe Brook Country, Interchurch Clergy. Address: Hackettstown, N.J.

TREXLER, Clifford H., surgeon; b. Mertztown, Pa., Aug. 2, 1902; s. Howard C. and Annie L. (Hertzog) T.; A.B., Muhlenberg Coll., Allentown, Pa., 1922; M.D., Jefferson Med. Coll., Phila., 1926; m. Helen R. Baynes, Buffalo, N.Y., Nov. 23, 1926. Interne, Episcopal Hosp., Phila., 1926-28; engaged in gen. practice of medicine at Allentown, Pa., since 1928, limited exclusively to surgery since 1935. Served as mem. Civil Service Commn., City of Allentown, since 1930; dir. pub. schs. Dir. Childrens Aid Soc. of Lehigh Co., Art Mus., Allentown. Fellow Am. Coll. Surgs.; mem. Phi Kappa Tau, Theta Kappa Psi. Republican. Reformed Ch. Mason, Elk. Club: Lehigh Country. Home: 349 N. 7th St., Allentown, Pa.

TREXLER, Frank M., judge; b. Allentown, Pa., Jan. 9, 1861; s. Edwin W. and Matilda Sauerbeck) T.; A.B., Muhlenberg Coll., Allentown, 1879, A.M., from same college, 1882, LL.D., 1910; m. Jennie R. Shelling, Nov. 7, 1889 (wife now dec.); children—Edwin W., Mrs. Dorothy Williams, Mrs. Frances Schmidt, Mrs. Marion Baldrige, Robert W. Began practice at Allentown, 1882; city solicitor, 11 yrs.; president judge, Lehigh County, Pa., 1902-13; elected associate justice of Superior Court of Pa., Feb. 1914, president judge, 1930-35, retired, January, 1935. President Allentown Young Men's Christian Association since 1890; mem. state com., Y.M.C.A. Mem. Pa. State Bar Assn., American Bar Assn., Hist. Soc. of Pa., Lehigh Co. Hist. Soc. (pres.), Pa. German Soc., Huguenot Soc., S.R. Republican. Presbyterian. Mason (33°), Odd Fellow. Home: 1115 Walnut St. Office: Commonwealth Bldg., Allentown, Pa.

TRIEBOLD, Howard O., prof. agrl. and biol. chemistry; b. Washington Co., Minn., Feb. 15, 1902; s. August and Mary (Stutzman) T.; ed. Hamline U., St. Paul, Minn., 1919-21; B.S., U. of Minn., 1923, M.S., 1926, Ph.D., 1929; m. Louise Korfhage, June 30, 1924; children—Marjorie Jeanne, Howard O., Jr. Instr. in agrl. and biol. chemistry, Dept. Agrl. Chemistry, Pa. State Coll., 1926-36, prof. since 1936. Mem. Am. Chem. Soc., Am. Assn. Cereal Chemists, Sigma Xi, Phi Lambda Upsilon, Gamma Sigma Delta, Alpha Zeta, Alpha Gamma Rho. Republican. Methodist. Home: 216 S. Patterson St., State College, Pa.

TRIGG, Ernest T., mfr.; b. Aurora, Ill., Aug. 12, 1877; s. Thomas and Anna M. (Anderson) T.; ed. pub. schs.; m. Alice Gibbons, June 19, 1901; children—Helen Alice (Mrs. Charles J. Swain, Jr., dec.), Ernest T., Jr. With Heath & Milligan Mfg. Co., Chicago, 1895-1908; gen. mgr. John Lucas & Co., mfrs. paints, Phila., 1908, v.p., 1912, pres. until 1933; now pres. Nat. Paint, Varnish and Lacquer Assn. and was chmn. Industry Recovery Bd.; dir. Bankers Bond and Mortgage Guaranty Corpn. of America, Bankers Securities Corpn., Lit Bros., The Warner Co. (Phila.). Dir. Bd. of City Trusts, Philadelphia; trustee Temple U. (chmn. exec. com.). Pres. Paint Mfrs. Assn., U.S., 1911, Phila. Paint, Oil and Varnish Club, 1918-21, Phila. Chamber Commerce, 1918-21; chmn. ednl. bur. Am. Paint and Varnish Mfrs. Assn. Member Pennsylvania Commission to San Francisco Expn., 1915; regional adviser War Industries Board; member President Wilson's Industrial Conference, 1919, President Harding's Unemployment Conf., 1921; chairman Pres. Hoover's Committee on Home Ownership and Home Building; chmn. of Federal Home Loan Bank, 3d Federal Reserve Dist. Republican. Episcopalian. Mason (Shriner). Clubs: Union League (Phila.); Chicago Athletic; Duquesne (Pittsburgh). Home: 270 S. 15th St., Philadelphia. Office: Land Title Bldg., Philadelphia, Pa.; and 2201 New York Av. N.W., Washington, D.C.

TRIMBLE, Harcourt Newell, iron and steel products; b. Pittsburgh, Pa., Feb. 27, 1878; s. Alexander Newell and Henrietta (Gerberding) T.; ed. Luckey Sch., Duquesne Heights, Pittsburgh, 1884-91; m. Blanche Clemene, July 9, 1902; children—Suzanne (Mrs. Robert H. Snyder), Harcourt Newell. Began as office boy, 1891; now merchant of iron and steel products under name of H. N. Trimble; v.p. and dir. Pittsburgh Bridge & Iron Works; treas. and trustee Ranco Mining Co. Republican. Lutheran. Mason (Consistory and Shrine). Clubs: Duquesne, Pittsburgh Athletic Assn., Pittsburgh Field (Pittsburgh). Home: 1307 Beechwood Boul. Office: Oliver Bldg., Pittsburgh, Pa.

TRIMBLE, Henry W.; judge 1st Dist. Ct. of Essex County, term expires 1940. Address: Montclair, N.J.

TRIMBLE, Rufus James, lawyer; b. Montclair, N.J., Oct. 10, 1888; s. James McNeil and Lucy Raymond (Weeks) T.; ed. Princeton U., 1906-08; A.B., Columbia U., 1912; LL.B., Columbia Law Sch., 1914; m. Verna Lee Rooney, June 26, 1916; children—Joan Weekes, Verna Rudd. Admitted to N.Y. bar, 1915; asso. with Cravath & Henderson, New York, N.Y., 1914-18; with Baker, Botts, Parker & Garwood, Houston, Tex., 1920; export legal work, Texas Co., at New York, 1921-23; in pvt. practice at New York, 1923-31; mem. firm Swiger, Scandrett, Chambers & Landon, N.Y. City, 1931-34; asst. counsel, Federal Res. Bank of N.Y. since 1934. Served in Air Service, U.S.N., 1918-19; asst. spl. rep. Sec. of War Baker, 1919; rep. in Eng., U.S. Liquidation Commn., 1919. Chmn. membership com. Am. Foreign Law Assn.; mem. Am. Bar Assn., Delta Kappa Epsilon, Phi Delta Phi. Democrat. Episcopalian. Club: Golf (Montclair). Home: 26 Westover Rd., Verona, N.J. Office: 33 Liberty St., New York, N.Y.

TRIMBLE, Thomas Patton, pres. judge; b. Allegheny City, Pa., June 17, 1869; s. William Foster and Margaret Ann (Freer) T.; A.B., Westminster Coll., New Wilmington, Pa., 1891, LL.D., 1918; m. Euphemia McNaugher, Sept. 29, 1898; children—Janet McNaugher (Mrs. Robert Peebles Rhodes), Thomas Patton, Frances, Euphemia, Mary Annetta (Mrs. Richard Stone Heller). Admitted to Allegheny Co. bar, 1894, and began practice in Pittsburgh; asst. solicitor for Allegheny Co., 1900-03; apptd. judge of Orphans Court, May 5, 1913, elected Nov. 1913, re-elected without opposition, 1923; commd. pres. judge Feb. 10, 1929, re-elected without opposition Nov. 1933. Mem. United Presbyterian Ch. Clubs: Duquesne, University. Home: 5927 Howe St. Office: 804 City-County Bldg., Pittsburgh, Pa.

TRINKS, C(harles) L(eopold) Willibald, prof. of mech. engring.; b. Berlin, Germany, Dec. 10, 1874; s. Wilhelm and Bertha (Obst) T.; M.S., Charlottenburg Inst. of Tech., 1897; m. 3d, Ruth Waxham. Came to U.S., 1899, naturalized, 1909. Junior engr., Dortmund, Germany, 1897-99; engr. Phila., East Pittsburgh, 1899-1902; chief engr. William Tod Co., Youngstown, O., 1902-05; prof. of mech. engring., Carnegie Inst. of Tech. since 1905; dir. Nat. Industrial Pub. Co., Tate, Jones & Co. Mem. Am. Soc. M.E., Am. Iron and Steel Inst., Assn. of Iron and Steel Engrs., Engrs. Soc. Western Pa., Soc. of Metals, V.D.I., V.D.E. Presbyterian. Club: Pittsburgh Athletic Assn. Home: 1016 Murray Hill Av., Pittsburgh, Pa.

TRINKS, Willibald, mechanical engr.; b. Berlin, Germany, Dec. 10, 1874; s. Wilhelm and Bertha (Obst) T.; grad. with honors, Charlottenburg Poly., 1897; m. 2d, Edith Moore, Aug. 8, 1910 (now dec.); 1 son, Harold Rodney (now dec.); m. 3d, Ruth Eudora Bittner, June 13, 1938. Came to U.S., 1899; chief mech. engr. William Tod Co., Youngstown, O., 1902-05; prof. mech. engring., Carnegie Inst. Tech., Pittsburgh, 1905—; cons. engr. Jones & Laughlin Steel Co., 1920—. Mem. Am. Soc. M.E., Engrs., Soc., Western Pa. Soc., Am. Iron and Steel Inst. Co-author: Trinks and Housum Shaft Governors, 1905. Author: Governors, and the Governing of Prime Movers, 1919; Industrial Furnaces, Vol. I, 1923, Vol. II, 1925; Industrieöfen, 1928; Roll Pass Design (3 vols.), 1933. Home: 1016 Murray Hill Av., Pittsburgh, Pa.

TRIPLETT, John Edwin, clergyman; b. Cynthiana, Ky., Oct. 14, 1880; s. Rev. John Edwin and Anna Carrie (Johnston) T.; grad. Shepherd Coll. State Normal Sch., Shepherdstown, W.Va., 1896; A.B., Hampden-Sydney Coll., 1900; A.M., Princeton, 1903; B.D., Princeton Theol. Sem., 1904; D.D., Richmond Coll., 1914; unmarried. Ordained Presbyn. ministry, 1904; pastor 2d Ch., N.Y. City, 1904-07, Bedford Park Ch., 1907-09, First Ch., Woodbury, N.J., 1909-20, Girard Av. Ch., Phila., since 1920; prof. Greek and N.T. lit., Temple U., since 1923. Mem. Phi Gamma Delta. Democrat. Presbyn. Mason, Odd Fellow. Lecturer on religious and lit. subjects. Home: 930 N. 15th St., Philadelphia, Pa.

TROSSBACH, Herman, physician; b. Carlstadt, N.J., June 23, 1881; s. Herman and Emilia (Giebner) T.; student Drake Bus. Coll., Jersey City, N.J., 1894-95; M.D., L.I.Sch. of Medicine, N.Y., 1907; grad. study Mayo Clinic and Johns Hopkins U., and Nat. Pathol. Labs., N. Y. City; m. Minnie M. Augustin, 1913; children—Julia Carolyn, Carolyn Emilia. Interne Englewood Hospital Englewood, N.J., 1907-08; in practice of medicine, Brooklyn Hills, N.Y., 1908-09; clin. asst. in internal medicine, N.Y. Polyclinic 1908; in practice Colorado Springs, Colo., 1909-17; clin. pathologist, N.Y. Medical College and Hospital for Women, 1917-18; in practice at Hasbrouck, N.J. 1919-25, and in Bogota, N.J. since 1925; past president medical board, Hackensack Hospital, Hackensack, N.J., now attdg. physician in medicine, now dir. of medicine, Hackensack Hosp. Fellow Am. Coll. Physicians. Mem. N.J. State Med. Soc., Bergen Co. Med. Soc. (past pres.). Republican. Unitarian. Home: 97 Palisade Av., Bogota, N.J.

TROSTEL, Louis Jacob, chem. engring.; b. Galion, O., Dec. 31, 1893; s. Jacob Michael and Mary Amelia (Lenhart) T.; B. Chem. Engring., Ohio State U., Columbus, O., 1918; Chem. Engr., Ohio State U., 1936; Ceramic Engr., Ohio State U., 1937; m. Katherine Fisher, June 2, 1925; children—Louis Jacob, Jr., Michael Frederick. Employed as steel examiner, British Ministry of Munitions, 1918; jr. engr., Standard Chem. Co., Pittsburgh, Pa., 1918-19; jr. chem., U.S. Bur. of Mines Exptl. Sta., Pittsburgh, Pa., 1920-21; asst. engr., U.S. Bur. Chemistry, Washington, D.C., 1921-23; chief chemist, General Refractories Co., Baltimore, Md. since 1923; awarded patents on refractory compositions and processes. Fellow Am. Ceramic Soc. (v.p. 1933-34). Mem. Am. Chem. Soc., Electro-chem. Soc.,

Am. Soc. for Testing Materials, Am. Refractories Inst., Am. Inst. Chem Engrs., Am. Inst. Ceramic Engrs. Joint Com. on Foundry Refractories of Am. Foundrymen's Assn. and Am. Ceramic Soc. since 1925, Spl. Research Com. on Boiler Furnace Refractories of Am. Soc. Mech. Engrs. since 1928, Alpha Chi Sigma. Lutheran. Mason (32°). Contbr. many sci. articles and papers to tech. mags. and proceedings of sci. socs. Home: 4302 Miami Pl. Office: General Refractories Co., Baltimore, Md.

TROTH, Celeste Heckscher (Mrs. Edward Osborne Troth), artist; b. Ambler, Pa., July 19, 1888; d. Austin Stevens and Celeste (Massey) Heckscher; ed. Farnum Sch., The Agnes Irwin Sch., Phila., Low & Heywood Sch., Stamford, Conn., 1903-04; m. Edwin Oscar Perrin, Sept. 3, 1912 (divorced); 1 dau., Isabelle Heckscher Perrin; m. 2d, Edward Osborne Troth, Dec. 3, 1922. Has followed profession as artist since 1929, specializing in portraits; exhibited at Warwick Galleries, Phila., Fellowship Acad. Fine Arts, Germantown Art League, Art Alliance, Cosmopolitan Club, McClees Galleries and Steinways, Phila.; symbolic painting "The Back of The Cross" permanently placed in P.E. Cathedral Church of Christ, Roxborough, Pa., was selected for cover design for Salvation Army "The War Cry," Easter issue, 1935. A Herald of Magna Charta Soc., Phila. Mem. bd. mgrs. Indigent Widows and Single Women's Soc., Phila.; mem. bd. mgrs. Germantown Relief Soc. Mem. Nat. Assn. Am. Composers and Conductors. Episcopalian. Clubs: Cosmopolitan, Art Alliance (Phila.); Federation of Arts (Washington, D.C.). Home: Chestnut Hill. Studio: 34 S. 16th St., Philadelphia, Pa.

TROTTER, Frank Butler, coll. prof.; b. Washington Co., O., Feb. 27, 1863; s. James and Elizabeth (Stock) T.; A.B., Roanoke Coll., Va., 1890 (highest grade in class), A.M., 1895, L. H.D., 1935; LL.D., W.Va. Wesleyan Coll., 1914; Harvard Grad Sch., 1891-92; m. Lillian List Steele, Aug. 22, 1895; 1 son, Lorentz Steele. Teacher in pub. schs. 4 yrs., and pvt. schs. 2 yrs., W. Va.; prof. Latin and modern langs., 1890-1907; vice-pres. 1894, acting pres., 1898, W.Va. Conf. Sem. (since 1902, W.Va. Wesleyan Coll.); prof. Latin 1907—, dean Coll. Arts and Sciences, 1911-16, acting pres., 1914-16, president, 1916-28, professor Latin, 1928-39, West Virginia Univ.; retired June 30, 1939. Republican. Methodist; del. Gen. Conf. M.E. Ch., 1900, 12, 16, 20. Mem. Phi Beta Kappa Phi Gamma Delta. Rotarian. Home: Morgantown, W.Va.

TROUPE, John Franklin, clergyman; b. Milroy, Pa., Apr. 24, 1890; s. Frank and Kathryn (Getz) T.; ed. Franklin and Marshall Coll., 1907-09; Ph.B., Syracuse U., 1911; grad. study Johns Hopkins U., 1911-12; A.M., Princeton, 1913; student Princeton Theol. Sem., 1912-15, grad. 1915; hon. D.D., Oscaloosa Coll., 1925; m. Alma Carolyn Sandel, Aug. 2, 1916; children—Mary Kathryn, Martha Elizabeth. Ordained to ministry Presbyn. Ch. U.S.A., 1915; pastor, New Park, Pa., 1915-20; Fremont, O., 1920-27, Giddings Presbyn. Ch., St. Louis, Mo., 1927-30, Second Presbyn. Ch., Wilkinsburg, Pa., 1930-36, Emmanuel Presbyn. Ch., Phila, Pa. since 1936; moderator Westminster Presbytery, 1919, Toledo Presbytery, 1925. Mem. Lambda Chi Alpha, Theta Beta Phi. Awarded N.T. Greek Fellowshop Princeton Theol. Sem., 1915. Republican. Presbyn. Mason. I.O.O.F. Author. Growth in Grace, 1915, 2d edit., 1932; Saint Paul and the Mystery Religions, 1917; Interviewing God, 1930. Contbr. to religious mags. and other journs. and newspapers. Home: Telford, Pa.

TROWBRIDGE, George Augustus, clergyman; b. Berlin, Germany, Aug. 12, 1897; s. Augustus and Sarah Esther (Fulton) T.; (parents Am. citizens); grad. Hill Sch., Pottstown, Pa., 1916; A.B., Princeton U., 1920; student Trinity Coll., Oxford, Eng., 1920-21; B.D., Va. Theol. Sem. 1924; m. Jean Whiting, June 8, 1926; children —Clinton Whiting, Katharine, Augustus. Ordained to ministry of P.E. Ch., 1924; master St. Paul's Sch., Concord, N.H., 1924-25; chaplain to Episcopal students, Yale, 1925-27; asst. minister All Angels Ch., New York, 1927-28, rector, 1928-38; rector St. Paul's Ch., Chestnut Hill, Phila., since 1939. Served with Am. Field Service, France, 1917; with Corps Engrs., U.S. Army, and O.T.S., Humphries, Va., 1917-18. Clubs: Sunnybrook, Philadelphia Cricket. Home: 18 E. Chestnut Av., Chestnut Hill, Philadelphia, Pa.

TRUE, Rodney Howard, botanist, physiologist; b. Greenfield, Sauk Co., Wis., Oct. 14, 1866; s. John M. and Mary Annie (Beede) T.; B.S., U .of Wis., 1890, univ. fellow in botany, 1890-92, M.S. 1892; student botany under Peffer at Liepzig, 1893-95, Ph.D., 1895; m. Katharine McAssey, July 1, 1896 (dec.); 1 son, Rodney Philip; m. 2d, Martha A. Griffith, Dec. 22, 1927. Taught common schs. in Wis. 2 yrs.; prin. Wis. Acad., Madison, 1892-93; instr. pharmacognosy, 1895-96, asst. prof. pharmacognosy, 1896-99, U. of Wis.; lectured at Harvard, winter, 1899-1900, and asst. Radcliffe College; lecturer in botany, Harvard, 1900-01; plant physiologist, U.S. Dept. Agr., 1901-20, in charge physiol. investigations; prof. botany and dir. Botanic Garden, Univ. of Pa., 1920-37, emeritus prof. of botany since 1937; dir. Morris Arboretum, U. of Pa., 1933—. Mem. gen. com. for revision of 9th U.S. Pharmacopœia; adv. council of Allegheny Forest Expt. Sta. since 1934, chmn. since 1936. Fellow A.A.A.S. (sec. com. one hundred on scientific research, 1925, mem. council, 1926); mem. Am. Assn. Univ. Profs. (council 1927), Bot. Soc. America (v.p. 1930), Ecol. Soc. America, Agrl. History Soc. (ex-pres.), Pa. Bot. Soc., Pa. Hort. Soc. (exec. council 1936-38), Pa. Forestry Assn. (v.p. 1937), Phila. Acad. Natural Sciences, American Philosophical Society, Society Naturalists, Phi Beta Kappa, Sigma Xi, Delta Upsilon. Episcopalian. Contbr. of papers on original research to Annals of Botany, Botanisches Centralblatt, and other scientific jours. and govt. bulls. Clubs: Lenape (Phila.); Cosmos (Washington, D.C.). Home: 4111 Baltimore Av., Philadelphia, Pa.

TRUITT, Ralph Purnell, M.D.; b. Snow Hill, Md., Aug. 4, 1885; s. George Worthington and Gertrude Duncan (Purnell) T.; grad. high sch., Snow Hill, student Washington Coll., Chestertown, Md.; M.D., U. of Md., 1910; m. Eleanor McConnell, Sept. 2, 1920; 1 son, James McConnell. Interne Univ. Hosp., Baltimore, 1909-10; jr. asst. physician N.J. State Hosp., Trenton, N.J., 1910-12; physician in chief City Hosp. (insane dept.), Baltimore, 1912; asst. resident psychiatrist Johns Hopkins Hosp., 1913-14; clin. dir. La. State Hosp., Jackson, La., 1915; sr. physician N.J. State Hosp., 1916-17; lt., capt. and maj. M.C., U.S.A., 1917-19; med. dir. Ill. Soc. for Mental Hygiene and asst. prof. neurology and psychiatry, U. of Ill. Med. Dept., 1919-23; dir. Child Guidance Clinic Demonstration under auspices Nat. Com. for Mental Hygiene, Los Angeles, Calif., 1924; dir. Div. on Prevention of Delinquency, Commonwealth Fund Program, 1925-27, New York; asso. prof. psychiatry and dir. psychiatric clinic, U. of Md., since 1927; cons. psychiatrist University and Union Memorial hosps.; hon. consultant Inst. of Pa. Hosp., Phila. Mem. Am. Psychiatric Assn., Am. Orthopsychiatric Assn. (pres. 1935-36), Phi Sigma Kappa. Contbr. to professional jours. Home: 3904 Canterbury Road. Office: 1014 St. Paul St., Baltimore, Md.

TRUITT, Reginald Van Trump, biol. lab. dir.; b. Snow Hill, Md., Sep. 12, 1891; s. George Wilmer and Gertrude (Purnell) T.; grad. Snow Hill (Md.) High Sch., 1910; A.B., U. of Md., College Park, 1914, M.S., 1920; Ph. D., Am. U., Washington, D.C., 1929; grad. work, Berlin (Germany) U., 1922; m. Mary Harrington, June 18, 1930; children—Virginia Harrington, Emerson Harrington, Gertrude Purnell. Teacher of science and prin., Sudlersville (Md.) High Sch., 1914-19; asst. prof. zoology, U. of Md., 1919-23, asso. prof., 1923-25; prof., 1925-26; dir. Chesapeake Biol. Lab., Solomons Island, Md., since 1926. Served as pursuit pilot (2d lt.) Air Corps, U.S. Army, during World War. Chmn. Md. State Planning Commn., Com. on Conservation; mem. Nat. Fisheries Advisory Bd. Mem. A.A.A.S., Am. Fisheries Soc., Nat. Shellfisheries Assn., Md. Acad. of Science (Fellow), Md. Natural History Soc. (hon. life), Ecological Soc. of America, Am. Soc. of Limnological Soc. Md. Game Protective Assn., Md. Outdoor Life Assn., N.E.A., Biol. Soc. of Washington, Audubon Soc. America (v.p. Dist. of Columbia), Am. Assn. Univ. Profs., Sigma Xi, Phi Kappa Phi, Kappa Alpha, Omicron Delta Kappa. Presbyterian. Club: Solomons Island (Md.) Yacht. Home: College Park, Md. Office: College Park, Md.; also Solomons Island, Md.

TRUMBULL, Charles Gallaudet, editor; b. Hartford, Conn., Feb. 20, 1872; s. Clay and Alice Cogswell, Gallaudet) T.; grad. Hamilton Sch., Philadelphia; A.B., Yale University, 1893; Litt.D., Wheaton College, 1928; m. Aline van Orden, Nov. 18, 1897. Has been with The Sunday School Times since 1893, and its editor since 1903; also v.p., sec., dir. The Sunday School Times Co.; for many years staff writer Toronto Globe: every week writer Phila. Evening Pub. Ledger, Sioux Falls (S.D.) Daily Argus-Leader, Long Beach (Calif.) Morning Sun, Bradenton (Fla.) Herald. Companion of 1st class Military Order Loyal Legion; associate member Victoria Inst., Eng.; member Palestine Exploration Fund, Eng., Archæol. Inst. America; fellow American Geog. Society; mem. Yale Club (Philadelphia), Psi Upsilon Fraternity. Presbyn. Treas. Belgian Gospel Mission; chmn. Pioneer Mission Agency, Keswick Colony of Mercy, council Victorious Life Testimony; v.p. World's Christian Fundamentals Assn. Author: A Pilgrimage to Jerusalem, 1904; Taking Men Alive, 1907, 1938; Men Who Dared, 1907; Genesis and Yourself, 1912, 26; Anthony Comstock, Fighter, 1913; What Is the Gospel?, 1918; Life Story of C. I. Scofield, 1920; Prophecy's Light on Today, 1937. Home: 7808 Cobden Road, Laverock, Chestnut Hill, Philadelphia. Office: Heid Bldg., 325 N. 13th St., Philadelphia, Pa.

TRUMP, Charles Croasdale, mech. and chem. engring.; b. Syracuse, N.Y., Aug. 19, 1886; s. Edward Needles and Katharine (Croasdale) T.; A.B., Harvard U., 1909; M.E., Cornell U., 1911; m. Rachel Bulley, Mar. 10, 1917; children—Peter Bulley, Rachel Harriet, Charles Edward. Engaged as sec. Humphrey Gas Pump Co., 1911-24; sec. Stumpf Una-Flow Engine Co., Inc., 1912-21; mgr. N.Y. Office, Fuller Lehigh Co., 1919-21; v.p. Humphrey Gas Pump Co. and Stumpf Una-Flow Engine Co., 1921-24; engr. tests, Atlantic Refining Co., 1924-27; asst. chem. engr., Supplee-Wills-Jones Milk Co., 1927-28; pres. Trump Corpn., 1928-38, pres. Jas. Spear Stove & Heating Co., 1931-38; v.p. and sales engr., Haverly Electric Co., Inc., East Syracuse, N.Y., and Sanitary Metal Cap Corpn., Syracuse, N.Y., located at Phila., Pa., office since 1938. Served as asst. Adminstrn. Engr., U.S. Fuel Adminstrn., N.Y. State, 1918. Served in N.Y.N.G., 1914-15. Specialist in air conditioning, cooling, heating, and drying as applied to human comfort and industrial processes. Mem. Tau Beta Pi, Delta Upsilon., Harvard Union. Republican. Mem. Religious Soc. Friends. Home: 503 Baird Rd., Merion Station, Pa. Office: 1823 Market St., Philadelphia, Pa.

TRUMP, Rachel Bulley (Mrs. Charles Croasdale Trump), artist; b. Canton, O., May 3, 1890; d. Reginald Hargreaves and Harriet Mary (Tanner) Bulley; grad. Goodyear Burlingame Sch., Syracuse, N.Y., 1908; B.P., Syracuse U., 1912; m. Charles Croasdale Trump, Mar. 10, 1917; children—Peter Bulley, Rachel Harriet, Charles Edward. Has followed profession as artist since 1912; specializing in painting of portraits; represented by portrait of Hon. Martin A. Knapp, judge of U.S. Circuit Ct. of Appeals, in Circuit Ct. of Appeals, Richmond, Va., and of Miss Frances Canby Ferris, in Haverford Friends Sch., Haverford, Pa.; noted especially for portraits of children. Awarded Gold Medal at Annual Oil Show of Plastic Club, 1939. Mem. Nat. Assn. Women Painters and Sculptors, Phila. Art Alliance, Gamma Phi Beta. Unitarian. Clubs: Plastic, Print (Philadelphia). Home: 503 Baird Rd., Merion, Pa.

TRUMPOUR, Frederick James, civil engr.; b. Meadville, Pa., Oct. 3, 1870; s. Frederick W. and Laura (Mackey) T.; B.S. in Engring., Alleghany Coll., Meadville, Pa., 1892; m. Jessie

W. Smith, M.D., Aug. 25, 1908. Began in-field work civil engring., 1886; wide variety of engring. engagements for r.r. cos., steel cos. and engring. co., 1893-1918; engr., engring. branch, constrn. div., U.S.A., office of Q.M.G. since 1918; designed and superintended constrn. of a deep sub-surface drainage project on Miss. River bluffs, Natchez, Miss., 1925; awarded number of patents for various inventions; developed methods and machine for continuous production of blue-prints, 1935. Served in Spanish-Am. War, 1898. Mem. A.A.A.S., Nat. Hist. Soc., Am. Geog. Soc., Washington Soc. Engrs., Soc. Am. Mil. Engrs., Am. Soc. Civil Engrs., U. Spanish War Vets., Second U.S. Cav. Vets. Assn., Nat. Rifle Assn., Sigma Alpha Epsilon. Mason. Contbr. pamphlet and articles on blue-printing. Home: Woodland Trails, Forest Glen, Md. Office: 2350 Munitions Bldg., Washington, D.C.

TRUSS, James Petheram, tax commr.; b. New Castle, Del., Nov. 5, 1896; s. William Marvin and Emma Rebecca (Steele) T.; A.B., U. of Del., 1921; m. Ethel Robinson, Sept. 5, 1922; children—Jean Riddle, Joan Robinson. Began as reporter and sports editor, 1920; became chief field dep., Internal Revenue Dept., Wilmington, 1921, chief income tax div., 1921-26; auditor State Tax Dept., 1926-34; asst. tax commr., 1934-37, state tax commr., Wilmington, since 1937. Mem. Del. Permanent Budget Commn. Mem. Chamber of Commerce, Nat. Assn. of Tax Adminstrs., Tax Policy League, Acad. of Polit. Science, Am. Legion (Lawrence Roberts Post 1, Del. Post 1), Brandywine Business Men's Assn., Sigma Phi Epsilon. Episcopalian. Clubs: University (Wilmington); Kennett Square (Pa.) Golf and Country. Home: 606 W. 29th St. Office: 843 King St., Wilmington, Del.

TRUXAL, John Calvin, banker; b. Greensburg, Pa., Jan. 11, 1905; s. Jacob Quimbly and Elizabeth (Gehr) T.; grad. Greensburg (Pa.) pub. schs., 1917, Greensburg High Sch., 1921; A.B., Franklin & Marshall Coll., Lancaster, Pa., 1925, A.M., 1926; studied Lancaster Theol. Sem., 1925-26; m. Edith Kathryn Smith, Dec. 28, 1926; children—John Calvin, Jacob Q., III, Jean Elaine, Joan Edith. Teacher Swarthmore (Pa.) Prep. Sch., 1926-27; with Lancaster County Nat. Bank, Lancaster, Pa., since 1927, beginning as clk., advanced through various positions, becoming v.p. and trust officer, 1935. Awarded Williamson Medal (Franklin & Marshall Coll.), 1926. Mem. Phi Kappa Psi, Phi Beta Kappa. Democrat. Reformed Ch. Club: Media Heights Golf. Home: 731 College Av. Office: Lancaster County Nat. Bank, Lancaster, Pa.

TSCHAN, Francis J(oseph), prof. of history; b. Germany, Jan. 1, 1881; s. Francis Joseph and Katherine (Tschan) T.; brought to U.S., 1881, naturalized, 1901; A.B., Loyola U., Chicago, 1901, A.M., 1902, LL.D., 1933; Ph.D., U. of Chicago, 1916; m. Anna Katherine Evert, Oct. 28, 1908; children—Margaret Elizabeth (Mrs. Hugh R. Riley, Jr.), Robert Evert. Asst. in history, U. of Chicago, 1912-14; instr. of history, Yale, 1914-18; asst. prof. of history, Carnegie Inst. Tech., 1919-25; with Pa. State Coll. since 1925 as asso. prof. of history, 1925-31, prof. of mediæval history since 1931; teacher summers, Cath. U. of America, 1932, U. of Pittsburgh, 1933, U. of Pa., 1939. Mem. Mediæval Acad. of America, Am. Hist. Assn., Am. Cath. Hist. Assn. (pres. 1928-29), Am. Assn. Univ. Profs. (mem. nat. council 1932-35; exec. com. nat. council 1934-35; organization and policy com. 1935-39; com. on chapters for Pa. and N.J. since 1935), Pa. Hist. Soc., Phi Eta Sigma (nat. council since 1937), Theta Kappa Phi, Pi Lambda Sigma. Roman Catholic. Club: Center Hills Country. Contbr. to Dictionary of Am. Biography, Cath. Encyclopedia, Helmold's Chronicle of the Slavs, Records of Civilization: Sources and Studies XXI, also articles to hist. jours. Home: 500 Pugh St., State College, Pa.

TSCHUDY, Estelle Waters; b. Smyrna, Del.; d. William Ely and Mary Jamison (Price) Waters; ed. Smyrna (Del.) Pub. Sch., pvt. schs., Phila., Swarthmore (Pa.) Coll.; m. Harry Carpenter Tschudy, July 11, 1900 (died 1937). State librarian, Dover, Del., 1925-27, 1933-37; mem. Del. Ho. of Reps., 1931. Mem. Rep. State Com., 1928-38, State Bd. Charities, 1932-36, Emergency Aid, Phila., 1917-19, Nat. Advisory Com. on Women's Participation N.Y. World's Fair, 1939. Mem. Taxpayers' Research League, Nat. Order Women Legislators. Republican. Clubs: Twentieth Century (Smyrna, Del.; pres. 1909); College, Modern (Phila., Pa.). Home: Smyrna, Del.; and Modern Club, Philadelphia, Pa.

TUBBS, Arthur Lewis ("Arthur Sylvester"), playwright; b. Glens Falls, N.Y., July 2, 1867; s. George W. and Mary L. (Lewis) T.; ed. Glens Falls High Sch.; studied music in Glens Falls and Syracuse, N.Y., and Phila.; unmarried. Engaged in newspaper work since 1885; was dramatic and musical critic for Philadelphia Evening Bulletin 38 years, retiring, July, 1935. Contributor of many poems and short stories to newspapers and magazines; writer of plays used by amateur theatrical cos. and also for professional stage. Plays: Cowslip Farm, The Fruit of His Folly; Followed by Fate; Valley Farm; Heart of a Hero; Willowdale; Penalty of Pride; The Country Minister; Miss Buzby's Boarders; Farm Folks; The Village Schoolma'am; For the Old Flag; Alias Miss Sherlock; Home Acres; Rose Lawn; etc. Address: Evening Bulletin, Philadelphia, Pa.

TUCKER, Gabriel, prof. bronchoscopy, laryngeal surgery, clin. bronchoscopy and esophagoscopy, U. of Pa. Address: U. of Pennsylvania, Philadelphia, Pa.

TUCKER, Katharine, prof. nursing edn. and dir. courses in same, U. of Pa. Address: U. of Pennsylvania, Philadelphia, Pa.

TUCKER, Katharine Dickinson (Mrs. Collingwood Tucker); b. Cumberland, Md., Mar. 18, 1873; d. Laurence Thomsen and Nannie Hill (Tidball) Dickinson; ed. pvt. schs. and under tutors; m. George Collingwood Tucker, May 3, 1893. Student of negro folk songs since childhood; has given lecture recitals in leading cities of U.S. and before many univs. and socs.; made phonographic records of many Afro-Am. folk songs for Harvard U. collection; sang with success in Paris. Democrat. Episcopalian. Address: Box 65, Lahaska, Pa.

TUCKER, Ray T(homas), magazine corr.; b. Holyoke, Mass., Aug. 28, 1893; s. Thomas Joseph and Teresa (Powers) T.; grad. high sch., Holyoke, 1910; A.B., Yale, 1915; m. Elizabeth Anne Flanagan, June 7, 1920; children—Donn, Joanne. Began as reporter Springfield (Mass.) Republican, 1915; later mem. staff Elizabeth (N.J.) Journal; then Sunday editor Waterbury (Conn.) Republican; magazine editor Hartford (Conn.) Courant, 1919-20; polit. editor New York Evening Post, 1920-24, Washington corr., 1924-27; polit. writer and Washington corr. New York Telegram (now World-Telegram), 1927-33; Washington corr. Collier's Weekly, 1933-34, McClure Newspaper Syndicate since 1935. With intelligence sec., inf., U.S.A., World War. Catholic. Clubs: Yale, National Press, Racquet, Congressional Country (Washington). Author: Mirrors of 1932, 1932; Sons of the Wild Jackass, 1932. Contbr. to mags. Home: 6308 Hillcrest Pl., Chevy Chase, Md. Office: National Press Bldg., Washington, D.C.

TUCKER, Raymond Adams, ins. broker; b. Hartford, Conn., July 14, 1897; s. Frederick Newton and Leila Adams (Seymour) T.; ed. pub. schs. and high sch., Hartford and West Hartford, 1903-13; m. Edith Bell, Jan. 1, 1921 (died 1922); 1 son, Raymond Adams, Jr.; m. 2d, Frances M. Bell, Sept. 6, 1924; 1 son, Bates Bell. Soprano soloist, Boys Choir of St. John's P.E. Ch., Hartford; began as mail boy with Travelers Ins. Co., Hartford, 1914, then sec. to pres. of co., later spl. agt. at Syracuse, N.Y., and asst. mgr. at Pittsburgh, Pa., 1919-24; ins. broker as mem. firm Tucker and Johnston since 1924; pres. and dir. Official Railway Guide Pub. Co. (founded 1889); dir. Pittsburgh Convention and Tourist Bur.; mem. firm D. Bates Bell Agency. Served as 2d lt. Air Corps, U.S.A. during World War. Sec. and mem. Allegheny Co. Aviation Bd.; mem. transportation Research Commn. of Pittsburgh; dir. Acad. Sci. and Art, Thornburg Pub. Sch. Bd. (sec.). Mem. Ins. Agts. Assn., Pittsburgh Life Underwriters Assn. Republican. Methodist. Mason. Clubs: Rotary, Aero (Pittsburgh); Village Players (Thornburg); Fellows. Home: 560 Hamilton Rd., Thornburg, Pittsburgh, Pa. Office: Chamber of Commerce Bldg., Pittsburgh, Pa.

TUCKER, Rufus Stickney, economist; b. Somerville, Mass., Nov. 14, 1890; s. Frank Pierce and Susan Matilda (White) T.; A.B., Harvard, 1911, A.M., 1912, Ph.D., 1914; m. Lucy Harriot Nash, Oct. 16, 1923; children—Harriot Nash, Martha Nash, Nancy Nash, Abigail Nash. Instr. economics and pub. finance, U. of Mich., 1915-17, Harvard, 1919-23; sr. economic analyst U.S. Dept. of Commerce, 1923-25; chief economic analyst, U.S. Treasury Dept., 1925-26; chief economist Am. Founders Corpn., 1926-32; economist Bancamerica-Blair Corpn., 1933; asso. economist Brookings Instn., 1934; asso. economist Twentieth Century Fund, 1934-35; dir. statis. research Rep. Nat. Com., 1936; asso. economist Gen. Motors Corpn. since 1936; dir. Republic Investors Fund, Sovereign Investors, Inc. Served as capt. inf., U.S. Army, 1918. Mem. Am. Econ. Assn., Am. Statis. Assn., Phi Beta Kappa. Republican. Mason. Club: Westfield (N.J.) Tennis. Author: Big Business, Its Growth and Place (with others), 1937; How Profitable Is Big Business (with others), 1937. Compiled a syllabus in public finance, 1916. Author of several govt. reports. Contbr. to business and economic jours. Home: 436 Hillside Av., Westfield, N.J. Office: General Motors Corpn., 1775 Broadway, New York, N.Y.

TUCKERMAN, Arthur, author; b. N.Y. City, Jan. 6, 1896; s. Fleming and Edith Adele (Cozzens) T.; prep. edn., Cutler Sch., N.Y. City, University Sch., Washington, D.C., and Cheltenham Sch., Eng.; B.A., Christ Ch., Oxford U., 1921; m. Elise Strother, Jan. 20, 1927. Author: Breath of Life, 1922; Galloping Dawns, 1924; Possible Husbands, 1926; High Walls, 1929. Writer short stories for Cosmopolitan, Saturday Evening Post, Collier's, Harper's Bazaar, etc. Home: Chateaula, Ruxton, Md. Address: care Bankers Trust Co., 16 Wall St., New York, N.Y.

TUFT, Louis, physician; b. Phila., Pa., Sept. 14, 1898; s. Harry and Edith (Kofsky) T.; M.D., U. of Pa., 1920; m. Carlyn Janet Manasses, July 1, 1930; children—Janet Louise, Elizabeth Ann, Harry Manasses. Resident jr. physician, Pittsburgh City Home and Hosps., 1921-23; active practice in Phila. since 1923; asso. in medicine, Mt. Sinai Hosp., Phila., 1923-28; instr. in medicine, U. of Pa. Med. Sch., 1924-31; visiting pathologist, Howard, Northwestern and Babies Hosps., Philadelphia, 1926-33; asst. pathologist, Grad. Hosp., Phila., 1928-32; research fellow, Research Inst. of Cutaneous Medicine, Phila., since 1928; chief, Clinic of Allergy and Applied Immunology, Temple U. Hosp., Phila., since 1931; asso. in immunology and medicine, Temple U. Sch. of Medicine, Phila., since 1931; dir. of Pa. State Health Labs., Phila., 1936-39. Fellow A.M.A., Phila. Coll. Physicians; mem. Soc. for Study of Asthma and Allied Conditions, Assn. for Study of Allergy, Am. Assn. of Immunologists, Soc. of Investigative Dermatology, Phila. Allergy Soc., Pathol. Soc. of Phila., Phi Lambda Kappa. Author: Clinical Allergy, 1937; numerous scientific and med. articles. Home: 4613 Larchwood Av. Office: 1530 Locust St., Philadelphia, Pa.

TUFTS, Joseph P(arker), housing and social work; b. Eskridge, Kan., Dec. 20, 1901; s. James Albert and Eva (Richardson) T.; grad. Abilene (Kan.) High Sch., 1919; A.B., Baker U., Baldwin, Kan., 1923; M.A., Boston U., 1928; grad. work at Harvard and U. of Pittsburgh; m. Edith Miller, Aug. 24, 1926. Supt. Brown Memorial Foundation, Abilene, Kan., 1927-28; instr. dept. of sociology, Dartmouth Coll., Hanover, N.H., 1928-29; asst. dir. Pittsburgh Housing Assn., 1929-34, exec. dir. since 1934; lecturer in economics and housing, Smith Coll. Sch. of Social Work, Northampton, Mass., and Sch. of Applied Social Sciences, U. of Pittsburgh; cons. Housing Authority, City of Pittsburgh; dir. Gen. Health Council, Pittsburgh; dir. Pa. Housing and Town Planning Assn.; chmn. housing com. and mem. program com. Nat. Conf. Social Work; mem. nat. exec. com. and chmn. Pa. div. Am. Assn. of Social Workers. Mem. Nat. Assn. Housing Officials, Am. Planning and Civic Assn., Am. Acad. Polit. and Social Sciences. Independent Democrat. Home: 3114 Iowa St. Office: 519 Smithfield St., Pittsburgh, Pa.

TULL, Mary Esther, journalist, poet; b. Frederick, Md.; d. Wesley Summerfield and Eleanor (Howard) Tull; student Hood Sem., Frederick, Md.; B.A., Hood Coll., Frederick, Md., 1924; unmarried. Mem. of staff The News-Post, Frederick, Md., since 1924, writing general news and feature articles; established the society section of both papers; columnist since 1927. Mem. Nat. League of Am. Pen Women, English Speaking Union, Hood Coll. Alumnae Assn., Hood Club, Frederick Co. Hist. Soc., Alpha Lambda Sigma Literary Soc. (Hood Coll.). Awarded gold prize for best short story appearing in Hood Herald, Hood Coll., 1924. Democrat. Protestant. Chmn. of judges in awarding Hood Coll. Alumnae Assn. literary prizes since 1931. Author: Stained Windows (verse), 1927; Quest (verse), 1932. Contbr. poems and articles for mags. and newspapers. Address: 119 Record St., Frederick, Md.

TULL, Rudulph F., life ins.; b. Elkton, Md., Sept. 20, 1881; s. Robert Francis and Mary (Ellis) T.; student Elkton (Md.) grammar and high schs.; student Washington Coll., 1898-99, Goldey Business Coll., Wilmington, Del., 1899-1900; m. Elizabeth Coale, Oct. 27, 1906; children—Elizabeth Ellis (Mrs. William Dorsey Hines), Harvey Coale. Stenographer in law office, Elkton, Md., 1900-02; with Fidelity Mutual Life Ins. Co., Phila., since 1902, stenographer, 1902-05, held junior position in New Business or Underwriting Dept., 1905-23, now exec. head of same, asst. sec. of company, 1923-24, sec. since Jan. 1924. Republican. Episcopalian. Clubs: Union League, Phila. Country (Phila.). Home: 24 Penarth Road, Bala-Cynwyd, Pa. Office: The Parkway at Fairmount Av., Philadelphia, Pa.

TULLER, Jesse D., pres. Tuller Constrn. Co.; b. Auburn, N.Y., Aug. 5, 1885; s. Watson D. and Alice (Ellison) T.; student pub. schs., Auburn, N.Y., 1897-1905; C.E., Cornell U., 1909; m. Sara Austin, Aug. 2, 1913; children—Margaret A., John (dec.). Began as civil engr., Cape Cod (Mass.) Canal, 1909; engaged in constrn. N.Y. State Barge Canal, Catskill Aqueduct, railroad constrn. in Wis., and waterworks, sewage disposal plants and bridge constrn. to 1923; pres. and treas. Tuller Constrn. Co., Red Bank, N.J., since 1923; dir. Second Nat. Bank & Trust Co. Republican. Mason. Clubs: Monmouth Country (Eatontown, N.J.); Cornell (New York); Cornell Engrs. (Ithaca, N.Y.). Home: 1 Silverwhite Av. Office: 95 Monmouth St., Red Bank, N.J.

TUMOLILLO, Joseph G.; elected judge Municipal Court of Phila. for 10 yr. term, 1933. Address: Municipal Court of Philadelphia, Philadelphia, Pa.

TUNNELL, James Miller, lawyer; b. Clarksville, Del., Aug. 2, 1879; s. Henry Maull and Rhoda Elizabeth (Bennett) T.; A.B., Franklin Coll. (now combined with Muskingum Coll., New Concord, O.), 1900; m. Sarah Ethel Dukes, Nov. 10, 1905; children—James Elisha (dec.), James Miller, Robert White. Began as teacher pub. sch., 1903, advancing to prin. Frankford and Ocean View schs.; admitted to Del. bar, 1907; mem. firm White & Tunnell, 1907-19; practiced alone, 1920-36; with James M. Tunnell, Jr., as Tunnell & Tunnell since 1936; pres. Georgetown Trust Co.; dir. First Nat. Bank of Frankford, Del. Chmn. Dem. County Com., Sussex Co., 1910-12 and 1914-18; del. Dem. Nat. Conv., 1916; Dem. nominee for U.S. senator, 1924; chmn. Dem. State Com. during campaigns of 1928 and 1930; mem. Dem. Nat. Com. since 1931. Pres. Bd. of Edn. Georgetown Spl. Sch., 1919-32. Presbyn. Mason (32°), Odd Fellow. Club: Rehoboth Beach (Del.) Country. Home: Georgetown, Del.

TUPPER, James Waddell, coll. prof.; b. Sheet Harbor, N.S., Mar. 31, 1870; s. John and Eliza Bedford (Waddell) T.; B.A., Dalhousie Coll., Halifax, N.S., 1891; Ph.D., Johns Hopkins, 1895; m. Mary Patterson Harmon, Dec. 30, 1903; 1 son, Harmon. Professor of English and of history, Western U., London, Ont., 1897-1900; asso. in English, Bryn Mawr Coll., 1900-02; instr. in English, Harvard, 1902-04; asso. prof. English lit., 1906-09, prof. since 1909, Lafayette Coll., Easton, Pa. Mem. Modern Lang. Assn. America, Phi Beta Kappa. Editor: D'Avenant's Love and Honour, and The Siege of Rhodes, 1909; Representative English Dramas (with Prof. Frederick Tupper), 1914; Narrative and Lyric Poems, 1927; English Poems from Dryden to Blake, 1933. Chmn. Conf. on English in the Central Atlantic States, 1914, 1917-19, 1931. Lecturer, summer sessions at Johns Hopkins, U. of Texas, Rutgers, New York U., etc. Address: 5 E. Campus, Easton, Pa.

TURCK, Charles Joseph, educator; b. New Orleans, La., Sept. 13, 1890; s. Charles Edwin and Louisa Bertha (Frank) T.; A.B., Tulane U., 1911; A.M., Columbia U., 1912, LL.B., 1913; LL.D., Ky. Wesleyan, 1928, Cumberland U., 1930, Tulane U., 1935; m. Emma Fuller, Sept. 28, 1914; children—Viola, Emma Louise. Admitted to bar, N.Y., 1913, later La., Tenn. and Ky.; practiced with Lord, Day & Lord, N.Y. City, until 1916; prof. law, Tulane U., 1916-20, Vanderbilt U., 1920-24, also sec. Law Sch.; prof. law and dean Law Sch.; U. of Ky., 1924-27; pres. Centre Coll., 1927-36; dir. dept. social edn. and action, Bd. of Christian Edn. Presbyn. Church, U.S.A., since 1936. Was educational dir. War Work Council, Y.M. C.A., Pensacola, Fla., and Parris Island, S.C., 1918-19. Mem. Com. on Instns. of Higher Learning, Southern Edn. Assn.; mem. exec. com. Nat. Commn. of Ch.-Related Colleges; mem. Ky. State Reorganization Commn., Ky. State Tax Commn.; mem. Dept. of Ch. Coöperation and Union, Presbyn. Ch. U.S.A.; mem. Federated Council Depts. of Social Service, Race Relations and Internat. Justice and Good Will; del. to World Conf. at Oxford and Edinburgh, 1937. Mem. Am. Soc. Internat. Law, Am. Polit. Science Assn., Am. Assn. Univ. Profs., Holland Soc., New York, Phi Beta Kappa, Sigma Nu, Phi Delta Phi. Democrat. Presbyn. Mason. Rotarian (gov. 18th dist. 1932-33). Editor of Anson on Contracts, 1929. Home: 6445 Greene St. Office: Witherspoon Bldg., Philadelphia, Pa.

TURNBULL, Agnes Sligh (Mrs. James Lyall Turnbull), writer; b. New Alexandria, Pa., Oct. 14, 1888; d. Alexander Halliday and Lucinda Hannah (McConnell) Sligh; prep. edn., Washington (Pa.) Sem.; grad. Indiana (Pa.) State Normal Sch., 1910; studied U. of Chicago 1 yr.; m. James Lyall Turnbull, July 27, 1918; 1 dau., Martha Lyall. First story pub. by Am. Mag., 1920; since contbr. stories to same and Woman's World, Country Gentleman, McCall's Mag., etc. Mem. Authors' League America, Authors' Guild, Pi Kappa Sigma. Republican. Presbyn. Author: Far Above Rubies, 1926; Wife of Pontius Pilate, 1928; In the Garden, 1929; The Four Marys, 1932; Old Home Town, 1933; This Spring of Love, 1934; The Rolling Years (novel), 1936; Remember the End (novel), 1938. Home: 46 Claremont Av., Maplewood, N.J.

TURNBULL, Arthur, broker; b. New York, N.Y., June 17, 1865; s. William and Helen M. (Stone) T.; grad. St. Marks Sch., Southboro, Mass., 1882; A.B., Columbia, 1886; m. Alice Winifred Post, Jan. 22, 1907; children—William, Arthur. Sec. to pres. Erie R.R., 1886-88; successively asst. treas., treas. and v.p. U.S. Mortgage & Trust Co., from its organization to 1902; partner Post & Flagg, New York Stock Exchange, since 1902; dir. Chem. Bank & Trust Co. Gov. New York Stock Exchange. Trustee Teachers Coll. of Columbia U. Mem. St. Andrews Soc., Delta Psi. Republican. Presbyn. Clubs: Union (New York); Somerset Hills Country (Bernardsville, N.J.). Home: Far Hills, N.J. Office: 49 Broad St., New York, N.Y.

TURNBULL, Barton P.; treasurer and dir. Rockefeller Centre Inc.; dir. Consolidated Coal Co. of Delaware, Chase Nat. Bank of New York. Home: 87 Hillcrest Av., Summit, N.J. Office: 30 Rockefeller Plaza, New York, N.Y.

TURNBULL, Margaret, author; b. Glasgow, Scotland; d. Thomas Easton and Jean (Craig) T.; brought to U.S. at age of 2; ed. pub. schs., Arlington, N.J., and by pvt. study. Mem. Soc. Am. Dramatists and Composers, New York, Authors' League, New York, Phillips Mill Community Assn. (dir.), Women's Nat. Rep. Club, New York. Presbyn. Author: W. A. G.'s Tale, 1913; Looking After Sandy, 1914; Handle with Care, 1916; The Close-Up, 1918; Madame Judas, 1925; Alabaster Lamps, 1925; The Left Lady, 1926; Rogues' March, 1928; The Handsome Man, 1928; A Monkey in Silk, 1931; The Return of Jenny Weaver, 1932; In the Bride's Mirror, 1934; The Coast Road Murder, 1934; also (plays), Genesee of the Hills (dramatization of Told in the Hills), prod. 1905; A Society Policeman, prod. Atlantic City, N.J., 1905; Classmates (with William C. de Mille), prod. New York, 1907; On the Square (with Hector H. Turnbull), prod. New York, 1913; The Deadlock, prod. Washington and New York, 1913; At the Mitre, prod. Fine Arts Theatre, Chicago, 1914; also author of many motion picture plays and scenarios; at least seven of Miss Turnbull's novels have a Buchs County, Pa., background. Home: New Hope, Pa.

TURNER, Bird Margaret, univ. prof.; b. Moundsville, W.Va.; d. John M. and Mary J. (Douglas) T.; A.B., U. of W.Va., Morgantown, W.Va., 1915, A.M., 1917; Ph.D., Bryn Mawr (Pa.) Coll., 1920; unmarried. Teacher mathematics High Sch., Moundsville, W.Va.; asst. dir. Model Sch., Bryn Mawr (Pa.) Coll., 1917-18; instr. mathematics, U. of Ill., Urbana, Ill., 1920-23; asst. prof. mathematics, U. of W.Va., Morgantown, 1923-25, asso. prof., 1925-31, prof. mathematics since 1931. Fellow A.A.A.S.; mem. Am. Math. Soc., Math. Assn. of America, Phi Beta Kappa, Kappa Kappa Gamma. Presbyterian. Address: 354 Spruce St., Morgantown, W.Va.

TURNER, Charles Franklin, physician; b. Wilkes-Barre, Pa., Mar. 6, 1896; s. Charles Simpson and Delphine Lydia (Huber) T.; student Princeton U., 1914-16; student Lafayette U., 1925; M.D., U. of Pa., 1929; m. Patience Laird Hughes, June 16, 1916; 1 son, James Hughes. Interne, Meth. Episcopal Hosp., Phila., 1929-30; practice of medicine, Montclair, N.J., since 1930; mem. staff Essex County Hosp., Belleville, N.J., and Mountainside Hosp. and Community Hosp., Montclair; school physician, Montclair. Served as 1st lt., Aviation, U.S. Army, 1917-19. Mem. A.M.A., Asso. Physicians of Montclair, William Pepper Med. Soc. of U. of Pa., Alpha Mu Pi Omega. Episcopalian. Club: Quadrangle (Princeton). Home: 72 Cambridge Rd. Office: 151 Grove St., Montclair, N.J.

TURNER, Charles Root, dean of Sch. of Dentistry, U. of Pa.; b. Raleigh, N.C., Nov. 3, 1875; s. Vines Edmund and Love Gales (Root) T.; grad. Raleigh Male Acad., 1891; A.B., U. of N.C., 1895; D.D.S., U. of Pa., 1898, Sc.D., 1933; M.D., Med. Coll. of Va., 1899, Sc.D., 1935; m. Sara Cameron Clark, June 21, 1906; 1 dau., Sara Clark. Began practice at Richmond, 1900; prof. prosthetic dentistry, U. of Pa., since 1902; dean Sch. of Dentistry, same univ., since 1917. Mem. A.M.A., Am. Dental Assn., Phi Beta Kappa, Sigma Xi, Phi Kappa Sigma, Delta Sigma Delta, Pi Mu. Democrat. Episcopalian. Club: University. Author: American Text Book of Prosthetic Dentistry, 1932. Home: 755 Beacom Lane, Merion, Pa.

TURNER, Creighton Hooker, physician; b. Montoursville, Pa., Nov. 17, 1883; s. William Acerly and Louisa (Blair) T.; grad. Muncy Normal, Pa., 1903; M.D., Jefferson Med. Coll., 1909; m. Mattie Allen, June 15, 1918; children—Creighton, Nancy Louise. Resident physician Jefferson Hosp., Phila., 1909-11, chief resident physician, 1911-12; med. chief outpatient dept., St. Agnes Hosp., Phila., 1912-22, visiting physician since 1922; gen. practice 1912-25; internist since 1925; asso. professor of medicine, Jefferson Med. Coll., since 1928. Mem. Phi Rho Sigma, Alpha Omega Alpha. Mason. Clubs: Rolling Green Golf (Delaware Co., Pa.); Medical (Phila.). Address: 1731 Pine St., Philadelphia, Pa.

TURNER, Ellwood Jackson, lawyer; b. Allegheny, Pa., Aug. 9, 1886; s. Frederick Fairthorn and Jennie (Short) T.; ed. Swarthmore Coll., 1904-05; LL.B., U. of Pa. Law Sch., 1908; m. Elizabeth Addis Downing, Nov. 8, 1911; children—Elizabeth Addis, William Howard, Ellwood Jackson, Frederick Fairthorn II, Anne Downing. Admitted to Pa. bar, 1909 and engaged in practice of law at Phila., 1909-13, at Chester, Pa., since 1913; mem. Pa. Ho. of Rep., 1925-38, re-elected for 8th term, 1938, now speaker; chmn. Interstate Commn. Del. River basin; mem. bd. mgrs., Council of State Govts.; served as solicitor for cities and twps. Served as sergt. Pa. Res. Mil., 1917-18. Mem. Pa. and Del. Co. bar assns., Phila. and Del. Co. lawyers clubs, Phi Sigma Kappa. Past vice-pres. Kiwanis Internat. and Gov. Pa. Dist. of Kiwanis. Republican. Presbyn. Club: Kiwanis of Chester (past pres.) Home: Idlewild Lane, Media, Pa. Office: 602 Crozer Bldg., Chester, Pa.

TURNER, Homer Griffield, geologist, chemist; b. Toronto, Can., Nov. 3, 1887; s. Berkley Griffield and Eleanor (Temple) T.; B.S., Syracuse U., 1912, M.S., 1914; student U. of Chicago, summer 1913; m. Nina Ida Cornish, Nov. 28, 1916; children—J. Eleanor, Erma Norine, Byron Berkley. Came to U.S., 1891, naturalized, 1903. Instr. mineralogy, Syracuse, 1913-16, asst. prof., 1916-18; asst. prof. geology, Lehigh U., 1918-26 and 1927-29, acting head dept. geology, 1926-27; dir. research Anthracite Inst. since 1929; research engineer Anthracite Equipment Corporation. Mem. Nat. Coal Classification Com. Fellow A.A.A.S.; mem. Am. Chem. Soc., Am. Inst. Mining & Metall. Engrs., Am. Water Works Assn., Pa. Acad. Science, Pa. Waterworks Operators' Assn., Pa. Sewage Works Assn., Alpha Chi Sigma, Sigma Xi, Sigma Beta. Republican. Methodist. Clubs: University, Lehigh Valley Engineers, Center County Engrs. (State College, Pa.); Coal Research (U.S. and Eng.). Author of numerous publs. on fundamental properties of anthracite and new uses of anthracite, also articles on design and operation of filters. Discoverer of method for showing micro-structure of anthracite. Home: 420 E. Hamilton Av., State College, Pa. Office: 19 Rector St., New York, N.Y.

TURNER, Hulett M., pres. Towanda Printing Co.; b. Towanda, Pa., Oct. 22, 1878; s. Dudley H. and Letitia (Breed) T.; ed. high sch.; m. Floy Lilley, June 4, 1908; children—Louise (Mrs. Paul A. Mitten), Frances (Mrs. J. Nevin Shaffer), David M. Pres. Towanda (Pa.) Printing Co. since 1927. Postmaster of Towanda, 2 terms, 1924-33. Republican. Presbyterian. Clubs: Rotary, Masonic (Towanda, Pa.). Home: Ontario Apts. Office: Main St., Towanda, Pa.

TURNER, John Patrick, physician; b. Raleigh, N.C., Nov. 1, 1886; s. Jesse Edward and Jennie Virginia (Edwards) T.; student Coll. of City of New York, 1900-03; M.D., Shaw Univ., Raleigh, N.C., 1906, LL.D., 1934; grad. course in surgery, U. of Pa., 1921; m. Marion Carmencita Harris, Apr. 15, 1909; 1 dau., Marion Virginia (wife of Frederick D. Stubbs, M.D.). Interne Douglass Hosp., Phila., 1906; practice as physician and surgeon, Phila., since 1907; chief of surgical staff Douglass Hosp. since 1918; elected pres. of staff Douglass Hosp., 1938; med. dir. and vice-pres. Keystone Aid Ins. Co.; med. inspr. Phila. Pub. Schs., 1912-30; police surgeon Phila. Police Department, since 1930. Mem. Metropolitan Bd., Y.M.C.A.; mem. bd. dirs. Crime Prevention Bureau of Phila.; mem. bd. dirs. Sesqui-Centennial, 1926; mem. Bd. of Pub. Edn., Phila., since 1935; mem. phys. edn. com. Y.M.C.A. of U.S.; trustee Shaw U., Raleigh, N.C., Berean Sch., Phila., Pa. Biol. Research Foundation. Served in Med. Reserve Corps, U.S. Army, during World War. Pres. Nat. Med. Assn., 1921; mem. A.M.A., Pa. State Med. Soc., Phila. County Med. Soc., Phila. Acad. Medicine, Sigma Pi Phi, Kappa Alpha Psi. Republican. Methodist. Mason (33°), Elk. Club: Citizens (Phila.). Author: Ringworm and Its Successful Treatment, 1921. Home: 1705 W. Jefferson St. Office: 1302 S. 18th St., Philadelphia, Pa.

TURNER, Louis Alexander, univ. prof.; b. Cleveland, O., Jan. 1, 1898; s. Elmer Canfield and Lucy (Mason) T.; student Buchtel Acad., Akron, O., 1911-15; A.B., A.M., Cornell U., 1920; Ph.D., Princeton U., 1923; m. Margaret Mather, July 20, 1931; children—Almon Richard, Elizabeth Chase. Instr. physics Princeton U., 1922,23, asst. prof., 1925-29, asso. prof. physics since 1929; nat. research fellow, Harvard, 1924-25; John Simon Guggenheim Memorial Fellow, Göttingen, 1929-30. Mem. Am. Phys. Soc., Am. Assn. Physics Teachers, Phi Beta Kappa, Sigma Xi, Delta Upsilon. Club: Nassau (Princeton, N.J.). Home: 179 Prospect Av. Office: Palmer Physical Laboratory, Princeton, N.J.

TURNER, Matilda Hutchinson, artist; b. Jerseyville, Ill.; d. Louis Henry and Mary Jane (Hutchinson) Turner; student Marietta (O.) Coll. for Women, Drexel Inst. Art Dept., Phila., 1901-03; Pa. Acad. Fine Arts under Hugh H. Breckenridge, Wm. Chase, Sargeant Kendall, Cecelia Beaux; miniature painting under A. Margaretta Archambault. Employed as research librarian, Dept. of History, Gen. Assem. of Presbyn. Ch., Phila., 1918-1939; retired, 1939; has followed profession of painting since 1916, especially in painting of miniatures; exhibited at Century of Progress, Chicago, Ill., and in many of the largest cities of the U.S. Mem. Speech Reading Club of Phila., Plastic Club of Phila.; life mem. Fellowship Pa. Acad. of the Fine Arts, Pa. Soc. Miniature Painters. Republican. Presbyterian. Author: Poems in anthology, Ring-A-Round by Mildred P. Harrington, and in Christmas Lyrics of 1937, Vol. II. Home: 3717 Hamilton St., Philadelphia, Pa.

TURNER, William Jay, lawyer; LL.B., U. of Pa., 1891. Practiced in Phila. since 1891; gen. counsel Lehigh Coal & Navigation Co., Lehigh & N.E. R.R. Co.; dir Phila. Nat. Bank. Mem. Am. Bar. Assn. Office: 1421 Chestnut St., Philadelphia, Pa.

TURP, James S., judge; b. Mayo Landing, N.J., Feb. 22, 1894; s. John and Isabella (McKandless) T.; prep. edn., business coll. and Emerson Inst., Washington, D.C.; LL.B., with distinction, George Washington U., 1920; m. Anna P. Hunsicker, May 21, 1921; children—Donald Leo, Maribelle Jean, David Henry, Ernest Burchard, Virginia Lois. Began as mill worker, 1908; variously employed to 1920; admitted to N.J. bar, 1920; asst. U.S. dist. atty., Dist. of N.J., 1925-28; judge Mercer County Court of Common Pleas, Trenton, since 1935. Formerly mayor of Hightstown, N.J. and sec. to pres. of State Senate. Received Boy Scout award for work among youth. Mem. Mercer County, N.J. State, Am. bar assns., Am. Legion, Hightstown Grange, Phi Delta Phi, Order of Coif. Republican. Presbyterian. Mason. Home: 314 S. Main St., Hightstown, N.J. Office: Broad Street Bank Bldg., Trenton, N.J.

TURPIN, C. Murray, ex-congressman; b. Kingston, Pa., March 4, 1878; grad. high sch., Kingston, and Wyoming Sem.; D.D.S., U. of Pa., 1904; m. Anna M. Manley, 1907 (died 1929); 4 children. Carpenter, grocery clk. and steamboat capt. before entering dental practice at Kingston; mem. Bd. of Edn., 6 yrs., burgess of Kingston 4 yrs., prothonotary of Luzerne Co., Pa., 4 yrs.; elected to 71st Congress, 1929, to fill vacancy; reëlected to 72nd to 74th Congresses (1933-37), 12th Pa. Dist. Corpl. Co. F, 9th Pa. Vol. Inf., Spanish-Am. War, later capt. Pa. N.G. Mem. Veteran Firemen's Assn., Jr. Order United Am. Mechanics, United Spanish War Vets., Am. Legion (certificate), Psi Omega, etc., also hon. life mem. various orgns. Republican. Clubs: Kiwanis, Wyoming Valley Automobile. Home: Kingston, Pa.

TUTELA, Luigi, music prof.; b. Grottaminarda, Italy, May 2, 1885; s. Generoso and Maria (Moschella) T.; student elementary pub. sch., Grottaminarda, 1890-95, Normal Inst., Avellino, 1895-98; studied violin, piano, harmony, under Signor Arturo Nutini (blind violinist and pianist), Prof. A. Penza, Dr. S. N. Penfield, New York, 1898-1905; grad. New York Coll. of Music, 1910; Diploma of Honor, Naples (Italy) Music Acad., 1925; came to U.S., 1898, naturalized, 1930; m. Concettina De Jeso, July 3, 1910; children—Marie (Mrs. Michael Vigliotta), Alfred, Robert, Olga. Began as organist, Olivet Chapel, Newark, N.J., 1910; has been teacher of music at Newark, N.J., since 1908. Winner of Neapolitan Song Contest (New York). Republican. Catholic. Composer: Le Trionfo, for band and orchestra; Sciara-Sciat Elegy, for violin and piano (2d Prize at Internat. Music Contest); Sinfonia Passionale; Sonata Tragica, for piano; Tresa, one act opera. Author: Cuore ed Arte (poems and novels), 1928. Address: 467 S. 14th St., Newark, N.J.

TUTTLE, Clarence E., chmn. bd., treas. and dir. Rustless Iron & Steel Corpn. Home: Garrison, Md. Office: 3400 E. Chase St., Baltimore, Md.

TUTTLE, James Horton, banking; b. Croton-on-Hudson, N.Y., Oct. 24, 1875; s. Nathaniel and Elanora Jordan (Clark) T.; student pub. and pvt. schs.; attended Coll. City of New York, 1892-96; LL.B., New York Law Sch., 1898; m. Elizabeth Norris, June 15, 1900; children—William Norris, Elizabeth Norris (Mrs. Donald E. Wilbur), Helen Norris. Admitted to New York bar, 1898, and in pvt. practice of law, N.Y. City, 1898-1908; became mem. staff Girard Trust Co., 1908, asst. v.p. since 1920; sec. and dir. Thos. Emery's Sons, Inc., Cincinnati; sec. and dir. Emery Holding Co., Cincinnati; dir. J. E. Caldwell & Co., Pa. Laundry Co., Phila. Served as 1st lt., 313th Inf., U.S. Army, 1917-19; now lt. col., Inf. Res. (313th Inf. Organized Reserves). Mem. Phila. Bar Assn., Mil. Order Fgn. Wars of U.S., Mil. Order World War, Am. Legion, Delta Kappa Epsilon. Republican. Mason. Clubs: Union League (Phila.); Merion Cricket (Haverford, Pa.). Home: County Line Road, Bryn Mawr, Pa. Office: Girard Trust Co., Philadelphia, Pa.

TUTWILER, Wirt Henry, investment securities; b. Lexington, Va., June 20, 1877; s. Ely Shores and Edmonia Preston (McClelland) T.; student Washington & Lee U., Lexington, Va., 1893; m. Virginia Moxter (died 1937); m. 2d, Elizabeth Parker Baird, Jan. 23, 1939. Salesman Kingan & Co., Richmond, Va., 1897-1921; salesman Harrison & Co., Phila., 1921-33, gen. partner since 1933. Mem. Pa. Hist. Soc., Art Alliance, Soc. Colonial Wars, S.R. (Pa.), Alpha Tau Omega. Republican. Presbyterian. Mason (32°, Shriner). Home: 303 Clwyd Rd., Bala-Cynwyd. Office: 123 S. Broad St., Phila., Pa.

TUVE, Merle Antony, research physicist; b. Canton, S.D., June 27, 1901; s. Anthony G. and Ida Marie (Larsen) T.; prep. edn. Augustana Acad., Canton, S.D., 1915-18; B.S. in elec. engring., U. of Minn., 1922, A.M., 1923; Ph. D., Johns Hopkins, 1926; m. Winifred Gray Whitman (M.D.), Oct. 27, 1927; children—Trygve Whitman, Lucy Winifred. Teaching fellow U. of Minn., 1922-23; instr. in physics, Princeton U., 1923-24, Johns Hopkins, 1924-26; asso. physicist, Carnegie Inst. of Washington, 1926, physicist, 1928-38, chief physicist since 1938. Received A.A.A.S. prize (with L. R. Hafstad and O. Dahl), 1931. Fellow Am. Phys. Soc.; mem. Philos. Soc., Washington Acad. Medicine, Tau Beta Pi, Sigma Xi, Gamma Alpha, Phi Beta Kappa. Democrat. Lutheran. Contbr. to Physical Review and other scientific jours. Home: 135 Hesketh St., Chevy Chase, Md. Office: 5241 Broad Branch Rd., Washington, D.C.

TWISS, William Bertrand; prof. English, Rutgers U. Address: Rutgers U., New Brunswick, N.J.

TWITCHELL, Earl Wagner, pres. E. W. Twitchell, Inc.; b. Haddonfield, N.J., Oct. 22, 1893; s. Oscar and Mary W. (James) T.; ed. Haddonfield pub. schs.; m. Pauline Hatch, Sept. 4, 1919; children—Nancy, Betsy Hatch. Active engaged in paper industry since 1911; employed by D. L. Ward Co., Philadelphia, 1911-13; organizer, 1913, and since pres. E. W. Twitchell, Inc.; dir. Camden Trust Co. (Haddonfield branch), John Estaugh Bldg. & Loan Assn. (Haddonfield). Trustee Bancroft Sch. Pres. Paper Twine Mfrs. Assn. Home: 273 Montwell Av., Haddonfield, N.J. Office: Third and Somerset Sts., Philadelphia, Pa.

TWITMYER, Edward Marvin, psychologist; b. Phila., Pa., Mar. 4, 1901; s. Edwin Burket and

Mary Elizabeth (Marvin) T.; A.B., U. of Pa., 1924, A.M., same, 1926, Ph. D., same, 1930; m. Elizabeth C. Bull, June 7, 1930; children; —Robert Yates, Thomas Marvin. Engaged as asst. instr. psychology, U. of Pa., 1924-26, instr. 1926-37; asst. personnel officer, U. of Pa. Coll., 1928-32; personnel adviser School of Nursing, Phila. Gen. Hosp., 1933-37, Presbyn. Hosp., 1935-37; lecturer and cons. psychologist since 1930; dir. Student Personnel, Girard Coll., Phila., Pa. since 1937. Fellow Am. Assn. Applied Psychology, A.A.A.S., Nat. Edn. Assn., Eastern Assn. Coll. Deans and Advisers of Men (sec.-treas.), Pa. Assn. Clin. Psychologists, Sigma Xi, Theta Delta Chi. Republican. Presbyn. Club: Lenape (Philadelphia). Home: Primos, Pa.

TWITMYER, Edwin Burket, prof. psychology; b. McElhattan, Pa., Sept. 14, 1873; s. George Wells and Johanna (Reese) T.; Ph.B., Lafayette Coll., Easton, Pa., 1896; Ph.D., U. of Pa., 1902; LL.D., Lafayette Coll., 1933; m. Mary E. Marvin, Dec. 26, 1907; children—Edward Marvin, Georgiana Jane. Instr. in psychology, U. of Pa., 1897-1907, asst. prof. psychology, 1907-14, prof. since 1914, also dir. Psychol. Lab. and Clinic and chief of Speech Clinic, U. of Pa. Trustee Pa. State Sch. for Feeble-Minded, Pa. Sch. for the Deaf, Delaware County Hosp. Fellow A.A.A.S., Am. Soc. for Study Disorders of Speech; mem. Am. Psychol. Soc., Sigma Xi, Theta Delta Chi. Democrat. Presbyn. Mason (32°). Club: University. Co-Author (with Nathanson): The Correction of Defective Speech, 1932. Contbr. to various mags. Home: Secane, Pa.

TWOMBLY, Clifford Gray, clergyman; b. Stamford, Conn., May 7, 1869; s. Alexander Stevenson and Abigail Quincy (Bancroft) T.; student Boston Latin Sch., 1880-86; B.A., Yale, 1891; B.D., Episcopal Theol. Sch., Cambridge, Mass., 1894; student Andover Theol. Sem., 1891-93; D.D. Franklin and Marshall Coll., 1916; m. Edith Cazenove Balch, July 1, 1897; children—Gray Huntington, Alexander Stevenson. Deacon, 1894, priest, 1895, P.E. Ch.; asst. minister Grace Ch., New Bedford, Mass., 1894-1897; rector St. Paul's Ch., Newton Highlands, Mass., 1897-1907; rector St. James' Ch., Lancaster, Pa., since 1907; canon St. Stephens' Cathedral, Harrisburg, Pa. Mem. exec. council of Harrisburg Diocese. Writer and lecturer on sociol. subjects, especially reform of the movies. Home: 115 N. Duke St., Lancaster, Pa.

TWOMBLY, Henry Bancroft, lawyer; b. Albany, N.Y., Nov. 10, 1862; s. Alexander Stevenson and Abigail Quincy (Bancroft) T.; grad. Boston Latin Sch., 1880; A.B., Yale, 1884; law, Harvard, 1884-86; m. Frances Doane, Sept. 12, 1889; 1 son, Edward Bancroft. Admitted to N.Y. bar, 1887, N.J. bar, 1894, Md. bar; sr. mem. Putney, Twombly & Hall; dir. and gen. counsel Internat. Salt Co., Retsof Mining Co., Detroit Rock Salt Mining Co., Avery Rock Salt Mining Co., Valvoline Oil Co., Lobsitz Mills Co., Sauquoit Silk Mfg. Co., Berkshire Industrial Farm. Sec. Neighborhood House, chmn. advisory board Lincoln Y.M.C.A., mem. Health Bd.—all of Summit. Referee of Children's Court of Union County. Mem. N.Y. State Bar Assn., New York Law Inst., N.Y. County Lawyers Assn., University Assn. (pres.), Playhouse Assn. (Summit), S.A.R., Phi Beta Kappa, Psi Upsilon, Skull and Bones. Republican. Presbyn. Clubs: Lawyers, Nat. Republican (New York); Athenaeum, Canoe Brook Country (Summit); Graduate (New Haven) Home: 226 Hobart Av., Summit, N.J. Office: 165 Broadway, New York, N.Y.

TWOMEY, M. Joseph, clergyman; b. Killarney, Ireland, Jan. 10, 1871; s. Timothy and Hannah (Conner) T.; B.Ph., Brown U., 1900, D.D., 1921; grad. Newton Theol. Instn., Newton Centre, Mass., 1903; LL.D., Temple University, Philadelphia, 1934; m. Ella Caroline Stanton, Nov. 4, 1903. Came to U.S., 1890, naturalized citizen, 1902. Ordained ministry Bapt. Ch., 1903; pastor Danielson, Conn., 1903-05, Portland, Me., 1905-14, Peddie Memorial Church, Newark, N.J., 1914-30, Baptist Temple, Philadelphia, 1930-35, North Orange Bapt. Ch., Orange, N.J., since 1937. Member executive com. Northern Baptist Conv., 1913-19, mem. Bd. of Am. Bapt. Foreign Mission Soc., 1922-37; pres. Bapt. Conv. of Pa., 1931-33; mem. bd. Me. Bapt. Conv., 1908-13, N.J. Bapt. Conv., 1916-30; pres. Me. Sunday Sch. Assn., 1913-14. Mem. Bd. trustees N.J. Baptist Conv. since 1937; trustee Va. Union Univ., Internat. Sem., Peddie Sch. Hebron (Me.) Acad., Eastern Bapt. Theol. Sem. (Phila.). Republican. Mason (32°). Club: Newark Athletic. Home: 189 Glenwood Av., East Orange, N.J.

TYDINGS, Millard E., senator; b. Havre de Grace, Md., Apr. 6, 1890; s. Millard F. and Mary B. (O'Neill) T.; B.S. in M.E., Md. Agrl. Coll. 1910; LL.B., U. of Md., 1913; LL.D. from Washington College in 1927; m. Eleanor Davies, 1935. Admitted to Maryland bar, 1913, and began practice at Havre de Grace; mem. Md. Ho. of Del., 1916-17, speaker 1920-22, Senate, 1922; mem. 68th and 69th Congresses (1923-27), 2d Md. District; elected mem. U.S. Senate 3 terms, 1927-45. Democrat. Served as private on Mexican border, 1916; with A.E.F., as officer, advancing to lt. col. 29th Div., Machine Gun Units; participated in Haute, Alsace, Meuse-Argonne offensive. Awarded D.S.M., D.S.C., 3 citations. Mem. Commn. on State War Memorial Bldg., Md. Mem. Am. Legion, Vets. of Foreign Wars. Episcopalian. Mason, Elk. Clubs: Maryland Club (Baltimore); Chevy Chase (Washington); Burning Tree; Havre de Grace Yacht. Home: Havre de Grace, Md.

TYLER, Charles A., newspaper pub.; b. Bristol, Pa., Oct. 14, 1877; s. George F. and Mary E. (Young) T.; student Drexel Inst., Phila.; m. Isabel Thompson, June 21, 1906. Manager steamship and travel cos., 1897-1914; v.p. Public Ledger, Phila., 1914-34; pres. and treas. The Philadelphia Inquirer since 1934; dir. Tradesmen's Nat. Bank & Trust Co., Liberty Mut. Ins. Co.; trustee Cyrus H. K. Curtis Estate. Republican. Episcopalian. Mason (32°). Clubs: Union League, Racquet, Phila. Country; Seaview Golf (Absecon, N.J.). Home: The Kenilworth, Germantown. Office: 400 N. Broad St., Philadelphia, Pa.

TYLER, Cornelius Boardman, lawyer; b. Plainfield, N.J., Nov. 15, 1875; s. Col. Mason Whiting and Eliza Margaret (Schroeder) T.; 9th generation from Gov. William Bradford of Mayflower; prep. edn., Williston Sem., Easthampton Mass.; A.B., Amherst, 1898; LL.B., Columbia, 1901 (studied physics and mathematics there also); m. Susan Tilden Whittlesey, Dec. 29, 1908; children—John, David, Caroline Boardman. Mem. firm Tyler & Tyler (with brother Wm. S.), New York; pres. Rossendale Reddaway Co. (Newark, N.J.); dir. and mem. exec. com. Plainfield Trust Co.; active in developing apple raising on Lake Chelan, Wash., and pres. Chelan Orchards; with brother owns and operates Wood Brook Farms (certified milk plant), Metuchen, N.J.; officer or dir. various other corpns. Pres. Plainfield Pub. Library, Community Chest of Plainfield, 1922-36. Chmn. Price Com. of Food Administration for N.J., World War. Active in affairs of Amherst Coll., chmn. alumni fund, 1926-28, chmn. exec. com. alumni council, 1933-34. Fellow Am. Geog. Soc.; mem., Mayflower Soc., Military Order Loyal Legion, Academy of Political Science, Shakespeare Society of Plainfield, Phi Beta Kappa, Psi Upsilon, Phi Delta Phi. Independent Republican. Presbyn. Clubs: The Century Association (New York); Country (Pittsfield). Author: Genealogical Appendix to Autobiography of W. S. Tyler, D.D., LL.D. (grandfather), 1912; (with Rollin U. Tyler) Tyler Genealogy (2 vols.), 1912. Has crossed the Am. continent 40 times and has traveled extensively in Europe and other parts of the world. One of founders Columbia Law Review. Home: 525 W. 7th St., Plainfield, N.J.; (summer) "Inwode," Pittsfield, Mass. Office: 165 Broadway, New York, N.Y.

TYLER, William Seymour, lawyer; b. Plainfield, N.J., Oct. 18, 1873; s. Mason Whiting and Eliza Margaret (Schroeder) T.; prep. edn., Williston Sem., Easthampton, Mass.; A.B., Amherst Coll., 1895; student Göttingen, Germany, 1896; LL.B., Columbia, 1899; m. Ethel Van Boskerck, Nov. 23, 1899; children—Margaret Rowe, William Seymour, 3d, Edith Edwards (Mrs. Henry B. Noss). Admitted to N.Y. bar, 1898, and since practiced in New York; mem. firm Tyler & Tyler; pres. Wood Brook Farms (N.J. business corpn.). Served as federal food adminstr. for N.J. during World War; dir. Am. Relief Adminstrn. European Children's Fund, 1918-19; mem. Common Council, City of Plainfield, N.J., 1902-08; pres. Bd. of Edn., Plainfield, N.J.; pres. Anti-Tuberculosis League, Plainfield, N.J.; mem. bd. visitors State Coll. of Agr., N.J., and mem. bd. mgrs. State Agrl. Expt. Sta. since 1926; pres. Plainfield Y.M.C.A., 1930-35. Mem. New England Soc. City of New York, Soc. Mayflower Descendants (gov. N.J. Soc., 1912-13), Psi Upsilon. Presbyterian (elder Crescent Av. Ch., Plainfield). Club: University (New York). Home: 520 W. 8th St., Plainfield, N.J. Office: 165 Broadway, New York, N.Y.

TYREE, Lewis, prof. of law; b. Salem, Va., May 18, 1892; s. Cornelius and Anne Taylor (Abrams) T.; student Fork Union (Va.) Mil. Acad., 1905-08; B.A., M.A., U. of Va., Charlottesville, Va., 1912; LL.B., Washington and Lee U., Lexington, Va., 1915; m. Winifred Scott West, July 28, 1921; children—Lewis, Mary West, Scott West. Admitted to Va. bar, 1915, and practiced at Richmond, Va., 1916-17; prof. law, Washington and Lee U., Lexington, Va., 1919-25, U. of Newark, N.J., since 1925. Served as ensign, U.S.N.R.F., 1917-19. Mem. Alpha Chi Rho, Phi Alpha Delta, Omicron Delta Kappa, Delta Sigma Rho. Democrat. Baptist. Mason. Club: Newark (N.J.) Athletic. Home: 16 Park Pl. Office: 40 Rector St., Newark, N.J.

TYRRELL, Henry Grattan, cons. engr.; b. Weston, Ont., Can., Nov. 8, 1867; s. William and Elizabeth (Burr) T.; grad. Sch. Practical Science, Toronto, 1886; C.E., U. of Toronto, 1894; m. Lilly Bryant, Jan. 1, 1890 (died Jan. 1906); children—George Grattan, William Bryant, Alicia; m. 2d, Mary Maude Knox, Nov. 7, 1907; 1 son, H. Grattan Knox. On exploration surveys in western Canada and on railroad construction, Quebec and Maine, 4 yrs.; design and constrn. bridges and bldgs., 1888-1904; spl. engr. bridges and bldgs., Harriman rys., 1906-08; consulting engr. since 1908; propr. Tyrrell Engring. Co.; gave services to U.S. Govt., World War, in designing, building and valuation of war plants. Has been connected with constrn. of many notable bridges and other structures in U.S. and foreign countries; reported on rebuilding the twice-destroyed line of ry. through Rainbow Canyon between Salt Lake City and Los Angeles; designed improved type of ry. crossing gates; also types of regulating gates for canals and waterways; plans for St. Clair Memorial Bridge, and high level crossings of rivers at Detroit, Montreal, Norfolk, Va., etc.; spanning 20 miles of Chesapeake Bay, from Baltimore to Eastern Shore; crossing Irish Channel from Ireland to Scotland by means of bridge and tunnel; prepared standard designs and estimated costs for bridges of ordinary span, steel and concrete, and published original charts and formulæ for weight and cost, now in general use; since World War has prepared engring. reports for constrn. (U.S. and foreign) to approximate value of $2,000,000,000. After World War bought large army camp for own use. Built hosp. bldgs. in N.E. for U.S. Govt. Member Soc. Promotion Engring. Education, Am. Assn. Engrs., Am. Soc. Engrs., A.A.A.S., Baltimore Association of Commerce. Clubs: Engineers, Civitan (Baltimore). Author: Mill Building Construction, 1900; Concrete Bridges and Culverts, 1909; Mill Buildings, 1910; History of Bridge Engineering, 1911; Artistic Bridge Design, 1912; Engineering of Shops and Factories, 1912. Assisted by his wife in publication of his books. Extensive contbr. to engring. and scientific jours. of America and Europe. Proprietor Grattan Tyrrell Co., Baltimore. Home: "Grattanwood," Catonsville, Md. Office: 5 Guilford Av., Baltimore, Md.*

TYSON, Anthony Morris, lawyer; b. Phila., Pa., July 17, 1866; s. Marshall and Catharine Ellen (Smith) T.; student Hopkinson's Private Classical Sch., Boston, 1880-86, Harvard Coll., Cambridge, Mass., 1886-88; LL.B., U. of Md. Law Sch., Baltimore, Md., 1891; m. Laura Lee

Packard, June 30, 1910 (died Oct. 4, 1925). Admitted to bar, 1891; since in gen. practice of law. Mem. Am. Bar Assn., Md. State Bar Assn., Baltimore City Bar Assn., Soc. Colonial Wars in State of Md., Md. Soc. S.A.R. Democrat. Episcopalian (vestryman Christ Ch., Baltimore). Club: University (Baltimore). Home: 206 Chancery Road. Office: 207 N. Calvert St., Baltimore, Md.

TYSON, Carroll Sargent, artist; b. Phila., Pa., Nov. 23, 1877; s. Carroll S. and Clara (Reeves) T.; student Forsyth's Sch., DeLancey Sch., Royal Acad. of Munich, Germany, 1899-1901; m. Helen Roebling, Oct. 16, 1912; children—Charles Roebling, Helen (Mrs. Louis Madeira). Has followed profession as artist since 1896, specializing in landscapes and birds; exhibited in N.Y., Boston, Phila., Wilmington, Washington, London, Eng.; dir. Phoenix Iron Co., Little Schuylkill Navigation and Coal Co., Del. & Bound Brook R.R. Co. Dir. Zool. Soc. of Phila., Fairmount Park Assn., Pa. Mus. Decorated with two medals Legion of Honor (France). Republican. Episcopalian. Clubs: Racquet, Art, Philadelphia, Sunnybrook (Phila.). Home: 8811 Towanda St., Chestnut Hill. Office: 319 Walnut St., Philadelphia, Pa.

TYSON, Floyd Thaddeus, univ. prof.; b. York, Pa., Nov. 10, 1898; s. Thaddeus and Anna (Koller) T.; B.S., Pa. State Coll., 1920; Ph.D., Yale, 1923; m. Verna Summerill, Sept. 1, 1928; children—Elizabeth, John, Thaddeus. Began as chemist and research fellow at Yale, 1920-23; asst. prof. chemistry, Temple U. Phila., 1924-33, asso. prof. since 1934. Served in S.A.T.C., 1917-18. Fellow A.A.A.S.; mem. Am. Chem. Soc., Sigma Xi, Phi Kappa Phi. Home: 222 Hewett Rd., Glenside, Pa.

TYSON, Francis Doughton, prof. economics; b. Odessa, Del., Aug. 21, 1888; s. William Green and Margaret Russell (Hallman) T.; grad. Central High Sch., Phila., Pa., 1906; A.B., U. of Pa., 1909, Ph.D., 1912, Harrison scholar, 1909-10; m. Helen Miller Glenn, June 15, 1917; children—Frances Elizabeth, Robert Glenn. Asst. in English, U. of Pa., 1910-11, instr. in economics, 1911-12; instr. in social economy, New York Sch. of Social Work, 1912-13; instr. and asst. prof. economics and sociology, U. of Pittsburgh, 1913-19, prof. economics since 1920. Spl. agt. U.S. Bur. Immigration, Dept. of Labor, 1917-20; sec. Home Service Com. and dir. Home Service Inst., Allegheny County Chapter Am. Red Cross, 1917-19; mem. Gov.'s Adv. Com. on Pub. Subsidies, 1922-23; Gov.'s Commn. on Unemployment Reserves, 1932-33; mem. State adv. council on employment service Pa. Dept. Labor and Industry; chmn. Allegheny Co. Advisory council; mem. bd. Legal Aid Soc., Internat. Inst., Housing Assn.; dir. Pa. Housing and Planning Assn.; mem. bd. and chmn. industrial com., Urban League; mem. state affairs commn. Chamber of Commerce. Mem. Am. Econ. Assn., Am. Acad. Polit. and Social Science, Am. Sociological Society, American Association University Profs., Phi Beta Kappa, Kappa Sigma, Omicron Delta Kappa. Mem. Soc. Friends. Clubs: Faculty, University, Civic of Allegheny Co. Contbr. to Am. Econ. Rev., Am. Jour. Sociology, New Republic, Survey; author of monographs on economics of the commercial theatre and motion pictures, and labor and immigration problems. Home: 4247 Bryn Mawr Rd., Pittsburgh, Pa.

TYSON, George Russell, prof. edn.; b. Odessa, Del., Aug. 24, 1890; s. Wm. Green and Margaret (Hallman) T.; ed. Phila. Sch. Pedagogy, 1909-11; B.S., U. of Pa., 1916, A.M., same, 1922, Ph.D., same, 1936; m. Helen Armor, June 27, 1928. Engaged in teaching, Phila., Pa., 1911-17; Harrison Fellow in Edn., U. of Pa., 1919-21; prof. edn. and dir. summer sch., Cornell Coll., 1921-27; prof. and head dept. edn., Ursinus Coll., Collegeville, Pa., since 1927. Served as psychologist, U.S.A., 1918-19; specialist in testing and grading, 1920. Mem. Nat. Edn. Assn., Phi Delta Kappa. Independent Republican. Methodist (trustee Ch. of the Advocate). Club: Morris Field (Philadelphia). Home: 4927 Morris St., Philadelphia, Pa. Office: Collegeville, Pa.

TYSON, Levering, college pres.; b. Reading, Pa., Apr. 9, 1889; s. Charles Hunter and Emma Lucy (Geise) T.; A.B., Gettysburg (Pa.) Coll., 1910, Litt.D., 1930; A.M., Columbia, 1911; m. Reba Pomeroy Kittredge, Dec. 31, 1914; children—James Levering, Reba Jane, David Otto. Gazeteer editor New Internat. Cyclo., 1912-15; alumni sec. and mng. editor Columbia Alumni News, 1914-20, editor, 1920-30; also served as sec. and pres. Assn. Alumni Secretaries; organizer, 1919, and first pres. Alumni Mags. Associated; apptd. fellow, 1927, Am. Alumni Council (combination of Assn. Alumni Socs. and Alumni Mags. Associated), also chmn. Aims and Policies Com.; asso. dir. university extension, Columbia U., 1920-30, organizing the home study dept.; conducted study of radio broadcasting in adult edn., 1929, for Am. Assn. for Adult Edn. and Carnegie Corpn. of New York; dir. Nat. Advisory Council on Radio in Education, Inc., 1930-37; president Muhlenberg College since 1937. Formerly alumni trustee Gettysburg Coll.; mem. council Am. Association for Adult Edn.; mem. Am. Polit. Science Assn., Acad. Polit. and Social Science, Acad. Polit. Science, Am. Acad. Air Law, A.L.A., World Assn. for Adult Edn., Progressive Edn. Assn., Am. Council on Edn., Institute of Pacific Relations, Am. Mus. Natural History, Phi Beta Kappa, Phi Delta Theta, Omicron Delta Kappa, Acacia. Lutheran. Democrat. Mason. Clubs: Livingston (Allentown); Uptown (New York); Mantoloking Yacht. Author: (brochures) Education Tunes In, 1930; What to Read About Radio, 1933; Where Is American Radio Heading?, 1934; also contbr. many papers on alumni activities, university extension, adult edn. and related subjects. Editor: Radio and Education (pub. by U. of Chicago), 1932-35. Home: 2401 Chew St., Allentown, Pa.

TYSON, Ralph Maguire, M.D., pediatrician; b. Montgomery, Pa., May 9, 1888; s. James Grier and Emma (Achenbach) T.; student Bucknell U.; M.D., Jefferson Med. Coll. (Phila.), 1915; m. Hazel Beeber, June 19, 1917; 1 son, Ralph Robert. Interne Jefferson Hosp., Phila.; prof. of pediatrics, Temple U. Sch. of Medicine, 1932-37; practicing physician in Phila. and specialist in pediatrics since 1922; consulting pediatrician Shriners' Hosp.; chief of pediatric dept., Pa. Hosp. since 1924; chief Med. Service St. Christopher's Children's Hosp., 1937-38. Served in Med. Corps, A.E.F., U.S.A., World War. Mem. A.M.A. (pediatric sect.), Pa. State Med. Soc. (pediatric edn. com.), Phila. Co. Med. Soc., Phila. Pediatric Soc., Coll. of Physicians of Phila., Am. Acad. of Pediatrics, Am. Bd. of Pediatrics, Doctors Golf Assn. of Phila., Sigma Alpha Epsilon, Alpha Kappa Kappa. Republican. Methodist. Clubs: Manufacturers and Bankers (Phila.); Manufacturers Golf and Country. Contbr. of papers on pediatrics to med. jours. Home: 6709 N. 8th St. Office: 255 S. 17th St., Philadelphia, Pa.

TYSON, William Perry, lawyer; b. Norristown, Pa., Sept. 7, 1895; s. Daniel Gross and Ellamanda (Scholl) T.; grad. pub. schs., Downingtown, Pa., 1912, West Chester (Pa.) Business Sch., 1913; m. Grace E. Keim, Dec. 27, 1922; 1 son, William Perry (died 1931). Began as clk. Worth Steel Co., 1912; asst. sta. agt., Reading Ry. Co., 1913-16; pur. agt. Phila. Brass Co., 1916-18; with production dept. E. G. Budd Co., 1919; dept. prothonotary, Chester Co., 1920-27, prothonotary, 1927-31; admitted to Pa. bar, 1929 and since 1931, engaged in gen. practice of law at West Chester, Pa.; v.p., trust officer and dir. First Nat. Bank of West Chester; dir. Lukens Steel Co., Downingtown Mfg. Co., Daily Local News Co. Served as pvt., Inf., U.S. Army, 1918. Mem. Am. Bar Assn., Chester Co. Bar Assn., Penna. Bar Assn. Republican. Methodist. Mason (K.T., Shriner), Odd Fellow, Moose, Patriotic Order Sons of America. Home: 322 Washington Av., Downingtown, Pa. Office: 11 N. High St., West Chester, Pa.

U

UDY, Stanley Hart, lawyer; b. Bartonsville, Pa., Apr. 7, 1889; s. William Hart and Clara Jane (Slutter) U.; Ph.B., U. of Chicago, 1916, J.D., 1919; m. Hilda Lestina Huse, Sept. 10, 1927; one son, Stanley Hart. Assistant secretary of Agency of U.S. in United States-Venezuela Arbitration, at The Hague, 1910; disbursing officer Commn. of Engrs., Costa Rica-Panama Boundary Arbitration, 1911-13; asst. prof. law, U. of Mo. Law Sch., 1920-21; asst. solicitor Dept. of State, 1921-22; asso. counsel for U.S. in U.S.-Norway Arbitration, May-Oct. 1922, also in Am.-British Claims Arbitration, 1922-25; asso. legal adviser to President, Plebiscitary Commn., Tacna-Arica Arbitration, 1926; counsel for U.S., General and Special Claims Commissions, United States and Mexico, 1927-30; practiced in New York City since Nov. 1930. Made special study of judicial system of State of Illinois, 1919-20, for Legislative Reference Bureau of Illinois, and wrote about half of bulletin on the judiciary, for use of delegates of Illinois Constitutional Conv. Served as 1st lt. U.S.A. on staff of Provost Marshal Gen. Crowder, Dec. 23, 1918-Jan. 31, 1919. Mem. Am. Bar Assn., Am. Soc. Internat. Law, Phi Sigma Kappa, Phi Delta Phi, Phi Beta Kappa, Order of the Coif. Republican. Mason (32°, Shriner). Clubs: University. Home: 33 Gilbert Pl., West Orange, N.J. Office: 33 W. 46th St., New York, N.Y.

UELAND, Elsa, educator; b. Minneapolis, Minn., Mar. 10, 1888; d. Andreas and Clara (Hampson) U.; B.A., U. of Minn., 1909; New York Sch. of Philanthropy, 1909-10; M.A., Columbia, 1911. Resident worker, Richmond Hill Settlement, N.Y. City, 1909-11; investigator, Vocational Guidance Assn., 1911-12, Vocational Edn. Assn., 1912-14; teacher pub. schs., Gary, Ind., 1914-16; organizer and pres. Carson Coll. (a progressive sch. for orphan girls), Phila., 1917—; mem. teaching staff Cooperative Sch. for Student Teachers, N.Y. City, 1934-35; supervisor of orns., Tygart Valley Homestead, W. Va., for U.S. Resettlement Adminstrn., 1935-36. Mem. N.E.A., Progressive Edn. Assn., Am. Assn. Social Workers, Pa. Hort. Soc., Phi Beta Kappa, Alpha Phi. Unitarian. Home: Flourtown, Pa.

UHLE, David John, v.p. Coplay Cement Mfg. Co.; b. Cleveland, O., Mar. 31, 1885; s. Otto and Caroline (Stieglitz) U.; ed. Cleveland pub. schs.; m. Davina W. Fyfe, July 5, 1909; children—Otto, John David, Helen Caroline, Marion Davina, Robert Goodwin, Theodore Thomas. Draftsman Van Dorn Iron Wks., 1903; mech. draftsman, Interstate Engr. Co., 1904-05; with American Bridge Co., 1905-15, as structural draftsman, 1905-06, structural checker, 1906-08, structural squad leader, 1908-11, structural designing engr., 1911-15; fabricating engr., Bethlehem Steel Co., 1915-16; chief engr., Atlas Cement Co., 1916-17, asst. plant mgr., 1917-25; v.p. in charge operations Coplay Cement Mfg. Co. since 1925; pres. and dir. Grudex Corpn. since 1934. Licensed professional engr., Pa. Mem. Am. Chem. Soc., Am. Mech. Engrs., Am. Soc. Testing Materials, Lehigh Valley Engring. Club, Nat. Soc. Professional Engrs. Christian Scientist. Mason (32°, K.T., Shriner). Club: Bethlehem Republican. Home: 203 S. 16th St., Allentown, Pa. Office: Coplay Cement Mfg. Co., Coplay, Pa.

UHLENHUTH, Eduard (Carl Adolph), univ. prof.; b. Wolkersdorf, nr. Vienna, Austria, July 19, 1885; s. Adolf Franz and Leopoldine Rosalie U.; came to U.S., 1914, naturalized, 1924; Ph.D., Univ. of Vienna, 1911; m. Elizabeth Baier, July 17, 1919; 1 son, Eberhard Henry. Research asst., Biol. Inst., Vienna, 1911-14; fellow and later asso., Rockefeller Inst. for Med. Research, 1914-24; guest, Dept. Anatomy, Johns Hopkins U., 1924-25; asso. prof. anatomy, U. of Md. Med. Sch., 1925-31, prof. gross anatomy, 1931-34, head and chmn. dept. gross anatomy since 1934. Fellow A.A.A.S. Mem. Am. Assn. of Anatomy, Soc. of Exptl. Biology and Medicine, Am. Assn. for Study Endocrinology, Harvey Soc., Am. Assn. Zoologists, Marine Biol. Labs., Woods Hole, Mass., U. of Md. Biol. Soc. (past pres.). Awarded VanMeter Prize of Am. Assn. for the Study of Goiter. Home: 4115 Westview Rd., Baltimore, Md.

UHLER, Claude, psychiatrist; b. Baltimore, Md., July 18, 1894; s. William J. and Anna (Wittig) U.; A.B., Johns Hopkins U., 1915; M.D., Johns Hopkins U. Med. Sch., 1919; m. Moment Clem, Sept. 28, 1928. House officer, Henry Phipps Psychiatric Clinic, Baltimore, Md., 1919-20; first resident physician, Baylor Univ. Hosp., Dallas, Tex., 1920-21; clin. psychiatrist, Baylor U. Med. Sch. and practicing psychiatrist, Dallas, Tex., 1921-29; sr. psychiatrist, Worcester State Hosp., Worcester, Mass., 1929-30; asst. psychiatrist, N.Y. State Dept. Mental Hygiene, 1930-31; clin. dir. Del. State Mental Hygiene and Child Guidance Clinics, Farnhurst, Del., since 1931. Served in U.S.A., 1918-19. Diplomate Am. Bd. Psychiatry. Fellow Am. Psychiatric Assn., A.M.A.; mem. Am. Orthopsychiatric Assn., Pa. Psychiatric Soc., Del. Acad. of Medicine, Phi Beta Pi. Presbyn. Club: New Castle (New Castle, Del.). Home: Farnhurst, Del.

UHLER, Stewart Mann, M.D., surgeon; b. Stockerton, Pa., Feb. 11, 1879; s. Hiram and Julia Ann (Mann) U.; A.M., Lafayette Coll.; M.D., Jefferson Med. Coll.; post-grad. study, New York and Germany, 1920-22; m. Ella M. Messinger, Dec. 1906; 1 dau., Ella M. Engaged in gen. practice of medicine, 1906-20; chief ear, nose and throat dept. Sacred Heart Hosp., Allentown, Pa., since 1922, Quakertown Community Hosp. since 1930; asso. surgeon eye, ear, nose and throat dept. Allentown Gen. Hosp. since 1924; dir. First Nat. Bank of Pen Angel. Fellow Am. Coll. Surgeons; mem. Am. Acad. Ophthalmology and Otolaryngology, A.M.A., Lehigh Valley Med. Assn., Lehigh County Med. Soc., Allentown Chamber of Commerce, S.A.R., Patriotic Order Sons of America. Mason, Odd Fellow, Elk. Clubs: Skytop, Irem Temple Country. Home: Bushkill Drive, Easton, Pa. Office: 104 N. 8th St., Allentown, Pa.

ULERICH, William Keener, newspaper editor; b. Latrobe, Pa., Apr. 18, 1910; s. William Wesley and Anna (Keener) U.; grad. Latrobe (Pa.) High Sch., 1926; A.B., Pa. State Coll., 1931; m. Edith Willis Orton, May 26, 1934. Reporter Huntingdon (Pa.) Daily News, 1931-32, State College (Pa.) Times, 1932-34; editor Centre Daily Times, State Coll., Pa., since establishment, Apr. 2, 1934; part time instr. in journalism, Pa. State Coll. Mem. Delta Upsilon, Sigma Delta Chi. Republican. Methodist. Home: 222 E. Irvin Av. Office: 110 W. College Av., State College, Pa.

ULLMAN, Alfred, surgeon; b. Baltimore, Md., Oct. 2, 1881; s. Samuel and Eliza (Millhauser) U.; M.D., Coll. Phys. and Surgs., Baltimore, 1902; m. Bertha Katz; children—Alfred, Elizabeth Sara, Jeanne Frances. In gen. practice of surgery for many years. Fellow Am. Coll. Surgeons; mem. Am. Bd. Surgery. Jewish religion. Mason, Elk. Club: Suburban. Home and Office: 1712 Eutaw Pl., Baltimore, Md.

ULLMANN, Harry Maas, coll. prof.; b. Springfield, Mo., Apr. 14, 1868; s. Ludwig and Sarah (Maas) U.; A.B., Johns Hopkins U., 1889, Ph.D., 1892; student Ecole des Mines, Paris, 1893-94; m. Rachel Barnett Mifflin, Aug. 21, 1919; children—Harriet Mifflin, Thomas Mifflin. Instr. in quantitative and industrial analysis, 1894-1904; asst. prof in chemistry, Lehigh U., 1904-10, asso. prof., 1910-14, prof. of chemistry and chem. engring. and head of dept. since 1914. Fellow London Chem. Soc.; mem. A.A.A.S., Am. Inst. Chem. Engrs., Am. Chem. Soc., Soc. for Promotion Engring. Edn., Societe Chimique de Paris, Deutsche Chemische Gesellschaft. Theta Delta Chi, Sigma Xi, Tau Beta Pi. Democrat. Episcopalian. Clubs: Bethlehem, Saucon Valley Country. Address: 20 W. Church St., Bethlehem, Pa.

ULLOM, Josephus Tucker, physician; b. Athens, O., Oct. 4, 1877; s. Andrew Wolf and Ellenor Jane (Tucker) U.; student Athens (O.) High Sch., 1891-94; A.B., Ohio U., Athens, O., 1898, M.A. (hon.), 1914; M.D., U. of Pa., 1901; m. Selena Patterson Hughes, Oct. 15, 1908; children—Margaret Jane (Mrs. Fred MacD. Richardson), Charlotte Bayard (Mrs. Wm. H. Haines, III), Selena Hughes, Josephine Tucker. Mem. of staff, Henry Phipps Inst. for Tuberculosis, Phila., 1903-13; visiting physician, Phila. Gen. Hosp., tuberculosis dept., 1904-07, Chestnut Hill Hosp., Phila., since 1907; instr. in medicine, U. of Pa., 1910-13; visiting physician, Germantown Hosp., Phila., since 1933. Fellow Am. Coll. Physicians, Phila. Coll. Physicians; mem. Phila. Co., Pa. State med. socs., A.M.A. Republican. Methodist. Author numerous med. articles. Address: 160 Carpenter Lane, Mt. Airy, Philadelphia, Pa.

ULLRICH, Elvin H(enry), lawyer; b. Newark, N.J., Feb. 22, 1907; s. August and Ida L. (Baerenrodt) U.; student U. of Newark, Newark, N.J.; LL.B., N.J. Law Sch., Newark; hon. Ph.D., Blue Ridge Coll., New Windsor, Md., 1937; m. Alice Pistor, Nov. 10, 1931. Admitted to N.J. bar as atty., 1929, as counselor, 1935; engaged in gen. practice of law at Elizabeth, N.J. since 1936; police recorder; judge dist. ct. of Union Co. since 1931; borough atty. Borough of Kenilworth, N.J., 1934-38. Mem. bd. visitors, Blue Ridge Coll., New Windsor, Md. Mem. Am. Bar Assn., Union Co. Bar Assn., Delta Theta Phi. Republican. Presbyn. Mason. Club: Canoe Brook Country (Summit). Home: 1085 Nicholas Av., Union. Office: 1143 E. Jersey St., Elizabeth, N.J.

ULMAN, Joseph N., judge; b. Baltimore, Md., Aug. 9, 1878; s. Nathan and Dina (Oppenheim) U.; A.B., Johns Hopkins, 1898; A.M., Columbia, 1900; m. Ella Guggenheimer June 23, 1903; children—Joseph N., Elinor. Admitted to Md. bar, 1901, and began practice at Baltimore; mem. firm Knapp, Ulman & Tucker, 1910-24; mem. faculty U. of Md. Law Sch., 1908-28; judge Supreme Bench of Baltimore since 1924. Pres. Md. Prisoners' Aid Assn., 1910-12, 1919-24, now dir.; treas. Montrose Sch. for Girls, 1920-24; pres. Hebrew Benevolent Soc., 1925-28; chmn. Com. on Prison Labor, apptd. by Nat. Industrial Recovery Bd., 1934; chmn. Prison Industries Reorganization Administrn., 1935-36, mem. of board since 1936; dir. and mem. exec. com. Community Fund of Baltimore, 1925-30; pres. Baltimore Urban League, 1931-34; v.p. Baltimore branch, Am. Jewish congress, since 1937; consultant Pub. Works Administrn. since 1938; dir. Nat. Probation Assn., Nat. Urban League, Legal Aid Bur. of Baltimore. Mem. Advisory Com. on Criminal Justice, Am. Law Inst., 1934, advisor criminal justice and youth since 1938. Mem. Am. Bar Assn. (mem. com. on edn. and practice of Criminal Law Sect. since 1938), Md. State Bar Assn., Baltimore City Bar Assn. (grievance com., 1914-15 and 1920-22), Am. Law Inst. (elected 1936), Am. Sociol. Soc., Md. Com. on Prison Labor, Johns Hopkins Alumni Assn. (past pres.), Phi Beta Kappa, Phi Alpha, Omicron Delta Kappa (hon. 1935). Democrat. Clubs: University, Chesapeake. Author: A Judge Takes the Stand, 1933; also wrote intro. to Marshall & May's The Divorce Court—Maryland, 1932, and "The Trial Judge's Dilemma," in Glueck's Probation and Criminal Justice, 1933. Contbr. chapter, "Law as a Creative Force in Social Welfare" to Lowry's Readings in Social Case Work, 1939. Contbr. to Year Book of Nat. Probation Assn., 1932-33, 1936, 1938; also articles to mags. Asso. editor Jour. Criminal Law and Criminology. Home: 2615 Talbot Road. Office: Court House, Baltimore, Md.

ULREY, Dayton, radio mfg. exec.; b. N. Manchester, Ind., Sept. 19, 1884; s. Stephen S. and Mary Jane (Tridle) U.; student Chester High Sch., N. Manchester, Ind., 1902-06; A.B., Ind. U., Bloomington, Ind., 1911; A.M., Indiana U., 1912; Ph.D., Leland Stanford U., 1917; m. Lela Rittenhouse, Nov. 29, 1912 (died Sept. 15, 1938); children—Elizabeth Jane, Karl Rittenhouse, Mary Anne, Richard Abbott, Barbara Louise. Began as physics teacher, Indiana U., 1911; physics instr., U. of Pittsburgh, 1912-15, asst. prof., 1917-18; grad. asst. in physics, Leland Stanford U., 1915-17; research physicist Westinghouse Electric & Mfg. Co., Pittsburgh, Pa., 1918-30, mgr. physics div., research dept., 1930-37; mgr. transmitting and special tubes div., research and engring. dept., RCA Radiotron Div., RCA Mfg. Corpn., Harrison, N.J., since 1937. Mem. Am. Phys. Soc., Am. Optical Soc., Inst. of Radio Engrs., Am. Inst. E.E. Home: 175 Forest Av., Glen Ridge, N.J. Office: RCA Mfg. Co., Inc., Harrison, N.J.

ULRICH, Elmer B., teacher of science; b. Brickerville, Pa., Apr. 5, 1880; s. Allen Corry and Lavina (Bixler) U.; B.Pd., M.Pd., West Chester (Pa.) State Normal Sch., 1899; B.S., Muhlenberg Coll., Allentown, Pa., 1907; Ph.D., U. of Pa., 1910; m. Ella Rice Hoffman, Sept. 9, 1908; children—Catharine Lavinia, Grace Elizabeth. County sch. teacher, Lebanon Co., Pa., 1896-1901; prin. Unionville (Pa.) High Sch., Chester Co., 1901-02, Luzerne Co., 1902-06; sch. teacher, Phila. schs. since 1908, now head science dept., Simon Gratz High Sch., Phila.; asst., U. of Pa. Grad. Sch., 1910-11. Fellow A.A.A.S.; mem. Pa. Bot. Soc., Sigma Xi. Republican. Lutheran. Mason. Home: 3717 Taylor Av., Drexel Hill. Office: 17th and Luzerne Sts., Philadelphia, Pa.

UMBEL, Robert Emeroy, lawyer; b. Henry Clay Twp., Fayette Co., Pa., July 11, 1863; s. Samuel C. and Martha L. (Brown) U.; prep. edn. Georges Creek Acad., Smithfield, Pa.; grad. Western Pa. Classical and Scientific Inst., Mt. Pleasant, Pa., 1885; m. Frances Grier White, Nov. 29, 1899; 1 dau., Margaret Grier (Mrs. Robert W. Leeds). Admitted to Pa. bar, 1887, and began practice at Uniontown; judge Courts of 14th Jud. Dist. of Pa., 1900-15; pres. Fayette Title & Trust Bldg.; v.p. and dir. White Swan Hotel Co. Am. Pa., Fayette Co. bar assns. Democrat. Presbyn. Mason (33°, Shriner). Clubs: Triangle (pres.), Uniontown Country. Home: 50 W. Main St. Office: Fayette Title & Trust Bldg., Uniontown, Pa.

UMBREIT, Samuel John, clergyman, editor; b. Manchester, Wis., Feb. 22, 1871; s. Henry E. and Sophie (Forcy) U.; Ph.B., North Central Coll., Naperville, Ill., 1898, Ph.M., 1907; student Chicago U., 1923, U. of Berlin, Germany, 1928; hon. D.D., Evang. Theol. Sem., Naperville, Ill., 1916; m. Amanda M. Bauernfeind, June 29, 1899 (dec. 1937); children—Kenneth Bernard, Lucile Burdella. Ordained to ministry Evang. Ch., 1898; served in Chicago and Wis.; served as missionary in Japan and supt. of mission, 13 yrs. and 3 yrs. supt. mission in China, 1905-21; bishop of European Area of Evang. Ch., 1926-34; editor The Christliche Botschafter, German organ Evang. Ch., Harrisburg, Pa., since 1934. Republican. Mem. Evang. Ch. Home: 3029 N. Fifth St., Harrisburg, Pa. Office: Third & Reily St., Harrisburg, Pa.

UMSTED, John Rittenhouse, lawyer; b. Germantown, Pa., 1871; grad. Central High Sch.; grad. U. of Pa. Law Sch., 1893. Engaged in gen. practice of law at Phila., specializing in decedents' estates and real property law; formerly v.p. Continental-Equitable Title & Trust Co.; now pres. Pa. Title Assn.; former chmn. of legal sect. Am. Title Assn.; dir. Wilson Line, Inc. Chmn. com. on law of decedents' estates and trusts, Pa. Bar Assn.; mem. Germantown Hist. Soc. Home: 214 Pelham Rd., Germantown, Philadelphia, Pa. Office: 501 Commercial Trust Bldg., Philadelphia, Pa.

UNANGST, Edward Jacob, merchant, banker; b. Seips, Pa., Jan. 11, 1859; s. John J. and Susan C. (Seip) U.; ed. Nazareth (Pa.) pub. schs.; m. Mary A. Helms, Nov. 26, 1885; children—Elwood John, Raymond, Helen Eliza, Mae Susan. Became associated with father in gen. store, Nazareth, Pa., 1874; became partner John J. Unangst & Son, 1883, sole owner, 1895; partner with sons, E. J. Unangst & Sons, 1917; dir. Second Nat. Bank of Nazareth since 1900, pres. since 1922; pres. Nazareth Planing Mill Co. Mem. Nazareth Bd. of Edn., 1888-97. Pres. Greenwood Cemetery Co. Treas. Northampton Co. Agrl. Soc., 1890-96. Lutheran (mem. bd. trustees, bldg. com. and Sunday Sch.; treas. St. John's Evangelical Lutheran Ch., 1879-1904). Home: 32 S. Broad St. Office: Broad and Belvidere Sts., Nazareth, Pa.

UNCAPHER, Andrew Gallagher, lawyer; b. Vandergrift, Pa., Sept. 23, 1901; s. Milton E. and Margaret E. (Gallagher) U.; grad. Vandergrift (Pa.) pub. schs., 1916, Culver (Ind.) Mil. Acad., 1919; B.S., U. of Pa., 1923; LL.B., U. of Pittsburgh, 1926; m. Mary Wilson

Jackson, Oct. 19, 1927; children—Carolyn Jackson, Andrew G. Admitted to Pa. bar, 1926 and since in gen. prac. at Greensburg, Pa.; solicitor Hyde Park Glove Co. since 1931, Vandergrift (Pa.) Svgs. & Tr. Co. since 1934, North Washington Coal Co. since 1928; special dep. atty. gen., Commonwealth of Pa.; treas. Westmoreland Co., 1931-35, sheriff since 1935; mem. Vandergrift Sch. Dist. since 1932, West Leechburg Sch. Dist. since 1934; partner Milton E. Uncapher Estate (real estate and ins.); dir. Vandergrift Svgs. & Trust Co., North Washington Coal Co. Republican county chmn. since 1934. Mem. Theta Delta Chi, Phi Delta Phi. Republican. Presbyterian. Mason, Elk, K.P. Club: University (Pittsburgh). Home: 245 Franklin Av. Office: 415 Bank & Trust Bldg., Greensburg, Pa.

UNDERHILL, Charles Reginald, electrical engr.; b. Chappaqua, N.Y., Nov. 2, 1874; s. of Joshua Bowron and Elizabeth (Green) U.; descendant of Capt. John U.; on account of deafness did not attend college; largely self-ed., specializing through corr. and text-books, in mathematics, physics, and engring.; m. Ella Howell Johnson, Apr. 6, 1898; children—Charles Reginald, Marguerite Allaire. Employed in inspection dept. Western Electric Co., N.Y. City, 1892-1900; chief elec. engr. Varley Duplex Magnet Co., Jersey City, N.J., and Providence, R.I., 1900-04; consulting elec. engr., N.Y. City, 1904-09; editor and tech. writer, Westinghouse Electric & Mfg. Co., Pittsburgh, 1909-10; chief engr., Am. Electric Fuse Co., Muskegon, Mich., 1910-11; chief elec. engr., Acme Wire Co., New Haven, Conn., 1911-21; cons. elec. engr., 1921-26; with Wappler Elec. Co., Inc., L.I. City, 1926-29, developing surg. and other high frequency machines. Has made extensive researches in the actions of electromagnets, the results of which have been published largely in Electrical World and Trans. Am. Inst. Electrical Engrs. Lectured on "Electromagnets," in leading colleges and univs. of U.S. Inventor of wireless telegraph printing system and other telegraphic and signaling devices. Commd. capt., Aviation Sect., Signal R.C., 1917; officer in charge radio tests in flight, Langley Field, on flying status; transferred to Air Service, 1918; served as radio officer, Sch. for Aerial Observers, Langley Field, also as radio statis. officer, Air Service Mil. Aeronautics, Washington. Fellow Am. Institute Elec. Engrs., A.A.A.S.; mem. Mil. Order World War, Am. Legion, Nat. Soc. Puritan Descendants, Pi Gamma Mu. Democrat. Author: The Electromagnet, 1903; Wireless Telegraphy and Telephony (with W.W. Massie), 1908; Solenoids, Electromagnets and Electromagnetic Windings, 1910; Magnets, 1924; Coils and Magnet Wire, 1925; Power Factor Wastes, 1926; Electrons at Work, 1933. Contbr. to Standard Handbook for Electrical Engineers since 1913. Discovered connection between elec. resistivity and specific heat. Address: Lower Bank, N.J.

UNDERHILL, Frederick Saunders, wholesale lumber mcht.; b. Montreal, Quebec, Can., Nov. 12, 1865; s. John and Annie (Ireland) U.; came to U.S., 1870, naturalized, 1888; student Phila. elementary schs., Keystone Grammar Sch., Phila., 1872-81, City Commercial Inst., Phila., 1883-85, also home study Chautauqua corr. course; m. Hattie Vollum Macartney, Sept. 1, 1917; children of sister adopted after her death —Rosalind Wortley (Mrs. Charles Barney Burt), Augustus Morley, Arthur Blackburn, Alma Clara (Raymond Hartman). Office boy Baldwin Locomotive Works, Phila., 1881-84; sec. to George McKelway, pharmacist, Phila., 1884-86; clk. and stenographer Thomas Potter Sons & Co., Phila., 1886-88; correspondent and order clk. James Strong & Co., Phila., 1888-98; local preacher in charge St. Matthew's M.E. Ch., Phila., 1887-93, ch. being built and dedicated free of debt during pastorate; partner Wistar, Underhill & Co., wholesale lumber mchts, Phila. since 1898; treas. Evergreen (N.C.) Lumber Co. since 1914, Penn-Sumter (S.C.) Lumber Co. since 1919, James Strong Lumber Co., Bristol, Tenn., since 1918, Unaka Lumber Corpn., Asheville, N.C., since 1920. Served as chmn. and organized Group 16 Liberty Loan Industrial Com., including 12 industries in Phila., 1917-19;

chmn. Eastern Delaware County War Work Council, Y.M.C.A., 1917-19. Mem. Central Com. on Lumber Standards, Washington, D.C., since 1927; dir. Lansdowne (Pa.) Pub. Schs. since 1903, pres. since 1925. Mem. Annual Conf. of Methodist Ch.; pres. bd. trustees Lansdowne (Pa.) Methodist Ch. since 1916; asso. supt. Lansdowne Methodist Sunday Sch. since 1910; pres. Del. Co. (Pa.) Christian Endeavor Union, 1912; 1st v.p. in charge finance Del. Co. Sabbath Sch. Assn., 1910-26; chmn. Social Service Commn. of Phila. since 1939; pres. Council of Lansdowne Choristers since 1937. Mem. Nat. Hardwood Lumber Assn. (dir.; 1st v.p. 1915-19, Nat.-Am. Wholesale Lumber Assn. (dir.; pres. 1927-30), Lumbermen's Exchange of Phila. (dir.; pres. 1916-18), Phila. Wholesale Lumberman's Assn. (dir.; pres. 1918-19), Union Athletic Assn. (Lansdowne; pres. 1917-18. Republican. Methodist. Mason (Washington Lodge 59, Worshipful Master, 1916). Home: 9 E. Plumstead Av., Lansdowne, Pa. Office: 1520 Locust St., Philadelphia, Pa.

UNDERWOOD, George B(oyle), mortgage banker; b. Brooklyn, N.Y., Mar. 2, 1903; s. George Patrick and Mary Ellen (Boyle) U.; grad. Marion (Ala.) Mil. Inst., 1921; Litt.B. Rutgers U., 1925; m. Priscilla Parker Earle, May 31, 1939. Began as newspaper reporter on Newark Ledger, 1925; later with N. Y. Evening Post and Associated Press; asso. state dir. Federal Housing Adminstrn., 1934-37; mortgage business since 1937; pres. and dir. Underwood-Frank Mortgage Co., mortgage financing Irvington, N.J., since 1937; vice-pres. and dir. Irvington Trust Co., Lake Paulinskill Development Co.; dir. Realty Investors. Pres. Mortgage Bankers Assn. of N.J. Mem. Delta Kappa Epsilon. Elk. Clubs: Crestmont Golf (West Orange, N.J.); Downtown, Bankers, Newark Athletic (Newark). Home: 125 Harrison St., East Orange, N.J. Office: 1000 Springfield Av., Irvington, N.J.

UNDERWOOD, Roy Reynolds, pres. Knox Glass Associates, Inc.; b. Fisher, Pa., July 27, 1887; s. H. A. and Ida (Smith) U.; student pub. schs.; m. Vesta N. Hosterman, May 10, 1910. Upon graduation, entered glass bottle mfg. plant as mould attendant, continuing through apprenticeship; began as mfr., 1914; pres. Knox Glass Associates, Inc., since 1935, now also dir.; dir. Knox (Pa.) Glass Bottle Co., Knox Glass Bottle Co. (Jackson, Miss.), Wightman Bottle & Glass Mfg. Co., Marienville Glass Co., Pa. Bottle Co., Oil City Glass Bottle Co., Metro Glass Bottle Co., Foxburg Bank. Mason, Odd Fellow. Clubs: Rotary, Foxburg Country. Home: Knox, Pa. Office: Veach Bldg., Oil City, Pa.

UNDERWOOD, William Edwin, editor and pub.; b. New Orleans, La., Nov. 8, 1860; s. Napoleon and Mary Elizabeth (Hogan) U.; ed. pub. schs. of New Orleans and pvt. tutors; m. Grace Cordell, Oct. 25, 1885; children—Jennie (dec.); Ruth, Lyon, Grace (dec.), Caroline (Mrs. W. L. Waite). Engaged in ins. bus. in various cities since starting as clk. in ins. agency, 1880; spl. agt. and gen. life ins., 1890-1900; asso. editor ins. mag., New Orleans, 1887-89; ins. journalism, New York, N.Y., 1902-27; prin. owner, editor and pub. "Insurance" a publ. identified with ins. bus., Newark, N.J. since 1927. Republican. Episcopalian. Home: 244 Washington St., Hasbrouck Heights, N.J. Office: 671 Broad St., Newark, N.J.

UNGER, Sidney Emanuel, rabbi; b. New York, N.Y., May 7, 1896; s. Adolph and Julia (Klein) U.; grad. DeWitt High Sch., New York; A.B. U. of Cincinnati, 1925; Rabbi, Hebrew Union Coll., Cincinnati, 1928; S.T.D., Temple U., Phila., 1936, Ed.M., 1939; unmarried. Asst. rabbi, Rodeph Shalom Congregation, 1928-33; rabbi, Temple Judea, since 1933. Served as 2d lt., Machine Gun Corps, U.S. Army, Hancock, Ga., during World War. Chaplain hdqrs. staff, 79th Div., Phila.; Eastern State Penitentiary, Phila. Mem. Am. Legion (chaplain), Phi Delta Epsilon, Mu Sigma, Pi Tau Pi. Mason. Clubs: Philmont Country, Ashbourne Country (Phila.). Home: Melrose Park, Pa. Address: 6835 York Rd., Philadelphia, Pa.

UNGER, William Hudson Roosevelt, lawyer and banking; b. Shamokin, Pa., Mar. 29, 1905; s. William Horace and Ella (Malick) U.; A.B., Dickinson Coll., 1927; LL.B., Dickinson Coll. Law Sch., 1929; m. Sarah Jane Tritt, Jan. 29, 1927; 1 son, William Hudson. Admitted to Pa. bar, 1929, and since engaged in gen. practice of law at Shamokin; sr. mem. firm W. H. Unger & Sons; asst. dist. atty., 1935-36; solicitor for co. controller since 1937; pres. and dir. Market Street Nat. Bank since 1937. Served in Officers Res. Corps., 1924-28. Mem. Phi Delta Theta. Republican. Methodist. Elk. Club: Shamokin Valley Country. Home: 22 No. 7th St. Office: 12 S. Market St., Shamokin, Pa.

UNTERMAN, Isaac, journalist; b. Warsaw, Poland, Oct. 15, 1889; s. Israel and Bessie (Wodka) U.; came to U.S., 1911, naturalized, 1917; D.D., Rabbinical Coll., Wilno, Poland, 1910; LL.B., Hamilton Coll. of Law, Chicago, 1916; Ph.D., Oskaloosa Coll., Ia., 1919; m. Lena Alkow, Oct. 15. 1911; children—Theodore Herzl, Ben Zion, Bessie (Mrs. Irving Wiener), Israel. Began career as journalist, 1911; editor and publisher, Jewish Morning Star, Newark, N.J. since 1921, Hudson Jewish News, Jersey City, N.J., 1921-32, Passaic Jewish Record, Passaic, N.J., 1930-35. Jewish religion. Author: The Feast of Esther, 1916; Jewish Holidays, 2 vols., 1938; History of Jews of Newark (in Yiddish), 3 vols., 1930; Feasts and Festivals (Yiddish), 2 vols., 1936; Jewish Education (Yiddish), 1916; Stories For Children (in Hebrew), 8 vols., Warsaw, 1920. Home: 163 Seymour Av., Newark, N.J.

UPDEGRAFF, William Barrett, mech. engineer; b. Connersville, Ind.; s. John F. and Luella (Rawls) U.; ed. Newburgh (N.Y.) Acad., 1896-99, Harvard, 1901-04; m. Mabelle Bond, July 10, 1906; children—Ross Bond, Joan. Successively marine engr., designing, operating, installing and testing marine machinery including turbines and submarine machinery and industrial engring., 1904-13; with Watson-Stillman Co., builders of hydraulic machinery, Roselle, N.J., since 1913, designing and selling, now v.p. and mgr. New York City sales. Mem. Harvard Engring. Soc. (past pres.), Am. Soc. Mech. Engrs. (past chmn. Plainfield, N.J., Sect.), Army Ordnance Assn. (v.p. New York Post). Republican. Presbyterian. Mason. Clubs: Harvard, Railroad-Machinery (New York). Has designed, patented and sold special equipment used in building subaqueous tunnels. Home: 384 El Mora Av., Elizabeth, N.J. Office: Roselle, N.J.; and 75 West St., New York, N.Y.

UPDEGROVE, Harvey Claude, physician; b. Easton, Pa., Oct. 16, 1886; s. Jacob Davidheiser and Susan S. (Beck) U.; A.B. with honors, Lafayette Coll., 1907; M.D., U. of Pa. Med. Sch., 1911; m. Gladys Rhodes Collins, Nov. 26, 1918; children—Elizabeth Collins, John Harvey, Charles David. Interne, German Hosp., Phila., 1911-14; engaged in gen. practice of medicine and surgery at Easton, Pa. since 1914; asso. surgeon Easton Hosp. since 1914. Served as lt. then capt. Med. Corps, R.A., 1917-19 with B.E.F.; wounded in action Apr. 12, 1918, in France; awarded Mil. Cross (Brit.). Mem. A.M.A., Lehigh Valley and Northampton Co. med. socs., Phi Beta Kappa, Alpha Omega Alpha, Delta Kappa Epsilon, Phi Alpha Sigma. Republican. Protestant. Clubs: Lehigh Valley Tennis (Easton); Hillcrest (Phillipsburg, N.J.). Noted as tennis player; Lehigh Valley Champion, 1920-22; Del. Valley Champion, 1916, 1919, 1920; Bethlehem Champion, 1925; Easton Champion, successively, 1907-34. Address: 420 Paxinosa Av., Easton, Pa.

UPP, John W., elec. engring.; b. Sandusky, O., Jan. 9, 1868; s. Henry B. and Elizabeth (Anderson) U.; M.E. in E.E., Cornell U., 1889; m. Elizabeth Sanman, Oct. 5, 1891; 1 son, John W., Jr. Asso. with General Electric Co. continuously, 1893-1933, mgr. switchgear dept. when retired, 1933. Mem. Am. Soc. Mech. Engrs., Am. Inst. Elec. Engrs., Phi Delta Theta. Republican. Congregationalist. Clubs: Union League, Racquet, Right Angle, Merion Cricket. Home: 220 Golfview Rd., Ardmore, Pa. Office: 1429 Walnut St., Philadelphia, Pa.

UPPVALL, Axel Johan, univ. prof.; b. Avelsäter, Värmland, Sweden, Jan. 2, 1872; s. Johan Jacob and Brita Kajsa (Persdotter) U.; grad. Hebron (Me.) Acad., 1901; student Gymnasium, Lund, Sweden, 1902-03, U. of Göttingen, 1903-04, 1905-06, U. of Nancy (France), summer 1904; B.A., Colby Coll., Waterville, Me., 1905; M.A., Harvard, 1907; Ph.D., Clark U., Worcester, Mass., 1919; studied U. of Berlin, summer, 1922; Jusserand Traveling scholar, U. of Pa. to Iceland, summers, 1923, 27; came to U.S., 1895, naturalized citizen, 1905; m. Alma Mathilda Johnson, Aug. 31, 1918. Instr. French, Hebron (Me.) Acad., 1907-08; instr. French and Latin, Philips Brooks Sch., Phila., 1908-09; instr. French, U. of New Brunswick, Can., 1909-10; instr. French, U. of Pa., 1910-11; chmn. dept. French and German, U. of New Brunswick, 1911-16; asst. prof. German, Clark U., Worcester, Mass., 1916-18; instr. French, U. of Pa., 1919-21, instr. German and Scandinavian languages, 1921-25, asst. prof., 1925-30, prof. Scandinavian languages since 1930. Acting recording sec. Council of Swedish Colonial Soc.; 1st sec. Swedish Am. Council; mem. publication bd. Am. Swedish Monthly; corr. mem. Riksföreningen, Gothenburg, Sweden; mem. Am. Assn. Univ. Profs., Modern Lang. Assn. America, Am. Soc. Swedish Engrs., New England Soc. Knight Royal Order of Vasa, 1st class, 1934. Republican. Lutheran. Author: August Strindberg, A Psychoanalytic Study, 1920; Strindberg the Man, 1920; Manual of Swedish Phonology, 1938; Swedish Grammar and Reader, 1938; etc. Home: 216 S. 43d St., Philadelphia, Pa.

UPSON, Maxwell Mayhew, engr.; b. Milwaukee, Wis., Apr. 22, 1876; s. Edwin M. and Kittie (Parsons) U.; A.B., U. of N. Dakota, 1896, Dr. Engring., 1931; M.E., Cornell U. 1899; m. Mary Shepard Barrett, Apr. 28, 1915; 1 dau., Jeanette. With Westinghouse, Church, Kerr & Co., N.Y. City, advancing to mng. engr., 1899-1905; asst. to pres. and chief engr. Hockanum Mills Co., Rockville, Conn., 1905-07; general manager, chief engr. and v.p. Raymond Concrete Pile Company, 1907-31, pres. of same company since 1931; chmn. bd. of dirs. Internat. Contractors Co.; pres. Barranquilla Port & Terminal Company. Is the holder of many patents controlling the placing of concrete piles with use of a permanent shell, and building of retaining walls, sea walls and subaqueous constrn. Trustee Cornell U. Mem. Am. Concrete Inst. (pres. 1926-28), Am. Soc. C.E., Am. Soc. M.E., Am. Soc. for Testing Materials. Republican. Presbyn. Clubs: Engineers, University, Bankers, Cornell U. Club of New York, Knickerbocker Country, Aldecress Country, Englewood Field; University (Chicago). Home: Mountain Rd., Englewood, N.J. Office: 140 Cedar St., New York, N.Y.

UPTON, Arthur Van Gorder, county supt. of schools; b. Harrison Co., W.Va., Feb. 26, 1901; s. Abram Van Gorder and Bertha Alice (Holden) U.; A.B., W.Va. Wesleyan Coll., Buckhannon, 1923; A.M., W.Va. Univ., Morgantown, 1937; Ped.D., W.Va. Wesleyan Coll., 1938; m. Louise Elizabeth Glenn, Aug. 4, 1926; children—Arthur Van Gorder, Jr., Robert Glenn. Employed as dir. W.Va. High Sch. State Basketball Tournament, 1922-23; teacher and athletic dir., Victory High Sch., Clarksburg, W. Va., 1923-26; playground dir., City of Clarksburg, 1925-26 summers; prin. Victory High Sch., Clarksburg, 1926-29; state dir. phys. edn. and asst. high sch. supervisor, W.Va. Bd. Edn., 1929-32; prin. high sch., Morgantown, W.Va., 1932-39; county supt. of schools, Harrison County, W.Va., since 1939. Mem. Clarksburg Library Bd., 1929. Pres. Monongalia Co. Safety Council, 1936. Mem. Boy Scout Council for Mountaineer Area, 1938. Mem. bd. trustees W.Va. Wesleyan Coll. since 1932. Mem. Nat. Edn. Assn., W.Va. State Edn. Assn. (mem. legislative com.), Nat. Assn. State Dirs. of Phys. Edn., W.Va. Assn. Secondary Sch. Prins. (sec. 1936, pres. 1937), Kappa Delta Pi, Kappa Alpha (province comdr. Hamilton Province). Republican. Methodist. Mason (K.T., S.R.). Odd Fellow. Club: Lake Floyd (Clarksburg). Lions Club (state sec.) 1926. Author: Manual of Physical Education for Elementary Schools, 1932. Home: Clarksburg, W.Va.

URBAN, Walter George, oral surgeon; b. Pittsburgh, Pa., Feb. 22, 1902; s. John and Mary (Diesing) U.; D.D.S., U. of Pittsburgh, 1929, M.S., 1931, Litt.M., 1938; unmarried. Gen. practice of dentistry, Pittsburgh, 1929-30, specializing in oral surgery since 1930; attending oral surgeon, Allegheny Co. Juvenile Court Detention Home, Pittsburgh, since 1930, dir. dental clinic since 1933. Fellow Internat. Coll. of Anesthetists; asso. fellow A.M.A.; mem. Am. Soc. Oral Surgeons and Exodontists, Soc. Am. Bacteriologists, Internat. Anesthesia Research Soc., Am. Dental Assn., Pa. State Dental Soc., Odontological Soc. of Western Pa. Home: 72 S. 19th St., Pittsburgh, Pa.

URBANSKI, Matthew F., surgeon; b. Perth Amboy, N.J., Aug. 8, 1891; s. Francis Xavier and Agnes U.; M.D., N.Y. Univ. Med. Sch., 1914; m. May Bond, 1930; 1 son, Francis Xavier. In practice of medicine at Perth Amboy, N.J.; pres. North Amboy (N.J.) Bldg. & Loan Assn. Formerly commr. pub. safety, Perth Amboy, N.J., med. dir. of schs. and pres. bd. of health. Fellow Am. Coll. of Surgeons. Catholic. Address: 314 Washington St., Perth Amboy, N.J.

UREY, Harold Clayton, chemistry; b. Walkerton, Ind., Apr. 29, 1893; s. Samuel Clayton and Cora Rebecca (Reinoehl) U.; B.S., U. of Mont., 1917; Ph.D., U. of Calif., 1923; Am. Scandinavian Foundation fellow to U. of Copenhagen, 1923-24; D.Sc., U. of Mont., also Princeton U., 1935; m. Frieda Daum, June 12, 1926; children—Gertrude Elizabeth, Frieda Rebecca, Mary Alice. Teacher rural schs., 1911-14; chemist Barrett Chem. Co., Phila., 1917-19; instr. chemistry, U. of Mont., 1919-21; asso. in chemistry, Johns Hopkins, 1924-29; asso. prof. chemistry, Columbia, 1929-34, prof. since 1934. Mem. A.A.A.S., Am. Acad. of Arts and Sciences, Am. Chem. Soc., Nat. Acad. Sciences, Académie Royale des Sciences, des Lettres et des Beaux Arts de Belgique, Am. Philos. Soc., Am. Physical Soc., Sigma Xi, Gamma Alpha, Phi Lambda Upsilon, Epsilon Chi. Awarded Willard Gibbs Medal by Chicago Sect. Am. Chem. Soc., 1934; Nobel prize in chemistry, 1934. Clubs: Faculty (Columbia U.), Cosmos. Author: (with A. E. Ruark) Atoms, Molecules and Quanta, 1930. Contbr. to a Treatise on Physical Chemistry (edited by H. S. Taylor), 1931. Editor Journal of Chemical Physics, 1933—. Contbr. to scientific jours. Has specialized in structure of atoms and molecules, thermodynamic properties of gases, absorption spectra, Raman spectra, Isotopes. Discoverer of hydrogen atom of atomic weight two. Home: 355 Highwood Av., Leonia, N.J.

URICH, Clair John, supervising prin. schs.; b. Patton, Pa., Aug. 9, 1903; s. John A. and Rose C. (Anna) U.; A.B., St. Francis Coll., Loretto, Pa., 1928; M.Ed., Pa. State Coll., 1938; m. Ethelene M. Lilly, Aug. 6, 1929; children—John Joseph (dec.), Cornelius F. Engaged in teaching mathematics and science, Hastings, Cambria Co., Pa., 1928-33; supervising prin. schs., Hastings Borough, Cambria Co., Pa., since 1933. Mem. Cambria Co. Prins. Assn. Democrat. Roman Catholic. K.C. (4°), Knight of St. George. Home: Beaver St., Hastings, Pa.

URMY, Ralph Brainerd, clergyman, editor; b. San Francisco, Calif., Feb. 27, 1867; s. Rev. William Smith and Emma Brainerd (Thomas) U.; Coll. of the Pacific, Stockton, Calif., 1883-86; Garrett Bibl. Inst., Evanston, Ill., 1892-93; B.D., Drew U., Madison, N.J., 1896; D.D., Allegheny Coll., Meadville, Pa., 1908; m. Marion Freer Saxe, June 30, 1897; children—Herbert Saxe (dec.), Thomas Van Orden, Ralph Brainerd, Keith Merwin, Marion Mabel. Pastor Sanford St. M.E. Ch., East Orange, N.J. 1896-97, Mendham, 1897-1900, Park Av. M.E. Ch., East Orange, 1900-04, Morristown, 1904-14, Centenary Ch., Newark, 1914-21, Bellevue Ch., Pittsburgh, 1921-28, 1932-34; editor Pittsburgh Christian Advocate, 1928-32; pastor 1st Ch., Westfield, N.J., 1934-38; pastor Lyndhurst Methodist Church since 1938. Sec. of Y.M.C.A., with 1st Div., U.S.A., France, 1917-18. Member of Newark Conf. M.E. Ch.; del. to Gen. Conf. M.E. Ch., 5 times; mem. bd. mgrs., Bd. Foreign Missions M.E. Church, 1912-24 and 1928-32; mem. World Service Commn., 1924-28. Mem. Phi Kappa Psi. Mason. Home: 307 Tontine Av., Lyndhurst, N.J.*

URNER, Hammond, judge; b. Frederick, Md., Dec. 4, 1868; s. Milton G. and Laura A. (Hammond) U.; A.B., Dickinson Coll., Pa., 1890, A.M., 1893; LL.D., St. John's Coll., Annapolis, 1918; m. Mary L. Floyd, May 3, 1893; children—George Floyd (dec.), Joseph Walker, Francis Hammond, Martin Jonas. Admitted to bar, 1891, and practiced at Frederick; mem. firm of Urner, Keedy & Urner, 1891-1901, Urner & Urner, 1901-09. City atty., Frederick, 1898-1901; Rep. candidate for atty.-gen. of Md., 1907; chief judge 6th Jud. Circuit of Md. and asso. judge Court of Appeals of Md., 1909-26, reëlected for 2d term of 15 yrs., 1926; retired from Bench, Dec. 4, 1938, at 70 years of age, under provision of Md. Constitution, and returned to practice of law. Republican. Methodist. Trustee Frederick City Hosp. Pres. Md. State Bar Assn., 1916. Home: 215 E. 2d St., Frederick, Md.

URQUHART, Paul Johnston, aluminum mfr.; b. Steubenville, O., Feb. 16, 1880; s. Moses Johnston and Susan (Copeland) U.; student pub. sch. and high sch., Steubenville, O., 1886-97, Duff's Commercial Coll., Pittsburgh, 1897-98; m. Ada McKee, Jan. 10, 1907 (dec.); m. 2d, Mary McKee, Apr. 15, 1916 (dec.); children—Ada McKee, Paul Johnston; m. 3d, Gertrude McKee, April 2, 1934. In employ various cos., 1898-1902; asso. with Aluminum Co. of America, Pittsburgh, and its subsidiaries continuously since 1902, successively bookkeeper, office mgr., credit mgr., traffic mgr., gen. auditor, controller and vice-pres. Aluminum Co. of America since 1931. Mem. Controllers Inst. of America (dir. and nat. pres. 1936-37); Nat. Assn. Cost Accountants. Republican. Presbyn. (trustee Shady Side Ch.). Mason (K.T., Shriner). Clubs: Duquesne, Pittsburgh Athletic (Pittsburgh); Pittsburgh Field (Aspinwall). Home: 605 Devonshire St. Office: 801 Gulf Bldg., Pittsburgh, Pa.

URSPRUNG, Charles William, surgeon; b. Lancaster, Pa., Apr. 23, 1896; s. Charles O. and Catherine (Strine) U.; M.D., Hahnemann Med. Coll. and Hosp. of Phila., 1919; m. Myrtle Witmer, June 25, 1924; 1 dau., Susanne. In practice as surgeon, Lancaster, Pa., since 1920; sec. med. staff St. Joseph's Hosp.; consulting surgeon Columbia Hosp., Columbia, Pa.; surgeon St. Joseph's Hosp., Rossmere Tuberculosis Sanitarium, Lancaster Co. Hosp. for Insane. Vice-pres. of bd. Thadeus Stevens Industrial Sch. Fellow Am. Coll. Surgeons; mem. Pi Upsilon Rho. Democrat. Catholic. K. of C., Elk. Clubs: Lions (past pres.), Hamilton (Lancaster); Manufacturers and Bankers (Phila.). Address: 415 James St., Lancaster, Pa.

UTLEY, Frederick Brown, physician; b. Rodman, N.Y., Mar. 15, 1880; s. Charles Albert and Mary Jane (Brown) U.; A.B., Yale, 1903; M.D., Coll. of Phys. and Surgs. of Columbia U., 1907; m. Florence Day, June 10, 1915; stepchildren—William M. Day, Elizabeth K. Day (Mrs. John W. Bracken, Jr.); children—Florence Day, Frederick Brown. Interne Presbyn. Hosp., New York, 1907-09, Sloane Maternity Hosp., N.Y., 1909; resident Reineman and Magee Hospitals, Pittsburgh, 1909-12; in practice internal medicine at Pittsburgh since 1912; instr. obstetrics, U. of Pittsburgh Med. Sch., 1909-11, instr. clin. microscopy, 1911, instr. medicine, 1912-19, asst. prof. medicine, 1919-34, asso. prof. since 1934; sr. staff mem. Magee Hosp., Pittsburgh, since 1921; asst. staff mem. St. Francis Hosp., 1912-21, asso., 1921-29, staff mem. since 1929; mem. consulting staff Eye & Ear Hosp. Served as capt. then maj., Med. Corps, U.S. Army, Camp Hancock, Ga., 1918-19. Fellow Am. Coll. Physicians; mem. Am., Pa. State, Allegheny Co. med. socs., A.A.A.S., Soc. for Biol. Research, Assn. for Study Internal Secretions, Pittsburgh Acad. of Medicine, Sigma Xi, Phi Beta Kappa. Republican. Presbyterian. Club: Harvard-Yale-Princeton, University (Pittsburgh). Home: 726 St. James St. Office: 121 University Pl., Pittsburgh, Pa.

UTTERBACK, William Irvin, coll. prof.; b. Crawfordsville, Ind., Oct. 11, 1872; s. John Walton and Martha H. (Miller) U.; B.S., Wabash Coll., Crawfordsville, Ind., 1901; A.M., U. of Mo., Columbia, 1915; m. Ruby Bessie Austin, June 14, 1905 (died 1938); children— William Irvin, Anna Martha (Mrs. Thomas L. Clendenning) U. Engaged in teaching rural schs., 1891-97; teacher in high schs., 1901-07; pres. The School of The Ozarks, Forsyth, Mo., 1907-08; instr. biology, Westminster Coll., Fulton, Mo., 1908-11; instr. biology in high schs. and coll., 1911-19; prof. zoology, Marshall Coll., Huntington, W.Va., since 1919, head dept. zoology since 1929. Fellow A.A.A.S. Mem. W.Va. Acad. Sci., Inst. Am. Genealogy, Chi Beta Phi, Epsilon Delta. Democrat. Presbyn. (elder). K. P. Clubs: Kiwanis, Rotary (Huntington.). Author: The Second Triangle, 1928; The Naiades of Missouri, 1916; The History and Genealogy of the Utterback Family in America (1620-1938), 1939. Contbr. three monographs. Home: 1810 Kite Av., Huntington, W.Va.

UTTLEY, William Willis, judge; b. Lewistown, Pa., Mar. 20, 1872; s. Thomas M. and Margaret Rebecca (Junkin) U.; student Lewistown (Pa.) pub. and high schs., 1878-1890; Ph.B., Dickinson Coll., Carlisle, Pa., 1890; m. Elizabeth Guyer, June 26, 1907; children—William W., John Guyer. Admitted to Mifflin Co. bar, 1896; since in gen. practice of law at Lewistown, Pa.; President judge Ct. of Common Pleas of Mifflin Co., 58th Pa. Judicial Dist., since 1932. Mem. exec. com. Mifflin Co. Community Fund; dir. Lewistown Y.M.C.A. Mem. Pa. Bar. Assn., Beta Theta Pi. Democrat. Presbyterian. Club: Rotary (Lewistown, Pa.). Home: 103 Academy Hill. Chambers: Court House, Lewistown, Pa.

UZZELL, Edward Foy, physician; b. Raleigh, N.C., June 20, 1892; s. William C. and Sophia (Nixon) U.; student U. of N.C.; M.D., Jefferson Med. Coll., 1916; m. Marion Gunter, Sept. 8, 1920; children—Marion Elizabeth, Edward Foy, Mary Jane, John Havelock Gunter, Joan. Physician, Atlantic City, N.J., since 1916; gynecological chief Atlantic City Hospital. Pres. Atlantic City Hosp. Staff, 1937. Fellow Am. Coll. Surgeons; mem. Atlantic County Med. Soc. (pres. 1939). Clubs: Stamp (dir.), Kiwanis (Atlantic City). Home: 112 S. Somerset Av. Office: 2703 Pacific Av., Atlantic City, N.J.

V

VACCARO, Leopold, M.D., chief med. advisor State Workmen's Ins. Fund, Dept. of Labor and Industry; b. Italy, Feb. 2, 1887; s. John and Rachel (Laus) V.; M.D., Medico-Chirurgical Coll. of Philadelphia, 1916; post-grad. student, U. of Rome, 1925; m. Pierina Chiera. Asst. surgeon E. I. duPont de Nemours, 1916-19; mem. staff genito-urinary dept. Pa. Hosp., 1919-23; asst. instr. medicine, U. of Pa., 1923-30; surgeon Nat. Stomach Hosp., 1925-32; mem. surg. staff Hahnemann Hosp., Broad St. Hosp., 1929-37; chief med. advisor Dept. of Labor and Industry since 1935. Regular Dem. candidate for coroner of Philadelphia County, 1933 (withdrew). Fellow College International de Chirurgiens (Geneva). Knighted by King Victor Emanuel III of Italy as Cavaliere Ufficiale for civic and philanthropic work, 1924; Knight Comdr., 1932. Mason (Past Master Golden Rule Lodge No. 748, F.&A.M.). Clubs: William Paca League (pres.), Safety Engineers. Author of biographies of Virgil, Dante, Leonardo da Vinci, Spallanzani and Ramazzini; also numerous surg. and med. papers and articles. Address: 1917 S. Broad St., Philadelphia, Pa.

VADEN, Claude Anderson, state mgr. Prudential Ins. Co. of America; b. Spring Garden, Va., May 29, 1886; s. James L. and Bettie Anderson (Ingram) V.; student pub. schs.; m. Henrietta Harper, June 1, 1914. Began as salesman when 14 yrs. old.; entered life ins. business at Richmond, Va., 1905; asso. with Prudential Ins. Co. continuously since 1907, mgr. at Wheeling, W.Va., 1908, mgr. for State W.Va. since 1908; vice-pres. and dir. Center Foundry & Machine Co., Wheeling, W.Va., since 1926; pres. Twelfth St. Garage. Served as mgr. Liberty Loan and Ohio Co. War Savings campaigns during World War. Organized and first pres. Wheeling Life Underwriters Assn., 1911. Republican. Presbyn. Club: Fort Henry (Wheeling.) Home: Cecil Place. Office. Wheeling Bank & Trust Bldg., Wheeling, W.Va.

VAIL, James Garrett, chemist; b. Phila., Pa. Nov. 16, 1886; s. Benjamin and Anna Garrett (McCollin) V.; student U. of Pa., Harvard, Technische Hochschule, Darmstadt, Germany; m. Ruth M. Russell, June 7, 1910; children—Benjamin, Garrett (dec.), Philip Cresson. Began as chemist with Phila. Quartz Co., mfrs. silicates of soda, and has spent entire career with company; v.p. and chem. dir. since 1933. Relief work in Germany with Am. Friends Service Commn., 1919-20. Chmn. exec. com. Westtown Sch.; mem. exec. com. Pendle Hill. Fellow Am. Ceramic Soc.; mem. Am. Inst. Chem. Engrs. (v.p., 1938), to Soc. Chem. Industry (chmn. Am. sect., 1936-37), Franklin Inst., Am. Chem. Soc. (chmn. Phila. sect., 1921-22), Dirs. of Industrial Research. Awarded Chem. Industry Medal, 1933. Society of Friends. Clubs: University (Phila.); Chemists (New York). Author: Am. Chem. Soc. monograph, Soluble Silicates in Industry, many papers on soluble silicates in tech. jours. U.S. rep. to World Chem. Engring. Congress, London, 1936. Home: 502 W. Front St., Media, Pa. Office: 121 S. 3d St., Philadelphia, Pa.

VAIL, William Penn, M.D.; b. Blairstown, N.J., Sept. 8, 1880; s. John Davis and Melissa (Gregory) V.; student Blair Acad., 1895-98; B.S., Princeton U., 1902, M.S., 1907; M.D., U. of Pa., 1906; m. Virginia Moore, of San Diego, Calif., Oct. 1, 1919 (divorced); 1 dau., Georgia Moore. Interne Children's Hosp., Philadelphia, 1906-07, Pennsylvania Hosp., Philadelphia, 1907-09; studied Paris and Vienna, 1910; oto-laryngologist Sch. for the Blind, Overbrook, Philadelphia, 1912-19; laryngologist dept. for tuberculosis Philadelphia Gen. Hosp., Blockley, 1914-19; in gen. practice at Blairstown, N.J., since 1920, specializing in treatment of eye, ear, nose and throat; physician Princeton Summer Camp since 1931; trustee Granger Trusts, Philadelphia. Served as lt. (j.g.) M.C., U.S.N. R.F., 1917-18, lt., 1918-19; med. exec. officer Naval Training Camp, Philadelphia Navy Yard, 1918-19. Pres. Blairstown Twp. Bd. of Edn., 1928-32. Fellow Coll. of Physicians of Philadelphia, Inst. Am. Genealogists; mem. A.M.A., N.J. State Med. Soc., Warren County Med. Soc., S.R., N.J. Geneal. Soc., Alpha Mu Pi Omega, Alpha Omega Alpha. Episcopalian. Mason. Clubs: Princeton (Philadelphia); Phi Gamma Delta (New York). Author: Syllabus on French Literature, 1902; Syllabus on Pathology, Parts I, II, III, 1906-07; Thomas Vail—Salem 1640 (geneal. record of descendants), 1937. Hobbies: millstones, old clocks and wood carving; carved and erected baldachin and rood screen, St. Luke's Cathedral, Orlando, Fla., 1938-39. Address: Blairstown, N.J.

VALE, Thomas Eyster, lawyer; b. East Pennsboro Twp., Cumberland Co., Jan. 16, 1866; s. Capt. Joseph G. and Sarah (Eyster) V.; grad. Carlisle (Pa.) High Sch., 1882; A.B., Dickinson Coll., Carlisle, Pa., 1887; LL.B., Dickinson Sch. of Law, 1891; m. Mary Murry Himes (d. Dr. Charles F. Himes, LL.D.), Sept. 21, 1905; children—Mary Himes, Sarah Elizabeth (Mrs. Frederick F. Rush). Prin. of high sch., Delta, York Co., Pa., 1887-89; admitted to Pa. bar, 1891, Pa. Supreme Court, 1902, Pa. Superior Court, 1905, U.S. Dist. Court, 1926; in gen. practice, Carlisle, Pa., since 1891; formerly instr. Dickinson Sch. of Law, 4 yrs.; borough solicitor several yrs.; dist. atty. Cumberland Co., 1902-05; now asso. with brother, Major E. Mode Vale, in law firm of Vale & Vale, Carlisle, Pa. Chief burgess, Burough of Carlisle, 3 yrs.; former mem. and sec. Bd. of Sch. Dirs., 13 yrs.; now sec. and solicitor Sch. Bd. of Carlisle. Mem. Pa. Bar Assn., Phi Beta Kappa, Phi Kappa Psi. Republican. Methodist. Mason, Elk, Odd Fellow. Clubs: Carlisle (Pa.) Country, Old Town Run Hunting and Fishing. Author: Vale Pennsylvania Digest (with Ruby R. Vale), 1908-13, revised 1938; History of the Public Schools of Carlisle, Pa., 1935. Home: 170 W. Louther St. Office: 12 N. Hanover St., Carlisle, Pa.

VALENTINE, Milton Henry, clergyman, editor, professor; b. Reading, Pa., Aug. 18, 1864; s. Milton and Margaret Grayson, (Galt) V.; student Gettysburg Acad., 1875-78; A.B., Gettysburg Coll., 1882, D.D., 1902; A.M., Gettysburg Theol. Sem., 1887; m. Evelyn M. Ladd, Feb. 1, 1888. Ordained to ministry of Luth. Ch., Dec. 1, 1887; pastor Trinity Luth. Ch., Bedford, Pa., 1887-92, Messiah Luth. Ch., Phila., 1892-99; editor Lutheran Observer, Phila., 1899-1915; prof. of English Bible, Gettysburg (Pa.) Coll., 1916-30, prof. emeritus since 1930. Home: 114 Springs Av., Gettysburg, Pa.

VALENTINE, W. Alfred, judge; b. Chester Co., Pa., s. William Alexander and L. Emma (Cave) V.; ed. pub. schs.; LL.B., Dickinson Sch. of Law, 1901; m. Mary I. Shoemaker, Oct. 22, 1902; children—William A., Mary E., Jonathan C., Margaret A. Admitted to bar of Supreme Ct. of Pa., 1902; dist. atty., Luzerne Co., 1910-11; solicitor for controller, Zuzerne Co., 1922-26; solicitor for sheriff, same co., 1927-28; local counsel D.L.& W. R.R., 1922-29, Pa. R.R., 1927-29; judge Ct. of Common Pleas since 1929; dir. Wyoming Nat. Bank. Pres. bd. incorporators Dickinson Sch. of Law. Mem. Wilkes-Barre Chamber of Commerce, Sons of America. Republican. Presbyterian. Clubs: Westmoreland, Craftsmen's. Elk. Home: 112 Charles St. Office: Court House, Wilkes-Barre, Pa.

VALK, William Eliadore, patent lawyer; b. Washington, D.C., Aug. 30, 1889; s. William Eliadore and Manette Lansing (Reeve) V.; Georgetown U. Sch. of Law, Washington, D.C., 1916; m. Myra E. McGrath, May 9, 1916; children—William Eliadore, John Garry. Patent atty. Curtiss Wright Corpn., Paterson, N.J., since 1916; pres., dir. Aircraft Cowling Corpn., Summit, N.J., since 1937; v.p. and dir. Mfrs. Aircraft Assn., New York, since 1931; sec. and dir. The Reed Propeller Co., Inc., New York, since 1928; dir. Atlantic Casting & Engring. Corpn. Mem. Inst. of Aeronautical Sciences, N.Y. Patent Law Assn., Phi Alpha Delta. Episcopalian. Club: Ridgewood Country (Ridgewood, N.J.). Home: 224 Heights Rd., Ridgewood, N.J. Office: Wright Aeronautical Corpn., Paterson, N.J.

VALL-SPINOSA, Arthur, mfr. metal specialties; b. Ponce, Porto Rico, Oct. 4, 1880; s. Zacharias and Caroline (Armstrong) V-S.; B.S., Kenyon Coll., Gambier, O., 1901; C.E., Lehigh U., Bethlehem, Pa., 1903; m. Alice Blanche Wigley, Sept. 15, 1909; children—Arthur Alan, Elaine, Ellsmore. Employed as civil engr. Bethlehem Steel Co., Bethlehem, Pa., 1903-04, McClintic Marshall Co., Pittsburgh, Pa., 1904-09; vice-pres., dir. and chief engr. Consolidated Expanded Metal Co., Braddock, Pa., 1909-25; vice-pres., dir. and chief engr., Penn Metal Company, Inc., mfrs., Parkersburg, W.Va., since 1925. Mem. American Society Civil Engineers, Archæol. Inst. of America, Alpha Delta Phi. Republican. Episcopalian. Mason. Home: 1333 Market St. Address: Box 1460, Parkersburg, W.Va.

VAN BEUREN, Frederick Theodore, Jr., surgeon; b. N.Y. City, Feb. 10, 1876; s. Frederick T. and Elizabeth A. (Potter) Van B.; A.B., Yale, 1898; M.D., Coll. Phys. and Surg. (Columbia), 1902; m. Jessica T., May 26, 1906; children—Frederick T. III, Jessica, Michael M. II, John M. Asso. in anatomy, 1905-13, asso. in surgery, 1920, asst. professor, 1922, asso. prof. clin. surgery since 1929, asso. dean, 1921-34, Coll. of Physicians and Surgeons (Columbia); pres. Morristown (N.J.) Memorial Hosp. since 1933; asst. attending surgeon, Lincoln Hosp., 1910-13, Roosevelt Hosp., 1913-21; attending surgeon Volunteer Hosp., 1915-17, Sloan Hosp. for Women, 1920—; asso.

visiting surgeon Presbyn. Hosp. Mem. Squadron A., N.G. N.Y., 1899-1910, resigned as capt.; 1st lt. M.R.C., U.S.A., 1910-18; capt. and maj. M.C., U.S.A., 1918-19; with A.E.F., July 1918-Feb. 1919; hon. discharged, Feb. 2, 1919; maj. M.R.C., U.S.A., 1920-35. Fellow Am. Coll. Surgeons, Am. Surg. Assn., Am. Foundation of Surgery; mem. Southern Surg. Soc., A.M.A., New York Surg. Soc., Acad. Medicine, Alpha Delta Phi, Wolf's Head. Republican. Presbyn. Clubs: Century, Players (New York); Morris Country Golf; Yeamans Hall. Home: Morristown, N.J. Office: 65 5th Av., New York, N.Y.

VAN BUREN, Charles Henry, stock broker; b. Brooklyn, N.Y., Dec. 15, 1861; s. Henry and Sarah Ann (Williams) V.; ed. Brooklyn schs.; m. Elvira L. Snyder, June 27, 1906; children—Josephine Day, Henry Foster, Charles Henry, Katharine Elisabeth (Mrs. Hampton Pierson Howell, Jr.), Frederick Snyder, Albert Williams. Mgr. with M. N. Day, stock broker, 1885-88; owner C. H. Van Buren & Co., members Consolidated Stock Exchange, 1888-1926, and New York Stock Exchange, 1926-31; spl. partner McClave & Co., members New York Stock Exchange, since 1931. Dir. and first v.p. Consolidated Stock Exchange of N.Y. Mem. bd. of mgrs. Williamsburg Y.M.C.A. (Brooklyn); trustee First Presbyn. Ch. of Williamsburg, Lee Avenue Congl. Ch. Republican. Episcopalian (vestryman St. Paul's Episcopal Ch. of Englewood, N.J.). Clubs: Holland Soc. of N.Y. (v.p.); Englewood Field. Home: 155 Chestnut St., Englewood, N.J.; (summer): Point O'Woods, Long Island, N.Y.

VAN BUSKIRK, Arthur B(ostwick), lawyer; b. Pottstown, Pa., Mar. 27, 1896; s. Charles C. and Florence A. (McKinley) Van B.; A.B., Yale, 1917; LL.B., U. of Pa. Law Sch., 1922; m. Katharine Jones, Oct. 17, 1925; children—George, Joseph, David. Admitted to Pa. bar, 1922 and engaged in gen. practice of law in Pittsburgh since 1924; law sec. to the Chief Justice of Pa., 1922-24; mem. firm, Reed, Smith, Shaw & McClay since 1934; dir. Pittsburgh & W.Va. Ry. Co., Allegheny Trust Co., Nat. Radiator Co. Served as 2d lt. F.A., U.S. A., 1917-19, with 79th Div. with A.E.F. in France. Dir. Pittsburgh Assn. for Improvement of Poor, Pub. Health Nursing Assn. Mem. Am. Bar Assn., Pa. Bar Assn., Allegheny County Bar Assn., Zeta Psi, Phi Delta Phi. Republican. Presbyn. Clubs: Duquesne, Fox Chapel Golf (Pittsburgh); Rolling Rock (Ligonier). Home: 5208 Pembroke Place. Office: Union Trust Bldg., Pittsburgh, Pa.

VANCE, John Thomas, librarian; b. Lexington, Ky., Aug. 24, 1884; s. John Thomas and Emily Chew (Gibney) V.; A.B., Ky. U. (now Transylvania Coll.), 1905; LL.B., U. of Mich., 1909, hon. LL.M., 1933; spl. work in civil law, U. of Santo Domingo, Dominican Republic, 1920-21; S.J.D., Catholic University of America, 1937; m. Margaret Scott Breckinridge, Mar. 1, 1917; children—John Thomas, Henry Breckinridge, Louise Ludlow Dudley. Admitted to Ky. bar, 1909, and practiced at Lexington, 1909-13, as mem. firm of Vance & Harbison; dep. gen. receiver Dominican customs Santo Domingo, 1913-19; mem. firm Lippitt & Vance, Santo Domingo, 1920-21, Washington, D.C., 1922-24; law librarian of Congress since 1924. Mem. Bd. of Curators, Transylvania Coll. A del. of A.L.A. to 1st World Library and Bibliog. Congress, Rome and Venice, 1929; member Second Pan American Congress of History and Geography (Washington, D.C.), 1935; pres. D.C. Library Assn., 1935-37; pres. Instituto de las Españas (Washington chapter), 1937-39. Mem. Am. Assn. Law Libraries (pres. 1933), Am. Law Inst., Am. Bar Assn. (sec. sect. on internat. and comparative law), Am. Soc. Internat. Law, Foreign Law Assn., Société de Legislation Comparée, Riccobono Seminar of Roman Law, Bibliog. Soc. Am., Kappa Alpha, Phi Delta Phi. Presbyn. Clubs: Chevy Chase, Cosmos. Author: Background of Hispanic American Law, 1936. Contbr. to legal periodicals. Home: 16 W. Irving St., Chevy Chase, Md. Address: Law Library, Library of Congress, Washington, D.C.

VANCE, Walter, high school prin.; b. Roaring, W.Va.; s. Elijah and Phebe Jane (Morral) V.; student Shepherd State Teachers Coll., W. Va., 1909-11; A.B., W.Va. U., 1917, A.M., 1924; A.M., Columbia, 1926, grad. student, summers, 1929-30; student Peabody Coll., summer, 1921; m. Marion Brooking, Aug. 17, 1926. Teacher of rural schools of Pendleton County, W.Va., 1903-09; prin. Man (W.Va.) High Sch., 1917-20, Hillsboro (W.Va.) High Sch., 1920-25; instr. Glenville State Teachers Coll., summer 1926; prin. Kermit (W.Va.) High Sch., 1926-27; asst. prin. and teacher, McDowell County, W.Va., 1927-37; prin. Richmond High Sch., Pear, W.Va., since 1937. Supt. Iaeger Meth. S.S., 1934-37. Mem. First Families of Virginia Assn., Inc., Sigma Delta Phi (W.Va. U.). Mem. Christian Ch. Mason (K.T., Shriner). Contbr. poems to several anthologies. Address: Hamlin, W.Va.

van de KAMP, Peter, coll. prof.; b. Kampen, Netherlands, Dec. 26, 1901; s. Lubbertus and Engelina Cornelia Adriana (van der Wal) van de K.; Doctorandus, U. of Utrecht, Netherlands, 1922; Ph.D., U. of Calif., Berkeley, Calif., 1925; Ph.D., U. of Groningen, Netherlands, 1926; came to U.S., 1923. Engaged as asst. in astronomy, Groningen, Netherlands, 1922-23; research asst. in astronomy, Leander McCormick Obs., U. of Va., Charlottesville, Va., 1923-24; Martin Kellogg Fellow, Lick Obs., Calif., 1924-25; instr. astronomy, U. of Va., 1925-28, asst. prof., 1928-37; asso. prof. astronomy, dir. Sproul Obs., Swarthmore (Pa.) Coll., since 1937. Mem. A.A.A.S., Am. Astron. Soc., Va. Acad. Science, Internat. Astron. Union, Netherlands Astron. Soc., Sigma Xi. Awarded President's and Visitors Prize, U. of Va., 1927, 1937, 1938. Office: Swarthmore College, Swarthmore, Pa.

VAN DEMARK, Ernest S., civil engr.; b. High Falls, N.Y., Nov. 21, 1888; s. Willet Irving and Carrie (Snyder) Van D.; student Kingston (N.Y.) Acad., 1902-06; B.S. in C.E., Tufts Coll., Medford, Mass., 1911; unmarried. Civil engr., B.&O. R.R. Co., 1911-15; civil engr. E. I. du Pont de Nemours & Co., Wilmington, Del., 1915-26; planning engr. City of Richmond, Va., 1926-27; city engr. and bldg. insp., City of Hopewell, Va., 1927-32; civil engr., E. I. du Pont de Nemours & Co., Wilmington, Del., 1933-37; partner Van Demark & Lynch, engrs., Wilmington, Del., since 1937. Mem. Nat. Soc. Professional Engrs., Am. Assn. Engrs., Alpha Kappa Pi. Republican. Dutch Reformed. Mason (Washington, Del., Lodge 1). Home: 707 W. 11th St. Office: 421 N. Broom St., Wilmington, Del.

VAN DEN BERG, Cornelius, Jr.; pres. W.Va. Water Service Co.; officer or dir. many companies. Address: Charleston, W.Va.

VANDERBILT, Arthur T., lawyer; b. Newark, N.J., July 7, 1888; s. Lewis and Alice H. (Leach) V.; A.B., Wesleyan U., Middletown, Conn., 1910, A.M., 1912; LL.B., Columbia, 1913; LL.D., Tulane, Wesleyan, Western Reserve, U. of British Columbia, 1938; m. Florence A. Althen, Sept. 12, 1914; children—Jean Althen, Virginia Elizabeth, Lois Dorothy, Robert Althen, William Runyon. Admitted to N.J. bar, 1913; prof. law, N.Y. Univ. Law Sch., since 1914; counsel, Essex Co., N.J., since 1921; chmn. Judicial Council, N.J., since 1930; dir. Savings Investment & Trust Co.; pres. Lincoln Mortgage Co.; chmn. bd. Pepsi-Cola Co. since 1938. Chairman Nat. Conf. of Judicial Councils, 1933-37, chmn. exec. com., 1937-39; chmn. U.S. atty. general's com. to confer with com. of senior circuit judges appointed by Chief Justice Hughes to draft the bill for the administrative office of the United States Courts, 1938-39; mem. of atty. general's com. on administrative procedure since 1939. Mem. Am. Bar Assn. (mem. gen. council 1932-34; chmn. ins. law sect. 1933-34; mem. exec. com. 1934-35; pres. 1937-38), N.J. State Bar Assn. (v.p. 1934-37), Am. Polit. Science Assn., Delta Kappa Epsilon, Phi Beta Kappa, Phi Delta Phi. Republican. Methodist. Clubs: University (New York); Baltusrol (Short Hills, N.J.); Essex, Down Town (Newark). Home: Hobart Av., Short Hills, N.J. Office: 744 Broad St., Newark, N.J.

VANDERBILT, Paul, librarian; b. Cambridge, Mass:, Mar. 5, 1905; s. Harold M. and Minnie (Miner) V.; ed. Amherst Coll., 1923-25; A.B., Harvard U., 1927; m. Julia M. Lloyd, Aug. 28, 1933. Began career as book salesman, 1927; librarian, Phila. Mus. Art since 1928; dir. Union Library Catalogue of Phila. Met. Area since 1936; dir. Bibliog. Planning Com. of Phila. since 1939; on interim leave of absence, spl. work for Henry E. Huntington Library, San Marino, Calif., 1931, and Library Company of Phila., 1938; European investigations, 1928-29, 1938. Dir. (of corpn.) Union Library Catalogue of Phila. Met. Area. Mem. Am. Library Assn., Internat. Fed. for Documentation, Alpha Delta Phi. Office: 1300 Locust St., Philadelphia, Pa.

VANDERBLUE, Homer Bews, economist; b. Hinsdale, Ill., Dec. 24, 1888; s. Frank J. and Mary (Bews) V.; A.B., Northwestern, 1911, A.M., 1912; Ph.D., Harvard, 1915; unmarried. Instr. economics, Harvard, 1914-15; asst. prof. transportation, 1915-16, asso. prof., 1916-20, prof., 1920-22, Northwestern U.; research dir. Denver Civic Commercial Assn., 1920-21; prof. business economics, Harvard U., 1922-29, also served as economist, Harvard U. com. on economic research, and dir. Harvard Economic Service; v.p. Tri-Continental Corpn., 1929-37; consulting economist Gen. Motors Corpn., 1938; Curator Kress Library of Business, Harvard, 1938-39; prof. of transportation, Northwestern U., since 1939. Honorary curator of early economic literature, Baker Library, Harvard University, since 1936. Student 1st O.T.C., Ft. Sheridan, Ill., 1917; hon. discharged as capt., Dec. 19, 1918. Chmn. Library Com., Coll. of William and Mary, since 1936; mem. Com. on Economic Bibliography of the British Acad., 1937. Mem. Am. Econ. Assn., Business Hist. Soc., Econ. History Soc., Sigma Nu. Clubs: Faculty (Cambridge); Harvard (New York). Author: Railroad Valuation, 1917; Railroad Valuation by the Interstate Commerce Commission, 1920; Railroads—Rates, Service, Management (with Kenneth F. Burgess), 1923; Problems in Business Economics, 1924, rev., 1929; The Iron Industry in Prosperity and Depression (with W. L. Crum), 1926; Economic Principles—A Case Book, 1927; The Florida Land Boom, 1927; Adam Smith and the Wealth of Nations, 1936; Pricing Policy in the Automobile Industry, 1939. Contbr. to economic and business publs. Home: Penwood Farm, Everett, Pa. Address: Baker Library, Soldiers Field, Boston, Mass.; Wieboldt Hall, 301 E. Chicago, Av., Chicago, Ill.

van der HOEVEN, Bernard Jacob Cornelis, chem. engring.; b. Hasselt, Netherlands, May 22, 1899; s. Willem and Neeltje A. (Visser) van der H.; Chem. E., Tech. Univ., Delft, Netherlands, 1922; came to U.S., 1923, naturalized, 1938; m. Annette E. Royle, Apr. 20, 1929; children—Willem Royle, Gertrude Neeltje, Bernard Jacob Cornelis. Began as asst. in Univ., Delft, 1922; research chemist, Lehn & Fink Co., Bloomfield, N.J., 1923, Rockefeller Inst., New York, N.Y., 1923-26; with Koppers Co., Pittsburgh, Pa. as research chemist, operating engr., operating supt. since 1926. Mem. Am. Chem. Soc., Am. Inst. Chem. Engrs., Am. Gas Assn., Netherlands Chem. Soc. Dutch Reformed Ch. Home: 90 Woodhaven Drive, Mt. Lebanon, Pa. Office: Koppers Bldg., Pittsburgh, Pa.

VANDERKLEED, Charles Edwin, chemist; b. Lafayette, Ind., Apr. 24, 1878; s. Charles and Elizabeth (Van Aalst) V.; Ph.G., Purdue U., Lafayette, Ind., 1895, Ph.C., 1896, B.Sc., 1899, A.C., 1901, D.Sc., 1934; Pharm.D., Medico-Chirurg. College, Philadelphia, 1908; Ph.M., Phila., Coll. of Pharm. and Science, 1929; m. Edith Parks, Sept. 18, 1901 (died 1937); children—Lois Lee (Mrs. H. Lester Haws), Eugene Parks (dec.); m. 2d, Carolyn G. Bailey, Jan. 20, 1939. Asst. Chemistry, Purdue, 1896-1901; chem.. expert, Ind. courts, 1899-1901; analyt. chemist, Sharp & Dohme, Baltimore, 1901-02; dir. chem. laboratories H. K. Mulford Co., Phila., 1902-17; prof. pharm. chemistry, 1908-14, prof. analytical chemistry, 1914-16, Medico-Chirurg. Coll., Phila.; lecturer on chem. control, Phila. Coll. Pharmacy, 1916-28; v.p. Markleed Chemical Corporation, 1917-18; chemist Hercules Powder Co., 1918-

19; sec., dir. Cellulose Silk Co. America, 1920-22; supt. of Robert McNeil Lab., Phila., 1920-33; now v.p. and scientific dir. McNeil Labs., Inc.; treas. and dir. Henry C. Blair Co. Fellow American Institute Chemists; mem. revision committee U.S. Pharmacopœia, 1910-20; mem. Am. Chem. Soc., Am. Pharm. Assn., A.A.A.S., Nat. Inst., Social Sciences, Phi Zeta Delta, Beta Phi Sigma, and Kappa Psi. Author: Course in Quantitative Chemical Analysis (with Julius W. Sturmer), 1898; Course in Qualitative Inorganic Chemistry (with Arthur L. Green), 1903; sect. on Strychnos Alkaloids, in Allen's Commercial Organic Analysis, 1912. Extensive contbr. to chemical and pharm. jours. Home: 200 Harvard Av., Collingswood, N.J., Office: 2900 N. 17th St., Philadelphia, Pa.

VANDERPOOL, Wynant Davis, banker, lawyer; b. Newark, N.J., Aug. 15, 1875; s. Wynant and Alice Wayland (Davis) V.; ed. Princeton, 1894-98, Harvard Law Sch., 1898-1901; m. Cornelia Willis, Oct. 17, 1905; children—Eugene, Mary Willis (Mrs. William W. Cochran), Wynant Davis. Admitted to N.J. bar, 1903; v.p. Howard Savings Inst., Newark, 1917, pres. since 1924; pres. and mem. bd. mgrs. Howard Savings Instn. of Newark; dir. Newark & Essex Banking Co., Am. Ins. Co., Mutual Benefit Life Ins. Co., Bankers Indemnity Ins. Co. (all of Newark), Nat. Biscuit Co. of New York, Morristown (N.J.) Trust Co., United N.J. R.R. and Canal Co. of Trenton. Capt. motor transport U.S.A., 1918. Trustee Morristown Memorial Hosp., Morristown Library, St. Barnabas Hosp. Mem. Am. and Essex Co. bar assns., Am. Inst. Banking, Harvard Law Sch. Assn., Holland Soc. of N.Y., N.J. Hist. Soc., Bond Club of N.J., Chamber of Commerce. Episcopalian. Home: 86 Miller Rd., Morristown. Address: P.O. Box 177, Newark, N.J.

VANDERVOORT, James W., lawyer; b. in Preston County, Va. (now W.Va.), May 7, 1855; s. Amos A. and Susan (Holmes) V.; ed. U. of W.Va.; studied law, U. of Va. (non-grad.); m. Maud Shuttleworth, June 7, 1882. Admitted to bar, 1877; practiced, Parkersburg, W.Va.; counsel for B.&O. R. R. Co. for many years; has served as city atty. and mayor, Parkersburg, and judge Criminal Ct. of Wood Co., W.Va.; spl. master in chancery. Rep. presdl. elector, 1896. Methodist. Mem. Am. Bar. Assn. (mem. nat. commn. on uniform state laws); Am. Law Inst.; pres. W.Va. State Bar Assn., 1915-16. Mem. Board of Law Examiners, 1921—. Elk. Home: Parkersburg, W.Va.

VANDERWART, Herman; pres. City Nat. Bank & Trust Co. Address: Hackensack, N.J.

VANDERWORT, John; prof. animal husbandry extension, Pa. State Coll. Address: Pennsylvania State College, State College, Pa.

VANDER ZALM, Lindley Edward, coll. prof.; b. Grand Haven, Mich., Nov. 8, 1893; s. James and Joanna (Mull) V-Z.; A.B., U. of Mich., Ann Arbor, 1916; A.M., Teachers Coll. of Columbia U., 1920; student U. of Chicago, summer 1921, Teachers Coll. of Columbia U., summer 1923, U. of Mich., 1927-28; m. Marie Elida Knudson, Aug. 4, 1931; 1 son, Robert Edward. Employed as head of dept. edn. and dir. of training, Concord State Teachers Coll., Athens, W.Va., 1920-26; prof. edn. Marshall Coll., Huntington, W.Va., since 1928. Served in Med. Corps, U.S.A., at Debarkation Hosp. 3, N.Y. City, during World War. Mem. Nat. Edn. Assn., W.Va. State Edn. Assn., Phi Delta Kappa, Kappa Delta Pi. Presbyn. Mason (K.T., Shriner). Contbr. ednl. jours. Home: 1347 Neel St., Huntington, W.Va.

VAN DEUSEN, Edwin Hicks, physician; b. Troy, N.Y., Mar. 12, 1860; s. Isaac and Josephine (Hicks) Van D.; A.B., Phila. High Sch., Phila., Pa., 1877; M.D., U. of Pa. Med. Sch., 1880; grad. study, U. of Vienna, Austria, 1888; m. Adelaide Parmalee Smith, Nov. 27, 1883; children—Edwin Parmalee (dec.), Robert Hicks, Frederick (killed in battle of Argonne, Oct. 1918). Dispensary service, throat, nose and ear dept. Hahnemann Hosp., Phila., 1882-91; obstetrician to Rosine Home, Phila., Pa., 1886-1911; mem. staff St. Luke's Hosp., Phila., Pa., 1890-1911, exec. officer, 1900-11, obstetrician, 1905-11; in practice at Vineland, N.J., since 1912; mem. staff of Vineland Hosp., 1911-24; mem. staff Newcomb Hosp., Vineland, N.J., since 1924; physician to Training Sch., Vineland, since 1925. Mem. Am., N.J. State, Cumberland Co. med. assns., Am. Inst. Homeopathy, Phila. Co. Homeopathic Med. Soc., Phila. Homeopathic Med. Club, Vineland Hist. Soc. Republican. Baptist. Home: 12 N. Seventh St., Vineland, N.J.

VAN DEUSEN, Henry Reed, lawyer; b. Laurens, N.Y., June 2, 1872; s. Henry Newton and Mary Jane (Porter) V.; A.B., Wesleyan U., Middletown, Conn., 1894; LL.B., U. of Pa. Law Sch., 1899; m. Jessie Lawrence Dimmick, Sept. 16, 1903; children—William Connell (dec.), Lawrence Reed, Henry Reed. Admitted to bar, 1899; since in gen. practice at Scranton, Pa.; chmn. bd. and dir. Scranton Pump Mfg. Co.; treas. and dir. Federal Coal Co. Mem. Delta Kappa Epsilon, Phi Beta Kappa. Republican. Methodist. Home: 420 Quincy Av. Office: Scranton Life Bldg., Scranton, Pa.

VAN DEVENTER, Harry Brown, prof. Latin, U. of Pa. Address: U. of Pennsylvania, Philadelphia, Pa.

VANDEWATER, William Collins, lawyer; b. Princeton, N.J., Mar. 3, 1886; s. William Collins and Emma (Mercer) V.; A.B., Princeton U., 1907; LL.B., Columbia U. 1910; m. Ruth G. Lyon, July 6, 1922; children—Phyllis Lyon, Eleanor, Anne Greenoak. Admitted to N.J. bar, 1911; in private practice of law since 1911; dir. and counsel Princeton Bank & Trust Co., Princeton Water Co.; asso. counsel Princeton U. Served as capt., Inf., U.S. Army, with A.E.F., World War. Mem. Mercer County, N.J. and Am. bar assns. Republican. Protestant. Clubs: Nassau; Pretty Brook; Springdale; Princeton Club of N.Y. Home: Springdale Road. Office: 90 Nassau St., Princeton, N.J.

VAN DOORN, William, general mgr. Holland Am. Line; b. Amsterdam, Holland, Feb. 13, 1872; s. Gerard Dirk and Adriana (Hoen) V.; ed. pub. and pvt. schs.; m. Henriette Van Breemen, Nov. 30, 1900; children—Henriette, William. With Holland Am. Line since 1892; mgr. Amsterdam office, 1904-06; asst. gen. mgr. New York office, 1906-12, becoming gen. mgr., 1912; now retired. Mem. bd. dirs. Netherland Chamber of Commerce, at New York. Knight Comdr., Order of Orange Nassau, Netherlands, 1923. Clubs: Whitehall, Lawyers', Netherlands. Home: 153 Park St., Montclair, N.J.

VAN DOREN, Lloyd, chemical consultant, patent law; b. Oldwick, N.J., Dec. 11, 1889; s. Benjamin and Emma Louisa (Miller) Van D.; B.S., Gettysburg Coll., 1909; Ph.D., Johns Hopkins U., 1912; M.S., Gettysburg Coll., 1913; m. Louisa W. VanTassell; children—Cecil, Lloyd, Jr. Instr. chem., Lowell Textile Sch., 1912-13; assst. prof., U. of Akron, 1913-14; prof. and head of dept., Earlham Coll., 1914-19; chem. adviser, Emery, Varney, Blair & Hoguet, 1919-20; cons. chemist and patent solicitor, The Chemical Foundation, 1920-22; cons. chemist and patent atty., Mayer, Warfield & Watson, 1922-29; patent dept., Allied Chem. & Dye Corp., 1929-31; cons. chemist and patent atty., Watson, Bristol, Johnson & Leavenworth since 1931. Served as 1st lt. C.W.S., U.S.A. during World War. Fellow A.A.A.S., Am. Inst. of Chemists. Mem. Am. Chem. Soc., Phi Gamma Delta, Phi Beta Kappa, Gamma Alpha. Republican. Presbyn. Mason. Club: Chemists (New York). Home: 340 Greenbrook Rd., North Plainfield, N.J. Business: Watson, Bristol, Johnson & Leavenworth, 6 East 45th Street, New York City.

VAN DUSEN, Lewis Harlow, judge; b. Philadelphia, July 19, 1876; s. Joseph B. and Ellenora C. (Richstein) VanD.; grad. William Penn Charter Sch., 1894; A.B., Princeton U., 1898; LL.B., U. of Pa., 1901; m. Muriel L. M. Lund, Apr. 13, 1909; children—Lewis H., Francis L., Muriel C., Alverta S., Rita Mary. Admitted to Philadelphia bar, 1901; member of firm of Scott, Van Dusen, Archbald & Johnson; Civil Service commr., Phila., 1911-16, 1920-24; apptd. judge Orphans' Court, 1st Judicial Dist. of Pa., 1924, elected for ten yr. term, 1926, reelected, 1936, president judge since Mar. 5, 1937. Commd. capt. U.S. Res. Corps, May 1917; lt. col., Oct. 1918; hon. disch. Apr. 1919. Legal advisor to Ordnance Dept. of U.S. Army on settlement of war claims. Mem. Am. Law Inst., Am. Judicature Soc., Phila., New York, Pa. and Am. bar assns., Law Acad. of Phila. (recorder, 1907, dep. prothonotary 1908-09, prothonotary 1909-10, v.p. 1910, pres. 1911), Am. Legion, Army Ordance Assn., Mil. Order of Foreign Wars of the U.S. (judge advocate), Mil. Order of the World War, Nat. Assembly of Civil Service Commrs., Nat. Civil Service Reform League, Civil Service Assn. of Pa. (mem. exec. com.), Nat. Probation Assn. (mem. Phila. com.), Founders and Patriots of America (states atty.), Colonial Soc., Sons of the Revolution, Hist. Soc. of Pa., The Netherlands Soc. (pres.), Memorial Church of St. Paul (Overbrook, Phila.), Union Lodge No. 121 F. & A.M., Franklin Inst., Pa. Museum of Arts, Pa. Acad. of Fine Arts. Republican. Episcopalian. Clubs: Constitutional, Lawyers, Sharswood Law, Union League, Princeton (Phila.); Army and Navy (Washington); University Cottage (Princeton). Home: 6071 Drexel Road. Office: Room 416 City Hall, Philadelphia, Pa.

VAN DYKE, Eugene Nelson, orthopedic surgeon; b. Marysville, Pa., June 27, 1893; s. Arthur D. and Laura J. (Leiby) Van D.; B.S., Princeton U., 1916; M.D., Johns Hopkins U. Med. Sch., 1920; unmarried. Interne Robert Parker Hosp., Sayre, Pa., 1920-21; interne Johns Hopkins Hosp., 1921-22, resident orthopedic surgeon, 1923-24; asst. orthopedic surgeon, U. of Ia. Hosp. and Med. Sch., Iowa City, Ia., 1922-23; orthopedic surgeon in Scranton, Pa., since 1924; with Hahnemann Hosp., Scranton, Pittston (Pa.) Hosp., Wayne Memorial Hosp., Hohnesdale, Pa. Served in S.A. T.C., 1917-18. Fellow Am. Acad. Orthopedic Surgeons; mem. A.M.A., Lackawanna Co. Med. Soc., Pa. State Med. Assn. Presbyterian. Club: Exchange (Scranton, Pa.). Home: 1519 Clay Av., Scranton, Pa. Office: Connell Bldg., Scranton, Pa.

VAN DYKE, George Malcolm, clergyman; b. Lowville, N.Y., May 7, 1901; s. George Bergen and Mary (Swain) Van D.; A.B., Central High Sch., Scranton, Pa., 1918; student Lawrenceville (N.J.) Acad., 1918-19; A.B., Princeton U., 1923, A.M., 1929; B.Th., Princeton Theol. Sem., 1929; m. Margaret G. Mahy, May 18, 1929; children—Louise Mahy, Eleanor Marie, Margaret Elizabeth. Ordained to ministry Presbyn. Ch. U.S.A., 1929; pastor, Palisades Park, N.J., 1929-35, Lansdowne, Pa., since 1935; instr. in English, Prep. Sch. of Am. Univ., Beirut, Syria, 1923-26; moderator Chester Presbytery, summer 1938; mem. deputation sent by Presbyn. Bd. Fgn. Missions to Syria for investigation and counsel, autumn 1938; mem. Bd. Fgn. Missions Presbyn. Ch. U.S.A. since 1931. Mem. Phi Beta Kappa. Republican. Presbyterian. Clubs: Canterbury, Cleric (Phila.). Home: 129 Owen Av., Lansdowne, Pa.

VAN DYKE, Harry Benjamin, pharmacologist; b. Des Moines, Ia., Jan. 31, 1895; s. Benjamin Isaac and Louise Viola (Bude) Van D.; S.B., U. of Chicago, 1918, Ph.D., 1921, M.D., Rush Med. Coll., 1924; m. Elizabeth Allan, Apr. 14, 1920; children—Jane Elizabeth, Arthur Cushny. Asst. in physiol. chemistry, U. of Chicago, 1918, anatomy, 1919, asso. in pharmacology, 1920-21, asst. prof. pharmacology, 1924, asso. prof., 1926-30, prof., 1930-32; prof. and head dept. pharmacology, Peking Union Med. Coll., China, 1932-38; honorary prof. of physiology, Rutgers U. and head div. of pharmacology, Squibb Inst. For Med. Research, New Brunswick, N.J., since 1938. Served in Med. Div., S.A.T.C., 1917-18. Mem. Am. Physiol. Soc., Biochem. Soc. (Great Britain), Phi Beta Kappa, Sigma Xi, Alpha Omega Alpha. Home: 30 N. 8th Av., Highland Park, N.J. Office: Squibb Inst. for Medical Research, New Brunswick, N.J.

VAN DYKE, J. W., oil official; chmn. bd. Atlantic Refining Co.; pres. Atlantic Oil Producing Co., Atlantic Oil Shipping Co., Keystone

Pipe Line Co., Atlantic Pipe Line Co., Atlantic Refining Co. of Brazil, of Spain, Atlantic West African Co., Colombian Atlantic Refin. Co., Venezuelan Atlantic Refining Co., Buffalo Pipe Line Co.; dir. First Nat. Bank of Phila., Monroe Coal Min. Co., First Trst. Co., Cambrian & Ind. R.R. Home: The Barclay. Office: 260 S. Broad St., Philadelphia, Pa.

VAN DYNE, Henry Bowers, pres. Van Dyne Oil Co., Inc.; b. Troy, Pa., Mar. 23, 1889; s. Edward Everett and Louise (Wilson) Van D.; student Troy Schs., 1895-1906, Lawrenceville (N.J.) Sch., 1906-08; B.S., Dartmouth Coll., Hanover, N.H., 1912; m. Dorothy Nearing, Oct. 10, 1912; children—Edward Everett, Mary Nearing. Junior partner E. Van Dyne's Sons, tanners, 1912-22; owner chain automobile stores, 1922-29; pres. Grange Nat. Bank, Troy, Pa., 1922-31; pres. Van Dyne Oil Co., Inc., since 1923 (offices at Troy, Pa., Athens, Pa., Elmira, N.Y., Binghampton, N.Y., Corning, N.Y., and Naples, N.Y.). Del. Rep. Nat. Conv., 1936. Trustee First Presbyn. Ch., Troy, Pa., Robert Packer Hosp., Sayre, Pa. Mem. Phi Sigma Kappa (Dartmouth Chapter). Republican. Mason (32°). Clubs: Rotary (Troy, Pa.); City, Elmira Country (Elmira, N.Y.); Corey Creek Golf (Mansfield, Pa.); Iram Temple Country (Wilkes-Barre, Pa.); Acacia (Williamsport, Pa.). Home: 176 Canton St. Office: 18 Canton St., Troy, Pa.

VAN ETTEN, Edwin Jan, clergyman; b. Rhinebeck, N.Y., Apr. 28, 1884; s. Cornelius M.D.) and Sarah Clarissa (Hill) V.; grad. high sch., Rhinebeck, 1900; Riverview Mil. Acad., 1901; B.A., Amherst, 1905; student Gen. Theol. Sem.; B.D., Episcopal Theol. Sch., Cambridge, Mass., 1911; D.D., University of Pittsburgh, 1923, Allegheny Coll., 1923; D.D., Amherst (Mass.) College, 1935; unmarried. Deacon and priest P.E. Ch., 1911; asst. minister Trinity Ch., Boston, 1911-14; rector Christ Ch., New York, 1914-17, Calvary Ch., Pittsburgh, Pa., since 1917. Pres. Pa. Assn. for the Blind, 1923-25. Mem. Holland Soc., Alpha Delta Phi, Phi Beta Kappa. Clubs: University, Rotary, Field. The pioneer (Jan. 1921) in broadcasting ch. services. Home: 315 Shady Av., Pittsburgh, Pa.

VAN HISE, Warren Karle, mortgage broker; b. East Quogue, N.Y., Sept. 3, 1907; s. Ernest S. and Ethelyn Jane (Corwin) V.; ed. Southampton (N.Y.) High Sch., 1925, Rider Coll., Trenton, N.J., 1927-29, and special courses New York U.; unmarried. Traveling auditor Internat. Telephone and Telegraph. Co., New York, 1929-33; accountant Fidelity Union Title and Mortgage Guaranty Co., Newark, N.J., 1933-34; accountant and investigator Federal Communications Commn., 1934-35; broker of mortgage and real estate securities, own business, Newark, N.J., since 1935. Mem. Nat. Assn. Real Estate Bds., Delta Sigma Pi. Republican. Clubs: Newark Athletic, Down Town (Newark). Home: 45 N. Fullerton Av., Montclair, N.J. Office: 24 Commerce St., Newark, N.J.

VAN HORN, Rollin Weber, pres. Van Horn & Son, Inc.; b. Phila., Pa., Feb. 18, 1882; s. Alfred Roland and Jennie Sophia (Miller) V.; student high sch. and Peddie Inst., Highstown, N.J.; m. Helen Vollmer Adler, Jan. 13, 1927; children—Beryl, Jane, Wilhelmina. Began as designer of costume and scenic equipment for theatres, pageants, mardi gras, etc.; gen. mgr. Van Horn & Son, Inc., theatrical costumers, Phila., 1908-20, v.p., 1920-26, pres. since 1926. Mem. Pa. State Chamber of Commerce, Philadelphia Chamber of Commerce, Pa. Retail Mrchts. Assn., Chestnut St. Assn. Universalist. Home: Media, Pa. Office: S.E. Corner 12th and Chestnut Sts., Philadelphia, Pa.

VAN HOUTEN, Lyman Henry, coll. prof. psychologist; b. Bismarck, N.D., Mar. 10, 1888; s. William and Aria Gertrude (Van Helden) V.; grad. Pella (Ia.) High Sch., 1904; A.B., Central Coll., Pella, Ia., 1908; student U. of Chicago, summers 1908, 1909, 1915; A.M., U. of Ia., 1913; Ph.D., Columbia, 1929; m. Olive Blanche Henderson, June 4, 1916; children—Margaret, Olive Blanche. Supt. of schools, Ainsworth, Ia., 1908-09, Winfield, Ia., 1909-12; asst. in edn., U. of Ia., 1912-13; supt. of schools, Toledo, Ia., 1913-16; prof. of edn., State Teachers Coll., Cedar Falls, Ia., 1916-18, U. of Wyoming, 1920-21; field sec. U.S. Chamber of Commerce, 1920; prof. of edn. and psychology, State Teachers Coll., Edinboro, Pa., since 1921; visiting lecturer Ohio Univ., summer 1939. Served as capt. Sanitary Corps, U.S. Army, psychol. service, 1916-18; ednl. reconstruction service in Army hospitals. Licensed public school psychologist in Pa. Mem. N.E.A., Pa. State Edn. Assn., Pa. Assn. Clin. Psychologists, Am. Assn. Applied Psychologists, Progressive Edn. Assn., Pa. Assn. for Edn. of Exceptional Children, Am. Legion, Grange, Phi Delta Kappa, Kappa Delta Pi. Republican. Presbyterian (elder). Mason (32°). Club: Rotary (Edinboro-Cambridge Springs). Address: Edinboro, Pa.

VAN LAEYS, Leon Joseph, newspaperman; b. Cowley Co., Kan., Aug. 4, 1886; s. Jerome E. and Frances (Bezeau) V.; ed. pub. schs.; m. Madge Reynolds Harvey, Aug. 1, 1911. Reporter Kansas City Star, P. F. Collier's and Capper publications, 1906-10; circulation mgr. Capper Publications, 1911-12; business mgr. Houston (Tex.) Chronicle, 1913-15; asst. gen. mgr., exec. v.p. Houston (Tex.) Post, 1916-23; asst. to Henry J. Allen, Wichita Beacon, 1923-28; gen. mgr. McKinley Pub. Co., Kansas City, Mo., 1928-30; gen. mgr. and treas. Wilkes-Barre (Pa.) Record since 1930. Clubs: Westmoreland, Elks, Rotary, Wyoming Valley Country. Home: 539 Ford Av., Kingston, Pa.

VAN LIERE, Edward Jerald, univ. dean; b. Kenosha, Wis., Oct. 30, 1896; s. Martin and Wilhelmina (Pieper) Van L.; A.B., Univ., of Wis., 1915, M.S., 1917; M.D., Harvard U. Med. Sch., 1920; Ph.D., U. of Chicago, 1927; m. Helen Kimmins, Nov., —, 1923 (died 1929); m. 2d Alice E. Hartley, Nov. 10, 1930; 1 dau., Alice Wilhelmina. Asst. in zoology, Univ. of Wis., 1916-17; asst. in physiology, U. of Chicago, 1917-18; prof. physiology, U. of S.D., Vermilion, 1920-21; prof. physiology, W.Va. Univ., Morgantown, W.Va., since 1921; dean of Med. Sch. W.Va. Univ. since 1935. Served as 2d lt. San. Corps, U.S.A., 1918. Fellow Am. Coll. Physicians. Mem. Am. Physiol. Soc., Soc. for Exptl. Medicine and Biology, A.M.A., W.Va. and Monongalia County med. socs., Phi Beta Pi. Republican. Congregationalist. Mason. Contbr. many articles on influence of high altitudes on bodily functions to med. jours. Home: 508 Jefferson St., Morgantown, W.Va.

VAN LOON, Emily Lois, physician; b. Phila., Pa., Oct. 5, 1898; d. Frank W. and Emily Katherine (Laubach) VanL.; A.B., Swarthmore Coll., 1918; M.D., Woman's Med. Coll., 1922; M.Sc. in Medicine, U. of Pa. Grad. Sch. Medicine, 1928. Interne Woman's Med. Coll. Hosp., Phila., 1922-23; in practice at Phila. since 1924, specializing in otolaryngology and bronchoscopy since 1926; chief in otolaryngology, Woman's Hosp. of Phila. since 1928; prof. otolaryngology, Woman's Med. Coll. of Pa. since 1931, prof. broncho-esophagology since 1939; asso. prof. bronchoscopy, Temple U. since 1930. Fellow Am. Coll. Surgs., Phila. Coll. Phys. Mem. Am. Bronch. Soc., Phila. Laryngol. Soc., Alpha Epsilon Iota. Clubs: (woman's, literary, social, etc.) Home: 4705 Disston St., Tacony, Pa. Office: 1930 Chestnut St., Philadelphia, Pa.

VAN MIDDLESWORTH, Tunis Wilson, pub. utility exec.; b. New Brunswick, N.J., Oct. 21, 1884; s. Peter Q. and Ida G. (Stothoff) Van M.; ed. pub. schs. and high sch., Coleman's Bus. Coll.; m. Elsie Alice Wilcox, Feb. 18, 1911; children—Alice Wilson (Mrs. Millard Fillmore Ross), Richard W. Asso. with Public Service Corpn. of N.J. continuously since entering its employ as stenographer, 1902, successively, sec. to treas., stock transfer agt., cashier, asst. treas., then treas.; dir. Fidelity Union Stock & Bond Co. Republican. Mem. Dutch Reformed Ch. Clubs: Union, Court, Laurence Brook Country (New Brunswick). Home: 264 Grant Av., Highland Park, N.J. Office: 80 Park Place, Newark, N.J.

VANN, Robert L., lawyer; b. Ahoskie, N.C.; grad. Waters Normal Inst., Winton, N.C., 1901, Va. Union U., 1903; A.B., U. of Pittsburgh, 1906, LL.B., 1909; LL.D., Va. Union U., 1926, Wilberforce (O.) U., 1934; m. Jessie Matthews, of Gettysburg, Pa., Feb. 17, 1910. Admitted to Pa. bar, 1909, and since in gen. practice in Pittsburgh; 4th asst. city solicitor, 1917-21; mem. Pittsburgh law dept., 1917-21; founded Pittsburgh Courier (nat.), 1910, and since editor; pres. and treas. Pittsburgh Courier Pub. Co.; special asst. atty. gen. of U.S., Washington, D.C., 1933-36, resigned. Began political activities in national politics at Rep. Nat. Conv., Chicago, 1920; del. at large Rep. Nat. Conv., Cleveland, 1924; active in election of Presidents Harding, Coolidge and Hoover; changed to Democrat, 1932; del. at large Dem. Nat. Conv., Phila., 1936; special adviser to Nat. Dem. Com. Mem. Virgin Islands Advisory Com.; mem. Governor's Com. to Codify Laws of Pa.; mem. Constl. Celebrations Com. of Pa.; mem. state advisory council Federal Writers Project for Pa.; mem. Governor's Com. Celebration 150th anniversary of adoption of State Constitution. Mason (33°). Author of pamphlet, Patriot or Partisan. Home: 14th St., Oakmont, Pa. Office: 2628 Center Av., Pittsburgh, Pa.

VAN NAME, Elmer Garfield, lawyer, college pres.; b. Camden, N.J., Mar. 29, 1888; s. Clarence Barrett and Xenia (Smith) Van N.; LL.B., Temple U., 1912, grad. student, 1915-16; LL.D., Grove City Coll., 1934; m. Emily Osler Paul, Mar. 29, 1916; children—David Engelbert, Xenia Elizabeth, Emily Paul (dec.). Worked as clk. and title examiner, 1903-11; admitted to N.J. bar, 1912; counsellor at law, 1915; in practice at Camden; master in chancery, 1915, U.S. Supreme Court, 1932, spl. master, 1933; apptd. commr. N.J. Supreme Court, 1935; mem. bd. dirs. several building and loan associations; pres. Coll. of South Jersey since 1927; dean South Jersey Law Sch. since 1926. Mem. Am. and N.J. State bar assns., Camden Co. Bar Assn. (treas. for 10 yrs.), Acad. Polit. Science of N.Y., N.J. Soc. of Pa., Huguenot Soc. of Washington (D.C.), Netherlands Soc. of Phila., S.R., Haddonfield Hist. Soc., Sigma Pi. Republican. Methodist. Mason (K.T., Shriner). Club: Manufacturers and Bankers (Phila.) Home: Haddonfield, N.J. Office: 300 Broadway, Camden, N.J.

VANNATTA, George Woodruff, surgeon; b. Trenton, N.J., Aug. 3, 1888; s. Levi De Witt and Annie Sherman (Woodruff) V.; student Glen Ridge (N.J.) Grammar Sch., 1897-1902, High Sch., 1902-06; M.D., N.Y. U. Med. Coll., 1913; m. Mabel Elizabeth Shorter, June 24, 1915. Began as physician, East Orange, 1913; interne Newark (N.J.) City Hosp., 1913-14, resident, 1915; asst. supt. N.Y. Hosp., 1916; in gen. practice, East Orange, N.J., since 1918; chief surg. service Montclair (N.J.) Community Hosp. since 1925. Served in M.C., U.S. Army, during World War. Trustee Grace Meth. Ch., East Orange, N.J. Fellow Am. Coll. Surgeons; mem. Essex Co. Med. Soc., N.J., State Med. Soc., A.M.A., Phi Alpha Sigma. Republican. Methodist Mason, Odd Fellow, Jr. Order United Am. Mechanics, Royal Arcanum. Home: 17 Bradford Av., West Orange, N.J. Office: 226 N. Park St., East Orange, N.J.

VANNEMAN, Edward C., Jr.; judge Passaic Dist. Court, term expires 1941. Address: Passaic, N.J.

VAN POOLE, Carl Marcellus, physician; b. Salisbury, N.C., Aug. 21, 1887; s. Chalmers M. and Mary E. (Linn) Van P.; student U. of N.C., Chapel Hill, N.C., 1908-10; M.D., U. of Md. Med. Sch., Baltimore, 1916; m. Edna M. Litchfield, Nov. 21, 1922; 1 dau., Doris Lucille. Engaged in gen. practice of medicine and surgery at Mount Airy, Md., 1919-24; in practice at China Grove, N.C., 1924-30; at Mount Airy, Md. since 1930. Served as 1st lt., Med. Corps, U.S.A., in base hosps., U.S., 1918-19. Asst. Chief Mt. Airy Fire Co. Mem. Chamber of Commerce, Mt. Airy. Mem. Med and Chirurg. Faculty of Md., Carroll Co. Med. Soc., Alpha Omega Delta. Republican. Methodist. Mason. Odd Fellow. Club: Izaak Walton (Sykesville). Home: Park Av., Mount Airy, Md.

VAN SANT, William L.; surgeon-in-charge Hinton Hosp.; cons. surgeon Raleigh Gen. Hosp.,

Beckley, W.Va. Address: Hinton Hosp., Hinton, W.Va.

VAN SCIVER, J. Howard, pres. Bethlehem Foundry & Machine Co.; b. Camden, N.J., July 16, 1888; s. George D. and Clara E. (Johnson) V.; ed. Drexel Inst. Tech.; married; children—Strelsa, George D. Draftsman Hainesport Mining & Transportation Co., 1908-12, asst. chief engr., 1912-16, chief engr., 1916-20; sec. Van Sciver Corpn., 1920-28; pres. Bethlehem Foundry & Machine Co. since 1929, now also dir.; dir. Oil Burner Inst. Mason (Shriner). Clubs: Penn Athletic, Tri-State Yacht, Colonial Yacht, Bethlehem. Home: 605 Ashbourne Road, Elkins Park, Pa. Office: 225 S. 15th St., Philadelphia, Pa.

VAN SCIVER, Joseph Bishop, Jr., furniture mfg.; b. Camden, N.J., Aug. 1, 1894; s. Joseph Bishop and Florence Groff (Keily) Van S.; ed. Chestnut Hill Acad., grad., 1914, Drexel Inst. Tech., 1914-16; m. Louise L. Eveland, Sept. 28, 1923; 1 son, Joseph Bishop III. Began bus. career as designer of furniture; vice-pres. and gen. mgr., J. B. Van Sciver Co., mfrs. and retail mchts. furniture, Camden, N.J., Trenton, N.J., and Allentown, Pa., since 1916; dir. First Camden Nat. Bank & Trust Co.; former dir. Atlantic City R.R., Knickerbocker Lime Co., Hainesport (N.J.) Mining & Transportation Co., Fairlamb Co., De Frain Sand Co., Van Sciver Corpn., and Chamber of Commerce, Camden, N.J. Republican. Baptist. Clubs: Union League, Penn Athletic, Racquet, Phila. Cricket, Pylon Aviation (Philadelphia). Home: 501 Westview Av., Germantown, Philadelphia, Pa. Office: Camden, N.J.

VAN SICKLE, Clarence L(ott), prof. accounting; b. Frankfort, Ind., Mar. 16, 1892; s. Samuel and Catherine (McDowell) Van S.; B.S. in Econs., U. of Pittsburgh, 1923, A.M., same, 1925; m. Della B. Tschappat, Apr. 9, 1921. Held various positions as accountant with r.r. cos., Chicago, Ill., 1910-17; instr. in accounting and econs., Carnegie Inst. Tech., 1923-24; prof. accounting, accounting dept., U. of Pittsburgh, since 1924. Served with U.S.Q.M.C., Camp Taylor, Louisville, Ky., 1917-18. Mem. Am. Accounting Assn., Nat. Assn. Cost Accountants (pres. Pittsburgh chapter, 1931-32), Theta Chi, Beta Gamma Sigma, Alpha Kappa Psi. Mem. M.E. Ch. Author: Accounting System Installation, 1934; Cost Accounting, Fundamentals and Procedures, 1938. Author: Accounting Principles for Engineers, (with Charles Reitell), 1936. Home: 405 Bevington Rd., Forest Hills, Wilkinsburg, Pa.

VAN TRIES, William Potter, clergyman; b. Pa. Furnace, Pa., June 29, 1879; s. Thomas Campbell and Jennie (Milligan) Van T.; A.B., Princeton U., 1903; ed. Princeton Theol. Sem., 1904-07; (hon.) D.D., Tennent Coll. of Christian Edn., Phila., 1935; m. Daisy Augusta Aiken, Dec. 28, 1911; children—Thomas Aiken, Eleanor Jane, Clara Louise, Wilson Poe (dec.). Ordained to ministry Presbyn. Ch., 1907; pastor, Berwyn, Pa., 1908-11, Altoona, Pa., 1911-16, Parkesburg, Pa., 1916-23, Chester, Pa., 1924-28, Rumson, N.J., 1928-30; pastor, Ch. of the Redeemer, Germantown, Phila., Pa. since 1930; prof. English, Tennent Coll. of Christian Edn., Phila., Pa. since 1934. Republican. Presbyn. Home: 723 Wister St., Philadelphia, Pa.

VAN VOORHIS, Walter Roe, mathematics, adminstrn. head; b. Monongahela, Pa., July 23, 1904; s. Charles Elmer and Sallie C. (McConnell) Van V.; A.B., Pa. State Coll., 1930, A.M., 1931; ed. California State Teachers Coll., 1925; m. Hannah Ellen Grove, Aug. 29, 1924. Engaged in teaching, pub. schs., Washington Co., 1925-27; instr. mathematics, Pa. State Coll., 1930-33; administrative head, Schuylkill Undergrad. Centre, Pa. State Coll., Pottsville, Pa. and asst. prof. mathematics, 1934-39. Mem. Phi Lambda Theta, Kappa Delta Pi, Psi Chi, Kappa Phi Kappa, Pi Mu Epsilon. Republican. Presbyn. Clubs: Rotary, Schuylkill County Schoolman's, Schuylkill Country (Pottsville). Author: Statistical Procedures and Their Mathematical Bases (with C.C. Peters), 1935. Contbr. statis. and ednl. articles to mags. Home: 111 Wolf St., Pottsville, Pa.

VAN WINKLE, Charles Arthur, banking, real estate and ins.; b. Rutherford, N.J., Dec. 26, 1880; s. Arthur W. and Cornelia (Winant) Van W.; ed. pub. schs. and high sch.; m. Helen Decker, Sept. 30, 1908; children—Carolyn, Arthur D. Asso. with A. W. Van Winkle & Co., real estate and ins., Rutherford, N.J., continuously since becoming mem. firm, 1899, pres. since 1931; pres. Rutherford Trust Co. since 1914; 1st v.p. and dir. East Rutherford Savings Loan & Bldg. Assn. since 1902; pres. Central Mortgage Guaranty & Title Co., Wincast Co.; 2nd vice-pres. Boiling Spring Bldg. & Loan Assn. Member Holland Society of New York. Republican. Presbyn. (trustee First Ch. since 1912). Elk. Clubs: Rotary (Rutherford); Athletic (Newark). Home: 85 E. Pierrefont Av., Rutherford, N.J. Office: Station Square, Rutherford, N.J.

VAN WINKLE, Charles Ingersoll, physician; b. Rutherford, N.J., Feb. 11, 1905; s. Charles and Susie Maria (Gill) V.; grad. Rutherford (N.J.) High Sch., 1922; B.S., Rutgers U., 1926; M.D., Coll. of Physicians and Surgeons, Columbia, 1930; m. Anor Gertrude Whiting, Oct. 17, 1933; 1 dau., Mary Sue. Interne Bellevue Hosp., New York, 1930-32; physician Rutherford, N.J., since 1932; mem. staff and dir. gastro-intestinal clinic, Hackensack Hosp.; physician to Rutherford Schools. Mem. Bergen County Med. Soc., Rutgers Alumni Assn., P. and S. Alumni Assn., Beta Theta Pi, Phi Chi. Republican. Presbyterian. Club: Kiwanis (Rutherford). Address: 79 Ridge Rd., Rutherford, N.J.

VAN WINKLE, Major Edward, patent atty., elec. and mech. engring.; b. Jersey City, N.J., Apr. 24, 1879; s. Edward and Mary Jane (Wandel) VanW.; ed. Stevens Inst. Tech., 1893-97, Columbia U., 1897-1900, C.E.; m. Sama LeRoy Baldorf Aug. 15, 1900; 1 dau., Gertrude. Asso. with large corpns. in various engring. capacities to gen. mgr., 1899-1904; registered patent atty. and patent counsel for well-known corpns., New York, N.Y., 1905-16, and since 1919. Served as capt. later maj. 24th Engrs. U.S.A., 1917-19, with A.E.F. in France, Belgium, Luxemburg, Germany; rgtl. engr. officer constrn. troops bldg. Is-sur-Tille largest engr. depot in advance sector. Organizing comdr. Am. Legion post. Mem. Soc. Older Grads. (Columbia), Forty-Niners, Theta Delta Chi (nat. pres. grand lodge); asso. mem. Canadian Soc. Civil Engrs.; former mem. Am. Soc. C.E.; Am. Soc. Mech. Engrs. Republican. Mem. Dutch Reformed Ch. Clubs: Engineers of Plainfield (vice-pres.); University of Hudson Co., N.J. (hon. mem.). Home: 501 New Market Rd., Dunellen, N.J. Office: 103 Park Av., New York, N.Y.

VAN WINKLE, Winant, casualty insurance; b. Rutherford, N.J., Mar. 17, 1879; s. Arthur Ward and Cornelia (Winant) V.; student Bordentown Mil. Inst., 1894-96; B.S., Rutgers U., 1900; m. Jessie W. Mucklow, May 24, 1905; children—Winifred (Mrs. Frank B. Vanderbeek), Edgar Walling. Special agt. and asst. mgr. accident and health dept., U.S. Casualty Co., New York), 1900-07; asst. gen. mgr. Norwich & London Accident Co., Boston, 1907-09; vice-pres. and gen. mgr. Union Nat. Accident Co., Phila., 1910-13; with Commercial Casualty Ins. Co., Newark, since 1913, successively as mgr. accident and health dept., sec., vice-pres. and dir.; vice-pres. Metropolitan Casualty Ins. Co.; dir. Rutherford Trust Co.; pres. Wincast Co. Mem. N.J. Senate from Bergen Co. since 1934; mem. judiciary, appropriations and interstate relations coms.; chmn. banking and ins., taxation, and economy and reorganization coms. Trustee Rutgers U., N.J. Coll. for Women, N.J. Coll. of Pharmacy. Mem. Beta Theta Pi. Republican. Presbyterian. Mason, Elk. Clubs: Arcola Country; Newark Athletic. Home: 145 W. Passaic Av., Rutherford, N.J. Office: 10 Park Pl., Newark, N.J.

VARNES, Samuel Kepner, mech. engring.; b. East Salem, Pa., May 21, 1885; s. Joseph Darwin and Mary Alice (Kepner) V.; B.S. in E.E., Pa. State Coll., 1906, M.E., 1913; m. Florence Virginia Snyder, Oct. 9, 1912; children—Clara Louise, Anna Barbara. Foreman, Standard Steel Works, Burnham, Pa., 1906-07; draftsman, Pennsylvania Steel Co., Steelton, Pa., 1907, mech. testing, 1908, exptl. engr. and supt. steam and power equipment, 1908-17, mech. engr. mech. expt. div., engring. dept., 1917-18; supervising engr. E.I. duPont de Nemours & Co., Wilmington, Del., 1918-25; chief engr. Lazote, Inc., and successor duPont Ammonia Co. later absorbed into parent co. as Ammonia Dept. of E. I. duPont de Nemours & Co. since 1925. Mem. Am. Soc. Mech. Engrs. Republican. Methodist. Mason (32°). Home: Rockwood Rd. & Whittier Rd., Wilmington, Del.

VARNEY, William Wesley, engr., lawyer; b. Boston, Mass., Sept. 17, 1864; s. William Henry (capt. U.S.N.) and Mary E. (Hoffman) V.; mech. engring. course, Mass. Inst. Tech., 1883-86; LL.B., U. of Md., 1893; m. Edith McDonnal, Sept. 6, 1899; children—William Henry, John Hoffman. Draftsman, superintending constructor's office, U.S.N., Cramp's Shipyard, Phila., 1886-89; draftsman in charge superintending constructor's office, U.S.N., Baltimore, 1889-92; admitted to bar, federal and state, 1893; constrn. engr., Baltimore, 1893-99; city commr., Baltimore, 1899-1900; also city engr., pres. Bd. Pub. Works and mem. Water Bd.; cons. engr., Baltimore City, 1903-17, harbor engr., 1917-18; also in practice as patent lawyer since 1895. Mem. Am. Soc. M.E. (Am. Engring. Council 1925-27), Am. Soc. C.E., Soc. Naval Architects and Marine Engrs. Mem. Christian (Disciples) Ch. Odd Fellow; Grand Master I.O.O.F. of Md., 1910. Club: Maryland Yacht. Pioneer in television; filed application for 2 patents, Jan. 1892, on method of elec. transmission of optical impressions, and transmission of moving pictures in natural colors from life as well as from films. Home: 6017 Bellona Av. Office: Calvert Bldg., Baltimore, Md.

VASS, Thurman Elroy, surgeon; b. Alderson, W.Va., Jan. 27, 1889; s. Phillip E. and Eliza (Green) V.; student Concord Coll., Athens, W.Va., 1904-09, W.Va. Univ., 1909-11; M.D., Coll. of Phys. & Surgs., Baltimore, Md., 1914; (hon.) M.D., U. of Md. Med. Sch., 1916; m. Lucy E. Obenchain, Nov. 10, 1934. Interne Sheltering Arms Hosp., Hansford, W.Va., 1914; resident St. Luke's Hosp., Bluefield, W.Va., 1915-17, asst. surgeon, 1919-24, surgeon since 1924; vice-pres. St. Luke's Hosp. since 1924. Served as 1st lt. Med. R.C., U.S.A., 1917-19, relief surgeon in U.S. and France. Fellow Am. Coll. Surgeons. Mem. Am. Med. Assn., W.Va. State and Mercer Co. med. socs., Kappa Alpha, Kappa Xi. Democrat. Episcopalian. Mason (32°, Shriner). Clubs: Kiwanis, University, Country (Bluefield). Home: 714 Edgewood Rd. Office: 1710 Bland St., Bluefield, W.Va.

VASTINE, Jacob H., II, physician, radiologist; b. Catawissa, Pa., Apr. 3, 1897; s. George Hughes and Nellie M. (Pfahler) V.; student Bloomsburg (Pa.) State Normal Sch., 1911-14, Cornell U., 1914-17; M.D., U. of Pa., 1923; m. Frances Baldwin Anderson, Jan. 31, 1925; children—Nelle Anderson, Jacob H. III, Jane Pfahler. Interne Easton (Pa.) Hosp., 1923-24; resident in radiology Peter Bent Brigham Hosp., Boston, 1925-26; now clin. prof. of radiology, Women's Med. Coll.; asst. prof. of radiology, Grad. Sch., U. of Pa.; radiologist St. Christophers Children Hosp., Women's Coll. Hosp. Served in S.A.T.C., 1917-18. Mem. Phila. Coll. Physicians, Phila. Roentgen Ray Soc., Phila. Co. Med. Soc., A.M.A., Am. Roentgen Ray Soc., Am. Coll. Radiology, Phi Sigma Kappa. Registered by Am. Bd. Radiology. Episcopalian. Mason. Clubs: Philadelphia Country, Physicians Golf Assn., Medical (Phila.). Home: 267 Kent Rd., Wynnewood, Pa. Office: Medical Arts Bldg., Philadelphia, Pa.

VATES, Charles William, physician, surgeon; b. Pittsburgh, Pa., Mar. 2, 1885; s. John Christian and Elizabeth (Hartman) V.; M.D., U. of Pittsburgh, 1912; grad. study in pediatrics, Johns Hopkins Med. Sch. and Hosp., 1915, Sorbonne U., Paris, France, 1919; m. Rose Elizabeth Stanley (M.D., U. of Pittsburgh, 1912), June 9, 1917; children—Charles William, Jr., Elizabeth Rose, Howard LeRoy, Helen Louise. Physician and surgeon, Pittsburgh, since 1912; v.p. and dir. First Federal Savings & Loan Assn. of Mount Oliver, Pa.; chmn. bd.

liquidating trustees, Summit Bldg. & Loan Assn. of Mount Oliver. Dir. Mt. Oliver pub. schs., 1928-34; dir. South Hills Branch Y.M.C.A. of Pittsburgh; treas. Mt. Oliver Community Center. Served as 1st lt., then capt. and later major, Med. Corps, U.S. Army, 1917-19; with 310th Inf., 78th Div., A.E.F. Decorated Purple Heart; received Gen. Hdqrs. citation. Mem. A.M.A., Pa. State and Allegheny County med. socs., Phi Rho Sigma. Republican. Protestant. Mason (32°, Shriner). Address: 803 Brownsville Rd., Mount Oliver, Pittsburgh, Pa.

VAUCLAIN, Samuel Matthews, chmn. bd. Baldwin Locomotive Works; b. Phila., May 18, 1856; s. Andrew C. and Mary A. (Campbell) V.; ed. pub. schs., Altoona, Pa.; Sc.D., U. of Pa., 1906, Worcester Poly. Inst., 1931; LL.D., Villanova Coll.; m. Annie Kearney, Apr. 17, 1879; children—Samuel Matthews (dec.), Mary (Mrs. Franklin Abbott), Jacques L., Anne, Charles Parry, Constance Marshall (Mrs. William H. Hamilton, dec.). With Pa. R.R. System, 1872-83; with The Baldwin Locomotive Works since 1883, v.p., 1911-19, pres., 1919-29, chmn. bd. since 1929; chmn. bd. Standard Steel Works Co., Baldwin-Southwark Corpn., The Whitcomb Locomotive Co., Federal Steel Foundry Co., Baldwin-Southwark Corpn., I. P. Morris & De La Vergne, Inc., De La Vergne Engine Co., Mfrs. Mutual Fire Ins. Co.; director Westinghouse Electric & Mfg. Co., Westinghouse Electric Internat. Co., Westinghouse Acceptance Corpn., Phila. Nat. Bank, Fidelity-Phila. Trust Co., Beneficial Savings Fund Soc. of Phila., Midvale Co., Gen. Steel Castings Corpn., Baldwin Locomotive Works of Brazil, Inc., Pelton Water Wheel Co., Cramp Brass & Iron Foundries Co., Phila. Locomotive Works. Chmn. locomotive and car comn., Council Nat. Defense, and chmn. spl. advisory com. on plants and munitions, War Industries Bd., World War. Chmn. Municipal Gas Commn., Phila.; mgr. Northern Liberties Hosp.; president and trustee Bryn Mawr Hospital. Mem. Am. Soc. M.E. (hon.), Am. Soc. C.E., Am. Inst. Mining and Metall. Engrs., Instn. Civ. Engrs. of Gt. Britain, Am. Ry. Assn., Traveling Engrs. Assn., Pa. Soc., U. of Pa. Mus., Franklin Inst. (mem. bd.), Hist. Soc. Pa., Pa. Acad. Fine Arts, Pa. Mus. and Sch. of Industrial Art, Geog. Soc. Phila., Am. Acad. Polit. and Social Science, Am. Mus. Natural History, Army Ordnance Assn., Pa. Hort. Soc., Acad. Natural Sciences of Phila., Am. Philos. Soc., Instn. Structural Engrs. (Great Britain), Am. Mus. Natural History, Phila. Chamber of Commerce, Am. Chamber of Commerce in France, John Scott Medal Fund Com., Nat. Foreign Trade Council, Blair County Hist. Soc. (life), China Society America, Sulgrave Instn., American Society of French Legion of Honor, Philadelphia, Polish-Am. Chamber of Commerce, Devon Horse Show Assn., Council on Foreign Relations, Phila. Bourse, Ry. and Locomotive Hist. Soc., Inc. (life), Newcomen Soc. of Eng. (Am. Br.), U. of P. Bicentennial Com. Awarded D.S.M. (U.S.), 1919; Il Cancelliere Order Crown of Italy, 1920; Order of Polonia Restituta, 1923; Chevalier Legion of Honor (France), 1919; John Scott medal, 1891, 1931. Republican. Episcopalian. Clubs: Union League, Engineers', Merion, Penn Athletic, Automobile (Phila.); Railway (Chicago); Railway (New York); Western Railway; Army Navy Country (Washington). Home: "Broadlawn," Rosemont, Delaware Co., Pa. Office: 123 S. Broad St., Philadelphia, Pa.

VAUGHN, Floyd Ellis (Arky), professional baseball player; b. Clifty, Ark., Mar. 9, 1912; s. Robert Michael and Laura Alice (Denny) V.; student grade sch. and high sch., Fullerton, Calif., grad. 1930; m. Margaret Ann Allen, Oct. 30, 1931; children—Patricia Anne, Michaela Elizabeth. Engaged in playing professional baseball since 1931; with Wichita, Kan., 1931; under contract to Pittsburgh National League Club since 1932 as shortstop; played on National League All-Star Team, 1937; proprietor sheep ranch, Potter Valley, Calif., since 1937. Home: Potter Valley, Calif. Address: Pittsburgh Nat. League Baseball Club, Pittsburgh, Pa.

VAWTER, Eugene Raymond, county supt. of schools; b. Ansted, W.Va., Dec. 18, 1893; s. John Elliot and Emily Kyle (Rudisill) V.; prep. edn. Richmond (Va.) High Sch., 1908-10, Montgomery Prep. Branch of W.Va. U., 1910-12; B.S., W.Va. U., 1916; grad. student Columbia, 1937; unmarried. Prin. Ansted (W.Va.) High Sch., 1922-23; county supt. of schools, Fayette County, W.Va., 1923-27; prin. Nuttall (W.Va.) High Sch., 1927-32; prin. Gauley Bridge (W.Va.) High Sch., 1932-34; asst. county supt. of schools, Fayette County, W.Va., 1934-35, county supt. of schools since July 1935. Democrat. Presbyterian. Club: Lions. Home: Ansted, W.Va. Office: Fayetteville, W.Va.

VEACH, Carl L., seafood packer; b. Bentonville, Va., Sept. 25, 1883; s. David L. and Addie (Fielding) V.; A.B., Shenandoah Coll., Reliance, Va., 1906; m. Alma V. Clayton, Feb. 3, 1909; 1 son, Olyn David (dec.). School teacher, Warren Co., Va., 1907-08; in employ Majestic Shirt Co., and predecessor company, Baltimore, 1908-14; mem. firm J.M. Clayton Co., seafood packers, Hoopersville, Md., since 1914 (business removed to Cambridge, Md., 1921); vice-pres. and dir. Farmers & Merchants Nat. Bank, Cambridge, Md., since 1926. Mem. Phi Sigma Tau. Democrat. Methodist (steward, chmn. bd. of trustees Grace Church, Cambridge). Mason, O.E.S. Clubs: Cambridge Rotary (pres. 1938-39), Cambridge County (dir.). Home: Glenburn Av. and Travers. Office: Foot Commerce St., Cambridge, Md.

VEACH, Robert Wells, clergyman; b. New Castle, Pa., Oct. 5, 1871; s. George W. and Laura C. (Burnett) V.; B.A., Westminster Coll., New Wilmington, Pa., 1896, M.A., 1909, D.D., 1911; Auburn Theol. Sem., 1897-98, 1899-1900; Union Theol. Sem., 1898-99; Columbia, 1898-99; U. of Pa., 1911; m. Harriett Rebecca McLaughry, Sept. 13, 1900 (died Oct. 30, 1924); children—Elizabeth C., Harriett. Ordained Presbyn. ministry, 1900; pastor Mt. Hor Ch., Rochester, 1900-08; prof. religious pedagogy, 1908-12, dean, 1910-12, Bible Teachers' Training Sch., New York; pastor North Ch., Rochester, N.Y., 1912-15; ednl. sec. Presbyn. Bd. Publ. and Sabbath-School Work, Phila., Dec. 1915-20; pastor First Presbyn. Ch., Ridgewood, N.J., Jan. 1921-30; lecture tour in Orient and Near East, 1931. Democrat. Mason. Author: The King and His Kingdom, 1908; The Friendship of Jesus, 1911; Principles of Teaching; The Sunday School, Its Organization and Management; The Meaning of the War for Religious Education, 1919; The Dream Magnificent, 1938. Editor The Christian Educator. On leave of absence to direct Army Y.M.C.A. religious work at Camp Dix; in France with A.E.F., April 22-Nov. 18, 1918. Clubs: New York Clergy, Ridgewood Country. Lecture tour around world, 1930-31. Contbr. on religious subjects. Lecturer. Home: 475 Fairway Road, Ridgewood, N.J.

VEASEY, Benjamin R.; chief proctology Wilmington Gen. Hosp. Address: 1116 King St., Wilmington, Del.

VEASEY, Milton L., lawyer, banker; b. Pocomoke City, Md., Apr. 7, 1877; s. Thomas Jefferson and Marietta (Richards) V.; grad. Pocomoke City (Md.) High Sch., 1893; A.B., Western Md. Coll., Westminster, Md., 1896, A.M., 1899; LL.B., U. of Pa., Law Sch., 1902; m. May Morris Young, Nov. 22, 1905; children—Wanda May (Mrs. John Augustus Bullard), Jane Young. Practicing atty. at Pocomoke City, Md., 1902-33; pres. Pocomoke City (Md.) Nat. Bank since 1938; president Community Development Corpn., Chain Stores Realty Corpn. of Md. Mem. House of Dels., Md. Gen. Assembly, 1914; mem. Md. State Senate, 1931-39. Trustee Western Md. Coll. Mem. Phi Delta Phi. Democrat. Methodist. Mason (32°, Shriner). Address: Pocomoke City, Md.

VEBLEN, Oswald, prof. mathematics; b. Decorah, Ia., June 24, 1880; s. Andrew A. and Kirsti (Hougen) V.; A.B., U. of Ia., 1898; A.B., Harvard, 1900; Ph.D., U. of Chicago, 1903; hon. D.Sc., Oxford, 1929; hon. Ph.D., U. of Oslo, 1929; m. Elizabeth M. D. Richardson, 1908. Asso. in mathematics, U. of Chicago, 1903-05; preceptor in mathematics, 1905-10, prof., 1910-32, Princeton; prof. Inst. for Advanced Study, Princeton, since 1932. Capt. and maj., Ordnance Dept., U.S.A., 1917-19. Fellow Am. Acad. Arts and Sciences, Am. Phys. Soc., A.A.A.S.; mem. Nat. Acad. Sciences, Am. Philos. Soc., Am. Math. Soc. (pres. 1923-24), London Math. Soc., Circolo Mathematico di Palermo, Société Mathématique de France. Author: Infinitesimal Analysis (with N.J. Lennes), 1907; Projective Geometry (Vol. I, with J. W. Young), 1910, Vol. II, 1918, Cambridge Colloquium Lectures on Analysis Situs, 1922; Invariants of Quadratic Differential Forms, 1927; Foundations of Differential Geometry (with J.H.C. Whitehead), 1932; Projektive Relativitätstheorie, 1933. Home: Princeton, N.J.

VEENSCHOTEN, Vincent V., v.p. Northern Equipment Co.; b. Muitzeskill, N.Y., June 21, 1885; s. William and Fanny H. (Collison) V.; B.S. in E.E., Pa. State Coll., 1907; m. Lillian Colby, Jan. 31, 1914; children—William Edwin, John Colby, David Van. Test engr. Gen. Electric Co., 1907-09; steam engr. Isthmian Canal Commn., 1909-12; chief engr. Northern Equipment Co. since 1912, v.p. since 1912. Mem. Am. Soc. Mech. Engrs. Republican. Presbyn. Home: 1950 South Shore Drive. Office: Delaware Av. and Grove Drive, Erie, Pa.

VEH, Raymond Michael, clergyman and editor; b. Gibsonburg, O., June 26, 1901; s. Michael George and Ella E. (Yeasting) V.; A.B., North Central Coll., Naperville, Ill., 1923; A.M., U. of Ill., 1925; grad. study, Cleveland Coll., Western Res. U., Nast Theol. Sem.; hon. D.D., Western Union Coll., LeMars, Ia., 1936; m. Helen P. Zimmermann, Nov. 17, 1928; 1 dau., Marguerite Anne. Dir. student activities, Pilgrim Foundation, U. of Ill., 1924-25; asst. prof. sociology, Evansville Coll., Evansville, Ind., 1925-27, asst. dean of men, 1926-27; editor The Evangelical Crusader, youth weekly Evang. Ch., Harrisburg, Pa., since 1927; dir. Pa. Christian Endeavor Union; trustee Internat. Soc. of Christian Endeavor; adult counselor Gen. Evang. Young People's Union. Mem. Gen. Bd. Christian Edn., Gen. Bd. Missions, Bur. Ch. Architecture, Dept. Bible Work, S.S. and Tract Union of Evang. Ch. Republican. Mem. Evang. Ch. Contbr. to religious jours. Frequent speaker at colls. convs., assemblies. Home: 3313 N. 3d St., Harrisburg, Pa. Office: 3d and Reily Sts., Harrisburg, Pa.

VEITCH, Fletcher Pearre, chemist; b. Baltimore, May 22, 1868; s. Fletcher Roberts and Caroline Virginia (Pearre) V.; B.S., Md. Agrl. Coll., 1891, D.Sc., 1914; M.S., George Washington U., 1899; m. Laura T. Boyle, May 12, 1896. Asst., Md. Agrl. Expt. Sta., 1891-92; chemist, with W. S. Powell & Co., Baltimore, 1892-93; asst. chemist, Md. Agrl. Coll., 1894-99; asst. soil physicist, Md. Agrl. Expt. Sta., 1899-1901; with Dept. Agr., Washington, since 1901; asst. chemist, Bur. of Soils, 1901-02; same, Bur. of Chemistry, 1902-04; chief of Leather and Paper Lab., 1904-14; chemist in charge same, 1914-27; chemist in charge division industrial farm products, Bureau Chemistry and Soils, 1927-35; chief naval stores division Food and Drug Administration and naval stores research division Bureau Chemistry and Soils, 1935-38. Fellow A.A.A.S.; member Am. Chemical Society, American Leather Chemists' Association (ex-pres.), Society Leather Trades Chemists, Am. Soc. Testing Materials (chmn. naval stores com.), Assn. Agrl. Chemists (president 1922). Democrat. Author of numerous bulls. and articles on soils, fertilizers, tanning materials, leathers, turpentine, wood products, paper and paper making materials. Mem. com. on leather of Nat. Research Council, 1917-18, div. research extension, 1919-24; chmn. com. on paper specifications to joint com. on printing, 1913-36; mem. paper tech. com. Federal Specifications Bd., 1923-36; v. chmn. div. leather and gelatine, Am. Chem. Soc., 1923. Home College Park, Md.

VENABLE, Charles Scott, dir. of research; b. Chapel Hill, N.C., Sept. 3, 1891; s. Francis Preston and Sally Charlton (Manning) V.; A.B., Univ. of N.C., Chapel Hill, N.C., 1910, M.A., 1911; Ph.D., Mass. Inst. Tech., 1917; m. Olive Elsie Bartlett, Sept. 18, 1920; children—Charles Scott, Harriet Griswold. Chemist, U. of Va., Charlottesville, Va., 1917; chemist Mass. Inst. Tech. Research Lab. of Applied Chemistry,

1919-22; dir. of research Am. Viscose Corpn., Marcus Hook, Pa., since 1922. Served as capt., Chem. Warfare Service, U.S. Army, 1918-19. Auditor Nether Providence Twp. since 1935. Mem. Am. Chem. Soc., Franklin Inst., Delta Kappa Epsilon, Alpha Chi Sigma, Phi Beta Kappa. Democrat. Presbyterian. Clubs: Rolling Green Golf (Media, Pa.). Home: Wallingford, Pa. Office: American Viscose Corpn., Marcus Hook, Pa.

VENABLE, William Mayo, engineer; b. Cincinnati, Feb. 14, 1871; s. William Henry and Mary Ann (Vater) V.; Woodward High School, Chickering Inst.; B.S., U. of Cincinnati, 1892; M.S. (electricity), 1893, C.E., 1909; m. Jessie Genevieve Tuckerman, Dec. 26, 1901; children—Henry, John Ellinwood, Emerson. Mgr. National Contracting Co., sect. A, East Boston Tunnel, and portion of New Orleans drainage system, 1900-04; mgr. Municipal Engring. Co. and Sanitary Engring. Co. of New York, 1904-06; div. engr. Fla. East Coast R.R. building Long Key Viaduct, 1906-08; in charge of sewer work for Ferro-Concrete Constrn. Co., 1908-09; mgr. Blackstaff Engring. Co., Louisville, 1909-10; engr. Blaw-Knox Co., Pittsburgh, 1912—. Mem. Am. Soc. C.E., A.A.A.S., Optical Soc. America; v.p. Am. Rights League, 1916. Author: The Second Regiment of United States Volunteer Engineers, 1899; Interior Wiring, 1900; Garbage Crematories in America, 1906; Methods and Devices for the Bacterial Purification of Sewage, 1908; The Sub-Atoms, 1933; also various engring. papers and contributions to knowledge of color, and of the structure of hydrogen and of helium. Home: 822 N. St. Clair St., Pittsburgh, Pa.

VERMEULE, Cornelius Clarkson, civil engr.; b. New Brunswick, N.J., Sept. 5, 1858; s. Adrian and Maria (Veghte) V.; B.Sc., Rutgers Coll., 1878, M.S., C.E., 1880; m. Carolyn Carpenter Reed, June 7, 1888; children—Cornelius Clarkson, Warren Carpenter. In charge topog. survey, State of N.J., 1878-88, and continued until 1918 as consulting engr. State Geol. Survey; in gen. practice at New York since 1888, as consulting or construction engr. for many cities and pvt. corpns., in the United States and Cuba, also to Cuban government; organized York Cliffs (Me.) Improvement Co., 1892; obtained action by U.S. Govt., 1908, in rehabilitation of the sanitation of Cienfuegos, Cuba, at cost of $3,000,000, the work having been interrupted by political disturbances; engr. in charge of dismantling and reconstruction of Morris Canal for State of N.J. Mem. N.J. Hist. Society, N.J. Sanitary Assn., Am. Water Works Assn., Am. Soc. C.E., S.A.R., Holland Soc., New York Geneal. and Biog. Soc., N.E. Soc. of New York, N.E. Soc. of Orange. Presbyterian. Has written various monographs upon topography, water supply, etc.; author of map of Manhattan Island as it existed in 1776, and of several hist. monographs. Home: E. Orange, N.J. Office: 38 Park Row, New York, N.Y.

VERMEULE, Cornelius Clarkson, Jr., cons. engr.; b. New York, N.J., Sept. 26, 1895; s. Cornelius Clarkson and Carolyn Carpenter (Reed) V.; student Carteret Acad., Orange, N.J., 1909-13; student Princeton U., 1914-16, 1917, 1919-20, B.S., 1918, War Certificate in C.E., 1917; m. Catherine Sayre Comstock, Dec. 3, 1921; children—Cornelius Clarkson, III. Began as asst. engr. with C. C. Vermeule, New York, 1920; in gen. practice, Eastern states, 1920-28; cons. and directing engr. Morris Canal & Banking Co., Northern N.J., 1928-32; cons. engr. for various corpns. and orgns., New York, 1930-33; state engr. Pub. Works Adminstrn., N.J., 1933-36, acting state dir., 1936; cons. engr. for pub. bodies, corpns. and industrial clients, Short Hills, N.J. and New York since 1937. Served as pvt., corp., sergt., 2d N.J. Inf., 1915-16; 2d lt., 1st lt., capt., Inf., U.S. Army, 1916-19, service in Picardy, Somme, St. Mihiel, Meuse Argonne offensives; successively capt., maj., lt. col., Inf. Officers Res. Corps, since 1919. Asso. mem. Am. Soc. C.E.; mem. Mil. Order of Fgn. Wars. Awarded Silver Star; Distinguished Service Medal, N.J., 1924; Victory Medal with 4 battle clasps, 1919. Presbyterian. Clubs: Holland Society (New York); Cloister Inn (Princeton, N.J.); Short Hills (N.J.); Stony Brook Hunt (Princeton, N.J.). Address: Coniston Rd., Short Hills, N.J. Office: 38 Park Row, New York, N.Y.

VERMILYE, William Moorhead, banker; b. Orange, N.J., Apr. 6, 1880; s. Daniel Babbitt and Mary Cornelia (Holmes) V.; prep. edn. Staten Island (N.Y.) Acad.; student Mass. Inst. Tech., 1897-99; m. Ethel Howard Simpson, of Hingham, Mass., Oct. 11, 1905; children—Mary Nazro (Mrs. Phillip E. McKenney), William Howard, Ethel Cornelia (Mrs. William Russell Eaton), Ridgeley Clare. Treas. Manhasset Mfg. Co., Providence, R.I., 1921-22; exec. v.p. Nat. Aniline & Chem. Co., New York, 1923-30; v.p. Thomaston (Ga.) Cotton Mills, 1931-32; treas. Knox Hat Co., and chmn. bd. Hat Corpn. of America, 1932-33; treas. Eitingon Schild Co., New York, 1933-35; pres. and chmn. Susquehanna Silk Mills, New York, 1936-37; v.p. Nat. City Bank of N.Y. since 1937; dir. Susquehanna Silk Mills, Mo.-Kan. Pipe Line Co., Am. Type Founders, Byrndum Corpn., Va.-Car. Chem. Corpn. Endorsed Vermilye medal (awarded biennally for contribution to industrial management by Franklin Inst.). Mem. Newcomen Soc., Holland Soc., St. Nicholas Soc., Huguenot Soc., Soc. Colonial Wars of N.J. Republican. Episcopalian. Clubs: Union League, Merchants, Recess (New York). Author of brochures: Power in the Textile Industry; Economic Trends in Manufacturing and Sales; Human Understanding in Industry. Home: 930 Madison Av., Plainfield, N.J. Office: 55 Wall St., New York, N.Y.

VERNON, Frank Lawrence, clergyman; B.A., Trinity Coll., Toronto, Can., 1893; B.D., Episcopal Theol. Sch.; Cambridge, Mass., 1896; (hon.) D.D., Trinity Coll.; (hon.) Litt.D., St. Stephen's Coll. Ordained to ministry P.E. Ch., deacon, 1896, priest, 1897; rector, N. Grafton, Mass., 1896-1902; dean Cathedral Ch. of St. Luke, Portland, Me., 1902-20; rector St. Mark's Ch., Phila., since 1920; mem. Cathedral Chapter in Diocese of Pa.; mem. bd. mgrs. Episcopal Hosp., Phila.; Prov. Superior, Confraternity of the Blessed Sacrament; chaplain gen. Community of St. Mary. Address: 1625 Locust St., Philadelphia, Pa.

VEST, Cecil Woods, visiting gynecologist Union Memorial Hosp., Church Home and Infirmary, Cambridge-Maryland Hosp. Address: 1014 St. Paul St., Baltimore, Md.

VEST, Walter Edward, M.D.; b. Floyd Co., Va., Jan. 20, 1882; s. William Madison and Mary Susan (Boone) V.; A.B., Coll. William and Mary, 1902; M.D., Med. Coll. Va., 1909, hon. D.Sc., 1939; m. Saddie Pearl Blankinship, May 26, 1910; 1 son, Walter Edward. Interne, Memorial Hosp., Richmond, Va., 1909-10; gen. practice at Meherrin, Va., 1910-15, Huntington, since 1916; practice limited to diagnosis and treatment of med. conditions; internist C.&O. Ry. Co., Chesapeake & Ohio Hosp.; attending physician St. Mary's Hospital. Chief of medical service, base hosp., Camp Wadsworth, S.C., 1918-19. President State Public Health Council; member Medical Advisory Board of Cabell County Public Schools. Fellow A.M.A. (mem. House of Dels.; mem. Com. of 7), Am. Coll. Physicians (W.Va. mem. bd. govs.), Am. Coll. Chest Physicians; mem. Southern Med. Assn. (ex-chmn. council; chmn. sect. gastroenterology 1935; pres. 1939), W.Va. State Med. Assn. (pres. 1930), Cabell Co. Med. Soc. (pres. 1936), W.Va. Hosp. Assn. (pres. 1932), Southern States Assn. Ry. Surgeons, Assn. of Surgeons of the C.&O. Ry. (president 1936), Nat. Tuberculosis Assn., W.Va. Tuberculosis Assn. (ex-pres.), Am. Therapeutic Soc., Alumni Assn. Coll. of William and Mary (ex-pres.), Alumni Soc., Med. Coll. of Va. (pres. 1931), Huntington Alumni Assn. (pres.), Phi Beta Kappa, Phi Beta Pi, Pi Gamma Mu. Democrat. Methodist. Mason (Shriner). Kiwanian. Editor W.Va. Medical Jour. Contributor to Ky. Medical Jour., Southern Med. Jour., Internat. Jour. Surgery, Social Science. Home: 1115 9th Av. Office: First Huntington National Bank Bldg., Huntington, W.Va.

VICARY, Arthur Charles, retired; b. LeRoy, N.Y., Oct. 3, 1882; s. Charles Newell Wood and Louise Haskins (Bailey) V.; grad. Canton (O.) Central High Sch., 1902; B.S. in Engring., Case School of Applied Science, 1906; m. Mary DeWolfe Wilmarth, of Glen Falls, N.Y., Oct. 6, 1908; children—James Wilmarth, Louise De-Wolfe. Began as mechanic, 1906; purchasing agent Dean Electric Co. (now Garford Mfg. Co.), Elyria, O., 1906-08; sales engr. Thew Shovel Co., Lorain, O., 1908-13; engr. and sales mgr. Ball Engine Co., Erie, Pa., 1913-20, v.p. Erie Steam Shovel Co., successors, 1920-27, Bucyrus-Erie Co., successors, 1927-29; retired, 1929, now dir.; dir. Morehouse Motor Co., Erie, Pa., The C. N. Vicary Co., Canton, O. Administrator CWA, Erie Co., 2 yrs. Pres. Erie Community Chest, 3 terms. Former mem. Am. Soc. M.E.; pres. Erie Chamber of Commerce, 2 terms; mem. Phi Delta Theta. Republican. Presbyterian (trustee Ch. of the Covenant, Erie). Mason (Shriner). Clubs: Erie, Kahkwa (Erie). Home: Appledore, R.D. No. 2, Erie, Pa.

VICKERS, Arnold Montgomery, lawyer; b. Montgomery, W.Va., Aug. 8, 1908; s. Chas. Milton and Helen (Montgomery) V.; LL.B., Washington & Lee Univ. Law Sch., Lexington, Va., 1931; m. Nettie Hess Vickers, Dec. 22, 1932. Admitted to W.Va. bar, 1931, and since engaged in gen. practice of law at Montgomery; mem. firm Montgomery & Vickers, Montgomery, W.Va., 1931-39; mem. firm Eary, Thompson & Vickers with offices at Montgomery, W.Va., and Fayetteville, W.Va., since 1939; served as city atty., Montgomery, W.Va., 1933-35; mem. W.Va. Ho. of Dels., 1934-35; mayor of Montgomery since 1937. Mem. Lambda Chi Alpha, Phi Alpha Delta. Democrat. Methodist. Mason. Moose. Club: Rotary of Montgomery. Home: 314 Sixth Av. Office: Merchants Nat. Bank Bldg., Montgomery, W.Va.

VICKERS, Enoch Howard, prof. economics; b. Washington Co., Md., Mar. 14, 1869; s. William and Jerusha (Mullen) V.; A.B., W.Va. U., 1890; A.B., Harvard, 1893, A.M., 1894; studied U. of Berlin, 1895-96, Paris, 1896-98; m. Kiyo Nellie Nishigawa, Dec. 20, 1899; children—Fanny Clay, Alethea Kate, Walter William Howard. Teacher English and Mathematics, Prep. Sch. W.Va. U., 1890-92; asst. in constl. law and govt., Harvard, 1894-95; Robert Treat Paine fellow, Harvard, and non-resident student, 1895-97; prof. economics, Keiogijuku U., Tokyo, Japan, 1899-1910; prof. economics, W.Va. U., since 1911; state supervisor of inventory of publicly owned land in W.Va., 1939. Liberty Loan speaker and four minute man, World War. Pres. State Conf. Charities and Correction, W.Va., 1916, 17. Mem. Am. Economic Assn., Am. Assn. for Labor Legislation, Am. Assn. Univ. Profs., Am. Acad. Polit. and Social Science, Asiatic Soc. of Japan (life), Phi Kappa Psi, Phi Beta Kappa. Decorated Order of Rising Sun (Japan). Republican. Episcopalian. Home: Morgantown, W.Va.

VIEHOEVER, Arno, coll. prof.; b. Wiesbaden, Germany, Nov. 3, 1885; s. Joseph and Franciska (Maldaner) V.; Pharm. Chemist, U. of Marburg, 1908, Food Chemist 1913, Ph.D., 1913; m. Mabel E. Johnson, Nov. 21, 1915; children —Arnold Joseph, Ellen Margaret, Kent. Asst. and instructor, Bot. Pharmacognostical Inst., Marburg, 1909-13; pharmacognosist and chemist in charge Pharmacognosy Lab., Bur. of Chemistry, U.S. Dept. Agr., Washington, 1913-23; prof. in charge dept. biology and pharmacognosy, Phila. Coll. Pharmacy and Science, 1923-32, research prof. and dir. biol. and biochemical research lab. since 1934, also curator, dir. micros. labs. and expt. gardens; director Hyper Humus Co., Newton, N.J., Phenolphtalein Research Inst.; scientific adviser to Ministry of Economic Affairs, Dept. of Science, Bangkok, Siam (on leave of absence), 1939. Composer of songs and marches. Naturalized citizen of U.S., 1919. Fellow A.A. A.S. Mem. Am. Chem. Soc., Am. Pharm. Assn., Phila. Acad. Science, Franklin Inst., Bot. Soc.; hon. mem. Kappa Psi; mem. Sigma Xi. Referee Daphnia Methods of Assn. of Agrl. Chemists. Home: 210 Rutgers Av., Swarthmore, Pa.

VIERHELLER, Albert Frank, horticulturist; b. Parkersburg, W.Va., Feb. 10, 1894; s. Frank Albert and Caroline Wilhelmina (Buehler) V.; grad. Parkersburg (W.Va.) High Sch., 1911;

student North Ga. Agrl. Coll., Dahlonega, Ga., Sept.-Dec. 1913; B.S. in Agr., W.Va. U., 1918; M.S. in Agr., U. of Md., 1923; m. Ethel May Smith, June 8, 1926. Instr. horticulture, U. of Md., 1921-24, extension horticulturist since 1924, asso. prof. horticulture since 1936; entomol. inspector, Delaware, U.S. Bur. Entomology, Apr.-July 1918; orchard foreman Chert Mt. Orchards, Rada, W.Va., Mar. 1920-Jan. 1921; asst. county agrl. agent, Wellsburg, W.Va., May-Sept. 1917. Served with Med. Dept., U.S. Army, 1918-20. Mem. Md. State Hort. Soc. (sec.-treas. since 1923), Am. Legion, Sigma Phi Epsilon. Democrat. Presbyn. Mason (K.T.; Royal Arch). Home: 5 University Road, Hyattsville, Md.

VIESER, Milford A(ugust), vice-pres. Franklin Mortgage & Title Guaranty Co.; b. Newark, New Jersey, January 2, 1903; s. William E. G. and Emma (Lange) Vieser; educated at Pace Inst., New York (4 yr. accounting and business course), also courses at New York U. and Rutgers U.; m. Vera Kniep, June 2, 1928; 1 son, William Milford. Examiner, staff of chief examiner. Banking and Ins. Dept., State of N.J., 1920-23, sr. examiner, 1923; asst. sec. and asst. treas. City Mortgage Guaranty Co., Newark, 1923-26; vice-pres. and dir. Franklin Mortgage & Title Guaranty Co., Newark, since 1926; vice-pres. and dir. Franklin Agency since 1931; trustee Ace Bldg. & Loan Assn., Newark, 1932-37. Pres. N.J. Mortgage Conf. since 1938; vice-pres. and trustee N.J. Title Assn. since 1938. Republican. Presbyterian. Mason. Home: 23 Bradford Av., West Orange, N.J. Office: 509 Orange St., Newark, N.J.

VIEWEG, Hermann Frederick, research chemist; b. Buffalo, N.Y., Sept. 12, 1900; s. Rudolf and Emma (Klein) V.; B. Chemistry, Cornell U., 1921, Ph.D., same, 1924; m. Dr. Alice McNulty, Sept. 1, 1925. Asst. in mineralogy, Cornell U., 1919, instr., 1920-24, actg. asst. prof., 1924-25; prof. chemistry, Muhlenberg Coll., 1925-27; instr. physics, Cornell U., 1927-29; research metallurgist, Aluminum Co. America, 1929-30; asso. prof. ceramics, Rutgers U., 1930-35, prof., 1935; research engr., Johns-Manville Corpn., Manville, N.J. since 1935. Served as maj. F.A. Res. since 1934. Fellow Am. Inst. Chemists. Mem. Am. Chem., Am. Ceramic, Am. Mineral. socs., Am. Assn. Univ. Profs., Sigma Xi, Phi Kappa Phi. Mem. Evangelical Ch. Club: Rutgers University Outing. Home: 323 Lawrence Av., Highland Park, N.J. Office: Johns-Manville Research Labs., Manville, N.J.

VILSACK, Carl G., pres. Pittsburgh, Brewing Co. and Tech Food Products Co.; b. Pittsburgh, Pa., Apr. 27, 1888; s. Leopold and Dorothy (Blank) V.; student Georgetown U., 1910; m. Mary Alice Johnston; Jan. 20, 1913; children—Carl G., William J., Mary Bell. Sec. E. End Sav. & Trust Co., 1916-20, later becoming pres.; Vilsack-Martin Real Estate Co., Lawler-Vilsack Inv. Co., Tech Food Products Co., Pittsburgh Brewing Co., also dir. of each and dir. Washington Tin Plate Co. Mem. East Liberty Chamber of Commerce. Clubs: Pittsburgh Field, Long Vue Country, Pittsburgh Athletic Assn. Home: 5867 Aylesboro Av. Office: 3340 Liberty Av., Pittsburgh, Pa.

VINCENT, George Clark, clergyman; b. Ligonier, Pa., Jan. 29, 1884; s. Hanna and Martha Jeanette (Jamison) V.; B.A., Westminster Coll., New Wilmington, Pa., 1904; Rhodes scholar from Ohio, Oxford U., Eng., 1904-07, B.A., 1907, Holwell exhibitioner, Queen's Coll., Oxford, 1908-09; studied Pittsburgh Theol. Sem., 1908; D.D., Monmouth (Ill.) Coll., 1925; m. Mary Lois McMichael, Mar. 25, 1913. Ordained ministry U. P. Ch., 1911; successively pastor Monmouth, Ill., Washington, Pa., South Park Presbyterian Ch., Newark, N.J., Shadyside Ch., Pittsburgh, Pa., until 1928, Union Congl. Ch., Upper Montclair, N.J., since 1928. Vice-pres. Bd. Home Missions of Congregational Ch. Trustee Newark Mus. Assn. Mem. Sigma Chi. Home: 160 Cooper Av., Upper Montclair, N.J.

VINCENT, Henry Bethuel, musical dir.; b. Denver, Colo., Dec. 28, 1872; s. Bethuel T. and M. Ella (Masters) V.; student Oberlin Coll., 1889-90, 1892-93; Bordentown (N.J.) Inst.; studied music with Paur, Sherwood, Behrend, etc., London and Paris. Dir. Vincent Studio, Erie, Pa., 1900-29; dir. Erie Choral Soc. and Conneaut Choral Soc., 1914-18; organist and choirmaster successively 1st Presbyn. Ch., St. Patrick's Ch., Simpson Ch., Jewish Temple to 1932; condr. Erie Symphony Orchestra; gen. dir. Erie Playhouse. Official organist Chautauqua Instn., 1904-23. Conductor, Federal Music Project Orchestra, 1936-37. Lecturer before many schs., univs. and clubs. Commodore Erie Yacht Club, 1923-24 and 1927-29. Composer: (oratorio) The Prodigal Son, 1902: (Oriental song cycle) The Garden of Kama, 1905; (operettas) Indian Days and Savageland; (opera) Esperanza, prod., Washington, D.C., 1906; over 100 songs, anthems and pieces for piano, organ and orchestra. Clubs: Yacht, University, Art. Home: Erie, Pa.

VINCENT-DAVISS, Cedric Arthur, chem. development mgr.; b. Smethwick, Staffordshire, Eng., Sept. 23, 1898; s. Arthur Robert and Lucy (Fowler) V-D.; came to U.S., 1931, naturalized, 1937; student George Dixon Secondary Sch., Birmingham, Eng., 1908-16, U. of Birmingham (Eng.), 1916-17; B.Sc., U. of Birmingham (Eng.), 1921, B.Sc. Hons. Chem., 1922; m. Laura Bradley, Mar. 26, 1925; 1 dau., Anne. Chemist Kramer Radio Active Applicators, Birmingham, England, 1922-24, Niagara Electrolytic Iron Co., Niagara Falls, N.Y., 1924-28; research chemist, Carborundum Co., Niagara Falls, N.Y., 1928-30; chm. engr. E. I. du Pont de Nemours & Co., Wilmington, Del., 1930 to 1936, development mgr. metal treatment and cyanide products div. since 1937. Served as lt., East Lancashire Regt., British Army, 1917-19. Mem. Inst. of Chem. Engrs., Am. Chem. Soc., Electro-Chem. Soc., Soc. of Metals, Iron and Steel Inst., Inst. of Chemists (Great Britain and Ireland). Presbyn. Clubs: du Pont Country, University (Wilmington, Del.); Concord Country (Concordville, Pa.). Home: 2327 Pennsylvania Av. Office: E. I. du Pont de Nemours & Co., 10th & Market Sts., Wilmington, Del.

VINING, Robert Edward, publicist; b. Hull, Mass., Aug. 22, 1901; s. Daniel and Lydia H. (Watson) V.; grad. Medill Sch. Journalism of Northwestern U., 1929; B.B.A., U. of Baltimore, 1937; spl. courses, Johns Hopkins U.; unmarried. Employed on editorial staffs newspapers in Phila., Boston, Chicago, 1923-26; chief publicity dept., Western Electric Co. Hawthorne Works, Chicago, Ill., 1926-29; publicity director Western Electric Co. Point Breeze Works, Baltimore, since 1929. Commd. sr. lt. U.S.N. Res.; vice chmn. Md. Navy Day Com. since 1934. Mem. Md. State Bd. Edn. Chmn. Md. Commn. on Prison Labor, 1935-37; 2d v.p. and mem. bd. dirs. Baltimore Criminal Justice Commn.; mem. bd. Legal Aid Bur. Baltimore; vice-chmn. pub. com. Baltimore Assn. Commerce since 1933; Md. rep. on Young Men's Council of U.S.; sec. Md. Commn. for Study of Unpaid Wages; exec. sec. Com. on Industrial Rehabilitation, Fifth Federal Res. Dist., 1932-33. Mem. Acad. Polit. Sci., Am. Geog. Soc., English Speaking Union, U.S. Naval Res. Officers' Assn., Navy League of U.S., U.S. Naval Acad. Alumni Assn., Baltimore (hon.), Blue Key, Sigma Delta Chi, Delta Sigma Pi. Mem. University Club (Baltimore.). Awarded "First Young Citizen of Baltimore" Scroll for having done the most for the city as private citizen, 1935. Republican. Episcopalian. Mason. Home: 3111 N. Charles St. Office: 2500 Broening Highway, Baltimore, Md.

VINTON, Stallo, lawyer, author; b. Indianapolis, Ind., Dec. 15, 1876; s. Merrick Eugene and Susan Vandeman (MacIntire) V.; ed. Butler Coll., Indianapolis, Ind., 1891-95; A.B., Columbia U., 1898, A.M., same, 1899; LL.B., Columbia U. Law Sch., 1900; unmarried. Admitted to N.Y. bar, 1900 and since engaged in gen. practice in New York City. Served in N.Y. Guard, 1918-19 and N.G.N.Y., 1920-21. Mem. Quivira Soc., Hudson's Bay Record Soc., Calif. Hist. Soc., Colo. Hist. Soc., S.R., Phi Delta Theta. Honored as adopted mem. Cheyenne Indian Tribe. Republican. Author: John Colter, Discoverer of Yellowstone Park, 1926; Joe Meek, the Mountain Man (in manuscript). Editor, Overland with Kit Carson, 1930; American Fur Trade, 1935, 2d edit. Home: 558 Park Av., Weehawken, N.J. Office: 150 Broadway, New York, N.Y.; also, 661 Main Av., Passaic, N.J.

VINUP, Frederick Henry, physician and surgeon; b. Parkersburg, W.Va., Oct. 6, 1885; s. Charles R. and Dora (Geisz) V.; M.D., U. of Md. Med. Sch., Baltimore, 1909; m. Marie Belle Murchison, June 14, 1913 (dec.); children—Dorothy Elizabeth (Mrs. Paul Harnish Myers), Kathleen Murchison. Interne and resident, Univ. Hosp., 1908-09, Bay View Hosp., 1909-10, Eudowood Hosp., 1910-11, Robert Garrett Hosp., 1911-13; engaged in gen. practice of medicine at Baltimore since 1912; med. dir. and mem. bd. dirs. Monumental Life Ins. Co., Baltimore, since 1920; mem. firm Drs. Vinup, Buchness and Buchness, industrial physicians since 1928. Served as capt. Med. Corps, U.S.A., on Mexican border, 1916-17, major with A.E.F., 1917-19; col. Med. Corps Md. N.G., comdg. officer 104th Med. Regt.; div. surgeon, 29th Div. (Pa., Va., D.C.). Mem. Baltimore City Health Dept., 1912-22; pres. Bd. of Police Examiners, 1922-35; mem. Md. Bd. of Welfare, 1927-35. Mem. A.M.A., Med. & Chirurg. Faculty of Md., Baltimore City Med. Soc., Radiol. Soc. America, Am. Assn. Industrial Physicians and Surgeons, Assn. of Mil. Surgeons of U.S. (pres. 1927-28), Phi Chi. Democrat. Episcopalian. Mason (32°). Clubs: Maryland, Merchants, Maryland Yacht (Baltimore); Army and Navy (Washington, D.C.). Home: 5017 Falls Rd. Office: 110 E. Lombard St., Baltimore, Md.

VIPOND, John S., pres. Citizens Nat. Bank; b. Hollidaysburg, Pa., Apr. 29, 1863; s. John and Susan (Stetler) V.; student pub. schs.; m. Ruth Clark, 1921; children—Addam, Edgar, Paul, Edith, Elizabeth. Pres. Citizens Nat. Bank, Hollidaysburg, Pa. Elk. Club: Hollidaysburg (Pa.). Home: Olde Home Farm. Office: Allegheny St., Hollidaysburg, Pa.

VISSCHER, Barent Lambert, lawyer; b. Syracuse, N.Y., Dec. 25, 1885; s. John Barent and Clara Frances (Simons) V.; student Syracuse (N.Y.) High Sch., 1899-1903; A.B., Hobart Coll., Geneva, N.Y., 1907; LL.B., Syracuse (N.Y.) U. Coll. of Law, 1910; m. Edith Frances Wagner, June 24, 1912; children—Sally, Ann Chapman, Ellen Wagner. Clerk Lee & Brewster, Syracuse, N.Y., 1910, Wilson, Cobb & Ryan, Syracuse, N.Y., 1910-12; pvt. practice of law at Union Springs, N.Y., 1912; legal dept., Royal Indemnity Co., New York, 1912-22; asso. with Hawkins, Delafield & Longfellow, New York, since 1922, partner since 1934; admitted to practice in New York, 1910, New Jersey, 1921. Trustee Hobart Coll., Geneva, N.Y. Mem. Am. Bar Assn., N.Y. State Bar Assn., Assn. of Bar of City of New York, Sigma Chi. Democrat. Episcopalian. Mason. Home: 60 Hanover Rd., Mountain Lakes, N.J. Office: 49 Wall St., New York, N.Y.

VITTOR, Frank Fabio, sculptor; b. Mozzate, Como, Italy, Jan. 6, 1888; s. Carlo and Teresa (Moroni) Vittori; came to U.S., 1906, naturalized, 1922; ed. Coll. of Saronno, Italy, 1901-03, Acad. of Brera, Italy, 1903-05; m. Ademia Humphreys, Oct. 1917; children—Charles Frank, Gloria Jane, Phoebe Katherine, Carla Teresa, Anthony Armand, Leander Alexander. Woodcarver, Italy, 1898; studied sculpture in Italy and France; professional sculptor, U.S., since 1906; teacher of sculpture, Carnegie Inst. Tech., 1920-21. Mem. Planning Commn., Pittsburgh. Works: more than 20 war memorials in Pittsburgh dist.; busts (from life) Theodore Roosevelt, Calvin Coolidge; busts of Lincoln, Harding, Wilson, Gen. Sherman, Dr. John A. Brashear, Mark Twain, Clyde Kelly, Joaquin Miller; gigantic statue Steel (90 ft. high), Phila. Sesqui-Centennial, 1926; 4 granite relief panels for Westinghouse Memorial Bridge, Allegheny Co., Pa.; 12 panels on pylons, marking historic places along highways, Allegheny Co.; winner of nat. competition for design of half-dollar to commemorate Blue and Grey Reunion at Gettysburg, 1938. Awards: Cross of Merit and Gold medal at Bologna Exposition, 1931, and grand prize, same, 1933. Home: Castle Shannon, Pa. Studio: 1828 5th Av., Pittsburg, Pa.

VLACHOS, Nicholas Panagis, prof. classics; b. Amsterdam, Holland, Feb. 15, 1875; s. Nicholas and Anna Maria Geertruida (de Leeuw) V.; student Univ. of Amsterdam, 1897-98, U. of Pa., 1898-1903, Ph.D., 1901; came to U.S., 1896, naturalized, 1924; m. Mary Jean Dailey, June 10, 1911; children—Mary Anna Josephine (Mrs. Richard Jerrell Westcott), Nicholas de Leeuw. Engaged as prof. Greek and Latin, Temple U., Phila., since 1903. Mem. Classical Assn. of Atlantic States, Classical League, Am. Assn. Univ. Profs., Classical Club Phila. Author: Hellas and Hellenism, 1936. Home: 1920 N. Park Av., Philadelphia, Pa.

VOELMLE, Herbert Somerville, mfr.; b. Philadelphia, Pa., Dec. 25, 1891; s. Edward Cady and Elizabeth (Smith) V.; B.S., Central High Sch., Philadelphia, 1909; studied Sch. of Pedagogy, Philadelphia, 1910-12; m. Celia M. Richards, June 20, 1931. Teacher pub. sch., Philadelphia, 1912-14; with Voelmle Bros. since 1914, became partner, 1920 and sole owner, 1929; v.p. and dir. Tioga Nat. Bank & Trust Co. Served as 2d lt., F.A., U.S. Army, 1918. Mem. Am. Legion. Republican. Presbyterian. Mason (Past Master). Home: 1563 E. Montgomery Av. Office: 1739-43 N. Front St., Philadelphia, Pa.

VOGEL, Charles W., U.S. Pub. Health Service; b. Baltimore, Md., Aug. 8, 1870; s. Philip R. and Maria M. (Mueller); grad. Knapp's Inst., Baltimore, 1886; Md. Coll. of Pharmacy, 1892; M.D., U. of Md., 1895; widower; one son. Commd. asst. surgeon U.S.P. H.S., 1899, passed asst. surgeon, 1904, surgeon, 1912, med. dir. 1930, retired, 1935. Mem. A.M.A., Baltimore Med. Soc., Assn. of Mil. Surgeons. Lutheran. Contbr. articles to med. jours. Home: 104 W. University Parkway, Baltimore, Md.

VOGLESON, John Albert, engr.; b. Columbiana, O., Oct. 6, 1871; s. George A. and Annie E. (Metzger) V.; C. E., Cornell U., 1900; m. Margaret Smiley, Sept. 20, 1916. Surveyor on irrigation and r.r. work, Pacific Coast, 1892-97; asst. engr. Michigan-Lake Superior Power Co., 1900-01; employed by Bureau of Filtration, Philadelphia, 1901-05; prin. asst. engr. for waterworks Dept. of Waterworks and Sewer Construction, Manila, P.I., 1905-06; asst. engr. Dept. of Water Supply, Gas and Electricity, N.Y. City, 1906-07; construction engr. Bureau of Water, Philadelphia, 1907-09; chief Bur. of Health, 1910-22 (except for army service); chief engr. Bur. of Surveys, 1922-24, chief engr. Bur. of Engring., 1925-28; engr. Day & Zimmermann, Inc., since 1928. Served as major, Sanitary Corps, U.S. Army, World War. Mem. Am. Soc. Civil Engrs., Cornell Soc. Engrs., Franklin Inst., Sigma Xi. Republican. Protestant. Mason. Clubs: Engineers (ex. pres., trustee, Philadelphia). Home: 2031 Locust St. Office: Packard Bldg., Philadelphia, Pa.

VOIGT, Arno Constantine, M.D.; b. Hawley, Pa., Jan. 14, 1878; s. Alexius F. and Emilia (Ott) V.; ed. Honesdale pub. schs., 1884-93; M.D., Jefferson Med. Coll., 1901; m. Elizabeth Shanley, Oct. 4, 1907; children—Arno A., Dorothy A.; m. 2d, Rachel Davies, Dec. 5, 1911; 1 son, Carl; m. 3d, Eleanor Croop, Jan. 18, 1918; children—Janet E., George B. Pharmacist, 1893-97; in gen. practice of medicine since 1901; mem. staff Wayne County Hosp., Memorial Hosp. (Honesdale, Pa.); asst. physician Hosp. for Insane Retreat, Pa., 1901-04; pres. and dir. First Nat. Bank, Hawley, Pa.; dir. Hawley Tile & Supply Co., Hawley-Wallenpaupack Chamber of Commerce. Formerly coroner, Wayne Co., Pa.; former mem. and sec.-treas. Hawley Sch. Bd. Mem. A.M.A., Pa. Med. Soc., Wayne Co. Med. Soc., N.Y, and New England Ry. Surgeons Assn. Democrat. Mason (32°), Odd Fellow. Clubs: Hawley Hunting and Fishing, Hawley Rod and Gun. Home and Office: Hawley, Pa.

VOLKMANN, John Emil, acoustic engr.; b. Chicago, Ill., July 26, 1905; s. Max Theodore and Louise Dorothy (Matthiesen) V.; B.S., U. of Ill., 1927, M.S., same, 1928; m. Dorothy Alma Johnson, Nov. 28, 1929. Asst. physicist, acoustic research sect., Tech. & Test. Lab., Radio Corpn. America, N.Y. City, 1928-29; acoustical engr., RCA Photophone, Inc., N.Y. City, 1929-32 and RCA Victor Co., Inc., Camden, N.J., 1932-33; engr. in charge acoustic development, Photophone & Spl. Apparatus Div., RCA Mfg. Co., Inc., Camden, N.J., 1933-36, supervisor acoustic development & design sect., Sound Engring. Div. since 1936. Served as 2d lt. O.R.C. Signal Corps, 1927-34. Scouter, Boy Scouts America, 1938. Mem. Acoustical Soc. America, Soc. Motion Picture Engrs., Inst. Radio Engrs., Sigma Xi, Sigma Tau, Scabbard & Blade, Pi Tau Pi Sigma. Ch. of Christ Sci. Home: 700 Station Av., Haddon Heights. Office: RCA Mfg. Co., Inc., Camden, N.J.

VOLLMER, Harry Frederick, Jr., aircraft mfg.; b. Wilmington, Del., Aug. 20, 1892; s. Harry F. and Emma (McKeever) V.; student pub. schs. and high sch.; m. Anna L. Roether, Oct. 7, 1913; children—Harry F. III, Alice L. Asso. with Glenn L. Martin Company, aircraft mfrs., Baltimore, Md. continously since 1917, successively tool room foreman, gen. foreman mfg. div., factory supt., factory mgr., then vice-pres. in charge mfg. since 1937, dir. of corpn. since 1936. Mem. Nat. Aeronautic Assn. Presbyterian. Clubs: Reciprocity (Baltimore); Rodgers Forge (Towson); Maryland Flying (Baltimore). Home: 5409 Purlington Way. Office: Glenn L. Martin Co., Baltimore, Md.

VOLPE, Santo, coal operator; b. Caltanessetta, Montedoro, Italy, Oct. 20, 1879; s. Gaetano (Milazzo) V.; ed. public schools in Italy; m. Doratea Licata, June 26, 1904; children—Gaetana (Mrs. Charles J. Bufalino), Stephanie, Angela, Alphonsina, Santo. Came to U.S., 1906, naturalized, 1913. Contractor in coal business, Pittston, Pa., 1913-22; coal operator since 1922; pres. Volpe Coal Co., Pittston, Pa.; pres. Lockport Brewing Co., Lock Haven, Pa.; treas. Daly & Volpe Constrn. Co., Scranton, Pa.; dir. West Side Bank, West Pittston, Pittston Hosp. Mem. Montedoro Soc., Christopher Columbo Soc. Republican. Roman Cathloic. Clubs: Scranton (Scranton); Elks (Pittston); Downtown Athletic (New York). Home: 215 Wyoming Av., West Pittston, Pa. Office: Volpe Coal Co., Pittston, Pa.

VON BONNHORST, William E., banking, retired; b. Pittsburgh, Pa., Nov. 2, 1852; s. Sidney F. and Mary von B.; student U. of Pittsburgh, 1862-79. Employed in various capacities over a number of yrs.; asso. with Dollar Savings Bank, Pittsburgh, Pa., continuously, 1910-39, senior v.p., 1935-37; retired from active work, 1939. Republican. Episcopalian. Club: Duquesne (Pittsburgh). Home: 399 W. Prospect Av. Office: 338 Fourth Av., Pittsburgh, Pa.

von der LUFT, Oscar, chem. engring.; b. Boston, Mass., Apr. 15, 1894; s. Alexander and Alma L.; B.S. in Chem. Engring., U. of Minn., 1917; m. Sue Wooddy, 1921; children—Alexander, Richard, Robert. Chem. engr. ordnance dept. U.S.A., 1917-22; asso. with National Aniline & Chemical Corpn., 1922-28; gen. supt. American Cyanamid and Chemical Corpn. (Selden Div.), Bridgeville, Pa. since 1928. Capt. U.S. Army Ordnance Res. Mem. Am. Chem. Soc., Am. Inst. Chem. Engrs., Alpha Chi Sigma, Phi Lambda Upsilon. Episcopalian. Home: 418 Serpentine Drive, Mt. Lebanon, Pittsburgh, Pa.

VON ELBE, Guenther Johannes Konrad, physical chemist; b. Potsdam, Germany, Nov. 27, 1903; s. Kurt and Käthe (von Richthofen) von E.; student Humanistic Gymnasium, Neuwied and Berlin, Germany, 1913-22, U. of Kiel, Germany, 1922-23; Ph.D., U. of Berlin, Germany, 1929; unmarried. Came to U.S., 1930, naturalized, 1938. Liebig and Notgemeinschaft research fellow, U. of Berlin, 1928-30; DuPont research fellow, U. of Va., Charlottesville, Va., 1930-32; cons. phys. chemist, U.S. Bureau of Mines, 1931-32; mem. coal research lab., Carnegie Inst. of Tech., since 1932. Mem. Am. Chem. Soc., Va. Acad. of Science, Economic Club of Pittsburgh, Sigma Xi. Author: Combustion, Flames and Explosions of Gases (with Bernard Lewis), 1938; also about 40 papers in scientific jours. Home: West Waldheim Rd., Fox Chapel Dist., Pittsburgh, Pa. Office: Carnegie Institute of Technology, Pittsburgh, Pa.

von MOSCHZISKER, Robert, lawyer; b. Phila., Mar. 6, 1870; s. Frank A. and Clara (Harrison) von M.; ed. pub. schs. and pvtly.; LL.D., Lafayette College, Dickinson College, Pa. Mil. Coll., Temple Univ., Univ. of Pa., 1922, Juniata College, 1928; at 13 entered office of Edward Shippen and later studied law under him; admitted to bar, 1896; m. Anne Macbeth, June 29, 1912; children—Kate, Bertha, Michael, Practiced with Edward Shippen, 1896-1902; asst. dist. atty., Phila. Dist., Pa., 1902-03; judge Ct. of Common Pleas, No. 3, Phila. Co., 1903-10; justice Supreme Court of Pa., 1910-21, and chief justice, 1921-30; now in practice with law firm Ballard, Spahr, Andrews & Ingersoll, Phila. Trustee U. of Pa.; mem. bd. of Incorporators Dickinson Sam Sch. Republican. Mem. Am. Bar Assn., Pa. State Bar Assn., Law Assn. of Phila., Law Acad., Hist. Soc. of Pa., Selden Soc., Veteran Corps 1st Regt. Pa. N.G., Old Washington Grays; hon. mem. Phi Beta Kappa, Delta Theta Phi, Sigma Nu Phi. Mason. Clubs: Art, Lawyers, Union League, Legal, Print, Rittenhouse (Phila.). Author: Trial by Jury; Judicial Review of Legislation; Legal Essays. Home: 2101 Le Lancey Pl., Philadelphia, Pa.

VON NEUMANN, John, mathematics; b. Budapest, Hungary, Dec. 28, 1903; s. Max and Margaret (Kann) V.; student Berlin U., 1921-23, Zurich U., 1923-25; Ph.D., Budapest, 1925; m. Mariette Kovesi, Jan. 1, 1930; 1 dau., Marina; m. 2d, Klara Dan, Dec. 18, 1938. Privatdozent mathematics, Berlin U., 1927; visiting prof. mathematical physics, Princeton U., 1930, prof., 1931-33, prof. Institute for Advanced Study, 1933. Fellow Am. Physical Soc.; mem. Am. Math. Soc., Am. Math. Assn., Nat. Acad. of Sciences, Sigma Xi. Club: Nassau. Contbr. articles on math. subjects. Editor of Annals of Mathematics (Princeton). Co-editor of Compositio Mathematica (Amsterdam, Holland). Address: Fine Hall, Princeton, N.J.

VOORHEES, Clifford Irving, lawyer; b. New Brunswick, N.J., Aug. 4, 1884; s. Abraham and Martha J. (Van Nostrand) V.; student Lawrenceville (N.J.) Sch., 1900-02; A.B., Princeton U., 1906; LL.B., New York Law Sch., 1909; m. Adelaide Bailey Parker, Apr. 5, 1915; children—Frances M., Willard P., Clifford Irving, Jr., Henrietta A. M. Admitted to N.J. bar, 1909; since in private practice of law at New Brunswick. Trustee Lawrenceville Sch.; pres. Francis E. Parker Memorial Home. Mem. Am. Bar Assn., N.J. State Bar Assn., Middlesex County Bar Assn., Holland Soc. of N.Y., Soc. Colonial Wars in N.J., St. Nicholas Soc. of N.Y. Republican. Presbyterian. (trustee 1st Ch., New Brunswick). Clubs: University (New York); Ivy (Princeton); Princeton (New York). Home: Rose Bank, Landing Lane. Office: 390 George St., New Brunswick, N.J.

VOORHEES, Louis A(ugustus), chemist; b. New Brunswick, N.J., Mar. 6, 1865; s. Charles Holbert (M.D.) and Charlotte (Bournonville) V.; A.B., Rutgers Coll., 1885, A.M., 1888; m. May Wilcox, Oct. 24, 1900. Began with N.J. State Agrl. Expt. Sta., 1885, and advanced to chief chemist, 1895; resigned and opened own lab., 1905; chemist to Dept. of Health, City of New Brunswick, since 1920. A pioneer in various agrl. investigations, 1885-1905. Mem. A.A.A.S., Am. Chem. Soc., Am. Pub. Health Assn., Assn. Official Agrl. Chemists, N.J. Chem. Soc., Am. Dairy Science Assn., Internat. Assn. of Milk Sanitarians, N.J. Health Officers Assn., N.J. Health and Sanitary Assn., New Brunswick Scientific Soc., S.A.R., Phi Beta Kappa, Delta Upsilon. Democrat. Mason, Elk. Home: 357 George St. Office: City Hall, New Brunswick, N.J.

VOORHEES, Oscar McMurtrie, clergyman; b. nr. Somerville, N.J., Dec. 29, 1864; s. Samuel S. and Elizabeth (McMurtrie) V.; A.B., Rutgers Coll., 1888, A.M., 1891; grad. Theol. Seminary Reformed Church, New Brunswick, N.J., 1891; D.D., Miami University, Oxford, Ohio, 1911; LL.D., College of William and Mary, 1927; m. Alice R. MacNair, Oct. 29, 1891; children—Helen McMurtrie, Frances Van Kleek, Ralph Whitaker (dec.), Marian MacNair (dec.); m. 2d, Martha S. Elmendorf, June 25, 1902. Ordained Reformed (Dutch) ministry, 1891; pastor

Three Bridges, N.J., 1891-1903, High Bridge, N.J., 1903-09, Mott Haven Church, New York, 1909-22. Secretary United Chapters of Phi Beta Kappa, 1901-31, treas., 1901-13, historian since 1931. Pres. Hunterdon Co. Hist. Soc., 1903-04; mem. Delta Upsilon. Author of Historical Sketch of Phi Beta Kappa Soc. and many hist. papers. Editor Phi Beta Kappa Key, 1910-31; editor Phi Beta Kappa General Catalog, 1923; Phi Beta Kappa senator since 1901; sec. Phi Beta Kappa Foundation, Inc., 1924-31, trustee since 1924. Chmn. War Service Commn. Reformed Ch. in America, 1917. Y.M.C.A. service, France, 1918-19, representing Phi Beta Kappa Alumni of New York. Wrote: Ralph and Elizabeth Rodman Voorhees—a Tribute, 1927. Compiler: A Condensed Genealogy of the Van Voorhees Family, 1932; The Historical Handbook of the Van Voorhees Family in the Netherlands and America, 1935. Home: 44 Sicard St., New Brunswick, N.J. Office: 12 E. 44th St., New York, N.Y.

VOORHEES, Stephen Hegeman, banker; b. Griggstown, N.J., Aug. 3, 1864; s. Alfred I. and Emily (Suydam) V.; ed. pub. schs., Griggstown, and Normal and Model Sch., Trenton, N.J.; m. Helen Walton Gray, Oct. 31, 1893; children —Ruth Suydam (Mrs. Edward Le Roy Voorhees), Helen (Mrs. L. Josselyn Young). Began in employ Mercantile Nat. Bank, New York, 1884; with Chase Nat. Bank, 1889-99; organizer, and agt. Royal Bank of Canada, at N.Y. City, 1899-1915; v.p. Nat. City Bank, 1915-24 (retired). Pres. Bd. of Health, Plainfield, N.J. Mem. St. Nicholas Soc., Holland Soc., Soc. of Colonial Wars, Acad. Polit. Science, New York Chamber of Commerce. Clubs: Plainfield Country; Dunedin (Fla.) Yacht (commodore); The Pilgrims of the U.S. Republican. Presbyn. Home: 943 Madison Av., Plainfield, N.J.

VOORHIS, Harold Oliver, sec. N.Y. Univ.; b. Kokomo, Ind., July 29, 1896; s. Warren R. and Edna (Curlee) V.; B.S., Colgate University, 1919; student Columbia University Law Sch., 1920; M.A., New York University, 1922; m. Rosalie Morris, June 30, 1921; children—Patricia, Joanna, Katrina. Surveyor's asst. Saskatchewan, Can., 1914-15; sec. to pres. Colgate Univ., 1916-19, sec. to pres. Chautauqua Instn., 1919; sec. to v.p. Nat. Bank of Commerce, N.Y. City, 1920; instr. in economics and exec. sec. to chancellor New York U., 1920-25, asst. to chancellor and sec. of university since 1925. Served as lt. F.A., U.S.A., instr. in O.T.S., comdg. officer Sch. H.Q. Co., Camp Taylor, Ky., 1918-19. Mem. Phi Beta Kappa, Pi Delta Epsilon, Beta Theta Pi, Holland Soc., N.Y. (pres., Union Co., N.J., branch since 1938). Republican. Presbyn. Clubs: Plainfield Country, Faculty (New York U.). Home: "Witch Hollow," Plainfield, N.J. Office: 100 Washington Sq., New York, N.Y.

VOORHIS, Warren Rollin, lawyer; b. Indianapolis, Ind., Dec. 6, 1873; s. William Manning and Anna Christine (Cox) V.; student Irvington High Sch., Central Normal Coll., Nat. U., Ind. Teachers Coll.; LL.B., Ind. Law Sch., 1896; m. Edna Curlee, June 22, 1895; children—Harold O., Manning C., Dorothy A. (Mrs. Alden DeHart), Margaret Virginia (Mrs. F. Willoughby Frost). Admitted to Ind. bar, 1896; also mem. Federal bar and N.Y. bar; gen. practice in Ind., 1896-1918; pros. atty. Howard Circuit Court, Ind., 1903-05; city atty., Kokomo, 1907-11; spl. practice of rate and valuation law for pub. utilities since 1918; v.p. and dir. Am. Water Works and Electric Co., Inc.; v.p. and dir. West Penn Electric Co.; dir. West Penn Power Co., Monongahela West Penn Pub. Service Co., Potomac Edison Co.; v.p. and dir. Medallic Art Co. Mem. Acad. Polit. Science, Soc. of Medalists. Republican. Presbyn. Mason. Clubs: City Midday (New York); Plainfield Country; Bohemian (San Francisco). Contbr. articles on finance and pub. utility management to jours. Home: Rahway Road, Plainfield, N.J. Office: 50 Broad St., New York, N.Y.

VORSANGER, Berthold, lawyer; b. Englewood, N.J., Mar. 24, 1902; s. Ferdinand and Bertha (Vorsanger) V.; A.B., Cath. Univ., Washington, D.C., 1925; student Yale U. Law Sch., 1925-27, Columbia U., 1927-28; unmarried. Admitted to New Jersey bar as attorney, 1928, as counselor, 1933; engaged in general practice of law as individual at Englewood, N.J.; served as mem. N.J. Ho. of Assembly, 1934-35; judge third dist. ct. since 1937. Mem. Am. Bar Assn., N.J. Bar Assn., Bergen Co. Bar Assn., Phi Alpha Delta. Republican. Mem. Temple Emanuel, Englewood. Mason. Elk. Club: Yale Alumni (Bergen Co.). Home: 165 Cambridge Av. Office: 1 Engle St., Englewood, N.J.

VOSE, Richard Shepard, chem. engr., technologist; b. Somerville, Mass., Jan. 16, 1898; s. Rev. Riley A. and Florence (Davis) V.; B.Sc., Rutgers U., 1920, Ph.D., Cornell U., 1923; m. Helen Delap, June 6, 1925; children—Richard, James Quentin. Engaged in electrode manufacture development Acheson Graphite Co. 1920, sesquicarbonate process development Solvay Process Co., 1922, development Cook Paint & Varnish Co., 1923; industrial fellow, Mellon Inst., 1924; research asso., U. of Chicago, 1924-26; organic research chemist Mallinckrodt Chem. Works, 1926-28; process development R. & H. Chemicals Dept., E. I. du Pont de Nemours & Co., 1928-31; petroleum technologist and chem. engr. Sun Oil Co. since 1931. Mem. A.A.A.S., Am. Inst. Chem. Engrs., Am. Chem. Soc., Delta Kappa Epsilon. Author numerous articles in Jour. of Am. Chem. Soc. and Jour. of Industrial and Engring. Chemistry. Developed new meat curing process approved of U.S. Dept. Agr.; inventor of process chemically refining of oil (petroleum); co-inventor of process catalytic cracking of oil (petroleum); numerous U.S. and foreign patents and applications. Home: 317 Barker St., Ridley Park, Pa. Office: Sun Oil Co., Marcus Hook, Pa.

VOSHELL, Allen Fiske, surgeon; b. Providence, R.I., Oct. 28, 1893; s. Jonathan Kersey and Evelyn Niles (Clarke) V.; A.B., Johns Hopkins U., 1915; M.D., Johns Hopkins U. Med. Sch., 1919; m. Louise DeLancey Barclay, Nov. 24, 1921; 1 son, Allen Fiske, Jr. House officer Johns Hopkins Hosp., 1919-20, resident orthopedic surgeon, 1920-21, asst. dispensary surgeon, 1920-21; instr. orthopedic surgery, Johns Hopkins U., 1920-21; instr. orthopedic surgery, U. of Va. Med. Sch., Charlottesville, 1921-23, asst. prof., 1923-26, asso. prof., 1926-31; prof. orthopedic surgery, U. of Md. Med. Sch., Baltimore, Md., since 1931; chief orthopedic service U. of Md. and Baltimore City hosps. since 1931; visiting orthopedist, Mercy, Womens, Union Memorial hosps.; dir. phys. therapy depts. U. of Md. Hosp. and Dispensary since 1931. Served as pvt. Med. Enlisted Res. Corps, 1918; lt. comdr. Med. Res. Corps U.S.N. Fellow Am. Coll. Surgeons, Am. Acad. Orthopedic Surgeons, A.M.A. Mem. Southern Med. Assn., Baltimore Co. and City Med. socs., Med. & Chirurg. Faculty of Md., Johns Hopkins Surg. Soc., Robert Jones Orthopedic Club, Am. Orthopedic Assn., Baltimore Orthopedic Club (pres. 1935), Omicron Delta Kappa, Phi Gamma Delta. Certified Am. Bd. Orthopedic Surgery. Democrat. Episcopalian. Clubs: Johns Hopkins (Baltimore); Gibson Island, Md. Home: 702 Belvedere Av. Office: Medical Arts Bldg., Baltimore, Md.

VOSS, A. Irvin, ins. official; b. Phila., Pa., Dec. 23, 1878; s. August and Mary (Evans) V.; student pub. schs. and Temple Coll.; m. Nellie W. Bird, Nov. 15, 1900. Employed by Fire Assn. of Phila., since 1898, beginning as jr. clerk, sec. since 1925; sec. Lumbermen's Reliance Ins. Co., Philadelphia Nat. Ins. Co. Home: 1015 Wilde Av., Drexel Hill. Office: 401 Walnut St., Philadelphia, Pa.

VOSS, Carl August, clergyman; b. Wheeling, W.Va., Aug. 17, 1876; s. Rev. Edward and Anna (Diederich) V.; g.g.s. Johann Heinrich Voss, German poet; prep. edn., high sch., Cincinnati, O.; student Elmhurst (Ill.) Coll.; grad. Meadville Theological Sch., 1896; post-grad. work, Lane Theological Sem. and University of Cincinnati; D.D., University of Pittsburgh, 1909; m. Lucy Wilms, Apr. 19, 1898; children—Edward Wilms, Victor Emanuel, Carl Hermann, Dorothy Cecile. Ordained ministry Evang. Prot. Ch., 1896, pastor Immanuel Ch., Fairmount, Cincinnati, 1897-1905; pastor German Evang. Prot. (Smithfield) Ch., Pittsburgh, since 1905. Conglist. Ex-trustee Meadville Theol. Sch.; mem. Congl. National Commission on Missions; pres. German Protestant Orphanage, Allegheny County Mothers' Pension League; dir. German Protestant Home for Aged; v.p. Allegheny County Milk and Ice Assn.; dir. Pub. Health Nurses Assn.; mem. advisory bd. Chicago Theol. School; pres. Evangelical Protestant Church, 1913-20. Mem. Pi Gamma Mu. Mason (K.T., 32°, Shriner). Clubs: Hungry, Agora, Rotary. Author: History of German Evangelical Protestant Smithfield Church of Pittsburgh (1782-1907), 1907, and (1782-1932), 1932; History of the German Protestant Orphanage, Pittsburgh, 1912; History of the German Protestant Home for Aged, Pittsburgh, 1913. Contbr. to theol. jours. Lecturer. Home: 239 Amber St., Pittsburgh, Pa.

VOSS, Elbert, univ. prof.; b. Hector, Ark., Aug. 31, 1900; s. John Morris and Agnes Isabella (Luna) V.; student Panhandle Agrl. & Mech. Coll., Goodwell, Okla., 1923-24; B.S., Okla. Univ., Norman, Okla., 1928, M.S., 1930; Ph.D., U. of Fla., Gainesville, Fla., 1935; unmarried. Engaged as prof. materia medica, Indianapolis (Ind.) Coll. of Pharmacy, 1930-33; asst. prof. botany and pharmacognosy, Duquesne U., Pittsburgh, 1935-36, prof. pharmacology and pharmacognosy since 1936. Mem. Am. Pharm. Assn., Rho Chi. Democrat. Methodist. Home: 907 Franklin Av., Wilkinsburg, Pa.

VREELAND, Albert Lincoln, lawyer, congressman; b. East Orange, N.J., July 2, 1901; s. James Henry and Martha (Blackmore) V.; ed. N.Y. Elec. Sch., to 1919, Peddie Sch., Hightstown, N.J., to 1922, N.J. Law Sch., 1922-25; m. Helen Aeschbach, June 27, 1923; children—Elizabeth Louise, James Albert. Admitted to N.J. bar as atty., 1927, counsellor, 1931; engaged in gen. practice of law at East Orange since 1927; mem. firm Vreeland & Aeschbach since 1938; spl. master in chancery, 1938; asst. city counsel, East Orange, 1931-34; judge East Orange Recorder's Ct., 1934-38; admitted to practice before the Supreme Ct. of the U.S., 1939; mem. 76th Congress, 11th Dist., N.J., since 1939. Served with A.R.C., Ambulance Corps, 1918; 1st lt. M.I. Res. Mem. Am. and Essex Co. bar assns., Delta Theta Phi, Res. Officers Assn. (past pres. Southern Essex Chapter), Nat. Sojourners (pres. Northern N.J. Chapter), Holland Soc., S.A.R. Republican. Baptist. Mason (K.T.). Elk. Home: 415 Prospect St. Office: 380 Main St., East Orange, N.J.

VREELAND, Clarence Le Fevre, physician; b. Jersey City, N.J., Nov. 12, 1877; s. Henry Richard and Elizabeth Jane (Musk) V.; student Jersey City (N.J.) High Sch., 1891-93, Hasbrouck Inst., Jersey City, N.J., 1894, N.Y. Prep. Sch., New York City, 1895; M.D., Columbia, Coll. Phys. and Surg., 1900; m. Ethel M. Van Blaricom, Feb. 8, 1905; children—Charles Willard, Lois (Mrs. Walter Bodycomb). Interne Hackensack (N.J.) Hosp., 1900-01; asst. surgeon, St. Francis Hosp., Jersey City, 1902-05; pvt. practice at Jersey City, N.J., 1901-14, Pompton Lakes, N.J., since 1914; mem. courtesy staff, St. Joseph's Hosp., Paterson, N.J., since 1925; surgeon, Pub. Service Co. of N.J., Passaic Co., since 1929, Artistic Weaving Co., Pompton Lakes, N.J., since 1930; physician Pompton Lakes Schs., 1938-40. Served as maj., Med. Corps, U.S. Army, 1917-22. Mem. Passaic Co., N.J. State Med. Socs., Am. Mechanics Assn. Republican. Mason. Examiner, N.Y. Life Ins. Co., Travelers Ins. Co., State Mutual Assurance Co. Address: 516 Wauaque Av., Pompton Lakes, N.J.

VREELAND, Williamson Updike, coll. prof.; b. Rocky Hill, N.J., Aug. 30, 1870; s. Jacob M. and Louisa (Updike) V.; A.B., Princeton, 1892, Boudinot fellow in modern langs., 1892-93, A.M., 1896; the Sorbonne, Paris, 1892-93; Faculties of Letters, Florence, Italy, and Madrid, Spain, 1893-94; Doctorat es Lettrès, U. of Geneva, Switzerland, 1901; m. Alice May Brown, May 9, 1900; 1 dau., May. Instr. French 1894-97, asst. professor, 1897-1903, Woodhull professor Romance languages and head modern language department, 1903-13, Princeton University. Mem. Société Jean-Jacques Rousseau of

Geneva. Presbyterian. Mem. Phi Beta Kappa. Clubs: Princeton (New York and Phila.). Author: Selections from Gil Blas, 1900; Jean-Jacques Rousseau et les rapports littéraires entre Genève et l'Angleterre, 1901; French Syntax and Composition (with Prof. William Koren), 1907; Anthology of French Prose and Poetry (with Prof. Régis Michaud), 1910; Anthology of 17th Century French Literature (in collaboration), 1927; Anthology of 18th Century French Literature (in collaboration), 1930. Home: Princeton, N.J.

VUILLEUMIER, Ernest Albert, prof. chemistry; b. New City, Rockland Co., N.Y., Mar. 1, 1894; s. Charles and Matilda (Barny) V.; B.S. in Chemistry, U. of Pa., 1914; grad. student, same, 1915-16; Ph.D., U. of Berne, Switzerland, 1918; m. Frances E. Smith, Dec. 27, 1924. Analytical and control chemist, Powers-Weightman-Rosengarten Co., Phila., 1914-15; instr. chemistry, Drexel Inst., Phila., 1915-16; Rosengarten traveling scholarship, U. of Pa., at Berne, 1916-18; research chemist Powers-Weightman-Rosengarten Co., 1919-20; head of department of chemistry, Dickinson Coll., since 1920, also dean of the junior class, 1927-28, the freshman class, 1928-33, acting dean of the college, 1933-35, dean since 1935. With American E. F. in France, 1918-1919. Acting Swiss consul, Pa., N.J., and Del., summer 1923. Fellow Am. Inst. Chemists, A.A.A.S.; mem. American Chem. Soc., American Electrochem. Soc., Verein für Chemiker der Universitaet Bern, Pa. Acad. of Science, Phi Beta Kappa, Omicron Delta Kappa. Republican. Methodist. Author of articles presenting investigations in electrodeposition, analysis of alcoholic liquids, etc. Inventor Dickinson alcohometer and Dickinson solids-hydrometer; co-inventor of contractometer for study of peeling of nickel-plating. Address: Dickinson College, Carlisle, Pa.

W

WACHTER, Henry, ins. agent; b. Monroe Co., O., May 20, 1873; s. Christian and Sophia (Barman) W.; student pub. schs., Pittsburgh, Pa., Duff's Bus. Coll.; m. Caroline E. Weidman, Apr. 4, 1900; 1 dau., Emma Carolyn. Employed in various ins. agencies, 1893-1904; asst. sec. Birmingham Fire Ins. Co., Pittsburgh, Pa., 1904-06; mgr. Keystone Underwriters, Pittsburgh, Pa., since 1906, Concordia Fire Ins. Co., Girard Fire & Marine Ins. Co.; pres. South View Bldg. & Loan Assn.; dir. The Carrick Bank. Republican. Lutheran. Mason (K.T.). Clubs South Hills Country. Home: 214 Hoodridge Drive, Mt. Lebanon, Pa. Office: 830 Grant Bldg., Pittsburgh, Pa.

WADDELL, Charles Walter, physician; b. Preston Co., W.Va., Nov. 24, 1877; s. Richard B. and Lucy Ann (Weyant) W.; A.B., W.Va. Univ., 1900; M.D., Harvard U. Med. Sch., 1907; m. Myrtle D. Shaw, Sept. 14, 1909; children—Jean Shaw (Mrs. L. E. Sample, Jr.), Mary Ann (Mrs. J. Rendle Thomas), Sara Jane. Engaged in gen. practice of medicine at Fairmont, W.Va., since 1907; internal medicine exclusively since 1922; member staff Cook Hosp., Fairmont, W.Va. Served as chmn. med. adv. bd. 9th W.Va. Dist. during World War. Mem. Adv. Bd. State Dept. of Pub. Assistance since 1938. Fellow Am. Coll. Physicians. Mem. Am. Med. Assn., W.Va. State Med. Assn. (pres. 1938), Phi Kappa Psi, Alpha Omega Alpha. Republican. Presbyn. Mason. Elk. Home: 726 Coleman Av. Office: 320 Jefferson St., Fairmont, W.Va.

WADDELL, Fred R., gasoline and oil distributor; b. Hurlock, Md., May 5, 1887; s. Columbus and Lavenia Isabell (Trice) W.; grad. Hurlock (Md.) High Sch., 1904; unmarried. Began as farmer, Hurlock, Md., 1906, and owner and operator several farms since 1911; pres. Dorchester Oil Co., Hurlock, Md., since 1929; v.p. County Trust Co. of Md., Hurlock, Md., since 1931; dir. Red Star Motor Coaches, Inc. Chmn. Rep. State Central Com. since 1928; mem. Gen. Assembly, Md., 1918; mem. bd. town commrs., Hurlock, 1918-20; judge Civic Court, Hurlock, 1912-16. Dir. Children's Welfare Bd., Hurlock. Mem. Hurlock Chamber of Commerce. Republican. Methodist. Mason (master comdr.; Shriner; received hon. mention, 1928). Clubs: Shrine (Baltimore, Md.); Country (Cambridge, Md.); Country (Wright Warf, Md.). Address: Hurlock, Md.

WADDINGTON, Edward Clifton, lawyer; b. Elsinboro Twp., Salem Co., N.J., Jan. 15, 1883; s. George Grier and Mary Buzby (Gaskill) W.; prep. edn., Woodstown (N.J.) High Sch., 1897-1900; B.S., U. of Pa., 1904, LL.B., Law Sch., 1907; m. Mary Robinson Allen, Oct. 1, 1910; children—Mildred R. (Mrs. John S. Carpenter), Elinor J. (Mrs. Edgar H. Holton), Mary A. (Mrs. Lewis Barnum), Edward Clifton, Alice V., Richard. Admitted to N.J. bar, 1907, and since practiced at Camden, N.J.; mem. firm Waddington & Mathews, Camden, since 1921. Judge Ct. of Common Pleas, Co. of Salem, N.J., 1911-21 (2 terms). Trustee George Sch. Newton, Pa. Mem. Patriotic Order Sons of America. Awarded Silver Beaver of Boy Scouts of America, 1939. Democrat. Soc. of Friends. Mason (Woodstown, N.J., Lodge), Odd Fellow. Club: Du Pont-Penns Grove (N.J.) Country. Home: Woodstown, N.J. Office: 500 Broadway, Camden, N.J.

WADE, Truman Diller, lawyer; b. Gibraltar, Berks Co., Pa., Sept. 5, 1877; s. Benjamin and Mary (Shirk) W.; ed. Perkiomen Sem., Pennsburg, Pa.; m. Stella Leopold, Aug. 10, 1901; children—Carolus Alton, Helen Justine. Admitted to Chester County bar, 1905; since in gen. practice of law; mem. law firm Wade, Reid & McKeone since 1930; asst. dist. atty., Chester Co., 1912-16, dist. atty., 1916-20; asst. U.S. dist. atty., 1921-23. Mem. Am. Guernsey Cattle Assn., Spring City Driving Assn. (pres.). Republican. Methodist. Odd Fellow, Moose, Eagle, Elk, Grange. Home: The Knoll, Phoenixville, Pa. Office: Woolworth Bldg., West Chester, Pa.

WADE, William Henry, utilities exec.; b. Wyncote, Pa., Aug. 7, 1893; s. Charles Weaver and Eva Abigail (Graham) W.; B.S. in E.E., U. of Pa., 1914; m. Ruth Stockton Kennedy, Jan. 4, 1917; children—Frances Virginia, Robert Graham, Richard Stockton. Power sales engr. Penn Central Light and Power Co. (now Pa. Edison Co.), Altoona, Pa., 1914-17, new business mgr., 1917-29, asst. to pres., 1929-30, v.p. since 1930; v.p. Municipal Service Co., Altoona, 1930-32, O. Electric Power Co., 1930-32, York Rys. Co., York, Pa., 1930-33, Keystone Pub. Service Co., Oil City, Pa., 1930-33; treas. Gen. Portfolios, Inc., Altoona, since 1932; v.p. and dir. Blair Engring. & Supply Co., Altoona, since 1935. Trustee Mercy Hosp., Altoona; dir. Hollidaysburg (Pa.) Y.M.C.A. Hollidaysburg (Pa.) Sch. Dist. Mem. Hollidaysburg and Altoona Chambers of Commerce (dir.), Pa. Electric Assn. (past pres.; dir.), Blair Co. Alumni Assn. of U. of Pa. (sec. and treas.). Republican. Presbyterian. Club: Blairmont County (gov.; Hollidaysburg). Home: 700 Clark St., Hollidaysburg, Pa. Office: 1200 11th Av., Altoona, Pa.

WADHAM, Harvey N., brokerage; b. Egremont, Mass., June 12, 1871; s. Lewis C. and Orcelia W.; student rural dist. schs., Egremont, Mass.; m. Katherine Redfield, June 6, 1901; children—Katherine (Mrs. Colvin Swan), Norman. Began as runner for Jas. B. Colgate & Co., members N.Y. Stock Exchange, New York, 1890-1900, cashier, 1900-03, mem. firm, 1903-39, retired from partnership 1939, retaining desk room; pres. and dir. North Valley Nat. Bank, Tenafly, N.J.; dir. Bergen Bldg. Block Co. Pres. Africa Inland Mission, James Slip Mission. Republican. Plymouth Brethren Ch. Clubs: Lawyers (New York); Forest Lake (Pa.). Home: 330 Engle St., Tenafly, N.J. Office: 44 Wall St., New York, N.Y.

WADSWORTH, John Frederic, cons. engineer; b. Erie, Pa., Nov. 22, 1889; s. Edward Lyman and Caroline (Fluke) W.; ed. Central High Sch., Erie, Pa., 1905-09; Ph.B., Yale, 1912; m. Sarah Alice Fownes, June 21, 1924; 1 dau., Caroline Fownes. Employed as structural engr. with various concerns, Erie, Pa., 1912-17; cons. engr. at Erie, Pa., since 1919; designed Union Storage Company at Erie and was sec. of co. Served as 2d lt. Adj. Gen's. office, U.S. Army, 1917-19, with A.E.F. in France. Vice chmn. bd. trustees Pa. Soldiers' and Sailors' Home, 1936. Mem. Am. Soc. M.E. (past chmn.), Am. Soc. Refrigerating Engrs., Tech. Fed., Engrs. Soc. of Northwestern Pa. (past chmn.), Pa. Soc. of Prof. Engrs. (past chmn.), Nat. Soc. Prof. Engrs., Am. Legion, 313th Machine Gun Batln. Club: University (Erie, Pa.). Home: 254 W. 8th St. Office: 818 Commerce Bldg., Erie, Pa.

WAESCHE, Frederick Seton, physician; b. Sykesville, Md., Nov. 5, 1901; s. Jerome Frederick and Sue Nettye (Aylestock) W.; A.B., Western Md. Coll., Westminster, Md., 1923; M.D., U. of Md. Med. Sch., Baltimore, Md., 1927; m. Nan Elizabeth Brimer, Apr. 11, 1936; 1 son, James Frederick. Interne Md. Gen. Hosp., Baltimore, 1927-28; resident in medicine, South Baltimore Gen. Hosp., Baltimore, Md., 1928-29; engaged in gen. practice of medicine at Snow Hill, Md., since 1930. Mem. Med. and Chirurg. Faculty of Md., Worcester County Med. Soc. (past sec., treas., pres.), Nu Sigma Nu. Democrat. Presbyn. (trustee Snow Hill Ch.). Mason. Club: Civic. Home: Morris St. Office: Green St., Snow Hill, Md.

WAGENHORST, Lewis Hoch, dir. of teacher education; b. Kutztown, Pa., Jan. 29, 1891; s. Henry Rothermel and Sara Ellen (Hoch) W.; grad. State Normal Sch., Kutztown, Pa., 1908; A.B., Franklin and Marshall Coll., Lancaster, Pa., 1914; A.M., Teachers Coll., Columbia, 1922, Ph.D., 1926; m. Mary Gochnauer, Jan. 1, 1914; children—George Willard, Evelyn Jane (dec.), Esther Ellen (Mrs. George Bilowich), Mary Elizabeth. Teacher in rural school, 1908-10; teacher, High Sch., Perkasie, Pa., 1914-15; supervising prin. of schools, Perkasie, 1915-23; dir. of Lab. Schs., State Teachers Coll., Slippery Rock, Pa., since 1925; visiting prof. of elementary edn., George Peabody Coll. for Teachers, Nashville, Tenn., summer 1929. Mem. N.E.A., Pa. State Edn. Assn. (pres. Midwestern Dist. 1937), Supervisors of Student Teaching, Nat. Teacher Placement Assn., Pa. Teacher Placement Assn., Assn. of State Teachers Coll. Faculties (pres. 1937-39). Presbyterian (elder, supt. Sunday Sch.). Clubs: Rotary, Slippery Rock Cable Tow (Slippery Rock, Pa.). Author: The Administration and Cost of High School Interscholastic Athletics, 1926; contbr. ednl. articles to professional jours. Home: 211 E. Cooper St. Office: Laboratory School, State Teachers College, Slippery Rock, Pa.

WAGERS, Arthur J., MD.; b. DeKalb Co., Mo.; s. James and Aria A. (Metzger) W.; M.D. Washington U. Med. Sch., 1911; m. Marguerite Devin, June 21, 1911. Asst. to Dr. D. Braden Kyle, 1913; visiting laryngologist Philadelphia Hosp. for Contagious Diseases, 1920-21; asst. prof. laryngology, U. of Pa. Grad. Sch., 1923-32; otologist Joseph Price Memorial Hosp. since 1920; asso. in otology, Jefferson Med. Coll., 1929-34, asst. prof. laryngology since 1937; chief Laryngol. Clinic, Jefferson Hosp., since 1937. Served as capt. U.S. Med. Corps, World War; in charge of ear, nose and throat sect., Base Hosp., Camp Mead, Md. Fellow Am. Coll. Surgeons, Coll. Physicians of Philadelphia; mem. Am. Acad. Ophthalmology and Otolaryngology. Home: 4638 Larchwood Av. Office: 1429 Spruce St., Philadelphia, Pa.

WAGNER, Charles Conroy, coll., prof.; b. Mt. Jewett, Pa., Nov. 23, 1893; s. William Thomas and Ida Britton (Bush) W.; B.S., Allegheny Coll., Meadville, Pa., 1917; A.M., Pa. State Coll., 1925; Ph.D., U. of Mich., Ann Arbor, Mich., 1931; m. Grace Marie Parks, May 4, 1918; 1 daughter, Dorothy Marian. Instr. mathematics, Pa. State Coll., 1919-23, asst. prof., 1923-25,, asso. prof., 1925-33, on leave of absence, 1928-31, prof. mathematics since 1933, asst. to dean, Sch. of Liberal Arts since 1936; part time instr., U. of Mich., Ann Arbor, Mich., 1928-30, instr. 1930-31. Served as pvt., U.S. Army, 1917-19, with A.E.F. in France. Mem. Am. Math. Assn., Am. Mathematics Soc., Sigma Xi, Alpha Chi Rho, Pi Mu Epsilon, Sigma Pi Sigma. Republican. Methodist. Home: 835 W. Foster Av., State College, Pa.

WAGNER, Charles Frederick, cons. transmission engr.; b. Pittsburgh, Pa., Mar. 20, 1895; s. Leonard and Elizabeth (Buente) W.; B.S., Carnegie Inst. Tech., 1917; m. Ada Hanna, Sept. 7, 1920; children—Charles, Leonard. With Westinghouse Electric & Mfg. Co., East Pittsburgh, Pa., continuously since 1918, successively in materials and process engring. dept., staff of cons. transmission engr., research dept. central station engring. dept., and cons. transmission engr. since 1938. Dir. and treas. St. Peter's Orphan Home. Mem. Am. Inst. E.E., Franklin Institute, A.A.A.S., Tau Beta Pi, Sigma Xi, Beta Theta Pi. Republican. Co-Author: Symmetrical Components; writer numerous tech. papers. Home: 1303 Macon Av., Swissvale, Pa. Office: Westinghouse Electric & Mfg. Co., East Pittsburgh, Pa.

WAGNER, Dwight Homans, pres. Wheeling Corrugating Co. Home: Howard Apts. Office: Wheeling Corrugating Co., Wheeling, W.Va.

WAGNER, Edward Stephen, paper mfg.; b. Phila., Pa., Nov. 6, 1891; s. George S. and Mary Houston (Cantrell) W.; ed. pub. sch. and high sch., Phila., Pa.; grad. Evening Sch. of U. of Pa.; m. Rhoda E. Root, Dec. 18, 1916; 1 dau., Rhoda E. Began as employee in office Cambria Steel Co., 1907; asso. with Scott Paper Co., Chester, Pa. since 1913, dir. since 1919, treas., 1921, and 1st vice pres. and treas. since 1927; treas. Nova Scotia Wood Pulp and Paper Co.; vice-pres., treas and dir. Brunswick Pulp & Paper Co.; dir. Delaware County Nat. Bank. Republican. Episcopalian. Clubs: Union League, Philadelphia Country, Undine Barge, Racquet. Home: 532 Lafayette Rd., Merion, Pa. Office: Scott Paper Co., Chester, Pa.

WAGNER, Frederick Runyon, clergyman; b. New Market, N.J., May 30, 1873; s. George William and Agnes (Runyon) W.; student Missionary Inst., Selinsgrove, Pa.; A.B., Wittenberg Coll., Springfield, O., 1898, A.M., 1901; B.D., Luth. Theol. Sem., Gettysburg, Pa., 1901; D.D., Susquehanna U., Selinsgrove, 1917; m. Sarah B. Toot, Oct. 10, 1901; children—Agnes Elizabeth (Mrs. Ralph A. Beebe), Harriet Frances (Mrs. W. F. Warren), John Frederick, Richard Harman. Ordained ministry Luth. Ch., 1901; pastor St. Pauls Luth. Ch., Frostburg, Md., 1901-10, St. James Luth. Ch., Huntingdon, Pa., 1910-20, St. Johns Luth. Ch., Martinsburg, W. Va., since 1920. Pres. Allegheny Synod Luth. Ch., 1916-18. Republican. Mason. Rotarian. Home: 305 W. Martin St., Martinsburg, W.Va.

WAGNER, Harvey Giedion, automobile dealer, asso. judge; b. Washingtonville, Pa., Oct. 17, 1880; s. Daniel L. and Sarah (Deitrick) W.; ed. pub. schs.; m. Mary Brown, Feb. 25, 1903. Employed in various lines of work in Pa. and N.Y. to 1904; propr. meat market, Danville, Pa., 1904-07, in livery business of horse-drawn vehicles, 1907-10, added automobiles for hire and started first taxi business in Danville, 1910-18, sales agency for automobiles and trucks since 1918; served as sheriff Montour Co., 1918-21; started Danville-Sunbury bus line, 1921, and bus line in Danville to replace street cars, 1925; asso. judge Montour Co. for term 1936-42; dir. Danville Community Loan Co. Served as pres. Bus. Mens Assn.; dir. Chamber of Commerce. Mem. Patriotic Order Sons of America. Democrat. Lutheran. Elk. Jr. O.A.M. Home: 283 Mill St., Danville, Pa.

WAGNER, Herbert Appleton, public utilities; b. Phila., Pa., Feb. 24, 1867; s. William and Clara W. (Appleton) W.; grad. Stevens Inst. Tech., 1887; (hon.) Dr. Engring. Johns Hopkins U., 1937; m. Rose Margaret Keller, Jan. 12 1920; 1 son, Herbert A. Began as constrn. engr. Westinghouse Elec. Co., Pittsburgh, Pa., 1887; installed for same co., at St. Louis, the first large alternating central sta. in the West, 1888; gen. supt. Mo. Edison Co., St. Louis, 1888-1900; organizer, 1891, and first pres. Wagner Electric Mfg. Co., developing the first successful alternating current single phase motor, and other elec. devices; settled in Baltimore, 1911; v.p. and dir. Consolidated Gas, Electric Light & Power Co. and affiliated cos., 1910-15, pres. and dir., 1915-39, chmn. of bd., pres. and dir. since Mar. 21, 1939; v.p. Safe Harbor Water Power Corpn.; dir. Porcelain Enamel & Mfg. Co., Savings Bank of Baltimore, Pa. Water & Power Co., Baltimore Nat. Bank, The Lyric Co. Trustee Union Memorial Hosp., Edison Electric Inst., Stevens Inst. Tech., Children's Hosp. Sch., Community Fund of Baltimore; mem. exec. com. Assn. of Edison Illuminating Cos. Mem. Am. Inst. Elec. Engrs., Md. Acad. Sciences (pres. and chmn. bd. trustees), Baltimore Assn. Commerce (dir.). Mem. Newcomen Soc. of Eng. Episcopalian. Clubs: Maryland, Engineers, Baltimore Press, Advertising, Baltimore Country, Green Spring Valley Hunt, Elkridge, Maryland Polo, Md. Jockey, Gibson Island, Chesapeake Club; Engineers (New York). Home: Chattolanee, Md. Office: Lexington Bldg., Baltimore, Md.

WAGNER, Hobson Charles, supt. city schs.; b. Jonestown, Pa., Jan. 11, 1899; s. Irwin Daniel and Emily (Himmelberger) W.; B.S., Albright Coll., Reading, Pa., 1922; A.M., Columbia U., 1929; grad. study, Pa. State U., 1936-38; m. Kathryn E. Eyer, Aug. 19, 1924; children—Daniel Hobson, Mary Alice, Nancy Eyer. Teacher of mathematics and athletic coach, high sch., Towanda, Pa., 1922-26; supervising prin. pub. schs., Towanda, Pa., 1926-34; supt. schs., Hollidaysburg, Pa., since 1934. Served in World War, July 1918-May 1920. Mem. N.E.A., Pa. State Edn. Assn., Nat. Assn. Sch. Adminstrs., Am. Legion, Phi Delta Kappa. Republican. Presbyterian. Club: Kiwanis (Hollidaysburg, Pa.). Home: 801 Walnut St., Hollidaysburg, Pa.

WAGNER, J. Ernest, prin. high sch.; b. Heshbon, Pa., May 21, 1892; s. H. L. and Anna (Foust) W.; B.S., Bradley Poly. Inst., Peoria, Ill., 1916; A.M., U. of Pittsburgh, 1930, Ed. D., 1938; m. Mabel Austin, June 5, 1919. Engaged as teacher in pub. schs., Johnstown, Pa., 1916-26, dir. vocational edn., 1926-34, prin. evening schs., 1926-34, prin. high sch. since 1934; lecturer in vocational edn., U. of Pittsburgh evening classes, 1938-39. Served as pvt., Inf., U.S. Army, 1918. Mem. N.E.A., Am. Vocational Assn., Pa. State Edn. Assn., Pa. Secondary Sch. Prins. Assn. (vice-pres.), Phi Delta Kappa, Iota Lambda Sigma, Am. Legion. Republican. Lutheran. Mason. Club: Rotary (Johnstown, Pa.). Home: 333 Strayer St., Johnstown, Pa.

WAGNER, James Elvin, clergyman; b. Savannah, Tenn., Oct. 6, 1873; s. William Mathias and Annie Josephine (Walker) W.; A.B., Parsons Coll., Veal's Station, Tex., 1893; A.B., Upper Ia. U., 1904, D.D., 1910; grad. study, Ill. Wesleyan U.; m. Mary Catherine Britt, Dec. 17, 1893; children—Alta Anne (Mrs. John Carmichael Clark), William Lowel, Eugene Palmer, Harry Hughes. Prin. pub. sch., Norman, Okla., 1893-94; pastor Cumberland Presbyn. Ch., Henrietta, Tex., 1894-96; joined M.E.Ch., 1898; pastor various charges until 1908; pastor Enid, Okla., 1908-13, Mason City, Ia., 1913-17, Newton Center, Mass., 1917-21, Wesley M.E. Ch., Worcester, Mass., 1921-23, Omaha, Neb., 1923-26, Wheeling, W.Va., 1926-29, Mt. Lebanon Ch., Pittsburgh, Pa., 1929-33, First Church, Greensburg, Pa., 1933-37; St. Luke's Church, Long Branch, N.J. since 1937. Lecturer on evangelism, education and homiletics, in college and univs. for M.E. Board of Home Missions, 1919-1922. Worked as carpenter, Fore River Ship Yard, building submarines, World War. Republican. Mason (K.T.). Clubs: Fort Henry (Wheeling); Kiwanis (Pittsburgh); Itinerant (Boston). Author: Rural Evangelism, 1921. Contbr. to Zion's Herald, Christian Advocate, Northwestern Christian Advocate. Home: Long Branch, N.J.

WAGNER, M. Channing, asst. supt. of schools; b. Celina, O., May 27, 1887; s. Noah B. and Claressa (Miller) W.; student Otterbein Coll., Westerville, O.; A.B., Wittenberg Coll., 1918; A.M., Columbia, 1923; m. Alice Dale Northrup, Dec. 31, 1913; children—Helen Arlene, Miles Channing, Charles Northrup, David Robert, Eleanor Jane. Mem. staff Westinghouse Electric Co., 1906-08; teacher of mathematics and athletics Urbana (O.) High Sch., 1911-13, science and athletics, London (O.) High Sch., 1913-16; same, McKinley High Sch., Canton, O., 1916-20, vice prin., 1920-23; with Public Schools, Wilmington, Del., since 1923, as prin. High Sch., 1923-29, asst. supt. in charge secondary education and health since 1929; instructor Teachers College, Columbia, summers 1924-30. Mem. N.E.A., Am. Assn. Sch. Adminstrs., Del. State Edn. Assn., Phi Delta Kappa, Kappa Delta Pi. Methodist. Mason. Clubs: Kiwanis, Torch, Wilmington Whist (Wilmington, Del.); Kenneth Square (Pa.) Country. Home: 2003 N. Harrison St. Office: 11th and Washington Sts., Wilmington, Del.

WAGNER, Paul Conner, trust officer, lawyer; b. Reading, Pa., July 1, 1893; s. George W. and Sarah Emma (Conner) W.; A.B., Franklin & Marshall Coll., 1913; LL.B., U. of Pa., 1916; unmarried. Admitted to Phila. bar, 1916; deputy atty. gen. of Pa., 1927-29; partner law firm Clark, Wagner, McCarthy & Hebard, 1927-37; trust officer Fidelity-Philadelphia Trust Co. since 1937; lecturer, U. of Pa. Law Sch., 1924, 32. Mem. Phi Beta Kappa, Order of Coif, Am., Pa. and Phila. bar. assns. Home: Paoli, Pa. Office: 135 S. Broad St., Philadelphia, Pa.

WAGONER, Claude Brower, lawyer; b. Spring City, Pa., Apr. 11, 1900; s. Charles Shalkop and Lillie Cora (Brower) W.; A.B., U. of Pa., 1921, LL.B., Law Sch., 1924; m. Kathryn Groff, Apr. 18, 1925; children—David Everett, Claude Brower, Jr. Admitted to Pa. bar, 1924, and since engaged in gen. practice of law at Phila.; mem. firm Wesley, Wagoner, Troutman & McWilliams since 1930; dir. Bellefonte Central R.R. Co.; v.p. and dir. Floyd-Wells Co.; pres. H. R. Aiken Co.; dir. Quaker City Cold Storage Co. Served in U.S. Navy during World War. Mem. Phila., Pa., Chester Co. bar assns. Sharswood Law Club, Phi Beta Kappa, Theta Xi, Phi Delta Phi. Republican. Lutheran. Mason. Club: Union League (Phila.). Home: Chestnut and Cedar Sts., Spring City. Office: 1000 Packard Bldg., Philadelphia, Pa.

WAGONER, George, orthopædic surgeon; b. Johnstown, Pa., Jan. 16, 1896; s. Dr. George W. and Gertrude (Suppes) W.; M.D., U. of Pa., 1922; grad. study, U. of Innsbruck, Austria, 1929, 1934; m. Marjorie Jefferies, M.D., Aug. 9, 1924 (now dec.); children—Frieda Suppes, Ann. Interne Phila. Gen. Hosp., 1922-24; associated with U. of Pa. Sch. of Medicine and Grad. Sch. of Medicine since 1925, as asso. pathologist since 1925, asst. prof. of orthopædic surgery since 1929, dir. lab. of orthopædic research since 1933, asst. prof. of orthopædic research since 1937; surgeon to Bryn Mawr Hosp., Grad. Hosps. of U. of Pa., Phila. Orthopædic Hosp. Served as pvt. U.S. Army, 1917-19; now lieut. comdr., med. corps, U.S.N.R. Fellow Coll. Phys. Phila., Acad. Surgery, Phila., Am. Orthopædic Assn., Am. Med. Assn., Halstead Club, Sigma Xi. Democrat. Lutheran. Author: Handbook of Experimental Pathology (with R. P. Custer), 1932. Contbr. over forty papers dealing with repair, growth, and diseases of bones. Home: Polo Rd., Bryn Mawr, Pa.

WAHL, Arthur Munzenmaier, research engr.; b. Churdan, Ia., Oct. 15, 1901; s. Otto A. and Caroline R. (Munzenmaier) W.; B.S. in M.E., Iowa State Coll., Ames, Ia., 1925; Ph.D., U. of Pittsburgh, 1932; m. Lillian U. Thiesen, June 20, 1928. Grad. student Westinghouse Electric & Mfg. Co., 1925; research engr. Westinghouse Research Labs., East Pittsburgh, since 1926. Mem. Am. Soc. M.E., A.A.A.S., Westinghouse Engrs. Soc. Republican. Methodist. Clubs: Westinghouse, Bryn Mawr (Pa.) Men's. Co-Author (with A. Nadai): Plasticity, 1931; Marks' Mechanical Engineers' Handbook, 1930; Contributions to Mechanics of Solids, 1938; contbr. to engring. jours. Home: 21 Hillcrest Road, Wilkinsburg, Pa. Office: Westinghouse Electric & Mfg. Co., East Pittsburgh, Pa.

WAILES, George Handy, clergyman, educator; b. Salisbury, Md., Aug. 22, 1866; s. Ebenezer Leonard and Annie (Todd) W.; A.B., magna cum laude, Princeton, 1894, A.M., 1896; grad. Princeton Theol. Sem., 1897; D.D., Ursinus Coll., 1913; m. Lucretia Mott Franklin, Oct. 8,

1902 (died Aug. 8, 1918). Ordained Presbyn. ministry, 1897; pastor Scots Ch., Phila., 1897-1908; Prof. English Bible and Greek lang., Ursinus Coll., 1908-19; prof. exegetical theology, Reformed Episcopal Theol. Sem., 1919—. Teacher Hebrew and English Bible, Temple U., many yrs. Mem. Phi Beta Kappa. Home: 517 S. 48th St., Philadelphia, Pa.

WAIN, Sidney, editor and pub.; b. New York, N.Y., Jan. 23, 1909; s. Morris and Sarah W.; student N.Y. Univ.; m. Thelma Berlow; children—Constance Riva, Barbara Dawn. Began newspaper career as reporter; pres. Inter-Boro Publishing Co., Inc., publishers The Daily Standard, Red Bank, N.J.; editor The Daily Standard. Mem. bd. dirs. Red Bank Chamber of Commerce. Mem. bd. govs. West Side Bd. of Trade. Elk. Clubs: Lions (Red Bank); Camera, Boat (Monmouth); Yacht (Fair Haven). Home: 122 Harrison Av. Office: 170 Monmouth St., Red Bank, N.J.

WAITE, Joseph Orin, judge; b. LeBoeuff Twp., Erie Co., Pa., July 5, 1873; s. Daniel and Martha (Arters) W.; grad. Edinboro State Normal Sch.; student Allegheny Coll.; m. Nina E. Maycock, Apr. 18, 1903; children—Lois, Gordon. Dist. atty., Erie County, 1912-16; president judge Orphans' Court of Erie Co. since Jan. 1932. Mason (32°, K.T., Shriner), Odd Fellow, Elk. Clubs: Shrine, Elks, Erie. Contbr. to Erie Co. Law Journal, Pa. Dist. and Co. Reporter. Home: 505 Myrtle St. Address: Court House, Erie, Pa.

WAITE, William J., business exec.; b. Kansas City, Mo., Sept. 12, 1894; s. John Frank and Maude (Whiting) W.; B.S. Chem. Engring., U. of Kan., Lawrence, Kan., 1917; unmarried. Chemist Hercules Powder Co., Parlin, N.J., 1917-18, chief chemist, 1918-23; sec.-treas., gen. mgr. A. Gusmer, Inc., exporters and importers, Woodbridge, N.J., since 1923, Schock Gusmer & Co., Inc., mfrs. ferrous and non-ferrous machinery for chem. and allied industries, Hoboken, N.J., since 1927, George Fott Co., Hoboken, N.J., since 1927; dir., mem. exec. com., chmn. trust com. Clinton Trust Co., New York, since 1929; dir., mem. exec. com. Realty Mortgage Corpn., New York. Mem. Am. Chem. Soc., Sigma Alpha Epsilon, Alpha Chi Sigma. Democrat. Baptist. Elk. Clubs: New York Athletic (New York); Canoe Brook Country (trustee since 1934; Summit, N.J.); Shawnee Country (trustee since 1937; Shawnee-on-Delaware, Pa.); Lake Sunapee Country (New London, N.H.). Home: 269 Maple Av., Rahway, N.J. Office: 816 Clinton St., Hoboken, N.J.

WAKELEE, Edmund Waring, pub. utility exec.; b. Kingston, N.Y., Nov. 21, 1869; s. Nicholas and Eliza C. (Ingersoll) W.; grad. Kingston Acad., 1887; LL.B., New York U., 1891; unmarried. Admitted to N.Y. bar, 1891, N.J. bar, 1896; v.p. Pub. Service Corpn. of N.J. and subsidiaries since 1917; v.p. Palisades Trust & Guaranty Co., Englewood, N.J.; dir. Fidelity Union Trust Co. (Newark). The Englewood (N.J.) Sewerage Co., Sedgwick Machine Works (N.Y. City). Mem. N.J. Gen. Assembly, 1899-1900, State Senate, 1901-10 (served as floor leader, pres. of Senate and acting gov.). Vice-pres. Palisades Interstate Park Commn. Mem. Am., N.J. State and Bergen Co. bar assns., New York Co. Lawyers' Assn., Edison Electric Inst., Am. Gas Assn., American Transit Assn., N.J. Hist. Soc., Bergen County Hist. Soc., Ulster County Soc. in City of New York, Nat. Assn. Motor Bus Operators (v.p. and dir.), Chamber of Commerce of U.S., N.J. State, Bergen Co. (chmn. bd.), Newark, Jersey City, Paterson, Englewood, Camden, Trenton chambers of commerce, Alumni Assn. New York U. Law Sch., Delta Upsilon, Phi Delta Phi. Republican. Presbyn. Mason (32°), Elk; mem. Jr. Order United Am. Mechanics. Clubs: Metropolitan, Lotos, Nat. Republican (New York); Essex (Newark); Carteret (Trenton); Englewood; Knickerbocker Country (Tenafly, N.J.); Arcola Country; Aldecress Country (Demarest). Home: Demarest, N.J.; also 825—5th Av., New York, N.Y. Office: 80 Park Pl., Newark, N.J.

WAKSMAN, Selman Abraham, univ. prof.; b. Priluka, Kiev, Russia, July 2, 1888; s. Jacob and Fradia (London) W.; came to U.S., 1910, naturalized, 1915; B.Sc., Rutgers U., 1915, M.Sc., same, 1916; Ph.D., U. of Calif., 1918; m. Bertha D. Mitnik, Aug. 5, 1916; 1 son, Byron H. Began as research asst. in soil microbiology, 1915; research biochemist, Cutter Labs., 1917-18; bacteriologist, Takamine Labs., 1919-20; lecturer soil microbiology, Rutgers U., 1918-24, asso. prof., 1924-30, prof. soil microbiology since 1930; microbiologist, N.J. Agrl. Expt. Sta., New Brunswick, N.J. since 1921. Fellow A.A.A.S.; mem. Soc. Am. Bacteriologists, Soil Sci. Soc., America, Am. Soc. Agronomy, Mycol. Soc., Soc. Exptl. Biology and Medicine, Internat. Soc. Soil Sci. (Pres., 3d comm.), Am. Chem. Soc., Sigma Xi, Phi Beta Kappa. Corr. mem. French Acad. Scis. Received Nitrate of Soda Research Award of Am. Soc. of Agronomy for 1930. Author: Principles of Soil Microbiology, 1927, 2d edit., 1932; Humus, 1936, 2d edit., 1938; Enzymes, 1926; The Soil and the Microbe (with R. L. Starkey), 1931. Contbr. many sci. papers to tech. jours. Home: 35 Walter Av., Highland Park, N.J.

WALCOTT, Harry Mills, artist; b. Torrington, Conn., July 16, 1870; s. Dana Mills and Elizabeth (Billings) W.; ed. Rutherford (N.J.) pub. sch., Nat. Acad. Design, New York, Académie Julian, Paris; m. Belle Havens, June 1, 1905. Awarded hon. mention, Paris Salon; Clark prize and 1st Hallgarten prize, Nat. Acad. Design; Shaw fund, Soc. Am. Artists; hon. mention Carnegie Inst., Pittsburgh; medals, Pan-Am. and St. Louis expns.; Wanamaker prizes, Am. Art Assn., Paris; Daniel G. Reid Purchase Fund, Richmond (Ind.) Art Assn.; silver medal, Panama P.I. Expn., 1915. Represented in the H. C. Frick, John Wanamaker, Samuel T. Shaw, and Salmagundi Club collections, New York; W. S. Stimmel collection, Pittsburgh; Richmond, Ind., and Erie, Pa., Art Assns., A.N.A.; mem. Am. Art Assn. (Paris). Republican. Home: 46 The Terrace, Rutherford, N.J.

WALDBAUM, Abraham B., certified public accountant; b. Manchester, Eng., Dec. 23, 1899; s. Harry and Pauline (Charlson) W.; came to U.S., 1911, naturalized on coming of age; ed. pub. schs. of Manchester and Phila.; C.P.A., Pennsylvania, 1924; m. Netta Sugar, Aug. 31, 1924; 1 son, Morton Donald. Began as pub. accountant, Phila., 1917, and since in practice; partner A. B. Waldbaum & Co., certified public accountants, Phila., since 1922. Mem. Pa. Inst. C.P.A.'s, Am. Inst. Accountants, Am. Savings & Loan Inst. Jewish religion. Mason. Home: 5936 Windsor Av. Office: 12 S. 12th St., Philadelphia, Pa.

WALDINGER, Fred James, wholesale grocer; b. Erie Co., Pa., Apr. 20, 1885; s. Ferdinand and Sybilla (Wolf) W.; ed. grade schs. in Erie Co., Pa.; m. Mary Franz, June 15, 1907; children—Helen Amelia, Paul Fred. Employed as grocery clk., 1900-05, in grocery business on own acct., 1905-18; engaged in wholesale grocery business, 1918-25, consolidated with S. M. Flickinger Co. of Buffalo, N.Y., 1925, v.p., dir. S. M. Flickinger Co. and mgr. Erie (Pa.) branch since 1925. Dir. Kiwanis State Park Harbor Commn. Republican. Roman Catholic. Elk. Club: Elks (Erie, Pa.). Home: 3808 State St. Office: 2001 Wallace St., Erie, Pa.

WALDMAN, Henry S., lawyer; b. New York, N.Y., Oct. 18, 1902; s. Max and Amelia (Deutsch) W.; LL.B., N.Y. Univ. Law Sch., 1923; m. Dorothy Welt, Nov. 28, 1926; 1 dau., Carol Welt. Admitted to N.J. bar as atty., 1924, as counselor, 1930; engaged in gen. practice of law at Elizabeth since 1924; judge Police Ct. Borough of Roselle Park, N.J., 1924-26; apptd. first judge of Juvenile and Domestic Relations Ct. of Union Co., served 1931-36 and now for term, 1936-41; former mem. Good Will Ct. on radio; has aided state legislatures in drafting modern delinquency and probation laws. Mem. Union County Bar Assn. Phi Sigma Delta. Republican. Jewish religion. Contbr. articles on marriage, divorce, and delinquency. Home: 952 Harding Rd. Office: 286 N. Broad St., Elizabeth, N.J.

WALDMAN, Jacob W., dir. Doak Co., Inc.; b. Latvia, July 11, 1890; s. Samuel and Rachel (Katz) W.; came to U.S., 1910, naturalized, 1918; Pharm.D., George Washington U., 1914; m. Bessie R. Sherby, June 6, 1916; children—Sylvia Rita, Gloria. Began as pharmacist, 1914; owner of drug store, Hyattsville, Md., 1918-27; with Doak Chem. Co., mfrs. medical specialties, Cleveland, O., since 1929, dir. since 1932. Mem. Am. Pharm. Assn., Dist. of Columbia Pharm. Assn., Md. Pharm. Assn., George Washington U. Alumni Assn. Democrat. Jewish religion. Mason (Scottish Rite, Shriner). Home: Hyattsville, Md. Office: Hyattsville, Md.; and 2132 E. 9th St., Cleveland, O.

WALDRON, Ralph Augustus, coll. prof.; b. Rochester, Mass., Apr. 28, 1888; s. Hiram Edmund Baylis and Annie Bennett (Coll) W.; student Grew Sch., Hyde Park, Mass., 1893-1901, Hyde Park (Mass.) High Sch., 1902-05; B.S., Mass. State Coll., Amherst, Mass., 1910; student Pa. State Coll., 1910-14, M.S., 1912; Ph.D., U. of Pa., 1918; m. Helen Hatch, Dec. 15, 1911; children—Priscilla, Esther Suzanne. Instr. botany, Pa. State Coll., 1910-14, U. of Pa., 1915-18; farmer and horticulturist, Marshfield, Mass., 1918-22; prof. biology and head dept., Thiel Coll., Greenville, Pa., 1922-24; prof. biology and head science depts., State Teachers Coll., Slippery Rock, Pa., since 1924; part time instr. botany, Hort. Coll. for Women, Ambler, Pa., 1917-18; visiting prof. biology and geology, Youngstown (O.) Coll., 1924-38; visiting prof. science edn., Cornell U., summer 1931. Fellow A.A.A.S.; mem. Nat. Com. on Science Teaching Problems, Pa. Acad. Science (mem. exec. com.), Biology Assn. (past pres.), Teachers Coll. Science Teachers Assn. (past pres.), Am. Genetic Assn., N.E.A., Pa. State Edn. Assn., Am. Nature Assn., Sigma Xi, U. of Pa. Beta. Independent Republican. Presbyterian. Club: Kiwanis (Butler, Pa.). Co-author: Educational Biology, 1930; author numerous articles in ednl. mags.; papers presented at A.A.A.S., Pa. Acad. Science meetings; contbg. editor, Science Education. Lecturer before coll. assemblies, teachers' insts., high schs., clubs, etc. Travel guide and organizer of tours into Mexico, New England, Gaspe, Bermuda, and the West. Address: Slippery Rock, Pa.

WALDRON, William Henry, army officer, author; b. Huntington, W.Va., June 28, 1877; s. William and Helena Frances (Thomas) W.; distinguished grad. Inf. and Cav. Sch., 1905; grad. Army Staff Coll., 1906, Army War Coll., 1911; m. Allie McClure Powell, Nov. 14, 1901; 1 son, William Henry. Enlisted as sergt. Co. E, 2d W.Va. Inf., June 24, 1898; 2d lt. 9th Inf., Apr. 10, 1899; 1st lt. 29th Inf., Feb. 2, 1901; capt. 23d Inf., Apr. 3, 1908; trans. to 29th Inf., Oct. 29, 1910; maj., June 24, 1917; lt. col. N.A., Aug. 17, 1917; col. N.A., Aug. 1, 1918; hon. disch. emergency commn., June 30, 1920; lt. col. U.S.A., July 1, 1920; col., May 7, 1924. Sec. U.S. Inf. Assn. and editor its journal, 1919-24. Service in Spanish-Am. War, 1898, Philippine Insurrection, 1899-1900, Boxer Rebellion, 1900; wounded at Ho-siwo, China, Aug. 24, 1900; assigned duty Gen. Staff, Dec. 20, 1917; in France with A.E.F., May 23, 1918-May 17, 1919; chief of staff, 80th Div., N.A., Aug. 17, 1917-June 5, 1919; participated in battles Artios sector, British front, June 10-Aug. 22, 1918, Battle of St. Mihiel salient, Sept. 12-16, 1918, battles of the Meuse-Argonne, Sept. 26-Oct. 12, Nov. 1-11, 1918. Chief of staff 100th Div. Org. Res., 1924-1927; comdg. 10th U.S. Inf., 1927-29; detailed Gen. Staff, July 1, 1929; chief of staff 5th Corps Area, July 1, 1929-Feb. 1, 1930; exec. officer Militia Bur., Washington, D.C., 1930-33; chief of staff 100th Div. Organized Reserves, 1933-37; also commanded the W.Va. Dist. of Civilian Conservation Corps, Apr. 1935-Nov. 1936; retired Jan. 31, 1938. Awarded D.S.M., 1922, "for distinguished service" in France; D.S.C., 1922, "for heroism" at battle of Tien Tsin, China, July 13, 1900; citation General Order 18, Headquarters 80th Division, also from comdr. in chief A.E.F.; decorated Officer Legion of Honor (France), Sept. 19, 1919. Author: Scouting and Patrolling, 1916; Tactical Walks, 1917; Company Administration,

1917; Army Physical Training, 1919; Platoon Training (2 vols.), 1919; Thirty Minute Talks (with Merch Brant Stewart), 1919; Terrain Exercises, 1922; The Old Sergeant's Conferences, 1930; Flags of America, 1935; America's Flags, 1938. Home: 530 13th Av., Huntington, W.Va.

WALK, George Everett, educator; b. Bethany, O., Jan. 5, 1876; s. Isaac Newton and Rachel (Warner) W.; B.A., Ohio Wesleyan, 1899; M.A., Teachers Coll. (Columbia), 1911; fellow, Sch. of Education, New York U., 1913-14, Ph.D., 1914; LL.D., Juniata Coll., 1935; m. Maudelle Germond, Sept 1, 1908; children—Everett Germond, Margaret Germond (Mrs. Dean A. Gordon). Teacher and prin. pub. schs. until 1895; teaching fellow, Ohio Wesleyan, 1898-1899; prof. ancient langs., W.Va. Wesleyan Coll., 1899-1901; dep. div. supt. pub. instrn., Philippines, 1901-02, div. supt., 1902-10; dir. of training and head dept. of edn., State Teachers Coll., Edinboro, Pa., 1911-13; asst. to dean Sch. of Edn., New York U., 1913-14; prin. training dept., State Teachers Coll., Paterson, N.J., 1914-18; lecturer on edn., Brooklyn Inst. Arts and Sciences, and New York U., 1914-18; dir. teacher placement, U.S. Office of Edn., 1918-19; dean Teachers Coll., Temple U., since its organization in 1919; elected pres. State Teachers Coll., Shippensburg, Pa., 1931, but declined. Mem. bd. trustees Eastern State Penitentiary, Phila., 1925-35. Mem. Am. Acad. Polit. and Social Science, Am. Assn. of Sch. Adminstrs., N.E.A., Nat. Soc. Coll. Teachers of Edn., Sigma Chi, Phi Epsilon Kappa, Phi Delta Kappa, Phi Beta Kappa. Republican. Methodist. Author: Professional Training of Teachers in the United States, 1914; A Neglected Factor in Education, 1926; Standards for Thesis Writing (with N. W. Uewsom), 1936. Contbr. on ednl. topics. Home: 5135 Newhall St., Philadelphia, Pa.

WALKER, Alexander Edward, vice-pres. National Supply Co.; b. Detroit, Mich., Nov. 12, 1886; s. John Walker and Isabella (Paton) W.; B.S., U. of Mich., 1910; m. Marie Gaston, June 1, 1912; children—Frances Marie, Alexander Edward, Jr. Timekeeper Riter-Connelly Co., Pittsburgh, 1910-11; salesman, La Belle Iron Works, Steubenville, O., 1911-16; salesman Republican Iron & Steel Co., 1916-19, asst. gen. mgr. of sales, 1919-28, gen. mgr. of sales, 1928-30; gen. mgr. of sales Republic Steel Corpn., 1930-36; exec. vice-pres. and dir. Pittsburgh Steel Co., 1937-39; vice-pres. and dir. The Nat. Supply Co., and pres., Spang Chalfant, Inc., since April 1, 1939; dir. Empire Sheet & Tin Plate Co. Mem. Chi Psi. Unitarian. Clubs: Duquesne, Pittsburgh Athletic, Oakmont Country (Pittsburgh); Union, Country, Pepper Pike (Cleveland); Cloud (New York); Youngstown Country and Youngstown (Youngstown). Home: Park Mansions, 5023 Frew Av. Office: Grant Bldg., Pittsburgh, Pa.

WALKER, Arthur Meeker, physician; b. Pittsfield, Mass., Sept. 26, 1896; s. James Ransom and Louise (Meeker) W.; A.B., Williams Coll., Williamstown, Mass., 1919; M.D., Harvard Med. Sch., 1923; m. Sylvia Cabot, Nov. 29, 1924; children—Peter, James Eliot Cabot, Philip Cabot, Maria Louise. Interne Mass. Gen. Hosp., Boston, 1923-25; instr. pharmacology, U. of Pa. Med. Sch., 1925-30, asst. prof., 1930-38, asso. prof. since 1938. Served as capt., Inf., U. S. Army, 1917-19, with A.E.F. Mem. Am. Physiol. Soc., Am. Soc. for Clin. Investigation, Kappa Alpha, Phi Beta Kappa, Alpha Omega Alpha. Awarded Order of Purple Heart (U.S.) Republican. Club: Penllyn (Penllyn, Pa.) Home: Gwynedd Valley, Pa. Office: Univ. of Pa. Medical School, Philadelphia, Pa.

WALKER, Elton David, prof. of engring.; b. Taunton, Mass., Mar. 8, 1869; s. Benjamin Dudley and Ruth Barrows (Cobb) W.; grad. High Sch., Taunton, Mass.; B.S. in Civil Engring., Mass. Inst. Tech., 1890; m. D. M. Louise Brownell, Sept. 2, 1896; children—Dudley Brownell (dec.). Robert Brownell (dec.). Began as surveyor and draftsman Associated. Factory Mutual Fire Ins. Cos., Boston, June 1890; asst. in civil engring., Mass. Inst. Tech., 1890-91; draftsman with Edward Busse, mill engr., Boston, June 1891; civil engr. Q.M. Dept., U. S. Army, Fort Sheridan, Ill., 1891-92; mem. firm Walker & Gallagher, engrs., Chicago, 1892-94; instr. in civil engring., Union Coll., Schenectady, N.Y., 1894-97, asst. prof., 1897-1900; resident hydrographer U.S. Geol. Survey, 1898-1900; with Pa. State Coll. since 1900, asst. prof. of civil engring., 1900-02, prof. of hydraulic and sanitary engring., 1902-39, prof. of civil engring. emeritus since 1939, acting head of dept., 1907-39, acting dean Sch. of Engring., 1913-15; cons. engr. since 1894. Served as capt., Corps of Engrs., U.S. Army, with A.E.F. during World War; now col., Inact.-Res. Fellow Am. Pub. Health Assn.; mem. Am. Soc. Civil Engrs., Soc. Promotion Engring. Edn., Am. Assn. Univ. Profs., Am. Water Works Assn., Pa. Water Works Operators Assn., New England Water Works Assn., Pa. Sewage Works Assn. (pres. emeritus), Am. Legion, Reserve Officers Assn., Scabbard and Blade, Delta Kappa Epsilon, Sigma Xi, Tau Beta Pi, Phi Kappa Phi, Chi Epsilon. Awarded citation by Gen. Pershing; decorated Purple Heart Medal. Republican. Episcopalian. Club: University (State College, Pa.). Author of various articles and bulletins. Home: 704 McKee St., State College, Pa.

WALKER, James French, prin. Westtown Sch.; b. Flushing, O., Nov. 1, 1889; s. Abel and Hannah L. (French) W.; ed. Westtown Sch., Westtown, Pa., 1906-08; B.Sc. in agr., O. State U., 1914; Ed.M., Harvard U., 1931; m. Alice Nicholson Bell, June 24, 1916; children—Robert Bell, Ruth Nicholson, Margaret Louise. Engaged as orchard mgr. and teacher agr., Westown Sch., Westtown, Pa., 1914-24, actg. prin., 1924-25, prin. since 1925. Served as pres. Westtown-Thornbury Sch. Bd. since 1935. Mem. Headmasters Club, Progressive Edn. Assn. Republican. Mem. Religious Soc. Friends. Club: Niblick Golf (Philadelphia). Home: Westtown, Pa.

WALKER, John Yates Gholson, financier; b. of Am. parents, Liverpool, Eng., Apr. 11, 1871; ed. pub. schs.; m. Elizabeth B. Almy, Feb. 19, 1919; children—Kenneth Stewart, Elizabeth Lee, Mabel B., John Yates Gholson, William Magruder. Partner Walker Brothers, brokers, New York City; dir. Continental Realty Investment Co.; mem. U.S. bd. finance Caledonian Instn.; chmn. finance com. North British & Mercantile Ins. Co.; 1st v.p., trustee Bank for Savings in City of New York, Central Hanover Bank and Trust Co.; dir. Commonwealth Ins. Co., Mercantile Ins. Co. of America, U.S. Guarantee Co., Caledonian-Am. Ins. Co. Clubs: Union, Down Town Assn., Racquet and Tennis, Turf and Field, Essex County Country. Home: Llewellyn Park, West Orange, N.J. Office: 71 Broadway, New York, N.Y.

WALKER, Marshall Starr, assayer and metall. research; b. Salt Lake City, U., June 20, 1882; s. Samuel Starr and Ida (McClellan) W.; B.S., Mich. Coll. of Mines, 1905, E.M., same, 1906; m. Maude Marriott, June 23, 1909; children—Marshall Starr, Jr., Alexander Marriott, Charles Dodsley. Mining, milling, assaying in Mexico and U.S., 1908-12; tech. asst. U.S. Assay Office, New York, 1912-15; experimental and maintenance for Thos. A. Edison, 1916; research and original improvements in sampling copper bullion; also metal sales and personnel work, Cerro De Pasco Copper Corpn., 1917-25; organized Walker & Whyte, Inc., representation, assaying, and technical investigations for shippers of ores and metals to smelters, New York, N.Y. and pres. and dir. since 1925. Served in home guard, Glen Ridge, N.J. during World War. Mem. Shade Tree Commn., Glen Ridge. Presidental appointment, U.S. Assay Commn., 1938. Mem. Am. Inst. Mining & Metall. Engrs., Mining & Metall. Soc. of America, S.A.R. Republican. Episcopalian. Club: Mining (New York). Home: 224 Bay Av., Glen Ridge, N.J. Office: 409 Pearl St., New York, N.Y.

WALKER, Milton Barratt, lawyer, corpn. exec.; b. Harford Co., Md., June 27, 1873; s. Jacob P. and Cornelia A. (Smith) W.; student Harford Co. (Md.) Pub. Schs., Johns Hopkins U., Baltimore; LL.B., Md. U. Law Sch., Baltimore, Md., 1898; m. Jessie Carroll, July 7, 1902. Admitted to Md. Bar, 1898, and since in practice at Baltimore, Md.; exec. v.p., mem. exec. com. and dir. U.S. Fidelity & Guaranty Co., Baltimore, Mem. U.S. War Risk Ins. Com., Seamen's Sect., 1917-18. Mem. Int. Claim Assn. (pres., 1915). Methodist. Author: Walker on Fidelity Bonds, 1908. Home: Catonsville, Md. Office: Calvert and Redwood Sts., Baltimore, Md.

WALKER, Robert Bell, physician; b. Phila. Pa., Aug. 17, 1884; s. Thomas Holmes and Jane (Bell) W.; B.S., Central High Sch., Phila., 1902, A.M., 1909; M.D., Medico-Chirurg. Coll., Phila., 1907; m. Helen Grave Young, June 8, 1935. Asst. chief resident, Phila. Gen. Hosp., 1909-10; visiting physician, Medico-Chirurg. Hosp., Phila., 1909-14, instr. in medicine, Medico-Chirurg. Coll., Phila., 1910-13; visiting physician, Am. Stomach Hosp., Phila., 1909-31, med. dir., 1931-35; chief physician, Northern Home for Friendless Children, Phila., 1910-25; visiting physician, Nat. Stomach Hosp., Methodist Episcopal Hosp., Phila., since 1935; interenist with special attention to digestive disorders. Fellow A.M.A.; mem. Phila. Co., Pa. State med. socs. Ind. Republican. Protestant. Club: Bala Golf (Phila.). Asso. editor Am. Jour. of Gastro-Enterology, 1911-15. Address: 1824 Wallace St., Philadelphia, Pa.

WALKER, Robert Byron, M.D., surgeon; b. Meyerdale, Pa., Feb. 4, 1889; s. Edward M. and Minerva J. (Bittner) W.; student Gettysburg (Pa.) Acad., 1908-09, U. of Pa., 1914-15; B.S., Pa. Coll., Gettysburg, Pa., 1913; M.D., U. of Cincinnati (O.) Med. Coll., 1920; m. Inez S. Acker, Jan. 3, 1925; 1 son, Robert Acker. Voluntary asst., N.Y. Post Grad. Hosp., 1926-27, clin. asst., 1927-29, asso. in gynecology, 1929-35; surgeon Middlesex Gen. Hosp., New Brunswick, N.J., since 1928, chief dept. of obstetrics and gynecology since 1930. Served as private Med. R.C., U.S. Army, 1916-17. Fellow Am. Coll. Surgeons; diplomate Am. Bd. of Obstetrics and Gynecology; mem. Phi Delta Theta, Alpha Kappa Kappa, Beta Beta Beta. Republican. Lutheran. Mason. Clubs: Rutgers, New Brunswick Boat (New Brunswick, N.J.). Author of numerous scientific papers on obstetrics and gynecology. Home: 118 S. 1st Av., Highland Park, N.J. Office: 108 Church St., New Brunswick, N.J.

WALKER, Robert Hunt, life ins. spl. agt.; b. Baltimore, Md., Oct. 23, 1882; s. Elisha Hunt and Lucy (Cooper) W.; B.S., Swarthmore Coll., Swarthmore, Pa., 1902; m. Amelia E. Himes, June 4, 1910; children—Talbott Hunt, Katharine Wirt, Morgan Cooper. Asso. with Baltimore office Provident Mutual Life Ins. Co. of Phila. continuously since entering its employ as clk., 1902, served as gen. agt., 1916-34, spl. agt. since 1934; dir. Central Savings Bank, Baltimore, Baltimore Equitable Soc., Friendly Inn Assn. Served as capt. Q.M.C., U.S.A. during World War. Trustee emeritus Swarthmore Coll., Swarthmore, Pa. Trustee Sheppard and Enoch Pratt Hosp. Past sec. and pres. Baltimore Life Underwriters Assn. Mem. Delta Upsilon. Republican. Mem. Religious Soc. Friends. Served as treas. Baltimore Yearly Meeting Religious Soc. Friends, 1904-30. Club: Howard County Hunt (past sec. and treas.). Home: York & Walker Rds., Baltimore Co. Office: Fidelity Bldg., Baltimore, Md.

WALKER, Rome H., surgeon Mountain State Hosp. Address: 240 Capitol St., Charleston, W.Va.

WALKER, Samuel DeBow, real estate and builder; b. Newark, N.J., Mar. 20, 1893; s. William and Mary (DeBow) W.; ed. pub. schs., Keyport, N.J., high sch. Newark, N.J.; m. Margaret Quinn Stewart, Apr. 1, 1916 (div. 1921); 1 dau., Margaret Stewart; m. 2d, Emma Schlegel, Jan. 25, 1923; children—Betsy Ann, Mary Lou. Began as real estate salesman, 1914; organized Morrisey & Walker, Inc., and sec. and treas. since 1915; pres. Cliffwood Beach Co., Cloverleaf Memorial Parks, Inc., Laurence Harbor Water Co.; exec. v.p. Spring Lake Securities Co.; sec. and treas. Laurence Harbor Heights Co.; dir. Keyport

Banking Co. Mem. Am. Inst. Real Estate Appraisers, N.J. Assn. Real Estate Bds. (past pres.), N.J. Advertising Council (dir.). Republican. Clubs: Yacht (Keyport); Newark Athletic (Newark); Yacht (West Palm Beach, Fla.). Home: 101 Atlantic St., Keyport, N.J. Office: 1 Church St., Keansburg, N.J.

WALKER, Thomas Glynn; born in Harrison, N.J., Dec. 7, 1899; s. Samuel Edward and Mary Agnes (Glynn) W.; ed. St. Benedicts Prep. Sch., Newark, N.J., Seton Hall Coll., South Orange, N.J., Fordham U., New York City; m. Elizabeth Kylmore Fissell, Aug. 15, 1934; 1 dau., Elizabeth Glynn. Atty. at law and counsellor at law, N.J.; supreme court commr., N.J.; spl. master in chancery; associated with the law firm Wolber and Gilhooly, Newark, N.J., 1925-29; partner firm Skeffington and Walker, Newark, N.J., 1929-39; judge Court of Errors and Appeals, N.J.; judge Hudson County Ct. of Common Pleas; prof. law, John Marshall Coll. of Law, Jersey City, N.J., 1933-37, Mercer Beasley Sch. of Law, Newark, 1935. Mem. Assembly of State of N.J., 1933-37, speaker, 1937. Clubs: Essex (Newark, N.J.); Essex County Country (West Orange, N.J.). Home: Arlington, N.J.

WALL, Albert Chandler, lawyer; b. Kingston, N.J., Jan. 24, 1866; s. Edward and Sara (Berry) W.; grad Stevens Sch., Hoboken, N.J., 1882; A.B., Princeton, 1886, A.M., 1889; studied Columbia Law Sch.; m. Maria Carey, Apr. 30, 1896; children—Mrs. Josephine W. Froelick, Albert Carey. Admitted N.J. bar, 1890, and began practice at Jersey City, N.J.; mem. firm, Wall, Haight, Carey & Hartpence since 1920; dir. and gen. counsel Federal Ins. Co.; dir. Prudential Ins. Co. of America, Commercial Trust Co. of N.J. Mem. State Bar Assn., N.J. (ex-pres.). Episcopalian. Clubs: Essex County Country; University (New York). Home: Llewellyn Park, West Orange, N.J. Office: 15 Exchange Pl., Jersey City, N.J.

WALL, Alexander James, librarian; b. N.Y. City, Oct. 25, 1884; ed. high sch. and spl. courses in French and Spanish; m. Lillian B. Hashagen, Nov. 25, 1907; 1 son, Alexander J. Began in library work, 1898; librarian, New York Hist. Soc., 1921-37, dir., 1937—, also sec. bd. trustees and editor Quarterly Bull., 1917-36. Mem. Am. Hist. Assn., A.L.A., Bibliographical Soc. America, N.Y. State Library Assn., New York Library Club, Am. Antiquarian Soc. Trustee Lynbrook Bd. of Edn., 1926-36; v.p. Asso. Sch. Bds., State of N.Y., 1929-31. Pres. Buck Hill Art Assn., 1933-38. Mem. Soc. of Friends. Clubs: Salmagundi, Grolier, New York Athletic. Wrote: List of New York Almanacs (1694-1850), 1921; Sketch of Samuel Loudon (1727-1813), 1922; Books on Architecture Printed in America (1775-1830), 1925; Wax Portraiture, a contribution towards the study of wax work done in America, 1925; The Story of the Convention Army (1777-1783), 1927; Sketch of the Life of Horatio Seymour (1810-1886), 1929; The Story of Time Stone Farm, 1936. Home: 390 West End Av., New York, N.Y.; also Buckhill Falls, Pa. Office: 170 Central Park W., New York, N.Y.

WALL, William Guy, consulting engr.; b. Baltimore, Md., Aug. 7, 1876; s. William Edward and Mary Catherine (Dade) W.; grad. in Civ. Engring., Va. Mil. Inst., 1894; B.S., Mass. Inst. Tech., 1896; m. Minnie Tyndall, 1909 (died 1931); m. 2d, Helen Wessel, of Washington, D.C., 1934. Practiced at Indianapolis since 1900; founder, v.p. and chief engr. Nat. Motor Car Co.; cons: engr. for several prominent automobile companies. Maj. and lt. col., U.S.A., World War; col. Res. Mem. Am. Soc. Mech. Engrs., Soc. Automotive Engrs. (ex-pres.), Am. Legion, Forty and Eight, Delta Tau Delta. Sec. Am. Legion Endowment Fund Corpn. Democrat. Episcopalian. Clubs: University, County, Athletic, Traders Point Hunt, Woodstock (Indianapolis); Army and Navy (Washington, D.C.); Manor (Boyd, Md.); Potomac Hunt (Md.). Home: 1431 N. Delaware St., Indianapolis, Ind.; and "Walldene," Boyd, Md.

WALLACE, Charles Carroll, lawyer; b. Baltimore, Md., Sept. 28, 1889; s. Charles Carroll and Priscilla (Renshaw) W.; student U. of Md. Law Sch., 1908-11; unmarried. Admitted to Md. bar, 1912, Md. Court of Appeals, 1912, U.S. Supreme Court, 1927; associated with late Edward M. Hammond, 1912-19; asst. city solicitor, Baltimore, 1924-26, city solicitor and chief of City Law Dept., 1926-27; codifier pub. local laws of Baltimore City, 1927; mem. Md. Tax Revision Commn. to revise Md. tax statutes, 1927; in gen. practice of law since 1912. Mem. Am. Bar Assn., Md. State Bar Assn. (v.p. 1926-27), Baltimore City Bar Assn. Democrat. Club: University (Baltimore). Home: 1641 E. North Av. Office: Union Trust Bldg., Baltimore, Md.

WALLACE, Earl Keeney, prof. chemistry; b. Newmanstown, Pa., May 1, 1897; s. Harry Peter and Lillie May (Keeney) W.; B.S., Pa. State Coll., 1919; ed. U. of Pa., 1921-22; A.M., Columbia U., 1923, Ph.D., 1925; m. Blanche May Strickler, June 18, 1921; children —Louise Hazel, Earl Keeney, Jr., Gene Blanche. Engaged as instr. chemistry, Pa. Mill. Coll., 1919-21, asst. prof., 1921-23; asst. in organic chemistry, Columbia U., 1923-25; prof. chem. istry, Pa. Coll. for Women since 1925. Served in Engrs. Res. Corps. Mem. Am. Chem. Soc. (chmn. elect, Pittsburgh Sect.), Am. Inst. Chemists, Pittsburgh Chemists Club (past pres.), Phi. Lambda Upsilon, Sigma Xi. Republican. Mem. Reformed Ch. Home: 5806 Murrayhill Pl., Pittsburgh, Pa.

WALLACE, George Selden, lawyer; b. nr. Greenwood Station, Va., Sept. 6, 1871; s. Charles Irving and Maria Logan (Sclater) W.; ed. pub. sch. and Mechanics' Institute, Richmond; LL.B., W.Va. U., 1897; m. Frances Bodine, d. John S. Gibson, D.D., of Huntington, W.Va., Oct. 4, 1905; children—Frances Gibson, Champe Carter, Elizabeth Logan (Mrs. J. A. Cook), Margaret Sclater (Mrs. Buel B. Whitehill), William, and George Selden. Began law practice, 1897; was dir., president and 1st vice-president Union Bank & Trust Company, Huntington, 30 years; president Ben Lomond Company; sec. and treasurer Blackberry, Ky., and B. W.Va., Coal & Coke Co.; etc. City atty., Central City, W.Va., 1902-04; pros. atty., Cabell Co., 1905-08; mem. Dem. city, co. and state coms.; del Dem. Nat. Conv. Baltimore, 1912; pres. Bd. Park Commrs., Huntington, since 1925. Served 2d and 1st lt. 2d W.Va. Vol. Inf., Spanish-Am. War, 1898-99; div. q.m., Dec. 1898-Apr. 1899; mem. W.Va.N.G., 1900-16, advancing to lt. col.; actg. J.A.G., 1912, in Paint and Cabin Creek troubles, and was adviser to the gov. and comdr. in chief N.G.; defended action of guard and gov. successfully before the courts; commd. maj. J.A.G., O.R.C., Nov. 8, 1916. Organized board and put Selective Service Act into effect in West Va., 1917; chief miscel. sect. J.A.G.'s office, Washington, D.C.; promoted lt. col.; went to France, June 1918; sr. asst. to acting J.A.G. for France; hon. discharged, June 16, 1919. Mem. Am. Bar Assn., Cabell Co. Bar Association (ex-president), Society of Cincinnati in Virginia, Phi Sigma Kappa, Democrat. Episcopalian. Clubs: Army and Navy, Army, Navy and Marine Corps Country (Washington, D.C.). Author: The Need, Basis and Propriety of Martial Law, 1916; Genealogical Data Pertaining to the Descendants of Peter Wallace and Elizabeth Woods; Cabell County Annals and Families; and Monograph on "The Sclater Family in Virginia." Home: Huntington, W.Va.

WALLACE, Lester, v.p. Maryland Trust Co. Office: N.W. Cor. Calvert and Redwood Sts., Baltimore, Md.

WALLACE, Oates Charles Symonds, clergyman; b. Canaan, N.S., Nov. 28, 1856; s. William John and Rachel Louisa Harris (Witter) W.; A.B., Acadia U., N.S., 1883, A.M., 1889; A.M., McMaster Univ., Ont., 1892; D.D., Acadia, 1897; LL.D., Mercer University, Ga., 1897, Queen's, Can., 1903. McMaster, 1909; D.Litt. from Acadia University in 1926; m. Leonette Crosby, May 30, 1885 (died June 1902); children—Rachel Leonette, Oates Crosby Saunders; June 30, 1904 (died May 20, 1917); m. 3d, Helen Moore, d. of Rev. John Wright Moore, of Folkestone, Eng., Mar. 2, 1919. Country schoolmaster at 15; home missionary preacher at 17; ordained Bapt. ministry, 1885; pastor First Ch., Lawrence, Mass., 1885-91, Bloor Street Ch., Toronto, Can., 1891-95; chancellor McMaster U., 1895-1905; pastor First Ch., Lowell, Mass., 1905-08, First Ch., Baltimore 1908-13, Westmount Bapt. Ch., Montreal, Can., 1913-21, Eutaw Pl. Bapt. Ch., Baltimore, Md., 1921-35, pastor emeritus since Jan. 1, 1936. Author: Life of Jesus; What Baptists Believe; Looking Towards the Heights; Clover, Brier, and Tansy; As Thorns Thrust Forth; Pastor and People. Editor: From Montreal to Vimy Ridge and Beyond. Was editorial writer Am. Bapt. Publ. Soc. many yrs. Address: 2223 Sulgrave Av., Baltimore, Md.

WALLACE, Robert Burns; emeritus prof. English, Temple U. Address: Broad St. and Montgomery Av., Philadelphia, Pa.

WALLACE, William James Lord, coll. prof.; b. Salisbury, N.C., Jan. 13, 1908; s. Thomas Walker and Lauretta Julia (Lawson) W.; B.S., U. of Pittsburgh, 1927; A.M., Columbia U., 1931; Ph.D., Cornell U., 1937; m. Eleanor Louise Taylor, Dec. 7, 1929; 1 dau., Louise Eleanor. Engaged as instr. chemistry, Livingstone Coll., Salisbury, N.C., 1927-32, Lincoln Univ., Jefferson City, Mo., 1932-33; instr. chemistry, W.Va. State Coll., Institute, W.Va., 1933-35, asst. prof., 1935-37, asso. prof. chemistry since 1937. Served in R.O.T.C., U. of Pittsburgh, 1927; 2d lt. inf. O.R.C., 1929-34. Mem. Am. Chem. Soc., Alpha Phi Alpha, Sigma Xi. Mem. Research Council at W.Va. State Coll. Awarded Gen. Edn. Bd. Fellowship, 1930-31; Sage Fellowship in chemistry, Cornell U., 1936-37. Methodist. Clubs: The Contemporaries of W.Va. State College, The W.Va. State College Chess Club. Home: Faculty Cottage G, The Ellipse, Institute, W.Va.

WALLENSTEIN, Sydney; chief of service, dept. of urology, West Baltimore Gen. Hosp.; attending urol. surgeon Mount Pleasant Sanatorium; visiting urol. surgeon Sinai and St. Joseph's hosps. Address: 2042 Eutaw Place, Baltimore, Md.

WALLER, Allen George, agrl. economist; b. Seneca Falls, N.Y., Sept. 20, 1892; s. George A. and Annie B. (Allen) W.; B.S., Rutgers U., New Brunswick, N.J., 1915, M.S., 1919; m. Constance Stroud, 1920; m. 2d, Ingrid Nelson, 1925; children—Constance, David A. Asst. specialist in agronomy, N.J. State Agrl. Coll., 1916-17; specialist in farm management research, N.J. Agr. Exptl. Sta., 1919-26; asso. agrl. economist, U.S. Dept. Agr., 1924-26; became chief, dept. of agrl. econs., Rutgers University, New Brunswick, N.J., and N.J. Agr. Exptl. Sta., 1926, now prof. of agrl. econs. Served in U. S. Army, 1917-19. Mem. Farm Econ. Assn., Am. Statis. Assn., National Municipal League. Republican. Presbyterian. Mason (Scottish Rite), Grange. Co-author: Farm Economics: Management and Distribution, 1938; author of numerous bulletins on management, taxation, etc. Address: 85 Adelaide Av., New Brunswick, N.J.

WALLER, Charles Buckalew, lawyer; b. Bloomsburg, Pa., Feb. 14, 1890; s. Levi Ellmaker and Alice Mary (Buckalew) W.; A.B., Yale, 1912; LL.B., Harvard Law Sch., 1915; m. Frances Alexander Phelps, Dec. 15, 1917; 1 dau., Margaretta Phelps. Admitted to Pa. bar, 1915 and since engaged in gen. practice of law at Wilkes-Barre, Pa.; mem. firm Bedford, Waller, Jones and Darling since 1925; dir. Second Nat. Bank, Wilkes-Barre Record, Haddock Mining Co., Stevens Coal Co., Glen Summit Springs Water Co., Howell & King Co. Served as capt., 307th F.A., U. S. Army, 1917-19, with A.E.F., 1918-19; maj., F.A., U.S Army Res., 1920-22. Pres. Wilkes-Barre-Wyoming Valley Chamber of Commerce, 1935-36, Wilkes-Barre City Planning Commn.; chmn. Luzerne Co. Emergency Relief Bd., 1932-33. Dir. Wilkes-Barre Y.W.C.A., Wilkes-Barre General Hosp.; trustee and v.p. Community Welfare Fed. Mem. Pa. and Luzerne Co. bar assns., Pa. Constitutional Commemoration Com., Wyoming Hist. & Geneal. Soc. (dir.), Delta Kappa Epsilon. Republican. Presbyterian. Clubs: Westmoreland, Wyoming Valley Country (Wilkes-Barre), North

Mountain (Benton, Pa.). Address: 832 Miners Bank Bldg., Wilkes-Barre, Pa.

WALLER, Clifford Ellison, asst. surgeon gen. U.S. Pub. Health Service; b. Bremond, Texas, Apr. 1, 1886; s. William Franklin and Sarah (Ellison) W.; M.D., George Washington U., 1910; m. Helen Stewart, 1910; children—Dorothy Stewart, William Franklin. Physician U.S. Indian Med. Service, 1910-13; asst. surgeon U.S. Pub. Health Service, 1914-18, passed asst. surgeon, 1918, surgeon, 1922, asst. surgeon gen., 1931; health officer Raleigh and Wake Cos., N.C., 1918-19; state commr. of health, N.M., 1919-21; dir. county health work, Ga. State Bd. of Health, 1922-25; now chief Domestic Quarantine Div. (states relations div.), U.S. Pub. Health Service. Mem. Assn. of Mil. Surgeons, A.M.A., Am. Pub. Health Assn., Phi Sigma Kappa. Home: Woodside, Silver Spring, Md. Address: U.S. Public Health Service, Washington, D.C.

WALLEY, Harold L., real estate and ins.; b. New Kensington, Pa., Nov. 7, 1903; s. Harry C. and Rebecca A. (Peters) W.; ed. Mercersburg Acad., 1920-24, Grove City Coll., 1924-25; m. Grace E. Rowe, June 26, 1926; children—Harry C., Richard Lee. Engaged as individual on own acct. in real estate and ins. bus., New Kensington, Pa., since 1925. (Business organized, 1898.) Pres. New Kensington Y.M.C.A. Republican. Presbyn. (trustee 1st Presbyn. Ch.). I.O.O.F. Knights of Malta. Clubs: Kiwanis of New Kensington (sec.), Hill Crest Country, New Kensington Field Trial (pres.). Home: 442 Riverview Drive, New Kensington, Pa. Office: 510 Logan Bank Bldg., New Kensington, Pa.

WALLHAUSER, Andrew, physician; b. Newark, N.J., Nov. 11, 1892; s. Henry J. F. and Rachel A. (Vogt) W.; student Cornell U., 1912; M.D., Jefferson Med. Coll., Phila., 1916; grad. study, Columbia U., 1919-21; m. Isabel Park, Mar. 4, 1923; children—Jane Rachel, Mary Isabel. Asst. pathologist, Newark (N.J.) City Hosp., 1920-25, serologist, 1920-25; pathologist, Meth. Hosp., Indianapolis, Ind., 1925-26; became asst. prof. pathology, U. of Pittsburgh, Med. Sch., 1926, asst. prof. medicine, 1939; pathologist Presbyn. Hosp. of Pittsburgh since 1926, Woman's Hosp. since 1939. Served in Med. Corps, N.J.N.G., on Mexican border, 1916; lt. M.C., U.S.A., 1917-19, maj. N.J.N.G., 1919-25. Fellow Am. Coll. Physicians; mem. Soc. for Biol. Research, Clin. and Pathol. Soc., Acad. of Medicine of Pittsburgh, Phi Alpha Sigma. Republican. Episcopalian. Mason, Elk. Club: Oakmont Boat. Home: 226 Shady Av. Office: University of Pittsburgh, Pittsburgh, Pa.

WALLIS, Everett Stanley, univ. prof.; b. Waitsfield, Vt., Dec. 17, 1899; s. George Wilbur and Georgia Adelle (Bragg) W.; B.Sc., U. of Vt., 1921, M.Sc., same, 1922; A.M., Princeton, 1924, Ph.D., same, 1925; m. Mary Fletcher Northrop, of Burlington, Vt., June 26, 1926; 1 son, Peter Bent Brigham Northrop. Asst. prof. chemistry, St. John's Coll., Annapolis, Md., 1925-26, asso. prof. and head dept. chemistry, 1926-29; asst. prof. chemistry, Princeton U., 1929-34, asso. prof. since 1934. Fellow Am. Inst. of Chemists, A.A.A.S. Mem. Am. Chem. Soc., Alpha Tau Omega, Phi Beta Kappa, Sigma Xi. Awarded Charlotte Elizabeth Procter Fellowship Princeton U., 1924-25. Republican. Episcopalian. Asso. editor The Journal of Organic Chemistry. Contbr. chapter to Treatise of Organic Chemistry, edited by Henry Gilman, 1938. Contbr. over forty papers in field of organic chemistry. Home: 5 College Rd., Princeton, N.J.

WALLIS, William Ballantyne, mfr. electric furnaces; b. Pittsburgh, Pa., Apr. 13, 1888; s. John Irwin and Frances (Giberson) W.; grad. Pittsburgh Central High Sch., 1906; B.S., Pa. State Coll., 1911; m. Nell Meese Conley, Nov. 12, 1913. On test floor Westinghouse Electric & Mfg. Co., East Pittsburgh, 1909-10; engr. Idaho power companies, 1911-13; with West Penn Power Co., Pittsburgh, 1913-15; with W. E. Moore & Co., consulting engrs., Pittsburgh, 1915-19; asst. to gen. mgr. Jessop Steel Co.,

Washington, Pa., 1919-20; with Pittsburgh Lectromelt Furnace Co. since 1920, pres. since 1930; mng. dir. Lectromelt Furnaces of Can., Ltd. Mem. Am. Electro Chem. Soc., Am. Iron and Steel Inst., Am. Foundrymen's Assn., Steel Treaters Soc., Kappa Sigma. Republican. Presbyterian. Mason (K.T., 32°, Shriner). Clubs: Pittsburgh Athletic, University, Chartiers Heights Country (Pittsburgh); Nittany Country (Bellefonte); Machinery (New York). Home: 444 E. 52d St., New York, N.Y. Office: Foot of 32d St., Pittsburgh, Pa.

WALLS, Edgar Perkins, univ. prof.; b. Barclay, Md., Sept. 3, 1882; s. George David and Mary Augusta (Perkins) W.; B.S., Md. Agrl. Coll., College Park, 1903, M.S., 1905; student Johns Hopkins U., 1905-06; Ph.D., U. of Md., College Park, 1935; m. Olive Shreve Kimberlin, Dec. 19, 1910; 1 dau., Frances Lee (dec.). Asst. agronomist, Md. Expt. Sta., College Park, 1903-05; asst. prof. botany and plant pathology, Md. Agrl. Coll., College Park, 1908-09; prof. horticulture, St. Lawrence U., Canton, N.Y., 1909-10; instr. botany and plant pathology, Ore. Agrl. Coll., Corvallis, Ore., 1910-14; county agrl. agt., Talbot Co., Md., 1914-27; with Commercial Farm Management Work, 1927-31; asst. canning crops and marketing, Md. Extension Service, 1931-35; state leader rural discussion groups, 1935-37; canning crops specialist and asso. prof. canning crops tech., U. of Md., 1937-38; canning crops specialist and prof. canning crops, Hort. Dept. U. of Md., College Park, Md., since 1938. Mem. Sigma Xi, Phi Kappa Phi, Epsilon Sigma Phi. Democrat. Odd Fellow, K.P. Home: 3 Holly St., College Heights, Hyattsville, Md.

WALLS, John Abbet, electrical engr.; b. Lewisburg, Pa., Sept. 5, 1879; s. William Cameron and Anna Frick (Slifer) W.; B.S. in E.E., Mass. Institute Technology, 1899; (hon.) D.Sc., Bucknell University, 1931; m. Emmie H. Harman, Oct. 10, 1907. Pres. Pa. Water & Power Co. and Safe Harbor Water Power Corpn. (Baltimore). Dir. Pa. Water & Power Co., Safe Harbor Water Power Corpn., Eastern Rolling Mill Co. (all of Baltimore), Shawinigan Water & Power Co. (Montreal, Can.). Fellow Am. Inst. E.E.; mem. Am. Soc. C.E.; asso. mem. Canadian Inst. E.E. Club: Maryland. Home: 4 Beechdale Rd., Roland Park, Baltimore. Office: Lexington Bldg., Baltimore, Md.; also 40 Wall St., New York, N.Y.

WALLS, William Cameron, banking; b. Lewisburg, Pa., Jan. 27, 1852; s. John and Margaret (Green) W.; ed. Hill Sch., Pottstown Pa.; 1867-69; A.B. and A.M., Bucknell U., 1873; m. Anna Slifer, Nov. 19, 1878; children—John A., Dr. E. Slifer (deceased), Dorothy (Mrs. Harry McCormick). Engaged in business and banking since 1888; pres. Lewisburg Nat. bank since 1890; pres. Lewisburg and Tyrone R.R. Bridge Corpn. Trustee Bucknell Univ. Mem. Pa. Soc. S.R., Sigma Chi. Democrat. Affiliated with the Presbyterian Church. Home: 26 S. Third St. Office: 404 Market St., Lewisburg, Pa.

WALN, Amos Miller, lawyer; b. Yardville, N.J., Apr. 26, 1892; s. Henry Clay and Anna Maria (Miller) W.; direct desc. Nicholas W., who came with Wm. Penn on ship Welcome, 1682, from Chapelcroft, Eng.; through greatgrandmother, Maria Middleton, direct desc. Arthur M., a signer Declaration of Independence; student Trenton High Sch., 1910-11, N.J. State Model Sch., Trenton, 1912-13; m. Mary Katherine Bogden, Sept. 10, 1927. Studied law offices of W. Holt Apgar, 1914-15, and William E. Blackman, 1915-16, Trenton; admitted to N.J. bar as atty., 1916, as counselor, 1919; master in chancery, 1919, spl. master in chancery, 1937; solicitor for Hamilton Twp., largest twp. in U.S. since Jan. 1939; in practice alone at Trenton, N.J., since 1916; atty. The Yardville (N.J.) Nat. Bank since 1938. Mem. Mercer Co. Bar Assn. Republican. Mem. Friends Meeting. Club: Hamilton Township Republican League (White Horse, N.J.). Home: Allentown Rd., Yardville. Office: 2 N. Broad St., Trenton, N.J.

WALNUT, T. Henry, lawyer; b. Riverton, N. J., Sept. 4, 1879; s. Thomas H. and Katherine

P. (Durnell) W.; grad. Central High Sch., Phila.; student U. of Pa.; m. Flora Elderton, 1923; children—Thomas Henry, Francis K. Formerly counsel for Pa. Civil Service Reform; special asst. U.S. dist. atty. for Eastern Dist. of Pa., 1917-22; chmn. Pa. State Workmen's Compensation Bd., 1923-27; chmn. Occupational Diseases Commn., 1932-33. Mem. Pa. Legislature, 1911, 13 (elected on Keystone and Washington parties tickets). Mem. University Club, Phila. Home: 1 Lehman Lane. Office: 1420 Walnut St., Philadelphia, Pa.

WALSER, Henry, editor and publisher, Plain Speaker and Standard Sentinel. Office: 23 N. Wyoming St., Hazleton, Pa.

WALSH, Arthur, v.p. Thomas A. Edison, Inc.; b. Newark, N.J., Feb. 26, 1896; s. Michael Joseph and Mary Ann (Shane) W.; ed. Newark pub. schs., pvt. tutor and New York U. Sch. of Commerce; m. Agnes Mulvey, June 8, 1920; 1 dau., Barbara Louise. Began as concert violinist, 1915; recording violinist for Thomas A. Edison, 1915, later became advertising mgr., v.p. and gen. mgr. phonograph div., 1924-31, v.p. on gen. staff and dir. since 1931; on leave served as N.J. dir. Federal Housing Adminstrn., 1934-35, dep. adminstr., Washington, D.C., later asst. adminstr. since 1935; v.p. and dir. Edison Splitdorf Corpn., Thomas Alva Edison Foundation; dir. Edison Wood Products, Thomas A. Edison Ltd. (Can. and London), Lawyers Title Corpn. Served in U.S. Marine Corps during World War; lt. U.S. Naval Reserve, 1929-32. Mem. Alpha Kappa Psi. Democrat. Roman Catholic. Elk. Clubs: Baltusrol Golf (Springfield, N.J.); Essex (Newark, N.J.); Metropolitan (New York). Contbr. to business papers. Home: 332 Redmond Rd., South Orange, N.J. Office: West Orange, N.J.

WALSH, Basil Sylvester, insurance; b. Philadelphia, Pa., June 13, 1878; s. Daniel John and Mary E. (O'Connor) W.; ed. pub. schs., Phila.; m. Margaret A. Howlett, Mar. 1, 1905; children—Basil Francis (dec.), Ann (dec.), Daniel John, William David, Margaret May. Entered office Daniel J. Walsh's Sons, 1895, treas. since 1910; pres. Home Life Ins. Co. of America since 1912; pres. Home Protective Co., Urbaine Corpn., Mutual Guarantee Bldg. & Loan Assn., City Investment Co.; v.p. and treas. Glen Willow Ice Mfg. Co. Mem. Cath. Philopatrian Lit. Inst., Friendly Sons of St. Patrick. Republican. Catholic. Clubs: Seaview Golf (Absecon, N.J.); Phila. Country, Penn Athletic, Germantown Cricket, Bala Golf, Downtown. Home: City and Maple Avs., Bala-Cynwyd, Pa. Office: 504 Walnut St., Philadelphia, Pa.

WALSH, James Magarge, life ins. exec.; b. Phila., Pa., Sept. 18, 1897; s. James Edward and Marie Louise (Magarge) W.; grad. Wm. Penn Charter Sch., 1916, U. of Pa., 1920; m. Gladys Clothier Le Maistre, Jan. 31, 1918; 1 son, William Magarge. Asso. with Home Life Ins. Co. of Phila., Pa., continuously since 1920, mgr. mortgage dept. since 1924; v.p. City Investment Co.; dir. Home Protective Co., Urbaine Corpn., Daniel J. Walsh's Sons, Inc., Mutual Guarantee Bldg. & Loan Assn. Mem. Delta Kappa Epsilon. Republican. Roman Catholic. Clubs: Union League, Germantown Cricket, Philadelphia Country (Phila.). Home: N.W. Corner Laurel and Mulberry Lanes, Haverford, Pa. Office: 506 Walnut St., Philadelphia, Pa.

WALSH, John E., judge Municipal Court of Phila. since 1921. Address: Municipal Court, Philadelphia, Pa.

WALSH, Joseph, M.D.; b. Parsons, Pa., Oct. 28, 1870; s. Martin J. and Bridget (Golden) W.; A.B., Fordham U. 1890, A.M., 1893; M.D., U. of Pa., 1895; spl. med. studies in London, Paris, Vienna, Berlin, 1896-98; unmarried. Instr. clin. medicine and pathology, U. of Pa., 1898-1902; med. dir. White Haven Sanatorium, 1914-35, visiting physician since 1902; med. dir. St. Agnes' Hosp., 1911-18; now engaged in gen. practice of medicine, specializing in pulmonary tuberculosis. Served as capt. U.S. Army Med. Corps, 1918; comnding. officer U.S. Army Hosp. No. 17, 1918-19. Dir. Nat. Tuberculosis Assn., 1906-12; pres. Pa.

WALSH, Soc. for Prevention of Tuberculosis, 1905-07; mgr. Internat. Anti-Tuberculosis Assn., 1908-14. Fellow A.M.A., Coll. Physicians of Philadelphia. Democrat. Catholic. Club: Penn Athletic. Writer numerous articles, treatises and papers on pulmonary tuberculosis, etc. Home: Penn Athletic Club, 225 S. 18th St. Office: 521 Medical Arts Bldg., 16th and Walnut Sts., Philadelphia, Pa.

WALSH, Lester A.; prof. exptl. therapeutics, Temple U. Address: Broad St. and Montgomery Av., Philadelphia, Pa.

WALSH, Matthew John, educator and adminstr.; b. Grand Rapids, Mich., March 3, 1872; s. Hugh and Lucy (Lynch) W.; A.B., U. of Mich., 1898; A.M., Columbia, 1916; hon. Pd.D., Westminster Coll., 1933; hon. Litt. D., St. Francis Coll., 1934; m. Mary Louise Gilchriese, June 28, 1910; 1 dau., Frances Mary. Engaged in teaching and as prin. high schs. and supt. schs. at various places in Mich., 1899-1915; prof. edn., Extension Dept. Ohio Univ., 1916-20; head dept. edn., State Normal Sch. and State Teachers Coll., Indiana, Pa., 1920-27; dean of instrn., State Teachers Coll., Indiana, Pa. since 1927, actg. pres., June-Dec. 1936; dir. First Nat. Bank. Mem. Nat. Edn. Assn., Nat. Soc. for Sci. Study Edn., Pa. Edn. Assn. Republican. Presbyn. Mason (32°, Shriner). Club: Rotary. Author: Teaching as a Profession; Its Ethical Standards, 1926; co-author (with Louise G. Walsh) History and Organization of Education in Pennsylvania, 1931. Contbr. arts. and book reviews. Home: 282 S. 7th St., Indiana, Pa.

WALSH, Richard John, author, pub.; b. Lyons, Kan., Nov. 20, 1886; s. Joseph H. and Elizabeth (Haslam) W.; A.B., Harvard, 1907; m. Ruby Hopkins Abbott, Sept. 26, 1908 (divorced, 1935); children—Natalie Abbott, Richard John, Elizabeth; m. 2d, Pearl Sydenstricker Buck, June 11, 1935; adopted children—Richard Stulting, John Stulting, Jean Comfort, Edgar Sydenstricker. Served as reporter Boston Herald, 1907-09; asst. sec. Boston Chamber of Commerce, 1909-12; promotion mgr. Curtis Pub. Co., 1912-16; adv. writer, 1917-22; editor Collier's Weekly, 1922-24; pres. John Day Co., pubs., 1926—; asso. editor Judge, 1927-33; editor Asia Mag., 1933 —; pres. Editorial Publications, Inc., 1935—. Mem. staff U.S. Food Administration, 1917-18. First pres. and hon. mem. Art Director's Club; mem. Council on Foreign Relations. Clubs: Harvard, Players, Century, Dutch Treat (New York). Author: Kidd (verse), 1922; The Making of Buffalo Bill (with Milton S. Salsbury), 1928; also articles and fiction in mags. Home: Hilltown Twp., Bucks Co., Pa. Office: 40 E. 49th St., New York, N.Y.

WALSH, Thomas Joseph, bishop; b. Parker's Landing, Butler Co., Pa., Dec. 6, 1873; s. Thomas and Helen (Curtin) W.; ed. College and Sem. of St. Bonaventure (Allegany, N.Y.), U. of St. Appolinaris, the Pontifical Roman Sem., Rome, Italy, receiving S.T.D. and J.C.D.; LL. D., St. Bonaventure, 1913. Ordained priest R. C. Ch., 1900; 3d asst. rector St. Joseph's Cathedral, Buffalo, N.Y., Jan.-June 1909; pvt. sec. to Bishops Quigley and Colton, 1900-15, also chancellor of the diocese; rector St. Joseph's old Cathedral, 1915-18, and reapptd. chancellor of the diocese upon installation of Bishop Dougherty, serving 1916-18; consecrated bishop Diocese of Trenton, July 25, 1918; made asst. at Pontifical Throne, Mar. 13, 1922; transferred to See of Newark, Mar. 7, 1928; apptd. first archbishop of Newark, Dec. 11, 1937. Address: 552 S. Orange Av., South Orange, N.J.*

WALSH, Van Wormer, travel lecturer; b. Ceres, N.Y., Oct. 5, 1893; s. Dr. Frank Alfred and Edith (Van Wormer) W.; B.S., Harvard, 1917; grad. student at U. of Pa., Cornell, U. of Chicago, Jefferson Med. Coll. (Phila.), U. of Cincinnati, Oxford U. (Eng.); m. Edith Weston, Aug. 17, 1917 (divorced); 1 son, Van Wormer. Has traveled in all countries of the world except Persia, Siam, Tibet; lectures before univs., museums, forums, schools and clubs. Served with A.E.F., in France, 1917-19. Mem. Pi Eta (Harvard), Nu Sigma Nu. Republican. Club: Art Alliance (Phila.). Contbr. to periodicals. Home: 128 E. 7th St., Erie, Pa. Office: 418 S. 20th St., Philadelphia, Pa.

WALSH, William Concannon, lawyer; b. Cumberland, Md., Apr. 2, 1890; s. William Edward and Mary (Concannon) W.; A.B., Mt. Saint Mary's Coll., Emmitsburg, Md., 1910; LL.B., Cath. Univ. Law Sch., Washington, D.C., 1913; (hon.) LL.D., Mt. Saint Mary's Coll., 1930; m. Sarah Elizabeth Nee, June 1, 1929; children—William, Sarah Elizabeth. Admitted to Md. bar 1913 and engaged in practice at Cumberland since 1913 except when otherwise engaged; served as city atty., 1920-21; asso. judge 4th jud. circuit Md., 1921, chief judge and mem. ct. appeals Md., 1924-26; mem. firm Walsh, Hughes, Heskett & Williams, 1922-24; state ins. commr. Md., 1931-35; atty. gen. Md. for term 1938-42; mem. bd. dirs. Liberty Trust Co., Cumberland, since 1922, counsel since 1935; dir. W. T. Coulehan & Bro., Inc., Cumberland. Served as pvt. and corpl. inf. Md. N.G. on Mexican border, 1916; sergt. to 1st lt. inf., U.S.A., 1917-19, with A.E.F. in France. Del. to Dem. Nat. Convs., 1924-32; chmn. Dem. state conv., 1922. Mem. exec. com. Cumberland Community Chest, 1930-32; mem. bd. dirs. Allegany Hosp., Cumberland, Md. Mem. Am., Md. State, Allegany Co. bar assns. Democrat. Roman Catholic. K.C. Elk. Club: Country. Home: 601 Washington St. Office: Liberty Trust Bldg., Cumberland, Md.

WALTEMYER, William Claude, clergyman, coll. prof.; b. Beckleysville, Md., Apr. 27, 1889; s. Joseph and K. Jane (Royston) W.; A.B., Gettysburg Coll., 1908; B.D., Gettysburg Theol. Sem., 1911; A.M., Am. Univ., Washington, D.C., 1925, Ph.D., 1929; m. Mildred Butzler, Sept. 5, 1911; children—Miriam Esther, M. Ruth (wife of Rev. Edward McHale), Charlotte L., William C., Jr., Grace V., Jeanne F. Ordained to ministry Lutheran Ch., 1911; pastor, Landisville, Pa., 1911-13, Butler, Pa., 1913-16, Thurmont, Md., 1916-23, Washington, D.C., 1923-29; asso. prof. philosophy, Gettysburg Coll., 1929-30, prof. English Bible since 1930. Served as chaplain, 1st lt., C.A.C., U.S.A., 1918-19, at coast defenses of Boston and with A.E.F. Mem. Phi Beta Kappa, Phi Sigma Kappa, Kappa Phi Kappa. Republican. Lutheran. Mason. Home: 251 Springs Av., Gettysburg, Pa.

WALTER, Francis Eugene, congressman; b. Easton, Pa., May 26, 1894; s. Robley D. and Susie E. W.; student Princeton Prep. Sch., 1910-12, Lehigh U., 1912-14; A.B., George Washington U.; LL.B., Georgetown U., 1919; m. May M. Doyle, Dec. 19, 1925; children—Barbara, Constance, Jane (dec.). Admitted Pa. bar, 1919; in practice at Easton, 1919-27; solicitor Northampton Co., 1928-33; mem. 73d to 76th Congresses (1933-41), 21st Pa. Dist. Ensign Naval Aviation Res. Corps. Trustee Easton Hosp. Mem. Delta Theta, Phi Alpha Delta. Democrat. Lutheran. Mem. Elks, I.O.O.F., Jr. Order United Am. Mechanics, Eagles. Home: 806 Hamilton St. Office: Drake Bldg., Easton, Pa.

WALTER, Howard Kelly, lawyer; b. Sharpsburg, Pa., June 16, 1891; s. George Leonard and Bella Sarah (Kelly) W.; student Kiskimmetas Sch., Saltsburg, Pa., 1906-10; A.B., Cornell U., 1914; LL.B., Harvard Law Sch., 1917; m. Alison McEldowney, Jan. 1, 1923; children—Allen Guthrie (dec.), George Leonard, Geoffrey Ransom, Gregory Philip. Admitted to Pa. bar, 1919, and since practiced at Pittsburgh. Served in U.S. Army with A.E.F., 1917-19. Dir. and v.p. Children's Aid Soc. of Allegheny Co., Allegheny Co. Industrial Training Sch. for Boys. Mem. Pa. Bar Assn., Allegheny Co. Bar Assn., Zeta Psi. Republican. Presbyterian. Mason (32°). Clubs: Duquesne, Pittsburgh Athletic, Harvard-Yale-Princeton, Cornell, Rolling Rock, Fox Chapel Golf (Pittsburgh); Camp Fire (New York). Home: 5256 Wilkins Av. Office: First Nat. Bank Bldg., Pittsburgh, Pa.

WALTER, Martha artist; b. Phila.; d. George H. and Martha (Crawford) W.; studied at Pa. Acad. Fine Arts, Phila.; Julian Acad., Paris; also pvtly., under masters abroad. Exhibited in Salon, Paris, 1909, and since in prin. ann. exhbns. in cities of U.S.; one-man exhbns. in most of museums of America; awarded Toppan prize and Cresson Traveling Scholarship, Pa. Acad. Fine Arts, Mary Smith prize, 1909, gold medal, Fellowship Pa. Acad. Fine Arts, 1923; awarded prize Nat. Assn. Women Painters and Sculptors Exhibition, 1915. Represented in Toledo (O.) Mus. of Art, Fellowship of Pa. Acad. Fine Arts permanent collection, Pa. Acad. of Fine Arts, Norfolk Art Soc., Cedar Rapids (Ia.) Art Mus., Milwaukee (Wis.) Art Mus., Art Inst. of Chicago, Luxembourg Mus., Paris, etc. Painter of many portraits, including Queen of Spain, and genre subjects, notably a historic series of Ellis Island subjects. Formerly teacher of portrait painting in N.Y. Sch. of Art in New York and in Paris; also taught classes in Brittany. Home: (summer) 7535 Mill Rd., Melrose Park, Pa. Address: Van Dyck Studios, 939 Eighth Av., New York, N.Y.

WALTER, Paul Chamberlain, physician; b. Harrisburg, Pa., June 25, 1897; s. Harry Bushey and Sarah Amelia (Chamberlain) W.; B.S., Princeton, 1919; M.D., Johns Hopkins Med. Sch., 1923; m. E. Gertrude Brenner, June 24, 1926; 1 son, Paul Chamberlain. Interne, Church Home and Infirmary, Baltimore, Md., 1923-24; in gen. practice of medicine and surgery at Harrisburg, Pa., since 1924; mem. surg. staff Harrisburg Hosp.; chief med. insp., pub. schs. Harrisburg, Pa. Served in F.A., Central Officers Training Sch., Camp Taylor, Ky., 1918. Mem. A.M.A., Pa. State and Dauphin Co. med. socs., Key and Seal of Princeton. Republican. Presbyterian. Mason (32°). Rowed on varsity crew at Princeton two yrs. Home: 1317 N. 3d St., Harrisburg, Pa.

WALTER, Valerie H(arrisse), sculptor; b. Baltimore, Md.; d. M. R. and Bertha (Ulman) W.; student Mrs. Lefevre's School Peabody Conservatory of Music, Md. Inst. of Art, Art Students' League; studied under Augustus Lukeman. Exhibited at San Francisco World Fair, 1922, Pa. Acad., Archl. League, Nat. Sculpture Soc., Southern Arts League, etc. Works: Dr. Nicholas Sbarounis (Greek Army), Gen. Umberto Nobile (designed and pilot Norge), Dr. Carl Von Noorden (Vienna physician), Dr. W. F. Swann (scientist), Dr. de Amezaga (Genoa, physician), Dr. Robert Underwood (former ambassador to Italy), Chief Justice William Howard Taft; many studies of Negroes, Indians; statuettes of Charley Paddock (runner), Bill Tilden (tennis champion), Dorothy Snell (skater), etc.; also fountains, animals, and decorative pieces. Awarded medal, Corcoran Gallery of Art, 1934. Served in First Nat. Service Sch., Washington, D.C., 1916, Mil. Intelligence, 1918. Clubs: L'Hirondelle, Hamilton Street, Ice (Baltimore). Home: Brightside Rd., Woodbrook, Baltimore, Md.

WALTERS, Albert W., mcht., lumber and bldg. materials; b. Johnstown, Pa., June 25, 1893; s. John W. and Emma (Krebs) W.; ed. Lawrenceville (N.J.) Sch., 1910-11; A.B., Princeton, 1915; m. Harriet Jacobs, of Akron, O., June 16, 1917; children—Phyllis E., John W. II. Engaged in lumber business since 1915; mem. firm John W. Walters Co., lumber and bldg. materials, Johnstown, Pa., since 1921; dir. United States Nat. Bank; vice-pres. and dir. Friendly City Federal Savings & Loan Assn., First Federal Savings & Loan Assn. Served in F.A., O.T.C., Camp Taylor, Ky., 1918. Dir. Johnstown Chamber of Commerce. Republican. Presbyn. (trustee Westmont Ch.). Mem. Am. Legion, Pa. Soc. of New York. Clubs: Sunnehanna Country (vice-pres.), Bachelor (Johnstown); Harvard-Yale-Princeton (Pittsburgh). Home: 432 Orchard St. Office: 407 Lincoln St., Johnstown, Pa.

WALTERS, Evan Whitelaw, pres. Phoenix Silk Corpn.; b. Catasauqua, Pa., Dec. 7, 1891; s. John E. and Adah (Matchette) W.; student Lehigh U., Bethlehem, Pa.; m. Alice Burgess, Apr. 30, 1913; children—Barbara B., Richard S., Evan Whitelaw. Sales engr., Scranton (Pa.) Electric Constrn. Co., 1915-23; engr., Phoenix Silk Mfg. Co., Allentown, Pa., 1923-26, v.p. and gen. mgr., 1926-34, pres., 1934-38; pres.

and dir., Phoenix Silk Corpn., Allentown, Pa., since 1938. Mason. Club: Lehigh Country. Home: 25 S. West St. Office: Race and Court Sts., Allentown, Pa.

WALTERS, John W., banker and lumber mcht.; b. Llangadock, Wales, Oct. 16, 1861; s. Rev. Philip and Magdalene (Thomas) W.; came to U.S., 1883, and naturalized citizen; student pub. schs. nr. Swansea Wales and Arnold Coll.; m. Emma Krebs, Dec. 20, 1888; children—Winifred M., Albert W., Margaret (wife of Dr. F. A. Hager), J. Philip. Engaged in lumber business since 1884; mem. firm Thomas & Walters, 1884-96, propr., 1896-1921, mem. firm with two sons as John W. Walters Co., lumber and bldg. materials, Johnstown, Pa., since 1921; pres. Penn. Traffic Co., 1911-32; pres. Friendly City Savings & Loan Assn., 1922-32; pres. United States Nat. Bank, Johnstown, Pa., since 1933; trustee Johnstown Savings Bank. Mem. exec. com. Pa. State Y.M.C.A.; treas. Johnstown Y.M.C.A.; dir. Conemaugh Valley Memorial Hosp. Republican. Presbyterian (elder Westmont Ch.). Clubs: Bachelors, Sunnehanna Country (Johnstown, Pa.). Nearest living desc. of the great Welsh hymnologist, William Williams, Pantyceln, Wales, author, among other hymns, of "Guide me, oh thou Great Jehovah." Home: 433 Orchard St. Office: 407 Lincoln St., Johnstown, Pa.

WALTERS, Rea Gillespie, prof. commerce; b. Baltimore, Md., Jan. 22, 1888; s. Jacob Harry and Emma (Shuman) W.; student U. of Pittsburgh; B.S. in commerce, U. of Cincinnati; m. Rose M. Schall, 1909; 1 dau., Rose Emma. Engaged as teacher in bus. schs., New York City and Albany, teacher and prin. high sch., Aspinwall, Pittsburgh, Pa., instr. marketing subjects, East Liberty Y.M.C.A., Pittsburgh, 1912-14; prof. commerce, Grove City Coll., 1919-27; instr. marketing subjects, Oil City and Butler Y.M.C.A., 1925-27; asst. sales mgr. and adv. mgr., South-Western Pub. Co., Cincinnati, O., 1927-30; lecturer in marketing, U. of Cincinnati, 1929-30; personnel officer, Grove City Coll., 1930-39. Former mem. Rep. State Com. past pres. Grove City Commercial Club. Pres. Grove City Rotary Club. Dir. Grove City Hosp. Former trustee Pa. Soldiers Orphan Sch. Past pres. Nat. Commercial Teachers Federation, tri State Commercial Edn. Assn., Nat. Assn. Commercial Teacher Training Instns. Mem. Eastern Commercial Teachers Assn., Pi Gamma Mu. Republican. Methodist. Mason. Author: High School Commercial Education, 1922; Fundamentals of Selling, 1928; One Hundred Lessons in Spelling, 1914; Fundamentals of Retailing (with E. J. Rowse), 1931; Word Studies, 1937. Contbr. nearly 75 articles to various ednl. jours. Home: 530 Stewart Av., Grove City, Pa.

WALTERSDORF, Maurice Cleveland, economics; b. Hanover, Pa., Feb. 15, 1888; s. John Franklin and Alverta Jane (Sterner) W.; grad. Shippensburg State Normal Sch. (now Shippensburg State Teachers Coll.), 1911; grad. Perkiomen Sch., 1914; A.B., Franklin and Marshall Coll., 1916; A.M., Princeton, 1922, Ph.D., 1925; m. Catherine Elizabeth Crapster, Sept. 13, 1924; 1 son, John Maurice. Teacher pub. schs., Pa., 1908-09; prin. Glendola (N.J.) Sch., 1911-13; instr. of English, Perkiomen Sch., 1913-14; instr. and asst. registrar Mercersburg Acad., 1916-21; instr. Hun Sch., Princeton, N.J., 1921-24; asst. prof. economics, Washington and Jefferson Coll., 1924-27, prof. and head of department since 1927, sec. of the faculty since 1928, also sec. of Athletic Council since 1937; assisted State Budget Bureau in making survey of state and local taxation in Pa., 1934. Mem. Washington-Greene Counties Council, Boy Scouts of America, 1928-32; mem. Nat. Com. on Economic Guidance, Lions Internat., 1933; mem. Advisory Bd., Am. Economic Foundation, 1935; mem. Nat. Fed. for Economic Stabilization. Mem. Am. Economic Assn., Am. Assn. for Advancement of Labor Legislation, Am. Assn. Univ. Profs., Pi Gamma Mu, Lambda Chi Alpha; hon. mem. Eugene Field Soc. Presbyn. Clubs: Fortnightly, Lions (formerly dir., v.p. and pres.). Author: Regulation of Public Utilities in New Jersey, 1935. Contbr. to Am. Economic Rev., Nat. Municipal Rev., Yale Law Jour., Social Science, Economic Jour. (Eng.), Bull. Nat. Tax Assn., Public Utility Fortnightly, and other mags., also the press. Home: 417 Locust Av., Washington, Pa.

WALTON, Charles Spittall, Jr., leather tanner; b. St. Davis, Pa., July 26, 1893; s. Charles Spittall and Martha (England) W.; grad. Haverford Sch., 1911; B.S., U. of Pa., 1915; m. May Potts, Apr. 1, 1915; children—Virginia, Barbara. Asso. with Chas. S. Walton & Co., Inc., tanners, Phila. and Baltimore, since 1915, now pres. and dir; dir. Philadelphia Bourse, Central-Penn Nat. Bank., Wayne (Pa.) Title & Trust Co., Am. Baptist Pub. Society (Phila.). Pres. and dir. Phila. Y.M.C.A.; dir. Neighborhood League; dir. and trustee Bapt. Orphanage, Phila.; dir. Garrett Williamson Home. Trustee and chmn. finance com. Eastern Bapt. Theol. Sem. (Phila.); trustee Evans Dental Inst. at U. of Pa.; life trustee Tanners Research Foundation at U. of Cincinnati. Mem. Polit. Science Acad., Colonial Soc. of Pa., Phi Delta Theta. Republican. Baptist (trustee Central Bapt. Ch., Wayne, Pa.). Mason. Clubs: Union League, Penn Athletic (Philadelphia); Merion Cricket (Haverford); Everglades (Palm Beach, Fla.). Home: St. Davids, Pa. Office: 306 N. 3d St., Philadelphia, Pa.

WALTON, George Arthur, educator; b. Cochranville, Pa., Aug. 23, 1883; s. Joseph Solomon and Dora Elizabeth (Brosius) W.; grad. Friends Central Sch., Phila., Pa. 1900; A.B., U. of Pa., 1904, A.M., 1907; grad. study, Columbia and Union Theol. Sem., 1906-07; m. Emily Williams Ingram, Sept. 20, 1906; children—Margaret Brosius (Mrs. Dan. H. L. Jensen), Alice Ingram (Mrs. Aymar K. Allison), Ruth Pusey (Mrs. C. Douglas Darling), Jean Brosius, Dora Elizabeth. Teacher Latin, history, Friends Sch., Wilmington, Del., 1904-06; instr. in English, U. of Pa., 1907-08; teacher of English, George Sch., Pa., 1908-12, prin. since 1912. Clerk Phila. Yearly Meeting, Soc. of Friends, 1926-32; vice chmn. Friends Council on Edn. since 1936; chmn. independent schools advisory com., Educational Records Bureau, since 1938. Mem. N.E.A., Headmasters' Assn., Headmasters' Club of Phila. Dist. Address: George School, Pa.

WALTON, George Willever, prof. botany and geology, coll. dean; b. Irvington, N.J., Oct. 9, 1892; s. Harry Ellsworth and Sarah Jane (Kingsbury) W.; Ph.B., Lafayette Coll., 1915; M.S., Cornell U., 1924; grad. study, Cornell U., 1928, U. of Pa., 1931 (both summers); (hon.) D.Sc., Albright Coll., 1936; m. Ada Mae Kreidler Oct. 19, 1917; children—Richard Kreidler, Margaret Jane. Engaged in teaching natural sci., high schl., Sunbury, Pa., 1915-17; prof. biology and geology, Albright Coll., 1917-28, prof. botany and geology and coll. dean since 1928. Fellow A.A.A.S. Mem. Eastern-Assn. Coll. Deans & Advisers of Men, Pa. Edn. Assn., Pa. Acad. Sci. (charter mem.), Rittenhouse Astron. Soc. Phila., Phi Beta Kappa (pres. Reading Chapter 1939). Republican. Mem. Evang. Ch. I.O.O.F. Club: Torch of Reading. Home: 1426 Palm St., Reading, Pa.

WALTON, James Farley, banker; b. Pittsburgh, Pa., Aug. 23, 1888; s. John Fawcett and Annie (Farley) W.; student Phillips Exeter Acad., Exeter, N.H., 1905-06; Ph.B., Sheffield Scientific Sch., Yale, 1909; m. Bessie Scott, Jan. 2, 1913; children—Betty Scott, James Scott. Began as apprentice Mackintosh-Hemphill Co., Pittsburgh, Pa., 1909, and successively with Fort Pitt Spring Works, Mesta Machine Co., Harbison-Walker Refractories Co.; with Fidelity Trust Co., Pittsburgh, since 1914, treas. since 1934; dir. Allegheny Valley Trust Co., Verona, Pa.; sec. and treas. North Maryland Coal Mining Co., Johnstown, Pa.; v.p. and dir. East Pittsburgh Improvement Co. Dir., v.p. and treas. Travelers Aid Soc.; asst. treas. and dir. Eye and Ear Hosp. Mem. Berzelius Soc. (Yale). Republican. Presbyterian. Clubs: Fox Chapel Golf, Harvard-Yale-Princeton (Pittsburgh); Shawnee Country (Shawnee-on-Delaware). Home: 5325 Ellsworth Av. Office: Fidelity Trust Co., Pittsburgh, Pa.

WALTON, Joseph T. J., pres. Samuel Walton Co.; b. Bellevue, Pa., Oct. 17, 1886; s. Samuel and Carrie M. (Johnston) W.; student East Liberty Acad., Rensselaer Poly. Inst. (Troy, N.Y.); m. Clare N. Hutchins, Sept. 26, 1931. Pres. and dir. Samuel Walton Co., Pittsburgh; trustee Estate of Samuel Walton, deceased. Served as lt. Q.M.C., U.S. Army, 1918, in office of Chief of the Forage Branch, Q.M. Gen.'s Office, Chicago, 1918. Mem. Bellevue (Pa.) Masonic Hall Assn. (pres. and dir.), Chi Phi. Mason. Home: 3 S. Euclid Av., Bellevue, Pa. Office: 608 Empire Bldg., Pittsburgh, Pa.

WALTON, William Randolph, entomologist; b. Brooklyn, N.Y., Sept. 23, 1873; s. Walter and Susan (MacArdell) W.; ed. pub. schs. and Stevenson Sch. of Art, Pittsburgh, Pa., 1904-05 (prize student); m. Mary Agnes Becher, June 9, 1904; children—Walter F., M. Margaret, Wm. R., Henry V., John M. Telegraph operator Erie R.R., 1890; later with engring. depts. various rys., N.Y. and Pa., and with engring, firms until 1906; specialist and artist, Pa. State Div. Economic Zoölogy, Harrisburg, Pa., 1906-10; with Bur. Entomology, U.S. Dept. Agr., since Oct. 1, 1910; entomologist in charge cereal and forage insect investigations, 1917-23, now sr. entomologist. Specializes in dipterology, families of Syrphidæ, Asilidæ, and Tachinidæ. Fellow Entomol. Soc. America, A.A.A.S.; mem. Entomol. Soc. Washington (editor), Am. Assn. Econ. Entomologists, Entomol. Soc. France. Author of many illustrated papers on taxonomy of the Muscoidean and other flies, including an illustrated glossary of terms used in describing them, also of publs. on insects affecting cereal and forage crops. Home: Hyattsville, Md. Address: U.S. Bureau Entomology and Plant Quarantine, Washington, D.C.

WALTZ, John Buckley, banking; b. Chicago, Ill., Jan. 27, 1886; s. Joseph and Hannah (Crabtree) W.; student pub. schs., Brown Prep. Sch.; m. Mary L. Roddy, July 31, 1914; children—Mary Louise, John Buckley, Jr., Donald Henry, Robert G. Began as clk. with Commonwealth Title Ins. and Trust Co., 1900; clk. Market St. Title and Trust Co., and successively asst. title officer, title officer, then exec. vice-pres., 1911-30; merged with Integrity Trust Co., 1930, and vice-pres. since 1930; dir. Commonwealth Title Co. of Phila. Republican. Union League (Philadelphia); Aronimink Golf (Newtown Square). Home: 220 Cedarbrook Rd., Merion Golf Manor, Ardmore, Pa. Office: 4 S. 52d St., Philadelphia, Pa.

WALTZINGER, Fredrick John, lawyer; b. Newark, N.J., Apr. 18, 1899; s. William Benjamin and Anna (Mutz) W.; A.B., Lafayette Coll., 1921; LL.B., N.J. Law Sch. now Newark U., 1925; A.M., Lafayette Coll., 1931; m. Edna Marie Scheller, Oct. 3, 1928; children—Fredrick John III, George William. Engaged in teaching, pub. schs., 1921-24, prin., 1922-23; admitted to N.J. bar as atty., 1924, counsellor, 1927; engaged in gen. practice of law at Newark since 1924. Mem. Am., N.J. State and Essex Co. bar assns., Delta Tau Delta. Mem. Alumni Council Lafayette Coll., Social Service Bureau, Newark (trustee). Republican. Presbyn. Mason. Clubs: Down Town of Newark (trustee); Rock Spring (West Orange). Author: New Jersey Probate Practice, 2 vols., 1931; Replevin in New Jersey, 1934. Editor, N.J. Advanced Reports & Weekly Law Review since 1930. Home: 9 Colgate Rd., Maplewood. Office: 810 Broad St., Newark, N.J.

WALZAK, LEO A.; prof. periodontia, U. of Md. Address: University of Maryland, College Park, Md.

WAMPOLE, Harry Ziegler, pres. Telford Nat. Bank; b. Lederach, Pa., Sept. 10, 1877; s. Henry Strunk and Elizabeth Thompson (Ziegler) W.; ed. West Chester Teachers' Coll.; m. Elura Myers Gerhart, Jan. 19, 1918; children—Catherine, Gladys, Harry K. Teacher country sch., Milford Twp., Bucks Co., Pa., 1895-96; prin. West Telford Schs., Montgomery Co., Pa., 1896-1910; postmaster, West Telford, 1910-30; pres. and dir. Telford Nat. since 1908; dir. and sec. Citizen's Bldg. & Loan Assn. Mem. Pa. Ho. of Reps., 1937-38. Republican. Mem. Reformed Ch. Mason (32°). Address: 182 W. Broad St., Telford, Pa.

WANTZ, James Pearre, banking; b. Westminster, Md., Apr. 30, 1879; s. Charles Valentine and Caroline Virginia (Pearre) W.; student Western Md. Coll., Westminster, 1894-98; m. Carrie E. Rinehart, Nov. 17, 1903; children—Caroline Rinehart (Mrs. David H. Taylor), James Pearre, Jr. Employed as bank clk., 1898-1900; gen. bookkeeper, Union Nat. Bank, Westminster, Md., 1900-13, cashier, 1913-39, pres. since 1939; gen. agt. Maryland Casualty Co. since 1903; dir. B. F. Shriver Co. Served as vice-pres. Western Md. Coll. since 1930. Pres. bd. edn. Carroll Co., 1916-32. Democrat. Methodist (mem. bd. stewards). Mason (K.T., Shriner). Clubs: Westminster Rotary, Westminster Chamber of Commerce (pres. 1939). Home: 179 W. Main St. Office: 111 E. Main St., Westminster, Md.

WAPPAT, Blanche King Smith (Mrs. Fred William Wappat), librarian; b. Pittsburgh, Pa., Sept. 19, 1889; d. James Alexander and Sue (Thompson) Smith; diploma, Carnegie Library Sch., Carnegie Inst., Pittsburgh, 1919; m. Fred William Wappat, Aug. 2, 1911. Library asst., Carnegie Library, Pittsburgh, 1910-13, Cleveland Pub. Library, 1910; librarian Sch. of Applied Design, Pittsburgh, 1913-19; librarian Carnegie Inst. Tech., 1920-29; spl. lecturer, Carnegie Library Sch., 1930-31. Mem. A.L.A., Spl. Library Assn., Pa. Library Assn., Pittsburgh Library Club. Episcopalian. Originator of spl. methods and details of administration for art libraries. Sec. 1st organized meeting of art reference librarians, A.L.A. Conf., 1924. Compiler: Bibliography of Mosaics, 1919. Contbr. to Special Libraries Mag. and other professional publs. Home: "Cleeve Hill," Macon Av., Pittsburgh, Pa.

WAPPAT, Fred William, mfr. electric tools; b. Pittsburgh, Pa., May 22, 1886; s. William and Isabell (Scarth) W.; ed. Pittsburgh public schools; m. Blanche King Smith, Aug. 2, 1911. Shop manager Fawcus Machine Co., 1909-13; factory mgr. Pittsburgh Gage & Supply Co., 1913-17; private research, 1917-18; pres. and mgr. Wappat Gear Works (later Wappat, Inc., now Fred W. Wappat), mfr. portable electric tools, since 1918; vice-pres. and dir. Waverly Oil Works Co.; dir. All Penn Oil & Gas Co. Republican. Episcopalian. Mason. Inventor of electrical domestic appliances, portable electric tools, pressure regulating and relief valves. Home: 967 Macon Av. Office: 7325 Penn Av., Pittsburgh, Pa.

WARBURTON, Clyde William, agronomist; b. Independence, Ia., Dec. 7, 1879; s. William Henry and Ellen Clarissa (Irvine) W.; B.S. in Agr., Ia. State Coll. Agr. and Mechanic Arts, 1902, D.Sc., 1925; m. Anne Eliza Draper, Oct. 16, 1907. With U.S. Dept. Agr. since 1903, except 1911-12; successively assistant agr., Office of Farm Management, 1903-07, in charge oat investigations, Bur. Plant Industry, 1907-10, and 1912-20, in charge cereal agronomy experiments, 1920-23, dir. extension work, U.S. Dept. Agr. since Sept. 1923; editor book dept. Webb Pub. Co., St. Paul, Minn., 1911-12. Fellow A.A.A.S.; mem. American Soc. Agronomy (sec. 1915-18, pres. 1925), Washington Academy Science, Washington Bot. Soc., Beta Theta Pi, Phi Kappa Phi, Gamma Sigma Delta (pres. Nat. Council, 1925-26). Episcopalian. Club: Cosmos. Author (with A. D. Wilson) Field Corps, 1912. Editor Jour. Am. Soc. Agronomy, 1915-21. Home: 20 W. Lenox St., Chevy Chase, Md.

WARD, Alger Luman, research chemist; b. Easthampton, Mass., May 4, 1890; s. Oscar and Ella Jeanette (Alexander) W.; grad. Williston Acad., Easthampton, 1910; B.S. in chemistry, Syracuse (N.Y.) U., 1914, M.S., 1915; m. Emma Undritz, June 5, 1915. Research chemist for E. I. du Pont de Nemours & Co., 1915-20, discovering processes for synthesis of acetic acid, acetone, alkyl anilines, ethylene glycol and glycerine, covered by basic Am. and foreign patents; research chemist for United Gas Improvement Co., Phila., 1920-34; mgr. chem. labs. United Gas Improvement Co. since 1934. Principal work in physical properties, separation and polymerization of hydrocarbons; cause and prevention of formation of liquid-phase and vapor-phase gums in gas distribution systems (basic Am. and foreign patents); metal corrosion. Discoverer and exponent (with S. S. Kurtz, Jr.) the Refractivity Intercept. Awarded Louis E. Levy medal Franklin Inst. 1938. Mem. Franklin Inst., Am. Chem. Soc., Am. Gas Assn., Am. Petroleum Inst., Soc. of Chem. Industry, Sigma Beta, Alpha Chi Sigma. Republican. Episcopalian (vestryman St. Clement's Ch., Phila.). Contbr. and hon. asso. editor The Science of Petroleum, 1938. Contbr. numerous tech. articles to professional jours. Home: 818 N. Ormond Av., Drexel Hill, Pa. Office: United Gas Improvement Co., 319 Arch St., Philadelphia, Pa.

WARD, Arthur Edward, music edn. dir.; b. Syracuse, N.Y., Feb. 19, 1893; s. Joseph Morton and Sarah Jane (Skelton) W.; student Solvay (N.Y.) High Sch., 1909-13, Cornell U., summer 1919, Eastman Sch., Rochester, N.Y., 1922-24, under Frederick Hayward (voice), New York, 1925-26; B.Ped., Syracuse (N.Y.) U., 1917; m. Florence Elizabeth Howard, Sept. 17, 1917; children—Elizabeth Mary, Howard Edward, Richard Arthur. Dir. choirs in Syracuse (N.Y.) chs., 1911-17; dir. of music, pub. schs. in Panama C.Z., 1918-19, Iron Mountain, Mich., 1919-20, Sault Ste. Marie, Mich., 1920-22; teacher of vocal music, East High Sch., Rochester, N.Y., 1922-24; dir. music edn. in pub. schs., Montclair, N.J., since 1924; teacher of music edn., Rutgers U., New Brunswick, N.J., summers 1923-36; community song leader, voice teacher, concert organizer, accompanist and critic, Montclair, N.J. Civil service, Panama Canal Zone, during World War. Mem. N.E.A., Mus. Edn. Nat. Conf., N.J. Edn. Assn., Essex Co. (N.J.) Music Edn. Assn. (pres.). Congregationalist. Mason. Author: The Singing Road, 1939; Music Education in the High School. Co-author: Norwegian Nights (operetta), 1936; numerous mag. articles. Lecturer on sch. music subjects. Home: 344 N. Fullerton Av., Upper Montclair, N.J. Office: 22 Valley Rd., Montclair, N.J.

WARD, Charles William, artist; b. Trenton, N.J., Jan. 24, 1900; s. Fred I. and Mary Ellen (Glover) W.; ed. Pa. Acad. Fine Arts, 1926-31; unmarried. Has followed profession as artist since 1925; specializes in painting landscapes, murals, lithographs, water colors; represented by murals in U.S. Post Offices at Trenton, N.J., Roanoke Rapids, N.C., and paintings in pvt. collections; exhibited at Corcoran Art Gallery, Washington, D.C., Pa. Acad. Fine Arts and other important exhbns.; one-man shows in New York City, Trenton, N.J., Scranton, Pa., Raleigh, N.C. Awarded Cresson Traveling Scholarship by Pa. Acad. Fine Arts, 1930. Home: Carversville, Pa.

WARD, Christopher Longstreth, lawyer, author; b. Wilmington, Del., Oct. 6, 1868; s. Henry and Martha Potter (Bush) W.; A.B., Williams Coll., 1890; LL.B., Harvard University, 1893; Litt.D., University of Delaware, 1934; m. Caroline Tatnall Bush, May 5, 1897; children—Christopher L., Esther (Mrs. Philip J. Kimball), Rodman, Alison. Admitted to Del. bar, 1893, and began practice at Wilmington; pres. Corpn. Service Co. since 1920. Exec. chmn. Del. Tercentenary Commn.; mem. United States Del. Valley Tercentenary Commn. Decorated Comdr. Royal Order Vasa, 2d class, by King Gustaf V of Sweden, June 17, 1938. Mem. Hist. Soc. of Del., Wilmington Fine Arts Soc., Soc. Colonial Wars (gov., Del.), Delta Kappa Epsilon. Clubs: University, Wilmington Country; University, Williams (New York). Author: The Triumph of the Nut, 1923; Gentleman Into Goose, 1924; Twisted Tales, 1924; Foolish Fiction, 1925; One Little Man, 1926; Starling, 1927; The Saga of Cap'n John Smith, 1928; The Dutch and Swedes on the Delaware, 1930; Strange Adventures of Jonathan Drew, 1932; A Yankee Rover, 1933; Sir Galahad and other Rimes, 1936; New Sweden on the Delaware, 1938; Delaware Tercentenary Almanack, 1938. Contbr. to Saturday Rev. of Literature. Home: Bramshott, Greenville, Del. Office: 900 Market St., Wilmington, Del.

WARD, Christopher Longstreth Jr., lawyer; b. Wilmington, Del., June 21, 1898; s. Christopher Longstreth and Caroline (Bush) W.; student Wilmington Friends Sch., 1907-13, Taft Sch., Watertown, Conn., 1913-16; A.B., Williams Coll., Williamstown, Mass., 1920; B.A. (Juria), Oxford U., Eng., 1923; m. Anna Rutherfourd Pearson, Oct. 24, 1936. Admitted to Del. bar, 1924, and since practiced at Wilmington; mem. firm Marvel, Morford & Ward and Marvel, Morford, Ward & Logan, Wilmington, 1929-38; in pvt. practice since 1938; pres. Del. Mutual Bldg. & Loan Assn., Wilmington, since 1932; dir. The F. H. Smith Co., Frank Schoonmaker, Inc. Served in Inf., O.T.S., Camp Lee, Va., 1918. Dir. Wilmington Music Sch. Mem. Del. State and Am. bar assns., Am. Juducature Soc., S.A.R., Delta Kappa Epsilon. Clubs: Wilmington; Williams (New York City). Editor four editions Marvel on Delaware Corporations and Receiverships. Home: Greenville, Del. Office: Delaware Trust Bldg., Wilmington, Del.

WARD, Freeman, geologist; b. Yankton, S.D., Aug. 9, 1879; s. Joseph and Sarah Frances (Wood) W.; Yankton College, 1898-1901; A.B., Yale University, 1903, Ph.D., 1908; Sc.D. from Yankton College, 1934; m. Daisy Lee Eyerly, 1906; 1 dau., Sarah Wood. Asst. Instr. and asst. prof. geology, Yale, 1903-15; prof. geology and head of dept., U. of S.D., also state geologist, 1915-26; prof. geology and head of dept., Lafayette Coll., Pa., 1926—. Field work Conn. State Survey, Pa. State Survey and U.S. Geol. Survey, various summers. Mem. A.A.A.S., Geol. Soc. America, Am. Assn. Petroleum Geologists, Sigma Xi. Republican. Conglist. Home: Easton, Pa.

WARD, George, state banking commr.; b. Huttonsville, W.Va., Sept. 19, 1894; s. Wirt Casselman and Rose (White) W.; student Greenbrier Mil. Sch., 1907-12, Washington and Lee U., Lexington, Va., 1912-15, Carnegie Inst. Tech., 1915-17; m. Flora Davisson, Nov. 17, 1920; children—Flavius D., Wirt C., George II, William S., Reuben Kump. Became clk. Bank of Mill Creek, W.Va., 1912, cashier, 1920-27, pres., 1927-34; commr. of banking of W.Va. since 1934 (now serving second reappointment); dir. Inter-Mountain Coal & Lumber Co., Ky. & W.Va. Coal & Mining Co. Trustee Davis and Elkins Coll., Elkins, W.Va. Mem. Sigma Nu. Democrat. Presbyterian. Elk. Club: Edgewood Country (Charleston, W.Va.). Home: Mill Creek, W.Va. Office: Charleston, W.Va.

WARD, Grant Eben, surgeon; b. Lorain Co., O., Aug. 28, 1896; s. Fletcher DeLay and Harriett Grace (Walker) W.; A.B., Baldwin-Wallace Coll., Berea, O., 1917; M.D., Johns Hopkins Med. Sch., 1921; m. Lillian Anderson Hersperger, Aug. 16, 1922; children—Mary Grace, Margaret Lucille. Resident house officer, Johns Hopkins Hosp., 1921-22; asso., Howard A. Kelly Hosp., Baltimore, 1922-27; instr. surgery, U. of Md. Med. Sch., 1930-35, associate in surgery, 1935-37, asso. prof. surgery since 1937; assst. in surgery, Johns Hopkins Med. Sch., 1927-32; instr. in surgery, 1932-38, asso. in surgery since 1938; asst. visiting surgeon Johns Hopkins Hosp. since 1935; lecturer oral oncology, Baltimore Coll. Dental Surgery, U. of Md. Dental Sch. since 1934. Served in S.A.T.C., 1918. Fellow Am. Coll. Surgeons, A.M.A. Certified by Am. Bd. Surgery. Mem. Phi Kappa Phi, Am. Acad. Phys. Medicine (v.p. 1930-32), Am. Congress Phys. Therapy (v.p. 1935). Republican. Methodist. Club: Faculty of Johns Hopkins Univ. Home: 602 W. University Parkway. Office: Medical Arts Bldg., Baltimore, Md.

WARD, Harry Frederick; b. London, Eng., Oct. 15, 1873; s. Harry and Fanny (Jeffery) W.; came to America, 1891; U. of Southern Calif.; A.B., Northwestern U., 1897; A.M., Harvard, 1898; m. Daisy Kendall, Apr. 20, 1899; children—Gordon Hugh, Lynd Kendall, Muriel. Head resident Northwestern U. Settlement, Chicago, 1898-1900; ordained M.E. ministry, 1899; pastor Wabash Av., 47th St., and Union Av. chs., Chicago, and Euclid Av. Ch., Oak Park, Ill., 1899-1912; a founder, 1907, editorial sec., 1907-11, gen. sec. since 1911, Meth. Federation of Social Service; also prof. social service, Boston University Sch. of Theology, 1913-18. Mem. Phi Beta Kappa, Delta Sigma Rho, Delta Tau Delta. Author: Social Creed of the Churches, 1913; Social Evangelism, 1915; Poverty and Wealth, 1915; The Bible and Social Living, 1916; The Labor Movement, 1917; Christianizing Community Life (with R. H. Edwards), 1917; The Gospel for a Working

World, 1918; The Opportunity for Religion, 1919; The New Social Order—Principles and Programs, 1919; The Profit Motive, 1924; Our Economic Morality, 1929; Which Way Religion?, 1931; In Place of Profit, 1933. Editor of Year Book of the Church and Social Service and of Social Service Bull. Professor Christian ethics, Union Theol. Sem., New York, 1918—. Home: Palisade, N.J. Office: 3041 Broadway, New York, N.Y.

WARD, Herbert H., Jr., lawyer; b. Wilmington, Del., Apr. 29, 1890; s. Herbert H. and Stella E. (Lewis) W.; A.B., Princeton U., 1912; Harvard Law Sch., 1914; m. Miriam Juliette Rice, Sept. 18, 1917; children—Herbert H., III, Stella Miriam, John Rice. In practice at Wilmington, Del., since 1917; mem. of firm Ward & Gray, Wilmington, Del., since 1917. Mem. Am., Del. State, New Castle Co. bar assns., Key and Seal Club (Princeton). Republican. Methodist. Mason. Clubs: University, Wilmington Country, Social Service, Young Man's Republican (Wilmington, Del.). Home: 1035 Clayton St. Office: Delaware Trust Bldg., Wilmington, Del.

WARD, Holcombe, retired textile mfr.; b. New York, N.Y., Nov. 23, 1878; s. Robert and Mary Elizabeth (Snedeker) W.; A.B., Harvard, 1900; m. Louise Palen Conway, of South Orange, N.J., Apr. 16, 1905; children—Elizabeth E., Helen L. (Mrs. Richard M. Hurd, Jr.). Began with French & Ward, textile mfrs., New York, 1900, mem. of firm to liquidation, 1938. Pres. U.S. Lawn Tennis Assn. Mem. Fly Club (Harvard). Republican. Episcopalian (vestryman St. Peters Ch., Galilee, N.J.). Clubs: Harvard (New York); Seabright (N.J.) Lawn Tennis & Cricket (pres.), Heights Casino of Brooklyn (hon.); Orange Lawn Tennis (hon.). Home: "Orchard Lane," Riverside Drive, Red Bank, N.J. Office: 120 Broadway, New York, N.Y.

WARD, John Chamberlain, bishop; b. Elmira, N.Y., Aug. 27, 1873; s. Hamilton and Mary Adelia (Chamberlain) W.; A.B., Harvard, 1896; B.D., Gen. Theol. Sem., 1899, S.T.D., 1923; D.D., Kenyon, 1922; unmarried. Deacon, 1899, priest, 1900, P.E. Ch.; rector St. Stephen's Ch., Buffalo, 1899-1902, Grace Ch., Buffalo, 1902-21; consecrated bishop of Erie, Pa., Sept. 22, 1921; mem. Spl. Com. on Budget and Program, P.E. Ch. Mem. Pa. State Commn. on Healing Arts, 1927; chmn. Citizens Relief Com., Erie, 1933. Chaplain 74th Inf, N.G.N.Y., on Mexican border, 1916; chaplain same, local guard duty and Wadsworth, S.C., 1917; chaplain 105th Machine Gun Batt., 107th Inf., and 108th Inf., 27th Div., A.E.F., 1918, serving 9 mos. overseas; wounded in action; hon. disch. Mar. 1918, rank of capt. Awarded D.S.C. (U.S.); M.C. (British). Mem. Am. Legion. Republican. Clubs: Harvard, University. Home: 437 W. 6th St., Erie, Pa.

WARD, Lynd Kendall, artist and illustrator; b. Chicago, June 26, 1905; s. Harry Frederick and Daisy (Kendall) W.; B.S., Teachers Coll. (Columbia), 1926; student Staatliche Akademie fuer Graphische Kunst, Leipzig, Germany, 1926-27; m. May Yonge McNeer, June 11, 1926; children—Nanda Weedon, Robin Kendall. Began as illustrator, 1927; mem. Equinox Coöperative Press, Inc., New York, book publishers, since 1932. Mem. American Artists Congress, Sigma Chi. Author-Illustrator: (novels in woodcuts) God's Man, 1929; Madman's Drum, 1930; Wild Pilgrimage, 1932; Prelude to a Million Years, 1933; Song Without Words, 1936; Vertigo, 1937. Home: 1132 Abbott Boul., Palisade, N.J.

WARD, Perley Erik, publisher; b. Chicago, Ill., Oct. 4, 1880; s. Cyrus Joseph and Rebecca Isadore (Steele) W.; ed. grammar schs., Chicago; m. Susanna Lewis Knight, Feb. 1, 1910; children—Susanne, Elizabeth, Robert Erik, Evelyn. Began with Constrn. News (mag.), Chicago, Ill., 1894; with the Rams Horn, 1897-1900, Orange Judd Co. and Phelps Pub. Co., 1900-18; asst. treas. Good Housekeeping Co., Springfield, Mass., 1913-18; asst. to pres. F. M. Lupton Co., pubs., N.Y. City, 1919-20; with Farm Journal since 1920, pres., 1927-35, now vice-pres. and dir. circulation. Dir. Nat. Pubs. Assn. (pres. and dir.); Agrl. Pubs. Assn. Republican. Presbyn. Mason. Clubs: Penn Athletic (Philadelphia); Union League (Chicago). Writer on credit unions and co-operative banking. Organized in Mass. the first chartered credit union in U.S., 1910. Home: Wyncote, Pa., and Stone Harbor, N.J. Office: 232 S. 7th St., Philadelphia, Pa.

WARD, Thomas Johnson, banker, broker; b. Baltimore, Md., June 28, 1886; s. Francis Xavier and Ellen Topham (Evans) W.; ed. high sch., Baltimore; m. Pansy Beale Bloomer, June 3, 1911; 1 son, Thomas Johnson. Began in banking and brokerage business with H. W. Noble & Co., Philadelphia, Pa., 1906; with Cassatt & Co., bankers and brokers, Phila., since 1911, partner 1913 to Jan. 15, 1935, pres. Cassatt & Co. Inc., since Jan. 15, 1935; also vice-pres. Merrill Lynch & Co. Inc., since Aug. 1938; dir. Franklin County Coal Co., Old Ben Coal Corpn., Spicer Mfg. Corpn. Mem. exec. com., first 2 Liberty Loan drives, 3d Federal Res. Dist.; maj. U.S.A., Gen. Staff, 1918-19. Republican. Episcopalian. Clubs: Racquet, Sunnybrook Golf (Phila.); Recess, Links (New York). Home: Merion, Pa. Office: Commercial Trust Bldg., Philadelphia, Pa.

WARD, Waldron Merry, lawyer; b. Newark, N.J., June 27, 1886; s. Alexander Spencer and Julia (Merry) W.; grad. Barringer High Sch., Newark, N.J., 1902; A.B., Princeton, 1907; LL.B., New York Law Sch., 1909; m. Aline Toppin Coursen, Oct. 22, 1912; children—Waldron Merry, John Spencer, Aileen, Roger Coursen. Became asso. with Pitney, Hardin & Skinner, lawyers, Newark, N.J., 1907, mem. of firm since 1914; admitted to N.J. bar, 1910; mgr. Howard Savings Instn.; dir. Weston Elec. Instrument Corpn., Taylor-Wharton Iron & Steel Co., Am. Colortype Co. Trustee Hosp. of St. Barnabas and for Women and Children, Newark. Mem. Am. Bar Assn., Essex Co. Bar Assn. Republican. Episcopalian. Clubs: Essex (Newark); Baltusrol Golf (Springfield, N.J.); Princeton (New York). Home: 74 Whittredge Rd., Summit, N.J. Office: 744 Broad St., Newark, N.J.

WARDEN, Clarence Arthur, lawyer; b. Phila. Pa., Mar. 21, 1878; s. William G. and Sarah W. (Bushnell) W.; grad. Hill Sch., 1896; Ph.B., Yale, 1899; LL.B., U. of Pa. Law Sch., 1902; m. Helen Corning, June 6, 1900; children—Clarence A., Jr., Adele (Mrs. Henry D. Paxson, Jr.). Admitted to Pa. bar, 1902 and asso. with firm Morgan and Lewis, 1902-10, in practice alone since 1910; former gen. counsel United Gas Improvement Co., Phila.; dir. Germantown Trust Co., Phila. and chmn. bd. dirs. since 1935; chmn. adv. com. The Pennsylvania Company for Insurances on Lives and Granting Annuities, Ardmore branch; pres. Superior Tube Co., Norristown, Pa. Pres. bd. trustees The Hill Sch., Pottstown, Pa., since 1920; former trustee Children's Hosp., and Welfare Assn. of Phila. Republican. Presbyterian. Clubs: Rittenhouse, Yale, Corinthian Yacht (Philadelphia); Merion Cricket (Haverford); Gulph Mills Golf (Gulph Mills); University, Yale (New York). Home: Haverford, Pa. Office: Witherspoon Bldg., Philadelphia, Pa.

WARE, Harriet, composer; b. Waupun, Wis.; d. Silas Edward and Emily (Sperry) W.; grad. Pillsbury Conservatory of Music, Owatonna, Minn., 1896; studied piano 2 yrs. with William Mason, of New York; piano, voice and harmony, Paris, France; piano, composition and voice, Berlin; m. Hugh Montgomery Krumbhaar, Dec. 8, 1913. Recognized among foremost women composers. Pres. Harriet Ware, Publishers, Inc., since 1926. Mem. League Am. Pen Women (pres. for N.J. 1924; nat. chmn. of music 1938), Am. Society Composers, Authors and Publishers. Mem. nat. com. of fine arts of Gen. Fed. of Women's Clubs since 1935; mem. music com. Paper-Mill Play House since 1939. Club: MacDowell (New York). Composer: (songs) Boat Song, 1908; Sunlight Waltz Song, 1908; The Cross (words by Edwin Markham), 1909; The Hindu Slumber Song, 1909; The Forgotten Land, 1909; The Princess of the Morning, 1911; Sir Oluf (cantata), 1911; Song of the Sea (piano solo), 1911; Wind and Lyre (poem by Edwin Markham), 1912; Undine (also given as 1-act opera, libretto by Edwin Markham), 1915; Stars, 1921; In An Old Garden (song cycle), 1921; Trees (chorus for women's voices), 1924; The White Moth (ballet), 1925; Mountain Pictures (suite for piano), 1927; Cycle for Children—A City Child in the Country, 1927; Woman's Triumphal March, 3 part chorus, made nat. song of Gen. Federation Women's Clubs of America, June 1927; The Artisan (tone poem, words by Edwin Markham), for symphony orchestra and voice, given by New York Symphony Orchestra, 1929; From India (sung by Mme. Jeritza), 1934; The Artisan (given by Philharmonic Symphony Orchestra, Los Angeles), 1934; Gladness, 1935; musical score of play, Storm Bird, 1935; Prelude for Piano, 1935; A Junk from India (song), 1939; A Toast to New York (song; wrote poem and music), 1939; Victory Prelude, To You, Midnight Waltz (piano), 1939. Concert tours, 1924, '26, '34; concert and lecture tour in West, 1937; lecturer Aeolian Hall, New York, 1936, '38. 1st tour coast to coast, 1929. Manuscript of Undine in Congl. Library, Washington, D.C. Home: Terrill Rd., Plainfield, N.J.

WARE, John H., Jr., pres. Citizens Gas & Fuel Co., Gas Oil Products, Inc.; b. Phila, Pa., Apr. 12, 1888; s. John H. and Alice (Van Meter) W.; m. Clara Edwards, Nov. 25, 1907; children—John H. III, Willard M. Pres. Farmers Electric Co., 1913-19, Eastern Power Co., 1918-26, Northern Md. Power Co. and Southern Pa. Power Co., 1919-26, Eastern Gas Co., 1925-35, Citizens Gas & Fuel Co. since 1925, Elkton Gas Co., 1925-29, Oxford Cement Products Co., 1928-36, Del. Valley Utilities Co. since 1930, Ware & Co., Inc. 1934-36, Gas Oil Products, Inc., since 1934, Del. Land Co. and Del. Housing Assn. since 1935; pres. of more than 30 affiliates of these corpns. Trustee Chester Co. (Pa.) Council, Boy Scouts of America. Clubs: Com. of One Hundred (Miami Beach, Fla); Mfrs. and Bankers (Phila.); Engrs. (Baltimore). Home: Star Island, Miami Beach, Fla. Office: 45 S. Third St., Oxford, Pa.

WARE, Paul Blackburn, lawyer; b. Belington, W.Va., Feb. 16, 1902; s. J. Blackburn and Tilla E. (Glenn) W.; A.B., W.Va. Univ., Morgantown, 1924; LL.B., W.Va. Univ. Law Coll., 1926; m. Ruth McBee, Nov. 14, 1925; children—Paul B., Jr., James Holland, Jerry Lyn. Admitted to W.Va. bar, 1926, and since engaged in gen. practice of law at Philippi; mem. firm Ware & Ware since 1926; served as city atty. Philippi, W.Va., since 1937; divorce commr. Barbour Co., 1929-37. Served in R.O.T.C., 1921-24. Dir. Philippi Pub. Library. Mem. W.Va., Barbour Co. and Am. bar assns., Phi Alpha Delta, Kappa Kappa Psi. Republican. Mem. U.B. Ch. Mason. Clubs: Kiwanis (past pres.), Masonic, Rod and Gun (Philippi). Home: 108 S. Walnut St. Office: 14 S. Main St., Philippi, W.Va.

WARE, Ralph Hartman, prof. of English; b. Greensburg, Pa., June 3, 1894; s. Frank Willis and Sarah Elizabeth (Kean) W.; A.B., Allegheny Coll., Meadville, Pa., 1920; A.M., Pa. State Coll., 1922; Ph.D., U. of Pa., 1930; m. Esther Etta Ellenberger, Sept. 30, 1922. Asst. instr. in history, Allegheny Coll., Meadville, Pa., 1919-20; instr. in English, Pa. State Coll., 1920-21; teacher of English, Girard Coll., Phila., 1921-28; with U. of Pittsburgh since 1928, as asst. prof. of English, 1928-31, asso. prof. since 1931. Served in U.S. Army, with A.E.F., May 1917-July 1919. Mem. Modern Lang. Assn., Phi Kappa Psi, Phi Beta Kappa. Home: 825 East End Av., Pittsburgh, Pa.

WARE, Romaine Baker, writer; b. Bridgeton, N.J., Apr. 18, 1886; grad. Bridgeton High Sch., 1904; student West Jersey Acad., 1905-06; m. Laura Rave, 1911 (divorced, 1927); m. 2d, Stella St. Jacque, Sept. 6, 1928; 1 son, William Romaine. Began writing on garden topics, 1923; writer for St. Paul Pioneer Press, 1923-26, Morning Oregonian, Portland, 1927-30; garden editor Nature Mag., 1933; owner Chart Pub. Co., New York, pubs. of garden charts, since 1935; pres. and gen. mgr. The Jelmeter Co., Bridgeton, since 1935; garden editor Ladies'

Home Journal, 1935. Mem. Theosophical Soc. Republican. Contbr. on gardens and horticulture to mags. Home: 31 Institute Pl., Bridgeton, N.J.

WAREHEIM, Eli C.; exec. v.p. and dir. Commercial Credit Co. Home: Severna Park P.O., Anne Arundel Co., Md. Office: First Nat. Bank Bldg., Baltimore, Md.

WARFEL, Harry Redcay, univ. prof.; b. Reading Pa., Mar. 21, 1899; s. Wyatt William and Kate (Redcay) W.; A.B., Bucknell U., Lewisburg, Pa., 1920, A.M., 1922; A.M., Columbia U., 1924; grad. student U. of N.C., 1924-25; Ph.D., Yale U., 1932; m. Ruth Evelyn Farquhar, Apr. 15, 1922. Master of English, St. John's Sch., Manlius, N.Y., 1920-21; instr. in English, Bucknell U., Lewisburg, Pa., 1921-25, asst. prof., 1925-33, asso. prof., 1933-35; Sterling research fellow, Yale U., 1934-35; prof. English, U. of Md., College Park, Md., since 1935; visiting prof., U. of Toledo, summer 1938; alumni sec., Bucknell U., 1923-24. Served in S.A.T.C. and F.A. C.O.T.C., 1918. Mem. Modern Lang. Assn., Am. Literature Group, Nat. Council of Teachers of English, Am. Assn. Univ. Profs., Pa. Hist. Assn., Pa. German Soc., Mark Twain Soc., Delta Sigma. Democrat. Baptist. Author: David Bruce, 1925; James Gates Percival, 1932; Noah Webster: Schoolmaster to America, 1936. Editor: The American Mind, 1937, Sketches of American Policy, 1937, Poems by Noah Webster, 1936, American Local-Color Stories, 1939. Founder and editor, annual Bucknell Verse, 1926-34. Contbr. to literary and professional mags. Home: 80 Wine Av., Hyattsville, Md.

WARFEL, Mary Sophia, concert mgr.; b. Lancaster, Pa., Oct. 20, 1888; d. John Girvin and Elizabeth A. (Bachler) W.; student Shippen Sch., Lancaster, Pa., 1902-05; music student Sacred Heart Acad., Lancaster, Pa., 1898-1905; Mus.B., St. Mary's Coll., Notre Dame, Ind., 1907; unmarried. Piano student under Constantin von Sternberg, 1907-11; harp student under Baseler, Salzedo, Sassoli, Schuecker, Salvi; concert harpist, 1910-20; concert mgr., Bethlehem and Lancaster, Pa., 1920-30; treas. Antoherbine Co., Ltd., herb medicine, Lancaster, Pa., since 1929; mgr. Student Nurses Chorus, St. Joseph's Hosp., Lancaster, Pa., 1937-39; mem. faculty, Linden Hall Jr. Coll., Lititz, Pa. (harp dept.); master class of pvt. pupils of harp. Commr. Lancaster Council Girl Scouts, Inc. Mem. Musical Art Soc. (hon.), Internat. Fed. of Catholic Alumnae (Lancaster, Pa., regent). Republican. Catholic. Clubs: (hon.) Iris, Quota (founder & 1st pres.), Country (Lancaster, Pa.). Musical editor for Lancaster (Pa.) newspapers, 1922-24. Address: 310 N. Lime St., Lancaster, Pa.

WARFIELD, Edwin, Jr., publisher; b. Baltimore, Md., June 28, 1891; s. Edwin and Emma (Nicodemus) W.; student Country Sch. for Boys, Baltimore, 1902-04, Johns Hopkins U. Grad. Sch., 1912; A.B., St. John's Coll., Annapolis, Md., 1909, M.A., 1912; LL.B., U. of Md., Baltimore, Md., 1912; m. Katharine Lawrence Lee, Apr. 20, 1920; children—Katharine McLane, Edwin III, Frances King, Louise, Robert McLane. Asst. sec. Fidelity & Deposit Co., Baltimore, 1913-17, asst. sec., 1916-17; pres. Daily Record Co., Baltimore, 1920-39; pres. Judicial Printing Co., New York City, since 1937; pres. Hillsboro-Queen Anne Cooperative Corpn., Baltimore, since 1935; dir. Daily Record Co., Arundel Corpn., Fidelity & Deposit Co., Colonial Trust Co., Southern States Cooperative Corpn. Served as 1st lt., F.A., Md. N.G., 1917-18; capt., U.S. Army, 1918-19; with A.E.F. Mem. Md. Racing Commn., 1931-37; chmn. Conservation Commn. of Md. since 1939. Trustee, mem. Bd. of Visitors and Govs., St. John's Coll., Annapolis, Md. Democrat. Club: Maryland (Baltimore, Md.). Home: Woodbine, Md. Office: 15 E. Saratoga St., Baltimore, Md.

WARFIELD, Henry Mactier, ins. exec.; b. Baltimore, Md., July 1, 1867; s. Henry M. and Anna (Emory) W.; ed. pvt. and pub. schs., Baltimore: m. Rebecca Carroll Denison, Feb. 10, 1892; 1 dau., Mrs. Zachary R. Lewis. Began as clk. with wholesale dry goods house, 1884; clk., Continental Ins. Co. of N.Y., 1884-85, Royal Ins. Co. of Liverpool, 1885-96, resident mgr., 1896-1923; president of Henry M. Warfield-Roloson Company, mgrs. Royal Insurance Company and ins. brokers; dir. Md. Trust Company, Eutaw Savings Bank, Baltimore Steam Packet Co., Chesapeake & Potomac Telephone Co. Mem. Md. N. G., 1885-1920, col., 1903-08, adj. gen., 1908-20; served as maj., Md. Vol. Inf., Spanish-Am. War. Pres. Baltimore Assn. Commerce, 1937-39; pres. Assn. of Fire Underwriters of Baltimore City. Democrat. Episcopalian. Clubs: Maryland, Merchants, Bachelors Cotillon. Home: Timonium, Md. Office: 201-203 E. Redwood St., Baltimore, Md.

WARFIELD, J(ohn) Ogle, clergyman; b. Frederick Co., Md.; s. Cecilius E. and Laura W. (Thomas) W.; A.B., Johns Hopkins U., 1893; S.T.B., Episcopal Theol. Sch., Cambridge, Mass., 1896; A.M., U. of Pa., 1909; (hon.) D.D., St. John's Coll., Annapolis, Md., 1922; m. Louyse Duvall Spragins, Oct. 26, 1898; children—John Ogle (M.D.), Edwin Spragins, Louyse Spragins (Mrs. Geo. G. Barclay), Elizabeth Hamilton, Cecilius Edwin, Stith Bolling (dec.). Ordained to ministry P.E. Ch., deacon 1896, priest, 1897; rector, Dubois, Pa., 1896-99; rector St. Michael's Parish, Md., 1897-1900; asst., St. Paul's Ch., Chestnut Hill, Phila., 1901-14; vicar, Holy Trinity Chapel, 1916-23; rector, St. David's Ch., Phila., since 1923. Mem. Phi Gamma Delta. Episcopalian. Home: St. David's Rectory, Manayunk, Philadelphia, Pa.

WARFIELD, Joshua N., pres. Eureka-Md. Assurance Co.; b. Florence, Md., Feb. 28, 1884; s. Joshua N. and Lucy W. (Hutton) W.; student U. of Md.; m. Mary Nicodemus, Mar. 6, 1909. Pres. Eureka-Md. Assurance Corpn. since 1927. Home: Woodbine, Md. Office: 10 E. Fayette St., Baltimore, Md.

WARGOVICH, Michael John, Jr., real estate and ins. brokerage; b. Czechoslovakia, Nov. 30, 1895; s. Michael John and Anna (Tutko) W.; brought to U.S., 1900 and naturalized citizen, 1919; ed. parochial schs. and high sch., McKeesport, Pa., 1901-14, State Coll., 1918-19; m. Mary Lucanish, Sept. 24, 1919; children—Mildred, Raymond, Dolores, Matthias. Employed as steel worker, inspr., and foreman, 1915-25; bank cashier, 1926, real estate and ins. as propr. Wargovich Agency since 1926. Served as mem. Mayor's Advisory Com. Mem. Nat. Rep. Program Com.; chmn. Pa. Rep. Slovak Politics. Chmn. bd. auditors First Cath. Slovak Union and dir. of same. Republican. Roman Catholic. K.C. First Cath. Slovak Union. Clubs: Slovak Educational, Croation Educational. Address: 140 Seventh Av., McKeesport, Pa.

WARK, Homer Ethan, clergyman, educator; b. Spencer, Ind., Aug. 1, 1875; s. George B. and Elizabeth Rachel (Miller) W.; B.A., Campbell Coll., Holton, Kan., 1900; M.A., Washburn Coll., Topeka, Kan., 1904; S.T.B., Boston U. Sch. of Theology, 1906; Ph.D., Boston U., 1908; m. Gertrude Eliza Beecher, Sept. 5, 1900. Entered M.E. ministry, in Kan., 1900; pastor at Topeka, Leavenworth and Kansas City, Kan., until 1912, Calcutta, India, 1912-15; prof. Bible, Southwestern Coll., Winfield, Kan., 1915-18; prof. history of religion, etc., Boston U., 1921-26; became pres. W.Va. Wesleyan Coll., 1926; now pastor First M.E. Ch., Clarksburg. Chaplain U.S.A., May 1917-Feb. 22, 1919; with 137th Inf. in France 1 yr. Mem. Acad. Polit. Science. Republican. Mason. Club: Rotary (Clarksburg). Author of volumes on "The Religion of a Soldier" and "New Era in Missions." Home: Clarksburg, W.Va.*

WARNER, Alfred du Pont Jr., business exec.; b. Wilmington, Del., Oct. 10, 1878; s. Alfred D. and Emalea (Pusey) W.; student Friends Sch., Wilmington, Del., 1888-96; B.S., Cornell U., 1900; m. Eleanor Betts, Apr. 30, 1902; children—Mary Tatnall (dec. wife of Junius A. Giles, M.D.), Alice, Alfred D. III. Asso. with Warner Co., building materials, Phila., since 1900, v.p., treas. and dir. since 1905; v.p. and dir. American Lime & Stone Co.; dir. Security Trust Co., Wilmington, Del., Wilmington Savings Fund Soc., Perpetual Savings & Loan Assn.; dir. Wilmington-Morris Plan Bank. Served in Intelligence Bur., U.S. Navy, 1917-18. Pres. Wilmington Chamber of Commerce, 1919-21; mem. exec. bd. Wilmington Boy Scouts since 1918; trustee Cornell U., 1928-35. Mem. Delta Tau Delta. Republican. Unitarian. Clubs: Midday (Phila.); Wilmington Country (Wilmington, Del.); Cornell (New York). Home: 1005 Broom St., Wilmington, Del. Office: 219 N. Broad St., Philadelphia, Pa.

WARNER, Charles, pres. Warner Co.; b. Wilmington, Del., Apr. 22, 1877; s. Alfred D. and Emalea (Pusey) W.; ed. Friends Sch., Wilmington, Stevens Inst. of Tech., Drexel Inst. of Tech.; m. Ethel Eden Bach, Jan. 4, 1900; children—Dorothy (Mrs. Edward M. Kenworthey, now deceased), Charles, Frederick. With Charles Warner Co., and successor Warner Co., since 1899, beginning as engr. and asst. to pres., became pres., spring 1915, pres. and chmn. of bd. at death of father, fall 1915; dir. and mem. exec. com. Atlas Powder Co.; dir. N. Am. Cement Corpn.; pres. and chmn. Am. Lime and Stone Co.; dir. Federal Home Loan Bank of Pittsburgh. Pres. Wilmington Bd. Harbor Commrs.; trustee Drexel Institute of Technology. Chmn. Del. Rep. State Com., 1920, 22; chmn. Delaware Republican Finance Committee, 1922. Member Acad. Political Science, Am. Academy Political and Social Science, Am. Planning and Civic Assn., Drexel Alumni. Unitarian. Clubs: Penn Athletic, Engineers, Midday, Sons of Delaware in Phila. (Phila.). Home: 1404 Gilpin Av., Wilmington, Del. Office: 210 N. Broad St., Philadelphia, Pa.

WARNER, Everett Longley, painter, etcher; b. Vinton, Ia., July 16, 1877; s. Horace Everett and Anna (Riggs) W.; pupil of the Art Students' League, New York; Académie Julian, Paris, France; m. Katharine Jordan Thomas, June 14, 1923; children—Stephen, James McIntosh, Thomas Everett. Awards: First Corcoran prize, Washington Water Color Club, 1902; Sesnan gold medal, Pa. Acad. Fine Arts, 1908; silver medal, Internat. Expn., Buenos Aires, 1910; 2d Hallgarten prize, Nat. Acad. Design, 1912; William T. Evans prize, Salmagundi Club, 1913; bronze medal, Soc. Washington Artists, 1913; silver and bronze medals, Panama P.I. Expn. 2nd Altman Landscape Prize, Nat. Acad. Design, 1937, Wm. O. Goodman Prize Lyme Art Assn., 1937. Represented in permanent collections of Corcoran Gallery, Washington, Pa. Acad. Fine Arts, Boston Mus. of Fine Arts, Toledo Mus., Syracuse Museum, City Art Museum, St. Louis, Art Inst., Chicago, and New York Pub. Library, Gibbes Gallery (Charleston, S.C.), Okla. Art League (Oklahoma City). Engaged in ship camouflage 1917—; originator of 1 of 5 systems of camouflage approved by ship protection com. of War Risk Bur. Apptd. lt., Construction Corps, U.S.N.R.F., Feb. 1918, in charge Sub-Sect. of Design, U.S. Naval Camouflage. A.N.A., 1913, N.A., 1937. Mem. Soc. Washington Artists, Washington Water Color Club, Associated Artists of Pittsburgh, Am. Water Color Soc. Club: Nat. Arts. Address: Carnegie Institute of Technology, Pittsburgh, Pa.

WARNER, George Coffing, lawyer; b. Salisbury, Conn., July 13, 1871; s. Milton J. and Maria Birch (Coffing) W.; student U. of Va., 1892-93; LL.B., Columbia, 1891; m. Maude Marshall Kelley, 1900 (died 1903); m. 2d, Florence Ruth Loring, 1905 (divorced 1925); children—George Coffing, Percy de Forest II, Ruth Loring, Gifford Dyer; m. 3d, Mary Elizabeth Ransom, 1933. Admitted to bar, Va. and N.Y., 1893, Mass., 1894, to practice before Supreme Court of United States, 1910; began practicing at Great Barrington, Mass.; specializes in corpn. law; of counsel in N.Y. as to riparian rights in litigation arising from constrn. N.Y. Barge Canal; originator and mgr. of syndicates which acquired control of Nat. Shoe & Leather, Merchants, Chatham and Phenix banks, also of Internat. Banking Corpn.; pres., treas. and dir. Litchfield Co.; dir. and gen. counsel Conn. Pub. Service Corpn. Known as "father of branch banking" in N.Y. City. As v.p. Nat. Soc. for Promotion Industrial Edn., aided in securing federal legislation for vocational edn.; originator of Salisbury Assn.; founder of Save-A-Coin-A-Day Movement; originator, chmn. organization committee and trustee Antiquarian and Landmarks Soc., Inc., of Conn. Congregationalist. Clubs: Columbia University, Pilgrims, Univ. of Va. Home: Salisbury, Conn.; New Hope, Pa.; and Winter Park, Fla. Office: 156 5th Av., New York, N.Y.; and Colorado Bldg., Washington, D.C.

WARNER, Irving, vice-pres. Warner Co.; b. Wilmington, Del., Dec. 23, 1882; s. Alfred D. and Emalea (Pusey) W.; ed. Wilmington Friends Sch.; M.E., Cornell U., 1904; m. Marian Tallman, Jan. 25, 1908; children—Anne Dickie, Irving, Jr., Emalea Pusey 2d, Marian Tallman 2d (wife of Rev. Jesse M. Trotter) and John. Associated with the Warner Company, lime, sand and gravel, Phila., Pa., since 1904; vice-pres. and gen. mgr. American Lime & Stone Co., Bellefonte, Pa., 1922-23; vice-pres. and dir. Warner Company; dir. American Lime & Stone Co. Served with Engrs. Corps, U.S.A., 1918-19, with A.E.F. Served as mem. City Council of Wilmington, Del. Trustee Church Farm Sch., Glen Loch, Pa. Republican. Unitarian. Club: Vicmead Hunt. Home: 1109 Broom St., Wilmington, Del. Office: 219 N. Broad St., Philadelphia, Pa.

WARNER, John C., pres. First Nat. Bank; b. Milford, Pa., Aug. 11, 1863; s. Ebenezer and Emily (Buchanan) W.; student High Sch., Monticello, N.Y., 1879-81, Eastman Business Coll., Poughkeepsie, N.Y., 1883-85; m. Ella N. Kipp, Dec. 12, 1899; children—John C., Jr., Ann (Mrs. Irvin W. Hoff), Dorothy. Engaged in farming, Milford, Pa., 1885-1901; with First Nat. Bank, Milford, Pa., since 1901, successively as asst. cashier and cashier and pres. since 1922, dir. since 1900; dir. Milford (Pa.) Water Co. Dir. Milford (Pa.) Independent Sch. Dist., 1924-39. Republican. Presbyterian. Address: Milford, Pa.

WARNER, J(ohn) C(hristian), univ. prof., chemist; b. Goshen, Ind., May 28, 1897; s. Elias and Addie (Plank) W.; A.B., Indiana U., Bloomington, Ind., 1919, A.M., 1920, Ph.D., 1923; student U. of Mich., summer 1933; m. Louise Hamer, June 17, 1925; children—William Hamer, Thomas Payton. Research chemist The Barrett Co., Phila., 1918, Cosden Co., Tulsa, Okla., 1920-21; instr. chemistry, Indiana U., Bloomington, 1921-24; research chemist Wayne Chemicals Corpn., Ft. Wayne, Ind., 1925-26; instr. chemistry, Carnegie Inst. Tech., 1926-28, asst. prof., 1928-33, asso. prof. theoretical chemistry, 1933-36, asso. prof. metallurgy, 1936-38, prof. chemistry and head dept. chemistry since 1938. Mem. Am. Chem. Soc. (councilor), Electrochem. Soc., Am. Inst. Mining and Metall. Engrs., Sigma Xi, Delta Upsilon, Alpha Chi Sigma, Phi Beta Kappa. Club: Chemists (Pittsburgh). Author (with T. P. McCutcheon and H. Seltz): General Chemistry, 3d edit., 1939; also author many papers on researches in phys. chemistry, electro-chemistry, metallurgy; cons. on industrial chem. problems. Home: 1344 Denniston Av. Office: Carnegie Institute of Technology, Pittsburgh, Pa.

WARNER, William (Richard) Jr., retired; b. Phila., Pa., Nov. 2, 1859; s. William R. and Frances Ann (Dulin) W.; prep. edn. Phila. pvt. and pub. schs.; Ph. G., Phila. Coll. of Pharmacy and Science, 1881; m. Sallie H. Hinkle, May 9, 1882; children—Alberta Hinkle (Mrs. Harold R. Aiken, dec.), Blanche Dulin (dec.), William Richard III, Frank Haine (dec.), Emijo (Mrs. Addis M. Shields). Entered father's business, Wm. R. Warner & Co., mfrs. pharmaceuticals, Phila., about 1878, and continued same until 1908 when business was sold to Pfeiffer Chem. Co., St. Louis, Mo.; pres. 13th and 15th Sts. Passenger Ry. Co., Phila., since 1924. Home: The Union League, Philadelphia, Pa.

WARNOCK, Arthur Ray, coll. dean; b. Mason City, Ill., Dec. 4, 1883; s. George William and Charlotta (Costain) W.; A.B., U. of Ill., Urbana, Ill., 1905; student U. of Ill. Law Sch., 1905-07, 1908-09; m. Geraldine Fouché, Sept. 4, 1915; children—Arthur Ray, John Fouché. Instr. English, U. of Ill., Urbana, Ill., 1905-07, 1908-10, asst. dean of men, 1910-19; admitted to Ill. bar, 1910; dean of men, Pa. State Coll., since 1919. Mem. Beta Theta Pi, Phi Delta Phi, Phi Beta Kappa. Republican. Methodist. Home: East Campus, State College, Pa.

WARREN, Charles Bradley, sculptor; b. Ben Avon, Pa., Dec. 19, 1903; s. Charles Arbothnot and Ida (Bradley) W.; student Carnegie Inst. Tech., 1921-24, (night) 1924-31, Beaux Arts Inst. Design, New York, 1931-33; m. Dorothy Floyd, Aug. 22, 1936. Decorator with firm, James Warren & Son, Pittsburgh, Pa., 1925-31; sculpture studio in N.Y., 1931-33; opened studios in Pittsburgh, 1933, and since located there. Mem. Asso. Artists of Pittsburgh (dir.), Soc. of Sculptors (Pittsburgh), Architectural League of N.Y., Lambda Chi Alpha. Awarded Art Soc. prize, 1936; 3 hon. mentions, Carnegie Inst. Works: Memorial to Edison and Marconi, Republic, Pa.; stone reliefs, Prospect High Sch., Pittsburgh; sculptures for county bldg., High Point, N.C.; bronze fountain figure, H. H. McClintic Gardens, Pittsburgh; aluminum spandrel, Scott Twp. High Sch., Pa., pediment, dept. of justice, Raleigh, N.C.; gold medal for Stephen Foster Memorial, Pittsburgh; terra cotta sculptures, Thaddeus Stevens Sch., Pittsburgh. Mem. United Presbyn. Ch. Home: 233 Ridge Av., Ben Avon. Studios: Ben Avon and McCartney St., Pittsburgh, Pa.

WARREN, George C., retired broker; b. Barnegat, N.J., Oct. 15, 1877; s. George C. and Sarah M. (Cranmer) W.; ed. Barnegat (N.J.) Pub. Schs., Pennington (N.J.) Sem., Centenary Collegiate Inst., Hackettstown, N.J. Bank clerk, First Nat. Bank, New York, 1895-1915, partner Loew & Co., New York Stock Exchange firm, 1915-33; retired, 1933. Served in Office of Naval Intelligence, during World War; lt. commdr., N.J. Naval Militia. Presidential elector, 1916, 1920; del. to Rep. Nat. Conv., 1936; v.chmn. Rep. State Com. (mem. from Union Co.); pres. Summit (N.J.) Rep. Club. Pres. N.J. Bd. of Fish and Game Commrs.; mem. Interstate Sanitation Commn., N.J. Council. Mem. Sons of the Revolution, Am. Forestry Assn., Nat. Geographic Soc., N.J. Vets. of All Wars Memorial Assn. Republican. Methodist. Mason. Clubs: Belmar (N.J.) Fishing; Newark (N.J.) Bait and Fly Casting; Circus Saints and Sinners (New York). Address: Summit, N.J.

WARREN, George Sessions, chief engr.; b. Worcester, Mass., Sept. 21, 1881; s. Charles G. and Mary (Sessions) W.; M.E., Cornell U., 1905; m. Jane Isenberg, Feb. 10, 1910; children—George Sessions, Mary E. Employed by Sharon (Pa.) Steel Corpn. since 1905, beginning as draftsman, chief engr. since 1908. Mem. City Planning Commn. Mem. Am. Iron & Steel Inst., Am. Soc. M.E., Engrs. Soc. of Western Pa., Iron & Steel Engrs., Chamber of Commerce. Republican. Club: Sharon (Pa.) Country. Home: 936 Alcoma St. Office: care Sharon Steel Corpn., Sharon, Pa.

WARREN, Howard Saunders, consulting elec. engr.; b. Oldtown, Me., Mar. 3, 1873; s. John and Emily (Saunders) W.; prep. edn., East Me. Conf. Sem., Bucksport, Me., 1887-90; A.B., Stanford U., 1898; m. Mary Lillian Mitchell, Aug. 31, 1918; children—Doron Mitchell, Quentin Leventon. Electrician, U.S. Fur Seal Commn., 1897; designer Standard Elec. Co. of Calif., May-June 1898; wireman Calif. State Bd. of Harbor Commrs., July-Sept. 1898; gen. engr. Nevada County Electric Power Co., 1898-99; with Am. Telephone & Telegraph Co. in telephone transmission development, 1899-1933, designed loading coil, used in open wire circuits, 1901, type used in cables, 1902, phantom circuit coil, 1904, in charge of reduction to practice of loading invention, 1903-09, in charge of protection against interference from railroad electrification, electric power systems, electrolysis, lightning, 1909-19, as protection development engr., 1919-33; dir. of protection development, Bell Telephone Labs., Inc., New York, 1934-38; consulting engr. since 1938. Chmn. Am. Research Com. on Grounding; chmn. research sub-com. of Am. Com. on Electrolysis, 1915-21; pres. Stanford Club of N.Y., N.J. and Conn., 1926-28. Fellow Am. Inst. Elec. Engrs. (mem. transmission and distribution com. and committee on safety; also member board of examiners); fellow A.A.A.S.; member National Fire Protection Assn. (mem. Elec. com.), Sigma Xi. Protestant. Clubs: Engineers (New York); Montclair Athletic (Montclair, N.J.); Braidburn Country (Madison, N.J.). Home: 18 Brunswick Rd., Montclair, N.J. Office: 420 Lexington Av., New York, N.Y.

WARREN, Lewis Eugene, pharmaceutical chemist; b. Hillsdale, Mich., Aug. 14, 1876; s. John Morris and Emily (White) W.; Ph.C., U. of Mich., 1903, B.Sc., 1907, hon. M.Sc., 1932; m. Florence Leonora Smith, Oct. 11, 1902 (died 1915); m. 2d, Florence Helen Wixson, Sept. 3, 1921; children—Emily Wixson (dec.), Margaret Wixson, Jane Wixson, Dorothy Dodge, Louise Ermina. Asst. chemist Merck & Co., N.Y. City, 1903-05; food and drug inspection chemist, Bur. of Chemistry, U.S. Dept. Agr., Washington, D.C., 1907-09; asso. chemist Am. Med. Assn., Chicago, 1909-17, and 1919-25; chief research chemist Warner & Co., New York City, 1917-19; pharm. chemist Food and Drug Adminstrn., U.S. Dept. Agr., 1925-28; sr. chemist U.S. Dept. Agr. since 1928; sec. U.S. Pharm. Conv. since 1930. Mem. Am. Pharm. Assn., Am. Chem. Soc., Hist. Science Society. Past pres. Chicago and Washington branches, Am. Pharm. Assn. Awarded Ebert prize, jointly with A. B. Stevens, by Am. Pharm. Assn., 1908, and with W. A. Pucker, 1911. Unitarian. Contbr. of numerous papers, reports, etc., on pharm., history of science, chem. and related subjects, also editorials, essays, and book revs. in mags. Mem. editorial com. Methods of Analysis and Jour. of Assn. of Official Agrl. Chemists. Home: 2 Raymond St., Chevy Chase, Md.

WARREN, Richard Fairfield, mfg. dental supplies; b. Phila., Pa., Oct. 14, 1894; s. Henry Mather and Ida Carey (White) W.; grad. De Lancey Sch., Phila., Pa., 1913; A.B., U. of Pa., 1917; m. Winifred W. Dunn, Oct. 14, 1925. Engaged as sec. and dir. Pittsburgh Clay Products Co., Pittsburgh, Pa., 1919-37, Walker Mills Stone & Brick Co., 1920-37; dir. The S. S. White Dental Mfg. Co., Phila., Pa., since 1926. Served as ensign, U.S.N.R.F., 1917-19, overseas 1 yr., promoted to lieut., (j.g.), U.S.N.R.F., 1919; lieut. comdr., U.S.N.R., since 1937. Justice of the peace since 1932. Dir. Chester Co. Council Boy Scouts; honored by award Silver Beaver. Pres. Devon Citizens Assn. Mem. Soc. of Colonial Wars, S.R., Mil. Order Fgn. Wars of U.S., Mil. Order of World War, Psi Upsilon. Republican. Episcopalian. Mason (32°). Clubs: Union League, Sword, Varsity, Automobile. Photographic illustrator many mag. arts. and features. Home: Devon, Pa. Office: 909 Otis Bldg., Philadelphia, Pa.

WARREN, Robert Legh, president Brockway Glass Co.; b. Vulcan, Mich., Aug. 12, 1889; s. George B. and Bessie (Beadle) W.; grad. Wyoming Sem., Kingston, Pa., 1908, Lafayette Coll., Easton, Pa., 1912; m. Marie B. Garner, June 9, 1914; children—Robert Legh, Marie G., George Henry. Mgr. Beadle & Co., general store, Brockway, Pa., 1912-22; supt. Beadle & McCauley Coal Co., Brockway, Pa., since 1921; pres. Brockway (Pa.) Crystal Water Co. since 1915, dir. since 1912; pres. Brockway Glass Co. since 1928; pres. and dir. Keystone Silver Black Fox Ranch, Inc.; treas. and dir. The Beadle Corp., Inc. Dir. Glass Container Assn. of America; mem. Bucktail Council of Boy Scouts of America. Mason (Lodge 559; Jaffa Shrine; Coudersport Consistory), Elk (Du Bois, Pa.). Club: The Pa. Soc. (N.Y.). Home: 1033 Main St. Office: Main St. and Fifth Av., Brockway, Pa.

WARRINER, Samuel Dexter, corpn. officer; b. Lancaster, Pa., Feb. 24, 1867; s. Rev. Edward A. and Louisa (Voorhis) W.; A.B., Amherst, 1888; B.S., Lehigh U., 1890, E.M., 1890, hon. Dr. Engring.; m. Stella Mercer Farnham, May 18, 1898; children—Farnham, Eloise (Mrs. Richard M. Ehret), R. Dexter, J. Dorrance. Chmn. bd. and mgr. Lehigh Coal & Navigation Co. (mgr. since 1912); chmn. bd. and dir. Lehigh & N.E.R.R. Co.; dir. Lehigh Navigation Coal Co., Allentown Iron Co., Allentown Terminal R.R. Co., Old Company's Lehigh, Inc., Cranberry Creek Coal Co., Admiralty Coal Corpn., Alliance Insurance Company, Crab Orchard Improvement Company, Parkway Company, Lehigh & Hudson River Railway Co., Lehigh Power Securities Corpn., Nat. Power & Light Co., Pa. Salt Mfg. Co., Stonega Coke & Coal Co., Va. Coal and Iron Co., Westmoreland Coal Co., Westmoreland, Inc., Indemnity Ins. Co. of N. America, Ins. Co. of N. America, Phila. Fire & Marine Ins. Co., Phila. Nat. Bank, Pa. Co. for Insurances on Lives and Granting Annuities, Blue Ridge Real Estate Company, Del. Div. Canal Co. of Pa., Campbell Hall Connecting R.R. Co., Pochuck R.R. Co., Amboy Lehigh Coal Co., Monroe Water Supply Co., Nesquehoning Valley R.R. Co., Panther Valley Water Co., Summit Hill Water Co., Tresckow R.R. Co., Wilkes-Barre & Scranton Ry. Co., Greenwood Corpn., 250 S. 18th St. Corpn. Trustee Penn Mutual Life Ins. Co., Lehigh U. Republican. Episcopalian. Clubs: Union League, Rittenhouse, Engineers, Midday, Philadelphia Country (Phila.); Railroad-Machinery (New York); Westmoreland (Wilkes-Barre); Merion Cricket, Boca Raton, Santee, Seaview Golf, Mahoning Valley Country, Montrose Country, North Mountain, Pohoqualine Fish Assn., Woodmont Rod and Gun, U.S. Seniors' Golf Assn., Newcomen Society. Home: "Fernheim," Montrose, Pa.; and 250 S. 18th St., Philadelphia, Pa. Office: 1421 Chestnut St., Philadelphia, Pa.

WARTH, Albin Henry, chemist; b. Stapleton, S.I., N.Y., Mar. 26, 1885; s. Henry and Mary Louise (Hendrickson) W.; B.S., Columbia U., 1907; D.Sc., Am. Internat. Acad., Baltimore, 1930; m. Josephine O'Connor, Sept. 28, 1915; children—George Albin, Henry Kent, Philip Roger, Albin Henry, Jr. Chemist Lackawanna Steel Co., Buffalo, N.Y., 1907, Proctor & Gamble Mfg. Co., Port Ivory, N.Y., 1908-10; chief chemist, J. L. Hopkins Co., New York, 1910-12; research chemist, General Electric Co., West Lynn, Mass., 1912-14; chief chemist, Celluloid Co., Newark, N.J., 1914-16; chem. dir. Crown Cork & Seal Co., Baltimore, Md., since 1918; provost Am. Internat. Acad., Baltimore, Md., since 1938. Fellow A.A.A.S., Am. Inst. Chemists, Am. Internat. Acad. Mem. Am. Chem. Soc., Md. Acad. Scis., Baltimore Philatelic Soc., Collectors Club of N.Y. Awarded, Internat. Double Wreath, Cross of Compassionate Heart, Cross St. Nicholas. Dmcrt. Catholic. Co-Author (with Sutermeister & Browne), Casein and Its Industrial Applications, 1939. Contbr. over 225 articles to trade and gen. publs. Patentee many articles and processes. Home: 29 York Ct. Office: Crown Cork & Seal Co., Baltimore, Md.

WARTHEN, William Horace Franklin, asst. commr. of health; b. Baltimore, Md., Dec. 8, 1897; s. Franklin Filmore and Minnie Lee (Blake) W.; grad. Baltimore City Coll., 1915; B.A., Johns Hopkins U., Baltimore, 1919, M.D., 1922, grad. work since 1938; m. Blenda Ellen Smith, Jan. 19, 1936; 1 son, William Horace Franklin. Resident house officer Harriet Lane Home, Johns Hopkins Hosp., Baltimore, 1922-23; resident physician Children's Hosp., Akron, O., 1923-24; dir. Bur. of Child Hygiene, Baltimore City Health Dept., 1924-34; asst. commr. of health of Baltimore since 1934; asso. in hygiene and pub. health, U. of Md. Sch. of Medicine, Baltimore, since 1934; lecturer in pub. health admstrn., Johns Hopkins Sch. of Hygiene and Pub. Health since 1938. Mem. Exec. Com. Babies' Milk Fund Assn. of Baltimore; mem. bd. Md. Soc. for Prevention of Blindness; mem. bd. Md. State Bd. of Funeral Dirs. and Embalmers. Served as pvt. 1st class, R.O.T.C., 1917-18, S.A.T.C., 1918. Fellow Am. Pub. Health Assn.; mem. Med. and Chirurg. Faculty of Md., Baltimore City Med. Soc., Md. Acad. of Medicine and Surgery, Gamma Alpha Pi. Democrat. Episcopalian. Mason (past master; Royal Arch). Home: 646 N. Augusta Av. Office: City Health Dept., Baltimore, Md.

WARWICK, C(harles) Laurence, engr.; b. Phila., Pa., July 29, 1889; s. Charles Firman and Emily N. (Meyers) W.; student Central Manual Training Sch., Phila., 1902-05; B.S. in C.E., U. of Pa., 1909, C.E., 1926; m. Mary E. Orem, Jan. 25, 1915; children—C. Laurence, Robert Orem, Mary Elizabeth. Instr. and asso. prof. structural engring., U. of Pa., 1909-19; asst. in editorial and tech. work Am. Soc. for Testing Materials, Phila., 1909-19, sec. and treas. since 1919. Commr. Radnor Twp., Delaware Co., Pa., since 1937. Mem. Am. Soc. for Testing Materials, A.A.A.S., Am. Soc. C.E., Am. Soc. for Metals, Sigma Xi. Republican. Presbyterian. Clubs: Engineers (Phila.; v.p.), St. Davids Golf. Home: 418 Woodland Av., Wayne, Pa. Office: 260 S. Broad St., Philadelphia, Pa.

WARWICK, Edward, artist; b. Philadelphia, Pa., Dec. 10, 1881; s. Charles F. and Katherine (Griesemer) W.; prep. edn., Friends Central Sch. and Delancy Sch., Phila.; student U. of Pa.; studied at Pa. Mus. and Sch. of Industrial Art; m. Ethel Herrick, June 19, 1912; 1 son, Edward Worthington. Became instr. Pa. Museum Sch. of Industrial Art, 1914, prin. since 1933; lecturer on period costume and furniture; has specialized on wood blocks, pen and ink, and pastels. Mem. Phila. Art Alliance, Phila. Water Color, Sketch and Print clubs, Arms and Armourers Club, N.Y. City, Phi Kappa Psi. Clubs: Art, Contemporary. Author: Early American Costume, 1929. Home: 222 W. Hortter St., Philadelphia, Pa.

WARWICK, Ethel Herrick (Mrs. Edward Warwick), artist; b. N.Y. City; d. George Lucius and Elmira (Thomas) Herrick; graduate Moore Institute, School of Design; student Pennsylvania Academy Fine Arts; m. Edward Warwick, June 19, 1912; 1 son, Edward Worthington. Has followed profession as artist since 1910, painter of portraits, decorations, interior of homes in oil, water color and pastels, also landscapes in various mediums; exhibited in many large cities in important showings; represented in private collections. Mem. The Fellowship of Pa. Acad. Fine Arts, Phila. Art Alliance, New Century Guild, Phila. Print Club, Plastic Club, Phila. Water Color Club, Awarded Horstman Scholarship from Moore Inst. Sch. of Design for Women, 1904; water color prize by Plastic Club, 1930; prize for best oil sketch by Phila. Art Alliance, 1916. Republican. Episcopalian. Home: 222 W. Hortter St., Germantown, Philadelphia, Pa.

WASHBURN, Benjamin Martin, bishop; b. Bethel, Vt., June 1, 1887; s. Seth Monroe and Kate Strong (Brooks) W.; A.B., Dartmouth, 1907, D.D., 1929; B.D., Gen. Theol. Sem. of the P.E. Ch., 1913, S.T.D., 1933; m. Henrietta Tracy de Selding, Apr. 19, 1917; 1 son, Seth. Ordained ministry P.E. Ch., 1912; curate Grace Ch. (New York), 1912-15, vicar, 1915-18; rector St. Paul's Ch., Kansas City, 1918-29, Emmanuel Ch., Boston, 1929-32; bishop coadjutor of the diocese of Newark, 1932-35, bishop since 1935. Trustee Gen. Theol. Sem. of the P.E. Ch., Church Pension Fund, Church Life Ins. Corpn., and Church Hymnal Corpn. Mem. Mayflower Soc., S.A.R., Sigma Alpha Epsilon. Clubs: Essex (Newark); Rock Springs Country; Dartmouth (N.Y.). Home: Orange, N.J. Address: 621 Berkeley Av., Orange, N.J.

WASHBURN, Cadwallader, artist; b. Minneapolis, Minn.; s. William Drew and Elizabeth M. (Muzzy) W.; B.A., Gallaudet Coll., Washington, D.C., 1890, D.Sc., 1924; course in architecture, Mass. Inst. Tech., class of '93; Art Students' League, New York; pupil of H. Siddons Mowbray, 1895-96; pvt. pupil William Merritt Chase; studied with Joaquin Sorolla, Madrid, 1896-98, and Albert Besnard, 1899-1900; unmarried. Was in Japan and Manchuria, 1904-05, during Russo-Japanese War, for a time acting war corr. at Newchwang; war corr. Chicago Daily News, Mexico, 1910-12, Madero revolution; writer, 1922-23; in the Marquesas Islands, collecting bird eggs and nests for Museum of Comparative Oölogy. Dir. Washburn Lignite Coal Company of N.D. Represented in British Museum, Victoria and Albert Museum (London), Musée du Luxembourg, Bibliotheque Nationale (Paris), Ryke Museum (Amsterdam), Honolulu Academy Arts. Gold medal, Panama P.I. Expn., 1915. Mem. American Fed. of Arts, Soc. Am. Etchers; fellow American Geog. Soc. Trustee Museum Comparative Oölogy, Santa Barbara, Calif. Clubs: University (Mexico City); National Arts (New York); Arts (Washington). Rep. at Minneapolis Inst. Art, Library of Congress, Washington, D.C., Corcoran Art Gallery, Washington, Calif. state collection, Minn. state collection. Home: Lakewood, N.J. Address: care Frederick Keppel & Co., 71 E. 57th St., New York, N.Y.

WASHBURN, Newell R.; mem. surg. staff Milford Emergency Hosp. Address: 6 Causey Av., Milford, Del.

WASHBURN, Philip Carter, physician; b. Cleveland, O., May 8, 1875; s. Alvan Hyde and Mary Arabella (Carter) W.; A.B., Trinity Coll., Hartford, Conn., 1896, A.M., 1900; M.D., Coll. Physicians and Surgeons, Columbia U., 1900; m. Elinor Lathrop Daniels, June 25, 1912; children—Griffith Bowen, Elisabeth Gale (Mrs. Walter Lee Sarell, Jr.). Interne Hartford Hosp., N.Y. State Hosp. Service, 1900; engaged in pvt. practice of gen. medicine at Cape May, N.J., since 1901; senior physician, N.J. State Hosp., Greystone Park, N.J., since 1922. Served as capt. Med. Corps, U.S.A., during World War. Mem. Am. Med. Assn., N.J. Med. Soc., Morris Co. Med. Soc., Alpha Delta Phi. Republican. Episcopalian. Mason. Home: Greystone Park, N.J.

WASHBURN, Stanley, war corr., author; b. Minneapolis, February 7, 1878; s. William Drew and Elizabeth M. (Muzzy) W.; A.B., Williams Coll., 1901, hon. Dr. Humane Letters, 1921; attended Harvard Law Sch., 1901; m. Alice Langhorne, Nov. 27, 1906; children—Fawan, Stanley, Langhorne. Police reporter Minneapolis Journal, 1901-02; on staff Minneapolis Times, 1902-04; war corr. Chicago Daily News, 1904-06. Covered Russo-Japanese War, operated dispatch boat "Fawan" 4 mos. outside Port Arthur, with Nogi's army before Port Arthur; served with 3d Japanese Army until end of war; organized news service in Far East and India; operated dispatch boat in Black Sea, Dec. 1905, carrying British and U.S. Govt. official dispatches, mail and refugees; covered Russian Revolution, Jan. 1906. Headed party to explore British Columbia, summer of 1909; summer of 1910, went through from Edmonton to Prince Rupert by pack-train and canoe, 1,000 miles, being first party to make trip over line of new G.T.P. R.R. route, with exception of engrs. Went to Europe, Aug. 1914, as corr. Collier's Weekly, to Russia, Sept. 1914, as corr. London Times; attached to Russian Army for 26 mos., was only American having access to whole Russian front; also with French at Verdun, Apr. 1916, and attached to Roumanian Army 2 mos., 1916. Commd. maj. Minn. N.G., Apr. 1915, col. Feb. 1916, as aide on gov.'s staff. Apptd. maj. of cav. O.R.C., May 5, 1917; active duty May 9, as mil. aide to John F. Stevens, advisory railroad mission to Russia; transferred at Vladivostok to the Root diplomatic mission to Russia as mil. aide and asst. sec. of mission; G2 of 26th Div., in France, Apr. 1, 1918; served in Toul and Chateau-Thierry sectors with that div.; invalided home, Sept. 1918; hon. discharged, service, Jan. 27, 1919; lt. col. Mil. Intelligence Dept., June 10, 1931. Before leaving for France, by request Russian Embassy, detailed by State and War depts. to make speaking tour through 35 states presenting case of Russia in the war. Decorated by Emperor of Japan with Order of the Imperial Crown, 1907; by Czar with Order of St. Anna, 1915; by Gen. Brussilov, Order of St. George, 1916; by King of Roumania. Commdr. Order of Crown. Mon. mem. Japanese Red Cross Soc. Del. Rep. Nat. Convention, Chicago, 1912. Author: The Cable Game, 1911; Trails, Trappers and Tenderfeet, 1912; Nogi—The Man Against the Background of a War, 1913; The Spirit of the Wilds, 1913; Two in the Wilderness, 1914; Field Notes from the Russian Front, 1915; The Russian Campaign, April to August, 1915; Victory in Defeat, 1916; The Russian Offensive, 1917; also play, "The Man in Hiding," prod. May 1914. Apptd. by State Dept. to the secretariat of Am. Delegation to the Disarmament Conf., Washington, 1921; now coal mine operator; pres. Washburn Lignite Coal Co., Wilton, N.D., 1926-29, now vice-pres. Pres. N.D. Coal Operators' Assn.; v.p. and nat. councillor Greater N.D. Assn.; dir. Nat. Security League; chmn. Russian com. Nat. Civic Federation; trustee Am. Defense Soc. Mason. Pres. Arden Sch., Lakewood, N.J., 1920-27. Elk. Clubs: University, Nat. Republican, Century (New York); Delta Psi, Minneapolis, Skylight, Six o'Clock (Minneapolis). Republican nominee for Congress (1932), defeated by vote of 62,000 to 59,000. Mem. Am. Legion, Vets. of Foreign Wars, Reserve Officers Assn., Reserve Intelligence Officers Assn. Pres.

Landon-Knox Club and chmn. of the affiliated Rep. Clubs, Lakewood, 1936. Has made 1000 speeches in 42 different states since 1917; has been either war corr. or soldier with 20 armies and covered approximately 100 battles since 1904. Home: 600 Forrest Av., Lakewood, N.J.

WASHBURN, Victor Duke, M.D.; b. N.Y. City, July 16, 1882; s. Charles H. and Carlotta (Sorino) W.; M.D., Atlantic Med. Coll., Baltimore, Md., 1905; m. 2d, Margaret A. Elliott, Oct. 26, 1915; children—(by 1st marriage) Ruth, (by 2d marriage) Elliott Sorino. Practiced at Wilmington, Del., since 1905; urologist Wilmington Homœ. Hosp., St. Francis Hosp. Served as 1st lt. M.C., U.S.A., 1917-19; maj. M.C., Del. N.G. Mem. Wilmington Bd. Pub. Edn., 1915-27, 1931-33 (pres. 1923-27); dir. Dept. Pub. Safety, 1927-30; dir. Del. Safety Council. Fellow A.M.A.; mem. Am. Inst. Homœopathy, Del. Acad. Medicine, Assn. Mil. Surgeons. Republican. Unitarian. Mason. Club: University. Home: 702 Blackshire Rd. Office: 822 Washington St., Wilmington, Del.

WASHINGTON, Elizabeth Fisher, artist in landscapes and miniature portraits; born Siegfried's Bridge, Pa.; d. George Lafayette and Ann Bull (Clemson) Washington; direct desc. Col. Samuel Washington, brother to Gen. George Washington; great great niece of Dolly Madison, wife of Pres. Madison; ed. privately at home; art student Pa. Acad. of Fine Arts, 4 years; also Hugh Breckenridge's Summer Sch. (Ft. Washington, Pa.), Fred Wagner's Summer School and European traveling summer scholarship from Pa. Acad. Fine Arts; unmarried. Exhibited in: Pa. Acad. Fine Arts; Corcoran Gallery, Washington, D.C.; Nat. Acad. of Design, New York; Carnegie Inst., Pittsburgh; Art Inst. of Chicago; City Art Museum, St. Louis; and many others. Awards: Mary Smith prize of Pa. Acad. Fine Arts, 1917 and 1934; fellowship prize of Pa. Acad. Fine Arts, 1917; 1st landscape prize, Chester Springs, Pa. Mem. Pa. Soc. Miniature Painters (treas.), Plastic Club. Fellowship of Pa. Acad. of Fine Arts (rec. sec.), Phila. Art Alliance, Print Club of Phila., Nat. Soc. of Magna Charta Dames (regent general), Colonial Dames of America. Home: 214 S. 43d St. Studio: 1714 Chestnut St., Philadelphia, Pa.

WASON, Robert Alexander, author; b. Toledo, O., Apr. 6, 1874; s. Robert Alexander and Gertrude Louise (Paddock) W.; high sch., Delphi, 1 yr.; m. Emma Louise Brownell, May 11, 1911; children—Charles Brownell, Jane, Robert Alexander. Clerk in gen. store 8 yrs., varied by tramping and "roughing it" in the West; served 9 mos. in Light Battery D, 5th U.S. Arty., 1898-99. Author: Babe Randolph's Turning Point, 1904; The Wolves, 1908; Nachette (with Ned Nye), 1909; Happy Hawkins, 1909; The Steering Wheel, 1910; The Knight Errant, 1911; The Dog and the Child and the Ancient Sailor Man, 1911; Friar Tuck, 1912; And Then Came Jean, 1913; Happy Hawkins in the Panhandle, 1914; Knute Ericson's Celebration, in The Grim Thirteen, 1917; also vaudeville sketches, a comic opera, and short stories in popular mags. Home: Mountain Lakes, N.J.

WASSELL, Harry B., lawyer; b. Pittsburgh, Pa., Dec. 1, 1877; s. William and Emma (Rowswell) W.; student Pittsburgh pub. schs., 1884-92; Ph.B., Bucknell U., Lewisburg, Pa., 1900; LL.B., U. of Pittsburgh Law Sch., 1903; m. Edith Taylor, Nov. 30, 1920. Admitted to Pa. bar, 1903, and since practiced in Pittsburgh and vicinity; dir. Wood Preserving Corpn., Am. Mono Nickel Co., Liberty Baking Co., Trustee Phi Gamma Delta fraternity. Republican. Baptist. Mason (K.T., Shriner). Clubs: Duquesne, University, Pittsburgh Athletic Assn., Oakmont Golf (Pittsburgh); Chevy Chase (Washington, D.C.); Everglades (Palm Beach, Fla.); Phi Gamma Delta (New York). Home: Schenley Apts. Office: 3106 Grant Bldg., Pittsburgh, Pa.

WASSERMAN, William Stix, investment trust exec.; b. Phila., Pa. Mar. 24, 1901; s. Joseph and Edith (Stix) W.; ed. The Taft Sch.; A.B., Princeton, 1922; m. Marion Fleisher, Dec. 22, 1923; children—Marie Blanche, William Stix, Jr., Joseph II, Steven Rice. Began as asst. to pres. Artloom Corpn., later asso. with Dillon, Read & Co.; pres. Investment Corpn. of Phila., 1929-38; pres. W. S. Wasserman Co. since 1932; one of organizers The Delaware Fund and pres. since 1937; dir. Ryan Oil Co., N.Y. Shipbuilding Corpn. Served as leader Am. Del. to World's Econ. Conf. in Berlin, 1931; adviser to Del. of U.S. to Internat. Labor Conf., Geneva, 1937. Mason. Clubs: Midday (Philadelphia); Bankers, Explorers (New York). Home: "Square Shadows," Whitemarsh, Pa. Office: 225 S. 15th St., Philadelphia, Pa.

WATERMAN, Julius Louis, urologist; b. Rochester, N.Y., Mar. 18, 1890; s. Louis and Rosa (Neuberger) W.; M.D., Cornell U., 1911; m. Mary Moore Daily, July 11, 1930; 1 dau., Mina Rose. House surgeon Bellevue Hosp., New York, 1912-14; attending urologist Monroe Co., Park Av. and Highland hosps., Rochester, N.Y., 1920-30; chief venereal clinics Baden St. Dispensary, Rochester, 1914-17, Highland Hosp., 1920-30; urologist-in-chief Bradford (Pa.) Hosp. since 1930; cons. urologist Kane (Pa.) Community Hosp. since 1931, Warren Gen. and Pa. State hosps., Warren, Pa., since 1933; chief Pa. State Venereal Clinic, Bradford, since 1932. Served as lt. (j.g.), M.C., U.S. Navy and lt., M.C., 1917-19; lt. comdr. M.C., U.S.N.R., 1929, comdr., 1938; commanding officer, Med. Specialist Unit 1, 4th Naval Dist., since 1935. Fellow Am. Coll. Surgeons, A.M.A.; mem. Am. Urol. Assn., McKean Co. Med. Soc. (pres., 1938), McKean Co. Tuberculosis Assn. (dir.), County Healing Arts Assistance Com. (chmn.); diplomate Am. Bd. Urology. Mason (32°). Clubs: Bradford (Pa.); Rochester (N.Y.); Army and Navy (Washington, D.C.); Kane (Pa.) Country. Home: Cotswold Hill, R.D. 2. Office: 2 Main St., Bradford, Pa.

WATERS, Daniel Vaughn, mech, engring.; b. Kingston, Pa., Sept. 27, 1891; s. William Austin and Martha (Cleveland) W.; ed. Internat. Corr. Sch., 1910-15, spl. tutor advanced subjects, 1918-22, mechanics of machinery, 1928-29, effective speaking, 1929-30, accounting, Chicago Coll. of Commerce, 1930-34; m. Florence Hebbe, May 6, 1914 (died 1933); children—Florence Evelyn, Mary Jean. Began as apprentice machinist, 1907; machinist, then foreman, C.R.R. of N.J., 1911-15; designer, Niles-Bement-Pond Co., 1915-16; engr. Bethlehem Steel Corpn., 1916-17; head designer, Gould & Eberhardt, 1917-20; asst. chief engr., Ivers-Lee Co., 1920-21; mech. engr. in charge engring. office, Gould & Eberhardt, 1921-26; mech. engr., Western Electric Co., Kearny, N.J., 1926-28, development engr. in charge machine design, 1928-31, mech. engr. since 1931; awarded 9 patents covering devices related to production equipment; instr. advanced machine design and engring. problems, Cooper Union Engring. Sch. since 1937. Mem. Am. Soc. Mech. Engrs., Nat. Soc. Professional Engrs. Republican. Presbyn. Mason. Club: Engineers (Plainfield). Contbr. articles to tech. publs. Home: 65 Randolph Pl., South Orange. Office: 100 Central Av., Kearny, N.J.

WATERS, Edward Gilmay, physician; b. Derby, Conn., Jan. 14, 1898; s. Edward T. and Bertha (Corcery) W.; Ph.B. cum laude, Yale U., 1919; M.D., Harvard U. Med. Sch., 1922; grad. study surgery, N.Y.U. Med. Sch. and Bellevue Hosp., 1927-29; m. Edna MacCabe, Oct. 28, 1924; children—Edward Gilmay 3d, Leighton Kinsley, Dean Allison, Shirley Ellen (dec.), Edna Elaine (dec.). Interne Brooklyn Hosp., 1922-23; resident, Bridgeport (Conn.) Hosp., 1923-24; chief res. surg., Jersey City Med. Center, 1924-27; asst. prof. clin. gynecology and obstetrics, Columbia U. since 1937; div. chief obstetrics, Margaret Hague Maternity Hosp.; attdg. surg., Christ and Fairmount hosps.; asso. surg. Jersey City Med. Center; dir. Fairmount Hosp., Teaneck Med. Group. Served in R.O.T.C., arty. and Med. Corps, 1918. Fellow Am. Coll. Surgs. Diplomate Nat. Bd. Med. Examiners, Am. Bd. Obstetrics and Gynecology. Mem. A.M.A., Am. Soc. Regional Anesthesia, N.Y. Obstet. Soc., Practitioners Club, Harvard Med. Club of N.Y., Alpha Chi Rho, Alpha Kappa Kappa. Club: Cartaret (Jersey City). Author: Civic Sanitation, 1923. Contbr. about 40 articles to jurs. Home: 39 Gifford Av., Jersey City, N.J.

WATERS, Robert Suppes, pres. The Nat. Radiator Co.; b. Johnstown, Pa., Apr. 9, 1893; s. John H. and Alice May (Suppes) W.; grad. Lawrenceville (N.J.) Prep. Sch., 1913; B.S. in Economics, U. of Pa., 1917; unmarried. Began as clerk mfg. dept. Nat. Radiator Co., Johnstown, Pa., 1919, later apptd. sec. and then gen. mgr. of mfg., elected dir. and v.p. in charge mfg., research and development Nat. Radiator Corpn. (consolidation of 6 cos., 1927); pres. The Nat. Radiator Co. since June 1, 1939; v.p. and dir. U.S. Nat. Bank in Johnstown; trustee Johnstown Savings Bank. Corporator and mem. bd. of mgrs. Conemaugh Valley Memorial Hosp.; mem. bd. of corporators Citizens Cemetery Assn. Enlisted as seaman U.S. N.R.F., May 1917; trans. to Naval Aviation; naval aviator, Pensacola, and Naval Air Stations, France; disch. Jan. 1919; now lt. comdr. U.S.N.R. Mem. Johnstown Chamber of Commerce, U.S. Chamber of Commerce, U.S. Naval Inst., Am. Legion, Chi Phi. Republican. Lutheran. Mason (K.T., Shriner). Clubs: Bachelors, Sunnehanna Country (Johnstown); Duquesne (Pittsburgh); Rolling Rock (Ligonier, Pa.). Home: Southmont, Johnstown, Pa. Office: 221 Central Av., Johnstown, Pa.

WATERSON, Karl William, corpn. exec.; b. Chelsea, Vt., Mar. 9, 1876; s. Charles Albert and Mary Elizabeth (Colby) W.; B.S. in elec. engring., Mass. Inst. Technology, 1898; m. Anne Darling, Nov. 28, 1928; children—Anne Elizabeth, Karl William. With Am. Bell Telephone Co., and its successor Am. Telephone & Telegraph Co., since 1898, became asst. in engring. dept., 1898, in charge central office engring., 1901, in charge traffic engring., 1905, engr. of traffic, 1909, asst. chief engr., 1919, asst. v.p. 1927, v.p. personnel relations since 1937; mem. Long Lines Dept. Bd.; dir. Bell Telephone Labs., Inc. Rep. of Bell System in arrangement with mil. authorities for special facilities and service at training camps, etc., during World War. Trustee Short Hills (N.J.) Country Day Sch. Fellow Am. Inst. Elec. Engrs. Republican. Conglist. Clubs: University, Railroad-Machinery, Technology (New York); Essex County Country (West Orange, N.J.); Short Hills (Short Hills, N.J.); Barre Country (Barre, Vt.). Home: 35 Ox Bow Lane, Summit, N.J. Office: 195 Broadway, New York, N.Y.

WATERWORTH, Samuel James, surgeon; b. Baltimore, Md., Sept. 10, 1873; s. James Murray and Catherine (Lee) W.; M.D., Coll. Phys. & Surgs. U. of Md., 1893; m. Catherine Cunningham, June 22, 1898; children—Mary Anne (dec.), Margaret (dec.), Catherine Lee, Julia A., Anne Susanne, S. James, Jr., Andrew Joseph, Louise (Mrs. Jerome McGinnis), Betty Clare. Asst. to mine surgeon, 1893-95; engaged in pvt. practice at Clearfield, Pa. since 1895, asst. to Dr. M. Gard Whittier, 1895-1901; organized Clearfield Hosp., 1901, and surgeon in chief and chief of staff since 1924; post grad. work and study at all leading clinics, and abroad, and med. soc. meetings, all average two months annually for 40 yrs.; mem. Credential Bd. for Pa., Am. Coll. Surgs. Dir. Pub. Charities Assn. of Pa. Fellow Am. Coll. Surgs. since 1917. Mem. Am. Assn. of Industrial Phys. and Surgs., Am. Soc. for Study Neoplastic Diseases, Am. Soc. for Study of Goiter, Am. Soc. for Control of Cancer, Pa. State Med. Soc. (chmn. surg. sect., 1933, Cancer Commn. 4 yrs.), Clearfield Co. Med. Soc. (past pres.). Democrat. Roman Catholic. Club: Rotary (hon.). Contbr. to surg. literature for many yrs. Home: 102 S. Second St., Clearfield, Pa. Office: 207 E. Cherry St., Clearfield, Pa.

WATKINS, Charles, educator; b. Morristown, Tenn., Nov. 11, 1885; s. Wirt Crampton and Catherine (King) W.; A.B., Washington and Lee, 1909; M.S., Vanderbilt, 1911; Ph.D., Johns Hopkins, 1915; m. Amelia Jackson, Feb. 1917; children—Charles Emil, Lee Kirk. Taught in Branham and Hughes Boys Sch., 1909-10; instr. Washington and Lee U., 1911-13; asst. to pres. Carnegie Inst. Tech. since 1930, also prof. chemistry and head dept. of science since 1917 and dir. since 1929, Margaret Morrison Carnegie Coll. Chmn. Com. on graduate studies, Beta Theta Pi, Gamma Alpha, Phi Beta Kappa,

Phi Kappa Phi. Home: 5664 Darlington Rd., Pittsburgh, Pa.

WATKINS, Charles Law, dir. art. sch.; b. Peckville, Pa., Feb. 11, 1886; s. Thomas Hamer and Elizabeth (Law) W.; A.B., Yale U., 1908; m. Marie Mathilde Bader, Feb. 22, 1919; children—Thomas Hamer II, Gladys Marie, Ann, Elizabeth Law. Served as pres. Watkins Coal Co., Barnesboro, Pa., 1910-22, merged with Pa. Coal Co. and vice-pres. in charge of operations Pa. Coal & Coke Corpn., 1922-29; resigned to become asso. dir. Phillips Memorial Gallery, Washington, D.C., 1929; founded Phillips Gallery Art Sch. and dir. since 1931. Served with Am. Ambulance, 1916-17; aspirant F.A., French Army, 1917-18; awarded Croix de Guerre. Mem. Delta Kappa Epsilon, Skull and Bones. Presbyterian. Clubs: Apawamis (Rye, N.Y.); Summit Country of Cresson, Pa. (hon. pres.). Home: 7040 Hampden Lane, Bethesda, Md. Office: 1600 21st St. N.W., Washington, D.C.

WATKINS, Donald Newell, pub. tech. steel mags.; b. Bradford, Pa., Mar. 13, 1894; s. Daniel S. and Francis E. (Ford) W.; C.E., George Washington U., 1918; m. Eva J. Cook, Feb. 5, 1921. Employed as civil engr. later supt., Jones & Laughlin Steel Co., 1918-23; western sales mgr. General Refractories Co., 1923-27; pres. and dir. Steel Publications, Inc., pubs. steel tech. bus. papers, Pittsburgh, since 1927. Mem. Engrs. Soc. of Western Pa., Am. Iron and Steel Inst., Theta Delta Chi. Republican. Presbyterian. Mason. Clubs: Pittsburgh Athletic, Pittsburgh Field (Pittsburgh); South Shore Country (Chicago). Home: RFD. No. 2, Belle Vernon. Office: 108 Smithfield St., Pittsburgh, Pa.

WATKINS, Franklin Chenault, artist; b. New York City, Dec. 30, 1894; s. Benjamin Franklin and Shirley (Chenault) W.; ed. Groton Sch. (Mass.), 1908-10, U. of Va., 1911-12, U. of Pa., 1912-13; ed. art, Pa. Acad. Fine Arts, at intervals, 1914-20; m. Fridolyn Gimbel, Oct. 2, 1925. Began career as commercial artist, 1920, later turned to more personal painting. Represented in Mus. Modern Art, Whitney Mus. Am. Art, Hamilton Coll., all New York, N.Y.; Corcoran Gallery of Art, Washington, D.C.; Phillips Memorial Gallery, Washington, D.C.; Smith Coll. Mus. Art, Northampton, Mass.; Rodin Mus., Pa. Acad. Fine Arts and Phila. Mus. Art., Phila.; Courtauld Collection, London, Eng. Awarded first prize and Lehman prize Carnegie Inst. Internat. Exhbn., 1931; 1st William A. Clark prize and gold medal at Corcoran Gallery of Art, 1939; 2d prize, unrestricted div., Golden Gate International Expn., 1939; also awards at Chicago Art Inst., Phila. Sketch Club, Art Club Phila.; bronze medal, Paris Expn., 1937; bronze medal, Musee du Jeu de Paume, Paris, 1938. Instr. in painting, Stella Elkins Tyler Sch. of Fine Arts of Temple U. Served in Camouflage Div., U.S.N., during World War. Home: 2322 Delancey St., Philadelphia, Pa.

WATKINS, Harry Evans, judge; b. Watson, W.Va., Nov. 6, 1898; s. Jesse T. and Mary (Evans) W.; Fairmount (W.Va.) State Coll., 1917; LL.B., W.Va. U., 1923; m. Margaret Lehman, Aug. 20, 1927; children—Sally, Linda. Admitted to W.Va. bar, 1923; practiced in Fairmont, 1923-27; judge U.S. Dist. Court of Northern and Southern Dists. of W.Va., since 1937. Dem. presidential elector for W.Va., 1936. Dir. Fairmont Community Chest. Served as pvt. 1st class Signal Corps, U.S.A., 1918-19. Mem. W.Va. Bar Assn. (v.p. 1935-36), Am. Legion, Forty and Eight, Sphinx, Delta Tau Delta, Phi Delta Phi. Democrat. Presbyterian. Mason (32°). Clubs: Lions (Fairmont); Good Will (Monongah, W.Va.). Home: Fairmount, W.Va.

WATKINS, J. R., editor Raleigh Register. Office: care Beckley Newspapers Corpn., Beckley, W.Va.

WATKINS, John Elfreth, newspaperman; b. Vincentown, N.J., Feb. 12, 1875; s. John Elfreth and Helen (Bryan) W.; grad. Central High Sch., Washington, 1892; m. Corinne C., d. Courtland C. Clements, June 1, 1899. Editor in chief of Review (pub. by 4 high schs. of Washington) at age of 17; worked in press galleries of Congress at 19 as assistant correspondent Chicago Daily News. Contributed, 1894-1914, to leading dailies the "Watkins Letter" on Washington events for 20 yrs., this column becoming nucleus of the Watkins Syndicate which supplied news and feature matter to Am. and foreign press; developed for Cyrus H. K. Curtis, The Ledger Syndicate of Philadelphia and New York, beginning Dec. 1916, and was also gen. mgr. Curtis' Post Syndicate from 1924, until its absorption by Ledger Syndicate, 1929; created and developed many notable features for Curtis newspapers; established June 1935, Watkins Syndicate, Inc., of which is pres.; dir. distribution of London Times Cable Service, U.S. and Can., World War; in charge press, bur. Nat. Capital Centennial, 1900; chmn. sub-com. on cables, Am. Publishers' Com. on Electrical Communications, 1920-21; mem. bd. govs. Assn. of Am. Newspaper Syndicates. Unitarian. Author of more than 100 mystery and detective stories, also many articles in mags.; author of screen features, "The Thread," "The Test." Home: 2011 Delancey St., Philadelphia, Pa., and Avalon, N.J. Office: 2214-24 Chestnut St., Philadelphia, Pa.

WATKINS, Ralph James, economist; b. San Marcos, Tex., Dec. 31, 1896; s. Calvert and Martha (Smith) W.; B.B.A., U. of Tex., 1921, A.B., 1922; M.S., Columbia, 1924, Ph.D., 1927; student Universidad Nacional de Mexico, summer 1921; m. Willye Ward, June 20, 1918; 1 son, Calvert. Instr. in business administrn., U. of Tex., 1924-25, prof. statistics, and statistician Bur. of Business Research, 1927-28; asst. prof. statis. research, Bur. of Business Research, Ohio State U., 1925-27, asso. prof., 1928-29; mem. of research staff, Nat. Bur. of Economic Research, New York, 1929-30; dir. of Bur. of Business Research and prof. of statistics, U. of Pittsburgh, since 1930, chmn. social science seminar, 1937-38. Served as 1st sergt. U.S. Army, in U.S. and France, 1917-19. Mem. tech. advisory com. on labor statistics to the sec. of labor and industry, Commonwealth of Pa., 1933-34; mem. adv. com. on statistics and research, Dept. of Labor and Industry, Commonwealth of Pa., since 1937; dir. Pittsburgh Personnel Assn. since 1932; mem. research staff, Com. on Gov. Statistics and Information Services of the Am. Statis. Assn., Washington, D.C., Feb.-June, 1934, and member of the Com., 1934-37; mem. com. on prices in the bituminous coal industry, Conf. on Price Research, since 1936; mem. Advisory Com. on Metropolitan Areas, Census Bureau, since 1938; mem. com. on chem. economics Nat. Research Council since 1938; U.S. del. Tech. Tripartite Meeting on Coal-Mining Industry, Geneva, Switzerland, 1938; consultant, to direct national energy resources survey, Nat. Resources Com., Washington, D.C., since June 1938. Mem. Am. Economic Assn., Am. Statis. Assn. (review editor of Jour.), Royal Economic Soc., Beta Gamma Sigma, Pi Sigma Alpha, Alpha Kappa Psi. Mason. Clubs: University, Faculty (Pittsburgh); Cosmos (Washington). Author: several research reports, 1926-29; contbr. to Pittsburgh Business Review and dir. of numerous research studies pub. since 1930. Home: 1162 S. Negley Av., Pittsburgh, Pa.

WATKINS, W. C.; editor Maryland Farmer. Office: 812 Fidelity Bldg., Baltimore, Md.

WATRES, Laurence Hawley, ex-congressman; b. Scranton, Pa.; s. Hon. Louis A. (lt. gov. Pa.) and Effie (Hawley) W.; A.B., Princeton, 1904; LL.B., Harvard, 1907; unmarried. In practice at Scranton, 1907; mem. 68th to 71st Congresses (1923-31), 11th Pa. Dist. Republican. Capt. 108th Machine Gun Batt.; 28th Div., later maj., World War; wounded in action nr. Vesle River; after close of war assisted in reorganizing 109th Regt. Inf., Pa. N.G., as lt. col. of rgt. Awarded D.S.C. (U.S.). Home: Elmhurst Boul. Office: 506 Spruce St., Scranton, Pa.

WATSON, Albert Leisenring, judge; b. Montrose, Pa., Dec. 6, 1876; s. Willoughby W. and Annie Maria (Kemmerer) W.; B.A., Amhurst, 1901; studied law in offices of Watson, Diehl, Hall & Kemmerer, Scranton, Pa.; m. Mabel E. Wheeler, Jan. 9, 1902 (died Nov. 30, 1923); children—Albert Leisenring, Willoughby Wheeler (dec.), Righter; m. 2d, Effie Bradshaw Woodville, Oct. 6, 1930. Admitted to Pa. bar, 1903, and began practice at Scranton; mem. firm Watson, Diehl, Kemmerer & Watson, 1903-08, Watson, Diehl & Watson, 1908-25; apptd. mem. Commn. for Investigating Systems of Recording Deeds, Mortgages, etc., 1917; apptd. counsel Workmen's Compensation Bur., Pa., 1923; judge Court of Common Pleas, Lackawanna Co., Pa., 1926-28; judge U.S. Dist. Court, Middle Dist. of Pa., since Jan. 11, 1930. Mem. New England Soc., Pa. Republican. Presbyn. Mason (K.T., Knight of Malta); mem. Jr. Order United Am. Mechanics, Patriotic Order Sons of America. Clubs: Waverly (Scranton); University (New York). Home: Clarks Summit, Lackawanna Co., Pa. Chambers: Federal Bldg., Scranton, Pa.

WATSON, Bruce Mervellon, educator, author; b. Windsor, N.Y., Feb. 28, 1860; s. Robert Bruce and Amanda R. (Porter) W.; grad. State Normal and Training Sch., Oswego, N.Y., 1885; studied Syracuse U.; m. Jennie E. Moore, June 28, 1894; children—Robert Bruce, Dorothy Moore (Mrs. D. H. Ecker), Helen Annette (Mrs. L. E. Steiner). Vice-principal Pulaski (N.Y.) Acad., 1885-86; principal Seymour School, Syracuse, 1887-1904; head of math. dept., Central High Sch., Syracuse, 1904-08; supt. schs., Spokane, Wash., 1908-16; mng. dir. Pub. Edn. and Child Labor Assn. of Pa., 1916-36. Admitted to New York bar, 1898. Pres. Inland Empire Teachers' Assn., 1912-13. Member Philadelphia Committee on Public Affairs. Mem. N. E.A. (mem. legislative commn. since 1931). Congregationalist. Mason. Author: Summary of Arithmetic, 1895; Heath Primary Arithmetic, 1901; Watson and White's Arithmetical Series (Charles Edward White), 3 books, 1907; Watson and White's Modern Arithmetics, 3 books, 1918; Watson's Simplified Arithmetics, 1924; Modern Practical Arithmetics, 1925; Junior High School Mathematics (3 vols.), 1931; The Mastery Mathematics, 3 vols. (with Bodley, Hayes and Gibson), 1935. Contbr. many articles on sch. adminstrn. and pedagogy. Editor: Pennsylvania's Children in School and at Work, semi-monthly, 1920-36. Home: 509 Woodland Court, Wayne, Pa.

WATSON, Charles Roger, educationalist; b. Cairo, Egypt, July 17, 1873; s. Andrew and Margaret (McVickar) W.; A.B., Princeton, 1894, A.M., 1896, D.D., 1931; spl. student Princeton Theol. Sem., 1895-96, Allegheny Theol. Sem., 1897-98; grad. Princeton Theol. Sem., 1899; m. Maria Elizabeth Powell, Nov. 20, 1902; children—M. Elisabeth, Edward T. P., Margaret M., Charles R. Teacher Ohio State U., 1894-95, Princeton U., 1895-96, Lawrenceville Sch., 1896-97; in charge Mission Ch., Allegheny, Pa., 1899-1900; ordained U.P. ministry, July 26, 1900; pastor First Ch., St. Louis, 1900-02; corr. sec. Board of Foreign Missions, U.P. Ch. of North America, 1902-16, hon. corr. sec., 1916-22; sec. and pres.-elect American Univ., at Cairo, 1914-22, pres. since 1922. Mem. continuation com. World's Missionary Conference, Edinburgh, 1910. Special rep. of fgn. mission bds. of N. America at Paris Peace Conf., 1919. Mem. Internat. Missionary Council. Visited mission fields of India, Egypt and the Sudan, 1903-04, Egypt to study ednl. and missionary problems, 1911-12, 15, 17; chmn. council com. for Western Asia and North Africa, 1924-26; mem. Jerusalem Conf., I.M.C., 1928. Apptd. mem. Nat. Commn. on Edn. in Egypt, 1931; mem. Near East Christian Council. Clubs: Princeton (New York); Guezireh Sporting Club, Rotary Internat. (Cairo). Author of several books and numerous articles in mags. Home: American University, Cairo, Egypt. Address: (in U.S.A.) 1000 Land Title Bldg., Philadelphia, Pa.*

WATSON, Clarence Wayland, ex-senator; b. Fairmont, W.Va., May 8, 1864; s. James Otis and Matilda (Lamb) W.; ed. pub. schs., Marion Co., W.Va.; m. Minnie Lee Owings, Oct. 10, 1894. Engaged in coal mining in W.Va. since early life; organized several cos. which were later consolidated as Consolidation Coal Co., mines in W.Va., Md., Pa., Ky., of which was pres. until 1911, and 1919-28 (chmn. bd.

1911-18); president Elk Horn Coal Corporation; dir. Beaver Creek Consolidated Coal Company; National Coal Assn. Del. to Dem. Nat. Convention, 1908, 20; elected U.S. senator from W.Va., Jan. 25, 1911, for unexpired term (1911-13) of Stephen B. Elkins, deceased. Commd. lt. col., Ordnance Dept., U.S.A., Mar. 25, 1918; hon. discharged, Jan. 23, 1919. Episcopalian. Mason (K.T.). Clubs: Metropolitan, Chevy Chase (Washington); Baltimore, Maryland (Baltimore); Manhattan, Whist (New York); Duquesne (Pittsburgh); Travellers (Paris); Portland (London). Home: Fairmont Farms, Fairmont, W.Va.*

WATSON, Earle Fontonore, v.p. Am. Surety Co. of N.Y.; b. Susquehanna, Pa., Nov. 2, 1869; s. William Hopkins and Harriet Alvina (Bonker) W.; ed. pub. schs. and Wallkill Acad., Middletown, N.Y., 1876-84, N.Y. City grammar schs., 1884-85, Coll. City of N.Y., 1886-87; LL.B., New York U. Law Sch., 1895; m. Jennie Louise Barkley, May 8, 1890; children—Leona Earle (Mrs. Wm. E. Turner), Beatrice (Mrs. Edward B. Esbach), Frances Elaine (Mrs. Charles J. Haight). Began as office boy, 1888; clerk and bookkeeper, 1889-93; stenographer and law clerk, 1894-97; admitted to New York bar, 1895; managing clerk of legal dept. Am. Surety Co. of N.Y., 1898-99; atty. for same and mgr. contract dept., 1899-1903; asst. gen. solicitor Nat. Cash Register Co., Dayton, O., 1903-04; v.p. Am. Surety Co. of N.Y. since 1914; pres. Dumont Nat. Bank, Dumont Realty Co.; v.p. N.Y. Casualty Co. Fellow Am. Mus. Natural History. Republican. Methodist. Clubs: Manhattan Rifle and Revolver Assn. (N.Y. City); Allendale (N.J.) Revolver. Home: 170 Washington Av., Dumont, N.J. Office: 100 Broadway, New York, N.Y.

WATSON, Elmer Everett, M.D.; b. Fellowsville, W.Va., Oct. 8, 1879; s. William A. and Nancy Jane (Sinclair) W.; student Preston County schs., 1886-1900; M.D., Eclectic Med. Coll., 1908; m. Martha Bell Robinson, Apr. 30, 1902; children—Lucille (Mrs. Andrew Bailey, V), Mary Elizabeth (dec.), James William. In gen. practice of medicine at Albright, W.Va., since 1909; pres. and dir. Albright Nat. Bank of Kingwood, W.Va. Formerly mem. W.Va. State Legislature. Served on local draft board, World War. Mem. W.Va. State Med. Soc., Tau Alpha Epsilon. Republican. Methodist. Mason (32°). Address: Albright, W.Va.

WATSON, Frank Dekker, prof. sociology; b. Philadelphia, Pa., June 28, 1883; s. Edward Hagner and Margaret (Halfman) W.; grad. Central High Sch., Philadelphia, 1902; B.S. in Economics, Wharton Sch. Finance and Commerce, U. of Pa., 1905; Ph.D., U. of Pa., 1911; m. Amey Brown Eaton, Mar. 19, 1913; children—Mason Hagner, Roger Eaton, Curtis Brown, Peter Dekker. Asst. prin. schs., Quakertown, Pa., 1905-06; inst., Wharton Sch. Finance and Commerce, 1906-11; acting instr., Swarthmore (Pa.) Coll., 1908-11; mem. permanent staff New York Sch. of Philanthropy, 1911-14; prof. sociology and social work, Haverford (Pa.) Coll., since 1914; dir. Pa. Sch. of Social Service, 1918-21; lecturer, Temple U., 1924-25. Dir. Red Cross institutes, southeast Pa. chapter, and mem. fuel commn., Delaware Co., Pa., World War. Trustee White-Williams Foundation, 1920-30, pres. bd., 1921-26; dir. Race Relations Inst., Swarthmore, Pa., 1935; special labor economist Dept. of Labor and Industry, Commonwealth of Pa., 1937-38; lecturer, Pub. Service Inst., Dept. of Pub. Instruction, Commonwealth of Pa., 1938-39. Mem. Am. Sociol. Soc., Am. Econ. Assn., Am. Assn. for Labor Legislation, Am. Acad. Polit. and Social Science (editor May 1918 Annals), Phi Beta Kappa, Sigma Phi Epsilon, Delta Sigma Rho, Pi Gamma Mu. Democrat. Quaker. Clubs: Haverford (Philadelphia); Mountain View Golf (Greensboro, Vt.). Author: Economics (with Scott Nearing); The Charity Organization Movement in the United States, 1922. Home: 773 College Av., Haverford, Pa.

WATSON, Frank L., supt. of schs.; b. Nebraska, Pa., Jan. 7, 1899; s. Walter Leon and Anna Laura (Silzle) W.; A.B., Pa. State Coll., 1922; M. Ed., U. of Pittsburgh, 1936; m. Wilda Merryman, May 25, 1926; children—Betty, Lin, Willard, James, Faith. Owner and mgr., Watsons Garage, Kellettville, Pa., 1926-34; teacher of math., English, history, Kingsley Twp. H.S., Kellettville, Pa., 1926-29, prin., 1929-34; Forest Co. (Pa.) Supt. of Schs. since 1934. Served in World War. Mem. Am. Legion, Phi Kappa Phi. Republican. Methodist. Mason, Odd Fellow. Address: Court House, Tionesta, Pa.

WATSON, Frank Rushmore, architect; b. Frankford, Phila., Pa., Feb. 28, 1859; s. Samuel and Anna (Brous) W.; B.A., Central High Sch., Phila., 1877, M.A., 1887, Dr. of Fine Arts, Muhlenberg Coll., 1931; m. Fannie Foulkroud, 1890 (died 1896); m. 2d, Rebecca Sharpless Collins, Feb. 1, 1900; 1 dau., Margaret Anna. Practiced at Phila. since 1883; associated with Samuel Huckel, Jr., 1902-17; practiced alone, 1917-22; mem. firm of Frank R. Watson, Edkins & Thompson, 1922-36; mem. present firm Frank R. Watson and William Heyl Thompson since 1936. Architect many churches, including Episcopal Cathedral, Diocese of Pennsylvania, etc. Hon. associate of American Guild of Organists; fellow A.I.A.; mem. Art Alliance Phila., Frankford Hist. Soc.; hon. mem. archtl. societies of Uruguay, Buenos Aires, Chile and Mexico; del. by apptmt. of U.S. Govt. and A.I.A. to Pan-Am. Congress of Architects at Santiago, Chile, 1923, Buenos Aires, 1927. Republican. Episcopalian. Clubs: Union League (Phila.); Science and Art Club (Germantown). Home: Chestnut Hill, Pa. Office: Architects Bldg., Philadelphia, Pa.

WATSON, Frederick, British Consul Gen.; b. England, May 19, 1880; B.A., Cantab., 1902; m. Mary Carlyon Vavasour (Durell), 1910; 1 son, 1 dau. In British Consular Service since 1906, serving successively in Chile, Roumania, Russia, Italy, San Francisco, New York; British Consul Gen. at Phila. since 1923. Awarded Order of British Empire, 1923; Silver Jubilee Medal, 1935; Companion of the Most Distinguished Order of St. Michael and St. George, 1937. Mem. Church of England. Club: Art Club (Phila.). Office: 12 S. 12th St., Philadelphia, Pa.

WATSON, George Linton, cons. civ. engr.; b. Mullica, N.J., Dec. 13, 1879; s. Edmund Richard and Henrietta (Griffith) W.; spl. student U. of Pa., 1900; C.E., New York U.; D. Eng., Rutgers U., 1928; m. Vera Null, Nov. 10, 1915. Asst. engr., Vinton Colliery Co., 1901-03; resident engr., Campion-McClellan Co., 1906; resident engr., bridge constrn., Camden and Rahway, N.J., 1907; engr. of constrn., sewer systems, N.J., 1908; city engr., Dover, Del., also chief engr. United Paving Co., Atlantic City, N.J., 1909; constrn. and supervising engr. for tunnels, sewer systems, paving, road bldg., harbor works, etc., N.J., Pa., Porto Rico, Ecuador, Mexico, etc.; cons. engr. since 1916; spl. expert for U.S. Govt., Republic of Panama, Boston, Mass., Morristown and Paterson, N.J., etc.; consulting engr. Hudson River Vehicular Tunnel; consulting engr. Port of New York Authority. Served as lt. col., Engr. Corps, U.S.A., 1917, maj., 1918, col., 1919; 10 major engagements, wounded 3 times. Mem. Am. Soc. C.E., Engring. Inst. of Can., Instn. C.E. (England). Winner of Telford gold medal, 1928. Decorated Officer Legion of Honor and Croix de Guerre with Palm and Star (France); Mil. Cross (England); Comdr. Order of Crown (Belgium); N.J. State Medal. Republican. Episcopalian. Clubs: Engineers (New York); Montclair (N.J.) Golf. Author: Reclamation of New Jersey Coast, 1910; The Atlantic City Water Supply, 1912; The Design and Construction of the Sewage Treatment Works of Trenton, N.J., 1928. Home: Maplewood, N.J. Office: 32 W. 40th St., New York, N.Y.

WATSON, Herbert L., exec. v.p. DeLaval Steam Turbine Co.; b. Terre Haute, Ind., Aug. 19, 1883; s. Joseph A. and Alice (Lockridge) W.; B.S., Rose Polytechnic Inst., 1905; m. Nelle B. Noland, Dec. 2, 1914; children—William J., John L. Student apprentice Allis Chalmers Mfg. Co., 1905-07, sales engr., 1907-13; gen. sales mgr. DeLaval Steam Turbine Co., 1913-34, exec. v.p. since 1934; pres. and dir. Am. Bauer Wach Corpn.; dir. Turbo Engring. Co. Republican. Presbyn. Clubs: Engineers (New York); Trenton, Trenton Country (Trenton). Home: 27 Whittier Av. Office: DeLaval Steam Turbine Co., Trenton, N.J.

WATSON, Jesse Paul; prof. economic research and asst. dir. Bur. Business Research, U. of Pittsburgh. Address: U. of Pittsburgh, Pittsburgh, Pa.

WATSON, Joseph De Noon, mfr. paint and glass; b. Woodsfield, O., Sept. 25, 1894; s. Henry Knox and Ida May (De Noon) W.; student Mercersburg (Pa.) Acad., 1910-12, Washington and Jefferson Coll., Washington, Pa., 1914; m. Elizabeth Vankirk Borland, Dec. 28, 1918; children—Elizabeth Vankirk, Henry Knox II. Asso. with Watson Paint & Glass Co., Pittsburgh, Pa., sales mgr. 1914-19, treas., 1919-24; v.p. Standard Plate Glass Co., 1924-30; pres. Watson-Standard Co., Pittsburgh, since 1930; v.p. and treas. H. K. and J. D. Watson, Inc.; pres. Eagle Paint & Varnish Works. Served as lt., F.A., U.S.R.C., 1918-19. Mem. Phi Gamma Delta. Republican. Presbyterian. Mason (K.T., Shriner). Clubs: Duquesne, Pittsburgh Athletic (Pittsburgh); Country (Oakmont, Pa.). Home: 1149 Shady Av. Office: 225 Galveston Av., Pittsburgh, Pa.

WATSON, Mabel Madison, musician and teacher; b. Elizabeth, N.J.; d. James Madison and Emma (Hopper) W.; ed. pvt. schs.; grad. Met. Coll. Music, N.Y. City; studied in Berlin, Paris, Prague; composition under Harry Rowe Shelley, New York; Am. Conservatory, Fontainebleau, France, summers 1937-38. Engaged in teaching piano and violin since 1901; started Univ. Settlement Mus. Sch., New York City, 1901, now merged with Settlement Music Sch.; founded and mgr. for six yrs. music dept. Shady Hill Country Day Sch., Germantown, Pa.; compositions include many piano pieces also larger works for violin and piano, trios, and books of instrn. both text and music. Mem. Music Teachers Nat. Assn., Piano Teachers Congress, Progressive Edn. Assn., Phila. Music Teachers Assn., Music Teachers Forum, Phila. Fellowship Divine Truth. Home and Studio: Dorset Rd., Devon, Pa.

WATSON, Ripley, lawyer; b. Jersey City, N.J., Mar. 15, 1886; s. Wm. Perry (M.D.) and Cornelia Elizabeth (Wortendyke) W.; A.B., Rutgers Coll., 1908; LL.B., N.Y. Law Sch., 1910; (hon.) A.M., Rutgers Coll., 1911; m. Hattie Brown, Nov. 12, 1912; children—Harriet, William Perry II, Cornelia Elizabeth, Ripley, Jr. Admitted to N.J. bar as atty., 1911, as counselor, 1914; engaged in gen. practice of law at Jersey City, N.J., and North Bergen, N.J., since 1911, specializing in chancery, title and probate work. Mem. Am. Bar Assn., N.J. State Bar Assn., Hudson Co. Bar Assn., Beta Theta Pi, Beta Phi. Democrat. Mem. Dutch Ref. Ch. Mason. Clubs: Kiwanis of North Hudson. Home: 40 Hickory Drive, Maplewood. Office: 646 Main St., North Bergen, N.J.

WATSON, Robert Edward, mfg. biscuits; b. MacGregor, Manitoba, Jan. 25, 1892; s. John Henry and Margaret (Lamb) W.; came to U.S., 1931, naturalized citizen; student pub. schs. and high sch. grad., 1910; m. Pauline E. Stimers, Aug. 30, 1919; children—Robert Pardo, William Ralph, John Frank. Employed as salesman, D. S. Perrin Co., London, Ont., 1912-15 and sales mgr., 1919-26; western mgr., Wm. Paterson, Ltd., 1926-28; western mgr. Geo. Weston, Ltd., Toronto, Can., at Winnipeg, Can., 1928-31, vice-pres. and gen. mgr. Geo. Weston, Ltd., mfrs. "English Quality Biscuits" plant at Passaic, N.J. since 1931, dir. Geo. Weston, Ltd., since 1932. Served as pvt. to lt. C.E.F., 1915-18; awarded Distinguished Conduct Medal at Battle of Amiens, Aug. 9, 1918. Presbyn. Mason. Clubs: Country (Upper Montclair); Canadian of New York (New York City). Home: 24 Alexander Av., Nutley. Office: Geo. Weston, Ltd., 2 Brighton Av., Passaic, N.J.

WATSON, Thomas, attorney, coal executive; born in Greenville, Pennsylvania, on December 31, 1878; son of Harry and Annie (Johnston) W.; A.B., Yale, 1900; LL.B., Pittsburgh Law Sch., 1903; m. Anita M. Flynn, Feb. 5, 1913. Vice-pres., sec. and dir. Hillman Coal & Coke Co., Pittsburgh; pres. and dir. Neville Coke

& Chem. Co.; v.p. and dir. Paden City Land Co.; sec. and dir. Hecla Coal & Coke Co., Ambridge Land Co., Hillman Gas Coal Co., J. H. Hillman & Sons Co., Hillman Transportation Co., Puritan Land Co., Revere Land Co., Waynesburg Gas Coal Co.; treas. and dir. Paden City Pottery Co.; dir. Hillman Supply Co., Ky. Natural Gas Corpn., Paden City Glass Co., Pa. Industries, Inc., Pa. Bankshares and Securities Corpn., Pittsburgh Coke and Iron Co. Trustee Shadyside Hosp. Clubs: Civic of Allegheny Co., Yale (past pres.; mem. exec. com.), Harvard-Yale-Princeton (past pres.; dir.), Duquesne, Longue Vue. Home: 1830 Wightman St. Office: Grant Bldg., Pittsburgh, Pa.

WATSON, Thomas John, officer corps.; b. Campbell, N.Y., Feb. 17, 1874; s. Thomas and Jane (White) W.; ed. Addison (N.Y.) Acad. and Elmira Sch. of Commerce; LL.D., Lafayette Coll. and Rutgers, 1934, Colgate U., 1936, Cumberland U., 1936; L.H.D., Rollins, Coll., 1935; D.Eng., Stevens Inst. Tech., 1936; D.Sc., Alfred U., 1936; m. Jeannette M. Kittredge, Apr. 17, 1913; children—Thomas J., Jane, Helen Mary, Arthur Kittredge. Connected for 15 yrs. with the Nat. Cash Register Co. as spl. rep. and gen. sales mgr.; pres. and dir. Internat. Business Machines Corpn., New York, since 1914; pres. Internat. Chamber of Commerce; dir. Federal Res. Bank of New York, Niagara Fire Ins. Co.; pres. and dir. Internat. Business Machines Co., Ltd. of Can.; councillor Nat. Industrial Conf. Bd., Inc.; hon. v.p. Pan-Am. Soc.; dir. at large U.S. Chamber Commerce; dir and chmn. advisory com. on foreign participation, New York World's Fair of 1939; commr. gen. of the U.S. to Paris Internat. Expn. of 1937; dir. Merchants Assn. of N.Y. (past pres.), Travelers Aid Soc., City & Suburban Homes Co., Nat. Foreign Trade Assn., France-America Soc., Internat. Auxiliary Lang. Assn., Swedish Chamber of Commerce. Trustee Carnegie Endowment for Internat. Peace, Citizens Budget Commn. of N.Y. City, Columbia U., Lafayette Coll., Roosevelt Hosp., Religious Edn. Foundation; mem. Business Advisory Council of Dept. of Commerce and chmn. Foreign Trade Com.; mem. Council New York U. Men of Finance Club, 1931-33; councillor of New York U., 1931-33; mem. Nat. Council Boy Scouts of America; mem. Foreign Policy Assn., Council on Foreign Relations; vice-pres. Ohio Soc. of N.Y.; mem. exec. com. Globe-Mermaid Assn. of England and America. Chevalier Legion of Honor (France), 1934; officer same, 1935; merit cross of German Eagle with star, 1937; Cross of Commendatore, Am. Soc. Royal Italian Orders, 1936; Knight of the Royal Order of the North Star, 1937; Insignia of the Yugoslav Crown, 2d degree, with star, 1936; Comdr. of Belgian Order of the Crown, 1937; Order of Yugoslavian Crown First Class, 1937; Comdr. of Order of Vasa (Sweden), 1937; Comdr. French Legion of Honor, 1937; Comdr., first class, Order of the White Rose (Finland), 1938. Clubs: Advertising, Bankers, Economic (exec. com.), Export Mgrs. Club, Lotos, Metropolitan, Met. Opera, Railroad and Machinery, Town Hall (dir.), Union, Sportsmanship Brotherhood (dir.), River, New York Yacht; Baltusrol; Binghamton (N.Y.) Country; Burnt Mills Polo (N. Branch, N.J.); Essex Fox Hounds (Peapack, N.J.); Jefferson Island (Sherwood, Md.); Jekyl Island (Brunswick, Ga.); Little Beach (Barnegat Bay, N.J.); Somerset Hills Country (Bernardsville, N.J.); Internat. Business Machines Corpn. Employees Country (Endicott, N.Y.); Wyandanch (Smithton, L.I.); Union Interalliée (Paris, France). Home: 778 Park Av., New York; and Hills and Dales Farm, Lebanon, N.J. Office: 590 Madison Av., New York, N.Y.

WATT, Charles Channing, Jr., M.D.; b. Pittsburgh, Pa., Nov. 23, 1886; s. Charles C. and Mary Belle (McClelland) W.; student DeLancey Sch., 1904; M.D., U. of Pa., 1909; m. Euphemia L. Coplin, Oct. 15, 1930. Interne physician Germantown Hosp., 1909-10; asst. visiting physician Philadelphia Orthopaedic Hosp. since 1917; med. dir. of med. service Germantown Hosp. since 1935. Served as 1st lt. U.S. Med. Res. Corps, 1917; commanding officer Field Hosp. No. 22, M.O.T.C., Fort Oglethorpe, Ga.; capt. Med. Res. Corps, 1918; mem. Disability Bd., Blois, France. Mem. A.M.A., Pa. State Med. Soc., Philadelphia Co. Med. Soc., Philadelphia Pediatric Soc., Philadelphia Neurol. Soc., Philadelphia Coll. Physicians and Surgeons, Phi Kappa Psi, Alpha Mu Pi Omega. Republican. Presbyterian. Clubs: Union League, Philadelphia Cricket. Address: 6605 Wayne Av., Mt. Airy, Philadelphia, Pa.

WATT, Homer Andrew, prof. English; b. Wilkes-Barre, Pa., Sept. 11, 1884; s. Andrew Eton and Clara Susan (Woodruff) W.; A.B., Cornell U., 1906; M.A., U. of Wis., 1908, Ph.D., 1909; m. Effie Margaret Whyte, June 23, 1910; children—Harold Woodruff, William Whyte, Florence Jean. Mary M. Adams fellow U. of Wis., 1907-08; instr. English, same, 1909-16; asst. prof. English, 1916-20, asso. prof., 1920-22, prof. since 1922, head dept. since 1938, New York U.; exchange prof. English, U. of Southern Calif., 1925-26; prof. English, Univ. of Va., summer 1928, Univ. of Colo., summer 1932. Member Modern Language Assn. America, Modern Humanities Research Assn., Nat. Council Teachers of English, Shakespeare Assn. America, Phi Beta Kappa, Eta Sigma Phi, Andiron Club (New York). Awarded diploma and decoration, Order of St. Sava (Jugoslavia). Republican. Conglist. Author: Gorboduc, or Ferrex and Porrex, 1910; The Composition of Technical Papers, 1917, '25; (with J. B. Munn) Ideas and Forms in English and American Literature, 1925, '32; Highways in College Composition (with Oscar Cargill), 1930; Outlines of Shakespeare's plays (with K. J. Holzknecht and Raymond Ross), 1934; The Literature of England (with George B. Woods and George K. Anderson), 1936. Editor: (with Prof. J. W. Cunliffe) Thackeray's English Humorists, 1911; Modern America Series of English Texts. Contbr. essays and tech. articles. Home: 19 Douglas Rd., Glen Ridge, N.J.

WATTERS, Thomas, clergyman; b. Rauross, Ireland, Sept. 13, 1860; s. John W. and Elizabeth (Devor) W.; A.B., New York U., 1884; grad. Union Theol. Sem., 1888; D.D., Cedarville (O.) Coll., 1899; m. Margaret E. Downs, Oct. 24, 1899. Ordained Reformed Presbyn. ministry, 1889; pastor First Ch., Brooklyn, 1889-92, First Ch., Pittsburgh, 1892-1906, Tabernacle Presbyn. Ch., Pittsburgh, 1906-1922. Moderator Gen. Synod Reformed Presbyn. Ch., 1894; mem. bd. of supts. Reformed Presbyn. Theol. Sem., Phila., 1891-1901; trustee Reformed Presbyn. Theol. Sem., Phila., 1904-06; sec. bd. trustees Cedarville Coll., 1898-1906. Pres. Bd. of Temperance and Moral Welfare, Presbyn. Ch., 1913; mem. Bd. of Christian Ed., 1923; pres. Pittsburgh Florence Crittenton Home, 1923. Home: 6861 Penn Av., Pittsburgh, Pa.

WATTS, Hansford, real estate; b. East Lynn, W.Va., Feb. 4, 1873; s. Harrison and Sarah (Maynard) W.; student pub. schs. and Wayne Acad., Wayne, W.Va.; m. Jennie Booton, July 20, 1899; children—Vickers Booton, Margaret Vivian (Mrs. Waldo Locke Shore). Employed as book agt., 1893-94; dep. U.S. Marshall, 1894-96; propr. hotel, Huntington, W.Va., 1896-1903; engaged in jewelry bus., Huntington, W.Va., 1903-07; engaged in real estate and ins. bus. at Huntington, W. Va., since 1907; pres. Hans Watts Realty Co., Acre Land Co., Big Four Realty Co., Campbell Park Land Co., Builders, Inc., Central Hotel Co., Foster-Thornburg Hardware Co., all of Huntington, W. Va.; vice-pres. Childers & Watts, Inc., Thornburg Ins. Agency, of Huntington. Served as chmn. W.Va. Real Estate Commn. since 1937. Dir. Huntington Union Mission. Pres. and trustee Foster Foundation. Democrat. Baptist. Elk. Clubs: Rotary, Guyandotte, Guyan Country (Huntington). Home: 741 S. Boul. Office: 414 11th st, Huntington, W.Va.

WATTS, Joseph Thomas, church official; b. Raleigh, N.C., Mar. 19, 1874; s. Josiah Turner and Annie Eliza (McIver) W.; ed. pub. schs. and business coll.; student Southern Baptist Theol. Sem., 1903-05; D.D., Wake Forest (N. C.) Coll., 1916; m. Neva Hawkins, July 2, 1895; 1 dau., Elizabeth (Mrs. W. Emory Trainham). Sec. to gen. freight agent, and traveling freight agt. I.C. R.R. until 1903; ordained ministry Bapt. Ch., 1903; pastor and asst. pastor successively Aberdeen, Miss., Louisville, and Ashland, Ky., Lexington, N.C., and S.S. sec., Ky., until 1908; S.S. and Bapt. Young People's Union sec., Va., 1909-27; co-dir. Bapt. Coöperative Program, 1919-27; gen. sec. Md. Bapt. Union Assn., Baltimore, since 1927. Democrat. Author: Convention Adult Bible Classes, 1914; Home and Extension Department, 1930 (revision 1936), The Growing Christian. Contbr. on religious subjects. Home: Homewood Apts. Office: 405 Hearst Tower Bldg., Baltimore, Md.

WATTS, Ralph L., horticulturist; b. Kerrmoor, Clearfield Co., Pa., June 5, 1869; s. Martin Overholser and Marian Elizabeth (Hoyt) W.; B.S. in Agr., Pa. State Coll., 1890, M.S., 1899; D.Agr., Syracuse U., 1916; D.Sc., R.I. State Coll., 1931; m. Hattie Searle, Jan. 1, 1895; children—Gilbert Searle, Curtis McClure, Grace Elizabeth. Horticulturist Tenn. Expt. Sta., 1890-99; lecturer farmers' institutes, 1899-1908; prof. horticulture, 1908-12, dean and dir. Sch. of Agr. and Expt. Sta., Nov. 1, 1912—, Pa. State Coll. Mem. Soc. for Hort. Science, Vegetable Growers' Assn. America (ex-pres.), A.A.A.S.; pres. Pa. State Conservation Council. Presbyn. Mem. Phi Kappa Phi, Gamma Sigma Delta, Alpha Zeta, Delta Theta Sigma, Sigma Pi. Author: Vegetable Gardening (coll. text book), 1912; The Vegetable Garden; Vegetable Forcing, 1917; Vegetable Growing Projects, 1921; Growing Vegetables, 1923; Rural Pennsylvania, 1925. Address: 225 E. Foster Av., State College, Pa.

WATTS, Sidney James, lawyer; b. Pittsburgh, Pa., Oct. 16, 1883; s. William Hubert and Margaret (Kredel) W.; student Harvard; m. Marjorie Loose, May 20, 1910; children—Sidney James, Mary Elizabeth. Admitted to bar, 1908; since engaged in gen. practice of law; partner law firm Baker & Watts since 1930. Mem. Edgewood Borough Council, 1928-32. Mem. Am. Bar Assn., Pa. State Bar Assn., Allegheny Co. Bar Assn. Clubs: University, Harvard-Yale-Princeton (Pittsburgh); Edgewood Country; Harvard (New York). Home: 220 Beech St., Edgewood. Office: 1128 Union Trust Co. Bldg., Pittsburgh, Pa.

WATTS, William Carleton, naval officer; b. Phila., Pa., Feb. 14, 1880; s. Ethelbert and Emily (Pepper) W.; grad., with honors, U.S. Naval Acad., 1898; m. Julia F. Scott, Apr. 16, 1902. Ensign, Apr. 4, 1900; promoted through grades to rear adm., Apr. 1, 1931. Served on U.S.S. Columbia during Spanish-Am. War; judge advocate gen. of Navy, with rank of capt., Jan. 6, 1917-Apr. 15, 1918; aptpd. comdr. U.S.S. Albany, Apr. 24, 1918; engaged on convoy escort duty to end of World War; now Comdr., Base Force, U.S. Fleet. Episcopalian. Clubs: Army and Navy, Chevy Chase (Washington); New York Yacht. Home: Philadelphia, Pa. Address: Navy Dept., Washington, D.C.

WAUGH, H(omer) Roy, lawyer; b. Upshur Co., W.Va., Jan. 4, 1879; s. Homer M. and Malissa (Jane) W.; A.B., W.Va., Wesleyan Univ., Buckhannon, 1901; student W.Va. Univ. Law Coll., 1903-05; m. Eliza P. Newlon, Oct. 17, 1905; children—Mary Newlon (Mrs. G. M. Wooddell), John H., Helen, Louise (dec.), Winston Pitt (dec.). Admitted to W.Va. bar, 1905 and since engaged in gen. practice of law at Buckhannon; mem. firm Waugh & Waugh since 1938; served as pros. atty. Upshur Co., W.Va., 1905-08; mem. W.Va. Ho. of Dels., 1909-11; U.S. dist. atty. for Northern Dist., W.Va., 1911-14; judge Circuit Ct., 1921-28. Trustee W.Va. Wesleyan Coll., Buckhannon, W.Va. Mem. Sigma Chi. Republican. Methodist. Mason. Home: 89 S. Kanawha St. Office: Main St., Buckhannon, W.Va.

WAUGH, Karl Tinsley, psychologist; b. of Am. parents, Cawnpore, India, Nov. 30, 1879; s. James Walter (D.D.) and Jennie Mary (Tinsley) W.; B.A., Ohio Wesleyan U., 1900, M.A., 1901, LL.D., 1927; studied Columbia; M.A., Harvard, 1906, Ph.D., 1907; m. Emily L. Sprightley, Sept. 4, 1912; children—Eleanor Tinsley, Charles MacCarthy. Prof. philosophy and mathematics, Claflin U., S.C., 1900-04; Weld fellow and assistant in philosophy to Professor William James, Harvard, 1906-07; associate in psychology, U. of Chicago, 1907-09; head dept. philosophy and psychology, Beloit Coll., 1909-18; dean and prof. psychology and philosophy, Berea (Ky.) Coll., Sept. 1919-23; dean Coll. Arts and Sciences, and prof. psychology, U. of Southern Calif., 1923-31; prof. psychology, chmn. div. psychology and edn., Long Island Univ., Brooklyn, N.Y., 1930-31; pres. Dickinson College, Carlisle, Pa., 1931-34; dean Charles Morris Price Sch., Phila., since 1934; deputy dir. in charge of edn., Nat. Youth Administrn. for Pa., 1935-37; exec. dir. Federal Coöperative Health Service during 1937. Ednl. and psychol. investigation in China and India, 1916-17; lecturer in psychology, University of Colorado, 1909, 1914, and Northwestern Univ., 1921. Served as 1st lt., capt. and maj. U.S.A., psychol. div., World War, Aug. 1917-Feb. 5, 1919; in Surgeon General's Office, Washington, D.C.; chief psychol. examiner at Camp Gordon, Ga., Camp McClellan, Ala., trans. to Ft. McPherson, Ga.; supervisor Fed. Bd. for Vocational Edn., 5th Dist., Feb.-Sept. 1919. Treated successfully, by suggestion, nervous disorder, hysterical blindness, stammering, shell shock, etc.; organized first university courses leading to motion picture careers, Los Angeles. Fellow A.A.A.S.; mem. Am. Psychol. Assn., Am. Acad. Polit. and Social Science, Ky. Acad. Science. Soc. Psychical Research, Eugenics Research Assn., Western Psychol. Assn., Psychol. Corpn. (pres. Calif. br.), Sigma Xi, Phi Beta Kappa, Phi Delta Theta, Phi Kappa Phi, Pi Gamma Mu, Acacia, Omicron Delta Kappa. Presbyterian. Mason. Clubs: Poor Richard, Schoolmen's, Mendelssohn, Blackstonian. Author of articles: Vision in Animals, 1910; Mental Diagnosis of College Students, 1915; Comparative Mentality of Oriental and American Students, 1920; Rational Empiricism Views Teleology, 1927; The Liberal Arts College Faces the Present Age, 1932; Psychology in Modern Industry, 1934; Personal Hurdles (with J. W. Irwin), 1936; The Humanizing of Psychology; "Saturday Night Thoughts," contributed to newspaper columns. Specialist in the writings of Rudyard Kipling; editor poetry sect. Artland Mag. and California Southland, 1925-30. Home: 648 W. Ellet St., Mt. Airy, Philadelphia. Office: 1319 Locust St., Philadelphia, Pa.

WAXTER, Thomas Jacob Shryock, social worker; b. Baltimore, Md., Oct. 13, 1898; s. William Deal and Daisy (Shryock) W.; student Baltimore pub. schs., 1905-14, Boys Latin Sch., Baltimore, 1914-17; B.S., Princeton U., 1921; studied Johns Hopkins U. Grad. Sch., 1921-22; LL.B., Yale U. Sch. of Law, 1924; m. Peggy Ewing, Feb. 27, 1930; children—Thomas J. S., Peggy E. Admitted to Md. bar, 1924; associated with law firm Cook, Chestnut & Marshall, 1924-29; judge Juvenile Ct., Baltimore, 1929-35; dir. pub. welfare, Baltimore, since 1935. Served in U.S. Army, Apr. 1917-Aug. 1917, discharged because of physical reasons; mem. S.A.-T.C., Princeton U., Sept. 1918-Jan. 1919. Pres. Baltimore Legal Aid Bureau; mem. bd. Morgan Coll., Family Welfare Assn., Henry Watson's Children's Aid Soc., Council Social Agencies. Mem. Alpha Delta Phi, Order of the Coif. Democrat. Presbyterian. Home: 4721 East Lane. Office: 327 St. Paul Place, Baltimore, Md.

WAY, Frederick, Jr., steamboat pilot, author; b. Sewickley, Pa., Feb. 17, 1901; s. Frederick and Mabel Louise (Nicols) W.; student U. of Cincinnati, 1920-21; m. Charlotte Lyon, Oct. 17, 1923; children—Frederick III, Bettie Byrne, James Courtney; m. Grace Gray Morrison, Apr. 6, 1934. Began as "cub pilot" on Kanawha River, 1920; purser on General Crowder in Pittsburgh-Cincinnati trade, 1923; formed Pittsburgh & Cincinnati Packet Line, 1929; pilot on passenger vessels on upper Ohio, 1934; pilot for Streckfus Steamers, Inc. and Green Line steamers; instigator of steamboat races between Betsy Ann and Chris Greene and Tom Greene run at Cincinnati, 1928, 1929, 1930; managed River Exposition, Pittsburgh, 1938. Presbyterian. Clubs: Propeller of Pittsburgh, Ohio & Kanawha Masters & Pilots Assn. Author: The Log of the Betsy Ann, 1934; contbr. to marine publs. and short stories to mags. Home: 121 River Av., Sewickley, Pa.

WAY, Warren Wade, clergyman; b. Irvington, Ill., Mar. 18, 1869; s. Newton Edward and Lizzie Heaton (Erwin) W.; A.B., Hobart Coll., 1897 (class honors and Phi Beta Kappa), LL.D., 1932; Gen. Theol. Sem., New York, 1899; A.M., U. of Chicago, 1924; D.D., U. of the South, Sewanee, Tenn., 1929; m. Louisa Atkinson Smith, June 18, 1903; children—Evelyn Lee, Warren Wade, Roger Atkinson. Deacon, 1892, priest, 1899, P.E. Ch.; asst. minister All Angels' Ch., New York, 1898-99; missionary, Diocese of Springfield, 1900; rector Grace Ch., Cortland, N.Y., 1901-14, St. Luke's Ch., Salisbury, N.C., 1914-18, St. Mary's Sch., Raleigh, N.C., 1918-32, St. James' Ch., Atlantic City, N.J., since 1932. Chmn. Salisbury Chapter A.R.C., July 1917-18. Club: Brigantine Country. Home: 105 S. North Carolina Av., Atlantic City, N.J.

WAYNE, Joseph, Jr., banker; b. Phila., Pa., Sept. 26, 1873; s. Stephen Simmons and Isabella (Ross) W.; ed. pub. schools, Philadelphia; LL.D., University of Pennsylvania, 1937; m. Laura B. Jayne, Apr. 16, 1902; children—Elizabeth B., Josephine, Laura J. Pres., 1914-26, Girard Nat. Bank, which was consolidated with Phila. Nat. Bank under title The Phila.-Girard Nat. Bank, which was consolidated with the Franklin-Fourth Street Nat. Bank in 1928 under title The Phila. Nat. Bank, of which has since been pres.; pres. Philadelphia Clearing House Assn.; dir. Federal Reserve Bank of Phila., Phila. Saving Fund Soc., Provident Mut. Life Ins. Co., Provident Trust Co., Pa. Fire Ins. Co., Ins. Co. of North America, Alliance Ins. Co., Indemnity Ins. Co. of North America, Phila. and Reading Coal & Iron Co., Phila. and Reading Coal & Iron Corpn., Midvale Co., Phila. Fire and Marine Ins. Co., Baldwin-Southwark Corpn., Commonwealth Title Co., Parkway Co., Pennroad Corpn., Pennsylvania Railroad Co., Pennsylvania Co. (Pa. R.R. lines west). Served as mem. executive com. in charge of loan drives, 3d Federal Reserve Dist., World War. Clubs: Union League, Rittenhouse, Racquet, Sunnybrook Golf, Germantown Cricket, Phila. Cricket. Home: 8200 St. Martins Lane, Chestnut Hill, Pa. Office: Philadelphia Nat. Bank, Philadelphia, Pa.

WEAR, Joseph W(alker), broker; b. St. Louis, Mo., Nov. 27, 1876; s. James Hutchinson and Nancy (Holliday) W.; prep. edn. Smith Acad., St. Louis, 1885-95; A.B., Yale, 1899; m. Adaline Coleman Potter, Apr. 14, 1903 (died Jan. 25, 1935); 1 son, William Potter. With Wear Bros., dry goods commn. business, St. Louis, 1904-14; v.p. and treas. Thomas Potter Sons & Co., linoleum mfrs., Phila., 1914-20; partner W. A. Harriman & Co., Inc., in charge Phila. office, 1920-30; partner E. A. Pierce & Co., brokers, Phila., since 1930. Del. to Bull Moose conv., Chicago, 1914; mem. Rep. State Com.; chmn. Rep. Finance Com. for Pa. since 1938. Trustee Jefferson Med. Coll. and Hosp.; mem. Yale Alumni Bd. (chmn. 1928-30). Mem. Pa. Commn. for New York World's Fair. Mem. U.S. Lawn Tennis Assn. (v.p.), Alpha Delta Phi, Scroll and Key (Yale). Presbyn. (trustee Second Presbyn. Ch., Phila.). Clubs: Racquet (pres.), Yale (past pres.), Penn Athletic (Phila.); Penllyn (Penllyn, Pa.). Doubles champion of U.S. in court tennis with Jay Gould, 6 yrs.; racquet doubles champion of U.S., 3 yrs.; chmn. U.S. Davis Cup Com., 1928-30; capt. Davis Cup Team, 1928, 1935. Home: Penllyn, Pa. Office: Commercial Trust Bldg., Philadelphia, Pa.

WEAVER, Albert Frederick, clergyman; b. Oriental, Pa., July 31, 1878; s. Riley B. and Lovina (Beachel) W.; ed. Freeburg Acad., Middleburg Normal, summers 1894-97; hon. D.D., Albright Coll., Myerstown, 1934; m. Mary Holibaugh (died 1913); children—Rowland H., Malura T. (Mrs. Marvin D. Thomas); m. 2d, Anna M. Crowell, Nov. 25, 1914; 1 son, James Frederick. Engaged in teaching pub. schs., 1896-98; ordained to ministry Evang. Ch., 1903 (licensed 1899); served as pastor, 1899-1926; dist. supt. Evang. Ch., 1927-39; sec. Commn. on Finance, Evang. Ch., 1922-38; exec. sec.-treas. of Administrative Council, Evang. Ch. since 1938. Trustee and mem. exec. com. of Albright Coll., Reading, Pa. Mem. Federal Council of Chs. (exec. com.), Pa. Council of Chs. (commn. on evangelism), Commn. on Ch. Federation and Union of Evang. Ch. Republican. Mem. Evang. Ch. Mason (K.T., 32°). Club: Cleric of York, Pa., Acacia of Williamsport, Pa. Home: 713 S. Queen St., York, Pa.

WEAVER, Alvin Monroe, supt. schs.; b. nr. Hughesville, Pa., May 12, 1879; s. Irvin G. and Mary M. (Kepner) W.; grad. Lycoming Co. Normal Sch., 1894-99; A.B., Bucknell U., 1905, A.M., 1915, hon. Pd.D., 1928; student Harvard U. Law Sch., 1908-10; m. Hazel B. Lundy, Nov. 15, 1919; 1 dau., Adele Janet. Engaged as teacher rural schs., 1894; now supt. schs., Williamsport, Pa. Mem. Phi Gamma Delta. Republican. Lutheran. Mason. Home: 918 Rural Av., Williamsport, Pa.

WEAVER, Frederick Pattison, coll. prof.; b. Millersburg, Pa., Nov. 7, 1882; s. Philip and Amelia (Daniel) W.; student pub. schs., Upper Paxton Twp., Pa., 1888-99; B.S., Pa. State Coll., 1914; M.S., Cornell U., 1923, student, 1924-25, Ph.D., 1930; m. Marjory Irene Barto, June 7, 1919; children—Jean Frances, Claire Louise. Teacher pub. schs., Dauphin Co., Pa., 1899-1904; commercial chemist, Steelton and Coalport, Pa., 1904-10; instr. agrl. chemistry, Pa. State Coll., 1910-15, asst. dir. agrl. extension, 1915-25, head dept. agrl. economics, 1925-38, prof. emeritus agrl. economics since 1938. Served as mem. coms. on rural housing and on taxation of Pres. Hoover's Housing Commn., 1930-32, as mem. Mineral and Forest Land Taxation Commn. of Pa., 1931-32. Dir. Farm Credit Adminstrn., Baltimore, Md., since 1933. Mem. Acacia, Alpha Zeta, Sigma Xi, Phi Kappa Phi, Pi Gamma Mu. Democrat. Presbyterian. Club: Centre Hills Country, University (State College, Pa.). Home: 409 S. Barnard St., State College, Pa.

WEAVER, J(oseph) Kennard, lawyer; b. Phila., Pa., Dec. 21, 1894; s. Joseph Kennard and Almira (Yahn) W.; student U. of Pa., 1915-16; LL.B., Dickinson Sch. of Law, Carlisle, Pa., 1920; m. Gertrude T. Christensen, Oct. 29, 1919; children—Douglas (dec.), Robert Lee, Joseph Kennard. Admitted to Pa. bar, 1920, and since in practice at Phila.; special dep. atty. gen. Commonwealth of Pa., 1926; asso. legal advisor Federal Prohibition Adminstr., 1928-29. Served in U.S. Army, Apr. 1917-Dec. 1918. Incorporator Dickinson Sch. of Law. Mem. Phila. Bar Assn., Delta Sigma Phi, Delta Theta Phi. Republican. Methodist. Mason. Clubs: Union League, Penn Athletic, Optimist (Phila.). Home: 2034 W. Venango St. Office: 2125 Land Title Bldg., Philadelphia, Pa.

WEAVER, Louis Schneider, surgeon; b. Washington, D.C., Aug. 30, 1877; s. Francis Heyer and Katharine Magdalene (Schneider) W.; A.B., Gettysburg (Pa.) Coll., 1899; A.B., Yale, 1900; M.D., Johns Hopkins Med. Sch., 1904; m. Romayne Marker, Dec. 5, 1907 (died 1936); children—Frank Marker (M.D.), Katharine Marker, Louis Schneider, Jr. Interne Rhode Island Hosp., 1904-05, resident surgeon, 1905-06; engaged in gen. practice of medicine and surgery at York, Pa., since 1906; chief surg. staff, York Hosp., since 1908; surgeon Pa. R.R. Co., Western Md. R.R. Co. Served as sergt., Pa. Vol. Inf., Spanish-Am. War, 1898; 1st lt., Med. Corps, U.S. Army, 1917-19, with A.E.F. in France; capt., Med. Corps Res. Trustee Gettysburg Coll. Fellow Am. Coll. Surgeons; mem. Am. Bd. Surgery (Founders Group), Am., Pa. State, and York Co. med. assns., York Med. Club, Am. Legion (past comdr. York Post), Phi Kappa Psi, Beta Beta Beta. Republican. Lutheran. Club: Country (York, Pa.). Home: 198 Peyton Rd. Office: 25 N. Duke St., York, Pa.

WEAVER, Robert Francis, surgeon; b. Pottsville, Pa., July 9, 1883; s. Robert Thomas and Annie Mary (Carr) W.; student St. Clair (Pa.) High Sch., 1897-1900, Pottsville High Sch., 1900-03; M.D., U. of Pa., 1907; m. Frances E. Haverty, July 22, 1915; children—Frances Virginia, Dorothy Elizabeth, Virginia Ellen, Robert Thomas. In practice as physician and surgeon, St. Clair, Pa., since 1907; mem. staff

Pottsville Hosp. Served as 1st lt. Med. Officers Training Corps during World War. Mem. A.M. A., Pa. State Med. Soc., Schuylkill Co. Med. Soc. Republican. Catholic. K. of C., Elk. Mem. Pottsville Club. Address: 50 N. 2d St., St. Clair, Pa.

WEAVER, Ruth Hartley, physician; b. Palmyra, N.J., May 30, 1892; d. James and Ellen (Lake) Hartley; grad. Phila. Girls' High Sch., 1912; student Wellesley (Mass.) Coll., 1912-13; M.D., Woman's Med. Coll. of Pa., 1917; m. Harry Sands Weaver, Sr., Mar. 12, 1924 (died 1938). Interne Phila. Gen. Hosp., 1917-19; child hygiene physician Dept. of Pub. Health, 1919-25; clin. prof. of surgery, Woman's Med. Coll., Phila., 1919-25; clinician dept. of prevention of diseases, Children's Hosp., Phila., 1922-38, asst. dir., 1938; chief in pediatrics, Woman's Hosp. of Phila., since 1920; epidemiologist Dept. of Pub. Health since 1937; asst. prof. preventive medicine, hygiene and pub. health, Temple U. Med. Sch., Phila. Mem. Phila. Co. Med. Soc., Pa. State Med. Soc., A.M.A., Phila. Pediatric Soc., Am. Acad. of Pediatrics. Address: The Embassy, 2100 Walnut St., Philadelphia, Pa.

WEAVER, William Abbott, surgeon; b. Wilkes-Barre, Pa., Apr. 19, 1900; s. Wm. Gwynne (M.D.) and Mary Elizabeth (Abbott) W.; student Wyoming Sem., 1916-18, Lehigh U., Bethlehem, Pa., 1918-20; M.D., Jefferson Med. Coll., Phila., 1925; m. Ruth Slater Mengel, Feb. 12, 1929; children—William Abbott, Samuel Perry Mengel, Sally Lou. Clin. asst. surgeon Wilkes-Barre (Pa.) Gen. Hosp., 1926-29, asso. surg. since 1929; asst. surgeon Lehigh Valley Coal Co. since 1926; physician Luzerne Co. Poor Dist., 1926-38; city physician, Wilkes-Barre, 1937. Served as pvt., Inf., U.S. Army, 1918; 1st lt., Med. Res. Corps, 1925-26; asst. surg. Med. Det. F.A., 1926-28; capt. Med. Corps, F.A., 1928-29; maj. and rgtl. surgeon, 109th F.A., 1928-29. Mem. Bd. Edn., Wilkes-Barre, Pa., 1933-39. Mem. Bd. dirs. Luzerne Co. Blind Assn. Fellow Am. Coll. Surgs., A.M.A.; mem. Lehigh Valley and Luzerne Co. med. socs., S.R., Am. Legion, United Sportsmen, Phi Chi, Kappa Sigma. Republican. Protestant. Mason (K.T., Shriner). Clubs: Franklin, Craftsmen, Root Hollow Rod and Gun. Home: 28 Academy St., Wilkes-Barre, Pa.

WEAVER, William Marion, clergyman; b. Birdsboro, Pa., June 30, 1872; s. Francis Marion and Mary S. (Mertz) W.; A.B., Muhlenberg Coll., 1896; A.M., U. of Pa., 1926; S.T.D., Temple U., 1933; ed. Luth. Theol. Sem., Phila., 1896-99; m. Bertha M. Arenburg, Petite Riviere, Nova Scotia, Oct. 23, 1901; children—Francis William, Pauline Mary, Ruth Elizabeth (Mrs. Harry Muschamp), George Arenburg, Amy Flora (Mrs. Richard M. Gillis). Ordained to ministry Luth. Ch., 1899; minister chs. in Nova Scotia and Pa., 1899-1922; missionary Phila. Luth. City Mission, 1922-31; pastor St. Luke's Luth. Ch., West Collingswood, N.J., since 1931; pres. Pa. Prison Soc., 1926-31; pres. Nova Scotia Synod of Luth. Ch., 1909-15; pres. N.J. Conf. Luth. Ch., 1933-37; delegate from the Ministerium of Pa. to the convs. of the United Luth. Ch., Savannah, 1934, Columbus, O., 1936, Baltimore, 1938. Republican. Lutheran. Editor and mgr. Nova Scotia Lutheran, 1912-15. Home: 708 Collings Av., Collingswood, N.J.

WEBB, Carleton B., lawyer; b. Haddonfield, N.J., July 21, 1891; s. James A. and Sara (Braddock) W.; LL.B., U. of Pa., 1917; m. Mary Lippincott, Apr. 21, 1921; 1 dau., Anne Caroline. In practice of law at Phila.; instr. of business law, Drexel Inst. Evening Sch., since 1921; prof. of corpn. law, South Jersey Law Sch., Camden, N.J., since 1927. Served in U.S. Army, 1917-18. Vice-pres. Haddonfield (N.J.), Bd. of Edn., 1929-34; recorder Borough of Haddonfield (N.J.) since 1933. Mem. Am. Legion. Mason. Club: Union League (Phila.). Home: 280 Jefferson Av., Haddonfield, N.J. Office: 1700 Walnut St., Philadelphia, Pa.

WEBB, Charles Grosvenor, lawyer; b. Wellsboro, Pa., Mar. 23, 1899; s. Clarence Warden and Mary Helen (Osgood) W.; student Wellsboro (Pa.) High Sch., 1913-16, Phillips Acad., Andover, Mass., 1916-18; A.B., Princeton U., 1922; student U. of Pa. Law Sch., 1923-26; m. Sarah Blanche Radcliffe, Apr. 23, 1930. Admitted to Pa. bar, 1926; practiced alone, Wellsboro, Pa., 1926-33; asso. with G. Mason Owlett, Wellsboro, 1933-38; partner firm Owlett & Webb since 1938. Served as seaman, Princeton Navy Unit, 1918. Dist. atty., Tioga Co., Pa., 1932-36. Dir. Green Free Library, Wellsboro, Pa. Mem. Chamber of Commerce, Am. Bar Assn., Pa. Bar Assn., Phi Delta Phi. Republican. Presbyn. Home: 18 West Av. Office: 19 Central Av., Wellsboro, Pa.

WEBB, Frederick Woolford Conway, lawyer; b. Vienna, Md., June 27, 1889; s. John W. T. and Anna Virginia (Conway) W.; student Vienna (Md.) pub. schs., 1896-1903, Gilman Country Sch., Baltimore, 1903-08, U. of Va. (Academic Dept.), 1908-09; LL.B., U. of Va. Law Sch., 1912; m. Sarah Y. Graham, Oct. 29, 1916; m. 2d, Margaret Smith, Nov. 30, 1921; 1 son, John Wm. Thompson, II. Admitted to Md. bar, 1913; associated with law firm Ellegood, Freeny & Wailes, Salisbury, Md., 1913-14; mem. firm Woodcock & Webb, 1914-35, Woodcock, Webb, Bounds & Travers since 1936. Member Maryland State Board Law Examiners. Director Salisbury National Bank. Director Peninsula Gen. Hosp.; trustee John B. Parsons-Salisbury Home for the Aged; pres. and dir. Wicomico Welfare Assn. Mem. Am. Bar Assn., Md. State Bar Assn. Wicomico County Bar Assn., Delta Tau Delta. Democrat. Episcopalian. Mason, Elk, K.P. Club: Maryland (Baltimore). Home: 705 N. Division St. Office: Salisbury Bldg. & Loan Bldg., Salisbury, Md.

WEBB, Harold Worthington, prof. physics; b. Ithaca, N.Y., July 27, 1884; s. John Burkitt and Mary Emeline (Gregory) W.; A.B., Columbia, 1905, Ph.D., 1909; m. Vivienne J. Mackenzie, Oct. 20, 1920; children—William Mackenzie, Gregory Worthington. Instr. in physics, Columbia, 1909-14, asst. prof., 1914-24, asso. prof., 1924-29, prof. since 1929. Served as capt., Signal Corps, U.S.A., 1917-19. Fellow Am. Physical Soc. (sec. 1923-28), A.A.A.S.; mem. Optical Soc. America, Phi Beta Kappa, Sigma Xi. Episcopalian. Club: New York Yacht. Home: Leonia, N.J.

WEBB, James Michael, ins. exec.; b. Hingham, Mass., Sept. 29, 1895; s. Francis Mauer and Mary Elizabeth (Barrett) W.; student Hingham (Mass.) High Sch., 1908-12, Alexander Hamilton Sch. (corr. course), 1923-24, Columbia U. (extension courses), 1930-31; m. Anne Margaret Roberts, Dec. 1, 1923. Clerk, Paine Webber & Co., stock brokers, Boston, Mass., 1912-13; cashier, Conn. Mutual Life Ins. Co., 1913-20; oil production, Tulsa, Okla., 1921-22; comptroller, R. M. Hollingshead Co., polishes and dressings, Camden, N.J., 1923-26; v.p. Bankers Nat. Life Ins. Co., Montclair, N.J., since 1928; sec.-treas. Collateral Finance Co.; sec. Bankers Nat. Thrift Club. Served as chief storekeeper, U.S. Navy, 1917-19. Mem. Boys Com., Montclair (N.J.) Y.M.C.A. Mem. Montclair (N.J.) Chamber of Commerce. Catholic. Clubs: Upper Montclair Country, Kiwanis (pres.; Montclair, N.J.). Home: 67 S. Munn Av., East Orange, N.J. Office: 26 Park St., Montclair, N.J.

WEBB, Phillips Watson, publisher; b. Salem, Md., Oct. 15, 1877; s. R. Watson and Marie E. (Hurley) W.; ed. Vienna pub. schs.; student Goldey Commercial Coll., Wilmington, Del., 9 mos., 1900-01; m. Mildred Woolford, June 17, 1908; 1 dau., Mildred Virginia. Began as sch. teacher, 1896; in newspaper business since 1905; sole owner Webb & Webb, publishers of The Daily Banner and The Cambridge Record, since 1910; v.p. and dir. Franklin Credit-Finance Corpn.; dir. County Trust Co. of Md., Cambridge Mfg. Co., Eastern Shore Public Service Co. Mem. Maryland State Roads Commission. Mem. bd. govs. Washington Coll., Chestertown, Md. Democrat. Episcopalian. Mason, Elk. Clubs: Cambridge Country, Cambridge Yacht. Home: 15 High St. Office: 112 High St., Cambridge, Md.

WEBB, Thomas Edward, pres. Webb Packing Co.; b. Crisfield, Md., Dec. 25, 1891; s. Thomas Jefferson and Hettie (Byrd) W.; grad. high sch., Crisfield, Md., 1909; student Bryant and Stratton Business Coll., Baltimore, Md.; m. Nina Tawes, Nov. 1, 1917; 1 dau., Lucille Tawes. Began as delivery boy in grocery store, 1905; now pres. Webb Packing Co., Salisbury; pres. The Marine Bank, Crisfield, Md. Served as pvt., U.S. Army, during World War. Mem. bd. govs. Delmarva Chamber of Commerce. Democrat. Methodist. Mason. Club: Rotary of Crisfield, Md. (hon. mem.). Home: Crisfield, Md. Office: Salisbury, Md.

WEBB, Walter Loring, engineer; b. Rye, N.Y., June 25, 1863; s. Edward Dexter and Emily (Loder) W.; B.C.E., Cornell U. 1884, C.E., 1889; m. Mary Tremaine Hubbard, Sept. 1, 1886. Instr. civ. engring., Cornell, 1888-92; asst. prof. civ. engring., U. of Pa., 1893-1901; cons. engr. since 1901. Mem. American Soc. Civil Engrs., Am. Railway Engring. Assn., Am. Concrete Inst., Sigma Xi, Tau Beta Pi; Companion Mil. Order Foreign Wars. Clubs: Engineers'; Cornell (Phila.). Author: Shades, Shadow and Perspective; Problems in the Use and Adjustment of Engineering Instruments, 5th edition, 1907; Railroad Construction, 9th edition, 1931; Economics of Railroad Construction, 2d edit., 1912, transl. into the Russian, 1921. Contbr. sect. 3 (railroads) to American Civil Engineers' Pocket Book; also contbr. to engring. and scientific periodicals. Maj. of engrs., U.S. A., 1917-20, in France as chief engr. of renting requisitions and claims service, in charge of valuations. Mason (32°). Awarded Fuertes graduate gold medal by Cornell Univ., 1932, in recognition of 9th edit., "Railroad Construction." Home: Lansdowne, Pa.

WEBER, Alfred Herman, prof. of physics; b. Phila., Pa., Jan. 15, 1906; s. Frank Curt and Anna Josephine (Kling) W.; A.B., St. Joseph's Coll., Phila., 1928, A.M., 1931; Ph.D., U. of Pa., 1936; m. Frances Theresa Lever, Dec. 26, 1932; children—Constance Marie, Judith Ann. Instr. in physics and mathematics, St. Joseph's Coll., Phila., 1928-34, asst. prof. of physics, 1934-36, prof. of physics and head of dept. since 1936. Mem. Am. Physical Soc., Am. Assn. Physics Teachers, Franklin Inst. Roman Catholic. Club: Physics (Phila.). Author: Outline of Laboratory Physics, 1936; also tech. papers on photoelectricity, laboratory experiments in physics, etc., to jours. Home: 2329 Belmont Av., Ardmore, Pa. Office: St. Joseph's College, Philadelphia, Pa.

WEBER, Bernis Bensley, civil engring.; b. Salamanca, N.Y., Nov. 18, 1881; s. Blanchard Benjamin and Lena (Ferrin) W.; C.E., Cornell U., 1904; m. Mary Morrison Cumming, June 6, 1917; children—Anna Margaret, Alexander Cumming. Employed in N.Y. State Engring. Dept., 1904-06; asst. city engr., Oil City, Pa., 1906-13, city engr. since 1913. Mem. Nat. Soc. of Professional Engrs., Am. Pub. Works Assn. Republican. Presbyterian. Mason. Club: Kiwanis (Oil City, Pa.). Home: 162 Halyday St. Office: City Bldg., Oil City, Pa.

WEBER, Charles Henry, pres. May Lumber Co.; b. Pittsburgh, Pa., May 2, 1881; s. Robert and Marie (Mertz) W.; student business coll.; m. Ida Geiss, Dec. 10, 1908; 1 son, Charles. Began as clk. in wholesale lumber co.; treas. Keystone Lumber Co., 1910-20, v.p. 1920-32; pres. May Lumber Co. since 1932. Dir. Lumber Inst. of Allegheny County, Western Pa. Lumber Dealers Assn. Republican. Methodist (trustee). Mason (Shriner). Club: Alcoma Country. Home: 1650 Chislett St. Office: 1201 Brighton Road, Pittsburgh, Pa.

WEBER, Clarence Scott Paul, banker; b. Middletown, Del., July 4, 1899; s. Paul and Rosa Katherine (Hettenbach) W.; student Middletown (Del.) High Sch., 1906-15, Goldey Coll., Wilmington, Del., 1915-16; unmarried. Bank clk. Citizens Nat. Bank, Middletown, Del., 1916-20; asst. mgr. Del. Trust Co. (successor to Citizens Nat. Bank), Middletown, Del. 1920-24, mgr. since 1924, dir. since 1934; sec.-treas. and dir. Crystal Beach Manor, Inc., Middletown, since 1928; dir. The Mutual Loan Assn.; town auditor, Middletown, Del., 1928-38. In Boy Scout work since 1912; treas. Camp Appoquinimink (Episcopal Ch. Camp for Boys), Middletown, since 1934. Awarded 20 Year Vet. Pin, Boy Scouts of America, 1938. Republican. Methodist. Mason (Union Lodge 5, Middletown, Del), Odd Fellow (Good Samaritan Lodge 9, Middletown). Home: 10 E. Green St. Office: 1 W. Main St., Middletown, Del.

WEBER, Emil William, clergyman; b. Tompkinsville, N.Y., Sept. 6, 1884; s. Frederick and Mina (Ahrens) W.; student Wagner Coll., 1900-04, Luth, Theol. Sem., Mt. Airy, Pa., 1904-07, U. of Erlangen, Germany, 1907-08, U. of Leipzig, Germany, 1908; D.D., Muhlenberg Coll., 1935; m. Bertha Behner, June 23, 1909; children—Hugo C. A., Emil William, Jr. Ordained to ministry Luth. Ch., 1908; pastor, Bridgeton, N.J., 1908-13, pastor, Yonkers, N.Y., 1913-17; pastor Trinity Luth. Ch., Pottsville, Pa., since 1925. Served as chaplain, 1st lt., U.S.A., 1917-22, capt., 1922-25, resigned, Dec. 18, 1925; maj. U.S.A. Res., 1926. Mem. exec. bd. Ministerium of Pa.; dir. Pottsville (Pa.) Hosp., Schuylkill County Mental Hosp.; trustee Luth. Theol. Sem. (Mt. Airy, Pa.). Republican. Lutheran. Home: 301 N. 2d St., Pottsville, Pa.

WEBER, John, mech. engr.; b. Pittsburgh, Oct. 20, 1885; s. John and Emma Wilson (Beitler) W.; M.E., U. of Pittsburgh, 1909; D.Sc.; m. Blanche J. Martin, March 21, 1912; children—John Martin, James Harold, Dorothy Ellen. With U. of Pittsburgh since 1909, except during war period; successively research asst., instr. in mech. engring., asst. prof., asso. prof., prof and hd. of dept., 1922-25, bus. mgr. and supervising engr. constructional work, 1926-36, sec. of Univ. since 1936. Served as capt. engrs., World War; mem. Vehicle Standardization Board and of Automotive Products Com., War Industries Bd. Now mem. bd. of managers of Juvenile Court Home of Allegheny County. Mem. Soc. for Promotion Engring. Edn., Delta Tau Delta, Omicron Delta Kappa, Sigma Tau, Scabbard and Blade. Republican. Mem. United Presbyn. Ch. Club: University (Pittsburgh). Home: 1317 Denniston St., Pittsburgh, Pa.

WEBER, Samuel Edwin, supt. of schs.; b. Ellis, Vernon Co., Mo., July 23, 1875; s. George Jacob and Elizabeth (Zilliox) W.; grad. Lock Haven Normal Sch., Pa., 1895; Ph.B., Lafayette Coll., 1901; Ph.D., U. of Pa., 1905; m. Mary Louisa Knarr, Aug. 7, 1901; 1 son, Orville Ethelbert. Teacher in elementary schs., 1894-97; fellow in pedagogy, U. of Pa., 1903-05; prin. North Wales (Pa.) High Sch., 1901-03; supt. Cortland Normal Training Sch., N.Y., 1905-07; state high sch. insp. of La., 1908-10; dean Sch. of Liberal Arts and prof. edn., Pa. State Coll., 1910-14, and dir. summer session for teachers same; supt. schs., Scranton, Pa., 1914-22; supt. of schs., Charleston, W.Va., 1922-29; associate superintendent schools, Pittsburgh, Pennsylvania, in charge personnel, since 1929. Prof. educational administration and supervision, U. of Pa., summer session, 1922-23. Presbyn. Mem. N.E.A., Pa. Ednl. Assn. Clubs: Literary, University (Pa. State Coll.). Author: Charity School Movement in Colonial Pennsylvania, 1905; A Course of Study for High Schools, 1909; Coöperative Administration and Supervision of the Teaching Personnel, 1937. Joint Author of Weber, Koch, and Moran Series of Arithmetics. Joint translator of Brumbaugh's "Christopher Dock," 1905. Home: 1206 Inverness St., Pittsburgh, Pa.

WEBER, William A., prof. religious edn.; b. Cincinnati, O., July 30, 1880; s. John and Frederique (Opperman) W.; A.B., Otterbein Coll., Ohio, 1906, D.D., 1919; B.D., Bonebrake Theol. Sem., Dayton, O., 1909; studied Berlin and Marburg univs., 1910-11, University of Chicago, summers, 1912-16, and Yale University, 1923-24; Ph.D., Yale University; m. Justina A. Lemmerman, Sept. 27, 1910; 1 son, Robert L. Ordained U.B. ministry, 1909; pastor in Cleveland and Dayton, O., 4 yrs.; prof. religious edn., Bonebrake Theol. Sem., 1911-25; prof. religious edn., Theol. Sem., New Brunswick, N.J., since 1925; teacher, summer sessions, Rutgers U., 1926-31, prof. extension courses since 1931. Member Internat. Council Religious Education, mem. bd. control Sunday Schools of U.B. Ch., 1920-29; chmn. com. Week Day Sch. Religion, Dayton, O.; mem. executive com. N.J. Council Religious Edn. (chmn. com. on week-day and vacation ch. schs.); also chmn. com. on ednl. program and policies); mem. and chmn. edn. com. Bd. of Publ. and Bible Sch. Work, Ref. Ch. in America; mem. board of edn., Dayton, O., 1921-25 (twice pres.); mem. Dept. of Internat. Justice and Goodwill, Federal Council of the Churches of Christ in America. Mem. Religious Edn. Assn., Am. Assn. Advancement of Sci., Phi Beta Kappa. Club. Clergy. Author: The Daily Vacation Bible School; (joint) The Progressive Training Course; Theological Education in the Reformed Church in America. Contbr. numerous articles in religious and ednl. journals. Home: Seminary Pl. Address: Hertzog Hall, New Brunswick, N.J.

WEBSTER, Alice Irving, city clerk; b. Wallingford, Conn., July 2, 1887; d. Charles Irving and Abby Thornton (Dodd) Webster; student (honor) East Orange (N.J.) High Sch., 1900-03, Rutgers U. Extension Courses in pub. admnstrn., New Brunswick, N.J., 1934, 1935; unmarried. Stenographer, Manhattan Life Ins. Co., New York, 1905-06, Diamond Match Co., New York, 1906-07; in city clerk's office, City of East Orange (N.J.), 1907-10, dep. city clerk (civil service), 1910-33, city clerk, appointive City Council, since 1933. Mem. Am. Legion Auxiliary (chapter 73; charter mem.), State Fed. of Business and Professional Women's Clubs (sec.), Chamber of Commerce of the Oranges and Maplewood. Republican. Congregationalist. Club: Business and Professional Women's of the Oranges (past pres.; charter mem.). Home: 676 Springdale Av. Office: City Hall, East Orange, N.J.

WEBSTER, Ralph Rayner, high sch. prin.; b. Deals Island, Md., Nov. 18, 1901; s. Lennie G. and Isadora F. (Daniel) W.; B.S., St. John's Coll., 1921; A.M., U. of Md., College Park, Md., 1929; m. Alberta V. Schramm, June 27, 1929. Employed as prin. high sch., Marion, Md., 1921-22; instr. Frederick (Md.) High Sch., 1922-25; prin. high sch., Grantsville, Md., 1925-27, high sch., Mt. Savage, Md., 1927-29, Beall high sch., 1929-34; prin. Allegany high sch., Cumberland, Md., since 1934. Mem. Nat. Edn. Assn., Kappa Phi Kappa. Democrat. Presbyterian. Mason (32°, Shriner). Club: Rotary of Cumberland (sec.). Home: 639 Sedgwick St., Cumberland, Md.

WEBSTER, Steacy E., life insurance; b. Strasburg, Pa., Aug. 9, 1896; s. J. Harold and Mary S. (Rhorer) W.; ed. Wesleyan U.; m. Eleanor Scott Smith, Apr. 12, 1918. Employed by Uniflow Boiler Co., 1919-20, Gulf Refining Co., 1920-21; with Provident Mutual Life Ins. Co. of Phila. since 1921, in York (Pa.) office, 1921-29, gen. agent, Pittsburgh, since 1930. Served as lt., U.S. Inf., World War; gassed in St. Mihiel Drive. Dir. Community Fund, Pittsburgh. Past pres. Pa. State Assn. Life Underwriters, Gen. Agents and Mgrs. Group in Pittsburgh; dir. and ex-pres. Pittsburgh Life Underwriters Assn.; mem. Mil. Order Foreign War. Clubs: University, Chartiers Country (Pittsburgh). Home: 858 Osage Road, Virginia Manor. Office: 2500 Koppers Bldg., Pittsburgh, Pa.

WECKSTEIN, Herman Bernard Joseph, lawyer; b. Newark, N.J., Mar. 26, 1898; s. Bernard and Rebecca (Roman) W.; LL.B., N. J. Law Sch., Newark, N.J., 1919; m. Cele Meyers, July 1, 1920; children—Norbert, Raymond, Donald. In practice at Newark, N.J., since 1919, specializing in practice before Interstate Commerce Commn. since 1935. Former treas. Nat. Amateur Journalists Assn. Mem. Newark Amateur Journalist Assn. (past pres.), Y.M.H.A., and Y.W.H.A. (former mem. bd. of dirs.), Order Sons of Zion-Nat., Jewish Nat. Fund-Nat. (former mem. bd. of dirs.), Jewish War Vets. of U.S. (past comdr. Newark Post, past state boycott chmn., now trustee and anti-communist chmn.), Lambda Alpha Phi (past pres.). Democrat. Jewish religion. Mason, Elk, K.P. (past pres.), Brith Sholom (past pres.). Club: Ben Hur, Inc. (Newark, N.J.; sec.; past pres.). Home: 394 Clinton Pl. Office: 1060 Broad St., Newark, N.J.

WEDDERBURN, Joseph Henry Maclagan, mathematician; b. Forfar, Scotland, Feb. 26, 1882; s. Alexander Stormonth Maclagan and Anne (Ogilvie) W.; M.A., Edinburgh U., 1903, D.Sc., 1908; studied Leipzig, Berlin and U. of Chicago; unmarried. Asst. in mathematics, Edinburgh U., 1905-09; asst. prof. mathematics, Princeton, 1909-21, asso. prof., 1921-28, prof. since 1928. Captain Seaforth Highlanders and capt. Royal Engrs., British Army, 1914-19. Fellow A.A.A.S., Royal Soc. (London), Royal Soc. (Edinburgh); mem. Am. Math. Soc., Circolo Matematico di Palermo. Presbyn. Author: Lectures on Matrices, 1934. Editor: Annals of Mathematics. Contbr. on scientific topics. Home: 134 Mercer St., Princeton, N.J.

WEDEBERG, S. M.; prof. accounting, U. of Md. Address: University of Maryland, College Park, Md.

WEECH, Charles Sewell, ins. exec.; b. Baltimore, Md., Aug. 15, 1894; s. Rev. Robert William Henry and Clara Elizabeth (Ashley) W.; A.B., Johns Hopkins U., Baltimore, Md., 1915; LL.B., U. of Md., Baltimore, Md., 1920; m. Audrey Allen, Nov. 20, 1926; 1 son, Charles Sewell. With New Amsterdam Casualty Co., Baltimore, Md., since 1915, successively as attorney, and asst. sec.; vice-pres. since 1928. Served in Italy and France as mem. Johns Hopkins Ambulance Unit, U.S. Army, 1917-19. Mem. Phi Beta Kappa, Phi Kappa Sigma. Republican. Methodist. Clubs: Johns Hopkins, Engineers' (Baltimore, Md.). Home: 1307 Park Av. Office: 227 St. Paul St., Baltimore, Md.

WEED, J. Spencer; b. Middletown, N.Y., Dec. 24, 1879; s. John Hollister and Mary Ann (Sharp) W.; Williams Coll., 1900-03; m. Hannah Broadley Bowman, Oct. 14, 1908 (deceased); children—Douglas Bowman, Janet Mary, J. Spencer; m. 2d, Ethel Randall Eddy, Dec. 1, 1934. Vice-pres. Great Atlantic & Pacific Tea Corpn., 1913-24; pres. Grand Union Co., Grand Union Tea Co., Grand Union Stores, Inc., Jones Bros. Tea Co., Inc., since 1924; dir. Summit Trust Co. Served on U.S. Food Administration, 1917-19. Pres. Nat. Horse Show Assn. of America, Ltd., 1932-38. Republican. Conglist. Clubs: Union League, The Leash, Williams, India House, Baltusrol Golf, Short Hills; Morris County Golf; Spring Valley Hounds. Home: Spring Valley Rd., Morristown, N.J. Office: 233 Broadway, New York, N.Y.

WEED, Lewis Hill, anatomist; b. Cleveland, O., Nov. 15, 1886; s. Charles Henry and Mary Frances (Lewis) W.; A.B., Yale, 1908, A.M., 1909; M.D., Johns Hopkins, 1912; Sc.D., U. of Rochester, 1929; LL.D., Duke, 1938; unmarried. Fellow in charge of Lab. of Surg. Research, Harvard Med. Sch., 1912-13; Arthur Tracy Cabot fellow, same sch., 1913-14; instr., asso. and asso. prof. anatomy, 1914-19, prof. since July 1, 1919, dean med. faculty, 1923-29, dir. School of Medicine since 1929, Johns Hopkins University. Served as captain, Med. Corps, U.S.A., Aug. 1917-May 1919; was mil. dir. Army Neuro-Surg. Lab. at Johns Hopkins Med. Sch. Research asso. Carnegie Instn. of Washington, 1922-35. Trustee Inst. for Advanced Study since 1930; trustee Carnegie Instn. of Washington since 1935; mem. Med. Fellowship Board, Nat. Research Council since 1935, chmn. Div. of Med. Sciences, same, since 1939. Mem. Am. Assn. Anatomists, Am. Soc. Zoölogists, A.A.A.S., Am. Physiol. Soc., Am. Assn. Pathologists and Bacteriologists, Am. Soc. Mammalogists, Am. Assn. Phys. Anthropologists, Am. Neurological Assn. (asso.). Author of monographs and original articles on anatom. and neurol. subjects. Research in experimental neurology. Clubs: Maryland, University (Baltimore). Home: 3908 N. Charles St. Address: Johns Hopkins Medical School, Baltimore, Md.

WEEDER, Stephen Dana, surgeon; b. Phila., Pa., Feb. 18, 1896; s. Stephen G. and Ella (Richardson) W.; M.D., U. of Pa., 1917; m. Caroline D. Nixon, Apr. 16, 1925; children—Dorothy Crispin, Caroline Nixon, Dana Nixon, Richard Stockton. Instr. anatomy, U. of Pa. Med. Sch., 1920-32; mem. staff Pa. Hosp.,

1921-25; surgeon Germantown (Pa.) Hosp. since 1923; asso. surgeon Chestnut Hill (Pa.) Hosp. since 1927. Mem. Med. Club of Philadelphia, Soc. Colonial Wars of N.J. Republican. Presbyterian. Clubs: Philadelphia Cricket (mem. bd. govs.), Philadelphia Doctors Golf Assn. Author: Bundy's Anatomy and Physiology (rev. edit.), 1939; also various surg. papers. Co-author: Davis' Applied Anatomy (rev. edit.), 1934. Address: 6110 Greene St., Germantown, Philadelphia, Pa.

WEEKS, Dorothy Walcott, coll. prof.; b. Phila., Pa., May 3, 1893; d. Edward Mitchell and Mary Dexter (Walcott) W.; student Western High Sch., Washington, D.C., 1908-12; B.A., Wellesley (Mass.) Coll., 1916; M.S., Mass. Inst. Tech., 1923, Ph.D., 1930; M.S., Simmons Coll., Boston, Mass., 1925; student Cornell U. Summer Sch., 1918 and 1919, Harvard Grad. Sch. of Edn., summer 1927, 1st semester, 1927-28; unmarried. Asst. examiner U.S. Patent Office, Washington, D.C., 1917-20; lab. asst. U.S. Bur. of Standards, Washington, D.C., 1920; asst. in physics, Mass. Inst. Tech., 1920-21, research asso., 1921-22, instr. physics, 1922-24; instr. physics and gen. science, Buckingham Sch., Cambridge, Mass., 1923-24; supervisor of women Jordan Marsh Co., Boston, Mass., 1925-27; instr. physics, Wellesley (Mass.) Coll., 1928-29, Horton-Hallowell Fellow of Wellesley Coll. Alumnæ Assn., 1929-30; prof. physics and head dept., Wilson Coll., Chambersburg, Pa., since 1930; expert tech. examiner Civil Service Commn., Washington, D.C., summer 1930. Fellow A.A.A.S.; mem. Am. Assn. Univ. Women (pres. Pa.-Del. div.), Am. Phys. Soc., Am. Assn. Physics Teachers, Am. Math. Soc., Washington Philos. Soc., Am. Assn. Univ. Profs., Shakespeare Soc. (Wellesley Coll.). Republican. Episcopalian. Club: College (Boston, Mass.). Spl. research in spectroscopy, at present making study of spectral lines emitted by neutral iron atom. Address: Wilson Coll., Chambersburg, Pa.

WEEKS, Ernest Frederick, mech. engr.; b. East Orange, N.J., May 19, 1901; s. Frederick Thomas and Christina (Mackay) W.; grad. East Orange (N.J.) High Sch., 1918; B.S. in M.E., U. of Mich., 1922; M.E., 1929; m. Jean Ellen McCue, Dec. 31, 1922; children—Jean Ellen, Richard Ernest. Cadet engr. gas dept. Pub. Service Electric & Gas Co., Newark, N.J., 1922-23, Trenton, N.J., 1923-25, asst. to engr., Harrison (N.J.) Gas Works, 1925-29, asst. supt. Paterson (N.J.) Gas Works, 1929-32, supt., 1932-38, engr. of mfr. Passaic (N.J.) Div. since 1938. Mem. Am. Gas Assn., N.J. Gas Assn., Nat. Soc. Professional Engrs., N.J. Soc. Professional Engrs. (1st v.p. since 1939), Passaic Co. Engring. Soc. Republican. Episcopalian. Mason (Ivanhoe Lodge 88, Paterson, N.J.). Clubs: Masonic (Paterson, N.J.); North Jersey Country (Paterson, N.J.). Home: North Haledon, N.J. Office: 200 E. 5th St., Paterson, N.J.

WEEKS, Ralph Emerson, educator, pub.; b. Skaneateles, N.Y., Feb. 9, 1878; s. William Thomas and Martha M. (Cuddeback) W.; ed. high schs., Skaneateles; m. Elizabeth Porter, Nov. 22, 1904; children—Clara Porter, John Porter, Eleanor Porter, Ann Porter. Pres. Ralph E. Weeks Corpn., Ralph E. Weeks Co., Internat. Textbook Co., Internat. Corr. Schs., Capouse Warehouse Co., John T. Porter Co., International Correspondence Schs., Canadian, Ltd., Haddon Press, Inc., Haddon Craftsmen, Inc.; v.p. Williams Bakery; treas. and dir. U.S. Lumber Co., Miss. Central R.R. Co., J. J. Newman Lumber Co.; dir. Internat. Educational Pub. Co., Internat. Corr. Schs., Ltd., London, Internat. Schs. Co. of Latin America, First Nat. Bank (Scranton), Scranton-Lackawanna Trust Co., Weeks Hardware Co., Wesel Mfg. Co., Syndicate Realty Co., Bell Telephone Co. of Pa. Pres. Scranton Bd. of Trade, 1913-14; chmn. Scranton Chapter Am. Red Cross, 1916-20; trustee Community Welfare Assn., 1921-33, Scranton Pub. Library (v.p.) Wyoming Sem. (v.p.), Community Chest, Scranton-Keystone Jr. Coll., Y.W.C.A., First M.E. Ch. (pres. bd. trustees); pres. and dir. Pa. State Chamber of Commerce; pres. Scranton Y.M.C.A.; dir. Am. Red Cross, Family Welfare Soc., Scranton Chamber of Commerce. Republican. Methodist. Clubs: Scranton, Scranton Country. Home: 544 Jefferson Av. Office: Wyoming Av. and Ash St., Scranton, Pa.

WEELANS, Charles H., referee in bankruptcy; b. Trenton, N.J., Sept. 3, 1885; s. Charles and Sarah Hellings (Whitaker) W.; A.B., Princeton U., 1908; LL.B., Harvard Law Sch., 1911; m. Elizabeth Willis Bowne, Oct. 23, 1912; 1 dau., Elizabeth Bowne. Practice of law at Trenton, N.J., 1911-30; referee in bankruptcy, Trenton, N.J., since 1930. Trustee William McKinley Memorial Hosp.; trustee, Third Presbyn. Ch. Mem. Mercer Co., N.J. State, Am. bar assns. Republican. Presbyterian. Mason. Clubs: Trenton Country, Princeton (Trenton, N.J.); Harvard (Phila.). Home: 20 S. Overbrook Av. Office: Post Office Bldg., Trenton, N.J.

WEGLEIN, David Emrich, supt. schs.; b. Baltimore, Md., June 10, 1876; s. Morris and Rosa (Emrich) W.; grad. Baltimore City Coll., 1894; A.B., Johns Hopkins, 1897, Ph.D., 1916; A.M., Columbia, 1912; unmarried. Asst. prin. elementary sch., Baltimore, 1897-1900; 1st asst., Teachers' Training Sch., Baltimore, 1900-02; teacher and head of pedagogical dept., Baltimore City Coll., 1902-06; prin. Western High Sch., Baltimore, 1906-20; instr. in edn., Johns Hopkins, 1917-21, asso. in edn., 1921-28, asso. prof. edn. since 1928; asst. supt. schs., Baltimore 1921-24, 1st asst., 1924-25, supt. since 1925. Mem. problems and plans com. of Am. Council of Education, 1930-35, now mem. exec. com.; mem. Middle States Assn. of Colls. and Secondary Schs. (pres. 1938; mem. exec. com.); mem. Nat. Advisory Com. of Nat. Youth Administration, 1935. Fellow A.A.A.S.; mem. N.E.A. and Dept. Superintendence (2d v.p. of latter, also mem. joint emergency commn.), Md. State Teachers Assn. (ex-pres.), Ednl. Soc. Baltimore (ex-pres.), Phi Beta Kappa, Phi Delta Kappa. Jewish religion; member board trustees Eutaw Pl. Temple. Mason. Rotarian. Clubs: Civitan, University, Johns Hopkins. Author: Correlation of Abilities of High School Pupils, 1916. Home: 2400 Linden Av. Office: 3 E. 25th St., Baltimore, Md.

WEHNER, Edward F.; mem. staff and gynecol. surg. service St. Mary's Hosp. Address: 321 W. Main St., Clarksburg, W.Va.

WEIDLEIN, Edward Ray, chemical engr.; b. Augusta, Kan., July 14, 1887; s. Edward and Nettie (Lemon) W.; B.A., University of Kan., 1909, M.A., 1910; hon. ScD., Tufts Coll., 1924; LL.D., University of Pittsburgh, 1930; (hon.) Sc.D., Rutgers University, 1937; m. Hazel I. Butts, April 24, 1915; children—Edward Ray, Robert Butts, John David. Industrial fellow, research on camphor, U. of Kan., 1909-10, research on ductless glands, 1910-12; sr. fellow, Mellon Inst. of Industrial Research, Pittsburgh, Pa., having charge of investigations on metallurgy and hydrometallurgy of copper, and also of the experimental plant, at Thompson, Nev., 1912-16; asst. dir. of the Inst. at Pittsburgh, July-Oct. 1916, asso. dir., 1916-21, actg. dir., 1918-19, and since 1921 dir. Mellon Inst., and v.p. bd. trustees same, since 1928; dir. Forbes Nat. Bank, Pittsburgh. Trustee U. of Pittsburgh, Shadyside Academy (Pittsburgh); mem. Greater Pa. Council, 1932. Served as chemical expert War Industries Bd., Mar. 1918-Jan. 1919; chmn. fuel com., Nat. Research Council, 1918, and mem. central petroleum com. of same as rep. div. chemistry and chem. tech., 1927-30, also mem. at large div. of engring. industrial research. Fellow A.A.A.S. since 1925, American Institute Chemists, Royal Soc. of Arts, London; mem. Am. Chem. Soc. (chmn. Pittsburgh Sect., 1923; councilor, 1924-29; councilor at large, 1929-34; pres., 1937), Am. Inst. Chem. Engineers (dir. 1924, 29; pres. 1927-29), Am. Inst. of Mining and Metall. Engrs., Electro-Chem. Soc., Engrs. Soc. Western Pa., National Education Assn., Pa. Acad. Science, Am. Acad. Pol. and Social Sciences, Kan. Acad. Science, Société de Chimie Industrielle, Franklin Inst., Washington Academy Sciences, Society Chemical Industry (executive committee American section), American Institute, Faraday Soc., Pa. Soc., Société Chimique de France, Deutsche Chemische Gesellschaft, Chamber of Commerce of Pittsburgh (dir., v.p. 1931-34), Sigma Tau, Pi Upsilon, Sigma Xi, Phi Lambda Upsilon, Alpha Chi Sigma, Sigma Gamma Epsilon; hon. mem. Pittsburgh Acad. Science and Art., Inst. Chem. Engrs. (Gt. Britain), Chem. and Metall. Mining Soc. (S. Africa); dir. Allegheny Council West of Boy Scouts America. Awarded Chem. Industry medal by Soc. of Chem. Industry, 1935. Republican. Clubs: Chemists (non-resident v.p.), Pittsburgh Faculty (pres. 1923), University (dir. 1925-28; sec. 1926-27; v.p. 1920-31; pres. 1931-33), Authors' of Pittsburgh, Oakmont Country, Longue Vue, Duquesne. Co-Author: Science in Action, 1931; Glances at Industrial Research, 1935. Contbr. numerous articles, especially on the direction, results and value of industrial research. Original research in development of processes for use of sulphur dioxide in hydrometallurgy; lab. management; application of science in industry, etc. Home: 325 S. Dallas Av., Pittsburgh, Pa.

WEIDMAN, Fred Deforest, physician; b. Bristol, Conn., Oct. 16, 1881; s. Herman Constantine and Eva Lucinda (Stone) W.; M.D., U. of Pa. Med. Sch., 1908; m. Florence Lafayette Krewson, Aug. 24, 1904 (died 1933); children—Dorothy Mary, Allen Frederick; m. 2d, Lillian Ensley Hawk, May 21, 1937. In general practice of medicine, 1908-13; prof. pathology, Woman's Med. Coll., Phila., 1914-17; asst. pathologist, Phila. Zool. Garden since 1910; prof. dermatol. research, U. of Pa., since 1923, prof. dermatology and vice-dean, Grad. Sch. of Medicine, since 1934. Pres. Sect. on Mycology, 3d Internat. Cong. for Microbiology, 1939. Mem. Am. Dermatol. Assn. (sec. since 1935), A.M.A., Phila. Path. Soc., Phila. Dermatol. Soc., Sigma Xi. Mason (Oriental Lodge 385). Home: 20 Tenby Rd., Llanerch, Pa. Office: Medical Laboratories, U. of Pa., 36 Hamilton Walk, Philadelphia, Pa.

WEIERBACH, John A., physician; b. Pleasant Valley, Pa., Jan. 14, 1883; s. Josiah S. and Amelia (Frey) W.; M.D., Medico Chirurg. Med. Coll., Phila., 1910; m. Bertha G. Hendricks, June 13, 1911; children—Gerald H., Janet May. Engaged in gen. practice of medicine and surgery, Quakertown, Pa., since 1910; dir. Best Made Silk Hosiery Co. since 1926; dir. Merchants Nat. Bank since 1935; chief of eye, ear, nose and throat dept., Quakertown Community Hosp. and Grand View Hosp., Sellersville, Pa. Dir. Grand View Hosp., Sellersville, Pa. Fellow Am. Coll. Surgeons; mem. A.M.A., Pa. Med. Soc., Phila. Laryngol. Soc. Democrat. Evang. Ch. Mason (32°, Shriner). Home: 1121 W. Broad St., Quakertown, Pa.

WEIHL, Fred Phillip, high sch. prin.; b. Marietta, O., Jan. 9, 1903; s. John and Mary Caroline (Grealey) W.; A.B., W.Va. Wesleyan U., Buckhannon, W.Va., 1926, A.M., 1934; m. Pauline Bender, June 21, 1928; 1 dau., Jo Ann. Employed as teacher and athletic coach, high sch., Buckhannon, W.Va., 1926-27; coach, high sch., Wellsburg, W.Va., 1928-29; coach, high sch., Weston, W.Va., 1930-34, prin. high sch. since 1934. Mem. W.Va. Prins. Assn., Central W.Va. Basketball Officials Assn. (pres.), W.Va. Football Officials Assn. Democrat. Methodist. Mason. Club: Rotary of Weston. Home: 618 Locust St., Weston, W.Va.

WEIL, Richard, Jr., pres. L. Bamberger & Co.; b. New York, N.Y., Dec. 5, 1907; s. Richard and Minnie (Straus) W.; student Hotchkiss Sch., 1921-25, Yale, 1925-28; m. Allene Hall, of New York, N.Y., Jan. 5, 1935; children—Richard, III, Martha. Began as merchant, 1928; with R. H. Macy & Co., 1928-36; v.p. L. Bamberger & Co., 1936-39, pres. since 1939. Home: 123 Hillside Av., Englewood, N.J. Office: care L. Bamberger & Co., Market St., Newark, N.J.

WEILER, Royal William, newspaper pub.; b. Emaus, Pa., Sept. 7, 1880; s. John Wilson and Mary Elizabeth (Schmale) W.; ed. pub. schs.; m. Hester Estella Binder, Aug. 16, 1900; 1 son, Fred Wilson. Teacher pub. schs., Emaus, 1900-10; reporter Allentown (Pa.) Democrat, 1900-13; gen. mgr. Allentown Democrat Pub. Co., 1913-19; pres. and mgr. Allentown Call Pub. Co. since 1919; pres. and mgr. Chronicle and News Publishing Co. since 1935. Mem. Allentown Police Pension Fund Commn. Rep. mem. Associated Press, Am. Newspaper Publishers'

WEILERSTEIN

Assn., Pa. Newspaper Publishers' Assn.; dir. Family Welfare Orgn.; dir. Boys' Haven, Inc., Lehigh County Hist. Soc., Lehigh County Humane Soc. Republican. Mem. Reformed Ch. Mason (33°), Shriner; mem. Tall Cedars of Lebanon, Odd Fellows, Elks, Eagles, Patriotic Order Sons of America, Brotherhood of America, Chamber of Commerce, Internat. Circulation Managers' Assn. Rotarian. Home: 1615 Linden St. Office: 101 N. 6th St., Allentown, Pa.

WEILERSTEIN, Baruch Reuben, rabbi; b. New York, N.Y., May 22, 1894; s. Abraham and Fannie (Pantinovitz) W.; B.A., N.Y.U., 1917; rabbi, Jewish Theol. Sem. of America, New York, 1919; m. Sarah Huyla Rose, June 29, 1920; children—Herschel, Judith, Deborah, Ruth. Rabbi, Temple Emanu-El of Borough Park, Brooklyn, N.Y., 1919-21, Congregation Petach Tikvah, Brooklyn, N.Y., 1921-29, Community Synagogue, Atlantic City, N.J., since 1929. Dir. Fed. of Jewish Charities; dir. Travellers Aid Soc.; mem. bd. of govs., Jewish Community Center. Mem. Rabbinical Assembly of Jewish Theol. Sem. Address: 216 S. Vermont Av., Atlantic City, N.J.

WEILL, Alfred Sigismund, lawyer; b. Buffalo, N.Y., Dec. 5, 1873; s. Louis and Emelia (Desbecker) W.; A.B., Harvard, 1895; LL.B., Harvard Law Sch., 1898; m. Louise Steele Young, Nov. 14, 1901; 1 dau., Louise (Mrs. Francis Otis Allen, Jr., died 1934). Admitted to New York bar, 1898, and practiced at Buffalo until 1901; moved to Phila. and admitted to practice in Pa. cts., 1902; spl. atty. in Solicitor's Office, Bur. Internal Revenue, Washington, D.C., 1918; specialized in federal taxation since 1918; sr. mem. law firms Weill, Nesbit & Lisenby (Phila.), Weill, Satterlee, Green & Morris (Washington, D.C.) and Satterlee & Green (N.Y. City). Mem. Am. Bar Assn., Pa. Bar Assn., Phila. Bar Assn. Republican. Jewish religion. Clubs: Harvard, Philadelphia Cricket, Penn Athletic (Phila.); Harvard (N.Y. City); Buffalo (Buffalo, N.Y.). Home: 201 W. Chestnut Av. Office: 1240 Land Title Bldg., Philadelphia, Pa.

WEIMER, Bernal Robinson, coll. prof.; b. Port Royal, Pa., Dec. 4, 1894; s. George McCullough and Ada Ruth (Robinson) W.; A.B., West Va. Univ., Morgantown, 1916, A.M., 1918; Ph.D., U. of Chicago, 1927; m. Margaret Grace Robinson, Aug. 31, 1918; children —John Robinson, Margaret Brown, George Alexander. Engaged as supervising prin. schs., Mifflintown, Pa., 1918-21; prof. biology, Bethany Coll., Bethany, W.Va., since 1921; instr. zoology, W.Va. Univ., summers 1924, 1932, U. of Chicago, summer 1927; chmn. sci. and mathematics group, Bethany Coll., since 1931, dean of faculty and prof. biology since 1936. Served in inf. and med. service, U.S.A., during World War. Mem. A.A.A.S., Am. Soc. Zoologists, Am. Assn. Biology Teachers, W.Va. Acad. Sci. (pres. 1928), W.Va. Biol. Survey (exec. com.), Com. State Dept. Edn. on Biol. Sci., Phi Beta Kappa, Sigma Xi, Am. Legion. Democrat. Mem. Disciples Ch. Mason. Co-author (with P. D. Strausbaugh), General Biology, 1938; A Manual for the Biology Laboratory, 1938. Contbr. to sci. and gen. mags. and journs. Home: Bethany, W.Va.

WEIMER, William G(ottlieb), meat packing; b. Wheeling, W.Va., Feb. 13, 1875; s. Fredrick H. and Marie (Schmidt) W.; student pub. schs. and pvt. sch., Wheeling, W.Va.; grad. Frazier Business Coll., Wheeling. m. Rose Biery, Jan. 11, 1899; children—Wilma (Mrs. Russell J. Foose), Helen (widow of Lewis C. Schaaf, dec.), Fredrick G. In employ Fredrick H. Weimer, meat packing, Wheeling, W.Va., 1893-1913; asso. with Weimer Packing Co., meat packers, Wheeling, W.Va. since 1913, pres. since 1913; dir. Fulton Bank & Trust Co., Wheeling. Trustee St. James Lutheran Church. Republican. Home: 42 Heiskell Av. Office: 1039 Main St., Wheeling, W.Va.

WEINBERG, Edwin David, physician; b. Lonaconing, Md., July 25, 1895; s. Joseph and Rosa (Fine) W.; grad. Central High Sch., Lonaconing, Md., 1913; A.B., Dickinson Coll., Carlisle, Pa., 1917, hon. M.A., 1926; M.D.,

Johns Hopkins U. Sch. of Medicine, Baltimore, Md., 1922; m. Edith May Rothschild, Sept. 2, 1926; children—Marjorie Rothschild, Alice Ann. Instr. in orthopaedic surgery, Johns Hopkins U., Baltimore, Md., 1930—; asst. visiting orthopaedic surgeon, Johns Hopkins Hosp., Baltimore, Md., 1930; attending orthopaedic surgeon, S. Baltimore Gen. Hosp., Baltimore; consultant, orthopaedic surgeon, U.S. Marine Hosp., Baltimore, Md.; asso. attending orthopaedic surgeon, Sinai Hosp., Baltimore; mem. staff, Woman's Hosp., Baltimore; attending orthopaedic surgeon, Hebrew Home for the Aged, Baltimore. Fellow Am. Acad. of Orthopaedic Surgeons, A.M.A.; mem. Editors' and Authors' Assn., Med. Research Club, Southern Med. Soc., Baltimore City Med. Soc., Med. and Chirurg. Faculty of Med., Johns Hopkins Surgical Soc., Phi Delta Theta. Democrat. Jewish religion. Club: Suburban Country (Baltimore County). Author of numerous papers on orthopaedic surgery. Home: "Wincrest," Pikesville, Md. Office: 1208 Eutaw Pl., Baltimore, Md.

WEINBERG, J(ames) Arthur, asst. in surgery, Johns Hopkins U.; asst. visiting surgeon John Hopkins Hosp.; mem. visiting staff Union Memorial, Sinai and West Baltimore Gen. hosps. and Hosp. for Women; surg. consultant Provident Hosp. Address: 1208 Eutaw Pl., Baltimore, Md.

WEINBERG, Max H., M.D., neurologist; b. Bessarabia, Russia, Mar. 16, 1883; s. Samuel and Rachel (Bernstein) W.; M.D., U. of Pittsburgh, 1912; m. Bessie Evelyn Sakon, Nov. 6, 1913. Came to U.S., 1901; naturalized citizen, 1909. Asst. pathologist Montefiore Hosp., Pittsburgh, 1913-15, chief pathologist, 1920-31; asst. bacteriologist and serologist Western Pa. Hosp., Pittsburgh, 1915-17, asst. in neurology, 1919-30, asso. neurologist since 1930; cons. neurologist U.S. Vets. Bur., Pittsburgh Dist. 1920-24; chief neurologist Ohio Valley Hosp. since 1923; cons. psychiat. U.S. Dist. Ct. since 1937; cons. neuropsychiatrist Pittsburgh Jewish Home of the Aged since 1920. Served as lt., Neuropsychiat. Corps, U.S. Army, 1918. Field sec. Peoples Jewish Relief, 1915-18; mem. med. council Montefiore Hosp., 1924-30; mem. Workmen's Circle, Pittsburgh. Ex-pres. Pittsburgh Med. Forum, Pittsburgh Neuro-psychiatric Soc. Club: Concordia (Pittsburgh). Published numerous short stories in Yiddish, 1905-13, humorous articles in Yiddish, 1913-17; also wrote many scientific articles on neuro-psychiatry since 1919. Translated: The Iron Hill (by Jack London) into Yiddish, 1913. Home: 5717 Pocusset St. Office: 6094 Jenkins Arcade, Pittsburgh, Pa.

WEINBERGER, Nelson S., M.D.; b. Quakertown, Pa., June 27, 1882; s. John G. and Sarah Ann (Shelly) W.; grad. West Chester State Teachers Coll., 1900, Perkiomen Sch., 1901; M.D., U. of Pa., 1905; m. Martine Rittenhouse Hartman, 1911; 1 son, John Joseph. House surgeon Wills Hosp., Philadelphia, 1909-10; chief of eye, ear, nose and throat Guthrie Clinic and Robert Packer Hospital since 1912; dir. Merchant's & Mechanics Bank of Sayre. Fellow Am. Coll. Surgeons; mem. A.M.A., Am. Acad. Ophthalmology and Otology; Am. Laryngol., Rhinol. and Otol. Soc., N.Y. and New England Ry. Surgeons. Mason. Club: Shepard Hills Country. Author: Secondary Glaucoma, 1932; Common Ground of the Physician and Dentist, 1933; Associated Problems of Internal Medicine, the Eye and the Ear, 1934; Oral Manifestations of Systemic Diseases, 1935; Chronic Recurrent Iritis, 1935; Primary Glaucoma, 1936; Common Colds in Children, 1937; Interstitial Keratitis, 1937; etc. Home: 209 S. Elmer Av. Address: Robert Packer Hosp., and Guthrie Clinic, Sayre, Pa.

WEINGAERTNER, Hans, artist; b. Kraiburg, Bavaria, Germany, Sept. 11, 1896; s. Johann and Anna (Boschner) W.; came to U.S., 1922; ed. Royal Acad., Munich, 1915-22, Royal Inst. Anatomy, 1915-17; m. Elsie F. Mitchel, June 28, 1930. Has followed profession as artist since 1919; exhibited in Brooklyn Museum, Art Institute of Chicago, Biennial Exhbn., Corcoran Gallery, Washington, D.C., State Museum, Trenton, N.J., Soc. of Ind. Artists (annually); represented in Newark Museum, Co-operative Gallery,

WEIRICK

Newark, N.J.; awards Am. Artists Professional League, honorable mention, State Exhbn., Montclair Museum, 1938. Mem. Modern Artists of N.J., New Haven Paint & Clay Club, Soc. of Independent Artists. Catholic. Home: 312 Lake Av., Lyndhurst, N.J.

WEINGARTNER, George T(orrence), lawyer; b. Lawrence Co., Pa., Aug. 24, 1875; s. George A. and Martha (Warnock) W.; student Rose Point (Pa.) Acad.; m. Anna Hazen, May 30, 1901; children—Martha (Mrs. Meryl B. Klinesmith), Elizabeth (Mrs. Bart Richards, Robert Aiken, Helen (Mrs. Robert E. Hoose). Admitted to Pa. bar, 1899 and since engaged in gen. practice of law at New Castle; mem. firm Weingartner and Mercer since 1914; served as mem. Pa. Ho. of Rep., 1904-08, mem. Pa. Senate, 1908-12 and 1924-32; county commr. Lawrence Co., 1920-25; dir. Lawrence Savings & Trust Co., Blair Strip Steel Co., New Castle Hotel Corpn. Served as chmn. Victory Liberty Loan Com. Mem. Lawrence Co. (Pa.) Bar Assn. Republican. Methodist. Home: Butler Road. Office: Lawrence Savings & Trust Co. Bldg., New Castle, Pa.

WEIR, Ernest Tener, mfr.; b. Pittsburgh, Pa., Aug. 1, 1875; s. James and Margaret (Manson) W.; educated public schools, Pittsburgh; m. Mary Kline, 1901; children—Mrs. Coleman C. Carter, Henry K. and Ernest T. (twins), m. 2d, Mrs. Aeola Dickson Siebert, 1926. Began in employ of Braddock Wire Co., 1891; became connected with Oliver Wire Co., 1922; apptd. chief clk. Monongahela Tin Plate Mills, 1901, later supt., also mgr. Monessen Mills, 1903, both belonging to the Am. Tin Plate Co.; associated with J. R. Phillips, 1905, in organizing the Phillips Sheet & Tin Plate Co. (Clarksburg, W.Va.), of which became pres., 1908, title changed, 1916, to the Weirton Steel Co., which became a subsidiary in 1929 of the Nat. Steel Corpn. of which he was founder and is now chmn. of bd. and chief executive; also chmn. bd. and dir. Weirton Steel Co., Great Lakes Steel Corpn., Hanna Iron Ore Co., Hanna Furnace Corpn., Midwest Steel Corpn., Weirton Coal Co., Bank of Weirton and numerous other corpns. Pres. Am. Iron and Steel Inst.; mem. advisory bd. Transportation Assn. America; dir. Pittsburgh Regional Planning Assn., mem. Pittsburgh Symphony Soc., Carnegie Inst., Engineers Soc. of Western Pa., Pittsburgh Chamber of Commerce, Fathers and Sons Golf Assn. of Western Pa.; mem. bd. dir. and exec. com. U. of Pittsburgh, Allegheny Gen. Hosp., Maurice and Laura Falk Foundation. Trustee East End Christian Ch. (Pittsburgh). Clubs: Bankers, Duquesne, Pittsburgh Field, Civic Club of Allegheny County, Pittsburgh Athletic Assn., Fox Chapel (Pittsburgh); Long Vue Club of Verona, Pa. (gov.); Williams Country (Weirton-Hollidays Cove, W.Va.); Woodmont Rod and Gun (Md.); Detroit Club (Detroit); Queen City (Cincinnati); Union League, Links, Cloud (New York); Congressional Country (Washington, D. C.); Mid Ocean, Anglers (Bermuda). Home: Schenley Apts. Office: Grant Bldg., Pittsburgh, Pa.

WEIR, Henry Kline, steel exec.; b. Pittsburgh, Pa., June 1, 1905; s. Ernest Tener and Mary (Kline) W.; student Phillips Exeter Acad., Exeter, N.H., Yale, Harvard Sch. Business Adminstrn.; m. Helen Denney Harmonson, June 21, 1935; 1 dau., Dorothy Denney. Served as asst. sec. and asst. treas. National Steel Corpn., Pittsburgh, since 1934; pres. Peoples Bank of Hollidays Cove, W.Va., since 1936; dir. Fidelity Trust Co., Pittsburgh, Pa., Union Fidelity Title Ins. Co., Bank of Weirton, W.Va. Mem. Alpha Delta Phi. Republican. Christian Scientist. Clubs: Duquesne, Fox Chapel Golf, Harvard-Yale-Princeton (Pittsburgh); Yale (New York City). Home: 5340 Maynard Street. Office: 2800 Grant Bldg., Pittsburgh, Pa.

WEIRICK, Joseph Charles, sch. supt.; b. Howard, Pa., Aug. 16, 1881; s. Zachary Taylor and Jennie (Neff) W.; grad. Bucknell U., 1917; grad. study, U. of Pa., 1920 and 1937, Columbia U., 1919; m. Marie Holmes, Oct. 23, 1907. Teacher and prin. schs. and high schs., Howard and Lock Haven, Pa., 1900-15; supt. schs.,

Ashland, Pa., 1916-18; prin. Sr. High Sch., Abington, Pa., 1918-34; supt. schs., Abington Twp., Montgomery Co., Pa., since 1934. Mem. advisory com. Crestmont Nursery Sch., Abington Y.M.C.A. Mem. Nat. Edn. Assn., Pa. State Edn. Assn., Am. Assn. Sch. Adminstrs., Am. Mus. Natural History, Am. Forestry Assn., Old York Rd. Hist. Soc., Old York Rd. Schoolmen's Club, Pa. State Fish & Game Protective Assn. Republican. Presbyn. (mem. session). Odd Fellow. Club: Keystone Automobile. Home: 408 York Rd. Office: Susquehanna Road, Abington, Pa.

WEISER, George Upp, iron mfr.; b. York, Pa., Oct. 28, 1861; s. John Augustus and May Jane (Upp) W.; student York Collegiate Inst., 1878-82; m. Sarah Catherine Eyster, York, Pa., Apr. 18, 1901; children—Charles Spangler, Sarah C. Eyster (Mrs. Henry B. Martin). Asso. with Eyster Weiser Co., mfrs. iron castings, York, Pa., since 1899, treas. since 1899; dir. York County Nat. Bank, York Water Co. Democrat. Presbyterian. Clubs: Lafayette, York Country; Manufacturers and Bankers (Phila.). Home: 105 W. Spingittsburg Av., York, Pa.

WEISGERBER, William Edwin, coll. prof.; b. Luthersburg, Pa., Nov. 10, 1881; s. Henry and Theresa (Schindele) W.; student State Teachers Coll., Lock Haven, Pa., 1902-05; B.S., Franklin & Marshall Coll., 1912, M.S., 1913; grad. study, Columbia U., summer 1914; M.S., U. of Pa., 1928; m. Margaret Kryder, June 10, 1914; children—Wilhemena Eloise (dec.), Wilma Elaine. Began as teacher pub. schs., Pa., 1901; successively asst., instr. and asst. prof. chemistry, Franklin & Marshall Coll., 1912-29, prof. chemistry since 1929, sec. of faculty since 1927. Treas and sec. Theta Chapter, Phi Beta Kappa since 1918. Mem. Am. Chem. Soc., Phi Beta Kappa, Phi Kappa Tau. Mem. Reformed Ch. Odd Fellow, Knight of Malta. Home: 830 Buchanan Av., Lancaster, Pa.

WEISS, David Harold, lawyer, state representative; b. Czechoslovakia, Aug. 3, 1905; s. Elias and Yetty (Stern) W.; student Monessen High Sch.; A.B., U. of Mich.; LL.B., U. of Pittsburgh; unmarried. Admitted to practice before Pa. cts., 1933; elected to House of Rep., Commonwealth of Pa., 1937, renominated on Dem. ticket, 1938. Elected sch. dir., City of Monessen, 6-yr. term, 1935, pres. of bd. since 1937. Mem. Westmoreland County Bar, Labor's Non-Partisan League, Tau Epsilon Rho, Pa. State Grange. K.P., B'nai B'rith. Club: Kiwanis (dir. 1936). Home: 1001 Athalia Av., Monessen, Pa. Offices: Bank and Trust Bldg., Greensburg, Pa.; and 423 Donner Av., Monessen, Pa.

WEISS, Ferenz, rabbi; b. Samson, Hungary, Feb. 26, 1884; s. Joseph and Rose (Weiss) W.; came to U.S., 1928, naturalized, 1933; student Pressburg (Tolcava, Gyor) Rabbinical Seminary, 1900-05, ordained rabbi, 1905; student University of Steiermark, Graz, Austria, 1901; married Rebecca Schwartz, February 24, 1906; children—Andrew, Elaine (wife of Dr. Joseph Lang), David, Ann, Joseph (dec.), Anton, Paul, Agnes. Began as rabbi, Wertesi, Hungary, 1906; rabbi Congregation Beth Mordecai, Perth Amboy, N.J., 1928-29, Congregation Beth Jacob, Perth Amboy, N.J., 1929-34, Congregation Ohav Sholom, Astoria, N.Y., 1934-35, Congregation Beth Jacob, Perth Amboy, N.J., since 1935. Field rabbi, Königgraetz, Böhmen, during World War. Mem. Rabbinical Assn. of U.S. and Can. (dir.), Col. Mihály De Kovatch Assn. (pres.), Rabbinical Assn. of N.J. (v.p.), Ahavath Achim Assn. (mem. bd. of dirs.). Author: "Song of Songs" and many Biblical and historical works. Hungarian orator; speaker at Roman Catholic and Reformed Churches. Home: 180 Brighton Av. Office: 396 Division St., Perth Amboy, N.J.

WEISS, Harry Bischoff, entomologist; b. Phila., Pa., Oct. 31, 1883; s. Harry Bender and Catharine Margaret (Bischoff) W.; student North East Manual Training Sch., Phila., 1898-1902, U. of Pa., 1902-06; m. Florence Haines Brown, Nov. 10, 1906; children—Viola Murdock (Mrs. Kenneth Q. Jennings), Harry Shelton. Began as entomology and chemist, Phila., 1906; asst. to state entomologist of N.J., Trenton, N.J., 1911-16; chief inspector N.J. Dept. of Agr., Trenton, N.J., 1916-20, chief Bur. of Plant Industry since 1920; lecturer in entomology, N.J. Agr. Coll., New Brunswick, N.J., 1911-16. Mem. Am. Assnciation Economic Entomologists (sec.-treas. Eastern branch since 1929), Am. Cranberry Growers' Assn. (statistician since 1923), N.Y. Entomol. Soc. (pres., 1923-25), Hist. of Science Soc., N.J. Migratory Child Commn. (sec., 1930-32), Bibliographical Soc. of America, Am. Statistical Assn., Washington Biological Soc.; fellow A.A. A.S., Entomol. Soc. of America, N.Y. Acad. of Sciences. Author: Thomas Say, Early American Naturalist, 1931; The Pioneer Century of American Entomology, 1936; Rafinesque's Kentucky Friends, 1936; numerous tech. papers. Editor Jour. N.Y. Entomol. Soc. since 1924, Am. Book Collector, 1932-34; asso. editor Jour. of Economic Entomology since 1937. Home: 19 N. 7th Av., Highland Park, N.J. Office: N.J. Dept. of Agr., Trenton, N.J.

WEISS, Louis, physician; b. Austria-Hungary, Jan. 6, 1877; s. Bernard and Miriam Rebecca (Kleinmann) W.; grad. Newark (N.J.) High Sch., 1896; M.D., Coll. of Physicians and Surgeons, Columbia, 1900; m. Henrietta Epstein, 1906; children—Harry Benjamin, Milton Willard, Beulah Miriam (Mrs. Jack Norman Masin). Began practice as physician, Newark, N.J., 1900; attended med. and surgical clinics, City Dispensary, Newark, N.J., 1900-06, dist. physician, 1906-12; specializes in diseases of eye, ear, nose and throat since 1914; school physician, eye clinics, 1914-19. One of the founders of Newark Maternity Hosp., 1910, also founder Beth Israel Clinic, both of which later joined Beth Israel Hosp.; now propr. of own hosp. Pres. Emanuel Community Center of Newark; mem. Essex County Med. Soc., N.J. State Med. Soc., A.M.A., B'nai B'rith, Ind. Order B'rith Abraham, Hungarian Jewish Benevolent Soc., Newark. Address: 519 Springfield Av., Newark, N.J.

WEISS, Paul, asso. prof. philosophy; b. New York, N.Y., May 19, 1901; s. Samuel and Emma (Rothschild) W.; B.S.S., Coll. City of N.Y., 1927; A.M., Harvard, 1928, Ph.D., 1929; m. Victoria Brodkin, Oct. 27, 1928; children—Judith Evelyn, Jonathan. Instr. and tutor in philosophy, Harvard and Radcliffe, 1930-31; asso. in philosophy, Bryn Mawr (Pa.) Coll., 1931-33, asso. prof. since 1933; mem. exec. bd. Journal of Symbolic Logic, 1934-35; mem. advisory bd. Philosophy of Science. Mem. Am. Philos. Assn. (mem. exec. com., 1937-40), Phi Beta Kappa. Jewish religion. An editor of the Collected Papers of C. S. Peirce, 6 vols., 1931-35; author Reality, 1938. Contbr. Am. Philosophy Today and Tomorrow; Philosophical Essays for A. W. Whitehead; also articles on logic, metaphysics and ethics in tech. jours. Contributing editor, Philosophical Abstracts. Home: Cartref, Bryn Mawr, Pa.

WEISS, William Erhard, chmn. of bd. Sterling Products, Inc.; b. Canton, O., Dec. 18, 1879; s. Erhard and Wilhelmina (Heil) W.; Ph.G., Phila. Coll. of Pharmacy and Science, 1896; Dr. of Philosophiae, honoris causa, U. of Cologne, Germany, 1928; m. Helena Schwertfeger, Oct. 16, 1901; children—Madelyn Elizabeth (Mrs. Henry Lane Kinnucan), William Erhard. Began as chemist and pharmacist, 1896; chmn. bd., gen. mgr. and dir. Sterling Products, also officer and dir. many subsid. cos.; pres. and dir. Bayer-Semesan Co.; dir. Am. I.G. Chem. Corpn. Trustee Linsley Inst., Wheeling, W.Va. Democrat. Episcopalian. Mason (32°, K.T., Shriner), Elk. Clubs: Union League, The Terrace (New York); Detroit Club; Fort Henry, Wheeling Country, Cedar Rocks Golf (Wheeling, W.Va.); Boca Raton (Fla.) Club; Everglades, Seminole Golf (Palm Beach, Fla.); Columbus Beach, Burt Lake Golf (Indian River, Mich.); Club de Peche Petit-Pabos, Inc., Quebec, Can. Home: Elmwood, Wheeling, W.Va. Office: 92-104 19th St., Wheeling, W.Va.; and 170 Varick St., New York, N.Y.

WEISSER, Edward A., ophthalmologist; b. Pittsburgh, Pa., Jan. 18, 1876; s. Joachim and Catherine (Wilhelm) W.; A.M., Mt. St. Mary's Coll.; M.D., U. of Pa.; m. Elizabeth Neary, Oct. 10, 1907; children—Edward A., C. William, Daniel Neary. Interne Germantown Hosp., Philadelphia; ophthalmologist St. Francis Hosp. since 1903, Rosalia Hosp. since 1904. Dir. Duquesne U. Fellow Am. Coll. Surgeons; mem. A.M.A., Am. Acad. Ophthalmology and Otolaryngology, Pa. Med. Soc., Pittsburgh Acad. Medicine, Allegheny Co. Med. Soc., Pittsburgh Ophthalmology Soc. Clubs: Civic, Pittsburgh Athletic Assn., Wildwood Country. Home: 431 Graham St. Office: 806 May Bldg., Pittsburgh, Pa.

WEITH, Archie James, chem. research dir.; b. La Harpe, Kan., Oct. 18, 1886; s. Stephen Henry and Ellen Jane (Shanklin) W.; grad. Iola (Kan.) High Sch., 1904; B.S., U. of Kan., Lawrence, Kan., 1908, M.S., 1910; m. Mabel Grace Ulrich, June 30, 1913; children—Archie James, Marjorie Jane, Kenneth Duncan, Evelyn Frances. Chief chemist Kan. State Water Supply, Lawrence, Kan., 1905-08; industrial fellow, U. of Kan., 1908-14; sec. Redmanol Chem. Products Co., Chicago, 1914-22; asso. dir. research and development, Bakelite Corpn., Bloomfield, N.J., 1922-35, acting dir., 1935-38, dir. since 1938; dir. Bakelite Dental Products Co., Bakelite Bldg. Products Co. Mem. Nat. Research Council (chmn. plastics com.), Am. Chem. Soc. (councilor), Am. Electrochem. Soc., Am. Phys. Soc., Soc. Chem. Industry, Inst. of Chemists, Boy Scouts of America, Alpha Chi Sigma, Acacia, Sigma Xi. Republican. Presbyterian. Club: Chemists (New York). Co-author: Polymarization, 1937. Contbr. numerous articles on plastics, phenol condensation, etc. to tech. mags. Home: 55 Grover Lane, Caldwell, N.J. Office: 230 Grove St., Bloomfield, N.J.

WEITZENKORN, Louis, playwright; b. Wilkes-Barre, Pa., May 28, 1893; s. Joseph K. and Jennie (Livingston) W.; student Pa. Military Coll., Chester, Pa., 1907-08; Columbia Univ., 1912; m. Ilse Lahn Lichtblau, 1932. Reporter, New York Tribune, 1914, New York Times, 1915; conductor of "The Guillotine," a column of verse in New York Call, 1916, 17; Sunday feature editor, The World, 1924-29; editor in chief New York Evening Graphic. With 302d batt. Tank Corps. U.S.A., France, 1918. Author: (plays) First Mortgage, prod. in Royale Theatre, New York, 1929; Five Star Final, prod. in Cort Theatre, New York, 1931; Two Bones and a Dog, 1934; And the Sun Goes Down, 1935; Name Your Poison (with Herbert C. Lewis), 1935; The Burglar Strike, 1937; also various motion pictures. Home: Neshamic, N.J.*

WELCH, Roy Dickinson, prof. music; b. Dansville, N.Y., Jan. 19, 1885; s. Enam Dickinson and Alice (Conable) W.; diploma U. of Mich. Sch. of Music, 1907; A.B., U. of Mich. Coll. of Literature, Science and Arts, 1909, hon. Mus.M., 1927; studied U. of Munich, 1930-31, U. of Vienna, 1931-32; m. Mildred Scott, Aug. 11, 1911 (died July 23, 1917); m. 2d, Sylvia Eastman Spencer, June 16, 1920; children—Anne Spencer, Catherine Conable, Spencer, Roy Dickinson. Instr. in piano, U. of Mich. Sch. of Music, 1907-10; instr. history and music and composition, same, 1912-14; asst. prof. music, Smith Coll., Northampton, Mass., 1914-18, asso. prof., 1918-21, prof., 1921-35, also chmn. dept. of music, 1923-30 and 1933-34; visiting prof. music, Harvard, summers 1923-34; visiting prof. music, Princeton U., 1934-35, prof. since Sept. 1935. Served as capt. Am. Red Cross in France, 1918-19. Mem. Music Teachers Nat. Assn., Am. Musicol. Soc., Am. Assn. Univ. Profs., Phi Beta Kappa, Trigon (U. of Mich.). Author: The Study of Music in the American College, 1925; The Appreciation of Music, 1927; also articles in mags. Home-Studio: Olden Manor, Olden Lane, Princeton, N.J.

WELD, Theodore Vance, v.p. Piper Aircraft Corpn.; b. Asheville, N.Y., Sept. 10, 1903; s. Clyde A. and Eleanor (Vance) W.; ed. Bliss Elec. and Engring. Sch., Washington, D.C.; m. H. Ena Johnson, Aug. 22, 1929. Salesman W. L. Nuttal & Son, Sherman, N.Y., Ford dealers, 1923, Third & Lafayette St. Garage, Jamestown,

WELDAY

N.Y., Hudson and Essex dealers, 1925-28; sales mgr. Turner Radio Shops, Jamestown, N.Y., Warren and Bradford, Pa., 1928-32; sales mgr. Taylor Aircraft Co., 1933-35, pres., 1935-37; v.p. Piper Aircraft Corpn. since 1937. Dir. Lock Haven Chamber of Commerce; mem. bd. govs. U.S. Aeronautical Chamber of Commerce. Methodist. Club: Rotary. Home: 215 N. Fifth St. Office: Bald Eagle St., Lock Haven, Pa.

WELDAY, Henry Alexander, clergyman; b. on farm nr. Bloomingdale, O., July 18, 1881; s. Samuel Smith and Mary (Deter) W.; desc. John Rickey of Pa., capt. in Colonial Army; A.B., O. Wesleyan U., 1909; student, Boston U. Sch. of Theology, 1912-15, S.T.B., 1915; D.D., O. Wesleyan U., 1937; m. Mary Parkin, June 15, 1916; children—Priscilla Grace, Robert James, Chester Oliver. Began as teacher pub. schs., 1901; ordained Methodist ministry, 1915, after serving on trial, Lowellville, O., 1910-12; pastor, Newell, W.Va., 1915-17, Ingomar, Pa., 1917-24, First Ch., New Brighton, Pa., 1924-28, Sewickley, Pa., 1928-33, North Av. Ch., Pittsburgh, Pa., since 1933. Pres. North Side Ministerial Assn. Mem. Community Club, New Brighton, Pa. Mem. Delta Sigma Rho. Democrat. Methodist. Mason (32°). Home: 112 W. North Av., Pittsburgh, Pa.

WELDIN, William Archie, professional engr.; b. Connellsville, Pa., Jan. 16, 1881; s. Lewis Cass and Mary Eva (Johnson) W.; C.E., U. of Pittsburgh, 1902; m. Nina Adams Eaton, Nov. 8, 1906. Employed as engr. in various capacities and for a number of different concerns, 1899-1910; with Pittsburgh-Buffalo Coal Co., 1910-14; proposal engr. Pittsburgh Coal Washer Co., 1914-16; mem. firm Blum, Weldin & Co., practicing engrs., Pittsburgh, since 1916. Mem. Am. Soc. C.E., Am. Inst. Mining and Metall. Engrs., Am. Mining Congress, Engrs. Soc. of Western Pa. (past dir.). Republican. Methodist (trustee Christ Ch.). Club: Rotary (Pittsburgh; past pres. and dir.). Home: 1938 Beechwood Boul. Office: 417 Grant St., Pittsburgh, Pa.

WELKER, George Ernest, natural gas engr.; b. Oil City, Pa., Oct. 24, 1888; s. George A. and Jennie R. (Ellsworth) W.; prep. edn., Mich. Mil. Acad., Orchard Lake; B.S. in C.E., Clarkson Coll. Tech., Potsdam, N.Y., 1909; B.S. in Mining Engring., Mich. Coll. Mines, 1910, E.M., 1910; m. Josephine Wilson Powell, July 14, 1917; children—George Wilson (dec.), Mary Joan. Civil engr. and geologist, United Fuel Gas Co., Charleston, W.Va., 1910-12; chief engr. and geologist, Iroquois Natural Gas Corpn., Buffalo, N.Y., 1912-17; with United Natural Gas Co., Oil City, since 1918, chief civ. engr. and geologist, 1918-24; also cons. engr. for affiliated cos. since 1918; vice pres. and cons. engr., United Natural Gas Co., Mars Co., 1924-27, pres. both cos. since 1927; pres. Ridgway Natural Gas Co., St. Mary's Natural Gas Co., The Sylvania Corpn., Smethport Natural Gas Co., Mercer County Gas Co. Mem. Nat. Gas Advisory Bd. Pa. State Coll.; dir. Oil City Y.M.C.A. Mem. advisory com. (past chmn.) natural gas dept., Am. Gas Assn. (past v.p.); mem. Pa. Natural Gas Men's Assn. (dir., ex-pres.), Oil City Chamber Commerce (dir.), Theta Tau, Omicron Pi Omicron. Republican. Presbyn. Clubs: Rotary (pres.), Wanango Country. He has acted as cons. engr. in many rate case proceedings before courts and pub. service commns. in U.S. and Can. Home: 420 W. 3d St. Office: 308 Seneca St., Oil City, Pa.

WELKER, John Stanley, banking; b. Wheatland, Pa., Sept. 25, 1891; s. George Carlon and Sydney (Hall) W.; student Wheatland and Sharon pub. schs.; m. Florence Reed, Oct. 22, 1912; 1 son, John Stanley. Began as deputy clk. of cts. of Mercer Co., 1909; deputy collector Internal Revenue, later asst. cashier First Nat. Bank, Farrell, Pa.; sec. and trust officer Farmers & Merchants Trust Co., Greenville, Pa., since 1922; dir. Board of Trade Bldg. & Loan Assn. Served as roll call chmn. Am. Red Cross, 1937, chmn. Mercer Co. Chapter, 1938; mem. advisory bd. Salvation Army. Democrat. Presbyn. Mason. Club: Greenville Country, Greenville Rotary (pres. 1934-35). Home: 396 S. Main St. Office: 201 Main St., Greenville, Pa.

941

WELLER, Curtis D., civil engr.; b. New London, Ia., Oct. 27, 1889; s. William Lee and Martha Melvina (Roberts) W.; grad. New London (Ia.) High Sch., 1907; B.S. in civil engring., Iowa State Coll., 1913; m. Anna Mary Hedges, Oct. 11, 1916; children—Sybil Louise, William Lee. Asst. engr. Compania Mexicana de Petroleo "El Aquila," Tampico, Mexico, 1913-14; asst. county engr. Guthrie County, Ia., 1914-16, county engr., 1916-20; resident engr. Ia. Highway Commn., 1920-21, asst. dist. engr., 1921-25; engr. with A.A. Davis Co., contractor, Kansas City, Mo., 1925; resident engr. with Harrington, Howard & Ash, consulting engrs., Kansas City, Mo., 1926-30; resident engr. with Ash, Howard, Needles & Tammen, consulting engrs., Kansas City, Mo., 1930-31; resident bridge engr. N.J. State Highway Dept., Trenton, since 1931. Mem. Am. Soc. Civil Engrs. Republican. Methodist. Mason. Home: 114 Poplar Av., Merchantville, N.J. Office: State House Annex, Trenton, N.J.

WELLER, Ovington E., ex-senator; b. Reisterstown, Md., Jan. 23, 1862; grad. U.S. Naval Acad., 1881; LL.B., Nat. U., Washington, D.C., 1887, LL.M., 1888; married. Resigned from Navy, 1883; with Post Office Dept., Washington, 1883-87. Active in politics since 1903; chmn. State Roads Commn. of Md., 1912-15 (expending $16,000,000 on pub. roads); Rep. candidate for gov. of Md., 1915; del. at large and chmn. Md. delegations, Rep. Nat. Conv. 1916-24, 36; elected treas. Nat. Senatorial Com., 1918; mem. U.S. Senate, 1921-27; chmn. Md. Pub. Service Commn. since 1935; mem. Rep. Nat. Com. from Md. Address: Tuscany Apt., Baltimore, Md.

WELLES, Henry Hunter, Jr.; b. Forty Fort, Luzerne Co., Pa., Jan. 21, 1861; s. Henry Hunter (D.D.) and Ellen Susanna (Ladd) W.; A.B., Princeton, 1882, A.M., 1885; Columbia Coll. Law Sch., 1884-85; m. Caroline S. McMurtry, Oct. 4, 1892; children—Katharine Ryerson, Charlotte Rose, Henry H., III. Admitted to Pa. bar, 1885, and practiced about 1 yr.; mgr. family estate, 1886-1908, developing suburban real estate, 1886-1917; field rep. Board of Nat. Missions of Presbyn. Ch. in U.S.A., 1920-26; mem. staff Presbyn. Pension Fund Campaign, 1927. Republican. Elder First Presbyterian Ch., New York. Clubs: Westmoreland (Wilkes-Barre, Pa.); Princeton (New York). Home: 2 E. 86th St., New York, N.Y., and (summer) Glen Summit Springs, Mountain Top P.O., Pa.

WELLINGTON, John Louis, artist, banking; b. Cumberland, Md., May 20, 1878; s. George Louis and Caroline (Lear) W.; grad. Allegany County Acad., Cumberland, 1897; B.S., Princeton U., 1901; m. Helen Gordon Wiley, Apr. 15, 1903; children—George Louis, Helen Huldah (Mrs. William Gaylord Swan), Louise Comley. Began as teller Citizens' Nat. Bank, 1901; later with Citizens' Savings Bank and Liberty Trust Co.; now asst. cashier and dir. Commercial Savings Bank, Cumberland. Artist in oils and water color. Exhibited: Washington, D.C., Water Color Club, annual exhbn., 1936-39; Md. Inst. Alumni, 1937; Am. Water Color Soc., New York, 1938; Allied Artists of America, New York, 1938; Pa. Acad. of Fine Arts, Phila., annual exhbn. water colors and miniatures, 1938. Republican. Mason, Elk. Club: Cumberland Country. Home. 303 Washington St. Office: Commercial Savings Bank, Cumberland, Md.

WELLIVER, Judson Churchill, corpn. executive; b. Aledo, Ill., Aug. 13, 1870; s. Morrison and Alpha (Harroun) W.; ed. pub. schs., Fort Dodge, Ia., Cornell Coll., Ia.; m. Jane Douglas Hutchins, July 3, 1899; children—Edward M., Allan J., Sarah H., Jane Douglas. Newspaper work, Sioux City Journal, Sioux City Tribune, Des Moines Leader; later polit. editor and editorial writer Washington Times, and Frank A. Munsey newspapers; sent to Europe by President Roosevelt, 1907, to report upon waterway systems of Europe and Great Britain, the companies' laws of Great Britain, and railroad situation in Europe, report pub. in Report Inland Waterways Commn., 1908; London corr. and

WELLS

European mgr. New York Sun, 1917-18; in charge publicity at Harding hdqrs., Marion O., during 1920 campaign, and attached to the White House organization after Mar. 4, 1921, occupying a confidential relation to Presidents Harding and Coolidge until Nov. 1, 1925, resigned; dir. public relations with Am. Petroleum Inst., 1925-27; editor The Herald, Washington, D.C., 1928; asst. to pres. of Pullman Co., 1928-31; dir. public relations Sun Oil Co., Phila. Clubs: Players (New York); Nat. Press (Washington); Pen and Pencil, Penn Athletic (Phila.). Contbr. to mags. Address: The Cambridge, Alden Park Manor, Philadelphia, Pa.*

WELLMAN, C. E.; editor Huntington Advertiser. Office: care Huntington Pub. Co., Huntington, W.Va.

WELLONS, Charles McCartney, engr.; b. Barnesville, O., June 27, 1893; s. James William and Eleanor (McCartney) W.; student pub. schs., Barnesville and Columbus, O., 1899-1907, East High Sch., Columbus, O., 1907-11; B.M.E., Ohio State U., Columbus, 1915; m. Ina Frances Waddell, June 27, 1918; children —Frank Waddell, Charles McCartney. Material man, transmission line constrn., Am. Gas & Electric Co., Wheeling, W.Va., 1915-17; inspector and draftsman U.S. Engrs. Office, Wheeling, 1917-19; supt. U.S. Engrs. Office, Pittsburgh, Pa., 1919-23, asst. engr., 1923-26, engr., 1926-31, sr. engr., 1931-32, prin. engr. since 1932. Mem. Sigma Phi Epsilon. Presbyn. Club: Highland Country (Bellevue, Pa.). Home: 19 Grant Av., Bellevue, Pa. Office: Federal Bldg., Pittsburgh, Pa.

WELLS, Edwin Webster; mem. law firm Wells & McCormick. Office: Fidelity Bldg., Baltimore, Md.

WELLS, George Harlan, M.D.; b. Elkton, Md., May 28, 1880; s. Joseph Lumm and Florence (Harlan) W.; grad. Elkton Acad., 1895; B.S., U. of Del., 1899; M.D., Hahnemann Med. Coll. of Phila., 1902; hon. Dr. Med. Science, Univ. of Delaware, 1934; m. Martha Parr Scott, Apr. 11, 1907 (died July 19, 1922); m. 2d, Emma E. Mertz, Feb. 12, 1925; children—William Henry Scott, Florence Harlan, Virginia. Began practice at Phila., 1902; instr. in medicine, Hahnemann Med. Coll. of Phila., 1902-16, asso. professor of medicine, 1916-25, professor of clinical medicine, 1925-31, professor of medicine since 1931; editor Hahnemann Monthly, 1913-18; physician in chief, Hahnemann Hospital since 1925. Contract surgeon, U.S.A., 1918. Fellow Am. Coll. Physicians; mem. Am. Inst. Homeopathy (expres.), Homœ. Med. Soc. Pa. (pres.), Homœ. Med. Soc. of Phila. (trustee), Pa. Hist. Soc. Republican. Presbyn. Clubs: Union League, Huntingdon Valley Country. Contbr. to Hahnemannian Monthly, Jour. Am. Inst. of Homeopathy. Home: 1627 Spruce St., Philadelphia, Pa.

WELLS, Harold B.; judge N.J. Court of Errors and Appeals, term expires 1942. Address: Bordentown, N.J.

WELLS, Ira J. K., sch. supervisor; b. Tamo, Ark., July 1, 1898; s. William James and Emma (Brown) W.; A.B., Lincoln U. of Pa., 1923; studied Columbia U., July 1931, Ohio State U., June-July 1936; m. Edna Virginia Clowden, July 26, 1935; children—Ira James Kohath, Edna Anita Vernetta. Engaged in welfare work, U. S. Steel Co., 1934; staff mem. Pittsburgh Courier, 1924; insurance salesman, Pa., 1925-26; head dept. sciences, Stratton High Sch., Beckley, W.Va., 1927-33; state supervisor Negro schools since 1933. Home: 1032 Bridge Road. Office: State House, Charleston, W.Va.

WELLS, Jacob Elbert, clergyman; b. Marion Co., W.Va., Nov. 27, 1873; s. Richard Daniel and Mary Jane (Atha) W.; A.B., W.Va. Wesleyan Coll., Buckhannon, 1907; S.T.B., Boston Univ. Sch. of Theology, 1910; hon. D.D., W.Va. Wesleyan Coll., 1923; m. Daisie Wells Furbee, June 29, 1910; children—Harriet Jane, Anna Virginia. Held various student pastorates, 1903-10; ordained to ministry Meth. Ch., 1910-24; dist. supt. Elkins Dist., 1924-29; pastor, Parkersburg, 1929-34, Huntington, 1934-35; dist. supt. Buckhannon Dist. since 1935; pres. W.Va. Conf. Epworth League, 1912-22; organized Epworth League Inst. at W.Va. Wesleyan Coll., 1917 and dean, 1917-21; chmn. W.Va. Wesleyan Coll. Semi-Centennial Celebration of 1940. Trustee W.Va. Wesleyan Coll., Buckhannon, W.Va. Republican. Methodist. Mason. Club: Rotary of Buckhannon. Contbr. to religious jours. Home: 25 College Av., Buckhannon, W.Va.

WELLS, Joseph Mahan, pottery mfr.; b. Steubenville, O., Apr. 6, 1889; s. William Edwin and Elizabeth Browning (Mahan) W.; student East Liverpool (O.) High Sch., 1902-06, Phillips Andover Acad., Andover, Mass., 1906-07, Yale, 1907-10; B.S., Bethany (W. Va.) Coll., 1912; m. Fern Hanna, Aug. 21, 1913; children—Virginia Rose, Joseph Mahan. Clk. W. I. Tebbutt Co., East Liverpool, O., 1912-14; bookkeeper Homer Laughlin China Co., Newell, W.Va., 1914-18, plant supt., 1923-30, sec. and gen. mgr. since 1930, dir. since 1928; asst. receiver Cartwright Bros. Co., East Liverpool, O., 1919-23; pres. The Lawrence Cooperage Co., Newell, W.Va., since 1924; dir. Newell Bridge & St. Ry Co., Newell Water & Power Co. Served as 2d lt., F.A., U.S. Army, during World War. Trustee East Liverpool (O.) Hosp., East Liverpool Y.M.C.A., East Liverpool Chamber of Commerce; dir. and mem. exec. com. W.Va. State Chamber of Commerce since 1928. Mem. Am. Ceramic Soc., Made in America Club (pres. and dir. since 1938), U. S. Potters Assn. (chmn. labor relations com. since 1928, chmn. tariff com. since 1930), Nat. Mfrs. Assn. (mem. labor relations com.), W.Va. Mfrs. Assn. (dir.), Sigma Nu. Republican. Presbyterian. Mason, Elk. Clubs: Duquesne, Oakmont Country (Pittsburgh); East Liverpool (O.) Country; North Hempsted (L.I., N.Y.) Country. Ohio State Golf Champion, 1924, 1926. Address: Newell, W.Va.

WELLS, Roger Hewes; asso. in economics and politics, Bryn Mawr Coll., 1923-27, asso. prof., 1927-33, prof., 1933-36, prof. polit. science since 1936. Address: Bryn Mawr Coll., Bryn Mawr, Pa.

WELLS, William Firth, biologist, sanitarian; b. Boston, Mass., Aug. 25, 1887; s. Obadiah Firth and Helen Marian (Deeds) W.; grad. Phillips Exeter Acad., 1905; B.Sc. in Biology and Pub. Health, Mass. Inst. Tech., 1910; m. Mildred Washington Weeks, Apr. 9, 1917; 1 son, William Firth. With Mass. and Conn. State bds. of health, also pub. health labs. of N.Dak., and Washington, D.C., Filtration Plant, 1910-12; with U. of Ill., 1912-13, U.S. P.H.S., 1913-17; apptd. to U.S. Bur. Fisheries, 1917; biologist and sanitarian, N.Y. State Conservation Commn., 1919-29; leave of absence with North Atlantic Oyster Farms, 1927-29; instr. in sanitary science, Harvard, 1930-37; asst. prof. sanitary engring., U. of Pa. Med. Sch., since 1937. Enlisted in U.S.A., 1917; commissioned 1st lt. San. Corps, 79th Div., Camp Meade, Md.; capt., May 24, 1918, 301st Water Tank Train; served in France; hon. discharged, Aug. 12, 1919. Episcopalian. Mason. Developed chlorination method of purifying oysters; first to artificially propagate oyster, quahaug, soft clam, scallop and mussel from egg. Invented air centrifuge for bacteriol. air analysis; demonstrated air-borne infection by droplet nuclei as vehicles of respired contagion; also sanitary ventilation by bactericidal irradiation of air with ultra-violet light as a practical means of control. Home: Media, Pa.

WELSH, Edward Burgett, clergyman; b. Lincoln, Tenn., Mar. 28, 1881; s. Rev. Edward Payson and Sarah (Burgett) W.; A.B., Coll. of Wooster (O.), 1901; B.D., Princeton Theol. Sem., 1906; student U. of Erlangen, Germany, 1906-07, U. of Basel, Switzerland, 1907; A.M., Columbia U., 1926; m. Mary Truman, June 3, 1922; children—Margaret Ann, Elizabeth Burgett, Elinor Truman. Engaged as teacher high sch., 1901, home missionary, Tenn. mountains, 1902-03; ordained to ministry Presbyn. Ch., 1907; pastor East Lake Ch., Wilmington, Del., 1907-10, Oil City, Pa., 1910-17, Ridgway, Pa., 1919-24; supply, Bellmore, L.I., N.Y., 1924-26; pastor, Corapolis, Pa., since 1927. Mem. Presbyn. Hist. Soc., Delta Sigma Rho. Awarded Fellowship in Systematic Theology, Princeton, 1906. Republican. Presbyterian. Home: 1208 Vance Av., Corapolis, Pa.

WELSH, George A., U.S. judge; b. Bay View, Cecil Co., Md., Aug. 9, 1878; s. George and Sarah (Pickering) W.; Temple U., 1892-94, LL.B., 1906; m. Nellie Ross Wolff, June 27, 1906 (died Feb. 18, 1920); children—William, Conwell; m. 2d, Helen Reed Kirk, Oct. 31, 1921; children—Margaret, Patrick, Deborah. Sec. to mayor of Philadelphia, 1904-06; assistant city solicitor of Philadelphia, 1906-07; assistant district attorney of Phila., 1907-22; mem. law firm Welsh & Bluett; mem. 68th to 72d Congresses (1923-33), 6th Pa. Dist.; resigned May 31, 1932, and has since served as U.S. dist. judge, Eastern Dist. of Pa. Dir. and sec. Temple U., 1914-38, v.p. since Dec. 21, 1938. Mem. Bd. of Edn., Phila. County, 11 yrs. Republican. Mason (K.T.), Elk. Home: 4105 Cambridge St., Philadelphia, Pa.

WELSH, Herbert, publicist, artist; b. Phila., Pa., Dec. 4, 1851; s. John and Mary W.; A.B., U. of Pa., 1871; LL.D., Washington and Lee U.; studied art in Phila., and 1873-74, in atelier of Bonnât, Paris; m. Fanny Frazer, April 1873. An organizer, 1882, and for 34 yrs. corr. sec. Indian Rights Assn., serving as president for 11 years, and now president emeritus. A leader in revolt against "boss rule" in Pa., 1890, which resulted in defeat of Delamater and election of Pattison as gov. Pres. of the Fellowship of the Pa. Academy of Fine Arts, 3 yrs.; mem. com. Nat. Civil Service Reform League; editor and pub. City and State, weekly, 1895-1904; lecturer and contbr. to mags. on the Indian question, civ. service reform, municipal govt., etc. Advocate of peaceable adjustment of all internat. disputes by arbitration, and ultimate universal peace policy; earnest opponent of the acquisition of the Philippine Islands by force, and prominent in movement to expose torture and other delinquencies of army there. Organized the movement which resulted in the preservation, by purchase, of forests on Sunapee Mountain, N.H., now a public park of 700 acres. Author: Civilization Among the Sioux Indians; Four Weeks Among Some of the Sioux Tribes; A Visit to the Navajo, Pueblo and Hualpais Indians; The Other Man's Country; The New Gentleman of the Road. Home: 5335 Baynton St., Germantown. Office: 301 S. 17th St., Phila., Pa.*

WELSH, J. Miller, pres. Peoples Nat. Bank; b. Long Valley, N.J., Oct. 30, 1883; s. Mathias T. and Mary Edith (Hager) W.; student German Valley (N.J.) Pub. Sch., Centenary Collegiate Inst., Hackettstown, N.J., 1899-1901, 1902-03, Bordentown (N.J.) Mil. Inst., 1901-02, Coleman's Business Coll., Newark, N.J., 1903-04; m. Pearle E. Welch, Oct. 18, 1910; children—J. Miller, Mathias T. (dec.). Became bookkeeper Peoples Nat. Bank, Hackettstown, N.J., 1906, now president. Dir. Hackettstown (N.J.) Bldg. & Loan Assn., Chamber of Commerce. Republican. Presbyterian. Clubs: Men's (charter mem.), Musconetcong Country (charter mem.; Hackettstown, N.J.). Home: 401 Church St. Office: 144 Main St., Hackettstown, N.J.

WELSH, Mark Frederick, state vet.; b. Saginaw, Mich., Nov. 22, 1895; s. Joseph and Anna (Stoddard) W.; D.V.M., Mich. State Coll., East Lansing, Mich., 1919; M.S., U. of Md., College Park, 1925; student George Washington U., Washington, D.C., 1926-28, Am. Univ., 1928-30; m. Claribel Pratt, Dec. 24, 1919. Asst. prof. bacteriology, U. of Md., College Park, 1919-29, insp. in charge, 1929-35; state vet., Md., since 1935; dir. First Md. Bldg. Assn., Riverdale, Md. Served as private, U.S. Army, 1917. Mem. U.S. Livestock Assn. (dir.), Chief Live Stock Officials (sec.), Alpha Tau Omega, Chi Psi Omega, Alpha Psi. Mason. Club: Kiwanis (Prince George's Co., Md.). Address: College Park, Md.

WELSH, Ralph Budd, banker; b. Long Valley, N.J., Sept. 29, 1897; s. Mathias Trimmer and Mary Edith (Hager) W.; student Hackettstown (N.J.) High Sch., 1911-15; A.B., Dartmouth Coll., Hanover, N.H., 1919; m. Leonora Titman, Sept. 1, 1920; children—Ralph Budd, Betty Jean, Marilyn Edith. Statistician Winchester Repeating Arms Co., New Haven, Conn., 1919-24; treas. and dir. Citizens Trust Co., Summit, N.J., 1924-37; sec.-treas. The Morris Co. Savings Bank, Morristown, N.J., since 1937; treas. and dir. Summit (N.J.) Mortgage and Finance Co. since 1925. Served as 2d lt., F.A., U.S. Army, 1918. Mem. Kappa Sigma. Republican. Presbyterian. Clubs: Dartmouth (New York); Canoe Brook Country (Summit, N.J.); Rotary (Morristown, N.J.). Home: 48 Oakland Pl., Summit, N.J. Office: 21 South St., Morristown, N.J.

WELSH, Robert Frazer, ry. pres.; b. Paris, France, Feb. 2, 1874; s. Herbert and Fanny (Frazer) W.; student Germantown Acad., St. Luke's Sch. and DeLancey Sch.; B.S., Trinity Coll., 1895; m. Frances Sewzuk, Aug. 5, 1933. Pres. Phila., Germantown & Norristown R.R. since 1932. Home: Laverock, Chestnut Hill. Office: 132 S. 4th St., Philadelphia, Pa.

WEMPLE, Charles Edwin, mfg. stone products; b. Lockport, N.Y., Oct. 23, 1878; s. McKinney and Eliza (Jakeway) W.; student pub. schs. and grad. high sch., Lockport, N.Y., 1898; m. Minnie B. Rignall, June 24, 1903; children—Martha Louise (Mrs. George B. Lukens), Ella-Kate (Mrs. Darcy Wilson), Priscilla (Mrs. William Butler), Philip Edwin. Began as stenographer and accountant Lockport Pulp Co. and Lockport Felt Co., 1898-1900; asst. mgr. Smallwood Stone Co., Empire, O., 1900, mgr., 1901-15; mgr. American Stone Co., mfrs. wood pulp grinding stones, Littleton, W.Va., since 1915, pres. since 1930, sole propr. since 1935; pres. Southern Lime Products Co., Wheeling, W.Va., since 1928; vice-pres. and treas. Vitro-Crete Co., Wheeling, W.Va., dir. Security Trust Co., Wheeling, W.Va., Glendale Lead & Zinc Co., Moundsville. Served as mem. city council, Toronto, O., 1912-14. Former mem. Wheeling Rotary Club (sec. 1925-27). Mem. Wild Life League of Ohio Co., Alumni Assn. of Boy Scouts. Democrat. Presbyn. (clk. of session Vance Memorial Ch.). Mason (K.T., 32°, Shriner). K.P. Club: Masonic. Home: 13 Laurel Av. Office: Hawley Bldg., Wheeling, W.Va.

WENCELIUS, Leon Georges, educator; b. Niederbronn les Bains, France, Oct. 9, 1900; s. Leon Gustave and Marie Frederique (Hoff) W.; came to U.S., 1926; B. es Lettres, U. de Nancy, 1917, B. es Sciences, 1917; B. en Theologie Protestante, U. de Strasbourg, 1925, Licencie es Lettres, 1929, Licencie en Theologie Protestante, 1932; S.T.M., Union Theol. Sem., N.Y. City, 1927, S.T.D., 1929; Dr. es Lettres, La Sorbonne, 1937; m. Marguerite Ann Grosjean, Aug. 20, 1927. Instr. French, New York U., 1927-28, Hunter Coll., 1928-30; asst. prof. French, Swarthmore Coll., 1930-37, asso. prof. since 1937; also Prof. au Centre d'Etudes Superieures Francaises, New York, N.Y., 1938-39; served as lay reader at Eglise Francaise du St. Sauveur, Phila., since 1931. Mem. Soc. des Profs. Francais en Amerique, Soc. de l'Histoire du Protestantisme Francais, Soc. Calviniste de France, Modern Lang. Assn. Author: La Philosophie de l'Art Chez les Néo-Scolastiques, 1932; L'Esthétique de Calvin, 1937; Calvin et Rembrandt, 1937. Contbr. to French publs.; also to mags. and publs. in U.S. Home: 211 College Av., Swarthmore, Pa.

WENDEL, Hugo Christian Martin, educator; b. Phila., Pa., Apr. 6, 1884; s. Hugo Rudolf and Louise (Freudenberger) W.; student Theol. Sem., Mt. Airy, Pa., 1904-07; student philosophy and history, U. of Erlangen, 1907-08, U. of Leipzig, May-Aug., 1908; A.B., Princeton, 1910; Ph.D., U. of Pa., 1918; studied at Sorbonne, Paris, and L'Institut des Hautes Études Marocaines, Rabat, Morocco, 1926; m. Marie Theodora Petersen-Enge (Dr. Jur., U. of Marburg), Aug. 18, 1927; 1 dau., Marie Louise. Instr. in history Lankenau Sch. for Girls, Phila., 1910-14; Harrison fellow in history, U. of Pa., 1915-16, 1917-18, asst. in history, 1916-17; instr. in history, New York U., 1918-20, asst. prof., 1920-28; prof. history, Long Island U., since 1928, also chmn. com. on instrn., dir. summer schs., since 1931; pres. Bronx Soc. Arts and Sciences, 1925-28. Research and travel in Europe and North Africa, various periods. Mem. Internat. Law Seminar of Carnegie Endowment U. of Mich., summer 1936. Instr. in history S.A.T.C., New York U., 1918; later maj., staff specialist, U.S.A. Res. Mem. bd. dirs. Mt. Airy Sem. Mem. Am. Hist. Assn., Foreign Policy Assn., Phi Beta Kappa, Delta Sigma Phi. Lutheran; v.p. Board of Edn., United Luth. Ch., 1926-32. Club: Andiron. Author: Democracy in the New German Constitution, 1920; The Evolution of Industrial Freedom, 1921; Mediterranean Menace, 1927; Proègé System in Morocco, 1930. Home: 5 Barry Pl., Fairlawn-Radburn, N.J.

WENDELL, Arthur Rindge, vice-pres., treas., gen. mgr., The Wheatena Corpn.; b. Quincy, Mass., Feb. 22, 1876; s. George Blunt and Mary Elizabeth (Thompson) W.; prep. education Greenleaf Street School, Quincy, 1881-87, Adams Acad., Quincy, 1887-92; A.B., Harvard, 1896; m. Grace Frances Peck, Nov. 8, 1902; 1 dau., Eleanor Sherburne. Office mgr. Health Food Co., New York, 1896-1903; treas. and dir. The Wheatena Co. since June 5, 1903, also vice-pres. since May 1918; vice-pres. and dir. Highspire Flour Mills, Inc., since 1920; pres. Quaker City Flour Mills, Inc., Phila.; trustee and mem. advisory com. Individual Underwriters since 1916; trustee and chmn. Fireproof Sprinklered Underwriters since 1925; trustee and mem. advisory com. Metropolitan Inter-Insurers since 1928; dir. Arex Indemnity Co. since 1936; dir. Rahway Savings Instn. since 1913, vice-pres. since 1921; pres. Industrial Bldg. & Loan Assn., Rahway, 1910-38. Commr. Union County Park Commn., Elizabeth, N.J., since 1921 (formerly sec., treas., vice-pres. and pres.; now vice-pres.); commr. Rahway Civic Commn., 1910; pres. Rahway Bd. of Trade, 1914-16; sinking fund commr. and treas., City of Rahway, 1916-25; chmn. Citizens' Com. for Rahway Valley trunk sewer since 1932. Formerly trustee Morristown (N.J.) Sch. Mem. U.S. Trade Mark Assn. (vice-pres., dir.), Holland Soc. of New York (pres., trustee), N.J. Soc. of Founders and Patriots of America (dep. gov.), St. Nicholas Soc. of New York, Sons Am. Revolution, Soc. of Colonial Wars, Colonial Order of the Acorn, N.Y., Pi Eta (Harvard). Republican. Unitarian. Mason (Royal and Select Master). Clubs: University, Harvard (New York); Harvard of N.J.; Baltusrol Golf (Springfield, N.J.); Colonia Country (Colonia, N.J.); Union Interalliee (Paris); Hurlingham (London). Home: Wendelsora, Summit, N.J. Office: The Wheatena Corpn., Rahway, N.J.

WENDELL, James Isaac, educator; b. Schenectady, N.Y., Sept. 3, 1890; s. Irving Wendell and Ida Van Hyming (Lamb) W.; prep. edn. Townsend Harris Hall; New York, 1903-06, Mt. Hermon Sch., Mass., 1906-09; B. A., Wesleyan U., Conn., 1913, hon. M.A., 1930; hon. M.A., Univ. of Pa., 1938; LL.D. Lafayette College, 1938; m. Marjorie Potts, June 11, 1915; children—James III, John Potts, Harlan Leonard Potts. With The Hill School since 1913, successively instr. in English, asst. headmaster, treas., dean of administration, asso. headmaster, to 1928, headmaster since 1928. Co-founder Business Officers' Assn. of Eastern States Prep. Schs. Trustee Wesleyan U. since 1931; mem. com. examination ratings and mem. exec. com., Coll. Entrance Examination Bd. Republican. Episcopalian. Joint holder of world's record in 220 yds. low hurdles, 1913-23; holder of intercollegiate record of 220 yds. low hurdles; mem. Am. Olympic Team (2d in 110 metre hurdles), Stockholm, 1912. Address: The Hill School, Pottstown, Pa.

WENDT, Edwin Frederick, consulting engr.; b. New Brighton (Pittsburgh), Pa., May 12, 1869; s. Christian Ihmsen (M.D.) and Agnes (Scott) W.; A.B., Geneva (Pa.) College, 1888, D.Sc., 1913; m. Helen Lawall Bentley, Nov. 11, 1931. Began with Pittsburgh & Lake Erie R.R. (N.Y. Central Lines), 1888; became asst. chief engr. in charge maintenance of way and constrn., 1898, and continued with the co. until 1913; rd. reconstructed during his service, and developed from single track to 4-track road; mem. N.Y. Central Lines Engring. Com., 1907-13; engr. in charge constrn. Lake Erie & Eastern R.R., 1911-13; mem. Govt. Commn. which inspected new Govt. R.R. under constrn. in Alaska, 1917; mem. Engring. Bd. (Interstate Commerce Commn.), 1913-21, which supervised preparation of engring. reports in connection with federal valuation of railroads, telegraphs and telephones under Section 19a of Interstate Commerce Act; also chief engr. in charge Eastern dist., Bur. of Valuation; cons. engr. since 1921, specializing in matters involving regulation of railroads and public utilities. Admitted to practice before interstate Commerce Commn., 1929. Mem. Am. Ry. Engring. Assn. (pres. 1913, mem. com. waterways and harbors), Am. Soc. C. E. (chmn. exec. com. engring. economics div., 1935, 36, 37; mem. com. on valuation procedure), Am. Inst. Consulting Engrs. (pres. 1936-37), Assembly of Am. Engring. Council, Engrs. Soc. of Western Pa., Washington Soc. of Engrs. (pres. 1918), A.A.A.S., Ry. Signal Assn., Am. Economic Assn., Washington Acad. Sciences. United Presbyn. Club: Cosmos (Washington). Author various tech. papers and repts. Home: New Brighton, Pa. Office: Union Trust Bldg., Pittsburgh, Pa.

WENDT, John Scott, lawyer; b. New Brighton, Pa., Mar. 29, 1868; s. Christian Ihmsen and Agnes (Scott) W.; A.B., Geneva Coll., Beaver Falls, Pa., 1887; m. Mary V. Peyton, June 7, 1920; 1 son, John Scott. Admitted to Pa. bar, 1890, and since engaged in gen. practice of law at Pittsburgh; mem. firm Wendt and Graver since 1934. Mem. Allegheny County, Pa. and Am. bar assns., Western Pa. Hist. Soc. Republican. Presbyterian. Clubs: Edgeworth, Allegheny Country (Sewickley, Pa.); Duquesne, Civic (Pittsburgh). Home: 539 Boundary St., Sewickley, Pa. Office: Union Trust Bldg., Pittsburgh, Pa.

WENNER, Thomas J(efferson), M.D., surgeon; b. Lebanon, Pa., May 4, 1894; s. Dr. Alfred J. and Katherine Ida (Laudermilch) W.; M.D., U. of Pa., 1918; m. Edith Claie Hicks, June 4, 1934. Demonstrator chemistry and toxicology, Medico-Chirurg. Coll., Phila., 1914-16; head pathol. dept. Nesbitt Memorial Hosp., Wilkes-Barre, Pa., since 1920, asst. surgeon, 1925-29; Designated Med. Examiner, Vets. Adminstrn., since 1927. Served with Med. Corps, U.S. Army, 1916-19; commd. officer Lab. Sect., 103d Med. Regt., 1920-25, Med. Dept., 109th F.A., 1923-26. Fellow A.M.A., Am. Soc. Clin. Pathologists; mem. Pa. State Med. Soc., Luzerne Co. Med. Soc., Lehigh Valley Med. Soc., Pa. German Soc., Am. Legion. Reformed Ch. Mason. Clubs: Irem Temple Country, Craftsmans (Wilkes-Barre, Pa.) Lectured before co. med. socs., hosps. and other med. orgns. Address: 150 S. Washington St., Wilkes-Barre, Pa.

WENRICH, Calvin Naftzinger, physicist; b. Bernville, Pa., Nov. 21, 1873; s. Isaac S. and Emalina (Naftzinger), W.; B.E., Keystone State Normal Sch., Kutztown, Pa., 1896, M.E., 1898; A.B., Franklin and Marshall Coll., 1902, A.M., 1904; Ph.D., U. of Pa., 1910; m. Ivah Patterson, Dec. 21, 1910. Teacher pub. schs., Pa., 3 yrs.; teacher physics and mathematics, Franklin and Marshall Acad., 1900-04, 1906-07; prof. physics, Carthage (Ill.) Coll., 1904-06; instr. physics, 1097-08, fellow in physics, 1908-10, U. of Pa.; instr. physics, 1910, asst. prof., 1912, prof. and head of dept., 1914-20, U. of Pittsburgh; research physicist, Armstrong Cork Co., 1920—. Trustee Franklin and Marshall Coll. Mem. Am. Phys. Soc., A.A.A.S., Sigma Xi. Republican. Home: 923 W. Walnut St., Lancaster, Pa.

WENRICH, David Henry, prof. zoölogy; b. Lecompton, Kan., June 29, 1885; s. Christian K. and Frances Charity (Lippy) W.; A.B., U. of Kan., 1911, A.M., 1912; Ph.D., Harvard, 1915; m. Myra E. Spangler, June 19, 1916; children—Frances Anne, David Henry. Teaching fellow, U. of Kan., 1911-12; Austin teaching fellow, Harvard, 1912-13, 1914-15; instr. in zoölogy, U. of Pa., 1915-19, asst. prof., 1919-28, prof. since 1928. Fellow A.A.A.S.; mem. Am. Assn. Univ. Profs., Am. Soc. Zoölogists, Am. Soc. Naturalists, Am. Genetic Assn., Ecol. Soc. America, Am. Soc. Parasitologists (v.p. 1937), Am. Soc. Tropical Medicine, Am. Micros. Soc. (pres. 1930), Phila. Acad. Natural Science, Limnological Soc. Am., Am. Nature Assn., Am. Mus. Natural History, Bermuda Biol. Sta. for Research, Nat. Geog. Soc., Marine Biol. Lab. (Woods Hole, Mass.), Sigma Xi. Club: Lenape (U. of Pa.). Home: 21 W. Hinckley Av., Ridley Park, Pa.

WENTZ, Abdel Ross, clergyman, educator; b. Black Rock, York Co., Pa., Oct. 8, 1883; s. John Valentine and Ellen Catharine (Tracy) W.; A.B., Pa. Coll., Gettysburg, Pa., 1904; B.D., Luth. Theol. Sem., Gettysburg, 1907; univs. of Leipzig, Berlin, Tübingen, 1907-10; Ph.D., Geo. Washington, 1914; D.D., Gettysburg, 1921; m. Mary Edna Kuhlman, Aug. 15, 1917; children—Valentine (died 1936), Frederick Kuhlman, Mary Louise. Ordained Luth. ministry, 1907; prof. history, Gettysburg Coll., 1909-16; prof. ch. history, Luth. Theol. Sem., since 1916; mem. exec. bd. of United Luth. Ch. in America; sec. Am. Assn. Theol. Schs., 1934-36, treas. since 1936; mem. exec. com. Luth. World Conv., since 1935; mem. exec. com. World's Conf. on Faith and Order; alternate mem. Com. of Fourteen to form World Council of Churches. Mem. Am. Soc. Church History (pres. 1931-32; sec. 1934-37), Lutheran Hist. Soc. (curator), Pa. German Soc. Republican. Author: The Beginnings of the German Element in York County, Pennsylvania, 1916; History of the Lutheran Synod of Maryland, 1920; When Two Worlds Met, 1921; The Lutheran Church in American History, 1923, 2d edit., 1933; History of the Gettysburg Theological Seminary, 1926; Fliedner the Faithful, 1936; A New Strategy for Theological Education, 1937. Co-Author: The Lutheran Churches of the World, 1929. Mem. Phi Beta Kappa. Home: Gettysburg, Pa.

WENTZ, Daniel Bertsch, Jr., coal operator; b. Big Stone Gap, Va., June 10, 1903; s. Daniel Bertsch and Louise (Finlay) W.; student Fay Sch. (Southborough, Mass.), St. Paul's Sch. (Concord), Harvard; m. Elizabeth Sewell, Oct. 1, 1927. President Virginia-Kentucky Coal Corporation; v.p. Gen. Coal Co., Stonega Coke & Coal Co., Va. Coal & Iron Co., Wentz Corpn.; dir. Admiralty Coal Corpn., Crab Orchard Improvement Co., Wentz Co., Whitehall Cement Mfg. Co. Interstate R.R. Co. Republican. Episcopalian. Clubs: Philadelphia, Pine Valley Country, Racquet (Phila.; Huntingdon Valley Country (Abington). Home: Pineville, Pa. Office: 123 S. Broad St., Philadelphia, Pa.

WENTZEL, William Francis H., dir. humane edn.; b. Jacksonwald, Pa., Mar. 2, 1879; s. Francis N. and Rebecca K. (Hiester) W.; grad. Perkiomen Seminary, Pennsburg, Pennsylvania, 1902; B.S., Pa. State Coll., 1908 (valedictorian), M.S., 1911; student Grad. Sch., University of Pittsburgh, 1924-26; LL.D., Allen University, Columbia S.C., 1938; m. Lillie May Eidel, Dec. 19, 1904 (she died April 22, 1933); children—Wm. Arthur E., Emma May Ruth (Mrs. Earl B. Buchanan), Earl Everett E. Began as teacher pub. schs.; prin. W. Nottingham Acad., Colora, Md., 1911-13; prof. pedagogy and science, South Western State Normal Sch., California, Pa., 1913-16, also v. prin. and dean summer sch.; field sec. and organizer N.Y. State Humane Socs., 1916-18; chief probation officer Juvenile Court, Wilmington, Del., 1918-19; industrial sec. Metropolitan Y.M.C.A., Buffalo, N.Y., 1919-21; dir. humane edn., Bd. of Temperance and Moral Welfare, Presbyn. Ch. of U.S.A., 1921-23; field rep. Am. Humane Edn. Soc., since 1923; instr. social science and dir. student govt., George Westinghouse Sch., Pittsburgh, Pa., 1924-26; executive sec. and ednl. dir. Western Pa. Humane Soc. since Feb. 1926; sec. Federated Humane Socs. of Pa.; humane edn. chmn. Pa. Congress of Parent Teacher Assns. Member American Humane Assn., Am. Red Star Animal Relief, N.E.A., Delta Sigma Rho, Phi Kappa Phi, Pi Gamma Mu. Mason. Writer tracts on kindness to animals, etc.; lecturer. Home: Crafton, Pa. Office: 832 Bigelow Boul., Pittsburgh, Pa.

WERNER, Edwin H., v.p. and gen. mgr. Metropolitan Edison Co.; b. Wernersville, Pa., Mar.

29, 1890; s. John A. and Kate A. (Knoll) W.; C.E., Pa. State Coll., 1911; m. Estella M. Kreisher, Sept. 17, 1910; children—Josephine (Mrs. Bell), June V. Engr. Pa. Steel Co. (now Bethlehem Steel Co.), 1911-13; Pittsburgh Rys. Co., 1913-15, Reading Transit & Light Co., 1915-23; asst. gen. mgr. Reading Transit & Light Co., 1923-29; pres. and gen. mgr. Reading Transit Co. and Reading Coach Co., 1930-33; v.p. and gen. mgr. Metropolitan Edison Co. since 1933. Home: R.D. No. 1, Sinking Spring, Pa. Office: 412 Washington St., Reading, Pa.

WERNER, William Louser, prof. English; b. Phila., Pa., Jan. 20, 1894; s. David Thomas and Susan (Louser) W.; A.B., Muhlenberg Coll., Allentown, Pa., 1915; study U. of Clermont-Fd., France, 1919; student U. of Pa., 1919-20; A.M., Pa. State Coll., 1922; grad. study, Columbia U., 1922-23; m. Katherine Davies Bowman, June 15, 1926; 1 son, Richard Stephen. Engaged in teaching, high schs., 1915-17, 1919-20; instr. English, Pa. State Coll., 1920-23, asst. prof., 1923-31, asso. prof., 1931-36, prof. since 1936. Served as corp., 316th Inf., U.S. Army, 1917-19, with A.E.F. in Meuse-Argonne offensive. Mem. State Advisory Bd., Federal Writers Project in Pa. Mem. Modern Lang. Assn., Am. Assn. Univ. Profs., Am. Federation Teachers, Pa. German Soc., Pa. German Folklore Soc. Republican. Lutheran. Contbr. to various mags. of nat. circulation. Included in a number of anthologies. Home: 217 E. Beaver Av., State College, Pa.

WERT, Wilson Alfred, lawyer; b. Jordon, Pa., Aug. 26, 1877; s. David and Mary Ann (Kern) W.; student Muhlenberg Coll., Allentown, Pa., 1895-97; A.B., A.M., Franklin & Marshall Coll., Lancaster, Pa., 1899; LL.B., U. of Pa., 1903; m. Clorinda H. DeFrehn, Apr. 15, 1903; children—Ilerda C., Viola M., Alfred D., Edward D., Margaret C. Admitted to Lehigh Co. bar, 1904; also to Superior Ct. of Pa. and Supreme Ct. of Pa.; now mem. firm Snyder, Wert & Wilcox, attys. at law, Allentown; pres. Kutztown Rural Telephone & Telegraph Co. Prothonotary, Lehigh Co., 1918-30. Mem. Prothonotarys Assn. of State of Pa. (pres. 1920-30). Democrat. Mem. Reformed Ch. Elk. Club: Manufacturers and Bankers (Phila.). Home: 1317 Turner St. Office: 510 Hamilton St., Allentown, Pa.

WERTENBAKER, Thomas Jefferson, author, educator; b. Charlottesville, Va., Feb. 6, 1879; s. Charles Christian and Frances Thomas (Leftwich) W.; B.A. and M.A., U. of Va., 1902, Ph.D., 1910; m. Sarah Rossetter Marshall, July 10, 1916; 1 son, Thomas Jefferson. Editor on Baltimore News, 1905-06; asso. prof. history and economics, Agrl. and Mech. Coll. of Tex., 1907-09; instr. Am. history, U. of Va., 1909-10; with Princeton since 1910, successively instr. Am. history, asst. prof., asso. prof., and since 1925, Edwards prof. Am. history, also chmn. dept., 1928-1936; visiting prof. U. of Göttingen, 1931, ehrenburger, 1931; Harold Vyyyan Harmsworth Prof. of Am. History, Oxford 1939-1940; Page-Barbour lecturer, Univ. of Va., 1937; editor on Evening Sun, New York, 1918-23. Mem. Am. Hist. Assn., Am. Assn. Univ. Profs., Mass. Hist. Soc., N.J. Hist. Soc., Southern Historical Association, The Newcomen Society, Phi Beta Kappa and Phi Kappa Psi. Author: Patrician and Plebeian in Virginia, 1916; Virginia under the Stuarts, 1914; Planters of Colonial Virginia, 1922; The American People—A History, 1926; The First Americans, 1927; The United States of America (with Dr. Donald E. Smith), 1931; Norfolk—Historic Southern Port, 1931; The Founding of American Civilization, 1938. Home: 164 Prospect Av., Princeton, N.J.

WERTH, Matthew Fontaine Maury, utilities exec.; b. Richmond, Va., July 22, 1882; s. James Rhodes and Mary Herndon (Maury) W.; ed. Va. Mil. Inst.; m. Sallie Anne Warfield Cockey, June 18, 1914; children—Virginia Lee Maury, Sallie Anne Warfield, Matthew Fontaine Maury. Supt. constrn. Gen. Electric Co., Baltimore, 1905-06, Witherbee Storage Battery Co., New York, 1907-08; elec. foreman of Mech.

dept. Mahoning & Shenango Ry. Co., Youngstown, O., 1908-11; asst. mech. supt. British Columbia Electric Ry. Co., Ltd., Vancouver, B.C., 1911-16; supt. power Detroit United Rys., 1916-22; supt. generation Pa. Power & Light Co., Allentown, Pa., 1923-25, supt. operation, 1925-30, gen. supt. since 1930. Mem. Sigma Alpha Epsilon. Episcopalian. Clubs: Livingston, Lehigh Country (Allentown, Pa.). Home: 28 N. 15th St. Office: 901 Hamilton St., Allentown, Pa.

WESCOTT, Blaine Benjamin, engr. of tests; b. Syracuse, N.Y., July 7, 1895; s. Fred C. and Hattie M. (Adams) W.; B.S. in Chemistry, Syracuse (N.Y.) U., 1917; M.S., U. of Pittsburgh, 1920, Ph.D., 1922; m. Anna R. Kelly, Dec. 21, 1918; 1 dau., Shirley Norene. Jr. phys. chemist U.S. Bur. of Mines, Pittsburgh, 1918; instr. chemistry dept., U. of Pittsburgh, 1918-22; industrial fellow Mellon Inst., Pittsburgh, 1922-29; engr. of tests Gulf Research & Development Co., Pittsburgh, since 1929. Mem. Am. Soc. Metals (mem. exec. com. Pittsburgh Sect. 1936), Am. Soc. M.E., Am. Petroleum Inst. (chmn. several coms.), Pittsburgh Chamber of Commerce, Alpha Chi Sigma, Phi Lambda Upsilon. Republican. Contbr. scientific publs. Home: 810 Hulton Road, Oakmont, Pa. Office: Gulf Research & Development Co., Pittsburgh, Pa.

WESCOTT, Glenway, author; b. Kewaskum, Wis., Apr. 11, 1901; s. Bruce Peters and Josephine (Gordon) W.; student U. of Chicago, 1917-19; unmarried. Author: The Apple of the Eye, 1924; The Grandmothers—A Family Portrait, 1927; Good-Bye Wisconsin, 1928; Fear and Trembling, 1932; A Calendar of Saints for Unbelievers, 1932. Home: Stone-blossom, Hampton, N.J.*

WESCOTT, Paul, artist and teacher; b. Milwaukee, Wis., Apr. 12, 1904; s. Earl and Harriet (Bolton) W.; ed. Milwaukee State Normal Sch., 1922-23, Art Inst. of Chicago, 1925-26, Pa. Acad. of Fine Arts, 1928-32; m. Alison Farmer, Oct. 28, 1933. Instr. in art, Pa. Acad. of Fine Arts, summer sch., 1929; instr. in charge art dept., The Hill Sch. for Boys, Pottstown, Pa., since 1932; specializes in landscapes; chosen by Am. Federation Arts for Nat. Tour of Pa. Acad. Fine Arts, 1938, 39; exhibited Nat. Acad. Annual Exhbns., New York, Walker Galleries, New York, the important exhbns. at Phila., Corcoran Biennial Exhbns., Washington, D.C., and many other cities; one man shows, Art Alliance, Phila., and at Scranton (Pa.) Mus. Mem. Fellowship Pa. Acad. Fine Arts, Art Alliance. Awarded Cresson Traveling Scholarship, 1930; Toppan Prize, 1932; hon. mentions, Phila. Sketch Club, 1934 and 1936; $100 Prize, Art Club, Phila., 1937. Republican. Episcopalian. Home: 429 King St., Pottstown, Pa.

WESCOTT, Ralph Wesley, lawyer; b. Haddonfield, N.J., Sept. 19, 1883; s. John Wesley and Frances Marie Louise Le Clerc (Pryor) W.; prep. edn., Williston Acad., Easthampton, Mass., 1898-1902; A.B., Yale, 1906; student Univ. of London, Eng., 1907-08, U. of Calif., 1908-09, Harvard Law, 1909-10, U. of Pa. Grad. Sch., 1934-37; m. Marion Sturges-Jones, Dec. 15, 1925; 1 son, Roger Williams. Admitted to N.J. bar as atty., 1910, as counsellor, 1916; Supreme Court commr., 1925; special master in chancery, 1933; bar of U.S. Supreme Court, 1932; began practice Camden, N.J., 1910; jr. partner Wescott & Weaver, Camden, 1914-17, asso., 1923-27; associated with Louis B. LeDuc, Camden, since 1929; comptroller of customs, Phila., 1934-38; instr. in torts, South Jersey Law Sch., since 1926; dir. Internat. Pulverizing Corpn. Served in U.S.N.R.F., 1917-21; overseas service, 1918. Exec. sec. Pro-League Independents, 1920-22; co-organizer and dir. speakers' bureau, League of Nations Assn., New York, 1921-23. Dir. Camden Y.M.C.A., Camden County Chamber of Commerce. Mem. Am., N.J. State, Camden County bar assns., Am. Acad. Polit. and Social Science, Am. Legion, Vets. of Foreign Wars. Democrat. Episcopalian (vestryman, Grace Ch., Haddonfield, since 1929). Clubs: Haddon Field; Yale Alumni Assn. of Phila.

(scholarship committee.). Author of "History of U.S. Customs Service in Phila." Contbr. to law jours. and newspapers; editorial writer Camden Daily Courier, 1919-20; polit. writer N.Y. Evening Post, 1920-22. Home: 43 Chestnut St., Haddonfield, N.J. Office: 130 N. Broadway, Camden, N.J.

WESHNER, David Engel, theater exec.; b. Brooklyn, N.Y., Nov. 11, 1894; s. Louis and Bertha (Jarress) W.; student Bushwick High Sch., Brooklyn, N.Y., 1909-13; A.B., New York U., 1917; m. Goldie White, Oct. 28, 1923; children — Theodore Stewart, Dorothy Ann. Teacher, Kohut Sch. for Boys, Riverdale, N.Y., 1917-19; spl. publicity and newspaper work, 1919-21; treas. Tanney Printing & Pub. Corpn., 1922; editor Motion Picture Post, 1923; pres. Wesher-Davidson Advertising Agency, N.Y. City, and handling publicity, advertising and exploitation for independent and nat. motion picture producers, 1924-26; publicity and advertising dir. for Johnny Hines, 1924-26; production mgr. Action Pictures, Hollywood, Calif., 1927; dir. advertising and publicity Stanley-Fabian Corpn., Newark, N.J., 1928; gen. mgr. Stanley-Fabian Corpn., 60 theaters, 1929-30; dir. advertising, publicity and exploitation Warner Bros. Theaters, Inc., 1930-33; zone mgr. Warner Bros. theaters in Wis. and upper Mich., 1933-34; zone mgr. since 1934 first-run and key-neighborhood theaters, Phila., including Aldine, Boyd, Earle, Karlton, Keiths, Stanley, Stanton, Palace, Victoria, Circle, Midway, 69th St., State, Tower, Nixon, Roosevelt and Uptown; mem. grievance bd., Code Authority, representing affiliated theaters, 1933-34. Initiated and supervised, in conjunction with Commr. Wm. J. Egan, delinquent tax campaign drive for City of Newark, N.J., 1933. Maj. N.G. of N.J. since 1932; adj. gen.'s dept. and aide-de-camp, mil. staff of Gov. A. Harry Moore of N.J., 1932-35. Dir. Foster Home for Jewish Children, Phila. Former mem. bd. dirs. Motion Picture Theater Owners of Wisconsin and Upper Michigan; mem. Asso. Motion Picture Advertisers. Pi Lambda Phi. Democrat. Clubs: Variety (dir. 1935-36; 1937-38 and 1938-39); Philmont Country (Phila.). Home: Rittenhouse Plaza Apts. Office: 1028 Market St., Philadelphia, Pa.

WESLEY, Charles Sumner, lawyer; b. Philadelphia, Pa., Feb. 23, 1878; s. John S. and Sarah J. (Wright) W.; B.S. in Economics, U. of Pa., 1899, LL.B., 1902; m. Laura Clark, Apr. 6, 1904; children—Eleanor Clark (Mrs. Latimer S. Stewart), Margaret Clark (Mrs. Samuel Eldredge), Clark. Admitted to Pa. bar, 1902, and has since conducted gen. law practice in Phila.; mem. firm Tustin & Wesley since 1902; advisor to Govt. in Selective Draft, 1917; counsel to banking dept., U.S. Dept. of Justice in matters relative to closed banks since 1933; pres. Bellefonte Central R.R. Co., Huntingdon & Broad Top Mt. R.R., Globe & Republic Insurance Co.; also officer or director numerous corpns. Dir. Glen Mills Schs. for Boys, Sleighton Farms Sch. for Girls, Big Brother Assn. Mem. Am. Bar Assn., Pa. Bar Assn., Phila. Bar Assn. (gov.), Am. Soc. Internat. Law, Am. Acad. Polit. and Social Science, Delta Upsilon. Republican. Episcopalian. Club: Union League. Home: The Kenilworth, Alden Park. Office: Packard Bldg., Philadelphia, Pa.

WEST, Andrew Fleming, dean grad. sch. Princeton; b. Allegheny, Pa., May 17, 1853; s. Rev. Nathaniel and Mary (Fleming) W.; A.B., Princeton, 1874, Ph.D., 1883; LL.D., Lafayette Coll., 1897; D.Litt., Oxford U., 1902; m. Lucy Marshall Fitz Randolph, May 9, 1889. Prof. Latin, 1883-1928, dean Grad. Sch., 1901-1928, Princeton. Trustee Am. Acad. in Rome and chmn. Commn. on Sch. of Classical Studies. Writer on univ. edn. particularly classical edn. Hon. pres. Am. Classical League; past pres. Am. Philol. Assn.; v.p. Archæol. Inst. America. Planned Graduate College of Princeton, opened 1913. Editor: Terence, 1888; The Philobiblon of Richard de Bury, 1889. Author: Alcuin and the Rise of the Christian Schools, 1893; Latin Grammar, 1902; The Proposed Graduate College of Princeton University, 1903; American Liberal Education, 1907; Education and the War, 1919; Presentations for Degrees, 1929; Stray Verses, 1931; American General Education, 1932. Home: Princeton, N.J.

WEST, Arthur, mechanical engr.; b. Milwaukee, Wis., Mar. 25, 1867; s. Hubbell and Helen (Roberts) W.; M.E., U. of Wis., 1887; m. Alice Florence Tourtellot, Dec. 22, 1900. Engr. Edward P. Allis Co., Milwaukee, 1887-98, asst. to chief engr., 1898-1900; asst. chief engr. Allis-Chalmers Co., Milwaukee, 1900-04, also mgr. pumping engine dept., 1901-04; chief engr. Westinghouse Machine Co., Pittsburgh, 1904-08, v.p., 1906-08; mgr. power dept., Bethlehem Steel Co., 1908-27, cons. engr. since 1927. Cons. mech. engr. New York, Bd. of Water Supply, 1903-08; lecturer Johns Hopkins, Lehigh U. and U.S. Naval Acad., 1909-27; cons. engr. Lake Placid Club, N.Y., since 1927. Mem. Am. Soc. Mech. Engrs. (v.p. 1905-07), Inventor's Guild (New York), Chi Psi. Republican. Club: Lake Placid (past mem. council). Address: First Nat. Bank and Trust Co., Bethlehem, Pa.*

WEST, Charles Converse, banking and investments; b. Yonkers, N.Y., June 7, 1860; s. William Gordon and Mary (Cooke) W.; ed. pub. sch., Brooklyn, N.Y. and pvt. sch., Yonkers, N.Y., 1866-77; m. Mary J. Parsons, of Troy, O., Apr. 19, 1887; children—Charles Parsons (dec.), Converse Dettmer, Helen Copland (Mrs. John McC. Chapman, Jr.), George Parsons, Robert Culbertson. Began as clk. Charles Head & Co., stock brokers, 1877, mem. firm, 1890-1914, when bus. consolidated with Keech, Loew & Co., later F. B. Keech & Co., and mem. firm, 1914-32, retired, 1932. Served on gov. com. bd. and chmn. finance com. Montclair Y.M.C.A.; first pres. Montclair Boy Scouts, 6 yrs., trustee 22 yrs.; awarded Silver Beaver of Boy Scouts of America. Trustee First Congl. Ch. Republican. Conglist. Clubs: Athletic (Montclair); Downtown Athletic (N.Y.); Sky Top; Mohawk Lake; Seigniory (Quebec, Can.). Home: 100 Upper Mountain Av., Montclair, N.J.

WEST, John Howell, physician; b. Hope, N.J., Oct. 4, 1885; s. Edwin J. and Margaret M. (Cooke) W.; Ph.B., Lafayette Coll., 1908; M.D., Medico-Chirurg. Coll., 1913; m. Rosemary J. Dougherty, 1923; children—Rosemary Howell, Joan Elizabeth. Formerly resident phys., Presbyn. Hosp., Phila., Pa.; pediatrician asso. with Dr. Charles Gilmore Kerley, 1919-31; now chief of pediatrics, Easton Hosp., Easton, Pa. Fellow Am. Acad. Pediatrics; mem. Am. Bd. Pediatrics, Pa. State Med. Soc., Northampton Co. Med. Soc. Mason. Author: Keeping the Baby Well, 1923. Contbr. articles and papers to Archives of Pediatrics, and med. jours. Home: 151 Parker Av. Office: 40 N. 3d St., Easton, Pa.

WEST, Leslie Elliott, civil and sanitary engr.; b. Buffalo, N.Y., Aug. 8, 1903; s. Joseph and Marguerite (Craft) W.; student Irvington (N.J.) High Sch., 1917-21; B.S., Rutgers U., New Brunswick, N.J., 1925, C.E., 1929; m. Vivian Wagner, July 14, 1934; 1 dau., Virginia Leslie. Surveyor and engr. I. J. Casey, Jr., Irvington, N.J., 1919-27, Casey & West, Irvington, N.J., 1928-32; maintenance engr. Joint Meeting Sanitary Dist. Essex and Union Counties, Elizabeth, N.J., 1933-36, maintenance engr. and supt., 1936-38, chief engr. since 1938. Mem. Professional Engrs. and Surveyors, Sewage Works Assn., Phi Beta Kappa, Delta Theta Sigma. Republican. Jr.O.U.A.M. Club: Kiwanis Internat. (Irvington, N.J.). Home: 118 S. Kingman Rd., South Orange, N.J. Office: Joint Meeting, Essex and Union Cos., Elizabeth, N.J.

WEST, Roscoe Lambert, coll. pres.; b. Wilton, Me., Feb. 20, 1892; s. Melvin Josiah and Sara (Ham) W.; diploma State Normal Sch., Farmington, Me., 1910; A.B., Harvard U., 1914; Ed.M., Harvard U., 1923; m. Edith F. Richardson, Sept. 2, 1915; children—Richard Fussell, Helen Lee, Evan Richardson, Janet Frances. Employed as supt. schs., Farmington and Wilton, Me., 1914-16, Rockland and Rockport, Me., 1916-19, Needham, Mass., 1919-21; dir. elementary edn., City of Trenton, N.J., 1921-26; asst. commr. edn., State of N.J., 1926-28, dir. teacher edn., 1928-30; pres. State Teachers Coll., Trenton, N.J., since 1930. Served as pres. Mercer Co. Health and Tuberculosis League. Mem. Phi Beta Kappa. Presbyterian. Home: 247 Hillcrest Av., Trenton, N.J.

WEST, Stanley Raphael, clergyman; b. Phila., Pa., Apr. 2, 1884; s. William Harvey and Elizabeth Jones (Short) W.; ed. Girard Coll., Phila., 1891-99, Brown Prep Sch., Phila., 1905-07; B.D., Divinity Sch. of P.E. Ch. in Phila., 1910; m. Mary Louise Dean, Nov. 19, 1912. Employed as clk. with Delaware Ins. Co., Phila., 1899-1907, prepared for ministry, evenings, 1905-07; ordained to ministry P.E. Ch., deacon, 1910, priest, 1911; curate, St. Matthews, Phila., 1910-13, rector, Pottstown, Pa., 1913-24; rector, Calvary Ch., Conshohocken, Pa., since 1924; dean Convocation of Norristown, 1924-36; chmn. Dept. of Social Service and Instns., Diocese of Pa., P.E. Ch., 1925-29. Served as chaplain and 1st lt., U.S. Army, 1918, at Camp Devens, Mass. Interested actively in Boy Scout movement; honored by Silver Beaver Award. Chmn. Conshohocken Civilian Relief Assn., 1933-36; mem. Montgomery Co. Emergency Relief Bd., 1935-37. Chaplain Conshohocken Post, Am. Legion, 1926-36. Mem. Clerical, Monday Evening, Parish Administration, clubs of Diocese of Pa. Republican. Episcopalian. Clubs: Rotary (Conshohocken, Pa.); Penn Athletic (Phila.). Home: 317 Fayette St., Conshohocken, Pa.

WEST, William Brady, physician; b. Huntingdon, Pa., Oct. 28, 1903; s. Charles F. and Myrtle (Caveny) W.; B.S., Juniata Coll., 1927; M.D., Jefferson Med. Coll., 1932; m. Helen C. McCall, Aug. 20, 1931; children—William James, Mary Elinore. Interne Altoona Hosp., Altoona, Pa., 1932-33; engaged in gen. practice at Everett, Pa., 1933-34, at Huntingdon since 1934; asst. in obstetrics and gynecology, J. C. Blair Memorial Hosp., 1935-39, pres. staff since 1939; post grad. study in pediatrics, N.Y. Post Grad. Hosp., N.Y. City, 1935; physician to Juniata Coll.; coroner Huntingdon Co. Served as 1st lt. Med. Res. Corps. Dir. Huntingdon Borough Schs. Mem. Am. Med. Assn., Pa. State Med. Soc., Huntingdon Co. Med. Soc. (pres. 1938), Phi Chi. Republican. Lutheran. K.P. Clubs: Kiwanis, Country. Home: 906 Mifflin St., Huntingdon, Pa.

WEST, W(illiam) Nelson L(oflin), lawyer; b. Phila., Pa., Mar. 19, 1871; s. William Nelson and Mary Pennell (Loflin) W.; student Haverford (Pa.) Coll., 1888-92, U. of Pa. Law Sch., 1892-95; m. Anna Ervina West, June 11, 1898; children—Elinor W. Cary, Wm. Nelson III, Anne Nelson. Admitted to Pa. bar, 1895, and since engaged in gen. practice of law at Phila.; asso. with Rufus E. Shapley and Ellis Ames Ballard, 1894-1914; in practice alone at Phila. since 1914. Mem. Am. Bar Assn., Pa. Bar Assn., Phila Bar Assn., Phila. Hist. Soc., Phila Geog. Soc., Phila Acad. Natural Sciences, Am. Acad. Polit. and Social Sciences, Phi Kappa Sigma. Republican. Home: 240 E. Lancaster Pike, Wynnewood, Pa. Office: 1104 Stock Exchange Bldg., Philadelphia, Pa.

WESTBURGH, Edward Martin, b. Mar. 22, 1899; s. George and Eva (Hoffman) W.; B.S., Wesleyan U., Middletown, Conn., 1922; Ph.D., U. of Edinburgh, 1932; m. Doris Julienne Gidley, Springfield, Mass., Aug. 26, 1926; children —Marcella Titus, Joyce Gidley. Research psychologist dept. mental diseases, Pa. Hosp., Phila., 1922-26, clin. and research psychologist, 1926-29, sr. psychologist dept. mental diseases and Inst. of Pa. Hosp., 1929-32; chief of psychological service since 1932; assistant instructor in psychology, U. of Pa., 1923-26; private practice as psychologist; consultant, Haverford Coll., Devereaux Schs., Agnes Irwin Sch., Carrier Engring. Corpn., RCA Victor Co. of Canada, Supplee Wills Jones, Inc., Philadelphia County Board of Law Examiners; member staff University of Pa. Med. School and Grad. School of Medicine. Dir. Del. County (eastern) Family Welfare Soc. Served in S.A.T.C., 1917. Mem. Brit. Psychol. Soc., Am. Ortho-psychiatric Soc., Am. Assn. Mental Deficiency, Pa. Assn. Clinic Psychologists. Ind. Repub. Club: Union League (Phila.). Author: Introduction to Clinical Psychology, 1937. Contbr. to sci. jours. Home: 82 E. Greenwood Av., Lansdowne, Pa. Office: Institute of Pennsylvania Hospital, 111 N. 49th St., Philadelphia, Pa.

WESTCOTT, Allan Ferguson, educator, writer; b. Alexandria Bay, N.Y., Nov. 22, 1882; s. Wilson Henry and Isabel (Thomson) W.; Ph. B., Brown U., 1903, A.M., 1904; Ph.D., Columbia, 1911; m. Mary Townsend, June 29, 1905 (died 1922); children—Lois Townsend, William Allan, Ruth Isabel; m. 2d, Elizabeth Craven, Aug. 25, 1923; children—Emily Craven, Allan Craven. Instr. English, Brown Univ., 1903-04, Columbia, 1906-11; instr. English, 1911-18, asso. prof., 1918-20, prof. since 1920, U.S. Naval Acad. Spl. duty hist. sect. Office of Naval Intelligence, Washington, summer 1918. Mem. and asst. editor Monthly Proc. of United States Naval Inst. Mem. Soc. Stukely Westcott Desc. America (pres.), Kappa Sigma, Phi Beta Kappa. Democrat. Mem. Dutch Ref. Ch. Author: (with Prof. W. O. Stevens) A History of Sea Power, 1920. Editor: New Poems, by James I of England, 1910 (the original MS. found by the editor in the British Museum); Mahan on Naval Warfare, 1918; Dana's Two Years Before the Mast; Southey's Life of Nelson; Four Centuries of Literature, 1925. Home: 1 Thompson St., Annapolis, Md.

WESTCOTT, John Howell, univ. prof.; b. Phila., Pa., Aug. 3, 1858; s. John Howell and Mary (Dunton) W.; A.B., Princeton, 1887, A.M., 1880, Ph.D., 1887; studied Leipzig, 1877-78, Paris 1878-79; law courses U. of Pa., 1879-81; m. Edith F. Sampson, July 9, 1895 (died Sept. 6, 1905); children—John Howell (dec.) Lilian Vaughan (Mrs. John Quincy Stewart), Mary Dunton (Mrs. H. T. Westbrook); m. 2d, Marian Bate, Mar. 25, 1908. Practiced law at Phila., 1881-85; tutor Latin, 1885-87, prof., 1889-1925, tutor Roman law, 1892-1925, prof. emeritus since 1925, Princeton. Editor: (editions of Latin classics) Livy, Books 1, 21, 22, 1891, 1904; Livy Book 1, selections 21-30, 1924. Fifty Stories from Aulus Gellius, 1893; One Hundred and Twenty Epigrams from Martial, 1894; Selected Letters of Pliny the Younger, 1898; Ceasar's Gallie War, 1902; Suetonius—Julius and Augustus (with E. M. Rankin), 1918. Address: Princeton, N.J.

WESTERMAIER, Francis Victor, engr. street lighting; b. Phila., Pa. Jan. 27, 1881; s. Adolph and Katharine Borell (Rothenhausler) W.; B.S., in M.E., U. of Pa., 1901; m. Arlena A. Hart, Aug. 7, 1907; children—Francis Victor, Jr., Laura Elizabeth. Employed as cadet engr. United Gas Improvement Co., 1901-02; chief engr. United Lighting & Heating Co., 1903-16; chief engr. Welsbach St. Illuminating Co., Phila., 1916-26, v.p. since 1926; Mem. Am. Soc. M.E., Am Gas Assn., A.A. A.S., I.E.S. Honored by award of silver medal at Panama Pacific Expn., 1915. Republican. Presbyterian. Clubs: Racquet, Engineers (Philadelphia); Bankers of America, University of Pa. (New York). Home: 400 Kings Highway E., Haddonfield, N.J. Office: 1500 Walnut St., Philadelphia, Pa.

WESTON, Charles Sidney, banker; b. Carbondale, Pa., Aug. 25, 1860; s. Edward W. and Susan Seeley (Moore) W.; student Granville Mil. Acad., 1876-78; C.E., Rensselaer Poly. Inst., 1882; m. Harriett Grace Storrs, Sept. 2, 1891. Engr. in employ Delaware & Hudson Co., 1882-85; asst. gen. real estate agt. and gen. real estate agt., same, 1885-1904; pres. Cherry River Paper Co., 1909-21; vice-pres. First National Bank, Scranton, Pa., 1912-13, pres., 1913-36, chmn. of the board since, June 30, 1936; chairman board Scranton First Nat. Corpn.; also chmn. of bd. Scranton-Lackawanna Trust Co.; mem. bd. mgrs. D. & H. Co.; dir. Internat. Correspondence Schools, Internat. Ednl. Pub. Co., Internat. Textbook Co., Scranton Correspondence Schools, Woman's Inst. Domestic Arts and Sciences, Technical Supply Co., Wyoming Shovel Works, Consumers Ice Co. (Scranton), Everglades Cypress Co., Scranton Lace Co., Hebard Cypress Co., Cherry River Paper Co., Andrews Hardwood Co., Cherry

River Broom & Lumber Co., D. & H. R.R. Corpn. (mem. exec. com.), N.Y. Lackawanna & Western Ry. Mem. Delta Phi. Republican. Presbyn. Clubs: Scranton, Country (Scranton); Waverly Country (Pennsylvania); Westmoreland (Wilkes-Barre, Pennsylvania); Union League, New York Yacht, Bankers, Railroad, City Midday (New York); Gatineau Rod and Gun (Quebec); Fox Hill Country (Pittston, Pa.); Oakmont Shooting (N.C.). Donor to City of Scranton of Weston Recreation Field and Community House. Home: 624 Monroe Av. Office: First Nat. Bank, Scranton, Pa.

WESTPHAL, Edward Pride, clergyman; b. Lansing, Mich., Dec. 17, 1893; s. Ludwig Waldemar and Callie A. (Pride) W.; A.B., Carroll Coll., 1917, D.D., 1937; B.D., McCormick Theol. Sem. (now Presbyn. Theol. Sem.), Chicago, 1920; A.M., U. of Chicago, 1924; m. Alice Edith Benson, June 4, 1918. Stated supply (while attending coll. and sem.), Chilton, Wis., 1914-16, Mauston, 1916-17, Berkeley, Ill., 1917-20; ordained ministry Presbyn. Ch., 1919 by the Presbyetry of Milwaukee; pastor Fulton, Ill., 1920-25; field rep. Bd. of Christian Edn. of the Presbyn. Ch. U.S.A., in Synod of Neb., 1925-29 (Synod of Ia. added to territory 1927); dir. adult edn. and men's work Bd. of Christian Edn., Presbyn. Ch. U.S.A. since 1929. Mem. Internat. Council of Religious Edn. (mem. ednl. commn.; mem. coms. on religious edn. for adults, family and parent edn., improved uniform lessons), Federal Council of Chs. of Christ in America (vice chmn. com. on marriage and the home). Republican. Author: Through the Bible Day by Day, 1931. Contbr. to religious jours. Home: 6831 Anderson St. Office: Witherspoon Bldg., Philadelphia, Pa.

WETHERILL, Robert, Jr. banking; b. Chester, Pa., Sept. 4, 1895; s. Robert and Mary B. (Gray) W.; student Tome Sch., Port Deposit, Md.; m. Barbara C. Bispham, Nov. 9, 1916; children—Robert 3d, Harrison Bispham, William Gray, Richard 2d, Edward Bispham, Rulon Eyre. Dir. Chester Cambridge Bank and Trust Co., Charleston Transit Co. Republican. Episcopalian. Mason. Clubs: Chester (Chester); Union League (Philadelphia); Seaview Golf (Absecon, N.J.); Springhaven (Wallingford, Pa.). Home: 20th and Providence Av., Chester, Pa.

WETHERILL, Samuel Price, pres. Wetherill Engring. Co., Hyper-Hymus Co.; b. Phila., Pa., 1880; s. Samuel P. and Christine (Northrop) W.; B.S., of Pa., 1903; LL.D., Upsala Coll., East Orange, N.J., 1938; m. Edith Bucknell, June 7, 1902. Pres. Wetherill Engring. Co. (Phila.), Hyper-Hymus Co. Mem. City Parks Assn. (past pres.; mem. bd.); mem. bd. Community Health and Civic Assn.; founder Regional Planning Fed. (past pres.; member exec. com.); mem. Phila. City Planning Commn. (past vice chmn.); mem. Univ. Mus. Trustee Am. Swedish Hist. Mus. Mem. Phila. Art Alliance (hon. pres.), Phila. Forum (gov.), Air Defense League (mem. bd.), Fairmont Park Art Assn. (mem. bd.), Phila. Chamber of Commerce (mem. bd. exec. com.), Phila. Inst. of Architects (hon.), Soc. Automotive Engrs. (past pres. Phila. chapter), Acad. Natural Sciences, Bryn Mawr Memorial and Community Assn., Pa. Acad. Fine Arts, Pa. Houring and Town Planning, Phila. Housing Assn., Playgrounds and Recreation Assn. of America, U.S. Chamber of Commerce, Pa. Museum of Art, Aero Club of Pa., Am. Forestry Assn., Am. Nature Assn., Bur. of Municipal Research, Mil. Order Foreign Wars, Nat. Econ. League, Pa. Parks Assn., Phila. Soc. for Promoting Agr., Soc. for Preservation of Landmarks, Franklin Inst., Am. Acad. Polit. and Social Science, Am. Philos. Soc., Friends of·Wissahickon, Mil. Order Loyal Legion, Nat. Bur. Econ. Research, Nat. Recreation Assn., Wistar Assn., Soc. Colonial Wars, Delta Psi, Sphinx Sr. Soc. Unitarian. Clubs: Union League, Rittenhouse, The Penn (pres., mem. bd.), Contemporary, Merion Cricket, Keystone Automobile, Phila.). Author: Interdependence, 1921; Mutualism; 1934. Holder various patents. Chmn. bd. Phila. Coll. of Pharmacy and Science. Home: 1830 Rittenhouse Sq. Office: Morris Bldg., Philadelphia, Pa.

WETHERILL, William Chattin, dir. student welfare; b. Bethlehem, Pa., Aug. 15, 1886; s. John Price and Alice Davis (Cortright) W.; grad. DeLancy Sch., 1905; B.S. in M.E., U. of Pa., 1910, M.S., 1923, M.E., 1924; m. Isabel Bartow Muller, June 25, 1910; children—W. Chattin, Cynthia, A. Frederic Muller, Isabel, Letitia. Asst. chief Bur. of Water, Phila., 1911-12; factory supt. Wetherill Dye Casting Co., 1912-14; v.p. Keystone Screw Co., 1914-20; asst. prof. mech. engring., U. of Pa., 1920-28; dir. metals utilization in campaign for elimination of industrial waste under Sec. of Commerce, Herbert Hoover, Washington, D.C., 1925-28; Phila. mgr. Washington Steel Form Co., 1928-31, v.p., 1931; dir. student welfare, U. of Pa., since 1931; dir. Goodall Rubber Co. Enlisted U.S. Navy, Aug. 1917; commd. ensign and sent to Mass. Inst. Tech. and subsequently to Curtis Aircraft Corpn., and Standard Aircraft Corpn. to take charge of contract for bldg. 150 flying boats for U.S. Navy; sent to Curtis Aircraft Corpn., Garden City, L.I. where flying boats NC-1, 2, 3 and 4 were built (NC-4 later made first trans-Atlantic flight); sent to Europe with Westervelt Bd. to investigate flying equipment for report to Washington; sent to League Island Navy Yard, Nov. 26, 1918; hon. discharged Feb. 1919. Trustee St. Christopher's Hosp. for Children, Bethesda Sch., Seybert Instn.; vice-pres. Franklin Institute. Member Loyal Legion of U.S., Pennsylvania Society S.R., Psi Upsilon. Republican. Episcopalian (Vestryman St. Paul's Church, Chestnut Hill). Clubs: Rittenhouse, Lenape, Mask and Wig, Contemporary, Sunnybrook Golf, Pohoqualine Fishing Assn. Home: 1673 E. Willow Grove Av., Chestnut Hill, Philadelphia, Pa.

WETJEN, Harry Carl, pres. Surdam & Co.; b. West New York, N.J., Jan. 29, 1895; s. Henry and Emma (Wetzel) W.; ed. Wharton Sch. (U. of Pa.); m. Hilda F. Weissenfluh, Oct. 11, 1919. Office boy and runner in bank, New York, 1910-11; bookkeeper and salesman elec. supplies, 1911-19; began as gen. office man Surdam & Co., securities, 1919, later becoming salesman and trader, dir. since 1925, v.p., 1929-36, pres. since 1936. Served as private Co. G, 316th Inf., U.S. Army, during World War, participating in St. Mihiel and Argonne offensives, wounded, 1918. Decorated Order of Purple Heart (U.S.). Mem. Scranton Community Chest. Mem. Am. Legion, Scranton Chamber of Commerce. Club: Lake Wallenpaupack Yacht. Home: 1632 Sanderson Av. Office: Mears Bldg., Scranton, Pa.

WETMORE, Edward Ditmars, corpn. official; b. Warren, Pa., Jan. 4, 1861; s. Lansing Ditmars and Maria (Shattuck) W.; B.S., Lafayette Coll., 1882; LL.D., Columbia, 1884; m. Helen Davenport, July 9, 1888 (died 1906); children —Beatrice Davenport (Mrs. D. Bryant Turner, now deceased), Rachel Weatherbee (dec.), Alice Cynthia (Mrs. Maurice R. Brann); m. 2d, Ella Leech, of Erie, Pa., Oct. 1, 1907. Admitted to Pa. bar, 1885; mgr. Wetmore Lumber Co., 1885-1909; pres. Warren Trust Co., 1912-24; chmn. of bd. Warren Bank & Trust Co. 1934-37; pres. Kinzua Lumber Co. since 1909, Kinzua Pine Mills Co. since 1927, Condon, Kinzua & Southern R.R. Co. since 1928, Wallowa Timber Co. since 1907, Tionesta Timber Co. since 1921; vice-pres. Pa. Gas Co.; chmn. bd. of trustees Struthers Library Bldg.; mem. bd. Warren Gen. Hosp., Warren Library Assn. Mem. Sigma Chi. Clubs: Conewango, Conewango Valley Country (Warren, Pa.); Santa Barbara (Santa Barbara, Calif.). Home: The Pines, Wetmore Farm, Warren. Office: 209 2d Av., Warren, Pa.

WETTACH, Charles Daniel, retired; b. Pittsburgh, Pa., Aug. 31, 1868; s. Chris and Elizabeth (Dellenbach) W.; B.S., U. of Pittsburgh, 1897; m. Louise Marie Mueller, Mar. 15, 1909; 1 son, William. Associated with W. W. Lawrence and Co., Inc., Pittsburgh, during active career, treas. and v.p., 1897-1916, pres., 1916-36, retired, 1936; dir. Pitt Nat. Bank; mem. bd. mgrs. Allegheny Co. Workhouse. Mem. City Council, N. S. Pittsburgh, 1903-06. Chmn. athletic council U. of Pittsburgh, 1925-38. Mem. Chamber of Commerce; founder, 1912, Alpha Kappa Psi, pres. 1912-14; pres. Nat. Paint, Oil & Varnish Assn., 1905-06. Republican. Clubs: Duquesne, University (Pittsburgh). Home: 6337 Walnut St., Pittsburgh, Pa.

WETTER, Charles Hart, lawyer; b. Phila., Pa., Apr. 21, 1889; s. Charles Griswold and Ann Mary (Lenny) W.; grad. Friends' Central Sch., Phila., 1906; A.B., Swarthmore Coll., 1909; LL.B., U. of Pa., 1912; m. Helen F. Brookfield, Nov. 4, 1925. Admitted to Pa. bar, 1913, and since in gen. practice in Phila. Served in Plattsburg, R.O.T.C., 1915; with 1st Troop, Phila. City Cav., Mexican Border Service, 1916; R.O.T.C., Ft. Niagara, 1917; commd. 2d lt. F.A., U.S. Army, 1917; capt., A.E.F., 1917-19. Hon. mem. First City Troop of Phila.; mem. Phi Kappa Psi, Phi Delta Phi. Republican. Presbyterian. Clubs: Merion Cricket (Haverford); Union League (Phila.). Home: Pembroke Rd., Bryn Mawr, Pa. Office: 1500 Walnut St., Philadelphia, Pa.

WETZEL, Walter, funeral dir.; b. Phila., Pa., Apr. 11, 1881; s. John Henry, Sr., and Caroline (Schadewald) W.; student pub. schs. and Pierce Bus. Coll.; studied embalming with H. S. Eckel & Co.; m. Amelia Elizabeth Newman, June 23, 1883; children—Walter Frederick, Alvin Frederick, Pearl Anna. Associated with Wetzel & Son, Inc., as pres. and treas. since 1925; dir. Wyoming Bank & Trust Co. Republican. Seventh Day Adventist. Mason. Home: 6902 Rising Sun Av. Office: 4710-12 N. 5th St., and 2328-30 Germantown Av., Philadelphia, Pa.

WETZEL, William Enos, investments; b. Pen Argyl, Pa., July 24, 1900; s. William A. and Velma (Wieand) W.; A.B., Wesleyan U., Middletown, Conn., 1921; married. President First Nat. Co. of Trenton; proprietor W. E. Wetzel & Co.; dir. Trenton Saving Fund Soc. Served in U.S.N. R.F., 1918-21. Member State Committee Y.M.C.A. Member Delta Kappa Epsilon, Phi Beta Kappa. Presbyterian. Home: 102 Buckingham Av. Office: 1 W. State St., Trenton, N.J.

WEYER, Edward Moffat, prof. philosophy; b. Portsmouth, O., Oct. 1, 1872; s. George W. and Mary Letitia (Marshall) W.; U. of Wis., 1891-93; B.A., Yale, 1895; Ph.D., U. of Leipzig, 1898; m. Julia Morris Ross, July 25, 1900 (died 1911); children—Elliott Ross, Edward Moffat; m. 2d, Mary Rodes Christie, Apr. 10, 1924. Prof. philosophy or psychology, Washington and Jefferson Coll., 1899—, and dean of the coll., dir. extension work, and prof. philosophy, 1922-30, dean and prof. of philosophy, 1930-35, dean of faculty and prof. philosophy since 1936. American Psychol. Assn., Am. Philos. Assn., Phi Delta Theta. Contbr. on philos. and psychol. topics to Internat. Journal of Ethics, Forum, Yale Review, Psychol. Review, etc. Republican. Presbyn. Home: Washington, Pa.

WEYFORTH, William Oswald, univ. prof.; b. Baltimore, Md., Sept. 1, 1889; s. William Oswald and Emma (Oberheim) W.; A.B., Johns Hopkins U., 1912, Ph.D., 1915; unmarried. Instr. polit. economy, Western Res. U., Cleveland, O., 1915-17; asso. in polit. economy, Johns Hopkins U., Baltimore, Md., 1919-22, asso. prof. polit. economy since 1922. Mem. Am. Econ. Assn., Am. Statis. Assn., Delta Upsilon, Delta Sigma Pi, Phi Beta Kappa. Lutheran. Club: Johns Hopkins (Baltimore). Author: The Organizability of Labor, 1917; The Federal Reserve Board, 1933. Home: 104 Thicket Rd., Baltimore, Md.

WEYGANDT, Cornelius, college prof.; b. Germantown, Phila., Dec. 13, 1871; s. Cornelius N. and Lucy E. (Thomas) W.; Germantown Acad., 1882-87; A.B., Univ. of Pa., 1891, Ph.D., 1901, Litt.D., 1931; Litt.D., Franklin and Marshall, 1930; LL.D., Susquehanna University, 1933; m. Sara Matlack Roberts, June 19, 1900; children—Cornelius N., Ann Matlack. Engaged in newspaper work with Phila. Record and Phila. Evening Telegraph, 1892-97; instr. English, 1897-1904, asst. prof., 1904-07, prof., 1907—, U. of Pa. Mem. Modern Lang. Assn. America, Am. Ornithologists' Union, Del. Valley Ornithological Club. Club: Franklin Inn (Phila.). Author: Irish Plays and Playwrights, 1913; A Century of the English Novel, 1925; Tuesdays at Ten, 1928; The Red Hills, 1929; The Wissahickon Hills, 1930; A Passing America, 1932; The White Hills, 1934; The Time of Tennyson, 1936; The Blue Hills, 1936; The Time of Yeats, 1937; New Hampshire Neighbors, 1937; Philadelphia Folks, 1938. Home: Wissahickon Av., Germantown, Philadelphia, Pa.

WEYL, Carrie Stein (Mrs. Maurice N. Weyl); b. Phila., Pa., July 7, 1870; d. Charles and Fannie (Kaufman) Stein; student pub. schs. and extension courses; m. Maurice N. Weyl, June 7, 1894 (dec.); children—Charles, Edward Stern. Devotes considerable time to peace movement and study of fgn. policy and internat. affairs; vice-pres. and chmn. govt. and fgn. policy of Phila. Co. League of Women Voters since 1930; mem. bd. and chmn. govt. and fgn. policy, Pa. League of Women Voters; mem. nat. exec. com. of Com. on Cause and Cure of War, 1935-39, also mem. Pan-Am. Commn., same, and delegate to all conferences; vice-chairman Eastern Pa. Com. on Cause and Cure of War; mem. exec. com. Pa. Branch, League of Nations Assn.; chmn. International Relations and mem. exec. com. Phila. Federation of Women's Clubs and Allied Orgns.; conducts study groups for three orgns. on international relations; v.p. Phila. Sect., Nat. Council of Jewish Women, 1928-36, now hon. vice chmn. and chmn. com. internat. relations, also mem. nat. steering com. on internat. relations. Mem. Am. Acad. Polit. and Social Science, Foreign Policy Assn. Jewish religion. Home: 6506 Lincoln Drive, Philadelphia, Pa.

WEYL, Charles, elec. engring.; b. Phila., Pa., May 22, 1896; s. Maurice N. and Carrie (Stein) W.; B.S. in E.E., U. of Pa., 1917, (hon.) M.S., 1927; m. Elinor Gittelson, Apr. 28, 1920; children—Elinor Jean, Doris Ann. Employed as apprentice elec. engr., Bell Telephone Co., 1917; instr. elec. engring., U. of Pa., 1920-25, asst. prof., 1925-36, asso. prof., 1936-37, prof. since 1937; asst. prof. radiol. physics, U. of Pa. Grad. Sch. of Medicine since 1938; cons. engr. on own acct., 1920-36; dir. and cons. engr. Internat. Resistance Co. elect. mfrs. since 1928; pres. Edward Stern & Co., Inc., printers and pubs., since 1936. Served as ensign, U.S.N.R.F., 1918-19. Dir. Moore Sch. X-Ray Lab. U. of Pa. Mcm. A.A.A.S., Am. Inst. E.E., Franklin Inst. Awarded Franklin Inst. Longstreth Medal, 1930. Co-author (with S. Reid Warren Jr.): Apparatus and Technique for Roentgenography of the Chest, 1935; contbr. many tech. papers on x-ray, acoustics and related tech. subjects. Home: 255 Harvey St. Office: 200 S. 33d St., Philadelphia, Pa.

WEYL, Hermann, mathematics; b. Elmshorn, Germany, Nov. 9, 1885; s. Ludwig and Anna (Dieck) W.; ed. univ. of Munich and Göttingen; Ph.D., Göttingen, 1908; hon. Dr. Philosophy, U. of Oslo, 1929; hon. Dr. Technology, Hochschule, Stuttgart, 1929; m. Helene Joseph, Sept. 1, 1913; children—Fritz Joachim, Michael. Privatdozent U. of Göttingen, 1910-13; prof. mathematics Tech. Hochschule, Zürich, 1913-30; Jones research prof. in mathematics, Princeton, 1928-29; prof. mathematics, U. of Göttingen, 1930-33; prof. mathematics Inst. for Advanced Study, Princeton, since Dec. 1, 1933. Mem. Am. Acad. Arts and Sciences, Am. Philos. Soc. Am. Math. Soc., and mem. or hon. mem. various European socs. Awarded Lobatschefsky prize, Kazan, 1925. Research work in differential equations, topology, relativity theory, infinitesimal geometry, group theory, philosophy of mathematics, etc. Author of 7 books pub. in Europe, and 3 books pub. in U.S.—The Open World, 1932; Mind and Nature, 1934; The Classical Group, 1939; also articles in mags. Home: 270 Mercer St., Princeton, N.J.

WEYL, Woldemar Anatol, coll. prof.; b. Darmstadt, Germany, June 13, 1901; s. Wladimir and Auguste (Blech) W.; came to U.S., 1937; Diplomingeniuer, Darmstadt Technische Hochschule, 1924; Dr. Ing., Aachen Tech. Hochsch., 1931; m. Ilse Rudow, Oct. 29, 1936; 1 dau., Karin Gisela. Research asst. in Kaiser Wilhelm Inst. for silicate research, Berlin-Dahlem, Germany, later head of the dept. of glass research, 1926-37; visiting prof. in U.S.A., 1937; prof. glass technology, Pa. State Coll. since 1938. Mem. Am. Ceramic Soc., various German socs., Sigma Xi. Home: 38 Orlando Apts., State College, Pa.

WEYMOUTH, George Tyler, investment broker; b. Garden City, N.Y., Dec. 4, 1904; s. Clarence Andrew and Margaret (Tyler) W.; student Montgomery Sch., Wynnewood, Pa., 1920-24; B.S., Yale, 1929; m. Deo du Pont, Sept. 27, 1930; children—Eugene Eleuthere du Pont, Patricia Bradford, George Tyler, Jr. Efficiency engr. Phila. Rubber Works, Oaks, Pa., 1929, asst. supt., 1929-30; mgr. investment trust dept. Laird, Bissel & Meeds, Wilmington, Del., 1930-32; organized Laird & Co., investment brokers, Wilmington, Del., 1932, and since managing partner. Purchased seat on N.Y. Stock Exchange, 1932; dir. Del. Trust Co. Chmn. finance com. Rep. State Com. since 1936; treas. Del. State Relief Com., 1932-33. Trustee Montgomery Sch., Wynnewood, Pa. Mem. Chamber of Commerce (dir.), Del. Steeple Chase Race Assn. (dir.), Del. Turf Club (dir.), St. Anthony Hall (Yale). Republican. Episcopalian. Clubs: Wilmington, Vicmead Hunt (treas. since 1937, gov. since 1937), Wilmington Country (Wilmington, Del.); Yale, Bankers, The Hangar (New York); Fox Catcher Farms Hunt (Fairhill, Md.). Home: Greenville, Del. Office: Nemours Bldg., Wilmington, Del.

WHALEN, Will Wilfrid, clergyman, author; b. nr. Mt. Carmel, Pa., May 7, 1886; s. Michael J. and Alice (Debo) W.; ed. St. Charles Sem., Overbrook, Pa., and Mt. St. Mary's Coll., Emmitsburg, Md. Served as singer and actor; writer and collaborator of plays; ordained priest R.C. Ch., 1911. Author: The Celibate Father, 1927; The Golden Squaw (the story of Mary Jemison), 3d edit., 1928; Give Me a Chance!, 1929; Co-Stars—Cecil Spooner and Oscar Wilde, 1930; also Twilight Talks to Quiet Hearts; The Ex-Seminarian; The Girl from Mine Run; The Forbidden Man; The Girl Who Fought; The Ex-Nun; (published plays) Scandal's Lash; What Priests Never Tell; The Irish Sparrow. Home: Orrtanna, Pa.

WHALEY, George P., oil producer; b. Chesterfield, Ill., Sept. 25, 1870; s. George W. and Elizabeth (Adderly) W.; ed. high sch., Emporia, Kan.; unmarried. Began with Standard Oil Co., Pittsburgh, Pa., 1889; mem. lubricating sales com., Standard Oil Co. of N.J., 1895-1907; dir. Vacuum Oil Co., 1903-07, v.p., 1907-24, pres., 1924-30; retired from active business. Republican. Episcopalian. Clubs: Metropolitan, Recess, Lawyers, Church; Essex County (N..J) Country; Short Hills (N.J.) Country; Rolling Rock Country (Ligonier, Pa.). Home: Short Hills, N.J.

WHALLON, Walter Lowrie, clergyman; b. Vincennes, Ind., Sept. 23, 1878; s. Edward P. (Rev. Dr.) and Margaret Ellen (Kitchell) W.; A.B., Hanover (Ind.) Coll., 1899, A.M., 1903, D.D., 1916; grad. Princeton Theol. Sem., 1903; m. Irene Snyder, Oct. 26, 1905; children—Edward Valentine, John Montgomery. Ordained ministry Presbyn. Ch. U.S.A., 1903; pastor Broad Av. Ch., Altoona, Pa. 1903-10, Central Ch., Zanesville, O., 1910-25, Roseville Av. Ch., Newark, N.J., since 1925; exchange preacher in London and England, 1928. Mem. Permanent Jud. Commn. of Presbyn. Ch., 1916-19; moderator Synod of Ohio, 1922; mem. Gen. Assembly's Com. on Princeton Theol. Sem., 1926-28; mem. bd. mgrs. and v.p. Lord's Day Alliance of U.S.; mem. bd. of Foreign Missions Presbyn. Ch., U.S.A. Trustee Coll. of Wooster (O.), 1916-25, Princeton and Bloomfield Theol. sems., Presbyn. Hosp., Newark. Mem. Princeton Theol. Sem. Alumni Assn. of N.Y. City and Vicinity (pres. 1927-28), S.A.R., Beta Theta Pi, Pi Gamma Mu. Mason (K.T.); Grand Chaplain Masonic Grand Lodge of N.J., 1931-32. Home: 30 Roseville Av., Newark, N.J.

WHARTON, Lawrence Richardson, surgeon; b. Harda, India, Oct. 11, 1887; s. Greene Lawrence and Emma Virginia (Richardson) W. (citizens of U.S.A.); Ph.B., Hiram Coll., Hiram, O., 1907; M.D., Johns Hopkins Med. Sch., 1915; m. Louise Wallace Hazelhurst, Jan. 10, 1922; children—Lawrence Richardson, Jr., Blagden Hazelhurst, John Gill. Interne Johns Hopkins Hosp., asst. resident and resident gynecologist, 1915-21; asso. in gynecology and asst. attending gynecologist, Johns Hopkins Hosp.; consulting gynecologist, Union Memorial, Women's of Md., Church Home, Sinai, and Provident hosps. Served as 1st lt. to capt. Med. Corps, U.S.A., 1917-19 with A.E.F. Mem. A.M.A., Am. Urol. Assn., Southern Med. Assn., Phi Beta Kappa. Episcopalian. Club: Maryland. Home: 4504 Roland Av. Office: 1201 N. Calvert St., Baltimore, Md.

WHEAT, Harry Grove, univ. prof.; b. Berkeley Springs, W.Va., Apr. 8, 1890; s. Alfred Asbury and Tamson Bell (Shockey) W.; A.B., W.Va. Univ., 1912; A.M., U. of Chicago, 1917; Ph.D., Columbia U., 1929; m. Florence Bodey, Aug. 20, 1919; 1 dau., Mary Eleanor. Engaged in teaching, high sch., Davis, W.Va., 1912-13; supt. schs., Williamstown, W.Va., 1913-16; instr. in edn., State Normal Sch., Glenville, W.Va., 1917, 1919-24; instr. in edn., State Teachers Coll., Milwaukee, Wis., 1924-25; prof. edn., Marshall Coll., Huntington, W.Va., 1925-35; prof. edn., W.Va. Univ., Morgantown, W.Va., since 1935. Served in F.A., U.S.A., 1918-19 with A.E.F.; grad. Saumur Arty. Sch, France, 1919. Mem. Nat. Edn. Assn., W.Va. State Edn. Assn., Am. Edn. Research Assn., Nat. Soc. for Study of Edn., Phi Beta Kappa, Phi Delta Kappa, Sigma Phi Epsilon. Republican. Methodist. Mason. Kiwanis. Author: The Teaching of Reading, 1923; The Relative Merits of Arithmetic Problems, 1929; The Psychology of the Elementary School, 1931; The Psychology and Teaching of Arithmetic, 1937; Wheat Practice Books for Arithmetic, 1936. Co-author (with R. L. Jones), Jones-Wheat Arithmetic, 1935. Home: 252 Park St., Morgantown, W.Va.

WHEATLEY, H. Winship, lawyer; b. Washington, D.C., Feb. 14, 1882; s. Joseph and Emma Phillippa (Taylor) W.; grad. Nat. Univ. Law Sch., Washington, D.C., 1903; m. Emma L. Kehoe, July 3, 1907; children—H. Winship, Jr., Joseph Matthew (dec.), Albert Paul, Francis Ira, Rosemary, Margaret Mary. Admitted to D.C. bar, 1903 and since engaged in gen. practice of law at Washington, also admitted to Md. bar, 1912 and in practice at Hyattsville since 1912, prof. law, Nat. Univ. Law Sch., Washington, D.C., since 1916; chem. local adv. com. for D.C. federal rules of civil procedure; chmn. com. on local rules civil procedure dist. ct. of U.S. for D.C., 1938. Mem. adv. bd. Notre Dame Coll. of Md., Baltimore, Md. Mem. Am., D.C., Md. State bar assns., Prince Georges Co. Bar Assn., Bar Assn. of Dist. of Columbia (former pres.). Democrat. Roman Catholic. Clubs: University, Corinthian Yacht (Washington); Gibson Island (Gibson Island, Md.). Home: Hyattsville, Md. Office: 1010 Vermont Av. N.W., Washington, D.C.; also 120 Maryland Av., Hyattsville, Md.

WHEATLEY, William Alonzo, educator; b. Verona, N.Y., Feb. 28, 1869; s. William and Lottie (Fry) W.; A.B., Syracuse U., 1894, A.M., 1897; Yale, 1904-05, 1911-12; m. Mabel Ballantine, Aug. 8, 1901; children—William Ballantine, Esther Mabel, John Carol. Principal Minoa (N.Y.) Grammar Sch., 1894; v-prin. East Syracuse (N.Y.) High Sch., 1895; prin. Andes (N.Y.) High Sch., 1896-97, Syracuse U. Prep. Sch., 1898-99, Chester (N.Y.) High Sch., 1900-04; supt. schs., Fairfield Conn., 1905, towns of Fairfield and Branford, Conn., 1906-10; prin. City High Sch., and supt. schs., Middletown, Conn., 1910-17; rep. War Camp Community Service, 1917-20; teacher Hartford (Conn.) High School, 1921-23; head of dept. of edn., State Teachers Coll., Edinboro, Pa., 1923-1936, dean of instruction since 1936. Organized community recreation for soldiers of Camp Greene, Charlotte, North Carolina. Member N.E.A. Commn. on the Reorganization of Secondary Edn., Phi Kappa Psi, Phi Beta Kappa, etc. Republican. Conglist. Author: German Declensions Made Easy for Beginners, 1895; (with Enoch B. Gowin) Occupations, a Text-book in Vocational Guidance,

1916; The Good Citizen, Sticking to the Main Issue, 1920; Teaching Aptitude Tests, 1927; (with Royce R. Mallory) Building Character and Personality, a Text-book in Orientation, 1936. Home: Edinboro, Pa.

WHEATON, Warren William, pub. relations; b. Brooklyn, N. Y., Nov. 14, 1892; s. Warren William and Catherine (Blayney) W.; ed. high sch., Albany, N.Y., Cathedral Acad. and Rensselaer Polytechnic Institute (non-graduate); m. Margaret Coyle, 1914; 1 dau., Marjorie; m. 2d, Anne Williams, Feb. 19, 1926. Began as reporter Albany Argus, 1914; then with Knickerbocker Press and New York Times; later with Internat. News Service, Washington. D.C.; Washington corr. Public-Ledger, Phila., 1924-34; dir. pub. relations Rep. Nat. Com. and Rep. Congl. and Senatorial campaign coms., 1934-37; dir. pub. relations Phila. Rep. Central Campaign Com. and Rep. State Com. since 1937. Clubs: National Press, Columbia Country, Burning Tree, Gridiron. Home: Alden Park Manor, Germantown, Pa. Address: Market St. Nat. Bank Bldg., Philadelphia, Pa.

WHEELER, Anna Pell (Mrs. Arthur L. Wheeler), mathematician; b. Hawarden, Ia., May 5, 1883; d. Andrew Gustav and Amelia (Frieberg) Johnson; A.B., U. of S.D., 1903; A.M., Radcliffe Coll., 1905; Göttingen, 1906-07; Ph.D., University of Chicago, 1910; hon. Sc.D., New Jersey College, 1932, and Mt. Holyoke College, 1937; m. Alexander Pell, July 19, 1907 (died 1921); m. 2d, Arthur L. Wheeler, July 6, 1925 (died 1932). Inst. mathematics, Mt. Holyoke Coll., 1911-14, asso. prof., 1914-18; asso. prof. mathematics, Bryn Mawr Coll., 1918-25; prof., 1925-26, non-resident prof., 1927-32, prof. since 1932. Mem. Am. Math. Soc., A.A.A.S., Sigma Xi. Contbr. to math. jours. Home: Bryn Mawr, Pa.

WHEELER, Frederic Collins, v.p. Fidelity-Philadelphia Trust Co.; b. Philadelphia, Pa., Mar. 30, 1894; s. Samuel Bowman and Laetitia Collins (Hulse) W.; ed. Protestant Episcopal Acad. (Philadelphia), St. Paul's Sch. (Concord, N.H.) and Yale U.; m. Leslie A. McCarten, Oct. 31, 1919; children—Arthur Ledlie, Frederic Collins. Mgr. Philadelphia office, Robins Conveying Belt Co., 1920-24, asst. gen. sales mgr., 1924-26; v.p. and gen. mgr. Mirkil, Valdes & Co., 1926-36; v.p. Fidelity-Philadelphia Trust Co. since 1936. First lt. First Troop, Philadelphia City Cavalry (transferred to honorary roll June 4, 1937). Home: 408 Mill Road, Wynnewood, Pa. Office: 135 S. Broad St., Philadelphia, Pa.

WHEELER, Herbert Eugene, advertising agency; b. Phila., Pa., June 17, 1884; s. Richard Isaac and Mary (Galbraith) W.; student pub. schs., Phila. Bus. Coll., 1902-04, Wharton Sch., of U. of Pa., evening dept., 1904-07; Temple U. Law Sch., Phila., 1907-08; m. Edna Virginia Morozzi, Sept. 14, 1912; 1 son, Herbert Eugene. Asso. with N.W. Ayer & Son, Inc., advertising agency, Phila., Pa. continuously since 1897, v.p. and treas. since 1936; dir. American Type Founders, Inc. Republican. Presbyterian. Clubs: Union League, Down Town, Rotary (Phila.); Aronimink Golf. Home: 441 S. 48th St. Office: 210 W. Washington Sq., Philadelphia, Pa.

WHEELER, Homer Jay, agrl. chemist; b. Bolton, Mass., Sept. 2, 1861; s. Jesse Brown and Martha Ann (Sykes) W.; B.S. from Mass. Agrl. Coll., also from Boston, University, 1883; A.M., Ph.D., University of Göttingen, 1889; Sc.D., Brown University, 1911; D.Sc., Massachusetts State Coll., 1933; m. at Brooklyn, Frieda H. F. Ruprecht, May 15, 1891; children—Carl Otto Jordan, William Edwin, Roland Arthur. Asst. chemist, Mass. Agrl. Expt. Sta., 1883-87; chief chemist, R.I. Agrl. Expt. Sta., 1889-1905, dir. and agronomist, agrl. expt. sta., Sept. 1, 1901-12, acting pres., 1902-03, prof. geology, 1893-1912, and agrl. chemistry, 1903-07, R.I. State Coll.; resigned as dir. agrl. expt. sta., 1912; chief agronomist The Am. Agrl. Chem. Co., until Dec. 1931. Ex-pres. Assn. Official Agrl. Chemists U.S.; mem. Am. Chem. Soc., A.A.A.S, Am. Geog. Soc., Am. Soc. Agronomy (ex-pres.). Author: Manures and Fertilizers; Citrus Culture in Florida; Citrus Culture in California. Chmn. during the World War of sub-com. on soils and fertilizers of Nat. Research Council. Home: 386 N. Fullerton Av., Upper Montclair, N.J.

WHEELER, Janet, portrait painter; b. Detroit, Mich.; d. Orlando B. and Amanda M. (Bennett) W.; pupil Pa. Acad. Fine Arts; Julian Acad. and Courtois, Paris, France. Has exhibited at Salon, Paris, and in all principal Am. exhbns. Awarded 1st Toppan prize, and Mary Smith prize, both Pa. Acad. Fine Arts; gold medal, Art Club, Phila.; silver medal, St. Louis Expn., 1904. Mem. bd. dirs. Fellowship of Pa. Acad. Fine Arts; mem. Federation of Arts (Washington), Art Alliance (Philadelphia), Soc. of the History of Art (Paris). Clubs: Cosmopolitan (bd. govs.), Plastic of Phila. (v.p.); Lyceum, Am. Woman's (London). Home: The Barclay, E. Rittenhouse Sq. Philadelphia, Pa.

WHEELER, John Franklin, pres. Pioneer Dime Bank; b. Pleasant Mount, Pa., July 23, 1858; s. Chauncey C. and Ann M. (Spencer) W.; student Common Sch.; married, Oct. 20, 1888; children—Paul, Malcolm, Catherine. Successively as office boy, clerk and accountant in supt's. office, 1871-1903; cashier Pioneer Dime Bank, Carbondale, Pa., 1903-23, pres. since 1924. Home: 70 Spring St. Office: 27 N. Main St., Carbondale, Pa.

WHEELER, Joseph Lewis, librarian; b. Dorchester, Mass., Mar. 16, 1884; s. Rev. George Stevens and Mary Jane (Draffin) W.; Ph.B., Brown U., 1906 (class of '73 prize), M.A., 1907; B.L.S., N.Y. State Library School, 1909, M.L.S., 1925; Litt.D., U. of Md., 1934, Brown Univ., 1936; m. Mabel Archibald, Oct. 20, 1910; children—John Archibald, Joseph Towne, Robert Reid, Mary Bethel. Asst. Providence Pub. Library and Brown U. Library, 1902-07; asst. librarian Pub. Library, Washington, D.C., 1909-11; librarian Jacksonville (Fla.) Pub. Library, 1911-12; asst. librarian Los Angeles Pub. Library, 1912-15; librarian Youngstown (O.) Pub. Library, 1915-26; librarian Enoch Pratt Free Library, Baltimore, since 1926. Mem. Md. Library Commn. Dir. A.L.A. exhibits, San Francisco and Phila. expns.; camp library dir., 1917-18. Trustee Peale Mus., Md. Acad. Sci. Pres. Ohio Library Assn., 1921; mem. A.L.A. (v.p. 1926-27; exec. bd. 1929-33; bd. of edn. for librarianship 1931-36), Am. Library Inst., Bibliog. Soc. America, N.E. A., Am. Sociol. Soc., Am. Hist. Assn., Am. Council on Edn., Nat. Council Social Studies, Maryland Historical Soc., Maryland Academy of Sciences; fellow A.A.A.S. (council). Member White House Conf. on Child Health, also on Housing. Clubs: Rotary, Torch (pres.). Author: The Library and the Community, 1924; (with others) My Maryland (sch. textbook), 1934. Editor series of science booklists for A.A.A.S., 1929-34 (one million distributed). Advisory editor Library Quarterly. Contbr. to mags. and Dictionary of Am. Biography. Recipient of Baltimore civic award in art and lit. for 1933. Del. 2d Internat. Library Congress, Madrid, 1935. Address: Enoch Pratt Free Library, Baltimore, Md.

WHEELER, William Archie, marketing specialist; b. Stockton, Minn., June 28, 1876; s. Charles Adams and Sylvia Maria (Allen) W.; B.Agr., U. of Minn., 1900, M.S., 1901; m. Harriet Maria Alden, June 3, 1901; children—Harold Alden, Helen, Margaret, Catherine, Harriet. Instr. botany, U. of Minn., 1898-1903; prof. botany and head of dept., S.D. State Coll., 1903-07; sec. and mgr. Dak. Improved Seed Co., Mitchell, 1907-16; specialist in charge seed marketing, Bur. of Markets, U.S. Dept. Agr., 1916-19; in charge marketing information, same bur., 1920-22; chief hay, feed and seed div., Bur. of Agrl. Economics, 1922—. Commd. by Sec. of Agr. Houston to investigate and report on seed conditions in Europe immediately following signing of Armistice, 1919-20; initiated and supervised the publication by the U.S. Dept. Agr., The Seed Reporter, 1918-19, and The Market Reporter, 1920-21; initiated and developed the field of broadcasting of official federal and state crop and market reports to agrl. interests by radio, 1920-21; U.S. Dept. Agr. rep. on Nat. Radio Service Commn.; apptd. by Secretary Wallace and P.M. General Hays to investigate use of radio for broadcasting information, 1921-22; rep. of U.S. Dept. of Agr. on 1st, 2d, 3d and 4th Nat. Radio confs., 1922-25. V.p. Nat. Corn Assn., 1908-11; mem. Nat. Assn. Marketing Officials, Am. Farm Economics Assn., Seed Council of North America, Internat. Crop Improvement Assn., Sigma Xi. Republican. Unitarian. Home: 5616 Grove St., Chevy Chase, Md.

WHEELWRIGHT, Robert, landscape architect; b. Jamaica Plain (Boston), Mass., Feb. 20, 1884; s. George William and Sophia Elizabeth (Bond) W.; grad. Hill Sch., Pottstown, Pennsylvania, 1902; A.B., Harvard, 1906, M.L.A., 1908; m. Attaresta Barclay Moon (nee De Silver), Nov. 6, 1920 (died 1933); m. 2d, Louise Nichols Goodin, Mar. 27, 1935 (divorced Jan. 1937); m. 3d, Ellen C. du Pont Meeds, Oct. 7, 1937. In New York office of Wilson Eyre, architect of Philadelphia, 1909-10; entered office of Charles Downing Lay, landscape architect, New York, 1910; mem. firm Lay & Wheelwright, 1916; called to Washington, D.C., June 1917, to work as war camp planner, and planned Camp Dodge (Des Moines), Camp Merritt (Tenafly, N.J.), and replanned Camp Mills (Garden City, L.I.) for wooden construction; discharged from service, Jan. 1, 1919; practiced alone in N.Y. City, 1919-20, Phila., 1920-26; mem. firm Wheelwright & Stevenson, Phila., since 1926; prof. landscape architecture, U. of Pa., since 1924. A founder, and editor Landscape Architecture, 1910-20. Mem. Am. Soc. Landscape Architects, Am. Civic Assn., Sigma Xi. Democrat. Unitarian. Clubs: Harvard, Century Assn. (New York). Home: Goodstay, Wilmington, Del. Office: 225 S. 15th St., Philadelphia, Pa.

WHELAN, George Leo, M.D.; b. Chicago, Ill., Apr. 27, 1900; s. Wm. Francis and Margaret (Goldric) W.; student LaSalle Sch., Chicago, 1904-14; M.D., U. of Pa., 1921, M.Sc. in medicine, 1925; unmarried. Interne St. Agnes Hosp., 1921, Phila. Gen. Hosp., 1923; engaged in practice of medicine at Phila., Pa., since 1926, specializing in diseases of ear, nose and throat; mem. staff Philadelphia Gen. Hosp., Eagleville Sanatorium, Rush Hosp. Fellow Phila. Coll. Phys.; mem. A.M.A., Pan-Am. and Phila. County med. socs., Am. Acad. Otolaryngology, Am. Laryngol., Rhinol. and Otol. Soc., Phila. Laryngol. Soc. Roman Catholic. Home: 2100 Walnut St., Philadelphia, Pa.

WHELEN, John Howard, Jr., securities broker; b. Phila., Pa., Apr. 4, 1897; s. John Howard and Josephine (Porter) W.; student P.E. Acad. of Phila., Hill Sch., Pottstown, Pa.; A.B., Princeton, 1921; married Alice Bennett, Feb. 10, 1933; children—William Ellison, Alexandra Porter. Partner Carstairs & Co., brokers and mems. various exchanges, Phila., since 1927, mem. firm since 1929; pres. and dir. Pa. Share Co.; dir. Fairmount Park Transit Co., John B. Ellisons & Sons Co., Inc. Served as ensign U.S.N. R.F. during World War. Treas. and dir. Geog. Soc. of Phila. Mem. Ivy Club, Princeton. Republican. Episcopalian. Mason (32°, Shriner). Clubs: Racquet, Gun (Phila.). Home: 1834 Delancey St. Office: 1421 Chestnut St., Philadelphia, Pa.

WHERRETT, Harry Scott, plate glass mfr.; b. Connersville, Ind., Oct. 24, 1876; s. William Henry and Belle Jane (Scott) W.; grad. high sch., Kokomo, Ind., 1891; m. Mary Amy Sprague, Sept. 2, 1907. Began as jr. clk., Diamond Plate Glass Co., Kokomo, 1891; clk., sales dept. Pittsburgh Plate Glass Co., 1896-1901, asst. sales mgr., 1901-05, sales mgr., 1905-17, chmn. commercial dept., 1916-20, v.p., 1920-28, pres. since 1928; v.p. Southern Alkali Corpn.; dir. Columbia Alkali Corpn., Ditzler Color Co., Westinghouse Elec. & Mfg. Co., Mellon Nat. Bank, Pittsburgh Br. of Federal Reserve Bank of Cleveland, Pres. Plate Glass Mfrs. of America; mem. Optical Glass Com., World War. Republican. Protestant. Clubs: Duquesne, Pittsburgh Athletic, Longue Vue Country (Pittsburgh); Rockefeller Center Luncheon (New York); Columbia Country (Md.). Home: Park Mansions, Frew Av. Office: Grant Bldg., Pittsburgh, Pa.*

WHERRY, Edgar (Theodore), ecologist; b. Phila., Sept. 10, 1885; s. Albert C. and Elizabeth S. (Doll) W.; B.S., U. of Pa., 1906, Ph.D., 1909; m. E. G. Smith, 1914. Formerly teacher of chemistry, mineralogy, geology and crystallography, Lehigh U.; asst. curator mineralogy, U. S. Nat. Mus., 1913-17; crystallographer, U. S. Bur. Chemistry, Washington, 1917-23, chemist in charge of crop chemistry, 1923-30; asso. prof. botany, Univ. of Pa., since 1930. Lecturer on chemistry, Wagner Free Inst., Phila., 1908-13. Fellow Geol. Soc. America, Mineral Soc. America (pres. 1923), A.A.A.S.; mem. Am. Chem. Soc. (pres. Washington sect., 1927), Pa. Acad. Science (pres. 1935), Phila. Mineral. Soc., Am. Fern Soc. (pres. 1934-38). Editor of American Mineralogist, 1919-21. Home: 27 Oberlin Av., Swarthmore, Pa.

WHETSELL, Harry E(dwin), coll. bus. mgr.; b. Terra Alta, W.Va., Feb. 9, 1897; s. George P. and Lillie (Hinebaugh) W.; student Davis and Elkins Coll., Elkins, W.Va., 1914-17; A.B., W.Va. U., Morgantown, 1918; student Columbia U., summer 1921; m. Marguerite Freeman, Sept. 2, 1922. Instr. mathematics, Davis and Elkins Coll., Elkins, W.Va., 1919-22, asst. prof., 1922-23, asso. prof., 1923-25, bus. mgr. since 1925; vice-pres. Financial Service Co., Elkins, W.Va., since 1938. Served in F.A. Officers' Training Sch., U.S.A., 1918. Delta Tau Delta. Democrat. Presbyn. Mason (K.T., Shriner), Elk. Club: Rotary of Elkins (past pres.); Club: Elkins Country. Home: College Drive, Elkins, W.Va.

WHETSTONE, Walter, pub. utilities exec.; b. Philadelphia, Pa., Apr. 12, 1876; s. Joseph and Elizabeth (Bray) W.; engineering dept., U. of Pa., 1899; m. Susie Hilt, Mar. 2, 1902; children—Dorothy (Mrs. Henry W. LeBoutillier), Walter, Joseph, Cornelius, Pearce, Wynn. Pres. United Utilities & Service Corpn., Southern Cities Utilities Co., The Whetstone Engring. Co., etc. Member Am. Society Polit. and Social Science, Acad. of Natural Sciences of Phila., Psi Upsilon. Republican. Mason. Clubs: Union League (Phila.); Bankers (New York). Home: Cambridge Apt., Alden Park, Philadelphia, Pa. Office: Fox Bldg., Philadelphia, Pa.

WHITAKER, Arthur Preston, prof. Am. history; b. Tuscaloosa, Ala., June 6, 1895; s. Walter Claiborne and Isabel Preston (Royall) W.; B.A., University of Tenn., 1915; Rhodes Scholar, Tenn., 1917; A.M., Harvard University, 1917, Ph.D. from same, 1924; student, Sorbonne, Paris, 1919; Amherst Memorial fellow, 1924; Guggenheim Memorial fellow, 1929; m. Alix Feild, Oct. 4, 1919; children—Ewing, Arthur Royall. Inst. in history U. of Tenn., 1919-20; Austin teaching fellow, Harvard, 1920-21; instr. in history, Simmons Coll., 1921-22, New York U., 1922-24; prof. history Fla. State Coll., 1926-27; visiting prof. history, Vanderbilt, 1927-28; lecturer U. of Wis., 1928, Columbia, 1930, N.Y. Univ., 1936, Princeton, 1937; Albert Shaw lecturer on diplomatic history, Johns Hopkins, 1938; asso. prof. history, Western Reserve U., 1928-30; prof. Am. history, Cornell U., 1930-36; prof. of Latin-Am. history, U. of Pa., since 1936. Served in F.A., U.S.A., 1917-19. Mem. Am. Hist. Assn., Am. Acad. Polit. and Social Science, Miss. Valley Hist. Assn., Hispanic Soc. of America (corr. mem.), Council on Foreign Relations (New York), Alpha Tau Omega. Episcopalian. Author: Spanish-American Frontier, 1927; The Mississippi Question (1795-1803), 1934. Contbr. chapter on "The New Latin America" in contemporary world affairs, 1939. Compiler: Documents Relating to Spanish Commercial Policy in the Floridas and Louisiana (1778-1808), 1931. Contbr. to Dictionary Am. Biography, also to hist. jours. Address: University of Pa., Philadelphia, Pa.

WHITCRAFT, Franklin Pierce, Jr., banking; b. Baltimore, Md., Oct. 22, 1887; s. Franklin Pierce and Sally Ann (McHarry) W.; A.B., Johns Hopkins U., 1909; m. Virginia Regester, Oct. 16, 1912; children—Franklin Pierce III, Edward Church Regester, Louise Virginia. Asso. with Eutaw Savings Bank, Baltimore, Md., continuously since entering its employ as clk., 1910, asst. treas., 1918-21, treas., 1921-27, 2d vice-pres. and treas., 1927-31, vice-pres. and dir. since 1931. Mem. Phi Gamma Delta. Republican. Methodist. Club: Baltimore Country. Home: Lutherville, Md. Office: 20 N. Eutaw St., Baltimore, Md.

WHITE, Albert Blakeslee, ex-governor; b. Cleveland, O., Sept. 22, 1856; s. Emerson E. and Mary Ann (Sabin) W.; A.B. (with honors), Marietta Coll., 1878, LL.D., W.Va. U., 1910, Marietta Coll., 1935; m. Agnes Ward, Oct. 2, 1879. Reporter and later mng. editor Lafayette (Ind.) Daily Journal, 1878-81; purchased State Journal, Parkersburg, W.Va., 1881, made it a daily, 1883, and remained its editor until retiring, July 1899. Collector internal revenue dist. W.Va., 1889-93, and 1897-1901, and 1921-25; gov. of W.Va., 1901-05; state tax commr., 1907-10; mem. Senate, 3d Dist., W.Va., term 1927-31; mem. State Bd. of Edn. since 1936; engaged in mfg. business. Pres. Nat. Editorial Assn., 1887-88. Y.M.C.A. war work overseas, 1918-19. Republican. Mem. Vets. of Foreign Wars. Emeriti member Imperial Council of Shrine A.A.O.N.M.S., 1937. Home: 1040 Murdock Av., Parkersburg, W.Va.

WHITE, Allen Hunter, lawyer; b. Springerton, Ill., April 13, 1896; s. John Monroe and Lee Jane (Hunter) W.; student U. of Cincinnati, 1915-17; LL.B., U. of Pa. Law Sch., 1922; m. Caroline Yale Crouter, Aug. 4, 1924; children—John Edgerton Hunter, Peter, Caroline Yale. Admitted to Pa. bar, 1922, and since engaged in gen. practice of law at Phila.; librarian and law sec., Supreme Ct. of Pa., 1922-25; asso. with firm Ballard, Spahr, Andrews and Ingersoll since 1925 and mem. firm since 1931. Served as field batt. sergt. maj., F.A., U.S. Army, 1917-19, with A.E.F. Mem. Am., Pa. State, and Phila. bar assns., Am. Law Inst., Am. Judicature Soc., Juristic Soc. of Phila. (past pres.), Hare Law Club, Nat. Econ. League, Sigma Alpha Epsilon, Phi Delta Phi. Republican. Clubs: University, Phila. Skating Club & Humane Soc. (Phila.); Merion Cricket (Haverford, Pa.). Home: St. Davids, Pa. Office: 1035 Land Title Bldg., Philadelphia, Pa.

WHITE, Alma, bishop Pillar of Fire Church; b. Lewis County, Kentucky, June 16, 1862; d. William Moncure and Mary Ann (Harrison) Bridwell; Millersburg (Ky.) Female Coll. 3 yrs., A.B.; studied lt. U. of Denver; A.M. and D.D., Alma White College; m. Kent White, Meth. clergyman, Dec. 21, 1887; children—Arthur Kent, Ray Bridwell. Founder, 1901, and pres. Pillar of Fire Ch. (organized 1901); founder Alma White Coll., Alma Prep. School, Zarephath Bible Sem. (all Zarephath, N.J.), Belleview Jr. Coll. and Alma Temple (Denver, Colo.), Galilean Training School (Los Angeles, Calif.), Eden Grove Acad. (Cincinnati, Ohio), Alma Bible College (London); pres. Pillar of Fire Corpn. Bds. of N.J., Colo.,-N.Y., O.; trustee Alma Bible Coll., London. Teacher pub. schs., 1879-87; evangelist, 1887-1900; incorporated Pillar of Fire Ch., Colo., 1902, came to N.J., 1905, and moved headquarters to Zarephath, 1908. Republican. Author: Looking Back from Beulah, 1902; Gems of Life (for children), 1907; Golden Sunbeams, 1909; The Chosen People, 1910; My Trip to the Orient, 1911; The New Testament Church, 1911; The Titanic Tragedy—God Speaking to the Nations, 1912; Truth Stranger than Fiction, 1913; Why I Do Not Eat Meat, 1915; Restoration of Israel, the Hope of the World, 1917; The Story of My Life and the Pillar of Fire (5 vols.), 1919-33; With God in the Yellowstone, 1920; My Heart and My Husband (poem), 1923; The Ku Klux Klan in Prophecy, 1925; The Voice of Nature (verse), 1927; Musings of the Past (verse), 1927; Hymns and Poems, 1931; Short Sermons, 1932; Radio Sermons and Lectures, 1936; Jerusalem, 1936; The Sword of the Spirit, 1937; also more than 150 hymns. Preacher, lecturer, nature artist. Editor Pillar of Fire, Rocky Mountain Pillar of Fire, Occidental Pillar of Fire, London Pillar of Fire; The British Sentinel (London); The Dry Legion; founder radio sta. KPOF, Denver, 1927, WAWZ, Zarephath, N.J., 1931; founder Woman's Chains. Address: Zarephath, N.J., also 1845 Champa St., Denver, Colo.

WHITE, Arthur Kent, clergyman, educator; b. Denver, Colo., Mar. 15, 1889; s. Kent and Mollie Alma (Bridwell) W.; A.B., Columbia, 1915; A.M., Princeton, 1921; D.D., Alma White College, 1927; m. Kathleen Merrill Staats, Sept. 6, 1915; children—Arlene Hart, Horace Merrill, Constance Juanita, Pauline Alma. Ordained ministry Pillar of Fire Church, 1910; nat. v.p. and asst. supt. Pillar of Fire Ch., also various offices in connection with publs. of the ch.; pres. Alma White Coll. and Preparatory Sch., Zarephath, N.J.; lecturer Belleview Jr. Coll., Denver, Colo. Lecturer over Radio Station WAWZ of Zarephath, N.J. and KPOF, Denver. Republican. Author: Your Home Your College, 1922; (with Ray Bridwell White) A Toppling Idol—Evolution, 1933; The Boys Made Good, 1936. Home: Zarephath, N.J.; also 1845 Champa St., Denver, Colo.

WHITE, Barclay, engring. and bldg.; b. Lansdowne, Pa., Aug. 2, 1887; s. Howard and Helen Trump (Comly) W.; A.B., Swarthmore (Pa.) Coll., 1906, C.E., 1909; m. Edith Spencer Lewis, Oct. 1, 1910; children—Mary Elma (wife of Dr. Chas. C. Price), Helen Deborah, Barclay, Margaret Spencer. Employed as engr. bldg. constrn., Truscon Steel Co., 1906-07; engr. Phila. Steel & Wire Co., 1908-09; engr. and bldg. supt., John R. Wiggins Co., 1910-12; pres. Barclay White Co., builders, Phila., since 1913; chmn. bd. Hotel Traymore Co., Atlantic City, N.J.; pres. and dir. Industrial Realty Corpn., Phila.; dir. Skytop Lodge, Inc., Skytop, Pa. Apptd. appraiser, 1935, by U.S. Dist. Ct. of properties approximate value $115,000,000, of bankrupt Phila. Co. for Guaranteeing Mortgages. Mem. bd. mgrs. Swarthmore Coll. Mem. Am. Soc. C.E., Sigma Xi, Delta Upsilon. Republican. Soc. of Friends. Clubs: Union League (Phila.); Rolling Green Golf (Media, Pa.; vice-pres.). Home: 120 Hilldale Rd., Lansdowne, Pa. Office: 22 N. 36th St., Philadelphia, Pa.

WHITE (John) Beaver, engineer; b. Milroy, Pa., June 10, 1874; s. Rev. John W. and Mary Miller (Beaver) W.; B.S. in M.E., Pa. State Coll., 1894; M.E. in E.E., Cornell, 1899; m. in Buckinghamshire, Eng., Harriet H. Stevens, June 9, 1904 (died Mar. 25, 1928); children—Harriet, Clarissa, Joan, Louise; m. 2d, Margery Thompson Sperry, July 25, 1934. Began with J. G. White & Company, engineers and builders, Baltimore, Md., 1894; gen. mgr. and engr. Eastchester Electric Co., Mt. Vernon, N.Y., 1896-98; practiced at Salisbury and Winston-Salem, N.C., 1899-1900; constructing electric light and power and street ry., San Juan, P.R., 1900-01; in Mandalay, Burma, and Hyderabad and Bombay, India, 1901-02; in charge street ry. constrn. in many cities in England, for J. G. White & Co., Ltd., 1902-04; financial dir. same company, in London, England, 1904-09; established firm Beaver White & Co., London, 1909; dir. Internat. Light & Power Co., Home and Foreign Securities Co., Foreign Trade Co., Ltd. Mem. Am. Relief Com., London, 1914-15; dir. Commn. for Relief in Belgium, in charge purchase and shipping, London, 1914-15, in America, 1915-16; was mem. Advisory Com. for Belgian Relief; assisted in preliminary work of U.S. Food Administration; representative of U.S. Food Administrator on Exports Administrative Bd.; mem. War Trade Bd., representing the food administrator, Oct. 1917-Feb. 1919. Chmn. Am. delegation to Internat. Communications Conf., Paris, 1925; apptd. by President Coolidge del. to Internat. Radio Conf., Washington, 1927; apptd. by President Hoover as mem. Annual Assay Commn., 1933. Officer Order of the Crown, Belgium, 1919. Studying economic conditions in Eng., France and Germany. Home: Villa Nova, Pa. Office: Land Title Bldg., Philadelphia, Pa.

WHITE, Charles Doughty, mayor; b. Denton, Md., July 8, 1875; s. Josiah and Mary Kirby (Allen) W.; ed. Swarthmore Coll., 1889-92, U. of Pa., 1892-96; m. Margaret Davis Fisher, Dec. 23, 1901; children—Bertha Deane (Mrs. John W. Nason), Esther Allen (Mrs. John P. Corry), Josiah 4th, Francis Fisher, Margaret Eliza. Admitted to Pa. bar and engaged in practice of law, 1897-1902; joined father and brothers in Marlborough Hotel enterprises, 1901; vice-pres. Josiah White & Sons Co., proprs. and operators Marlborough-Blenheim Hotel since 1906; pres. Guarantee Bank & Trust Co. since 1933; served as councilman Atlantic City, 1909-12, dir. sts. and pub. improvements, 1912-16; served as mem. N.J. Senate, 1917-20; drafted to fill unexpired term of former mayor and Mayor of Atlantic City since 1935. Trustee Atlantic City Hosp. Mem. Chamber of Commerce, Hotel Men's Assn., N.J. Bankers' Assn., N.J. State Hotel Men's Assn., A.A.A.S., Delta Upsilon. Republican. Mem. Religious Soc. Friends. Club: Rotary, Country, Seaview Golf (Atlantic City). Home: 138 N. Harrisburg Av., Atlantic City, N.J. Office: City Hall; also Marlborough-Blenheim Hotel, Atlantic City, N.J.

WHITE, Charles Edward, prof. inorganic chemistry; b. College Park, Md., Nov. 4, 1901; s. Thomas Herbert and Annie Louise (Round) W.; B.S., U. of Md., 1923, M.S., same, 1924, Ph.D., same, 1926; grad. study, U. of Ill., summer 1926; m. Helen Trent Rose, of Hyattsville, Md., Aug. 20, 1925; children—Helen Elizabeth, Frances Ann. Instr. inorganic chemistry, U. of Md., 1926-28, asst. prof., 1928-30, asso. prof., 1930-38, prof. since 1938. Served as 2d lt. Inf. Res., 1923-28; 1st lt. C.W.S. Res., 1928-38. Mem. Am. Chem. Soc., Sigma Xi, Alpha Chi Sigma, Alpha Tau Omega, Phi Kappa Phi. Democrat. Episcopalian. Contbr. articles to chem. jours. Home: 9 Beech St., College Heights, Hyattsville, Md.

WHITE, Charles P., mem. staff Delaware and Wilmington Gen. hosps.; ophthalmologist Delaware State Hosp. for Insane, Farnhurst, Del. Address: 925 Market St., Wilmington, Del.

WHITE, Edith Grace, coll. prof.; b. Boston, Mass., May 16, 1890; d. Joseph Adie and Elizabeth (Kelly) W.; student Washington Allston Grammar Sch., 1896-1904, Brighton High Sch. (both of Boston), 1904-08; A.B., Mount Holyoke Coll., South Hadley, Mass., 1912; A.M., Columbia U., 1913, Ph.D., 1918; unmarried. Research asst., Princeton U., 1915-16; head biology dept., Heidelberg U., Tiffin, O., 1918-20, Shorter Coll., Rome, Ga., 1920-23; prof. biology and head dept., Wilson Coll., Chambersburg, Pa., since 1923; research asso. in ichthyology, Am. Mus. Natural History, N.Y. City, since 1933. Mem. A.A.A.S., N.Y. Acad. of Sciences, Am. Genetics Assn., Am. Eugenics Soc., Am. Soc. Ichthyologists, Phi Beta Kappa, Pi Gamma Mu. Republican. Author: Textbook of General Biology, 1928, 2d edit., 1937; Laboratory Manual of General Biology, 1934, 2d edit., 1937; Textbook of Genetics, 1939; Phylogeny of the Elasmobranch Fishes, 1937; many short articles on ichthyology, etc., since 1918. Research at Imperial U., Tokyo, Japan, 1930, Laboratorium voor Het, Batavia, Java, 1931. Home: 1312 Edgar Av. Address: Wilson Coll., Chambersburg, Pa.

WHITE, Elizabeth Brett, prof. history; b. Yorktown, N.Y., Jan. 17, 1880; d. Henry and Sarah (Dickerman) W.; grad. high sch., Passaic, N.J., 1897; A.B., Cornell U., 1904; A.M., U. of Wis., 1917; Ph.D., Clark U., Worcester, Mass., 1920; unmarried. Welfare work under Presbyn. Bd. of Home Missions, Walnut Spring, N.C., 1904-06; professor history, Pa. Coll. for Women, Pittsburgh, 1912-24; dean of women and prof. history, Ursinus Coll., Collegeville, Pa., 1924-1938; head dept. of history since 1924. Mem. Am. Hist. Assn., Am. Assn. Univ. Women, Am. Assn. Univ. Profs., Foreign Policy Assn., Tau Kappa Alpha. Awarded Justin Winsor prize, Am. Hist. Assn., for Manuscript, Franco-American Relations, 1924. Republican. Reformed Ch. Author: American Opinion of France, 1927. Home: Shepherdstown, Pa. Address: Ursinus Coll., Collegeville, Pa.

WHITE, Francis, diplomat; b. Baltimore, Md., Mar. 4, 1892; s. Miles, Jr., and Virginia Purviance (Bonsal) W.; Ph.B., Sheffield Scientific Sch. (Yale), 1913; post-grad. work, univs. of Grenoble and École Libre des Sciences Politiques, Paris, France, and U. of Madrid and Real Academia, Madrid; m. Nancy Brewster, June 28, 1920. Entered diplomatic service as sec., July 28, 1915, and assigned to Peking,

China; trans. to Teheran, Persia, 1918, Havana, Cuba, 1919, Buenos Aires, Argentina, 1920, acting during various periods as chargé d'affaires; trans. to Dept. of State, Mar. 1922; in charge Div. of Latin Am. Affairs, 1922-26; counselor of Embassy, Madrid, Spain, 1926-27; asst. sec. of State, 1927-33; E.E. and M.P. to Czechoslovakia, July-Dec. 1933. Pres. of Foreign Bondholders Protective Council, Inc. Trustee Johns Hopkins Univ. Episcopalian. Clubs: Metropolitan, Chevy Chase (Washington); Brook, India House (New York). Home: 4603 Kerneway, Baltimore, Md. Office: 90 Broad St., New York, N.Y.

WHITE, Frank, ex-treas. of U.S.; b. Stillman Valley, Ill., Dec. 12, 1856; s. Joshua and Lucy Ann (Brown) W.; B.S., U. of Ill., 1880 (LL.D., 1904); m. Elsie Hadley, Sept. 19, 1894. Mem. N.D. Ho. of Rep., 1891-93, Senate, 1893-99; maj. 1st N.D. Vol. Inf., May 2, 1898-Sept. 25, 1899; served in Philippines; col. of inf., 41st Div., July 18, 1917-June 12, 1919, 14 months in France. Gov. of N.D., 1901-05; treas. of U.S., 1921-28. Republican. Congregationalist. Past Grand Comdr. Knights Templars in N.D. Mem. S.A.R. Home: 6804 Meadow Lane, Chevy Chase, Md.

WHITE, George Loring, clergyman; b. Lake Co., Ill., Feb. 15, 1872; s. Andrew J. and Abbie Chase (Smith) W.; A.B., University of Chicago, 1898, B.D. from same, 1903, A.M., 1904; D.D., Grand Island (Neb.) Coll., 1925; m. Edna C. Pollock, Mar. 1, 1900; 1 son, Loring Pollock; m. 2d, Josephine Upton, of S. Pasadena, Calif., June 8, 1920; children—Grace Upton, Frank Gwinn, Kenneth Harry. Ordained Baptist ministry, 1900; pastor McCook, Nebraska, 1900-03, Harvey, Ill., 1903-04; supt. Bapt. missions in Utah and Wyo., 1907-11; supt. work for Am. Bapt. Pub. Soc. in western states, 1911-19; joint sec., states west of Miss. River for Am. Bapt. Publ. Soc. and Am. Bapt. Home Mission Soc., 1919-23; western rep. Am. Bapt. Publ. Soc.; dir. Northern Bapt. Corr. Sch., 1923-27; western sec. Bapt. Ministers and Missionaries Benefit Bd., 1927-28; asso. sec. Bapt. Ministers and Missionaries Benefit Bd. since 1928. Mem. Delta Tau Delta. Republican. Home: 56 Hillside Av., Tenafly, N.J.

WHITE, Gerald Taylor, editor and naval architect; b. New York, N.Y., Dec. 24, 1887; s. Walter William and Cornelia (Taylor) W.; student N.Y. Pub. Sch. 28, 1896-1903; m. Edith Barker, Sept. 23, 1910; 1 dau., Marjorie (dec.). Began as boatbuilder, Chas. L. Seabury & Co., New York, 1903; editor The Dinghy Mag., New York, 1910; writer on boating subjects since 1910; naval architect and plant supt. Eastern Motor Sales Co., New York, 1912-17; naval architect Tams, Lemoine & Crane, New York, 1917-20; instr. naval architecture, Cooper Inst. of Arts and Sciences, New York, 1917-20; editor The Rudder, New York, 1920-28; chief naval architect Fairchild Boats, Inc., New York, 1928; editor Motor Boat Mag., New York, naval architect Westlawn Associates, tech. dir. Westlawn Sch. of Yacht Design., Montville, N.J., since 1930. Mem. Soc. of Automotive Engrs. Hon. mem. Broad Channel Yacht Club (Long Island, N.Y.); Red Bank (N.J.) Yacht Club, Palm Beach (Fla.) Yacht Club, Illinois Valley Yacht Club, (Peoria, Ill.), Traverse City (Mich.) Boat Club, Nat. Speed Boat Club. Contbr. tech. articles on boating to mags. in U.S., Can., Europe. Designer Miss Broadway series of hydroplanes, Grey Dawn series of auxiliaries and specialist in design motor and small boats for amateur builders. Address: Montville, N.J.

WHITE, Grace Yoke (Mrs. W. H. S. White), dramatic coach, poet; b. Weston, Lewis County, W.Va., Nov. 11, 1884; d. Solomon Gordon and Helen Ann (Wolverton) Yoke; student Morgantown High School, 1899-1903, W.Va. Univ., Morgantown, 1903-07; m. Wilson H. S. White, Aug. 22, 1908, children—Roy Laban (dec.), Dorothy Jo (Mrs. William Harold Cunningham), Wilson H. S., Jr., Helinda Elizabeth, James Solomon, Patricia Grace. Dramatic entertainer and public speaking instr. since 1930. First poet laureate W.Va. Federated Women's Clubs; first poet laureate N.S.D.A.R. (W.Va.); first poet laureate Nat. Wolverton Club, Washington,

D.C.; mem. nat. bd. of dirs. Nat. Poetry Center, Radio City, N.Y. City. Represented W.Va. at New York World's Fair in Nat. Poetry Book. Mem. W.Va. Federated Women's Clubs (past state chmn. of poetry; past fine arts chmn., past pres. of President's Club); mem. Daughters of the Confederacy, W.Va. Garden Club, D.A.R. (state v. regent), League Am. Pen Women, Bookfellow, Alpha Psi Omega, Phi Chi, Delta Psi Omega (nat. v.p.), Eastern Star, Rebecca, White Shrine of Jerusalem. Democrat. Methodist. Has written poetry which has been included in state, national and international anthologies, also in state and national magazines. Address: Box 65, Shepherdstown, W.Va.

WHITE, Harold Edwards, cons. engr.; b. Buffalo, N.Y., Apr. 24, 1893; s. Charles William and Katharine Margaret (Lang) W.; E.M., Lehigh U., Bethlehem, Pa., 1916; m. Stella Haeberle, Jan. 16, 1919; children—Charles Haeberle, Joyce Carleton. Research asst. Norton Co., Niagara Falls, N.Y., 1916; mem. exploration party to Guiana, S.A., 1917; asst. supt. Norton Co., Chippawa, Can., 1917-18; mgr. electric furnace plant, Deutsche Norton Gesellschaft, Grosswelzheim, Bavaria, Germany, 1919-21; research engr. Norton Co., Niagara Falls, N.Y., 1921; operating supt. Southern Manganese Corpn., Anniston, Ala., 1921-27; ceramic engr. and v.p., Lava Crucible Co., Pittsburgh, since 1927. Fellow Am. Ceramic Soc.; mem. Am. Inst. Mining & Metall. Engrs., Am. Inst. Chem. Engrs., Deutsche Keramichen Gesellschaft, Tau Beta Pi, Psi Upsilon. Episcopalian. Clubs: University (Pittsburgh), Rotary (Zelienople, Pa.); University (Niagara Falls, N.Y.). Home: 308 Beaver St., Zelienople, Pa.

WHITE, Jacob Reese, pres. Houston-White Co.; b. Millsboro, Del., Aug. 8, 1901; s. William Jacob Peter and Georgiana Tilney (Godwin) W.; student Cheshire (Conn.) Sch., 1915-17, Tome Sch., Port Deposit, 1917-19; m. Sarah Hoyt Carpenter, Oct. 8, 1921; children—Jacob Reese, Mary Tilney, Virginia Thomas. Office boy and laborer, Houston-White Co., Millsboro, 1919-21; sales mgr. Houston-White Co., mfrs. bldg. materials and wood packages, Millsboro, Del., 1921-23, sec. and treas., 1923-25, v.p. and treas., 1925-36, pres. since 1936; pres. Houston Lumber Co., Houston, Del., since 1925, Baltimore Package Co. since 1934; v.p. Millsboro Trust Co. since 1936; dir. Farmers Bank, Kent County Mutual Ins. Co. Pres. commrs. of Millsboro, Del., since 1929, Millsboro Fire Co., 1924-34. Pres. Order United Am. Mechanics Cemetery, Inc., since 1935, Laymen's League of Sussex Co., 1934-35; mem. exec. com. or council P.E. Diocese of Del. since 1930; jr. warden St. Mark's P.E. Vestry, Millsboro, since 1936, supt. Sunday Sch. since 1925. Mem. Middle Atlantic Lumberman's Assn. (dir.). Democrat. Episcopalian. Mason (Franklin Lodge 12, Georgetown, Del.; St. John's Commandery, Wilmington, Del.; Shriner, LuLu Temple, Phila.), United Order Am. Mechanics (Millsboro, Del.). Club: Rehobeth Beach (Del.) Country. Address: Millsboro, Del.

WHITE, James Dugald, investment banker; b. Kearney, Neb., May 7, 1889; s. James Gilbert and Kathleen Victoria Maud (Mullon) W.; A.B., Cornell U., 1911; m. Dorothy Owen, May 4, 1912. With Engineering Securities Corpn., New York, 1911-15; mem. Hemphill, White & Chamberlain, 1915-19; v.p. J. G. White & Co. 1919-30, pres. since 1930; dir. The J. G. White Engineering Corpn., Osceola Cypress Co., New England Concrete Pipe Corpn., Foreign Light & Power Co., Gen. Reinsurance Corpn., Upper Columbia Co., North Star Ins. Co., Am. Yugoslav Electric Co., Danube Products, Inc., Internat. Public Service Co., Second Av. R.R. Corpn., Industrial Brownhoist Corpn. Mem. S.R., Delta Phi. Served as capt. inf., U.S.A., 1917-19. Clubs: University, Cornell, City Mid-Day (New York); Bay Head (N.J.) Yacht; Manasquan River Golf (Brielle, N.J.). Home: 463 Main Av., Bay Head, N.J. Office: 37 Wall St., New York, N.Y.

WHITE, John Baker, lawyer; b. Romney, W. Va., Aug. 24, 1868; s. Christian Streit (capt. C.S.A.) and Eliza J. (Schultze) W.; student pub. sch. and high sch., Romney, W.Va.; studied law under pvt. tutors; unmarried. Employed as clk. in office sec. of state, 1886-92, chief clk., 1892-93; sec. to gov., 1893-97; admitted to W.Va. bar, 1897 and engaged in gen. practice of law at Charleston; mem. Bd. of Affairs (commn. govt.), Charleston, 1907-11; supt. Kanawha Co. Law and Order League, 1921-22; mem. W.Va. Bd. of Control since 1932, has served as treas., pres., and now sec. since 1939. Served as capt. inf., 1st W.Va. Vols., Spanish-Am. War, 1898-99; maj. and lt. col. Judge Adv. Gen. Dept., U.S.A., 1917-19; judge adv. Am. troops in Gt. Britain; also in France and Army of Occupation on Rhine; promoted to col. U.S.A. Auxiliary Res., Aug. 1932. Awarded D.S.O. (Brit.) and decorated by King George V. Democrat. Presbyn. Mason (32°, Shriner). Clubs: Army and Navy; American Officers, Athenaeum, Lincoln's Inn, Grey's Inn, Middle Temple (London, Eng.). Home: Cavalier Apts. Office: Capitol Bldg., Charleston, W.Va.

WHITE, Jonathan W(inborne), soil research chemist; b. Greenville, N.C., Mar. 28, 1883; s. Jonathan and Laura Milton (Hudgins) W.; B.S., in chemistry, N.C. State Coll., 1903; M.S. in agrl. chemistry, U. of Ill., 1912; m. Helen Frances Smith, Jan. 1, 1916; children—Jonathan Winborne, Helen Frances, Harry Donald, Philip Louis. Dye chemist, 1903-05; mine chemist, 1905-06; asst. chemist Pa. Agrl. Expt. Station, 1906-12; soil research chemist, Pa. State Coll., 1912-20, prof. soil tech. since 1920. Mem. Am. Soc. Agronomy, Acacia, Phi Kappa Phi, Gamma Sigma Delta, Phi Lambda Upsilon, Sigma Xi, Alpha Zeta. Elected first research lecturer, Pa. State Coll.. (research award). Democrat. Methodist. Mason. Contbr. articles on soil science to Jour. Am. Soc. Agronomy, etc.; author of agrl. bulls. Home: 524 S. Allen St., State College, Pa.

WHITE, Luke Matthews, clergyman; b. Huntsville, Ala., Oct. 18, 1877; s. David Irvine and Lucy (Matthews) W.; B. A., U. of Va., 1902, M.A., 1902; D.D., Va. Theol. Sem., Alexandria, Va., 1905; m. Jane Tucker, June 27, 1905; children—Beverley Tucker, David Irvine, Luke Matthews. Ordained to ministry P.E. Ch., 1905; rector St. John's Ch., Warsaw, Va., 1905-06, Christ Ch., Pulaski, Va., 1906-10, St. Mark's Ch., Shreveport, La., 1910-16, St. Luke's Ch., Montclair, N.J., since 1916. Club: University (New York). Home: 75 S. Fullerton Av., Montclair, N.J.

WHITE, Marsh William, asso. prof. physics; b. Claremont, N.C., Apr. 22, 1896; s. Wm. Franklin and Dora (Marsh) W.; A.B., Park Coll., Parkville, Mo., 1917; M.S., Pa. State Coll., 1920, Ph.D., 1926; m. Stella Steele, Fairfax Mo., Sept. 12, 1917; children—Laurence Marsh, Kenneth Steele, Malcolm Arthur. Instr. physics, Pa. State Coll., 1918, asst. prof., 1920-26, asso. prof. physics since 1926. Fellow A.A.A.S.; mem. Am. Assn. Univ. Profs., Delta Chi, Sigma Pi Sigma, Pi Mu Epsilon, Sigma Xi. Republican. Methodist. Author: Experimental College Physics, 1932. Contbr. scientific papers to tech. jours. Home: 511 E. Prospect Av., State College, Pa.

WHITE, Ray Bridwell, clergyman, educator; b. Morrison, Colo., Aug. 24, 1892; s. Kent and (Mollie) Alma (Bridwell) W.; A.B., Columbia, 1917; A.M., Princeton, 1921; D.D., Alma White College, 1928; student University of Denver (leave of absence from Columbia Univ.), 1915-16; m. Grace Eaton Miller, Aug. 29, 1916. Ordained ministry Pillar of Fire Ch., 1913; nat. officer of the ch. since 1918, also a teacher, an editor of publications, and sec. Pillar of Fire Corpn., Colo.; pres. Belleview Jr. (formerly Westminster) Coll. and Bible Sem., Colo., since 1921; pres. Zarephath Bible Sem.; co-mgr. and broadcaster radio stations WAWZ and KPOF. Founder Collegiate Legion of Honor. Republican. Author: The King's Message (sermons), 1916; The Doctrines and Discipline of the Pillar of Fire Church, 1918; A Challenge from the Pulpit (sermons), 1920; The Legend of Manitousa, Hank, Poems and Sketches, 1926; By What Authority, or Why the Pillar of Fire, 1928; The Truth Concerning Infallible Popes, 1929; The Trail of the Desert Sun, 1931; The Plaster of Paris Christ, 1933; (with Arthur K. White) A Toppling Idol—Evolution, 1933; The Book of God, 1935; Pulpit and Pen (sermons, lectures, essays), 1937; Eternal Security Insecure—or The Heresy of Once in Grace Always in Grace, 1939. Address: 1845 Champa St., Denver, Colo.; and Zarephath, N.J.

WHITE, Robert McKinney, lawyer; b. Grove City, Pa., June 11, 1886; s. William Morehead and Minnie Madavell (McBride) W.; B.S., Washington & Jefferson Coll., 1908, M.S., 1911; J.D., U. of Mich., 1912; m. Luola Jackson Little, Dec. 29, 1909; children—Jack Little, Robert McKinney, II. Instr. high sch., New Castle, Pa., 1908-10; prof. mathematics, Geneva Coll., Beaver Falls, Pa., 1910-11; admitted to Pa. bar, 1912, and since engaged in gen. practice of law at New Castle; asst. city solicitor, New Castle, Pa., 1918-24, city solicitor, 1924-36; lecturer in law, Westminster Coll., 1932-34. Mem. Am., Pa. State, and Lawrence Co. bar assns., Beta Theta Pi. Republican. Presbyn. Home: 320 Hazelcroft Av. Office: 17 E. North St., New Castle, Pa.

WHITE, Robert V., surgeon; b. Scranton, Pa., Aug. 28, 1877; s. Robert E. and Mary B. (Talley) W.; student Scranton (Pa.) High Sch., 1891-94, Sch. of the Lackawanna, Scranton, Pa., 1894-96; M.D., Hahnemann Med. Coll., Phila., 1901; m. Ella Emily Walter, Dec. 7, 1905; children—Robert E., Eleanor E., Walter K. Surgeon, Hahnemann Hosp., Scranton, Pa., 1905-30, chief surgeon since 1930; consulting surgeon, Wyoming Valley Hosp., Wilkes-Barre, Pa., since 1910; chief surgeon, Lackawanna and Wyoming Valley R.R., Scranton, Pa., since 1910; consulting surgeon, Wayne Co. Memorial Hosp., Honesdale, Pa., since 1934. Mem. Pa. State Homœo. Med. Soc. (pres. 1939), Hahnemann Med. Coll. Alumni Assn. (pres. 1927), Phi Alpha Gamma (grand pres. 1939-40). Republican. Episcopalian. Club: Scranton (Pa.) Country. Home: 1006 Linden St. Office: 434 Spruce St., Scranton, Pa.

WHITE, Roscoe Rostin, surgeon; b. Logan, W.Va., June 14, 1901; s. Charles Bruce and Victoria (Zirkles) W.; student Washington and Lee Univ., Lexington, Va., 1919-21; M.D., Jefferson Med. Coll., Phila., Pa., 1925; m. Jean Ercie Oplinger, May 21, 1932. Interne O. Valley Gen. Hosp., Wheeling, W.Va., 1925-26; grad. study in surgery and resident surgeon, Locust Mountain Hosp., Shenandoah, Pa., 1926-29; engaged in gen. practice of surgery at Somers Point, N.J., since 1929; chief surgeon, Atlantic Shores Hosp., Somers Point, N.J., since 1930; dir. Seashore Bldg. & Loan Assn., Ocean City, N.J. Served as 1st lt. Med. Res., U.S.A. since 1925. Mem. bd. edn. City of Somers Point, N.J.; mem. bd. health, Somers Point, N.J. Mem. A.M.A., N.J. State Med. Soc., Phi Chi. Democrat. Presbyterian. Mason. Club: Ocean City Country (Somers Point). Home: 644 Shore Rd., Somers Point, N.J.

WHITE, Roy Barton, pres. Western Union Telegraph Co.; b. Metcalf, Ill., Aug. 8, 1883; s. John Marshall and Anna (Maxfield) W.; ed. high sch.; m. Flora E. Auman, Aug. 4, 1908; children—Frances Jane (Mrs. E. B. Young), Roy Barton. Began, 1902, telegraph operator and agt. Ind., Decatur & Western Ry.; train dispatcher C.,H.&D. Ry., at Indianapolis, 1902-08, chief train dispatcher, 1908-09; chief clk. to gen. supt. same ry., at Cincinnati, 1909-10, and supt. at Indianapolis, 1910-15; supt. with B.&O. R.R. at Flora, Ill., 1915-16, Seymour, Ind., 1916-17, Phila. and Baltimore, 1917-21, gen. supt. at Baltimore, 1921-23, gen. mgr. at N.Y. City, 1923-26; joined Central R.R. of N.J. as sr. v.p., 1926, pres., 1926-33; pres. Western Union Telegraph Co. since June 1, 1933; dir. and mem. exec. com. Lehigh & Hudson River Ry. Co., Central R.R. Co. of N.J. Dir. Great American Ins. Co., Am. Express Co.; trustee Bank of New York. With U.S. R.R. Administration during period of World War. Presbyn. Mason (32°, Shriner). Clubs: Metropolitan, Recess, Cloud, Railroad (New York); Traffic and Chicago (Chicago); Raritan Valley Country (Somerville, N.J.); Metropolitan (Washington, D.C.); Bohemian (San Francisco). Home: Beaver Brook Farm, Annandale, N.J. Office: 60 Hudson St., New York, N.Y.

WHITE, Theophilus, chmn. bd. Calvert Mortgage Co.; officer or dir. many companies. Home: 5502 Roland Av. Office: 215 N. Calvert St., Baltimore, Md.

WHITE, Thomas Raeburn, lawyer; b. Dublin, Ind., Aug. 30, 1875; s. William Wilson and Mary Abigail (White) W.; B.L., Earlham Coll., 1896; LL.B., U. of Pa., 1899; LL.D., Earlham College, Richmond, Ind., 1935; m. Elizabeth Wilson, June 12, 1901 (died Jan. 25, 1921); children—Mary Louise, William Wilson, Thomas Raeburn; m. 2d, Agnes Dorothy Shipley, Jan. 12, 1924; children—David, Dorothy Shipley, Stephen Prevost. Admitted to Pa. bar and U.S. Courts, 1899; lecturer, 1899-1904, asst. prof. law, 1904-05, U. of Pa. Trustee Bryn Mawr Coll.; chmn. Com. of 70, 1920-30. Clubs: University, Union League, Rittenhouse, Sunnybrook Golf, Penllyn Country. Author: Some Recent Criticism of Gelpcke vs. Dubuque, 1899; Business Law, 1901; Oaths in Judicial Proceedings and Their Effect upon the Competency of Witnesses, 1903; Commentaries on the Constitution of Pennsylvania, 1907. Home: 1807 DeLancey Place, Phila.; (summer) Penllyn, Pa. Office: Land Title Bldg., Philadelphia, Pa.

WHITE, Wallace Earl, prof. of wood utilization; b. Hyde Park, Boston, Mass., Mar. 6, 1899; s. Harry Wallace and Floretta Myrtle (Jones) W.; B.S., U. of Vt., Burlington, Vt., 1925, M.S., 1926; Ph.D., Yale, 1929; m. Charlotte Margaret Pettit, Aug. 23, 1930; children—Margaret Jane, Rosalie Mary Muir. Asst. botanist, Vt. Exptl. Sta., 1926-27; instr. in botany, Pa. State Coll. Dept. of Forestry, Mont Alto, Pa., 1929-31; asst. prof. of wood utilization, Pa. State Coll., 1931-35, asso. prof., 1935-38, prof. of wood utilization since 1938. Mem. Soc. Am. Foresters, Alpha Zeta, Phi Beta Kappa, Sigma Xi, Xi Sigma Pi, Tau Phi Delta. Republican. Christian Scientist. Club: University (State Coll., Pa.). Home: 330 E. Prospect Av., State College, Pa.

WHITE, Walter Rhoads, lawyer; b. Phila., Pa., Jan. 7, 1887; s. George Foster and Mary Jeanes (Walter) W.; A.B., U. of Pa., 1908; LL.B., U. of Pa. Law Sch., 1911; m. Eleanor May Kellogg, June 7, 1916; children—Nancy May, Joyce Harper, Daniel Doughty, Marilyn Cottrell, Christopher. Admitted to Pa. bar, 1911 and asso. with Lewis Lawrence Smith, 1911-18; trust officer Lansdowne Trust Co., 1918-31; sec. Lansdowne Bldg. & Loan Assn., 1925-35; in gen. practice of law specializing in estate and real estate law, Lansdowne, Pa., since 1935. Mem. Am. Bar Assn., Delaware Co. Bar Assn., Baronial Order of Runnemede (sec.), Kappa Alpha. Republican. Soc. of Friends. Club: Darby Lansdowne Rotary (past pres.). Home: Westtown, Pa. Office: 240 N. Wycombe Av., Lansdowne, Pa.

WHITE, William Renwick, asso. prof. agrl. edn.; b. Grove City, Pa., Apr. 22, 1878; s. David Porter and Eliza (Rainey) W.; A.B., Geneva Coll., 1901; B.S., Pa. State Coll., 1907, M.S., same, 1913, A.M., same, 1917; grad. study, U. of Minn., 1918-19; m. Isabella Waddell, Aug. 22, 1928. Engaged in teaching, in rural sch., Pa., 1901-02; civil engr., P.& L. E. R.R., 1902-05; farm supt., Allegheny Co., Pa., 1907-11; instr. agrl. edn., Pa. State Coll., 1911-13, asst. prof., 1913-22, asso. prof. since 1922. Has been active in work among boys and boy scouts; awarded Silver Beaver of Boy Scouts of America for Distinguished Service to Boyhood. Mem. Am. Assn. Univ. Profs., Pa. Edn. Assn. Reformed Presbyn. Contbr. edn. articles on various subjects to mags. and jours. Home: 734 McKee St., State College, Pa.

WHITE, William Wilson, lawyer; b. Philadelphia, Pa., Feb. 23, 1906; s. Thomas Raeburn and Elizabeth (Wilson) W.; grad. Germantown Friends Sch., 1923; A.B. magna cum laude, Harvard U., 1927; LL.B., cum laude, U. of Pa., 1933; m. Mary Lowber Sailer, Dec. 27, 1932; 1 son, William Wilson. Admitted to bar, 1933; since in gen. practice of law; partner White & Staples; dir. Pa. Joint Stock Land Bank, Barrett Automatic Keyless Lock Co. Mem. Philadelphia Bar Assn., Juristic Soc., Phi Kappa Sigma, Order of the Coif. Republican. Club:

University (Philadelphia). Editor U. of Pa. Law Review, 1932, editor-in-chief, 1933. Home: 612 W. Arbutus St. Office: 1930 Land Title Bldg., Philadelphia, Pa.

WHITE, Wilson Henry Stout, educator; b. Lewis Co., W.Va., Dec. 1, 1881; s. Remington Breckenridge and Malinda Ellen (Knight) W.; grad. Glenville (W.Va.) Normal Sch., 1904; A.B., W.Va. Univ., 1912, A.M., 1921; studied Johns Hopkins U.; Ped.D. from Salem (W.Va.) College, 1933; m. Grace Eliza Yoke, Aug. 22, 1908; children—Dorothy Jo., Wilson Henry Stout, James Solomon, Helinda Elizabeth, Patricia Grace. Principal Cowen (W.Va.) High Sch., 1908-09; supt. schs., Kingwood, 1910-11; supt. Piedmont dist. and city schs., 1913-18; supt. schs., Logan City, 1918-19; pres. Shepherd State Teachers College since 1920. Alderman on Shepherdstown City Council; mem. Jefferson Co. Relief Adminstrn. Mem. N.E.A., W.Va. Ednl. Assn. (pres. 1927), Am. Assn. Teachers' Colleges, S.A.R., Pi Kappa Alpha, Phi Beta Kappa. Chmn. Eastern Panhandle of W.Va. Bicentennial Commn. for Celebration of 200th Anniversary of Birth of George Washington. Democrat. Methodist. Mason (K.T., 32°, K.C.C.H.); Master Grand Lodge A.F. and A.M. of W.Va., 1937. Odd Fellow, Kiwanian (gov. W.Va. Dist. 1930). Home: Shepherdstown, W.Va.

WHITE, Winton John, supt. of schs.; b. Columbia, Pa., Jan. 8, 1883; s. Amos Sickles and Anna Mary (Geltmacher) W.; student Columbia (Pa.) High Sch., 1896-1900; A.B., U. of Pa., 1904, A.M., 1905, grad. student, 1905-07; student Columbia U., 1907-18; m. Gertrude May Van Zandt, Oct. 21, 1910; children—Winton John, Marion Helene (dec.), Robert Currier, David Craig. Head lang. dept., Wilmington (Del.) High Sch., 1905-07; head mathematics dept., Englewood (N.J.) High Sch., 1907-08, prin., 1908-18; supt. of schs., Englewood, N.J., since 1918. Trustee Social Service Fed. of Englewood, Englewood Library. Mem. N.J. State Edn. Assn. (v.p.), N.J. Schoolmasters Club (ex-gov.), N.J. Council of Edn. (ex-pres.), Philomathean Soc., Phi Beta Kappa. Republican. Presbyterian. Mason. Club: Rotary of Englewood (ex-pres.). Home: 88 Knickerbocker Rd. Office: Dwight Morrow High Sch., Englewood, N.J.

WHITEHEAD, Harvey Fisk, business exec.; b. Trenton, N.J., Dec. 17, 1867; s. Charles and Mary Chambers (McKean) W.; student State Model Sch., Trenton, N.J., 1874-85; m. Belle MacCrellish, Oct. 21, 1908; children—William McKean, Harvey Fisk. Clk. Hamilton Rubber Co., Trenton, N.J., 1885-92; asst. to treas. The Trenton (N.J.) Potteries Co., 1893-1907, asst. treas., 1907-25, treas., 1925-33, sec., treas. since 1933, dir. since 1938; dir. United Bldg. & Loan Assn., Trenton. Trustee 1st Presbyn. Ch., Trenton, 3 yrs. Served as home guard, Trenton, during World War. Borough councilman, Yardley, Pa., 1924-30. Dir. Yardley (Pa.) Pub. Library since 1935. Republican. Presbyterian. Home: Yardley, Pa. Office: The Trenton Potteries Co., Trenton, N.J.

WHITEHEAD, Howard Highberger, lawyer; b. Manor, Pa., June 4, 1885; s. Simon P. and Elizabeth (Highberger) W.; ed. Greensburg (Pa.) Sem., 1901-03; A.B., Franklin and Marshall Coll., Lancaster, Pa., 1907; m. Clara E. Mathias, July 27, 1916; children—Howard Mathias, Simon Wayne. Studied law and admitted to Pa. bar, 1910, and since engaged in gen. practice of law at Greensburg, Pa.; mem. firm Crowell and Whitehead since 1910; admitted to practice before Pa. Superior and Supreme cts. and U.S. Dist. Ct. Mem. Pa. and Westmoreland Co. bar assns., Lambda Chi Alpha. Democrat. Evang. and Reformed Ch. Mason (32°, Shriner). Home: Manor, Pa. Office: Bank & Trust Bldg., Greensburg, Pa.

WHITEHEAD, John Boswell, elec. engr.; b. Norfolk, Va., Aug. 18, 1872; s. Henry Colgate and Margaret Walke (Taylor) W.; E.E., Johns Hopkins, 1893, A.B., 1898, Ph.D., 1902; m. Mary Ellen Colston, Apr. 14, 1903; children—Clara (dec.), Margaret Walke, Joan Boswell. Elec engr., Westinghouse Electric & Mfg. Co., 1893-96, Niagara Falls (N.Y.) Power Co., 1896-97; instr. applied electricity, 1897-1900, asso., 1901-04, asso. prof., 1904-10, prof., 1910—, dean, 1919—, dir. Sch. of Engring., 1938—, Johns Hopkins Univ.; exchange prof. to France, 1926-27. Lab. asst., U.S. Bur. Standards, 1902; research asst., Carnegie Instn. Washington, 1902-05. Democrat. Episcopalian. Fellow Am. Inst. Elec. Engrs., Am. Physical Soc., A.A.A.S.; mem. Am. Inst. E.E. (pres. 1933-34), Nat. Acad. Sciences, Nat. Research Council, Société Française des Electriciens, Phi Beta Kappa (hon.), Tau Beta Pi, Delta Phi. Commd. maj. Engr. R.C., 1917. Clubs: Maryland, Johns Hopkins. Author: Electric Operation of Steam Railways, 1909; Dielectric Theory and Insulation, 1927; Impregnated Paper Insulation, 1935; Electricity and Magnetism, 1939; also many researches in field of high voltage insulation. Home: 19 W. Cold Spring Lane, Baltimore, Md.

WHITEHILL, Buell B(urton), lawyer; b. Brookville, Pa., Jan. 27, 1881; s. Stewart Herbert and Mary Ann (Shepherd) W.; student Brookville High Sch., 1895-97, Allegheny Coll., 1900-03; m. Lee May Snook, June 26, 1907; 1 son, Buell B., Jr. Court reporter Jefferson Co., 1901-16, Clarion Co., 1905-06, Indiana Co., 1906-11; studied law in office of father and Judge John W. Reed, Brookville, Pa.; admitted to Pa. Supreme Ct. Bar, 1912; law reporter, Boston, Mass., 1916-18; in charge safety work Bay State St. Ry. Co., Boston, 1918; admitted to Mass. Supreme Judicial Ct. Bar, 1916, Ohio Supreme Ct. Bar, 1919; mem. law firm Snook & Whitehill, Paulding, O., 1919-20; court reporter, Uniontown, Pa., 1920-24; mem. law firm Morrow & Whitehill, 1924-25, Jones, Whitehill & Lane, 1926-35, Whitehill & Lane since 1935. Sch. dir., 1911-16. Mem. Am. Bar Assn., Pa. Bar Assn., Fayette Co. Bar Assn. (sec. since 1921), Phi Gamma Delta. Republican. Presbyterian (elder since 1922). Mason (Lodge, Chapter, Commandery, Consistory, Shrine). Club: Shakespeare (Uniontown, Pa.). Home: 112 Union St. Office: 4 W. Main St., Uniontown, Pa.

WHITEHILL, Cyrus Guy, city treas.; b. Helen Furnace, Clarion Co., Pa., Nov. 11, 1893; s. James P. and Sarah Katherine (Dolby) W.; student business and teacher's colls.; m. Mae Marie Mahle, June 17, 1920; children—Richard Harold, Ramon Eugene. Teacher pub. sch., 1913-17; sec.- treas. Whitehill Yellow Cab Co., Inc., 1923-32; treas., Oil City, since 1932. Served as capt. 112th Inf., U.S. Army, World War. Dir. Y.M.C.A. Mem. Am. Legion, Vets. of Foreign Wars. Republican. Methodist. Club: Kiwanis (dir.). Home: 207 E. 7th St. Office: City Bldg., Oil City, Pa.

WHITEHORNE, Earl, editor, author; b. Verona, N.J., Nov. 8, 1881; s. Henry Bayard and Mary Elizabeth (Riker) W.; ed. pub. schs.; m. Earlena Taunt, Oct. 7, 1908; 1 dau., Mary Jane. Active in commercial development of the electrical industry since 1907; a founder, and mng. editor Electrical Merchandising, 1907-14; advertising business on own account, 1914-21, also contributing editor Electrical World and Electrical Merchandising; with McGraw-Hill Publishing Co. since 1921; commercial editor Electrical World and editorial dir. Electrical Merchandising, and Radio Retailing; now editor Electrical Contracting and editorial dir. of Wholesalers Salesman. Member Electrical Association of New York (president 1930-31), New York Electrical League (president 1928-30), Electrical Bd. of Trade of New York (pres. 1929-30), American Management Association (dir.), Illuminating Engring. Soc., N.Y. Elec. Soc., Nat. Electric Light Assn. Republican. Episcopalian. Club: Lake Valhalla Country (pres. 1931). Author: Supercargo (novel), 1939. Home: 135 Mountain Av., Caldwell, N.J. Office: 330 W. 42d St., New York, N.Y.

WHITEHOUSE, William Edwin, horticulturist; b. Somerville, Mass., Aug. 29, 1893; s. Edwin Ezra and Lillian Pearl (McAllister) W.; B.S. in Agr., Ore. Agrl. Coll., Corvallis, Ore., 1915; M.S. in Horticulture, Ia. State Coll., Ames, Ia., 1920; Ph.D., in horticulture, U. of Md., 1928; m. Helen A. Rosenbusch, Nov. 24, 1928; children—Barbara Anne, Donna Marie. Research asst., Iowa State Coll., 1917-20; asst. mgr. sales ednl. work Capital City Nurseries, 1920-21; asst. prof. pomology, U. of Md., 1921-29; agrl. explorer Div. of Plant Exploration and Introduction, Bur. of Plant Industry, U.S. Dept. Agr., 1929-30, horticulturist, 1930-33, sr. horticulturist since 1933. Enlisted as private, 1st class, Air Service, Nov. 1917; commnd. 2d lt., July 27, 1928; apptd. 2d lt. Air Corps Reserve, Feb. 1919; hon. discharged, 1929. Mem. Gamma Sigma Delta, Phi Kappa Phi, Sigma Xi. Republican. Protestant. Home: 8 University Road, Calvert Hills, Hyattsville, Md. Address: U.S. Dept. of Agriculture, Washington, D.C.

WHITELEY, Emily Stone (Mrs. James Gustavus Whiteley); b. Chicago, Ill.; d. Isaac Dulin and Sophia (Bainbridge) Stone; ed. pvt. schs. and spl. instrs., Baltimore, Md.; m. James Gustavus Whiteley (q.v.), Dec. 16, 1896. Member Md. Dem. State Central Com., 1934; del. Dem. Nat. Conv., Phila., 1936; apptd. by Pres. Roosevelt mem. Annual Assay Commn., 1937. Decorated by Belgian Govt. with Médaille de la Reine Elisabeth and accorded special honors by the Dutchess of Vendome for war work. Democrat. Episcopalian. Author: General Washington and his Aides-de-Camp, 1936. Contbr. articles on Am. history to jours. and periodicals. Home: 223 W. Lanvale St., Baltimore, Md.

WHITELEY, James Gustavus, writer; b. nr. Baltimore, July 9, 1866; s. William Stevens and Emmeline (Holmes) W.; ed. at pvt. schs. and under pvt. tutors; m. Emily Baily Stone, Dec. 16, 1896; 1 dau., Sophia Bainbridge (Mrs. Bayard Pintard Fonda). Unofficial rep. of Pres. of U.S. at The Hague, 1898, at Le Congrès Internat. d'Histoire Diplomatique, of which was v.p. and a founder. Mem. Internat. Com. which organized Le Congrès International d'Histoire Comparée, Paris, 1900; official del. of U.S. Govt. to same; apptd. consul of the Congo Free State by H.M. Leopold II, 1904, consul-gen., Sept. 1. 1905; apptd. consul of Belgium at Baltimore, Dec. 1916; attached to Belgian spl. mission to U.S. during its visit, June-Aug. 1917; hon. attaché to Belgian Mil. Mission, 1918-19. Knighted by H. M. Leopold, 1909, and created Chevalier de l'Ordre de la Couronne (of Belgium); created Commander de l'Ordre de Leopold II, Nov. 1917, for service to Belgian mission; fellow Royal Hist. Soc. (Eng.); mem. Inst. Internat. Colonial; v.p. Belgian League of Honor; mem. Am. Soc. Internat. Law; hereditary companion Mil. Order Foreign Wars; hon. mem. (with medal) Royal·Zoöl. Soc. of Antwerp; pres. Consular Assn. of Baltimore. Sec. Nat. Com. of U.S. for the Restoration Univ. of Louvain; sec.-gen. of Central Com. of Belgian Relief Fund, which organized Belgian relief cons. in 33 states; consul gen. of Belgium, at Baltimore since 1928. Chevalier de l'Ordre de Leopold, 1924; promoted Comdr. of Order of the Crown, 1931; Officer of Ordre de l'Etoile Africaine (Belgium). Episcopalian. Clubs: Maryland (Baltimore). Extensive contbr. to principal American and foreign revs. on subjects of internat. law, diplomatic history and foreign affairs. Address: 223 W. Lanvale St., Baltimore, Md.

WHITELY, Paul LeRoy, prof. psychology; b. Summitville, Ind., Dec. 31, 1893; s. Josiah B. and Dora E. (Smith) W.; A.B., Earlham Coll., Richmond, Ind., 1920; A.M., U. of Chicago, 1923, Ph.D., 1927; m. Esther R. Risser, Oct. 26, 1934; 1 son, James Lowell. Engaged in teaching pub. schs. of Ind., 1912-14; prof. psychology and edn., Neb. Central Coll., 1920-22; instr. psychology, Washington U., St. Louis, Mo., 1923-26; asso. prof. psychology, Colgate U., Hamilton, N.Y., 1927-30; prof. psychology, Franklin and Marshall Coll., Lancaster, Pa., since 1930; prof. psychology, summer sessions, Washington U., St. Louis, 1924-26, Emory U., Atlanta, Ga., 1928-29, U. of Ark., Fayetteville, Ark., 1930, N.D. Agrl. Coll., Fargo, N.D., 1931. Fellow A.A.A.S.; mem. Am. Psychol. Assn., Eastern Psychol. Assn., Am. Assn. Univ. Profs. (pres. local chapter), Sigma Xi, Pi Gamma Mu, Lambda Chi Alpha, Soc. of Friends. Clubs: Torch of Lancaster (pres.), Cliosophic Soc. Contbr. scientific articles to psychol. jours. Home: 519 State St., Lancaster, Pa.

WHITEMAN, Thomas Moorhead, newspaper editor; b. Latrobe, Pa., Mar. 12, 1877; s. Geary B. and Effie (Moorhead) W.; Ph.B., Dickinson Coll., Carlisle, Pa., 1899, A.M., 1900; LL.B., Columbia Sch. of Law, New York, 1902; LL.D., St. Vincent Coll., Latrobe, 1938; unmarried. Admitted to N.Y. State bar, 1902; pres. and mng. editor Latrobe Printing & Pub. Co., pubs. Latrobe Bulletin (daily) and job printers since 1902. Mem. Pa. Legislature, 1919-25. Awarded Distinguished Service Certificate by Am. Legion, Dept. of Pa., for service rendered Latrobe Post, 1936; presented testimonial by Latrobe Rotary Club as Latrobe's leading citizen, 1936. Pres. Latrobe Hosp., Latrobe Pub. Library. Mem. Phi Kappa Sigma, Phi Beta Kappa. Republican. Methodist. Clubs: Rotary, Latrobe Country. Home: 1301 Ligonier St. Office: 1215 Ligonier St., Latrobe, Pa.

WHITFIELD, Theodore Marshall, coll. prof.; b. Richmond, Va., May 24, 1905; s. James Morehead and Mary G. (Mathews) W.; A.B., Univ. of Richmond, Va., 1926; Ph.D., Johns Hopkins U., 1929; m. Elizabeth Denny Dixon, Sept. 2, 1931; children—Mary Emma, Margaret Denny, Theodore M., Jr. Engaged as asso. prof. history, Western Md. Coll., Westminster, Md., 1929-30, prof. history since 1930. Mem. Am. Hist. Soc., Va. Hist. Soc., Md. Hist. Soc., Carroll County Hist. Soc. (mem. bd. govs.), Phi Beta Kappa. Awarded Mrs. Simon Baruch univ. prize of U.D.C., 1929, on "Slavery Agitation in Virginia, 1829-32." Methodist. Home: 33 Ridge Rd., Westminster, Md.

WHITHAM, Lloyd B.; cons. ophthalmologist Church Home and Infirmary. Address: 700 N. Charles St., Baltimore, Md.

WHITING, Anna Rachel, prof. of biology; b. Saugerties, N.Y., Feb. 19, 1892; d. Robert Ernest and Cora Adele (Sickles) Young; A.B., Smith Coll., Northampton, Mass., 1916; student Yale, 1917-18; Ph.D., U. of Ia., Iowa City, Ia., 1924; m. Phineas Wescott Whiting, June 29, 1918. Teacher of biology, New Haven (Conn.) High Sch., 1916-18; asso. prof. of biology, Catawba Coll., Salisbury, N.C., 1927-28; prof. and head dept. of biology, Pa. Coll. for Women, Pittsburgh, 1928-36; now guest investigator in genetics, dept. of zoölogy, U. of Pa. Fellow A.A.A.S.; mem. Am. Soc. Zoölogists, Am. Naturalists, Genetics Soc. America, Gamma Phi Beta, Sigma Xi. Democrat. Episcopalian. Author of 28 scientific papers dealing with research in genetics. Home: 1016 S. 45th St., Philadelphia, Pa.

WHITING, Borden Durfee, lawyer; b. St. Louis, Mo., Jan. 3, 1876; s. Joseph Carey and Katherine Lippitt (Cady) W.; Ph.B., Brown U., 1898; LL.B., New York Law Sch., 1900; m. Emily Louise Clark, Jan. 9, 1901; 1 son, Myles. Began practice in office of Carter, Hughes & Dwight, New York, 1900; practiced in R.I., 1902-03; asst. atty. and asst. gen. atty., D., L.&W. R.R., 1903-07; apptd. mem. of N.J. Railroad Commn., 1907 (pres. of bd. 1909); mem. firm Whiting & Moore, Newark, N.J. Mem. N.G.N.Y., 1898-1900; elected mem. R.I. Ho. of Rep., Nov. 1903; city counsel, City of East Orange, 1911-14; organized Roosevelt State League for presdl. primary, 1912; elected mem. Rep. Nat. Com., at June conv., 1912; mem. Prog. Nat. Com., 1912-16. Trustee Orange Free Library; mem. Nat. Council Economic League. Mem. N.J. Legal Aid Soc. (ex-pres.), Am. and N.J. State bar assns., Assn. Bar City of New York, Essex County Lawyers' Club. Clubs: Essex, Essex County Country. Episcopalian. Home: Llewellyn Park, West Orange, N. J. Office: Essex Bldg., Newark, N.J.

WHITING, Francis Brooke, lawyer; b. Moorfield, W.Va., Oct. 18, 1873; s. James S. and Sydney C. (Hutton) W.; student Fishburne Mil. Acad., 1889-93, U. of Va., 1893-95; LL.B., U. of Md., 1898; m. Ruth White, Nov. 26, 1912; children—Anne Frances, Francis Brooke, II. Admitted to Md. bar, 1898; since in gen. practice of law; became pres. German Brewing Co., 1931; now pres. Western Md. Bldg. & Loan Assn.; v.p. Cumberland Savings Bank; dir. Cumberland & Westernport Transit Co. Served as lt., Spanish-Am. War. Mem. Am. Bar Assn., Md. State Bar Assn., Allegany County Bar Assn., Mil. and Naval Order Spanish-Am. War, Phi Delta Theta. Republican. Mason, Elk, Eagle. Clubs: Cumberland (Md.) Country; Maryland (Baltimore). Home: 632 Washington St. Office: Law Bldg., Cumberland, Md.

WHITING, George Armistead, pres. Standard Wholesale Phosphate & Acid Works, Inc.; b. Baltimore, Md., Nov. 3, 1879; s. Clarence Carlyle and Marian (Armistead) W.; m. Mary Gay Butler, 1900. Pres. Standard Wholesale Phosphate & Acid Works, Inc. Office: Mercantile Trust Bldg., Baltimore, Md.

WHITING, John Talman, pres. Alan Wood Steel Co.; b. Detroit, Mich., Aug. 1, 1887; s. Alexander Talman and Louise (Martine) W.; student pub. schs., Chicago, Ill., and Lewis Inst., 1901-05; M.E., U. of Mich., 1909; m. Ruth Clare, July 6, 1918; children—John Talman, III, William Bradford. Employed with Illinois Steel Co., South Chicago, Ill., 1909, and successively asst. supt., supt. blast furnaces, with various large concerns; v.p. and gen. mgr. Hamilton Coke & Iron Co., Hamilton, O., 1927-31; v.p. Alan Wood Steel Co., Conshohocken, Pa., 1932-35, exec. v.p. and dir., 1935-39, pres. since 1939; v.p. Rainey Wood Coke Co., Palmyra Quarry Co. Mem. Iron & Steel Inst., Mining & Metall. Engring. Soc., Eastern States Blast Furnace & Coke Oven Assn., Delta Kappa Epsilon. Republican. Presbyn. Clubs: Union League (Phila.); Golf (St. Davids, Pa.). Home: Radnor, Pa. Office: care Alan Wood Steel Co., Conshohocken, Pa.

WHITING, Louis Elliott, telephone co. exec.; b. Driftwood, Pa., May 11, 1886; s. Melvin Philip and Fidelia (Arnold) W.; student Syracuse U., 1906-08, Du Bois Bus. Coll., 1908-09; m. Irene Lindhome, June 18, 1910; children—Elizabeth Irene, Gifford Elliott. Engaged in teaching sch., 1909-11; entered telephone business at Ridgway, Pa., 1911-14, and at Jamestown, N.Y., 1914-23; at Meadville, Pa., since 1923, mgr. and dir. Meadville Telephone Co.; pres. Cochranton Telephone Co.; dir. Home Telephone Co. Mem. Meadville Sch. Bd., 1936-37; mem. Meadville Chamber of Commerce. Past pres. Meadville Kiwanis Club. Republican. Mem. M.E. Ch. Clubs: Kiwanis, Round Table. Home: 736 Maple St. Office: 229 Arch St., Meadville, Pa.

WHITLINGER, Frederick T., credit supervisor; b. Apollo, Pa., Nov. 21, 1879; s. John Finley and Julia Anne (Truby) W.; student Apollo (Pa.) High Sch., Kiskiminetas Springs Sch., Saltsburg, Pa., Allegheny Coll., Meadville, Pa., and Duff's Coll., Pittsburgh, Pa.; m. Edna Margaret Matthews, June 30, 1917; children—Frederick Kenneth, Hamilton Matthews, Anne Louise, Virginia Hamilton. Credit and collections supervisor Westinghouse Electric & Mfg. Co., East Pittsburgh, Pa.; dir. Homewood Bank (Pittsburgh); Matthews Bros. Constrn. Co. Mem. Credit Assn. of Western Pa., Calvary Beneficial Soc., Westinghouse Clerks Assn. Republican. Presbyn. (trustee Third United Presbyn. Ch.). Mason, Royal Order of Zebras. Clubs: Westinghouse, Churchhill Valley Golf (Wilkinsburg, Pa.); Automobile (Pittsburgh). Home: 6925 Rosewood St., Pittsburgh, Pa. Office: Westinghouse Electric & Mfg. Co., East Pittsburgh, Pa.

WHITMAN, Edwin A, prof. mathematics; b. Venice, N.Y., Oct. 5, 1887; s. Aaron Clarke and May (Alley) W.; A.B., Yale, 1910; A.M., U. of Pittsburgh, 1915; grad. study, U. of Mich., Ann Arbor, Mich., summers, 1920, 1921, 1927; m. Elsie Van Duyne, Dec. 30, 1914; children—Philip Martin, Robert Van Duyne. Engaged in teaching secondary schs., Winchester Sch., Pittsburgh, 1910-12, Rockville, Conn., 1912-13, Wilkinsburg, Pa., 1913-18, Pittsburgh, 1918-19; instr. mathematics, Carnegie Inst. Tech., Pittsburgh, 1919-25, asst. prof., 1925-31, asso. prof. since 1931. Mem. Am. Math. Assn., Am. Math. Soc., Phi Beta Kappa, Sigma Xi. Republican. Presbyterian. Mason. Co-author (with J. B. Rosenbach), Plane Trigonometry, 1929; College Algebra, 1933, revised edit., 1939; (with J. B. Rosenbach and David Moskovitz), Trigonometry, 1937; Mathematical Tables, 1937. Home: 521 Locust St., Edgewood, Pittsburgh, Pa.

WHITMAN, Ezra Bailey, consulting engr.; b. Baltimore, Md., Feb. 19, 1880; s. Ezra B. and Belle Cross (Slingluff) W.; student Baltimore City Coll.; C.E., Cornell University, 1901; m. Fanny Glenn, October 15, 1906; children—Fanny Glenn (Mrs. T. Brian Parsons), Ezra B., John Glenn. Member firm of Williams & Whitman, New York, 1902-06; division engineer on design and constrn. Baltimore Sewage Disposal Plant, 1906-11; chief engr. Baltimore Water Dept. (design and constrn. Filtration Plant and Loch Raven Dam), 1911-14; mem. firm Greiner & Whitman, 1914-16, Norton, Bird & Whitman, 1916-25; member of Whitman, Requardt & Smith, engineers, since 1925. Mem. and chmn. Pub. Service Com. of Md., 1921-27; mem. Engring. Bd. of Review of Chicago in lake level controversy, 1924-25; chmn. Efficiency and Economy Commn., apptd. by mayor to reorganize city govt. Baltimore; chmn. Efficiency and Economy Commn., Pittsburgh. Major of Construction Division, U.S.A., Sept. 1917-Mar. 1919; constructing quartermaster and utilities officer at Camp Mead, Md. Chmn. State Road Commn. of Md. Trustee Cornell U. Mem. Am. Soc. C.E. (exdir.), American Soc. Mech. Engrs., American Institute Electrical Engineers, American Water Works Assn., N.E. Water Works Assn., Am. Pub. Health Assn., Sigma Xi, Tau Beta Pi, Delta Upsilon. Democrat. Episcopalian. Mason. Clubs: Elkridge, Engineers', Merchants (Baltimore); Cornell (N.Y.). Home: 139 W. Lanvale St. Office: West Biddle St. at Charles St., Baltimore, Md.

WHITMARSH, David Carothers, clergyman; b. Savannah, O., May 20, 1885; s. William O. and Sarah (Carothers) W.; A.B., Washington and Jefferson Coll., Washington, Pa., 1906, (hon.) D.D., 1938; A.M., Princeton, 1908; student Princeton Theol. Sem., 1906-09; m. Mary V. Parsons, June 14, 1917; children—David Carothers, Jean Eleanor. Ordained to ministry Presbyn. Ch., 1909; pastor Presbyn. chs., Cumberland, O., New Castle, Pa., Barnesville, O.; pastor, McKeesport, Pa., 1921-29, Sheraden Ch., Pittsburgh, since 1932. Served with Y.M.C.A. with A.E.F. during World War. Mem. bd. trustees, Presbytery of Pittsburgh. Presbyterian. Mason (K.T.). Home: 3112 Landis St., Pittsburgh, Pa.

WHITMORE, Frank Clifford, prof. organic chemistry; b. N. Attleboro, Mass., Oct. 1, 1887; s. Frank Hale and Lena Avilla (Thomas) W.; A.B., Harvard U., 1911, A.M., 1912, Ph.D., in organic chemistry, 1914; (hon.) Sc.D., Franklin & Marshall Coll., 1937, Univ. of Delaware, 1937, Allegheny Coll., 1938; m. Marion Gertrude Mason, June 22, 1914; children—Frank C., Mason, Harry Edison, Marion Mason II, Patricia Joan (dec.). Instr. organic chemistry, Williams, 1916-17, Rice Inst., Houston, Tex., 1917-18; asst. prof. organic chemistry, U. of Minn., 1918-20; prof. organic chemistry, 1920—, actg. head chemical dept., 1924-25, head, 1925-29, Northwestern U., dean Sch. of Chemistry and Physics, Pa. State Coll. since 1929. Mem. advisory com. Chem. Warfare Service U.S. Army. Mem. Nat. Res. Council (chmn. div. chemistry and chmn. technology, 1927-28 and central petroleum com. 1928-31). Fellow A.A. A.S. (v. p. 1932; chmn. Sect. C); mem. Am. Chem. Soc. (councilor, 1926-28; dir. since 1928, pres. 1938), Am. Inst. Chem. Engineers, Inst. of Chemistry (dir. 1928), Am. Inst. of New York, Chem. Soc. London, Deutsche Chemische Gesell., Sigma Xi, Alpha Chi Sigma, Phi Lambda Upsilon, Phi Kappa Phi, Sigma Pi Sigma, Alpha Epsilon Delta, Phi Beta Kappa. Awarded Wm. H. Nichols Medal, 1937. Clubs: Chemists (Chicago); Chemists (New York); Cosmos (Washington, D.C.); Center Hills Country (State College, Pa.). Author: Organic Compounds of Mercury, 1921; Organic Chemistry, 1937. Mem. editorial bd. Chemical Bulletin, 1923-28, Organic Synthesis, 1925—(editor in chief Vol. 7, 1927, Vol. 12, 1932). Home: State College, Pa.

WHITMOYER, Raymond Britton, teacher and chemist; b. Beaver Lake, Pa., Sept. 29, 1888; s. William James and Sarah Ann (Britton) W.; student Hughesville, Pa. High Sch., 1903-06,

Lycoming Co. Normal Sch., Muncy, Pa., 1907; A.B., Dickinson Sem., Williamsport, Pa., 1911; A.B., Dickinson Coll., Carlisle, Pa., 1913, A. M., 1914; Ph.D., Columbia U., 1933; m. Mary Helen Lehman, of Shippensburg, Pa., Mar. 27, 1915. Teacher Pennsdale, Pa., 1907-08, Tivoli, Pa., 1909-10, South Williamsport (Pa.) High Sch., 1910-11, Conway Hall Prep. Sch., Carlisle, Pa., 1913-14; science teacher high sch., Atlantic City, N.J., 1914-18; research chemist Jackson Lab., Du Pont Co., Deep Water Point, N.J., 1918-19; head science dept. Sr. High Sch., Atlantic City, N.J., since 1919. Mem. N.E.A., N.J. State Teachers Assn., N.J. Science Teachers Assn. (pres. 1934-36), Am. Chem. Soc., Phi Beta Kappa, Sigma Xi, Kappa Delta Pi, Phi Kappa Sigma, Dickinson Coll. Alumni Assn. of Atlantic City (pres. 1934). Republican. Presbyterian. Club: Fortnightly (Atlantic City, N.J.; pres. 1928-30). Author article on sugar chemistry which later was sent on request to editor Gmelins Handbuch der anorganischen Chemie. Home: 43 N. Aberdeen Pl. Office: Albany and Atlantic Avs., Atlantic City, N.J.

WHITNER, Thomas C(obb), Jr., chemist, pres. Ellis Labs., Inc.; b. Atlanta, Ga., Feb. 7, 1893; s. Thomas Cobb and Emily Lou (Tichenor) W.; B.S. in textile engring., Ga. Sch. Tech., Atlanta, Ga., 1914, B.S. in Chem., 1916; Ph.D. (chem.), Johns Hopkins U., 1920; m. Mary Mendenhall, Sept. 9, 1921; chemist Southern Cotton Oil Co., Savannah, Ga., 1916-17, 1920-21; instr. chemistry, Johns Hopkins U., 1921-25, asso., 1925-27; research chemist Standard Oil Co. of N.J., Elizabeth, N.J., 1927-31; supervising chemical research Ellis Labs., Montclair, N.J., since 1931, pres. since 1938, engaged in chem. research, development work, consulting. Mem. Am. Chem. Soc., A.A.A.S., Sigma Phi Epsilon, Gamma Alpha. Republican. Presbyterian. Home: 136 Parker Rd., Elizabeth, N.J. Office: 98 Greenwood Av., Montclair, N.J.

WHITNEY, Alfred Rutgers, constructing engr.; b. N.Y. City, June 16, 1868; s. Alfred R. and Adeline Peers (Nesbitt) W.; prep. edn., Greylock Inst. Mil. Sch., South Williamstown, Mass., and Columbia Grammar Sch., N.Y. City; M.E., Stevens Inst. Tech., 1890, E.D., 1921; unmarried. With Portage Iron Co., Duncansville, Pa., 1890-91; gen. mgr., later v.p. Puget Sound Wire Nail and Steel Co., Everett, Wash., 1891-94, also gen. mgr. and elec. engr. Everett R.R. and Electric Co. and cons. engr. Puget Sound Pulp and Paper Co., Everett & Monte Cristo R.R., 1891-94; rep. Carnegie Steel Co., in Japan, 1894; mem. firm A. R. Whitney, iron and steel mfrs. and contractors, New York, 1894-96; organizer, 1896, A. R. Whitney, Jr. & Co., inc., 1899, as The Whitney Co., of which was pres. and treas. until 1926, chairman board, 1926-29; retired from active business, 1929. Company constructors of Great Am. Ins. Co. Bldg., W. R. Grace & Co. Bldg., Iron Age Bldg., New York; Masonic Temple and Central Branch Y.M.C.A., Brooklyn; Stock Exchange Bldg., Baltimore; Wentworth Inst., Boston; Amherst (Mass.) Coll. Library; International Trust Co. Building, Denver; Smith Building, Seattle, Wash., etc. War correspondent in Ethiopia, 1930. Director Morristown Trust Company. Mem. Squadron A, cav., N.Y.N.G., 1897; maj. staff Gov. Frank W. Higgins, 1905, and of Gov. John Alden Dix, 1911; brevet maj., 1911, successively capt. and regtl. adj., maj. and brigade adj. gen., 1912-16; aide to rear admiral Nathaniel R. Usher, 1913-17; aide Bur. of Naval Intelligence, World War. Mem. Am. Soc. C.E., N.E. Soc., Am. Geographic Society, S.R., Delta Tau Delta. Republican. Episcopalian. Clubs: Union League, University, Downtown Assn., Metropolitan Opera, Piping Rock, New York Yacht, Seawanhaka-Corinthian Yacht, Cruising Club of America, Anglers' (New York); Traveler, Explorer, Angler, Yachtsman and Navigator. Writer on engring., travel, cruising, fishing, etc. Designer and builder of the "Ruffhouse," original of now universally accepted type of Fla. houseboat. Home: Morristown, N.J., and 137 E. 66th St., New York, N.Y.

WHITNEY, E. Arthur, physician; b. Northampton, Mass., Oct. 20, 1895; s. Daniel W. and Jennie Mae (Longeway) W.; student Tufts Coll. Pre-Med. Sch., Medford, Mass., 1916-18, M.D., Med. Sch., 1922; m. Sarah A. Porter, June 25, 1924. Interne Booth Maternity Hosp., Boston, Jan.-June 1922, Springfield (Mass.) Hosp., 1922-23; resident in medicine and surgery New York Hosp., 1923-24; practice in Suffern, N.Y., 1924-26; asst. supt. Elwyn (Pa.) Training Sch. (private instn. for mentally retarded, organized 1852), 1926-30, supt. since 1930; instr. in psychiatry, U. of Pa. Med. Sch., Phila. Sch. of Occupational Therapy; staff mem. Chester (Pa.) Hosp. Vice-pres. and dir. Delaware Co. Welfare Council; dir. Delaware Co. Children's Camp. Served as pvt., U.S. Army, 1918. Mem. Delaware Co. Med. Soc. (dir.), Pa. Med. Soc., A.M.A., Am. Psychiatric Assn. (fellow), Am. Assn. on Mental Deficiency (nat. sec.), Philadelphia Commission for Study of Mental Deficiency, Epilepsy, and Delinquency (chairman committee for comprehensive plan, 1939). Assn. of Supts. and Trustees Pa. Instns. (pres. 1938), Phi Chi. Republican. Presbyterian. Mason. Club: Tufts (Phila.). Contbr. many articles on medicine, psychiatry and mental retardation to med jours. Address: Elwyn, Pa.

WHITNEY, Gerald DeForrest, educator; b. Bradley, Mich., Mar. 8, 1884; s. Frank G. and Edith A. (Hoyt) W.; student High Sch. and Kalamazoo (Mich.) Normal Sch.; B.S., Carnegie Inst. Tech., 1917; M.A., Columbia U., 1926; D.Sc., Stout Inst., 1927; m. Enola Erath, Apr. 16, 1916; children—Mary Edith, Jean, William. Teacher Pittsburgh pub. schs., 1909-19; dir. vocational edn., Altoona, Pa., 1919-20; supervisor vocational edn., Dept. of Pub. Instrn., Harrisburg, Pa., 1920-24; prof. and head dept. vocational teacher training, U. of Pittsburgh, 1924-36; deputy supt., Dept. of Pub. Instrn., Harrisburg, 1936-37; asso. supt. in charge secondary edn., Pittsburgh Pub. Schs., since 1938. Mem. N.E.A., Am. Vocational Assn., Pa. State Edn. Assn., Pittsburgh Personnel Assn. (dir.), Iota Lambda Sigma (past pres. Grand Chapter), Phi Delta Kappa, Kappa Phi Kappa. Democrat. Episcopalian. Clubs: Faculty (U. of Pittsburgh), Kiwanis (Pittsburgh). Contbr. to professional mags. Home: Notre Dame Place. Office: Board of Public Education, Pittsburgh, Pa.

WHITNEY, Philip Richardson, retired educator; b. Council Bluffs, Ia., Dec. 31, 1878; s. William Lambert and Alpa Matilda (Nutt) W.; student Newton (Mass.) pub. schs.; grad. Mass. Inst. Tech., 1902, post-grad. study in architecture, 1902-03; studied and traveled abroad, 6 mos., 1903; m. Helen Reed Jones, Apr. 17, 1906; children—Reed, Alpa Whitney Shelton. Collaborated with Prof. William Rotch Ware on several text books, 1903-04; instr. architecture, U. of Pa., 1904-10, asst. prof. graphics, 1910-20, prof. graphics, Sch. of Fine Arts, 1920-36; retired, 1936. Mem. Pa. Chapter Sigma Xi. Republican. Episcopalian. Clubs: Art, Water Color (Phila.); Players (Swarthmore, Pa.). Home: Orchard Av., Moylan, Pa.

WHITNEY, Russell Wayne, v.p. The Hinde & Dauch Paper Co.; b. Versailles, O., Jan. 16, 1889; s. Charles T. and Clara B. (Gulick) W.; ed. pub. sch.; m. Elsa Graefe, June 3, 1924; 1 son, Philip Graefe. Began as apprentice with The Hinde & Dauch Paper Co., Sandusky, O., 1910, advanced through various positions, becoming v.p., 1934. Served in U.S. Army, World War, 21 mos. Republican. Episcopalian. Home: 75 Prospect Av., Montclair, N.J. Office: 550 Ninth St., Hoboken, N.J.

WHITNEY, Will Alvah, journalist; b. Wakefield, Mass., July 10, 1902; s. George Augustus and Minnieville Whitney (Woodward) W.; grad. Taunton (Mass.) High Sch., 1920; B.S., Mass. Agrl. (now State) Coll., Amherst, Mass., 1924; unmarried. Asst. scientific aide U.S. Dept. of Agr., Washington, D.C., 1924-26, jr. pathotogist, 1926-33; mem. Washington Post dramatic dept., 1929-37; became Washington corr. for Nat. Exhibitor and Jay Emanuel publs., 1933; Washington corr. for Motion Picture Daily, 1934-38; asst. to mng. editor Jay Emanuel Publs., Inc. (motion picture trade jours.), Phila., since 1938. Life mem. Am. Phytopathol. Soc.; founder Am. Phytopathol. Soc. Press, editor in chief, 1929-32. Co-author several scientific papers. Home: 1623 Pine St. Office: 1225 Vine St., Philadelphia, Pa.

WHITRIDGE, William, banker, broker; b. Baltimore, Md., Aug. 9, 1869; s. John A. and Elen Ward (Henderson) W.; ed. private sch., Baltimore, U. of Berlin (Germany), 1890-91; A.B., Johns Hopkins U., 1890; m. Marie Louise Perin, Oct. 14, 1916; 1 dau., Gladys Perin. With Baltimore (Md.) Trust & Guarantee Co., 1893-98; v.p. Citizens' Trust Co., and Union Trust Co., Baltimore; mem. of firm John A. Whitridge Son bankers and brokers, Baltimore, Md., since 1908; dir. Western Nat. Bank, Md. Life Ins. Co. Served with Red Cross in France during World War. Mem. staff of Gov. Philips Lee Goldsborough, 1912-16. Mem. Delta Phi. Republican. Episcopalian. Clubs: Bachelors' Cotillion, Maryland, Elkridge, Merchants' (Baltimore). Home: Hotel Belvedere. Office: Garrett Bldg., Baltimore, Md.

WHITSIT, Lyle Antrim, hydro-elec. engring.; b. Decatur, Ill., May 15, 1881; s. Charles William and Laura (Chipman) W.; B.S. in engring., high sch., Ann Arbor, Mich., 1900; B.S. in C.E., U. of Mich., 1904, B.S. in Mar. Engring., same, 1905; m. Ruby Evans, Oct. 1, 1907 (now dec.); m. 2d, Marguerite Shaffer, Oct. 31, 1916; children—Keith Antrim, Florence Jean. Began as designer structural steel, 1906-10; has followed profession hydro-elec. engr. since 1910; prin. asst. engr. and res. engr. Aluminum Co. America, 1910-12; designer on N.Y. City Subway, 1913; dist. engr. Forest Service, 1914-18; cons. engr. to Japan for Aluminum Co. America, 1919; hydraulic engineer Superpower Survey, 1920; hydraulic engr. Adirondack P. & L. Corpn., 1921-24; hydraulic engr. Electric Bond and Share Co., 1925-26; hydraulic engr. United Engrs. & Constructors, Phila., 1927-35; prin. engr. U.S. Corps Engrs. in charge Div. No. 3 Passamoquoddy Project, Eastport, Me., 1935; cons. hydraulic engr. Ebasco Services, Inc., New York City, since 1935. Served as capt. Engrs. during World War; maj. U.S. Engrs. Res., 1920-30. Mem. Am. Soc. Civil Engrs., Am. Inst. Elec. Engrs., Am. Soc. Mech. Engrs. Republican. Episcopalian. Contbr. articles to sci. mags. and publs. Home: 615 Elm Av., Swarthmore, Pa. Office: No. 2 Rector St., New York, N.Y.

WHITTAKER, Clyde Malcolm, mfg. exec.; b. Ellwood City, Pa., Jan. 6, 1900; s. Elmer Ellsworth and Jessie (Ward) W.; student New Castle (Pa.) High Sch., U. of Mich.; m. Elisabeth Virginia Stadelhofer, Nov. 21, 1925; 1 son, Richard Ellsworth. Auditor, Universal Sanitary Mfg. Co., 1923-29, sec., treas. and dir., 1929-37, v.p., treas. and dir. since 1937. Dir. New Castle (Pa.) Sch. Bd. since 1936, v.p. since 1937. Home: 203 Englewood Av. Office: P.O. Box 391, New Castle, Pa.

WHITTEMORE, Clark McKinley, lawyer, banker; b. N.Y. City, May 2, 1876; s. Clark F. and Annie (McKinley) W.; ed. high sch., Elizabeth, N.J.; m. Regina G. Baremore, June 12, 1915; children—Patricia, Jean, Ann Randel, Clark McKinley, Margaret, John Rae. Admitted to N.J. bar, 1897, and began practice at Elizabeth; mem. Whittemore & McLean since 1922; pres. Union County Trust Company, 1922-34, now chmn. bd.; vice-pres. El Mora Realty Co.; dir. Linden Trust Co., Am. Gas Accumulator Co., Highway Lighthouse Co. Judge District Court, Elizabeth, 1908-13. Mem. Am. Bar Assn., N.J. State Bar Assn., Union County Bar Assn. (pres. 2 yrs.), N.J. Bankers Assn. Republican. Episcopalian. Mason. Clubs: Rotary, Elizabeth Town and Country. Home: 225 W. Jersey St. Office: 125 Broad St., Elizabeth, N.J.

WHITTEMORE, Laurens Ellis, radio engring.; b. Topeka, Kan., Aug. 20, 1892; s. Luther Denny and Frances Dean (Davis) W.; A.B., Washburn Coll., Topeka, 1914; A.M., U. of Kan., 1917; m. Gladys Ruth Walford, Oct. 14, 1919; children—Chester Davis, Nancy Walford, Jean Lytle. Instr. physics, U. of Kan., 1915-17; asst. and asso. physicist, radio lab. U.S. Bur. of Standards, Washington, D.C., 1917-24; sec. interdept. radio adv. com., U.S. Dept. Commerce, Washington, D.C., 1924; with Am.

Telephone & Telegraph Co., New York City since 1925; sec. Internat. Radio Conf., Washington, D.C., 1927. Fellow Inst. Radio Engrs.; mem. Am. Inst. Elec. Engrs., Washington Acad. Scis., Sigma Xi. Republican. Methodist. Clubs: Cosmos (Washington, D.C.). Home: 29 Berkeley Rd., Maplewood, N.J. Office: 195 Broadway, New York, N.Y.

WHITTEN, Charles E., judge; b. Burrell Twp., Westmoreland Co., Pa., Jan. 17, 1869; s. Alexander and Elizabeth (Martin) W.; grad. Indiana State Teachers Coll.; post-grad. course, Slippery Rock State Normal Sch.; m. Bessie G. Perdue, Apr. 6, 1898; children—Elizabeth H., Katherine M. Successively teacher pub. schs., Rice Collegiate Inst. and Markle Normal Acad.; studied law under Judge A. D. McConnell; admitted to bar, 1893; partner with J. R. Smith, 1893-1907; became partner Gaither & Whitten, 1907; apptd. judge Ct. of Common Pleas of Westmoreland Co., 10th Judicial Dist. of Pa., May 1921, elected for term of 10 yrs., Nov. 1921, re-elected, 1931, commd. president judge by gov., 1937. Mem. Pa. State Legislature, 1903-07. Mason (Dist. Deputy Grand Master). Served as elder, Presbyn. Ch., Sunday Sch. supt. and teacher Men's Bible Class. Author: Life of Alexander Hamilton. Home: 401 N. Main St. Address: Court House, Greensburg, Pa.

WHITTEN, Thomas E., lawyer; b. Wilkinsburg, Pa., May 24, 1903; s. Thomas and Georgia Savannah (Robbins) W.; grad. Wilkinsburg High Sch., 1921; student U. of Pittsburgh, 1921-23; LL.B., Dickinson Sch. of Law, 1926; m. Mildred R. Buckley, Dec. 18, 1937; 1 dau., Mildred Buckley. Admitted to Pa. bar, 1927; and since practiced in Pittsburgh; in office of U.S. atty., 1927-28; asst. solicitor, Allegheny Co., 1932-35; gen. counsel Rep. Com., Allegheny Co., 1935-38; associated with J. P. Fife and Douglas, Fife & Young; vice-pres. Acme Ash Co. Mem. Bd. for Assessment and Revision of Taxes of Allegheny Co., 1935; councilman, Borough of Wilkinsburg, 1930-33 and 1938-41. Mem. Alpha Chi Rho. Republican. Presbyn. Mason. Club: Youghiogheny Country. Home: 939 Trenton Av., Wilkinsburg, Pa. Office: 818 Frick Bldg., Pittsburgh, Pa.

WHITTLESEY, Charles Raymond, economist; b. Roseburg, Ore., Sept. 24, 1900; s. Charles Terrill and Penelope (Skinner) W.; A.B., Philomath Coll., 1921; ed. Occidental Coll., 1919-20; A.M., Am. Univ., Beirut, Syria, 1924; ed. U. of Wash., 1924-25; Ph.D., Princeton, 1928; m. Mary Weaver Fox, June 19, 1929; 1 dau., Margaret Terrill. Engaged in teaching, Am. Univ. of Beirut, Syria, 1921-24, with Near East Relief, Athens, Greece, 1923; economist, U.S. Tariff Commn., Washington, D.C., 1928; instr. econs., Princeton U., 1928-29, asst. prof., 1929-34, asso. prof. econs. since 1934; fellow Social Sci. Research Council in Europe, 1935-36; mem. Hines-Kemmerer Commn. to Turkey, 1934. Author: Governmental Control of Crude Rubber, 1931; International Monetary Issues, 1937. Contbr. articles on economic subjects to Encyclopaedia of Social Sciences and American and foreign learned journals. Mem. Am. Econs. Assn., Royal Econ. Soc. Democrat. Mem. Religious Soc. of Friends. Home: 48 Patton Av., Princeton, N.J.

WHITTLESEY, Federal Eliphalet, mgr. Raymond Mfg. Co.; b. Petroleum Center, Pa., June 4, 1870; s. Henry E. and Elizabeth (Wilson) W.; ed. high sch.; m. Flora E. Heath, Dec. 27, 1892; children—Louise E., Florence May, Federal Lee. Mgr. Raymond Mfg. Co., Corry, Pa., since 1891; v.p. and dir. Associated Spring Corpn., Bristol, Conn. Mem. Corry (Pa.) Sch. Bd., 1912-23, pres., 1919-23. Mem. Am. Soc. M.E., Am. Soc. Metals, Soc. Automotive Engrs. Prohibition Party. Presbyterian. Home: 202 W. Church St. Office: 226 S. Center St., Corry, Pa.

WHITTLESEY, Frederick Rendell, physician, univ. prof.; b. Shanghai, China, Jan. 30, 1901; s. Roger Burrell, citizen of U.S., and Annie (Withey) W.; A.B., Coll. of Wooster, O., 1921; M.D., Western Reserve U. Med. Sch., 1925; m. Helen Sperry, June 26, 1926; children—Clare, Ann. Interne Lakeside Hosp., Cleveland, O., 1925-26; resident physician Cleveland City Hosp., 1926-27, medical supt., 1927-29; engaged in practice internal medicine, Tulsa, Okla., 1929-30; physician, student health service, W.Va. Univ., Morgantown, W.Va. since 1930, dir. dept. since 1932; asso. prof. medicine, W.Va. Univ. Med. Sch., since 1935. Fellow Am. Med. Assn. Asso. Am. Coll. Physicians. Mem. W.Va. State Med. Assn., Monongalia Co. Med. Soc., Alpha Omega Alpha, Nu Sigma Nu. Asso. editor W.Va. State Medical Journal since 1939. Home: 100 Jackson Av., Morgantown, W.Va.

WHITTON, John Boardman, law educator; b. Oakland, Calif., Feb. 25, 1892; s. Charles Francis and Helen (Blakeslee) W.; A.B., U. of Calif., 1916, J.D., 1920; student in Paris, (Am. Field Service Fellow), The Hague, Geneva, 1923-26; Diplomé en Droit Internat., U. of Paris, 1926; m. Dangla de Laplane Laguerre, 1926; 1 dau., Hélène Andrée. Admitted to Calif. bar, 1919, and practiced in San Francisco, 1920-23; instr. internat. law, Princeton U., 1927-28, asst. prof., 1928-30, asso. prof. since 1930; dir. Geneva Research Center (on leave from Princeton U.), 1936-38; lecturer Institut des Hautes Etudes Internationales, Paris, 1927, 32, 34, at Acad. of Internat. Law, The Hague, 1927, 34, at Geneva Inst. of Internat. Relations, 1935, at Grad. Inst. of Internat. Studies, Geneva, 1936-38. Mem. bd. advisors Research in Internat. Law, Harvard, since 1929; dir. Legal Research Com. on Economic Sanctions, Twentieth Century Fund, 1930-31; mem. editorial bd. Revue Internationale Française du Droit des Gens since 1936. Served with American Ambulance Field Service, Am. Red Cross and French Army, 1917-1919. Decorated Knight of the Legion of Honor. Mem. Académie Diplomatique Internationale, Institut International d'Histoire Constitutionnelle, Am. Soc. Internat. Law, Alpha Delta Phi, Phi Delta Phi. Clubs: Princeton (New York); Nassau (Princeton). Author: Neutralité et la Societé des Nations, 1928; Doctrine de Monroe, 1933; La Règle pacta sunt servanda, 1935. Contbr. to Am. and European jours. Radio news commentator, Franco-Am. exchange, 1935-36. Home: 18 Edgehill St. Address: Dickinson Hall, Princeton, N.J.

WHITWORTH, John Burton, utility exec.; b. Piedmont, W.Va., Oct. 23, 1888; s. Edwin Walter and Laura Virginia (Burton) W.; ed. pub. schs. and Bliss Elec. Sch. (Washington); m. Alice Crooks, Sept. 16, 1914; children—John Burton, Elizabeth, Laura Virginia. Supt. of distribution Schuylkill div., Pa. Power & Light Co., 1911-12; mgr. Lykens Valley Light & Power Co., 1913-23; v.p. Gen. Utilities & Operating Co., 1918-35; gen. mgr. Peoples (Miami Beach) Gas Co., 1931-32; pres. Compania Electria De Santo Domingo, 1930-32; pres. Am. States Pub. Service Co., 1932-36; chmn. bd. Am. States Utilities Corpn. since 1936, also pres. since July 1938. Republican. Episcopalian. Club: Chester River Yacht and Country. Home: Radcliffe Hall, Chestertown, Md. Office: 833 Market St., Wilmington, Del.

WHOLEY, Cornelius Collins, neuropsychiatrist; b. Staunton, Va., May 4, 1875; s. William and Hannah (Collins) W.; A.B., Rock Hill Coll., Md., 1893, (hon.) A.M., 1895; M.D., U. of Va., 1899; grad. student Univ. of Vienna, 1899-1900; Johns Hopkins Med. Sch., 1900-02; m. Alice M. Douthitt, Dec. 28, 1908; m. 2d, Lillian Smith, May 26, 1933. In gen. practice of medicine, Baltimore and Pittsburgh, 1902-12; in practice of neuropsychiatry, Pittsburgh, since 1912; mem. psychiatric staff St. Francis Hosp. since 1910; neurologic staff Western Pa. Hosp. since 1914; consultant Homestead Hosp. since 1923; consultant Allegheny Co. Hosp. for Insane since 1920; psychiatrist Western State Penitentiary since 1923; lecturer on psychology, U. of Pittsburgh, since 1930; instr. in psychiatry, U. of Pittsburgh Sch. of Medicine, 1915-21, asst. prof., 1921-35, asso. prof. since 1935; consultant psychiatrist Federal Dist. Court of Pittsburgh since 1937. Served as capt., Med. Corps, U.S. Army, 1918-19. Diplomate in psychiatry and neurology; fellow Am. Coll. Physicians, A.M.A.; mem. Psychiat. Assn., Psychopathol. Assn., Psychoanalytic Assn. (pres. 1921), Pittsburgh Neuropsychiat. Assn. (pres. 1921-23). Clubs: University, Agora, Polygon (Pittsburgh). Home: Alder Court Apts. Office: 121 University Place, Pittsburgh, Pa.

WIBLE, Elmer E., physician; b. Greensburg, Pa., Jan. 8, 1867; s. William E. and Elizabeth (Truxal) W.; ed. Greensburg Sem., 1886-89; M.D., U. of Pittsburgh Med. Sch., 1891; m. Mary K. Cooper, June 16, 1903; children—William P., Betty, Jane T. (Mrs. Wm. Eberhardt II). Engaged in teaching sch. 1884-86; in gen. practice of medicine at Homestead, Pa., since 1891, specializing in ophthalmology since 1908; dir. Monongahela Trust Co.; pres. staff Homestead Hosp. Dir. Reformed Ch. Orphans Home. Mem. Am., Pa. State, Allegheny Co. and Pittsburgh ophthal. socs. Republican. Reformed Ch. Mason (K.T., 32°, Shriner). Club: Edgewood. Home: 416 Maple Av., Edgewood, Pa. Office: 238 E. 8th Av., Homestead, Pa.

WIBLE, Robert Edward, U.S. commr.; b. Gettysburg, Pa., Sept. 10, 1867; s. J. Edward and C. Rebecca (Belch) W.; B.S., Pa. Coll. (now Gettysburg Coll.), Gettysburg, Pa., 1889, M.S., 1891; m. Jean S. Cope, Jan. 14, 1902; children—R. Edward, Ralph Cope, E. Bradley, Joseph Belch, Charles L., H. Emley. Burgess City of Gettysburg, 1894-97; dist. atty. Adams Co. (Pa.), 1903-16; U.S. commr., Middle Dist. of Pa., since 1916. Republican. Lutheran. Mason (K.T.), Elk, Moose. Address: Mummasburg Rd., Gettysburg, Pa.

WICK, George DeWitte, lawyer; b. Slippery Rock, Pa., May 17, 1888; s. Alonzo S. and Margaret (Gill) W.; A.B., Grove City Coll., 1911; LL.B., U. of Pittsburgh, 1917; m. Margaret Ingersoll, Nov. 25, 1914; children—Kathryn, George, Ruth. Admitted to practice before cts. of Pa., Oct. 12, 1914; member of firm of Wick & Donley, 1914-17; with law firm Reed, Smith, Shaw & McClay, Pittsburgh, 1917-31; mem. firm Campbell, Wick, Houck & Thomas since 1931; admitted to practice before U.S. Supreme Ct., Oct. 24, 1932. Mem. Am. Bar Assn., Pa. State Bar Assn., Allegheny County Bar Assn. Clubs: Duquesne, Oakmont Country, University of Pittsburgh, Pittsburgh Athletic Assn. Home: 4754 Wallingford St. Office: 11th Floor, Peoples Bank Bldg., 307 Fourth Av., Pittsburgh, Pa.

WICKER, Samuel Evaristus, clergyman, educator; b. Altoona, Pa., Mar. 10, 1892; s. John Henry and Alice Regina (Wilt) W.; student Altoona (Pa.) High Sch., 1905-09, Gettysburg (Pa.) Theol. Sem., 1914-17; A.B., Gettysburg (Pa.) Coll., 1914; M.A., U. of Pa., 1923; S.T.D., Temple U., Phila., Pa., 1925; m. Orpah Christina Ashby, Dec. 12, 1918. Pastor St. Mark's Lutheran Ch., Oakland, Md., 1917-20; head social sciences Oakland (Md) High Sch., 1917-19; pastor Holy Trinity Lutheran Ch., Wilmington, Del., 1920-26; exec. sec. Wilmington Council of Chs., 1924-26; prof. religious edn., Temple U., Phila., 1924-25; prof. English and history, Wilmington High Sch., 1926-28, 1929-35; prof. religious edn., Cedar Crest Coll., Allentown, Pa., 1928-29; prof. of English, Wilmington Vocational Sch., 1930-32, religious edn., Lutheran Sch. of Christian Edn., Phila., 1930-38, social sciences, Pierre S. du Pont High Sch., Wilmington, Del., since 1935; prof. O.T., psychology, humanities and social sciences, Am. Theol. Sem. and Wilmington Bible Coll., Wilmington, since 1936, pres. since 1937; dir. religious edn., St. Stephen's Luth. Ch., Wilmington, since 1935. Served as Four Minute Man, United War Work Campaign, 1917-19; chmn. Garrett Co. (Md.) Jr. Red Cross, 1917-20, Trustee Am. Theol. Sem. since 1936. Mem. N.E.A., Religious Edn. Assn., Internat. Council Religious Edn., Druids, Sigma Beta, Phi Kappa Sigma. Republican. Lutheran. Mason (Blue Lodge, Chapter, Commandery, Consistory). Address: 719 W. 32d St., Wilmington, Del.

WICKERSHAM, Frank Borbridge, lawyer, judge; b. Newberry Twp., York Co., Pa., Apr. 7, 1863; s. Joseph and Hanna Cadwallader (Squibb) W.; ed. pub. schs. of York Co., 1869-81; M. Edn., Cumberland Valley State Normal Sch., 1884; hon. A.M., Gettysburg Coll., 1913, hon. LL.D., 1923; hon. LL.D., Albright Coll., 1928; m. Mary Fencil, Mar. 19, 1889 (died 1906); children—Frank Breyster, Robert Cadwallader, James Hopkins; m. 2d, Ruby S. Seacrest, May 4, 1910. Engaged in teaching in pub. schs., York Co. and Dauphin Co., 1881-88; admitted to

Pa. bar, 1888 and engaged in gen. practice at Harrisburg; mem. firm Wickersham and Metzger, 1911-20; asst. dist. atty., 1900-08 and 1912-20; County Solicitor, 1920; apptd. Judge Ct. of Common Pleas, 1920, elected for term 1922-32 and re-elected for term 1932-42. Mem. Phi Sigma Kappa. Republican. Lutheran. Mason (K.T., 32°, Shriner). I.O.O.F., K.P. Home: 2709 N. Front St. Office: Court House, Harrisburg, Pa.

WICKERSHAM, John Hough, engring. and construction; b. Lancaster, Pa., Oct. 11, 1881; s. J. Harold and Jessie W. (Hough) W.; Science Diploma, Phillips Acad., Andover, Mass., 1898; Ph.B., Sheffield Scientific Sch. (Yale U.), 1901; m. Marian S. Burroughs, Jan. 18, 1911; children—Marianne B., Joan H. Began in engring. and construction work, N.Y. City, 1901; night supt. Hudson Tunnels, New York, N.Y.; inspector under water, Hartford, Conn.; engaged in engring. and construction on own acct., Lancaster, Pa. since 1906; prop. Greenland Farms; pres. Conestoga Transportation Co.; dir. Farmers Bank & Trust Co. Served as capt., later col., engrs. U.S.A., World War. Decorated Purple Heart with Oak Cluster. Dir. Lancaster Gen. Hosp., Shippen Sch. Professional Engr. and Land Surveyor in Pa. Mem. Am. Soc. Civil Engrs., Am. Soc. Mech. Engrs., Am. Soc. Refrigerating Engrs., Am. Soc. for Testing Materials, Am. Concrete Inst., Nat. Fire Protection Assn., Theta Xi. Presbyn. (trustee 1st Ch). Clubs: Lancaster Country (dir.), Hamilton (Lancaster); Engineers and Yale of Philadelphia (dir. of both); Yale (New York); Army and Navy (Washington). Home: R.F.D. No. 4. Office: 14 S. Duke St., Lancaster, Pa.

WICKLINE, Robert Liddell, tax and business counselor; b. Glasgow, O., Dec. 1, 1880; s. Joseph Reynolds Coates and Susan Rebecca (Boyce) Wickline; graduate public high school, Sharpsburg, Pa., 1896, Pittsburgh Business College, 1899; married Bessie Headrick Clark, September 4, 1906 (died 1924); married 2d, Myrtle Irene Smith, May 26, 1927. Employed with Pa. R.R. Co. in passenger and freight offices, 1896-99; sec. to gen. supt., A. V. Ry., 1899-1901; auditor and sec. to pres., Peoples Nat. Bank, Pittsburgh, Pa., 1901-07; cashier Home Life Ins. Co. of N.Y., Pittsburgh, Pa., 1907-09; also organized Wickline Ins. Agency and propr. since 1907; supervisor of agts., Pittsburgh Life & Trust Co., 1909-17; with U.S. Treasury Dept. in various capacities, 1917-20; organized and pres. Corporation Audit Company, Pittsburgh, since 1920; asst. supervisor, U. S. Census, West Pa., 1930; individually specializes in estate management and as bus. and tax counselor; dir. Pittsburgh Cobalt Silver Co. Served as auditor Mt. Lebanon Twp. Trustee and sec. Centenary Fund Soc. of Pittsburg Conf. Republican. Methodist (pres. and trustee Mt. Lebanon Ch.). Mason (K.T., 32°, Shriner). Clubs: Pennsylvania Society of New York; Pittsburgh Motor (dir.), Insurance, Y.M.C.A., Methodist Social Union (Pittsburgh). Radio speaker on vital questions of the day since 1920; pub. speaker to large gatherings. Contbr. articles on current events and topics. Home: 200 Cedar Boul., Mt. Lebanon, Pa. Office: 4151 Jenkins Arcade, Pittsburgh, Pa.

WICKS, Elverton Hazlett, lawyer; b. Elizabeth, Pa., Apr. 17, 1884; s. Silas Monroe and Anna N. (Scott) W.; A.B., Washington and Jefferson Coll., Washington, Pa., 1909; LL.B., U. of Pittsburgh Law Sch., 1912; m. Grace C. Daughaday, June 30, 1914; children—Helen Roberta, William Hazlett. Admitted to Pa. bar, 1912, and since in gen. practice at Pittsburgh; atty. and dir. Treesdale Laboratories, Inc. Served as pres. Bellevue Sch. Bd., 6 yrs. Pres. Allied Bds. of Trade, 1 yr., Bellevue Bd. of Trade, 2 yrs.; chmn. com. on offenses of Ct. of Common Pleas of Allegheny Co. and of the Allegheny Co. Bar Assn. since 1934 and chmn. spl. investigating com. apptd. by Ct. Order, July 7, 1938. Mem. Allegheny Bar Assn., Phi Kappa Psi. Republican. Methodist. Club: Highland Country. Home: R.F.D. No. 3, Bellevue, Pa. Office: 1200 Jones Law Bldg., Pittsburgh, Pa.

WICKS, John Oliver, lawyer; b. Gill Hall, Pa., Feb. 4, 1880; s. Silas M. and Anna N. (Scott) W.; B.S., Washington & Jefferson Coll., Washington, Pa., 1906; LL.B., Harvard Law Sch., 1910; m. Eleanor O. Graham, June 29, 1921; children—John O., Virginia Louise. Admitted to Supreme Court bar, 1911 and since engaged in gen. practice of law; mem. law firm Weller, Wicks & Wallace, Pittsburgh, since 1921. Pres. M. E. Hosp. and Home for Aged since 1937. Mem. Am. Bar Assn., Pa. State Bar Assn., Allegheny Co. Bar Assn., Phi Kappa Psi. Methodist (pres. bd. trustees since 1925). Clubs: Duquesne, Harvard-Yale-Princeton (Pittsburgh); Highland Country. Home: 11 N. Howard St., Bellevue, Pa. Office: 915 Park Bldg., Pittsburgh, Pa.

WICKS, Robert Russell, clergyman; b. Utica, N.Y., June 3, 1882; s. Russell Haywood and Mary (Head) W.; B.A., Hamilton Coll., 1904, M.A., 1908; grad. Union Theol. Sem., 1908; D.D., Hamilton, 1919, Williams, 1925, Yale, 1926, Rutgers U., 1937; m. Eleanor MacMaster Hall, Oct. 18, 1910; children—Janet Lansing, Alden MacMaster, David Douglas, Robert Stewart, Margaret Cuthbert, Mary Boyd (dec.). Ordained Congl. ministry, 1908; pastor Arlington Av. Presbyn. Ch., East Orange, N.J., 1908-14, Second Congl. Ch., Holyoke, Mass., 1914-28, also chaplain Mt. Holyoke Coll., 1925-28; dean of Chapel, Princeton U., since Oct. 1929. Y.M.C.A. service, 6 mos., World War. Mem. bd. dirs Union Theol. Sem. Mem. Alpha Delta Phi. Author: The Reason for Living, 1934. Home: Princeton, N.J.

WICOFF, John Van Buren, lawyer; b. Plainsboro, N.J., June 9, 1878; s. John and Catharine Lucretia (Britton) W.; prep. edn. State Model Sch., Trenton, N.J., 1891-96; A.B., Princeton, 1900; student New York Law Sch., 1900-01, Jan.-June 1903; m. Lavinia Ely Applegate, June 8, 1904; children—John Edward, Douglas Britton, Dorothy Applegate (Mrs. W. M. Bennett), Catharine Lavinia, Evelyn Elizabeth, Marjorie Frances, Lavinia Applegate. Admitted to N.J. bar, 1903, and practiced as partner of late Judge William M. Lanning, until his appmt. to U.S. Dist. Court, 1904; practiced alone, 1904-11; mem. firm of Wicoff & Lanning since 1911; has served as atty. for Cranbury, Monroe, South Brunswick townships, Middlesex County and for Lawrence and West Windsor, Mercer County; president, dir. and counsel Broad St. Nat. Bank of Trenton; pres. and dir. Trenton Bone Fertilizer Co.; dir. Trenton Savings Fund Soc.; counsel and dir. Walker-Gordon Lab. Co., Inc. Mem. twp. com. Cranbury Twp., 1911-13; chmn. twp. com. Plainsboro Twp. since 1922. Rep. candidate for state senator from Middlesex Co., 1936. Mem. Bd. of Edn., Cranbury Twp., 1908-19; pres. Bd. of Edn., Plainsboro Twp. since 1919; mem. Middlesex Co. Vocational Sch. Bd. since 1914. Chmn. Mercer Co. Com. on Character and Fitness of Bar Candidates through Supreme Court Appmt. since 1923. During World War served as Federal food adminstr., Mercer Co., N.J., and City of Trenton; chmn. War Savings Stamp Com. and chmn. Y.M.C.A. War Fund Drive Com. of Plainsboro; mem. legal advisory bds. Mem. Am., N.J. State, and Mercer Co. Bar Assns., N.J Soc. of Sons of the Revolution (former chancellor), N.J. Soc. Colonial Wars (treas. since 1930), N.J. Soc. Order of Founders and Patriots of America (former gov.), Holland Soc. of N.Y. (vice-pres.), St. Nicholas Soc. of City of New York. Republican. Presbyterian. Mason (K.T., Shriner). Clubs: Rotary, Trenton, Princeton (Trenton); Nassau (Princeton). Home 1900 Princeton Rd., Plainsboro, N.J. Office: 143 E. State St., Trenton, N.J.

WIDENER, George Dunton; b. Philadelphia, Pa., Mar. 11, 1889; s. George Dunton and Eleanor (Elkins) W.; ed. DeLancey Sch.; m. Jessie Sloane, Mar. 20, 1917. Dir. Land Title Bank & Trust Co., Phila. Traction Co. V.p. and trustee Phila. Museum of Art; trustee Zool. Soc., Acad. Natural Sciences. Clubs: Philadelphia, Racquet (Phila.). Home: Chestnut Hill, Pa. Office: Land Title Bldg., Philadelphia, Pa.

WIDENER, Joseph E., capitalist; grad. U. of Pa. Sch. of Architecture; m. Ella H. Pancoast, (dec.). Dir. B.&O. R.R. Co., Phila. Nat. Bank, Fidelity-Phila. Trust Company, Land Title Bank and Trust Co., Reading Co., Electric Storage Battery Co., etc. Interested in horse racing; maintains stud near Lexington, Ky., and Chantilly, France; prin. owner Belmont Park Race track, Hialeah Park Race Track of Miami Jockey Club Owner of notable art collection, some 300 paintings, including 16 Rembrandts, Titians, Raphaels, Gainsboroughs, Van Dycks, Holbeins, Millets. Home: Elkins Park, Philadelphia. Office: Land Title Bldg., Philadelphia, Pa.

WIEDEFELD, Mary Theresa, coll. pres.; b. Baltimore, Md., Feb. 2, 1886; d. William Jenkins and Frances (Johnston) W.; diploma Md. State Normal Sch., Baltimore, Md., 1904; B.S., Johns Hopkins Univ., 1925, D.Ed., 1935. Engaged in teaching, elementary grades, Baltimore Co., Md., 1904-11, supervisor of primary grades, 1911-14; teacher of practice, Md. State Normal Sch., 1914-16, prin. training sch., 1916-19; supervisor elementary schs., Anne Arundel Co., Md., 1919-24; state supervisor elementary schs. of Md., 1924-38; pres. State Teachers Coll., Towson, Md., since 1938. Mem. Pi Lambda Theta. Democrat. Roman Catholic. Home: Glen Esk, Towson, Md.

WIEMAN, Elton Ewart, football coach; b. Orosi, Calif., Oct. 4, 1896; s. William Henry and Alma Florence (Morgan) W.; A.B., U. of Mich., 1921, grad. student, 1929; m. Margaret Gates Vogel, Dec. 22, 1922; children—Robert Allan, Helen Elizabeth. Line coach, U. of Mich., 1921-26, head coach of football, 1927-28, asst. dir. of athletics, 1923-29, dir. professional training in phys. edn. and athletics, 1929-30; part time line coach, U. of Minn., 1930-31; part time line coach, Princeton U., 1932-37, head coach of football since 1938; with State Mutual Life Assurance Co. of Worcester, Mass., 1930-38, as dist. agent, Grand Rapids, Mich., special agent, Ann Arbor, Mich., asso. gen. agent, Phila. Served in Air Service, U.S. Army, 1917-19; commd. 2d lt., 1919; mem. Am. Football Coaches Assn., Phi Beta Kappa, Kappa Sigma. Republican. Presbyn. Clubs: Nassau (Princeton); Princeton (New York). Author: Football Technique, 1929; Practical Football (with H. O. Crisler), 1934. Contbr. to mags. Home: 19 Maple St. Office: 88 Nassau St., Princeton, N.J.

WIENER, William, weather observer; b. Newark, N.J., Jan. 19, 1867; s. Oscar Wiener and Elizabeth (Frank) W.; A.B., Columbia U., 1888, A.M., 1889; Ph.B., Sch. of Mines, Columbia U., 1891; LL.B., N.J. Law Sch., Newark, 1929; m. Minnie Myers, Jan. 19, 1892; children—Theodora Marie (Mrs. Mortimer Lowy), Mervin Gerald. Head of sci. dept., Newark High Sch. and Barringer High Sch., Newark, N.J., 1893-1912; prin. Central High Sch., Newark, N.J., 1912-38; dean Newark Jr. Coll. since 1938; weather observer for Newark and vicinity since 1906; weather recorder for Newark Evening News and Newark Sunday Call since 1906; court expert in science and weather. Hebrew religion. Mason. Elks. Clubs: Schoolmens, Newark Athletic. Writer of a series of letters to parents on edn. and guidance of edn. of high sch. boys and girls, continuously since 1912. Home: 476 Ridge St. Office: Kresge Dept. Store, Newark, N.J.

WIESE, Kurt, artist; b. Minden, Germany, Apr. 22, 1887; s. Heinrich and Charlotte (Bekemeier) W.; m. Gertrude Hansen, June 26, 1930; came to U.S., 1927, naturalized, 1939. Journeyed through Russia, Siberia, Gobi Desert, Manchuria to China, 1909; merchant in China, 1909-14; made prisoner of war by Japanese at outbreak World War, delivered to British, and prisoner, Hongkong, 1914-16. Australia, 1916-19; while prisoner in Australia engaged in writing and drawing; making books for children, Germany, 1919-23; designer of settings, John Hagenbeck Film Co., Berlin, Germany, 1921-23; travelling, writing and illustrating books for S. Am. children, Brazil, 1923-27; New York, since 1927. Author and illustrator: The Chinese Ink Stick, Joe Buys Nails, Ella the Elephant, Wallie the Walrus, The Parrot Dealer, Liang and Lo; illustrator Young Fu, Ho-ming, Girl of New China, Good Wind and Good Water, His Excellency and Peter; illustrator with animal drawings Little Ones, Valiant, Silver Chief, Alexander—the Tale of a Monkey, Wagtail, The White Leopard, Goldfish Under the Ice, Freddy the Detective. Home: R.F.D. 1, Frenchtown, N.J.

WIESEN, Louis John, lawyer; b. Sharon, Pa., July 1, 1893; s. John L. Wiesen and Mary (Day) W.; ed. George Washington U., Washington, D.C., and U. of Pittsburgh Law Sch.; m. Virginia Boal Perkinson, Aug. 15, 1918; 1 son, John W. Admitted to practice before Pa. Bar, 1919, and since in practice at Sharon; pres. Sharon Coal & Ice Co., 1934-37; pres. First Federal Savings & Loan Assn. since 1934; dir. McDowell Nat. Bank since 1927; dir. Mercer Tube Co., Sharon; asst. dist. atty., Mercer Co., Pa., 1921-22. Trustee, F. H. Buhl Charitable Assn. Mem. Am. Legion (past comdr. Sharon Post), Sharon Chamber of Commerce (vice-pres.), Mercer Co. Bar Assn. (past pres.), Pa. Bar Assn. (past v.p.), U.S. Bldg. and Loan League (vice-chmn., pub. relations com.). Clubs: Buhl (past pres.), Sharon Country (past pres.). Home: 219 Case Av. Office: E. State St., Sharon, Pa.

WIEST, William Irvine, lawyer; b. Shamokin, Pa., July 25, 1903; s. William James and Rosanna Christina (Simmendinger) W.; student Shamokin (Pa.) High Sch., 1917-21; A.B., Dickinson Coll., Carlisle, Pa., 1925, M.A., 1927, LL.B., Dickinson Sch. of Law, 1927; m. Grace Iona Schleif, July 30, 1930; children—Grace Iona, Barbara Carolyn. Admitted to Pa. bar, 1928, and since practiced under own name at Shamokin, Pa.; dir. and solicitor Anthracite Mutual Fire Ins. Co., Domestic Mutual Fire Ins. Co.; dir. and sec. Heitzman Safety Blasting Plug Corpn. Solicitor to co. controller, Northumberland Co., 1929-34. Trustee Masonic Home Assn., Shamokin, Pa. Mem. Am. Bar Assn., Pa. Bar Assn., Northumberland Co. Bar Assn., Woolsack Soc., Sigma Chi. Republican. Reformed Ch. Mason (Shamokin Lodge 225, Chapter 264 Royal Arch, Commandery 77 K.T.; Mt. Moriah Council 10; Williamsport Consistory, Scottish Rite), Elk (Shamokin Lodge 355), Odd Fellow (Black Diamond Lodge, Shamokin Council), Junior Order United American Mechanics, Patriotic Order Sons of America (Washington Camp 30). Clubs: Rotary, Temple (Shamokin, Pa.); Acacia (Williamsport, Pa.). Home: 35 E. Sunbury St. Office: 4 W. Independence St., Shamokin, Pa.

WIEST, William James, mgr. The Kulp Co.; b. Klingerstown, Pa., Dec. 12, 1876; s. Felix Klinger and Sara (Williamson) W.; valedictorian, Shamokin (Pa.) High Sch., 1894; student Shamokin Bus. Coll., 1894-95; valedictorian, Mercersburg Acad., 1899; m. Rosanna C. Simmendinger, June 18, 1902; children—William Irvine, Sara Lea (Mrs. Joseph C. Hall), Rose Anna and John Robert (twins), Ruth Ethel, Helen Myrtle (dec.). Asso. with The Kulp Lumber Co., Shamokin, Pa., continuously since 1895, successively, bookkeeper, sec., and mgr. since 1928; sec. and dir. Anthracite Mutual Fire Ins. Co., Domestic Mutual Fire Ins. Co.; vice-pres. and dir. Sun Bldg. and Loan Assn. Mem. Bd. Edn., Shamokin, Pa. Sch. Dist., 1919-31; supt. Salem Evang. and Reformed Ch. Sch. since 1900; member and deacon, St. John's Evang. and Reformed Church; registered 20-yr. Vet. Scout, Boy Scouts of America. Awarded Varden Gold Medal, 1st Honor, Mercersburg Acad. Biographer of Rev. Charles B. Schneder, D.D. (1861-1931), 1939. Mem. Patriotic Order Sons of America. Republican. Asst. editor Silent Worker, monthly pub. St. John's Evang.-Ref. Ch. Home: 715 E. Dewart St., Shamokin, Pa. Office: 316 E. Independence St., Shamokin, Pa.

WIGGINS, William D., civil engr.; b. Richmond, Ind., Apr. 28, 1873; s. Philamon and Henrietta (McCullough) W.; was graduated Rose Poly. Inst., Terre Haute, Ind., 1895; m. Lula J. Daft, 1910; children—Jane Wiggins Spencer, William D., Jr. Entered service of Pa. Lines West of Pittsburgh, engring. dept., 1895; has held various positions including div. engr., div. supt., valuation engr., chief engr. maintenance of way, chief engr. Central Region, acting chief engr., and chief engr. Pa. R.R. since Oct. 1935. Mem. Am. Soc. C.E., Am. Ry. Engring. Assn. Republican. Episcopalian. Clubs: Union League, Merion Cricket (Phila.). Home: Merion, Pa. Office: Broad St. Sta. Bldg., Philadelphia, Pa.

WIGHT, E(dward) Van Dyke, clergyman; b. New Hamburg, N.Y., May 13, 1869; s. Rev. Joseph Kingsbury and Elizabeth (Van Dyke) W.; A.B., Princeton U., 1892, M.A., 1895; student Chicago Theol. Sem., 1892-94; grad. Princeton Theol. Sem., 1895; short summer course, Chicago U.; D.D., Hastings Coll., 1903; m. Kate O. Wilkerson, Aug. 28, 1897; children—Edward V. D., Elizabeth A., William K. Ordained Presbyn. ministry, 1895; pastor Wayne, Neb., 1896-97, Hastings, Neb., 1897-1907, also pres. Hastings Coll., 1898-1907 (secured $100,000 endowment); pastor Webb Horton Memorial Presbyn. Ch., Middletown, N.Y., 1907-36, pastor emeritus 1936—. Served in Y.M.C.A., France, World War. Moderator Synod of New York, 1915; mem. bd. of ch. erection. Republican. Clubs: University, Rotary. Author of "Revelation in Stained Glass" and a number of religious paper articles; lecturer at Evangelical Sem., San Juan, Puerto Rico, 1933. Home: Snowden Lane, Princeton, N.J.

WIGMAN, Harry F., v.p. Peoples Pittsburgh Trust Co.; b. Pittsburgh, Pa., Sept. 16, 1873; s. William and Carolina (Logeman) W.; ed. pub. and high sch.; m. Alma H. Hamm, Oct. 19, 1897; children—Ruth H., Helen B., Harry W. Employed by M. & M. Ins. Co., 1891-99, Nat. Fire Ins. Co. of Allegheny, 1899-1901; junior officer Peoples Trust Co. of Pittsburgh, 1901-04, sec. and treas., 1904-24, pres., 1924-30; name changed to Peoples Pittsburgh Trust Co., 1930, since v.p. Home: 307 Orchard Pl. Office: 1736 Carson St., Pittsburgh, Pa.

WIGNER, Eugene Paul, univ. prof.; b. Budapest, Hungary, Nov. 17, 1902; s. Anthony and Elizabeth (Einhorn) W.; Chem. Engr. and Dr. Engring., Technische Hochschule, Berlin; came to U.S., 1930, naturalized, 1937; m. Amelia L. Frank, Dec. 23, 1936 (died 1937). Lecturer, Princeton U., 1930, half-time prof. mathematical physics, 1931-37, Jones prof. since 1938; prof. of physics, U. of Wisconsin, Madison, Wis., 1937-38. Mem. Am. Phys. Soc., Am. Math. Soc., A.A.A.S., Am. Geog. Soc., Sigma Xi. Address: 120 Prospect Av., Princeton, N.J.

WIKANDER, Oscar Ragnar, mech. engr.; b. Goteberg, Sweden, Nov. 9, 1876; s. Gustav Oskar and Cecilia Christina (Malmstrom) W.; M.E., Tech. Acad. Chemnitz, Saxony, 1895; E.E., Tech. U., Karlsruhe, Germany, 1899; m. Mary Edna Gerdes, Feb. 8, 1908; children—Rosalind, Lawrence Einar, Frederick Gerdes. In charge elec. lab. Société Decauville, Corbeil, S.&O., 1899-1900; elec. engr. Campagnie d'Electricité Thomson-Houston de la Mediterranée, Paris, 1900-01; engaged in aeronautical engring., Paris and Stockholm, 1901-02; asst. chief electrician Nat. Tube Co., McKeesport, Pa., 1903-04; elec. engr. Westinghouse Electric & Mfg. Co., East Pittsburgh, 1909-11; chief exptl. dept. Gen. Electric Co., Sweden, 1905-06; commercial attaché Swedish Legation, Buenos Aires, 1906-09; successively designing and sales engr. and sales mgr., Hall Steam Pump Co., Pittsburgh, 1911-18; cons. engr. S. K. F. Industries, Inc., New York, 1918-21; cons. engr. New York, 1922-25; mech. engr. Ring Spring Dept., Edgewater Steel Co., Pittsburgh, since 1925. Mem. Am. Soc. M.E., Engrs. Soc. Western Pa., John Ericsson Soc. Awarded Melville Medal, 1935. Republican. Episcopalian. Club: Pittsburgh Railway. Holder 29 patents, 3 more pending. Writer of scientific articles. Home: 900 S. Negley Av., Pittsburgh, Pa. Office: Oakmont, Pa.

WILBER, Charles Parker, state forester and dir.; b. New Brunswick, N.J., Oct. 23, 1883; s. Francis Augustus and Laura Birge (Parker) W.; grad. Rutgers Prep. Sch., New Brunswick, N.J., 1900; A.B., Rutgers U., 1905, M.A., 1908; M.F., Yale Forestry Sch., 1907; m. Evelyn Beer Beasley, June 10, 1918; step children—Frederick Bartling Beasley, Evelyn Clark Beasley. With William M. Ritter Lumber Co., Maben, W.Va., 1907-08; forest asst. U.S. Forest Service, Dist. IV, Ogden, Ut., 1908-10; asst. forester N.J. Forest Commn., Trenton, N.J., 1910-11, asst. forester and state firewarden, 1911-15; asst. forester and state firewarden N.J. Dept. Conservation and Development, Trenton, N.J., 1915-21, state forester and chief div. forests and parks, 1922-37, state forester and dir. since 1937. Mem. N.J. State Planning Bd. since 1934, N.J. Council since 1937, N.J. State Soil Conservation Com. since 1937. Deacon 2d Reformed Ch., New Brunswick, N.J., 1914-18; elder 1st Presbyn. Ch., Trenton, N.J., since 1919, leader Mens Bible Class, 1920-22, pres. Mens Assn., 1921, supt. Sunday Sch., 1927-28; pres. Mens Bible Class Union, New Brunswick, 1917, Trenton Council of Chs., 1922-25; trustee New Brunswick Presbytery, Presbyn. Ch., U.S., since 1929; commr. gen. assembly, Presbyn. Ch., U.S., 1926. Mem. Soc. of Am. Foresters (pres. Allegheny Sect. 1928), State Foresters Assn. (pres. 1930), Nat. Council State Parks (N.J. rep. since 1928), Allegheny Forest Experiment Sta. (mem. advisory council since 1930), Trenton Hort. Soc., N.J. Advisory Com. on Pub. Recreation (pres. since 1936), Y.M.C.A. of Trenton (dir. since 1939), Am. Forestry Assn., Nat. Geog. Soc., N.J. Fish and Game Conservation League, N.J. Fed. of Shade Tree Commns., Washington Crossing Vol. Fire Co., Del. Valley Protective Assn. (dir. 1934), Rutgers Alumni Assn. (class sec. 1910-30), Rutgers Alumni Council (class rep. 1910-30), Yale Forest Sch. Alumni Assn. (pres. 1937-38), Alumni Assn. of Rutgers Coll. (trustee 1925-29), Yale Forest Sch. Robin Hood Soc., Chi Psi. Clubs: Rutgers (pres. 1922-25), Rotary (dir. 1931-33), Rutgers Varsity, Rutgers Outing (New Brunswick, N.J.); mem. Trenton Torch Club, 1925-26, Engineers Club, 1912-26 (dir. 1924-26, v.p. 1926). Author of numerous bulletins, leaflets, newspaper and mag. articles on forestry, forest fires, parks, land use and related subjects. Home: R.D. 6. Office: State House Annex, Trenton, N.J.

WILBUR, John Milnor, clergyman, educator; b. Charleston, S.C., Jan. 30, 1870; s. Theodore Augustus and Mary Bee (Cuttino) W.; prep. edn. University Sch., Charleston; Th.G., Southern Bapt. Theol. Sem., 1892; D.D., Richmond (Va.) Coll., 1912; m. Emma Comey Ellison, Sept. 2, 1924; children—John Milnor, Frances Comey. Ordained Bapt. ministry, 1891; asst. Eutaw Pl. Ch., Baltimore, 1892-93; pastor North Av. Ch., Baltimore, and later asso. pastor Eutaw Pl. Ch., until 1902; pastor Narberth, Pa., and Central Ch., Trenton, N.J., until 1909; prof. Bapt. Inst. for Christian Workers, Phila., 1909-11, pres. 1911-37, now pres. emeritus. Pres. Bd. of Edn. Northern Bapt. Conv., 1925-27; editor The Baptist Commonwealth, Phila., 5 yrs. Trustee Bapt. Inst. Mem. Beta Theta Pi. Home: Hohokus, N.J.

WILCOX, Clair, prof. economics; b. Cuba, N.Y., Jan. 29, 1898; s. Frederick Lown and Estelle W.; B.S., U. of Pa., 1919; A.M., O. State U., Columbus, O., 1922; Ph.D., U. of Pa., 1927; m. Florence Chapman, June 10, 1923; children—Andrea Chapman, Carolyn. Instr. econs., Lafayette Coll., Easton, Pa., 1919-20; asst. prof. econs., O. Wesleyan U., Delaware, O., 1920-23; instr. econs., U. of Pa., 1923-27; asst. prof. econs., Swarthmore (Pa.) Coll., 1927-29, asso. prof., 1929-31, prof. since 1931. Served as sec. Pa. State Parole Commn., 1926-27; dir. research, Nat. Commn. on Law Observance and Enforcement, 1930-31; mem. Gen. Code Authority, spl. adviser Consumers Advisory Bd., mem. Advisory Council, chief Code Adminstrn. Studies Unit, NRA, 1934-35; cons. economist, Social Security Bd., 1936; chmn. Phila. Chapter, League for Industrial Democracy, 1931-33; chmn. Econ. Problems Com., Soc. of Friends since 1937. Mem. bd. The Sch. in Rose Valley, 1933-35. Mem. Am. Econ. Assn., Am. Assn. Univ. Profs., Sphinx Sr. Soc., Theta Xi. Soc. of Friends. Author: Rate Limitation and the General Property Tax, 1922; The Parole of Adults from State Penal Institutions, 1927. Editor: America's Recovery Program, 1934. Contrib. editor, St. Louis Post-Dispatch, 1930-35. Contbr. to various publs. Home: 510 Ogden Av., Swarthmore, Pa.

WILCOX, Earley Vernon, author and lecturer; b. Busti, N.Y., Feb. 16, 1869; s. Abram F. and Sally Maria (Mead) W.; brother of Edwin Mead Wilcox; A.B., Otterbein Univ., 1890; A.B., Harvard Univ., 1892, A.M., 1894, Ph.D., 1895, Litt. D., 1932; m. Mabel Ruth Owens,

June 30, 1897; 1 dau., Ruth Evans (dec.). Asst. entomologist, Ohio Agrl. Expt. Sta., 1890-91; prof. biology and state entomologist, Bozeman, Mont., 1896-99; editor on Expt. Sta. Record, Dept. Agr., 1899-1908; spl. agent in charge U.S. Agrl. Expt. Sta., H.T., July 1, 1908-Dec. 31, 1914; administrative asst. States Relation Service, Jan. 1, 1915-Feb. 1, 1917; agrlist. in charge of investigations on tenancy and farm labor, Office of Farm Management, U.S. Dept. Agr., Feb. 1, 1917-Dec. 31, 1919; staff of Country Gentleman, Jan. 1, 1920-37. Pres. Shakespeare Soc. of Washington; pres. Columbia System Inc. Author: Farmer's Cyclopedia of Agriculture, 1904; Handbook of Meat Inspection, 1904; Handbook of Milk Inspection, 1912; Cyclopædia of Live Stock, 1907; Hawaii, Its Agricultural Possibilities, 1909; Lights and Shadows in Hawaii, 1913; Tropical Agriculture, 1916; Tama Jim, 1930. Contbr. bulls. and articles on tech. subjects. Home: 33 W. Irving St., Chevy Chase, Md. Office: 220 Southern Bldg., Washington, D.C.

WILCOX, Emily, newswriter; b. Wyoming, Pa., Jan. 7, 1889; d. William A. and Katherine Maria (Jenkins) Wilcox; student Wilkes-Barre (Pa.) Inst., 1908-09, Mount Holyoke Coll., South Hadley, Mass., 1909-10; unmarried. Editor Woman's Page, Scranton (Pa.) Times since 1919; teacher of parliamentary law since 1914. Sec.-treas. Wyoming Commemorative Assn. since 1918; hon. mem. Am. Assn. Univ. Women; mem. Soc. of Mayflower Descendants, Pa. Soc. Colonial Dames, D.A.R., Daughters of 1812, New England Women. Democrat. Presbyterian. Clubs: Scranton Quota (charter mem., pres.), Century (Scranton, Pa.). Author: Parliamentary Law Aids, 1917, 3d edit. 1934. Home: 819 Sunset St. Office: Scranton Times, Scranton, Pa.

WILCOX, William Jenkins, lawyer; b. Wyoming, Pa., Mar. 17, 1886; s. William Alonzo and Katherine Maria (Jenkins) W.; A.B., A.M., Hamilton Coll., Clinton, N.Y., 1909; LL.B., Washington & Lee U., 1912; m. Kitty Minor Rogers, Jan. 23, 1917; children—Eleanor Rogers, William J., John Rogers. Admitted to Pa. bar, 1913; engaged in gen. practice at Scranton, 1913-16, Harrisburg, 1919-23; counsel Pa. Power & Light Co., Allentown, Pa., 1923-34; in gen. practice at Allentown since 1934; now mem. firm Snyder, Wert and Wilcox; lecturer on govt. regulation of business, U. of Pa., 1914-18. Served in Pa. N.G., Mexican border, 1916-17; asst. adj. and capt. 153d Depot Brigade, U.S.A., Camp Dix, N.J., 1917-18, adj. and maj., 1918-19. Mem. Lehigh County Bar Assn. (librarian), Assn. of Practitioners before the Interstate Commerce Commn., S.R., Soc. of Cincinnati, Alpha Delta Phi, Phi Delta Phi. Democrat. Presbyn. Author: various hist. monographs and mag. articles. Asso. editor Torch Mag. Home: 127 S. West St. Office: 510 Hamilton St., Allentown, Pa.

WILDE, Bertram Merbach, business exec.; b. Philadelphia, Pa., Dec. 28, 1898; s. James T. and Anna E. (Pressler) W.; student pub. schs.; m. Helen E. Beale, Apr. 26, 1922. With Janney & Co., Phila., since 1915, beginning as office boy, successively asst. treas., asst. sec., treas. and sec., and v.p. and dir. since 1935; dir. Boone County Coal Corpn. Republican. Lutheran. Clubs: Rolling Green Golf, Bond (Phila.). Home: 5060 City Line Av. Office: 1529 Walnut St., Philadelphia, Pa.

WILDE, Earle Irving, coll. prof.; b. Taunton, Mass., June 17, 1888; s. Samuel Augusta and Mary Ellen (Lincoln) W.; B.S., Mass. State Coll., 1912; M.S., Pa. State Coll., 1917; Ph.D., Cornell U., 1929; m. Laura Kempton Wheeler, Aug. 26, 1914; children—Earle Irving, Richard Arnold, Helen Elizabeth, Ruth Ellen. Began as asst. in horticulture, Pa. State Coll., 1912, prof. ornamental horticulture since 1924. Served as 2d lt. Q.M. Corps, U.S.A., 1917-19. Mem. Pa. Hort. Soc., Northwestern Pa. Florists Assn., Kappa Sigma, Pi Alpha Xi, Am. Legion, Forty and Eight. Republican. Methodist. Club: Center Hills Country. Contbr. articles and bulls. on horticulture. Home: 123 S. Gill St., State College, Pa.

WILDER, Henry Lincoln, editor and publisher; b. Hingham, Mass., June 6, 1883; s. Isaac Henry and Maria Elizabeth (Waters) W.; student U. of Rochester, N.Y., 1903-05; A.B., Lebanon Valley Coll., Annville, Pa., 1908; B.S., Dickinson Coll., Carlisle, Pa., 1909; A.M., Columbia U., 1915; m. Ruth Arbelyn Schropp, Dec. 12, 1911; children—Adam Schropp, Arbelyn Elizabeth (Mrs. Joseph R. Sansone), John Henry. Engaged as football coach and athletic dir., 1905; coach and athletic dir. Lebanon Valley Coll., Annville, Pa., 1906-08, 1911-12; athletic dir., instr. mathematics, geology, Conway Hall, 1908-09; football coach Lebanon Valley Coll., 1906-07, 1911-12, 1921-22, Lebanon High Sch., 1913-19, 1928-30; chemist Pa. Steel Co., Steelton, Pa., 1909-12; supt. Pa. State Highway Dept., 1912-20; twp. engr., 1920-21; sec. Lebanon News Pub. Co., publishers daily and semi-weekly papers and gen. printers, since 1921; editor Lebanon Daily News-Times, Lebanon Semi Weekly News, since 1924; dir. Lebanon County Trust Co. Served as mem. Lebanon Civil Service Commn. since 1928, pres. to 1938. Mem. Chamber of Commerce; past chmn. Salvation Army Gen. Com.; 1st pres. Lebanon High Sch. Athletic Assn. Former asso. mem. Am. Soc. C.E.; mem. Theta Delta Chi. Republican. United Brethren. Mason (32°, Shriner), Elk. Clubs: Country, Lions (Lebanon, Pa.; 1st pres.); Riding (Quentin, Pa.). Home: 38 Berwyn Park. Office: Lebanon News, Lebanon, Pa.

WILDES, Harry Emerson, literary editor; b. Middletown, Del., Apr. 3, 1890; s. Albert Adams and Rhoda Catherine (Foster) W.; A.B., Phila. Central High Sch., 1909; A.B., cum laude in Economics, Harvard, 1913; A.M., U. of Pa., 1922, Ph.D., 1927; m. Helen Jaquette, June 27, 1919. Asst. traffic engr. Bell Telephone Co. of Pa., 1913-15; newspaper work, Phila. Press, Bulletin, North American, 1915-19; teacher social sciences, Phila. high schs., 1915-24 and 1925-30; lit. editor Phila. Public Ledger, 1930-34, of the Philadelphia Forum Magazine since 1933; columnist daily book column, "Of Making Many Books." Prof. economics and social sciences, Keio U., Tokyo, Japan, 1924-25. Mem. Council, Brigantine, N.J., 1922-23; mem. Sch. Bd. Tredyffrin Dist., Chester Co., Pa. Mem., Hist. Soc. of Pa., Asiatic Soc. of Japan (Tokyo), Am. Sociol. Soc. Clubs: Union League, Franklin Inn, Contemporary. Author: Social Currents in Japan, 1927; Japan in Crisis, 1934 (banned in Japan as prejudicial to public peace); Aliens in the East, 1937; Valley Forge, 1938. World traveler; made researches on social problems in Japan, China and Mexico. Home: Valley Forge, Pa. Address: 8th St. and Lehigh Av., Philadelphia, Pa.

WILES, Charles Peter, clergyman, editor; b. Lewistown, Md., Jan. 27, 1870; s. Americus G. P. and Sarah S. (Hummer) W.; ed. Millersville (Pa.) Normal Sch.; student Luth. Theol. Sem., Gettysburg, Pa., 1893-96; hon. A.M., Pa. Coll., Gettysburg, 1906; D.D., Carthage Coll., 1913; m. M. Alice Miller, June 10, 1896. Ordained Luth. ministry, 1896; pastor Rossville, Pa., 1896-1901, Pittsburgh, 1901-08, Washington, D.C., 1908-13; editor Lutheran Publ. Soc., Phila., 1913-18, United Luth. Publ. House, Phila., 1918—. Home: 259 Harvey St., Germantown. Office: Muhlenberg Bldg., Phila., Pa.

WILEY, Joseph Burton, supt. of schools; b. Colora, Md., Oct. 17, 1879; s. Andrew T. and Margaret (Fryer) W.; prep. edn., West Nottingham (Md.) Acad., 1894-99; A.B., Lafayette Coll., Easton, Pa., 1905; A.M., Columbia, 1935; m. Katharine Pettett, 1917; children—Margaret Pettett, Joseph Burton, Jackson Brainerd, Andrew Thompson, Stephen Bradford. Became teacher, 1905; supervising prin. public schools, Morristown, N.J. Trustee Morristown Pub. Library. Mem. N.E.A., N.J. Edn. Assn., Delta Upsilon. Presbyterian. Mason. Clubs: Morristown Rotary, N.J. Schoolmasters. Address: 17 Georgian Rd., Morristown, N.J.

WILEY, Roy William, supt. city schs.; b. Lawrence Co., Pa., Feb. 9, 1897; s. W. H. and Laura (Shannon) W.; B.S., Grove City (Pa.) Coll., 1918; A.M., U. of Pittsburgh, 1928, Ed.D., 1938; m. Marie Borland, June 10, 1925; children—Robert William, Richard Borland. Teacher and prin. high sch., Midland, Pa., 1918-22; prin. high sch., New Brighton, Pa., 1922-33; teacher in Geneva Coll. Summer Sch., 1921-33; prin. sr. high sch., Butler, Pa., 1933-37, supt. pub. schs., Butler, since 1937. Mem. Pa. State Edn. Assn., N.E.A., Phi Delta Kappa. Republican. United Presbyterian. Mason. Club: Rotary (Butler, Pa.). Home: 554 Third St. Office: Gibson Senior High School, Butler, Pa.

WILHELM, Charles Philip, lawyer; b. Baltimore, Md., Apr. 14, 1899; s. Charles Latoison and Minnie (Weller) W.; B.S., Univ. of Md., College Park, 1921, M.S., 1922; LL.B., W. Va. Univ. Law Coll., Morgantown, 1927; grad. student Harvard U. Law Sch., 1933-34; m. Cecile Watson, June 25, 1923. Engaged as instr. and athletic coach, high sch., W.Va., 1922-24; admitted to W.Va. bar, 1927 and engaged in gen. practice of law at Kingwood; admitted to practice before W.Va. Supreme Ct., 1929, U.S. Circuit Ct. of Appeals, 1936, and before Supreme Ct. of U.S., 1937; librarian, Coll. of Law, W.Va. Univ., 1928; instr. Coll. of Law, W.Va. Univ., 1934-35. Served as pvt. inf., U.S.A. during World War; now capt. inf. res. Chmn. Rep. Exec. Com. Preston Co. Mem. W.Va. Bar Assn., Order of Coif, Alpha Zeta, Theta Chi, Am. Legion. Republican. Episcopalian. Mason. Rotarian. Club: Press (Baltimore). Home: Near Bruceton, Grant District, Preston Co., W.Va. Office: Price St., Kingwood, W.Va.

WILKINSON, Bernard Waldo, physician, surgeon; b. Cottageville, W.Va., Aug. 31, 1902; s. Amous and Virginia (Gorrell) W.; B.S. in mdcne., W.Va. U., 1927; M.D. Med. Coll of Va., 1929; m. Ollie L. Conner, June 10, 1930; children—Barnard Waldo, Constance Lorraine, Carolyn Jane. Interne Med. Coll. of Va. Hosp., 1929-30, asst. resident surgeon, 1930-31, resident surgeon, 1931-32; practice as physician and surgeon, Clarksburg, W.Va., since 1932; visiting surgeon and mem. staff St. Mary's and Union Protestant hosps. Fellow Am. Coll. Surgeons; mem. Harrison County Med. Soc., W. Va. Med. Soc., A.M.A. Club: Aviation. Contbr. to Archives of Surgery, Am. Jour. Surgery. Home: 359 Tyler Av. Office: Union Bank Bldg., Clarksburg, W.Va.

WILKINSON, Kenneth Lawrence, engr., personnel exec.; b. Rochester, N.Y., Nov. 10, 1890; s. Lafayette Avery and Louella (Van Buskirk) W.; student Central Manual Training High Sch., Phila., 1905-08; B.S. in E.E., U. of Pa., 1912, E.E., 1937; m. Norma Elizabeth Schmidt, Sept. 9, 1913; children—Kenneth Lawrence, Robert Sheldon, Edith Louella. Engring. asst., Am. Telephone & Telegraph Co., New York, 1912-14, engring. supervisor, engring. dept., 1914-19, engring. supervisor, development and research dept., 1919-21, engring. supervisor, operation and engring. dept., 1921-22, engr. on foreign wire relations, operation and engring. dept., 1922-27, gen. operating results engr., operation and engring. dept., 1927-37, asst. v.p., personnel relations dept., since 1937. Chmn. of finance com., Stony Wold Sanitarium; council v.p., Boy Scouts of America. Fellow Am. Inst. E.E. Clubs: Braidburn Country (Madison, N.J.); Sussex Co. Country (Newton, N.J.). Home: 754 Irving Terrace, Orange, N.J. Office: 195 Broadway, New York, N.Y.

WILKINSON, Robert J., Jr., newspaperman; b. Huntington, W.Va., Feb. 23, 1917; s. Robert J. (M.D.) and Elizabeth (Richmond) W.; prep. edn., Tenn. Mil. Acad., Sweetwater, and Va. Presbyn. Sch., Danville, Va.; student Marshall Coll., Huntington, 1935-39; unmarried. With Internat. Nickel Co., Watts Ritter Co. and Huntington Baseball Club of Mid-Atlantic League, 1933-37; organized a drug company, sold interests, 1938; reporter and sports editor Wayne County Press and Ceredo Advance since 1938. One of founders Huntington Jr. Chamber of Commerce, 1938, chmn. health and sanitation com. Honor mem. Cabell County Pre-Med. Soc.; mem. Y.M.C.A. Democrat. Presbyterian. Home: 240 North Boul. Office: 1119 6th Av., Huntington, W.Va.

WILKINSON, Robert Johnson, surgeon; b. Campbell County, Va., July 12, 1888; s. Beverly Jasper and Jennie (Traylor) W.; prep. edn., Mary Agnes Inst., Brookneal, Va., under pvt. tutor and in pub. sch.; M.D. Med. Coll. of Va., 1912; m. Elizabeth Lewis Richmond, Apr. 6, 1916; children—Robert J., Elizabeth Traylor, Walter Richmond. Telegraph opr. Southern Ry. Co. 1904-07; owner of gen. mdse. business, Lynchs, Va., 1907-08; Interne Memorial Hosp., Richmond, 1912-13; asso. in gen. surgery of Dr. C.C. Coleman, Richmond, 1913-15; surgeon in charge Chesapeake & Ohio (R.R.) Hosp., Huntington, W.Va., since 1915; senior surgeon Wilkinson Surgical Clinic; asst. chief surgeon Chesapeake & Ohio Ry. Employees Hosp. Assn. Served in 1st Vt. Med. Corps, U.S.A., World War. Fellow Am. Coll. Surgeons; mem. A.M.A., Southern Med. Assn., W.Va. State Med. Soc., Cabell County Med. Soc. (ex-pres.), Chesapeake & Ohio Ry. Surgeons (ex-pres.). Democrat. Southern Methodist. Mason (32°, Shriner), Elk Club: Guyan Country. Contbr. articles on surg. diseases and treatment to W.Va. State Med. Jour., etc. Home: 240 N. Boul. Office: Wilkinson Surgical Clinic, 1119 6th Av., Huntington, W.Va.

WILKINSON, William Albert, prof. education; b. Buffalo, Mo., Mar. 4, 1873; s. Joseph S. and Margaret Anne (Stanley) W.; B.Pd., M.Pd., State Normal Sch., Warrensburg, Mo., 1907; B.S. in Edn., U. of Mo., 1910, A.M., 1911., A.M., Tehrs. Coll. (Columbia), 1918; m. Grace Greenwood Speaker, Sept. 5, 1918. Teacher Mo. rural schs., 4 yrs.; county commr. schs., Dallas Co., Mo., 1894-96; prin. schs. Buffalo, Mo., 1897-1901, Alton, 1901-06; supt. schs. Holden, 1907-09; head dept. edn. State Normal Sch., Mayville, N.D., 1911-17; prof. edn. and dir. Sch. of Edn., U. of Del., since 1918. Mem. N.E.A., Nat. Assn. Coll. Teachers of Edn., Nat. Soc. for Study of Edn., Delaware State Educational Assn. (pres. 1925-26), Phi Delta Kappa, Phi Kappa Phi. Republican. Methodist. Author: Rural School Management, 1917. Home: Newark, Del.

WILKS, Samuel S(tanley), math. statistician; b. Little Elm, Tex., June 17, 1906; s. Chance and Bertha (Gammon) W.; student Denton (Tex.) High Sch., 1920-23; B.A., North Tex. State Teachers Coll., Denton, Tex., 1926; M.A., U. of Tex., Austin, Tex., 1928; Ph.D., State U. of Ia., Iowa City, Ia., 1931; m. Gena Orr, Sept. 1, 1931; 1 son, Stanley Neal. Nat. research fellow mathematics, Columbia U., 1931-32, U. of London, Cambridge U., Eng., 1932-33; instr. mathmematics, Princeton U., 1933-36, asst. prof., 1937-38, asso. prof. mathematics since 1938. Mem. Am. Math. Soc., Am. Statis. Assn., Inst. of Math. Statistics (v.p. 1937-39), Econometric Soc., Psychometric Soc. Author: Numerous articles on math. theory statistics, statis. inference; research associate Coll. Entrance Exam. Bd. since 1937; editor Annals of Math. Satistics since 1938. Address: 210 Moore St., Princeton, N.J.

WILL, Homer C(hristian), prof. of biology; b. Timberville, Va., May 28, 1898; s. Samuel Gordon and Sallie Virginia (Hollar) W.; grad. Dayton (Va.) High Sch., 1916; A.B., Bridgewater (Va.) Coll., 1920; A.M., U. of Va., Charlottesville, Va., 1922; student U. of Mich., Ann Arbor, Mich., summers 1928-30; Ph.D.; U. of Pittsburgh, 1932; m. Ethel Fay Bauman, June 14, 1936. Teacher, Smithfield (W.Va.) High Sch., 1922-24, Lost Creek (W.Va.) High Sch., 1924-27; teacher of biology, Juniata Coll., Huntingdon, Pa., 1927-29, prof. biology since 1931; asst. in entomology, Carnegie Museum, Pittsburgh, 1929-31. Mem. Phi Sigma, Sigma Delta Psi. Democrat. Ch. of Brethren. Home: 301 18th St., Huntingdon, Pa.

WILLAMAN, John James, chemist; b. Brodhead, Wis., Oct. 7, 1889; s. John Henry and Eldora (Scoville) W.; B.S., U. of Wis., Madison, Wis., 1912, M.S., 1914; Ph.D., U. of Chicago, 1919; m. Leola Lorenz, June 25, 1915; children—Dorothy Ellen, Janet Leola. Instr.

chemistry, U. of Minn., Minneapolis, Wis., 1914-17, asst. prof., 1917-22, asso. prof., 1922-26, prof. 1926-29; head of chemistry dept., Geneva (N.Y.) Agr. Expt. Sta., 1929-30; dir. biochem. research, Rohm & Haas Co., Inc., Bristol, Pa., since 1930. Mem. Am. Chem. Soc., Phi Beta Kappa, Sigma Xi, Phi Lambda Upsilon. Club: Exchange (Bristol, Pa.) Home: Fairview Lane. Office: Rohm and Haas, Bristol, Pa.

WILLARD, Bradford, geologist; b. New York, N.Y., May 17, 1894; s. Gates and Katrina (Haff) W.; B.A., Lehigh U., 1921; A.M., Harvard U., 1922, Ph.D., 1923; m. Elise Krassa, June 22, 1923; children—Gates, Elizabeth B. Asst. prof. geology, Brown U., 1923-30; paleontologist S.D. Geol. Survey, summer, 1934; geologist Ill. Geol. Survey, summer, 1926; instr. geology, Harvard Summer Sch., 1927; asst. prof. geology, Lehigh U., 1st semester, 1937; asst. geologist Pa. Topographical & Geol. Survey, summer, 1929, and 1930-39; prof. geology and head dept., Lehigh U., since Sept. 1939. Mem. A.A.A.S., Geol. Soc. America, Paleontol. Soc., Pa. Acad. Science (press sec.), N.Y. Acad. Science, Field Conf. of Pa. Geologists, Am. Mus. Natural History, Bermuda Biol. Station for Research, Sigma Xi, etc. Club: Torch. Writer on scientific subjects. Home: Langhorne Av., Bethlehem, Pa.

WILLARD, Daniel, railway pres.; b. N. Hartland, Vt., Jan. 28, 1861; s. Daniel Spaulding and Mary Anna (Daniels) W.; grad. Windsor (Vt.) High Sch., 1878; student Mass. Agrl. Coll., 1878-79; LL.D., U. of Md., 1914, Dartmouth, 1915, U. of W.Va., 1919, Ohio U., 1927, Pa. Mil. Coll., 1928, U. of Pa., 1931, Middlebury Coll., 1931, Mass. State Coll., 1932, U. of Rochester, 1932; Dr. Bus. Administrn., Syracuse University, 1927; m. Bertha Leone Elkins, Mar. 2, 1885. Entered ry. service 1879; in various duties on different rys. until 1899; asst. gen. mgr. B.&O. R.R., 1899-1901; asst. to the pres., later 3d v.p., and 1st v.p. and gen. mgr. Erie R.R., 1901-04; 2d v.p., C.,B.&Q. R.R., 1904-10; also pres. Colo. Midland Ry. Co., and v.p. C. & S. Ry. Co, 1909-10; pres. B.&O. R.R. Co. since Jan. 15, 1910; pres. Alton R.R. Co.; chmn. bd. Buffalo, Rochester & Pittsburgh R.R., Reading Co., B.&O. Chicago Terminal R.R. Co.; pres. Buffalo & Susquehanna R.R.; dir. Am. Telephone & Telegraph Co., Mutual Life Ins. Co. of N.Y., Richmond, Fredericksburg & Potomac R.R. Co., Richmond-Washington Co. Pres. Am. Ry. Assn., 1911-13; dir. and mem. exec. com. Assn. of Am. Railroads. Mem. President's Orgn. on Unemployment Relief, 1931. Mem. Phi Sigma Kappa Fraternity. Clubs: Chicago (Chicago); Duquesne (Pittsburgh); Maryland, Baltimore Country, Merchants', University (Baltimore); Elkridge (Md.); Century, Recess (New York); Cosmos, Metropolitan (Washington). Mem. bd. trustees Johns Hopkins University, 1914—, pres. bd. since 1926; trustees Johns Hopkins Hosp. Apptd. mem. Advisory Commn. of Council Nat. Defense, Oct. 1916, and chmn., Mar. 1917; apptd. chmn. War Industries Bd., Nov. 17, 1917; resigned 1918. Commd. col. Engrs., U.S.A., Nov. 2, 1918; hon. adviser to Army Industrial Coll., 1925. Home: 206 Goodwood Gardens. Address: B. & O. R.R. Co., Baltimore, Md.

WILLARD, DeForest Porter, orthopedic surgeon; b. Phila., Pa., Feb. 20, 1884; s. DeForest and Elizabeth M. (Porter) W.; grad. Penn Charter Sch., 1901; B.S., U. of Pa., 1905, M.D., 1908; grad. study Mayo Clinic, Rochester, Minn., 1909-10; m. Margaretta Miller, Dec. 11, 1926. Orthopedic surgeon since 1910; asst. orthopedic dept. Univ. Hosp., and Orthopedic Hosp., Phila., 1910-17; prof. of orthopedic surgery, Grad. Sch. of Medicine, U. of Pa. since 1920; orthopedic surgeon to Graduate, Orthopedic, Bryn Mawr and Abrington hospitals, consultant orthopedic surgeon to Pennsylvania, Shriners and Babies hospitals. Served as 1st lt., Med. Corps, U.S. Army, 1917-19; with A.E.F. attached to Brit. Army, Apr.-Dec. 1917, U.S. Army, Jan. 1918-May 1919; hon. disch. as lt. col., July 1919. Mem. Am. Orthopedic Assn.

(sec. 1920-34; pres. 1935), Am. Surg. Assn., Am. Acad. Orthopedic Surgeons, Internat. Orthopedic Soc., Delta Psi. Republican. Presbyterian. Clubs: Philadelphia, University (Phila.); Merion Cricket (Haverford, Pa.); Gulph Mills Golf. Contbr. of many articles on orthopedic surgery to jours. Home: 633 Winsford Rd., Bryn Mawr, Pa. Office: 1726 Spruce St., Philadelphia, Pa.

WILLARD, Edgar Harold, physician; b. Frederick Co., Md., Mar. 27, 1887; s. Charles F. and Ann (Hoskinson) W.; student Washington and Lee U., 1903-04; M.D., U. of Md. Med. Sch., 1908; m. Mary Louise Gittings, 1910; children—Catherine Rebecca (Mrs. Guy W. Arnold), Edgar Harold, Jr., William Gittings, Jack. Engaged in gen. practice of medicine in Frederick Co., Md., 1909-22; then in practice at Berkeley Springs, W.Va.; supt. Berkeley Springs Sanatorium; mem. med. Staff, City Hosp., Martinsburg, W.Va. Past pres. Eastern Panhandle Med. Assn. Mem. Alpha Omega Delta. Democrat. Club: Morgan County Kiwanis. Office: 210 N. Washington St., Berkeley Springs, W.Va.

WILLARD, Frederic Wilson, pres. Nassau Smelting & Refining Co. Inc.; b. Houghton, N.Y., Apr. 16, 1881; s. Ephraim and Lucy Mae (Wilson) W.; A.B., U. of Mich., 1906, hon. A.M., 1929; m. Maude Myrtle Foote, Jan. 5, 1909; children—Harriet Aylene, Ruth Margaret. With Western Electric Co., 1906-31, analytical and research chemist, Chicago and New York, 1906-11, engr. of mfg. methods, Chicago, 1913-15, operating supt. Hawthorne Works, 1915-19, supt. Phila. instrument shop, 1919-21, div. supt. of installation, Phila., 1921-23, asst. engr. of mfg. Hawthorne Works, 1923-26, personnel dir., New York, 1926-29, asst. works mgr. Kearney Works, 1921-31; exec. v.p. Nassau Smelting & Refining Co., Inc., New York, 1931-37, pres. since 1937. Mem. Zoning Bd. of Adjustment, Summit, N.J., 1932-34; mem. Bd. of Edn., Summit, 1934, 1937-38, pres. 1937. Mem. Nat. Research Council, chmn. div. of chemistry and chem. technology, 1933-36, mem. grants-in-aid bd., 1933-36, mem. exec. bd., 1935-38, chmn. patent com. Served as lt. col. Chem. Warfare Service, O.R.C., 1925-36. Mem. Am. Chem. Soc. (chmn. Chicago sect. 1920; chmn. coll. and univ. accrediting com. 1936), Am. Inst. Chem. Engrs. (dir. 6 yrs.), Sigma Xi. Clubs: Chemists, Bankers (New York). Home: 12 Hawthorne Pl., Summit, N.J. Office: 50 Church St., New York, N.Y.

WILLCOX, Joseph Taney, ry. official; b. Glen Mills, Pa., Sept. 15, 1886; s. James Mark and Kate H. (Taney) W.; student R.C. High Sch., St. Joseph's Prep. Sch., Notre Dame Acad.; m. Ruth Channing Odiorne, Oct. 3, 1923; children —Ruth Channing, Catherine Taney, Joseph Taney, Jr., Thomas Odiorne, Ann Louisa. Studied law in office Ex-Sen. George Wharton Pepper; admitted to Pa. bar, 1907, and asso. with law offices of Thomas DeWitt Cuyler, 1909-10; asst. to sec. Pa. R.R. Co., 1910-12, asst. sec., 1912-17, 1919-25; asst. sec. and transfer agt., 1925-29, sec. since 1929; dir. Northern Trust Co.; mgr. Elmira & Williamsport R.R. Co. Served as capt. Q.M.R.C., 1917, Embarkation Service, Washington, D.C.; capt. transportation corps, 1918, as sec. Am. Sect. of Inter-Allied Transportation Council, A.E.F., under Brig. Gen. W. W. Atterbury, Dir. Gen. Transportation. Pres. The Glen Mills (Pa.) Sch. Republican. Roman Catholic. Clubs: Rittenhouse (Phila.), Rolling Green Golf (Springfield). Home: Wawa, Pa. Office: 1940 Broad St., Station Bldg., Philadelphia, Pa.

WILLCOX, Oswin W(illiam), chemist and agrobiologist; b. Austin, Tex., Oct. 11, 1870; s. Oswin and Phillippina (Bothmer) W.; B.S., U. of Tex., Austin, Tex., 1901; Ph.D., U. of Chicago, 1904; m. Margaret Kostenbauder, Oct. 25, 1906; children—Margaret Isabel, Ortrude Elizabeth, Oswin Burr. School teacher, Comanche Co., Tex., 1893-1900; asst. in soils, Iowa State Coll., 1904; chemist, U.S. Army Ordnance Dept., 1905-08; mgr. Scientific Station for Pure Products, 1909-15; chem. dir. Aetna Explosives Co., Mt. Union, Pa.; supt. Am. Zeolite Co., Paterson, 1918-23; tech. editor, Facts About

Sugar, and consulting agrobiologist since 1923. Mem. Am. Soc. of Agronomy, Sigma Xi. Mason. Author: Principles of Agrobiology, 1930; Nations Can Live At Home, 1935; Reshaping Agriculture, 1934; Can Industry Govern Itself?, 1936; A.B.C. of Agrobiology, 1937; has conducted investigations in scientific agrobiology and the social-economics of the world sugar industry. Address: 197 Union St., Ridgewood, N.J.

WILLET, Anne Lee (Mrs. William Willet), artist, lecturer, teacher; b. at Bristol, Pa.; d. of Rev. Henry Flavel and Anne Townsend (Cooper) Lee; ed. Acad. of Fine Arts, Phila., also under pvt. teachers and abroad; m. William Willet (artist), June 30, 1896 (died 1921); children—Rachel W. (Mrs. Thomas Hopkins English), Henry Lee, Elizabeth L'Estrange (Mrs. Murray Forst Thompson). Exhibited at Metropolitan Museum and Architectural League, New York; Pa. Academy Fine Arts; Boston Academy Fine Arts; Newport Art Assn.; Congressional Library, Washington; Boston Mus. Art; Art Inst., Chicago; Carnegie Inst.; Architectural League, New Haven; High Museum, Atlanta, Ga.; Ney Museum of Art, Austin, Tex. Designer and maker with William Willet of all windows, U.S. Mil. Chapel, West Point, N.Y.; great west window, Grad. Coll., Princeton; sanctuary window, St. Johns of Lattington, Locust Valley, L.I.; windows Holy Nativity Memorial Ch., Rockledge, Pa.; Greenwood Cemetery Chapel, Brooklyn; Harrison Memorial Holy Trinity Ch., Rittenhouse Sq., Phila.; Berry Memorial, Jefferson Av. Presbyn. Ch., Detroit; Potter Memorial, Jamestown, R.I.; Pardee Memorial, Lake Placid, N.Y.; marble sanctuary, altar, mosaic, etc., Trinity P.E. Ch., Miami, Fla.; "Journeyings of the Pilgrims," Hilton Devotional Chapel, Chapel and Library, Chicago Theol. Sem.; du Pont Memorial sanctuary and façade, St. John's Cathedral, Wilmington, Del.; Harrison Memorial, Calvary P.E. Ch., Phila.; Wilson Memorial, Ch. of the Savior, San Gabriel, Calif.; sanctuary, façade and transepts, First Presbyn. Ch. and Ch. of the Atonement, Chicago; windows Grace Church, Oak Park, Ill., Trowbridge Memorial, Santa Fe, N.M., Ch. of Blessed Sacrament, Detroit, Metropolitan M.E. Ch., Detroit; St. Andrews Ch. (Elyria, O.), First Presbyn. Ch. (Kalamazoo, Mich.), All Saints' Ch. (Austin, Tex.), St. Aloysius Ch. (Detroit, Mich.), Grosse Pointe (Mich.) Memorial Ch., Ch. of the Resurrection (Rye, N.Y.). Mem. Am. Federation Arts, Acad. Fine Arts, The Edward MacDowell Assn. Founders and Patriots of America. Republican. Home-Studio: 2310 Spruce St., Philadelphia, Pa.

WILLET, Henry Lee, stained glass artist; b. Pittsburgh, Pa., Dec. 7, 1899; s. William and Anne (Lee) W.; student Princeton, 1918-20, Wharton Sch. of U. of Pa., 1920-21; study and research in Europe, 1924-27; m. Muriel Crosby, Oct. 22, 1927; children—E. Crosby, Ann Lee, Zoe. Designer of stained glass since 1920; propr. Willet Stained Glass Co. Rep. by windows in Washington Cathedral, U.S. Mil. Acad., St. Paul's Episcopal Cathedral (Detroit), Northwestern U., Valley Forge Mil. Acad., Grosse Pointe (Mich.) Memorial Ch., First Unitarian Ch. (New Orleans), Cathedral Ch. of St. John (Wilmington), Trinity Memorial Ch. (Detroit), St. Katharine's Ch. (Baltimore), St. Mary's Sch. (Glens Falls, N.Y.), McCartney Library (Beaver Falls, Pa.), Duncan Memorial Chapel (Floydsburg, Ky.), Westminster Presbyn. Ch. (Minneapolis), First Presbyn. Ch. (Ardmore, Pa.), Christ Episcopal Ch. (Greensburg, Pa.), Trinity Ch. (Washington, D.C.), St. Paul's Cathedral (Erie, Pa.), Chapel of the Mediator (Phila.), Danforth Chapel (Berea, Ky.), East Liberty Presbyn. Ch. (Pittsburgh), Co-Cathedral of Christ the King (Atlanta, Ga.). Mem. Archtl. League of N.Y., Fairmount Park Art Assn., Phila. Art Alliance, Pa. Mus. of Art, Stained Glass Assn. of America (mem. exec. com.), Medieval Acad. of America, Am. Federation of Art, T Square (Phila.). Exhibited in the leading art galleries and lectured extensively on the art and craft of stained glass. Presbyterian. Home: Ambler, Pa. Studio: 3900 Girard Av., Philadelphia, Pa.

WILLETTS, Ernest Ward, M.D.; b. Pittsburgh, Pa., Sept. 20, 1879; s. Jesse and Sarah (Dunn) W.; M.D., U. of Pa., 1902; grad. study U. of Vienna, Austria, 1902-03, 1904-05; m. Anne Beattie, May 10, 1905; children—Agnes Beville, Ernest, Arthur T. Interne U. of Pa. Hosp., Phila., 1903-04; pathologist Pittsburgh Hosp., 1905-07, Columbia Hosp., 1906-09, Western Pa. Hosp., 1906-14, St. Francis Hosp., 1909-11, Pittsburgh Eye and Ear Hosp., 1906-24, Dixmont Hosp., 1908-12; med. consultant St. Margaret's Hosp.; mem. med. staff Allegheny Gen. Hosp.; consultant Pittsburgh Eye and Ear Hosp.; asso. in pathology, U. of Pittsburgh Med. Sch., 1910-11. Fellow Am. Coll. Physicians, Am. Soc. Clin. Pathologists; mem. A.M.A., Assn. Am. Bacteriologists, Med. Soc. State of Pa. (ex-v.p.), Allegheny Co. Med. Soc. (ex-pres.), Pittsburgh Acad. Medicine (ex-pres.). Club: University. Home: Saltsburg Rd., R.D. 1, Verona, Pa. Office: 429 Penn Av., Pittsburgh, Pa.

WILLEVER, John Calvin, telegraph official; b. Montana, N.J., Mar. 9, 1865; s. Jacob H. and Ellen F. (Rush) W.; educated public schs. Began as telegraph operator with Western Union Telegraph Co., 1882, and advanced to commercial gen. mgr., 1914, v.p. in charge commercial dept. since 1915, 1st v.p. since 1925; v.p. Am. Dist. Telegraph Co. of N.J., Atlantic & Pacific Tel. Co., Gold and Stock Tel. Co., Pacific & Atlantic Tel. Co., N.Y. Mut. Tel. Co., Southern & Atlantic Telegraph Co.; also dir. 37 telegraph cos. Democrat. Home: Millburn, N.J. Office: 60 Hudson St., New York, N.Y.

WILLEY, James Emory, pres. Peninsula Oil Co. of Seaford; b. Seaford, Del., Oct. 16, 1885; s. John E. and Emma (Brown) W.; grad. Seaford (Del.) High Sch.; m. Edna E. Hearn, June 5, 1909; children—James E., John E. Formerly sec. and treas. Del. Shipbuilding Co.; now pres. Peninsula Oil Co. Inc. of Seaford, Del.; v.p. and dir. Seaford Trust Co.; dir. Seaford Bldg. & Loan Assn. Postmaster, Seaford, Del., for 12 yrs. Club: Kiwanis of Seaford, Del. (ex-pres.). Address: Seaford, Del.

WILLEY, John Heston, clergyman; b. St. Michaels, Maryland; s. Edward and Susanna (Hambleton) W.; B.D., Drew Theological Seminary, 1882; Ph.B., Ill. Wesleyan U., 1886; Ph.M., Syracuse U., 1887, Ph.D., 1888, S.T.D., 1908; studied Christ Ch. Coll. ((Oxford U.), Eng., 1896; m. Ella M. Stickney, Apr. 27, 1892. Ordained ministry M.E. Ch., 1880; pastor successively Snow Hill, Md., Delaware City, Del., Milford, Del., Chestertown, Md., and College Church, Syracuse until 1896; pastor Nostrand Av. Ch., Brooklyn, 1898-1902, St. Mark's Ch., Brooklyn, 1902-10, Christ Ch., Pittsburgh, Pa., 1910-16, First Bapt. Ch., Montclair, N.J., since 1919. Pres. Lord's Day Alliance of the U.S. since 1930. Trustee Beaver Coll., Wilmington Acad., Syracuse U. Mem. N.Y. State Hist. Soc., Art Collectors League N.J., S.A.R. (chaplain since 1920), Montclair Art Mus., Am. Inst. Sacred Lit., Audubon Soc., Optimist Internat. (lt. gov.), Phi Kappa Phi. Del. to Gen. Conf. M.E. Ch., 1916. Mason (32°, K.T. Prelate Commandery since 1930). Clubs: Authors Club America, Journalist, Clergy, Essex Fells Country. Author: Back to Bethlehem, 1905; John Chrysostom, 1906; Midsummer Nights with the Great Dreamer, 1908; Joshua the Warrior Prince, 1913; God's Age-Old Purpose, 1918; Between Two Worlds, 1919; The World War and Tomorrow, 1920; Early Church Portraits, 1927; Humanity at Its Climax, 1928; Swords Bathed in Heaven, 1937. Home: 16 Upper Mountain Av., Montclair, N.J. Office: 156 5th av., New York, N.Y.

WILLGING, Eugene Paul, coll. librarian; b. Dubuque, Ia., Aug. 17, 1909; s. Edgar Henry and Anna G. (Kerper) W.; prep. edn., Columbia Acad., Dubuque, Ia., 1923-27; A.B., Columbia Coll. (now Loras Coll.), 1931; A.B. in library science, U. of Mich., 1932; grad. work U. of Mich., 1934, Columbia U., 1937; m. Mildred M. Stoffel, Dec. 26, 1933; children—Mary Ann, John Joseph, Elizabeth Jane. Cataloging librarian, Cath. Univ., 1932-33; head librarian, U. of Scranton (formerly St. Thomas Coll.), since 1933. Sec.-treas. Catholic Library Assn.; mem. Am. Library Assn. Editor of Catholic Library World (official organ of Catholic Library Assn.). Compiler of Index to Am. Catholic Pamphlets, 1937; Supplement 1, 1938; Supplement 2, 1939. Contbr. to Catholic jours. Home: 912 Madison Av., Scranton, Pa.

WILLIAMS, Albert S.; col. inf., U.S. Army; prof. mil. science and tactics, U. of Pa. Address: U. of Pennsylvania, Philadelphia, Pa.

WILLIAMS, Alford Joseph, Jr., aviator; b. New York, N.Y., July 26, 1896; s. Alford Joseph and Emma Elizabeth (Madden) W.; A.B., Fordham (N.Y.) U., 1915; LL.B., Georgetown U., Washington, D.C., 1926; m. Florence Hawes Selby, July 3, 1926. Pitcher for N.Y. Giants, Nat. League baseball team, 1916-17; enlisted as aviator, U.S. Navy, 1917, and remained with same as research aviator until 1930, attaining rank of lt.; tested planes, developed aerial acrobatics for air combat, specialized in high speed research; held Am. speed record 8 consecutive yrs.; developed improvements for standard combat plane; lecturer in aeronautical engring., U. of Pittsburgh; mgr. aviation dept. Gulf Oil Corpn. since 1933; maj. U.S. Marine Corps Res. since Apr. 1935. Admitted to N.Y. bar, 1926; mem. N.Y. State Bar Assn. Awarded Distinguished Flying Cross by U.S. Navy Dept., 1929, also trophy of Am. Soc. Mech. Engrs., 1929. Comr. of Scripps-Howard Jr. Aviators, numbering 400,000. Writes daily aviation column for Scripps-Howard newspapers. Frequent contbr. to Nat. popular periodicals and aeronautical jours. Address: Gulf Oil Corpn., 7th & Grant St., Pittsburgh, Pa.

WILLIAMS, Alfred Hector, coll. dean; b. Horatio, Pa., Feb. 28, 1893; s. Joseph and Elizabeth (Powell) W.; B.S. in economics, U. of Pa., 1915, A.M., 1916, Ph.D., 1924; m. Mabel Baker Fisher, of Phila., Nov. 26, 1918. Instr. in industry, U. of Pa., 1915-16; asst. gen. mgr. J. Franklin Miller, Inc., Philadelphia, 1916-17; special expert, research div., U.S. Shipping Bd., 1919; asst. prof., Wharton Sch. of Finance and Commerce, U. of Pa., 1920-21, prof. since 1921, and dean since 1939; asst. dir. consumers advisory bd., NRA, 1933; exec. sec. Automobile Labor Bd., 1934; dir. (Class C) Federal Reserve Bank of Phila. Served as 2d lt. Ordnance Dept., U.S. Army, 1917-19; with A.E.F. Dir. Nat. Bureau Econ. Research, Pa. Sch. for Social Work. Mem. Am. Econ. Assn., Am. Acad. Polit. and Social Science (dir.), Alpha Tau Omega. Republican. Methodist. Clubs: University, Lenape, Rolling Green Golf (all Phila.). Author: Analysis of Production of Worsted Sales Yarns (with A. M. Brunbaugh and H. S. Davis), 1929. Editor: The Marketing of Textiles, 1938; Textile Costing, 1938; Management of Textile Business, 1938; The Textile Industries—An Economic Analysis. Home: Providence Rd., Wallingford, Pa. Office: Wharton School of Finance and Commerce, Univ. of Pennsylvania, Philadelphia, Pa.

WILLIAMS, Alvin John, mcht. steel products; b. Pittsburgh, Pa., Jan. 27, 1893; s. David John and Emma E. (Klein) W.; A.B., Washington and Jefferson Coll., Washington, Pa., 1915; m. Clarissa C. Cochran, Aug. 26, 1915; children—Henry Cochran, David John II, Franklyn McClure, Clarissa Ellen, Susan Emma, Alvin John. Began as clk. in Mellon Nat. Bank, then clk. sales dept. Nat. Tube Co.; asso. with Chandler-Boyd Company, distributors industrial supplies and stainless steels, Pittsburgh, since 1922, salesman, then mgr., and v.p. and mgr. since 1925. Mem. Phi Kappa Psi. Democrat. Unitarian. Mason. Clubs: Duquesne, Metropolitan (Pittsburgh). Home: 45 Acad. Av., Mt. Lebanon, Pa. Office: 51 Terminal Way, South Side, Pittsburgh, Pa.

WILLIAMS, Anna Wessels, M.D.; b. Hackensack, N.J., Mar. 17, 1863; d. William and Jane Amelia (Van Saun) W.; M.D., Women's Med. Coll., New York Infirmary, 1891; grad. study Germany, Pasteur Inst., Paris, Marine Biol. Lab. and Columbia. Began practice at N.Y. City, 1895; asst. to chair of pathology and hygiene, New York Infirmary for Women and Children, 1891-96, pathologist, 1902-05; bacteriologist, N.Y. City Bur. of Labs., 1895-1905; asst. dir. labs., Health Dept. of N.Y. City, 1905-1934; served as lecturer New York U. Med. Bd. and as scientific asst. U.S. Pub. Health Service. Mem. A.A.A.S., Am. Pub. Health Assn., Soc. Am. Bacteriologists, Am. Assn. Immunologists, Am. Social Hygiene Assn., Women's Med. Assn. (pres.

1914), N.Y. Acad. Medicine, N.Y. Pathol. Soc. Club: Pascack Women's (N.J.). Author: Pathogenic Microörganisms, 1905, 10th edit., 1933; Who's Who Among the Microbes (with Dr. William H. Park), 1929; Streptococci in Relation to Man, 1932. Contbr. many bulls. to publs. Health Dept. N.Y. City and papers to Jour. Exptl. Medicine, etc. Home: Woodcliff Lake, N.J.

WILLIAMS, Benjamin Harrison, polit. science; b. Eugene, Ore., Mar. 23, 1889; s. John Monroe and Jennie Mary (Gwin) W.; A.B., U. of Ore., 1910, A.M., 1912; student Harvard Law Sch., 1912-13; Ph.D., U. of Calif., 1921; m. Helen Frances Ogsbury, Nov. 18, 1917; children—Patricia Gwynne, Stanton Monroe. Statistician Ore. State Industrial Accident Commn., 1914-16; sec. social welfare, U. of Ore. Extension Div., 1916-17; teaching fellow in polit. science, U. of Calif., 1920-21; instr. polit. science, U. of Pa., 1921-23, lecturer politics, Bryn Mawr Coll., 1923; asst. prof., U. of Pittsburgh, 1923-27, asso. prof. 1927-30, prof. since 1930; visiting prof. U. of Ore., summers 1921, 23, 25, 27; Sec. U. of Ore. Alumni Assn., 1914. Served as 1st lt. arty., U.S.A., with A.E.F., 1918-19. Mem. Am. Polit. Science Assn., Am. Soc. Internat. Law, Am. Assn., Univ. Profs., Pi Sigma Alpha. Democrat. Author: Economic Foreign Policy of the United States, 1929; The London Naval Conference, 1930; The United States and Disarmament, 1931; American Diplomacy—Policies and Practice, 1936. Asso. editor The Scholastic, 1927-28; contbr. to jours. Home: 3135 Breckenridge St., Pittsburgh, Pa.

WILLIAMS, Charles Alexander, lumber mcht.; b. Pittsburgh, Pa., May 16, 1897; s. William Hasson and Sarah Ann (Ireland) W.; ed. Washington pub. sch., 1910-13, Reno Business Coll., 1913-15; m. Anna Rimlinger, July 4, 1921. Engaged in lumber business continuously since 1912; with West Va. Lumber Co., Pittsburgh, Pa., 1912-16; salesman Ricks McCreight Lumber Co., 1916-25; pres. Williams Bros. Lumber Co., Inc., since 1925. Home: Pleasant Hills. Address: P.O. Box 5926, Station 10, Pittsburgh, Pa.

WILLIAMS, Charles Sumner, exec. v.p. Thomas A. Edison, Inc.; b. San Francisco, Calif., July 20, 1889; s. Rear Admiral Charles Sumner and Anne Emily (Bayard) W.; ed. Mass. Inst. Tech., 1907-09; A.B., Harvard, 1912; m. Juliet Capers Branham, Apr. 30, 1924; children—Anne Bayard, Charles Sumner, Jr., Mary Grace Gwynne, Hugh Branham. Began as scenario writer, Thomas A. Edison, Inc., 1913-14; vice-pres. Motion Picture Splty. Corpn., 1914-15; free lance writer, 1915-16; scenario writer, Thomas A. Edison, Inc., 1916-17; asst. to vice-pres. Thomas A. Edison, Inc., 1919-23, v.p. in charge of purchasing, 1923-31, exec. v.p. since 1931, dir. since 1931; dir. Thomas A. Edison, Ltd. of London; pres. and dir. Edison Splitdorf Corpn., Edison Wood Products, Inc.; exec. v.p. and dir. Edison Cement Corpn. Served as 1st lt. inf. promoted to capt. then maj. inf., U.S.A., 1917-19. Fellow Am. Geog. Soc. Mem. Mil. Order Fgn. Wars, Delta Psi. Trustee Short Hills Pvt. Sch. Episcopalian. Clubs: Rock Spring Country (West Orange); Harvard, Bankers of America (New York); Army and Navy (Washington). Home: Minnisink Rd., Short Hills, N.J. Office: Thomas A. Edison, Inc., Orange, N.J.

WILLIAMS, Clarence Oscar, educator; b. Russellville, Mo., Dec. 7, 1895; s. Robert Thomas and Effie Jane (Stevenson) W.; grad. High Sch., Russellville, Mo., 1914; B.S., State Teachers Coll., Warrensburg, Mo., 1921; A.M., Teachers Coll., Columbia, 1928; Ed.D., Sch. of Education, New York U., 1936; m. Ruth Vena Vesta Marr, Feb. 10, 1923; children—Jack Stevenson (dec.), Beverly Jean, Marilyn Ruth. Supt. of schools, Tipton, Mo., 1919-21; prin. Boonville (Mo.) High Sch., 1921-23, Jefferson City (Mo.) High Sch., 1923-26; asst. prof. of edn., Pa. State Coll., 1926-33, asso. prof., 1933-38; asst. dir. of teacher edn. and certification, State Dept. Pub. Instrn., Harrisburg, Pa., since 1938. Served as sergt. maj., 12th Replacement Batt., Camp MacArthur, Tex., 1918-19. Mem. N.E.A., Pa. State Edn. Assn., Am. Assn. Univ. Profs., Nat. Soc. Coll. Teachers of Edn., Phi Sigma Pi, Phi Delta Kappa, Kappa Phi Kappa. Democrat. Presbyterian. Mason (K.T.). Club: University (State College, Pa.). Author: Education in a Democracy, 1937. Home: 135 W. Park Av., State College, Pa.

WILLIAMS, Clement Clarence, univ. president; b. Bryant, Ill., Feb. 21, 1882; s. Isaac Greenbury and Martha Ann (Davis) W.; B.S., Southern Ia. Normal Sch., 1900; B.S. in C.E., U. of Ill., 1907; C.E., U. of Colo., 1909; LL.D., Lafayette, 1935; Eng. D., Northeastern Univ., 1936; Eng.D. Bucknell U., 1937; Sc.D., Hahnemann Med. Coll., 1938; m. Grace Josephine Black, Aug. 31, 1910 (died Feb. 3, 1917); m. 2d, Ora Louella Webb, June 8, 1921; children—Ora Louise, Ellen Webb, Clement Webb. Formerly engaged in railway, bridge, munl. and highway engring. work; instructor, assistant professor and acting prof. civil engring., U. of Colo., 1907-14; prof. ry. engring., 1914-18, prof. civ. engring., 1918-22, U. of Kan.; prof. civil engring. and head of the dept., U. of Ill., 1922-1926; dean Coll. of Engring., U. of Ia., 1926-35; pres. Lehigh U. since 1935. Supervising engr. War Dept., in construction of explosive plants, 1918-19. Member Am. Soc. C.E., Am. Ry. Engring. Assn., Iowa Engring. Soc., Soc. Promotion Engring. Edn. (pres. 1934-35), Tau Beta Pi, Sigma Xi, Sigma Tau; fellow A.A.A.S., Royal Society of Arts. Republican. Methodist. Club: University. Author: Design of Railway Location, 1917; Design of Masonry Structures and Foundations, 1921; Building and Engineering Career, 1934; Foundations, 1934; also various bulls. and articles in engring. mags. Home: Bethlehem, Pa.

WILLIAMS, Curtis Chandler, Jr., univ. prof.; b. Columbus, O., May 2, 1896; s. Curtis Chandler and Margaret Mary (Owen) W.; A.B., Princeton U., 1917; LL.B., Harvard U., 1925, S.J.D., 1931; m. Margrethe Cramer, July 29, 1924; 1 son, Curtis Chandler, III. Sec. Am. Embassy, London, England, 1917-21; sec. of legation and charge d'affaires ad interim, Am. Legation, Bangkok, Siam, 1921-22; admitted to Ohio bar, 1926; in gen. practice of law, New York, N.Y., 1925-26, Columbus, O., 1927-31; prof. law, Tulane U., 1931-32, W.Va. U. since 1932. Mem. Am. Soc. Internat. Law, Am. and W.Va. bar assns., Phi Beta Kappa, Phi Delta Phi. Presbyn. Mason, K.P. Clubs: Columbus, Columbus Athletic (Columbus, O.). Home: 112 Wagner Road, Morgantown, W.Va.

WILLIAMS, David Gordain, engr.; b. Northampton Co., Pa., Nov. 22, 1887; s. James Monroe and Mary Elizabeth (Schertzinger) W. student Slatington (Pa.) pub. schs., 1894-1905, Bethlehem (Pa.) Prep. Sch., 1905-06; M.E., Lehigh U., Bethlehem, Pa., 1910; m. Norma Rice Misson, Feb. 17, 1916; children—David Gordain, Howard Misson. Asst. to shop foreman York Safe & Lock Co., 1910; associated with DuPonts as fire and safety inspector, later on plant constrn., 1911-14; with Trojan Powder Co., Allentown, Pa., since 1914, beginning as engr., chief engr. since 1915; registered professional engr., State of Pa. Mem. Am. Soc. M.E., Army Ordnance Assn., Tau Beta Pi. Republican. Lutheran. Clubs: Engineers, Torch (Lehigh Valley); Brookside Country. Home: 118 S. 16th St. Office: 17 N. 7th St., Allentown, Pa.

WILLIAMS, Edmund, banking; b. Ferndale, Pa., Aug. 31, 1883; s. Edmund James and Drusilla (Hansberry) W.; ed. Girard Coll., Phila., 1890-98, Temple U., Phila., 1902-07; m. Sara B. Hargreaves, June 30, 1908; children—Richard H., Edmund. Engaged in banking business since 1898; in employ Third Nat. Bank, Phila., 1898-1901; with Tradesmens Nat. Bank, Phila., 1901-10, asst. cashier, 1910-18, cashier, 1918-19, v.p. and cashier, 1919-28; v.p. Tradesmens Nat. Bank & Trust Co., Phila., since 1928; sec.-treas. Chelten Corpn. since 1928; sec. Chelten Title Co. since 1928; dir. Morris Plan Co. of Phila. since 1935, Morris Plan Bank of Phila. since 1938. Republican. Presbyterian. Mason (32°). Clubs: Union League (Phila.); Old York Road Country (Jenkintown, Pa.). Home: 6421 N. 11th St. Office: 320 Chestnut St., Philadelphia, Pa.

WILLIAMS, Edward R., pres. Vulcan Mold & Iron Co.; b. Sharon, Pa., Apr. 8, 1900; s. Edward H. and Effie B. (Reel) W.; grad. Sheffield Scientific Sch. (Yale U.), 1921; m. Julia Lee Cox, March 1930; 1 daughter, Elizabeth U. With Valley Mould and Iron Corporation, 1921-22; Youngstown Sheet & Tube Co., 1922-23; pres. and chmn. bd. Vulcan Mold & Iron Co., Latrobe, since 1932. Dir. Latrobe Community Chest. Mem. Am. Soc. Metals, Am. Iron & Steel Inst., Yale Engring. Assn., Latrobe Chamber Commerce. Clubs: Yale, Pittsburgh Athletic Assn., Latrobe Country. Holder 4 U.S. and foreign patents. Home: 938 Hamilton Av. Office: Vulcan Mold & Iron Co., Latrobe, Pa.

WILLIAMS, Edwin Bucher, prof. Romanic langs.; b. Columbia, Pa., Sept. 20, 1891; s. Thomas Allison and Alice Jane (Bucher) W.; grad. Reading (Pa.) High Sch., 1910; student U. of Dijon, France, 1911; A.B., U. of Pa., 1914, A.M., 1916, Ph.D., 1924; m. Leonore Rowe, Jan. 29, 1921. Asst. prof. Romanic langs., U. of Pa., 1925-32, prof. since 1932, chmn. of dept., 1931-38; dean of Grad. Sch. of Arts and Sciences since 1938; visiting prof. U. of Colo., 1935. Served as pvt. and sergt. M.C., U.S. Army, Camp Greenleaf, Ga., 1918-19, World War. Mem. Mediæval Acad. America, Linguistic Soc. America, Modern Lang. Assn. America, Am. Assn. Teachers of Spanish, Phi Beta Kappa. Methodist. Mason. Author: Life and Dramatic Works of Gertrudis Gomez de Avellaneda, 1924; From Latin to Portuguese (Historical Phonology and Morphology of the Portuguese Lang.), 1938. Editor: Technical and Scientific French, 1926; Don Alvaro of the Duque de Rivas (with C. J. Winter), 1928; Aucassin et Nicolette, 1933; French Short Stories of the 19th Century, 1933; Maupassant for Rapid Reading, 1934; Jean Servien of Anatole France, 1935; Lettres de mon Moulin of Daudget, 1936. Contributor philological articles, particularly Portuguese. In charge Spanish sect. annual Am. Bibliography of Modern Lang. Assn. America; business mgr. Hispanic Review. Home: 224 St. Mark's Sq., Philadelphia, Pa.

WILLIAMS, Elizabeth Chew, club woman; b. Baltimore, Md; d. Henry and Georgeanna (Weems) W.; student Mrs. Wilson Cary Sch., 1883-84, Bryn Mawr Sch., Baltimore, Md., 1885-90. Chmn. Golden Jubilee Celebration Nat. Soc. Colonial Dames, 1941; regent for Md., bd. of regents Gunston Hall, Va. (home of George Mason, author of Bill of Rights); hon. pres. Md. Soc. Colonial Dames; past sec. Nat. Soc. Colonial Dames of America; past vice-pres. gen. for Md. Nat. Soc. D.A.R.; mem. order of Descs. of Colonial Govs., Nat. Soc. of Daughters of Runnemeade, order of First Families of Va., English Speaking Union. Episcopalian. Clubs: Amateur Gardeners (Baltimore); Club of Colonial Dames (Washington). Home: 108 W. 39th St., Baltimore, Md.

WILLIAMS, Elmer Grant, banker; b. Kellersburg, Pa., Feb. 10, 1866; s. Jacob and Elizabeth (Duckett) W.; grad. Clarion State Normal Sch., 1891; m. Jennie Maria Fredenburg, Dec. 24, 1894; children—Edna Gertrude, Margaret Audrey. Teacher Ridgway (Pa.) Borough Sch., 1886-93, supt. schs., 1892-93; treas. Elk Tanning Co., 1893-1914; pres. Ridgway Nat. Bank since 1914; pres. Ellinger Taylor Corpn.; sec. and dir. People's Bldg. & Loan Assn., Elk Bldg. & Loan Assn; dir. Grimsby Natural Gas. Co. Served as councilman and sch. dir., Ridgway, Pa. Dir., former treas., Ridgway Chamber Commerce. Republican. Methodist. Mason (K.T.; Eminent Comdr.; Past Master; Past High Priest). Club: Elk County Country. Home: 133 South St. Office: 216 Main St., Ridgway, Pa.

WILLIAMS, Frank Argyle, orthopedic surgeon; b. Lockbourne, O., Oct. 6, 1891; s. Isaac and Lovina (Seeds) W.; student Ohio State U., Columbus, O., 1909-10, 1910-11; B.S., U. of Chicago, 1914, M.D., Rush Med. Coll., Chicago, 1917; m. Elizabeth Neely, Oct. 12, 1929; children—Alice Ann, Mary Elizabeth. Interne N.Y. Post Grad. Med. Sch. Hosp., 1920-22; resident surgeon Hotel Pa., New York, 1922-23; practicing surgeon, Elizabeth, N.J., since 1924; attending orthopedic surgeon Elizabeth (N.J.) Gen. Hosp. since 1934, St. Elizabeth's Hosp., Elizabeth, N.Y., since 1935. Served as lt., M.C., U.S., Navy, 1917-20, in Azores Islands and Constantinople, Turkey; hon. disch., 1920. Fellow Am. Coll. Surgeons; mem. N.J. State Surg. Soc., A.M.A., Alpha Kappa Kappa, Chi Phi. Presbyterian. Clubs: Kiwanis, Elmora Country (Elizabeth, N.J.). Address: 324 W. Jersey St., Elizabeth, N.J.

WILLIAMS, Frank Ernest, univ., prof.; b. Liberty, Ill., May 4, 1877; s. Peter and Angeline (Hulse) W.; A.B., U. of Wis., 1910fi A.M., 1912, Ph.D., 1928; student U. of Chicago, summer, 1914; m. Lillian Emily Coapman, Sept. 17, 1913; children—Frank Coapman, Mary Emily, Jane Ann. Instr. in geography, U. of Wis., 1910-15, asst. prof., 1915-20; asst. prof. geography, U. of Pa., 1920-29, prof. since 1929; also geographer Inst. of Politics, 1928-32. Instr. summer sessions various univs. Capt. Mil. Intelligence Div., U.S.A., 1918-19. Expert for U.S. Shipping Bd., Caribbean Region, 1919; pres. Council of Geography Teachers of Pa., 1924-25; mem. regional com. for Pa., U.S. George Washington Bicentennial Commn., 1932. Mem. Nat. Research Council. Mem. advisory com. Pan-Am. Inst. of Geography and History. Mem. of Assn. Am. Geographers (v.p. 1930, sec. 1932-36), Geog. Soc. of Phila. (pres. 1936-38), Nat. Council of Geography Teachers, Am. Legion, Phi Beta Kappa, Sigma Xi, Gamma Alpha, Acacia. Democrat. Mem. Christian Ch., Mason. Co-Author: A Laboratory Manual of College Geography, 1913; Business Geography, 1922; Economic and Social Geography, 1933; also many articles on geog. subjects. Home: 25 Amherst Av., Swarthmore, Pa. Address: Univ. of Pa., Philadelphia, Pa.

WILLIAMS, Frank Harry Mead, teacher; b. Demos, O., Jan. 17, 1896; s. William A. and Mary E. (Lanning) W.; A.B., Central High Sch., Phila., 1913; A.B., U. of Pa., 1917, M.A., 1921, grad. student (part time), 1921-27; m. Pearl E. Pickup, June 30, 1925; children—Marilyn Virginia (dec.), Donald Merrill. Instr., Phila. Central High Sch., 1917-18; part time instr., Acad. of the Sisters of Mercy, Phila., 1917-18; instr. Drexel Inst. of Tech., 1918-28, asst. prof., 1928-37, asso. prof. mathematics since Jan. 1937, sec. of faculty of Engring. Sch.; instr., Phila. Central Y.M.C.A., June-Sept. 1918; instr. in S.A. T.C., Drexel Inst., 1918. Mem. Soc. for Promotion Engring. Edn., Phi Beta Kappa, Sigma Xi. Winner of 4-year scholarship to U. of Pa. granted by Phila. Bd. of Pub. Edn., 1913; scholarship to Grad. Sch., U. of Pa., 1919-20. Democrat. Presbyn. Mason. Mem. Drexel Men's Faculty Club. Home: 35 Llanberris Road, Bala-Cynwyd, Pa.

WILLIAMS, Franklin Grandey, coll. prof.; b. Bridport, Vt., May 17, 1893; s. Henry Keeler and Minnie Adele (Grandey) W.; A.B., Middlebury (Vt.) Coll., 1913; A.M., Pa. State Coll., 1923; Ph.D., Cornell U., 1929; grad. study, U. of Pa., 1932-33; m. Sarah Hila Lewis, June 17, 1919 (dec.); 1 dau., Ellen Lewis. Engaged in teaching high. schs., prep. sch. and acad., 1913-20; instr. Pa. State Coll., 1920-27; instr. mathematics, Cornell U., 1927-29; prof. mathematics, Susquehanna U., Selinsgrove, Pa., 1929-32; prof. mathematics, Pa. Mil. Coll., Chester, Pa., since 1933, registrar since 1934; headmaster Pa. Mil. Prep. Sch. since 1934. Mem. Am. Math. Soc., Math. Assn. of America, Kappa Delta Rho, Sigma Xi, Phi Mu Alpha, Phi Kappa Phi. Republican. Congregationalist. Home: 649 N. Chester Rd., Swarthmore, Pa. Office: Pennsylvania Military College, Chester, Pa.

WILLIAMS, Fred Mortimer, telephone engr.; b. Elk River, Minn., Oct. 11, 1883; s. John Howard and Amanda (Snow) W.; A.B., U. of Minn., Minneapolis, Minn., 1905, E.E., 1909; m. Elsie Switzer, June 25, 1912; children—Howard Switzer, Raymond Everett, Roger Morton (dec.), John Dinsdale. Began as apprentice, Western Electric Co., Chicago, Ill., 1909; engr. Western Electric Co., Chicago, 1910-19, chief equipment engring. div., 1919-23, supt. equipment engring. div., 1923-27, gen. installation engr., N.Y. since 1927. Mem. Am. Inst. Elec. Engrs., N.Y. Elec. Soc., Phi Beta Kappa, Sigma Xi, Tau Beta Pi. Republican. Methodist. Home: 1 Primrose Pl., Summit, N.J. Office: 395 Hudson St., New York, N.Y.

WILLIAMS, Frederick Ballard, artist; b. Brooklyn, Oct. 21, 1871; s. John K. and Jennie C. (Williams) W.; ed. pub. schs., Bloomfield and Montclair, N.J.; art edn. in Cooper Inst., New York Inst., Artists and Artisans, Nat. Acad. Design, etc., under John Ward Stimson. William Hamilton Gibson, C.Y. Turner, Edgar M. Ward; m. Marion Gerry Duncan, Oct. 16, 1901; children—Duncan B., F. Ballard. Landscape and figure painter; exhibitor at important art exhbns. in U.S. and in London, Paris, Venice and Rome. Pictures in Met. Mus. of Art (New York), Nat. Art Gallery (Washington), Brooklyn Inst. Arts and Sciences (purchased N.A.D. figure picture, 1909), Herron Inst. (Muskegon, Mich.), St. Louis Mus., Albright Gallery (Buffalo), Arnot Gallery (Elmira, N.Y.), Los Angeles Mus., Nat. Arts Club, Lotos Club, Engineers' Club (New York), Art Inst. Chicago, Montclair (N.J.) Art Mus., Milwaukee Art Inst., Grand Rapids Art Assn., Ft. Worth Museum of Art, National Gallery (Lima, Peru), etc. Bronze medal, Pan-American Exposition; Inness prize, Salmagundi Club; Isador gold medal, National Acad. Design, 1909. N.A., 1909; mem. New York Water Color Club; mem. council Nat. Acad. Design, 1910-11, asst. treas., 1930-38; nat. chmn. Am. Artists Professional League; pres. Montclair (N.J.) Art Assn., 1919-21. Mem. Mayors Municipal Art Com. of 100 for New York City. Clubs: Lotos, Salmagundi (pres. 4 terms), Nat. Arts, Glen Ridge Country. Home: Glen Ridge, N.J. Studio: 152 W. 57th St., New York, N.Y.

WILLIAMS, G. Alvin, vice-pres. United Carbon Co.; b. Weston, W.Va., Feb. 7, 1890; s. James and Lena (Bailey) W.; student Episcopal High Sch. of Va., 1906-08, Eastman Business Coll., 1909; m. Frances Whitehead, Oct. 16, 1916; children—Frances Cabbell, G. Alvin, Jr., Virginia Lee. Student industrial course at Yale & Towne Mfg. Co. plant, Stamford, Conn., jr. salesman in N.Y. City, later sr. salesman in Can., 1909-15; became mgr. Fuel City Mfg. Co., 1915; organized and then mgr. Liberty Carbon Co., Louisiana Carbon Co. and Midas Carbon Co., these with other cos, merged into United Carbon Co., mfrs. carbon black, gasoline and producers natural gas, Charleston, W.Va.; now first v.p.; v.p. Consolidated Supply Co. Republican. Mason, Elk. Home: Clarksburg, W. Va. Office: Charleston, W.Va.

WILLIAMS, George Philip, missionary sec.; b. Columbus, O., May 13, 1859; s. Robert Philip and Sarah Margaret W.; B.D., McCormick Theological Seminary, 1891; D.D. from Emporia (Kan.) College, 1904; m. Esther DeVine, June 2, 1891. Missionary, Am. S.S. Union, 1884-88; ordained Presbyn. ministry, 1891; pastor Emerald Av. Ch., Chicago, 1891-94; supt. Presbyn. Missions, Chicago Presbytery, 1894-1907; Northwestern Dist. supt. Am. S.S. Union, 1907-10; nat. sec. of missions, same, 1910-30; resigned on account of ill health. Republican. Club: City (Phila.). Home: 734 Yale Av., Swarthmore, Pa.

WILLIAMS, George Van Siclen, lawyer; b. Rockland, Sullivan Co., N.Y., June 6, 1869; s. Cornelius Crispell and Mary Jenette (Jocelyn) W.; ed. pub. schs.; LL.B., Albany Law Sch., 1890; m. Mae Louise Carll, Apr. 14, 1896; 1 son, George Carll. Practiced in New York, mem. firm Williams & Richardson, 1892-1920; counsel for Brooklyn City R.R. and Brooklyn Rapid Transit Co., 10 yrs.; chief counsel Conservation Commn. State of N.Y., 1911-12; pub. service commr. State of N.Y., Apr. 1, 1912-16. Pres. MacCoy Pub. & Masonic Supply Co. Formerly chmn. Dem. Co. Com. Kings County, and chmn. Law Com. Kings County Dem. Organization. Presbyn. Home: Mountain Lakes, N.J. Office: 35 W. 32d St., New York, N.Y.

WILLIAMS, George Washington, judge; b. Fredericktown, Cecil Co., Md., Dec. 12, 1885; s. George Washington and Caroline (Cohee) W.; LL.B., Baltimore Law Sch. (now dept. U. of Md.), 1908; m. Ewin Lamar Davis, May 3, 1927. Practiced in Baltimore, 1907-21; police judge, 1912; asst. city solicitor, 1918; mem. Park Bd., 1915-19; legal adviser to Govt. of Virgin Islands 1921-24; municipal judge, St. Thomas, 1921-24; U.S. dist. judge of V.I., Aug. 14, 1924-30. Mem. Am., Md. and Baltimore City bar assns., Soc. Colonial Wars, S.A.R., Soc. War of 1812, Eastern Shore Soc. Protestant. Democrat. Mason. Writer on legal topics. Home: 805 St. Paul St. Office: New Amsterdam Bldg., Baltimore, Md.

WILLIAMS, Gurdon Hunter, elec. engring.; b. New York City, Aug. 7, 1897; s. William Henry and Susan Rowland (Hunter) W.; A.B., Columbia U., 1920, E.E., same, 1922; m. Doris Alice Boyd, Dec. 22, 1926; children—Richard Tracy, Tracy Alice. Began as radio specialist, Westinghouse Electric & Mfg. Co., East Pittsburgh, Pa., 1922, installation and service engr. St. Louis Dist. Office, 1922-24, installation and development engr. on carrier current power line communication equipment at East Pittsburgh plant, 1924-28; communication engr., Ala. Power Co., Birmingham, Ala., 1928-30; with RCA Mfg. Co., Inc., Camden, N.J., since 1930, in charge elec. and phys. testing labs., 1930-35, in charge research, design and mfg. radio transmitting capacitors since 1935. Served in S.A. T.C., F.A., and O.T.C., 1918. Episcopalian. Home: 262 New Jersey Av., Collingswood. Office: RCA Mfg. Co., Camden, N.J.

WILLIAMS, Harvey Durrell, banker; b. Dorchester Co., Md., Dec. 19, 1884; s. William Spry and Mary Elizabeth (Hackett) W.; student pub. sch., Worchester Co., Md., 1890-99, high sch., Federalsburg, Md., 1899-1902; m. Mary Estella Towers, Oct. 9, 1912; children—Mary Elizabeth, William Robert. Eastern Shore Trust Co., Federalsburg, asst. cashier, 1902-20; v.p. and cashier The Sussex Trust Co., Laurel, Del., since 1920, dir. since 1925. V.p. bd. trustees Laurel (Del.) Spl. Sch. Dist. since 1937. Republican. Methodist. Mason (Nanticoke Lodge, Federalsburg, Md.). Home: Central Av. Office: Market St. and Central Av., Laurel, Del.

WILLIAMS, Homer W.; mem. law firm Williams & Williams. Address: Clarksburg, W.Va.

WILLIAMS, Horace James, otologist, laryngologist; b. Chincoteague, Va., July 2, 1885; s. James and Georgia (Pepper) W.; student, Dover Acad., Delaware Coll. and Jefferson Med. Coll.; unmarried. Otologist and laryngologist Germantown Dispensary and Hosp. since 1919; asso. in otolaryngology, Grad. Sch. of Medicine, U. of Pa., since 1919; otologist and laryngologist, Lutheran Orphanage in Germantown and Philadelphia Hosp. for Contagious Diseases since 1922, Memorial Hosp. since 1923; prof. otology, Jefferson Med. Coll. since 1937; otologist Jefferson Hosp. since 1937. Fellow Am. Otol. Soc., Coll. Phys. of Phila., Am. Laryngol. Soc., Phila. Laryngol. Soc., Am. Coll. Surgeons, Am. Laryngol., Rhinol. and Otol. Soc., Am. Acad. Ophthalmology and Otolaryngology; mem. A.M.A., Pa. State Med. Soc., Philadelphia County Med. Soc., Mil. Order Foreign Wars, Kappa Alpha, Phi Beta Pi. Clubs: Corinthian Yacht, Art, Union League of Phila., Phila. Cricket, Germantown Cricket. Author numerous med. articles. Address: 5908 Greene St., Germantown, Philadelphia, Pa.

WILLIAMS, Horace Oscar, M.D.; b. Yerkes, Pa., Jan. 25, 1875; s. Jacob and Hannah (Cook) W.; A.B., Ursinus Coll., Collegeville, Pa., 1896; M.D., Hahnemann Med. Coll., Phila., 1899; M.H.D., Hahnemann Med. Coll., 1899; m. Eva Ray Horton, Apr. 22, 1903; 1 son, Hugh Horton. In pvt. practice of medicine specializing in treatment of eye, ear, nose and throat, Lansdale, Pa., since 1899; physician Lansdale Bd. Health since 1910; med. examiner for leading life ins. cos. since 1902; pres. Equitable Pub. Co. since 1927; dir. First Nat. Bank since 1912; dir. and first v.p. Lansdale Thrift Corpn. since 1930; v.p. Lansdale Consumer Discount Co., 1938. Pres. Lansdale Chautauqua Assn., 1915-28, Lansdale Memorial Park Assn., 1919-34. Mem. Am. Inst. of Homeopathy, Pa. State Homoeo.-Med. Soc., Tri-County Med. Soc. (past pres.), Montgomery Co. Med. Soc. Republican. Lutheran (mem. council Trinity Ch. 21 yrs.). Mason (32°), Odd Fellow, Golden Eagle, Moose. Club: Rotary (pres.

1929-30). Contbr. articles and verse. Home and Office: 34 Green St., Lansdale, Pa.

WILLIAMS (George) Huntington, M.D., health commr.; b. Baltimore, Md., Dec. 16, 1892; s. George Huntington and Mary Clifton (Wood) W.; A.B., Harvard, 1915; M.D., Johns Hopkins, 1919, Dr.P.H., 1921; m. Mary Camilla McKim, Oct. 21, 1922; children—Mary Camilla, Huntington, Cynthia, McKim. Staff mem. League of Red Cross Socs., Geneva, Switzerland, 1920; dist. health officer N.Y. State Health Dept., 1921-30, sec. dept., 1931; asso. in medicine, in charge pub. health courses, Albany Med. Coll. (Union U.), 1927-31; conducted survey pub. health administration, City of Albany, 1931; dir. of health, Baltimore, 1931-33, commr. of health since 1933; prof. hygiene and pub. health, Med. Sch. U. of Md.; lecturer pub. health adminstrn., sch. hygiene and pub. health, Johns Hopkins. Mem. State Bd. of Health; mem. Baltimore City Welfare Bd. Fellow Am. Pub. Health Assn. (mem. exec. bd. 1935-38); mem. A.M.A., Med. and Chirurg. Faculty of Md., Baltimore City Med. Soc., Delta Omega (pres. 1936). Clubs: Merchants, Lake Placid. Author various articles on med. and publ. health subjects. Home: 620 W. Belvedere Av. Address: City Health Dept., Baltimore, Md.

WILLIAMS, Ira Jewell, lawyer; b. Pennsville, Pa., Nov. 20, 1873; s. David and Magdalen (Herr) W.; student DeLand (now Stetson) U., DeLand, Fla., 1885-87; LL.B., U. of Pa., 1897; m. Mary Harton Jones, of Pittsburgh, Pa., Feb. 17, 1898; children—Ira Jewell, David Alexander (deceased). Practiced, Phila. since 1896; mem. firm of Brown & Williams since 1899; chmn. bd. F. H. White Co.; dir. Fidelity Mutual Life Ins. Co., Chester Lace Mills, Central-Penn Nat. Bank, Northern Liberties Gas Co. Mem. Am., Pa. and Phila. bar assns., Assn. Bar City of New York, Lawyers' Club. Chmn. com. on judicial authority, Pa. Bar Assn.; mem. bd. dir. English-Speaking Union; mem. exec. com. Sentinels of the Republic; mem. com. on public affairs, Union League of Phila.; chmn. Constitution Defense Com.; chmn. John Marshall Memorial Com.; chmn. James Madison Anniversary Com.; mem. Advisory Board, Phila. Home for Incurables. Author of: "Actions by Trustees in Bankruptcy," "Contribution among Joint Tort Feasors," "What are a Man's Rights?" "John Marshall and Philadelphia," "The Inextinguishable Will to be Free," "Righteousness in Government," "The Chief Pillar of the Republic." Republican. Clubs: University, Union League, Art, Phila. Cricket, Sunnybrook, Pine Valley. Home: 444 W. Chestnut Av. Office: 1421 Chestnut St., Philadelphia, Pa.

WILLIAMS, James Peter, Jr., pres. Koppers Coal Co., b. Henrico Co., Va., Apr. 13, 1884; s. James Peter and Anna Page (Kinckle) W.; student U. of Va., 1903-05; m. Virginia Watkins Carrington, Sept. 4, 1912; children—James Peter, III, Nancy Carrington, Nell Baskerville. Mining and cons. engr. since 1905; pres. Koppers Coal Co.; v.p. and trustee Koppers United Co., Eastern Gas & Fuel associates. Dir. Nat. Coal Assn.; mem. Am. Inst. of Mining and Metall. Engrs., Am. Mining Congress. Democrat. Episcopalian. Clubs: Duquesne, Fox Chapel Golf (Pittsburgh); Pittsburgh Golf. Home: 621 S. Linden Av. Office: Koppers Bldg., Pittsburgh, Pa.

WILLIAMS, Jarvis, Jr., pres. Standard Cap & Seal Corpn., b. Foxboro, Mass., Mar. 18, 1884; s. Jarvis and Elizabeth (Plumridge) W.; B.S., Worcester Poly. Inst., 1907; m. Dorothy McCurrach, Jan. 31, 1931. Pres. Standard Cap & Seal Corpn. since 1929. Home: Ocean Av. Monmouth Beach, N.J. Office: 150 Bay St., Jersey City, N.J.

WILLIAMS, John Elmer, banker; b. Clifton, Pa., Jan. 29, 1887; s. J. Walter and Kate (Wilcox) W.; student common sch. and business coll.; m. Anna Hand Williams, Oct. 27, 1910; children—John Elmer, Jane Erskine, Jean Elizabeth (Mrs. Rupert Bowen Harris), Joseph Walter, Martha Ann. Clerk Hudson Coal Co., 1903-06; clerk Third Nat. Bank & Trust Co., Scranton, Pa., 1906-12, asst. cashier, 1912-25, cashier, 1925-31, v.p. and dir. since 1931; dir. South Mountrose (Pa.) Mfg. Co., Scranton Industrial Development Co. Treas. and dir. Scranton Chamber of Commerce; treas. New England Soc. of N.E. Pa., Lackawanna Hist. Soc. Republican. Presbyn. (pres. bd. trustees Westminster Ch.). Mason (32°, Shriner). Clubs: Wynooska Hunting (sec.-treas.), Irem Temple Country, Scranton (Scranton). Home: 821 N. Irving Av. Office: 120 Wyoming Av., Scranton, Pa.

WILLIAMS, John Lauris Blake, editor; b. Orange, N.J., June 21, 1893; s. Frederick Herbert and Elizabeth (Housell) W.; A.B., Princeton, 1914, A.M., 1915; unmarried. Mem. editorial dept. D. Appleton & Co. and D. Appleton-Century Co., Inc., since 1919, editor since 1935. Served in U.S. Army, 1918-19, World War. Republican. Episcopalian. Clubs: Princeton, Players (New York); Nassau (Princeton). Translator: (from the French of Stephanne Lauzanne) Fighting France, 1918; also from same, Great Men and Great Days, 1921. Home: 366 Carteret Pl., Orange, N.J. Office: 35 W. 32d St., New York, N.Y.

WILLIAMS, Marshall, mfg. exec.; b. Blackwood, N.J., July 24, 1873; s. Benjamin and Abigail (Turner) W.; grad. Rutgers Prep. Sch., 1890; B.S., Rutgers U., New Brunswick, N.J., 1894; m. Nellie Edna Steck, Oct. 15, 1907 (dec.); children—Elizabeth, Martha. Employed by Haupt & Franklin, engrs., 1895-96; inspector Pittsburgh Testing Labs., Ltd., 1896-98; with A. P. Roberts Co. and Am. Bridge Co., 1898-1901; asst. to operating mgr. Am. Bridge Co., 1901, mem. president's staff, 1901-02, operating mgr. Pittsburgh div., 1902-04, special assignment, 1904-05, asst. operating mgr. Pittsburgh div., 1905-13, operating mgr., 1913-17, asst. to pres., 1917-27, asst. gen. operating mgr., 1927-31, asst. to pres., Pittsburgh, since 1931. Mem. Am. Inst. Steel Construction, Am. Soc. C.E., Am. Welding Soc., Pittsburgh Chamber Commerce. Republican. Clubs: Metropolitan (Pittsburgh); Stanton Heights Golf, Schenley Matinee. Home: 6105 Howe St. Office: Frick Bldg., Pittsburgh, Pa.

WILLIAMS, Mary Wilhelmine, asst. prof. history, Goucher Coll., 1915-19, asso. prof., 1919-20, prof. since 1920. Address: Goucher College, Baltimore, Md.

WILLIAMS, Percy (Richmond), assessor; b. Pittsburgh, Pa., Jan. 5, 1887; s. Thomas M. and Ida (Richmond) W.; student pub. schs. and Actual Business College, Pittsburgh; m. Elizabeth Hausenberger, July 6, 1922; children—Thomas Jefferson, Elizabeth Bernice. Private stenographer to sec. and auditor Bell Telephone Co., Pittsburgh, 1903-12; exec. sec. Christian Social Service Union, Pittsburgh, 1913-15, Land Value Taxation League of Pa., 1915-17, Pittsburgh Real Estate Bd., 1918-21; mem. Pittsburgh Bd. of Assessors, 1922-25; exec. sec. and trustee Henry George Foundation since 1926; chief assessor of Pittsburgh since 1934; active in civic and economic reform movements especially in scientific methods of taxation. Mem. Nat. Assn. Assessing Officers (state chmn. 1938-39), Econ. Democracy Alliance of Pittsburgh (pres.), Pittsburgh Real Estate Bd. Clubs: Henry George (sec.), Civic, Hungry (Pittsburgh). Author: Pittsburgh's Graded Tax in Full Operation (Nat. Municipal Review), 1925; A Practical Program for Tax Reduction (monograph), 1929; Pittsburgh's Progress in Tax Reform (Kiwanis Mag.), 1927. Home: 201 Madeline St. Office: 504 City-County Bldg., Pittsburgh, Pa.

WILLIAMS, Philip Francis, M.D., gynecologist; b. Martin's Ferry, O., Oct. 20, 1884; s. Brady O'Neill and Mary Armistead (Grove) W.; Ph.B., Lafayette Coll., Easton, Pa., 1905; M.D., U. of Pa., 1909; m. Catherine Toland Stewart, June 2, 1923; children—Cay Stewart, Jeremiah, Eleanor Shelby. Began as physician, 1912, and since practiced in Philadelphia, specializing in obstetrics and gynecology; asst. prof. obstetrics, School of Medicine and Grad. Sch. of Medicine U. of Pa., since 1927; gynecologist and obstetrician Phila. Gen. Hosp., Jewish Hosp.; obstetrican Presbyterian Hosp.; cons. obstetrician Preston Retreat; consultant to Children's Bur., U.S. Dep. of Labor. Served as maj. M.C., U.S. Army, A.E.F., 1917-19, World War. Dir. Am. Com. on Maternal Welfare, Inc. Fellow Am. Coll. Surgeons, Am. Gynecol. Soc., Coll. Physicians of Phila.; diplomat Am. Bd. Obstetrics and Gynecology; mem. A.M.A., Phila. Obstet. Soc. (ex-pres.), Welsh Soc. of Phila., Pa. Soc. S.R., Nu Sigma Nu. Received Strittmater award, for research in maternal mortality, Phila., 1934. Republican. Presbyn. Mason. Clubs: Medical, Bala Golf, Doctors' Golf Assn. Reviser of Shear's Normal and Operative Obstetrics. Contbr. numerous professional articles to encys., text books and mags. Mem. Adv. Editorial Bd. Am. Jour. of Obstetrics and Gynecology. Home and Office: 2206 Locust St., Philadelphia, Pa.

WILLIAMS, Ralph Chester, pub. health service; b. Uchee, Russell Co., Ala., July 24, 1888; s. Arthur R. and Susan B. (Tatum) W.; B.S., Ala. Poly. Inst., Auburn, 1907; M.D., U. of Ala., 1910; m. Annie W. Perry, Feb. 26, 1913; 1 son, Ralph Chester. Pvt. practice, Ala., 1910-13; field dir. sanitation, Ala. State Health Dept., 1913-17; with U.S.P.H.S. since Mar. 1917; epidemic duty New Orleans and Tampico, Mex., in connection with outbreak of bubonic plague; asst. personnel officer P.H.S., 1923-27; asst. surgeon gen. in charge div. of sanitary reports and statistics and editor Pub. Health Repts. 1927-36, Med. Dir. Farm Security Adminstrn. since June 1936. Mem. Assn. Mil. Surgeons of U.S. (pres.), Theta Kappa Psi (nat. pres., nat. editor), Tau Kappa Epsilon, pres. Professional Interfraternity Conf., 1930-31, rep. U.S. Govt. at 6th Internat. Congress of Mil. Medicine and Pharmacy, The Hague, June 1931. Mem. S.A.R. Democrat. Baptist. Clubs: Cosmos, Columbia Country. Contbr. pub. health subjects. Compiler of Health Almanac for 1919 and 1920, also of Miners' Safety and Health Almanac for 1920, 21 and 22. Home: 6 Aspen St., Chevy Chase, Md. Address: Public Health Service, Washington, D.C.

WILLIAMS, Robert, lawyer and publisher; b. Paterson, N.J., Jan. 27, 1892; s. Robert and Alice Winslow (Ingham) W.; A.B., Princeton, 1915; LL.B., N.J. Law Sch., 1920; m. Margaret Brinkerhoff, November 20, 1918; children—Robert Jr., Helena; m. 2d, Frances A. Roche, Jan. 1, 1938. Admitted to N.J. bar, 1920, counsellor-at-law, 1923; and engaged in practice at Paterson; newspaperman, 1915-17; vice-pres. Call Printing & Pub. Co., publishing Paterson Morning Call, Paterson, N.J., 1919-20, sec.-treas., 1920-23, pres. and chmn. bd. dirs. since 1923. Served at Plattsburgh T.C. 1916; O.T.C., 1917; capt. 2d N.J.F.A., 1918. Del. to Rep. Nat. Conv., 1928. Dir. Paterson Y.M.C.A. Trustee Free Pub. Library System, Paterson since 1927; dir. Paterson Natural History Mus. First v.p. N.J. Assn., Amateur Athletic Union. Mem. N.J. Press Assn., N.J. Library Assn., Passaic Co. Bar Assn., Friends of Princeton Univ. Library, Friends of Rutgers Univ. Library. Served as asst. boxing coach Princeton U., 1934-37. Pres. Passaic Co. Bd. Taxation, 1926-36. Republican. Presbyn. Clubs: Forum, Exchange, North Jersey Country (Paterson). Author: Animal Ancestry and its Relation to Primitive Man, 1919; In Fields Afar, 1927; Rare Books from an Old Library, 1930; Pageant of Printing in Picture and Prose, 1938. Home: 555 E. 27th St., Paterson, N.J. Office: 33 Church St., Paterson, N.J.

WILLIAMS, Robert R., chemist; b. Nellore, India, of Am. parents, Feb. 16, 1886; s. Robert Runnels and Alice Evelyn (Mills) W.; std. Ottawa (Kan.) U., 1905; B.S., of Chicago, 1907, M.S., 1908, post grad. study, 1911-12; SeD., Ottawa U., 1935, Ohio Wesleyan U., 1938; m. Augusta C. Parrish, Mar. 27, 1912; children—Robert Reynolds, Elizabeth Alice, Jean Parrish, June Augusta. Began as teacher in Philippines, 1908; chemist Bur. of Science, Manila, 1909-15, Bur. of Chemistry, Washington, D.C., 1915-18, Western Electric Co. 1919-24; chem. dir. Bell Telephone Labs., N.Y. City, since 1925; research asso. Teachers Coll. (Columbia) and Carnegie Instn., 1923-34. Engaged in Chem. Warfare Service and Air Service research, Washington, D.C., 1918, World War. Mem. Am. Chem. Soc., Soc. Exptl. Biology and Medicine, Soc. Biol. Chemistry, Soc. for Testing Materials. Baptist. Inventor of processes for making submarine and textile insulation, etc. Author of many researches on antineuritic vitamin. Contbr. tech. articles to mags. Awarded Willard Gibbs medal, 1938. Home: 297 Summit Av., Summit, N.J. Office: 463 West St., New York, N.Y.

WILLIAMS, Robert Wood, lawyer; b. Baltimore, Md., May 29, 1890; s. George H. and Mary C. (Wood) W.; grad. Groton Sch., Groton, Mass., 1907; student Lycée Descartes, Tours, France, 1908; A.B., Harvard Coll., 1912, A.M., 1913; LL.B., Harvard Law Sch., 1915; m. Helen M. Gibbs, Apr. 26, 1924; children—Cornelia G., Robert W., George H., Rufus Macqueen. Admitted to Md. bar, 1915; mem. law firm Ritchie, Janney, Ober & Williams since 1917; dir. Colonial Trust Co. Trustee Johns Hopkins U., Enoch Pratt Free Pub. Libr. Church Home and Infirmary, all Baltimore. Served as capt., Intelligence Div., Gen. Staff, 1917-18. Pres. Family Welfare Soc., 1934-37. Mem. Am., Md. and Baltimore bar assns., Maritime Law Assn., Phi Beta Kappa. Democrat. Episcopalian. Clubs: Elkridge, Gibson Island, Merchants. Home: 917 Poplar Hill road. Office: Baltimore Trust Bldg., Baltimore, Md.

WILLIAMS, Roger Brian, lawyer; b. Baltimore, Md., Sept. 15, 1894; s. John F. and Lucy J. (Sanderson) W.; A.B., Princeton U., 1915; LL.B., U. of Md. Law Sch, Baltimore, 1918; m. Marybel Gill, June 2, 1925. Admitted to Md. bar, 1918 and since engaged in gen. practice of law at Baltimore; mem. firm Hershey, Donaldson, Williams & Stanley since 1925; served as asst. city solicitor Baltimore, 1926-27. Served as ensign U.S.N.R.F., 1917-19. Mem. Am. Bar Assn., Md. State Bar Assn., Baltimore City Bar Assn., Phi Kappa Sigma. Democrat. Presbyn. Clubs: Merchants, Wranglers Law (Baltimore); Wollaston Manor (Charles Co., Md.). Home: 3209 N. Charles St. Office: First Nat. Bank Bldg., Baltimore, Md.

WILLIAMS, Samuel Baker, tech. mag. editor; b. Orinoke, Norton Co., Kan., Aug. 2, 1889; s. James Walker and Margaret Agnes (McCulloch) W.; Litt.B., Princeton U., 1912, E.E., 1914; m. Catherine S. Williams, Dec. 26, 1913 (died 1926); 1 dau., Barbara (dec.); m. 2d, Katherine Abbott, June 22, 1928; children—Anne, Jean. Editorial asst. Electrical World, McGraw-Hill Pub. Co., New York, 1914-19, asst. managing editor, 1919-22, managing editor, 1936-38, editor since 1938; managing editor Elec. Record, New York, 1922-23, editor, 1923-24; editor and mgr. The Electragist, New York, 1924-28; editor and gen. mgr. Elec. Contracting, Chicago, 1928-36. Mem. bd. dirs. Chicago Business Pubs. Assn., 1934-35, Chicago Editorial Conf., 1934-35; mem. Am. Inst. E.E., Illuminating Engring. Soc. (chmn. editorial and pubs. com.). Democrat. Club: Rock Spring Country (West Orange, N.J.). Home: 2 West Rd., Short Hills, N.J. Office: 330 W. 42d St., New York, N.Y.

WILLIAMS, Samuel Howard, zoölogy; b. Connellsville, Pa., Oct. 17, 1893; B.S., Waynesburg (Pa.) Coll., 1915; U. of Pittsburgh, Fredrich Wilhelm U., Breslau, Germany; m. Helen Wellde, June 1933. Teacher pub. schs., Pa., 1915-19, Slippery Rock (Pa.) State Teachers Coll., 1919-23; with U. of Pittsburgh since 1923, prof. of zoölogy since 1924, and asso. dir. University Lake Lab.; leader of four expdns. to jungles between Amazon and Orinoco rivers in S. America, 1925-32; studies of insects in interior of Haiti, summer 1938. Mem. Pa. Game Commn., Internat. Game Policy Com.; v.p. Pittsburgh Zoöl. Soc.; mem. Pittsburgh Zoo Commn.; mem. Pymatuning Conservation Commn. Mem. Entomol. Soc. America, A.A.A.S. Am. Assn. Zoölogists, Am. Soc. Mammalogists, Pa. Acad. Science (pres.), New York Zoöl Soc. (research staff), Sigma Xi, Omicron Delta Kappa, Chi Rho Nu, Phi Sigma, Delta Sigma Phi. Lecturer Linnean Soc., London. Author: Outlines of Laboratory Zooölogy (with R. T. Hance), 1928; Mammals of Pennsylvania, 1928; A River Dolphin from Kartabo, 1928; Spring—The Naturalist Afield, 1924; The Living World, 1937; A Field and Laboratory Guide to Biology, 1938; also numerous papers and contributions on scientific subjects. Home: 5844 Northumberland St., Pittsburgh, Pa.

WILLIAMS, Sidney Clark, editor; b. Wells, Me., Mar. 2, 1878; s. S. Sumner and Ellen M. (Clark) W.; ed. pub. schs. and private pvt. tutors; unmarried. Began as spl. writer on Lewiston (Me.) Journal; later reporter Portland (Me.) Evening Express; editorial paragrapher Boston Evening Record, 1908-14; lit. editor and dramatic critic Boston Daily Advertiser, 1902-14; lit. editor Boston Herald, 1914-19, Phila. North American, Apr. 1920-25; lit. editor Philadelphia Inquirer since May 1925. Clubs: Union Boat, Papyrus, Newspaper (Boston); The Players, Dutch Treat, Century Assn. (New York); Univ. Barge, Franklin Inn Club, Phila. Art Alliance (Phila.). Author: A Reluctant Adam, 1915; The Eastern Window, 1918; An Unconscious Crusader, 1920; The Body in the Blue Room, 1922; In the Tenth Moon, 1923; Mystery in Red, 1925; The Drury Club Case, 1927; The Murder of Miss Betty Sloan, 1935; The Aconite Murders, 1936. Home: 2100 Walnut St. Address: The Inquirer, Phila., Pa.

WILLIAMS, W. Gordon, wholesale grocer; b. Wilkes-Barre, Pa., July 6, 1885; s. David S. and Mary Frances (Lucas) W.; student high sch. and Pierce Sch. of Business; m. Anna D. Lang, July 20, 1916; children—Gordon L., Frances K., Helen Grace. Clerk Corn Exchange Bank, Philadelphia, 1902-04; returned to Wilkes-Barre, 1905, and entered wholesale grocery business with Williams Bros. & Co.; dir. Miners Nat. Bank, Wilkes-Barre. Dir. Wyoming Valley Crippled Child.'s Assn., Wilkes-Barre Y.M.C.A. Mason (32°, Shriner). Club: Wilkes-Barre Rotary. Home: 1900 Wyoming Av., Forty Fort, Pa. Office: 81 S. Pennsylvania Av., Wilkes-Barre, Pa.

WILLIAMS, William Carlos, author, M.D.; b. Rutherford, N.J., Sept. 17, 1883; s. William George and Raquel Helène (Hobeb) W.; prep. edn., Horace Mann High Sch., N.Y. City; student Chateau de Lancy, Geneva, Switzerland; M.D., U. of Pa., 1906; post-grad. work in pediatrics, U. of Leipzig, 1 yr.; m. Florence Herman, Dec. 12, 1912; children—William Eric, Paul Herman. Practiced at Rutherford since 1910. Mem. Bergen County (N.J.) Med. Assn. Club: Univ. of Pa. Club (New York). Author: The Tempers, 1913; Al Que Quiere, 1917; Kora In Hell, 1920; Sour Grapes, 1921; Spring and All, 1922; Great American Novel, 1923; In the American Grain, 1925; A Voyage to Pagany, 1928; Translator; The Last Nights of Paris, by Philippe Soupault, 1929; The Knife of the Times and Other Stories, 1932; Novelette and Other Prose, 1932; Collected Poems, 1934; An Early Martyr, 1935; Adam & Eve and The City, 1936; White Mule, 1937; Life Along the Passaic River, 1938; Complete Collected Poems, 1938. Awarded Dial prize of $2,000 for services to Am. literature, 1926; Guarantors prize (poetry) of $100, 1931. Home: 9 Ridge Rd., Rutherford, N.J.

WILLIAMSON, Clarence Joseph, prof. ch. history; b. Bellefontaine, O., Aug. 13, 1879; s. John and Ella Martha (White) W.; A.B., Tarkio (Mo.) Coll., 1898; B.Th., Pittsburgh Theol. Sem., 1905; D.D., Geneva Coll., Beaver Falls, Pa., 1920; m. Jean MacClure Hill, Nov. 30, 1906 (died 1927); 1 dau., Lois Eleanore (Mrs. John Meally Robinson); m. 2d, Elizabeth Gilmore Manor, June 21, 1930; 1 dau., Barbara Gilmore. Principal Marissa (Ill.) Acad., 1898-99; instr. Assiut Coll., Egypt, 1899-1902; ordained ministry U.P. Ch., 1905; pastor Caledonia, N.Y., 1905-11, New Brighton, Pa., 1911-17, Highland Ch., New Castle, Pa., 1917-32; prof. ch. history, and govt., Pittsburgh-Xenia Theol. Sem., since 1932. Republican. Asso. editor The United Presbyn. Home: 5909 Hampton St. Office: 616 W. North Av., Pittsburgh, Pa.

WILLIAMSON, E. B.; editor York Dispatch. Office: 15-17 E. Philadelphia St., York, Pa.

WILLIAMSON, John Finley, choir conductor; b. Canton, O., June 23, 1887; s. William and Mary (Finley) W.; grad. Otterbein Conservatory of Music, Westerville, O., 1911; studied under Herbert Wilber Greene, David Bispham and Herbert Witherspoon; hon. Mus.D., Wooster U., 1928; hon. LL.D., Otterbein Coll., Westerville, 1935; m. Rhea Parlette, June 20, 1912; children—Delight, John Finley, Jean Parlette. Founder, 1921, and dir. Westminster Choir (40 voices), and has given concerts with the choir in principal cities of U.S. and Europe; also founder, 1926, and pres. Westminster Choir Coll., Princeton, N.J. Mem. Nat. Assn. Organists, Phi Mu Alpha, Sinfonia; hon. mem. Am. Hymn Soc. Republican. Presbyn. Editor Westminster Series. Home: 4 Hawthorne Av., Princeton, N.J.

WILLIAMSON, Oliver Robison, ch. official; b. Covington, O., May 6, 1871; s. Oliver and Sarah (Robison) W.; mainly self-educated; m. Nina Marie Bolt, June 26, 1895 (died Sept. 4, 1935); 1 dau., Ruth (Mrs. E. E. Ackland); m. 2d, Sally Ferry. Printer, writer, country newspapers, Ohio, Alabama, Indiana; reporter and editorial writer daily papers; mng. editor The Continent, 1910, pub. same, and sec. and manager McCormick Pub. Co., 1912-26; gen. dir. Department of Church Relations, Presbyn. Ch. in U.S.A., 1929-36; dir. production and purchases since 1936. President Chicago Presbyn. Social Union, 1914; chairman Inter-Church War Work Committee of Chicago during World War; organizer religious press for Federal Food Administration; commr. to Gen. Assembly Presbyn. Ch., 1910, 21, 23; chmn. advisory commn. Chicago Ch. Federation, 1917-26; mem. Federal Council Chs. of Christ in America; chmn. publicity com. World Alliance Presbyn. Chs.; one of founders publicity dept. Presbyn. Ch. DIR. The Layman Co. Mem. S.A.R. Republican. Club: Manufacturers' and Bankers' (Phila.). Author: (with C. E. Laughlin) The Complete Home, 1909. Home: The Drake. Office: Witherspoon Bldg., Philadelphia, Pa.

WILLIAMSON, Willie C., clergyman; b. Evergreen, N.C., June 7, 1883; s. Benjamin and Tena (Flowers) W.; student Thompson Inst., Lumberton, N.C., and private studies; m. Carrie G. Whitted, Dec. 18, 1912. Ordained Baptist ministry, 1904; served as pastor of following churches, successively, until 1934; Ebenezer Ch., Marietta, N.C.; Little Mt. Zion Ch., Lakeview, S.C.; Friend-Ship Ch., Nichols, S.C.; Holy Swamp Ch., Lumberton, N.C.; Jerusalem Ch., Hartsville, S.C., and Mt. Vernon Ch., Durham, N.C.; pastor White Rock Baptist Ch. since Oct. 1934. Dir. Citizens & Southern Bank & Trust Co. since 1935. Treas. Nat. Econ. and Social Service Counsel. Chmn. Evangelist Bd. of Pa. Baptist State Conv. since 1937, Bd. of Evangelism of Gen. Baptist Conv. of N.C., 1927-29 and 1930-34; moderator Lumber River Assn. of N.C. since 1930. Mem. exec. com. Foreign Mission Bd., Nat. Baptist Conv. of America, Inc., since 1936. Inter-Racial Com., 1917-20; mem. exec. bd. Lott-Cary Foreign Mission Soc., 1929-34. Elected pres. Wood Home and Day Nursery, 1939. Organized thrift movement among negro children of Philadelphia, 1935, with banking headquarters at Citizens & Southern Bank & Trust Co. Visited Europe, 1937, on Christian fellowship tour, as guest of Young Baptist of England, and as a del. to Young People's Internat. Congress held in Zurich, Switzerland. Republican. Home: 5218 Race St. Office: 52d and Arch Sts., Philadelphia, Pa.

WILLIGEROD, Alice, librarian; b. Newark, N.J.; d. Oscar and Ella (Dodd) W.; ed. Dearborn-Morgan Sch., Orange, N.J., Rye Sem., Rye, N.Y., and Pratt Sch. Library Sci., Brooklyn, N.Y., 1910-11. Asst., Chatham Square Branch, New York Pub. Library, 1908-10; chief of circulation and reference depts., pub. library, East Orange, N.J., 1911-13; librarian, pub. library, Hazleton, Pa., since 1913. Exec. dir. Sugarloaf Hist. Assn., Hazleton, Pa. Mem. Am. Library Assn., Pa. Library Assn., Pa. Library Club, New York Library Club, Grads. Assn. Pratt Inst. Sch. Library Science, English Speaking Union, Nat. Travel Club. Democrat. Episcopalian. Clubs: Women's Civic, Garden (Hazleton, Pa.). Home: 59 N. Church St., Hazleton, Pa.

WILLING, John Thomson, artist; b. Toronto, Ont., Can., Aug. 5, 1860; s. Thomas and Jessie Thomson (Gillespie) W.; ed. Model Sch., Toronto; studied Ont. Art Sch.; m. Charlotte Van der Veer, Nov. 18, 1886 (died 1930); children—Jessie Gillespie, Vander Veer (dec.), Elizabeth Hunnewell (wife of Rev. Orrin F. Judd). Editor Gravure Service Corpn. Asso. Royal Canadian Acad., 1884; pres. Am. Institute Graphic Arts, 1921-23. Clubs: Franklin Inn (Phila.); Shakespeare, Nat. Arts (New York). Author: Some Old Time Beauties, 1894; Dames of High Degree, 1895. Home: 76 Irving Place, New York; also Henryville, Monroe Co., Pa. Address: Graybar Bldg., New York, N.Y.

WILLIS, John Wirt, v.p. Allied Kid Co.; b. Galena, Md., 1875; s. James L. and Mary A. W.; ed. pub. schs. and business coll.; m. Mary Russell Holston, June 17, 1896. V.p. New Castle Leather Mfg. Co., 1919-33, Allied Kid Co., successors, since 1933. Home: Rodney Court Apts. Office: 11th and Poplar Sts., Wilmington, Del.

WILLISON, James Russell, real estate and ins.; b. Wheeling, W.Va., Sept. 13, 1895; s. Addison Ames and Imelda May (Smouse) W.; student Shady Side Acad., Pittsburgh; B.S. in Econ., U. of Pittsburgh, 1917; m. Florence I. Miller, Nov. 25, 1919; 1 son, Robert Miller. Asso. with C. C. McKallip & Co., Pittsburgh, Pa., 1919-21; with Wilkinsburg (Pa.) Real Estate & Trust Co. since 1921, president and dir. since 1938; sec., treas. and dir. Wilkinsburg Real Estate & Ins. Agency; dir. Wilkinsburg Hotel Co. Served in U.S. Navy during World War, ensign (T); lt. (j.g.) U.S.N.R.F. Mem. Am. Legion, Forty and Eight, Phi Delta Theta, Omicron Delta Kappa. Republican. Methodist. Mason. Clubs: University, Edgewood Country (Pittsburgh); Lions (Wilkinsburg, Pa.). Home: 511 S. Richland Lane, Pittsburgh, Pa. Office: 1001 Wood St., Wilkinsburg, Pa.

WILLITS, Joseph Henry, univ. prof.; b. Ward, Delaware Co., Pa., June 16, 1889; s. Francis Parvin and Elizabeth Anna (Paschall) Willits; A.B., Swarthmore College, 1911, A.M., 1912, LL.D., 1937; Ph.D., University of Pa., 1916; m. Ruth Clement Sharp, May 3, 1913; children — Barbara Kinsey, Clement Paschall, Robin Dana. Instr. geography and industry, 1912-17, asst. prof., 1919-20, prof. since 1920, Univ. of Pa., dean Wharton School of Finance and Commerce since 1933. Expert in study of unemployment for Phila., 1915; sec. and v.p. Phila. Assn. for Discussion of Employment Problems, 1915-21; employment superintendent U.S. Naval Aircraft Factory, 1917-19; director of the Industrial Research Department, Univ. of Pennsylvania, since 1921; expert in charge of studies in labor relations, U.S. Coal Commn., 1922-23; mem. ednl. advisory Bd. John Simon Guggenheim Memorial Foundation, 1924-1928; mem. exec. com. Personnel Research Fed.; former member State Industrial Bd. of Pa. Mem. President's Emergency Com. for Employment, 1930-31; pres. Nat. Bur. of Economic Research, 1933 (exec. dir. since 1936); mem. Federal Advisory Council of U.S. Employment Service. Mem. Am. Economic Assn., American Management Assn., Taylor Soc. Author: The Unemployment in Philadelphia, 1915; (with others) What the Coal Commission Found, 1925; Studies of Labor Relations for the U.S. Coal Commission; also various brochures on labor subjects. Editor 3 vols. of Annals of Am. Acad. Polit. and Social Sciences. Home: Ogden Av., Swarthmore, Pa.

WILLMAN, Leon Kurtz, clergyman; b. Pottstown, Pa., July 26, 1873; s. Mabery Ebling and Esther Guldin (Dry) W.; A.B., Wesleyan U., Conn., 1897, D.D., 1914; student Drew Theol. Sem., Madison, N.J., 1897-98; m. Anne Lydia Judkins, Jan. 17, 1901. Ordained M.E. ministry, 1898; pastor Waterbury, Vt., 1898-1902, Montpelier, Vt., 1902-04; instructor Bible history, The Hill School, Pottstown, Pa., 1904-07; pastor Spring Garden St. Ch., Phila., 1907-14, 1st Ch., Asbury Park, N.J., 1914-18; asso. field dir. Am. Red Cross, Army Hospitals, 1918-19; pastor Broadway Ch., Camden, N.J., 1919-20, First Ch. of Wilkes-Barre, Pa., since 1920. Mem. Phila. Social Service Commn., 1911-14; chmn. social service commn. Pa. Council of Chs., 1927-1935; lecturer Bible courses N.J. S.S. Assn., 1915-19; del. Gen. Conf. M.E. Ch., 1932. Mem. Phi Beta Kappa, Psi Upsilon. Republican. Mason; Grand Chaplain Knight Templars of Pa., 1930. Rotarian. Author: Men of the Old Testament; Pastor's Vade Mecum. Contbr. to Christian Advocate, etc. Home: 63 N. Franklin St., Wilkes-Barre, Pa.*

WILLNER, Irving, physician; b. New York, N.Y., Mar. 6, 1894; s. Morris and Anna (Willner) W.; student N.Y. Univ., 1913-14; M.D., N.Y. Univ. & Bellevue Hosp. Med. Coll., 1918; unmarried. Interne Bellevue Hosp., N.Y. City, 1918, Christ Hosp., Jersey City, N.J., 1918-19; engaged in gen. practice of medicine at Newark since 1919; connected with Dept. Health of Newark since 1919, now asst. dir. Div. of Tuberculosis; pres. med. bd. Dept. Health of Newark and chmn. exec. com. since 1938; asso. phthysiologist, Newark City and Beth Israel hosps.; courtesy staff St. Michaels, Presbyn. and St. James hosps.; pres. Yankee Bldg. & Loan Assn. Served as enlisted mem. Med. Res. Corps during World War. Mem. A.M.A., N.J. State and Essex Co. med. socs., Acad. Medicine of Northern N.J., Am. Legion. Mason (32°, Shriner), Elk. Home: 18 Waverly Av., Newark, N.J.

WILLOCK, Charles Edward, pres. Wolfe Brush Co.; b. Mifflin Twp., Allegheny Co., Pa., Dec. 25, 1870; s. William A. and Mary Elizabeth (McRoberts) W.; ed. common sch.; m. Ada Margaret Fife, Sept. 9, 1897; 1 son, Charles Edward. Employed by Fidelity Trust Co., Pittsburgh, 1890-1913, beginning as messenger, advanced through various positions becoming asst. treas., 1898, treas., 1902; pres. and dir. Wolfe Brush Co. since 1913; v.p. and dir. United States Glass Co. Mem. Nat. Assn. Mfrs. of U.S., Pittsburgh Chamber of Commerce, Pittsburgh Better Business Bureau. Clubs: Duquesne, Pittsburgh Athletic Assn. Home: 346 Maple Av., Edgewood. Office: Pennsylvania Av. and Bidwell St. N.S., Pittsburgh, Pa.

WILLS, George Stockton, educator; b. in Halifax Co., N.C., Apr. 3, 1866; s. Richard Henry and Ann Louisa (Norman) W.; Ph.B., U. of N.C., 1889, Ph.M., 1896; A.M., Harvard, 1898; Litt.D. from Western Maryland College, 1935; m. Georgia M., d. Holdridge Chidester, June 24, 1903; children—Katharine Walker (dec.), Richard Norman, Merillat Chidester (Mrs. A. Vail Frost, Jr.). Taught in pvt. boys' acads., 1889-94, 1900-01; instr. English, U. of N.C., 1894-96, and summer term, 1900; prof. English, Western Md. Coll., 1898-1900, 1901-04, and Sept. 1, 1922—; prof. English, Greensboro Woman's Coll., N.C., 1904-07; instr. English, Baltimore Poly. Inst., 1907-12, and 1914-22, actg. head dept. of English and German, 1911-12, head of dept., 1914, head dept. of English, 1920-22. News editor Atlantic Ednl. Jour., Baltimore, 1908-11. Spl. instr. English, U. of Md., 1918-20. Mem. Modern Lang. Assn. America, Am. Assn. Univ. Profs., S.A.R., Phi Beta Kappa, Sigma Nu. Wrote sketch of life and bibliography of works of Sidney Lanier, 1899; papers on Southern history and literature to Publs. of Southern History Assn., and to Ashe and Van Noppen's Biographical History of North Carolina. Author: (with D. W. Hendrickson and J. D. Makosky) Freshman Handbook in English. Episcopalian. Home: 42 Longwell Av., Westminster, Md.

WILLSON, Edward Acheson, pres. Grafo Colloids Corpn.; b. Youngstown, O., Apr. 6, 1893; s. John R. and Jean Wishart (Acheson) W.; A.B., Pa. State Coll., 1916; m. Katherine Beazel Kennedy, Sept. 26, 1917 (died 1922); children—Mary Jane, Katherene Kennedy; m. 2d, Lillian Anne Inboden, Aug. 31, 1926. Works mgr. Acheson Oildag Co., 1918-32; pres. Grafo Colloids Corpn. (formerly Grafo Lubricants Corpn.), Sharon, Pa., since 1934; dir. J. M. Willson & Sons. Mem. Pa. Soc. for Crippled Children, Chamber of Commerce. Republican. Presbyterian. Mason. Club: Rotary (Sharon, Pa.). Author: Colloidal Graphite Lubrication. Home: 388 Forker Boul. Office: 310 Wilkes Pl., Sharon, Pa.

WILLSON, Frederick Newton, univ. prof.; b. Brooklyn, Dec. 23, 1855; s. T. Newton and Mary Caroline (Evarts) W.; C.E., Rensselaer Poly. Inst., 1879; hon. A.M., Princeton, 1896; m. Mary H. Bruere, May 22, 1884 (died Mar. 28, 1893); children—Mary Louise, Grace Bruere, Edith Evarts, Alice Holmes; m. 2d, Anna R. Albertson, July 28, 1895; children—Elizabeth, Albert Newton. Started dept. of graphics in John C. Green Sch. of Science, Princeton, Dec. 1880; professorship created, 1883, and prof. descriptive geometry, stereotomy and tech. drawing, Princeton U., till June 1923, since then emeritus. Fellow A.A.A.S.; mem. Am. Soc. C.E., Am. Soc. M.E., Am. Math. Soc., Phi Beta Kappa (Princeton), Sigma Xi (Rensselaer). Presbyn. elder. Author of a series of text-books on descriptive geometry and its applications; also, Graphics and Faith, 1936. Crossed, on their catwalks, Brooklyn Bridge, 1878, George Washington Bridge, 1929, Golden Gate Bridge, Dec. 23, 1935. Home: Princeton, N.J.

WILLSON, Harold Edwin, consulting engr. (coal mining), registered professional engr.; b. Lykens, Pa., Sept. 12, 1887; s. Edwin Henry and Susan (Keiser) W.; prep. edn., Baltimore City Coll.; B.S., U. of Ill., 1916; m. Mabel Ruth Luke, June 1, 1923; children—Betty Sue, Harold Luke, Edwin Thomas, Frederick Metcalf, Mildred Ruth, Calvin Ashuelot. Began as engineer's helper, Kilsyth, W.Va., 1906; chief engr. McKell Coal & Coke Co., Glen Jean, 1908-14, chief engr. Mission Mining Co., Danville, Ill., 1917-18; supt. Rothwell Coal Co., Winona, W.Va., 1918-19, Cadle Ridge Coal Co., Thurmond, W.Va., 1920-21; mgr. Fire Creek Pocahontas Fuel Co., Thurmond, 1921-23; chief engr. and owner H. E. Willson Engring. Co., Oak Hill, W.Va., since 1919; sec.-treas. Stafford Coal Co., Elsiecoal, Ky., 1923-26. Arbitrator encroachment case of Md. New River Coal Co. vs. New River Export Smokeless Coal Co., 1929; commr. for Kanawha Circuit Court in royalty dispute N. S. Blake vs. Winding Gulf Colliery Co., 1930. Mem. City Council of Oak Hill. Mem. Am. Inst. Mining and Metall. Engrs., Am. Mining Congress, Alumni Assn. of U. of Ill., Soc. Professional Engrs. of W.Va. Republican. Episcopalian (trustee St. Andrews Ch.). Mason (32°). Address: Box 144, Oak Hill, W.Va.

WILMETH, James Lillard; b. Chewalla, McNairy Co., Tenn., Oct. 10, 1870; s. Benjamin F. and Isabella Bruce (DePoyster) W.; student Christian Coll., Howard Co., Ark., 1890-93; LL.B., Nat. U., Washington, D.C., 1906; m. Alpha B. Moore, Nov. 5, 1896; children—James L., Clyde Fairfax, Janice Louise. Became connected with office of auditor of Post Office Dept., Washington, D.C., 1895; lawyer in office of comptroller of the Treasury, 1906-10; chief clk. of Treasury Dept., 1910-17; dir. Bur. of Engraving and Printing, 1917-22. As chief clk. assisted in reorganizing the Treasury Dept.; directed the making of moneys, bonds and securities for financing the war; visited Europe at outbreak of the war, in charge of relief voted by Congress for Am. citizens. Mem. Nat. Fraternal Congress (past pres. press sect.). Mem. Pa. Acad. Fine Arts, Pa. Hist. Soc., Geneal. Soc. of Pa., Sigma Nu Phi, Legal, Manufacturers Club. Mem. of Christian (Disciples) Church; pres. Pa. Christian Missionary Society. Mason, Modern Woodman; Nat. sec. Jr. O.U.A.M. since June 1923, and editor Junior American. Democrat. Home: 108 Englewood Road, Upper Darby, Pa.

WILSON, Albert Harris; prof. mathematics, Haverford Coll. Address: Haverford Coll., Haverford, Pa.

WILSON, Alvin Chesley, chem. engr.; b. Calvert Co., Md., Nov. 11, 1890; s. Eliel and Fanny Hall (Gott) W.; B.E., N.C. State Coll., Raleigh, 1913; m. Mildred Dashiell, May 4, 1918; children—Alvin Chesley, Jr., Elizabeth Dashiell. Student engr., General Electric Co., Schenectady, N.Y., 1913-16; elec. engr. operating dept. Pa. water & Power Co., Baltimore, 1916-21; dir. research Davison Chem. Co., heavy chemicals, Baltimore, Md. since 1930. Served as 1st lt. Engr. Corps, U.S.A., 1917-19. Democrat. Episcopalian. Home: 324 St. Dunstan's Rd. Office: 20 Hopkins Pl., Baltimore, Md.

WILSON, Archer Alexander, physician; b. Cluster Springs, Va., Nov. 23, 1894; s. Thornton Samuel and Frances (Owen) W.; A.B., Hampden Sydney Coll., Hampden Sydney, Va., 1917; M.D., Med. Coll. of Va., Richmond, 1923; m. Elva Beveridge, July 16, 1930; children—Frances Owen, Archer Alexander, II, Margaret Beveridge. Interne, Sheltering Arms Hosp., Richmond, 1923-24; post grad. work in neurology and neurologic surgery, Hosp. Div. of Med. Coll. of Va., Richmond, 1929-31, and Boston (Mass.) City Hosp., 1930; specializing in neurological surgery in Charleston, W.Va., since 1931. Served in U.S.N., 1917-19, overseas service. Trustee Charleston Gen. Hosp., Charleston, W.Va. Fellow Am. Coll. Surgeons, Am. Med. Assn. Mem. W.Va. State Med. Soc., Phi Chi, Kappa Sigma. Democrat. Presbyterian. Mason (32°, Shriner). Clubs: Edgewood Country, Kanawha Country (Charleston). Home: 1001 Highland Rd. Office: Professional Bldg., Charleston, W.Va.

WILSON, Arthur Herman, prof. English; b. Camden, N.J., Feb. 24, 1905; s. Clarence and Edna (Ehrlinger) W.; A.B., U. of Pa., 1927, A.M., 1929, Ph.D., 1931; m. Ella Oberdorf, Dec. 26, 1935; 1 dau., Anne Elizabeth. Asst. instr. English Dept., U. of Pa., 1927-31; prof. English, Susquehanna U., Selinsgrove, Pa. since 1931, dir. Summer Sch., 1939. Mem. Phi Mu Delta, Phi Beta Kappa. Republican. Lutheran. Club: Rotary (Selinsgrove, Pa.). Author: History of the Philadelphia Theatre 1835 to 1855, 1935. Editor, Susquehanna University Studies since 1936. Home: 205 S. Market St., Selinsgrove, Pa.

WILSON, Benjamin James, research engr.; b. Pittston, Pa., Nov. 29, 1895; s. George Korah and Katherine (Zimmerman) W.; B.S., Bucknell U., Lewisburg, Pa., 1919, M.S., 1921; M.S., U. of Ill., Urbana, Ill., 1927, M.E., 1928; m. Louella Mae Dorcas, of Lebanon, Pa. Aug. 25, 1925; children—Kathryn Elizabeth, James Korah. Asst. master mechanic, elec. dept., Bethlehem Steel Co., Sparrow Point Md., 1919-20; instr. in mech. engring., Bucknell U. Lewisburg, Pa., 1920-24, asst. prof., 1924-28; research engr. Leeds & Northrup Co., Phila., 1928-35, chief of mech. div., Research Dept. since 1935. Mem. A.A.A.S., Am. Soc. M. E., Am. Soc. Metals, Franklin Inst. Sigma Xi. Presbyterian. Co-author: A Simple Method of Determining Stress in Curved Flexual Members; Flow of Air through Circular Orifices with Rounded Approaches (U. of Ill. Bulletins). Inventor of control system, fluid measuring system, method and system of motor control. Home: 136 E. Gorgas Lane. Office: 4901 Stenton Av., Philadelphia, Pa.

WILSON, David Wright, prof. physiol. chemistry; b. Knoxville, Ia., Jan. 4, 1889; s. James Ewing and Katherine (Wright) W.; B.S., Grinnell (Ia.) Coll., 1910; M.S., U. of Ill. Urbana, Ill., 1912; Ph.D., Yale, 1914; m. Helene Connet, Nov. 24, 1921; children—John Ewing (dec.), Thomas Hastings, Juliet Connet. With Johns Hopkins Med. Sch., 1914-22, successively as asst., asso. and asso. prof. of physiol. chemistry; Benjamin Rush professor of physiol. chemistry, U. of Pa. Med. Sch., since 1922. Served as 1st lt., later capt., Chem. Warfare Service, U.S. Army, during World War. Mem. Am. Soc. Biol. Chemists, Am. Physiol. Soc., Soc. for Exptl. Biology and Medicine, A.A.A.S., Physiol. Soc. of Phila., Phi Beta Kappa, Sigma Xi. Home: 5 Hathaway Circle, Wynnewood, Pa.

WILSON, Don McAuly, corpn. official; b. Bradford, Pa., Mar. 15, 1890; student Bradford (Pa.) High Sch.; unmarried. Asso. with Columbia Gas & Electric Corpn. and subsidiaries since 1910; pres. Atlantic Seaboard Corpn., Amere Gas Utilities Co., Va. Gas Distribution Corpn., Va. Gas Transmission Corpn.; dir. Eastern Pipe Line Co., Northern Gas Co., Northern Industrial Gas Co., Home Gas Co., Keystone Gas Co., Inc., Cincinnati Gas Transportation Co., Central Ky. Natural Gas Co., Huntington Development & Gas Co., Point Pleasant Natural Gas Co., United Fuel Gas Co., Warfield Natural Gas Co., Am. Fuel & Power Co. Mem. U.S. N.R.F., 1917-19. Mem. Am. Gas Assn., Am. Petroleum Assn. Republican. Presbyterian. Mason (32°, Shriner), Elk. Clubs: Athletic, Field (Pittsburgh). Home: Schenley Apts. Office: Union Trust Bldg., Pittsburgh, Pa.

WILSON, Edgar Kennard, hydraulic engr.; b. Southington, Conn., Nov. 14, 1878; s. Joseph Kennard and Lucy Stone (Taylor) W.; student Worcester (Mass.) Acad., 1893-97, U. of Me., Orono, Me., 1903-05; m. Ida May Pinkham, Sept. 15, 1909; 1 dau., Elizabeth (Mrs. Dura Shaw Bradford). Began as chainman, Portland, Me., 1898; successively chainman, instrumentman, surveyor for land surveying, railroad location and constrn.; with Rumford Falls (Me.) & Rangeley Lakes R.R. extension, 1901; location and constrn. work Phila. & Western R.R., Pa., 1903 and 1905-06; transitman to asst. engr. Central Div., Panama Canal, 1906-09; private practice, Elgin, Ill., 1909-11; Construction water main, Portland (Me.) Water Dist., 1911; with Pitometer Co., Inc., New York, since 1912 successively as field engr., office engr., chief engr. since 1925, on hydraulic investigations for municipal water works, leakage surveys, etc., treas. since 1930; v.p. and dir. The Pitometer Log Corpn., New York, since 1929. Served as captain, Engineers, U.S. Army, 1918. Mem. Essex Co. (N.J.) Mosquito Extermination Commn. since 1931. Mem. Am. Water Works Assn. (trustee N.Y. Sect. since 1938), Am. Soc. C.E., N.E. Water Works Assn., Montclair Soc. of Engrs., Sigma Chi. Republican. Congregationalist. Clubs: Rotary (New York); Railroad-Machinery (New York). Home: 54 Carolin Rd., Upper Montclair, N.J. Office: 50 Church St., New York, N.Y.

WILSON, Edwin Mood, educator; b. Lenoir, N.C., July 26, 1872; s. J. R. and Louisa (Round) W.; Wilson Acad. and Finley High Sch., Lenoir; A.B., Guilford Coll., N.C., 1892; A.B., U. of N.C., 1893; A.M., Haverford Coll., 1894, U. of Pa., 1927; Sc.D., Dickinson Coll., 1933; Litt.D., Rutgers U., New Brunswick, N. J., 1934; m. Alice Green, June 16, 1904 (died June 21, 1921). Connected with Haverford Sch., since Sept. 1895, now head master emeritus. Mem. Head Masters' Club of Phila. (pres. 1926), Head Masters' Assn. Presbyn. Address: 2031 Locust St., Phila., Pa.

WILSON, Ephraim King, v.p. and gen. counsel Fidelity & Deposit Co. of Md. Home: 527 W. 40th St. Office: Charles & Lexington Sts., Baltimore, Md.

WILSON, Ernest Carey, mfg. pig iron; b. Houston, Del., Aug. 28, 1890; s. Samuel Benjamin and Ella (Marvel) W.; ed. Goldey Coll., Wilmington, Del., 1908-09, U. of Pa. Wharton Sch., 1912-13; m. Sarah Cochrane, June 14, 1924 (died 1938). Employed with Eastern Malleable Iron Co., Wilmington, Del., 1909-11, E. I. Du Pont de Nemours & Co., 1911-13; with Delaware River Steel Co., Chester, Pa. since 1913, asst. sec. and asst. treas. since 1917, acting sec. and treas. during World War, dir. since 1920; sec., treas., and dir. Victoria Gypsum Mining & Mfg. Co.; treas. and dir. Iron Workers Bldg. Assn. Republican. Episcopalian. Home: 206 W. 23d St. Office: Delaware River Steel Co., Chester, Pa.

WILSON, Findley McClurkin, clergyman; b. Freeland, O., Aug. 26, 1872; s. James Renwick and Jane E. (Thompson) W.; A.B., Muskingum Coll., 1895, D.D., 1914; B.Th., Reformed Presbyn. Theol. Sem., 1898; D.D., Geneva Coll., 1914; m. Laura A. Anderson, July 17, 1900. Ordained to ministry Reformed Presbyn. Ch., 1899; pastor, Youngstown, O., 1899-1901, Parnassus, Pa., 1901-10; Winchester, Kansas, 1910-12; pastor Third Ch. of Covenanters, Phila., since 1912; also served as corr. sec. bd. fgn. missions of Reformed Presbyn. Ch. in N.A. since 1915; visited missions in Syria, Turkey, Cyprus, Egypt and Palestine, 1931. Pres. bd. corporators Geneva Coll.; mem. bd. supts. Reformed Presbyn. Theol. Sem., Pittsburgh, Pa. Moderator Nat. Synod Reformed Presbyn. Ch. in N.A., 1919-20. Republican. Club: Union League. Home: 2410 N. Marshall St., Philadelphia, Pa.

WILSON, Frank Minium, surgeon; b. Cumberland, Md., Nov. 7, 1890; s. Jacob Jones and Maria Josephine (McCormick) W.; student U. of Va., 1909-10; M.D., U. of Med. Med Sch., Baltimore, Md., 1914; m. Fannie Curtis Roberts, June 20, 1920; children—Fannie Roberts, Frank Minium, Jr., William McCormick. Interne St. Alexis Hosp., Cleveland, O., 1914-15; engaged in gen. practice of medicine and surgery at Cumberland, Md. since 1914; one of chief surgeons, Memorial Hosp., Cumberland, Md. since 1929. Served as capt. Med. Corps, U.S.A., 1917-19, with A.E.F. in France. Fellow Am. Coll. Surgeons. Mem. Am. Med. Assn., Medico-Chirurg. Faculty of Md., Alleganey-Garrett Co. Med. Soc. Republican. Presbyterian. Mason (K.T., 32°, Shriner). Club: Deep Creek Yacht of Garrett Co. (commodore). Home: 654 Washington St. Office: 122 S. Center St., Cumberland, Md.

WILSON, Fred T., mayor; b. Leas Springs, Tenn., Dec. 18, 1896; s. Marcus F. and Ellen (Courm) W.; ed. Leas Springs pub. schs.; m. Eva L. Pickens, July 3, 1920; children—Fred Edward, Mary Ellen, Ralph Clark. Employed on farm, 1910-12; engaged in saw mill and timber work, 1912-13; boiler maker apprentice in r.r. shops, 1914-17; mechanic in shops in various locations, 1917-18; mechanic B.&O. R. R., 1918-35; operated gen. ins. agency on parttime basis, Fairmont, W.Va., 1928-35; elected mayor of Fairmont, 1935, re-elected 1939. Enlisted, 1918, in U.S. Army, rejected because of physical disability. Mem. bd. Community Chest, Family Welfare Soc.; v.p. Union Mission Bd. Pres. W.Va. League of Municipalities, 1938, now dir.; serving 4th term as president Marion County Safety Council. Republican. Methodist. Elk, Moose (Dist. Deputy Supreme Dictator 2d term). Club: Lions (Fairmont). Sponsored many youth programs, safety programs and ideas and many civic improvement projects. Home: 109 Highland Av. Office: City Bldg., Fairmont, W.Va.

WILSON, George Harmon, lawyer; b. Barbourville, Ky., Feb. 16, 1876; s. Thomas Sanford and Catharine Frances (Gibson) W.; A.B., Union Coll., Barbourville, 1895, A.M., 1902, LL.D., 1938; LL.B., Harvard, 1907; m. Sarah Elizabeth Lock, of Barbourville, Jan. 2, 1909. Teacher of Greek and Latin, Union Coll., 1895-1904; admitted to the bars of Mass., Ohio and Mo.; practiced in Mass., 1907-08, Cleveland, O., 1909-10, Kansas City, Mo., 1910-14; gen. counsel Fidelity Mutual Ins. Co., Phila., since 1914, v.p. and dir. since 1929. Mem. Assn. Life Ins. Counsel, Acad. Polit. and Social Science. Republican. Methodist (chmn. bd. trustees Meth. Ch., Cynwyd, Pa.). Club: Union League (Phila.). Home: Gray's and Laurel Lanes, Haverford, Pa. Office: Parkway at Fairmount Av., Philadelphia, Pa.

WILSON, G(eorge) Lloyd, prof. transportation and public utilities; b. Phila., Pa., July 10, 1896; s. George Pepper and Margaretta R. (Duckett) W.; A.B., Swarthmore (Pa.) Coll., 1918; A.M., U. of Pa., 1924, Ph.D., 1925. M.B.A., 1926; grad. in transportation law, Temple U., 1929; m. Florence Platt Cornman, June 29, 1918; children— G(eorge) Lloyd, Marjorie Eleanor. Began as industrial traffic mgr., 1918; served as traffic mgr. Chester Shipbuilding Co., Ltd., and Merchant Shipbuilding Corpn.; was commercial agt. Southern S.S. Co., research dir. Nat. Freight & Delivery Co., and lecturer Temple U.; mem. faculty U. of Pa. since 1920, instr. in transportation, 1922-25, asst. prof., 1925-28, prof. since 1928, also dir. bur. pub. affairs, U. of Pa. since 1935; consultant to federal coördination of transportation cons. transportation economist. Mem. Asso. Traffic Clubs of America (v.p.; chmn. coms. edn. and research; editor publs.), Atlantic States Shippers Advisory Board (chmn. coll. relations com.), Transporation Soc., Am. Econ. Assn., Am. Acad. Polit. and Social Science, Assn. of Practitioners before Interstate Commerce Commission, Industrial Transportation Assn. (England), Book and Key, Kwink, Phi Beta Kappa, Beta Gamma Sigma, Phi Sigma Kappa, Pi Gamma Mu, Pi Alpha Epsilon, Alpha Lambda Sigma, Institut Scientifique d'Etudes des Communications et des Transport (France). Baptist. Mason. Club: Traffic. Author: Organization and Management Industrial and Commercial Traffic, 1925; Traffic Management, 1926; (with E. R. Johnson and G. G. Huebner) Principles of Transportation, 1928; Motor Traffic Management, 1928; Coördinated Motor-Rail-Steamship Transportation, 1930; The Transportation Crisis, 1933; Public Utility Industries (with J. M. Herring and R. B. Eustler), 1936; Public Utility Regulation, (with J. M. Herring and R. B. Eustler) 1938. Also series of 35 monographs on Industrial Traffic. Management, 1931, and 12 monographs on Railroad Freight Services, 1926-36. Editor: (with F. C. James) Banking and Transportation Problems, 1934. Editor, "Railroads and Government," Am. Acad. Polit. and Social Science, 1936. Contbr. many articles to transportation and traffic pubs. Home: 474 Gerhard St., Roxborough, Philadelphia, Pa.

WILSON, Harrison Betts, physician; b. Hardin, O., Dec. 7, 1891; s. Ernest Clyde and Grace Adeline (Wilson) W.; student Sidney (O.) High Sch., 1907-11; B.S.A., Ia. State Coll., Ames, Ia., 1915; B.A., South Dakota U., Vermilion, S.D., 1922; M.B., M.D., Minn. U., Minneapolis, Minn., 1926; m. Florence M. Richardson, Oct. 10, 1917 (died 1936); m. 2d, Lillian M. Wait, Mar. 29, 1937. Teacher high sch., Belmont, Ia., 1916-17; expert for U.S. Dept. Agr., Flandreau, S.D., 1917-20, Manitoba Dept. Agr., Winnipeg, 1920-21; began practice of medicine, Hackensack, N.J., 1927; asso. dir. dept. obstetrics Hackensack Hosp. since 1933, attending gynecologist since 1927. Fellow Am. Coll. Surgeons, N.J. Soc. Surgeons; mem. Bergen Co. Med. Soc., N.J. State Med. Soc., A.M.A., Royal Soc. Obstetricians and Gynecologists (Edinburgh, Scotland), N.J. Maternal Welfare Commn. Dutch Reformed. Mason. Club: Oritani Field (Hackensack, N.J.). Home: Tallmans, N.Y. Office: 430 Union St., Hackensack, N.J.

WILSON, Harry Ross, lawyer; b. Clarion, Pa., Sept. 3, 1864; s. Theophilus and Amanda L. (Lowry) W.; ed. Clarion (Pa.) Normal Sch.; B.S., Lafayette Coll., Easton, Pa., 1884, M.S., 1887; m. Hattie D. Davie, Oct. 24, 1894 (dec.); children—Harold Reed, Lawrence E., Harriette (Mrs. Harold S. Hayes), Geraldine (dec.); m. 2d, Anne S. Shirley, July 6, 1929; 1 dau., Ellen. Admitted Pa. bar, 1886, and since engaged in gen. practice at Clarion, Pa.; pres. judge Pa. 18th Judicial Dist., 1902-11; mem. firm Wagner & Wilson, timber and lumber mfg., 1890-1918; pres. and dir. First Nat. Bank, 1934-36. Served as del. Rep. Nat. Convs., 1896 and 1916, and presdl. elector, 1900. Mem. Pa. Bar Assn., Clarion Bar Assn., Sigma Chi. Republican. Presbyterian. Mason. Club: Pine Crest Country (Brookville, Pa.). Home: 1 Park Square. Office: 406 Main St., Clarion, Pa.

WILSON, Henry F., Jr., investment counsel; b. Brooklyn, N.Y., Nov. 4, 1882; s. Henry F. and Ellen C. (Diller) W.; ed. pub. schs. and Boys High Sch., 1900-04; m. Ruth G. Ludlow, Nov. 9, 1910 (died 1937). Employed as clk. with brokerage houses while atdg. sch.; clk. Bankers Trust Co., New York, N.Y., 1904-10, asst. sec., 1910-16, vice-pres., 1916-34; chmn. of bd., Fiduciary Counsel, Inc., Estate Planning Corpn., Economic Analysts, Inc. since 1934; dir. American Elevator & Machine Co. An organizer and pres. Corporate Fiduciaries Assn. of N.Y. City, 1925-28. For many yrs. active in trust confs. of Am. Bankers Assn. Republican. Episcopalian. Clubs: Glee, Republican (Montclair); Bankers (New York); Rockaway River Country (Mountain Lakes, N.J.). Home: 301 Valley Rd., Montclair, N.J. Office: 921 Bergen Av., Jersey City, N.J.

WILSON, Henry Isaiah, lawyer; b. Wellsboro, Pa., Apr. 10, 1869; s. Daniel M. and Lydia (Stickley) W.; student Warner's Business Coll., Elmira, N.Y., 1888; read law in offices of Elliott & Watson, Wellsboro, Pa.; m. Blanche Bacon, Apr. 4, 1893; children—Lavelle A., Cudray L. Admitted to bar, 1893; specialist in Pa. Workmen's Compensation Law, legal rep. of several major coal mfrs. Mem. from Jefferson Co., Pa. State Ho. of Rep., 1899-1900, 1911-15, 1916-38. Mem. Pa. Self Insurers' Assn. of Phila. (dir.), Pa. State Chamber of Commerce. Odd Fellow. Address: Pennsylvania Av., Big Run, Pa.

WILSON, Henry V. P.; chief of surg. staff Kent Gen. Hosp. Address: Loockerman St. and Park Drive, Dover, Del.

WILSON, Howard Mitchell, pres. Taylor-Wilson Mfg. Co.; b. Pittsburgh, Pa., May 26, 1900; s. Howard and Fairene (Stone) W.; A.B., Pa. State Coll., 1923; m. Mary McKinney, Apr. 1927. With Taylor-Wilson Mfg. Co., holding various positions including engring. and sales managerships, dir. since 1925, pres. since 1932. Councilman, Borough of Ingram. Pres. Pittsburgh Foundrymen's Assn., 1937-38; mem. Am. Inst. Mining and Metallurgical Engrs., Engineers Soc. of Western Pa., Ingram Board of Trade. Clubs: Rotary, Metropolitan (Pittsburgh). Home: 7 Sterling St., Ingram, Pittsburgh, Pa. Office: Thompson Av., McKees Rocks, Pa.

WILSON, Howard Russell, dentist; b. Ingram, Pa., Dec. 16, 1894; s. John Purdy and Margaret (Campbell) W.; D.D.S., U. of Pittsburgh Dental Coll., 1916; grad. student Columbia U., post-grad. Child Psychology, 1920; m. Mary Rowene Griffith, Aug. 16, 1917; children—John Howard, Howard Russell. Engaged in gen. practice of dentistry at Carnegie, Pa., since 1916; dir. First Federal Savings & Loan Assn., Carnegie Thrift & Loan Bank. Served as 1st lt., Dental Corps, U.S. Army, during World War. Pres. and dir. Carnegie Bd. of Edn.; chmn. Salvation Army Advisory Bd. Past pres. and dir. Carnegie Chamber of Commerce, Carnegie Rotary Club. Mem. Am. Pa., and Allegheny Co. dental socs., Delta Sigma Delta. Republican. United Presbyterian. Mason (K.T., 32°, Shriner). Club: Rotary (Carnegie, Pa.). Supt. of S.S. and has missed but one service at S.S. in 40 yrs. Home: 738 Washington Av. Office: Masonic Bldg., Carnegie, Pa.

WILSON, J. E.; v.p. and trust officer First Nat. Bank. Office: Fifth Av. and Wood St., Pittsburgh, Pa.

WILSON, James Caswell, banker; b. Hope, Ark., Nov. 6, 1888; s. Thomas Edwin and Adele (Stuart) W.; student grade sch., Little Rock, Ark., 1894-1904, Ark. Coll., Batesville, Ark., 1904-05, U. of Ark., Fayetteville, Ark., 1905-08; m. Anne Breckenridge Greenwood, June 15, 1922; children—James Caswell, Thomas Edwin, William Breckinridge. Messenger boy bank of Commerce, Little Rock, Ark., 1908-10; dept. mgr. Federal Reserve Bank, Little Rock, 1919-21, asst. mgr. 1921-25; state bank examiner, Ark., 1925-26; v.p. Bankers Trust Co., Little Rock, 1926-27; organized Camden (Ark.) Bank & Trust Co., 1927, exec. v.p., 1928-29; v.p. Exchange Bank & Trust Co., El Dorado, Ark., 1929-32; examiner R.F.C., Washington, D.C., 1932-34, asst. chief examining div., 1934-37; pres. First Bank & Trust Co., Perth Amboy, N.J., since 1937. Served as pvt., Central O.T.S., Camp Pike, Ark., during World War. Mem. Sigma Nu. Democrat. Presbyterian. Club: Rotary (Perth Amboy, N.J.). Home: 829 Mountain Av., Westfield, N.J. Office: 214 Smith St., Perth Amboy, N.J.

WILSON, John Graham, M.D.; b. Factoryville, Pa., Feb. 9, 1869; s. Giles S. and Helen (Dean) W.; M.D., U. of Mich., 1892; postgrad. work, London, England, 1913; student of psychiatry, U. of Pa., 1923; m. Louise Kent, Nov. 24, 1897. Engaged in gen. practice of medicine, Montrose, Pa., 1892-1918; chief Tuberculosis Clinic, 1909-18; physician Norristown State Hosp., Norristown, Pa., 1920-27 and 1931-36. Mem. Bd. of Health. Served as sch. dir., 1936-38; President Susquehanna Co. Med. Soc., 1902; hon. librarian Susquehanna Co. Hist. Soc. and Free Library Assn., 1916-18; mem. A.M.A., Am. Psychiatric Soc., Philadelphia Psychiatric Soc., Colonial Order of The Crown (descs. of Emperor Charlemagne), Soc. Mayflower Descendants of Pa., Civic Club of Factoryville. Odd Fellow (Past Grand Warren Lodge, Montrose, Pa., 1895), Mason (Past Master Warren Lodge No. 240, Montrose, 1903). Author: The Country Doctor; Emergency Abdominal Surgery; Home Laboratory Work for Physicians; The Psychological Approach to Religion; Our Children—Their Evaluation; Adult Opportunity Schools; Junior Colleges in Every Country; My Home College; Camp Arcola. Address: College Av., Factoryville, Pa.

WILSON, John Haden, lawyer, judge; b. Nashville, Tenn.; s. Andrew Henderson and Jane Graham (Spiers) W.; ed. Grove City Coll., 1888-91; hon. LL.D., Grove City Coll., 1936; m. Catherine Elizabeth Levis, Oct. 26, 1899; children—John Levis, Robert Stewart. Engaged in teaching pub. schs., 1885-96; admitted to Pa. bar, 1896, and since engaged in gen. practice at Butler; solicitor City of Butler for 27 yrs.; elected to 66th Congress of U.S. on Dem. ticket, Mar. 4, 1919; pres. judge Cts. of Butler Co., Pa., since 1934. Served as del. to Dem. Nat. Conv., 1916 and 1932. Democrat. Presbyterian. Clubs: Butler Country, University (Pittsburgh). Home: 212 E. Pearl St. Address: Court House, Butler, Pa.

WILSON, John Hunt, prof. physical chemistry, Lafayette Coll. Address: Lafayette Coll., Easton, Pa.

WILSON, John McCalmont, pres. Nat. Supply Co.; b. Franklin, Pa., Mar. 17, 1876; s. Henry Medary and Mary (Funk) W.; A.B., Bucknell U., 1897; LL.B., Harvard, 1900; m. Rachel Brundred, Apr. 12, 1910. Pres. Nat. Supply Co. since 1924; also pres. Spang Chalfant, Inc.; dir. First Nat. Bank, of Pittsburgh, Peoples-Pittsburgh Trust Co., Sharon Steel Corpn. Trustee Bucknell U. Mem. Phi Gamma Delta, Baptist, Mason. Clubs: Duquesne, Pittsburgh Golf, Fox Chapel Golf, Rolling Rock, Ligonier (Pittsburgh); University (New York). Home: 5021 Castleman St. Office: Grant Bldg., Pittsburgh, Pa.

WILSON, John Reid, supt. schs.; b. Bloomfield, N.J., Apr. 30, 1874; s. Alexander S. and Anna F. (Hopwood) W.; student State Normal Sch., Trenton, N.J., 1890-93; student Columbia U., 1903-05, B.S., 1913. Teacher rural schs., villages and towns, 1893-1901; prin. graded schs., Paterson, N.J., 1901-06, supt. schs. since 1906. Trustee Paterson Pub. Library; dir. Y.M.C.A. Mem. N.E.A., A.A.A.S., Soc. for Study of Edn., Am. Geog. Assn., N.J. State Teachers Assn, N.J Council of Edn., N.J. Hist. Soc., N.J. and N.Y. Schoolmasters' Clubs. Episcopalian. Elk. Clubs: Hamilton, North Jersey Country. Home: 10 Manor Rd. Office: City Hall, Paterson, N.J.

WILSON, J(oseph) Frank, newspaper editor and mgr.; b. Woodbury, N.J., Nov. 7, 1884; s. Joseph Frank and Mary (Dail) W.; desc. from colonial settlers; student pub. schs., Woodbury, N.J., Peirce Sch. of Bus., Phila., Pa.; m. Fannie Hendrickson, July 3, 1914; children—J. Frank, Jr. (dec.), Marian Frances, Harry Fairman. Asso. with Woodbury Daily Times continuously since entering its employ, 1897 (when owned by father and uncle), editor and mgr. since 1918, mem. firm owning and operating this paper since 1905; dir. Woodbury Trust Co. since 1918. Served in N.J. N.G., 11 yrs. Mem. Nat. Editorial Assn. Patriotic Order Sons of America. Republican. Methodist. Odd Fellow. Club: Kiwanis of Woodbury (pres. 1937). Home: 349 Glover St. Office: 47 Cooper St., Woodbury, N.J.

WILSON, Joseph James, librarian; b. Phila., Pa., June 21, 1879; s. John Harrison and Sarah (Prutzman) W.; student Central High Sch., Phila., 1892-96; m. Sadie Roseman, Mar. 26, 1906; children—Norman Miles, Herbert Joseph. Employed as asst. librarian Free Library of Phila., 1896-1917; librarian, Jefferson Med. Coll., Phila., since 1917. Mem. Am. Library Assn., Med. Library Assn., Booksellers Assn., Am. Assn. of the History of Medicine, Patriotic Order Sons of America. Republican. Presbyterian. Club: Penn Athletic (Phila.). Home: 5414 Baltimore Av., Philadelphia, Pa. Office: 1025 Walnut St., Philadelphia, Pa.

WILSON, Joseph Robert, lawyer; b. Liverpool, Eng., Sept. 6, 1866; s. Joseph and Mary Amanda Victoria (Hawkes) W.; Alsopps' Prep. Sch. Hoylake, Cheshire, Eng.; Liverpool Inst.; Dr. Steele's Strathallan Hall, Douglas, Isle of Man; LL.B., U. of Pa., 1902; m. Cora Irene, d. Thomas Shaw, Shawmont, Phila., May 14, 1890; children—Mary Michelet (Mrs. P. E.

Dieperveen, Rotterdam, Holland), John Hawkes, Sydney Violet (Mrs. Francis Thibault Boyd), Cora B. H. (Mrs. Horace T. Greenwood, Jr.). In engring. business with Thomas Shaw, prior to admission to bar, 1902; since practiced at Phila. Trustee Am. Oncologic Hosp. Mem. Am. Acad. Polit. and Social Science, Trans-Atlantic Soc. America (gov. 1909-21), Hist. Soc. Pa., Am. Bar Assn., Pa. Bar Assn., Philadelphia Bar Assn., Law Acad., Phila., Law Alumni Soc. U. of Pa. (bd. mgrs. 1906-16), Miller Law Club U. of Pa. (pres.), Delta Upsilon, Acacia Fraternity (nat. pres. 1908-10, chmn. trustees U. of Pa. Chapter, hon. mem. Harvard, Yale and Columbia Chapters), etc. Chmn. Legal Advisory Bd. for the Selective Service, 20th Div., Phila., 1917-18; spl. Registrar for Selective Service, U. of Pa., 1917-18; spl. counsel Ordnance Department, Phila. and mil. dir. for Manayunk and Roxborough Dist., Phila., 1917-18; chmn. War Savings Div. Treasury Dept., Bernalillo County, N.M., 1919. Dir. education and social economy, Sesquicentennial Internat. Expn., 1925-26. Officer Order of White Lion (Czechoslovakia), 1929; Comdr. Royal Order Isabel la Catolica (Spain), 1930; Comdr. Royal Order Crown of Italy, 1931. Clubs: Lawyers, Cosmopolitan, Univ. of Pa. Club, Nat. Sojourners (pres. Phila. Chap. 1935-36), Church Club of Phila. (bd. govs. 1934-38), Delta Upsilon (dir.), Acacia, Philobiblon, Poor Richard (Phila.); University (Washington, D.C.). Author: A Chapel in Every Home, 1898, 1922, 1936; The Santa Fe Trail, 1921. Office: 427 Walnut St., Philadelphia, Pa.

WILSON, Levi Thomas, coll. prof.; b. Jonesboro, Ark., Dec. 24, 1885; s. George W. and Sarah (Stroud) W.; A.B., Washington and Lee U., Lexington, Va., 1909, A.M., 1910; student U. of Va., Charlottesville, 1910-11; A.M., Columbia U., 1913; Ph.D., Harvard U., 1915; m. Barbara Belle Smohl, Apr. 28, 1917; children—Martha Sarah, Thomas George; m. 2d, Hazel Edith Schoonmaker, July 14, 1938. Instr. mathematics, Washington and Lee U., 1909-10; instr. mathematics, U. of Va., 1910-11; instr. mathematics, Columbia U., 1911-12, asst. in mathematics, 1912-13; instr. mathematics, Harvard U., 1913-15, U. of Ill., 1915-17; instr. mathematics, U.S. Naval Acad., Annapolis, Md., 1917-20, asst. prof., 1920-25, asso. prof., 1925-35, prof. mathematics since 1935. Sec.-treas. Annapolis Y.M.C.A. Trustee Annapolis Y.W.C.A. Mem. Am. Math. Soc., Raven Soc., Phi Beta Kappa. Democrat. Baptist. Mason. Clubs: Harvard, Naval Academy Officers. Co-author: (with Guy Roger Clements) Analytical and Applied Mechanics, 1935; Manual of Mathematics and Mechanics, 1937. Home: 20 Thompson St., Annapolis, Md.

WILSON, Louis Lafayette, pres. Union Mfg. Co.; b. Burrillville, R.I., May 21, 1875; s. George Lafayette and Eliza Jane (Ham) W.; student Danielson (Conn.) High Sch., 1888-90, Snell Business Coll., Putnam, Conn., 1891-92, Lowell (Mass.) Textile Inst., 1902-04; m. Etta Elizabeth Cole, June 21, 1899; children—Dorothea Alwilda (Mrs. James Heinlein Harris), Priscilla Avis (Mrs. Charles Worthington Ross, III). Began as mem. of firm H. E. Wilson & Co., hosiery mfg., Danielson, Conn., 1893-1901; foreman Lawrence Mfg. Co., Lowell, Mass., 1901-06; supt. Fay Stocking Co., Elyria, O., 1906-09, Ohio Penitentiary Knit Goods Mills, 1912-17, Am. Textiles Corpn., Bay City, Mich., 1919-22; pres. and mgr. Union Mfg. Co., Frederick, Md., since 1922; dir. and sec. Western Md. Trust Co. Mem. of Bd. Frederick Co. Children's Aid Soc., Frederick Co. Community Chest. Pres. Salvation Army Adv. Bd.; treas. Frederick Co. Council on Religious Edn.; v.p. Frederick Council Boy Scouts. Mem. Frederick (Md.) Chamber of Commerce, S. R. Republican. Methodist. Mason, DeMolay (adv. bd.). Club: Frederick (Md.) Kiwanis (past pres.). Home: 214 Rockwell Terrace. Office: 340 E. Patrick St., Frederick, Md.

WILSON, Lytle Murray, sch. supt.; b. Clearfield Co., Pa., Aug. 29, 1892; s. Ashley Hill and Mabel Viola (Murray) W.; grad. Lock Haven State Teachers Coll., 1913; B.S., Bucknell U., 1927; A.M., U. of Pittsburgh, 1931; m. Martha Evelyn Bovaird, May 24, 1917; children—James, Walter. Teacher and prin. various schs. in Pa., 1909-29; supervising prin. pub. sch., Aliquippa, Pa., 1929-35, business mgr. borough, 1935-37, prin. jr. high sch., 1937, supt. borough schs. since 1937. Served as mem. bd. dirs. local Relief Bd.; mem. Library Bd.; director Beaver County Chapter Am. Red Cross; mem. bd. trustees Beaver County Childrens Home. Mem. Phi Delta Kappa. Republican. Presbyn. Mason, Grange. Clubs: Exchange, Fraternity. Home: 1006 Irwin St., Aliquippa, Pa.

WILSON, Milburn Lincoln, under secretary of Agriculture; b. Atlantic, Ia., Oct. 23, 1885; s. John Wesley and Mary E. (Magee) W.; B.S.A., Iowa State College, Ames, Ia., 1907; M.S., Univ. of Wis., 1920; hon. D.Sc., Montana State College, 1935; m. Ida Elizabeth Morse, Dec. 17, 1913; children—Elizabeth, Virginia. Began as farmer, 1907; asst. agronomist, Mont. State Coll., 1910-12, extension agrl. economist, 1922-24, prof. and head dept. of agrl. economics since 1926; county agent, Custer County, Mont., 1913; state extension agent leader, 1914-22; in charge div. farm management and cost accounting, U.S. Dept. Agr., 1924-26; mgr. Fairway Farms Corpn. (an endowed research orgn.). Chief Wheat Production Sect., Agrl. Adjustment Adminstrn., U.S. Dept. of Agr., May 16-Sept. 1, 1933; dir. Div. of Subsistence Homesteads, U.S. Dept. Interior, Sept. 1, 1933-June 30, 1934; asst. sec. of Agr., 1934-37; under sec. of agr. since Jan. 1, 1937. Chmn. sub-com. in support of voluntary domestic allotment plan, U.S. Chamber of Commerce. Mem. Am. Econ. Assn., A.A.A.S., Am. Farm Economic Assn. (pres. 1925), Epsilon Sigma Phi (v.p.), Phi Kappa Phi, Alpha Zeta. Unitarian. Club: Cosmos. Author: Farm Relief and the Domestic Allotment Plan, 1933; etc. Home: 14 Rosemary St., Chevy Chase, Md. Address: U.S. Dept. of Agriculture, Washington, D.C.

WILSON, Norman W., paper mfg.; b. Erie, Pa., Jan. 31, 1885; ed. pub. sch. and high sch.; m. Flora Nick, Aug. 18, 1906; 1 son, Norman Douglas. Asso. with Hammermill Paper Co., mfrs., Erie, Pa., since 1901, first vice-pres. and gen. mgr. since 1914; pres. Grays Harbor Pulp and Paper Co., Hoquiam, Wash.; dir. U.S. Envelope Co., Springfield, Mass., since 1928, Rayonier, Inc., San Francisco, Calif., First Nat. Bank, Erie, Pa., Erie Co. Electric Co. Mem. bd. corporators Hamot Hosp., St. Vincent's Hosp. Mem. bd. dirs. Erie Community Chest. Mem. Pa. State Park & Harbor Commn., Erie, Pa. Mem. Am. Paper & Pulp Assn. (v.p., 1923-24, pres., 1925-26, exec. com. since 1934), U.S. Pulp Producers Assn. (v.p. 1934-36), Writing Paper Mfrs. Assn. (pres. 1921-23), Import Com. of Paper Industry (since 1924), Adv. Com. for U.S. Forest Products Lab., Nat. Com. on Wood Utilization, Quebec Forest Industries Assn., Ltd., Can. (bd. dirs. since 1927), Hoover Export Com., 1928. Republican. Episcopalian. Mem. St. Paul's Cathedral Chapter. Clubs: Kahkwa (dir.), Erie, University (Erie); Princeton (New York City). Home: 502 Hammermill Rd., Erie, Pa.

WILSON, Otis Guy, college dean; b. Ritchie Co., W.Va.; s. William Martin and Mary Jane (Nay) W.; A.B., W.Va. U., 1907, A.M., 1911; student U. of Chicago, summer 1908, Columbia, summer 1909, Harvard, summer 1922, U. of Pittsburgh, 1930-31, summer 1931; hon. Pd.D., Salem Coll., 1936; m. Helen Vance, Erie, Pa., 1913; children—William Guy, Vance Nay. Supt. of schools, Elkins, W.Va., 1908-15, Fairmont, W.Va., 1915-30; head dept. of edn., Glenville (W.Va.) State Teachers Coll., 1931-35; dean, Teachers Coll., Marshall Coll., Huntington, W.Va., since 1935. Pres. W.Va. Edn. Assn., 1914. Mem. N.E.A., Assn. Coll. Teachers of Edn., Phi Beta Kappa. Presbyterian. Address: Huntington, W.Va.

WILSON, Paul Hays, surgeon; b. New Castle, Pa., Sept. 15, 1902; s. Loyal Wilbur (M.D.) and Emma (Weitz) W.; A.B., Amherst (Mass.) Coll., 1924; M.D., Harvard Med. Sch., 1928; m. Margaret Frushour, June 12, 1937. Interne Mercy Hosp., Pittsburgh, 1928-29; surg. house officer, Boston City Hosp.; 1930-32; mem. surg. staff Jameson Memorial Hosp., New Castle Hosp., since 1929. Fellow Am. Coll. Surgeons; mem. Aesculapian Club of Boston, Lawrence Co. Med. Soc., Beta Theta Pi, Nu Simga Nu. Republican. Presbyterian. Mason (32°). Clubs: Rotary, Castle Field (New Castle, Pa.). Home: 211 Edison Av. Office: 211 N. Jefferson St., New Castle, Pa.

WILSON, Philip Johnson, Jr., chem. engr.; b. New York, N.Y., July 7, 1896; s. Philip Johnson and Louisa (Wilkinson) W.; B.S. in Chem. Engring., U. of Mich, Ann Arbor, Mich., 1918; post-grad. study, U. of Pittsburgh, 1935-40; m. Virginia Eaglesfield, Dec. 31, 1924; children— Phoebe, Judith, Virginia. Chem. engr. Semet Solvay Co., Syracuse, N.Y., 1918-21; chief recorder Cambria Steel Co., Johnstown, Pa., 1921-23; chief chemist in charge of by-product and benzol plants Ind. Coke & Gas Co., 1923-26; chem. engr. Semet-Solvay Co., New York, 1926-28, Koppers Research Corpn., Pittsburgh, 1928-32; sr. industrial fellow, Mellon Inst. of Industrial Research, Pittsburgh, since 1933. Mem. Am. Inst. Chem. Engrs. (sec.-treas. Pittsburgh sect.). Unitarian: Club: Pittsburgh Chemists. Writer tech. papers on gas and by-product industries. Home: 1426 Wightman St. Office: Mellon Inst. of Industrial Research, Pittsburgh, Pa.

WILSON, Richard Henry, research engring.; b. Bolton, Lancashire, Eng., Feb. 11, 1891; s. William and Jane (Whittingham) W.; came to U.S., 1914, naturalized, 1922; B.Sc., Victoria Univ., Manchester, Eng., 1913, M.Sc., same, 1923; m. Susan Agnes Pasley of Manchester, England, Aug. 31, 1916; children—Margaret Jane, Harry Pasley (dec.), Patricia Sue, Cicely Ann, Richard Whittingham, John Pasley. Engaged as asst., Toronto Univ., 1913-14; with research dept. Western Electric Co., 1914-25, and Bell Telephone Labs., Inc., since 1925, engaged in expts. in radio, 1914-19, head of research service dept., 1919-39; gen. service mgr. since 1939; awarded patents on devices; pres. Engineers Royalties, Inc., N.Y. City; professional engr. N.Y. State. Republican. Episcopalian. Contbr. articles to Harvard Business Review. Home: 540 Ridgewood Rd., Maplewood, N.J. Office: 463 West St., New York, N.Y.

WILSON, Robert Lee, elec. and mech. engr.; b. Shelbyville, Ill., Jan. 29, 1871; s. William G. (M.D.) and Frances Anna (Lee) W.; student State U. Ia., 1 yr.; B.S. in M.E., Rose Poly. Inst., Terre Haute, Ind., 1892; post-grad. work in elec. engring., Johns Hopkins, 1894; m. Fanny Hampton Jeffers Kennard, Nov. 15, 1900; children—Robert L., Eloise Hampton. With Gen. Electric Co., Schenectady, N.Y., 1892; with Westinghouse Electric & Mfg. Co. since 1894, successively as engineer, supt., gen. supt., works mgr., asst. v.p. and gen. mgr., assistant to president; superintended original electrification of the Manhattan Elevated R.R. and New York Subway; built and installed equipment for electrification of N.Y., N.H.&H. R.R., and the St. Clair Tunnel of Grand Trunk R.R.—the first two important alternating current r.r. electrifications in the U.S.; directed mfg. operations of Westinghouse Electric & Mfg. Co. at East Pittsburgh, 1914-31, then consultant to same; retired Jan. 1938. Fellow Am. Inst. E.E.; mem. Engrs'. Soc. Western Pa., E.A.R. Republican. Methodist. Clubs: University, Edgewood Country (Pittsburgh); Engineers' (New York). one of the first to advocate elective representation in works councils (joint conf. committees); frequent speaker upon industrial relations. Home: Cathedral Mansions, Pittsburgh, Pa.; also Bel Air, Md.

WILSON, Robert Monighan, real estate and ins. brokerage; b. Milton, Vt., Sept. 15, 1891; s. Henry George and Emogene (Comstock) W.; student high sch. Atlantic City, N.J., 1906-09, U. of Pa. Evening Sch. of Accts. & Finance, 1912-15; m. Sarah Sophia Brown, Oct. 25, 1924. Employed with Second Nat. Bank, Atlantic City, N.J., in various capacities, 1909-12; financial sec. with Col. Louis J. Kolb, 1912-17; asso. with Quaker City Corpn., exporters and importers, Phila., Pa., 1919-21; with Albert M. Greenfield & Co., real estate and ins. agency brokers, Phila., since 1921, v.p. and treas. since 1935; pres. Merchants Parcel Delivery. Served as chief petty officer, then ensign, U.S.O.R.F., 1917-18. Vice-pres., chmn. finance com., Pa. Real Estate Assn.; mem. bd. govs., chmn. finance com., Phila. Real Estate Bd. Mem. Delta Sigma Phi. Republican. Episcopalian. Mason. Clubs: Penn Athletic, Art, Philadelphia Country (Phila.). Home: 17 Shirley Rd., Narberth, Pa. Office: 200 Bankers Securities Bldg., Philadelphia, Pa.

WILSON, Samuel Milliken, M.D.; b. Philadelphia, Pa., Aug., 1867; s. James Foster (M.D.) and Louisa (Milliken) W.; student pub. schs.; M.D., U. of Pa., 1889; unmarried. Engaged in gen. practice of medicine since 1889. Mem. Phila. Coll. Physicians, A.M.A., Phila. Pathol. Soc., Pa. Med. Soc. Republican. Episcopalian. Mason. Clubs: Aesculapian, Medical, Malta Boat (Philadelphia). Home: 1205 Spruce St. Office: 1930 Chestnut St., Philadelphia, Pa.

WILSON, Samuel Taylor, ednl. adminstr.; b. Rising Sun, Md., Oct. 11, 1868; s. Thomas J. and Adeline H. (Kirk) W.; student West Nottingham Acad., 1887-90; C.E., Lafayette Coll., Easton, Pa., 1893; m. Anna W. Bryan, Oct. 2, 1895. Employed as civil engr. for Tippett & Wood, Phillipsburg, N.J., 1893-1903, pres. and gen. mgr., 1903-26, sec., dir. Tippett & Wood, Inc.; treas. Lafayette Coll., Easton, Pa., 1926-32, field rep. since 1932; dir., mem. exec. com. Easton Trust Co.; trustee N.J. Mfrs. Assn., Trenton, N.J.; dir. N.J. Mfrs. Assn. Casualty Ins. Co., N.J. Mfrs. Assn. Fire Ins. Co. Served as first pres. Easton, Pa., Community Chest, 1922-25 and mem. exec. com. since 1922; dir. Easton Y.M.C.A.; trustee Easton Y.W.C.A., Easton Children's Home; dir. N.J. Mfrs. Assn. Hosp., Inc.; life trustee Lafayette Coll. Mem. Delta Upsilon. Republican. Methodist (pres. bd. trustees, Easton Methodist Ch.). Home: 322 Reeder St. Office: Lafayette Coll., Easton, Pa.

WILSON, Stanley Moscript, elec. engr.; b. Chicago, Ill., Feb. 7, 1885; s. Thomas Hall and Jane Ellen (Bush) W.; student East Aurora (Ill.) grade sch., 1892-97, high sch., 1897-1901; m. Gertrude May Porteous, June 1, 1906; children—Stanmore Van Ness, Robert Porteous. Telephone maintenance man, Ill. Bell Telephone Co., Chicago, 1902-05, mgr. local exchanges, 1905-06; elec. work U.S. Govt., Chicago, 1907-10; telephone engr., supervisor, asst. supt., Western Electric Co., Hawthorne Works, Chicago, 1911-25; supt., 1925-26, gen. supt., 1927-35, and mgr. central office div., 1936-39, Western Electric Co., Kearny (N.J.) Works; engr. of mfr. Western Electric Co., New York, since 1939. Mem. Am. Inst. Elec. Engrs., Newark (N.J.) Chamber of Commerce, Jersey City (N.J.) Chamber of Commerce, West Hudson Mfrs. Assn. Republican. Presbyterian. Mason. Clubs: Canoe Brook Country (Summit, N.J.); Maplewood County (Maplewood, N.J.). Home: 41 Maplewood Av., Maplewood, N.J. Office: 195 Broadway, New York, N.Y.

WILSON, Theodore Halbert, educator, clergyman; b. Middletown, Conn., Feb. 11, 1885; s. Edwin Horace and Jane Amelia (Bidwell) W.; grad. Cambridge (Mass.) Latin School, 1902; A.B., Harvard, 1907, A.M., 1908, Ed.M., 1928, Ed.D., 1935; B.D., Union Theol. Sem., 1911; m. Faith Evelyn Harris, July 31, 1919; children—Faith Evelyn, Theodore Halbert, Carolyn Elsie. Ordained Congregational ministry, 1910; asst. pastor Flatbush (N.Y.) Ch., 1909; asst. dir. Student Christian Work, Union Theol. Sem., 1908-11; prin. Union Sch. of Religion, N.Y. City, 1910-11; asso. pastor 1st Ch., Montclair, N.J., 1911-12; pastor Skowhegan, Me., 1912-15, Olivet, Mich., 1916-18; prof. religion, 1916-18, pres., 1918-19, Olivet Coll.; field representative Congl. Nat. Council Commn. on Pilgrim Memorial Fund, Sept.-Dec. 1919, also mem. of Council; surveyor of theol. seminaries and training schs. for Interch. World Movement of N. America, Jan.-June 1920; prin. St. Johnsbury (Vt.) Acad., 1920-30; pres. Chevy Chase School, Washington, D.C., Aug. 1930-June 1932; dir. Nat. Park Sem., Forest Glen, Md., 1932-35; ednl. advisor McDonogh (Md.) Sch. since Sept. 1935, University of Baltimore since May 1937. Mem. Vt. Educational Survey Commn., 1928-30. Mem. N.E.A., Delta Upsilon. Phi Delta Kappa. Club: Harvard (Maryland). Home: 113 Oakdale Av., Catonsville, Md.

WILSON, Theophilus Lowry, lawyer; b. Clarion, Pa., Apr. 7, 1875; s. Theophilus Strattan and Amanda (Lowry) W.; ed. Clarion State Normal Sch. and Indiana U.; unmarried. Now engaged in private practice of law; dir. Citizens Trust Co., Lake Erie, Franklin & Clarion R.R. Co., Clarion, Pa., and Glenray Lumber Co., Alderson, W.Va. Presidential elector, 27th Congressional Dist. of Pa., 1908; president judge, 18th Judicial Dist. of Pa., July 1912-Jan. 1914; elected to represent 27th Congressional Dist. in Proposed Pa. Constitutional Conv., 1921 (grandfather, Samuel Wilson, mem. Constitutional Conv. 1873). Served as corpl. Co. D, 15th Regt., Pa. Vol. Inf., Spanish-Am. War; became capt. Co. D, 15th Regt., Pa. Nat. Guard, 1899. Life mem. Am. Red Cross. Mem. Clarion Co. Bar Assn., Pa. Forestry Assn. (life). Clubs: Wanango Country, Pittsburgh Athletic Assn. Author: Seventy-Five Year History of First Presbyterian Church of Clarion, Pa. (pub. in local papers); Roads and Highways of Clarion County; etc. Address: 10 Grant St., Clarion, Pa.

WILSON, Thomas William, pres. Del. Electric Power Co.; b. New York, N.Y., May 9, 1872; s. David and Frances Harriett (Crichton) W.; C.E., Lehigh U., 1894; m. Anna Beatrice Wilson, Sept. 1905. Engr. Pa. Steel Co., 1894-96; chief engr. Charleston City Ry. Co., 1896-98; chief engr. Internat. Ry. Co., 1898-1905, gen. mgr., 1905-12; v.p. and gen. mgr. Wilmington & Phila. Traction Co., 1912-27; pres. Del. Electric Power Co. since 1927; pres. Del. Power & Light Co., Del. Bus. Co., Southern Pa. Bus Co.; dir. Wilmington Trust Co.; mem. Wilmington Savings Fund Soc. Nat. Councillor, U.S. Chamber of Commerce; dir. Wilmington Chamber of Commerce, Del. Safety Council; chmn. for Del., Nat. advisory com., N.Y. World's Fair, 1939. Trustee Group Hosp. Service, Inc. Republican. Episcopalian. Clubs: Union League, Midday (Phila.); University (Buffalo); Seaview Golf (Absecon, N.J.); Wilmington, Vicmead Hunt, Rotary (Wilmington); Chester (Chester, Pa.); Wilmington Country. Home: Hotel du Pont. Office: 600 Market St., Wilmington, Del.

WILSON, William Pannell, mfg. exec.; b. Wheeling, W.Va., Jan. 6, 1872; s. William A. and Texanna W.; student pub. schs.; m. Ellen Wright, Oct. 19, 1898; children—George Taylor, William Pannell, Ellen Wright (Mrs. William L. Burt). Prin. partner W. A. Wilson & Son, wholesale millwork; pres. Ohio Valley Industrial Corpn., Wheeling, W.Va.; dir. Nat. Bank of W.Va. Chmn. Wheeling Park Commn. Dir. Ohio Valley Hosp. Assn. Presbyterian. Mason. Club: Wheeling Country, Fort Henry (Wheeling, W. Va.); Metropolitan (Washington, D.C.). Home: Highland Park, W.Va. Office: 1409 Main St., Wheeling, W.Va.

WILSON, William Riley; b. at Fair Haven, Preble Co., O., Sept. 5, 1860; s. David Sturgous and Mary Jane (Orr) W.; A.B., Washington and Jefferson Coll., Washington, Pa., 1886; grad. Allegheny (now Pittsburgh-Xenia) Theol. Sem., 1889; D.D., Westminster and Grove City colls., 1906; LL.D., Muskingum Coll., 1934; m. Lily Jane Brownlee, July 31, 1890; children—John Brownlee, David Porter, Robert McWatty (dec.), Ross Stevenson, Martha Ashton (Mrs. Alfred A. Hart), Mary Orr (Mrs. Christian F. Kenneweg), Lu Ellen Sutton (Mrs. James O. Paisley). Ordained ministry United Presbyn. Ch., 1889; pastor North Shenango Ch., Espyville Sta., Pa., 1889-92, 2d Ch., Mercer, Pa., 1892-99, 10th Ch., Allegheny, Pittsburgh, Pa., June 1899-1902, 1st Ch., Carnegie, Pa., 1902-06; prof. pastoral theology and homiletics, Pittsburgh-Xenia Theol. Sem., since 1906. Mem. Phi Gamma Delta. Home: Ben Avon, Pa.

WILSON, Wirt Bunten, physician; b. Frenchton, W.Va., May 27, 1881; s. John Westley and Hattie (Bunten) W.; student W.Va. Wesleyan Coll., Buckhannon, W.Va., 1909, U. of the South, Sewanee, Tenn., 1908; M.D., Md. Med. Coll., Baltimore, 1911; m. Margaret Arnold, Aug. 18, 1915. Interne Franklin Sq. Hosp., Baltimore, 1911-12, supt. 1912; post-grad. work Chicago Polyclinic Hosp., 1925, asst. to Dr. George Suker, 1925; chief Eye, Ear, Nose and Throat Clinic, Charleston (W.Va.) Gen. Hosp., 1926-28, chief of service, since 1929. Aeronautical examiner Dept. of Commerce, Charleston, since 1929. Fellow Am. Coll. Surgeons; mem. A.M.A., W.Va. State Med. Assn., Kanawha County Med. Soc. Republican. Methodist. Mason (32°). Home: 1568 Washington St. Office: Professional Bldg., Charleston, W.Va.

WIMER, Arthur C., newspaper corr.; b. New Castle, Pa., May 19, 1904; U. of Fla., 1923-25; B.Litt., Columbia, 1927; m. Mildred E. Hill, Sept. 1, 1928. Began as reporter New Castle News, 1922; with New York Times, 1926-27; reporter Griffin News Bur., Washington, D.C., 1927-29; mng. editor same, 1929-31; Washington corr. Hartford (Conn.) Courant since 1931. Mem. Sigma Delta Chi, Delta Chi. Club: Nat. Press. Home: 130 E. Bradley Lane, Chevy Chase, Md. Office: National Press Bldg., Washington, D.C.

WINCHELL, Alexander Vaughn, M.D.; b. Butte, Mont., Oct. 10, 1904; s. Alexander Newton and Edith Clare (Christello) W.; A.B. in geology, U. of Wis., 1925; A.M. in neurology, U. of Wis. Med. Sch., 1929; M.D., Rush Med. Sch. (U. of Chicago), 1931; m. Anne Pierson Forsyth, July 9, 1932; 1 son, Henry Forsyth. Interne Western Pa. Hosp., Pittsburgh, 1931-32, asst. radiologist, 1932-35; instr. U. of Rochester (N.Y.) Med. Sch., 1935-37; asst. radiologist Strong Memorial Hosp., Rochester, N.Y., 1935-37, Rochester Municipal Hosp., 1935-37; radiologist Am. Oncologic Hosp., Phila., Pa., since 1937, asst. med. dir. since 1937. Diplomate Am. Bd. Radiology; fellow A.M.A.; mem. A.A.A.S., Radiol. Soc. of N.A., Internat. Cancer Round Table, Pa. State Med. Soc., Phila. Co. Med. Soc., Physiol. Soc. Phila., Nu Sigma Nu, Beta Theta Pi. Presbyn. Home: Penn & Station Rds., Wynnewood, Pa. Office: 3234 Powelton Av., Philadelphia, Pa.

WINCHELL, Lawrence Romie, supt. of schools; b. Soledad, Calif., Feb. 25, 1898; s. Wallace William and Ida May (Harris) W.; grad. Newark (N.J.) State Normal Sch., 1923; B.S., Coll. of City of New York, 1925; A.M., Columbia, 1929; Ed.D., Rutgers U., 1937; m. Jane Davis, June 25, 1924; children—Lawrence Romie, Margaret June. Supervising prin., New Providence, N.J., 1923-34; supt. of schools, Vineland (including Landis Twp.), N.J., since 1934; sec. Bd. of Edn., New Providence, 1927-34; prin. Elementary and Junior High Sch., Newark, N.J., summers 1924-30; lecturer and extension prof. in teacher training, Rutgers U., 1929-39; prof. of edn., State U. of N.J., summers 1929-39. Mem. N.J. State Com. of Kiwanis Vocational Guidance; mem. N.J. State Course of Study Com. for Arithmetic, 1930, for Health and Safety, 1932; demonstration teacher of social studies in high school before N.J. State Teachers Assn. Mem. Vineland Library Assn., County Health Com., County Boy Scout Com. Served with 147th Co., U.S. Marines, during World War. Mem. N.J. Visual Assn. (sec.-treas. 1923-28; vice-pres. 1928; pres. 1930). Mem. Am. Legion, Sons Am. Revolution, N.J. Council of Edn., Beta Theta Pi, Phi Delta Kappa. Clubs: Kiwanis (pres.), Schoolmasters of South Jersey. Contbr. to ednl. jours.; doctor's thesis, A Proposed Plan for State Department of Visual Instruction for New Jersey. Home: 1101 New Pear St. Office: School Administration Bldg., 6th and Plum Sts., Vineland, N.J.

WINCHESTER, Edith May, coll. prof.; b. Charlottetown, Prince Edward Island, Sept. 6, 1896; d. Edward John and Mary (Dunderdale) W.; brought to U.S., 1897, citizen through father's naturalization, 1898; B.S., Simmons Coll., Boston, Mass., 1919; Ed.M., Harvard, 1932; unmarried. Instr. in secretarial studies, Margaret Morrison Carnegie Coll., Pittsburgh, 1919-25, asst. prof., 1925-27, prof. since 1937, acting head of Secretarial Dept., 1926-29, head since 1929; sec. of faculty, Carnegie Inst. Tech., 1926-35, 1937-38, chmn. of faculty, 1938-39. Dir. Nat. Assn. of Commercial Teacher-Training

Instns. Mem. N.E.A., Eastern Commercial Teachers Assn., Tri-State Commercial Edn. Assn., Simmons Coll. Alumnae Assn., Harvard Alumni Assn., Phi Kappa Phi; hon. mem. and faculty advisor Cwens, Mortar Board. Clubs: Simmons College (Pittsburgh); Women's (Carnegie Inst. Tech.). Home: Cathedral Mansions, Pittsburgh, Pa.

WINCHESTER, George, prof. physics, Rutgers U. Address: Rutgers U., New Brunswick, N.J.

WINCHESTER, James Price, chmn. bd. Wilmington Trust Co.; mgr. Artisans Savings Bank. Address: Wilmington, Del.*

WINDER, Ambrose Jones, real estate, appraisals, ins.; b. Phila., Pa., May 13, 1899; s. John and Lydia (Walton) W.; student pub. schs. and high sch., 1905-14, various evening schs., bus. courses, real estate law; m. Eleanor M. Schramm, Aug. 21, 1922 (divorced); 1 dau., Laura Schramm; m. 2d, Grace V. Klotz, July 30, 1937. Employed as stenographer, Reading R.R., 1912-17, and 1919; with real estate dept. Chelten Trust Co., 1919-21; employed in real estate bus., Phila., 1921-29; real estate officer, Chelten Title Co. and Tradesmens Nat. Bank & Trust Co., Phila., 1930-36; engaged in real estate bus. on own acct. specializing in appraisals, also ins., Phila., Pa., since 1936; has appraised many thousand pieces of real estate in past five yrs. for financial and pub. instns., attys. and pvt. parties; field dir. appraisal course, Wharton Sch. U. of Pa. and Am. Inst. Real Estate Appraisers. Served as chief yeoman, U.S.N., 1917-18, naval intelligence and high power radio detachment in France. Mem. Am. Inst. Real Estate Appraisers, Nat. Assn. Real Estate Bds., Phila. Real Estate Bd., Germantown Real Estate Bd., Vets. Fgn. Wars. Republican. Methodist. Club: Near Deer (Phila., Pa.). Home: 322 Meehan Av., Mt. Airy. Office: 1420 Walnut St., Philadelphia, Pa.

WINDISCH, Reuben, retired importer; b. Phila., Pa., Mar. 27, 1868; s. Frederick B. and Anna Marie W.; student pub. schs. and Pierce's Bus. Coll., Phila.; m. Mary L. Ramshasel, Oct. 16, 1889 (died 1934); children—Katherine L. (Mrs. Frank L. Olmes), Elma (Mrs. W. L. Schofield), Anna M. (dec. wife of Gilbert Daley); m. 2d, Elsa M. Freese, June 20, 1936. In employ of co. of which later became pres., 1883-1908; organizer and mem. firm R. Windisch & Co., later pres. R. Windisch & Co., Inc., Phila., importers and dealers, raw wool, hair etc., 1908-33; many yrs. dir. Nat. Security Bank, later Security Bank & Trust Co. Pres. German Baptist Home for the Aged in Phila. Republican. Baptist. Clubs: Fortnightly (pres. for 7 yrs.), Union League (Phila.; former mem. 20 yrs.). Home: 7023 Rising Sun Av., Philadelphia, Pa.

WINDLE, William Butler, judge; b. West Chester, Pa., Aug. 4, 1886; s. William Seal and Mary (Butler) W.; A.B., Haverford (Pa.) Coll., 1907; LL.B., U. of Pa., 1910; m. Eleanor Landis Porcher, June 27, 1917. Admitted to Pa. bar, 1910, and since practiced in West Chester, Pa.; dist. atty., Chester Co., 1920-24; judge Court of Common Pleas, Chester Co., since 1927, pres. judge since 1935. Served as maj., asst. judge advocate, 28th Div., U.S. Army, 1917-19. Dir. Chester Co. Hosp. Mem. Am. Bar Assn., Pa. Bar Assn., Sharswood Law Club, Am. Legion, Phi Kappa Sigma. Republican. Episcopalian. Elk. Clubs: West Chester (Pa.) Golf and Country; University (Phila.). Home: 132 W. Virginia Av. Address: Court House, West Chester, Pa.

WINE, Edgar Plaine, designing engr.; b. nr. Staunton, Va., June 21, 1886; s. John Samuel and Flora Catherine (Plaine) W.; student Staunton (Va.) Mil. Acad., 1901-05; m. Natalie Elizabeth Rossman, Jan. 12, 1916; children—Robert Edgar, Dorothy Elizabeth, John Albert. Entered employ Landis Tool Co., Waynesboro, Pa., 1909; in drafting dept. Frick Co., Waynesboro, 1909-12; draftsman, designer, engr. and exec., Landis Tool Co., Waynesboro, Pa., 1912-20, supt. factory, same, Greencastle, Pa., 1920-26, exptl. designer and in charge new development work, same, Waynesboro, Pa., since 1926; v.p. Greencastle Realty Co. Mem. Southern Engring. Soc. Served as dir. Greencastle Sch. Dist. Republican. Lutheran. Home: 454 E. Baltimore St., Greencastle, Pa. Office: Waynesboro, Pa.

WINEBRENNER, David Charles 3d, lawyer; b. Frederick, Md., June 16, 1897; s. David Charles, Jr. and Eleanor Nelson (Ritchie) W.; ed. St. Paul's Sch., Concord, N.H., 1911-16, Princeton U., 1916-17; LL.B., U. of Md. Law Sch., 1922; unmarried. Admitted to Md. bar, 1922 and since engaged in gen. practice of law at Frederick; pres. and dir. New Citizen Pub. and Mfg. Co.; dir. Potomac Edison Co., Frederick Hotel Co.; Dem. candidate for Congress, 1924; sec. of state of Md., 1925-35; chmn. Dem. State Central Com. for Frederick Co. since 1938. Served with American Field Service in France, 1917, in A.S., 1918. Mem. Am. and Md. State bar assns., S.A.R., Md. Hist. Soc., Phi Kappa Sigma. Democrat. Episcopalian. B.P.O.E. Clubs: Cotillion (Frederick); Chesapeake (Baltimore). Home: 110 Court St. Office: 100 W. Church St., Frederick, Md.

WING, Henry J(oseph), chemist; b. Steele City, Neb., Nov. 28, 1898; s. Henry Joseph and Kate Asenath (Faxon) W.; B.Sc., U. of Neb., Lincoln, Neb., 1921, M.Sc., 1925; Ph.D., State U. of Ia., Iowa City, Ia., 1929; m. Esther Leone Jackson, Aug. 25, 1925; 1 son, Henry Joseph. High sch. teacher, Neb. schools 1921-24; asst. prof. chemistry, Doane Coll., Crete, Neb., 1924-26, South Dakota State Coll., Brookings, S.D., 1926-28; asso. chemist U.S. Bur. of Standards, Washington, D.C., 1929-33; research chemist Antioch Industrial Research Inst., Yellow Springs, O., 1934, E. I. du Pont de Nemours & Co., Parlin, N.J., 1935-38; development chemist Johnson & Johnson, New Brunswick, N.J., since 1939. Served as apprentice seaman, U.S.N.R.F., 1918, 1st lt., C.W.S. Res. since 1926. Fellow, Am. Inst. Chemists, A.A.A.S.; mem. Am. Chem. Soc. (sec. N.J. Sect. since 1937), Alpha Chi Sigma, Sigma Tau, Phi Lambda Upsilon, Sigma Xi. Republican. Methodist. Mason. Club: Lions (Milltown, N.J.; pres. 1937-38). Home: 21 Elm Pl., Milltown, N.J. Office: Johnson & Johnson, New Brunswick, N.J.

WING, Herbert, Jr., coll. prof.; b. Minneapolis, Minn., Dec. 8, 1889; s. Herbert and Elizabeth Davis (Potter) W.; A.B., Harvard Coll.; A.M., and Ph.D., U. of Wis.; m. Helen Leonard Gilman, June 10, 1916; 1 son, Herbert Gilman. Asst. in European history, U. of Wis., 1910-12 and 1914-15; asso. prof., later prof., Greek Lang. and Lit., Dickinson Coll., since 1915, also dir. freshman course in history and chmn. debate council and head coach of debate since 1923; visiting asso. prof. history, U. of Mich., summer, 1917. Historian, ex-pres. Wing Family of America. Mem. Am. Hist. Assn., Archaeol. Inst. America, Am. Philol. Assn., Soc. for Promotion of Hellenic Studies (British), Tau Kappa Alpha (exec. sec. Pa. Dist.), Phi Beta Kappa. Mason. Author: Epeiros-Albania Boundary Dispute; Tribute Assessments in the Athenian Empire; also numerous hist. reviews and geneal. papers. Home: 429 W. South St. Address: Denny Hall, Carlisle, Pa.

WINGERD, Charles Beam, clergyman; b. Chambersburg, Pa., June 4, 1878; s. Abram M. and Catherine (Beam) W.; A.B., Lebanon Valley Coll., Annville, Pa., 1897, A.M., 1900; B.D., Union Theol. Sem., 1900; Ph.D., Ill. Wesleyan U., Bloomington, Ill., 1910; m. Leah Hartz, Oct. 15, 1900; children—Lowell H. Joyce (Mrs. John R. Cooper). Ordained to ministry Presbyn. Ch., 1900; served two pastorates, Pittsburgh, Pa., 1900-16, Martins Ferry, O., 1916-25; pastor Central Presbyn. Ch., New Castle, Pa., since 1925; pres. Presbyn. Hdqrs. Chautauqua, N.Y.; head of U. Promotion of Shenango Presbytery; mem. Presbytery of Shenango. Republican. Presbyterian. Contbr. to current jours. and to ch. papers. Home: 328 Park Av., New Castle, Pa.

WINGERD, Edmund Culbertson, lawyer; b. Reading, Pa., Mar. 27, 1886; s. Daniel Henry and Nancy Purviance (Culbertson) W.; grad. Chambersburg (Pa.) Acad., 1902; A.B., Franklin and Marshall Coll., Lancaster, Pa., 1906; LL.B., U. of Pa., 1910; m. Margaret Frances Coleman, Nov. 12, 1914; children—Edmund Culbertson, Joseph Coleman, William Noble, Daniel Henry, Robert Aitken. Admitted to Pa. bar, 1910, and since practiced at Chambersburg, Pa.; dir. The Nat. Bank of Chambersburg, Pa. Mem. Chi Phi. Republican. Presbyterian. Home: Edgar Av. and Riddle Rd. Office: Chambersburg Trust Co. Bldg., Chambersburg, Pa.

WINNE, Walter Griffen, lawyer; b. Brooklyn, Feb. 18, 1889; s. George T. and Agnes (Goff) W.; Litt.B., Rutgers Coll., 1910; LL.B., New York Law Sch., 1912; m. Althea M. Sharp, June 8, 1916; children—Eleanor Anne, Barbara. Began practice at Hackensack, N.J., 1912; now mem. firm Winne & Banta; mem. N.J. Ho. of Assembly, 1916-20; U.S. atty., Dist. of N.J., by apptmt. of President Harding, 1922-27. Mem. Chi Psi. Republican. Methodist. Club: Golf. Home: Hackensack, N.J.

WINNER, Harry E., educator; b. Sandy Lake, Pa., Jan. 30, 1878; s. James A. and Sarah C. W.; Ph.B., Grove City Coll., 1901, A.M., 1903; Ph.M., U. of Wis., 1921; LL.D., Grove City Coll., 1926; m. Florence Stoner, June 19, 1901 (dec.); 1 son, E. J.; m. 2d, Mae Stoner, July 3, 1914 (dec.); m. 3d, Adeline W. Mollenauer, Dec. 14, 1915; 1 son, Hal M. Successively teacher in rural and graded schs., high sch. prin. and supervising prin., 1895-1901; supervising prin., Pittsburgh, Pa., 1906-17; prin. South Hills High Sch. since 1917. Trustee representing alumni of Grove City Coll., 1931-34. Life mem. N.E.A.; mem. Pa. State Edn. Assn., Secondary Sch. Prins. Assn., High Sch. Prins. Club of Pittsburgh. Republican. Presbyn. Mason (Past Master). Home: 426 Eureka St., Pittsburgh, Pa.

WINSER, Beatrice, librarian; b. Newark, N.J., d. Henry and Edith (Cox) W. Librarian Newark Pub. Library; dir. and trustee Newark Mus.; trustee Univ. of Newark, Am. Library Inst.; mem. Am. Library Assn., N.J. Library Assn. (hon.). Episcopalian. Home: 666 Highland Av. Address: Public Library, Newark, N.J.

WINSLOW, Clinton Ivan; instr. polit. science, Goucher Coll., 1923-26, asst. prof., 1926-30, prof. since 1933. Address: Goucher College, Baltimore, Md.

WINSLOW, Eugene Hale, banker; b. Punxsutawney, Pa., Oct. 10, 1881; s. J. Carleton and Martha (Hughes) W.; student Cheltenham Mil. Acad., St. Paul's Sch.; A.B., Yale, 1904; m. Margaret Rinn, Nov. 25, 1907; children—Samuel R., John C., Anna Martha. Began as acct. in coal office, 1905; engaged as coal operator; with Punxsutawney (Pa.) Nat. Bank since 1920, pres. and chmn. bd. since 1937. Republican. Methodist. Home: Punxsutawney, Pa.

WINSLOW, Leon Loyal, educator; b. Brockport, N.Y., Jan. 20, 1886; s. William Ney and Carrie Thomas (Van Eps) W.; diploma, Pratt Inst., Brooklyn, 1908, Teachers College (Columbia), 1912; B.S., Columbia, 1912; M. S., Pa. State Coll., 1937; m. Lois Esther Crawford, Oct. 10, 1918; children—Kenelm Crawford, Armour Crawford, Anne Crawford, Louise Crawford. Supervisor art, pub. schs., Niagara Falls, 1908-11; scholar in industrial arts, Teachers Coll. (Columbia), 1911-12; teacher industrial arts, New Rochelle, N.Y., 1912; instr. same, U. of Pittsburgh, 1913; head of the industrial arts dept. of the Bowling Green State Coll., Ohio, 1914-18; supervisor of art and industrial arts edn., State of N.Y., 1918-24; sec. Federated Council on Art Edn., 1925-36; mem. bd. of govs., Nat. Assn. Art Edn., since 1936; mem. yearbook com. Nat. Soc. for Study of Edn., 1937. Dir. art, Baltimore Department of Education, since 1924; special service adviser on arts to Carnegie Corporation, New York City, 1926-1930. Lecturer on art education, Summer School, Univ. of Mich., 1925, University of Wis., 1927; in charge dept. of art, summers, Pa. State Coll., since 1927. Member N.E.A., Am. Federation Arts, Eastern Arts Assn., Md. States Teachers' Assn., Eastern Arts Association (pres. 1936-37), Ednl. Society Baltimore (ex-pres.), Phi Delta Kappa, Theta Delta Chi, Acacia. Author: Elementary Industrial Arts, 1921; Art and Industrial Arts (hand-

WINSLOW

book), 1921; (with Charles DeGarmo) Essentials of Design, 1923; Organization and Teaching of Art, 1925; Art Education Charts, 1929; (with Walter H. Klar) Art Education in Principle and Practice, 1933; The Integrated School Art Program, 1939. Contbr. to educational and art jours. Home: 324 Tunbridge Rd., Homeland, Baltimore. Office: 3 E. 25th St., Baltimore, Md.

WINSLOW, Ola E., instr. English, Goucher Coll., 1914-17, asst. prof., 1917-20, asso. prof., 1920-30, prof. since 1930, asst. dean, 1919-21. Address: Goucher College, Baltimore, Md.

WINSOR, James Davis, Jr., sr. partner Biddle, Whelen & Co.; b. Radnor, Pa., Sept. 6, 1876; s. James D. and Rebecca (Chapman) W.; B.A., U. of Pa., 1897; m. Marion Harding Curtin, June 16, 1904; children—Curtin, James D. III, Marion (Mrs. Henry D. Mirick). Sr. partner Biddle, Whelen & Co., Phila.; mgr. Phila. Saving Fund Soc.; dir. Ins. Co. of North America, Alliance Ins. Co., Indemnity Ins. Co., Philadelphia Fire & Marine Ins. Co., Nat. Security Ins. Co. of Omaha, Westmoreland Coal Co.; trustee Mutual Assurance Co. Pres. Merchants Fund, Oliver Fund. Republican. Episcopalian. Clubs: Rittenhouse (Phila.); Gulph Mills Golf. Home: Ardmore, Pa. Office: 1606 Walnut St., Philadelphia, Pa.

WINTER, Emil, banker; pres. Workingman's Savings Bank & Trust Co., Pittsburgh; also pres. Am. Magnesium Metals Corpn., Am. Refractories Co. of Pa., Austro-Am. Magnesite Corpn., Am. Austrian Magnesite Corpn.; dir. Magnesium Products, Inc. Trustee Mercy Hosp.; dir. Tuberculosis League. Home: "Lyndhurst," Beechwood Boul. Office: 800 E. Ohio St., Pittsburgh, Pa.

WINTER, John Calvin, pres. Vallamont Planing Mill Co.; b. Loyalscock Twp., Pa., Aug. 24, 1868; s. John and Christina (Shanbacher) W.; student Eagle Sch., 1874-84; m. Mary Elizabeth Glosser, Mar. 10, 1892; children—Harry Albert, Ora Marion (Mrs. Lawrence E. Waltz), Wilbur Glosser. m. 2d, Minnie M. Musser, May 26, 1938. Engaged in farming until 1887; carpenter, 1887-91; architect, builder and contractor, 1891-1933; pres. and treas. Vallamont Planing Mill Co. since 1898. Dir. Evang. Homes, Inc., Lewisburg, Pa. Trustee Central Pa. Bible Conf. Soc., Central Pa. Evang. Conf.; mem. Bd. of Ch. Extension of Evang. Ch., Bd. of Architects of Evang. Ch., Bd. on Ch. Union of Evang. and United Brethren Chs.; pres. bd. trustees First Evang. Ch., Williamsport, Pa. Republican. Home: 1001 Market St. Office: Rear 417 W. Third St., Williamsport, Pa.

WINTER, John E., univ. prof.; b. Holland, Mich., Feb. 28, 1878; s. Eije and Reka (Smits) W.; A.B., Hope Coll., Holland, Mich., 1902; A.B., U. of Mich., Ann Arbor, 1906, A.M., 1910, Ph.D., 1917; m. Lema Mokma, Dec. 24, 1906 (dec.); children—James Edwin (died 1939), John Lawrence. Teacher Greek and English, Northwestern Classical Acad., Orange City, Ia., 1906-08; supt. of schools, Cass City, Mich., 1908-11; prof. of philosophy and psychology, Goshen (Ind.) College, Goshen, 1913-15; asst. prof. of psychology, U. of N.D., 1915-16; prof. of psychology and edn., Parsons Coll., Fairfield, Ia., 1917-21; prof. psychology, W.Va. Univ., Morgantown, since 1921. Head of dept. of philosophy and psychology since 1929. Mem. A.A.A.S., Am. Psychol. Assn., Southern Soc. for Philosophy and Psychology (pres. 1934-35), W.Va. Acad. Sci., Pi Kappa Phi. Republican. Presbyn. Odd Fellow. Club: Kiwanis of Morgantown. Home: 324 Grandview Av., Morgantown, W.Va.

WIRES, Hazel K., artist; b. Oswego, N.Y., Feb. 16, 1903; d. Willard Augustus and Augusta Belle (Cooke) Kitts; student St. John's Sch., Boonton, N.J., 1915-19, Mary A. Burnham Sch., Northampton, Mass., 1919-21, Nat. Park Sem., Forest Glen, Md., 1921-22, Corcoran Gallery Sch. of Art, Washington, D.C., 1922-26, summer schs., Rockport and Gloucester, Mass., 1923-28, Louis Comfort Tiffany Foundation, Oyster Bay, N.Y., 1927; m. Alden Choate Wires, Aug. 4, 1928; children—Alden Choate, Willard Harrison. Artist Am. Red Cross Headquarters, Washington, D.C., 1925-27, Bur. of Art Exhibits, Washington, 1926-28, doing government displays in oils for county, state and internat. shows; free lance designer textiles, wrapping papers, painter landscapes, marines, 1928-35. Mem. Soc. of Washington Artists, Ridgewood (N.J.) Art Assn., Bergen Co. (N.J.) Artists Guild. Awarded 1st prize and scholarship, Corcoran Art Gallery, 1926, gold medal for still life, Soc. of Washington Artists, 1937. Republican. Episcopalian. Home: Sylvan Place, Haworth, N.J.

WIRT, George Herman, chief forest fire warden; b. McVeytown, Pa., Nov. 28, 1880; s. Jacob Rupp and Sarah Elizabeth (Reifsnyder) W.; B.Eng., Juniata Coll., Huntingdon, Pa., 1898, (hon.) M. Eng., 1903, M.S., 1928; B. Forestry, Biltmore (N.C.) Forest Sch., 1901; extension work U. of Pa. and U. of Chicago; m. Anna M. Avery, Oct. 1907; 1 dau., Mary Duncan; m. 2d, Bertha Belle Sellers, Feb. 2, 1912; children—Blanche Elizabeth, George Jacob, Julia Belle. Began as first state forester of Pa., 1901; forester in charge Mont Alto Forest, 1902-10; established first State Forest Tree Nursery of Pa., 1902; first dir. State Forest Acad., Mont Alto, 1903-10; chief forester for Pa., 1908-15; chief forest fire warden of Pa. since 1915. Mem. exec. com. Harrisburg Area, Boy Scouts of America, also chief forest guide. Mem. Soc. Am. Foresters, Pa. Forestry Assn., Am. Forestry Assn., Canadian Forestry Assn., Keystonians of Pa., Xi Sigma Pi. Republican. Presbyterian (elder). Author of forestry bulletins. Home: 215 N. 17th St., Camp Hill. Office: Educational Bldg., Harrisburg, Pa.

WISE, Henry Morris, lawyer; b. New York, N.Y., May 23, 1880; s. Morris S. and Katie (Harris) W.; student Horace Mann Sch., New York, 1894-97; A.B., Columbia, 1901, LL.B., 1903; m. Mildred F. Whyte, 1909 (she died 1925); children—Frances (Mrs. Edward J. Portley), Andrew Edward; m. 2d, Margaret I. Portley, 1926; children—Henry Portley, Patricia. Admitted to N.Y. bar, 1903, and since practiced in New York; now mem. firm of Wise, Shepard, Houghton & Lebett; dir. Continental Bank and Trust Co. of New York, Continental Safe Deposit Co., I.T.C. Corpn.; pres. and dir. Potrero Sugar Co.; v.p. and dir. A. N. Stollwerck, Inc.; treas. and dir. Wall St. Shares Corpn. Mem. Am. and N.Y. State bar assns., Assn. of the Bar City of New York. Republican. Roman Catholic. K.C. Clubs: Lawyers, Columbia University (New York); Arcola Country (Arcola, N.J.). Home: Hillsdale, N.J. Office: 30 Broad St., New York, N.Y.

WISE, John Laing, newspaper editor and pub.; b. Butler, Pa., Apr. 13, 1893; s. Levi Moyer and Bertha Rebecca (Laing) W.; ed. U. of Wis., Madison, Wis., 1912-13; A.B., Allegheny Coll., Meadville, Pa., 1916; m. Ruth Clark, Jan. 17, 1922; children—Marilyn C., John Laing, Jr. Newspaper man asso. with Butler (Pa.) Eagle since 1916; pres. Eagle Printing Co., Inc.; dir. Butler Co. Nat. Bank & Trust Co. Served in U.S. Army during World War. Trustee Slippery Rock State Teachers Coll., Butler Methodist Church. Mem. Am. Legion, Delta Tau Delta. Republican. Methodist. Rotarian. Clubs: Rotary (past pres.), Country (Butler, Pa.); University (Pittsburgh). Home: 515 N. Main St. Office: 116 W. Diamond St., Butler, Pa.

WISE, John Shreeve, Jr., pres. Pa. Power & Light Co.; b. Philadelphia, Pa., July 17, 1877; s. John Shreeve and Mary Anne (Switzer) W.; student Eastburn Acad., Philadelphia, 1888-94; B.S. in E.E., U. of Pa., 1898; m. Adele Shapley, Oct. 22, 1902; children—John Shreeve, III, Cooper Shapley, James Seymour, Florence Adele, Mary Annette. Held various positions Edison, Powellton, Callowhill and Columbia Steam-Electric stations, Philadelphia, Sept. 1898-Jan. 1899; student Gen. Electric Co., Feb. 1899; employed in testing dept., Schenectady, N.Y., later Lynn, Mass., until 1901; meter reader, tester, collector and later bookkeeper Atlantic City Electric Light Co., summer, 1901; asst. supt. Auburn (N.Y.) Light, Heat & Power Co., 1901, supt., 1902-06; became mgr. Harwood Power Co. and Harwood Electric Co., Hazleton, Pa., 1906; gen. mgr. and dir. Harwood Electric Co., 1907-20; gen. mgr. Lehigh Navigation Electric Co., 1913-20; became operating mgr. Pa. Power & Light Co. upon organization, June 1920, pres. and dir. since Nov. 2, 1928; pres. and dir. several affiliated cos. Mem. local com. on industrial preparedness, Naval Consulting Bd. of the U.S., World War. Served on State Registration Bd. for Professional Engrs., State of Pa., Dec. 1927-Nov. 1931. Mem. bd. trustees Sacred Heart Hosp. Assn., Inc., Allentown, Pa. Pres. Pa. Electric Assn., 1927-28; chmn. Pa. Joint Com. on Rural Electrification, 1927-36; mem. Am. Inst. Elec. Engrs., Mu Phi Alpha Engring. Soc. of U. of Pa., Phi Delta Theta. Elk. Clubs: Union League, Engineers', Lehigh Country, Livingston; College Boat and Varsity clubs of U. of Pa. Home: 3003 Turner St. Office: 901 Hamilton St., Allentown, Pa.

WISE, Walter Dent, surgeon; b. Patuxent Beach, Md., May 18, 1885; s. Walter Hanson Briscoe Stone and Martha Jane (Dent) W.; ed. pvt. schs.; M.D., U. of Md., 1906; m. Agnes Gordon Whiting, Oct. 20, 1914 (died 1919); children—Marian Gordon Armistead (dec.), Agnes Whiting; m. 2d, Josephine Warfield McMillan, July 27, 1921. Practiced in Baltimore since 1906; prof. clin. surgery, U. of Md. since 1931; professor Surgery, U. of Md. since 1937; chief surgeon Mercy Hosp.; visiting surgeon Union Memorial, Women's, South Baltimore Gen. hosps. Fellow Am. Coll. Surgeons, Am. Surgical Assn., Southern Surg. Assn.; mem. Am., Md. State and Baltimore med. assns., Phi Beta Pi; elected sec. Med. and Chirurg. Faculty of Md., 1931. Democrat. Episcopalian. Clubs: Maryland, Gibson Island, Elkridge. Contbr. articles on surgery. Home: 8 Charlecote Pl. Office: 1120 St. Paul St., Baltimore, Md.

WISEMAN, Robert Joseph, elec. engring.; b. Cambridge, Mass., July 18, 1890; s. Thomas Joseph and Mary (Spillane) W.; B.S., Mass. Inst. Tech., 1912, D.Sc., 1915; m. Agnes Ruth Troy, Oct. 29, 1930. Asst. instr., Mass. Inst. Tech., 1912-13, research asst., 1915-17; with engring. dept., Western Union Telegraph Co., 1917-18; asst. wire and cable engr., Nat. Conduit & Cable Co., Hastings-on-Hudson, N.Y., 1918-20, engr., 1920-21; research engr. The Okonite Co., Passaic, N.J., 1921-28, chief engr. since 1928. Fellow Am. Inst. Elec. Engrs. Mem. Am. Soc. for Testing Materials, Nat. Research Council, Insulated Power Cable Engrs. Assn., Electric Inst., Passaic Co. Engring. Soc. Awarded Saltonstall fellowship at M.I.T., 1914-15. Republican. Roman Catholic. Clubs: Technology of Northern N.J. (Newark, N.J.); Engineers (New York); Electric (Chicago). Home: 466 E. 39th St., Paterson. Office: The Okonite Co., Passaic, N.J.

WISHART, John Miller, clergyman; b. Guernsey Co., O., Aug. 10, 1877; s. James and Margaret Ann (Miller) W.; A.B., Muskingum Coll., New Concord, O., 1905; B.D., Pittsburgh Theol. Sem., 1908; hon. D.D., Monmouth Coll., 1916; m. Flora Bell Wallace, Aug. 19, 1909; children—Josephine Margaret, Florabel, John Wallace. Ordained to ministry Presbyn. Ch., 1908; minister, Gibson Heights Ch., St. Louis, Mo., 1908-13, Washington, Ia., 1913-21, Crerar Memorial Presbyn. Ch., Chicago, Ill., 1921-23, First Presbyn. Ch., Carnegie, Pa., since 1923. Republican. Presbyn. Home: 526 Beechwood Av., Carnegie, Pa.

WISHART, William Liggitt, clergyman; b. Pittsburgh, Pa., Jan. 6, 1894; s. William Irvine and Martha E. (Liggitt) W.; A.B., Muskingum Coll., New Concord, O., 1914; student Western Reserve U. Law Sch., 1914-15; post grad. study, U. of Pittsburgh, Sch. of Philosophy, 1915-16; grad. Pittsburgh Theol. Sem., 1919, Th.M., 1924; student U. of Edinburgh Divinity Sch., 1923-24; D.D., Washington and Jefferson Coll., 1934; m. Sara Louise Beggs, July 1920. Ordained Presbyn. ministry, 1919; pastor Unity United Presbyn. Ch., Unity, Pa., 1919-24, Second United Presbyn. Ch., Washington, Pa., 1924-31, First Presbyn. Ch., Sharon, Pa., since 1931. Dir. Mercer County Red Cross, Mercer

County Boy Scouts, Budd Orphans Home, Haywood Home. Mem. Tau Kappa Alpha. Republican. Clubs: Rotary, Ashler (Sharon). Home: 44 Ormond Av., Sharon, Pa.

WISTER, John Caspar, landscape architect; b. Germantown, Pa., Mar. 19, 1887; s. William Rotch and Mary (Eustis) W.; grad. Hackley Sch., Tarrytown, N.Y., 1905; A.B., Harvard, 1909; student Harvard Sch. Landscape Architecture, 1906-10; unmarried. Employed as landscape architect with C. N. Lowrie, New York, N.Y., and Sears & Wendell, Phila., Pa., 1910-16; in practice on own acct. since 1916; dir. North Pa. R.R. Co. Served in U.S. Army in France, 1917-19, 1st sergt. Advance Ordnance Depot No. 4 with A.E.F. Dir. Arthur Hoyt Scott Hort. Foundation, Swarthmore Coll. Pres. Am. Iris Soc., 1920-34; v.p. John Bartram Assn. since 1929; sec. Am. Rose Soc., 1921-23; sec. Pa. Hort. Soc. since 1929; mem. over 25 hort. socs. in U.S. and abroad. Honored by medals from Pa. Hort. Soc., Mass. Hort. Soc., Am. Iris Soc., English Iris Soc., Scott Foundation. Unitarian. Author: The Iris, 1927; Lilac Culture, 1930; Bulbs for American Gardens, 1930; Four Seasons in Your Garden, 1936; contbr. numerous arts. to mags. and jours. Home: Wister and Clarkson Av., Germantown, Philadelphia, Pa.

WITHAM, Ernest C., educator; b. West Gray, Me., Oct. 6, 1880; s. Alphonso Nelson (M.D.) and Mary Lizzie (Pennell) W.; B.S., Tufts Coll., 1904; M.A., New York U., 1933; m. Lillian Emma Davis, Dec. 24, 1908; children—Pennell Davis, Elizabeth Clair. Prin. John A. Andrew Sch., Windham, Me., 1904-05; submaster Hudson (Mass.) High Sch., 1905-06; prin. boys' dept. Perkins Instn. for the Blind, Mass., 1906-09; supt. schs. Conway-Bartlett-Madison Dist., N.H., 1909-12; supt. schs., Southington, Conn., 1912-22; supt. schs., Putnam, Conn., 1922; dir. of research, pub. schs. of Wilmington, Del., 1922-29; instr. N.H. State Normal Sch., Keene and Plymouth, several summers; instr. U. of Del. Summer School, 1927; now asso. prof. edn., Rutgers Univ., and sec., of School of Edn. faculty. Pvt. Conn. State Guard, 1917-19. Mem. N.E.A., Dept. of Superintendence, Ednl. Research Assn., Nat. Soc. for Study of Edn., Theta Delta Chi, Phi Delta Kappa (treas. of Alpha Pi chapter), Kappa Phi Kappa. Republican. Mem. Reformed (Dutch) Ch. Mason. Author: Standard Geography Tests; Witham's Silent Reading and English Vocabulary Tests; Standard Arithmetic Tests; Witham's Fraction Drill Cards (oral); Hall of Fame Test; Standardized History Tests; New Series of Witham Geography Tests; School Administration Forms; Tests on Essential Language Habits; series of ten articles on Types of School Administration in the various states, 1934-35; Problem Studies in School Administration, 1936; also numerous essays and articles on edn. and other subjects. Home: Central Av., Stelton, N.J. Address: Rutgers University, New Brunswick, N.J.

WITHEROW, William Porter, steel mfr.; b. Pittsburgh, Pa., Apr. 15, 1888; s. William and Alice May (Douglass) W.; grad. St. Paul's Sch., Concord, N.H., 1905; Ph.B., Yale, 1908; m. Dorothy Dilworth, Dec. 3, 1913; children—William Porter, Virginia Crossan. With Jones & Laughlin Steel Co., Pittsburgh, 1908-10; mem. firm Irvin & Witherow, engrs., 1910-14; pres. Witherow Steel Corpn., 1914-29; chmn. bd. Donner Steel Co., 1929-30; v.p. Republic Steel Corpn., 1930; pres. and dir. Blaw-Knox Co. Pittsburgh, since 1937; pres. and dir. Steel Products Co.; trustee Dollar Savings Bank; dir. First Nat. Bank of Pittsburgh, Pittsburgh and W.Va. R.R., Pittsburgh Coal Co., Peoples-Pittsburgh Trust Co., Sun Drug Co. Dir. Pittsburgh Chamber of Commerce, Internat. Chamber of Commerce. Chmn. Citizens Com. on Taxation, Pittsburgh, 1932; tech. adviser Internat. Labor Conf., Geneva, 1936; dir. Nat. Industrial Recovery Bd., Washington, 1935. Dir. Community Fund of Pittsburgh, Nat. Community Chests. Trustee Carnegie Inst., Carnegie Inst. of Tech.; v.p. and dir. Pittsburgh Y.M.C.A. Mem. Yale Club of Pittsburgh (pres.) Engrs. Soc. of W.Pa., Soc. Automotive Engrs., Yale Engrs. Soc., Delta Psi. Republican. Presbyterian. Clubs: Duquesne, Fox Chapel Golf, Harvard-Yale-Princeton, Pittsburgh Golf (Pittsburgh); Bankers (N.Y. City); Allegheny Country (Sewickley, Pa.); Rolling Rock Hunt (Greensburg, Pa.). Home: 5448 Northumberland St. Office: Farmers Bank Bldg., Pittsburgh, Pa.

WITHERS, Robert Edwin, manufacturer; b. Danville, Va., Mar. 13, 1865; s. Robert Enoch and Mary Virginia (Royall) W.; grad. high sch., Richmond, Va., Va. Mil. Inst., Lexington, Va., 1885; m. Mary Cloyd Kent, June 2, 1892; children—Robert Edwin, Kent Cloyd. Dir., v.p., treas. Aluminum Co. of America; treas. Aluminum Ore Co., Aluminum Seal Co., U.S. Aluminum Co., Knoxville Power Co., Carolina Aluminum Co., St. Lawrence River Power Co. President and trustee Arnold Sch.; trustee Family Welfare Assn. of Pittsburgh. Mem. Sigma Chi. Episcopalian. Mason. Clubs: University, Duquesne, Oakmont Country. Home: 924 South Aiken Av. Office: Gulf Bldg., Pittsburgh, Pa.

WITMAN, John (Jacob), mcht. elec. fixtures; b. Reading, Pa., July 22, 1882; s. Joseph and Magdalena F. (Kuebler) W.; grad. high sch., Reading, Pa., 1901; m. Katie L. Adams, Dec. 12, 1905. Employed in office, 1901-04; purchased half interest in Reading (Pa.) Electric Co., 1904, and sole propr. since 1907; organizer and propr. Reading Chandelier Works since 1910; propr. Maidencreek Orchards since 1920; dir. Reading City Bank & Trust Co., Reading Fair Co. Pres. and dir. Maidencreek Fish and Game Club. Republican. Mason (Consistory, 32°, Shriner). Elk. Clubs: Berkshire Country (dir.), Wyomissing (Reading, Pa.). Home: 434 Windsor St. Office: 503 Penn St., Reading, Pa.

WITMER, Charles Howard, M.D.; b. Neffsville, Pa., Jan. 5, 1885; s. Dr. Elias H. and Ella (Sutton) W.; student Millersville (Pa.) State Normal Sch., 1900-02; M.D., U. of Pa., 1909; m. Ethyl Howell, Oct. 20, 1915; children—Robert Howell, Richard Howell. Began gen. practice of medicine, 1912; county med. dir. State Dept. of Health, 1918-24; chief med. staff St. Joseph's Hosp., Lancaster, Pa., since 1915; pres. and dir. Lancaster and Suburban Elec. & Inspection Co. since 1931; dir. Lancaster Co. Nat. Bank. Pres. bd. dirs. Manheim Twp. Sch. Dist. since 1929. Pres. and dir. Lancaster Welfare Federation, 1930; pres. Lancaster Co. Tuberculosis Soc. since 1915; dir. Lancaster Chamber of Commerce, 1930-33. Mem. Lancaster County Medical Soc. (pres. 1939-40); Pa. State Medical Soc., Am. Med. Assn. Mem. Rotary Internat. (past dist. gov.). Republican. Lutheran (pres. council St. Peter's Ch. since 1926). Mason (Past Master Lamberton Lodge No. 476; Past Thrice Potent Master Lancaster Lodge of Perfection). Clubs: Hamilton, Shrine of Lancaster County, Lancaster (Pa.) Rotary. Home: Breeze Hill. Office: 126 E. Chestnut St., Lancaster, Pa.

WITMER, Francis Potts, civil engr.; b. Phila., Pa., Apr. 2, 1873; s. Ambrose E. and Imogene B. (Potts) W.; A.B., Central High Sch., Phila., 1891; B.S., U. of Pa., 1893, C.E., 1894; m. Minnie Sears Barr, June 24, 1897; children—Dorothy Imogene (dec.), Francis Potts. Instr. in civil engring., U. of Pa., 1894; draftsman and designer Phoenix Bridge Co., 1897-1900; engr. in charge bridge design, Am. Bridge Co., Phila. office, later New York office, 1901-13; structural engr. New York, Municipal Ry. Corpn. (Brooklyn Rapid Transit System), 1913-20; cons. engr., associated with Howard C. Baird, New York, since 1920; dir. civ. engring. dept. and prof. civ. engring., U. of Pa., since 1924. Collaborated with Mr. Baird in constrn. of Bear Mountain Bridge over Hudson River, 1922-24. Mem. Am. Soc. C.E., Am. Soc. for Testing Materials, Am. Concrete Inst., Soc. for Promotion Engring. Edn., Engineers Club (Phila.), Franklin Inst., Sigma Xi, Tau Beta Pi, Phi Beta Kappa. Republican. Episcopalian. Home: The Orchard, Bala-Cynwyd, Pa. Office: 95 Liberty St., New York, N.Y.; and U. of Pa., Philadelphia, Pa.

WITMEYER, Paul E(ugene), supt. city schs.; b. Annville, Pa., Apr. 15, 1896; s. John A. and Sarah (Snoke) W.; A.B., Lebanon Valley Coll., Annville, Pa., 1916; A.M., Columbia U., 1923; Ed.D., N.Y. Univ., 1938; m. Kathryn Bender, June 25, 1924; 1 dau., Janet Ellen. Employed as prin. high sch., Columbia, Pa., 1920-23; supt. schs., Columbia, Pa., 1923-30; supt. schs., Shamokin, Pa., since 1930; instr., Sch. of Edn., Bucknell U., 1938, Sch. of Edn., New York U., 1939. Served as 2d lt., Inf., U.S. Army, during World War. Vice chmn. com. on edn. Pa. Dept. of Am. Legion, 1938-39. Mem. Pa. State Edn. Assn. (pres. northeastern conv. dist. 1935-36), N.E.A.; dist. gov. Rotary, 1936-37. Republican. Lutheran. Mason. Home: 7th and Church Sts., Shamokin, Pa.

WITTREICH, Andrew O., lawyer; b. Union City, N.J., May 25, 1900; s. Otto and Ellen Josephine (Buchanan) W.; student Cornell U., 1919-20; LL.B., Fordham U., New York, 1923; m. Muriel Viola Wilson, Aug. 25, 1925; children—Ronald Andrew, Warren James, Paul Edward. Admitted to bar, 1924, and since practiced at Jersey City, N.J.; treas. Roffmann Beer Equipment Co., Crown Sanitary Products, Inc. Formerly city atty., Union City, N.J., asst. prosecutor of pleas, Hudson Co., N.J., and commr. of selections, Hudson Co. Pres. Camp Winape. Club: Lambs (New York City). Home: 212 Palisade Av., Union City, N.J. Office: 26 Journal Sq., Jersey City, N.J.

WOERNER, Paul Leslie, dir. athletics; b. Bridgeport, Conn., Sept. 22, 1905; s. Paul Henry and Laura Augusta (Layer) W.; student Swarthmore Coll., 1923-25; grad. U.S. Naval Acad., Annapolis, Md., 1929, B.S., 1937; student Halsey-Stuart Sch. Finance, Chicago, 1930-31, Cornell U. Coaching Sch., summer, 1938; m. June Marion Watson, Nov. 20, 1936. Served as ensign U.S.N., 1929-30; with Halsey-Stuart & Co., investment banking, Newark, N.J., 1930-32; mgr. properties Prudential Life Ins. Co., Newark, N.J., 1932-34; dir. athletics and football coach, Upsala Coll., East Orange, N.J., since 1934. Served as lt. U.S.N. Res. since 1935. Mem. U.S. Naval Res. Officers Assn., Naval Acad. Grads. Assn., Navy Athletic Assn., Am. Football Coaches Assn., Kappa Sigma. Swedish Luth. Ch. Home: 56 Fairview Av., Chatham, N.J.

WOHL, Michael G(erschon), physician; b. Ukrania, Feb. 19, 1889; s. Gerschon and Sarah (Block) W.; came to U.S., 1907, naturalized, 1915; M.D., Medico-Chirurgical Coll., Phila., 1912; grad. student Columbia, 1923, Univ. of Vienna, Med. Sch., 1927-28; m. Reisa Gillerson, June 15, 1914; children—George Theodore, Joseph, Milton. Began practice as physician, Phila., 1912; prof. of pathology and bacteriology, Temple U. Med. Sch., Phila., 1915-16; asso. prof. clin. pathology, Creighton U. Sch. of Medicine, Omaha, Neb., 1917-26; dir. metabolic diseases and clin. lab., Mercy Hosp., Council Bluffs, Ia., 1918-27; dir. clin. lab. Methodist Hosp., Omaha, Neb., 1922-1925; chief of med. staff, Paxton Memorial Hosp., Omaha, Neb., 1924-26; chief diagnostic clinic, Mt. Sinai Hosp., Phila., 1930-33; asso. prof. of exptl. medicine, Temple U., 1928-32, asso. prof. of medicine and chief endocrine clinic, Temple University Medical School, Phila., since 1932; asst. physician Phila. Gen. Hosp. since 1932; physician Northern Liberties Hosp. Fellow Phila. Coll. of Physicians, A.M.A.; mem. Am. Therapeutic Assn., Internat. and Spanish Speaking Assn. of Physicians, Dentists and Pharmacists (hon. mem.); Phila. Pathol. Soc., Med. League of Phila. (pres.), Phi Delta Epsilon. Mason (32°, Shriner). Author: Bedside Interpretations of Laboratory Findings, 1930; contbr. to Cyclopedia of Medicine; also articles to med. jours. Home: 1727 Pine St., Philadelphia, Pa.

WOLDMAN, Norman E., metall. engr.; b. Cleveland, O., July 22, 1899; s. Morris and Frances (Halper) W.; ed. Western Res. U., 1916-18; B.Sc., Case Sch. Applied Sci., Cleveland, O., 1921; M.S., O. State U., 1922; Ph.D., Columbia U., 1925; unmarried. Instr. chemistry, U. of Me., 1922-23; instr. metallurgy, U. of Ill., 1923-24; prof. chemistry and metallurgy, U.S. Naval Acad., 1925-29; research metallurgist, Westinghouse Electric & Mfg. Co., 1929-34; chief metall. engr., Naval Gun Factory, 1934-36; chief metall. engr. Eclipse Aviation Div., Bendix Aviation Corpn., Bendix, N.J., since 1936; cons. metallurgist, Crystal Engring. Labs. Served as lt. comdr., U.S.N.R.F. Mem. A.A.A.S, Am. Soc. for Metals. Author: Physical Metallurgy, 1930; Engineering Alloys, 1936. Home: 100 Prospect Av., Hackensack, N.J.

WOLF, Carl George, clergyman; b. Stony Ridge, O., July 20, 1885; s. George and Marie (Raukopf) W.; A.B., Capital Univ., Columbus, O., 1907; student Luth. Sem., Columbus, O., 1907-10; A.M., Johns Hopkins U., 1921, Ph.D., 1933; m. Margaret D. Umhau, Oct. 8, 1913; children—Carl Umhau, Herbert Christian. Ordained to ministry Luth. Ch., 1910; pastor, Aberdeen, Md., 1910-13; pastor, Grace Luth. Ch., Baltimore, Md., since 1913; mem. bd. dirs. Inner Mission Soc., 1924-32, Council of Chs., Baltimore, Md., 1935-39; pres. local conf., 1924-26; sec. Eastern Dist. of Am. Luth. Ch., 1925-26. Lutheran. Author: The Peacock in Classical Civilization (doctor's thesis); The Way of Discipleship, 1928. Home: 5205 Harford Rd., Baltimore, Md.

WOLF, David Ober, steel mfr.; b. Highspire, Pa., July 9, 1889; s. Franklin L. and Catherine E. (Ober) W.; student Mercersburg (Pa.) Acad. and Lafayette Coll. (Easton, Pa.); m. Marian Steele, Apr. 7, 1923; children—Marjorie Ann, Marian Elizabeth. Asst. Eastern sales mgr. Apollo (Pa.) Steel Co., 1914-18, asst. gen. mgr. sales, 1919-23, gen. mgr. sales since 1923, v.p. in charge of sales and dir. since 1936; dir. P. Wall Mfg. Supply Co., Pittsburgh. Served as corp., Ordnance Dept., U.S. Army, overseas, 1918-19. Mem. Delta Upsilon. Republican. Lutheran. Mason (Consistory and Shrine), Elk. Clubs: Alcoma Golf (Wilkensburg, Pa.); Pittsburgh Athletic. Home: R.D. 3, Irwin, Pa. Office: Apollo, Pa.

WOLF, Irwin Damasius, merchant; b. Paragould, Ark., July 8, 1894; s. Joseph and Ida (Goldman) W.; grad. high sch., Paragould, 1908, Western Mil. Acad., Alton, Ill., 1910; student Washington U., St. Louis, 1910-11; m. Martha C. Kaufmann, June 26, 1917; children —Irwin Damasius, John Morris, Betty Kaufmann. Began as retail clk. for S. L. Joseph Mercantile Co., Paragould, 1911, advancing to gen. mgr.; partner Wolf and Bascho Cotton Co., also chmn. bd. S. L. Joseph Mercantile Co., 1919-22; with Kaufmann Dept. Stores, Pittsburgh, since 1922, v.p. since 1935; v.p. Investment Land Co., Kaufmann Securities Corpn., Joseph Plantation Co. Served as 2d lt. Signal Corps, later capt. Air Service, World War; maj. Res. A.S. Dir. Community Fund of Pittsburgh; pres. Allegheny County Boy Scouts of America; mem. bd. Montefiore Hosp., Pittsburgh; trustee Irene Kaufmann Settlement; dir. Jewish Federation Philanthropies, Young Men's and Women's Hebrew Assn., Jewish Social Service Bur. (pres.). Mem. Am. Management Assn. (v.p.), Nat. Retail Dry Goods Assn. (chmn. vendors relations com.). Annual Packaging Conf. (originator and donor of annual award for best package design). Democrat. Hebrew. Mason. Clubs: Concordia, Westmoreland. Author: (with W. J. Donald) Handbook of Business Administration, 1931. Contbr. to business publs. Home. Pasadena Drive, Aspinwall, Pa. Office: Kaufmann Dept. Stores, Inc., 400 5th Av., Pittsburgh, Pa.

WOLF, Luther Benaiah, clergyman; b. Abbottstown, Adams Co., Pa., Nov. 29, 1857; s. John George and Eleanor Catherine (Bittinger) W:; A.B., Pa. Coll., Gettysburg, 1880; B.D., Gettysburg Theol. Sem., 1883; D.D., Wittenberg, 1903; fellow Madras U.; 1893; m. Alice Catherine Benner, July 3, 1883; children—Mrs. Edith Norris Crigler, Mrs. Eleanor Stewart, Anna Dryden, Paul Benner. Ordained Luth. ministry, 1883; prin. Am. Evang. Luth. Mission Coll., Guntur, India, 1883-1907; after merger of Luth. chs. as United Lutheran Church in America, served as sec.-treas. of its Bd. of Foreign Missions, and as home base sec. from 1928; retired from active service July 1, 1933. Author: After Fifty Years (historical sketch of the Guntur Mission), 1895; Missionary Heroes of the Lutheran Church, 1911. Home: 2212 South Av., Baltimore, Md.

WOLF, William A., musician, composer; b. Lancaster, Pa.; s. John Philip and Elizabeth (Bomberger) W.; Mus.B., Univ. of N.Y., 1903; hon. Mus.M., same, 1905, Mus.D., 1908; Ph.D., Webster Univ., 1929; studied under Massah M. Warner and Minton Pyne (Phila.), Dr. William Mason, Rafael Joseffy, A. J. Goodrich and Homer N. Bartlett (New York), Feruccio Busoni (Berlin), Herman Scholtz (Dresden), Dr. Hugo Reimann and Dr. Carl Piutti (Leipzig Conservatory); m. Frances Fairlamb Harkness, pianist. Founder, 1913, since dir. Wolf Institute of Music, Lancaster. Mem. executive committee 27 years Nat. Assn. Organists (founder Pa. council and pres. since 1920); active mem. Hymn Soc. America. Republican. Mem. Ch. of England. Elk (chmn. musical activities and library cons., B.P.O.Elks); founder and dir. Am. Guild of Master-singers. Club: Lancaster Travel (dir.). Author of numerous compositions (many pub. nom-de-plume) for piano, also many sacred works, including a Magnificat and Nunc Dimittis in D and Magnificat and Nunc Dimittis in G; compositions include work of every phase of musical endeavor, conspicuous of which are anthems, canticles, hymn-tunes, carols, chorales and works for the pianoforte, organ, and voice; a festival anthem, "He that Dwelleth," composed in commemoration of the 450th anniv. of birth of Dr. Martin Luther, has won wide acclaim. Recent works include Organ Solo, "When Jack Frost Paints a Picture"; two chorale preludes; anthem, "Go Thou, in Life's Fair Morning," "I Will Magnify the Lord" (Lorenz anthem contest); vocal solos, "God Is Love," "A Sacramental Song," "The Nativity," "The Kings Highway," "The King of Love," "The Triumph of Righteousness," "The Piper"; pianoforte works include two modern compositions in dance forms, "The Jaunting Car" and "A French Country Dance," and "The Fancy Skater," "High Jinks," "Dance Espagnol," "A Courtly Dance." Contbr. to Diapason, Am. Organist; former editor and critic of music dept. Lancaster New Era-Examiner. Home: 423 W. Chestnut St., Lancaster, Pa.

WOLFE, Bernard C., banker; b. Wilkes-Barre, Pa., Oct. 30, 1898; s. Charles F. and Antoinette (Laubach) W.; grad. Benton (Pa.) High Sch., 1917; m. Alice Z. Houseworth, July 25, 1917; children—Margaret, Mary, Helen, Charles. Employed as clk. Col. Co. Nat. Bank, Benton, Pa., 1923-28; cashier Farmers State Bank, Shickshinny, Pa., 1928-31; exec. vicepres. First Nat. Bank, Towanda, Pa., 1931-35, pres. since 1935; sec. and dir. Towanda Bldg. & Loan Assn. Dir. Towanda pub. schs. Republican. Methodist. Mason. Clubs: Union Masonic, Towanda Country (Towanda, Pa.). Home: 312 Second St., Office: 312 Main St., Towanda, Pa.

WOLFE, Bertram Kimball, lawyer; b. Phila., Pa., Mar. 20, 1894; s. William S. and Mabel (Kimball) W.; A.B., Central High Sch., Phila., 1913; LL.B., Temple U., Phila., 1917; m. Jane Staggers, Nov. 30, 1936. Admitted to Pa. bar, 1916, and since in gen. practice, Phila.; prof. of law, Temple U. since 1919. Served in Chem. Warfare Service, U.S. Army, during World War. Mem. Am. Legion, Founders and Patriots of America. Republican. Baptist. Clubs: Union League, Penn Athletic (Phila.). Contbr. legal articles to Temple Univ. Law Quarterly. Home: 1417 Spruce St. Office: 123 S. Broad St., Philadelphia, Pa.

WOLFE, Edgar Briant, outdoor advertising; b. Newark, N.J., Aug. 2, 1881; s. Charles M. and Martha L. (Briant) W.; ed. high sch., Newark, N.J., 1895-99; m. Elizabeth O. Winans, Oct. 29, 1907 (dec.); 1 son, Robert Winans; m. 2d, Bertha E. Tuite, Apr. 21, 1931. Designer electric displays, Electrical Motor and Equipment Co., then, supt., sales mgr. same, 1902-11; vice-pres. and gen. mgr., Nat. Electric Sign Co., 1911-15; vice-pres. dir., United Adv. Corpn. and Federal Adv. Corpn., since 1915; dir. Lehigh Adv. Corpn.; vice-pres. and dir., Am. Outdoor Adv. Service. Republican. Presbyn. Mason. Clubs: Country (Essex Fells); Down Town, Newark Athletic (Newark). Home: Essex Fells, N.J. Office: 354 Park Av., Newark, N.J.

WOLFE, Edward Inman, M.D.; b. Muhlenburg, Pa., May 10, 1894; s. Edward I. and Anne (Bloss) W.; ed. Wyoming Sem. and Cornell U.; M.D., Jefferson Med. Coll.; m. Mary Nicholson, July 3, 1918; children—Betty N., John N., Anne B., Edward I. Asso. in medicine on staff Wilkes-Barre Gen. Hosp. since 1925. Served as 1st lt. Med. Corps, U.S. Army, 1917-19. Fellow Am. Coll. Physicians; mem. A.M.A., Pa. State Med. Soc., Lehigh Valley Med. Assn. (v.p. 1937-38), Luzerne Co. Med. Soc., Alpha Omega Alpha, Nu Sigma Nu. Address: 1110 Wyoming Av., Forty Fort, Pa.

WOLFE, Frank Byron, certified pub. accountant; b. Rockland Lake, N.Y., July 10, 1884; s. Phillip and Louisa (Baumann) W.; student pub. sch. and high sch., Brooklyn, N.Y., evening and extension study Cooper Union, New York, N.Y., and pvt. commercial schs.; m. Mazie Parlaman Mock, Sept. 20, 1906; children—Emma Louise (dec.), Valerie (dec.), Frank Byron. Employed in clerical capacity, 1902-12; since 1912, engaged in professional accounting and industrial engineering work, and as mfg. exec.; received C.P.A. certificate in Mass., 1918, and in Mich., 1927; asso. in exec. capacity 4 yrs. with General Motors Corpn.; dir. and v.p., Pittsburgh Equitable Meter Co.; dir., v.p., treas., Merco Nordstrom Valve Co.; dir., v.p., Standard Steel Spring Co., H. A. Smith Machine Co. Dir. Pittsburgh Athletic Assn. Mem. Am. Inst. of Accountants, Nat. Assn. Cost Accountants. Republican. Baptist. Mason. Clubs: Fellows, Pittsburgh Athletic. Home: 725 S. Negley Av. Office: 400 N. Lexington Av., Pittsburgh, Pa.

WOLFE, Oliver Howard, banker; b. Phila. Pa., Jan. 7, 1882; s. Oliver and Anna (Moyer) W.; ed. Radnor (Pa.) pub. schs.; m. Elizabeth Roehm, Sept. 4, 1920; children — Marjorie Louise, Katharine Elizabeth. With Phila. Nat. Bank, 1899-1911, cashier since 1915; with Am. Bankers' Assn., 1911-15; mgr. Phila. loan agency, Reconstruction Finance Corpn., Feb.-June, 1932. With Y.M.C.A. in France, 1918-19; served with 1st Div., A.E.F., later chief of Bur. of Personnel, Paris hdqrs. Republican. Episcopalian. Mason. Clubs: Union League, Rotary (Phila.). Author of various textbooks on banking used by Am. Inst. Banking and by corr. schs. Member faculty Grad. Sch. of Banking, Rutgers Univ. Home: Radnor, Pa. Office: 421 Chestnut St., Philadelphia, Pa.

WOLFE, Russell, lawyer; b. Montgomery Co., Pa., Aug. 4, 1882; s. Dr. Samuel and Emma (Seipt) W.; A.B., Yale, 1906; LL.B., U. of Pa., 1909; m. Irvel Myers, June 30, 1927 (died 1938); children—Elinor Jane, Patricia Anne. Admitted to N.Y. bar, 1909, Pa. bar, 1911; practiced in New York City, 1909-17, in Phila. since 1920; lecturer on code pleading, U. of Pa. Law Sch., 1912-16; principal hearing examiner Pa. Pub. Service Commn., 1925-37; asst. trust officer Land Title Bank & Trust Co., Phila., 1920-22; trust officer Corn Exchange Nat. Bank & Trust Co., Phila., 1923-24. Served with Military Intelligence Division, U.S. Army, 1917-19. Mem. Sharswood Law Club, Alpha Delta Phi, Phi Delta Phi. Episcopalian. Home: Brookside Av. and Askin Rd., St. Davids, Pa. Office: 1400 S. Penn Square, Philadelphia, Pa.

WOLFE, William Henry, lawyer; b. Parkersburg, W.Va., Mar. 3, 1879; s. William Henry and Joanna M. (Cook) W.; A.B., Marietta (O.) Coll., 1899; A.M., Columbia, 1901, LL.B., 1902; m. Katharine W. White, Feb. 16, 1905; children—Elizabeth, Albert B., Agnes W. (dec.). Admitted to N.Y. bar, 1902, and began practice at N.Y. City; in practice at Parkersburg since 1903; pres. 2d Nat. Bank of Parkersburg, 1910-27; v.p. and atty. First Nat. Bank of Parkersburg since 1927. Atty. Parkersburg, 1909-11. Trustee Marietta Coll., Davis and Elkins Coll., Elkins, W.Va. Mem. Am. Bar Assn., Phi Beta Kappa. Republican. Presbyn. Mason, Elk. Club: Parkersburg Country. Home: 1360 Market St. Office: 214 4th St., Parkersburg, W.Va.

WOLFENDEN, James, congressman; b. Cardington, Delaware Co., Pa., July 25, 1889; ed. pub. schs. and academy. Elected to 70th Congress, 1928, to fill vacancy caused by death of Thomas S. Butler, and reëlected to 71st to 76th Congresses (1929-41), 8th Pa. Dist. Republican. Home: Upper Darby, Pa.

WOLFERTH, Charles Christian, M.D.; b. Clarksboro, N.J., May 18, 1887; s. John C. and Mary Wolferth (Rode) W.; A.B., Princeton U., 1908; M.D., U. of Pa., 1912; m. Mary Beatrice Comber, July 26, 1922; children —Mary Beatrice, Charles Christian, Caroline Grau. Physician since 1912; with Sch. of Medicine, U. of Pa., since 1917, successively as instr., associate, asst. prof. and, since 1935, prof. clin. medicine. Served as maj. Med. Reserve Corps, U.S. Army, World War. Mem. Assn. Am. Physicians, Am. Soc. for Clin. Investigation, Am. Clin. and Climatol. Soc., Phi Beta Kappa, Sigma Xi, Alpha Omega Alpha. Club: Philadelphia Country. Home: 26 Raynham Rd., Merion, Pa.

WOLFF, Charles Edgar, furniture mcht.; b. Waynesboro, Pa., June 11, 1882; s. James Patterson and Sarah Alice (Funk) W.; student high sch., Waynesboro, Pa., 1889-1900, Waynesboro Bus. Coll., 1900-02; m. Elizabeth V. Brubaker, Nov. 29, 1904; children—Mary Eleanor (Mrs. John C. L. Brown), James Patterson, Isabelle Anderson. Employed as salesman Wolff & McKoun, Waynesboro, Pa., retail furniture and floor coverings, 1902-04, mem. firm since 1904; dir. Citizens Nat. Bank & Trust Co. of Waynesboro. Trustee Waynesboro Y.M. C.A.; dir. Waynesboro Hosp. Republican. Methodist. Mason. Club: Masonic (Waynesboro, Pa.). Home: 136 Clayton Av. Office: E. Main St., Waynesboro, Pa.

WOLFF, Thomas Conrad, physician; b. Montreal, P.Q., Apr. 24, 1891; s. Conrad Emil and Mary Margaret (Mackay) W.; came to U.S., 1922; Litt.B., Laval Univ., Montreal, Canada, 1911; M.D., C.M., McGill University Medical Department, Montreal, P.Q., 1917; m. Edith Dorothy Stewart, September 26, 1922; children —Thomas Conrad, Jr., Stewart Mackay, Dorothy Barry. On resident staff Montreal General Hospital, 1920-21; resident physician, Laurentian Sanatorium, Ste. Agathe, P.Q., 1921-22; engaged in gen. practice of medicine, Adamsville, R.I., 1922-27; grad. study in cardiology, Johns Hopkins Hosp., 1927-28; dispensary physician and asst. vis. physician, Johns Hopkins Hosp., 1928-39; dir. heart clinics, Mercy and South Baltimore Gen. hosps. since 1930; med. dir. Home for Incurables, Baltimore since 1938; asst. in medicine, U. of Md. Med. Sch., Baltimore, 1928-1930, instr. medicine, 1930-31, asso., 1931-36, asst. prof. medicine since 1936; asst. and instr. medicine Johns Hopkins U. Med. Sch. since 1928. Served as lt. then capt. Med. Corps, Canadian Army, 1917-19, with C.E.F. Mem. A.M.A., Md. State and Baltimore City med. socs., Nu Sigma Nu. Club: Johns Hopkins. Home: 1032 E. 36th St. Office: 11 E. Chase St., Baltimore, Md.

WOLFFE, Joseph Barnett, physician; b. Wilno, Poland, Apr. 25, 1896; s. Barnett and Jennie (Gershuni) W.; came to U.S., 1915, naturalized, 1920; student Univ. of Glasgow, Scotland, 1913-15; M.D., Temple U., Phila., 1919; m. Evelyn Rose Leedes, Aug. 1936; children— Leonard Lee, Marian Frances Jennie. Physician, Phila., since 1919; asso. in medicine and charge cardiac clinic, Mt. Sinai Hosp., Phila., 1921-29; clin. asst. in medicine, Temple U. Hosp., Phila., 1923-26, cardiologist, 1926-39; cardiologist, Temple U. Med. Sch., since 1926, asso. prof. in medicine, since 1929; cardiologist to Willow Crest, convalescent home; consultant to Eastern Penitentiary. Lt. comdr., U.S.N.R. specialist corps. Mem. A.M.A. and county and state med. socs., Am. Coll. Physicians (asso.), Am. Therapeutic Soc., Phila., Pa. State and Am. Heart Assns., Assn. Mil. Surgeons Am. Bd. of Internal Medicine. Mason. Clubs: Officers (Phila. Navy Yard); Physicians Square (Phila.). Contbr. many articles on med. subjects, especially regarding the heart, to med. jours. Home: R.F.D., No. 4, Fairton, N.J. Office: 1829 Pine St., Philadelphia, Pa.

WOLFROM, Ralph Theodore, newspaper publisher; b. Bellevue, O., Mar. 4, 1883; s. Fred and Mary (Sutter) W.; student Bellevue (O.) pub. schs. and Capital U., Columbus, O., 1902-03; m. Gertrude Ramsdell, Sept. 8, 1909; children—Eleanor Louise (Mrs. Richard Taylor), Richard Ramsdell. Began as store clerk, 1897; bookkeeper for telephone company, 1904, later sec. and treas. Local Telephone Co., Bellevue Home Telephone Co., Crestline Local Telephone Co., Wood County Telephone Co. until 1924; newspaper publishing business, Millburn and Maplewood, N.J., 1924-26; pres. News-Chronicle Co., Shippensburg, Pa., since 1926. Lutheran. Mason, Elk. Home: Baltimore Rd. Office: 6 N. Penn St., Shippensburg, Pa.

WOLFSKEIL, William D.; judge N.J. Ct. of Errors and Appeals, term expires 1941. Address: Elizabeth, N.J.

WOLGEMUTH, Daniel Musser, mcht., feed and coal; b. nr. Mt. Joy, Pa., Apr. 26, 1895; s. Hiram E. and Martha M. (Musser) W.; student East Donegal Twp. schs., Lancaster Co., Pa.; m. Ella N. Heisey, May 3, 1917; children— D. Jay, Donald H. Engaged in farming, 1912-15; teller in bank, 1915-19; mem. firm Wolgemuth Bros., mchts. in feed, grain, and coal since 1919; one of liquidating trustees of Florin Trust Co., Mt. Joy, Pa.; dir. First Nat. Bank & Trust Co., Mt. Joy, Pa. Served as sch. dir. of East Donegal Twp. Schs., Lancaster Co., Pa., 1926-32. Republican. Mem. Brethren in Christ Ch. Home: Florin, Pa.

WOLK, Samuel, rabbi; b. Baltimore, Md., Mar. 12, 1899; s. Simon and Mary (Kahan) W.; grad. Baltimore City Coll., 1916; B.A., U. of Cincinnati, 1920; Rabbi, Hebrew Union Coll., 1923; M.A., Harvard U., 1928; student summer session Johns Hopkins U. and U. of Heidelberg; m. Mary Cohen, Mar. 18, 1934; 1 son, Daniel Simon. Asst. rabbi Temple Israel, Boston, Mass., 1923-29; rabbi Temple B'nai B'rith, Wilkes-Barre, Pa., since 1929. Trustee Bucknell Jr. Coll., Wilkes-Barre. Mem. Phi Beta Kappa. Home: 36 Mallery Place, Wilkes-Barre, Pa.

WOLLAK, Theodore, M.D.; b. Baltimore, Md., July 6, 1904; s. Armin and Sophie (Steinitz) W.; grad. DeWitt Clinton High Sch., New York, 1920; B.S., Md. State Coll., 1923; M. D., Coll. of Physicians and Surgeons, Baltimore, 1927; m. Martha Trauger, Oct. 5, 1934; 1 step-dau., Alice May. Interne Protestant Hosp., Norfolk, Va., 1927-28; chief resident physician, U. of Md. Hosp., Baltimore, 1928-29, Sinai Hosp., Baltimore Jan.-June, 1929; asst. physician Norristown (Pa.) State Hosp., June-July, 1929, Spring Grove State Hosp., July 1929-Dec. 1930; asst. physician Torrance (Pa.) State Hosp., Dec. 1930-Aug. 1934, supt. since Oct. 1935. Mem. Pa. Med. Soc., Am. Psychiatric Assn. Mem. Greek Catholic Ch. Address: Torrance State Hospital, Torrance, Pa.

WOLMAN, Abel, sanitary engr.; b. Baltimore, Md., June 10, 1892; s. Morris and Rose (Wachsman) W.; A.B., Johns Hopkins U., 1913, B.S. in Engring., 1915; m. Anne Gordon, June 10, 1919; 1 son, Markley Gordon. Began as asst. engr., U.S. Pub. Health Service, 1914; chief engr. Dept. of Health, Md., 1922-39; lecturer and prof. san. engring., Johns Hopkins Sch. of Hygiene and Pub. Health, also at Harvard, Princeton, U. of Chicago and other univs.; cons. engr. City of Baltimore and Baltimore County; acting state dir. for Md. and Del., Federal Emergency Pub. Works Adminstrn. Chmn. Md. State Planning Commn., Md. Water Resources Commn., Water Resources Com. of Nat. Resources Com. Mem. Am. Soc. C.E., Am. Water Works Assn., Am. Pub. Health Assn. (pres. 1939), A.A.A.S., Faraday Soc. (Eng.), Royal Inst. Pub. Health (Eng.). Home: 3213 N. Charles St. Address: Johns Hopkins University, Baltimore, Md.

WOLMAN, Samuel, M.D.; b. Poland, June 17, 1880; s. Morris and Yetta (Wacksman) W.; brought to U.S., 1885; grad. pub. schs., 1894, Baltimore City Coll., 1899; A.B., Johns Hopkins U., 1902, M.D., 1906; m. Adele Kempner, 1910; children—Judith (Mrs. Herbert Har-

ris), Margaret. In gen. practice of medicine since 1906; asso. in medicine, Johns Hopkins U., since 1930. Mem. Phi Beta Kappa. Dir. Nat. Tuberculosis Assn.; Pres. Md. Tuberculosis Assn. Home: 2444 Eutaw Place, Baltimore, Md.

WOLSEY, Louis, rabbi; b. Midland, Mich., Jan. 8, 1877; s. William and Frances (Krueger) W.; A.B., University of Cincinnati; rabbi, Hebrew Union College, Cincinnati, 1899; grad. study U. of Chicago, Western Reserve U. and U. of Pa.; m. Florence Helen Wiener, June 12, 1912; children—Allon L., Jonathan L. Rabbi Congregation B'nai Israel, Little Rock, Ark., 1899-1907, Euclid Av. Temple, Cleveland, 1907-25, Congregation Rodeph Shalom, Phila., Pa., since 1925. Chaplain Ark. N.G., 1906-07. Mem. Bd. of Edn., Little Rock, 1906-07. Mem. Central Conf. Am. Rabbis (pres. 1925-27; chmn. revision of Union Hymnal), Fed. Jewish Charities of Phila. (trustee), Am. Oriental Soc., Soc. Bibl. Lit. Mem. exec. bd. Commn. on Jewish Edn. Chmn. Mayor's Crime Commn., Phila., 1937. Clubs: Philmont, Ashbourne. Home: 8210 Old York Rd., Elkins Park, Pa. Office: 615 N. Broad St., Philadelphia, Pa.

WOLVERTON, Charles A., congressman; b. Camden, N.J., Oct. 24, 1880; s. Charles S. and Martha W.; grad. high sch., 1897; LL.B., U. of Pa., 1900; m. Sara May Donnell, M.D., June 25, 1907; 1 son, Donnell Knox. Admitted to N.J. bar, 1901, and began practice at Camden; asst. city solicitor, Camden, 1904-06; asst. prosecutor Camden County, 1906-13; spl. asst. atty. gen., N.J., 1913-14; mem. N.J. Ho. of Assembly, 1915-18 (speaker of House, 1918); prosecutor of pleas, Camden County, 1918-23; alternate del. at large Rep. Nat. Conv., 1920; dir. and asso. counsel First Camden Nat. Bank & Trust Co.; mem. 70th to 76th Congresses (1927-41), 1st N.J. Dist. Federal food administrator Camden County, 1917-19. Mem. Am. Bar Assn., N.J. Soc. of Pa. Methodist. Mason (32°, K.T., Shriner), Elk, L.O.O.M. Home: Merchantville, N.J.

WOLVERTON, John Marshall, ex-congressman; b. Bigbend, W.Va., Jan. 31, 1872; s. James S. and Eliza Ann (Ferrell) W.; student Glenville (W.Va.) State Normal Sch. and Fairmount State Normal Sch.; LL.B., W.Va. U., 1901; m. Laura V. Herold, Dec. 20, 1907; children—Helen N., James H., Barbara Ruth. Admitted to W.Va. bar, 1901, and began practice at Richwood. Pros. atty. Nicholas Co., W.Va., 1913-17, 1921-25; mayor of Richwood, 1918-19; mem. 69th and 71st Congresses (1925-27, 1929-31), 3d W.Va. Dist.; now mem. law firm Wolverton & Callaghan. Home: Richmond, W.Va.

WONER, George Irvin, printing and pub.; b. Wooster, O., June 13, 1870; s. Jeremiah David and Rebecca (Irvin) W.; student Baldwin-Wallace Coll., Berea, O., 1886-88; Ph.B., Wooster (O.) Coll., 1894; Ph.M., Wooster U., 1897; m. Lucretia Peebles, Nov. 6, 1896; 1 son, George Irvin (dec.); m. 2d, Laura Blanche McClung, June 6, 1911. Engaged in newspaper work 1894-98; editor and mgr. Daily Republican, Painesville, O., 1898-1906; mng. editor Butler (Pa.) Eagle, 1906-11; editor and mgr. Butler (Pa.) Citizen, 1911-13; head of The Ziegler Printing Co., publishers, Butler, Pa., 1913-37; pres. Oakville Realty Co. Served as mem. Pa. Ho. of Rep., 1919-25, author of first Prohibition Law Enforcement Act in Pa., 1921. Past pres. Butler Commercial Club; pres. Men's Fellowship Club, Butler Presbytery; chmn. bd. trustees Butler Co. S.S. Assn. Republican. Presbyn. Mason (32°), Odd Fellow. Home: 1017 Center Av. Office: The Diamond, Butler, Pa.

WONSETLER, John Charles, artist and teacher; b. Camden, N.J., Aug. 25, 1900; s. John Bean and Bertha (Bridge) W.; ed. Phila. Mus. Sch. Industral Art, 1921-25; m. Adelaide Hill, June 29, 1929. Has executed mural commns. in N.J., Pa., N.Y., Md., Del. and Va. since 1925, including Fackenthal Library, Franklin and Marshall Coll., Ch. of St. Mary Magdalen de Pazzi, R.C., Phila., Pa., St. John's English Luth. Ch., Tamaqua, Pa., Warwick Hotel, Phila., Pa.,

Belvedere Hotel, Baltimore, Md., and theatres and pvt. homes; exhibited one-man show, Art Alliance, Phila., 1930; Phila. Mus. Sch. Industrial Art, 1931; Am. Inst. Architects, 1939; instr. drawing from cast and model, Phila. Mus. Sch. Industrial Art, 1926-31. Home: 864 N. 27th St., Camden, N.J. Studio: Vernon Lane, Rose Valley, Moylan, Pa.

WOOD, Alan 3d, retired mech. engr. and steel mfr.; b. Conshohocken, Pa., Mar. 1, 1875; s. Howard and Mary (Biddle) W.; B.S. and M.E., U. of Pa., 1895; m. Elizabeth F. Read, Oct. 20, 1910; children—Harleston Read, Catherine Vaux. Asso. with Alan Wood Iron & Steel Co. since 1895, clerical and mill supervisor 4 yrs., engring. and designing, 14 yrs., dir. Alan Wood Steel Co. since 1937; dir. Edw. G. Budd Mfg. Co. Mem. Franklin Inst., Am. Soc. for Testing Materials, Pa. Soc. Sons of the Revolution. Republican. Episcopalian (sec. and treas. S.S., Ch. of Redeemer). Club: Little Egg Harbor Yacht (Beach Haven, N.J.). Home: 615 Pembroke Rd., Bryn Mawr, Pa.

WOOD, Albert Gerard, prof. biology; b. Waynetown, Ind., Jan. 20, 1881; s. Wm. Heath and Sarah Margaret (Swank) W.; B.S., Valparaiso U., 1904, B.Ped., 1905; A.B., Ind. Univ., 1909; A.M., U. of Neb., 1916; grad. study, U. of Chicago, various, 1916-27; m. Bessie French, June 20, 1911; 1 dau., Doris Elizabeth. Began as teacher rural sch., Ind., 1900; teacher high schs., Ind. and Colo., 1904-16; prof. of biology, Trinity Univ., Tex., 1916-19, Baker Univ., Kan., 1916-26; prof. of biology, Grove City Coll., Grove City, Pa., since 1927. Served as city bacteriologist, Baker, Kan., 1919-26. Mem. A.A.A.S., Sigma Xi, Pi Gamma Mu, Phi Delta Kappa. Republican. Methodist. Home: 426 Poplar St., Grove City, Pa.

WOOD, Alfred C(onard), surgeon; b. Hatboro, Pa., June 17, 1863; s. Comly and Geraldine (Shoemaker) W.; student Hatboro pub. schs. and Friends' Central Sch., Phila.; Ph.G., Phila. Coll. Pharmacy, 1885; M.D., U. of Pa. Med. Sch., 1888; m. Dorothy Donnelly, 1922; 1 son, Alfred Conard. Interne Hosp. of U. of Pa., 1888-89; mem. med. faculty, U. of Pa., 1890-1928, with title of asst. prof. surgery; retired, 1928; formerly surgeon Hosp. of U. of Pa., Philadelphia Gen. Hosp., Howard (since merged with U. of Pa.), Rush Hosp., Memorial Hosp.; cons. surgeon to hosps. in Norristown and Coatesville, Pa., and Wilmington, Del., etc. Fellow Am. Surg. Assn., Am. Coll. Surgeons, Philadelphia Acad. Surgery, Coll. Physicians of Philadelphia, etc. Republican. Clubs: Union League, Penn Athletic. Contbr. to med. books and jours. Address: 2035 Walnut St., Philadelphia, Pa.

WOOD, Augustus I(dell), banking; b. Hoboken, N.J., May 17, 1859; s. Newman A. and Margaret R. (Idell) W.; student pub. sch., Phillipsburg, N.J.; m. Jennie E. Davis, Feb. 16, 1887 (dec.); children—Nelson H. (dec.), Everett I. (dec.), Anna G. Employed as clk., Phillipsburg (N.J.) Nat. Bank, 1876-87; sec. Frankford Trust Co., Phila., 1887-90; sec. and treas. West Phila. Title & Trust Co., 1890-1907, pres., 1907-29, when merged with Integrity Trust Co. and dir. latter since 1929. Trustee Wesley Foundation; trustee and pres. M.E. Home for Aged, Phila., Pa. Republican. Methodist. Home: 334 Louella Av., Wayne, Pa. Office: S.E. Cor. Walnut St., Philadelphia, Pa.

WOOD, Austin Hislop; instr. clin. urology, Johns Hopkins U.; urologist St. Agnes, Maryland Gen., Bon Secours and South Baltimore Gen. hosps.; visiting urologist Johns Hopkins U. Sch. of Medicine. Address: 101 W. Read St., Baltimore, Md.

WOOD, Earl LeRoy, physician; b. Chester, Pa., Oct. 8, 1894; s. Thomas Jefferson and Mary Ella (Miller) W.; student Newark (N.J.) pub. schs., 1901-13; M.D., N.Y. Homeopathic Med. Coll. and Flower Hosp., 1917; M.Sc. (Med.), U. of Pa. Grad. Sch. of Medicine, 1928; student U. of Vienna, Austria, 1926, Ecole de Medicine, Paris, 1930; m. Flora Helen Assmann, Oct. 9, 1924; 1 son, Francis Assmann. Interne Newark (N.J.) City Hosp., 1919-21; in gen. practice, Newark, 1921-25, specialist in otolaryngology, Newark, since 1925. Served as 1st lt., 1917-19, and capt., 1919, Med. Corps, U.S. Army, with A.E.F.; capt. 102d Cav. (Essex Troop) N.J. Nat. Guard, 1921-24; maj., 302d Cav., U.S. Army, 1924-34; lt. col., surgeon, Med. Res., 61st Cav. Div., since 1934. Mem. Am. Acad. Otolaryngology, Am. Coll. Surgeons, Am. Laryngol., Rhinol., and Otol. Soc., A.M.A., Acad. of Medicine of Northern N.J., Soc. of Surgeons of N.J., Order of Founders and Patriots of America, Soc. of Colonial Wars, S.A.R. Awarded Purple Heart, U.S. Army, 1933. Republican. Presbyterian. Clubs: U. of Pa. (New York); Essex Co. Country (West Orange, N.J.). Home: 225 Ballantine Parkway. Office: 160 Roseville Av., Newark, N.J.

WOOD, Edith Elmer, author; b. Portsmouth, N.H., Sept. 24, 1871; d. Comdr. Horace (U.S.N.) and Adele (Wiley) Elmer; B.L., Smith College, 1890; A.M., Columbia, 1917, Ph.D., 1919; grad. N.Y. Sch. of Social Work, 1917; m. Lt. Albert Norton Wood, U.S.N., June 24, 1893; children—Horace Elmer (dec.), Thurston Elmer (dec.), Horace Elmer II, Albert Elmer. Writer since 1890. Founder, 1906, pres., 1906, 07, 09, hon. pres., 1908—, Anti-Tuberculosis League of Porto Rico; del. Internat. Congress Tuberculosis, 1908. Chmn. national com. on housing, Am. Assn. University Women, 1917-29; in charge courses in housing, Columbia Univ. extension, 1926-30, Teachers College, summer sessions, 1925-32, 36, 37; consultant, housing div. Pub. Works Adminstr., 1933-37; consultant U.S. Housing Authority since 1938; mem. N.J. State Housing Authority, 1934-35; vice-pres. National Public Housing Conference, 1932-36, dir. 1936—; mem. exec. com. International Housing Assn., 1931-37, Phi Beta Kappa. Author: Her Provincial Cousin, 1893; Shoulder Straps and Sunbonnets, 1901; The Spirit of the Service, 1903; An Oberland Châlet, 1910; The Housing of the Unskilled Wage Earner, 1919; Housing Progress in Western Europe, 1923; Recent Trends in American Housing, 1931; Slums and Blighted Areas in the United States (Housing Div. Bull.), 1935. Contbr. to mags. and newspapers. Home: Cape May Court House, N.J.

WOOD, Edith Longstreth (Mrs. W. S. Wood), artist; b. Phila., Pa.; d. Samuel Noble and Mary Hance (Cook) Longstreth; grad. Friends Central Sch., Phila., 1901; A.B., Bryn Mawr Coll., 1905; student Woodbrook Settlement near Birmingham, England, 1906, Pa. Acad. of Fine Arts, 1922-28; also Paris, France, and summer schools in Chester Springs, Pa., and Colorado Springs, Colo.; m. William Stroud Wood, Oct. 18, 1912 (died 1922). Artist and painter. Works in permanent collections in La France Art Inst., Phila., Lambert Fund Collection of Pa. Acad. Fine Arts, also in private collections. Awards: Cresson Traveling scholarship by Pa. Acad. Fine Arts, 1928. Mem. Bryn Mawr Coll. Alumnae Assn., North Shore Art Assn., Gloucester, Mass.; fellow Pa. Acad. Fine Arts. Mem. Soc. of Friends. Clubs: Phila. Art Alliance, Print, Plastic, Phila. Water Color (Phila.). Home: 2139 Cypress St. Studio: 354 Middle City Bldg., 34 S. 17th St., Philadelphia, Pa.

WOOD, Edmund Bacon McAlister, clergyman; b. Staten Island, N.Y., Nov. 30, 1896; s. Rev. A. L. and Fanny Hay (Brand) W.; A.B., St. Stephen's Coll., 1921; student Gen. Theol. Sem., New York; m. Frances McKean Bayard, May 7, 1927; children—Judith Bayard, Edmund Bacon, Fanny Hay. Ordained to ministry P.E. Ch., deacon, 1924, priest, 1925; asst. at St. Timothy's Ch., Roxborough, Phila., 1924-27; rector, Clark Mills, N.Y., 1927-32; chaplain Donaldson Sch., Ilchester, Md., 1932; rector, Ch. of the Advent, Cape May, N.J., 1933; rector, St. Timothy's Ch., Roxborough, Phila., Pa., since 1934. Served as dir. United Campaign in 21st Ward of Phila., 1937. Mem. Kappa Gamma Chi. Episcopalian. Home: St. Timothy's Rectory, 5720 Ridge Av., Roxborough, Philadelphia, Pa.

WOOD, Eric Fisher, author, architect; b. N.Y. City, Jan. 4, 1889; s. William B. (M.D.) and Frances (Fisher) W.; Ph.B., Sheffield Scientific Sch. (Yale), 1910; A.B., Yale, 1910; studied Columbia U. Sch. of Architecture, and École des Beaux Arts Paris; m. Vera de Ropp, Apr. 20, 1918; children—Eric Fisher, Eleanor Morton, Peter de Ropp, Alec Laughlin. Propr. firm Eric Fisher Wood & Co., architects; with H. Hornbostel, won competition and selection as architects for Warren G. Harding Memorial at Marion, O. Civil attaché at the Am. Embassy, Paris, under Ambassador Herrick, 1914; officer Am. Ambulance Corps. in France, 1915; maj. British Army, 1917, wounded at Battle of Arras; maj. U.S.N.A., Aug. 14, 1917, and asst. chief of staff, 83d Div.; lt. col. G.S. asst. chief of staff, 88th Div.; wounded in Meuse-Argonne; col. 107th U.S. (1st Pa. Regt.) Field Arty. V.p. Nat. Security League, 1915-16; a founder Am. Legion, 1919, and elected its 1st national adjutant; member Society Beaux Arts Architects, Engring. Society of Western Pa., Soc. Colonial Wars. Officer Legion of Honor (France). Chmn. Pa. Rep. State Exec. Com., 1926-28; sec. Pa. Delegation Rep. National Convention, 1928. Clubs: Duquesne (Pittsburgh); Union League (Phila.). Author: Note Book of an Attaché, 1915; The Writing on the Wall, 1916; The Note Book of an Intelligence Officer, 1918; Biography of Leonard Wood, 1920; Basic Manual Field Artillery, 1934; also articles, Century Magazine, The Outlook, Saturday Evening Post. Home: 5260 Center Av., Pittsburgh; and R. 1, Bedford, Pa. Office: 233 Oliver Av., Pittsburgh, Pa.

WOOD, Ernest Richard, educator; b. Del Norte, Colo., July 19, 1891; s. George Edward and Minnie Leah (Pruden) W.; A.B., Ohio U., Athens, O., 1916, B.S. in Edn., 1916; A.M., Clark U., 1917; Ph.D., Univ. of Chicago, 1923; m. Alice Hazel Gettles, Dec. 25, 1917 (died Nov. 22, 1934); children—John Francis, Gerald David; m. 2d, Pearle Felicia Stone, June 13, 1936; 1 dau., Edna Beth. Teacher rural schs., Athens County, O., 1908-11; superintendent schools Chauncey, O., 1911-13; assistant in dept. of psychology, Ohio University, 1915-16; prin. Univ. High Sch., Lexington, Ky., 1919-21; prof. psychology, Kan. State Teachers Coll., 1922-29; dir. Bur. of Standards and Measurements, 1924-29; dir. Ohio scholarship tests and instructional research, State Dept. of Edn., Columbus, O., 1929-32; prof. education, Ohio State U., summers, 1930, 31, 32; asso. prof. ednl. psychology, New York U., since 1932. Served as psychol. examiner, U.S.A., 1917-18. Mem. Am. Ednl. Research Assn., Am. Psychol. Assn., Am. Statis. Assn., Nat. Soc. for Study of Edn., Phi Delta Kappa, Kappa Delta Pi. Conglist. Originated the "Every Pupil Test," Gen. Scholarship Test, also many statistical devices. Author of reports of results of scholarship tests. Co-author: Educational Psychology, 1936; The Every Pupil Series—Language Trails, 1938; Arithmetic Books, 1939; Health and Play, 1939; Safety Series, 1939. Chmn. in charge of construction of Nationwide Every Pupil U.S. Constitution Tests for the Sesquicentennial Commn. Contbr. articles to ednl. jours. Home: 167 Watchung Av., Montclair, N.J. Office: New York University, Washington Square East, New York, N.Y.

WOOD, Francis Clark, M.D.; b. of Am. parents, Wellington, Cape Colony, South Africa, Oct. 1, 1901; s. Clinton Tyler and Jennie Stoddard (Clark) W.; grad. Wooster (O.) Acad., 1918; A.B., Princeton U., 1922; M.D., U. of Pa., 1926; m. Mary Louise Woods, June 4, 1926; children—Francis Clark, Elizabeth Vance, Lawrence Crane. Interne Hosp. of U. of Pa., 1926-28; instr. in medicine Med. Sch., U. of Pa., 1928-33, asso. in medicine since 1933; fellow of Robinette Foundation for Study of Cardiovascular Disease, U. of Pa. Hosp., since 1928. Fellow Am. Coll. Physicians, Phila. Coll. Physicians; mem. A.M.A., Phila. Co. Med. Soc., Am. Soc. for Clin. Investigation. Presbyterian. Club: Princeton (Phila.). Home: Laurel Lane, Haverford, Pa. Office: 256 S. 21st St., Philadelphia, Pa.

WOOD, Frederick William, consulting engr.; b. Lowell, Mass., Mar. 16, 1857; s. William and Elizabeth French (Kidder) W.; B.S., Mass. Inst. Tech., 1877; m. Caroline Peabody Smith, Jan. 24, 1884; children—Frederick Brayton, Dorothy, Elizabeth (Mrs. Clarke Farwell Freeman), Helen, Caroline (Mrs. Carl Billings Willard), Richard Minot. Began with Pa. Steel Co. at Baldwin (now Steelton), Pa., 1877, gen. supt., 1884-89, gen. mgr., 1889-91, 2d v.p., 1893; pres. Md. Steel Co., 1891-1916; in charge of same after purchase by Bethlehem Steel Co., 1916-18; v.p. Am. Internat. Shipbuilding Corpn., 1918-21; dir. Consol. Gas Electric Light & Power Co. of Baltimore, Pa. Water & Power Co., Eastern Rolling Mill Co., Savings Bank of Baltimore. Mem. Claims Commn. of U.S. Shipping Bd., Emergency Fleet Corpn., 1921-23; term mem. of Corpn. Mass. Inst. Tech., 1906-11; trustee Johns Hopkins U.; dir. Md. Inst. Mem. Am. Inst. Mining and Metall. Engrs., Am. Soc. M.E., Am. Soc. Naval Architects and Marine Engrs., Am. Iron and Steel Institute, A.A.A.S. Republican. Unitarian. Clubs: University, Maryland, Merchants (Baltimore); Cosmos (Washington, D.C.); Engineers' (New York). Originated improvements in mfr. of steel which have been generally adopted in the industry. Home: 2429 Keyworth Av., Baltimore, Md.

WOOD, Harold Bacon, M.D.; b. Camden, N. J., Mar. 23, 1878; s. James F. and Mary L. (Collins) W.; M.D., U. of Pa., 1901, Dr.P.H., 1910; m. Edith Gray, Apr. 16, 1907 (dec.); children—Merrill, Barbara; m. 2d, Adessa F. Kistler, Oct. 11, 1930. Engaged in pub. health work since 1910; developed State Lab., Miss. State Bd. of Health, 1910-12; asst. commr. of health, State of W.Va., 1913; epidemiologist N.Y. State Dept. of Health during World War; city health officer, Bloomington, Ill., 1923; epidemiologist Pa. State Dept. of Health, Harrisburg, Pa., 1925-33. Dir. Harrisburg Natural History Soc. Charter fellow Am. Pub. Health Assn.; fellow A.M.A.; asso. mem. Am. Ornithologists' Union; mem. Dauphin Co. Med. Soc., Wilson Ornithol. Club, Eastern Bird-Banding Assn. Republican. Presbyterian. Author: Sanitation Practically Applied, 1917 (later translated into Spanish); also more than 250 articles on pub. health and ornithology. Home: 3016 N. Second St., Harrisburg, Pa.

WOOD, Horace Elmer II, univ. prof.; b. Portland, Ore., Feb. 6, 1901; s. Albert Norton and Edith (Elmer) W.; A.B., Princeton U., 1921; A.M., Columbia, 1923, Ph.D., 1927; m. Florence Dowden, Dec. 7, 1925; 1 son, Thurston Elliott. Teacher Poly. Prep. Country Day Sch., Brooklyn, N.Y., 1921-23; instr. biology, Washington Sq. Coll., N.Y.U., 1923-28, asst. prof. geology, 1928-32; prof. biology and chmn. dept., Dana Coll., Newark, N.J., 1931-35, U. of Newark, N.J., since 1935. Fellow Geol. Soc. of America, The Paleontological Soc., A.A.A.S., N.Y. Acad. of Sciences (v.p. since 1939); mem. Phi Beta Kappa, Sigma Xi. Author fifty scientific pubs. ranging from notes to monographs. On field expdns. in Cenozoic fossil fields of western North America, 1923, 1928, 1931, 1932, 1933, 1934, 1938. Home: 3916 45th St., Long Island City, N.Y. Office: U. of Newark, Newark, N.J.

WOOD, Horatio Charles, M.D., Ph.M.; b. Phila., Pa., Feb. 26, 1874; s. Horatio C. and Eliza H. (Longacre) W.; grad. William Penn Charter Sch., Phila., 1890; student lit. dept. U. of Pa. 2 yrs.; M.D., U. of Pa., 1896; research work, U. of Berne, 1897-98, U. of Turin, 1898; m. Alice L. Lovell, Dec. 19, 1899; children—Horatio C. III, Florence L. Demonstrator in pharmacodynamics, U. of Pa., 1898-1907; asso. prof. pharmacol., 1907-10; prof. pharmacol. and therapeutics, Medico-Chirurg. Coll., Phila., 1910-16; prof. same, U. of Pa., since 1916; prof. materia medica, Phila. Coll. of Pharmacy and Science since 1921. Asst. visiting phys. to Phila. General Hosp., 1904-08; mem. Com. on Revision of U.S. Pharmacopœia, since 1910. Fellow A.A.A.S.; mem. American Soc. Pharmacology, Am. Pharm. Assn. Presbyn. Editor: Therapeutics, Its Principles and Practice, 11th to 13th edits. (with father), 1899; United States Dispensatory, 20th edit., 1907, and 21st edit., 1926, 22d edit., 1937. Author: A Text Book of Pharmacology, 1912. Home: 319 S. 41st St., Philadelphia, Pa.

WOOD, Loren Newton, lawyer; b. Cambridge, Ill., Dec. 30, 1876; s. Henry DeLos and Emma (Harper) W.; B.S., Carleton Coll., Northfield, Minn., 1899; A.M., Columbia, 1902, LL.B., 1902; m. Elizabeth Thompson, June 17, 1908; children—Janet, Loren Thompson, Howard Stuart, Robert DeLos. Admitted to N.Y. bar, 1902, to all Federal Courts, 1902-04; mem. law firm of Wood, Molloy & France; pres. and dir. First Nat. Bank of Bound Brook, N.J.; dir. and gen. counsel Wessel Duval & Co., Maltbie Chem. Co., Inland Tar Co., Tar Distilling Corpn., Novadel-Agene Corpn., Trustee Somerset Hosp., Somerville, N.J. Mem. Am. and N.Y. State bar assns,, Phi Rho Sigma. Conglist. Clubs: Midday (New York); Raritan Valley Country (gov.). Home: Bound Brook, N.J. Office: 25 Broad St., New York, N.Y.

WOOD, Robert Williams, physicist; b. Concord, Mass., May 2, 1868; s. Dr. Robert Williams and Lucy J. (Davis) W.; A.B., Harvard, 1891; Johns Hopkins, 1891-92; U. of Berlin, 1892-94; LL.D., Clark, 1909, U. of Birmingham, 1913, Edinburgh, 1921; Ph.D., honoris causa, University of Berlin, 1931; m. Gertrude Ames, Apr. 19, 1892; children—Margaret, Robert Williams, Elizabeth, Bradford (dec.). Instr. physics, 1897-99, asst. prof., 1899-1901, U. of Wis.; prof. experimental physics, Johns Hopkins, since 1901, research prof., 1938. In 1898 originated method now in general use of thawing frozen street mains and service pipes by passing an electric current through them. Awarded John Scott Legacy premium and medal, Franklin Inst., Phila., for color-photography; Rumford premium, a gold and a silver medal, by Am. Acad., 1909, for researches on theory of light; silver medal, London Soc. Arts for color-photog. process; gold medal for physics for 1918, Societa Italiana delle Scienze (detta dei XL), Rome; Ives's medal, Optical Society of America, 1933; Rumford gold medal by Royal Society of London, 1938. Commd. maj., Signal O.R.C., Aug. 1917; with A.E.F.; developed methods for secret signaling. Foreign mem. Royal Soc., London; hon. fellow Royal Micros. Soc., London; hon. mem. London Optical Soc.; corr. mem. Königliche Akademie der Wissenschaften zu Göttingen; foreign asso. Accademia dei Lincei, Rome; foreign mem. Acad. of Science, Leningrad; fellow Am. Acad. Arts and Sciences; member Nat. Acad. Sciences, Am. Philos. Soc., Am. Physical Soc. (pres. 1935)); hon. mem. Royal Instn., London; foreign mem. Royal Swedish Acad., 1932; hon. foreign mem. Indian Assn. for Cultivation of Science, Calcutta, 1931; hon. fellow London Physical Soc., 1933. Author: Physical Optics, 1905, rev. edits, 1911, 34; Researches in Physical Optics, 2 vols.; also fiction, The Man who Rocked the Earth, and the Moon-Maker (with Arthur Train), 1915. Illustrated nonsense verses, How to Tell the Birds from the Flowers, and other wood-cuts. Researches in optics, spectroscopy, atomic and molecular radiation, supersonics recorded in some 240 papers in European and Am. tech. jours. Home: 1023 St. Paul St., Baltimore, Md.

WOOD, Thomas, lawyer; b. Muncy, Pa., June 5, 1883; s. William J. and Elizabeth (Peterman) W.; A.M., Bucknell U., Lewisburg, Pa., 1907; LL.B., U. of Mich., Ann Arbor, Mich., 1907; m. Blanche Stoner, June 2, 1910; children—William H., Fannie R., Thomas, Harry P., James S. Admitted to Pa. bar, 1911, and since in gen. practice of law; mem. law firm Reading and Wood, Williamsport, Pa.; pres. and treas. Robinson Mfg. Co. Dir. Lycoming Co. Community Chest; mem. Lycoming Co. Boy Scout Council. Mem. Phi Gamma Delta. Democrat. Presbyterian. Mason, Odd Fellow. Author: Practical Grammar and Composition, 1910. Home: Muncy, Pa. Office: 120 W. Fourth St., Williamsport, Pa.

WOODBRIDGE, Freeman, lawyer; b. Saratoga Springs, N.Y., June 2, 1866; s. John and Helen (Freeman) W.; student Rutgers Prep. Sch., Hill Sch., Pottstown, Pa.; A.B., N.Y.U., 1889; m. Nettie March, Oct. 15, 1902. Admitted to N.J. bar, Nov. 1892, and since in practice at New Brunswick, N.J. Pres. New Brunswick (N.J.) Bd. of Aldermen, 1900-05; judge, New Brunswick (N.J.) Dist. Court, 1911-26. Dir. St. Peter's Hosp., New Brunswick, N.J.; mem. New Brunswick (N.J.) Pub. Library Bd. Mem. Zeta Psi. Democrat. Presbyterian. Mason, Odd Fellow. Club: Union of New Brunswick (N.J.). Home: 43 Mine St. Office: 390 George St., New Brunswick, N.J.

WOODBRIDGE, Richard George, Jr., chem. dir.; b. Iowa City, Ia., Mar. 18, 1886; s. Rev Richard George and Anna Amelia (Rode) W.; B.S. in Chem., Mass. Inst. Tech., 1907; m. Ethel Lytle Whall, July 5, 1911; children—Richard George III, Margaretta Lytle. Research asst. in cellulose, Mass. Inst. Tech., 1907-08; research chemist and div. head smokeless powder div., Exptl. Sta., E. I. du Pont de Nemours & Co., Wilmington, Del., 1908-15, smokeless powder operating dept., Carney's Point Staff, 1915-16, div. head smokeless and black powder, Exptl. Sta., 1916-20, mgr. cellulose div. chem. dept., 1920-21, dir. Brandywine Lab., smokeless powder dept., 1921-27, chem. dir. smokeless powder dept., 1927-38, asst. chem. dir. explosives dept. since 1938. Mem. Am. Chem. Soc., Am. Inst. Chem. Engrs., Army Ordnance Assn. Republican. Episcopalian. Club: Wilmington (Del.) Country. Holder numerous patents on improvements in smokeless powder. Home: 2407 W. 17th St. Office: E.I. du Pont de Nemours & Co., Wilmington, Del.

WOODBURY, Walter E., clergyman; b. Nashua, N.H., May 7, 1886; s. Edgar Charles and Eva Jane (Wheeler) W.; A.B., Brown U., 1906, A.M., 1908; student Harvard, 1908-09; B.D., Newton Theol. Inst., Newton Centre, Mass., 1911; hon. D.D., Northern Baptist Sem., Chicago, Ill., 1938; m. Maude Alice Rideout, Aug. 2, 1911 (now dec.); children—Dorothy Maude, David Walter, Newton Edgar, Roger Fiske; m. 2d, Gladys Rose Roberts, of Boston, Aug. 5, 1930; children—James Roberts, Geraldine Eva. Ordained to ministry Baptist Ch., 1911; minister Bristol Ch., Bristol, Conn., 1911-15, Worthen Street Ch., Lowell, Mass., 1915-20, Trinity Ch., Minneapolis, 1920-23, 1st Ch., Melrose, Mass., 1924-30; dir. of promotion and field sec. Southern Calif. Baptist Conv., 1930-36; sec. of evangelism Am. Baptist Home Mission Soc., N.Y. City, since 1936. Ednl. sec. Y.M.C.A., Camp Devens, Mass., 1918. Mem. Ministers' Council of Northern Baptist Conv., Phi Beta Kappa, Phi Kappa Psi. Home: 7 Daisy Pl., Tenafly, N.J. Office: 23 E. 26th St., New York, N.Y.

WOODBURY, Wesley Kimball, lawyer; b. Sweden, Me., Feb. 21, 1855; s. Enoch W. and Sallie Ludlow (Kimball) W.; student Gould's Acad., Bethel, Me.; m. Anna Belle Belville, June 21, 1882; children—Isabella Mitchell, Robert Belville. Admitted to Schuylkill Co. bar, 1881; since in gen. practice of law; now mem. law firm Woodbury and Woodbury; formerly v.p. and dir. Schuylkill Trust Co.; now sec.-treas. and dir. Thompson Realty Co., Inc.; sec. and dir. Pardee Land Co., Inc.; legal adviser Safe Deposit Bank of Pottsville; solicitor Pottsville Community Hotel. Pres. Pottsville Free Public Library, Benevolent Assn.'s Home for Children. Clubs: Schuylkill Country (Pottsville); Wallops Island (Accomac Co., Va.). Home: 1023 Mahantongo St. Office: 408 Thompson Bldg., Pottsville, Pa.

WOODCOCK, Amos Walter Wright, lawyer; b. Salisbury, Md., Oct. 29, 1883; s. Amos Wilson and Julia Ann Harris (Wright) W.; grad. Wicomico High Sch., Salisbury, Md., 1899; B.A., St. John's Coll., Annapolis, Md., 1903; LL.B., U. of Md., 1910; M.A., Harvard, 1912; LL.D., Washington, 1932, St. John's, 1937; unmarried. Began practice at Salisbury, 1912; mem. firm Woodcock & Webb since 1914. Asst. atty. gen. of Md., 1920-22; U.S. atty., Dist. of Md., 1922-30; director of United States Bureau of Prohibition, 1930-33; apptd. special assistant to atty. gen. of U.S., Apr. 1, 1933, and continues to represent U.S. in various cases; pres. St. John's College, Annapolis, Md., 1934-37; director Salisbury National Bank. Served as captain Company I, 1st Maryland Infantry, Mexican border, 1916; capt., maj., lt. col., 115th Inf. A.E.F., World War; participated in defense Centre Sector, Haute-Alsace, Aug. 13-Sept. 25, 1918; Meuse-Argonne, Oct. 8-29; comdr. batt. in capture Rechene Hill, North of Verdun, Oct. 10; cited and promoted "for gallantry in action"; brig. gen. comdg. 58th Brigade, Md. N.G., since Dec. 1, 1936. Mem. Am. and Md. bar assns., Am. Legion (dept. comdr., 1921-22), Phi Sigma Kappa. Republican. Methodist. Clubs: Nat. Press (Washington, D.C.); Annapolitan, University (Baltimore); Naval Acad. Officers. Home: Salisbury, Md. Address: Salisbury, Md.

WOODCOCK, Floyd W.; v.p. Crescent Pub. Service Co.; officer or dir. many companies. Home: Du Pont Hotel. Office: Delaware Trust Bldg., Wilmington, Del.

WOODCOCK, William Irwin, Jr., lawyer; b. Hollidaysburg, Pa., Mar. 12, 1893; s. William Irwin and Elizabeth (Unangst) Woodcock; Ph.B., Lafayette Coll., 1916; LL.B., U. of Pa., 1921; m. Helen Ewing Campbell, Jan. 2, 1929; 1 dau., Frances Elizabeth. Admitted to Pa. bar, 1921; gen. solicitor Reading Co., 1929-36, gen. counsel since Jan. 10, 1936; gen. counsel and dir. Pa.-Reading Seashore Lines; gen. solicitor and dir. Ironton R.R. Co. Mem. Philadelphia Bar Assn., Phi Kappa Psi. Presbyterian. Club: Union League (Phila). Home: 6312 Overbrook Av. Office: 415 Reading Terminal Bldg., Philadelphia, Pa.

WOODFORD, John Wallace, business exec.; b. Centreville, Md., Feb. 1, 1891; s. William J. and Ida (Cole) W.; ed. Centreville (Md.) High Sch., Baltimore Business Coll.; m. Eva Hazel, Mar. 21, 1916. Began as stenographer, 1909; sec. and dir. Richardson & Robbins Co., packers food products, Dover, Del., since 1932; dir. Eastern Shore Pub. Service Co., Del. R.R. Co. Mayor of Dover, Del., 1924-39. Democrat. Congregationalist. Mason (33°). Address: Dover, Del.

WOODRING, Edwin Stephen, clergyman; b. Lehigh Co., Pa., Feb. 17, 1872; s. John Joseph and Mary Ann (Acker) W.; A.B., Muhlenberg Coll., Allentown, Pa., 1894, A.M., 1897, hon. D.D., 1930; pastor's course, Moody Bible Inst., Chicago, Ill., 1894-96; m. Lulu E. Koons, Oct. 13, 1896; children—Mark Thomas (dec.), Philip Wendell. Ordained to ministry U. Evang. Ch., 1896; served chs. in Ill., 1896-1907; served chs. in Pa., 1907-21; presiding elder, 1921-26; name of ch. changed to Evang. Congl. and served as Bishop for term, 1926-35; presiding elder Eastern Dist. of East Pa. Conf. of Evang. Congl. Ch. since 1935; mem. of all ch. bds. Trustee Burd and Rogers Memorial Home for the Aged, Herndon, Pa. Republican. Evang. Conglist. Ch. Home: 116 S. 15th St., Allentown, Pa.

WOODRING, Wendell Phillips, geologist; b. Reading, Pa., June 13, 1891; s. James Daniel and Margaret (Hurst) W.; A.B., Albright Coll., Myerstown, Pa., 1910; Ph.D., Johns Hopkins U., 1916; m. Josephine Jamison, Feb. 9, 1918; children—Judy Worth, Jane Hurst. Research fellow Johns Hopkins U., 1916-17; geol. explorations in Central America, 1917-18; geologist U.S. Geol. Survey, 1919-1927 and since 1930; in charge of geol. survey of Republic of Haiti, 1920-24; prof. invertebrate paleontology, Calif. Inst. Tech., 1927-30. Served with 74th Engrs., U.S.A., 1918-19. Fellow Geol. Soc. of America., A.A.A.S., Paleontological Soc.; mem. Calif. Acad. of Science, Geol. Soc. of Washington, Phi Beta Kappa, Sigma Xi. Author: Geology of Republic of Haiti, 1924; Miocene Mollusks from Bowden, Jamaica, 1925, 1928; also 2 books, Carnegie Inst., Washington, 1925, 1928; also publs. on geology and paleontology of West Indies, Central and South America, and Calif. Home: 202 Raymond St., Chevy Chase, Md. Office: U.S. Geological Survey, Washington, D.C.

WOODROE, William May, lawyer; b. Charleston, W.Va., Jan. 21, 1906; s. James David and Jane (May) W.; student Charleston grade and high schs., 1912-22; LL.B., W.Va. U., Morgantown, W.Va., 1927; m. Isabel Tomasa Clark, Dec. 21, 1929. Admitted to W.Va. bar, 1927; associate firm Coleman & Thompson, Charleston, 1927-32, MacCorkle, Clark & MacCorkle, Charleston, 1932-35; mem. Clark, Woodroe & Butts, Charleston, since 1935; dir. Virginian Mortgage Co. Mem. Am. Bar Assn., W.Va. Bar Assn., Charleston Bar Assn., Sigma Chi, Phi Delta Phi. Democrat. Episcopalian. Club: Pioneer (Charleston, W.Va.). Home: 513 Linden Rd. Office: 1400 Union Bldg., Charleston, W.Va.

WOODRUFF, Clinton Rogers, lawyer; b. Phila., Dec. 17, 1868; s. Charles H. and Rachel A. (Pierce) W.; A.B., Central High Sch., Phila., 1886; Ph.B., U. of Pa., 1889, LL.B., 1892; m. Anna F. Miller, 1890; 1 dau., Mrs. Edwin S. Dixon, Jr.; m. 2d, Florence V. Stilwell, 1921. Chairman joint com. on electoral reform in Pa.; spl. Indian commr. (with Charles J. Bonaparte), 1903-04, to investigate charges of fraud; sec. Phila. Municipal League, 1891-97, and counsel, 1897-1903; counsel Am. Acad. Polit. and Social Science; pres. Union Benevolent Assn.; chairman Phila. Com. for Active Citizenship. Mem. Pa. legislature 2 terms; author of "personal registration" amendment to Pa. Constitution; pres. Bd. Personal Registration Commrs. for Phila., 1906-16 and 1919-20; pres. Civil Service Commission, Phila., 1920-24; became spl. asst. city solicitor, 1924; now dir. of pub. welfare, City of Philadelphia. Pres. Am. Ch. Union, Christian Social Union, Churchmen's Alliance, Boys' Club of Phila. Mem. Am. Econ. Assn., Am. Polit. Science Assn., Nat. Civ. Service Reform League (council), Ednl. Club of Pa. (hon.), Am. Park and Outdoor Art Assn. (pres., 1902-04), Am. Civic Assn. (1st v.p., 1904-19; treas. 1920—), Pa. Salary Survey Com. (chmn. bd.), Union Benevolent Assn., Public Charities Assn. (pres. and mem. exec. com.). Editor Proc. of Nat. Conf. for Good City Government, 1894-1911; sec. National Municipal League, 1894-1920; honorary secretary since 1920, and editor Nat. Municipal Review. Chmn. diocesan social service com. and mem. joint commn. social service, P.E. Ch. Trustee Free Library, Phila.; trustee St. Stephen's Coll., Gen. Theol. Sem. of P.E. Ch. Author: City Government by Commission. Asso. Editor The Living Church. Editor the Nat. Municipal League Series; Municipal Encyclopædia; A New Municipal Program. Contbr. to reviews and mags. Chmn. Local Exemption Bd., 1917-18; mem. War Commn. Diocese of Pa., and of advisory com. Nat. Council Defense. Order Crown of King of Roumania, 1923. Home: 2219 Spruce St., Philadelphia, Pa.

WOODRUFF, Eugene Cyrus, prof. elec. ry. engring., Pa. State Coll. Address: Pa. State Coll., State College, Pa.

WOODRUFF, John Irwin, univ. prof.; b. Selinsgrove, Pa., Nov. 24, 1864; s. Henry and Barbara Elizabeth ((Klingler) W.; grad. Susquehanna U., 1888; A.B., Bucknell U., 1890, A.M., 1893; Litt.D., Wittenberg Coll., 1902; LL.D., Waynesburg Coll., 1921; m. Annie Margaret Moyer, 1892; children—Ralph W., Mrs. Mary Elizabeth Martin. Teacher pub. schs., 1881-83; prof. philosophy, Susquehanna U. since 1892, organized coures in Latin, English, education and philosophy and built curricula in same, acting pres., 1901-04. Mem. Pa. Ho. of Reps., 1919-22. Pres., dir. and one of organizers Snyder County Trust Co. of Selinsgrove. Republican. Lutheran. Mason. Club: Selinsgrove Rotary (charter mem.). Writer of a number of poems and sermons.. Lecturer on ednl., philos., sociol. and popular subjects. Home: 305 W. Walnut St. Address: Susquehanna University, Selinsgrove, Pa.

WOODRUFF, Robert Winship, mfr.; b. Columbus, Ga., Dec. 1889; s. Ernest and Emily (Winship) W.; prep. edn., Ga. Mil. Acad.; student Emory U., 1908-10; m. Nell Hodgson, Oct. 17, 1912. Mechanic and city salesman, Gen. Fire Extinguisher Co., Atlanta, 1910-11; purchasing agt. Atlantic Ice & Coal Corpn., 1911-13; became connected with White Motor Co., Cleveland, O., 1913, advancing to pres.; pres. The Coca-Cola Company since 1923. Dir. The Coca-Cola Co. and subsidiaries, Continental Gin Co. (Birmingham), Nat. Fgn. Trade Council (N.Y.), Homeopathic Hosp. (Wilmington), Mem. Business Adv. Council Dept. of Commerce. Trustee Emory Univ. (Atlanta), Ga. Mil. Acad. (College Park, Ga.) Martha Berry School (Rome, Ga.). Served as capt. and maj. Ordnance Dept., U.S.A., World War. Clubs: Athletic, Capital City, Piedmont Driving (Atlanta); Wilmington, Wilmington Country, Vicmead Hunt (Wilmington); Links, N.Y. Southern, Recess (N.Y.); National Golf (Augusta); Biltmore Forest (Asheville); Burning Tree (Washington); Maryland (Baltimore); Union (Cleveland). Office: 101 W. 10th St. Wilmington, Del., and 310 North Av., Atlanta, Ga.

WOODRUFF, Stanley Rogers, urologist; b. Orange, Conn., Dec. 3, 1875; s. George Edson and Sarah (Rogers) W.; Ph.G., Brooklyn Coll. of Pharmacy, 1894; M.D., Yale Univ. Med. Dept., 1897; m. Marguerite Clinton, Sept. 18, 1906. Engaged in gen. practice of medicine at Derbey, Conn., 1898, then, Bayonne, N.J., 1899-1912; practice of urology at Jersey City, N.J. since 1912; prof. urology, N.Y. Polyclinic Med. Sch. since 1938; asso. attending urologist N.Y. Post Grad. Hosp.; attending urologist Christ Hosp., Jersey City, Bayonne Hosp. Served as surgeon N.J.N.G., 1902-08. Pres. Bd. Edn., Bayonne, N.J. since 1934. Treas. and dir. Bayonne Y.M.C.A. Fellow Am. Coll. Surgeons, N.Y. Acad. of Medcine; mem. A.M. A. and County and State Med. Socs.; Am. Urol. Assn.; hon. mem. Italian Urol. Soc. Democrat. Reformed Ch. Clubs: Yale (New York; Baltusrol Golf. Author: Urographic Urology, 1932. Home: 691 Av. C, Bayonne. Office: 16 Enos Pl., Jersey City, N.J.

WOODRUFF, Wesley Ellsworth, lawyer and editor; b. Salem, Pa., June 1, 1867; s. Rev. James Oscar (D.D.) and Eliza (Townley) W.; student Norwich (N.Y.) Free Acad., 1879-81, Wyoming Sem., 1881-83; A.B., Wesleyan U., Middletown, Conn., 1884, hon. A.M., Wesleyan U., 1886; Litt.D., Susquehanna U., 1926; m. Mary C. Davis, June 7, 1905. Successively reporter, city editor, feature writer, editorial writer, Times Leader, Wilkes-Barre, Pa., now asso. editor; editor and mgr. Luzerne Legal Register since 1905; studied law and admitted to Pa. bar, 1905, and since engaged in gen. practice of law at Wilkes-Barre; served as sec. Luzerne Co. Bar Assn. since 1915; well known as music critic and reviewer; lecturer on topics English lit. and Am. history; lecturer on Gothic eccles. architecture. Mem. Civic Art Jury; dir. Little Theatre, Wilkes-Barre Symphony and Bach Festival. Mem. S.R., Pa. State Bar Assn. Wesleyan Alumni Council, Delta Kappa Epsilon. Republican. Episcopalian; del. Diocesan Conv. Diocese of Bethlehem. Clubs: Westmoreland, Wyoming Valley Country (Wilkes-Barre); Sankaty Head Golf (Nantucket, Mass.). Home: 78 West Union St. Office: 1412 Deposit Bank Bldg., Wilkes-Barre, Pa.

WOODS, Alan Churchill, ophthalmologist; b. Baltimore, Md., Aug. 20, 1889; s. Hiram and Laura (Hall) W.; prep. edn. Boys Latin Sch., Baltimore, 1900-06; A.B., Johns Hopkins, 1910, M.D., 1914; m. Ann Powel Dyrd, of Gloucester County, Va., June 19, 1917; children—Alan Churchill, Ann Byrd, Jacquelin Ambler. House officer Peter Bent Brigham Hosp., Boston, 1914-15; fellow in research medicine and asst. in ophthalmology, U. of Pa., 1915-17; instr. in ophthalmology, Johns Hopkins Med. Sch., 1919-22, asso., 1922-26, asso. prof., 1926-34, Acting prof. of ophthalmology, 1934, dir. of dept., 1937; ophthalmologist in chief, Johns Hopkins Hosp., since 1937. Served as 1st lt. Med. Corps, U.S. Army, Mexican Punitive Expdn., 1916; capt. and maj., 1917-18; with A.E.F. Mem. Am. Ophthal. Soc., Assn. Am. Immunologists, A.M.A., Phi Kappa Psi, Sigma Xi. Presbyn. Clubs: Maryland, Elkridge Hunt Hamilton Street (Baltimore); Gibson Island (Gibson Island, Md.). Author: Allergy and Immunology in Ophthalmology, 1933. Contbr. numerous articles to ophthal. jours. Home: 103 Millbrook Rd. Office: Johns Hopkins Hospital, Baltimore, Md.

WOODS, Albert Fred, dir. grad. scientific work; b. Belvidere, Ill., Dec. 25, 1866; s. Fred M. and Eliza O. (Eddy) W.; B.Sc., Univ. of Nebraska, 1890, A.M., 1892, D.Agr., 1913; LL.D., St. John's Coll., Annapolis, Md., 1922; ScD., University of Maryland, 1932; m. Bertha Gerneaux Davis, June 1, 1898; children —Charles Frederick (dec.), Albert Frederick (dec.), Mark Winton, Winton de Ruyter. Asst. botanist, Univ. of Neb., 1890-93; asst. chief and 1st asst. pathologist, Div. Vegetable Psysiology and Pathology, 1893-1900; pathologist and physiologist and asst. chief Bur. of Plant Industry, 1900-10, U.S. Dept. Agr.; dean Minn. State Agrl. Coll. and dir. of Expt. Sta., 1910-17; exec. officer Md. State Bd. of Agr. and pres. Md. State Coll. of Agr., July 1917-20; pres. University of Maryland, 1920-26; director of scientific work, U.S. Dept. Agr., 1926-34; dir. Grad. Sch. Dept. Agr. since 1926; prin. pathologist Bur. Plant Industry since July 1934. U.S. delegate International Inst. of Agr., Rome, 1905, Internat. Bot. Congress, Vienna, 1905. Gen. chmn. coms. on food production and conservation Md. Council of Defense, 1917. Pres. First Inter-Am. Conf. on Agr., Forestry and Animal Husbandry, Washington, 1930. Mem. Internat. Commn. for Intellectual Coöperation since 1930. Fellow A.A.A.S., Bot. Soc. America, Soc. Morphology and Physiology, Am. Soc. Naturalists, Am. Acad. Polit. and Social Sci., Bot. Soc. Washington, Washington Acad. Sciences; mem. Nat. Research Council (chmn. com. on fertilizers, 1917-18; chmn. dir. of State Relations, 1923-24), Am. Hort. Soc. (ex-pres.), Land Grant Colleges Assn. of U.S. (pres. 1925), Gamma Sigma Delta, Sigma Xi. Alpha Zeta; life mem. Nat. Farmers' Congress. Clubs: Cosmos, University (Washington). Wrote Plant Pathology in Ency. Americana, numerous reports and articles in publs. of Dept. of Agr. and scientific jours., etc. Home: Berwyn, Md. Address: U.S. Dept Agriculture, Washington, D.C.

WOODS, Bertha Gerneaux (Davis), writer; b. Penn Yan, N.Y.; d. Charles W. and Harriet (Winton) Davis; ed. pub. and high schs., Washington; m. Albert Fred Woods, educator, June 1, 1898; children—Charles Frederick (dec.), Albert Frederick (dec.), Mark Winton, Winton de Ruyter. Mem. League Am. Pen Women, Catholic Poetry Soc. of America. Presbyterian. Clubs: Progress, Faculty of U. of Md. Contbr. poems and short stories. Author: Verses, 1908; Verses by Three Generations (with Harriett Winton Davis and Mark Winton Woods), 1921; The Guest and Other Verse, 1926; The Patient Scientists and Other Verse, 1928; The Little Gate (poems), 1935. Awarded Near East Relief prize for Golden Rule Sunday poem published in Youth's Companion, 1925. Home: Berwyn, Maryland.

WOODS, Charles Albert, lawyer; b. Pittsburgh, Pa., Aug. 21, 1868; s. George (LL.D.) and Ellen C. (Crane) W.; A.B., Princeton U., 1890, A.M., 1893; student Harvard Law Sch., 1893; m. Martha S. Taylor, Oct. 4, 1898; children—Mary Taylor Heath, Charles A., Jr., John Gardiner. Admitted to Allegheny Co. bar, 1892; v.p., gen. counsel, dir. Edward A. Woods Co., Pittsburgh, since 1928. Solicitor Allegheny County controller, 1907-13, Sewickley (Pa.) Borough, 1896-1936, burgess, 1938-42. Mem. for Pa., Panama-Pacific Expn., 1913-14; mem. bd. law examiners, Allegheny Co., 1936-42; v.p. Allegheny Co. Rep. Exec. Com., 1911. Counsel Sewickley Valley Hosp. State Chancellor S.A.R., 1933-37; mem. Phi Beta Kappa. Presbyterian. Mason (32°). Clubs: Duquesne, Allegheny Country, Edgeworth, Harvard-Yale-Princeton (Pittsburgh). Home: 224 Thorn St., Sewickley, Pa. Office: 2415 Grant Bldg., Pittsburgh, Pa.

WOODS, Elmer B(illingfelt), lawyer; b. Reading, Pa., Aug. 29, 1886; s. Wellington G. and Emma D. (Kreider) W.; A.B., Bucknell U., Lewisburg, Pa., 1910; LL.B., Temple U. Law Sch., Phila., Pa., 1918; m. Anna L. Kline, Oct. 12, 1907; children—Wellington C., Katharine (Mrs. Charles F. Skinner), Elmer B. II. Employed as prin. high sch., Red Bank, N.J., 1910-12; supervising prin. schs., Glassboro, N. J., 1913-21; admitted to N.J. bar as atty., 1921, as counselor, 1925; engaged in gen. practice of law at Pitman, N.J. since 1933; judge common pleas ct., Gloucester Co. since 1934; solicitor for Elk, Franklin, Washington twps., Newfield Borough, Chestnut Ridge Bldg. & Loan Assn.; recorder, borough of Glassboro, N.J. Served in Ednl. Corps, U.S.A., 1919; with A.E.F. in France. Mem. exec. com. Boy Scouts of America, Gloucester-Salem Dist. Dem. State Committeeman, 1932-34. Dir. Am. Automobile Assn. of Southern N.J. Mem. Am. Bar Assn., Phi Kappa Psi. Democrat. Mason (K. T., Shriner), Jr. O.U.A.M., Odd Fellow, Maccabee. Club: Rotary of Glassboro. Address: 519 N. Broadway, Pitman, N.J.

WOODS, Eugene, banker; b. Curllsville, Pa., Feb. 11, 1891; s. George B. and Ada (Armagost) W.; student Grove City (Pa.) Coll., 1910-11, Eastman Bus. Coll., Poughkeepsie, N.Y., 1911-12; m. Marjorie Logue, Sept. 8, 1915. Asso. with Sligo (Pa.) Nat. Bank continuously since starting as asst. cashier, 1912, cashier, 1913-22, v.p., 1922-38, pres. since 1938; v.p. First Nat. Bank, Rimersburg, Pa., 1922-38, pres. since 1938; dir. First Nat. Bank, New Bethlehem, Pa., since 1936. Democrat. Methodist. Mason (32°, Shriner), Odd Fellow. Home: Sligo, Pa.

WOODS, John Mitchell, lawyer; b. New Castle, Pa., Nov. 1, 1869; s. Francis Marion and Julia M. (Junkin) W.; student Martinsburg (W.Va.) Schs., 1879-86, Pantops Acad., Charlottesville, Va., 1886-88, Washington and Jefferson College, Washington, Pa., 1888-89; B.L., Washington and Lee Univ., Lexington, Va., 1892; m. Eleanor Tabb, Oct. 16, 1901; children—Virginia Tabb (Mrs. William Ashman Palmer), John Mitchell. Admitted to W.Va. bar, 1892; partner in law practice with Col. Robert W. Monroe, Romney, W.Va., 1892-96, with J. Nelson Wisner Martinsburg, W.Va., 1896-98, with Senator Charles J. Faulkner and Stewart W. Walker, Martinsburg, 1899-1913; judge circuit court, 23d Judicial Circuit of W.Va., 1912-25; mem. firm Price, Smith & Spilman, Charleston, since 1925. Home: Brookland Court. Office: Kanawha Banking & Trust Co. Bldg., Charleston, W.Va.

WOODS, Luther Eugene, coal operator; b. York Co., Pa., Jan. 24, 1883; s. Albert and Elizabeth (Frey) W.; student Millersville State Normal Sch., Pa., 1902-03, Pa. Bus. Coll., Lancaster, Pa., 1904; m. Nettie Nora Bicking, June 21, 1910; children—Luther Eugene, Jr., Ella Elizabeth (Mrs. Hugh Smith Daniel). Employed as sec. to gen. supt., U.S. Coal & Coke Co., Gary, W.Va., 1904-15; pres. and dir. Crystal Block Coal & Coke Co. and Crystal Block Mining Co., Huntington, W.Va., since 1915; pres. Central Pocahontas Coal Co., 1915-29; pres. Am. Coal Cleaning Corpn., 1920-29; pres. Red Jacket Coal Corpn., 1937-39; vice chmn. and dir. Bituminous Coal Producers Bd. for Dist. 8 under Nat. Bituminous Coal Act. Served as mem. W.Va. Senate, 1924-32. Dir. Nat. Coal Assn. Republican. Methodist. Mason (Shriner). Club: Rotary of Welch (past pres.). Home: 438 6th Av. Office: West Virginia Bldg., Huntington, W.Va.

WOODS, Robert William, clergyman; b. Blain, Pa., May 30, 1873; s. William Wharton and Catherine Jane (Loy) W.; A.B., Gettysburg (Pa.) Coll., 1898, A.M., 1901, (hon.) D.D., 1926; B.D., Luth. Theol. Sem., 1901; m. Martha Ella Douds, June 30, 1909; children—Catherine Margaret (R.N.), Rev. Wayne Robert, Martha Louise. Ordained to ministry Luth. Ch., 1901, and pastor Luth. Ch. of the Redeemer, Pittsburgh, continuously since its founding in 1901; dean of East End Ministers, Pittsburgh; del. to World's S.S. Conv., Glasgow, Scotland, 1924, and later toured Europe; on Seminar Tour through Europe and Near East, 1930; pres. Pittsburgh Synod of Gen. Synod, 1916-17; pres. Pittsburgh-Perry Co. Peoples Assn.; pres. Homewood-Brushton Council of Chs. since 1916; pres. Union Ministerial Assn. Pittsburgh, 1920-37. Mem. bd. trustees Luth. Theol. Sem., Gettysburg, Pa.; dir. Homewood-Brushton Y.M.C.A. Republican. Lutheran. Mason (32°), Odd Fellow, K.P. Desc. from Nicholas Loy, served under Gen. Washington in Revolution, and g.g. son Michael Loy for whom Loysville (Pa.) was named. Home: 7146 Upland St., Pittsburgh, Pa.

WOODS, Roy Cleo, coll. prof.; b. Oskaloosa, Ia., Apr. 17, 1891; s. Elmer Ellsworth and Emma (Barkley) W.; A.B., Penn Coll., Oskaloosa, Ia., 1918, M.S., 1919; A.M., State Univ. of Ia., Iowa City, 1924, Ph.D., 1927; m. Florence Maxwell, Aug. 12, 1920; children—Cleo Arlene, Elmer Maxwell, Donald Roy. Engaged in teaching, high sch., Sigourney, Ia., 1919-21; supt. schs., Olds, Ia., 1921-23; supt. city schs., Nashua, Ia., 1924-27; asso. prof. edn., Marshall Coll., Huntington, W.Va., 1927-29, prof. edn. since 1929; pres. Marshall Coll. Publication Soc. Served with Am. Red Cross in France, 1918-19; awarded Medaille Commerative de la Grand Guerre (vol. clasp) and Medaille Interallie (France). Mem. N.E.A., Am. Edn. Research Assn., Nat. Soc. for Study of Edn., Nat. Soc. of Coll. Teachers of Edn., Nat. Soc. of Teachers of Ednl. Measurements, W.Va. State Edn. Assn., W.Va. Acad. of Sci., Kappa Delta Pi, Phi Delta Kappa. Republican. Presbyn. Mason. Clubs: Kiwanis (Huntington); Penn Letter (Oskaloosa, Ia.). Contbr. articles to ednl. mags. and jours. Home: 848 Ninth Av., Huntington, W.Va.

WOODS, William Johnson, pres. Pa. Glass Sand Corpn.; b. Lewistown, Pa., Dec. 11, 1888; s. Joseph Milliken and Sarah E. (Johnson) W.; A.B., Princeton U., 1911; m. Myrtle E. Sebrell, Nov. 1914; children—Margaret Sebrell, William J., Jr., Ann Witherspoon. Asso. with Pa. Glass Sand Corpn., Lewistown, Pa., continuously since 1911, successively laborer, asst. foreman, foreman, salesman, asst. gen. mgr., gen. mgr., pres. since 1927; pres. Pa. Pulverizing Co. New York Feldspar Corpn.; dir. Consolidated Feldspar Corpn. Dir. Y.M.C.A., Lewistown, Pa. Mem. Tiger Inn Club, Princeton. Republican. Presbyn. Clubs: Union League (Philadelphia); Duquesne (Pittsburgh). Home: Lewistown, Pa.

WOODSIDE, Robert E., Jr., lawyer; b. Millersburg, Pa., June 4, 1904; s. Robert E. and Ella (Neitz) W.; A.B., Dickinson Coll., Carlisle, Pa., 1926; LL.B., Dickinson Sch. of Law, 1928; m. F. Fairlee Habbart, July 11, 1931; children—William Edward, Robert James. Page in Pa. Senate, 1921 and 1923; admitted to Pa. bar, 1928, and since engaged in gen. practice of law at Harrisburg, Pa.; asso. with Paul L. Hutchison and Phillips Brooks Scott; admitted to practice before Supreme and Superior cts. and Dist. Ct. of the U.S. Served as mem. Pa. Ho. of Rep., 1932-39; majority (Rep.) floor leader, 1939. Mem. Pa. and Dauphin Co. bar assns., Phi Kappa Sigma, Tau Kappa Alpha. Republican. Evang. Ch. Mason (32°, Shriner), Ind. Order Red Men, Royal Arcanum. Home: 276 North St., Millersburg, Pa. Office: Union Trust Bldg., Harrisburg, Pa.

WOODWARD, Carl Raymond, sec. Rutgers Univ.; b. Tennent, N.J., July 20, 1890; s. William Henry and Edith (Reid) W.; B.S., Rutgers U., 1914, A.M., 1919; Ph.D., Cornell U., 1926; m. Lulu Altha Ryno, Apr. 5, 1916; children—Carl Raymond, Jr., Mildred Ryno, William VanNeste. Engaged in teaching rural schs., 1908-10, high schs., Madison, N.J., 1914-15; asso. with N.J. Agr. Expt. Sta. and Rutgers Univ. since 1915; editor and librarian, Agr. Expt. Sta., 1915-16, editor and sec., 1916-27; instr. English, Rutgers U., 1920-26, asst. prof., 1926-28, alumni assn. work, 1927-28, asst. to pres., 1928-36, dir. ednl. research, 1930-32, sec. Rutgers Univ. since 1936. Mem. N.J. State Bd. Edn. since 1936. Past pres. New Brunswick Community Chest. Mem. Agrl. History Soc. (v.p.), New Brunswick Sci. Soc., N.J. and New Brunswick hist. socs.), N.J. Health and San. Assn., Phila. Soc. for Promoting Agr., Phi Gamma Delta, Phi Beta Kappa, Phi Delta Kappa. Hon. mem. N.J. Press Assn., Future Farmers of Am. Republican. Presbyn. Mason, Grange. Clubs: Kiwanis, Rutgers (New Brunswick). Author: The Curriculum of the College of Agriculture, 1921; The Development of Agriculture in New Jersey, 1640-1880, (pub.) 1927. Co-author (with Frank App), The Farmer and His Farm, 1924. Co-author (with I. N. Waller), New Jersey's Agricultural Experiment Station, 1880-1930, (pub.) 1932. Contbr. chapters on agr. to book, New Jersey—a History, edited by I. S. Kull, 1930. Home: 253 Lawrence Av., New Brunswick, N.J.

WOODWARD, Charles William, judge; b. Jackson, Ga., Feb. 21, 1895; s. William Jefferson and Stella (Moore) W.; student U. of

Ga., Athens, 1912-13; LL.B., George Washington U. Law Sch., Washington, D.C., 1922; m. Clarine Fletchall, Aug. 25, 1917; children—Charles William, Jr., Arthur Fletchall. Admitted to Md. bar, 1923, and engaged in gen. practice of law at Rockville, Md., since 1923; judge Montgomery Co. police ct., 1928-32; apptd. asso. judge 6th jud. circuit, 1932, elected, 1934 for 15 yr. term, 1934-49. Served as sergt. inf., Ga. N.G., 1916-17; capt. inf., U.S.A., 1917-19. Dir. Rockville Boys Club. Mem. Md. State Bar Assn., Montgomery Co. Bar Assn. Democrat. Methodist. Mason. Club: Rotary of Rockville. Home: N. Van Buren St., Rockville, Md.

WOODWARD, George, M.D.; b. Wilkes-Barre, Pa., June 22, 1863; s. Stanley and Sarah (Butler) W.; A.B., Yale, 1887, Ph.B., 1888; M.D., U. of Pa., 1891; m. Gertrude Houston, Oct. 9, 1894; children—Henry Howard Houston (killed in action, World War), George, Stanley, Charles H., Gertrude Houston (deceased). Member Philadelphia Board of Health, 1897-1900; member Committee of 70; member Permanent Relief Committee; president Children's Aid Soc., Bur. Municipal Research; trustee Chestnut Hill Acad. (sec., treas.). Mem. Pa. State Senate, 1918-38. Episcopalian. Republican. Clubs: University, City. Mem. Phila. Art Alliance (v.pres.), Art Alliance of America (v.p.), Yale Alumni Assn. (ex-pres.). Home: Mermaid, cor. McCallum St. Office: Girard Trust Bldg., Phila., Pa.

WOODWARD, Graham Cox, lawyer; b. Washington, D.C., Sept. 6, 1880; s. Dr. Joseph Janvier and Blanche (Wendell) W.; student Central High School, Washington, D.C., 1895-96, Northwestern Acad., Evanston, Ill., 1896-97, Germantown Acad., Phila., 1897-98; B.S., U. of Pa., 1902, LL.B., 1904; m. Alice Weber, Nov. 24, 1909; children—Mary Wendell, Elizabeth Cox, Elise Weber (Mrs. Anthony Cuthbert Hopkins). Admitted to Pa. bar, 1904; asso. in law office of John G. Johnson, Phila., 1902-07; mng. clerk Read & Pettit, 1907-11; engaged in practice of law alone at Phila. since 1911; dep. mercantile appraiser City of Phila., 1936-37; atty. for city treas., 1935-36. Candidate for justice of Supreme Court of Pa., 1931. Served as mem. local draft bd., Phila., during World War. Mem. representative com. Phila. Yearly Meeting of Religious Soc. of Friends since 1936; mem. com. of Phila. Quarterly Meeting's Boarding Home for Friends since 1937. Mem. Bar Assn. of Phila. Republican. Soc. of Friends. Author: Office and Duties of Coroners in Pennsylvania (received Peter Stephen Duponceau prize of Law Acad. of Phila., 1911; prize has not been awarded since and awarded only 7 times since 1783); Pennsylvania Law and Procedure in Replevin, 1929; Motions and Rules in Pennsylvania with Forms, 1934; contbr. many articles to legal mags., chapters in legal textbooks, etc. Home: 1304 Pine St. Office: Land Title Bldg., Philadelphia, Pa.

WOODWARD, Herbert P(reston), geologist; b. Batavia, N.Y., Aug. 13, 1899; s. Herbert P. and Bertha Lorraine (Johnson) W.; A.B., U. of Rochester, 1921; A.M., Columbia U., 1926, Ph.D., same, 1927; 1 dau., Faith Lorraine. Instr. of geography, Columbia U., 1924-28; instr. of geology, Barnard Coll., 1927, Hunter Coll., 1928; prof. pre-legal dept., N.J. Law Sch., 1928-32, Dana Coll., Newark, 1932-35; prof. geology and dir. division of natural science, U. of Newark, N.J., since 1935; field expert in geology, N.Y. State Mus., 1920; asst. in geol. Am. Mus. National History, 1925; field geologist, Va. Geol. Survey, since 1926; geologist, W.Va. Geol. Survey since 1937. Contbr. to various geol. publs. Served in S.A.T.C., 1918. Fellow A.A.A.S., Geol. Soc. of America. Mem. Am. Assn. Univ. Profs., Sigma Xi. Republican. Home: 15 Summit St., East Orange, N.J.

WOODWARD, Thompson Elwyn, dairy husbandman; b. Brunswick, Mo., Jan. 10, 1884; s. Joseph and Agnes (Smutz) W.; B.S., U. of Mo., Columbia, Mo., 1907, M.S., 1911; m. Ethel Cora Chappel, Apr. 10, 1915; children—Elwyn Chappel, Miriam, Albert Davis. Employed as dairyman, U.S. Dept. Agr., Hammond, La., 1907-08; asst. prof. in charge dairy dept., Utah Agrl. Coll., Logan, Utah, 1908-10; dairy husbandman, U.S. Dept. Agr. since 1911, sr. dairy husbandman, Bur. Dairy Industry, Beltsville, Md., since 1928. Mem. A.A.A.S., Am. Soc. of Animal Production, Am. Dairy Sci. Assn., Sigma Xi. Home: 2 Pine St., Hyattsville, Md.

WOODY, Walter Thomas, prof. history of education; b. Thorntown, Ind., Nov. 3, 1891; s. Mahlon and Matilda (Shafer) W.; A.B., Ind. U., 1913; A.M., Columbia, 1916, Ph.D., 1918; m. Wilhelmine A. Lawton, June 12, 1920; children—Elinore Marie, Mary Cranston. Teacher of German, high sch., Warsaw, Ind., 1913-15; asst. in history of edn., Columbia, 1916-17; asst. prof. history of edn., U. of Pa., 1919-24, prof. since 1924; prof. history of edn., U. of Calif., summers, 1923, 29, 33, U. of Ill., summers, 1938, 39; Guggenheim fellowship in ednl. research, 1929-30; lecturer on edn., Swarthmore College, 1931-32, 1935-36 and at Johns Hopkins Univ., 1933-34. Sec. Internat. Com. Y.M.C.A., in charge relief work in Russia and prison camps in France, 1917-19. Mem. N.E.A., A.A.A.S., Am. Hist. Assn., Nat. Soc. Coll. Teachers of Edn., Am. Assn. Univ. Profs., National Society for Study of Education, American Geog. Society of N.Y., Am. Ethmol. Society, Friends' Historical Society, Phi Delta Kappa, Kappa Phi Kappa. Quaker. Author: Early Quaker Education in Pennsylvania, 1920; Fürstenschulen in Germany After the Reformation, 1920; Quaker Education in the Colony and State of New Jersey, 1923; History of Women's Education in the United States, 1929; Educational Views of Benjamin Franklin, 1931; New Minds, New Men—The Emergence of the Soviet Citizen, 1932. Contbr. to Dictionary of Am. Biography, Ednl. Outlook, Jour. Ednl. Research, etc. Home: 35 Kent Rd., Upper Darby, Pa.

WOODYARD, Henry Chapman, Jr., newspaper pub.; b. Spencer, W.Va., June 6, 1899; s. Henry Chapman and Emma (Douglas) W.; student Davis & Elkins Coll., Elkins, W.Va., 1913-17, W.Va. Univ., Morgantown, 1917-21; m. Ida Moore, Nov. 1922; children—Lois, Emma D., Jane. Engaged as newspaper pub. at Spencer, W.Va., since 1925; pres. Woodyard Publications, Spencer, W.Va., since 1937; sec. and treas. Woodyard Publications of Del., Newark, Del., since 1936; treas. Woodyard Associates, 247 Park Av., N.Y. City, since 1939; treas. New Trojan Gas Co., Spencer, W.Va., since 1938; dir. Calhoun Oil & Gas Co., Spencer, W.Va.; treas. Fayette Newspapers, Fayetteville, W.Va., since 1937; treas. Tyler Star News, Sistersville, W.Va., since 1938; treas. Boone Natural Gas Co. since 1939. Republican. Presbyterian. Mason. Address: Spencer, W.Va.

WOODYARD, William, newspaper pub.; b. Spencer, W.Va., Sept. 13, 1894; s. Henry Chapman and Emma (Douglas) W.; student Nazareth Hall Mil. Acad., Nazareth, Pa., 1909-11, W. Va. Univ., Morgantown, 1912-16; m. Frances Huddleston, Nov. 22, 1926; 1 son, William Henry. Employed as bus. mgr. Times-Record, Spencer, W.Va., 1920-23; v.p. Woodyard Publs. Inc., Spencer, W.Va., since 1929; pres. Roane County Bank, Spencer, W.Va., since 1934. Served as 1st lt. Ord. Res. Corps, to capt. finance dept. U.S.A., 1917-19. Mem. W.Va. Ho. of Dels., 1926-28; mem. W.Va. Senate, 1929-33. Mem. Phi Kappa Psi. Republican. Presbyn. Mason. Elk. Home: Ravenswood Road. Office: 101 Record St., Spencer, W.Va.

WOOFTER, Emory Judson, clergyman, coll. pres.; b. Troy, W.Va., Apr. 25, 1867; s. Calvin and Susan (Vannoy) W.; student Transylvania U., Lexington, Ky., 1887-89; Th.G., Southern Baptist Theol. Sem., Louisville, Ky., 1892; hon. D.D., Salem Coll., Salem, W.Va., 1921; m. Alice Gay Bush, July 18, 1905; children—Yvone Mildred, Mary Bush (Mrs. Key Dickinson), Susan Madolin (Mrs. Samuel Kistler). Ordained to ministry Bapt. Ch., 1893; pastor, Glenville, W.Va., 1893-1894; Troy and asso. chs., Troy, W.Va., 1895-1903, Harrisville and Simpson, W.Va., 1903-07, Salem, W.Va., 1907-37; instr. Christian psychology, Salem Coll., 1930-37; pres. Alderson-Broaddus Coll., Philippi, W.Va., since 1938; exec. sec. and trustee W.Va. Bapt. Edn. Soc. since 1921. Served as dir. publicity and active as salesman govt. bonds during World War. Baptist. Mason (K.T.), Odd Fellow. Club: Kiwanis of Salem. Contbr. many articles and tracts to religious jours. Home: 1802 19th St., Parkersburg, W.Va.

WOOLERY, William Kirk, coll. prof.; b. Bethany, W.Va., July 20, 1888; s. William Henry and Linnie (Kirk) W.; A.B., Bethany Coll., Bethany, W.Va., 1908; A.M., U. of Calif., Berkeley, 1915; Ph.D., Johns Hopkins, 1926; m. Edna Welling, June 17, 1927; children—Nancy Elizabeth, Lucretia Ann, Margaret Ellen, Wilson Kirk. Engaged as prin. high sch., Flushing, O., 1909-10; instr. State Teachers Coll. Athens, W.Va., 1910-12; instr. high sch., Benicia, Calif., 1912-15, Palo Alto, Calif., 1916-19; asst. prof. of history, Bethany (W. Va.) Coll., 1921-25, prof., 1925-29, dean, 1930-36, provost since 1936. Served as mem. council town of Bethany, W.Va., 1924-37. Mem. Am. Hist. Assn., Am. Polit. Sci. Assn., Southern Hist. Soc., Upper Ohio Valley Hist. Soc. (v.p.), Beta Theta Pi, Pi Gamma Mu. Democrat. Ch. Disciples of Christ. Mason. Home: Bethany, W.Va.

WOOLEVER, Harry, retired cement mfr.; b. Allentown, Pa., Dec. 26, 1862; s. Adam and Ella Ann (Saylor) W.; ed. Muhlenberg Coll. 1881-83, Lehigh U. Prep. Sch., 1879-80; m. Eliza May Hartman, Jan. 17, 1884 (dec.); children—Harry A. (dec.), C.A. (dec.), May E.; m. 2d, Nellie Henderson Weaver, Feb. 7, 1900; children—Bertha Louise (Mrs. Richard H. Shuford), Harry A., Charles Weaver. Began as employee morning newspaper in Allentown, Pa., 1876; asso. with Coplay Cement Co. and was pres. of same; dir. Coplay Cement Mfg. Co. Mem. Pa. Soc., Phi Gamma Delta. Republican. Lutheran. Mason. Home: 1009 S. 49th St., Philadelphia, Pa.; (summer) 337 Wesley Av., Ocean City, N.J.

WOOLLEY, Edward Mott, author; b. Milwaukee, Feb. 25, 1867; s. James T. and Mary A. (Shearman) W.; grad. high sch., Homer, Mich., 1883; m. Milwaukee, Anna Lazelle Thayer, Dec. 20, 1898; children—Catherine Lazelle, Marion. Engaged in mercantile business, 1883-93; entered newspaper and lit. work, 1893; reporter San Francisco Examiner, 1894; reporter and writer Chicago Herald and Times-Herald, 1895-1901; writer, lit. editor and editorial writer, Chicago Journal, 1901-04; editor Fuel, Chicago, 1905; editorial staff Chicago Post, 1906, System Mag., Chicago, 1907-09, since spl. writer for Saturday Evening Post, Collier's Weekly, McClure's Mag., Scribner's Magazine, World's Work, Everybody's, American, Good Housekeeping and other mags.; spl. writer for newspaper syndicates. Noms de plume, "Robert Bracefield," "Richard Bracefield." Mem. Authors' League America. Club: City (New York). Author: Pluck Will Win, 1903; Roland of Altenburg, 1904; A Minister of War, 1906; The Art of Selling Goods, 1907; The Castle of Gloom, 1908; Miss Huntington, 1908; The Real America in Romance (3 vols.), 1909-10; The Winning Ten, 1910; Donald Kirk Series, 1912-13; The Junior Partner, 1912; Addison Broadhurst, Master Merchant, 1913; The Cub Reporter, 1913; Free-Lancing for Forty Magazines, 1927; Writing for Real Money, 1928; The Curve, 1929; 100 Paths To a Living, 1931; also Romances of Small Business (500), serially in newspapers, 1923-25. Spl. research in occupational fields for syndicates; spl. war work for Com. Pub. on Information, etc. Home: 71 Park Av., Passaic, N.J.

WOOLLEY, Herbert Codey, M.D.; b. Monmouth Co., N.J., Aug. 27, 1881; s. Levi L. and Nellie (Codey) W.; grad. high sch., Asbury Park, N.J., 1896; Temple U. 1900; M.D., Jefferson Med. Coll., Phila., 1904; m. Agnes Higinbotham, Aug. 24, 1908; children—Richard George, Herbert Codey; m. 2d, Henrietta Croft Beman, of Va., Apr. 3, 1937. Began practice at Phila., 1909; clin. dir. St. Elizabeth's Hosp., 1924-29, asst. supt., 1929-37; supt. Pennhurst State School, 1937-38; supt. Phila. State Hosp. since Oct. 1938. Commd. 1st lieutenant M.R.C., U.S.A., 1908, and promoted through grades to col.; served as post surgeon Ft. Davis, Alaska, and Ft. Sill, Okla.; federal examiner State of Okla., June 20-Oct. 1, 1917; training officer personnel 35th Div. (Med. Dept.); organized and comd. 110th Sanitary Train; comd. 1st Sanitary Train, 1st Div., A.E.F.; mil. comdr. Hilschid and Syne areas in occupied Germany; comdg. officer 364th Med. Regt.; col. U.S. Army Reserve. Fellow Am. Psychiatric Assn.; mem. Washington Soc. Mental and Nervous Diseases (ex-pres.), U.S. Power Squadron, Am. Legion (past comdr.), Jefferson Med. Coll. Alumni Assn. (ex-pres.), Chester Co. and Pa. State Med. socs., Am. Med. Assn., Am. Assn. on Mental Deficiency, Soc. of First Division, U.S.A., Phi Beta Pi. Republican. Methodist. Clubs: Army and Navy, Army-Navy Country, Internat. Med. Club, Washington Yacht. Address: Philadelphia State Hospital, Philadelphia, Pa.

WOOLLEY, Lawrence Foss, physician; b. Ann Arbor, Mich., Sept. 29, 1895; s. Jed F. and Agnes (Forsyth) W.; A.B., U. of Utah., Salt Lake City, Utah, 1922; M.D., Johns Hopkins Med. Sch., 1926; m. Fannie Christiana Haines, M.D., Dec. 24, 1924; children—Barbara, Ruth, John Lawrence, Anna Christine. Interne U. of Md. Hosp., Baltimore, 1926-27; asst. physician, resident psychiatrist, Colo. Psychopathic Hosp., Denver, Colo., 1927-30; instr. and asst. prof. psychiatry, U. of Colo. Med. Sch., 1927-30; psychiatrist, Child Guidance Clinic, Inc., Cleveland, O., 1930-32; clin. dir. Sheppard and Enoch Pratt Hosp., Towson, Md., since 1932; asst. prof. then asso. prof. psychiatry, U. of Md. since 1935. Served as pvt. to sergt. 1st class, Med. Corps, U.S.A., 1917-19. Fellow A.M.A., Am. Psychiatric Assn.; asso. Am. Coll. Phys.; mem. A.A.A.S., Am. Orthopsychiatric Assn., Central Neuropsychiatric Assn., Southern Med. Assn., Med. and Chirurg. Faculty of Md., Baltimore City, Md. Soc., Phi Beta Kappa, Sigma Xi, Alpha Omega Alpha, Theta Kappa Psi. Certified by Nat. Bd. Neurology and Psychiatry. Democrat. Home: 6 Dixie Drive, Towson, Md.

WOOLLEY, Victor Baynard, judge; b. Wilmington, Del., Mar. 29, 1867; s. Augustus S. and Sarah (Baynard) W.; B.S., Delaware Coll., 1885, LL.D., 1913; student Harvard Law Sch., 1889-90; m. Mildred Clark, July 28, 1904; children—Victor Clark (dec.), John Augustus. Admitted to Del. bar, 1880; prothonotary, Superior Court, New Castle Co., Del., 1895-1901; asso. judge, Supreme Court of Del., 1909-14; judge U.S. Circuit Court of Appeals for the 3d Circuit, by appmt. of President Wilson, since Aug. 12, 1914. Lecturer on Delaware practice, U. of Pa. Law Dept. Trustee Univ. of Del.; mem. Soc. of Colonial Wars. Democrat. Episcopalian. Author: Woolley on Delaware Practice, 1906. Clubs: Wilmington, Wilmington Country. Home: 1309 Rodney St., Wilmington, Del.

WOOLMAN, Henry Newbold; b. Philadelphia, Pa.,Pa., Sept. 3, 1875; s. Edward W. and Rebecca S. (Townsend) W.; student William Penn Charter Sch., 1886-92; B.S., U. of Pa., 1896, hon. Sc.D., 1930; m. Mary S. C. Boude, Nov. 19, 1902; 1 son, Henry Newbold. Clerk in father's milk business, 1896; joined Supplee Wills Jones Milk Co. (now merged with Nat. Dairy Products Corpn.), 1919, now sec. and vice-pres.; pres. Mantua Bldg. Assn. No. 2; sec. Powelton Bldg. Assn.; dir. Nat. Dairy Products Corpn., Edw. W. Woolman Bldg. & Loan Assn. Mem. Dairy Industry Com., Washington. Dir. of exhibits Sesqui-Centennial Commn. of State of Pa., 1926. Life trustee, mem. exec. bd., chmn. Valley Forge Bd., U. of Pa.; overseer William Penn Charter Sch.; nat. dir. Am. Youth Hostel Assn.; dir. Wharton Sch. Alumni Soc. of U. of Pa. (pres. 1927-35), Gen. Alumni Soc. of U. of Pa. (president 1926-30); mem. Hist. Soc. of Pa., Friends Hist. Soc., Am. Acad. Polit. and Social Science, Phila. Milk Exchange (pres. 1914), Internat. Assn. of Milk Dealers, Phila. Chamber of Commerce, Psi Upsilon. Republican. Mem. Soc. of Friends. Clubs: Union League, University, Penn Athletic, Horse-Shoe Trail (pres.). Home: 132 St. George's Rd., Ardmore, Pa. Office: 1523 N. 26th St., Philadelphia, Pa.

WOOLSEY, Lester Hood, lawyer; b. Stone Ridge, N.Y., Aug. 3, 1877; s. Luther and Rachel (Hood) W.; A.B., magna cum laude, Harvard, 1901; LL.B., George Washington, 1908. grad. work, Harvard and George Washington; m. Grace Hamblin, June 4, 1903; children—Ruth, Beth. Asst. geologist U.S. Geol. Survey, 1902-07, examining and reporting on mining dists. east of Sierra Nev. Mts.; examiner of claims, U.S. Land Office, 1908-09; instr. law, Washington Coll. Law, 1909-10, George Washington U. Law Sch., 1910-11; sec. on behalf of U.S. Internat. Fur Seal Conf., Washington, D. C., 1911; atty. Dept. of State, Washington, D.C., 1909-13; asst. solicitor, same, in office of the counselor, 1913-15, attached to office of sec. of state, 1915-16; law adviser Dept. of State, 1916-17; solicitor for Dept. of State, 1917-20; technical del. U.S. Peace Conf., Paris, 1919; practicing law in partnership with Hon. Robert Lansing, 1920-28, since then, Lansing & Woolsey, internat. law; internat. law expert for Chinese Government in Conf. on Limitation of Armament, including Pacific and Far Eastern questions; prof. internat. law, Am. Univ., 1921; counsel for Chile in Tacna-Arica arbitration before President of U.S., 1923-24. Mem. Bar of D.C. and Supreme Court of United States; mem. editorial board & treas. Am. Soc. Internat. Law; mem. editorial bd. of "World Affairs"; legal adviser to Pan-American Union, Washington, D. C.; special counsel of U.S., U.S.-Mexican General Claims Commn., 1936. Decorated Comdr. Order White Elephant, by King of Siam, for services on treaty between U.S. and Siam, 1920; Order of Chia-Ho (golden grain), China, for services in connection with Conf. on Limitation of Armament, 1922; Officer of the Order of Al Merito, Chile, 1936. Clubs: Cosmos, Harvard. Author of numerous articles and editorials on internat. law, also various geol. repts., pub. by U.S. Geol. Survey. Home: 7007 Brookville Rd., Chevy Chase, Md. Office: 726 Jackson Pl., Washington, D.C.

WOOLWORTH, Charles Sumner, merchant; b. Rodman, N.Y., Aug. 1, 1856; s. John Hubbell and Fanny (McBrier) W.; ed. pub. schs.; m. Anna E. Ryals, June 2, 1886 (died 1913); children—Ethel W., Fred E., Richard W. Began in five and ten cent stores on own account, at Scranton, P., 1880, later opening many branch stores in various parts of the country; business merged, 1912, with other concerns forming the F. W. Woolworth Co., of which is now chmn. bd.; v.p. U.S. Lumber Co., Miss. Central R.R. Co.; dir. First Nat. Bank (Scranton), Internat. Textbook Co., Scranton-Lackawanna Trust Co. Trustee Syracuse U., Wyoming (Pa.) Seminary, Scranton Y.M.C.A., Scranton Y.W.C.A., Mercy Hosp. Mem. advisory bd. George F. Geisinger Memorial Hosp., Danville, Pa., Johnson's Manual Training Sch.; dir. Internat. Corr. Schs. Republican. Methodist. Clubs: Scranton, Country (Scranton); Everglades, Gulf Stream (Palm Beach). Home: 520 Jefferson Av. Office: Scranton Life Bldg., Scranton, Pa.

WOOLWORTH, Chester McNutt, pres. Animal Trap Co. of America; b. Niagara Falls, N.Y., May 21, 1893; s. Felix M. and Morelli (Kingsley) W.; grad. Dartmouth Coll., 1916; m. May Gorton, Jan. 17, 1924; children—Sylvia Gorton, Richard. Employed in office Oneida Community, Ltd., Chicago, Ill., 1919-20, dist. sales mgr. at Phila., Pa., 1920-24; sec.-treas. Animal Trap Co. of America, mfrs. steel animal and rodent traps, hand garden tools, duck decoys and gunstocks, 1924-27, pres. since 1927. Served as provisional 1st lieut., U.S.A., World War. Republican. Episcopalian. Clubs: Hamilton, Country (Lancaster). Home: 1 Jackson Drive, Lancaster, Pa. Office: N. Locust St., Lititz, Pa.

WOOSTER, Harold Abbott, librarian; b. Northfield, Conn., Sept. 29, 1892; s. Levi S. and Louise A. (Morse) W.; A.B., Wesleyan U., 1914, A.M., 1915; m. Violet Scriver, Sept. 15, 1917; children—Harold A., Jr., Warren Scriver, Margaret Louise. Librarian Atheneum (Free Pub. Library), Westfield, Mass., 1919-25; librarian Pub. Library, Brockton, Mass., 1925-30; librarian Scranton Pub. Library, Scranton, Pa., since 1930. Served in U.S.N.R.F., 1917-18, ensign, 1918; library war service, A.L.A., 1919. Mem. Pa. Library Assn. (pres. 1937). Presbyterian. Contbr. articles to library jours. Home: 536 Wheeler Av., Scranton, Pa. Office: Scranton Public Library, Scranton, Pa.

WORDEN, Albert W.; b. Asbury Park, N.J., Sept. 18, 1891; s. Albert W. and Annie C. (Woodward) W.; ed. pub. schs., Red Bank, N.J., 1898-1906, Renouard Training Sch. for Embalmers, New York, N.Y., 1917; m. Sara E. Fay, Dec. 12, 1912; children—Harry C. F., James A., Robert F., Christa Joyce. Employed in mech. and reportorial depts. newspapers, 1906-16; engaged as funeral dir. and sr. mem. firm Worden Funeral Home, Red Bank, N.J., since 1916; vice-pres. Red Bank Bldg. & Loan Assn.; dir. Merchants Trust Co. Mem. Bd. Edn. Red Bank, 6 yrs. Coroner Monmouth Co., 1918-21. Dir. Red Bank Y.M.C.A. Mem. Am. Inst. Funeral Dirs., Nat. Funeral Dirs. Assn., N.J. State Funeral Dirs. Assn (past v.p.). Democrat. Presbyn. Mason (32°), Elk, Moose, I.O.O.F., K.P., Jr. O.U.A.M. Clubs: Lions (past pres.), Swimming River Golf, Monmouth Boat (dir.), North Shrewsbury Ice Yacht and Boat. Home: 66 E. Front St., Red Bank, N.J. Office: 60 E. Front St., Red Bank, N.J.

WORDEN, Charles Beatty, occupational medical work; b. Steubenville, O., Apr. 26, 1874; s. James Avery (D.D.) and Mary Reeder (Hendrickson) W.; A.B., Princeton, 1894; M.D., Med. Sch., Univ. of Pa., 1898; univs. of Berlin and Vienna 1 yr.; m. Ora Otis Williams, Dec. 18, 1907; children—Ora Otis, James Avery II, Philip Monroe. Began practice at Philadelphia, 1898; resident physician Presbyterian Hosp., 1899-1900; asst. surgeon orthopædic dept., Univ. Hosp., and asso. prof. diseases of stomach, Polyclinic Hosp., 1900-07; mem. staff Phipps Inst., 1905-07; specialized in occupational med. work; med. dir. John Wanamaker Stores, New York and Phila., since 1906. Capt. U.S. Med. Corps, 1918-19. Fellow A.M.A., Coll. Physicians, Phila.; mem. Phila. Co. Med. Soc., Loyal Legion. Republican. Presbyn. Clubs: Princeton (Phila.); Nassau (Princeton, N.J.). Home: Rosedale Rd., Princeton, N.J. Office: 13th and Market Sts., Philadelphia, Pa.

WORDEN, Edward Chauncey, I, chemist; b. at Ypsilanti, Mich., April 17, 1875; s. Chauncey Perry and Elvira Mabel (Brainerd) W.; Ph.C., U. of Mich., 1896; B.S., New York U., 1907, M.A., 1909, D.Sc., 1921; m. Anna Wilhelmina Breitsman, Sept. 25, 1901; children—Marian Alice (Mrs. De Witt Bell), Edward Chauncey II, Anna Lois, Waite Warren, Loanna. Served as chemist at N.Y. Agrl. Expt. Station, Geneva, 1896-97; mem. firm of Crane & Worden, chemists, New York, 1899-1900; chemist Celluloid Zapon Co., Springfield, N.J., 1900-02, Clark Thread Co., Newark, 1902-14, Worden Lab., Milburn, N.J., 1914—. Chmn. com. on airplane coatings, Nat. Research Council, 1916; edition Report 10382 and 13228 (5000 pages) "Aviation Chemistry, 1914-18," prepared for U.S. Army Air Service; chief of airplane wing coating sect., Bur. of Aeronautics, Washington, D.C., 1916-18, crossing Atlantic 14 times for U.S. Govt. Fellow Chem. Soc., London, and French Acad., Paris; mem. Am. Chem. Soc.; Soc. Chem. Industry, Chem. Soc., France. Mason (32°, K.T., Shriner). Clubs: Chemists' (New York); Racquet (Washington, D.C.). Author: Nitrocellulose Industry, 2 vols., 1911; Cellulose Acetate, 1915; Technology of Cellulose Esters, Vol. 1 (3,709 pages), 1921; Chemical Patents Index (United States), 1915-1924, 5 vols. 1927; (with Edward C. Worden, II) Technical Dict. of Chemistry (containing over 400,000 separate headings in alphabetical arrangement). Asso. editor Kunstoffe, also of La Coutchoue et la Guttapercha. Contbr. Journal Soc. Chem. Industry. Home: Milburn, N.J.; Laboratory and Library, Wyoming, N.J.*

WORK, William Roth, prof. elec. engineering; b. Steelton, Pa., May 4, 1881; s. Joseph Alexander and Alice Anna (Lupfer) W.; student Wittenberg Acad., Springfield, O., 1895-98; A.B., Wittenberg Coll., 1902, hon. D.Sc., 1920; M.E. in E.E., Ohio State U., 1905; m. Ola Frank

Kautzman, June 27, 1907; children—Alice Myers, William Worthington. With Carnegie Inst. Tech. since 1906, head of dept. elec. engring. since 1921. Mem. Com. on Edn. and Special Training, General Staff, War Dept., 1918. Fellow A.A.A.S.; mem. Am. Inst. Elec. Engrs., Engrs. Soc. of Western Pa., Soc. for Promotion of Engring. Edn., Am. Assn. Univ. Profs., Beta Theta Pi, Sigma Xi, Tau Beta Pi, Eta Kappa Nu. Republican. Presbyn. Home: 5702 Beacon St., Pittsburgh, Pa.

WORKER, Joseph Garfield, mech. engr.; b. Stewart, Ia., Aug. 16, 1881; s. Joseph James and Georgia Belle (Swingle) W.; M.E., U. of Ill., Urbana, Ill., 1904; m. Maybelle Edna Sampson, May 20, 1909; 1 dau., Josephine Georgine (Mrs. Kenneth Fungston Thomas). In employ Deere & Company, Moline, Ill., 1904-05, Westinghouse Machine Company, 1905-07, Calumet Steel Co., Chicago Heights, Ill., 1907-08, Westinghouse Machine Co., 1908-15, Westinghouse Electric & Mfg. Co., East Pittsburgh, Pa., 1915-23; with Am. Engring. Co., Phila., since 1923, asst. to pres., 1923-27, dir. and gen. sales mgr., 1927-39; pres. and dir. Affiliated Engring. Corpns., Ltd., Montreal, Can., 1927-39. Mem. Am. Soc. M. E., Stoker Mfrs. Assn. (past pres.), Franklin Inst., Electric Hoist Mfrs. Assn. (past chmn.), Delta Upsilon. Republican. Christian. Clubs: Manufacturers Golf and Country (Phila.); Engineers (New York). Co-Author (with Thos. A. Peebles): Mechanical Stokers, 1922. Address: 305 Summit Av., Jenkintown, Pa.

WORTH, Charles Lester, supervising prin. schs.; b. Asbury Park, N.J., June 18, 1909; s. Harry and Viola (Van Middlesworth) W.; diploma Trenton Teachers Coll., Trenton, N.J., 1930; B.S., Rutgers U., New Brunswick, N.J., 1935; grad. study N.Y. Univ., 1935-39; m. Lois Windeler, June 18, 1928; children—Lois Joy, Charles John, David Ward. Teaching prin., Bedminster, N.J., 1930-31, New Bedford, N.J., 1931-32; prin., Avon, N.J., 1932-37; supervising prin., Point Pleasant Borough, N.J., 1937-38; supervising prin. schs., Lambertville, N.J., since 1938. Dir. City Library Bd., Supervisors Round Table, Credit Union, all of Lambertville, N.J. Mem. N.J. Edn. Assn., Nat. Sch. Adminstrs. Assn., N.E.A. Methodist. Club: Rotary. Home: Belmont Apts., Church St., Lambertville, N.J.

WORTHING, Archie Garfield, physicist; b. LeRoy, Wis., Feb. 6, 1881; s. Arthur James and Loella (McKnight) W.; grad. State Normal Sch., Oshkosh, Wis., 1900; B.A., U. of Wis., 1904; State U. of Ia., 1908-09; Ph.D., U. of Mich., 1911; m. Exie Lillian Witherbee, June 23, 1905; children—Marion Witherbee, Helen Witherbee, Robert Witherbee. Teacher grammar sch., Brandon, Wis., 1900-01; asst. in physics, U. of Wis., 1904-06; acting instr. physics, State U. of Ia., 1906-09; asso. physicist Physical Lab. of Nat. Lamp Works, Cleveland, O., 1910-14; physicist Nela Research Labs., Cleveland, 1914-25; head of physics dept. U. of Pittsburgh, 1925-37, prof. physics since 1925. Fellow Am. Phys. Soc.; mem. Am. Optical Soc., Am. Assn. Physics Teachers, Phi Beta Kappa, Sigma Xi. Unitarian. Contbr. to scientific and tech. jours. Determined the true temperature scale of tungsten and other metals and their emissivities at incandescent temperatures. Home: 1372 N. Sheridan Av., Pittsburgh, Pa.

WORTHINGTON, Arthur Whittemore, business exec.; b. Steubenville, O., Apr. 26, 1885; s. Henry Daniel and Mary Florence (Hill) W.; B.S., Rose Poly. Inst., Terre Haute, Ind., 1906, C.E., 1913; unmarried. Asst. on engring. corps, later engr. in charge construction Pa. R.R., 1906-15; erecting engr. Koppers Co., 1915-17; consulting engr., Cleveland, O., 1920; with Pittsburgh Limestone Corpn. (subsidiary of U.S. Steel Corpn.) since 1921, successively as asst. to gen. mgr., gen. mgr., and v.p., gen. mgr. and dir. since 1932. Served as lt., later capt., Corps Engrs., U.S. Army, with A.E.F. (chief engr. maintenance of way, Am. Rys., in advance sect.), 1917-19. Mem. Am. Inst. Mining and Metall. Engrs., Rose Poly. Inst. Alumni Assn. (past v.p.). Republican. Congregationalist. Clubs: University (past pres.), Traffic (Pittsburgh). Home: University Club. Office: 512 Frick Bldg., Pittsburgh, Pa.

WORTHINGTON, Charles Campbell, mech. engr., retired; b. Brooklyn, N.Y., Jan. 6, 1854; s. Henry Rossiter and Sara (Newton) W.; gen. engring. course, Columbia; m. Julia A. Hedden, 1879 (dec.); children—Julia Hedden (Mrs. Edmund Monroe Sawtelle), Henry Rossiter (dec.), Chas. Campbell (dec.), Edward Hedden, Reginald Stuart; m. 2d, Maude C. Rice, of N.Y. City, June 7, 1906; children—Sara Newton (Mrs. Robert Lord Holt), Alice Rice (Mrs. Bishop Perkins Hill). Owner and pres. Henry R. Worthington Corpn., mfrs. steam pumps, 1875-1900 (retired); consultant and chmn. of bd. Worthington Mower Co., Stroudsburg, Pa. Inventor of Worthington high duty water works engine and hydraulic machinery now in use in principal countries of the world. Invented, 1913, and introduced the Worthington gang lawn mower, in general use on golf courses. Mem. Am. Soc. M.E. (ex-mem. council). Republican. Episcopalian. Clubs: Engineers', New York Athletic; Racquet and Tennis, Chevy Chase (Washington, D.C.). Home: Shawnee-on-Delaware, Pa.

WORTHINGTON, Ellicott Hewes, investment banker; b. Baltimore, Md., Feb. 17, 1877; s. Joseph Muse and Caroline Krebs (Hewes) W.; student private sch., Annapolis, Md., 1883-89, St. John's Coll., prep. dept., Annapolis, Md., 1889-92, coll. dept., 1892-93; m. Katharine Graham Frick, Apr. 24, 1915 (died, 1927). Clerk Baltimore (Md.) Warehouse Co., 1893-98, McKim & Co., bankers, Baltimore, Md., 1898-1907, Fidelity Trust Co., 1907-13; treas. Munsey Trust Co. (now Equitable Trust Co.), Baltimore, Md., 1913-17; mem. of firm W. W. Lanahan & Co., investment bankers, Baltimore, Md., since 1917. Served as pvt., 5th Md. Regt., U.S.V., in Spanish-Am. War, 1898. Pres. Instructive Visiting Nurse Assn. of Baltimore City. Independent Democrat. Episcopalian. Clubs: Maryland (Baltimore, Md.); Gibson Island (Md.). Home: 1531 Bolton St. Office: Calvert Bldg., Baltimore, Md.

WORTHINGTON, Frank Dallam; mem. staff Frederick City Hosp. Address: 228 N. Market St., Frederick, Md.

WORTHLEY, Harlan Noyes, coll. prof.; b. Boston, Mass., Feb. 6, 1895; s. James Noyes and Florence Currier (Stickney) W.; B.S., Mass. State Coll., 1920, M.S., 1923; student Ohio State U., 1937-38; m. Ruth Stewart Woodbridge, Dec. 2, 1917; children—Florence May, Harlan Woodbridge. Investigator in economic entomology, Mass. Agrl. Expt. Sta., 1920-24, asst. prof., 1924-25; asst. prof. of entomology extension, Pa. State Coll., 1925-27, asst prof., 1927-31, asso. prof., 1931-35, prof. since 1935. Served in O.T.C., Plattsburg, N.Y., Aug.-Nov. 1917; 2d Corps Sch., Chatillon-sur-Seine, France, Jan.-Mar. 1918; 1st lt., 166th Inf., U.S. Army, 42d Div., Mar.-Nov. 1918; hon. dicharged Apr. 1919. Mem. Borough Council, State College, Pa., 1935-37. Fellow A.A.A.S.; mem. Am. Soc. of Econ. Entomology (v.p. 1937), Entomol. Soc. America, Pa. Acad. of Science, Phi Kappa Phi, Sigma Xi, Gamma Sigma Delta, Kappa Sigma. Independent Republican. Methodist. Contbr. articles on results of research to Jour. Econ. Entomology; author of bulletins of Mass. and Pa. Agrl. Expt. stations. Home: 501 E. Hamilton Av., State College, Pa.

WOTRING, Clayton Warren, supt. twp. schs.; b. Bittners Corner, Pa., June 14, 1894; s. Orville A. and Cora A.R. (George) W.; A.B., Franklin and Marshall Coll., Lancaster, Pa., 1916; A.M., Columbia U. Teachers Coll., 1923; Ph.D., N.Y.U. Sch. of Edn., 1932; m. Katie M. Hunsberger, Dec. 8, 1917. Engaged as teacher and prin. pub. and high sch., 1910-18; supervising prin. schs. East Greenville, 1919-26; supt. schs. Mauch Chunk Twp., Nesquehoning, Pa., since 1926. Served as corp., Co. M, 316th Inf., 79th Div., U.S. Army, at Camp Meade, during World War. Vice chmn. traffic safety com. Am. Legion Dept. of Pa.; v.p. Mauch Chunk Twp. Tuberculosis Soc. Mem. N.E.A., Pa. State Edn. Assn. (past pres. local branch), Carbon Co. Schoolmens Assn. (pres.), Pa. State Teachers League, Nat. Cong. of Parents and Teachers, Pa. Soc. for Crippled Children, Inc., Nesquehoning Hose Co., Am. Legion, Forty and Eight, Phi Kappa Tau (Xi Chapter, Lancaster, Pa.), Phi Delta Kappa (Rho Chapter, N.Y.). Reformed Ch. Mason (East Greenville, Pa.), Knight of Pythias (East Greenville, Pa.). Clubs: Lehigh Valley Motor (Allentown, Pa.; dir.); Rotary (Nesquehoning, Pa.; past pres.). Home: 233 W. Catawissa St. Office: 90 E. Catawissa St., Nesquehoning, Pa.

WRAY, Chester Burton, lawyer; b. Altoona, Pa., Oct. 19, 1889; S. George H. and Annie Belle (Lafferty) W.; Ph.B., Franklin and Marshall Coll., Lancaster, Pa., 1913; B.S., 1917; LL.B., U. of Mich., Ann Arbor, Mich., 1917; m. Margaret Riddell, Nov. 29, 1919 (died Oct. 21, 1921); m. 2d, Rae Davis, Sept. 1, 1926; children—Anna Jane, Dorothy Louise. In employ Pa. R.R., as clerk, 4 yrs., chemist, 6 yrs.; admitted to Pa. bar, 1918, and since in gen. practice of law at Altoona, Pa. Mem. staff of Atty. Gen. of Pa., 1931-34; dist. atty. Blair Co., Pa. since 1936. Mem. Pa. Bar Assn., Blair Co. Lawyers Guild, Patriotic Order Sons of America, Chi Phi. Republican. Presbyterian. Mason (K.T., Shriner), K.P., D.O.O.K. Club: Shrine (Altoona, Pa.). Home: 3412 Oneida Av. Office: Central Trust Bldg., Altoona, Pa.

WRENN, Harold Holmes, architect, artist; b. Norfolk, Va., Apr. 27, 1887; s. William A. and Mary (Woodward) W.; student U. of Va., 1904-05; student Archtl. Sch. of Columbia U., 1905-06; m. Elizabeth Cheeney Jencks, Nov. 29, 1919; children—John Haughton, Mary Haughton, Elizabeth Platt Jencks. Employed as archtl. draftsman, Ferguson & Calrow, architects, Norfolk, Va., 1906-12; mem. firm Ferguson, Calrow & Wrenn, 1913-18, Calrow, Wreen & Tazewell, 1919-21, Calrow & Wrenn, 1921-23; in individual practice in Baltimore, Md., 1925-30, mem. firm Wrenn, Lewis & Jencks since 1930, serving now only in advisory capacity, actively engaged in profession of painting; one-man exhbns. of paintings in New York, Paris, Baltimore, Richmond and other cities; exhibited in museums, Cleveland, Indianapolis and many other cities including Corcoran Biennial, Washington, and World's Fair, N.Y. City; represented in permanent collections, Baltimore Mus. of Arts, Va. Mus. Fine Arts, many others including pvt. collections. Served as 1st lt. F.A., U.S.A., 1918-19, with A.E.F.; wounded in Meuse-Argonne; invalided home after Armistice; awarded citation for bravery by Gen. Pershing. Former mem. Am. Inst. Architects. Mem. Artists Union, Am. Fed. Arts, Provincetown Art Assn., American Legion, Beta Theta Pi. Democrat. Clubs: Batchelors Cotillon, Chester Yacht. Home: 1 W. Mt. Vernon Pl. Office: 113 W. Mulberry St., Baltimore, Md.

WRENSCH, Frank Albert, editor; b. Montclair, N.J., Feb. 1, 1898; s. Albert and Pauline (Fentzlaff) W.; Ph.B., Sheffield Scientic Sch. (Yale), 1919; unmarried. Associated with Turner Construction Co., 1919-20; with Air Reduction Sales Corpn., 1920-21; with Angus Publishing Co. as managing editor of The Spur, 1921-35, editor, 1935-36. On editorial staff The Sportsman, Jan. to Oct. 1937. Served in United States Naval Res., 1918-22. Mem. Phi Gamma Delta. Republican. Clubs: Yale, Town Hall (New York). Author and editor, Horses in Sport, 1937. Home: 266 Claremont Av., Montclair, N.J.; (summer) Mile Creek Rd., Old Lyme, Conn. Office: 50 Vanderbilt Av., New York, N.Y.

WRIGHT, Albert Bayard, economist; b. Wenona, Ill., Dec. 28, 1885; s. Frank and Charlotte Belle (Evans) W.; B.S., Ill. Wesleyan U., 1907; student law dept. same university, 1907-08, 1909-10, M.A. in Economics, 1910; M.A. in Political Science, University of Illinois, 1914; Dr. Commercial Science, Duquesne U., 1927; m. Lucie Estabrook Newman (M.A., Columbia, 1910), June 18, 1913 (died July 1, 1937); children—Charlotte Evans, Janet Estabrook, Albert Bayard, Priscilla Bromley. Teacher of science, high sch., Marysville, Mo., 1908-09; prof. chemistry, U. of Puget Sound, 1910-12; research asst. to dean of Grad. Sch., U. of Ill., 1912-14; instr. polit. science, U. of Pittsburgh,

1914, asst. prof., 1916, asso. prof., 1917, prof. 1918-20, prof. public and business administration, 1920-24, U. of Pittsburgh, also dean Sch. of Economics, 1918-23 (leave of absence, 1923-24); research asso. Sch. of Commerce, U. of Chicago, 1923-24; prof. economics, Sch. of Commerce, Duquesne U., since 1924, also dir. grad. div., 1927-31, head dept. of business administration, 1931—, dean Sch. of Business Administration, 1932—, also dir. Downtown Evening Div., 1933—; lecturer in social edn., Pa. State Coll., 1924-31. Mem. Nat. Econ. League, Sigma Chi, Phi Alpha Delta, Alpha Kappa Psi, Omicron Delta Kappa, Beta Gamma Sigma, Phi Kappa Phi. Home: 5649 Woodmont St., Pittsburgh, Pa.

WRIGHT, Alexander Holland, prof. chemistry; b. Allegheny City, Pa., Nov. 23, 1874; s. Charles Bingley and Margaret (Holland) W.; A.B., Washington and Jefferson Coll., Washington, Pa., 1898; A.M., 1901, (hon.) D.Sc., 1939; grad. study, Chicago U., 3 summers; Ph.D., Columbia U., 1919; m. Mary McElroy, Dec. 26, 1901; 1 son, Arthur Alexander. Engaged in teaching high sch., 1898-1901; supt. pub. schs., Greenville, Pa., 1901-03; prof. chemistry, Muskingum Coll., 1903-16; instr., Coll. City of N.Y., also Columbia U., 1916-19; instr. Queen's Univ., Can., 1919-20; prof. chemistry, head of dept. chemistry, Washington and Jefferson Coll., Washington, Pa., 1920-39, prof. emeritus since 1939. Trustee United Presbyn. Ch., New Concord, Pa.; trustee 2d United Presbyn. Ch., Washington, Pa., since 1928. Fellow Am. Inst. Chemists, A.A.A.S.; mem. Am. Chem. Soc., Am. Assn. Univ. Profs., Sigma Xi. Republican. United Presbyterian. Home: McElree Rd., Washington, Pa.

WRIGHT, Alfred Edward, life ins. dist. mgr.; b. Sharon, Pa., Mar. 10, 1887; s. John and Eliza (Meikle) W.; B.S., Westminster Coll., New Wilmington, Pa., 1911; m. Katherine Jane Beighley, Nov. 24, 1917; children—Alfred Edward, Robert Beighley, Samuel Cochran. Engaged as prin. high sch. North Union Twp., Uniontown, Pa., 1911-17, Uniontown High Sch., Uniontown, Pa., 1917-21; investment banker, 1922-33; dist. mgr. Mutual Life Ins. Co. of N.Y., at Uniontown, Pa., since 1933; dir. Cochran Coal & Coke Co., Morgantown, W.Va. Mem. bd. trustees Bethany (W.Va.) Coll. Republican. Presbyn. Mason. Club: Rotary of Uniontown, Pa. Home: 22 N. Mt. Vernon Av., Uniontown, Pa.

WRIGHT, Bruce Simpson, clergyman; b. Eldred, Pa., Feb. 24, 1879; s. Albert Josiah and Bertha (Simpson) W.; A.B., Allegheny Coll., Meadville, Pa., 1905, D.D., 1920; m. Margarette Catherine Armstrong, Oct. 30, 1907; children—Harriet Esther, Elizabeth Anne, Robert Bruce. Pastor First M.E. Ch., Fredonia, N.Y., 1905-12, Simpson M.E. Ch., Erie, Pa., 1912-15, American Ch., Manila, P.I., 1915-18, Trinity M.E. Ch., Albany, N.Y., 1918-20, Asbury-Delaware M.E. Ch., Buffalo, N.Y., 1920-33, Old Stone M.E. Ch., Meadville, Pa., 1934-36, First M.E. Ch., Erie, Pa., since 1936. Chmn. Am. Defense Com., P.I., World War. Dean of Summer Grad. Sch. for Ministers, Silver Lake, N.Y. Exchange preacher to Brit. Isles, 1923-26. Mem. Commn. on World Peace of M.E. Ch. Trustee Allegheny Coll.; mem. advisory council Am. Brotherhood for the Blind. Mem. Y.M.C.A., Phi Delta Theta, Internat. Soc. Theta Phi. Republican. Mason (32°, K.T.). Clubs: University, Round Table, Rotary, Literary Union. Author: Americans Away, 1916; Moments of Devotion, 1921; The Life in the Spirit, 1927; God, the Greatest Poet—Man, His Greatest Poem, 1928; The House of Happiness, 1928; The Symphony of Faith, 1929; Pentecost Day by Day, 1930; Girded with Gladness, 1931; Steps Into the Sanctuary, 1932; Chancel Windows, 1933; Lenten Gallery, 1938. Contbr. to Christian Century, New York Christian Advocate, David C. Cook Publications, etc. Home: 717 Sassafras St., Erie, Pa.; and "Wright-Wood," Kane, Pa. Study: 707 Sassafras St., Erie, Pa.

WRIGHT, Carroll Spaulding, dermatologist; b. Freeport, Mich., Dec. 27, 1895; s. Ernest and Inez (Spaulding) W.; grad. high sch., Conneaut, Ohio, 1913; B.S., U. of Mich., 1916, M.D., 1919; m. Helen Cutting Shaw, June 23, 1923; children—Janet Joan, Juliana. Began practice, 1919; instr. dermatology, U. of Mich., 1920-22; asst. prof. dermatology, Grad. Sch. of Medicine, U. of Pa., 1923-25, asso. prof., 1925-35; prof. dermatology and syphilology Temple U. Med. Sch., Phila., since 1931; cons. dermatologist Municipal Hosp. of Phila., Shriners Hosp., Pa. Inst. for Blind, Elwyn Training Sch. Pres. Temple Univ. Hosp. staff, 1938-39. Trustee Research Inst. of Cutaneous Medicine. Served in U.S. Med. R.C., 1917-18, World War. Mem. Am. Dermatol. Assn., Acad. of Dermatology and Syphilology, Soc. for Investigative Dermatology, Nu Sigma Nu, Sigma Xi. Republican. Conglist. Mason. Clubs: Rotary Internat., Medical, Phila. Country. Author (with Dr. J. F. Schamberg): Diseases of the Skin, 1898, revised edit., 1934; (with same) Treatment of Syphilis, 1932. Contbr. to cyclos. and tech. mags. Home: Moreno Rd., Wynnewood, Pa. Office: 1402 Spruce St., Philadelphia, Pa.

WRIGHT, Catharine Morris (Mrs. Sydney Longstreth Wright, Jr.), artist; b. Phila., Jan. 26, 1899; d. Harrison Smith and Anna (Wharton) Morris; ed. pvt. schs., Phila. Sch. of Design for Women, 1916-18; m. Sydney Longstreth Wright, Feb. 28, 1925; children—Anna Wharton, William Redwood, Harrison Morris, Ellicott. Began career as artist, 1918. Hon. mention Phila. Art Club, 1924, Gimbel award, 1932; Mary Smith prize, Pa. Acad. Fine Arts, 1933; 2d Hallgarten prize, Nat. Acad. Design, 1933; Greenough memorial prize, Newport Art Assn., 1933; Germantown Art League Prize, 1936. Represented in Pa. Acad. of Fine Arts. Asso. Nat. Acad., 1933; mem. Am. Water Color Soc., N.Y., Phila., Washington and Baltimore water color clubs, Allied Artists of America. Author: The Simple Nun (verse), 1929. Home: Endsmeet Farm, Glenside, Pa.

WRIGHT, Chauncey B.; attending surgeon Huntington Memorial and St. Mary's hosps. Address: 517 Ninth St., Huntington, W.Va.

WRIGHT, Charles Adshead, prof. journalism; b. Rutledge, Pa., Oct. 8, 1899; s. Joseph Hetherington and Henrietta O. (Humphries) W.; B.S. in Econs., U. of Pa. Wharton Sch., 1922, A.M., Grad. Sch., 1931; m. Helen Turner McCormack, Oct. 10, 1923; children—Charles Alan, Jean. Employed in various jobs between high sch. and coll., 1917-18; part time and summer jobs while at coll., free lance contbr., Phila. Ledger and Record, 1919-22; reporter Lancaster Av. News, Phila., 1922, continuing part time to 1931, mng. editor; copy writer adv. agency, 1922-23; reporter and radio editor, Phila. Evening Bulletin, 1923-25; instr. then asst. prof. journalism, and dir. undergrad. publs., Temple U., Phila., since 1926. Served as pvt., S.A.T.C., 1918. Active in Boy Scouts, parent teachers assn., and civic assn. Mem. adv. bd. Asso. Collegiate Press; past exec. sec. Intercollegiate Newspaper Assn. Mem. Am. Assn. Univ. Profs., Am. Assn. Teachers of Journalism, Elbeetian Legion (former Lone Scouts), Blue Key, Sigma Delta Chi, Alpha Delta Sigma, Sigma Phi Epsilon. Awarded $500 Mergenthaler Prize for radio script, Salute to the Modern Newspaper, 1936, since pub. in book form. Republican. Presbyterian. Contbr. to newspapers and mags. Began writing at age 16 for Lone Scout mag. and high sch. mag. Home: 2743 Belmont Av., Ardmore, Pa.

WRIGHT, Daniel Thew, judge; b. Riverside, Hamilton Co., O., Sept. 24, 1864; s. D. Thew and Juliet Frances (Rogers) W.; grad. Hughes High Sch., Cincinnati, 1885; LL.B., Cincinnati Law Sch., 1887; m. Alice Williams, Oct. 26, 1887; children—Gladys Marie, Claire, Alice Liston, Daniel Thew III; m. 2d, Lou Price Hinton, Oct. 27, 1932. Admitted to bar, 1887; practiced at Cincinnati; specialist as trial lawyer; village solicitor of Riverside, 1888-90; mayor of Riverside, 1890-93; 2d asst., 1888-90, and 1st asst. pros. atty., Hamilton Co., 1890-93; elected and served as judge Court of Common Pleas, Hamilton Co., O., 1893-98; justice Supreme Court of D.C., Nov. 6, 1903-Nov. 1, 1914; resigned to resume practice of law. Republican. Home: Fenwick, Md.*

WRIGHT, Eliza G(rumman), club woman; b. Lewistown, Pa., July 26, 1879; d. William H. and Catharine McCay (Buoy) Bratton; ed. pub. sch., Sterling, N.D., 1885-96, pvt. tutors, N.D. Agrl. Coll., Fargo, N.D., 1896-97; m. Roy V. Wright, October 7, 1901; children—Catharine Louisa (Mrs. William C. Menninger), Dorothy Elizabeth, (Mrs. Henry E. Sharpe), Esther McCay (dec.), Josephine Anne. Pres. Sheltered Workroom (for aiding physically handicapped women) since 1939. Dir. women's div. Primary Campaign Dwight W. Morrow for Senator, 1930; nat. chmn. women's div. Engrs. Hoover for Pres. Campaign, 1928, 1932; mem. bd. recreation, East Orange, N.J., since 1934. Trustee East Orange (N.J.) Gen. Hosp.; dir. Orange Y.W.C.A.; mem. women's bd. mgrs. East Orange Gen. Hosp., pres. 1935-39; pres. women's auxiliary Upsala Coll., 1930-31; pres. women's auxiliary Am. Soc. Mech. Engrs., 1925-28. Republican. Presbyterian. Clubs: Engineering Woman's (New York); pres. 1936-38, dir. since 1929); Charlotte Emerson Brown Sheltered Workroom. Republican (East Orange, N.J.); Round Table of Oranges (East Orange, N.J.); Cosmopolitan (Montclair). Co-author (with Roy V. Wright): How to be a Responsible Citizen, 1938. Address: 398 Walnut St., East Orange, N.J.

WRIGHT, Eugene B.; mem. surg. staff Union Protestant and St. Mary's hosps. Address: 127 W. Main St., Clarksburg, W.Va.

WRIGHT, Frank Ayres, architect; b. Liberty, Sullivan Co., N.Y., Nov. 19, 1854; s. A. B. and M. J. W.; A.B., Cornell, 1879; m. Elizabeth Hanford, Jan. 9, 1883; children—Mrs. Carile Hanford Middleditch, Mrs. Frances Hanford Poillon, Mrs. Elizabeth Juliette Slosson, Ehrick Hanford. In practice of architecture since 1879. One of founders and sec., 1885, Architectural League of New York; fellow Am. Inst. Architects. Trustee village S. Orange, N.J., 1887; dir. in various clubs. Mem. N.E. Soc., Orange (N.J.) Architectural League. Clubs: Nat. Arts, Cornell (New York); Canoe Brook Country, Baltusrol Golf, Waterwitch. Author: Modern House Painting, 1880; Architectural Perspective for Beginners, 1882. Home: Summit, N.J.

WRIGHT, Fred William, portrait painter; b. Crawfordsville, Ind., Oct. 12, 1880; s. Charles Wm. and Virginia (Bromley) W.; student John Herron Art Inst., Indianapolis, Ind., 1904-06, Julian's Acad., Paris, and Studio P. Marcel Baronneau, Paris, France, 1906-07, Art Students League, N.Y. City and Cooper Union Art Sch., N.Y. City, 1908; m. F. May Blue, Sept. 23, 1903; 1 dau. died in infancy. Has followed profession as artist specializing in portraits in oil, also pastel, and water colors on ivory at New York, N.Y., 1910-38, at Cambridge, Md., since 1938; represented by many portraits in pub. bldgs. including State Capitol, Law Sch., Albany, N.Y., Union, Catholic, and Nat. Dem. clubs, N.Y. City, N.Y. Co. Lawyers Assn., Waldorf Astoria Hotel, Columbia Univ.; 8 portraits in DuPont bd. room, Wilmington, Del., 6 portraits Dunn & Bradstreet bd. room, N.Y. City; many portraits of well known people in offices and pvt. homes. Mem. Soc. of Cincinnati of Va. Methodist. Club: Salmagundi (New York). Address: Box 387, Cambridge, Md.

WRIGHT, Gifford King, lawyer; b. Greenville, Pa., Mar. 19, 1874; s. Rev. John Eliot (D.D.), and Ellen M. (Kerr) W.; A.B., Haverford Coll., 1893; m. Elizabeth Ball, of Lock Haven, Pa., Apr. 19, 1900 (died 1919); m. 2d, Louise Graff, of Sewickley, Pa., Mar. 6, 1930. Admitted to Pa. Bar, 1897, and since engaged in general practice of law at Pittsburgh; mem. firm Alter, Wright & Barron since 1920. Mem. Pa. Bar Assn. (president 1939-40), Am. Bar Assn., Bar Assn. of the City of New York, Allegheny County Bar Assn., Am. Law Inst. Republican. Presbyterian. Clubs: Edgeworth, Allegheny Country (Sewickley); Duquesne (Pittsburgh); Bankers of America (New York). Home: 39 Thorn St., Sewickley, Pa. Office: 2201 First Nat. Bank Bldg., Pittsburgh, Pa.

WRIGHT, Guier Scott, educator; b. Stamford, Conn., July 31, 1891; s. George Lathrop and Florence Guier (Scott) W.; ed. Haverford (Pa.) Sch., 1902-06; diploma, High Sch., Pottstown, Pa., 1909; student Sheffield Scientific Sch. (Yale), 1909-10; m. Dorothy F. Battles, June 27, 1925; children—Dorothy Alden, Guier Scott, Patricia Locke. With F. W. Welsh & Co., bonds, Phila., 1913, F. J. Lisman & Co., 1913-14; salesman in San Francisco for Phila. Specialty Sales Co., machine specialties, 1915; teacher and athletic dir., Montgomery Sch., Wynnewood, Pa., 1916-17; asst. to principal, Miss Wright's Sch. (founded by sister), Bryn Mawr, 1920-30, director and principal since 1930; pres. Lloyd Gliem, Inc., auto sales; pres. Aurora Products, Inc. With Y.M.C.A. at Camp Meade, Md., 1917-18; joined 314th Inf., 79th Div., U.S.A., 1918; overseas, July 1918-May 1919; served as color sergt. Trustee Bryn Mawr Memorial Assn. Mem. Am. Geog. Soc., Am. Legion (post comr.). Republican. Episcopalian. Club: Merion Cricket (Haverford, Pa.). Home: Roberts Rd., Bryn Mawr, Pa.*

WRIGHT, Hamilton Mercer, writer; b. New Haven, Conn., Dec. 29, 1875; s. Hamilton M. and Anne Dana (Fitzhugh) W.; student U. of Mich., 1895, U. of Colo., 1896, LL.B., 1899; m. Cora Elizabeth Pease, 1900; children—Hamilton Mercer, Eugene Pease, Richard Wm., Peter Craig. Instr. Law Sch. U. of Southern Calif., 1899-1900; on staffs Los Angeles Times, Herald, Saturday Post, until 1903; with Bur. Information Calif. Promotion Com., 1903-05; with Pacific Commercial Mus. in Philippine Islands, 1905-06; editor Overland Monthly, 1907; staff San Francisco Examiner, 1907-11; editor in chief San Francisco Expn., 1911-15 (gold medal of honor); toured Central and S. America, contributing to Pan-Am. Union, 1916-17; corr. in France, 1918; information dir. Fla. E. Coast Railway, 1922-29, Government of Egypt, 1932-38, City of Miami, Fla., 1927-31; v.p. Fla. State Chamber of Commerce, 1931-32 and 1933-34; toured Nile Valley Basin (describing govt. irrigation scheme), 1933-35. Republican. Episcopalian. Author: Handbook of Philippines, 1905; America Across the Seas (with John F. Stevens and others), 1912. Regular contbr. to mags. and newspapers. Home: 144 W. Newell Av., Rutherford, N.J. Office: 30 Rockefeller Plaza, New York, N.Y.*

WRIGHT, Horace Wetherill, univ. prof.; b. Phila., Pa., Aug. 5, 1884; s. William Harry and Aubertine (Woodward) W.; A.B., U. of Wis., Madison, Wis., 1908; Ph.D., U. of Pa., 1917; fellow Am. Acad. of Rome (Italy), 1914-15; unmarried. Instr. in Latin, U. of Mo., Columbia, Mo., 1917-18; asst. prof. of Latin, Oberlin (O.) Coll., 1918-19; asso. in Latin, Bryn Mawr (Pa.) Coll., 1919-21; prof. of Latin, Lehigh U., Bethlehem, Pa., since 1921, head of dept. since 1921. Mem. Archaeol. Inst. of America (recorder, 1930-32; sec.-treas., Bethlehem, Pa., chapter, since 1925), Am. Philol. Assn., Classical Assn. of the Atlantic States (v.p., 1930-32), Classical League of the Lehigh Valley (pres., 1925-26), Am. Classical League, Eta Sigma Phi. Republican. Unitarian. Author: The Sacra Idulia In Ovid's Fasti (doctoral thesis), 1917; The Janus Shrine of the Forum and numerous other articles in classical pubs. Address: 447 Heckewelder Pl., Bethlehem, Pa.

WRIGHT, Howard V., chem. engring.; b. Indianola, Ia., June 4, 1892; s. Isaac C. and Belle (Hastie) W.; A.B., Simpson Coll., Indianola, Ia., 1917; M.S., Ia. State Coll., Ames, Ia., 1921, Ch.E., 1926; m. Mildred Kennedy, Dec. 25, 1918; children—Ernest Charles, Alice Wright (dec.). Instr. Ia. State Coll., 1919-20, asst. prof. chem. engring., 1921-25; chief, plants dept., Edgewood Arsenal, Md., C.W.S., 1925-32, asst. chief and chief, munitions div. since 1932; sec. Md. Gladiolus Soc., Inc. Mem. Am. Chem. Soc., Am. Inst. Chem. Engrs., Alpha Tau Omega. Methodist. Club: Kiwanis of Havre de Grace, Md. Home: Edgewood Arsenal, Md.

WRIGHT, Isaac Miles, prof. education; b. Scio, N.Y., Mar. 7, 1879; s. John S. and Belle E. (Saunders) W.; grad. high sch., Belmont, N.Y., 1899; B.S., Alfred (N.Y.) U., 1904; Pd.M., New York U., 1914, Pd.D., 1916; m. Maude Goff Paul, June 24, 1909. Teacher rural sch., Belmont, N.Y., 1898-99; prin. grammar sch., Scio, N.Y., 1900-01; asst. in high sch., 1904-07; prin. high sch., Elliottville, 1907-10, Lawrence, 1910-13; teacher Dwight Sch., N.Y. City, 1913-17; prof. edn., Muhlenberg Coll., since 1917, also dir. Sch. of Edn., and of Summer Sch. of Muhlenberg Coll., increasing attendance at latter from 37 to 1,114 in 6 yrs. Pres. Board of Edn., Allentown. Mem. N.E.A., also Dept. of Superintendence, same, Am. Assn. Univ. Profs., Nat. Council Geography Teachers, Nat. Soc. Coll. Teachers of Edn., Pa. Soc. S.R., Pa. State Teachers' Assn., Phi Kappa Tau (grand pres. 1928-30), Phi Delta Kappa, Kappa Phi Kappa, Omicron Delta Kappa. Republican. Episcopalian. Mason (K.T., Shriner). Clubs: Oakmont, Brookside, Rotary. Home: Allentown, Pa.

WRIGHT, J. Merrill, lawyer; b. Pittsburgh, Pa., Jan. 9, 1876; s. Joseph E. and Ella R. (Diehl) W.; A.B., Allegheny Coll., A.M., 1895; LL.B., U. of Pittsburgh, 1897; m. Laura Arons Pearce, June 12, 1901; children—Laura Wright Hoster, Henry Pearce, J. Merrill, Jr. Admitted to bar, 1898; partner law firm McKelvey & Wright, 1901-15, Stone, Wright & Chalfant, 1918-20, Wright, Chalfant & McCandless, 1920-23, Wright & Rundle since 1923; pres. and dir. Franklin Cotton Mill Co. (Cincinnati), Alpha Coal Co.; pres. and dir. Tarentum, Brackenridge Street Railway Company, Brackenridge Bus Co.; president and director Brackenridge - McKelvy Land Co.; organizer and dir. Monongahela Trust Co., Homestead; dir. Alicia Supply Co., Grays Landing Ferry Co. Clubs: Pittsburgh, Pittsburgh Golf, Duquesne, Fox Chapel, Allegheny Country (Pittsburgh); Queen City (Cincinnati); University (New York); Rolling Rock. Home: 1552 Beechwood Boul. Office: 624 Frick Bldg., Pittsburgh, Pa.

WRIGHT, John Calvin, vocational edn.; b. Elkhart Co., Ind., June 24, 1876; s. John J. and Hannah (Postma) W.; grad. Kan. State Normal Sch., Emporia, Kan., 1900, Latin course, 1901; B.S. in Edn., U. of Mo., 1918, A.M., 1919; Sc.D. in Edn., Stout Inst., Menominee, Wis., 1926; m. Cordelia D. Bennett, June 4, 1903; children—Nadia Virginia, Genevieve Grace, Dale Jokshan. Began as teacher rural schs., 1895; teacher high sch. and supt. schs., Belleville, Kan., 1900-04; teacher high schs., Kansas City, Mo., 1904-14; dir. vocational instrn. same city, 1913-18; with Fed. Bd. Vocational Edn. from 1917, dir., 1922-33; now asst. commr. for vocational edn., U.S. Office of Edn. Architect and builder in Kansas City, 6 yrs. Corpl. Co. H, 22d Kan. Vols., Spanish-Am. War, 1898; spl. agt. for war training, 1918. Mem. N.E.A., Am. Vocational Assn.; charter mem. Boone Family Assn., Am. Order of Pioneers. Presbyn. Mason. Author: Automotive Repair (4 vols.); Co-Author: Automotive Construction and Operation; Supervision of Vocational Education; Administration of Vocational Education; Efficiency in Education; Efficiency in Vocational Education; You and Your Job. Editor Trade Series of John Wiley & Sons. Made survey of pulp and paper industry. Home: 5624 Western Av., Chevy Chase, Md. Office: Dept. of Interior, Office of Education, Washington, D.C.

WRIGHT, John Pilling, pres. Continental-Diamond Fibre Co.; b. Newark, Del., May 17, 1881; s. Samuel J. and Isabel (Pilling) W.; m. Elizabeth Johnson, Sept. 9, 1908. Pres. Continental-Diamond Fibre Co. since 1929. Office: S. Chapel St., Newark, Del.

WRIGHT, Joseph Purdon, lawyer; b. Colorado Springs, Colo., June 10, 1884; s. Richard William and Sarah Louise (Carter) W.; LL.B., U. of Md. Law Sch., 1905; A.B., Johns Hopkins U., 1908; m. Lucy Agnes Wright, June 24, 1914; children—Margaret Louise, Joseph Purdon, Jr., Richard Armstrong. Admitted to Md. bar, 1909, and since engaged in gen. practice of law at Baltimore; admitted to bar U.S. Dist. Ct., Md., 1913; admitted to practice before Supreme Ct. of U.S., 1920; served as asst. atty. gen. Md., 1920-24; first supt. Md. State Police, 1935; gen. counsel Pub. Service Comm. since 1935; Commr. of Uniform State Laws for Md.; dir. Bartgis Brothers Co.; U.S. Fidelity & Guaranty Co., Homestead Fire Ins. Co., Baltimore Broadcasting Co. Served as sergt. cav. Md. N.G. on Mexican border, 1915-16; pvt. inf., U.S.A., 1917-19. Trustee Univ. of Baltimore. Mem. Am., Md. State, Baltimore City bar assns., Am. Law Inst., Commercial Law League of America (past pres.), Phi Gamma Delta. Republican. Episcopalian. Mason (K.T., 32°, Shriner, past potentate Boumi Temple). I.O.O.F. Club: Merchants. Home: Lake Station. Office: Baltimore Trust Co., Baltimore, Md.

WRIGHT, Katharine Hays Law, M.D.; b. Erie, Pa., Aug. 20, 1877; d. Stephen John and Ella Florence (Kimball) Law; grad. Lowell (Mass.) High Sch., 1896, Lowell (Mass.) Training Sch. for Teachers, 1898; M.D., Woman's Med. Coll. of Pa., 1904; m. John W. Wright, M.D., Jan. 1, 1913 (died 1926); 1 dau., Virginia Law. Teacher Lowell Training Sch. for Teachers, 1898-1900; interne New England Hosp., Boston, 1904-05; practice of medicine, Boston, 1904-09, Erie, Pa., since 1909; mem. staff Hamot Hosp., 1909-38; chief Pa. State Tuberculosis Clinic since 1918; specialized in ear, nose, throat and chest diseases since 1909. Mem. advisory bd. Erie Co. Tuberculosis Hosp. Mem. Erie County Med. Soc. (pres.), Mass. Med. Soc., A.M.A., Erie Co. Health and Tuberculosis Soc. Republican. Episcopalian. Clubs: Erie Garden (pres.), Erie Business and Professional Women's. Address: 4220 Sunnydale Boul., Erie, Pa.

WRIGHT, Norris N., v.p. Continental-Diamond Fibre Co.; b. Newark, Del., Mar. 29, 1886; s. Samuel J. and Isabel (Pilling) W.; student U. of Del.; m. Fleta Robertson, June 3, 1921; children—Eugenia Isabel, Martha. V.p. and dir. Continental-Diamond Fibre Co. since 1929. Office: S. Chapel St., Newark, Del.

WRIGHT, Richard Robert, educator, banker; b. Dalton, Ga., May 16, 1855; s. Robert Waddell and Harriet (Lynch) W.; A.B., Atlanta U., 1876, A.M., 1879; LL.D., Wilberforce, 1899; m. Lydia Elizabeth Howard, June 7, 1877; children—Richard Robert, Julia O., Mrs. Essie W. Thompson, Mrs. Lillian M. Clayton, Dr. W. H., Edwina M., Mrs. Harriet W. Lemon, Emanuel C. Prin. Ware High Sch., 1880-91; pres. Ga. State Industrial Coll., 1891-1921; pres. Citizens & Southern Bank & Trust Company of Philadelphia, since 1921. Served in the Spanish-American War as an additional paymaster with the rank of major vols., Aug. 3-Dec. 1, 1898. Organizer and pres. Ga. State Agrl. and Industrial Assn., 1907; anniversary speaker Am. Missionary Assn., 1880-1898; trustee Atlanta U. Del. 4 nat. Rep. convs.; declined appmt. E.E. and M.P. to Liberia, tendered by Pres. McKinley. Traveled extensively in Europe. Methodist. Mason (33°), Elk. Mem. Am. Acad. Polit. and Social Science. Pres. Nat. Assn. of Presidents of A. and M. Colleges for Negroes, 1900-06; pres. Nat. Assn. Teachers in Colored Schs., 1908-12; pres. Nat. Negro Bankers Association. Secured passage of an act by U.S. Senate for appropriation of $250,000 to promote Semi-Centennial Emancipation Exhibition, 1913. Appointed by gov. Ga. chmn. Colored Association Council of Food Production and Conservation; apptd. by gov. of Ga. as Negro historian of enlisted colored troops in France, and visited Eng., France and Belgium to collect hist. data for the archives of Ga. and for a book on the Negro in the Great War. Mem. Spanish-Am. War Veterans, Phila. Business League (pres.). Apptd. by Gov. J. S. Fisher of Pa. mem. commn. to erect a statue in memory of the colored soldiers in all Am. wars. Promoter of Youths' Thrift Clubs. Home: 554 N. 58th St. Office: 1849 South St., Philadelphia, Pa.

WRIGHT, Ross Pier, mfr.; b. Westfield, N.Y., Aug. 22, 1874; s. Reuben G. and Emma Cora (Pierce) W.; prep. edn., high sch. Westfield, and Phillips Acad., Andover, Mass.; Ph.B., Yale, 1896; m. Mabel Eliza Woodward, June 9, 1903; children—Theron Woodward, Allyn Seymour, Richard Pier. Associated with brothers in purchasing control of Eastman Machine Co., Buffalo, and was made sec., treas. and mgr. of same; sold out, 1902, and with brothers purchased the Reed Manufacturing Company, manufacturers of small tools (Erie, Pa.), of which is sec., treas. and plant manager; director Erie Systematic Building & Loan Assn. (now First Federal Savings & Loan Assn.); manager Wright Brothers Farm; member board directors Federal Reserve Bank, Cleveland, Ohio, since 1917. Member bd. corporators Hamot Hosp. (Erie). Vice-pres. Erie Chamber of Commerce, Anti-Tuberculosis Soc.; dir. Erie Mfrs.' Assn., Niagara Assn. of Erie; treas. Pa. Hist. Assn.; mem. N.Y. State Archæol. Soc. (dir.), Pa. Archæol. Soc. (pres.), Erie Social Hygiene Assn. (dir.); mem. advisory council Am. Social Hygiene Assn. (New York); chmn. Com. of Sixteen; mem. Federation Pennsylvania Historical Socs. (v.p.), Pennsylvania Historical Commn., Erie County Hist. Soc., Chautauqua County (N.Y.) Hist. Soc. Mem. Am. Soc. Mech. Engrs., Theta Delta Chi. Republican. Presbyn.; trustee Ch. of the Covenant. Clubs: University, Erie, Kahkwa, Rotary, Erie Motor, Erie Art (Erie); Bankers (Cleveland and Pittsburgh). Home: 235 W. 6th St. Office: Reed Mfg. Co., Erie, Pa.

WRIGHT, Roydon Vincent, editor; b. Red Wing, Minn., Oct. 8, 1876; s. Reuben Andrus and Louisa Anna (Schaefer) W.; prep. edn., high sch., St. Paul; M.E., U. of Minn., 1898; hon. Dr. Engring., Stevens Inst., Tech., 1931; m. Eliza Grumman Bratton, Oct. 7, 1901; children—Catharine Louisa (Mrs. William Claire Menninger), Dorothy Elizabeth (Mrs. Henry Edwards Sharpe), Esther McCay (dec.), Josephine Anne. Machinist apprentice, C.,M.&St.P. Ry., 1898-99; spl. apprentice, etc., C.G.W. Ry., 1899-1901; mech. engr. P.&L.E. R.R., 1901-04; asso. editor American Engineer and Railroad Journal, 1904-05, editor, 1905-10; mech. dept. editor Railway Age, and editor Railway Mechanical Engineer, since Dec. 1911; v.p. and sec. Simmons-Boardman Pub. Corpn.; also editor Locomotive Cyclopedia, Car Builders' Cyclopedia, Material Handling Cyclopedia; lecturer on citizenship, Newark, Coll. of Engring. Dir. Ampere (N.J.) Bank & Trust Co. Mem. John Fritz Medal Board (1932-35; pres. 1935). Fellow Am. Soc. Mech. Engrs. (v.p. 1926-27; pres. 1931); mem. United Engring. Soc. (trustee; pres. 1928-29), treas. Associated Business Papers, Inc.; pres. Nat. Conf. of Business Paper Editors; mem. N.Y. Railroad Club (exec. com.), Silver Bay Assn. (trustee), Franklin Inst., Newcomen Society, Sigma Xi, Beta Theta Pi, Pi Tau Sigma (hon.). Vice-pres. Y.M.C.A. of Oranges; mem. transportation, industrial and program services coms., Nat. Council Y.M.C.A.; chmn. Silver Bay Industrial Conf., 1936-37; mem. administration bd., Com. on Friendly Relations among Foreign Students. Mem. advisory bd. Dept. of Smoke Regulation, Hudson County, N.J.; freeholder, Essex County, N.J., 1935-37. Republican. Presbyn. Clubs: Engineers, Railroad-Machinery. Author of a manual on citizenship (for Am. Soc. Mech. Engrs.). Co-Author (with Eliza G. Wright): How to Be A Responsible Citizen." Contbr. to "Toward Civilization," 1930. Home: 398 N. Walnut St., East Orange, N.J. Office: 30 Church St., New York, N.Y.

WRIGHT, Sydney L(ongstreth), chemistry, education; b. Germantown, Phila., Pa., Oct. 9, 1896; s. William Redwood and Letitia Ellicott (Carpenter) W.; prep. edn., Episcopal Acad., Phila., 1909-14; B.S., Princeton U., 1918, A.M., 1920, Ph.D., 1928; m. Catharine (Wharton) Morris, Feb. 28, 1925; children—Anna Wharton, William Redwood, Harrison Morris, Ellicott. Research chemist, Barrett Co., Phila., 1919-21; chemist Ayer Clin. Lab. of Pa. Hosp., 1923-28; Nat. Research fellow in medicine, 1928-30; Porter fellow, U. of Pa., 1930-32, instr. medicine, 1931-34, Girvin fellow, 1932-33, instr. physiol. chemistry, 1932-36; asso. dir. Franklin Inst. since 1934, dir. of membership since 1936, asst. to sec. since 1939. Trustee Wagner Free Inst. of Science since 1931, sec. since 1935; dir. Library Co. of Phila. since 1937; pres. Meadowbrook Sch. since 1938; mem. bd. of dirs. Pa. Acad. Fine Arts since 1939. Served as private in U.S. Army in France, 1917-19. Mem. Franklin Inst., Am. Soc. Biol. Chemists, Am. Chem. Soc. Clubs: Tower (Princeton);

Franklin Inn, Princeton, University Barge (Phila.). Author: The Story of The Franklin Institute, 1938; also numerous tech. papers. Editor of Bulletin of Wagner Free Inst. Home: Endsmeet Farm, Glenside, Pa. Office: The Franklin Insitute, Philadelphia, Pa.

WRIGHT, Thomas Archibald, cons. metall. chemist and engr.; b. New York, N.Y., Feb. 25, 1887; s. Thomas Henry and Margaret Irene (Bell) W.; student Battin High Sch., Elizabeth, N.J., 1899-1903; m. Eva Caroline Frederick, 1908; children—Margaret Irene (Mrs. Harold J. Mobus), Frederick Henderson, Thomas Archibald. Clk. Am. Agrl. Chem. Co., Carteret, N.J., 1903-04; asst. assayer Delamar Copper Works, Carteret, N.J., 1904-07; assayer U.S. Lead Refining Co., Grasselli, Ind., 1907-08; chemist Dr. Lucius Pitkin, New York, 1908-16; chief chemist Lucius Pitkin, Inc., commercial lab., cons. chemists and engrs., New York, 1916-21, sec. and tech. dir. since 1921; pres. Buffalo Testing Labs., commercial lab., Buffalo, N.Y., since 1930; sec. 47 Fulton St. Corpn. since 1925; licensed professional engr. N.J., and N.Y. Mem. bd. edn., Piscataway Twp., N.J. 1924-27; mem. ct. of honor Boy Scouts of America, Plainsfield, N.J., since 1937. Fellow Am. Inst. Chemists; mem. Assn. Cons. Chemists and Chem. Engrs. (pres. 1935-37, dir.), Am. Council Commercial Labs. (dir.), Am. Chem. Soc., Am. Inst. Mining and Metall. Engrs., Mining and Metall. Soc. of America, Brit. Inst. of Metals, Electrochem. Soc., Plainfield (N.J.) Mineral. Soc. (pres. since 1938), Mineral. Soc. of America, Am. Soc. for Testing Materials. Republican. Congregationalist. Clubs: Mining (New York); Engineers (Plainfield, N.J.). Home: 1161 Stillman Av., Plainfield, N.J. Office: Pitkin Bldg., 47 Fulton St., New York, N.Y.

WRIGHT, Walter Livingston, univ. pres.; b. Juliustown, N.J., Feb. 3, 1872; s. Walter L. and Elizabeth (Gaskill) W.; B.A., Princeton (science fellowship), 1892, M.A., 1895; LL.D., Lincoln U. (Pa.), 1933; m. Jean Carr, July 3, 1895; children—Walter Livingston, George Carr, Jean Gray. Prof. mathematics, Lincoln U., 1893-1936, v.p., 1926-36, pres. since Feb., 1936. Served in Y.M.C.A. ednl. work at Brest, France, World War. Mem. Math. Assn. America, Phi Beta Kappa. Rotarian. Address: Lincoln University, Pa.

WRIGHT, W(illiam) A(lbert) Earl, dean; b. Bendersville, Pa., Nov. 26, 1900; s. Scott Stewart and Flora M. (Webb) W.; B.S., Gettysburg Coll., 1923, M.S., 1928; Ed.D., George Washington U., 1935; m. Mary L. Archibald, June 12, 1929. Teacher senior high sch., New Kensington, Pa., 1923-24; Blairsville, Pa., 1924-27, Reading, Pa., 1927-28; dean of men, State Teachers Coll., Shippensburg, Pa., since 1928. Mem. N.E.A., Pa. State Edn. Assn., Pa. Acad. Sciences, Phi Delta Kappa. Republican. Lutheran. Clubs: Rotary (Shippensburg); Carlisle (Pa.) Country. Wrote many articles on ednl. subjects. Address: State Teachers Coll., Shippensburg, Pa.

WRIGHT, William Jenks, investment banker; b. St. Davids, Pa., Aug. 8, 1896; s. Menturn Tatum and Ethel Story (Jenks) W.; grad. Middlesex Sch., Concord, Mass., 1914; student Haverford (Pa.) Coll., 1914-17; m. Alberte Vawter Bicknell, Oct. 4, 1920; children—William Jenks, Ernest Bicknell, Charlotte. Asso. with Graham Parsons & Co., investment bankers, Phila., 1920-26; v.p. Blair & Co., bankers, 1926-28; partner Janney & Co., Phila., 1928-31; mgr. Phila. office Salomon Bros. & Hutzler since 1932. Served as volunteer Am. Field Service with French Army, Mar.-Sept., 1919, U.S. Army Abulance Corps, 1917-19. Treas. and chmn. finance com., com. of Seventy, Phila. Decorated Croix de Guerre (France) and Am. overseas medal. Republican. Presbyterian. Clubs: Racquet, Philadelphia Cricket (Phila.); Ribault (Jacksonville, Fla.). Home: 140 W. Chestnut Av. Office: 123 S. Broad St., Philadelphia, Pa.

WRIGHT, Winthrop Robins, prof. physics; b. Trenton, N.J., May 11, 1888; s. William Robins and Fannie (Bailey) W.; A.B., U. of Mich., Ann Arbor, Mich., 1909, Ph.D., 1917; grad. study, Columbia U., 1912-15; grad. study,

Cambridge U., Eng., 1925-26; m. Bertha W. Fisher, Oct. 30, 1915 (died 1932); children—John Fisher, Naomi Fisher; m. 2d, Ruth A. Cline, Nov. 9, 1934; 1 son, Winthrop Robins. Began as instr. mathematics, Ga. Sch. Tech., 1909-12; instr. U. of Mich., 1915-17; asst. physicist, U.S. Bur. of Standards, 1917-19; asst. prof. physics, Swarthmore (Pa.) Coll., 1919-24, asso. prof. 1924-29, prof. since 1929. Fellow A.A.A.S., Am. Phy. Soc.; mem. Franklin Inst., Sigma Xi. Presbyterian. Home: 4 Whittier Place, Swarthmore, Pa.

WRISTON, Robert, physician and surgeon; b. Kincaid, W.Va., Aug. 23, 1879; s. Isaac G. and Alice (Stanley) W.; student Concord Normal Sch., Athens, W.Va., 1896-1900; M.D., Coll. of Physicians and Surgeons, Baltimore, Md., 1901-05; m. Minnie Davis, May 11, 1910; children—Mary Alice (Mrs. James G. Rizos), June, Marjorie, Martha Vane. Teacher public schools of Raleigh County, W.Va., 1896-1900; began as physician and surgeon, Beckley, W.Va., 1905; treas. Raleigh Gen. Hosp., Beckley, W. Va., since 1928; v.p. Raleigh County Bank, Beckley, W.Va., since 1925, Beckley Newspaper Corpn. since 1932; dir. Beckley Water Co., Homeseekers Bldg. & Land Co. Served as med. examiner, Raleigh County Draft Bd., during World War. Mem. city council, Beckley, 1914-18, 1928-30; mayor, Beckley, 1936-37. Mem. Raleigh County Med. Soc., W.Va. Med. Assn., Southern Med. Assn. Republican. Methodist. Mason (Chapter, Commandry, Shriner). Home: 202 Neville St. Office: Raleigh County Bank Bldg., Beckley, W.Va.

WROTH, James Stewart, mining engr.; b. Albuquerque, N.M., Oct. 13, 1885; s. James Henry and Ella Forrest (Burke) W.; student U. of N.M., 1901-02; B.S., U. of Calif., 1906; m. Marion Churchill van Haagen, Oct. 5, 1923; children—Mary Elizabeth, James Henry, William Fabyan, Robert Stewart. Gen. engring., Western U.S. and Mex., 1906-13; successively chief mine engr., asst. mine supt., asst. to cons. engr. Chile Copper Co., Chile, 1913-18; independent practice as cons. mining engr., New York, 1919-25; with U.S. Bureau of Mines in charge of potash investigations in N.M., Tex. and in Europe, 1926-29; mining engr. Internat. Mining Corpn., New York, since 1929. Served as 1st lt., Engrs., U.S. Army, 1918. Mem. Am. Inst. of Mining and Metall. Engrs., Mining and Metall. Soc of America, S.A.R., Pi Kappa Alpha. Republican. Episcopalian. Mason (Shriner). Club: Mining (New York). Home: 602 Prospect St., Westfield, N.J. Office: 630 5th Av., New York, N.Y.

WROTH, Peregrine Jr., chief surgeon Potomac Edison Co.; surgeon Western Md. R.R.; cons. surgeon Md. Tuberculosis Sanatorium, Washington County Hosp. and Waynesboro (Pa.) Hosp. Address: 131 W. Washington St., Hagerstown, Md.

WRY, Orlin Vincent, physician; b. Fairfield, Vt., Apr. 7, 1901; s. Ila Anthony and Ora Winfred (Hibbard) W.; M.D., U. of Vt. Med. Sch., 1925; m. Grace Marion Dickinson, June 16, 1928; children—Orlin Vincent, Charles Anthony, Ora Elizabeth, Mary Grace. Interne Bishop De Goesbriand Hosp., Burlington, Vt., 1924-25, Bayonne Hosp., Bayonne, N.J., 1925-26; engaged in gen. practice of medicine at East Rutherford, N.J., since 1926; Vanderbilt Clinic, N.Y. City, 1928-31; asst. surgeon, St. Mary's Hosp., Passaic, N.J., since 1931, chief 3d div. obstetrics since 1939, mem. bd. govs. since 1939; police surgeon, East Rutherford, 1927-32; dir. Boiling Springs Bldg. & Loan Assn., East Rutherford, N.J. Served as 1st lt. Med. Res. Corps, U.S.A., 1925-35. Mem. bd. edn. East Rutherford since 1935. Mem. Am. Med. Assn., N.J. State and Bergen County med. socs. Roman Catholic. Elk. Club: Elks of Rutherford. Home: 95 High St., East Rutherford, N.J.

WUNDER, Clarence Edmond, architect, engr.; b. Phila., Nov. 14, 1886; s. Otto and Katherine (Dirks) W.; ed. Central Manual Training Sch., Phila., and pvt. instrn.; m. Elizabeth I. Geissel, Oct. 18, 1910; children—Clarence Edmond, Katherine Elizabeth, Richard Paul. Draftsman with Kurt W. Peuckert, architect and engr., Phila., 1905-10; mem. firm Peuckert & Wunder, 1910-14, alone since 1914; designer of Penn-

WURDACK sylvania Hotel, Temple Univ. Stadium, Bonwit, Teller & Co.'s Store, George Allen Store, Cuneo Eastern Press, Inc., Keebler Weyl Baking Co., also many aptmt. houses, industrial plants, institutional bldgs. etc. Mem. Am. Inst. Architects. Mason. Clubs: Merion Cricket, Union League (Phila.). Home: Dodds Lane, Ardmore, Pa. Office: Architects Bldg., Philadelphia, Pa.

WURDACK, John Herman, univ. prof.; b. Pittsburgh, Pa., Sept. 10, 1888; s. John Joseph and Maria Martha (Lockau) W.; Ph.G., U. of Pittsburgh Sch. of Pharmacy, 1909, Pharm.D., 1910; m. Mary Elizabeth McMahon, Jan. 20, 1919; children—John, Mary, Paul, Rose. Employed as pharmacist, 1909-10; instr. in chemistry, U. of Pittsburgh Sch. of Medicine, 1910-11; instr. post grad. courses, U. of Pittsburgh Sch. of Pharmacy since 1911, instr. chemistry, physics, and Latin, 1914-21, asst. prof. chemistry, 1921-23, asso. prof., 1923-25, prof. since 1925. Mem. Am. Chem. Soc., Am. and Pa. Pharm. socs., Nat. Geog. Soc., Phi Delta Chi. Asso. in revision U.S. Pharmacopoeia IX and Nat. Formulary IV and VI. Republican. Catholic. Abstracter for yearbooks of Am. Pharm. Assn., 1914-16 and 1927. Author: Pharmaceutical Latin, 1927. Contbr. articles to pharm. jours. Home: 312 McKinley St. Office: 1431 Boul. of the Allies, Pittsburgh, Pa.

WURTS, Charles Stewart, Jr., securities brokerage; b. Phila., Pa., May 27, 1901; s. Charles Stewart and Elizabeth (Wister) W.; ed. Prot. Episcopal Acad., Phila., Pa., 1909-19; C.E., Princeton, 1923. Unmarried. Began as civil engr., Phila. Electric Co., 1924-25; mem. firm Coles & Wurts, brokers stocks and bonds, Phila., 1926-31; propr. C. S. Wurts & Co., successors, since 1931. Trustee P. E. Acad., Phila., Pa. Republican. Episcopalian. Clubs: Rittenhouse, Whitemarsh Valley Hunt (Phila.); Chester Yacht (Chester, N.S.); Nassau, Charter (Princeton, N.J.); Royal N.S. Yacht Squadron (Halifax, N.S.). Home: 926 Spruce St. Office: 1327 Walnut St., Philadelphia, Pa.

WURZBACH, J. A.; editor Dispatch-Herald. Office: 12th and French Sts., Erie, Pa.

WYATT, Joseph M.; mem. law firm Wyatt, Jones & Reardon. Office: Keyser Bldg., Baltimore, Md.

WYCKOFF, Everett Bailey, lawyer; b. Grafton, W.Va., July 21, 1906; s. Ole Everett and Mayme (Bailey) W.; LL.B., W.Va. Univ. Law Coll., Morgantown, 1930; m. Beulah N. Reardon, Aug. 2, 1932; 1 dau., Carolyn Jeanne. Admitted to W.Va. bar, 1930 and since engaged in gen. practice of law at Grafton; mem. firm Wyckoff and Wyckoff since 1930. Past pres. Taylor Co. Bd. of Trade. Mem. W.Va. State Bar Assn., Sigma Nu. Republican. Baptist. Mason. Home: 329 W. Washington St. Office: Professional Bldg., Grafton, W.Va.

WYER, Ramon, accountant, engr.; b. Columbus, O., Jan. 16, 1912; s. Samuel S. and Pauline LeFevre (Conover) W.; B.I.E., O. State U., Columbus, O., 1931; M.B.A., Harvard, 1935; unmarried. Analyst, Allied Chem. & Dye Corpn., New York City, 1935-36; v.p. May Oil Burner Corpn., Baltimore, since 1936. Mem. Tau Beta Pi, Chi Phi. Author: Fact and Fallacy on the St. Lawrence. Home: 3203 N. Charles St. Office: May Oil Burner Corpn., Baltimore, Md.

WYETH, Newell Convers, artist; b. Needham, Mass., Oct. 22, 1882; s. Andrew Newell and Henriette (Zirngiebel) W.; ed. Mechanics Arts High Sch., Mass. Normal Art Sch., Eric Pape's Art Sch., all of Boston; studied with C. W. Reed and Howard Pyle; m. Carolyn Brenneman Bockius, Apr. 16, 1906; children—Henriette Zirngiebel, Carolyn Brenneman, Nathaniel Convers, Ann, Andrew. Principal works: Decorations of grill room, Traymore Hotel, Atlantic City, N.J.; large panels, Mo. State Capitol, representing two battles of Civil War; two historic panels, Federal Reserve Bank and 5 large murals in New First National Bank, Boston; triptych in dining room of Hotel Roosevelt, N.Y. City; 5 panels in Hubbard Memorial Bldg., Nat. Geographic Soc., Washington; large mural in Franklin Savings Bank, N.Y. City; mural panel, Penn Mut. Life Ins. Co. Bldg., Phila.; triptych for the reredos of the Chapel of the Holy Spirit, Nat. Episcopal Cathedral, Washington, D.C.; a mural depicting the Builders of St. Andrews School, St. Andrews Episcopal School for Boys, Middletown, Del. Awarded gold medal, San Francisco Expn., 1915; Beck prize, Pa. Acad. Fine Arts, 1910; 4th Clark prize, for painting, Corcoran Art Gallery, Washington, D.C., 1932. Has illustrated 20 juvenile classics. Mem. Soc. Illustrators, Phila. Water Color Club, Fellowship Pa. Acad. Fine Arts. Republican. Unitarian. Home: Chadds Ford, Pa.

WYLIE, James Beall, farming, stock raising; born in Cumberland Township, Greene County, Pennsylvania, September 24, 1862; son of Robert (6 ancestors in Colonial Army) and Elizabeth (Beall, 10th generation b. in U.S.) W.; A.B., Washington and Jefferson Coll., Washington, Pa., 1882; m. Helen Roseborough, June 24, 1890; children—Marion Margaret (Mrs. Robert M. Murphy), L. Jean Gaston (Mrs. John A. Harrison), capt. Garvin R. Asso. with father in farming and wool commission business (established in 1840) and propr. after death of father; closed wool business, 1918; v.p. and dir. Peoples Nat. Bank. Served as Vol. State Police, commd. by Gov. of Pa., 1917-19; sch. supervisor and rd. supervisor for 40 yrs. without salary or fees. Dir. The Washington Sem. (founded 1840). Hon. mem. Luther Burbank Soc.; mem. Nat. Grange, Washington Hist. Soc. Republican. United Presbyterian. Home: R.F.D. No. 3, Washington, Pa.

WYLIE, James Renwick, Jr., partner Huntley & Huntley; b. Wilkinsburg, Pa., Sept. 12, 1897; s. James Renwick and Laura A. (Steele) W.; B.S., Dartmouth Coll., 1919; M.S., U. of Pittsburgh, 1921; m. Alice Virginia Bell, Feb. 27, 1927; children—Virginia Bell, James Renwick, III, John Sheridan. Employed by R. E. Davis, engr., 1921-26; partner Huntley & Huntley, petroleum geologists and engrs., since 1926. Mem. Am. Assn. Petroleum Geologists. Republican. United Presbyn. Home: 1501 Marion Av., Wilkinsburg, Pa. Office: 2711 Grant Bldg., Pittsburgh, Pa.

WYLIE, Robert Morris, M.D.; b. Trenton, O., Oct. 23, 1883; s. Robert and Adelia (Jadden) W.; A.B., Denison U., Granville, O., 1904, A.M., 1909; M.D., Johns Hopkins Med. Sch., Baltimore, 1923; m. Grace Felton, July 31, 1913. Prof. physics and chemistry, Marshall Coll., Huntington, W.Va., 1909-19; interne Johns Hopkins Hosp., 1923-24; in gen. practice of medicine at Huntington since 1924; mem. staff Huntington Memorial Hosp., St. Marys Hosp. Fellow Am. Coll. Physicians; mem. A.M.A., W.Va. State Med. Soc., Phi Gamma Delta, Nu Sigma Nu. Republican. Presbyn. Mason (Scottish Rite). Clubs: Guyan Country, Executives (Huntington). Home: 1351 13th St. Office: 955 4th Av., Huntington, W.Va.

WYMAN, Levi Parker, prof. chemistry; b. Skowhegan, Me., July 12, 1873; s. Augustine H. and Sarah (Parker) W.; grad. high sch. Skowhegan, 1891; A.B., Colby Coll., 1896, A.M., 1899; Ph.D., U. of Pa., 1902; Sc.D., Pa. Mil. Coll., 1930; m. Ida M. Rich, Dec. 31, 1896; 1 son, Newton Augustine. Teacher pub. schs. of Mass. 4 yrs., Pa. State Coll., 1903-04; prof. chemistry, Pa. Mil. Coll., since 1905, dean since 1920, v.p. since 1930. Lt. col. Pa. N.G., 1930. Mem. Phi Delta Theta. Republican. Baptist. Author: The Golden Boys Series (9 vols.), 1920; The Lakewood Boys Series (5 vols.), 1924; The Hunniwell Boys Series (7 vols.), 1929-30; Donald Price's Victory, 1930; The Mystery of Eagle Lake, 1931. Home: 115 West 24th St., Chester, Pa.

WYNN, I(saac) N(ewton) Earl, lawyer; b. West Chester, Pa., Dec. 15, 1888; s. I. Newton and Ella E. (Bishop) W.; A.B., Swarthmore, 1910; m. E. Irene Ingram, Oct. 20, 1917; children—Virginia I., Betty B. Admitted to Chester County (Pa.) bar, 1916, Pa. state bar, 1930; engaged in gen. practice of law at West Chester since 1916; trust officer of Nat. Bank of Chester Co. & Trust Co., 1919-35, now dir. and sec. bd.; pres. and dir. Chester County Thrift Corpn. Trustee and sec.-treas. Oaklands Cemetery; dir. West Chester Y.M.C.A. Mem. Chester Co. Bar Assn., Pa. Bar Assn., Phi Sigma Kappa. Republican. Presbyn. (trustee First Presbyn. Ch.). Mason. Club: Rotary. Home: 404 Price St. Office: 13 N. High St., West Chester, Pa.

WYNN, James Henry, investment banker; b. Phila., Pa., Dec. 18, 1901; s. James Maurice and Jennie (Pratt) W.; B.S., Lafayette Coll., 1924; m. Marian Sloan, Sept. 20, 1929; 1 dau., Jane Morris. Associated with J. W. Sparks & Co., bankers and brokers, Phila., since 1924, mem. firm since 1929. Mem. Theta Delta Chi. Republican. Clubs: Union League, Merion Cricket. Home: Rose Lane, Haverford, Pa. Office: 1510 Chestnut St., Philadelphia, Pa.

WYNN, John Sparks, investment banking; b. West Chester, Pa., Aug. 2, 1899; s. J. Maurice and Jennie (Pratt) W.; B.S., Lafayette Coll., Easton, Pa., 1922; m. Helen Van Dusen, Apr. 24, 1926; children—John Sparks, Barbara Anne. Asso. with J. W. Sparks & Co., bankers and brokers, mem. N.Y. Stock Exchange, Phila., since 1922, mem. firm since 1929. Served in arty., O.T.C., Camp Zachary Taylor, 1918. Mem. Theta Delta Chi. Republican. Presbyterian. Club: Union League (Phila.). Home: 223 Winding Way, Merion, Pa. Office: 1510 Chestnut St., Philadelphia, Pa.

WYTHES, William Henry, high school prin.; b. Altoona, Pa., Dec. 20, 1894; s. George Washington and Matilda (Allport) W.; student Evening Sch. of Accounts and Finance, U. of Pa., 1913-16; B.S. in edn., U. of Pa., 1928, A.M., 1932; m. Marion Paul Lukens, Nov. 23, 1921; children—Jack Lukens, Richard Allport, Paul Morrison. Stenographer Pa. R.R., Camden, N.J., 1913-14; bank clerk Broadway Trust Co., Camden, 1914-16; teacher Camden High Sch., 1916-33; prin. Woodrow Wilson High Sch., Camden, N.J., since 1933. Served with 224th Aero Service Squadron, U.S. Army, 1918; disch. sergt. 1st class. Mem. Phi Delta Kappa. Episcopalian. Club: Camden County Pennsylvania. Home: 265 Merion Av., Haddonfield, N.J. Office: Woodrow Wilson High School, Camden, N.J.

Y

YAEGER, Christian G(eorge), physician; b. Phila., Pa., June 30, 1872; s. Christian and Christina (Stauth) Y.; A.B., Central High Sch., Phila., 1892; M.D., U. of Pa., 1895; m. Mary Ann Sommers, Nov. 20, 1901; 1 stepson, Raymond Lock Sommers, M.D. In practice of medicine, Phila., since 1895, gen. practice 1895-1920, specializing in internal medicine since 1920. Mem. Phila. Co. Med. Soc., Med. Club of Phila., Physicians Motor Club. Republican. Episcopalian. Mason (32°, Shriner). Club: Old York Road Country (Montgomery Co., Pa.). Home: 619 Chelten Av., Oaklane. Office: 2403 E. York St., Philadelphia, Pa.

YAGGY, Edward Esher, Jr., mfg. oil burners; b. Hutchinson, Kas., Apr. 13, 1909; s. Edward Esher and Laura (Reed) Y.; A.B., Yale U., 1931; M.B.A., Harvard U. Grad. Sch. Bus. Adminstrn., 1935; m. Elizabeth Ross Duncan, Dec. 14, 1935; 1 son, Duncan. Began as apple salesman Yaggy Plantation Co., 1925; student commercial dept., Pub. Service Electric & Gas Co. N.J., Newark, N.J., 1931-34; in statis. dept. Kidder, Peabody & Co., N.Y. City, 1935-36; pres. and dir. May Oil Burner Corpn., mfrs. oil burners, Baltimore, Md., since 1936; pres. and dir. May Fuel Oil Corpn., Baltimore. Sec. and dir. Md. Soc. for Prevention of Blindness. Mem. Beta Theta Pi. Democrat. Episcopalian. Clubs: Rotary, Merchants, Maryland, Chesapeake, Baltimore Country (Baltimore); Elkridge. Home: 4604 Charles St. Office: 1501 Maryland Av., Baltimore, Md.

YAHRES, John M., mfr. screws and bolts; b. Etna, Pa., Aug. 26, 1890; s. Samuel H. and Susan A. (Taylor) Y.; ed. pub. schs., Etna, Pa., and Duff's Business Coll.; m. Inde D. Moore, Mar. 1, 1916; children—Robert M., John M. In employ Nat. Bolt and Nut Co., Pittsburgh, Pa., 1907-10; with Pittsburgh Screw and Bolt Corpn. since 1910, now exec. v.p. Presbyn. Mason (K.T., 32°, Shriner). Clubs: Highland Country (Bellevue); Duquesne (Pittsburgh); Country (Oakmont). Home: 71 N. Euclid Av., Bellevue, Pa. Address: P.O. Box 1708, Pittsburgh, Pa.

YANT, William Parks, chemist; b. East Sparta, O., Nov. 12, 1894; s. James Alpheus and Sarah Elizabeth (Parks) Y.; B.S., Wooster (Ohio) Coll., 1918; spl. course in chemistry, U. of Pittsburgh; m. Elizabeth M. Grossman, July 29, 1933. Instr. in organic chemistry, Wooster Coll., 1919, 20; jr. chemist Gas Lab., U.S. Bur. of Mines, Pittsburgh Expt. Sta., 1921, continuing successively as asst. chemist, chemist in charge of lab., supervising chemist of Health Lab. sect., supervising engr. U.S. Bur. Mines, Pittsburgh Expt. Sta. and chief chemist Health Div., U.S. Bur. of Mines, since 1936, dir. of research and development Mine Safety Appliances Co., Pittsburgh, Pa. Chem. Warfare Service, 1918; research on gas masks. Fellow A.A.A.S.; mem. Am. Chem. Soc. (chmn. Pittsburgh sect. 1933), Am. Inst. Mining and Metall. Engrs., American Public Health Association, Coal Mining Institute of America. Mason. Contbr. many articles in Govt. publs. and in tech. press, in the field of applied gas chemistry and engring., with particular reference to problems of health and safety from industrial gases, vapors and dusts. Address: Mine Safety Appliances Co., Braddock and Thomas Boul., Pittsburgh, Pa.

YARDLEY, Farnham, mfr. valves; b. Yonkers, N.Y., Aug. 8, 1868; s. Charles Burleigh and Margaret Tufts (Swan) Y.; grad. Ashland High Sch., East Orange, N.J., 1885, Phillips Acad., Andover, Mass., 1886; m. Harriet Mullett Jenkins, Apr. 2, 1907; 1 son, Alfred Jenkins. Formerly insurance broker, N.Y. City; elected v.p. Jenkins Bros., 1911, pres. since 1917; pres. Jenkins Bros. Ltd., Montreal, Can.; chmn. of Bd. First Nat. Bank (West Orange), Bartlett Carry Realty Co.; dir., sec. Llewellyn Park Improvement Co.; mayor of West Orange, 1915-17; councilman, East Orange, 1902-06, also chmn. water com. Rep. presdl. elector, N.J., 1924. Paymaster U.S.S. Portsmouth, Spanish-Am. War; was aide to comdg. officer N.R.N.J., rank of lt. j.g., now on retired list. Active in World War work; chmn. Defense Com., West Orange; federal food administrator of Oranges; chmn. or vice chmn. various Liberty Loan Campaigns, West Orange; etc. Pres. West Orange Sinking Fund Commn.; trustee West Orange High School Scholarship Fund, Llewellyn Park (West Orange), Marcus L. Ward Home (Maplewood, N.J.), House of Good Shepherd (Orange, N.J.), The Record Ambulance (ex-pres.). Member Academy of Political Science, Association for Protection of Adirondacks (trustee and vice-pres.), N.J. Historical Society, N.E. Soc. of Oranges; Founders and Patriots America, Soc. Colonial Wars (ex-gov. N.J. Soc.), S.A.R., Chamber Commerce State of N.Y., Chamber Commerce and Civics of the Oranges and Maplewood, N.J., Welfare Fed. of the Oranges (ex-pres.), Assn. Residents of Upper Saranac Lake (pres.), Am. Supply and Machinery Mfrs. Assn. (ex-pres., mem. advisory bd.). Episcopalian; warden Ch. of the Holy Innocents, West Orange; member advisory and financial com. Diocese of Newark. Clubs: Essex County Country, Rock Springs (N.J.); Union, Merchants, Racquet and Tennis (New York). Home: Llewellyn Park, West Orange, N.J. Office: 80 White St., New York, N.Y.

YARDLEY, Richard Quincy, cartoonist; b. Baltimore, Md., Mar. 11, 1902; s. Richard Turner and Alice (Hall) Y.; ed. Md. Inst., Baltimore; m. Margaret Bruening, of Pittsburgh, Oct. 4, 1927. Mem. staff Baltimore Evening Sun, 1923-24; cartoonist Baltimore Morning Sun since 1934. Clubs: University (Baltimore); National Press (Washington, D.C.). Home: 2647 N. Charles St. Office: Baltimore Sun, Baltimore, Md.

YARNALL, Charlton, banker; b. Phila., Pa., Aug. 1, 1864; s. Ellis and Margaret (Harrison) Y.; student Haverford Coll., 1880-82; m. Anna Brinton Coxe, May 23, 1889; children—Alexander Coxe, Mrs. Margaret Newbold, Mrs. Yarnall Jacobs, Agnes, LePage. Mem. firm Ellis, Yarnall & Son, mchts., Phila., 1885-1935; dir. Phila. Nat. Bank since 1910; dir. Buffalo & Susquehanna R R. Corpn.; chmn. bd. Phila. Contributionship for Insurance of Houses from Loss by Fire; dir. Hale & Kilburn Corpn.; mgr. Phila. Saving Fund Soc.; dir. The Church Life Ins. Corpn., The Church Properties Fire Ins. Corpn. Trustee Univ. of Pa., Phila. Museum of Art, Estate Alexander B. Coxe, Ch. Pension Fund, Bryn Mawr Hospital, Welfare Federation of Philadelphia. Dir. and pres. Newtown Twp. Sch. Dist. since 1929. Member English-Speaking Union (vice-president and dir.). Republican. Episcopalian. Clubs: Philadelphia, Rittenhouse, Radnor Hunt, Franklin Inn, New York Yacht. Home: Devon, Pa. Office: 1528 Walnut St., Philadelphia, Pa.

YARNALL, D. Robert, mechanical engr.; b. Delaware Co., Pa., June 28, 1878; s. Edward S. and Sidney S. (Garrett) Y.; B.S. in M.E., U. of Pa., 1901, M.E., 1905; m. Elizabeth R. Biddle, 1923; children—D. Robert, James Biddle, Nancy Hutton. With Coatesville Boiler Works, 1902-07, Stokes & Smith Co., 1907-12; v.p., gen. mgr. Nelson Valve Co., Phila., 1912-18; organizer, 1912, and member firm Yarnall-Waring Co., mfrs. power plant specialties; director and v.p. Pullenlite Company, James G. Biddle Co. Mem. Commn. in Europe having charge of feeding German children, 1920, and chmn. during latter part of time with hdqrs. in Berlin, again in 1924 for the American Friends Service Company and the Gen. Allen Com.; mem. Austrian Refugee Commn., 1938. Dir. Am. Engring. Council, 1928-34; vice-pres. Engring. Foundation; dir. United Engineering Trustees (pres. 1938-39); mem. Am. Soc. M.E. (mgr. 1917-20), Franklin Inst., Engineers' Club of Phila. (pres. 1929-30), Am. Friends Service Com., Sigma Xi. Chmn. com. Westtown Sch.; pres. and dir. Pendle Hill. Republican. Quaker. Clubs: Engineers, Phila. Cricket; Engineers (New York). Home: 42 W. Upsal St., Germantown. Office: Chestnut Hill, Philadelphia, Pa.

YARNALL, Stanley Rhoads, educator; b. Phila., Pa., Aug. 29, 1871; s. Hibberd and Mary Ashbridge (Rhoads) Y.; A.B., Haverford (Pa.) Coll., 1892 (Phi Beta Kappa), A.M., 1893; A.M., Univ. of Pa., 1925; special courses in edn., Columbia, Cornell U., Harvard; m. Susan Ashbridge Roberts, Aug. 9, 1917; children— Stanley Rhoads, Richard Ashbridge. With Porter & Coates, later Henry T. Coates & Co., publs., Phila., 1893-98; teacher, Latin, Greek and ancient history, Germantown Friends Sch., 1898-1906, actg. prin., same, 1906-07, prin., 1907—. Mem. bd. mgrs. Haverford Coll.; sec. bd. mgrs. Cheney Training Sch. for Teachers, 1905-22; v.p. Dunwoody Home for the Convalescent. Mem. Coll. Entrance Examining Bd., 1914-24; pres. Headmasters' Assn. of U.S., 1930; treas. Assn. Colls. and Preparatory Schs. of Middle States; mem. Edn. Council Soc. of Friends, 1933-36; vice-pres. Phila. Council Boy Scouts of America; pres. Richard Humphrey Foundation. Pres. Science and Art Club, Germantown. Home: 5337 Knox St., Germantown, Philadelphia, Pa.

YATES, Cullen, artist; b. Bryan, O., Jan. 24, 1866; s. Franklin B. and Lavinia A. (Punches) Y.; ed. under William M. Chase, Leonard Ochtman, etc., Acad. Design, N.Y., Acad. Julian, École des Beaux Arts, Paris; m. Mabel Taylor, May 27, 1911; children—Richard C., Lavinia. Specialty landscapes; represented in Phila. Art Club, Lotos Club, William T. Evans collection, Nat. Gallery, Washington, Montclair (N.J.) Gallery, Brooklyn Inst. Arts and Sciences, St. Louis Mus., Seattle Gallery, Nat. Arts Club (New York), Mus. of History, Science and Art (Los Angeles, Calif.), Youngstown (O.) Museum of Art, Phila. Art Club, Westfield (Mass.) Art Collection, Portland (Ore.) Art Galleries, Buck Hill (Pa.) Art Assn. (purchase prize), Newark (N.J.) Museum of Art, and many private collections. Bronze medal, St. Louis Exposition, 1904; George Inness, Jr., prize, Salmagundi Club; Joseph Isidor prize, same, 1921; Nat. Arts Club medal, 1932. A.N.A., 1908, N.A., 1919. Mem. New York Society of Painters, American Water Color Society, New York Water Color Club, Allied Artists America, Artists' Aid Soc. Clubs: Lotos, Salmagundi, Nat. Arts, Century Assn. (New York). Home: Shawnee on Delaware, Monroe Co., Pa. Address: National Arts Club, 15 Gramercy Park, New York, N.Y.

YATES, Henry A., fire ins. exec.; b. Jacksonville, Ill.; student U. of Mich.; married; 1 dau., Margaret. Asst. mgr. Western Dept. Aetna Fire Ins. Co., at Chicago, Ill.; v.p. Southern Fire Ins. Co., St. Louis, Mo.; v.p. and dir. Nat. Union Fire Ins. Co., Pittsburgh, since 1931; v.p. and dir. Birmingham Fire Ins. Co., Nat. Union Indemnity Co. Republican. Episcopalian. Home: 4107 Bigelow Boul. Office: 139 University Pl., Pittsburgh, Pa.

YATES, William Oswald, clergyman; b. Zelienople, Pa., May 10, 1884; s. Rudolph Clay and Ida (Oswald) Y.; student New Windsor Coll., 1902-04; A.B. and A.M., Princeton; student Princeton Theol. Sem., 1906-09; m. Barbara Schulze, Dec. 25, 1914; children—Helen Ruth, William Benjamin. Ordained to ministry Presbyn. Ch.; asst. N.Y. Av. Presbyn. Ch., Washington, D.C., 1908; missionary to Siam, 1909-14; pastor Westminster Ch., Allentown, Pa., 1915-21; pastor Swissvale Presbyn. Ch., Swissvale, Pa., since 1921. Served as chaplain Central O.T.C., 1917-18. Mem. Alpha Tau Epsilon. Republican. Presbyn. Clubs: Rotary (Swissvale); Alpha Tau Epsilon(Pittsburgh). Home: 1803 Monongahela Av., Swissvale, Pa.

YEAGER, George Herschel, instr. surgery, U. of Med.; mem. surg. staff University Hosp.; jr. consultant Bon Secours Hosp. Address: 101 W. Read St., Baltimore, Md.

YEAGER, James Franklin, Jr., entomologist; b. Plymouth, N.C., Apr. 9, 1899; s. James Franklin and Lena Caroline (Rigby) Y.; Ph.B., Yale U., 1924; A.M., Columbia U., 1926; Ph.D., N.Y. Univ., 1929; m. Ruby I. Chapman, June 2, 1920; 1 son, Bertram Jackson. Instr. biology, N.Y. Univ., 1924-29, asst. prof., 1929-30; asst. prof. biology, Ia. State Coll., Ames, 1930-31, asso. prof., 1931-36; entomologist, insect physiology, U.S. Dept. Agr., Nat. Agrl. Research Center, Beltsville, Md., 1936-37, sr. entomologist, research in insect physiology, since 1937; lecturer in insect physiology, U. of Md., College Park, Md., since 1936. Mem. A.A.A.S., Soc. Exptl. Biology and Medicine, Am. Assn. Econ. Entomologists, Entomol. Soc. of America, Am. Genetics Assn., Am. Soc. Zoologists, Entomol. Soc. Washington, Biol. Soc. Washington, N.Y. Acad. Sci., Sigma Xi. Home: 8909 Fairview Rd., Silver Spring, Md.

YEAGER, William Allison, univ. prof.; b. Kimberton, Pa., Apr. 28, 1889; s. Allison E. and Esther Clara (Beerbower) Y.; A.B., Ursinus Coll., 1914; A.M., U. of Pa., 1918, Ph.D., 1929; m. Edna M. Krout, Nov. 25, 1914; 1 son, Kennett William; m. 2d, Alice Y. Danehower, Jan. 1, 1932. Teacher in pub. and high schs. and supt. pub. schs., 1914-27; head dept. edn., Kutztown State Teachers Coll., 1927-30; with Teacher Div., Dept. Pub. Instrn., Harrisburg, Pa., 1930-34; prof. edn. and dir. courses in sch. administrn., U. of Pittsburgh, since 1934. Mem. Nat. and Pa. edn. assn., Am. Assn. Sch. Administrs., Phi Delta Kappa, Kappa Phi Kappa. Republican. Methodist. Mason. Author: Home-School-Community Relations, 1939. Contbr. articles, reports and researches to ednl. jours. Home: 3510 Iowa St., Pittsburgh, Pa.

YEAGER, William Howard, physician; b. Bear Gap, Northumberland Co., Pa., Sept. 26, 1881; s. Simon Swank and Mahala Jane (Adams) Y.; grad. Coal Twp. (Pa.) High Sch., 1900; M.D., U. of Md., Baltimore, 1912; m. Mary Agnes Bunting, July 1, 1919; children—Mary Agnes, William Howard. Salesman, 1900-06; physician in chief Baltimore City Tuberculosis Hospital, 1912-13; first assistant physician Maryland State Sanatorium, 1913-17; in practice at Hagerstown, Md., since 1920. Served as 1st lt., U.S. Army Med. Corps, 1917, capt., 1917-18, major, 1918-19. Mem. A.M.A., Washington Co., Southern, Cumberland Valley Med. Socs., Phi Chi, Phi Sigma Kappa. Republican. Episcopalian. Elk. Clubs: Potomac Game and Fish (Williamsport, Md.); Cumberland Valley Field Trial, Conococheague (Hagerstown, Md.); Monteray Hunt and Rifle (Pa.). Home: 1024 The Terrace. Office: Professional Arts Bldg., Hagerstown, Md.

YEALY, Dorsey Weston, investments; b. Derry, Pa., June 24, 1880; s. David M. and

Minerva (Crissinger) Y.; grad. Derry (Pa.) High Sch., 1896; m. Emma Kerr, Jan. 18, 1905; 1 dau., Isobel Wells (wife of Jerome K. Fisher, M.D.). Began as sch. teacher, 1896; banker 1900-30, successively bank clerk, asst. cashier, cashier, v.p. and pres.; partner New York Stock Exchange firm, 1930-34; v.p. Capitol Saving Plan, Phila., 1934-38; v.p. Independence Fund of North America, Inc., creators and mgrs. living trusts, Pittsburgh, since 1929; dir. Braeburn Alloy Steel Corpn.; sales mgr. Phillips, Schmertz & Co., investment dealers. Republican. Methodist. Mason (32°, Shriner). Clubs: Rotary (hon.), Breakfast, Pittsburgh Athletic Assn. (Pittsburgh). Home: 5445 Beacon St. Office: 497 Union Trust Bldg., Pittsburgh, Pa.

YEANY, Ralph Waldo, clergyman; b. Shannondale, Pa., May 12, 1878; s. John H. and Maria (Keck) Y.; student Thiel Prep. Sch. and Coll., 1896-1901; A.B., Allegheny Coll., 1903, A.M., 1907; student Lutheran Theol. Sem., Phila., 1903-06; m. Della Rinker, June 12, 1906; children—John Francis, Elizabeth Rinker. Ordained Lutheran ministry, 1906; pastor, Sioux Falls, S.D., 1906-08, Freeport, Pa., 1908-09, Evans City, Pa., 1909-18, Brick Church, Pa., 1918-20; founded, 1920, and since supt. Bethseda Home, Meadville, Pa., now also sec.-treas. Pres. Kittanning Conf. of Pittsburgh Synod, 1916-19. Served as mem. Co. B, 16th Regt., Pa. Nat. Guard, 1900-03. Mem. Sigma Alpha Epsilon. Republican. Mason (32°). Club: Rotary of Meadville (mem. boys' work com.). Address: N. Main Extension, Meadville, Pa.

YEARICK, Ralph O., corpn. exec.; b. Jacksonville, Pa., Feb. 15, 1891; s. Harvey S. and Katherine (Stover) Y.; m. Margaret McCormick, Oct. 14, 1914; 1 son, Ralph M. With Westinghouse Air Brake Co. since 1909, as stenographer, 1909-11, private sec., 1911-18, asst. to gen. mgr., 1918-25, asst. sec., 1925-26, sec., 1926, acting v.p. and sec. since 1927; acting v.p. and sec. Wilmerding Corpn.; asst. sec. Union Switch & Signal Co.; dir. Pitt Nat. Bank. Republican. Mem. Reformed Ch. Mason. Club: Edgewood Country. Home: 736 North Av., Wilkinsburg, Pa. Office: Wilmerding, Pa.

YEARLEY, Mary Smith (Mrs. Thomas B.C.Y.), club woman; b. Baltimore, Md., Mar. 28, 1875; d. William H. V. and Eliza Jane (Judik) Smith; student Visitation Convent, Baltimore, Md.; m. Harry M. Benzinger, Jan. 12, 1918 (dec.); m. 2d, Thomas B. C. Yearley, Oct. 17, 1935 (dec.). Served as sec. Nat. Council of Catholic Women, 1920-24; pres. Internat. Fed. of Catholic Alumnae, 1922-26, chmn. dept. of edn. since 1932. Democrat. Roman Catholic. Club: Baltimore Country. Home: 100 W. University Parkway, Baltimore, Md.

YEATMAN, Georgina P(ope), architect; b. Ardsley, N.Y., June 26, 1902; d. Pope and Georgie Claibourne (Watkins) Y.; A.B., U. of Pa., 1922; student U. of Pa. Dept. Fine Arts, 1922-24; B.S. in Architecture, Mass. Inst. Tech., 1925; hon. B.Arch., U. of Pa., 1937. Employed as draftsman, Bissell & Sinkler, Phila., Pa., 1928-29, asso. with firm as architect, 1929; engaged in practice of architecture on own acct., Phila., Pa., since 1929; registered as architect in Pa., N.J., and W.Va.; apptd. dir. Dept. of City Architecture, Phila. for term, 1936-40; mem. and sec. Zoning Board of Adjustment for terms, 1936-41; consultant to Moore Inst. of Art, Sci. and Industry; dir. Octavia Hill Assn.; dir. Phila. Housing Assn. Trustee Darrow Sch., New Lebanon, N.Y. Mem. Am. Inst. Architects, Pa. Assn. Architects, Phila. Art Alliance, Kappa Kappa Gamma, Pi Mu Epsilon. Democrat. Clubs: Women's City, Acorn, Cosmopolitan (Philadelphia); Philadelphia Aviation Country (Ambler). Home: 520 East Gravers Lane, Chestnut Hill. Office: Architects Bldg., 17th & Sansom Sts., Philadelphia, Pa.

YEATMAN, Pope, mining engr.; b. St.Louis, Aug. 3, 1861; s. Thomas and Lucretia (Pope) Y.; M.E., Washington U., St. Louis, 1883; m. Georgie Claiborne Watkins, June 28, 1894; children—Jane Bell (Mrs. Ernest C. Savage), Georgina Pope, Pope. In mining in Mexico, Mo., N.M., Colo., 1883-95; mining engr. Consolidated Gold Fields of S. Africa, Ltd., and mgr. Robinson Deep Gold Mining Co., Johannesburg, S. Africa, 1895-99; also gen. mgr. Simmer and Jack Proprietary Gold Mining Co., Ltd., 1899; gen. mgr. and consulting engr. Randfontein Estates Gold Mining Co., Ltd., Transvaal, S. Africa, 1899-1904; consulting engr. M. Guggenheim's Sons Co., and Guggenheim Exploration Co.; also consulting engr. Nev. Consolidated Copper Co., Steptoe Valley Smelting & Mining Co., Chile Exploration Co., of Chile, Braden Copper Co., of Chile, 1906-16; independent consulting practice, 1916—. Mem. Am. Inst. Mining Egnrs., Am. Soc. C.E., Instn. Mining and Metallurgy (London), Engrs.' Society St. Louis, Mining and Metallurgical Society of America. Awarded D.S.M., 1921. Republican. Vol. for service of U.S. in World War, Aug. 1917; cons. engr., later chief non-ferrous metals div. War Industries Bd., Washington, D.C., until Jan. 1919; resumed practice. Home: 520 East Gravers Lane, Chestnut Hill, Philadelphia, Pa. Office: 165 Broadway, New York, N.Y.

YEAWORTH, Irvin Shortess, clergyman; b. Relay, Md., Jan. 14, 1899; s. Irvin C. and Anna E. (Shortess) Y.; A.B., Johns Hopkins U., 1920; A.M., Princeton U., 1922; Th.B., Princeton Theol. Sem., 1923; grad. study, U. of Berlin, 1923-26; m. Liv Alfsen, Aug. 6, 1924; children—Irvin Shortess, David Victor, Betty Jean, James Thomas, Lillian Margaret. Ordained to ministry Presbyn. Ch., 1923; pastor, Am. Ch. in Berlin, Germany, 1923-26; pastor, Olyphant, Pa., 1927-29, Aurora, Ill., 1929-33; pastor, 1st Presbyn. Ch., Homestead, Pa., since 1933. Served as pvt., Inf., U.S. Army, 1918. Mem. bd. dirs. New Covenant Mission, Keystone Sch. of the Bible, Boy Scout Council; trustee Presbytery of Pittsburgh. Mem. Alpha Tau Epsilon. Clubs: Rotary, Outlook (Homestead, Pa.). Home: 2044 West St. Office: 908 Ann St., Homestead, Pa.

YELLIN, Samuel, metal worker; b. Poland, Mar. 2, 1885; s. Zacharias and Kate (Weintraub) Y.; began studying art at the age of 11 and studied in schs. throughout European countries; m. Leah Josephs, Dec. 25, 1913; children—Ethel, Harvey. Came to U.S., 1906, naturalized citizen, 1924. Conducts business in own name as designer and executer of decorative metal work; credited witth revival of good design and craftsmanship in metal work in America. Works: (metal) Harkness Memorial, Quadrangle, Yale U.; Carillon Tower, Mountain Lake, Fla.; Nat. Cathedral, Washington, D.C.; Federal Reserve Bank, Equitable Trust Co., New York; McKinlock Memorial, Northwestern U.; Hall of Fame, New York U.; W. K. Vanderbilt residence, Northport, L.I.; Cathedral of St. John the Divine, New York; Grace Cathedral, San Francisco; U. of Pittsburgh; Metropolitan Mus. Cloister, New York; etc. Adviser to Pa. Mus. of Art. Awarded medal, Art Institute Chicago, 1918; medal Am. Inst. Architects, 1920; Boston Architectural medal, 1920; gold medal, Architectural League, New York, 1922; Bok civic award, Phila., 1925; Americanization prize, Art Exhbn., Phila., 1916; alumni medal Pa. Mus. and Sch. of Industrial Art, 1930. Mem. American Federation of Arts, Am. Inst. Architects, Architectural League of New York, Art Alliance of America, Soc. of Arts and Crafts of Boston, Pa. Mus. and Sch. Industrial Arts, Phila. Art Alliance, Architects Club of Chicago, Am. Association Museums, Fairmount Park Art Association, Société des Ames dé Louvre, Paris, etc. Clubs: Art in Trades Club, Pa. Athletic, Phila. Sketch, T-Square. Contbr. to art jours. and mags.; lecturer at universities and colleges; collector of old iron work. Contbr. Theory, Modern Technique and Practice on Decorative Metal Work to 14th edit. Ency. Britannica. Home: 331 E. Lancaster Pike, Wynnewood, Pa. Office: 5520 Arch St., Philadelphia, Pa.

YENSEN, Trygve D(ewey), research engr.; b. Drammen, Norway, Jan. 30, 1884; s. Jens Carl and Josephine (Rögeberg) Jensen; came to U.S., 1903, naturalized 1912; student Kristiania (Norway) Kathedral Sch., 1900-03; B.S. in elec., engring., U. of Ill., Urbana, Ill., 1907; M.S., 1912; Ph.D. in physics, Calif. Inst. of Tech., 1927; m. Louise Dewey, June 30, 1910; 1 son, Arne Dewey. Elec. engr., Gen. Electric Co., Schnectady, N.Y., 1907-08; instr., elec. dept., U. of Ill., 1908-09; elec. engr. Shawinigan Water & Power Co., Montreal, Can., 1909-10; asst., U. of Ill. Engring Exptl. Sta., 1910-13, 1st asst., 1913-15, research asst. prof., 1915-16; engr. research labs., Westinghouse Electric & Mfg. Co., East Pittsburgh, 1916-25, sect. engr., 1927-29, div. mgr. since 1929. Fellow Am. Phys. Soc.; mem. Am. Inst. E.E., Am. Inst. Mining and Metall. Engrs., Am. Soc. for Metals, Pittsburgh Phys. Soc., Science of Metals Club, Tau Beta Pi, Sigma Xi, Eta Kappa Nu. Awarded Edison medal diploma of merit by Am. Inst. E.E., 1908, Howe medal by Am. Soc. for Metals, 1935. Republican. Unitarian. Specialty: magnetism and magnetic materials. Home: 10 Hillcrest Rd., Forest Hills, Pittsburgh 21, Pa. Office: Westinghouse Research Labs., East Pittsburgh, Pa.

YEOMANS, Earl Raymond, dir. athletics; b. Phila., Pa., July 24, 1895; s. George Yost and Alice (Witcher) Y.; B.S., Temple U., 1917, M.S., same, 1929; m. Irene Pearce, Nov. 29, 1917. Engaged as dir. phys. edn., Phila. Bd. Edn., 1917-20; met. dir. phys. edn., Phila. Y.M.C.A., 1920-27; dir. athletics, Temple U. since 1927. Mem. Eastern Intercollegiate Boxing Assn. (past pres.), Eastern Intercollegiate Basketball Assn. (past pres.), Eastern Intercollegiate Athletic Assn. (dir.), Phi Epsilon Kappa, Sigma Pi, Zeta Lambda Phi. Kappa Kappa Psi, Phi Delta Kappa. Republican. Baptist. Club: Penn Athletic (Philadelphia). Home: 502 Murdoch Rd., Mt. Airy, Philadelphia, Pa.

YERKES, Leonard A.; b. Phila., Pa., Sept. 11, 1880; s. Augustus A. and Ella (Ehret) Y.; student St. Paul's Sch. and U. of Pa.; m. Helen Jayne Joyce, Apr. 30, 1905; children—Leonard A., William J., Mrs. Robert A. Ramsdell, Mrs. James Provost Smith, Mrs. Ludlow Elliman, Helen Remsen. Gen. mgr. and dir. rayon dept. E. I. du Pont de Nemours & Co. since 1936. Home: Greenville, Del. Office: Wilmington, Del.

YINGLING, Herbert Francis, chemist; b. Burnham, Pa., Aug. 18, 1904; s. David Milton and Julia (Bigelow) Y.; grad. Phila. Coll. of Pharmacy & Science, 1926; m. Helen Price, Aug. 19, 1929; 1 son, David Bigelow. Employed with Standard Steel Works, 1923; employed in drug stores, Phila. and Lewistown, 1926-30; chemist with Am. Viscose Co. since 1930. Mem. Dem. County Com. since 1934, chmn. since 1936. Mem. Upsilon Sigma Phi. Democrat. Lutheran. Mason. Home: Logan Boul., Burnham, Pa. Office: Duquesne Way, Lewistown, Pa.

YOAKAM, Gerald Alan, educator, author; b. Eagle Grove, Ia., Nov. 18, 1887; s. Eugene George and Olive Louisa (Mason) Y.; Tama (Ia.) High Sch., 1902-06; A.B., U. of Iowa, 1910, A.M., 1919, Ph.D., 1922; m. Helen Marie Swain, Aug. 2, 1911; children—Barbara Jeane, Richard David. Prin. supt. and co. supt. schs. in Iowa, 1910-18; prin. U. of Ia. Elementary Sch., 1919-20; dir. teacher training State Teachers Coll., Kearney, Neb., 1920-23; prof. edn. and head dept. elementary edn., U. of Pittsburgh, 1923-32, prof. edn. and dir. of courses since 1932. Mem. N.E.A., Nat. Soc. for Study of Edn., Am. Assn. Univ. Profs., Phi Kappa Phi, Phi Delta Kappa. Methodist. Clubs: Faculty, University. Author: Effect of a Single Reading, 1924; Reading and Study, 1928; Improvement of the Assignment, 1932 (translated into Polish, 1936); Directed Study and Observation of Teaching, 1934; (with R.G. Simpson) An Introduction to Teaching and Learning, 1934; (with Bagley and Knowlton) Reading to Learn, 1935. Contbr. ednl. jours. Asso. editor, Journal of Educational Research; mem. Yearbook Com. Nat. Soc. of Edn., 36th Yearbook, Par I, 1936. Home: 6711 Beacon St., Pittsburgh, Pa.

YODER, Paul Daniel, clergyman; b. Womelsdorf, Pa., Feb. 16, 1879; s. Henry and Sarah Anna (Leiss) Y.; M.Ed., Kutztown State Teachers Coll., 1898; A.B., Franklin and Marshall Coll., Lancaster, Pa., 1907, (hon.) D.D., 1932; B.D., Theol. Sem., Lancaster, Pa., 1910; student U. of Chicago, summer 1909, U. of Wis., summer 1925; m. Kittie Horton Huff, Aug. 9, 1911; children—Paul Henry, Sarah Kathryn

(Mrs. O. Bruce Thomason), Margaret Lorraine (wife of Rev. Darwin X. Gass), Sallie Elizabeth, Edna Leona, Stewart Aylmer. Ordained to Christian ministry, 1910 and pastor, Gary, Ind., 1910-12; pastor various chs., 1912-20; pastor Evang. and Ref. Ch., Codorus, Pa., since 1920; teacher Community Sch. of Religion, York, Pa., 1927-34; instr. rural sociology and ch. work, Theol. Sem., Lancaster, Pa., since 1930; sec. Dept. Town and Country Chs., Pa. Council Chs. since 1938; mem. exec. com. Gen Synod Ref. Ch., 1933-36. Served as pres. Bd. Edn., Codorus, Pa., 1922-36; dir. bd. edn. Potomac Synod Evang. & Ref. Ch. since 1918, Pen-Mar Ref. Reunion Bd. since 1918. Mem. Pa. German Soc. Sigma Pi. Democrat. Evang. and Ref. Ch. Mason, Odd Fellow, K.P. Club: White Rose. Author: Soul of the Rural Church, 1927. Home: Codorus, Pa.

YOHE, Curtis Miller, railway official; b. Connellsville, Pa., Sept. 22, 1887; s. James Buchanan and Mary Margaret (Sykes) Y.; LL.B., Cornell U., 1910; m. Elsie May Close, Dec. 15, 1914; children—Curtis Miller (dec.), Barbara Close, Mary Ann, Elsie May, Curtis Miller, III. Purchasing agt. Pittsburgh & Lake Erie R.R., 1921-28, v.p. since 1929; asst. to pres. N.Y.C. Lines, 1928-29; officer and dir. various r.r.'s and subsidiary properties; dir. Mellon Nat. Bank. Trustee Dollar Savings Bank. Mem. Carnegie Hero Fund Commn.; dir. Pa. State and Pittsburgh chambers of commerce. Mem. Zeta Psi. Methodist. Clubs: Duquesne, Oakmont Country, Rolling Rock Country; Cornell (New York). Home: 6665 Kinsman Rd. Office: Pittsburgh & Lake Erie, Railroad, Pittsburgh, Pa.

YOHLIN, Mordecai, rabbi; b. Beliatzerkov, Russia, Mar. 1881; s. Hersch and Betty (Schriber) Y.; studied in Russia; m. Ester Pessie Sererbria, Sept. 1902; children— Betty (Mrs. Morris Potash), Mary (Mrs. Meyer Brown), Rose, Rae, Harry, Sylvia. Came to U.S., 1925, naturalized, 1931. Rabbi, Beliatzerkov, Russia, 1908-25; rabbi, Phila., since 1925, Atereth Israel, since 1938. Exec. mem. Vad Hakashris (body to see dietary laws are observed by Jewish meat firms); mem. exec. bd. Union of Orthodox Rabbis of U.S. and Canada; mem. exec. com. Am. Jewish Congress; mem. Jewish Nat. Fund; mem. sponsoring com. Palastinian Pavilion at New York's World's Fair; mem. Mizrachi (orthodox Zionist orgn.). Author: Kihilath Mordechi (commentary on Old Testament), Vol. 1, 1912, Vol. 2, 1933. Home: 1530 S. 6th St., Philadelphia, Pa.

YOLLES, Ephraim Elieser, rabbi, lecturer; b. Sambor, Galicia, Jan. 14, 1894; s. Sholom and Esther (Teicher-Luria) Y.; grad. as rabbi Rabbinical Coll. of Stanislau, 1912; qualified expert on Talmudical problems, 1915; m. Betty Weissblum, 1912 (died 1924); 1 dau., Sara; m. 2d, Pepi Pollak, Aug. 1932; children— Esther, Shoshana. Came to U.S., 1921, naturalized, 1927. Asst.-rabbi to his father, Head of Rabbinate of Jewish community, Stryi, Galicia, 1912-14; asst. in Chief Rabbi's office, Budapest, Hungary, 1914-15; chaplain Austria-Hungary, Army, 1916-18; lecturer on Talmud, Hebrew High Sch., Stryi, Poland, 1918-21; rabbi United Orthodox Congregations, Strawberry Mansion, Phila., since 1921. Chmn. exec. bd. United Rabbinate of Phila.; pres. Orthodox Zionist Organization of Phila.; v.p. Phila. Council, Am. Jewish Congress. Contbr. to rabbinical monthly Hapardes; author of essays pub. in Poland. Home: 3233 W. Berks St., Philadelphia, Pa.

YORK, Harlan Harvey, prof. botany; b. nr. Plainfield, Ind., Sept. 8, 1875; s. Pleasant McPherson and Elizabeth (Hornaday) Y.; Ph.B., DePauw U., Greencastle, Ind., 1903; A.M., Ohio State U., 1905; student Columbia, 1905-06; Ph.D., Johns Hopkins, 1911; m. Edith Thayer Cline, Aug. 26, 1908; 1 son, James Thayer; m. 2d, Minnie White Taylor, of Little Compton, R.I., June 23, 1934. Fellow in botany, Ohio State U., 1903-04, asst. in botany, 1904-05; fellow in botany, Columbia, 1905-06; asst. in U.S. Nat. Herbarium, 1906; instr. of botany, U. of Tex., 1906-09; asst. in botany, Johns Hopkins, 1909-10, fellow, 1910-11; asst. prof. of botany, Brown U., 1911-19; prof. of botany, W.Va. Univ., 1919-23; pathologist div. of forest pathology, U.S. Dept. Agr., 1923; forest pathologist N.Y. State conservation Dept., 1923-30; prof. of botany, U. of Pa., since 1930; asst. in cryptogemic botany, Biol. Lab., Cold Spring Harbor, L.I., summers, 1906-11, instr. in charge, summers 1912-15; pathologist div. of forest pathology, U.S. Dept. Agr., summers 1916-22; special investigator and cons. pathologist N.Y. Conservation Dept., summers since 1930. Mem. A.A.A.S., Phytopathological Soc., Torrey Bot. Club, Am. Foresters, Phi Beta Kappa, Sigma Xi, Gamma Alpha, Sigma Nu. Mason, K. of P. Clubs: Lenape (U. of Pa.); McAlpine Street (Phila.). Contbr. to Jour. of Phytopathology, Science. Home: 4201 Pine St., Philadelphia, Pa.

YORK, James Arthur, physician; b. Rose, Tenn., July 31, 1893; s. James Milton and Emma Caroline (Schubert) Y.; student Union (W.Va.) Acad., 1908-12; A.B., Randolph-Macon Coll., Ashland, Va., 1916; M.D., Johns Hopkins Med. Sch., 1923; m. Josephine H. Pront, Aug. 28, 1924; children—Douglas Hamilton, Mary Caroline. Interne, Hosp. for Women of Md., Baltimore, 1923-24, asst. resident, 1924-25, resident surgeon, 1925-26. Served as 2d lt., 28th Div., U.S. Army, 1917-19. Mem. of bd. of trustees, Randolph-Macon Coll., Ashland, Va., Randolph-Macon Woman's Coll., Lynchburg, Va., Randolph-Macon Acad., Front Royal, Va., since 1932; trustee Gaithersburg Home for Aged and Orphans. Mem. Med. and Chirurg. Faculty of Md., Phi Chi. Democrat. Methodist. Mason. Clubs: Bonnie View Golf, Johns Hopkins (Baltimore, Md.). Home: 2601 Talbot St. Office: 1107 St. Paul St., Baltimore, Md.

YORK, Minnie (White) Taylor, (Mrs. Harlan Harvey Y.), forest pathologist, librarian; b. Little Compton, R.I., Oct. 18, 1890; d. Andrew Simeon and Mary Priscilla (White) Taylor; A.B., Brown U., Providence, R.I., 1913, A.M., 1916; m. Harlan Harvey York, June 23, 1934. Asst.: Providence (R.I.) Pub. Library, 1909-15; collaborator, U.S. Dept. Agr., 1913-16, spl. agt., 1916-17, asst. in forest pathology, 1917-22, junior pathologist, 1922-24; librarian, Cleveland Mus. of Natural History, Cleveland, O., 1924-34. Fellow A.A.A.S.; mem. Am. Assn. Univ. Women, Brown Alumnae Club of Eastern Pa., Sigma Delta Epsilon. Republican. Club: Women's University (Phila.). Contbr. articles in tech. and library publs. Home: 4201 Pine St., Philadelphia, Pa.

YORK, Wilbur Heskett, physician, univ. prof.; b. Chattanooga, Tenn., Oct. 31, 1895; s. James Milton and Emma C. (Schubert) Y.; A.B., Randolph-Macon Coll., Ashland, Va., 1916; student U. of Va. Med. Sch., Charlottesville, 1917-18; M.D., Johns Hopkins, 1924; m. Virginia E. Franke, Dec. 20, 1928 (dec.); 1 son, James Milton II; m. 2d, Helen H. Whitlock, July 17, 1931; 1 dau., Anne Virginia. Asso. prof. physiol. chemistry, Emory Univ., Atlanta, Ga., 1918-22; medical adviser, Cornell U., 1926-36; chmn. dept. of health and phys. edn., Princeton U., since 1936. Served as mem. Med. Enlisted Res. Corps, 1917-18. Fellow Nat. Council on Religion in Higher Edn. Mem. Am. Med. Assn., Am. Student Health Assn., Kappa Sigma, Phi Rho Sigma, Phi Beta Kappa. Democrat. Presbyn. Clubs: Nassau, Springdale Golf (Princeton). Home: 87 Battle Rd., Princeton, N.J.

YORKE, Edward W., pub. service exec.; b. Newtown, Pa., Oct. 24, 1874; s. James and Frances M. (Dawson) Y.; student Oil City (Pa.) Bus. Coll., 1895-96; Elec. Engr., Scranton Correspondence Sch., 1906; m. Margaret V. Meade, Corry, Pa., Sept. 7, 1910; children —Edward W., Florence M., Mary E., Margaret F., Helen R. Began as oil well operator, 1890; asso. with Keystone Pub. Service, Oil City, Pa., continuously since 1898, successively, st. ry. operator, sub station operator, central station engr., chief engr., supt. of power plants, and vice-pres. and asst. gen. mgr. in charge of production and equipment, and dir. since 1933; vice-pres. and dir. Citizens Transit Co., Reno Bridge Co. Mem. Pa. State Chamber of Commerce, Oil City Chamber of Commerce. Mem. Pa. Electric Assn. Republican. Roman Catholic. Clubs: Knights of Columbus, Rotary, Wanango Country (Oil City, Pa.). Home: 505 Central Av. Office: Keystone Public Service, Oil City, Pa.

YOST, Calvin Daniel, librarian, coll. prof.; b. Schuylkill Co., Pa., Nov. 5, 1866; s. Daniel J. and Lydia (Bretney) Y.; A.B., Ursinus Coll., Collegeville, Pa., 1891, A.M., 1895, B.D., 1907; grad. student Ursinus Sch. of Theology, 1891-93, Yale Divinity Sch., 1893-94; (hon.) D.D., Heidelberg Coll., Tiffin, O., 1925; m. Sara Ida Wagner, Aug. 28, 1894 (dec.); 1 son, Merrill Wagner (dec.); m. 2d, Amelia K. Wagner, July 14, 1897 (dec.); children—Ethelbert Bretney, Margaret Amelia, Calvin Daniel. Engaged in teaching in pub. schs. 1883-87; ordained to ministry Evang. and Reformed Ch., 1894; pastor, 1894-96 and 1901-07; prin. high sch., Mahanoy City, Pa., 1896-1901; field sec., Ursinus Coll., Collegeville, Pa., 1907-10, librarian since 1910, instr., later prof. German since 1910. Served as pres. Collegeville Borough Council, 1922-34; Burgess, 1938. Dir. Ursinus Coll. since 1916; sec. of bd. since 1923. Mem. Nat. and Pa. edn. assns., A.L.A., M.L.A., Pa. German Soc., Pa. German Folklore Soc. Republican. Mason. Home: 33 Sixth Av., Collegeville, Pa.

YOST, Ellis A(sby), lawyer, b. Fairview, W. Va., Dec. 12, 1872; student Ohio Northern U., 1891-92, Wilmington Conf. Acad., Dover, Del., 1903-04, Ohio Wesleyan U., 1897; LL.B., W.Va. U., 1908; m. Lenna Lowe, Sept. 26, 1899; 1 son, Leland Lowe. Admitted to W. Va. bar and U.S. Supreme Court; extensive experience in real estate business and many years with oil and gas promotion and development companies; dep. state tax commr. of W.Va., 1921-22; asst. U.S. atty., Southern Dist. of W.Va., 1922-30; chief examiner Federal Radio Commn., 1930-33; mem. of bd. and head of land dept., Gordon Oil Co., Grand Rapids, Mich. Mayor of Fairview, W.Va., at age of 23; mem. W.Va. Legislature, 1909-11, 1913-15. Lay del. to Gen. Conf. Meth. Ch., Kansas City, 1928. Mem. Am., W.Va. State, Cabell County and Huntington bar assns. Republican. Methodist. Mason (Shriner). Club: Kiwanis (past pres.). Home: Huntington, W.Va.

YOST, Gaylord, violinist, composer; b. Fayette, O., Jan. 28, 1888; s. Charles E. and Ada Virginia (Purcell) Y.; student Toledo Conservatory of Music, 1903-04, Detroit Conservatory of Music, 1905-06, later in Berlin, Germany, with Issay Barmas; self-taught in composition; Mus.B. from Detroit Conservatory of Music, 1931; Mus.D. from Waynesburg (Pa.) Coll., 1936; m. Rose Natalie Strėbe, Apr. 18, 1917; m. 2d, Ruth Margaret Steuernagel, Mar. 30, 1931. Concert tours in Europe, Central America and U.S., 1907-11; head of violin dept. Ind. Coll. of Music and Fine Arts, Indianapolis, 1915-21; also appears frequently as soloist. Composer: (violin and piano) Reverie; Abendlied; Serenade; Novellette; American Rhapsody; Berceuse; Canzonetta; Humoresque; Danse Characterisque; La Coquette; From the South; Evening; Firefly; Farfalls; Nostromo; Prelude; Song and Dance; also transcriptions of famous composers and pedagogical works; (piano) Prelude Solonnelle, Improvisation; Etude; Caprice Excentrique; Vistas; (songs) A Love Note; Love's Count; My Heart Must Break; (orchestra) Louisiana Suite; many manuscript compositions. Head of violin dept. Pittsburgh Musical Institute since Sept. 1921. Founded the Yost String Quartet, 1925, and also an annual chamber music series of concerts in Pittsburgh. Made revolutionary discoveries regarding violin technic in 1932, incorporated in a book, "The Yost System." Joint recitals with Barre Hill, 1935-36. Studio: Pittsburgh Musical Institute, Pittsburgh, Pa.

YOST, John Stevenson Long, lawyer; b. Baltimore, Md., May 18, 1892; s. William Franklin and Eleanor Bonner (Long) Y.; A.B., Johns Hopkins U., 1914; LL.B., U. of Md. Law Sch., Baltimore, Md., 1917; m. Helen B. Gatchell, 1930; 1 son, Stevenson; m. 2d Clarissa Tilghman Goldsborough, Nov. 25, 1933; 1 dau. Julia

Goldsborough. Began as teacher Gilman Sch., Baltimore, Md., 1914; studied law while teaching and admitted to Md. bar, 1916; asso. with Frank, Emory & Beeuweskes, Baltimore, Md., 1917; served as spl. asst. to sec. of state, Washington, D.C., 1918-19; mem. firm Maloy, Brady, Howell & Yost, Baltimore, Md., 1920-26; mem. firm Maloy, Brady & Yost, 1926-38, asso. with Maloy & Brady since 1939; chief atty. U.S. Dept. Agr., 1933-35; spl. asst. to atty. gen. of U.S. since 1935. Mem. Am. Bar Assn., Baltimore Bar Assn., Wednesday Law Club of Baltimore, Alpha Delta Phi. Democrat. Episcopalian. Club: Bachelors' Cotillon (Baltimore). Home: 1308 John St. Office: Fidelity Bldg., Baltimore, Md.

YOST, Lenna Lowe (Mrs. Ellis A.); b. Basnettville, W.Va., Jan. 25, 1878; d. Jonathan and Columbia (Basnett) Lowe; ed. W.Va. Wesleyan Coll. and Ohio Northern U.; L.H.D. from W.Va. Wesleyan Coll., 1929; m. Ellis A. Yost, 1899; 1 son, Leland Lowe. Past pres. W.Va. Equal Suffrage Assn. and as chmn. of com. directed campaign for ratification of the 19th Amendment; nat. rep. and corr. in Washington, 1918-30; past pres. W.Va. Woman's Christian Temperance Union. First woman teller Rep. Nat. Conv., 1920; first woman to preside over a Rep. State Conv., and first woman to serve as chmn. Platform Com. in a Rep. State Conv.; chmn. Rep. Women's Exec. Com. of W.Va., 1920-22; mem. Rep. Nat. Com., 1924-32, exec. com., 1928-32; director women's div. Rep. Nat. Committee, 1930-35. Mem. State Bd. of Edn., W.Va., 1921-23; trustee W.Va. Wesleyan Coll. Del. to Internat. Congress Against Alcoholism, Lausanne, Switzerland, 1921, Copenhagen, Denmark, 1923. Mem. Am. Assn. University Women, League of Am. Pen Women, D.A.R., Woman's Nat. Farm and Garden Assn. (exec. com.), Pi Sigma Alpha. Club: Nat. Woman's Country. Home: Huntington, W.Va.

YOUNG, Barton Rogers, prof. roentgenology, Temple U. Address: Broad St. and Montgomery Av., Philadelphia, Pa.

YOUNG, Charles Duncanson, ry. official; b. Washington, D.C., May 19, 1878; s. Thomas H. and Annie Cowden ((Forster) Y.; M.E., Cornell, 1902; m. Florence Booth, June 8, 1904; children—John R., Marjorie B. (Mrs. Drew W. Hiestand), Anne F. (Mrs. Nelson Y. Ruth). Began as spl. apprentice, Columbus (O.) shops, Pa. R.R., 1900; successively asst. motive power inspector, asst. master mechanic, asst. engr. motive power, engr. tests, supt. motive power, div. supt., gen. supervisor stores, stores mgr., gen. purchasing agt., asst. v.p., v.p. in charge purchases, stores and ins. 1932-38, v.p. in charge real estate, purchases and ins. since 1938; inventor many devices asso. with mech. arts; pres. and dir. Enola Sewerage Co., Harborside Warehouse Co., Manor Real Estate & Trust Co., Pa. Terminal Real Estate Co., Stuyvesant Real Estate Co.; trustee Associates of Jersey Co.; dir. Pa. R.R. Co., Mutual Fire, Marine & Inland Ins. Co., Norfolk & Western Ry. Co., Pocahontas Coal & Coke Co., Chicago Union Sta. Co., Merchants Warehouse Co., Pittsburgh Joint Stock Yards Co.; mgr. Lykens Valley R.R. & Coal Co.; v.p. and dir. various subsidiary r.r. and water supply companies, dir. and mem. exec. com. In U.S.N., Spanish-Am. War; lt. col. U.S.A. Transportation Corps, World War. Awarded Edward Longstreth medal by Franklin Inst. 1915, for work on locomotive superheaters. Trustee Drexel Inst. of Tech. Mem. Am. Soc. for Testing Materials (chmn. various coms. 1913-21, pres. 1921-22), Am. Ry. Assn. (chmn. Div. VI, purchases and stores, 1925), S.A.R., Pa. Scotch-Irish Soc. (dir. and mem. Council), Pa. Soc. New York, Mil. Order of World War, Am. Mil. Engrs., Beta Theta Pi, Sphinx Head, Aleph Semach. Republican. Episcopalian. Clubs: Racquet, Union League (Phila.). Home: Haverford, Pa. Office: Broad St. Station Bldg., Philadelphia, Pa.

YOUNG, Charles Francis, supt. city schs.; b. Aurora, Mo., June 4, 1893; s. Charles and Elizabeth (Riggs) Y.; A.B., Friends U., Wichita, Kan., 1915; B.S., U. of Pittsburgh, 1922, A.M., 1927, Ph.D., 1936; m. Katherine U. Kepler, Aug. 15, 1920; 1 son, Earl S. Teacher and sch. supt. in Okla. and Kan., 1911-16; supervising prin., Mt. Jewett, Pa., 1922-24; prin. high sch., Swissvale, 1924-29; supt. schs., East Pittsburgh, since 1929. Mem. N.E.A., Nat. Soc. for Study of Edn., Am. Assn. Sch. Administrs., Acad. of Polit. Sci., Phi Delta Kappa. Republican. Methodist. Club: Rotary (East Pittsburgh, Pa.). Home: 523 Ridge Av., East Pittsburgh, Pa.

YOUNG, Charles Morris, artist; b. Gettysburg, Pa., Sept. 23, 1869; s. Christopher Baughman and Anna Louise Y.; ed. pub. schs. and tutors; Pa. Acad. Fine Arts, 1891-95; under Colarossi, Paris, 1897-98; m. Eliza Middleton Coxe, Nov. 18, 1903; children—Arthur Middleton, Christopher, Alexander Coxe (dec.), Philip Francis, Brinton Coxe. Splty. landscapes and portraits; hon. mention, and Tappan prize, Pa. Acad. Fine Arts, 1893, 1894; hon. mention, Buffalo Expn., 1901; silver medal, Charlestown Expn., 1904, St. Louis Expn., 1904; gold medal, Art Club, Phila., 1908; hon. mention, Carnegie Inst., Internat. Exhbn., 1910; silver medal, Buenos Aires, 1910; gold medal, Panama P.I. Expn., 1915; Sesnan gold medal, Pa. Acad. Fine Arts, 1921; Stotesbury prize, 1925; awarded Olympian medal, Amsterdam, Holland, 1928. Represented in the permanent collections of Pa. Acad. Fine Arts, Boston Art Club, St. Louis Club, Nat. Gallery (Budapest, Hungary), Albright Gallery (Buffalo Mus.), Nat. Mus. (Santiago, Chile), Corcoran Gallery (Washington, D.C.), Memorial Art Gallery, Rochester, N.Y., Reading (Pa.) Art Gallery, and many pvt. collections. A.N.A., 1913. Club: Art (Phila.). Address: Radnor, Pa.

YOUNG, Charles Raymond, lawyer; b. Coatesville, Pa., June 28, 1889; s. Samuel S. and Sallie P. (Hammond) Y.; Ph.B., Dickinson Coll., 1909, A.M. (post-grad. work), 1911; student Dickinson Sch. of Law; m. Elizabeth B. Arnold, Sept. 20, 1915; 1 dau., Suzanne A. Admitted to Supreme Court of Pa. and Chester Co. bar, 1912; practiced law, West Chester, Pa., 1912-21, Coatesville, Pa., since 1921; dir. Citizens Bldg. & Loan Assn. of Coatesville, Coatesville Airport; pres. Honey Brook Trust Co. (now in voluntary liquidation), 1924. Dir. Coatesville Chamber of Commerce; mem. Pa. Bar Assn., Chester County Bar Assn. Republican. Presbyterian. Mason. Home: 562 E. Lincoln Highway. Office: 242 E. Lincoln Highway, Coatesville, Pa.

YOUNG, Edgar Charles, clergyman; b. Jamaica, B.W.I., Jan. 31, 1887; s. Charles James and Elizabeth Ernestine (Henriquez) Y.; came to U.S., 1906, naturalized, 1935; student Gen. Theol. Sem., New York, 1912-15, B.D., 1917; M.A., New York U., 1915; B.S. in Edn., Temple U., 1920; S.T.M., Phila. Divinity Sch., 1922, Th.D., 1931; m. Myra Jeannette Reynolds, Oct. 5, 1908; children—Dorothy Ernestine, Kenneth Edgar Reynolds, Harold Alan, Louise Jeannette, Stanley Norman, Donald Arthur. Began as timekeeper, Internat. Harvester Co., Hamilton, Can., 1909; pastor Episcopal Neighborhood House, Sept. 1, 1915-Apr. 30, 1916; vicar Phillips Brooks Memorial Chapel (Holy Trinity Parish) since May 1, 1916; lecturer in Old and New Testament lit., Southwest Training Sch. for Religious Teachers, Phila., 1933; mem. of Commn. on Ch. Schs., Episcopal Diocese of Pa., 1937, Dept. of Religious Edn., 1938, Social Service Dept., 1934. Voluntary chaplain of Douglass and Mercy hosps., 1915-25. Awarded Ward Prize for Pub. Reading, Gen. Theol. Sem., New York, 1915. Mem. Soc. of Biblical Exegesis, Am. Bible Teachers Assn. Episcopalian. Home: 200 N. 50th St. Office: 1925 Lombard St., Philadelphia, Pa.

YOUNG, George, Jr., banker; b. Clifton, N.J., Jan. 12, 1892; s. George and Mary Catherine (McNamara) Y.; B.S., Dartmouth Coll., 1914; M.C.S., Amos Tuck Sch. of Administration and Finance, Hanover, N. H., 1915; m. Bertha Bennett, Apr. 28, 1922; 1 son, George III. Sec. Bd. of Trade, Passaic, N.J., 1915-17; with Passaic Nat. Bank and Trust Co. since 1920, dir. since 1932, pres. since 1935. Served as capt. 33d Arty. Brig., U.S.A., 1917-19. Vice chmn. Passaic Am. Red Cross; v.p. Passaic Gen. Hosp. Mem. Delta Tau Delta. Presbyterian. Mason. Clubs: Arcola Country (Ridgewood, N.J.); Bankers (N.Y. City). Office: 657 Main Av., Passaic, N.J.

YOUNG, George John, physician; b. Brooklyn, N.Y., Oct. 16, 1898; s. George Jobson and Matilda (Geiss) Y.; grad. Boys' High Sch., Brooklyn, N.Y., 1917; A.B., Cornell U., Ithaca, N.Y., 1923; M.D., Cornell Univ. Med. Coll., New York City, 1926; m. Mildred Truslow, Nov. 3, 1922; 1 son, George John. Interne Morristown Memorial Hosp., 1926-27, pathologist, 1927-33, and since 1938, attending physician since 1929; instr. in clinical medicine, physician to out-patients, New York Hosp., 1930-38; visiting pathologist All Souls Hosp., Morristown, N.J., since 1935, Newton Memorial Hosp. since 1932, Dover Gen. Hosp. since 1936. Served with U.S. Navy, May 1917-Aug. 1919; over-seas duty, Oct. 1917-July 1919. Fellow Am. Coll. Physicians, Am. Heart Assn., A.M.A.; mem. N.J. Soc. Clinical Pathologists, Med. Soc. N.J. (treas.), Theta Delta Chi, Nu Sigma Nu. Clubs: Spring Brook Country (Morristown, N.J.); Cornell (New York). Address: 60 Maple Av., Morristown, N.J.

YOUNG, George Pervus, pres. Wood Ridge Nat. Bank; b. Wood Ridge, N.J., Dec. 9, 1875; s. James and Emma (Simpson) Y.; ed. Wood Ridge public schools; m. Jennie L. Vandalinda, Nov. 31, 1899; children—Evelyn Louise, George Pervus. Jeweler, N.Y., 1888-1914; organized business trucking wholesale and retail grain, Wood Ridge, N.J., 1914, sold business, 1922; insp. Portland Cement Assn., Bergen County, 1922-23; and partner in Wholesale Truck Parts Co., East Rutherford, 1923-28; pres. Wood Ridge Nat. Bank on orgn., June 1929, and since served as pres.; v.p. Ridge Investment Corpn., Carlstadt, N.J., since 1927; dir. Carlstadt Bldg. & Loan Assn. Freeholder Bergen County, 1908-14; councilman, Wood Ridge, 1895-1907, mayor, 1907-10; pres. Sinking Fund Commn., 1910-27; fire chief, 1899-1905. Republican. Presbyterian. Mason (Boiling Spring Lodge 152; Lebanon Chapter 42, Royal Arch, Rutherford, N.J.), Elk (Rutherford Lodge 547). Club: Wood Ridge (N.J.) Masonic. Home: 533 Anderson Av. Office: Wood Ridge Bank Bldg., Wood Ridge, N.J.

YOUNG, Hugh Hampton, surgeon; b. San Antonio, Tex., Sept. 18, 1870; s. Gen. William Hugh and Frances Michie (Kemper) Y.; A.B., A.M., U. of Va., 1893, M.D., 1894; Johns Hopkins, 1894-95; D.Sc., Queen's University, Belfast, 1933; m. Bessy Mason Colston, June 4, 1901 (died May 21, 1928); children—Frances Kemper (Mrs. Wm. Francis Rienhoff), Frederick Colston, Helen Hampton (Mrs. Bennett Crain), Elizabeth Campbell (Mrs. Warren Russell Starr). Pathologist to Thomas Wilson Sanitarium, 1895; successively asst. resident surgeon, 1895-98, head of dept. urol. surgery, and asso. surgeon Johns Hopkins Hospital, and clinical professor of urology, Johns Hopkins U. Pres. Md. State Lunacy Commn. Pres. Am. Assn. Genito-Urinary Surgeons, 1909, Am. Urol. Assn., 1909, Medico-Chirurgical Faculty of Md., 1912—; dir. urology A.E.F., 1917; sr. consultant in same, A.E.F., 1918; col. Med. Corps U.S.A. Mem. Internat. Assn. Congres Internationale d'Urologie (pres. 1927); corresponding mem. Association Française d'Urologie, Deutsche Gesellschaft für Urology, Sociedad de Cirujia de Buenos Aires, Societa Italiana di Urologia, Chi Phi and Nu Sigma Nu fraternities; fellow Am. College of Surgeons, Royal College of Surgeons of Ireland. Clubs: Maryland, Elkridge, Gibson Island, Baltimore Country, Johns Hopkins, Bachelors Cotillon. Author: studies in Urological Surgery (Vol. VIII, Johns Hopkins Hosp. Repts.), 1906; Hypertrophy and Cancer of the Prostate (Vol. XIV, Johns Hopkins Reports), 1906; Young's Practice of Urology (2 vols.); Urological Roentgenology; Genital Abnormalities, Hermaphroditism and Related Adrenal Diseases. Founder and editor Jour. of Urology. Has contributed over 350 papers to Am. and foreign med. jours. Home: 100 W. Cold Spring Lane, Baltimore, Md.

YOUNG, J. Elmer, banker; b. Pine Grove Mills, Pa., Jan. 31, 1873; s. David H. and Cathrine (Carper) Y.; student Juniata Coll.; m. Mary Guisler, Mar. 23, 1897; children—Mrs. Frances L. Rupert, Mrs. Mary Alma Johnson.

Engaged in milling business, 1893-1902, mercantile business, 1903-38, hardware business, 1910-12, automobile business, 1914, establishing first automobile service station in Petersburg; one of incorporators first bank in Petersburg, 1905, operated as a private bank; dir. First Nat. Bank since organization, 1913, pres. since 1931; pres. and dir. Huntingdon Wholesale Grocery Co. Pres. and mem. Petersburg Borough Council, 1908-15. Treas. and mem. Petersburg Sch. Bd. Pres. Huntingdon Co. Sch. Dirs. Assn., 1935-37; dir. Huntingdon Co. Library Assn.; mem. exec. com. Huntingdon Co. Sunday Sch. Assn. Mem. Huntingdon Co. Game, Fish and Forestry Assn. Mason (32°), Odd Fellow, Woodman, Maccabee, Hartslog Grange, Patrons of Husbandry (Alexandria). Club: Huntingdon County Motor (v.p. and dir.). Address: Petersburg, Pa.

YOUNG, James Howard, chem. engr.; b. Kansas City, Kan., Jan. 5, 1892; s. James Andrew and Mary E. (Farr) Y.; A.B. in Engring., Kansas State Coll., Manhattan, Kan., 1914; M.Sc., O. State U., Columbus, O., 1916, Ph.D., 1918; m. Mildred Morse, Sept. 1916; children—James Donald, Virginia Morse, David Hall, Richard Aldrich. Industrial Fellow, Mellon Inst., Pittsburgh, 1918-21, Sr. Industrial Fellow since 1921; v.p. and dir. H. H. Robertson Co., Pittsburg, Pa., since 1929. Served in C.W.S., U.S.A. on research in war gases, 1916-18. Mem. Am. Inst. Chem. Engrs., Am. Chem. Soc., Sigma Xi, Phi Lambda Upsilon. Republican. Methodist. Mason. Clubs: Pittsburgh, University, Duquesne (Pittsburgh); St. Clair Country. Home: 370 Jefferson Drive. Office: Farmers' Bank Bldg., Pittsburgh, Pa.

YOUNG, James Thomas, college prof.; b. Phila., Sept. 23, 1873; s. Andrew J. and Louisa A. Y.; Ph.B., U. of Pa., 1893; Ph.D., U. of Halle, 1895. Dir. of the Wharton School Finance and Commerce, 1904-12; now prof. pub. administration, U. of Pa. Mem. Am. Philos. Soc., Am. Polit. Science Assn., Am. Acad. Polit. and Social Science (dir.), Phi Beta Kappa. Clubs: Lenape, Merion Cricket. Author: The New American Government and Its Work, 1915, 3d edit., 1933; also articles on government, pub. regulation of business in various jours. and procs. Address: Wharton School, Univ. of Pa., Philadelphia, Pa.

YOUNG, Joseph Samuel, pres. Lehigh Portland Cement Co.; b. Allentown, Pa., June 15, 1898; s. Edward Mark and Kate (Anewalt) Y.; A.B., Princeton, 1919; LL.B., Columbia, 1923; m. Marion I. Johnson, Sept. 16, 1926; 1 son, William Johnson. Entered employ Lehigh Portland Cement Co., 1923, v.p. and asst. to pres., 1926, pres. since 1932; pres. various subsidiary corporations; partner M. S. Young & Co. Pres. and dir. Allentown Steam Heating and Power Co.; dir. Pennsylvania Water and Power Co. Instr. Machine Gun O.T.S., Camp Hancock, Ga., 1917-19. Trustee Cement Inst.; dir. Portland Cement Assn. Republican. Presbyn. Clubs: Livingston, Lehigh Country (Allentown); University Cottage (Princeton, N.J.); Princeton (New York). Home: Allentown, Pa.

YOUNG, Percy Sacret, chmn. exec. com. Pub. Service Corpn. of N.J.; b. London, England, Dec. 19, 1870; s. Richard and Sarah Ann (Sacret) Y.; ed. English Pub. Sch., England; B.C.S., New York U., 1908; m. Grace Whiting Mason, Dec. 7, 1904; children—Percy Sacret, Dorothy, George Wooldridge, William Clements, Thomas Rumsey, Gertrude Mary, Katharine, Sarah Sacret. Came to U.S., 1886, naturalized citizen, 1918. Collector Omaha Gas Co., 1890-95; traveling auditor United Gas Improvement Co., 1895-98, asst. agent Jersey City office, 1898-99; asst. treas., later sec., Hudson Co. Gas Co., 1899-1903; comptroller Public Service Corpn. of N.J., 1903-14, treas., 1914-17, v.p. 1917-39, chmn. exec. com. since Apr. 18, 1939, now also dir. same and its subsidiaries; dir. Firemen's Ins. Co., Fidelity Union Trust Co., Brighton Mills. Mem. council New York U.; mem. bd. trustees U. of Newark, St. Barnabas Hosp., Hosp. for Women and Children. Republican. Episcopalian. Clubs: Essex, Newark Athletic (Newark); Montclair (N.J.) Golf, Plymouth (Mass.) Country; Yeamans Hall (Charleston, S.C.). Home: 97 Warren Pl., Montclair, N.J. Office: 80 Park Pl., Newark, N.J.

YOUNG, Robert Anewalt, pres. Lehigh Valley Trust Co.; b. Allentown, Pa., Nov. 2, 1894; s. Edward Mark and Kate Rebecca (Anewalt) Y.; student Allentown Prep. Sch., 1909-11, Pa. Mil. Coll., Chester, Pa., 1911-15; m. Eleanor Caroline Soleliac, June 23, 1923; children—Barbara, Richard Edward. Asso. with Lehigh Valley Trust Co., Allentown, Pa., since 1915, pres. and dir. since 1932; pres. and dir. Greenleaf Realty Co.; v.p. Allentown Steam Heat and Power Co.; mem. firm M. S. Young & Co., hardware mchts.; dir. Lehigh Portland Cement Co., Lehigh Valley Transit Co. Served with Pa. N.G. on Mexican border, 1915-16; with 149th Machine Gun Batln., U.S.A., 1917-19. Dir. Sacred Heart Hosp., Cedarcrest Coll., Muhlenberg Coll. Republican. Presbyterian. Mason, Elk, Moose. Clubs: Lehigh Country, Livingston, Shrine (Allentown, Pa.). Home: 45 S. Fulton St. Office: 634 Hamilton St., Allentown, Pa.

YOUNG, Rowland Lawrence, elec. engr.; b. Phila., Pa., Oct. 3, 1886; s. William Rowland and Kate (Lawrence) Y.; grad. Germantown (Pa.) Acad., 1903; B.S. in E.E., U. of Pa., 1907, E.E., 1928; m. Elizabeth Darlington Cope, Sept. 2, 1911; children—William Cope, Lawrence Darlington, Katherine Ingram, Margaret Lawrence. Grad. engring. apprentice Westinghouse Electric and Mfg. Co., 1907-09; instr. in mathematics, Carnegie Inst. Tech., 1909; engring. rep. McGraw Pub. Co., Pittsburgh Dist., 1909-10; editorial staff Electrical World, N.Y., 1910; asst. mgr. Metall. and Chem. Engring., N.Y., 1910; in charge power sect. of engring. dept. Am. Telephone anl Telegraph Co., 1911-19, dept. development and research, 1919-34; Power Maintenance Engr. Bell Telephone Labs., 1934-35, power maintenance, safety and standards since 1935. Rep. of Telephone Group on standards Council of Am. Standards Assn. since 1932; rep. Telephone Group on Am. Inst. E.E. Standards Com.; mem. Nat. Safety Council. Professional Engr., Univ. of State of N.Y., 1936. Fellow A.A.A.S.; mem. Am. Inst. E.E., Am. Soc. Safety Engrs., Telephone Pioneers of America, Nat. Geog. Soc., A.R.C. Life Saving Corps, Sigma Xi. Republican. Club: Univ. of Pennsylvania (New York). Presbyn. Joint author series of Bell System Practices—Power Plants; also author of tech. papers on telephone power plants published by Bell System and Am. Inst. Elec. Engrs. Holder of patents for power systems in general use in manual and dial telephone offices. Home: 447 N. Maple Av., East Orange, N.J. Office: 463 West St., New York, N.Y.

YOUNG, William Robins, coll. prof.; b. Mifflinburg, Pa., Apr. 16, 1896; s. Harry Berryhill and Margaret Eloise (Robins) Y.; B.S., Pa. State Coll., 1918, M.E., Engring. Sch., 1925; m. Evelyn Hester Hutchins, Mar. 4, 1924; children—William Robins, Jr., Richard Hutchins. Instr. engring. extension, Pa. State Coll., 1919-22, asst. prof., 1922-35, supervisor corr. instrn. div. since 1935. Served in O.T.S. and 2d lt. U.S. Army, 1918; O.R.C., U.S.A. since 1919, now lt. col. Mem. State College Borough Planning Commn. since 1933, pres., 1934-36, sec. since 1937. Trustee Alumni Assn., Upsilon Chapter, Alpha Sigma Phi, 1924-28 and since 1930, pres. since 1935, grand corr. sec., 1932-36. Mem. Pa. State Assn. for Adult Edn., Pa. Vocational Assn., Res. Officers Assn. (pres. Pa. Dept., 1935, III Corps pres., 1936-37), Am. Legion, Centre Co. Engrs. Soc. of Pa., Conservation Assn. Republican. Presbyterian. Mason (32°, Shriner). Clubs: University, Centre Hills Country (State College, Pa.); Army and Navy (Washington, D.C.). Home: 255 E. Hamilton Av., State College, Pa.

YOUNGELSON, Irving, lawyer; b. Mountain View, N.J., June 2, 1903; s. Max and Bella (Passmonick) Y.; student U. of Pa., 1920-22; LL.B., Fordham U. Law Sch., 1926; m. Celia Silverstein, Oct. 1, 1929; children—Joan, James Frank. Admitted to N.J. bar as atty., 1927, as counselor, 1931; engaged in gen. practice of law at Dover, N.J., since 1927; judge second jud. dist. ct. for Morris Co. since 1933; supreme ct. commr. since 1935. Served as chmn. and pres. Dover Dem. Club, 1929-33. Mem. Morris Co. Bar Assn. Democrat. Hebrew religion. Mason. Elk. Home: 10 N. Elk Av. Office: 6 E. Blackwell St., Dover, N.J.

YOUNGER, John Elliott, engr., prof. engring.; b. Canyon, Tex., Mar. 7, 1892; s. James Beauregard and Mary Ella (Elliott) Y.; student West Tex. State Teachers Coll., 1911-12, U. of Tex., 1914-15; B.S., U. of Calif., 1923, M.S., 1924, Ph.D., 1925; m. Nancy Brunette Francis, June 3, 1919; children—John Francis, Nancy Ella. Prin. Abernathy (Tex.) High Sch., 1912-14; teacher Philippine Islands, 1914-17; teacher of mech. engring., U. of Calif., 1923-27; sr. aeronautical engr. U.S. Army Air Corps, 1927-29; prof. of mech. engring., U. of Calif., 1929-38; prof. mech. engring. and head of dept., U. of Md., since 1938. Served as 2d lt., Res. mil. aviator, Air Service, U.S.A., 1917-19. Studied aeronautical developments in round-the-world tour, 1936; lectured before Royal Aeronautical Soc. of Great Britain, London, on high altitude flying, 1938. Fellow Inst. Aeronautical Sciences (mem. advisory bd.); mem. Am. Soc. Mech. Engrs., Soc. for Promotion Engring. Edn., Am. Assn. of Univ. Profs., Nat. Soc. of Prof. Engrs., A.A.A.S., Sigma Xi. Author: Dynamics of Airplanes (with B. M. Woods), 1931; Airplane Construction and Repair, 1931; Structural Design of Metal Airplanes, 1935; Airplane Maintenance (with A. F. Bonnalie and N. F. Ward), 1937; Mechanics for Engineering Students, 1938. Contbr. many papers to jours. of scientific socs. Home: 510 Rolling Road, Chevy Chase, Md.

YOUNGMAN, John Crawford, lawyer; b. Williamsport, Pa., Jan. 25, 1903; s. Charles Worman and Margaret Maud (Porter) Y.; grad. Curtin Grammar Sch. (Williamsport), 1916, Williamsport High Sch., 1920; B.S. in Economics, Wharton Sch. (U. of Pa.), 1924; LL.B., Harvard U. Law Sch., 1927; m. Ruth Young Allen, Feb. 7, 1933; children—John Crawford, Charles Van Patten, Margaret Allen. Admitted to Pa. bar, 1927; associated in gen. practice with Hon. Max L. Mitchell, Williamsport, 1927-38, with Malcolm Muir since 1938; dist. atty. Lycoming Co., Pa., 1932-35; served as spl. counsel for Commonwealth of Pa. in injunction suits to eliminate stream pollution. Mem. Flood Control Council of Susquehanna Drainage Area. Mem. Am. Bar Assn., Pa. Bar Assn., Kappa Sigma. Republican. Presbyn. Mason (32°, K.T.), Elk, Moose. Clubs: Ross, Williamsport Wheel, Highland Lake Manor, Young Men's Republican (Williamsport). Active in work of organized sportsmens assns.; pres. Pa. Federation of Sportsmens Club, 1939. Home: 54 Roderick Road. Office: 21 W. Third St., Williamsport, Pa.

YOUNT, John Arndt, clergyman; b. Bridgewater, Nova Scotia, Feb. 15, 1881; s. Rev. Adolphus LeRoy (D.D.) and Leah Eleanor (Henkel) Y., citizens of U.S.; A.B., Roanoke Coll., Salem, Va., 1901; ed. Luth. Theol. Sem., Mt. Airy, Phila., Pa., 1901-04; A.M., W.Va. U., Morgantown, W.Va., 1910; S.T.M., Western Theol. Sem., Pittsburgh, Pa., 1925; grad. study U. of Pittsburgh, 1922-25; m. Mary Elizabeth Steele, Oct. 1, 1908; children—John Armstrong, James Steele. Ordained to ministry Lutheran Ch., 1904; pastor various Luth. chs. in Pa., 1904-17; pastor St. Johns Luth. Ch., Pittsburgh, Pa., 1917-27; pastor Calvary Reformed Ch., Turtle Creek, Pa., 1927-31; resident chaplain and recreational dir., Pittsburgh City Home and Hosp., Mayview, Pa., since 1935; mem. firm Banksville Coal Co., Pittsburgh, 1931-35; supervisor and treas., Mayview Cooperative Store, Mayview, Pa.; editor News Bulletin (weekly), Mayview, Pa. Mem. Evang. and Reformed Ministerial Assn., Pittsburgh, Pa., Sigma Chi. Democrat. Evang. and Reformed Ch. Home: 166 Crane Rd., Crafton, Pittsburgh, Pa. Office: Mayview, Pa.

YUENGLING, Frank Dohrman, banker, corpn. exec.; b. Pottsville, Pa., Sept. 27, 1876; s. Frederick George and Minna (Dohrman) Y.; student Phillips Acad., Andover, Mass., 1894-96, Princeton, 1896-98; m. Augusta C. Roseberry, Apr. 24, 1907; children—Augusta Roseberry (Mrs. Louis N. Ulmer), Frederick George, Frank

YUNGEL

Dohrman, Richard Lee, David G. Began as mem. firm D. G. Yuengling & Son, brewing, Pottsville, Pa., 1898, pres. D. G. Yuengling & Son, Inc., since 1914; pres. Pa. Nat. Bank & Trust Co., Yuengling Realty Co., Pottsville Feed Co., Yuengling Securities Corpn.; treas. Pottsville Hotel & Realty Co. Republican. Episcopalian. Mason (K.T., 32°, Shriner). Elk. Clubs: Pottsville, Country, Motor (Pottsville); Princeton, Racquet (Philadelphia). Home: 15th and Mahantongo Sts. Office: 5th and Mahantongo Sts., Pottsville, Pa.

YUNGEL, Joseph P., mfr. shoes; b. Stuttgart, Germany, Feb. 19, 1867. Pres. Devine & Yungel Shoe Mfg. Co.; dir. Allison East End Trust Co. Mem. Harrisburg Chamber of Commerce. Mason (Shriner). Club: Rotary of Harrisburg. Home: 1738 Market St. Office: 16th and Elm Sts., Harrisburg, Pa.

YUSTER, Samuel Terrill, chemist, petroleum engr.; b. Manchester, England, Dec. 21, 1903; s. Tobias and Fanny Bell (Goldstone) Y.; came to U.S. 1909, naturalized, 1914; grad. high school, Fargo, N.D., 1922; B.S. in Chemistry, N.D. State Coll., Fargo, N.D., 1926; Ph.D., U. of Minn., Minneapolis, Minn., 1934; m. Rose Bernice Goldich, Dec. 9, 1934; children—Louis Howard, Frances Anne. Instr. in science and mathematics, Oberon (N.D.) High Sch., 1926-27; chemist U.S. Bur. of Standards, San Francisco, 1927-29; teaching asst., fellow and research asso. in chemistry dept., U. of Minn., Minneapolis, Minn., 1929-34; asso. prof. of petroleum and natural gas engring. and in charge of water flooding research, Sch. of Mineral Industries, Pa. State Coll., since 1934. Mem. Am. Chem. Soc., Am. Petroleum Inst., Sigma Xi, Phi Lambda Upsilon, Phi Kappa Phi, Sigma Gamma Epsilon. Jewish religion. Home: 1029 W. Beaver Av., State College, Pa.

Z

ZABRISKIE, Abram Josiah, mcht. coal and bldg. supplies; b. Hackensack, N.J., May 7, 1875; s. Josiah A. and Mary Ellen (Van Gieson) Z.; student Business Coll., Paterson, N.J., 1889-90; m. Amy Bowman, Oct. 20, 1896. Began as mgr. Zabriskie & L'Hommedieu, Inc., East Stroudsburg, Pa., coal and bldg. supplies, since 1903, pres., treas., and dir. since 1923; pres., treas., and dir. Home Realty Co. of Monroe; pres. and dir. Colonial Securities Corpn.; v.p. and dir. First-Stroudsburg Nat. Bank; dir. Monroe Silk Mills. Treas. Monroe Co. Boy Scouts. Dir. Stroudsburg Y.M.C.A. Mem. Holland Soc. of New York. Republican. Presbyterian. Mason. Club: Kiwanis (Stroudsburg, Pa.). Home: 551 Thomas St., Stroudsburg, Pa. Office: 270 S. Courtland St., East Strouds burg, Pa.

ZAHNISER, Charles Reed; b. Mercer County, Pa., May 30, 1873; s. William Arthur and Jane (Bromley) Zahniser; A.B., Grove City Coll., Grove City, Pa., 1896, A.M., 1896, Ph.D., 1909; S.T.B., University of Chicago, Chicago, Ill., 1900; m. Pearl Stroud, 1896; children—Virgil Stroud, Pearl Charline (dec.), Chalmers Flath. Student pastor Presbyn. Ch. in U.S.A., Chicago, 1898-1900; pastor Sorrento, Ill., 1900-01, Pittsburgh, Pa., 1901-14; sec. Pittsburgh Council of Chs., 1914-29; survey dir. Pittsburgh Area, Interchurch World Movement, 1919-20; mem. editorial staff Presbyterian Advance, 1904-12; editor Pittsburgh Christian Outlook, 1914-29; extension lecturer Federal Council Chs. since 1929; prof. social science and applied Christianity, Boston U., since 1929. Trustee Pa. Penitentiary, 1923-29. Presbyn. Mason. Author: The Zahnisers—A Family History, 1904; Social Christianity, 1911; Casework Evangelism, 1927; Interchurch Community Programs, 1932; The Soul Doctor, 1938. Home: 253 S. St. Clair St., Pittsburgh, Pa.

ZAHNISER, William John, mgr. Finance Adjustment Co.; b. Clinton Co., Ia., May 12, 1857; s. Jacob Wright and Caroline (Bolton) Z.; ed. Washington pub. sch., 1867-77; m. Anna Mary Hines, Apr. 15, 1880 (died 1906); m. 2d, Edna Marshall, Oct. 15, 1925; children—Miriam Jane (Mrs. William Price Filbert),

Elizabeth Caroline and William James (twins). Engaged as bldg. contractor, 1883-1908; pres. Metropolitan Nat. Bank, 1908-24; pres. Metropolitan Trust Co., 1912-18; now mgr. Finance Adjustment Co.; sec. and treas. Hulton Land Co.; pres. Butler Highfields Co., Butler Land & Development Co. Served as mem. City Council, 1900-04; mem. bd. mgrs. Allegheny Co. Workhouse, sec. 18 yrs., supt. 2 yrs. Pres. East Liberty Bd. of Trade, 3 yrs.; mem. Oakmont Borough Council, 2 yrs. Republican. Presbyn. Home: 5460 Penn Av., Pittsburgh, Pa.

ZANGE, Otto A., real estate and ins.; b. Baltimore, Md., Sept. 23, 1876; s. Max and Louise (Strattman) Z.; ed. pub. schs. Wilkinsburg, Pa.; m. Catherine E. Wilde, June 26, 1902. In employ Geo. S. Davis Co., McKees Rocks, Pa., real estate, ins. and mortgages, 1907-23, propr. since 1923; dir. Hankey Baking Co. Served as corp., 18th regt. Pa. vol. inf. during Spanish-American War. Republican. Lutheran. Mason (K.T., 32°, Shriner). Elk, Eagle, Moose. Club: Lions (McKees Rocks, Pa.). Home: 1146 Wayne Av. Office: 522 Chartiers Av., McKees Rocks, Pa.

ZANTZINGER, Clarence Clark, architect; b. Phila., Aug. 15, 1872; s. Alfred (M.D.) and Sarah Crawford (Clark) Z.; Ph.B., Yale, 1892; B.S., in Architecture, U. of Pa., 1895; A.D.G., École des Beaux Arts, Paris, 1901; m. Margaret S. Buckley, Oct. 24, 1903. Practiced, Phila., 1901—; mem. Zantzinger & Borie. Fellow Am. Inst. Architects, 1911; mem. Am. Federation of Arts, T-Square Club, Soc. Beaux Arts Architects, Société des Architects Diplomés, Pa. Soc. Sons of the Revolution, Soc. Colonial Wars in State of Pa. Officier Legion d' Honneur (France). Clubs: Yale, Penn Athletic (Phila.), Century Assn. (New York); Graduate (New Haven). Home: 8500 Seminole Av., Chestnut Hill, Pa. Office: Architects Bldg., Philadelphia, Pa.

ZAPPALA, Frank J., lawyer; b. Italy, May 24, 1898; s. Joseph and Marmela (Penna) Z.; A.B., and LL.B., Duquesne U., Pittsburgh; m. Josephine Andolina, July 10, 1930; children—Frank J., Stephen A., Richard Allen. Sec. to Harold Rosenbush, banker, New York City, 1915-16; export mgr. Butler Bros., New York City, 1916-18, foreign rep. to Central and South Americas, 1918-20; teacher of foreign languages, Pittsburgh, 1920-26; spl. interpreter of French, Spanish and Italian in Allegheny Co. (Pa.) Courts, 1920-26; admitted to Allegheny Co. bar, 1928, and since in practice at Pittsburgh; mem. bars Supreme, Superior, U.S., Dist. Cts. Mem. Pa. State Hse. of Rep. since 1934. Mem. Squirrel Hill Board of Trade (dir.; past v.p.), Homewood-Brushton Bd. of Trade, Tau Delta Phi. Democrat. Elk, K.C. Club: Itamerica (Pittsburgh; founder, past pres.). Home: 5401 Hobart St., Office: 1119 Plaza Bldd., Pittsburgh, Pa.

ZARTMAN, Ira Forry, prof. physics; b. Lancaster Co., Pa., Dec. 18, 1899; s. Eli Kline and Sarah Elser (Forry) Z.; B.S., Muhlenberg Coll., Allentown, Pa., 1923; M.S., N.Y. U., 1925; Ph.D., U. of Calif., Berkeley, Calif., 1930; m. Edith Grace Wenger, June 5, 1924; 1 son, Ira William. Engaged as instr. physics, N.Y. Univ., 1924-27; Whiting research fellow, U. of Calif., Berkeley, Calif., 1928-29; prof. physics, head of dept. of physics, Muhlenberg Coll., Allentown, Pa., since 1930. Served as pvt., Inf., U.S. Army, during World War. Mem. Am. Phys. Soc., Am. Assn. Physics Teachers, Sigma Xi, Phi Kappa Tau. Republican. Lutheran. Home: 200 Parkview Av., Allentown, Pa.

ZAVITZ, Edwin Cornell, headmaster; b. Ilderton, Ont., Can., July 4, 1892; s. Jonah Daniel and Emily (Cornell) Z.; brought to U.S., 1906; B.A., U. of Mich., 1914; M.A., Teachers Coll. (Columbia University), 1931; m. Francis Marion John, February 22, 1919; children—John James Cornell, Peter Kirk Cornell. Teacher Sidwells Friends Sch., Washington, D.C., 1914-20, Moraine Pk. Sch., Dayton, O., 1920-24; headmaster Antioch Sch., Yellow Springs, O., 1924-27; prof. edn., Antioch Coll, 1924-27; headmaster Chateau de Bures nr. Paris, France, 1928-30. Univ. Sch. Cincinnati, O., 1931-35, Baltimore Friends Sch. since 1935.

ZELLER

Served with American Friends Service Com. and Am. Red Cross, in France, 1917-18. Dir. Foreign Policy Assn. of Cincinnati. Mem. N.E.A., Dept. of Superintendance, Progressive Edn. Assn., Phi Delta Kappa. Mem. Soc. of Friends. Clubs: Torch (Baltimore); Torch (Cincinnati); North Baltimore Kiwanis. Address: Baltimore Friends School, Homeland, Baltimore, Md.

ZEIGLER, Earl Frederick, clergyman, educator; b. Barnard, Kan., Jan. 13, 1889; s. Frank and Marietta (Finney) Z.; A.B., Ohio Northern U., 1913, D.D., 1933; B.D., Presbyn. Theol. Sem. of Chicago, 1918; A.M., U. of Chicago, 1926; m. Mabel E. Faulkner, June 28, 1911; children—Mary Margaret, Ruth, Earl Frederick, James Faulkner. Teacher and superintendent of various schools in Ohio, 1907-16; ordained ministry Presbyterian Church, 1918; pastor Pullman (Ill.) Church, 1916-18, First Ch., Rochelle, Ill., 1918-22, Union Ch. and Berea Coll., Berea, Ky., 1922-29; dean Presbyn. Coll. of Christian Edn., 1929-37; asso. Editor Bd. of Christian Edn., Presbyn. Ch. U.S.A., since 1937. Awarded Blacktsone Fellowship in New Testament, Presbyn. Theol. Sem., Chicago, 1918; also preaching prize same inst., 1918. Republican. Mason. Author: Toward Understanding Adults, 1931; The Way of Adult Education, 1938. Contbr. to religious jours. Home: 5 Windsor Av., Narberth, Pa. Office: 910 Witherspoon Bldg., Philadelphia, Pa.

ZEITLIN, Solomon, coll prof.; b. Vitebsk, Russia, May 31, 1892; s. Joel and Esther (Levit) Z.; student Univ. of Paris, 1913-14; Th.D., École Rabbinque, Paris, 1914; Ph.D., Dropsie Coll., Phila., 1917; unmarried. Came to U.S., 1914, naturalized, 1922. Fellow Dropsie Coll., 1915-17; instr. in Jewish history, Rabbinical Coll., New York, 1917-25; prof. and head rabbinical dept., Dropsie Coll., Phila., since 1925; prof. of Jewish history, Yeshiva Coll., New York, since 1930. Mem. Am. Hist. Soc., Bibl. Soc., Societe des Etudes Juives, Paris; fellow Am. Acad. for Jewish Research. Clubs: Judeans (New York); Oriental (Phila.). Author: Megillat Tanrith, 1922; Studies in the Beginnings of Christianity, 1924; Josephus on Jesus, 1931; Canonization of the Hebrew Scriptures, 1933; History of the Second Jewish Commonwealth, 1933; Maimonides—A Biography, 1935; The Jews: Race, Nation or Religion, 1936; The Pharisees and the Gospels, 1938; The Book of Jubilees, 1939; contbr. to Hebrew, German, French and English scientific publs. Home: Hotel Sylvania, Philadelphia, Pa.

ZELLER, Harry A., gen. mgr. W.Va. Rail Co.; b. Girard, O., Oct. 25, 1871; s. Louis and Rosina (Hahn) Z.; ed. pub. and high sch., Girard; m. Evalyn May Probst, Oct. 15, 1896; children—Sylvia, Margaret (dec.). Clk. in store Girard, 1885-88; asst. postmaster, Girard, 1888-90; office boy and yard clk. Trumbull Iron Co. 1890-92; paymaster Union Iron & Steel Co., 1892-93; shipping clk. same and Pomeroy (O.) Iron & Steel Co., 1893-99; supt. Am. S. H. Carnegie Stel Co., 1899-1902, Schonthal Iron & Steel Co., Cumberland, Md., 1902-05; gen. supt. Md. Rail Co., Cumberland, 1905-06; traveled for Schonthal Iron Co., Columbus, O., 1906-07; organizer, 1907, treasurer and general manager The W.Va. Rail Co., 1907-12; v.p. and gen. mgr. since 1912. Dist. chmn. four-minute men, 2d tr. camp, Ft. Benjamin Harrison; mem. War Labor and War Resource bds., Council of Defense, Liberty Loan, Thrift Stamps, Am. Red Cross, Salvation Army, Y.M. C.A., Jewish and Catholic drives, World War; chmn. Citizen's Corpn. com., 'flu' epidemic, 1918; formerly dir. Community Chest, Park Bd., Boys' Work; dir. Salvation Army Bd., Y.M.C.A. Bd., Cabell Co. War Memorial Arch Association. Mem. W.Va. Mfrs. Association (dir.), Jobbers and Mfrs. Bureau (dir., expresident), Huntington Chamber Commerce (expres.), W.Va. State Chamber Commerce (dir.). Republican. Episcopalian. Elk. Clubs: Rotary (ex-pres.), Guyandot, Guyan Country. Home: 1434 5th Av. Office: care The West Virginia Rail Co., Huntington, W.Va.*

ZELLER, Samuel Charles, prof. German and New Testament; b. London, Wis., May 25, 1905; s. Rev. Franz and Constance (Venter)

Z.; A.B., Moravian Coll., Bethlehem, Pa., 1927; B.D., Moravian Theol. Sem., 1929; A.M., U. of Pa., 1932; student Episcopal Divinity Sch., 1934-35, since 1939; m. Frida Helene Kramer, June 1, 1929; children—Karl F. W., Gerhard D. Instr. German, Moravian Coll., Bethlehem, Pa., 1929 to 1933, asst. prof., since 1933; prof. N.T., Moravian Theol. Sem., Bethlehem, Pa., since 1937; actg. prof. Greek, Lehigh U., 1935-36; acting pastor, College Hill Moravian Ch., Bethlehem, Pa., 1930-31; ordained to Christian Ministry of Moravian Ch., 1931. Mem. Soc. Bib. Lit. and Exegesis, Moravian Hist. Soc. Moravian. Collaborated in translation of diaries and letters of the White River Indian Mission, pub. under title The Moravian Indian Mission on White River, by Ind. Hist. Bur., 1938. Home: 42 S. Broad St., Nazareth, Pa. Office: Moravian College, Bethlehem, Pa.

ZENTMAYER, William, M.D.; b. Phila., Pa., Oct. 28, 1864; s. Joseph and Catharine (Bluim) Z.; M.D., U. of Pa., 1886; unmarried. Professor diseases of the eye, Graduate School of Medicine, University of Pa.; cons. surgeon to Wills (Eye) Hospital, St. Mary's Hospital and Glen Mills School. Fellow A.M.A. (chairman section ophthalmology, 1916-17), Coll. Physicians of Phila. (chmn. sect. on ophthalmology, 1909-10); mem. Am. Ophthal. Soc. (pres. 1926-27), Acad. Ophthalmology and Oto-Laryngology, Acad. Nat. Sciences, Pa. Acad. Fine Arts, Ophthal. Soc. of United Kingdom (British), A.A.A.S.; pres. local Med. Alumni Soc. of U. of Pa., 1922-23; chmn. sect. on eye, ear, nose and throat, Med. Soc. of State of Pa., 1935-36. Asso. editor Archives of Ophthalmology. Dir. of Nat. Soc. for Prevention of Blindness. Home: 265 Forrest Av., Merion, Pa. Office: 1930 Chestnut St., Philadelphia, Pa.

ZERBE, Amos Walter, sch. supt.; b. Pinegrove Twp., Schuylkill Co., Pa., Aug. 11, 1878; s. Jacob and Elizabeth (Wenrich) Z.; grad. Pinegrove Borough High Sch., Keystone State Teachers Coll., 1905; B.S. in Edn., Lebanon Valley Coll., 1925; M.S. in Edn., Pa. State Coll., 1935; m. Lillian May Spancake, Dec. 1905 (dec.); children—Jay Stuart (dec.), Robert Bruce. Teacher twp. schs., 1897-1901; supervising prin. schs., East Greenville, Pa., 1905-07, Reilly Twp., Pa., 1907-12, Tremont Borough, Pa., 1929-30; asst. co. supt. of schs., Schuylkill Co., Pa., 1930-37, co. supt. since July 1937. Exec. officer Schuylkill Co. Bd. of Sch. Dirs. Pres. Schuylkill Co. Anti-Tuberculosis Soc. since 1938; dir. Schuylkill Co. Nat. Youth Projects; county administrator Nat. Youth Administration. Mem. N.E.A., Pa. State Edn. Assn., Am. Automobile Assn., Phi Delta Kappa. Mason, Odd Fellow (Past Officer). Clubs: Schuylkill County Schoolmen's, Schuylkill County Motor, Tremont Borough Civic, Rotary International, Roedersville Game and Fish Assn., Tremont Borough Gun. Home: 14 S. Pine St., Tremont, Pa. Office: Administration Bldg., 2d and Minersville Sts., Pottsville, Pa.

ZERBE, Farran, numismatist; b. Tyrone, Pa., Apr. 16, 1871; s. James Albert and Bridget McAvoy) Z.; ed. pub. and pvt. schs.; m. Gertrude Mahoney, Sept. 10, 1932. Mercantile business until 1900; chief numismatist, St. Louis Expn., 1904, Portland Expn., 1905-06; editor and pub. The Numismatist, 1909-10; exhibitor and lecturer, "Money of the World," 1907-14 and 1920-28; chief of numismatic department San Francisco Expn., 1915-16. Mem. U.S. Assay Com., 1909, 1923. Mem. Am. Numismatic Assn. (pres. 1907-09 and of Pacific Coast Soc., 1918-23), Am. Numismatic Soc. (New York), Numismatic Club (New York), Tyrone Club, Elks. Contbr. numerous articles on numismatics and finance. Collected over 50,000 specimens of mediums of exchange, ranging over 5,000 yrs., and of an extensive library on the subject; sold collection and library to Chase Nat. Bank, New York, 1928, and became curator and numismatist for the bank. Home: Tyrone, Pa. Address: 46 Cedar St., New York, N.Y.

ZETLIN, Emanuel Roman, violinist, teacher; b. St. Petersburg, Russia, Sept. 17, 1900; s. Dr. Nathan S. and Catherine (Banck) Z.; B.A. in music, Imperial Conservatory, St. Petersburg, Russia, 1916; (hon.) Mus.D., Washington Coll. of Music, 1936; m. Gitta Dezsö, (div. 1939); 1 son, Guy Edward. Came to U.S., 1923, naturalized, 1930. Concert violinist since 1916; concertmaster symphony orchestra, Frankfort-on-Main, Germany, 1920; prof., Curtis Inst. of Music, Phila., Pa., 1924-28; mem. Flesh-Zetlin-Bailly-Salmond String Quartet, 1925-28; head violin dept., Washington Coll. of Music, Washington, D.C., since 1928, Phila. Settlement Music Sch. since 1928, Christodora House, N.Y. City, 1930-36, Manhattan Music Sch. since 1929, Bronx House and Music Sch. Settlement since 1936; prof. chamber music dept. Inst. Musical Art, Juilliard Sch. of Music, N.Y. City, since 1938; appeared as soloist with symphonies in Europe, N.Y. Symphony Orchestra and others. Mem. Nat. Music Teachers Assn. Lutheran. Home: 416 Queen St., Philadelphia, Pa. Office: 120 Claremont Av., New York, N.Y.

ZETZER, Rose Sylvan, lawyer; b. Baltimore, Md., Jan. 13, 1904; d. Jacob Lewis and Baila (Hendler) Z.; grad. Eastern High Sch., Baltimore, 1921; LL.B., U. of Md. Sch. of Law, 1925, student Sch. of Commerce, 1922-23; student Baltimore Hebrew Coll., 1935-38, spl. courses John Hopkins U., 1926-29; unmarried. Admitted to Md. bar, 1925; to Supreme Ct. of Dist. of Columbia, 1933, and practiced in Baltimore since 1925, in Washington, D.C., since 1933. Mem. Nat. Assn. Women Lawyers (v.p. for Md., 1935-37; chmn. uniform divorce laws com., 1937-38), Women's Bar Assn. of Baltimore (v.p. since 1939), Jr. Council of Jewish Women (v.p. and me. exec. bd., 1936-38), Business and Professional Women's Council of Md. (pres. 1934-36), Women Lawyers' Luncheon Club (pres. 1934-37), Nat. Woman's Party (corr. sec. Md. branch since 1935), Eastern High Sch. Alumnae Assn. (recording sec. 1935-37; mem. exec. bd. since 1935), Hadassah (mem. exec. bd. Baltimore chapter). Democrat. Jewish religion. Home: 2808 Berwick Av. Office: 209 E. Fayette St., Baltimore, Md.; 416 Fifth St. N.W., Washington, D.C.

ZIEGLER, Howard Gordon; b. Pittsburgh, Pa., Dec. 14, 1900; s. William and Sarah (MacAfee) Z.; grad. Friendship Grade Sch., 1915, Peabody High Sch., 1919; B.S., U. of Pittsburgh, 1923; m. Dorothy M. McGee, Aug. 8, 1928; children—Nancy Dorothy, Joan Sarah. Auditor Duquesne Construction Co., 4 mos., 1919; teacher evening high schs., 1919-22; pres. C. & W. Ziegler, Inc. (organized by father and uncle 1881) since 1923. Vice-pres. U. of Pittsburgh Alumni of Business Adminstrn. Sch.; mem. Pittsburgh Credit Assn., Pittsburgh Conv. Bureau. Mem. Pittsburgh Purveyors Assn., Delta Sigma Phi, Beta Gamma Sigma. Republican. Catholic. Clubs: Pittsburgh Athletic Assn., Wildwood Country (Pittsburgh). Home: 380 Morrison Drive, Mt. Lebanon, Pa. Office: 108 Boul. of Allies, Pittsburgh, Pa.

ZIEGLER, Louis Charles, dentist; b. Hungary, Mar. 27, 1894; s. Bernard and Rose (Bresh) B.; came to U.S., 1908, naturalized, 1913; D.D.S., U. of Louisville (Ky.) Dental Sch., 1920; m. Ruth Meyers, June 8, 1922; children—Bernadine, Louis Charles. Engaged in practice of dentistry at Louisville, Ky., 1920-24, and at Bethlehem, Pa., since 1924. Served in R.O.T.C., 1916-18. Pres. Sch. Bd., Bethlehem, Pa., 1936-37. Pres. B'rith Sholom Community Center, 1937-40. Mem. Am. Legion. Democrat. Jewish religion. Mason, K.P. Home: 307 E. 4th St., Bethlehem, Pa.

ZIEGLER, Percival Thomas, prof. animal husbandry; b. Lederach, Pa., Sept. 11, 1891; s. Irvin B. and Katharine (Koons) Z.; B.S., Pa. State Coll., 1913, M.S., 1922; m. Erma Ann Abegglen, June 14, 1914 (dec.); 1 dau., Geneva Carolyn. Employed as mgr. Walnut Hill Farm, Washington, Pa., 1914-19; instr. poultry husbandry, Pa. State Coll., 1919-20, instr. animal husbandry, 1920-26, asst. prof., 1926-31, prof. since 1931. Mem. Soc. of Animal Production, Delta Sigma Phi. Republican. Methodist. Club: Center Hills Country (State College, Pa.). Contbr. circulars and bulls. on animal husbandry. Home: 218 Highland Av., State College, Pa.

ZIEGLER, Samuel Horning, prof. of psychology and edn.; b. Malvern, Ill., Jan. 11, 1880; s. Jesse and Hannah (Horning) Z.; grad. West Chester State Teachers Coll., 1902; A.B., Ursinus Coll., Collegeville, Pa., 1910, A.M., 1912; Ph.D., U. of Pa., 1923; m. Sadie Florence Brownmiller, June 8, 1904; children—Frederick Ephriam, Harold Jesse. Teacher in country schools, Montgomery Co., Pa., 1898-1901; teacher in pub. schools, Lancaster, Pa., 1902-05; teacher of history, Boys High Sch., Reading, Pa., 1908-14, West Phila. High Sch. for Boys, 1914-18; dir. of social studies in secondary schools, Cleveland, O., 1918-26; prof. of edn. and psychology, Cedar Crest Coll., Allentown, Pa., since 1926. Mem. N.E.A., Pa. State Edn. Assn., Phi Delta Kappa, Pi Gamma Mu. Republican. Brethren Ch. Club: Torch, Lehigh Valley (Allentown, Pa.). Author of Social Studies in the Junior High School; co-author: Our Community, Choosing an Occupation. Home: 1820 Pennsylvania St., Allentown, Pa.

ZIEMER, Harry Stork, M.D.; b. Adamstown, Pa., June 25, 1893; s. Henry Heber and Alice (Stork) Z.; B.S., Muhlenberg Coll.; M.D., U. of Pa.; m. Henrietta Siemens, Nov. 26, 1919; children—Marion, Catherine, Dorothy, Janet. Engaged in gen. practice of medicine, Adamstown, Pa., since 1921; Lancaster Co. med. dir. since 1934. Dir. Wyomissing Valley Bank. Mem. Lancaster Co. Welfare Federation Com. Pres. Lancaster Co. and City Med. Soc., 1938, Federation of Democratic Clubs, 1937; trustee Am. Legion (Cocalico Post); mem. State Chamber of Commerce (Lancaster Co. Council). Mason. Clubs: Lions (dir.), Wyomissing. Address: 2 E. Main St., Adamstown, Pa.

ZIMMERMAN, Charles Fishburn, banker; b. Duncannon, Pa., June 21, 1878; s. Lucien Calvin and Clara Reed (Steele) Z.; A.B., Princeton, 1900, grad. work, 1901; m. Eleanor Graydon Hinckley (direct desc. of Elder William Brewster of the Mayflower), Sept. 10, 1903; children—Charles Hinckley, Edward Bailey, Eleanor Graydon. Clerk First Nat. Bank, Harrisburg, Pa., 1901, Steelton (Pa.) Trust Co., 1902-07, treas., 1907-12; treas. Lebanon County (Pa.) Trust Co., 1912-26; pres. First Nat. Bank, Huntingdon, Pa., since 1926. Mem. Pa. Bankers Assn. (pub. edn. commn., 1924-31; econ. policy commn., 1931-36; exec. com. nat. bank div., 1931-36; com. on banking studies, 1934-36; exec. council 1936-37; administrative com., 1937-38; research council, 1937-38). Dir. Pa. State Chamber of Commerce, 1938, U.S. Chamber of Commerce, 1938. Mem. Delta Upsilon. Republican. Presbyn. Mason. Address: First Nat. Bank, Huntingdon, Pa.

ZIMMERMAN, Charles Samuel, pres. The I. W. Scott Co.; b. Bellevue, Pa., July 20, 1892; s. George Henry and Ida (Luster) Z.; student U. of Pittsburgh, 1914-16; m. Lily West, Sept. 3, 1920; children—Charles West, Joan West. Entire business career with The I. W. Scott Co., seed and implement dealers, Pittsburgh, pres. and dir. since 1929. Republican. Home: 1527 Center St., Wilkinsburg, Pa. Office: 500 Liberty Av., Pittsburgh, Pa.

ZIMMERMAN, David William, high school prin.; b. Walkersville, Md., Sept. 8, 1901; s. Harry Elmer and Fannie Louise (Hoke) Z.; prep. edn. Walkersville (Md.) High Sch., 1915-16, Boys' High Sch., Frederick, Md., 1916-19; A.B., Franklin and Marshall Coll., Lancaster, Pa., 1923; A.M., Columbia, 1927; grad. student Johns Hopkins, summer 1931, U. of Chicago, summer 1935; m. Ethel Jane Birely, June 27, 1929; 1 dau., Ethel Ann. Prin. Walkersville (Md.) Jr. High Sch., 1923-24, Frederick (Md.) Jr. High Sch., 1924-26, Thurmont (Md.) Sr. High Sch., 1926-32, Kenwood High Sch., Raspeburg Post Office, Md., 1932-34; prin. Catonsville (Md.) High Sch. since 1934. Mem. N.E.A., Dept. of Secondary Sch. Prins., Lambda Chi Alpha. Presbyterian. Mason. Club: Catonsville Rotary. Home: 104 Bloomsbury Av., Catonsville, Md.

ZIMMERMAN, Elinor Carr, artist; b. St. Louis, Mo., Dec. 14, 1878; d. Benjamin Waters and Ellen Powell (Carr) Z.; B.S., Washington U., St. Louis, Mo., 1907, B.Arch., 1912; student Phila. Sch. Miniature Painting, Pa. Acad. Fine Arts, both since 1936. Began as miniature painter in Phila. Sch. Miniature Painting, 1936; first work accepted for exhbn. by Pa. Soc. Miniature Painters at Pa. Acad. Fine Arts, 1936; work in other exhbns., Washington, Chicago, Phila., 1937, Chicago, Los Angeles, 1938, Asbury Park, N.J., Pa. Soc. Miniature Painters at Art Alliance, Phila., 1939; present work in exbn. Pa. Soc. Miniature Painters at Phila. Museum. Mem. Pa. Soc. Miniature Painters, Am. Artists Professional League, Washington U. Alumni Assn., Am. Soc. for the Hard of Hearing, League for the Hard of Hearing, of St. Louis and of Phila. Democrat. Episcopalian. Home: 2038 Race St., Philadelphia, Pa.

ZIMMERMAN, Frederic Martin, banking; b. Brooklyn, N.Y., May 6, 1897; s. August and Katherine (Behrens) Z.; ed. Commercial High Sch., Brooklyn, N.Y., Columbia U., New York, Am. Institute of Banking, New York; wife: Hermine; children—Claire, Alan. Stenographer Fourth Nat. Bank, New York, 1912-14; correspondence clerk Bank of New York, New York, 1914-16; credit man Guaranty Securities Corpn., New York, 1917-21; gen. mgr. Auto Brokerage Co., New York, 1921-26; branch mgr. Commercial Credit Co., Phila., 1926-28; exec. vice-pres. and dir. Automobile Bnkg. Corpn., Phila., since 1928; vice-pres. and dir. A.B.C. Credit, Inc., A.B.C. Credit Corpn. Writer and lecturer on econ. subjects. Home: 1416 Knox Rd., Wynnewood, Pa. Office: Market St. National Bank Bldg., Philadelphia, Pa.

ZIMMERMAN, Louis S., v.p. Maryland Trust Co. Home: Severna Park, Anne Arundel Co., Pa. Office: Maryland Trust Bldg., Baltimore, Md.

ZIMMERMAN, O., pres. Union Screw and Mfg. Co.; b. Glenfield, Pa., Jan. 30, 1894; s. George H. and Ida May (Luster) Z.; ed. pub. schs. and high sch.; m. Jean Wickersham, Sept. 3, 1920; children—Stuart Hays, Helen Clare. Pres. with Union Screw & Mfg. Co. Republican. Presbyn. Mason. Rotarian. Club: Rotary. Home: 33 Castle Shannon Boul., Mt. Lebannon, Pa. Office: 207 S. Main St., Pittsburgh, Pa.

ZIMMERMAN, W. F.; chmn. bd., pres. and trust officer Montgomery Nat. Bank. Address: Norriston, Pa.

ZIMMERMANN, Charles Conrad, surgeon; b. Cumberland, Md., Apr. 27, 1899; s. Charles Philip and Laura Belle (Kelley) Z.; student St. Johns Coll., Anapolis, Md., 1918, Randolph Macon Coll., Ashland, Va., 1919-21; M.D., U. of Md. Med. Sch., Baltimore, Md., 1925; m. Anna Kathryn Whitlock, Sept. 28, 1928; children—Conrad Bay, Judith. Interne Md. Gen. Hosp., Baltimore, 1925-28, St. Joseph's Hosp., Baltimore, 1928-29; engaged in practice of medicine and surgery at Cumberland, Md. since 1929, specializing in surgery since 1929; member surgical staff Allegany Hosp., Memorial Hosp. Served in S.A.T.C., 1918. Fellow Am. Coll. Surgeons; mem. Randolph Winslow Surgical Soc., Allegany-Garrett County, Med. Soc., Chi Beta Pi, Phi Beta Pi. Democrat. Lutheran. Mason, Elk. Club: Elks (Cumberland.) Home: 941 Braddock Rd., Cumberland, Md.

ZIMMERMANN, George Floyd, dean; b. in Montoursville, Pa., May 17, 1891; s. George Andrews and Mary Elizabeth (Else) Z.; graduate high sch., Williamsport, Pa., 1911; Ph.B. Dickinson Coll., 1915, A.M., 1918; S.T.B., Boston U. Sch. of Theology, 1918; M.R.E., Boston U. Sch. Religious Edn. and Social Service, 1920; D.D. from Atlanta Theological Seminary, 1929; m. Florence, d. Frank Venn, May 22, 1920; 1 son, George Floyd. Ordained ministry M.E. Ch., 1918; dir. religious edn., Sixth Presbyn. Ch., Pittsburgh, Pa., 1920-21; dir. religious edn. Albion (Mich.) M.E. Ch., and head dept. of economics and finance, Albion Coll., 1921-22; asso.-pastor Cass Av. Ch., Detroit, 1922-23; treas. and head dept. economics, dean of summer sessions, Atlanta U., 1923-26; dean and head dept. religious edn., 1926-1931, of Atlanta Theol. Sem., now Atlanta Theol. Sem. Foundation, affiliated with Vanderbilt U. Sch. of Religion, Nashville; dean, prof. philosophy and religious edn., Temple U. Sch. of Theology, Phila., since 1931. Mem. Phila. conference Methodist Episcopal Ch. Grad. First Chaplain Tr. Sch., U.S. Army, Camp Zachary Taylor, Louisville, Ky., 1918; 1st lt., chaplain, May 29, 1918; served as chaplain 109th Inf., 28th Div., and of Base Hosp. No. 11, A.E.F., Nantes, France, and Base Hosp. No. 101, St. Nazaire; hon. discharged July 10, 1919. Awarded Victory Medal with 5 bars, World War Chaplain's medal, Purple Heart. Trustee Bapt. Inst., Phila. (v.p.). Mem. Alpha Chi Rho, Phi Delta Kappa, Pi Gamma Mu. Republican. Mason. Methodist. Editor of Temple Theologian. Home: 533 W. Hortter St., Germantown, Philadelphia, Pa.

ZIMMERMAN, John Edward, mechanical engr.; b. Buenos Aires, Argentine Republic, Jan. 31, 1874; s. John C. and Anna C. (MacKinley) Z.; B.A., Nat. Coll. of Buenos Aires, 1894; studied U. of Buenos Aires and U. of Pa.; m. Sarah Ann Frazier, June 5, 1900; children—Harriet F. (Mrs. Gerald W. Caner), Anna Cecilia (Mrs. Kenneth Van Strum), Helena (Mrs. Reinhardt Wildbolz), Audrey (Mrs. George Davis Gammon), Jean (Mrs. Edward L. Marshall). Served as interpreter with City Troop of Philadelphia, Porto Rican campaign, Spanish-American War; supt. of manufacture, American Pulley Company, Philadelphia, 1899-1901, sec., 1901-07; formerly mem. Dodge & Day, now Day & Zimmerman, Inc., pres. until 1929; pres. United Gas Improvement Co. since 1929; dir. Philadelphia Electric Co., Am. Pulley Co., United Gas Improvement Co., Conn. Electric Service Co., Phila. Steam Co., Conn. Light & Power Co., Pa. R.R. Trustee U. of Pa. Mem. Am. Soc. Mech. Engrs., Franklin Inst. Clubs: University, Racquet, Rittenhouse, Engineers, Philadelphia, Midday, Bankers of America, Sunnybrook Golf, Sea View Golf, Boca Raton, Corinthian Yacht; N.Y. Yacht. Home: 25 E. Summit St., Chestnut Hill. Office: 1401 Arch St., Philadelphia, Pa.

ZINN, John Brown, prof. of chemistry; b. Gettysburg, Pa., Aug. 20, 1888; s. Merville Eugene and Margaret Ellen (Brown) Z.; B.S., Gettysburg (Pa.) Coll., 1909; Ph.D., Johns Hopkins, 1913; m. Effie Matilda Miller, Jan. 1, 1913; children—Margaret Elizabeth, John Brown. Instr. in chemistry, Amherst (Mass.) Coll., 1913-15, asso. prof., 1915-19; prof. of chemistry, Worcester (Mass.) Poly. Instr., 1919-24; prof. and head chemistry dept., Gettysburg (Pa.) Coll. since 1924. Mem. Am. Chem. Soc., Am. Assn. Univ. Profs., Phi Beta Kappa, Gamma Alpha, Sigma Xi, Alpha Tau Omega. Republican. Lutheran. Mason. Home: 201 W. Broadway, Gettysburg, Pa.

ZINN, Waltman Farnsworth; clin. prof. otorhinolaryngology, U. of Md.; prof. bronchoscopy and esophagoscopy, Georgetown University; rhinolaryngologist Mercy Hosp.; attending otorhinolaryngologist South Baltimore General Hosp.; laryngologist Church Home and Infirmary, Union Memorial Hosp. and Hosp. for Women of Md.; bronchoscopist Mercy Hosp., Baltimore, and Georgetown U. Hosp., Washington, D.C. Address: 101 W. Read St., Baltimore, Md.

ZINSSER, John Sharman, chemical engr.; b. New York, N.Y., Aug. 30, 1894; s. Frederick G. and Emma (Sharman) Z.; prep. edn. MacKenzie Sch., 1901-10; B.S., Harvard, 1915; A.M., Columbia U., 1917; m. Isabella Wadsworth, July 10, 1920; children—Ellen, John Sharman, Thomas Wood. Chem. engr. Zinsser & Co., Hastings, N.Y., 1920-33, dir. since 1920; with Bankers Trust Co., New York, 1933-34; with Merck & Co., Inc., Rahway, N.J., 1934-35; pres. Sharp & Dohme, Inc., Phila., since 1935; dir. Girard Trust Co., Phila. Served as capt. Chem. Warfare Service, U.S. Army, 1919. Dir. Haverford (Pa.) Sch., Babies Hosp., Phila. Mem. Am. Chem. Soc., Chemist's Club of New York, Am. Soc. Chem. Engrs. Clubs: Harvard, Merion Cricket, Rittenhouse (Phila.). Home: Spring Mill Rd., Bryn Mawr, Pa. Office: 640 N. Broad St., Philadelphia, Pa.

ZINZOW, W(illiam) A(ugust), research physicist; b. Ripon, Wis., Nov. 22, 1890; s. John F. T. and Augusta (Lueck) Z.; student Ripon (Wis.) High Sch., 1904-08, Northwestern Colt., Naperville, Ill., 1912-13; A.B., Ripon (Wis.) Coll., 1915; M.S., U. of Pittsburgh, 1925; m. Helen Page, 1916; children—Kathryn Louise, William Alan. Teacher physics, Wausau (Wis.) High Sch., 1915-20; lab. asst. physics Westinghouse Electric and Mfg. Co., East Pittsburgh, Pa., 1920-21; instr. physics, U. of Pittsburgh, 1921-22; head physics dept., Muskingum Coll., New Concord, O., 1922-26; research physicist Bakelite Corpn., Bloomfield, N.J., 1926-33, chief physicist since 1933. Mem. Am. Phys. Soc., Am. Soc. for Testing Materials. Methodist. Mason. Home: 42 Cleveland Rd., Caldwell, N.J. Office: 230 Grove St., Bloomfield, N.J.

ZIRKE, Conway, prof. botany, U. of Pa. Address: U. of Pennsylvania, Philadelphia, Pa.

ZOLLER, Edwin Walter, artist and coll. prof.; b. Pittsburgh, Pa., May 29, 1900; s. Charles Henry and Elizabeth Margarite (Richter) Z.; ed. U. of Pittsburgh, 1917-18; A.B., Pa. State Coll., 1921; student Carnegie Inst. Teach., 1921-24; study in Italy, 1924, painting in Paris, 1927-28; m. Lucille A. Lang, July 2, 1927. Teacher of art in various high schs., 1921-31; studio of painting, Pittsburgh, 1931-33; lecturer in art and instr. in design, Pittsburgh Center and Altoona Summer Session of Pa. State Coll., 1927-33; studio of painting and instr. in art Pa. State Coll. Center, Towanda, 1933-34; administrative head and asst. prof. fine arts, DuBois Undergrad. Center, Pa. State Coll., DuBois, Pa., since 1935; exhibited in Paris, France; Florence, Italy; New York City; Pittsburgh; and other cities; represented in pvt. collections and in Pittsburgh Pub. Schs. Served in S.A.T.C., 1917-18. Mem. Asso. Artists of Pittsburgh; Pi Kappa Alpha. Lutheran. Traveled in Spain and northern Africa, 1928. Lecturer on art and history of art since 1925. Home: 131 E. DuBois Av., DuBois, Pa.

ZOOK, Ralph Taylor, petroleum producer; b. Newville, Pa., Oct. 5, 1889; s. Eli J. and Rebecca Jane (Huey) Z.; ed. mech. elec. engring., Williamson Sch., Delaware Co., Pa., 1906-09; m. Imogen Leuffer, Mar. 6, 1918 (died Oct. 19, 1922); 1 son, Edward Leuffer (dec.); m. 2d. Martha Bannon Jones, Feb. 16, 1927; adopted daughters, Sally, Polly. Designing and erecting, gas producers and engines, steam turbines, oil engines, mech. sales engr. on gas engines and gasoline plants, 1909-14; formed partnership with Wm. J. Sloan to organize co. to manufacture liquid hydrocarbons from natural gas, later same partnership organized cos. for producing Pa. grade oil by water flood methods and refining. Dir., vice-pres. for Pa., and chmn. membership com. of Independent Petroleum Assn. of America. Republican. Presbyn. Mason (32°, Shriner). Clubs: Bradford, Country, Valley Hunt. Home: Hedgehog Road, Office: 101 Main St., Bradford, Pa.

ZOUCK, Frank H., banking; b. Beckleysville, Md., June 13, 1865; s. Henry C. and Mary Ann (Fowble) Z.; grad. Reisterstown High Sch., 1881; ed. Bryant & Stratton Bus. Coll., Baltimore, 1882-83; m. Alice A. Chick, Mar. 14, 1888; children—Alice Marguerite, Ada E. (Mrs. Edward H. German), Dorothy A. (Mrs. Wm. A. Merrick). Began as clk. Western Md. R.R. 1883; chmn. Md. State Rds. Commn., 1916-20; now pres. Reisterstown Savings Bank. Home: Reisterstown, Md.

ZUBAK, Matthew F. C., attending oculist and aurist Ohio Valley Gen. and Wheeling hosps. Address: 1126 Market St., Wheeling, W.Va.

ZUCKER, Adolf Edward, coll. prof.; b. Ft. Wayne, Ind., Oct. 26, 1890; s. Friedrich and Marie (Kremmer) Z.; prep. edn., Concordia Coll., Ft. Wayne; A.B., U. of Ill., 1912, A.M., 1913; Ph.D., University of Pa., 1917; studied Sorbonne, Paris, and Unversities of Munich and Berlin; m. Lois Miles, Sept. 6, 1916; 1 son, John Miles. Instr. German, U. of Pa., 1916-17; instr. modern langs., Tsing Hua Coll., Peking, China, 1917-18; asst. prof. English, Peking Union Med. Coll., 1918-22; prof. modern langs. and comparative lit., U. of Md., 1923-35; prof. German lit., University of N.C., 1935-37; prof.

of German Lit., and head of dept., Indiana U., 1937-38; chmn. div. of humanities, U. of Md., since 1938. Member Modern Lang. Assn. America, Modern Humanities Research Assn., Soc. for Advancement Scandinavian Studies, Am. Assn. Univ. Profs., Gesellschaft für Theatergeschichte (Berlin), Goethe Soc. of Weimar, Soc. for History of Germans in Md. Author: Robert Reitzel, 1917; The Chinese Theater, 1925; Ibsen, the Master Builder, 1929 (transl. into French). Editor: Western Literature from Homer to Shaw, 1922; The Romantic Poets, 1926; Middle Nineteenth Century Poets, 1927; Thoma's Lokalbahn, 1931. Translator: The Redentin Easter Play (with H. H. Russell), 1939. Asso. editor of Studies in Philology, 1935-37; contbr. to philol. jours. Home: Riverdale, Md.

ZUCKER, Saul Joseph, lawyer; b. Newark, N.J., Jan. 22, 1901; s. Morris Joseph and Rose (Kirsch) Z.; A.B., Columbia U., 1921; LL.B., Columbia U. Law Sch., 1923; m. Alice Levy, Dec. 20, 1933; 1 son, Morris Robert. Admitted to N.J. bar as atty., 1924, as counselor, 1927; admitted to practice before the Supreme Ct. of the U.S., 1931; supreme ct. commr. of N.J. since 1933; engaged in gen. practice of law at Newark, N.J., since 1924; mem. firm Kristeller and Zucker since 1939. Mem. Essex County, N.J., State and Am. bar assns., Columbia Law Alumni Assn., Zeta Beta Tau. Jewish religion. Clubs: Mountain Ridge Country (West Caldwell); Lawyers (New York). Home: 329 Turrell Av., South Orange. Office: 744 Broad St., Newark, N.J.

ZUERNER, Frank DeWitt, sch. supt.; b. North Braddock, Pa., June 28, 1888; s. Philip and Lyda (Braznell) Z.; A.B., Otterbein Coll., 1910; student O. State U., summers, 1911-12; A.M., U. of Pittsburgh, 1930, grad. study, 1930-34; LL.D., Westminster Coll., 1934; m. Alberta Zinn, No. 24, 1937. Teacher and supervising prin. schs., Blairsville, Pa., 1910-17; teacher, North Braddock, Pa., 1920-28; prin. North Braddock Jr. High Sch., 1928-29; supt. schs., North Braddock, since 1929; dir. First Nat. Bank, Braddock Community Discount. Served in Med. Corps, U.S.A., 1918-20. Mem. bd. dirs. Carnegie Library of Braddock. Mem. Pa. State Edn. Assn. (past pres. Western Conv. Dist.), Braddock Bd. of Trade (dir.), Rotary Internat. (past gov. dist.), Pi Delta Kappa. Started W.P.A. Project for Adult Edn. on coll. level in North Braddock. United Presbyn. Mason (Shriner). Home: 825 Bell Av., North Braddock, Pa.

ZUGSMITH, Robert, prof. physiology and embryology, U. of Pittsburgh. Address: U. of Pittsburgh, Pittsburgh, Pa.

ZUMBRUNNEN, Thomas Michael, clergyman; b. Monroe Co., O., May 16, 1887; s. Christian and Mary (Thomas) Z.; A.B., W.Va. Wesleyan Coll., Buckhannon, W.Va., 1917; B.D., Drew Theol. Sch., Madison, N.J., 1924; hon. D.D., W.Va. Wesleyan Coll., 1934; m. Elizabeth Conaway, June 19, 1919; children—Charles Edward, Mary Elizabeth. Ordained to ministry Meth. Ch., 1918; minister, East Grafton, Pruntytown, Middlehope, N.Y., Pennsboro, Grafton, Charleston, W.Va., 1912-28; minister, Edgewood Park, Wheeling, W.Va., 1928-36; minister, First Ch., Elkins, W.Va., since 1936. Chmn. Randolph Co. Chapter Red Cross since 1937. Trustee W.Va. Wesleyan Coll., Buckhannon, since 1930. Republican. Methodist. Mason. K.P. Club: Rotary. Home: 317 Kerens Av., Elkins, W.Va.

ZUNDEL, George Lorenzo Ingram, educator; b. Brigham City, Utah, Dec. 23, 1885; s. Abraham and Mary Ellenor (Ingram) Z.; grad. Brigham Young Coll., Logan, Utah, 1909; B.S. in Agr., Utah Agrl. Coll., Logan, 1911; M.S. in Agr., Cornell U., 1915; Ph.D., Yale U., 1929; m. Rose Mae Bell, of Logan, Utah, Sept. 14, 1910; 1 son, Robert Clayburn. Student asst. in botany, Utah State Agrl. Coll., 1909-11, instr. in botany, 1911-12; teacher Box Elder High Sch., Brigham City, 1912-13; asst. prof. biology, Brigham Young Coll., Logan, 1915-17; spl. research on potato diseases for U.S. Dept. Agr., Jerome, Ida., summer, 1916; asst. plant pathologist in charge of cereal disease control in State of Washington for U.S. Dept. Agr., 1917-20; extension plant pathologist, Washington State Coll., 1919-26; asst. botanist to George Perkins Clinton (authority on Ustilaginales and other fungi), Conn. Agrl. Expt. Station, New Haven, 1926-28; asst. prof. plant pathology, Agrl. Extension Service, Pa. State Coll., since 1928. Known as authority on the Ustilaginales or smuts (smut fungi). Fellow A.A.A.S.; mem. Am. Phytopathol. Soc., Mycol. Soc. America, British Mycol. Soc., Inst. Am. Genealogy (Chicago), Soc. Genealogist (London), Nat. Geneal. Soc. (Washington, D.C.). Progressive Republican. Mem. Ch. of Latter Day Saints. Author: Wheat Smut Control, 1919; A New Corn Smut in Washington (with B. F. Dana), 1920; Some Ustilaginales of the State of Washington, 1920; The Effects of Treatment for Bunt on the Germination of Wheat, 1921; Smuts and Rusts of Northern Utah and Southern Idaho, 1921; The Dusting of Wheat and Oats for Smut (with F. D. Heald and L. W. Boyle), 1923; Notes on the Ustilaginales of Washington, 1926; Notes on Pennsylvania Ustilaginales, 1930; Monographic Studies on the Ustilaginales Attacking Andropogon, 1930; Notes on New Species of Ustilaginales, 1931; New and Rare North and South American Ustilaginales, 1933; The Ustilaginales of Pennsylvania, 1933; Miscellaneous Notes on the Ustilaginales, 1937; George Perkins Clinton, 1867-1937 (life sketch), 1938; Notes on Some Ustilaginales from India (with G. P. Clinton), 1938; A New Smut from Southern Chili, 1938. Home: State College, Pa. Address: 616 Sunset Rd.; or 203 Botany Bldg., Pa. State College, State College, Pa.

ZWEMER, Samuel Marinus, missionary, author; b. Vriesland, Mich., Apr. 12, 1867; s. Adrian and Katharina (Boon) Z.; A.B., Hope College, Holland, Mich., 1887, A.M., 1890; New Brunswick (N.J.) Theol. Sem., 1890; D.D., Hope, 1904, Rutgers, 1919; LL.D., Muskingum Coll., 1918; ordained clergyman, Reformed Ch. in America, 1890; m. Bagdad, Arabia, Amy E. Wilkes, May 18, 1896; children —Nellie Elizabeth (Mrs. Claude L. Pickens, Jr.), Kathrina (dec.), Ruth (dec.), Raymund L., Amy Ruth (Mrs. Homer N. Vioiette), Mary Moffatt. Missionary at various stations in Arabia, 1891-1912, and at Cairo, Egypt, 1913-29. Has traveled extensively; crossed Oman Peninsula; visited Sanaa in Yemen twice, during Arab rebellion, 1892, 1904; visited Hofhoof in Hassa, East Arabia, twice, etc.; chmn. and organizer Mohammedan Missionary Conference, Cairo, Egypt, 1906. Now prof. of the history of religion and Christian missions, Princeton Theological Seminary. Editor of the Moslem World (quar. rev.), New York; president Am. Christian Lit. Soc. for Moslems. Author: Arabia, the Cradle of Islam, 1902; Topsy Turvy Land (with Mrs. Amy E. Zwemer), 1902; Raymund Lull, 1904; Moslem Doctrine of God, 1906; Islam— A Challenge to Faith; The Moslem World, 1907; The Moslem Christ, 1911; The Unoccupied Mission Fields, 1910; Zigzag Journeys in the Camel Country, 1912; Childhood in Moslem World, 1915; Mohammed or Christ, 1915; The Disintegration of Islam, 1917; Influence of Animism on Islam, 1920; A Moslem Seeker After God, 1920; Christianity the Final Religion, 1921; Call to Prayer, 1923; The Law of Apostasy in Islam, 1924; Across the World of Islam, 1928; The Glory of the Cross, 1928; Thinking Missions with Christ, 1933; The Origin of Religion, 1935. Fellow Royal Geog. Soc., Victoria Inst.; mem. Royal Asiatic Soc.; hon. Phi Beta Kappa (N.J. Chapter, 1923). Home: 80 Alexander St., Princeton, N.J. Office: 156 Fifth Av., New York, N.Y.

ZWORYKIN, Vladimir Kosma, dir. research lab.; b. Russia, July 30, 1889; E.E., Petrograd Inst., Tech., 1912; student Coll. de France, Paris, 1912-14; Ph.D., U. of Pittsburgh, 1926; D.Sc., Brooklyn Poly. Inst., 1938; m. Tatiana Vasilieff, 1915; children—Nina, Elain. Came to U.S., 1919, naturalized, 1924. Research with Westinghouse Elec. and Mfg. Co., 1920-29; with R.C.A. Mfg. Co. since 1929, dir. electronic research lab. since 1934. Awarded Morris Liebmann Memorial Prize (for contbns. to development of television), 1934. Served in Radio Corps of Russian Army during World War. Mem. Inst. of Radio Engrs., Am. Inst. Elec. Engring., Am. Phys. Soc., Soc. of Motion Picture Engrs., Sigma Xi. Author: Photocells and Their Applications, 1932. Home: Taunton Lakes, N.J. Office: R.C.A. Mfg. Co., Inc., Camden, N.J.

INDEX BY STATES

This index groups by states all sketches appearing in this book

DELAWARE

Afflerbach, Calvin E., Georgetown, 5
Aikman, Everett M., Edge Moor, 6
Allen, Ned B., Newark, 10
Allen, Rena, Newark, 11
Allen, William F., Seaford, 11
Allison, James W., Wilmington, 11
Anderson, Clarence E., Bridgeville, 14
Anderson, Daniel G., Rehoboth Beach, 14
Arthurs, Stanley M., Wilmington, 24
Bailey, Arthur L., Wilmington, 32
Bailey, Henry J., Wilmington, 33
Baker, Charles W., Jr., Greenville, Wilmington, 34
Baker, Thomas A., Newark, 36
Bancroft, John, Jr., Wilmington, 40
Banton, Conwell, Wilmington, 40
Bates, Daniel M., Wilmington, 49
Bausman, Robert O., Newark, 51
Bayard, Thomas F., Wilmington, 51
Bayliss, Charles W., Edge Moor, 51
Beebe, James, Lewes, 56
Beebe, Richard C., Lewes, 56
Bell, Max S., Wilmington, 60
Bellanca, Frank M., New York, N. Y., 60
Bellanca, Giuseppe M., Rockland, New Castle, 60
Benner, Claude L., Wilmington, 62
Bennett, Hiram R., Wilmington, 63
Bent, Leavitt N., Hollyoak, Wilmington, 64
Bergland, Eric L., Wilmington, 64
Berl, Eugene E., Wilmington, 65
Bigelow, Charles A., Wilmington, 70
Biggs, John, Jr., Wilmington, 70
Binder, Walter J., Wilmington, 71
Bird, Samuel B., Centerville, Wilmington, 72
Bird, William E., Wilmington, 72
Bissell, Alfred E., Wilmington, 74
Bissell, George F., Wilmington, 74
Black, J. Leon, Milton, 75
Blatz, John B., Wilmington, 79
Blatz, William C., Wilmington, 79
Blumberg, Leo, Wilmington, Newark, 81
Bolton, Elmer K., Wilmington, 84
Boyce, William H., Dover, 91
Boykin, S. F., Wilmington, 93
Bradley, Aubrey O., Wilmington, 95
Brentlinger, John M., Wilmington, 100
Brittingham, Thomas E., Jr., Wilmington, 104
Brown, Benjamin N., Wilmington, 108
Brown, Harry F., Wilmington, 109
Brown, J. Thompson, Montchanin, Wilmington, 110
Brown, Karl K., Seaford, 110
Brubaker Merlin M., Wilmington, 114
Buck, Clayton D., Wilmington, 117
Burdick, C. Lalor, Wilmington, 120
Burkholder, Eberly P., Dover, 122
Burnett, Marguerite H., Wilmington, 122
Burr, Samuel E., II, New Castle, 123
Bush, Henry T., Wilmington, 125
Byam, Edwin C., Newark, 128
Calvarese, Flaviano, Wilmington, 131
Candee, Charles L., Wilmington, 133
Cann, John P., Newark, Wilmington, 134
Cantwell, Garrett R., Wilmington, 134
Carpenter, Robert R. M., Montchanin, Wilmington, 138
Carpenter, Walter S., Jr., Wilmington, 138
Carter, George, Smyrna, 140
Chambers, Arthur D., Wilmington, 145
Chilton, Thomas H., Wilmington, 151
Cohen, Harry, Wilmington, 164
Conover, Elisha, Jr., Newark, 173
Cooch, Francis A., Wilmington, 174
Cooper, Richard W., Newark, 176
Cordie, Cornell H., Wilmington, 178

Corkran, Wilbur S., Rehoboth Beach, Lewes, 178
Cornbrooks, Thomas M., Wilmington, 178
Craig, Harry E., Wilmington, 184
Crane, Jasper E., Wilmington, 185
Crooks, Ezra B. Newark, 190
Cryder, James W., Wilmington, 193
Curtis, Charles M., Wilmington, 196
Danby, H. Gregg, Wilmington, 200
Daugherty, John F., Newark, 202
Daugherty, Martin M., Newark, 202
Davidson, Hobart O., Wilmington, 203
Davis, Carl H., Wilmington, 203
Davis, Henry, Wilmington, 205
Davis, James R., Wilmington, 206
Day, Cyrus L., Newark, 209
DeKnight, Edward W., Wilmington, 212
Denney, Oswald E., Smyrna, 215
Denney, William du H., Dover, 215
Detjen, Louis R., Newark, 217
Dietrich, Daniel W., Wilmington, 222
Dillon, Samuel M., Wilmington, 223
Dolliver, Alan K., Bellevue, Wilmington, 227
Donohue, Francis M., Greenville, Wilmington, 229
Drake, Quaesita C., Newark, 233
Drew, Thomas B., Wilmington, 234
Duane, Howard, Wilmington, 235
Duffy, Charles E., Wilmington, 236
Dunham, Russell H., Wilmington, 238
Du Pont, A. Felix, Wilmington, 240
Du Pont, Alfred V., Greenville, Wilmington, 240
Du Pont, E. Paul, Montchanin, 240
Du Pont, Ernest, Wilmington, 240
Du Pont, Francis V., Wilmington, 240
Du Pont, Irénée, Granogue, Wilmington, 240
Du Pont, Lammot, Wilmington, 240
Du Pont, Pierre S., Wilmington, 240
Du Pont, William, Jr., Wilmington, 240
Dutton, George E., Newark, 241
Earley, Albert, Georgetown, 244
Eastman, Albert S., Newark, 244
Eaton, Harry B., Wilmington, 245
Echols, Angus B., Wilmington, 245
Edge, James B. D., Wilmington, 247
Eliason, James B., Wilmington, 252
Elley, Harold W., Wilmington, 253
Errigo, Joseph A., Marshallton, Wilmington, 261
Everitt, Frank B., Rehoboth Beach, 265
Falion, William M., Wilmington, 268
Finkelstein, Isaac B., Wilmington, 280
Fitzmaurice, Edmond J., Wilmington, 284
Foulk, William H., Centreville, Wilmington, 292
Foulke, Willing B., Wilmington, 293
Fowler, Burton P., Wilmington, 293
Frame, Thomas C., Dover, 295
Fulmer, Clarence A., Wilmington, 304
Gallo, Anthony J., Wilmington, 307
Gant, Charles H., Wilmington, 308
Garretson, Cornelius D., Wilmington, 310
Gassaway, Frederic G., Cragmere, Wilmington, 311
Golder, Marjory S., Newark, 327
Goodrich, Edgar J., Rehoboth Beach, 330
Gottlieb, Albert S., Harrington, 332
Grant, William T., Ashland, Wilmington, 335
Grasselli, Thomas S., Wilmington, 336
Green, Percy W., Wilmington, 339
Greenewalt, Mary H., Wilmington, 340
Grier, Albert O. H., Wilmington, 342

Griffenberg, Elbert D., Wilmington, 343
Grossley, Richard S., Dover, 347
Groves, John S., Wilmington, 348
Gunby, Walter E., Wilmington, 350
Hallam, Clement B., Wilmington, 357
Hallman, Ernest C., Laurel, 357
Hammond, Bernice W., Dover, 360
Handforth, Thomas, Wilmington, 362
Hargis, David H., Wilmington, 366
Harrington, William W., Dover, 369
Harrington, Willis F., Wilmington, 369
Harris, Henry C., Newark, 369
Harris, Marian D., Wilmington, 370
Harter, George A., Newark, 372
Harvey, Lewis B., Wilmington, 375
Haskell, Harry G., Wilmington, 375
Hastings, Daniel O., Wilmington, 376
Hayes, Ralph, Wilmington, 380
Heald, William H., Wilmington, 382
Hebard, Benjamin M., Wilmington, 383
Heckert, Winfield W., Ardentown, Wilmington, 383
Heim, Raymond W., Newark, 385
Hering, George C., Wilmington, 391
Higgins, Charles A., Wilmington, 396
Hill, Roy L., Wilmington, 399
Hirsch, Daniel, Milford, 402
Hoff, Preston, Wilmington, 405
Holley, Ella J., Wilmington, 408
Hollis, Charles M., Seaford, 409
Holloway, Harry V., Dover, 409
Holt, Lee C., Wilmington, 411
Holzman, Mark B., Hockessin, 411
Homsey, Samuel E., Wilmington, 412
Hope, William M., Dover, 413
Horsey, Harold W., Dover, Wilmington, 416
Houghton, Clinton O., Newark, 417
Howard, Edward G., Wilmington, 418
Hughes, James H., Dover, 423
Hullihen, Walter, Newark, 424
Huntington, Park W., Wilmington, 428
James, Albert W., Wilmington, 440
Jessup, John B., Wilmington, 445
Jones, Harrison, Wilmington, 453
Jones, Lawrence J., Wilmington, 454
Joslin, Theodore G., Greenville, 455
Jost, Arthur C., Dover, 456
Kann, James J., Wilmington, 458
Kemp, Robert D., Wilmington, 467
Kennedy, Matthew G., Wilmington, 468
Killoran, Clair J., Wilmington, 473
Kleffman, Albert H., Wilmington, 479
Kleitz, George, Wilmington, 480
Kniffen, Frederick, Hollyoak, Wilmington, 482
Koerber, George A., Newark, 485
Koester, Edwin F., Wilmington, 485
Kurtz, Charles C., Wilmington, 494
Laird, Walter J., Wilmington, 496
Lamb, Richard W., Wilmington, 497
La Motte, William O., Wilmington, 498
Lawrence, James C., Wilmington, 504
Layton, Caleb S., Wilmington, 505
Layton, Daniel J., Georgetown, 505
Lee, Henry H., Wilmington, 507
Levy, Benjamin E., Wilmington, 515
Lewis, William D., Newark, 519
Lincoln, Edmond E., Wilmington, 521
Lodge, George, Claymont, Wilmington, 528
Long, Cuth W., Selbyville, 530
Longendyke, William F., Seaford, 531
Lyon, Leland, Wilmington, 540
MacCollum, Isaac J., Wyoming, 541
MacLeod, Donald C., Wilmington, 545
MacRae, Allan A., Wilmington, 546

Maguire, John F., Wilmington, 548
Marshall, John, Wilmington, 556
Marshall, Samuel M. D., Milford, 557
Martin, Joseph H., Wilmington, 559
Mayerberg, Emil R., Wilmington, 567
Maynard, Edward W., Wilmington, 567
McCue, C. A., Newark, 577
McDermott, Frank A., Wilmington, 579
McKinstry, Arthur R., Wilmington, 586
McMullen, Richard C., Dover, Wilmington, 588
McSweeny, James L., Wilmington, 591
Melson, Elwood F., Wilmington, 595
Metten, William F., Wilmington, 599
Metten, William M., Wilmington, 599
Miller, Ashby, Wilmington, 602
Miller, Edgar R., Wilmington, 603
Miller, Jay W., Wilmington, 605
Morford, James R., Wilmington, Marshallton, 620
Morris, Harold H., Wilmington, 623
Morris, Hugh M., Newark, Wilmington, 623
Morris, John J., Jr., Wilmington, 624
Morton, Nellie, Wilmington, 626
Mullin, James P., Wilmington, 631
Mullin, John H., Wilmington, 631
Mylrea, Thomas D., Newark, 638
Nelson, George M., Delmar, 641
Nields, John P., Wilmington, 647
Nixon, Anson B., Hollyoak, Wilmington, 648
Nollau, Edgar H., Wilmington, 649
Norman, George M., Wilmington, 650
Nowland, Otho, Wilmington, 652
Overdeer, Frank N., Wilmington, 664
Owens, Charles A., Wilmington, 665
Palmer, Charles C., Newark, 667
Parker, Frank W., Wilmington, 670
Parsons, Louis S., Wilmington, 672
Patterson, Gordon D., Wilmington, 674
Paynter, Rowland G., Georgetown, 676
Pearson, George B., Jr., Newark, Wilmington, 678
Peets, Orville H., Millsboro, 679
Pell, Walden, 2d, Middletown, 680
Pettingill, William L., Wilmington, 686
Philips, Earle S., Wilmington, 687
Pickard, Frederick W., Greenville, Wilmington, 690
Pierson, John C., Wilmington, 691
Polk, Albert F., Wilmington, 696
Poole, William, 6th, Wilmington, 698
Powell, Walter A., Dover, 702
Preston, Howard K., Newark, 704
Preyer, William Y., Wilmington, 705
Prickett, Clifford D., Wilmington, 706
Prickett, William, Wilmington, 706
Purdy, Willard G., Wilmington, 708
Raskob, William F., Wilmington, 715
Rea, Robert W., Wilmington, 717
Records, Victor C., Laurel, 718
Reese, Charles L., Wilmington, 721
Reese, Charles L., Jr., Wilmington, 721
Regestein, Walter P., Wilmington, 722
Rheuby, Gould G., Wilmington, 728
Rhoads, Philip G., Wilmington, 729
Rhodes, William W., Wilmington, 729
Richards, Charles S., Georgetown, 731
Richards, Leonard, Wilmington, 731
Richards, Robert H., Wilmington, 731

DELAWARE

Richards, Robert H., Jr., Wilmington, 732
Richardson, Lunsford, Wilmington, 733
Ridgely, Charles du P., Camden, 734
Ridgely, Henry, Dover, 735
Robinson, Edmund G., Wilmington, 744
Robinson, Robert P., Wilmington, 745
Robinson, Winifred J., Newark, 746
Rodney, Richard S., New Castle, Wilmington, 747
Rogers, Russell D., Wilmington, 749
Rose, Robert E., Wilmington, 753
Ryan, Leon H., Newark, New Castle, 764
Ryden, George H., Newark, 764
Samonisky, Harris, Wilmington, 767
Satterthwaite, Reuben, Jr., Wilmington, 769
Saville, Joseph H., Wilmington, 770
Sawin, Ellen Q., Wilmington, 770
Schoonover, Frank E., Wilmington, 779
Schulson, Solomon, Wilmington, 781
Schuster, George L., Newark, 782
Schutt, Harold S., Greenville, Wilmington, 782
Shands, Alfred R., Jr., Wilmington, 792
Sharp, Hugh R., Wilmington, 793
Shilling, John, Dover, 799
Simon, Morris, Dover, 807
Simons, Frank K., Newark, 807
Simonton, Fagan H., Wilmington, 807
Sipple, William V., II, Milford, 810
Smith, Lemon L., Wilmington, 821
Southerland, Clarence A., Wilmington, 830
Speakman, Frank L., Wilmington, 832
Speer, William H., Wilmington, 832
Spencer, Francis E., Wilmington, 833
Spencer, Robert L., Newark, 834
Springer, Harold L., Centreville, Wilmington, 836
Springer, Willard, Jr., Rockland, Wilmington, 836
Stayton, William H., Smyrna, 842
Stearns, Louis A., Newark, 843
Stephenson, Gilbert T., Wilmington, 846
Stillman, Jesse W., Wilmington, 851
Stine, Charles M. A., Wilmington, 851
Stine, Milton H., Wilmington, 852
Stirling, James S., Wilmington, 852
Stouffer, Samuel M., Wilmington, 857
Stradley, Wilmer, Wilmington, 858
Strikol, Albert J., Wilmington, 861
Stull, Philip B., Wilmington, 864
Sturges, Gertrude C., Newark, 864
Swenehart, John, Wilmington, 871
Sypherd, Wilbur O., Newark, 873
Tanberg, Arthur P., Wilmington, 875
Tarumianz, Mesrop A., Farnhurst, 876
Taylor, Cornelia H., Dover, 877
Thaddeus, Victor, Arden, 883
Tiffany, Harold E., Newark, Wilmington, 891
Tisdale, Wendell H., Wilmington, 893
Townsend, G. Marshall, Milford, 895
Townsend, John G., Jr., Selbyville, 895
Townsend, Sylvester D., Wilmington, 896
Truss, James P., Wilmington, 900
Tschudy, Estelle W., Smyrna, 900
Tunnell, James M., Georgetown, 901
Uhler, Claude, Farnhurst, 905
Van Demark, Ernest S., Wilmington, 909
Varnes, Samuel K., Wilmington, 912
Veasey, Benjamin R., Wilmington, 913
Vincent-Daviss, Cedric A., Wilmington, 915
Wagner, M. Channing, Wilmington, 919
Ward, Christopher L., Greenville, Wilmington, 926
Ward, Christopher L., Jr., Greenville, Wilmington, 926
Ward, Herbert H., Jr., Wilmington, 927
Warner, Alfred Du P., Jr., Wilmington, 928
Warner, Charles, Wilmington, 928
Warner, Irving, Wilmington, 929
Washburn, Newell R., Milford, 930
Washburn, Victor D., Wilmington, 931
Weber, Clarence S. P., Middletown, 936
Weymouth, George T., Greenville, Wilmington, 947
Wheelwright, Robert, Wilmington, 948
White, Charles P., Wilmington, 950
White, Jacob R., Millsboro, 950
Whitworth, John B., Wilmington, 955
Wicker, Samuel E., Wilmington, 955
Wilkinson, William A., Newark, 959
Willey, James E., Seaford, 960
Williams, Harvey D., Laurel, 962
Willis, John W., Wilmington, 965
Wilson, Henry V. P., Dover, 967
Wilson, Thomas W., Wilmington, 969
Winchester, James P., Wilmington, 970
Woodbridge, Richard G., Jr., Wilmington, 976
Woodcock, Floyd W., Wilmington, 977
Woodford, John W., Dover, 977
Woodruff, Robert W., Wilmington, 977
Woolley, Victor B., Wilmington, 980
Wright, John P., Newark, 983
Wright, Norris N., Newark, 983
Yerkes, Leonard A., Greenville, Wilmington, 987

MARYLAND

Abercrombie, Ronald T., Baltimore, 1
Abeshouse, Benjamin S., Baltimore, 2
Adams, Leason H., Bethesda, 3
Adams, Rowland K., Baltimore, 4
Addicks, Lawrence, Bel Air, 4
Addison, Joseph, Glenn Dale, Baltimore, 4
Adkins, William H., Easton, 5
Adler, Charles, II, Baltimore, 5
Aiken, Gerald R., Catonsville, Baltimore, 6
Albinson, J. Warren, Elkton, 6
Albright, William F., Baltimore, 7
Alcock, John L., Towson, Baltimore, 7
Alden, Carroll S., Annapolis, 7
Alderman, Lewis R., Chevy Chase, 7
Alexander, Ralph I., Cumberland, Frostburg, 8
Allen, Hervey, Oxford, 10
Allen, Leah B., Frederick, 10
Allen, Wendell D., Baltimore, 11
Allison, James B., Chevy Chase, 11
Allner, F. A., Baltimore, 12
Ames, Joseph S., Baltimore, 13
Anderson, Thomas B. H., Baltimore, 16
Andrews, Donald H., Baltimore, 17
Andrews, Ethan A., Baltimore, 17
Andrews, Mary R., Baltimore, 17
Andrews, Matthew P., Baltimore, 17
Andrus, Edwin C., Baltimore, 17
Apple, Joseph H., Frederick, 20
Apple, Miriam R., Frederick, 20
Appleby, Paul H., Chevy Chase, 20
Appleman, Charles O., College Park, 20
Armstrong, Alexander, Ruxton, Hagerstown, Baltimore, 21
Arrowsmith, Harold N., Baltimore, 23
Ashbrook, Frank G., Bethesda, 24
Ashbury, Howard E., Baltimore, 24
Ashman, Louis S., Baltimore, 25
Atwill, Lionel, Eccleston, 27
Auchter, Eugene C., College Park, 27
Avery, Charles D., Takoma Park, 27
Aycock, Thomas B., Baltimore, 29
Bachrach, Walter K., Bethesda, 30
Baetjer, Edwin G., Baltimore 31
Bagby, Alfred J., Baltimore, 31
Bagby, Anne C., Baltimore, 31
Bagby, Cecil H., Baltimore, 31
Bagley, Charles, Jr., Baltimore, 31
Bahlke, George W., Baltimore 31
Bahn, Walter D., Baltimore, 31
Bailey, Garland H., Baltimore, 32
Bailey, Levin C., Salisbury, 33
Baker, George H., Aberdeen, 35
Baker, Henry F., Baltimore, 35
Baker, Henry S., Baltimore, 35
Baker, Holmes D., Frederick, 35
Baker, John H., Buckeystown, Baltimore, 35
Baker, Joseph R., Kensington, 35
Baker, Oliver E., College Park, 36
Baker, William G., Jr., Towson, Baltimore, 36
Baldwin, Calvin B., Bethesda, 38
Baldwin, William L., Baltimore, 38
Ballard, Wilson T., Ruxton, Baltimore, 39
Bamberger, Florence E., Baltimore, 39
Bamford, Ronald, Hyattsville, 39
Bancroft, Milton B., Sandy Spring, 40
Bandel, John M., Linthicum, Baltimore, 40
Bardette, Charles M., Baltimore, 40
Bard, Philip, Baltimore, 41
Bardgett, Edward R., Baltimore, 42
Barker, Lewellys F., Baltimore, 42
Barkley, Frederick R., Bethesda, 42
Barnes, George O., Chevy Chase, 43
Barnes, Grace, Forest Glen, 43
Barnett, George E., Baltimore, 44
Barnhart, John L., Baltimore, 44
Barnhart, William R., Frederick, 45
Barr, Stringfellow, Annapolis, 45
Barrett, Arthur G., Baltimore, 45
Barroll, Lewin W., Baltimore, 46
Bartlett, J. Kemp, Baltimore, 47
Barton, Carlyle, Towson, Baltimore, 47
Barton, Randolph, Jr., Pikesville, Baltimore, 47
Barton, Vola P., Baltimore, 47
Baskervill, William M., Baltimore, 48
Bauer, John C., Baltimore, 50
Bauernschmidt, Marie O. von H., Baltimore, 50
Baur, J. Fred, Baltimore, 51
Bawden, George A., Baltimore, 51
Bay, Robert P., Baltimore, 51
Bayley, Francis R., Baltimore, 51
Baylor, C. N., Hagerstown, 52
Baylor, John W., Baltimore, 52
Beall, J. Glenn, Baltimore, 53
Bearden, Joyce A., Baltimore, 54
Beardsley, Wilfred A., Baltimore, 54
Beatty, Joseph M., Jr., Baltimore, 54
Beck, Harvey G., Baltimore, 55
Beck, Solomon S., Chestertown, 55
Beeuwkes, C. John, Baltimore, 57
Beirne, Francis F., Ruxton, Baltimore, 58
Beisser, Paul T., Baltimore, 58
Bell, William H., Chevy Chase, 60
Bennett, George E., Baltimore, 62
Bergey, James R., Baltimore, 64
Bergland, John M., Baltimore, 64
Bernheim, Bertram M., Pikesville, Baltimore, 65
Berry, Edward W., Baltimore, 66
Bertholf, Lloyd M., Westminster, 66
Besley, Fred W., Baltimore, 67
Best, William H., Baltimore, 67
Bethel, Walter A., Chevy Chase, 67
Billig, Thomas C., Chevy Chase, 71
Bingley, George A., Annapolis, 72
Birdseye, Claude H., Chevy Chase, 72
Birely, Morris A., Thurmont, 72
Biser, Daniel B., Baltimore, 73
Bisgyer, Gustave, Baltimore, 73
Bishopp, Fred C., Silver Spring, 73
Bispham, William N., Baltimore, 74
Bixler, Edward C., New Windsor, 74
Bjorlee, Ignatius, Frederick, 74
Black, Luther A., University Park, 75
Black, Samuel D., Towson, 75
Blackwell, Jefferson D., Salisbury, 76
Blades, Webster S., Baltimore, 76
Blake, Charles F., Baltimore, 77
Blakeman, William H., Baltimore, 78
Bland, Richard H., Catonsville, Baltimore, 78
Bliss, William J. A., Baltimore, 80
Blocher, Nellie K., Frederick, 80
Blum, William, Chevy Chase, 81
Boas, George, Baldwin, 82
Boeckel, Richard M., Norbeck, 82
Boggs, Samuel W., Chevy Chase, 83
Bolgiano, Louis P., Sr., Baltimore, 83
Bolgiano, Ralph, Towson, Baltimore, 84
Bolwell, Robert W., Silver Spring, 84
Bond, Carroll T., Baltimore, 84
Bond, Edward J., Baltimore, 84
Bonnell, Robert O., Baltimore, 85
Bordley, James, Baltimore, 87
Boston, William T., Cambridge, 88
Bosworth, Edwin C., Bethesda, 88
Bouve, Clement L., Chevy Chase, 88
Bovey, William H., Hagerstown, 89
Bowe, Dudley P., Baltimore, 89
Bowen, Josiah S., Baltimore, Towson, 89
Bower, Elizabeth B., Frederick, 89
Bowie, Clarence K., Baltimore, 90
Bowman, Ethel, Baltimore, 90
Bowman, Isaiah, Baltimore, 90
Boyce, Charles P., Baltimore, 91
Boyce, Fred G., Jr., Baltimore, 91
Boyce, Heyward E., Baltimore, 91
Boyce, William G., Baltimore, 91
Boyd, J. Cookman, Baltimore, 92
Boyd, Kenneth B., Baltimore, 92
Boyd-Carpenter, Chevy Chase, 92
Boyer, George M., Damascus, 93
Boylan, James E., Jr., Westminster, 93
Bradley, William C., Hurlock, 95
Brady, George M., Baltimore, 96
Brady, S. Proctor, Baltimore, 96
Bramble, Charles C., Annapolis, 96
Brandes, Elmer W., Chevy Chase, 97
Brannan, William F., Ruxton, Baltimore, 98
Bratney, Bertrand H., Glenelg, Baltimore, 98
Braunlich, Alice F., Baltimore, 98
Breg, W. Roy, Bethesda, 99
Breitstein, Moses L., Baltimore, 100
Brewer, William R., Cumberland, 101
Brewster, Benjamin H., Jr., Stevenson, Baltimore, 101
Brewster, Benjamin H., III, Brooklandville, Baltimore, 101
Bridge, Edward M., Baltimore, 101
Bridge, Josiah, Takoma Park, 101
Bridges, Henry P., Hancock, 101
Bridges, William A., Towson, 101
Brindle, Harry, Hagerstown, 102
Briscoe, Philander B., Baltimore, 103
Broedel, Max, Baltimore, 104
Broening, William F., Baltimore, 105
Brombacher, William G., Chevy Chase, 105
Bromwell, Richard E., Baltimore, 105
Brooks, Earl H., Baltimore, 106
Brooks, Rodney J., Baltimore, 106
Broughton, Levin B., College Park, 107
Brown, Charles W., Baltimore, 108
Brown, Donaldson, Port Deposit, 108
Brown, Edgar, Lanham, 108
Brown, Edgar F., Baltimore, 108
Brown, Ford K., Annapolis, 108
Brown, Harry J., Chevy Chase, 109
Brown, Helen E., Baltimore, 109
Brown, Hylton R., Silver Spring, 110
Brown, Lillian O., Frederick, 111
Brown, Theodore F., Westminster, 112
Brown, Thomas R., Baltimore, 112
Brown, Warren W., Baltimore, 112
Brown, Wilson, Annapolis, 113
Brown, Zenith J., Annapolis, 113
Bruce, Howard, Elkridge, Baltimore, 114
Bruce, James, Eccleston, 114
Bruce, Louise E., Baltimore, 114
Bruce, W. Cabell, Ruxton, 114
Brumbach, Lynn H., Hagerstown, 115
Brune, Herbert M., Jr., Ruxton, Baltimore, 115
Brush, Warren D., Chevy Chase, 115
Bryan, Charles E., Havre de Grace, 115
Bryan, J. Wallace, Baltimore, 115
Buchanan, Scott, Annapolis, 116
Buchholz, Heinrich E., Baltimore, 116
Bucholtz, Carl, Longgreen, 117
Buchwald, Leona C., Baltimore, 117
Buck, Charles H., Baltimore, 117
Buck, Elizabeth C., Reisterstown, Baltimore, 117
Buck, Walter H., Brooklandville, Baltimore, 117
Buckingham, Edgar, Chevy Chase, 117
Buckler, H. Warren, Baltimore, 118

MARYLAND

Budnitz, Edmund, Baltimore, 118
Bullard, Dexter M., Rockville, 119
Bullis, William F., Silver Spring, 119
Bunting, George A., Baltimore, 120
Bunting, John J., Salisbury, 120
Burbage, E. E., Sr., Berlin, 120
Burkart, Joseph A., Chevy Chase, 121
Burke, Edmund S., Cumberland, 121
Burky, Earl L., Loch Raven, Baltimore, 122
Burnam, Curtis F., Baltimore, 122
Burnett, Paul M., Baltimore, 122
Burns, F. Highlands, Baltimore, 123
Burton, Charles W., Jr., Baltimore, 124
Bush, Edgar M., Hampstead, 125
Bussey, Gertrude C., Baltimore, 125
Butler, John M., Baltimore, 126
Byrd, Harry C., College Park, 128
Cadwalader, Thomas F., Joppa, Baltimore, 129
Cairnes, Laura J., Baltimore, 129
Caldwell, Joseph S., Riverdale, Beltsville, 130
Calloway, Walter B., Baltimore, 130
Calverton, Victor F., Baltimore, 131
Campbell, Harry G., Towson, 132
Canning, Joseph A., Baltimore, 134
Cannon, Burdelle S., Baltimore, 134
Cantwell, Harry A., North East, 134
Carey, Andrew C., Owings Mills, Baltimore, 135
Carey, Francis J., Baltimore, 136
Carey, Francis K., Baltimore, 136
Carey, James, 3d, Baltimore, 136
Carlson, C. Allen, Crisfield, 136
Carrington, Edward C., Loreley, 138
Carroll, Benjamin S., Bel Air, 138
Carroll, Charles, Jr., Ellicott City, 138
Carroll, Douglas G., Brooklandville, Baltimore, 139
Carson, John, Chevy Chase, 139
Carter, Allan, Baltimore, 139
Carter, John D., Denton, 140
Carty, Virginia, Frederick, 140
Casbarian, Harvey T., College Park, 141
Casey, William J., Baltimore, 142
Caskie, Marion M., Chevy Chase, 142
Casler, Dewitt B., Baltimore, 142
Castle, Elizabeth M., Baltimore, 143
Chaffinch, James R., Denton, 144
Chalmers, Henry, Chevy Chase, 144
Chambers, D. B., Baltimore, 145
Chambers, Thomas R., Baltimore, 145
Chapman, James W., Jr., Baltimore, 147
Chapman, Katharine A., Kensington, 147
Chapman, Ross M., Towson, 147
Chappell, Ralph H., Kensington, 148
Cheek, Leslie, Jr., Baltimore, see Addenda
Cheslock, Louis, Baltimore, 149
Chesney, Alan M., Baltimore, 149
Chesnut, William C., Baltimore, 150
Chideckel, Maurice, Baltimore, 150
Childs, Marquis W., Chevy Chase, 151
Chisolm, James J., Baltimore, 152
Chisolm, Oliver B., Baltimore, 152
Christie, Alexander G., Baltimore, 152
Churchill, George M., Bethesda, 153
Ciotti, Hector J., Baltimore, see Addenda
Clapp, Clyde A., Baltimore, 154
Clapp, Earle H., Chevy Chase, 154
Clapper, Raymond, Chevy Chase, 154
Clare, Robert D., Baltimore, 154
Clark, Charles C., Chevy Chase, 154
Clark, Ernest J., Baltimore, 155
Clark, Janet H., Baltimore, 155
Clark, John B., Cumberland, 155
Clark, Lindley D., Sandy Spring, 156
Clark, Taliaferro, Germantown, 156
Clark, Thomas W. Y., Baltimore, 156
Clark, Walter L., Baltimore, 156
Clark, William M., Baltimore, 157
Clarke, Carl D., Ruxton, Baltimore, 157
Clarke, Marjorie R., Ruxton, 157
Claus, William, Cumberland, 158
Clayton, Alexander B., Chevy Chase, 158
Cleaveland, Allan, Baltimore, 158
Clemen, Rudolf A., Chevy Chase, 159
Clements, Guy R., Annapolis, 159

Clephane, Walter C., Chevy Chase, 159
Cloud, William W., Baltimore, 161
Clough, Paul W., Baltimore, 161
Coad, Joseph A., Leonardtown, Baltimore, 161
Coady, Charles P., Jr., Baltimore, 161
Coale, James J., Annapolis, 161
Cobb, Stanwood, Chevy Chase, 162
Coblentz, Emory L., Middletown, Frederick, 162
Coblentz, Leslie N., Middletown, Frederick, 162
Coblentz, Richard G., Baltimore, 162
Coburn, Fred L., Havre de Grace, 162
Coe, Conway P., Chevy Chase, 162
Coe, Ward B., Riderwood, Baltimore, 163
Cohen, Barnett, Baltimore, 164
Cohen, Lee, Pikesville, 164
Cohen, Louis, Bethesda, 164
Cohill, Edmund P., Hancock, 164
Cohn, Charles M., Baltimore, 165
Cohn, L. Clarence, Baltimore, 165
Cole, Charles W., Towson, 165
Cole, Norman B., Baltimore, 165
Cole, William P., Jr., Towson, Fork, 166
Coleman, William C., Eccleston, Baltimore, 166
Collins, Charles W., Oxon Hill, 168
Collins, Clarence E., Crisfield, 168
Collitz, Klara M., Baltimore, 168
Colston, J. A. Campbell, Woodbrook, Baltimore, 169
Coman, Dana, Baltimore, 169
Combs, Hugh D., Baltimore, 169
Cone, Sydney M., Pikesville, 170
Conover, Julian D., Chevy Chase, 173
Constable, William P., Baltimore, 173
Cook, Albert S., Towson, 174
Cook, Orator F., Jr., Lanham, 174
Cook, Vernon, Baltimore, 175
Coombes, Ethel R., Chevy Chase, 176
Coop, Jesse J., Chesterton, 176
Coriell, Louis D., Baltimore, 178
Cornwell, John J., Baltimore, 179
Corrington, Julian D., Chestertown, 180
Cort, William W., Baltimore, 180
Cory, Ernest N., College Park, 180
Cotterman, Harold F., College Park, 181
Cotton, Alburtus, Baltimore, 181
Cotton, William E., Beltsville, 181
Coulbourn, George C., Marion Station, 181
Councill, Wilford A. H., Baltimore, 182
Cover, Harry R., Westminster, 182
Cowherd, Joseph K., Cumberland, 182
Cowles, Rheinart P., Baltimore, 183
Crabbe, George W., Baltimore, 185
Crane, Esther, Baltimore, 185
Crane, Harley L., Hyattsville, Beltsville, 185
Crawford, Arthur B., Beltsville, 186
Crockett, James M., Pocomoke City, 189
Croker, Maria B., Baltimore, 189
Crooks, Esther J., Baltimore, 190
Cross, Charles W., Chevy Chase, 190
Crowe, Samuel J., Baltimore, 191
Crowther, Gwynn, Lutherville, Baltimore, 192
Cullen, Thomas S., Baltimore, 193
Cullen, Victor F., State Sanatorium, 194
Cummins, Charles A., Baltimore, 195
Cunningham, John H., Westminster, 195
Curley, Michael J., Baltimore, 195
Curran, William, Baltimore, 196
Curry, Robert G., Bethesda, 196
Curtis, Eugene N., Baltimore, 196
Curtis, Harvey L., Chevy Chase, 197
Curtiss, Charles D., Chevy Chase, 197
Cushwa, David K., Sr., Williamsport, 197
Cutchin, Esther, Baltimore, 198
Cutler, George C., Garrison, Baltimore, 198
Dale, Frederick A., Baltimore, 199
Dalzell, George W., Chevy Chase, 199
Dandy, Walter E., Baltimore, 199
Dantzig, Tobias, Hyattsville, College Park, 200
Darling, Ira A., Sykesville, 201
Darrin, Marc de L., Baltimore, 201

Darton, Nelson H., Chevy Chase, 201
Davis, Arthur L., Chestertown, 203
Davis, E. Asbury, Baltimore, 204
Davis, Francis A., Baltimore, 204
Davis, Hoagland C., Baltimore, 205
Davis, Irene M., Baltimore, 205
Davis, John S., Baltimore, 206
Davis, Paul B., Baltimore, 206
Davis, Roy T., Forest Glen, 207
Davis, Russell S., Cambridge, 207
Davis, Samuel G., Jr., Baltimore, 207
Dawson, Thomas L., Rockville, 208
Dawson, Walter W., Oakland, 208
Day, Arthur L., Bethesda, 209
Day, John H., Baltimore, 209
Dearing, Arthur H., Annapolis, 210
Deaton, John L., Baltimore, 210
Decker, Alonzo G., Towson, 211
Decker, Josef B., Elkton, 211
Defandorf, Francis M., Chevy Chase, 212
Delaplaine, Edward S., Frederick, Annapolis, 212
Delaplaine, Robert E., Frederick, Braddock Heights, 212
Delaplaine, William T., Frederick, 212
De Lauter, Henry K., Braddock Heights, Frederick, 213
Dellinger, John H., Chevy Chase, 213
Denmead, Garner W., Baltimore, 215
Dennis, George R., Jr., Frederick, 215
Dennis, Samuel K., Baltimore, 215
Deschler, Lewis, Bethesda, 217
De Vault, Samuel H., Hyattsville, College Park, 218
Devilbiss, Wilbur, Brunswick, 218
De Witt, George A., Bethesda, 219
Dickerson, Edwin T., Baltimore, 219
Dickinson, John, Trappe, 220
Dieffenbach, Rudolph, Garrett Park, 221
Diehl, Charles F., Baltimore, 221
Dieke, Gerhard H., Baltimore, 221
Dielman, Louis H., Baltimore, 221
Diener, Louis, Baltimore, 221
Dippel, Adelbert L., Baltimore, 223
Dixon, James, Easton, 224
Dobbs, Edward C., Baltimore, 225
Dobson, Edgar F., Baltimore, 225
Dobson, Frank M., College Park, 225
Dodd, Francis J., Emmitsburg, 225
Dohme, Alfred R. L., Baltimore, 227
Dole, Esther M., Chestertown, 227
Donn, Edward W., Jr., Chevy Chase, 228
Donnell, Harold E., Baltimore, 228
Donoho, Edmond S., Baltimore, 229
Dorsey, John L., Baltimore, 230
Douglas, William O., Silver Spring, 231
Douglass, Louis H., Baltimore, 232
Douw, Henry deP., Annapolis, 232
Doyle, Henry G., Chevy Chase, 233
Doyle, Marion W., Chevy Chase, 233
Dozier, Herbert L., Cambridge, 233
Drach, John G. P., Baltimore, 233
Dryden, Raymond C., Pocomoke City, 235
Duckett, Thomas H., Hyattsville, 235
Duffy, Edmund, Baltimore, 236
Duffy, Edward, Baltimore, 236
Dugdale, Horace K., Baltimore, 236
Duke, Charles C., Baltimore, 237
Du Mez, Andrew G., Baltimore, 237
Dumont, Paul E., Baltimore, 237
Dunbar, Paul B., Chevy Chase, 238
Duncan, Alexander E., Baltimore, 238
Dunford, Edward B., Riverdale, 238
Dunkle, John L., Frostburg, 239
Dunn, Edward K., Baltimore, 239
Dunn, Herbert L., Baltimore, 239
Dunning, Henry A. B., Baltimore, 240
Dunning, J. H. Fitzgerald, Baltimore, 240
Dunnington, Virginius G., Baltimore, 240
Dunton, William R., Jr., Catonsville, 240
Durbin, Joseph W., 2d, Baltimore, 240
Eager, Auville, Baltimore, 242
Earle, Swepson, Baltimore, 243
Easter, James M., Owings Mills, Baltimore, 244
Eastman, Nicholson J., Baltimore, 244
Eaton, George O., Baltimore, 244
Eaton, Herbert N., Chevy Chase, 245

Ebeling, Herman L., Baltimore, 245
Ebeling, Karl W., Baltimore, 245
Edgett, Eugene A., Baltimore, 247
Edmunds, Page, Baltimore, 247
Edwards, Carolyn H., Glen Echo, 248
Edwards, Charles R., Baltimore, 248
Edwards, Monte, Baltimore, 248
Eells, Walter C., Bethesda, 249
Einarsson, Stefán, Baltimore, 251
Ekaitis, George L., Kennedyville, Chestertown, 252
Ekin, John J., Towson, Baltimore, 252
Eldridge, Francis R., Bethesda, 252
Elgin, William W., Towson, 252
Eliasberg, Louis E., Baltimore, 252
Ellicott, Valcoulon LeM., Bethesda, Rockville, 253
Elliott, Foster F., Chevy Chase, 254
Ellis, Francis A., Baltimore, 254
Emery, Harland C., Baltimore, 256
Emery, James A., Chevy Chase, 257
Emmett, Paul H., Baltimore, 257
Enders, Martin L., Baltimore, 258
England, Charles W., University Park, College Park, 258
Englar, George M., Baltimore, 258
Engle, Benjamin, Towson, Baltimore, 258
Epstein, Jacob, Baltimore, 260
Esterson, Albert A., Baltimore, 262
Etchison, Bates, Gaithersburg, 262
Evans, George H., Jr., Baltimore, 263
Evans, Silliman, Baltimore, 264
Everett, Houston S., Baltimore, 265
Every, William F., Baltimore, 265
Ewing, Jack S., Lutherville, Baltimore, 265
Ezekiel, Mordecai J. B., Bethesda, 267
Fadum, Ernest F., Baltimore, 267
Fagin, Nathan B., Baltimore, 267
Fahrney, Henry L., Frederick, 267
Fairbank, Herbert S., Baltimore, 268
Falk, Isidore S., Chevy Chase, 268
Falls, William F., Hyattsville, 269
Fargo, Lee K., Baltimore, 270
Farley, Frederic H. M. S., Baltimore, 270
Farquhar, Allan, Sandy Spring, 271
Fast, Gustave, Annapolis, Baltimore, 271
Feise, Ernst, Baltimore, 273
Feldmeyer, George T., Annapolis, 273
Fell, Edgar T., Baltimore, 273
Felton, Holden S., Frederick, 273
Fenhagen, George C., Baltimore, 274
Fenhagen, James C., Baltimore, 274
Fenlon, John F., Baltimore, 274
Fenn, Don F., Baltimore, 274
Fenning, Karl, Gaithersburg, 274
Ferguson, John B., Hagerstown, 275
Ferree, Clarence E., Baltimore, 276
Ferris, Walter E., Easton, 276
Fesperman, Harvey A., Hagerstown, 276
Fetrow, Ward W., Chevy Chase, 277
Field, Carter, Chevy Chase, 277
Field, Isaac S., Baltimore, 278
Field, Richard S., Rockville, 278
Fieser, James L., Bethesda, 278
Finan, Joseph B., Cumberland, 279
Finch, George A., Chevy Chase, 279
Finch, John W., Chevy Chase, 279
Fink, A. J., Mt. Washington, Baltimore, 279
Finney, George G., Eccleston, Baltimore, 280
Finney, John M. T., Baltimore, 280
Finney, John M. T., Ruxton, Baltimore, 280
Firor, Whitmer B., Baltimore, 280
Fisher, Frank, Jr., Govanstown, 281
Fisher, John W., Westernport, 282
Fisher, Samuel J., Baltimore, 282
Fisher, William A., Baltimore, 282
Fiske, Charles, Baltimore, 282
Fitch, Edgar K., Mt. Washington, Baltimore, 283
Fitzpatrick, Clarke J., Catonsville, Baltimore, 284
Flack, Horace E., Mt. Washington, Baltimore, 284
Flaherty, E. P., Baltimore, 284
Fleck, Harvey K., Baltimore, 284
Fleischmann, Edwin M., Baltimore, Lansdowne, 284
Fleming, John A., Chevy Chase, 285
Flynn, Bernard J., Baltimore, 287
Foley, Charles J., Havre de Grace, 288
Follis, Richard H., Sr., Baltimore, 288
Fontaine, Edgar C., Chestertown, Baltimore, 288

Foote, Mark, Chevy Chase, 288
Footner, Hulbert, Lusby, 289
Ford, William W., Woodbrook, 289
Forsythe, William H., Sykesville, Ellicott City, 290
Foss, Wilson P., Jr., Centreville, 291
Fowler, Laurence H., Baltimore, 293
Fox, H. P., Salisbury, 293
Fox, John L., Baltimore, 294
France, Jacob, Baltimore, 295
France, Mary A., St. Mary's City, 295
Frank, Eli, Baltimore, 295
Frank, Eli, Jr., Baltimore, 295
Frank, Grace, Baltimore, 295
Fraser, John F., Baltimore, 297
Frazer, Joseph C. W., Baltimore, 297
Freeman, Allen W., Baltimore, 298
Freeman, Elmer B., Baltimore, 298
French, John C., Baltimore, 299
French, William C., Gaithersburg, 299
Fried, Hiram, Baltimore, 300
Friedenwald, Edgar B., Baltimore, 300
Friedenwald, Harry, Baltimore, 300
Friedenwald, Jonas S., Baltimore, 300
Friedenwald, Julius, Baltimore, 300
Frobisher, Martin, Jr., Baltimore, 301
Frohman, Philip H., Gibson Island, 302
Fulton, Chester A., Baltimore, 304
Fulton, John C., Brooklandville, Baltimore, 304
Funkhouser, Elmer N., Hagerstown, 304
Gallagher, Edward J., Jr., Baltimore, 306
Gallagher, Katharine J., Baltimore, 306
Galloway, Charles W., Baltimore, 307
Galvin, Thomas K., Baltimore, 307
Gamble, Cary B., Jr., Baltimore, 307
Gambrill, James H., Jr., Frederick, 308
Gans, Hilary W., Baltimore, 308
Gantert, Frank A., Baltimore, 308
Gardner, Henry A., Chevy Chase, 308
Gardner, Irvine C., Chevy Chase, 309
Gardner, William S., Baltimore, 309
Garey, Enoch B., Oakland, 309
Garnett, Leslie C., Chevy Chase, 310
Garrett, John W., Baltimore, 310
Garrett, Robert, Baltimore, 310
Gary, E. Stanley, Catonsville, Baltimore, 311
Gary, James A., Jr., Baltimore, 311
Gascoyne, William J., Baltimore, 311
Gassaway, Louis D., Annapolis, 311
Gatley, H. Prescott, Chevy Chase, 312
Gay, Leslie N., Baltimore, 313
Genter, Albert L., Baltimore, 315
Geppert, William L., Cumberland, 315
Geraghty, William R., Baltimore, 315
German, Arthur R., Baltimore, 316
Germuth, Frederick A., Halethorpe, Baltimore, 316
Geschickter, Charles F., Baltimore, 316
Ghent, Pierre M., Baltimore, 317
Ghingher, J. J., Baltimore, 317
Gibson, David C., Baltimore, 318
Gibson, Kasson S., Chevy Chase, 319
Gieske, Alfred W., Catonsville, Baltimore, 319
Gift, Foster U., Baltimore, 319
Gill, Robert J., Baltimore, 321
Gillis, Alexander J., Baltimore, 322
Gilson, C. Albert, Frederick, 323
Girdwood, John, Baltimore, 323
Gish, Oliver H., Chevy Chase, 323
Goddard, Eunice R., Baltimore, 326
Goldbach, Leo J., Baltimore, 327
Goldenweiser, Emanuel A., Chevy Chase, 327
Goldsborough, Felix V., Sr., Baltimore, 327
Goldsborough, Phillips L., Baltimore, 327
Goldsborough, T. Alan, Denton, 327
Goldsmith, Harry, Baltimore, 327
Goldstein, Albert E., Baltimore, 328
Golomb, Elhanan H., Baltimore, 328
Goodloe, Don S. S., Bowie, 329
Goodloe, Jane F., Baltimore, 329
Goodman, Alexander, Baltimore, 329
Goodman, Morris H., Baltimore, 329
Goodnow, Frank J., Baltimore, 329

Goodrich, Donald W., Baltimore, 329
Goodwin, Thomas C., Baltimore, 330
Gordon, Douglas H., Baltimore, 330
Gordy, William S., Jr., Salisbury, 331
Goresline, Harry E., Silver Spring, 331
Gorman, Lawrence C., Baltimore, 332
Goss, Albert S., Chevy Chase, 332
Gottschall, Andrew W., Chevy Chase, 332
Gould, Clarendon I. T., Baltimore, 333
Gould, Frank, Towson, Baltimore, 333
Gould, Justinus, Baltimore, 333
Gracie, William A., Cumberland, 334
Graham, Albert D., Lutherville, Baltimore, 334
Graham, William C., Rising Sun, 335
Gray, Edith S., Chevy Chase, 337
Gray, John B., Jr., Prince Frederick, 337
Gray, John C., Annapolis, 337
Gray, Lewis C., Chevy Chase, 337
Green, Harry J., Baltimore, 338
Green, Joseph C., Chevy Chase, 338
Greene, Herbert E., Baltimore, 340
Greene, Laurence, Baltimore, 340
Greene, L. Wilson, Aberdeen, 340
Greenfield, Kent R., Baltimore, 341
Greer, William R., Baltimore, 341
Greiner, John E., Ruxton, Baltimore, 342
Grice, John C., Hagerstown, 342
Griffin, Bulkley S., Chevy Chase, 343
Griffin, Isabel K., Chevy Chase, 343
Griggs, Robert F., Chevy Chase, 344
Grimes, William H., Catonsville, Baltimore, 344
Grimsley, George P., Baltimore, 345
Grinnalds, Jefferson C., Baltimore, 345
Griswold, Alexander B., Baltimore, 345
Griswold, Benjamin H., Jr., Baltimore, 345
Griswold, Robertson, Baltimore, 345
Grosvenor, Gilbert H., Bethesda, 350
Guttmacher, Alan F., Baltimore, 351
Guttmacher, Manfred S., Baltimore, 351
Haas, John F., Baltimore, 351
Haas, Michael S., Baltimore, 351
Hacker, Theodore W., Baltimore, 352
Hackney, H. Hamilton, Finksburg, Baltimore, 352
Haile, LeRoy Y., Towson, 354
Hale, Charles B., Hyattsville, 355
Hall, Robert L., Pocomoke City, 356
Hall, Sidney, Baltimore, 356
Hall, Thomas J., 3d, Tracys Landing, 356
Hallgren, Mauritz A., Glenwood, 357
Hamburger, Louis P., Baltimore, 358
Hamill, William H., Crisfield, 359
Hamilton, William T., Hagerstown, 360
Hamlet, Harry G., Chevy Chase, 360
Hamlin, Percy G., Cambridge, 360
Hamman, Louis, Baltimore, 360
Hanrahan, Edward M., Ruxton, Baltimore, 363
Hanson, Elisha, Bethesda, 363
Hardcastle, Alexander, Baltimore, 364
Harding, Constance, Frederick, 364
Hardinge, Harold, Jr., Baltimore, 365
Hardwick, H. J., Annapolis, 365
Hardy, Charles O., Silver Spring, 365
Haring, Malcolm M., Riverdale, 366
Harlan, Henry D., Baltimore, 367
Harlow, Richard C., Westminster, 367
Harman, Susan E., Hyattsville, College Park, 367
Harne, Oliver G., Baltimore, 367
Harr, William R., Chevy Chase, 368
Harrington, Emerson C., Cambridge, 369
Harris, Lynn H., New Windsor, 370
Harris, Milton, Bethesda, 370
Harris, W. Hall, Jr., Baltimore, 371
Harrison, Edmund P. H., Jr., Baltimore, 371
Harrison, H. Norris, Centreville, 371
Harry, David G., Pylesville, 371
Hart, Robert S., Baltimore, 372

Hartman, Carl G., Baltimore, 373
Hartman, Ralph E., Frederick, 373
Hartson, Joseph T., Baltimore, 373
Hartung, Walter H., Baltimore, 374
Harwood, Charles M., Baltimore, 375
Hasse, Adelaide, Silver Spring, 375
Hathaway, Harrison R., Bethesda, 377
Havens, Charles W., Westminster, 378
Havens, Raymond D., Baltimore, 378
Hawes, Raymond P., Baltimore, 378
Hawken, J. A., Hagerstown, 378
Hawkins, Arthur H., Cumberland, 378
Hawkins, Harry C., Chevy Chase, 378
Hawks, Rachel M., Ruxton, 379
Hayden, Reynolds, Annapolis, 379
Hayes, John W., North Beach, 380
Hazard, Robert C., Baltimore, 381
Hazlett, Adam J., Baltimore, 381
Healy, James P., Baltimore, 382
Heaps, William J., Baltimore, 382
Heath, Louise R., Frederick, 382
Heath, William P., Baltimore, 382
Heatwole, Timothy O., Baltimore, 383
Hechter, Carl A., Sr., Riverdale, Hyattsville, 383
Hecht, Lee I., Baltimore, 383
Hedrich, Arthur W., Baltimore, 384
Hegner, Robert W., Baltimore, 384
Helfner, Gordon G., Baltimore, 385
Heisey, Victor D., Cumberland, 385
Helfenstein, Edward T., Baltimore, 386
Helm, William P., Riverdale, 386
Henderson, George, Cumberland, 388
Henderson, Walter C., Chevy Chase, 388
Hennighausen, Frederick H., Baltimore, 389
Hepbron, James M., Baltimore, 390
Heskett, Charles Z., Cumberland, 393
Hewitt, Charles T., Baltimore, 395
Highe, Edgar C., Bethesda, 396
Higgins, Nathan B., Ruxton, Baltimore, 396
Hildt, Thomas, Baltimore, 397
Hilgenberg, Carl G., Baltimore, 397
Hill, Bancroft, Baltimore, 397
Hill, Eben C., Baltimore, 398
Hill, James W., Jr., Baltimore, 398
Hill, J. B. P. Clayton, Annapolis, 398
Hill, Lewis B., Baltimore, 399
Hiller, Grace, Baltimore, 400
Himes, Joseph H., Frederick, 400
Himstead, Ralph E., Chevy Chase, 400
Hines, Frank B., Chestertown, 401
Hinkley, John, Baltimore, 401
Hintz, Carl W. E., College Park, 402
Hirsch, Isaac, Cumberland, 402
Hockley, Chester F., Hydes, Baltimore, 404
Hodge, Mary A., Baltimore, 404
Hoehling, Adolph A., Chevy Chase, 405
Hoff, Charles W., Baltimore, 405
Hoffberger, Harry, Baltimore, 405
Hoffman, James I., Chevy Chase, 406
Hoffmeier, Frank N., Hagerstown, 406
Hoffrogge, Fred W., Baltimore, 406
Hogan, John F., Baltimore, 406
Hogan, Joseph V., Baltimore, 406
Hoisington, Gregory, Baltimore, 407
Holdcraft, Paul E., Hagerstown, 407
Holden, Edwin C., Baltimore, 407
Holland, Paul L., Baltimore, 408
Hollander, Jacob H., Baltimore, 408
Hollander, Sidney, Baltimore, 408
Hollister, Joseph H., Chevy Chase, 409
Holloway, Fred G., Westminster, 409
Hollyday, Guy T. O., Baltimore, 410
Hollyday, John D., Funkstown, Hagerstown, 410
Holmes, Dwight O. W., Baltimore, 410
Holtman, Dudley F., Chevy Chase, 411
Holzapfel, Henry, Jr., Hagerstown, 411
Homer, Harry L., Riderwood, 411
Honoré, Paul, Port Deposit, 412
Hood, Ethel P., Baltimore, 412
Hooker, Donald R., Baltimore, 412
Hooper, Elizabeth, Baltimore, 412
Hooper, James E., Ruxton, Baltimore, 413
Hopkins, Annette B., Baltimore, 413
Hopkins, James S., Bel Air, 414

Hopkins, Robert M., Ruxton, Baltimore, 414
Hopkins, Walter C., Catonsville, Baltimore, 414
Horn, Edgar G., Baltimore, 414
Horner, Charles F., Chevy Chase, 415
Horney, William R., Centreville, 415
Hornsby, Rogers, Baltimore, 415
Houston, G. Porter, Baltimore, 417
Howard, Charles M., Baltimore, 417
Howard, John D., Baltimore, 418
Howard, Phillip W., Baltimore, 418
Howard, William T., Baltimore, 418
Howell, A. Brazier, Ruxton, 419
Howell, Clewell, Towson, 419
Howell, Roger, Baltimore, 419
Howell, William H., Baltimore, 420
Howell, William R., Chestertown, 420
Hoyt, Ray, Hyattsville, 421
Hoyt, Sidney M., Baltimore, 421
Hubbard, John C., Baltimore, 421
Hubbard, Thomas F., Baltimore, see Addenda
Hubbard, Wilbur R., Chestertown, 421
Huber, Frederick R., Baltimore, 421
Hudgins, Herbert E., Baltimore, 422
Huff, Wilbert J., Silver Spring, 422
Hughes, James W., Elkton, 423
Hulburt, Lorain S., Baltimore, 424
Hummel, Arthur W., Chevy Chase, 425
Humphrey, George S., Hagerstown, 426
Humphrey, Harry B., Cabin John, 426
Hundley, John M., Jr., Baltimore, 426
Hunner, Guy L., Pasadena, Baltimore, 426
Hunter, Albert C., Silver Spring, 427
Hunter, Oscar B., Chevy Chase, 428
Huston, Harland W., Salisbury, 429
Hutchins, Amos F., Baltimore, 430
Hutchins, Elliott H., Baltimore, 430
Hutzler, Albert D., Pikesville, Baltimore, 430
Hyde, Roscoe R., Baltimore, 431
Hynson, William G., Ruxton, 431
Hyslop, James A., Silver Spring, 431
Ickes, Harold L., Olney, 431
Iglehart, Francis N., Stevenson, Baltimore, 432
Iglehart, Joseph A. W., Lutherville, 432
Ijams, George E., Baltimore, 432
Ikeler, Kenneth C., College Park, 432
Ingberg, Simon H., Bethesda, 432
Ingle, William, Baltimore, 433
Insley, Herbert, Chevy Chase, 434
Insley, T. S., Cambridge, 434
Isanogle, Alvey M., Westminster, 435
Isanogle, Anna H., Westminster, 435
Israel, Edward L., Baltimore, 435
Jack, William G., Port Deposit, 436
Jackson, Charles S., Baltimore, 436
Jackson, Elmer M., Jr., Annapolis, 437
Jackson, Hartley H. T., Chevy Chase, 437
Jackson, Howard W., Baltimore, 437
Jacobs, Disston W., Snow Hill, 438
Jacobs, Henry B., Baltimore, 438
Jacobs, Thomas M., Baltimore, 439
James, Albert E., Chevy Chase, 440
Janney, Stuart S., Garrison, Baltimore, 441
Jarman, G. W., Salisbury, 442
Jeffries, Charles S., Frostburg, 443
Jenkins, John G., College Park, 443
Jenkins, T. Courtenay, Baltimore, 443
Jennings, Frank L., Baltimore, 444
Jennings, Herbert S., Baltimore, 444
Jett, Ewell K., Chevy Chase, 445
Jett, Page C., Prince Frederick, 445
Johnson, Arthur N., Baltimore, 446
Johnson, Benjamin A., Salisbury, 446
Johnson, Buford J., Baltimore, 446
Johnson, Charles W. L., Baltimore, 447
Johnson, Edward S., Baltimore, 447
Johnson, Gerald W., Baltimore, 448
Johnson, Philander C., Rockville, 449
Johnson, Robert W., Jr., Baltimore, 449
Johnson, Robert W., Baltimore, 449

MARYLAND

Johnston, Richard H., Silver Spring, 450
Jones, Charles B., Baltimore, 452
Jones, E. Ray, Annapolis, 452
Jones, Edgar A., Princess Anne, 452
Jones, Emmett L., Cumberland, 452
Jones, Ernest R., Oakland, 452
Jones, Harry C., Baltimore, 453
Jones, Henry A., Hyattsville, Beltsville, 453
Jones, J. S. William, Chestertown, 453
Jones, Kenneth B., Cambridge, 454
Jory, Herbert G., Baltimore, 455
Joslin, Charles L., Baltimore, 455
Joyce, Hazleton A., Severna Park, Baltimore, 456
Justice, Daniel W., Baltimore, 456
Kamens, Benjamin M., Cumberland, 458
Kanner, Leo, Baltimore, 458
Katenkamp, William E., Baltimore, 459
Katz, Sidney H., Edgewood, 459
Katzenelbogen, Solomon, Bethesda, 459
Kavanaugh, E. P., Baltimore, 460
Kearney, Francis X., Baltimore, 461
Keating, Thomas J., Centerville, 461
Keech, Edward P., Jr., Baltimore, 461
Keefer, Arthur C., Mt. Rainier, 461
Keefer, Clarence E., Baltimore, 461
Keenan, Joseph B., Chevy Chase, 462
Kelley, Louise, Baltimore, 464
Kelly, Evander F., Texas, 465
Kelly, Howard A., Baltimore, 465
Kemler, Joseph I., Baltimore, 466
Kemp, William B., College Park, 467
Kennedy, Ambrose J., Baltimore, 467
Kent, Frank R., Baltimore, 468
Kerlin, Robert T., Cumberland, 469
Kibler, Alton L., Baltimore, Edgewood Arsenal, 471
Kibler, John T., Chestertown, 471
Kiefer, Paul J., Annapolis, 472
Kieffer, Richard F., Baltimore, 472
Kile, Orville M., Glen Echo Heights, 472
Kilpatrick, Ellen P., Baltimore, 473
Kilpatrick, Mary G., Baltimore, 473
Kimberly, George M., Catonsville, Baltimore, 473
King, Henry S., Baltimore, Riderwood, 474
King, Howell A., Baltimore, 474
King, Jessie L., Baltimore, 474
King, John T., Baltimore, 474
King, Warren T., Towson, Baltimore, 475
Kinsolving, Arthur B., Baltimore, 476
Kinsolving, Sally B., Baltimore, 476
Kiplinger, Willard M., Bethesda, 476
Kirby, Francis J., Baltimore, 477
Kirk, Harris E., Baltimore, 477
Knotts, Earle P., Denton, 483
Knotts, James O., Denton, 483
Knox, Charles W., Laurel, 483
Kohler, Milton, Hagerstown, 485
Koon, Thomas W., Cumberland, 486
Koontz, Amos R., Baltimore, 486
Koontz, Paul R., Baltimore, 487
Kopp, Charles L., Cumberland, 487
Koppelman, Walter, Baltimore, 487
Korner, Jules G., Jr., Chevy Chase, 487
Kouwenhoven, Frank W., Baltimore, 488
Kouwenhoven, William B., Baltimore, 488
Krabill, Verlin C., Pocomoke City, 488
Krantz, John C., Jr., Baltimore, 488
Kratz, John A., Baltimore, 489
Krause, Allen K., Baltimore, 489
Krieger, Abraham, Baltimore, 491
Kudner, Arthur H., Grasonville, 492
Kummer, Frederic A., Baltimore, 493
Kurrelmeyer, William, Baltimore, 493
Lahey, Richard, Baltimore, 496
Lambert, William V., Silver Spring, 497
Lamborn, Louis E., McDonogh, 498
Lanahan, William W., Towson, Baltimore, 498
Lancaster, Henry C., Baltimore, 498
Lane, Frederick W., Edgewood, 499
Lane, William P., Jr., Hagerstown, 500
Lang, George F., Baltimore, 500
Lange, Edward H., Baltimore, 500

Langford, George S., College Park, 500
Lankford, Henry M., Princess Anne, 501
Lardner, John J., Baltimore, 501
Laroque, Herbert E., Baltimore, 501
Latimer, Thomas E., Hyattsville, 502
Lauchheimer, Sylvan H., Baltimore, 502
Lauritzen, John I., Chevy Chase, 503
Lazaron, Morris S., Pikesville, 505
Leach, Paul R., Chevy Chase, 506
Leake, Lowell L., Chevy Chase, 506
Lebherz, William B., Frederick, 506
Le Brun, Pierre N., Port Deposit, 506
Lederer, Lewis G., Baltimore, 507
Lee, Blair, Silver Spring, 507
Lee, Frederic P., Bethesda, 507
Lee, Howard H. M., Baltimore, 507
Lee, Philip F., Frederick, Baltimore, 508
Leetch, Robert G., Baltimore, 508
Legg, Thomas H., Union Bridge, 509
Leighton, Alan, Cottage City, 510
Lemmi, Charles W., Baltimore, 511
Lenhard, Raymond E., Baltimore, 512
Lentz, Valentine, Arnold, 512
Leonhart, James C., Baltimore, 513
Leopold, Eugene J., Baltimore, 513
Leser, Oscar, Baltimore, 513
Le Van, Gerald W., Boonsboro, 514
Levering, Edwin W., Jr., Ruxton, Baltimore, 514
Levering, J. P. Wade, Ruxton, Baltimore, 514
Levin, Harry O., Baltimore, 514
Levin, Jack, Takoma Park, 514
LeViness, Charles T., Baltimore, 515
Levy, Herbert, Baltimore, 515
Levy, Raphael, Baltimore, 516
Lewald, James, Laurel, 516
Lewin, John H., Baltimore, see Addenda
Lewis, Charles L., Annapolis, 517
Lewis, David J., Cumberland, 517
Lewis, Dean, Baltimore, 517
Lewis, Elizabeth F., Arnold, 517
Lewis, Florence P., Baltimore, 517
Lewis, George W., Chevy Chase, 517
Lewis, H. H. Walker, Baltimore, 518
Lewis, Lloyd G., Riderwood, Baltimore, 518
Lewis, Warren H., Baltimore, 519
Lewton, Frederick L., Takoma Park, 520
Lilly, Austin J., Baltimore, 521
Lindsay, George E., Baltimore, 522
Litsinger, Elizabeth C., Baltimore, 524
Little, Lawrence C., Westminster, 524
Littlepage, Thomas P., Bowie, 525
Livingood, Frederick G., Chestertown, 526
Livingston, Burton E., Riderwood, Baltimore, 526
Lloyd, Howard H., Baltimore, 526
Lloyd, Morton G., Chevy Chase, 526
Locher, Roy W., Baltimore, 527
Lockhart, Henry, Jr., Longwoods, 527
Long, Breckinridge, Laurel, 529
Long, C. W., Salisbury, 529
Long, Edgar F., Hyattsville, 529
Long, Perrin H., Baltimore, 530
Longcope, Warfield T., Baltimore, 531
Lonn, Ella, Baltimore, 531
Looper, Edward A., Baltimore, 531
Love, William S., Jr., Baltimore, 534
Lovejoy, Arthur O., Baltimore, 534
Lowndes, Tasker G., Cumberland, 535
Lowndes, W. Bladen, Baltimore, 535
Lowndes, William B., Jr., Baltimore, 535
Lowry, Edward G. Jr., Towson, Baltimore, 535
Lucas, Harry P., Brooklandville, 536
Lucas, James C. M., Baltimore, 536
Luckett, Thomas J., Capitol Heights, 536
Luhn, John A., Baltimore, 537
Lynn, Frank S., Baltimore, 539
Lyon, James A., Rockville, 540
Lyon, Leverett S., Cabin John, 540
Mac Callum, William A., Baltimore, 541
Macgowan, Birkhead, Baltimore, 543

Machen, Arthur W., Ruxton, Baltimore, 543
Macht, Ephraim, Baltimore, 543
Mackall, Robert M., Baltimore, 544
Mackert, Charles L., Hyattsville, 544
MacLean, Angus L., Baltimore, 545
MacMurray, John Van A., Brooklandville, 545
Magness, John R., Takoma Park, Beltsville, 547
Magoon, Charles A., Beltsville, Riverdale, 547
Magraw, James F., Perryville, 548
Magruder, Warren K., Baltimore, 548
Mahon, John D., Ellicott City, Baltimore, 548
Mahoney, Charles H., College Park, 548
Makover, Abraham V., Baltimore, 549
Malcolm, Ola P., Bethesda, 549
Malone, Kemp, Baltimore, 550
Maloy, William M., Baltimore, 550
Manzetti, Leo P., Roland Park, 552
Marble, John P., Chevy Chase, 552
Marburg, Theodore, Baltimore, 552
Marbury, Ogle, Laurel, Baltimore, 552
Marbury, William L., Jr., Baltimore, 553
Maril, Herman, Baltimore, 553
Markey, D. John, Frederick, 554
Marsalis, Thomas, Queenstown, 555
Marshall, Berry C., Baltimore, 556
Marshall, E. Kennerly, Jr., Baltimore, 556
Marshall, Leon C., Chevy Chase, 556
Marshall, R. E., Baltimore, 557
Marti, Fritz, Chevy Chase, College Park, 557
Martien, James C., Baltimore, 557
Martin, Florence A. D., Baltimore, 558
Martin, Glenn L., Baltimore, 558
Martin, J. Willis, Annapolis, 558
Martin, William E., Randallstown, 560
Martinet, Marjorie D., Baltimore, 560
Marvel, N. Clyde, Baltimore, 560
Mason, F. Van Wyck, Riderwood, 561
Mason, S. Blount, Jr., Baltimore, 561
Mast, Samuel O., Baltimore, 562
Mathews, Edward B., Baltimore, 563
Mathias, Charles M., Frederick, 563
Mathiesen, Anna, Baltimore, 563
Matré, Joseph B., Silver Spring, 563
Mattern, Johannes, Baltimore, 564
Matthai, Joseph F., Baltimore, 564
Matthai, William H., Baltimore, 564
Matthews, Joshua M., Phoenix, Baltimore, 565
Matthews, Thomas S., Ellicott City, Baltimore, 565
Mattoon, Wilbur R., Takoma Park, 565
Maxcy, Kenneth F., Baltimore, 566
Maxson, Charles W., Baltimore, 566
May, Peter H., Baltimore, 567
Mayer, Erwin E., Baltimore, 567
Mayer, Fred S., Baltimore, 567
Maynard, Theodore, Westminster, 567
McAdams, Thomas B., Baltimore, 568
McBurney, John W., Chevy Chase, 569
McCall, Arthur G., College Park, 570
McCall, Max A., Chevy Chase, 570
McCardell, Adrian N., Frederick, 571
McCasland, Selby V., Baltimore, 572
McCollum, Elmer V., Baltimore, 574
McComas, Henry C., Roland Park, 574
McCord, Joseph, Boonsboro, 575
McCormack, Frederick O., Brooklandville, Baltimore, 575
McCormick, Charles P., Baltimore, 575
McCulloch, Duncan, Jr., Glencoe, 577
McCulloch, James E., Silver Spring, 577
McDougle, Ivan E., Baltimore, 580
McElfish, A. G., Cumberland, 580
McElwain, Howard B., Baltimore, 580
McFall, John M., Ruxton, Baltimore, 581
McFarland, Frieda W., Hyattsville, 581

McGlannan, Alexius, Baltimore, 582
McGrew, Dallas D. L., Bethesda, 583
McKenney, Frederic D., Kensington, 585
McKenzie, William R., Baltimore, 586
McLanahan, Austin, Baltimore, 587
McLanahan, James C., Baltimore, 587
McLanahan, Samuel, Baltimore, 587
McNaughton, Edna B., College Park, 589
McNeil, Marshall, Silver Spring, 590
McReynolds, Frederick W., Ashton, 590
McSherry, William C., Frederick, 590
McWilliams, William A., Annapolis, 591
Mead, Gilbert W., Chestertown, 591
Meade, DeVoe, College Park, 591
Medford, Richard C., Williamsport, Hagerstown, 592
Meeks, Benjamin W., Frederick, 592
Megraw, Herbert A., Baltimore, 593
Meier, Fred C., Chevy Chase, 593
Melvin, Ridgely P., Annapolis, 595
Mencken, August, Baltimore, 595
Mencken, Henry L., Baltimore, 595
Mendenhall, Walter C., Chevy Chase, 595
Mercer, Beverly H., Baltimore, 596
Meredith, Carey L., Annapolis, 596
Meriam, Lewis, Kensington, 596
Merrick, Robert G., Woodbrook, Baltimore, 597
Merrill, Melvin C., Takoma Park, 597
Merriman, Harry M., St. Michaels, 597
Metz, Charles W., Baltimore, 599
Metzerott, Oliver, Hyattsville, 599
Metzger, Frederick E., Lutherville, 599
Metzger, Jacob E., College Park, 599
Meyer, Adolf, Baltimore, 600
Michaels, Urlwin O., Baltimore, 600
Middendorf, Harry S., Baltimore, 601
Miles, Clarence W., Baltimore, 602
Miles, Eugene L., Baltimore, 602
Miles, Hooper S., Salisbury, 602
Miles, L. Wardlaw, Baltimore, 602
Miller, Anna I., Baltimore, 602
Miller, Charles R., Baltimore, 603
Miller, C. Wilbur, Cockeysville, Baltimore, 603
Miller, Edward T., Easton, 603
Miller, George E., Edgewood Arsenal, 604
Miller, Jesse I., Chevy Chase, 605
Miller, Joshua A., College Park, 606
Miller, Laurence M., Baltimore, 607
Miller, Lawrence V., Baltimore, 607
Miller, Leo H., Hagerstown, 607
Miller, Sydney R., Baltimore, 608
Miller, Theodore E., Baltimore, 608
Miller, Victor D., Hagerstown, 608
Milloy, James S., Chevy Chase, 609
Millspaugh, Arthur C., Bethesda, 609
Milholm, William H., Towson, 610
Mish, Joseph D., Hagerstown, 611
Mitchell, Broadus, Baltimore, 611
Mitchell, George W., Baltimore, 611
Mitchell, Walter J., La Plata, 612
Moehle, Frederick L. W., Baltimore, 612
Moffett, George M., Queenstown, 612
Moller, Mathias P., Jr., Hagerstown, 614
Moment, Gairdner B., Baltimore, 614
Montgomery, Edward G., Chevy Chase, 615
Moore, Joseph E., Baltimore, 618
Moore, William E., Baltimore, 618
Moore, William H., 3d, Baltimore, Lutherville, 619
Morey, George W., Chevy Chase, 620
Morgan, Philip S., Baltimore, 621
Morgan, Theophilous J., Forest Glen, 622
Morreale, Eugenio, Baltimore, 622
Morrill, Dorothy I., Frederick, 622
Morris, Frank K., Baltimore, 623
Morris, George, Harwood, 623
Morrison, Theodore H., Baltimore, 625
Morrissy, Elizabeth, Baltimore, 625
Morrow, Emerson B., Baltimore, 625

MARYLAND

Morsell, H. Tudor, Chevy Chase, 626
Morton, Samuel P., Jr., Baltimore, 626
Moser, Herman M., Baltimore, 627
Mount, Myrl M., College Park, 628
Muller, Julius F., Catonsville, Baltimore, 630
Mullikin, Addison E., Baltimore, 631
Mullikin, Oliver S., Easton, 631
Munson, G. Kibby, Chevy Chase, 632
Murnaghan, Francis D., Baltimore, 633
Murphy, Frederic V., Chevy Chase, 633
Murphy, J. Edwin, Baltimore, 633
Murphy, Louis S., Chevy Chase, 633
Murray, Joseph H., Towson, 634
Myers, Paul F., Chevy Chase, 637
Nachlas, William, Baltimore, 638
Nagell, Frank J., Baltimore, Towson, 638
Nance, Oran H., Baltimore, 638
Nash, Ogden, Baltimore, 638
Neill, William, Jr., Baltimore, 640
Nelson, Boyd, Baltimore, 640
Nelson, Elnathan K., Silver Spring, 641
Nelson, Frederic C., Baltimore, 641
Nelson, George M., Salisbury, 641
Nelson, J. Arthur, Baltimore, 641
Nelson, James W., Arbutus, Baltimore, 641
Nelson, John R., Bethesda, 641
New, Archey C., Baltimore, 643
Newell, Horatio W., Baltimore, 643
Ney, Grover C., Baltimore, 645
Nice, Harry, Baltimore, 645
Nichols, Firmadge K., Baltimore, 645
Nicodemus, Frank M., Monkton, Baltimore, 646
Nicodemus, Kent C., Walkersville, 646
Nicolet, Ben H., Riverdale, 647
Niles, Emory H., Baltimore, 647
Niles, Henry E., Baltimore, 647
Nitchie, Elizabeth, Baltimore, 648
Noble, William D., Easton, 649
Nock, Randolph M., Salisbury, 649
Nolting, William G., Glencoe, Baltimore, 649
Norcross, Theodore W., Chevy Chase, 649
Norment, William M., Hagerstown, 650
Norris, Walter B., Annapolis, 650
Norton, John B. S., College Park, 651
Nourse, Edwin G., Chevy Chase, 652
Novak, Emil, Baltimore, 652
Novey, M. Alexander, Baltimore, 652
Nyburg, Sidney L., Baltimore, 653
Ober, Frank B., Baltimore, 654
Ober, J. Hambleton, Baltimore, 654
O'Connor, James E., Baltimore, 656
O'Conor, Herbert R., Annapolis, 656
Odenheimer, Cordelia P., Baltimore, 656
O'Donovan, Charles, Baltimore, 657
O'Dunne, Eugene, Baltimore, 657
Offutt, Thiemann S., Towson, 657
Ogden, Harry F., Baltimore, 658
Oliver, John R., Baltimore, 659
Olivier, Stuart, Baltimore, 660
Onderdonk, Adrian H., St. James School, 661
Oosterling, James, Baltimore, 661
Opie, Reginald S., Baltimore, 661
O'Rourke, Lawrence A., Chevy Chase, 662
Ortmann, Otto R., Baltimore, 662
Oswald, Edward J., Hagerstown, 664
Ott, Mary C., Frederick, 664
Owens, Hamilton, Riderwood, Baltimore, 665
Owens, John W., Baltimore, 665
Oxley, John E., Rockville, 665
Page, Charles G., Baltimore, 666
Page, William C., Ruxton, Baltimore, 666
Page, William T., Chevy Chase, 666
Pagon, W. Watters, Baltimore, 666
Painter, Sidney, Baltimore, 667
Palmer, William N., Easton, 668
Palmisano, Vincent L., Baltimore, 668
Pancoast, Elinor, Baltimore, 668
Pangborn, Thomas W., Hagerstown, 668
Park, Edwards A., Towson, Baltimore, 669
Parke, Francis N., Westminster, 669
Parker, Edward C., Chevy Chase, 669
Parker, William A., Baltimore, 670

Parson, Willard S., Baltimore, 671
Partridge, Emelyn N., Baltimore, 672
Partridge, George E., Baltimore, 672
Pasma, Henry K., Rockville, 672
Paton, Stewart, Baltimore, 673
Patrick, Walter A., Mt. Washington, 673
Patten, Harrison E., Silver Spring, 673
Patterson, Harry J., College Park, 674
Patterson, J. Milton, Baltimore, 674
Patterson, Marjorie, Baltimore, 674
Patterson, Paul C., Baltimore, 674
Pattison, John R., Cambridge, 675
Pattrell, Arthur E., Towson, 675
Paulson, Moses, Baltimore, 675
Payne, Lewis, Salisbury, 676
Peabody, J. Winthrop, Chevy Chase, 676
Peacock, James C., Chevy Chase, 676
Pearl, Raymond, Baltimore, 677
Pearre, Albert A., Frederick, 677
Pearre, Sifford, Baltimore, Gibson Island, 677
Peelle, Stanton C., Chevy Chase, 679
Peirce, William H., Baltimore, 679
Penniman, George D., Baltimore, 681
Perdew, Frank A., Cumberland, 682
Perkins, Edward E., Springfield, Bowie, 682
Perkins, Milo R., Bethesda, 682
Perkins, Walter F., Baltimore, 682
Perring, Henry G., Baltimore, 683
Perry, C. Alfred, Towson, Baltimore, 683
Pessagno, Daniel J., Baltimore, 684
Peter, Arthur, Bethesda, 684
Peter, Robert, Rockville, 684
Peter, T. V., Baltimore, 684
Peter, V. J., Baltimore, 684
Peters, William J., Chevy Chase, 685
Pfaffenbach, George A., Havre de Grace, 686
Pfeiffer, Karl E., Baltimore, 686
Pfund, A. Herman, Baltimore, 687
Phelps, Winthrop M., Baltimore, 687
Phillips, Albanus, Cambridge, 688
Phillips, Albanus, Jr., Cambridge, 688
Phillips, Charles L., Baltimore, 689
Phillips, Levi B., Cambridge, 689
Phillips, Percy W., Chevy Chase, 689
Phillips, Ralph W., Beltsville, 689
Phillips, Samuel E., Hagerstown, 689
Phillips, Theodore, Cambridge, 689
Pierson, Charles J., Hyattsville, 691
Pierson, Leon D., Salisbury, Snow Hill, 691
Pillsbury, Harold C., Baltimore, 692
Pincoffs, Maurice C., Baltimore, 692
Piper, James, Baltimore, 693
Pleasants, J. Hall, Baltimore, 695
Plummer, Frederick B., Hagerstown, 695
Plummer, William E., Baltimore, 696
Poe, Edgar A., Garrison, Baltimore, 696
Poe, Edgar A., Jr., Baltimore, 696
Pollitt, Levin I., Baltimore, 696
Poole, John, Chevy Chase, 697
Porter, Frederick S., Baltimore, 698
Porter, John J., Hagerstown, 699
Post, A. H. S., Baltimore, 699
Potter, Henry B., Washington, Baltimore, 700
Pouder, George B., Baltimore, 701
Pound, John C., Baltimore, 701
Powell, Fred W., Chevy Chase, 701
Prather, Perry F., Hagerstown, 703
Preinkert, Alma H., College Park, 703
Prentis, Morton M., Baltimore, 704
Prescott, Stedman, Rockville, 704
Preston, Walter W., Bel Air, 704
Prettyman, E. Barrett, Chevy Chase, 704
Prettyman, Forrest J., Rockville, 705
Prince, Sydney R., Chevy Chase, 706
Pryor, James C., Sherwood Forest, 707
Pugh, James H., Chevy Chase, Rockville, 708
Pullen, Thomas G., Jr., Catonsville, 708
Purdum, Smith W., Hyattsville, 708
Purnell, William C., Baltimore, 708
Pyle, Charles S., Rising Sun, 709
Quaintance, Altus L., Silver Spring, 709
Radcliffe, George L., Baltimore, 710
Ragatz, Lowell J., Bethesda, 711
Rakeman, Carl, Chevy Chase, 711
Raleigh, George P., Baltimore, 711

Ralston, Oliver C., Hyattsville, 712
Ranck, James B., Frederick, 712
Ranck, Than V., Easton, 712
Rand, Gertrude, Baltimore, 713
Randall, Blanchard, Baltimore, 713
Randall, Blanchard, Jr., Baltimore, 713
Raskin, Moses, Baltimore, 715
Rasko, John J., Centreville, 715
Ratcliff, Thomas C., Baltimore, 715
Rawls, Fletcher H., Silver Spring, 716
Rawls, William L., Baltimore, 716
Rebert, G. Nevin, Frederick, 718
Reddick, Olive I., Frederick, 718
Redwood, John, Jr., Ruxton, Baltimore, 719
Reed, Lowell J., Baltimore, 720
Reed, Merle R., Chevy Chase, 720
Reed, Wendell M., Welcome, 720
Reeder, J. Dawson, Baltimore, 720
Rees, Charles W., Silver Spring, 721
Reese, Matthias F., Baltimore, 721
Reeside, John B., Jr., Hyattsville, 721
Reiblich, George K., Baltimore, 723
Reid, E. Emmet, Baltimore, 723
Reid, Harry F., Baltimore, 724
Reid, Legh W., Highfield, 724
Reier, Adam W., Dundalk, 724
Reifschneider, Charles A., Baltimore, 724
Reifsnyder, Miles S., Westminster, 724
Rempe, P. J., Hagerstown, 726
Requardt, John M., Baltimore, 726
Rever, R. Rossiter, Baltimore, 727
Reynolds, Walter F., Baltimore, 728
Rice, Herbert L., Pikesville, 730
Rich, Benjamin S., Baltimore, 730
Rich, Charles S., Baltimore, 730
Rich, Edward N., Baltimore, 730
Richards, Esther L., Baltimore, 731
Richards, Thomas L., Cumberland, 732
Richardson, Edward H., Baltimore, 732
Richardson, John H., Stemmer's Run, Baltimore, 733
Riddick, Carl W., Riva, 734
Ridgely, Irwin O., Baltimore, 735
Riely, Compton, Baltimore, 735
Rieman, Charles E., Baltimore, 735
Rienhoff, William F., Jr., Baltimore, 736
Riepe, Harry U., Jr., Baltimore, 736
Ries, Ferdinand A., Baltimore, 736
Rigger, William L., Baltimore, 736
Riggs, Jesse B., Baltimore, 736
Rightor, Chester E., Chevy Chase, 736
Riley, John L., Snow Hill, 737
Riley, Robert H., Catonsville, Baltimore, 737
Rintoul, James L., Mount Washington, Baltimore, 737
Ritter, Alonzo W., Hagerstown, 738
Rivkin, Harvey, Baltimore, 739
Rizer, Richard T., Frostburg, Cumberland, 739
Roberts, John W., Beltsville, 741
Roberts, W. Frank, Baltimore, 741
Robertson, Benjamin P., Hyattsville, 741
Robertson, David A., Baltimore, 742
Robertson, John, Baltimore, 742
Robertson, John T., Baltimore, 742
Robertson, Robert H., Pocomoke City, 742
Robertson, Thomas E., Chevy Chase, 742
Robins, Stanley G., Salisbury, 743
Robinson, David M., Baltimore, 743
Robinson, Edward L., Baltimore, 744
Robinson, G. Canby, Baltimore, 744
Robinson, Harry M., Baltimore, 744
Robinson, J. Ben, Baltimore, 744
Robinson, Samuel M., Norbeck, 745
Robinson, William, Silver Spring, 746
Robison, Samuel S., Clifton, 746
Roe, Dudley G., Sudlersville, 748
Rogers, Harry L., Baltimore, 749
Rolker, John G., Baltimore, 750
Roop, William E., Westminster, 751
Root, Ralph E., Annapolis, 751
Rose, Albert C., Chevy Chase, 752
Rosenau, William, Baltimore, 754
Rosenbaum, Morris, Cumberland, 754
Rosenblatt, Samuel, Baltimore, 755
Rosenthal, Lewis J., Baltimore, 755
Rossmann, Louis, Baltimore, 757
Rothschild, Felix, Baltimore, 758
Rothschild, Solomon, Baltimore, 758
Rothschild, Stanford Z., Baltimore, 758
Roulston, Robert B., Baltimore, 758
Rouse, John G., Baltimore, 758

Rowe, John I., Baltimore, 759
Rowe, Joseph E., Baltimore, 759
Rowland, James M. H., Baltimore, 759
Royal, William C., Frederick, 760
Rubenstein, Frank J., Baltimore, 760
Rudolph, Joseph, Baltimore, 761
Ruehle, Godfrey L. A., Silver Spring, 761
Ruff, John K., Randallstown, Baltimore, 761
Ruge, Edwin G. W., Baltimore, 761
Rupp, Paul B., Fort Howard, 762
Ruzicka, Charles, Baltimore, 764
Rytina, Anton G., Baltimore, 765
Sachs, Louis, Baltimore, 765
Sadler, John D., Bethesda, 765
Saltzman, Charles M., Silver Spring, 766
Samuel, Albert H., Baltimore, 767
Samuels, Abram, Baltimore, 767
Samuelson, Herman, Baltimore, 767
Sanford, Raymond L., Chevy Chase, 768
Satterlee, Herbert L., Sotterley, 769
Sayler, J. Abner, Baltimore, 770
Scarborough, James B., Annapolis, 771
Schaefer, Otto, Baltimore, 772
Schlenger, Leo, Baltimore, 776
Schluderberg, William F., Baltimore, 777
Schmick, William F., Baltimore, 777
Schmitt, Richard B., Baltimore, 778
Schnauffer, Patrick M., Frederick, 778
Schofield, Samuel B., Westminster, 779
Schrader, Albert L., Chevy Chase, College Park, 780
Schrader, Frank C., Bethesda, 780
Schreiner, Oswald, Chevy Chase, 780
Schuler, Hans, Baltimore, 781
Scofield, Carl S., Lanham, 784
Scott, Wirt S., Bozman, 786
Sears, Julian D., Chevy Chase, 787
Seegar, J. King B. E., Baltimore, 788
Segall, Jacob B., Annapolis, 788
Semmes, John E., Baltimore, 790
Sexsmith, Edgar A., Baltimore, 790
Sexton, Roy L., Chevy Chase, 791
Shaffer, George W., Baltimore, 791
Shaw, Edward D., Chevy Chase, 793
Shepard, Donald D., Silver Spring, 796
Shields, George R., Silver Spring, 798
Shipley, A. Earl, Westminster, 799
Shipley, Arthur M., Baltimore, 799
Shipley, George, Easton, 799
Shipley, Richard L., Baltimore, 799
Shockley, Orlando M., Showell, 800
Shook, Myron G., Baltimore, 801
Short, Oliver C., College Park, 801
Shrier, Albert F., Baltimore, 802
Shriver, Alfred J., Baltimore, 802
Shriver, George G., Baltimore, 802
Shriver, George M., Pikesville, 802
Shriver, Henry, Cumberland, 802
Shriver, Samuel H., Pikesville, Baltimore, 802
Shuff, Benjamin H., Frederick, 802
Shuger, Leroy W., Baltimore, 803
Shull, J. Marion, Chevy Chase, 803
Shure, R. Deane, Takoma Park, 804
Shure, Ralph G., Takoma Park, 804
Siegel, Isadore A., Baltimore, 804
Sigerist, Henry E., Baltimore, 805
Silberman, David, Baltimore, 805
Silverman, Sam M., Baltimore, 806
Simmons, George R., Baltimore, 807
Simpson, Edward R., Ruxton, Baltimore, 808
Simpson, Iona J., Baltimore, 808
Simpson, Kirke L., Chevy Chase, 808
Singewald, H. Elmer, Baltimore, 809
Singewald, Joseph T., Jr., Baltimore, 809
Singley, Frederick J., Baltimore, 809
Sippel, Bettie M., Baltimore, 810
Skinner, Clarence A., Kensington, 811
Skinner, Homer L., Baltimore, 811
Skutch, Alexander F., Baltimore, 812
Skutch, Rachel F., Baltimore, 812
Slack, Harry R., Jr., Baltimore, 812
Slack, Henry R., Jr., Baltimore, 812

MARYLAND

Slaybauth, J. Paul, Colora, 812
Slingluff, Jesse, Baltimore, 813
Sloan, Duncan L., Cumberland, 813
Small, Mary L., Baltimore, 814
Smith, Albert V. D., Baltimore, 815
Smith, Arthur F., Lonaconing, 815
Smith, Charles S., Port Tobacco, 816
Smith, Daniel C. W., Baltimore, 816
Smith, Edward P., Baltimore, 816
Smith, H. Webster, Baltimore, 818
Smith, Harold C., Rockville, 818
Smith, Horace T., Baltimore, 819
Smith, Howard C., Baltimore, 819
Smith, J. Brookes, Baltimore, 819
Smith, Michael P., Reisterstown, Baltimore, 821
Smith, Richard P., Hagerstown, 822
Smith, Thomas H., Queenstown, Baltimore, 823
Smith, Wilbur F., Baltimore, 823
Smith, William H., Hagerstown, 823
Smith, William M., Frederick, 823
Smith, Winford H., Baltimore, 824
Smoot, Merrill C., Hagerstown, 824
Snow, Chester, Chevy Chase, 826
Snyder, A. Cecil, Baltimore, 826
Snyder, Charles D., Baltimore, 826
Snyder, Jesse O., Hagerstown, 827
Sobeloff, Simon E., Baltimore, 828
Solter, George A., Baltimore, 829
Somerville, Thomas, III, Chevy Chase, Muirkirk, 829
Sonneborn, Siegmund B., Baltimore, 829
Soper, Morris A., Baltimore, 829
Southgate, Hugh M., Chevy Chase, 830
Soyster, Hale B., Chevy Chase, 830
Sparks, William S., Cumberland, 831
Speer, J. Ramsey, Trappe, 832
Speer, Talbot T., Lutherville, Baltimore, 832
Speers, Thomas G., Baltimore, 833
Spencer, Eleanor P., Baltimore, 833
Spencer, Hazelton, Baltimore, 834
Spencer, Jervis, Jr., Baltimore, 834
Spencer, Roscoe R., Chevy Chase, 834
Spitman, Edwin A., Baltimore, 835
Spitzer, Leo, Baltimore, 835
Spitznas, James E., Cumberland, Baltimore, 835
Spiva, William B., Princess Anne, 835
Sprowls, Jesse W., Hyattsville, College Park, 836
Squire, Frank C., Chevy Chase, 837
Stahr, Henry I., Frederick, 838
Stamp, Adele H., College Park, 839
Stanley, William, Laurel, 840
Stauffen, Frederick C., Baltimore, 841
Steele, John D., Baltimore, 843
Stein, Charles F., Baltimore, 844
Steinberg, Samuel S., College Park, 845
Stevens, Charles L., Baltimore, 848
Stevens, Wayne M., College Park, 848
Stewart, Arthur B., Baltimore, 849
Stewart, George A., Baltimore, 849
Stickney, Louis R., Baltimore, 850
Stimson, Arthur M., Chevy Chase, 851
Stimson, Dorothy, Baltimore, 851
Stockbridge, Enos S., Govans, Baltimore, 852
Stone, Harvey B., Baltimore, 855
Strahorn, John S., Jr., Baltimore, 858
Strange, Miriam, Annapolis, 858
Straughn, James H., Baltimore, 859
Strauss, George A., Baltimore, 859
Strauss, Myer, Baltimore, 859
Streeter, George L., Baltimore, 860
Strickland, Frederick H., Baltimore, 860
Strobel, Peyton B., Baltimore, 861
Strube, Gustav, Baltimore, 862
Stryker, Goss L., Timonium, 863
Stultz, D. E., Frederick, 864
Sullivan, William C., Chevy Chase, 866
Supplee, Frederick M., Baltimore, 866
Swain, Robert L., Baltimore, 868
Swann, Samuel D., Baltimore, 869
Swanson, Neil H., Baltimore, 869
Swartz, Charles K., Baltimore, 869
Swartz, Joel H., Baltimore, 869
Sweeney, Richard H., Hagerstown, 870

Swick, Clarence H., Capitol Heights, 871
Swisher, Carl B., Baltimore, 872
Swope, Harry F., Baltimore, 872
Swope, John L., Baltimore, 872
Sybert, Cornelius F., Elkridge, Ellicott City, 872
Sykes, Philip L., Baltimore, 872
Symington, Donald, Darlington, Baltimore, 873
Symmonds, Charles J., Chevy Chase, 873
Symons, Thomas B., College Park, 873
Szold, Henrietta, Baltimore, 873
Tabak, Israel, Baltimore, 873
Tabler, Homer E., Hancock, 874
Taliaferro, Thomas H., College Park, 875
Tall, Lida L., Baltimore, 875
Tall, Webster C., Baltimore, 875
Tappan, Benjamin, Baltimore, 875
Tarun, William, Baltimore, 876
Tawes, John M., Crisfield, Annapolis, 876
Taylor, Aubrey E., Chevy Chase, 876
Taylor, Charles H., Baltimore, 877
Taylor, John C., Baltimore, 878
Taylor, John T., Chevy Chase, 878
Taylor, Oliver G., Chevy Chase, 879
Taylor, S. N., Baltimore, 879
Taylor, William A., Baltimore, 880
Teel, Rolland M., Severna Park, 880
TeLinde, Richard W., Baltimore, 880
Temple, Charles E., Hyattsville, College Park, 881
Tewksbury, William D., Chevy Chase, 882
Thalheimer, Alvin, Baltimore, 883
Thatcher, Howard R., Baltimore, 883
Thawley, Wesley E., Denton, 883
Thomas, Frederic L., Ashton, Sandy Spring, 884
Thomas, Henry B., Jr., Baltimore, 885
Thomas, John C., Easton, 885
Thomas, Martha C., Frederick, 886
Thomas, Ralph L., Baltimore, 886
Thomas, Royle P., Hyattsville, 886
Thomas, Woodlief, Chevy Chase, 886
Thompson, Eustis H., Baltimore, 887
Thompson, Lewis R., Chevy Chase, 888
Thompson, Richard H., Baltimore, 888
Thompson, Robert C., Towson, Baltimore, 888
Thomsen, Iloszel C., Baltimore, 889
Thorn, George W., Baltimore, 890
Thorpe, Merle, Bethesda, 890
Tiemeyer, Arthur C., Baltimore, 891
Tiffany, Herbert T., Baltimore, 891
Tilghman, Harrison, Easton, 892
Tilghman, William B., Salisbury, 892
Titus, Harry W., Beltsville, 893
Tobias, William A., Hagerstown, 893
Tolson, Howard C., Cumberland, 894
Tompkins, Raymond S., Baltimore, 894
Torrence, Robert M., Baltimore, 895
Toulson, William H., Baltimore, 895
Trageser, Charles A., Baltimore, 896
Traver, Amos J., Frederick, 897
Treille, Marguerite, Frederick, 897
Trostel, Louis J., Baltimore, 898
Truitt, Ralph P., Baltimore, 899
Truitt, Reginald V. T., College Park, Solomons Island, 899
Trumpour, Frederick J., Forest Glen, 899
Tucker, Ray T., Chevy Chase, 900
Tuckerman, Arthur, Ruxton, 900
Tull, Mary E., Frederick, 901
Tuttle, Clarence E., Garrison, Baltimore, 902
Tuve, Merle A., Chevy Chase, 902
Tydings, Millard E., Havre de Grace, 903
Tyrrell, Henry G., Catonsville, Baltimore, 903
Tyson, Anthony M., Baltimore, 903
Uhlenhuth, Eduard, Baltimore, 904
Ullman, Alfred, Baltimore, 905
Ulman, Joseph N., Baltimore, 905
Urner, Hammond, Frederick, 907
Vance, John T., Chevy Chase, 909

Van Poole, Carl M., Mount Airy, 911
Varney, William W., Baltimore, 912
Veach, Carl L., Cambridge, 913
Veasey, Milton L., Pocomoke City, 913
Veitch, Fletcher P., College Park, 913
Vest, Cecil W., Baltimore, 914
Vierheller, Albert F., Hyattsville, 914
Vining, Robert E., Baltimore, 915
Vinup, Frederick H., Baltimore, 915
Vogel, Charles W., Baltimore, 916
Vollmer, Harry F., Jr., Baltimore, 916
Voshell, Allen F., Baltimore, 917
Waddell, Fred R., Hurlock, 918
Waesche, Frederick S., Snow Hill, 918
Wagner, Herbert A., Chattolanee, Baltimore, 919
Waldman, Jacob W., Hyattsville, 920
Walker, Milton B., Catonsville, Baltimore, 921
Walker, Robert H., Baltimore, 921
Wall, William G., Boyd, 922
Wallace, Charles C., Baltimore, 922
Wallace, Lester, Baltimore, 922
Wallace, Oates C. S., Baltimore, 922
Wallenstein, Sydney, Baltimore, 922
Waller, Clifford E., Silver Spring, 923
Walls, Edgar P., Hyattsville, 923
Walls, John A., Baltimore, 923
Walsh, William C., Cumberland, 924
Walter, Valerie H., Baltimore, 924
Walton, William R., Hyattsville, 925
Walzak, Leo A., College Park, 925
Wantz, James P., Westminster, 926
Warburton, Clyde W., Chevy Chase, 926
Ward, Grant E., Baltimore, 926
Wareheim, Eli C., Severna Park, Baltimore, 928
Warfel, Harry R., Hyattsville, 928
Warfield, Edwin, Jr., Woodbine, Baltimore, 928
Warfield, Henry M., Timonium, Baltimore, 928
Warfield, Joshua N., Woodbine, Baltimore, 928
Warren, Lewis E., Chevy Chase, 929
Warth, Albin H., Baltimore, 930
Warthen, William H. F., Baltimore, 930
Watkins, Charles L., Bethesda, 932
Watkins, W. C., Baltimore, 932
Watts, Joseph T., Baltimore, 934
Waxter, Thomas J. S., Baltimore, 935
Webb, Frederick W. C., Salisbury, 936
Webb, Phillips W., Cambridge, 936
Webb, Thomas E., Crisfield, Salisbury, 936
Webster, Ralph R., Cumberland, 937
Wedeberg, S. M., College Park, 937
Weech, Charles S., Baltimore, 937
Weed, Lewis H., Baltimore, 937
Weglein, David E., Baltimore, 938
Weinberg, Edwin D., Pikesville, Baltimore, 939
Weinberg, J. Arthur, Baltimore, 939
Weller, Ovington E., Baltimore, 941
Wellington, John L., Cumberland, 941
Wells, Edwin W., Baltimore, 941
Welsh, Mark F., College Park, 942
Westcott, Allan F., Annapolis, 945
Weyforth, William O., Baltimore, 946
Wharton, Lawrence R., Baltimore, 947
Wheatley, H. Winship, Hyattsville, 947
Wheeler, Joseph L., Baltimore, 948
Wheeler, William A., Chevy Chase, 948
Whitcraft, Franklin P., Jr., Lutherville, Baltimore, 949
White, Charles E., Hyattsville, 950
White, Francis, Baltimore, 950
White, Frank, Chevy Chase, 950
White, Theophilus, Baltimore, 951
Whitehead, John B., Baltimore, 952
Whitehouse, William E., Hyattsville, 952
Whiteley, Emily S., Baltimore, 952
Whiteley, James G., Baltimore, 952
Whitfield, Theodore M., Westminster, 953

Whitham, Lloyd B., Baltimore, 953
Whiting, Francis B., Cumberland, 953
Whiting, George A., Baltimore, 953
Whitman, Ezra B., Baltimore, 953
Whitridge, William, Baltimore, 954
Whitworth, John B., Chestertown, 955
Wiedefeld, Mary T., Towson, 956
Wilcox, Earley V., Chevy Chase, 957
Willard, Daniel, Baltimore, 959
Williams, Elizabeth C., Baltimore, 961
Williams, George W., Baltimore, 962
Williams, Huntington, Baltimore, 963
Williams, Mary W., Baltimore, 963
Williams, Ralph C., Chevy Chase, 963
Williams, Robert W., Baltimore, 964
Williams, Roger B., Baltimore, 964
Wills, George S., Westminster, 965
Wilson, Alvin C., Baltimore, 965
Wilson, Ephraim K., Baltimore, 966
Wilson, Frank M., Cumberland, 966
Wilson, Levi T., Annapolis, 968
Wilson, Louis L., Frederick, 968
Wilson, Milburn L., Chevy Chase, 968
Wilson, Robert L., Bel Air, 968
Wilson, Theodore H., Catonsville, 969
Wimer, Arthur C., Chevy Chase, 969
Winebrenner, David C., 3d, Frederick, 970
Winslow, Clinton I., Baltimore, 970
Winslow, Leon L., Baltimore, 970
Winslow, Ola E., Baltimore, 971
Wise, Walter D., Baltimore, 972
Wolf, Carl G., Baltimore, 973
Wolf, Luther B., Baltimore, 973
Wolff, Thomas C., Baltimore, 974
Wolman, Abel, Baltimore, 974
Wolman, Samuel, Baltimore, 974
Wood, Austin H., Baltimore, 975
Wood, Frederick W., Baltimore, 975
Wood, Robert W., Baltimore, 976
Woodcock, Amos W. W., Salisbury, 976
Woodring, Wendell P., Chevy Chase, 977
Woods, Alan C., Baltimore, 977
Woods, Albert F., Berwyn, 977
Woods, Bertha G., Berwyn, 978
Woodward, Charles W., Rockville, 978
Woodward, Thompson E., Hyattsville, 979
Woolley, Lawrence F., Towson, 980
Woolsey, Lester H., Chevy Chase, 980
Worthington, Ellicott H., Baltimore, 981
Worthington, Frank D., Frederick, 981
Wrenn, Harold H., Baltimore, 981
Wright, Daniel T., Fenwick, 982
Wright, Fred W., Cambridge, 982
Wright, Howard V., Edgewood Arsenal, 983
Wright, John C., Chevy Chase, 983
Wright, Joseph C., Baltimore, 983
Wroth, Peregrine, Jr., Hagerstown, 984
Wyatt, Joseph M., Baltimore, 985
Wyer, Ramon, Baltimore, 985
Yaggy, Edward E., Jr., Baltimore, 985
Yardley, Richard Q., Baltimore, 986
Yeager, George B., Baltimore, 986
Yeager, James F., Jr., Silver Spring, 986
Yeager, William H., Hagerstown, 986
Yearley, Mary S., Baltimore, 987
York, James A., Baltimore, 988
Yost, John S. L., Baltimore, 988
Young, Hugh H., Baltimore, 989
Younger, John E., Chevy Chase, 990
Zavitz, Edwin C., Baltimore, 991
Zetzer, Rose S., Baltimore, 992
Zimmerman, David W., Catonsville, 992
Zimmerman, Louis S., Baltimore, 993
Zimmermann, Charles C., Cumberland, 993
Zinn, Waltman F., Baltimore, 993
Zouck, Frank H., Reisterstown, 993
Zucker, Adolf E., Riverdale, 993

NEW JERSEY

Aaronson, Robert H., Jr., Bordentown, 1
Abbett, Leon, Hoboken, 1
Abell, Frank D., Morristown, 1
Abrams, Dorothy A., Hawthorne, Paterson, 2
Abrams, Lawrence B., Glen Ridge, 2
Abramson, Maurice, Bayonne, 2
Acker, Eleanor B., Collingswood, 2
Ackerman, Garret N., Woodcliff Lake, Westwood, 3
Ackerson, Henry E., Jr., Jersey City, 3
Ackley, David B., Trenton, 3
Adamic, Louis, Milford, 3
Adams, Edwin P., Princeton, 3
Adams, Jessie F., Atlantic City, 3
Adams, Paul D., Essex Fells, Upper Montclair, 4
Adams, Rayford K., Skillman, 4
Adams, Russell V., Maplewood, Newark, 4
Addis, Charles M., Mountain Lakes, 4
Ader, Kenneth L., Rahway, 5
Agar, William M., Lakewood, 5
Agee, Howard H., Newark, 5
Agger, Eugene E., New Brunswick, 6
Albion, Robert G., Princeton, 6
Albright, Louis F., Spring Lake, 7
Albright, William H., Woodbury, 7
Aldrin, Edwin E., Upper Montclair, 8
Alexander, James W., Princeton, 8
Alford, Leon P., Montclair, 8
Allen, Charles L., New Brunswick, 9
Allen, Edward R., Summit, Newark, 10
Allen, James M., Passaic, 10
Allen, Junius, Summit, 10
Allen, Rena, Woodbridge, 11
Allen, Roy M., Bloomfield, 11
Allison, James B., Jr., Highland Park, 11
Allman, David B., Atlantic City, 11
Ambruster, Howard W., Westfield, 13
Ames, Louis A., Essex Fells, 13
Amick, Chester A., Bound Brook, 13
Ammann, Othmar H., Boonton, 13
Anderson, Charles D., Pennington, 14
Anderson, J. Fisher, Jersey City, 15
Anderson, John F., New Brunswick, 15
Anderson, Paul L., East Orange, 15
Anderson, Robert van V., Upper Montclair, 16
Anderson, William A., Princeton, Trenton, 16
Andrew, Harriet W. F., Trenton, 16
Andrew, Seymour L., Orange, 17
Andrews, Benjamin R., Edgewater, 17
Andrews, Clarence L., Atlantic City, 17
Angela, Emilio P., Chatham, 18
Anson, Edward H., Shrewsbury, 18
Anthony, Harold E., Englewood, 18
Anthony, Irvin, Seaside Park, 18
Anthony, James T., South Orange, 19
Antopol, William, Newark, 19
App, Frank, Bridgeton, 19
Appel, Joseph, Paterson, 19
Applebaum, Samuel, Newark, 20
Appleby, J. Randolph, Jr., South River, 20
Applegate, J. Arthur, Perth Amboy, 20
Applegate, John B., Hoboken, 20
Archer, Franklin M., Haddonfield, Camden, 21
Archer, Franklin M., Jr., Moorestown, Camden, 21
Arentz, Fred B., Short Hills, Newark, 21
Arlitz, William J., Hoboken, 21
Armour, Allison V., Princeton, 21
Armstrong, Edward C., Princeton, 22
Armstrong, Frederic P., Keyport, 22
Armstrong, Thomas R., Jersey City, 22
Armstrong, William P., Princeton, 22
Arnold, Arthur D., Passaic, 22
Arnold, Frank A., Upper Montclair, 23

Arny, Henry V., Upper Montclair, 23
Ash, Arthur F., Weehawken, 24
Ash, Frank W., Paterson, 24
Ashen, David J., Rutherford, 24
Askew, Sarah B., Trenton, 25
Atchley, Dana W., Englewood, 25
Atkin, Isaac C. R., Short Hills, 26
Atkins, Paul M., Upper Montclair, 26
Atkinson, Ralph W., Westfield, Perth Amboy, 26
Atkinson, Willard S., Westmont, 26
Atwood, Edward A., Paterson, 27
Auerbacher, Louis J., Newark, 27
Auf Der Heide, Oscar L., West New York, 27
Auten, James E., Barber, 27
Avis, John B., Woodbury, Camden, 28
Babbott, Frank L., Bernardsville, 28
Babcock, Charles C., Atlantic City, 29
Babcock, George W., Hackensack, 29
Bacharach, Isaac, Brigantine, Atlantic City, 29
Bacheller, Joseph H., Newark, 29
Backes, Peter, Trenton, 30
Bacon, Clarence E., Montclair, 30
Bacon, George M., Millstone, 30
Bacon, Raymond C., Bound Brook, 30
Badgley, Theo. A., Newark, 30
Baer, William J., East Orange, 31
Baeseman, R. Winfield, Asbury Park, 31
Bagg, Linus W., Newark, 31
Bahney, Luther W., Elizabeth, Carteret, 32
Bahnsen, Henry, Passaic, 32
Bailey, Alanson Q., Collingswood, 32
Bailey, Arthur S., Upper Montclair, 32
Bailey, Austin, Maplewood, 32
Bailey, Calvin W., East Orange, Newark, 32
Bailey, Ethel H., Montclair, 32
Bailey, George B., Newark, 32
Bailey, George C., Elizabeth, Perth Amboy, 32
Bailey, Neil P., Highland Park, New Brunswick, 33
Bailey, Ralph W., Westfield, 33
Bailey, Stacy P., Highlands, 33
Baird, David, Jr., Marlton, Camden, 34
Baker, Charles W., Montclair, 34
Baker, Elsworth F., Marlboro, 34
Baker, Frederick V. V., Mountain Lakes, 34
Baker, John S., Short Hills, 35
Baker, Maclyn F., Irvington, 35
Baker, Maurice E., Camden, 35
Baker, Moses N., Montclair, 36
Baker, Philip W., High Bridge, 36
Baker, Ralph D., Haddonfield, Camden, 36
Baker, S. Josephine, Princeton, 36
Baker, William E., Tenafly, 36
Baketel, H. Sheridan, Jersey City, 37
Baldrey, Haynsworth, Newton, 37
Baldwin, Arthur J., East Orange, 38
Baldwin, Clifford A., Merchantville, Camden, 38
Baldwin, Edward H., Newark, 38
Ballantine, Stuart, Boonton, 38
Balz, George A., Perth Amboy, 39
Bamberger, Edgar S., West Orange, 39
Bamberger, Louis, South Orange, Newark, 39
Barber, Charles W., Short Hills, 41
Barbour, John C., Clifton, Hackensack, 41
Barbour, W. Warren, Locust, Red Bank, 41
Barclay, Isaiah D., Cranbury, 41
Barison, Morris E., Jersey City, 42
Barker, Harry, Montclair, 42
Barkhorn, Charles W., Newark, 42
Barkhorn, Henry C., Newark, 42
Barling, Eugene H., West Orange, Newark, 42
Barlow, De Witt D., Plainfield, 42
Barnard, Chester I., South Orange, Newark, 42
Barnard, Glenn H., Bayonne, 43
Barnert, Meyer, Paterson, 43
Barnes, Morton A., Long Branch, 44
Barnes, William J., Englewood, 44

Barney, Charles N., Harrison, 44
Barron, Jacob T., Newark, 46
Barrow, Henry Y., Cranford, 46
Barrows, Arthur M., Trenton, 46
Barry, Herbert, West Orange, 46
Bartlett, John W., New Brunswick, 47
Bartlett, Robert W., Ventnor, 47
Bartol, George E., Jr., Camden, 47
Barton, John H., South Orange, Harrison, 47
Barton, Warren H., Madison, 47
Bassett, Carroll P., Summit, 48
Bassett, Lavern C., Dunellen, 48
Bataille, Edward F., Maplewood, Newark, 48
Bateman, John, Haddonfield, Camden, 49
Bates, Madison C., Maplewood, Newark, 49
Bauer, John, Montclair, 50
Baum, Felix, Newark, 50
Baumann, John R., Rahway, 51
Bayles, Edwin A., Short Hills, 51
Bayles, Theodore F., New Brunswick, 51
Baylis, Chester, Dover, 51
Beach, George R., Montclair, Sussex, Jersey City, 52
Beach, H. Prescott, Montclair, 52
Beach, Sylvester W., Princeton, 52
Bean, Albert M., Haddonfield, Camden, 53
Bean, Arthur N., Newark, 53
Beard, William M., Westfield, 54
Beardslee, John W., Jr., New Brunswick, 54
Beason, Ross, Jersey City, 54
Beattie, Robert B., East Orange, 54
Beatty, Albert M., Nutley, 54
Beatty, Henry T., Hoboken, 54
Beattys, George D., Westfield, 55
Beaver, Harry C., Harrison, 55
Bechtold, Frank, Jr., Cranford, Garwood, 55
Becker, Edgar A., Ridgewood, 55
Becker, Leo V., Paterson, 56
Becker, Mrs. William A., Summit, 56
Beckley, Quitman F., Princeton, 56
Beckwith, Charles S., Pemberton, 56
Bedford, Bruce, Trenton, 56
Bedford, Henry P., Irvington, 56
Beers, Clifford W., Englewood, 57
Beers, George P., Glen Rock, 57
Beers, Louis J., Newark, 57
Beggs, Frederic, Paterson, 57
Beggs, George E., Princeton, 57
Begley, Thomas D., Burlington, 57
Beisler, Henry, Union City, Belleville, 58
Beisler, Lawrence G., Hillside, 58
Belcher, Arthur W., Maplewood, 58
Belcher, Donald R., Westfield, 58
Belford, Ralph J., Princeton, 59
Beling, Christopher P., Montclair, Newark, 59
Belknap, Fredericka, New Brunswick, 59
Bell, Enid, North Bergen, 59
Bell, John H., South Orange, 59
Bell, William T., Glen Ridge, 60
Bellamy, Charles R., Caldwell, 60
Bellis, Horace D., Trenton, 60
Bellows, Brian C., Maplewood, 60
Ben-Asher, Soloman, Jersey City, 60
Bender, Fred W., Elizabeth, Jersey City, 61
Bender, Harold H., Princeton, 61
Bender, Howard L., Bloomfield, 61
Benet, Hugh, Montclair, Harrison, 61
Benjamin, Harold C., Jersey City, 62
Bennett, Earle O., Asbury Park, 62
Bennett, M. Katharine J., Englewood, 63
Bensinger, Noel E., Madison, 63
Bensley, Maynard G., Summit, 63
Benson, Byron D., Passaic, 63
Benson, C. Wesley, Paterson, 63
Benson, Charles E., Montclair, 63
Bentley, David F., Jr., Camden, 64
Benton, Thaddeus Q., Orange, 64
Berger, Nathan H., East Orange, Newark, 64
Berkey, Charles P., Palisade, 64
Berkow, Samuel G., Perth Amboy, 65
Berlin, Joseph I., Jersey City, 65
Bernard, Ted B., Princeton, 65
Berner, John N., Ventnor, Atlantic City, 65
Berrien, Cornelius R., Upper Montclair, 66
Berry, David W., Millville, 66

Berry, Maja L., Toms River, 66
Besler, William G., Plainfield, 67
Besson, Harlan, Hoboken, 67
Best, Howard R., Cranford, 67
Bestor, Paul, Glen Ridge, Newark, 67
Bettman, Clarence A., Rumson, 67
Betts, George W., Jr., Englewood, 67
Betts, Philander, 3d, Belmar, 67
Bevan, Lynne J., Montclair, 68
Beyer, Jesse W., Rutherford, 68
Bianchi, Angelo R., Newark, 68
Bianchi, Ovidio, Orange, 68
Biddulph, Howard, Bloomfield, Newark, 69
Biehl, George, Teaneck, Union City, 70
Bigelow, John O., Newark, 70
Bigelow, Robert L., Jersey City, 70
Bigelow, William F., Roselle Park, 70
Bilder, Nathaniel, East Orange, Newark, 70
Bill, Alfred H., Princeton, 70
Billetdoux, Edmond W., New Brunswick, 71
Bilofsky, Maxwell M., North Bergen, 71
Binder, Louis R., Paterson, 71
Binder, Walter J., Trenton, 71
Bingham, Arthur W., East Orange, 71
Birch, Stephen, Mahwah, 72
Birch, William D., Boonton, Dover, 72
Birch, William F., Dover, 72
Birely, Morris F., Ridgewood, 72
Bishop, Carl, Plainfield, 73
Bishop, Howard B., Summit, 73
Bissell, Archibald H., Montclair, 74
Black, Archibald, Montclair, 74
Black, Charles C., Jersey City, 74
Black, Helen N., Jersey City, 75
Black, Hugh, Upper Montclair, 75
Blackwell, Enoch, Trenton, 76
Blackwood, Andrew W., Princeton, 76
Blair, Augustine W., New Brunswick, 76
Blair, John E., Leonia, 76
Blair, William R., Red Bank, 77
Blake, Clinton H., Englewood, 77
Blake, George H., Newark, 77
Blakeslee, Myra A., East Orange, 78
Blanchard, Charles L., Dover, 78
Blauvelt, Bula C., Jersey City, 79
Bleakly, Edwin G. C., Camden, 79
Bleakney, Walker, Princeton, 79
Bliss, Elmer J., Jr., Morristown, 80
Bloch, Chaim I., Jersey City, 80
Blumberg, Harry S., Jersey City, 81
Blumberg, Jacob, Elizabeth, 81
Board, Fred Z., Ridgewood, 82
Boardman, Gordon C., Millville, 82
Boardman, Samuel W., Jr., Cedar Grove, Newark, 82
Boas, Franz, Grantwood, 82
Bock, Frank J., Newark, 82
Bodine, Joseph L., Trenton, 82
Boettger, Theodore, Lodi, 83
Boggs, John F. L., Newark, Bay Head, 83
Bolte, G. Arthur, Atlantic City, 84
Bonnell, Charles A., Cape May Court House, 85
Bonner, Francis A., Upper Montclair, 85
Bonomo, Michael J., Newark, 85
Bookstaver, Barnet S., Teaneck, 86
Booth, John A., Essex Fells, Montclair, 86
Booth, Winfield S., Rutherford, Newark, 86
Boozan, William E., Elizabeth, 86
Borden, Albert G., South Orange, 86
Borden, Bertram H., Rumson, 87
Borden, William S., Trenton, 87
Borg, John H., Englewood, Hackensack, 87
Borg, John, Hackensack, 87
Borloso, Alfred N., Paterson, 87
Borow, Benjamin, Bound Brook, 87
Borow, Maurice, Bound Brook, 87
Bortone, Frank, Jersey City, 87
Boswell, John E., Ocean City, 88
Boughton, Fred G., Woodbury, 88
Bowden, Garfield A., East Orange, Jersey City, 88
Bower, Joseph A., Montclair, 89
Bowerman, Arthur L., Newark, 89
Bowes, Edward, Rumson, 90
Bowlby, Harry L., East Orange, 90
Bowles, Harry H., Summit, 90
Bowman, Robert T., Trenton, 90

Bowman, Willard E., Orange, Newark, 90
Bowne, C. B., Montclair, 91
Boyce, Gray C., Princeton, 91
Boyd, Clare M. C. S., Summit, 91
Boyd, Elmer B., New Brunswick, 91
Boyd, Fiske, Summit, 91
Boyd, James O., Upper Montclair, Newark, 92
Boyd, Pliny A., Bloomfield, 92
Boyden, Alan A., Stelton, 92
Boyer, John R. C., Basking Ridge, 93
Boyle, Alexander R. M., Bloomfield, 93
Boynton, Henry C., Trenton, 94
Braddock, Harold, Montclair, 94
Bradley, James A., Union, 95
Bradley, Luke C., Jersey City, 95
Bradley, Robert H., Newark, 95
Bradley, Vincent P., Trenton, 95
Bradley, Will, Short Hills, 95
Bradshaw, John H., Orange, 95
Braitmayer, Otto E., Ridgewood, 96
Bramhall, Fay B., New Brunswick, 96
Brandt, Joseph A., Princeton, 97
Bransome, Edwin D., Rumson, 98
Bratney, John F., Glen Ridge, 98
Bray, Mabel E., Trenton, 98
Breckenridge, John E., Woodbridge, 99
Breder, Charles M., Jr., Mahwah, 99
Breed, Charles H., Blairstown, 99
Breen, Frank J., Trenton, 99
Brennan, John P., Merchantville, Camden, 100
Brennan, Kenneth, Burlington, 100
Brentano, Arthur, East Orange, 100
Bressler, Harry S., West Englewood, 100
Brestell, Rudolph E., Merchantville, 100
Brewer, Charles P., Vineland, 100
Brewer, Frank D., Glen Ridge, 101
Briggs, Frankland, Newark, 102
Briggs, George W., Madison, 102
Brigham, Carl C., Princeton, 102
Brightman, Harold W., Glen Ridge, Newark, 102
Brisco, Norris A., Summit, 103
Bristol, Edward N., Montclair, 103
Bristol, Leverett D., Montclair, 103
Britten, Edwin F., Jr., Orange, 104
Brock, Thomas S., Trenton, 104
Brodesser, Frederick A., Elizabeth, 104
Brody, Morton S., New Brunswick, 104
Broek, John Y., Plainfield, 105
Brogan, Thomas J., Jersey City, 105
Brokaw, Christopher A., Elizabeth, 105
Brown, Arlo A., Madison, 107
Brown, Arthur H., Ridgewood, 107
Brown, Carleton, Upper Montclair, 108
Brown, Chester T., New Brunswick, Newark, 108
Brown, Frederick L., New Brunswick, 109
Brown, George E., Ocean City, 109
Brown, George H., Haddonfield, Camden, 109
Brown, Henry S., Princeton, 109
Brown, J. Douglas, Princeton, 110
Brown, Jane H., May's Landing, 110
Brown, John J., Cranford, 110
Brown, Lawrence G., Elizabeth, 111
Brown, Margaret C., East Orange, 111
Brown, Perc S., Glen Ridge, Harrison, 111
Brown, Ralph L., Montclair, 111
Brown, Raymond J., South Orange, 111
Brown, Stanley C., Camden, 112
Brown, Thomas H., Jersey City, 112
Brown, Wade H., Princeton, 112
Brown, Willard D., Closter, 112
Brown, Zaidee, Upper Montclair, 113
Browne, Charles, Princeton, 113
Bruen, James H., Morristown, 114
Bruhns, George F. W., Cranford, 114
Brunstetter, Max R., Rutherford, 115
Brunyate, William L., South Orange, Newark, 115
Brush, Alvin G., Jersey City, 115
Bryan, Joseph H., Asbury Park, 116
Bryan, Robert R., Paterson, 116
Bryan, Wilbur A., South River, 116
Bryant, Donald R., Trenton, 116
Buchanan, Malcolm G., Princeton, Trenton, 116
Bucher, John E., Fort Lee, 116
Buck, Leonard J., Far Hills, Jersey City, 117
Buck, Oscar M., Madison, 117
Buckley, Oliver E., Maplewood, 118

Buddington, Arthur F., Princeton, 118
Buermann, Robert, Lakewood, 119
Buffum, Douglas L., Princeton, 119
Bugbee, Newton A. K., Trenton, 119
Bull, Ernest M., Montclair, 119
Burger, Edward K., Allendale, 120
Burk, Paul H., Beverly, Riverside, 121
Burke, Daniel, Summit, 121
Burke, Kenneth, Andover, 121
Burke, Louis F., South Orange, 121
Burke, Robert E., Morristown, 121
Burlew, Frederick M., Matawan, 122
Burlington, Harry J., Montvale, 122
Burnap, Robert S., South Orange, Harrison, 122
Burns, Vincent G., Palisade, 123
Burris, William P., Short Hills, 124
Burritt, Norman W., Chatham, Summit, 124
Burtis, Philip B., Merchantville, 124
Burton-Opitz, Russell, Palisade, 125
Buser, Raymond C., Paterson, 125
Bushnell, Asa S., Princeton, 125
Bushnell, Henry D., Montclair, 125
Butler, Elmer G., Princeton, 126
Butler, Eustace C., Caldwell, 126
Butler, George V., East Orange, Newark, 126
Butler, William M., Maplewood, 127
Butt, Howard, Morristown, 127
Buttenheim, Harold S., Madison, 127
Button, Forrest C., New Brunswick, 127
Byrne, Joseph M., Jr., Newark, 128
Byrne, Sister Marie José, Convent Station, 128
Cadbury, Benjamin, Moorestown, 129
Cade, Seeley, Jersey City, 129
Caffery, Edwin C., South Orange, 129
Cafiero, Anthony J., Wildwood, 129
Cain, David E., Princeton, 129
Cairns, Alexander, Newark, 129
Calder, Alexander, Montclair, 130
Caley, Earle R., Princeton, 130
Calvert, Bruce, Mountain, 131
Cameron, A. Guyot, Princeton, 131
Cameron, Norman W., Garfield, 131
Campbell, George A., Upper Montclair, 132
Campbell, Luther A., Trenton, Jersey City, 132
Campbell, William, South Orange, East Orange, 133
Campbell, William H., Jr., Maplewood, Newark, 133
Campbell, William M., Garwood, 133
Canada, William J., Mountain Lakes, 133
Cann, Jessie Y., Newark, 133
Canright, Cyril M., Cranford, 134
Cannon, Florence V., Camden, 134
Capen, Charles E., West Orange, Newark, 134
Capen, William H., Mountain Lakes, 134
Caplan, Albert J., Camden, 134
Capps, Edward, Princeton, 135
Carbin, Edward F., Jersey City, 135
Cardwell, Edgar P., Newark, 135
Carey, Lawrence B., Plainfield, 136
Carlander, Oswald R., Camden, 136
Carlson, Oscar L., Upper Montclair, Montclair, 136
Carlson, Robert C., New Brunswick, 136
Carman, Charles B., Metuchen, 136
Carpenter, Edmund H., Woodbury, 137
Carpenter, Hedwig K., Elizabeth, 137
Carpenter, William S., Princeton, 138
Carr, Gene, Englewood, 138
Carrington, William J., Ventnor, Atlantic City, 138
Carroll, Walter R., Camden, 139
Carson, Edwin S., Ridgewood, 139
Carter, Emmett B., Tenafly, 139
Carter, Samuel T., Jr., Plainfield, 140
Carty, May M., Jersey City, 140
Carvin, Frank D., Summit, Newark, 141
Cary, Lewis R., Princeton, 141
Case, Clarence E., Somerville, 141
Case, J. Herbert, Plainfield, 141
Casey, Frank I., Trenton, 142
Casselman, Arthur J., Camden, Trenton, 142
Cater, Douglas A., East Orange, 143
Cathcart, Charles S., New Brunswick, 143

Catlin, Joseph P., Plainfield, 143
Cavicchia, Peter A., Newark, 144
Cavinato, Lawrence A., Fort Lee, 144
Chafey, James H., Bay Head, 144
Chaffee, Maurice A., New Brunswick, 144
Chambellan, Rene P., Grantwood, 145
Chamberlain, George A., Quinton, 145
Chamberlain, Wilbur, Orange, 145
Chambers, Charles E., Roselle, 145
Chambers, Franklin S., New Lisbon, 145
Chance, Edwin M., Mantoloking, 146
Chandler, Alfred N., Newark, 146
Chandler, William H., Montclair, 146
Chandless, Ralph W., Hackensack, 147
Chapline, George F., Paterson, 147
Chapman, Charles S., Leonia, 147
Chapman, Ira T., Elizabeth, 147
Charles, Robert S., West Orange, 148
Charlton, C. Coulter, Atlantic City, 148
Chase, Burr L., Madison, 148
Chase, Lawrence S., Montclair, Newark, 148
Cheney, Elliott W., Washington, 149
Chenoweth, Arthur S., Somers Point, Atlantic City, 149
Childers, Robert J., Plainfield, 151
Childs, Harwood L., Princeton, 151
Chiles, Harry L., Orange, 151
Chinard, Gilbert, Princeton, 151
Chipman, Ralph N., Chatham, Mound Brook, 151
Christ, Clarence C., Summit, Newark, 152
Christian, Benjamin D., Montclair, Ampere, 152
Christy, William G., Weehawken, Jersey City, 152
Chrysler, Minton A., New Brunswick, 153
Chubb, Hendon, Orange, 153
Church, Alonzo, Princeton, 153
Church, Franklin H., Salem, 153
Church, W. J., Kearny, 153
Chute, Charles L., Mountain Lakes, 154
Ciampaglia, Carlo, Middle Valley, 154
Clapp, Alfred C., Montclair, Newark, 154
Clapp, Edward A., Montclair, Newark, 154
Clark, Arthur, West Orange, 154
Clark, Charles P., Summit, Newark, 154
Clark, Franklin J., Montclair, 155
Clark, J. Harold, New Brunswick, 155
Clark, John B., Bedminster, Newark, 155
Clark, Joseph F., Wildwood, 156
Clark, Ralph A., Phillipsburg, 156
Clark, William, Princeton, Newark, 157
Clarke, Charles W., Caldwell, 157
Clarke, William H. C., Mountain Lakes, 157
Clarken, Joseph A., Newark, 158
Clay, Thomas A., Paterson, 158
Clayton, N. W., South River, 158
Cleary, Frank L., Somerville, 158
Clee, Frederick E., Jersey City, 158
Clee, Lester H., Newark, 158
Clement, John K., Montclair, 159
Clement, Lewis M., Camden, 159
Clement, Ray A., Cranford, 159
Clevenger, William M., Atlantic City, 160
Clift, John W., Summit, 160
Clinchy, Everett R., Madison, 160
Clippinger, Richard D., Vineland, 160
Clothier, Robert C., New Brunswick, 161
Cloud, Albert W., Englewood, 161
Clovis, James R., Highland Park, Newark, 161
Coad, Oral S., New Brunswick, 161
Cobb, Ebenezer B., Elizabeth, 162
Cobham, James L., Jersey City, 162
Cochran, Henry J., Plainfield, 163
Cochran, Jean C., Plainfield, 163
Coes, Harold V., Upper Montclair, 163
Coffman, Joe W., Hackensack, 163
Coggeshall, Murray H., Morristown, 163
Cohn, Joseph E., Newark, 165
Cohn, Morris M., Paterson, 165
Cohn, Saul, Newark, 165
Colby, Everett, West Orange, 165

Cole, David L., Paterson, 165
Cole, Felix, Montclair, 165
Cole, William H., New Brunswick, 166
Coleman, Bernard S., Newark, 166
Coleman, Joseph G., Hamburg, 166
Coleman, Susan M., Newark, 166
Coleman-Norton, Paul R., Princeton, 167
Colgate, Robert B., Jersey City, 167
Colgate, Russell, West Orange, Jersey City, 167
Colgate, S. Bayard, Orange, Jersey City, 167
Colie, F. R., Newark, 167
Colin, Philip G., Bayonne, 167
Collester, Donald G., Clifton, 167
Collins, Arthur J., Jr., Moorestown, 168
Collins, Charles H., Somers Point, 168
Collins, Charles W., Morristown, 168
Collins, G. Rowland, Newark, 168
Collins, Henry, Tenafly, 168
Collins, Laurence M., Greystone Park, 168
Colpitts, Edwin H., Orange, 168
Colpitts, Walter W., Princeton, 168
Colton, Ethan T., Upper Montclair, 169
Colton, Isadore H., South Orange, Newark, 169
Colver, Alice R., Tenafly, 169
Colvin, Charles H., Morristown, 169
Colvin, Fred H., Point Pleasant, 169
Colyer, Morrison C., Newark, 169
Comando, Harry N., Newark, 169
Comen, Louis M., North Bergen, Union City, 170
Comstock, Louis K., Montclair, 170
Conard, William R., Burlington, 170
Conaway, Walt P., Atlantic City, 170
Conklin, Edwin G., Princeton, 171
Conklin, Franklin, Jr., Newark, 171
Conklin, Lewis R., Ridgewood, 171
Conley, Brooks L., Fanwood, North Plainfield, 171
Connelly, John A., Trenton, 172
Conner, John G., Trenton, 172
Connett, Eugene V., 3d, South Orange, 172
Conning, John S., Upper Montclair, 172
Connolly, John J., Newark, 172
Connolly, John E., Elizabeth, 172
Connolly, T. Vincent, Paterson, 172
Connors, Charles H., Highland Park, 173
Conover, Elbert M., Westfield, 173
Constant, Frank H., Princeton, 173
Conty, Anthony J., Union City, 173
Conwell, Walter L., Montclair, 173
Cook, Edmund D., Princeton, 174
Cook, George R., 3d, Princeton, 174
Cook, John H., Passaic, Paterson, 174
Cook, Sidney A., New Brunswick, 175
Cooke, Hereward L., Princeton, 175
Coombs, John B., Somerville, 176
Cooney, John R., Maplewood, Newark, 176
Cooper, Drury W., Montclair, 176
Cope, William C., Glen Ridge, Newark, 177
Copeland, Wilbur F. D., Alpine, 177
Corbin, Arthur S., Passaic, 178
Corbin, Horace K., West Orange, Newark, 178
Corn, David, Ridgefield Park, 178
Cornelison, Robert W., Somerville, Plainfield, 179
Cornell, William B., Montclair, 179
Cornish, Hubert R., Paterson, 179
Corradini, Robert E., Madison, 179
Corwin, Edward S., Princeton, 180
Corwin, Margaret T., New Brunswick, 180
Cosgrove, Samuel A., Jersey City, 181
Costabile, Vincent, Lyndhurst, 181
Costello, William F., Dover, 181
Costikyan, S. Kent, Montclair, 181
Coughtry, Frank G., Orange, 181
Coult, Joseph, Newark, 181
Coulter, James A., Jersey City, 182
Couse, William J., Asbury Park, 182
Couse, William P., Asbury Park, 182
Cowles, David O., East Orange, 183
Cowperthwait, William D., Medford, 183
Cox, Douglas F., West Orange, 183
Cox, John C., Maplewood, 183
Cox, Philip W. L., Maplewood, 183

Cox, William H. D., Short Hills, Newark, 184
Cox, William W., Montclair, 184
Coxson, Harold P., Stratford, 184
Cozzens, James G., Lambertville, 184
Craig, Robert, Maplewood, 185
Craig, Samuel G., Princeton, 185
Crain, William E., Mt. Ephraim, Woodbury, 185
Crane, Frederick L., Elizabeth, 185
Crane, Norman T., Plainfield, 185
Craven, Charles E., Montclair, 186
Craven, D. Stewart, Salem, 186
Crecca, William D., Newark, 187
Creese, James, Hoboken, 187
Crescente, Fred J., Hawthorne, Paterson, 187
Cressman, Henry M., Egg Harbor City, 187
Croasdale, Francis E., Ventnor City, Atlantic City, 189
Crocco, Anthony E., Ridgewood, 189
Croll, Morris W., Princeton, 189
Cromwell, Doris D., Somerville, 190
Crooks, Richard, Sea Girt, 190
Crooks, Thomas L. R., Maplewood, Newark, 190
Cross, William R., Bernardsville, 191
Crossfield, Henry C., South Orange, East Orange, 191
Crossley, George C., Trenton, 191
Crossley, Moses L., Plainfield, Bound Brook, 191
Crouch, Richard C., Millburn, 191
Crouch, Robert P., Trenton, Jersey City, 191
Crow, Charles S., New Brunswick, 191
Crowe, John J., Westfield, Jersey City, 191
Crowley, James A., Passaic, 192
Crowther, Rae, Haddonfield, 192
Croxton, Frederick E., Leonia, 192
Crum, Ralph W., Upper Montclair, Passaic, 192
Crumley, Thomas R., Eatontown, Asbury Park, 192
Crump, James I., Oradell, 192
Cudlipp, William C., Jersey City, 193
Culin, Walter A., Madison, 193
Cullimore, Allan R., South Orange, 194
Culp, Cordie J., New Brunswick, 194
Culver, Edward P., Princeton, 194
Cumberland, William N., Englewood, 194
Cummings, Harold N., Belleville, Newark, 194
Cummins, Annie B. T., Belvidere, 195
Cunliffe, Rex B., Stelton, New Brunswick, 195
Cuppia, Jerome C., Montclair, 195
Currie, Edward W., Matawan, 196
Currie, Norman W., Plainfield, 196
Currier, Richard D., Montclair, 196
Curry, Edward T., Camden, 196
Curtis, Leona, Plainfield, 197
Curtis, Richard, Haddonfield, 197
Curtiss, William J., Montclair, 197
Cutler, Bertram, Greens Village, 198
Cutting, Charles S., Gladstone, 198
Cutts, Henry E., Tenafly, 198
Daggett, Edwin H., Plainfield, 199
Daggett, Parker H., New Brunswick, 199
Dahlgren, Ulric, Princeton, 199
Dana, Charles A., Bernardsville, 200
Dane, Charles, South Orange, 200
Darling, Benjamin J., Jersey City, 201
Darlington, Hart, Maplewood, 201
David, Abraham J., Roselle, Elizabeth, 202
Davidson, Adeline T., East Orange, 202
Davidson, Max D., Perth Amboy, 203
Davies, Thomas R., East Orange, 203
Davis, Benjamin W., Princeton, 203
Davis, Chester M., Rahway, 203
Davis, David R., Upper Montclair, 204
Davis, Edward L., Orange, 204
Davis, Edwin B., New Brunswick, 204
Davis, Francis B., Camden, 204
Davis, Harvey N., Hoboken, 205
Davis, Helen C. M., Hoboken, 205
Davis, Howard L., Upper Montclair, 205
Davis, J. Warren, Lawrenceville, 205

Davis, Richard S., Palisade-on-Hudson, North Bergen, 206
Davis, William C., Haddon Heights, 207
Davis, William H., Orange, 207
Davisson, Clinton J., Short Hills, 208
Davy, Ralph, Morris Plains, 208
Dawkins, George E., Newark, 208
Dawley, Clarence A., Plainfield, 208
Dawson, Coningsby, Newark, 208
Dawson, Edward, Passaic, 208
Day, Joseph P., Short Hills, 209
Day, Sarah J., Englewood, 209
Dean, Ernest W., Westfield, 210
Deans, William, Ridgewood, 210
Dear, Joseph A., Ridgewood, Jersey City, 210
Debevoise, Thomas, Green Village, 210
De Graw, John, Montague, Newark, 212
De Knight, Edward W., Passaic, 212
Delchamps, Harold J., Mountain Lakes, 213
de Leeuw, Adele L., Plainfield, 213
De Lorenzo, William, Hackensack, 214
Demarest, Charles S., Ridgewood, 214
Demarest, William H. S., New Brunswick, 214
Dengler, Calvin F., Woodbridge, Carteret, 215
Denise, Garret A., Freehold, 215
Dennis, George P., Hightstown, 215
Dennis, Paul G., Plainfield, 215
Deppeler, John H., Weehawken, 216
Derby, Harry L., Montclair, 216
de Regt, Albert C., New Brunswick, 216
Derick, Clarence G., Sewaren, 216
De Visme, Alice W., New Brunswick, 218
Devoe, William B., Montclair, 218
Dewing, Henry B., Princeton, 218
DeWitt, John D., Nutley, 219
Diament, George E., Cedarville, Bridgeton, 219
Dickey, Edward T., Camden, 220
Dickinson, C. Roy, East Orange, 220
Dickinson, Neville S., Maplewood, Newark, 220
Diefenbach, Carl M., Collingswood, 221
Diffendorfer, Ralph E., Madison, 222
Dillon, Howard W., South Amboy, 223
Dinsmore, Carlos M., West Englewood, 223
Dittmar, Charles F., Freehold, 224
Dix, William F., South Orange, 224
Dixon, Frank H., Princeton, 224
Dixon, John E., East Orange, 225
Dobbs, Joseph, Bernardsville, 225
Dodd, Howard S., Glen Ridge, Montclair, 225
Dodd, William E., Beach Haven, 225
Dodds, Harold W., Princeton, 226
Dodge, M. Hartley, Madison, 226
Dodgen, Lily M., Trenton, 226
Doe, Charles L., Long Valley, Glen Ridge, Montclair, 226
Doersam, Charles H., Palisade, 226
Dolan, Albert H., Englewood, 227
D'Olier, Franklin, Morristown, Newark, 227
Doll, Edgar A., Vineland, 227
Dolliver, Charles M., North Plainfield, Plainfield, 227
Donelson, Earl T., Trenton, 228
Donges, Ralph W. E., Camden, 228
Doniger, Simon, East Orange, Newark, 228
Donnelly, Marcus E., North Bergen, Jersey City, 229
Donovan, Edward F., West Englewood, 229
Doolittle, Lewis J., Maplewood, 229
Dorau, Herbert B., Ridgewood, 229
Dorety, Sister Helen Angela, Convent, 229
Dorrance, Arthur C., Camden, 230
Dougall, John B., Summit, 231
Dougan, James E., Caldwell, Newark, 231
Dougherty, Gregg, Princeton, 231
Douglas, Robert S., Elizabeth, 231
Douglass, H. Paul, Upper Montclair, 231
Douglass, Mabel S., New Brunswick, 232
Douty, Daniel E., Englewood, Hoboken, 232
Downing, Charles T., Newton, 232

Dreyfuss, Leonard, Essex Fells, Newark, 234
Drittler, Max W., Boonton, 234
Drukker, Dow H., Passaic, 235
Drukker, Dow H., Jr., Passaic, 235
Drushel, J. Andrew, Westfield, 235
DuBois, Charles G., Englewood, 235
Duckworth, George E., Princeton, 235
Duffy, John, Point Pleasant, 236
Dugan, Raymond S., Princeton, 236
Duke, Charles W., Cape May, 237
Duke, Nathaniel, West Orange, 237
Duke, Roy F., East Orange, Newark, 237
Dumper, Arthur, Newark, 237
Dumper, Arthur S., Newark, 237
Dunaway, John A., Maplewood, 237
Duncan, Charles M., Freehold, 238
Dunham, Frederic G., Ridgewood, 238
Dunham, Henry B., Blackwood, 238
Dunlop, Walter S., Camden, 239
Dunne, Edward F., Convent, Rockaway, 239
Dunsmore, John W., Hoboken, 240
Durand, Frank, Sea Girt, Spring Lake, 240
Dutcher, Edward M., Newton, 241
Dyer, Frank L., Ventnor, 242
Eagleton, Wells P., Newark, 242
Eakin, Frank, Short Hills, 243
Eakin, Mildred O. M., Short Hills, 243
Earle, Beatrice L., Princeton, 243
Earle, Edgar P., Mantoloking, 243
Earle, Edward M., Princeton, 243
Earle, Murray, Mantoloking, 243
Earp, Edwin L., Basking Ridge, 244
Easley, George A., Morristown, 244
Easterly, George R., Short Hills, 244
Eaton, Charles A., Plainfield, 244
Eberhardt, Fred L., Maplewood, Newark, 245
Echols, Charles P., Englewood, 245
Eckelmann, Luis E., Newark, 246
Eddy, Henry S., Westfield, 246
Edge, Walter E., Ventnor, 247
Edison, Charles, West Orange, 247
Edison, Theodore M., West Orange 247
Edris, Warren P., Mountain Lakes, 248
Edwards, Paul K., Maplewood, Newark, 248
Egan, Charles M., Jersey City, 249
Egbert, Lester D., Montclair, 249
Eglin, James M., Glen Rock, 249
Egner, Arthur F., South Orange, Newark, 249
Ehnes, Morris W., Leonia, 249
Eichelberger, Percy S., Collingswood, 250
Eichler, George M., Weehawken, Jersey City, 250
Eichner, Laurits C., Bloomfield, 250
Eidmann, Frank L., Princeton, 250
Eikenberry, William L., Trenton, 251
Einstein, Albert, Princeton, 251
Eisenhart, Luther P., Princeton, 251
Eisner, Mortimer, Newark, 251
Elder, Alexander H., Glen Ridge, 252
Elder, Walter T., Highland Park, New Brunswick, 252
Elderkin, George W., Princeton, 252
Elgin, Joseph C., Princeton, 252
Elk, Benjamin R., Garfield, 252
Elkinton, Thomas W., Moorestown, 253
Ellenstein, Meyer C., Newark, 253
Ellerhusen, Florence C., Towaco, 253
Ellerhusen, Ulrich H., Towaco, 253
Elliott, Charles H., New Brunswick, Trenton, 253
Ellis, Carleton, Montclair, 254
Ellis, William J., Trenton, 254
Ellmaker, Lee, Haddonfield, 255
Ellsberg, Edward, Westfield, 255
Elmen, Gustaf W., Leonia, 255
Elmore, Carl H., Englewood, 255
Elsasser, Theodore H., North Bergen, 255
Elson, Henry W., Plainfield, 256
Elwood, Robert A., Absecon, 256
Ely, William H. J., Rutherford, 256
Embree, William D., Tenafly, 256
Emerson, Linn, Orange, 257
Emhardt, William C., Longport, 257
Engels, William H., Rahway, 258
England, Herbert K., Roselle, 258
English, Ada J., New Brunswick, 259
English, Charles R., Red Bank, 259
English, Conover, Summit, Newark, 259
English, John T., Irvington, 259

Englund, Carl R., Holmdel, 259
Ennis, Joseph, Paterson, 259
Ennis, William D., Wyckoff, 260
Erdman, Charles R., Princeton, 260
Erler, Eugene W., South Orange, 260
Erskine, Archibald M., Chatham, Newark, 261
Escher, Franklin, Englewood, 261
Estabrook, Edward L., West Orange, 262
Etzkorn, Leo R., Paterson, 263
Eustace, Bartholomew J., West Collingswood, Camden, 263
Evans, John F., Paterson, 264
Evans, William A. D., Summit, Hoboken, 264
Evans, William W., Paterson, 265
Exton, William G., Newark, 266
Fagan, Arthur, Hoboken, 267
Fair, James H. S., Far Hills, 268
Fairbanks, Benjamin, Newark, 268
Fake, Guy L., Newark, 268
Fales, David, Jr., New Brunswick, 268
Falk, Louis A., Jersey City, 269
Falkner, Roland P., East Orange, 269
Falls, Laurence E., Maplewood, Newark, 269
Fankhauser, Gerhard, Princeton, 269
Fardelmann, John H., Jr., Montclair, 269
Farley, Arthur J., New Brunswick, 270
Farmer, Vincent, Hackensack, 270
Farmer, Walter D., Allentown, 270
Farnam, George O., Trenton, Bordentown, 270
Farny, George W., Morris Plains, 271
Farquhar, Thomas L., Maplewood, 271
Farr, Irving L., Montclair, 271
Farr, Walter J., Teaneck, 271
Farrand, Wilson, Princeton, 271
Farrell, Charles L., Newark, 271
Farrell, John J., Westfield, Short Hills, 271
Farwell, Hermon W., Leonia, 272
Fassett, Harvey L., Newark, 272
Fast, Louis A., Newark, 272
Featherston, Daniel F., Asbury Park, 273
Feller, Alexander, Highland Park, Newark, New Brunswick, 273
Fenias, Edward, Newark, 274
Fenner, Clarence N., Clifton, 274
Ferguson, John W., Paterson, 275
Ferguson, Smith F., Short Hills, 275
Fernald, Henry B., Upper Montclair, 276
Ferry, Leland F., Teaneck, 276
Fetter, Frank A., Princeton, 277
Fettinger, Theodore S., Newark, 277
Fetzer, Karl R., Rutherford, 277
Fey, Harold E., Leonia, 277
Field, Frank L., Far Hills, 278
Field, William J., Jersey City, 278
Fielder, James F., Montclair, Jersey City, 278
Fielding, William J., Newark, 278
Files, Ellery K., East Orange, Newark, 278
Filmer, Robert S., Stelton, New Brunswick, 279
Findley, Alvin I., Montclair, 279
Finke, George W., Hackensack, 280
Finkler, Rita S., Newark, 280
Finley, Charles W., Montclair, 280
Fireman, Peter, Lambertville, 280
Firth, Norman C., Maplewood, 281
Fischelis, Robert P., Trenton, 281
Fishler, Franklin, Ridgewood, 282
Fite, Warner, Hopewell, 283
Fithian, J. Herbert, Bridgeton, 283
Fitzhugh, Percy K., Oradell, 283
Flagg, Herbert J., Ridgewood, Newark, 284
Fleming, Charles L., Penn's Grove, 285
Fleming, Eric, New Brunswick, 285
Fletcher, Arthur, Montclair, Newark, 286
Fletcher, Charles W., Newark, 286
Flexner, Abraham, Princeton, 286
Flexner, Anne C., Princeton, 286
Flitcroft, William, Paterson, 286
Flood, Henry, Jr., Rahway, 286
Florcyk, Edward M., Rockaway, 286
Focarino, Vincent C., Lodi, 287
Foerster, Robert F., Princeton, 287
Fokker, Anthony H. G., Alpine, Clifton, 288
Foley, Gerald T., West Orange, Newark, 288
Folger, Oliver H., Maywood, Hackensack, 288
Folwell, Amory P., Montclair, 288

NEW JERSEY

Forbes, B. C., Englewood, 289
Ford, L. Stanley, Leonia, Hackensack, 289
Forman, Philip, Trenton, 290
Forrest, Henry O., Teaneck, 290
Forstall, Alfred E., Montclair, 290
Fort, Leslie R., Plainfield, 290
Foster, Lloyd E., East Orange, 291
Foster, Ronald M., Westfield, 292
Foster, Sadie L., Newark, 292
Foster, Solomon, Newark, 292
Foster, Thomas J., Ridgewood, 292
Foster, Warren D., Westwood, Ridgewood, 292
Foster, William E., Hackensack, 292
Foulhoux, Jacques A., Short Hills, 292
Foulkes, William H., Newark, 293
Fournier, Louis F., East Paterson, 293
Fox, Henry, Cape May Court House, 294
Fox, John P., Maplewood, 294
Fradkin, Elvira E., Montclair, 294
Frank, Fritz J., Madison, 295
Frank, Morris, Bayonne, 296
Frankel, Emil, Trenton, 296
Franklin, Curtis, Mountain Lakes, Jersey City, 296
Franklin, Neil S., Belmar, Asbury Park, 296
Frantz, Samuel G., Princeton, 296
Frazer, Spaulding, Bernardsville, Newark, 297
Frederick, Halsey A., Mountain Lakes, 298
Freeman, Forster W., Paterson, 298
Freeman, Forster W., Jr., Paterson, 298
Freeman, Richard D., South Orange, 298
Frelinghuysen, Joseph S., Far Hills, 299
French, Walter B., Ridgewood, 299
Freygang, Walter H., Essex Falls, Bloomfield, 300
Friedland, Jacob, Jersey City, 301
Friedman, Theodore, North Bergen, 301
Friedrich, F. A., Paterson, 301
Frohling, Edward A., Princeton, 302
Frolich, Per K., Westfield, Elizabeth, 302
Frost, Inglis F., Chester, Morristown, 302
Fry, Morton H., Montclair, 302
Fry, Thornton C., Wyoming, 303
Fryer, Jane E., Merchantville, 303
Fuchs, William W., Jersey City, 303
Fuhlbruegge, Edward, Newark, 303
Fuld, Leonhard F., Jersey City, 303
Fuller, Caroline M., Lakewood, 303
Fuller, Earl W., Morris Plains, 303
Fuller, Ralph B., Leonia, 304
Fulper, William H., Jr., Trenton, 304
Funk, Wilfred J., Montclair, 304
Furman, Franklin DeR., Hoboken, 305
Furman, N. Howell, Princeton, 305
Furst, George, Newark, 305
Gabrielson, Guy G., Bernardsville, 305
Gag, Wanda, Milford, 305
Galanti, Marinus C., Lodi, 306
Gallagher, Ralph P., Elizabeth, 306
Gallup, George H., Princeton, 307
Gallup, Wallace L., Newark, 307
Gerard, Ira D., New Brunswick, 308
Gardner, Horace J., Grenloch, 308
Gardner, Wallace J., Trenton, 309
Gardner, Walter P., Jersey City, 309
Garis, Howard R., East Orange, Newark, 309
Garis, Lilian C., East Orange, 309
Garretson, Leland B., Morristown, 310
Garrett, Garet, Tuckahoe, 310
Garrison, Samuel F., Bordentown, 311
Gaskill, Burton A., May's Landing, Atlantic City, 311
Gaskill, Thomas L., Camden, 311
Gates, Caleb F., Princeton, 311
Gaugler, Jos. F., Ridgewood, 312
Gaunt, Carl G., New Brunswick, 312
Gaunt, Harold G., Atlantic City, 312
Gauss, Christian, Princeton, 313
Gaylord, Franklin A., West Englewood, 313
Gebhardt, William R., Clinton, 314
Gee, Howard J., Montclair, 314
Gehman, Henry S., Princeton, 314
George, Charles A., Elizabeth, 315
George, John J., New Brunswick, 315
Gerould, Gordon H., Princeton, 316
Gerould, Katharine F., Princeton, 316
Gherardi, Bancroft, Short Hills, 317
Ghezzi, Victor, Deal, 317

Giacomantonio, Archimedes A. M., Jersey City, 317
Gibbons, Helen D., Princeton, 317
Gibbons, Willis A., Montclair, Passaic, 318
Gibbs, Alfred T., Montclair, 318
Gibson, George H., Montclair, 318
Giglio, Alphonsus S. V., Elizabeth, 319
Gilbert, William M., Madison, 320
Gilbreth, Lillian M., Montclair, 320
Gildersleeve, Nelson B., East Orange, 320
Gill, Elizabeth, Mendham, 321
Gill, John G., Trenton, 321
Gillespie, William, Princeton, 321
Gillmore, Quincy A., Rumson, 322
Gilman, Charles, Plainfield, 322
Gilman, James B., New Brunswick, 322
Ginsberg, Louis, Paterson, 323
Glazebrook, Francis H., Morristown, 324
Glenn, Alfred T., Jr., Margate City, Atlantic City, 325
Glenn, Earl R., Upper Montclair, Montclair, 325
Glintenkamp, Hendrik, Sparta, 325
Gluckman, Isaac E., Newark, 326
Gnichtel, Frederick W., Trenton, 326
Goeller, Jacob, Irvington, 326
Goldmann, Sidney, Trenton, 327
Goldstein, Hyman I., Camden, 328
Goodall, Charles E., Roselle, Newark, 328
Goodell, Edwin B., Montclair, 329
Goodkind, Morris, New Brunswick, Trenton, 329
Goodwin, William N., Jr., Newark, 329
Gordon, Benjamin L., Atlantic City, 330
Gordon, Joseph B., Marlboro, 331
Gordon, Myron B., Montclair, Paterson, 331
Gordon, Ralph F., Mahwah, 331
Gore, John K., Orange, 331
Gottlief, Solomon, Hoboken, 332
Gough, John F., Jersey City, 332
Gould, Beatrice B., Hopewell, 333
Gould, Charles B., Hopewell, 333
Gould, Laura S., Atlantic City, 333
Goulden, Harold D., West Orange, Roselle, 333
Grabach, John R., Irvington, 333
Grace, John F., Harrison, 334
Graham, Frank D., Princeton, 334
Graham, Kelley, Jersey City, 335
Grainger, Isaac B., Montclair, 335
Grammer, Carl E., Summit, 335
Graves, Charles C., Jr., Marlboro, 336
Graves, Harold T., Jr., Summit, 336
Graves, William S., Shrewsbury, 336
Gray, Arthur W., Westfield, 336
Gray, Charles M., Vineland, 336
Gray, Edward W., Newark, 337
Grece, Philip W., Jersey City, 337
Green, Charles H., Ridgewood, 338
Green, Florence T., Long Branch, 338
Green, Francis H., Pennington, 338
Green, Harold D., Paterson, 338
Green, Robert M., Essex Fells, Newark, 339
Green, Samuel, Trenton, 339
Green, Wyman R., Madison, 339
Greenan, John T., East Orange, 339
Greenberg, Joseph, Hoboken, 339
Greene, Arthur M., Jr., Princeton, 339
Greene, Bartlett, Margate, 340
Greene, Richard T., Montclair, 340
Greenwood, Harry D., Elizabeth, 341
Gregg, Albert E., Audubon, 341
Gregg, William C., Hackensack, 341
Gregory, Waylande, Bound Brook, 342
Gregory, William S., Orange, 342
Greifinger, Marcus H., Newark, 342
Grieve, Lucia C. G., Ocean Grove, 343
Griffin, William V., Peapack, 343
Griffith, Frederic R., Belmar, 343
Griffith, Stephen C., Jr., Morristown, 344
Grimshaw, Robert, Leonia, 345
Griscom, John M., Moorestown, 345
Groel, Frederick H., East Orange, Newark, 345
Gross, Edward R., New Brunswick, 346
Grossman, Max, Atlantic City, 347
Grossnickle, Foster E., Nutley, Jersey City, 347
Groves, Hannah C., Haddonfield, 348
Grubbs, Henry A., Princeton, 348
Gruger, Frederic R., Chester, 348

Guertin, Arthur H., North Haledon, Paterson, 349
Guilfoil, Paul H., Maplewood, Newark, 349
Guion, Edward, Northfield, 349
Guldahl, Ralph, Braidburn, 349
Gulliver, Robert H., Trenton, 349
Gunn, Thomas M., Paulsboro, Woodbury, 350
Gunther, Charles O., Hoboken, 350
Guntrum, Emilie I., Elizabeth, 350
Haber, Isador, Weehawken, Union City, 351
Hackett, E. Byrne, Bound Brook, 352
Hadley, Charles F., Merchantville, 352
Hagar, Ivan D., Tenafly, 352
Hagedorn, Hermann, Montclair, 353
Hageman, Aaron M., Verona, Bloomfield, 353
Haggerty, Cecil J., Teaneck, 353
Hague, Frank, Jersey City, 353
Hahn, Frederick C., Upper Montclair, Arlington, 353
Hahn, Lew, Ridgewood, 354
Haight, Clarence M., Franklin, 354
Haight, Thomas G., Englewood, Jersey City, 354
Haines, Thomas H., Montclair, 354
Haire, Frances H., East Orange, 355
Halbach, Robert M., Toms River, 355
Haldenstein, Alfred A., Plainfield, 355
Hale, George C., Dover, 355
Hall, Clyde W., Trenton, 356
Hall, Frank H., Englewood, 356
Hall, Fred S., Upper Montclair, 356
Hall, Frederick W., Newark, Bound Brook, 356
Hall, Walter P., Princeton, 357
Halliday, Ernest M., Mountain Lakes, Denville, 357
Halliday, William R., Morristown, Hoboken, 357
Halprin, Harry, Caldwell, 358
Ham, William F., Bay Head, 358
Hamblen, Emily S., Stanhope, 358
Hamill, James A., Jersey City, 358
Hamilton, Charles W., Upper Montclair, 359
Hamilton, Clyde C., Highland Park, 359
Hamilton, Francis M., Leonia, 359
Hamilton, Frank W., Dover, 359
Hamilton, Willard I., Maplewood, 360
Hammer, Edwin W., South Orange, 360
Hammond, Ogden H., Bernardsville, Jersey City, 361
Hand, George T., Denville, 361
Hand, Molly W., Roselle, Elizabeth, 361
Hand, Thomas M., Cape May, 362
Haneman, Frederick T., Brigantine, 362
Haneman, Vincent S., Brigantine, Atlantic City, 362
Haney, Lewis H., Maplewood, 362
Hanlon, John, Pennington, 362
Hanna, Charles A., Montclair, 362
Hannoch, Herbert J., South Orange, Newark, 363
Hanscom, Clarence D., Denville, 363
Hanson, Ernest R., Bloomfield, 363
Hanzsche, William T., Trenton, 363
Hardenbergh, John G., Princeton, Plainsboro, 364
Hardenbergh, William A., Ridgewood, 364
Hardin, Charles R., Newark, 364
Hardin, John R., Newark, 364
Harding, Ernest A., Princeton, Trenton, 364
Harding, William B., South Orange, Newark, 365
Harney, Julia C., Jersey City, 368
Harper, George M., Princeton, 368
Harper, Harry C., Hackensack, 368
Harrington, Marshall C., Chatham, Madison, 369
Harris, Harvey E., Bloomfield, 369
Harrison, Benjamin V., Montclair, 371
Harrop, George A., Jr., Princeton, 371
Hart, Cecil A., Hackensack, 372
Hart, Edward J., Jersey City, 372
Hartley, Fred A., Jr., Kearny, 372
Hartley, Ralph V. L., Summit, 372
Hartman, Albert L., Upper Montclair, Montclair, 372
Hartridge, Emelyn B., Plainfield, 373
Hartshorne, Richard, East Orange, Newark, 373
Hartt, George M., Passaic, 373
Hartwell, H. Ameroy, Weehawken, 374

Hartwell, Oliver W., Trenton, 374
Harvey, Alexander, Hackensack, 374
Harvey, Edmund N., Princeton, 374
Harvey, John S. C., Camden, 375
Harvey, Zarina H., Maplewood, 375
Haslam, Robert T., Short Hills, 375
Hasler, Frederick E., Little Silver, 375
Hassard, Charles T., Union, 375
Hastings, Walter S., Princeton, 376
Hatch, Roy W., Upper Montclair, 376
Hatfield, Nina, Hoboken, 376
Hauck, Anthony M., Jr., Hampton, Clinton, 377
Hauschka, Carola S., Princeton, 377
Hausman, Leon A., New Brunswick, 377
Havemeyer, Henry O., Mahwah, 377
Hawkes, Edward M. Z., Newark, 378
Hawkes, Stuart Z., Newark, 378
Hawkins, Alfred C., New Brunswick, 378
Hay, George A. F., Ridgewood, 379
Hayes, Albert O., Highland Park, New Brunswick, 379
Hayes, Lydia Y., Far Hills, Newark, 380
Hayhow, Edgar C., East Orange, Paterson, 380
Hayne, Coe, Dumont, 380
Hayward, William G., East Orange, 381
Hazelton, William H., Salem, 381
Hazen, Joseph C., Summit, 381
Hazen, Joseph N., Lambertville, 381
Head, Walter D., Montclair, 382
Headlee, Thomas J., Dayton, New Brunswick, 382
Heck, Robert C. H., New Brunswick, 383
Heely, Allan V., Lawrenceville, 384
Heermance, Radcliffe, Princeton, 384
Heffner, Roy J., Morristown, 384
Heher, Harry, Trenton, 384
Heilner, Van Campen, Spring Lake Beach, 385
Hein, Carl, Woodcliff Lake, 385
Heising, Raymond A., Summit, 386
Heiss, Charles A., Pottersville, 386
Heller, Edgar W., Newark, 386
Heller, Leighton J., Clementon, Camden, 386
Helyar, Frank G., Stelton, New Brunswick, 387
Henderson, Leon, Millville, 388
Hendrickson, Harold A., Red Bank, 388
Hendrickson, John H., Keyport, 388
Henninger, G. Ross, Haworth, 389
Heppenheimer, Ernest J., Tenafly, Jersey City, 390
Herb, Charles O., Summit, 390
Hermann, John H., Orange, 391
Herr, Dougal, Essex Fells, Elizabeth, 392
Herrman, William G., Deal, Asbury Park, 392
Hersh, Edward S., Elizabeth, 393
Herzberg, Max J., South Orange, Newark, 393
Hess, Arleigh P., Mullica Hill, 393
Hess, Henry L., Pleasantville, 394
Hess, Sara M., Hillsdale, 394
Hessert, Edmund C., Collingswood, Camden, 394
Hetrick, Samuel L., Deal, Jersey City, 394
Heustis, Charles H., Longport, 395
Hewett-Thayer, Harvey W., Princeton, 395
Hewitt, George, Paterson, 395
Heyl, Lawrence, Princeton, 395
Heyliger, William, Ridgefield Park, 395
Hibben, Samuel G., Montclair, 395
Hickman, Joseph N. K., New Brunswick, 396
Hickok, Paul R., Newark, 396
Hicks, Ami M., Scotch Plains, 396
Hildebrandt, Emanuel H. C., Upper Montclair, 397
Hildum, Clayton E., Plainfield, 397
Hill, E. Rowland, East Orange, 398
Hill, Harry S., Hightstown, Trenton, 398
Hill, Percival S., Nutley, 399
Hill, Roscoe R., Leonia, 399
Hillman, Julian A., Atlantic City, 400
Hills, Frederic W., East Orange, 400
Hinck, Claus F., Jr., Montclair, 401
Hine, Willard F., Westfield, 401
Hines, Earl G., West Milford, 401
Hinrichsen, Arthur F., Mountain Lakes, 401
Hinsdale, Katharine L., Lakewood, 402

NEW JERSEY

Hird, Emerson F., Bound Brook, 402
Hirschthal, Meyer, Hoboken, 402
Hitchcock, Clarence C., Hasbrouck Heights, 403
Hite, Omar, Glen Rock, 403
Hitti, Philip K., Princeton, 403
Hitz, Ralph, Pittstown, 403
Hixson, Arthur W., Leonia, 403
Hoadley, Frederick, Upper Montclair, Newark, 404
Hobein, Charles A., Montclair, 404
Hocker, Carl D., East Orange, 404
Hoddeson, Samuel I., New Brunswick, 404
Hoehn, Matthew A., Newark, 405
Hoelzer, Virginia, Bloomfield, 405
Hoffman, Arthur G., Orange, 405
Hoffman, Harold G., South Amboy, 405
Hoffman, Milton J., New Brunswick, 406
Hollander, Edward, Weehawken, Union City, 408
Holley, Alfred T., Hackensack, 408
Holliday, Robert C., Stillwater, 409
Hollinger, D. Wilson, Trenton, 409
Hollingshead, W. Stewart, Riverton, Camden, 409
Hollingsworth, Herman H., Clifton, 409
Hollinshed, Ralph K., Westville, 409
Holmes, Henry D., Summit, 410
Holsopple, James Q., Titusville, Trenton, 411
Holzmann, Albert W., New Brunswick, 411
Homan, J. Albert, Trenton, 411
Homrighausen, Elmer G., Princeton, 412
Hooper, Franklin H., Montclair, 413
Hopkins, Carleton R., Collingswood, 413
Hopper, Elmer F., Maplewood, Newark, 414
Hopson, Howard C., Jersey City, 414
Horne, Herman H., Leonia, 415
Horsch, William G., Woodbury, Paulsboro, 415
Hotchkiss, Charles H. B., Hohokus, 416
Hotelling, Harold, Mountain Lakes, 416
Hough, Lynn H., Madison, 416
Houghton, William M., Plainfield, 417
Hovey, George R., Upper Montclair, 417
Howard, John T., Glen Ridge, 418
Howard, Philip E., Moorestown, 418
Howard, Stanley E., Princeton, 418
Howe, Edward L., Princeton, 418
Howe, John C., Newark, 419
Howe, Samuel B., Cranberry Lake, Newark, 419
Howell, Benjamin F., Princeton, 419
Howell, Corwin, Maplewood, Newark, 419
Howell, Robert W., Trenton, 419
Howley, Bartholomew M., Highland Park, New Brunswick, 420
Hoy, Charles W., Glassboro, 420
Hubbard, Francis A., Maplewood, 421
Huber, Charles J., Ridgewood, Hoboken, 421
Huckin, LeRoy B., Englewood, 422
Hudson, Hoyt H., Princeton, 422
Hughes, Frederic J., Plainfield, 423
Hughes, Harold L., Plainfield, 423
Hughes, Howard L., Trenton, 423
Hughes, John V., Passaic, 423
Hughes, Percy, Belvidere, 423
Hulett, George A., Princeton, 424
Hull, Lewis M., Boonton, 424
Hullinger, Edwin W., Atlantic Highlands, 425
Hulsart, John, Manasquan, 425
Humes, Ralph H., Shrewsbury, 425
Hummel, Ernest G., Camden, 425
Hummer, Harry D., Bordentown, 425
Humphrey, Harold P., Washington, 426
Hun, John G., Princeton, 426
Hungerford, Churchill, Sr., Wenonah, Clayton, 426
Hunsaker, Herbert C., Newark, 426
Hunt, Harriet L., Summit, 427
Hunt, Theodore B., Metuchen, 427
Hunt, William S., South Orange, Newark, 427
Hunter, Arthur, Montclair, 427
Hunter, James G., Orange, 428
Hunter, Joseph, Bloomfield, 428
Huntsman, Robert F. R., Plainfield, 429

Hurtzig, William G., Morristown, 429
Hurwitz, Max Z., Jersey City, Hoboken, 429
Husselton, Thomas L., Atlantic City, 429
Huston, McCready, Keswick Grove, 429
Hutchinson, Charles P., Trenton, 430
Hutchison, Charles E., East Orange, 430
Hutson, Frederick L., Princeton, 430
Hyatt, Harriet R., Princeton, 431
Hyatt, Ralph W., Short Hills, Newark, 431
Hyde, Louis K., Plainfield, 431
Iams, Samuel H., Princeton, 431
Ill, Edward J., Newark, 432
Imbrie, Andrew C., Princeton, 432
Inch, Sydney R., South Orange, 432
Ingebritsen, Otis C., Montclair, 433
Ingersoll, William H., Maplewood, 433
Ingham, John A., Leonia, 433
Ingmanson, John H., Rahway, 433
Ingram, William A., High Bridge, 433
Ireland, Clarence E., Rochelle Park, Jersey City, 434
Irvin, Robert R., Bloomfield, Belleville, 434
Irwin, James B., Belleville, 434
Irwin, Robert B., Upper Montclair, 435
Ittner, Martin H., Jersey City, 435
Ives, Herbert E., Montclair, 435
Ivins, Haddon, Englewood, Union City, 436
Jack, Horace W., Haddonfield, Camden, 436
Jackson, Frederick J. F., Englewood, 437
Jackson, Frederick W., Summit, 437
Jackson, Halliday R., Salem, 437
Jackson, Harold P., Montclair, Newark, 437
Jackson, Ralph G., Woodbury, 438
Jacobs, Harry S., Newark, 438
Jacobs, Max, Hampton, 439
Jacobson, Lewis S., Woodbridge, Perth Amboy, 439
Jacobus, David D., Bernardsville, Hoboken, 439
Jacobus, David S., Montclair, 439
Jacobus, George R., Ridgewood, 439
Jaeger, Hans, Princeton, 440
Jagels, Claus H. C., Summit, Hoboken, 440
Jameson, Robert W., Jersey City, 441
Jamieson, Crawford, Trenton, Princeton, 441
Janes, Robert B., Rutherford, Harrison, 441
Jannelli, Vincent, Newark, 441
Jarrett, Cora N., Princeton, 442
Jeffers, Henry W., Plainsboro, 442
Jeffers, Horace C., Morristown, 442
Jeffery, Frank M., Ocean Grove, 442
Jeffery, Oscar W., Englewood, 442
Jencks, Millard W., Upper Montclair, 443
Jenks, Josephine, Morristown, 444
Jepsen, Glenn L., Princeton, 444
Jewett, Fannie F., Short Hills, 445
Jewett, Frank B., Short Hills, 445
Johnsen, Sigurd W., Montclair, Passaic, 445
Johnson, Albert R., New Brunswick, 445
Johnson, Allan J., Princeton, 446
Johnson, Eldridge R., Moorestown, Camden, 447
Johnson, Helgi, New Brunswick, 448
Johnson, John B., Maplewood, 448
Johnson, Kate B., Trenton, 448
Johnson, Laurence B., East Orange, Newark, 448
Johnson, Lewis H., Madison, 449
Johnson, Norman G., Wenonah, Gibbstown, 449
Johnson, Robert W., Princeton, New Brunswick, 449
Johnson, William H., Princeton, 450
Johnston, Emma L., Paterson, Campgaw, 450
Johnston, Henry R., Essex Fells, 450
Johnston, John, Short Hills, 450
Johnston, John H., Highland Park, 450
Johnston, Lemuel R., East Orange, 450
Johnston, Percy H., Montclair, 450

Johnstone, S. Paul, Westfield, 450
Johnstone, Edward L., Woodbine, 451
Johnstone, Edward R., Vineland, 451
Johnstone, Henry W., Short Hills, Rahway, 451
Jones, Charles S., Newark, 452
Jones, Frank C., Montclair, Passaic, 452
Jones, Franklin T., Madison, 452
Jones, H. Ennis, Merchantville, 453
Jones, Loren F., Camden, 454
Jones, Mark M., Princeton, 454
Jones, Paul R., Palmyra, 454
Jones, Reginald L., Summit, 454
Jones, Thomas R., Summit, Elizabeth, 455
Joy, James R., Plainfield, 456
Judge, William J., Montclair, 456
Kagan, Louis R., Jersey City, 457
Kahler, Hugh M., Princeton, 457
Kalichevsky, Vladimir A., Woodbury, 457
Kaliski, Jesse, Jersey City, 457
Kaltman, David L., Englewood, Jersey City, 457
Kappes, Charles W., Union City, 459
Karcher, Joseph T., Sayreville, 459
Katz, Daniel, Princeton, 459
Katzenbach, G. A., Trenton, 459
Kaufman, Anton, Newark, 459
Kaufman, Reuben, Paterson, 460
Kaufman, Samuel, Newark, 460
Kaufmann, Helen L., Hampton, 460
Kays, Henry T., Newton, 460
Kean, Hamilton F., Ursino, 460
Kearns, William J., Newark, 461
Keffer, Frances A., Hillsdale, 462
Kehoe, Arthur H., Ridgewood, 462
Keim, George de B., Edgewater Park, 462
Kelcey, Guy, Westfield, 463
Keller, Harry H., Ventnor, 463
Keller, Henry, Jr., New Brunswick, 463
Kelley, James F., South Orange, 464
Kelly, Mervin J., Short Hills, 466
Kelsey, Frederick T., South Orange, 466
Kemmerer, Edwin W., Princeton, 466
Kemmerer, John L., Short Hills, Jersey City, 466
Kemp, Archie B., Westwood, 467
Kemp, Hal, Dover, 467
Kennedy, Charles W., Princeton, 467
Kennedy, Paul S., Glen Ridge, Newark, 468
Kennedy, R. Lewis, Bayonne, 468
Kennel, Louis, Dumont, North Bergen, 468
Kenney, John A., Montclair, Newark, 468
Kern, Howard L., Newark, 470
Kerney, James, Jr., Trenton, 470
Kerr, Wilbur F., Princeton, 470
Kessler, Henry H., Newark, 470
Kidde, Walter, Montclair, 471
Kieb, Ormonde A., Maplewood, Newark, 472
Kilduffe, Robert A., Margate, Atlantic City, 472
Kiley, Moses E., Trenton, 472
Killian, John A., Englewood, 472
Killian, John C., Trenton, 473
Kilmer, Aline, Stillwater, 473
Kim, Gay B., Paterson, 473
Kind, Paul A., Audubon, Camden, 473
King, Charles D., Summit, 474
King, Robert W., Short Hills, 475
King, Victor L., Bound Brook, 475
King, Willard V., Convent, 475
Kingdon, Frank, West Orange, Newark, 475
Kingman, Russell B., Orange, West Orange, 475
Kingsbury, Edwin F., Rutherford, 475
Kingsbury, Franklin L., Fair Haven, 475
Kinkead, Eugene F., South Orange, 475
Kinsley, Carl, Plainfield, 476
Kip, Frederic E., Montclair, 476
Kipp, Walter A., Rutherford, 476
Kirby, Allan P., Convent, Jersey City, 476
Kircher, Edward A., Plainfield, 477
Kircher, Ellis C., Oaklyn, Camden, 477
Kirk, James T., Elizabeth, 477
Kirk, William, Pennsgrove, 477

Kirkpatrick, Martin G., Collingswood, 478
Kirkpatrick, Sidney D., Millburn, 478
Kirkwood, Maclean, Towaco, 478
Kiryen, Frank D., Glen Ridge, 478
Kissam, Philip, Princeton, 478
Kitson, Arthur, Jr., Margate City, 478
Kittredge, Arthur E., Audubon, 479
Klain, Zora, Stelton, 479
Klarmann, Emil G., Bloomfield, 479
Klausner, David M., Jersey City, 479
Klein, Jacob M., Perth Amboy, 480
Kline, Burton, Westfield, 480
Kline, Earl K., Madison, 480
Klosky, Simon, New Brunswick, Newark, 481
Klosterman, Julius A., Bogota, 481
Klotz, John R. M., Montclair, 481
Kluge, Albert C., Pompton Lakes, 482
Knevels, Gertrude, West Orange, 482
Kniffin, Herbert R., New Brunswick, 482
Knight, Augustus S., Far Hills, 482
Knowlton, Daniel C., Montclair, 483
Knox, Samuel L. G., Englewood, 484
Knox, Stuart K., Montclair, 484
Koch, Frank, Arlington, 484
Kocher, Edward H., Boonton, 484
Kohman, Girard T., Summit, 485
Kollmorgen, Frederick L. G., Mountain Lakes, 486
Konvitz, Joseph, Newark, 486
Konvitz, Milton R., Newark, 486
Koons, Tilghman B., Plainfield, 486
Koop, William H., Essex Fells, 487
Koopman, John R., Denville, 487
Korb, Robert T., Audubon, 487
Kraemer, Joseph, Newark, 488
Kraemer, Manfred, Newark, 488
Krehbiel, Otto F., Shrewsbury, Red Bank, 489
Kreutzinger, Edmund P., Montclair, Clifton, 490
Kristeller, Lionel P., Newark, 491
Krueger, Wabun C., Dayton, 491
Kruse, William C., Jr., South Orange, Newark, 492
Kuhn, C. John, Upper Montclair, 492
Kuizenga, John E., Princeton, 492
Kull, Irving S., Highland Park, New Brunswick, 492
Kummel, Henry B., Trenton, 493
Kunkel, Louis O., Princeton, 493
Kurth, Wilfred, Ridgewood, 493
Kussy, Nathan, East Orange, Newark, 494
Labatut, Jean, Princeton, 494
Labrecque, Theodore J., Red Bank, 494
Ladenburg, Rudolf W., Princeton, 495
Lamb, Charles R., Cresskill, 497
Lamb, Ella C., Cresskill, 497
Lamb, Karl B., Tenafly, 497
Lambdin, Henry L., Summit, 497
Lambert, Gerard B., Princeton, 497
La Mer, Victor K., Leonia, 498
Lamme, Maurice A., Maplewood, 498
Lamont, William H. F., New Brunswick, 498
Lanahan, Henry, Short Hills, West Orange, 498
Landau, Hyman J., Orange, 499
Landers, Howe S., Glen Ridge, Newark, 499
Landes, William S., East Orange, Newark, 499
Lane, Robert R., Summit, Newark, 499
Lang, Leon S., Newark, 500
Langfeld, Herbert S., Princeton, 500
Langmuir, Dean, Englewood, 500
Lankard, Frank G., Madison, 501
Lardner, Henry A., Montclair, 501
Larrabee, Albert S., Lakewood, 501
La Rue, Edwin D., Verona, Montclair, 502
La Salle, Dorothy M., East Orange, 502
Lasser, Aaron, Maplewood, Newark, 502
Lasser, Jacob K., South Orange, 502
Latham, Harold S., Arlington, 502
Laughlin, Ledlie I., Princeton, 503
Law, Harrison, Nutley, 503
Lawrence, Charles L., Linden, 504
Lawrence, Joseph S., Newton, 504
Lawrence, Josephine, Newark, 504
Lawson, Evald B., East Orange, 505
Lawson, Octo G., Madison, 505

NEW JERSEY

Lawson, Walter E., Woodbury, Gibbstown, 505
Leander, Hugo A., Short Hills, 506
Leary, Lewis G., West Milford, 506
Leber, Charles T., Upper Montclair, 506
Lebson, Abram A., Englewood, 506
Lee, Elsworth M., Paterson, 507
Lee, Henry, Hopatcong, 507
Lee, James A., East Orange, 507
Lee, John, Nutley, 507
Lee, Linwood L., New Brunswick, 508
Lefevre, Edwin, Atlantic City, 509
Lefschetz, Solomon, Princeton, 509
Legg, Clarence A., Newark, Fair Haven, 509
Leich, Chester, Leonia, 510
Leichter, Walter, Weehawken, Union City, 510
Leiper, Henry S., Leonia, 510
Leitch, Alexander, Princeton, 511
Leman, G. W., Bogota, 511
Lenfestey, Nathan C., Summit, 511
Lent, Frederick, East Orange, 512
Lentz, Maxwell J., Clifton, Passaic, 512
Lenz, Charles O., Newark, 512
Leonard, Lester C., Little Silver, Red Bank, 512
Lerrigo, Peter H. J., Summit, 513
Leubuscher, Frederic C., Essex Fells, 514
Leuthauser, Theodore C., Newark, 514
Levenson, Joseph, Woodbine, 514
Levin, Louis, Trenton, 515
Levine, Joseph, Plainfield, 515
Levine, Philip, Newark, 515
Levine, William, Newark, 515
Levinsohn, Sandor A., Paterson, 515
Lewin, William, Newark, 516
Lewis, Allen, Basking Ridge, 516
Lewis, Arthur W., Riverton, Camden, 516
Lewis, Burdette G., Princeton, 516
Lewis, Edwin, Madison, 517
Lewis, George F., Essex Fells, 517
Lewis, Harry L., Westfield, Elizabeth, 518
Lewis, Harry J., Belmar, 518
Lewis, Marion L., Nutley, 518
Lewis, Vivian M., Paterson, 519
Lichtenthal, Daniel, Riverside, 520
Liddell, Donald M., Elizabeth, 520
Lieberman, Abraham, Weehawken, Union City, 520.
Lieblich, Joseph T., Paterson, 520
Lilly, Edwin B., Ridgewood, 521
Lincoln, Charles M., Montclair, 521
Lindback, Christian R., Ventnor, 522
Lindeman, Eduard C., High Bridge, 522
Lindquist, Raymond I., Orange, 522
Linson, Corwin N., Atlantic Highlands, 523
Linton, Morris A., Moorestown, 523
Lippitt, Walter O., Westwood, 524
Littauer, Kalman, Union City, 524
Littel, Charles L., Teaneck, 524
Litter, David H., South Orange, 524
Little, E. H., Jersey City, 524
Little, Ernest, Highland Park, Newark, 524
Little, Marou B., Rahway, 525
Littledale, Clara S., Short Hills, 525
Liva, Paolo F., Lyndhurst, 525
Livengood, Horace R., Elizabeth, 525
Livingston, Herman, Plainfield, Elizabeth, 526
Llewellyn, Frederick B., Montclair, 526
Lloyd, Frank T., Merchantville, Camden, 526
Lloyd, Frank T., Jr., Merchantville, Camden, 526
Lobeck, Armin K., Englewood, 527
Loblein, Eldon L., New Brunswick, Bay Head, Point Pleasant, 527
Lockhart, Henry, Jr., Camden, 527
Lockwood, Charlotte M., Murray Hill, 528
Loetscher, Frederick W., Princeton, 528
Loizeaux, Charles E., Plainfield, 529
Lomax, Paul S., Maplewood, 529
London, William, Perth Amboy, 529
Loomis, Nathaniel E., Westfield, 531
Loomis, Ruth, Lakewood, 531
Lord, Edward T. S., Glen Ridge, 532
Lord, Edwin B., Arlington, Jersey City, 532
Lord, Ernest A., Northfield, Atlantic City, 532

Lord, William A., Maplewood, Newark, Orange, 532
Loree, Leonor F., West Orange, 532
Losche, George F., Teaneck, Hackensack, 532
Loser, Paul, Trenton, 532
Lotka, Alfred J., Red Bank, 532
Lott, Leigh M., Bridgeton, 532
Lotte, Charles W., Paterson, 533
Loud, Frederick E., Collingswood, 533
Loutrel, Cyrus H., South Orange, Newark, 533
Loveland, Henry M., Bridgeton, 534
Lovell, Earl B., Montclair, 534
Lovell, Ralph L., Cranford, 534
Lowe, Boutelle E., Hasbrouck Heights, 534
Lowe, Elias A., Princeton, 534
Lowrie, Walter, Princeton, 535
Lowry, Oscar R., West Orange, 535
Lowy, Harry P., Newark, 535
Lucas, Francis F., East Orange, 536
Lucas, William A., Elizabeth, 536
Lucioni, Luigi, Union City, 536
Ludlow, Theodore R., South Orange, Orange, 536
Ludlow, William O., Madison, Summit, 536
Luftman, Harry I., Hillside, Newark, 537
Lum, George V., Chatham, Summit, 537
Lum, Hermann A., Haddonfield, 537
Lum, Ralph E., Chatham, Newark, 537
Lunas, Lawrence J., Verona, Newark, 538
Luscombe, Albert P., Nutley, Belleville, 538
Lutz, Edwin G., Dumont, 538
Lutz, Frank E., Ramsey, 538
Lutz, Harley L., Princeton, 538
Lyford, Oliver S., Englewood, 539
Lynch, Charles F., Paterson, Newark, 539
Lyon, Adrian, Perth Amboy, 539
Lyon, Howard R., Somerville, 540
MacClintock, Paul, Princeton, 541
MacDonald, Harry B., Plainfield, 542
MacDowell, John L., Perth Amboy, 542
MacFadden, Bernarr, Newark, 542
Macfarland, Charles S., Mountain Lakes, 542
MacGinnis, Henry R., Trenton, 543
MacGregor, Lawrence J., Chatham, Summit, 543
Mackay, John A., Princeton, 544
Mackay, William A., Coytesville, 544
MacKellar, James M., Tenafly, 544
Mackenzie, Alastair St. C., Weehawken, 544
Mackenzie, Donald, Princeton, 544
Mackey, Richard J., Verona, Jersey City, 544
MacKinney, Paul R., Essex Fells, 545
MacLaren, Malcolm, Princeton, 545
MacMillan, Charles W., Montclair, 545
MacMillan, Edward A., Princeton, 545
Macpherson, Elwood H., Millburn, 546
Madden, John T., Orange, 546
Magee, Russell S., Audubon, 547
Mager, Gus, South Orange, 547
Magie, David, Princeton, 547
Maihl, Viola R., Elizabeth, Linden, 548
Major, James A., Maywood, Hackensack, 548
Major, Randolph T., Plainfield, Rahway, 548
Malcolm, Talbot M., Westfield, 549
Mallett, Daniel T., Hackensack, 549
Mallett, John P., Elizabeth, South Kearny, 549
Mallory, Clifford D., Jersey City, 550
Mallory, Virgil S., East Orange, 550
Malmar, Ruth M., Montclair, 550
Mancusi-Ungaro, Lodovico, Newark, 551
Mancusi-Ungaro, Themistocles, Newark, 551
Mann, Manley B., Boonton, 551
Marburg, Louis C., Montclair, 552
Margaretten, Morris, Perth Amboy, 553
Mark, Joseph S., Woodbridge, 554
Marlatt, Clyde D., Essex Fells, Newark, 554
Marquis, Dean W., Short Hills, East Orange, 555
Marquis, Sarah, Jamesburg, 555
Marsh, Anne S., Essex Fells, 555

Marsh, Theodore M., East Orange, Newark, 555
Marshall, Charles H., Short Hills, 556
Marshall, Edward W., Haddonfield, 556
Martin, Edgar S., East Orange, 558
Martin, Jay R., Yardville, 559
Martin, Kingsley L., Montclair, 559
Martin, LeRoy A., Madison, 559
Martin, Luther, 3d, Morristown, 559
Martin, Paul, Princeton, 559
Martin, William H., New Brunswick, 560
Martland, Harrison S., Newark, 560
Marts, Arnaud C., Plainfield, 560
Marvin, Dwight E., Summit, 560
Marvin, Walter S., Montclair, 560
Marvin, Walter T., New Brunswick, 560
Marx, Harry S., Ridgewood, 560
Marzulli, Olindo, Newark, 561
Mason, Alpheus T., Princeton, 561
Mason, Clarence E., Jr., Atlantic City, 561
Mason, James H., 3d, Atlantic City, 561
Mason, Lois M., Atlantic City, 561
Mason, Warren P., West Orange, 562
Massa, Frank, Audubon, Camden, 562
Mathews, Frank A., Jr., Riverton, Camden, 563
Matlock, Isaiah, Interlaken, Asbury Park, 563
Matte, Hubert P., Harrison, 564
Matthews, Frank E., Trenton, 564
Matthews, Fred E., Leonia, 564
Matthews, Paul, Princeton, 565
Matthews, William F., Montclair, 565
Matthews, William R., Princeton, 565
Matzal, Leopold C., Newark, 565
Maurer, Charles L., Camden, 565
Maurice, Arthur B., Elizabeth, 565
Maveety, Donald J., Millburn, 566
Maxcy, Charles J., Rutherford, 566
Maxfield, J. P., Madison, 566
Mayham, Ray E., Westfield, Newark, 567
McAfee, Joseph E., Summit, 568
McBride, William M., Passaic, 569
McCabe, David A., Princeton, 569
McCain, C. Curtice, East Orange, 570
McCarter, Robert H., Rumson, Newark, 571
McCarter, Thomas N., Rumson, Newark, 571
McCloy, John, Leonia, 573
McClure, Charles F. W., Princeton, 573
McClure, Grace L. J., Princeton, 573
McConathy, Osbourne, Glen Ridge, 574
McCormack, William J., West Orange, Orange, 575
McCormick, Howard, Leonia, 575
McCreary, Lewis W., East Orange, 577
McCurdy, Ralph G., Englewood, 578
McDonough, Andrew L., Plainfield, 579
McDonough, Roger H., New Brunswick, 580
McDouall, Leslie G., East Orange, Newark, 580
McDowell, Samuel J., Metuchen, Keasbey, 580
McElroy, George, Elizabeth, Trenton, 580
McFeely, Percy R., Bogota, 581
McGalliard, David C., Rutherford, 581
McGarvey, Robert J., Elizabeth, 581
McGovern, John F., Jr., New Brunswick, 582
McGowan, James, Jr., Beach Haven, Camden, 582
McGraw, James H., Jr., Madison, 583
McIntire, Carl, Collingswood, 584
McKenny, Luke M., East Orange, 585
McKenzie, Kenneth, Princeton, 586
McKinney, Howard D., New Brunswick, 586
McKinney, James F., Englewood, 586
Mclaughlin, Thomas H., Paterson, 587
McLean, Donald H., Hillside, Elizabeth, 587
McLellan, George A., East Orange, 587
McLellan, Roy D., Woodbridge, Perth Amboy, 588

McMahon, John R., Little Falls, 588
McManus, Ambrose, Elizabeth, 588
McMaster, John D., Jersey City, 588
McMillen, Wheeler, Hopewell, 588
McNaughton, John, Wanaque, Pompton Lakes, 589
McNicol, Donald M., Roselle Park, 590
McRae, George W., Maplewood, Newark, 590
McSpadden, Joseph W., Montclair, 590
Mead, Frank S., Chatham, 591
Meader, Stephen W., Moorestown, 591
Meder, Albert E., Jr., Westfield, New Brunswick, 592
Medsger, Oliver P., Arlington, 592
Meese, Alfred H., Little Falls, 592
Megargee, Edwin, Dunellen, 592
Meier, Mahlon M., Glen Ridge, Newark, 593
Meinzer, Martin S., Perth Amboy, 593
Meister, Walter F., Elizabeth, South Amboy, 594
Melcher, Frederic G., Montclair, 594
Meloney, Lester F., Clifton, 595
Menzies, Alan W. C., Princeton, 596
Merck, George W., West Orange, Rahway, 596
Meredith, Albert B., Cranford, 596
Meritt, Benjamin D., Princeton, 596
Merity, Howard E., South Orange, 597
Merrey, Edward F., Sr., Paterson, 597
Merrill, Earle A., Westfield, 597
Merritt, Carroll B., Madison, 597
Merz, August, East Orange, Bound Brook, 598
Meserole, Clinton V., Englewood, 598
Messick, Charles P., Trenton, 598
Mestice, Francis P., Newark, 598
Metz, Russell K., Hopewell, 599
Metzenheim, Henry H., Hillside, Newark, 599
Metzger, Fraser, New Brunswick, 599
Meyer, Henry C., Jr., Montclair, 600
Meyerson, Samuel C., South Orange, Dover, 600
Meyrowitz, Ernest duP., South Orange, 600
Middleton, Elliott, Montclair, 601
Middleton, Harry C., Moorestown, 601
Middleton, Melbourne F., Jr., Moorestown, 601
Middleton, William, Bloomfield, 601
Miessner, Benjamin F., Short Hills, Millburn, 601
Miller, Alten S., Princeton, 602
Miller, Anthony P. M., Pleasantville, Atlantic City, 602
Miller, Arthur B., Montclair, 602
Miller, Edmund F., Jersey City, 603
Miller, Edward F., Maywood, 603
Miller, Floyd L., Roselle Park, Elizabeth, 604
Miller, George J., Perth Amboy, 604
Miller, Gerald H., Cranbury, 604
Miller, John A., Glen Ridge, 606
Miller, John S., Rahway, Perth Amboy, 606
Miller, Norman C., New Brunswick, 607
Miller, Spencer, Jr., South Orange, 607
Miller, William A., Clifton, 608
Milligan, Charles H., Westfield, 608
Mills, Frederick C., Englewood, 609
Mills, Gail A., Princeton, 609
Mills, John, Maplewood, 609
Milnor, Joseph W., Maplewood, 609
Milstead, John O., Vineland, 610
Milton, John, Jersey City, 610
Minahan, Daniel F., Orange, Newark, 610
Minard, Duane E., Newark, 610
Mindnich, Frank C., Newark, 610
Missonellie, William, Hawthorne, 611
Mitchell, James A., Englewood, 611
Mitchell, William A., Millburn, 612
Mitrany, David, Princeton, 612
Moe, Alfred K., Elizabeth, 612
Moffat, Barclay W., Red Bank, 612
Moffett, Ernest C., Woodbridge, 613
Moffett, Louis B., Woodbury, 613

Molina, Edward C. D., East Orange, 613
Molitor, Hans, Elizabeth, Rahway, 613
Moment, John J., Plainfield, 614
Mones, Leon, Newark, 614
Monro, Hugh R., Montclair, 614
Monroe, Andrew P., Short Hills, Newark, 615
Moodie, William C., Montclair, 616
Moody, Lewis F., Princeton, 616
Mook, Charles C., Metuchen, 616
Mooney, Melvin, Lake Hiawatha, Passaic, 616
Moore, Arthur H., Jersey City, 616
Moore, Charles S., Atlantic City, 617
Moore, Edward T., Passaic, 617
Moore, Frank F., Woodlynne, 617
Moore, Franklin F., Trenton, 617
Moore, George R., Manasquan, Asbury Park, 617
Moore, Harry W., Flemington, 617
Moore, Ira C., Jr., Millburn, Newark, 617
Moore, Perry M., East Orange, Bloomfield, 618
Moore, Ralph L., Woodbury, 618
Moore, William G., Haddonfield, Camden, 619
Moorfield, Amelia B., Newark, Nutley, 619
Morales, Franklin E., Toms River, 619
Moran, Léon, Plainfield, 619
Moreau, Charles E., Bloomfield, 619
Moreau, Daniel H., Flemington, 619
Morehouse, Lyman F., Montclair, 620
Morey, Charles R., Princeton, 620
Morgan, Alfred P., Upper Montclair, 620
Morgan, Carl H., Haddonfield, 621
Morgan, Jerome J., Maplewood, 621
Morgan, John D., South Orange, 621
Morgan, Ora S., Leonia, 621
Morgan, Sherley W., Princeton, 622
Morgan, Tali E., Asbury Park, 622
Morgan, William L., Newark, Brielle, 622
Moroso, John A., Cresskill, 622
Morrell, Joseph A., New Brunswick, 622
Morris, Edward A., Trenton, 623
Morris, George F., Shrewsbury, 623
Morris, Robert H., Haddonfield, 624
Morrison, Caldwell, Newark, 625
Morrison, Robert H., Trenton, 625
Morrow, Mrs. Dwight W., Englewood, 625
Morse, Alfred H. C., Jersey City, 626
Morse, Anson E., Princeton, 626
Morse, David A., Far Hills, Newark, 626
Morse, Gilbert L., Montclair, 626
Morton, James F., Paterson, 626
Morvay, Leonard S., Newark, 627
Moss, Harry J., East Orange, 627
Moss, Randolph M., East Orange, 627
Mott, Joseph W., Atlantic City, 628
Mott, William E., Burlington, 628
Mount, Walter B., Montclair, 628
Mueller, Carl F., Montclair, 629
Muir, Malcolm, Short Hills, 630
Munn, Wilbur, Orange, 632
Munn, William F., West Orange, 632
Munro, Dana G., Princeton, 632
Munsick, Donald B., Maplewood, Newark, 632
Murdock, George J., Newark, 632
Murphy, Ray D., Upper Montclair, see Addenda
Murray, Albert F., Haddonfield, 633
Murray, C. Edward, Jr., Princeton, Trenton, 633
Murray, George W., Newark, 634
Murray, Harold A., Newark, 634
Murray, Sister Teresa Gertrude, Elizabeth, 634
Murray, William D., Plainfield, 634
Musgrove, Eugene R., East Orange, Newark, 635
Musser, Benjamin F. B., Atlantic City, 635
Muta, Samuel A., West Orange, 636
Myatt, Leslie E., Bridgeton, 636
Myers, Charles A., Englewood, Bayonne, 636
Myers, Chester G., Sparta, 636
Myers, Frank C., Caldwell, 637
Myers, Lanning, Wildwood, 637
Myers, William S., Princeton, 637
Nadell, Harry, Montclair, Paterson, 638
Nadworney, Devora, Bayonne, 638

Nary, Thomas D., Sea Girt, Asbury Park, 638
Naylor, John A., Matawan, 638
Nearing, Scott, Ridgewood, 639
Neeser, Robert W., Rumson, 639
Neff, Elmer H., Montclair, 639
Nelden, Robert J., Paterson, 640
Nelson, Alexander H., Atlantic City, 640
Nelson, Cyril A., New Brunswick, 640
Nelson, George C. E., Ridgewood, 641
Nelson, John B., Princeton, 641
Nelson, Mrs. William S., Orange, 642
Neubauer, Frank N., Westfield, 642
Neulen, Leon N., Woodbury, Camden, 642
Neuscheler, Albert W., Newark, 643
Newcomb, Bryant B., Long Branch, 643
Newell, Sara M., Atlantic City, 643
Newkirk, Samuel F., Jr., Elizabeth, 644
Newman, Jacob L., Newark, 644
Newman, Jarvis E., Belmar, Asbury Park, 644
Newton, John E., Highland Park, 645
Nichols, Charles W., West Orange, 645
Nichols, Isabel M., Atlantic City, 645
Nicholson, Kenyon, Stockton, 646
Nicol, Alexander R., Summit, 646
Niedermeyer, Frederick D., Perth Amboy, 647
Nims, Albert A., Bloomfield, Newark, 647
Nixon, Lewis, Nixon, 648
Noble, G. Kingsley, Englewood, 648
Nordgaard, Martin A., East Orange, 650
North, Charles E., Montclair, 650
North, Eric M., Summit, 650
Northey, F. H., Bound Brook, 651
Northrop, John H., Princeton, 651
Northrup, Edwin F., Princeton, Trenton, 651
Northwood, Arthur, Newark, 651
Norton, Mary T., Jersey City, 651
Novotny, Joseph, East Orange, 652
Noyes, Morgan P., Upper Montclair, 652
Nugent, Albert W., Newark, 653
Nugent, Barbara B., Newark, 653
Nugent, James A., Jersey City, 653
Nunn, William L., Newark, Radburn, 653
Nutt, Arthur, Upper Monclair, Paterson, 653
Nyiri, William A., Newark, 653
Oberholser, Robert M., Bordentown, 654
Obert, Josiah E., New Egypt, 655
O'Brien, Charles F., Jersey City, 655
O'Brien, J. Charles, Maplewood, South Orange, 655
O'Brien, Patrick M., Morristown, Newark, 655
O'Brien, Seumas, Glen Ridge, 655
O'Brien, Thomas G., Jersey City, 655
O'Brien, William A., Jersey City, 655
Ockford, John W., Ridgewood, Jersey City, 656
O'Connor, Dennis F., South Orange, Newark, 656
O'Connor, Johnson, Hoboken, 656
O'Connor, Maurice E., Belleville, 656
Odlum, Floyd E., Jersey City, 656
O'Donnell, Stewart H., Trenton, 657
Oesterle, Eric A., Collingswood, 657
Ogburn, Sihon C., Jr., Westfield, 657
O'Gorman, William D., Montclair, Newark, 658
O'Hanlon, Edward P., Madison, 658
Okin, Irving, Passaic, 659
Olinger, Nathaniel A., Bloomfield, 659
Oliphant, A. Dayton, Princeton, Trenton, 659
Olson, Harry F., Haddon Heights, Camden, 660
Olson, Karl J., East Orange, 660
Onderdonk, John C., Jr., Englewood, Newark, 661
O'Neill, Edward L., Newark, 661
O'Neill, James L., Short Hills, 661
Orbe, Lorenzo F., Passaic, Clifton, 661
Orben, C. Milford, Millburn, Newark, 661

Orchard, William J., Maplewood, Belleville, 661
Orcutt, Daniel P., Plainfield, 661
Orcutt, Louis E., Demarest, 661
Orelup, John W., Short Hills, Jersey City, 661
Ormsby, Alexander F., Jersey City, 662
Osborn, Albert S., Montclair, 662
Osborn, George A., New Brunswick, 662
Osborne, Harold S., Upper Montclair, 663
Osborne, William H., Newark, 663
Osgood, Charles G., Princeton, 663
Pacsu, Eugene, Princeton, 666
Paine, Harold W., Upper Montclair, Arlington, 666
Palmer, Albert R., Madison, 667
Palmer, Avery R., Ridgefield Park, 667
Palmer, Dwight R. G., South Orange, 667
Palmer, Edgar, Princeton, 667
Palmer, V. Claude, Mount Holly, 668
Panofsky, Erwin, Princeton, 668
Pantaleone, Joseph, Trenton, 668
Paquin, Samuel S., Teaneck, 668
Parker, Charles W., Morristown, 669
Parker, Henry G., New Brunswick, 670
Parker, Terry, East Orange, 670
Parkin, Francis R., Bound Brook, 670
Parr, Joseph G., Englewood, Jersey City, 671
Parrish, Herbert, New Brunswick, 671
Parrish, Morris L., Pine Valley, 671
Parrot, Raymond T., Summit, Elizabeth, 671
Parrott, Thomas M., Lawrenceville, 671
Parson, Hubert T., West End, 671
Parsons, Theodore D., Little Silver, Red Bank, 672
Partch, Clarence E., Stelton, 672
Patch, James B., Millville, 672
Paterson, John, Madison, 672
Paterson, Robert, Newark, 672
Paton, William K., Paterson, 673
Patrick, W. Burton, Orange, 673
Patterson, Edwin W., Leonia, 673
Patterson, Frank A., Palisades Park, 673
Patterson, John R., Short Hills, Millburn, 674
Paul, Alice, Moorestown, 675
Paul, Joseph C., South Orange, Newark, 675
Paul, Sarah W., Summit, 675
Payne, Elizabeth S., East Orange, 676
Peacock, Robert, Brigantine, Mount Holly, 676
Pearce, Charles S., Jersey City, 676
Pearce, Henry A., West Orange, 677
Pearce, Louise, Princeton, 677
Pearson, Peter H., East Orange, 678
Pease, Lucius C., Maplewood, Newark, 678
Peaslee, Amos J., Clarksboro, Mantoloking, 678
Pedersen, Robert H., Orange, 678
Peer, Alfred J., Newark, 679
Peet, Gerald D., Montclair, Belleville, 679
Penfield, Thornton B., Englewood, 680
Penn, Marion, South Orange, Newark, 681
Perham, Roy G., Hasbrouck Heights, 682
Perham, Roy G., Jr., Hasbrouck Heights, 682
Perkins, Kenneth, Atlantic Highlands, 682
Perkins, William R., Upper Montclair, 682
Perlman, Samuel, Bayonne, 683
Perrine, Van Dearing, Maplewood, 683
Perry, Arthur L., Rahway, 683
Perry, Lawrence, Glen Ridge, 683
Perry, Thomas D., Moorestown, 684
Perskie, Joseph B., Atlantic City, 684
Petry, Walter B., Trenton, 685
Pettersen, Anton L., Passaic, 685
Petty, Nelson L., Trenton, 686
Pfister, Joseph C., Newark, 687
Phelps, John J., Hackensack, 687
Phillips, Alexander R., Montclair, 688
Phillips, Ethel C., Nutley, 688

Phillips, George W. M., Elizabeth, 688
Phillips, Irene C., Nutley, 689
Phillips, Mary C., Washington, 689
Pickering, David B., East Orange, 690
Pierce, Clay A., Rumson, 690
Pierce, Edward L., Princeton, 690
Pierson, Delavan L., Montclair, 691
Pierson, Ellis L., Pennington, Trenton, 691
Pierson, John D., Weehawken, Hoboken, 691
Pigott, Albert W., Skillman, 691
Pike, Wilbert V., Haddonfield, Camden, 692
Pilling, Norman B., Westfield, Bayonne, 692
Pistor, George E. J., Upper Montclair, 693
Pitkin, Walter B., Dover, 694
Pitman, Earle C., Red Bank, Parlin, 694
Pitney, Shelton, Morristown, Newark, 694
Platt, John, Westfield, 695
Plumer, Richard C., East Orange, Newark, 695
Plympton, Frank B., Hackensack, 696
Plympton, George F., Hackensack, 696
Poe, John P., Princeton, 696
Polowe, David, Paterson, 697
Pomeroy, Daniel E., Englewood, 697
Pond, James B., Denville, 697
Pons, Carlos A., Allenhurst, Asbury Park, 697
Poole, DeWitt C., Princeton, 697
Pooley, Joseph E., Madison, 698
Poore, Henry R., Orange, 698
Pope, Bentley H., Newark, 698
Pope, Clifford H., Chatham, 698
Pope, Frederick A., Somerville, 698
Porter, Henry J., Montclair, Newark, 698
Porter, James M., Montclair, Newark, 699
Porter, Newton H., Montclair, 699
Porter, William S., Summit, 699
Ports, Earl G., Livingston, Newark, 699
Post, Claude C., Butler, 699
Post, Robert C., Englewood, 700
Post, William S., Bernardsville, 700
Potter, Benjamin P., Teaneck, Jersey City, 700
Potter, Ellen C., Trenton, 700
Potter, Francis M., Metuchen, 700
Potter, Maurice A., Long Branch, 700
Potter, Philip A., Hohokus, 700
Potter, Pitman B., Long Branch, 700
Potter, Raymond T., East Orange, 701
Potter, Thomas P., Teaneck, 701
Powell, Alvin L., Glen Ridge, 701
Powell, Lyman P., Mountain Lakes, 701
Powell, Richard R. B., Englewood, 702
Power, Archie D., Caldwell, Harrison, 702
Power, Florence D. S., Caldwell, 702
Powers, David L., Trenton, 702
Powers, Donald H., Moorestown, 702
Powers, Mary S., Tenafly, 702
Powers, Walter P., Ampere, Sparta, Spring Lake, 702
Pratt Arthur H., South Orange, Newark, 703
Pratt, Auguste G., Englewood, 703
Pratt, Carroll C., New Brunswick, 703
Pratt, Frank R., New Brunswick, 703
Pratt, Henry B., Hackensack, 703
Prentice, William K., Princeton, 704
Prescott, Amos N., Passaic, 704
Preston, Frances F., Princeton, 704
Price, Miles O., Leonia, 705
Price, Thomas B., Morristown, 705
Price, Winfield S., Camden, 705
Priest, George M., Princeton, 706
Prince, Arthur L., New Brunswick, 706
Prince, John D., Ringwood Manor, 706
Probst, Everett W., Rutherford, Arlington, 707
Proctor, George N., Verona, 707
Proctor, Haydn, Asbury Park, 707
Proctor, James W., Tenafly, 707
Prosser, Seward, Englewood, 707
Pulsifer, Lawson V., Kearny, 708

Pyle, Wallace, Orange, Jersey City, 709
Quigley, Margery C., Montclair, 709
Quinn, George E., Bogota, 710
Quinn, John J., Rahway, 710
Quinn, John J., Red Bank, 710
Rabe, Rudolph F., Basking Ridge, 710
Rachlin, Israel J., South Orange, Newark, 710
Radcliffe, Amos H., Paterson, 710
Raisin, Max, Paterson, 711
Rake, Geoffrey W., Kingston, New Brunswick, 711
Ramsey, Will W., Perth Amboy, 712
Randolph, Corliss Fitz, Maplewood, 713
Ranger, Richard H., Newark, 714
Ranken, Howard B., Cranford, 714
Rankin, Edward S., Glen Ridge, Newark, 714
Rankin, Walter M., Princeton, 714
Ranson, Marius, Orange, East Orange, 714
Rapalje, de Witt, Plainfield, 714
Rapelje, Walter S., Jersey City, 715
Rathbone, Henry B., Newark, 715
Raul, Josephine G., East Orange, 716
Rautenstrauch, Walter, Palisade, 716
Raven, John H., New Brunswick, 716
Ray, G. J., Summit, 716
Ray, Harold, Trenton, 717
Raycroft, Joseph E., Princeton, 717
Read, William T., New Brunswick, 717
Rearick, Allan C., Summit, 717
Rector, Thomas M., Morristown, Hoboken, 718
Redman, Lawrence V., Caldwell, Bloomfield, 718
Reed, Donald W., New Brunswick, 719
Reed, Henry D., East Orange, 719
Reed, Louis F., Orange, 719
Reed, Rufus O., Upper Montclair, 720
Rees, Albert H., Lawrenceville, Trenton, 720
Reese, Mitchell, Trenton, 721
Reeve, Charles S., Leonia, Edgewater, 721
Reeve, Irving S., Englewood, 721
Reeves, Hugh L., Bridgeton, 722
Reeves, John M., Summit, 722
Reger, John F., Somerville, 722
Regestein, Walter P., Penns Grove, 722
Reich, Henry, Newark, 723
Reich, Jerome J., Hillside, 723
Reichard, Gladys A., Grantwood, 723
Reid, A. Duncan, Montclair, 723
Reilly, William B., Newark, 724
Reimold, Abraham G. H., Orange, Harrison, 725
Reinfeld, Abraham G., Newark, 725
Remer, Daniel F., Mt. Holly, 725
Remsen, Gerard T., Upper Montclair, 726
Rentschler, Harvey C., East Orange, 726
Reoch, Alexander E., South Orange, 726
Replogle, Delbert E., Ridgewood, Paterson, 726
Rescigno, Peter J., Paterson, 726
Reussille, Leon, Jr., Red Bank, 727
Revere, Clinton T., Westfield, 727
Reynard, Grant, Leonia, 727
Reynolds, Charles B., Mountain Lakes, 727
Reynolds, Charles L., Newark, 727
Reynolds, Samuel R. M., Cranford, 728
Reynolds, William W., Haddonfield, 728
Reznikoff, Elias J., Long Branch, 728
Rhoads, Samuel N., Haddonfield, 729
Rhodes, Edward E., Newark, 729
Rhodes, George I., Glen Ridge, 729
Rich, Stephen G., Verona, 730
Richards, Charles G., Verona, 731
Richards, Emerson L., Atlantic City, 731
Richards, Samuel H., Haddonfield, Camden, 732
Richardson, Charles A., Closter, 732
Richardson, Ernest C., Princeton, 732
Richardson, George P., Maplewood, Newark, 733
Richardson, Marion B., Livingston, 733
Richardson, Willard S., Montclair, 733

Richardson, William P., Morristown, 733
Rickaby, Mary W., Paterson, 734
Riddle, Malcolm G., Ventnor, Atlantic City, 734
Ridgeway, William W., Camden, 735
Ridgway, S. Paul, Atlantic City, 735
Riefler, Winfield W., Princeton, 735
Rieman, Aloysius P., Jersey City, 735
Riggins, John A., Haddonfield, Camden, 736
Riley, Mark R., Maplewood, Orange, 737
Riley, Russell W., Trenton, 737
Rimkufsky, Benjamin A., Atlantic City, 737
Rinear, Earl H., Highland Park, New Brunswick, 737
Ringold, James, Trenton, 737
Rinkenbach, William H., Dover, 737
Riordan, Joseph A., Harrison, 737
Ripley, Edward W., Montclair, 738
Rippel, Julius S., Newark, 738
Ripps, A. V., Bayonne, 738
Ritchie, John W., Flemington, 738
Ritter, William H., Jr., Bridgeton, 738
Robb, Hunter, Burlington, 739
Robbins, Charles D., Maplewood, Newark, 739
Robbins, Edmund Y., Princeton, 739
Robbins, Leonard H., Montclair, 740
Roberts, Austin L., Cranford, Jersey City, 740
Roberts, E. Weston, Wyoming, 740
Roberts, Edward H., Princeton, 740
Roberts, Helen F., Irvington, Bayonne, 740
Roberts, Kate L., South Orange, 741
Roberts, Newell W., South Orange, 741
Robertson, Campbell, Roselle, Perth Amboy, 741
Robertson, Frank A., Washington, 742
Robertson, W. Spencer, Madison, 742
Robie, Theodore R., Montclair, East Orange, 743
Robinson, Chalfant, Princeton, 743
Robinson, Edward M., Convent, 744
Robinson, Edwin A., Chatham, Harrison, 744
Robinson, Lindsay E., Newark, 745
Robinson, Stewart M., Elizabeth, 746
Robison, Samuel S., Tom's River, 746
Rockwell, Frederick F., Ridgefield, 746
Rockwell, William L., East Orange, 747
Rodes, Lester A., South River, 747
Roe, John J., North Bergen, 748
Roebling, Ferdinand W., III, Trenton, 748
Roeder, Arthur, Short Hills, 748
Roemer, Charles H., Paterson, 748
Rogan, Fred L., Montclair, 748
Rogers, Charles I., Princeton, 748
Rogers, Harry L., Riverton, 749
Rogers, Harvey E., Trenton, Hamilton Square, 749
Rogers, Lawrence H., Trenton, 749
Rogers, Milton B., Montclair, 749
Rohrer, Albert L., Maplewood, 750
Rolfe, Stanley H., Newark, 750
Rooke, Robert L., Westfield, 751
Roon, Leo, South Orange, Elizabeth, 751
Root, Robert K., Princeton, 751
Roper, Lewis M., Jersey City, 752
Rose, Arthur F., Maplewood, 752
Rose, Edward C., Harbourton, Newark, 752
Rose, Grace D., Morristown, 753
Rose, Henry R., Newark, 753
Rose, Mary D. S., Edgewater, 753
Rose, Russell K., Belleville, Harrison, 753
Rose, Willis M., Maplewood, Hillside, 753
Rosecrans, Egbert, Blairstown, Belvidere, 754
Rosenbach, Abraham S. W., Strathmere, 754
Rosinger, Alfred, Paterson, 756
Ross, Sanford, 3d, Rumson, 757
Ross, Walter C., Ridgewood, Jersey City, 757
Rossi, Louis M., Perth Amboy, 757
Rost, Henry L., Westfield, 757
Roth, Frederick G. R., Englewood, 757

Rothschild, Karl, New Brunswick, 758
Rounds, Charles R., Trenton, 758
Roye, Harry F., Haddonfield, Camden, 760
Rudolfs, Willem, New Brunswick, 760
Rule, Arthur R., Westfield, 761
Rumery, Ralph R., Short Hills, 761
Rumsey, Herbert, Sr., Passaic, 761
Runyon, Frederick O., Maplewood, Newark, 762
Runyon, Harry, Belvidere, 762
Runyon, Laurance, New Brunswick, 762
Runyon, Melcolm E., Maplewood, Newark, 762
Russell, Franklin F., Mahwah, 763
Russell, Henry N., Princeton, 763
Russell, James E., Trenton, 763
Russell, Norman F. S., Edgewater Park, Burlington, 763
Russell, Walter C., Metuchen, 763
Rutstein, Leo, Maplewood, Newark, 763
Ryan, Frederick B., Short Hills, 764
Ryan, Heber H., Upper Montclair, 764
Ryan, Will C., Nutley, 764
Sage, Dean, Bernardsville, 765
Salsbury, Nate, Caldwell, 766
Sampson, Edward, Princeton, 767
Sampson, Harry O., Highland Park, New Brunswick, 767
Samuelson, Sidney E., Newton, 767
Sander, Frank V., New Brunswick, 768
Sanderson, Sidney, Highland Park, 768
Sands, Alexander H., Jr., Montclair, 768
Sanford, Olive C., Nutley, 768
Sangster, Margaret E., Tenafly, 768
Satz, David M., South Orange, Newark, 769
Saunders, Wilbour E., Hightstown, 769
Savage, Henry L., Princeton, 770
Savitz, Jerohn J., Wenonah, 770
Sawders, James C., Nutley, 770
Scammell, Frank G., Trenton, 771
Scarborough, Harland J., Upper Montclair, Newark, 771
Scarff, Paul B., Westfield, 771
Schaaf, Edward O., Newark, 772
Schaaf, Royal A., Newark, 772
Schaffer, Harry, Newark, 773
Schaffle, Albert E. F., Bound Brook, New Brunswick, 773
Schanck, Thomas E., New Brunswick, 773
Schaphorst, William F., Atlantic Highlands, Newark, 773
Schenck, Frederick P., West Orange, East Orange, 774
Scherer, William J., Irvington, 775
Schermerhorn, Richard, Jr., Montclair, 775
Schicks, George C., Upper Montclair, 775
Schiff, Edmund, Verona, 775
Schiffer, Herbert M., Leonia, 775
Schleicher, George B., Clementon, 776
Schlesinger, Joel L., West Orange, Newark, 776
Schlesinger, Louis, West Orange, Newark, 776
Schlesman, Carleton H., Paulsboro, 776
Schley, Kenneth B., Far Hills, 776
Schley, Reeve, Far Hills, 776
Schlink, Frederick J., Washington, 777
Schlosser, Frank G., Hoboken, 777
Schluter, Frederic E., Princeton, 777
Schmidt, Frederick W., Jersey City, Newark, 777
Schmidt, George P., New Brunswick, 777
Schneiderman, J. Jerome, Bayonne, 778
Schofield, Graham L., Bridgeton, 779
Schomp, Albert L., Plainfield, 779
Schor, Charles, North Bergen, Jersey City, 779
Schroeder, Lloyd L., West Englewood, Hackensack, 781
Schucker, Paul F., Jersey City, 781
Schuetz, Frederick F. du F., South Orange, 781
Schulz, Leo, Woodcliff Lake, 781
Schumann, John J., Jr., Upper Montclair, 782
Schwacha, George, Jr., Orange, 782
Schwartz, Joseph B., Perth Amboy, 782
Schwarz, Berthold T. D., Montclair, Jersey City, 783

Schwed, Irving, Somerville, 783
Schwep, Charles F., Plainfield, 784
Scoon, Robert, Princeton, 784
Scott, Campbell, Montclair, 784
Scott, William B., Princeton, 785
Scranton, Charles W., East Orange, 786
Scribner, Charles, Far Hills, 786
Scudder, Antoinette Q., Newark, 786
Scudder, Edward W., Rumson, Newark, 786
Scudder, Frank D., Montclair, 786
Seabrook, Byron M., Merchantville, Camden, 787
Seaman, Augusta H., Seaside Park, 787
Seaman, Otis R., Long Branch, Freehold, 787
Seaman, William, Bound Brook, 787
Searles, Thomas M., South Orange, 787
Seeley, Mildred L., Morristown, 788
Seger, George N., Passaic, 788
Segoine, Harold R., New Brunswick, 788
Seguine, William M., Kenvil, 788
Seidensticker, Charles A., Princeton, 789
Seifert, Edwin A., Glen Ridge, 789
Seiffert, Morgan R., Highland Park, New Brunswick, 789
Selinger, Samuel, West New York, 789
Senior, Frank S., Montclair, 790
Sergeant, Edgar, Nutley, 790
Shackleton, Samuel P., Maplewood, 791
Shaffer, Elmer L., Trenton, 791
Shanks, Carrol M., Montclair, Newark, 792
Shanley, Joseph S., Rumson, Newark, 792
Shannon, Floyd B., Summit, Kearny, 792
Shannon, Joseph G., Jersey City, 792
Sharp, Charles E., Port Norris, 792
Sharpe, Francis R., Ocean City, 793
Sharpe, John C., Blairstown, 793
Shaw, Alfred E., Bartley, 793
Shaw, Charles G., Spring Lake, 793
Shaw, George R., Verona, Harrison, 794
Shaw, Ralph M., Jr., Beverly, 794
Shay, Samuel M., Merchantville, 794
Shear, Theodore L., Princeton, 795
Sheddan, William B., Princeton, 795
Shenstone, Allen G., Princeton, 796
Shepard, Fred E., Elizabeth, 796
Shepard, Stanley, Jr., New Brunswick, 796
Sherman, Edith B., South Orange, 797
Sherman, Henry J., Moorestown, Camden, 797
Sherwin, Robert S., Newark, 798
Sherwood, Edward L., Ridgewood, 798
Shewhart, Walter A., Mountain Lake, 798
Shipler, Guy E., Chatham, 799
Shipman, Jehiel G., Newark, 800
Shipps, Hammell P., Delanco, Camden, 800
Shope, Edward P. L., Haddonfield, Camden, 801
Shotwell, Fred C., Franklin, 801
Shreeve, Herbert E., Maplewood, 802
Shull, George H., Princeton, 803
Shulman, Abraham, Paterson, 803
Shurtleff, Flavel, Montclair, 804
Sickles, Frederick J., New Brunswick, 804
Siegmund, Humphreys O., West Orange, 805
Sielke, Albert V., Westwood, 805
Silk, Charles I., Perth Amboy, 805
Sill, John B., Trenton, 805
Silliman, Reuben D., East Orange, 805
Silver, Arthur E., Upper Montclair, 806
Silverman, O. Jay, Atlantic City, 806
Silvers, Earl R., Rahway, 806
Silzer, George S., Metuchen, Newark, 806
Simeone, Peter A., Jersey City, Union City, 806
Simpson, John R., Englewood, 808
Simpson, Maxwell S., Elizabeth, 808
Sinclair, Archibald G., Bloomfield, 808
Sinn, Francis D., Montclair, 809
Sinnott, Arthur J., Newark, 809
Sisson, Edgar G., Montclair, 810

NEW JERSEY

Sisson, Nelson W., West Orange, East Orange, 810
Sitterly, Charles F., Madison, 810
Skelley, William C., New Brunswick, 810
Skinker, Murray F., Montclair, 811
Skinner, Charles E., Madison, 811
Skinner, Charles W., Newfield, 811
Slade, James J., Jr., New Brunswick, 812
Slater, John E., Upper Montclair, 812
Slaughter, Evans G., Wildwood Gardens, 812
Sloan, Harold P., Interlaken, 813
Sloan, Harold S., Montclair, 813
Sloane, T. O'Conor, South Orange, 813
Slocum, Chester A., Long Branch, 813
Slocum, Harry B., Long Branch, 813
Sloman, Joseph, Union City, 814
Slotkin, Samuel, Elberon, 814
Small, Frederick P., Ridgefield, Harvey Cedars, 814
Smalley, Harry C., Bridgeton, 814
Smathers, William H., Margate City, Atlantic City, 814
Smith, Carroll D., Jr., Essex Fells, Orange, 815
Smith, Charles H., Short Hills, 815
Smith, Earl B., Princeton, 816
Smith, Frank A., Elizabeth, 817
Smith, Frank W., Ridgewood, 817
Smith, Frederic W., Maplewood, Newark, 817
Smith, George T., Jersey City, 818
Smith, H. Alexander, Princeton, 818
Smith, H. Arthur, Lawrenceville, Trenton, 818
Smith, Harold M., Bordentown, 818
Smith, Harry L., Washington, 819
Smith, James G., Princeton, 819
Smith, J. Spencer, Tenafly, 820
Smith, Joseph L., Newark, 820
Smith, Marshall M., East Orange, 821
Smith, Paul E., Plainfield, 821
Smith, Peter A., South Orange, East Orange, 821
Smith, Powell R., Salem, 822
Smith, Preston H., Bayonne, 822
Smith, Rauland P., Pennington, 822
Smith, Thomas A., Jr., West Caldwell, Newark, 822
Smith, Vann H., Burlington, 822
Smith, William A., Sea Girt, 823
Smith, William T., South Orange, 823
Smithers, Ernest L., East Orange, 824
Smithers, William W., Spring Lake, 824
Smyth, Charles P., Princeton, 824
Smyth, Henry D., Princeton, 824
Snader, David L., Hoboken, 825
Snedecor, Spencer T., Hackensack, 825
Snevily, Robert S., Westfield, 825
Snider, Luther C., Leonia, 825
Snook, H. Clyde, Summit, 826
Snyder, Burdett E., Montclair, Hoboken, 826
Somerndike, John M., South Orange, 829
Sommer, Frank H., Newark, 829
Sommer, George N. J., Trenton, 829
Sommers, Paul B., Maplewood, Newark, 829
Sontag, Raymond J., Princeton, 829
Sooy, Leslie T., Pitman, 829
Sooy, Walter C., Woodcrest, 829
Sooy, William F., Atlantic City, 829
Sosman, Robert B., Westfield, Kearny, 830
Southworth, George C., Red Bank, 830
Spaeth, J. Duncan, Princeton, 831
Spargo, John A., Nutley, 831
Sparks, John B., Plainfield, 831
Spaulding, Edward G., Princeton, 832
Speare, Charles F., Bound Brook, 832
Speers, James M., Montclair, 832
Spencer, James H., Jr., Franklin, 834
Spencer, Kenneth, Montclair, 834
Sperr, Frederick W., Jr., Vineland, 834
Spingarn, Samuel, Union City, 835
Spinks, Lewis, Highland Park, Nixon, 835
Spofford, William B., Middletown, 835
Sprague, George C., Englewood, 835
Sprague, Harry A., Upper Montclair, 836

Sprague, Howard B., New Brunswick, 836
Springer, William M., Maplewood, Hillside, 836
Spurgeon, Dorset L., Newton, 837
Spurling, Oliver C., Upper Montclair, 837
Stace, Walter T., Princeton, 837
Stacey, Alfred E., Jr., Essex Fells, 837
Stafford, Geoffrey W., Madison, 838
Stahler, Harry S., Union City, 838
Stahler, Horace C., Seaside Park, 838
Stalnaker, John M., Princeton, 838
Stalter, Charles C., Hohokus, Paterson, 839
Stam, Jacob, Paterson, 839
Stangé, Emilé, North Hackensack, 839
Stanger, George H., Vineland, 839
Stanley, Edward O., Jr., Orange, Newark, 839
Stanley, Wendell M., Princeton, 840
Stanoyevich, Milivoy S., Montclair, 840
Stanton, Albert H., Maplewood, Newark, 840
Starke, Emory P., New Brunswick, 840
Starr, Lewis A., Woodbury, Camden, 841
Staton, Harry, Beachwood, 841
Staub, Albert W., Ridgewood, 841
Staub, Walter A., Short Hills, 841
Stauffen, Ernest, Jr., Englewood, 841
Stauffer, Donald A., Princeton, 841
Stauffer, Milton T., New Brunswick, 842
Stavitsky, Michael A., Murray Hill, Newark, 842
Stearns, Harry L., Woodbury, 842
Stedman, John W., Morristown, Newark, 843
Steel, Charles L., Jr., West Englewood, Teaneck, 843
Stein, LeRoy B., Newark, 845
Stein, Martin H., Elizabeth, 845
Steinbach, Jacob, Jr., Long Branch, 845
Stephens, Marsena P., Summit, 846
Stephens, Stephen D., Maplewood, Newark, 846
Stephenson, David T., Madison, 846
Stern, David, 3d, Haddonfield, 847
Stern, Julius D., Haddonfield, Camden, 847
Stevens, David H., Montclair, 848
Stevens, Donald R., Ridgewood, Passaic, 848
Stevens, Ernest, Montclair, 848
Stevens, George M., Collingswood, 848
Stevens, J. Thompson, Montclair, 848
Stevens, Leslie, Montclair, Newark, 848
Stevens, Wilbur A., Clifton, Newark, 848
Stevenson, George S., Red Bank, 849
Stevenson, J. Ross, Princeton, 849
Stewart, John Q., Princeton, 850
Stewart, Percy H., Plainfield, 850
Stewart, Vernon T., Montclair, 850
Stewart, Walter W., Far Hills, Princeton, 850
Stickney, Fernald S., West Caldwell, Newark, 850
Stickney, George H., East Orange, 850
Stifler, Francis C., Summit, 851
Stillman, Albert L., Plainfield, Jersey City, 851
Stillman, Edwin A., Gladstone, Roselle, 851
Stillman, W. Paul, Newark, 851
Stillwell, Lewis B., Princeton, 851
Stillwell, Richard, Princeton, 851
Stivers, Earl R., Rockaway, 852
Stock, Wallace T., Orange, 852
Stockton, Richard, VI, Trenton, Newark, 852
Stockwell, Frank C., Hoboken, 853
Stockwell, Henry F., Moorestown, Camden, 853
Stokes, Edward C., Trenton, 853
Stokes, Howard G., East Orange, 854
Stokes, Joseph, Moorestown, 854
Stone, Mildred F., Bloomfield, Newark, 855
Storey, Walter R., Teaneck, 856
Storrs, Cleveland H., Orange, 856
Story, Walter S., Maplewood, 857
Stout, Charles F. C., Camden, 857
Stout, Henrietta V., Short Hills, 857
Stoutenburgh, Robert B., Montclair, Newark, 857

Stowe, Walter H., New Brunswick, 858
Stragnell, Gregory, Millburn, Bloomfield, 858
Strange, Robert, South Orange, 858
Straughn, Clinton C., Middletown, Red Bank, 859
Street, Frank, Leonia, 860
Street, J. Fletcher, Beverly, 860
Streeter, Donald D., Iona, 860
Streeter, Thomas W., Morristown, 860
Strieby, Maurice E., Maplewood, 861
Stringer, Arthur, Mountain Lakes, 861
Stringfellow, George E., Montclair, West Orange, 861
Strombach, Victor H., New Vernon, Irvington, 862
Strong, Solomon C., West Orange, 862
Strong, Wendell M., Glen Ridge, 862
Stroud, Clara, Pt. Pleasant, 862
Strunk, William, Princeton, 863
Stryker, Josiah, South Orange, Newark, 863
Stuart, Donald C., Princeton, 863
Stuart, Duane C., Princeton, 863
Stuart, Harry G., Bernardsville, 863
Stuhr, William S., Weehawken, Hoboken, 864
Stull, Eugene S., Jr., Rutherford, Jersey City, 864
Stutesman, John H., New Brunswick, 865
Stutsman, Martin B., Plainfield, 865
Subin, Harry, Ventnor, Atlantic City, 865
Sullivan, Mark A., Jersey City, 866
Summerill, John M., Jr., Penns Grove, Salem, 866
Summerill, Joseph J., Jr., Woodbury, Camden, 866
Summerill, Thomas G., Salem, 866
Sumner, William A., Pompton Plains, Paterson, 866
Sutphen, William G. V. T., Morristown, 867
Sutphin, William H., Matawan, 867
Sutton, Erastus W., Lebanon, 867
Swan, Herbert S., Upper Montclair, 868
Swan, John J., Montclair, 868
Swartwout, Mary C., Montclair, 869
Sweeney, Thomas W., Maplewood, 870
Sweeney, William J., Elizabeth, Bayway, 870
Sweet, Albert W., Red Bank, Freehold, 870
Swift, Clement K., Camden, 871
Swingle, Wilbur W., Princeton, 871
Sykes, M'Cready, Plainfield, 872
Szerlip, Leopold, Newark, 873
Taber, Norman S., South Orange, 873
Taft, Frank, Montclair, 874
Talbot, Herbert R., Ridgewood, Carlstadt, 874
Talbot, George H., Clifton, Passaic, 874
Talcott, J. Frederick, Rumson, 874
Tarbell, Martha, East Orange, 875
Tarr, Frederick C., Princeton, 876
Tate, William, Closter, 876
Tatem, Henry R., Jr., Audubon, 876
Taylor, Archibald W., Westfield, 876
Taylor, Garvin P., Montclair, 877
Taylor, Harold E., Irvington, Newark, 878
Taylor, Harold W., Englewood, 878
Taylor, Hugh S., Princeton, 878
Taylor, Raymond A., Lakewood, 879
Taylor, Thomas S., Caldwell, 880
Teall, Edna A. W., Bloomfield, 880
Teall, Edward N., Maplewood, 880
Teaze, Moses H., Bloomfield, 880
Teeters, Wilbur O., Cresskill, 880
Tenbroeck, Carl, Princeton, 881
Tennant, George G., Jersey City, 881
Tenney, Dwight, Verona, Bloomfield, 882
Terhune, Albert P., Pompton Lakes, 882
Terhune, Anice, Pompton Lakes, 882
Terhune, Beekman R., Plainfield, 883
Tetor, Frederick A., Ridgewood, 882
Thom, William T., Jr., Princeton, 883
Thomas, Eugene P., Plainfield, 884
Thomas, George B., Maplewood, 884
Thomas, Harrison M., Princeton, 885

Thomas, Harry G., Asbury Park, 885
Thomas, John P., Allendale, 885
Thomas, Richard S., Bordentown, 886
Thompson, Fred C., Little Falls, Paterson, 887
Thompson, James V., Madison, 888
Thompson, Lloyd, Mountainside, Westfield, 888
Thompson, Mary W., Hohokus, 888
Thompson, Willard C., New Brunswick, 889
Thompson, William P., English Creek, West Atlantic City, 889
Thomson, John S., Jersey City, Glen Rock, 889
Thomson, McLeod, Atlantic City, 889
Thomson, Philip L., Glen Ridge, 889
Threlkeld, Archie L., Montclair, 890
Thurston, Alice M., Princeton, 891
Thurston, Henry W., Montclair, 891
Thygeson, Phillips, Tenafly, 891
Tiffany, J. Raymond, Montclair, Hoboken, 892
Tilghman, George H., Morristown, 892
Tilton, George I., Trenton, 892
Tinker, Charles P., Madison; 892
Tischler, Saul, Newark, 893
Titus, Norman E., Rumson, 893
Tobey, Franklin J., Newark, 893
Todd, John R., Summit, 894
Tomlinson, Norman B., Morristown, 894
Tomlinson, Paul G., Princeton, 894
Tomlinson, Roy E., Montclair, 894
Toolan, John E., Perth Amboy, 894
Totzauer, Josef, Ridgewood, 895
Townsend, Marion E., Glen Ridge, Newark, 896
Travaline, Frank M., Jr., Collingswood, Camden, 897
Tremaine, Charles M., Westfield, 897
Trenchard, Thomas W., Trenton, 897
Trevorrow, Robert J., Hackettstown, 898
Trimble, Henry W., Montclair, 898
Trimble, Rufus J., Verona, 898
Trossbach, Herman, Bogota, 898
Tucker, Rufus S., Westfield, 900
Tuller, Jesse D., Red Bank, 901
Turnbull, Agnes S., Maplewood, 901
Turnbull, Arthur, Far Hills, 901
Turnbull, Barton P., Summit, 901
Turner, Charles F., Montclair, 901
Turner, Louis A., Princeton, 902
Turp, James S., Hightstown, Trenton, 902
Tutela, Luigi, Newark, 902
Twiss, William B., New Brunswick, 902
Twitchell, Earl W., Haddonfield, 902
Twombly, Henry B., Summit, 903
Twomey, M. Joseph, East Orange, 903
Tyler, Cornelius B., Plainfield, 903
Tyler, William S., Plainfield, 903
Tyree, Lewis, Newark, 903
Udy, Stanley H., West Orange, 904
Ullrich, Elvin H., Union, Elizabeth, 905
Ulrey, Dayton, Glen Ridge, Harrison, 905
Underhill, Charles R., Lower Bank, 906
Underwood, George B., East Orange, Irvington, 906
Underwood, William E., Hasbrouck Heights, Newark, 906
Unterman, Isaac, Newark, 906
Updegraff, William B., Elizabeth, Roselle, 906
Upson, Maxwell M., Englewood, 907
Urbanski, Matthew F., Perth Amboy, 907
Urey, Harold C., Leonia, 907
Urmy, Ralph E., Lyndhurst, 907
Uzzell, Edward F., Atlantic City, 908
Vail, William P., Blairstown, 908
Valk, William E., Ridgewood, Paterson, 908
Van Beuren, Frederick T., Jr., Morristown, 908
Van Buren, Charles H., Englewood, 909
Vanderbilt, Arthur T., Short Hills, Newark, 909
Vanderkleed, Charles E., Collingswood, 909
Vanderpool, Wynant D., Morristown, Newark, 910
Vanderwart, Herman, Hackensack, 910

Van Deusen, Edwin H., Vineland, 910
Vandewater, William C., Princeton, 910
Van Doorn, William, Montclair, 910
Van Doren, Lloyd, Plainfield, 910
Van Dyke, Harry B., Highland Park, New Brunswick, 910
Van Hise, Warren K., Montclair, Newark, 911
Van Middlesworth, Tunis W., Highland Park, Newark, 911
Van Name, Elmer G., Haddonfield, Camden, 911
Vannatta, George W., West Orange, East Orange, 911
Vanneman, Edward C., Passaic, 911
Van Sciver, Joseph B., Jr., Camden, 912
Van Winkle, Charles A., Rutherford, 912
Van Winkle, Charles I., Rutherford, 912
Van Winkle, Major Edward, Dunellen, 912
Van Winkle, Winant, Rutherford, Newark, 912
Veach, Robert W., Ridgewood, 913
Veblen, Oswald, Princeton, 913
Vermeule, Cornelius C., East Orange, 914
Vermeule, Cornelius C., Jr., Short Hills, 914
Vermilye, William M., Plainfield, 914
Vieser, Milford A., West Orange, Newark, 915
Vieweg, Hermann F., Highland Park, Manville, 915
Vincent, George C., Upper Montclair, 915
Vinton, Stallo, Weehawken, Passaic, 915
Visscher, Barent L., Mountain Lakes, 915
Volkmann, John E., Haddon Heights, Camden, 916
Von Neumann, John, Princeton, 916
Voorhees, Clifford I., New Brunswick, 916
Voorhees, Louis A., New Brunswick, 916
Voorhees, Oscar M., New Brunswick, 916
Voorhees, Stephen H., Plainfield, 917
Voorhis, Harold O., Plainfield, 917
Voorhis, Warren E., Plainfield, 917
Vorsanger, Berthold, Englewood, 917
Vreeland, Albert L., East Orange, 917
Vreeland, Clarence L., Pompton Lakes, 917
Vreeland, Williamson U., Princeton, 917
Waddington, Edward C., Woodstown, Camden, 918
Wadham, Harvey N., Tenafly, 918
Wagner, James E., Long Branch, 919
Wain, Sidney, Red Bank, 920
Waite, William J., Rahway, Hoboken, 920
Wakelee, Edmund W., Demarest, Newark, 920
Waksman, Selman A., Highland Park, 920
Walcott, Harry M., Rutherford, 920
Waldman, Henry S., Elizabeth, 920
Walker, John Y. G., West Orange, 921
Walker, Marshall S., Glen Ridge, 921
Walker, Robert B., Highland Park, New Brunswick, 921
Walker, Samuel D., Keyport, Keansburg, 921
Walker, Thomas G., Arlington, 922
Wall, Albert C., West Orange, Jersey City, 922
Waller, Allen G., New Brunswick, 922

Wallis, Everett S., Princeton, 923
Waln, Amos M., Yardville, Trenton, 923
Walsh, Arthur, South Orange, West Orange, 923
Walsh, Thomas J., South Orange, 924
Waltzinger, Frederick J., Maplewood, Newark, 925
Ward, Arthur E., Upper Montclair, Montclair, 926
Ward, Harry F., Palisade, 926
Ward, Holcombe, Red Bank, 927
Ward, Lynd K., Palisade, 927
Ward, Perley E., Stone Harbor, 927
Ward, Waldron M., Summit, Newark, 927
Ware, Harriet, Plainfield, 927
Ware, Romaine B., Bridgeton, 927
Warren, George C., Summit, 929
Warren, Howard S., Montclair, 929
Washburn, Benjamin M., Orange, 930
Washburn, Cadwallader, Lakewood, 930
Washburn, Philip C., Greystone Park, 930
Washburn, Stanley, Lakewood, 930
Wason, Robert A., Mountain Lakes, 931
Waters, Daniel V., South Orange, Kearny, 931
Waters, Edward K., Jersey City, 931
Waterson, Karl W., Summit, 931
Watkins, John E., Avalon, 932
Watson, Earle F., Dumont, 933
Watson, George L., Maplewood, 933
Watson, Herbert L., Trenton, 933
Watson, Ripley, Maplewood, North Bergen, 933
Watson, Robert E., Nutley, Passaic, 933
Watson, Thomas J., Lebanon, 934
Watt, Homer A., Glen Ridge, 934
Way, Warren W., Atlantic City, 935
Weaver, William M., Collingswood, 936
Webb, Harold W., Leonia, 936
Webb, James M., East Orange, Montclair, 936
Weber, William A., New Brunswick, 937
Webster, Alice I., East Orange, 937
Weckstein, Herman B. J., Newark, 937
Wedderburn, Joseph H. M., Princeton, 937
Weed, J. Spencer, Morristown, 937
Weeks, Ernest F., North Haledon, Paterson, 938
Weelans, Charles H., Trenton, 938
Weil, R. J., Jr., Englewood, Newark, 938
Weilerstein, Baruch R., Atlantic City, 939
Weingaertner, Hans, Lyndhurst, 939
Weiss, Ferenz, Perth Amboy, 940
Weiss, Harry B., Highland Park, Trenton, 940
Weiss, Louis, Newark, 940
Weist, Archie J., Caldwell, Bloomfield, 940
Weitzenkorn, Louis, Neshanic, 940
Welch, Roy D., Princeton, 940
Weller, Curtis D., Merchantville, Trenton, 941
Wells, Harold B., Bordentown, 941
Welsh, J. Miller, Hackettstown, 942
Welsh, Ralph B., Summit, Morristown, 942
Wendel, Hugo C. M., Fairlawn, 942
Wendell, Arthur R., Summit, Rahway, 943
Wertenbaker, Thomas J., Princeton, 944
Wescott, Glenway, Hampton, 944
Wescott, Ralph W., Haddonfield, Camden, 944
West, Andrew F., Princeton, 944
West, Charles C., Montclair, 945

West, Leslie E., South Orange, Elizabeth, 945
West, Roscoe L., Trenton, 945
Westcott, John H., Princeton, 945
Westermaier, Francis V., Haddonfield, 945
Wetzel, William Enos, Trenton, 946
Weyl, Hermann, Princeton, 947
Whaley, George P., Short Hills, 947
Whallon, Walter L., Newark, 947
Wheeler, Homer J., Upper Montclair, 948
White, Alma, Zarephath, 949
White, Arthur K., Zarephath, 949
White, Charles D., Atlantic City, 949
White, George L., Tenafly, 950
White, Gerald T., Montville, 950
White, James D., Bay Head, 950
White, Luke M., Montclair, 951
White, Ray B., Zarephath, 951
White, Roscoe R., Somers Point, 951
White, Roy B., Annandale, 951
White, Winton J., Englewood, 952
Whitehead, Harvey F., Trenton, 952
Whitehorne, Earl, Caldwell, 952
Whiting, Borden D., West Orange, Newark, 953
Whitmoyer, Raymond B., Atlantic City, 953
Whitner, Thomas C., Jr., Elizabeth, Montclair, 954
Whitney, Alfred R., Morristown, 954
Whitney, Russell W., Montclair, Hoboken, 954
Whittemore, Clark M., Elizabeth, 954
Whittemore, Laurens E., Maplewood, 954
Whittlesey, Charles R., Princeton, 955
Whitton, John B., Princeton, 955
Wicks, Robert R., Princeton, 956
Wicoff, John V. B., Plainsboro, Trenton, 956
Wieman, Elton E., Princeton, 956
Wiener, William, Newark, 956
Wiese, Kurt, Frenchtown, 956
Wight, E. Van Dyke, Princeton, 957
Wigner, Eugene P., Princeton, 957
Wilber, Charles P., Trenton, 957
Wilbur, John M., Hohokus, 957
Wiley, Joseph B., Morristown, 958
Wilkinson, Kenneth L., Orange, 958
Wilks, Samuel S., Princeton, 958
Willard, Frederic W., Summit, 959
Willcox, Oswin W., Ridgewood, 959
Willever, John C., Millburn, 960
Willey, John H., Montclair, 960
Williams, Anna W., Woodcliff Lake, 960
Williams, Charles S., Short Hills, Orange, 961
Williams, Frank A., Elizabeth, 961
Williams, Fred M., Summit, 962
Williams, Frederick B., Glen Ridge, 962
Williams, George V. S., Mountain Lakes, 962
Williams, Gurdon H., Collingswood, Camden, 962
Williams, Jarvis, Jr., Monmouth Beach, Jersey City, 963
Williams, John L. B., Orange, 963
Williams, Robert, Paterson, 963
Williams, Robert R., Summit, 963
Williams, Samuel R., Short Hills, 964
Williams, William C., Rutherford, 964
Williamson, John F., Princeton, 964
Willner, Irving, Newark, 965
Willson, Frederick N., Princeton, 965
Wilson, Edgar K., Upper Montclair, 966
Wilson, Harrison B., Hackensack, 967

Wilson, Henry F., Jr., Montclair, Jersey City, 967
Wilson, James C., Westfield, Perth Amboy, 967
Wilson, John R., Paterson, 967
Wilson, J. Frank Woodbury, 967
Wilson, Richard H., Maplewood, 968
Wilson, Stanley M., Maplewood, 969
Winchell, Lawrence R., Vineland, 969
Winchester, George, New Brunswick, 970
Wing, Henry J., Milltown, New Brunswick, 970
Winne, Walter G., Hackensack, 970
Winser, Beatrice, Newark, 970
Wires, Hazel K., Haworth, 971
Wise, Henry M., Hillsdale, 971
Wiseman, Robert J., Paterson, Passaic, 971
Witham, Ernest C., Stelfon, New Brunswick, 972
Wittreich, Andrew O., Union City, Jersey City, 972
Woerner, Paul L., Chatham, 972
Woldman, Norman E., Hackensack, 972
Wolfe, Edgar B., Essex Fells, Newark, 973
Wolffe, Joseph B., Fairton, 974
Wolfskeil, William D., Elizabeth, 974
Wolverton, Charles A., Merchantville, 974
Wonsetler, John C., Camden, 974
Wood, Earl L., Newark, 975
Wood, Edith E., Cape May Court House, 975
Wood, Ernest R., Montclair, 975
Wood, Horace E., II, Newark, 976
Wood, Loren N., Bound Brook, 976
Woodbridge, Freeman, New Brunswick, 976
Woodbury, Walter E., Tenafly, 976
Woodruff, Stanley R., Bayonne, Jersey City, 977
Woods, Elmer B., Pitman, 978
Woodward, Carl R., New Brunswick, 978
Woodward, Herbert P., East Orange, 979
Woolever, Harry, Ocean City, 979
Woolley, Edward M., Passaic, 979
Worden, Albert W., Red Bank, 980
Worden, Charles B., Princeton, 980
Worden, Edward C., I, Millburn, Wyoming, 980
Worth, Charles L., Lambertville, 981
Wrensch, Frank A., Montclair, 981
Wright, Eliza G., East Orange, 982
Wright, Frank A., Summit, 982
Wright, Hamilton M., Rutherford, 983
Wright, Royden V., East Orange, 984
Wright, Thomas A., Plainfield, 984
Wroth, James S., Westfield, 984
Wry, Orlin V., East Rutherford, 984
Wythes, William H., Haddonfield, Camden, 985
Yardley, Farnham, West Orange, 986
York, Wilbur H., Princeton, 988
Young, George, Jr., Passaic, 989
Young, George J., Morristown, 989
Young, George P., Wood Ridge, 989
Young, Percy S., Montclair, Newark, 990
Young, Rowland L., East Orange, 990
Youngelson, Irving, Dover, 990
Zinzow, W. A., Caldwell, Bloomfield, 993
Zucker, Saul J., South Orange, Newark, 994
Zwemer, Raymond M., Princeton, 994
Zworykin, Vladimir K., Taunton Lakes, Camden, 994

PENNSYLVANIA

Aaron, Marcus, Pittsburgh, 1
Aaron, Sister Mary Cyril, Greensburg, 1
Abbott, Alfred T., Philadelphia, 1
Abbott, Edwin M., Philadelphia, 1
Abbott, Fred W., Philadelphia, 1
Abel, R. L., Pittsburgh, 1
Abell, Richard G., Philadelphia, 1
Aberle, Gustave C., Jenkintown, Philadelphia, 1
Aberle, Harry C., Jenkintown, Philadelphia, 2
Aberly, John, Gettysburg, 2
Abersold, John R., Lansdowne, Philadelphia, 2

Abraham, James W., Uniontown, 2
Abraham, Paul J., Greensburg, 2
Abrahams, Robert D., Philadelphia, 2
Acheson, Alexander W., Washington, 2
Acheson, Marcus W., Jr., Pittsburgh, 2
Ackley, Clarence E., Pittsburgh, Harrisburg, 3
Adair, Watson B., Sewickley, Pittsburgh, 3
Adams, Comfort A., Philadelphia, 3
Adams, Edwin W., Philadelphia, 3
Adams, Enoch H., Bellefonte, 3

Adams, George J., Philadelphia, 3
Adams, Harold, Lancaster, 3
Adams, John S., Philadelphia, 3
Adams, Marjorie N., Swarthmore, 4
Adams, Martin E., Lancaster, 4
Adams, Viers W., Johnstown, 4
Addie, Charles E. B., Philadelphia, 4
Addison, William H. F., Philadelphia, 4
Ade, Lester K., Harrisburg, 4
Aderton, Alphonso L., Harrisburg, 5
Adler, Cyrus, Philadelphia, 5
Adler, Francis H., Philadelphia, 5
Adolphe, Albert J., Philadelphia, 5

Affelder, Estelle M., Pittsburgh, 5
Ahl, A. William, Selinsgrove, 6
Aiken, William J., Pittsburgh, 6
Aikens, H. Hayes, Llanerch, Upper Darby, 6
Ailman, Mildred A., State College, New Wilmington, 6
Aires, Benjamin H., Mt. Lebanon, Pittsburgh, 6
Aitkin, Austin K., Bala-Cynwyd, Philadelphia, 6
Akeley, Archibald P., Coudersport, 6
Akers, Oscar P., Meadville, 6
Albig, Reed H., McKeesport, 6
Albright, Charles, Harrisburg, 6

PENNSYLVANIA

Albright, Denton M., Crafton, 7
Albright, Raymond W., Reading, 7
Album, Leon, Philadelphia, 7
Alden, Ezra H., Philadelphia, 7
Alderfer, Harold F., State College, 7
Alexander, Fay K., Philadelphia, 8
Alexander, James H., Warren, 8
Alexander, John H., Pittsburgh, 8
Alexander, Maitland, Sewickley, 8
Alexander, Park J., Pittsburgh, 8
Alexander, William E., Lancaster, 8
Alford, Newell G., Pittsburgh, 9
Algeo, Albert M., Washington, 9
Allbeck, Montraville M., Scottdale, 9
Alderdice, Norman, Sewickley Heights, 9
Alleman, Frank, Lancaster, 9
Alleman, Gellert, Wallingford, 9
Alleman, Herbert C., Gettysburg, 9
Allen, Albert L., Harrisburg, 9
Allen, Alexander J., Swarthmore, 9
Allen, Clarence E., Warren, 9
Allen, David K., Johnstown, 9
Allen, Edward M., Scranton, 9
Allen, George H., Easton, 10
Allen, Henry B., Philadelphia, 10
Allen, Henry E., Easton, 10
Allen, Leslie, Pittsburgh, 10
Allen, Philip M., Blue Bell, Philadelphia, 11
Allen, Robert G., Greensburg, 11
Allen, Samuel S., Jr., Pittsburgh, 11
Allen, William G., Erie, 11
Allis, Oswald T., Philadelphia, 11
Allis, Paul M., Milroy, Lewistown, 11
Allison, Jonathan D., Roaring Branch, 11
Allison, Wesley L., Pittsburgh, 11
Allman, Drue N., Philadelphia, 11
Allman, Justin P., Philadelphia, 12
Allport, James H., Barnsboro, 12
Allwein, A. Francis, Philadelphia, 12
Almond, Linda S., Philadelphia, 12
Alpers, Bernard J., Merion, Philadelphia, 12
Alsentzer, Harry A., Jr., Philadelphia, 12
Alston, Robert S., Philadelphia, 12
Alter, George E., Pittsburgh, 12
Altmeyer, George, McKeesport, 12
Altmeyer, Walter S., McKeesport, 12
Altmiller, Charles H., Hazleton, 12
Alvin, G. W., Wilkinsburg, Pittsburgh, 12
Alwyne, Horace, Rosemont, Bryn Mawr, 12
Amadon, Roger S., Philadelphia, 12
Amberg, Richard H., Oil City, 12
Amerman, Ralph A., Scranton, 13
Ames, Frank N., Corry, 13
Ames, J. Wilson, Honesdale, 13
Ames, William H., Carlisle, 13
Amos, Thyrsa W., Pittsburgh, 14
Amram, David W., Bryn Mawr, Philadelphia, 14
Amram, Philip W., Feasterville, Philadelphia, 14
Anders, Howard S., Philadelphia, 14
Anders, Stanley S., Norristown, 14
Anderson, Archer E., Narberth, 14
Anderson, Camilla V., Philadelphia, 14
Anderson, Carlotta A., Upper Darby, 14
Anderson, Claire A., Westmont, Johnstown, 14
Anderson, Dwight M., Donora, 15
Anderson, Edmund A., Palmerton, 15
Anderson, Edwin J. A., State College, 15
Anderson, H. M., Muddy Creek Forks, York, 15
Anderson, Hjalmar S., Titusville, 15
Anderson, Horace B., Johnstown, 15
Anderson, Hugh C., Pittsburgh, 15
Anderson, Hurst R., Meadville, 15
Anderson, J. H., Grove City, 15
Anderson, James T., Beaver, 15
Anderson, John U., Mt. Lebanon, Pittsburgh, 15
Anderson, Mildred M., Pittsburgh, 15
Anderson, Ralph S., Philadelphia, 15
Anderson, Robert F., West Chester, 15
Anderson, Robert R., Brackenridge, 16
Anderson, Russell S., Erie, 16
Anderson, Thomas L., Washington, 16
Anderson, Troyer S., Swarthmore, 16
Anderson, Walter I., Elmwood, York, 16

Anderson, William B., Philadelphia, 16
Anderson, William D., Philadelphia, 16
Anderson, William K., Johnstown, 16
Anderson, William S., Philadelphia, 16
Andorn, Alvin M., Philadelphia, Chester, 16
Andrews, Carl W., Ridgway, St. Marys, 17
Andrews, Charles E., Jr., New Bethlehem, 17
Andrews, Dickson, Meadville, 17
Andrews, H. G., Johnstown, 17
Andrews, James H. M., Philadelphia, 17
Andrews, Schofield, Philadelphia, 17
Andruss, Harvey A., Bloomsburg, 17
Angelo, Emidio, Philadelphia, 18
Anglada, Joseph A., Jenkintown, 18
Angloch, Milton C., Pittsburgh, 18
Annenberg, Moses L., Philadelphia, 18
Anschutz, C. W., Philadelphia, 18
Anspach, Brooke M., Ardmore, Philadelphia, 18
Anspach, Marshall R., Williamsport, 18
Anstadt, Henry, Chambersburg, 18
Anstaett, Herbert B., Lancaster, 18
Anstine, Harry B., York, 18
Anthony, Harry W., Strausstown, 18
Anthony, James T., Philadelphia, 19
Anthony, Luther B., Easton, Raubsville, 19
Anthony, Richard L., Lewisburg, 19
Anthony, Roy D., State College, 19
Aponick, John J., West Nanticoke, Wilkes-Barre, 19
App, Austin J., Scranton, 19
Appel, Kenneth E., Haverford, Philadelphia, 19
Appel, Theodore B., Lancaster, 19
Appel, Thomas R., Lancaster, 19
Apple, Henry H., Lancaster, 19
Apple, Ulysses A., Lebanon, 20
Appleby, John W., Harrisburg, 20
Appleton, Joseph L. T., Philadelphia, 20
Appleyard, Joseph, Lancaster, 20
Arbuthnot, Charles, 3d, Pittsburgh, 21
Arbuthnot, Thomas S., Pittsburgh, 21
Archambault, A. Margaretta, Philadelphia, 21
Areford, G. Carl, Uniontown, 21
Arensberg, Francis I., Pittsburgh, Swissvale, 21
Armor, James C., Pittsburgh, 21
Armstrong, C. Dudley, Lancaster, 22
Armstrong, Clyde A., Pittsburgh, 22
Armstrong, Dwight L., Lancaster, 22
Armstrong, Thomas F., Philadelphia, 22
Arner, Calvin E., Allentown, 22
Arner, Maurice R., McKees Rocks, 22
Arnett, John H., Philadelphia, 22
Arnhold, George L., Philadelphia, 22
Arnold, Benjamin L., Kittanning, 22
Arnold, C. Russell, Lansdowne, Philadelphia, 22
Arnold, Clifford H., Ardmore, 22
Arnold, Harrison N., State College, 23
Arnold, Jesse O., Philadelphia, 23
Arnold, John C., Clearfield, 23
Arnold, John H., Harrisburg, Vanderbilt, 23
Arnold, Robert S. L., Philadelphia, 23
Arnovich, Morris, Philadelphia, 23
Aronoff, Max, Upper Darby, Philadelphia, 23
Aronson, Harvey M., Pittsburgh, 23
Aronson, I. Leonard, Pittsburgh, 23
Arter, Theodore, Altoona, 23
Arthur, Edmund W., Ben Avon, Pittsburgh, 23
Arthur, Herbert S., McKeesport, 23
Arthur, J. Howard, Pittsburgh, 23
Arthur, Samuel J., Erie, 24
Arthur, William C., Meadville, 24
Arthurs, Ann C., Philadelphia, 24
Arzt, Max, Scranton, 24
Ash, William C., Philadelphia, 24
Ashcraft, Charles E., Jr., Pittsburgh, 24
Ashcraft, Leon T., Philadelphia, 24
Ashe, Edmund M., Pittsburgh, 24
Ashford, Thomas F., Jr., Mt. Lebanon, Pittsburgh, 24

Ashley, George H., Harrisburg, 24
Ashley-Montagu, Montagu F., Philadelphia, 24
Ashton, Dorothy L., Swarthmore, 25
Ashton, Ethel V., Philadelphia, 25
Ashton, Leonard C., Swarthmore, Philadelphia, 25
Asplundh, Griffith, Bryn Athyn, Jenkintown, 25
Aston, James, Pittsburgh, 25
Aston, John G., State College, 25
Atchison, Clyde S., Washington, 25
Atchison, Thomas C., Washington, 25
Atherholt, Gordon M., Pittsburgh, 25
Atherton, Benjamin R., Jersey Shore, 25
Atherton, Fred B., Scranton, 25
Atherton, Thomas H., Philadelphia, 26
Atkins, Jacob T., York, 26
Atkins, Paul S., York, 26
Atkinson, Sterling K., Glenside, Philadelphia, 26
Atkinson, Willard S., Philadelphia, 26
Atlee, Edward D., Ardmore, Philadelphia, 26
Atlee, John L., Bausman, Lancaster, 26
Atlee, Washington L., Chester, 26
Atwell, Samuel P., Washington, 26
Atwell, Loyal P., Beaver Falls, 26
Atwood, Arthur R., Mt. Lebanon, Pittsburgh, 27
Aubrey, George W., Allentown, 27
Aufhammer, Charles H., Coatesville, 27
Aurand, Orris H., Steelton, 27
Austin, Charles R., State College, 27
Austin, James H., Jr., Sewickley, Pittsburgh, 27
Austin, James H., Bala-Cynwyd, Philadelphia, 27
Austin, Richard L., Philadelphia, 27
Austin, Shirley P., Allison Park, Pittsburgh, 27
Auten, James E., Overbrook, 27
Averett, Leonard, Philadelphia, 28
Avery, George A., Philadelphia, 28
Avinoff, Andrey, Pittsburgh, 28
Ayars, R. D., Pittsburgh, 28
Aydelotte, Frank, Swarthmore, 28
Ayer, Joseph C., Philadelphia, 28
Ayers, Hobart B., Pittsburgh, 28
Ayers, Joseph W., Easton, 28
Ayres, Arthur U., Philadelphia, 28
Ayres, James D., Pittsburgh, 28
Babasinian, V. S., Bethlehem, 28
Babb, Maurice J., Ardmore, 28
Babbitt, James A., Haverford, Philadelphia, 28
Babcock, Edward V., Pittsburgh, 29
Babcock, Harry F., State College, 29
Babcock, William W., Bala-Cynwyd, Philadelphia, 29
Bach, George W., Erie, 29
Bacharach, Herman I., Philadelphia, 29
Bachman, Albert, Gettysburg, 29
Bachman, Benjamin B., Ardmore, 29
Bachman, David M., Philadelphia, 29
Bachman, Frank H., Rydal, Philadelphia, 29
Bachman, Rowland W., Allentown, 29
Bachmann, Ernest F., Philadelphia, 29
Backenstoe, Gerald S., Emmaus, 30
Bæckstrand, Clifford J., Lancaster, 30
Bacon, Allen E., Wilkes-Barre, 30
Bacon, Arthur D., Harrisburg, 30
Bacon, Earl D., Sharon, 30
Bacon, Harry E., Merion, Philadelphia, 30
Bacon, John F., York, 30
Bacon, Leslie D., Lansdowne, Philadelphia, 30
Bacon, Lewis H., Pottsville, 30
Bacon, Walter A., Pottsville, 30
Badura, Bernard, New Hope, 31
Badura, Faye R. S., New Hope, 31
Baer, George H., Pottstown, 31
Baer, Harry A. D., Allentown, 31
Bagger, Henry H., Pittsburgh, 31
Bagnell, Robert, Philadelphia, 31
Bailey, Emmett E., Oil City, 32
Bailey, Ervin G., Easton, 32
Bailey, Frank R., Pittsburgh, 32
Bailey, George A., Narberth, Philadelphia, 32
Bailey, George R., Harrisburg, 32
Bailey, James B., Bryn Mawr, Philadelphia, 33

Bailey, Stacy P., DuBois, 33
Bailey, Weldon, Philadelphia, 33
Bailey, William S., Harrisburg, 33
Baily, William L., Haverford, 33
Bain, Edgar C., Pittsburgh, 33
Bains, Edward, Philadelphia, 33
Bair, George F., Pittsburgh, 33
Bair, Henry S., York, 33
Bair, Lawrence E., Lancaster, 34
Baird, Joseph S., Pittsburgh, 34
Baish, Henry H., Harrisburg, 34
Baker, Allen L., State College, 34
Baker, Arthur M., Philadelphia, 34
Baker, Colley S., Harrisburg, 34
Baker, Donald G., Collegeville, 34
Baker, Everett M., Valencia, Pittsburgh, 34
Baker, Frank E., Bala-Cynwyd, Philadelphia, 34
Baker, Horace F., Sewickley, Pittsburgh, 35
Baker, Mary N., Wilkes-Barre, 35
Baker, Milton G., Wayne, 35
Baker, Morris H., Montrose, 35
Baker, Moses H., Pittsburgh, 35
Baker, Samuel, Scranton, 36
Baker, Thomas S., Pittsburgh, 36
Baker, Ulysses S. G., Susquehanna, 36
Baker, Walter H., Washington, Bridgeville, 36
Baker, William F., Philadelphia, 36
Baker, William H., York, 36
Bakewell, Donald C., Sewickley, Pittsburgh, 37
Bakken, Herman E., Pittsburgh, New Kensington, 37
Balano, Paula H., Philadelphia, 37
Balcom, Max F., Emporium, 37
Balderston, C. Canby, Drexel Hill, 37
Baldinger, Albert H., Pittsburgh, 37
Baldridge, Robert M., McKeesport, 37
Baldrige, Thomas J., Hollidaysburg, 37
Baldrige, William L., Hollidaysburg, 37
Baldwin, Arthur C., Philadelphia, 38
Baldwin, Elizabeth G., Hollidaysburg, 38
Baldwin, Frank E., Austin, 38
Baldwin, Harrison R., Erie, 38
Baldwin, Henry W., Saegerstown, 38
Baldwin, James H., Philadelphia, 38
Ball, Michael V., Warren, 38
Ballagh, James C., Philadelphia, 38
Ballantyne, Nathaniel W., Pittsburgh, 39
Ballard, F. L., Philadelphia, 39
Ballentine, Floyd G., Lewisburg, 39
Ballinger, Robert I., Philadelphia, 39
Balsbaugh, Edward M., Annville, 39
Balsley, Charles H., Connellsville, 39
Balthaser, Jennie M., Sinking Spring, 39
Bamberger, Henry F., Philadelphia, 39
Bamberger, Leo, Philadelphia, 39
Bancroft, George R., Drexel Hill, Philadelphia, 40
Bancroft, Wilfred, Haverford, Philadelphia, 40
Bancroft, William W., Collegeville, 40
Bane, David E., Uniontown, 40
Bane, James C., Washington, 40
Bange, Guy W., Hanover, 40
Banghart, Harold L., Warren, 40
Banks, William H., Mifflintown, 40
Bankson, Ellis E., Pittsburgh, 40
Banner, Franklin C., State College, 40
Bannerot, Frederick G., Pittsburgh, 40
Barach, Joseph H., Pittsburgh, 40
Barber, Charlie R., Erie, 41
Barber, J. Thomas, Lancaster, 41
Barber, Samuel, West Chester, 41
Barber, Theodore S., Wilkes-Barre, 41
Barbey, John E., Reading, 41
Barbour, Marshall R., Pittsburgh, 41
Barchus, John L., Salisbury, 41
Barclay, John, Jr., Greensburg, 41
Barclay, William K., Haverford, Philadelphia, 41
Barclay, William K., Jr., Wynnewood, Philadelphia, 41
Bard, Guy K., Denver, Lancaster, 41
Barker, Albert W., Moylan, 42

PENNSYLVANIA

Barker, H. C., Philadelphia, 42
Barker, Rodman, Foxboro, Philadelphia, 42
Barnard, J. Lynn, Collegeville, 43
Barnard, Julian W., Norristown, 43
Barnes, Demass E., Pittsburgh, 43
Barnes, George E., Philadelphia, 43
Barnes, G. H. Edgar, Philadelphia, 43
Barnes, Horace R., Lancaster, 43
Barnes, Howard M., Doylestown, 43
Barnes, Ira W., Philadelphia, 43
Barnes, James, Haverford, Philadelphia, 44
Barnes, James A., Philadelphia, 44
Barnes, John H., Devon, Philadelphia, 44
Barnes, Morgan, Grove City, 44
Barnes, T. Ellis, Haverford, 44
Barnes, W. Harry, Philadelphia, 44
Barnett, Frank R., Waynesboro, 44
Barnhart, Frank P., Johnstown, 44
Barnhart, Paul S., Greensburg, 44
Barnhouse, Donald G., Philadelphia, 45
Barr, Floyd W., Beaver Falls, 45
Barr, Joseph W., Oil City, 45
Barraclough, Henry, Elkins Park, Philadelphia, 45
Barratt, Stanley, Wilcox, 45
Barrett, Anthony P., Drexel Hill, Harrisburg, 45
Barrett, Arthur, Bellevue, Pittsburgh, 45
Barrett, Benjamin B., Norristown, 45
Barrett, Charles S., Pittsburgh, 45
Barrett, Don C., Haverford, 45
Barrett, Dulin A., Pittsburgh, 45
Barrett, Michael T., Philadelphia, 45
Barrett, William A., Pittsburgh, 46
Barringer, Brandon, Philadelphia, 46
Barringer, D. Moreau, Jr., Philadelphia, 46
Barrow, William E., Franklin, 46
Barsel, Solomon M., Philadelphia, 46
Barth, Carl G., Philadelphia, 46
Barthold, William G., Bethlehem, 46
Bartholomew, Tracy, Pittsburgh, 46
Bartle, Harvey, Philadelphia, 46
Bartle, Henry J., Ardmore, Philadelphia, 47
Bartlett, Alden E., West Chester, 47
Bartlett, George G., Philadelphia, 47
Bartlett, North E., Philadelphia, 47
Bartol, George E., Jr., Wynnewood, 47
Barton, George, Philadelphia, 47
Barton, Olive R., Gettysburg, 47
Barton, Samuel G., Philadelphia, 47
Barton, Samuel V. D., Castle Shannon, 47
Bartow, Harry E., Collingdale, Philadelphia, 48
Bascom, Florence, Bryn Mawr, 48
Bascom, Harry F., Allentown, 48
Bashioum, H., Pittsburgh, 48
Baskett, George T., Retreat, 48
Baskett, Olive T., Retreat, 48
Bass, Lawrence W., Pittsburgh, 48
Batcheller, Hiland G., Pittsburgh, 48
Batdorf, Grant D., Harrisburg, 48
Batdorf, Harvey S., Easton, 48
Bateman, William, Philadelphia, 49
Bates, Daniel M., Philadelphia, 49
Bates, Edward I., Meadville, 49
Bates, Harry H., Ridley Park, Philadelphia, 49
Bates, Joseph S., Swarthmore, 49
Bates, Robert S., Meadville, 49
Bates, William N., Philadelphia, 49
Baton, George S., Pittsburgh, 49
Batt, William L., Wyncote, Philadelphia, 49
Battaglia, Pasquale M., Philadelphia, 49
Batten, Harry A., Bryn Mawr, Philadelphia, 50
Batten, Loring W., Swarthmore, 50
Battle, John R., Ardmore, Philadelphia, 50
Battles, William W., Newton Square, Philadelphia, 50
Bauer, Elmer G., Glenshaw, Pittsburgh, 50
Bauer, William G., St. Marys, 50
Bauer, William J., Pittsburgh, 50
Baugh, Albert C., Philadelphia, 50
Baugher, Jacob I., Hershey, 50
Baughman, George W., Jr., Pittsburgh, Swissvale, 50

Baughman, Harry F., Philadelphia, 50
Baum, Henry J., Altoona, 51
Baum, Walter E., Sellersville, 51
Bausman, J. W. B., Lancaster, 51
Bayard, Edwin S., Pittsburgh, 51
Bayless, Stanley C., Austin, 51
Bayley, Paul L., Bethlehem, 51
Bayliss, Charles W., Wayne, 51
Bayliss, Ella H., Titusville, 51
Bazard, Walter S., Midland, 52
Bazett, Henry C., Haverford, 52
Bazley, James R., Pottsville, 52
Bazzoni, Charles B., Wallingford, 52
Beal, Carleton D., Biglerville, 52
Beal, Frederick W., Philadelphia, 52
Beal, George D., Pittsburgh, 52
Beal, Walter H., Wynnewood, 53
Beale, Leonard T., Philadelphia, 53
Beale, Wilson T. M., Philadelphia, 53
Beall, Charles R., Edgewood, Swissvale, 53
Beall, John T., Jr., Pittsburgh, 53
Beals, C. Wearne, Sabula, Du Bois, St. Marys, 53
Beam, Adam L., State College, 53
Beaman, J. Frank, Lansdowne, Philadelphia, 53
Beaman, William W., Troy, 53
Beamish, Richard J., Harrisburg, 53
Bean, Oscar O., Doylestown, 53
Beane, Theodore L., Norristown, 53
Beane, John G., Pittsburgh, 54
Bear, Raymond R., Allentown, 54
Beard, John A., Mifflinburg, 54
Beard, Myrtle H., Reading, 54
Beardslee, Claude G., Bethlehem, 54
Beardsley, Edward J. G., Philadelphia, 54
Beardwood, Matthew, Philadelphia, 54
Beattie, Lester M., Pittsburgh, 54
Beatty, John D., Valencia, 54
Beatty, Ralph P., Uniontown, 55
Beaver, J. Lynford, Bethlehem, 55
Beaver, William H., Haverford, Philadelphia, 55
Bechtold, Gustavus H., Philadelphia, 55
Beck, Charles E., Portland, 55
Beck, Charles W., Jr., Wyncote, Philadelphia, 55
Beck, Herbert H., Lancaster, 55
Beck, Jean-Baptiste, Bryn Mawr, 55
Beck, John A., Karns City, 55
Beck, Paul R., Butler, 55
Becker, John B., Philadelphia, 55
Becker, Joseph, Pittsburgh, 56
Becker, Sylvanus A., Bethlehem, 56
Beckley, Clarence W., Warren, 56
Beckman, Irland M., Philadelphia, 56
Beckwith, Frank C., Lancaster, 56
Beckwith, J. S., Pittsburgh, 56
Bedford, Paul, Wilkes-Barre, 56
Bedrossian, Edward H., Drexel Hill, Philadelphia, 56
Bee, Charles H., Indiana, 56
Beede, Victor A., State College, 56
Beegle, Clifford H., Beaver Falls, 56
Beegle, May, Pittsburgh, 57
Beehler, George W., Jr., Philadelphia, 57
Beer, Phares G., Allentown, 57
Beery, Pauline G., State College, 57
Beery, Vincent D., Philadelphia, 57
Beeson, Charles E., Pittsburgh, 57
Behan, Richard J., Pittsburgh, 57
Behney, Charles A., Wynnewood, Philadelphia, 57
Behrend, Ernst H., Erie, 58
Behrend, Moses, Philadelphia, 58
Beideman, Joseph E., Audubon, Norristown, 58
Beidelman, Harry H., Hanover, 58
Beierschmitt, Gerald A., Mt. Carmel, 58
Beiler, Irwin R., Meadville, 58
Beitler, Harold B., Bryn Mawr, Philadelphia, 58
Beitler, S. Wilmer, Butler, 58
Belcher, Wallace E., Philadelphia, 59
Belin, G. d'Andelot, Waverly, Scranton, 59
Belin, Henry, 3d, Waverly, Scranton, 59
Belknap, John H., Wilkinsburg, Pittsburgh, 59
Bell, Albert H., Greensburg, 59
Bell, C. Ray, Lebanon, 59
Bell, Charles H., Devon, Philadelphia, 59
Bell, Frank B., Pittsburgh, 59

Bell, Harry C., Pittsburgh, 59
Bell, Jesse S., Williamsport, 59
Bell, John F., Jenkintown, 59
Bell, Laurence S., Wilkinsburg, Pittsburgh, 60
Bell, Samuel K., Wyncote, Jenkintown, 60
Beltram, Basil R., Philadelphia, 60
Bemis, Royal W., Philadelphia, 60
Bencker, Ralph B., Haverford, Philadelphia, 60
Bender, Arthur J., Ardmore, Philadelphia, 61
Bendiner, Irvin, Philadelphia, 61
Benedict, Daniel N., Waynesboro, 61
Benedito, Sidney L., Pittsburgh, 61
Benedum, Michael L., Pittsburgh, 61
Benét, Laura, Westtown, 61
Benjamin, Charles D., Philadelphia, 62
Benjamin, Frank P., Scranton, 62
Benn, John K., Mt. Lebanon, Pittsburgh, 62
Benner, Thomas M., Pittsburgh, 62
Benner, Winthrop W., Arcola, Conshohocken, 62
Bennett, Charles E., Pittsburgh, 62
Bennett, Charles W., Pittsburgh, 62
Bennett, Claude E., Wellsboro, 62
Bennett, George E., Corry, 62
Bennett, George W., Washington, 62
Bennett, Gershon S., New Castle, 62
Bennett, Newman H., Pittsburgh, 63
Bennett, Virgil E., Beaver, Pittsburgh, 63
Bennett, William C., Indiana, 63
Benney, George A., Sewickley, Pittsburgh, 63
Bennis, David A., Philadelphia, 63
Bensinger, C. Raymond, East Stroudsburg, Stroudsburg, 63
Benson, Charles P., Aspinwall, 63
Benson, Francis C., Jr., Philadelphia, 63
Benson, Joseph P., Punxsutawney, 64
Benswanger, William E., Pittsburgh, 64
Bent, Quincy, Bethlehem, 64
Bentley, Franklin L., State College, 64
Benton, Herbert E., Philadelphia, 64
Beresford, Frank M., Ardmore, Philadelphia, 64
Berg, Gustav F., Pittsburgh, 64
Berg, John D., Glen Osborne, Pittsburgh, 64
Berg, Ragnar, Mt. Lebanon, Pittsburgh, 64
Berger, Andrew B., Pittsburgh, 64
Berger, G. George R. B., Pittsburgh, 64
Berger, G. Fred, Philadelphia, Norristown, 64
Bergstresser, Ira F., Allentown, 64
Bergstrom, Albert R., Coatesville, 64
Berk, Ira L., Pittsburgh, 65
Berkheimer, Frank E., Lemoyne, 65
Berl, Ernst, Pittsburgh, 65
Berlin, John C., Knox, 65
Berman, Aaron, Drexel Hill, Philadelphia, 65
Bernd-Cohen, Max, West Chester, 65
Bernhard, John J., Allentown, 65
Bernhardy, Harry W., Rochester, 65
Bernheim, Oscar F., Allentown, 65
Bernheimer, Leo G., Philadelphia, 66
Bernreuter, Robert G., State College, 66
Bernstein, Mitchell, Elkins Park, Philadelphia, 66
Bernstein, Ralph, Philadelphia, 66
Bernstine, J. Bernard, Philadelphia, 66
Berry, Herman C., Philadelphia, 66
Bert, Otto F. H., Washington, 66
Bertolet, John A., Philadelphia, 66
Bertolet, William S., Reading, 66
Bervinchak, Nicholas, Pottsville, 67
Best, Harvey P., Philadelphia, 67
Best, William E., Pittsburgh, 67
Betts, Emmett A., State College, 67
Betz, LeRoy D., Meadowbrook, Philadelphia, 68
Beury, Charles E., Philadelphia, 68
Beutner, Reinhard H., Philadelphia, 68
Beye, William, Pittsburgh, 68
Beyer, Alvin D., Norristown, 68
Beymer, Albert S., Allison Park, Pittsburgh, 68
Bezanson, Anne, Philadelphia, 68

Biagi, Ernest L., Philadelphia, 68
Bialas, Joseph F., Pittsburgh, 68
Biben, Joseph H., Philadelphia, 68
Bickel, H. Rank, Lebanon, 68
Bickel, William F., Aspinwall, Pittsburgh, 69
Biddle, A. J. Drexel, Philadelphia, 69
Biddle, Charles J., Andalusia, Philadelphia, 69
Biddle, Edward M., Ardmore, Philadelphia, 69
Biddle, Francis, Philadelphia, 69
Biddle, Gertrude B., Philadelphia, Carlisle, 69
Biddle, John H., Huntingdon, 69
Biddle, Moncure, Devon, Philadelphia, 69
Biddle, Nicholas, Noble, Philadelphia, 69
Bidwell, Charles C., Riegelsville, 69
Bidwell, Marshall S., Pittsburgh, 69
Bieber, Milton J., Philadelphia, 69
Bierly, Robert N., West Pittston, Wilkes-Barre, 70
Biester, Edward G., Doylestown, 70
Biestech, Charles F., Pittsburgh, 70
Bigelow, Fred A., Wyomissing, Reading, 70
Bigelow, Frederick S., Haverford, 70
Bigger, Frederick, Pittsburgh, 70
Biggs, John Q., Johnstown, 70
Bikle, Henry W., Strafford, Philadelphia, 70
Billhartz, William H., Pittsburgh, 71
Billheimer, Stanley, Palmyra, 71
Billikopf, Jacob, Philadelphia, 71
Billings, John H., Ardmore, 71
Binford, Oriel J., Butler, 71
Bingham, Eugene C., Easton, 71
Bining, Arthur C., Drexel Hill, 72
Binkerd, Robert S., Philadelphia, 72
Binns, Benjamin G., Monongahela, Donora, 72
Birch, Raymond E., Mt. Lebanon, Pittsburgh, 72
Birdsong, Henry E., Philadelphia, 72
Birkmann, Charles J., Philadelphia, 72
Birney, Hoffman, Glen Mills, 73
Birrell, George W., Lancaster, 73
Biscoe, Alvin B., Lewisburg, 73
Bish, Eugene W., Brockway, 73
Bishop, Arthur V., Carlisle, 73
Bishop, Frederic L., Pittsburgh, 73
Bishop, Frederick J., Scranton, 73
Bishop, Herman L., Lansdale, 73
Bishop, Howard B., Easton, 73
Bishop, R. E., Philadelphia, 73
Bishop, Ward L., Bethlehem, 73
Bitting, William T., Wynnewood, Philadelphia, 74
Bitzer, Newton E., Lancaster, 74
Bixby, Edward W., Wilkes-Barre, 74
Black, Arthur O., Butler, 74
Black, Burton A., Grove City, 74
Black, Eleanor S., Pittsburgh, 74
Black, George S., Chambersburg, 74
Black, Harold L., New Wilmington, 74
Black, Matthew W., Berwyn, 75
Black, Ned, Mechanicsburg, Harrisburg, 75
Black, Robert M., Pittsburgh, 75
Black, Russell V. N., New Hope, 75
Blackburn, Albert E., Merion, 75
Blackburn, George S., Bryn Mawr, 75
Blackburn, James B., Pittsburgh, 75
Blackburn, Lesley, Everett, 75
Blackburn, Morris A., Philadelphia, 75
Blackman, John H., Jr., Dallas, Scranton, 75
Blackmore, George A., Perrysville, Swissvale, Wilmerding, 76
Blackwood, James M., New Castle, 76
Blackwood, Oswald, Pittsburgh, 76
Bladel, Edward L., Crafton, Pittsburgh, 76
Blai, Boris, Elkins Park, 76
Blair, John L., Warren, 76
Blair, Mortimer W., Philadelphia, 76
Blair, Orland R., Clarks Summit, 77
Blair, Parr D., Meadville, 77
Blair, Ross M., Mt. Lebanon, Pittsburgh, 77
Blair, Thomas M. H., Pittsburgh, State College, 77
Blair, Walter A., Chester, 77
Blair, William W., Pittsburgh, 77

Blaisdell, George G., Bradford, 77
Blake, Francis F. E., Philadelphia, 77
Blakeley, George H., Bethlehem, 77
Blanchard, Maria G., Pittsburgh, 78
Blanchet, Paul R., State College, 78
Bland, Pascal B., Bala-Cynwyd, Philadelphia, 78
Blanning, Wendell Y., Williamstown, 78
Blanshard, Brand, Swarthmore, 78
Blanshard, Frances B., Swarthmore, 78
Blanton, Darrell E., Pittsburgh, 78
Blasband, Alfred, Philadelphia, 79
Blasingame, Ralph U., State College, 79
Blass, Charles A., Erie, 79
Blatt, A. S., Easton, 79
Blatz, John B., Philadelphia, 79
Blatz, William C., Fairville, 79
Blauch, Victor R., Leechburg, 79
Blaxter, Henry V., Pittsburgh, 79
Blazek, Paul Pittsburgh, 79
Bleakney, Edward M., Pittsburgh, 79
Blenko, Walter J., Allison Park, Pittsburgh, 79
Blew, Michael J., Philadelphia, 80
Blinn, Charles P., Jr., Ardmore, Philadelphia, 80
Bliss, Robert P., Harrisburg 80
Bliss, Sydney R., Scranton, 80
Bloch, Julius, Malvern, Philadelphia, 80
Block, Frank B., Philadelphia, 80
Blodgett, Francis B., Erie, 80
Blondheim, Adolphe W., New Hope, 80
Blough, Elijah R., Pittsburgh, 81
Blouin, Sister Marie Elise, Greensburg, 81
Bluett, Thomas, Philadelphia, 81
Blum, Louis P., Pittsburgh, 81
Blumberg, Nathan, Philadelphia, 81
Blumenthal, Hart, Philadelphia, 81
Blumer, Max A., Pittsburgh, 81
Boal, Pierre de L., Boalsburg, 81
Bockius, Morris R., Philadelphia, 82
Bode, Frederick W., Pittsburgh, 82
Bodine, Helen K., Newtown Square, 82
Bodine, John R., Catawissa, 82
Bodine, Marc W., Williamsport, 82
Bodine, William B., Philadelphia, 82
Bodine, William W., Villanova, Philadelphia, 82
Boenning, Henry D., Philadelphia, 83
Boericke, Garth W., Merion, Philadelphia, 83
Boettcher, Henry F., Pittsburgh, 83
Bogardus, James F., Swarthmore, 83
Boger, Robert C., Philadelphia, 83
Bohlen, Francis H., Philadelphia, 83
Bok, Curtis, Philadelphia, 83
Bok, Mary L. C., Merion Station, 83
Boland, Patrick J., Scranton, 83
Bolard, John A., Cambridge Springs, 83
Boles, Russell S., Narberth, Philadelphia, 83
Bolger, James H., Bangor, 83
Bolger, Robert V., Philadelphia, 83
Boliman, William H., Lancaster, 84
Bolton, Thaddeus L., Narberth, 84
Bombassei-Frascani, Giorgio M., Pittsburgh, 84
Bomberger, Christian M., Jeannette, 84
Bomberger, Richard W., Lancaster, 84
Bond, Charles M., Lewisburg, 84
Bond, Earl D., Bryn Mawr, Philadelphia, 84
Bond, Frank A., Pittsburgh, 84
Bond, Walter L., York, 85
Bond, William S., York, 85
Bonine, Chesleigh A., State College, 85
Bonner, John J., Philadelphia, 85
Bonnert, O. G. F., Ridgway, 85
Bonnet, Frederic, Jr., Ridley Park, Marcus Hook, 85
Bonniwell, Eugene C., Philadelphia, 85
Boocock, Cornelius B., Haverford, 85
Book, William I., Philadelphia, 85
Bookstaber, Philip D., Harrisburg, 85
Bookwalter, George R., Franklin, 86
Boomhower, William G., Philadelphia, 86
Boone, Charles G., Natrona, 86

Booth, Albert E., Bradford, 86
Booth, Cecil O., Pittsburgh, 86
Booth, George, Pittsburgh, 86
Booth, Isaac W., Philadelphia, 86
Booth, Miriam B., Erie 86
Booth, William W., Pittsburgh, 86
Boothby, Willard S., Philadelphia, 86
Borie, Charles L., Rydal, Philadelphia, 87
Borland, Andrew A., State College, 87
Borneman, Henry S., Philadelphia, 87
Bornscheuer, Albert A., Pittsburgh, 87
Borst, George H., Wayne, Philadelphia, 87
Borton, George W., Philadelphia, 87
Bortz, Edward L., Philadelphia, 87
Bosler, Lester C., Philadelphia, 88
Bossard, James H. S., Lansdowne, 88
Bostock, Edward C., Bryn Athyn, Philadelphia, 88
Bostwick, Roy G., Wilkinsburg, Pittsburgh, 88
Boswell, George E., Bristol, 88
Bothwell, Edgar C., Pittsburgh, 88
Bothwell, Edward G., Pittsburgh, 88
Botset, Holbrook G., Pittsburgh, 88
Boughton, Guy C., Erie, 88
Boulden, Philip A., Philadelphia, 88
Boulton, Harry, Clearfield, Philadelphia, 88
Boving, Charles B., Pittsburgh, 89
Bowen, John C., Allentown, 89
Bowen, Samuel B., Philadelphia, 89
Bower, Catharine R., Philadelphia, 89
Bower, John O., Philadelphia, 89
Bowers, Archibald C., Greensburg, Jeannette, 89
Bowers, Charles H., Nanty Glo, 89
Bowers, Frank L., Point Marion, 89
Bowman, Addison M., Camp Hill, Carlisle, 90
Bowman, Harry L., Drexel Hill, Philadelphia, 90
Bowman, John G., Pittsburgh, 90
Bowman, John W., Harrisburg, 90
Bowman, Joseph H., Pittsburgh, 90
Bown, Charles E., Pittsburgh, 90
Boyd, Charles P., Kennett Square, Philadelphia, 91
Boyd, D. Knickerbacker, Philadelphia, 91
Boyd, David H., Pittsburgh, 91
Boyd, George M., Philadelphia, 92
Boyd, Harry B., Indiana, 92
Boyd, Julian P., Merion, Philadelphia, 92
Boyd, Marcus, Coraopolis, Pittsburgh, 92
Boyd, Richard N., Allentown, 92
Boyd, Roy M., Philadelphia, 92
Boyd, Thomas Y., Honesdale, 92
Boyer, Calvin S., Doylestown, 92
Boyer, Carl, Philadelphia, 92
Boyer, Carl W., Allentown, 92
Boyer, Daniel B., Boyertown, 92
Boyer, Emery H., Johnstown, 93
Boyer, E. Albert, Northampton, Easton, 93
Boyer, Francis, Norristown, Philadelphia, 93
Boyer, Frank P., Mifflinburg, 93
Boyer, Philip A., Philadelphia, 93
Boyer, Robert, Philadelphia, 93
Boyer, Samuel P., Johnstown, 93
Boylan, Matthew A., Scranton, 93
Boyle, Charles J., Johnstown, 93
Boyle, H. Cotter, Allentown, 93
Boyle, Hugh C., Pittsburgh, 93
Boyle, Orrin E., Allentown, 93
Braceland, Francis J., Philadelphia, 94
Bracken, John R., State College, 94
Bradbury, Robert H., Wayne, 94
Bradbury, Samuel, Philadelphia, 94
Bradford, Avery J., Pittsburgh, 94
Bradford, Charles E., McKeesport, 94
Bradford, Frederick A., Bethlehem, 94
Bradford, Louis J., State College, 94
Bradford, Mark A., Pittsburgh, 94
Bradfute, John H., Mt. Lebanon, Pittsburgh, 94
Bradley, Edward S., Philadelphia, 95
Bradley, Francis A., Philadelphia, 95
Bradley, Michael J., Philadelphia, 95
Bradley, Paul R., Pittsburgh, 95
Bradley, William N., Pittsburgh, 95

Bradshaw, Guy R., Greenville, 95
Bradshaw, Thompson, Beaver, 95
Bradshaw, William A., Sr., Pittsburgh, 95
Bradway, Florence D., Philadelphia, 96
Braham, William W., New Castle, 96
Brainard, Edward H., Pittsburgh, 96
Brainerd, Arthur A., Norwood, Philadelphia, 96
Braisted, William C., West Chester, 96
Brakeley, George A., Philadelphia, 96
Bram, Israel, Upland, Philadelphia, 96
Bramer, Samuel E., Pittsburgh, Glassport, 96
Branch, Edward D., Pittsburgh, 97
Brand, Millen, New Hope, 97
Brand, Thurlow W., Pittsburgh, 97
Brandes, George H., Allentown, 97
Brandon, J. Campbell, Butler, 97
Brandon, James B., Scranton, 97
Brandon, John W., Butler, 97
Brandon, Washington D., Butler, 97
Brandt, David D., Mechanicsburg, 97
Bransfield, John W., Philadelphia, 98
Braude, Bennett A., Westmont, Johnstown, 98
Brauff, Herbert D., Vandergrift, 98
Braun, Arthur E., Pittsburgh, 98
Braun, Carl J., Jr., Pittsburgh, 98
Braun, Ernest R., Jr., Avalon, Pittsburgh, 98
Braun, Herbert, Philadelphia, 98
Braunstein, Baruch, Philadelphia, 98
Brazer, Clarence W., Chester, 99
Breakey, Edward P., Oakmont, Pittsburgh, 99
Bream, Henry T., Gettysburg, 99
Breeden, Waldo, Pittsburgh, 99
Breene, Edmond C., Oil City, 99
Brégy, Edith M., Philadelphia, 99
Brégy, Katherine M. C., Philadelphia, 99
Brehman, A. Balfour, Philadelphia, 99
Breitigan, James H., Lititz, 99
Breitwieser, Thomas J., East Stroudsburg, 100
Breneman, Paul B., State College, 100
Brengle, Henry G., Radnor, Philadelphia, 100
Brennan, Cornelius P., Philadelphia, 100
Bretherick, Arthur P., Darby, Philadelphia, 100
Brevillier, Edwin H., Erie, 100
Brewer, Ralph E., Wilkinsburg, Pittsburgh, 101
Brewer, Robert W. A., Huntingdon Valley, 101
Brewster, C. Barton, Philadelphia, 101
Brewster, Ethel H., Swarthmore, 101
Bricker, Sacks, Philadelphia, 101
Brien, Donald G., Pittsburgh, 101
Briggs, Charles A., Scottdale, 102
Briggs, Leon W., Pittsburgh, 102
Bright, Alan, Ensworth, Pittsburgh, 102
Bright, Stanley, Reading, 102
Brilhart, David H., Bethlehem, 102
Brinker, William E., Jr., Wilkinsburg, 102
Brinkmann, Heinrich W., Swarthmore, 102
Brinley, Charles E., Philadelphia, 102
Brinton, Anna S. C., Wallingford, 102
Brinton, Caleb B., Carlisle, 103
Brinton, Christian, West Chester, 103
Brinton, Clarence C., Philadelphia, 103
Brinton, Henry L., West Chester, 103
Brinton, Howard H., Wallingford, 103
Brinton, Jasper Y., Philadelphia, 103
Bristow, William H., Shippensburg, 103
Britan, Joseph T., Philadelphia, 104
Britt, Lillian A., Philadelphia, 104
Brittain, James A., Philadelphia, 104
Brockbank, John I., DuBois, 104
Brockway, Chauncey E., Sharon, 104
Broden, Edwin H., Swissvale, Pittsburgh, 104

Brodhead, George M., Philadelphia, 104
Brodstein, Ellis, Reading, 104
Bromer, Edward S., Lancaster, 105
Bronk, Detlev W., Media, Philadelphia, 105
Bronk, Isabelle, Swarthmore, 105
Bronk, Mitchell, Philadelphia, 105
Bronstein, Jesse B., Allentown, 105
Brooke, Francis M., Bryn Mawr, Philadelphia, 105
Brooke, George, Ithan, Birdsboro, 105
Brooke, George, 3d, Birdsboro, 105
Brooke, John A., Philadelphia, 105
Brooke, Robert E., Birdsboro, 106
Brooks, Betty W., Pittsburgh, 106
Brooks, Edward S., York, 106
Brooks, Frank F., Pittsburgh, Shields, 106
Brooks, George G., Scranton, 106
Brooks, Harold K., Pittsburgh, 106
Brooks, John B., Erie, 106
Brooks, John H., Scranton, 106
Brooks, Robert C., Swarthmore, 106
Brooks, Stanley T., Pittsburgh, 106
Brooks, Thomas R., Scranton, 106
Broome, Edwin C., Philadelphia, 107
Broomell, I. Norman, Philadelphia, 107
Brosky, Frank J., Pittsburgh, 107
Brotemarkle, Robert A., Philadelphia, 107
Brough, Charles Y., Hanover, 107
Brown, Arthur E., Harrisburg, 107
Brown, Arthur E., Philadelphia, 107
Brown, Bishop, Ingomar, 108
Brown, Charles L., Merion, Philadelphia, 108
Brown, Charles L., Philadelphia, 108
Brown, Clarence M., Philadelphia, 108
Brown, Ellis Y., Jr., Downington, 108
Brown, Francis S., Philadelphia, 109
Brown, Francis S., Jr., Philadelphia, 109
Brown, Gabriel S., Easton, 109
Brown, George A., Dormont, Pittsburgh, 109
Brown, George W., Jr., Philadelphia, 109
Brown, Henry P., Jr., Philadelphia, 109
Brown, Henry W., Punxsutawney, 109
Brown, Herbert V., Johnstown, 109
Brown, Howard S., Philadelphia, 110
Brown, James R., Esterly, 110
Brown, James T., Sewickley, Pittsburgh, 110
Brown, John A., Philadelphia, 110
Brown, John D. M., Allentown, 110
Brown, John T., Jr., Wyncote, Philadelphia, 110
Brown, Joseph B., Pittsburgh, 110
Brown, Joseph J., Philadelphia, 110
Brown, Kenneth R., Tamaqua, 111
Brown, Lewis S., Narberth, Philadelphia, 111
Brown, Mace, Pittsburgh, 111
Brown, Neill S., 3d, Shields, Pittsburgh, 111
Brown, Oscar, Philadelphia, 111
Brown, Owen C., Lansdowne, Philadelphia, 111
Brown, Paul G., Philadelphia, 111
Brown, Ralph N., Warren, 111
Brown, Revelle W., Philadelphia, 112
Brown, Richard L., Allentown, 112
Brown, Richard P., Philadelphia, 112
Brown, Samuel H., Jr., Bala-Cynwyd, Philadelphia, 112
Brown, Samuel T., Pittsburgh, 112
Brown, Sydney M., Bethlehem, 112
Brown, Thomas J., Philadelphia, 112
Brown, Thomas K., Jr., Swarthmore, Philadelphia, 112
Brown, Thomas M., Mt. Lebanon, Pittsburgh, 112
Brown, W. Norman, Moylan, Philadelphia, 113
Brown, Wyatt, Harrisburg, 113
Brownback, John H., Collegeville, 113
Brownback, Russell J., Norristown, 113
Browne, Vere B., Tarentum, Breckenridge, 113
Brownell, Eleanor O., Bryn Mawr, 113
Brownlee, Roy H., Pittsburgh, 113

Brownmiller, Roy E., Pottsville, Harrisburg, 113
Broyles, William A., State College, 114
Broza, Stanley A., Devon, Philadelphia, 114
Bruck, Samuel, Philadelphia, 114
Brumbach, Claude A., Esterly, 114
Brumbach, William D., Esterly, 114
Bruner, John W., Bloomsburg, 115
Brunner, Henry S., State College, 115
Brunot, John B., Greensburg, 115
Brust, William T., Erie, 115
Bruton, Paul W., Wayne, Philadelphia, 115
Bruun, Johannes H., Swarthmore, Norwood, 115
Bryans, Henry B., Norristown, Philadelphia, 116
Bryson, John F., Girardville, 116
Buccieri, Agostino R., Pittsburgh, 116
Buchanan, David R., Washington, 116
Buchanan, Edwin P., Pittsburgh, 116
Buchanan, Mary, Philadelphia, 116
Buchanan, Robert H., Scranton, 116
Bucher, George H., Mt. Lebanon, Pittsburgh, 116
Buchman, Frank N. D., Allentown, 117
Buck, Charles A., Bethlehem, 117
Buck, Pearl S., Perkasie, 117
Bucke, Jacob E. A., Shamokin, 117
Buckingham, Guy E., Meadville, 118
Buckley, Albert C., Philadelphia, 118
Buckner, Chester A., Pittsburgh, 118
Buckwalter, Isaac Z., Lancaster, 118
Budahn, Louis A., Pottsville, 118
Budd, Edward G., Philadelphia, 118
Budd, Thomas A., Merion, Philadelphia, 118
Budke, John F., Franklin, 118
Buell, Marjorie H., Frazer, Malvern, 118
Buenting, Otto W., Pittsburgh, Wilmerding, 118
Buerger, Charles B., Pittsburgh, 119
Bufalino, Charles J., Pittston, 119
Buffington, Joseph, Philadelphia, 119
Bughman, Henry C., Jr., Sewickley, Pittsburgh, 119
Buka, Alfred J., Pittsburgh, 119
Bulleit, Eugene V., Gettysburg, 119
Bullinger, Clarence E., State College, 119
Bullock, Charles A., Canton, 119
Bumpus, Lester W., Pittsburgh, 119
Bunce, Earl H., Palmerton, 120
Bunn, John F., Jr., Philadelphia, 120
Bunting, Martha, Philadelphia, 120
Burch, Henry R., Philadelphia, 120
Burchfield, Albert H., Pittsburgh, 120
Burchfield, Albert H., Jr., Pittsburgh, 120
Burchinal, William J., Smithfield, 120
Burden, Verne G., Wynnewood, Philadelphia, 120
Burgess, Arthur S., Wyncote, Philadelphia, 120
Burgess, John S., Wyncote, 121
Burgess, Thomas, Philadelphia, 121
Burgess, William, Jr., Morrisville, 121
Burgwin, Hill, Pittsburgh, 121
Burke, Alexander E., Philadelphia, 121
Burke, Patrick J., Locust Gap, 121
Burke, Robert B., Philadelphia, 121
Burkett, Philip H., Philadelphia, 122
Burkholder, Henry C., Lancaster, 122
Burki, Albert H., Gibsonia, Pittsburgh, 122
Burnett, Loutellus A., Pittsburgh, 122
Burnett, Mary C., Pittsburgh, 122
Burnett, W. Emory, Philadelphia, 122
Burnham, E. Lewis, Berwyn, Philadelphia, 122
Burnley, Harry, Marple, Media, 123
Burns, Jesse E., Oil City, 123
Burns, Kelvin, Pittsburgh, 123
Burns, Stillwell C., Philadelphia, 123
Burns, Vincent L., Philadelphia, 123

Burnside, Robert E., Washington, 123
Burpee, David, Doylestown, Philadelphia, 123
Burpee, W. Atlee, Jr., Philadelphia, 123
Burr, Anna R., Bryn Mawr, 123
Burr, Charles W., Philadelphia, 123
Burr, M. Vashti, Ebensburg, Harrisburg, 123
Burr, Walter H., Coatesville, 124
Burrell, David de F., Williamsport, 124
Burrell, George A., Pittsburgh, 124
Burstein, David I., Philadelphia, 124
Burt, James C., Pittsburgh, 124
Burt, William N., Jr., Edgewood, Pittsburgh, 124
Burtis, Philip B., Philadelphia, 124
Burton, Carroll, Johnstown, 124
Burton, Horace M., Primos, Philadelphia, 125
Burtt, Howard, Philadelphia, 125
Busch, Henry P., Philadelphia, 125
Busch, Miers, Philadelphia, 125
Bushong, Robert G., Reading, 125
Busser, Frank S., Philadelphia, 125
Butcher, Howard, Jr., Ardmore, Philadelphia, 125
Butler, Arthur G., Pittsburgh, 126
Butler, Frank A., State College, 126
Butler, LaFayette L., Hazleton, 126
Butler, Mary, Philadelphia, Uwchland, 126
Butler, Philo W., Scranton, 126
Butler, Ralph, Philadelphia, 126
Butler, Rock L., Wellsboro, 126
Butler, Smedley D., Newtown Square, 126
Butler, Will G., Blossburg, 126
Butler, William L., Drexel Hill, Philadelphia, 127
Butt, William E., State College, 127
Butterfield, Thomas E., Bethlehem, 127
Butterweck, Joseph S., Philadelphia, 127
Butterworth, Gordon, Abington, Philadelphia, 127
Butts, Allison, Bethlehem, 127
Butts, Donald C., Philadelphia, 127
Butz, Charles A., Bethlehem, 128
Butz, Reuben J., Allentown, 128
Buzzard, Josiah F., Altoona, 128
Bycroft, John S., Jr., Sharon, 128
Bye, Raymond P., Moylan, Philadelphia, 128
Byerly, John L., Ohl, Summerville, 128
Byers, John F., Sewickley, 128
Byron, Robert J., Philadelphia, 129
Cabeen, David C., Drexel Hill, 129
Cadbury, Benjamin, Philadelphia, 129
Cadbury, William E., Philadelphia, 129
Cadot, John J., York, 129
Cadwalader, Williams B., Villa Nova, Philadelphia, 129
Cadwallader, James A., Mt. Lebanon, Pittsburgh, 129
Cadwallader, William H., Pittsburgh, Swissvale, 129
Calderwood, Alva J., Grove City, 130
Caldwell, Albert O., Titusville, 130
Caldwell, William J., New Castle, 130
Caldwell, William T., Philadelphia, 130
Callahan, Jeremiah J., Pittsburgh, 130
Callenbach, Ernest W., Boalsburg, State College, 130
Callender, Clarence N., Merion, Philadelphia, 130
Calvert, George H., Glenshaw, Pittsburgh, 131
Calvert, Philip P., Cheyney, 131
Calvin, Everett Y., Beaver Falls, 131
Cameron, Donald W., Pittsburgh, 131
Cameron, James R., Philadelphia, 131
Camp, Chauncey F., Johnstown, 131
Campbell, Aaron P., Reading, Wyomissing, 131
Campbell, Arthur R., Lancaster, 131
Campbell, C. William, Coraopolis, Pittsburgh, 131
Campbell, Clyde S., Connellsville, 132
Campbell, David B., Canonsburg, 132
Campbell, Edward H., Wynnewood, Philadelphia, 132
Campbell, Edward W., Philadelphia, 132

Campbell, Ethan A., Chester, 132
Campbell, George J., Wildwood, Pittsburgh, 132
Campbell, James A. G., Chester, 132
Campbell, James H., Bellevue, Pittsburgh, 132
Campbell, Lawrence W., Johnstown, 132
Campbell, LeRoy B., Warren, 132
Campbell, Paul E., Pittsburgh, 132
Campbell, William F., New Wilmington, 133
Campbell, Wilson A., Sewickley, Aliquippa, 133
Campion, John L., Philadelphia, 133
Campman, Clarence C., West Middlesex, 133
Canan, William T., Altoona, 133
Cancelmo, J. James, Philadelphia, 133
Cannon, Florence V., Chester Springs, 134
Cannon, Russell A., Wynnewood, Birdsboro, 134
Cantarow, Abraham, Philadelphia, 134
Cantor, Aaron S., Scranton, 134
Caplan, Albert J., Elkins Park, 134
Caplan, Harry N., Allentown, 135
Capolino, Gertrude R., Philadelphia, 135
Capolino, J. Joseph, Philadelphia, 135
Cappabianca, John B. C. A., Erie, 135
Capper, Aaron, Philadelphia, 135
Capper, Howard M., Camp Hill, 135
Caputo, Eugene A., Ambridge, 135
Caraher, Edward P. M., Loretto, 135
Carey, Bruce A., Narberth, Philadelphia, 135
Carleton, Francis J., Philadelphia, 136
Carling, George F., Sayre, 136
Carlisle, William A., DuBois, 136
Carlock, John B., Pittsburgh, 136
Carlson, H. C., Braddock, Pittsburgh, 136
Carmichael, Thomas H., Philadelphia, 136
Carney, Francis T., Johnstown, 137
Carney, William J., Erie, 137
Carothers, John A., Pittsburgh, 137
Carothers, Neil, Bethlehem, 137
Carpenter, Aaron E., Philadelphia, 137
Carpenter, Charles A., Pittsburgh, 137
Carpenter, Edmund N., Wilkes-Barre, 137
Carpenter, Howard C., Philadelphia, 137
Carpenter, James D., Harrisburg, 137
Carpenter, Joseph R., Jr., Philadelphia, 137
Carpenter, Rhys, Downingtown, 137
Carr, Harry C., Rosemont, Philadelphia, 138
Carr, James O., Pittsburgh, Brackenridge, 138
Carr, John R., Philadelphia, see Addenda
Carr, Walter R., Uniontown, 138
Carr, William A., Philadelphia, 138
Carrell, John B., Hatboro, 138
Carrigg, Joseph L., Susquehanna, Montrose, 138
Carringer, Marion A., Tionesta, 138
Carroll, Joseph H., Pittsburgh, 139
Carroll, Mitchell, Lancaster, 139
Carroll, Thomas B., Pittsburgh, 139
Carroll, Wayne T., Kaylor, 139
Carson, David R., Lansdowne, Philadelphia, 139
Carson, Edwin R., Pittsburgh, 139
Carson, John R., New Hope, 139
Carson, Norma B., Philadelphia, 139
Carson, Roy I., Charleroi, 139
Carson, Waid E., Pittsburgh, 139
Carter, Boake, Philadelphia, 139
Carter, Ephraim C., Pittsburgh, 140
Carter, George H., Philadelphia, 140
Carter, Harvey L., Collegeville, 140
Carter, J. Frank, Brookline, Upper Darby, 140
Carter, James, Lincoln University, 140
Carter, John H., Lancaster, 140
Carter, William J., Harrisburg, 140
Carter, William T., 2d, Bryn Mawr, Philadelphia, 140
Cartwright, John H., Ridgway, 140
Cartwright, Richard A., Ridgway, 140
Carver, Clarence J., Carlisle, 141

Carver, George, Pittsburgh, 141
Carwile, Preston B., Bethlehem, 141
Cary, Charles R., Philadelphia, 141
Cary, Dale E., Lancaster, 141
Cary, Page, Philadelphia, 141
Case, Andrew W., State College, 141
Case-Blechschmidt, Dorothy, Philadelphia, 141
Casey, Daniel N., Camp Hill, Harrisburg, 141
Casey, Helen B. N., Philadelphia, 142
Casey, John F., Jr., Pittsburgh, 142
Cash, William E., Philadelphia, 142
Cashman, Bender Z., Pittsburgh, 142
Cassatt, Robert K., Rosemont, Philadelphia, 142
Casselberry, Russel D., State College, 142
Casselman, Arthur V., Reading, Philadelphia, 142
Cassidy, H. Creighton, Lewistown, 143
Cassidy, Lewis C., Pittsburgh, 143
Castallo, Mario A., Philadelphia, 143
Castle, Alfred W., Harrisburg, Mechanicsburg, 143
Casto, Theodore D., Philadelphia, 143
Catherwood, Cummins, Bryn Mawr, Philadelphia, 143
Catlin, Sheldon, Radnor, Philadelphia, 143
Cattanach, Lachlan M., Wilkes-Barre, 143
Cattell, Jaques, Lancaster, 143
Cauffman, Stanley H., Wissahickon, 143
Caum, Samuel L., Bethlehem, 144
Cavalcante, Anthony, Uniontown, 144
Caveiti, John E., Meadville, 144
Cawthra, W. H., DuBois, 144
Chadwick, E. Wallace, Chester, 144
Chaffee, Carl F., Swarthmore, Philadelphia, 144
Chaffee, Orel N., Erie, 144
Chalfant, Charles E., Mt. Lebanon, Pittsburgh, 144
Chalfant, P. Floyd, Waynesboro, 144
Chalfant, Sidney A., Pittsburgh, 144
Challis, David A., Sewickley, 144
Chamberlain, W. Edward, Philadelphia, 145
Chamberlin, Ralph E., Palmerton, 145
Chamberlin, William B., Torresdale, 145
Chambers, Francis S., Lancaster, 145
Chambers, Francis T., Penllyn, Philadelphia, 145
Chambers, Will G., State College, 145
Champion, John B., Philadelphia, 146
Champlin, Carroll D., State College, 146
Champlin, Helen K., State College, 146
Chance, Burton, Radnor, Philadelphia, 146
Chance, Edwin M., Philadelphia, 146
Chandlee, Grover C., State College, 146
Chandler, Paul G., Clarion, 146
Chandler, Paul V., Philadelphia, 146
Chandler, Percy M., Philadelphia, 146
Chandler, Swithin, Strafford, Philadelphia, 146
Chaney, George S., Washington, 147
Chaney, Newcomb K., Moylan, Philadelphia, 147
Chapin, Edward D., Milton, 147
Chapin, Katherine G., Philadelphia, 147
Chaplin, James C., Sewickley, Pittsburgh, 147
Chapman, Charles H., Philadelphia, 147
Chapman, Ernest T., New Kensington, 147
Chapman, Everett, Marshallton, Coatesville, 147
Chapman, Walter H., Philadelphia, 147
Charles, Christian E., Lancaster, 148
Charles, Rollin L., Lancaster, 148
Charlesworth, James C., Pittsburgh, 148
Chase, Charles T., Bala-Cynwyd, Philadelphia, 148
Chase, Eugene P., Easton, 148

PENNSYLVANIA

Chase, Eugene W., Oil City, 148
Chase, James M., Clearfield, 148
Chase, Philip H., Bala-Cynwyd, Philadelphia, 148
Chase, Walter D., Bethlehem, 149
Chase, William C., Clearfield, 149
Chatto, Byron H., Pittsburgh, East Pittsburgh, 149
Chenault, Roy L., Verona, Pittsburgh, 149
Cheney, Edith, Philadelphia, 149
Cherrington, George H., Pittsburgh, 149
Cherry, C. Waldo, Harrisburg, 149
Chesnutt, Nelson A., Upper Darby, 149
Chester, John N., Pittsburgh, 149
Chesterman, Francis J., Pittsburgh, 149
Cheston, J. Hamilton, Penllyn, Philadelphia, 150
Cheston, James, 3d, Philadelphia, 150
Chew, Oswald, Radnor, Philadelphia, 150
Chew, Robert E., Pittsburgh, 150
Chew, Samuel C., Bryn Mawr, 150
Chew, Tobias O., Indiana, 150
Cheyney, Edward P., Media, 150
Cheyney, Edward Ralph, Media, 150
Chidester, John Y., Uniontown, 150
Chidsey, Andrew D., Jr., Easton, 150
Chidsey, Harold R., Easton, 150
Chidsey, Thomas M., Easton, 150
Child, Harry C., Sayre, 151
Childs, Louis M., 2d, Norristown, 151
Childs, Randolph W., Bryn Athyn, Philadelphia, 151
Childs, William St. C., Pittsburgh, 151
Chipman, Charles, Easton, 151
Chipman, John S., Easton, 151
Chorlton, William H., Philadelphia, 152
Christiansen, Oscar A., McKees Rocks, 152
Christman, Charles E., Mt. Lebanon, Pittsburgh, 152
Christman, Howard L., Washington, 152
Christman, Paul S., Schuylkill Haven, 152
Christy, George L., Pittsburgh, 152
Chrostwaite, Thomas F., Hanover, 153
Chubb, Charles F., Coraopolis, Pittsburgh, 153
Chubb, Lewis W., Pittsburgh, 153
Church, Charles F., Drexel Hill, Philadelphia, 153
Church, Helen L., Philadelphia, 153
Church, Nathan W., Ulysses, 153
Church, Samuel H., Pittsburgh, 153
Church, Walter H., McKees Rocks, 153
Churchill, H. V., New Kensington, 153
Churchill, Herman R., Drexel Hill, 154
Clapper, Samuel M. D., Philadelphia, 154
Clark, Donald G., Pittsburgh, McKeesport, 154
Clark, Dora M., Chambersburg, 154
Clark, Edward R., Kingston, Scranton, 155
Clark, Edwin M., Indiana, 155
Clark, Eliot R., Philadelphia, 155
Clark, Frederic L., Philadelphia, 155
Clark, Harry E., Pittsburgh, 155
Clark, Heath M., Indiana, 155
Clark, Henry A., Erie, 155
Clark, Herbert L., Haverford, Philadelphia, 155
Clark, Jefferson H., Wyncote, Philadelphia, 155
Clark, Joseph S., Wayne, Philadelphia, 156
Clark, L. J., Philadelphia, 156
Clark, Laurence, Philadelphia, 156
Clark, Lelt. V., Latrobe, 156
Clark, Norman E., Washington, 156
Clark, Percy H., Bala-Cynwyd, Philadelphia, 156
Clark, Ralph A., Easton, 156
Clark, Sydney P., Norristown, Philadelphia, 156
Clark, Walter G., Westfield, Wellsboro, 156
Clarke, A. Vinton, Philadelphia, 157
Clarke, Charles M., Pittsburgh, 157
Clarke, Charles W. E., Penn Valley, 157
Clarke, Eugene C., Chambersburg, 157

Clarke, Francis P., Philadelphia, 157
Clarke, Harold V., Philadelphia, 157
Clarke, Robert, Beaver Falls, 157
Clarke, William A., Wallingford, Philadelphia, 157
Clarkson, Edward R., Pittsburgh, 158
Clause, Robert L., Sewickley, Pittsburgh, 158
Clausen, Bernard C., Pittsburgh, 158
Clawson, John L., Philadelphia, 158
Clawson, John W., Collegeville, 158
Clay, Joseph V. F., Philadelphia, 158
Claycomb, David L., Altoona, Harrisburg, 158
Cleaveland, Winfield M., Camp Hill, Harrisburg, 158
Cleaves, Benjamin F., Altoona, 158
Cleeton, Glen U., Pittsburgh, 158
Cleland, Charles S., Philadelphia, 159
Cleland, William E., Beaver Falls, 159
Clement, John S., Jenkintown, Philadelphia, 159
Clement, Lewis M., Philadelphia, 159
Clement, Martin W., Rosemont, Philadelphia, 159
Clements, Rex S., Bryn Mawr, 159
Clemmer, Leon, Philadelphia, 159
Clerf, Louis H., Philadelphia, 159
Cleveland, Arthur, Merion, Philadelphia, 159
Cleven, Nels A. N., Pittsburgh, 160
Clewell, Clarence E., Philadelphia, 160
Climenhaga, Asa W., Grantham, 160
Cline, Thomas L., Gettysburg, 160
Clinger, William F., Warren, 160
Clipman, William H., Lewisburg, 160
Cloak, Andrew B., Freedom, Rochester, 160
Cloak, Frank V. C., Philadelphia, 160
Cloetingh, Arthur C., State College, 160
Cloonan, John J., Bangor, 160
Cloos, Wilmot D., Lake Ariel, 160
Close, Ralph, Mt. Lebanon, Pittsburgh, 160
Clothier, Isaac H., Jr., Radnor, Philadelphia, 161
Clothier, Morris L., Villa Nova, Philadelphia, 161
Clothier, William J., Valley Forge, Philadelphia, 161
Cloud, Samuel P., West Chester, 161
Clouting, Elmer S., Philadelphia, 161
Clutz, Frank H., Gettysburg, 161
Clyde, Arthur W., State College, 161
Coakley, Thomas F., Pittsburgh, 162
Coar, Stanley F., Scranton, 162
Coates, George M., Philadelphia, 162
Coates, George W., Beaver Falls, 162
Cobau, William D., New Castle, 162
Coburn, Frederick W., Birdsboro, 162
Cochran, George G., Dawson, 163
Cochran, Harry A., Glenside, Philadelphia, 163
Cochran, Thomas C., Mercer, 163
Cocks, Orrin G., Wellsboro, 163
Cogill, Lida S., Philadelphia, 164
Cohen, A. B., Scranton, 164
Cohen, Abraham, Reading, Philadelphia, 164
Cohen, Herman B., Philadelphia, 164
Cohen, Lester, Doylestown, 164
Cohen, Louis, Mt. Carmel, 164
Cohen, Mortimer J., Philadelphia, 164
Cohen, Solomon S., Philadelphia, 164
Cohill, Maurice B., Ben Avon, Pittsburgh, 164
Cohn, Arthur, Philadelphia, 164
Coit, Charles W., Narberth, 165
Colbert, Charles F., Jr., Pittsburgh, 165
Coldren, Daries D-W., Schuylkill Haven, 165
Coldren, Ira B., Uniontown, 165
Cole, Henry E., Pittsburgh, 165
Cole, Lloyd G., Blossburg, 165
Cole, Thomas P., Greensburg, 166

Cole, Versa V., Philadelphia, 166
Coleman, Harry S., Pittsburgh, 166
Coleman, John, Beaver Falls, 166
Coleman, Ralph P., Jenkintown, Philadelphia, 166
Coleman, William H., Lewisburg, 166
Coleman, William J., Pittsburgh, 167
Coler, Carl S., Wilkinsburg, East Pittsburgh, 167
Colgan, Howard O., Donora, 167
Colket, Edward B., Philadelphia, 167
Coll, Edward B., Mt. Lebanon, Pittsburgh, 167
Colletti, Ferdinando, Reading, 167
Colley, Robert H., Philadelphia, 167
Collier, Bryan C., Allentown, 167
Collier, William E., Philadelphia, 167
Collins, Alexander T., Greensburg, 168
Collins, Herman L., Philadelphia, 168
Collins, J. M., Philadelphia, 168
Collins, John B., Pittsburgh, 168
Collins, Philip S., Wyncote, Philadelphia, 168
Colt, Martha C., Harrisburg, 169
Colvin, William H., Pittsburgh, 169
Colwell, Alexander H., Pittsburgh, 169
Comfort, Howard, Haverford, 170
Comfort, William W., Haverford, 170
Compton, Earl V., Harrisburg, 170
Comroe, Bernard I., Philadelphia, 170
Comstock, Glen M., Beaver, Pittsburgh, 170
Conard, Charles W., Lansdowne, Philadelphia, 170
Condon, Harry R., Pittsburgh, 170
Confrey, Burton, Pittsburgh, 170
Congdon, Clement R., Philadelphia, 170
Congdon, Wray H., Bethlehem, 171
Conger, William H., Jr., Philadelphia, 171
Conkling, Edwin G., Philadelphia, 171
Conkling, Wallace E., Philadelphia, 171
Conlen, William J., Philadelphia, 171
Conley, Bernard, Altoona, 171
Conley, Clarence A., Clarion, 171
Conley, Claude E., Dormont, 171
Conn, Charles F., Wayne, Philadelphia, 172
Connell, William B., State College, 172
Connell, William H., Philadelphia, 172
Connelley, Clifford B., Pittsburgh, 172
Connelly, John R., Bethlehem, 172
Connett, Harold, Haverford, Philadelphia, 172
Connole, Joseph V., Wilkes-Barre, 172
Connolly, H. J., Clarks Summit, Scranton, 172
Connor, William L., Allentown, 173
Connors, Garrett A., Sharon, 173
Conrad, William Y., Devon, Reading, 173
Converse, John W., Rosemont, Edystone, 173
Conway, G. W., New Castle, 173
Conway, Lester H., Sewickley, 173
Conway, Thomas, Jr., Philadelphia, 173
Conyngham, William H., Wilkes-Barre, 174
Cook, Arthur N., Glenside, 174
Cook, Ernest F., Swarthmore, 174
Cook, Frank H., Athens, Sayre, 174
Cook, Graham, Reading, 174
Cook, Gustavus W., Wynnewood, Chester, 174
Cook, Lora H., Cooksburg, 174
Cook, Thomas W., Allentown, 175
Cooke, Donald E., Philadelphia, 175
Cooke, James F., Bala-Cynwyd, Philadelphia, 175
Cooke, Jay, Philadelphia, 175
Cooke, Merritt T., Jr., Philadelphia, 175
Cooke, Morris L., Philadelphia, New Hope, 175
Cooley, Arthur S., Bethlehem, 175
Coolidge, George G., Pittsburgh, 175
Coombs, James N., Philadelphia, 175
Coon, Philip L., Beaver Falls, 176
Coon, William E., Erie, 176
Coons, Albert, Lebanon, 176

Cooper, Alex S., Harrisburg, 176
Cooper, Arthur E., Landisville, Lancaster, 176
Cooper, David A., Wynnewood, Philadelphia, 176
Cooper, Howell C., Pittsburgh, 176
Cooper, Maurice D., Pittsburgh, 176
Cooper, Roy C., Pittsburgh, 177
Cooper, Stuart, Philadelphia, 177
Cooper, Thomas Y., Hanover, 177
Cooperman, Morris B., Philadelphia, 177
Coover, Carson, Paxtang, Harrisburg, 177
Coover, Melanchthon, Gettysburg, 177
Cope, Henry N., Mont Alto, 177
Cope, Thomas D., Wayne, 177
Copeland, Dean B., Butler, 177
Copeland, Joseph F., Drexel Hill, 177
Coppedge, Mrs. Fern I., Philadelphia, 177
Coppock, Walter J., Moylan, Philadelphia, 177
Coppolino, John F., Philadelphia, 178
Corbiere, Anthony S., Allentown, 178
Corcoran, Sanford W., Dormont, Pittsburgh, 178
Cordes, Frank, Pittsburgh, 178
Cordray, Albert T., New Wilmington, 178
Cornbrooks, Thomas M., Springfield, 178
Cornell, Walter S., Philadelphia, 179
Cornfeld, Harry G., Collingdale, 179
Cornish, Samuel D., Collegeville, 179
Cornwell, Martha J., West Chester, 179
Corr, Patrick J., Pittsburgh, 179
Corrado, Gaetano, Connellsville, 179
Corrado, Guy, Connellsville, 179
Corrigan, James A., Hazleton, 180
Corrin, Kenneth M., Philadelphia, 180
Corser, John B., Scranton, 180
Corson, Fred P., Carlisle, 180
Corson, George C., Wyncote, Norristown, 180
Cort, John S., Pittsburgh, 180
Cosgrove, John C., Johnstown, 180
Costain, Thomas B., Bethayres, 181
Costello, James P., Hazleton, 181
Côté, Joseph L., Jr., Greensburg, 181
Cotton, Jarvis M., Pittsburgh, 181
Cotton, Robert W., Pittsburgh, McKees Rocks, 181
Cottrell, James E., Philadelphia, 181
Coughlin, Alfred G., Athens, 181
Coulter, James A., New Hope, 182
Coulter, Richard, Greensburg, 182
County, Albert J., St. Davids, 182
Courtice, Thomas R., McKeesport, 182
Cousens, Theodore W., Easton, 182
Cousley, Stanley W., Wynnewood, Philadelphia, 182
Covell, William E. R., Pittsburgh, 182
Covert, William C., Philadelphia, 182
Cowan, Carl B., Philadelphia, 182
Cowin, Roy B., Bethlehem, 182
Cox, Edward H., Swarthmore, 183
Cox, John L., Philadelphia, 183
Cox, Reavis, Swarthmore, Philadelphia, 184
Coyle, William R., Bethlehem, 184
Craig, Albert B., Sewickley, Pittsburgh, 184
Craig, Earl B., Elkins Park, Philadelphia, 184
Craig, Earle M., Beaver, Freedom, 184
Craig, Frank A., Philadelphia, 184
Craig, George L., Sewickley, Pittsburgh, 184
Craig, George R., Pittsburgh, 184
Craig, J. Reed, Erie, 184
Craig, Josiah K., Pittsburgh, 184
Craig, Mark R., Sewickley, Pittsburgh, 185
Craig, Samuel G., Philadelphia, 185
Craine, W. M. C., Altoona, 185
Crampton, George S., Philadelphia, 185
Crane, Clifford F., Harrisburg, 185
Crane, Judson S., Pittsburgh, 185
Crane, Utley E., Philadelphia, 185
Cranmer, Clyde W., Kittanning, 185
Craven, Henry T., Philadelphia, 186
Crawford, Benjamin F., Carnegie, **186**

PENNSYLVANIA

Crawford, Daniel, Jr., Philadelphia, 186
Crawford, Glenn M., Meadville, 186
Crawford, Harry J., Emlenton, 186
Crawford, James P. W., Philadelphia, 186
Crawford, James S., Pittsburgh, 186
Crawford, Matthew A., Brookville, 187
Crawford, Ralston, Chadds Ford, 187
Crawford, Stanton C., Pittsburgh, 187
Crawford, William R., Philadelphia, 187
Creighton, Edward B., Media, Philadelphia, 187
Creighton, Henry J. M., Swarthmore, 187
Creighton, William J., Pittsburgh, 187
Creitz, Charles E., Easton, 187
Crenshaw, James L., Bryn Mawr, 187
Creskoff, Jacob J., Philadelphia, 187
Cressman, Paul L., Mechanicsburg, Harrisburg, 188
Cressman, W. D., Norristown, 188
Cresswell, Donaldson, Bryn Mawr, Philadelphia, 188
Cret, Paul P., Philadelphia, 188
Cretcher, Leonard H., Pittsburgh, 188
Cribbs, Charles C., Pittsburgh, 188
Crichton, Andrew B., Johnstown, 188
Cridland, Harry L., Altoona, 188
Crispin, M. Jackson, Berwick, 188
Criss, Nicholas R., Pittsburgh, 189
Crist, Richard H., Pittsburgh, 189
Crist, Samuel S., Columbia, 189
Critchfield, Margaret E., Lancaster, 189
Crocker, Walter J., Philadelphia, 189
Crofoot, George E., Philadelphia, 189
Croll, Edward E., Jenkintown, Philadelphia, 189
Croll, Philip C., Womelsdorf, 189
Crolly, John W., Scranton, 189
Cromer, Clinton O., State College, 190
Cromie, William J., Philadelphia, 190
Crooks, Forrest C., Solebury, 190
Crosby, Charles N., Meadville, 190
Crosby, Henry L., Philadelphia, 190
Croskey, John W., Philadelphia, 190
Croskey, Ralph S., Villa Nova, Philadelphia, 190
Crosland, Edward S., Lancaster, 190
Crothers, Wesley G., Chester, 191
Crouse, Charles C., Greensburg, 191
Crow, Arthur E., Uniontown, 191
Crow, William J., Uniontown, 191
Crowe, Montgomery F., Stroudsburg, East Stroudsburg, 191
Crowell, Daniel V. B., Greensburg, 191
Crownfield, Gertrude, Philadelphia, 192
Crowther, Ernest, Crafton, 192
Crowther, Henry L., Philadelphia, 192
Crowther, Rae, Philadelphia, 192
Cruikshank, Burleigh, Philadelphia, 192
Crum, Earl L., Bethlehem, 192
Crum, Rolfe P., Philadelphia, 192
Crumlish, James C., Philadelphia, 192
Crump, Edward, Jr., Pittsburgh, 192
Crumrine, Clarence A., Washington, 192
Crumrine, Ernest S., Washington, 193
Crumrine, Lucius M., Washington, 193
Crumrine, Norman R., Beaver, 193
Crutchfield, James S., Sewickley, Pittsburgh, 193
Cryder, Donald S., State College, 193
Cubbon, Walter E., Oil City, 193
Culbertson, Andrew A., Edinboro, Erie, 193
Culbertson, Leland J., Meadville, 193
Culbertson, Stuart A., Meadville, 193
Culbertson, William S., Charmian, 193
Culley, David E., Pittsburgh, 194
Cullinan, T. W., Philadelphia, 194
Culp, John F., Harrisburg, 194
Culver, Charles M., Towanda, 194
Culver, Montgomery M., Edgewood, 194
Cummings, Herbert W., Sunbury, 194

Cummings, James H., Jr., Berwyn, Philadelphia, 194
Cummings, Robert A., Pittsburgh, 194
Cuneo, Edmund R., Latrobe, 195
Cunningham, Jesse E. B., Philadelphia, 195
Cunningham, Joseph A., Philadelphia, Harrisburg, 195
Cunningham, Samuel K., Pittsburgh, 195
Cupp, John E., Williamsport, 195
Curran, James, Pottsville, 195
Curran, Thomas A., Chester, 196
Currie, Barton W., Bala-Cynwyd, 196
Currie, D. Angus, Erie, 196
Currier, Arnold J., State College, 196
Curry, Charles H., Coraopolis, Swissvale, 196
Curry, Glendon E., Pittsburgh, 196
Curry, Grant, Pittsburgh, 196
Curry, Haskell B., State College, 196
Curry, P. H., Pittsburgh, 196
Curry, W. Lawrence, Jenkintown, 196
Curtin, Eugene A., Scranton, 196
Curtis, George B., Bethlehem, 197
Curtis, Lawrence, Philadelphia, 197
Curtis, Melville G., Philadelphia, 197
Curtis, Richard, Philadelphia, 197
Curtis, Samuel P., Philadelphia, 197
Curtis, William F., Allentown, 197
Curtiss, Elliott, Jr., Ivyland, Philadelphia, 197
Curtze, Alban W., Erie, 197
Curtze, Frederick F., Erie, 197
Cushman, Edward F., Philadelphia, 197
Cusick, Martin E., Sharpsville, Sharon, 198
Custer, Christopher R. C., Narberth, Ardmore, 198
Custer-Shoemaker, Dacia, Pittsburgh, 198
Custis, John T., Philadelphia, 198
Cuthbert, Virginia L., Pittsburgh, 198
Cutler, Jacob W., Philadelphia, 198
Cyr, Howard M., Palmerton, 198
Czarniecki, Myron J., Aspinwall, Pittsburgh, 198
Dahle, Chester D., State College, 199
Dailey, Elmer M., Butler, 199
Daker, Jess O., Pittsburgh, 199
Daland, Elliot, Philadelphia, 199
Daly, Edwin K., Philadelphia, 199
Daly, J. Burrwood, Philadelphia, 199
Daly, Thomas A., Philadelphia, 199
Dalzell, Robert D., Pittsburgh, 199
Dambach, John, Pittsburgh, 199
Dambach, L. Earl, Duquesne, 199
Danforth, Irving W., Pittsburgh, 200
Daniel, Channing W., St. David's, Philadelphia, 200
Daniel, Todd, Philadelphia, 200
Daniels, Frank C., Curwensville, 200
Dann, Alexander W., Sewickley, Pittsburgh, 200
Dannehower, William F., Norristown, 200
Dannenberg, Arthur M., Philadelphia, 200
Danton, J. Periam, Philadelphia, 200
Dantzscher, Walter F., State College, 200
Darbaker, L. K., Wilkinsburg, Pittsburgh, 200
Darling, Chester A., Meadville, 201
Darling, Ira A., North Warren, 201
Darlington, Isabel, West Chester, 201
Darms, John M. G., Philadelphia, 201
Darrah, Leon C., Reading, 201
Darrow, George P., Philadelphia, 201
Dartt, Henry H., Dalton, Scranton, 201
D'Ascenzo, Nicola, Philadelphia, 201
Dashiell, Philip T., Glenmoore, Philadelphia, 202
Daughenbaugh, Paul J., Wrightstown, 202
Daugherty, Carroll R., Pittsburgh, 202
Daugherty, Harry K., Grove City, 202
Daume, Edward F., Pittsburgh, 202
Davey, Wheeler P., State College, 202

David, Charles W., Rosemont, Bryn Mawr, 202
David, William M., Philadelphia, 202
Davidson, Arthur J., Philadelphia, 202
Davidson, Hobart O., Swarthmore, 203
Davies, Arthur W., Pittsburgh, 203
Davies, George R., Pittsburgh, 203
Davies, Tom, Scranton, 203
Davis, Alan B., New Wilmington, 203
Davis, Andrew J., Drexel Hill, Philadelphia, 203
Davis, Arthur G., Erie, 203
Davis, Arthur V., Pittsburgh, 203
Davis, Austin W., Philadelphia, 203
Davis, Clarence E., Ebensburg, 204
Davis, Daniel E., Sewickley, Pittsburg, 204
Davis, Daniel L., Lancaster, 204
Davis, David M., Haverford, Philadelphia, 204
Davis, Earle C., North East, 204
Davis, Elwood C., State College, 204
Davis, Frank G., Lewisburg, 204
Davis, Fred W., East Stroudsburg, 204
Davis, George E., Pittsburgh, 204
Davis, George T. B., Philadelphia, 205
Davis, Holmes A., Pittsburgh, 205
Davis, Horace N., Bristol, 205
Davis, Howard A., Philadelphia, 205
Davis, Howard B. F., Downingtown, 205
Davis, Howard C., Erie, 205
Davis, Hugh H., Sewickley, Pittsburgh, 205
Davis, James E., Swarthmore, Philadelphia, 206
Davis, James J., Pittsburgh, 206
Davis, John W., Lewisburg, 206
Davis, Jonathan R., Kingston, Wilkes-Barre, 206
Davis, J. Lawrence, Bangor, 206
Davis, Nelson F., Lewisburg, 206
Davis, Nelson P., Pittsburgh, 206
Davis, Paul A., 3d, Philadelphia, 206
Davis, Robert C., Johnstown, 206
Davis, Shelby C., Haverford, Philadelphia, 207
Davis, T. Carroll, Philadelphia, 207
Davis, Warren S., Philadelphia, 207
Davis, William H., Kane, 207
Davis, William P., Jr., Bryn Mawr, Philadelphia, 207
Davison, George S., Pittsburgh, 207
Davison, Joseph H., Ashland, 207
Davison, Watson P., Chambersburg, 208
Davison, William R., Greencastle, 208
Day, Ewing W., Pittsburgh, 209
Day, Gardiner M., Wilkes-Barre, 209
Day, Kenneth M., Pittsburgh, 209
Dayhoff, Harry O., Harrisburg, 209
Deal, Erastus C., Wilkes-Barre, 209
Dean, Willis L., Kingston, 210
Deane, Philip B., York, 210
Deans, William, Philadelphia, 210
Deardorff, Merle N., Warren, 210
Dearolf, Walter S., Reading, 210
Dearth, Walter A., Pittsburgh, 210
Deasy, John F., Wynnewood, Philadelphia, 210
De Blasio, James, Dunbar, 210
De Blois, Austen K., Philadelphia, 210
DeCamp, Joseph E., State College, 211
Dechant, Miles B., Reading, 211
de Charms, George, Bryn Athyn, 211
Dechert, Philip, Philadelphia, 211
Dechert, Robert, Bridgeport, Philadelphia, 211
Deck, Luther J., Allentown, 211
Deck, Roy, Lancaster, 211
Decker, Harry R., Pittsburgh, 211
Decker, Oliver J., Williamsport, 211
Decker, Philip H., Williamsport, 211
Deemer, Bert, Philadelphia, 211
Deemer, William R., Williamsport, 211
Deer, Roy B., Philadelphia, 211
Deitrick, George A., Sunbury, 212
DeJuhasz, Kalman J., State College, 212
De Land, Clyde O., Philadelphia, 212
De Laney, Lewis E., Sayre, 212
Delaney, William E., Jr., Williamsport, 212
Delany, Joseph R. K., Philadelphia, 212

Delbridge, Thomas G., Drexel Hill, Philadelphia, 212
de Leo de Laguna, Grace M. A., Bryn Mawr, 213
Delk, Edwin H., Philadelphia, 213
Della Cioppa, Thomas E., Philadelphia, 213
Dellinger, Martin C., Lancaster, 213
Dellplain, Morse, Rosemont, Philadelphia, 213
Del Manzo, Milton C. E., New Hope, 213
DeLong, Berton H., Reading, West Lawn, 213
DeLong, Calvin M., East Greenville, 213
De Long, Irwin H., Lancaster, 213
De Long, Roy A., Philadelphia, 213
De Long, Vaughn R., Oil City, 214
De Long, Warren, Ardmore, Philadelphia, 214
Demaree, David R., Pittsburgh, 214
de Merlier, Franz, Pocopson, Philadelphia, 214
Demmler, Oscar W., Pittsburgh, 214
Demmy, Maurice C., Lititz, 214
de Moll, Carl, Swarthmore, Philadelphia, 214
Dempwolf, Frederick G., York, 214
Dende, Peter J., Pittsburgh, 214
Dende, John, Scranton, 214
Dengler, Robert E., State College, 215
Denig, Fred, Pittsburgh, 215
Denman, David N., Latrobe, 215
Denman, Mary T., Latrobe, 215
Denney, John D., Columbia, 215
Dennis, Charles J., Bradford, 215
Dennis, William V., State College, 215
Dennison, Boyd C., Pittsburgh, 215
Denton, David W., Rochester, Beaver Falls, 216
Denworth, Hugh F., Swarthmore, Philadelphia, 216
Denworth, Katharine M., Swarthmore, Bradford, 216
Denworth, Raymond K., Swarthmore, Philadelphia, 216
De Pierro, M. Salvador, Freeland, 216
Depp, Walter M., Pittsburgh, 216
Depta, Michael, Pittsburgh, 216
Dereume, Raymond J., Pittsburgh, Punxsutawney, 216
Derickson, Samuel H., Annville, 216
de Rivas, Damaso, Lansdowne, Philadelphia, 217
Dermitt, H. Marie, Pittsburgh, 217
DeRoy, Mayer S., Pittsburgh, 217
Derr, Amnon I., Dormont, Pittsburgh, 217
Derr, Ralph B., Oakmont, New Kensington, 217
Derrick, William H., Portage, 217
Dershuck, J. R., Hazleton, 217
Dery, D. George, Catasauqua, 217
de Schweinitz, Paul, Bethlehem, 217
Detlefsen, John A., Swarthmore, 217
Detweiler, George H., Swarthmore, Philadelphia, 217
Detweiler, W. Frank, Brackenridge, 218
Devens, Henry F., Pittsburgh, 218
Devereux, Robert T., West Chester, 218
DeVitis, Michael A., Swissvale, 218
Devitt, William, Allenwood, 218
Devlin, Thomas F., Langhorne, 218
De Walt, Horace E., Mt. Lebanon, Pittsburgh, 218
Dewees, Lovett, Glen Mills, Ardmore, 218
Dewey, Ralph S., Corry, 218
De Witt, John H., Sunbury, 219
De Witt, John P., Dallas, Wyoming, 219
de Young, Bertram I., Philadelphia, 219
Diamond, Herbert M., Bethlehem, 219
Diamond, Norman H., New Castle, 219
Dice, J. Howard, Pittsburgh, 219
Dick, George A., Upper Darby, Philadelphia, 219
Dicke, Henry F., Allentown, 219
Dickerson, Roy E., Philadelphia, 219
Dickey, Charles D., Philadelphia, 219
Dickey, Charles E., Pittsburgh, 220
Dickey, Edward T., Philadelphia, 220
Dickey, Elmer L., Oil City, 220
Dickey, Samuel, Oxford, 220
Dickie, J. Roy, Pittsburgh, 220
Dickinson, Everett H., Philadelphia, 220
Dickinson, John, Philadelphia, 220

Dickinson, Oliver B., Chester, Philadelphia, 220
Dickson, Conway W., Berwick, 220
Dickson, Halsey E., Reading, 220
Dickson, Harold E., State College, 221
Dickson, John M., Gettysburg, 221
Dickson, R. R., Pittsburgh, 221
Dickson, Reid S., Philadelphia, 221
Dickson, Thomas S., York, 221
di Domenica, Angelo, Philadelphia, 221
Diebel, Alfred H., Philadelphia, 221
Diefenderfer, Alpha A., Bethlehem, 221
Diefendorf, Adelbert, Pittsburgh, 221
Diegel, Leo, Philmont, 221
Diehl, Jacob, Lock Haven, 221
Diemand, John A., Philadelphia, 221
Dierolf, Claude O., Philadelphia, 222
Dieter, Clarence D., Washington, 222
Dietrich, Daniel W., Philadelphia, 222
Dietrich, Harvey O., Norristown, 222
Dietz, Alvin F., Shamokin, 222
Dietz, William R., Reading, 222
Diez, Max, Bryn Mawr, 222
Diffenderfer, George M., Carlisle, 222
Diffenderffer, Charles H., Wynnewood, Philadelphia, 222
Di Genova, John, Upper Darby, Philadelphia, 222
Dilks, Walter H., Jr., Philadelphia, 222
Dill, George C., East Pittsburgh, 222
Dillen, John H., Altoona, 222
Diller, Mary B., Lancaster, 222
Diller, Theodore, Pittsburgh, 223
Dillinger, Gregg A., Pittsburgh, 223
Dillon, Edward S., Penn Valley, Philadelphia, 223
Dillon, Walter S., Lincoln Park, Reading, 223
Dilser, F. Harry, Pottstown, 223
Dimmitt, Luther M., Swarthmore, Philadelphia, 223
Dines, Lloyd L., Pittsburgh, 223
Dintenfass, Henry, Philadelphia, 223
Dippell, Victor W., Lancaster, 223
Disque, Robert C., Swarthmore, 223
Dissinger, Chester B., Milford, 224
Disston, Henry, Philadelphia, 224
Distler, Theodore A., Easton, 224
Dithrich, W. Heber, Coraopolis, Pittsburgh, 224
Ditter, J. William, Ambler, 224
Dively, G. Nevin, Altoona, 224
Dively, M. Augustus, Altoona, Hollidaysburg, 224
Diven, John, Philadelphia, 224
Dix, Edgar H., Jr., Oakmont, New Kensington, 224
Dixon, Charles F., St. David's, Philadelphia, 224
Dixon, John W., Wilkinsburg, 225
Dixon, Mary Q. A., Philadelphia, 225
Dixon, Russell W., Butler, 225
Doak, Frank F., Pittsburgh, 225
Doan, Francis J., State College, 225
Doan, Gilbert E., Bethlehem, 225
Doane, Joseph C., Philadelphia, 225
Dodds, John H., Mt. Lebanon, Pittsburgh, 226
Dodds, Robert J., Pittsburgh, 226
Dodds, William P., Pittsburgh, 226
Dodge, Arthur B., Lancaster, 226
Dodge, Kern, Philadelphia, 226
Dodson, Alan C., Bethlehem, 226
Dodworth, James R., Jr., Pittsburgh, 226
Dodworth, Paul K., Bellevue, Pittsburgh, 226
Doering, Alois H., Pittsburgh, 226
Doggett, Alexander A., State College, 226
Dohan, Edith H., Darling, 227
Doherty, Robert E., Pittsburgh, 227
Doherty, T. A., Susquehanna, 227
Dolfinger, Henry, Merion, Philadelphia, 227
Doll, Albert M., Erie, 227
Dolman, John, Jr., Swarthmore, 227
Domville, Paul C. K., Philadelphia, 227
Donahoe, Thomas A., Scranton, 228
Donahue, Frank R., Philadelphia, 228
Donaldson, Holland H., Pittsburgh, 228
Donaldson, John A., Harrisburg, 228
Donaldson, John C., Pittsburgh, 228
Donaldson, John S., Pittsburgh, 228
Donaldson, Walter F., Pittsburgh, 228
Donato, Giuseppe, Philadelphia, 228
Doney, Paul H., Carlisle, 228
Doney, Willis F., Duquesne, 228
Donnally, H. R., Pittsburgh, 228
Donoghue, Daniel C., Philadelphia, 229
Donovan, William M., Scranton, 229
Doolittle, Harold, Pittsburgh, 229
Dooner, Emilie Z., Merion, Philadelphia, 229
Dooner, Richard T., Merion, Philadelphia, 229
Dorasavage, William C., Pottsville, 229
Dorman, George R., Pittsburgh, 229
Dorn, Forest D., Bradford, 229
Dorr, John H., Monongahela, 229
Dorrance, Anne, Dallas, 229
Dorrance, Arthur C., Ardmore, 230
Dorrance, Frances, Kingston, 230
Dorrance, George M., Philadelphia, 230
Dorrance, Gordon, Philadelphia, 230
Dorrance, Harold J., Pittsburgh, 230
Dorrance, Roy G., Pittsburgh, 230
Dorsey, Frank J. G., Philadelphia, 230
Dotterer, Ray H., State College, 230
Doty, Robert W., Butler, 230
Doty, Robert W., Harrisburg, 230
Doty, William S., Ben Avon, Pittsburgh, 230
Doubman, John R., Philadelphia, 231
Dougherty, Denis J., Philadelphia, 231
Dougherty, Joseph F., Upper Darby, 231
Doughton, Isaac, Mansfield, 231
Doughty, Howard E., Clarks Summit, Dickson, 231
Douglas, George W., Philadelphia, 231
Douglass, Alfred E., Catasauqua, 231
Douglass, Earl L., Philadelphia, 231
Douglass, Herbert W., New Brighton, 232
Douthett, Walter R., Darby, 232
Doutrich, Isaac H., Harrisburg, 232
Douty, Nicholas, Elkins Park, Philadelphia, 232
Dovey, Clayton D., Johnstown, 232
Down, Sidney G., Pittsburgh, Wilmerding, 232
Downs, Charles B., Philadelphia, 232
Downs, William F., Philadelphia, 232
Doxsee, Carll W., Pittsburgh, 232
Doyle, Bartley J., Philadelphia, 233
Doyle, Michael F., Philadelphia, 233
Doyle, Thomas L., Philadelphia, 233
Drake, Charles L., Stroudsburg, 233
Drake, J. Frank, Pittsburgh, 233
Drant, Patricia, Westtown, Philadelphia, 233
Drasher, Clark L., Hazleton, Scranton, 234
Drayton, John W., Penllyn, Philadelphia, 234
Dreifus, Charles, Pittsburgh, 234
Drennen, William J., Narberth, 234
Dresden, Arnold, Swarthmore, 234
Drew, Ira W., Philadelphia, 234
Drew, James B., Pittsburgh, 234
Drew, Thomas B., Kennett Square, 234
Drexel, George W. C., Bryn Mawr, Philadelphia, 234
Dreyer, Ashley E., Philadelphia, 234
Drinker, Henry S., Merion, Philadelphia, 234
Driscoll, Denis J., St. Marys, Harrisburg, 234
Driver, Leootis L., Harrisburg, 234
Drozeski, Edward H., Erie, 235
Druck, Samuel, Scranton, 235
Duane, Morris, Rosemont, Philadelphia, 235
Dubell, Charles B., Philadelphia, 235
Du Bois, John E., Jr., Du Bois, 235
DuBois, John L., Doylestown, 235
Du Bois, William F., Coudersport, 235
Dudley, Adolphus M., Oakmont, East Pittsburgh, 235
Dudley, Ed, Jr., Philadelphia, 236
Dudley, Wray, Pittsburgh, 236
Duer, John V. B., Narberth, Philadelphia, 236
Duff, James H., Carnegie, Pittsburgh, 236
Duff, John T., Jr., Pittsburgh, 236
Duff, Samuel E., Ben Avon, Pittsburgh, 236
Duff, William H., 2d, Pittsburgh, 236
Duff, William M., Ben Avon, Bellevue, Pittsburgh, 236
Duffy, James T., Jr., York, 236
Duggan, Frank L., Pittsburgh, 236
Duke, Charles W., Upper Darby, 237
Dulles, Heatly C., Villa Nova, Philadelphia, 237
Dumbauld, George L., Pittsburgh, 237
Dumbauld, Horatio S., Uniontown, 237
Du Mont, Francis M., State College, 237
Dumont, Frederick T. F., Ronks, 237
Dunaway, Wayland F., State College, 237
Dunbar, James C., Mt. Lebanon, Pittsburgh, 238
Duncan, David C., State College, 238
Duncan, Garfield G., Philadelphia, 238
Duncan, Harry A., Philadelphia, 238
Duncan, Ralph W., Lansdowne, 238
Dunham, James M., Philadelphia, 238
Dunkelberger, George F., Selinsgrove, 238
Dunkerley, Charles A., Beaver Falls, 238
Dunmire, Glenn D., Pittsburgh, 239
Dunn, David, Harrisburg, 239
Dunn, Emmett R., Haverford, 239
Dunn, F. Eldred, Philadelphia, 239
Dunn, H. Stewart, Pittsburgh, 239
Dunn, Matthew A., Mount Oliver, 239
Dunn, Thomas P., Harbourcreek, Erie, 239
Dunn, Wilbur L., Uniontown, 239
Dunnells, Clifford G., Pittsburgh, 239
Dunsford, Jan R., Edgeworth, Pittsburgh, 240
Durant, Frederick C., Jr., Philadelphia, 240
Durham, Fred S., Catasauqua, Allentown, 241
Durham, Hannah M., Allentown, 241
Durham, Joseph E., Jr., Allentown, 241
Dusham, Edward H., State College, 241
Dutcher, Raymond A., State College, 241
Dutton, Charles J., Erie, 241
Dutton, Lewis R., Jenkintown, 241
Duy, Albert W., Bloomsburg, 241
Dwier, W. Kirkland, Philadelphia, 241
Dwyer, Frank P., Renovo, 241
Dwyer, Vincent C., Pittsburgh, 242
Dyche, Howard E., Wilkinsburg, Pittsburgh, 242
Dye, William S., Jr., State College, 242
Dyer, Charlotte L., New Hope, 242
Dyer, Dorothy T., Lewisburg, 242
Dyer, George, New Hope, 242
Dyer, John H., Scranton, 242
Dyer, William E. S., Noble, Philadelphia, 242
Dyson, John M., Hazleton, 242
Eaby, Charles W., Lancaster, 242
Ealy, Charles H., Somerset, 243
Earhart, Will, Pittsburgh, 243
Earle, Edgar P., Philadelphia, 243
Earle, George H., Haverford, Harrisburg, 243
Earle, Murray, Philadelphia, 243
Earle, Ralph, Philadelphia, 243
Earnest, William H., Harrisburg, 244
Eastell, Richard T., Pittsburgh, 244
Eastwood, Sidney K., Pittsburgh, 244
Eaton, Alice R., Harrisburg, 244
Eaton, Charles C., Erie, 244
Eaton, Paul B., Easton, 245
Eavenson, Howard N., Pittsburgh, 245
Eberhard, William N., Allentown, 245
Eberharter, Herman P., Pittsburgh, 245
Eberlein, Harold D., Philadelphia, 245
Eberly, Isaac C., Reading, 245
Ebert, Charles E., Merion, Philadelphia, 245
Ebrey, Glen O., Oil City, 245
Eby, Frank H., Springfield, 245
Eck, Lee, Richland, 246
Eckels, John P., Conneaut Lake, Meadville, 246
Eckert, Charles R., Beaver, 246
Eckert, Clyde J., Erie, 246
Eckert, Frank E., Bradford, 246
Eckert, William H., Crafton, Pittsburgh, 246
Eckfeldt, Howard, Bethlehem, 246
Eckhardt, Engelhardt A., Pittsburgh, 246
Eckhardt, Henry P., Pittsburgh, 246
Eckles, Robert A., New Castle, 246
Eddy, Milton W., Carlisle, 246
Eddy, William W., Easton, 246
Edelman, Samuel, Philadelphia, 246
Eder, Charles E., Philadelphia, 246
Edgcomb, Ervin R., Philadelphia, 246
Edgecombe, Arthur C., Beaver Falls, 247
Edgerly, Beatrice, Bushkill, 247
Edmonds, Franklin S., Whitemarsh, Philadelphia, 247
Edmonds, George W., Philadelphia, 247
Edmondson, David E., Danville, 247
Edmunds, Albert J., Cheltenham, 247
Edmundson, George L., McKeesport, 247
Edrehi, Isaac C., Philadelphia, 247
Edrop, Arthur N., Radnor, Philadelphia, 248
Edwards, A. L., Osceola Mills, Harrisburg, 248
Edwards, Bateman, Bethlehem, 248
Edwards, Boyd, Mercersburg, 248
Edwards, Edward T., Latrobe, 248
Edwards, Eugene, Latrobe, 248
Edwards, George J., Jr., Philadelphia, 248
Edwards, Henry B., Pittsburgh, 248
Edwards, Lester R., Bradford, 248
Edwards, Ogden M., Jr., Pittsburgh, 248
Edwards, Vere B., Coraopolis, Pittsburgh, 249
Edwards, Walter H., Bethlehem, 249
Edwards, William G., State College, 249
Effing, Gerald H., Lancaster, 249
Egan, John P., Pittsburgh, 249
Egbert, Seneca, Wayne, 249
Eggers, Clifford R., Bellevue, Pittsburgh, 249
Eggleston, Charles F., Glenolden, Philadelphia, 249
Ehlers, Henry E., Philadelphia, 249
Ehrenfeld, Frederick, Philadelphia, 250
Ehrhart, Oliver T., Lancaster, 250
Ehrhart, Victor H., Jamestown, 250
Eibeck, John, Avalon, Pittsburgh, 250
Eichenauer, John B., Pittsburgh, 250
Eicher, Alex, Jr., Greensburg, 250
Eicher, C. Ward, Greensburg, 250
Eicher, Charles G., Mt. Lebanon, McKees Rocks, 250
Eicher, HuBert C., Harrisburg, 250
Eichley, Roy O., Dormont, Pittsburgh, 250
Eichler, George A., Northampton, 250
Eilenberger, William B., Stroudsburg, 251
Einstein, Jacob R., Kittanning, 251
Eisaman, Howard G., East Springfield, Harrisburg, 251
Eisele, Richard O., Pittsburgh, 251
Eisemann, Harry O., Bangor, 251
Eisenberg, J. Linwood, Shippensburg, 251
Eisenhart, Jacob C., York, Hanover, 251
Eisenhart, William S., York, 251
Eisenhart, Willis W., Tyrone, 251
Eisenhauer, John H., Reading, 251
Eldredge, Laurence H., Bryn Mawr, Philadelphia, 252
Eliason, Eldridge L., Philadelphia, 252
Elkan, Henri, Philadelphia, 253
Elkin, Cortlandt W. W., Pittsburgh, 253
Elkin, Curtis E., Indiana, 253
Elkins, William M., Philadelphia, 253
Elkinton, J. Passmore, Moylan, Philadelphia, 253
Elkinton, Thomas W., Philadelphia, 253
Ellenbogen, Henry, Pittsburgh, 253

Elliott, George W., Philadelphia, 254
Elliott, William J., Lansdowne, Philadelphia, 254
Ellis, Charles C., Huntingdon, 254
Ellis, Furey, Philadelphia, 254
Ellis, Mell B., Ardmore, Philadelphia, 254
Ellis, William T., Philadelphia, 255
Ellis, William T., Swarthmore, 255
Ellmaker, Lee, Philadelphia, 255
Ellson, John V., Jr., Philadelphia, 255
Elmer, Manuel C., Pittsburgh, 255
Elmer, Robert P., Wayne, 255
Elmer, Walter G., Philadelphia, 255
Elmes, Frank C., Berwick, 255
Else, Frank L., Ardmore, Philadelphia, 255
Eltonhead, Frank, Hatboro, Philadelphia, 256
Elverson, Howard W., Bellevue, New Brighton, 256
Elverson, Lew, Swarthmore, 256
Ely, Sumner B., Pittsburgh, 256
Ely, William N., Jr., Ambler, Bridgeport, 256
Embery, Frank, Philadelphia, 256
Embery, Joseph R., Philadelphia, 256
Emerson, Edith, Philadelphia, 256
Emery, Chester A., Pittsburgh, 257
Emery, R. Edson, Pittsburgh, Washington, 257
Emhardt, William C., Philadelphia, 257
Emig, William H., Pittsburgh, 257
Emlen, John T., Philadelphia, 257
Emmerich, Mary A. P., Hazleton, 257
Emmet, Herman L., Erie, 257
Emmons, Peter K., Scranton, 257
Emrich, John O., Pittsburgh, 257
Enck, Schuyler C., Harrisburg, 257
Endean, M. P., New Kensington, 258
Enders, Robert A., Harrisburg, 258
Enders, Robert K., Swarthmore, 258
Endsley, Andrew D., Tarentum, 258
Endsley, James W., Somerfield, 258
Endsley, Louis E., Pittsburgh, 258
Engard, Charles I., Philadelphia, Harrisburg, 258
Engel, Gilson C., Philadelphia, 258
Engelder, Carl J., Pittsburgh, 258
Engh, Harry M., Edinboro, Erie, 258
Englander, Samuel, Philadelphia, 258
Engle, John R., Palmyra, 259
Englerth, Louis D., Philadelphia, 259
English, Charles H., Erie, 259
English, E. Schuyler, Philadelphia, 259
English, James H., Grove City, 259
English, Kenneth J., Pittston, 259
English, Oliver S., Philadelphia, 259
Englund, A. Helmer, Philadelphia, 259
Enright, John J., Pittsburgh, 260
Enslin, Morton S., Chester, 260
Eppinger, John G., Chambersburg, 260
Erb, Elmer E., Harrisburg, 260
Erb, John W., Easton, 260
Erb, Russell C., Conshohocken, Philadelphia, 260
Erdly, Calvin V., Lewistown, 260
Erdman, Wilton A., Stroudsburg, 260
Ernst, James E., Mohrsville, 261
Erskine, Bernard G., Emporium, 261
Erskine, Laurie Y., New Hope, 261
Ersner, Matthew S., Philadelphia, 261
Ervin, Carl E., Camp Hill, Harrisburg, 261
Ervin, James S., Mt. Lebanon, Pittsburgh, 261
Ervin, Spencer, Bala-Cynwyd, Philadelphia, 261
Esenwine, William A., Salona, Mill Hall, 261
Esbach, Ovid W., Glenside, 261
Eshelman, Fayette C., Hazleton, 261
Esherick, Wharton, Paoli, 261
Eshner, Augustus A., Philadelphia, 261
Essick, Charles R., Reading, 262
Essig, Norman S., Philadelphia, 262
Estep, Harry A., Pittsburgh, 262
Estep, Thomas G., Jr., Pittsburgh, 262
Esterly, Charles J., Sally Ann Furnace, Reading, 262
Esterly, John E., Reading, 262
Estermann, Immanuel, Pittsburgh, 262

Estes, William L., Bethlehem, 262
Estes, William L., Jr., Bethlehem, 262
Etter, Harry B., Shippensburg, 262
Etting, Emlen, Haverford, Philadelphia, 262
Ettinger, Amos A., Bethlehem, 263
Ettinger, George T., Allentown, 263
Eubank, Weaver K., Philadelphia, 263
Euler, Ralph S., Sewickley, Pittsburgh, 263
Evans, Anna L., Pittsburgh, 263
Evans, Cadwallader, Jr., Waverly, Scranton, 263
Evans, Charles, Philadelphia, 263
Evans, Charles C., Berwick, 263
Evans, Edward W., Philadelphia, 263
Evans, Harold, Philadelphia, 263
Evans, Harold G., West Lawn, Reading, 263
Evans, Henry B., Merion, 263
Evans, J. Ray, Donora, 264
Evans, John B., Pottstown, 264
Evans, John C., Reading, 264
Evans, John H., Sharon, 264
Evans, John J., Lancaster, 264
Evans, Louis H., Pittsburgh, 264
Evans, Owen D., Ridley Park, Philadelphia, 264
Evans, Powell, Haverford, Mahoney City, 264
Evans, Raymond L., Sayre, 264
Evans, Robert D., Pittsburgh, East Pittsburgh, 264
Evans, Roy S., Pittsburgh, Butler, 264
Evans, Rulison, Kingston, Wilkes-Barre, 264
Evans, Thomas, Philadelphia, 264
Evans, William B., Darby, Chester, 265
Evans, William D., Pittsburgh, 265
Evans, William R., Yeadon, Lansdowne, 265
Everard, Joshua G., Huntingdon, 265
Everett, Edith M., Flourtown, Philadelphia, 265
Everett, Harold A., State College, 265
Eves, William, 3d, George School, 265
Ewald, Louis, Bryn Athyn, Philadelphia, 265
Ewan, Stacy N., Jr., Lansdowne, 265
Ewers, John R., Pittsburgh, 265
Ewing, John M., Ligonier, 266
Ewing, Joseph N., Valley Forge, Philadelphia, 266
Ewing, Lucy E. L., Philadelphia, 266
Ewing, Warren W., Bethlehem, 266
Exley, Gordon R., Philadelphia, 266
Eyerly, Paul R., Bloomsburg, 266
Eyman, Elmer V., Drexel Hill, Philadelphia, 266
Eyman, William G., Pittsburgh, 266
Eyre, Louisa, Philadelphia, 266
Eyre, Wilson, Philadelphia, 266
Eysmans, Julien L., Philadelphia, 266
Eyster, William H., Lewisburg, 266
Ezickson, William J., Narberth, Philadelphia, 267
Fabel, Harry E., Meadville, 267
Fackenthal, Benjamin F., Jr., Riegelsville, 267
Fackler, Charles L., York, 267
Faddis, Charles I., Waynesburg, 267
Fagan, Frank N., State College, 267
Fagan, Patrick T., Pittsburgh, 267
Fahnestock, Murray, Philadelphia, 267
Fair, Frederick, Oil City, 267
Fair, Marvin L., Elkins Park, 268
Fairchild, Mildred, Bryn Mawr, 268
Fairfield, Erle, Wilkinsburg, 268
Fairing, John W., Greensburg, 268
Fairless, Benjamin F., Pittsburgh, 268
Falck, Frederick M., Philadelphia, 268
Falk, Leon, Jr., Pittsburgh, 268
Falk, Maurice, Pittsburgh, 269
Fall, Gilbert H., Philadelphia, 269
Farage, D. James, Carlisle, 269
Faragher, Helen M., Pittsburgh, 269
Faragher, Paul V., Oakmont, Pittsburgh, 269
Faragher, Warren F., Swarthmore, Philadelphia, 269
Faris, Paul P., Haverford, Philadelphia, 270
Farley, Eugene B., Wilkes-Barre, 270
Farley, Richard B., Eddington, Philadelphia, 270
Farmer, Clarence R., Lancaster, 270

Farmer, William R., Pittsburgh, 270
Farnham, George W., Clarks Summit, Scranton, 270
Farnham, Robert, Philadelphia, 270
Farnsworth, Philo T., Philadelphia, 271
Farquhar, Francis, York, 271
Farquhar, Harold B., Bethlehem, 271
Farr, Clifford B., Bryn Mawr, Philadelphia, 271
Farr, Edward B., Tunkhannock, 271
Farrell, John T., Jr., Philadelphia, 271
Farrell, Thomas F., Wilkes-Barre, 272
Faunce, Benjamin F., Johnstown, 272
Fauset, Joseph H., Woodville, Pittsburgh, 272
Fausold, Samuel, Indiana, 272
Faust, J. Frank, Chambersburg, 272
Fawcett, William H., Pittsburgh, 272
Fawley, James L., Philadelphia, 272
Fay, Frank L., Greenville, 273
Feaser, George W., Middletown, 273
Feather, Harry E., Philadelphia, 273
Fedigan, Edward J., Pittsburgh, 273
Fee, George E., Belle Vernon, 273
Feick, Harry W., Avalon, 273
Feirer, William A., Philadelphia, 273
Felix, Anthony G., Merion, Philadelphia, 273
Felix, Otto F., Pittsburgh, 273
Fell, Frank J., Jr., Phoenixville, Philadelphia, 273
Fellner, Felix J., Latrobe, 273
Fels, Samuel S., Philadelphia, 273
Fene, William J., Pittsburgh, 273
Fenerty, Clare G., Philadelphia, 274
Fenno, George F., Swarthmore, Philadelphia, 274
Fenton, Beatrice, Philadelphia, 274
Fentress, Helena D., Devon, 274
Fenwick, Charles G., Bryn Mawr, 274
Ferguson, Arthur W., York, 275
Ferguson, James W., Pittsburgh, 275
Ferguson, John M., Pittsburgh, 275
Ferguson, Lewis K., Narberth, Philadelphia, 275
Ferguson, Melville F., Philadelphia, 275
Ferguson, Nancy M., Philadelphia, 275
Ferguson, Walter D., Philadelphia, 275
Ferguson, William H., Reading, 276
Fernald, Ernest M., Easton, 276
Fernberger, Samuel W., Philadelphia, 276
Fernley, George A., Plymouth Meeting, Philadelphia, 276
Ferris, Edythe, Philadelphia, 276
Ferris, Seymour W., Alden, Philadelphia, 276
Fetherolf, Fred A. P., Allentown, 276
Fetter, Elwood M., Lewisburg, 277
Fetter, Frank W., Berwyn, 277
Fetterhoof, Chester D., Huntingdon, 277
Fetterman, Henry H., Allentown, 277
Fichman, Meyer E., Harrisburg, 277
Fickes, Edwin S., Pittsburgh, 277
Fielding, Mantle, Philadelphia, 278
Fife, Joseph P., Pittsburgh, 278
Filbert, B. Ludwig S., Bala-Cynwyd, Philadelphia, 278
Filer, Enoch C., Erie, 278
Fillion, Ferdinand, Pittsburgh, 279
Finch, Francis E., York, 279
Finck, Furman J., Philadelphia, 279
Findley, Frank D., McConnellsburg, 279
Fink, Clarence H., Pittsburgh, Haysville, 279
Fink, Cornelius W., Carlisle, 279
Fink, Scott, Irwin, Greensburg, 279
Fink, William L., Oakmont, 279
Finlon, Frank T., Braddock, 280
Finn, Albert E., Hatboro, 280
Finney, Theodore M., Pittsburgh, 280
Finney, William P., Philadelphia, 280
Fischer, Carl C., Philadelphia, 281
Fischer, Emil E., Philadelphia, 281
Fish, Harry S., Sayre, 281
Fisher, Charles A., Pittsburgh, 281
Fisher, Clarence C., Pittsburgh, 281
Fisher, Frank P., Pittsburgh, 281

Fisher, George C., Pittsburgh, 281
Fisher, Gordon, Pittsburgh, 281
Fisher, Grant E., New Castle, 281
Fisher, Henry, Philadelphia, 282
Fisher, Isaac C., Lebanon, 282
Fisher, J. Wilmer, Reading, 282
Fisher, John S., Indiana, 282
Fisher, Mahlon L., Williamsport, 282
Fisher, Ralph F., York, 282
Fisher, Robert M., Indiana, 282
Fisher, William H., Chambersburg, 282
Fiss, Ira T., Shamokin Dam, 283
Fister, H. Ray, Dalton, Scranton, 283
Fitch, William K., Pittsburgh, 283
Fiterman, Morris, Philadelphia, 283
Fitzgerald, Rufus H., Pittsburgh, 283
Fitzgerald, Thomas, Pittsburgh, 283
Fitz-Hugh, Thomas, Jr., Wynnewood, Philadelphia, 283
Fitzpatrick, Helena M., Philadelphia, 284
Fitzpatrick, John J., Drexel Hill, Philadelphia, 284
Flannery, J. Harold, W. Pittston, 284
Flannery, John R., Pittsburgh, 284
Fleck, Wilbur H., Kingston, 284
Fleisher, Alexander, Churchville, 284
Fleisher, Louis M., Philadelphia, 284
Fleisher, Samuel S., Philadelphia, 284
Fleming, Alenson R., Wellsboro, 285
Fleming, Mervin R., Red Lion, 285
Fleming, Montgomery W., Bellefonte, 285
Fletcher, Stevenson W., State College, 286
Flight, John W., Haverford, 286
Flinn, Alexander R., Pittsburgh, 286
Flint, Homer L., Crafton, Pittsburgh, 286
Flock, Herman F. W., Williamsport, 286
Floersheim, Berthold, Pittsburgh, 286
Flood, Gerald F., Philadelphia, 286
Flory, Clyde R., Sellersville, 287
Flosdorf, Earl W., Lansdowne, 287
Flounders, Charles L., Chester, 287
Foelsch, Charles, Sunbury, 287
Foerderer, Percival E., Bryn Mawr, Philadelphia, 287
Foering, Howard A., Bethlehem, 287
Fogel, Edwin M., Fogelsville, 287
Fogg, John M., Philadelphia, 288
Foley, Michael A., Philadelphia, 288
Folinsbee, John F., New Hope, 288
Follmer, Frederick V., Milton, 288
Folwell, William H., Merion, Philadelphia, 288
Folz, Stanley, Philadelphia, 288
Foote, Paul D., Pittsburgh, 288
Foote, Percy W., Harrisburg, 289
Foraker, Forest A., Pittsburgh, 289
Forbes, Ernest B., State College, 289
Ford, Adelbert, Bethlehem, 289
Ford, Charles A., Philadelphia, 289
Ford, Thomas H., Reading, 289
Forker, John N., Pittsburgh, 289
Forman, Max L., Philadelphia, 290
Fornance, Joseph K., Norristown, 290
Forrest, Earle R., Washington, 290
Forrey, Harry N., York, 290
Forsht, Ruth, Pittsburgh, 290
Forstall, Walton, Rosemont, 290
Forster, William H., Erie, 290
Fort, Tomlinson, Bethlehem, 291
Fortenbaugh, Robert, Gettysburg, 291
Fortescue, Horace, Philadelphia, 291
Fosa, Joseph W., State College, 291
Fosnot, Walter, Lewistown, 291
Foss, George E., Harrisburg, 291
Foss, Harold L., Danville, 291
Foster, Alexander, Jr., Jenkintown, Philadelphia, 291
Foster, Laurence, Lincoln University, 291
Foster, Major B., Cheltenham, 291
Foulk, Paul L., Altoona, 292
Foulke, Roland R., Ardmore, Philadelphia, 293
Foulke, Thomas A., Ambler, 293
Foulke, Willie B., Media, 293
Foust, Leslie A., Washington, 293
Foust, Madeleine S., Pittsburgh, 293
Fowle, Lester P., Lewisburg, 293

Fowler, William H., Sewickley, Pittsburgh, 293
Fox, Herbert, Philadelphia, 294
Fox, John E., Harrisburg, 294
Fox, John H., Pittsburgh, 294
Fox, Robert T., Hummelstown, Harrisburg, 294
Fox, Will S., Pine Grove, 294
Fox, William J., Philadelphia, 294
Frack, William A., Easton, 294
Fraim, Samuel R., Lancaster, 294
Frampton, James V., Oil City, 295
Francis, Richard S., Philadelphia, Haverford, 295
Francis, Thomas, Scranton, 295
Francis, Vida H., Philadelphia, 295
Franck, Harry A., New Hope, 295
Frank, Grace, Bryn Mawr, 295
Frank, William K., Pittsburgh, 296
Frankenfield, Clyde S., Northampton, Catasauqua, 296
Franklin, James H., Chester, 296
Franklin, Walter S., Ardmore, Philadelphia, 296
Frantz, Jacob P., Clearfield, 296
Frantz, Oswin S., Lancaster, 296
Frary, Francis C., Oakmont, 297
Fraser, Albert G., Upper Darby, Philadelphia, 297
Fraser, Donald M., Bethlehem, 297
Fraser, Herbert F., Wallingford, 297
Fraser, James W., New Bethlehem, 297
Frazer, John, Philadelphia, 297
Frazer, John G., Pittsburgh, 297
Frazier, Chauncey E., Washington, 297
Fear, Frank A., Montrose, 298
Fredman, Samuel, Philadelphia, 298
Freed, Cecil F., Reading, 298
Freedman, Abraham L., Philadelphia, 298
Freehof, Solomon B., Pittsburgh, 298
Freeman, Charles, New Wilmington, 298
Freeman, Edgar W., Merion, Philadelphia, 298
Freeman, Jonathan W., Pittsburgh, 298
Freeman, Norman E., Wynnewood, Philadelphia, 298
Freihofer, Stanley H., Merion, Philadelphia, 299
French, Clifford W., Harrisburg, 299
French, James H., Collegeville, Harrisburg, 299
Frescoln, Leonard D., Philadelphia, 299
Fretz, Floyd C., Bradford, 299
Fretz, Franklin K., Easton, 299
Fretz, John E., Easton, 299
Fretz, William F., Pipersville, Doylestown, 299
Frevert, Harry L., Philadelphia, 299
Frew, William, Pittsburgh, 300
Frey, Alexander H., Radnor, Philadelphia, 300
Frey, Herbert O., Philadelphia, 300
Frey, John W., Pittsburgh, 300
Frey, Oliver W., Allentown, 300
Frey, Victor M., York, 300
Frick, Ezra, Waynesboro, 300
Frick, John A., Allentown, 300
Fries, Irvin A., Philadelphia, 301
Frisesell, H. Edmund, Murrysville, Pittsburgh, 301
Frink, Orrin, Jr., State College, 301
Frishmuth, Harriet W., Philadelphia, 301
Fritsch, Joseph L., Crafton, Pittsburgh, 301
Fritsch, Robert R., Allentown, 301
Fritz, F. Herman, Chester, 301
Frizzell, John H., State College, 301
Frocht, Max M., Pittsburgh, 302
Fronefield, Joseph M., Wayne, 302
Frost, Ellis M., Pittsburgh, 302
Frost, Frank R., Pittsburgh, 302
Frost, Stuart W., State College, 302
Fry, George A., Pittsburgh, 302
Fry, Guy E., Thornton, Philadelphia, 302
Fry, Howard M., Lancaster, 302
Fry, William C., Jr., Reiffton, 303
Frye, Edwin G., Harrisburg, 303
Fryer, Eugénie M., Philadelphia, 303
Fryling, George R., Erie, 303
Fuchs, Walter, State College, 303
Fuelhart, William C., Tidioute, Endeavor, 303
Fuller, Edward, Philadelphia, 303
Fuller, Edward L., Dalton, Scranton, 303
Fuller, Merton O., Bethlehem, 303
Fuller, Walter D., Penn Valley, Philadelphia, 304

Fulper, William H., Jr., Washington Crossing, 304
Fulton, Clarence E., Tarentum, Creighton, 304
Fulton, Dorothy, Lititz, 304
Fulton, James G., Pittsburgh, 304
Funk, Nevin E., Philadelphia, 304
Furey, Francis J., Immaculata, 305
Furlong, Thomas F., Jr., Ardmore, 305
Furman, Roy E., Waynesburg, 305
Fussell, Robert, Media, 305
Gabbert, Mont R., Pittsburgh, 305
Gabel, Arthur B., Merion, 305
Gadsden, Philip H., Philadelphia, 305
Gage, Albert H., Pittsburgh, 306
Gage, Hy, Philadelphia, 306
Gageby, Frank A., Crafton, 306
Galbally, Edward J., Philadelphia, 306
Galbraith, Wilbur F., Coal Center, Pittsburgh, 306
Galbreath, Robert F., New Wilmington, 306
Galiardi, Philip, Connellsville, 306
Gallager, Herbert V. B., Haverford, Philadelphia, 306
Gallagher, Sister Miriam, Dallas, 306
Gallaher, Sarah M., Ebensburg, 306
Gallup, William D., Bradford, 307
Gamble, Guy P., McKeesport, 307
Gamble, John T., Greenville, 307
Gamble, Robert B., Meadville, 307
Gamble, Samuel C., Butler, 307
Gamble, William D., Sharon, 307
Ganey, J. Cullen, Bethlehem, 308
Gannett, Farley, Harrisburg, 308
Gannon, John M., Erie, 308
Garber, Daniel, Lumberville, 308
Garber, Eli L., Lititz, Lancaster, 308
Garber, Ralph J., State College, 308
Gardner, Ashton, Hollidaysburg, 308
Gardner, Frank D., State College, 308
Gardner, Horace J., Philadelphia, 309
Gardner, Paul, Lancaster, 309
Gardner, Theodore R., Emmaus, Allentown, 309
Gardner, Walter, Philadelphia, 309
Garlach, Elsie A., Gettysburg, 309
Garland, Fred M., Pittsburgh, 309
Garland, Robert, Pittsburgh, 309
Garman, Harry F., Barnesboro, 309
Garner, James B., Pittsburgh, 310
Garrett, Arthur S., Drexel Hill, Philadelphia, 310
Garrett, Erwin C., Philadelphia, 310
Garrey, George H., Philadelphia, 310
Garrison, F. Lynwood, Philadelphia, 310
Gartman, George E., York, 311
Garver, Francis M., Ivyland, 311
Garver, Ivan E., Roaring Spring, 311
Gaskill, Joseph F., Llanerch, Philadelphia, 311
Gaston, John M., Aspinwall, Pittsburgh, 311
Gates, Theodore J., State College, 312
Gates, Thomas S., Philadelphia, 312
Gateson, Daniel W., Philadelphia, 312
Gauger, Alfred W., State College, 312
Gaul, Harriet A., Pittsburgh, 312
Gaul, Harvey B., Pittsburgh, 312
Gay, Hiram B., Haverford, Philadelphia, 313
Gay, Walter A., Jr., Philadelphia, 313
Gazzam, Joseph M., Jr., Philadelphia, 313
Gearhart, Ephraim M., Erie, 313
Gearhart, Ethan A., Allentown, 313
Gearhart, Robert H., Jr., Philadelphia, 313
Geary, Alexander B., Wallingford, Chester, 313
Geary, Theodore C., Lansdowne, Philadelphia, 313
Gebert, Herbert G., Greenville, 314
Gebhardt, Neil H., Erie, 314
Gechtoff, Leonid, Philadelphia, 314
Geegan, James G., Pittsburgh, Canonsburg, 314
Geisinger, Arch L., Carnegie, Pittsburgh, 314
Gellert, Nathan H., Meadowbrook, Philadelphia, 314
Gelstharp, Frederick, Tarentum, Creighton, 314

Gemmill, Benjamin M., Hartsville, 314
Gemmill, Charles W., New Cumberland, 315
Gemmill, Paul F., Swarthmore, 315
George, Forney P., Harrisburg, Carlisle, 315
George, Henry W., Middletown, 315
George, Homer, South Fork, 315
George, Howard, Philadelphia, 315
George, Walter L., Apollo, 315
George, William D., Sewickley, Pittsburgh, 315
Gerberich, Albert H., Carlisle, 315
Gerberich, Enos S., Harrisburg, Mount Joy, 315
Gerheim, Mearl F., Salina, 316
Gernerd, Fred B., Allentown, 316
Gerson, Felix N., Philadelphia, 316
Gerwig, George W., Pittsburgh, 316
Gest, Margaret R., Philadelphia, 316
Gethoefer, Louis H., Pittsburgh, 316
Getson, Philip, Philadelphia, 316
Getty, Frank D., Philadelphia, 316
Getty, George A., Summerville, Brookville, 317
Geyelin, Antony L., Villa Nova, Philadelphia, 317
Giarth, David I., Ford City, Kittanning, 317
Gibble, Phares B., Palmyra, 317
Gibbon, John H., Philadelphia, 317
Gibbons, George R., Pittsburgh, 317
Gibbons, Paul W., Philadelphia, 317
Gibbons, Walter B., Bala-Cynwyd, Philadelphia, 318
Gibbs, Ferry L., Pittsburgh, 318
Gibbs, George, Rosemont, 318
Gibbs, Harrison, Rosemont, 318
Gibbs, Raymond S., Scranton, 318
Gibson, George G., Edgewood, Wilkinsburg, 318
Gibson, James E., Philadelphia, 318
Gibson, Robert J., Bellevue, Pittsburgh, 319
Gibson, Robert M., Pittsburgh, see Addenda
Gibson, Robert W., Pittsburgh, 319
Gibson, William H., Philadelphia, 319
Giddens, Paul H., Meadville, 319
Gideon, Henry J., Philadelphia, 319
Giesecke, Albert A., West Philadelphia, 319
Gilbert, Ernest M., Wyomissing, Reading, 319
Gilbert, Henderson, Harrisburg, 320
Gilbert, John, Rydal, Philadelphia, 320
Gilbert, Keller H., Philadelphia, 320
Gilbert, Richard H., Tyrone, 320
Gilbert, Ross K., Chambersburg, 320
Gilbertson, Catherine P., Lansford, 320
Gildea, James H., Coaldale, 320
Giles, Raymond C., Mt. Lebanon, Pittsburgh, 320
Gilkyson, Hamilton H., Jr., Mont Clare, Coatesville, Phoenixville, 320
Gilkyson, Phoebe H., Mont Clare, 320
Gill, Arthur B., Merion, Philadelphia, 321
Gill, James P., Latrobe, 321
Gill, John D., Bala-Cynwyd, Philadelphia, 321
Gill, Wilson L., Philadelphia, 321
Gillespie, James E., State College, 321
Gillespie, Mary E., Annville, 321
Gillespie, Stanley A., Greenville, 321
Gillet, Joseph E., Bryn Mawr, 321
Gillet, Stanley A., Jenkintown, Philadelphia, 321
Gillette, Ninde T., Corry, 322
Gillingham, Clinton H., Glenside, Philadelphia, 322
Gillingham, Harrold E., Philadelphia, 322
Gilman, Robert L., Moylan-Rose Valley, Philadelphia, 322
Gilmer, Albert H., Easton, 322
Gilmore, Edward R., Pittsburgh, 322
Gilpin, Sherman F., Port Washington, Philadelphia, 322
Gilroy, Helen T., Noble, 323
Gilson, James F., Pittsburgh, 323
Gimbel, Ellis A., Philadelphia, 323
Gingery, Don, Clearfield, 323
Gingrich, Christian C., Lawn, Palmyra, 323
Gingrich, Christian R., Annville, 323

Gingrich, Felix W., Reading, 323
Ginter, Robert M., Pittsburgh, 323
Ginther, Mrs. Pemberton, Buckingham, 323
Gipson, Lawrence H., Bethlehem, 323
Gish, Warren F., Stony Creek Mills, 324
Githens, Thomas S., Philadelphia, Glenolden, 324
Gitt, Josiah W., Hanover, York, 324
Gittings, J. Claxton, Philadelphia, 324
Gladfelter, Millard E., Philadelphia, 324
Glahn, Albert T., Forty Fort, 324
Glahn, Mark M., Kingston, Forty Fort, 324
Glasner, Samuel, Uniontown, 324
Glass, Leopold C., Philadelphia, 324
Glasser, Norman L., Carnegie, 324
Glatfelter, Philip H., Spring Grove, 324
Gleason, Rutherford E., Philadelphia, 325
Glendening, John, Philadelphia, 325
Glenn, Herbert R., State College, 325
Glenn, John G., Gettysburg, 325
Glenn, Oliver E., Lansdowne, 325
Glover, David L., Mifflinburg, 325
Glover, Robert H., Philadelphia, 325
Gluck, Arthur, Castle Shannon, Pittsburgh, 325
Godcharles, Frederic A., Milton, 326
Goddard, Harold C., Swarthmore, 326
Godfrey, Edward, Pittsburgh, 326
Godshalk, Clarence A., Ardmore, Philadelphia, 326
Godshall, Wilson L., Bethlehem, 326
Goetz, A. John, Monessen, 326
Goetzenberger, Ralph L., Philadelphia, 326
Gold, John S., Lewisburg, 327
Goldbacher, Lawrence, Philadelphia, 327
Goldberger, Henry R., Altoona, 327
Golden, Charles O., Bushkill, 327
Goldenberg, John B., Merion, Philadelphia, 327
Golder, Benjamin M., Philadelphia, 327
Goldman, David H., Pittsburgh, 327
Goldsmith, Clifford, Westtown, 327
Goldsmith, Lester M., Philadelphia, 327
Goldsmith, Malcolm, Pittsburgh, Braddock, 328
Goldsmith, Maurice F., Pittsburgh, 328
Goldstein, Hyman I., Philadelphia, 328
Goldstein, William K., Scranton, 328
Goldsworthy, George W., Jr., Pittsburgh, 328
Gollmar, Frank I., West View, Pittsburgh, 328
Golz, Walter, Chambersburg, 328
Good, John D., McKeesport, 328
Good, Oscar E., Progress, Harrisburg, 328
Goodale, Stephen L., Pittsburgh, 328
Goodall, Herbert W., Philadelphia, 329
Goodell, William N., Philadelphia, 329
Goodling, Cletus L., Farm School, 329
Goodman, Nathan G., Philadelphia, 329
Goodrich, Charles F., Mt. Lebanon, Pittsburgh, 329
Goodrich, Herbert F., Philadelphia, 330
Goodspeed, Arthur W., Philadelphia, 330
Gordon, Alfred, Philadelphia, 330
Gordon, Burgess L., Philadelphia, 330
Gordon, Clarence M., Easton, 330
Gordon, Franklin F., Coatesville, 330
Gordon, Irwin L., Bywood, Philadelphia, 331
Gordon, John K., Chambersburg, 331
Gordon, Maude W., Erie, 331
Gordon, Seth, Harrisburg, 331
Gordy, Urie L., Chambersburg, 331
Gorham, Donald R., Philadelphia, 331
Gorham, Robert C., Pittsburgh, 331
Gorrell, John J. N., Pittsburgh, 332

Gossling, John H., Philadelphia, 332
Gotshall, Roy J., Lansdowne, Philadelphia, 332
Gott, Estep T., Sewickley, Pittsburgh, 332
Gottlieb, Maxim B., Philadelphia, 332
Gottlieb, Moritz M., Allentown, 332
Gotwals, John E., Phoenixville, 332
Gould, Beatrice B., Philadelphia, 333
Gould, Charles B., Philadelphia, 333
Gould, George, Mt. Lebanon, Pittsburgh, 333
Gould, Ralph R., Pittsburgh, 333
Gould, William D., Carlisle, 333
Gourley, W. Clyde, Glenside, Willow Grove, 333
Gow, J. Steele, Pittsburgh, 333
Gowen, James E., Philadelphia, 333
Graber, Henry, Royersford, 333
Grace, Eugene G., Bethlehem, 334
Graf, Julius E., Avalon, Pittsburgh, 334
Graff, F. Malcolm, Blairsville, 334
Graff, George W., York, 334
Graff, Richard M., Worthington, 334
Grafly, Dorothy, Philadelphia, 334
Graham, Arthur K., Philadelphia, Jenkintown, 334
Graham, Ben G., Pittsburgh, 334
Graham, Edwin E., Philadelphia, 334
Graham, John C., Butler, 334
Graham, John H., Glenside, Philadelphia, 335
Graham, Louis E., Beaver, 335
Graham, Robert X., Wilkinsburg, 335
Gramley, Dale H., Bethlehem, 335
Granowitz, Abram M., Johnstown, 335
Grant, Catharine E., Philadelphia, Harrisburg, 335
Grant, William H., St. Marys, 335
Graper, Elmer D., Pittsburgh, 335
Grapin, Camille, Pittsburgh, 335
Gravell, James H., Ambler, 336
Graves, Arthur R., Bethlehem, 336
Graves, Harold F., State College, 336
Graves, W. Brooke, Ardmore, 336
Gray, David J., Scranton, 337
Gray, James H., Pittsburgh, 337
Gray, Jessie, Philadelphia, 337
Gray, John S., Wilkinsburg, Pittsburgh, 337
Gray, Joseph, Spangler, Barnesboro, 337
Gray, Joseph B., Pittsburgh, 337
Grebe, Melvin H., Philadelphia, 337
Green, Clyde C., New Castle, 338
Green, G. Edward, Edgewood, Pittsburgh, 338
Green, George R., State College, 338
Green, Harry, Allentown, Bethlehem, 338
Green, John F. C., McKeesport, 338
Green, Otis F., Philadelphia, 339
Greenawalt, Emerson G., Susquehanna, 339
Greenbaum, Frederick R., Philadelphia, 339
Greenbaum, Sigmund S., Philadelphia, 339
Greenberg, Reynold H., Philadelphia, 339
Greenberg, Simon, Philadelphia, 339
Greene, Edward M., Huntingdon, 340
Greene, Floyd L., St. Davids, Philadelphia, 340
Greene, Lloyd B., Philadelphia, 340
Greenewalt, Mary H., Philadelphia, 340
Greenfield, Albert M., Philadelphia, 340
Greenslade, Grover R., Pittsburgh, Bridgeville, 341
Greenstone, Julius H., Philadelphia, 341
Greenway, Walter B., Jenkintown, 341
Greenzweig, Oscar A., Wind Gap, 341
Greer, Charles C., Johnstown, 341
Greer, Robert B., Media, 341
Gregory, Ralph A., Scranton, 342
Gregory, Thomas B., Emlenton, Pittsburgh, 342
Greisheimer, Esther M., Philadelphia, 342
Greiss, George A., Allentown, 342

Gress, Ernest M., Camp Hill, Harrisburg, 342
Greth, Morris S., Temple, 342
Grier, George W., Ben Avon, Pittsburgh, 342
Grier, Thomas C., Birmingham, 343
Griffin, Frederick R., Haverford, Philadelphia, 343
Griffin, Joseph A., Dickson, Scranton, 343
Griffing, Curtis A., Linesville, 343
Griffith, Beatrice F., Merion, 343
Griffith, Edward, Kingston, Scranton, 343
Griffith, George W., Ebensburg, 343
Griffith, Helen S., Philadelphia, 344
Griffith, Ivor, Elkins Park, Philadelphia, 344
Griffith, James A., Pittsburgh, 344
Griffith, J. P. Crozer, Philadelphia, 344
Griffiths, Hall M., Philadelphia, 344
Grim, George A., Nazareth, 344
Grimes, William C., West Alexander, 344
Grimm, Herbert L., Gettysburg, 344
Grimm, Karl J., Gettysburg, 344
Gring, Wilbur D., Newport, 345
Griscom, John M., Philadelphia, 345
Griscom, Rodman E., Haverford, Philadelphia, 345
Grizzell, E. Duncan, Philadelphia, 345
Groblewski, Casimir C., Plymouth, 345
Groce, William M., Selinsgrove, 345
Groff, June G., Philadelphia, 346
Groff, Robert A., Bala-Cynwyd, Philadelphia, 346
Groff, Wilmer K., Berwyn, 346
Groh, John L., Lebanon, 346
Grondalski, Lars O., Pittsburgh, Swissvale, 346
Grone, Robert Y., Danville, 346
Groover, Clair, Lewisburg, 346
Grose, C. Herman, Erie, 346
Grosh, Miriam, Beaver Falls, 346
Gross, John H., Lansdowne, Philadelphia, 346
Gross, John M., Bethlehem, 347
Gross, Juliet K., Philadelphia, Sellersville, 347
Gross, Malcolm W., Allentown, 347
Grossman, Samuel L., Harrisburg, 347
Groton, Nathanael B., Whitemarsh, 347
Grove, Harry A., Greencastle, 347
Grove, Robert E., Pittsburgh, 348
Groves, Frederick B., Pittsburgh, 348
Groves, Hannah C., Philadelphia, 348
Grubb, William R., Bangor, 348
Grubbs, Barton, 2d, Edgewood, Pittsburgh, 348
Gruber, Charles M., Bala-Cynwyd, Philadelphia, 348
Gruenberg, Frederick P., Philadelphia, 348
Grumbine, Harvey C., Lebanon, 348
Grundy, Joseph R., Bristol, 348
Gruver, Elbert A., Philadelphia, 348
Gubb, Larry E., Philadelphia, 348
Guckert, William L., Pittsburgh, 348
Guerin, John J., Philadelphia, 349
Guerrisi, Girolamo, Lebanon, 349
Guffey, Joseph F., Pittsburgh, 349
Guild, Lawrence R., Pittsburgh, 349
Guillet, George L., State College, 349
Gulick, Lee N., Bala-Cynwyd, 349
Gulliksen, Finn H., Pittsburgh, East Pittsburgh, 349
Gumaer, Alfred H., Philadelphia, 349
Gummey, Henry R., Jr., Philadelphia, 350
Gummo, Blanchard S., Lock Haven, Lewisburg, 350
Gunnison, Sisson B., Erie, Girard, 350
Gunster, Joseph F., Scranton, 350
Guthrie, Charles C., Pittsburgh, 350
Guthrie, Charles E., Coudersport, 350
Guthrie, Donald, Sayre, 350
Guthrie, Walter J., Pittsburgh, 351
Gutmueller, William G., Pottstown, 351
Gyger, Furman H., Kimberton, 351
Haas, Alfred M., Philadelphia, 351
Haas, Francis B., Harrisburg, 351
Haas, Harry J., Haverford, Philadelphia, 351
Haas, Robert E., Allentown, 351

Haber, Vernon R., State College, 351
Habgood, Robert P., Bradford, 351
Hackemann, Louis F., Allentown, 352
Hackenberg, Joseph L., Windber, 352
Hackett, James L., Emporium, 352
Hackett, Samuel E., Pittsburgh, 352
Hackney, Henry E., Pittsburgh, 352
Hadden, Samuel B., Philadelphia, 352
Haddock, John C., Wilkes-Barre, 352
Haddon, Harry H., Northumberland, Sunbury, 352
Hadley, Samuel H., Sharon, 352
Hadzsits, George D., Philadelphia, 352
Hafey, William J., Scranton, 352
Haffner, Thomas N., Allentown, Bath, 353
Hagan, James, Pittsburgh, 353
Hager, William H., Lancaster, 353
Hagert, Henry, Philadelphia, 353
Hague, William W., Library, Pittsburgh, 353
Hagy, Henry B., Reading, 353
Hahn, Frank E., Philadelphia, 353
Hahn, Frederick E., Philadelphia, 354
Hahn, Theodore F., Scranton, 354
Haig, Alfred R., Philadelphia, 354
Haines, Amena P., Bryn Athyn, 354
Haines, Arthur S., Library, Pittsburgh, 354
Haines, Benjamin W., West Chester, 354
Haines, Harold A., Philadelphia, 354
Haines, Harry L., Red Lion, 354
Haiston, Frank, Pottstown, 355
Halberg, Elmer J., Kittanning, 355
Halbert, LeRoy, Sharon, 355
Haldeman, Paul C., Coatesville, 355
Haldeman-Jefferies, Don, Chalfont, Harrisburg, Philadelphia, 355
Halderman, J. Leonard, Doylestown, 355
Half, Rudolph S., Pittsburgh, 355
Hall, Clarence A., Philadelphia, 355
Hall, John A. F., Harrisburg, 356
Hall, John H., Philadelphia, 356
Hall, Lyle G., Ridgway, St. Mary's, 356
Hall, Mary B., Bethlehem, 356
Hall, Ralph E., Pittsburgh, 356
Hall, Robert W., Bethlehem, 356
Hall, William S., Easton, 357
Hall, Wrayburn B., Coudersport, 357
Hallett, George H., West Chester, 357
Hallett, Winslow N., Allentown, 357
Hallowell, A. Irving, Philadelphia, 357
Hallowell, Henry R., Philadelphia, 358
Hallowell, Howard T., Jenkintown, 358
Halpern, Leon A., Philadelphia, 358
Haluska, John J., Patton, 358
Ham, Ernest L., Rochester, 358
Ham, William R., Boalsburg, State College, 358
Hambock, Leonard C., Philadelphia, 358
Hamer, Alfred, Pittsburgh, 358
Hamill, Samuel M., Philadelphia, 359
Hamilton, George E., Meadville, 359
Hamilton, Harry D., Washington, 359
Hamilton, Hughbert C., Philadelphia, 359
Hamilton, James W., Ben Avon, Pittsburgh, 359
Hamilton, J. Taylor, Bethlehem, 359
Hamilton, Milton W., Reading, 360
Hamilton, William J., Carbondale, 360
Hamlin, Orlo J., Smethport, 360
Hamm, Homer A., Meadville, 360
Hammett, Frederick S., Philadelphia, 360
Hammond, Frank C., Philadelphia, 360
Hammond, Harry P., State College, 360
Hamor, William A., Oakmont, Pittsburgh, 361
Hampson, Harold S., Warren, 361
Hamsher, Mervin H., Harrisburg, 361
Hanauer, Albert M., Pittsburgh, 361
Hance, Robert T., Pittsburgh, 361

Hand, Alfred, Philadelphia, 361
Hand, George T., Bethlehem, 361
Haney, John L., Philadelphia, 362
Hankey, William L., New Kensington, Wilmerding, 362
Hankins, James H., Uniontown, 362
Hanley, Edward J., Tarentum, Brackenridge, 362
Hanna, Bernard F., Rockwood, 362
Hanna, Clinton R., Pittsburgh, 363
Hanna, Meredith, Philadelphia, 363
Hanny, William F., Swarthmore, 363
Hansell, John L., Ambler, 363
Hanselman, William L., Meadville, 363
Hanson, Henry W. A., Gettysburg, 363
Harbeson, John F., Philadelphia, 363
Harbeson, William P., Philadelphia, 364
Harbison, Francis R., Fox Chapel, Pittsburgh, 364
Harbison, Ralph W., Sewickley, Pittsburgh, 364
Harbold, Peter M., Lancaster, 364
Harcum, Edith H., Bryn Mawr, 364
Hardcastle, John D., Mt. Lebanon, Pittsburgh, 364
Harding, George, Wynnewood, 365
Hardinge, Harlowe, York, 365
Harker, Frank M., Bryn Mawr, Philadelphia, 365
Hardt, John W., Philadelphia, 365
Hardt, Walter K., Haverford, 365
Hardy, Fred N., Port Allegany, 365
Hare, Amory, Media, 365
Hare, Jay V., Trevose, Philadelphia, 366
Hare, Mollie W., Langhorne, 366
Harger, George D., Pittsburgh, 366
Hargest, William M., Harrisburg, 366
Hargroves, Vernon C., Philadelphia, 366
Haring, Albert, Bethlehem, 366
Haring, Fred A., Pittsburgh, 366
Harker, Samuel A., Bloomsburg, 366
Harkey, William F., Washington, 366
Harkins, John F., State College, 366
Harkins, Melvin R., Philadelphia, 366
Harkness, Reuben E. E., Chester, 366
Harlan, Clarence E., Renovo, 366
Harlan, Orla K., State College, 367
Harley, John P., Williamsport, 367
Harllee, Chauncey M. D., Philadelphia, 367
Harman, J. Paul, Greensburg, 367
Harmeson, Glen W., Bethlehem, 367
Harmon, George D., Bethlehem, 367
Harms, John H., Philadelphia, 367
Harner, Nevin C., Lancaster, 368
Harnwell, Gaylord P., Wynnewood, 368
Harper, Francis, Swarthmore, Philadelphia, 368
Harpst, Clifford W., Sharon, 368
Harr, Luther, Philadelphia, 368
Harré, T. Everett, Wrightsville, 369
Harris, Arthur E., Philadelphia, 369
Harris, Burtt, Pittsburgh, 369
Harris, Charles W., Easton, 369
Harris, Clinton L., State College, 369
Harris, Francis W., Coatesville, 369
Harris, George R., Perrysville, Pittsburgh, 369
Harris, John H., Camp Hill, Harrisburg, 370
Harris, John H., Pittsburgh, 370
Harris, John T., Bryn Mawr, Philadelphia, 370
Harris, Philip H., Johnstown, 370
Harris, Stanley E., Lansdowne, Philadelphia, 370
Harris, Stephen, Philadelphia, 370
Harris W. Carlton, Philadelphia, 371
Harrison, Bruce, Mt. Lebanon, Pittsburgh, 371
Harrison, Charles C., Jr., Philadelphia, 371
Harrison, Charles J., Jr., Somerset, 371
Harrison, Earl G., Moylan, Philadelphia, 371
Harrison, Francis G., Gladwyne, Philadelphia, 371
Harrison, H. Norris, Philadelphia, 371
Harrison, Joseph F. X., Philadelphia, 371

PENNSYLVANIA

Harrison, Thomas R., Wyncote, Philadelphia, 371
Harry, Carolus P., Norristown, 371
Harry, Philip W., Lancaster, 372
Hart, Charles, Media, Chester, 372
Hart, John F., Philadelphia, 372
Hart, Thomas, Wynnewood, Philadelphia, 372
Hart, U. Shuman, Hollidaysburg, 372
Harter, Nathan W., Greenville, 372
Hartgen, Frederick A., Erie, 372
Hartman, Edwin M., Lancaster, 373
Hartman, Galen C., Pittsburgh, 373
Hartman, Guy N., Somerset, Meyersdale, 373
Hartman, Roland C., Hanover, 373
Hartman, Thomas H., New Castle, 373
Hartman, William E., Carlisle, 373
Hartmann, William V., Pittsburgh, 373
Hartung, Charles A., Pittsburgh, 374
Hartz, Robert E., Palmyra, 374
Hartzog, Herbert J., Bethlehem, 374
Harvey, Adelbert W., Pittsburgh, 374
Harvey, Charles W., Philadelphia, 374
Harvey, E. Marshall, Media, 374
Harvey, Frederic A., Pittsburgh, 374
Harvey, John S. C., Radnor, 374
Harvey, Lewis B., Newtown Square, 375
Harvey, McLeod, Waynesburg, 375
Harvey, Walter B., Pittsburgh, 375
Hasek, Carl W., State College, 375
Haslam, George S., Palmerton, 375
Hasley, Thomas O., Pittsburgh, 375
Hassler, Jacob P., Grove City, 375
Hassold, Carl F. R., Philadelphia, 376
Hastings, Glen B., Montoursville, Williamsport, 376
Hastings, Penn G., Philadelphia, Milton, 376
Hastings, Willard S., Elkins Park, Philadelphia, 376
Haswell, John R., State College, 376
Hatch, David A., Easton, 376
Hatfield, Charles J., Philadelphia, 376
Hathaway, Charles M., Jr., Olyphant, 376
Hathaway, Harle W., Philadelphia, 377
Hathway, Marion, Pittsburgh, 377
Hauber, Alois J., St. Marys, 377
Hauberger, George H., Philadelphia, 377
Haudenshield, John E., Carnegie, Pittsburgh, 377
Haupt, William S., Shamokin, 377
Hause, Nathan E., Harrisburg, 377
Hauser, Conrad A., Upper Darby, Philadelphia, 377
Hausman, William A., Jr., Allentown, 377
Havenhill, Robert S., Beaver, Monaca, 378
Havens, Paul S., Chambersburg, 378
Haviland, James T., Wayne, Philadelphia, 378
Haviland, Walter W., Lansdowne, 378
Hawes, Edward M., Norristown, 378
Hawkes, William F., Philadelphia, 378
Hawks, Edward, Philadelphia, 378
Hawley, William C., Pittsburgh, Wilkinsburg, 379
Hay, George, Johnstown, 379
Hay, Homer W., Somerset, 379
Hay, Malcolm, Sewickley, Pittsburgh, 379
Hay, Southard, Pittsburgh, 379
Hayes, E. V., Pittsburgh, 379
Hayes, J. Carroll, West Chester, 379
Hayes, John R., Embreeville, 379
Hayes, Norman T., Rosemont, Philadelphia, 380
Haynes, Roy A., Philadelphia, 380
Hays, Harry C., Fredonia, 380
Hays, Jo, State College, 380
Hays, John L., Pittsburgh, 380
Haythorn, Samuel R., Pittsburgh, 381
Hayward, Nathan, Wayne, Philadelphia, 381
Hazard, Spencer P., Philadelphia, 381
Hazen, Carl M., Titusville, 381
Hazlehurst, Thomas H., Jr., Bethlehem, 381
Head, Leon O., Center Ridge, 381
Headings, Donald N., Norristown, 382
Heald, Kenneth C., Pittsburgh, 382

Healy, Fred A., Ardmore, Philadelphia, 382
Heard, Drayton, Sewickley, Pittsburgh, 382
Heard, James D., Pittsburgh, 382
Heath, Edwin J., Bethlehem, 382
Heathcote, Charles W., West Chester, 382
Hebard, Benjamin M., Narberth, 383
Hechler, F. G., State College, 383
Hecht, Edward, Lock Haven, 383
Heckel, George B., Philadelphia, 383
Heckscher, Maurice, Washington, Philadelphia, 383
Hedenburg, Oscar F., Pittsburgh, 383
Hedley, Evalena, Philadelphia, 383
Heffner, Edward H., Philadelphia, 384
Heilbron, Tillie T., Media, Philadelphia, 384
Heilbrunn, Lewis V., Philadelphia, 384
Heilman, Eugene A., Philadelphia, 384
Heilman, Harry A., Kittanning, 384
Heilman, Russell H., Pittsburgh, 384
Heimerdinger, Leo H., Philadelphia, 385
Heine, H. Eugene, Philadelphia, 385
Heinly, Charles B., York, 385
Heintzelman, C. H., Coatesville, 385
Heinz, Howard, Pittsburgh, 385
Heiserman, Clarence B., Haverford, Philadelphia, 385
Heisey, Herman B., Lewistown, 385
Heisler, Roland C., Wynnewood, Philadelphia, 386
Heiss, Elwood D., East Stroudsburg, 386
Heissenbuttel, Ernest G., Greenville, 386
Helbert, George K., Philadelphia, 386
Held, Jacob B., Erie, 386
Held, Omar C., Pittsburgh, 386
Helferich, Donald L., Lansdowne, 386
Hellmund, Rudolph E., Swissvale, 386
Helmbold, Theodore R., Pittsburgh, 387
Helme, J. Burn, State College, 387
Helriegel, Florence J., Scranton, 387
Helson, Harry, Narberth, 387
Helton, Roy A., Upper Darby, Harrisburg, 387
Hemingway, Reginald S., Bloomsburg, 387
Hemphill, John, Philadelphia, 387
Hemphill, Marguerite F., Beaver Falls, 387
Henderson, Adelbert A., Wilkinsburg, Pittsburgh, 387
Henderson, Davis W., Uniontown, 387
Henderson, Earl F., New Castle, 387
Henderson, Joseph H., Shiremanstown, Harrisburg, 388
Henderson, Joseph W., Philadelphia, 388
Henderson, Katharine C., Altoona, 388
Henderson, Robert H., Huntingdon, 388
Hendricks, William C., Brookville, 388
Hendrickson, David, New Hope, 388
Henke, Frederick G., Meadville, 388
Henn, Arthur W., Pittsburgh, 388
Hennessey, John J., Philadelphia, 389
Henning, Stanley R., Trucksville, Wilkes-Barre, 389
Henning, William L., State College, 389
Henninger, Frank L., Sunbury, 389
Henretta, James E., Kane, 389
Henrici, Max, Coraopolis, Pittsburgh, 389
Henry, Arnold K., Philadelphia, 389
Henry, George M., Berwyn, Philadelphia, 389
Henry, John T., Martha Furnace, 389
Henry, Wilbur F., Washington, 390
Hensel, George W., Jr., Quarryville, 390
Hensler, Carl P., Pittsburgh, 390
Hepburn, Joseph S., Philadelphia, see Addenda
Heppenstall, Charles W., Pittsburgh, 390
Heppenstall, Robert B., Pittsburgh, 390
Herbach, Joseph, Philadelphia, 390
Herben, Stephen J., Haverford, 390
Herber, E. C., Carlisle, 390

Herbert, Robert B., Greensburg, 390
Herbst, Josephine F., Erwinna, 390
Herd, John V., Philadelphia, 391
Herdic, Carl W., Williamsport, 391
Hergesheimer, Ella S., Reading, 391
Hergesheimer, Joseph, West Chester, 391
Herman, Albert, Philadelphia, 391
Herman, John W., Coatesville, 391
Herman, Leonora O., Philadelphia, 391
Herman, Samuel S., West Chester, Philadelphia, 391
Herman, Stewart W., Harrisburg, 391
Herman, Theodore F., Lancaster, 391
Hermann, Burke M., Boalsburg, 391
Herndon, Edward L., Pottsville, 391
Herndon, John G., Jr., Haverford, 391
Herpst, Martha J., Titusville, 392
Herr, Benjamin B., Lancaster, 392
Herr, Benjamin M., Pittsburgh, 392
Herr, Herbert T., Jr., Pittsburgh, 392
Herr, John D., Philadelphia, 392
Herr, John K., Lancaster, 392
Herrick, Cheesman A., Philadelphia, 392
Herrman, Clinton S., Philadelphia, 392
Herron, David C., Monongahela, 392
Herron, Samuel D., Sewickley, Pittsburgh, 393
Hershey, Ezra F., Hershey, 393
Hershey, Milton S., Hershey, 393
Hershner, Newton W., Mechanicsburg, 393
Hertzler, Jacob O., Erie, 393
Hertzler, William, Port Royal, 393
Hervey, John G., Upper Darby, Philadelphia, 393
Herzog, Eugene, Pittsburgh, 393
Heselbarth, Thomas K., Pittsburgh, 393
Hess, Arleigh P., Philadelphia, 393
Hess, Elam G., Manheim, 393
Hess, Elmer, Erie, 394
Hess, George H., Uniontown, 394
Hess, H. Lloyd, Lancaster, 394
Hess, Henry L., Philadelphia, 394
Hess, Herbert W., Philadelphia, 394
Hess, Leslie E., Drexel Hill, Philadelphia, 394
Hesse, Frank M., Pittsburgh, 394
Hetrick, William H., Connellsville, 394
Hetzel, Frederic V., West Chester, 394
Hetzel, Ralph D., State College, 394
Heuer, Russell P., Bryn Mawr, Philadelphia, 394
Hewitt, Arthur C., Bellefonte, 395
Heywood, Harry B., Jenkintown, Conshohocken, 395
Hibbs, Ben, Narberth, Philadelphia, 395
Hibshman, Edward K., State College, 395
Hibshman, Eugene E., Altoona, 395
Hickerson, Ainslee E., Narberth, Ardmore, 396
Hickey, David F., Bradford, 396
Hicks-Bruun, Mildred M., Swarthmore, Norwood, 396
Hiers, Glen S., Bala-Cynwyd, Philadelphia, 396
Higbee, Donald M., Connellsville, 396
Higbee, William S., Philadelphia, 396
Higgins, Henry B., Sewickley, Pittsburgh, 396
Higgins, John M., Sayre, 396
Higgins, Robert A., State College, 396
Higgins, Ruth L., Jenkintown, 397
Higgins, Thomas J., Philadelphia, 397
High, Samuel H., Horsham, Norristown, 397
Highberger, Elmer, Jr., Oil City, 397
Hildenberger, Martin J., Bethlehem, 397
Hildner, Richard C., Pittsburgh, 397
Hill, Calvin F., Neffs, 397
Hill, Charles C., Carlisle, 398
Hill, Edward Y., Philadelphia, 398
Hill, Grace L., Swarthmore, 498
Hill, Henry C., Lewisburg, 398
Hill, J. Ben, State College, 398
Hill, J. Bennett, Wynnewood, Marcus Hook, 399
Hill, Minot J., Bristol, 399
Hill, Samuel S., Wernersville, 399
Hill, Theodore C., North East, Erie, 399
Hill, Walter L., Scranton, 400

Hillegass, Charles E., Pennsburg, 400
Hillegass, Foster C., Pennsburg, Norristown, 400
Hillegass, Jonathan B., Norristown, 400
Hilles, Robert L., Philadelphia, 400
Hilliard, Thomas J., Sharpsburg, Pittsburgh, 400
Hillman, John H., Jr., Pittsburgh, 400
Hillstrom, David A., Corry, 400
Himebaugh, John W., Erie, 400
Himes, Leslie R., New Bethlehem, 400
Hinchman, William R., Pittsburgh, 401
Hindman, James E., Wilkinsburg, Pittsburgh, 401
Hindman, William B., Uniontown, 401
Hipsher, Edward E., Philadelphia, 402
Hipwell, Harry H., Pittsburgh, 402
Hires, Charles E., Jr., Wynnewood, Philadelphia, 402
Hires, Harrison S., Berwyn, Philadelphia, 402
Hirsch, Albert C., Pittsburgh, 402
Hirsch, Isaac E., Pittsburgh, 402
Hirsch, Joseph, Philadelphia, 402
Hirschwald, Rudolph M., Philadelphia, 403
Hirsh, Harry B., Philadelphia, 403
Hirsh, Sidney, Pittsburgh, 403
Hirst, Lester L., Pittsburgh, 403
Hirt, William E., Erie, 403
Hirtzel, Orris C., North East, 403
Hitchens, William F., Pittsburgh, 403
Hitchler, Walter H., Carlisle, 403
Hittle, James M., Greenville, 403
Hoag, Clarence G., Haverford, 404
Hoban, Thomas L., Scranton, 404
Höber, Rudolf O. A., Philadelphia, 404
Hoblitzelle, Harrison, Ithan, Eddystone, 404
Hodge, Charles, 4th, Philadelphia, 404
Hodges, Clarence A., Philadelphia, 404
Hodges, Fletcher, Jr., Pittsburgh, 404
Hodges, Harry, Philadelphia, 405
Hodges, Leigh M., Doylestown, Philadelphia, 405
Hodgkiss, Harold E., State College, 405
Hoechst, Coit R., Pittsburgh, 405
Hoeveler, John A., Mt. Lebanon, Pittsburgh, 405
Hoffman, Dean M., Harrisburg, 405
Hoffman, George W., Upper Darby, 405
Hoffman, Harry C., Connellsville, 405
Hoffman, Harry F., Allentown, 406
Hoffman, James F., Wilkinsburg, 406
Hoffman, Leon H., Punxsutawney, 406
Hoffman, Luther S., East Stroudsburg, 406
Hoffman, William S., State College, 406
Hofmann, Josef, Merion, Philadelphia, 406
Hofstetter, William A., Philadelphia, 406
Hogan, Charles V., Pottsville, 406
Hogan, Franklin E., Kane, 406
Hogg, Harold K., Lancaster, 407
Holbrook, Arthur A., East Stroudsburg, Stroudsburg, 407
Holbrook, Elmer A., Pittsburgh, 407
Holcomb, Richmond C., Upper Darby, 407
Holcombe, John L., Pittsburgh, 407
Holden, Hale, Jr., Haverford, Philadelphia, 407
Holden, Robert F., Haverford, Philadelphia, 407
Holland, J. Burnett, Norristown, 407
Holland, Leicester B., Philadelphia, 407
Holland, Moorhead B., Pittsburgh, 408
Holland, Rupert S., Wayne, 408
Holland, Stanley H., McKeesport, 408
Hollander, Lester, Pittsburgh, 408
Hollinger, John A., Allison Park, Pittsburgh, 409
Hollingsworth, Charles B., Greensburg, 409
Hollinshead, Byron S., La Plume, 409

PENNSYLVANIA

n, Samuel L., Mars, 533
n, Edward W., Altoona, 533
ner, Josiah R., Emlenton, 533
ridge, Jonathan E., Philahia, 533
an, James S., Beaver Falls,

Charles H., Easton, 533
Estelle L., Wynnewood,
ladelphia, 534
John W., Washington, 534
nd, Charles N., Wilkes-Barre,

Henry, Langhorne, 534
John V., Philadelphia, 534
gard, Leon, Harrisburg, 534
thal, Alexander, Pittsburgh,

s, John B., Philadelphia, 535
e, Robert N., North Bradk, Braddock, 535
ht, Wallace J., Center
ey, 535
Ellsworth, Butler, 535
H. H., Pittsburgh, 535
W. Norwood, Lewisburg,

Alexander, Pittsburgh, 535
man, Howard B., Pittsburgh,

Edwin A., Villa Nova,
adelphia, 536
Emil A., Washington, York,

e, Walter W., Philadelphia,

Bente S., Beaver Falls, 536
n, Seymour D., Philadelphia,
wyne, 536
ag, Frederick W., Swarth-
, 537
Augustine, St. Marys, 537
ach, Frank K., Tyrone, 537
, Edward C., Philadelphia,

Francis D. W., Balayd, Philadelphia, 537
, Hiram S., Philadelphia,

Robert M., Philadelphia,
Iermann A., Philadelphia,

s, Katharine, Philadelphia,

C. Harrison, Erie, 538
Frederick H., Philadelphia,

William E., Haverford, 538
Romeo A., Philadelphia,

lbert C., Moosic, 538
oland B., Abington, 538
Villiam F., Ambler, 538
Richard T., Bala-Cynwyd,

Robert R., Coudersport,

Clay F., Greensburg,
ale, 539
Clyde A., Annville, 539
Ralph, Sharpsburg, Pitts-
, 539
Edward J., Scranton, 539
William R., Scranton, 539
. B. Vincent, Rosemont,
delphia, 539
ohn D., Sewickley, Pittsilian M., Ardmore, 540
ouis W., Pittsburgh, 540
William P., Pittsburgh, 540
Thomas M., Pittsburgh, 540
ur, Angus, Pittsburgh, 541
ey, Clarence E. N., Pitts-
-Dexter, Edith, Sharon,

am, John A., Philadelphia,

er, William J., Jr., Ridley
Chester, 541
ey, James E., Jr.,
rgh, 541
Alexander, Philadelphia,

William L., Philadelphia,

lie, William T., Lewisburg,

, Albert D., Chester,
542
Harry, Wyncote,
lphia, 542
d, Robert, Jr., Phila-
, 542
, Mary E., West Chester,

e, Roy S., Drexel Hill,

MacFarland, George A., Jenkintown, Philadelphia, 543
Macfarlane, Catherine, Philadelphia, see Addenda
Macfarlane, Charles E., Edgewood, Wilmerding, 543
MacGillivray, Charles D., Drexel Hill, Philadelphia, 543
MacGilvary, Norwood, Pittsburgh, 543
MacIntosh, Aden B., Lancaster, 543
MacIntosh, Mark, Swarthmore, 543
Mack, Connie, Philadelphia, 543
Mack, John S., McKeesport, 543
Mack, Warren B., State College, 544
Mackall, Paul, Bethlehem, 544
Mackay, Robert W., Warren, 544
Mackenzie, George W., Philadelphia, 544
Mackie, Alexander, Philadelphia, 545
MacKinnon, George V., Jenkintown, Philadelphia, 545
Macklin, John F., Philadelphia, 545
Maclay, Robert B., Belleville, 545
MacLennan, Alexander G., Pittsburgh, 545
MacMillan, Hugh R., Bradford, 545
Macneill, Norman M., Philadelphia, 546
MacQueen, Lawrence I., Pittsburgh, 546
Madden, Francis J., Duquesne, 546
Madden, Joseph W., Pittsburgh, 546
Maddox, William P., Philadelphia, 546
Madeira, Percy C., Ogontz, Philadelphia, 546
Madeira, Percy C., Jr., Philadelphia, 546
Maeder, LeRoy M. A., Philadelphia, 547
Magaw, Elden S., Upper Darby, Philadelphia, 547
Magee, F, Earle, Oil City, 547
Magee, James M., Pittsburgh, 547
Magee, John F., Easton, 547
Magenau, John M., Erie, 547
Magidson, Frank, Pittsburgh, 547
Magill, Frank S., Chambersburg, 547
Magill, James P., Philadelphia, 547
Magill, Walter H., Philadelphia, 547
Magrady, Frederick W., Mt. Carmel, 548
Maguire, Frank P., East Stroudsburg, Harrisburg, 548
Mahoney, Bertha W., Erie, 548
Mainzer, Francis S., Huntingdon, 548
Mairs, Thomas I., State College, 548
Malcherek, Karl A., Pittsburgh, Hollidaysburg, 549
Malcolm, Gilbert, Boiling Springs, 549
Male, Arthur J., Allentown, 549
Malick, Robert E., Shamokin, 549
Mallalieu, Wilbur V., Harrisburg, 549
Mallery, Otto T., Philadelphia, 549
Mallon, Henry N., Bradford, 549
Mallon, Joseph, Philadelphia, 549
Malone, Clarence F., Beaver, Rochester, 550
Malone, Watson, Haverford, Philadelphia, 550
Maloney, Clifton, Philadelphia, 550
Man, E. Lester, Scranton, 550
Manchester, Charles, Franklin, 550
Mancill, Frank H., Merion Station, Philadelphia, 551
Manges, Edmund A., Huntingdon, 551
Mann, Alexander, Pittsburgh, 551
Mann, Thomas A., Philadelphia, 551
Manning, Frank L., Collegeville, 551
Manning, Helen H. T., Bryn Mawr, 551
Mansfield, Donald B., Philadelphia, 551
Mansfield, J. Clark, Pittsburgh, 551
Mansfield, Myron G., Pittsburgh, 551
Mansfield, William D., McKeesport, 552
Manson, Frederic E., Williamsport, 552
Mansuy, John L., Ralston, 552
Mantnband, Charles, Williamsport, 552
Marbaker, Edward E., Pittsburgh, 552
Marble, Dean R., State College, 552
Marceau, Henri, Philadelphia, 553

March, Matthias L., Norristown, Bridgeport, 553
March, William A., Norristown, Bridgeport, 553
Marcks, Frederick A., Nazareth, 553
Margie, Peter M., West Pittston, Kingston, Pittston, Wilkes-Barre, 553
Margiotti, Charles J., Pittsburgh, 553
Margolis, Jacob, Pittsburgh, 553
Marinaro, Carmen V., Butler, 553
Maris, Albert B., Lansdowne, Philadelphia, 553
Markell, William O., Pittsburgh, 554
Markle, David L., State College, 554
Markle, Donald, Jeddo, 554
Markle, John, 2d, Camp Hill, Harrisburg, 554
Marks, Harold K., Allentown, 554
Marks, Lewis H., Paoli, Philadelphia, 554
Marks, Mary H., Pittsburgh, 554
Marlier, Raymond M., Ingram, Pittsburgh, 554
Marlin, Harry H., New Castle, 554
Marquard, William B., Easton, 554
Marquardt, Carl E., State College, 555
Marriner, Guy V. R., Philadelphia, 555
Marriott, Ross W., Swarthmore, 555
Marsella, Loreto, Norristown, 555
Marsh, James I., Pittsburgh, 555
Marsh, Ritchie T., Erie, 555
Marsh, Robert P., Gettysburg, 555
Marshall, Charles D., Pittsburgh, 556
Marshall, Charles H., Philadelphia, 556
Marshall, Edward W., Philadelphia, 556
Marshall, James E., Butler, 556
Marshall, John, Swarthmore, 556
Marshall, John G., Beaver, 556
Marshall, Loyal S., Springdale, 556
Marshall, Mortimer P., Lancaster, 556
Marshall, Roy K., Pittsburgh, 557
Marshall, Thomas R., Melrose Park, Philadelphia, 557
Matteney, Charles W., Ridley Park, 557
Martin, Adam M., York, 557
Martin, Adam O., Doylestown, 557
Martin, Alfred, Brackenridge, Verona, 557
Martin, Arthur C., Greensburg, Pittsburgh, 557
Martin, Asa E., State College, 557
Martin, Carl N., Anselma, Philadelphia, 557
Martin, Charles E., Bellefonte, 557
Martin, Christian F., Nazareth, 558
Martin, Edward, Washington, 558
Martin, Francis C., Johnstown, 558
Martin, George C., Clymer, 558
Martin, George E., Pittsburgh, 558
Martin, Hershel R., Philadelphia, 558
Martin, James P., Lancaster, 558
Martin, James S., Beaver Falls, 558
Martin, John C., Philadelphia, 559
Martin, Joseph B., Paxtang, Harrisburg, 559
Martin, Mildred P., Philadelphia, 559
Martin, Newton P., Leola, 559
Martin, Renwick H., Beaver Falls, Pittsburgh, 559
Martin, Robert W., Quakertown, 559
Martin, Sydney E., Upper Roxborough, Philadelphia, 559
Martino, Antonio P., Philadelphia, 560
Marts, Arnaud C., Lewisburg, 560
Masland, Frank E., Jr., Carlisle, 561
Mason, Edgar D., Pittsburgh, 561
Mason, Francis C., Gettysburg, 561
Mason, George M., Erie, 561
Mason, J. Alden, Berwyn, Philadelphia, 561
Mason, Mary S. T., Philadelphia, 561
Mason, Thomas W., State College, 562
Massingham, Sherman, Pittsburgh, 562
Massol, Merwin B., Pittsburgh, 562
Masten, Fred C., Pittsburgh, 562
Master, Henry B., Devon, 562
Masters, Frank M., Harrisburg, 562
Masters, Harry G., Pittsburgh, 562
Masters, Harry V., Reading, 562
Mates, James W., Pittsburgh, 562
Mather, Frank J., Jr., Washington Crossing, 562

Mather, Thomas R., Benton, 563
Mathesius, Walther E. L., Pittsburgh, 563
Mathews, Charles H., Jr., Paoli, Philadelphia, 563
Matt, C. David, Philadelphia, 564
Mattas, Clyde L., Scranton, 564
Mattes, Philip V., Scranton, 564
Matthews, Archibald M., Somerset, 564
Matthews, Arthur P., Scranton, 564
Matthews, H. Alexander, Philadelphia, 564
Matthews, Isaac G., Chester, 564
Mattox, Edgar E., Pittsburgh, 565
Matzer, Robert L., Lewisburg, 565
Maurer, Felix O., Frackville, 565
Maurer, James H., Reading, 565
Maxey, George W., Scranton, Philadelphia, 566
Maxey, Paul H., Scranton, 566
Maxfield, Ezra K., Washington, 566
Maxfield, Jane C., Washington, 566
Maxwell, Charles F., Greensburg, 566
Maxwell, Charles P., Easton, 566
May, Edwin C., Pittsburgh, 567
May, Herbert A., Pittsburgh, 567
May, Kenneth F., Pittsburgh, 567
Mayer, Edward E., Pittsburgh, 567
Mayes, William E., Brockway, 567
Mays, Jacob H., Weiser Park, 568
Mays, Paul K., Bryn Athyn, 568
Mayser, Charles W., Lancaster, 568
Maywood, Armour A., Pittsburgh, 568
Mazer, Charles, Philadelphia, 568
McAdoo, Henry M., Fort Washington, 568
McAfee, W. Keith, New Castle, 568
McAlister, David I., Washington, 568
McAlister, John B., Harrisburg, 568
McAndrew, Mary B., Carbondale, 568
McAndrew, Paul C., Scranton, 569
McBride, F. Scott, Philadelphia, 569
McBride, John B., Canonsburg, Pittsburgh, 569
McBride, Lois M., Bradford Woods, Pittsburgh, 569
McBride, Milford L., Grove City, 569
McBride, William, Sewickley, Pittsburgh, 569
McBride, William K., Harrisburg, 569
McBurney, James H., Canonsburg, 569
McCabe, Thomas B., Swarthmore, Chester, Philadelphia, 569
McCabe, Warren L., Pittsburgh, 569
McCafferty, Ernest D., Allison Park, Pittsburgh, 569
McCaffrey, Thomas Jr., Pittsburgh, 569
McCague, Robert R., Sewickley, Pittsburgh, 569
McCahan, David, Swarthmore, Philadelphia, 570
McCahill, David I. B., Pittsburgh, 570
McCain, Samuel H., Kittanning, 570
McCamey, Harold E., Fox Chapel, Pittsburgh, 570
McCance, Pressly H., Pittsburgh, 570
McCandless, James F., Pittsburgh, 570
McCandless, Lee C., Butler, 570
McCandless, Milton C., Rochester, 571
McCandless, Lester C., Pittsburgh, 571
McCann, Minnie A., Reading, 571
McCarter, Henry, Philadelphia, 571
McCarthy, Anna L., Mayfield, 571
McCarthy, Daniel J., Philadelphia, 571
McCarthy, Louise C., Ridley Park, 571
McCartney, James L., Philadelphia, 571
McCarty, Harriet D., Pittsburgh, 571
McCarty, Roy A., Drexel Hill, Philadelphia, 571
McCaslin, Murray F., Pittsburgh, 572
McCauley, Thomas A., North East, 572
McClain, Harry C., Hustontown, 572
McClean, Lee D., Meadville, 572
McCleary, Thomas G., Braddock, 572
McClellan, George E., Bellefonte, 572
McClellan, Robert P., Irwin, 572

PENNSYLVANIA

Holloway, Edward S., Philadelphia, 409
Holman, Edward L., New Bloomfield, 410
Holman, William K., Ithan, Philadelphia, 410
Holmes, Ernest G. N., Bethlehem, 410
Holmes, Henry K., Pittsburgh, 410
Holmes, Jesse H., Moylan, 410
Holroyd, Roland, Philadelphia, 410
Holsinger, Virgil C., Millvale, 410
Holton, Charles R., Bethlehem, 411
Holtzapple, George E., York, 411
Holtzman, Herbert P., West Reading, 411
Homsher, Howard N., Bartville, 412
Hoober, John A., York, 412
Hood, Alexander B., Connellsville, 412
Hood, Jean, State College, 412
Hood, Richard, Philadelphia, 412
Hook, John I., Waynesburg, 412
Hooker, Davenport, Pittsburgh, 412
Hoon, Merle R., Pittsburgh, 412
Hooper, Robert P., Philadelphia, 413
Hoopes, Darlington, Reading, 413
Hoover, Herbert N., Solebury, 413
Hoover, Benjamin A., Wrightsville, 413
Hoover, Clyde W., Enola, 413
Hoover, Harvey D., Gettysburg, 413
Hoover, Samuel E., Jenkintown, Philadelphia, 413
Hope, Richard, Pittsburgh, 413
Hopkins, James B., Easton, 413
Hopkinson, Edward, Jr., Philadelphia, 414
Hopper, Harry B., Merion, Philadelphia, 414
Hopwood, Josephine L. R., Primos, Philadelphia, 414
Horelick, Samuel, Pittsburgh, 414
Horn, Clarence A., Reading, 414
Horn, Robert C., Allentown, 414
Hornbostel, Henry, Pittsburgh, 415
Horne, S. Hamill, Bryn Mawr, Philadelphia, 415
Horner, Meyers B., Washington, 415
Horner, Walter W., Pittsburgh, 415
Horner, William S., Pittsburgh, 415
Horrow, Benjamin, Philadelphia, 415
Horton, Clayton R., Portland, Johnsonville, 416
Hosford, Charles F., Jr., Aspinwall, 416
Hosking, Herbert T., Jr., Lansdowne, Philadelphia, 416
Hotson, Leslie, Haverford, 416
Houck, Maurice, Berwick, 416
Houck, Samuel C., Boyertown, 416
Houghten, Ferry C., Pittsburgh, 416
Houghton, Frederick P., Bala-Cynwyd, Philadelphia, 417
House, Edward J., Pittsburgh, 417
Houser, Karl M., Narberth, Philadelphia, 417
Housman, William F., Steelton, 417
Houston, James G., Pittsburgh, 417
Houston, Samuel F., Philadelphia, 417
Houtz, Harry D., Selinsgrove, 417
Houze, Roger J. J., Point Marion, 417
Hovde, Brynjolf J., Pittsburgh, 417
Howard, Edgar B., Bryn Mawr, 418
Howard, Frederick A., Chester, 418
Howard, Philip E., Philadelphia, 418
Howard, William E., Pittsburgh, 418
Howat, John B., Sharon, 418
Howe, George, Philadelphia, 419
Howe, Thomas D., Pittsburgh, 419
Howell, John C., Philadelphia, 419
Hower, Harry, Pittsburgh, 420
Howland, Alice G., Bryn Mawr, 420
Howland, Anne W., Philadelphia, 420
Howland, Arthur C., Swarthmore, 420
Howland, Fred B., Titusville, 420
Howland, Harry W., Galeton, 420
Howorth, John, Wilkes-Barre, 420
Howson, Furman S., Wayne, Philadelphia, 420
Hoy, Charles W., Philadelphia, 420
Hoyler, Cyril N., Bethlehem, 420
Hoyt, Creig S., Grove City, 420
Hubach, Louis A., Pittsburgh, 421

Hubbard, Charles G., Smethport, 421
Hubbard, John W., Pittsburgh, 421
Hubbs, Robert C., Philadelphia, 421
Huber, Charles F., Wilkes-Barre, 421
Huber, Charles H., Gettysburg, 421
Huber, John F., Wynnewood, Philadelphia, 421
Hudnut, Herbert B., Bellevue, 422
Hudson, Thomas H., Uniontown, 422
Huebner, Grover G., Upper Darby, 422
Huebner, Solomon S., Merion, 422
Huff, William K., Philadelphia, 422
Hufferd, Ralph W., Bradford, 423
Hufnagel, Frederick B., Pittsburgh, 423
Hufnagel, Henry M., Clarion, 423
Hughes, Don E., Dushore, 423
Hughes, Fred A., Dickson City, Scranton, 423
Hughes, I. Lamont, Pittsburgh, 423
Hughes, John H., Brookville, 423
Hughes, Ray O., Pittsburgh, 424
Hulbert, Gustavus A., Henryville, 424
Hull, Robert A., Waverly, Scranton, 424
Hull, William I., Swarthmore, 424
Hulley, Elkanah B., Wilkinsburg, Pittsburgh, 424
Hulme, Norman, Swarthmore, Philadelphia, 425
Hulme, Thomas W., Haverford, 425
Hulse, Shirley C., Bedford, 425
Hulton, John G., Latrobe, 425
Humes, E. Lowry, Pittsburgh, 425
Humes, Samuel H., Williamsport, 425
Humke, Herman C., Punxsutawney, 425
Humphrey, Arthur F., Greensburg, Pittsburgh, 426
Humphrey, Arthur L., Pittsburgh, Wilmerding, 426
Humphreys, Warren R., Philadelphia, 426
Hunsicker, Charles O., Allentown, 426
Hunt, Bruce A., Williamsport, 426
Hunt, Everett L., Swarthmore, 426
Hunt, Frank R., Easton, 427
Hunt, Henry F., Danville, 427
Hunt, Levi C., Schuylkill Haven, 427
Hunt, Percival, Pittsburgh, 427
Hunt, Rachel M. M., Pittsburgh, 427
Hunt, Roy A., Pittsburgh, 427
Hunt, Theodore B., Easton, 427
Hunt, Willis R., Easton, 427
Hunter, Charles W., Haverford, Philadelphia, 427
Hunter, Frances T., Philadelphia, 428
Hunter, James N., Pittsburgh, 428
Hunter, John R., Jr., Hollidaysburg, Altoona, 428
Hunter, Lillian A., Tidionte, 428
Hunter, Thomas H., Sewickley, McKees Rocks, 428
Huntley, George W., Jr., Emporium, 428
Huntley, Louis G., Pittsburgh, 428
Hunton, Ella G., Greenville, 428
Huot, Constant J., Swissvale, 429
Hurd, Peter, Chadds Ford, 429
Hurevitz, Meyer, Philadelphia, 429
Hurley, Emmet D., Erie, 429
Hurwitz, Abraham, Reading, 429
Husek, Joseph, Palmyra, 429
Husemen, Lewis E., Wilkinsburg, 429
Huston, Charles L., Coatesville, 430
Huston, Stewart, Coatesville, 430
Hutchinson, Bennett W., Pittsburgh, 430
Hutchinson, Paul E., Pittsburgh, 430
Hutchinson, Robert P., Bethlehem, 430
Hutchison, Albert W., State College, 430
Hutchison, Ralph C., Washington, 430
Hutchison, Stuart N., Pittsburgh, 430
Hutchisson, Elmer, Pittsburgh, 430
Hutton, A. J. White, Chambersburg, 430
Hyatt, Frank K., Chester, 431
Hyde, Walter W., Philadelphia, 431
Ihrig, Roscoe M., Pittsburgh, 432
Illingworth, Ralph W., Jr., Pine Grove Mills, 432

Illman, Adelaide T., Philadelphia, 432
Illman, George M., Philadelphia, 432
Ingersoll, C. Jared, Washington, Philadelphia, 433
Ingersoll, Frank B., Sharpsburg, Pittsburgh, 433
Ingersoll, Robert S., Penllyn, Philadelphia, 433
Ingham, Charles T., Pittsburgh, 433
Inglis, William W., Scranton, 433
Ingram, Martha B., Sharon, 433
Innes, William T., Philadelphia, 434
Irland, George A., Lewisburg, 434
Irvin, Charles H., Big Run, 434
Irvin, Richard, Pittsburgh, 434
Irving, Laurence, Swarthmore, 434
Irwin, Harold S., Carlisle, 434
Irwin, Orlando W., Pittsburgh, 435
Irwin, William W., Farrell, 435
Isaacs, Asher, Pittsburgh, 435
Isherwood, James E., Waynesburg, 435
Isherwood, James H., Allegany, 435
Itter, Harry A., Easton, 435
Iverson, Lorenz, Pittsburgh, 435
Ivy, Robert H., Lansdowne, Philadelphia, 436
Jack, James E., Titusville, 436
Jackson, Albert A., Philadelphia, 436
Jackson, Arthur C., Swarthmore, Philadelphia, 436
Jackson, Chevalier, Schwenkville, Philadelphia, 436
Jackson, Eugene J., St. Mary's, 437
Jackson, Frank S., Punxsutawney, 437
Jackson, Frederick B., Warren, 437
Jackson, J. Roy, Beaver, 437
Jackson, James R., Philadelphia, 438
Jackson, John J., Pittsburgh, 438
Jackson, Joseph, Philadelphia, 438
Jackson, Lloyd E., Pitcairn, Pittsburgh, 438
Jackson, Ralph G., Philadelphia, 438
Jackson, Samuel M., 2d, Pittsburgh, 438
Jackson, William H., Pittsburgh, 438
Jacob, Frederick M., Pittsburgh, 438
Jacobs, Melvin L., Paradise, Harrisburg, 439
Jacobs, Merkel H., Media, 439
Jacobs, Myrl L., Bethlehem, 439
Jacobs, Nathan B., Pittsburgh, 439
Jacobs, Robert L., Carlisle, 439
Jacoby, Wilmer M., Pittsburgh, 439
Jaekel, Frederic B., Doylestown, Philadelphia, 440
Jaffe, Israel M., Butler, 440
James, Alfred P., Pittsburgh, 440
James, Arthur E., West Chester, Philadelphia, 440
James, Arthur H., Plymouth, 440
James, Frank C., Philadelphia, 440
James, Frederic, Wynnewood, 440
James, Henry D., Pittsburgh, 440
James, Joseph H., Pittsburgh, 441
James, Ralph E., Allentown, 441
James, Reese D., Bridgeport, Philadelphia, 441
Jamieson, Lewis C., Warren, 441
Jamison, David L., St. Davids, 441
Jamison, Jay N., McDonald, Pittsburgh, 441
Janeway, Augustine S., Harrisburg, 441
Janney, Walter C., Bryn Mawr, Philadelphia, 441
Janssen, Henry, Wyomissing, Reading, 442
Jaquette, Henrietta S., Swarthmore, 442
Jarrett, Benjamin, Farrell, 442
Jarvis, Anna, Philadelphia, 442
Jaspan, Harry J., Philadelphia, 442
Jayne, Horace H. F., Wallingford, Philadelphia, 442
Jefferis, J. Walter, Kennett Square, 442
Jeffery, John F., Erie, 442
Jeffery, Edward M., Philadelphia, 443
Jefferys, William H., Rosemont, Philadelphia, 443
Jeffrey, Lon C., Pittsburgh, 443
Jenckes, Earl S., Wyomissing, Shillington, 443
Jenkins, Arthur H., Jenkintown, Philadelphia, 443
Jenkins, Charles F., Philadelphia, 443

Jenkins, George H., Gwynedd, Norristown, 443
Jenkins, John C., Union City, 443
Jenkins, Thomas C., Pittsburgh, 443
Jenkinson, Richard D., Bellevue, 444
Jenks, John S., Philadelphia, 444
Jenks, Morton, Philadelphia, 444
Jennings, Burgess H., Bethlehem, 444
Jennings, Dale C., Pittsburgh, 444
Jennings, O. E., Pittsburgh, 444
Jensen, Cyril D., Bethlehem, 444
Jepson, Paul N., Philadelphia, 444
Jewett, Arthur C., Pittsburgh, 445
Jiuliante, Jessamine, Erie, 445
Jockers, Ernst, Doylestown, 445
Johnson, Albert W., Lewisburg, 445
Johnson, Albert W., Jr., Williamsport, 446
Johnson, Alfred H., Pittsburgh, 446
Johnson, Amandus, Philadelphia, 446
Johnson, Benjamin M., Pittsburgh, 446
Johnson, Charles M., Drexel Hill, Philadelphia, 446
Johnson, Charles M., Pittsburgh, 446
Johnson, Clarence R., Lahaska, 447
Johnson, Elizabeth F., Bryn Mawr, 447
Johnson, Elmer E. S., Hereford, Pennsburg, 447
Johnson, Emma, Philadelphia, 447
Johnson, Emory R., Philadelphia, 447
Johnson, Frederick G., Wilkes-Barre, 447
Johnson, George, Lincoln University, 447
Johnson, George B., West Chester, 447
Johnson, Guy R., Harrisburg, 448
Johnson, Herbert, Huntingdon Valley, 448
Johnson, Holgar J., Pittsburgh, 448
Johnson, Howard C., Moylan, Philadelphia, 448
Johnson, John C., West Chester, 448
Johnson, Josiah B., Ligonier, 448
Johnson, Lester F., York, 449
Johnson, Ralph C., Washington, 449
Johnson, Robert L., Philadelphia, 449
Johnson, Russell C., Collegeville, 449
Johnson, Theodore, Erie, 449
Johnson, Thomas H., Westtown, Swarthmore, 449
Johnson, Virgil L., Philadelphia, 449
Johnston, Alfred M., Freeport, 450
Johnston, Archibald, Bethlehem, 450
Johnston, Cecil C., Meadville, 450
Johnston, Harry L., Altoona, 450
Johnston, Howard M., Clarion, 450
Johnston, John, Pittsburgh, 450
Johnstone, Arthur L., Wilkes-Barre, 451
Johnstone, Burton K., State College, 451
Jones, Addison, Washington, 451
Jones, Adrian H., West Hazleton, Hazleton, 451
Jones, Arthur J., Swarthmore, 451
Jones, Barclay L., Upper Darby, Philadelphia, 451
Jones, Benjamin C., Tyrone, 451
Jones, Benjamin C., 3d, Sewickley, Pittsburgh, 451
Jones, Benjamin R., Jr., Wilkes-Barre, 452
Jones, Burwell W., Delta, 452
Jones, Charles S., Washington Crossing, 452
Jones, Clement R., Pittsburgh, 452
Jones, David R., Greenville, 452
Jones, Edward R., State College, 452
Jones, Edward S., Blakely, Scranton, 452
Jones, George E., Pittsburgh, 453
Jones, Harold W., Wynnewood, Philadelphia, 453
Jones, Harry A., Washington, 453
Jones, Henry W., Pittsburgh, 453
Jones, H. Ennis, Philadelphia, 453
Jones, Horace C., Conshohocken, 453
Jones, John L., Johnstown, Ebensburg, 453
Jones, John P., Drexel Hill, Upper Darby, 454
Jones, Lawrence E., Philadelphia, 454

PENNSYLVANIA

Jones, Livingston E., Philadelphia, 454
Jones, Loren F., Philadelphia, 454
Jones, Marshall J. H., Philadelphia, 454
Jones, Montfort, Pittsburgh, 454
Jones, Owen, Scranton, 454
Jones, Robert, Ben Avon, Pittsburgh, 454
Jones, Rufus M., Haverford, 454
Jones, Russell N., Johnsonburg, 455
Jones, Vincent, Philadelphia, 455
Jones, Walter A., Pittsburgh, 455
Jones, Webster N., Pittsburgh, 455
Jordan, Frank C., Pittsburgh, 455
Jordan, George, York, 455
Jordan, James S., Scranton, 455
Joseph, Charles H., Pittsburgh, 455
Joseph, Emrys S., Harrisburg, 455
Joyce, Harry B., Erie, 456
Joyce, John St. G., Highland Park, 456
Judge, Wade W., Mansfield, 456
Judkins, Malcolm F., McKeesport, 456
Julian, Alvin F., Allentown, 456
Jump, Henry D., Philadelphia, 456
Kabakjian, Dicran H., Lansdowne, Philadelphia, 456
Kaemmerling, Effie B., Erie, 457
Kaercher, George H., Pottsville, 457
Kagan, Pescha, Washington, 457
Kahler, Arthur D., Carlisle, 457
Kain, George H., York, 457
Kalbfus, Edward C., State College, 457
Kallenbach, Walter D., Drexel Hill, 457
Kallok, John, West Aliquippa, 457
Kalodner, Harry E., Philadelphia, 457
Kamman, William F., Pittsburgh, 458
Kane, E. Kent, Kushequa, Kane, 458
Kane, Evan O'N., Kane, 458
Kane, Francis F., Philadelphia, 458
Kann, Gustave H., Pittsburgh, 458
Kann, James J., Chadds Ford, 458
Kantner, Franklin E., Reading, 458
Kaplan, Eliah, New Castle, 458
Kaplan, Frank R. S., Pittsburgh, 458
Kapp, Cecil A., Philadelphia, 458
Kappel, John F., Pittsburgh, 458
Kappel, William J., Pittsburgh, 458
Karr, Robert M., Pittsburgh, 459
Kase, Paul G., Reading, 459
Kasel, Frank V., Columbia, 459
Katz, David, Philadelphia, 459
Kaufman, Daniel, Scottdale, 459
Kaufman, Charles M., Tower City, 459
Kaufman, David E., Philadelphia, 459
Kaufman, George S., Holicong, 460
Kaufman, Harry K., Philadelphia, 460
Kaufman, Morgan S., Scranton, 460
Kaufmann, Albert G., Brentwood, Pittsburgh, 460
Kaufmann, Arthur C., Ardmore, Philadelphia, 460
Kaufmann, Edgar J., Pittsburgh, 460
Kay, James, Philadelphia, 460
Kay, J. LeRoy, Pittsburgh, 460
Kay, Robert G., Philadelphia, 460
Keagy, Gula B., New Castle, 460
Kean, John S., Philadelphia, 460
Keane, Raymond R., Philadelphia, 460
Kearney, George F., Philadelphia, 461
Keath, Charles K., Lititz, 461
Keator, Alfred D., Reading, 461
Keboch, Frank D., Pittsburgh, 461
Keeble, Glendinning, Pittsburgh, 461
Keech, Finley, Harrisburg, 461
Keedy, Edwin R., Philadelphia, 4
Keefe, David A., Athens, 461
Keefer, Brua C., Jr., Williamsport, 461
Keeler, Harold R., Drexel Hill, Philadelphia, 461
Keen, Edward O., York, 461
Keen, John H., Philadelphia, 462
Keenan, J. Hilary, Greensburg, 462
Keenan, James F., Pittsburgh, 462
Keenan, Peter, Edison, 462
Keener, Martin M., Lampeter, Lancaster, 462
Keevil, Charles S., Lewisburg, 462
Kegel, Will C., Ellwood City 462
Keiper, Charles A., Stroudsburg, East Stroudsburg, 462
Keirns, May E., Huntingdon, 463
Keiser, Clarence E., Lyon Station, 463
Keister, Clinton L., Harrisburg, 463

Keister, John R., Greensburg, 463
Keith, John D., Gettysburg, 463
Kellam, Frederic J., Indiana, 463
Kellenberger, Keith E., Edgewood, Swissvale, 463
Keller, Edward L., State College, 463
Keller, Frederick E., Philadelphia, 463
Keller, Harry H., Jenkintown, Philadelphia, 463
Keller, Hiram H., Doylestown, 463
Keller, John C., Allentown, 464
Keller, John O., State College, 464
Keller, Joseph S., Merion, Philadelphia, 464
Keller, Joseph W., Merion, Philadelphia, 464
Keller, Oliver J., Pittsburgh, 464
Keller, William H., Lancaster, 464
Kellett, Donald S., Collegeville, 464
Kellett, William W., Philadelphia, 464
Kelley, Arthur P., Landenberg, 464
Kelley, Augustine B., Greensburg, 464
Kelley, Richard C., Philadelphia, 464
Kellogg, Herbert M., Lopez, 465
Kelly, Frances H., Pittsburgh, 465
Kelly, Frances M., Philadelphia, 465
Kelly, Herbert T., Philadelphia, 465
Kelly, J. Howard, Monessen, 465
Kelly, John A., Haverford, 465
Kelly, Lewis H., Pittsburgh, 465
Kelly, Thomas C., Philadelphia, 466
Kelly, Thomas K., Haverford, 466
Kelsey, Albert, Philadelphia, 466
Kelsey, Carl, Mendenhall, 466
Kelso, James A., Pittsburgh, 466
Kelso, James L., Pittsburgh, 466
Kemner, E. Fred, Philadelphia, 466
Kemp, Alvin F., Mertztown, Reading, 467
Kempel, Arthur B., East Brady, 467
Kendall, John W., Myersdale, Pittsburgh, 467
Kendig, H. Evert, Philadelphia, 467
Kendrick, W. Freeland, Philadelphia, 467
Kennedy, Andrew M., Sewickley, 467
Kennedy, John B., Columbia, 467
Kennedy, O'Neil, Uniontown, 468
Kennedy, Reid, Pittsburgh, Homestead, 468
Kennedy, Thomas, Hazleton, 468
Kennell, Henry B., Lehighton, 468
Kent, A. Atwater, Ardmore, Philadelphia, 468
Kent, Clarence H., State College, 468
Kent, Donald W., White Marsh, Philadelphia, 468
Kent, Everett, Bangor, 468
Kent, Everett L., Merion, Clifton Heights, 468
Kent, John I., Meadville, 468
Kent, Orville C., Meadville, 469
Kent, Roland G., Philadelphia, 469
Kent, Russell D., Swarthmore, Clifton Heights, 469
Kenworthey, Charles E., Ardmore, Philadelphia, 469
Kenworthy, J. Miller, Philadelphia, 469
Kenyon, Elmer, Pittsburgh, 469
Kephart, Alvin E., Yerkes, Philadelphia, 469
Kephart, John W., Ebensburg, 469
Keppel, Alvin R., Drexel Hill, Philadelphia, 469
Kerigan, Florence, Haverford, Philadelphia, 469
Kern, Frank D., State College, 469
Kern, John D., Philadelphia, 470
Kern, Richard A., Wynnewood, Philadelphia, 470
Kern, William F., Pittsburgh, 470
Kerr, Charles M., Jr., York, 470
Kerr, Duncan J., Sayre, Bethlehem, 470
Kerr, Hugh T., Pittsburgh, 470
Kerr, Samuel L., Philadelphia, 470
Kerstetter, Daniel C., Hamburg, 470
Ketchum, Carlton G., Pittsburgh, 470
Ketchum, George, Pittsburgh, 471
Ketels, Luther H., Reading, 471
Ketler, Frank C., Elkins Park, 471
Ketler, Weir C., Grove City, 471
Ketterer, Lillian H., Philadelphia, 471
Keylor, Josiah C., Cochranville, 471
Keyworth, William A., York, 471
Kiehl, Eugene P., Brookline, Philadelphia, 472
Kift, Jane L., Philadelphia, 472

Kilborn, William T., Pittsburgh, Bridgeville, 472
Kilker, Adrian J., Berwyn, 472
Killian, John C., Philadelphia, 473
Kimball, Fiske, Philadelphia, 473
Kimbrough, Robert A., Jr., Wynnewood, Philadelphia, 473
Kincaid, William M., Philadelphia, 473
Kinder, James S., Pittsburgh, 473
King, Caroline B., Philadelphia, 474
King, Charles G., Pittsburgh, 474
King, Helen D., Bryn Mawr, 474
King, James W., Kittanning, 474
King, Joseph T., Lawrenceville, 474
King, Karl C., Morrisville, 474
King, LeRoy A., Narberth, 474
King, Morland, Easton, 474
King, Wyncie, Bryn Mawr, 475
Kingsbury, Dana W., Nanticoke, 475
Kingsbury, Susan M., Bryn Mawr, 475
Kinnard, Leonard H., Wynnewood, Philadelphia, 476
Kinney, Antoinette B., Pittsburgh, 476
Kinsley, John F., Pittsburgh, 476
Kinsloe, Charles L., State College, 476
Kinzer, J. Roland, Lancaster, 476
Kiracofe, Edgar S., Huntingdon, 476
Kirby, C. Valentine, Harrisburg, 477
Kirby, Dunne W., Philadelphia, 477
Kirby, Fred M., Wilkes-Barre, 477
Kirby, R. S., State College, 477
Kirk, Mabel E., State College, 477
Kirkbride, Mabelle M., Norristown, 478
Kirkpatrick, Alton, Lansdowne, Philadelphia, 478
Kirkpatrick, Harlow B., Pittsburgh, 478
Kirkpatrick, Martin G., Philadelphia, 478
Kirkpatrick, William H., Easton, 478
Kirner, Walter R., Pittsburgh, 478
Kiser, Robert W., Pittsburgh, 478
Kiskaddon, J. Fulton, North East, 478
Kisner, Ralph, Danville, 478
Kitson, Arthur, Jr., Philadelphia, 478
Kitto, Charles W., Philadelphia, 479
Kittredge, Arthur E., Philadelphia, 479
Kizis, Andrew C., West Pittston, Pittston, 479
Klaer, Harvey, Philadelphia, 479
Kleeb, Henry A., Pittsburgh, 479
Klein, Arthur W., Bethlehem, 479
Klein, Charles, Philadelphia, 479
Klein, Charles H., Pittsburgh, 479
Klein, Frederic S., Lancaster, 479
Klein, Harry M. J., Lancaster, 480
Klein, John W., Reading, 480
Klein, Louis A., Moylan, Philadelphia, 480
Klein, William H., Easton, Nazareth, 480
Klieforth, Alfred W., Boalsburg, 480
Klimm, Lester E., Philadelphia, 480
Kline, Emanuel, Philadelphia, 480
Kline, J. Clinton, Sunbury, 480
Kline, J. Simpson, Sunbury, 480
Kline, John R., Swarthmore, 481
Kline, Sidney D., West Lawn, Reading, 481
Kline, Whorten A., Collegeville, 481
Klinedinst, David P., York, 481
Klingel, Joseph W., Philadelphia, 481
Klingelhofer, Edward K., Sewickley, Pittsburgh, 481
Klinginsmith, John G., Pittsburgh, 481
Klonower, Henry, Philadelphia, Harrisburg, 481
Klonowski, Henry T. T., Scranton, 481
Klopp, Henry I., Allentown, 481
Knandel, Herman C., State College, 482
Knapp, Harry B., Wellsboro, 482
Knapp, Rolla S., Easton, 482
Knauer, Wilhelm F., Philadelphia, 482
Knight, Harry S., Sunbury, 482
Knight, Seymour N., Penfield, Philadelphia, 482
Kniseley, John B., Pittsburgh, 483
Kniskern, Philip W., Swarthmore, Philadelphia, 483
Kniss, C. Asher, Mifflinburg, 483
Knowles, Archibald C., Philadelphia, 483

Knowles, Frank R., Johnstown, 483
Knowles, Richard, Philadelphia, 483
Knowles, William G., Philadelphia, 483
Knox, Harry E., Philadelphia, 483
Knox, Paul W., Philadelphia, 483
Knox, Robert W., Washington, 484
Knox, William F., Pittsburgh, 484
Knutsen, Martin H., State College, 484
Koch, Alfred, Latrobe, 484
Koch, Carl E., Pittsburgh, 484
Koch, Carleton S., Edgewood, McKeesport, 484
Koch, Caspar P., Pittsburgh, 484
Koch, Julius A., Pittsburgh, 484
Kochin, Elihu W., Pittsburgh, 485
Kohler, Charles H., Philadelphia, 485
Kohler, Edwin L., Allentown, 485
Köhler, Wolfgang, Swarthmore, 485
Kohlstedt, Edward D., Philadelphia, 485
Kohn, Bernard, Philadelphia, 485
Kolb, Louis J., Philadelphia, 485
Kolbe, Parke R., Philadelphia, 485
Koller, Edmund L., Scranton, 485
Koller, James R., Myerston, Lebanon, 486
Kolmer, John A., Bala-Cynwyd, Philadelphia, 486
Konkle, Burton A., Swarthmore, Philadelphia, 486
Konrad, Henry R., Port Carbon, 486
Konzelmann, Frank W., Philadelphia, 486
Koontz, Norman C., Indiana, 486
Kopf, Harry D., Warren, 487
Kopp, John W., Williamstown, 487
Korb, Carl R., Pittsburgh, 487
Korb, Robert T., Philadelphia, 487
Korns, Charles B., Sr., Sipesville, 487
Koser, John M., Ardmore, 487
Kossler, Herman S., Crafton, Pittsburgh, 487
Kothny, Gottdank L., Strafford, Philadelphia, 487
Kotzen, Earl L., Reading, 488
Kovacs, Koloman, Duquesne, 488
Koyl, George S., Philadelphia, 488
Kraft, John F., Washington, 488
Kramer, Clarence R., Clearfield, 488
Kramer, Roland L., Drexel Hill, Philadelphia, 488
Kraner, Hobart M., Bethlehem, 488
Kratz, Albert R., Berkshire Heights, Reading, 489
Krause, George D., Lebanon, 489
Krause, Maxwell, Lebanon, 489
Krauss, Franklin B., State College, 489
Krausz, Charles E., Philadelphia, 489
Krebs, Frank P., Tamaqua, 489
Krebs, W. W., Johnstown, 489
Kreider, Charles D., Nazareth, 490
Kreider, Henry K., Campbelltown, 490
Kreider, William E., Palmyra, 490
Kreider, William H., Philadelphia, 490
Kreidler, William A., Upper Darby, Philadelphia, 490
Kremer, David N., Philadelphia, 490
Kremp, Laura A. M., Reading, 490
Kremp, Marie E. M., Reading, 490
Kresge, Elijah E., Lancaster, 490
Kressley, George S., Reading, 490
Kretschmann, Theodore W., Selinsgrove, 490
Kribs, David A., Chambersburg, State College, 490
Krick, Charles S., St. Davids, 491
Kriebel, William P., Moylan, Philadelphia, 491
Kriss, Max, State College, 491
Krivobok, Vsevolod N., Pittsburgh, 491
Krogh, Detlef M. F., Philadelphia, 491
Krohn, Israel, Easton, 491
Krouse, Luther A., Pottstown, 491
Krumbhaar, E. B., Philadelphia, 491
Krupp, Harry Z., Lansdale, Philadelphia, 491
Kruse, Theophile K. T., Mt. Lebanon, Pittsburgh, 491
Krusen, Wilmer, Media, Philadelphia, 492
Krut, John A., McKeesport, 492
Kuehner, Quincy A., Glenside, 492
Kuhlmann, G. Edward, Oil City, 492
Kuiper, Rienk B., Philadelphia, 492
Kulp, Clarence A., Upper Darby, Philadelphia, 492

PENNSYLVANIA

Kun, Joseph L., Philadelphia, 493
Kunkel, Beverly W., Easton, 493
Kunkel, George, Harrisburg, 493
Kunkel, John C., Harrisburg, 493
Kunkelman, Merle R., Leetsdale, 493
Kurniker, Max W., Pittsburgh, 493
Kurtz, Charles T., Clearfield, 494
Kurtz, Jacob B., Altoona, 494
Kurtz, John F., Harrisburg, 494
Kurtz, John R., Vandergrift, 494
Kuykendall, Clark P., Towanda, 494
Kuznets, Simon S., Media, Philadelphia, 494
Kyle, Frank P., Red Lion, Burnham, 494
Kyle, William J., Waynesburg, 494
Kynett, Alpha G., Philadelphia, 494
Kynett, Harold H., Wayne, Philadelphia, 494
La Brum, J. Harry, Philadelphia, 495
Lackey, Sylvester J., Clarion, 495
Lacy, George R., Mt. Lebanon, Pittsburgh, 495
Ladd, George T., Coraopolis, Pittsburgh, 495
Ladner, Albert H., Jr., Philadelphia, 495
Ladner, Grover C., Philadelphia, 495
Laessle, Albert, Jenkintown, 495
LaFavre, Harry B., Springfield, Philadelphia, 495
Lafean, Edward C., Pittsburgh, 495
Lafferty, Theodore T., Nazareth, 496
Laffoon, Carthrae M., Irwin, East Pittsburgh, 496
Laidley, Lowell T., Carmichaels, 496
Laird, George S., Abington, Philadelphia, 496
Laird, John B., Philadelphia, 496
Laird, John W., Philadelphia, 496
Laird, Richard D., Greensburg, 496
Laird, Robert M., Hanover, York, 496
Laird, Warren P., Philadelphia, 496
Lake, Kirsopp, Haverford, 496
Lakin, Harry A., Harrisburg, 497
Lally, J. P., Mt. Lebanon, Pittsburgh, 497
Lamb, Carl S., Wilkinsburg, Pittsburgh, 497
Lamb, Hugh L., Philadelphia, 497
Lamb, Richard W., Kennett Square, 497
Lamb, William H., Wynnewood, Philadelphia, 497
Lamberton, Chess, Franklin, 497
Lamberton, Robert, Franklin, 498
Lambie, Joseph S., Wilkinsburg, Pittsburgh, 498
Lammers, Martin W., Jenkintown, Philadelphia, 498
Lampe, William E., Philadelphia, 498
Lamsa, George M., Philadelphia, 498
Lancaster, Edward L., Lancaster, 498
Land, John N., Hamburg, 499
Lander, William P. S., Rosemont, 499
Landes, William G., Lansdowne, 499
Landis, Mark H., Waynesboro, 499
Landis, William F., Ardmore, 499
Landis, William W., Carlisle, 499
Lane, Nathaniel F., Philadelphia, 499
Lane, Otho E., Westtown, Philadelphia, 499
Lanfear, Vincent W., Pittsburgh, 500
Lang, Harold L., Fox Chapel, Pittsburgh, 500
Lange, Ernest O. A., Swarthmore, Philadelphia, 500
Lange, Linda B., Philadelphia, 500
Laning, Harris, Philadelphia, 500
Lanning, Robert L., Dormont, Pittsburgh, 501
Laplace, Louis B., Philadelphia, 501
Laramy, Robert E., Bethlehem, 501
Larer, Richard W., Philadelphia, 501
Larkin, Charles R., Bethlehem, 501
Larkin, Fred V., Bethlehem, 501
Larner, Chester W., Philadelphia, 501
Larrabee, Don M., Williamsport, 501
La Rue, Daniel W., East Stroudsburg, 502
La Rue, Mabel G., East Stroudsburg, 502
Lathem, Abraham L., Chester, 502

Latta, Harrison W., Philadelphia, 502
Laubenstein, Franklin J., Ashland, 502
Laudenslager, Ray V., Weatherly, 502
Lauer, Conrad N., Penllyn, Philadelphia, 503
Lauffer, George N., Kittanning, 503
Lauffer, Vada D. K., Upper Darby, 503
Laughlin, George, Jr., Pittsburgh, 503
Laughlin, Irwin, Pittsburgh, 503
Laughlin, Sara E., West Philadelphia, Philadelphia, 503
Laurie, Frank A., Bryn Mawr, 503
Laverty, Elizabeth S., Merion, 503
Law, Margaret L., Chestnut Hill, 504
Law, Marie H., Philadelphia, 504
La Wall, Elmer H., Wilkes-Barre, Scranton, 504
LaWall, Harold J., Haverford, Philadelphia, 504
Lawrence, David L., Pittsburgh, 504
Lawrence, Granville A., Philadelphia, 504
Lawrence, James C., Moylan, 504
Lawrie, Ritchie, Jr., Harrisburg, 504
Laws, Bertha M., Philadelphia, Wynnewood, 504
Laws, George M., Philadelphia, 504
Lawson, George B., Lewisburg, 505
Lawson, James H., McKeesport, 505
Laycock, Charles W., Kingston, Wilkes-Barre, 505
Layng, Frank R. S., Jr., Greenville, 505
Leach, Henry G., Villanova, 505
Leach, Howard S., Bethlehem, 505
Leach, Walter, Mansfield, Jersey Shore, 506
Leaf, Leonard, Pottstown, 506
Leaman, William G., Jr., Philadelphia, 506
Leathermann, Clarence G., Hummelstown, 506
Leattor, William L., Riegelsville, 506
Leavitt, Frederic H., Ardmore, Philadelphia, 506
LeClere, John B., Allison Park, Pittsburgh, 507
Lederer, Erwin R., Bradford, 507
Lederer, Lucy C. K., State College, 507
Lee, Charles M., Beaver Falls, 507
Lee, Harry W., Reading, 507
Lee, Henry H., Moylan, 507
Lee, John C., Pottsville, 508
Lee, John H., Philadelphia, 508
Lee, John M., Philipsburg, 508
Lee, Manning de V., Ambler, Philadelphia, 508
Lee, Walter E., Philadelphia, 508
Lee, William P., Glenside, 508
Leech, Carl G., Media, 508
Leech, Edward T., Mt. Lebanon, Pittsburgh, 508
Leech, George L., Harrisburg, 508
Leeds, Morris B., Philadelphia, 508
Lees, George C., Pottstown, 508
Lefever, Clarence N., Erie, 509
LeFevre, Laura Z., Philadelphia, 509
Lefferts, Walter, Philadelphia, 509
Leffler, George L., State College, 509
Leffler, Ross L., McKeesport, Pittsburgh, 509
Legrain, Leon, Philadelphia, 509
LeGrys, Herbert J., St. Marys, 509
Leh, Howard H., Nazareth, Bath, 509
Leh, John, Allentown, 509
Leh, John H., Allentown, 509
Lehman, George M., Pittsburgh, 509
Lehman, James A., Philadelphia, 510
Lehn, Homer M. B., Grove City, 510
Lehr, Anna M. M., Bryn Mawr, 510
Leibensperger, George F., Kutztown, 510
Leighton, Henry, Wilkinsburg, Pittsburgh, 510
Leinbach, Paul S., Philadelphia, 510
Leisenring, Edward B., Ardmore, Philadelphia, 511
Leiser, Andrew A., Jr., Lewisburg, 511
Leister, John S., State College, 511
Leith, Hugh, Mt. Lebanon, 511
Leith-Ross, Harry, New Hope, 511
Leitzel, Frank D., Pittsburgh, 511
LeMon, Melvin W., Lewisburg, 511
Lengler, Frederick K., Scranton, 512
Lenhert, George R., Jr., Philadelphia, 512
Lenning, Frederick, 6th, Philadelphia, 512

Lentz, Edwin W., Philadelphia, 512
Lentz, William J., Philadelphia, 512
Leonard, Adna W., Pittsburgh, 512
Leonard, Joseph S., Bethlehem, 512
Leonard, Walter C., Pittsburgh, 512
Leonards, Thomas C., Bryn Mawr, Philadelphia, 512
Leopold, Samuel, Melrose Park, Philadelphia, 513
Leroux, Jules, Philadelphia, 513
Lesh, John A., Philadelphia, 513
Lesher, Amos Y., Ambler, Philadelphia, 513
Lesher, Carl E., Pittsburgh, 513
Lesley, Frank W., York, 513
Lessenberry, David D., Pittsburgh, 513
Letchworth, George E., Jr., Philadelphia, 514
Leuba, James H., Bryn Mawr, 514
Leukel, George A., Kennett Square, 514
Levengood, Brooklyn B., Bellwood, 514
Lever, John H., Philadelphia, 514
Levering, William W., Jenkintown, Philadelphia, 514
Levin, Leonard S., Pittsburgh, 514
Levin, Max, Mayview, 515
Levinthal, Abraham A., Philadelphia, 515
Levinthal, Bernard L., Philadelphia, 515
Levinthal, Louis E., Philadelphia, 515
Levitsky, Louis M., Wilkes-Barre, 515
Levy, Leon, Philadelphia, 515
Levy, Maurice A., Williamsport, 516
Lewellyn, Charles L., Uniontown, 516
Lewis, Arthur M., Philadelphia, 516
Lewis, Charles B., Philadelphia, 516
Lewis, Charles F., Pittsburgh, 517
Lewis, Edwin J., Corry, 517
Lewis, Edwin O., Philadelphia, 517
Lewis, Francis A., Bryn Mawr, Philadelphia, 517
Lewis, George, Philadelphia, 517
Lewis, H. Edgar, Pittsburgh, 518
Lewis, Harry R., Warren, 518
Lewis, Herbert F., Conneaut Lake, 518
Lewis, James E., Pittsburgh, 518
Lewis, Leicester C., Philadelphia, 518
Lewis, Ludwig C., Villa Nova, Philadelphia, 518
Lewis, Mahlon E., Ben Avon, Pittsburgh, 518
Lewis, Margaret S., York, 518
Lewis, Mary F. W., Philadelphia, 518
Lewis, Mary R. H., Media, Philadelphia, 519
Lewis, Orville G., Washington, 519
Lewis, Robert T., Pittsburgh, 519
Lewis, Thomas M., Plymouth, Wilkes-Barre, 519
Lewis, Willard P., State College, 519
Lewis, William D., Lansdowne, 519
Lewis, William D., Philadelphia, 519
Lewis, William M., Easton, 519
Lewith, Edward L., Wilkes-Barre, 520
Lewy, Frederic H., Philadelphia, 520
Lichliter, Levi G., Harrisburg, 520
Lichtenberger, James B., Haverford, Philadelphia, 520
Lichtenberger, James P., Philadelphia, 520
Lichtenthaler, Henry P., Pittsburgh, 520
Lick, Maxwell J., Erie, 520
Lifter, Morris, Philadelphia, 520
Liggett, Sidney S., Sewickley, 521
Light, Harry F., Lebanon, Avon, 521
Light, V. Earl, Annville, 521
Lightcap, John S., Jr., Latrobe, 521
Lilly, Scott B., Swarthmore, 521
Lincoln, Joseph C., Villa Nova, Pittsburgh, 522
Lincoln, Rollo B., Wilkinsburg, Pittsburgh, 522
Lindback, Christian R., Philadelphia, 522
Lindborg, Carl, Lansdowne, Philadelphia, 522
Lindenmuth, Anson W., Allentown, 522
Lindley, Ernest H., Erwinna, 522
Lindsay, Alexander P., Pittsburgh, 522
Lindsay, George L., Philadelphia, 522
Lindsey, Edward S., Warren, 523
Linen, James A., Jr., Waverly, Scranton, 523

PENNSYLVANIA

McClellan, William S., Spring Grove, 572
McClelland, Clark R., Kutztown, 572
McClelland, Ellwood H., Pittsburgh, 572
McClelland, George W., Merion, Philadelphia, 572
McClintic, Robert H., Pittsburgh, 572
McClintock, Charles A., Pittsburgh, 572
McClintock, Gilbert S., Wilkes-Barre, 573
McClintock, Walter, Pittsburgh, 573
McClintock, Walter J., Meadville, 573
McCloskey, Edward W., Philadelphia, 573
McCloskey, Robert F., Pittsburgh, Blawnox, 573
McCloskey, Thomas D., Pittsburgh, 573
McClung, Clarence E., Wallingford, 573
McClung, Frank A., Butler, 573
McClure, George W., Braddock, Pittsburgh, 573
McClure, James F., Lewisburg, 574
McClure, John J., Chester, 574
McClure, Norman E., Collegeville, 574
McCluskey, Frank P., Easton, 574
McCollim, Frances, Philadelphia, 574
McCollough, A. E., Lancaster, 574
McConnell, Alexander, Greensburg, 574
McConnell, Malcolm F., Munhall, 574
McConnell, Robert S., Philadelphia, 575
McConnell, William C., Shamokin, 575
McCord, Frederick A., Wayne, Philadelphia, 575
McCord, John L. E., State College, 575
McCord, Ralph B., North East, Erie, 575
McCormick, Arthur B., Oil City, 575
McCormick, John H., Williamsport, 576
McCormick, Louis P., Connellsville, 576
McCormick, Seth T., Jr., Williamsport, 576
McCormick, Vance C., Harrisburg, 576
McCormick, William W., Beaver Falls, 576
McCouch, Grayson P., Media, 576
McCown, Edward C., Pittsburgh, 576
McCoy, Frank R., Lewistown, 576
McCracken, Charles C., Ardmore, Philadelphia, 576
McCracken, Lee A., Oil City, Franklin, 576
McCracken, Robert T., Philadelphia, 576
McCracken, Samuel, Wilkes-Barre, 576
McCrady, Edward, Jr., Wilkinsburg, Braddock, 576
McCrady, John B., Wilkinsburg, Pittsburgh, 577
McCrea, Lowrain E., Bala-Cynwyd, Philadelphia, 577
McCready, J. Homer, Pittsburgh, 577
McCready, Robert T. M., Sewickley, Pittsburgh, 577
McCreary, George B., Pittsburgh, 577
McCreary, Robert E., Monaca, Beaver, 577
McCreath, Lesley, Harrisburg, 577
McCreight, Israel, DuBois, 577
McCrory, William B., Pittsburgh, 577
McCulloch, Joseph P., Newville, 578
McCullough, Clarence E., Washington, 578
McCune, Joseph C., Edgewood, Wilmerding, 578
McCurdy, Alexander, Jr., Philadelphia, 578
McCutchen, Robert T., South Mountain, 578
McCutcheon, Thomas P., Jr., Philadelphia, 578
McDaniel, Walton B., Philadelphia, 578
McDermott, John J., Lebanon, 579
McDivitt, Michael M., Kittanning, 579
McDonald, Edward, McDonald, 579
McDonald, Ellice, Swarthmore, Philadelphia, 579

McDonald, Harl, St. Davids, 579
McDonald, John N., McDonald, 579
McDonald, Michael F., Ashley, Wilkes-Barre, 579
McDonald, Peter, Philadelphia, 579
McDonnell, Frank J., Scranton, 579
McDonnell, John W., Sunbury, 579
McDonnell, Patrick J., Scranton, 579
McDonough, John E., Media, 580
McDowell, Harry B., Sharon, 580
McDowell, Milton S., State College, 580
McElroy, William S., Pittsburgh, 580
McElroy, Margaret J., Doylestown, 580
McElroy, Samuel F., Latrobe, 580
McElwee, William, Jr., New Wilmington, New Castle, 580
McEntire, Lloyd, Saylorsburg, 581
McFall, William B., Pittsburgh, 581
McFarland, J. Horace, Harrisburg, 581
McFarland, Joseph, Philadelphia, 581
McFarland, William W., Pittsburgh, 581
McGarrah, Albert F., Swarthmore, Pittsburgh, 581
McGeary, William R., Pittsburgh, 582
McGee, William L., Media, Philadelphia, 582
McGill, Earl W., Meadville, 582
McGinley, Thomas A., Sewickley, Pittsburgh, 582
McGinness, Samuel W., Pittsburgh, 582
McGinnis, Bernard B., Pittsburgh, 582
McGinnis, Claude S., Wyncote, 582
McGovern, Edward F., Wilkes-Barre, 582
McGranery, James P., Philadelphia, 582
McGrath, John B., Houtzdale, 582
McGraw, Thomas H., Jr., Oakmont, Braeburn, 583
McGregor, James C., Washington, 583
McGuire, Hugh E., Pittsburgh, 583
McGurl, John B., Minersville, Pottsville, 583
McHenry, Donald B., Danville, 583
McIlhattan, William H., Greensburg, 583
McIlvain, Greer, Pittsburgh, 583
McIlvaine, William A. H., Washington, 583
McIlwain, Knox, Philadelphia, 583
McInerney, William I., Midland, 583
McIntyre, George I., Beaver, 584
McIntyre, John T., Philadelphia, 584
McIntyre, Joseph D., Drexel Hill, Philadelphia, 584
McIver, Joseph, Philadelphia, 584
McKaig, Edgar S., Radnor, Philadelphia, 584
McKay, Leo H., Sharon, 584
McKay, Marion K., Pittsburgh, 584
McKay, William S., Grove City, 584
McKee, Captain William, New Wilmington, 584
McKee, Edward D., Villanova, 584
McKee, Joel S., New Castle, 584
McKee, Paul H., Latrobe, 584
McKee, Samuel H., Pittsburgh, 585
McKeehan, Hobart D., Huntingdon, 585
McKeehan, Joseph P., Carlisle, 585
McKelvy, Eugene A., Ardmore, Philadelphia, 585
McKelvy, Francis G., Easton, 585
McKelvy, William M., Pittsburgh, 585
McKenna, J. Frank, Pittsburgh, 585
McKenna, Philip M., Latrobe, 585
McKenna, Roy C., Latrobe, Pittsburgh, 585
McKenrick, Paul L., Kittanning, 585
McKenzie, Carl H., Erie, 585
McKenzie, Fayette A., Huntingdon, 585
McKenzie, Mrs. R. Tait, Philadelphia, 586
McKernan, Frank J., Johnstown, 586
McKenney, Paul V., Pittsburgh, 586
McKinney, William W., Ambridge, 586
McKinstry, Edwin L., West Chester, 586
McKnight, Robert J. G., Wilkinsburg, Pittsburgh, 587
McKnight, Robert W., Sewickley, Pittsburgh, 587
McKoy, Thomas H., Jr., Philadelphia, 587

McLaughlin, Joseph C., Butler, 587
McLaughlin, Mary M., Freeport, 587
McLean, Eugene L., Philadelphia, 587
McLean, Robert, Ft. Washington, Philadelphia, 587
McLeod, Malcolm, Pittsburgh, 588
McLure, Norman R., Radnor, Philadelphia, 588
McMarlin, John G., Butler, 588
McMath, Robert E., Bethlehem, 588
McMillen, Clayton L., Etna, 588
McMillen, Wheeler, Philadelphia, 588
McMillion, Theodore M., Beaver Falls, 588
McMullen, Joshua W., Oxford, 588
McMurray, John B., Washington, 588
McMurray, Thomas E., Pittsburgh, Wilkinsburg, 589
McMurtrie, Edith, Philadelphia, 589
McNair, Harold V., Middletown, Harrisburg, 589
McNair, William N., Pittsburgh, 589
McNall, James M., Woodville, 589
McNally, Thomas F., Jenkintown, 589
McNamara, Edward P., State College, 589
McNary, Carl W., Erie, 589
McNaugher, John, Pittsburgh, 589
McNaugher, William H., Pittsburgh, 589
McNaul, James F., Pittsburgh, 590
McNeil, Sister Marie Gertrude, Greensburg, 590
McNeil, Robert L., Philadelphia, 590
McNett, William B., Narberth, 590
McNutt, George D., Canonsburg, 590
McNutt, William R., Chester, 590
McShane, John J., Jr., Pittsburgh, 590
McSparran, John A., Greene, 590
McSweeney, John J., Wilkes-Barre, 591
McVay, Sister Mary Stanislaus, Greensburg, 591
McVicar, Nelson, Tarentum, Pittsburgh, 591
McWilliams, James B., Pittsburgh, 591
Mead, Douglass S., State College, 591
Mead, Edward S., Philadelphia, 591
Meade, Richard H., Jr., Miquon, Philadelphia, 591
Meader, Stephen W., Philadelphia, 591
Meanor, Harold H., Coraopolis, 592
Mechling, Benjamin F., Flowertown, Philadelphia, 592
Mecluskey, John F., Philadelphia, 592
Medill, George H., York, 592
Meeker, George H., Philadelphia, 592
Meeser, Spencer B., Pittsburgh, 592
Megargel, Harold J., Scranton, 593
Mehl, Robert F., Pittsburgh, 593
Meigs, Arthur I., Radnor, Philadelphia, 593
Meigs, Cornelia L., Bryn Mawr, 593
Meigs, John, Wynnewood, Philadelphia, 593
Meilicke, Carl A., Bethlehem, 593
Meinel, William J., Huntingdon Valley, Philadelphia, 593
Meisel, Emanuel G., Pittsburgh, 593
Meisenhelder, Edmund W., York, Dover, 593
Meisle, Kathryn, Philadelphia, 594
Meldrum, William B., Haverford, 594
Melhorn, Nathan R., Philadelphia, 594
Meliodon, Jules A., Philadelphia, 594
Meller, Harry B., Pittsburgh, 594
Mellon, Fred S., Jeannette, Pittsburgh, 594
Mellon, Ralph R., Pittsburgh, 594
Mellon, Richard K., Pittsburgh, 594
Mellon, Thomas A., Pittsburgh, 594
Mellon, William L., Pittsburgh, 594
Mellon, John H., Rochester, 594
Mellor, Walter, Philadelphia, 594
Mellor-Gill, Margaret W., Philadelphia, 595
Meloy, Luella P., Washington, 595
Meminger, James W., Lancaster, 595
Memming, Gerrit H. R., Reading, 595
Mendenhall, Thomas E., Johnstown, 595

Mengel, Charles H., Allentown, 595
Mengel, Levi W., Reading, 595
Mengert, Ulric J., Philadelphia, 596
Menges, Franklin, York, 596
Menten, Maud L., Pittsburgh, 596
Mercer, Eugene L., Swarthmore, 596
Meredith, C. H., Hanover, 596
Merker, Ralph K., Erie, 597
Merkle, Frederick G., State College, 597
Merrick, Frank A., Pittsburgh, 597
Merrick, James K., Philadelphia, 597
Merriman, Robert, Clarks Summit, Scranton, 597
Merriman, Roger B., Jr., Pittsburgh, 597
Mershon, Oliver F., Philadelphia, 598
Merten, William J., Pittsburgh, 598
Mertz, John E., Easton, 598
Mertz, William F., Nazareth, 598
Messler, Eugene L., Pittsburgh, 598
Metcalf, William, Jr., Sewickley, Pittsburgh, 598
Metheny, C. Brainerd, Beaver Falls, Pittsburgh, 598
Metz, Robert C., Ashley, 599
Metzger, Fritz L., Bellevue, Pittsburgh, 599
Metzger, Irvin D., Pittsburgh, 599
Metzger, Leon D., Harrisburg, 599
Metzger, Maurice R., Middletown, Harrisburg, 599
Metzger, William P., Zelienople, New Brighton, 599
Metzler, Sankey W., Uniontown, 599
Meyer, Charles A., Pittsburgh, 600
Meyer, George Y., Pittsburgh, 600
Meyers, Charles E., Lancaster, 600
Meyers, Meredith, Lewiston, 600
Meyers, Milton K., Philadelphia, 600
Mezger, Fritz, Bridgeport, 600
Michaels, Frank B., East Stroudsburg, Stroudsburg, 600
Michels, Nicholas A., Hatfield, Philadelphia, 601
Michels, Walter C., Strafford, 601
Michener, Albert O., Philadelphia, 601
Michie, Thomas J., Pittsburgh, 601
Middleton, Harry C., Philadelphia, 601
Middleton, Melbourne F., Jr., Philadelphia, 601
Miel, Charles J., Wayne, Philadelphia, 601
Mikell, William E., Philadelphia, 602
Millar, Albert S., Philadelphia, 602
Millar, Charles C., Butler, 602
Millener, William S., Williamsport, 602
Miller, Adam F., Lebanon, 602
Miller, Anne M. M., Ridley Park, 602
Miller, Benjamin L., Bethlehem, 602
Miller, Bruce J., Lewisburg, 603
Miller, Carl I., Pittsburgh, East Pittsburgh, 603
Miller, Charles H., Butler, 603
Miller, Charles L., Lancaster, 603
Miller, David A., Allentown, 603
Miller, D. Roy, Chester Springs, 603
Miller, Donald E., Pittsburgh, 603
Miller, E. Clarence, Melrose Park, Philadelphia, 603
Miller, Emma G., Slippery Rock, 604
Miller, F. Dean, Bradford, 604
Miller, Floyd H., Waynesburg, 604
Miller, Frank P., Meadville, 604
Miller, Fred Z., New Hope, 604
Miller, George C., Butler, 604
Miller, George E., Gettysburg, 604
Miller, Harry H., Steelton, Harrisburg, 604
Miller, Henry J., Pittsburgh, 604
Miller, Henry R., Ben Avon, Pittsburgh, 605
Miller, Herbert L., Bryn Mawr, 605
Miller, Howard D., Summit Hill, 605
Miller, Jacob K., Philadelphia, 605
Miller, James C., Philadelphia, 605
Miller, James H., Pittsburgh, 605
Miller, James M., Central City, 605
Miller, James S., Hazleton, 605
Miller, Jere E., Chambersburg, 605
Miller, John A., Nazareth, 606
Miller, John A., Wallingford, 606
Miller, John D., Thompson, 606
Miller, John F., Pittsburgh, Wilmerding, 606
Miller, John K., Pittsburgh, 606
Miller, John O., Pittsburgh, 606
Miller, John S., Somerset, 606

PENNSYLVANIA

Miller, Joseph R., Ambridge, 606
Miller, Joshua H., New Castle, 606
Miller, Julius F., Franklin, 606
Miller, Karl G., Upper Darby, 606
Miller, L. Earle, Indiana, 607
Miller, M. Valentine, Philadelphia, 607
Miller, Moore R., Saltsburg, 607
Miller, Nathan, Pittsburgh, 607
Miller, Park H., Drexel Hill, Philadelphia, 607
Miller, Philip S., Lincoln University, 607
Miller, Raymond C., Lyon Station, 607
Miller, Samuel W., Blairsville, 607
Miller, T. Grier, Narberth, Philadelphia, 608
Miller, Walter L., Susquehanna, 608
Miller, William B., Sewickley, Pittsburgh, 608
Millgram, Abraham E., Philadelphia, 608
Milligan, Orlando H., Pittsburgh, 608
Milligan, Samuel C., Pittsburgh, 608
Milliken, Howard E., Harrisburg, 608
Milliken, Lorenzo F., Drexel Hill, Philadelphia, 608
Milward, Carl L., Milton, 609
Milne, Caleb J., Jr., Philadelphia, 609
Milne, John L., Drexel Hill, Philadelphia, 609
Milner, Byron A., Philadelphia, 609
Milnor, Mark T., Harrisburg, 610
Miner, Charles H., Wilkes-Barre, 610
Miner, Robert C., Wilkes-Barre, 610
Minick, James W., Camp Hill, Harrisburg, 610
Minner, Ralph J., Catasauqua, 610
Minnick, John H., Philadelphia, 610
Minton, Wilson P., Milroy, 610
Mitchell, Claude, West Newton, 611
Mitchell, David E., Pittsburgh, 611
Mitchell, David R., State College, 611
Mitchell, Harry L., Pittsburgh, 611
Mitchell, Howard H., Merion, 611
Mitchell, Howard W., Pittsburgh, 611
Mitchell, J. West, Sewickley, Pittsburgh, 611
Mitchell, John M., Rosemont, 611
Mitchell, Ruth C., Pittsburgh, 611
Mitchell, Viola, Pittsburgh, 612
Mitchell, William R. K., Conshohocken, Philadelphia, 612
Mitten, Arthur A., Philadelphia, 612
Mock, Charles A., Reading, 612
Mockridge, John C. H., Philadelphia, 612
Moffatt, Earl B., Scranton, 612
Moffet, Horace C., Pittsburgh, 612
Moffitt, George R., Harrisburg, 613
Moffitt, Harold F., Altoona, 613
Mogel, Charles L., Millersburg, 613
Mohler, Roy W., Bala-Cynwyd, Philadelphia, 613
Mohler, Samuel L., Lancaster, 613
Moise, Albert L., Philadelphia, 613
Molarsky, Maurice, Philadelphia, 613
Moll, Lloyd A., Allentown, 614
Molloy, J. Carroll, Pineville, Doylestown, 614
Monaghan, James, Philadelphia, 614
Monahan, Lawrance P., Gibsonia, Pittsburgh, 614
Mong, George L. W., Somerset, Harrisburg, 614
Monks, Frederick C., Kittanning, 614
Monrad, Carl C., Mt. Lebanon, Pittsburgh, 614
Monro, Charles B., Pittsburgh, 614
Monro, William L., Pittsburgh, 614
Monroe, George K., Clairton, 615
Montanye, Edwin Y., Philadelphia, 615
Monteverde, Louis W., Pittsburgh, 615
Montgomery, Frank S., Charleroi, 615
Montgomery, Howard D., Pittsburgh, 615
Montgomery, James A., Philadelphia, 615
Montgomery, James S., Philadelphia, 615
Montgomery, Thaddeus L., Bala-Cynwyd, Philadelphia, 615
Montgomery, Walter C., Waynesburg, 615

Montgomery, Walter L., Harrisburg, 616
Mook, Harold F., Erie, 616
Moon, Seymour B., Coraopolis, Pittsburgh, 616
Moon, Virgil H., Bryn Mawr, 616
Mooney, James E., Five Points, Jenkintown, 616
Mooney, William R., Rosemont, Bryn Mawr, 616
Moore, Bruce V., State College, 617
Moore, Darius C., Beaver, 617
Moore, Edward C., Erie, 617
Moore, Frederic T., Williamsport, 617
Moore, Frederick L., Scranton, 617
Moore, James C., Jr., Philadelphia, 617
Moore, James M., Lititz, 618
Moore, John P., Philadelphia, 618
Moore, John T., Wernersville, Reading, 618
Moore, J. Hampton, Philadelphia, 618
Moore, Joseph L., Ridley Park, 618
Moore, Merrill M., Bethlehem, 618
Moore, Robert, Danville, 618
Moore, William E., Pittsburgh, 619
Moorhead, Forest G., Beaver, 619
Moorhead, Hugh M., Erie, 619
Moorhead, Stirling W., Philadelphia, 619
Moorhead, William S., Pittsburgh, 619
Mordell, Albert, Philadelphia, 619
Morehead, James C., Pittsburgh, 620
Morehouse, J. Stanley, Upper Darby, 620
Moreno, Manuel E., Philadelphia, 620
Morey, Frank R., Swarthmore, 620
Morgan, Albert T., Pittsburgh, 620
Morgan, Angela, Rydal, 620
Morgan, Carl F., Philadelphia, 621
Morgan, Charles E., 3d, Newtown, Philadelphia, 621
Morgan, Edward M., Tyrone, 621
Morgan, F. Corlies, Philadelphia, 621
Morgan, James H., Carlisle, 621
Morgan, Sister M. Sylvia, Scranton, 621
Morgan, Marshall S., Malvern, Philadelphia, 621
Morgan, Peto W., Pittsburgh, Wilmerding, 621
Morgan, T. Frank, Philadelphia, 622
Moritz, Theodore L., Pittsburgh, 622
Morledge, Joseph S., Pittsburgh, 622
Morningstar, Samuel R., Philipsburg, 622
Morris, Charles M., Newtown, Langhorne, 622
Morris, David, Washington, 622
Morris, Edward S., Philadelphia, 623
Morris, Galloway C., Wayne, Philadelphia, 623
Morris, George B., Bradford, 623
Morris, George D., New Castle, 623
Morris, Harrison S., Philadelphia, 623
Morris, Homer L., Wallingford, 623
Morris, Lawrence J., West Chester, Philadelphia, 624
Morris, Paul L., Pottstown, 624
Morris, Robert M., Punxsutawney, 624
Morris, Roland S., Philadelphia, 624
Morris, Samuel Dalton, 624
Morris, Sarah I., Philadelphia, 624
Morris, Vlon N., Philadelphia, 624
Morris, Walter E., Punxsutawney, 624
Morris, William F., Jr., Pittsburgh, 625
Morrison, Charles M., Ivyland, Philadelphia, 625
Morrison, Frank G., Mt. Lebanon, Pittsburgh, 625
Morrison, Thomas, Pittsburgh, 625
Morrissey, Richard V., Swissvale, Williamsport, 625
Morrow, John D. A., Shields, Pittsburgh, 625
Morrow, John S., Pittsburgh, 625
Morrow, S. John, Uniontown, 625
Morse, Adrian O., State College, 626
Morse, Anson E., Philadelphia, 626
Morse, Benjamin F., Hazleton, Sugar Loaf, 626
Morse, Edwin K., Pittsburgh, 626
Morse, Louis S., York, 626
Morton, Earl A., Pittsburgh, 626
Moser, Guy L., Douglasville, 627

Moser, Ralph E., Pittsburgh, 627
Moser, Wallace G., Scranton, 627
Moser, Walter L., Pittsburgh, 627
Moses, Elbert B., Pittsburgh, 627
Moses, Harry M., Pittsburgh, 627
Moses, Thomas, Pittsburgh, 627
Moses, Walter, Philadelphia, 627
Moskovitz, Harry S., Philadelphia, 627
Mott, Joseph W., Greentown, 628
Moul, Clayton E., York, Spring Grove, 628
Mountford, Leslie, Mercer, 628
Mowls, John N., Uniontown, 628
Mowrey, Raymond G., Quincy, Chambersburg, 628
Moyer, Edward T., Philadelphia, 628
Moyer, Gabriel H., Lebanon, 628
Moyer, Harry C., Lebanon, Schaefferstown, 628
Moyer, James A., Philadelphia, 629
Moyer, Tilghman H., Allentown, 629
Mudd, Stuart, Haverford, 629
Mudge, Edmund W., Pittsburgh, 629
Mudge, Lewis S., Bryn Mawr, Philadelphia, 629
Mueller, Fred W., Philadelphia, 629
Mueller, William A., Philadelphia, 630
Muend, Charles J., Philadelphia, 630
Muir, Charles M., Pittsburgh, 630
Muir, William W., Warren 630
Muldoon, Hugh C., Pittsburgh, Dushore, 630
Mullen, Edward A., Philadelphia, 630
Mullen, Philip H. R., Pittsburgh, 630
Muller, George P., Philadelphia, 630
Muller, Valentin K. R., Bryn Mawr, 631
Müller-Munk, Peter, Pittsburgh, 631
Mullin, Charles E., Huntingdon, 631
Mullison, Olin R., Kingston, Wilkes-Barre, 631
Mumford, Edward W., Philadelphia, 631
Mumma, Anna E. D., Lancaster, 631
Mummart, Clarence A., Greencastle, 631
Munch, James C., Lansdowne, Upper Darby, 631
Munger, George A., Philadelphia, 631
Munger, James S., Nazareth, 631
Munn, Matthew G., Erie, 631
Munn, Ralph, Pittsburgh, 632
Muñoz, Gonzalo C., Philadelphia, 632
Munroe, Robert, Jr., Pittsburgh, 632
Munroe, Robert, 3d, Pittsburgh, 632
Munroe, Thomas W., Derry, 632
Murdoch, Alexander, Pittsburgh, 632
Murdoch, William M., Pittsburgh, 632
Murdock, D. Ray, Greensberg, 632
Murphy, Eugene C., Philadelphia, 633
Murphy, Louis E., Philadelphia, 633
Murphy, Miles, Merion, 633
Murphy, Raymond E., Lemont, 633
Murray, Alfred L., Lansdale, 633
Murray, Elsie, Athens, 633
Murray, Harry D., Grove City, 634
Murray, John A., Patton, 634
Murray, Philip, Pittsburgh, 634
Murray, Samuel, Philadelphia, 634
Murray, William W., Canonsburg, 634
Murrelle, Harlan G., Sayre, 634
Murrie, William F. R., Hershey, 635
Murrin, James A., Franklin, 635
Murrin, James B., Scranton, 635
Murrin, John B., Butler, 635
Murrin, Joseph S., Scranton, Carbondale, 635
Muschat, Maurice, Philadelphia, 635
Musgrave, John K., Pittsburgh, 635
Muskat, Morris, Oakmont, 635
Musser, Alfred J., Indiana, 635
Musser, Florence A., Lansdowne, 635
Musser, Paul H., Drexel Hill, Philadelphia, 636
Mutch, Andrew, Wynnewood, 636
Myers, Albert C., Moylan, 636

Myers, C. Randolph, Ebensburg, 636
Myers, Charles, St. Davids, Philadelphia, 636
Myers, Charles E., State College, 636
Myers, Chester G., Hellan, 636
Myers, Clarence E., Philadelphia, 636
Myers, Helen E., Annville, 637
Myers, Jerome I., Scranton, 637
Myers, John D., Merion, Philadelphia, 637
Myers, John E., Lemoyne, 637
Myers, Robert L., Jr., Lemoyne, 637
Myers, Walter L., Dormont, Pittsburgh, 637
Myers, William H., Jr., St. Davids, Philadelphia, 637
Myers, William K., Merion, Philadelphia, 637
Nadai, Arpad L., Wilkinsburg, East Pittsburgh, 638
Nagle, Clarence F., Scranton, 638
Nagle, Edgar C., Northampton, 638
Nagorski, Francis T., Erie, 638
Navarro, Rocco A., Pittsburgh, 638
Neale, James R., New Wilmington, 639
Neel, Gregg L., Pittsburgh, 639
Neeley, John H., Pittsburgh, 639
Neely, William H., Harrisburg, 639
Neff, Jonathan C., Philadelphia, 640
Neilson, Harry R., St. Davids, Philadelphia, 640
Neilson, Lewis, St. Davids, 640
Neilson, Thomas R., Philadelphia, 640
Neisser, Hans P., Swarthmore, 640
Neisser, Rittenhouse, Chester, 640
Nell, Raymond B., Selinsgrove, 640
Nelley, Thomas J., Steelton, Harrisburg, 640
Nelson, A. A., Ebensburg, 640
Nelson, Byron, Reading, 640
Nelson, Harley A., Palmerton, 641
Nelson, James A., Bethlehem, 641
Nelson, John E., Pittsburgh, 641
Nelson, John E., Pittsburgh, 641
Nelson, Robert F., Bryn Mawr, West Conshohocken, 642
Nelson, William L., Philadelphia, 642
Neprash, Jerry A., Lancaster, 642
Netting, M. Graham, Pittsburgh, 642
Nettleton, Lewis L., Oakmont, Pittsburgh, 642
Neuman, Abraham A., Philadelphia, 642
Neville, Harvey A., Bethlehem, 643
Nevin, David W., Easton, 643
Nevin, Gordon B., New Wilmington, 643
Nevin, William L., Philadelphia, 643
Newburger, Frank L., Jr., Elkins Park, Philadelphia, 643
Newbury, Frank D., Pittsburgh, East Pittsburgh, 643
Newcomb, Thomas H., Pittsburgh, 643
Newcomer, Lester W., Lancaster, 643
Newhall, Blackwell, Bryn Mawr, Philadelphia, 644
Newhall, C. Stevenson, Philadelphia, 644
Newhall, Thomas, Philadelphia, 644
Newlon, Homer T., Pittsburgh, 644
Newman, Bernard J., Philadelphia, 644
Newman, John G., Philadelphia, 644
Newman, Philip F., Allentown, 644
Newpher, James A., Harrisburg, 644
Newsom, Nathan W., Philadelphia, 645
Newton, Joseph F., Philadelphia, 645
Niblo, James M., Norristown, 645
Nichols, Joseph K., Philadelphia, 645
Nichols, Isabel M., Philadelphia, 645
Nichols, Jeannette P., Swarthmore, 645
Nichols, Pierrepont H., Slippery Rock, 645
Nichols, Roy F., Swarthmore, 646
Nicholson, Percival, Ardmore, 646
Nicholson, William R., Wynnewood, Philadelphia, 646
Nicholson, William H., Jr., Philadelphia, 646
Nick, Edwin W., Erie, 646
Nickel, James E., Erie, 646

PENNSYLVANIA

Nicklas, John B., Jr., Mt. Lebanon, Pittsburgh, 646
Nicodemus, Edwin A., Harrisburg, 646
Nicodemus, Roy E., Danville, 646
Niemann, Kenneth E., Pittsburgh, 647
Niesley, Howard G., State College, 647
Nietz, John A., Pittsburgh, 647
Niles, Henry C., York, 647
Niles, John S., Carbondale, 647
Nimick, Thomas H., Pittsburgh, 647
Nimkoff, Meyer F., Lewisburg, 647
Nissler, Christian W., Philadelphia, 648
Nissley, Walter B., State College, 648
Nitrauer, William E., Mount Joy, 648
Nitzsche, Elsa K., Philadelphia, 648
Nitzsche, George E., Philadelphia, 648
Noble, David A., Philadelphia, 648
Noble, Urbane A., Scranton, 648
Nolan, James B., Reading, 649
Noll, Charles F., State College, 649
Nolte, John F., Altoona, 649
Noonan, James P., Mahanoy City, 649
Noonan, Joseph F., Mansfield, 649
Noone, Ernest L., Drexel Hill, 649
Norcross, Wilbur H., Carlisle, 649
Norden, N. Lindsay, Philadelphia, 650
Nordstrom, John A., Grove City, 650
Norman, George M., Fairville, 650
Norris, Charles C., Bryn Mawr, Philadelphia, 650
Norris, George W., Gwynedd Valley, Philadelphia, 650
Norris, George W., Dimock, 650
Norris, Henry, Bryn Mawr, 650
North, Henry B., York, 651
Northart, Paul R., Mt. Lebanon, Pittsburgh, 651
Northrup, Harry B., State College, 651
Norton, Albert R., Pittsburgh, 651
Norton, Theodore E., Easton, 651
Norton, Warren P., Meadville, 652
Noss, John V., Lancaster, 652
Novotny, E. E., Prospectville, Philadelphia, 652
Noyes, Arthur P., Norristown, 652
Nugent, Gerald P., Philadelphia, 653
Nungesser, Fred L., Mt. Lebanon, Pittsburgh, 653
Nurick, Gilbert, Harrisburg, 653
Nusbaum, Lee, Philadelphia, 653
Nusbaum, Louis, Philadelphia, 653
Nuse, Roy C., Rushland, 653
Oakley, Albert C., Pittsburgh, 653
Oakley, Amy, Villanova, 653
Oakley, Cletus O., Haverford, 654
Oakley, Thornton, Villanova, 654
Oakley, Violet, Philadelphia, 654
Ober, Bert F., Latrobe, 654
Ober, Henry K., Elizabethtown, 654
Oberdorf, Harvey A., Columbia, 654
Oberly, Henry S., Upper Darby, Philadelphia, 654
Obermanns, Henry F., Erie, 655
Obermayer, Leon J., Philadelphia, 655
Obernauer, Harold, Pittsburgh, 655
Oberrender, John S., White Haven, Freeland, 655
O'Brien, Edward J., Pittsburgh, 655
O'Brien, J. Vick, Pittsburgh, 655
O'Brien, James A., Rosemont, Philadelphia, 655
O'Connell, C. Leonard, Pittsburgh, 656
O'Connell, James J., Belle Vernon, 656
O'Connell, John M., Jeannette, 656
O'Connor, Martin J., Scranton, 656
Odgers, Merle M., Philadelphia, 656
O'Donnell, Francis T., Wilkes-Barre, 657
O'Donnell, Leo D., Pittsburgh, 657
O'Donnell, Raymond, State College 657
O'Donoghue, Michael J., Philadelphia, 657
Oerlein, Karl F., California, 657
Oesterling, Adolph L., Butler, 657
Offermann, Henry F., Philadelphia, 657
Ogden, Rachel C., Hadley, 658
Oglesby, Warwick M., Harrisburg, 658
Ogrodowska-Ridpath, Johanna, Merion, Philadelphia, 658
O'Hare, Bernard V., Shenandoah, 658

O'Harra, Margaret T., Philadelphia, 658
Ohl, Jeremiah F., Philadelphia, 658
Okeson, Walter R., Old Zionsville, Bethlehem, 659
Old, Marcus C., Collegeville, 659
Olds, Edwin G., Pittsburgh, 659
O'Leary, Patrick E., Hollidaysburg, Altoona, 659
Olewine, James H., State College, 659
Oliensis, Abraham E., Philadelphia, 659
Oliphant, James O., Lewisburg, 659
Oliver, Augustus K., Pittsburgh, 659
Oliver, Bennett, Pittsburgh, 659
Oliver, George S., Pittsburgh, 659
Oliver, John W., Pittsburgh, 660
Oliver, Joseph H., Scranton, 660
Oliver, L. Stauffer, Philadelphia, 660
Olivier, Charles P., Upper Darby, 660
Olmes, Mildred Y., Titusville, 660
Olmstead, Robert H., State College, 660
Olmstead, Frederick L., Brockway, 660
Olmsted, George W., Ludlow, 660
Olsen, Thorsten Y., Philadelphia, 660
O'Malley, Charles P., Scranton, 661
Oppenheimer, Oscar W., Pittsburgh, 661
Oresek, Charles W., South Brownsville, 661
Ormandy, Eugene, Philadelphia, 661
Orndoff, Jessie M., Waynesburg, 662
Ornstein, Leo, Philadelphia, 662
Orr, George P., Berwyn, Philadelphia, 662
Orr, John, New Wilmington, 662
Orr, John A., Pittsburgh, 662
Ortner, Elmer A., Pittsburgh, 662
Osborn, Robert R., Philadelphia, 663
Osbourn, Samuel E., Philadelphia, 663
Osbourne, Alfred S., Pittsburgh, 663
Osgood, Harlow S., New Wilmington, 663
Osol, Arthur, Philadelphia, 663
Ostermayer, Robert W., Clairton, 663
Osthaus, Carl E., Overton, 663
Ostheimer, Maurice, Whitford, 663
Ostrolenk, Bernhard, Solebury, 663
Oswald, Charles S., Lynnport, 664
Othmer, Donald F., Coudersport, 664
Ott, Frank H., Towanda, 664
Otto, Henry H., Scranton, 664
Otto, Louisa B., Allentown, 664
Ourbacker, George J., Wynnewood, Philadelphia, 664
Overberger, Edwin W., Cresson, 664
Overholts, Lee O., State College, 664
Ovrebo, Paul J., Selinsgrove, 664
Owen, Hubley R., Philadelphia, 664
Owen, Ralph D., Llanerch, 665
Owen, W. B., Kittanning, 665
Owens, Edith H., Parkesburg, 665
Owens, Frederick W., State College, 665
Owens, William G., Lewisburg, 665
Owings, Capers B., Philadelphia, 665
Owlett, Gilbert M., Wellsboro, 665
Oyler, Richard S., Altoona, 665
Packard, Francis R., Philadelphia, 665
Packard, John H., 3d, Philadelphia, 665
Packard, Kent, Paoli, Philadelphia, 666
Padden, John F., Scranton, 666
Paddock, Frank, Philadelphia, 666
Padgett, Frederick H., Sunbury, 666
Page, Robert P., Jr., Ardmore, 666
Painter, Clark H., Butler, 666
Painter, Frank H., Jersey Shore, Williamsport, 666
Painter, George E., Mt. Lebanon, Pittsburgh, 666
Painter, Howard I., Butler, 666
Paist, Theresa W., Wayne, 667
Palmer, Charles E., McKeesport, 667
Palmer, Charles S., Pittsburgh, 667
Palmer, Frederic, Jr., Haverford, 667
Palmer, Gordon, Wynnewood, Philadelphia, 667
Palmer, Philip M., Bethlehem, 668
Palmer, Samuel C., Swarthmore, 668

Palmer, Walter, Media, Chester, 668
Palmquist, Elim A. E., Narbrook, Philadelphia, 668
Pancoast, Henry K., Merion, Philadelphia, 668
Papánek, Ján, Pittsburgh, 668
Parcell, Malcolm S., Washington, 669
Pardee, C. Marvin, Hazleton, 669
Pardoe, William S., Philadelphia, 669
Parente, Antonio, Monessen, 669
Pargny, Eugene W., Pittsburgh, 669
Parish, Benjamin D., North Hills, Philadelphia, 669
Park, Marion E., Bryn Mawr, 669
Park, Theodore, Chester, 669
Parker, Andrew M., Glenside, Philadelphia, 669
Parker, Dorothy R., Pipersville, 669
Parker, Edward W., Philadelphia, 670
Parker, Frank, Philadelphia, 670
Parker, Frank C., Norristown, 670
Parker, J. Brooks B., Strafford, Philadelphia, 670
Parker, Roswell J., Scranton, 670
Parker, William A., West Philadelphia, 670
Parker, William M., Oil City, 670
Parker, William N., Philadelphia, 670
Parkin, William, Pittsburgh, 670
Parkins, George V., Elizabeth, McKeesport, 670
Parkinson, Chauncey W., Waynesburg, 670
Parkinson, William N., Philadelphia, 671
Parks, Joseph W., Altoona, 671
Parks, Lytle R., State College, 671
Parks, Samuel M., Jr., Pittsburgh, 671
Parlin, Wellington A., Carlisle, 671
Parrish, Joseph A., Bellefonte, 671
Parrish, Morris L., Philadelphia, 671
Parry, Florence F., Pittsburgh, 671
Parry, George G., Philadelphia, 671
Parsons, Lewis M., Haverford, Pittsburgh, 672
Patch, Richard H., Jenkintown, Philadelphia, 672
Paternostro, Francis H., Williamsport, 672
Patrick, Ruth, Philadelphia, 673
Patterson, Alexander E., Paoli, Philadelphia, 673
Patterson, Catherine N., Philadelphia, 673
Patterson, Clarence A., New Castle, 673
Patterson, Clifford S., Monongahela, 673
Patterson, Ernest M., Philadelphia, 673
Patterson, Gaylard H., Carlisle, 674
Patterson, Graham C., Ardmore, Philadelphia, 674
Patterson, S. Howard, Philadelphia, 674
Patterson, Thomas M., Wayne, Philadelphia, 674
Patterson, William W., Jr., Sewickley, Pittsburgh, 675
Pattison, John O., Elkland, 675
Patton, Hugh M., Pittsburgh, 675
Patton, Katharine, Philadelphia, 675
Paul, Harold L., Port Carbon, Pottsville, 675
Paul, John D., Philadelphia, 675
Paul, John R., Philadelphia, 675
Paul, Theodore S., Philadelphia, 675
Payne, Frank, Harrisburg, 676
Payne, John G., Oil City, 676
Peabody, Gertrude D., Philadelphia, 676
Peacock, Ralph W., Houston, Washington, 676
Peake, Walter L., Corry, 676
Peale, Rembrandt, Jr., St. Benedict, 676
Pearce, McLeod M., Beaver Falls, 677
Pearce, William, Titusville, 677
Pearce, William T., Narberth, Philadelphia, 677
Pearlman, Martin M., Philadelphia, 677
Pearsall, David E., Allison Park, 678
Pearson, Gerald H. J., Drexel Hill, Philadelphia, 678
Pearson, Joseph C., Allentown, 678
Pearson, Joseph T., Jr., Huntingdon Valley, 678
Pearson, William A., Narberth, 678
Peartree, Armand J., Bala-Cynwyd, Philadelphia, 678

Pease, Henry H., Philadelphia, 678
Pebly, Harry E., Sharpsville, 678
Peck, Staunton B., Philadelphia, 678
Peery, Rob R., Merion, Philadelphia, 679
Peery, Thomas B., Philadelphia, 679
Peffley, William E., Lemoyne, Harrisburg, 679
Peinado Vallejo, Juan, Narberth, 679
Peirce, Bertha C., Jenkintown, 679
Peirce, Frederick, Wynnewood, Philadelphia, 679
Peirce, Mary B., Philadelphia, 679
Peirce, Thomas M., Jr., Philadelphia, 679
Peirce, Willis M., Palmerton, 680
Pelser, Kurt, Philadelphia, 680
Pelouze, Percy S., Drexel Hill, Philadelphia, 680
Pemberton, Ralph, Paoli, Philadelphia, 680
Pence, Leland H., Philadelphia, 680
Pender, Harold, Philadelphia, 680
Pendergrass, Eugene P., Wynnewood, Philadelphia, 680
Pendleton, Joseph S., Calcium, Reading, 680
Pendleton, Louis, Bryn Athyn, 680
Pennell, Edred J., Mifflintown, 681
Penniman, Josiah H., Philadelphia, 681
Pennypacker, Isaac A., Ardmore, Philadelphia, 681
Penrose, Charles, West Chester, Philadelphia, 681
Pent, Rose M., Jenkintown, 681
Pentz, James G., Harrisburg, 681
Pepper, George W., Devon, Philadelphia, 681
Pepper, John O., State College, 682
Pepper, O. H. Perry, Ithan, Philadelphia, 682
Pepper, William, Philadelphia, 682
Perkins, John D., Conshohocken, 682
Perkins, William W. C., Langhorne, 683
Perley, George A., Wyncote, Philadelphia, 683
Perot, T. Morris, Jr., Philadelphia, 683
Perrin, Oliver W., Ardmore, Philadelphia, 683
Perry, David R., Altoona, 683
Perry, John L., Pittsburgh, 683
Perry, Lynn, Easton, 683
Perry, Thomas D., Philadelphia, 684
Pershing, Avra N., Greensburg, 684
Pershing, Louise, Crafton, 684
Person, John E., Williamsport, 684
Pessolano, Frank J., New Kensington, 684
Peter, Luther C., Philadelphia, 684
Peters, Albert G., Philadelphia, 684
Peters, Charles C., State College, 684
Peters, Errol K., Allentown, 684
Peters, John F., Pittsburgh, 685
Peters, Martin L., Phoenixville, 685
Peters, Roy S., Saegertown, Meadville, 685
Peters, Sidney N., Philadelphia, 685
Peters, Stacy E., Lancaster, 685
Peterson, Herbert G., Mansfield, 685
Peterson, Rudolph, Lewisburg, 685
Petry, Howard K., Harrisburg, 685
Pettibon, Arthur W., Rochester, 685
Petty, David M., Bethlehem, 686
Pew, J. Howard, Ardmore, 686
Pfaelzer, Elsie L., Philadelphia, 686
Pfaff, Will, McKeesport, 686
Pfahler, George E., Philadelphia, 686
Pfahler, Robert G., Windber, 686
Pfaltzgraff, George W., York, 686
Pfatteicher, Ernst P., Philadelphia, 686
Pfefferle, George H., Bradford, 686
Pfeifle, Robert, Bethlehem, 687
Pfund, Harry W., Haverford, 687
Phelps, Andrew M., Mt. Lebanon, Pittsburgh, 687
Phelps, Harold A., Pittsburgh, 687
Philbrick, Francis S., Swarthmore, 687
Philips, Earle S., Kennett Square, 687
Philips, S. Jones, Kennett Square, 688
Phillips, Benjamin D., Butler, 688
Phillips, Charles H., Trucksville, Wilkes-Barre, 688
Phillips, Frank R., Mt. Lebanon, Pittsburgh, 688

Phillips, Harriet D., Pittsburgh, 688
Phillips, John M., Carrick, Pittsburgh, 689
Phillips, Leslie, Pittsburgh, 689
Phillips, Linn V., Uniontown, 689
Phillips, Marie T., Pittsburgh, 689
Phillips, Samuel M., Sharon, 689
Phillips, Thomas W., Jr., Butler, 689
Phillips, William H., Glenshaw, Pittsburgh, 689
Piatt, John E., Wyoming, 689
Picard, Henry, Hershey, 690
Pickett, Clarence E., Wallingford, Philadelphia, 690
Piekarski, Frank A., Pittsburgh, 690
Pielemeier, W. H., State College, 690
Pierce, Appleton H., Coatesville, 690
Pierce, Frederick W., State College, 690
Pierce, James H., Scranton, 690
Piercy, Samuel K., Allentown, 691
Piersol, George M., Huntingdon Valley, Philadelphia, 691
Pigossi, Dante, Bridgeville, 691
Pigott, Reginald J. S., Pittsburgh, 691
Pike, Clayton W., Philadelphia, 692
Pilcher, Lewis F., Philadelphia, Harrisburg, 692
Pilling, William S., Philadelphia, 692
Pillsbury, Donald M., Narberth, Philadelphia, 692
Pilsbry, Henry A., Philadelphia, 692
Pinchot, Cornelia B., Milford, 692
Pinchot, Gifford, Milford, 692
Pinola, Frank L., Kingston, Pittston, Wilkes-Barre, 692
Pinto, Salvatore, Philadelphia, 693
Piper, Joseph D., Pittsburgh, 693
Piper, William T., Lock Haven, 693
Pirson, Sylvain J. G., State College, 693
Pitcairn, Harold F., Bryn Athyn, Philadelphia, 693
Pitcairn, Raymond, Philadelphia, 693
Pitcher, Charles S., Rome, Philadelphia, 693
Pitfield, Robert L., Philadelphia, 693
Pitkin, Francis A., Harrisburg, 694
Pitman, John H., Swarthmore, 694
Pitman, Ralph W., South Ardmore, Philadelphia, 694
Pittenger, Paul S., Philadelphia, 694
Pittman, Hobson, Upper Darby, 694
Pitz, Henry C., Plymouth Meeting, Philadelphia, 694
Pitzonka, Walter W., Bristol, 694
Pivirotto, Arthur M., Pittsburgh, 694
Plack, William L., Philadelphia, 694
Plank, William E., Easton, 695
Platt, Charles A., Grove City, 695
Platt, Haviland H., Philadelphia, 695
Platt, John O., Paoli, Philadelphia, 695
Pleasants, Henry, Jr., West Chester, 695
Pleasants, Henry, 3d, Philadelphia, 695
Plumer, John S., Pittsburgh, 695
Plummer, Wilbur C., Upper Darby, Philadelphia, 696
Poling, Daniel A., Philadelphia, 696
Pollock, Thomas C., Philadelphia, 697
Pollock, Walter W., Philadelphia, 697
Pontius, S. Gilmore, Lancaster, 697
Pontzer, Robert F., Ridgway, 697
Pool, Joseph H., 3d, Kingston, Wilkes-Barre, 697
Pope, Francis H., Philadelphia, 698
Pope, Harry E., Pittsburgh, 698
Popp, Henry W., State College, 698
Porkess, William, Wilkinsburg, 698
Porter, Horace C., Philadelphia, 698
Porter, James W., Jr., Sewickley, Pittsburgh, 699
Portnoff, Alexander, Philadelphia, 699
Portser, Robert K., Greensburg, 699
Post, Harold F., Greensburg, 699
Post, Joseph W., Wyncote, Philadelphia, 699
Post, Levi A., Haverford, 699

Potteiger, Clarence R., Upper Darby, Philadelphia, 700
Potter, John W., Carlisle, 700
Potter, Kenneth G., Waynesboro, 700
Powell, Alfred R., Mt. Lebanon, Pittsburgh, 701
Powell, Edith W., Devon, Harrisburg, 701
Powell, William A., Merion, Philadelphia, 702
Powell, William M., Dallas, Wyoming, 702
Powers, Donald H., Philadelphia, 702
Powers, Philip H., Pittsburgh, 702
Prall, Charles E., Pittsburgh, 702
Prather, Ralph C., Philadelphia, 703
Pratt, Carl D., Tamaqua, 703
Pratt, Henry S., Haverford, 703
Pray, Kenneth L. M., Narberth, Philadelphia, 703
Preisler, Kenneth L., Watsontown, 703
Prendergast, James, Philadelphia, 703
Prentis, Henning W., Jr., Lancaster, 704
Prentiss, Harriet D., Philadelphia, 704
Pressman, Ralph, Philadelphia, 704
Prettyman, Cornelius W., Carlisle, 704
Prewitt, Richard H., Lansdowne, Philadelphia, 705
Price, Frank J., Lackawaxen, 705
Price, Franklin H., Philadelphia, 705
Price, John V., Norristown, 705
Price, William G., Jr., Chester, 705
Price, William N., Philadelphia, 706
Priestman, Glyndon, Philadelphia, 706
Printz, Stanley V., Allentown, 706
Prinz, Hermann Lansdowne, 706
Pritchard, John P., Washington, 706
Prizer, William M., Haverford, Philadelphia, 707
Prosch, Frederick, Philadelphia, 707
Prothero, John C., Jeannette, 707
Prothro, James T., Philadelphia, 707
Prugh, Byron E. P., Harrisburg, 707
Pugh, David B., State College, 707
Pugh, Emerson M., Pittsburgh, 708
Pugh, William B., Wallingford, Philadelphia, 708
Pugh, William S., Pottsville, 708
Puglese, Sebastian C., Pittsburgh, 708
Pullinger, Herbert, Philadelphia, 708
Purvis, Joseph D., Butler, 708
Purvis, William E., Grove City, 709
Putman, Dwight F., Gettysburg, 709
Putnam, Earl B., Philadelphia, 709
Putnam, Francis J., Pittsburgh, 709
Putts, B. Swayne, Erie, 709
Pyle, Milton C., West Grove, 709
Pyle, Robert, West Grove, 709
Quier, Edwin A., Reading, 709
Quigley, Francis P., Philadelphia, 709
Quinn, Arthur H., Bala-Cynwyd, 709
Quinn, James L., Braddock, 710
Quinn, Josephine T., Lansford, 710
Quinn, Lawrence R., Pittsburgh, 710
Quinn, Mary A., Aspinwall, Braddock, 710
Radasch, Henry E., Gladwyne, Philadelphia, 710
Rader, Frank S., Neumanstown, Myerstown, 710
Raditz, Lazar, Philadelphia, 710
Raff, A. Raymond, Philadelphia, 710
Rafter, Joseph L., Harrisburg, 711
Raiguel, George E., Philadelphia, 711
Raine, Wendell P., Philadelphia, 711
Raker, John H., Allentown, 711
Raker, William W., Kutztown, 711
Rall, Charles R., Pittsburgh, 711
Ralston, Cameron, Point Marion, 711
Rambo, Ormond, Jr., Merion Station, Philadelphia, 712
Ramsburg, C. J., Sewickley, Pittsburgh, 712
Ramsey, William H. C., Bryn Mawr, 712
Ranck, Clayton H., Philadelphia, 712
Ranck, Dayton L., Lewisburg, 712
Ranck, Lee R., Milton, 712
Randall, Alexander, Philadelphia, 713
Randall, Roland R., Philadelphia, 713

Randles, Andrew J., Pittsburgh, 713
Randolph, Edward Fitz, Lansdowne, 713
Randolph, Evan, Philadelphia, 713
Rankin, James L., Chester, 714
Rankin, John H., Penllyn, Philadelphia, 714
Rankin, Lynn M., Upper Darby, Philadelphia, 714
Rankin, Matthew, Chester, 714
Ransley, Harry C., Philadelphia, 714
Rapking, Aaron H., Philadelphia, 715
Rasbridge, Emerson B., Stony Creek Mills, Reading, 715
Raschen, John F. L., Pittsburgh, 715
Rassweiler, Clifford F., Swarthmore, 715
Ratzlaff, Carl J., Easton, 715
Rau, Albert G., Bethlehem, 715
Rauh, Bertha F., Pittsburgh, 715
Raul, Harry L., Easton, 715
Rausch, Herbert S., Girardville, 715
Ravdin, I. S., Philadelphia, 716
Ray, Daniel P., Johnstown, 716
Ray, Joseph W., Jr., Uniontown, 717
Ray, R. H., Indiana, 717
Raymond, Walter C., Johnstown, 717
Raynolds, James W., Pittsburgh, 717
Raynor, George E., Bethlehem, 717
Rea, Robert W., Devon, 717
Read, Charles W., New Castle, 717
Read, Conyers, Merion, Philadelphia, 717
Read, Harry M., York, 717
Readio, Wilfred A., Pittsburgh, 717
Rearick, William M., Mifflinburg, 718
Reath, Theodore W., Ardmore, Philadelphia, 718
Rebbeck, Elmer W., Pittsburgh, 718
Rebmann, G. Ruhland, Jr., Haverford, Philadelphia, 718
Reckord, Frank F. D., Harrisburg, 718
Redding, Charles S., Jenkintown, Philadelphia, 718
Redfield, Edward W., New Hope, 718
Reed, Alexander P., Pittsburgh, 719
Reed, David A., Pittsburgh, 719
Reed, DeVeaux H., McKeesport, 719
Reed, Earl F., Pittsburgh, 719
Reed, George L., Harrisburg, 719
Reed, Gordon W., Bradford, 719
Reed, Henry M., Ben Avon, 719
Reed, James C., Pittsburgh, 719
Reed, John E., Erie, 719
Reed, Luther D., Philadelphia, 720
Reed, Marjorie E., Plymouth, 720
Reeder, Frank, Jr., Easton, 720
Reeder, Harry T., Glenside, Philadelphia, 720
Rees, John G., Scranton, 721
Reese, Daniel R., Scranton, 721
Reese, Frederick S., Carlisle, 721
Reese, Warren S., Philadelphia, 721
Reeser, Dick M., New Kensington, 721
Reeve, William F., III, Newtown Square, Philadelphia, 721
Reeves, Francis B., Jr., Blue Bell, Philadelphia, 722
Reeves, James A. W., Greensburg, 722
Reeves, John R., Coudersport, 722
Reeves, Rufus S., Philadelphia, 722
Regner, Sidney L., Reading, 722
Rehm, William C., Lancaster, 722
Rehn, James A. G., Philadelphia, 722
Reiber, Aaron E., Butler, 723
Reiber, Richard H., Pittsburgh, 723
Reich, Max I., Newtown, 723
Reich, Nathaniel J., Philadelphia, 723
Reichel, John, Wynnewood, Glenolden, 723
Reichold, Ralph G., Mt. Lebanon, Pittsburgh, 723
Reid, Dana B., Meadville, 723
Reid, James J., State College, 724
Reid, William J., Jr., Pittsburgh, 724
Reider, Joseph, Philadelphia, 724
Reif, Edward C., Bellevue, 724
Reiff, Elmer P., Merion, Philadelphia, 724
Reighard, John P., Shamokin, 724
Reiley, Henry B., Somerset, 724
Reilly, Paul, Philadelphia, 724
Reilly, George W., Harrisburg, 724
Reimann, Hobart A., Merion, 725

Reimann, Stanley P., Philadelphia, 725
Reimensnyder, John M., Milton, 725
Reimer, Rudolph E., Bradford, 725
Reimert, William D., Allentown, 725
Reinhold, Paul B., Pittsburgh, 725
Reiter, Howard R., Bethlehem, 725
Reiter, Manoah R., Morrisville, 725
Reiter, Murray C., Pittsburgh, 725
Reitz, Walter R., Oil City, 725
Remak, Gustavus, Jr., Philadelphia, 725
Remick, Walter L., Hazleton, 725
Rench, Walter F., Philadelphia, 726
Renfro, Charles H., Allentown, 726
Reno, Claude T., Allentown, Harrisburg, 726
Rentz, Frederick L., New Castle, 726
Repass, Ellis A., Columbia, 726
Repplier, Agnes, Philadelphia, 726
Repplier, Sidney J., Philadelphia, 726
Retan, George A., Mansfield, 726
Reuter, Frederick B., Sewickley, Pittsburgh, 727
Reynolds, Frank W., Genesee, 727
Reynolds, John E., Meadville, 727
Reynolds, Joseph B., Bethlehem, 727
Reynolds, William N., Wilkes-Barre, 728
Rhoad, Hiram F., Lancaster, 728
Rhoads, C. Brewster, Huntingdon Valley, Philadelphia, 728
Rhoads, Charles J., Bryn Mawr, 728
Rhoads, John S., Stoystown, 728
Rhoads, Joseph H., Philadelphia, 729
Rhode, William S., Kutztown, 729
Rhodes, Chester H., Stroudsburg, 729
Rhodes, George P., Pittsburgh, 729
Rhodes, John C., Wyncote, Jenkintown, 729
Rhodes, Walter K., Lewisburg, 729
Rhodes, William W., Westtown, 729
Rhone, Mortimer C., Williamsport, 729
Rhyne, Sidney W., Philadelphia, 729
Rice, Charles P., York, 730
Rice, John, Easton, 730
Rice, John S., Gettysburg, Biglerville, 730
Rice, John W., Lewisburg, 730
Rice, Philip X., State College, 730
Rice, Stuart A., Philadelphia, 730
Rich, Robert F., Woolrich, 730
Rich, Thaddeus, Philadelphia, 730
Richard, Irwin, Red Hill, 731
Richards, Alfred N., Bryn Mawr, 731
Richards, Alvin S., Norristown, West Conshohocken, 731
Richards, Florence H., Philadelphia, 731
Richards, George W., Lancaster, 731
Richards, Horace C., Philadelphia, 731
Richards, Ralph S., Edgeworth, Pittsburgh, 731
Richards, Samuel M., Freeport, 732
Richards, William J., Pottsville, 732
Richardson, Channing A., Philadelphia, 732
Richardson, Clarence H., Lewisburg, 732
Richardson, Edgar S., Reiffton, Reading, 732
Richardson, Ernest G., Philadelphia, 733
Richardson, Harry B., Beaver, Aliquippa, 733
Richardson, Joseph A., Pittsburgh, 733
Richardson, Leo D., Knox, 733
Richardson, Russell, Philadelphia, 733
Richardson, William E., Reading, 733
Richardson, William W., Mercer, 733
Richie, Gustavus A., Annville, 733
Richley, John W., York, 733
Richmond, Samuel M., Sewickley, 734
Richter, William B., Philadelphia, 734
Richter, Wilmer S., Upper Darby, 734
Rickard, LeRoy R., Mercer, 734
Rickert, Glennis H., Kane, 734
Ricketson, John H., III, Pittsburgh, 734
Ricketts, George A., Osceola Mills, 734

Rickey, James W., Pittsburgh, 734
Riddle, Henry A., Jr., Lewistown, 734
Riddle, Melvin W., Chambersburg, 734
Ridenour, Chauncey O., State College, 734
Ridgway, William D., Bethayres, Jenkintown, 735
Ridgway, William H., Coatesville, 735
Ridinger, Charles W., Pittsburgh, 735
Ridpath, Robert F., Merion, Philadelphia, 735
Rieger, Charles L. W., Glenside, Philadelphia, 735
Rieman, George F., Connellsville, 735
Riemer, Guido C. L., Kutztown, 735
Rieser, Jacob L., Reading, 736
Riesman, David, Philadelphia, 736
Riggs, Norman C., Pittsburgh, 736
Riggs, Robert, Philadelphia, 736
Rigling, Alfred, West Philadelphia, 737
Riker, Charles R., Mt. Lebanon, Pittsburgh, 737
Rinehart, Daniel, Waynesboro, 737
Riordan, Frank S., Lansford, 737
Ristine, Charles S., Strafford, Philadelphia, 738
Ristine, Frederick P., Wayne, Philadelphia, 738
Riston, Paul, Warren, 738
Ritenbaugh, George F., Pittsburgh, 738
Ritenour, Joseph P., State College, 738
Ritter, Ella N., Williamsport, 738
Ritter, Thomas E., Allentown, 738
Ritter, Verus T., Merion, Philadelphia, 738
Ritter, Walter L., Altoona, 738
Rittman, Walter F., Pittsburgh, 738
Ritts, Elias, Butler, 739
Ritzman, Michael E., Reading, 739
Rivas, Damaso de, Lansdowne, 739
Rivenburg, Romeyn H., Lewisburg, 739
Robb, Edmond E., McKeesport, 739
Robb, Eugene K., Bedford, 739
Robb, Marshall V., Reading, 739
Robbins, Edward R., Philadelphia, 739
Robbins, Frank A., Jr., Steelton, 740
Robbins, Frederick R., Bryn Mawr, Philadelphia, 740
Robbins, Harry W., Lewisburg, 740
Roberts, Emerson B., Wilkinsburg, Pittsburgh, 740
Roberts, Frank C., Wynnewood, Philadelphia, 740
Roberts, George L., Sayre, Towanda, 740
Roberts, Graham, Bala-Cynwyd, 740
Roberts, Harold C., Ambler, Philadelphia, 740
Roberts, Isaac W., Bala-Cynwyd, Philadelphia, 740
Roberts, John H. R., Merion Station, Philadelphia, 741
Roberts, Kenneth, Philadelphia, 741
Roberts, Warren R., Bethlehem, Harrisburg, 741
Robertshaw, John A., Greensburg, Youngwood, 741
Robertson, Andrew W., Clairton, Pittsburgh, 741
Robertson, Charles E., Scranton, 741
Robertson, Harold F., Philadelphia, 742
Robertson, Stuart, Philadelphia, 742
Robertson, William E., Philadelphia, 742
Robertson, William J., Easton, 742
Robins, Edward, Philadelphia, 743
Robins, Henry R., Philadelphia, 743
Robinson, Alexander C., Sewickley, Pittsburgh, 743
Robinson, Charles K., Pittsburgh, 743
Robinson, Dwight P., St. Davids, Philadelphia, 743
Robinson, Edwin C., Pittsburgh, McKeesport, 744
Robinson, George T., Johnstown, 744
Robinson, Harold M., Philadelphia, 744
Robinson, J. French, Pittsburgh, 745
Robinson, James R., Zelienople, 745
Robinson, John J., Philadelphia, 745
Robinson, Joseph A., New Bethlehem, 745
Robinson, Louis N., Swarthmore, 745

Robinson, Lucius W., Pittsburgh, Indiana, 745
Robinson, Maurice R., Wilkinsburg, Pittsburgh, 745
Robinson, Ovid D., Coraopolis, Pittsburgh, 745
Robinson, Stewart M., Philadelphia, 745
Robinson, Victor, Philadelphia, 745
Robinson, William C., Sewickley, Pittsburgh, 746
Robinson, Wilton H., Pittsburgh, 746
Rock, Katharine H., Greenville, 746
Rockhold, Kenneth E., York, 746
Rockwell, Albert, Warren, 746
Rockwell, Edward H., Easton, 746
Rockwell, Rena V., Forest Hills, 746
Rockwell, Willard F., Pittsburgh, 747
Rodale, Jerome I., Allentown, Emmaus, 747
Roddy, Harry J., Conestoga, Lancaster, 747
Rodefer, Onward A., Waynesburg, 747
Rodenbaugh, Henry N., Wynnewood, Philadelphia, 747
Rodgers, Charles C., Irwin, 747
Rodgers, Frank E., Scranton, 747
Rodgers, Henry C. F., Pittsburgh, 747
Rodgers, William B., Pittsburgh, 747
Rodman, John S., Philadelphia, 747
Roeder, Jesse N., Palmerton, 748
Roemer, Henry A., Pittsburgh, Sharon, 748
Roessing, Frank M., Pittsburgh, 748
Roessing, Mrs. Jennie B., Pittsburgh, 748
Rogers, Donald S., Scottdale, 748
Rogers, Elizabeth F., Lansdowne, Chambersburg, 748
Rogers, Forrest G., Howard, Bellefonte, 748
Rogers, Herbert W., Easton, 749
Rogers, Karl H., Merion, Narberth, 749
Rogers, Mildred, New Castle, 749
Rogers, William, Jr., Philadelphia, 749
Rohlfing, Charles C., Media, 749
Rohrbach, Quincy A. W., Kutztown, 749
Rohrbaugh, Lewis G., Carlisle, 749
Rohrbeck, Edwin H., State College, 750
Rojahn, Isaiah H., Dallastown, 750
Rolfe, Alfred G., Pottstown, 750
Rolfe, John C., Philadelphia, 750
Romera-Navarro, Miguel, Philadelphia, 750
Roney, Harold A., Lumberville, 750
Ronco, Gerald, Philadelphia, 750
Rook, Charles A., Pittsburgh, 751
Rooney, Arthur J., Pittsburgh, 751
Roose, Robert L., Pitcairn, 751
Roosevelt, Nicholas G., Ambler, Philadelphia, 751
Root, Harriet T., Bethlehem, 751
Root, Thomas S., Somerton, Philadelphia, 751
Root, William T., Valencia, 751
Rorer, Jonathan T., Philadelphia, 752
Rorer, Virgil E., Elkins Park, 752
Rosanoff, Martin A., Mt. Lebanon, Pittsburgh, 752
Rose, Charles B., Philadelphia, Eddystone, 752
Rose, Don, Sewickley, Pittsburgh, 752
Rose, Donald F., Bryn Athyn, Philadelphia, 752
Rose, Edward, Wynnewood, Philadelphia, 752
Rose, Goodman A., Pittsburgh, 752
Rose, Harold J., Pittsburgh, 753
Rose, Howard S., Oil City, 753
Rose, Ivan M., Merion, Philadelphia, 753
Rose, Philip S., Ardmore, Philadelphia, 753
Rose, Roy, Sewickley, Pittsburgh, 753
Rose, William P., Cambridge Springs, 753
Roseboro, Francis B., Philadelphia, 753
Rosen, Ben, Elkins Park, Philadelphia, 754
Rosen, Theodore, Philadelphia, 754
Rosenbach, Abraham S. W., Philadelphia, 754
Rosenbach, Joseph B., Pittsburgh, 754
Rosenbaum, Leon, Philadelphia, 754

Rosenbaum, Samuel R., Philadelphia, 754
Rosenberg, Albert S., Scranton, 754
Rosenberg, Jacob E., Pittsburgh, 754
Rosenberg, Milton M., Scranton, 755
Rosenberg, Samuel, Pittsburgh, 755
Rosenberger, Randle C., Rahns, 755
Rosenberry, M. Claude, Camp Hill, Harrisburg, 755
Rosenblatt, Maurice C., Philadelphia, 755
Rosengarten, Walter E., Philadelphia, Ardmore, 755
Rosenkrans, Carl B., East Stroudsburg, 755
Rosenthal, Albert, New Hope, 755
Rosenthal, Arthur G., Punxsutawney, 755
Rosenthal, S. Leonard, Philadelphia, 755
Rosenwald, Lessing J., Jenkintown, Philadelphia, 755
Rosewater, Victor, Philadelphia, 755
Rosica, James V., Philadelphia, 756
Rosin, Harry, Philadelphia, 756
Rosoff, Martin A., Philadelphia, 756
Ross, Carmon, Edinboro, 756
Ross, Clarence F., Meadville, 756
Ross, Edgar S., Bala-Cynwyd, Marcus Hook, 756
Ross, F. Clair, Harrisburg, 756
Ross, Fred E., Erie, 756
Ross, George, Doylestown, Philadelphia, 756
Ross, McElwee, McKeesport, 756
Ross, Thomas, Doylestown, 757
Rosser, Edward M., Kingston, 757
Rosskam, William B., Philadelphia, 757
Rossheim, Irving D., Rydal, Philadelphia, 757
Rossiter, Frank S., Swissvale, 757
Rossiter, James P., Erie, Harrisburg, 757
Rossman, John G., Warren, 757
Rotan, Ellwood J., Valley Forge, Philadelphia, 757
Roth, John E., Pittsburgh, 757
Rothermel, Abraham B., Stony Creek Mills, Reading, 758
Rothermel, Amos S., Kutztown, 758
Rothman, Maurice M., Philadelphia, 758
Rothrock, H. H., Forest Hills, Pittsburgh, 758
Rothrock, Col. William P., State College, 758
Roush, Gar A., Bethlehem, 758
Rowan, Charles A., Pittsburgh, Wilmerding, 759
Rowand, Harry H., Pittsburgh, 759
Rowland, Albert S., Shippensburg, 759
Rowland, Charles J., State College, 759
Rowland, Ewart G., Washington, 759
Rowland, Roger W., New Castle, 759
Rowland, Theodore S., Philadelphia, 759
Rowland, Wilfred E., Pittsburgh, Beaver Falls, 759
Rowley, Edith, Meadville, 759
Rowley, George H., Greenville, Mercer, 759
Rowley, Myron E., Aliquippa, 759
Rowley, Thomas J., Vandergrift, 760
Rowntree, Leonard G., Philadelphia, 760
Roxby, John B., Philadelphia, 760
Roy, William M., Towanda, 760
Royer, B. Franklin, Chambersburg, Tunkhannock, 760
Royer, Galen E., Huntingdon, 760
Ruddock, William M., Indiana, 760
Ruddy, John F., Scranton, 760
Rudisill, Earl S., Greenville, 760
Rudolphy, Jay R., Philadelphia, 761
Rue, Francis J., Philadelphia, 761
Ruhe, Percy R., Vera Cruz, Allentown, 761
Ruhl, Charles R., Millmont, 761
Runk, Louis B., Philadelphia, 761
Runkle, Erwin W., State College, 762
Rupert, Frank F., Pittsburgh, 762
Rupley, David R., Bradford, 762
Rupp, Charles A., State College, 762
Rupp, George A., Allentown, 762
Rusca, Felix St. E., Philadelphia, 762
Rush, Benjamin, Kirkland, Philadelphia, 762
Rush, Eugene, Philadelphia, 762
Rush, Raymond W., Oil City, 762

Russ, William A., Jr., Selinsgrove, 762
Russell, Dallmeyer, Pittsburgh, 762
Russell, Frank H., Newtown, 762
Russell, Karl M., Franklin, 763
Ruth, Franklin W., Bernville, 763
Ruth, Stephen E., Philadelphia, 763
Rutherford, Albert G., Honesdale, 763
Rutter, William M., Pine Forge, Philadelphia, 764
Ryan, Hugh J., Bradford, 764
Ryan, John T., Pittsburgh, 764
Ryan, Michael J., Philadelphia, 764
Ryan, Michael J., Mahanoy City, 764
Ryland, Alban S., Pottsville, 764
Ryland, George B., Pittsburgh, 765
Rys, C. F. W., Pittsburgh, 765
Saalbach, Louis, Pittsburgh, 765
Sabatini, Raphael, Philadelphia, 765
Saby, Rasmus S., Gettysburg, 765
Sackett, Robert L., State College, 765
Sacks, Leon, Philadelphia, 765
Sacks, Samuel I., Philadelphia, 765
Sadler, Cornelius R., Beaver Falls, 765
Safford, Elisha, Darby, 765
Safford, Frederick R., Philadelphia, 765
Sagebeer, Joseph E., Berwyn, 766
Sagendorph, Frank E., 2d, Lansdowne, Philadelphia, 766
Saint, Lawrence, Huntingdon Valley, 766
Saint-Gaudens, Homer S., Pittsburgh, 766
Saklatwalla, Beram D., Pittsburgh, 766
Saleeby, Eli R., Philadelphia, 766
Salkeld, Howard B., Zelienople, Conneaut Lake, 766
Salko, Samuel, Philadelphia, 766
Salter, Charles E. W., Franklin, 766
Saltus, Samuel M., Philadelphia, 766
Salzedo, Carlos, Philadelphia, 767
Sample, Paul L., McKeesport, 767
Samson, Harry G., Pittsburgh, 767
Samuel, Bunford, Philadelphia, 767
Samuel, Edmund R., Mt. Carmel, 767
Samuel, Snowden, St. Davids, Philadelphia, 767
Sanborn, G. Walter, Pittsburgh, 767
Sanborn, Walter L., Lansdale, 768
Sanders, Charles F., Gettysburg, 768
Sando, Edwin M., Hanover, 768
Sandston, Leonard M., Pittsburgh, 768
Sandy, William C., Harrisburg, 768
Sanville, Henry F., Melrose Park, Philadelphia, 768
Sappington, Samuel W., Philadelphia, 769
Sartain, Paul J., Philadelphia, 769
Sassaman, Ira S., Williamsport, 769
Satterthwaite, Linton, Jr., Philadelphia, 769
Satterthwaite, William H., Jr., Doylestown, 769
Sauereisen, Christian F., Aspinwall, Pittsburgh, 769
Saul, Maurice B., Moylan, Philadelphia, 769
Saul, Walter B., Philadelphia, 769
Saunders, Lawrence, Bryn Mawr, Philadelphia, 769
Sausser, Irvin E., Valley View, 770
Sautter, Albert C., Philadelphia, 770
Savage, Leona H., Benton, Harrisburg, 770
Savidge, Myron B., Turbotville, 770
Savige, Laurence D., Peckville, Scranton, 770
Sawyer, Paul B., Pocono Lake, 770
Sayers, John C., Reynoldsville, 770
Saylor, Harold D., Philadelphia, 770
Saylor, Melvin A., Philadelphia, 771
Saylor, Owen W., Johnstown, 771
Sayre, Frank G., Philadelphia, 771
Sayres, Gardner A., Lancaster, 771
Scaife, Alan M., Pittsburgh, 771
Scaife, James V., Jr., Pittsburgh, Oakmont, 771
Scanlan, LeRoy J., Johnstown, 771
Scarl, Jackson E., Bethlehem, Harrisburg, Allentown, 771
Scattergood, Alfred G., Philadelphia, 771
Scattergood, J. Henry, Villanova, Philadelphia, 772

PENNSYLVANIA

Schabacker, Martin J., Erie, 772
Schacterle, George K., Philadelphia, 772
Schaefer, Frederic, Pittsburgh, 772
Schaeffer, Asa A., Philadelphia, 772
Schaeffer, Charles E., Philadelphia, 772
Schaeffer, E. Carroll, Reading, 772
Schaeffer, Edwin E., Kittanning, 772
Schaeffer, Harold F., Waynesburg, 772
Schaeffer, Herbert O., Middletown, Harrisburg, 772
Schaeffer, J. Parsons, Philadelphia, 772
Schaeffer, John A., Lancaster, 773
Schaeffer, John N., Lancaster, 773
Schaeffer, Paul N., Reading, 773
Schaeffer, Robert C., Allentown, 773
Schaeffer, William B., Mountaintop, Wilkes-Barre, 773
Schaffer, William I., Haverford, Philadelphia, 773
Schall, R. R., Norristown, Philadelphia, 773
Schaller, Grover L., Harrisburg, 773
Schamberg, Gilbert F., Philadelphia, 773
Schatz, Harry A., Philadelphia, 774
Schatz, William J., Allentown, 774
Schaum, George F., Lancaster, 774
Scheeline, Isaiah, Hollidaysburg, Altoona, 774
Scheeline, Julia S., Hollidaysburg, 774
Scheer, Edward W., Rydal, Philadelphia, 774
Scheffey, Lewis C., Merion, Philadelphia, 774
Scheide, John H., Titusville, 774
Schell, Frank C., Ardmore, 774
Schelling, Felix E., Lumberville, 774
Schenck, Eunice M., Bryn Mawr, 774
Schenck, Harry P., Wynnewood, Philadelphia, 775
Schiedt, Richard C. F., Lancaster, 775
Schifano, Emanuel F., Pittsburgh, Harrisburg, 775
Schildknecht, Page M., Lancaster, 775
Schiller, Morgan B., Sewickley, Pittsburgh, 776
Schindel, Jeremiah J., Philadelphia, 776
Schinz, Albert, Philadelphia, 776
Schlacks, Charles H., Bryn Mawr, 776
Schlegel, Albert G. W., Red Lion, 776
Schlegel, H. Franklin, Easton, 776
Schleicher, George B., Philadelphia, 776
Schlesman, Carleton H., Allentown, 776
Schlosser, Ralph W., Elizabethtown, 777
Schluraff, Helen M., Erie, 777
Schmehl, Luther C., Reading, 777
Schmidt, Carl F., Narberth, 777
Schmidt, Franklin J., Nazareth, 777
Schmidt, Henry D., York, 777
Schmidt, Henry K., Pittsburgh, 777
Schmidt, Otto, Philadelphia, 778
Schmidt, William H., Philadelphia, 778
Schmucker, Samuel C., West Chester, 778
Schnabel, Walter M., Pittsburgh, 778
Schnader, William A., Philadelphia, 778
Schnur, George H., Jr., Erie, 778
Schnure, William M., Selinsgrove, 778
Scholsinger, George, Swarthmore, 778
Schoch, Marion S., Selinsgrove, 778
Schoch, Silas H., Philadelphia, 778
Schoen, Max, Pittsburgh, 778
Schoff, Hannah K., Philadelphia, 779
Schofield, W. Richison, Philadelphia, 779
Scholz, Karl W. H., Media, 779
Schoonmaker, Frederic P., Bradford, 779
Schoonmaker, William P., Philadelphia, 779
Schott, Carl P., State College, 779
Schott, Edwin D., Galeton, 780
Schotte, Karl B., Kittanning, 780
Schrag, William A., Philadelphia, 780
Schramm, Gustav I., Mt. Lebanon, Pittsburgh, 780

Schramm, Henry C., Williamsburg, 780
Schramm, Jacob R., Philadelphia, 780
Schramm, William E., Butler, 780
Schreiner, Samuel A., Mt. Lebanon, Pittsburgh, 780
Schrenk, Helmuth H., Pittsburgh, 780
Schrepfer, Frank A., Narberth, Philadelphia, 780
Schreyer, Charles A., Williamsport, 780
Schroeder, Elmer A., Philadelphia, 781
Schroeder, Elmer F., Philadelphia, 781
Schropp, John K. R., Lebanon, 781
Schuette, Walter E., Sewickley, 781
Schultz, John R., Meadville, 781
Schultz, William C., Waynesboro, 781
Schumaker, Albert J. R., Philadelphia, 782
Schumann, Edward A., Philadelphia, 782
Schutt, Harold S., Philadelphia, 782
Schuyler, Elmer L., Williamsport, 782
Schuyler, William H., Wilkes-Barre, 782
Schwab, Charles M., Bethlehem, Loretto, 782
Schwartz, Edwin G., Allentown, 782
Schwartz, Walter M., Philadelphia, 782
Schwarz, Lawrence T., Greensburg, 783
Schwarz, William T., Merion, 783
Schwarze, William N., Bethlehem, 783
Schweinitz, George E. de, Philadelphia, 783
Schweinitz, Karl de, Philadelphia, 783
Schweitzer, Paul H., State College, 783
Schweizer, J. Otto, Philadelphia, 783
Schwenk, Elwood, Lebanon, 783
Sciotto, Bruce A., Johnstown, 784
Scott, Edgar, Villa Nova, Philadelphia, 784
Scott, Frank D., Jenkintown, 784
Scott, Garfield, Philadelphia, 784
Scott, George S., Pittsburgh, 784
Scott, Henri, Philadelphia, 784
Scott, Herbert, Pittsburgh, 784
Scott, James N., Waynesburg, 785
Scott, John C., Philadelphia, 785
Scott, Joseph P., Langhorne, Bristol, 785
Scott, Kenneth S., Oakbourne, 785
Scott, Margaretta M., Philadelphia, 785
Scott, Merit, State College, 785
Scott, Samuel B., Philadelphia, 785
Scott, Samuel H., Coatesville, 785
Scott, William R., Pittsburgh, 786
Scott, Wirt S., Philadelphia, 786
Scoville, Samuel, Jr., Haverford, Philadelphia, 786
Scranton, Marion M. W., Scranton, 786
Scranton, Worthington, Dalton, Scranton, 786
Scribner, Henry S., Pittsburgh, 786
Scribner, Joseph A., Sewickley, Pittsburgh, 786
Scudder, Townsend, III, Swarthmore, 786
Scully, Cornelius D., Pittsburgh, 786
Seal, Ethel D., Philadelphia, 787
Searles, Thomas M., Philadelphia, 787
Seaton, Lewis H., Chambersburg, 787
Sebring, Lawrence M., Beaver, 787
Sechrist, Elizabeth H., Red Lion, 787
Sechrist, William C., Blossburg, Mont Alto, 787
Seddon, Scott, Haverford, Philadelphia, 787
Seder, Willard J., Swissvale, Rankin, 788
Seegers, John C., Philadelphia, 788
Seely, Leslie B., Philadelphia, 788
Seelye, Theodore E., Ambler, Philadelphia, 788
Segal, Bernard G., Philadelphia, 788
Seibel, George, Pittsburgh, 788
Seibert, Florence B., Philadelphia, 788
Seifriz, William, Chester Springs, Philadelphia, 789
Seil, Gilbert E., Bala-Cynwyd, Norristown, 789

Seilikovitch, Solomon, Philadelphia, 789
Seipp, Alice, Scranton, 789
Seiver, Louis M., Drexel Park, Philadelphia, 789
Sekol, Severin W., Scranton, 789
Selden, Edwin V. D., Oil City, 789
Sellers, Coleman, III, Berwyn, Philadelphia, 789
Sellers, Monroe D., Sellersville, 789
Sellers, Montgomery P., Carlisle, 789
Sellin, Thorsten, Philadelphia, 789
Seltz, Harry, Pittsburgh, 790
Seltzer, Albert P., Philadelphia, 790
Semenow, Robert W., Pittsburgh, 790
Senn, Alfred, Bala-Cynwyd, 790
Sennett, Bernard W., Erie, 790
Sensenich, Chester G., Irwin, 790
Sensenich, Louis E., Irwin, Greensburg, 790
Senter, Ralph T., Philadelphia, 790
Serena, John N., Philadelphia, 790
Sewall, Arthur W., Philadelphia, 790
Seybold, Roscoe, Pittsburgh, 791
Seyfert, Stanley S., Bethlehem, 791
Seymour, Frederick E., Ardmore, 791
Shafer, Glenn M., Carlisle, 791
Shafer, Stewart S., Stroudsburg, Mt. Pocono, 791
Shaffer, Frederick B., Somerset, 791
Shaffer, Isaac A., Jr., Lock Haven, 791
Shaffer, Laurance F., Mt. Lebanon, Pittsburgh, 791
Shaffer, William W., Meadville, 791
Shaler, Charles B., Pittsburgh, 791
Shallcross, Samuel M., Bellefonte, 791
Shallcross, Thomas, Jr., Merion, Philadelphia, 792
Shambach, Jesse Y., Camp Hill, Harrisburg, 792
Shanaman, Forrest R., Reading, 792
Shand, William, Lititz, Lancaster, 792
Shankweiler, Fred L., Allentown, 792
Shankweiler, John V., Allentown, 792
Shannon, Paul E. V., York, 792
Sharfsin, Joseph, Philadelphia, 792
Sharp, Raymond, South Temple, Reading, 793
Sharpe, John M., 3d, Chambersburg, 793
Sharpless, Frederic C., Rosemont, 793
Shattuck, Harold B., State College, 793
Shaw, Arthur E., Philadelphia, 793
Shaw, Charles B., Springdale, 793
Shaw, Charles B., Swarthmore, 793
Shaw, Farnham H., Wellsboro, 794
Shaw, Harold N., Erie, 794
Shaw, John J., Philadelphia, Harrisburg, 794
Shaw, Ralph M., Jr., Philadelphia, 794
Shaw, Reuben T., Philadelphia, 794
Shay, Harry, Philadelphia, 794
Shay, Howell L., Moylan, Philadelphia, 794
Shea, C. Bernard, Pittsburgh, 794
Sheafer, Arthur W., Pottsville, 794
Sheafer, Clifton W., Pottsville, 794
Sheafer, Henry, Pottsville, 794
Sheaffer, Charles M., Wayne, Philadelphia, 795
Sheaffer, Daniel M., Wayne, Philadelphia, 795
Shearer, J. Harry, Altoona, 795
Sheddan, Boyd R., Harrisburg, 795
Shedden, Leon B., Sayre, 795
Sheeder, Franklin I., Jr., Collegeville, 795
Sheedy, Morgan J., Altoona, 795
Sheedy, Morgan M., Altoona, 795
Sheely, W. C., Gettysburg, 795
Sheetz, Ralph A., Mechanicsburg, Harrisburg, Enola, 795
Shelley, Carl B., Steelton, Harrisburg, 796
Shelly, Percy V. D., Glenside, 796
Shelton, Whitford H., Swissvale, Pittsburgh 796
Shenk, Hiram H., Annville, 796
Shenton, Edward, Westtown, Philadelphia, 796
Shepard, Donald D., Pittsburgh, 796
Shepard, Jesse S., Philadelphia, 796
Shepherd, Riley M., Kittanning, 796
Sheppard, Lawrence B., Hanover, 797

Sheppard, Thomas T., Pittsburgh, 797
Sheppard, Walter L., Philadelphia, 797
Sheppard, William H. C., Philadelphia, 797
Shepperson, Sister Mary Fides, Pittsburgh, 797
Sheraw, George F., Altoona, 797
Sherbondy, Henry S., Smithton, 797
Sheridan, John E., Philadelphia, 797
Sherk, Abraham L., Chambersburg, 797
Sherk, Earl J., Shillington, Reading, 797
Sherman, George H. W., Oil City, 797
Sherman, William O., Pittsburgh, 797
Shero, Lucius R., Swarthmore, 798
Shero, William F., Greensburg, 798
Sherriff, John C., Pittsburgh, 798
Sherrill, Richard E., Pittsburgh, 798
Shetlock, William, Coplay, 798
Shibli, Jabir, State College, 798
Shick, Robert P., Philadelphia, 798
Shields, John F., Philadelphia, 798
Shields, Thomas E., Philadelphia, 798
Shigley, James F., State College, 799
Shinn, Owen L., Swarthmore, Philadelphia, 799
Shipley, Charles R., Rosemont, Philadelphia, 799
Shipley, Grant B., Pittsburgh, 799
Shipley, Harold A., Pittsburgh, 799
Shipley, Walter P., Philadelphia, 799
Shipley, William S., York, 799
Shively, Charles S., Huntingdon, 799
Shockley, Frank W., Pittsburgh, 800
Shoemaker, Dora A., Bala-Cynwyd, Philadelphia, 800
Shoemaker, Edna C., Media, 800
Shoemaker, Frank D., Scranton, 800
Shoemaker, Henry W., McElhattan, 800
Shollenberger, Clarence L., Merion, 800
Shollenberger, Darius W., Montgomery, 800
Shoop, Irvin E., Elizabethtown, 801
Shorey, Katherine A., York, 801
Short, Albert, Philadelphia, 801
Short, Samuel M., Port Royal, Mifflintown, 801
Shortess, George S., Elizabethtown, 801
Shortlidge, Jonathan C., West Chester, 801
Shotz, Charles S., Philadelphia, 801
Shoudy, Royal A., Bethlehem, 801
Shreiner, Charles W., Glen Loch, 802
Shreve, Lyman C., Erie, 802
Shreve, Milton W., Erie, 802
Shryock, John K., Philadelphia, 802
Shryock, Joseph G., Philadelphia, 802
Shryock, Richard H., Merion, 802
Shugert, Stanley P., Philadelphia, 803
Shull, George S., Pittsburgh, 803
Shull, Samuel E., Stroudsburg, 803
Shuman, George H., Pittsburgh, 803
Shuman, Warren N., Jersey Shore, 803
Shumberger, John C., Allentown, 803
Shumway, Daniel B., Bryn Mawr, 803
Shumway, Edward A., Merion, Philadelphia, 804
Shuster, Benjamin H., Philadelphia, 804
Shutack, George A., Nesquehoning, Lehighton, 804
Sibbald, Reginald S., Collegeville, 804
Sickman, Albert S., Lock No. 4, 804
Siebert, Christian L., Camp Hill, Harrisburg, 804
Siedle, Theodore A., California, 804
Siegel, Harry L., Lewistown, 804
Siglin, H. O., Shamokin, 805
Sigman, James G., Philadelphia, 805
Sigmund, Benjamin J., Philadelphia, 805
Silin, Isaac J., Erie, 805
Silk, Joseph M., Ingomar, Pittsburgh, 805
Silliman, Harry I., Pottsville, 805

Silsley, John C., Greensburg, 805
Silverblatt, Jacob, Wilkes-Barre, Pittston, 806
Silverman, Alexander, Pittsburgh, 806
Silverman, Isaac H., Philadelphia, 806
Silverman, Meyer H., Rydal, Philadelphia, 806
Silverstone, Seymour S., Johnstown, 806
Simmons, Charles W., Bethlehem, 806
Simmons, Lucretia V., State College, 807
Simon, Edward P., Philadelphia, 807
Simon, Grant M., Philadelphia, 807
Simon, Israel A., Pittsburgh, 807
Simon, Joseph A., Lock Haven, 807
Simons, Erwin W., Mt. Lebanon, Pittsburgh, 807
Simons, Joseph H., State College, 807
Simpson, Alexander C., Philadelphia, 807
Simpson, David W., Indiana, 808
Simpson, F. M., Lewisburg, 808
Simpson, Harold E., Pittsburgh, 808
Simpson, John C., Norristown, 808
Simpson, Warren B., Huntingdon, 808
Sims, Charles A., Philadelphia, 808
Sims, Joseph P., Philadelphia, 808
Simsohn, Julian S., Elkins Park, Philadelphia, 808
Sinclair, John S., Philadelphia, 809
Singer, Edgar A., Jr., Philadelphia, 809
Singley, John D., Pittsburgh, 809
Singmaster, Elsie, Gettysburg, 809
Sinkler, John P. B., Philadelphia, 809
Sinnock, John R., Philadelphia, 809
Sipe, Chester H., Freeport, Butler, 809
Sipes, Dwight R., Everett, 809
Siple, Paul A., Erie, 810
Skariatina, Irina, St. Davids, 810
Skelly, Daniel J., Oil City, 810
Skillern, Samuel R., Jr., Bala-Cynwyd, Philadelphia, 810
Skillington, James E., Bloomsburg, 810
Skillman, David B., Easton, 810
Skillman, Thomas J., Ardmore, Philadelphia, 810
Skinner, Charles E., Wilkinsburg, 811
Skinner, Clifford W., Meadville, 811
Skinner, Laila, Meadville, 811
Skinner, William A., Scranton, 811
Skinner, William S., Philadelphia, 811
Skoss, Solomon L., Philadelphia, 811
Skweir, John, McAdoo, 812
Slack, Norris H., West Chester, 812
Slantz, Fred W., Easton, 812
Slemons, John A., Philadelphia, 812
Slepian, Joseph, Pittsburgh, 812
Slesinger, Hyman A., Windber, 813
Slifer, Henry F., North Wales, 813
Sloan, Marianna, Philadelphia, 813
Sloan, William A., Philadelphia, 813
Sloane, Joseph, Philadelphia, 813
Sloat, Charles A., Gettysburg, 813
Slocum, George W., Milton, 813
Slocum, Stephen E., Ardmore, 813
Slocum, Winthrop W., Wilkinsburg, Pittsburgh, 814
Slosser, Gaius J., Pittsburgh, 814
Smail, Lloyd L., Bethlehem, 814
Small, James C., Ardmore, Philadelphia, 814
Small, Ray A., Lewisburg, Mill Hall, 814
Smathers, Charles B., Scotland, 814
Smeltzer, Clarence H., Glenside, 814
Smeltzer, William C., Bellefonte, 815
Smelzer, Donald C., Bala-Cynwyd, Philadelphia, 815
Smiley, E. Kenneth, Bethlehem, 815
Smiley, Helen A., Philadelphia, 815
Smillie, Frederick B., Gulph Mills, Norristown, 815
Smith, Albert H., Topton, 815
Smith, A. Burton, Wyoming, 815
Smith, Bela B., Kingston, 815
Smith, Carolin H., Ardmore, 815
Smith, Charles C., Bridgeport, 815
Smith, Charles R., Homestead, 816
Smith, Clarence J., Allentown, 816
Smith, Claude C., Swarthmore, Philadelphia, 816
Smith, Edward B., Jr., Edgemont, Philadelphia, 816
Smith, Eliza K., Pittsburgh, 816

Smith, Elva S., Pittsburgh, 817
Smith, Ernest G., Wilkes-Barre, 817
Smith, Ethelbert W., Pittsburgh, 817
Smith, F. Raymond, State College, 817
Smith, Frank W., Butler, 817
Smith, Frederick C., Philadelphia, 817
Smith, Frederick O., Wilkes-Barre, 818
Smith, Geoffrey S., Fort Washington, Philadelphia, 818
Smith, George M. B., Selinsgrove, 818
Smith, George S., Kane, 818
Smith, George V., Ardmore, Philadelphia, 818
Smith, Harold E., Pittsburgh, 818
Smith, Harradon S., Forty Fort, Wilkes-Barre, 818
Smith, Harriet L., Philadelphia, 818
Smith, Harry L., Jersey Shore, 819
Smith, Harvey F., Fort Hunter, Harrisburg, 819
Smith, Harvey H., Pittsburgh, 819
Smith, Henry B., Philadelphia, 819
Smith, Hervey B., Bloomsburg, 819
Smith, Howard W., Ardmore, 819
Smith, Jacob C., Tarentum, 819
Smith, James E., Beaver Falls, 819
Smith, J. Willison, Philadelphia, 820
Smith, John A., Reading, 820
Smith, John F. D., Philadelphia, 820
Smith, John P., Pittsburgh, 820
Smith, J. Russell, Swarthmore, 820
Smith, Lauren H., Bryn Mawr, Philadelphia, 820
Smith, Laurence D., Pittsburgh, McKeesport, 820
Smith, Lawrence W., Huntingdon Valley, Philadelphia, 820
Smith, Lemon L., Johnstown, 821
Smith, Lloyd W., Coraopolis, Pittsburgh, 821
Smith, Louis A., Aliquippa, 821
Smith, Louis C., Harrisburg, 821
Smith, Lynn A., Pittsburgh, 821
Smith, Matthew J. A., Fleetwood, 821
Smith, Maurice A., Jeannette, 821
Smith, Melton A., Oakmont, 821
Smith, Miles W., Jenkintown, Philadelphia, 821
Smith, Oscar F., Boalsburg, State College, 821
Smith, Paul G., Harrisburg, 821
Smith, Ralph C., Baden, Ambridge, 822
Smith, Ralph H., Pittsburgh, 822
Smith, Ralph R., Lansdale, 822
Smith, Robert M., Bethlehem, 822
Smith, Sidney E., Merion, Philadelphia, 822
Smith, Sion B., Bellevue, Pittsburgh, 822
Smith, Theodore F., Pittsburgh, 822
Smith, Thomas B., Philadelphia, 823
Smith, Valentine, Waynesboro, 823
Smith, Wade C., Philadelphia, 823
Smith, W. Hinckle, Bryn Mawr, Philadelphia, 823
Smith, William M., Easton, 823
Smith, William N., Reading, 823
Smith, William S. A., Philadelphia, 823
Smith, William W., Pittsburgh, 824
Smithers, William W., Philadelphia, 824
Smoley, Constantine K., Scranton, 824
Smukler, Max E., Philadelphia, 824
Smyers, Bertrand H., Pittsburgh, 824
Smyth, Callender S., Philadelphia, 824
Smyth, Calvin M., Philadelphia, 824
Smyth, Henry F., Lansdowne, Philadelphia, 824
Smyth, Thomas, Indiana, 825
Smyth, Thomas L., Allentown, 825
Snader, Edward R., Jr., Wynnewood, Philadelphia, 825
Snavely, Benjamin F., Lampeter, Lancaster, 825
Snavely, Edwin R., Stroudsburg, 825
Snell, Henry B., New Hope, 825
Snelling, Walter O., Allentown, 825
Snively, Samuel F., Pittsburgh, 825
Snoke, James S., Leetsdale, 826
Snowden, Chauncey E., Philadelphia, 826
Snowden, Roy R., Mt. Lebanon, Pittsburgh, 826

Snyder, Abram E., New Milford, 826
Snyder, Charles E., Greensburg, 826
Snyder, Claude E., Altoona, 826
Snyder, Corson C., Bethlehem, 826
Snyder, Daniel J., Greensburg, 826
Snyder, Edward D., Haverford, 827
Snyder, Frank E., Liberty, 827
Snyder, Harmon M., Glenside, Philadelphia, 827
Snyder, Harry O., Ben Avon, Pittsburgh, 827
Snyder, Henry S., Bethlehem, 827
Snyder, Irving R., York, 827
Snyder, James W., Slatington, 827
Snyder, Jeremiah G., Port Trevorton, 827
Snyder, J. Buell, Perryopolis, 827
Snyder, Lewis N., Sellersville, Perkasie, 827
Snyder, Luther D., Littlestown, 827
Snyder, Oscar J., Narberth, Philadelphia, 827
Snyder, Peter W., Dormont, Pittsburgh, 828
Snyder, Q. Sheldon, Pittsburgh, 828
Snyder, Walter J., West Philadelphia, 828
Snyder, Warren P., Bristol, 828
Snyder, Wayne L., Brookville, 828
Snyder, William C., Jr., Sewickley, Pittsburgh, 828
Sobel, Isador, Erie, 828
Sobel, Jeffrey M., Erie, 828
Soffel, Sara M., Pittsburgh, 828
Soliday, David S., Merion, Philadelphia, 828
Solis-Cohen, J., Jr., Elkins Park, Philadelphia, 828
Solis-Cohen, Myer, Philadelphia, 828
Sollenberger, Michael E., Waynesboro, 829
Sommer, Henry J., Selinsgrove, 829
Sones, Warren W. D., Pittsburgh, 829
Sorensen, Andrew J., Edgewood, Swissvale, 830
Sorg, John H., Mt. Lebanon, Pittsburgh, 830
Sotter, Alice B., Holicong, 830
Sotter, George W., Phoenixville, 830
Soulen, Henry J., Phoenixville, 830
Souser, Kenneth, Philadelphia, 830
South, Furman, Jr., Pittsburgh, 830
Sowden, Lee, Philadelphia, 830
Spaeth, Edmund B., Philadelphia, 830
Spahr, Boyd L., Haverford, Philadelphia, 831
Spahr, Murray H., Jr., Rosemont, Philadelphia, 831
Spahr, Richard R., Mechanicsburg, 831
Spangler, Charles C., York, 831
Spangler, Cleon P., Pittsburgh, 831
Spangler, Penn S., Bellevue, Pittsburgh, 831
Spare, J. E., Pottstown, 831
Spare, Ralph H., Jr., Pottstown, 831
Spatola, Joseph, Sr., Philadelphia, 832
Speck, Frank G., Swarthmore, 832
Speer, Clyde C., Allison Park, Pittsburgh, 832
Speer, Hugh B., Erie, 832
Speer, J. Ramsey, Pittsburgh, 832
Speer, Joseph A., West Chester, 832
Speicher, John W., Reading, 833
Speight, Francis W., Philadelphia, 833
Speight, Harold E. B., Swarthmore, 833
Speiser, Ephraim A., Philadelphia, 833
Speller, Frank N., Pittsburgh, 833
Spellissy, Frederic F., Philadelphia, 833
Spellmire, Walter B., Pittsburgh, 833
Spence, George K., Johnsonburg, 833
Spencer, Edith L., Huntingdon, 833
Spencer, Herbert L., Pittsburgh, 834
Spencer, Judah C., Erie, 834
Sperring, William F., Lock Haven, 834
Spiegel, Ernest A., Philadelphia, 834
Spiegel-Adolf, Anna S., Philadelphia, 834
Spiller, Robert E., Swarthmore, 834
Spiller, William G., Philadelphia, 835
Spofford, Thomas W., Erie, 835
Spooner, Thomas, Wilkinsburg, East Pittsburgh, 835
Spotts, Charles D., Lancaster, 835
Sprague, Wheeler S., Swarthmore, 836

Spriggs, Joseph C., Washington, 836
Springer, Eva, Philadelphia, 836
Sproul, John R., Chester, Philadelphia, 836
Sproul, Thomas J., Media, Philadelphia, 836
Squier, Harold N., Scranton, 837
St. Peter, Wilfred N., Pittsburgh, 837
Staats, J. Riley, California, 837
Stabler, Evert F., Clairton, 837
Stabler, Walter B., Philadelphia, 837
Stack, Michael J., Philadelphia, 837
Stackhouse, Daniel M., Johnstown, 837
Stackpole, Albert H., Dauphin, Harrisburg, 837
Stackpole, Edward J., Jr., Dauphin, Harrisburg, 837
Stadie, William C., Radnor, 838
Stadtfeld, Joseph, Pittsburgh, 838
Stahl, K. F., Pittsburgh, 838
Stahl, Nicholas, Allentown, 838
Stahler, Horace C., Philadelphia, 838
Stahlman, Thomas M., Pittsburgh, 838
Stainsby, Wendell J., Danville, 838
Stalford, Martin R., Wyalusing, 838
Stamm, John S., Harrisburg, 839
Stamm, Raymond T., Gettysburg, 839
Stanford, Edward V., Villanova, 839
Stang, William H., Allentown, 839
Stanier, Elmer S., Mt. Lebanon, Pittsburgh, 839
Stanley, Clarence, Pittsburgh, 839
Stanton, E. Dean, Westtown, West Chester, 840
Staples, Philip C., Ardmore, Philadelphia, 840
Starr, Edward, Jr., Philadelphia, 840
Starr, Isaac, Philadelphia, 840
Starr, James, Philadelphia, 840
Starrett, C. V., Pittsburgh, 841
Staudenmeier, Charles W., Ashland, 841
Stauffer, B. Grant, Lancaster, 841
Stauffer, Charles M., Bethlehem, Allentown, 841
Stauffer, Edgar E., Reading, 842
Stauffer, Gertrude F., Lancaster, 842
Stauffer, Nathan P., Rosemont, Philadelphia, 842
Stauffer, Randolph, Reading, 842
Stavely, Earl B., State College, 842
Stayer, J. Clyde, Huntingdon, 842
Stead, John, Bethlehem, Easton, 842
Stead, Robert, Philadelphia, 842
Stearne, Allen M., Philadelphia, 842
Stearns, Frederick W., Philadelphia, 842
Stebbins, George E., Pittsburgh, 843
Steber, Raymond W., Warren, 843
Steele, Charles, Northumberland, 843
Steele, David M., Newtown Square, 843
Steele, Donald M., Jenkintown, Philadelphia, 843
Steele, Frank J., Meadville, Lancaster, 843
Steele, Frederick A., Easton, 843
Steele, Joseph M., Philadelphia, 843
Steele, Robert M., California, 843
Steele, Robert T. S., Williamsport, 844
Steele, William, 3d, Philadelphia, 844
Steen, John W., Belle Vernon, 844
Steere, Douglas V., Haverford, 844
Steere, Jonathan M., Haverford, Philadelphia, 844
Steese, James G., Mt. Holly Springs, 844
Steever, Miller D., Easton, 844
Stegeman, Gebhard, Pittsburgh, 844
Steidle, Edward, State College, 844
Stein, James R., Philadelphia, 844
Steiner, Melvin A., Pittsburgh, 845
Steiner, Williams K., Pittsburgh, 845
Steinfurth, Albert W., Wilkinsburg, 845
Steininger, Cloyd, Lewisburg, 845
Steininger, Russell F., Monessen, 845
Steinman, James H., Lancaster, 845
Steinman, John F., Lancaster, 845
Steinmetz, Philip J., Elkins Park, 845
Stellman, Louis H., Drexel Hill, Philadelphia, 845

Stempel, Guido H., Jr., Pittsburgh, 846
Stengel, Frederick W., Lititz, 846
Stengle, Faber A., Collingdale, 846
Stephan, Elmer A., Pittsburgh, 846
Stephano, Constantine S., Elkins Park, Philadelphia, 846
Stephens, Maynard M., State College, 846
Stephenson, Franklin W., Pittsburgh, 846
Sterling, Ernest A., Montrose, 846
Stern, Benjamin S., Philadelphia, 847
Stern, David, 3d, Philadelphia, 847
Stern, Elizabeth G., Media, Philadelphia, 847
Stern, Horace, Philadelphia, 847
Stern, Howard E., Philadelphia, 847
Stern, Julius D., Philadelphia, 847
Stern, Leon T., Media, Philadelphia, 847
Stern, Oscar I., Philadelphia, 847
Sternfeld, Harry, Philadelphia, 847
Sterrett, Frank W., Bethlehem, 847
Sterrett, James R., Pittsburgh, 847
Sterrett, Thomas G., Erie, 848
Stetson, John B., Jr., Elkins Park, 848
Stevens, Richard K., Philadelphia, 848
Stevenson, George B., Lock Haven, 849
Stevenson, John A., Philadelphia, 849
Stevenson, William L., Harrisburg, 849
Stewart, David H., Dormont, 849
Stewart, George A., Clearfield, 849
Stewart, Harold A., Latrobe, 849
Stewart, James R., Philadelphia, 849
Stewart, John L., Washington, 850
Stewart, Paul R., Waynesburg, 850
Stewart, Reid T., Pittsburgh, 850
Stewart, Rowe, Philadelphia, 850
Stewart, William C., Parkers Landing, 850
Stickle, John W., Quakertown, 850
Stiefel, Ralph C., Jr., Ellwood City, 850
Stifler, Francis M., Sewickley, Pittsburgh, 851
Stinchcomb, James, Pittsburgh, 851
Stineman, Oliver M., Johnstown, 852
Stinson, John W., Jr., Pittsburgh, 852
Stirling, Warren, Philadelphia, 852
Stitt, Harry C., York, 852
Stitzel, Jonas W., Hollidaysburg, 852
Stock, Harry B., Carlisle, 852
Stock, McClean, York, 852
Stocker, Frederick P., Bethlehem, 852
Stockton, Charles T., Sharon, 852
Stockwell, John W., Jr., Philadelphia, 853
Stoddard, Alice K., Philadelphia, 853
Stoddard, Harold F., Pittsburgh, 853
Stoddard, William B., Carbondale, 853
Stoddart, Charles W., State College, 853
Stoeber, John B., Greenville, 853
Stofflet, Clinton F., Pen Argyle, 853
Stokes, Claude N., Philadelphia, 853
Stokes, Edward L., Haverford, Philadelphia, 853
Stokes, Francis J., Philadelphia, 853
Stokes, Henry W., Media, 854
Stokes, John H., Philadelphia, 854
Stokes, John S., Huntingdon Valley, Philadelphia, 854
Stokes, Joseph, Jr., Philadelphia, 854
Stokes, Walter, St. Davids, Philadelphia, 854
Stokley, James, Pittsburgh, 854
Stoll, I. V., Rome, 854
Stoltz, Glenn E., Pittsburgh, 854
Stone, Carleton E., Coraopolis, Pittsburgh, 854
Stone, Charles H., South Coatesville, Coatesville, 855
Stone, Charles R., Munhall, 855
Stone, Edmund C., Mt. Lebanon, Pittsburgh, 855
Stone, Elinore C., Pittsburgh, 855
Stone, Elton C., Easton, 855
Stone, Morris D., Pittsburgh, 855
Stone, Ralph W., Harrisburg, 855
Stone, Warren M., Warren, 855
Stone, Witmer, Philadelphia, 855
Stoneback, Robert S., Emmons, 855

Stonecipher, Alvin H. M., Annville, 856
Stonecipher, Frank W., Pittsburgh, 856
Stonehouse, Ned B., Glenside, 856
Stoner, Edward G., Pittsburgh, 856
Stoner, Frank R., Jr., Edgeworth, Pittsburgh, 856
Stoner, James M., Jr., Sewickley, 856
Stonesifer, Joseph R., Stroudsburg, 856
Stonesifer, Paul N., Chambersburg, 856
Storer, Norman W., Pittsburgh, 856
Storey, Douglass D., Carlisle, Harrisburg, 856
Stork, Charles W., Philadelphia, 856
Stotz, Edward, Jr., Pittsburgh, 857
Stoudt, John B., Allentown, 857
Stouffer, Christian S., Pottstown, Stowe, 857
Stoughton, Bradley, Bethlehem, 857
Stout, Charles F. C., Ardmore, 857
Stout, Oliver, Philadelphia, 857
Stout, Wesley W., Ambler, Philadelphia, 857
Stover, Ross H., Philadelphia, 857
Stowell, Jay S., Philadelphia, 858
Stradley, Leighton P., Philadelphia, 858
Straessley, Edward C., Beaver Falls, 858
Stranahan, James A., Mercer, 858
Strassburger, Eugene B., Pittsburgh, 858
Strassburger, Ralph B., Norristown, 858
Strassburger, William J., Pittsburgh, 858
Stratman, Herman, Pittsburgh, Hopewell, 858
Stratton, Alfred J., Stony Creek Mills, Reading, 859
Stratton, John J., Philadelphia, 859
Stratton, Leon D., Ridley Park, Philadelphia, 859
Straub, Howard F., Selinsgrove, 859
Straub, James M., Pittsburgh, McKees Rocks, 859
Straub, Theodore A., Jr., Canonsburg, McKees Rocks, 859
Strauss, Abram, Elkins Park, Philadelphia, 859
Strauss, Jerome, Pittsburgh, Bridgeville, 859
Strawbridge, Anna E., Philadelphia, 859
Strawbridge, Anne W., Philadelphia, 859
Strawbridge, Edward R., Philadelphia, 860
Strawbridge, Frederic H., Philadelphia, 860
Strayer, Lloyd W., New Castle, 860
Streamer, A. Camp, Wilkinsburg, Pittsburgh, 860
Strecker, Edward A., Philadelphia, 860
Streeper, Amanda, Philadelphia, 860
Street, Edward T., Downingtown, 860
Street, J. Fletcher, Philadelphia, 860
Strickland, Charles G., Erie, 860
Strickler, Daniel B., Lancaster, 861
Strickler, Homer H., Hummelstown, Harrisburg, 861
Striegel, John G., Altoona, 861
Strock, Henry B., Lancaster, 861
Strod, Arvid I., Mt. Lebanon, Pittsburgh, 861
Strodach, Paul Z., Gwynedd Valley, Philadelphia, 861
Stroh, Dorothy E., Milford, 861
Strong, George V., Philadelphia, 862
Strong, Nathan L., Brookville, 862
Strong, William W., Mechanicsburg, 862
Stroud, Morris N., Philadelphia, Villanova, 862
Stroud, William D., Villanova, Philadelphia, 862
Stroup, Philip T., New Kensington, 862
Strub, Henry M., Williamsport, 862
Struck, F. Theodore, State College, 863
Strumia, Max M., Bryn Mawr, 863
Stuart, Joseph C., Blairsville, 863
Stuart, Kenneth J., Philadelphia, 863
Stuart, Milton C., Bethlehem, 863
Stuart, Robert L., Allentown, 863
Stubbs, Evan L., Lansdowne, Philadelphia, 864
Stubbs, Ralph S., Philadelphia, 864

Stuck, Harry C., Mifflinburg, Millmont, 864
Stuckert, Howard M., Philadelphia, 864
Stull, Arthur M., Johnstown, Ebensburg, 864
Stull, Howard W., Johnstown, 864
Stump, J. Henry, Reading, 864
Sturgeon, William E., Glenside, 864
Sturges, Lillian, Pittsburgh, 864
Sturgis, Margaret C., Ardmore, Philadelphia, 864
Sturgis, Russell D., Collegeville, 864
Strum, Rolland G., New Kensington, 864
Sturtevant, Charles N., Philadelphia, 865
Sturtevant, Percy G., Erie, 865
Stutzman, Rachel, Bellefonte, 865
Stutz, George F. A., Palmerton, 865
Styer, Freas, Norristown, 865
Styri, Haakon, Philadelphia, 865
Sudell, Harold, Upper Darby, Philadelphia, 865
Sugden, William H., Wilkes-Barre, 865
Sullivan, Francis W., Philadelphia, 865
Sullivan, John J., Philadelphia, 865
Sultzbach, Daniel I., Valley View, 866
Sunderman, F. William, Philadelphia, 866
Sundheim, Harry G., Philadelphia, 866
Sundheim, Joseph H., Philadelphia, 866
Super, John H., Wilkes-Barre, 866
Surdam, Truman A., Scranton, 866
Susman, Milton K., Pittsburgh, 866
Sussman, Samuel, Philadelphia, 866
Sutch, William P., Norristown, 867
Suter, Francis L., Lancaster, 867
Sutherland, Abby A., Ogontz School, 867
Sutherland, Hale, Bethlehem, 867
Sutherland, John B., Pittsburgh, 867
Sutherland, Robert L., Lewisburg, 867
Sutherland, Walter C., West Pittston, Pittsburgh, 867
Sutliff, Stephen D., Shippensburg, 867
Suttle, Clifford B., Bala-Cynwyd, Philadelphia, 867
Sutton, Isaac C., Philadelphia, 867
Sutton, John B., Pittsburgh, 868
Sutton, Thomas, Indiana, 868
Suydam, Richard S., Pittsburgh, 868
Swain, James E., Allentown, 868
Swain, James R., Philadelphia, 868
Swan, Thomas N., Pittsburgh, 868
Swaney, Homer H., Beaver Falls, 868
Swaney, Walter G., Pittsburgh, 868
Swank, Calvin P., Philadelphia, 868
Swann, William F. G., Swarthmore, 869
Swanson, William F., Pittsburgh, 869
Sward, Keith, New Kensington, 869
Swartley, Stanley S., Meadville, 869
Swartz, Aaron S., Norristown, 869
Swartz, Frank M., State College, 869
Swartz, Leon E., Lewistown, 869
Swartz, Morris E., York, 869
Swartzel, Karl D., Pittsburgh, 869
Swayze, George A., Drexel Hill, Philadelphia, 870
Sweadner, Charles A., Pittsburgh, 870
Sweeney, Stephen B., Lansdowne, 870
Sweeny, E. Arthur, Greensburg, 870
Sweet, Alfred H., Washington, 870
Sweet, Ellingham T., Scranton, 870
Sweet, William H., Blairsville, 870
Swick, J. Howard, Beaver Falls, 871
Swift, Archie D., Wayne, Philadelphia, 871
Swift, Clement K., Brookline, 871
Swift, Raymond W., State College, 871
Swigart, Paul J., Alexandria, 871
Swigart, William E., Huntingdon, 871
Swindler, James A., New Wilmington, 871
Swindler, Mary H., Bryn Mawr, 871
Swing, R. Hamill D., Philadelphia, 871
Swiren, David B., Philadelphia, 872
Swope, Charles S., West Chester, 872
Swope, Guy J., Harrisburg, 872
Swope, Joseph R., Johnstown, 872

Swope, Wilbur D., State College, 872
Swoyer, Alfred E., Honesdale, 872
Sykes, Charles H., Bala-Cynwyd, Philadelphia, 872
Sykes, Frank H., Bala-Cynwyd, Philadelphia, 872
Syling, John C., New Castle, 873
Sylvester, Mildred L., Philadelphia, 873
Syme, M. Herbert, Philadelphia, 873
Symonds, Nathaniel G., Pittsburgh, 873
Sztark, Heliodor, Pittsburgh, 873
Tabor, Edward O., Pittsburgh, 874
Taft, Julia J., Flourtown, Philadelphia, 874
Taggart, Marion A., Harrisburg, 874
Taggart, Matthew H., Harrisburg, 874
Taggart, Ralph E., Radnor, Philadelphia, 874
Taitt, Francis M., Chester, Philadelphia, 874
Talbot, Walter L., Philadelphia, 874
Talley, Mabel, Linwood, Marcus Hook, 875
Talley, Randal E., Irwin, Pittsburgh, 875
Talone, Leonard A., Conshohocken, 875
Tanger, Jacob, State College, 875
Tanger, Landis, Millersville, 875
Tanner, Henrietta T., Philadelphia, 875
Tanner, Sheldon C., State College, 875
Tappert, Carl R., Philadelphia, 875
Tarshish, Allan, Hazleton, 876
Tassman, Isaac S., Philadelphia, 876
Tate, John M., Jr., Sewickley, Pittsburgh, 876
Taylor, Allyn C., West Lawn, Reading, 876
Taylor, Charles A., Philadelphia, 876
Taylor, Clement N., Philadelphia, 877
Taylor, Clyde C., Pittsburgh, 877
Taylor, Cyril S., New Kensington, 877
Taylor, Earl H., Swarthmore, Philadelphia, 877
Taylor, Elmer B., Harrisburg, 877
Taylor, Emily D., Philadelphia, 877
Taylor, Francis R., Cheltenham, Philadelphia, 877
Taylor, Freeman P., Llanerch, Philadelphia, 877
Taylor, George, Jr., Wilkinsburg, 877
Taylor, George W., Jenkintown, Philadelphia, 877
Taylor, Gilbert H., New Wilmington, 878
Taylor, H. Birchard, Bryn Mawr, Philadelphia, 878
Taylor, Henry W., Chester, Philadelphia, 878
Taylor, Henry W., Quakertown, 878
Taylor, Joshua C., Chester, 878
Taylor, Katharine H., York, 878
Taylor, Lily R., Bryn Mawr, 879
Taylor, Merritt H., Ardmore, Upper Darby, 879
Taylor, Mills J., Upper Darby, Philadelphia, 879
Taylor, Nelson W., State College, 879
Taylor, Oscar T., Pittsburgh, 879
Taylor, Roland L., Gwynedd Valley, Philadelphia, 879
Taylor, Samuel A., Wilkinsburg, Pittsburgh, 879
Taylor, Thomas G., Westmoreland, Greensburg, 879
Taylor, William R., Lumberville, 880
Taylor, William R., Philadelphia, 880
Teagarden, Florence M., Pittsburgh, 880
Teahan, Roscoe W., Meadowbrook, Philadelphia, 880
Teal, Harvey D., Clairton, 880
Teed, Harold W., West Pittston, 880
Teller, Sidney A., Pittsburgh, 881
Temple, Edward B., Swarthmore, Philadelphia, 881
Temple, Henry W., Washington, 881
Temple, William G., Philadelphia, 881
Templeton, Edwin S., Greenville, 881
Templin, Richard J. W., Dallas, West Pittston, 881

PENNSYLVANIA

Templin, Richard L., New Kensington, 881
Tennent, David H., Bryn Mawr, 881
Textor, Gottleib P., Wilkinsburg, 882
Thackray, George E., Bethlehem, 882
Thatcher, Charles G., Swarthmore, 883
Thayer, Frederick M., Newtown Square, Philadelphia, 883
Thayer, Horace R., State College, 883
Theis, Edwin R., Bethlehem, 883
Theiss, Lewis E., Lewisburg, 883
Thomas, Albert L., Meadville, 883
Thomas, Alfred D., Hazleton, 884
Thomas, Alfred K., Harrisburg, 884
Thomas, A. Russell, Doylestown, 884
Thomas, Donald S., Aspinwall, Pittsburgh, 884
Thomas, Edmund W., Gettysburg, 884
Thomas, Emma E., Philadelphia, 884
Thomas, Harold A., Pittsburgh, 885
Thomas, J. Earl, Philadelphia, 885
Thomas, John F., Sharon, 885
Thomas, John M., Pittsburgh, 885
Thomas, John S. L., Philadelphia, 885
Thomas, Lawrence E., Kittanning, Ford City, 886
Thomas, Lida L., Wayne, 886
Thomas, Perry C., Pittsburgh, 886
Thomas, Stanley J., Bethlehem, 886
Thomas, Theodore, Greensburg, Scottdale, 886
Thomas, Walter, State College, 886
Thomas, Walter H., Merion, Philadelphia, 886
Thomas, Wilbur K., Lansdowne, Philadelphia, 886
Thomas Aquinas, Sister Mary, Immaculata, 886
Thompson, Albert E., Washington, 886
Thompson, Alexander M., Gibsonia, Pittsburgh, 887
Thompson, A. Paul, Pittsburgh, 887
Thompson, Allen D., Carlisle, 887
Thompson, Charles I., Philadelphia, 887
Thompson, C. Seymour, Rutledge, 887
Thompson, Donald, Edgeworth, Pittsburgh, 887
Thompson, Donald C., Meadville, 887
Thompson, Edward J., Philipsburg, 887
Thompson, Elias W., Factoryville, 887
Thompson, F. Raymond, Jr., Philadelphia, 887
Thompson, James G., Middleburg, 888
Thompson, John V., Pittsburgh, 888
Thompson, J. Whitaker, Philadelphia, 888
Thompson, Lorin H., Jr., Pittsburgh, 888
Thompson, Paul, Haverford, Philadelphia, 888
Thompson, Robert M., Harrisburg, 888
Thompson, Russell I., Carlisle, 889
Thompson, Ruth P., West Philadelphia, 889
Thompson, W. Robert, Waynesburg, 889
Thompson, Wm. C., Elkins Park, Philadelphia, 889
Thomson, McLeod, Philadelphia, 889
Thomson, O. R. Howard, Williamsport, 889
Thorington, James, Philadelphia, 889
Thornburg, Charles L., Bethlehem, 890
Thornbury, Sedgley, Huntingdon, 890
Thorne, Thomas R., Greenville, 890
Thornton, E. Quin, Philadelphia, 890
Thornton, Mary B., Philadelphia, 890
Thornton, Thomas A., Pittsburgh, 890
Thorp, Charles M., Pittsburgh, 890
Thrush, Morris C., Philadelphia, 890
Thudium, William J., Haverford, Philadelphia, 890
Thun, Ferdinand, Wyomissing, 890
Thurston, Lee M., Pittsburgh, 891
Thwing, Charles B., Philadelphia, 891

Thwing, John B., Philadelphia, 891
Tibbens, Clyde E., Washington, 891
Tibbens, Perry M., Beech Creek, 891
Tibbott, Harry, Ebensburg, 891
Tideswell, Albert F., Erie, 891
Tiffany, Joseph E., Pittsburgh, 891
Tilberg, Wilbur E., Gettysburg, 892
Tilden, Marmaduke, Jr., Blue Bell, Philadelphia, 892
Tillotson, Edwin W., Pittsburgh, 892
Tilton, Elvin J., Aliquippa, 892
Tily, Herbert J., Bala-Cynwyd, Philadelphia, 892
Tingley, Edrick K., Marietta, 892
Tinker, Wesley R., Sr., Pittsburgh, 893
Tippetts, Charles S., Pittsburgh, 893
Titsworth, William A., Montrose, 893
Titus, Paul, Pittsburgh, 893
Titus, Robert R., Villanova, Oaks, 893
Titzell, George G., Kittanning, 893
Tobias, Clarence E., Jr., Pennsburg, 893
Todd, Chester W., Sunbury, 893
Todd, F. Phelps, Wyncote, Philadelphia, 893
Todd, Kirkland W., Pittsburgh, 894
Todd, Walter E. C., Beaver, Pittsburgh, 894
Tolley, William P., Meadville, 894
Tolmachoff, Innokenty P., Pittsburgh, 894
Tomb, James W., Indiana, 894
Tomlinson, Charles S., Milton, 894
Tomlinson, George M., Philadelphia, 894
Toole, Thomas A., Wilkes-Barre, 895
Toothaker, Charles R., Philadelphia, 895
Topanelian, Edward, Jr., Verona, Pittsburgh, 895
Torrence, Frank M., State College, 895
Toth, Alexander, Lancaster, 895
Tower, Carl V., Collegeville, 895
Town, Charles M., Philadelphia, 895
Towne, Robert D., Philadelphia, 895
Townsend, John M., Beaver Falls, New Brighton, 895
Towson, Charles E., Philadelphia, 896
Trabue, Marion R., State College, 896
Tracy, Lee, Trucksville, 896
Tracy, Martha, Philadelphia, 896
Traister, Harold W., Beaver Falls, 896
Transue, Stanley F., Bethlehem, 896
Tranter, Henry, Pittsburgh, 896
Trasoff, Abraham, Philadelphia, 896
Travaline, Frank M., Jr., Philadelphia, 897
Traylor, Samuel W., Allentown, 897
Traynor, Harold, Pittsburgh, 897
Treder, Oscar F. R., Harrisburg, Bedford, 897
Trees, Joe C., Gibsonia, Pittsburgh, 897
Trescher, Maud B., Jeannette, 897
Tress, John S., Beaver Falls, 897
Tressler, Frank E., New Bloomfield, 898
Trexler, Clifford H., Allentown, 898
Trexler, Frank M., Allentown, 898
Triebold, Howard O., State College, 898
Trigg, Ernest T., Philadelphia, 898
Trimble, Harcourt N., Pittsburgh, 898
Trimble, Thomas P., Pittsburgh, 898
Trinks, Willibald, Pittsburgh, 898
Triplett, John E., Philadelphia, 898
Troth, Celeste H., Philadelphia, 899
Troupe, John F., Pittsburgh, 899
Trowbridge, George A., Philadelphia, 899
True, Rodney H., Philadelphia, 899
Trumbull, Charles G., Philadelphia, 899
Trump, Charles C., Merion Station, Philadelphia, 899
Trump, Rachel B., Merion, 899
Truxal, John C., Lancaster, 900
Tschan, Francis J., State College, 900
Tschudy, Estelle W., Philadelphia, 900
Tubbs, Arthur L., Philadelphia, 900
Tucker, Gabriel, Philadelphia, 900
Tucker, Katharine, Philadelphia, 900
Tucker, Katharine D., Lahaska, 900

Tucker, Raymond A., Pittsburgh, 900
Tuft, Louis, Philadelphia, 900
Tufts, Joseph P., Pittsburgh, 900
Tull, Rudolph F., Bala-Cynwyd, Philadelphia, 901
Tumolillo, Joseph G., Philadelphia, 901
Tupper, James W., Easton, 901
Turck, Chares J., Philadelphia, 901
Turnbull, Margaret, New Hope, 901
Turner, Charles R., Merion, 901
Turner, Creighton H., Philadelphia, 901
Turner, Ellwood J., Media, Chester, 902
Turner, Homer G., State College, 902
Turner, Hulett M., Towanda, 902
Turner, John P., Philadelphia, 902
Turner, Matilda H., Philadelphia, 902
Turner, William J., Philadelphia, 902
Turpin, C. Murray, Kingston, 902
Tuttle, James H., Bryn Mawr, Philadelphia, 902
Tutwiler, Wirt H., Bala-Cynwyd, Philadelphia, 902
Twitchell, Earl W., Philadelphia, 902
Twitmyer, Edward B., Primos, 902
Twitmyer, Edwin B., Secane, 903
Twombly, Clifford G., Lancaster, 903
Tyler, Charles A., Philadelphia, 903
Tyson, Carroll S., Philadelphia, 903
Tyson, Floyd T., Glenside, 904
Tyson, Francis D., Pittsburgh, 904
Tyson, George R., Philadelphia, Collegeville, 904
Tyson, Levering, Allentown, 904
Tyson, Ralph M., Philadelphia, 904
Tyson, William P., Downingtown, West Chester, 904
Ueland, Elsa, Flourtown, 904
Uhle, David J., Allentown, Coplay, 904
Uhler, Stewart M., Easton, Allentown, 905
Ulerich, William K., State College, 905
Ullmann, Harry M., Bethlehem, 905
Ullom, Josephus T., Philadelphia, 905
Ulrich, Elmer B., Drexel Hill, Philadelphia, 905
Umbel, Robert E., Uniontown, 905
Umbreit, Samuel J., Harrisburg, 905
Umsted, John R., Philadelphia, 905
Unangst, Edward J., Nazareth, 905
Uncapher, Andrew G., Greensburg, 905
Underhill, Frederick S., Lansdowne, Philadelphia, 906
Underwood, Roy R., Knox, Oil City, 906
Unger, Sidney E., Melrose Park, Philadelphia, 906
Unger, William H. R., Shamokin, 906
Updegrove, Harvey C., Easton, 906
Upp, John W., Ardmore, Philadelphia, 906
Uppvall, Axel J., Philadelphia, 907
Urban, Walter G., Pittsburgh, 907
Urich, Clair J., Hastings, 907
Urquhart, Paul J., Pittsburgh, 907
Urspring, Charles W., Lancaster, 907
Utley, Frederick B., Pittsburgh, 907
Uttley, William W., Lewistown, 908
Vaccaro, Leopold, Philadelphia, 908
Vail, James G., Media, Philadelphia, 908
Vale, Thomas E., Carlisle, 908
Valentine, Milton H., Gettysburg, 908
Valentine, W. Alfred, Wilkes-Barre, 908
Van Buskirk, Arthur B., Pittsburgh, 909
van de Kamp, Peter, Swarthmore, 909
Vanderbilt, Paul, Philadelphia, 909
Vanderblue, Homer B., Everett, 909
van der Hoeven, Bernard J. C., Mt. Lebanon, Pittsburgh, 909
Vanderkleed, Charles E., Philadelphia, 909
Vanderwort, John, State College, 910
Van Deusen, Henry R., Scranton, 910
Van Deventer, Harry B., Philadelphia, 910
Van Dusen, Lewis H., Philadelphia, 910
Van Dyke, Eugene N., Scranton, 910

Van Dyke, George M., Lansdowne, 910
Van Dyke, J. W., Philadelphia, 910
Van Dyne, Henry B., Troy, 911
Van Etten, Edwin J., Pittsburgh, 911
Van Horn, Rollin W., Media, Philadelphia, 911
Van Houten, Lyman H., Edinboro, 911
Van Laeys, Leon J., Kingston, 911
Van Loon, Emily L., Tacony, Philadelphia, 911
Vann, Robert L., Oakmont, Pittsburgh, 911
Van Sciver, J. Howard, Elkins Park, Philadelphia, 912
Van Sciver, Joseph B., Jr., Philadelphia, 912
Van Sickle, Clarence L., Wilkinsburg, 912
Van Tries, William P., Philadelphia, 912
Van Voorhis, Walter R., Pottsville, 912
Vastine, Jacob H., II, Wynnewood, Philadelphia, 912
Vates, Charles W., Pittsburgh, 912
Vauclain, Samuel M., Rosemont, Philadelphia, 913
Vaughan, Floyd E., Philadelphia, 913
Veenschoten, Vincent V., Erie, 913
Veh, Raymond M., Harrisburg, 913
Venable, Charles S., Wallingford, Marcus Hook, 913
Venable, William M., Pittsburgh, 914
Vernon, Frank L., Philadelphia, 914
Vicary, Arthur C., Erie, 914
Viehoever, Arno, Swarthmore, 914
Vilsack, Carl G., Pittsburgh, 915
Vincent, Henry B., Erie, 915
Vipond, John S., Hollidaysburg, 915
Vittor, Frank F., Castle Shannon, Pittsburgh, 915
Vlachos, Nicholas P., Philadelphia, 916
Voelmle, Herbert S., Philadelphia, 916
Vogleson, John A., Philadelphia, 916
Voigt, Arno C., Hawley, 916
Volpe, Santo, West Pittston, Pittston, 916
Von Bomhorst, William E., Pittsburgh, 916
von der Luft, Oscar, Pittsburgh, 916
Von Elbe, Guenther J. K., Pittsburgh, 916
von Moschzisker, Robert, Philadelphia, 916
Vose, Richard S., Ridley Park, Marcus Hook, 917
Voss, A. Irvin, Drexel Hill, Philadelphia, 917
Voss, Carl A., Pittsburgh, 917
Voss, Elbert, Wilkinsburg, 917
Vuilleumier, Ernest A., Carlisle, 918
Wachter, Henry, Mt. Lebanon, Pittsburgh, 918
Wade, Truman D., Phoenixville, West Chester, 918
Wade. William H., Hollidaysburg, Altoona, 918
Wadsworth, John F., Erie, 918
Wagenhorst, Lewis H., Slippery Rock, 918
Wagers, Arthur J., Philadelphia, 918
Wagner, Charles C., State College, 918
Wagner, Charles F., Swissvale, East Pittsburgh, 919
Wagner, Edward S., Merion, Chester, 919
Wagner, Harvey G., Danville, 919
Wagner, Hobson C., Hollidaysburg, 919
Wagner, J. Ernest, Johnstown, 919
Wagner, Paul C., Paoli, Philadelphia, 919
Wagoner, Claude B., Spring City, Philadelphia, 919
Wagoner, George, Bryn Mawr, 919
Wahl, Arthur M., Wilkinsburg, East Pittsburgh, 919
Wailes, George H., Philadelphia, 919
Waite, Joseph O., Erie, 920
Walbaum, Abraham B., Philadelphia, 920
Waldinger, Fred J., Erie, 920
Waldron, Ralph A., Slippery Rock, 920
Walk, George E., Philadelphia, 921
Walker, Alexander E., Pittsburgh, 921

PENNSYLVANIA

Walker, Arthur M., Gwynedd Valley, Philadelphia, 921
Walker, Elton D., State College, 921
Walker, James F., Westtown, 921
Walker, Robert B., Philadelphia, 921
Wall, Alexander J., Buckhill Falls, 922
Wallace, Earl K., Pittsburgh, 922
Wallace, Robert B., Philadelphia, 922
Waller, Charles B., Wilkes-Barre, 922
Walley, Harold L., New Kensington, 923
Wallhauser, Andrew, Pittsburgh, 923
Wallis, William B., Pittsburgh, 923
Walls, William C., Lewisburg, 923
Walnut, T. Henry, Philadelphia, 923
Walser, Henry, Hazleton, 923
Walsh, Basil S., Bala-Cynwyd, Philadelphia, 923
Walsh, James M., Haverford, Philadelphia, 923
Walsh, John E., Philadelphia, 923
Walsh, Joseph, Philadelphia, 923
Walsh, Lester A., Philadelphia, 924
Walsh, Matthew J., Indiana, 924
Walsh, Richard J., Hilltown, 924
Walsh, Van Wormer, Erie, Philadelphia, 924
Waltemyer, William C., Gettysburg, 924
Walter, Francis E., Easton, 924
Walter, Howard K., Pittsburgh, 924
Walter, Martha, Melrose Park, 924
Walter, Paul C., Harrisburg, 924
Walters, Albert W., Johnstown, 924
Walters, Evan W., Allentown, 924
Walters, John W., Johnstown, 925
Walters, Rea G., Grove City, 925
Waltersdorf, Maurice C., Washington, 925
Walton, Charles S., Jr., St. Davids, Philadelphia, 925
Walton, George A., George School, 925
Walton, George W., Reading, 925
Walton, James F., Pittsburgh, 925
Walton, Joseph T. J., Bellevue, Pittsburgh, 925
Waltz, John B., Ardmore, Philadelphia, 925
Wampole, Harry Z., Telford, 925
Wappat, Blanche K. S., Pittsburgh, 926
Wappat, Fred W., Pittsburgh, 926
Ward, Alger L., Drexel Hill, Philadelphia, 926
Ward, Charles W., Carversville, 926
Ward, Freeman, Easton, 926
Ward, John C., Erie, 927
Ward, Perley E., Wyncote, Philadelphia, 927
Ward, Thomas J., Merion, Philadelphia, 927
Warden, Clarence A., Haverford, Philadelphia, 927
Ware, John H., Jr., Oxford, 927
Ware, Ralph H., Pittsburgh, 927
Warfel, Mary S., Lancaster, 928
Warfield, J. Ogle, Philadelphia, 928
Wargovich, Michael J., Jr., McKeesport, 928
Warner, Alfred du P., Jr., Philadelphia, 928
Warner, Charles, Philadelphia, 928
Warner, Everett L., Pittsburgh, 928
Warner, George C., New Hope, 928
Warner, Irving, Philadelphia, 929
Warner, John C., Milford, 929
Warner, J. C., Pittsburgh, 929
Warner, William, Jr., Philadelphia, 929
Warnock, Arthur R., State College, 929
Warren, Charles B., Ben Avon, Pittsburgh, 929
Warren, George S., Sharon, 929
Warren, Richard J., Devon, Philadelphia, 929
Warren, Robert L., Brockway, 929
Warriner, Samuel D., Montrose, Philadelphia, 929
Warwick, C. Laurence, Wayne, Philadelphia, 930
Warwick, Edward, Philadelphia, 930
Warwick, Ethel H., Philadelphia, 930
Washington, Elizabeth F., Philadelphia, 931
Wassell, Harry B., Pittsburgh, 931
Wasserman, William S., Whitemarsh, Philadelphia, 931
Waterman, Julius L., Bradford, 931
Waters, Robert S., Johnstown, 931

Waterworth, Samuel J., Clearfield, 931
Watkins, Charles, Pittsburgh, 931
Watkins, Donald N., Belle Vernon, Pittsburgh, 932
Watkins, Franklin C., Philadelphia, 932
Watkins, John E., Philadelphia, 932
Watkins, Ralph J., Pittsburgh, 932
Watres, Laurence H., Scranton, 932
Watson, Albert L., Clarks Summit, Scranton, 932
Watson, Bruce M., Wayne, 932
Watson, Charles R., Philadelphia, 932
Watson, Frank D., Haverford, 933
Watson, Frank L., Tionesta, 933
Watson, Frank R., Philadelphia, 933
Watson, Frederick, Philadelphia, 933
Watson, Jesse P., Pittsburgh, 933
Watson, Joseph D., Pittsburgh, 933
Watson, Mabel M., Devon, 933
Watson, Thomas, Pittsburgh, 933
Watt, Charles C., Jr., Philadelphia, 934
Watters, Thomas, Pittsburgh, 934
Watts, Ralph L., State College, 934
Watts, Sidney J., Pittsburgh, 934
Watts, William C., Philadelphia, 934
Waugh, Karl T., Philadelphia, 934
Way, Frederick, Jr., Sewickley, 935
Wayne, Joseph, Jr., Philadelphia, 935
Wear, Joseph W., Penllyn, Philadelphia, 935
Weaver, Albert F., Williamsport, York, 935
Weaver, Alvin M., Williamsport, 935
Weaver, Frederick P., State College, 935
Weaver, J. Kennard, Philadelphia, 935
Weaver, Louis S., York, 935
Weaver, Robert F., St. Clair, 935
Weaver, Ruth H., Philadelphia, 936
Weaver, William A., Wilkes-Barre, 936
Webb, Carleton B., Philadelphia, 936
Webb, Charles G., Wellsboro, 936
Webb, Walter L., Lansdowne, 936
Weber, Alfred H., Ardmore, Philadelphia, 936
Weber, Bernis B., Oil City, 936
Weber, Charles H., Pittsburgh, 936
Weber, Emil W., Pottsville, 937
Weber, John, Pittsburgh, 937
Weber, Samuel E., Pittsburgh, 937
Webster, Steacy E., Pittsburgh, 937
Weeder, Stephen D., Philadelphia, 937
Weeks, Dorothy W., Chambersburg, 938
Weeks, Ralph E., Scranton, 938
Weidlein, Edward R., Pittsburgh, 938
Weiman, Fred D., Llanerch, Philadelphia, 938
Weierbach, John A., Quakertown, 938
Weiler, Royal W., Allentown, 938
Weill, Alfred S., Philadelphia, 939
Weinberg, Max H., Pittsburgh, 939
Weinberger, Nelson S., Sayre, 939
Weingartner, George T., New Castle, 939
Weir, Ernest T., Pittsburgh, 939
Weir, Henry K., Pittsburgh, 939
Weirick, Joseph C., Abington, 939
Weiser, George U., York, 940
Weisgerber, William E., Lancaster, 940
Weiss, David H., Monessen, Greensburg, 940
Weiss, Paul, Bryn Mawr, 940
Weisser, Edward A., Pittsburgh, 940
Weld, Theodore V., Lock Haven, 940
Welday, Henry A., Pittsburgh, 941
Weldin, William A., Pittsburgh, 941
Welker, George E., Oil City, 941
Welker, John S., Greenville, 941
Welles, Henry H., Jr., Mountaintop, 941
Welliver, Judson C., Philadelphia, 941
Wellons, Charles M., Bellevue, Pittsburgh, 941
Wells, George H., Philadelphia, 941
Wells, Roger H., Bryn Mawr, 942
Wells, William F., Media, 942
Welsh, Edward B., Coraopolis, 942
Welsh, George A., Philadelphia, 942
Welsh, Herbert, Philadelphia, 942

Welsh, Robert F., Philadelphia, 942
Wencelius, Leon G., Swarthmore, 942
Wendell, James I., Pottstown, 943
Wendt, Edwin F., New Brighton, Pittsburgh, 943
Wendt, John S., Sewickley, Pittsburgh, 943
Wenner, Thomas J., Wilkes-Barre, 943
Wenrich, Calvin N., Lancaster, 943
Wenrich, David H., Ridley Park, 943
Wentz, Abdel R., Gettysburg, 943
Wentz, Daniel B., Jr., Pineville, Philadelphia, 943
Wentzel, William F. H., Crafton, Pittsburgh, 943
Werner, Edwin H., Sinking Spring, Reading, 943
Werner, William L., State College, 944
Wert, Wilson A., Allentown, 944
Werth, Matthew F. M., Allentown, 944
Wescott, Blaine B., Oakmont, Pittsburgh, 944
Wescott, Paul, Pottstown, 944
Weshner, David E., Philadelphia, 944
Wesley, Charles S., Philadelphia, 944
West, Arthur, Bethlehem, 945
West, John H., Easton, 945
West, Stanley R., Conshohocken, 945
West, William B., Huntingdon, 945
West, W. Nelson L., Wynnewood, Philadelphia, 945
Westburgh, Edward M., Lansdowne, Philadelphia, 945
Westermaier, Francis V., Philadelphia, 945
Weston, Charles S., Scranton, 945
Westphal, Edward P., Philadelphia, 946
Wetherill, Robert, Jr., Chester, 946
Wetherill, Samuel P., Philadelphia, 946
Wetherill, William C., Philadelphia, 946
Wetjen, Harry C., Scranton, 946
Wetmore, Edward C., Warren, 946
Wettach, Charles D., Pittsburgh, 946
Wetter, Charles H., Bryn Mawr, Philadelphia, 946
Wetzel, Walter, Philadelphia, 946
Weyer, Edward M., Washington, 946
Weygandt, Cornelius, Philadelphia, 946
Weyl, Carrie S., Philadelphia, 947
Weyl, Charles, Philadelphia, 947
Weyl, Woldemar A., State College, 947
Whalen, Will W., Orrtanna, 947
Wheatley, William A., Edinboro, 948
Wheaton, Warren W., Philadelphia, 948
Wheeler, Anna P., Bryn Mawr, 948
Wheeler, Frederic C., Wynnewood, Philadelphia, 948
Wheeler, Herbert E., Philadelphia, 948
Wheeler, Janet, Philadelphia, 948
Wheeler, John F., Carbondale, 948
Wheelwright, Robert, Philadelphia, 948
Whelan, George L., Philadelphia, 948
Whelen, John H., Jr., Philadelphia, 948
Wherrett, Harry S., Pittsburgh, 948
Wherry, Edgar, Swarthmore, 949
Whetstone, Walter, Philadelphia, 949
Whitaker, Arthur P., Philadelphia, 949
White, Allen H., St. Davids, Philadelphia, 949
White, Barclay, Lansdowne, Philadelphia, 949
White, Beaver, Villanova, Philadelphia, 949
White, Edith G., Chambersburg, 950
White, Elizabeth B., Shepherdstown, Collegeville, 950
White, Harold E., Zelienople, 950
White, Jonathan W., State College, 951
White, Marsh W., State College, 951
White, Robert M., New Castle, 951
White, Robert V., Scranton, 951
White, Thomas R., Penllyn, Philadelphia, 951
White, Wallace E., State College, 951

White, Walter R., Westtown, Lansdowne, 951
White, William R., State College, 951
White, William W., Philadelphia, 951
Whitehead, Harvey F., Yardley, 952
Whitehead, Howard H., Manor, Greensburg, 952
Whitehill, Buell B., Uniontown, 952
Whitehill, Cyrus G., Oil City, 952
Whitely, Paul L., Lancaster, 952
Whiteman, Thomas M., Latrobe, 953
Whiting, Anna R., Philadelphia, 953
Whiting, John T., Radnor, Conshohocken, 953
Whiting, Louis E., Meadville, 953
Whitinger, Frederick T., Pittsburgh, East Pittsburgh, 953
Whitman, Edwin A., Pittsburgh, 953
Whitmarsh, David C., Pittsburgh, 953
Whitmore, Frank C., State College, 953
Whitney, E. Arthur, Elwyn, 954
Whitney, Gerald D., Pittsburgh, 954
Whitney, Philip R., Moylan, 954
Whitney, Will A., Philadelphia, 954
Whitsit, Lyle A., Swarthmore, 954
Whittaker, Clyde M., New Castle, 954
Whitten, Charles E., Greensburg, 955
Whitten, Thomas E., Wilkinsburg, Pittsburgh, 955
Whittlesey, Federal E., Corry, 955
Wholey, Cornelius C., Pittsburgh, 955
Wible, Elmer E., Edgewood, Homestead, 955
Wible, Robert E., Gettysburg, 955
Wick, George D., Pittsburgh, 955
Wickersham, Frank B., Harrisburg, 955
Wickersham, John H., Lancaster, 956
Wickline, Robert L., Mt. Lebanon, Pittsburgh, 956
Wicks, Elverton H., Bellevue, Pittsburgh, 956
Wicks, John O., Bellevue, Pittsburgh, 956
Widener, George D., Philadelphia, 956
Widener, Joseph E., Philadelphia, 956
Wiesen, Louis J., Sharon, 957
Wiest, William I., Shamokin, 957
Wiest, William J., Shamokin, 957
Wiggins, William D., Merion, Philadelphia, 957
Wigman, Harry F., Pittsburgh, 957
Wikander, Oscar R., Pittsburgh, Oakmont, 957
Wilcox, Clair, Swarthmore, 957
Wilcox, Emily, Scranton, 958
Wilcox, William J., Allentown, 958
Wilde, Bertram M., Philadelphia, 958
Wilde, Earle I., State College, 958
Wilder, Henry L., Lebanon, 958
Wildes, Harry E., Valley Forge, Philadelphia, 958
Wiles, Charles F., Philadelphia, 959
Wiley, Roy W., Butler, 958
Will, Homer C., Huntingdon, 959
Willaman, John J., Bristol, 959
Willard, Bradford, Bethlehem, 959
Willard, DeForest F., Bryn Mawr, Philadelphia, 959
Willcox, Joseph T., Wawa, Philadelphia, 959
Willet, Anne L., Philadelphia, 960
Willet, Henry L., Ambler, Philadelphia, 960
Willetts, Ernest W., Verona, Pittsburgh, 960
Willging, Eugene P., Scranton, 960
Williams, Albert S., Philadelphia, 960
Williams, Alford J., Jr., Pittsburgh, 960
Williams, Alfred H., Wallingford, Philadelphia, 960
Williams, Alvin J., Mt. Lebanon, Pittsburgh, 960
Williams, Benjamin H., Pittsburgh, 961
Williams, Charles A., Pittsburgh, 961
Williams, Clarence O., State College, 961
Williams, Clement C., Bethlehem, 961
Williams, David G., Allentown, 961
Williams, Edmund, Philadelphia, 961

PENNSYLVANIA

Williams, Edward R., Latrobe, 961
Williams, Edwin B., Philadelphia, 961
Williams, Elmer G., Ridgway, 961
Williams, Frank E., Swarthmore, Philadelphia, 962
Williams, Frank H. M., Bala-Cynwyd, 962
Williams, Franklin G., Swarthmore, Chester, 962
Williams, George P., Swarthmore, 962
Williams, Horace J., Philadelphia, 962
Williams, Horace O., Lansdale, 962
Williams, Ira J., Philadelphia, 963
Williams, James P., Jr., Pittsburgh, 963
Williams, John E., Scranton, 963
Williams, Marshall, Pittsburgh, 963
Williams, Percy, Pittsburgh, 963
Williams, Philip F., Philadelphia, 963
Williams, Samuel H., Pittsburgh, 964
Williams, Sidney C., Philadelphia, 964
Williams, W. Gordon, Forty Fort, Wilkes-Barre, 964
Williamson, Clarence J., Pittsburgh, 964
Williamson, E. B., York, 964
Williamson, Oliver R., Philadelphia, 964
Williamson, Willie C., Philadelphia, 964
Willigerod, Alice, Hazleton, 964
Willing, John T., Henryville, 965
Willison, James R., Pittsburgh, Wilkinsburg, 965
Willits, Joseph H., Swarthmore, 965
Willman, Leon K., Wilkes-Barre, 965
Willock, Charles E., Pittsburgh, 965
Willson, Edward A., Sharon, 965
Wilmeth, James L., Upper Darby, 965
Wilson, Albert H., Haverford, 965
Wilson, Arthur H., Selinsgrove, 966
Wilson, Benjamin J., Philadelphia, 966
Wilson, David W., Wynnewood, 966
Wilson, Don M., Pittsburgh, 966
Wilson, Edwin M., Philadelphia, 966
Wilson, Ernest C., Chester, 966
Wilson, Findley M., Philadelphia, 966
Wilson, George R., Haverford, Philadelphia, 966
Wilson, G. Lloyd, Philadelphia, 966
Wilson, Harry R., Clarion, 967
Wilson, Henry I., Big Run, 967
Wilson, Howard M., Pittsburgh, McKees Rocks, 967
Wilson, Howard R., Carnegie, 967
Wilson, J. E., Pittsburgh, 967
Wilson, John G., Factoryville, 967
Wilson, John R., Butler, 967
Wilson, John H., Easton, 967
Wilson, John M., Pittsburgh, 967
Wilson, Joseph J., Philadelphia, 967
Wilson, Joseph R., Philadelphia, 967
Wilson, Lytle M., Aliquippa, 968
Wilson, Norman W., Erie, 968
Wilson, Paul H., New Castle, 968
Wilson, Philip J., Jr., Pittsburgh, 968
Wilson, Robert L., Pittsburgh, 968
Wilson, Robert M., Narberth, Philadelphia, 968
Wilson, Samuel M., Philadelphia, 969
Wilson, Samuel T., Easton, 969
Wilson, Theophilus L., Clarion, 969
Wilson, William R., Ben Avon, 969
Winchell, Alexander V., Wynnewood, Philadelphia, 969
Winchester, Edith M., Pittsburgh, 969
Winder, Ambrose J., Philadelphia, 970
Windisch, Reuben, Philadelphia, 970
Windle, William B., West Chester, 970
Wine, Edgar P., Greencastle, Waynesboro, 970
Wing, Herbert, Jr., Carlisle, 970

Wingerd, Charles B., New Castle, 970
Wingerd, Edmund C., Chambersburg, 970
Winner, Harry E., Pittsburgh, 970
Winslow, Eugene H., Punxsutawney, 970
Winsor, James D., Jr., Ardmore, Philadelphia, 971
Winter, Emil, Pittsburgh, 971
Winter, John C., Williamsport, 971
Wirt, George H., Camp Hill, Harrisburg, 971
Wise, John L., Butler, 971
Wise, John S., Jr., Allentown, 971
Wishart, John M., Carnegie, 971
Wishart, William L., Sharon, 971
Wister, John C., Philadelphia, 972
Witherow, William P., Pittsburgh, 972
Withers, Robert E., Pittsburgh, 972
Witman, John, Reading, 972
Witmer, Charles H., Lancaster, 972
Witmer, Francis P., Bala-Cynwyd, Philadelphia, 972
Witmeyer, Paul E., Shamokin, 972
Wohl, Michael G., Philadelphia, 972
Wolf, David O., Irwin, Apollo, 973
Wolf, Irwin D., Aspinwall, Pittsburgh, 973
Wolf, William A., Lancaster, 973
Wolfe, Bernard C., Towanda, 973
Wolfe, Bertram K., Philadelphia, 973
Wolfe, Edward I., Forty Fort, 973
Wolfe, Frank B., Pittsburgh, 973
Wolfe, Oliver H., Radnor, Philadelphia, 973
Wolfe, Russell, St. Davids, Philadelphia, 973
Wolfenden, James, Upper Darby, 974
Wolferth, Charles C., Merion, 974
Wolff, Charles E., Waynesboro, 974
Wolfe, Joseph B., Philadelphia, 974
Wolfrom, Ralph T., Shippensburg, 974
Wolgemuth, Daniel M., Florin, 974
Wolk, Samuel, Wilkes-Barre, 974
Wollak, Theodore, Torrance, 974
Wolsey, Louis, Elkins Park, Philadelphia, 974
Woner, George I., Butler, 974
Wonsetler, John C., Moylan, 974
Wood, Alan, 3d, Bryn Mawr, 975
Wood, Albert G., Grove City, 975
Wood, Alfred C., Philadelphia, 975
Wood, Augustus I., Wayne, Philadelphia, 975
Wood, Edith L., Philadelphia, 975
Wood, Edmund B. M., Philadelphia, 975
Wood, Eric F., Bedford, Pittsburgh, 975
Wood, Francis C., Haverford, Philadelphia, 975
Wood, Harold B., Harrisburg, 976
Wood, Horatio C., Philadelphia, 976
Wood, Thomas, Muncy, Williamsport, 976
Woodbury, Wesley K., Pottsville, 976
Woodcock, William I., Jr., Philadelphia, 977
Woodring, Edwin S., Allentown, 977
Woodruff, Clinton R., Philadelphia, 977
Woodruff, Eugene C., State College, 977
Woodruff, John I., Selinsgrove, 977
Woodruff, Wesley E., Wilkes-Barre, 977
Woods, Charles A., Sewickley, Pittsburgh, 978
Woods, Eugene, Sligo, 978
Woods, Robert W., Pittsburgh, 978
Woods, William J., Lewistown, 978
Woodside, Robert E., Jr., Millersburg, Harrisburg, 978
Woodward, George, Philadelphia, 979
Woodward, Graham C., Philadelphia, 979
Woody, Walter T., Upper Darby, 979

Woolever, Harry, Philadelphia, 979
Woolley, Herbert C., Philadelphia, 980
Woolman, Henry N., Ardmore, Philadelphia, 980
Woolworth, Charles S., Scranton, 980
Woolworth, Chester M., Lancaster, Lititz, 980
Wooster, Harold A., Scranton, 980
Worden, Charles B., Philadelphia, 980
Work, William R., Pittsburgh, 980
Worker, Joseph G., Jenkintown, 981
Worthing, Archie G., Pittsburgh, 981
Worthington, Arthur W., Pittsburgh, 981
Worthington, Charles C., Shawnee-on-Delaware, 981
Worthley, Harlan N., State College, 981
Wotring, Clayton W., Nesquehoning, 981
Wray, Chester B., Altoona, 981
Wright, Albert B., Pittsburgh, 981
Wright, Alexander H., Washington, 982
Wright, Alfred E., Uniontown, 982
Wright, Bruce S., Erie, Kane, 982
Wright, Carroll S., Wynnewood, Philadelphia, 982
Wright, Catharine M., Glenside, 982
Wright, Charles A., Ardmore, 982
Wright, Gifford K., Sewickley, Pittsburgh, 982
Wright, Guier S., Bryn Mawr, 983
Wright, Horace W., Bethlehem, 983
Wright, Isaac M., Allentown, 983
Wright, J. Merrill, Pittsburgh, 983
Wright, Katharine H. L., Erie, 983
Wright, Richard R., Philadelphia, 983
Wright, Ross P., Erie, 983
Wright, Sydney L., Glenside, Philadelphia, 984
Wright, Walter L., Lincoln University, 984
Wright, W. A. Earl, Shippensburg, 984
Wright, William J., Philadelphia, 984
Wright, Winthrop R., Swarthmore, 984
Wunder, Clarence E., Ardmore, Philadelphia, 984
Wurdack, John H., Pittsburgh, 985
Wurts, Charles S., Jr., Philadelphia, 985
Wurzbach, J. A., Erie, 985
Wyeth, Newell C., Chadds Ford, 985
Wylie, James B., Washington, 985
Wylie, James B., Jr., Wilkinsburg, Pittsburgh, 985
Wyman, Levi P., Chester, 985
Wynn, I. N. Earl, West Chester, 985
Wynn, James H., Haverford, Philadelphia, 985
Wynn, John S., Merion, Philadelphia, 985
Yaeger, Christian G., Philadelphia, 985
Yahres, John M., Bellevue, Pittsburgh, 985
Yant, William P., Pittsburgh, 986
Yarnall, Charlton, Devon, Philadelphia, 986
Yarnall, D. Robert, Philadelphia, 986
Yarnall, Stanley R., Philadelphia, 986
Yates, Cullen, Shawnee-on-Delaware, 986
Yates, Henry A., Pittsburgh, 986
Yates, William O., Swissvale, 986
Yeager, William J., Pittsburgh, 986
Yealy, Dorsey W., Pittsburgh, 986
Yeany, Ralph W., Meadville, 987
Yerick, Ralph O., Wilkinsburg, Wilnerding, 987
Yeatman, Georgina P., Philadelphia, 987
Yeatman, Pope, Philadelphia, 987
Yeaworth, Irvin S., Homestead, 987
Yellin, Samuel, Wynnewood, Philadelphia, 987

Yensen, Trygve D., Pittsburgh, East Pittsburgh, 987
Yeomans, Earl R., Philadelphia, 987
Yingling, Herbert F., Burnham, Lewistown, 987
Yoakam, Gerald A., Pittsburgh, 987
Yoder, Paul D., Codorus, 987
Yohe, Curtis M., Pittsburgh, 988
Yohlin, Mordecai, Philadelphia, 988
Yolles, Ephraim E., Philadelphia, 988
York, Harlan H., Philadelphia, 988
York, Minnie T., Philadelphia, 988
Yorke, Edward W., Oil City, 988
Yost, Calvin D., Collegeville, 988
Yost, Gaylord, Pittsburgh, 988
Young, Barton R., Philadelphia, 989
Young, Charles D., Haverford, Philadelphia, 989
Young, Charles F., East Pittsburgh, 989
Young, Charles M., Radnor, 989
Young, Charles R., Coatesville, 989
Young, Edgar C., Philadelphia, 989
Young, J. Elmer, Petersburg, 989
Young, James H., Pittsburgh, 990
Young, James T., Philadelphia, 990
Young, Joseph S., Allentown, 990
Young, Robert A., Allentown, 990
Young, William R., State College, 990
Youngman, John C., Williamsport, 990
Yount, John A., Pittsburgh, Mayview, 990
Yuengling, Frank D., Pottsville, 990
Yuengling, Joseph P., Harrisburg, 991
Yuster, Samuel T., State College, 991
Zabriskie, Abram J., Stroudsburg, East Stroudsburg, 991
Zahniser, Charles R., Pittsburgh, 991
Zahniser, William J., Pittsburgh, 991
Zange, Otto A., McKees Rocks, 991
Zantzinger, Clarence C., Philadelphia, 991
Zappala, Frank J., Pittsburgh, 991
Zartman, Ira F., Allentown, 991
Zeigler, Earl F., Narberth, Philadelphia, 991
Zeitlin, Solomon, Philadelphia, 991
Zeller, Samuel C., Nazareth, Bethlehem, 991
Zentmayer, William, Merion, Philadelphia, 992
Zerbe, Amos W., Tremont, Pottsville, 992
Zerbe, Farran, Tyrone, 992
Zetlin, Emanuel R., Philadelphia, 992
Ziegler, Howard G., Mt. Lebanon, Pittsburgh, 992
Ziegler, Louis C., Bethlehem, 992
Ziegler, Percival T., State College, 992
Ziegler, Samuel H., Allentown, 992
Ziemer, Harry S., Adamstown, 992
Zimmerman, Charles F., Huntingdon, 992
Zimmerman, Charles S., Wilkinsburg, Pittsburgh, 992
Zimmerman, Elinor C., Philadelphia, 992
Zimmerman, Frederic W., Wynnewood, Philadelphia, 993
Zimmerman, O., Mt. Lebanon, Pittsburgh, 993
Zimmerman, W. F., Norristown, 993
Zimmermann, George F., Philadelphia, 993
Zimmermann, John E., Philadelphia, 993
Zinn, John B., Gettysburg, 993
Zinsser, John S., Bryn Mawr, Philadelphia, 993
Zirke, Conway, Philadelphia, 993
Zoller, Edwin W., DuBois, 993
Zook, Ralph T., Bradford, 993
Zuerner, Frank D., North Braddock, 994
Zugsmith, Robert, Pittsburgh, 994
Zundel, George L. I., State College, 994

WEST VIRGINIA

Abersold, George W., Wheeling, 2
Adams, Earl D., Wheeling, 3
Adams, Herbert C., Parkersburg, 3
Albert, Charles E., Elkins, 6
Alderson, Joseph N., Charleston, 7
Aldrich, Moriel S., Charleston, 7

Alexander, Andrew S., Charleston, 8
Alexander, George M., Fairmont, 8
Alexander, William F., Charles Town, 8
Allebach, Leroy, Charleston, 9
Allen, Fred C., Marlinton, 10

Allen, Howard B., Morgantown, 10
Allen, James E., Huntington, 10
Allen, Wilbert M., Wheeling, 11
Allen, William W., South Charleston, Charleston, 11
Ambler, Charles H., Morgantown, 12

Ambler, Mason G., Parkersburg, 13
Anderson, Henry R., Charleston, 15
Anderson, Randolph L., Charleston, 15
Anderson, William B., Jr., Huntington, 16

WEST VIRGINIA

Angel, Philip, Charleston, 18
Arbuckle, Howard B., Maxwelton, 20
Archer, Charles H., Athens, Princeton, 21
Armentrout, Aubrey W., Martinsburg, 21
Armentrout, Walter W., Morgantown, 21
Arnold, Arthur, Piedmont, 22
Arnold, D. H. Hill, Elkins, 23
Ashworth, Ben H., Beckley, 25
Aspinall, Richard, Morgantown, 25
Atwood, Horace, Morgantown, 27
Avis, S. B., Charleston, 28
Bachmann, Carl G., Wheeling, 29
Bacon, Frank N., Fayetteville, 30
Bacon, Lee F., Huntington, 30
Baer, Ira P., Huntington, 31
Bailey, R. D., Pineville, 33
Bailey, Russell B., Wheeling, 33
Baker, Charles G., Morgantown, 34
Baker, John M., Spencer, 35
Baker, William E., Elkins, 36
Baldwin, Robert D., Morgantown, 38
Banner, Roy R., Logan, 40
Barker, Oliver D., Parkersburg, 42
Barnes, Arnold A., Charleston, 43
Beans, Robert T., Wheeling, 54
Beckwith, Frank J., Charles Town, 56
Bell, Robert P., Point Pleasant, Grafton, 60
Bell, Samuel P., Spencer, 60
Beneke, George C., Wheeling, 61
Benfield, William A., Sinks Grove, 62
Bennett, Carey M., Glenville, 62
Bennett, Isaac L., Franklin, 63
Bennett, Lyle H., Charleston, 63
Bergy, Gordon A., Morgantown, 65
Bess, Thomas, Keyser, 67
Bias, Randolph, Williamson, 68
Black, Albert F., Hamlin, 74
Black, W. P., Charleston, 75
Blackford, George A., Wheeling, 75
Blackwell, Ashby C., Charleston, 76
Blackwood, Edwin N., Charleston, 76
Blagg, Donald O., Charleston, 76
Bland, Robert, Logan, 78
Blanton, James L., Fairmont, 78
Blaydes, James E., Bluefield, 79
Bleininger, Albert V., Newell, 79
Blessing, Riley A., Charleston, 79
Blizzard, Reese, Parkersburg, 80
Bloch, Jesse A., Wheeling, 80
Bloss, James R., Huntington, 80
Blue, Frederick O., Charleston, 81
Blue, William F., Charleston, 81
Blundon, Joseph P., Keyser, 81
Bobbitt, Lee O., Summersville, 82
Bobbitt, Ray M., Huntington, 82
Boggs, L. G., Fairmont, 83
Bomberger, John H. A., II, Wheeling, 84
Bond, Harley D., Salem, 84
Bond, Sirus O., Salem, 85
Bonnesen, Charles H., Wheeling, 85
Boomsliter, George P., Morgantown, 86
Booth, Leland, Morgantown, 86
Booth, Osborne, Bethany, 86
Bouchelle, J. F., Charleston, 88
Bowen, Harry Freeman, 89
Bowers, Elsworth V., Huntington, 89
Bowie, William C., Point Pleasant, 90
Bracey, Altamont H., Welch, 94
Brackett, William S., South Charleston, 94
Bradford, Thomas N., Wheeling, Triadelphia, 94
Bradley, Joseph G., Dundon, 95
Brady, Alfred S., Jr., Charleston, 96
Brammer, Fred E., Huntington, Dehue, 96
Brand, Franklin M., Morgantown, 97
Brannan, Dorsey, Morgantown, 97
Brast, Edwin A., Parkersburg, 98
Brennan, John H., Wheeling, 100
Brewster, William, Charleston, 101
Bridges, Henry P., Berkeley Springs, 101
Brile, Lawrence M., Fairmont, 102
Broaddus, Randolph G., Hinton, Beckley, 104
Brooke, Francis J., Jr., Charleston, 105
Brooks, Alonzo B., Wheeling, 106
Brooks, William E., Morgantown, 106
Brouzas, Christopher G., Morgantown, 107
Brown, Benjamin B., Charleston, 108
Brown, James R., Huntington, 110
Brown, John F., Elkins, 110
Brown, Martin, Moundsville, 111
Brown, Ralph C., Buckhannon, 111
Brown, William A., Hinton, 113

Brown, William G., Summersville, 113
Brugh, Benjamin F., Montgomery, 114
Bruns, William F., Ceredo, 115
Buckey, William E., Fairmont, 117
Buford, Robert K., Charleston, 119
Burgess, Frances C., Huntington, 121
Burt, David A., Wheeling, 124
Bush, R. G., Elkins, 125
Butts, Henry P., Charleston, 128
Byrer, Harry H., Martinsburg, 128
Byrne, Amanda A., Charleston, 128
Byrnside, Marshall A., Madison, 128
Cabell, Charles A., Charleston, Carbon, 129
Cadden, Anthony V., Hopemont, 129
Caldwell, Joseph R., Wheeling, 130
Caldwell, William A., Wheeling, 130
Calhoun, Harlan M., Moorefield, 130
Callaghan, Glenn S., Charleston, 130
Callahan, James M., Morgantown, 130
Campbell, John E., Charleston, 132
Campbell, Rolla D., Huntington, 133
Campbell, Strother A., Charleston, 133
Canady, Herman G., Institute, 133
Cannaday, John E., Charleston, 134
Carlin, Leo, Morgantown, 136
Carney, Chesney M., Clarksburg, 137
Carter, Carl J., Fairmont, 139
Cato, Henry S., Charleston, 143
Cavins, Lorimer V., Charleston, 144
Chambers, Bernard B., Beckley, 145
Chambers, Chester C., Logan, 145
Chambers, Orlando C., Madison, 145
Charter, Lena M., Ravenswood, Charleston, 148
Chilton, William E., Jr., Charleston, 151
Chitwood, Oliver P., Morgantown, 152
Chrisman, Lewis H., Buckhannon, 152
Christie, Samuel A., Keystone, 152
Christie, Sidney L., Keystone, 152
Churchman, Vincent T., Jr., Charleston, 154
Clagett, Thomas H., Bluefield, 154
Clark, Friend E., Morgantown, 155
Clark, Hubert G., Williamson, 155
Clark, Lawrence E., Bethany, 156
Clark, T. S., Charleston, 156
Clark, Walter E., Charleston, 156
Clendenin, J., Huntington, 159
Cline, William P., Charleston, 160
Clinton, James B., Fairmont, 160
Clovis, Elijah E., Wheeling, 161
Coffey, Aubrey J., Logan, 163
Cole, Delbert E., Ravenswood, 165
Cole, Irving D., Clarksburg, 165
Coleman, James E., Fayetteville, Gauley Bridge, 166
Coleman, William S., Lewisburg, 167
Collett, Armand R., Morgantown, 167
Colwell, Robert C., Morgantown, 169
Conley, George T., Sr., Williamson, 171
Conley, James S., Charleston, 171
Conley, Philip M., Charleston, 171
Conley, William G., Charleston, 172
Cook, Leslie L., Elkins, 174
Cook, Roy B., Charleston, 174
Core, Earl L., Core, 178
Cornwell, John J., Romney, 179
Cottle, Brooks, Morgantown, 181
Cowden, William K., Huntington, 182
Cox, F., Morgantown, 183
Cox, Floyd B., Morgantown, 183
Cox, John H., Morgantown, 183
Cox, Norman W., Huntington, 183
Coyle, George L., Charleston, 184
Craddock, Bantz W., Glenville, 184
Cramblet, Wilbur H., Bethany, 185
Crawford, David B., Parkersburg, 186
Crawford, John M., Parkersburg, 186
Crichton, Walter G., Charleston, 188
Crichton, William, Jr., Charleston, Crichton, 188
Crockett, Joseph M., Welch, 189
Culp, Earl J., Harrisville, 194
Cuppett, David E., Thomas, 195
Curd, Thomas H. S., Welch, 195
Custer, Ruhl S., Weirton, 198
Cuthbert, Frank E., Morgantown, 198
Cutlip, James E., Sutton, 198

Dadisman, Andrew J., Morgantown, 199
Darby, Arleigh L., Morgantown, 201
Davidson, Edwin L., Parkersburg, 203
Davies, Earl C. H., Morgantown, 203
Davis, George G., Sutton, 205
Davis, Harvey G., Charleston, 205
Davis, Innis C., Charleston, 205
Davis, John A., Jr., Parkersburg, 206
Davis, John T., Elkins, 206
Davis, John W., Institute, 206
Davis, Roland J., Morgantown, 206
Davis, Staige, Charleston, 207
Davis, T. Edward, Salem, 207
Davisson, George I., Weston, 208
Dawson, Daniel B., Charleston, 208
Dawson, H. Donald, Bethany, 208
Dawson, William M. O., 2d, Charleston, 208
Dayton, Arthur S., Charleston, 209
Deahl, Jasper N., Morgantown, 209
Deison, Edward B., Clarksburg, 212
DeNoon, Anna L., Huntington, 216
Dent, Herbert W., Grafton, 216
Dickinson, Edmund C., Morgantown, 220
Dickinson, John L., Charleston, 220
Dillinger, Harvey E., Charleston, 223
Dillon, Charles W., Fayetteville, 223
Dodds, Gideon S., Morgantown, 226
Dodrill, Draco, Clarksburg, 226
Donley, Edward G., Morgantown, 228
Donley, Robert T., Morgantown, 228
Dorrance, Charles, Fairmont, 230
Dotson, Beril A., St. Marys, 230
Dougherty, George, Morgantown, 231
Downs, William S., Morgantown, 232
Draper, John W., Morgantown, 233
Dunlap, Emma W., Hinton, 239
Dunn, Raymond H., South Charleston, 239
Durig, William E., New Martinsville, 241
Dustman, Robert B., Morgantown, 241
Dyer, Luther L., Webster Springs, 242
Easley, David M., Bluefield, 244
Easley, Frank S., Bluefield, 244
East, Clyde H., South Charleston, Charleston, 244
Echols, Leonard S., Charleston, 245
Edmiston, Andrew, Weston, 247
Edwards, Levi A., St. Albans, Charleston, 248
Edwards, Rowland H., Welch, 248
Eiesland, John, Morgantown, 250
Elbin, Paul N., West Liberty, 252
Elkins, Davis, Morgantown, 253
Elliott, Grace Y., Philippi, 254
Elliott, John W., Philippi, 254
Elswick, Walter A., Hinton, 256
England, Welch, Charleston, 258
Ernst, James E., Keyser, 261
Escue, Henry M., St. Albans, 261
Evans, D. Bargar, Moundsville, 263
Evans, Lamotte, Charleston, 264
Evans, Samuel J., Princeton, 264
Everett, Hermon D., Charleston, 265
Farnsworth, Floyd F., Milton, 270
Farren, Oran B., St. Marys, 272
Fawcett, Ivan, Wheeling, 272
Ferguson, Charles W., Wayne, 275
Ferguson, Daniel L., Jr., Institute, 275
Ferrell, Harrison H., Institute, 276
File, William H., Beckley, 278
Fischer, John W., Parkersburg, 281
Fisher, Charles F., Clarksburg, 281
Fisher, Jake, Sutton, 282
Fitzpatrick, Herbert, Huntington, 283
Fleming, Allison S., Edgemont, Fairmont, 285
Fleming, Brooks, Jr., Fairmont, 285
Fleming, Wallace B., Buckhannon, 286
Flournoy, Harry L., Charleston, 287
Flournoy, Patrick W., Charleston, 287
Flynn, Clarence E., Arbovale, Marlinton, 287
Flynn, John P., Sistersville, 287
Ford, O. Rex, Morgantown, 289
Forman, Alexander H., Morgantown, 290
Forrer, Charles D., Parkersburg, 290
Foss, Feodore F., Wheeling, 291
Foster, Thomas V., Spencer, 292
Fox, Fred L., Charleston, 293

Fox, J. Francke, Bluefield, 294
Frame, Arch M., Charleston, 294
Frame, Nat T., Wheeling, 295
Francis, James D., Huntington, 295
Franzheim, Edward B., Wheeling, 296
Frasure, Carl M., Morgantown, 297
Friedman, Harry, Grafton, 301
Fulton, William S., Wheeling, 304
Gaines, Joseph H., Charleston, 306
Gaines, Ludwell E., Fayetteville, 306
Galpin, Sidney L., Morgantown, 307
Garden, George A., Wheeling, 308
Garrett, Harold M., Bridgeport, Clarksburg, 310
Gates, Charles B., Charleston, 311
Gay, Frank E., Bethany, 313
Geary, W. B., Charleston, 314
Gebhardt, Homer, Huntington, 314
Geiger, Marlin G., Charleston, South Charleston, 314
Gericke, Oscar C., Fairmont, 316
Gibson, Alva J., Charleston, 318
Gibson, Philip P., Huntington, 319
Gilbert, Frank A., Huntington, 320
Gill, Richard D., Wheeling, 321
Gilliam, Marion W., Williamson, 322
Giltinan, David M., Charleston, 323
Given, Walter M., Charleston, 324
Glass, Alexander, Wheeling, 324
Glauner, George L., Buckhannon, 324
Glenn, Marshall, Morgantown, 325
Gocke, William T., Clarksburg, 326
Goff, William R., Parkersburg, 327
Gohen, Charles M., Huntington, 327
Golden, Benjamin I., Elkins, 327
Goodman, Horace L., Ronceverte, 329
Goodrich, Edgar J., Charleston, 330
Goodwin, Russell B., Wheeling, 330
Goodykoontz, Wells, Williamson, 330
Gore, Howard M., Clarksburg, 331
Gott, Ernest F., Charleston, 332
Gould, Arthur B., Buckhannon, Salem, 332
Gould, Arthur M., Adrian, Buckhannon, 332
Gravatt, William A., Charleston, 336
Gray, Bernard E., Keyser, 336
Gray, Howard L., Rainelle, 337
Gray, William R., Mount Hope, 337
Green, Irvin T., Bethany, 338
Greene, Harry W., Institute, 340
Greene, John H., Williamson, 340
Greenleaf, William E., Huntington, 341
Greer, Herbert C., Morgantown, 341
Grimes, William C., Wheeling, 344
Grose, Logan S., Buckhannon, 346
Grove, John B., Petersburg, 347
Guilher, James M., Clarksburg, 349
Gullickson, Otto A., Huntington, 349
Gunning, Harold D., Ronceverte, 350
Hackney, Lilian, Huntington, 352
Hall, Arthur A., Morgantown, 355
Hall, Kent B., Wheeling, 356
Hall, Sobisca S., Clarksburg, 356
Hall, Van Byron, Sutton, 356
Hall, William M., Institute, 357
Hallam, William A., Buckhannon, 357
Hallanan, Walter S., Charleston, 357
Halley, Albert R., Huntington, 357
Hamlin, Adolph P., Institute, 358
Hamilton, Bryan, Elkins, 359
Hamilton, Dewey D., Mannington, 359
Hamilton, Henry A., Elkins, 359
Hamric, Edwin L., Parkersburg, 361
Hancock, Walter E., Salem, 361
Hanlin, Fred A., Weirton, 362
Hannum, Alberta P., Moundsville, 363
Hardman, Thomas P., Morgantown, 365
Harman, William M., Parsons, 367
Harman, Roy L., Beckley, 367
Harper, Jacob M., Spencer, 368
Harper, Samuel W., Wheeling, 368
Harris, Mary B., Alderson, 370
Harris, Thomas L., Morgantown, 370
Harris, Virgil B., Gassaway, Sutton, 370
Hart, Walter L., Morgantown, 372
Harte, Richard, Parkersburg, 372
Harvey, Agnes L., Huntington, 374
Hatcher, John H., Charleston, 376
Hatfield, Henry D., Huntington, 376
Haught, Thomas W., Buckhannon, 377
Hayes, Augustus W., Huntington, 379

Hayes, Leslie D., Morgantown, 380
Hayman, Joseph L., Morgantown, 380
Haymond, Frank C., Fairmont, 380
Hazlett, Robert, Wheeling, 381
Hedrick, Charles E., Huntington, 384
Hedrick, G. C., Beckley, 384
Henderson, Cam, Huntington, 387
Henderson, Harry O., Morgantown, 388
Hendrix, Nevins B., Martinsburg, 388
Hennen, Ray V., Morgantown, 389
Henry, James A., Weirton, 389
Herbert, James C., Fairmont, 390
Hereford, John W., Huntington, 391
Hess, Henry N., Wheeling, 394
Hill, Arthur M., Charleston, 397
Hill, Lawrence B., Morgantown, 399
Hines, Cary S., Sutton, 401
Hines, John L., White Sulphur Springs, 401
Hines, W. E., Sutton, 401
Hinsdale, Guy, White Sulphur Springs, 401
Hoblitzell, John D., Jr., Parkersburg, 404
Hodge, Williard W., Morgantown, 404
Hoff, William B., Parkersburg, 405
Hoffheimer, G. M., Clarksburg, 405
Hoffman, John G., 3d, Wheeling, 406
Hoffman, Joseph C., Charleston, 406
Hoge, Ernest K., Wheeling, 407
Hogsett, Everett L., Huntington, 407
Holloway, William W., Wheeling, 409
Holmes, Howard A., Fairmont, 410
Holstine, Russell M., Montgomery, 411
Holt, Homer A., Fayetteville, Charleston, 411
Holt, Rush D., Weston, 411
Hoover, J. M., Webster Springs, 413
Hopkins, Andrew D., Parkersburg, 413
Horner, Vaughan, Parkersburg, 415
Howard, Benjamin F., Welch, 417
Howard, G. W., Welch, 418
Howard, LeRoy D., Fairmont, 418
Howell, Harry R., Charleston, 419
Hron, Ralph P., Huntington, 421
Hudelson, Earl, Morgantown, 422
Hughes, Alvaroe G., Kingwood, 423
Hughes, William T., Jr., Morgantown, 424
Hugus, Wright, Wheeling, 424
Hull, Bruce H., Institute, 424
Hunter, Glenn, Morgantown, 428
Hunter, J. Ross, Charleston, 428
Hutchinson, John O., Beckley, 430
Hyde, Richard E., Charleston, 431
Hyma, Nicholas, Buckhannon, 431
Hymes, Myron B., Buckhannon, 431
Ireland, Ritchie A., Charleston, 434
Irvine, William B., Elm Grove, Wheeling, 434
Irwin, Grattan G., Charleston, 434
Jablonski, Joseph S., Huntington, 436
Jackson, Earle G., Chester, 436
Jackson, James A., Institute, Charleston, 438
Jackson, Naaman, Logan, 438
Jacob, William F., Wellsburg, 438
Jacobson, Carl A., Morgantown, 439
James, Ernest K., Charleston, 440
Jarrett, Clarence L., Charleston, 442
Jarrett, Cora H., Shepherdstown, 442
Jarvis, Hugh, Clarksburg, 442
Jeffers, Charles W., Wheeling, 442
Jefferson, Miles M., Canty's Institute, Institute, 442
Jenkins, John E., Huntington, 443
Jennings, Ivan F., Welch, 444
Jepson, Edwin C., Wheeling, 444
John, William S., Morgantown, 445
Johns, Vernon, Charleston, 445
Johnson, Benjamin S., Bluefield, 446
Johnson, Charles B., Clarksburg, 446
Johnson, David D., Morgantown, 447
Johnson, George W., Parkersburg, 448
Johnson, Henry R., Fairmont, 448
Johnson, Lewis E., Alderson, 449
Johnson, Louis A., Clarksburg, 449
Jones, Archbold M., Parkersburg, 451
Jones, Clement R., Morgantown, 452
Jones, Edmund L., Wheeling, 452
Jones, Harrison T., Fairmont, 453
Jones, James S., Wheeling, 453
Jones, Lloyd M., Morgantown, 454
Jordan, Emory V., Charleston, 455

Joyce, Claude A., Logan, 456
Judson, James E., Buckhannon, 456
Kahn, David H., Parkersburg, 457
Kappes, William C., Huntington, 459
Karickhoff, Oda E., Buckhannon, 459
Kay, Robert H. C., Charleston, 460
Kee, John, Bluefield, 461
Keister, H. S., Fairmont, 463
Kelly, Lon H., Charleston, 465
Kelly, Michael B., Wheeling, 466
Kemp, Anna M., Bethany, 467
Kemper, A. Judson, Lost Creek, Clarksburg, 467
Kenna, Joseph N., Charleston, 467
Kennedy, John A., Clarksburg, Elkins, 467
Kessel, Oliver D., Ripley, 470
Kessel, Russel, Ripley, Charleston, 470
Ketchum, Dickerson A., Charleston, 471
Keyser, W. R., Welch, 471
Kimball, Charles N., Sistersville, 473
Kincaid, Wallace P., Summersville, 473
Kingdon, Arthur F., Bluefield, 475
Kirby, David, Charleston, 477
Kirkpatrick, Forrest H., Bethany, 478
Kittle, Frank G., Philippi, 479
Klausner, Bertram, Fairmont, 479
Klinger, Allen C., Huntington, 481
Klumpp, James S., Huntington, 482
Knight, Edward W., Charleston, 482
Koehler, Walter A., Morgantown, 485
Koontz, Arthur B., Charleston, 486
Kraybill, David B., Montgomery, 489
Krebs, Charles E., Charleston, 489
Krumpelmann, John T., Huntington, 491
Kuhn, Ernest G., Grafton, 492
Kump, Herman G., Elkins, 493
Laing, John, Charleston, 496
Laird, William R., Montgomery, 496
Lambert, Oscar D., Buckhannon, 497
Largent, Robert J., Huntington, 501
Laughlin, Samuel O., Jr., Wheeling, 503
Law, Clyde O., Wheeling, 503
Lawall, Charles E., Morgantown, 504
Lawson, Aubrey F., Weston, 505
Lee, Howard B., Charleston, 507
Lehman, William P., Fairmont, 510
Leitch, Andrew, Bethany, 511
Lemmon, Lyman N., Wheeling, 511
Leonian, Leon N., Morgantown, 513
Levering, Howard A., Huntington, 514
Lewis, H. V., Charleston, 518
Lincoln, John J., Elkhorn, 521
Linsz, Henri P., Wheeling, 523
Little, Arthur W., White Sulphur Springs, 524
Litz, Moroni A., Charleston, 525
Lively, Frank, Charleston, 525
Lively, William T., Charleston, 525
Livesay, Edward A., Morgantown, 526
Locke, Albert W., St. Marys, 527
Logan, Thomas, Parkersburg, 529
Long, Joseph H., Huntington, 530
Louchery, Charles W., Clarksburg, 533
Love, Charles M., Jr., Charleston, 533
Love, George, Fayetteville, 534
Lovins, William T., Huntington, 534
Lowndes, William B., Jr., Clarksburg, 535
Loy, A. Clinton, Romney, 535
Loy, Melvin P., Huntington, 535
Lublinger, Abram J., Bluefield, 536
Lutz, Athey R., Parkersburg, 538
Lutz, George W., Elm Grove, 538
Lynch, Lawrence R., Clarksburg, 539
Lyon, George M., Huntington, 540
Magill, William S., Morgantown, 547
Mahaffey, Pearl, Bethany, 548
Mahan, C. E., Jr., Fayetteville, 548
Mahood, Alexander M., Charleston, 548
Mann, Fletcher W., Beckley, 551
Marcum, John R., Huntington, 553
Marsh, Joseph F., Athens, 555
Marsh, Ray S., Morgantown, 555
Marshall, John, Parkersburg, 556
Martens, James H. C., Morgantown, 557
Martin, Clarence E., Martinsburg, 558

Martin, Thomas W., Martinsburg, 560
Mason, W. H., Elkins, 562
Matheus, John F., Institute, 563
Mathews, William B., Charleston, 563
Matthews, Howard D., Wheeling, 564
Matthews, John C., Huntington, 565
Maxwell, Earl L., Elkins, 566
Maxwell, Frank J., Clarksburg, 566
Maxwell, George R., Morgantown, 566
Maxwell, Haymond, Charleston, 567
McAdams, Laura J., Elkins, 568
McCamic, Charles, Moundsville, Wheeling, 570
McCamic, Jay T., Wheeling, 570
McCauley, William D., Moorefield, 572
McClintic, Clifton F., Williamsburg, 572
McClintic, George W., Charleston, 572
McClue, Arthur E., Charleston, 573
McClung, James, Richmond, 573
McClure, Walter H., Wheeling, 574
McConnell, John C., Triadelphia, Wheeling, 574
McCrum, Arlington B., Charleston, 577
McCulloch, John H., Beckley, 578
McCullough, F. Witcher, Huntington, 578
McCuskey, Roy, Buckhannon, 578
McCuskey, William C. D., Wheeling, 578
McDaniel, Leon S., Charleston, 578
McDavid, John E., Charleston, 579
McDonald, Orville L., Clarksburg, 579
McDowell, Ted G., Beckley, 580
McFarland, Archie J., Wheeling, 581
McGee, Lemuel C., Elkins, 582
McGinnis, Bernard C., Huntington, 582
McGinnis, J. H., Beckley, 582
McGuire, Patrick J., Wellsburg, 583
McGuire, Thomas W., Carbon, 583
McHenry, Jesse P., Wheeling, 583
McKay, John J., Sistersville, 584
McKenzie, John E., Beckley, 586
McKenzie, Loratius L., Institute, 586
McKown, Gilbert C., Martinsburg, 587
McMillan, William A., Charleston, 588
McNash, John H., Wheeling, 589
McNeer, Selden S., Huntington, 589
Meador, Palma G., Charleston, 591
Meadows, Clarence W., Beckley, Charleston, 591
Meek, John H., Huntington, 592
Meredith, James A., Fairmont, 596
Meredith, J. Harper, Fairmont, 596
Merry, Frieda K., Charleston, 597
Merry, Ralph V., Charleston, 598
Miller, Henry N., Bethany, 604
Miller, Hugh, Charleston, 605
Miller, Irving, Elkins, 605
Miller, Lewis H., Ripley, 607
Miller, Roy B., Parkersburg, 607
Millsop, Thomas E., Weirton, 609
Moats, Francis P., Parkersburg, 612
Mohler, D. N., Charleston, 613
Moist, Ronald F., Clarksburg, 613
Molby, Fred A., Morgantown, 613
Monroe, Verne, Cameron, 615
Montague, Margaret P., Sulphur Springs, 615
Montgomery, Julian E., Wheeling, 615
Moore, Ben W., Charleston, 617
Moore, Houston B., Lewisburg, 617
Moore, Junius W., Charleston, 618
Moore, Thomas W., Huntington, 618
Moos, Jean C., Bethany, 619
Morris, Earle H., Charleston, 623
Morris, Samuel, Morgantown, 624
Morris, Samuel J., Morgantown, 624
Morris, Stanley C., Charleston, 624
Morris, Warren F., Wheeling, 625
Moyer, Earl B., Parkersburg, 628
Mudge, William A., Huntington, 629
Mueller, Harry E., Huntington, 630
Murray, Irvin L., South Charleston, Charleston, 634
Murray, Mrs. Irvin L., Charleston, 634
Musgrave, F. G., Point Pleasant, 635
Musser, Harry P., Charleston, 635
Naylor, Joseph R., Wheeling, 639
Naylor, Roy B., Wheeling, 639
Neal, B. T., Jr., Parkersburg, 639
Neal, George I., Huntington, 639
Neely, Matthew M., Fairmont, 639

Neff, Charles T., Jr., Morgantown, 639
Nelson, Oscar, Charleston, 641
Nesbitt, Frank W., Wheeling, 642
Nesbitt, Russell G., Wheeling, 642
Neuenschwander, Paul W., Sistersville, 642
Newcomb, James F., Huntington, 643
Noer, Ruth D., Morgantown, 649
Northcott, Elliott, Le Sage, 651
Norvell, George W., Huntington, 652
Nowlin, Robert A., Elkhorn, 652
Nutter, Trevey, Fairmont, 653
Oates, Theodore K., Martinsburg, 654
O'Brien, Frank A., Wheeling, 655
O'Brien, J. J. P., Wheeling, 655
O'Brien, William S., Charleston, 656
O'Connor, Robert E., Charleston, 656
Ogden, Chester B., Clarksburg, 658
Ogden, Herschel C., Wheeling, 658
Ogden, Marshall W., Fairmont, 658
Ogden, Rachel C., Buckhannon, 658
Oliver, Rosa V., Huntington, 660
Orton, Clayton R., Morgantown, 662
Otey, Ernest G., Bluefield, 664
Page, Basil L., Buckhannon, 666
Palmer, John C., Jr., Wheeling, 667
Palmer, John C., 3d, Wheeling, 668
Paris, Auguste J., Jr., Charleston, 669
Parsons, Dickson W., Morgantown, 672
Pauli, Lee C., Wheeling, 675
Peairs, Leonard M., Morgantown, 676
Pennybacker, Everett B., Vienna, Parkersburg, 681
Percival, Walter C., Morgantown, 682
Permar, Robert, Wheeling, 683
Peterkin, William G., Parkersburg, 684
Peters, Charles G., Charleston, 685
Peyton, Thomas W., 4th, Barboursville, Huntington, 686
Pharr, Walter W., Mt. Hope, 687
Phillips, Daniel E., Shepherdstown, 688
Phillips, Edward M., Wheeling, 688
Pickett, Justus C., Morgantown, 690
Picklesimer, Hayes, Charleston, 690
Pierce, Carleton C., Kingwood, 690
Pierce, Willis E., Moundsville, 691
Pierre, William H., Morgantown, 691
Piggott, Harold W., Parkersburg, 691
Pinckard, H. R., Huntington, 692
Pitt, William P., Huntington, 694
Plant, Albert C., Wheeling, 695
Plate, Blair, Parkersburg, 695
Poffenbarger, George, Charleston, 696
Poffenbarger, Nathan S., Charleston, 696
Pohlman, George G., Morgantown, 696
Point, Walter W., Charleston, 696
Poland, John R., Martinsburg, 696
Pollock, Bruce H., Point Pleasant, 697
Pollock, Rebecca L., Morgantown, 697
Porterfield, Allen W., Morgantown, 699
Posey, Thomas E., Institute, 699
Posten, Hale J., Morgantown, 700
Potts, Louis R., Moundsville, 701
Powell, Francis W., Elkins, 701
Power, Francis R., Charleston, 702
Preston, Alfred D., Beckley, 704
Preston, John J. D., Charleston, 704
Preysz, Louis R. F., Elkins, 705
Price, Paul H., Morgantown, 705
Price, Samuel, Lewisburg, 705
Price, T. Brooke, Charleston, 705
Prichard, Lucy E., Huntington, 706
Pride, C. Benjamin, Morgantown, 706
Prince, Elmer W., Morgantown, 706
Pritchard, Robert H., Weston, 706
Pritt, Thaddeus, Elkins, 707
Purdum, R. B., Elkins, 708
Purinton, Edward E., Morgantown, 708
Radenbaugh, Frances I., Parkersburg, 710
Rafferty, Russell, Wheeling, 711
Ramage, Chesney M., Fairmont, 712
Ramsay, Robert L., Wellsburg, 712
Randal, Boyd, Williamson, 713
Randolph, Jennings, Elkins, 714
Rankin, John O., Wheeling, 714
Rapking, Aaron H., Lost Creek, 715
Rasmussen, Torlock, Grafton, 715
Ray, Charles A., Pocotaligo, Charleston, 716
Ray, John V., Charleston, 717

Reass, Joseph H., Wheeling, 718
Reed, Louis, Grantsville, 719
Reed, Perley I., Morgantown, 720
Reed, Robert J., Wheeling, 720
Reed, Robert J., Jr., Wheeling, 720
Reeder, Benjamin G., Morgantown, 720
Reeder, Franklin H., Jr., Charleston, 720
Reese, Albert M., Morgantown, 721
Reger, David B., Morgantown, 722
Reid, Edgar A., Charleston, 724
Reuter, Otto K., Bellepoint, Hinton, 727
Revercomb, William C., Charleston, 727
Reynolds, C. J., Bluefield, 727
Reynolds, Clarence N., Jr., Morgantown, 727
Rhawn, Heister G., Clarksburg, 728
Rhead, Frederick H., Newell, 728
Rhinehart, N. Porter, Charleston, 728
Rice, Lacy I., Martinsburg, 730
Richards, William A., Bluefield, 732
Richardson, George, Jr., Bluefield, 733
Riggleman, Leonard, Charleston, 736
Riley, James B., Wheeling, Charleston, 737
Riley, Thomas S., Wheeling, 737
Ritchie, Charles, Charleston, 738
Ritz, Harold A., Charleston, 739
Roberts, Emmett E., Bethany, 740
Robertson, Sidney H., Clendenin, 742
Robinson, Benjamin O., Parkersburg, 743
Robinson, Howard L., Clarksburg, 744
Robinson, Ira E., Philippi, Clarksburg, 744
Robinson, Jedidiah W., Grafton, 745
Rodgers, Decatur R., Martinsburg, see Addenda
Rogers, Harold F., Fairmont, 749
Rohrbough, Edward G., Glenville, 750
Rollins, Lawrence E., Charleston, 750
Romer, Isadore B., Huntington, 750
Rosenbloom, Benjamin L., Wheeling, 755
Rosier, Joseph, Fairmont, 756
Ross, Cecil B., Buckhannon, 756
Roudebush, Russell I., Huntington, 758
Rouzer, Paul C., Keyser, 758
Rowley, Walter N., Huntington, 760
Ruf, Casper A., Parkersburg, 761
Russell, Henry M., Wheeling, 763
Sale, William G., Jr., Welch, 766
Salton, Russell A., Williamson, 766
Salvati, Raymond E., Holden, 767
Sammons, William P., Wheeling, 767
Samworth, Fred W., Huntington, 767
Sanders, Carlton C., Beckley, 768
Sanders, Jos. M., Bluefield, 768
Sands, Harry S., Wheeling, 768
Sayre, Everett, Beckley, 771
Sayre, Floyd M., Beckley, 774
Scherr, Harry, Huntington, 775
Schiffer, Andrew C., Wheeling, 775
Schmidt, Carl O., Wheeling, 777
Scholz, Carl, Charleston, 779
Schoolcraft, Arthur A., Buckhannon, 779
Schoolfield, George C., Charleston, 779
Schuck, Charles J., Wheeling, 781
Schwinn, Jacob, Wheeling, 784
Scott, Charles M., Bluefield, 784
Scott, Henry D., Wheeling, 784
Scott, Hugh B., Wheeling, 784
Scott, Isaac M., Wheeling, 785
Scott, James E., Wheeling, 785
Scott, Paul W., Huntington, 785

Scott, William E., Maxwelton, Lewisburg, 785
Sell, William D., Charleston, 789
Shaffer, Harry G., Madison, 791
Shannon, Ernest S., Williamstown, 792
Shaver, Clement L., Fairmont, 793
Shaw, Craig, Moundsville, 793
Shawhan, Hubbard W., Charleston, 794
Shawkey, Arthur A., Charleston, 794
Shawkey, Morris P., Charleston, 794
Shedan, George, Parkersburg, 795
Sheldon, John L., Morgantown, 796
Shelton, Harry L., Elkins, 796
Shepherd, Walton S., Charleston, 796
Shipman, James F., Moundsville, 799
Shortridge, Wilson P., Morgantown, 801
Shott, Hugh I., Bluefield, 801
Shreve, Francis, Fairmont, 802
Shuff, William D., Princeton, 803
Shuman, Albert, Morgantown, 803
Simmons, Sattis, Ripley, 807
Simmons, William B., Berkeley Springs, 807
Simpson, John N., Morgantown, 808
Slaven, Lant R., Williamson, 812
Smith, Clarence E., Fairmont, 816
Smith, Edward G., West Milford, Clarksburg, 816
Smith, Fred M., Morgantown, 817
Smith, Gilbert, Fayetteville, 818
Smith, Harrison B., Charleston, 819
Smith, James L., Elizabeth, 820
Smith, Joe L., Beckley, 820
Smith, Levin, Parkersburg, 821
Smith, Mortimer W., Jr., Charleston, 821
Smith, Robert E., Huntington, 822
Smith, Wallace H., Glendale, 823
Snead, Samuel J., White Sulphur Springs, 825
Snyder, Harry L., Charleston, 827
Snyder, Melvin C., Kingwood, 827
Somerville, E. J., Point Pleasant, 829
Somerville, G. G., Point Pleasant, 829
Spangler, Robert C., Morgantown, 833
Sperry, Melvin G., Clarksburg, 834
Spiker, Claude C., Morgantown, 834
Spilman, Robert S., Charleston, 835
Spilman, Robert S., Jr., Charleston, 835
Sprague, John H. C., Huntington, 836
Spray, Robb S., Morgantown, 836
Spurr, A. C., Fairmont, 837
St. Clair, Otis E., Welch, 837
St. Clair, Wade H., Bluefield, 837
Stallard, Clint W., Montgomery, 838
Stalnaker, Elizabeth M., Morgantown, 838
Stambaugh, Fred M., Charleston, 839
Stark, Lyda A., Clarksburg, 840
Stathers, Madison, Morgantown, 841
Stathers, William G., Clarksburg, 841
Staunton, Frederick M., Charleston, 842
Steed, Robert D., Charleston, 843
Stemple, Forrest W., Morgantown, 846
Steptoe, Philip P., Charleston, 846
Stevenson, Charles A., Morgantown, 849
Stevenson, Olla, Huntington, 849
Stewart, Melville, Charleston, 850
Stifel, Arthur C., Wheeling, 850
Stifel, Edward W., Wheeling, 851
Stoken, Norman, Beckley, 853
Stone, Arthur G., Charleston, 854

Stone, Harry E., Morgantown, 855
Strader, George S., Bluefield, 858
Strange, William W., Huntington, 858
Straub, George L., Welch, 859
Strausbaugh, P. D., Morgantown, 859
Strider, Robert E. L., Wheeling, 861
Strother, Dan J. F., Welch, 862
Stroup, Thomas A., Omar, 862
Stubblefield, Edward, Princeton, 863
Stutler, Boyd B., Charleston, 865
Sullivan, Frank H., Charleston, 865
Sutherland, Howard, Elkins, 867
Sutton, George M., Bethany, 867
Swart, Howard A., Charleston, 869
Swartz, Osman E., Charleston, 869
Swint, Benjamin H., Charleston, 871
Swint, John J., Wheeling, 871
Sydnor, Giles G., Charles Town, 872
Sydnor, Henry M., Charles Town, 872
Talbot, S. Benton, Elkins, 874
Taylor, Britton P., Huntington, 876
Taylor, Charles T., Huntington, 877
Taylor, James A., Fayetteville, 878
Tetrick, W. Guy, Clarksburg, 882
Thomas, Frank A., Charleston, 884
Thomas, Frederick L., Charleston, 884
Thomas, Harry V., Clarksburg, 885
Thomas, James H., Wheeling, 885
Thomas, James K., Charleston, 885
Thomas, Robert B., Huntington, 886
Thomas, Wesley C., Huntington, 886
Thompson, Alden W., Morgantown, 887
Thompson, Ernest, Charleston, 887
Thompson, French W., Lewisburg, 887
Thompson, Hugh G., Charleston, 888
Tieche, Albert U., Beckley, 891
Todd, Gordon L., Princeton, 894
Tomassene, Raymond A., Wheeling, 894
Townsend, T. C., Charleston, 896
Trail, Grover C., Beckley, 896
Trainer, G. H., Salem, 896
Traugh, George H., Fairmont, 897
Trembly, Charles E., Terra Alta, 897
Trent, William W., Charleston, 897
Trotter, Frank B., Morgantown, 899
Turner, Bird M., Morgantown, 901
Upton, Arthur V. G., Clarksburg, 907
Utterback, William I., Huntington, 908
Vaden, Claude A., Wheeling, 908
Vall-Spinosa, Arthur, Parkersburg, 908
Vance, Walter, Hamlin, 909
Van Den Berg, Cornelius, Jr., Charleston, 909
Vandervoort, James W., Parkersburg, 910
Vander Zalm, Lindley E., Huntington, 910
Van Liere, Edward J., Morgantown, 911
Van Sant, William L., Beckley, Hinton, 911
Vass, Thurman E., Bluefield, 912
Vawter, Eugene R., Ansted, Fayetteville, 913
Vest, Walter E., Huntington, 914
Vickers, Arnold M., Montgomery, 914
Vickers, Enoch M., Morgantown, 915
Waddell, Charles W., Fairmont, 918
Wagner, Dwight H., Wheeling, 919

Wagner, Frederick R., Martinsburg, 919
Waldron, William H., Huntington, 920
Walker, Rome H., Charleston, 921
Wallace, George S., Huntington, 922
Wallace, William J. L., Institute, 922
Ward, George, Mill Creek, Charleston, 926
Ware, Paul B., Philippi, 927
Wark, Homer E., Clarksburg, 928
Watkins, Harry E., Fairmont, 932
Watkins, J. R., Beckley, 932
Watson, Clarence W., Fairmont, 932
Watson, Elmer E., Albright, 933
Watts, Hansford, Huntington, 934
Waugh, H. Roy, Buckhannon, 934
Wehner, Edward F., Clarksburg, 938
Weihl, Fred P., Weston, 938
Weimer, Bernal R., Bethany, 939
Weimer, William G., Wheeling, 939
Weiss, William E., Wheeling, 940
Wellman, C. E., Huntington, 941
Wells, Ira J. K., Charleston, 941
Wells, Jacob E., Buckhannon, 941
Wells, Joseph M., Newell, 942
Wemple, Charles E., Wheeling, 942
Wheat, Harry G., Morgantown, 947
Whetsell, Harry I., Elkins, 949
White, Albert B., Parkersburg, 949
White, Grace Y., Shepherdstown, 950
White, John B., Charleston, 950
White, Wilson H. S., Shepherdstown, 952
Whittlesey, Frederick R., Morgantown, 955
Wilhelm, Charles P., Kingwood, 958
Wilkinson, Bernard W., Clarksburg, 958
Wilkinson, Robert J., Jr., Huntington, 958
Wilkinson, Robert J., Huntington, 959
Willard, Edgar H., Berkeley Springs, 959
Williams, Curtis C., Jr., Morgantown, 961
Williams, G. Alvin, Clarksburg, Charleston, 962
Williams, Homer W., Clarksburg, 962
Willson, Harold E., Oak Hill, 965
Wilson, Archer A., Charleston, 966
Wilson, Fred T., Fairmont, 966
Wilson, Otis G., Huntington, 968
Wilson, William P., Highland Park, Wheeling, 969
Wilson, Wirt B., Charleston, 969
Winter, John E., Morgantown, 971
Wolfe, William H., Parkersburg, 973
Wolverton, John M., Richman, 974
Woodroe, William M., Charleston, 977
Woods, John M., Charleston, 978
Woods, Luther E., Huntington, 978
Woods, Roy C., Huntington, 978
Woodyard, Henry C., Jr., Spencer, 979
Woodyard, William, Spencer, 979
Woofter, Emory J., Parkersburg, 979
Woolery, William K., Bethany, 979
Wright, Chauncey B., Huntington, 982
Wright, Eugene B., Clarksburg, 982
Wriston, Robert, Beckley, 984
Wyckoff, Everett B., Grafton, 985
Wylie, Robert M., Huntington, 985
Yost, Ellis A., Huntington, 988
Yost, Lenna L., Huntington, 989
Zeller, Harry A., Huntington, 991
Zubak, Matthew F. C., Wheeling, 993
Zumbrunnen, Thomas M., Elkins, 994

Jones, Livingston E., Philadelphia, 454
Jones, Loren F., Philadelphia, 454
Jones, Marshall J. H., Philadelphia, 454
Jones, Montfort, Pittsburgh, 454
Jones, Owen, Scranton, 454
Jones, Robert, Ben Avon, Pittsburgh, 454
Jones, Rufus M., Haverford, 454
Jones, Russell N., Johnsonburg, 455
Jones, Vincent, Philadelphia, 455
Jones, Walter A., Pittsburgh, 455
Jones, Webster N., Pittsburgh, 455
Jordan, Frank C., Pittsburgh, 455
Jordan, George, York, 455
Jordan, James S., Scranton, 455
Joseph, Charles H., Pittsburgh, 455
Joseph, Emrys S., Harrisburg, 455
Joyce, Harry B., Erie, 456
Joyce, John St. G., Highland Park, 456
Judge, Wade W., Mansfield, 456
Judkins, Malcolm F., McKeesport, 456
Julian, Alvin F., Allentown, 456
Jump, Henry D., Philadelphia, 456
Kabakjian, Dicran H., Lansdowne, Philadelphia, 456
Kaemmerling, Effie B., Erie, 457
Kaercher, George H., Pottsville, 457
Kagan, I'escha, Washington, 457
Kahler, Arthur D., Carlisle, 457
Kain, George H., York, 457
Kalbfus, Edward C., State College, 457
Kallenbach, Walter D., Drexel Hill, 457
Kallok, John, West Aliquippa, 457
Kalodner, Harry E., Philadelphia, 457
Kamman, William F., Pittsburgh, 458
Kane, E. Kent, Kushequa, Kane, 458
Kane, Evan O'N., Kane, 458
Kane, Francis F., Philadelphia, 458
Kann, Gustave H., Pittsburgh, 458
Kann, James J., Chadds Ford, 458
Kantner, Franklin R., Reading, 458
Kaplan, Eliah, New Castle, 458
Kaplan, Frank R. S., Pittsburgh, 458
Kapp, Cecil A., Philadelphia, 458
Kappel, John F., Pittsburgh, 458
Kappel, William J., Pittsburgh, 458
Karr, Robert M., Pittsburgh, 459
Kase, Paul G., Reading, 459
Kasel, Frank V., Columbia, 459
Katz, David, Philadelphia, 459
Kauffman, Daniel, Scottdale, 459
Kaufman, Charles M., Tower City, 459
Kaufman, David E., Philadelphia, 459
Kaufman, George S., Holicong, 460
Kaufman, Harry K., Philadelphia, 460
Kaufman, Morgan S., Scranton, 460
Kaufmann, Albert G., Brentwood, Pittsburgh, 460
Kaufmann, Arthur C., Ardmore, Philadelphia, 460
Kaufmann, Edgar J., Pittsburgh, 460
Kay, James, Philadelphia, 460
Kay, J. Leltoy, Pittsburgh, 460
Kay, Robert G., Philadelphia, 460
Keagy, Gula B., New Castle, 460
Kean, John S., Philadelphia, 460
Keane, Raymond R., Philadelphia, 461
Kearney, George F., Philadelphia, 461
Keath, Charles K., Lititz, 461
Keator, Alfred D., Reading, 461
Keboch, Frank D., Pittsburgh, 461
Keeble, Glendinning, Pittsburgh, 461
Keech, Finley, Harrisburg, 461
Keedy, Edwin R., Philadelphia, 1
Keefe, David A., Athens, 461
Keefer, Brua C., Jr., Williamsport, 461
Keeler, Harold R., Drexel Hill, Philadelphia, 461
Keen, Edward O., York, 461
Keen, John H., Philadelphia, 462
Keenan, J. Hilary, Greensburg, 462
Keenan, James F., Pittsburgh, 462
Keenan, Peter, Edison, 462
Keener, Martin M., Lampeter, Lancaster, 462
Keevil, Charles S., Lewisburg, 462
Kegel, Will C., Ellwood City 462
Keiper, Charles A., Stroudsburg, East Stroudsburg, 462
Keirns, May E., Huntingdon, 463
Keiser, Clarence E., Lyon Station, 463
Keister, Clinton L., Harrisburg, 463

Keister, John R., Greensburg, 463
Keith, John D., Gettysburg, 463
Kellam, Frederic J., Indiana, 463
Kellenberger, Keith E., Edgewood, Swissvale, 463
Keller, Edward L., State College, 463
Keller, Frederick E., Philadelphia, 463
Keller, Harry H., Jenkintown, Philadelphia, 463
Keller, Hiram H., Doylestown, 463
Keller, John C., Allentown, 464
Keller, John O., State College, 464
Keller, Joseph S., Merion, Philadelphia, 464
Keller, Joseph W., Merion, Philadelphia, 464
Keller, Oliver J., Pittsburgh, 464
Keller, William H., Lancaster, 464
Kellett, Donald S., Collegeville, 464
Kellett, William W., Philadelphia, 464
Kelley, Arthur P., Landenberg, 464
Kelley, Augustine B., Greensburg, 464
Kelley, Richard C., Philadelphia, 464
Kellogg, Herbert M., Lopez, 465
Kelly, Frances L., Pittsburgh, 465
Kelly, Frances M., Philadelphia, 465
Kelly, Herbert T., Philadelphia, 465
Kelly, J. Howard, Monessen, 465
Kelly, John A., Haverford, 465
Kelly, Lewis H., Pittsburgh, 465
Kelly, Thomas C., Philadelphia, 466
Kelly, Thomas R., Haverford, 466
Kelsey, Albert, Philadelphia, 466
Kelsey, Carl, Mendenhall, 466
Kelso, James A., Pittsburgh, 466
Kelso, James L., Pittsburgh, 466
Kemner, E. Fred, Philadelphia, 466
Kemp, Alvin F., Mertztown, Reading, 467
Kempel, Arthur B., East Brady, 467
Kendall, John W., Myersdale, Pittsburgh, 467
Kendig, H. Evert, Philadelphia, 467
Kendrick, W. Freeland, Philadelphia, 467
Kennedy, Andrew M., Sewickley, 467
Kennedy, John B., Columbia, 467
Kennedy, O'Neil, Uniontown, 468
Kennedy, Reid, Pittsburgh, Homestead, 468
Kennedy, Thomas, Hazleton, 468
Kennell, Henry B., Lehighton, 468
Kent, A. Atwater, Ardmore, Philadelphia, 468
Kent, Clarence H., State College, 468
Kent, Donald W., White Marsh, Philadelphia, 468
Kent, Everett, Bangor, 468
Kent, Everett L., Merion, Clifton Heights, 468
Kent, John I., Meadville, 468
Kent, Orville C., Meadville, 469
Kent, Roland G., Philadelphia, 469
Kent, Russell H., Swarthmore, Clifton Heights, 469
Kenworthey, Charles E., Ardmore, Philadelphia, 469
Kenworthy, J. Miller, Philadelphia, 469
Kenyon, Elmer, Pittsburgh, 469
Kephart, Alvin E., Yerkes, Philadelphia, 469
Kephart, John W., Ebensburg, 469
Keppel, Alvin R., Drexel Hill, Philadelphia, 469
Kerigan, Florence, Haverford, Philadelphia, 469
Kern, Frank D., State College, 469
Kern, John D., Philadelphia, 470
Kern, Richard A., Wynnewood, Philadelphia, 470
Kern, William F., Pittsburgh, 470
Kerr, Charles M., Jr., York, 470
Kerr, Duncan J., Sayre, Bethlehem, 470
Kerr, Hugh T., Pittsburgh, 470
Kerr, Samuel L., Philadelphia, 470
Kerstetter, Daniel C., Hamburg, 470
Ketchum, Carlton G., Pittsburgh, 470
Ketchum, George, Pittsburgh, 471
Ketels, Luther H., Reading, 471
Ketler, Frank C., Elkins Park, 471
Ketler, Weir C., Grove City, 471
Ketterer, Lillian H., Philadelphia, 471
Keylor, Josiah B., Cochranville, 471
Keyworth, William A., York, 471
Kiehl, Eugene P., Brookline, Philadelphia, 472
Kift, Jane L., Philadelphia, 472

Kilborn, William T., Pittsburgh, Bridgeville, 472
Kilker, Adrian J., Berwyn, 472
Killian, John C., Philadelphia, 473
Kimball, Fiske, Philadelphia, 473
Kimbrough, Robert A., Jr., Wynnewood, Philadelphia, 473
Kincaid, William M., Philadelphia, 473
Kinder, James S., Pittsburgh, 473
King, Caroline B., Philadelphia, 474
King, Charles G., Pittsburgh, 474
King, Helen D., Bryn Mawr, 474
King, James W., Kittanning, 474
King, Joseph T., Lawrenceville, 474
King, Karl C., Morrisville, 474
King, LeRoy A., Narberth, 474
King, Morland, Easton, 474
King, Wyncie, Bryn Mawr, 475
Kingsbury, Dana W., Nanticoke, 475
Kingsbury, Susan M., Bryn Mawr, 475
Kinnard, Leonard H., Wynnewood, Philadelphia, 476
Kinney, Antoinette B., Pittsburgh, 476
Kinsley, John F., Pittsburgh, 476
Kinsloe, Charles L., State College, 476
Kinzer, J. Roland, Lancaster, 476
Kiracofe, Edgar S., Huntingdon, 476
Kirby, C. Valentine, Harrisburg, 477
Kirby, Dunne W., Philadelphia, 477
Kirby, Fred M., Wilkes-Barre, 477
Kirby, R. S., State College, 477
Kirk, Mabel E., State College, 477
Kirkbride, Mabelle M., Norristown, 478
Kirkpatrick, Alton, Lansdowne, Philadelphia, 478
Kirkpatrick, Harlow B., Pittsburgh, 478
Kirkpatrick, Martin G., Philadelphia, 478
Kirkpatrick, William H., Easton, 478
Kirner, Walter R., Pittsburgh, 478
Kiser, Robert W., Pittsburgh, 478
Kiskaddon, J. Fulton, North East, 478
Kisner, Ralph, Danville, 478
Kitson, Arthur, Jr., Philadelphia, 478
Kitto, Charles W., Philadelphia, 479
Kittredge, Arthur E., Philadelphia, 479
Kizis, Andrew C., West Pittston, Pittston, 479
Klaer, Harvey, Philadelphia, 479
Kleeb, Henry A., Pittsburgh, 479
Klein, Arthur W., Bethlehem, 479
Klein, Charles, Philadelphia, 479
Klein, Charles H., Pittsburgh, 479
Klein, Frederic S., Lancaster, 479
Klein, Harry M. J., Lancaster, 480
Klein, John W., Reading, 480
Klein, Louis A., Moylan, Philadelphia, 480
Klein, William H., Easton, Nazareth, 480
Klieforth, Alfred W., Boalsburg, 480
Klimm, Lester E., Philadelphia, 480
Kline, Emanuel, Philadelphia, 480
Kline, I. Clinton, Sunbury, 480
Kline, J. Simpson, Sunbury, 480
Kline, John R., Swarthmore, 481
Kline, Sidney D., West Lawn, Reading, 481
Kline, Whorten A., Collegeville, 481
Klinedinst, David P., York, 481
Klingel, Joseph W., Philadelphia, 481
Klingelhofer, Edward K., Sewickley, Pittsburgh, 481
Klinginsmith, John G., Pittsburgh, 481
Klonower, Henry, Philadelphia, Harrisburg, 481
Klonowski, Henry T. T., Scranton, 481
Klopp, Henry I., Allentown, 481
Knandel, Herman C., State College, 482
Knapp, Harry B., Wellsboro, 482
Knapp, Rolla S., Easton, 482
Knauer, Wilhelm F., Philadelphia, 482
Knight, Harry S., Sunbury, 482
Knight, Seymour H., Penfield, Philadelphia, 482
Kniseley, John B., Pittsburgh, 483
Kniskern, Philip W., Swarthmore, Philadelphia, 483
Kniss, C. Asher, Mifflinburg, 483
Knowles, Archibald C., Philadelphia, 483

Knowles, Frank R., Johnstown, 483
Knowles, Richard, Philadelphia, 483
Knowles, William G., Philadelphia, 483
Knox, Harry E., Philadelphia, 483
Knox, Paul W., Philadelphia, 483
Knox, Robert W., Washington, 484
Knox, William F., Pittsburgh, 484
Knutsen, Martin H., State College, 484
Koch, Alfred, Latrobe, 484
Koch, Carl E., Pittsburgh, 484
Koch, Carleton S., Edgewood, McKeesport, 484
Koch, Caspar P., Pittsburgh, 484
Koch, Julius A., Pittsburgh, 484
Kochin, Elihu W., Pittsburgh, 485
Kohler, Charles H., Philadelphia, 485
Kohler, Edwin L., Allentown, 485
Köhler, Wolfgang, Swarthmore, 485
Kohlstedt, Edward D., Philadelphia, 485
Kohn, Bernard, Philadelphia, 485
Kolb, Louis J., Philadelphia, 485
Kolbe, Parke R., Philadelphia, 485
Koller, Edmund L., Scranton, 485
Koller, James R., Myerston, Lebanon, 486
Kolmer, John A., Bala-Cynwyd, Philadelphia, 486
Konkle, Burton A., Swarthmore, Philadelphia, 486
Konrad, Henry R., Port Carbon, 486
Konzelmann, Frank W., Philadelphia, 486
Koontz, Norman C., Indiana, 486
Kopf, Harry D., Warren, 487
Kopp, John W., Williamstown, 487
Korb, Carl R., Pittsburgh, 487
Korb, Robert T., Philadelphia, 487
Korns, Charles B., Sr., Sipesville, 487
Koser, John M., Ardmore, 487
Kossler, Herman S., Crafton, Pittsburgh, 487
Kothny, Gottdank L., Strafford, Philadelphia, 487
Kotzen, Earl L., Reading, 488
Kovacs, Koloman, Duquesne, 488
Koyl, George S., Philadelphia, 488
Kraft, John F., Washington, 488
Kramer, Clarence R., Clearfield, 488
Kramer, Roland L., Drexel Hill, Philadelphia, 488
Kraner, Hobart M., Bethlehem, 488
Kratz, Albert R., Berkshire Heights, Reading, 489
Krause, George D., Lebanon, 489
Krause, Maxwell, Lebanon, 489
Krauss, Franklin B., State College, 489
Krausz, Charles E., Philadelphia, 489
Krebs, Frank P., Tamaqua, 489
Krebs, W. W., Johnstown, 489
Kreider, Charles D., Nazareth, 490
Kreider, Henry K., Campbelltown, 490
Kreider, William E., Palmyra, 490
Kreider, William H., Philadelphia, 490
Kreider, William A., Upper Darby, Philadelphia, 490
Kremer, David N., Philadelphia, 490
Kremp, Laura A. M., Reading, 490
Kremp, Marie A. M., Reading, 490
Kresge, Elijah E., Lancaster, 490
Kressley, George S., Reading, Philadelphia, 490
Kretschmann, Theodore W., Selinsgrove, 490
Kribbs, David A., Chambersburg, State College, 490
Krick, Charles S., St. Davids, 491
Kriebel, William F., Moylan, Philadelphia, 491
Kriss, Max, State College, 491
Krivobok, Vsevolod N., Pittsburgh, 491
Krogh, Detlef M. F., Philadelphia, 491
Krohn, Israel, Easton, 491
Krouse, Luther A., Pottstown, 491
Krumbhaar, E. B., Philadelphia, 491
Krupp, Harry Z., Lansdale, Philadelphia, 491
Kruse, Theophile K. T., Mt. Lebanon, Pittsburgh, 491
Krusen, Wilmer, Media, Philadelphia, 492
Krut, John A., McKeesport, 492
Kuehner, Quincy A., Glenside, 492
Kuhlmann, G. Edward, Oil City, 492
Kuiper, Rienk B., Philadelphia, 492
Kulp, Clarence A., Upper Darby, Philadelphia, 492

Holloway, Edward S., Philadelphia, 409
Holman, Edward L., New Bloomfield, 410
Holman, William K., Ithan, Philadelphia, 410
Holmes, Ernest G. N., Bethlehem, 410
Holmes, Henry K., Pittsburgh, 410
Holmes, Jesse H., Moylan, 410
Holroyd, Roland, Philadelphia, 410
Holsinger, Virgil C., Millvale, 410
Holton, Charles R., Bethlehem, 411
Holtzapple, George E., York, 411
Holtzman, Herbert P., West Reading, 411
Homsher, Howard N., Bartville, 412
Hoober, John A., York, 412
Hood, Alexander B., Connellsville, 412
Hood, Jean, State College, 412
Hood, Richard, Philadelphia, 412
Hook, John I., Waynesburg, 412
Hooker, Davenport, Pittsburgh, 412
Hoon, Merle R., Pittsburgh, 412
Hooper, Robert P., Philadelphia, 413
Hoopes, Darlington, Reading, 413
Hooven, Herbert N., Solebury, 413
Hoover, Benjamin A., Wrightsville, 413
Hoover, Clyde W., Enola, 413
Hoover, Harvey D., Gettysburg, 413
Hoover, Samuel E., Jenkintown, Philadelphia, 413
Hope, Richard, Pittsburgh, 413
Hopkins, James B., Easton, 413
Hopkinson, Edward, Jr., Philadelphia, 414
Hopper, Harry B., Merion, Philadelphia, 414
Hopwood, Josephine L. R., Primos, Philadelphia, 414
Horelick, Samuel, Pittsburgh, 414
Horn, Clarence A., Reading, 414
Horn, Robert C., Allentown, 414
Hornbostel, Henry, Pittsburgh, 415
Horne, S. Hamill, Bryn Mawr, Philadelphia, 415
Horner, Meyers B., Washington, 415
Horner, Walter W., Pittsburgh, 415
Horner, William S., Pittsburgh, 415
Horrow, Benjamin, Philadelphia, 415
Horton, Clayton R., Portland, Johnsonville, 416
Hosford, Charles F., Jr., Aspinwall, 416
Hosking, Herbert T., Jr., Lansdowne, Philadelphia, 416
Hotson, Leslie, Haverford, 416
Houck, Maurice, Berwick, 416
Houck, Samuel C., Boyertown, 416
Houghten, Ferry C., Pittsburgh, 416
Houghton, Frederick P., Bala-Cynwyd, Philadelphia, 417
House, Edward J., Pittsburgh, 417
Houser, Karl M., Narberth, Philadelphia, 417
Housman, William F., Steelton, 417
Houston, James G., Pittsburgh, 417
Houston, Samuel F., Philadelphia, 417
Houtz, Harry D., Selinsgrove, 417
Houze, Roger J. J., Point Marion, 417
Hovde, Brynjolf J., Pittsburgh, 417
Howard, Edgar B., Bryn Mawr, 418
Howard, Frederick A., Chester, 418
Howard, Philip E., Philadelphia, 418
Howard, William E., Pittsburgh, 418
Howat, John B., Sharon, 418
Howe, George, Philadelphia, 419
Howe, Thomas D., Pittsburgh, 419
Howell, John C., Philadelphia, 419
Hower, Harry, Pittsburgh, 420
Howland, Alice G., Bryn Mawr, 420
Howland, Anne W., Philadelphia, 420
Howland, Arthur B., Swarthmore, 420
Howland, Fred B., Titusville, 420
Howland, Harry W., Galeton, 420
Howorth, John, Wilkes-Barre, 420
Howson, Furman S., Wayne, Philadelphia, 420
Hoy, Charles W., Philadelphia, 420
Hoyler, Cyril N., Bethlehem, 420
Hoyt, Creig S., Grove City, 420
Hubach, Louis A., Pittsburgh, 421

Hubbard, Charles G., Smethport, 421
Hubbard, John W., Pittsburgh, 421
Hubbs, Robert C., Philadelphia, 421
Huber, Charles F., Wilkes-Barre, 421
Huber, Charles H., Gettysburg, 421
Huber, John F., Wynnewood, Philadelphia, 421
Hudnut, Herbert B., Bellevue, 422
Hudson, Thomas M., Uniontown, 422
Huebner, Grover G., Upper Darby, 422
Huebner, Solomon S., Merion, 422
Huff, William K., Philadelphia, 422
Hufferd, Ralph W., Bradford, 423
Hufnagel, Frederick B., Pittsburgh, 423
Hufnagel, Henry M., Clarion, 423
Hughes, Don E., Dushore, 423
Hughes, Fred A., Dickson City, Scranton, 423
Hughes, I. Lamont, Pittsburgh, 423
Hughes, John H., Brookville, 423
Hughes, Ray O., Pittsburgh, 424
Hulbert, Gustavus A., Henryville, 424
Hull, Robert A., Waverly, Scranton, 424
Hull, William I., Swarthmore, 424
Hulley, Elkanah B., Wilkinsburg, Pittsburgh, 424
Hulme, Norman, Swarthmore, Philadelphia, 425
Hulme, Thomas W., Haverford, 425
Hulse, Shirley C., Bedford, 425
Hulton, John G., Latrobe, 425
Humes, E. Lowry, Pittsburgh, 425
Humes, Samuel H., Williamsport, 425
Humke, Herman C., Punxsutawney, 425
Humphrey, Arthur F., Greensburg, Pittsburgh, 426
Humphrey, Arthur L., Pittsburgh, Wilmerding, 426
Humphreys, Warren R., Philadelphia, 426
Hunsicker, Charles O., Allentown, 426
Hunt, Bruce A., Williamsport, 426
Hunt, Everett L., Swarthmore, 426
Hunt, Frank R., Easton, 427
Hunt, Henry F., Danville, 427
Hunt, Levi C., Schuylkill Haven, 427
Hunt, Percival, Pittsburgh, 427
Hunt, Rachel M. M., Pittsburgh, 427
Hunt, Roy A., Pittsburgh, 427
Hunt, Theodore B., Easton, 427
Hunt, Willis R., Easton, 427
Hunter, Charles W., Haverford, Philadelphia, 427
Hunter, Frances T., Philadelphia, 428
Hunter, James N., Pittsburgh, 428
Hunter, John R., Jr., Hollidaysburg, Altoona, 428
Hunter, Lillian A., Tidionte, 428
Hunter, Thomas H., Sewickley, McKees Rocks, 428
Huntley, George W., Jr., Emporium, 428
Huntley, Louis G., Pittsburgh, 428
Hunton, Ella G., Greenville, 428
Huot, Constant J., Swissvale, 429
Hurd, Peter, Chadds Ford, 429
Hurevitz, Meyer, Philadelphia, 429
Hurley, Emmet D., Erie, 429
Hurwitz, Abraham, Reading, 429
Husek, Joseph, Palmyra, 429
Husemen, Lewis E., Wilkinsburg, 429
Huston, Charles L., Coatesville, 430
Huston, Stewart, Coatesville, 430
Hutchinson, Bennett W., Pittsburgh, 430
Hutchinson, Paul E., Pittsburgh, 430
Hutchinson, Robert P., Bethlehem, 430
Hutchison, Albert W., State College, 430
Hutchison, Ralph C., Washington, 430
Hutchison, Stuart N., Pittsburgh, 430
Hutchisson, Elmer, Pittsburgh, 430
Hutton, A. J. White, Chambersburg, 430
Hyatt, Frank K., Chester, 431
Hyde, Walter R., Philadelphia, 431
Ihrig, Roscoe M., Pittsburgh, 432
Illingworth, Ralph W., Jr., Pine Grove Mills, 432

Illman, Adelaide T., Philadelphia, 432
Illman, George M., Philadelphia, 432
Ingersoll, C. Jared, Washington, Philadelphia, 433
Ingersoll, Frank B., Sharpsburg, Pittsburgh, 433
Ingersoll, Robert S., Penllyn, Philadelphia, 433
Ingham, Charles T., Pittsburgh, 433
Inglis, William W., Scranton, 433
Ingram, Martha B., Sharon, 433
Innes, William T., Philadelphia, 434
Irland, George A., Lewisburg, 434
Irvin, Charles H., Big Run, 434
Irvin, Richard, Pittsburgh, 434
Irving, Laurence, Swarthmore, 434
Irwin, Harold S., Carlisle, 434
Irwin, Orlando W., Pittsburgh, 435
Irwin, William W., Farrell, 435
Isaacs, Asher, Pittsburgh, 435
Isherwood, James E., Waynesburg, 435
Isherwood, James H., Allegany, 435
Itter, Harry A., Easton, 435
Iverson, Lorenz, Pittsburgh, 435
Ivy, Robert H., Lansdowne, Philadelphia, 436
Jack, James E., Titusville, 436
Jackson, Albert A., Philadelphia, 436
Jackson, Arthur C., Swarthmore, Philadelphia, 436
Jackson, Chevalier, Schwenkville, Philadelphia, 436
Jackson, Eugene J., St. Mary's, 437
Jackson, Frank S., Punxsutawney, 437
Jackson, Frederick B., Warren, 437
Jackson, J. Roy, Beaver, 437
Jackson, James R., Philadelphia, 438
Jackson, John J., Pittsburgh, 438
Jackson, Joseph, Philadelphia, 438
Jackson, Lloyd E., Pitcairn, Pittsburgh, 438
Jackson, Ralph G., Philadelphia, 438
Jackson, Samuel H., 2d, Pittsburgh, 438
Jackson, William H., Pittsburgh, 438
Jacob, Frederick M., Pittsburgh, 438
Jacobs, Melvin L., Paradise, Harrisburg, 439
Jacobs, Merkel H., Media, 439
Jacobs, Myrl L., Bethlehem, 439
Jacobs, Nathan B., Pittsburgh, 439
Jacobs, Robert L., Carlisle, 439
Jacoby, Wilmer M., Pittsburgh, 439
Jaekel, Frederic B., Doylestown, Philadelphia, 440
Jaffe, Israel M., Butler, 440
James, Alfred P., Pittsburgh, 440
James, Arthur E., West Chester, 440
James, Arthur H., Plymouth, 440
James, Frank C., Philadelphia, 440
James, Frederic, Wynnewood, 440
James, Henry D., Pittsburgh, 440
James, Joseph H., Pittsburgh, 441
James, Ralph E., Allentown, 441
James, Reese D., Bridgeport, Philadelphia, 441
Jamieson, Lewis C., Warren, 441
Jamison, David L., St. Davids, 441
Jamison, Jay N., McDonald, Pittsburgh, 441
Janeway, Augustine S., Harrisburg, 441
Janney, Walter C., Bryn Mawr, Philadelphia, 441
Janssen, Henry, Wyomissing, Reading, 442
Jaquette, Henrietta S., Swarthmore, 442
Jarrett, Benjamin, Farrell, 442
Jarvis, Anna, Philadelphia, 442
Jaspan, Harry J., Philadelphia, 442
Jayne, Horace H. F., Wallingford, Philadelphia, 442
Jefferis, J. Walter, Kennett Square, 442
Jeffery, John F., Erie, 442
Jeffery, Edward M., Philadelphia, 443
Jefferys, William H., Rosemont, Philadelphia, 443
Jeffrey, Lon C., Pittsburgh, 443
Jenckes, Earl S., Wyomissing, Shillington, 443
Jenkins, Arthur H., Jenkintown, Philadelphia, 443
Jenkins, Charles F., Philadelphia, 443

Jenkins, George H., Gwynedd, Norristown, 443
Jenkins, John C., Union City, 443
Jenkins, Thomas C., Pittsburgh, 443
Jenkinson, Richard D., Bellevue, 444
Jenks, John S., Philadelphia, 444
Jenks, Morton, Philadelphia, 444
Jennings, Burgess H., Bethlehem, 444
Jennings, Dale C., Pittsburgh, 444
Jennings, O. E., Pittsburgh, 444
Jensen, Cyril D., Bethlehem, 444
Jepson, Paul N., Philadelphia, 444
Jewett, Arthur C., Pittsburgh, 445
Jiuliante, Jessamine, Erie, 445
Jockers, Ernst, Doylestown, 445
Johnson, Albert W., Lewisburg, 445
Johnson, Albert W., Jr., Williamsport, 446
Johnson, Alfred H., Pittsburgh, 446
Johnson, Amandus, Philadelphia, 446
Johnson, Benjamin M., Pittsburgh, 446
Johnson, Charles M., Drexel Hill, Philadelphia, 446
Johnson, Charles M., Pittsburgh, 446
Johnson, Clarence R., Lahaska, 447
Johnson, Elizabeth F., Bryn Mawr, 447
Johnson, Elmer E. S., Hereford, Pennsburg, 447
Johnson, Emma, Philadelphia, 447
Johnson, Emory R., Philadelphia, 447
Johnson, Frederick G., Wilkes-Barre, 447
Johnson, George, Lincoln University, 447
Johnson, George B., West Chester, 447
Johnson, Guy R., Harrisburg, 448
Johnson, Herbert, Huntingdon Valley, 448
Johnson, Holger J., Pittsburgh, 448
Johnson, Howard C., Moylan, Philadelphia, 448
Johnson, John C., West Chester, 448
Johnson, Josiah B., Ligonier, 448
Johnson, Lester F., York, 449
Johnson, Ralph G., Washington, 449
Johnson, Robert L., Philadelphia, 449
Johnson, Russell C., Collegeville, 449
Johnson, Theodore, Erie, 449
Johnson, Thomas H., Westtown, Swarthmore, 449
Johnson, Virgil L., Philadelphia, 449
Johnston, Alfred M., Freeport, 450
Johnston, Archibald, Bethlehem, 450
Johnston, Cecil C., Meadville, 450
Johnston, Harry L., Altoona, 450
Johnston, Howard M., Clarion, 450
Johnston, John, Pittsburgh, 450
Johnstone, Arthur E., Wilkes-Barre, 451
Johnstone, Burton K., State College, 451
Jones, Addison, Washington, 451
Jones, Adrian H., West Hazleton, Hazleton, 451
Jones, Arthur J., Swarthmore, 451
Jones, Barclay L., Upper Darby, Philadelphia, 451
Jones, Benjamin F., Tyrone, 451
Jones, Benjamin F., 3d, Sewickley, Pittsburgh, 451
Jones, Benjamin R., Jr., Wilkes-Barre, 452
Jones, Burwell W., Delta, 452
Jones, Charles S., Washington Crossing, 452
Jones, Clement P., Pittsburgh, 452
Jones, David R., Greenville, 452
Jones, Edward H., State College, 452
Jones, Edward S., Blakely, Scranton, 452
Jones, George E., Pittsburgh, 453
Jones, Harold W., Wynnewood, Philadelphia, 453
Jones, Harry A., Washington, 453
Jones, Henry W., Pittsburgh, 453
Jones, H. Ennis, Philadelphia, 453
Jones, Horace C., Conshohocken, 453
Jones, John L., Johnstown, Ebensburg, 453
Jones, John P., Drexel Hill, Upper Darby, 454
Jones, Lawrence E., Philadelphia, 454

PENNSYLVANIA

Harrison, Thomas R., Wyncote, Philadelphia, 371
Harry, Carolus P., Norristown, 371
Harry, Philip W., Lancaster, 372
Hart, Charles, Media, Chester, 372
Hart, John F., Philadelphia, 372
Hart, Thomas, Wynnewood, Philadelphia, 372
Hart, U. Shuman, Hollidaysburg, 372
Harter, Nathan W., Greenville, 372
Hartgen, Frederick A., Erie, 372
Hartman, Edwin M., Lancaster, 373
Hartman, Galen C., Pittsburgh, 373
Hartman, Guy N., Somerset, Meyersdale, 373
Hartman, Roland C., Hanover, 373
Hartman, Thomas H., New Castle, 373
Hartman, William E., Carlisle, 373
Hartmann, William V., Pittsburgh, 373
Hartung, Charles A., Pittsburgh, 374
Hartz, Robert E., Palmyra, 374
Hartzog, Herbert J., Bethlehem, 374
Harvey, Adelbert W., Pittsburgh, 374
Harvey, Charles W., Philadelphia, 374
Harvey, E. Marshall, Media, 374
Harvey, Frederic A., Pittsburgh, 374
Harvey, John S. C., Radnor, 375
Harvey, Lewis B., Newtown Square, 375
Harvey, McLeod, Waynesburg, 375
Harvey, Walter B., Pittsburgh, 375
Hasek, Carl W., State College, 375
Haslam, George S., Palmerton, 375
Hasley, Thomas O., Pittsburgh, 375
Hassler, Jacob P., Grove City, 375
Hassold, Carl F. R., Philadelphia, 376
Hastings, Glen B., Montoursville, Williamsport, 376
Hastings, Penn G., Philadelphia, Milton, 376
Hastings, Willard S., Elkins Park, Philadelphia, 376
Haswell, John R., State College, 376
Hatch, David A., Easton, 376
Hatfield, Charles J., Philadelphia, 376
Hathaway, Charles M., Jr., Olyphant, 376
Hathaway, Harle W., Philadelphia, 377
Hathway, Marion, Pittsburgh, 377
Hauber, Alois J., St. Marys, 377
Hauberger, George H., Philadelphia, 377
Haudenshield, John R., Carnegie, Pittsburgh, 377
Haupt, William S., Shamokin, 377
Hause, Nathan E., Harrisburg, 377
Hauser, Conrad A., Upper Darby, Philadelphia, 377
Hausman, William A., Jr., Allentown, 377
Havenhill, Robert S., Beaver, Monaca, 378
Havens, Paul S., Chambersburg, 378
Haviland, James T., Wayne, Philadelphia, 378
Haviland, Walter W., Lansdowne, 378
Hawes, Edward M., Norristown, 378
Hawkes, William F., Philadelphia, 378
Hawks, Edward, Philadelphia, 378
Hawley, William C., Pittsburgh, Wilkinsburg, 379
Hay, George, Johnstown, 379
Hay, Homer W., Somerset, 379
Hay, Malcolm, Sewickley, Pittsburgh, 379
Hay, Southard, Pittsburgh, 379
Hayes, E. V., Pittsburgh, 370
Hayes, J. Carroll, West Chester, 379
Hayes, John R., Embreeville, 379
Hayes, Norman T. Rosemont, Philadelphia, 380
Haynes, Roy A., Philadelphia, 380
Hays, Harry C., Fredonia, 380
Hays, Jo, State College, 380
Hays, John L., Pittsburgh, 380
Haythorn, Samuel R., Pittsburgh, 381
Hayward, Nathan, Wayne, Philadelphia, 381
Hazard, Spencer P., Philadelphia, 381
Hazen, Carl M., Titusville, 381
Hazlehurst, Thomas H., Jr., Bethlehem, 381
Head, Leon O., Center Ridge, 381
Headings, Donald M., Norristown, 382
Heald, Kenneth C., Pittsburgh, 382

Healy, Fred A., Ardmore, Philadelphia, 382
Heard, Drayton, Sewickley, Pittsburgh, 382
Heard, James D., Pittsburgh, 382
Heath, Edwin J., Bethlehem, 382
Heathcote, Charles W., West Chester, 382
Hebard, Benjamin M., Narberth, 383
Hechler, F. G., State College, 383
Hecht, Edward, Lock Haven, 383
Heckel, George B., Philadelphia, 383
Heckscher, Maurice, Washington, Philadelphia, 383
Hedenburg, Oscar F., Pittsburgh, 383
Hedley, Evalena, Philadelphia, 383
Heffner, Edward H., Philadelphia, 384
Heilbron, Tillie T., Media, Philadelphia, 384
Heilbrunn, Lewis V., Philadelphia, 384
Heilman, Eugene A., Philadelphia, 384
Heilman, Harry A., Kittanning, 384
Heilman, Russell H., Pittsburgh, 384
Heimerdinger, Leo H., Philadelphia, 385
Heine, H. Eugene, Philadelphia, 385
Heinly, Charles B., York, 385
Heintzelman, C. H., Coatesville, 385
Heinz, Howard, Pittsburgh, 385
Heiserman, Clarence B., Haverford, Philadelphia, 385
Heisey, Herman B., Lewistown, 385
Heisler, Roland C., Wynnewood, Philadelphia, 386
Heiss, Elwood D., East Stroudsburg, 386
Heissenbuttel, Ernest G., Greenville, 386
Helbert, George K., Philadelphia, 386
Held, Jacob B., Erie, 386
Held, Omar C., Pittsburgh, 386
Helfferich, Donald L., Lansdowne, 386
Hellmund, Rudolph E., Swissvale, 386
Helmbold, Theodore R., Pittsburgh, 387
Helme, J. Burn, State College, 387
Helriegel, Florence J., Scranton, 387
Helson, Harry, Narberth, 387
Helton, Roy A., Upper Darby, Harrisburg, 387
Hemingway, Reginald S., Bloomsburg, 387
Hemphill, John, Philadelphia, 387
Hemphill, Marguerite F., Beaver Falls, 387
Henderson, Adelbert A., Wilkinsburg, Pittsburgh, 387
Henderson, Davis W., Uniontown, 387
Henderson, Earl F., New Castle, 387
Henderson, Joseph H., Shiremanstown, Harrisburg, 388
Henderson, Joseph W., Philadelphia, 388
Henderson, Katharine C., Altoona, 388
Henderson, Robert H., Huntingdon, 388
Hendricks, William C., Brookville, 388
Hendrickson, David, New Hope, 388
Henke, Frederick G., Meadville, 388
Henn, Arthur W., Pittsburgh, 388
Hennessey, John J., Philadelphia, 389
Henning, Stanley R., Trucksville, Wilkes-Barre, 389
Henning, William L., State College, 389
Henninger, Frank L., Sunbury, 389
Henretta, James E., Kane, 389
Henrici, Max, Coraopolis, Pittsburgh, 389
Henry, Arnold K., Philadelphia, 389
Henry, George M., Berwyn, Philadelphia, 389
Henry, John T., Martha Furnace, 389
Henry, Wilbur F., Washington, 390
Hensel, George W., Jr., Quarryville, 390
Hensler, Carl P., Pittsburgh, 390
Hepburn, Joseph S., Philadelphia, see Addenda
Heppenstall, Charles W., Pittsburgh, 390
Heppenstall, Robert B., Pittsburgh, 390
Herbach, Joseph, Philadelphia, 390
Herben, Stephen J., Haverford, 390
Herber, E. C., Carlisle, 390

Herbert, Robert B., Greensburg, 390
Herbst, Josephine F., Erwinna, 390
Herd, John V., Philadelphia, 391
Herdic, Carl W., Williamsport, 391
Hergesheimer, Ella S., Reading, 391
Hergesheimer, Joseph, West Chester, 391
Herman, Albert, Philadelphia, 391
Herman, John W., Coatesville, 391
Herman, Leonora O., Philadelphia, 391
Herman, Samuel S., West Chester, Philadelphia, 391
Herman, Stewart W., Harrisburg, Philadelphia, 391
Herman, Theodore F., Lancaster, 391
Hermann, Burke M., Boalsburg, 391
Herndon, Edward L., Pottsville, 391
Herndon, John G., Jr., Haverford, 391
Herpst, Martha J., Titusville, 392
Herr, Benjamin B., Lancaster, 392
Herr, Benjamin M., Pittsburgh, 392
Herr, Herbert T., Jr., Pittsburgh, 392
Herr, John D., Philadelphia, 392
Herr, John K., Lancaster, 392
Herrick, Cheesman A., Philadelphia, 392
Herrman, Clinton S., Philadelphia, 392
Herron, David C., Monongahela, 392
Herron, Samuel D., Sewickley, Pittsburgh, 393
Hershey, Ezra F., Hershey, 393
Hershey, Milton S., Hershey, 393
Hershner, Newton W., Mechanicsburg, 393
Hertzler, Jacob O., Erie, 393
Hertzler, William, Port Royal, 393
Hervey, John G., Upper Darby, Philadelphia, 393
Herzog, Eugene, Pittsburgh, 393
Heselbarth, Thomas K., Pittsburgh, 393
Hess, Arleigh P., Philadelphia, 393
Hess, Elam G., Manheim, 393
Hess, Elmer, Erie, 394
Hess, George H., Uniontown, 394
Hess, H. Lloyd, Lancaster, 394
Hess, Henry L., Philadelphia, 394
Hess, Herbert W., Philadelphia, 394
Hess, Leslie E., Drexel Hill, Philadelphia, 394
Hesse, Frank M., Pittsburgh, 394
Hetrick, William H., Connellsville, 394
Hetzel, Frederic V., West Chester, 394
Hetzel, Ralph D., State College, 394
Heuer, Russell P., Bryn Mawr, Philadelphia, 394
Hewitt, Arthur C., Bellefonte, 395
Heywood, Harry B., Jenkintown, Conshohocken, 395
Hibbs, Ben, Narberth, Philadelphia, 395
Hibshman, Edward K., State College, 395
Hibshman, Eugene E., Altoona, 395
Hickerson, Ainslee E., Narberth, Ardmore, 396
Hickey, David F., Bradford, 396
Hicks-Bruun, Mildred M., Swarthmore, Norwood, 396
Hiers, Glen S., Bala-Cynwyd, Philadelphia, 396
Higbee, Donald M., Connellsville, 396
Higbee, William S., Philadelphia, 396
Higgins, Henry B., Sewickley, Pittsburgh, 396
Higgins, John M., Sayre, 396
Higgins, Robert A., State College, 396
Higgins, Ruth L., Jenkintown, 397
Higgins, Thomas J., Philadelphia, 397
High, Samuel H., Horsham, Norristown, 397
Highberger, Elmer, Jr., Oil City, 397
Hildenberger, Martin J., Bethlehem, 397
Hildner, Richard C., Pittsburgh, 397
Hill, Calvin F., Neffs, 397
Hill, Charles C., Carlisle, 398
Hill, Edward Y., Philadelphia, 398
Hill, Grace L., Swarthmore, 498
Hill, Henry C., Lewisburg, 398
Hill, J. Ben, State College, 398
Hill, J. Bennett, Wynnewood, Marcus Hook, 399
Hill, Minot A., Bristol, 399
Hill, Samuel S., Wernersville, 399
Hill, Theodore C., North East, Erie, 399
Hill, Walter L., Scranton, 400

Hillegass, Charles E., Pennsburg, 400
Hillegass, Foster C., Pennsburg, Norristown, 400
Hillegass, Jonathan B., Norristown, 400
Hilles, Robert L., Philadelphia, 400
Hilliard, Thomas J., Sharpsburg, Pittsburgh, 400
Hillman, John H., Jr., Pittsburgh, 400
Hillstrom, David A., Corry, 400
Himebaugh, John W., Erie, 400
Himes, Leslie R., New Bethlehem, 401
Hinchman, William R., Pittsburgh, 401
Hindman, James E., Wilkinsburg, Pittsburgh, 401
Hindman, William B., Uniontown, 401
Hipsher, Edward E., Philadelphia, 402
Hipwell, Harry H., Pittsburgh, 402
Hires, Charles E., Jr., Wynnewood, Philadelphia, 402
Hires, Harrison S., Berwyn, Philadelphia, 402
Hirsch, Albert C., Pittsburgh, 402
Hirsch, Isaac E., Pittsburgh, 402
Hirsch, Joseph, Philadelphia, 402
Hirschwald, Rudolph M., Philadelphia, 403
Hirsh, Harry B., Philadelphia, 403
Hirsh, Sidney, Pittsburgh, 403
Hirst, Lester L., Pittsburgh, 403
Hirt, William E., Erie, 403
Hirtzel, Orris C., North East, 403
Hitchens, William F., Pittsburgh, 403
Hitchler, Walter H., Carlisle, 403
Hittle, James M., Greenville, 403
Hoag, Clarence G., Haverford, 404
Hoban, Thomas L., Scranton, 404
Höber, Rudolf O. A., Philadelphia, 404
Hoblitzelle, Harrison, Ithan, Eddystone, 404
Hodge, Charles, 4th, Philadelphia, 404
Hodges, Clarence A., Philadelphia, 404
Hodges, Fletcher, Jr., Pittsburgh, 404
Hodges, Harry, Philadelphia, 405
Hodges, Leigh M., Doylestown, Philadelphia, 405
Hodgkiss, Harold E., State College, 405
Hoechst, Coit R., Pittsburgh, 405
Hoeveler, John A., Mt. Lebanon, Pittsburgh, 405
Hoffman, Dean M., Harrisburg, 405
Hoffman, George W., Upper Darby, 405
Hoffman, Harry C., Connellsville, 405
Hoffman, Harry F., Allentown, 406
Hoffman, James F., Wilkinsburg, 406
Hoffman, Leon H., Punxsutawney, 406
Hoffman, Luther S., East Stroudsburg, 406
Hoffman, William S., State College, 406
Hofmann, Josef, Merion, Philadelphia, 406
Hofstetter, William A., Philadelphia, 406
Hogan, Charles V., Pottsville, 406
Hogan, Franklin E., Kane, 406
Hogg, Harold K., Lancaster, 407
Holbrook, Arthur A., East Stroudsburg, Stroudsburg, 407
Holbrook, Elmer A., Pittsburgh, 407
Holcomb, Richmond C., Upper Darby, 407
Holcombe, John L., Pittsburgh, 407
Holden, Hale, Jr., Haverford, Philadelphia, 407
Holden, Robert F., Haverford, Philadelphia, 407
Holland, J. Burnett, Norristown, 407
Holland, Leicester B., Philadelphia, 407
Holland, Moorhead B., Pittsburgh, 408
Holland, Rupert S., Wayne, 408
Holland, Stanley H., McKeesport, 408
Hollander, Lester, Pittsburgh, 408
Hollinger, John A., Allison Park, Pittsburgh, 408
Hollingsworth, Charles B., Greensburg, 409
Hollinshead, Byron S., La Plume, 409

PENNSYLVANIA

Gossling, John H., Philadelphia, 332
Gotshall, Roy J., Lansdowne, Philadelphia, 332
Gott, Estep T., Sewickley, Pittsburgh, 332
Gottlieb, Maxim B., Philadelphia, 332
Gottlieb, Moritz M., Allentown, 332
Gotwals, John E., Phoenixville, 332
Gould, Beatrice B., Philadelphia, 333
Gould, Charles B., Philadelphia, 333
Gould, George, Mt. Lebanon, Pittsburgh, 333
Gould, Ralph R., Pittsburgh, 333
Gould, William D., Carlisle, 333
Gourley, W. Clyde, Glenside, Willow Grove, 333
Gow, J. Steele, Pittsburgh, 333
Gowen, James E., Philadelphia, 333
Graber, Henry, Royersford, 333
Grace, Eugene G., Bethlehem, 334
Graf, Julius E., Avalon, Pittsburgh, 334
Graff, F. Malcolm, Blairsville, 334
Graff, George W., York, 334
Graff, Richard M., Worthington, 334
Grafly, Dorothy, Philadelphia, 334
Graham, Arthur K., Philadelphia, Jenkintown, 334
Graham, Ben G., Pittsburgh, 334
Graham, Edwin E., Philadelphia, 334
Graham, John C., Butler, 334
Graham, John H., Glenside, Philadelphia, 335
Graham, Louis E., Beaver, 335
Graham, Robert X., Wilkinsburg, 335
Gramley, Dale H., Bethlehem, 335
Granowitz, Abram M., Johnstown, 335
Grant, Catharine E., Philadelphia, Harrisburg, 335
Grant, William H., St. Marys, 335
Graper, Elmer D., Pittsburgh, 335
Grapin, Camille, Pittsburgh, 335
Gravell, James H., Ambler, 336
Graves, Arthur F., Bethlehem, 336
Graves, Harold F., State College, 336
Graves, W. Brooke, Ardmore, 336
Gray, David J., Scranton, 337
Gray, James H., Pittsburgh, 337
Gray, Jessie, Philadelphia, 337
Gray, John S., Wilkinsburg, Pittsburgh, 337
Gray, Joseph, Spangler, Barnesboro, 337
Gray, Joseph R., Pittsburgh, 337
Grebe, Melvin H., Philadelphia, 337
Green, Clyde C., New Castle, 338
Green, G. Edward, Edgewood, Pittsburgh, 338
Green, George R., State College, 338
Green, Harry, Allentown, Bethlehem, 338
Green, John F. C., McKeesport, 338
Green, Otis H., Philadelphia, 339
Greenawalt, Emerson G., Susquehanna, 339
Greenbaum, Frederick R., Philadelphia, 339
Greenbaum, Sigmund S., Philadelphia, 339
Greenberg, Reynold H., Philadelphia, 339
Greenberg, Simon, Philadelphia, 339
Greene, Edward M., Huntingdon, 340
Greene, Floyd L., St. Davids, Philadelphia, 340
Greene, Lloyd B., Philadelphia, 340
Greenewalt, Mary H., Philadelphia, 340
Greenfield, Albert M., Philadelphia, 340
Greenslade, Grover R., Pittsburgh, Bridgeville, 341
Greenstone, Julius H., Philadelphia, 341
Greenway, Walter B., Jenkintown, 341
Greenzweig, Oscar A., Wind Gap, 341
Greer, Charles C., Johnstown, 341
Greer, Robert B., Media, 341
Gregory, Ralph A., Scranton, 342
Gregory, Thomas B., Emlenton, Pittsburgh, 342
Greisheimer, Esther M., Philadelphia, 342
Greiss, George A., Allentown, 342
Gress, Ernest M., Camp Hill, Harrisburg, 342
Greth, Morris S., Temple, 342
Grier, George W., Ben Avon, Pittsburgh, 342
Grier, Thomas C., Birmingham, 343
Griffin, Frederick R., Haverford, Philadelphia, 343
Griffin, Joseph A., Dickson, Scranton, 343
Griffing, Curtis A., Linesville, 343
Griffith, Beatrice F., Merion, 343
Griffith, Edward, Kingston, Scranton, 343
Griffith, George W., Ebensburg, 343
Griffith, Helen S., Philadelphia, 344
Griffith, Ivor, Elkins Park, Philadelphia, 344
Griffith, James A., Pittsburgh, 344
Griffith, J. P. Crozer, Philadelphia, 344
Griffiths, Hall M., Philadelphia, 344
Grim, George A., Nazareth, 344
Grimes, William C., West Alexander, 344
Grimm, Herbert L., Gettysburg, 344
Grimm, Karl J., Gettysburg, 344
Gring, Wilbur D., Newport, 345
Griscom, John M., Philadelphia, 345
Griscom, Rodman E., Haverford, 345
Grizzell, E. Duncan, Philadelphia, 345
Groblewski, Casimir C., Plymouth, 345
Groce, William M., Selinsgrove, 345
Groff, June G., Philadelphia, 346
Groff, Robert A., Bala-Cynwyd, Philadelphia, 346
Groff, Wilmer K., Berwyn, 346
Groh, John L., Lebanon, 346
Grondahl, Lars O., Pittsburgh, Swissvale, 346
Grone, Robert Y., Danville, 346
Groover, Clair, Lewisburg, 346
Grose, C. Herman, Erie, 346
Grosh, Miriam, Beaver Falls, 346
Gross, John H., Lansdowne, Philadelphia, 346
Gross, John M., Bethlehem, 347
Gross, Juliet P., Philadelphia, Sellersville, 347
Gross, Malcolm W., Allentown, 347
Grossman, Samuel L., Harrisburg, 347
Groton, Nathanael B., Whitemarsh, 347
Grove, Harry A., Greencastle, 347
Grove, Robert E., Pittsburgh, 348
Groves, Frederick P., Pittsburgh, 348
Groves, Hannah C., Philadelphia, 348
Grubb, William R., Bangor, 348
Grubbs, Barton, 2d, Edgewood, Pittsburgh, 348
Gruber, Charles M., Bala-Cynwyd, Philadelphia, 348
Gruenberg, Frederick P., Philadelphia, 348
Grumbine, Harvey C., Lebanon, 348
Grundy, Joseph R., Bristol, 348
Gruver, Elbert A., Philadelphia, 348
Gubb, Larry E., Philadelphia, 348
Guckert, William L., Pittsburgh, 348
Guerin, John J., Philadelphia, 349
Guerrisi, Girolamo, Lebanon, 349
Guffey, Joseph F., Pittsburgh, 349
Guild, Lawrence R., Pittsburgh, 349
Guillet, George L., State College, 349
Gulick, Lee N., Bala-Cynwyd, 349
Gulliksen, Finn H., Pittsburgh, East Pittsburgh, 349
Gumaer, Alfred H., Philadelphia, 349
Gummey, Henry R., Jr., Philadelphia, 350
Gummo, Blanchard S., Lock Haven, Lewisburg, 350
Gunnison, Sisson B., Erie, Girard, 350
Gunster, Joseph F., Scranton, 350
Guthrie, Charles C., Pittsburgh, 350
Guthrie, Charles E., Coudersport, 350
Guthrie, Donald, Sayre, 350
Guthrie, Walter J., Pittsburgh, 351
Gutmueller, William G., Pottstown, 351
Gyger, Furman N., Kimberton, 351
Haas, Alfred M., Philadelphia, 351
Haas, Francis B., Bloomsburg, 351
Haas, Harry J., Haverford, Philadelphia, 351
Haas, Robert E., Allentown, 351
Haber, Vernon R., State College, 351
Habgood, Robert P., Bradford, 351
Hackemann, Louis F., Allentown, 352
Hackenberg, Joseph L., Windber, 352
Hackett, James L., Emporium, 352
Hackett, Samuel E., Pittsburgh, 352
Hackney, Henry E., Pittsburgh, 352
Hadden, Samuel B., Philadelphia, 352
Haddock, John C., Wilkes-Barre, 352
Haddon, Harry H., Northumberland, Sunbury, 352
Hadley, Samuel H., Sharon, 352
Hadzsits, George D., Philadelphia, 352
Hafey, William J., Scranton, 352
Haffner, Thomas N., Allentown, Bath, 353
Hagan, James, Pittsburgh, 353
Hager, William H., Lancaster, 353
Hagert, Henry, Philadelphia, 353
Hague, William W., Library, Pittsburgh, 353
Hagy, Henry B., Reading, 353
Hahn, Frank E., Philadelphia, 353
Hahn, Frederick E., Philadelphia, 354
Hahn, Theodore F., Scranton, 354
Haig, Alfred R., Philadelphia, 354
Haines, Amena P., Bryn Athyn, 354
Haines, Arthur S., Library, Pittsburgh, 354
Haines, Benjamin W., West Chester, 354
Haines, Harold A., Philadelphia, 354
Haines, Harry L., Red Lion, 354
Halston, Frank, Pottstown, 355
Halberg, Elmer J., Kittanning, 355
Halbert, LeRoy, Sharon, 355
Haldeman, Paul C., Coatesville, 355
Haldeman-Jefferies, Don, Chalfont, Harrisburg, Philadelphia, 355
Halderman, J. Leonard, Doylestown, 355
Half, Rudolph S., Pittsburgh, 355
Hall, Francis J., Philadelphia, 355
Hall, John A. F., Harrisburg, 356
Hall, John H., Philadelphia, 356
Hall, Lyle G., Ridgway, St. Mary's, 356
Hall, Mary B., Bethlehem, 356
Hall, Ralph E., Pittsburgh, 356
Hall, Robert W., Bethlehem, 356
Hall, William S., Easton, 357
Hall, Wrayburn B., Coudersport, 357
Hallett, George H., West Chester, 357
Hallett, Winslow N., Allentown, 357
Hallowell, A. Irving, Philadelphia, 357
Hallowell, Henry R., Philadelphia, 358
Hallowell, Howard T., Jenkintown, 358
Halpern, Leon A., Philadelphia, 358
Haluska, John J., Patton, 358
Ham, Ernest L., Rochester, 358
Ham, William R., Boalsburg, State College, 358
Hamblock, Leonard C., Philadelphia, 358
Hamer, Alfred, Pittsburgh, 358
Hamill, Samuel M., Philadelphia, 358
Hamilton, George E., Meadville, 359
Hamilton, Harry D., Washington, 359
Hamilton, Hughbert C., Philadelphia, 359
Hamilton, James W., Ben Avon, Pittsburgh, 359
Hamilton, J. Taylor, Bethlehem, 359
Hamilton, Milton W., Reading, 360
Hamilton, William J., Carbondale, 360
Hamlin, Orlo J., Smethport, 360
Hamm, Homer A., Meadville, 360
Hammett, Frederick S., Philadelphia, 360
Hammond, Frank C., Philadelphia, 360
Hammond, Harry P., State College, 360
Hamor, William A., Oakmont, Pittsburgh, 361
Hampson, Harold S., Warren, 361
Hamsher, Mervin H., Harrisburg, 361
Hanauer, Albert M., Pittsburgh, 361
Hance, Robert T., Pittsburgh, 361
Hand, Alfred, Philadelphia, 361
Hand, George T., Bethlehem, 361
Haney, John L., Philadelphia, 362
Hankey, William L., New Kensington, Wilmerding, 362
Hankins, James H., Uniontown, 362
Hanley, Edward J., Tarentum, Brackenridge, 362
Hanna, Bernard F., Rockwood, 362
Hanna, Clinton R., Pittsburgh, 363
Hanna, Meredith, Philadelphia, 363
Hanny, William F., Swarthmore, 363
Hansell, John L., Ambler, 363
Hanselman, William L., Meadville, 363
Hanson, Henry W. A., Gettysburg, 363
Harbeson, John F., Philadelphia, 363
Harbeson, William P., Philadelphia, 364
Harbison, Francis R., Fox Chapel, Pittsburgh, 364
Harbison, Ralph W., Sewickley, Pittsburgh, 364
Harbold, Peter M., Lancaster, 364
Harcum, Edith H., Bryn Mawr, 364
Hardcastle, John D., Mt. Lebanon, Pittsburgh, 364
Harding, George, Wynnewood, 365
Hardinge, Harlowe, York, 365
Hardt, Frank M., Bryn Mawr, Philadelphia, 365
Hardt, John W., Philadelphia, 365
Hardt, Walter K., Haverford, 365
Hardy, Fred N., Port Allegany, 365
Hare, Amory, Media, 365
Hare, Jay V., Trevose, Philadelphia, 366
Hare, Mollie W., Langhorne, 366
Harger, George D., Pittsburgh, 366
Hargest, William M., Harrisburg, 366
Hargroves, Vernon C., Philadelphia, 366
Haring, Albert, Bethlehem, 366
Haring, Fred A., Pittsburgh, 366
Harker, Samuel A., Bloomsburg, 366
Harkey, William F., Washington, 366
Harkins, John F., State College, 366
Harkins, Melvin R., Philadelphia, 366
Harkness, Reuben E. E., Chester, 366
Harlan, Clarence E., Renovo, 366
Harlan, Orla K., State College, 367
Harley, John P., Williamsport, 367
Harllee, Chauncey M. D., Philadelphia, 367
Harman, J. Paul, Greensburg, 367
Harmeson, Glen W., Bethlehem, 367
Harmon, George D., Bethlehem, 367
Harms, John L., Philadelphia, 367
Harner, Nevin C., Lancaster, 367
Harnwell, Gaylord P., Wynnewood, 367
Harper, Francis, Swarthmore, Philadelphia, 368
Harpst, Clifford W., Sharon, 368
Harr, Luther, Philadelphia, 368
Harré, T. Everett, Wrightsville, 368
Harris, Arthur E., Philadelphia, 369
Harris, Burtt, Pittsburgh, 369
Harris, Charles W., Easton, 369
Harris, Clinton L., State College, 369
Harris, Francis W., Coatesville, 369
Harris, George R., Perrysville, Pittsburgh, 369
Harris, John H., Camp Hill, Harrisburg, 370
Harris, John H., Pittsburgh, 370
Harris, John T., Bryn Mawr, Philadelphia, 370
Harris, Philip H., Johnstown, 370
Harris, Stanley E., Lansdowne, Philadelphia, 370
Harris, Stephen, Philadelphia, 370
Harris W. Carlton, Philadelphia, 371
Harrison, Bruce, Mt. Lebanon, Pittsburgh, 371
Harrison, Charles C., Jr., Philadelphia, 371
Harrison, Charles J., Jr., Somerset, 371
Harrison, Earl G., Moylan, Philadelphia, 371
Harrison, Francis G., Gladwyne, Philadelphia, 371
Harrison, H. Norris, Philadelphia, 371
Harrison, Joseph F. X., Philadelphia, 371

PENNSYLVANIA

Kun, Joseph L., Philadelphia, 493
Kunkel, Beverly W., Easton, 493
Kunkel, George, Harrisburg, 493
Kunkel, John C., Harrisburg, 493
Kunkelman, Merle R., Leetsdale, 493
Kurniker, Max W., Pittsburgh, 493
Kurtz, Charles T., Clearfield, 494
Kurtz, Jacob B., Altoona, 494
Kurtz, John F., Harrisburg, 494
Kurtz, John R., Vandergrift, 494
Kuykendall, Clark P., Towanda, 494
Kuznets, Simon S., Media, Philadelphia, 494
Kyle, Frank P., Red Lion, Burnham, 494
Kyle, William J., Waynesburg, 494
Kynett, Alpha G., Philadelphia, 494
Kynett, Harold H., Wayne, Philadelphia, 494
La Brum, J. Harry, Philadelphia, 495
Lackey, Sylvester J., Clarion, 495
Lacy, George R., Mt. Lebanon, Pittsburgh, 495
Ladd, George T., Coraopolis, Pittsburgh, 495
Ladner, Albert H., Jr., Philadelphia, 495
Ladner, Grover C., Philadelphia, 495
Laessle, Albert, Jenkintown, 495
LaFavre, Harry B., Springfield, Philadelphia, 495
Lafean, Edward C., Pittsburgh, 495
Lafferty, Theodore T., Nazareth, 496
Laffoon, Carthrae M., Irwin, East Pittsburgh, 496
Laidley, Lowell T., Carmichaels, 496
Laird, George S., Abington, Philadelphia, 496
Laird, John B., Philadelphia, 496
Laird, John W., Philadelphia, 496
Laird, Richard D., Greensburg, 496
Laird, Robert M., Hanover, York, 496
Laird, Warren P., Philadelphia, 496
Lake, Kirsopp, Haverford, 496
Lakin, Harry A., Harrisburg, 497
Lally, J. P., Mt. Lebanon, Pittsburgh, 497
Lamb, Carl S., Wilkinsburg, Pittsburgh, 497
Lamb, John L., Philadelphia, 497
Lamb, Richard W., Kennett Square, 497
Lamb, William H., Wynnewood, Philadelphia, 497
Lamberton, Chess, Franklin, 498
Lamberton, Robert, Franklin, 498
Lambie, Joseph S., Wilkinsburg, Pittsburgh, 498
Lammers, Martin W., Jenkintown, Philadelphia, 498
Lampe, William E., Philadelphia, 498
Lamsa, George M., Philadelphia, 498
Lancaster, Edward L., Lancaster, 498
Land, John N., Hamburg, 499
Lander, William P. S., Rosemont, 499
Landes, William G., Lansdowne, 499
Landis, Mark H., Waynesboro, 499
Landis, William P., Ardmore, 499
Landis, William W., Carlisle, 499
Lane, Nathaniel F., Philadelphia, 499
Lane, Otho E., Westtown, Philadelphia, 499
Lanfear, Vincent W., Pittsburgh, 500
Lang, Harold L., Fox Chapel, Pittsburgh, 500
Lange, Ernest O. A., Swarthmore, Philadelphia, 500
Lange, Linda B., Philadelphia, 500
Laning, Harris, Philadelphia, 500
Lanning, Robert L., Dormont, Pittsburgh, 501
Laplace, Louis B., Philadelphia, 501
Laramy, Robert E., Bethlehem, 501
Larer, Richard W., Philadelphia, 501
Larkin, Charles R., Bethlehem, 501
Larkin, Fred V., Bethlehem, 501
Larner, Chester W., Philadelphia, 501
Larrabee, Don M., Williamsport, 501
La Rue, Daniel W., East Stroudsburg, 502
La Rue, Mabel G., East Stroudsburg, 502
Lathem, Abraham L., Chester, 502

Latta, Harrison W., Philadelphia, 502
Laubenstein, Franklin J., Ashland, 502
Laudenslager, Ray V., Weatherly, 502
Lauer, Conrad N., Penllyn, Philadelphia, 503
Lauffer, George N., Kittanning, 503
Lauffer, Vada D. K., Upper Darby, 503
Laughlin, George, Jr., Pittsburgh, 503
Laughlin, Irwin, Pittsburgh, 503
Laughlin, Sara E., West Philadelphia, Philadelphia, 503
Laurie, Frank A., Bryn Mawr, 503
Laverty, Elizabeth S., Merion, 503
Law, Margaret L., Chestnut Hill, 504
Law, Marie H., Philadelphia, 504
La Wall, Elmer H., Wilkes-Barre, Scranton, 504
LaWall, Harold J., Haverford, Philadelphia, 504
Lawrence, David L., Pittsburgh, 504
Lawrence, Granville A., Philadelphia, 504
Lawrence, James C., Moylan, 504
Lawrie, Ritchie, Jr., Harrisburg, 504
Laws, Bertha M., Philadelphia, Wynnewood, 504
Laws, George M., Philadelphia, 504
Lawson, George B., Lewisburg, 505
Lawson, James H., McKeesport, 505
Laycock, Charles W., Kingston, Wilkes-Barre, 505
Layng, Frank R. S., Jr., Greenville, 505
Leach, Henry G., Villanova, 505
Leach, Howard S., Bethlehem, 505
Leach, Walter, Mansfield, Jersey Shore, 506
Leaf, Leonard, Pottstown, 506
Leaman, William G., Jr., Philadelphia, 506
Leathernan, Clarence G., Hummelstown, 506
Leattor, William L., Riegelsville, 506
Leavitt, Frederic H., Ardmore, Philadelphia, 506
LeClere, John B., Allison Park, Pittsburgh, 507
Lederer, Erwin R., Bradford, 507
Lederer, Lucy C. K., State College, 507
Lee, Charles M., Beaver Falls, 507
Lee, Harry W., Reading, 507
Lee, Henry H., Moylan, 507
Lee, John C., Pottsville, 508
Lee, John H., Philadelphia, 508
Lee, John M., Philipsburg, 508
Lee, Manning de V., Ambler, Philadelphia, 508
Lee, Walter E., Philadelphia, 508
Lee, William P., Glenside, 508
Leech, Carl G., Media, 508
Leech, Edward T., Mt. Lebanon, Pittsburgh, 508
Leech, George L., Harrisburg, 508
Leeds, Morris E., Philadelphia, 508
Lees, George C., Pottstown, 508
Lefever, Clarence H., Erie, 509
LeFevre, Laura Z., Philadelphia, 509
Lefferts, Walter, Philadelphia, 509
Leffler, George L., State College, 509
Lefler, Ross L., McKeesport, Philadelphia, 509
Legrain, Leon, Philadelphia, 509
LeGrys, Herbert J., St. Marys, 509
Leh, Howard H., Nazareth, Bath, 509
Leh, John, Allentown, 509
Leh, John H., Allentown, 509
Lehman, George M., Pittsburgh, 509
Lehman, James M. B., Philadelphia, 510
Lehn, Homer M. B., Grove City, 510
Lehr, Anna M. M., Bryn Mawr, 510
Leibensperger, George F., Kutztown, 510
Leighton, Henry, Wilkinsburg, Pittsburgh, 510
Leinbach, Paul S., Philadelphia, 510
Leisenring, Edward B., Ardmore, Philadelphia, 511
Leiser, Andrew A., Jr., Lewisburg, 511
Leister, John S., State College, 511
Leith, Hugh, Mt. Lebanon, 511
Leith-Ross, Harry, New Hope, 511
Leitzel, Frank O., Pittsburgh, 511
LeMon, Melvin W., Lewisburg, 511
Lengler, Frederick E., Scranton, 512
Lenhert, George R. Jr., Philadelphia, 512
Lenning, Frederick, 6th, Philadelphia, 512

Lentz, Edwin W., Philadelphia, 512
Lentz, William J., Philadelphia, 512
Leonard, Adna W., Pittsburgh, 512
Leonard, Joseph S., Bethlehem, 512
Leonard, Walter C., Pittsburgh, 512
Leonards, Thomas C., Bryn Mawr, Philadelphia, 512
Leopold, Samuel, Melrose Park, Philadelphia, 513
Leroux, Jules, Philadelphia, 513
Lesh, John A., Philadelphia, 513
Lesher, Amos Y., Ambler, Philadelphia, 513
Lesher, Carl E., Pittsburgh, 513
Lesley, Frank W., York, 513
Lessenberry, David D., Pittsburgh, 513
Letchworth, George E., Jr., Philadelphia, 514
Leuba, James H., Bryn Mawr, 514
Leukel, George A., Kennett Square, 514
Levengood, Brooklyn B., Bellwood, 514
Lever, John H., Philadelphia, 514
Levering, William W., Jenkintown, Philadelphia, 514
Levin, Leonard S., Pittsburgh, 514
Levin, Max, Mayview, 515
Levinthal, Abraham A., Philadelphia, 515
Levinthal, Bernard L., Philadelphia, 515
Levinthal, Louis E., Philadelphia, 515
Levitsky, Louis M., Wilkes-Barre, 515
Levy, Leon, Philadelphia, 515
Levy, Maurice A., Williamsport, 516
Lewellyn, Charles L., Uniontown, 516
Lewis, Arthur M., Philadelphia, 516
Lewis, Charles B., Philadelphia, 516
Lewis, Charles F., Pittsburgh, 517
Lewis, Edwin J., Corry, 517
Lewis, Edwin O., Philadelphia, 517
Lewis, Francis A., Bryn Mawr, Philadelphia, 517
Lewis, George, Philadelphia, 517
Lewis, H. Edgar, Pittsburgh, 518
Lewis, Harry R., Warren, 518
Lewis, Herbert F., Conneaut Lake, 518
Lewis, James E., Pittsburgh, 518
Lewis, Leicester C., Philadelphia, 518
Lewis, Ludwig C., Villa Nova, Philadelphia, 518
Lewis, Mahlon E., Ben Avon, Pittsburgh, 518
Lewis, Margaret S., York, 518
Lewis, Mary F. W., Philadelphia, 518
Lewis, Mary R. H., Media, Philadelphia, 519
Lewis, Orville G., Washington, 519
Lewis, Robert T., Pittsburgh, 519
Lewis, Thomas M., Plymouth, Wilkes-Barre, 519
Lewis, Willard P., State College, 519
Lewis, William D., Lansdowne, 519
Lewis, William D., Philadelphia, 519
Lewis, William M., Easton, 519
Lewith, Edward L., Wilkes-Barre, 520
Lewy, Frederic H., Philadelphia, 520
Lichliter, Levi G., Harrisburg, 520
Lichtenberger, James B., Haverford, Philadelphia, 520
Lichtenberger, James P., Philadelphia, 520
Lichtenthaler, Henry P., Pittsburgh, 520
Lick, Maxwell J., Erie, 520
Lifter, Morris, Philadelphia, 520
Liggett, Sidney S., Sewickley, 521
Light, Harry L., Lebanon, Avon, 521
Light, V. Earl, Annville, 521
Lightcap, John S., Jr., Latrobe, 521
Lilly, Scott B., Swarthmore, 521
Lincoln, Joseph C., Villa Nova, 521
Lincoln, Rollo B., Wilkinsburg, Pittsburgh, 522
Lindback, Christian R., Philadelphia, 522
Lindborg, Carl, Lansdowne, Philadelphia, 522
Lindemuth, Anson W., Allentown, 522
Lindley, Ernest K., Erwinna, 522
Lindsay, Alexander P., Pittsburgh, 522
Lindsay, George L., Philadelphia, 522
Lindsey, Edward S., Warren, 523
Linen, James A., Jr., Waverly, Scranton, 523

Lingelbach, Anna L., Philadelphia, 523
Lingelbach, William E., Philadelphia, 523
Lininger, Frederick F., State College, 523
Linn, William B., Philadelphia, 523
Linton, Edwin, Philadelphia, 523
Linton, Frank B. A., Philadelphia, 523
Linton, Morris A., Philadelphia, 523
Lippincott, Horace M., Philadelphia, 523
Lippincott, Joseph W., Bethayres, Philadelphia, 524
Lippincott, J. Bertram, Philadelphia, 524
Lippincott, Martha S., West Philadelphia, 524
Lisle, Clifton, Wayne, 524
Lisse, Martin W., State College, 524
Little, Peter J., Ebensburg, 525
Lively, Chauncy C., Waynesburg, 525
Liversidge, Horace P., Bala-Cynwyd, Philadelphia, 525
Livingston, A. E., Wayne, Philadelphia, 526
Livingston, Benjamin T., Philadelphia, 526
Livingston, Philip A., Narberth, 526
Livingstone, Roy M., Philadelphia, 526
Lizza, Bedy, Dunbar, 526
Llewellyn, Lee, Pittsburgh, 526
Lloyd, Stacy B., Ardmore, Philadelphia, 527
Loane, William P. C., Drexel Hill, 527
Lobb, Hugh R., Mechanicsburg, 527
Lobingier, Ella H., Bradford Woods, Pittsburgh, 527
Locke, Alfred C., Franklin, 527
Locke, Charles A., Pittsburgh, 527
Locke, John H., Villanova, Eddystone, 527
Lockley, Lawrence C., Philadelphia, 528
Lockwood, Dean P., Haverford, 528
Loeb, Arthur, Philadelphia, 528
Loeb, Howard A., Elkins Park, Philadelphia, 528
Loeb, Oscar, Philadelphia, 528
Loechel, Lloyd O., Columbia, 528
Loesche, William H., Philadelphia, 528
Loewer, Charles H., Hazleton, 528
Logan, Frank A., Norristown, Bridgeport, 528
Logan, Harry A., Warren, 528
Logan, James J., York, 529
Logue, James G., Williamsport, 529
Lohr, William S., Easton, 529
Loman, Harry J., Drexel Hill, Philadelphia, 529
Long, Charles E., Chester, 529
Long, Clarence E., Pittsburgh, 529
Long, Daniel E., Fayetteville, Chambersburg, 529
Long, Esmond R., Philadelphia, 530
Long, John C., Bethlehem, 530
Long, John R., Kittanning, Tarentum, 530
Long, John W., Williamsport, 530
Long, Mason, State College, 530
Long, Newell B., Bellefonte, 530
Long, Theodore K., New Bloomfield, 530
Long, William F., Lancaster, 530
Longacre, David F., Boyertown, 530
Longaker, John H., Pottstown, 530
Longsdorf, Harold H., Dickinson, 531
Longstreth, Walter C., Philadelphia, 531
Look, Arnold E., Newtown Square, 531
Loose, Jacob C., East Mauch Chunk, Mauch Chunk, 531
Loose, Katharine R., Reading, 531
Lopatto, John S., Wilkes-Barre, 531
Lopez, Aaron M., Warren, 532
Lord, Charles S., Reynoldsville, 532
Lorimer, Graeme, Conshohocken, 532
Lorimer, Sarah M., Conshohocken, 532
Lott, Howard R., New Hope, Philadelphia, 532
Louchheim, William S., Philadelphia, 533
Loucks, William N., Merion, 533
Loud, Frederick E., Philadelphia, 533
Louden, Adelaide B., Quakertown, Philadelphia, 533

PENNSYLVANIA

Louden, Samuel L., Mars, 533
Loudon, Edward W., Altoona, 533
Loughner, Josiah R., Emlenton, 533
Loughridge, Jonathan E., Philadelphia, 533
Louthan, James S., Beaver Falls, 533
Love, Charles H., Easton, 533
Love Estelle L., Wynnewood, Philadelphia, 534
Love, John W., Washington, 534
Loveland, Charles N., Wilkes-Barre, 534
Lovett, Henry, Langhorne, 534
Lovitt, John V., Philadelphia, 534
Lowengard, Leon, Harrisburg, 534
Lowenthal, Alexander, Pittsburgh, 535
Lownes, John B., Philadelphia, 535
Lowrie, Robert N., North Braddock, Braddock, 535
Lowright, Wallace J., Center Valley, 535
Lowry, Ellsworth, Butler, 535
Lowry, H. H., Pittsburgh, 535
Lowry, W. Norwood, Lewisburg, 535
Lowy, Alexander, Pittsburgh, 535
Loxterman, Howard E., Pittsburgh, 535
Lucas, Edwin A., Villa Nova, Philadelphia, 536
Lucas, Emil A., Washington, York, 536
Lucasse, Walter W., Philadelphia, 536
Luce, Bente S., Beaver Falls, 536
Ludlum, Seymour D., Philadelphia, Gladwyne, 536
Luehring, Frederick W., Swarthmore, 537
Luhr, Augustine, St. Marys, 537
Lukenbach, Frank K., Tyrone, 537
Lukens, Edward C., Philadelphia, 537
Lukens, Francis D. W., Bala-Cynwyd, Philadelphia, 537
Lukens, Hiram S., Philadelphia, 537
Lukens, Robert M., Philadelphia, 537
Lum, Hermann A., Philadelphia, 538
Lummis, Katharine, Philadelphia, 538
Lund, C. Harrison, Erie, 538
Lund, Frederick H., Philadelphia, 538
Lunt, William E., Haverford, 538
Luongo, Romeo A., Philadelphia, 538
Lutz, Albert C., Moosic, 538
Lutz, Roland B., Abington, 538
Lutz, William F., Ambler, 538
Lyford, Richard T., Bala-Cynwyd, 539
Lyman, Robert R., Coudersport, 539
Lynch, Clay F., Greensburg, Scottdale, 539
Lynch, Clyde A., Annville, 539
Lynch, Ralph, Sharpsburg, Pittsburgh, 539
Lynett, Edward J., Scranton, 539
Lynett, William R., Scranton, 539
Lyon, B. B. Vincent, Rosemont, Philadelphia, 539
Lyon, John D., Sewickley, Pittsburgh, 540
Lyon, Julian M., Ardmore, 540
Lyons, Louis W., Pittsburgh, 540
Lytle, William T., Pittsburgh, 540
Mabon, Thomas M., Pittsburgh, 540
MacArthur, Angus, Pittsburgh, 541
Macartney, Clarence E. N., Pittsburgh, 541
MacBride-Dexter, Edith, Sharon, 541
MacCallum, John A., Philadelphia, 541
MacCarter, William J., Jr., Ridley Park, Chester, 541
MacCloskey, James E., Jr., Pittsburgh, 541
MacColl, Alexander, Philadelphia, 541
MacCoy, William L., Philadelphia, 541
MacCreadie, William T., Lewisburg, 542
MacDade, Albert D., Chester, Media, 542
MacDonald, Harry, Wyncote, Philadelphia, 542
MacDonald, Robert, Jr., Philadelphia, 542
MacElree, Mary E., West Chester, 542
MacElwee, Roy S., Drexel Hill, 542

MacFarland, George A., Jenkintown, Philadelphia, 543
Macfarlane, Catherine, Philadelphia, see Addenda
Macfarlane, Charles E., Edgewood, Wilmerding, 543
MacGillivray, Charles D., Drexel Hill, Philadelphia, 543
MacGilvary, Norwood, Pittsburgh, 543
MacIntosh, Aden B., Lancaster, 543
MacIntosh, Mark, Swarthmore, 543
Mack, Connie, Philadelphia, 543
Mack, John B., McKeesport, 543
Mack, Warren B., State College, 544
Mackall, Paul, Bethlehem, 544
Mackay, Robert W., Warren, 544
Mackenzie, George W., Philadelphia, 544
Mackie, Alexander, Philadelphia, 545
MacKinnon, George V., Jenkintown, Philadelphia, 545
Macklin, John F., Philadelphia, 545
Maclay, Robert B., Belleville, 545
MacLennan, Alexander G., Pittsburgh, 545
MacMillan, Hugh R., Bradford, 545
Macneill, Norman M., Philadelphia, 546
MacQueen, Lawrence I., Pittsburgh, 546
Madden, Francis J., Duquesne, 546
Madden, Joseph W., Pittsburgh, 546
Maddox, William P., Philadelphia, 546
Madeira, Percy C., Ogontz, Philadelphia, 546
Madeira, Percy C., Jr., Philadelphia, 546
Maeder, LeRoy M. A., Philadelphia, 546
Magaw, Elden S., Upper Darby, Philadelphia, 547
Magee, F. Earle, Oil City, 547
Magee, James M., Pittsburgh, 547
Magee, John F., Easton, 547
Magenau, John M., Erie, 547
Magidson, Frank, Pittsburgh, 547
Magill, Frank S., Chambersburg, 547
Magill, James P., Philadelphia, 547
Magill, Walter H., Philadelphia, 547
Magrady, Frederick W., Mt. Carmel, 548
Maguire, Frank P., East Stroudsburg, Harrisburg, 548
Mahoney, Bertha W., Erie, 548
Mainzer, Francis S., Huntingdon, 548
Mairs, Thomas I., State College, 548
Malcherek, Karl A., Pittsburgh, Hollidaysburg, 549
Malcolm, Gilbert, Boiling Springs, 549
Male, Arthur J., Allentown, 549
Malick, Robert E., Shamokin, 549
Mallalieu, Wilbur V., Harrisburg, 549
Mallery, Otto T., Philadelphia, 549
Mallon, Henry N., Bradford, 549
Mallon, Joseph, Philadelphia, 550
Malone, Clarence F., Beaver, Rochester, 550
Malone, Watson, Haverford, Philadelphia, 550
Maloney, Clifton, Philadelphia, 550
Man, E. Lester, Scranton, 550
Manchester, Charles, Franklin, 550
Mancill, Frank H., Merion Station, Philadelphia, 551
Manges, Edmund L., Huntingdon, 551
Mann, Alexander, Pittsburgh, 551
Mann, Thomas A., Philadelphia, 551
Manning, Frank L., Collegeville, 551
Manning, Helen H. T., Bryn Mawr, 551
Mansfield, Donald B., Philadelphia, 551
Mansfield, J. Clark, Philadelphia, 551
Mansfield, Myron G., Pittsburgh, 551
Mansfield, William D., McKeesport, 552
Manson, Frederic E., Williamsport, 552
Mansuy, John L., Ralston, 552
Mantinband, Charles, Williamsport, 552
Marbaker, Edward E., Pittsburgh, 552
Marble, Dean R., State College, 552
Marceau, Henri, Philadelphia, 553

March, Matthias L., Norristown, Bridgeport, 553
March, William A., Norristown, Bridgeport, 553
Marcks, Frederick A., Nazareth, 553
Margie, Peter M., West Pittston, Kingston, Pittston, Wilkes-Barre, 553
Margiotti, Charles J., Pittsburgh, 553
Margolis, Jacob, Pittsburgh, 553
Marinaro, Carmen V., Butler, 553
Maris, Albert B., Lansdowne, Philadelphia, 553
Markell, William O., Pittsburgh, 554
Markle, David L., State College, 554
Markle, Donald, Jeddo, 554
Markle, John, 2d, Camp Hill, Harrisburg, 554
Marks, Harold K., Allentown, 554
Marks, Lewis H., Paoli, Philadelphia, 554
Marks, Mary H., Pittsburgh, 554
Marlier, Raymond M., Ingram, Pittsburgh, 554
Marlin, Harry H., New Castle, 554
Marquard, William B., Easton, 554
Marquardt, Carl E., State College, 555
Marriner, Guy V. R., Philadelphia, 555
Marriott, Ross W., Swarthmore, 555
Marsella, Loreto, Norristown, 555
Marsh, James I., Pittsburgh, 555
Marsh, Ritchie T., Erie, 555
Marsh, Robert P., Gettysburg, 555
Marshall, Charles D., Pittsburgh, 556
Marshall, Charles H., Philadelphia, 556
Marshall, Edward W., Philadelphia, 556
Marshall, James E., Butler, 556
Marshall, John, Swarthmore, 556
Marshall, John G., Beaver, 556
Marshall, Loyal S., Springdale, 556
Marshall, Mortimer V., Lancaster, 556
Marshall, Roy K., Pittsburgh, 557
Marshall, Thomas R., Melrose Park, Philadelphia, 557
Marteney, Charles W., Ridley Park, 557
Martin, Adam H., York, 557
Martin, Adam O., Doylestown, 557
Martin, Alfred, Brackenridge, Verona, 557
Martin, Arthur C., Greensburg, Pittsburgh, 557
Martin, Asa E., State College, 557
Martin, Carl N., Anselma, Philadelphia, 557
Martin, Charles E., Bellefonte, 557
Martin, Christian F., Nazareth, 558
Martin, Edward, Washington, 558
Martin, Francis C., Johnstown, 558
Martin, George C., Clymer, 558
Martin, George E., Pittsburgh, 558
Martin, Hershel R., Philadelphia, 558
Martin, James P., Lancaster, 558
Martin, James S., Beaver Falls, 559
Martin, John C., Philadelphia, 559
Martin, Joseph B., Paxtang, Harrisburg, 559
Martin, Mildred P., Philadelphia, 559
Martin, Renwick H., Beaver Falls, Pittsburgh, 559
Martin, Robert W., Quakertown, 559
Martin, Sydney E., Upper Roxborough, Philadelphia, 559
Martino, Antonio P., Philadelphia, 560
Marts, Arnaud C., Lewisburg, 560
Masland, Frank E., Jr., Carlisle, 561
Mason, Edgar D., Pittsburgh, 561
Mason, Francis C., Gettysburg, 561
Mason, George M., Erie, 561
Mason, J. Alden, Berwyn, Philadelphia, 561
Mason, Mary S. T., Philadelphia, 561
Mason, Thomas W., State College, 562
Massingham, Sherman, Pittsburgh, 562
Massol, Merwin B., Pittsburgh, 562
Masten, Fred C., Pittsburgh, 562
Master, Henry B., Devon, 562
Masters, Frank M., Harrisburg, 562
Masters, Harry G., Pittsburgh, 562
Masters, Harry V., Reading, 562
Mates, James W., Pittsburgh, 562
Mather, Frank J., Jr., Washington Crossing, 562

Mather, Thomas R., Benton, 563
Mathesius, Walther E. L., Pittsburgh, 563
Mathews, Charles H., Jr., Paoli, Philadelphia, 563
Matt, C. David, Philadelphia, 564
Mattas, Clyde L., Scranton, 564
Mattes, Philip V., Scranton, 564
Matthews, Archibald M., Somerset, 564
Matthews, Arthur P., Scranton, 564
Matthews, H. Alexander, Philadelphia, 564
Matthews, Isaac G., Chester, 564
Mattox, Edgar E., Pittsburgh, 565
Matz, Robert L., Lewisburg, 565
Maurer, Felix G., Frackville, 565
Maurer, James H., Reading, 565
Maxey, George W., Scranton, Philadelphia, 566
Maxey, Paul H., Scranton, 566
Maxfield, Ezra K., Washington, 566
Maxfield, Jane C., Washington, 566
Maxwell, Charles F., Greensburg, 566
Maxwell, Charles P., Easton, 566
May, Edwin C., Pittsburgh, 567
May, Herbert A., Pittsburgh, 567
May, Kenneth F., Pittsburgh, 567
Mayer, Edward E., Pittsburgh, 567
Mayes, William H., Brockway, 567
Mays, Jacob H., Weiser Park, 568
Mays, Paul K., Bryn Athyn, 568
Mayser, Charles W., Lancaster, 568
Maywood, Armour A., Pittsburgh, 568
Mazer, Charles, Philadelphia, 568
McAdoo, Henry M., Fort Washington, 568
McAfee, W. Keith, New Castle, 568
McAlister, David I., Washington, 568
McAlister, John B., Harrisburg, 568
McAndrew, Mary B., Carbondale, 568
McAndrew, Paul C., Scranton, 568
McBride, F. Scott, Philadelphia, 569
McBride, John B., Canonsburg, Pittsburgh, 569
McBride, Lois M., Bradford Woods, Pittsburgh, 569
McBride, Milford L., Grove City, 569
McBride, William, Sewickley, Pittsburgh, 569
McBride, William K., Harrisburg, 569
McBurney, James H., Canonsburg, 569
McCabe, Thomas B., Swarthmore, Chester, Philadelphia, 569
McCabe, Warren L., Pittsburgh, 569
McCafferty, Ernest D., Allison Park, Pittsburgh, 569
McCaffrey, Thomas J., Pittsburgh, 569
McCague, Robert H., Sewickley, Pittsburgh, 569
McCahan, David, Swarthmore, Philadelphia, 570
McCahill, David I. B., Pittsburgh, 570
McCain, Samuel H., Kittanning, 570
McCamey, Harold E., Fox Chapel, Pittsburgh, 570
McCance, Pressly H., Pittsburgh, 570
McCandless, James F., Pittsburgh, 570
McCandless, Lee C., Butler, 570
McCandless, Milton L., Rochester, 571
McCandliss, Lester C., Pittsburgh, 571
McCann, Minnie A., Reading, 571
McCarter, Henry, Philadelphia, 571
McCarthy, Anna L., Mayfield, 571
McCarthy, Daniel J., Philadelphia, 571
McCarthy, Louise F., Ridley Park, 571
McCartney, James L., Philadelphia, 571
McCarty, Harriet D., Pittsburgh, 571
McCarty, Roy A., Drexel Hill, Philadelphia, 571
McCaslin, Murray F., Pittsburgh, 572
McCauley, Thomas A., North East, 572
McClain, Harry C., Hustontown, 572
McClean, Lee D., Meadville, 572
McCleary, Thomas G., Braddock, 572
McClellan, George E., Bellefonte, 572
McClellan, Robert P., Irwin, 572